MARTINDALE-HUBBELL®

BAR REGISTER OF PREEMINENT LAWYERS™ 2000

VOLUME I

ALABAMA–MICHIGAN

EIGHTY-FOURTH EDITION

MARTINDALE-HUBBELL
A Member of LEXIS Publishing™

LEXIS Publishing™

LEXIS-NEXIS • MARTINDALE-HUBBELL
MATTHEW BENDER • MICHIE • SHEPARD'S

121 Chanlon Road, New Providence, NJ 07974 • 1-800-526-4902
Email: info@martindale.com • www.martindale.com

Published by Martindale-Hubbell®, A Member of LEXIS® Publishing™

Louis J. Andreozzi, President and Chief Executive Officer
Carol D. Cooper, Publisher, Senior Vice President, Marketing and Product Development
Larry D. Thompson, Senior Vice President, U.S. Sales and Customer Relations
Andrew W. Meyer, Vice President, Administration
Vera Lang, Vice President and Chief Financial Officer
Dean Hollister, Vice President, Database Production
John Roney, Vice President, Chief Information Officer

International Standard Book Number: 1-56160-424-0 (set)

Printed and bound in the United States of America
by Quebecor World Book Services
Taunton, Massachusetts

ISBN 1-56160-424-0

9 781561 604241

TABLE OF CONTENTS

TABLE OF CONTENTS — *Continued*

PRACTICE AREAS SECTION, VOLUME II (Minnesota–Wyoming, Canada, International)

FOREWORD

We are pleased to present the 84th edition of the **Martindale-Hubbell® Bar Register of Preeminent Lawyers™**, the definitive guide to America's leading lawyers and law firms.

The **Martindale-Hubbell Bar Register** lists only the most distinguished law practices – those that have achieved the highest "AV®" rating in the **Martindale-Hubbell Law Directory**. The "A" signifies the highest levels of legal ability, while the "V" denotes "very high" adherence to professional standards of conduct, ethics, reliability and diligence. This rating is the result of a peer review system based upon the confidential opinions of practicing attorneys and members of the judiciary.

The 2000 **Bar Register** contains concise listings and full contact data for more than 9,000 sole practitioners and law firms in the United States and Canada. It lists lawyers and firms excelling in 61 practice areas, from Administrative Law to Workers Compensation. Five new Practice Areas are included this year – Education Law, Elder Law, Franchise Law, Legal Malpractice, and Nonprofit & Tax Exemption Organizations. Also with this edition, Probate, Trusts and Estate Planning is now Trusts and Estates, Wills and Probate.

We believe you will find the **Bar Register** invaluable whenever you need to identify today's most highly regarded law firms in a particular geographic location or area of expertise. In addition, your **Bar Register** status is noted in your professional listing emphasizing your firm's prestige and standing. Your listing on *martindale.com* will feature an icon to instantly alert potential clients to your **Bar Register** status.

As always, we invite you to contact us with any suggestions for new practice areas or ideas to further improve the next edition.

Thank you for your support.

Louis J. Andreozzi
President and Chief Executive Officer

MARTINDALE-HUBBELL®/LEXIS®-NEXIS® LEGAL ADVISORY BOARD

The Martindale-Hubbell/LEXIS-NEXIS Legal Advisory Board was formed to ensure that Martindale-Hubbell and LEXIS-NEXIS are responsive to the constantly changing needs of the legal profession. The following lawyers selected from the private, corporate and international sectors of the profession comprise the 1999-2000 Board.

MARTHA W. BARNETT of Holland & Knight, Tallahassee, Florida. Ms. Barnett is a former Chair of the House of Delegates of the American Bar Association, the first woman lawyer to be so honored, and has served on the ABA's Board of Governors. Currently, she is the President-Elect of the American Bar Association, to serve as such from August 1999 to July 2000, and to serve as President from July 2000 to August 2001.

ALLEN E. BRENNECKE of Harrison, Brennecke, Moore, Smaha & McKibben, Marshaltown, Iowa. Mr. Brennecke has served as a Member of the Board of Directors of the National Judicial College, President of the Iowa State Bar Association, a Member of the ABA House of Delegates since 1975 and its Chair, 1984-1986. His prior service to the ABA also includes four years on the Board of Governors and three years as Chair of the IOLTA Commission. He previously served on the Board of Editors of the American Bar Association Journal and served as Chair from 1989 to 1995.

BENJAMIN R. CIVILETTI of Venable, Baetjer, Howard & Civiletti, Washington, D.C. and Baltimore, Maryland. Mr. Civiletti is a former Attorney General of the United States under President Carter, 1979-1981. He is the former Chairman of the ABA Litigation Section and has been a member of the ABA House of Delegates since 1991. He also serves as the ABA Representative to the United Nations. He is the Chairman of Venable. Mr. Civiletti is a Fellow of the American College of Trial Lawyers and the American Law Institute.

DOUGLAS B. HENDERSON is the Founding and Senior Partner of Finnegan, Henderson, Farabow, Garrett & Dunner, Washington, D.C. Mr. Henderson is a Member of the Advisory Council of the United States Court of Federal Claims, and a Member of the Board of the Federal Circuit Bar Association. He was formerly Chairman of the Patent Division and Member of Council of the Section of Intellectual Property Law of the American Bar Association. He was the Founder of the Federal Circuit Bar Association, a co-founder of the U.S. Court of Federal Claims Bar Association, and a co-founder of the ITC Trial Lawyers Association.

THOMAS G. HEINTZMAN, O.C., Q.C., of McCarthy Tétrault, Toronto, Ontario, is a past President of the Canadian Bar Association (1994-1995). He is a member of the International Bar Association and the past Canadian member of the Council. Mr. Heintzman is a Fellow of the International Academy of Trial Lawyers, and the American College of Trial Lawyers and the past Chair of its Canadian Judiciary Committee. He is an Officer of the Order of Canada.

THOMAS J. KLITGAARD, formerly Senior Vice President and General Counsel of Sega of America, Inc., is now a partner with Dillingham & Murphy, San Francisco. He is a former Chairman of the California State Bar's Committee on the Maintenance of Professional Competence. He is a member of the panel of technology arbitrators of the American Arbitration Association in New York and a member of the Advisory Board of the Southwestern Legal Foundation in Dallas. He is currently the chairman of a graduate business management program in Shanghai, China.

RALPH I. LANCASTER, JR. of Pierce Atwood, Portland, Maine is currently serving as Independent Counsel, In Re Herman, by appointment of the Special Division of the D.C. Court of Appeals. He previously served as Counsel for the United States before the International Court of Justice in a case concerning delimitation of the Maritime Boundary in the Gulf of Maine and as Special Master by appointment of the Untied States Supreme Court in State of New Jersey vs. State of Nebraska. Mr. Lancaster began his legal career as a law clerk to the Honorable Edward T. Gignoux. He is a Past-President of the Maine State Bar Association and a former member of the House of Delegates of the American Bar Association. He served as Chair of the Standing Committee on Federal Judiciary of the ABA. He is a Fellow of the American College of Trial Lawyers and served as its President, 1989-1990.

JERALYN E. MERRITT, a sole practitioner from Denver, Colorado, is an author and frequent lecturer on criminal defense. She was selected by Chairman Bill McCollum, House Judiciary Committee, Subcommittee on Crime, to present oral and written congressional testimony on federal marijuana sentencing laws on behalf of the National Association of Criminal Defense Lawyers (NACDL) on March 6, 1996, in Washington, D.C. She served as Chair from 1995-1996 while a judicially appointed member of the Standing Committee on the Criminal Justice Act for the United States District Court for the District of Colorado from 1994-1996. Ms. Merritt is currently a member of the Board of Directors and Chair of the Advisory Board for the National Association of Criminal Defense Lawyers, the Director of the Cyberspace Bar Association and a member of the Board of Governors for the American Board of Criminal Lawyers.

HARRIET E. MIERS, Co-Managing Partner of Locke Liddell & Sapp LLP, has previously served as President and director of the State Bar of Texas as well as President and Chairman of the Board of Directors for the Dallas Bar Association. She is currently a member of the House of Delegates for the American Bar Association and State Delegate for the State of Texas. Ms. Miers also serves as a Trustee of the Southwestern Legal Foundation, a member of the Executive Board for the Southern Methodist University School of Law and Chair of the Texas Lottery Commission.

WILLIAM G. PAUL of Crowe & Dunlevy, Oklahoma City, Oklahoma. Mr. Paul is the former Senior Vice President & General Counsel, Phillips Petroleum Company, Bartlesville, Oklahoma. In February 1998, he was nominated to be President-Elect of the American Bar Association, to serve as such from August 1998 to August 1999, and is now the President to serve as such from August 1999 to July 2000. He has served as President of the Oklahoma State Bar Association, President of the National Conference of Bar Presidents, a Member of the American Bar Association, House of Delegates 1975-1999 and is a Fellow in the American College of Trial Lawyers.

FERNANDO POMBO, Founder and Senior Partner of Gomez-Acebo & Pombo, Madrid, Spain, has contributed to and authored several publications in the field of international business law. Currently, he is the International Bar Association Chairman of SLP. Mr. Pombo has been a visiting professor at the Institute on International Legal Studies in Salzburg, Austria since 1985. He is also a former President of LES International and a member of the Spanish Arbitration Court. He is fluent in Spanish, English, French and German.

WM. REECE SMITH, JR. of Tampa, Florida, is the senior member of Carlton, Fields, Ward, Emmanuel, Smith & Cutler, P.A. A Rhodes Scholar at Oxford University, England, he was later President of The Florida Bar (1972-73), the American Bar Association (1980-81), and the International Bar Association (1988-90). He is a Fellow of the American College of Trial Lawyers and the International Academy of Trial Lawyers and serves on the Council of the American Law Institute. He received the American Bar Association's Gold Medal for "exceptionally distinguished service to the cause of American Jurisprudence."

WALTER H. WHITE, JR. is a Partner of Bryan Cave L.L.P. in London, England. Mr. White previously has served as a Partner of Steptoe & Johnson L.L.P. in Washington, D.C. and as the Managing Director of its Moscow office. Mr. White is a former Commissioner of Securities for the State of Wisconsin 1988-1991. He has served as a member of the ABA House of Delegates, as the Chair of the Section of Individual Rights and Responsibilities and as chair of the Young Lawyers Division. Mr. White has also been a member of the State Bar of Wisconsin Board of Governors, on the Board of the Milwaukee Foundation and is currently a Board member of the Central-Asian-American Enterprise Fund by appointment of President Clinton.

USER'S GUIDE

The **Martindale-Hubbell Bar Register of Preeminent Lawyers** is a two-volume registry of firms and attorneys of significant stature. The 2000 edition presents sixty-one alphabetically sequenced practice area sections and an index to the firms listed in each practice area.

This **Subscriber Locator**, arranged alphabetically by subscriber name, will assist the user in identifying those practice areas and geographic location(s) where the subscriber lists.

A typical entry appears as follows:

Firm Name *Practice Areas*

LEWANDOWSKI & BERRY, P.C.
Roseland, NJ . . . . . .Banking Law; Bankruptcy Law; Civil Trial Practice; General Practice; Tax Law
New York, NY . . . . .Banking Law; Bankruptcy Law; Tax Law

Geographic Location

The **Practice Areas Section** clearly lists the practice area at the top of the page, along with the geographic location. Listings for the United States and Canada are arranged in alphabetic sequence by state (or Canadian province) and within state (or Canadian province) by city name and finally by listee name. For countries other than the United States and Canada, alphabetic country name is the major sequence, followed by city and then listee name.

A typical section entry appears as follows:

Practice Area *Geographic Location*

County Seat Indicator

GENERAL PRACTICE **NEW YORK—AMSTERDAM**

AMSTERDAM,* Montgomery Co.

Firm Name **LETTERMAN AND KOLACKOVSKY, P.C.** (AV) *Firm Rating*

Contact Information

46 Rose Street, P.O. Box 2429, 12010
Telephone: 515-214-9291
Fax: 515-214-6153
Email: postmaster@lettkol.com *URL:* http://www.lettkol.com

Mitchell J. Letterman John Kolackovsky

——— *Associate Indicator*

Megan Brett Ann Kolackovsky
Doris Vayda

Clients

Representative Clients: New York Home Security, Inc.; American Flight School, Inc.; East Coast Recycling Center, New York Casualty, Inc.; American Fire Insurance Corp.
Reference: Atlantic National Bank.

For full biographical listings, see the Martindale-Hubbell Law Directory.

Martindale-Hubbell Professional Biographies Reference

For additional help or explanation, please call Martindale-Hubbell Customer Relations, at (800) 526-4902.

INDEX SECTION

AAFEDT, FORDE, GRAY & MONSON, P.A.
Minneapolis, MN....................Insurance Defense

AARON, WILLIAM
Miami, FL....................Criminal Trial Practice

AARONS LAW FIRM, P.C.
Santa Fe, NM....................Criminal Trial Practice

AARONSON, EDWARD D., A LAW CORPORATION
Encino, CA....................Real Estate Law

ABBATE, LAWRENCE & WORDEN, P.C.
Melville, NY....................Medical Malpractice; Product Liability Law

ABBEY, WEITZENBERG, HOFFMAN & EMERY, A PROFESSIONAL CORPORATION
Santa Rosa, CA....................Banking Law; Bankruptcy Law; Business Law; Civil Trial Practice; Construction Law; Labor and Employment Law; Medical Malpractice; Personal Injury; Real Estate Law

ABBOT, MURPHY AND HARVEY, P.C.
Louisville, GA....................Business Law; General Practice

ABBOTT, C. MICHAEL, P.C.
Atlanta, GA....................Appellate Practice; Criminal Trial Practice

ABBOTT, NICHOLSON, QUILTER, ESSHAKI & YOUNGBLOOD, P.C.
Detroit, MI....................Business Law; Civil Trial Practice; Employment Benefits Law; Family Law; Labor and Employment Law; Municipal and Zoning Law; Real Estate Law; Tax Law; Trust and Estates, Wills and Probate

ABBOTT & NOLEN
Sacramento, CA....................Civil Trial Practice; Insurance Defense

ABDO AND ABDO, P.A.
Minneapolis, MN....................Appellate Practice; Business Law; Civil Trial Practice; Environmental Law; General Practice; Real Estate Law; Securities Law; Sports and Entertainment Law; Trust and Estates, Wills and Probate

ABELE & SANDERSON, L.L.C.
St. Louis, MO....................Personal Injury; Product Liability Law; Workers Compensation

ABEL, MUSSER, SOKOLOSKY, MARES & KOURI
Oklahoma City, OK....................Personal Injury

ABELSON LAW FIRM, THE
Washington, DC....................Medical Malpractice

ABEYTA-NELSON P.C.
Yakima, WA....................Personal Injury; Product Liability Law

ABLONDI, FOSTER, SOBIN & DAVIDOW, P.C.
Washington, DC....................International Trade Law

ABOWITZ, RHODES & DAHNKE, P.C.
Oklahoma City, OK....................Civil Trial Practice; Insurance Defense; Personal Injury; Securities Law

ABRAHAMS KASLOW & CASSMAN
Omaha, NE....................General Practice

ABRAHAMSON, REED & ADLEY
Hammond, IN....................Civil Trial Practice; Commercial Litigation; Insurance Defense; Transportation Law

ABRAMOWITZ & POMERANTZ, P.A.
Fort Lauderdale, FL....................Medical Malpractice; Personal Injury

ABRAMS, GORELICK, FRIEDMAN & JACOBSON, P.C.
New York, NY....................Civil Trial Practice; Insurance Defense

ABRAMS & SMITH, A PROFESSIONAL ASSOCIATION
Minneapolis, MN....................Civil Trial Practice; Insurance Defense; Personal Injury; Product Liability Law

ABRAMSON & FOX
Chicago, IL....................Civil Trial Practice

ABRAMSON & FREEDMAN, L.L.C.
Philadelphia, PA....................Administrative Law; Civil Trial Practice; Commercial Litigation

ABRAMSON & MAGIDSON, P.A.
Miami, FL....................Admiralty/Maritime Law; Personal Injury; Workers Compensation

ABRAMSON, REIS, BROWN & DUGAN
Manchester, NH....................Medical Malpractice; Personal Injury

ACKER, LAWRENCE J., P.C.
Bloomfield Hills, MI....................Medical Malpractice; Professional Liability

ACKERMAN, JAMES H. LAW OFFICES OF
Long Beach, CA....................Admiralty/Maritime Law; General Practice

ACKERMAN & ACKERMAN, P.C.
Troy, MI....................Eminent Domain

ACKERMAN, ALLAN A., P.C.
Chicago, IL....................Appellate Practice; Criminal Trial Practice

ACKERMAN, LEE B., P.C., LAW OFFICES OF
Los Angeles, CA....................Legal Malpractice

ACKERMAN, LINK & SARTORY, P.A.
West Palm Beach, FL....................Business Law; Real Estate Law; Securities Law

ACKERMAN & TERRY, LLC
Westbury, NY....................Bankruptcy Law; Commercial Litigation

ACKMAN, MAREK & BOYD, LTD.
Kankakee, IL....................Civil Trial Practice; Insurance Defense; Medical Malpractice
Watseka, IL....................General Practice

ADAMI, GOLDMAN & SHUFFIELD, INCORPORATED
San Antonio, TX....................Insurance Defense

ADAMO AND NEWMAN
Westerly, RI....................Criminal Trial Practice; Family Law; Personal Injury

ADAMS & ADAMS
Miami, FL....................Civil Trial Practice; General Practice

ADAMS & ASSOCIATES
Oklahoma City, OK....................Civil Trial Practice; Criminal Trial Practice; Personal Injury

ADAMS, BARFIELD, DUNAWAY & HANKINSON, LLP
Thomaston, GA....................General Practice

ADAMS, COOGLER, WATSON & MERKEL, P.A.
West Palm Beach, FL....................Civil Trial Practice; Commercial Litigation; Insurance Defense; Medical Malpractice; Personal Injury; Product Liability Law; Workers Compensation

ADAMS, GALLINAR, IGLESIAS & MEYER, P.A.
Miami, FL....................Aviation Law; Banking Law; International Business Law; Real Estate Law

ADAMS & GRAHAM, L.L.P.
Harlingen, TX....................Appellate Practice; Civil Trial Practice; Insurance Defense; Medical Malpractice; Product Liability Law; Professional Liability; Workers Compensation

ADAMS AND JOHNSTON, A PROFESSIONAL LAW CORPORATION
New Orleans, LA....................Civil Trial Practice

ADAMS, LYNCH & LOFTIN, P.C.
Bedford, TX....................Banking Law; Business Law; Labor and Employment Law; Real Estate Law

ADAMS AND REESE LLP
New Orleans, LA....................General Practice

ADAMS, WESTON, LAW FIRM
Columbia, SC....................General Practice

ADDISON, MICHAEL C.
Tampa, FL....................Antitrust Law; Civil Trial Practice; Construction Law; Product Liability Law; Securities Law

ADDUCI, MASTRIANI & SCHAUMBERG, L.L.P.
Washington, DC....................Administrative Law; International Trade Law; Patent, Trademark, Copyright and Unfair Competition

ADELMAN LAVINE GOLD AND LEVIN, A PROFESSIONAL CORPORATION
Philadelphia, PA....................Bankruptcy Law; Corporate Law; Real Estate Law

ADELMAN, ROBERT A., A LAW CORPORATION
Beverly Hills, CA....................Family Law

ADELSON, GOLDEN, LORIA & SIMONS, P.C.
Boston, MA....................Real Estate Law

ADINAMIS & ADINAMIS, ATTORNEYS, A PROFESSIONAL CORPORATION
Indianapolis, IN....................Tax Law; Trust and Estates, Wills and Probate

ADKINS & KELSTON, P.C.
Boston, MA....................Commercial Litigation; Criminal Trial Practice

ADKINS, POTTS & SMETHURST, L.L.P.
Salisbury, MD....................Civil Trial Practice; Environmental Law; Municipal and Zoning Law; Real Estate Law

ADKISON, CYNTHIA, P.C.
Bloomfield Hills, MI....................Insurance Defense; Labor and Employment Law

ADKISON, NEED, GREEN & ALLEN
Bloomfield Hills, MI....................Banking Law; Business Law; Commercial Litigation; Communications Law; Computer Law; Corporate Law; Family Law; General Practice; Land Use Law; Municipal and Zoning Law

ADKISSON & JACKSON, L.L.P.
San Antonio, TX....................Medical Malpractice; Personal Injury; Product Liability Law

ADLER, ALAN R.
Morristown, NJ....................Tax Law

ADLER, DAVID W.
Phoenix, AZ....................Family Law; Trust and Estates, Wills and Probate

ADLER, JOHN S., A PROF. CORP., LAW OFFICES OF
San Diego, CA....................Labor and Employment Law

ADOLPH & BINTINGER, P.S.
Seattle, WA....................Civil Trial Practice

AGAPAY, LEVYN & HALLING, A PROFESSIONAL CORPORATION
Los Angeles, CA....................Civil Trial Practice

AGINS HAAZ & SEIDEL, L.L.P.
Philadelphia, PA....................Personal Injury

AGNEW & BRUSAVICH
Torrance, CA....................Civil Trial Practice; Medical Malpractice; Personal Injury; Product Liability Law

AHLERS, COONEY, DORWEILER, HAYNIE, SMITH & ALLBEE, P.C.
Des Moines, IA....................General Practice

AHMUTY, DEMERS & MCMANUS
New York, NY....................Civil Trial Practice; Insurance Defense

AIKIN, WENDY L., P.A.
Winter Park, FL....................Commercial Litigation; Family Law; Personal Injury

AIKINS, MACAULAY & THORVALDSON
Winnipeg, MB, Canada....................Business Law; Civil Trial Practice; General Practice; Insurance Defense; Personal Injury; Tax Law; Trust and Estates, Wills and Probate

AINSA PARTNERS, LLP
El Paso, TX....................Banking Law; Business Law; Commercial Litigation; Construction Law; Corporate Law; Eminent Domain; Government Contracts; Land Use Law; Municipal and Zoning Law; Real Estate Law

AINSWORTH, SULLIVAN, TRACY, KNAUF, WARNER & RUSLANDER, P.C.
Albany, NY....................Appellate Practice; General Practice; Insurance Defense; Product Liability Law

AIRD & BERLIS
Toronto, ON, Canada....................General Practice

AITKEN, SCHAUBLE, PATRICK, NEILL & RUFF
Pullman, WA....................Trust and Estates, Wills and Probate

AJALAT, POLLEY & AYOOB
Los Angeles, CA....................Tax Law

AKIN, GUMP, STRAUSS, HAUER & FELD
Brussels, Belgium....................General Practice
Washington, DC....................General Practice
Austin, TX....................General Practice
Dallas, TX....................General Practice
Houston, TX....................General Practice
San Antonio, TX....................General Practice

AKINS, JEFFREY R.
San Antonio, TX....................Civil Trial Practice

ALBERT, WARD & JOHNSON, P.C.
Greenwich, CT....................Business Law; Civil Trial Practice; Construction Law; Corporate Law; General Practice; Municipal and Zoning Law; Real Estate Law; Trust and Estates, Wills and Probate

ALBERT, WEILAND & GOLDEN
Costa Mesa, CA....................Appellate Practice; Bankruptcy Law; Civil Trial Practice; Commercial Litigation; Creditors Rights; Real Estate Law

ALBERT, WHITEHEAD & MCGAUGH, P.C.
Chicago, IL....................Business Law; Civil Trial Practice; Labor and Employment Law

ALBRIGHT BROWN & GOERTEMILLER, LLC
Baltimore, MD....................Civil Trial Practice; Criminal Trial Practice

ALBRIGHT, STODDARD, WARNICK & ALBRIGHT, A PROFESSIONAL CORPORATION
Las Vegas, NV....................Appellate Practice; Banking Law; Bankruptcy Law; Civil Trial Practice; Commercial Law; Construction Law; Family Law; General Practice; Insurance Defense; Real Estate Law; Trust and Estates, Wills and Probate

ALBRITTONS, CLIFTON, ALVERSON & MOODY, P.C.
Andalusia, AL....................Civil Trial Practice; General Practice; Insurance Defense; Product Liability Law; Professional Liability; Tax Law; Trust and Estates, Wills and Probate; Workers Compensation

ALCORN, JOHN R. LAW OFFICES OF
Irvine, CA....................Immigration and Naturalization

ALDEN ARONOVSKY & SAX LLP
San Francisco, CA....................Civil Trial Practice; Commercial Litigation; Environmental Law

ALDERMAN AND ALDERMAN
Syracuse, NY....................Family Law; Real Estate Law; Trust and Estates, Wills and Probate

ALDRICH & BONNEFIN, P.L.C.
Irvine, CA....................Banking Law

ALEXANDER & CLEAVER, P.A.
Annapolis, MD....................Business Law; Commercial Law; Personal Injury

ALEXANDER, HAWES & AUDET
San Jose, CA....................Antitrust Law; Civil Trial Practice; Personal Injury; Product Liability Law; Toxic Torts

ALEXANDER, HOLBURN, BEAUDIN & LANG
Vancouver, BC, Canada....................General Practice; Insurance Defense; Labor and Employment Law

ALEXANDER RALSTON, SPECKHARD & SPECKHARD, L.L.P.
Greensboro, NC....................Civil Trial Practice; Commercial Law; Corporate Law; Medical Malpractice; Personal Injury; Real Estate Law; Trust and Estates, Wills and Probate; Workers Compensation

ALEXANDER, TOM, & ASSOCIATES
Houston, TX....................Civil Trial Practice; Family Law

ALEXANDER & VANN, LLP
Thomasville, GA....................General Practice

ALFERS & CARVER, LLC
Denver, CO....................International Business Law; Natural Resources Law; Oil and Gas Law

ALFORD, E. GREGORY
San Diego, CA....................Family Law

ALFORD & KALIL, P.A.
Jacksonville, FL....................Product Liability Law; Professional Liability; Toxic Torts

ALHADEFF CANNON ROSE SOLAR & PARKS, LLP
San Diego, CA....................Bankruptcy Law; Business Law; Civil Trial Practice; Labor and Employment Law; Tax Law; Trademark, Copyright and Unfair Competition; Trust and Estates, Wills and Probate

ALI, PAPPAS & COX, P.C.
Syracuse, NY....................Civil Trial Practice; Commercial Litigation; Creditors Rights; General Practice; Real Estate Law

ALKON, RHEA & HART
Christiansted, St. Croix, VI....................Civil Trial Practice; Personal Injury

ALLAN & SHIPP, P.A.
St. Petersburg, FL....................General Practice; Securities Law; Trust and Estates, Wills and Probate

ALLE, JAMES
Grosse Pointe, MI....................Family Law

ALLEN, RICHARD E.
Augusta, GA....................Civil Trial Practice; Criminal Trial Practice; Family Law; General Practice

ALLEN, ALLEN, ALLEN & ALLEN, A PROFESSIONAL CORPORATION
Richmond, VA....................Personal Injury; Product Liability Law

ALLEN, ALLEN, BOERNER & BREELAND
Brookhaven, MS....................Banking Law; Civil Trial Practice; Commercial Law; Family Law; General Practice; Insurance Defense; Labor and Employment Law; Personal Injury; Real Estate Law; Trust and Estates, Wills and Probate

ALLEN, BRINTON, SIMMONS & MCCARTHY, P.A.
Jacksonville, FL....................Business Law; Civil Trial Practice; Commercial Litigation; Construction Law

ALLEN, COOLEY & ALLEN
Lawrence, KS....................General Practice

ALLEN, DELL, FRANK & TRINKLE, P.A.
Tampa, FL....................Civil Trial Practice; Family Law; General Practice

ALLEN, DYER, DOPPELT, MILBRATH & GILCHRIST
Orlando, FL....................Commercial Litigation; Intellectual Property Law; Patent, Trademark, Copyright and Unfair Competition; Trademark, Copyright and Unfair Competition

ALLEN & FLATT INCORPORATED
Newport Beach, CA....................Personal Injury

ALLEN, GLENN K., A PROFESSIONAL ASSOCIATION
Jacksonville, FL .... Civil Trial Practice; Family Law; Medical Malpractice; Personal Injury; Professional Liability

ALLEN GUTHRIE & MCHUGH
Charleston, WV .... Administrative Law; Appellate Practice; Civil Trial Practice; Criminal Trial Practice; Health Care Law; Tax Law

ALLEN, JOHNSON, ALEXANDER & KARP, P.A.
Washington, DC .... Civil Trial Practice; General Practice; Insurance Defense; Product Liability Law
Baltimore, MD .... Civil Rights; Civil Trial Practice; General Practice; Insurance Defense; Product Liability Law

ALLEN AND KIMBELL, LLP
Santa Barbara, CA .... General Practice

ALLEN LAW FIRM, A PROFESSIONAL CORPORATION
Little Rock, AR .... Banking Law; Commercial Litigation; Insurance Defense; Securities Law

ALLEN, MATKINS, LECK, GAMBLE & MALLORY LLP
Irvine, CA .... General Practice
Los Angeles, CA .... General Practice; Public Utilities Law
San Diego, CA .... General Practice
San Francisco, CA .... General Practice

ALLEN & MOORE, L.L.P.
Raleigh, NC .... Administrative Law; Business Law; Civil Trial Practice

ALLEN AND PINNIX, P.A.
Raleigh, NC .... Administrative Law; Antitrust Law; Immigration and Naturalization; International Business Law

ALLEN, POLGAR, PROIETTI & FAGALDE
Merced, CA .... Civil Trial Practice; General Practice

ALLEN & PRICE, P.L.C.
Phoenix, AZ .... Antitrust Law; Civil Trial Practice; Health Care Law; Patent, Trademark, Copyright and Unfair Competition; Trademark, Copyright and Unfair Competition

ALLEN, SCRUGGS, SOSSAMAN & THOMPSON, P.C.
Memphis, TN .... Business Law; Labor and Employment Law; Workers Compensation

ALLEN, VAHRENWALD & JOHNSON, LLC
Fort Collins, CO .... General Practice

ALLEN, VAUGHN, COBB & HOOD, P.A.
Gulfport, MS .... Banking Law; Business Law; Civil Trial Practice; Corporate Law; General Practice; Insurance Defense; Personal Injury; Product Liability Law; Real Estate Law; Workers Compensation

ALLEN, W. RILEY, P.A.
Orlando, FL .... Civil Trial Practice

ALLEN, YURASEK & MERKLIN
Marysville, OH .... General Practice

ALLEY, RAYMOND A., JR., P.A.
Tampa, FL .... Family Law

ALLISON & BASSETT, L.L.P.
Austin, TX .... Criminal Trial Practice

ALLISON, MACKENZIE, HARTMAN, SOUMBENIOTIS & RUSSELL, LTD.
Carson City, NV .... General Practice

ALLMAN SPRY LEGGETT & CRUMPLER, P.A.
Winston-Salem, NC .... General Practice

ALLOTT, ANN, A PROFESSIONAL CORPORATION
Denver, CO .... Immigration and Naturalization

ALLRED, BACON, HALFHILL, LANDAU & YOUNG, PC
Fairfax, VA .... General Practice

ALLRED, JOEL M., P.C.
Salt Lake City, UT .... Appellate Practice; Aviation Law; Civil Trial Practice; Medical Malpractice; Personal Injury; Product Liability Law

ALLRED LAW FIRM, THE
Jackson, MS .... Insurance Defense

ALPER & MCCULLOCH
San Francisco, CA .... Civil Trial Practice; Commercial Litigation

ALPERT, BARKER & RODEMS, P.A.
Tampa, FL .... Civil Trial Practice; Commercial Litigation; General Practice; Insurance Defense; Securities Law

ALPERT, BUTLER & SANDERS, P.C.
West Orange, NJ .... Antitrust Law; Banking Law; Commercial Litigation; Communications Law; Trademark, Copyright and Unfair Competition

ALSCHULER GROSSMAN STEIN & KAHAN LLP
Los Angeles, CA .... General Practice

AL-SHUBAIKI, TORKI A., LEGAL ADVISORS
Riyadh, Saudi Arabia .... General Practice

ALSTON & JONES
Jackson, MS .... Antitrust Law; Civil Trial Practice; Communications Law; General Practice; Natural Resources Law; Tax Law

ALTHEIMER & GRAY
Chicago, IL .... General Practice

ALTHOUSE & MCDONOUGH
Upland, CA .... Business Law; Civil Trial Practice; General Practice; Trust and Estates, Wills and Probate

ALTICK & CORWIN CO., L.P.A.
Dayton, OH .... General Practice

ALTMAN, JAMES J.
New Port Richey, FL .... Trust and Estates, Wills and Probate

ALTMAN, LAWRENCE J.
Chesterfield, MO .... Labor and Employment Law

ALTMAN, D. DAVID CO., A LEGAL PROFESSIONAL ASSOCIATION
Cincinnati, OH .... Environmental Law

ALTMAN, KRITZER & LEVICK, P.C.
Atlanta, GA .... General Practice; Real Estate Law; Tax Law

ALTON, WALTER G., JR., & ASSOCIATES, P.C.
New York, NY .... Medical Malpractice; Personal Injury

ALVARADO, SMITH & SANCHEZ, A PROFESSIONAL CORPORATION
Los Angeles, CA .... Business Law; Civil Trial Practice; Commercial Litigation; Corporate Law; Environmental Law; International Business Law; Real Estate Law

ALVERSON, TAYLOR, MORTENSEN, NELSON & SANDERS
Las Vegas, NV .... Administrative Law; Banking Law; Bankruptcy Law; Business Law; Civil Trial Practice; Commercial Law; Commercial Litigation; Construction Law; Immigration and Naturalization; Insurance Defense; International Business Law; Medical Malpractice; Municipal Bond/Public Authority Financing; Real Estate Law; Trust and Estates, Wills and Probate

AMADO, HONEY KESSLER
Beverly Hills, CA .... Appellate Practice

AMBROSE, WILSON, GRIMM & DURAND
Knoxville, TN .... Civil Trial Practice; General Practice; Insurance Defense

AMELUNG, WULFF & WILLENBROCK, P.C.
St. Louis, MO .... Insurance Defense

AMES & AMES
Onancock, VA .... General Practice

AMLONG & AMLONG, P.A.
Fort Lauderdale, FL .... Family Law; Labor and Employment Law

AMSTER, ROTHSTEIN & EBENSTEIN
New York, NY .... Patent, Trademark, Copyright and Unfair Competition

AMUNDSEN, MOORE & TORPY
Tallahassee, FL .... Environmental Law; Health Care Law

ANAPOL, SCHWARTZ, WEISS, COHAN, FELDMAN AND SMALLEY, P.C.
Philadelphia, PA .... Civil Trial Practice; Commercial Litigation; Environmental Law; Medical Malpractice; Personal Injury; Professional Liability; Toxic Torts

ANCEL & DUNLAP, LLP
Indianapolis, IN .... Bankruptcy Law

ANDERLINI, FINKELSTEIN & EMERICK, A PROFESSIONAL CORPORATION
San Mateo, CA .... Commercial Litigation; Personal Injury

ANDERSEN, BERKSHIRE, LAURITSEN & BROWER
Omaha, NE .... General Practice; Labor and Employment Law

ANDERSEN, DAVIDSON & TATE, P.C.
Lawrenceville, GA .... Banking Law; Business Law; Civil Trial Practice; Family Law; General Practice; Real Estate Law

ANDERSON, JEFFREY C. LAW OFFICES OF
San Antonio, TX .... Medical Malpractice

ANDERSON, MICHAEL J.
Sacramento, CA .... Trust and Estates, Wills and Probate

ANDERSON, ABLON, LEWIS & GALE, LLP
Los Angeles, CA .... Commercial Litigation; Insurance Defense; Real Estate Law

ANDERSON, ADLER, COHEN & HARVEY LLP
Boston, MA....Civil Trial Practice; Labor and Employment Law; Medical Malpractice; Product Liability Law

ANDERSON & ASSOCIATES, P.A.
Columbia, SC....Bankruptcy Law

ANDERSON, BRODY, LEVINSON, WEISER & HORWITZ, P.A.
Phoenix, AZ....General Practice; Real Estate Law

ANDERSON, COE & KING, L.L.P.
Baltimore, MD....Civil Trial Practice; Product Liability Law

ANDERSON, DANIEL & COXE
Wrightsville Beach, NC....Insurance Defense

ANDERSON, GALLOWAY & LUCCHESE, A PROFESSIONAL CORPORATION
Walnut Creek, CA....Civil Trial Practice; Insurance Defense; Medical Malpractice; Product Liability Law

ANDERSON & GILBERT
St. Louis, MO....Civil Trial Practice; General Practice

ANDERSON, JOHNSON, LAWRENCE, BUTLER & BOCK
Fayetteville, NC....Insurance Defense

ANDERSON KILL & OLICK, L.L.P.
Washington, DC....Civil Trial Practice; General Practice

ANDERSON KILL & OLICK, P.C.
New York, NY....Antitrust Law; Civil Trial Practice

ANDERSON, MURPHY & HOPKINS, L.L.P.
Little Rock, AR....Insurance Defense; Medical Malpractice; Product Liability Law; Workers Compensation

ANDERSON & QUINN
Rockville, MD....Civil Trial Practice; Commercial Litigation; General Practice; Insurance Defense; Medical Malpractice; Personal Injury; Product Liability Law; Workers Compensation

ANDERSON, SHANNON, O'BRIEN, RICE & BERTZ
Stevens Point, WI....General Practice

ANDERSON & STEVENS, P.A.
Jacksonville, FL....Tax Law; Trust and Estates, Wills and Probate

ANDERSON, THOMAS T., P.C.
Indio, CA....General Practice

ANDERSON, TIMOTHY G., P.A.
Tampa, FL....Civil Trial Practice; Personal Injury; Product Liability Law

ANDERSON, WALKER & REICHERT, LLP
Macon, GA....General Practice; Insurance Defense; Tax Law; Trust and Estates, Wills and Probate

ANDERSON, ZEIGLER, DISHAROON, GALLAGHER & GRAY, PROFESSIONAL CORPORATION
Santa Rosa, CA....Business Law; Corporate Law; General Practice; Tax Law; Trust and Estates, Wills and Probate

ANDRADE & ASSOCIATES
Irvine, CA....Construction Law; Insurance Defense; Labor and Employment Law

ANDRE, BLAUSTEIN & GREEN, L.L.P.
Atlanta, GA....Trust and Estates, Wills and Probate

ANDRE, MORRIS & BUTTERY, A PROFESSIONAL LAW CORPORATION
San Luis Obispo, CA....Business Law; Civil Trial Practice; Corporate Law; Environmental Law; Labor and Employment Law; Land Use Law; Mergers and Acquisitions; Real Estate Law; Trust and Estates, Wills and Probate

ANDRES & BERGER, A PROFESSIONAL CORPORATION
Haddonfield, NJ....Medical Malpractice

ANDREWS, SALLY S.
Houston, TX....Trust and Estates, Wills and Probate

ANDREWS DAVIS LEGG BIXLER MILSTEN & PRICE, A PROFESSIONAL CORPORATION
Oklahoma City, OK....Antitrust Law; Banking Law; Bankruptcy Law; Civil Trial Practice; General Practice; Health Care Law; Labor and Employment Law; Real Estate Law; Securities Law; Tax Law; Trust and Estates, Wills and Probate

ANDREWS & KURTH L.L.P.
Los Angeles, CA....General Practice
Washington, DC....General Practice
New York, NY....General Practice
Dallas, TX....General Practice
Houston, TX....General Practice

ANDREWS LAW OFFICES
Syracuse, NY....Civil Trial Practice; Insurance Defense; Product Liability Law

ANDRUS, SCEALES, STARKE & SAWALL, LLP
Milwaukee, WI....Patent, Trademark, Copyright and Unfair Competition

ANESI, FRANK J.
Durango, CO....Commercial Law; General Practice; Real Estate Law

ANESI, OZMON, RODIN, NOVAK & KOHEN, LTD.
Chicago, IL....Civil Trial Practice; Personal Injury; Workers Compensation

ANGELO, KILDAY & KILDUFF
Sacramento, CA....Civil Rights; Labor and Employment Law

ANGINO & ROVNER, P.C.
Harrisburg, PA....Appellate Practice; Civil Trial Practice; Medical Malpractice; Personal Injury; Product Liability Law; Professional Liability

ANGLE, CARLSON, GOLDRICK & ROBERTS
Santa Barbara, CA....Appellate Practice; Bankruptcy Law; Commercial Litigation; Family Law; Personal Injury; Real Estate Law; Trust and Estates, Wills and Probate

ANGLE, MURPHY, VALENTINO & CAMPBELL, P.C.
York, NE....General Practice

ANGONES, HUNTER, MCCLURE, LYNCH & WILLIAMS, P.A.
Miami, FL....Civil Trial Practice; General Practice; Insurance Defense; Medical Malpractice

ANNINO, DRAPER & MOORE, P.C.
Springfield, MA....Construction Law; Elder Law; Environmental Law; Health Care Law; Real Estate Law

ANSBACHER, BARRY B., P.A.
Jacksonville, FL....Real Estate Law

ANSPACH & ASSOCIATES
Chicago, IL....Environmental Law

ANSPACH & SERRAINO
Toledo, OH....General Practice

ANSTANDIG, MCDYER, BURDETTE & YURCON, P.C.
Pittsburgh, PA....Civil Trial Practice; General Practice; Insurance Defense

ANTHENELLI & OTWAY
Salisbury, MD....Civil Trial Practice; Criminal Trial Practice; Personal Injury

ANTHONY, ANDREW J., P.A.
Miami, FL....Civil Rights; Insurance Defense; Personal Injury; Product Liability Law

ANTHONY & CARLSON, LLP
Oakland, CA....Civil Trial Practice; Insurance Defense; Labor and Employment Law; Medical Malpractice; Personal Injury; Professional Liability

ANTIN, MICHAEL, A LAW CORPORATION
Los Angeles, CA....Employment Benefits Law; Tax Law; Trust and Estates, Wills and Probate

ANTON, BRUCE
Dallas, TX....Criminal Trial Practice

ANTONELLI, TERRY, STOUT & KRAUS, LLP
Arlington, VA....Intellectual Property Law; Patent, Trademark, Copyright and Unfair Competition

ANWYL, SCOFFIELD, STEPP & UNIVERSAL
Sacramento, CA....Insurance Defense

ANZALONE LAW OFFICES
Wilkes-Barre, PA....Personal Injury

APFELBAUM, APFELBAUM & APFELBAUM
Sunbury, PA....Business Law; Trust and Estates, Wills and Probate

APICELLA AND TRAPP
Cleveland, OH....Medical Malpractice; Personal Injury

APPLE AND APPLE, A PROFESSIONAL CORPORATION
Pittsburgh, PA....Bankruptcy Law; Commercial Law; Creditors Rights

APRUZZESE, MCDERMOTT, MASTRO & MURPHY, A PROFESSIONAL CORPORATION
Liberty Corner, NJ....Commercial Law; Labor and Employment Law
Newark, NJ....Commercial Law; Labor and Employment Law
Springfield, NJ....Commercial Law; Labor and Employment Law

ARAGON, RAYMOND GEORGE
Chula Vista, CA....Criminal Trial Practice

ARAGON, BURLINGTON, WEIL & CROCKETT, P.A.
Miami, FL....Commercial Litigation; Criminal Trial Practice

ARBES, JAKE
Atlanta, GA .... Appellate Practice; Criminal Trial Practice

ARCHER, DAVID G., P.C.
Cartersville, GA .... Civil Trial Practice; Labor and Employment Law; Municipal and Zoning Law

ARENT FOX KINTNER PLOTKIN & KAHN, PLLC
Washington, DC .... Intellectual Property Law

ARESTY INTERNATIONAL LAW OFFICES, P.C.
Boston, MA .... International Business Law

ARIANO, ANDERSON, HARDY & CASTILLO, P.C. A PROFESSIONAL CORPORATION
Elgin, IL .... General Practice

ARKIN, HARRY L., & ASSOCIATES, P.C.
Denver, CO .... Arbitration; Business Law; International Business Law; Trust and Estates, Wills and Probate

ARKIN SCHAFFER & KAPLAN LLP
New York, NY .... Appellate Practice; Arbitration; Civil Trial Practice; Criminal Trial Practice; Labor and Employment Law; Securities Law

ARLEN, ROBERT M., P.A.
Delray Beach, FL .... Tax Law; Trust and Estates, Wills and Probate

ARMBRECHT, JACKSON, DEMOUY, CROWE, HOLMES & REEVES, L.L.C.
Mobile, AL .... Administrative Law; Admiralty/Maritime Law; Antitrust Law; Banking Law; Bankruptcy Law; Business Law; Civil Trial Practice; Commercial Litigation; Employment Benefits Law; General Practice; Insurance Defense; Labor and Employment Law; Medical Malpractice; Natural Resources Law; Securities Law; Tax Law

ARMOR, G. W.
Laverne, OK .... Trust and Estates, Wills and Probate

ARMSTRONG, E. ALAN
Atlanta, GA .... Aviation Law

ARMSTRONG ALLEN PREWITT GENTRY JOHNSTON & HOLMES, PLLC
Memphis, TN .... Antitrust Law; Banking Law; Bankruptcy Law; Business Law; Civil Trial Practice; Commercial Law; Commercial Litigation; Communications Law; Computer Law; Employment Benefits Law; Environmental Law; Family Law; General Practice; Health Care Law; Insurance Defense; Labor and Employment Law; Medical Malpractice; Municipal Bond/Public Authority Financing; Personal Injury; Product Liability Law; Real Estate Law; Securities Law; Tax Law; Trademark, Copyright and Unfair Competition; Trust and Estates, Wills and Probate; Workers Compensation

ARMSTRONG & ARMSTRONG, P.A.
Smithfield, NC .... Family Law; Medical Malpractice; Personal Injury

ARMSTRONG, DONOHUE, CEPPOS & VAUGHAN, CHARTERED
Rockville, MD .... Civil Trial Practice; Criminal Trial Practice; Insurance Defense; Medical Malpractice; Personal Injury

ARMSTRONG, GARRISON, LAW CORPORATION
San Diego, CA .... Pension and Profit Sharing; Tax Law

ARMSTRONG & MEJER, P.A.
Miami, FL .... Admiralty/Maritime Law; Business Law; Civil Trial Practice; Insurance Defense

ARMSTRONG TEASDALE LLP
Kansas City, MO .... General Practice
St. Louis, MO .... Antitrust Law; Civil Trial Practice; Environmental Law; General Practice; Labor and Employment Law; Tax Law

ARNETT, DRAPER & HAGOOD
Knoxville, TN .... Civil Trial Practice; General Practice; Labor and Employment Law

ARNOLD, RICHARD P.
Greenbelt, MD .... Criminal Trial Practice

ARNOLD & ANDERSON
Atlanta, GA .... Labor and Employment Law

ARNOLD, ANDERSON & DOVE, P.L.L.P.
Minneapolis, MN .... Business Law; Civil Trial Practice; Family Law; General Practice; Personal Injury; Real Estate Law

ARNOLD GALLAGHER SAYDACK PERCELL & ROBERTS, P.C.
Eugene, OR .... General Practice

ARNOLD & PORTER
Washington, DC .... General Practice

ARNOLD WHITE & DURKEE, A PROFESSIONAL CORPORATION
Menlo Park, CA .... Patent, Trademark, Copyright and Unfair Competition
Washington, DC .... Patent, Trademark, Copyright and Unfair Competition
Chicago, IL .... Patent, Trademark, Copyright and Unfair Competition
Minneapolis, MN .... Patent, Trademark, Copyright and Unfair Competition
Austin, TX .... Patent, Trademark, Copyright and Unfair Competition
Houston, TX .... Patent, Trademark, Copyright and Unfair Competition

ARONBERG GOLDGEHN DAVIS & GARMISA
Chicago, IL .... Appellate Practice; Banking Law; Civil Trial Practice; Commercial Litigation; Corporate Law; Family Law; General Practice; Health Care Law; Insurance Defense; Labor and Employment Law; Real Estate Law; Trust and Estates, Wills and Probate

ARONSOHN WEINER, A PROFESSIONAL CORPORATION
Hackensack, NJ .... Commercial Litigation; Family Law

ARONSON, ROBERT H.
Chicago, IL .... Criminal Trial Practice

ARSENEAULT & FASSETT
Chatham, NJ .... Appellate Practice; Civil Trial Practice; Criminal Trial Practice

ARTER & HADDEN LLP
Los Angeles, CA .... General Practice
Washington, DC .... General Practice
Cleveland, OH .... General Practice; Labor and Employment Law; Tax Law
Columbus, OH .... General Practice

ARTHUR AND PERLMUTTER
Denver, CO .... Creditors Rights

ARTZ, WILLIAM E., A PROFESSIONAL CORPORATION
Arlington, VA .... Medical Malpractice; Personal Injury

ASBILL, JUNKIN & MOFFITT, CHTD.
Washington, DC .... Civil Trial Practice; Criminal Trial Practice

ASHBY & GEDDES
Wilmington, DE .... Civil Trial Practice; General Practice

ASHCRAFT, WILLIAM E., LAW OFFICE, P.A.
Fort Lauderdale, FL .... Real Estate Law

ASHCROFT WILES, LLP
Salem, OR .... Insurance Defense; Trust and Estates, Wills and Probate

ASHE, TANNER, WRIGHT & KELLEY, P.C.
Tuscumbia, AL .... Civil Trial Practice; Insurance Defense; Medical Malpractice; Personal Injury; Product Liability Law; Workers Compensation

ASHLEY, ASHLEY & ARNOLD
Dyersburg, TN .... Construction Law; Government Contracts

ASHMORE, JOSEPH E., JR., P.C.
Dallas, TX .... Banking Law; General Practice; Health Care Law; Trust and Estates, Wills and Probate

ASKER, CHAPP & CLOS, P.C.
Westland, MI .... Business Law; Commercial Litigation; Real Estate Law; Sports and Entertainment Law; Trust and Estates, Wills and Probate

ASKEW & ARCHBOLD, A PROFESSIONAL CORPORATION
Stockton, CA .... Business Law

ASPEY, WATKINS & DIESEL, P.L.L.C.
Flagstaff, AZ .... Criminal Trial Practice; Personal Injury

ASTOR WEISS KAPLAN & ROSENBLUM, LLP
Philadelphia, PA .... Business Law; Commercial Litigation; Family Law; General Practice; Personal Injury; Real Estate Law; Trust and Estates, Wills and Probate

ASTUNO, JOHN JR.
Denver, CO .... Medical Malpractice; Personal Injury

ASWAD & INGRAHAM
Binghamton, NY .... Civil Trial Practice; Criminal Trial Practice; Labor and Employment Law; Medical Malpractice; Real Estate Law

ATCHISON, CROSBY, SAAD & BEEBE, P.C.
Mobile, AL .... Business Law; Civil Trial Practice; Construction Law; Corporate Law; Environmental Law; Personal Injury; Product Liability Law; Toxic Torts

ATCHLEY, RUSSELL, WALDROP & HLAVINKA, L.L.P.
Texarkana, TX .... Civil Trial Practice; General Practice

ATER WYNNE LLP
Portland, OR............General Practice

ATES & ASSOCIATES, A PROFESSIONAL LAW CORPORATION
New Orleans, LA............General Practice

ATHERTON & ALLEN
Chula Vista, CA............General Practice; Trust and Estates, Wills and Probate

ATHERTON & HUTH
Emporia, KS............General Practice

ATKINS & COHEN
Philadelphia, PA............Civil Trial Practice

ATKINSON, HAMILL & BARROWCLOUGH, P.C.
Phoenix, AZ............Bankruptcy Law; Commercial Litigation; Real Estate Law

ATKINSON, HASKINS, NELLIS, BOUDREAUX, HOLEMAN, PHIPPS & BRITTINGHAM, A PROFESSIONAL CORPORATION
Tulsa, OK............Antitrust Law; Appellate Practice; Aviation Law; Bankruptcy Law; Business Law; Civil Rights; Civil Trial Practice; Commercial Litigation; Environmental Law; Insurance Defense; Medical Malpractice; Personal Injury; Product Liability Law

ATKINSON & KELSEY, P.A.
Albuquerque, NM............Family Law

ATKINSON, PERRY, ATKINSON & BALHOFF, L.L.C.
Baton Rouge, LA............Environmental Law; Insurance Defense; Personal Injury

ATLAS & HALL, L.L.P.
McAllen, TX............General Practice

ATLASS PROFESSIONAL CORPORATION
Denver, CO............Tax Law; Trust and Estates, Wills and Probate

ATLEE, HALL & BROOKHART, L.L.P.
Lancaster, PA............Medical Malpractice; Personal Injury; Product Liability Law

ATTERBURY & RILEY, S.C.
Madison, WI............Medical Malpractice; Personal Injury; Product Liability Law

ATWOOD & CHERNY
Boston, MA............Civil Trial Practice; Family Law

ATWOOD, MALONE, TURNER & SABIN, A PROFESSIONAL ASSOCIATION
Roswell, NM............Insurance Defense; Medical Malpractice

ATWOOD, RONALD W., P.C.
Portland, OR............Workers Compensation

AUBERT & PAJARES, L.L.C.
Covington, LA............Insurance Defense; Product Liability Law

AUERBACH, MARSHALL J., & ASSOCIATES, LTD.
Chicago, IL............Family Law

AUERBACH, PHILIP G., A PROFESSIONAL CORPORATION
Red Bank, NJ............Appellate Practice; Civil Trial Practice; Criminal Trial Practice; General Practice; Medical Malpractice; Personal Injury; Product Liability Law

AUGUST & KULUNAS, P.A.
West Palm Beach, FL............Tax Law; Trust and Estates, Wills and Probate

AULTMAN, TYNER, RUFFIN & YARBOROUGH, LTD., A PROFESSIONAL LAW CORPORATION
Columbia, MS............Admiralty/Maritime Law; Banking Law; Civil Trial Practice; Commercial Law; Environmental Law; General Practice; Insurance Defense
Gulfport, MS............Admiralty/Maritime Law; Banking Law; Civil Trial Practice; Commercial Law; Environmental Law; General Practice; Insurance Defense
Hattiesburg, MS............Admiralty/Maritime Law; Banking Law; Civil Trial Practice; Commercial Law; Environmental Law; General Practice; Insurance Defense

AUSLEY & ALGERT, L.L.P.
Austin, TX............Family Law

AUSLEY & MCMULLEN, P.A.
Tallahassee, FL............General Practice

AUSTIN, PEIRCE & SMITH, P.C.
Aspen, CO............Appellate Practice; Civil Trial Practice; General Practice; Municipal and Zoning Law; Real Estate Law

AUSTIN & PEPPERMAN
Leesburg, FL............Appellate Practice; Civil Trial Practice; General Practice

AUTREY, D. ROBERT, JR., P.C.
Marietta, GA............Civil Trial Practice

AVERY & ASSOCIATES
San Francisco, CA............Tax Law; Trust and Estates, Wills and Probate

AVERY, WHIGHAM & WINESETT, P.A.
Fort Myers, FL............Trust and Estates, Wills and Probate

AVIS & AVIS, P.A.
Palm Beach, FL............Commercial Litigation; Corporate Law; Real Estate Law

AWSUMB, R. A., & ASSOCIATES, PLC
St. Paul, MN............Personal Injury; Product Liability Law

AXE, JOHN R. AND ASSOCIATES
Grosse Pointe Farms, MI............Municipal Bond/Public Authority Financing

AXELROD, GOODMAN, STEINER & BAZELON
Chicago, IL............Transportation Law

AXLEY BRYNELSON, LLP
Madison, WI............Civil Trial Practice; Commercial Law; Environmental Law; General Practice; Insurance Defense; Medical Malpractice; Personal Injury; Trust and Estates, Wills and Probate

AYABE, CHONG, NISHIMOTO, SIA & NAKAMURA
Honolulu, HI............Construction Law; Insurance Defense; Legal Malpractice; Medical Malpractice; Personal Injury; Real Estate Law

AYCOCK, HORNE & COLEMAN
Franklin, LA............General Practice

AYE LAW FIRM, P.A.
Tampa, FL............Labor and Employment Law

AYRES, JENKINS, GORDY & ALMAND, P.A.
Ocean City, MD............Civil Trial Practice; Criminal Trial Practice

AZAR & AZAR, L.L.C.
Montgomery, AL............General Practice

BABIN, SEEGER, CROW & MANWELL, LLP
Santa Rosa, CA............Business Law; Insurance Defense

BABST, CALLAND, CLEMENTS AND ZOMNIR, A PROFESSIONAL CORPORATION
Pittsburgh, PA............Commercial Law; Construction Law; Environmental Law; Labor and Employment Law; Municipal and Zoning Law

BACALSKI, BYRNE & KOSKA
San Diego, CA............Civil Trial Practice; General Practice

BACHMAN & LAPOINTE, P.C.
New Haven, CT............Patent, Trademark, Copyright and Unfair Competition

BACHMANN, HESS, BACHMANN & GARDEN, P.L.L.C.
Wheeling, WV............General Practice; Insurance Defense; Personal Injury

BACINO, BIRGER GREG, APC, THE LAW OFFICES OF
San Diego, CA............Aviation Law; Elder Law; Personal Injury; Product Liability Law; Toxic Torts

BACKER & BACKER, A PROFESSIONAL CORPORATION
Indianapolis, IN............Business Law; Commercial Law; Construction Law; Real Estate Law

BACKES & HILL
Trenton, NJ............Civil Trial Practice; General Practice

BACKMAN & BLUMEL, P.S.
Spokane, WA............Medical Malpractice; Personal Injury

BACKUS, LELAND EUGENE, & ASSOCIATES LTD.
Las Vegas, NV............Construction Law; Insurance Defense; International Business Law

BACON & DEAR, PLC
Phoenix, AZ............Employment Benefits Law; Immigration and Naturalization

BACON & MILLS, LLP
Brea, CA............Corporate Law; Trust and Estates, Wills and Probate
Los Angeles, CA............Business Law; Insurance Defense

BADDOUR, PARKER & HINE, PROFESSIONAL CORPORATION
Goldsboro, NC............General Practice

BADGER, DAVID R., P.A.
Charlotte, NC............Bankruptcy Law

BADGER, DOLAN, PARKER & COHEN
Boston, MA............Commercial Law; Insurance Defense; Product Liability Law

BADGLEY - MULLINS
Seattle, WA .... Commercial Litigation

BADIAK WILL & RUDDY
New York, NY .... Admiralty/Maritime Law; Aviation Law; Civil Trial Practice; General Practice; Insurance Defense; Transportation Law

BAER MARKS & UPHAM LLP
New York, NY .... Civil Trial Practice; General Practice

BAGGETT, MCCALL & BURGESS, A PROFESSIONAL LAW CORPORATION
Lake Charles, LA .... Personal Injury; Toxic Torts

BAI, POLLOCK AND COYNE, P.C.
Bridgeport, CT .... Civil Trial Practice; Insurance Defense; Medical Malpractice; Personal Injury; Product Liability Law

BAILEY & BROWN
Sacramento, CA .... Insurance Defense

BAILEY & DIXON, L.L.P.
Raleigh, NC .... Appellate Practice; Civil Trial Practice; Insurance Defense; Personal Injury; Product Liability Law; Public Utilities Law

BAILEY LAW FIRM
Mountain Home, AR .... Medical Malpractice

BAILEY & MYERS, P.A.
Maitland, FL .... Medical Malpractice; Personal Injury; Product Liability Law

BAILEY, PATTERSON, CADDELL, HART, MILLIKEN & BAILEY, P.A.
Charlotte, NC .... Civil Trial Practice; Criminal Trial Practice; Personal Injury; Tax Law

BAILEY & PETERSON, P.C.
Denver, CO .... General Practice

BAILEY, RALPH, P.A.
Greenville, SC .... Patent, Trademark, Copyright and Unfair Competition

BAILEY & STOCK
Cheyenne, WY .... Civil Trial Practice

BAIN, TROY E.
Shreveport, LA .... Civil Trial Practice; Medical Malpractice; Personal Injury

BAIN & MCRAE
Lillington, NC .... General Practice

BAINTON MCCARTHY & SIEGEL, LLC
New York, NY .... Civil Trial Practice

BAIRD, BAIRD, BAIRD AND JONES, P.S.C.
Pikeville, KY .... General Practice

BAIRD, WILLIAMS, DAVIS & SMITH
Phoenix, AZ .... Commercial Litigation; Real Estate Law

BAISE, MILLER & FREER, P.C.
Washington, DC .... Environmental Law

BAKAS, JOHN W. JR.
Tampa, FL .... Commercial Litigation; Construction Law; Government Contracts

BAKER, J. NORMAN
Mountain View, CA .... Family Law

BAKER, BAKER & TWOMEY, P.A.
Baltimore, MD .... Civil Trial Practice

BAKER BOTTS, L.L.P.
Washington, DC .... Administrative Law; Business Law; Civil Trial Practice; Commercial Law; Environmental Law; General Practice; Natural Resources Law; Patent, Trademark, Copyright and Unfair Competition; Tax Law; Trademark, Copyright and Unfair Competition
New York, NY .... Business Law; Civil Trial Practice; Commercial Law; General Practice; Patent, Trademark, Copyright and Unfair Competition; Tax Law; Trademark, Copyright and Unfair Competition
Austin, TX .... Administrative Law; Banking Law; Bankruptcy Law; Business Law; Civil Trial Practice; Commercial Law; Environmental Law; General Practice; Patent, Trademark, Copyright and Unfair Competition; Real Estate Law; Trademark, Copyright and Unfair Competition
Dallas, TX .... Administrative Law; Antitrust Law; Banking Law; Bankruptcy Law; Business Law; Civil Trial Practice; Commercial Law; General Practice; Labor and Employment Law; Patent, Trademark, Copyright and Unfair Competition; Personal Injury; Real Estate Law; Trademark, Copyright and Unfair Competition
Houston, TX .... Administrative Law; Admiralty/Maritime Law; Antitrust Law; Banking Law; Bankruptcy Law; Business Law; Civil Trial Practice; Commercial Law; Environmental Law; General Practice; Labor and Employment Law; Patent, Trademark, Copyright and Unfair Competition; Personal Injury; Real Estate Law; Tax Law; Trust and Estates, Wills and Probate

BAKER & BOYAN, P.L.L.C.
High Point, NC .... General Practice

BAKER, CAMPBELL & PARSONS
Nashville, TN .... General Practice

BAKER & DANIELS
Washington, DC .... General Practice
Elkhart, IN .... General Practice
Fort Wayne, IN .... General Practice
Indianapolis, IN .... General Practice
South Bend, IN .... General Practice
Qingdao, China .... General Practice

BAKER, DONELSON, BEARMAN & CALDWELL
Jackson, MS .... Civil Trial Practice; Commercial Litigation; Environmental Law; General Practice; Health Care Law; Insurance Defense; Labor and Employment Law; Tax Law; Trust and Estates, Wills and Probate
Chattanooga, TN .... Commercial Litigation; General Practice; Health Care Law; Immigration and Naturalization; Intellectual Property Law; Labor and Employment Law; Real Estate Law; Securities Law; Tax Law; Trust and Estates, Wills and Probate
Huntsville, TN .... Civil Trial Practice; General Practice
Johnson City, TN .... Civil Trial Practice; Commercial Litigation; General Practice; Labor and Employment Law; Securities Law
Knoxville, TN .... Civil Trial Practice; Environmental Law; General Practice; Securities Law; Tax Law
Memphis, TN .... Banking Law; Bankruptcy Law; Business Law; Civil Trial Practice; Environmental Law; General Practice; Health Care Law; Immigration and Naturalization; Insurance Defense; Labor and Employment Law; Municipal Bond/Public Authority Financing; Securities Law; Tax Law
Nashville, TN .... Antitrust Law; Bankruptcy Law; Civil Trial Practice; Corporate Law; Environmental Law; General Practice; Health Care Law; Labor and Employment Law; Mergers and Acquisitions; Real Estate Law; Securities Law; Tax Law

BAKER, DUBLIKAR, BECK, WILEY & MATHEWS
Canton, OH .... Civil Trial Practice; Insurance Defense

BAKER, ELIZABETH S., P.A., LAW OFFICES OF
Miami, FL .... Family Law

BAKER & HOSTETLER LLP
Long Beach, CA .... Admiralty/Maritime Law; General Practice
Los Angeles, CA .... Admiralty/Maritime Law; Bankruptcy Law; Civil Trial Practice; Environmental Law; General Practice; Labor and Employment Law; Real Estate Law; Trademark, Copyright and Unfair Competition
Denver, CO .... Civil Trial Practice; Environmental Law; General Practice
Washington, DC .... Administrative Law; Antitrust Law; Banking Law; Civil Trial Practice; Communications Law; Environmental Law; General Practice; Labor and Employment Law; Tax Law; Trademark, Copyright and Unfair Competition; Transportation Law
Orlando, FL .... Civil Trial Practice; Construction Law; General Practice; Municipal Bond/Public Authority Financing; Real Estate Law; Tax Law
Cleveland, OH .... Antitrust Law; Banking Law; Bankruptcy Law; Civil Trial Practice; Communications Law; Construction Law; Employment Benefits Law; Environmental Law; General Practice; Immigration and Naturalization; Labor and Employment Law; Municipal Bond/Public Authority Financing; Real Estate Law; Tax Law; Trademark, Copyright and Unfair Competition; Trust and Estates, Wills and Probate
Columbus, OH .... Bankruptcy Law; Civil Trial Practice; Employment Benefits Law; General Practice; Labor and Employment Law; Tax Law; Transportation Law
Houston, TX .... Civil Trial Practice; General Practice

BAKER AND JACOBSON, A PROFESSIONAL CORPORATION
Los Angeles, CA .... Bankruptcy Law; Civil Trial Practice; Construction Law; Real Estate Law

BAKER, JENKINS, JONES & DALY, P.A.
Ahoskie, NC .... Insurance Defense

BAKER, KEENER & NAHRA, LLP
Santa Monica, CA .... Commercial Litigation; Construction Law; Labor and Employment Law; Legal Malpractice; Medical Malpractice; Personal Injury; Product Liability Law; Professional Liability; Toxic Torts

BAKER, LANCIANESE, CAMPBELL & CONATY
Huntington, WV ..... Bankruptcy Law; Creditors Rights; Health Care Law; Insurance Defense; Labor and Employment Law; Medical Malpractice; Product Liability Law; Professional Liability; Real Estate Law; Toxic Torts

BAKER LAW FIRM, THE
Little Rock, AR ..... Civil Trial Practice; Personal Injury

BAKER, MANOCK & JENSEN, A PROFESSIONAL CORPORATION
Fresno, CA ..... General Practice

BAKER & MAXHAM, A PROFESSIONAL CORPORATION
San Diego, CA ..... Patent, Trademark, Copyright and Unfair Competition

BAKER & MCKENZIE
Palo Alto, CA ..... General Practice
San Diego, CA ..... General Practice
San Francisco, CA ..... General Practice
Washington, DC ..... General Practice
Miami, FL ..... General Practice
Chicago, IL ..... General Practice
New York, NY ..... General Practice
Dallas, TX ..... General Practice
Houston, TX ..... General Practice
Toronto, ON, Canada ..... General Practice
Buenos Aires, Argentina ..... General Practice
Melbourne, Victoria, Australia ..... General Practice
Sydney, New South Wales, Australia ..... General Practice
Baku, Azerbaijan ..... General Practice
Manama, Bahrain ..... General Practice
Brussels, Belgium ..... General Practice
Santiago, Chile ..... General Practice
Beijing, China ..... General Practice
Hong Kong, China ..... General Practice
Prague, Czech Republic ..... General Practice
Cairo, Egypt ..... General Practice
Paris, France ..... General Practice
Milan, Italy ..... General Practice
Rome, Italy ..... General Practice
Almaty, Kazakhstan ..... General Practice
Ciudad Juarez, Chihuahua, Mexico ..... General Practice
Mexico, D.F., Mexico ..... General Practice
Monterrey, Nuevo León, Mexico ..... General Practice
Tijuana, Baja California, Mexico ..... General Practice
Moscow, Russia ..... General Practice
St. Petersburg, Russia ..... General Practice
Singapore, Singapore ..... General Practice
Barcelona, Spain ..... General Practice
Madrid, Spain ..... General Practice
Zürich, Switzerland ..... General Practice
Hsinchu, Taiwan ..... General Practice
Taipei, Taiwan ..... General Practice
Bangkok, Thailand ..... General Practice
Kyiv (Kiev), Ukraine ..... General Practice
Caracas, Venezuela ..... General Practice
Valencia, Venezuela ..... General Practice
Hanoi, Vietnam ..... General Practice
Ho Chi Minh City, Vietnam ..... General Practice
Geneva, Switzerland ..... General Practice
Stockholm, Sweden ..... General Practice
Warsaw, Poland ..... General Practice
Berlin, Germany ..... General Practice
Düsseldorf, Germany ..... General Practice
Frankfurt/Main, Germany ..... General Practice
Munich, Germany ..... General Practice

BALCH & BINGHAM LLP
Birmingham, AL ..... General Practice

BALCOMB & GREEN, P.C.
Glenwood Springs, CO ..... General Practice

BALDWIN & HASPEL, L.L.C.
New Orleans, LA ..... Business Law; Product Liability Law; Real Estate Law; Tax Law

BALFOUR MOSS
Regina, SK, Canada ..... Civil Trial Practice; Commercial Law; General Practice

BALISLE & ROBERSON, S.C.
Madison, WI ..... Appellate Practice; Family Law; Trust and Estates, Wills and Probate

BALK, OXFELD, MANDELL & COHEN, A PROFESSIONAL CORPORATION
Newark, NJ ..... General Practice; Labor and Employment Law

BALL, ANDREW D., P.C.
Rockville, MD ..... Trust and Estates, Wills and Probate

BALLARD, ROSENBERG & GOLPER
Universal City, CA ..... Arbitration; Labor and Employment Law

BALLARD SPAHR ANDREWS & INGERSOLL, LLP
Denver, CO ..... Civil Trial Practice; Commercial Law; Environmental Law; General Practice; Municipal Bond/Public Authority Financing; Natural Resources Law; Real Estate Law; Securities Law
Washington, DC ..... General Practice; Municipal Bond/Public Authority Financing; Real Estate Law; Tax Law
Baltimore, MD ..... Banking Law; Bankruptcy Law; Civil Trial Practice; Commercial Law; Real Estate Law
Philadelphia, PA ..... Antitrust Law; Banking Law; Bankruptcy Law; Civil Trial Practice; Commercial Law; Employment Benefits Law; Environmental Law; General Practice; Health Care Law; Labor and Employment Law; Municipal Bond/Public Authority Financing; Real Estate Law; Tax Law; Trust and Estates, Wills and Probate
Salt Lake City, UT ..... Municipal Bond/Public Authority Financing; Real Estate Law

BALL, BALL, MATTHEWS & NOVAK, P.A.
Montgomery, AL ..... Civil Trial Practice; Corporate Law; General Practice; Insurance Defense; Product Liability Law

BALL, BARDEN & BELL, P.A.
Asheville, NC ..... Insurance Defense

BALL, BARTON & HOFFMAN, A PROFESSIONAL ASSOCIATION
Monticello, AR ..... General Practice

BALL, EGGLESTON, BUMBLEBURG, MCBRIDE, WALKEY & STAPLETON, PC
Lafayette, IN ..... Appellate Practice; Civil Trial Practice; General Practice; Insurance Defense; Municipal and Zoning Law; Personal Injury; Real Estate Law; Trust and Estates, Wills and Probate

BALL JANIK LLP
Portland, OR ..... General Practice

BALL & KOONS
Bay Minette, AL ..... Criminal Trial Practice

BALL, MCDONOUGH & ARTZ, P.C.
Binghamton, NY ..... Personal Injury; Real Estate Law

BALL & MOURTON, LTD., PLLC
Fayetteville, AR ..... Business Law; General Practice; Tax Law; Trust and Estates, Wills and Probate

BALLON STOLL BADER & NADLER, P.C.
New York, NY ..... General Practice

BAMBERGER & FEIBLEMAN
Indianapolis, IN ..... Bankruptcy Law; Civil Rights; Commercial Law; International Business Law

BANDER, FOX-ISICOFF & ASSOCIATES, P.A.
Miami, FL ..... Immigration and Naturalization

BANGEL, BANGEL & BANGEL, L.L.P.
Portsmouth, VA ..... Personal Injury

BANGS, MCCULLEN, BUTLER, FOYE & SIMMONS, L.L.P.
Rapid City, SD ..... Civil Trial Practice; Corporate Law; General Practice; Health Care Law; Labor and Employment Law; Personal Injury; Trust and Estates, Wills and Probate

BANKS & UNDERHILL, P.C.
Portland, OR ..... Business Law; Civil Rights; Professional Liability; Securities Law

BANKSTON & RICHARDSON, L.L.P.
Austin, TX ..... Appellate Practice; Civil Trial Practice

BANNER & WITCOFF, LTD.
Washington, DC ..... Patent, Trademark, Copyright and Unfair Competition; Trademark, Copyright and Unfair Competition
Chicago, IL ..... Patent, Trademark, Copyright and Unfair Competition; Trademark, Copyright and Unfair Competition
Boston, MA ..... Patent, Trademark, Copyright and Unfair Competition
Portland, OR ..... Patent, Trademark, Copyright and Unfair Competition

BANNIGAN & KELLY, P.A.
St. Paul, MN ..... Civil Trial Practice; Labor and Employment Law; Municipal and Zoning Law

BANTA, HOYT, EVERALL & FARRINGTON, L.L.C.
Englewood, CO ....Civil Trial Practice; General Practice; Real Estate Law

BANTZ, GOSCH, CREMER, PETERSON & SOMMERS
Aberdeen, SD ....Banking Law; Business Law; Insurance Defense

BANZET, BANZET & THOMPSON
Warrenton, NC ....General Practice

BARASH & STOERZBACH, P.C.
Galesburg, IL ....General Practice; Trust and Estates, Wills and Probate

BARBAS WEED KOENIG NUÑEZ & WHEELEY
Tampa, FL ....Personal Injury; Workers Compensation

BARBER, JAMES C. LAW OFFICES OF
Dallas, TX ....Medical Malpractice; Personal Injury

BARBER, EMERSON, SPRINGER, ZINN & MURRAY, L.C.
Lawrence, KS ....General Practice

BARBER, HAMILTON & SHOULDERS
Evansville, IN ....General Practice

BARBER, MCCASKILL, JONES & HALE, P.A.
Little Rock, AR ....Commercial Law; General Practice; Health Care Law; Insurance Defense; Legal Malpractice; Medical Malpractice; Personal Injury; Product Liability Law; Toxic Torts; Trust and Estates, Wills and Probate; Workers Compensation

BARBERA, CLAPPER, BEENER, RULLO & MELVIN
Somerset, PA ....General Practice

BARBIERI, CHRISTINA J. & ASSOCIATES
Philadelphia, PA ....Workers Compensation

BARBOSA GARCIA LLP
Los Angeles, CA ....Business Law; Commercial Litigation; Construction Law; Eminent Domain; Labor and Employment Law; Mergers and Acquisitions; Municipal and Zoning Law

BARCLAY & GOERING, P.C.
Phoenix, AZ ....Health Care Law

BARDENWERPER & LOBB, PLLC
Louisville, KY ....Land Use Law; Municipal and Zoning Law; Real Estate Law

BARFORD, BURNS F. JR.
Valatie, NY ....General Practice; Municipal and Zoning Law; Real Estate Law; Trust and Estates, Wills and Probate

BARGER, HERMANSEN, MCKIBBEN & VILLARREAL, L.L.P.
Corpus Christi, TX ....Appellate Practice; Civil Trial Practice; Insurance Defense

BARHAM & ARCENEAUX, A PROFESSIONAL LAW CORPORATION
New Orleans, LA ....Appellate Practice; Civil Trial Practice

BARISH, MARVIN I., LAW OFFICES, A PROF. CORP.
Philadelphia, PA ....Admiralty/Maritime Law; Civil Trial Practice; Medical Malpractice; Personal Injury; Transportation Law

BARKATS & ASSOCIATES, CHARTERED, ATTORNEYS AND COUNSELORS AT LAW
Washington, DC ....Aviation Law; Computer Law; Intellectual Property Law; International Business Law; Trademark, Copyright and Unfair Competition

BARKER, BROWN, BUSBY, CHRISMAN & THOMAS, A PROFESSIONAL CORPORATION
Las Vegas, NV ....Civil Trial Practice; Commercial Litigation; Insurance Defense; Labor and Employment Law

BARKER THOMAS & WALTERS, A PROFESSIONAL LAW CORPORATION
San Diego, CA ....Commercial Litigation; Construction Law; Labor and Employment Law

BARKLEY, ALICE SUET YEE
San Francisco, CA ....Environmental Law; Land Use Law

BARKLEY & KENNEDY, CHARTERED
Rockville, MD ....Bankruptcy Law; Commercial Litigation; Creditors Rights

BARLEY, SNYDER, SENFT & COHEN, LLC
Chambersburg, PA ....Business Law; General Practice; Health Care Law
Hanover, PA ....Commercial Litigation; General Practice; Labor and Employment Law
Harrisburg, PA ....Commercial Litigation; General Practice; Tax Law
Lancaster, PA ....Commercial Litigation; General Practice; Health Care Law
Reading, PA ....General Practice; Intellectual Property Law; Labor and Employment Law
York, PA ....Commercial Litigation; General Practice; Health Care Law

BARLOW & DERBY
Troy, MI ....Business Law; Health Care Law; Labor and Employment Law

BARLOW AND HARDTNER L.C.
Shreveport, LA ....Administrative Law; Appellate Practice; Business Law; Civil Trial Practice; Commercial Law; Communications Law; Construction Law; Environmental Law; General Practice; Insurance Defense; Land Use Law; Natural Resources Law; Product Liability Law; Public Utilities Law; Real Estate Law; Tax Law; Transportation Law; Trust and Estates, Wills and Probate

BARMANN, KRAMER & BOHLEN, P.C.
Kankakee, IL ....Commercial Law; Commercial Litigation; General Practice; Health Care Law; Personal Injury

BARNES, ALFORD, STORK & JOHNSON, L.L.P.
Columbia, SC ....Appellate Practice; Arbitration; Banking Law; Construction Law; General Practice; Insurance Defense; Legal Malpractice; Medical Malpractice; Product Liability Law; Real Estate Law; Tax Law; Workers Compensation

BARNES, CROSBY, FITZGERALD & ZEMAN LLP
Irvine, CA ....Civil Trial Practice

BARNES, F. SMITH, P.C.
Oklahoma City, OK ....Business Law; Trust and Estates, Wills and Probate

BARNES & THORNBURG
Washington, DC ....General Practice
Chicago, IL ....Bankruptcy Law; Creditors Rights; General Practice
Elkhart, IN ....Bankruptcy Law; Creditors Rights; General Practice
Fort Wayne, IN ....Bankruptcy Law; Creditors Rights; General Practice
Indianapolis, IN ....Bankruptcy Law; Creditors Rights; General Practice
South Bend, IN ....Bankruptcy Law; Creditors Rights; General Practice

BARNETT, LYNN D.
St. Louis, MO ....Workers Compensation

BARNETT, BARCLAY & SPRINGMANN, P.A.
Orlando, FL ....Criminal Trial Practice; Family Law

BARNETT • MATTICE
Fairfield, CA ....Personal Injury

BARNETT, SCOTT F., CHARTERED
Tampa, FL ....Trust and Estates, Wills and Probate

BARNEY, GROSSMAN, DUBOW & MARCUS
Ithaca, NY ....General Practice

BARNHART, STEVEN D., & ASSOCIATES, P.C.
Atlanta, GA ....Civil Trial Practice; Labor and Employment Law

BARNWELL WHALEY PATTERSON & HELMS, LLC
Charleston, SC ....Civil Trial Practice; Construction Law; Health Care Law; Insurance Defense; Labor and Employment Law; Product Liability Law

BAROKAS, MARTIN, AHLERS & TOMLINSON
Seattle, WA ....Business Law; Construction Law

BARON, SAR, GOODWIN, GILL & LOHR
Sioux City, IA ....General Practice

BAROUSSE & CRATON
Crowley, LA ....Civil Trial Practice; General Practice

BARR, BURT, & ASSOCIATES, L.L.P.
Dallas, TX ....Insurance Defense; International Business Law

BARR, DUGAN, & ASSOCIATES
Redding, CA ....Aviation Law; Civil Trial Practice; Personal Injury; Product Liability Law

BARR, JOSEPH J., JR., A PROFESSIONAL CORPORATION
San Diego, CA ....Civil Trial Practice; Insurance Defense

BARR, MURMAN, TONELLI, HERZFELD & RUBIN
Tampa, FL ....Civil Trial Practice; Commercial Litigation; Insurance Defense; Medical Malpractice; Personal Injury; Workers Compensation

BARR, UNGER AND MCINTOSH, L.L.C.
Charleston, SC ....Civil Trial Practice; Criminal Trial Practice

BARRACK, RODOS & BACINE
Philadelphia, PA ....Antitrust Law; Securities Law

BARRAN LIEBMAN LLP
Portland, OR ....Labor and Employment Law

BARRET, HAYNES, MAY, CARTER AND ROARK, P.S.C.
Hazard, KY ....General Practice

BARRETT, DANIEL R. LAW OFFICES OF
Fort Worth, TX ....Medical Malpractice

BARRETT & ASSOCIATES
Cambridge, MA ....Business Law; Mergers and Acquisitions; Securities Law

BARRETT BURKE WILSON CASTLE DAFFIN & FRAPPIER, L.L.P.
Addison, TX....................Banking Law; Bankruptcy Law; Civil Trial Practice; Corporate Law; Real Estate Law

BARRETT & DEACON, A PROFESSIONAL ASSOCIATION
Jonesboro, AR ....Civil Trial Practice; General Practice; Insurance Defense

BARRETT GILMAN & ZIKER
Seattle, WA ....Commercial Litigation; Environmental Law

BARRETT GRAVANTE CARPINELLO & STERN LLP
New York, NY....................Appellate Practice; Civil Trial Practice; Criminal Trial Practice

BARRETT & WEBER, A LEGAL PROFESSIONAL ASSOCIATION
Cincinnati, OH ....Administrative Law; Municipal and Zoning Law; Real Estate Law; Trust and Estates, Wills and Probate

BARRIS, SOTT, DENN & DRIKER, P.L.L.C.
Detroit, MI....................Civil Trial Practice; Real Estate Law

BARRON & BERRY, L.L.P.
Greensboro, NC ....Civil Trial Practice; Medical Malpractice; Personal Injury

BARRON & STADFELD, P.C.
Boston, MA....................Banking Law; Business Law; Civil Trial Practice; Environmental Law; General Practice; Personal Injury; Real Estate Law

BARROW GADDIS GRIFFITH & GRIMM, A PROFESSIONAL CORPORATION
Tulsa, OK....................Bankruptcy Law; Business Law; Civil Trial Practice; Tax Law

BARROW, SIMS & LEE, A PROFESSIONAL CORPORATION
Savannah, GA ....Insurance Defense

BARRY, MCTIERNAN & MOORE
New York, NY....................Civil Trial Practice; Insurance Defense

BARRY, RICHARD, AND SHARON MAH
San Rafael, CA....................Family Law

BARTEL ENG LINN & SCHRODER
Sacramento, CA ....Securities Law; Tax Law

BARTELS & FEUREISEN, LLP
White Plains, NY ....General Practice

BARTHOLOMEW, WASZNICKY & MOLINARO LLP
Sacramento, CA ....Family Law

BARTIMUS, FRICKLETON & PRESLEY, A PROFESSIONAL CORPORATION
Kansas City, MO....................Aviation Law; Health Care Law; Medical Malpractice; Personal Injury; Product Liability Law

BARTKO, ZANKEL, TARRANT & MILLER, PROFESSIONAL CORPORATION
San Francisco, CA ....Civil Trial Practice; Commercial Litigation; Real Estate Law

BARTLETT, BARBARA ANN
Tulsa, OK....................Family Law

BARTLETT, MCDONOUGH, BASTONE & MONAGHAN, LLP
Mineola, NY....................Medical Malpractice; Personal Injury

BARTON, KLUGMAN & OETTING LLP
Los Angeles, CA ....Civil Trial Practice

BARTON, RICHARDSON, CANSECO & WHITNEY, L.L.P.
New Orleans, LA ....Commercial Litigation

BARTON & SCHNEIDER, L.L.P.
San Antonio, TX....................Real Estate Law

BARTON AND STREVER, P.C.
Newport, OR....................Personal Injury

BASILE, PAUL L. JR.
Los Angeles, CA ....Business Law; Tax Law; Trust and Estates, Wills and Probate

BASILE & TESTA, A PROFESSIONAL CORPORATION
Vineland, NJ....................Civil Trial Practice; General Practice

BASKIN, RICHARD J. LAW OFFICES OF
Oakland, CA ....Personal Injury; Product Liability Law

BASKIN, BENNETT & KOMKOV, L.L.P.
Austin, TX ....Commercial Litigation; Construction Law

BASS, SUZANNE
Jacksonville, FL ....Criminal Trial Practice

BASS, BERRY & SIMS PLC
Nashville, TN....................Antitrust Law; Bankruptcy Law; Environmental Law; Health Care Law; Labor and Employment Law; Municipal Bond/Public Authority Financing; Securities Law; Tax Law

BASS & CARLSON, P.A.
Minneapolis, MN ....Personal Injury

BASS, JAMES R., INC., LAW OFFICES OF
San Antonio, TX....................Civil Trial Practice; Family Law; Trust and Estates, Wills and Probate

BASSETT LAW FIRM
Fayetteville, AR ....Civil Trial Practice; General Practice

BASSFORD, LOCKHART, TRUESDELL & BRIGGS, P.A.
Minneapolis, MN....................Civil Trial Practice; Environmental Law; General Practice; Insurance Defense; Personal Injury

BASTEDO STEWART SMITH
Toronto, ON, Canada....................Family Law

BASTIANELLI, BROWN & KELLEY, CHARTERED
Washington, DC....................Admiralty/Maritime Law; Government Contracts

BASTONE ASSOCIATES
Boston, MA....................Immigration and Naturalization

BASYE & GOLDEN
San Mateo, CA....................Trust and Estates, Wills and Probate

BATES, PHILIP A.
Pensacola, FL....................Business Law; Commercial Litigation; Creditors Rights

BATES & CASEY
Fort Worth, TX ....Criminal Trial Practice

BATES MECKLER BULGER & TILSON
Chicago, IL....................Civil Trial Practice; Commercial Law; Insurance Defense; Labor and Employment Law; Product Liability Law

BATHGATE, WEGENER & WOLF, P.C.
Lakewood, NJ ....Civil Trial Practice; Environmental Law; General Practice; Municipal Bond/Public Authority Financing

BATJER & WAGSTAFF, P.C.
Abilene, TX....................General Practice; Insurance Defense

BATSEL, MCKINLEY, ITTERSAGEN, GUNDERSON & BERNTSSON, P.A.
Englewood, FL....................Real Estate Law; Trust and Estates, Wills and Probate
Port Charlotte, FL ....Real Estate Law

BATSON, NOLAN, BRICE, HARVEY & WILLIAMSON, PLLC
Clarksville, TN....................Commercial Litigation; General Practice; Insurance Defense

BATTLE FOWLER LLP
New York, NY....................General Practice

BATZAR & WEINBERG, A PROFESSIONAL CORPORATION
Rockville Centre, NY ....Bankruptcy Law; Commercial Law; Commercial Litigation

BAUDLER, BAUDLER, MAUS & BLAHNIK
Austin, MN....................General Practice
Spring Valley, MN....................General Practice

BAUER, BERNARD K., CO., L.P.A.
Findlay, OH ....Personal Injury

BAUER, CRIDER & PELLEGRINO
Clearwater, FL ....Criminal Trial Practice
Tampa, FL ....Criminal Trial Practice

BAUGHER, METTLER & SHELTON
Palm Beach, FL....................Real Estate Law; Tax Law; Trust and Estates, Wills and Probate

BAUM & ASSOCIATES
Bloomfield Hills, MI....................Criminal Trial Practice

BAUMEISTER & SAMUELS, P.C.
Morristown, NJ ....Aviation Law; Civil Trial Practice; Environmental Law; Medical Malpractice; Personal Injury; Product Liability Law; Toxic Torts
New York, NY....................Aviation Law; Civil Trial Practice; Environmental Law; Medical Malpractice; Personal Injury; Product Liability Law; Toxic Torts

BAUM, HEDLUND, ARISTEI, GUILFORD & DOWNEY, A PROFESSIONAL CORPORATION
Los Angeles, CA....................Aviation Law; Personal Injury; Product Liability Law

Washington, DC .... Aviation Law; Personal Injury; Product Liability Law

BAUS, HAMMOND & DALY, L.L.P.
New Orleans, LA .... Insurance Defense

BAVOL, BUSH & SISCO, P.L.L.C.
Tampa, FL .... Commercial Litigation; Medical Malpractice; Product Liability Law

BAXLEY, DILLARD, DAUPHIN & MCKNIGHT
Birmingham, AL .... Administrative Law; Criminal Trial Practice; Personal Injury

BAXTER, JENSEN, PAYNE, YOUNG & SMITH
Benton, AR .... Civil Trial Practice; Insurance Defense

BAYARD, FORREST S.
Chicago, IL .... Family Law

BAYER, THEODORE R.
Miami, FL .... Arbitration

BAYER, KARL
Austin, TX .... Appellate Practice; Civil Trial Practice; Computer Law; Medical Malpractice; Patent, Trademark, Copyright and Unfair Competition; Personal Injury; Product Liability Law

BAYKO GIBSON CARNEGIE HAGAN SCHOONMAKER & MEYER LLP
Houston, TX .... Appellate Practice; Civil Trial Practice; General Practice; Labor and Employment Law

BAYLESS & STOKES
Houston, TX .... Civil Trial Practice; Commercial Litigation; Creditors Rights; Trust and Estates, Wills and Probate

BAYLOR, EVNEN, CURTISS, GRIMIT & WITT
Lincoln, NE .... General Practice

BAYS, DEAVER, HIATT, LUNG & ROSE
Honolulu, HI .... Commercial Law; Construction Law; Real Estate Law

BEACH, BURCKE, HELFERS, MITTLEMAN AND STEWART, L.L.C.
St. Louis, MO .... Civil Trial Practice

BEACH LAW FIRM, P.A.
Columbia, SC .... Commercial Law; Public Utilities Law; Securities Law

BEAHM AND GREEN
New Orleans, LA .... Health Care Law; Medical Malpractice; Professional Liability

BEAM, BROBECK & WEST
Santa Ana, CA .... Employment Benefits Law; General Practice; Insurance Defense; Medical Malpractice; Product Liability Law

BEAN, KINNEY & KORMAN, A PROFESSIONAL CORPORATION
Arlington, VA .... Banking Law; Family Law; Personal Injury

BEARD, RUSSELL C. (RUSTY)
Abilene, TX .... Commercial Litigation; Insurance Defense

BEARDEN, BRECKENRIDGE & GIDLOW
St. Louis, MO .... Labor and Employment Law

BEARD, STEVEN L., P.C.
Marietta, GA .... Medical Malpractice; Personal Injury

BEASLEY, ALLEN, CROW, METHVIN, PORTIS & MILES, P.C.
Montgomery, AL .... Commercial Litigation; Personal Injury; Product Liability Law

BEASLEY, CASEY & ERBSTEIN
Philadelphia, PA .... General Practice

BEASLEY, LEACOCK & HAUSER, P.A.
West Palm Beach, FL .... Appellate Practice; Business Law; Commercial Litigation

BEATIE AND OSBORN LLP
New York, NY .... Civil Trial Practice; Commercial Law; Commercial Litigation; Environmental Law; Insurance Defense; Product Liability Law; Securities Law

BEATTIE PADOVANO, LLC
Montvale, NJ .... Civil Trial Practice; Commercial Law; General Practice

BEATTY, THOMAS D.
Las Vegas, NV .... Appellate Practice; Civil Trial Practice; Criminal Trial Practice

BEATTY, CRAMP, KAUFFMAN & LINCKE
Media, PA .... Corporate Law; General Practice; Insurance Defense; Medical Malpractice; Municipal and Zoning Law; Trust and Estates, Wills and Probate

BECK, PAUL A. & ASSOCIATES
Pittsburgh, PA .... Intellectual Property Law; Patent, Trademark, Copyright and Unfair Competition

BECK, CHAET, MOLONY & BAMBERGER, S.C.
Milwaukee, WI .... Corporate Law; Health Care Law; Labor and Employment Law

BECK, DE CORSO, DALY, BARRERA & KREINDLER, A PROFESSIONAL LAW CORPORATION
Los Angeles, CA .... Administrative Law; Business Law; Civil Trial Practice; Criminal Trial Practice

BECKER, GLYNN, MELAMED & MUFFLY LLP
New York, NY .... General Practice

BECKER, HICKS, IRVING & HADEED, P.C.
Springfield, VA .... Business Law; Civil Trial Practice; Criminal Trial Practice; Family Law; Immigration and Naturalization

BECKER & KAPLAN LLC
Chicago, IL .... Business Law; Civil Trial Practice; Commercial Litigation; Construction Law; Franchise Law; Labor and Employment Law; Real Estate Law

BECKER LAW OFFICE
San Francisco, CA .... Bankruptcy Law

BECKER, STEVEN A., A PROFESSIONAL LAW CORPORATION
San Bernardino, CA .... Family Law

BECKERMAN & BECKERMAN, LLP
Rochester, NY .... Family Law; General Practice

BECKES, KATHERINE F.
Denver, CO .... Tax Law

BECKHAM & BECKHAM, P.A.
North Miami Beach, FL .... Appellate Practice; Transportation Law

BECKLEY, JAMES F., P.A.
Albuquerque, NM .... Trust and Estates, Wills and Probate

BECKLEY & MADDEN
Harrisburg, PA .... Construction Law; General Practice; Labor and Employment Law

BECKMAN LAWSON, LLP
Fort Wayne, IN .... Bankruptcy Law; General Practice; Labor and Employment Law; Land Use Law; Real Estate Law

BECKMAN, MILLMAN & SANDERS, LLP
New York, NY .... Business Law

BECK, REDDEN & SECREST
Houston, TX .... Appellate Practice; Civil Trial Practice; Commercial Litigation

BEDZOW, KORN, BROWN, MILLER & ZEMEL, P.A.
Aventura, FL .... Commercial Litigation

BEELER, JOSEPH, P.A.
Miami, FL .... Criminal Trial Practice

BEEMER & BEEMER
Clarks Summit, PA .... Civil Trial Practice

BEEM & MANN, PROFESSIONAL CORPORATION
Denver, CO .... Civil Trial Practice; Commercial Litigation; Personal Injury

BEER & TOONE, P.C.
Phoenix, AZ .... Aviation Law; Insurance Defense

BEERY & SPURLOCK CO., L.P.A.
Columbus, OH .... Transportation Law

BEGAM, LEWIS, MARKS & WOLFE
Phoenix, AZ .... Civil Trial Practice; Medical Malpractice; Personal Injury; Product Liability Law; Professional Liability

BEGGS & LANE
Pensacola, FL .... General Practice

BEGLEY, CARLIN & MANDIO
Bristol, PA .... Civil Trial Practice; General Practice
Langhorne, PA .... Civil Trial Practice; General Practice

BEHR, MANTOVANI, MCCARTER & POTTER, P.C.
St. Louis, MO .... Insurance Defense

BEIER HOWLETT, PROFESSIONAL CORPORATION
Bloomfield Hills, MI .... Commercial Litigation; Corporate Law; Family Law; Insurance Defense; Municipal and Zoning Law; Trust and Estates, Wills and Probate

BEIL, JACOB
Columbus, GA .... Commercial Law

BEIRNE, MAYNARD & PARSONS, L.L.P.
Houston, TX .... Civil Trial Practice; General Practice

BELAIR & EVANS LLP
New York, NY .... Civil Trial Practice; Legal Malpractice; Medical Malpractice

BELANGER & PLIMPTON
Lovelock, NV .... Civil Trial Practice; General Practice; Personal Injury

BELCHER, HENZIE & BIEGENZAHN, A PROFESSIONAL CORPORATION
Los Angeles, CA .... Aviation Law; General Practice; Insurance Defense; Product Liability Law

BELDEN, BELDEN, PERSIN & JOHNSTON
Greensburg, PA .... Criminal Trial Practice; General Practice; Workers Compensation

BELDOCK LEVINE & HOFFMAN LLP
New York, NY .... Civil Trial Practice; Criminal Trial Practice; Family Law

BELES, ROBERT J.
Oakland, CA .... Criminal Trial Practice

BELETIC, ANNE TURNER
Dallas, TX .... Family Law

BELGRADE AND O'DONNELL, A PROFESSIONAL CORPORATION
Chicago, IL .... Admiralty/Maritime Law; Insurance Defense; Transportation Law

BELIN LAMSON MCCORMICK ZUMBACH FLYNN, A PROFESSIONAL CORPORATION
Des Moines, IA .... Civil Trial Practice; General Practice

BELIN RAWLINGS & BADAL LLP
Los Angeles, CA .... Antitrust Law; Business Law; Commercial Litigation

BELLAMY, RUTENBERG, COPELAND, EPPS, GRAVELY & BOWERS, P.A.
Myrtle Beach, SC .... Appellate Practice; Business Law; Civil Trial Practice; Commercial Law; General Practice; Insurance Defense; Labor and Employment Law; Personal Injury; Product Liability Law; Real Estate Law; Trust and Estates, Wills and Probate

BELLAND, STANTON P., P.C.
Los Angeles, CA .... International Trade Law

BELL & ASSOCIATES, P.A.
Madison, MS .... Business Law; Family Law; Medical Malpractice; Personal Injury; Toxic Torts

BELLATTI, FAY, BELLATTI & BEARD
Jacksonville, IL .... General Practice

BELL, CHARLES M., A PROFESSIONAL ASSOCIATION
Ellicott City, MD .... Aviation Law

BELL, DAVIS & PITT, P.A.
Winston-Salem, NC .... General Practice

BELL, LEEPER & ROPER, P.A.
Orlando, FL .... Insurance Defense

BELL, ORROCK & WATASE, LLP
Riverside, CA .... Insurance Defense; Personal Injury

BELL, RYNIKER & LETOURNEAU, P.C.
Houston, TX .... Admiralty/Maritime Law; Government Contracts; Insurance Defense; International Business Law

BELL, STANLEY J., A PROFESSIONAL CORPORATION
San Francisco, CA .... Construction Law; Personal Injury; Product Liability Law

BELSKY & ASSOCIATES
San Diego, CA .... Insurance Defense; Medical Malpractice

BELTRAN & ASSOCIATES
Atlanta, GA .... Professional Liability

BELTZ, EDWARDS & SABO, L.L.P.
Colorado Springs, CO .... Business Law; Civil Trial Practice; Construction Law; Family Law; General Practice; Personal Injury; Real Estate Law; Securities Law; Trust and Estates, Wills and Probate; Workers Compensation

BELZ & JONES, P.C.
St. Louis, MO .... Corporate Law

BENCKENSTEIN, NORVELL & NATHAN, L.L.P.
Beaumont, TX .... Civil Trial Practice; Insurance Defense; Personal Injury

BENCKENSTEIN & OXFORD, L.L.P.
Beaumont, TX .... Admiralty/Maritime Law; Civil Trial Practice; Environmental Law; General Practice; Natural Resources Law

BENCOMO & ASSOCIATES
New Orleans, LA .... Admiralty/Maritime Law; Personal Injury; Toxic Torts

BENDER, HAROLD J.
Charlotte, NC .... Criminal Trial Practice

BENDURE & THOMAS
Detroit, MI .... Appellate Practice; Civil Trial Practice; Tax Law

BENEDICT AND ALTMAN
New Brunswick, NJ .... Appellate Practice; Criminal Trial Practice

BENETAR BERNSTEIN SCHAIR & STEIN
New York, NY .... Labor and Employment Law

BENJAMIN & BENSON
Cambridge, MA .... Family Law

BENJAMIN, MICHAEL D., P.C.
Philadelphia, PA .... Medical Malpractice

BENNARDO, JACK A.
Merrick, NY .... Real Estate Law; Tax Law; Trust and Estates, Wills and Probate

BENNETT, EDMUND C.
Providence, RI .... Tax Law; Trust and Estates, Wills and Probate

BENNETT, LEON F.
Woodland Hills, CA .... Family Law; Sports and Entertainment Law

BENNETT & BENNETT
Eaton, OH .... Civil Trial Practice; Criminal Trial Practice; General Practice; Trust and Estates, Wills and Probate

BENNETT BENNETT AND TROIANO, P.A.
Portland, ME .... Business Law; Civil Trial Practice; Employment Benefits Law; General Practice; Labor and Employment Law; Mergers and Acquisitions; Real Estate Law; Tax Law; Trust and Estates, Wills and Probate

BENNETT BIGELOW & LEEDOM, P.S.
Seattle, WA .... Health Care Law

BENNETT, BOEHNING & CLARY
Lafayette, IN .... General Practice

BENNETT, CARMICHAEL & KENNEDY, L.L.P.
Scottsdale, AZ .... Business Law; Civil Trial Practice; Personal Injury; Real Estate Law

BENNETT & GUTHRIE, P.L.L.C.
Winston-Salem, NC .... Commercial Litigation; Construction Law; Environmental Law; Insurance Defense; Medical Malpractice; Workers Compensation

BENNETT & HALL, L.L.P.
Fort Worth, TX .... Insurance Defense

BENNETT JONES
Calgary, AB, Canada .... Appellate Practice; Banking Law; Business Law; Civil Trial Practice; Commercial Law; Employment Benefits Law; Environmental Law; General Practice; Health Care Law; International Business Law; Medical Malpractice; Natural Resources Law; Public Utilities Law; Real Estate Law; Securities Law; Trust and Estates, Wills and Probate
Edmonton, AB, Canada .... General Practice
Toronto, ON, Canada .... General Practice

BENNETT LOTTERHOS SULSER & WILSON, P.A.
Jackson, MS .... Bankruptcy Law; Commercial Litigation; Environmental Law; Insurance Defense

BENNETT, SAMUELSEN, REYNOLDS AND ALLARD, A PROFESSIONAL CORPORATION
Oakland, CA .... Civil Trial Practice; Insurance Defense; Personal Injury; Toxic Torts

BENOIT, ALEXANDER, SINCLAIR, HARWOOD & HIGH, L.L.P.
Twin Falls, ID .... Insurance Defense

BENSINGER, COTANT, MENKES & AARDEMA, P.C.
Gaylord, MI .... Civil Trial Practice; Insurance Defense; Legal Malpractice; Medical Malpractice; Product Liability Law; Professional Liability
Grand Rapids, MI .... Insurance Defense; Legal Malpractice; Medical Malpractice; Product Liability Law; Professional Liability
Marquette, MI .... Insurance Defense; Legal Malpractice; Medical Malpractice; Patent, Trademark, Copyright and Unfair Competition; Product Liability Law; Professional Liability

BENSON, JAMES R. JR.
Denver, CO .... Commercial Litigation

BENTON & CENTENO, L.L.P.
Birmingham, AL ..... Bankruptcy Law; Commercial Litigation

BENTON CLARK & TAYLOR, P.C.
San Antonio, TX ..... Banking Law; Corporate Law; Real Estate Law; Tax Law; Trust and Estates, Wills and Probate

BERCHEM, MOSES & DEVLIN, A PROFESSIONAL CORPORATION
Milford, CT ..... Commercial Law; General Practice; Labor and Employment Law

BERENBAUM, WEINSHIENK & EASON, P.C.
Denver, CO ..... Appellate Practice; Banking Law; Bankruptcy Law; Business Law; Civil Trial Practice; Environmental Law; Health Care Law; Labor and Employment Law; Real Estate Law; Securities Law; Tax Law; Trademark, Copyright and Unfair Competition; Trust and Estates, Wills and Probate

BERENS & TATE, P.C.
Omaha, NE ..... Employment Benefits Law; General Practice; Labor and Employment Law

BERENSTEIN, MOORE, BERENSTEIN, HEFFERNAN & MOELLER, L.L.P.
Sioux City, IA ..... General Practice; Tax Law; Trust and Estates, Wills and Probate

BERESFORD, BOOTH, DEMARAY & TROMPETER, INC., P.S.
Seattle, WA ..... Commercial Litigation

BERESKIN & PARR
Toronto, ON, Canada ..... Business Law; Patent, Trademark, Copyright and Unfair Competition

BERESTON, MICHAEL H., P.A.
Annapolis, MD ..... Medical Malpractice

BERG & ANDROPHY
Houston, TX ..... Civil Trial Practice; Commercial Litigation; Criminal Trial Practice; Medical Malpractice; Personal Injury; Product Liability Law

BERGER, FRANCES C. LAW OFFICES OF
New York, NY ..... Immigration and Naturalization

BERGER, GARY D. LAW OFFICES OF
San Francisco, CA ..... Trust and Estates, Wills and Probate

BERGER AND BERGER
Evansville, IN ..... Civil Trial Practice; Labor and Employment Law; Personal Injury; Product Liability Law

BERGER DAVIS & SINGERMAN
Fort Lauderdale, FL ..... Bankruptcy Law; Business Law; Civil Trial Practice; Creditors Rights; Real Estate Law; Tax Law

BERGER & MONTAGUE, P.C.
Philadelphia, PA ..... Antitrust Law; Securities Law

BERGER & NORTON, A LAW CORPORATION
Santa Monica, CA ..... Eminent Domain; Land Use Law; Real Estate Law

BERGER STERN & WEBB, LLP
New York, NY ..... Intellectual Property Law

BERGER & ZAVESKY CO., L.P.A.
Cleveland, OH ..... Personal Injury

BERGERON, PARADIS & FITZPATRICK, LLP
Burlington, VT ..... Personal Injury

BERGERT & BERGERT
Arlington, VA ..... Intellectual Property Law; Patent, Trademark, Copyright and Unfair Competition

BERGESON & ELIOPOULOS, LLP
San Jose, CA ..... Civil Trial Practice; Commercial Litigation; Intellectual Property Law; Securities Law

BERGHOLTZ, RICHARD S., P.A.
Mount Dora, FL ..... Construction Law

BERGMAN & BARRETT
Princeton, NJ ..... Arbitration; Civil Trial Practice; Commercial Law; Commercial Litigation; Family Law; Labor and Employment Law; Personal Injury; Trust and Estates, Wills and Probate; Workers Compensation

BERGMAN, WEDNER & DACEY, INC.
Los Angeles, CA ..... Business Law; Civil Trial Practice; Construction Law; Labor and Employment Law; Product Liability Law; Real Estate Law

BERGSTEDT & MOUNT
Lake Charles, LA ..... Admiralty/Maritime Law; Banking Law; Civil Trial Practice; General Practice; Insurance Defense; Real Estate Law

BERGSTRESSER AND ASSOCIATES, P.C., LAW OFFICES
Boston, MA ..... Medical Malpractice; Personal Injury

BERICK, PEARLMAN & MILLS, A LEGAL PROFESSIONAL ASSOCIATION
Cleveland, OH ..... General Practice

BERKE, ROBERT LAW OFFICES OF
Santa Monica, CA ..... Criminal Trial Practice

BERKEY, JON H., P.C.
Bloomfield Hills, MI ..... Commercial Law; Environmental Law; Real Estate Law

BERKOWITZ, LEFKOVITS, ISOM & KUSHNER, A PROFESSIONAL CORPORATION
Birmingham, AL ..... Antitrust Law; Business Law; Civil Trial Practice; General Practice; Health Care Law; Intellectual Property Law; Labor and Employment Law; Real Estate Law; Securities Law; Tax Law; Trust and Estates, Wills and Probate

BERKOWITZ, TRAGER & TRAGER, LLC
Westport, CT ..... Corporate Law

BERLACK, ISRAELS & LIBERMAN LLP
New York, NY ..... Administrative Law; Bankruptcy Law; Business Law; Civil Trial Practice; Employment Benefits Law; Energy Law; Public Utilities Law; Securities Law; Tax Law; Trust and Estates, Wills and Probate

BERLAND, ALLAN M.
Kentfield, CA ..... Real Estate Law

BERLINER, CANDON & JIMISON
Washington, DC ..... Administrative Law

BERLINER ZISSER WALTER & GALLEGOS, A PROFESSIONAL CORPORATION
Denver, CO ..... Arbitration; Corporate Law; Mergers and Acquisitions; Real Estate Law; Securities Law

BERMAN, DAVID
Medford, MA ..... Civil Trial Practice

BERMAN, BOURNS & CURRIE, LLC
West Hartford, CT ..... Civil Trial Practice; Family Law; General Practice; Real Estate Law; Trust and Estates, Wills and Probate

BERMAN, DAVID C., A PROFESSIONAL CORPORATION
Morristown, NJ ..... Commercial Litigation

BERMAN, DAVID M., P.A., LAW OFFICES OF
Miami, FL ..... Tax Law

BERMAN, DEVALERIO, PEASE & TABACCO, LLP
San Francisco, CA ..... Antitrust Law; Securities Law

BERMAN, ELIHU H., P.A.
Clearwater, FL ..... Business Law; Civil Trial Practice; Personal Injury

BERMAN, GAUFIN, TOMSIC, SAVAGE & CAMPBELL, A PROFESSIONAL CORPORATION
Salt Lake City, UT ..... Civil Trial Practice

BERMAN, PALEY, GOLDSTEIN & KANNRY, LLP
New York, NY ..... Construction Law; Environmental Law

BERMAN & WEISS
Palm Desert, CA ..... Medical Malpractice; Personal Injury; Product Liability Law

BERMAN WOLFE RENNERT VOGEL & MANDLER, P.A.
Miami, FL ..... Commercial Litigation; Real Estate Law; Securities Law

BERNARD, CASSISA, ELLIOTT & DAVIS, A PROFESSIONAL LAW CORPORATION
Metairie, LA ..... General Practice; Product Liability Law; Toxic Torts

BERNARD, HAFFEY & BOHNERT CO., L.P.A.
Cleveland, OH ..... Business Law; Civil Trial Practice; Commercial Litigation; Criminal Trial Practice; General Practice

BERNAUER, THOMAS A., A PROFESSIONAL CORPORATION
Newport Beach, CA ..... Family Law

BERNKOPF, GOODMAN & BASEMAN LLP
Boston, MA ..... Business Law; General Practice; Real Estate Law

BERNSTEIN, BRENDA JOY, P.C.
Atlanta, GA ..... Criminal Trial Practice

BERNSTEIN LITOWITZ BERGER & GROSSMANN LLP
New York, NY ..... Antitrust Law; Civil Rights; Securities Law

BERNSTEIN, SHUR, SAWYER & NELSON, A PROFESSIONAL CORPORATION
Portland, ME ..... General Practice

BERNSTEIN, STAIR & MCADAMS LLP
Knoxville, TN ....Business Law; Civil Trial Practice; Commercial Litigation; Construction Law; Creditors Rights; Family Law; General Practice; Product Liability Law

BERRIGAN, PATRICK J., (P.L.C.)
Slidell, LA ....Commercial Litigation; Real Estate Law

BERRY, THOMAS A. & ASSOCIATES
Bloomington, IN ....Civil Trial Practice

BERRY & BERRY, A PROFESSIONAL CORPORATION
Oakland, CA ....Civil Trial Practice

BERRY, KELLEY & HANSEN
Lincoln, NE ....Appellate Practice; Criminal Trial Practice

BERTHOLD, TIANO & O'DELL
Charleston, WV ....Aviation Law; Medical Malpractice; Product Liability Law

BERTINE, HUFNAGEL, HEADLEY, ZELTNER, DRUMMOND & DOHN, LLP
Scarsdale, NY ....Corporate Law

BERTZ, MICHAEL A.
Los Angeles, CA ....Securities Law

BESHARA, EDWARD C., P.A.
Winter Park, FL ....Immigration and Naturalization

BESS KUNZ, A PROFESSIONAL CORPORATION
Phoenix, AZ ....Civil Trial Practice; Insurance Defense; Personal Injury; Product Liability Law

BEST & ANDERSON, P.A.
Crystal River, FL ....Civil Trial Practice; Medical Malpractice; Personal Injury
Melbourne, FL ....Civil Trial Practice; Medical Malpractice; Personal Injury
Orlando, FL ....Civil Trial Practice; Environmental Law; Medical Malpractice; Personal Injury

BEST KOEPPEL, A PROFESSIONAL LAW CORPORATION
New Orleans, LA ....Admiralty/Maritime Law; General Practice; Insurance Defense; Toxic Torts; Workers Compensation

BEST & SHARP, A PROFESSIONAL CORPORATION
Tulsa, OK ....Civil Trial Practice; Insurance Defense; Medical Malpractice; Personal Injury; Professional Liability; Workers Compensation

BESUNDER, HARVEY B. LAW OFFICES OF
Hauppauge, NY ....Commercial Litigation; Real Estate Law

BETTERMAN & DIXON
Omaha, NE ....Commercial Litigation

BETTS & HOLT
Washington, DC ....Energy Law

BETTS, PATTERSON & MINES, P.S.
Seattle, WA ....General Practice

BEUS, GILBERT & DEVITT, P.L.L.C.
Phoenix, AZ ....Commercial Litigation; Municipal and Zoning Law; Professional Liability; Real Estate Law

BEVERIDGE & DIAMOND, P.C.
Washington, DC ....General Practice
New York, NY ....General Practice

BEVERIDGE & DIAMOND LLP
San Francisco, CA ....General Practice

BEYERS, COSTIN & CASE, A PROFESSIONAL CORPORATION
Santa Rosa, CA ....Real Estate Law

BIALAC, JAMES T.
Phoenix, AZ ....General Practice

BIANCO & MURPHY
San Francisco, CA ....Civil Trial Practice; Labor and Employment Law; Personal Injury

BIBLE, HOY & TRACHOK, A PROFESSIONAL CORPORATION
Reno, NV ....Appellate Practice; Business Law; Commercial Litigation; Construction Law

BICKEL & ASSOCIATES
Piedmont, CA ....Real Estate Law

BICKEL & BREWER
Dallas, TX ....Civil Trial Practice; General Practice

BICKFORD, HARRY L. LAW OFFICE
Ardmore, OK ....Civil Trial Practice; General Practice; Workers Compensation

BIDNA & KEYS, A PROFESSIONAL LAW CORPORATION
Newport Beach, CA ....Business Law

BIEBEL & FRENCH, A LEGAL PROFESSIONAL ASSOCIATION
Dayton, OH ....Patent, Trademark, Copyright and Unfair Competition

BIEN & SUMMERS LLP
Novato, CA ....Appellate Practice

BIENSTOCK & CLARK
Santa Monica, CA ....Civil Trial Practice

BIERI & AMES
Detroit, MI ....Real Estate Law

BIERMAN & BIERMAN, P.C.
Grinnell, IA ....General Practice

BIERMAN, SHOHAT, LOEWY & KLEIN, PROFESSIONAL ASSOCIATION
Miami, FL ....Appellate Practice; Criminal Trial Practice; General Practice; International Business Law

BIESER, GREER & LANDIS
Dayton, OH ....Civil Trial Practice; General Practice

BIGGS AND BATTAGLIA
Wilmington, DE ....Civil Trial Practice; Criminal Trial Practice; General Practice

BIGHAM ENGLAR JONES & HOUSTON
New York, NY ....Insurance Defense

BILLET & CONNOR
Philadelphia, PA ....Civil Trial Practice

BILLING, COCHRAN, HEATH, LYLES & MAURO, P.A.
Fort Lauderdale, FL ....Insurance Defense; Medical Malpractice

BILLINGS, CUNNINGHAM, MORGAN & BOATWRIGHT, PROFESSIONAL ASSOCIATION
Orlando, FL ....Medical Malpractice; Personal Injury

BILLINGS & SOLOMON, P.C.
Houston, TX ....Admiralty/Maritime Law

BILZIN SUMBERG DUNN PRICE & AXELROD LLP
Miami, FL ....General Practice

BINDERMAN, WILLIAM N.
New York, NY ....General Practice
Philadelphia, PA ....General Practice

BINGAMAN, HESS, COBLENTZ & BELL, A PROFESSIONAL CORPORATION
Reading, PA ....Banking Law; Bankruptcy Law; Civil Trial Practice; Creditors Rights; General Practice

BINGHAM DANA LLP
Hartford, CT ....General Practice
Washington, DC ....General Practice
Boston, MA ....General Practice
London, England ....General Practice

BINKLEY & ASSOCIATES
Birmingham, MI ....Civil Trial Practice

BINKLEY, MICHAEL W., P.C.
Nashville, TN ....Family Law; Personal Injury; Workers Compensation

BINNING, J. BOYD
Columbus, OH ....Personal Injury

BINSTOCK, TORCHINSKY AND ASSOCIATES, P.C., LAW OFFICES OF
Washington, DC ....Tax Law; Trust and Estates, Wills and Probate
Chevy Chase, MD ....Tax Law; Trust and Estates, Wills and Probate

BIOFF SINGER AND FINUCANE, LLP
Kansas City, MO ....Civil Trial Practice; Labor and Employment Law

BIRCH, STEWART, KOLASCH & BIRCH, LLP
Falls Church, VA ....Patent, Trademark, Copyright and Unfair Competition

BIRD, ELIZABETH ANNE LAW OFFICES OF
San Francisco, CA ....Trust and Estates, Wills and Probate

BIRD, FRANCIS M. JR.
Atlanta, GA ....General Practice; Trust and Estates, Wills and Probate

BIRD & BIRD, A LAW CORPORATION
Torrance, CA ....Criminal Trial Practice

BIRD, SVENDSEN, BROTHERS, SCHESKE & PATTISON, P.C.
Sturgis, MI ....General Practice

BIRDWELL, JANKE & DURANDO, LLP
Portland, OR..........Patent, Trademark, Copyright and Unfair Competition

BIRD, WILLIAM Q., AND ASSOCIATES, P.C.
Atlanta, GA..........Civil Trial Practice; Medical Malpractice; Personal Injury; Product Liability Law

BIREN & KATZMAN
Los Angeles, CA..........Personal Injury; Product Liability Law; Professional Liability

BIRGE & MAYERS, P.C.
Denver, CO..........Arbitration; Commercial Law; Criminal Trial Practice; Securities Law

BIRKA-WHITE, DAVID M. LAW OFFICES OF
Alamo, CA..........Construction Law; Product Liability Law

BIRNKRANT & BIRNKRANT, P.C.
Farmington Hills, MI..........Commercial Litigation; Insurance Defense; Product Liability Law

BISCEGLIE & FRIEDMAN, LLC
Newark, NJ..........Labor and Employment Law

BISGYER, BERT NEIL LAW OFFICES OF
Washington, DC..........Labor and Employment Law

BISHOP, JAMES A. LAW OFFICES OF
Brunswick, GA..........General Practice

BISHOP, BARRY, HOWE, HANEY & RYDER, A PROFESSIONAL CORPORATION
Emeryville, CA..........Arbitration; Aviation Law; Civil Trial Practice; Construction Law; Environmental Law; Insurance Defense; Product Liability Law; Real Estate Law; Trust and Estates, Wills and Probate

BISHOP & BISHOP
Ashdown, AR..........General Practice

BISHOP, COLVIN, JOHNSON & KENT
Birmingham, AL..........General Practice; Personal Injury; Trust and Estates, Wills and Probate

BISHOP & HEINTZ, P.C.
Traverse City, MI..........Business Law; Corporate Law; Patent, Trademark, Copyright and Unfair Competition; Personal Injury

BISHOP, PAYNE, HARVARD & KAITCER, L.L.P.
Fort Worth, TX..........Civil Trial Practice; Real Estate Law

BISHOP, ROSSI & SCARLATI, LTD.
Oakbrook Terrace, IL..........Business Law; Tax Law

BITTMAN, HOWARD
Boulder, CO..........Civil Trial Practice; Criminal Trial Practice; Family Law; Real Estate Law

BLACHLY, TABOR, BOZIK & HARTMAN
Valparaiso, IN..........Civil Trial Practice; General Practice; Personal Injury; Real Estate Law; Trust and Estates, Wills and Probate

BLACK, A. CLIFTON
Kissimmee, FL..........Civil Trial Practice

BLACK, MICHAEL V.
Phoenix, AZ..........Criminal Trial Practice

BLACKARD, WILLIAM R. JR.
Jacksonville, FL..........Tax Law; Trust and Estates, Wills and Probate

BLACK & BLACK
Port Arthur, TX..........General Practice

BLACK COMPEAN & HALL, A LIMITED LIABILITY PARTNERSHIP
Los Angeles, CA..........Appellate Practice; Civil Trial Practice; Insurance Defense

BLACK HELTERLINE, LLP
Portland, OR..........Banking Law; Bankruptcy Law; Civil Trial Practice; Commercial Law; Environmental Law; General Practice; Immigration and Naturalization; Natural Resources Law; Real Estate Law; Tax Law

BLACK, MCCUSKEY, SOUERS & ARBAUGH, A LEGAL PROFESSIONAL ASSOCIATION
Canton, OH..........Civil Trial Practice; General Practice; Labor and Employment Law

BLACK & MCLAREN, A PROFESSIONAL CORPORATION
Memphis, TN..........Civil Trial Practice

BLACKMON & SNELLINGS, LLP
Sacramento, CA..........Criminal Trial Practice

BLACKMORE & BLACKMORE
Fort Lauderdale, FL..........Criminal Trial Practice; Insurance Defense; Personal Injury

BLACK, NOLAND & READ, P.L.C.
Staunton, VA..........General Practice

BLACK, RICHARD A., P.C.
Phoenix, AZ..........Medical Malpractice; Product Liability Law

BLACKWELL & WHITE
Gulfport, MS..........Corporate Law; Eminent Domain; General Practice; Municipal Bond/Public Authority Financing

BLAIR CONAWAY BOGRAD & MARTIN, P.A.
Charlotte, NC..........Commercial Litigation; Construction Law

BLAIR AND PARSONS
Pell City, AL..........Civil Trial Practice; General Practice; Insurance Defense

BLAIR, SCHAEFER, HUTCHISON & WOLFE, LLP
Vancouver, WA..........General Practice

BLAIR, STROUD & DAVIDSON
Batesville, AR..........General Practice

BLAKE, CASSELS & GRAYDON LLP
Calgary, AB, Canada..........General Practice
Vancouver, BC, Canada..........General Practice
Ottawa, ON, Canada..........General Practice
Toronto, ON, Canada..........General Practice
Beijing, China..........General Practice
London, England..........General Practice

BLAKE, KIRCHNER, SYMONDS, MACFARLANE, LARSON & SMITH, P.C.
Detroit, MI..........Insurance Defense

BLAKESLEE, WESLEY D.
Westminster, MD..........General Practice

BLANC WILLIAMS JOHNSTON & KRONSTADT, LLP
Los Angeles, CA..........Business Law; Commercial Litigation; Computer Law; Intellectual Property Law; Labor and Employment Law; Sports and Entertainment Law

BLANCHARD, ROBERTSON, MITCHELL & CARTER, P.C.
Joplin, MO..........General Practice; Insurance Defense

BLANCHARD, WALKER, O'QUIN & ROBERTS, A PROFESSIONAL LAW CORPORATION
Shreveport, LA..........Appellate Practice; Bankruptcy Law; Civil Trial Practice; Commercial Law; Commercial Litigation; Criminal Trial Practice; Energy Law; Environmental Law; General Practice; Insurance Defense; Labor and Employment Law; Natural Resources Law; Real Estate Law; Tax Law; Trust and Estates, Wills and Probate

BLANCO TACKABERY COMBS & MATAMOROS, P.A.
Winston-Salem, NC..........Bankruptcy Law; Commercial Law

BLANEY MCMURTRY LLP
Toronto, ON, Canada..........General Practice

BLANK, CHRISTOPHER L.
Newport Beach, CA..........Bankruptcy Law; Business Law

BLANKINGSHIP & KOOMEY, P.C.
Alexandria, VA..........Commercial Litigation

BLANK ROME COMISKY & MCCAULEY LLP
Philadelphia, PA..........General Practice

BLANTON, EDWARD L., JR., P.A., LAW OFFICE OF
Baltimore, MD..........Bankruptcy Law; Civil Trial Practice; Corporate Law; Tax Law

BLASINGAME, BURCH, GARRARD, BRYANT & ASHLEY, P.C,
Athens, GA..........Civil Trial Practice; General Practice; Insurance Defense; Product Liability Law

BLATT, FRANKLIN R. LAW OFFICES OF
Harrisonburg, VA..........Family Law

BLATT, HAMMESFAHR & EATON
Chicago, IL..........Admiralty/Maritime Law; Civil Trial Practice; Construction Law; Corporate Law; Environmental Law; Government Contracts; Health Care Law; Insurance Defense; Labor and Employment Law; Medical Malpractice; Product Liability Law; Professional Liability; Toxic Torts; Transportation Law
New York, NY..........Banking Law; Civil Trial Practice; International Business Law

BLAUGRUND, HERBERT & MARTIN, INCORPORATED
Dublin, OH..........Administrative Law; Appellate Practice; Banking Law; Bankruptcy Law; Business Law; Civil Rights; Civil Trial Practice; Environmental Law; Family Law; Labor and Employment Law; Land Use Law; Municipal and Zoning Law; Nonprofit and Tax Exempt Organizations; Personal Injury; Real Estate Law; Tax Law; Trust and Estates, Wills and Probate; Workers Compensation

BLAU, KRAMER, WACTLAR & LIEBERMAN, P.C.
Jericho, NY ....Corporate Law; Real Estate Law; Securities Law

BLAZZARD, GRODD & HASENAUER, P.C.
Westport, CT............................General Practice; Securities Law; Tax Law; Trust and Estates, Wills and Probate

BLECHER & COLLINS, A PROFESSIONAL CORPORATION
Los Angeles, CA........................Antitrust Law; Appellate Practice; Business Law; Civil Trial Practice; Trademark, Copyright and Unfair Competition

BLEDSOE & BLEDSOE, P.L.L.C.
Charlotte, NC............................General Practice; Real Estate Law

BLEDSOE, SCHMIDT, LIPPES, MOONLY & ROBERSON, P.A.
Jacksonville, FL........................Civil Trial Practice

BLEIER LAW FIRM, THE
Folsom, CA...............................Civil Trial Practice; Commercial Litigation; Communications Law; Eminent Domain; Environmental Law; Real Estate Law

BLEUEL & MUIRHEAD
Ventura, CA...............................Trust and Estates, Wills and Probate

BLEY AND BLEY
San Francisco, CA......................Family Law; Personal Injury; Professional Liability

BLISH & CAVANAGH
Providence, RI...........................Antitrust Law; Civil Trial Practice; Commercial Law; Commercial Litigation; Construction Law; Environmental Law; General Practice; Labor and Employment Law; Medical Malpractice; Municipal Bond/Public Authority Financing; Personal Injury

BLISS & WILKENS, LLC
Anchorage, AK...........................Aviation Law; Civil Trial Practice; Health Care Law

BLOCK & COLUCCI, P.C.
Buffalo, NY...............................Banking Law; Corporate Law; Real Estate Law

BLOND & ALLISON, P.C., LAW OFFICES OF
Kansas City, MO........................Family Law

BLOOM & BUELL
Boston, MA................................Civil Trial Practice; General Practice; Health Care Law; Insurance Defense

BLOOM, DAVID B., A PROF. CORP., LAW OFFICES OF
Los Angeles, CA........................Banking Law; Bankruptcy Law; Business Law; Civil Trial Practice; Commercial Law; Construction Law; General Practice; International Business Law; Personal Injury; Real Estate Law; Sports and Entertainment Law

BLOOM, LEONARD, & ASSOCIATES, LLC
Towson, MD..............................Patent, Trademark, Copyright and Unfair Competition

BLOOM & WITKIN
Boston, MA................................Sports and Entertainment Law; Tax Law

BLOOSTON, MORDKOFSKY, JACKSON & DICKENS
Washington, DC.........................Communications Law

BLUE & EDWARDS, P.A.
Towson, MD..............................Trust and Estates, Wills and Probate

BLUM, EDWARD L.
Oakland, CA..............................Commercial Law; Real Estate Law

BLUM, LORIN B. LAW OFFICES OF
Oakland, CA..............................Family Law

BLUM, BAMBI G., P.A.
Miami, FL..................................Appellate Practice

BLUMENFELD, NORMAN L. LAW OFFICES OF
Washington, DC.........................Personal Injury

BLUMENFELD & COHEN
Washington, DC.........................Antitrust Law; Communications Law; Computer Law

BLUNT & ASSOCIATES, P.C.
Scottsdale, AZ...........................Trust and Estates, Wills and Probate

BLUT, JEROME L., CHARTERED
Las Vegas, NV...........................Tax Law; Trust and Estates, Wills and Probate

BOBO, SPICER, CIOTOLI, FULFORD, BOCCHINO & DEBEVOISE, P.A.
North Palm Beach, FL...............Health Care Law; Insurance Defense; Medical Malpractice
Orlando, FL...............................Health Care Law; Insurance Defense; Medical Malpractice

BOBROFF, HESSE, LINDMARK & MARTONE, P.C.
St. Louis, MO............................Labor and Employment Law

BOCK, JOHN GORDON
Houston, TX..............................Civil Trial Practice; Family Law

BODDINGTON & BROWN, CHARTERED
Kansas City, KS.........................General Practice

BODELL, GERALD E.
Bridgeport, CT...........................Appellate Practice; Civil Rights; Civil Trial Practice; Criminal Trial Practice

BODMAN, LONGLEY & DAHLING LLP
Ann Arbor, MI...........................Intellectual Property Law
Cheboygan, MI..........................Banking Law
Detroit, MI................................Administrative Law; Antitrust Law; Appellate Practice; Banking Law; Bankruptcy Law; Business Law; Civil Trial Practice; Commercial Law; Communications Law; Construction Law; Creditors Rights; Environmental Law; General Practice; Health Care Law; Intellectual Property Law; Labor and Employment Law; Mergers and Acquisitions; Municipal and Zoning Law; Municipal Bond/Public Authority Financing; Natural Resources Law; Pension and Profit Sharing; Product Liability Law; Professional Liability; Real Estate Law; Securities Law; Tax Law; Trademark, Copyright and Unfair Competition; Trust and Estates, Wills and Probate

BODYFELT, MOUNT, STROUP & CHAMBERLAIN
Portland, OR.............................Civil Trial Practice; Insurance Defense

BOEGGEMAN, GEORGE, HODGES & CORDE, P.C.
White Plains, NY.......................Appellate Practice; Arbitration; Civil Trial Practice; Commercial Litigation; Construction Law; Corporate Law; Insurance Defense; Medical Malpractice; Product Liability Law; Transportation Law

BOEHL STOPHER & GRAVES
Lexington, KY...........................Civil Trial Practice; General Practice; Workers Compensation
Louisville, KY...........................Civil Trial Practice; General Practice; Workers Compensation
Paducah, KY.............................Civil Trial Practice; General Practice

BOELTER & ASSOCIATES
Seattle, WA...............................Tax Law

BOESCHE, MCDERMOTT & ESKRIDGE
Tulsa, OK..................................Banking Law; Bankruptcy Law; Civil Trial Practice; Commercial Litigation; Employment Benefits Law; Energy Law; General Practice; Health Care Law; International Business Law; International Trade Law; Mergers and Acquisitions; Natural Resources Law; Oil and Gas Law; Pension and Profit Sharing

BOGENSCHUTZ & DUTKO, P.A.
Fort Lauderdale, FL..................Criminal Trial Practice

BOGGS, LOEHN & RODRIGUE
New Orleans, LA.......................Environmental Law; Health Care Law; Insurance Defense; Medical Malpractice

BOGIN, PATTERSON & BOHMAN LLP
Dayton, OH...............................Bankruptcy Law; Business Law

BOGUE KOURY & MARYLANDER LLC
Denver, CO...............................Medical Malpractice; Personal Injury; Product Liability Law

BOKELMAN & BENJAMIN, A PROFESSIONAL LAW CORPORATION
San Francisco, CA.....................Medical Malpractice; Personal Injury

BOLEN & ERWIN, LTD., A PROF. LAW CORP.
Alexandria, LA..........................Insurance Defense; Product Liability Law

BOLEN, FRANSEN & BOOSTROM LLP
Fresno, CA................................Business Law; Real Estate Law; Trust and Estates, Wills and Probate

BOLSON KUNTZ & SEREMBE
San Bernardino, CA..................Workers Compensation

BONAPARTE & MIYAMOTO, A PROFESSIONAL LAW CORPORATION
Los Angeles, CA.......................Immigration and Naturalization

BONDURANT, MIXSON & ELMORE, LLP
Atlanta, GA...............................Antitrust Law; Appellate Practice; Civil Trial Practice; Commercial Litigation; Constitutional Law; Criminal Trial Practice; Environmental Law; Professional Liability; Trademark, Copyright and Unfair Competition

BONE, BILL, P.A., THE LAW OFFICE OF
West Palm Beach, FL...............Personal Injury

BONEZZI SWITZER MURPHY & POLITO, CO. L.P.A.
Cleveland, OH...........................Medical Malpractice; Toxic Torts

BONINA & BONINA, P.C.
Brooklyn, NY............................Civil Trial Practice; Medical Malpractice; Personal Injury; Product Liability Law

BROWN, HAROLD & ASSOCIATES, LAW OFFICES OF
Boston, MA....Antitrust Law; Franchise Law

BROWN, KENT MASTERSON LAW OFFICES OF
Danville, KY....Appellate Practice; Civil Trial Practice

BROWN AND AMODIO, A LEGAL PROFESSIONAL ASSOCIATION
Medina, OH....General Practice

BROWN, BEMILLER, MURRAY & MCINTYRE
Mansfield, OH....General Practice; Insurance Defense

BROWN & BOLAND
San Francisco, CA....Insurance Defense

BROWN AND BROWN
St. Ignace, MI....General Practice

BROWN, BROWN & BROWN, A PROFESSIONAL ASSOCIATION
Bel Air, MD....Civil Trial Practice; Criminal Trial Practice; Family Law; Personal Injury; Real Estate Law; Trust and Estates, Wills and Probate; Workers Compensation

BROWN CLARK, A PROFESSIONAL ASSOCIATION
Sarasota, FL....Commercial Litigation; Construction Law; Workers Compensation

BROWN & CONNERY, LLP
Camden, NJ....Admiralty/Maritime Law; Civil Trial Practice; General Practice; Insurance Defense
Westmont, NJ....Admiralty/Maritime Law; Civil Trial Practice; General Practice; Insurance Defense

BROWN, CUMMINS & BROWN CO., L.P.A.
Cincinnati, OH....Business Law; Civil Trial Practice; Health Care Law; Labor and Employment Law; Securities Law

BROWN, DREW & MASSEY, LLP
Casper, WY....Administrative Law; Appellate Practice; Banking Law; Bankruptcy Law; Business Law; Civil Trial Practice; Commercial Law; Construction Law; Creditors Rights; Environmental Law; Family Law; General Practice; Insurance Defense; Labor and Employment Law; Natural Resources Law; Public Utilities Law; Real Estate Law; Trust and Estates, Wills and Probate

BROWN, ELLYN L., CHARTERED
Towson, MD....Franchise Law; Securities Law

BROWN ENVIRONMENTAL LAW GROUP, P.C., THE
Chicago, IL....Environmental Law

BROWN, ERNEST, & COMPANY, A PROFESSIONAL CORPORATION
San Francisco, CA....Construction Law; International Business Law

BROWN & GREEN, P.A.
Orlando, FL....Labor and Employment Law

BROWN, HAY & STEPHENS
Springfield, IL....Business Law; General Practice

BROWN, JAMES E., & ASSOCIATES, P.C.
Denver, CO....Business Law; Civil Trial Practice; Real Estate Law; Securities Law

BROWN, JEFFERIES AND BOULWARE
Barnwell, SC....General Practice

BROWN & KELLY, L.L.P.
Buffalo, NY....Business Law; Commercial Litigation; Criminal Trial Practice; Insurance Defense; Labor and Employment Law; Personal Injury; Real Estate Law; Trust and Estates, Wills and Probate

BROWN, KINSEY & FUNKHOUSER, P.L.C.
Mason City, IA....General Practice

BROWN LAW FIRM, P.C.
Billings, MT....General Practice; Insurance Defense; Medical Malpractice; Tax Law; Trust and Estates, Wills and Probate

BROWN, MALCOLM H., P.C.
Bismarck, ND....Commercial Law

BROWN RAYSMAN MILLSTEIN FELDER & STEINER LLP
New York, NY....Civil Trial Practice; General Practice

BROWN, ROSETA, LONG, MCCONVILLE, KILCULLEN & CARLSON
Eugene, OR....Insurance Defense

BROWN SCHWARTZ PATTERSON & ANKERS, P.C.
Troy, MI....Civil Rights; Labor and Employment Law

BROWN, SIMS, WISE & WHITE, A PROFESSIONAL CORPORATION
Houston, TX....Admiralty/Maritime Law; Insurance Defense

BROWN, TERRELL, HOGAN, ELLIS, MCCLAMMA & YEGELWEL, P.A.
Jacksonville, FL....Civil Rights; Environmental Law; Labor and Employment Law; Medical Malpractice; Personal Injury; Toxic Torts

BROWN, WARD & HAYNES, P.A.
Waynesville, NC....Business Law

BROWN, WARD, SALZMAN & WEISS, P.A.
Orlando, FL....Administrative Law; Business Law; Civil Trial Practice; Commercial Litigation; Government Contracts; Labor and Employment Law; Product Liability Law

BROWN, WATT & BUCHANAN, P.A.
Biloxi, MS....Corporate Law; Environmental Law; Insurance Defense; Product Liability Law; Transportation Law; Workers Compensation
Pascagoula, MS....Corporate Law; Environmental Law; Insurance Defense; Product Liability Law; Transportation Law; Workers Compensation

BROWN & WICHMER, P.C.
St. Louis, MO....Immigration and Naturalization

BROWN, WINFIELD & CANZONERI, INCORPORATED
Los Angeles, CA....Municipal and Zoning Law; Real Estate Law

BROWN, WINICK, GRAVES, GROSS, BASKERVILLE AND SCHOENEBAUM, P.L.C.
Des Moines, IA....General Practice

BROWN & WOOD LLP
Washington, DC....General Practice
New York, NY....General Practice

BROWNING BUSHMAN, A PROFESSIONAL CORPORATION
Houston, TX....Patent, Trademark, Copyright and Unfair Competition

BROWNING, KALECZYC, BERRY & HOVEN, P.C.
Helena, MT....Administrative Law; Commercial Law; Environmental Law; Health Care Law; Immigration and Naturalization; Insurance Defense; Natural Resources Law

BROWNING & LIPTON
Dallas, TX....Insurance Defense

BROWNING & TANKSLEY, LLP
Marietta, GA....Banking Law; Civil Trial Practice; Family Law; Medical Malpractice; Personal Injury; Product Liability Law; Trust and Estates, Wills and Probate

BROWNSTEIN HYATT & FARBER, P.C.
Denver, CO....Administrative Law; Business Law; Civil Trial Practice; Commercial Litigation; Corporate Law; Environmental Law; General Practice; Labor and Employment Law; Land Use Law; Municipal Bond/Public Authority Financing; Real Estate Law; Securities Law; Tax Law

BROYLES & PRATT, A PROFESSIONAL CORPORATION
Austin, TX....Civil Trial Practice; Insurance Defense; Public Utilities Law
Corpus Christi, TX....Civil Trial Practice; Insurance Defense; Legal Malpractice; Public Utilities Law

BRUCKER MORRA & HILTUNEN, A PROFESSIONAL CORPORATION
Los Angeles, CA....Employment Benefits Law

BRUCKNER & SYKES, L.L.P.
Houston, TX....Labor and Employment Law

BRUDER, GENTILE & MARCOUX, L.L.P.
Washington, DC....Administrative Law; Energy Law; Public Utilities Law

BRUINOOGE & ASSOCIATES
Rutherford, NJ....Land Use Law; Real Estate Law

BRUNENKANT & HASKELL, LLP
Washington, DC....Administrative Law; Energy Law; Natural Resources Law; Public Utilities Law

BRUNN & FLYNN, A PROFESSIONAL CORPORATION
Modesto, CA....Civil Trial Practice; Insurance Defense; Real Estate Law; Trust and Estates, Wills and Probate

BRUNO, FREDERIC & ASSOCIATES
Minneapolis, MN....Criminal Trial Practice

BRYAN CAVE LLP
St. Louis, MO....General Practice

BRYAN, NELSON, SCHROEDER, CASTIGLIOLA & BANAHAN
Pascagoula, MS....Business Law; Civil Trial Practice; Corporate Law; Insurance Defense

BRYANT AND HIGBY, CHARTERED
Panama City, FL....General Practice

BRYANT LAW OFFICES
Wilmington, OH....General Practice

BRYANT, LOVLIEN & JARVIS, P.C.
Bend, OR................................General Practice

BRYCE, WILLIAM D.
Georgetown, TX ....Business Law

BRYDGER, GORDON C., P.A.
Fort Lauderdale, FL...............Family Law

BRYDGES, MAHAN, O'BRIEN & FRUCCI, P.C.
Virginia Beach, VA...............Civil Trial Practice; Criminal Trial Practice; Family Law; Medical Malpractice; Personal Injury; Product Liability Law

BRYDON, SWEARENGEN & ENGLAND, PROFESSIONAL CORPORATION
Jefferson City, MO................General Practice

BUCCI, BAILEY & JAVINS, L.C.
Charleston, WV......................Medical Malpractice; Personal Injury; Product Liability Law

BUCHANAN, DOUGLAS
Bishop, CA.............................Criminal Trial Practice; General Practice; Trust and Estates, Wills and Probate

BUCHANAN, ROBERT L. JR.
Aiken, SC ....Civil Trial Practice

BUCHANAN, JURDEM & ZULAUF, P.C.
Denver, CO ....Personal Injury

BUCHANAN, SILVER & BECKERING, P.L.C.
Grand Rapids, MI ....Civil Trial Practice; Commercial Litigation; Medical Malpractice; Personal Injury; Product Liability Law

BUCK & BUCK
Smithville, TN.........................General Practice

BUCK & GORDON LLP
Seattle, WA ....Environmental Law; Municipal and Zoning Law; Real Estate Law

BUCKINGHAM, HOLZAPFEL, ZEIHER, WALDOCK & SCHELL CO., L.P.A.
Sandusky, OH ....Commercial Law; General Practice

BUCKLEY FIRM, THE, P.C.
Mission Viejo, CA...................Bankruptcy Law; Civil Trial Practice; General Practice; Real Estate Law

BUCKLEY & HAYES, L.L.P.
New Orleans, LA....................Civil Trial Practice; Health Care Law; Insurance Defense; Medical Malpractice; Personal Injury; Workers Compensation

BUCKLEY KING & BLUSO, A LEGAL PROFESSIONAL ASSOCIATION
Cleveland, OH.........................Civil Trial Practice

BUCKLEY, MENDLESON & CRISCIONE, P.C.
Albany, NY..............................Workers Compensation

BUCKLEY, NAGLE, GENTRY, BRION, MCGUIRE & MORRIS
West Chester, PA....................General Practice; Municipal and Zoning Law; Trust and Estates, Wills and Probate

BUCKNELL STEHLIK
Seattle, WA ....Commercial Law

BUDNER, BRUCE A. & ASSOCIATES
Dallas, TX...............................Legal Malpractice; Personal Injury

BUESSER, BUESSER, BLACK, LYNCH, FRYHOFF & GRAHAM, P.C.
Bloomfield Hills, MI..............Family Law; General Practice

BUFALINI, DAVID A., P.S., INC.
Tacoma, WA ....Personal Injury

BUHLER LAW FIRM, THE
Memphis, TN..........................Corporate Law; Securities Law

BUIST, MOORE, SMYTHE & MCGEE, P.A.
Charleston, SC ....Admiralty/Maritime Law; Bankruptcy Law; Civil Trial Practice; Commercial Law; Construction Law; Environmental Law; General Practice; Health Care Law; Insurance Defense; Labor and Employment Law; Product Liability Law; Real Estate Law

BULLARD, ANDERSON & ANDERSON, PLLC
Clarkston, MI..........................Arbitration; Aviation Law; Business Law; Civil Trial Practice; International Business Law; Real Estate Law

BULLARD, KORSHOJ, SMITH & JERNSTEDT, A PROFESSIONAL CORPORATION
Portland, OR...........................Labor and Employment Law

BULL, HOUSSER & TUPPER
Vancouver, BC, Canada..........General Practice

BULLOCK, CHILDS, PENDLEY, REED, HERZFELD & RUBIN
Jacksonville, FL ....Civil Trial Practice; Insurance Defense

BULUA, STANLEY E., ATTORNEY AT LAW, LLC
Scarsdale, NY..........................Tax Law

BUMP AND BUMP
Chadron, NE...........................General Practice

BUNCH & BROCK
Lexington, KY ....Bankruptcy Law

BUNGER & ROBERTSON
Bloomington, IN ....Banking Law; Business Law; Civil Trial Practice; General Practice; Health Care Law; Insurance Defense; Personal Injury; Real Estate Law; Trust and Estates, Wills and Probate

BUONAURO, ROBERT J., P.A.
Orlando, FL ....Criminal Trial Practice

BURAK ANDERSON & MELLONI, PLC
Burlington, VT ....General Practice

BURBIDGE AND MITCHELL
Salt Lake City, UT.................Commercial Litigation; Personal Injury

BURCH & CRACCHIOLO, P.A.
Phoenix, AZ ....Appellate Practice; Bankruptcy Law; Civil Trial Practice; Commercial Law; Criminal Trial Practice; Environmental Law; Family Law; General Practice; Insurance Defense; Medical Malpractice; Personal Injury; Product Liability Law; Real Estate Law; Tax Law; Trust and Estates, Wills and Probate

BURCH, PORTER & JOHNSON
Memphis, TN..........................General Practice

BURD MAGATHAN LOZANO & ZACHERL, L.L.P.
Miami, FL ....Aviation Law; Civil Trial Practice

BURD & NAYLOR
Santa Ana, CA........................Bankruptcy Law

BURESH, FREDRIC C., P.A.
Fort Lauderdale, FL...............Bankruptcy Law; Business Law

BURESH, KAPLAN, JANG & FELLER
Berkeley, CA ....Insurance Defense

BURG SIMPSON ELDREDGE & HERSH, P.C.
Englewood, CO ....Civil Trial Practice; Commercial Law; Insurance Defense

BURGE, DAVID A., CO., L.P.A.
Cleveland, OH........................Patent, Trademark, Copyright and Unfair Competition

BURGER, WILLIAM KENNERLY
Murfreesboro, TN..................Civil Trial Practice

BURGER & BENNETT, P.C.
McCook, NE...........................Civil Trial Practice; Real Estate Law

BURGETT & ROBBINS
Jamestown, NY ....Civil Trial Practice; Family Law; General Practice; Personal Injury; Product Liability Law

BURGE & WETTERMARK, P.C.
Birmingham, AL ....Personal Injury; Transportation Law

BURGOYNE, MICHAEL H., P.A., LAW OFFICE OF
Towson, MD...........................General Practice

BURKE, DANIEL V.
Carlsbad, CA..........................Family Law

BURKE COSTANZA & CUPPY LLP
Merrillville, IN ....General Practice

BURKE, MARLIN W., P.C.
Denver, CO ....Health Care Law

BURKE & MAYER, A PROFESSIONAL LAW CORPORATION
New Orleans, LA...................Admiralty/Maritime Law; Environmental Law

BURKE, THOMAS M., P.C., LAW OFFICES
St. Louis, MO.........................Personal Injury; Workers Compensation

BURKERT & HART
Fort Myers, FL.......................Personal Injury

BURK LAW FIRM, THE, A PROFESSIONAL CORPORATION
Austin, TX..............................Civil Trial Practice; Commercial Litigation

BURK & SEATON, P.A.
Minneapolis, MN...................Labor and Employment Law

BURLEIGH, LAWRENCE K., LTD., A PROF. LAW CORP.
Lafayette, LA ....Admiralty/Maritime Law; Aviation Law; Personal Injury

BURNHAM & BROWN, A PROFESSIONAL CORPORATION
Oakland, CA ....General Practice

BURNS ANDERSON JURY & BRENNER, L.L.P.
Austin, TX ....Insurance Defense; Transportation Law; Workers Compensation

BURNS, BRYANT, HINCHEY, COX & ROCKEFELLER, P.A.
Dover, NH ....Insurance Defense; Medical Malpractice; Personal Injury

BURNS, CUNNINGHAM & MACKEY, P.C.
Mobile, AL...............................Commercial Law; Medical Malpractice; Personal Injury; Product Liability Law; Toxic Torts

BURNS, DOANE, SWECKER & MATHIS, L.L.P.
Alexandria, VA ....Patent, Trademark, Copyright and Unfair Competition; Trademark, Copyright and Unfair Competition

BURNS & FARREY
Worcester, MA.........................Insurance Defense

BURNS & LEVINSON LLP
Boston, MA..............................Business Law; Corporate Law; Creditors Rights; General Practice

BURNS, MCDONALD, BRADFORD, PATRICK & TINSLEY, L.L.P.
Greenwood, SC ....Civil Trial Practice; General Practice

BURNS RAY & DELANO, PROFESSIONAL ASSOCIATION
Portland, ME ....Business Law; Commercial Litigation; Construction Law; General Practice; Insurance Defense; Labor and Employment Law; Product Liability Law; Securities Law

BURNSIDE, WALL, DANIEL, ELLISON & REVELL
Augusta, GA ....Civil Trial Practice; Commercial Litigation; General Practice; Municipal and Zoning Law; Personal Injury

BURR & FORMAN LLP
Birmingham, AL ....Antitrust Law; Banking Law; Business Law; Civil Trial Practice; Communications Law; Environmental Law; General Practice; Labor and Employment Law; Municipal Bond/Public Authority Financing; Real Estate Law; Tax Law; Trust and Estates, Wills and Probate
Huntsville, AL..........................Banking Law; Business Law; Real Estate Law; Trust and Estates, Wills and Probate

BURR, JEFFREY L., & ASSOCIATES
Las Vegas, NV ....Trust and Estates, Wills and Probate

BURRIS, MACMILLAN, PEARCE & MAYER, L.L.P.
Charlotte, NC...........................Real Estate Law

BURROUGHS, HEPLER, BROOM, MACDONALD & HEBRANK
Edwardsville, IL.......................Civil Trial Practice

BURROW & PARROTT, L.L.P.
Houston, TX ....Civil Trial Practice; Personal Injury; Toxic Torts

BURSTEIN, HERTOGS & MCFARLAND, P.A.
Minneapolis, MN.....................General Practice

BURT, ROBERT G., P.C.
Portland, OR............................Business Law; General Practice; Mergers and Acquisitions; Tax Law; Trust and Estates, Wills and Probate

BURTON, JOHN C.
Pasadena, CA...........................Appellate Practice; Civil Rights; Civil Trial Practice; Medical Malpractice; Personal Injury

BURTON, R. NICHOLAS
Decatur, IL...............................Tax Law; Trust and Estates, Wills and Probate

BURTON & MURPHY
Tampa, FL ....Commercial Litigation; Computer Law

BURTON & SUE, L.L.P.
Greensboro, NC ....Civil Trial Practice; Insurance Defense; Personal Injury; Workers Compensation

BURTON, VOLKMANN & SCHMAL, LLP
Santa Cruz, CA........................Insurance Defense

BUSCH AND BUSCH, LLP
North Brunswick, NJ...............Business Law; Civil Trial Practice; Family Law; General Practice; Insurance Defense; Municipal and Zoning Law; Personal Injury; Real Estate Law; Trust and Estates, Wills and Probate

BUSCH PROFESSIONAL CORPORATION
Golden, CO ....General Practice

BUSCHMANN, CARR & SHANKS, PROFESSIONAL CORPORATION
Indianapolis, IN.......................Bankruptcy Law; Civil Trial Practice; Commercial Law; Creditors Rights; Labor and Employment Law; Workers Compensation

BUSER, PAUL J.
Scottsdale, AZ..........................Business Law; Elder Law; Family Law; Trust and Estates, Wills and Probate

BUSH CRADDOCK & RENEKER, L.L.P.
Dallas, TX................................Civil Trial Practice; Personal Injury

BUSH, HAUDER & ADKERSON
Dallas, TX................................Insurance Defense; Workers Compensation

BUSH, JAMES, P.C., LAW OFFICES OF
Phoenix, AZ ....Commercial Litigation

BUSSART, WEST, ROSSETTI, PIAIA & TYLER, P.C.
Rock Springs, WY ....Civil Trial Practice; General Practice

BUSTO & JENNINGS, PROFESSIONAL ASSOCIATION
Miami, FL ....Commercial Litigation

BUTKUS & REIMER, P.C.
Albuquerque, NM....................Insurance Defense; Medical Malpractice

BUTLER, JACK A. LAW OFFICES OF
Nashville, TN...........................Personal Injury

BUTLER BURNETTE PAPPAS
Miami, FL ....Insurance Defense
Tallahassee, FL ....Insurance Defense
Tampa, FL ....Insurance Defense

BUTLER, HICKY & LONG
Forrest City, AR......................Aviation Law; Civil Trial Practice; General Practice; Insurance Defense; Medical Malpractice; Trust and Estates, Wills and Probate

BUTLER & HOSCH, P.A.
Orlando, FL ....Banking Law; Bankruptcy Law; Real Estate Law

BUTLER, JAMES T., & ASSOCIATES, P.A.
Tampa, FL ....Personal Injury

BUTLER & MACDOUGALD
Atlanta, GA ....Personal Injury; Product Liability Law

BUTLER, SNOW, O'MARA, STEVENS & CANNADA, PLLC
Jackson, MS ....General Practice

BUTLER, WOOTEN, OVERBY, FRYHOFER, DAUGHTERY & SULLIVAN
Atlanta, GA ....Civil Trial Practice; Medical Malpractice; Personal Injury; Product Liability Law
Columbus, GA ....Civil Trial Practice; Medical Malpractice; Personal Injury; Product Liability Law

BUTT, THORNTON & BAEHR, P.C.
Albuquerque, NM....................Civil Trial Practice; Insurance Defense; Labor and Employment Law; Product Liability Law

BUTTERMAN KAHN & GARDNER, LLP
New York, NY..........................Family Law

BUTZ DUNN DESANTIS & BINGHAM, A PROFESSIONAL CORPORATION
San Diego, CA ....Civil Trial Practice

BUTZEL LONG, A PROFESSIONAL CORPORATION
Ann Arbor, MI ....Antitrust Law; Appellate Practice; Banking Law; Commercial Litigation; Constitutional Law; Intellectual Property Law
Birmingham, MI.......................Commercial Litigation; Family Law; Municipal and Zoning Law; Real Estate Law; Trust and Estates, Wills and Probate
Detroit, MI...............................Administrative Law; Antitrust Law; Appellate Practice; Business Law; Civil Trial Practice; Commercial Litigation; Constitutional Law; Construction Law; Employment Benefits Law; Environmental Law; Health Care Law; Immigration and Naturalization; Intellectual Property Law; International Business Law; Labor and Employment Law; Mergers and Acquisitions; Professional Liability; Real Estate Law; Tax Law; Trademark, Copyright and Unfair Competition
Okemos, MI ....Administrative Law; Construction Law; Public Utilities Law

BYE, GOFF & ROHDE, LTD.
River Falls, WI.........................Personal Injury

BYERS, FRITZ
Toledo, OH ....Appellate Practice; Civil Trial Practice; Communications Law; Labor and Employment Law

BYERS CASGRAIN
Montreal, QU, Canada ....General Practice

BYNUM, ARLEN DEAN SPIDER, P.C., LAW OFFICES OF
Dallas, TX................................Insurance Defense

BYRD, BYRD, ERVIN, WHISNANT, MCMAHON & ERVIN, P.A.
Morganton, NC.........................Criminal Trial Practice; General Practice; Personal Injury; Trust and Estates, Wills and Probate

BYRD, DAVIS AND EISENBERG, L.L.P.
Austin, TX .... Aviation Law; Medical Malpractice; Personal Injury; Product Liability Law

BYRD, MISCHE, BEVIS, BOWEN, JOSEPH & O'CONNOR, P.C.
Fairfax, VA .... Family Law

BYRNE, BENESCH & WALSMA, P.C.
Yuma, AZ .... Real Estate Law

BYRNE, EDWARD O., & ASSOCIATES P.C.
Denver, CO .... International Business Law

BYRNE, JAMES B., JR., P.A.
Longwood, FL .... Civil Trial Practice

BYRNE, KIELY & WHITE, LLP
Denver, CO .... Aviation Law; Insurance Defense; Product Liability Law

BYSSHE, FREDERICK H. JR., LAW OFFICES OF
Ventura, CA .... Medical Malpractice; Personal Injury; Product Liability Law

CABANISS, JOHNSTON, GARDNER, DUMAS & O'NEAL
Birmingham, AL .... Civil Trial Practice; General Practice
Mobile, AL .... Civil Trial Practice; General Practice

CABANISS, MCDONALD, SMITH & WIGGINS, P.A.
Orlando, FL .... Civil Trial Practice; Product Liability Law

CABELL, ROBERT & ASSOCIATES
Richmond, VA .... Criminal Trial Practice

CACACE, TUSCH & SANTAGATA
Stamford, CT .... Business Law; Civil Trial Practice; Commercial Litigation; Corporate Law; Municipal and Zoning Law; Personal Injury; Real Estate Law; Trust and Estates, Wills and Probate

CACCIATORE, RONALD K., P.A.
Tampa, FL .... Criminal Trial Practice

CACHERIS, PLATO, LAW OFFICES OF
Washington, DC .... Criminal Trial Practice
Alexandria, VA .... Criminal Trial Practice

CADES SCHUTTE FLEMING & WRIGHT
Honolulu, HI .... Banking Law; Civil Trial Practice; General Practice; Patent, Trademark, Copyright and Unfair Competition; Real Estate Law; Trust and Estates, Wills and Probate
Kailua-Kona, HI .... Civil Trial Practice; General Practice

CADWALADER, WICKERSHAM & TAFT
New York, NY .... General Practice

CAESAR, RIVISE, BERNSTEIN, COHEN & POKOTILOW, LTD.
Philadelphia, PA .... Computer Law; Intellectual Property Law; Patent, Trademark, Copyright and Unfair Competition

CAHALANE, VINCENT P., P.C.
Brockton, MA .... Arbitration; Civil Trial Practice; Construction Law; Insurance Defense; Personal Injury; Product Liability Law

CAHILL, CHRISTIAN & KUNKLE, LTD.
Chicago, IL .... Commercial Litigation; Construction Law; Environmental Law; Intellectual Property Law; Product Liability Law

CAHILL GORDON & REINDEL
Washington, DC .... General Practice
New York, NY .... General Practice; Municipal Bond/Public Authority Financing
Paris, France .... General Practice

CAHILL, KATHLEEN, LLC, THE LAW OFFICES OF
Baltimore, MD .... Labor and Employment Law; Medical Malpractice; Personal Injury

CAHILL LAW OFFICES
Nevada, IA .... General Practice; Trust and Estates, Wills and Probate

CAHILL & MARQUART, P.A.
Moorhead, MN .... General Practice
Fargo, ND .... General Practice

CAHN WISHOD & KNAUER, LLP
Melville, NY .... Banking Law; Business Law; Commercial Litigation; Corporate Law; Environmental Law; Municipal and Zoning Law

CALAFELL, RAY, JR., P.A.
Tampa, FL .... Civil Trial Practice

CALAWAY, STEPHEN G.
Winston-Salem, NC .... Real Estate Law

CALBOM & SCHWAB, P.S.C.
Moses Lake, WA .... Personal Injury; Workers Compensation

CALCUTT CUNNINGHAM DAVISON ROGERS BOYNTON & PETTERSON, P.L.L.C.
Traverse City, MI .... Corporate Law

CALDWELL, BERNER & CALDWELL
Woodstock, IL .... Civil Trial Practice; General Practice

CALDWELL & PACETTI
Palm Beach, FL .... General Practice; Municipal Bond/Public Authority Financing

CALFEE, HALTER & GRISWOLD LLP
Cleveland, OH .... General Practice; Trademark, Copyright and Unfair Competition
Columbus, OH .... General Practice

CALHOUN, FAULK, WATKINS & FAIRCLOTH, L.L.C.
Troy, AL .... Civil Trial Practice; General Practice; Insurance Defense

CALHOUN, KADEMENOS & HEICHEL CO., L.P.A.
Mansfield, OH .... General Practice

CALHOUN & STACY
Dallas, TX .... Appellate Practice; Banking Law; Bankruptcy Law; Business Law; Civil Trial Practice; Commercial Law; Commercial Litigation; Communications Law; Construction Law; Corporate Law; Environmental Law; General Practice; Health Care Law; Insurance Defense; Labor and Employment Law; Medical Malpractice; Municipal and Zoning Law; Patent, Trademark, Copyright and Unfair Competition; Personal Injury; Product Liability Law; Real Estate Law; Securities Law; Tax Law; Transportation Law; Trust and Estates, Wills and Probate

CALKINS & CALKINS
Eugene, OR .... General Practice; Insurance Defense

CALLAHAN & BLAINE, A PROFESSIONAL LAW CORPORATION
Santa Ana, CA .... Business Law; Commercial Litigation; Construction Law; Environmental Law; General Practice; Patent, Trademark, Copyright and Unfair Competition; Real Estate Law

CALLAHAN & DEACON
Sacramento, CA .... Civil Trial Practice; Personal Injury

CALLAHAN LAW FIRM
Tallahassee, FL .... Insurance Defense; Medical Malpractice; Personal Injury

CALLAHAN, REBECCA, A PROFESSIONAL LAW CORPORATION
Newport Beach, CA .... Appellate Practice; Bankruptcy Law; Civil Trial Practice; Commercial Litigation

CALLAN, REGENSTREICH, KOSTER & BRADY
New York, NY .... Civil Trial Practice; Criminal Trial Practice; Insurance Defense; Medical Malpractice; Personal Injury; Product Liability Law

CALLENDER, JOHN F.
Jacksonville, FL .... Commercial Litigation; Personal Injury

CALLISTER NEBEKER & MCCULLOUGH, A PROFESSIONAL CORPORATION
Salt Lake City, UT .... Antitrust Law; Banking Law; Bankruptcy Law; Business Law; Civil Trial Practice; Commercial Law; Corporate Law; Employment Benefits Law; Environmental Law; General Practice; Labor and Employment Law; Municipal Bond/Public Authority Financing; Natural Resources Law; Nonprofit and Tax Exempt Organizations; Pension and Profit Sharing; Personal Injury; Real Estate Law; Securities Law; Tax Law; Trust and Estates, Wills and Probate

CALLOWAY, NORRIS & BURDETTE
Dallas, TX .... Trust and Estates, Wills and Probate

CALLOWAY, S. MARCUS, P.C.
Atlanta, GA .... Real Estate Law

CALVERT, MELANIE A.
Pasadena, CA .... Labor and Employment Law

CAMERON, MARRIOTT, WALSH, HODGES & COLEMAN, P.A.
Orlando, FL .... Civil Trial Practice; Insurance Defense

CAMERON MCKENNA LLP
Washington, DC .... Energy Law; Public Utilities Law

CAMERON & MITTLEMAN LLP
Providence, RI .... Business Law; Health Care Law

CAMERON, PEARLSON & GALE
Long Beach, CA .... Banking Law; Civil Trial Practice; Environmental Law; Labor and Employment Law; Land Use Law; Real Estate Law; Toxic Torts

CAMNER, LIPSITZ AND POLLER, PROFESSIONAL ASSOCIATION
Miami, FL ....Corporate Law; General Practice; Real Estate Law

CAMP & CAMP, P.A.
Fort Lauderdale, FL ....Real Estate Law; Trust and Estates, Wills and Probate

CAMP CHURCH & ASSOCIATES
Vancouver, BC, Canada ....Administrative Law; Aviation Law; Commercial Litigation

CAMPANA, VIEH, SHORE, OWENS & LOEB
Scottsdale, AZ ....Commercial Litigation; Family Law; Medical Malpractice; Personal Injury; Real Estate Law

CAMPBELL, JAMES M.
Orlando, FL ....Criminal Trial Practice; Family Law

CAMPBELL, ARELLANO & RICH
Charlotte Amalie, St. Thomas, VI ....Appellate Practice; Bankruptcy Law; Commercial Litigation; Environmental Law

CAMPBELL, BLACK, CARNINE, HEDIN, BALLARD & MCDONALD, P.C.
Mount Vernon, IL ....Civil Trial Practice; General Practice; Insurance Defense

CAMPBELL, DILLE AND BARNETT P.L.L.C.
Puyallup, WA ....Civil Trial Practice

CAMPBELL, LEA, MICHAEL, MCCONNELL & PIGOT
Charlottetown, PE, Canada ....Administrative Law; Business Law; Civil Trial Practice; General Practice; Insurance Defense; Personal Injury

CAMPBELL & LEVINE, LLC
Pittsburgh, PA ....Bankruptcy Law; Commercial Law

CAMPBELL, MCCRANIE, SISTRUNK, ANZELMO & HARDY, P.C.
Metairie, LA ....Appellate Practice; Civil Trial Practice; Commercial Law; Medical Malpractice; Professional Liability

CAMPBELL, O'BRIEN & MISTELE, P.C.
Troy, MI ....Business Law; General Practice; Real Estate Law; Trust and Estates, Wills and Probate

CAMPBELL, WALLER & MCCALLUM, L.L.C.
Birmingham, AL ....Commercial Litigation; Personal Injury

CAMPBELL, WOODS, BAGLEY, EMERSON, MCNEER & HERNDON, P.L.L.C.
Charleston, WV ....General Practice
Huntington, WV ....General Practice

CAMPEAU & THOMAS, A LAW CORPORATION
San Jose, CA ....Bankruptcy Law; Civil Trial Practice; Commercial Law

CAMPNEY & MURPHY
Vancouver, BC, Canada ....General Practice

CAMRUD, MADDOCK, OLSON & LARSON, LTD.
Grand Forks, ND ....General Practice

CANALES & SIMONSON, P.C.
Corpus Christi, TX ....Appellate Practice; Civil Trial Practice; Commercial Litigation; Criminal Trial Practice

CANGES, IWASHKO & BETHKE, A PROFESSIONAL CORPORATION
Denver, CO ....Civil Trial Practice; Commercial Litigation; Criminal Trial Practice; Family Law

CANNON & DUNPHY, S.C.
Brookfield, WI ....Personal Injury; Professional Liability

CANNON, MEYER VON BREMEN & GOSS, LLP
Albany, GA ....Civil Trial Practice; Personal Injury; Product Liability Law; Real Estate Law

CANO, KRISTIN M.
Newport Beach, CA ....Corporate Law; Securities Law

CANSLER, LOCKHART, CAMPBELL, EVANS, BRYANT & GARLITZ, P.A.
Charlotte, NC ....Business Law; Commercial Litigation; Insurance Defense

CANTEY & HANGER
Dallas, TX ....General Practice; Insurance Defense; Personal Injury
Fort Worth, TX ....General Practice; Insurance Defense; Labor and Employment Law; Personal Injury; Tax Law
Austin, TX ....Administrative Law; Insurance Defense; International Business Law; Tax Law

CANTOR, DAVID MICHAEL, P.C., LAW OFFICES OF
Mesa, AZ ....Criminal Trial Practice

CANTRILL, SKINNER, SULLIVAN & KING
Boise, ID ....General Practice; Insurance Defense

CAPITELLI & WICKER
New Orleans, LA ....Admiralty/Maritime Law; Civil Trial Practice; Criminal Trial Practice; Medical Malpractice; Personal Injury

CAPLAN, BUCKNER, ROHRBAUGH & KOSTECKA, CHTD.
Bethesda, MD ....General Practice

CAPLIN & DRYSDALE, CHARTERED
Washington, DC ....Business Law; Civil Trial Practice; Criminal Trial Practice; Tax Law; Trust and Estates, Wills and Probate
New York, NY ....Business Law; Civil Trial Practice; Criminal Trial Practice; Trust and Estates, Wills and Probate

CAPRETZ & ASSOCIATES
Newport Beach, CA ....Business Law; Civil Trial Practice; Commercial Law; Commercial Litigation; Construction Law; General Practice; Product Liability Law; Toxic Torts

CAPUTO, ANTHONY J., P.C.
White Plains, NY ....Civil Trial Practice; Insurance Defense

CAPUTO, JOHN A., & ASSOCIATES
Pittsburgh, PA ....Medical Malpractice; Personal Injury; Product Liability Law

CARB, LURIA, COOK & KUFELD, LLP
New York, NY ....Commercial Litigation; Real Estate Law; Trust and Estates, Wills and Probate

CARDELLI HEBERT, P.C.
Royal Oak, MI ....Commercial Law; Insurance Defense; Product Liability Law

CARDILLO & CORBETT
New York, NY ....Admiralty/Maritime Law; Corporate Law

CARELLA, BYRNE, BAIN, GILFILLAN, CECCHI, STEWART & OLSTEIN, A PROFESSIONAL CORPORATION
Roseland, NJ ....General Practice; Municipal Bond/Public Authority Financing; Patent, Trademark, Copyright and Unfair Competition

CAREY, AUSTIN, JR., P.C.
Hartford, CT ....Environmental Law

CAREY & HILBERT
Clearwater, FL ....Personal Injury

CAREY, O'MALLEY, WHITAKER & MANSON, P.A.
Tampa, FL ....Commercial Litigation; Construction Law; Environmental Law

CARIDDI, MEE, RUÉ, AVOCATS ASSOCIÉS À LA COUR DE PARIS
Paris, France ....General Practice

CARLBERG, GWENDOLYN JO M.
Alexandria, VA ....Family Law

CARLIN, HELLSTROM & BITTNER
Davenport, IA ....General Practice

CARLIN, MADDOCK, FAY & CERBONE, P.C.
Florham Park, NJ ....Civil Trial Practice; Commercial Litigation; Environmental Law; General Practice; Labor and Employment Law; Product Liability Law

CARLIN & VASVARI, LLC
Youngstown, OH ....Civil Trial Practice

CARLINER, REMES AND MIRBAGHERI-SMITH, P.C.
Washington, DC ....Immigration and Naturalization

CARLOCK, DAVID, P.C.
Dallas, TX ....Family Law

CARLSMITH BALL
Los Angeles, CA ....General Practice
Washington, DC ....General Practice
Hilo, HI ....General Practice
Honolulu, HI ....Administrative Law; Admiralty/Maritime Law; Antitrust Law; Appellate Practice; Arbitration; Banking Law; Bankruptcy Law; Business Law; Civil Trial Practice; Commercial Law; Commercial Litigation; Construction Law; Corporate Law; Creditors Rights; Employment Benefits Law; Energy Law; Environmental Law; General Practice; Government Contracts; Health Care Law; Immigration and Naturalization; Intellectual Property Law; International Business Law; Labor and Employment Law; Land Use Law; Mergers and Acquisitions; Nonprofit and Tax Exempt Organizations; Patent, Trademark, Copyright and Unfair Competition; Pension and Profit Sharing; Public Utilities Law; Real Estate Law; Securities Law; Tax Law; Trust and Estates, Wills and Probate; Workers Compensation
Kailua-Kona, HI ....General Practice
Wailuku, HI ....General Practice
Hagåtña, GU ....General Practice
Saipan, TT ....General Practice
Mexico, D.F., Mexico ....General Practice

CARLSON, HAMMOND & PADDOCK, L.L.C.
Denver, CO .... Environmental Law

CARLSON WENDLER & ASSOCIATES, P.C.
Edwardsville, IL .... Personal Injury

CARLTON, FIELDS, WARD, EMMANUEL, SMITH & CUTLER, P.A.
Miami, FL .... General Practice
Orlando, FL .... General Practice
Pensacola, FL .... General Practice
St. Petersburg, FL .... General Practice
Tallahassee, FL .... General Practice
Tampa, FL .... General Practice
West Palm Beach, FL .... General Practice

CARMAN, BEAUCHAMP, SANG & TOPKIN, P.A.
Deerfield Beach, FL .... Insurance Defense

CARMAN, CALLAHAN & INGHAM
Farmingdale, NY .... Banking Law; Commercial Law; Insurance Defense; Trust and Estates, Wills and Probate

CARMICHAEL & POWELL, PROFESSIONAL CORPORATION
Phoenix, AZ .... Administrative Law; Bankruptcy Law; Construction Law; Personal Injury; Real Estate Law

CARMODY LAW OFFICES
Albuquerque, NM .... Family Law

CARMODY & TORRANCE LLP
New Haven, CT .... General Practice
Waterbury, CT .... General Practice

CARNEY BADLEY SMITH & SPELLMAN, P.S.
Seattle, WA .... General Practice

CARON & STEVENS/BAKER & MCKENZIE
Amsterdam, Netherlands .... General Practice

CAROSELLI, BEACHLER, MCTIERNAN & CONBOY, LLC
Pittsburgh, PA .... Personal Injury; Workers Compensation

CARPENTER & ASSOCIATES
Houston, TX .... Civil Trial Practice; Criminal Trial Practice; Legal Malpractice

CARPENTER, BENNETT & MORRISSEY
Newark, NJ .... Admiralty/Maritime Law; Antitrust Law; Appellate Practice; Banking Law; Civil Trial Practice; Commercial Law; Employment Benefits Law; Environmental Law; General Practice; Health Care Law; Labor and Employment Law; Personal Injury; Real Estate Law; Tax Law; Trust and Estates, Wills and Probate; Workers Compensation

CARPENTER & CHÂVEZ, LTD.
Albuquerque, NM .... Aviation Law; Civil Trial Practice; Medical Malpractice; Personal Injury; Product Liability Law

CARPENTER & KLATSKIN, P.C.
Denver, CO .... Commercial Law; Real Estate Law

CARPENTER & NIXON, LLP
Santa Fe, NM .... Natural Resources Law; Public Utilities Law

CARPENTER & O'CONNOR
Knoxville, TN .... General Practice; Insurance Defense

CARPONELLI & KRUG
Chicago, IL .... Civil Trial Practice

CARR, ALFORD, CLAUSEN & MCDONALD, L.L.C.
Mobile, AL .... Appellate Practice; Civil Trial Practice; Health Care Law; Insurance Defense; Product Liability Law; Professional Liability

CARR, ALLISON, PUGH, HOWARD, OLIVER & SISSON, P.C.
Birmingham, AL .... Civil Trial Practice; Insurance Defense; Labor and Employment Law; Product Liability Law; Transportation Law; Workers Compensation

CARR GOODSON WARNER, A PROFESSIONAL CORPORATION
Washington, DC .... Environmental Law; General Practice; Insurance Defense; Labor and Employment Law

CARR, HUNT & JOY L.L.P.
Lubbock, TX .... Appellate Practice; Commercial Law; Family Law; General Practice; Insurance Defense

CARR, KENNEDY, PETERSON & FROST, A LAW CORPORATION
Redding, CA .... Civil Trial Practice; General Practice

CARR & LISTON
Boston, MA .... Civil Trial Practice; Labor and Employment Law

CARR, MCCLELLAN, INGERSOLL, THOMPSON & HORN, PROFESSIONAL CORPORATION
Burlingame, CA .... General Practice

CARR, TABB & POPE
Atlanta, GA .... Civil Trial Practice

CARRINGTON, COLEMAN, SLOMAN & BLUMENTHAL, L.L.P.
Dallas, TX .... Antitrust Law; General Practice; Tax Law

CARROLL, MICHAEL BROOKS
San Francisco, CA .... Antitrust Law

CARROLL, CARROLL, DAVIDSON & YOUNG, P.C.
Syracuse, NY .... Civil Trial Practice; General Practice; Personal Injury; Trust and Estates, Wills and Probate

CARROLL, KELLY & MURPHY
Providence, RI .... Civil Trial Practice; General Practice

CARROW, ROBERT D.
San Francisco, CA .... Civil Trial Practice; Construction Law; Criminal Trial Practice; Personal Injury

CARRUTHERS & ROTH, P.A.
Greensboro, NC .... Civil Trial Practice; General Practice

CARSON, CHARLES T.
Phoenix, AZ .... Insurance Defense

CARSON, LESLIE J. JR.
Philadelphia, PA .... Trust and Estates, Wills and Probate

CARSON & COIL, P.C.
Jefferson City, MO .... Appellate Practice; Bankruptcy Law; Civil Trial Practice; Family Law; Insurance Defense; Medical Malpractice; Personal Injury; Real Estate Law; Trust and Estates, Wills and Probate; Workers Compensation

CARTER & COLEMAN
Alexandria, VA .... Civil Trial Practice; Employment Benefits Law; Health Care Law; Insurance Defense; Labor and Employment Law; Sports and Entertainment Law

CARTER, NOLAN, P.A.
Orlando, FL .... Medical Malpractice; Personal Injury

CARTER & THOMAS LLP, LAW OFFICES OF
Boca Raton, FL .... Civil Trial Practice; Elder Law; Personal Injury; Real Estate Law; Trust and Estates, Wills and Probate

CARTON, WITT, ARVANITIS & BARISCILLO, L.L.C.
Asbury Park, NJ .... Banking Law; Civil Trial Practice; Corporate Law; General Practice; Insurance Defense
Manasquan, NJ .... Banking Law; Civil Trial Practice; Corporate Law; General Practice; Insurance Defense

CARTWRIGHT, DRUKER & RYDEN
Marshalltown, IA .... General Practice

CARUANA AND LORENZEN, P.A.
Miami, FL .... Commercial Litigation; Family Law

CARUSO, BURLINGTON, BOHN & COMPIANI, P.A.
West Palm Beach, FL .... Appellate Practice

CARUSO & GEORGETTI
Toledo, OH .... Personal Injury

CARVER, DARDEN, KORETZKY, TESSIER, FINN, BLOSSMAN & AREAUX, L.L.C.
New Orleans, LA .... Banking Law; Oil and Gas Law

CARY, WELCH & HICKMAN, L.L.P.
Hannibal, MO .... General Practice

CASARINO, CHRISTMAN & SHALK
Wilmington, DE .... Civil Trial Practice; Insurance Defense; Personal Injury; Product Liability Law; Workers Compensation

CASASSA AND RYAN
Hampton, NH .... Corporate Law; General Practice; Real Estate Law; Trust and Estates, Wills and Probate

CASE & DUSTERHOFF, LLP
Beaverton, OR .... Insurance Defense; Product Liability Law

CASEY, DONALD C.
Alexandria, VA .... Patent, Trademark, Copyright and Unfair Competition

CASEY, JOHN F.
Columbus, OH .... Business Law

CASEY & BARNETT, LLC
New York, NY .... Admiralty/Maritime Law

CASEY, GENTZ & SIFUENTES, L.L.P.
Austin, TX .... Communications Law

CASEY, GERRY, REED & SCHENK
San Diego, CA .... Business Law; Civil Trial Practice; Personal Injury; Product Liability Law

CASEY & RICHARDS
Newport Beach, CA .... Trust and Estates, Wills and Probate

CASH JONES, L.L.P.
Houston, TX .... Civil Trial Practice; Real Estate Law

CASKIE & FROST, A PROFESSIONAL CORPORATION
Lynchburg, VA .... General Practice

CASNER & EDWARDS, LLP
Boston, MA .... Business Law; Civil Trial Practice; General Practice

CASPER AND CASPER
Middletown, OH .... Personal Injury; Workers Compensation

CASPER & DE TOLEDO LLC
Stamford, CT .... Civil Trial Practice; Labor and Employment Law; Personal Injury

CASPER, MEADOWS & SCHWARTZ, A PROFESSIONAL CORPORATION
Walnut Creek, CA .... Personal Injury

CASSADY, FULLER & MARSH, LLP
Enterprise, AL .... Civil Trial Practice; General Practice; Insurance Defense

CASSELS BROCK & BLACKWELL LLP
Toronto, ON, Canada .... General Practice

CASSIDAY, SCHADE & GLOOR
Chicago, IL .... General Practice

CASSIDY, SEAN
Greensburg, PA .... Oil and Gas Law

CASSIDY, BRUCE G., & ASSOCIATES, P.A.
Philadelphia, PA .... Civil Trial Practice; Criminal Trial Practice; International Business Law; Personal Injury

CASSIDY & MUELLER
Peoria, IL .... Civil Trial Practice; General Practice; Insurance Defense

CASSIDY, MYERS, COGAN, VOEGELIN & TENNANT, L.C.
Wheeling, WV .... Civil Trial Practice; Labor and Employment Law; Personal Injury

CASSIDY, WARNER, LANE & WINSTEAD, A PROFESSIONAL CORPORATION
Santa Ana, CA .... Civil Trial Practice; Environmental Law; Insurance Defense; Product Liability Law

CASSTEVENS, HANNER, GUNTER & CONRAD, P.A.
Charlotte, NC .... General Practice

CASTELLO, WAYNE P.
Gainesville, FL .... Real Estate Law; Trust and Estates, Wills and Probate

CATALDO LAW OFFICES, LLP
Franklin, MA .... Criminal Trial Practice; Family Law

CATAPANO-FRIEDMAN, ROBERT S., P.C.
Albany, NY .... Employment Benefits Law; Labor and Employment Law; Tax Law

CATES & HOLLOWAY
Scottsdale, AZ .... Patent, Trademark, Copyright and Unfair Competition

CATHEY & STRAIN
Cornelia, GA .... Civil Trial Practice; Personal Injury; Product Liability Law

CATRI, HOLTON, KESSLER & KESSLER, P.A.
Fort Lauderdale, FL .... Appellate Practice; Civil Trial Practice; Insurance Defense; Personal Injury; Product Liability Law

CATRON, CATRON & SAWTELL, A PROFESSIONAL ASSOCIATION
Santa Fe, NM .... Appellate Practice; Banking Law; Civil Trial Practice; Commercial Law; General Practice; Real Estate Law; Tax Law; Trust and Estates, Wills and Probate

CATTERTON, KEMP & GREENBERG, P.A.
Rockville, MD .... Civil Trial Practice; Criminal Trial Practice

CATTS, AUSTIN E.
Brunswick, GA .... Civil Trial Practice; Personal Injury

CAUDLE & SPEARS, P.A.
Charlotte, NC .... Civil Trial Practice; Commercial Litigation; Environmental Law; General Practice; Insurance Defense; Personal Injury; Tax Law

CAULFIELD, DAVIES & DONAHUE
Sacramento, CA .... Construction Law; Insurance Defense; Personal Injury; Product Liability Law

CAUSEY, CAYWOOD, TAYLOR, MCMANUS & BAILEY
Memphis, TN .... Criminal Trial Practice; Family Law; General Practice; Trust and Estates, Wills and Probate

CAVAZOS, HENDRICKS, POIROT & DEWEY, P.C.
Dallas, TX .... Bankruptcy Law; Creditors Rights

CAVEY, NANCY L.
St. Petersburg, FL .... Workers Compensation

CAYER, KILSTOFTE & CRATON, A PROFESSIONAL LAW CORPORATION
Long Beach, CA .... Banking Law; Civil Trial Practice; General Practice

CEARLEY LAW FIRM, P.A.
Little Rock, AR .... Civil Trial Practice; General Practice

CEBALLOS, M. ALAN, P.A.
Jacksonville, FL .... Criminal Trial Practice

CELLA, MCKEON & WILLIAMS, P.C.
North Haven, CT .... Insurance Defense

CELLI, SCHLOSSBERG & DIAMOND, L.L.C.
Morristown, NJ .... Civil Trial Practice; Family Law

CENATIEMPO & DITTA, LLP
Houston, TX .... Trust and Estates, Wills and Probate

CERRATO, DAWES, COLLINS, SAKER & BROWN, A PROFESSIONAL CORPORATION
Freehold, NJ .... Civil Trial Practice; General Practice; Personal Injury

CERTILMAN BALIN ADLER & HYMAN, LLP
East Meadow, NY .... Bankruptcy Law; Civil Trial Practice; General Practice; Municipal and Zoning Law; Real Estate Law; Securities Law; Tax Law; Trust and Estates, Wills and Probate

CERUSSI & SPRING, A PROFESSIONAL CORPORATION
White Plains, NY .... Civil Trial Practice; Insurance Defense

CERVANTES & ASSOCIATES
St. Louis, MO .... Personal Injury

CESARANO, MARILYN J. W., P.A.
Miami, FL .... Family Law

CESARI AND MCKENNA, L.L.P.
Boston, MA .... Antitrust Law; Patent, Trademark, Copyright and Unfair Competition; Trademark, Copyright and Unfair Competition

CETRULO, ROBERT C., P.S.C.
Covington, KY .... Civil Trial Practice

CHADBOURNE & PARKE
London, England .... General Practice
Los Angeles, CA .... General Practice
Washington, DC .... General Practice
New York, NY .... General Practice
Hong Kong, China .... General Practice
Moscow, Russia .... General Practice

CHADWELL, STEELE R.
Princeton, NJ .... Health Care Law; Trust and Estates, Wills and Probate

CHAFFE, MCCALL, PHILLIPS, TOLER & SARPY, L.L.P.
New Orleans, LA .... Admiralty/Maritime Law; Commercial Litigation; General Practice; Labor and Employment Law; Natural Resources Law

CHAIKIN & SHERMAN, P.C.
Washington, DC .... Medical Malpractice; Personal Injury

CHAIREZ & ASSOCIATES
Irvine, CA .... Civil Trial Practice

CHALAT LAW OFFICES, P.C.
Denver, CO .... Medical Malpractice; Personal Injury

CHALIF, JOHN L. J.D., LL.M.
West Palm Beach, FL .... Securities Law

CHAMBERS, JOY S.
Alexandria, VA .... Trust and Estates, Wills and Probate

CHAMBERS LAW GROUP, PROFESSIONAL ASSOCIATION
St. Petersburg, FL .... Medical Malpractice; Personal Injury; Product Liability Law

CHAMPION, JAN
San Jose, CA .... Civil Trial Practice; Medical Malpractice; Personal Injury; Product Liability Law

CHANCE & MADDOX
Calhoun, GA..........General Practice

CHANDLER & BRITT, LLC
Buford, GA..........Criminal Trial Practice; General Practice

CHANDLER LAW OFFICES
Lufkin, TX..........Personal Injury

CHANDLER, TULLAR, UDALL & REDHAIR, L.L.P.
Tucson, AZ..........Civil Trial Practice; Commercial Law; Environmental Law; General Practice; Insurance Defense; Natural Resources Law; Personal Injury; Real Estate Law

CHANFRAU, CHANFRAU & BOUCK
Daytona Beach, FL..........Medical Malpractice; Personal Injury

CHANG, CHRISTOPHER E. LAW OFFICES OF
New York, NY..........Criminal Trial Practice

CHAPIN SHEA MCNITT & CARTER, A PROFESSIONAL CORPORATION
San Diego, CA..........Business Law; Civil Trial Practice; Commercial Law; Insurance Defense; Product Liability Law

CHAPMAN, MICHAEL L.
Atlanta, GA..........Commercial Law; Construction Law

CHAPMAN, BYRHOLDT & YON
Anderson, SC..........Criminal Trial Practice; Personal Injury; Workers Compensation

CHAPMAN AND CUTLER
Chicago, IL..........General Practice; Municipal Bond/Public Authority Financing
Salt Lake City, UT..........General Practice

CHAPMAN, GLUCKSMAN & DEAN, A PROFESSIONAL CORPORATION
Los Angeles, CA..........Construction Law; Insurance Defense

CHAPMAN, LEWIS & SWAN
Clarksdale, MS..........General Practice; Personal Injury

CHAPPANO WOOD PLL
Columbus, OH..........International Business Law

CHAPPELL, E. HUGH, JR., P.A.
Fort Lauderdale, FL..........Personal Injury

CHAPPELL, PARMELEE, JOHNSON & HILL, P.C.
Fort Worth, TX..........Civil Trial Practice; Education Law; General Practice

CHAR SAKAMOTO ISHII LUM & CHING
Honolulu, HI..........Civil Trial Practice

CHARAPP, DEESE & WEISS, LLP
Washington, DC..........Commercial Litigation; Corporate Law; Government Contracts; Labor and Employment Law

CHARFOOS, REITER, PETERSON, HOLMQUIST & PILCHAK, P.C.
Detroit, MI..........Civil Rights; Employment Benefits Law; Labor and Employment Law; Workers Compensation
Farmington Hills, MI..........Civil Rights; Employment Benefits Law; Labor and Employment Law; Workers Compensation

CHARITON & SCHWAGER
Wilkes-Barre, PA..........Business Law; Civil Trial Practice

CHARLSON BREDEHOFT, P.C.
Reston, VA..........Labor and Employment Law

CHARLSON, MARBEN & JORGENSON, P.A.
Thief River Falls, MN..........General Practice

CHARTERS, HECK, O'DONNELL, PETRULIS & ZORZA, P.C.
Troy, MI..........General Practice

CHARWAT, MARK S., P.C.
Garden City, NY..........Trust and Estates, Wills and Probate

CHASON & CHASON, P.C.
Bay Minette, AL..........General Practice

CHATHAM LAW FIRM
Hernando, MS..........General Practice; Medical Malpractice

CHATTERTON, ROBERT D.
Orange, CA..........Criminal Trial Practice

CHATTMAN, GAINES & STERN
Cleveland, OH..........Commercial Litigation; Corporate Law; Labor and Employment Law; Trust and Estates, Wills and Probate

CHAUNCEY, HARRISON K., JR., P.A., LAW OFFICES OF
Palm Beach, FL..........Business Law; Real Estate Law; Tax Law; Trust and Estates, Wills and Probate

CHAVEZ, THEODORE R.
Campbell, CA..........Real Estate Law

CHEADLE & CHEADLE
Nashville, TN..........Commercial Litigation; Creditors Rights

CHEATHAM, ESTES & HOLLMAN, P.C.
West Bloomfield, MI..........Civil Trial Practice; Environmental Law; Insurance Defense; Medical Malpractice; Product Liability Law; Trust and Estates, Wills and Probate

CHEEK & ZEEHANDELAR, LLP
Columbus, OH..........Creditors Rights

CHEHARDY, SHERMAN, ELLIS, BRESLIN & MURRAY, L.L.P.
Metairie, LA..........General Practice

CHEN, WALSH, TECLER & MCCABE, L.L.P.
Rockville, MD..........General Practice; Real Estate Law

CHENEY & CHENEY, P.C.
Reidsville, GA..........General Practice; Personal Injury

CHERNAU, CHAFFIN & BURNSED, PLLC
Nashville, TN..........Banking Law; Civil Trial Practice; Labor and Employment Law; Real Estate Law; Trademark, Copyright and Unfair Competition

CHERNIN & GOLD, LLP
Binghamton, NY..........General Practice

CHERNOFF, VILHAUER, MCCLUNG & STENZEL, LLP
Portland, OR..........Patent, Trademark, Copyright and Unfair Competition

CHERNOV, STERN & KRINGS, S.C.
Milwaukee, WI..........Appellate Practice; Commercial Law; Commercial Litigation; Corporate Law; Creditors Rights; Product Liability Law; Real Estate Law; Trust and Estates, Wills and Probate

CHERWIN, GLICKMAN & THEISE, LLP
Boston, MA..........Business Law; Commercial Law; General Practice

CHESNUT, LIVINGSTON & PYE, P.C.
Doraville, GA..........General Practice

CHESNUTT, CHARLES R.
Dallas, TX..........Bankruptcy Law

CHESTER, WILLCOX AND SAXBE LLP
Columbus, OH..........Bankruptcy Law; Business Law; Civil Trial Practice; International Business Law; Public Utilities Law; Real Estate Law; Securities Law; Trust and Estates, Wills and Probate

CHICOINE & HALLETT, P.S.
Seattle, WA..........Tax Law

CHIERICI, CHIERICI & SMITH, A PROFESSIONAL CORPORATION
Moorestown, NJ..........Appellate Practice; Civil Trial Practice; Commercial Litigation; General Practice; Insurance Defense; Medical Malpractice; Personal Injury; Product Liability Law; Toxic Torts

CHILVERS & TAYLOR, PC
Emeryville, CA..........Commercial Litigation; Health Care Law

CHIMEL DORADO
New York, NY..........Corporate Law; International Business Law; Real Estate Law

CHIMICLES & TIKELLIS LLP
Haverford, PA..........Civil Trial Practice

CHING, YUEN & MORIKAWA
Honolulu, HI..........Banking Law; Real Estate Law; Tax Law

CHINN & ASSOCIATES, PLLC
Jackson, MS..........Family Law

CHINNERY, CARL, & ASSOCIATES, P.C.
Lee's Summit, MO..........Business Law; Real Estate Law; Trust and Estates, Wills and Probate

CHISENHALL, NESTRUD & JULIAN, P.A.
Little Rock, AR..........Civil Trial Practice; Corporate Law; Environmental Law; Public Utilities Law

CHITWOOD & HARLEY
Atlanta, GA..........Antitrust Law; Securities Law

CHOATE, HALL & STEWART
Boston, MA..........General Practice

CHOPIN, WAGAR, COLE, RICHARD, REBOUL & KUTCHER, LLP
Metairie, LA..........General Practice

CHORCHES & NOVAK, P.C.
Wethersfield, CT..........Bankruptcy Law

COOPER, SPONG & DAVIS, P.C.
Portsmouth, VA....................Environmental Law; General Practice; Health Care Law

COOPER & STIELER
New Providence, NJ................Intellectual Property Law; Patent, Trademark, Copyright and Unfair Competition

COOPER & TUERK, LLP
Baltimore, MD....................Personal Injury; Product Liability Law

COOPER & WOLFE, P.A.
Miami, FL....................Appellate Practice

COOPER & WOODRUFF, A LAW CORPORATION
Abbeville, LA....................General Practice

COOPERMAN LEVITT WINIKOFF LESTER & NEWMAN, P.C.
New York, NY....................Civil Trial Practice; Corporate Law; General Practice

COOVER & COOVER
Corpus Christi, TX....................Family Law

COPE, JOSEPH ADAMS
Boulder, CO....................Civil Trial Practice; Natural Resources Law

COPELAND COOK TAYLOR & BUSH, A PROFESSIONAL ASSOCIATION
Jackson, MS....................Banking Law; Civil Trial Practice; Commercial Law; Insurance Defense; Natural Resources Law; Tax Law

COPELAND, LANDYE, BENNETT AND WOLF, LLP
Portland, OR....................Bankruptcy Law; Business Law; Environmental Law; Real Estate Law; Securities Law

COPP & BERALL, LLP
Hartford, CT....................Tax Law; Trust and Estates, Wills and Probate

COPPLE, CHAMBERLIN, BOEHM & MURPHY, P.C.
Phoenix, AZ....................Appellate Practice; Insurance Defense; Medical Malpractice; Personal Injury

CORBAN & GUNN
Biloxi, MS....................Business Law; General Practice; Insurance Defense

CORBETT CROCKETT & LECKRONE
Nashville, TN....................Commercial Law; Commercial Litigation; Real Estate Law; Tax Law

CORBETT GORDON & ASSOCIATES, P.C.
Portland, OR....................Labor and Employment Law

CORBIN SILVERMAN & SANSEVERINO LLP
New York, NY....................Banking Law; Corporate Law; Securities Law

CORBITT & JOHNSON, P.C.
Tulsa, OK....................Family Law

CORBOY & DEMETRIO, P.C.
Chicago, IL....................Civil Trial Practice; Medical Malpractice; Personal Injury

CORCORAN, WILLIAM E.
McAllen, TX....................Family Law; Personal Injury

CORCORAN, ROBERT T., P.C.
Hackensack, NJ....................Appellate Practice; Family Law

CORDA, WILLIAM J.
Lakeland, FL....................Personal Injury

CORDRAY & GOODRICH, PROFESSIONAL CORPORATION
Houston, TX....................Business Law; Mergers and Acquisitions; Real Estate Law; Tax Law; Trust and Estates, Wills and Probate

CORETTE POHLMAN & KEBE, A PROFESSIONAL CORPORATION
Butte, MT....................General Practice

CORKERN & CREWS, L.L.C.
Natchitoches, LA....................Insurance Defense

CORLEY, MONCUS & WARD, P.C.
Birmingham, AL....................Bankruptcy Law; General Practice; Insurance Defense; Real Estate Law; Trust and Estates, Wills and Probate

CORNBLATT, BENNETT, PENHALLEGON & ROBERSON, P.A.
Baltimore, MD....................Insurance Defense; Medical Malpractice; Product Liability Law; Workers Compensation

CORNELIUS & COLLINS, LLP
Nashville, TN....................Civil Trial Practice; General Practice

CORNELL & GOLLUB
Boston, MA....................Civil Trial Practice; General Practice; Insurance Defense; Medical Malpractice

CORRERO FISHMAN HAYGOOD PHELPS WALMSLEY & CASTEIX, L.L.P.
New Orleans, LA....................Banking Law; Business Law; Commercial Litigation; Corporate Law; Mergers and Acquisitions; Real Estate Law; Securities Law; Trust and Estates, Wills and Probate

CORSI, MARIO D.
Dover, OH....................Real Estate Law; Trust and Estates, Wills and Probate

CORTEZ MACAULAY BERNHARDT & SCHUETZE LLC
Denver, CO....................Arbitration; Business Law; Civil Trial Practice; Commercial Litigation; Labor and Employment Law; Personal Injury; Product Liability Law

CORWIN, BRENT E., P.C.
Scottsdale, AZ....................Commercial Litigation; Personal Injury

CORY, TIMOTHY S. & ASSOCIATES, LAW OFFICES OF
Las Vegas, NV....................Bankruptcy Law

CORY, KENNETH C., A PROFESSIONAL CORPORATION
Las Vegas, NV....................Civil Trial Practice; Criminal Trial Practice; Personal Injury

CORY, MEREDITH, WITTER, ROUSH & CHENEY, A LEGAL PROFESSIONAL ASSOCIATION
Lima, OH....................General Practice

COSGRAVE, VERGEER & KESTER, L.L.P.
Portland, OR....................General Practice

COSTELLO COONEY & FEARON, LLP
Syracuse, NY....................Bankruptcy Law; Civil Trial Practice; Corporate Law; General Practice; Health Care Law; Labor and Employment Law; Real Estate Law; Tax Law; Trademark, Copyright and Unfair Competition

COSTILLA, FRANK, JR., P.L.L.C.
Brownsville, TX....................Personal Injury

COTHRAN, JAMES C. JR.
Spartanburg, SC....................Civil Trial Practice

COTKIN, COLLINS & GINSBURG, A PROFESSIONAL CORPORATION
Los Angeles, CA....................General Practice
Santa Ana, CA....................General Practice

COTNEY, HUGH, P.A.
Jacksonville, FL....................Criminal Trial Practice; Personal Injury; Product Liability Law

COTSIRILOS, JOHN G.
San Diego, CA....................Criminal Trial Practice

COTTER, COTTER AND SOHON, P.C.
Bridgeport, CT....................Insurance Defense; Workers Compensation

COTTINGHAM & PORTER, P.C.
Douglas, GA....................General Practice

COTTON, JOHN H., & ASSOCIATES, LTD.
Scottsdale, AZ....................Civil Trial Practice; Commercial Litigation; Medical Malpractice

COUCH WHITE, LLP
Albany, NY....................Administrative Law; Construction Law; Energy Law; General Practice; Health Care Law; Public Utilities Law

COUGHLIN & GERHART, L.L.P.
Binghamton, NY....................Civil Trial Practice; General Practice

COULOMBE LAW FIRM, THE, A PROFESSIONAL CORPORATION
Costa Mesa, CA....................Civil Trial Practice

COUNCIL, BARADEL, KOSMERL & NOLAN, P.A.
Annapolis, MD....................Business Law; Civil Trial Practice; Environmental Law; Family Law; Insurance Defense; Labor and Employment Law; Municipal and Zoning Law; Personal Injury; Real Estate Law; Trust and Estates, Wills and Probate

COURBOIS, FRANCIS
Oklahoma City, OK....................Criminal Trial Practice

COURTLAND, ROBERT D., CHARTERED
Bethesda, MD....................Tax Law

COUSINEAU, MCGUIRE & ANDERSON, CHARTERED
Minneapolis, MN....................Insurance Defense

COUZENS, LANSKY, FEALK, ELLIS, ROEDER & LAZAR, P.C.
Farmington Hills, MI....................Bankruptcy Law; Business Law; Civil Trial Practice; Commercial Law; Corporate Law; Employment Benefits Law; General Practice; Labor and Employment Law; Pension and Profit Sharing; Real Estate Law; Tax Law; Trust and Estates, Wills and Probate

COVINGTON & BURLING
Washington, DC....General Practice

COVINGTON & CROWE LLP
Ontario, CA....Civil Trial Practice; Employment Benefits Law; Family Law; General Practice; Real Estate Law

COVINGTON, PATRICK, HAGINS, STERN & LEWIS, P.A.
Greenville, SC....Civil Trial Practice; Product Liability Law

COWAN, DENNIS K.
Redding, CA....Bankruptcy Law

COWARD, HICKS & SILER, P.A.
Sylva, NC....Civil Trial Practice; Real Estate Law; Trust and Estates, Wills and Probate

COWART, ROY N., P.C.
Warner Robins, GA....Corporate Law; General Practice

COWLES & THOMPSON, A PROFESSIONAL CORPORATION
Dallas, TX....Civil Trial Practice; Commercial Law; General Practice; Insurance Defense; Municipal and Zoning Law
McKinney, TX....General Practice
Tyler, TX....General Practice

COX, GOUDY, MCNULTY & WALLACE, P.L.L.P.
Minneapolis, MN....Civil Trial Practice; Commercial Law; Personal Injury

COX HANSON O'REILLY MATHESON
Fredericton, NB, Canada....Administrative Law; Appellate Practice; Banking Law; Bankruptcy Law; Civil Trial Practice; Commercial Law; Construction Law; Environmental Law; Family Law; General Practice; Insurance Defense; Labor and Employment Law; Real Estate Law; Tax Law
Saint John, NB, Canada....Tax Law
St. John's, NF, Canada....General Practice; Insurance Defense
Halifax, NS, Canada....General Practice

COX, LEVAN, SPRADER & PATTON, P.L.L.C.
Nashville, TN....Insurance Defense; Transportation Law

COX & MOYER, A PROFESSIONAL CORPORATION
San Francisco, CA....Antitrust Law; Aviation Law; Civil Trial Practice; Medical Malpractice; Personal Injury; Product Liability Law

COX PADMORE SKOLNIK & SHAKARCHY
Denver, CO....Commercial Litigation; International Business Law
New York, NY....General Practice

COX & SMITH INCORPORATED
San Antonio, TX....Antitrust Law; Banking Law; Bankruptcy Law; Business Law; Civil Trial Practice; Computer Law; General Practice; Health Care Law; Labor and Employment Law; Natural Resources Law; Patent, Trademark, Copyright and Unfair Competition; Real Estate Law; Securities Law; Tax Law; Trust and Estates, Wills and Probate

COX, ZWERNER, GAMBILL & SULLIVAN
Terre Haute, IN....Banking Law; Civil Trial Practice; General Practice; Insurance Defense; Real Estate Law; Trust and Estates, Wills and Probate

COY, GILBERT & GILBERT
Richmond, KY....General Practice

COYNE, NIESS, SCHULTZ, BECKER & BAUER, S.C.
Madison, WI....Civil Trial Practice

COZEN AND O'CONNOR, A PROFESSIONAL CORPORATION
Philadelphia, PA....Civil Trial Practice; Commercial Law; General Practice; Insurance Defense; Personal Injury

CRABBE, BROWN, JONES, POTTS & SCHMIDT
Columbus, OH....Civil Trial Practice; General Practice; Insurance Defense

CRABTREE, SCHMIDT, ZEFF, JACOBS & FARRAR
Modesto, CA....General Practice

CRACKEN, HARKEY & PAYNE, LLP
Dallas, TX....Civil Trial Practice; Medical Malpractice; Personal Injury; Product Liability Law

CRADDICK, CANDLAND & CONTI, PROFESSIONAL CORPORATION
Danville, CA....Business Law; Civil Trial Practice; Insurance Defense; Medical Malpractice

CRAFT, PATRICIA J., P.C.
Decatur, GA....Labor and Employment Law

CRAIG, RANDALL K. LAW OFFICES OF
Evansville, IN....Business Law; Tax Law; Trust and Estates, Wills and Probate

CRAIG & CRAIG
Mattoon, IL....Banking Law; Business Law; Civil Trial Practice; Commercial Law; Environmental Law; General Practice; Labor and Employment Law; Land Use Law; Medical Malpractice; Natural Resources Law; Product Liability Law; Public Utilities Law; Real Estate Law; Trust and Estates, Wills and Probate; Workers Compensation

CRAIG AND MACAULEY, PROFESSIONAL CORPORATION
Boston, MA....Banking Law; Bankruptcy Law; Business Law; Commercial Litigation; General Practice; Insurance Defense

CRAIGE, BRAWLEY, LIIPFERT & WALKER, L.L.P.
Winston-Salem, NC....General Practice; Insurance Defense; Trust and Estates, Wills and Probate

CRAMER & ANDERSON LLP
Litchfield, CT....General Practice

CRAMER LAW FIRM, THE
Jacksonville, FL....Insurance Defense; Labor and Employment Law; Personal Injury; Workers Compensation

CRAMER, MULTHAUF & HAMMES, LLP
Waukesha, WI....Business Law

CRANFILL, SUMNER & HARTZOG, L.L.P.
Raleigh, NC....Insurance Defense; Personal Injury

CRANMORE, FITZGERALD & MEANEY
Hartford, CT....Banking Law; Civil Trial Practice; Real Estate Law

CRARY, HUFF, INKSTER, HECHT & SHEEHAN, P.C.
Sioux City, IA....General Practice

CRAVATH, SWAINE & MOORE
New York, NY....General Practice
Hong Kong, China....General Practice
London, England....General Practice

CRAWFORD, B. HAYDEN
Tulsa, OK....Civil Trial Practice

CRAWFORD, JOHN A. JR.
San Diego, CA....Criminal Trial Practice

CRAWFORD, RUSSELL E.
Orlando, FL....Criminal Trial Practice

CRAWFORD & MCKINNEY
Houston, TX....Personal Injury; Professional Liability

CREEDON & FELICIANI, P.C.
Norristown, PA....Civil Trial Practice; Medical Malpractice; Personal Injury; Product Liability Law

CREMEN, FRANK J.
Las Vegas, NV....Criminal Trial Practice

CREMINS & ASSOCIATES, P.C.
Fairfax, VA....Appellate Practice; Civil Trial Practice; Health Care Law; Medical Malpractice

CRENSHAW, DUPREE & MILAM, L.L.P.
Lubbock, TX....Insurance Defense; Medical Malpractice; Trust and Estates, Wills and Probate

CREWS & HANCOCK, P.L.C.
Richmond, VA....Business Law; Commercial Law; Health Care Law; Medical Malpractice

CREWS & KLEIN, P.C.
Charlotte, NC....Insurance Defense

CRIBBS & MCFARLAND, A PROFESSIONAL CORPORATION
Arlington, TX....General Practice

CRIMMINS, ROBERT C.
Riverhead, NY....Civil Trial Practice; Commercial Litigation

CRISLIP, PHILIP & ASSOCIATES
Memphis, TN....General Practice

CRISP PAGE & CURRIN, L.L.P.
Raleigh, NC....Communications Law

CRIST, SCHULZ, BIORN & SHEPHERD, A PROFESSIONAL CORPORATION
Palo Alto, CA....Trust and Estates, Wills and Probate

CRISTE, VIRGINIA S. LAW OFFICES OF
Indian Wells, CA....Family Law

CRISTE, PIPPIN & GOLDS
Palm Desert, CA....Bankruptcy Law; Business Law; Civil Trial Practice; Real Estate Law

CRITTENDEN • MARTIN
Birmingham, AL....Family Law

CRITTENDEN & CRITTENDEN, P.A.
Winter Haven, FL....................General Practice

CROCKETT, DAVID G., P.C.
Atlanta, GA ....Bankruptcy Law; Civil Trial Practice; Commercial Law; Creditors Rights; Real Estate Law

CROCKETT & MYERS, LTD., A PROFESSIONAL CORPORATION
Las Vegas, NV ....Medical Malpractice; Personal Injury; Workers Compensation

CROFTS, CALLAWAY & JEFFERSON, A PROFESSIONAL CORPORATION
San Antonio, TX......................Appellate Practice

CROLEY, DAVIDSON & HUIE
Knoxville, TN ....Real Estate Law

CROMWELL, MARGRIT E. LAW OFFICE OF
Tucson, AZ ....Family Law

CRONIN, FRIED, SEKIYA, KEKINA & FAIRBANKS, ATTORNEYS AT LAW, A LAW CORPORATION
Honolulu, HI...........................Admiralty/Maritime Law; Aviation Law; Medical Malpractice; Personal Injury; Product Liability Law; Professional Liability

CRONIN & STANEWICH
Phoenix, AZ ....Insurance Defense; Medical Malpractice; Personal Injury; Product Liability Law

CROSS, MURPHY, SMUCK & HOUSTON
Washington, DC......................Tax Law; Trust and Estates, Wills and Probate

CROSSETT, EDGAR L., III, P.C.
Atlanta, GA ....Personal Injury

CROW AND CROW
Pomeroy, OH ....General Practice

CROWE & DUNLEVY
Norman, OK ....Banking Law; Bankruptcy Law; Civil Trial Practice; Commercial Law; Corporate Law; General Practice; Health Care Law; Labor and Employment Law; Municipal Bond/Public Authority Financing; Real Estate Law
Oklahoma City, OK................Antitrust Law; Appellate Practice; Banking Law; Bankruptcy Law; Civil Trial Practice; Commercial Law; Commercial Litigation; Corporate Law; General Practice; Health Care Law; Intellectual Property Law; Labor and Employment Law; Municipal Bond/Public Authority Financing; Oil and Gas Law; Patent, Trademark, Copyright and Unfair Competition; Real Estate Law; Securities Law; Tax Law; Workers Compensation
Tulsa, OK.................................Banking Law; Bankruptcy Law; Civil Trial Practice; Commercial Law; Commercial Litigation; Corporate Law; General Practice; Health Care Law; Intellectual Property Law; Labor and Employment Law; Municipal Bond/Public Authority Financing; Oil and Gas Law; Real Estate Law; Securities Law; Workers Compensation

CROWE & SCOTT, P.A.
Phoenix, AZ ....Civil Trial Practice; Criminal Trial Practice

CROWELL, WILLIAM D.
Harwich Port, MA...................Real Estate Law

CROWELL & MORING
London, England ....General Practice
Irvine, CA................................General Practice
Washington, DC......................General Practice

CROWELL AND OWENS, L.L.C.
Alexandria, LA ....Business Law; Tax Law; Trust and Estates, Wills and Probate

CROWELL, SUSICH, OWEN & TACKES, LTD., A PROF. LAW CORP.
Carson City, NV ....Administrative Law; Business Law

CROWLEY BARRETT & KARABA, LTD.
Chicago, IL..............................Commercial Litigation

CROWLEY, HAUGHEY, HANSON, TOOLE & DIETRICH, P.L.L.P.
Billings, MT ....Administrative Law; Banking Law; Bankruptcy Law; Business Law; Civil Trial Practice; Commercial Law; Criminal Trial Practice; Employment Benefits Law; Environmental Law; Family Law; General Practice; Health Care Law; Immigration and Naturalization; Insurance Defense; Labor and Employment Law; Medical Malpractice; Municipal Bond/Public Authority Financing; Natural Resources Law; Personal Injury; Product Liability Law; Public Utilities Law; Real Estate Law; Securities Law; Tax Law; Trademark, Copyright and Unfair Competition; Transportation Law; Trust and Estates, Wills and Probate; Workers Compensation

CROWSON & INGRAM
El Paso, TX.............................Banking Law; Bankruptcy Law; Business Law; Civil Trial Practice; Commercial Law; Commercial Litigation; Creditors Rights; General Practice; Real Estate Law

CRUMP, TOLSON & PAGE LLP
Tulsa, OK................................Commercial Litigation; Environmental Law; General Practice

CRUMPLER O'CONNOR & WYNNE
El Dorado, AR ....General Practice

CRUSE, FIRETAG & BOCK, P.C.
Phoenix, AZ ....Banking Law; Commercial Law; Real Estate Law

CRUSE, SCOTT, HENDERSON & ALLEN, L.L.P.
Houston, TX ....Civil Trial Practice; Medical Malpractice; Professional Liability

CRUTSINGER & BOOTH
Dallas, TX...............................Patent, Trademark, Copyright and Unfair Competition

CRYSTAL, HEYTOW & WARNICK, P.C.
Chicago, IL..............................Insurance Defense

CUCCIO AND CUCCIO
Hackensack, NJ.......................General Practice

CULBERTSON, THOMAS A.
Santa Ana, CA ....Civil Trial Practice

CULBRETH, STEPHEN E.
Wilmington, NC......................Appellate Practice; Criminal Trial Practice; Personal Injury; Workers Compensation

CULLEN LAW FIRM, LTD.
Minneapolis, MN ....Civil Trial Practice

CULP ELLIOTT & CARPENTER, P.L.L.C.
Charlotte, NC..........................Tax Law

CULVER, SHERIDAN, KNOWLTON, EVEN & FRANKS, P.C.
Muskegon, MI.........................Business Law; Commercial Litigation; General Practice; Real Estate Law

CUMMINGS & SNYDER, P.A.
Fort Lauderdale, FL ....Administrative Law; Construction Law; Government Contracts
Tallahassee, FL ....Administrative Law; Construction Law; Government Contracts

CUMMINS, BERNARD F.
Martinez, CA...........................General Practice

CUNEO LAW GROUP, THE, P.C.
Washington, DC......................Administrative Law; Antitrust Law; Commercial Litigation; Corporate Law; Securities Law

CUNNINGHAM, BLACKBURN, FRANCIS, BROCK & CUNNINGHAM
Grand Island, NE ....General Practice

CUNNINGHAM, BOUNDS, YANCE, CROWDER & BROWN, L.L.C.
Mobile, AL..............................Admiralty/Maritime Law; Aviation Law; Civil Trial Practice; General Practice; Medical Malpractice; Personal Injury; Product Liability Law; Professional Liability; Transportation Law

CUNNINGHAM, CLARK & GREIWE, P.A.
Tampa, FL ....Civil Trial Practice; General Practice; Medical Malpractice; Personal Injury; Product Liability Law

CUNNINGHAM DALMAN, P.C.
Holland, MI ....Banking Law; Business Law; Civil Trial Practice; Environmental Law; Family Law; General Practice; Insurance Defense; Personal Injury; Real Estate Law; Trust and Estates, Wills and Probate

CUNNINGHAM, DARLOW, ZOOK & CHAPOTON, LLP
Houston, TX ....Antitrust Law; Commercial Litigation; Intellectual Property Law; Securities Law

CUNNINGHAM LAW FIRM
Phoenix, AZ ....Personal Injury

CURAN, MICHAEL E., P.C., THE LAW OFFICES OF
New York, NY.........................Administrative Law; Civil Trial Practice; Insurance Defense; Personal Injury

CURET & BARRON
Hammond, LA.........................General Practice

CURIALE DELLAVERSON HIRSCHFELD KELLY & KRAEMER, LLP
Los Angeles, CA ....Labor and Employment Law
San Francisco, CA ....Labor and Employment Law

CURLEY & CURLEY, P.C.
Boston, MA.............................Civil Trial Practice; General Practice; Insurance Defense

CURRAN, DENNIS J.
Boston, MA.............................Civil Trial Practice; Personal Injury

CURRAN & CURRAN
Fort Lauderdale, FL ....Corporate Law

CURRAN, JAMES, P.A.
Fort Lauderdale, FL.....Administrative Law

CURRAN & PARRY
Las Vegas, NV.....Construction Law; Municipal and Zoning Law; Real Estate Law

CURRAN AND WATSON
Fullerton, CA.....Criminal Trial Practice

CURRIE JOHNSON GRIFFIN GAINES & MYERS, PLLC
Jackson, MS.....Civil Trial Practice; General Practice; Insurance Defense; Medical Malpractice

CURRIE KENDALL POLASKY MEISEL, PLC
Midland, MI.....Banking Law; Civil Trial Practice; Family Law; General Practice; Real Estate Law; Tax Law
Saginaw, MI.....Banking Law; Civil Trial Practice; Family Law; General Practice; Real Estate Law; Tax Law

CURRY, MORIN AND GOUDARZI, P.C.
Marshall, TX.....Aviation Law; Civil Trial Practice; Personal Injury

CURTIN & HEEFNER, LLP
Morrisville, PA.....General Practice

CURTIN, MURPHY & O'REILLY, P.C.
Boston, MA.....Civil Trial Practice; Insurance Defense

CURTIS, BRINCKERHOFF & BARRETT, P.C.
Stamford, CT.....Administrative Law; Business Law; Civil Trial Practice; Commercial Law; Commercial Litigation; Corporate Law; Elder Law; Eminent Domain; Family Law; General Practice; Land Use Law; Personal Injury; Real Estate Law; Tax Law; Trust and Estates, Wills and Probate

CURTIS & LAMBERT, A PROFESSIONAL LAW CORPORATION
Lafayette, LA.....Admiralty/Maritime Law; Personal Injury

CURTIS LAW OFFICE
Oshkosh, WI.....Civil Trial Practice; Personal Injury; Trust and Estates, Wills and Probate; Workers Compensation

CURTIS, MALLET-PREVOST, COLT & MOSLE
Mexico, D.F., Mexico.....General Practice
Washington, DC.....General Practice
Newark, NJ.....General Practice
New York, NY.....Admiralty/Maritime Law; Bankruptcy Law; Civil Trial Practice; Criminal Trial Practice; International Business Law; Real Estate Law; Tax Law; Trust and Estates, Wills and Probate
London, England.....General Practice
Paris, France.....General Practice
Frankfurt/Main, Germany.....General Practice

CUSHING, PETER
Orlando, FL.....Family Law

CUSHING, MORRIS, ARMBRUSTER & JONES, LLP
Atlanta, GA.....Business Law

CUSTER & HILL, P.C.
Marietta, GA.....Family Law; General Practice; Trust and Estates, Wills and Probate

CUTHBERT LAW OFFICES, A PROFESSIONAL CORPORATION
Petersburg, VA.....Personal Injury

CUTLER, LAURENCE J.
Morristown, NJ.....Family Law

CUTLER & STANFIELD, L.L.P.
Denver, CO.....Transportation Law
Washington, DC.....Aviation Law; Energy Law; Environmental Law; Municipal and Zoning Law; Natural Resources Law; Transportation Law

CUTRIGHT & CUTRIGHT
Chillicothe, OH.....General Practice; Real Estate Law; Trust and Estates, Wills and Probate

CUYLER BURK
Parsippany, NJ.....Appellate Practice; Arbitration; Banking Law; Business Law; Civil Trial Practice; Commercial Litigation; Corporate Law; Environmental Law; General Practice; Insurance Defense; Personal Injury; Real Estate Law; Toxic Torts

CYPERT, CROUCH, CLARK & HARWELL
Springdale, AR.....Commercial Litigation; General Practice; Insurance Defense

CYRIL & CROWLEY LLP
San Francisco, CA.....Civil Trial Practice; Insurance Defense; Product Liability Law

CZYGIER, JOHN M. JR.
Riverhead, NY.....Trust and Estates, Wills and Probate

DAAR & NEWMAN, PROFESSIONAL CORPORATION
Los Angeles, CA.....General Practice; Insurance Defense; International Business Law

D'AGOSTINO, KRACKELER, BAYNES & MAGUIRE, P.C.
Albany, NY.....General Practice

DAHL, JAMES E. & ASSOCIATES
Chicago, IL.....Civil Trial Practice

DAHLGREN AND CLOSE
Washington, DC.....International Business Law

DAILEY, GARRETT C.
Oakland, CA.....Family Law

DAILY & WOODS, P.L.L.C.
Fort Smith, AR.....Civil Trial Practice; General Practice; Insurance Defense; Oil and Gas Law

DALEIDEN & TREMAINE, LTD.
Arlington Heights, IL.....General Practice

DALE & KLEIN, L.L.P.
McAllen, TX.....Civil Trial Practice; Family Law; Insurance Defense

D'ALESSANDRO, JACOVINO & GERSON
Florham Park, NJ.....Civil Trial Practice; General Practice; Insurance Defense; Medical Malpractice

DALEY, BLACK & MOREIRA
Halifax, NS, Canada.....General Practice

DALLER GREENBERG & DIETRICH, LLP
Fort Washington, PA.....Commercial Litigation; Construction Law; Environmental Law; Labor and Employment Law; Product Liability Law; Toxic Torts

DALNEKOFF & MASON, P.A.
Annapolis, MD.....Civil Trial Practice; Criminal Trial Practice; Family Law

DALTON, TREASURE & MOWRER
Kennett, MO.....General Practice

DALY LAVERY & HALL
Ossining, NY.....General Practice

D'AMATO & LYNCH
New York, NY.....Civil Trial Practice; Insurance Defense

DAMON KEY LEONG KUPCHAK HASTERT, ATTORNEYS AT LAW, A LAW CORPORATION
Honolulu, HI.....General Practice

DAMON & MOREY LLP
Buffalo, NY.....Civil Trial Practice; Commercial Litigation; Health Care Law; Insurance Defense; Intellectual Property Law; Labor and Employment Law

DAMON, OOSTERHOUSE & WITTE, L.L.P.
Grand Rapids, MI.....Business Law

DAMRELL, NELSON, SCHRIMP, PALLIOS & LADINE, A PROFESSIONAL CORPORATION
Modesto, CA.....Civil Trial Practice; General Practice

DANAHER, TEDFORD, LAGNESE & NEAL, P.C.
Hartford, CT.....Insurance Defense

DANIEL, CLAMPETT, POWELL & CUNNINGHAM, L.L.C.
Springfield, MO.....Civil Trial Practice

DANIEL & DANIEL
Pawleys Island, SC.....General Practice; Personal Injury

DANIEL, LAWSON, TUGGLE & JERLES, L.L.P.
Perry, GA.....General Practice

DANIEL & OBERMAN
Knoxville, TN.....Civil Trial Practice; Criminal Trial Practice

DANIELS, FINE, ISRAEL & SCHONBUCH, LLP
Los Angeles, CA.....Construction Law; Insurance Defense; Toxic Torts

DANIELS, KASHTAN & FORNARIS, P.A.
Miami, FL.....Construction Law; Workers Compensation

DANIELS LAW OFFICES, P.C.
Boston, MA.....Bankruptcy Law; Commercial Litigation; Creditors Rights

DANIELS, SANDERS, PIANOWSKI, TODD & THOMAS
Elkhart, IN.....Civil Trial Practice; Corporate Law; Labor and Employment Law

DANIELSON HARRIGAN & TOLLEFSON, LLP
Seattle, WA.....Admiralty/Maritime Law; Civil Trial Practice; Commercial Litigation; Construction Law

DANKENBRING GREIMAN OSTERHOLT & HOFFMANN, P.C.
St. Louis, MO....................Real Estate Law; Tax Law; Trademark, Copyright and Unfair Competition

DANKNER & MILSTEIN, P.C.
New York, NY....................Civil Trial Practice

DANN, DORFMAN, HERRELL AND SKILLMAN, A PROFESSIONAL CORPORATION
Philadelphia, PA....................Computer Law; Intellectual Property Law; Patent, Trademark, Copyright and Unfair Competition

DANNING, GILL, DIAMOND & KOLLITZ, LLP
Los Angeles, CA....................Bankruptcy Law

DANZIGER & MARKHOFF LLP
White Plains, NY....................Pension and Profit Sharing

DAPEER, ROSENBLIT & LITVAK, LLP
Los Angeles, CA....................Civil Trial Practice; Municipal and Zoning Law; Professional Liability

DARBY, PEELE, BOWDOIN, PAYNE & KENNON
Lake City, FL....................General Practice

DARCHE, GARY M.
Kew Gardens, NY....................Civil Trial Practice

DARK, CLAYTON E. JR.
Lufkin, TX....................General Practice; Insurance Defense

DARLING, HALL & RAE, LLP
Los Angeles, CA....................Business Law; Civil Trial Practice; Corporate Law; Real Estate Law; Trust and Estates, Wills and Probate

DART ADAMSON DONOVAN & HANSON
Salt Lake City, UT....................Commercial Litigation; Construction Law; Family Law; Municipal and Zoning Law; Personal Injury; Real Estate Law

DASCHBACH, COOPER, HOTCHKISS & CSATARI, PROFESSIONAL ASSOCIATION
Lebanon, NH....................General Practice

DASILVA, HILOWITZ & MCEVILY LLP
Garden City, NY....................Family Law; Trust and Estates, Wills and Probate

DATSOPOULOS, MACDONALD & LIND, P.C.
Missoula, MT....................Business Law; Commercial Litigation

DAUER & THOMPSON
Sacramento, CA....................Administrative Law; Appellate Practice; Construction Law; Government Contracts

DAUGHERTY, DAVID H.
Huntington, WV....................Trust and Estates, Wills and Probate

DAVENPORT, EVANS, HURWITZ & SMITH, L.L.P.
Sioux Falls, SD....................Banking Law; Bankruptcy Law; Business Law; Civil Trial Practice; General Practice; Insurance Defense; Personal Injury; Real Estate Law; Tax Law

DAVENPORT, FILES & KELLY, L.L.P.
Monroe, LA....................Criminal Trial Practice; General Practice; Insurance Defense

DAVEY & BROGAN, P.C.
Norfolk, VA....................Admiralty/Maritime Law; Insurance Defense; Transportation Law

DAVID, ANTHONY P., A PROFESSIONAL CORPORATION
San Francisco, CA....................Commercial Litigation; Personal Injury

DAVIDOFF, PAUL F., A PROFESSIONAL CORPORATION
Kalamazoo, MI....................Bankruptcy Law; Commercial Litigation

DAVIDSON, THOMAS M.
McLean, VA....................Business Law; Corporate Law; Mergers and Acquisitions

DAVIDSON, DAVIDSON & KAPPEL, LLC
New York, NY....................Patent, Trademark, Copyright and Unfair Competition

DAVIDSON, MEAUX, SONNIER, MCELLIGOTT & SWIFT
Lafayette, LA....................Aviation Law; Business Law; Civil Trial Practice; Commercial Litigation; General Practice; Insurance Defense

DAVIDSON, NIX & JONES, A PROFESSIONAL LAW CORPORATION
Shreveport, LA....................Business Law; Labor and Employment Law; Oil and Gas Law

DAVIDSON, WIGGINS, JONES & COLEMAN, P.C.
Tuscaloosa, AL....................Civil Trial Practice; General Practice; Insurance Defense

DAVIES & HUMPHREYS
Nashville, TN....................Insurance Defense; Medical Malpractice; Product Liability Law; Workers Compensation

DAVIES MCFARLAND & CARROLL, P.C.
Pittsburgh, PA....................Civil Trial Practice; General Practice; Insurance Defense; Medical Malpractice; Product Liability Law; Workers Compensation

DAVIES, WARD & BECK
Toronto, ON, Canada....................Antitrust Law; Banking Law; Business Law; Civil Trial Practice; Commercial Law; Computer Law; Environmental Law; General Practice; Real Estate Law; Securities Law; Tax Law

DAVIS, JAMES MARTIN
Omaha, NE....................Criminal Trial Practice; Personal Injury

DAVIS, STEPHEN J.
Minneapolis, MN....................Real Estate Law

DAVIS, BROWN, KOEHN, SHORS & ROBERTS, P.C.
Des Moines, IA....................General Practice; Patent, Trademark, Copyright and Unfair Competition; Tax Law

DAVIS AND BUJOLD
Manchester, NH....................Patent, Trademark, Copyright and Unfair Competition

DAVIS & CANNON
Sheridan, WY....................Civil Trial Practice

DAVIS & CARICO LLP
Manhattan Beach, CA....................Trust and Estates, Wills and Probate

DAVIS, CEDILLO & MENDOZA, INCORPORATED
San Antonio, TX....................Commercial Litigation

DAVIS & CERIANI, P.C.
Denver, CO....................Arbitration; Bankruptcy Law; Civil Trial Practice; Commercial Litigation; Legal Malpractice; Professional Liability; Real Estate Law

DAVIS & COMPANY
Vancouver, BC, Canada....................General Practice

DAVIS, COX & WRIGHT, PLC
Fayetteville, AR....................Civil Trial Practice; Commercial Law; Commercial Litigation; General Practice; Insurance Defense; Product Liability Law

DAVIS & DAVIS, P.C.
Austin, TX....................Administrative Law; Civil Trial Practice; General Practice; Health Care Law; Insurance Defense

DAVIS, DAVIS & KAAR
Milton, PA....................General Practice

DAVIS FIRM, THE
Seattle, WA....................Admiralty/Maritime Law; Medical Malpractice; Personal Injury; Product Liability Law

DAVIS & FOX
Los Angeles, CA....................Business Law; Civil Trial Practice; General Practice; Insurance Defense; Real Estate Law

DAVIS, GORDON & DONER, P.A.
West Palm Beach, FL....................Medical Malpractice; Personal Injury; Product Liability Law

DAVIS, GRAHAM & STUBBS LLP
Denver, CO....................General Practice

DAVIS & HAMRICK, L.L.P.
Winston-Salem, NC....................General Practice

DAVIS, HOWARD M., P.C.
West Orange, NJ....................Civil Trial Practice; Commercial Law; General Practice

DAVIS & KUELTHAU, S.C.
Milwaukee, WI....................Admiralty/Maritime Law; Business Law; Environmental Law; Labor and Employment Law; Municipal Bond/Public Authority Financing; Real Estate Law; Tax Law; Trust and Estates, Wills and Probate

DAVIS & LOWE, P.C.
Phoenix, AZ....................Bankruptcy Law; Creditors Rights

DAVIS, MURRELLE & LUMSDEN, P.A.
Beaufort, NC....................Admiralty/Maritime Law; Civil Trial Practice; Personal Injury

DAVIS, ORETSKY & GUILFOYLE, P.C.
Houston, TX....................Commercial Litigation; Insurance Defense; Labor and Employment Law; Personal Injury; Professional Liability; Toxic Torts

DAVIS POLK & WARDWELL
Washington, DC....................General Practice
New York, NY....................General Practice
London, England....................General Practice
Paris, France....................General Practice

DAVIS, PUNELLI & KEATHLEY LLP
Newport Beach, CA .... Business Law; Civil Trial Practice; Real Estate Law

DAVIS, STURGES & TOMLINSON
Louisburg, NC .... General Practice; Insurance Defense

DAVIS, TUPPER & GRIMSLEY, L.L.P.
Beaufort, SC .... Arbitration; Corporate Law; Family Law; Insurance Defense; Medical Malpractice; Product Liability Law; Real Estate Law; Trust and Estates, Wills and Probate

DAVIS, WALTER LEE, JR., A PROFESSIONAL CORPORATION
Johnson City, TN .... Trust and Estates, Wills and Probate

DAVIS & WEISMAN, P.C.
St. Louis, MO .... Creditors Rights

DAVIS & WILKERSON, P.C.
Austin, TX .... Civil Trial Practice; Commercial Litigation; Health Care Law; Insurance Defense; Labor and Employment Law; Medical Malpractice

DAVIS & YOUNG
Cleveland, OH .... General Practice; Insurance Defense; Medical Malpractice; Product Liability Law

DAWDA, MANN, MULCAHY & SADLER, P.L.C.
Bloomfield Hills, MI .... Business Law; Civil Trial Practice; Commercial Litigation; Corporate Law; Environmental Law; Labor and Employment Law; Mergers and Acquisitions; Real Estate Law; Tax Law; Trust and Estates, Wills and Probate

DAWSON, JOHN B., JR., P.C.
Mineola, NY .... Trust and Estates, Wills and Probate

DAWSON, SODD & BEARD, P.C.
Corsicana, TX .... Civil Trial Practice

DAY, BERRY & HOWARD LLP
Hartford, CT .... General Practice
Stamford, CT .... General Practice
Boston, MA .... General Practice

DAY, EDWARDS, FEDERMAN, PROPESTER & CHRISTENSEN, P.C.
Oklahoma City, OK .... Appellate Practice; Arbitration; Banking Law; Bankruptcy Law; Business Law; Civil Trial Practice; Commercial Law; Commercial Litigation; Construction Law; Corporate Law; Creditors Rights; Energy Law; Environmental Law; General Practice; Health Care Law; Insurance Defense; Intellectual Property Law; International Business Law; Labor and Employment Law; Natural Resources Law; Oil and Gas Law; Product Liability Law; Real Estate Law; Securities Law; Toxic Torts; Workers Compensation

DAY & SAWDEY, A PROFESSIONAL CORPORATION
Grand Rapids, MI .... Corporate Law

DEAN, KRISTI WEILER LAW OFFICES OF
Encino, CA .... Insurance Defense

DEAN & GIBSON, L.L.P.
Charlotte, NC .... Aviation Law; Civil Trial Practice; Commercial Litigation; Insurance Defense

DEANER, DEANER, SCANN, MALAN & LARSEN
Las Vegas, NV .... Civil Trial Practice; Commercial Litigation; General Practice; Real Estate Law

DEARTH, MARKHAM & JACK, CHARTERED
Parsons, KS .... General Practice

DEASEY, MAHONEY & BENDER, LTD.
Philadelphia, PA .... Civil Trial Practice; Insurance Defense

DEASON, CHARLES A. JR.
El Paso, TX .... Personal Injury; Product Liability Law

DEASON, EDWARD J.
Torrance, CA .... Personal Injury

DEASON, MARSHALL C. JR.
Tampa, FL .... Real Estate Law

DEATON, DAVISON & KESSINGER, A PROFESSIONAL CORPORATION
Ada, OK .... General Practice; Insurance Defense

DEBEVOISE & PLIMPTON
Washington, DC .... General Practice
New York, NY .... General Practice
Hong Kong, China .... General Practice
London, England .... General Practice
Paris, France .... General Practice
Moscow, Russia .... General Practice

DE BLASIO, FIGMAN, EPSTEIN & LA ROCCA, P.C.
New York, NY .... Civil Trial Practice; Legal Malpractice; Medical Malpractice; Personal Injury; Product Liability Law

DEBOEST, KNUDSEN, STOCKMAN, WISEMAN, DECKER & DRYDEN, P.A.
Fort Myers, FL .... Appellate Practice; Business Law; Civil Trial Practice; Professional Liability; Real Estate Law; Trust and Estates, Wills and Probate

DEBRUYN, JOHN LAW OFFICES
Denver, CO .... Tax Law; Trust and Estates, Wills and Probate

DEBUS KAZAN & WESTERHAUSEN, LTD.
Phoenix, AZ .... Criminal Trial Practice; Personal Injury

DECARLO, CONNOR & SELVO, A PROFESSIONAL CORPORATION
Los Angeles, CA .... Employment Benefits Law; Labor and Employment Law

DECAROLIS, SAENZ & TROPE, LLP
Los Angeles, CA .... Civil Trial Practice; Family Law

DECHERT PRICE & RHOADS
Washington, DC .... General Practice
Boston, MA .... General Practice
Princeton, NJ .... General Practice
New York, NY .... General Practice
Harrisburg, PA .... General Practice
Philadelphia, PA .... General Practice
Brussels, Belgium .... General Practice
London, England .... General Practice
Paris, France .... General Practice

DECKER, JONES, MCMACKIN, MCCLANE, HALL & BATES, A PROFESSIONAL CORPORATION
Fort Worth, TX .... Business Law; Civil Trial Practice; Commercial Litigation; Corporate Law; General Practice; Insurance Defense; Intellectual Property Law; Medical Malpractice; Mergers and Acquisitions; Oil and Gas Law; Real Estate Law; Tax Law; Toxic Torts; Trademark, Copyright and Unfair Competition; Trust and Estates, Wills and Probate; Workers Compensation

DECUBELLIS & MEEKS, P.A.
Orlando, FL .... Business Law; Civil Trial Practice; General Practice; Real Estate Law

DEEGAN & DEEGAN, L.L.P.
Hempstead, NY .... Civil Trial Practice; General Practice; Insurance Defense; Professional Liability

DEEHL, DAVID L., P.A.
Miami, FL .... Personal Injury

DEENER, FEINGOLD & STERN, A PROFESSIONAL CORPORATION
Hackensack, NJ .... Administrative Law; Business Law; Civil Trial Practice; Commercial Law; General Practice; Tax Law; Trust and Estates, Wills and Probate

DEEP & WOMACK
Henderson, KY .... Civil Trial Practice; General Practice; Insurance Defense

DEES, J. GORDON, A PROFESSIONAL CORPORATION
Houston, TX .... Criminal Trial Practice

DEETH WILLIAMS WALL, LLP
Toronto, ON, Canada .... Computer Law; Intellectual Property Law; Patent, Trademark, Copyright and Unfair Competition

DEFINO, MICHAEL G.
Media, PA .... Criminal Trial Practice; Personal Injury

DEFOREST & KOSCELNIK
Pittsburgh, PA .... Civil Trial Practice; Commercial Law; Labor and Employment Law

DEFREES & FISKE
Chicago, IL .... Public Utilities Law

DE GRANDPRÉ CHAIT
Montreal, QU, Canada .... Civil Trial Practice; Construction Law; General Practice; Real Estate Law

DEGRAVELLES, PALMINTIER & HOLTHAUS
Baton Rouge, LA .... Civil Trial Practice; Personal Injury

DE GROOT, KELLER, VINCENT & ALMASSIAN, P.L.C.
Grand Rapids, MI .... Bankruptcy Law; Civil Trial Practice; Commercial Law; Commercial Litigation; Personal Injury

DEGUERIN & DICKSON
Houston, TX .... Criminal Trial Practice

DEHAY & ELLISTON, L.L.P.
Dallas, TX .... Civil Trial Practice; Insurance Defense; Personal Injury; Product Liability Law

DEKLE, PATRICK H., P.A.
Tampa, FL ....Civil Trial Practice; Medical Malpractice; Personal Injury

DE LA GARZA, BILL, & ASSOCIATES, P.C.
Houston, TX ....Family Law; Real Estate Law

DELANEY AND O'CONNOR LLP
Syracuse, NY ....Elder Law; Health Care Law; Trust and Estates, Wills and Probate

DELANEY & SUMNER
Rapid City, SD ....Civil Trial Practice; Family Law; Insurance Defense; Oil and Gas Law; Personal Injury

DELANEY, WILES, HAYES, GERETY, ELLIS & YOUNG, INC.
Anchorage, AK ....Environmental Law; General Practice; Insurance Defense; Labor and Employment Law; Medical Malpractice; Natural Resources Law; Product Liability Law

DELANOY, ENGLISH, SCHUETZE & MCGAHA, A PROFESSIONAL CORPORATION
Las Vegas, NV ....Commercial Litigation; Insurance Defense

DELAP, HERBERT A., & ASSOCIATES, P.C.
Denver, CO ....General Practice

DE LA PARTE, GILBERT & BALES, PROFESSIONAL ASSOCIATION
Tampa, FL ....Commercial Litigation; Environmental Law

DELBELLO DONNELLAN WEINGARTEN & TARTAGLIA, LLP
White Plains, NY ....Banking Law; Commercial Litigation; Environmental Law; Insurance Defense; Land Use Law; Real Estate Law

DELEON, BOGGINS & ICENOGLE, A PROFESSIONAL CORPORATION
Austin, TX ....Administrative Law; Civil Trial Practice; Insurance Defense

DELGADO, ACOSTA, BRADEN & JONES, P.C.
El Paso, TX ....General Practice

D'ELIA & CAVANAUGH
Orleans, MA ....Trust and Estates, Wills and Probate

DELISIO MORAN GERAGHTY & ZOBEL, P.C.
Anchorage, AK ....Business Law; Civil Trial Practice; Insurance Defense

DELLECKER, WILSON & KING, P.A.
Orlando, FL ....Medical Malpractice; Personal Injury; Product Liability Law

DEL SOLE & DEL SOLE, L.L.P.
New Haven, CT ....Civil Trial Practice

DELSTON, ROSS S.
Washington, DC ....Banking Law

DEL TORO & SANTANA
San Juan, PR ....Civil Trial Practice

DEMA, JOHN K., P.C., LAW OFFICES OF
Christiansted, St. Croix, VI .....Environmental Law

DEMAKIS LAW OFFICES, P.C.
Lynn, MA ....Civil Trial Practice; Commercial Law; Personal Injury; Real Estate Law

DEMARIA ELLIS & BAUCH L.L.C.
Newark, NJ ....Labor and Employment Law

DEMARTINI, D'AQUILA & VOLK, A PROFESSIONAL LAW CORPORATION
Kenner, LA ....Commercial Litigation

DE MARTINO FINKELSTEIN ROSEN & VIRGA
Washington, DC ....Business Law; Securities Law

DEMENT AND MARQUARDT, P.L.C.
Kalamazoo, MI ....Trust and Estates, Wills and Probate

DEMENT, VANDIVORT AND DEMENT
Sikeston, MO ....Civil Trial Practice

DEMERSSEMAN JENSEN, L.L.P.
Rapid City, SD ....General Practice

DEMET & DEMET, S.C.
Milwaukee, WI ....Corporate Law

DEMETRIOU, DEL GUERCIO, SPRINGER & MOYER, LLP
Los Angeles, CA ....Administrative Law; Business Law; Civil Trial Practice; Commercial Law; Eminent Domain; Environmental Law; Health Care Law; Natural Resources Law; Real Estate Law; Tax Law; Trust and Estates, Wills and Probate

DEMING, PARKER, HOFFMAN, GREEN & CAMPBELL, P.C.
Norcross, GA ....Civil Trial Practice; Corporate Law; Criminal Trial Practice; Personal Injury; Workers Compensation

DEMPSEY & SASSO
Orlando, FL ....Antitrust Law; Civil Trial Practice; Construction Law; Criminal Trial Practice; Labor and Employment Law

DENHAM & KING, PLLC
Ocean Springs, MS ....Personal Injury

DENIUS, FRANKLIN W.
Austin, TX ....Civil Trial Practice

DENLINGER, ROSENTHAL & GREENBERG, A LEGAL PROFESSIONAL ASSOCIATION
Cincinnati, OH ....Labor and Employment Law

DENMEAD & MALONEY
Columbus, OH ....Civil Trial Practice; General Practice; Personal Injury

DENNIN, TIMOTHY J., P.C.
New York, NY ....Securities Law

DENNIS, HARRY D. JR.
Pompano Beach, FL ....Civil Trial Practice; Family Law

DENNIS, CORRY & PORTER, L.L.P.
Atlanta, GA ....Aviation Law; Civil Trial Practice; General Practice; Insurance Defense; Personal Injury; Product Liability Law; Transportation Law

DENTON & CARY
Bolivar, TN ....General Practice

DENTON & KEULER
Paducah, KY ....Admiralty/Maritime Law; Banking Law; Commercial Litigation; General Practice; Public Utilities Law

DENTON & LOPEZ
Las Vegas, NV ....Civil Trial Practice; General Practice; Trust and Estates, Wills and Probate

DE ORCHIS, WALKER & CORSA, LLP
New York, NY ....Admiralty/Maritime Law; Civil Trial Practice; Commercial Law; Insurance Defense; Product Liability Law; Transportation Law

DEPEW AND GILLEN, L.L.C.
Wichita, KS ....Aviation Law; Business Law; Civil Trial Practice; Corporate Law; Environmental Law; General Practice; Insurance Defense; Natural Resources Law; Personal Injury; Trust and Estates, Wills and Probate

DERBES LAW FIRM, THE, L.L.C.
Metairie, LA ....Commercial Litigation; Tax Law

DERICKSON, DAVID G., P.C.
Phoenix, AZ ....Criminal Trial Practice; Health Care Law

DERR, ALLEN
Boise, ID ....Personal Injury

DERR, DAILEY J., P.A.
Durham, NC ....Construction Law

DESANTO, JAMES J., A PROFESSIONAL CORPORATION
Libertyville, IL ....Commercial Litigation; Labor and Employment Law; Personal Injury

DESHAZO, GARY F. & ASSOCIATES
Austin, TX ....Civil Trial Practice; Legal Malpractice

DESJARDINS DUCHARME STEIN MONAST
Montreal, QU, Canada ....General Practice
Quebec, QU, Canada ....General Practice

DESSEN, MOSES & SHEINOFF
Philadelphia, PA ....Civil Trial Practice

DETISCH & CHRISTENSEN
San Diego, CA ....Civil Trial Practice; General Practice

DEUSCHLE, BRIAN C., CHARTERED
Fort Lauderdale, FL ....Commercial Law; Commercial Litigation

DEUTCH & FALK, A PROFESSIONAL CORPORATION
Woodbridge, NJ ....Construction Law; Health Care Law; Securities Law

DEUTSCH & BLUMBERG, P.A.
Miami, FL ....Civil Trial Practice; Medical Malpractice; Personal Injury; Product Liability Law

DEUTSCH, DAVID M., CO., L.P.A.
Dayton, OH ....Medical Malpractice; Personal Injury; Product Liability Law

DEUTSCH WILLIAMS BROOKS DERENSIS HOLLAND & DRACHMAN, P.C.
Boston, MA ....Civil Trial Practice
Nantucket, MA ....Civil Trial Practice

DEVEAU, COLTON & MARQUIS
Atlanta, GA .... Patent, Trademark, Copyright and Unfair Competition

DEVEREUX, MURPHY, STRILER, BRICKEY & SHER, L.L.C.
St. Louis, MO .... Commercial Litigation; Real Estate Law

DE VINE & KOHN, PLLC
Southfield, MI .... Business Law; Construction Law; Tax Law; Trust and Estates, Wills and Probate

DEVINE, MILLIMET & BRANCH, PROFESSIONAL ASSOCIATION
Manchester, NH .... General Practice

DEVLIN, JOHN GERARD, & ASSOCIATES, P.C.
Philadelphia, PA .... Civil Trial Practice; Environmental Law; Insurance Defense; Product Liability Law; Transportation Law

DEVORSETZ STINZIANO GILBERTI HEINTZ & SMITH, P.C.
Syracuse, NY .... Environmental Law; Land Use Law

DE VRIES, PRICE & DAVENPORT, A PROFESSIONAL CORPORATION
Mason City, IA .... Insurance Defense

DEWEY BALLANTINE LLP
Washington, DC .... General Practice
New York, NY .... General Practice; Municipal Bond/Public Authority Financing

DEWITT ROSS & STEVENS S.C.
Madison, WI .... General Practice; Patent, Trademark, Copyright and Unfair Competition

DEWOSKIN, ALAN E., P.C.
St. Louis, MO .... Commercial Litigation; Family Law

DEYOE HEISSENBUTTEL, L.L.C.
Wayne, NJ .... Appellate Practice; Civil Trial Practice; Environmental Law; Family Law; General Practice; Insurance Defense; Legal Malpractice; Personal Injury; Product Liability Law; Professional Liability

DIAMOND AND DIAMOND, P.A.
Fort Myers, FL .... Workers Compensation

DIAMOND RASH GORDON & JACKSON, P.C.
El Paso, TX .... Civil Trial Practice; Municipal Bond/Public Authority Financing

DIAMOND & SCHARNBERGER
Woodland Hills, CA .... Business Law; Personal Injury; Real Estate Law

DICERBO & PALUMBO
Olean, NY .... General Practice

DICKENSON, MURDOCH, REX AND SLOAN, CHARTERED
Boca Raton, FL .... Real Estate Law; Trust and Estates, Wills and Probate

DICKERSON, DICKERSON, CONSUL & POCKER
Las Vegas, NV .... Civil Trial Practice; Commercial Litigation; Family Law; Personal Injury

DICK AND HARRIS
Chicago, IL .... Intellectual Property Law; Patent, Trademark, Copyright and Unfair Competition

DICKIE, MCCAMEY & CHILCOTE, A PROFESSIONAL CORPORATION
Pittsburgh, PA .... General Practice

DICKINSON & GIBBONS, P.A.
Sarasota, FL .... Civil Trial Practice; General Practice; Insurance Defense; Medical Malpractice; Real Estate Law; Trust and Estates, Wills and Probate

DICKINSON, MACKAMAN, TYLER & HAGEN, P.C.
Des Moines, IA .... Banking Law; Labor and Employment Law; Tax Law; Trust and Estates, Wills and Probate

DICKINSON WRIGHT PLLC
Washington, DC .... General Practice; Patent, Trademark, Copyright and Unfair Competition
Bloomfield Hills, MI .... General Practice
Detroit, MI .... Civil Trial Practice; Environmental Law; General Practice; Labor and Employment Law; Municipal Bond/Public Authority Financing
Grand Rapids, MI .... General Practice
Lansing, MI .... General Practice

DICKSTEIN SHAPIRO MORIN & OSHINSKY LLP
Washington, DC .... General Practice

DIDONATO & WINTERHALTER, P.C.
Philadelphia, PA .... Bankruptcy Law; Commercial Law; Commercial Litigation; Creditors Rights; Municipal and Zoning Law

DIEPENBROCK & COSTA
Sacramento, CA .... Environmental Law; Insurance Defense

DIETRICH, EDWARD H.
Westport, CT .... Trust and Estates, Wills and Probate

DIETRICH, THOMAS W.
Phoenix, AZ .... Trust and Estates, Wills and Probate

DIETRICH, GLASRUD, MALLEK & AUNE
Fresno, CA .... Commercial Litigation; Corporate Law; Pension and Profit Sharing; Real Estate Law; Tax Law; Trust and Estates, Wills and Probate

DIKE, BRONSTEIN, ROBERTS & CUSHMAN, LLP
Boston, MA .... Patent, Trademark, Copyright and Unfair Competition; Trademark, Copyright and Unfair Competition

DIKMAN AND DIKMAN
Lake Success, NY .... Criminal Trial Practice; Family Law; Personal Injury; Real Estate Law; Trust and Estates, Wills and Probate

DILL, MATTHEW T.
Wilmington, NC .... Trust and Estates, Wills and Probate

DILLARD & GALLOWAY, LLC
Atlanta, GA .... Family Law; Municipal and Zoning Law

DILLARD AND KATONA
Tappahannock, VA .... General Practice

DILLINGHAM & MURPHY, LLP
San Francisco, CA .... Insurance Defense; Intellectual Property Law

DILLON MCCANDLESS KING COULTER & GRAHAM L.L.P.
Butler, PA .... General Practice

DILL & SHOWLER
Redlands, CA .... General Practice

DILWORTH & BARRESE
Uniondale, NY .... Patent, Trademark, Copyright and Unfair Competition

DILWORTH PAXSON LLP
Philadelphia, PA .... General Practice

DIMASCIO, JOHN P. THE LAW OFFICES OF
Garden City, NY .... Family Law

DIMITRIOU, EMMANUEL H., P.C.
Pottsville, PA .... Criminal Trial Practice
Reading, PA .... Criminal Trial Practice

DIMMICH, GULDIN, DINKELACKER & BRIENZA, P.C.
Orefield, PA .... Civil Trial Practice

DIMOCK STRATTON CLARIZIO
Toronto, ON, Canada .... Computer Law; Patent, Trademark, Copyright and Unfair Competition; Trademark, Copyright and Unfair Competition

DIMURO, GINSBERG & MOOK, P.C.
Alexandria, VA .... Commercial Litigation; General Practice

DINES, GROSS & ESQUIVEL, P.C.
Albuquerque, NM .... Communications Law; Health Care Law; Insurance Defense; Labor and Employment Law; Professional Liability

DINGEMAN, DANCER & CHRISTOPHERSON, P.L.C.
Traverse City, MI .... Business Law; Civil Trial Practice; Commercial Litigation; Corporate Law; Environmental Law; Health Care Law; Personal Injury; Real Estate Law; Trust and Estates, Wills and Probate

DINN, HOCHMAN AND POTTER, LLC
Cleveland, OH .... Labor and Employment Law

DINSE, KNAPP & MCANDREW, P.C.
Burlington, VT .... Civil Trial Practice; General Practice; Health Care Law; Insurance Defense; Labor and Employment Law

DIONNE & GASS
Boston, MA .... Business Law; Real Estate Law

DIORIO & SERENI, LLP
Media, PA .... Civil Trial Practice; Family Law; General Practice; Personal Injury

DI RENZO AND BOMIER, LLC
Neenah, WI .... Business Law; General Practice; Insurance Defense

DIRMANN, JAMES R., P.A.
Sarasota, FL .... Criminal Trial Practice

DIVER, GRACH, QUADE & MASINI
Waukegan, IL .... Banking Law; Civil Trial Practice; Family Law; Municipal and Zoning Law; Real Estate Law; Trust and Estates, Wills and Probate

DJORDJEVIC, MICHAEL M., CO. LPA
Akron, OH ....Medical Malpractice; Professional Liability

DOBBERTEEN & LUNA
Los Angeles, CA ....Bankruptcy Law

DOBSON & BROWN, P.A.
St. Augustine, FL....Commercial Litigation; Environmental Law

DODD AND DENNIS, P.C.
Valdosta, GA ....Civil Trial Practice; Criminal Trial Practice; Family Law; Personal Injury

DODDS, KIDD, RYAN & MOORE
Little Rock, AR ....Personal Injury

DODGE, DAVID A., P.C.
Grand Rapids, MI ....Criminal Trial Practice

DODSON AND ASSOCIATES, P.C.
Denver, CO ....Commercial Litigation

DOERING, STEVEN B.
Garnett, KS ....General Practice

DOERNER, SAUNDERS, DANIEL & ANDERSON, L.L.P.
Tulsa, OK....General Practice; Labor and Employment Law; Natural Resources Law; Securities Law

DOFFERMYRE, SHIELDS, CANFIELD, KNOWLES & DEVINE
Atlanta, GA ....Civil Trial Practice; Medical Malpractice; Personal Injury; Product Liability Law

DOHERTY & SHERIDAN, L.L.P.
Fairfax, VA ....Insurance Defense; Trust and Estates, Wills and Probate

DOHERTY & VENEZIA, A PROFESSIONAL CORPORATION
Phoenix, AZ ....Insurance Defense; Workers Compensation

DOHERTY, WALLACE, PILLSBURY AND MURPHY, P.C.
Springfield, MA....General Practice; Patent, Trademark, Copyright and Unfair Competition

DOK, LEVY & PERRIN
San Jose, CA ....Family Law

DOLAN AND DOLAN, P.A. A PROFESSIONAL CORPORATION
Newton, NJ ....General Practice

DOLE, COALWELL, CLARK, MOUNTAINSPRING & MORNARICH, P.C.
Roseburg, OR ....Civil Trial Practice; General Practice

DOLIN, NORMAN M. LAW OFFICES OF
Beverly Hills, CA....Family Law

DOLIN & ASSOCIATES, P.C.
Rochester, NY....Civil Trial Practice; Labor and Employment Law

DOLLINGER, GONSKI & GROSSMAN
Carle Place, NY ....Civil Trial Practice; Commercial Law; General Practice; Real Estate Law

DOMENGEAUX WRIGHT & ROY, A PROFESSIONAL LAW CORPORATION
Lafayette, LA ....Admiralty/Maritime Law; Civil Trial Practice; Personal Injury; Product Liability Law

DOMESTICO & BARRY
Framingham, MA ....Civil Trial Practice; Commercial Litigation; Labor and Employment Law

DOMINA LAW PC
Omaha, NE ....Civil Trial Practice; Criminal Trial Practice; Personal Injury

DOMINICK, FLETCHER, YEILDING, WOOD & LLOYD, P.A.
Birmingham, AL....Civil Trial Practice; General Practice; Real Estate Law; Tax Law

DONAHOE, PECARO & VOLLENDER, P.A.
Fort Lauderdale, FL....Civil Trial Practice; Insurance Defense; Personal Injury

DONAHOO, BALL & MCMENAMY, P.A.
Jacksonville, FL....Real Estate Law; Tax Law; Trust and Estates, Wills and Probate

DONAHUE & DONAHUE, ATTORNEYS, P.C.
Lowell, MA ....Business Law; General Practice; Insurance Defense; Trust and Estates, Wills and Probate

DONAHUE MESEREAU & LEIDS L.L.P.
Los Angeles, CA....Business Law; Corporate Law; Securities Law

DONAHUE, WOOD, LOVING & VOGEL
Sacramento, CA ....Civil Trial Practice; Insurance Defense

DONALD, RANDALL, DONALD & TIPTON
Tuscaloosa, AL ....General Practice; Insurance Defense

DONALDSON, BELL & PICKETT, P.C.
Albany, GA....Criminal Trial Practice; General Practice

DONAU & BOLT
Tucson, AZ ....Criminal Trial Practice; Family Law

DONENFELD, JACK A., A LEGAL PROF. ASSN., LAW OFFICES OF
Cincinnati, OH ....Securities Law

DONLEVY-ROSEN & ROSEN, PROFESSIONAL ASSOCIATION
Miami, FL ....Trust and Estates, Wills and Probate

DONNELLY, DANIEL
Garrison, NY ....Civil Trial Practice

DONOHUE, JAMES F.
White Plains, NY ....Administrative Law; Criminal Trial Practice; Personal Injury

DONOHUE, MARY SUE
Boca Raton, FL ....Trust and Estates, Wills and Probate

DONOHUE AND DONOHUE
Philadelphia, PA ....Administrative Law; Corporate Law; Criminal Trial Practice; International Trade Law

DONOHUE, SABO, VARLEY & ARMSTRONG, P.C.
Albany, NY....Civil Trial Practice; Insurance Defense

DONOVAN, MARTIN K.
Providence, RI....Civil Trial Practice; General Practice; Insurance Defense; Personal Injury

DONOVAN PARRY CARBIN MCDERMOTT & RADZIK
New York, NY....Insurance Defense

DONOVAN, PAUL F., PROFESSIONAL CORPORATION
Lancaster, NH....General Practice

DONOVAN AND ROBERTS, P.C.
Wheaton, IL....Civil Trial Practice; Commercial Litigation; General Practice; Personal Injury

DORAMUS, TRAUGER & NEY
Nashville, TN....Business Law; Civil Trial Practice

DORAN • BLACKMOND LLP
South Bend, IN ....Bankruptcy Law; Civil Trial Practice; Commercial Law; Environmental Law; Insurance Defense; Personal Injury; Product Liability Law

DORAN & NOWALIS
Wilkes-Barre, PA ....Bankruptcy Law

DORF & DORF, A PROFESSIONAL CORPORATION
Rahway, NJ....Labor and Employment Law

DORITY & MANNING, P.A.
Greenville, SC....Patent, Trademark, Copyright and Unfair Competition

DORNAN, DONALD C. JR.
Biloxi, MS....Civil Trial Practice

DORR, CARSON, SLOAN & BIRNEY, P.C.
Denver, CO ....Patent, Trademark, Copyright and Unfair Competition; Trademark, Copyright and Unfair Competition

DORSEY & WHITNEY LLP
Minneapolis, MN....General Practice

DORWART, FREDERIC
Tulsa, OK....Banking Law; Natural Resources Law; Oil and Gas Law

DOSTART CLAPP & COVENEY, LLP
San Diego, CA ....Business Law

DOTY & SHAPIRO, P.C.
Boulder, CO ....Business Law; Trust and Estates, Wills and Probate

DOUGHERTY, HILDRE, DUDEK & HAKLAR
San Diego, CA ....Admiralty/Maritime Law; Personal Injury; Product Liability Law

DOUGLAS, ALEXA, KOEPPEN & HURLEY
Valparaiso, IN....General Practice

DOUGLAS, DENHAM, ROGERS & HOOD
Portland, ME ....General Practice

DOUGLAS, ROBINSON, LEONARD & GARVEY, P.C.
Concord, NH ....Civil Trial Practice; Family Law; Labor and Employment Law; Personal Injury; Trust and Estates, Wills and Probate

DOVER & DIXON, P.A.
Little Rock, AR....General Practice

DOW, COGBURN & FRIEDMAN, P.C.
Houston, TX ....Real Estate Law

DOW, EINHAUS & MATTISON, P.A.
Owatonna, MN ....General Practice

DOW, LOHNES & ALBERTSON, PLLC
Washington, DC ....Antitrust Law; Communications Law; General Practice; Tax Law

DOWD & DOWD, LTD.
Chicago, IL ....Appellate Practice; Insurance Defense; Transportation Law

DOWLER, ROBERT W.
Fairfax, VA ....Civil Trial Practice

DOWLING, AARON & KEELER, INCORPORATED
Fresno, CA ....Bankruptcy Law; Business Law; Civil Trial Practice; Commercial Law; Environmental Law; General Practice; Health Care Law; Insurance Defense; Municipal Bond/Public Authority Financing; Professional Liability; Real Estate Law; Securities Law; Sports and Entertainment Law; Tax Law; Trademark, Copyright and Unfair Competition; Trust and Estates, Wills and Probate

DOWNEY, BRAND, SEYMOUR & ROHWER LLP
Sacramento, CA ....Environmental Law; General Practice; Natural Resources Law

DOWNEY & CLEVELAND, LLP
Marietta, GA ....Civil Trial Practice; General Practice; Insurance Defense; Medical Malpractice; Personal Injury

DOWNEY, WILLIAM J., P.C.
Phoenix, AZ ....Civil Trial Practice; Insurance Defense; Personal Injury

DOYLE & HARRIS, A PROFESSIONAL CORPORATION
Tulsa, OK ....Antitrust Law; Civil Trial Practice; Securities Law

DOYLE, LEWIS & WARNER
Toledo, OH ....Appellate Practice; Business Law; Civil Trial Practice; Corporate Law; General Practice; Insurance Defense; Real Estate Law; Tax Law; Transportation Law; Trust and Estates, Wills and Probate

DOYLE & NELSON
Augusta, ME ....Administrative Law

DOYLE & WINTHROP, P.C.
Phoenix, AZ ....Construction Law; Health Care Law; Insurance Defense; Medical Malpractice; Personal Injury

DOZIER, MILLER, POLLARD & MURPHY
Charlotte, NC ....Bankruptcy Law; Business Law; Civil Trial Practice; Criminal Trial Practice; Family Law; Immigration and Naturalization; Personal Injury; Trust and Estates, Wills and Probate

DRAGE, DE BEAUBIEN, KNIGHT, SIMMONS, MANTZARIS & NEAL
Orlando, FL ....Civil Trial Practice

DRAKE & DRAKE
Cullman, AL ....Personal Injury; Workers Compensation

DRAKE, SOMMERS, LOEB, TARSHIS & CATANIA, PLLC
Newburgh, NY ....General Practice

DRANOFF & GOLDSCHMIDT, L.L.P.
Pearl River, NY ....Family Law

DRATH, CLIFFORD, MURPHY, WENNERHOLM & HAGEN, A PROFESSIONAL CORPORATION
San Francisco, CA ....Civil Trial Practice; Insurance Defense

DRAUGELIS & ASHTON, L.L.P.
Plymouth, MI ....Business Law; Civil Trial Practice; General Practice; Insurance Defense; Personal Injury; Trust and Estates, Wills and Probate

DREHER LANGER & TOMKIES L.L.P.
Mandeville, LA ....Banking Law
Columbus, OH ....Banking Law

DREILING, BIEKER & HOFFMAN, LLP
Hays, KS ....General Practice

DRENDEL TATNALL, A PROFESSIONAL CORPORATION
Batavia, IL ....General Practice

DRENNER & STUART, L.L.P.
Austin, TX ....Real Estate Law

DRESNICK & ELLSWORTH, P.A.
Miami, FL ....Health Care Law

DRESSER, DRESSER, GILBERT & HAAS, P.C.
Sturgis, MI ....General Practice

DRESSLER, ROBERT A.
Fort Lauderdale, FL ....Trust and Estates, Wills and Probate

DREW, COOPER & ANDING
Grand Rapids, MI ....Civil Rights; Civil Trial Practice; Personal Injury

DREYER, BABICH, BUCCOLA & CALLAHAM, LLP
Sacramento, CA ....Personal Injury

DRIGGERS, SCHULTZ & HERBST, A PROFESSIONAL CORPORATION
Troy, MI ....Business Law

DRINKA, LEVINE & MASSON, S.C.
Milwaukee, WI ....Corporate Law; Family Law; Real Estate Law; Tax Law; Trust and Estates, Wills and Probate

DRINKER BIDDLE & REATH LLP
Washington, DC ....General Practice
Philadelphia, PA ....General Practice

DRINKER BIDDLE & SHANLEY LLP
Florham Park, NJ ....Banking Law; Bankruptcy Law; Civil Trial Practice; Corporate Law; Environmental Law; General Practice; Health Care Law; Labor and Employment Law; Real Estate Law; Tax Law

DRISCOLL, TALARICO, FRIZZELL, OLIVO & DRISCOLL
Danbury, CT ....Civil Trial Practice; Commercial Law; Corporate Law; Real Estate Law; Trust and Estates, Wills and Probate

DROBNY LAW OFFICES
Sacramento, CA ....Business Law; Tax Law; Trust and Estates, Wills and Probate

DROLET, FREEMAN, COTTON & NORRIS, P.C.
Bloomfield Hills, MI ....Business Law; Construction Law; Real Estate Law; Trust and Estates, Wills and Probate

DRUBNER, HARTLEY, O'CONNOR & MENGACCI
Waterbury, CT ....Commercial Litigation; Health Care Law

DRUMMOND & DRUMMOND, LLP
Portland, ME ....General Practice

DRUMMOND & DUCKWORTH
Newport Beach, CA ....Intellectual Property Law; Patent, Trademark, Copyright and Unfair Competition

DRUMM & THORNTON
Sikeston, MO ....Civil Trial Practice; General Practice; Trust and Estates, Wills and Probate

DUANE, W. FORD
Orlando, FL ....Criminal Trial Practice

DUANE, MORRIS & HECKSCHER LLP
San Francisco, CA ....General Practice
Wilmington, DE ....General Practice
Washington, DC ....General Practice
Miami, FL ....General Practice
Palm Beach, FL ....General Practice
Boston, MA ....General Practice
Cherry Hill, NJ ....General Practice
Newark, NJ ....General Practice
New York, NY ....General Practice
Allentown, PA ....General Practice
Harrisburg, PA ....General Practice
Philadelphia, PA ....General Practice
Wayne, PA ....General Practice

DUBÉ & GOODGAL, P.C.
Baltimore, MD ....Labor and Employment Law

DUBE, PATRICIA KAY, P.C.
Houston, TX ....Civil Trial Practice; Construction Law; Health Care Law; Insurance Defense; Product Liability Law

DUBOIS BILLIG LOUGHLIN CONATY & WEISMAN
Mineola, NY ....Medical Malpractice

DUCKOR SPRADLING & METZGER, A LAW CORPORATION
San Diego, CA ....Civil Trial Practice; Commercial Law; Securities Law

DUDLEY, DUDLEY & WINDLE
El Paso, TX ....Insurance Defense; Personal Injury

DUDLEY, GALUMBECK & NECESSARY
Tazewell, VA ....Civil Trial Practice; Criminal Trial Practice; Personal Injury

DUÉ, CABALLERO, PRICE & GUIDRY, (A PROFESSIONAL ASSOCIATION)
Baton Rouge, LA ....Admiralty/Maritime Law; Personal Injury

DUFF, DUBBERLY, TURNER, WHITE & BOYKIN, L.L.C.
Columbia, SC .... Labor and Employment Law

DUFFORD & BROWN, P.C.
Denver, CO .... Antitrust Law; Bankruptcy Law; Business Law; Commercial Law; Energy Law; Environmental Law; General Practice; Labor and Employment Law; Natural Resources Law; Real Estate Law; Trademark, Copyright and Unfair Competition

DUFFY, VIRGINIA M.
Jenkintown, PA .... Real Estate Law

DUFFY & GREEN
West Chester, PA .... Criminal Trial Practice; General Practice; Personal Injury

DUGAN & JAKUBOWSKI, P.A.
Timonium, MD .... Medical Malpractice; Product Liability Law

DUKE GERSTEL SHEARER, LLP
San Diego, CA .... Appellate Practice; Business Law; Construction Law; Elder Law; Personal Injury; Product Liability Law; Professional Liability; Real Estate Law; Securities Law

DUKES, DUKES, KEATING AND FANECA, P.A.
Gulfport, MS .... Administrative Law; Admiralty/Maritime Law; Bankruptcy Law; Business Law; Civil Trial Practice; Commercial Law; Commercial Litigation; Construction Law; Corporate Law; Environmental Law; General Practice; Insurance Defense; Labor and Employment Law; Land Use Law; Municipal and Zoning Law; Personal Injury; Product Liability Law; Real Estate Law; Transportation Law; Workers Compensation

DULANY & LEAHY, LLP
Westminster, MD .... General Practice; Trust and Estates, Wills and Probate

DUMOUCHEL, DAVID F., P.C.
Detroit, MI .... Appellate Practice; Criminal Trial Practice; Professional Liability

DUNAWAY & CROSS, A PROFESSIONAL CORPORATION
Washington, DC .... Administrative Law; Antitrust Law

DUNCAN, GREEN, BROWN, LANGENESS & ECKLEY, A PROFESSIONAL CORPORATION
Des Moines, IA .... General Practice

DUNCAN, JOHN A., A PROFESSIONAL CORPORATION
Orange, CA .... Trust and Estates, Wills and Probate

DUNCAN & RAINWATER, TRIAL LAWYERS, A PROF. ASSN.
Little Rock, AR .... Civil Trial Practice; Medical Malpractice; Personal Injury; Product Liability Law

DUNCAN, THOMASSON, LEONARD & SHATTUCK
La Grange, GA .... General Practice

DUNHAM, BOMAN & LESKERA
Belleville, IL .... Civil Trial Practice; General Practice; Insurance Defense; Trust and Estates, Wills and Probate
Collinsville, IL .... Civil Trial Practice; Criminal Trial Practice; General Practice; Insurance Defense; Trust and Estates, Wills and Probate

DUNLAP & BURDICK, A PROFESSIONAL LAW CORPORATION
Santa Cruz, CA .... Personal Injury; Product Liability Law

DUNLAP, CODDING & ROGERS, P.C.
Oklahoma City, OK .... Patent, Trademark, Copyright and Unfair Competition

DUNLAP & SEEGER, P.A.
Rochester, MN .... General Practice

DUNN, ABPLANALP & MAURIELLO, P.C.
Vail, CO .... Civil Trial Practice; General Practice; Real Estate Law

DUNN, FRANKLIN & MURPHY
Lexington, KY .... Land Use Law; Municipal and Zoning Law

DUNN, JAMES F., & ASSOCIATES, P.A.
St. Paul, MN .... Civil Trial Practice

DUNN, KACAL, ADAMS, PAPPAS & LAW, A PROFESSIONAL CORPORATION
Houston, TX .... Civil Trial Practice; Medical Malpractice

DUNN, MACDONALD & COLEMAN, P.C.
Knoxville, TN .... General Practice; Insurance Defense

DUNN, NUTTER, MORGAN & SHAW
Texarkana, AR .... Civil Trial Practice; Commercial Litigation; General Practice; Medical Malpractice; Natural Resources Law; Product Liability Law

DUNN, ROGASKI, PREOVOLOS & WEBER
Vallejo, CA .... General Practice; Insurance Defense

DUNN, STANCZAK & WILLARD
Bloomington, IL .... Commercial Litigation; Education Law; General Practice

DUNN & WEATHERED, P.C.
Corpus Christi, TX .... Appellate Practice; Civil Trial Practice; Insurance Defense

DUNNAM & DUNNAM, L.L.P.
Waco, TX .... Civil Trial Practice; Criminal Trial Practice; Family Law; General Practice; Real Estate Law

DUNTON, SIMMONS & DUNTON, L.L.P
White Stone, VA .... Civil Trial Practice; General Practice

DUNWODY WHITE & LANDON, P.A.
Miami, FL .... Commercial Litigation; Trust and Estates, Wills and Probate

DUPLASS, ZWAIN & BOURGEOIS, A PROFESSIONAL LAW CORPORATION
Metairie, LA .... Civil Trial Practice

DUPONT AND RADLAUER, L.L.P.
New London, CT .... Business Law; Civil Trial Practice; Trust and Estates, Wills and Probate

DURANDO, BIRDWELL & JANKE, LLP
Tucson, AZ .... Intellectual Property Law

DURBIN, LARIMORE & BIALICK, P.C.
Oklahoma City, OK .... Commercial Law; Insurance Defense; Real Estate Law

DURHAM, EDWARD D.
Montrose, CO .... Civil Trial Practice; Family Law; General Practice

DURHAM JONES & PINEGAR, A PROFESSIONAL CORPORATION
Salt Lake City, UT .... Business Law; Civil Trial Practice; Real Estate Law; Securities Law; Tax Law

DURKIN & BOGGIA
Ridgefield Park, NJ .... Civil Trial Practice

DURKIN, THOMAS ANTHONY, P.C.
Chicago, IL .... Criminal Trial Practice

DUSHOFF & MCCALL, A PROFESSIONAL CORPORATION
Phoenix, AZ .... Civil Trial Practice; Commercial Litigation; Eminent Domain; Land Use Law; Municipal and Zoning Law; Real Estate Law

DUTEL, WILLIAM J., LAW OFFICES OF
Covington, LA .... Commercial Law; Commercial Litigation; Corporate Law; Real Estate Law; Trust and Estates, Wills and Probate

DUTTON, BRAUN, STAACK & HELLMAN, P.L.C.
Waterloo, IA .... General Practice

DUVALL & DUVALL, L.L.P.
Salisbury, MD .... Civil Trial Practice; Criminal Trial Practice; General Practice; Health Care Law

DUVIN, CAHN & HUTTON, A LEGAL PROFESSIONAL ASSOCIATION
Cleveland, OH .... Appellate Practice; Civil Trial Practice; Employment Benefits Law; Labor and Employment Law; Workers Compensation

DWORKEN & BERNSTEIN CO., L.P.A., A PROFESSIONAL CORPORATION
Painesville, OH .... Corporate Law; Real Estate Law

DWORKIN, MICHAEL L. AND ASSOCIATES
San Mateo, CA .... Aviation Law; Transportation Law

DWORSKY, TAMARA L.
Scottsdale, AZ .... Trust and Estates, Wills and Probate

DWYER & BLACK, P.C.
Olean, NY .... Personal Injury

DWYER, DALY, BROTZEN & BRUNO, LLP
Los Angeles, CA .... Appellate Practice; Aviation Law; Civil Trial Practice

DWYER, HUDDLESON & RAY, P.C.
Fort Collins, CO .... General Practice

DWYER, SMITH, GARDNER, LAZER, POHREN, ROGERS & FORREST
Omaha, NE .... Bankruptcy Law; Business Law; Civil Trial Practice; Commercial Law; Computer Law; Corporate Law; General Practice; Health Care Law; Labor and Employment Law; Personal Injury; Tax Law; Trust and Estates, Wills and Probate

DWYER & WHITE
Atlanta, GA .... Medical Malpractice; Personal Injury

DYE, TUCKER, EVERITT, LONG & BREWTON, A PROFESSIONAL ASSOCIATION
Augusta, GA ... Bankruptcy Law; Business Law; Civil Trial Practice; General Practice; Insurance Defense; Medical Malpractice; Real Estate Law

DYER, GAROFALO, MANN & SCHULTZ, A LEGAL PROFESSIONAL ASSOCIATION
Dayton, OH ... Personal Injury

DYER & WHITE LLP
Menlo Park, CA ... Civil Trial Practice; Labor and Employment Law; Personal Injury; Product Liability Law

DYKAS, FRANK J., P.A.
Boise, ID ... Patent, Trademark, Copyright and Unfair Competition

DYKEMA GOSSETT PLLC
Washington, DC ... General Practice
Chicago, IL ... General Practice
Ann Arbor, MI ... General Practice
Bloomfield Hills, MI ... General Practice
Detroit, MI ... Antitrust Law; Civil Trial Practice; Environmental Law; General Practice; Health Care Law; International Business Law; Labor and Employment Law; Municipal Bond/Public Authority Financing; Patent, Trademark, Copyright and Unfair Competition; Personal Injury; Real Estate Law; Tax Law
Grand Rapids, MI ... General Practice
Lansing, MI ... General Practice

DYTRYCH, TERRENCE F., P.A., THE LAW OFFICE OF
West Palm Beach, FL ... Commercial Litigation; Personal Injury

EAGAN, MICHAEL Q.
San Francisco, CA ... Commercial Litigation

EAGLETON, EAGLETON AND HARRISON, INC.
Tulsa, OK ... Business Law; Employment Benefits Law; Family Law; Pension and Profit Sharing; Tax Law; Trust and Estates, Wills and Probate

EARDLEY LAW OFFICES, P.C.
Cannonsburg, MI ... Personal Injury

EARL, BLANK, KAVANAUGH & STOTTS, PROFESSIONAL ASSOCIATION
Miami, FL ... Environmental Law; Natural Resources Law
Sarasota, FL ... Environmental Law; Natural Resources Law

EARL, CURLEY & LAGARDE, P.C.
Phoenix, AZ ... Land Use Law; Municipal and Zoning Law

EARLE & PATCHEN, PROFESSIONAL ASSOCIATION
Miami, FL ... Eminent Domain

EARLEY, JACK M. LAW OFFICE OF, THE
Costa Mesa, CA ... Criminal Trial Practice

EARLY, LENNON, PETERS & CROCKER, P.C.
Kalamazoo, MI ... Business Law; Corporate Law; General Practice; Insurance Defense; Real Estate Law; Tax Law; Trust and Estates, Wills and Probate; Workers Compensation

EARLY, LUDWICK & SWEENEY, L.L.C.
New Haven, CT ... Product Liability Law; Toxic Torts

EARLY, S. ALLEN, & ASSOCIATES
Detroit, MI ... Criminal Trial Practice; Labor and Employment Law

EARP COHN P.C.
Westmont, NJ ... Business Law; Civil Trial Practice; Real Estate Law

EASTLAND, HENRY B., P.C.
Colorado Springs, CO ... Trust and Estates, Wills and Probate

EASTMAN & SMITH LTD.
Toledo, OH ... Banking Law; Business Law; Civil Trial Practice; Environmental Law; General Practice; Health Care Law; Insurance Defense; Labor and Employment Law; Real Estate Law; Tax Law; Trust and Estates, Wills and Probate; Workers Compensation

EASTON, W. DOUGLAS LAW OFFICES OF
Costa Mesa, CA ... Medical Malpractice; Personal Injury

EASTON & SCHIFF
Los Angeles, CA ... Corporate Law; Real Estate Law; Trust and Estates, Wills and Probate

EATON, MARTINEZ & HART, P.C.
Albuquerque, NM ... Civil Trial Practice; Medical Malpractice; Personal Injury; Product Liability Law

EATON, PEABODY, BRADFORD & VEAGUE, P.A.
Bangor, ME ... Administrative Law; Antitrust Law; Banking Law; Business Law; Civil Trial Practice; Environmental Law; General Practice; Health Care Law; Insurance Defense; Labor and Employment Law; Municipal and Zoning Law; Municipal Bond/Public Authority Financing; Personal Injury; Real Estate Law; Trust and Estates, Wills and Probate

EAVES, BARDACKE, BAUGH KIERST & KIERNAN, P.A.
Albuquerque, NM ... Antitrust Law; Banking Law; Civil Trial Practice; Commercial Law; Commercial Litigation; Employment Benefits Law; Environmental Law; Insurance Defense; Oil and Gas Law

EBERLE, BERLIN, KADING, TURNBOW & MCKLVEEN, CHARTERED
Boise, ID ... Antitrust Law; Civil Trial Practice; General Practice; Natural Resources Law; Securities Law; Tax Law

ECKER, LOEHR, ECKER & ECKER, L.L.P.
Yonkers, NY ... Civil Trial Practice; Corporate Law; Family Law; Personal Injury; Real Estate Law

ECKER & STANDISH, CHARTERED
Las Vegas, NV ... Family Law

ECKERT KOST & VOCKE
Rhinelander, WI ... Appellate Practice; Civil Trial Practice; General Practice; Insurance Defense

ECKERT SEAMANS CHERIN & MELLOTT, LLC
Washington, DC ... General Practice
Harrisburg, PA ... General Practice
Pittsburgh, PA ... General Practice; Patent, Trademark, Copyright and Unfair Competition

ECKHOFF & HOPPE
San Francisco, CA ... Patent, Trademark, Copyright and Unfair Competition

ECKSTEIN, MICHAEL L., ATTORNEY AT LAW, A PROF. CORP.
New Orleans, LA ... Business Law; Mergers and Acquisitions; Sports and Entertainment Law; Tax Law; Trust and Estates, Wills and Probate

EDERER & PRICE, L.L.C.
San Antonio, TX ... Criminal Trial Practice; General Practice

EDGARTON, ST. PETER, PETAK, MASSEY & BULLON
Fond du Lac, WI ... General Practice

EDMONSON, BIGGS & MOZINGO, P.A.
Jackson, MS ... Banking Law; Commercial Law; Insurance Defense

EDMUNDS MAKI VERGA & THORN
Honolulu, HI ... Commercial Law; Criminal Trial Practice; Personal Injury; Trademark, Copyright and Unfair Competition

EDMUNDS & WILLIAMS, P.C.
Lynchburg, VA ... General Practice

EDSON, LAPLANTE & SPINELLI
Sacramento, CA ... Insurance Defense

EDWARDS & ANGELL, LLP
Providence, RI ... Antitrust Law; Civil Trial Practice; Communications Law; Environmental Law; General Practice; Labor and Employment Law; Municipal Bond/Public Authority Financing; Natural Resources Law; Tax Law; Trademark, Copyright and Unfair Competition

EDWARDS & ANTHOLIS, P.C.
Morristown, NJ ... Commercial Law; Tax Law

EDWARDS, BALLARD, BISHOP, STURM, CLARK & KEIM, P.A.
Spartanburg, SC ... Employment Benefits Law; Environmental Law; Immigration and Naturalization; Labor and Employment Law; Workers Compensation

EDWARDS, SOOY & BYRON, A PROFESSIONAL CORPORATION
San Diego, CA ... Civil Trial Practice; Insurance Defense
Las Vegas, NV ... Civil Trial Practice; Commercial Litigation; Construction Law; Insurance Defense; Product Liability Law

EDWARDS, TOLSTEDT & FRICKLE
Billings, MT ... Personal Injury

EDWARDS & WINTERTON, CHTD.
Las Vegas, NV ... Bankruptcy Law; Commercial Litigation; Corporate Law; Real Estate Law; Tax Law; Trust and Estates, Wills and Probate

EFFRON, WAYNE D., P.C.
Greenwich, CT ... Family Law; Personal Injury

EFMAN & OBEDIN
Central Islip, NY ... Criminal Trial Practice

EGAN, FLANAGAN AND COHEN, P.C.
Springfield, MA ... General Practice

EGAN & MAZZARA, PLLC
Troy, MI ... Commercial Litigation

EGAN, THOMAS F., P.A.
Orlando, FL ... Commercial Litigation; Criminal Trial Practice

EGERTON, MCAFEE, ARMISTEAD & DAVIS, P.C.
Knoxville, TN .... Banking Law; Civil Trial Practice; Health Care Law; Tax Law; Trust and Estates, Wills and Probate; Workers Compensation

EGGER & TALMADGE
San Diego, CA .... Insurance Defense; Workers Compensation

EHLINGER & KRILL, S.C.
Milwaukee, WI .... Business Law; Civil Trial Practice; Health Care Law

EHMANN & HILLER, P.C.
Phoenix, AZ .... Employment Benefits Law; Tax Law; Trust and Estates, Wills and Probate

EHRENBERG & FROST, P.C.
Chicago, IL .... Bankruptcy Law; Commercial Litigation

EHRENPREIS, RALPH, A PROFESSIONAL LAW CORPORATION
Los Angeles, CA .... Immigration and Naturalization

EHRLICH, FRAZER & FELDMAN
Garden City, NY .... Labor and Employment Law

EIDSON & ASSOCIATES, P.C.
Atlanta, GA .... Civil Trial Practice

EIG AND SCHWARTZ, CHARTERED
Bethesda, MD .... Business Law; Trust and Estates, Wills and Probate

EIKENBURG & STILES, P.C.
Houston, TX .... General Practice

EISEN & JOHNSTON
Sacramento, CA .... Appellate Practice

EISENBERG, ANDERSON, MICHALIK & LYNCH, L.L.P.
New Britain, CT .... Labor and Employment Law

EISENBERG & FINK, LLP
Irvine, CA .... Commercial Litigation; Construction Law; Personal Injury

EISENBERG & KIRSCH
Liberty, NY .... Insurance Defense

EISENBERG, SUE ELLEN, P.C.
Bloomfield Hills, MI .... Arbitration; Labor and Employment Law

EISENBUD, FREDERICK
Hauppauge, NY .... Environmental Law

EISENHART & EISENHART
Cambridge, NE .... General Practice

EISENSTAT, GABAGE, BERMAN & FURMAN, A PROFESSIONAL CORPORATION
Vineland, NJ .... Civil Trial Practice; General Practice; Insurance Defense

EISENSTEIN, GWEN M.
Dallas, TX .... Real Estate Law

EISFELDER, ROBERT W., P.C., LAW OFFICES OF
Los Angeles, CA .... Civil Trial Practice; Family Law

EISNER & HUBBARD, P.C.
New York, NY .... Labor and Employment Law

ELAM & BURKE, A PROFESSIONAL ASSOCIATION
Boise, ID .... Antitrust Law; Banking Law; Bankruptcy Law; Business Law; Civil Trial Practice; Commercial Law; Environmental Law; General Practice; Insurance Defense; Labor and Employment Law; Municipal Bond/Public Authority Financing; Natural Resources Law; Real Estate Law; Securities Law; Trust and Estates, Wills and Probate; Workers Compensation

ELAM & GLASGOW
Union City, TN .... General Practice; Insurance Defense

ELARBEE, THOMPSON & TRAPNELL, LLP
Atlanta, GA .... Employment Benefits Law; Immigration and Naturalization; Labor and Employment Law

ELDEN LAW FIRM, THE
Chicago, IL .... Health Care Law

ELDER, KURZMAN & VACCARELLA, P.A.
Miami, FL .... Construction Law

ELLENBOGEN & GOLDSTEIN, P.C.
New York, NY .... Family Law

ELLIFF, KEYSER, OBERLE & DANCEY, P.C.
Pekin, IL .... Business Law; Municipal and Zoning Law; Trust and Estates, Wills and Probate

ELLIN AND BAKER
Baltimore, MD .... Civil Trial Practice; Medical Malpractice; Personal Injury; Product Liability Law

ELLIOTT & BLACKBURN
Valdosta, GA .... Civil Trial Practice; General Practice

ELLIOTT REIHNER SIEDZIKOWSKI & EGAN, P.C.
Blue Bell, PA .... Civil Trial Practice; Commercial Law

ELLIS, RONALD D.
Torrance, CA .... Commercial Law

ELLIS, HOOPER, WARLICK & MORGAN, LLP
Jacksonville, NC .... General Practice

ELLIS LAW FIRM
Benton, AR .... Civil Trial Practice; Insurance Defense

ELLIS, LI & MCKINSTRY PLLC
Seattle, WA .... Commercial Litigation

ELLIS & MORGAN
Stillwater, OK .... Commercial Law; Trust and Estates, Wills and Probate

ELLIS & RAPACKI
Boston, MA .... Civil Trial Practice; Personal Injury; Product Liability Law

ELLISON & HINKLE, A PROFESSIONAL LAW CORPORATION
Ventura, CA .... Personal Injury

ELLISTON & ORMESHER, L.L.P.
Dallas, TX .... Civil Trial Practice; Criminal Trial Practice

ELLMAN, BURKE, HOFFMAN & JOHNSON, A PROFESSIONAL CORPORATION
San Francisco, CA .... Civil Trial Practice; Land Use Law; Municipal and Zoning Law; Real Estate Law

ELMAN & ASSOCIATES, A PROFESSIONAL CORPORATION
Media, PA .... Patent, Trademark, Copyright and Unfair Competition

ELMAN & EHARDT, LTD.
Harvard, IL .... General Practice

ELMORE, ELMORE & WILLIAMS, P.A.
Asheville, NC .... Criminal Trial Practice; Medical Malpractice; Personal Injury; Workers Compensation

ELROD & MASCHER, P.C.
Indianapolis, IN .... Municipal and Zoning Law; Tax Law; Trust and Estates, Wills and Probate

ELSENER & CADENHEAD, P.C.
Seminole, OK .... Civil Trial Practice; General Practice

ELSTEIN AND ELSTEIN, P.C.
Bridgeport, CT .... Business Law; Personal Injury; Real Estate Law

ELWOOD, O'DONOHOE, O'CONNOR & STOCHL
Charles City, IA .... General Practice
Cresco, IA .... General Practice
New Hampton, IA .... General Practice

ELY AND TRUE
Batavia, OH .... Insurance Defense

EMANUEL AND DUNN
Raleigh, NC .... Business Law

EMCH, SCHAFFER, SCHAUB & PORCELLO CO., L.P.A.
Toledo, OH .... Intellectual Property Law; Patent, Trademark, Copyright and Unfair Competition

EMERY CUTI BRINCKERHOFF & ABADY PC
New York, NY .... Appellate Practice; Civil Rights; Civil Trial Practice; Commercial Litigation; Constitutional Law; Criminal Trial Practice

EMERY JAMIESON
Edmonton, AB, Canada .... Civil Trial Practice; General Practice; Patent, Trademark, Copyright and Unfair Competition

EMISON, DOOLITTLE, KOLB & ROELLGEN
Vincennes, IN .... General Practice; Insurance Defense

EMMANUEL, SHEPPARD & CONDON
Pensacola, FL .... Civil Trial Practice

EMMETT, COBB, WAITS, KESSENICH & O'NEIL, A PROFESSIONAL LAW CORPORATION
New Orleans, LA .... Admiralty/Maritime Law; Medical Malpractice

EMMOTT, JACK H. III, & ASSOCIATES, P.C.
Houston, TX .... Civil Trial Practice; Family Law

EMOND & VINES
Birmingham, AL .... Antitrust Law; Commercial Litigation; Medical Malpractice; Personal Injury; Product Liability Law

ENGINEER, RUMI LAW OFFICES OF
Denver, CO .... Immigration and Naturalization

ENGLAND & COHEN, LLP
Oxnard, CA .... General Practice

ENGLAND, WHITFIELD, SCHRÖEDER & TREDWAY, L.L.P.
Oxnard, CA .... Business Law; Construction Law; Education Law; Land Use Law; Real Estate Law; Tax Law

ENGLISH & VAN HORNE, P.C.
Detroit, MI .... Immigration and Naturalization

ENGLISH & WOOD, P.C.
Tulsa, OK .... Bankruptcy Law

ENNIS, CHARLES W.
Denver, CO .... Trust and Estates, Wills and Probate

ENTERPRISE COUNSEL GROUP THE
Irvine, CA .... Civil Trial Practice; Computer Law; Labor and Employment Law

ENTWISTLE & CAPPUCCI LLP
New York, NY .... Securities Law

ENWALL & GRANT, L.L.C.
Boulder, CO .... Civil Trial Practice; Criminal Trial Practice

EPPERSON & RENCHER, A PROFESSIONAL CORPORATION
Salt Lake City, UT .... Medical Malpractice

EPPS AND EPPS, LAW OFFICE OF
Johnson City, TN .... Construction Law; General Practice; Land Use Law; Municipal and Zoning Law

EPSTEIN BECKER & GREEN, P.C.
New York, NY .... General Practice

EPSTEIN, SHAPIRO & EPSTEIN
Philadelphia, PA .... Tax Law

EPTING & HACKNEY
Chapel Hill, NC .... Civil Trial Practice; Family Law; General Practice; Personal Injury; Real Estate Law

ERHARD, RUEBEL & JENNINGS, A PROFESSIONAL CORPORATION
Dallas, TX .... Civil Trial Practice; Corporate Law; Labor and Employment Law

ERICKSON, DAVIS, MURPHY, JOHNSON, GRIFFITH & WALSH, LTD.
Decatur, IL .... Commercial Litigation; Insurance Defense

ERICKSON & SEDERSTROM, P.C.
Lincoln, NE .... Civil Trial Practice; General Practice; Health Care Law; Insurance Defense; Labor and Employment Law; Municipal and Zoning Law; Personal Injury; Real Estate Law; Trust and Estates, Wills and Probate
Omaha, NE .... Bankruptcy Law; Civil Trial Practice; Environmental Law; General Practice; Insurance Defense; Labor and Employment Law; Personal Injury; Securities Law; Tax Law; Trust and Estates, Wills and Probate

ERICKSON, THORPE & SWAINSTON, LTD.
Reno, NV .... Civil Trial Practice; Construction Law; General Practice; Insurance Defense; Labor and Employment Law; Medical Malpractice; Product Liability Law

ERICKSON, WEBB & SCOLTON
Jamestown, NY .... Corporate Law; General Practice; Personal Injury; Real Estate Law; Trust and Estates, Wills and Probate

ERLACH, RAYMOND N. STELLA
San Francisco, CA .... Business Law; Civil Trial Practice; Securities Law; Tax Law

ERMAN, TEICHER, MILLER, ZUCKER, FREEDMAN & GORDON, A PROFESSIONAL CORPORATION
Southfield, MI .... Bankruptcy Law

ERNSTROM & DRESTE, LLP
Rochester, NY .... Commercial Litigation; Construction Law

ERSKINE & ERSKINE
Worcester, MA .... Trust and Estates, Wills and Probate

ERSKINE & MCMAHON, L.L.P.
Longview, TX .... Personal Injury; Product Liability Law; Toxic Torts

ERWIN THOMPSON & HASCHEFF
Reno, NV .... Business Law; Civil Trial Practice; Corporate Law; Labor and Employment Law; Natural Resources Law; Real Estate Law

ESDAILE, BARRETT & ESDAILE
Boston, MA .... Civil Trial Practice; General Practice; Personal Injury

ESLER & LINDIE, P.A.
Fort Lauderdale, FL .... Business Law; Civil Trial Practice; Commercial Litigation; General Practice; Insurance Defense; Personal Injury

ESPY, ALAN C., P.A.
West Palm Beach, FL .... Insurance Defense; Personal Injury

ESSEN, ESSEN, SUSANECK, CANET & LIPSON, P.A.
Miami, FL .... Criminal Trial Practice

ESTES, HOYT & HANSEN, A PROFESSIONAL CORPORATION
San Diego, CA .... Bankruptcy Law; Civil Trial Practice

ETHERIDGE, MOSER, GARNER AND BRUNER, P.A.
Laurinburg, NC .... General Practice

ETNIRE, GEOFFREY C.
Pleasanton, CA .... Real Estate Law

EUBANKS, HILYARD & BOGAN, P.A.
Orlando, FL .... Aviation Law; Civil Trial Practice; General Practice; Insurance Defense; Medical Malpractice; Personal Injury; Workers Compensation

EVANS, CARTER, KUNES & BENNETT, P.A.
Charleston, SC .... Tax Law; Trust and Estates, Wills and Probate

EVANS AND CLESI, A PROFESSIONAL LAW CORPORATION
New Orleans, LA .... Insurance Defense

EVANS & DIXON, L.L.C.
St. Louis, MO .... Civil Trial Practice; Insurance Defense; Workers Compensation

EVANS, GANDY, DANIEL & MOORE
Fort Worth, TX .... Criminal Trial Practice

EVANS, JOHN F., & ASSOCIATES
Hamilton, ON, Canada .... Civil Trial Practice

EVANS, JONES & REYNOLDS, A PROFESSIONAL CORPORATION
Nashville, TN .... General Practice

EVANS, KAREN, LITIGATION RESOLUTION, INC.
Miami, FL .... Commercial Law; Labor and Employment Law

EVANS, KEANE LLP
Boise, ID .... General Practice
Kellogg, ID .... General Practice

EVANS, OSBORNE & KREIZMAN
Ocean Township, NJ .... Admiralty/Maritime Law; Civil Trial Practice; Corporate Law; General Practice; Insurance Defense

EVANS & PETREE
Memphis, TN .... Banking Law; Civil Trial Practice; Commercial Law; Criminal Trial Practice; General Practice; Insurance Defense; Tax Law

EVANS, PORTNOY & QUINN
Pittsburgh, PA .... Legal Malpractice; Medical Malpractice; Personal Injury; Product Liability Law

EVERETT, JAMES J., P.C., LAW OFFICES OF
Phoenix, AZ .... Tax Law; Trust and Estates, Wills and Probate

EVERSON, WHITNEY, EVERSON & BREHM, S.C.
Green Bay, WI .... General Practice; Insurance Defense; Medical Malpractice; Product Liability Law

EWING, DIETZ, TURNER & KEHOE, PROFESSIONAL ASSOCIATION
Easton, MD .... Civil Trial Practice; Commercial Litigation; Family Law; General Practice; Municipal and Zoning Law; Real Estate Law; Trust and Estates, Wills and Probate

EWING & EWING, P.C.
Denver, CO .... Personal Injury

EWING & HOBEROCK
Nevada, MO .... General Practice

EWING, JOHNSON, GRAVES & DRISKILL, PROFESSIONAL LAW CORPORATION
El Centro, CA .... General Practice

EYSTER, KEY, TUBB, WEAVER & ROTH
Decatur, AL .... General Practice; Insurance Defense; Medical Malpractice; Product Liability Law; Tax Law

FABRICANT & YESKOO, LLP
New York, NY .... Commercial Litigation; Patent, Trademark, Copyright and Unfair Competition

FAEGRE BENSON HOBSON AUDLEY
London, England ....General Practice

FAEGRE & BENSON LLP
Denver, CO ....General Practice
Minneapolis, MN...................General Practice

FAGELBAUM & HELLER, LLP
Los Angeles, CA ....Civil Trial Practice; Commercial Litigation

FAGEL & HABER
Chicago, IL.............................Banking Law; Bankruptcy Law; Real Estate Law; Securities Law; Tax Law

FAIN, MAJOR, WILEY & BRENNAN, P.C.
Atlanta, GA ....Civil Trial Practice; General Practice; Insurance Defense; Labor and Employment Law; Medical Malpractice; Personal Injury; Product Liability Law; Workers Compensation

FAIRCHILD, HANEY & BUCK, P.A.
Topeka, KS.............................General Practice

FAIRCHILD, PRICE, THOMAS, HALEY & WILLINGHAM, L.L.P.
Center, TX.............................General Practice; Insurance Defense; Medical Malpractice; Product Liability Law; Professional Liability; Real Estate Law; Toxic Torts
Houston, TX ....General Practice; Insurance Defense; Medical Malpractice; Product Liability Law; Professional Liability; Real Estate Law; Toxic Torts
Nacogdoches, TX....................General Practice; Insurance Defense; Medical Malpractice; Product Liability Law; Professional Liability; Real Estate Law; Toxic Torts

FAIRFIELD, FARROW, FLOWERS, PIERSON & STROTZ, P.C.
Albuquerque, NM...................Commercial Litigation; Government Contracts; Real Estate Law

FAIRFIELD & FREEMAN
Ventura, CA ....Trust and Estates, Wills and Probate

FAIRFIELD, JEFFREY J., P.C.
Herndon, VA...........................Commercial Law

FAKES, ARTHUR, P.C.
Chicago, IL.............................Computer Law; International Business Law
Lombard, IL...........................Computer Law; Intellectual Property Law; International Business Law

FALK LAW FIRM, THE, PLLC
Washington, DC.....................Government Contracts; Health Care Law; Insurance Defense; Labor and Employment Law; Trust and Estates, Wills and Probate

FALK & SIEMER, LLP
Buffalo, NY ....General Practice

FANCHER, C. LARRY
La Habra, CA ....Family Law

FANT, PHILIP A.
San Francisco, CA ....Admiralty/Maritime Law

FARACI & LANGE, LLP
Rochester, NY........................Medical Malpractice; Personal Injury; Product Liability Law; Real Estate Law

FARAGE, MCBRIDE & RUGGIERI
Philadelphia, PA ....Civil Trial Practice; Medical Malpractice; Product Liability Law

FARBER, STEVEN G.
Santa Fe, NM.........................Criminal Trial Practice; Personal Injury

FARBER, SEGALL & PAPPALARDO
White Plains, NY ....Commercial Litigation

FARISH, FARISH & ROMANI
West Palm Beach, FL ....Civil Trial Practice; Family Law; Personal Injury; Real Estate Law

FARMER, KELLEY, BROWN AND WILLIAMS
London, KY ....Banking Law; Civil Trial Practice; General Practice; Insurance Defense; Medical Malpractice; Product Liability Law; Real Estate Law

FARMER, PRICE, HORNSBY & WEATHERFORD, L.L.P.
Dothan, AL.............................Commercial Litigation; Personal Injury

FARMER & WATLINGTON, L.L.P.
Yanceyville, NC ....General Practice

FARNSWORTH & VONBERG
Houston, TX ....Business Law; Commercial Law; Natural Resources Law

FARR, DAVIS & FITZE
Tunkhannock, PA ....Civil Trial Practice; General Practice; Real Estate Law; Trust and Estates, Wills and Probate

FARR, FARR, EMERICH, SIFRIT, HACKETT AND CARR, P.A.
Punta Gorda, FL ....General Practice

FARRELL, J. MICHAEL
Philadelphia, PA ....Civil Trial Practice

FARRELL, FARRELL & FARRELL, L.C.
Huntington, WV ....Commercial Litigation

FARRIS, MATHEWS, BRANAN & HELLEN, P.L.C.
Memphis, TN ....Administrative Law; Admiralty/Maritime Law; Banking Law; Civil Trial Practice; Communications Law; General Practice; Insurance Defense; Municipal and Zoning Law; Real Estate Law

FARRIS, VAUGHAN, WILLS & MURPHY
Vancouver, BC, Canada..........General Practice

FARRIS, WARFIELD & KANADAY, PLC
Nashville, TN ....General Practice

FARRISH, JOHNSON & MASCHKA, P.L.L.P.
Mankato, MN ....Civil Trial Practice; General Practice; Insurance Defense

FARRUGIA, VICTOR R., A PROFESSIONAL LAW CORPORATION
New Orleans, LA....................Labor and Employment Law

FARUKI GILLIAM & IRELAND P.L.L.
Dayton, OH............................Commercial Litigation

FASKEN MARTINEAU DUMOULIN
Vancouver, BC, Canada..........General Practice
Toronto, ON, Canada.............General Practice; Trademark, Copyright and Unfair Competition
Montreal, QU, Canada ....General Practice
Quebec, QU, Canada ....General Practice
London, England ....General Practice

FAUST, HARRELSON, FULKER, MCCARTHY & SCHLEMMER
Troy, OH ....General Practice

FAVOUR, MOORE & WILHELMSEN, A PROFESSIONAL ASSOCIATION
Prescott, AZ ....Appellate Practice; Business Law; Civil Trial Practice; Commercial Law; Family Law; General Practice; Real Estate Law; Trust and Estates, Wills and Probate

FAVRET, DEMAREST, RUSSO & LUTKEWITTE, A PROFESSIONAL LAW CORPORATION
New Orleans, LA....................Civil Trial Practice; General Practice

FAW, FOLGER, JOHNSON & CAMPBELL, L.L.P.
Mount Airy, NC ....General Practice

FAY, SHARPE, FAGAN, MINNICH & MCKEE, LLP
Cleveland, OH........................Intellectual Property Law; Patent, Trademark, Copyright and Unfair Competition; Trademark, Copyright and Unfair Competition

FEARER, NYE, AHLBERG & CHADWICK
Rochelle, IL............................General Practice

FEATHERSTONE DESISTO LLP
Denver, CO ....Commercial Litigation

FEATHERSTONHAUGH, CONWAY, WILEY & CLYNE, L.L.P.
Albany, NY ....Administrative Law; Business Law; Commercial Litigation; Corporate Law; Labor and Employment Law; Medical Malpractice; Personal Injury; Product Liability Law

FECHTER & DICKSON, P.A.
Tampa, FL ....Civil Rights; Labor and Employment Law

FECZKO AND SEYMOUR
Pittsburgh, PA ....Civil Trial Practice; Personal Injury; Trust and Estates, Wills and Probate

FEDER LAW OFFICE, P.A.
Phoenix, AZ ....Criminal Trial Practice; Medical Malpractice; Personal Injury

FEDERLEIN & KERANEN, P.C.
Bloomfield Hills, MI...............Civil Trial Practice; Commercial Litigation; Construction Law; Insurance Defense; Land Use Law

FEENEY KELLETT WIENNER & BUSH, PROFESSIONAL CORPORATION
Bloomfield Hills, MI...............Civil Trial Practice; Commercial Law; Product Liability Law

FEINBERG GROUP, THE, LLP
Washington, DC......................Business Law; Civil Trial Practice; Commercial Law; Construction Law; Employment Benefits Law; General Practice; Insurance Defense; Labor and Employment Law; Medical Malpractice; Patent, Trademark, Copyright and Unfair Competition; Product Liability Law

FEINGERTS & ASSOCIATES, A PROFESSIONAL LAW CORPORATION
New Orleans, LA....................General Practice; Government Contracts

FEINGOLD, EUGENE M. LAW OFFICES OF
Munster, IN....................Civil Trial Practice; General Practice; Municipal and Zoning Law

FEINGOLD & ALPERT, L.L.P.
New York, NY....................Tax Law

FEIRICH/MAGER/GREEN/RYAN
Carbondale, IL....................General Practice

FEIWELL & HANNOY, PROFESSIONAL CORPORATION
Indianapolis, IN....................Bankruptcy Law; Commercial Law; Real Estate Law

FELDERSTEIN WILLOUGHBY & PASCUZZI LLP
Sacramento, CA....................Bankruptcy Law

FELDESMAN, TUCKER, LEIFER, FIDELL & BANK LLP
Washington, DC....................Business Law; Family Law; Health Care Law

FELDHAKE, AUGUST & ROQUEMORE
Costa Mesa, CA....................Appellate Practice; Banking Law; Bankruptcy Law; Business Law; Civil Trial Practice; Commercial Law; Commercial Litigation; Environmental Law; General Practice; International Business Law; International Trade Law; Mergers and Acquisitions; Real Estate Law; Securities Law; Trust and Estates, Wills and Probate

FELD, HYDE, LYLE, WERTHEIMER & BRYANT, P.C.
Birmingham, AL....................Tax Law; Trust and Estates, Wills and Probate

FELDMAN & FIORELLO
Wayne, NJ....................Family Law

FELDMAN, FRANDEN, WOODARD & FARRIS
Tulsa, OK....................Civil Trial Practice; Medical Malpractice

FELDMAN GALE & WEBER, P.A.
Miami, FL....................Commercial Litigation; Medical Malpractice; Patent, Trademark, Copyright and Unfair Competition; Product Liability Law

FELDMAN, JOEL H., P.A.
Boca Raton, FL....................Family Law

FELDMAN, KIEFFER & HERMAN, LLP
Buffalo, NY....................Civil Trial Practice; Environmental Law; Health Care Law; Insurance Defense; Medical Malpractice; Product Liability Law

FELDMAN, KLEIDMAN & COFFEY, L.L.P.
Fishkill, NY....................Personal Injury

FELDMAN & ORLANSKY
Anchorage, AK....................Appellate Practice; Civil Trial Practice; Criminal Trial Practice

FELDSTEIN GRINBERG STEIN & MCKEE, A PROFESSIONAL CORPORATION
Pittsburgh, PA....................Business Law; Civil Trial Practice; Employment Benefits Law; Family Law; Health Care Law; Insurance Defense; Personal Injury

FELHABER, LARSON, FENLON & VOGT, PROFESSIONAL ASSOCIATION
Minneapolis, MN....................General Practice; Labor and Employment Law
St. Paul, MN....................General Practice

FELLERS, SNIDER, BLANKENSHIP, BAILEY & TIPPENS, A PROFESSIONAL CORPORATION
Oklahoma City, OK....................General Practice
Tulsa, OK....................General Practice

FELLOWS, PIPER & SCHMIDT
Milwaukee, WI....................Insurance Defense

FELSMAN, BRADLEY, GUNTER & DILLON, LLP
Fort Worth, TX....................Patent, Trademark, Copyright and Unfair Competition

FENDIG, MCLEMORE, TAYLOR, WHITWORTH & DURHAM, P.C.
Brunswick, GA....................Civil Trial Practice; General Practice; Insurance Defense; Legal Malpractice; Medical Malpractice; Personal Injury; Product Liability Law

FENDLER, OSCAR
Blytheville, AR....................General Practice

FENDON, DON A., P.C.
Phoenix, AZ....................Workers Compensation

FENNEMORE CRAIG, A PROFESSIONAL CORPORATION
Phoenix, AZ....................Administrative Law; Antitrust Law; Appellate Practice; Banking Law; Bankruptcy Law; Business Law; Civil Trial Practice; Commercial Law; Commercial Litigation; Communications Law; Computer Law; Constitutional Law; Construction Law; Criminal Trial Practice; Employment Benefits Law; Environmental Law; General Practice; Health Care Law; Immigration and Naturalization; Insurance Defense; Intellectual Property Law; International Business Law; Labor and Employment Law; Land Use Law; Medical Malpractice; Mergers and Acquisitions; Municipal and Zoning Law; Natural Resources Law; Patent, Trademark, Copyright and Unfair Competition; Pension and Profit Sharing; Personal Injury; Product Liability Law; Professional Liability; Public Utilities Law; Real Estate Law; Securities Law; Sports and Entertainment Law; Tax Law; Trademark, Copyright and Unfair Competition; Transportation Law; Trust and Estates, Wills and Probate; Workers Compensation
Tucson, AZ....................General Practice; Labor and Employment Law

FENTON, CHAPMAN, FENTON, SMITH & KANE, P.A.
Bar Harbor, ME....................Civil Trial Practice; Corporate Law; Environmental Law; General Practice; International Business Law; Personal Injury; Real Estate Law; Trust and Estates, Wills and Probate

FERENCIK, LIBANOFF, BRANDT & BUSTAMANTE, P.A.
Fort Lauderdale, FL....................Construction Law; Real Estate Law

FERGUSON, CASE, ORR, PATERSON & CUNNINGHAM LLP
Ventura, CA....................Civil Trial Practice; Real Estate Law

FERGUSON, NEWBURN & WESTON, A PROFESSIONAL CORPORATION
La Jolla, CA....................Trust and Estates, Wills and Probate

FERGUSON, SCHETELICH & HEFFERNAN, P.A.
Baltimore, MD....................Admiralty/Maritime Law; Aviation Law; Civil Trial Practice; Construction Law; Environmental Law; Insurance Defense; Labor and Employment Law; Tax Law; Transportation Law; Trust and Estates, Wills and Probate

FERGUSON, STEIN, WALLAS, ADKINS, GRESHAM & SUMTER, P.A.
Charlotte, NC....................Appellate Practice; Civil Rights; Civil Trial Practice; Criminal Trial Practice; Education Law; Labor and Employment Law; Medical Malpractice; Personal Injury

FERNANDEZ, JOHN D., P.A.
Clearwater, FL....................Criminal Trial Practice; Personal Injury

FERNANDEZ & KNEBEL, A PROFESSIONAL CORPORATION
Dallas, TX....................Civil Trial Practice; Commercial Litigation; Corporate Law; Health Care Law; Real Estate Law

FERRARA, FIORENZA, LARRISON, BARRETT & REITZ, P.C.
Syracuse, NY....................Education Law; Labor and Employment Law

FERRARO & ASSOCIATES, P.A.
Miami, FL....................Civil Trial Practice; Personal Injury

FERRARO, RUSSELL J., JR. AND ASSOCIATES, P.A.
Stuart, FL....................Family Law

FERRELL, WAYNE E. JR.
Jackson, MS....................Aviation Law

FERRELLE, JOHN R., P.C.
Brunswick, GA....................Medical Malpractice

FERRELL SCHULTZ CARTER & FERTEL, P.A.
Miami, FL....................Civil Trial Practice; Criminal Trial Practice

FERRERI, FOGLE & PICKLESIMER
Lexington, KY....................Insurance Defense; Workers Compensation
Louisville, KY....................Insurance Defense; Workers Compensation

FERRETTE & SLATER, A LAW CORPORATION
San Diego, CA....................Real Estate Law; Trust and Estates, Wills and Probate

FERRIS & BRITTON, A PROFESSIONAL CORPORATION
San Diego, CA....................Antitrust Law; Banking Law; Business Law; Civil Trial Practice; Commercial Law; Communications Law; General Practice; Insurance Defense; Labor and Employment Law; Real Estate Law; Securities Law; Tax Law; Trademark, Copyright and Unfair Competition

FERRIS & SALTER, P.C.
Ann Arbor, MI....................Criminal Trial Practice; Medical Malpractice; Personal Injury

FERRO LABELLA LOGERFO & ZUCKER, A PROFESSIONAL CORPORATION
Hackensack, NJ....................Banking Law; Commercial Law; Real Estate Law; Trust and Estates, Wills and Probate

FERRUZZO & FERRUZZO
Santa Ana, CA....................Business Law

FERRY, WARREN D., P.C.
Butler, PA....................Civil Trial Practice

FETTERLY & GORDON, P.A.
Minneapolis, MN....................Civil Trial Practice; Insurance Defense; Personal Injury

FIDDLER GONZÁLEZ & RODRÍGUEZ, LLP
San Juan, PR....................Antitrust Law; Banking Law; Bankruptcy Law; Civil Trial Practice; Commercial Law; Environmental Law; General Practice; Immigration and Naturalization; Insurance Defense; Labor and Employment Law; Municipal Bond/Public Authority Financing; Real Estate Law; Tax Law; Trademark, Copyright and Unfair Competition

FIEDELMAN & MCGAW
Jericho, NY....................Insurance Defense

FIELD & FIELD, P.C.
Kalamazoo, MI ....Personal Injury

FIELD & GOLAN
Chicago, IL..............................Banking Law; Business Law; Commercial Litigation; Mergers and Acquisitions; Real Estate Law

FIELD, RICHARDSON & WILHELMY
Walnut Creek, CA ....Construction Law; Real Estate Law

FIELDS, JOHN W., P.A.
Seneca, SC ....Real Estate Law

FIGARI DAVENPORT & GRAVES, L.L.P.
Dallas, TX ....Business Law; Civil Trial Practice; General Practice; Insurance Defense; Labor and Employment Law

FIGLIULO & SILVERMAN, P.C.
Chicago, IL..............................Civil Trial Practice; Commercial Litigation; Eminent Domain; Land Use Law; Legal Malpractice

FILDEW HINKS, P.L.L.C.
Detroit, MI ....Civil Trial Practice; General Practice; Real Estate Law; Tax Law; Trust and Estates, Wills and Probate

FILE, PAYNE, SCHERER & FILE
Beckley, WV ....Banking Law; General Practice; Insurance Defense; Real Estate Law

FILICE, BROWN, EASSA & MCLEOD, LLP
Oakland, CA ....Civil Trial Practice; Environmental Law; General Practice; Product Liability Law

FILION, WAKELY & THORUP
Toronto, ON, Canada ....Labor and Employment Law

FILLEY, G. WILLIAM
San Francisco, CA ....Family Law; Trust and Estates, Wills and Probate

FINCH, MONTGOMERY & WRIGHT
Palo Alto, CA ....Trust and Estates, Wills and Probate

FINCK, KEVIN W. LAW OFFICES OF
San Francisco, CA ....Business Law; Commercial Law; International Business Law

FINE & FAURE
Albuquerque, NM ....Personal Injury

FINE & HATFIELD, A PROFESSIONAL CORPORATION
Evansville, IN..........................Appellate Practice; Bankruptcy Law; Business Law; Civil Trial Practice; Environmental Law; Health Care Law; Insurance Defense; Labor and Employment Law; Product Liability Law; Real Estate Law; Tax Law; Trust and Estates, Wills and Probate

FINER, KIM & STEARNS
Torrance, CA...........................Bankruptcy Law; Business Law; Civil Trial Practice; Environmental Law; General Practice; Real Estate Law; Trust and Estates, Wills and Probate

FINESTONE & MORRIS
Atlanta, GA ....Commercial Litigation; Criminal Trial Practice

FINK, DAVID E.
Baltimore, MD ....Civil Trial Practice

FINKBOHNER AND LAWLER, L.L.C.
Mobile, AL...............................Bankruptcy Law; Civil Trial Practice; Commercial Law; General Practice; Municipal and Zoning Law; Personal Injury; Product Liability Law

FINKEL & ALTMAN, L.L.C.
Columbia, SC ....Bankruptcy Law; Civil Trial Practice; Commercial Law; Construction Law; Criminal Trial Practice; Insurance Defense; Personal Injury; Real Estate Law; Tax Law

FINKEL GOLDSTEIN BERZOW ROSENBLOOM & NASH, LLP
New York, NY.........................Bankruptcy Law; Commercial Litigation; Creditors Rights

FINKELMEIER & FARRELL
Cincinnati, OH ....Workers Compensation

FINLAYSON, MAC D., P.C.
Tulsa, OK ....Bankruptcy Law; Creditors Rights

FINLEY, WARREN
Laguna Beach, CA ....General Practice

FINLEY, ALT, SMITH, SCHARNBERG, CRAIG, HILMES & GAFFNEY, P.C.
Des Moines, IA ....Appellate Practice; Banking Law; Business Law; Civil Trial Practice; Construction Law; Employment Benefits Law; General Practice; Health Care Law; Insurance Defense; Labor and Employment Law; Medical Malpractice; Personal Injury; Product Liability Law; Real Estate Law; Tax Law; Transportation Law; Trust and Estates, Wills and Probate; Workers Compensation

FINMAN, SHELDON E., P.A.
Fort Myers, FL ....Family Law

FINNEGAN, HENDERSON, FARABOW, GARRETT & DUNNER, L.L.P.
Washington, DC......................Patent, Trademark, Copyright and Unfair Competition; Trademark, Copyright and Unfair Competition

FINNERTY & FINNERTY
Boston, MA.............................Insurance Defense; Product Liability Law

FINNERTY & LAROCCA, P.C.
Paramus, NJ............................Appellate Practice; Civil Trial Practice; Family Law

FINNEY, DANIEL P. JR.
St. Louis, MO..........................Personal Injury

FIORE LAW GROUP, LLP
San Jose, CA ....Tax Law; Trust and Estates, Wills and Probate

FIORETTI, MICHAEL D.
Philadelphia, PA ....Family Law

FISCH, SPIEGLER, GINSBURG, LADNER & ATTARIAN, A PROFESSIONAL LAW CORPORATION
San Diego, CA ....Business Law; Civil Trial Practice; Labor and Employment Law; Real Estate Law; Trust and Estates, Wills and Probate

FISCHER, BESSETTE & MULDOWNEY, L.L.P.
Malone, NY.............................Civil Trial Practice; Insurance Defense; Personal Injury

FISCHER, BROWN & GUNN, P.C.
Fort Collins, CO ....General Practice

FISCHETTE, OWEN, HELD & MCBURNEY
Jacksonville, FL ....Bankruptcy Law; Commercial Litigation

FISH, EMANUEL S. LAW OFFICES OF
Maplewood, NJ ....Civil Trial Practice; Personal Injury; Product Liability Law

FISH & NEAVE
Palo Alto, CA ....Patent, Trademark, Copyright and Unfair Competition
New York, NY.........................Patent, Trademark, Copyright and Unfair Competition

FISHBACH, HERTAN & IVES
New York, NY.........................Commercial Law; Commercial Litigation

FISHEL, GRACE J.
St. Louis, MO..........................Patent, Trademark, Copyright and Unfair Competition

FISHER, ARTHUR W., III, P.A.
Tampa, FL ....Intellectual Property Law; Patent, Trademark, Copyright and Unfair Competition

FISHER, BOYD, BROWN, BOUDREAUX & HUGUENARD, L.L.P.
Houston, TX ....Aviation Law; Commercial Litigation; Personal Injury; Product Liability Law

FISHER CLINARD & CRAIG, PLLC
High Point, NC........................General Practice

FISHER, FISHER & BERGER
New York, NY.........................Civil Trial Practice; Commercial Litigation; Construction Law; Corporate Law; General Practice

FISHER LAW OFFICE
St. Joseph, MI ....Trust and Estates, Wills and Probate

FISHER & NEWSOM, P.C.
Austin, TX ....Municipal Bond/Public Authority Financing

FISHER, OLSON, DALEY & BATA, LTD.
Grand Forks, ND ....General Practice

FISHER, PATTERSON, SAYLER & SMITH, L.L.P.
Overland Park, KS..................Civil Rights; Civil Trial Practice; Commercial Law; Insurance Defense; Labor and Employment Law; Medical Malpractice; Product Liability Law
Topeka, KS..............................Appellate Practice; Bankruptcy Law; Civil Rights; Civil Trial Practice; Commercial Law; General Practice; Insurance Defense; Labor and Employment Law; Legal Malpractice; Personal Injury; Product Liability Law; Workers Compensation

FISHER & PHILLIPS LLP
Newport Beach, CA................Labor and Employment Law
Redwood City, CA ....Labor and Employment Law
Fort Lauderdale, FL ....Labor and Employment Law
Atlanta, GA ....Employment Benefits Law; Labor and Employment Law
New Orleans, LA....................Labor and Employment Law
Houston, TX ....Labor and Employment Law

FISHER THURBER LLP
La Jolla, CA .... Securities Law

FISHER WAYLAND COOPER LEADER & ZARAGOZA L.L.P.
Washington, DC .... Communications Law; General Practice; Intellectual Property Law

FISHMAN & JAKLITSCH
Upper Marlboro, MD .... Personal Injury

FISHMAN & MORGENTHAL
Carlisle, PA .... Commercial Law; Land Use Law; Municipal and Zoning Law; Trust and Estates, Wills and Probate

FITCH, EVEN, TABIN & FLANNERY
San Diego, CA .... Patent, Trademark, Copyright and Unfair Competition
Washington, DC .... Patent, Trademark, Copyright and Unfair Competition
Chicago, IL .... Patent, Trademark, Copyright and Unfair Competition

FITE & O'BRIEN, LTD.
McLean, VA .... Family Law

FITZGERALD, HENRY ST. JOHN
Arlington, VA .... Appellate Practice; Commercial Litigation

FITZGERALD, ABBOTT & BEARDSLEY LLP
Oakland, CA .... General Practice

FITZGERALD & ASSOCIATES
Palm Springs, CA .... Labor and Employment Law

FITZGERALD, J. PATRICK, P.A.
Miami, FL .... Real Estate Law

FITZGERALD LAW FIRM, THE
Cheyenne, WY .... Civil Trial Practice; Medical Malpractice; Personal Injury; Product Liability Law

FITZGERALD MORRIS BAKER FIRTH
Glens Falls, NY .... Business Law; Civil Trial Practice; Trust and Estates, Wills and Probate

FITZGIBBONS, JOHN M.
Sarasota, FL .... Criminal Trial Practice
Tampa, FL .... Criminal Trial Practice

FITZGIBBONS & ANDERSON
Las Vegas, NV .... Civil Trial Practice

FITZGIBBONS BROTHERS
Estherville, IA .... General Practice

FITZPATRICK, BLACKEY & DEVANIE
La Crosse, WI .... General Practice; Product Liability Law

FITZPATRICK, CELLA, HARPER & SCINTO
Washington, DC .... Patent, Trademark, Copyright and Unfair Competition
New York, NY .... Patent, Trademark, Copyright and Unfair Competition

FITZPATRICK, F. EMMETT, P.C.
Philadelphia, PA .... Appellate Practice; Civil Trial Practice; Commercial Law; Commercial Litigation; Computer Law; Criminal Trial Practice; General Practice; International Business Law; International Trade Law; Real Estate Law

FITZPATRICK & WATERMAN
Bayonne, NJ .... General Practice; Municipal Bond/Public Authority Financing; Tax Law
Secaucus, NJ .... General Practice; Municipal Bond/Public Authority Financing; Tax Law

FITZSIMMONS, LAURA WIGHTMAN
Las Vegas, NV .... Eminent Domain

FITZSIMMONS RINGLE & JACOBS, P.C.
Newark, NJ .... Civil Trial Practice; Criminal Trial Practice; Personal Injury; Product Liability Law

FIXEL & MAGUIRE
Orlando, FL .... Eminent Domain
Tallahassee, FL .... Eminent Domain

FJELDAL & ASSOCIATES, A PROFESSIONAL CORPORATION
Houston, TX .... Civil Trial Practice; Insurance Defense

FLAHERTY, MEISLER & COURTNEY
Vernon, CT .... Civil Trial Practice; Criminal Trial Practice; General Practice; Personal Injury

FLAHERTY, SENSABAUGH & BONASSO, P.L.L.C.
Charleston, WV .... Civil Trial Practice; Product Liability Law; Professional Liability

FLAHIVE, OGDEN & LATSON, A PROFESSIONAL CORPORATION
Austin, TX .... Workers Compensation

FLANAGAN, BOOTH, UNGER & MOSES
Glendale, CA .... Criminal Trial Practice; Personal Injury

FLANAGAN, MANIOTIS & BERGER, P.A.
West Palm Beach, FL .... Insurance Defense

FLASTER/GREENBERG, P.C.
Cherry Hill, NJ .... Business Law; Commercial Law; Commercial Litigation; Health Care Law; Labor and Employment Law; Land Use Law; Pension and Profit Sharing; Real Estate Law; Tax Law; Trust and Estates, Wills and Probate

FLAXMAN, NEIL, PROFESSIONAL ASSOCIATION
Miami, FL .... Administrative Law; Labor and Employment Law

FLEISCHMANN, ROGER JUSTICE LAW OFFICES OF
San Francisco, CA .... Business Law

FLEISSNER, PHILLIP A., PLLC
Chattanooga, TN .... Civil Trial Practice; Environmental Law; Labor and Employment Law; Product Liability Law

FLEMING & ASSOCIATES, L.L.P.
Houston, TX .... Aviation Law; Environmental Law; Personal Injury; Product Liability Law

FLEMING & CURTI
Tucson, AZ .... Trust and Estates, Wills and Probate

FLEMING, JOSEPH Z., P.A.
Miami, FL .... Communications Law; Environmental Law; Labor and Employment Law; Natural Resources Law

FLEMING, PATTRIDGE & RUNNERSTROM, P.C.
Golden, CO .... General Practice

FLETCHER, HARLEY & FLETCHER
Augusta, GA .... Corporate Law; General Practice; Government Contracts; Tax Law

FLETCHER, HEALD & HILDRETH, P.L.C.
Washington, DC .... Communications Law

FLETCHER, SIBELL & MIGATZ, P.C.
Manhasset, NY .... General Practice

FLETCHER, TILTON & WHIPPLE, P.C.
Worcester, MA .... General Practice

FLEURIET SCHELL LAW FIRM, THE, LLP
Harlingen, TX .... Civil Trial Practice

FLICKER & KERIN
Palo Alto, CA .... Business Law; Family Law; Real Estate Law

FLIGELTAUB, WILLIAM H.
Seattle, WA .... Criminal Trial Practice; Personal Injury

FLORES, CASSO & PETTITT, L.L.P.
McAllen, TX .... General Practice; Personal Injury; Product Liability Law

FLORIN, ROEBIG, WALKER, HUDDLESTUN & ROGERS, P.A.
Palm Harbor, FL .... Labor and Employment Law; Medical Malpractice; Personal Injury

FLOYD LAW FIRM, P.C.
Norman, OK .... Municipal Bond/Public Authority Financing
St. Louis, MO .... Personal Injury; Product Liability Law

FLOYD LAW FIRM, THE, PC
Surfside Beach, SC .... General Practice

FLYNN, DELICH & WISE
Long Beach, CA .... Admiralty/Maritime Law; Civil Trial Practice; Insurance Defense; International Business Law; Patent, Trademark, Copyright and Unfair Competition; Toxic Torts
San Francisco, CA .... Admiralty/Maritime Law; Civil Trial Practice; Insurance Defense; International Business Law; Patent, Trademark, Copyright and Unfair Competition; Toxic Torts

FLYNN & GASKINS, L.L.P.
Minneapolis, MN .... Civil Trial Practice; Insurance Defense; Labor and Employment Law; Product Liability Law

FLYNN MCKENNA WRIGHT & KARSH
Colorado Springs, CO .... Banking Law; Commercial Law; Commercial Litigation; International Business Law; Real Estate Law; Tax Law

FLYNN, PALMER & TAGUE
Champaign, IL .... General Practice

FLYNN & PHILLIPS, LLP
San Rafael, CA....Real Estate Law

FLYNN, PY & KRUSE, A LEGAL PROFESSIONAL ASSOCIATION
Sandusky, OH....General Practice

FOGARTY COHEN SELBY & NEMIROFF LLC
Greenwich, CT....Business Law; Civil Trial Practice; Corporate Law; General Practice

FOGEL, FELDMAN, OSTROV, RINGLER & KLEVENS, A LAW CORPORATION
Santa Monica, CA....Civil Trial Practice; Labor and Employment Law; Personal Injury

FOGEL, JO BENSON, P.A.
Rockville, MD....Family Law

FOGEL, LAMBER & BRONNENKANT, PROFESSIONAL ASSOCIATION
Phoenix, AZ....Appellate Practice; Arbitration; Business Law; Civil Trial Practice; Commercial Litigation; Personal Injury

FOGG, FOGG & HANDLEY
El Reno, OK....Civil Trial Practice

FOLEY, COGNETTI, COMERFORD & CIMINI
Scranton, PA....Insurance Defense

FOLEY & FOLEY
Palmyra, NY....Medical Malpractice; Personal Injury; Product Liability Law; Workers Compensation

FOLEY, HOAG & ELIOT LLP
Washington, DC....General Practice
Boston, MA....General Practice; Labor and Employment Law; Tax Law

FOLEY & JONES
Las Vegas, NV....Civil Trial Practice; Construction Law; Personal Injury

FOLEY & JUDELL, L.L.P.
New Orleans, LA....Municipal Bond/Public Authority Financing

FOLEY & LARDNER
Los Angeles, CA....Health Care Law
San Diego, CA....General Practice
San Francisco, CA....General Practice
Denver, CO....General Practice
Washington, DC....General Practice
Jacksonville, FL....General Practice
Orlando, FL....General Practice; Labor and Employment Law
Tallahassee, FL....General Practice
Tampa, FL....General Practice
West Palm Beach, FL....General Practice
Chicago, IL....General Practice
Annapolis, MD....General Practice
Madison, WI....General Practice
Milwaukee, WI....Antitrust Law; General Practice; Tax Law

FOLEY, MCLANE, FOLEY, MCDONALD & MACGREGOR
Scranton, PA....Medical Malpractice; Personal Injury; Product Liability Law

FOLGER LEVIN & KAHN LLP
San Francisco, CA....General Practice

FOLKESTAD & FAZEKAS, P.C.
Castle Rock, CO....General Practice; Municipal and Zoning Law; Real Estate Law

FOLLICK & BESSICH, P.C.
Huntington Station, NY....International Trade Law

FOLLIN & OVERFIELD, L.L.P.
Greensboro, NC....Bankruptcy Law

FONDA, HILBERMAN & FRASER LLP
Los Angeles, CA....Insurance Defense

FONZONE & ASHLEY
Allentown, PA....General Practice; Insurance Defense; Municipal and Zoning Law

FORAN & SCHULTZ
Chicago, IL....Civil Trial Practice; Construction Law; Criminal Trial Practice; Eminent Domain; Health Care Law; Municipal and Zoning Law; Trademark, Copyright and Unfair Competition

FORBES & BOWMAN
Savannah, GA....Insurance Defense; Labor and Employment Law; Product Liability Law

FORCHELLI, CURTO, SCHWARTZ, MINEO, CARLINO & COHN, LLP
Mineola, NY....Civil Trial Practice; Real Estate Law

FORD, JON R.
Enid, OK....Family Law

FORD, FRANCIS A., P.C.
Worcester, MA....Personal Injury

FORD & HARRISON LLP
Los Angeles, CA....Labor and Employment Law
Miami, FL....Labor and Employment Law
Tampa, FL....Civil Trial Practice; Labor and Employment Law
Atlanta, GA....Labor and Employment Law
Memphis, TN....Labor and Employment Law

FORD AND HOWARD, P.C.
Gadsden, AL....Civil Trial Practice; General Practice; Insurance Defense

FORD LAW FIRM, THE
Los Angeles, CA....Appellate Practice; Civil Trial Practice

FORD MARRIN ESPOSITO WITMEYER & GLESER, L.L.P.
New York, NY....Business Law; Civil Trial Practice; Corporate Law; General Practice

FORD & RICHARDSON
Lewisburg, WV....General Practice

FORD & SINCLAIR, P.A.
Miami, FL....Medical Malpractice

FORD, WALKER, HAGGERTY & BEHAR, PROFESSIONAL LAW CORPORATION
Long Beach, CA....Civil Trial Practice; Commercial Litigation; Construction Law; General Practice; Insurance Defense; Product Liability Law

FOREMAN, BOUDREAUX, SMITH & JOHNSON
Dallas, TX....Personal Injury; Product Liability Law

FORE, MILLER & SCHWARTZ
Louisville, KY....Business Law; Commercial Law; General Practice; Real Estate Law; Securities Law

FORMAN HOLT & ELIADES LLC
Rochelle Park, NJ....Banking Law; Bankruptcy Law; Commercial Litigation; Real Estate Law

FORSYTH, HOWE, O'DWYER, KALB & MURPHY, P.C.
Rochester, NY....Banking Law; Bankruptcy Law; Commercial Law; Creditors Rights; Eminent Domain; Real Estate Law

FORTINO, PLAXTON, MOSKAL & COSTANZO, P.C.
Alma, MI....General Practice; Insurance Defense

FORTNEY & KLINGSHIRN
Akron, OH....Construction Law; Labor and Employment Law

FORTUNE, JOHNNY, P.A.
Fort Walton Beach, FL....Trust and Estates, Wills and Probate

FOSSETT & BRUGGER, CHARTERED
Greenbelt, MD....Civil Trial Practice; Land Use Law; Real Estate Law

FOSTER, FOSTER, ALLEN & DURRENCE, P.C.
Chattanooga, TN....Civil Trial Practice; Construction Law; Environmental Law; General Practice; Insurance Defense; Medical Malpractice; Personal Injury; Real Estate Law; Securities Law

FOSTER, MEADOWS & BALLARD, P.C.
Detroit, MI....Admiralty/Maritime Law; Transportation Law

FOSTER PEPPER & SHEFELMAN PLLC
Seattle, WA....General Practice

FOSTER, PURDY, ALLAN, PETERSON & DAHLIN, LLP
Medford, OR....General Practice

FOSTER, SWIFT, COLLINS & SMITH, P.C.
Lansing, MI....Banking Law; Civil Trial Practice; Employment Benefits Law; Environmental Law; General Practice; Health Care Law; Immigration and Naturalization; Insurance Defense; International Business Law; Labor and Employment Law; Patent, Trademark, Copyright and Unfair Competition; Personal Injury; Real Estate Law; Transportation Law; Trust and Estates, Wills and Probate

FOULKROD, S. WALTER III & ASSOCIATES
Harrisburg, PA....Administrative Law; Civil Trial Practice

FOULSTON & SIEFKIN L.L.P.
Dodge City, KS....Business Law; Civil Trial Practice; General Practice; Tax Law; Trust and Estates, Wills and Probate
Topeka, KS....Administrative Law; Business Law; Employment Benefits Law; Tax Law; Transportation Law
Wichita, KS....Administrative Law; Antitrust Law; Banking Law; Bankruptcy Law; Business Law; Civil Trial Practice; Commercial Law; Construction Law; Employment Benefits Law; Environmental Law; General Practice; Health Care Law; Insurance Defense; International Business Law; Labor and Employment Law; Medical Malpractice; Natural Resources Law; Personal Injury; Real Estate Law; Securities Law; Tax Law; Trademark, Copyright and Unfair Competition; Trust and Estates, Wills and Probate

FOURNARIS & SANET, P.A.
Miami, FL .... Medical Malpractice; Personal Injury

FOURNET, M. MICHELE
Baton Rouge, LA .... Criminal Trial Practice

FOWLER, MEASLE & BELL, L.L.P.
Lexington, KY .... Bankruptcy Law; Insurance Defense

FOX, MAURICE F.
Denver, CO .... Real Estate Law

FOX, RENEE ISLA
Washington, DC .... Trust and Estates, Wills and Probate

FOX & FOX, L.L.P.
Stamford, CT .... Real Estate Law; Trust and Estates, Wills and Probate

FOX, GROVE, ABBEY, ADAMS, BYELICK & KIERNAN
St. Petersburg, FL .... Insurance Defense

FOX HORAN & CAMERINI LLP
New York, NY .... Civil Trial Practice; International Business Law; Securities Law

FOX, OLDT & BROWN
Easton, PA .... Elder Law; Personal Injury; Trust and Estates, Wills and Probate

FOX, ROTHSCHILD, O'BRIEN & FRANKEL, LLP
Trenton, NJ .... General Practice
Philadelphia, PA .... General Practice; Real Estate Law; Tax Law

FRALEY & FRALEY, L.L.P.
Dallas, TX .... Civil Trial Practice; Commercial Litigation; Health Care Law; Insurance Defense; Medical Malpractice; Personal Injury; Professional Liability

FRAMME LAW FIRM, PLC
Richmond, VA .... Civil Trial Practice

FRAMPTON, WILLIAMS & LITTLE, A PROFESSIONAL ASSOCIATION
Fresno, CA .... Labor and Employment Law

FRANCHISE LAW TEAM
Rancho Santa Margarita, CA .... Franchise Law

FRANCZEK SULLIVAN P.C.
Chicago, IL .... Arbitration; Civil Trial Practice; Education Law; Employment Benefits Law; Labor and Employment Law

FRANKE, RAINEY & SALLOUM, PLLC
Gulfport, MS .... Admiralty/Maritime Law; Civil Trial Practice; Commercial Law; Environmental Law; General Practice; Insurance Defense; Real Estate Law; Trust and Estates, Wills and Probate; Workers Compensation

FRANKE & SCHULTZ, A PROFESSIONAL CORPORATION
Kansas City, MO .... Civil Trial Practice; Insurance Defense; Personal Injury; Product Liability Law

FRANK LAW FIRM, THE, L.L.P.
St. Louis, MO .... Personal Injury

FRANKLIN, CARDWELL & JONES
Houston, TX .... Civil Trial Practice; Commercial Litigation; Medical Malpractice; Personal Injury

FRANKLIN, COOPER & MARCUS, PLLC
Chattanooga, TN .... Civil Trial Practice; Insurance Defense; Labor and Employment Law; Personal Injury; Product Liability Law

FRANKLIN, GORDON & HOBGOOD
Madisonville, KY .... Insurance Defense; Medical Malpractice

FRANKLIN AND HANCE, P.S.C.
Louisville, KY .... Civil Trial Practice; Medical Malpractice; Personal Injury; Product Liability Law

FRANKOVITCH, ANETAKIS, COLANTONIO & SIMON
Weirton, WV .... General Practice; Personal Injury

FRANKS, E. BEN LAW OFFICES OF
Texarkana, TX .... Civil Trial Practice

FRANSEN & HARDIN, A P.L.C.
New Orleans, LA .... Admiralty/Maritime Law

FRANTZ, MCCONNELL & SEYMOUR, LLP
Knoxville, TN .... Civil Trial Practice; Commercial Litigation; General Practice; Insurance Defense; Labor and Employment Law

FRASER MILNER
Vancouver, BC, Canada .... General Practice
Ottawa, ON, Canada .... General Practice
Toronto, ON, Canada .... General Practice

FRASER, STRYKER, VAUGHN, MEUSEY, OLSON, BOYER & BLOCH, P.C.
Omaha, NE .... Banking Law; Commercial Law; Environmental Law; General Practice; Insurance Defense; Labor and Employment Law; Real Estate Law; Tax Law

FRASER TREBILCOCK DAVIS & FOSTER, P.C.
Lansing, MI .... Civil Trial Practice; Employment Benefits Law; Environmental Law; Health Care Law; Insurance Defense; Labor and Employment Law; Medical Malpractice; Product Liability Law; Real Estate Law; Trust and Estates, Wills and Probate

FRASIER, FRASIER & HICKMAN
Tulsa, OK .... Personal Injury; Product Liability Law; Workers Compensation

FRATES, WILLIAM S., II P.A.
Vero Beach, FL .... Product Liability Law

FRAZER, S. STEWART
Dallas, TX .... General Practice

FRAZER, GREENE, UPCHURCH & BAKER, L.L.C.
Mobile, AL .... Civil Trial Practice; Commercial Litigation; Insurance Defense; Medical Malpractice; Product Liability Law; Professional Liability

FRAZER SCHAPIRO & RICH, S.C.
Milwaukee, WI .... Environmental Law; Tax Law

FRAZIER & FRAZIER, ATTORNEYS AT LAW, P.A.
Jacksonville, FL .... Tax Law; Trust and Estates, Wills and Probate

FREDERICKS, BARRY I.
Englewood Cliffs, NJ .... Civil Trial Practice; Intellectual Property Law

FREEARK, HARVEY, MENDILLO, DENNIS, WULLER & CAIN, P.C.
Belleville, IL .... Commercial Litigation; Insurance Defense

FREEBURG, JUDY & NETTELS
Pasadena, CA .... Civil Trial Practice; Environmental Law; Insurance Defense; Medical Malpractice

FREEDMAN BOYD DANIELS HOLLANDER GOLDBERG & CLINE P.A.
Albuquerque, NM .... Antitrust Law; Appellate Practice; Civil Rights; Civil Trial Practice; Commercial Litigation; Criminal Trial Practice; Securities Law

FREEDMAN AND FISH
New York, NY .... Elder Law; Trust and Estates, Wills and Probate

FREEDMAN, LEVY, KROLL & SIMONDS
Washington, DC .... General Practice

FREELAND & FREELAND
Oxford, MS .... Banking Law; Bankruptcy Law; Civil Trial Practice; Commercial Law; Commercial Litigation; Constitutional Law; Insurance Defense; Product Liability Law; Real Estate Law

FREEMAN, FREEMAN & SALZMAN, P.C.
Chicago, IL .... Antitrust Law; Commercial Litigation; Securities Law

FREEMAN, LOFTUS & MANLEY
New City, NY .... Banking Law; Real Estate Law; Trust and Estates, Wills and Probate

FREEMAN MATHIS & GARY, LLP
Atlanta, GA .... Civil Rights; Construction Law; Insurance Defense; Labor and Employment Law

FREEMAN & SUPRAN, P.A.
West Palm Beach, FL .... Medical Malpractice; Personal Injury

FREEMAN, WOLFE & GREENBAUM, P.A.
Towson, MD .... Civil Trial Practice; Criminal Trial Practice

FREEMAN, WRIGHT & HERMAN
Atlanta, GA .... Civil Trial Practice; Environmental Law; Labor and Employment Law; Personal Injury; Product Liability Law

FREISHTAT & SANDLER
Baltimore, MD .... Civil Trial Practice; Commercial Litigation; Construction Law; Professional Liability

FREITAS, MCCARTHY, MACMAHON & KEATING, LLP
San Rafael, CA .... Insurance Defense

FRENCH & STONE, P.C.
Boulder, CO .... Civil Trial Practice; Commercial Law; Personal Injury

FREUND, FREEZE & ARNOLD, A LEGAL PROFESSIONAL ASSOCIATION
Dayton, OH .... Civil Trial Practice; Commercial Law; Construction Law; Insurance Defense; Medical Malpractice; Product Liability Law

FRIDAY, ELDREDGE & CLARK
Little Rock, AR .... Antitrust Law; Banking Law; Civil Trial Practice; General Practice; Insurance Defense; Labor and Employment Law; Municipal Bond/Public Authority Financing; Personal Injury; Securities Law; Tax Law

FRIED & ASSOCIATES, P.C.
Livonia, MI .... Tax Law; Trust and Estates, Wills and Probate

FRIEDBERG, JOSEPH S., CHARTERED
Minneapolis, MN .... Criminal Trial Practice

FRIED, BIRD & CRUMPACKER, A PROFESSIONAL CORPORATION
Los Angeles, CA .... Banking Law; Commercial Litigation; Labor and Employment Law; Real Estate Law

FRIED, FRANK, HARRIS, SHRIVER & JACOBSON
Washington, DC .... General Practice; Tax Law
New York, NY .... General Practice
London, England .... General Practice
Paris, France .... General Practice

FRIEDLOB SANDERSON RASKIN PAULSON & TOURTILLOTT, LLC
Denver, CO .... Civil Trial Practice; Corporate Law; Environmental Law; Natural Resources Law; Securities Law; Transportation Law

FRIEDMAN, AVERY S.
Cleveland, OH .... Civil Rights

FRIEDMAN, BARRY A. & ASSOCIATES
Mobile, AL .... Creditors Rights

FRIEDMAN & ATHERTON
Boston, MA .... Civil Trial Practice; Family Law; General Practice

FRIEDMAN & BABBITT CO., L.P.A.
Columbus, OH .... Family Law

FRIEDMAN BABCOCK & GAYTHWAITE
Portland, ME .... Civil Trial Practice; Environmental Law; Health Care Law; Insurance Defense; Personal Injury; Product Liability Law

FRIEDMAN, C. MARSHALL, A PROFESSIONAL CORPORATION
St. Louis, MO .... Civil Trial Practice

FRIEDMAN, COLLARD, CUTTER & PANNETON, PROFESSIONAL CORPORATION
Sacramento, CA .... General Practice; Personal Injury

FRIEDMAN, DOMIANO & SMITH CO., L.P.A.
Cleveland, OH .... Medical Malpractice; Personal Injury; Product Liability Law

FRIEDMAN AND FRIEDMAN, P.A.
Miami, FL .... Medical Malpractice; Personal Injury

FRIEDMAN KAPLAN & SEILER LLP
New York, NY .... Business Law; Civil Trial Practice; Commercial Litigation; Labor and Employment Law; Securities Law

FRIEDMAN, LEAK & BLOOM, P.C.
Birmingham, AL .... Insurance Defense; Product Liability Law

FRIEDMAN, LEVY & GOLDFARB, P.C.
New York, NY .... Medical Malpractice; Personal Injury

FRIEDMAN, OLIVE, MCCUBBIN, SPALDING, BILTER, ROOSEVELT & MONTGOMERY, A PROFESSIONAL CORPORATION
San Francisco, CA .... Trust and Estates, Wills and Probate

FRIEDMAN, WITTENSTEIN & HOCHMAN, A PROFESSIONAL CORPORATION
New York, NY .... Civil Trial Practice; Corporate Law; General Practice

FRIEDRICH & FRIEDRICH, P.A.
Fort Lauderdale, FL .... Trust and Estates, Wills and Probate

FRIELING, LEONARD I., P.C.
Boulder, CO .... Criminal Trial Practice

FRIEND, KARL E.
Allentown, PA .... Bankruptcy Law
Reading, PA .... Bankruptcy Law

FRIEND & ASSOCIATES, L.L.P.
Houston, TX .... Medical Malpractice

FRIERSON & WATSON
Stuart, FL .... Criminal Trial Practice; Personal Injury

FRIJOUF, RUST & PYLE, P.A.
Tampa, FL .... Patent, Trademark, Copyright and Unfair Competition

FRILOT, PARTRIDGE, KOHNKE & CLEMENTS, L.C.
New Orleans, LA .... Admiralty/Maritime Law; Environmental Law; General Practice; Insurance Defense; Product Liability Law

FRINK, FOY & YOUNT, P.A.
Shallotte, NC .... General Practice
Southport, NC .... General Practice

FRISK, FRANK W., JR., P.C.
Washington, DC .... Natural Resources Law

FRISTOE, TAYLOR & SCHULTZ, LTD., P.S.
Olympia, WA .... General Practice

FROELICH & WEPRIN CO. LPA
Dayton, OH .... Business Law; Real Estate Law

FROHNMAYER, DEATHERAGE, PRATT, JAMIESON, CLARKE & MOORE, P.C.
Medford, OR .... Commercial Litigation; General Practice; Insurance Defense

FROIMSON, JEROME L.
Phoenix, AZ .... Labor and Employment Law

FROMME SCHWARTZ NEWMAN & CORNICELLO, LLP
New York, NY .... Commercial Litigation; Corporate Law; Real Estate Law

FROMMER LAWRENCE & HAUG LLP
New York, NY .... Patent, Trademark, Copyright and Unfair Competition

FROSS ZELNICK LEHRMAN & ZISSU, P.C.
New York, NY .... Trademark, Copyright and Unfair Competition

FROST & JACOBS LLP
Cincinnati, OH .... Antitrust Law; Banking Law; Bankruptcy Law; Civil Trial Practice; Commercial Law; Communications Law; Environmental Law; General Practice; Health Care Law; Intellectual Property Law; Labor and Employment Law; Patent, Trademark, Copyright and Unfair Competition; Real Estate Law; Tax Law
Middletown, OH .... General Practice

FROST & SAUNDERS, P.A.
Bartow, FL .... Civil Trial Practice; Commercial Litigation; General Practice; Medical Malpractice; Personal Injury

FRUE LAW FIRM, THE, L.L.P.
Asheville, NC .... Real Estate Law

FRYER & ROSS
New York, NY .... Civil Trial Practice

FTHENAKIS, BASIL P.
Palo Alto, CA .... Antitrust Law; Civil Trial Practice; Patent, Trademark, Copyright and Unfair Competition

FUCHSBERG & FUCHSBERG
New York, NY .... Civil Trial Practice; Medical Malpractice; Personal Injury; Product Liability Law

FUCHSBERG, JACOB D., THE, LAW FIRM
New York, NY .... Medical Malpractice; Personal Injury

FUENTES AND KREISCHER
Tampa, FL .... Real Estate Law

FUJIYAMA, DUFFY & FUJIYAMA, ATTORNEYS AT LAW, A LAW CORPORATION
Honolulu, HI .... Civil Trial Practice; General Practice

FUKUNAGA MATAYOSHI HERSHEY & CHING
Honolulu, HI .... Civil Trial Practice; Insurance Defense; Intellectual Property Law; Product Liability Law

FULBRIGHT & JAWORSKI L.L.P.
Houston, TX .... General Practice

FULCHER, HAGLER, REED, HANKS & HARPER, LLP
Augusta, GA .... General Practice

FULLENWEIDER & ASSOCIATES
Houston, TX .... Family Law

FULLER, BECTON, SLIFKIN & BELL, P.A.
Raleigh, NC .... Medical Malpractice; Personal Injury

FULLER HOLSONBACK & BIVINS, P.A.
Tampa, FL .... Commercial Litigation; Mergers and Acquisitions; Securities Law; Trust and Estates, Wills and Probate

FULLER, JOHNSON & FARRELL, P.A.
Pensacola, FL .... Civil Trial Practice; Product Liability Law
Tallahassee, FL .... Civil Trial Practice; Product Liability Law

FULLER, TELLINGHUISEN, GORDON & PERCY, P.C.
Lead, SD....................Administrative Law; Business Law; Civil Trial Practice; Corporate Law; Criminal Trial Practice; Family Law; General Practice; Personal Injury; Trust and Estates, Wills and Probate; Workers Compensation

FULLER, VAUGHN AND GOTT
Kingsport, TN....................Insurance Defense

FULLER-JACOBS, NANCY & ASSOCIATES
San Diego, CA....................Immigration and Naturalization; International Business Law; International Trade Law

FULTON, PHILIP J. & ASSOCIATES
Columbus, OH....................Workers Compensation

FULWIDER PATTON LEE & UTECHT, LLP
Los Angeles, CA....................Patent, Trademark, Copyright and Unfair Competition

FUNDERBURK & ANDREWS
Baton Rouge, LA....................Insurance Defense

FUNK & BOLTON, A PROFESSIONAL ASSOCIATION
Baltimore, MD....................Administrative Law; Appellate Practice; Business Law; Insurance Defense; Municipal Bond/Public Authority Financing

FURBEE, AMOS, WEBB & CRITCHFIELD
Fairmont, WV....................Civil Trial Practice; Commercial Litigation; General Practice; Insurance Defense; Real Estate Law
Morgantown, WV....................General Practice

FUREY & FUREY, P.C.
Hempstead, NY....................Civil Trial Practice

FUREY, KERLEY, WALSH, MATERA & CINQUEMANI, A PROFESSIONAL CORPORATION
Mineola, NY....................Appellate Practice; Insurance Defense

FURGANG & ADWAR, LLP
New York, NY....................Intellectual Property Law

FURIA AND TURNER
Philadelphia, PA....................Civil Trial Practice; Medical Malpractice; Personal Injury; Product Liability Law; Real Estate Law; Trust and Estates, Wills and Probate; Workers Compensation

FURR AND COHEN, P.A.
Boca Raton, FL....................Bankruptcy Law; Creditors Rights; Family Law; Real Estate Law

FURR AND HENSHAW
Myrtle Beach, SC....................Civil Trial Practice; Medical Malpractice; Personal Injury

FUSCO LEGAL GROUP, THE, L.C.
Morgantown, WV....................Antitrust Law; Civil Trial Practice; Commercial Litigation; General Practice; Health Care Law; Mergers and Acquisitions

FUTERFAS, ALAN S. LAW OFFICES OF
New York, NY....................Criminal Trial Practice

GABEL INTERNATIONAL LAW FIRM
Burlington, VT....................International Business Law

GABLER & ASSOCIATES, P.C.
Pittsburgh, PA....................Employment Benefits Law

GABROY, ROLLMAN & BOSSÉ, P.C.
Tucson, AZ....................Civil Trial Practice; General Practice; Personal Injury; Tax Law; Trust and Estates, Wills and Probate

GACA MATIS BAUM & RIZZA, A PROFESSIONAL CORPORATION
Pittsburgh, PA....................Civil Trial Practice

GADSBY & HANNAH LLP
Boston, MA....................Civil Trial Practice; General Practice

GAGER & PETERSON, LLP
Waterbury, CT....................General Practice

GAGE & WILLIAMS LAW FIRM
Muskogee, OK....................Civil Trial Practice; General Practice

GAILOR & ASSOCIATES, P.L.L.C.
Raleigh, NC....................Family Law

GAINES & HELINGER
Clearwater, FL....................Eminent Domain

GAINSBURGH, BENJAMIN, DAVID, MEUNIER & WARSHAUER
New Orleans, LA....................Admiralty/Maritime Law; Criminal Trial Practice; Environmental Law; General Practice; Medical Malpractice; Personal Injury; Product Liability Law

GAIR, GAIR, CONASON, STEIGMAN & MACKAUF
New York, NY....................Civil Trial Practice; General Practice; Personal Injury

GALATZ, EARL, & ASSOCIATES
Las Vegas, NV....................Civil Trial Practice; Medical Malpractice; Personal Injury; Product Liability Law

GALFAND BERGER, LLP
Philadelphia, PA....................Labor and Employment Law; Medical Malpractice; Personal Injury; Product Liability Law; Toxic Torts; Trust and Estates, Wills and Probate; Workers Compensation

GALFIN & PASSON, LLP
Irvine, CA....................Business Law; Commercial Litigation; Real Estate Law

GALLAGHER & CALISTRO
New Haven, CT....................Appellate Practice; Civil Trial Practice; General Practice; Medical Malpractice; Personal Injury; Product Liability Law; Professional Liability

GALLAGHER, EVELIUS & JONES, LLP
Baltimore, MD....................Banking Law; Business Law; Civil Trial Practice; Commercial Law; Commercial Litigation; Corporate Law; Education Law; Health Care Law; Nonprofit and Tax Exempt Organizations; Real Estate Law; Securities Law; Tax Law; Trust and Estates, Wills and Probate; Workers Compensation

GALLAGHER GOSSEEN FALLER KAPLAN & CROWLEY
Garden City, NY....................Civil Trial Practice; Employment Benefits Law; General Practice; Insurance Defense; Labor and Employment Law; Personal Injury; Product Liability Law

GALLAGHER, JAMES J., LAW OFFICES OF
Fort Lauderdale, FL....................Insurance Defense

GALLAGHER, JOHN J., P.C., LAW OFFICES OF
Philadelphia, PA....................Business Law; Civil Trial Practice; Commercial Litigation; Personal Injury; Public Utilities Law

GALLAGHER & LATHROP, A PROFESSIONAL CORPORATION
San Francisco, CA....................Patent, Trademark, Copyright and Unfair Competition

GALLAGHER, REILLY, LACHAT & EGBERT, P.C.
Philadelphia, PA....................Insurance Defense

GALLAGHER, SHARP, FULTON & NORMAN
Cleveland, OH....................Civil Trial Practice; Environmental Law; General Practice; Insurance Defense; Medical Malpractice; Product Liability Law; Professional Liability

GALLAGHER, WALKER, BIANCO & PLASTARAS
Mineola, NY....................Business Law; Insurance Defense; Medical Malpractice; Product Liability Law

GALLAGHER, YOUNG, LEWIS, HAMPTON & DOWNEY, L.L.P.
Houston, TX....................Aviation Law; Civil Trial Practice; Commercial Law; Environmental Law; Medical Malpractice; Personal Injury; Product Liability Law

GALLAS & SCHULTZ
Kansas City, MO....................Bankruptcy Law

GALLAWA • BROWN • KROESCH, A PROFESSIONAL CORPORATION
Sacramento, CA....................Insurance Defense; Personal Injury

GALLET DREYER & BERKEY, LLP
New York, NY....................Civil Trial Practice; Real Estate Law; Trust and Estates, Wills and Probate

GALLIGAN & NEWMAN
McMinnville, TN....................General Practice

GALLIGAN, TULLY, DOYLE & REID, P.C.
Des Moines, IA....................Medical Malpractice

GALLIHER, KEITH E., JR., CHARTERED
Las Vegas, NV....................Personal Injury

GALLION, BAKER & BRAY, P.S.C.
Lexington, KY....................Civil Trial Practice; Medical Malpractice

GALLNER, SHELDON, P.C.
Council Bluffs, IA....................Family Law; Personal Injury; Workers Compensation

GALLON, E. S., & ASSOCIATES
Dayton, OH....................Administrative Law; Personal Injury; Product Liability Law; Workers Compensation

GALLOP, JOHNSON & NEUMAN, L.C.
St. Louis, MO....................General Practice

GALLOWAY, SMITH, WETTERMARK & EVEREST, LLP
Mobile, AL....................Insurance Defense; Trust and Estates, Wills and Probate

GALTON & HELM LLP
Los Angeles, CA ..... Civil Trial Practice; Health Care Law; Insurance Defense

GAMBERG, JAY M., P.A.
Hollywood, FL ..... Bankruptcy Law

GAMBRELL & STOLZ, L.L.P.
Atlanta, GA ..... Civil Trial Practice; General Practice

GAMMILL, WARREN P.
Miami, FL ..... Business Law; Real Estate Law

GANDIN, SCHOTSKY, RAPPAPORT, GLASS & GREENE, LLP
Melville, NY ..... Civil Trial Practice; Medical Malpractice; Personal Injury; Product Liability Law

GANDY, FRANCIS I. JR.
Corpus Christi, TX ..... Civil Trial Practice

GANNON, COTTRELL & WARD, P.C.
Alexandria, VA ..... Civil Trial Practice; Family Law
Fairfax, VA ..... Family Law

GAONA MOORE, P.C.
Phoenix, AZ ..... Construction Law; Labor and Employment Law

GARAN, LUCOW, MILLER & SEWARD, P.C.
Ann Arbor, MI ..... Civil Trial Practice; General Practice; Insurance Defense; Product Liability Law
Detroit, MI ..... Civil Trial Practice; General Practice; Insurance Defense; Product Liability Law
Grand Blanc, MI ..... Civil Trial Practice; General Practice; Insurance Defense; Product Liability Law
Grand Rapids, MI ..... Civil Trial Practice; General Practice; Insurance Defense; Product Liability Law
Lansing, MI ..... Civil Trial Practice; General Practice; Insurance Defense; Product Liability Law
Mount Clemens, MI ..... Civil Trial Practice; General Practice; Insurance Defense; Product Liability Law
Port Huron, MI ..... Civil Trial Practice; General Practice; Insurance Defense; Product Liability Law
Traverse City, MI ..... Civil Trial Practice; General Practice; Insurance Defense; Product Liability Law
Troy, MI ..... Civil Trial Practice; General Practice; Insurance Defense; Product Liability Law

GARBARINI & SCHER, P.C.
New York, NY ..... Medical Malpractice; Product Liability Law

GARCIA, MANUEL D. LAW OFFICES OF
Honolulu, HI ..... International Business Law; Real Estate Law; Tax Law

GARDERE & WYNNE, L.L.P.
Dallas, TX ..... General Practice

GARDNER, BARROW & SHARPE, A PROFESSIONAL CORPORATION
Danville, VA ..... General Practice; Personal Injury

GARDNER BOND TRABOLSI ST. LOUIS & CLEMENT, PLLC
Seattle, WA ..... Insurance Defense

GARDNER, CARTON & DOUGLAS
Chicago, IL ..... General Practice

GARDNER & CHARNEY, P.L.L.P.
Boise, ID ..... Insurance Defense; Workers Compensation

GARDNER, GARDNER, BARROW & SHARPE, A PROFESSIONAL CORPORATION
Martinsville, VA ..... General Practice; Personal Injury

GARDNER, MIDDLEBROOKS, FLEMING, GIBBONS & KITTRELL, P.C.
Mobile, AL ..... Insurance Defense; Labor and Employment Law; Workers Compensation

GARFINKLE & ASSOCIATES, LAW OFFICES OF
Washington, DC ..... Family Law; Intellectual Property Law; Trust and Estates, Wills and Probate

GARFINKLE, MCLEMORE & WALKER, PLLC
Nashville, TN ..... Bankruptcy Law; Personal Injury

GARFUNKEL, WILD & TRAVIS, P.C.
Great Neck, NY ..... Health Care Law

GARGARO, WILLIAM J., JR., A PROFESSIONAL CORPORATION
Los Angeles, CA ..... Medical Malpractice

GARIPPA AND DAVENPORT, A PROFESSIONAL CORPORATION
Montclair, NJ ..... Civil Trial Practice; Real Estate Law; Tax Law

GARLAND, SAMUEL & LOEB, P.C.
Atlanta, GA ..... Appellate Practice; Civil Trial Practice; Criminal Trial Practice; Labor and Employment Law; Medical Malpractice; Personal Injury; Product Liability Law

GARLINGTON, LOHN & ROBINSON, PLLP
Missoula, MT ..... General Practice

GARMON & GOODMAN
Glasgow, KY ..... Bankruptcy Law; General Practice; Real Estate Law; Trust and Estates, Wills and Probate

GARNER & STEIN, LLP
Amarillo, TX ..... Civil Trial Practice; Commercial Law; Personal Injury

GARNIER & GARNIER, P.C.
Falls Church, VA ..... Insurance Defense

GARRAHAN, BARBIERI & GARRAHAN, P.C.
Framingham, MA ..... Real Estate Law

GARRETT & GARRETT, A PROF. CORP., LAW OFFICES
Bedford, VA ..... General Practice

GARRETT & GILLIARD
Augusta, GA ..... Appellate Practice; Criminal Trial Practice

GARRETT & JENSEN
Santa Ana, CA ..... Insurance Defense; Personal Injury

GARRIGLE, PALM AND THOMASSON
Cherry Hill, NJ ..... General Practice

GARSON GERSPACH DECORATO & COHEN, LLP
New York, NY ..... Civil Trial Practice; Insurance Defense; Medical Malpractice

GARTNER, BENNETT & SCHUPP, P.C.
Minneapolis, MN ..... Civil Trial Practice; Personal Injury; Product Liability Law

GARTNER & YOUNG, A PROFESSIONAL CORPORATION
Los Angeles, CA ..... Labor and Employment Law

GARVER LAW OFFICES, P.C.
Reston, VA ..... Civil Trial Practice; Criminal Trial Practice; Medical Malpractice; Personal Injury

GARVEY, ANDERSON, JOHNSON, GABLER & GERACI, S.C.
Eau Claire, WI ..... General Practice; Insurance Defense

GARVEY, SCHUBERT & BARER
Portland, OR ..... General Practice
Seattle, WA ..... Admiralty/Maritime Law; General Practice

GARVIN, DAVID M., P.A.
Miami, FL ..... Criminal Trial Practice; Tax Law

GARVIN & TRIPP, A PROFESSIONAL ASSOCIATION
Fort Myers, FL ..... Appellate Practice; Commercial Litigation; Personal Injury

GARWOOD, MCKENNA, MCKENNA & WOLF, P.A.
Orlando, FL ..... Labor and Employment Law

GARY & GOODMAN LIMITED
Vienna, VA ..... Business Law; Commercial Law; Corporate Law; Mergers and Acquisitions; Real Estate Law; Tax Law

GARZA & GARZA, L.L.P.
Brownsville, TX ..... Civil Trial Practice

GARZA, REGAN & ROSENBLATT, P.C.
Rockville, MD ..... Bankruptcy Law; Commercial Litigation

GASSMAN, STEPHEN, LAW OFFICES OF
Garden City, NY ..... Civil Trial Practice; Family Law

GATES LAW OFFICE
Columbia City, IN ..... Trust and Estates, Wills and Probate

GATHRIGHT & HARDY
Louisville, KY ..... Real Estate Law

GATLIN & BIRCH, P.A.
Tampa, FL ..... Business Law; Commercial Litigation; Real Estate Law

GATZKE, DILLON & BALLANCE
Carlsbad, CA ..... Aviation Law; Civil Trial Practice; Environmental Law

GAULEY & CO.
Saskatoon, SK, Canada ..... Civil Trial Practice; Commercial Law; General Practice; Labor and Employment Law

GAULT DAVISON, A PROFESSIONAL SERVICE CORPORATION
Flint, MI ..... Business Law; Civil Trial Practice; Commercial Law; Corporate Law; Environmental Law; Insurance Defense; Labor and Employment Law; Trust and Estates, Wills and Probate

GAUNTLETT & ASSOCIATES
Irvine, CA....Appellate Practice; Intellectual Property Law

GAVIN LAW FIRM
Belleville, IL....Admiralty/Maritime Law; Commercial Litigation; Environmental Law

GAW, VAN MALE, SMITH, MYERS & MIROGLIO, A PROFESSIONAL LAW CORPORATION
Napa, CA....Business Law; Civil Trial Practice; Family Law; Land Use Law; Real Estate Law; Tax Law; Trust and Estates, Wills and Probate

GAWTHROP, GREENWOOD & HALSTED, A PROFESSIONAL CORPORATION
West Chester, PA....Business Law; General Practice; Health Care Law; Municipal and Zoning Law; Trust and Estates, Wills and Probate

GAY & CHACKER, A PROFESSIONAL CORPORATION
Philadelphia, PA....Personal Injury

GAYLORD, MCNALLY, STRICKLAND & SNYDER, L.L.P.
Greenville, NC....Business Law; Commercial Litigation; General Practice; Insurance Defense; Personal Injury; Real Estate Law

GEAN, GEAN & GEAN
Fort Smith, AR....Bankruptcy Law; Corporate Law; Real Estate Law

GEARHISER, PETERS, LOCKABY & TALLANT, PLLC
Chattanooga, TN....Business Law; Civil Trial Practice; General Practice; Tax Law; Trust and Estates, Wills and Probate

GEARY, WILLIAM L.
Columbus, OH....Family Law

GEARY, PORTER & DONOVAN, P.C.
Dallas, TX....Civil Trial Practice; Eminent Domain; Family Law; Real Estate Law; Trust and Estates, Wills and Probate

GEBHARDT, JOSEPH D., P.C.
Washington, DC....Civil Rights; Labor and Employment Law

GEBHARDT & KIEFER, P.C.
Clinton, NJ....General Practice

GEDNEY, SEAMAN & HILGENDORFF
Florham Park, NJ....General Practice; Tax Law; Trust and Estates, Wills and Probate

GEESLIN, JOSEPH D. JR.
Indianapolis, IN....Tax Law

GEHLHAUSEN, JOHN, P.C.
Lamar, CO....Civil Trial Practice; Personal Injury

GEHRING, ROBERT J., CO., L.P.A.
Cincinnati, OH....Civil Trial Practice; Insurance Defense; Personal Injury; Product Liability Law; Professional Liability

GEIMER LAW FIRM, S.C.
Green Bay, WI....Trust and Estates, Wills and Probate

GELB & GELB LLP
Boston, MA....Civil Trial Practice; Family Law; Intellectual Property Law; Securities Law

GELERMAN, CASHMAN & DONAHUE
Dedham, MA....Civil Trial Practice; General Practice

GELLES, PETER A.
Los Angeles, CA....International Business Law; Real Estate Law

GELT, PADDISON & ASSOCIATES P.C.
Denver, CO....Tax Law

GEMRICH, MOSER, BOWSER, MURPHY & GRAHAM, LLP
Kalamazoo, MI....Corporate Law

GENDERS, CURT, P.A.
Tampa, FL....Personal Injury; Trust and Estates, Wills and Probate

GENDRY & SPRAGUE, P.C.
San Antonio, TX....Aviation Law; Insurance Defense

GENN, JONATHAN M.
Silver Spring, MD....Corporate Law

GENNET, KALLMANN, ANTIN & ROBINSON, A PROFESSIONAL CORPORATION
Parsippany, NJ....Appellate Practice; Civil Trial Practice; Insurance Defense; Personal Injury

GENOVA, BURNS & VERNOIA
Livingston, NJ....Administrative Law; Appellate Practice; Civil Trial Practice; Environmental Law; Health Care Law; Insurance Defense; Labor and Employment Law

GENTRY & HASKINS LLP
Colorado Springs, CO....Criminal Trial Practice

GENTRY, NICHOLAS R., L.L.C., LAW OFFICES OF
Albuquerque, NM....Civil Trial Practice

GENTRY, PHILLIPS AND HODAK, P.A.
Jacksonville, FL....Civil Trial Practice; Medical Malpractice; Personal Injury

GEORGE & DONALDSON, L.L.P.
Austin, TX....Appellate Practice; Civil Trial Practice

GEORGE, EDWARD P., JR., INC., A PROF. CORP.
Long Beach, CA....Appellate Practice; Civil Trial Practice; Criminal Trial Practice; Personal Injury

GEORGE AND GEORGE, LTD., A PROFESSIONAL LAW CORPORATION
Baton Rouge, LA....Admiralty/Maritime Law; Personal Injury

GEORGE, HARTZ, LUNDEEN, FLAGG & FULMER
Miami, FL....Insurance Defense; Medical Malpractice

GEORGE, J. K., & ASSOCIATES
Los Osos, CA....Tax Law; Trust and Estates, Wills and Probate

GEORGE, J.K., & ASSOCIATES
San Luis Obispo, CA....Tax Law; Trust and Estates, Wills and Probate

GEORGE & SHIELDS, LLP
Irvine, CA....Business Law; Civil Trial Practice; Labor and Employment Law

GEORGESON, THOMPSON & ANGARAN, CHARTERED
Reno, NV....Insurance Defense

GEORGE, THOMAS, P.C.
Austin, TX....Civil Trial Practice; Health Care Law

GERAGHTY, O'LOUGHLIN & KENNEY, PROFESSIONAL ASSOCIATION
St. Paul, MN....Civil Trial Practice; Construction Law; Insurance Defense; Labor and Employment Law; Medical Malpractice

GERAGHTY, PATRICK E., A PROFESSIONAL ASSOCIATION
Fort Myers, FL....Civil Rights; Civil Trial Practice; Commercial Law; Personal Injury

GERAGOS & GERAGOS
Los Angeles, CA....Criminal Trial Practice

GERALDS, JONES, SHERROW, SCHRADER & RICE, P.S.C.
Lexington, KY....General Practice; Insurance Defense; Real Estate Law

GERARD SINGER & LEVICK, P.C.
Addison, TX....Bankruptcy Law; Business Law; Civil Trial Practice; Commercial Litigation; Insurance Defense

GERBER & BATEMAN, A PROFESSIONAL ASSOCIATION
Santa Fe, NM....Family Law; Trust and Estates, Wills and Probate

GERBER & GERBER
Blue Bell, PA....Business Law; Civil Trial Practice; Criminal Trial Practice; Eminent Domain; General Practice; Personal Injury; Real Estate Law

GERBER & SAMSON, L.L.C.
Wayne, NJ....Civil Trial Practice; Labor and Employment Law; Municipal and Zoning Law

GERDING & O'LOUGHLIN, P.C.
Farmington, NM....Civil Trial Practice

GERLING LAW OFFICES, PROFESSIONAL CORPORATION
Evansville, IN....Medical Malpractice; Personal Injury; Product Liability Law

GERRITY AND BURRIER
Columbus, OH....Family Law; Personal Injury

GERSON, GREKIN & WYNHOFF, ATTORNEYS AT LAW, A LAW CORPORATION
Honolulu, HI....Real Estate Law; Trust and Estates, Wills and Probate

GERSTEIN GRAYSON, LLP
Haddonfield, NJ....General Practice

GERSTEIN, JOE W., P.C.
Doraville, GA....General Practice

GERTNER & GERTNER
Columbus, OH....Civil Trial Practice; Criminal Trial Practice; Personal Injury

GESSLER, HUGHES & SOCOL, LTD.
Chicago, IL....Civil Rights; Civil Trial Practice; Commercial Litigation; Health Care Law; Immigration and Naturalization; Insurance Defense; Labor and Employment Law; Medical Malpractice; Personal Injury; Professional Liability

GETMAN LAW FIRM
Oneonta, NY .... General Practice; Real Estate Law; Trust and Estates, Wills and Probate

GETNICK & GETNICK
New York, NY .... Business Law; Civil Trial Practice; Commercial Litigation; Criminal Trial Practice

GHOLSON, HICKS & NICHOLS, A PROFESSIONAL ASSOCIATION
Columbus, MS .... General Practice

GIACOMINI, J. ANTHONY, PC
Klamath Falls, OR .... General Practice

GIANELLI & FORES, A PROFESSIONAL LAW CORPORATION
Modesto, CA .... Business Law; Commercial Litigation; Trust and Estates, Wills and Probate

GIAUQUE, CROCKETT, BENDINGER & PETERSON, A PROFESSIONAL CORPORATION
Salt Lake City, UT .... Antitrust Law; Commercial Law

GIBBES GRAVES MULLINS HORTMAN HARLOW MARTINDALE & JONES, PLLC
Laurel, MS .... Environmental Law; General Practice; Insurance Defense; Real Estate Law

GIBBONS, JOHN B.
Cleveland, OH .... Criminal Trial Practice

GIBBONS, WILLIAM P.
Cleveland, OH .... Business Law

GIBBONS, SMITH, COHN & ARNETT, A PROFESSIONAL ASSOCIATION
Tampa, FL .... General Practice

GIBBS & BRUNS, L.L.P.
Houston, TX .... Civil Trial Practice; Commercial Law

GIBBS & HOLMES
Charleston, SC .... Labor and Employment Law

GIBBS AND SCHWARTZMAN
San Antonio, TX .... Tax Law; Trust and Estates, Wills and Probate

GIBNEY, ANTHONY & FLAHERTY, LLP
New York, NY .... General Practice; Tax Law

GIBSON, DUNN & CRUTCHER LLP
Los Angeles, CA .... General Practice

GIBSON, HAGLUND & PAULSEN
Irvine, CA .... Securities Law

GIBSON, HOTCHKISS, ROACH & DAVENPORT
Wichita Falls, TX .... Banking Law; Business Law; Civil Trial Practice; Construction Law; General Practice; Trust and Estates, Wills and Probate

GIBSON, LEFLER & ASSOCIATES
Princeton, WV .... Banking Law; Civil Trial Practice; Criminal Trial Practice; Medical Malpractice; Personal Injury; Product Liability Law; Workers Compensation

GIBSON, MCCLURE & WALLACE, L.L.P.
Dallas, TX .... Civil Trial Practice; Commercial Litigation; Insurance Defense; Labor and Employment Law

GIBSON, OCHSNER & ADKINS, LLP
Amarillo, TX .... General Practice

GIBSON, RICHARD H., A PROF. CORP., LAW OFFICES OF
Los Angeles, CA .... Bankruptcy Law; Civil Trial Practice

GIFFEN LEE
Kitchener, ON, Canada .... Civil Trial Practice; Family Law; Insurance Defense; Personal Injury; Trust and Estates, Wills and Probate

GIFFIN, WINNING, COHEN & BODEWES, P.C.
Springfield, IL .... Bankruptcy Law; Civil Trial Practice; General Practice; Insurance Defense

GIGNILLIAT, SAVITZ & BETTIS
Columbia, SC .... Employment Benefits Law; Labor and Employment Law

GILBERT, MICHAEL L.
Denver, CO .... Elder Law; Trust and Estates, Wills and Probate

GILBERT, HARRELL, GILBERT, SUMERFORD & MARTIN, P.C.
Brunswick, GA .... Civil Trial Practice; General Practice; Insurance Defense

GILBERT, MCGLOAN, GILLIS
Saint John, NB, Canada .... Business Law; Civil Trial Practice; General Practice; Insurance Defense

GILBREATH LAW FIRM
Fort Smith, AR .... Medical Malpractice; Product Liability Law

GILCHRIST & RUTTER, PROFESSIONAL CORPORATION
Los Angeles, CA .... Labor and Employment Law
Santa Monica, CA .... Bankruptcy Law; Business Law; Creditors Rights; Real Estate Law

GILCREASE, GLYNN W. JR., LAW OFFICES OF
Tempe, AZ .... Personal Injury

GILDEMEISTER, WILLIA, KEANE, STAHLE & ANDREASEN, L.L.P.
Sioux City, IA .... General Practice

GILKEY, STEPHENSON & WEESE, P.A.
Albuquerque, NM .... Labor and Employment Law

GILLARY, RANDALL J., P.C.
Troy, MI .... Commercial Litigation

GILL AND BALDWIN
Glendale, CA .... Business Law; Civil Trial Practice; Construction Law; Trust and Estates, Wills and Probate

GILLESPIE, GOLDMAN & KRONENGOLD
Fort Lauderdale, FL .... Civil Trial Practice; Commercial Litigation; Personal Injury

GILLESPIE, HART, ALTIZER & WHITESELL, P.C.
Tazewell, VA .... General Practice

GILLESPIE, JAMES R., P.A.
Boise, ID .... General Practice

GILLESPIE, ROZEN & WATSKY, P.C.
Dallas, TX .... Labor and Employment Law

GILLILAND & ASSOCIATES
Covington, KY .... Health Care Law; Labor and Employment Law

GILLILAND & HAYES, P.A. A PROFESSIONAL ASSOCIATION
Hutchinson, KS .... Civil Trial Practice; Commercial Litigation; Construction Law; Employment Benefits Law; General Practice; Health Care Law; Insurance Defense; Labor and Employment Law; Medical Malpractice; Real Estate Law; Tax Law; Trust and Estates, Wills and Probate; Workers Compensation

GILLIN, JACOBSON, ELLIS & LARSEN
Orinda, CA .... Civil Trial Practice; Commercial Litigation; Labor and Employment Law; Personal Injury

GILLIS, NORMAN B. JR.
Mc Comb, MS .... General Practice

GILLIS & ANGLEY
Hingham, MA .... Corporate Law; General Practice

GILLIS & SLOGAR
Houston, TX .... Bankruptcy Law; Business Law; Civil Trial Practice; Commercial Law; Real Estate Law; Tax Law

GILLOCK, MARKLEY & KILLEBREW
Las Vegas, NV .... Medical Malpractice; Personal Injury

GILLOTTI, CAPRISTO & BECK, P.C.
Pittsburgh, PA .... Family Law

GILL PROFESSIONAL CORPORATION
Denver, CO .... Trust and Estates, Wills and Probate

GILMAN, MCLAUGHLIN & HANRAHAN, LLP
Boston, MA .... General Practice

GILMER, SADLER, INGRAM, SUTHERLAND & HUTTON
Blacksburg, VA .... General Practice; Insurance Defense; Personal Injury
Pulaski, VA .... General Practice; Insurance Defense; Personal Injury

GILMORE, R. PATRICK
Chandler, OK .... Civil Trial Practice

GILMORE & BELL, A PROFESSIONAL CORPORATION
Kansas City, MO .... Municipal Bond/Public Authority Financing

GILMORE, REES & CARLSON, P.C.
Franklin, MA .... Tax Law; Trust and Estates, Wills and Probate

GILPIN, PAXSON & BERSCH
Houston, TX .... Appellate Practice; Banking Law; Bankruptcy Law; Civil Trial Practice; Construction Law; Environmental Law; Insurance Defense; Personal Injury; Product Liability Law; Real Estate Law

GILREATH & ASSOCIATES
Knoxville, TN .... Aviation Law; Environmental Law; Medical Malpractice; Personal Injury; Product Liability Law

GILSTRAP, WILLIAM G.
Albuquerque, NM .... Personal Injury

GINGELL & JENKINS, P.C.
Silver Spring, MD .... General Practice; Real Estate Law; Trust and Estates, Wills and Probate

GINSBERG, EUGENE S.
Garden City, NY.....Arbitration; Labor and Employment Law; Real Estate Law

GINSBERG & BROOME
New York, NY.....Civil Trial Practice; Medical Malpractice; Personal Injury; Product Liability Law

GIOFFRE & GIOFFRE, PROFESSIONAL CORPORATION
Purchase, NY.....General Practice; Real Estate Law; Trust and Estates, Wills and Probate

GIORDANO, HALLERAN & CIESLA, A PROFESSIONAL CORPORATION
Middletown, NJ.....General Practice

GIRARDI AND KEESE
Los Angeles, CA.....Civil Trial Practice; Commercial Litigation; Medical Malpractice; Personal Injury; Product Liability Law; Professional Liability; Toxic Torts

GISLASON & HUNTER, LLP
Mankato, MN.....Civil Trial Practice
Minneapolis, MN.....Civil Trial Practice
New Ulm, MN.....Civil Trial Practice; General Practice

GITLIN, GARY M., A PROFESSIONAL LAW CORPORATION
Calabasas, CA.....Real Estate Law

GITTLER, AMY J., PLC
Phoenix, AZ.....Civil Trial Practice; Commercial Litigation; Labor and Employment Law

GLASER, HAROLD I.
Baltimore, MD.....Civil Trial Practice; Criminal Trial Practice

GLASGOW AND VEAZEY
Nashville, TN.....Insurance Defense

GLASS, JOSEPH G.
Louisville, KY.....General Practice

GLASSMAN, JETER, EDWARDS & WADE, P.C.
Memphis, TN.....Civil Trial Practice; Construction Law; Insurance Defense; Labor and Employment Law; Personal Injury; Product Liability Law

GLATSTEIN & O'BRIEN, LLP
Denver, CO.....Trust and Estates, Wills and Probate

GLAZE & GLAZE, P.C.
Jonesboro, GA.....Banking Law; Commercial Litigation; Corporate Law; Trust and Estates, Wills and Probate

GLEASON, FLYNN & EMIG, CHARTERED
Rockville, MD.....Insurance Defense

GLEAVES SWEARINGEN LARSEN POTTER SCOTT & SMITH, LLP
Eugene, OR.....General Practice

GLEICHER & PATEK, P.C.
Detroit, MI.....Health Care Law; Medical Malpractice; Personal Injury

GLENN, MILLS & FISHER, P.A.
Durham, NC.....Civil Rights; Civil Trial Practice; Personal Injury

GLENN MURPHY GRAY & STEPP, L.L.P.
Columbia, SC.....Civil Trial Practice; Commercial Litigation; Criminal Trial Practice; General Practice; Personal Injury; Product Liability Law

GLENNON, GOODMAN, LUBELEY, VAUGHN & WALKER, L.L.P.
Reston, VA.....General Practice

GLICKMAN, SUGARMAN, KNEELAND & GRIBOUSKI
Worcester, MA.....Criminal Trial Practice; General Practice

GLICK & RETAMAR
Boca Raton, FL.....Medical Malpractice; Personal Injury

GLOSSER & SHREVE
Pittsburgh, PA.....Bankruptcy Law; Commercial Law; Creditors Rights; Real Estate Law

GLOVER, ANDERSON, LEWIS & PREBEG P.C., PROFESSIONAL CORPORATION
Houston, TX.....Appellate Practice; Civil Trial Practice; Personal Injury; Product Liability Law

GLOVER & DAVIS, P.A.
Newnan, GA.....Bankruptcy Law; Business Law; Civil Trial Practice; Construction Law; General Practice; Municipal and Zoning Law; Personal Injury; Real Estate Law; Trust and Estates, Wills and Probate

GLOVER & VAN COTT, A PROFESSIONAL ASSOCIATION
Phoenix, AZ.....Commercial Litigation

GLOVER, YOUNG, WALTON, PHILLIPS & TUCKER, PLLC
Meridian, MS.....Civil Trial Practice; General Practice; Insurance Defense; Labor and Employment Law; Real Estate Law; Trust and Estates, Wills and Probate

GOBER, GARY R. THE LAW OFFICE OF
Nashville, TN.....Personal Injury

GOCKERMAN, WILSON, SAYLOR & HESSLIN, P.C.
Manistee, MI.....Civil Trial Practice; Municipal and Zoning Law; Real Estate Law

GODARD, WEST & ADELMAN, P.C.
Fairfax, VA.....Insurance Defense

GODDARD & GODDARD, P.C.
Denver, CO.....Trust and Estates, Wills and Probate

GODFREY & ASSOCIATES, PROFESSIONAL CORPORATION
Denver, CO.....Civil Trial Practice; Product Liability Law

GODFREY FIRM, THE, A PROFESSIONAL LAW CORPORATION
New Orleans, LA.....Civil Trial Practice; General Practice; Municipal Bond/Public Authority Financing; Tax Law

GODFREY & KAHN, S.C.
Green Bay, WI.....General Practice
Madison, WI.....General Practice
Milwaukee, WI.....General Practice
Oshkosh, WI.....General Practice

GODFREY, VANDOVER & BURNS, INC., A PROFESSIONAL CORPORATION
St. Louis, MO.....Insurance Defense

GODLOVE, MAYHALL, DZIALO, DUTCHER & ERWIN, A PROFESSIONAL CORPORATION
Lawton, OK.....General Practice

GODWIN WHITE & GRUBER, A PROFESSIONAL CORPORATION
Dallas, TX.....Banking Law; Bankruptcy Law; Civil Trial Practice; Commercial Law; General Practice; Insurance Defense; Labor and Employment Law; Tax Law; Trust and Estates, Wills and Probate

GOEDERT, HUNTINGTON & DEBOER
Oak Park, IL.....Business Law; Trust and Estates, Wills and Probate

GOERING, ROBERTS, BERKMAN, RUBIN & BROGNA, P.C.
Tucson, AZ.....Civil Trial Practice; General Practice; Insurance Defense; Medical Malpractice; Personal Injury

GOFF AND GOFF
Ruston, LA.....Product Liability Law

GOFFSTEIN, RASKAS, POMERANTZ, KRAUS, SHERMAN, RUTHMEYER & SUSMAN, L.L.C.
St. Louis, MO.....Insurance Defense

GOICOECHEA & DI GRAZIA, LTD., A PROF. CORP., LAW OFFICES
Elko, NV.....Business Law; Civil Trial Practice; General Practice

GOINS, UNDERKOFLER, CRAWFORD & LANGDON, L.L.P.
Dallas, TX.....Business Law; Construction Law

GOLD, ESTELLA S.
Moorestown, NJ.....Civil Trial Practice; Computer Law; Intellectual Property Law; Trademark, Copyright and Unfair Competition

GOLD, SALLY B. LAW OFFICES OF
Baltimore, MD.....Family Law

GOLD & ASSOCIATES
New York, NY.....International Business Law; International Trade Law

GOLD BENNETT CERA & SIDENER LLP
San Francisco, CA.....Securities Law

GOLDBERG & CONNOLLY
Rockville Centre, NY.....Construction Law

GOLDBERG, GRUENER, GENTILE, HOROHO & AVALLI, P.C.
Pittsburgh, PA.....Family Law

GOLDBERG, JAY, P.C.
New York, NY.....Civil Trial Practice; Criminal Trial Practice; Real Estate Law

GOLDBERG, JEFFREY M., & ASSOCIATES, LTD.
Chicago, IL.....Aviation Law; Medical Malpractice; Personal Injury; Product Liability Law

GOLDBERG, KATZMAN & SHIPMAN, P.C.
Harrisburg, PA.....Antitrust Law; Business Law; Civil Trial Practice; Commercial Law; Criminal Trial Practice; Family Law; General Practice; Insurance Defense; Medical Malpractice; Municipal and Zoning Law; Municipal Bond/Public Authority Financing; Personal Injury; Product Liability Law; Real Estate Law; Tax Law; Trust and Estates, Wills and Probate

GOLDBERG, KOHN, BELL, BLACK, ROSENBLOOM & MORITZ, LTD.
Chicago, IL.....Real Estate Law

Milan, Italy............................General Practice

GRAHAM LAW FIRM, THE
St. Louis, MO..........................Civil Trial Practice

GRAHAM, MARJORIE GADARIAN, P.A.
Palm Beach Gardens, FL.........Appellate Practice

GRAMPP, GLENN A.
Evansville, IN..........................Criminal Trial Practice

GRANAHAN, THOMAS F., P.A.
Tampa, FL ....Criminal Trial Practice; Insurance Defense; Personal Injury

GRANNAN, WILLIAM JOSEPH LAW OFFICE OF
Arlington, MA ....Real Estate Law; Trust and Estates, Wills and Probate

GRANT, RUSSELL P. JR.
Jackson, MS ....Natural Resources Law

GRANT, FRIDKIN, PEARSON, ATHAN & CROWN, P.A.
Naples, FL...............................General Practice

GRANT & GRANT, LLP
Longmont, CO ....General Practice

GRANT, LEATHERWOOD & PITTS, P.A.
Greenville, SC..........................Civil Trial Practice; Commercial Litigation; Environmental Law; Insurance Defense; Product Liability Law

GRANTHAM, KIRK, P.A.
West Palm Beach, FL...............Real Estate Law; Trust and Estates, Wills and Probate

GRATCH JACOBS & BROZMAN, P.C.
New York, NY..........................Bankruptcy Law; Commercial Litigation; Corporate Law

GRATTAN & GALATI
Sacramento, CA ....Administrative Law; Energy Law; Environmental Law; Land Use Law; Natural Resources Law

GRAVEL AND SHEA, A PROFESSIONAL CORPORATION
Burlington, VT ....Antitrust Law; Appellate Practice; Banking Law; Business Law; Civil Trial Practice; Commercial Law; Criminal Trial Practice; Environmental Law; General Practice; Immigration and Naturalization; Municipal and Zoning Law; Real Estate Law; Tax Law; Trust and Estates, Wills and Probate

GRAVES, DOUGHERTY, HEARON & MOODY, A PROFESSIONAL CORPORATION
Austin, TX ....General Practice

GRAY CARY WARE & FREIDENRICH LLP
El Centro, CA ....General Practice
La Jolla, CA............................General Practice
Palo Alto, CA ....General Practice
San Diego, CA ....General Practice
San Francisco, CA ....General Practice

GRAY & GILLILAND, P.C.
Atlanta, GA ....Aviation Law; Bankruptcy Law; Civil Trial Practice; Family Law; Insurance Defense; Land Use Law; Real Estate Law

GRAY LAW FIRM, THE, A PROFESSIONAL LAW CORPORATION
Lake Charles, LA.....................Commercial Litigation; Eminent Domain; Oil and Gas Law; Trust and Estates, Wills and Probate

GRAY, SOWLE & IACCO, A PROFESSIONAL CORPORATION
Mount Pleasant, MI.................Medical Malpractice; Personal Injury; Workers Compensation

GRAY, YORK & DUFFY LLP
Los Angeles, CA......................Business Law; Civil Trial Practice; Construction Law; Insurance Defense

GREBEN & ASSOCIATES
Sacramento, CA ....Commercial Litigation; Environmental Law

GRECO, MOLLIS & O'HARA, A PROFESSIONAL CORPORATION
Irvine, CA................................Business Law; Tax Law; Trust and Estates, Wills and Probate

GREEN, JOHN R.
Duncan, OK ....General Practice

GREEN, BRUCE DAVID, P.A.
Fort Lauderdale, FL ....Aviation Law

GREEN CORDONNIER & HOUSE, LLP
St. Louis, MO..........................Family Law

GREEN LAW OFFICES
Boise, ID.................................Civil Trial Practice; General Practice; Real Estate Law

GREEN, LUNDGREN & RYAN, A PROFESSIONAL CORPORATION
Cherry Hill, NJ ....General Practice; Insurance Defense

GREEN, SCHAAF & JACOBSON, P.C.
St. Louis, MO..........................Business Law; Commercial Litigation; Securities Law

GREENBAUM, ROWE, SMITH, RAVIN, DAVIS AND HIMMEL LLP
Woodbridge, NJ ....Bankruptcy Law; Civil Trial Practice; General Practice; Real Estate Law; Tax Law

GREENBERG, GARY J.
New York, NY..........................Commercial Litigation

GREENBERG DAUBER EPSTEIN & TUCKER, A PROFESSIONAL CORPORATION
Newark, NJ ....Banking Law; Civil Trial Practice; Commercial Law; Criminal Trial Practice; General Practice; Tax Law

GREENBERG GLUSKER FIELDS CLAMAN & MACHTINGER LLP
Los Angeles, CA ....General Practice; Tax Law; Trust and Estates, Wills and Probate

GREENBERG & PLEBAN
St. Louis, MO..........................Criminal Trial Practice; Medical Malpractice; Personal Injury; Product Liability Law

GREENBERG & SCHULMAN
Woodbridge, NJ ....Tax Law; Trust and Estates, Wills and Probate

GREENBERG, STEWART G., P.A.
Miami, FL ....Personal Injury

GREENBLATT, JAY H., & ASSOCIATES, A PROF. CORP.
Vineland, NJ...........................Civil Trial Practice; General Practice; Insurance Defense; Personal Injury; Product Liability Law; Professional Liability

GREENE, BROILLET, TAYLOR, WHEELER & PANISH, LLP
Santa Monica, CA...................Personal Injury

GREENE & CURTIS, L.L.P.
Springfield, MO......................Business Law

GREENE, CYNTHIA L., P.A.
Miami, FL ....Family Law

GREENE AND LETTS
Chicago, IL..............................Insurance Defense; Labor and Employment Law

GREENE, RALEIGH "LEE", III
St. Petersburg, FL...................Commercial Litigation; Family Law

GREENE AND REID
Syracuse, NY...........................Insurance Defense; Personal Injury

GREENE & ZINNER, P.C.
White Plains, NY ....Civil Trial Practice; Commercial Litigation; Corporate Law; General Practice

GREENEBAUM DOLL & MCDONALD PLLC
Louisville, KY ....General Practice; Labor and Employment Law

GREENFELDER, MANDER, HANSON, MURPHY & DWYER
Dade City, FL.........................Criminal Trial Practice; Personal Injury

GREENFIELD, BREWER, BAILOR & KAY
Pittsburgh, PA ....Civil Trial Practice; Criminal Trial Practice

GREENHAW & GREENHAW
Fayetteville, AR ....Insurance Defense

GREENLEE, WINNER AND SULLIVAN, P.C.
Boulder, CO ....Patent, Trademark, Copyright and Unfair Competition

GREENMAN, GOLDBERG, RABY & MARTINEZ, PROFESSIONAL CORPORATION
Las Vegas, NV ....Personal Injury; Workers Compensation

GREENSPAN & GREENSPAN
White Plains, NY ....Civil Trial Practice; Criminal Trial Practice; Securities Law; Tax Law

GREENSPUN, PETER D., & ASSOCIATES, P.C.
Fairfax, VA ....Civil Trial Practice; Criminal Trial Practice; Personal Injury

GREENWALD, GREENWALD, POWERS & WINSOR LLP
Milford, MA............................Civil Trial Practice; Municipal and Zoning Law; Personal Injury; Real Estate Law; Trust and Estates, Wills and Probate

GREENWALD, HOFFMAN, MEYER & MONTES, L.L.P.
Glendale, CA...........................Business Law; Real Estate Law; Trust and Estates, Wills and Probate

GREENWALD, STEVEN I., P.A.
Boca Raton, FL ....Real Estate Law; Trust and Estates, Wills and Probate

GREER, HERZ & ADAMS, L.L.P.
Galveston, TX........Commercial Litigation; General Practice

GREESON & ASSOCIATES
Greensboro, NC........Medical Malpractice; Personal Injury

GREFE & SIDNEY, P.L.C.
Des Moines, IA........Civil Trial Practice; General Practice; Insurance Defense; Tax Law; Trust and Estates, Wills and Probate

GREGG & FARRIS
Batesville, AR........Banking Law; Commercial Litigation; Insurance Defense

GREGG & GREGG, P.C.
Houston, TX........Civil Trial Practice; General Practice; Municipal and Zoning Law; Real Estate Law

GREGORIO, SAM N., A PROFESSIONAL LAW CORPORATION
Shreveport, LA........Personal Injury

GREGORY, CHRISTY & MANIKLAL
Cordele, GA........Civil Trial Practice

GREGORY, EASLEY AND COURTNEY
Murray, KY........General Practice; Personal Injury

GREINES, MARTIN, STEIN & RICHLAND LLP
Beverly Hills, CA........Appellate Practice

GRELL, CHRISTOPHER E. LAW OFFICES OF
San Francisco, CA........Personal Injury

GRENADIER, SIMPSON & DUFFETT, P.C.
Alexandria, VA........Family Law

GRESENS & GILLEN LLP
Buffalo, NY........Commercial Litigation; Construction Law

GRESHAM, DAVIS, GREGORY, WORTHY & MOORE, A PROFESSIONAL CORPORATION
San Antonio, TX........Corporate Law; General Practice

GREVE, CLIFFORD, WENGEL & PARAS, LLP
Sacramento, CA........Civil Trial Practice; Insurance Defense

GRIEM, DAVID
Detroit, MI........Civil Trial Practice; Criminal Trial Practice
Mount Clemens, MI........Civil Trial Practice; Criminal Trial Practice

GRIFFIN COCHRANE & MARSHALL, A PROFESSIONAL CORPORATION
Atlanta, GA........Construction Law

GRIFFIN, COOGAN & VENERUSO, P.C.
Bronxville, NY........Banking Law; Business Law; Civil Trial Practice; Corporate Law; Real Estate Law; Tax Law

GRIFFIN & FLETCHER
Cincinnati, OH........Real Estate Law

GRIFFIN & GOULKA
Boston, MA........Insurance Defense; Personal Injury

GRIFFIN & LINDER, P.A.
Orlando, FL........Personal Injury

GRIFFITH & GRIFFITH
Cleveland, MS........Civil Rights; Civil Trial Practice; Insurance Defense; Natural Resources Law

GRIFFITH LAW OFFICES
Rome, NY........General Practice; Real Estate Law; Trust and Estates, Wills and Probate

GRIFFITH & NIXON, P.C.
Dallas, TX........Business Law; Construction Law; Real Estate Law

GRIFFITHS & CASTLE, INC.
Palo Alto, CA........Construction Law

GRIMES GOEBEL GRIMES HAWKINS & GLADFELTER, P.A.
Bradenton, FL........Civil Trial Practice; Eminent Domain; Land Use Law; Personal Injury; Real Estate Law; Trust and Estates, Wills and Probate

GRIMES & WARWICK
San Diego, CA........Criminal Trial Practice

GRIMMER, EDWARD P.
Crown Point, IN........Civil Trial Practice; Commercial Litigation

GRISI & RIEGLER
Akron, OH........Personal Injury

GRISSIM & HODGES
Nashville, TN........Real Estate Law

GRISWOLD, LASALLE, COBB, DOWD & GIN, L.L.P.
Hanford, CA........General Practice

GRODSKY, IRVIN, P.C.
Mobile, AL........Bankruptcy Law; Commercial Litigation

GROGAN, GRAFFAM, MCGINLEY & LUCCHINO, P.C.
Pittsburgh, PA........General Practice

GROSMAN & GROSMAN
Millburn, NJ........Appellate Practice; Family Law

GROSS, MCGINLEY, LABARRE & EATON, LLP
Allentown, PA........Civil Trial Practice; Communications Law

GROSS, MINSKY, MOGUL & SINGAL, P.A.
Bangor, ME........Banking Law; Bankruptcy Law; Civil Trial Practice; Corporate Law; Criminal Trial Practice; General Practice; Health Care Law; Medical Malpractice; Real Estate Law; Trust and Estates, Wills and Probate

GROSS, NEMETH & SILVERMAN, P.L.C.
Detroit, MI........Appellate Practice

GROSS SHUMAN BRIZDLE & GILFILLAN, P.C.
Buffalo, NY........General Practice

GROSSBART, ROBERT N., P.A.
Baltimore, MD........Bankruptcy Law

GROSSMAN, KRUTTSCHNITT, HEAVEY & JACOB, A PROFESSIONAL CORPORATION
Brick, NJ........Insurance Defense; Medical Malpractice

GROSSMAN LAW OFFICES
Columbus, OH........Family Law

GROSSMAN & WALDMAN, L.L.P.
Houston, TX........Personal Injury

GROWE & BUCHHOLZ
St. Louis, MO........Personal Injury

GROWER, KETCHAM, MORÉ, RUTHERFORD, NOECKER, BRONSON, SIBONI & EIDE, P.A.
Orlando, FL........Aviation Law; Insurance Defense; Workers Compensation

GRUCCIO, PEPPER, GIOVINAZZI, DESANTO & FARNOLY, P.A.
Vineland, NJ........Banking Law; Bankruptcy Law; Civil Trial Practice; General Practice; Insurance Defense; Labor and Employment Law; Municipal and Zoning Law; Personal Injury; Trust and Estates, Wills and Probate

GRUEL, MILLS, NIMS AND PYLMAN
Grand Rapids, MI........Civil Trial Practice; Commercial Law; Commercial Litigation; Environmental Law; General Practice; Health Care Law; Medical Malpractice; Personal Injury

GRUND & BRESLAU, P.C.
Denver, CO........Aviation Law; Commercial Law; Insurance Defense; Product Liability Law; Real Estate Law

GRUNERT STOUT & BRUCH
Charlotte Amalie, St. Thomas, VI........Aviation Law; Banking Law; Business Law; Civil Rights; Civil Trial Practice; Commercial Law; General Practice; Insurance Defense; International Business Law; Personal Injury; Real Estate Law; Tax Law; Trust and Estates, Wills and Probate

GRUNSKY, EBEY, FARRAR & HOWELL, A PROFESSIONAL CORPORATION
Watsonville, CA........General Practice

GRZECA, JEROME G., S.C.
Milwaukee, WI........Immigration and Naturalization

GUDMUNDSON, SIGGINS, STONE & SKINNER, LLP
San Francisco, CA........Insurance Defense

GUEBERT & YEOMANS, P.C.
Albuquerque, NM........Civil Trial Practice; Commercial Litigation; Insurance Defense; Personal Injury; Product Liability Law

GUICE, JUDY M., A PROFESSIONAL ASSOCIATION
Biloxi, MS........Admiralty/Maritime Law; Civil Trial Practice; Medical Malpractice; Personal Injury; Product Liability Law

GUIDA & EAGAN, P.A.
Columbia, MD........Civil Trial Practice; Personal Injury

GUILD, RUSSELL, GALLAGHER & FULLER, LTD.
Reno, NV........Administrative Law; Business Law; Civil Trial Practice; Corporate Law; General Practice; Trust and Estates, Wills and Probate

GUILLORY & MCCALL, L.L.C.
Lake Charles, LA....................Insurance Defense; Toxic Torts

GUILLOT, GREGORY H., CHARTERED
Washington, DC....................Communications Law; Trademark, Copyright and Unfair Competition

GULICK, JOHN N. JR.
San Francisco, CA....................Civil Trial Practice

GULLAHORN & HARE, P.C.
Albertville, AL....................Banking Law; Civil Trial Practice; General Practice; Municipal Bond/Public Authority Financing

GULLETT, COMBS, REED & BOWLING
Hazard, KY....................Civil Trial Practice; General Practice; Natural Resources Law; Personal Injury; Real Estate Law

GUMBINER & ESKRIDGE LLP
Walnut Creek, CA....................Commercial Litigation

GUM & HILLIER, P.A.
Asheville, NC....................Bankruptcy Law; Family Law

GUMP, RICHARD A., JR., P.C., LAW OFFICES OF
Dallas, TX....................Immigration and Naturalization

GUNDERSON, MICHAEL A.
Detroit, MI....................Insurance Defense

GUNDERSON, BRENT M., P.C.
Mesa, AZ....................Immigration and Naturalization; Trust and Estates, Wills and Probate

GUNDLACH, LEE, EGGMANN, BOYLE & ROESSLER
Belleville, IL....................General Practice

GUNHUS, GRINNELL, KLINGER, SWENSON & GUY, LTD.
Moorhead, MN....................Civil Trial Practice; General Practice
Fargo, ND....................General Practice

GUNSBERG & BRESKIN, P.C.
Bloomfield Hills, MI....................Arbitration; Civil Rights; Civil Trial Practice; Labor and Employment Law

GUNSTER, YOAKLEY, VALDES-FAULI & STEWART, P.A.
West Palm Beach, FL....................General Practice

GUNTA & REAK, S.C.
Milwaukee, WI....................Admiralty/Maritime Law; Constitutional Law; Construction Law

GURNEY & HANDLEY, P.A.
Orlando, FL....................Civil Trial Practice; General Practice

GUSRAE, KAPLAN & BRUNO
New York, NY....................Securities Law

GUTGLASS ERICKSON & BONVILLE, S.C.
Milwaukee, WI....................Insurance Defense

GUTHERY & RICKLES, P.C.
Denver, CO....................Nonprofit and Tax Exempt Organizations; Pension and Profit Sharing; Tax Law; Trust and Estates, Wills and Probate

GUTMAN & GUTMAN LLP
Mineola, NY....................Commercial Law; Commercial Litigation; Creditors Rights; Real Estate Law

GUTTERMAN, CARLTON & HECKENBACH, L.L.P.
Lone Tree, CO....................Family Law

GWIN, LEWIS & PUNCHES, LLP
Natchez, MS....................General Practice; Insurance Defense
Woodville, MS....................General Practice

HAASIS & GOODIN
San Diego, CA....................Civil Trial Practice; Insurance Defense

HABBESHAW, KALMANS & SCHWARTZ, P.C.
San Antonio, TX....................Bankruptcy Law; Commercial Litigation

HABEDANK, CUMMING, BEST & SAVAGE
Sidney, MT....................General Practice

HABUSH, HABUSH, DAVIS & ROTTIER, S.C.
Appleton, WI....................Medical Malpractice; Personal Injury; Product Liability Law
Green Bay, WI....................Medical Malpractice; Personal Injury; Product Liability Law
Lake Geneva, WI....................Medical Malpractice; Personal Injury; Product Liability Law
Madison, WI....................Medical Malpractice; Personal Injury; Product Liability Law
Milwaukee, WI....................Medical Malpractice; Personal Injury; Product Liability Law
Racine, WI....................Medical Malpractice; Personal Injury; Product Liability Law
Rhinelander, WI....................Medical Malpractice; Personal Injury; Product Liability Law
Waukesha, WI....................Medical Malpractice; Personal Injury; Product Liability Law
Wausau, WI....................Medical Malpractice; Personal Injury; Product Liability Law

HACKARD, HOLT & HELLER
Gold River, CA....................Commercial Litigation; Environmental Law; Product Liability Law

HACKETT & MAXWELL, P.C.
Troy, MI....................Antitrust Law; Business Law; Civil Trial Practice; Commercial Litigation; Corporate Law; General Practice; Transportation Law

HACKMAN HULETT & CRACRAFT, LLP
Indianapolis, IN....................Administrative Law; General Practice; Real Estate Law

HACK, PIRO, O'DAY, MERKLINGER, WALLACE & MCKENNA, P.A.
Florham Park, NJ....................Bankruptcy Law; Civil Trial Practice; Environmental Law; General Practice; Insurance Defense; Personal Injury; Product Liability Law; Professional Liability; Real Estate Law; Trust and Estates, Wills and Probate; Workers Compensation

HADDAD, SUSAN CHRISTINE
Chicago, IL....................Family Law

HADDLETON & COLLINS, P.C.
Hyannis, MA....................Trust and Estates, Wills and Probate

HADDOCK PROFESSIONAL ASSOCIATION
Winter Park, FL....................Business Law; Education Law; Real Estate Law

HADIPUTRANTO, HADINOTO & PARTNERS
Jakarta, Indonesia....................General Practice

HAGEN, DYE, HIRSCHY & DILORENZO, P.C.
Portland, OR....................Business Law; Commercial Law; Real Estate Law; Tax Law; Trust and Estates, Wills and Probate

HAGERTY, JOHNSON, ALBRIGHTSON & BEITZ, P.A.
Minneapolis, MN....................Civil Trial Practice; Real Estate Law; Trust and Estates, Wills and Probate

HAGGARD, PARKS & STONE, P.A.
Miami, FL....................Aviation Law; Civil Trial Practice; Personal Injury

HAGOORT, NICHOLAS H., JR., P.A.
Boynton Beach, FL....................Trust and Estates, Wills and Probate

HAHN, MCCLURG, WATSON, GRIFFITH & BUSH, P.A.
Lakeland, FL....................Commercial Litigation; General Practice; Real Estate Law; Trust and Estates, Wills and Probate

HAIGHT, BROWN & BONESTEEL, L.L.P.
Riverside, CA....................Bankruptcy Law; Civil Trial Practice; Commercial Law; Constitutional Law; Labor and Employment Law; Municipal and Zoning Law; Personal Injury; Product Liability Law; Professional Liability; Public Utilities Law
San Diego, CA....................Civil Trial Practice; Commercial Litigation; Corporate Law; Environmental Law; Health Care Law; Insurance Defense; International Business Law; Labor and Employment Law; Personal Injury; Product Liability Law
San Francisco, CA....................Civil Trial Practice; Commercial Litigation; Computer Law; Creditors Rights; Environmental Law; Health Care Law; Insurance Defense; Labor and Employment Law; Product Liability Law; Professional Liability; Toxic Torts
Santa Ana, CA....................Civil Trial Practice; Commercial Litigation; Insurance Defense; Personal Injury
Santa Monica, CA....................Appellate Practice; Bankruptcy Law; Civil Trial Practice; Commercial Litigation; Environmental Law; Health Care Law; Insurance Defense; Intellectual Property Law; Labor and Employment Law; Personal Injury; Product Liability Law; Professional Liability; Toxic Torts; Trust and Estates, Wills and Probate

HAIGHT GARDNER HOLLAND & KNIGHT
New York, NY....................General Practice

HAILEY, MCNAMARA, HALL, LARMANN & PAPALE, L.L.P.
Metairie, LA....................Admiralty/Maritime Law; General Practice; Insurance Defense; Professional Liability

HAIMS, MACGOWAN, VALENTINO & PEEBLES, L.L.P.
Oakland, CA....................Civil Trial Practice; Construction Law; Environmental Law; General Practice; Health Care Law; Insurance Defense; Personal Injury; Product Liability Law

HAINER & BERMAN, P.C.
Troy, MI....................Business Law; Civil Trial Practice; Environmental Law; Labor and Employment Law; Real Estate Law; Trust and Estates, Wills and Probate

HAINES, MARTIN L., III, CHARTERED
Lake Park, FL........Family Law

HALABY CROSS & SCHLUTER
Denver, CO........Civil Trial Practice; General Practice; Insurance Defense

HALE AND DORR LLP
Washington, DC........General Practice
Boston, MA........General Practice

HALE, FOGLEMAN & ROGERS
West Memphis, AR........Civil Trial Practice; Personal Injury

HALE & HAMLIN
Ellsworth, ME........Civil Trial Practice; Real Estate Law; Trust and Estates, Wills and Probate

HALE HEADRICK DEWEY & WOLF, PLLC
Memphis, TN........Antitrust Law; Bankruptcy Law; Business Law; Commercial Litigation; Communications Law; Construction Law; Corporate Law; Creditors Rights; Criminal Trial Practice; Eminent Domain; Health Care Law; Medical Malpractice; Mergers and Acquisitions; Personal Injury; Product Liability Law; Tax Law

HALE, KINCAID & SKINNER, P.C.
Liberty, MO........General Practice

HALE LANE PEEK DENNISON HOWARD AND ANDERSON
Carson City, NV........Business Law; Corporate Law; General Practice; Real Estate Law
Las Vegas, NV........Administrative Law; Bankruptcy Law; Commercial Litigation; Corporate Law; General Practice; Health Care Law; Real Estate Law; Tax Law; Trust and Estates, Wills and Probate
Reno, NV........Bankruptcy Law; Business Law; Commercial Litigation; Corporate Law; General Practice; Health Care Law; Natural Resources Law; Real Estate Law; Securities Law; Tax Law; Trust and Estates, Wills and Probate

HALE LAW FIRM
St. Louis, MO........Insurance Defense

HALE & WAGNER, S.C.
Milwaukee, WI........Commercial Litigation

HALEY BADER & POTTS P.L.C.
Arlington, VA........Communications Law; Trademark, Copyright and Unfair Competition

HALEY, PURCHIO, SAKAI & SMITH
Hayward, CA........General Practice; Land Use Law

HALICZER, PETTIS & WHITE, P.A.
Fort Lauderdale, FL........Appellate Practice; Civil Trial Practice; Insurance Defense; Medical Malpractice; Workers Compensation

HALIO & HALIO
Charleston, SC........Civil Trial Practice

HALIW SICILIANO AND MYCHALOWYCH
Farmington Hills, MI........Business Law; Commercial Litigation; Insurance Defense

HALKIDES & MORGAN, A PROFESSIONAL CORPORATION
Redding, CA........Insurance Defense

HALL, H. GLENN JR.
Austin, TX........Banking Law; Real Estate Law

HALL, THOMAS J.
Reno, NV........Real Estate Law

HALL, ANSLEY, RODGERS & CONDRY, A PROFESSIONAL CORPORATION
Springfield, MO........Insurance Defense

HALL, BLOCH, GARLAND & MEYER
Macon, GA........Banking Law; Business Law; Civil Trial Practice; General Practice; Insurance Defense; Personal Injury; Tax Law

HALL, BOOTH, SMITH & SLOVER, A PROFESSIONAL CORPORATION
Atlanta, GA........Civil Trial Practice; Insurance Defense; Medical Malpractice

HALL & BROGDEN, P.C.
Indianapolis, IN........Business Law; Trust and Estates, Wills and Probate

HALL, CASHWELL & SULLIVAN, L.L.P.
Wilmington, NC........Criminal Trial Practice; Personal Injury

HALL, CONERLY, MUDD & BOLVIG, P.C.
Birmingham, AL........General Practice; Insurance Defense

HALL, DAVID AND JOSEPH, P.A.
Miami, FL........Civil Trial Practice; Commercial Law; Family Law; Personal Injury

HALL, DAVID W., ATTORNEY AT LAW, A LAW CORPORATION
Honolulu, HI........Civil Trial Practice; Criminal Trial Practice

HALLENBECK, LASCELL, NORRIS & HELLER
Rochester, NY........Civil Trial Practice; Commercial Litigation; Medical Malpractice; Personal Injury; Product Liability Law

HALL, ESTILL, HARDWICK, GABLE, GOLDEN & NELSON, A PROFESSIONAL CORPORATION
Tulsa, OK........General Practice

HALL & EVANS, L.L.C.
Colorado Springs, CO........General Practice
Denver, CO........General Practice

HALL & HALL
Staten Island, NY........Banking Law

HALL, JOHN WESLEY, JR., A PROFESSIONAL CORPORATION
Little Rock, AR........Appellate Practice; Constitutional Law; Criminal Trial Practice

HALL AND LEWIS, P.C.
Mount Pleasant, MI........General Practice

HALL & MULLINS, P.C.
Augusta, GA........Business Law; Real Estate Law

HALLORAN & SAGE LLP
Hartford, CT........General Practice
Middletown, CT........General Practice

HALL, PARTENHEIMER & KINKLE
Princeton, IN........General Practice; Natural Resources Law; Real Estate Law

HALL, RENDER, KILLIAN, HEATH & LYMAN, PROFESSIONAL SERVICES CORPORATION
Indianapolis, IN........Health Care Law; Medical Malpractice; Tax Law; Trust and Estates, Wills and Probate
Louisville, KY........Construction Law; Health Care Law; Insurance Defense; Labor and Employment Law

HALL AND SICKELS, P.C.
Reston, VA........General Practice; Personal Injury

HALVERSON & APPLEGATE, P.S.
Yakima, WA........General Practice

HALVERSON, WATTERS, DOWNS, REYELTS & BATEMAN, LTD.
Duluth, MN........General Practice; Insurance Defense

HAMEL LAW FIRM, THE
Amesbury, MA........Business Law; Commercial Law; General Practice; Personal Injury; Trust and Estates, Wills and Probate
Charlotte, NC........General Practice

HAMILTON, BROOK, SMITH & REYNOLDS, P.C.
Lexington, MA........Patent, Trademark, Copyright and Unfair Competition

HAMILTON AND FAATZ, A PROFESSIONAL CORPORATION
Denver, CO........Business Law; Civil Trial Practice; Corporate Law; General Practice

HAMILTON, GIBSON, NICKELSEN, RUSH & MOORE
Honolulu, HI........General Practice

HAMILTON & LINDER
Meridian, MS........General Practice; Personal Injury; Workers Compensation

HAMILTON, PEATROSS, WRIGHT & POU
Shreveport, LA........Real Estate Law

HAMMAN & BENN
Chicago, IL........Commercial Law; Computer Law; Intellectual Property Law

HAMMER, BILL C., & ASSOCIATES
Las Vegas, NV........Administrative Law; Corporate Law; Real Estate Law

HAMMER & JACOBS
San Jose, CA........Family Law

HAMM, MILBY & RIDINGS
London, KY........General Practice; Insurance Defense; Product Liability Law; Workers Compensation

HAMMOND AND CLARK
Loveland, CO........General Practice

HAMMOND & SEWARDS
Columbus, OH........Commercial Litigation; Insurance Defense; Medical Malpractice

HAMPTON & ROYCE, L.C.
Salina, KS.................General Practice

HANCOCK & ESTABROOK, LLP
Syracuse, NY.................General Practice; Municipal Bond/Public Authority Financing; Tax Law

HANCOCK ROTHERT & BUNSHOFT LLP
San Francisco, CA.................General Practice

HANDLIN & ASSOCIATES
Houston, TX.................Insurance Defense

HANDY & ROBINSON, P.C.
Fort Worth, TX.................Personal Injury

HANEN, ALEXANDER, JOHNSON & SPALDING, L.L.P.
Houston, TX.................Civil Trial Practice; Commercial Litigation; Insurance Defense; Medical Malpractice; Product Liability Law

HANEY, PHILIP S., ASSOCIATES
Tulsa, OK.................Nonprofit and Tax Exempt Organizations

HANFLIK, HENRY M., P.C., LAW OFFICES OF
Flint, MI.................Personal Injury

HANFT, FRIDE, O'BRIEN, HARRIES, SWELBAR & BURNS, P.A.
Duluth, MN.................Civil Trial Practice; General Practice; Insurance Defense; Trust and Estates, Wills and Probate

HANIFY & KING, PROFESSIONAL CORPORATION
Boston, MA.................Antitrust Law; Bankruptcy Law; Civil Trial Practice; Commercial Law; Real Estate Law

HANKIN, THEODORE M.
Newport Beach, CA.................Business Law; Trust and Estates, Wills and Probate

HANKIN, HANIG, STALL, CAPLICKI, REDL & CURTIN, LLP
Poughkeepsie, NY.................General Practice; Labor and Employment Law; Personal Injury; Real Estate Law; Trust and Estates, Wills and Probate

HANLEY, CHRISTINE D., & ASSOCIATES, P.A.
West Palm Beach, FL.................Labor and Employment Law

HANLEY & DEJORAS, P.A.
Minneapolis, MN.................Criminal Trial Practice

HANLON & LAVIGNE, A PROFESSIONAL CORPORATION
Edison, NJ.................Civil Trial Practice; Labor and Employment Law; Product Liability Law

HANNA, KERNS & STRADER, A PROFESSIONAL CORPORATION
Portland, OR.................Real Estate Law; Tax Law; Trust and Estates, Wills and Probate

HANNA & PLAUT, L.L.P.
Austin, TX.................Insurance Defense

HANNAFAN, MICHAEL T., & ASSOCIATES, LTD.
Chicago, IL.................Antitrust Law; Civil Trial Practice; Commercial Litigation; Intellectual Property Law; Product Liability Law; Professional Liability

HANNIG LAW FIRM LLP
Redwood City, CA.................Civil Trial Practice; Corporate Law; Real Estate Law

HANOVER & SCHNITZER
San Bernardino, CA.................Bankruptcy Law

HANOVER, WALSH, JALENAK & BLAIR, PLLC
Memphis, TN.................General Practice

HANSEN, JOEL F. & ASSOCIATES
Las Vegas, NV.................Civil Trial Practice; Insurance Defense

HANSEN, HUBBARD & SWANSON
Sturgis, SD.................General Practice

HANSEN, MCCLINTOCK & RILEY
Des Moines, IA.................Civil Trial Practice; General Practice; Insurance Defense; Legal Malpractice; Workers Compensation

HANSEN, MEAGHER, SHAMBEAU & MARONEY, S.C.
Waupaca, WI.................General Practice

HANSON, BRIDGETT, MARCUS, VLAHOS & RUDY, LLP
San Francisco, CA.................General Practice

HANSON, CURRAN, PARKS & WHITMAN
Providence, RI.................Admiralty/Maritime Law; Appellate Practice; Civil Trial Practice; Environmental Law; General Practice; Insurance Defense; Labor and Employment Law

HANSON & HANSON
McCook, NE.................General Practice

HANSON, LULIC & KRALL
Minneapolis, MN.................Insurance Defense

HANSON MAREK BOLKCOM & GREENE, LTD.
Minneapolis, MN.................Civil Trial Practice; Product Liability Law

HARAD, GITTLEMAN, GREENBERG, BRUNNER & LOVE
Philadelphia, PA.................Insurance Defense

HARALSON, MILLER, PITT & MCANALLY, P.L.C.
Tucson, AZ.................Aviation Law; Civil Trial Practice; General Practice; Medical Malpractice; Personal Injury

HARBINSON, TUNE, MANGOLD & KASSELIK, A PROFESSIONAL CORPORATION
San Francisco, CA.................Workers Compensation

HARBISON, KESSINGER, LISLE & BUSH
Lexington, KY.................General Practice

HARBOLD, R. CHRIS AND ASSOCIATES
Columbus, OH.................Family Law

HARDIG, LEE AND GROVES, PROFESSIONAL ASSOCIATION
South Bend, IN.................Medical Malpractice; Personal Injury

HARDIG PARSONS PEDERSEN & STOUT, PLLC
Bloomfield Hills, MI.................Business Law; Civil Trial Practice; Corporate Law; Family Law; Insurance Defense

HARDIMAN & CARROLL, A LAW PARTNERSHIP
San Francisco, CA.................Civil Trial Practice; Insurance Defense; Professional Liability

HARDIN, HAL D.
Nashville, TN.................General Practice

HARDIN, KUNDLA, MCKEON, POLETTO & POLIFRONI, P.A., A PROFESSIONAL CORPORATION
Springfield, NJ.................Civil Trial Practice; Commercial Litigation; Construction Law; Environmental Law; Health Care Law; Insurance Defense; Medical Malpractice; Product Liability Law; Transportation Law

HARDING, BASS, FARGASON, BOOTH & ST. CLAIR, L.L.P.
Lubbock, TX.................General Practice

HARDT, FREDERICK W.
Moorestown, NJ.................Government Contracts; Land Use Law; Municipal and Zoning Law; Real Estate Law; Trust and Estates, Wills and Probate

HARDWICK & HARRIS
Baltimore, MD.................Insurance Defense

HARDWICK, HAUSE & SEGREST
Dothan, AL.................Civil Trial Practice; Education Law; General Practice; Insurance Defense

HARDWICK LAW FIRM
Renton, WA.................Personal Injury

HARDY, BISSETT & TEICHNER, P.A.
Miami, FL.................Civil Trial Practice; General Practice; Insurance Defense; Product Liability Law

HARDY ERICH BROWN & WILSON, A PROFESSIONAL CORPORATION
Sacramento, CA.................Bankruptcy Law; Civil Trial Practice; Construction Law; Environmental Law; Insurance Defense; Labor and Employment Law; Medical Malpractice; Personal Injury; Product Liability Law; Real Estate Law

HARDY, G.P., III, P.C.
Houston, TX.................Civil Trial Practice; Commercial Law; Personal Injury

HARE, WYNN, NEWELL AND NEWTON
Birmingham, AL.................Civil Trial Practice; Medical Malpractice; Personal Injury; Product Liability Law

HARGAN, MARK C.
Newport Beach, CA.................Construction Law

HARGRAVES, KARB, WILCOX & GALVANI, LLP
Framingham, MA.................Family Law; Land Use Law; Real Estate Law; Trust and Estates, Wills and Probate

HARGROVE, PESNELL & WYATT, A P.L.C.
Shreveport, LA.................Civil Trial Practice; Natural Resources Law

HARHAI, STEPHEN J.
Denver, CO.................Family Law

HARKAVY, SHAINBERG, KOSTEN, KAPLAN & DUNSTAN, PC
Memphis, TN.................Business Law; Environmental Law; General Practice; Labor and Employment Law; Municipal and Zoning Law; Real Estate Law; Trust and Estates, Wills and Probate

HARKLEROAD & HERMANCE, A PROFESSIONAL CORPORATION
Atlanta, GA ....Administrative Law; Banking Law; Business Law; International Business Law; Tax Law

HARLAN & FLORA, P.C.
Norfolk, VA ....Aviation Law; Medical Malpractice; Personal Injury; Product Liability Law

HARLEY & BROWNE
New York, NY..........................Civil Trial Practice; Medical Malpractice

HARLIN, PARKER, ALCOTT & CHAUDOIN, P.S.C.
Bowling Green, KY ....Civil Trial Practice; General Practice; Insurance Defense; Product Liability Law

HARLOW, ADAMS & FRIEDMAN, P.C.
Milford, CT..............................Bankruptcy Law; General Practice; Real Estate Law; Trust and Estates, Wills and Probate

HARMAN, CLAYTOR, CORRIGAN & WELLMAN, A PROFESSIONAL CORPORATION
Richmond, VA.........................Insurance Defense

HARMAN, OWEN, SAUNDERS & SWEENEY, A PROFESSIONAL CORPORATION
Atlanta, GA ....Business Law; Insurance Defense

HARMATA LAW OFFICES
Sacramento, CA ....Administrative Law; Construction Law; General Practice; Government Contracts

HARMON, STEVEN L.
Riverside, CA.........................Criminal Trial Practice

HARMON, SUSAN M.
Bala Cynwyd, PA.....................Trust and Estates, Wills and Probate

HARNED, BACHERT & DENTON
Bowling Green, KY ....Business Law; Civil Trial Practice; Workers Compensation

HARNESS, DICKEY & PIERCE, P.L.C.
Washington, DC.......................Intellectual Property Law; Patent, Trademark, Copyright and Unfair Competition
Ann Arbor, MI ....Intellectual Property Law; Patent, Trademark, Copyright and Unfair Competition
Troy, MI...................................Computer Law; Intellectual Property Law; Patent, Trademark, Copyright and Unfair Competition

HARNISH, JENNEY, MITCHELL AND RESH
Waltham, MA ....Civil Trial Practice; General Practice; Real Estate Law; Trust and Estates, Wills and Probate

HARPER, DAVID W.
Louisville, KY.........................Mergers and Acquisitions

HARPER, EDWARD J. II
Greenville, NC ....Bankruptcy Law; Commercial Litigation

HARPER, FERGUSON & DAVIS
Louisville, KY.........................Municipal Bond/Public Authority Financing

HARPER, HORNBAKER, ALTENHOFEN & OPAT, CHARTERED
Junction City, KS...................Civil Trial Practice

HARPER LAW FIRM, THE, P.A.
Greenville, SC........................Commercial Litigation; Construction Law

HARRANG LONG GARY RUDNICK P.C.
Eugene, OR.............................General Practice

HARRAY & LINKER
Monterey, CA ....Appellate Practice; Civil Trial Practice; Insurance Defense; Medical Malpractice

HARRELL AND HARRELL
Trenton, TN ....Criminal Trial Practice; Personal Injury

HARRELL & LINDSEY, P.A.
Camden, AR ....General Practice; Trust and Estates, Wills and Probate

HARRINGTON, THOMAS S.
Eden, NC.................................General Practice
Wentworth, NC.......................General Practice

HARRINGTON, HOPPE & MITCHELL, LTD.
Warren, OH.............................General Practice
Youngstown, OH ....Bankruptcy Law; General Practice

HARRINGTON, THOMPSON, ACKER & HARRINGTON, LTD.
Chicago, IL.............................Civil Trial Practice; Personal Injury

HARRIS, DAVID J.
Wilkes-Barre, PA ....Bankruptcy Law

HARRIS, CADDELL & SHANKS, P.C.
Decatur, AL ....Civil Trial Practice; Corporate Law; General Practice; Insurance Defense; Product Liability Law; Tax Law

HARRIS, CLECKLER & HOLLIS
Birmingham, AL......................Civil Trial Practice; Insurance Defense; Medical Malpractice; Personal Injury; Product Liability Law

HARRIS, DOWELL, FISHER & HARRIS, L.C.
St. Louis, MO..........................Labor and Employment Law

HARRIS, FEARS, DAVIS, LYNCH & MCDANIEL
Norfolk, VA ....Insurance Defense

HARRIS • GINSBERG LLP
Los Angeles, CA.....................Family Law

HARRIS & HARRIS
Austin, TX ....Administrative Law; Civil Trial Practice; Workers Compensation

HARRIS AND HARRIS, A PROFESSIONAL CORPORATION
Warrington, PA.......................Civil Trial Practice; Municipal and Zoning Law

HARRIS, JOHN D., P.C.
Phoenix, AZ ....Business Law; Commercial Litigation

HARRIS, LAMBERT, HOWERTON & DORRIS
Marion, IL...............................Personal Injury; Workers Compensation

HARRIS, LAVERN D., ATTORNEY AT LAW, P.C.
Kerrville, TX...........................Civil Trial Practice

HARRIS, MIDYETTE & DARBY, P.A.
Lakeland, FL...........................General Practice

HARRIS, NANCY HUTCHESON, P.A.
Tampa, FL ....Family Law

HARRIS, PALUMBO, POWERS & CUNNINGHAM, P.L.L.C.
Phoenix, AZ ....Insurance Defense; Medical Malpractice; Personal Injury

HARRIS, SHELTON, DUNLAP AND COBB, P.L.L.C.
Memphis, TN..........................Criminal Trial Practice; Environmental Law; General Practice; Health Care Law; Insurance Defense; Mergers and Acquisitions

HARRIS, TIM L., AND ASSOCIATES
Charlotte, NC.........................Medical Malpractice; Personal Injury; Workers Compensation
Gastonia, NC ....Medical Malpractice; Personal Injury
Monroe, NC ....Personal Injury

HARRIS, TRIMMER & THOMPSON
Reno, NV ....Environmental Law; Natural Resources Law

HARRIS, WELSH & LUKMANN
Chesterton, IN ....General Practice

HARRISON, JOSEPH
Boca Raton, FL ....Administrative Law; Health Care Law

HARRISON, BRENNECKE, MOORE, SMAHA & MCKIBBEN
Marshalltown, IA....................General Practice; Trust and Estates, Wills and Probate

HARRISON & HUGHES, P.C.
Alexandria, VA ....Civil Trial Practice

HARRISON & RIAL, L.L.P.
Austin, TX ....Commercial Litigation; Natural Resources Law; Product Liability Law

HARRISON, ROBERT, & ASSOCIATES
Bloomfield Hills, MI...............Civil Trial Practice; Commercial Litigation; Criminal Trial Practice; Labor and Employment Law; Trademark, Copyright and Unfair Competition

HARRISON, TUCKER & HYDE, LLP
Springfield, MO......................Medical Malpractice; Personal Injury; Product Liability Law; Workers Compensation

HARRISON & WALL
Eastman, GA...........................General Practice

HARRISON, WHITE, SMITH, HAYES & COGGINS, P.A.
Spartanburg, SC.....................Civil Trial Practice; Personal Injury; Workers Compensation

HART, RICHARD H. JR., LAW OFFICES
Milwaukee, WI.......................Corporate Law

HART, BROOK, ATTORNEY AT LAW, A LAW CORPORATION
Honolulu, HI..........................Criminal Trial Practice

HART & CALLEY, P.C.
Alexandria, VA ....Municipal and Zoning Law

HART, GEORGE W., P.C.
Atlanta, GA ....Medical Malpractice; Personal Injury

GOLDBERG, MUFSON & SPAR, A PROFESSIONAL CORPORATION
West Orange, NJ......................Business Law; Civil Trial Practice; Tax Law; Trust and Estates, Wills and Probate

GOLDBERG & SIMPSON, P.S.C.
Louisville, KY..........................Bankruptcy Law; Civil Trial Practice; Corporate Law; Insurance Defense; Securities Law

GOLDBERG, STINNETT, MEYERS & DAVIS, A PROFESSIONAL CORPORATION
San Francisco, CA..................Bankruptcy Law

GOLDBERGER AND DUBIN, P.C.
New York, NY..........................Appellate Practice; Criminal Trial Practice; Insurance Defense

GOLDBLATT, LIPKIN & COHEN, P.C.
Norfolk, VA..............................Bankruptcy Law; Commercial Law; Family Law; Personal Injury; Trust and Estates, Wills and Probate; Workers Compensation

GOLDEN, TAYLOR & POTTERFIELD
Columbia, SC...........................Civil Trial Practice; Family Law

GOLDEN, WEXLER & SARNESE, P.C.
Garden City, NY.....................General Practice

GOLDFARB, BERNARD S.
Cleveland, OH..........................Business Law; Commercial Litigation; Labor and Employment Law

GOLDFEIN & JOSEPH, A PROFESSIONAL CORPORATION
Philadelphia, PA.....................Civil Trial Practice; Commercial Litigation; Insurance Defense; Medical Malpractice; Product Liability Law; Professional Liability; Workers Compensation

GOLD & GOLD
Plano, TX.................................Civil Trial Practice; Creditors Rights

GOLDING HOLDEN COSPER POPE & BAKER, L.L.P.
Charlotte, NC...........................Civil Trial Practice; Insurance Defense

GOLD LANGE & MAJOROS, P.C.
Southfield, MI..........................Bankruptcy Law; Creditors Rights

GOLD, LAWRENCE M., P.C.
Atlanta, GA.............................Mergers and Acquisitions

GOLDMAN, LAURENCE R.
Woodland Hills, CA...............Family Law

GOLDMAN ANTONETTI & CÓRDOVA
San Juan, PR...........................Banking Law; Civil Trial Practice; Commercial Law; Environmental Law; General Practice; Labor and Employment Law; Municipal Bond/Public Authority Financing; Natural Resources Law; Real Estate Law; Tax Law

GOLDMAN & CURTIS, P.C.
Lowell, MA..............................Business Law; General Practice

GOLDMAN & HAFETZ
New York, NY..........................Civil Trial Practice; Criminal Trial Practice

GOLDMAN & KAGON, LAW CORPORATION
Los Angeles, CA......................Family Law; General Practice; Real Estate Law

GOLDMAN, LEONARD A., & ASSOCIATES
Los Angeles, CA......................Bankruptcy Law; Civil Trial Practice; Commercial Law; Real Estate Law

GOLDMAN & ROSEN, LTD.
Akron, OH................................Bankruptcy Law; Family Law; Tax Law; Trust and Estates, Wills and Probate

GOLD MORRISON & LAUGHLIN PC
Alexandria, VA........................Bankruptcy Law

GOLDNER, SOMMERS, SCRUDDER & BASS
Atlanta, GA.............................Civil Trial Practice; Commercial Law; General Practice; Health Care Law; Insurance Defense; Labor and Employment Law; Legal Malpractice; Medical Malpractice; Personal Injury; Product Liability Law; Professional Liability; Workers Compensation

GOLDSHORE & WOLF, P.C.
Plainsboro, NJ..........................Environmental Law

GOLDSMITH & BURNS
Los Angeles, CA......................Insurance Defense; Trust and Estates, Wills and Probate

GOLDSTEIN, BERTRAM M., & ASSOCIATES, P.A.
Baltimore, MD.........................Medical Malpractice; Product Liability Law

GOLDSTEIN, BUCKLEY, CECHMAN, RICE & PURTZ, P.A.
Fort Myers, FL........................Commercial Law; Construction Law; General Practice; Personal Injury; Product Liability Law; Workers Compensation

GOLDSTEIN, FLANZ & FISHMAN
Montreal, QU, Canada............Banking Law; Bankruptcy Law; Civil Trial Practice; Commercial Law; Real Estate Law

GOLDSTEIN, GOLDSTEIN AND HILLEY
San Antonio, TX......................Criminal Trial Practice

GOLDSTEIN, KENNEDY & PETITO
Los Angeles, CA......................Labor and Employment Law

GOLDSTEIN, MCGRODER & WOODS, LTD. A PROFESSIONAL CORPORATION
Phoenix, AZ.............................Appellate Practice; Civil Trial Practice; Medical Malpractice; Personal Injury; Product Liability Law

GOLDSTEIN & MORRIS, LLP
New York, NY..........................Civil Trial Practice; Commercial Litigation; Labor and Employment Law; Sports and Entertainment Law

GOLDSTEIN & MUSTO, A PROFESSIONAL CORPORATION
San Francisco, CA..................Civil Trial Practice

GOLDSTEIN AND PECK, P.C.
Bridgeport, CT........................General Practice; Real Estate Law
Westport, CT...........................General Practice; Real Estate Law

GOLDSTEIN AND PRICE, L.C.
St. Louis, MO..........................Admiralty/Maritime Law

GOLDSTEIN, RICHARD S., P.C., LAW OFFICES OF
New York, NY..........................Immigration and Naturalization

GOLDSTEIN, STUART
Phoenix, AZ.............................Medical Malpractice; Personal Injury

GOLD & VANARIA, P.C.
Springfield, MA.......................Commercial Litigation; Creditors Rights

GOLD, WEEMS, BRUSER, SUES & RUNDELL, A PROFESSIONAL LAW CORPORATION
Alexandria, LA........................General Practice; Tax Law

GOLENBOCK, EISEMAN, ASSOR & BELL
New York, NY..........................Civil Trial Practice; Commercial Law; Corporate Law; General Practice; Securities Law

GOLOB, MICHAEL H.
Farmington Hills, MI..............Civil Trial Practice; Commercial Law; Family Law

GOLOMB, DAVID B. LAW OFFICES OF
New York, NY..........................Medical Malpractice; Personal Injury; Product Liability Law; Professional Liability

GOLOMB, GEORGE E.
Baltimore, MD.........................Civil Rights; Labor and Employment Law

GOMEZ, ROLAND H.
Miami, FL................................Insurance Defense; Personal Injury

GOMEZ, DAVID F., A PROFESSIONAL CORPORATION
Phoenix, AZ.............................Civil Trial Practice; Labor and Employment Law

GONANO, HARRELL & FERGUSON
Fort Pierce, FL........................Land Use Law; Real Estate Law

GONZALEZ, MARCE JR.
Merrillville, IN........................Appellate Practice; Criminal Trial Practice; Personal Injury

GONZALEZ-MIRANDA, NOEL S.
San Juan, PR...........................Commercial Law

GOODELL, DEVRIES, LEECH & GRAY, LLP
Baltimore, MD.........................Insurance Defense; Medical Malpractice; Product Liability Law

GOODELL, STRATTON, EDMONDS & PALMER, L.L.P.
Topeka, KS..............................Arbitration; Bankruptcy Law; Civil Trial Practice; Communications Law; Corporate Law; Elder Law; Environmental Law; General Practice; Health Care Law; Insurance Defense; Labor and Employment Law; Legal Malpractice; Nonprofit and Tax Exempt Organizations; Securities Law; Tax Law; Trust and Estates, Wills and Probate

GOODING & DODSON, P.C.
Texarkana, TX.........................Civil Trial Practice; Insurance Defense

GOODING, HUFFMAN, KELLEY & BECKER
Lima, OH.................................Civil Trial Practice; Insurance Defense

GOODLETTE, COLEMAN & JOHNSON, P.A.
Naples, FL...............................Real Estate Law

GOODMAN, EARLE GARY
Beverly Hills, CA....................Real Estate Law

GOODMAN CHESNOFF & KEACH, A PROFESSIONAL CORPORATION
Las Vegas, NV.........................Constitutional Law; Criminal Trial Practice; Personal Injury

GOODMAN & CLARK
Arlington, TX....................Family Law

GOODMAN & GOODMAN, A LEGAL PROFESSIONAL ASSOCIATION
Cincinnati, OH....................Family Law; Health Care Law; Labor and Employment Law; Personal Injury; Real Estate Law; Trust and Estates, Wills and Probate

GOODMAN, MCGUFFEY, AUST & LINDSEY, LLP
Atlanta, GA....................Civil Trial Practice; Insurance Defense; Workers Compensation

GOODMAN PHILLIPS & VINEBERG
Montreal, QU, Canada....................General Practice
Hong Kong, China....................General Practice

GOODMAN, ROBERT U., P.L.C.
Shreveport, LA....................Business Law; Civil Trial Practice; Commercial Law

GOODMAN WEISS MILLER LLP
Cleveland, OH....................Business Law; Civil Trial Practice; Securities Law

GOODSILL ANDERSON QUINN & STIFEL
Honolulu, HI....................Admiralty/Maritime Law; Banking Law; Civil Trial Practice; Commercial Litigation; Communications Law; Construction Law; Environmental Law; General Practice; Health Care Law; Immigration and Naturalization; Insurance Defense; Intellectual Property Law; International Business Law; Labor and Employment Law; Mergers and Acquisitions; Product Liability Law; Professional Liability; Real Estate Law; Securities Law; Tax Law; Trust and Estates, Wills and Probate

GOODSON, MANLEY & DURFEE, P.L.C.
Phoenix, AZ....................Business Law; General Practice; Trust and Estates, Wills and Probate

GOODWIN & GOODWIN
Charleston, WV....................Civil Trial Practice; Corporate Law; General Practice; Government Contracts; Labor and Employment Law; Municipal Bond/Public Authority Financing; Personal Injury
Parkersburg, WV....................General Practice
Ripley, WV....................General Practice

GOODWIN, PROCTER & HOAR LLP
Boston, MA....................General Practice

GOODY, W. KEITH
Jackson, WY....................Criminal Trial Practice; Family Law; Personal Injury

GOOLD PATTERSON DEVORE ALES & ROADHOUSE
Las Vegas, NV....................Commercial Law; Commercial Litigation; General Practice; International Business Law; Real Estate Law

GORANSON, BAIN & LARSEN, L.C.
Dallas, TX....................Family Law

GORDON, ARATA, MCCOLLAM, DUPLANTIS & EAGAN, L.L.P.
Lafayette, LA....................Oil and Gas Law
New Orleans, LA....................Environmental Law; General Practice; Oil and Gas Law

GORDON, EDELSTEIN, KREPACK, GRANT, FELTON & GOLDSTEIN
Los Angeles, CA....................Construction Law; Environmental Law; Medical Malpractice; Personal Injury; Product Liability Law; Toxic Torts; Workers Compensation

GORDON & EINSTEIN, LTD.
Chicago, IL....................Business Law; Real Estate Law

GORDON & HENESON, P.A.
Baltimore, MD....................Civil Trial Practice

GORDON LAW FIRM, THE
Hartwell, GA....................Civil Trial Practice; General Practice; Real Estate Law

GORDON, MUIR AND FOLEY, LLP
Hartford, CT....................Banking Law; Civil Trial Practice; Commercial Law; Construction Law; General Practice; Insurance Defense; Medical Malpractice; Real Estate Law; Trust and Estates, Wills and Probate

GORDON, SIEGEL, MASTRO, MULLANEY, GORDON & GALVIN, P.C.
Latham, NY....................Corporate Law

GORDON, SILBERMAN, WIGGINS & CHILDS, P.C.
Birmingham, AL....................Banking Law; Bankruptcy Law; Business Law; Civil Rights; Civil Trial Practice; Commercial Law; Employment Benefits Law; General Practice; Labor and Employment Law; Personal Injury; Real Estate Law; Tax Law; Trust and Estates, Wills and Probate

GORHAM & WALDREP, P.C.
Birmingham, AL....................Business Law; Civil Rights; Civil Trial Practice; Criminal Trial Practice; Family Law; General Practice; Labor and Employment Law; Municipal and Zoning Law; Municipal Bond/Public Authority Financing; Natural Resources Law; Personal Injury; Real Estate Law; Trust and Estates, Wills and Probate

GORMAN, WASZKIEWICZ, GORMAN & SCHMITT
Utica, NY....................Civil Trial Practice; General Practice

GORNBEIN, HENRY S.
Bloomfield Hills, MI....................Family Law

GORSUCH KIRGIS LLP
Denver, CO....................Business Law; Commercial Litigation; Communications Law; Computer Law; Construction Law; Corporate Law; Environmental Law; Government Contracts; Health Care Law; Insurance Defense; Intellectual Property Law; Labor and Employment Law; Land Use Law; Mergers and Acquisitions; Municipal and Zoning Law; Natural Resources Law; Public Utilities Law; Securities Law; Tax Law; Trademark, Copyright and Unfair Competition; Trust and Estates, Wills and Probate

GOSMA & GALLAGHER, P.L.C.
Davenport, IA....................Banking Law; Business Law; Commercial Litigation; General Practice; Real Estate Law; Trust and Estates, Wills and Probate

GOSNEY, CLIFF B. JR.
Port Orange, FL....................Civil Trial Practice

GOTT, YOUNG & BOGLE, P.A.
Wichita, KS....................General Practice

GOTTLIEB & PEARSON
Montreal, QU, Canada....................International Trade Law

GOUBEAUX & GOUBEAUX
Greenville, OH....................General Practice

GOUGH, SHANAHAN, JOHNSON & WATERMAN
Helena, MT....................General Practice

GOULD, COOKSEY, FENNELL, O'NEILL, MARINE & CARTER, PROFESSIONAL ASSOCIATION
Vero Beach, FL....................Civil Trial Practice; General Practice; Trust and Estates, Wills and Probate

GOULD, KILLIAN & WYNNE
Hartford, CT....................Business Law; General Practice; Insurance Defense; Trust and Estates, Wills and Probate

GOURVITZ, ELLIOT H., P.A.
Springfield, NJ....................Family Law

GOUVEIA & MILLER
Merrillville, IN....................Bankruptcy Law; Personal Injury

GOVERNALI, JOSEPH P.
White Plains, NY....................Commercial Litigation; Family Law; General Practice

GOVERNO AND KAVANAGH LLP
Boston, MA....................Civil Trial Practice; Insurance Defense; Toxic Torts

GOZIGIAN, WASHBURN & CLINTON
Cooperstown, NY....................General Practice; Personal Injury; Real Estate Law; Trust and Estates, Wills and Probate

GRACE, JOHN PHILIP, P.C.
Phoenix, AZ....................Personal Injury

GRACE, UNRUH & PRATT, L.C.
Wichita, KS....................Civil Trial Practice; Commercial Litigation; Insurance Defense; Labor and Employment Law; Product Liability Law

GRADY & ASSOCIATES, LEGAL PROFESSIONAL ASSOCIATION
Naples, FL....................Securities Law

GRAHAM & ARCENEAUX
New Orleans, LA....................Real Estate Law

GRAHAM, CAMPAIGN, P.C.
New York, NY....................Computer Law; Intellectual Property Law; Nonprofit and Tax Exempt Organizations; Trademark, Copyright and Unfair Competition

GRAHAM, CLARK, JONES, BUILDER, PRATT & MARKS
Winter Park, FL....................Civil Trial Practice; Real Estate Law

GRAHAM, CURTIN & SHERIDAN, A PROFESSIONAL ASSOCIATION
Morristown, NJ....................General Practice

GRAHAM & DUNN PC
Seattle, WA....................General Practice

GRAHAM AND GRAHAM, LTD.
Springfield, IL....................General Practice

GRAHAM & JAMES LLP
Los Angeles, CA....................General Practice
Palo Alto, CA....................General Practice
San Francisco, CA....................Admiralty/Maritime Law; General Practice
Washington, DC....................General Practice

HART AND HART
Benton, IL .... Civil Trial Practice; General Practice

HART & HORAN, P.C.
Fairfax, VA .... Construction Law

HARTE, WILLIAM J., LTD.
Chicago, IL .... Civil Trial Practice; Commercial Law; Securities Law

HARTLEY, DENNIS W., P.C., PROFESSIONAL CORPORATION
Colorado Springs, CO .... Criminal Trial Practice

HARTLEY, WALL & NORMAN
Orlando, FL .... Civil Trial Practice; Commercial Litigation

HARTNETT LAW FIRM, THE
Dallas, TX .... Trust and Estates, Wills and Probate

HARTSELL, HARTSELL & WHITE, PA
Concord, NC .... Insurance Defense

HARTZELL, GLIDDEN, TUCKER AND HARTZELL
Carthage, IL .... General Practice

HARTZOG CONGER & CASON, A PROFESSIONAL CORPORATION
Oklahoma City, OK .... Banking Law; Civil Trial Practice; Commercial Law; General Practice; Health Care Law; Labor and Employment Law; Real Estate Law; Securities Law; Tax Law; Trust and Estates, Wills and Probate

HARTZOG, SILVA & DAVIES
Franklin, TN .... General Practice

HARVEY & BATTEY, P.A.
Beaufort, SC .... Commercial Litigation; Elder Law; Environmental Law; Family Law; General Practice; Municipal and Zoning Law; Personal Injury; Real Estate Law; Tax Law; Trust and Estates, Wills and Probate

HARVEY AND MUMFORD
Albany, NY .... Appellate Practice; Arbitration; Civil Trial Practice; Commercial Litigation; General Practice; Medical Malpractice; Personal Injury; Product Liability Law; Professional Liability

HARVEY, PENNINGTON, CABOT, GRIFFITH & RENNEISEN, LTD.
Philadelphia, PA .... General Practice

HARVIN, WESLEY R., P.A.
Stuart, FL .... Commercial Litigation

HARWELL & PLANT
Lawrenceburg, TN .... Insurance Defense; Real Estate Law

HARWICK, MAURICE
North Hollywood, CA .... Civil Trial Practice

HASH & O'BRIEN, PLLP
Kalispell, MT .... General Practice; Insurance Defense; Real Estate Law; Tax Law

HASKELL & PERRIN
Chicago, IL .... Civil Trial Practice; Insurance Defense; Medical Malpractice; Product Liability Law; Professional Liability

HASKELL SLAUGHTER & YOUNG, L.L.C.
Birmingham, AL .... Antitrust Law; Banking Law; Business Law; Civil Trial Practice; Commercial Law; General Practice; Health Care Law; Labor and Employment Law; Municipal Bond/Public Authority Financing; Tax Law

HASKELL SLAUGHTER YOUNG & GALLION, L.L.C.
Montgomery, AL .... Civil Trial Practice; General Practice; Labor and Employment Law

HASLAM FIRM, THE
Fort Worth, TX .... Civil Trial Practice; Personal Injury

HASPEL & MEISELMAN, CHARTERED
Rockville, MD .... Family Law

HASS, D. WINTHROP, S.C.
Milwaukee, WI .... Corporate Law; Mergers and Acquisitions

HASSENFELD & LEDERMAN
Boston, MA .... Commercial Law

HASSETT & DONNELLY
Worcester, MA .... Insurance Defense

HATCH AND PARENT
Santa Barbara, CA .... Land Use Law

HATCHER, B. PAUL
Chattanooga, TN .... Real Estate Law

HATCHER, STUBBS, LAND, HOLLIS & ROTHSCHILD
Columbus, GA .... Banking Law; Bankruptcy Law; Commercial Law; Employment Benefits Law; General Practice; Insurance Defense; Municipal Bond/Public Authority Financing; Real Estate Law; Tax Law; Trust and Estates, Wills and Probate

HATTER, DONOVAN & MCFAUL, LLP
Mineola, NY .... Civil Trial Practice; Insurance Defense; Personal Injury; Trust and Estates, Wills and Probate

HATTERY, SIMPSON & WEST
Galesburg, IL .... General Practice; Personal Injury; Trust and Estates, Wills and Probate

HAUER, HARVEY I., P.C.
Bingham Farms, MI .... Family Law

HAUGEN LAW FIRM, PLLP
Minneapolis, MN .... International Business Law; Patent, Trademark, Copyright and Unfair Competition

HAUGH & HAUGH, P.C.
Charlottesville, VA .... Civil Trial Practice; Criminal Trial Practice

HAUPTMAN & RICHMOND, P.A.
West Orange, NJ .... Tax Law; Trust and Estates, Wills and Probate

HAURY, WILLIAM W. JR.
Fort Lauderdale, FL .... Civil Trial Practice; Commercial Litigation

HAUSHALTER, HARRY
Hamilton Square, NJ .... Civil Trial Practice; Tax Law

HAVERSTOCK, GARRETT AND ROBERTS
St. Louis, MO .... Patent, Trademark, Copyright and Unfair Competition

HAWKINS • BLICK
San Jose, CA .... Civil Trial Practice; Legal Malpractice; Medical Malpractice; Personal Injury

HAWKINS, MOODY, BINGHAM, MILLER & ASSOCIATES, P.C.
Kingsport, TN .... Medical Malpractice; Personal Injury; Product Liability Law; Workers Compensation

HAWKINS & NORRIS
Des Moines, IA .... Antitrust Law; Business Law; Civil Trial Practice; Personal Injury

HAWKINS & PARNELL, LLP
Atlanta, GA .... Civil Rights; Civil Trial Practice; Commercial Law; Environmental Law; General Practice; Municipal and Zoning Law; Product Liability Law; Professional Liability; Sports and Entertainment Law; Transportation Law

HAWKINS, SCHNABEL, LINDAHL & BECK, LLP
Los Angeles, CA .... Civil Trial Practice; Insurance Defense

HAWLEY, HUDSON & HAWLEY
Mt. Vernon, IN .... Natural Resources Law

HAWORTH RIGGS
High Point, NC .... General Practice

HAYDEN AND MILLIKEN, P.A.
Miami, FL .... Admiralty/Maritime Law; Business Law; Corporate Law; Insurance Defense
Tampa, FL .... Admiralty/Maritime Law; Business Law; Corporate Law; Insurance Defense

HAYDEN, THOMAS C., JR., P.A.
La Plata, MD .... General Practice

HAYDUK, ANDREWS & HYPNAR, P.C.
Detroit, MI .... Civil Trial Practice; Environmental Law; Insurance Defense; Labor and Employment Law; Product Liability Law; Trust and Estates, Wills and Probate

HAYES, J. MICHAEL
Buffalo, NY .... Civil Trial Practice; Personal Injury

HAYES, HARKEY, SMITH & CASCIO, L.L.P.
Monroe, LA .... Civil Trial Practice; General Practice; Insurance Defense; Medical Malpractice

HAYES LORENZEN, PLC
Iowa City, IA .... Medical Malpractice

HAYES, PHILLIPS & MALONEY, P.C.
Denver, CO .... Municipal and Zoning Law

HAYGOOD, LYNCH, HARRIS & MELTON
Forsyth, GA .... General Practice
Monticello, GA .... General Practice

HAYNES AND BOONE, LLP
Dallas, TX .... General Practice

HAYNES, HULL, RIEDER & EWELL, P.A.
Tullahoma, TN....................General Practice

HAYNSWORTH BALDWIN JOHNSON & GREAVES LLC
Jacksonville, FL....................Labor and Employment Law
Tampa, FL....................Labor and Employment Law
Charlotte, NC....................Labor and Employment Law
Greensboro, NC....................Labor and Employment Law
Raleigh, NC....................Labor and Employment Law
Columbia, SC....................Labor and Employment Law
Greenville, SC....................Labor and Employment Law

HAYNSWORTH, MARION, MCKAY & GUÉRARD, L.L.P.
Charleston, SC....................Administrative Law; Business Law; Civil Trial Practice; Employment Benefits Law; General Practice; Health Care Law; Insurance Defense; Medical Malpractice; Municipal Bond/Public Authority Financing; Product Liability Law; Real Estate Law; Securities Law; Tax Law; Trust and Estates, Wills and Probate
Columbia, SC....................Administrative Law; Banking Law; Bankruptcy Law; Business Law; Civil Trial Practice; Employment Benefits Law; Environmental Law; General Practice; Insurance Defense; Medical Malpractice; Municipal Bond/Public Authority Financing; Product Liability Law; Public Utilities Law; Real Estate Law; Securities Law
Greenville, SC....................Administrative Law; Banking Law; Bankruptcy Law; Business Law; Civil Trial Practice; Construction Law; Employment Benefits Law; Environmental Law; General Practice; Health Care Law; Insurance Defense; Medical Malpractice; Municipal Bond/Public Authority Financing; Patent, Trademark, Copyright and Unfair Competition; Product Liability Law; Real Estate Law; Tax Law; Trust and Estates, Wills and Probate; Workers Compensation

HAYNSWORTH, PERRY, BRYANT, MARION & JOHNSTONE
Greenville, SC....................General Practice

HAYS, MCCONN, RICE & PICKERING
Houston, TX....................Banking Law; Civil Trial Practice; Insurance Defense; Personal Injury

HAZLETT & WILKES
Tucson, AZ....................General Practice; Insurance Defense; Medical Malpractice

HEAD, HEAD & HEAD
Carrollton, GA....................Family Law; Personal Injury; Trust and Estates, Wills and Probate

HEAD, SEIFERT & VANDER WEIDE, A PROFESSIONAL ASSOCIATION
Minneapolis, MN....................Commercial Litigation; General Practice; Securities Law

HEAD, THOMAS & WEBB, LLC
Atlanta, GA....................Criminal Trial Practice

HEALTH LAW FIRM, THE
Little Rock, AR....................Health Care Law

HEALY, GEORGE W. IV
New Orleans, LA....................Admiralty/Maritime Law; Personal Injury

HEALY & BAILLIE, LLP
Stamford, CT....................Admiralty/Maritime Law; General Practice
New York, NY....................Admiralty/Maritime Law; General Practice

HEALY & STUDWELL LAW FIRM, P.C.
Tucson, AZ....................Medical Malpractice; Personal Injury; Product Liability Law

HEARD LINEBARGER GRAHAM GOGGAN BLAIR PEÑA & SAMPSON, LLP
San Antonio, TX....................Criminal Trial Practice; Family Law; General Practice; International Business Law

HEARN, BRITTAIN & MARTIN, P.A.
Conway, SC....................Criminal Trial Practice; Family Law; Personal Injury

HEARNE, EPPRIGHT & GEST, A PROFESSIONAL CORPORATION
Austin, TX....................Civil Trial Practice; General Practice

HECHT, SOLBERG, ROBINSON & GOLDBERG, LLP
San Diego, CA....................Business Law; Land Use Law; Real Estate Law

HECKER & HARRIMAN
Los Angeles, CA....................Patent, Trademark, Copyright and Unfair Competition

HECTOR & HARKE LLP
Miami, FL....................Commercial Litigation

HEDEEN, HUGHES, WETERING & KNESS
Worthington, MN....................General Practice

HEDLAND, BRENNAN, HEIDEMAN & COOKE, A PROFESSIONAL CORPORATION
Anchorage, AK....................Civil Trial Practice

HEDRICK, DEWBERRY & REGAN, P.A.
Jacksonville, FL....................Civil Trial Practice; Commercial Litigation; Construction Law; Labor and Employment Law

HEENAN BLAIKIE
Montreal, QU, Canada....................General Practice

HEENEY, ARMSTRONG & HEENEY
Rockville, MD....................Criminal Trial Practice

HEIDELL, PITTONI, MURPHY & BACH, LLP
Stamford, CT....................Medical Malpractice
New York, NY....................Insurance Defense; Medical Malpractice

HEIDMAN, REDMOND, FREDREGILL, PATTERSON, PLAZA & DYKSTRA, L.L.P.
Sioux City, IA....................Civil Trial Practice; General Practice; Insurance Defense; Workers Compensation

HEILIG, MCKENRY, FRAIM & LOLLAR, A PROFESSIONAL CORPORATION
Norfolk, VA....................Insurance Defense

HEILIGENSTEIN & BADGLEY, PROFESSIONAL CORPORATION
Belleville, IL....................Personal Injury

HEIN, SMITH, BEREZIN, MALOOF & JACOBS, L.L.C.
Hackensack, NJ....................Business Law; Civil Trial Practice; Commercial Law; Employment Benefits Law; General Practice; Insurance Defense; Medical Malpractice; Personal Injury; Product Liability Law; Real Estate Law; Workers Compensation

HEINRICH GORDON HARGROVE WEIHE & JAMES, P.A.
Fort Lauderdale, FL....................Civil Trial Practice; General Practice; Personal Injury

HEINTZMAN, WARREN, WISE & FORNELLA, P.C.
Pittsburgh, PA....................Admiralty/Maritime Law; Civil Trial Practice; Insurance Defense; Medical Malpractice; Product Liability Law

HEISE MARKARIAN P.A.
Miami, FL....................Civil Trial Practice

HEISERMAN, ROBERT G., P.C.
Denver, CO....................Immigration and Naturalization

HELEIN & ASSOCIATES, P.C.
McLean, VA....................Communications Law

HELFREY, SIMON & JONES, P.C.
St. Louis, MO....................Criminal Trial Practice; Intellectual Property Law; International Business Law; Mergers and Acquisitions; Real Estate Law

HELLER, DRAPER, HAYDEN & HORN, L.L.C.
New Orleans, LA....................Bankruptcy Law

HELLER, STEPHEN H., A PROFESSIONAL CORPORATION
Encino, CA....................Medical Malpractice; Personal Injury; Product Liability Law

HELLRING LINDEMAN GOLDSTEIN & SIEGAL LLP
Newark, NJ....................Antitrust Law; Appellate Practice; Bankruptcy Law; Civil Trial Practice; Commercial Litigation; Criminal Trial Practice; Environmental Law; Family Law; General Practice; Intellectual Property Law; Labor and Employment Law; Natural Resources Law; Real Estate Law; Securities Law; Tax Law; Trust and Estates, Wills and Probate

HELM & ASSOCIATES
Anchorage, AK....................Medical Malpractice

HELMKE, BEAMS, BOYER & WAGNER
Fort Wayne, IN....................Bankruptcy Law; Civil Trial Practice; Creditors Rights; General Practice; Municipal and Zoning Law; Trust and Estates, Wills and Probate

HELMS, HANRAHAN & MYERS
Arcadia, CA....................Family Law; General Practice; Trust and Estates, Wills and Probate

HELMSING, SIMS & LEACH, P.C.
Mobile, AL....................Aviation Law; Civil Trial Practice; Commercial Law; Commercial Litigation; Criminal Trial Practice; General Practice; Insurance Defense; Personal Injury; Trust and Estates, Wills and Probate

HELSELL FETTERMAN LLP
Seattle, WA....................General Practice

HEMENWAY & BARNES
Boston, MA....................Business Law; General Practice; Trust and Estates, Wills and Probate

HENDERSON, THOMAS W.
Newport Beach, CA................Trust and Estates, Wills and Probate

HENDERSON & BRENNAN
White Plains, NY....................Civil Trial Practice

HENDERSON & BUTLER
Huntsville, AL.........................Insurance Defense

HENDERSON, FRANKLIN, STARNES & HOLT, PROFESSIONAL ASSOCIATION
Fort Myers, FL.........................Business Law; Civil Trial Practice; Corporate Law; General Practice; Insurance Defense; Personal Injury; Real Estate Law; Tax Law; Trust and Estates, Wills and Probate

HENDERSON, HANEMANN & MORRIS, A PROFESSIONAL LAW CORPORATION
Houma, LA...............................Admiralty/Maritime Law; Insurance Defense; Product Liability Law; Workers Compensation

HENDREN AND ANDRAE
Jefferson City, MO.................General Practice; Insurance Defense

HENDRICK, PHILLIPS, SCHEMM & SALZMAN, A PROFESSIONAL CORPORATION
Atlanta, GA............................Construction Law

HENDRICKS, NATHAN V. III
Atlanta, GA............................Municipal and Zoning Law

HENDRICKS & HENDRICKS
Coral Gables, FL....................Trust and Estates, Wills and Probate

HENDRICKSON, RAY
Irvine, CA...............................Family Law

HENDRY, STONER, SAWICKI & BROWN, P.A.
Orlando, FL.............................International Trade Law; Real Estate Law; Tax Law

HENICAN, JAMES & CLEVELAND
Metairie, LA............................Corporate Law; Mergers and Acquisitions; Real Estate Law; Tax Law; Trust and Estates, Wills and Probate

HENINGER, BURGE, VARGO AND DAVIS, LLP
Birmingham, AL......................Medical Malpractice; Personal Injury

HENINGER AND HENINGER, PROFESSIONAL CORPORATION
Davenport, IA..........................General Practice; Medical Malpractice

HENKE-BUFKIN, A PROFESSIONAL ASSOCIATION
Clarksdale, MS.......................Insurance Defense; Product Liability Law

HENNENBERG & ASSOCIATES
Cleveland, OH........................Civil Rights; Criminal Trial Practice; Real Estate Law; Trust and Estates, Wills and Probate

HENNENHOEFER, JAMES A., A PROFESSIONAL CORPORATION
Vista, CA.................................Family Law

HENNIGAN, MERCER & BENNETT
Los Angeles, CA.....................Antitrust Law; Bankruptcy Law; Civil Trial Practice; Commercial Litigation; Securities Law

HENRICKSEN & HENRICKSEN, INC.
El Reno, OK............................General Practice

HENRY & BEAVER LLP
Lebanon, PA............................Civil Trial Practice; General Practice

HENRY, BUCHANAN, HUDSON, SUBER & CARTER, P.A.
Tallahassee, FL......................Civil Trial Practice; General Practice; Insurance Defense

HENRY, MCCORD, BEAN & MILLER, P.L.L.C.
Tullahoma, TN........................General Practice

HENSHAW, TODD MAXWELL
Tulsa, OK................................Bankruptcy Law

HENSLEE, FOWLER, HEPWORTH & SCHWARTZ, L.L.P.
Austin, TX...............................Insurance Defense

HENSLEY & HENSLEY
Raymore, MO..........................Criminal Trial Practice; Family Law; Personal Injury; Workers Compensation

HENSON & EFRON, P.A.
Minneapolis, MN.....................Commercial Litigation; Environmental Law; Family Law; General Practice; Product Liability Law; Securities Law

HENSON AND FUERST, P.A.
Rocky Mount, NC....................Medical Malpractice; Personal Injury

HENSON & HENSON, L.L.P.
Greensboro, NC......................Civil Trial Practice; Insurance Defense; Personal Injury

HENSON, HENSON, HENSON, MARSHALL & MILBURN, LLP
Shawnee, OK..........................General Practice

HEPFER, CHERYL LYNN
Rockville, MD..........................Family Law

HERBERT & HERBERT
Glasgow, KY............................Civil Trial Practice; Family Law; General Practice; Personal Injury; Real Estate Law

HERBOLSHEIMER, LANNON, HENSON, DUNCAN AND REAGAN, P.C.
La Salle, IL..............................Appellate Practice; Civil Trial Practice; General Practice; Insurance Defense; Medical Malpractice; Professional Liability; Real Estate Law; Workers Compensation

HERLOCKER, ROBERTS & ST. PETER, L.L.C.
Winfield, KS............................General Practice

HERMAN, GOLDSTEIN & FORSYTH, P.C.
Scottsdale, AZ........................Civil Trial Practice; Insurance Defense; Personal Injury

HERMAN, HERMAN, KATZ & COTLAR, L.L.P.
New Orleans, LA.....................Civil Trial Practice; General Practice

HERMAN & HOWRY, L.L.P.
Austin, TX...............................Civil Trial Practice; Commercial Litigation

HERMANN, CAHN & SCHNEIDER
Cleveland, OH........................Business Law; Civil Trial Practice; Family Law; Insurance Defense; Personal Injury; Product Liability Law

HERMENZE & MARCANTONIO
Westport, CT...........................Trust and Estates, Wills and Probate

HERNER, DONALD A. LAW OFFICES OF
Stamford, CT...........................Business Law; Corporate Law

HEROLD AND HAINES, PROFESSIONAL ASSOCIATION
Warren, NJ...............................General Practice

HERRERA, LONG & POUND, P.A.
Santa Fe, NM..........................Civil Trial Practice; Health Care Law; Insurance Defense; Land Use Law; Municipal and Zoning Law; Product Liability Law; Real Estate Law

HERRICK LAW OFFICE, S.C.
Fond du Lac, WI......................Insurance Defense

HERRING, D. JEFFERSON
Nashville, TN..........................Tax Law; Trust and Estates, Wills and Probate

HERRMANN, LAWRENCE M.
Jackson Heights, NY..............Criminal Trial Practice

HERSH, NEAL RAYMOND LAW OFFICES OF
Beverly Hills, CA....................Family Law

HERSH FAMILYLAW PRACTICE, A PROFESSIONAL CORPORATION
San Francisco, CA..................Family Law

HERSHEWE & GULICK, P.C.
Joplin, MO...............................Medical Malpractice; Personal Injury

HERSHNER, HUNTER, ANDREWS, NEILL & SMITH, LLP
Eugene, OR.............................General Practice

HERTEN, BURSTEIN, SHERIDAN, CEVASCO, BOTTINELLI & LITT, L.L.C.
Hackensack, NJ......................Appellate Practice; Civil Trial Practice; Land Use Law; Product Liability Law

HERTZ, SCHRAM & SARETSKY, P.C.
Bloomfield Hills, MI.................Banking Law; Bankruptcy Law; Business Law; Commercial Law; Commercial Litigation; Family Law; Securities Law; Tax Law

HERTZBERG, RICHARD J.
Phoenix, AZ............................Civil Trial Practice; Criminal Trial Practice

HERZFELD & RUBIN, P.C.
New York, NY..........................General Practice

HERZOG, CREBS & MCGHEE, LLP
St. Louis, MO..........................Civil Trial Practice

HERZOG, FISHER, GRAYSON & WOLFE, A LAW CORPORATION
Beverly Hills, CA....................Business Law; Commercial Litigation; Health Care Law; Insurance Defense

HERZOG AND O'CONNOR, P.C.
Phoenix, AZ............................Insurance Defense; Personal Injury; Workers Compensation

HESLIN & ROTHENBERG, P.C.
Albany, NY..............................Intellectual Property Law; Patent, Trademark, Copyright and Unfair Competition

HESSIAN & MCKASY, P.A.
Minneapolis, MN....................Bankruptcy Law; Labor and Employment Law; Municipal and Zoning Law; Real Estate Law

HESSION & BEKOFF
Mineola, NY....................Criminal Trial Practice; Personal Injury

HESTER, GRADY, HESTER, GREENE & PAYNE
Elizabethtown, NC....................General Practice

HESTER, JON L., P.C., A PROFESSIONAL CORPORATION
Oklahoma City, OK....................Family Law

HEWITT, JAMES W.
Lincoln, NE....................General Practice

HEWLETT, COLLINS AND ALLARD
Wilmington, NC....................Criminal Trial Practice

HEYL, ROYSTER, VOELKER & ALLEN, PROFESSIONAL CORPORATION
Edwardsville, IL....................Insurance Defense
Peoria, IL....................Insurance Defense
Rockford, IL....................Insurance Defense
Springfield, IL....................Insurance Defense
Urbana, IL....................Insurance Defense

HICKEY, MACKEY, EVANS & WALKER
Cheyenne, WY....................Banking Law; Civil Trial Practice; Commercial Law; Criminal Trial Practice; General Practice; Personal Injury; Public Utilities Law

HICKS, H. MELVILLE JR.
New York, NY....................Commercial Law

HICKS & ANDERSON, P.A.
Miami, FL....................Appellate Practice; General Practice

HICKS, BRAMS & SCHER
West Palm Beach, FL....................Civil Trial Practice

HICKS & LUCKY, A PROFESSIONAL CORPORATION
El Paso, TX....................Civil Trial Practice; Insurance Defense; Medical Malpractice; Personal Injury

HICKSON, DAVID L.
San Diego, CA....................Trust and Estates, Wills and Probate

HIENTON FRY, P.C.
Phoenix, AZ....................Real Estate Law

HIERING, DUPIGNAC & STANZIONE, A PROFESSIONAL CORPORATION
Toms River, NJ....................General Practice

HIGBEE, JENSEN & MACFARLANE, P.C.
Cedar City, UT....................General Practice; Personal Injury

HIGGINS, CAVANAGH & COONEY
Providence, RI....................Civil Trial Practice; General Practice; Insurance Defense

HIGGS, FLETCHER & MACK LLP
San Diego, CA....................Banking Law; Civil Trial Practice; General Practice

HIGH, STACK, LAZENBY, PALAHACH & FEILER
Miami, FL....................Civil Trial Practice; Personal Injury

HIGH, SWARTZ, ROBERTS & SEIDEL, LLP
Norristown, PA....................General Practice

HIGHSAW, MAHONEY & CLARKE, P.C.
Washington, DC....................Labor and Employment Law

HIGHTOWER, ROBERT S.
Tallahassee, FL....................Corporate Law; Mergers and Acquisitions; Tax Law; Trust and Estates, Wills and Probate

HILBRECHT & ASSOCIATES, CHARTERED
Las Vegas, NV....................Administrative Law; General Practice; Personal Injury

HILBURN, CALHOON, HARPER, PRUNISKI & CALHOUN, LTD.
Little Rock, AR....................Civil Trial Practice; General Practice; Labor and Employment Law; Securities Law; Tax Law

HILDER, PHILIP H., & ASSOCIATES, P.C.
Houston, TX....................Criminal Trial Practice

HILL, JOHN E. LAW OFFICES OF
San Francisco, CA....................Civil Trial Practice

HILL & BARLOW, A PROFESSIONAL CORPORATION
Boston, MA....................General Practice

HILL AND BLEIBERG
Atlanta, GA....................Medical Malpractice; Personal Injury; Product Liability Law

HILLENCAMP & ALVAREZ, P.A.
Miami, FL....................Medical Malpractice; Personal Injury

HILL, EVANS, DUNCAN, JORDAN & DAVIS
Greensboro, NC....................Civil Trial Practice; General Practice

HILL, FARRER & BURRILL LLP
Los Angeles, CA....................Appellate Practice; Civil Trial Practice; Eminent Domain; General Practice; Labor and Employment Law; Real Estate Law; Tax Law

HILL & HILL
Houston, TX....................General Practice

HILL, HILL, CARTER, FRANCO, COLE & BLACK, P.C.
Montgomery, AL....................Civil Trial Practice; General Practice

HILLIARD, FRANK P.
Louisville, KY....................Civil Trial Practice; General Practice; Insurance Defense

HILLIS CLARK MARTIN & PETERSON, A PROFESSIONAL SERVICE CORPORATION
Seattle, WA....................General Practice

HILLMAN, FORMAN, NELSEN CHILDERS, LINGO & MCCORMACK
Omaha, NE....................General Practice

HILL & PARKER, A PROFESSIONAL CORPORATION
Houston, TX....................Civil Trial Practice; Personal Injury

HILL AND PONTON, PROFESSIONAL ASSOCIATION
Orlando, FL....................Aviation Law; Civil Trial Practice; Medical Malpractice; Personal Injury; Product Liability Law

HILL, REIS, ADAMS, HALL & SCHIEFFELIN, P.A.
Orlando, FL....................Antitrust Law; Appellate Practice; Civil Trial Practice; General Practice; Health Care Law; Insurance Defense; Medical Malpractice; Personal Injury; Product Liability Law; Professional Liability

HINCKLEY, ALLEN & SNYDER LLP
Boston, MA....................Banking Law; Bankruptcy Law; Business Law; Commercial Law; Commercial Litigation; Computer Law; Construction Law; Creditors Rights; Employment Benefits Law; Energy Law; General Practice; Health Care Law; Intellectual Property Law; International Business Law; International Trade Law; Labor and Employment Law; Mergers and Acquisitions; Municipal and Zoning Law; Municipal Bond/Public Authority Financing; Patent, Trademark, Copyright and Unfair Competition; Pension and Profit Sharing; Product Liability Law; Public Utilities Law; Real Estate Law; Securities Law; Tax Law; Trademark, Copyright and Unfair Competition; Trust and Estates, Wills and Probate; Workers Compensation
Providence, RI....................Banking Law; Bankruptcy Law; Business Law; Commercial Law; Commercial Litigation; Computer Law; Construction Law; Creditors Rights; Employment Benefits Law; Energy Law; General Practice; Health Care Law; Intellectual Property Law; International Business Law; International Trade Law; Labor and Employment Law; Mergers and Acquisitions; Municipal and Zoning Law; Municipal Bond/Public Authority Financing; Patent, Trademark, Copyright and Unfair Competition; Pension and Profit Sharing; Product Liability Law; Public Utilities Law; Real Estate Law; Securities Law; Tax Law; Trademark, Copyright and Unfair Competition; Trust and Estates, Wills and Probate; Workers Compensation

HINDMAN, GOLDSTEIN & HARDER, P.C.
Columbia, MO....................Civil Trial Practice

HINDS, ROBERT T., JR. AND ASSOCIATES, P.C.
Greenwood Village, CO....................Family Law

HINES & THOMAS
San Francisco, CA....................Insurance Defense

HINKLEY & GIUNTA
Midland, TX....................Personal Injury

HINMAN, HOWARD & KATTELL, LLP
Binghamton, NY....................Civil Trial Practice; Corporate Law; General Practice; Labor and Employment Law; Municipal Bond/Public Authority Financing; Natural Resources Law; Oil and Gas Law; Tax Law

HINMAN, STRAUB, PIGORS & MANNING, P.C.
Albany, NY....................Health Care Law; Labor and Employment Law

HINSHAW & CULBERTSON
Chicago, IL....................General Practice

HINTON & ALFERT, A PROFESSIONAL CORPORATION
Walnut Creek, CA....................Aviation Law; Civil Trial Practice; Commercial Litigation; Personal Injury; Product Liability Law

HIRSCH LAW OFFICE, P.C.
Phoenix, AZ....................Bankruptcy Law; Family Law

HIRSCHHORN, AUSTIN, P.C.
Troy, MI....Bankruptcy Law; Business Law; Civil Trial Practice; Commercial Law; General Practice; Real Estate Law

HIRSCHHORN, JOEL, P.A.
Coral Gables, FL....Appellate Practice; Criminal Trial Practice

HIRSH, BJORGAARD & ROGERS, P.L.C.
Tucson, AZ....Criminal Trial Practice

HIRSON WEXLER PERL & STARK, A PROFESSIONAL CORPORATION
Newport Beach, CA....Immigration and Naturalization

HIRST & APPLEGATE, A PROFESSIONAL CORPORATION
Cheyenne, WY....Civil Trial Practice; Real Estate Law; Trust and Estates, Wills and Probate

HISCOCK & BARCLAY, LLP
Syracuse, NY....Banking Law; Business Law; Commercial Litigation; General Practice

HISHON FIRM, THE, LLC
Atlanta, GA....Business Law; Civil Trial Practice; General Practice; Tax Law

HOAGLAND, LONGO, MORAN, DUNST & DOUKAS
New Brunswick, NJ....Business Law; Civil Trial Practice; Construction Law; Environmental Law; Insurance Defense

HOBBS & HAIN, P.C.
Selma, AL....General Practice

HOBBS, HARRY M., P.A.
Tampa, FL....Real Estate Law

HOBBS, LARRY F., P.C.
Denver, CO....Labor and Employment Law

HOBSON, CADY & CADY
Hampton, IA....Civil Trial Practice; General Practice

HOCHMAN, SALKIN, RETTIG, TOSCHER & PEREZ, A PROFESSIONAL CORPORATION
Beverly Hills, CA....Business Law; Corporate Law; Criminal Trial Practice; Real Estate Law; Tax Law; Trust and Estates, Wills and Probate

HOCKEMA, TIPPIT & ESCOBEDO, L.L.P.
Edinburg, TX....Commercial Litigation; Personal Injury

HODGDEN, HALLREN, SMITHTON & HODGDEN, P.L.L.C.
Woodward, OK....General Practice

HODGES, CHARLES R., P.C.
Dallas, TX....Family Law

HODGES & DAVIS, P.C.
Merrillville, IN....Civil Trial Practice; Commercial Law; General Practice; Health Care Law; Real Estate Law
Portage, IN....Civil Trial Practice; Commercial Law; General Practice; Health Care Law; Real Estate Law

HODGES & LEVERETT, L.L.C.
Elberton, GA....General Practice

HODGSON, RUSS, ANDREWS, WOODS & GOODYEAR, LLP
Albany, NY....General Practice
Buffalo, NY....Civil Trial Practice; General Practice; Immigration and Naturalization; Labor and Employment Law; Patent, Trademark, Copyright and Unfair Competition; Tax Law

HODOSH, SPINELLA & ANGELONE
Providence, RI....Civil Trial Practice

HOEFFNER, JAMES V.
Austin, TX....Bankruptcy Law

HOEPPNER WAGNER & EVANS LLP
Merrillville, IN....General Practice; Insurance Defense; Labor and Employment Law; Product Liability Law
Valparaiso, IN....Employment Benefits Law; General Practice; Insurance Defense; Labor and Employment Law; Product Liability Law; Real Estate Law

HOFELICH & KING
Cleveland, OH....Civil Trial Practice

HOFF, CURTIS, PACHT, CASSIDY & FRAME, P.C.
Burlington, VT....General Practice

HOFFERT & ASSOCIATES, P.C.
Southfield, MI....Tax Law

HOFFINGER FRIEDLAND DOBRISH & STERN, P.C.
New York, NY....Appellate Practice; Civil Trial Practice; Commercial Litigation; Corporate Law; Criminal Trial Practice; Family Law; Real Estate Law; Securities Law; Tax Law

HOFFMAN, JAMES P. LAW OFFICES OF
Keokuk, IA....Personal Injury; Workers Compensation

HOFFMAN DREWRY HANCOCK & SIMMONS
Indianapolis, IN....Commercial Law; Commercial Litigation; Construction Law; Government Contracts

HOFFMAN & FOWLER, LLP
Atlanta, GA....Business Law; Civil Trial Practice; Family Law; Personal Injury; Tax Law; Trust and Estates, Wills and Probate

HOFFMAN & HERTZIG, P.A.
Miami, FL....Aviation Law; Business Law; Civil Trial Practice

HOFFMAN & LYONS, P.C.
Rockville, MD....Commercial Litigation

HOFFMAN POLLOK & PICKHOLZ LLP
New York, NY....Criminal Trial Practice; Securities Law

HOFFMAN, WACHTELL, KOSTER & MAIER
White Plains, NY....Civil Trial Practice; General Practice; Municipal and Zoning Law; Real Estate Law; Workers Compensation

HOFFMANN & BARON, LLP
Parsippany, NJ....Intellectual Property Law; Patent, Trademark, Copyright and Unfair Competition
Syosset, NY....Intellectual Property Law; Patent, Trademark, Copyright and Unfair Competition

HOFFMANN & MCCONKEY, P.L.C., LAW OFFICES OF
Des Moines, IA....Workers Compensation

HOFLER, HAYES, & ASSOCIATES, P.A.
Durham, NC....Civil Trial Practice; Construction Law; Personal Injury

HOGAN, THOMAS R. LAW OFFICES OF
San Jose, CA....Business Law; Civil Trial Practice; Construction Law; General Practice

HOGAN DUBOSE & TOWNSEND, L.L.P.
Houston, TX....Appellate Practice; Civil Trial Practice

HOGAN & HARTSON
Prague, Czech Republic....General Practice
Colorado Springs, CO....General Practice
Denver, CO....General Practice
Washington, DC....General Practice
Baltimore, MD....General Practice
Rockville, MD....General Practice
McLean, VA....General Practice
Brussels, Belgium....General Practice
London, England....General Practice
Paris, France....General Practice
Moscow, Russia....General Practice
Warsaw, Poland....General Practice

HOGAN & HOGAN
East Providence, RI....General Practice

HOGAN, PALACE & SCULLY
Hackensack, NJ....Civil Trial Practice; Commercial Litigation; Real Estate Law; Trust and Estates, Wills and Probate

HOGAN & SARZYNSKI, L.L.P.
Binghamton, NY....Arbitration; Education Law; Labor and Employment Law; Municipal and Zoning Law

HOGAN, SMITH & ALSPAUGH, P.C.
Birmingham, AL....Civil Trial Practice; Environmental Law; Medical Malpractice; Personal Injury; Product Liability Law

HOGG, RYCE & HUDSON
West Palm Beach, FL....Labor and Employment Law

HOGUE, HILL, JONES, NASH AND LYNCH, L.L.P.
Wilmington, NC....Civil Trial Practice; General Practice; Insurance Defense

HOGUE & LANNIS
Pittsburgh, PA....Business Law; Commercial Litigation

HOHMANN & TAUBE, L.L.P.
Austin, TX....Banking Law; Bankruptcy Law; Civil Trial Practice; Insurance Defense

HOHN & SCHEÜERLE
Philadelphia, PA....Civil Trial Practice

HOIDAL & HANNAH, P.L.C.
Phoenix, AZ....Criminal Trial Practice

HOLAHAN, GUMPPER & DOWLING
Fairfield, CT....Civil Trial Practice

HOLAHAN, MALLOY, MAYBAUGH, MONNICH & DELIE
Troy, MI................................Civil Trial Practice; Environmental Law; Insurance Defense; Medical Malpractice; Personal Injury; Product Liability Law; Professional Liability; Trust and Estates, Wills and Probate

HOLBROOK, HEAVEN & OSBORN, P.A.
Kansas City, KS.......................Civil Trial Practice; General Practice; Insurance Defense

HOLBROOK & PITT
Ashland, KY...........................Real Estate Law

HOLCOMB DUNBAR, A PROFESSIONAL ASSOCIATION
Clarksdale, MS.........................Civil Trial Practice; Commercial Law; General Practice; Insurance Defense; Trust and Estates, Wills and Probate; Workers Compensation
Oxford, MS..............................Bankruptcy Law; Civil Trial Practice; Commercial Law; General Practice; Insurance Defense; Labor and Employment Law
Southaven, MS.........................Civil Trial Practice; Commercial Law; General Practice; Insurance Defense

HOLCOMBE, BOMAR, GUNN AND BRADFORD, P.A.
Spartanburg, SC.......................Civil Trial Practice; General Practice; Medical Malpractice; Product Liability Law

HOLDER, HOLLY I., P.C.
Denver, CO.............................Environmental Law; Natural Resources Law

HOLDMANN, LEE F., CHARTERED
Bethesda, MD..........................Arbitration; Trust and Estates, Wills and Probate

HOLLAND & BONZAGNI, P.C.
Springfield, MA........................Patent, Trademark, Copyright and Unfair Competition

HOLLAND & HART LLP
Denver, CO.............................General Practice

HOLLAND KAUFMANN & BARTELS, LLC
Greenwich, CT.........................Business Law; Civil Trial Practice; Commercial Litigation; Family Law; General Practice; Land Use Law; Real Estate Law; Trust and Estates, Wills and Probate

HOLLAND & KNIGHT LLP
San Francisco, CA....................General Practice
Washington, DC.......................General Practice
Fort Lauderdale, FL..................General Practice
Jacksonville, FL......................General Practice
Lakeland, FL...........................General Practice
Melbourne, FL.........................General Practice
Miami, FL...............................General Practice
Orlando, FL............................General Practice
St. Petersburg, FL....................General Practice
Tallahassee, FL.......................General Practice
Tampa, FL..............................General Practice
West Palm Beach, FL................General Practice
Atlanta, GA.............................General Practice
Falls Church, VA......................General Practice

HOLLEMAN, BOYCE, A PROFESSIONAL CORPORATION
Gulfport, MS............................Business Law; Civil Trial Practice; Corporate Law; Criminal Trial Practice; Family Law; General Practice; Government Contracts; Medical Malpractice; Personal Injury; Product Liability Law; Workers Compensation

HOLLEY, ALBERTSON & POLK, P.C.
Golden, CO.............................Civil Trial Practice; Construction Law; Land Use Law; Real Estate Law

HOLLIMAN LANGHOLZ RUNNELS FORSMAN & SELLERS, A PROFESSIONAL CORPORATION
Tulsa, OK...............................General Practice; Natural Resources Law

HOLLINS, SCHECHTER, FEINSTEIN & CONDAS, A PROFESSIONAL CORPORATION
Orange, CA.............................Insurance Defense

HOLLINS, WAGSTER & YARBROUGH, P.C.
Nashville, TN..........................Civil Trial Practice; Criminal Trial Practice; Insurance Defense

HOLLIS AND JOHNSON
Chicago, IL.............................Banking Law; Bankruptcy Law; Business Law; Commercial Law; Commercial Litigation; Real Estate Law

HOLLISTER & BRACE, A PROFESSIONAL CORPORATION
Santa Barbara, CA....................Business Law; Civil Trial Practice; Energy Law; Environmental Law; Land Use Law; Natural Resources Law; Real Estate Law

HOLLOMAN, CHARLES R., P.A.
Ocala, FL...............................Criminal Trial Practice

HOLLORAN LAW FIRM, THE, P.C.
St. Louis, MO..........................Medical Malpractice; Personal Injury; Product Liability Law

HOLLOWAY, DOBSON, BACHMAN & JENNINGS, A PROFESSIONAL CORPORATION
Oklahoma City, OK...................Civil Trial Practice

HOLLOWAY ODEGARD & SWEENEY, P.C.
Phoenix, AZ............................Insurance Defense

HOLLOWAY & ROWLEY, P.C.
Houston, TX............................Civil Trial Practice

HOLLOWELL, PEACOCK & MEYER, P.A.
Raleigh, NC............................Health Care Law

HOLLSTEIN KEATING CATTELL JOHNSON & GOLDSTEIN, P.C.
Philadelphia, PA......................Admiralty/Maritime Law; Commercial Litigation; Product Liability Law; Toxic Torts

HOLME ROBERTS & OWEN LLP
Boulder, CO............................General Practice; Intellectual Property Law
Colorado Springs, CO................General Practice; Intellectual Property Law; Nonprofit and Tax Exempt Organizations
Denver, CO.............................Banking Law; Civil Trial Practice; Environmental Law; General Practice; Health Care Law; Intellectual Property Law; International Business Law; Labor and Employment Law; Municipal Bond/Public Authority Financing; Natural Resources Law; Nonprofit and Tax Exempt Organizations; Patent, Trademark, Copyright and Unfair Competition; Real Estate Law; Securities Law; Tax Law; Trust and Estates, Wills and Probate
Salt Lake City, UT....................General Practice; Nonprofit and Tax Exempt Organizations
London, England......................General Practice

HOLMES FIRM, THE, A PROFESSIONAL CORPORATION
Dallas, TX..............................Real Estate Law

HOLMES WEDDLE & BARCOTT, A PROFESSIONAL CORPORATION
Anchorage, AK.........................General Practice
Seattle, WA.............................General Practice

HOLMES, WOODS & GARZA
Dallas, TX..............................Family Law; Trust and Estates, Wills and Probate

HOLMSTROM & KENNEDY, P.C.
Rockford, IL............................General Practice

HOLPER, WELSH & MITCHELL, LTD.
Phoenix, AZ............................Bankruptcy Law; Business Law; Commercial Litigation; Real Estate Law
Minneapolis, MN......................Bankruptcy Law; Business Law; Commercial Litigation; Real Estate Law

HOLT, LONGEST, WALL & BLAETZ, P.L.L.C.
Burlington, NC.........................General Practice

HOLT NEY ZATCOFF & WASSERMAN, LLP
Atlanta, GA.............................Business Law; Civil Trial Practice; Commercial Law; Communications Law; Environmental Law; General Practice; Municipal and Zoning Law; Real Estate Law; Tax Law

HOLT & WATT
Reidsville, NC..........................Real Estate Law

HOLT YORK MCDARRIS, LLP
Raleigh, NC............................Municipal and Zoning Law

HOLTON HOWARD & GOODMAN, P.C.
Nashville, TN..........................Tax Law; Trust and Estates, Wills and Probate

HOLTORF, KOVARIK, ELLISON & MATHIS, P.C.
Gering, NE..............................General Practice; Insurance Defense

HOLTZMAN, ERIC H.
Hauppauge, NY........................Civil Trial Practice; Commercial Law; Commercial Litigation; Environmental Law; General Practice; Product Liability Law

HOLTZMAN, KRINZMAN, EQUELS & FURIA
Miami, FL...............................Administrative Law; Bankruptcy Law; Civil Trial Practice; Commercial Litigation; Corporate Law; Real Estate Law

HONEYCHURCH AND FINKAS
Fairfield, CA...........................Criminal Trial Practice

HONIGMAN MILLER SCHWARTZ AND COHN
Detroit, MI..............................Antitrust Law; Bankruptcy Law; Civil Trial Practice; Communications Law; Criminal Trial Practice; Environmental Law; General Practice; Health Care Law; Labor and Employment Law; Municipal Bond/Public Authority Financing; Natural Resources Law; Real Estate Law; Tax Law
Lansing, MI.............................Civil Trial Practice; Environmental Law; General Practice; Insurance Defense; Natural Resources Law; Tax Law; Transportation Law

HOOD LAW FIRM
Charleston, SC ....Civil Trial Practice; General Practice; Insurance Defense; Medical Malpractice; Personal Injury; Product Liability Law; Professional Liability

HOOD, L. PAUL, JR., A PROFESSIONAL LAW CORPORATION
Covington, LA ....Tax Law; Trust and Estates, Wills and Probate

HOOD & RAYNOLDS, P.C.
Tulsa, OK ....Family Law

HOOKER & RODRIGUEZ
Tucson, AZ ....Criminal Trial Practice

HOOPER, HATHAWAY, PRICE, BEUCHE & WALLACE
Ann Arbor, MI ....Business Law; Civil Trial Practice; Commercial Litigation; Corporate Law; Criminal Trial Practice; Employment Benefits Law; Environmental Law; Family Law; General Practice; Labor and Employment Law; Medical Malpractice; Personal Injury; Real Estate Law; Trust and Estates, Wills and Probate

HOOPER, LUNDY & BOOKMAN, INC.
Los Angeles, CA ....Health Care Law

HOOVER, ROBERT D., P.L.C., LAW OFFICES OF
Baton Rouge, LA ....Insurance Defense; Personal Injury

HOPGOOD, CALIMAFDE, KALIL & JUDLOWE LLP
New York, NY ....Intellectual Property Law; Patent, Trademark, Copyright and Unfair Competition

HOPKINS & CARLEY, A LAW CORPORATION
San Jose, CA ....Commercial Law; Corporate Law; Environmental Law; General Practice; Patent, Trademark, Copyright and Unfair Competition; Real Estate Law; Tax Law; Trust and Estates, Wills and Probate

HOPKINS, CRAWLEY, BAGWELL & UPSHAW, P.L.L.C.
Gulfport, MS ....Civil Trial Practice; Environmental Law; Insurance Defense; Personal Injury; Product Liability Law; Workers Compensation

HOPKINS LAW FIRM, A PROFESSIONAL ASSOCIATION
Little Rock, AR ....Commercial Law

HOPKINS RODEN CROCKETT HANSEN & HOOPES, PLLC
Boise, ID ....General Practice
Idaho Falls, ID ....General Practice

HOPKINS & SUTTER
Washington, DC ....General Practice; Tax Law
Chicago, IL ....Commercial Litigation; General Practice; Tax Law; Trust and Estates, Wills and Probate

HOPPE & STOKES, P.A.
Miami, FL ....Admiralty/Maritime Law; Medical Malpractice; Personal Injury

HOPPEL, MAYER & COLEMAN
Washington, DC ....Admiralty/Maritime Law

HOPPER, GALLIHER & TUCKER, P.C.
Indianapolis, IN ....Bankruptcy Law; Commercial Litigation; Creditors Rights

HOPSON AND HABENICHT, LTD.
Chester, VA ....Civil Trial Practice

HORGER, BARNWELL & REID, L.L.P.
Orangeburg, SC ....General Practice

HÖRGER, HÖRGER, LANIER & KNIGHT, L.L.P.
Orangeburg, SC ....Civil Trial Practice

HORLICK, MICHAEL D., P.A.
Venice, FL ....Corporate Law; Trust and Estates, Wills and Probate

HORN, JEROLD I.
Peoria, IL ....Trust and Estates, Wills and Probate

HORN, ARTHUR S., P.A.
Nutley, NJ ....Real Estate Law; Trust and Estates, Wills and Probate

HORNBERGER, GHAZARIANS & BREWER
Los Angeles, CA ....Civil Trial Practice

HORNE, BISTROW & DULBERG, P.C.
Phoenix, AZ ....Civil Trial Practice; Commercial Litigation; Construction Law; Intellectual Property Law; Personal Injury

HORNE, FOY S., JR., P.C.
Athens, GA ....Personal Injury; Workers Compensation

HORNE, HOLLINGSWORTH & PARKER, A PROFESSIONAL ASSOCIATION
Little Rock, AR ....General Practice

HORNECKER, COWLING, HASSEN & HEYSELL, L.L.P.
Medford, OR ....General Practice

HORNSBY, WATSON & MEGINNISS
Huntsville, AL ....Civil Trial Practice; Personal Injury; Product Liability Law; Workers Compensation

HORNTHAL, RILEY, ELLIS & MALAND, L.L.P.
Elizabeth City, NC ....Civil Trial Practice; General Practice

HOROWITZ, EDWARD J., A PROFESSIONAL CORPORATION
Los Angeles, CA ....Appellate Practice

HOROWITZ, FORAN & SONNTAG, P.A.
Greenbelt, MD ....Medical Malpractice; Personal Injury

HORRIGAN & GOEHRS, L.L.P.
Houston, TX ....Trust and Estates, Wills and Probate

HORTON, KNOX, CARTER & FOOTE
El Centro, CA ....General Practice; Insurance Defense; Trust and Estates, Wills and Probate

HORTY, SPRINGER & MATTERN, P.C.
Pittsburgh, PA ....Health Care Law

HORVITZ & LEVY, LLP
Los Angeles, CA ....Appellate Practice; Commercial Litigation; Health Care Law; Insurance Defense; Intellectual Property Law

HORWATT, MICHAEL, & ASSOCIATES P.C.
McLean, VA ....Business Law; Commercial Law; Real Estate Law

HORWITZ & FUSSELL, A PROF. ASSN., LAW OFFICES OF
Orlando, FL ....Criminal Trial Practice

HOSKIN, FARINA, ALDRICH & KAMPF, PROFESSIONAL CORPORATION
Grand Junction, CO ....General Practice

HOSTAK, HENZL & BICHLER, S.C.
Racine, WI ....General Practice

HOSTETLER & KOWALIK, P.C.
Indianapolis, IN ....Bankruptcy Law; Commercial Law; Creditors Rights

HOTTELL, DENNIS M. & ASSOCIATES
Fairfax, VA ....Family Law

HOTZ & ASSOCIATES, P.C.
Tucker, GA ....Banking Law; Civil Trial Practice

HOURIGAN, KLUGER & QUINN, A PROFESSIONAL CORPORATION
Wilkes-Barre, PA ....General Practice; Labor and Employment Law; Medical Malpractice; Personal Injury; Real Estate Law; Trust and Estates, Wills and Probate

HOUSE, KINGSMILL & RIESS, L.L.C.
New Orleans, LA ....Civil Trial Practice

HOUSSIERE, DURANT & HOUSSIERE, LLP
Houston, TX ....Medical Malpractice; Product Liability Law; Securities Law

HOUSTON, PHILLIP C., P.A.
West Palm Beach, FL ....Personal Injury

HOVDE LAW FIRM
Indianapolis, IN ....Construction Law; Medical Malpractice; Personal Injury; Product Liability Law

HOVEY & KIRBY, A PROFESSIONAL CORPORATION
San Diego, CA ....Bankruptcy Law; Business Law; Civil Trial Practice; Commercial Law; Construction Law; Environmental Law; Municipal and Zoning Law; Real Estate Law

HOWARD, JOHN H.
Ventura, CA ....Civil Trial Practice

HOWARD, BRENNER & NASS, P.C.
Philadelphia, PA ....Civil Trial Practice; Toxic Torts

HOWARD, CARSWELL & BENNETT, P.C.
Jesup, GA ....General Practice; Insurance Defense

HOWARD, DAVIS & BUNT, P.C.
Tyler, TX ....Medical Malpractice

HOWARD, GREEN & MCDARRIS, L.L.P.
Raleigh, NC ....Family Law; General Practice

HOWARD & HOWARD ATTORNEYS, P.C.
Peoria, IL ....Banking Law; Business Law; Commercial Litigation; Communications Law; Environmental Law; General Practice; Labor and Employment Law; Municipal Bond/Public Authority Financing; Public Utilities Law

HOWARD & HOWARD ATTORNEYS, P.C. — *Continued*

Bloomfield Hills, MI..........Antitrust Law; Banking Law; Bankruptcy Law; Business Law; Commercial Litigation; Environmental Law; General Practice; Immigration and Naturalization; Labor and Employment Law; Municipal Bond/Public Authority Financing; Patent, Trademark, Copyright and Unfair Competition; Real Estate Law; Securities Law; Tax Law

Kalamazoo, MI..........Banking Law; Bankruptcy Law; Business Law; Commercial Litigation; General Practice; Real Estate Law; Securities Law

Lansing, MI..........Administrative Law; Banking Law; Business Law; Commercial Litigation; General Practice; Labor and Employment Law; Municipal Bond/Public Authority Financing; Real Estate Law; Tax Law

HOWARD, LEGGANS, PIERCY & HOWARD

Mount Vernon, IL..........General Practice

HOWARD, MACKIE

Calgary, AB, Canada..........General Practice

HOWARD ROME MARTIN & RIDLEY LLP

Redwood City, CA..........Civil Trial Practice; Insurance Defense

HOWD & LUDORF

Hartford, CT..........General Practice; Insurance Defense

HOWE, EDWIN A., P.C., THE LAW FIRM OF

Denver, CO..........Civil Trial Practice; Medical Malpractice; Personal Injury

HOWE, GEDNEY M., III, P.A.

Charleston, SC..........Civil Trial Practice; Criminal Trial Practice; Personal Injury; Product Liability Law

HOWE, WATERS & CARPENTER, P.A.

Hendersonville, NC..........General Practice; Real Estate Law

HOWELL, JOEL W. III

Jackson, MS..........Civil Trial Practice

HOWELL & HAFERKAMP, L.C.

St. Louis, MO..........Patent, Trademark, Copyright and Unfair Competition

HOWELL, LEMBHARD G., P.S., LAW OFFICES OF

Seattle, WA..........Personal Injury

HOWES, JOHN R., A PROFESSIONAL ASSOCIATION

Fort Lauderdale, FL..........Criminal Trial Practice

HOWETT, KISSINGER & MILES, P.C.

Harrisburg, PA..........Family Law

HOWIE & SWEENEY, L.L.P.

Dallas, TX..........Aviation Law; Medical Malpractice; Personal Injury; Product Liability Law

HOWLAND, DAVID R. LAW OFFICES OF

Miami, FL..........Insurance Defense

HOWREY & SIMON

Washington, DC..........General Practice

HOWSER, NEWMAN & BESLEY, L.L.C.

Columbia, SC..........Insurance Defense; Product Liability Law; Professional Liability; Workers Compensation

HOWSON & HOWSON

Spring House, PA..........Patent, Trademark, Copyright and Unfair Competition

HOYLE, MORRIS & KERR LLP

Philadelphia, PA..........Civil Trial Practice; General Practice

HOYLE, WILLIAM V., JR., P.C.

Newport News, VA..........Civil Trial Practice

HRONES AND GARRITY

Boston, MA..........Criminal Trial Practice

HUANG & MITCHELL, A PROFESSIONAL LAW CORPORATION

Los Angeles, CA..........Commercial Litigation

HUBBARD, CATES & LONG

Roxboro, NC..........General Practice

HUBBARD, SMITH, MCILWAIN, BRAKEFIELD & BROWDER, P.C.

Tuscaloosa, AL..........Banking Law; Bankruptcy Law; Business Law; Civil Trial Practice; General Practice; Tax Law

HUBER, BOOK, CORTESE, HAPPE & BROWN, P.L.C.

Des Moines, IA..........Civil Trial Practice; Creditors Rights; Insurance Defense; Legal Malpractice; Personal Injury; Product Liability Law; Professional Liability; Workers Compensation

HUBER AND WALDRON

Allentown, PA..........Criminal Trial Practice; Personal Injury

HUCKABAY, MUNSON, ROWLETT & TILLEY, P.A.

Little Rock, AR..........Civil Trial Practice; Insurance Defense; Medical Malpractice; Personal Injury; Product Liability Law; Workers Compensation

HUCKABY, FLEMING, FRAILEY, CHAFFIN, CORDELL, GREENWOOD & PERRYMAN, L.L.P.

Oklahoma City, OK..........Civil Trial Practice; Insurance Defense

HUDDLESTON, BOLEN, BEATTY, PORTER & COPEN

Charleston, WV..........General Practice

Huntington, WV..........General Practice

HUDGINS LAW FIRM

Alexandria, VA..........Civil Trial Practice; Insurance Defense

HUERTA, MARCELINO J., III, P.A.

Tampa, FL..........Criminal Trial Practice

HUFF LAW OFFICES

Harlan, KY..........General Practice; Insurance Defense; Labor and Employment Law

HUFF, MORAN & ORRON

Cranbury, NJ..........Elder Law

HUFFAKER & CONWAY, A PROFESSIONAL CORPORATION

Albuquerque, NM..........Antitrust Law; Commercial Litigation; Insurance Defense

Santa Fe, NM..........Administrative Law; Antitrust Law; Appellate Practice; Commercial Litigation; Environmental Law; Insurance Defense; Natural Resources Law

HUFFAKER, GREEN & HUFFAKER

Tahoka, TX..........General Practice

HUFFINE, DAVID E., P.A.

Wilmington, NC..........Real Estate Law

HUFFORD, HORSTMAN, MONGINI, PARNELL & MCCARTHY, P.C.

Flagstaff, AZ..........Arbitration; Commercial Law; Family Law; Labor and Employment Law; Municipal and Zoning Law; Real Estate Law; Trust and Estates, Wills and Probate

HUGHES, AMYS

Toronto, ON, Canada..........Insurance Defense

HUGHES LAW OFFICES

Sioux Falls, SD..........Business Law; Civil Trial Practice; Health Care Law; Municipal and Zoning Law; Personal Injury; Real Estate Law

HUGHES & LUCE, L.L.P.

Dallas, TX..........Arbitration; Banking Law; Bankruptcy Law; Business Law; Civil Trial Practice; Commercial Law; Criminal Trial Practice; Employment Benefits Law; Energy Law; General Practice; Intellectual Property Law; Labor and Employment Law; Real Estate Law; Securities Law; Sports and Entertainment Law; Tax Law; Trust and Estates, Wills and Probate

HUGHES, MATHEWS & DIDIER, P.A.

St. Cloud, MN..........Business Law; Civil Trial Practice; Commercial Law; Health Care Law; Labor and Employment Law

HUGHES & NUNN

San Diego, CA..........Insurance Defense

HUGHES & SCHACHT, P.S.

Bellingham, WA..........Patent, Trademark, Copyright and Unfair Competition

HUGHES & STRUMOR, LTD. CO.

Albuquerque, NM..........Municipal Bond/Public Authority Financing; Securities Law

HUGHEY, FLICK & CATANIA

Media, PA..........Criminal Trial Practice; Personal Injury

HUGIE, ELDON R.

Bakersfield, CA..........Business Law; Trust and Estates, Wills and Probate

HUIE, FERNAMBUCQ AND STEWART, LLP

Birmingham, AL..........Civil Trial Practice; Medical Malpractice; Product Liability Law

HULL, NORMAN LINDER, P.A.

Orlando, FL..........Bankruptcy Law; Business Law; Civil Trial Practice; Commercial Litigation; Construction Law

HULL, TOWILL, NORMAN, BARRETT & SALLEY, A PROFESSIONAL CORPORATION

Augusta, GA..........Arbitration; Business Law; Civil Trial Practice; Construction Law; Corporate Law; Environmental Law; General Practice; Insurance Defense; Real Estate Law; Securities Law; Tax Law; Trust and Estates, Wills and Probate

HULLVERSON & HULLVERSON, L.L.C.
St. Louis, MO..........................Medical Malpractice; Personal Injury

HULLVERSON LAW FIRM, THE
St. Louis, MO..........................Admiralty/Maritime Law; Medical Malpractice; Personal Injury; Product Liability Law

HULL, WEBBER & REIS, LLP
Rutland, VT..........................General Practice

HULTSTRAND, CHARLES, P.C.
Mesa, AZ..........................Commercial Litigation

HUMMEL & COAN
Louisville, KY..........................Insurance Defense; Personal Injury

HUMPHREYS DUNLAP WELLFORD ACUFF & STANTON, A PROFESSIONAL CORPORATION
Memphis, TN..........................General Practice

HUNEGS, STONE, KOENIG, LENEAVE & KVAS, P.A.
Minneapolis, MN..........................Admiralty/Maritime Law; Aviation Law; Civil Trial Practice; Medical Malpractice; Personal Injury; Product Liability Law

HUNT, DAVID E.
Portland, ME..........................Trust and Estates, Wills and Probate

HUNT, RUSSELL DAVID
Waco, TX..........................Criminal Trial Practice

HUNT, COOK, RIGGS, MEHR & MILLER, P.A.
Boca Raton, FL..........................Family Law; General Practice; Trust and Estates, Wills and Probate

HUNT & ROSS, A PROFESSIONAL ASSOCIATION
Clarksdale, MS..........................Administrative Law; General Practice; Municipal and Zoning Law; Natural Resources Law; Public Utilities Law; Real Estate Law

HUNTER, RICHARD S. JR.
Raleigh, NC..........................Personal Injury

HUNTER, BLAZIER, O'DOWD & MORENO, A PROFESSIONAL LAW CORPORATION
Lake Charles, LA..........................Tax Law; Trust and Estates, Wills and Probate

HUNTER, JOHNSTON, ELAM & BENJAMIN, PLLC
Greensboro, NC..........................General Practice

HUNTER, MACLEAN, EXLEY & DUNN, P.C.
Savannah, GA..........................Business Law; Civil Trial Practice; Environmental Law; General Practice; Labor and Employment Law; Tax Law; Trust and Estates, Wills and Probate

HUNTER RICHEY DI BENEDETTO & BREWER, LLP
Sacramento, CA..........................Business Law; Civil Trial Practice; Construction Law; Environmental Law; Health Care Law; Land Use Law; Mergers and Acquisitions; Patent, Trademark, Copyright and Unfair Competition; Real Estate Law; Trademark, Copyright and Unfair Competition

HUNTER, SMITH & DAVIS, LLP
Johnson City, TN..........................General Practice
Kingsport, TN..........................Banking Law; Civil Trial Practice; Environmental Law; General Practice; Labor and Employment Law; Municipal Bond/Public Authority Financing; Tax Law

HUNTON & WILLIAMS
Richmond, VA..........................General Practice

HUPPERT & SWINDLEHURST, P.C.
Livingston, MT..........................General Practice

HUPY, MICHAEL F., & ASSOCIATES, S.C.
Milwaukee, WI..........................Personal Injury

HURLEY, FOX, SELIG & KELLEHER
Stony Point, NY..........................Civil Trial Practice; Commercial Law; General Practice; Land Use Law; Municipal and Zoning Law; Personal Injury; Product Liability Law; Real Estate Law

HURLEY, JOSEPH A., P.A.
Wilmington, DE..........................Criminal Trial Practice

HURLEY, LYNCH & RE, P.C.
Bend, OR..........................Civil Trial Practice; General Practice

HURTUK & DAROFF CO., L.P.A.
Cleveland, OH..........................Real Estate Law

HUSKEY, DOW T.
Dothan, AL..........................Business Law

HUSTEAD LAW FIRM, THE, A PROFESSIONAL CORPORATION
Denver, CO..........................Commercial Litigation; Insurance Defense; Labor and Employment Law

HUTCHINS & ASSOCIATES, LLC
Denver, CO..........................Trust and Estates, Wills and Probate

HUTCHINS, WHEELER & DITTMAR, A PROFESSIONAL CORPORATION
Boston, MA..........................General Practice

HUTCHISON, MAMELE & COOVER, P.A.
Sanford, FL..........................Family Law

HUTCHISON & MASON PLLC
Raleigh, NC..........................Business Law

HUTTON & HUTTON
Wichita, KS..........................Medical Malpractice; Personal Injury; Product Liability Law

HUTTON, LAURY, YOUNG & LIETZ
Danville, IL..........................Civil Trial Practice; General Practice; Insurance Defense

HWANG & ASSOCIATES, P.C.
Philadelphia, PA..........................Civil Trial Practice

HYATT & HYATT, P.C.
Decatur, GA..........................General Practice; Personal Injury; Workers Compensation

HYATT, PETERS & WEBER
Annapolis, MD..........................Banking Law; Civil Trial Practice; Commercial Law; Family Law; Insurance Defense; Medical Malpractice; Real Estate Law

HYDE, MILLER, OWEN & TROST, A PROFESSIONAL CORPORATION
Sacramento, CA..........................Government Contracts; Municipal and Zoning Law

HYMAN LIPPITT, P.C.
Birmingham, MI..........................Bankruptcy Law; Business Law; Civil Trial Practice; Commercial Law; Commercial Litigation; Corporate Law; Family Law; General Practice; International Business Law; Labor and Employment Law; Land Use Law; Mergers and Acquisitions; Municipal and Zoning Law; Real Estate Law; Securities Law; Tax Law; Trust and Estates, Wills and Probate

HYMAN, STUART I., P.A.
Orlando, FL..........................Criminal Trial Practice

ICE MILLER DONADIO & RYAN
Indianapolis, IN..........................Antitrust Law; Banking Law; Bankruptcy Law; Civil Trial Practice; Commercial Law; Communications Law; Construction Law; Creditors Rights; Employment Benefits Law; Environmental Law; General Practice; Health Care Law; Immigration and Naturalization; International Trade Law; Labor and Employment Law; Medical Malpractice; Municipal Bond/Public Authority Financing; Natural Resources Law; Personal Injury; Real Estate Law; Securities Law; Tax Law; Trademark, Copyright and Unfair Competition; Trust and Estates, Wills and Probate

ICENOGLE, NORTON & SETER, A PROFESSIONAL CORPORATION
Greenwood Village, CO..........................Civil Trial Practice; Municipal and Zoning Law; Transportation Law

IFSHIN & FRIEDMAN, P.L.L.C.
Washington, DC..........................Civil Trial Practice

IMAI, TADLOCK & KEENEY, LLP
San Francisco, CA..........................Insurance Defense

INDIANO, WILLIAMS & WEINSTEIN-BACAL
San Juan, PR..........................Bankruptcy Law; Civil Trial Practice; Commercial Law; Construction Law; Personal Injury

INGBER & ARONSON, P.A.
Minneapolis, MN..........................Immigration and Naturalization

INGERMAN & HORWITZ, L.L.P.
Baltimore, MD..........................Personal Injury

INGE, TWITTY & DUFFY
Mobile, AL..........................Civil Trial Practice; General Practice; Insurance Defense; Professional Liability

INGHAM, SAMUEL D. III
Los Angeles, CA..........................Natural Resources Law; Real Estate Law; Tax Law; Trust and Estates, Wills and Probate

INGLESBY, FALLIGANT, HORNE, COURINGTON & NASH, A PROFESSIONAL CORPORATION
Savannah, GA..........................Bankruptcy Law

INGLIS, LEDBETTER & GOWER
Los Angeles, CA..........................Corporate Law

INGLISH & MONACO, P.C.
Jefferson City, MO..........................Civil Trial Practice; General Practice; Insurance Defense

INGRAM YUZEK GAINEN CARROLL & BERTOLOTTI, LLP
New York, NY........................Appellate Practice; Banking Law; Business Law; Civil Trial Practice; Commercial Law; Construction Law; General Practice; Insurance Defense; Real Estate Law; Tax Law

INTERNATIONAL LAW FIRM, THE
Riyadh, Saudi Arabia..............General Practice

INZER, HANEY, JOHNSON & MCWHORTER, P.A.
Gadsden, AL..............................Civil Trial Practice; Corporate Law; General Practice

IRELAND, CARROLL & KELLEY, P.C.
Tyler, TX...................................Appellate Practice; Bankruptcy Law; Civil Trial Practice; Insurance Defense

IRELL & MANELLA LLP
Los Angeles, CA........................General Practice

IRESON & WEIZEL, P.C.
Houston, TX..............................Personal Injury; Product Liability Law

IRVIN, STANFORD & KESSLER, LLP
Atlanta, GA...............................Labor and Employment Law

ISAACSON & ISAACSON
Greensboro, NC.........................Business Law; Commercial Law; General Practice; Municipal and Zoning Law; Real Estate Law

ISEMAN, CUNNINGHAM, RIESTER & HYDE, LLP
Albany, NY.................................Civil Trial Practice; Commercial Litigation; Construction Law; Corporate Law; Health Care Law; Nonprofit and Tax Exempt Organizations; Personal Injury; Real Estate Law; Tax Law; Toxic Torts

ISICOFF & RAGATZ, P.A.
Miami, FL...................................Trademark, Copyright and Unfair Competition

ISOM, DAVID K. LAW OFFICES
Salt Lake City, UT....................Commercial Litigation

ISRAELSON, SALSBURY, CLEMENTS & BEKMAN, L.L.C.
Baltimore, MD...........................Admiralty/Maritime Law; Civil Trial Practice; Medical Malpractice; Personal Injury; Product Liability Law

IVENER & HOLT LLP
Los Angeles, CA........................Immigration and Naturalization

IVERSON, YOAKUM, PAPIANO & HATCH
Los Angeles, CA........................Appellate Practice; Business Law; Civil Trial Practice; Environmental Law; General Practice; Labor and Employment Law; Product Liability Law

IVEY, BARNUM & O'MARA, LLC
Greenwich, CT...........................General Practice

IVEY, MCCLELLAN, GATTON & TALCOTT, L.L.P.
Greensboro, NC.........................Bankruptcy Law; General Practice

IVINS, PHILLIPS & BARKER, CHARTERED
Washington, DC.........................Tax Law; Trust and Estates, Wills and Probate

IVONE, DEVINE & JENSEN, LLP
Lake Success, NY......................Civil Trial Practice; Insurance Defense; Medical Malpractice

JABURG & WILK, P.C.
Phoenix, AZ...............................Bankruptcy Law; Business Law; Commercial Litigation; Trust and Estates, Wills and Probate

JACKS, ADAMS & WESTERFIELD, P.A.
Cleveland, MS...........................General Practice; Insurance Defense; Product Liability Law

JACKSON & CAMPBELL, P.C.
Washington, DC.........................General Practice

JACKSON HARRIS BURLINGAME & HUBERT, LLC
Danielson, CT............................General Practice

JACKSON & JESSUP, P.C.
Arlington, VA.............................Transportation Law

JACKSON & KELLY
Washington, DC.........................General Practice
Lexington, KY............................General Practice
Charleston, WV..........................Administrative Law; Admiralty/Maritime Law; Antitrust Law; Banking Law; Bankruptcy Law; Civil Trial Practice; Commercial Law; Construction Law; Criminal Trial Practice; Employment Benefits Law; Environmental Law; General Practice; Health Care Law; Insurance Defense; Labor and Employment Law; Municipal Bond/Public Authority Financing; Natural Resources Law; Public Utilities Law; Real Estate Law; Securities Law; Tax Law; Transportation Law; Trust and Estates, Wills and Probate; Workers Compensation
Martinsburg, WV........................General Practice
Morgantown, WV........................General Practice
New Martinsville, WV...............General Practice

JACKSON, LEWIS, SCHNITZLER & KRUPMAN
White Plains, NY.......................Labor and Employment Law

JACKSON, O'KEEFE AND PHELAN
Hartford, CT.............................Appellate Practice; Civil Trial Practice; Family Law; General Practice; Insurance Defense; Medical Malpractice; Personal Injury

JACKSON WALKER L.L.P.
Austin, TX.................................Administrative Law; Business Law; Communications Law; Environmental Law; General Practice; Health Care Law; Labor and Employment Law
Dallas, TX.................................Appellate Practice; Business Law; Civil Trial Practice; Communications Law; Computer Law; General Practice; Health Care Law; Insurance Defense; International Business Law; Labor and Employment Law; Patent, Trademark, Copyright and Unfair Competition; Personal Injury; Product Liability Law; Real Estate Law; Tax Law
Fort Worth, TX..........................Civil Trial Practice; General Practice; Insurance Defense; Labor and Employment Law; Real Estate Law
Houston, TX..............................Business Law; Civil Trial Practice; Communications Law; Energy Law; Environmental Law; General Practice; Insurance Defense; International Business Law; Personal Injury
San Angelo, TX.........................Civil Trial Practice; General Practice
San Antonio, TX........................Civil Trial Practice; General Practice; Health Care Law; Insurance Defense; Labor and Employment Law; Patent, Trademark, Copyright and Unfair Competition; Personal Injury

JACKSON WHITE GARDNER WEECH & WALKER, P.C.
Mesa, AZ...................................Business Law; Commercial Litigation; Construction Law; Elder Law; Labor and Employment Law; Municipal and Zoning Law; Personal Injury; Real Estate Law; Tax Law; Trust and Estates, Wills and Probate

JACOB, ARTHUR LAW OFFICES OF
Hackensack, NJ.........................Patent, Trademark, Copyright and Unfair Competition

JACOB & WEINGARTEN
Troy, MI....................................Commercial Litigation; Creditors Rights; Real Estate Law

JACOBOWITZ, GARFINKEL & LESMAN
New York, NY............................Insurance Defense

JACOBOWITZ, GRABELLE, DEFINO, MCGOUGHRAN & LATIMER
Oakhurst, NJ.............................Family Law

JACOBS, REX W.
Long Beach, CA.........................Personal Injury

JACOBS, DARLEEN M., A PROFESSIONAL LAW CORPORATION
New Orleans, LA.......................Admiralty/Maritime Law; Personal Injury

JACOBS, GRUDBERG, BELT & DOW, P.C.
New Haven, CT..........................Civil Trial Practice; General Practice

JACOBS & JACOBS
New Haven, CT..........................Civil Trial Practice; Medical Malpractice; Personal Injury; Product Liability Law

JACOBS AND SLAWSKY, P.A.
Atlanta, GA...............................Labor and Employment Law

JACOBSON AND GOLDBERG, LLP
Garden City, NY........................Administrative Law; Health Care Law

JACOBSON, PRICE, HOLMAN & STERN, PLLC
Washington, DC.........................Patent, Trademark, Copyright and Unfair Competition

JACOBSON & SCHWARTZ
Rockville Centre, NY................Appellate Practice; Insurance Defense; Product Liability Law

JAECKLE FLEISCHMANN & MUGEL, LLP
Buffalo, NY...............................General Practice

JAFFE AND CLEMENS
Beverly Hills, CA......................Family Law

JAFFE, RAITT, HEUER & WEISS, PROFESSIONAL CORPORATION
Detroit, MI.................................Bankruptcy Law; Business Law; Civil Trial Practice; Commercial Litigation; Employment Benefits Law; Environmental Law; Family Law; General Practice; Health Care Law; Municipal and Zoning Law; Municipal Bond/Public Authority Financing; Real Estate Law; Securities Law; Tax Law; Trust and Estates, Wills and Probate
Southfield, MI...........................General Practice

JAMES, GARY J.
Oklahoma City, OK................Criminal Trial Practice

JAMES, DENECKE, URRUTIA, MARMADUKE & LAWSON, P.C.
Portland, OR................Business Law; Civil Trial Practice; Mergers and Acquisitions; Real Estate Law

JAMES, GOLDMAN & HAUGLAND, P.C. A PROFESSIONAL CORPORATION
El Paso, TX................Banking Law; Bankruptcy Law; General Practice; Insurance Defense

JAMES, GRAY, BRONSON & SWANBERG, P.C.
Great Falls, MT................Civil Trial Practice

JAMES, POTTS AND WULFERS, INC.
Tulsa, OK................Business Law; Commercial Law; Real Estate Law; Tax Law; Trust and Estates, Wills and Probate

JAMIESON, MOORE, PESKIN & SPICER, A PROFESSIONAL CORPORATION
Princeton, NJ................General Practice

JAMIN, EBELL, SCHMITT & MASON, A PROFESSIONAL CORPORATION
Kodiak, AK................General Practice

JANET, WILLOUGHBY & GERSHON, LLC
Baltimore, MD................Medical Malpractice; Personal Injury; Product Liability Law

JANIK & FORBES
Cleveland, OH................Appellate Practice; Civil Trial Practice; Construction Law; Environmental Law; General Practice; Insurance Defense; Labor and Employment Law; Personal Injury; Product Liability Law; Securities Law; Trademark, Copyright and Unfair Competition

JANUSZEWSKI, MCQUILLAN AND DENIGRIS
New Britain, CT................General Practice

JARDINE & PAGANO, A PROFESSIONAL CORPORATION
Springfield, NJ................Labor and Employment Law; Trust and Estates, Wills and Probate

JAVERBAUM WURGAFT HICKS & ZARIN, A PROFESSIONAL CORPORATION
Springfield, NJ................Civil Trial Practice; Commercial Litigation; Medical Malpractice; Personal Injury; Product Liability Law; Professional Liability

JEANSONNE & REMONDET, L.L.C.
Lafayette, LA................Civil Trial Practice; Insurance Defense

JEFFCOAT, PIKE & NAPPIER, LLC
Myrtle Beach, SC................Trust and Estates, Wills and Probate

JEFFER, HOPKINSON & VOGEL
Hawthorne, NJ................Business Law; Civil Trial Practice; General Practice; Municipal and Zoning Law; Municipal Bond/Public Authority Financing; Real Estate Law

JEFFERS & BANACK, INCORPORATED
San Antonio, TX................Appellate Practice

JEFFERS, DANIELSON, SONN & AYLWARD, P.S.
Wenatchee, WA................General Practice

JEFFRIES, OLSON, FLOM & BULLIS, P.A.
Moorhead, MN................Civil Trial Practice; General Practice
Fargo, ND................Civil Trial Practice; General Practice

JELLIFFE, FERRELL, MORRIS, DOERGE & FOSTER
Harrisburg, IL................Civil Trial Practice; General Practice; Insurance Defense; Workers Compensation

JENKENS & GILCHRIST, A PROFESSIONAL CORPORATION
Dallas, TX................General Practice

JENKINS, GOODMAN & NEUMAN
San Francisco, CA................Commercial Law

JENKINS & KLING, P.C.
St. Louis, MO................Criminal Trial Practice; Real Estate Law

JENKINS MARZBAN LOGAN
Vancouver, BC, Canada................Arbitration; Civil Trial Practice; Commercial Litigation; Construction Law; Family Law; Real Estate Law

JENKINS & NELSON, P.C.
Cartersville, GA................General Practice

JENKINS & WILSON, P.A.
Durham, NC................Intellectual Property Law; Patent, Trademark, Copyright and Unfair Competition

JENNE, SCOTT & JENNE
Cleveland, TN................Civil Trial Practice; Construction Law; Medical Malpractice; Personal Injury; Product Liability Law; Workers Compensation

JENNER & BLOCK
Chicago, IL................General Practice

JENNINGS, HAUG & CUNNINGHAM, L.L.P.
Phoenix, AZ................Business Law; Civil Trial Practice; Construction Law; Personal Injury

JENNINGS, STROUSS & SALMON, P.L.C.
Phoenix, AZ................Banking Law; Bankruptcy Law; Civil Trial Practice; Environmental Law; General Practice; Health Care Law; Insurance Defense; Labor and Employment Law; Medical Malpractice; Municipal Bond/Public Authority Financing; Natural Resources Law; Personal Injury; Real Estate Law; Securities Law; Tax Law; Trademark, Copyright and Unfair Competition; Trust and Estates, Wills and Probate

JENSEN BAIRD GARDNER & HENRY
Kennebunk, ME................General Practice
Portland, ME................Banking Law; Civil Trial Practice; Environmental Law; General Practice; Real Estate Law; Trust and Estates, Wills and Probate

JENSEN, JACQUELINE M., INC.
Irvine, CA................Trust and Estates, Wills and Probate

JENSEN & KELLEY, P.A.
Phoenix, AZ................Family Law

JEPPSON, H. ROY, A PROFESSIONAL CORPORATION
Los Angeles, CA................Business Law; Commercial Litigation; Labor and Employment Law
Oxnard, CA................Business Law; Commercial Litigation; Labor and Employment Law

JESSOP & COMPANY, P.C.
Denver, CO................Bankruptcy Law

JESTER, MICHAEL H.
San Diego, CA................Patent, Trademark, Copyright and Unfair Competition

JETER & WILLIAMS, P.A.
Columbia, SC................Business Law

JEWELL, COLLINS & DELAY
Norfolk, NE................General Practice

JG, P.C. BUSINESS & CORPORATE LAW
Pleasanton, CA................Business Law; Corporate Law

JIMÉNEZ, GRAFFAM & LAUSELL
San Juan, PR................Admiralty/Maritime Law; Civil Trial Practice; Construction Law; Environmental Law; General Practice; Insurance Defense; Labor and Employment Law; Medical Malpractice; Personal Injury; Product Liability Law; Transportation Law

JIMENEZ, JORGE R., LAW OFFICES
San Juan, PR................Antitrust Law; Banking Law; Civil Trial Practice; Commercial Law; General Practice; Real Estate Law

JINKERSON, GUYTON N.
San Jose, CA................Criminal Trial Practice

JOANIS LAW GROUP, THE
Minneapolis, MN................Bankruptcy Law

JOANNES, JOHN A., A PROFESSIONAL CORPORATION
Los Angeles, CA................Immigration and Naturalization

JOENS, TIMOTHY L., & ASSOC., A PROF. CORP.
Irvine, CA................Appellate Practice; Business Law; Civil Trial Practice

JOHNS & CHRISTENSEN, A PROFESSIONAL CORPORATION
San Rafael, CA................Appellate Practice; Civil Trial Practice; Commercial Litigation; Insurance Defense; Legal Malpractice

JOHNS, FLAHERTY & RICE, S.C.
La Crosse, WI................General Practice

JOHNSON, DONALD L.
Chicago, IL................Professional Liability

JOHNSON, JAMES M.
Minden, LA................Business Law; Civil Trial Practice; Criminal Trial Practice; Family Law; Personal Injury

JOHNSON, JAY M.
Ventura, CA................Criminal Trial Practice; Family Law

JOHNSON AND ANGELO
Cleveland, OH................Environmental Law; Insurance Defense; Labor and Employment Law

JOHNSON, AYERS & MATTHEWS
Roanoke, VA................Insurance Defense

JOHNSON, BARRY L., P.A.
Hilton Head Island, SC .... Bankruptcy Law; Business Law; Commercial Litigation; Personal Injury; Real Estate Law

JOHNSON & BELL, LTD.
Chicago, IL .... Civil Trial Practice; Environmental Law; Insurance Defense; Medical Malpractice

JOHNSON, BLAKELY, POPE, BOKOR, RUPPEL & BURNS, P.A.
Clearwater, FL .... General Practice
Tampa, FL .... General Practice

JOHNSON & BOWEN
El Paso, TX .... General Practice

JOHNSON, BUNCE & NOBLE, P.C.
Peoria, IL .... General Practice

JOHNSON, CLIFTON, LARSON & CORSON, P.C.
Eugene, OR .... Personal Injury; Product Liability Law

JOHNSON & EDWARDS LLP
San Diego, CA .... Civil Trial Practice

JOHNSON EIESLAND HUFFMAN & CLAYBORNE LAW FIRM, LLP
Rapid City, SD .... Commercial Law; Insurance Defense; Medical Malpractice

JOHNSON, FERGUSON & PIPKIN
Houston, TX .... Personal Injury; Toxic Torts

JOHNSON, FLODMAN, GUENZEL, ESKE & WIDGER
Lincoln, NE .... Civil Trial Practice; Family Law; Health Care Law; Insurance Defense; Trust and Estates, Wills and Probate

JOHNSON, GARY C., P.S.C.
Pikeville, KY .... Commercial Law; Personal Injury

JOHNSON, GAVER & LEACH, LLP
Monterey, CA .... Trust and Estates, Wills and Probate

JOHNSON, GREEN, MILLER & GIBSON, P.A.
Milton, FL .... General Practice

JOHNSON, GRUSIN, KEE & SURPRISE, P.C.
Memphis, TN .... General Practice; Real Estate Law

JOHNSON, HESTER, WALTER & BRECKENRIDGE, L.L.P.
Ottumwa, IA .... General Practice

JOHNSON & HOULIHAN, S.C.
Rhinelander, WI .... General Practice

JOHNSON, JEAN E., JR., P.C.
Marietta, GA .... Medical Malpractice; Personal Injury

JOHNSON & JOHNSON, LAW OFFICES
Las Vegas, NV .... Trust and Estates, Wills and Probate

JOHNSON & JOHNSON, P.L.C.
Newport, KY .... Personal Injury

JOHNSON, JOHNSON, BARRIOS & YACOUBIAN, A PROFESSIONAL LAW CORPORATION
New Orleans, LA .... Admiralty/Maritime Law; Insurance Defense; Workers Compensation

JOHNSON, KENNEDY, DAHL & WILLIS
Wichita, KS .... General Practice; Insurance Defense

JOHNSON & LAMBETH
Wilmington, NC .... Criminal Trial Practice; Insurance Defense

JOHNSON LAW GROUP, THE
Seattle, WA .... Business Law; Commercial Law

JOHNSON & MCPHERSON, P.L.C.
Grosse Pointe Farms, MI .... Business Law; Real Estate Law; Trust and Estates, Wills and Probate

JOHNSON & OLIVER, A LEGAL PROFESSIONAL ASSOCIATION
Portsmouth, OH .... General Practice; Trust and Estates, Wills and Probate

JOHNSON & ROCHE
McLean, VA .... Personal Injury

JOHNSON, RODNEY G., LTD.
Phoenix, AZ .... Labor and Employment Law

JOHNSON, SCHACHTER & COLLINS, A PROFESSIONAL CORPORATION
Sacramento, CA .... Civil Trial Practice; Insurance Defense; Personal Injury; Product Liability Law; Professional Liability

JOHNSON, SIMMERMAN & BROUGHTON, L.C.
Clarksburg, WV .... Civil Trial Practice; Construction Law; Environmental Law; Medical Malpractice; Personal Injury; Tax Law; Trust and Estates, Wills and Probate

JOHNSON SMITH PENCE & HEATH LLP
Indianapolis, IN .... Administrative Law; Banking Law; Bankruptcy Law; Civil Trial Practice; Commercial Law; Environmental Law; General Practice; Health Care Law; Insurance Defense; Intellectual Property Law; Real Estate Law; Securities Law

JOHNSON & SYLVAN, P.C.
Dallas, TX .... Insurance Defense; Medical Malpractice

JOHNSON & TAYLOR
Pontiac, IL .... Real Estate Law; Tax Law; Trust and Estates, Wills and Probate

JOHNSON & WARD
Atlanta, GA .... Aviation Law; Business Law; Civil Trial Practice; General Practice; Personal Injury; Product Liability Law; Professional Liability

JOHNSON & WEBBERT, L.L.P.
Augusta, ME .... Aviation Law; Insurance Defense; Labor and Employment Law; Product Liability Law

JOHNSON & YANG, P.C.
Wheaton, MD .... Immigration and Naturalization

JOHNSTON, ALLISON & HORD, P.A.
Charlotte, NC .... Construction Law; General Practice

JOHNSTON, ARONSON & DIAMOND, A PROFESSIONAL CORPORATION
Harrisburg, PA .... Employment Benefits Law; Labor and Employment Law; Pension and Profit Sharing

JOHNSTON BARTON PROCTOR & POWELL LLP
Birmingham, AL .... Banking Law; Commercial Litigation; Communications Law; Construction Law; Health Care Law; Labor and Employment Law; Product Liability Law; Real Estate Law; Sports and Entertainment Law

JOHNSTON & DODD, P.L.C.
Phoenix, AZ .... Administrative Law; Civil Trial Practice; Health Care Law

JOHNSTON, HINESLEY, FLOWERS & CLENNEY, P.C., A PROFESSIONAL CORPORATION
Dothan, AL .... Mergers and Acquisitions; Securities Law; Tax Law

JOHNSTON, HOLROYD & ASSOCIATES
Princeton, WV .... General Practice; Personal Injury

JOHNSTON, POTTERFIELD & NATHANSON, P.C.
Iowa City, IA .... Bankruptcy Law; Civil Trial Practice; Commercial Law; Criminal Trial Practice; Family Law; Personal Injury; Trust and Estates, Wills and Probate

JOHNSTON • TOBEY, P.C.
Dallas, TX .... Legal Malpractice; Professional Liability

JOHNSTONE, ADAMS, BAILEY, GORDON AND HARRIS, L.L.C.
Mobile, AL .... Admiralty/Maritime Law; Antitrust Law; Banking Law; Bankruptcy Law; Business Law; Civil Trial Practice; Construction Law; Employment Benefits Law; Environmental Law; General Practice; Health Care Law; Insurance Defense; Labor and Employment Law; Natural Resources Law; Real Estate Law; Tax Law; Trust and Estates, Wills and Probate

JOHNSTONE, ADAMS, BAILEY, GORDON AND HARRIS, L.L.C.
Bay Minette, AL .... Business Law; Civil Trial Practice; General Practice

JOLLEY, URGA, WIRTH & WOODBURY
Las Vegas, NV .... Administrative Law; Appellate Practice; Banking Law; Bankruptcy Law; Business Law; Civil Trial Practice; Commercial Law; Commercial Litigation; Construction Law; Environmental Law; Family Law; General Practice; Labor and Employment Law; Municipal and Zoning Law; Natural Resources Law; Personal Injury; Real Estate Law; Transportation Law; Trust and Estates, Wills and Probate

JONAS & LASORTE
West Palm Beach, FL .... Commercial Litigation; Real Estate Law

JONASSEN, WILLIAM S., P.A.
Largo, FL .... Medical Malpractice; Personal Injury

JONES, JIM
Sallisaw, OK .... General Practice

JONES, O. F. III, LAW OFFICE OF
Victoria, TX .... Civil Trial Practice

JONES, RANDOLPH B.
Nashville, TN .... Arbitration; Commercial Law; Corporate Law; General Practice

JONES & BAHRET, CO., L.P.A.
Holland, OH .... Civil Trial Practice; Insurance Defense

JONES, BLECHMAN, WOLTZ & KELLY, P.C.
Newport News, VA ....General Practice

JONES, CHARTERED
Pocatello, ID ....General Practice

JONES, CORK & MILLER, LLP
Macon, GA ....General Practice

JONES, DAY, REAVIS & POGUE
Irvine, CA................................Civil Trial Practice; General Practice
Los Angeles, CA ....Antitrust Law; Bankruptcy Law; Civil Trial Practice; General Practice; Insurance Defense; Labor and Employment Law; Patent, Trademark, Copyright and Unfair Competition; Tax Law; Trademark, Copyright and Unfair Competition
Washington, DC.......................Antitrust Law; Civil Trial Practice; Criminal Trial Practice; General Practice; Labor and Employment Law; Municipal Bond/Public Authority Financing; Tax Law
Atlanta, GA ....Antitrust Law; Civil Trial Practice; General Practice; Labor and Employment Law; Municipal Bond/Public Authority Financing; Tax Law
Chicago, IL...............................Antitrust Law; Civil Trial Practice; Criminal Trial Practice; General Practice; Labor and Employment Law; Municipal Bond/Public Authority Financing; Tax Law
New York, NY.........................Civil Trial Practice; Criminal Trial Practice; General Practice; Insurance Defense; Municipal Bond/Public Authority Financing; Patent, Trademark, Copyright and Unfair Competition; Trademark, Copyright and Unfair Competition
Cleveland, OH..........................Antitrust Law; Civil Trial Practice; Criminal Trial Practice; General Practice; Insurance Defense; Labor and Employment Law; Municipal Bond/Public Authority Financing; Patent, Trademark, Copyright and Unfair Competition; Real Estate Law; Tax Law; Trademark, Copyright and Unfair Competition
Columbus, OH ....Civil Trial Practice; General Practice; Labor and Employment Law; Municipal Bond/Public Authority Financing
Pittsburgh, PA ....Civil Trial Practice; General Practice; Insurance Defense; Labor and Employment Law
Dallas, TX................................Antitrust Law; Civil Trial Practice; General Practice; Labor and Employment Law; Municipal Bond/Public Authority Financing; Tax Law
Sydney, New South Wales, Australia ....General Practice
Brussels, Belgium ....General Practice
Hong Kong, China....................General Practice
London, England ....General Practice; Tax Law
Paris, France.............................General Practice
Frankfurt/Main, Germany ......General Practice
Tokyo, Japan............................General Practice
Geneva, Switzerland................General Practice
Taipei, Taiwan..........................General Practice

JONES, E. STEWART
Troy, NY...................................Civil Trial Practice; Criminal Trial Practice; General Practice; Medical Malpractice; Personal Injury; Product Liability Law

JONES, GALLIGAN, KEY & LOZANO, L.L.P.
Weslaco, TX.............................Civil Trial Practice; General Practice

JONES, GARY L., CO., L.P.A.
Columbus, OH ....Administrative Law

JONES, GIVENS, GOTCHER & BOGAN, A PROFESSIONAL CORPORATION
Tulsa, OK.................................Business Law; General Practice

JONES, HEWSON & WOOLARD
Charlotte, NC...........................General Practice

JONES, JACKSON & MOLL, PLC
Fort Smith, AR.........................Civil Trial Practice; Insurance Defense

JONES AND JONES
Hackensack, NJ........................Banking Law; Commercial Law; Trust and Estates, Wills and Probate

JONES & JONES
Garden City, NY ....Civil Trial Practice; General Practice; Trust and Estates, Wills and Probate
Marshall, TX.............................Civil Trial Practice; Personal Injury

JONES, JONES & LUSHBAUGH, PLC
Fayetteville, AR ....Insurance Defense

JONES, JONES, VINES & HUNKINS
Wheatland, WY.........................General Practice

JONES, KEY, MELVIN & PATTON, P.A.
Franklin, NC ....General Practice

JONES, MCGLASSON & BENCKART, P.C.
Bloomington, IN ....Business Law; Personal Injury; Transportation Law; Trust and Estates, Wills and Probate

JONES OBENCHAIN, LLP
South Bend, IN ....General Practice

JONES, OSTEEN, JONES & ARNOLD
Hinesville, GA..........................General Practice; Personal Injury; Product Liability Law

JONES, ROGERS & NAVARRO
San Antonio, TX......................Insurance Defense

JONES, SNEAD, WERTHEIM, WENTWORTH & JARAMILLO, P.A.
Santa Fe, NM...........................Commercial Litigation

JONES & TROUSDALE
Florence, AL ....Insurance Defense; Medical Malpractice; Personal Injury; Product Liability Law

JONES, WALKER, WAECHTER, POITEVENT, CARRÈRE & DENÈGRE, L.L.P.
New Orleans, LA ....General Practice

JONES & WYATT
Enid, OK ....Civil Trial Practice; Criminal Trial Practice

JORDAN & BRISTOL
Brunswick, GA.........................Insurance Defense; Product Liability Law

JORDAN AND HAMBURG
New York, NY.........................Patent, Trademark, Copyright and Unfair Competition

JORDAN, HYDEN, WOMBLE & CULBRETH, P.C.
Corpus Christi, TX ....Bankruptcy Law; Commercial Litigation

JORDAN PRICE WALL GRAY JONES & CARLTON
Raleigh, NC..............................Construction Law; General Practice

JORDON, WAYNE A.
Alamogordo, NM ....General Practice

JORGENSON, SIEGEL, MCCLURE & FLEGEL, LLP
Menlo Park, CA.......................General Practice

JORY, PETERSON, WATKINS & SMITH
Fresno, CA ....Civil Trial Practice; Labor and Employment Law

JOSCELYN, MCNAIR AND JEFFREY, P.C.
Ann Arbor, MI ....General Practice

JOSE, HENRY, BRANTLEY & KELTNER, L.L.P.
Fort Worth, TX ....Appellate Practice; Civil Trial Practice; Medical Malpractice; Personal Injury; Product Liability Law

JOSEPH, RAYMOND & ASSOCIATES
East Lansing, MI ....Civil Trial Practice; Insurance Defense; Product Liability Law

JOSEPH, GREENWALD AND LAAKE, P.A.
Greenbelt, MD ....Commercial Litigation

JOSEPH & JOSEPH
Columbus, OH ....Family Law; Real Estate Law

JOSEPHS, BONNIE P.
New York, NY.........................Civil Trial Practice

JOSEPHS, JACK & GAEBE, P.A.
Miami, FL ....Civil Trial Practice; Commercial Litigation; Insurance Defense; Personal Injury; Professional Liability

JOSEPHSON, LOVELL & DRINGMAN
Big Timber, MT ....Real Estate Law; Trust and Estates, Wills and Probate

JOSLYN KEYDEL & WALLACE, LLP
Detroit, MI...............................Tax Law; Trust and Estates, Wills and Probate

JUDICE & ADLEY, A PROFESSIONAL LAW CORPORATION
Lafayette, LA ....Insurance Defense

JULIAN & PERTZ, P.C.
Utica, NY ....Civil Trial Practice; Medical Malpractice; Personal Injury; Product Liability Law

JULIEN & SCHLESINGER, P.C.
New York, NY..........................Civil Trial Practice; Medical Malpractice; Personal Injury; Product Liability Law

JUNEAU FIRM, THE, A PROFESSIONAL LAW CORPORATION
Lafayette, LA ....Admiralty/Maritime Law; Insurance Defense

KABALA & GEESEMAN, A PROFESSIONAL CORPORATION
Pittsburgh, PA ....General Practice

KAHN, DEES, DONOVAN & KAHN, LLP
Evansville, IN...........................Admiralty/Maritime Law; Banking Law; Civil Trial Practice; Corporate Law; Environmental Law; General Practice; Health Care Law; Insurance Defense; Labor and Employment Law; Real Estate Law; Tax Law

KAHN, KLEINMAN, YANOWITZ & ARNSON CO., L.P.A.
Cleveland, OH..........General Practice

KAHN, SMITH & COLLINS, P.A.
Baltimore, MD..........Administrative Law; Labor and Employment Law; Medical Malpractice; Personal Injury

KAHRS, NELSON, FANNING, HITE & KELLOGG L.L.P.
Wichita, KS..........Business Law; Civil Trial Practice; Commercial Litigation; Corporate Law; General Practice; Insurance Defense; Natural Resources Law; Product Liability Law; Real Estate Law

KAISER, JACK I. LAW OFFICES
San Francisco, CA..........Immigration and Naturalization

KAJAN MATHER AND BARISH, A PROFESSIONAL CORPORATION
Beverly Hills, CA..........Tax Law

KALCHEIM, SCHATZ & BERGER
Chicago, IL..........Family Law

KALEEL & KALEEL, P.A.
St. Petersburg, FL..........Civil Trial Practice

KALISON, MCBRIDE & JACKSON, P.A.
Liberty Corner, NJ..........Health Care Law; Mergers and Acquisitions; Tax Law; Trust and Estates, Wills and Probate

KALOW, SPRINGUT & BRESSLER LLP
New York, NY..........Intellectual Property Law

KAMBERG, BERMAN, P.C.
Springfield, MA..........Bankruptcy Law; Commercial Law; Commercial Litigation

KAMER & ZUCKER
Las Vegas, NV..........Labor and Employment Law

KANE, DONLEY & JOHNSON, P.C.
Colorado Springs, CO..........Civil Trial Practice; Family Law; General Practice; Insurance Defense

KANE, RUSSELL, COLEMAN & LOGAN, A PROFESSIONAL CORPORATION
Dallas, TX..........Bankruptcy Law; Civil Trial Practice; General Practice; Real Estate Law; Tax Law

KANE & SILVERMAN, PROFESSIONAL CORPORATION
Philadelphia, PA..........Civil Trial Practice; Medical Malpractice; Personal Injury; Product Liability Law

KANIA, LINDNER, LASAK AND FEENEY
Bala Cynwyd, PA..........Business Law; Civil Trial Practice; Commercial Law; Commercial Litigation; Corporate Law; Mergers and Acquisitions; Real Estate Law

KANTROVITZ, MARTIN LAW OFFICES OF
Boston, MA..........Personal Injury; Product Liability Law

KANTROW, SPAHT, WEAVER & BLITZER, A PROFESSIONAL LAW CORPORATION
Baton Rouge, LA..........Civil Trial Practice; Commercial Law; General Practice; Real Estate Law; Trust and Estates, Wills and Probate

KAPETAN MEYERS ROSEN & LOUIK, P.C.
Pittsburgh, PA..........Medical Malpractice; Personal Injury; Product Liability Law

KAPLAN, JOEL S.
Garden City, NY..........Civil Trial Practice; General Practice

KAPLAN, BEGY & VON OHLEN
Chicago, IL..........Commercial Litigation; Construction Law; Insurance Defense; Labor and Employment Law; Product Liability Law; Securities Law

KAPLAN, HOWARD GORDON, LTD.
Chicago, IL..........Business Law; Employment Benefits Law; Real Estate Law; Tax Law

KAPLAN, STRANGIS AND KAPLAN, P.A.
Minneapolis, MN..........General Practice

KAPLIN STEWART MELOFF REITER & STEIN, PROFESSIONAL CORPORATION
Blue Bell, PA..........Bankruptcy Law; Civil Trial Practice; Commercial Law; Health Care Law; Real Estate Law; Tax Law

KAPNER, LEWIS, P.A.
West Palm Beach, FL..........Civil Trial Practice; Family Law

KARASZKIEWICZ, KIRK T., & ASSOCIATES, P.C.
Philadelphia, PA..........Criminal Trial Practice

KARGIANIS WATKINS WERNER, L.L.P., P.S.
Seattle, WA..........Personal Injury; Product Liability Law

KARIC, STEVEN S., A PROF.CORP., LAW OFFICES OF
Los Angeles, CA..........Civil Trial Practice; Commercial Litigation; Trademark, Copyright and Unfair Competition

KARNS & KARABIAN
Los Angeles, CA..........Administrative Law

KARP, DAVID I.
Van Nuys, CA..........Civil Trial Practice

KARP, FROSH, LAPIDUS, WIGODSKY & NORWIND, P.A.
Bethesda, MD..........Commercial Litigation; Medical Malpractice; Personal Injury; Product Liability Law; Toxic Torts

KARR, CHARLES, P.A., LAW OFFICES OF
Fort Smith, AR..........Medical Malpractice

KARSMAN, BROOKS & CALLAWAY, P.C.
Savannah, GA..........Bankruptcy Law; Business Law; Civil Trial Practice; Commercial Law; Insurance Defense; Labor and Employment Law; Product Liability Law; Workers Compensation

KASDAN, SIMONDS, MCINTYRE, EPSTEIN & MARTIN
Irvine, CA..........Construction Law; Real Estate Law

KASDIN, PETER D., LTD.
Chicago, IL..........Medical Malpractice; Personal Injury

KASDORF, LEWIS & SWIETLIK, S.C.
Milwaukee, WI..........Aviation Law; Insurance Defense; Labor and Employment Law; Product Liability Law; Professional Liability; Workers Compensation

KASS LAW FIRM
Portsmouth, VA..........Personal Injury

KATARINCIC & SALMON
Pittsburgh, PA..........Civil Trial Practice; Securities Law

KATSKEE, HENATSCH & SUING
Omaha, NE..........Civil Trial Practice; General Practice; Insurance Defense; Professional Liability

KATTEN MUCHIN & ZAVIS
Chicago, IL..........General Practice

KATZ, BARRON, SQUITERO, FAUST & BERMAN, P.A.
Miami, FL..........Commercial Litigation; Insurance Defense; Real Estate Law

KATZ, GREENBERGER & NORTON
Cincinnati, OH..........General Practice

KATZ, KANTOR & PERKINS
Bluefield, WV..........General Practice

KATZ & KLEIN
White Plains, NY..........General Practice

KATZ, KUTTER, HAIGLER, ALDERMAN, BRYANT & YON, PROFESSIONAL ASSOCIATION
Tallahassee, FL..........Administrative Law

KATZ, LOOK & MOISON, PROFESSIONAL CORPORATION
Denver, CO..........Business Law; Civil Trial Practice; Commercial Litigation; Real Estate Law; Tax Law; Trust and Estates, Wills and Probate

KATZ & MANKA, LTD.
Minneapolis, MN..........Family Law

KATZ, STEVEN M., P.A.
Rockville, MD..........Business Law; Trust and Estates, Wills and Probate

KATZ, TELLER, BRANT & HILD, A LEGAL PROFESSIONAL ASSOCIATION
Cincinnati, OH..........Banking Law; Bankruptcy Law; Business Law; Civil Trial Practice; Employment Benefits Law; Environmental Law; Family Law; General Practice; Health Care Law; Labor and Employment Law; Municipal and Zoning Law; Real Estate Law; Securities Law; Tax Law; Trust and Estates, Wills and Probate

KAUFFMAN, EARL G.
Philadelphia, PA..........Criminal Trial Practice

KAUFMAN & CANOLES, A PROFESSIONAL CORPORATION
Chesapeake, VA..........General Practice
Newport News, VA..........General Practice
Norfolk, VA..........General Practice
Virginia Beach, VA..........General Practice
Williamsburg, VA..........General Practice

KAUFMAN, COREN, RESS & WEIDMAN, P.C.
Philadelphia, PA..........Civil Trial Practice; Commercial Litigation

KAUFMAN & CUMBERLAND CO., L.P.A.
Cleveland, OH..........Antitrust Law; Business Law; Civil Trial Practice; Commercial Litigation; Municipal Bond/Public Authority Financing; Product Liability Law; Real Estate Law

KAUFMAN & FLORENCE
Lebanon, OH..........General Practice

KAUFMAN & GREEN, L.L.P.
Wilmington, NC......................Banking Law; Creditors Rights; Health Care Law; Real Estate Law

KAUFMAN & LOGAN LLP
San Francisco, CA......................Appellate Practice; Bankruptcy Law; Civil Trial Practice; Commercial Litigation; Environmental Law

KAUFMAN AND PAYTON
Farmington Hills, MI......................Insurance Defense

KAUFMAN & ROTHFEDER, P.C.
Montgomery, AL......................Bankruptcy Law; Business Law; Commercial Law; Commercial Litigation; Environmental Law; Health Care Law; Real Estate Law; Tax Law; Trust and Estates, Wills and Probate

KAUFMAN, SCHNEIDER & BIANCO, LLP
Jericho, NY......................Employment Benefits Law; Labor and Employment Law

KAUFMAN & YOUNG, A PROFESSIONAL CORPORATION
Beverly Hills, CA......................Family Law

KAVALLER, MILES L., A PROFESSIONAL LAW CORPORATION
Beverly Hills, CA......................Transportation Law

KAVANAGH, SCULLY, SUDOW, WHITE & FREDERICK, P.C.
Galesburg, IL......................General Practice
Peoria, IL......................Civil Trial Practice; General Practice; Labor and Employment Law

KAWACHIKA & OSAKI
Honolulu, HI......................Civil Trial Practice

KAY, J. BENJAMIN III
Augusta, GA......................Bankruptcy Law; Corporate Law; Creditors Rights

KAY & ANDERSEN, S.C.
Madison, WI......................Civil Trial Practice; Construction Law; Environmental Law; Insurance Defense

KAY CASTO & CHANEY PLLC
Charleston, WV......................Civil Trial Practice; General Practice

KAY & MERKLE
San Francisco, CA......................Business Law; Real Estate Law; Sports and Entertainment Law; Tax Law

KAYE, ALLEN E., P.C.
New York, NY......................Immigration and Naturalization

KAYE, ROSE & PARTNERS, LLP
Los Angeles, CA......................Admiralty/Maritime Law
San Diego, CA......................Admiralty/Maritime Law
San Francisco, CA......................Admiralty/Maritime Law
Miami, FL......................Admiralty/Maritime Law

KAYE, SCHOLER, FIERMAN, HAYS & HANDLER, LLP
Los Angeles, CA......................General Practice
Washington, DC......................General Practice
New York, NY......................General Practice
Hong Kong, China......................General Practice

KAYLOR, ROBERT W., P.A.
Raleigh, NC......................Public Utilities Law

KAZAN, MCCLAIN, EDISES, SIMON & ABRAMS, A PROFESSIONAL LAW CORPORATION
Oakland, CA......................Civil Trial Practice; Personal Injury; Workers Compensation

KAZEE, KINNER & CHAFIN
Prestonsburg, KY......................General Practice; Insurance Defense; Natural Resources Law

KEAN, MILLER, HAWTHORNE, D'ARMOND, MCCOWAN & JARMAN, L.L.P.
Baton Rouge, LA......................Admiralty/Maritime Law; Civil Trial Practice; Commercial Law; Environmental Law; Health Care Law; Intellectual Property Law; Labor and Employment Law; Public Utilities Law; Tax Law

KEANE & BEANE, P.C.
White Plains, NY......................Commercial Law; Environmental Law; General Practice; Labor and Employment Law; Municipal and Zoning Law; Personal Injury; Real Estate Law

KEANE, REESE & VESELY, P.A.
St. Petersburg, FL......................Civil Trial Practice

KEANE, WILLIAM T., P.C.
Phoenix, AZ......................Personal Injury

KEARNEY, GARY W.
Pasadena, CA......................Family Law

KEARNEY & WESTFALL
Fort Worth, TX......................Criminal Trial Practice

KEATING JONES BILDSTEIN & HUGHES, P.C.
Portland, OR......................Insurance Defense

KEATING, MUETHING & KLEKAMP, P.L.L.
Cincinnati, OH......................Banking Law; Bankruptcy Law; Civil Trial Practice; Environmental Law; General Practice; Insurance Defense; Medical Malpractice; Real Estate Law; Securities Law; Tax Law; Trademark, Copyright and Unfair Competition

KEATS, JOHN A.
Fairfax, VA......................General Practice

KEEFER, O'REILLY & FERRARIO
Las Vegas, NV......................Business Law; Civil Trial Practice

KEEFER WOOD ALLEN & RAHAL, LLP
Harrisburg, PA......................Civil Trial Practice; General Practice; Health Care Law; Tax Law

KEEGAN, RAYMOND J., & ASSOC., LLP
White Plains, NY......................Personal Injury

KEELEY, HAYES, DUDLEY & GARRETT
Boca Raton, FL......................Real Estate Law; Trust and Estates, Wills and Probate

KEENER DOUCHER CURLEY & PATTERSON, A LEGAL PROFESSIONAL ASSOCIATION
Columbus, OH......................Civil Trial Practice; Insurance Defense; Personal Injury; Product Liability Law

KEENER & KEENER
Centre, AL......................General Practice

KEGLER, BROWN, HILL & RITTER
Columbus, OH......................Administrative Law; Banking Law; Bankruptcy Law; Business Law; Civil Trial Practice; Construction Law; Employment Benefits Law; Environmental Law; General Practice; Health Care Law; Immigration and Naturalization; Labor and Employment Law; Municipal and Zoning Law; Natural Resources Law; Public Utilities Law; Real Estate Law; Tax Law; Trademark, Copyright and Unfair Competition; Trust and Estates, Wills and Probate

KEHART, SHAFTER & WEBBER, P.C.
Decatur, IL......................General Practice; Insurance Defense

KEHOE, DENNIS J., A LAW CORPORATION
Aptos, CA......................Environmental Law

KEILP, JOE, P.C.
Phoenix, AZ......................Criminal Trial Practice

KEIL & WEINKAUF
Washington, DC......................Patent, Trademark, Copyright and Unfair Competition

KEISER, LARRY S.
Wilkes-Barre, PA......................Civil Trial Practice; Personal Injury

KEITGES & BANGLE, A PROFESSIONAL LAW CORPORATION
Sacramento, CA......................Insurance Defense

KEITH, DARRELL, P.C., LAW FIRM OF
Fort Worth, TX......................Legal Malpractice; Medical Malpractice

KEKER & VAN NEST, L.L.P.
San Francisco, CA......................Civil Trial Practice

KELAHER, CONNELL & CONNOR, P.C.
Surfside Beach, SC......................Civil Trial Practice; Personal Injury

KELAHER LAW OFFICES, P.A.
Orlando, FL......................Medical Malpractice; Personal Injury

KELEHER & MCLEOD, P.A.
Albuquerque, NM......................Insurance Defense; Trust and Estates, Wills and Probate

KELL, ALTERMAN & RUNSTEIN, LLP
Portland, OR......................Admiralty/Maritime Law; Bankruptcy Law; Business Law; Civil Trial Practice; Corporate Law; Creditors Rights; Family Law; Labor and Employment Law; Mergers and Acquisitions; Personal Injury; Real Estate Law; Tax Law; Trust and Estates, Wills and Probate

KELLER, JENNIFER L. LAW OFFICES OF
Newport Beach, CA......................Criminal Trial Practice

KELLER AND CURTIN CO., L.P.A.
Cleveland, OH......................Business Law; Civil Trial Practice; Corporate Law; Environmental Law; Insurance Defense; Product Liability Law

KELLER & HOUCK, A PROFESSIONAL ASSOCIATION
Miami, FL......................Admiralty/Maritime Law

KELLER, REYNOLDS, DRAKE, JOHNSON & GILLESPIE, P.C.
Helena, MT .... Civil Trial Practice; Insurance Defense

KELLER, THOMA, SCHWARZE, SCHWARZE, DUBAY & KATZ, P.C.
Detroit, MI .... Arbitration; Civil Trial Practice; Employment Benefits Law; General Practice; Insurance Defense; Labor and Employment Law; Trust and Estates, Wills and Probate; Workers Compensation

KELLER, WAHLBERG & MORRATO, P.C.
Denver, CO .... Personal Injury

KELLEY, BELCHER & BROWN, A PROFESSIONAL CORPORATION
Bloomington, IN .... Civil Trial Practice; Insurance Defense; Personal Injury; Product Liability Law

KELLEY DRYE & WARREN LLP
New York, NY .... General Practice

KELLEY, HERMAN & SMITH
Fort Lauderdale, FL .... Real Estate Law; Trust and Estates, Wills and Probate

KELLEY, JAMES C., P.A.
Miami, FL .... Insurance Defense

KELLEY, JASONS, MCGUIRE & SPINELLI, L.L.P.
Philadelphia, PA .... Civil Trial Practice; Commercial Law; Insurance Defense; Personal Injury; Product Liability Law; Toxic Torts

KELLEY, KRONENBERG, KELLEY, GILMARTIN, FICHTEL & WANDER, P.A.
Fort Lauderdale, FL .... Insurance Defense; Workers Compensation

KELLEY, MCCANN & LIVINGSTONE, LLP
Cleveland, OH .... Appellate Practice; Bankruptcy Law; Business Law; Civil Trial Practice; Environmental Law; Family Law; General Practice; Labor and Employment Law; Municipal and Zoning Law; Real Estate Law

KELLEY & MURPHY
Blue Bell, PA .... Administrative Law; Business Law; Civil Trial Practice; Commercial Law; Commercial Litigation; Corporate Law; General Practice; Insurance Defense; Labor and Employment Law; Personal Injury; Real Estate Law; Workers Compensation

KELLEY, WEBER, PIETZ & SLATER, S.C.
Wausau, WI .... Civil Trial Practice

KELL & FLACH
St. Charles, MO .... Personal Injury

KELLUM & JONES, P.A.
New Bern, NC .... Civil Trial Practice; Personal Injury; Workers Compensation

KELLY AFFLECK GREENE
Toronto, ON, Canada .... Administrative Law; Antitrust Law; Banking Law; Civil Trial Practice; Commercial Litigation; Construction Law; Environmental Law; Insurance Defense; Intellectual Property Law; Medical Malpractice; Municipal and Zoning Law; Patent, Trademark, Copyright and Unfair Competition; Personal Injury; Product Liability Law; Professional Liability

KELLY, BAUERSFELD, LOWRY & KELLEY, LLP
Woodland Hills, CA .... Patent, Trademark, Copyright and Unfair Competition

KELLY & HAMMERS, A PROFESSIONAL CORPORATION
Santa Monica, CA .... Family Law

KELLY, HART & HALLMAN, A PROFESSIONAL CORPORATION
Fort Worth, TX .... General Practice

KELLY, RODE & KELLY, LLP
Mineola, NY .... Insurance Defense

KELLY, TIMOTHY F., LAW OFFICES OF
Munster, IN .... Civil Trial Practice; General Practice; Insurance Defense; Labor and Employment Law; Medical Malpractice; Personal Injury; Product Liability Law

KELSCH KELSCH RUFF & KRANDA
Mandan, ND .... Environmental Law; General Practice

KEMP, DUCKETT, SPRADLEY, CURRY & ARNOLD
Little Rock, AR .... General Practice

KEMP, SMITH, DUNCAN & HAMMOND, A PROFESSIONAL CORPORATION
El Paso, TX .... Antitrust Law; General Practice; Labor and Employment Law; Tax Law

KEMPE, JOSEPH C., PROFESSIONAL ASSOCIATION
Jupiter, FL .... Tax Law; Trust and Estates, Wills and Probate
Stuart, FL .... Tax Law; Trust and Estates, Wills and Probate
Vero Beach, FL .... Tax Law; Trust and Estates, Wills and Probate

KEMPER & BARLOW
Madison, IN .... General Practice

KENDALL, HUGH F., ATTORNEY, P.C.
Chattanooga, TN .... Real Estate Law; Tax Law; Trust and Estates, Wills and Probate

KENDRICKS BORDEAU, P.C.
Marquette, MI .... General Practice

KENNEDY, JAMES L. JR.
Ketchum, ID .... Environmental Law; Natural Resources Law; Real Estate Law

KENNEDY & CHRISTOPHER, P.C.
Denver, CO .... Civil Trial Practice; Medical Malpractice

KENNEDY, CICCONETTI & KNOWLTON, L.P.A.
Wooster, OH .... Civil Trial Practice; Trust and Estates, Wills and Probate

KENNEDY COVINGTON LOBDELL & HICKMAN, L.L.P.
Charlotte, NC .... General Practice
Raleigh, NC .... General Practice
Rock Hill, SC .... General Practice

KENNEDY, FULTON, KOONTZ & FARINASH
Chattanooga, TN .... Bankruptcy Law

KENNEDY, JOHNSON, D'ELIA & GILLOOLY
New Haven, CT .... Civil Trial Practice; Medical Malpractice; Personal Injury; Product Liability Law; Professional Liability; Workers Compensation

KENNEDY, NERVIG & CARLISLE, LLP
Wadena, MN .... General Practice

KENNEDY, RICHARD R., A PROFESSIONAL LAW CORPORATION
Lafayette, LA .... Admiralty/Maritime Law; Appellate Practice; Civil Trial Practice; Personal Injury

KENNELLY, DENNIS LAWRENCE LAW OFFICE OF
Menlo Park, CA .... Labor and Employment Law

KENNERSON SCHWARTZ SEMERDJIAN & HAILE LLP
San Diego, CA .... Business Law; Civil Trial Practice; Commercial Law; Construction Law; Corporate Law; Insurance Defense; Intellectual Property Law; Labor and Employment Law; Personal Injury; Product Liability Law; Professional Liability; Real Estate Law; Trademark, Copyright and Unfair Competition; Trust and Estates, Wills and Probate

KENNEY & KEARNEY LLP
Cherry Hill, NJ .... Civil Trial Practice; Commercial Litigation; Environmental Law; Labor and Employment Law

KENNY, BRIMMER, MELLEY & MAHONEY
Hartford, CT .... General Practice; Insurance Defense; Medical Malpractice; Personal Injury; Product Liability Law

KENNY NACHWALTER SEYMOUR ARNOLD CRITCHLOW & SPECTOR, PROFESSIONAL ASSOCIATION
Miami, FL .... Antitrust Law; Civil Trial Practice; General Practice; Trademark, Copyright and Unfair Competition

KENNY & STEARNS
Newark, NJ .... Admiralty/Maritime Law; Civil Trial Practice
New York, NY .... Admiralty/Maritime Law; Civil Trial Practice; Insurance Defense

KENT, HAZZARD, JAEGER, GREER, WILSON & FAY
White Plains, NY .... Corporate Law; General Practice; Real Estate Law; Trust and Estates, Wills and Probate

KENT & MCBRIDE, P.C.
Philadelphia, PA .... Civil Trial Practice

KENT, WORSHAM & SMART
Savannah, GA .... Civil Trial Practice; Insurance Defense

KENYON & KENYON
Washington, DC .... Patent, Trademark, Copyright and Unfair Competition
New York, NY .... Patent, Trademark, Copyright and Unfair Competition

KEPLEY, GILLIGAN & EYRICH, A LEGAL PROFESSIONAL ASSOCIATION
Cincinnati, OH .... Business Law; Civil Trial Practice; Personal Injury; Real Estate Law; Workers Compensation

KERKAM, STOWELL, KONDRACKI & CLARKE, P.C.
Falls Church, VA .... Patent, Trademark, Copyright and Unfair Competition

KERN & GONZALEZ, A PROFESSIONAL CORPORATION
Los Angeles, CA .... Civil Trial Practice; Insurance Defense; Labor and Employment Law; Medical Malpractice; Product Liability Law

KERR, ANN LOUGHRIDGE
Clearwater, FL ....Family Law
Tampa, FL ....Family Law

KERR, IRVINE, RHODES & ABLES, A PROFESSIONAL CORPORATION
Oklahoma City, OK................Administrative Law; Civil Trial Practice; Corporate Law; Environmental Law; General Practice; Insurance Defense; Labor and Employment Law

KERR MCDONALD, LLP
Baltimore, MD ....Civil Trial Practice

KERR & WARD, L.L.P.
Midland, TX ....Business Law; Civil Trial Practice; General Practice; Health Care Law; Natural Resources Law

KERRICK, GRISE & STIVERS
Bowling Green, KY ....Banking Law; Business Law; Civil Trial Practice; Commercial Law; General Practice; Health Care Law; Insurance Defense; Labor and Employment Law; Medical Malpractice; Personal Injury; Product Liability Law; Professional Liability; Real Estate Law; Trademark, Copyright and Unfair Competition; Workers Compensation

KERRIGAN, ESTESS, RANKIN & MCLEOD
Pensacola, FL..........................Civil Trial Practice; Medical Malpractice; Personal Injury

KERSTEN & MCKINNON, S.C.
Milwaukee, WI ....Antitrust Law; Business Law; Civil Trial Practice; Personal Injury

KESSLER, COHEN & ROTH, A PROFESSIONAL CORPORATION
Philadelphia, PA ....Civil Trial Practice; Medical Malpractice; Personal Injury; Product Liability Law

KESSLER, DOUGLAS W., P.C.
Atlanta, GA ....Business Law

KESSLER & KESSLER, A LAW CORPORATION
Los Angeles, CA ....Commercial Litigation; Corporate Law; Real Estate Law; Tax Law; Trust and Estates, Wills and Probate

KESSLER & SCHWARZ, P.C.
Atlanta, GA ....Family Law

KESSNER DUCA UMEBAYASHI BAIN & MATSUNAGA, ATTORNEYS AT LAW, A LAW CORPORATION
Honolulu, HI...........................Banking Law; Bankruptcy Law; Insurance Defense; Product Liability Law; Workers Compensation

KESTENBAUM, HAROLD L., P.C.
Garden City, NY ....Franchise Law

KETCHAM & KETCHAM
Columbus, OH ....Criminal Trial Practice; Trust and Estates, Wills and Probate

KETCHEY HORAN, P.A.
Tampa, FL ....Bankruptcy Law; Business Law; Commercial Litigation; Corporate Law; Creditors Rights; Real Estate Law; Trust and Estates, Wills and Probate

KEULING-STOUT, P.C.
Big Stone Gap, VA ....Civil Trial Practice; General Practice

KEYSER MASON BALL
Mississauga, ON, Canada........Banking Law

KEZIAH, GATES & SAMET, L.L.P.
High Point, NC.......................General Practice

KICKHAM LAW OFFICES
Brookline, MA ....Real Estate Law; Trust and Estates, Wills and Probate

KIENBAUM, KAREN SMITH & ASSOCIATES
Detroit, MI..............................Arbitration; Labor and Employment Law

KIENBAUM OPPERWALL HARDY & PELTON, P.L.C.
Birmingham, MI......................Labor and Employment Law
Detroit, MI..............................Labor and Employment Law

KIERNAN, PLUNKETT & REDIHAN
Providence, RI.........................Civil Trial Practice

KIESEWETTER WISE KAPLAN SCHWIMMER & PRATHER, PLC
Memphis, TN ....Labor and Employment Law

KIESLER & BERMAN
Chicago, IL..............................Civil Trial Practice; Insurance Defense

KIGER & ALPERN
Pittsburgh, PA ....Civil Trial Practice; Insurance Defense; Medical Malpractice; Personal Injury; Product Liability Law

KILBORNE, ROBERT S. IV, LAW OFFICES OF
Rancho Santa Fe, CA.............Business Law; Civil Trial Practice; Medical Malpractice; Personal Injury

KILBURN, JONES, GILL & CAMPBELL, L.L.P.
Houston, TX ....Civil Trial Practice; Oil and Gas Law

KILCULLEN, WILSON AND KILCULLEN, CHARTERED
Washington, DC......................Construction Law; Government Contracts

KILE MCINTYRE HARBIN & LEE
Washington, DC......................Intellectual Property Law

KILGORE, DONALD C.
Portsmouth, VA ....Commercial Law; General Practice

KILGORE & KILGORE, A PROFESSIONAL CORPORATION
Dallas, TX ....Civil Trial Practice; General Practice; Labor and Employment Law; Natural Resources Law

KILLEEN & FIERRO
Houston, TX ....Admiralty/Maritime Law; Civil Trial Practice; Energy Law; Insurance Defense

KILLIAN, DONOHUE & SHIPMAN, LLC
Hartford, CT ....Administrative Law; Energy Law; Land Use Law; Municipal and Zoning Law

KILLIAN & GEPHART, LLP
Harrisburg, PA........................Administrative Law; Civil Trial Practice; Criminal Trial Practice; Environmental Law; Labor and Employment Law

KILLWORTH, GOTTMAN, HAGAN & SCHAEFF, L.L.P.
Dayton, OH.............................Patent, Trademark, Copyright and Unfair Competition

KILPATRICK, AUD & WILLIAMS, L.L.P.
Little Rock, AR ....Insurance Defense; Legal Malpractice; Medical Malpractice; Product Liability Law; Professional Liability; Workers Compensation

KIMBLE, NELSON, AUDILETT, MCDONOUGH & MOLLA, P.C.
Tucson, AZ ....Insurance Defense; Product Liability Law

KIMERER & LAVELLE, P.L.C.
Phoenix, AZ ....Antitrust Law; Civil Trial Practice; Commercial Litigation; Criminal Trial Practice; Environmental Law; Personal Injury

KINCAID, TAYLOR & GEYER
Zanesville, OH........................General Practice

KINERK, BEAL, SCHMIDT & DYER, P.C.
Tucson, AZ ....Medical Malpractice; Personal Injury; Product Liability Law; Professional Liability; Sports and Entertainment Law

KING, JEAN LEDWITH
Ann Arbor, MI ....Family Law

KING & ATTRIDGE
Rockville, MD.........................Commercial Litigation; Construction Law

KING & BALLOW
San Diego, CA ....General Practice
Nashville, TN..........................Antitrust Law; Civil Trial Practice; Communications Law; General Practice; Labor and Employment Law; Tax Law; Trademark, Copyright and Unfair Competition

KING, BLACKWELL & DOWNS, P.A.
Orlando, FL ....Civil Trial Practice; Commercial Litigation; Personal Injury

KING & KING
Greeneville, TN.......................Family Law

KING AND KING, L.L.C.
Jackson, WY............................Civil Trial Practice; Personal Injury

KING LAW FIRM
Oklahoma City, OK................Civil Trial Practice; Insurance Defense; Product Liability Law

KING, PAGANO & HARRISON
Washington, DC......................Antitrust Law; Civil Trial Practice; Criminal Trial Practice; Health Care Law; Intellectual Property Law; Labor and Employment Law
New York, NY.........................Civil Trial Practice; Health Care Law; Intellectual Property Law; Labor and Employment Law

KING • PETERSON • DYMOND LLP
Englewood, CO ....Civil Trial Practice; Commercial Law

KING AND SCHICKLI
Lexington, KY ....Intellectual Property Law; Patent, Trademark, Copyright and Unfair Competition

KING & VERNON, P.A.
Columbia, SC ....Civil Trial Practice; Criminal Trial Practice; Family Law; General Practice

KINGCADE, THOMAS E., PROFESSIONAL ASSOCIATION
West Palm Beach, FL............Civil Trial Practice; Commercial Litigation; Personal Injury

KINGERY DURREE WAKEMAN & RYAN, ASSOC.
Peoria, IL............Civil Trial Practice; General Practice; Medical Malpractice

KINGSLEY, JOHN P., P.C.
Catskill, NY............Insurance Defense

KINNARD, CLAYTON & BEVERIDGE
Nashville, TN............Medical Malpractice

KINNEY, KEMP, SPONCLER, JOINER & THARPE
Dalton, GA............Insurance Defense; Workers Compensation

KINSEY VINCENT PYLE, P.A.
Daytona Beach, FL............Construction Law

KIPLE, KIPLE, DENEFE, BEAVER & GARDNER, L.L.P.
Ottumwa, IA............General Practice

KIPNIS TESCHER LIPPMAN & VALINSKY
Fort Lauderdale, FL............Commercial Litigation; Creditors Rights; Securities Law

KIPP AND CHRISTIAN, P.C.
Salt Lake City, UT............Civil Trial Practice; General Practice; Insurance Defense; Personal Injury

KIRBY, PATRICK M.
Flint, MI............General Practice

KIRBY & HOLT, L.L.P.
Raleigh, NC............Medical Malpractice; Personal Injury

KIRCH, DAVID W., P.C.
Aurora, CO............Trust and Estates, Wills and Probate

KIRCHER, C. WILLIAM, JR., A PROF. CORP., LAW OFFICES OF
Irvine, CA............Business Law

KIRKENDALL & ISGUR
Houston, TX............Bankruptcy Law

KIRKLAND & ELLIS
Los Angeles, CA............Criminal Trial Practice; General Practice
Washington, DC............General Practice
Chicago, IL............General Practice
New York, NY............General Practice
London, England............General Practice

KIRKPATRICK & LOCKHART LLP
Pittsburgh, PA............General Practice

KIRLIN, CAMPBELL & KEATING
New York, NY............Admiralty/Maritime Law

KIRSCHNER AND VENKER, P.C.
Atlanta, GA............Medical Malpractice; Personal Injury

KIRSCHNIK, JAMES L., S.C.
Milwaukee, WI............Construction Law

KIRSHENBAUM LAW ASSOCIATES
Warwick, RI............Civil Trial Practice; Family Law; Personal Injury

KIRSHMAN, HARRIS & BRANTON, A PROFESSIONAL CORPORATION
Beverly Hills, CA............Business Law
Las Vegas, NV............Civil Trial Practice; Labor and Employment Law

KIRTON & MCCONKIE, A PROFESSIONAL CORPORATION
Salt Lake City, UT............Civil Trial Practice; Commercial Law; General Practice; Insurance Defense; Personal Injury; Real Estate Law; Trust and Estates, Wills and Probate

KIRVEN & KIRVEN, P.C.
Buffalo, WY............General Practice; Real Estate Law; Trust and Estates, Wills and Probate

KIRWAN & BARRETT, P.C.
Bozeman, MT............Appellate Practice; Banking Law; Business Law; Civil Trial Practice; Commercial Law; Construction Law; Labor and Employment Law; Municipal and Zoning Law; Personal Injury; Real Estate Law; Trust and Estates, Wills and Probate

KISSOON, CLUGG, LINDER & DITTBERNER, LTD.
Edina, MN............Family Law

KITCH DRUTCHAS WAGNER DENARDIS & VALITUTTI, A PROFESSIONAL CORPORATION
Ann Arbor, MI............General Practice
Detroit, MI............Civil Trial Practice; Environmental Law; General Practice; Health Care Law; Insurance Defense; Labor and Employment Law; Medical Malpractice; Personal Injury
Grand Rapids, MI............General Practice
Lansing, MI............General Practice
Mount Clemens, MI............General Practice

KITCHEN, JUDKINS, SIMPSON & HIGH
Tallahassee, FL............Civil Trial Practice; Commercial Litigation; Criminal Trial Practice; Personal Injury

KITCHENS, BENTON, KITCHENS & WARREN, A PROFESSIONAL LAW CORPORATION
Minden, LA............General Practice

KITCHIN, NEAL, WEBB, WEBB & FUTRELL, P.A.
Rockingham, NC............General Practice

KITRICK, MARK, CO., L.P.A.
Columbus, OH............Civil Trial Practice; Personal Injury

KITTAY, GOLD & GERSHFELD, P.C.
New York, NY............Bankruptcy Law; Commercial Litigation

KITTREDGE, DONLEY, ELSON, FULLEM & EMBICK, LLP
Philadelphia, PA............Commercial Litigation; Environmental Law; Insurance Defense; Labor and Employment Law

KIVITZ & LIPTZ, LLC
Chevy Chase, MD............Civil Trial Practice

KIZER AND BLACK
Maryville, TN............Civil Trial Practice

KIZER, HOOD & MORGAN, L.L.P.
Baton Rouge, LA............Bankruptcy Law; Real Estate Law

KIZER & NEU
Bremen, IN............General Practice
Plymouth, IN............General Practice

K.K.M., P.A.
Bethesda, MD............Business Law

KLAMANN & HUBBARD, P.A.
Overland Park, KS............Civil Trial Practice

KLAUBER & JACKSON
Hackensack, NJ............Patent, Trademark, Copyright and Unfair Competition; Trademark, Copyright and Unfair Competition

KLEHR, HARRISON, HARVEY, BRANZBURG & ELLERS LLP
Philadelphia, PA............General Practice

KLEIN, HOWARD BRUCE LAW OFFICES OF
Philadelphia, PA............Criminal Trial Practice

KLEIN, DENATALE, GOLDNER, COOPER, ROSENLIEB & KIMBALL, LLP
Bakersfield, CA............Bankruptcy Law; Business Law; Civil Trial Practice; Commercial Law; Construction Law; Corporate Law; Environmental Law; General Practice; Labor and Employment Law; Personal Injury; Real Estate Law; Tax Law; Trust and Estates, Wills and Probate

KLEIN, JOEL, & ASSOCIATES
San Antonio, TX............Commercial Law; Creditors Rights

KLEINBARD, BELL & BRECKER LLP
Philadelphia, PA............Business Law; Commercial Litigation; Corporate Law; Creditors Rights; Environmental Law; General Practice; Labor and Employment Law; Mergers and Acquisitions; Municipal and Zoning Law; Pension and Profit Sharing; Securities Law; Toxic Torts

KLEINFELD, KAPLAN AND BECKER
Washington, DC............Administrative Law

KLEINPETER & KLEINPETER
Baton Rouge, LA............Civil Trial Practice; Commercial Litigation; Insurance Defense

KLENDA, MITCHELL, AUSTERMAN & ZUERCHER, L.L.C.
Wichita, KS............General Practice

KLIEWER, BREEN, GARATONI, PATTERSON & MALONE, INCORPORATED
San Antonio, TX............Tax Law

KLINE, JOHN R., P.C.
Helena, MT............Tax Law; Trust and Estates, Wills and Probate

KLINE & SPECTER, P.C.
Philadelphia, PA............Civil Trial Practice

KLINEDINST, FLIEHMAN & MCKILLOP, A PROFESSIONAL CORPORATION
San Diego, CA............Civil Trial Practice; Commercial Litigation; Construction Law; Labor and Employment Law; Professional Liability

KLUGER, PERETZ, KAPLAN & BERLIN, P.A.
Fort Lauderdale, FL............Civil Trial Practice
Miami, FL............Civil Trial Practice

KLUMPP AND BARNATT
Lake Charles, LA....................Tax Law; Trust and Estates, Wills and Probate

KLUNDER, CARL J.
Irvine, CA....................Insurance Defense

KLUTTZ, REAMER, BLANKENSHIP, HAYES & RANDOLPH, L.L.P.
Salisbury, NC....................General Practice; Insurance Defense

KNAPP, MARSH, JONES & DORAN, L.L.P.
Los Angeles, CA....................General Practice

KNECHT, MICHAEL C., & ASSOCIATES, P.A.
Palm Beach Gardens, FL.........Civil Trial Practice; Personal Injury

KNEE & ROSS, LLP
Los Angeles, CA....................Labor and Employment Law

KNEELAND, KORB, COLLIER & LEGG
Ketchum, ID....................Family Law; Real Estate Law

KNIGHT, JOHN DAVID
Cullman, AL....................General Practice

KNIGHT & FISHER
Macon, GA....................Medical Malpractice

KNIGHT, FORD, ATWILL, PARSHALL & BAKER
Columbia, MO....................General Practice; Insurance Defense

KNIGHT, MANZI, NUSSBAUM & LAPLACA, P.C.
Upper Marlboro, MD..............Administrative Law; Banking Law; Business Law; Civil Trial Practice; Commercial Law; Criminal Trial Practice; Family Law; General Practice; Municipal Bond/Public Authority Financing; Real Estate Law

KNOLL, JAMES L.
Portland, OR....................Arbitration; Construction Law

KNOPFLER & ROBERTSON, LLP
Los Angeles, CA....................Business Law; Construction Law; Corporate Law; Environmental Law; Labor and Employment Law; Oil and Gas Law; Product Liability Law; Real Estate Law; Toxic Torts

KNOTT, JOHN K. JR.
Cheshire, CT....................Municipal and Zoning Law

KNOWLES, JOHN L.
Geneva, AL....................General Practice

KNOWLES & ASSOCIATES, LLC
Carmel, IN....................Business Law; Civil Trial Practice; Criminal Trial Practice; Trust and Estates, Wills and Probate

KNOX MCLAUGHLIN GORNALL & SENNETT, P.C.
Erie, PA....................General Practice

KNOX AND SWAN
Thomson, GA....................General Practice

KNUDSEN, BERKHEIMER, RICHARDSON & ENDACOTT
Lincoln, NE....................General Practice

KOBAYASHI, SUGITA & GODA
Honolulu, HI....................Business Law; Commercial Law; General Practice; Real Estate Law

KOBLENTZ & KOBLENTZ
Cleveland, OH....................Civil Trial Practice; Criminal Trial Practice; Family Law

KOCH & HARRINGTON, P.A.
Clearwater, FL....................Family Law

KOCH, RON, P.A.
Albuquerque, NM....................Criminal Trial Practice

KODNER, WATKINS, MUCHNICK & DUNNE, L.C.
St. Louis, MO....................Securities Law

KOENIGSBERG, JAY, P.A.
Miami, FL....................Real Estate Law

KOEPKE, KARL O.
Orlando, FL....................Medical Malpractice; Personal Injury

KOEPPEL MARTONE LEISTMAN & HERMAN, L.L.P.
Mineola, NY....................Municipal and Zoning Law; Real Estate Law

KOFF, HOWARD M., P.C.
Albany, NY....................Tax Law

KOFF, WENDOLOWSKI, FERGUSON & MANGAN, P.C.
Wilkes-Barre, PA....................Labor and Employment Law

KOHLER & HART
Milwaukee, WI....................Criminal Trial Practice

KOHN, MICHAEL G.
Cincinnati, OH....................Civil Trial Practice

KOHN, KOHN & COLAPINTO, P.C.
Washington, DC....................Labor and Employment Law

KOHN PARTNERSHIP, THE, L.P.
St. Louis, MO....................Mergers and Acquisitions; Tax Law

KOHN, SHANDS, ELBERT, GIANOULAKIS & GILJUM, LLP
St. Louis, MO....................Antitrust Law; Labor and Employment Law; Tax Law

KOHNER, MANN & KAILAS, S.C.
Milwaukee, WI....................Banking Law; Bankruptcy Law; Business Law; Civil Trial Practice; Commercial Law; Commercial Litigation; Construction Law; Creditors Rights

KOHRS & FISKE
Santa Monica, CA....................Insurance Defense

KOLCZYNSKI, PHILLIP J., LAW CORPORATION
Santa Ana, CA....................Aviation Law

KOLESAR & LEATHAM, CHARTERED
Las Vegas, NV....................Banking Law; Bankruptcy Law; Business Law; Commercial Litigation; Real Estate Law; Trust and Estates, Wills and Probate

KOLEY, JESSEN, DAUBMAN & RUPIPER, PROFESSIONAL CORPORATION
Omaha, NE....................General Practice

KOLLIN, GARY, P.A.
Fort Lauderdale, FL....................Criminal Trial Practice

KOLLMAN & SHEEHAN, P.A.
Baltimore, MD....................Business Law; Commercial Law; Construction Law; Labor and Employment Law

KOLODINSKY, SEITZ & TRESHER
Daytona Beach, FL....................Medical Malpractice; Personal Injury
New Smyrna Beach, FL..........Medical Malpractice; Personal Injury

KOLODNY & ANTEAU
Beverly Hills, CA....................Family Law

KOLVOORD, OVERTON AND WILSON
Essex Junction, VT....................General Practice

KOMPA, MARK A. LAW OFFICES OF
Newport Beach, CA....................Bankruptcy Law; Real Estate Law

KONCILJA & ASSOCIATES, P.C.
Denver, CO....................Civil Trial Practice; Commercial Litigation

KONIG, RICHARD W.
Stockton, CA....................Trust and Estates, Wills and Probate

KONOWIECKI & RANK LLP
Los Angeles, CA....................Corporate Law; Health Care Law; Mergers and Acquisitions; Securities Law

KOO, LARRABEE & LAU-KEE, LLP
Ardsley, NY....................Corporate Law

KOONS, FULLER, VANDEN EYKEL & ROBERTSON, A PROFESSIONAL CORPORATION
Dallas, TX....................Family Law
Plano, TX....................Family Law

KOONS, STEPHEN R., P.A.
West Palm Beach, FL....................Personal Injury

KOONZ, MCKENNEY, JOHNSON, DEPAOLIS & LIGHTFOOT
Washington, DC....................Personal Injury

KOOPERSMITH & BROWN, LLP
Lake Success, NY....................Family Law

KOPELMAN AND PAIGE, P.C.
Boston, MA....................Civil Trial Practice; Environmental Law; General Practice; Insurance Defense; International Business Law; Municipal and Zoning Law

KOPELOWITZ, HARVEY G.
Boca Raton, FL....................Business Law; Commercial Litigation; Real Estate Law

KOREY, SWEET, MCKINNON, SIMPSON & VUKELJA
Ormond Beach, FL....................General Practice; Real Estate Law

KORMEIER & WALTERS
Houston, TX....................Trust and Estates, Wills and Probate

KORN, ANDREW R., P.C.
Dallas, TX....................Commercial Litigation

KORN & COHN, PROFESSIONAL CORPORATION
Plymouth Meeting, PA...........Construction Law

KORNBERG, HOWARD CRAIG
Los Angeles, CA .... Personal Injury

KORNIEVSKY, GEORGE M., A PROF. CORP., LAW OFFICES OF
Irvine, CA .... Family Law

KORTHALS, JOHN L.
Pompano Beach, FL .... Real Estate Law; Trust and Estates, Wills and Probate

KOSKI, ARTHUR C., P.A., LAW OFFICES OF
Boca Raton, FL .... Construction Law; Public Utilities Law

KOSKOFF, KOSKOFF & BIEDER, P.C.
Bridgeport, CT .... Aviation Law; Civil Rights; Commercial Litigation; Health Care Law; Medical Malpractice; Personal Injury; Product Liability Law; Toxic Torts

KOSTELANETZ & FINK, LLP
New York, NY .... Appellate Practice; Civil Trial Practice; Commercial Litigation; Criminal Trial Practice; Intellectual Property Law; Securities Law; Tax Law; Trust and Estates, Wills and Probate

KOZYAK TROPIN & THROCKMORTON, P.A.
Miami, FL .... Bankruptcy Law

KRAEMER, BURNS, MYTELKA, LOVELL & KULKA, P.A.
Springfield, NJ .... Business Law; Civil Trial Practice; Commercial Litigation

KRAGE & JANVEY, L.L.P.
Dallas, TX .... Appellate Practice; Civil Trial Practice; Commercial Litigation; Corporate Law; Creditors Rights; Real Estate Law; Securities Law; Tax Law

KRAMER, GILDA L.
Philadelphia, PA .... Civil Trial Practice

KRAMER, DILLOF, TESSEL, DUFFY & MOORE
New York, NY .... Civil Trial Practice; Medical Malpractice; Personal Injury

KRAMER, FEINGOLD & CASTROVINCI, PLLC
Commack, NY .... Civil Trial Practice; Family Law

KRAMER & FRANK, P.C.
St. Louis, MO .... Commercial Litigation; Creditors Rights

KRAMER LEVIN NAFTALIS & FRANKEL LLP
New York, NY .... Civil Trial Practice; General Practice

KRAMER, RAYSON, LEAKE, RODGERS & MORGAN, LLP
Knoxville, TN .... General Practice

KRAMON & GRAHAM, P.A.
Baltimore, MD .... General Practice

KRAMSKY, ELLIOTT N. LAW OFFICES OF
Woodland Hills, CA .... Patent, Trademark, Copyright and Unfair Competition

KRATHEN, DAVID, A PROF. ASSOC., THE LAW OFFICES OF
Fort Lauderdale, FL .... Medical Malpractice

KRATZIG, PAUL G. LAW OFFICES OF
Corpus Christi, TX .... Commercial Litigation; Criminal Trial Practice

KRAUS, SHERRY S.
Rochester, NY .... Tax Law

KRAVIT, GASS, HOVEL & LEITNER S.C.
Milwaukee, WI .... Insurance Defense

KRAVITZ, SCHNITZER & SLOANE, CHARTERED, A PROFESSIONAL CORPORATION
Las Vegas, NV .... Banking Law; Bankruptcy Law; Civil Trial Practice; Commercial Litigation; Insurance Defense; Real Estate Law

KREDER, BROOKS, HAILSTONE & LUDWIG
Scranton, PA .... Banking Law; Business Law; Civil Trial Practice; General Practice; Insurance Defense; Personal Injury; Product Liability Law

KREHBIEL, BANNERMAN & HORN, P.A.
Albuquerque, NM .... Commercial Law; Commercial Litigation; Health Care Law; Natural Resources Law

KREINDLER & KREINDLER
New York, NY .... Aviation Law; Medical Malpractice; Personal Injury; Product Liability Law

KREIS, ENDERLE, CALLANDER & HUDGINS, A PROFESSIONAL CORPORATION
Battle Creek, MI .... Banking Law; Bankruptcy Law; Business Law; Civil Trial Practice; Commercial Law; Construction Law; Corporate Law; Employment Benefits Law; Environmental Law; Family Law; General Practice; Health Care Law; Immigration and Naturalization; Labor and Employment Law; Mergers and Acquisitions; Municipal and Zoning Law; Real Estate Law; Tax Law; Trust and Estates, Wills and Probate
Kalamazoo, MI .... Banking Law; Bankruptcy Law; Business Law; Civil Trial Practice; Commercial Law; Construction Law; Corporate Law; Employment Benefits Law; Environmental Law; Family Law; General Practice; Health Care Law; Immigration and Naturalization; Labor and Employment Law; Mergers and Acquisitions; Municipal and Zoning Law; Real Estate Law; Tax Law; Trust and Estates, Wills and Probate

KREITZMAN, MORTENSEN, SIMON & IRGANG
New York, NY .... Labor and Employment Law

KREMBS & ALKIRE LLP
Cleveland, OH .... Commercial Litigation; Medical Malpractice; Personal Injury; Product Liability Law

KRETSCHMAN, KAREN L.
Austin, TX .... Family Law

KREUSLER-WALSH, JANE, P.A.
West Palm Beach, FL .... Appellate Practice

KREVOLIN & HORST, LLC
Atlanta, GA .... Business Law; Civil Trial Practice; Commercial Litigation; Corporate Law; Personal Injury; Real Estate Law

KRIEGER, ALBERT J., P.A.
Miami, FL .... Criminal Trial Practice

KRIEGER & KRIEGER
Omaha, NE .... Immigration and Naturalization

KRIGER, MARK J.
Detroit, MI .... Criminal Trial Practice

KRIST LAW FIRM, THE, P.C.
Houston, TX .... Civil Trial Practice; Personal Injury

KRISZTAL, RUBEN J.
Overland Park, KS .... Medical Malpractice

KRIVCHER MAGIDS PLC
Memphis, TN .... Bankruptcy Law; Commercial Law; Family Law; General Practice; Insurance Defense; Real Estate Law; Trust and Estates, Wills and Probate

KROLL, RUBIN & FIORELLA LLP
New York, NY .... General Practice

KROLOFF, BELCHER, SMART, PERRY & CHRISTOPHERSON
Stockton, CA .... General Practice

KRONEY • MINCEY, INC.
Dallas, TX .... Business Law; Trust and Estates, Wills and Probate

KRONTZ, KENNETH W., P.C.
Douglasville, GA .... Criminal Trial Practice; Family Law; Personal Injury

KROVITZ LAW FIRM, THE, P.C.
Englewood, CO .... Real Estate Law

KRUCHKO & FRIES
Baltimore, MD .... Labor and Employment Law
McLean, VA .... Labor and Employment Law

KRUEGER, JAMES, ATTORNEY AT LAW, A LAW CORPORATION
Honolulu, HI .... Civil Trial Practice; Medical Malpractice; Personal Injury; Product Liability Law
Lihue, HI .... Civil Trial Practice; Medical Malpractice; Personal Injury; Product Liability Law
Wailuku, HI .... Civil Trial Practice; Medical Malpractice; Personal Injury; Product Liability Law

KRUGER, ALLEN J., P.A.
Laurel, MD .... Family Law

KRUGLIAK, WILKINS, GRIFFITHS & DOUGHERTY CO., L.P.A.
Canton, OH .... General Practice

KRUGMAN & KAILES LLP
Saddle Brook, NJ .... Civil Trial Practice; Commercial Law; Commercial Litigation; Corporate Law; Environmental Law; General Practice; International Business Law; Securities Law; Tax Law; Trust and Estates, Wills and Probate

KRUKOWSKI & COSTELLO, S.C.
Milwaukee, WI .... Labor and Employment Law

KRUM, MARK JAY
Philadelphia, PA .... Civil Trial Practice; Criminal Trial Practice

KRUPIN GREENBAUM & O'BRIEN, LLC
Washington, DC .... Immigration and Naturalization; Labor and Employment Law

KRUPNICK CAMPBELL MALONE ROSELLI BUSER SLAMA HANCOCK MCNELIS LIBERMAN & MCKEE, P.A.
Fort Lauderdale, FL ... Admiralty/Maritime Law; Aviation Law; Civil Trial Practice; Environmental Law; General Practice; Medical Malpractice; Personal Injury; Product Liability Law; Toxic Torts

KRYS BOYLE FREEDMAN & SAWYER, P.C.
Denver, CO ... Securities Law

KUBASIAK, CREMIEUX, FYLSTRA, REIZEN & ROTUNNO, PROFESSIONAL CORPORATION
Chicago, IL ... Commercial Litigation

KUBICKI DRAPER
Fort Lauderdale, FL ... Insurance Defense
Miami, FL ... Insurance Defense
West Palm Beach, FL ... Insurance Defense

KUBOVCIK & KUBOVCIK
Washington, DC ... Intellectual Property Law

KUHN & BELZ
Laguna Niguel, CA ... Personal Injury

KUMMER KAEMPFER BONNER & RENSHAW
Las Vegas, NV ... Civil Trial Practice; Commercial Law; Insurance Defense; Securities Law

KUNIHOLM, ELIZABETH F.
Raleigh, NC ... Medical Malpractice

KUNKEL MILLER & HAMENT
Fort Myers, FL ... Labor and Employment Law
Sarasota, FL ... Labor and Employment Law
Tampa, FL ... Labor and Employment Law

KUPFER, RICHARD A., P.A.
West Palm Beach, FL ... Appellate Practice

KURLBAUM STOLL SEAMAN & MUSTOE, P.C.
Kansas City, MO ... Commercial Law; Corporate Law

KURRUS, THOMAS W.
Gainesville, FL ... Criminal Trial Practice

KURZMAN & EISENBERG, LLP
White Plains, NY ... Trust and Estates, Wills and Probate

KUSSMAN & WHITEHILL
Los Angeles, CA ... Medical Malpractice; Personal Injury; Product Liability Law

KUTAK ROCK
Denver, CO ... General Practice
Washington, DC ... General Practice
Atlanta, GA ... General Practice
Omaha, NE ... General Practice

KUTNER, RUBINOFF, BUSH & LERNER
Miami, FL ... Civil Trial Practice; General Practice

KUVIN & STETTIN, P.A.
Fort Lauderdale, FL ... Medical Malpractice; Personal Injury

KWALL, SHOWERS & COLEMAN, P.A.
Clearwater, FL ... Administrative Law; Business Law; Civil Rights; Commercial Litigation; Criminal Trial Practice; General Practice; Labor and Employment Law; Personal Injury

KYNES, MARKMAN & FELMAN, P.A.
Tampa, FL ... Appellate Practice; Criminal Trial Practice

LABARRE, JEROME, A PROFESSIONAL CORPORATION
Portland, OR ... Civil Trial Practice; Securities Law

L'ABBATE, BALKAN, COLAVITA & CONTINI, L.L.P.
Garden City, NY ... Civil Trial Practice; General Practice; Insurance Defense; Product Liability Law; Toxic Torts

LABE, ROBERT B., P.C.
Southfield, MI ... Business Law; Tax Law; Trust and Estates, Wills and Probate

LABER, EDWARD HARRIS, LTD.
Tucson, AZ ... Civil Trial Practice; Criminal Trial Practice

LACEY & JONES, LLP
Birmingham, MI ... Civil Trial Practice; Insurance Defense; Labor and Employment Law; Workers Compensation

LACKEY, NUSBAUM, HARRIS, RENY & TORZEWSKI, A LEGAL PROFESSIONAL ASSOCIATION
Toledo, OH ... Admiralty/Maritime Law; Family Law; Labor and Employment Law; Personal Injury; Product Liability Law

LACKEY, RODGERS, PRICE AND SNEDEKER
Nashville, TN ... Civil Trial Practice

LACY, KATZEN, RYEN & MITTLEMAN, LLP
Rochester, NY ... Bankruptcy Law; Family Law; General Practice; Personal Injury; Trust and Estates, Wills and Probate

LADAR & LADAR
San Francisco, CA ... Criminal Trial Practice

LADENDORF, MARK C. & ASSOCIATES
Indianapolis, IN ... Medical Malpractice; Personal Injury

LADNER DOWNS
Vancouver, BC, Canada ... General Practice; Real Estate Law

LAFF STEIN CAMPBELL TUCKER & DELANEY, LLP
Denver, CO ... Business Law; Real Estate Law

LAFF, WHITESEL & SARET, LTD., A PROFESSIONAL CORPORATION
Chicago, IL ... Patent, Trademark, Copyright and Unfair Competition

LAFLEUR BROWN
Montreal, QU, Canada ... General Practice

LAGARENNÉ, LAWRENCE E.
Monticello, NY ... Civil Trial Practice

LAGERLOF, SENECAL, BRADLEY, GOSNEY & KRUSE, LLP
Los Angeles, CA ... Civil Trial Practice; General Practice
Pasadena, CA ... Administrative Law; Bankruptcy Law; Civil Trial Practice; Environmental Law; Municipal and Zoning Law; Natural Resources Law; Real Estate Law; Trust and Estates, Wills and Probate

LAGUE, NEWMAN & IRISH, A PROFESSIONAL CORPORATION
Muskegon, MI ... Business Law; Civil Trial Practice; Corporate Law; Environmental Law; General Practice; Health Care Law; Medical Malpractice; Real Estate Law

LAHIVE & COCKFIELD, LLP
Boston, MA ... Patent, Trademark, Copyright and Unfair Competition

LAIRD, DALLAS J.
Casper, WY ... Civil Trial Practice

LAKE TINDALL, LLP
Greenville, MS ... Admiralty/Maritime Law; General Practice

LAKE, TOBACK & YAVITZ
Chicago, IL ... Family Law

LALOS & KEEGAN
Washington, DC ... Patent, Trademark, Copyright and Unfair Competition

LAMAR, BURGESS, HALE, MILLER, NORRIS & FELDMAN, P.C.
Birmingham, AL ... Civil Trial Practice

LAMARCA & LANDRY, P.C.
West Des Moines, IA ... Civil Trial Practice; Commercial Law; Commercial Litigation; Medical Malpractice; Personal Injury; Professional Liability; Workers Compensation

LAMB & BARNOSKY, LLP
Melville, NY ... Administrative Law; Appellate Practice; Banking Law; Business Law; Civil Trial Practice; Commercial Law; Computer Law; Corporate Law; Environmental Law; Health Care Law; International Business Law; Labor and Employment Law; Land Use Law; Mergers and Acquisitions; Municipal and Zoning Law; Real Estate Law; Securities Law; Tax Law; Trust and Estates, Wills and Probate

LAMBDIN, JOHNSON, HERLOCKER, SODERBERG & LAMBDIN, CHARTERED
Wichita, KS ... Family Law

LAMBERT, JAY
Louisville, KY ... Criminal Trial Practice

LAMBERT, PAUL WATSON
Tallahassee, FL ... Health Care Law

LAMBERT & ROFFMAN, L.L.C.
Madison, GA ... General Practice

LAMBERTH, BONAPFEL, CIFELLI & STOKES, P.A.
Atlanta, GA ... Bankruptcy Law; Business Law; Creditors Rights

LAMBOS & JUNGE
New York, NY ... Admiralty/Maritime Law; Civil Trial Practice; Labor and Employment Law

LAMKIN, VAN EMAN, TRIMBLE, BEALS & ROURKE
Columbus, OH ... Civil Trial Practice; Medical Malpractice; Personal Injury; Product Liability Law

LAMMERS, LAMMERS & KLEIBACKER, L.L.P.
Madison, SD....General Practice

LAMPF, LIPKIND, PRUPIS, PETIGROW & LABUE, A PROFESSIONAL CORPORATION
West Orange, NJ....Tax Law; Trust and Estates, Wills and Probate

LANDAU, JULIE ELLEN LAW OFFICE OF
Baltimore, MD....Family Law

LAND, CLARK, CARROLL, MENDELSON & BLAIR, P.C.
Alexandria, VA....General Practice

LANDELS RIPLEY & DIAMOND, LLP
San Francisco, CA....General Practice

LANDERS & PARSONS
Tallahassee, FL....Energy Law; Environmental Law

LANDIS, GRAHAM, FRENCH, HUSFELD, SHERMAN & FORD, P.A.
Daytona Beach, FL....Criminal Trial Practice; General Practice; Personal Injury; Trust and Estates, Wills and Probate
DeLand, FL....General Practice; Personal Injury; Trust and Estates, Wills and Probate
Deltona, FL....General Practice; Trust and Estates, Wills and Probate

LANDOE, BROWN, PLANALP, BRAAKSMA & REIDA, P.C.
Bozeman, MT....General Practice

LANDRUM & LANDRUM
Jasper, GA....General Practice

LANDRUM & SHOUSE
Lexington, KY....Appellate Practice; General Practice; Insurance Defense
Louisville, KY....Civil Rights; Civil Trial Practice

LANDRY & WATKINS
New Iberia, LA....General Practice; Insurance Defense

LANDSMAN, RON M., P.A.
Bethesda, MD....Trust and Estates, Wills and Probate

LANDWEHR & HOF
New Orleans, LA....Bankruptcy Law; Trust and Estates, Wills and Probate

LANE, AITKEN & MCCANN, L.L.P.
Washington, DC....Patent, Trademark, Copyright and Unfair Competition

LANE & EHRLICH, LTD.
Phoenix, AZ....Business Law; Tax Law; Trust and Estates, Wills and Probate

LANE, FERTITTA, JANNEY & THOMAS
Baton Rouge, LA....Insurance Defense; Medical Malpractice; Personal Injury; Product Liability Law

LANE, GANNON & TALIAFERRO, L.L.P.
San Antonio, TX....Aviation Law; Commercial Litigation; Insurance Defense; Product Liability Law

LANE & LANE
Chicago, IL....Medical Malpractice; Personal Injury

LANE, LANE AND KELLY
Braintree, MA....General Practice

LANE, MARC J., A PROF. CORP., THE LAW OFFICES OF
Chicago, IL....Business Law; Tax Law

LANE POWELL SPEARS LUBERSKY LLP
Portland, OR....Antitrust Law; General Practice; Labor and Employment Law
Seattle, WA....Antitrust Law; Bankruptcy Law; Civil Trial Practice; Environmental Law; General Practice; Labor and Employment Law; Land Use Law; Real Estate Law; Tax Law

LANE, REESE, AULICK, SUMMERS & FIELD, P.A.
Coral Gables, FL....Admiralty/Maritime Law; Appellate Practice; Civil Trial Practice; Insurance Defense; Professional Liability

LANE, TROHN, BERTRAND & VREELAND, P.A.
Lakeland, FL....Civil Trial Practice; General Practice

LANE & WATERMAN
Rock Island, IL....General Practice
Davenport, IA....General Practice

LANER, MUCHIN, DOMBROW, BECKER, LEVIN AND TOMINBERG, LTD.
Chicago, IL....Employment Benefits Law; Labor and Employment Law

LANG MICHENER
Ottawa, ON, Canada....General Practice
Toronto, ON, Canada....General Practice

LANG & MORGERA, L.L.P.
Boston, MA....Medical Malpractice; Personal Injury; Product Liability Law

LANG, RICHERT & PATCH, A PROFESSIONAL CORPORATION
Fresno, CA....Bankruptcy Law; Civil Trial Practice; Construction Law; Environmental Law; General Practice; Labor and Employment Law; Medical Malpractice; Personal Injury; Real Estate Law

LANGAN, DEMPSEY AND BRODIGAN
Boston, MA....Civil Trial Practice; Construction Law

LANGLAIS & SCHUMACHER, P.A.
Hastings, MN....Real Estate Law; Tax Law

LANIER, PARKER & SULLIVAN, P.C.
Houston, TX....Appellate Practice; Commercial Litigation; Medical Malpractice; Personal Injury; Product Liability Law

LANKLER SIFFERT & WOHL LLP
New York, NY....Appellate Practice; Civil Trial Practice; Commercial Litigation; Criminal Trial Practice

LANO, NELSON, O'TOOLE & BENGTSON, LTD.
Grand Rapids, MN....Civil Trial Practice; Insurance Defense

LANSDEN, MITCHELL BAYLOR
Houston, TX....Criminal Trial Practice

LAPPAS, SPERO T. THE LAW OFFICES OF
Harrisburg, PA....Criminal Trial Practice; Personal Injury

LAPPIN & KUSMER LLP
Boston, MA....Patent, Trademark, Copyright and Unfair Competition

LAPUYADE, WASHINGTON & MOLK, LLC
Denver, CO....Commercial Litigation; Professional Liability

LARA, ART B. JR.
Amarillo, TX....Civil Trial Practice; General Practice

LARKY, SHELDON G.
Bingham Farms, MI....Family Law

LAROE, WINN, MOERMAN & DONOVAN
Washington, DC....Transportation Law

LA ROSSA & ROSS
New York, NY....Criminal Trial Practice; General Practice

LARSON, RONALD F., P.C.
Sun City, AZ....Trust and Estates, Wills and Probate

LARSON & TAYLOR
Alexandria, VA....Patent, Trademark, Copyright and Unfair Competition

LASCHER & LASCHER, A PROFESSIONAL CORPORATION
Ventura, CA....Appellate Practice; International Business Law

LASER, WILSON, BUFFORD & WATTS, P.A.
Little Rock, AR....Civil Trial Practice; Education Law; General Practice; Insurance Defense; Medical Malpractice; Workers Compensation

LASH & GOLDBERG LLP
Miami, FL....Commercial Litigation

LASKY, HAAS & COHLER, PROFESSIONAL CORPORATION
San Francisco, CA....Civil Trial Practice

LASPADA, ANTHONY J., P.A.
Tampa, FL....Criminal Trial Practice; Personal Injury

LASSER, MYRON G., P.C.
Staten Island, NY....Personal Injury

LASTER, G. A.
San Mateo, CA....Business Law; Municipal Bond/Public Authority Financing

LATHAM & WATKINS
Los Angeles, CA....General Practice

LATHROP & CLARK, LLP
Madison, WI....General Practice; Patent, Trademark, Copyright and Unfair Competition; Trademark, Copyright and Unfair Competition

LATHROP & RUTLEDGE, A PROFESSIONAL CORPORATION
Cheyenne, WY....Civil Trial Practice; General Practice; Insurance Defense

LAUB & FRANCHINO, L.L.C., LAW OFFICES OF
Raritan, NJ....Insurance Defense; Product Liability Law

LAUCHENGCO, JOSÉ Y. JR.
Los Angeles, CA....................Civil Trial Practice; Criminal Trial Practice; Personal Injury

LAUER, PHILIP D., P.C.
Easton, PA....................Civil Trial Practice; Criminal Trial Practice

LAUFMAN, ALAN K., J.D., M.D., A PROF. CORP., LAW OFFICES OF
Dallas, TX....................Medical Malpractice; Personal Injury; Product Liability Law

LAUGHLIN AND BOWEN
Hilton Head Island, SC....................Admiralty/Maritime Law; Civil Trial Practice; Construction Law

LAUGHLIN, PETERSON & LANG
Omaha, NE....................Civil Trial Practice; General Practice; Real Estate Law; Tax Law; Trust and Estates, Wills and Probate

LAURO, JOHN F., P.A.
Tampa, FL....................Commercial Litigation; Criminal Trial Practice

LAUTSCH LAW CORPORATION
Newport Beach, CA....................Business Law

LAVELLE, WILLIAM A.
Athens, OH....................Trust and Estates, Wills and Probate

LAVERY, DE BILLY
Montreal, QU, Canada....................General Practice
Quebec, QU, Canada....................General Practice

LAVIN, COLEMAN, O'NEIL, RICCI, FINARELLI & GRAY
New York, NY....................Civil Trial Practice; Insurance Defense; Product Liability Law
Philadelphia, PA....................Civil Trial Practice; Insurance Defense; Product Liability Law

LAW, SNAKARD & GAMBILL, A PROFESSIONAL CORPORATION
Fort Worth, TX....................Business Law; Commercial Litigation; General Practice

LAWING SHARPLESS & STAVOLA, P.A.
Greensboro, NC....................Civil Trial Practice; General Practice; Medical Malpractice

LAWLER, ANDREW M., P.C.
New York, NY....................Criminal Trial Practice

LAWRENCE, WILLIAM V.
Craig, CO....................Trust and Estates, Wills and Probate

LAWRENCE, BACA & DONOHUE PLLC
Houston, TX....................Bankruptcy Law

LAWRENCE FIRM, THE, L.P.A.
Cincinnati, OH....................Medical Malpractice; Personal Injury; Product Liability Law

LAWRENCE, KAMIN, SAUNDERS & UHLENHOP
Chicago, IL....................Civil Trial Practice; Construction Law; Corporate Law; Labor and Employment Law; Securities Law

LAWRENCE AND LAWRENCE
Louisville, KY....................Trust and Estates, Wills and Probate

LAWRENCE AND WALSH, P.C.
Hempstead, NY....................Business Law

LAWRENCE, WERNER, KESSELRING, SWARTOUT & BROWN, LLP
Rochester, NY....................Banking Law; Bankruptcy Law; Commercial Law; Commercial Litigation; Creditors Rights; Municipal and Zoning Law; Trust and Estates, Wills and Probate

LAWS & MURDOCH, P.A.
Russellville, AR....................General Practice

LAWSON, KIPP, FORBES & AYRES
Fairfax, VA....................Civil Trial Practice

LAWSON LUNDELL LAWSON & MCINTOSH
Vancouver, BC, Canada....................General Practice

LAWSON, WILLIAM M., JR., P.A.
Phoenix, AZ....................Real Estate Law

LAWTON & CATES, S.C.
Madison, WI....................Civil Trial Practice; Construction Law; Criminal Trial Practice; Labor and Employment Law; Personal Injury

LAXALT & NOMURA, LTD.
Reno, NV....................Civil Trial Practice

LAYDEN & LAYDEN
Lafayette, IN....................Civil Trial Practice; General Practice

LAZARUS, PAUL D.
Miami, FL....................Criminal Trial Practice

LAZARUS & ASSOCIATES, A PROFESSIONAL CORPORATION
Phoenix, AZ....................Land Use Law; Municipal and Zoning Law

LAZZARO AND KRAUS
Cleveland, OH....................Family Law

LEA, ARDEN J. LAW OFFICES OF
Fort Walton Beach, FL....................Admiralty/Maritime Law; Insurance Defense

LEACH, RAY
San Antonio, TX....................Civil Trial Practice; Personal Injury

LEACH, KENNETH C., P.C.
Albuquerque, NM....................Business Law; Corporate Law; Oil and Gas Law; Real Estate Law; Trust and Estates, Wills and Probate

LEACH, MCGREEVY & BAUTISTA, LLP
San Francisco, CA....................Construction Law; Environmental Law; Insurance Defense; Medical Malpractice; Product Liability Law; Workers Compensation

LEACH, SULLIVAN, SULLIVAN & WATKINS
Duncan, OK....................General Practice; Trust and Estates, Wills and Probate

LEAHEY & JOHNSON, P.C.
New York, NY....................Civil Trial Practice; Construction Law; Insurance Defense; Medical Malpractice; Product Liability Law

LEAHY & DENAULT, LLP
Claremont, NH....................General Practice

LEAKE, ANDERSSON & MANN, L.L.P.
New Orleans, LA....................Civil Trial Practice; Commercial Law; Construction Law; General Practice; Insurance Defense

LEARY, BRIDE, TINKER & MORAN, A PROFESSIONAL CORPORATION
Cedar Knolls, NJ....................Civil Trial Practice; Construction Law; Environmental Law; Insurance Defense; Product Liability Law

LEATH, BOUCH & CRAWFORD, L.L.P.
Charleston, SC....................Construction Law; Creditors Rights; Environmental Law; Toxic Torts

LEATHERMAN, WITZLER, DOMBEY & HART
Perrysburg, OH....................General Practice; Trust and Estates, Wills and Probate

LEATHERWOOD WALKER TODD & MANN, P.C.
Greenville, SC....................Antitrust Law; Bankruptcy Law; Civil Trial Practice; Construction Law; Environmental Law; General Practice; Health Care Law; Insurance Defense; Patent, Trademark, Copyright and Unfair Competition; Real Estate Law; Tax Law; Transportation Law
Spartanburg, SC....................Civil Trial Practice; General Practice; Insurance Defense

LEAVELL, JEFFREY, S.C.
Racine, WI....................Civil Trial Practice; Environmental Law; Insurance Defense

LEAVY, SCHULTZ, DAVIS & FEARING, P.S.
Kennewick, WA....................General Practice

LEBEAU, CHARLES P. LAW OFFICES OF
San Diego, CA....................Business Law; International Business Law; Tax Law

LEBLANC & YOUNG
Portland, ME....................Tax Law; Trust and Estates, Wills and Probate

LEBOVITS & DAVID, A PROFESSIONAL CORPORATION
Los Angeles, CA....................Aviation Law; Civil Trial Practice; Personal Injury; Product Liability Law

LECLAIR RYAN, A PROFESSIONAL CORPORATION
Richmond, VA....................Administrative Law; Appellate Practice; Bankruptcy Law; Business Law; Civil Trial Practice; Health Care Law; Immigration and Naturalization; Labor and Employment Law; Patent, Trademark, Copyright and Unfair Competition; Product Liability Law; Real Estate Law; Securities Law; Tax Law

LEDBETTER, COGBILL, ARNOLD & HARRISON, LLP
Fort Smith, AR....................General Practice; Insurance Defense; Medical Malpractice; Product Liability Law; Workers Compensation

LEDGEWOOD LAW FIRM, A PROFESSIONAL CORPORATION
Philadelphia, PA....................Trust and Estates, Wills and Probate

LEDY-GURREN & BLUMENSTOCK, L.L.P.
New York, NY....................Insurance Defense; Product Liability Law; Toxic Torts

LEE, DAVID L. LAW OFFICES OF
Chicago, IL.............................Labor and Employment Law

LEE, ROTAN E.
Philadelphia, PA ....Corporate Law; Municipal Bond/Public Authority Financing

LEE, BLACK, SCHEER & HART, P.C.
Savannah, GA ....Business Law; Civil Trial Practice; General Practice; Real Estate Law

LEE, DUROCHER, KISNER, WALKER & REID
Oklahoma City, OK.................Civil Trial Practice; Insurance Defense; Medical Malpractice; Personal Injury; Product Liability Law; Professional Liability

LEE, EADON, ISGETT AND POPWELL, P.A.
Columbia, SC ....Medical Malpractice; Personal Injury; Product Liability Law; Workers Compensation

LEE, ERTER, WILSON, HOLLER & SMITH, L.L.C.
Sumter, SC..............................Civil Trial Practice; Criminal Trial Practice; Family Law; Insurance Defense

LEE, FUTRELL & PERLES, L.L.P.
New Orleans, LA ....Admiralty/Maritime Law; Civil Trial Practice; Energy Law; General Practice; Insurance Defense; Toxic Torts

LEE, GODDARD & DUFFY LLP
Irvine, CA...............................Business Law; Civil Trial Practice

LEE, JOHN PETER, LTD.
Las Vegas, NV ....Bankruptcy Law; Business Law; Civil Trial Practice; Commercial Litigation; General Practice; Real Estate Law; Trust and Estates, Wills and Probate

LEE, LEE & GARNER
Whiteville, NC.........................General Practice

LEE, MARTIN, GREEN & REITER, INC.
Bellefonte, PA ....General Practice
State College, PA ....General Practice

LEE & MCINISH
Dothan, AL..............................Civil Trial Practice; General Practice; Insurance Defense; Product Liability Law

LEE, ROBERT W., & ASSOCIATES, P.C.
Birmingham, AL ....Personal Injury

LEE, SMART, COOK, MARTIN & PATTERSON, P.S., INC.
Seattle, WA ....Insurance Defense

LEESFIELD, LEIGHTON, RUBIO & MAHFOOD, P.A.
Miami, FL ....Civil Trial Practice; General Practice

LEFEBVRE, BARRON & VIVONE, CHTD.
Las Vegas, NV ....Civil Trial Practice; Construction Law; Insurance Defense; Personal Injury; Product Liability Law; Toxic Torts

LEFEBVRE, FRANCIS, BUREAU
New York, NY.........................Business Law; Tax Law

LEFFLER, HYLAND & THOMPSON, A PROFESSIONAL CORPORATION
Fairfax, VA ....Civil Trial Practice; Criminal Trial Practice; Labor and Employment Law; Real Estate Law

LEFTWICH & DOUGLAS, P.L.L.C.
Washington, DC.......................General Practice

LEGAL STRATEGIES GROUP
Emeryville, CA.........................Civil Trial Practice; General Practice; Intellectual Property Law

LEGER & MESTAYER
New Orleans, LA ....Admiralty/Maritime Law

LEGROS LAW PARTNERS, P.C.
Berwyn, PA ....Environmental Law

LEHMAN & EILEN, LLP
Uniondale, NY ....Business Law; Civil Trial Practice; Securities Law; Trademark, Copyright and Unfair Competition

LEHNER, MITCHELL, RODRIGUES AND SEARS
Portland, OR...........................Insurance Defense

LEHR MIDDLEBROOKS PRICE & PROCTOR, P.C.
Birmingham, AL ....Labor and Employment Law

LEIB & KATT, S.C.
Milwaukee, WI ....Civil Trial Practice

LEIBOWITZ & COHEN
Knoxville, TN ....Business Law; Civil Trial Practice; Construction Law; Criminal Trial Practice; Labor and Employment Law; Land Use Law; Medical Malpractice; Personal Injury; Trust and Estates, Wills and Probate

LEIBOWITZ, MARTIN L., P.A.
Jacksonville, FL ....Workers Compensation

LEIBY CONSTRUCTION LAW FIRM, PROFESSIONAL ASSOCIATION
Fort Lauderdale, FL...............Construction Law; Government Contracts

LEICK, HAMMONS AND BRITTAIN
Corbin, KY ....General Practice

LEINOFF, ANDREW M., & ASSOCIATES, P.A.
Miami, FL ....Family Law

LEISAWITZ HELLER ABRAMOWITCH PHILLIPS, P.C.
Wyomissing, PA......................Bankruptcy Law; Commercial Litigation; Mergers and Acquisitions; Personal Injury; Real Estate Law

LEITER, WILLIAM
Tulsa, OK................................Trust and Estates, Wills and Probate

LEITNER, WILLIAMS, DOOLEY & NAPOLITAN, PLLC
Chattanooga, TN ....General Practice
Knoxville, TN ....General Practice
Memphis, TN ....General Practice
Nashville, TN..........................General Practice

LELAND, PARACHINI, STEINBERG, MATZGER & MELNICK, L.L.P.
San Francisco, CA ....General Practice

LEMON, ARMEY, HEARN & LEININGER
Warsaw, IN ....Civil Trial Practice; Corporate Law; Product Liability Law; Trust and Estates, Wills and Probate

LEMON, SHEARER, EHRLICH, PHILLIPS & GOOD, A PROFESSIONAL CORPORATION
Perryton, TX..........................Civil Trial Practice; General Practice; Natural Resources Law

LENAHAN & DEMPSEY, A PROFESSIONAL CORPORATION
Scranton, PA..........................Civil Trial Practice; General Practice; Insurance Defense; Personal Injury; Securities Law; Workers Compensation

LEON, AMBERSON & CARROLL, L.L.P.
San Antonio, TX.....................Civil Trial Practice; Criminal Trial Practice

LEONARD FELKER ALTFELD GREENBERG & BATTAILE, P.C.
Tucson, AZ ....Bankruptcy Law; Civil Trial Practice; Commercial Litigation; Real Estate Law

LEONARD & MORRISON
Fort Lauderdale, FL...............Real Estate Law; Trust and Estates, Wills and Probate

LEONARD, STREET AND DEINARD, PROFESSIONAL ASSOCIATION
Minneapolis, MN....................General Practice

LEONE, LAWRENCE E.
Los Angeles, CA ....Family Law

LEOPOLD, PETRICH & SMITH, A PROFESSIONAL CORPORATION
Los Angeles, CA ....Civil Trial Practice; Trademark, Copyright and Unfair Competition

LEPLEY, PATRICK H.
Bellevue, WA..........................Personal Injury

LEPRELL, SAMUEL L.
Jacksonville, FL ....Business Law; Real Estate Law

LERNER, DAVID, LITTENBERG, KRUMHOLZ & MENTLIK
Westfield, NJ ....Patent, Trademark, Copyright and Unfair Competition

LERUM, NORMAN J.
Chicago, IL.............................Appellate Practice; Civil Trial Practice; Commercial Litigation

LESLIE & SMITH, P.C.
El Paso, TX............................Bankruptcy Law

LESS, GETZ & LIPMAN
Memphis, TN..........................Construction Law

LESSER & SOBEL, P.C.
Bridgeport, CT ....Civil Trial Practice; Personal Injury; Real Estate Law

LEUPP, WACHOB & WOODALL
Auburn, CA ....Criminal Trial Practice; Insurance Defense

LEVENE, NEALE, BENDER & RANKIN L.L.P.
Los Angeles, CA ....Bankruptcy Law

LEVENS, WILLIAM P.
Tampa, FL ....Personal Injury; Workers Compensation

LEVENTHAL LAW FIRM, THE, P.C.
Denver, CO ....Civil Trial Practice; Medical Malpractice; Personal Injury

LEVENTHAL & SLAUGHTER, P.A.
Orlando, FL ....Criminal Trial Practice

LEVERTY & ASSOCIATES LAW, CHARTERED
Reno, NV ....Administrative Law; Civil Trial Practice

LEVETT ROCKWOOD P.C.
Westport, CT........Business Law; General Practice; Health Care Law; Labor and Employment Law; Patent, Trademark, Copyright and Unfair Competition; Tax Law

LEVIN, MARK
Roseland, NJ........Tax Law; Trust and Estates, Wills and Probate

LEVIN, FISHBEIN, SEDRAN & BERMAN
Philadelphia, PA........Admiralty/Maritime Law; Antitrust Law; Civil Trial Practice; Commercial Litigation; Environmental Law; General Practice; Medical Malpractice; Product Liability Law; Securities Law

LEVIN & GILLEY
Beaufort, SC........General Practice; Real Estate Law; Trust and Estates, Wills and Probate

LEVIN, MARMAROS & CHARMS CO., L.P.A.
Cleveland, OH........Commercial Litigation; Medical Malpractice; Personal Injury; Product Liability Law

LEVIN, MICHAEL I., AND ASSOCIATES, P.C.
Huntingdon Valley, PA........Labor and Employment Law

LEVINE, AARON M. & ASSOCIATES
Washington, DC........Medical Malpractice; Personal Injury; Product Liability Law

LEVINE & ASSOCIATES
Los Angeles, CA........Business Law

LEVINE, BLASZAK, BLOCK & BOOTHBY, LLP
Washington, DC........Communications Law

LEVINE, BUSCH, SCHNEPPER & STEIN, P.A.
Miami, FL........Medical Malpractice; Personal Injury; Workers Compensation

LEVINE, CARL S., & ASSOCIATES, P.C.
Roslyn, NY........Commercial Litigation

LEVINE, HIRSCH, SEGALL & BRENNAN, P.A.
Tampa, FL........Civil Trial Practice; Criminal Trial Practice; Family Law; Personal Injury

LEVINE & PARTNERS, P.A.
Miami, FL........Commercial Litigation; General Practice; Insurance Defense

LEVINE, STEINBERG & MILLER
San Diego, CA........Civil Trial Practice; Personal Injury

LEVINE SULLIVAN & KOCH, L.L.P.
Washington, DC........Communications Law; Intellectual Property Law

LEVINE AND YATES, P.C.
Arlington, VA........Immigration and Naturalization

LEVINGSTON & LEVINGSTON
Cleveland, MS........Bankruptcy Law; Corporate Law

LEVIT, MANN & HALLIGAN, P.C.
Richmond, VA........Labor and Employment Law

LEVY, HERBERT MONTE
New York, NY........Appellate Practice

LEVY, ANGSTREICH, FINNEY, BALDANTE, RUBENSTEIN & COREN, P.C.
Philadelphia, PA........Civil Trial Practice; Commercial Litigation

LEVY, EHRLICH & PETRIELLO, A PROFESSIONAL CORPORATION
Newark, NJ........General Practice; Tax Law; Trust and Estates, Wills and Probate

LEVY, JAMES L., P.C.
St. Albans, VT........Personal Injury

LEVY & LAMBDIN, P.C.
Denver, CO........Civil Trial Practice; Commercial Litigation; Environmental Law; Insurance Defense

LEVY, STEVEN B., LTD.
Naperville, IL........Civil Trial Practice; Medical Malpractice; Personal Injury
Wheaton, IL........Civil Trial Practice; Medical Malpractice; Personal Injury

LEWALLEN, JO BETSY LAW OFFICES OF
Austin, TX........Family Law

LEWANDOWSKI LAW FIRM, THE, A PROFESSIONAL CORPORATION
Kansas City, MO........Transportation Law

LEWIS, JOHN B.
Sacramento, CA........Civil Trial Practice

LEWIS & ALLEN, P.C.
Kalamazoo, MI........Business Law; Commercial Law; Commercial Litigation; Corporate Law; Family Law; General Practice; Labor and Employment Law; Real Estate Law; Trust and Estates, Wills and Probate

LEWIS & ASSOCIATES
Beaumont, TX........Civil Trial Practice; Insurance Defense

LEWIS, BABCOCK & HAWKINS, L.L.P.
Columbia, SC........Civil Trial Practice

LEWIS, D'AMATO, BRISBOIS & BISGAARD LLP
Los Angeles, CA........General Practice

LEWIS, FISHER, HENDERSON & CLAXTON, LLP
Memphis, TN........Labor and Employment Law

LEWIS & GREER, P.C.
Poughkeepsie, NY........Construction Law; Municipal and Zoning Law; Public Utilities Law; Real Estate Law

LEWIS & KAPPES, PROFESSIONAL CORPORATION
Indianapolis, IN........General Practice; Immigration and Naturalization; Public Utilities Law

LEWIS, KULLMAN & STERBCOW
New Orleans, LA........Admiralty/Maritime Law; Medical Malpractice; Personal Injury

LEWIS LAW FIRM, THE, A PROFESSIONAL CORPORATION
Washington, DC........Family Law

LEWIS & MUNDAY, A PROFESSIONAL CORPORATION
Washington, DC........Environmental Law; Municipal Bond/Public Authority Financing; Securities Law
Boston, MA........Municipal Bond/Public Authority Financing; Securities Law
Detroit, MI........Banking Law; Business Law; Civil Trial Practice; Environmental Law; Health Care Law; Municipal Bond/Public Authority Financing; Real Estate Law; Securities Law; Transportation Law

LEWIS & PRESTON
Elizabethtown, KY........General Practice

LEWIS, RICE & FINGERSH
St. Louis, MO........Admiralty/Maritime Law; Antitrust Law; Civil Trial Practice; General Practice; Labor and Employment Law; Municipal Bond/Public Authority Financing; Tax Law

LEWIS & ROBERTS, P.L.L.C.
Raleigh, NC........Construction Law; Insurance Defense; Workers Compensation

LEWIS AND ROCA, LLP
Phoenix, AZ........Antitrust Law; Banking Law; Bankruptcy Law; Business Law; Civil Trial Practice; Commercial Law; Criminal Trial Practice; Environmental Law; General Practice; Health Care Law; Labor and Employment Law; Real Estate Law; Securities Law; Tax Law; Trademark, Copyright and Unfair Competition
Tucson, AZ........Real Estate Law

LEWIS, ROGERS & KUDRLE, P.C.
Plattsburgh, NY........Banking Law; Corporate Law; General Practice; Municipal and Zoning Law; Trust and Estates, Wills and Probate

LEWIS, TAYLOR, TODD & DIXON, P.C.
La Grange, GA........General Practice

LEYDIG, VOIT & MAYER, LTD.
Washington, DC........Patent, Trademark, Copyright and Unfair Competition
Chicago, IL........Patent, Trademark, Copyright and Unfair Competition
Rockford, IL........Patent, Trademark, Copyright and Unfair Competition

LIBERT, JACK L. LAW OFFICES OF
Garden City, NY........Municipal and Zoning Law

LIBERT, VICTOR E., LAW OFFICE OF
Simsbury, CT........Patent, Trademark, Copyright and Unfair Competition

LICATA, ARTHUR F., P.C.
Boston, MA........Civil Trial Practice

LICCARDO, ROSSI, STURGES & MCNEIL, A PROFESSIONAL LAW CORPORATION
San Jose, CA........Personal Injury; Product Liability Law; Real Estate Law; Trust and Estates, Wills and Probate

LICHTENAUER, ROBERT A.
Indianapolis, IN....................Tax Law; Trust and Estates, Wills and Probate

LIDDLE & ROBINSON, L.L.P.
New York, NY....................Civil Trial Practice; Family Law; Labor and Employment Law

LIEBER & LIEBER
New York, NY....................Insurance Defense; Product Liability Law

LIEBERMAN, MAX L. & ASSOCIATES
Fort Washington, PA....................Real Estate Law

LIEBERMAN, DODGE, SENDROW & GERDING, LTD.
Phoenix, AZ....................Commercial Litigation; Real Estate Law

LIEBERMAN, MARTIN, P.C.
Phoenix, AZ....................Criminal Trial Practice

LIEBERMAN & NOWAK, LLP
New York, NY....................Patent, Trademark, Copyright and Unfair Competition

LIEBERTHAL, DAVID H.
Tucson, AZ....................Family Law

LIEFF, CABRASER, HEIMANN & BERNSTEIN, LLP
San Francisco, CA....................Antitrust Law; Civil Trial Practice; Environmental Law; Labor and Employment Law; Product Liability Law; Securities Law

LIGGIO, BENRUBI & WILLIAMS, P.A.
West Palm Beach, FL....................Civil Trial Practice; Health Care Law; Personal Injury

LIGHTCAP, ROBERT P.
Latrobe, PA....................Construction Law

LIGHTFOOT, FRANKLIN & WHITE, L.L.C.
Birmingham, AL....................Antitrust Law; Appellate Practice; Civil Trial Practice; Commercial Litigation; Construction Law; Environmental Law; Labor and Employment Law; Personal Injury; Product Liability Law; Securities Law

LIGHTMAN, MANOCHI & KORNILOWICZ
Philadelphia, PA....................Civil Trial Practice

LIGMAN, MARTIN & EVANS, P.L.
Miami, FL....................Commercial Law; Insurance Defense

LILES, GAVIN & COSTANTINO
Jacksonville, FL....................Civil Trial Practice; Commercial Litigation; Medical Malpractice; Personal Injury; Product Liability Law

LILLY, ANDERSON, MORGAN
Toronto, ON, Canada....................Insurance Defense

LIMANDRI, CHARLES S.
Rancho Santa Fe, CA....................Civil Trial Practice

LIMBACH & LIMBACH, L.L.P.
San Francisco, CA....................Patent, Trademark, Copyright and Unfair Competition

LIM, RUGER & KIM, LLP
Los Angeles, CA....................Civil Trial Practice

LINDABURY, MCCORMICK & ESTABROOK, P.A.
Westfield, NJ....................Banking Law; Civil Trial Practice; Commercial Law; Construction Law; General Practice; Health Care Law; Labor and Employment Law; Municipal Bond/Public Authority Financing; Public Utilities Law; Real Estate Law; Tax Law

LINDER & HOLLOWELL, A PROFESSIONAL CORPORATION
Indianapolis, IN....................Insurance Defense

LINDHORST & DREIDAME CO., L.P.A.
Cincinnati, OH....................Civil Trial Practice; General Practice; Insurance Defense; Medical Malpractice

LINDLEY, SCALES & CORBETT, A PROFESSIONAL CORPORATION
San Diego, CA....................Banking Law; Business Law; Civil Trial Practice; Commercial Law; Commercial Litigation; Creditors Rights; Health Care Law; Professional Liability; Real Estate Law

LINDNER & MARSACK, S.C.
Milwaukee, WI....................Labor and Employment Law

LINDOW & TREAT, L.L.P.
San Antonio, TX....................Insurance Defense

LINDSAY, HART, NEIL & WEIGLER, LLP
Portland, OR....................Admiralty/Maritime Law; Antitrust Law; Labor and Employment Law

LINES, HINSON AND LINES
Quincy, FL....................General Practice

LINIAK, BERENATO, LONGACRE & WHITE, LLC
Bethesda, MD....................Patent, Trademark, Copyright and Unfair Competition

LINNE, WILLIAM V.
Pensacola, FL....................Tax Law; Trust and Estates, Wills and Probate

LINOWES AND BLOCHER LLP
Silver Spring, MD....................Bankruptcy Law; Business Law; Commercial Litigation; Environmental Law; General Practice; Land Use Law; Municipal and Zoning Law; Real Estate Law

LIONEL SAWYER & COLLINS
Las Vegas, NV....................Bankruptcy Law; Civil Trial Practice; General Practice; Labor and Employment Law; Land Use Law; Real Estate Law
Reno, NV....................General Practice

LIPKIN, STANLEY G.
Denver, CO....................Family Law

LIPKIN, MARSHALL, BOHORAD & THORNBURG, A PROFESSIONAL CORPORATION
Pottsville, PA....................General Practice

LIPMAN, ANTONELLI, BATT, DUNLAP, WODLINGER & GILSON, A PROFESSIONAL CORPORATION
Vineland, NJ....................Civil Trial Practice; General Practice

LIPMAN & KATZ, P.A.
Augusta, ME....................Civil Trial Practice; Commercial Litigation; Labor and Employment Law; Personal Injury

LIPPE & ASSOCIATES, LAW OFFICES OF
Dallas, TX....................Appellate Practice; Civil Trial Practice

LIPPMAN, MAHFOUZ & MARTIN
Morgan City, LA....................General Practice; Personal Injury

LIPSCHUETZ, JESSE N., P.C.
Denver, CO....................Real Estate Law

LIPSCOMB, J. RANDOLPH
Columbus, MS....................Civil Trial Practice

LIPSHUTZ, GREENBLATT & KING
Atlanta, GA....................Civil Trial Practice; General Practice; Real Estate Law

LIPSIG, SHAPEY, MANUS & MOVERMAN, P.C.
New York, NY....................Personal Injury; Product Liability Law

LIPSTET & HIRSCH, L.L.P.
Houston, TX....................Commercial Law; Family Law; International Business Law

LIRTZMAN, NEHLS & HEPNER, A PROFESSIONAL CORPORATION
Boulder, CO....................Bankruptcy Law; Real Estate Law

LISS AND ASSOCIATES, P.C.
Bloomfield Hills, MI....................Civil Trial Practice; Commercial Law; Personal Injury

LISTON/LANCASTER
Grenada, MS....................Civil Trial Practice; General Practice
Jackson, MS....................Civil Trial Practice; General Practice
Winona, MS....................Civil Trial Practice; General Practice

LITCHFORD & CHRISTOPHER, PROFESSIONAL ASSOCIATION
Orlando, FL....................Antitrust Law; Appellate Practice; Civil Trial Practice; Commercial Litigation; General Practice

LITE, DE PALMA, GREENBERG & RIVAS, LLC
Newark, NJ....................Admiralty/Maritime Law; Appellate Practice; Civil Trial Practice; Criminal Trial Practice; Environmental Law

LITMAN, ASCHE & GIOIELLA, LLP
New York, NY....................Civil Trial Practice; Criminal Trial Practice; Personal Injury

LITMAN, KRAAI AND BROWN, L.L.C.
Kansas City, MO....................Patent, Trademark, Copyright and Unfair Competition

LITMAN LAW OFFICES, LTD.
Arlington, VA....................Patent, Trademark, Copyright and Unfair Competition

LITMAN LITMAN HARRIS & BROWN, P.C.
Pittsburgh, PA....................Civil Trial Practice

LITTEN & SIPE, L.L.P.
Harrisonburg, VA....................General Practice

LITTLE, GILMAN & VELASQUEZ, P.A.
Albuquerque, NM....................Family Law

LITTLE, LITTLE, LITTLE, WINDEL & COPPEDGE
Madill, OK ....General Practice

LITTLE, PARSLEY & CLUVERIUS, P.C.
Richmond, VA ....Environmental Law; Real Estate Law; Trust and Estates, Wills and Probate

LITTLER MENDELSON, A PROFESSIONAL CORPORATION
San Francisco, CA ....General Practice

LITTNER, DESCHLER & LITTNER
Allentown, PA ....General Practice; Real Estate Law; Trust and Estates, Wills and Probate
Bethlehem, PA ....General Practice; Real Estate Law; Trust and Estates, Wills and Probate
Easton, PA ....General Practice; Real Estate Law; Trust and Estates, Wills and Probate

LITVAK, LITVAK, MEHRTENS & EPSTEIN, PROFESSIONAL CORPORATION
Denver, CO ....Family Law

LIVINGSTON & MATTESICH, LAW CORPORATION
Sacramento, CA ....Administrative Law; Appellate Practice; Business Law; Civil Trial Practice; Commercial Litigation; Construction Law; Eminent Domain; Energy Law; Environmental Law; General Practice; Health Care Law; Intellectual Property Law; Labor and Employment Law; Natural Resources Law; Patent, Trademark, Copyright and Unfair Competition; Product Liability Law; Real Estate Law

LLOYD, DINNING, BOGGS & DINNING
Demopolis, AL ....General Practice

LLOYD, GOSSELINK, BLEVINS, ROCHELLE, BALDWIN & TOWNSEND, P.C.
Austin, TX ....Environmental Law

LLOYD, SCHREIBER & GRAY, P.C.
Birmingham, AL ....Civil Trial Practice; Insurance Defense

LOBEL & OPERA LLP
Irvine, CA ....Bankruptcy Law; Commercial Law; Commercial Litigation

LOBRANO & KINCAID, P.L.
Jacksonville, FL ....Business Law; Commercial Litigation; Construction Law; Real Estate Law; Trust and Estates, Wills and Probate

LOCKE & HERBERT
New York, NY ....Civil Trial Practice; Insurance Defense

LOCKE LIDDELL & SAPP LLP
Dallas, TX ....General Practice

LOCKE REYNOLDS LLP
Indianapolis, IN ....Banking Law; Civil Trial Practice; Construction Law; General Practice; Health Care Law; Insurance Defense; Labor and Employment Law; Medical Malpractice; Patent, Trademark, Copyright and Unfair Competition; Personal Injury; Product Liability Law; Securities Law; Tax Law

LOE, WARREN, ROSENFIELD, KAITCER & HIBBS, A PROFESSIONAL CORPORATION
Fort Worth, TX ....Business Law; Family Law

LOEB & LOEB LLP
Los Angeles, CA ....Antitrust Law; Appellate Practice; Banking Law; Bankruptcy Law; Civil Trial Practice; Environmental Law; General Practice; Intellectual Property Law; Labor and Employment Law; Real Estate Law; Tax Law; Trademark, Copyright and Unfair Competition; Trust and Estates, Wills and Probate
New York, NY ....Antitrust Law; Appellate Practice; Banking Law; Bankruptcy Law; Civil Trial Practice; General Practice; Real Estate Law; Tax Law; Trademark, Copyright and Unfair Competition; Trust and Estates, Wills and Probate
Rome, Italy ....General Practice

LOEWY, STEVEN A., P.A.
Bethesda, MD ....Real Estate Law

LOFTON, LIONEL S.
Charleston, SC ....Criminal Trial Practice

LOGAN, CHARLES E.
San Jose, CA ....Bankruptcy Law

LOGAN, GARY
Las Vegas, NV ....Aviation Law; Medical Malpractice; Personal Injury

LOGGANS, SUSAN E., & ASSOCIATES, P.C.
Chicago, IL ....Civil Trial Practice; Medical Malpractice; Personal Injury; Product Liability Law

LOHF, SHAIMAN & JACOBS, P.C.
Denver, CO ....Business Law; Natural Resources Law; Real Estate Law; Tax Law

LOMBARDI, LOPER & CONANT, LLP
Oakland, CA ....Civil Trial Practice; Education Law; Insurance Defense; Medical Malpractice; Product Liability Law; Professional Liability

LOMELL, MUCCIFORI, ADLER, RAVASCHIERE, AMABILE & PEHLIVANIAN, A PROFESSIONAL CORPORATION
Toms River, NJ ....Civil Trial Practice; Environmental Law; General Practice; Insurance Defense; Municipal and Zoning Law; Personal Injury; Product Liability Law; Toxic Torts; Workers Compensation

LOMMEN, NELSON, COLE & STAGEBERG, P.A.
Minneapolis, MN ....Business Law; Civil Trial Practice; Insurance Defense; Real Estate Law

LONDON FISCHER LLP
New York, NY ....Admiralty/Maritime Law; Appellate Practice; Civil Trial Practice; Construction Law; Insurance Defense; Product Liability Law

LONG ALDRIDGE & NORMAN LLP
Atlanta, GA ....Administrative Law; Antitrust Law; Appellate Practice; Bankruptcy Law; Business Law; Civil Trial Practice; Communications Law; Computer Law; Creditors Rights; Employment Benefits Law; Environmental Law; Family Law; General Practice; Health Care Law; Immigration and Naturalization; Labor and Employment Law; Municipal Bond/Public Authority Financing; Public Utilities Law; Real Estate Law; Securities Law; Sports and Entertainment Law; Tax Law; Trust and Estates, Wills and Probate

LONG, BURNER, PARKS & SEALY, A PROFESSIONAL CORPORATION
Austin, TX ....Administrative Law; Insurance Defense

LONG & JAUDON, P.C.
Denver, CO ....Civil Trial Practice; General Practice; Insurance Defense; Labor and Employment Law; Legal Malpractice; Medical Malpractice

LONG LAW FIRM, L.L.P.
Baton Rouge, LA ....Commercial Litigation; Insurance Defense; Professional Liability; Public Utilities Law

LONG & LEVIT LLP
San Francisco, CA ....General Practice

LONG & LONG
Chapel Hill, NC ....Civil Trial Practice; Family Law

LONG, PARKER, WARREN & JONES, P.A.
Asheville, NC ....Civil Trial Practice; Criminal Trial Practice

LONG, TUMINELLO, BESSO, SELIGMAN, QUINLAN & WERNER
Bay Shore, NY ....Civil Trial Practice; Criminal Trial Practice; Personal Injury

LONG & WILLIAMSON, A PROFESSIONAL CORPORATION
Santa Ana, CA ....Insurance Defense

LOOMIS, EWERT, PARSLEY, DAVIS & GOTTING, P.C.
Lansing, MI ....Commercial Litigation; Corporate Law

LOONEY & GROSSMAN LLP
Boston, MA ....Bankruptcy Law; Business Law; Civil Trial Practice; General Practice

LOONEY, NICHOLS & JOHNSON, PLLC
Oklahoma City, OK ....Civil Trial Practice; General Practice

LOPEZ, DAVID T. & ASSOCIATES
Houston, TX ....Arbitration; Labor and Employment Law

LOPEZ, SCOTT P. LAW OFFICE OF
Boston, MA ....Civil Trial Practice; Criminal Trial Practice

LOPEZ, HODES, RESTAINO, MILMAN & SKIKOS, A LAW CORPORATION
Newport Beach, CA ....Civil Trial Practice; Labor and Employment Law; Medical Malpractice; Personal Injury; Product Liability Law; Toxic Torts

LORD, BISSELL & BROOK
Los Angeles, CA ....General Practice
Atlanta, GA ....General Practice
Chicago, IL ....General Practice
Rockford, IL ....General Practice

LORD & WHIP, A PROFESSIONAL ASSOCIATION
Baltimore, MD ....General Practice; Workers Compensation

LORENZO & GIANVITO, P.C.
Punxsutawney, PA ....Civil Trial Practice; Commercial Litigation; Personal Injury

LORUSSO & LOUD
Boston, MA ....Patent, Trademark, Copyright and Unfair Competition

LOSKAMP, ALVIN N., A LAW CORPORATION
Burbank, CA .... Business Law; Trust and Estates, Wills and Probate

LOTT, FRANKLIN, FONDA & FLANAGAN
Greenwood, MS .... General Practice

LOVE, THORNTON, ARNOLD & THOMASON, P.A.
Greenville, SC .... Civil Trial Practice; Corporate Law; Criminal Trial Practice; Environmental Law; General Practice; Insurance Defense; Medical Malpractice; Product Liability Law; Real Estate Law

LOVELESS, CURTIS M.
Denton, TX .... Family Law

LOVELL & STEWART, LLP
New York, NY .... Antitrust Law; Civil Trial Practice; Commercial Law; Corporate Law; Criminal Trial Practice; Securities Law

LOVETT, THOMAS G. JR.
Minneapolis, MN .... Bankruptcy Law; General Practice; Trust and Estates, Wills and Probate

LOVICH & PENN
Los Angeles, CA .... Insurance Defense

LOVITZ AND GOLD, P.C.
Philadelphia, PA .... Civil Trial Practice; Labor and Employment Law

LOW & CHILDERS, P.C.
Phoenix, AZ .... Administrative Law

LOWE, BRYAN A, & ASSOCIATES, A PROF. LAW CORP.
Las Vegas, NV .... Elder Law; Real Estate Law; Trust and Estates, Wills and Probate

LOWE • EKLUND • WAKEFIELD CO., L.P.A.
Cleveland, OH .... Business Law; Commercial Litigation; Medical Malpractice; Personal Injury; Product Liability Law

LOWE, MOBLEY & LOWE
Haleyville, AL .... Insurance Defense

LOWE, STEIN, HOFFMAN, ALLWEISS & HAUVER, L.L.P.
New Orleans, LA .... Administrative Law; Business Law; Civil Trial Practice; Commercial Law; Corporate Law; Family Law; General Practice; Insurance Defense; Labor and Employment Law; Personal Injury; Tax Law; Trust and Estates, Wills and Probate

LOWENBAUM PARTNERSHIP, THE, L.L.C.
St. Louis, MO .... Commercial Litigation; Corporate Law; Health Care Law; Labor and Employment Law; Securities Law

LOWENHAUPT & CHASNOFF, L.L.C.
St. Louis, MO .... General Practice; Tax Law

LOWENTHAL, BETTY L.
Sylvan Lake, MI .... Family Law

LOWER, JOYCE Q.
Bloomfield Hills, MI .... Trust and Estates, Wills and Probate

LOWTHORP, RICHARDS, MCMILLAN, MILLER, CONWAY & TEMPLEMAN, A PROFESSIONAL CORPORATION
Oxnard, CA .... Corporate Law; Real Estate Law; Trust and Estates, Wills and Probate

LOWY, RONALD S. THE LAW OFFICES OF
Miami, FL .... Commercial Litigation; Criminal Trial Practice; Personal Injury

LUBIN & ENOCH, P.C.
Phoenix, AZ .... Labor and Employment Law

LUBIN, RICHARD G., P.A.
West Palm Beach, FL .... Criminal Trial Practice

LUCAS, HENRY C. III
Philadelphia, PA .... Admiralty/Maritime Law; Commercial Litigation

LUCAS BOWKER & WHITE
Edmonton, AB, Canada .... Civil Trial Practice; Commercial Law; Environmental Law; General Practice

LUCAS, HOLCOMB & MEDREA
Merrillville, IN .... General Practice

LUCAS LAW FIRM, THE
San Francisco, CA .... Civil Trial Practice; Labor and Employment Law

LUCAS & TONN, P.C.
Miles City, MT .... General Practice

LUCCO BROWN & MUDGE
Edwardsville, IL .... Civil Trial Practice; Criminal Trial Practice

LUCE, FORWARD, HAMILTON & SCRIPPS LLP
La Jolla, CA .... Trust and Estates, Wills and Probate
San Diego, CA .... Banking Law; Bankruptcy Law; Business Law; Environmental Law; Family Law; General Practice; Insurance Defense; Intellectual Property Law; International Business Law; Labor and Employment Law; Municipal Bond/Public Authority Financing; Personal Injury; Product Liability Law; Real Estate Law; Securities Law; Tax Law

LUCKETT LAW FIRM, A PROFESSIONAL ASSOCIATION
Clarksdale, MS .... General Practice; Insurance Defense

LUDENS, POTTER & BURCH
Morrison, IL .... General Practice

LUDWIG GOLDBERG & KRENZEL, A PROFESSIONAL CORPORATION
San Francisco, CA .... Employment Benefits Law

LUEDEKA, NEELY & GRAHAM, P.C.
Knoxville, TN .... Computer Law; Intellectual Property Law; Patent, Trademark, Copyright and Unfair Competition

LUEDERS, ROBERTSON & KONZEN
Granite City, IL .... Commercial Litigation; Energy Law; General Practice; Public Utilities Law; Trust and Estates, Wills and Probate

LUFFEY, JOHN L. JR.
Monroe, LA .... Tax Law

LUGENBUHL, BURKE, WHEATON, PECK, RANKIN & HUBBARD, A LAW CORPORATION
New Orleans, LA .... Admiralty/Maritime Law; Commercial Litigation; Environmental Law

LUNDEEN, DAVID F.
Fergus Falls, MN .... Elder Law; Employment Benefits Law; General Practice; Pension and Profit Sharing; Real Estate Law; Tax Law; Trust and Estates, Wills and Probate

LUNDIN, JOHN W., P.S.
Seattle, WA .... Criminal Trial Practice; Environmental Law

LUNDY & ASSOCIATES, P.C.
Fort Wayne, IN .... Patent, Trademark, Copyright and Unfair Competition
Indianapolis, IN .... Patent, Trademark, Copyright and Unfair Competition

LUNDY & DAVIS, L.L.P.
Lake Charles, LA .... Admiralty/Maritime Law; Personal Injury

LUPO, DAVID G., P.C.
St. Louis, MO .... Elder Law

LUPO & KOCZKUR, P.C.
Detroit, MI .... Insurance Defense; Product Liability Law

LUSK, FRALEY, MCALISTER & SIMMS, P.C.
Birmingham, AL .... Civil Trial Practice; Commercial Litigation; Employment Benefits Law; Insurance Defense; Medical Malpractice; Personal Injury; Product Liability Law; Professional Liability; Transportation Law; Workers Compensation

LUSK & LUSK
Guntersville, AL .... General Practice; Insurance Defense

LUSTBADER, PHILIP M., & DAVID LUSTBADER, A PROFESSIONAL CORPORATION
Livingston, NJ .... Appellate Practice; Civil Trial Practice; Insurance Defense; Medical Malpractice; Personal Injury; Product Liability Law; Workers Compensation

LUTHER, ANDERSON, PLLP
Chattanooga, TN .... Insurance Defense

LUTY, ROBERT L., A PROFESSIONAL CORPORATION
Los Angeles, CA .... Medical Malpractice; Personal Injury; Product Liability Law

LUXAN & MURFITT
Helena, MT .... General Practice

LUXENBERG, GARBETT, KELLY & SAPIENZA, P.C.
New Castle, PA .... Insurance Defense; Personal Injury

LYKKEBAK, DONALD A.
Orlando, FL .... Criminal Trial Practice

LYLES, DARR & CLARK
Spartanburg, SC .... General Practice

LYNBERG & WATKINS, A PROFESSIONAL CORPORATION
Los Angeles, CA .... Civil Trial Practice

LYNCH & ASSOCIATES, P.L.L.C.
Boise, ID .... General Practice; Insurance Defense; Product Liability Law

LYNCH, CHAPPELL & ALSUP, A PROFESSIONAL CORPORATION
Midland, TX .... General Practice; Natural Resources Law; Tax Law

LYNCH, DALLAS, SMITH & HARMAN, P.C.
Cedar Rapids, IA .... Civil Trial Practice; General Practice

LYNCH, GALLAGHER, LYNCH & MARTINEAU, P.L.L.C.
Mount Pleasant, MI .... Environmental Law; General Practice; Natural Resources Law; Oil and Gas Law

LYNCH, MARTIN, KANE, KUPER, KEEFE & BARTELS, LLC
North Brunswick, NJ .... Civil Trial Practice; General Practice; Insurance Defense; Personal Injury; Product Liability Law

LYNN, FULKERSON, NICHOLS AND KINKEL, PLLC
Lexington, KY .... Insurance Defense; Medical Malpractice; Workers Compensation

LYNN, JACKSON, SHULTZ & LEBRUN, P.C.
Rapid City, SD .... Civil Trial Practice; General Practice; Personal Injury

LYNN LAW OFFICE
Syracuse, NY .... Civil Trial Practice; Criminal Trial Practice; Personal Injury; Trust and Estates, Wills and Probate

LYNN STODGHILL MELSHEIMER & TILLOTSON, L.L.P.
Dallas, TX .... Commercial Law

LYON & ARTZ PLC
Bloomfield Hills, MI .... Intellectual Property Law; Patent, Trademark, Copyright and Unfair Competition
Southfield, MI .... Intellectual Property Law; Patent, Trademark, Copyright and Unfair Competition

LYON, FERRITER & FITZPATRICK, LLP
Holyoke, MA .... Business Law; Corporate Law; General Practice; Trust and Estates, Wills and Probate

LYON KIRWIN, P.A.
Winter Park, FL .... Commercial Law; Commercial Litigation; Construction Law; Government Contracts

LYON & LYON LLP
Los Angeles, CA .... Antitrust Law; Patent, Trademark, Copyright and Unfair Competition

LYON, WEIGAND & GUSTAFSON, P.S.
Yakima, WA .... General Practice

LYONS, BRANDT, COOK & HIRAMATSU
Honolulu, HI .... Civil Trial Practice; Insurance Defense

LYONS LAW FIRM, THE
Wilmington, DE .... Criminal Trial Practice; Personal Injury

LYONS, PIPES & COOK, P.C.
Mobile, AL .... Admiralty/Maritime Law; Appellate Practice; Banking Law; Bankruptcy Law; Civil Trial Practice; Commercial Law; Environmental Law; General Practice; Labor and Employment Law; Municipal Bond/Public Authority Financing; Natural Resources Law; Pension and Profit Sharing; Product Liability Law; Professional Liability; Real Estate Law; Tax Law; Trust and Estates, Wills and Probate

LYONS & RHODES, P.C.
San Antonio, TX .... Medical Malpractice; Personal Injury

LYTAL, REITER, CLARK, FOUNTAIN & WILLIAMS
West Palm Beach, FL .... Medical Malpractice; Personal Injury; Product Liability Law

LYTLE, THOMAS F.
Sacramento, CA .... Civil Trial Practice; Personal Injury

MACCABE & MCGUIRE
Chicago, IL .... Civil Trial Practice; Insurance Defense; Transportation Law

MACCARTHY, POJANI & HURLEY, LLP
Worcester, MA .... Banking Law; Civil Trial Practice; General Practice; Insurance Defense

MACCARTNEY, MACCARTNEY, KERRIGAN & MACCARTNEY
Nyack, NY .... General Practice; Insurance Defense

MACCORKLE LAVENDER & CASEY PLLC
Charleston, WV .... Product Liability Law

MACDONALD & ASSOCIATES
San Francisco, CA .... Bankruptcy Law

MACDONALD, FITZGERALD & MACDONALD, P.C.
Flint, MI .... General Practice; Personal Injury; Product Liability Law; Workers Compensation

MACDONALD, ILLIG, JONES & BRITTON LLP
Erie, PA .... General Practice

MACELREE, HARVEY, GALLAGHER, FEATHERMAN & SEBASTIAN, LTD.
Exton, PA .... General Practice
Kennett Square, PA .... General Practice
West Chester, PA .... Banking Law; Civil Trial Practice; General Practice; Personal Injury

MACEY, WILENSKY, COHEN, WITTNER & KESSLER, LLP
Atlanta, GA .... Bankruptcy Law; Civil Trial Practice; Creditors Rights; General Practice; Real Estate Law

MACIE, JAMES J.
Jonesboro, GA .... Family Law

MACINNIS, DONNER & KOPLOWITZ
San Francisco, CA .... Business Law; Family Law; Trust and Estates, Wills and Probate

MACKALL, CROUNSE & MOORE, PLC
Minneapolis, MN .... General Practice; Patent, Trademark, Copyright and Unfair Competition

MACKALL, MACKALL & GIBB, A PROFESSIONAL CORPORATION
Fairfax, VA .... Real Estate Law; Trust and Estates, Wills and Probate

MACKENZIE FUJISAWA BREWER STEVENSON
Vancouver, BC, Canada .... General Practice

MACKOFF KELLOGG LAW FIRM
Dickinson, ND .... General Practice

MACLEAN & JACQUES, LTD.
Phoenix, AZ .... Appellate Practice; Commercial Law; Family Law; Real Estate Law; Trust and Estates, Wills and Probate

MACLEAY, LYNCH, GREGG & LYNCH, P.C.
Washington, DC .... Civil Trial Practice; Insurance Defense; Workers Compensation

MACPHERSON LESLIE & TYERMAN
Regina, SK, Canada .... Administrative Law; Appellate Practice; Banking Law; Bankruptcy Law; Business Law; Civil Trial Practice; Commercial Law; Commercial Litigation; Construction Law; Criminal Trial Practice; Employment Benefits Law; Environmental Law; Family Law; General Practice; Health Care Law; Insurance Defense; Labor and Employment Law; Medical Malpractice; Natural Resources Law; Professional Liability; Real Estate Law; Securities Law; Tax Law; Trust and Estates, Wills and Probate; Workers Compensation

MACRAE, GERALD C.
Los Angeles, CA .... Civil Trial Practice

MACVEAN, LEWIS, SHERWIN & MCDERMOTT, P.C.
Middletown, NY .... Banking Law; General Practice; Insurance Defense; Personal Injury; Real Estate Law; Trust and Estates, Wills and Probate

MADDEN, FRANK, & ASSOCIATES
Plymouth, MN .... Employment Benefits Law

MADDEN, MADDEN AND DEL DUCA, P.A.
Haddonfield, NJ .... General Practice

MADDEN, POLIAK, MACDOUGALL & WILLIAMSON
Seattle, WA .... Admiralty/Maritime Law; Insurance Defense

MADDIN, HAUSER, WARTELL, ROTH, HELLER & PESSES, P.C.
Southfield, MI .... Banking Law; Business Law; Civil Trial Practice; Employment Benefits Law; Pension and Profit Sharing; Real Estate Law; Tax Law; Trust and Estates, Wills and Probate

MADDOX, THOMAS E., JR., P.C.
Atlanta, GA .... Civil Rights; Criminal Trial Practice; Medical Malpractice

MADEWELL, JARED & HALFACRE
Cookeville, TN .... Civil Trial Practice; General Practice; Insurance Defense

MADIGAN & SCOTT, INC.
Springfield, VA .... Business Law; Civil Trial Practice; Real Estate Law

MADISON, HARBOUR, MROZ & BRENNAN, P.A.
Albuquerque, NM .... Commercial Litigation; Insurance Defense; Medical Malpractice; Product Liability Law

MADORSKY, MARSHA G.
Miami, FL .... Trust and Estates, Wills and Probate

MADORY, ZELL AND PLEISS, A PROFESSIONAL CORPORATION
Tustin, CA .... Medical Malpractice

MADSON & METCALF, A PROFESSIONAL CORPORATION
Salt Lake City, UT .... Intellectual Property Law; Patent, Trademark, Copyright and Unfair Competition

MAEDER, JEROME A., LAW OFFICES, S.C.
Wausau, WI............................Medical Malpractice; Personal Injury

MAGAÑA, CATHCART & MCCARTHY
Los Angeles, CA.....................Personal Injury

MAGEE AND ISHERWOOD, L.L.P.
Wall Township, NJ...............Civil Trial Practice; General Practice; Insurance Defense; Municipal and Zoning Law; Personal Injury

MAGER LAW FIRM, THE, P.C.
Philadelphia, PA.....................Labor and Employment Law

MAGGIO & KATTAR, P.C.
Washington, DC.......................Immigration and Naturalization

MAGIE, ANDRESEN, HAAG, PACIOTTI, BUTTERWORTH & MCCARTHY, P.A.
Duluth, MN...........................Civil Trial Practice; General Practice; Insurance Defense; Real Estate Law

MAGINNIS & HURLEY, A PROFESSIONAL LAW CORPORATION
New Orleans, LA.....................Admiralty/Maritime Law; Insurance Defense; Product Liability Law

MAGRUDER & SUMNER
Rome, GA...............................Civil Trial Practice

MAGUIRE & KRESS, P.C.
Pocatello, ID...........................Insurance Defense

MAHASSNI, HASSAN, LAW OFFICE OF
Jeddah, Saudi Arabia..............General Practice

MAHER, GIBSON AND GUILEY, A PROF. ASSN. OF LAWYERS
Orlando, FL............................Medical Malpractice; Personal Injury; Product Liability Law

MAHER & MAHER, LLP
Irvine, CA...............................Environmental Law; General Practice

MAHL REHON WALWORTH & ROBERTS, A PROFESSIONAL CORPORATION
San Jose, CA...........................Banking Law; Commercial Litigation; Construction Law

MAHON & FARLEY, P.A.
Jacksonville, FL......................Family Law; Personal Injury

MAHONEY, DOUGHERTY AND MAHONEY, P.A. PROFESSIONAL ASSOCIATION
Minneapolis, MN.....................Civil Trial Practice; Insurance Defense

MAIN, JOHN W., P.C.
Phoenix, AZ............................Workers Compensation

MAIN, RONALD, P.C.
Tulsa, OK...............................Business Law; Civil Trial Practice; Family Law; General Practice; Real Estate Law

MAINERO, MARIO W., JR., INC.
Newport Beach, CA.................Civil Trial Practice

MAINES & LOEB, PLLC
Washington, DC.......................Appellate Practice

MAINOR & HARRIS
Las Vegas, NV.........................Construction Law; Medical Malpractice; Personal Injury; Product Liability Law

MAIRE, MANSELL & BEASLEY, A LAW CORPORATION
Redding, CA............................Insurance Defense; Personal Injury

MAJESTIC, PARSONS, SIEBERT & HSUE, A PROFESSIONAL CORPORATION
San Francisco, CA...................Intellectual Property Law; Patent, Trademark, Copyright and Unfair Competition

MALFITANO CAMPBELL & DICKINSON
Jacksonville, FL......................Labor and Employment Law
Tampa, FL...............................Labor and Employment Law

MALIN, HALEY & DIMAGGIO, P.A.
Fort Lauderdale, FL................Patent, Trademark, Copyright and Unfair Competition
Miami, FL...............................Patent, Trademark, Copyright and Unfair Competition
West Palm Beach, FL..............Patent, Trademark, Copyright and Unfair Competition

MALLINCKRODT & MALLINCKRODT
Salt Lake City, UT...................Patent, Trademark, Copyright and Unfair Competition

MALLOY & MALLOY, P.A.
Miami, FL...............................Intellectual Property Law; Patent, Trademark, Copyright and Unfair Competition; Trademark, Copyright and Unfair Competition

MALLOY & SULLIVAN, LAWYERS PROFESSIONAL CORPORATION
Hingham, MA..........................Communications Law

MALNICK, DAVID, A PROFESSIONAL CORPORATION
San Jose, CA...........................Civil Trial Practice; Personal Injury; Product Liability Law

MALONE, THOMAS WILLIAM
Atlanta, GA.............................Medical Malpractice; Personal Injury

MALONE, THOMAS P., & ASSOCIATES, P.C.
Denver, CO.............................Family Law

MALONEY, HUENNEKENS, PARKS, GECKER & PARSONS, A PROFESSIONAL CORPORATION
Richmond, VA.........................Bankruptcy Law; Business Law; Commercial Law; Commercial Litigation; Construction Law; General Practice; Labor and Employment Law; Personal Injury; Securities Law; Workers Compensation

MALONEY & MALONEY
Aberdeen, SD..........................Construction Law; Employment Benefits Law; Labor and Employment Law; Personal Injury

MALONEY & YURACHEK, P.C.
Falls Church, VA.....................Trust and Estates, Wills and Probate

MALOON, JERRY L., CO., L.P.A.
Columbus, OH.........................Medical Malpractice

MANAHAN, PIETRYKOWSKI, BAMMAN & DELANEY
Toledo, OH.............................Commercial Litigation; Insurance Defense

MANATT, PHELPS & PHILLIPS, LLP
Los Angeles, CA.....................General Practice

MANCHESTER, BENNETT, POWERS & ULLMAN, A LEGAL PROFESSIONAL ASSOCIATION
Youngstown, OH.....................General Practice

MANCHESTER LAW OFFICES, PROFESSIONAL CORPORATION
Burlington, VT........................Civil Trial Practice; Commercial Law; Environmental Law; Medical Malpractice; Personal Injury

MANCHESTER & PIGNATO, P.C.
Oklahoma City, OK.................Civil Rights; Insurance Defense

MANCHESTER & WILLIAMS
San Jose, CA...........................Criminal Trial Practice

MANCKE, WAGNER, HERSHEY AND TULLY
Harrisburg, PA........................Civil Trial Practice; Criminal Trial Practice; General Practice; Personal Injury; Transportation Law

MANDELBAUM, SALSBURG, GOLD, LAZRIS, DISCENZA & STEINBERG, P.A.
West Orange, NJ.....................General Practice

MANDEL, LIPTON AND STEVENSON LIMITED
Chicago, IL.............................Civil Trial Practice; Family Law; General Practice; Immigration and Naturalization

MANDELL LAW FIRM, THE, A PROFESSIONAL CORPORATION
Vienna, VA.............................Business Law

MANDELSTAMM, JEROME R.
St. Louis, MO.........................Business Law; Real Estate Law; Trust and Estates, Wills and Probate

MANEY, DAMSKER & JONES, P.A.
Tampa, FL...............................Appellate Practice; Civil Trial Practice; Commercial Litigation; Criminal Trial Practice; Family Law; Tax Law; Trust and Estates, Wills and Probate

MANEY & GORDON, P.A.
Tampa, FL...............................Immigration and Naturalization

MANGUM, WALL, STOOPS & WARDEN, P.L.L.C.
Flagstaff, AZ..........................Business Law; Civil Trial Practice; Commercial Law; Construction Law; Corporate Law; Family Law; General Practice; Insurance Defense; Labor and Employment Law; Personal Injury; Real Estate Law; Trust and Estates, Wills and Probate

MANLEY, BURKE, LIPTON & COOK, A LEGAL PROFESSIONAL ASSOCIATION
Cincinnati, OH.......................Land Use Law; Municipal and Zoning Law

MANLEY, TRAEGER, PERRY & STAPP
Demopolis, AL........................General Practice

MANN, FREDERICK R., JR., P.A.
Winter Park, FL......................Criminal Trial Practice

MANN, KENNETH L., P.A.
Orlando, FL............................Appellate Practice; Arbitration; Civil Trial Practice; Commercial Litigation; Legal Malpractice

MANN LAW FIRM
Terre Haute, IN......................Civil Trial Practice; Personal Injury

MANN & MITCHELL
Providence, RI..........................Civil Rights; Criminal Trial Practice

MANN & WOOLDRIDGE, P.C.
Newnan, GA..........................General Practice

MANNES, MICHAEL H., P.A.
Baltimore, MD..........................Real Estate Law

MANNING & CROUCH
Raleigh, NC..........................Civil Trial Practice; Criminal Trial Practice

MANNING CURTIS BRADSHAW & BEDNAR, LLC
Salt Lake City, UT..........................General Practice

MANNING, FULTON & SKINNER, P.A.
Raleigh, NC..........................General Practice

MANOS, MARTIN, PERGRAM & DIETZ, L.P.A.
Delaware, OH..........................General Practice

MANSFIELD TANICK & COHEN, P.A.
Minneapolis, MN..........................Bankruptcy Law; Civil Trial Practice; Labor and Employment Law; Trust and Estates, Wills and Probate

MANSOUR, GAVIN, GERLACK & MANOS CO., L.P.A.
Cleveland, OH..........................Civil Trial Practice

MANTA AND WELGE, A PROFESSIONAL CORPORATION
Philadelphia, PA..........................Commercial Law; Commercial Litigation; Environmental Law; Insurance Defense; Labor and Employment Law; Product Liability Law

MANWELL & MILTON
San Francisco, CA..........................Business Law; Securities Law

MAPOTHER & MAPOTHER
Louisville, KY..........................Banking Law; Bankruptcy Law; Creditors Rights; Real Estate Law

MARAN & MARAN
Newark, NJ..........................Legal Malpractice; Medical Malpractice; Product Liability Law; Professional Liability

MARCH & LILEY, P.C.
Fort Collins, CO..........................General Practice

MARCOUX, ALLEN, ABBOTT, SCHOMER & BOWER, P.C.
Jackson, MI..........................Banking Law; Civil Trial Practice; Corporate Law; General Practice; Insurance Defense; Labor and Employment Law; Tax Law

MARCUS, GOULD & SUSSMAN, LLP
White Plains, NY..........................Commercial Litigation; Real Estate Law; Trust and Estates, Wills and Probate

MARCUS, GRYGIEL & CLEGG, P.A.
Portland, ME..........................Banking Law; Bankruptcy Law; Business Law; Commercial Law; Commercial Litigation; General Practice; Health Care Law

MARCUS & SHAPIRA LLP
Pittsburgh, PA..........................Antitrust Law; Bankruptcy Law; Civil Trial Practice; Commercial Law; Corporate Law; General Practice; Insurance Defense; Labor and Employment Law; Personal Injury; Real Estate Law; Securities Law; Tax Law; Trust and Estates, Wills and Probate; Workers Compensation

MARDEROSIAN, OREN & PABOOJIAN, A PROFESSIONAL CORPORATION
Fresno, CA..........................Business Law; Insurance Defense; Labor and Employment Law

MAREADY, WILLIAM F. THE LAW OFFICES OF
Winston-Salem, NC..........................Aviation Law; Product Liability Law

MARGER, JOHNSON & MCCOLLOM, P.C.
Portland, OR..........................Intellectual Property Law; Patent, Trademark, Copyright and Unfair Competition; Trademark, Copyright and Unfair Competition

MARGOLIS & CASSIDY
Milwaukee, WI..........................Family Law

MARGULIS GRANT & MARGULIS, P.C.
St. Louis, MO..........................Criminal Trial Practice

MARISCAL, WEEKS, MCINTYRE & FRIEDLANDER, P.A.
Phoenix, AZ..........................Bankruptcy Law; Commercial Litigation; Family Law; General Practice; Real Estate Law

MARK & BURKHEAD
Mission, KS..........................Workers Compensation
Kansas City, MO..........................Workers Compensation

MARKLE, RAMOS & ZITO, A PROFESSIONAL CORPORATION
Houston, TX..........................Insurance Defense; Medical Malpractice; Personal Injury

MARKOW, WALKER & REEVES, P.A.
Jackson, MS..........................Environmental Law; Insurance Defense; Medical Malpractice

MARKOWITZ, DAVIS, RINGEL & TRUSTY, P.A.
Miami, FL..........................Bankruptcy Law; Commercial Litigation; Creditors Rights; Real Estate Law; Trust and Estates, Wills and Probate

MARK & PEARLSTEIN, P.A.
Phoenix, AZ..........................Family Law; Insurance Defense; Medical Malpractice; Personal Injury

MARKS GRAY
Jacksonville, FL..........................General Practice

MARKS, MADSEN & HIRSCHBACH
Sioux City, IA..........................General Practice

MARKS, O'NEILL, REILLY, O'BRIEN & COURTNEY, P.C.
Philadelphia, PA..........................Civil Trial Practice; Environmental Law; Insurance Defense; Medical Malpractice; Personal Injury; Product Liability Law; Toxic Torts; Workers Compensation

MARKUSON, GLORIA CROWLEY
Scarsdale, NY..........................General Practice; Trust and Estates, Wills and Probate

MARKUSSON, GREEN & JARVIS, P.C.
Denver, CO..........................Civil Trial Practice; Environmental Law; Insurance Defense; Product Liability Law; Toxic Torts

MARLIN & SALTZMAN, A PROFESSIONAL LAW CORPORATION
Santa Ana, CA..........................Business Law; Insurance Defense

MARR HIPP JONES & PEPPER
Honolulu, HI..........................Labor and Employment Law

MARRINER, JONES & FITCH
Washington, PA..........................General Practice

MARRONE ROBINSON FREDERICK & FOSTER, PROFESSIONAL CORPORATION
Burbank, CA..........................Insurance Defense

MARRS, MICHAEL D., A PROFESSIONAL CORPORATION
St. Joseph, MI..........................Personal Injury

MARS, RICHARD D., P.A.
Bartow, FL..........................Criminal Trial Practice

MARSH, RICKARD & BRYAN, P.C.
Birmingham, AL..........................Personal Injury; Product Liability Law

MARSH, SPAEDER, BAUR, SPAEDER & SCHAAF, LLP
Erie, PA..........................General Practice; Insurance Defense; Tax Law

MARSHACK SHULMAN & HODGES LLP
Irvine, CA..........................Bankruptcy Law; Commercial Litigation

MARSHALL, MARILYN J.
Tallahassee, FL..........................General Practice

MARSHALL CONWAY & WRIGHT, P.C.
New York, NY..........................Insurance Defense

MARSHALL HILL CASSAS & DE LIPKAU
Reno, NV..........................Civil Trial Practice; Corporate Law; Natural Resources Law

MARSHALL LAW FIRM
New York, NY..........................Intellectual Property Law; Trademark, Copyright and Unfair Competition

MARSHALL, O'TOOLE, GERSTEIN, MURRAY & BORUN
Chicago, IL..........................Intellectual Property Law; Patent, Trademark, Copyright and Unfair Competition

MARSHALL, WILLIAMS & GORHAM, L.L.P.
Wilmington, NC..........................Admiralty/Maritime Law; Civil Trial Practice; General Practice

MARSTILLER, PHILIP S., P.C.
Richmond, VA..........................Labor and Employment Law; Product Liability Law

MARTEN & BROWN LLP
Seattle, WA..........................Environmental Law

MARTENS DUNAJ MARLOWE DAVIS & MARLOWE
Miami, FL..........................Commercial Litigation; Computer Law

MARTIN, ADE, BIRCHFIELD & MICKLER, P.A.
Jacksonville, FL..........................General Practice

MARTIN & ASSOCIATES, L.L.C.
Phoenix, AZ..........................Real Estate Law

MARTIN & ASSOCIATES, P.A.
Minneapolis, MN..........................Business Law; Nonprofit and Tax Exempt Organizations; Real Estate Law; Tax Law; Trust and Estates, Wills and Probate

MARTIN, BACON & MARTIN, P.C.
Mount Clemens, MI..........Civil Trial Practice; Insurance Defense; Medical Malpractice; Personal Injury; Product Liability Law

MARTIN, BROWNE, HULL & HARPER, P.L.L.
Springfield, OH..........General Practice

MARTIN, CHARLES L., LAW OFFICES OF
Decatur, GA..........Administrative Law

MARTIN, CHURCHILL, BLAIR, HILL, COLE & HOLLANDER, CHARTERED
Wichita, KS..........Labor and Employment Law

MARTIN & GLASER, CHARTERED
Sarasota, FL..........Personal Injury; Product Liability Law

MARTIN, GUNN & MARTIN, A PROFESSIONAL CORPORATION
Westmont, NJ..........Civil Trial Practice

MARTIN, JOHN O., P.C.
Denver, CO..........Medical Malpractice

MARTIN, JUSTICE & VINCENT
Ashland, KY..........Civil Trial Practice; General Practice; Insurance Defense; Personal Injury

MARTIN LAW FIRM, THE
Chicago, IL..........Environmental Law

MARTIN LAW OFFICE
Oklahoma City, OK..........Criminal Trial Practice

MARTIN, LIPSKY, KAUFMAN & WEINSTEIN, P.A.
Miami Lakes, FL..........Medical Malpractice; Personal Injury; Product Liability Law

MARTIN, MAGNUSON, MCCARTHY & KENNEY
Boston, MA..........General Practice; Insurance Defense

MARTIN & MARTIN, P.A.
Lakeland, FL..........General Practice

MARTIN, MARTIN & WOODARD, LLP
Syracuse, NY..........Bankruptcy Law; Civil Trial Practice; Commercial Law; Personal Injury; Trust and Estates, Wills and Probate

MARTIN & MEHAFFY, LLC
Boulder, CO..........Insurance Defense

MARTIN, RONALD T., P.A.
Boca Raton, FL..........Pension and Profit Sharing; Tax Law; Trust and Estates, Wills and Probate

MARTIN, SHOWERS, SMITH & MCDONALD, L.L.P.
Hillsboro, TX..........General Practice

MARTIN, SHUDT, WALLACE, DILORENZO & JOHNSON
Troy, NY..........Commercial Law; Corporate Law; Real Estate Law; Trust and Estates, Wills and Probate

MARTIN, SNYDER & BERNSTEIN, P.A.
Baltimore, MD..........Civil Trial Practice; Criminal Trial Practice; Tax Law

MARTIN, TATE, MORROW & MARSTON, P.C.
Memphis, TN..........General Practice

MARTIN, VAN DE WALLE, DONOHUE, MCGAHAN, CATALANO & FAIRGRIEVE
Jericho, NY..........Banking Law; Civil Trial Practice; Commercial Litigation; Insurance Defense; Personal Injury; Real Estate Law; Trust and Estates, Wills and Probate

MARTIN, WILSON & MACDOWELL, A PROFESSIONAL CORPORATION
Santa Ana, CA..........Civil Trial Practice

MARTÍNEZ ODELL & CALABRIA
San Juan, PR..........Banking Law; Bankruptcy Law; Civil Trial Practice; Commercial Law; Environmental Law; General Practice; Labor and Employment Law; Municipal Bond/Public Authority Financing; Real Estate Law; Tax Law

MARTONYI ÉS KAJTÁR BAKER & MCKENZIE
Budapest, Hungary..........General Practice

MARTSON DEARDORFF WILLIAMS & OTTO, A PROFESSIONAL CORPORATION
Carlisle, PA..........General Practice

MARTZELL & BICKFORD
New Orleans, LA..........Commercial Litigation; Criminal Trial Practice; Environmental Law; Medical Malpractice; Oil and Gas Law; Personal Injury; Toxic Torts

MARVIN, DOUGLAS R., P.C.
Fairfax, VA..........International Business Law

MARX & MARX
Atlanta, GA..........Civil Trial Practice; Labor and Employment Law
New York, NY..........Civil Trial Practice; Labor and Employment Law

MARZIK, ROBERT K., P.C., LAW OFFICES OF
Stratford, CT..........Admiralty/Maritime Law

MASERITZ, GUY B.
Columbia, MD..........Business Law

MASKALERIS & ASSOCIATES
Morristown, NJ..........Civil Trial Practice

MASON, GRIFFIN & PIERSON, A PROFESSIONAL CORPORATION
Princeton, NJ..........Civil Trial Practice; Real Estate Law; Trust and Estates, Wills and Probate

MASON, J. CHENEY, P.A.
Orlando, FL..........Criminal Trial Practice; Family Law

MASON, JOHN, PARTNERS, LTD.
Stateline, NV..........Sports and Entertainment Law

MASON, SLOVIN & SCHILLING CO., L.P.A.
Cincinnati, OH..........Banking Law; Commercial Law; Creditors Rights

MASON STEINHARDT JACOBS PERLMAN & PESICK, PROFESSIONAL CORPORATION
Southfield, MI..........Commercial Law; Corporate Law; Environmental Law; General Practice; Land Use Law; Municipal and Zoning Law; Real Estate Law; Tax Law; Trust and Estates, Wills and Probate

MASON, STEVEN A., P.A.
Hollywood, FL..........Civil Trial Practice; Commercial Litigation; Family Law; Real Estate Law

MASON & THOMAS
Sacramento, CA..........Civil Trial Practice; Insurance Defense; Personal Injury

MASSA, PATRICK C., P.A., LAW OFFICES OF
North Palm Beach, FL..........Civil Trial Practice; Personal Injury

MASTAGNI, HOLSTEDT & CHIURAZZI, A PROFESSIONAL CORPORATION
Sacramento, CA..........Labor and Employment Law; Personal Injury; Workers Compensation

MASTERS & TAYLOR, L.C.
Charleston, WV..........Personal Injury

MASTERSON, THOMAS A., & ASSOCIATES, P.C.
Norristown, PA..........Arbitration

MASTRIANA & CHRISTIANSEN, PROFESSIONAL ASSOCIATION
Fort Lauderdale, FL..........Business Law; Real Estate Law

MASUD, GILBERT & PATTERSON, P.C.
Saginaw, MI..........Labor and Employment Law

MATHENY SEARS LINKERT & LONG, LLP
Sacramento, CA..........Appellate Practice; Business Law; Civil Trial Practice; Employment Benefits Law; Insurance Defense; Personal Injury; Product Liability Law; Real Estate Law

MATHEW & MATHEW, P.C.
Phoenix, AZ..........Criminal Trial Practice

MATHEWS, COLLINS, SHEPHERD & GOULD, A PROFESSIONAL CORPORATION
Princeton, NJ..........Intellectual Property Law; Trademark, Copyright and Unfair Competition

MATHEWS, STANTON T., & ASSOCIATES, A LAW CORP.
Laguna Hills, CA..........Elder Law; Labor and Employment Law; Medical Malpractice; Personal Injury; Product Liability Law

MATHIS, MARIFIAN, RICHTER & GRANDY, LTD.
Belleville, IL..........Tax Law; Trust and Estates, Wills and Probate

MATISON, CHARLES A., P.C., THE LAW OFFICES OF
Northfield, NJ..........Family Law

MATKOV, SALZMAN, MADOFF & GUNN
Chicago, IL..........Labor and Employment Law

MATSEN, JEFFREY R. & ASSOCIATES
Newport Beach, CA..........Business Law; International Business Law; Trust and Estates, Wills and Probate

MATTHEWS, EDWIN R., P.C.
Short Hills, NJ..........Commercial Law; Environmental Law; Insurance Defense; Municipal and Zoning Law; Product Liability Law

MATTHEWS & STEEL
Atlanta, GA..........Civil Trial Practice; Commercial Litigation; Medical Malpractice; Personal Injury; Product Liability Law

MATTHIAS & BERG LLP
Los Angeles, CA .... Business Law; Commercial Litigation; International Business Law; Mergers and Acquisitions; Securities Law; Tax Law

MATTHIESEN, CHASE & ERWIN, L.L.P.
Houston, TX .... Civil Trial Practice; Insurance Defense

MATTIMOE, THOMAS E., LLC
Atlanta, GA .... Corporate Law; Real Estate Law

MATTIONI, LTD.
Philadelphia, PA .... Admiralty/Maritime Law; Civil Trial Practice; Environmental Law; General Practice

MATTOCH, IAN L., LAW OFFICES OF
Honolulu, HI .... Personal Injury; Product Liability Law

MATTOX & MATTOX
New Albany, IN .... General Practice; Medical Malpractice; Personal Injury

MATTSON, RICKETTS, DAVIES, STEWART & CALKINS
Lincoln, NE .... General Practice

MATZ, JEFFREY A. LAW OFFICES OF
Los Angeles, CA .... Civil Trial Practice

MAUPIN TAYLOR & ELLIS, P.A.
Raleigh, NC .... General Practice; Labor and Employment Law

MAURER, EUGENE J., JR., P.A.
Wilmington, DE .... Criminal Trial Practice

MAURER LAW FIRM
La Jolla, CA .... Civil Trial Practice

MAURO, GOLDBERG & LILLING
Great Neck, NY .... Appellate Practice

MAUTZ BAUM & O'HANLON, LLP
Pendleton, OR .... General Practice

MAUZY LAW FIRM
Minneapolis, MN .... Criminal Trial Practice

MAXIE RHEINHEIMER STEPHENS & VREVICH, LLP
San Diego, CA .... Construction Law; Labor and Employment Law; Professional Liability

MAY, MICHAEL P.
Baltimore, MD .... General Practice

MAY, MICHAEL R.
Des Moines, IA .... Public Utilities Law

MAY, ADAM, GERDES & THOMPSON, L.L.P.
Pierre, SD .... General Practice

MAY AND MAY, PROFESSIONAL CORPORATION
Detroit, MI .... Trust and Estates, Wills and Probate
Southfield, MI .... Trust and Estates, Wills and Probate

MAYALL, HURLEY, KNUTSEN, SMITH & GREEN, A PROFESSIONAL CORPORATION
Stockton, CA .... Insurance Defense

MAYER, BROWN & PLATT
Los Angeles, CA .... General Practice
Washington, DC .... General Practice
Chicago, IL .... General Practice
New York, NY .... General Practice
Charlotte, NC .... General Practice
Houston, TX .... General Practice
London, England .... General Practice
Berlin, Germany .... General Practice
Cologne, Germany .... General Practice
Bishkek, Kyrgyzstan .... General Practice
Ashgabat, Turkmenistan .... General Practice
Tashkent, Uzbekistan .... General Practice

MAYER, FRIEDLICH, SPIESS, TIERNEY, BROWN & PLATT
Chicago, IL .... General Practice

MAYER & RISER, PLLC
Highlands, NC .... General Practice

MAYER, SMITH & ROBERTS, L.L.P.
Shreveport, LA .... Civil Trial Practice; General Practice; Insurance Defense; Medical Malpractice; Professional Liability; Workers Compensation

MAYFIELD & PERRENOT, P.C.
El Paso, TX .... Banking Law; General Practice; Immigration and Naturalization; Insurance Defense; International Trade Law; Trust and Estates, Wills and Probate

MAYNARD, O'CONNOR, SMITH & CATALINOTTO, LLP
Albany, NY .... Appellate Practice; Insurance Defense; Medical Malpractice; Personal Injury

MAYNE & MAYNE
Sioux City, IA .... Civil Trial Practice; Insurance Defense; Labor and Employment Law; Workers Compensation

MAYNES, BRADFORD, SHIPPS & SHEFTEL LLP
Durango, CO .... General Practice

MAYOCK, W. MICHAEL
Pasadena, CA .... Appellate Practice; Criminal Trial Practice

MAYOR, DAY, CALDWELL & KEETON, L.L.P.
Austin, TX .... General Practice
Houston, TX .... General Practice

MAYS, KARBERG & WACHTER
Cleveland, OH .... Real Estate Law

MAZUR, CARP & RUBIN, P.C.
New York, NY .... Civil Trial Practice; Construction Law; Trust and Estates, Wills and Probate

MCAFEE & TAFT, A PROFESSIONAL CORPORATION
Oklahoma City, OK .... Employment Benefits Law; General Practice; Labor and Employment Law; Natural Resources Law; Patent, Trademark, Copyright and Unfair Competition; Tax Law

MCALLISTER & ABROMOVITZ
Phoenix, AZ .... Insurance Defense; Product Liability Law

MCALLISTER, HYBERG & WHITE
Northfield, NJ .... Civil Trial Practice; Insurance Defense; Personal Injury; Product Liability Law

MCALOON & FRIEDMAN, P.C.
New York, NY .... Civil Trial Practice; Health Care Law; Medical Malpractice; Personal Injury; Real Estate Law

MCANDREW, THOMAS J., ESQ., LTD.
Providence, RI .... Labor and Employment Law

MCANGUS, GOUDELOCK & COURIE, L.L.C.
Columbia, SC .... Civil Trial Practice; Workers Compensation

MCBRIDE BAKER & COLES
Chicago, IL .... Antitrust Law; Banking Law; Business Law; Commercial Litigation; Computer Law; Employment Benefits Law; Environmental Law; General Practice; Intellectual Property Law; Labor and Employment Law; Real Estate Law; Securities Law; Tax Law; Trust and Estates, Wills and Probate
Oakbrook Terrace, IL .... Banking Law; Business Law; Commercial Litigation; General Practice; Real Estate Law; Trust and Estates, Wills and Probate

MCBRIDE AND MCBRIDE, P.C.
Grove City, PA .... General Practice

MCCABE, COLLINS, MCGEOUGH & FOWLER, LLP
Mineola, NY .... Insurance Defense

MCCABE & MACK LLP
Poughkeepsie, NY .... General Practice

MCCABE O'DONNELL, A PROFESSIONAL ASSOCIATION
Phoenix, AZ .... Commercial Litigation; Real Estate Law; Tax Law; Trust and Estates, Wills and Probate

MCCAFFREY & TAWWATER
Oklahoma City, OK .... Civil Trial Practice; Labor and Employment Law; Medical Malpractice; Personal Injury; Workers Compensation

MCCAHILL, JOHN A.
Washington, DC .... Criminal Trial Practice

MCCALLAR AND ASSOCIATES
Savannah, GA .... Bankruptcy Law; Civil Trial Practice; Commercial Litigation

MCCALLA, THOMPSON, PYBURN, HYMOWITZ & SHAPIRO
New Orleans, LA .... General Practice; Labor and Employment Law

MCCALL, DOUGHTON & BLANCATO, P.L.L.C.
Winston-Salem, NC .... Corporate Law

MCCALL & RITCHIE, LLP
Austin, TX .... Oil and Gas Law

MCCAMPBELL & YOUNG, A PROFESSIONAL CORPORATION
Knoxville, TN .... General Practice

MCCANDLISH & LILLARD, A PROFESSIONAL CORPORATION
Fairfax, VA .... Banking Law; Business Law; Civil Trial Practice; Commercial Litigation; Computer Law; General Practice; Health Care Law; Intellectual Property Law; Medical Malpractice; Real Estate Law; Trust and Estates, Wills and Probate

MCCANNA, KONZ, DUDAS, KEWLEY & PAPENDORF, S.C.
Appleton, WI .... Civil Trial Practice; Insurance Defense

MCCARROLL, NUNLEY & HARTZ
Owensboro, KY .... General Practice; Insurance Defense

MCCARTER & ENGLISH, LLP
Wilmington, DE .... General Practice
Cherry Hill, NJ .... Civil Trial Practice; General Practice
Newark, NJ .... Admiralty/Maritime Law; Antitrust Law; Banking Law; Bankruptcy Law; Civil Trial Practice; Commercial Law; Communications Law; Computer Law; Employment Benefits Law; Family Law; General Practice; Health Care Law; Insurance Defense; International Business Law; Labor and Employment Law; Municipal Bond/Public Authority Financing; Natural Resources Law; Personal Injury; Real Estate Law; Securities Law; Tax Law; Trademark, Copyright and Unfair Competition; Transportation Law; Trust and Estates, Wills and Probate
Philadelphia, PA .... General Practice

MCCARTHY, JOHN C.
Claremont, CA .... Civil Trial Practice; Labor and Employment Law

MCCARTHY & COSTELLO, L.L.P.
Lanham, MD .... General Practice; Personal Injury

MCCARTHY, LEBIT, CRYSTAL & HAIMAN CO., L.P.A.
Cleveland, OH .... Tax Law

MCCARTHY, LEONARD, KAEMMERER, OWEN, LAMKIN & MCGOVERN, L.C.
St. Louis, MO .... Business Law; Labor and Employment Law

MCCARTHY & MASSEY, P.C.
Manassas, VA .... Commercial Litigation; Labor and Employment Law; Medical Malpractice; Workers Compensation

MCCARTHY, PALMER, VOLKEMA & THOMAS, A LEGAL PROFESSIONAL ASSOCIATION
Columbus, OH .... Appellate Practice; Civil Trial Practice; Medical Malpractice; Personal Injury; Product Liability Law

MCCARTHY AND SCHATZMAN, P.A.
Princeton, NJ .... Appellate Practice; Banking Law; Business Law; Civil Trial Practice; Commercial Law; Creditors Rights; Family Law; General Practice; Municipal and Zoning Law; Real Estate Law; Trust and Estates, Wills and Probate

MCCARTHY, SUMMERS, BOBKO, MCKEY, WOOD & SAWYER, P.A.
Stuart, FL .... Banking Law; Civil Trial Practice; Commercial Law; Commercial Litigation; Construction Law; Corporate Law; Family Law; General Practice; Land Use Law; Real Estate Law; Trust and Estates, Wills and Probate

MCCARTHY TÉTRAULT
Calgary, AB, Canada .... General Practice
Vancouver, BC, Canada .... General Practice
London, ON, Canada .... General Practice
Ottawa, ON, Canada .... General Practice
Toronto, ON, Canada .... General Practice
Montreal, QU, Canada .... General Practice
Quebec, QU, Canada .... General Practice
London, England .... General Practice

MCCAUGHAN, WILLIAM P. LAW OFFICE OF
Miami, FL .... General Practice; Real Estate Law

MCCAUGHEY & METOS
Salt Lake City, UT .... Criminal Trial Practice

MCCAULEY & ASSOCIATES ALC
Newport Beach, CA .... Business Law; Civil Trial Practice

MCCLAIN, RAY P., ATTORNEY, P.A.
Charleston, SC .... Labor and Employment Law; Personal Injury

MCCLELLAN & BROWN, A PROFESSIONAL CORPORATION
San Diego, CA .... Civil Trial Practice; Personal Injury; Product Liability Law

MCCLELLAN, POWERS, EHMLING & DIX, P.C.
Gallatin, TN .... Civil Trial Practice; Insurance Defense

MCCLELLAND & ANDERSON, L.L.P.
Lansing, MI .... Commercial Law; Commercial Litigation; Construction Law; Land Use Law; Real Estate Law

MCCLUNG, PETERS AND SIMON
Albany, NY .... Banking Law; Commercial Litigation; General Practice

MCCOLLOUGH & ASSOCIATES, P.C.
Austin, TX .... Communications Law; Public Utilities Law

MCCOLLOUGH, TERRY L., P.A.
Orlando, FL .... Civil Trial Practice; Commercial Litigation; Personal Injury

MCCOLLUM, CROWLEY, VEHANEN, MOSCHET & MILLER, LTD.
Minneapolis, MN .... Insurance Defense

MCCONAUGHEY & GOFF
Decatur, GA .... Trust and Estates, Wills and Probate

MCCONNAUGHHAY, DUFFY, COONROD, POPE & WEAVER, P.A.
Tallahassee, FL .... Civil Trial Practice; Workers Compensation

MCCONNELL AND FINNERTY
North Vernon, IN .... General Practice

MCCONNELL VALDÉS
San Juan, PR .... General Practice

MCCORKLE, PEDIGO & JOHNSON, LLP
Savannah, GA .... General Practice

MCCORMACK & EPSTEIN
Boston, MA .... Civil Trial Practice; Insurance Defense; Personal Injury

MCCORMICK AND CHRISTOPH, P.C.
Boulder, CO .... Criminal Trial Practice; Personal Injury

MCCORMICK, HOFFMAN, REES, FAUBION, VAN BUSKIRK, JOHNSON & SCHUMOCK, P.S.
Lakewood, WA .... General Practice

MCCORMICK, KIDMAN & BEHRENS, LLP
Costa Mesa, CA .... Civil Trial Practice; Eminent Domain; Environmental Law; General Practice; Natural Resources Law; Trust and Estates, Wills and Probate

MCCORMICK & MITCHELL, A PROFESSIONAL CORPORATION
San Diego, CA .... Arbitration; Construction Law; Insurance Defense; Product Liability Law

MCCORMICK, PAULDING & HUBER, LLP
Hartford, CT .... Intellectual Property Law
Springfield, MA .... Intellectual Property Law

MCCORMICK & PRIORE, P.C.
Philadelphia, PA .... Civil Trial Practice; Environmental Law; Insurance Defense; Medical Malpractice; Product Liability Law; Toxic Torts

MCCORRISTON MIHO MILLER MUKAI
Honolulu, HI .... Business Law; Civil Trial Practice; General Practice; Insurance Defense; International Business Law; Real Estate Law; Tax Law

MCCOY & ASSOCIATES, P.C.
Philadelphia, PA .... Civil Rights; Labor and Employment Law

MCCOY ROBERTS BEGNAUD & FRIEDMAN, A LAW CORPORATION
Natchitoches, LA .... General Practice

MCCOY, WEAVER, WIGGINS, CLEVELAND & RAPER, PLLC
Fayetteville, NC .... General Practice

MCCOY & WEST
Lexington, KY .... Civil Trial Practice; Criminal Trial Practice

MCCOY, WILKINS, STEPHENS & TIPTON, P.A.
Jackson, MS .... Insurance Defense

MCCULLOUGH SHERRILL, LLP
Atlanta, GA .... Business Law; Civil Trial Practice; General Practice; Immigration and Naturalization; International Business Law; Labor and Employment Law; Real Estate Law

MCCULLOUGH, SMITH, WRIGHT & KEMPE, P.A.
St. Paul, MN .... Family Law; Personal Injury

MCCURDY & CANDLER, L.L.C.
Decatur, GA .... General Practice

MCCURLEY, KINSER, MCCURLEY & NELSON, L.L.P.
Dallas, TX .... Family Law

MCCUTCHEN, BLANTON, RHODES & JOHNSON, L.L.P.
Columbia, SC .... Appellate Practice; Civil Trial Practice; General Practice; Insurance Defense

MCCUTCHEN, DOYLE, BROWN & ENERSEN, LLP
Los Angeles, CA .... General Practice
San Francisco, CA .... General Practice
Walnut Creek, CA .... General Practice
Taipei, Taiwan .... General Practice

MCCUTCHEON, MCCUTCHEON & BAXTER, P.A.
Conway, SC .... Civil Trial Practice; General Practice; Insurance Defense; Medical Malpractice

MCDADE, FOGLER, MAINES & LOHSE, L.L.P.
Houston, TX .... Civil Trial Practice

MCDANIEL, DUKE A.
Petersburg, WV .... General Practice

MCDANIEL & MARSH
Baltimore, MD .... Appellate Practice; Civil Trial Practice; Commercial Litigation; Criminal Trial Practice

MCDANIEL & WELLS, P.A.
Jonesboro, AR .... Personal Injury

MCDAVID, TERRY
Lake City, FL .... Real Estate Law

MCDERMOTT & MCGEE
Millburn, NJ .... Appellate Practice; Civil Trial Practice; General Practice; Insurance Defense; Medical Malpractice; Personal Injury; Professional Liability

MCDONALD, E. DANDRIDGE
Charleston, WV .... Public Utilities Law

MCDONALD, BROWN & FAGEN
Dallas Center, IA .... General Practice

MCDONALD CARANO WILSON MCCUNE BERGIN FRANKOVICH & HICKS LLP
Las Vegas, NV .... Civil Trial Practice; Commercial Law; Construction Law; General Practice; Municipal and Zoning Law; Real Estate Law; Tax Law; Trust and Estates, Wills and Probate
Reno, NV .... Administrative Law; Civil Trial Practice; Commercial Law; Construction Law; Employment Benefits Law; Environmental Law; General Practice; Intellectual Property Law; Labor and Employment Law; Municipal and Zoning Law; Real Estate Law; Tax Law; Trust and Estates, Wills and Probate; Workers Compensation

MCDONALD, FRANCES B., P.C.
Denver, CO .... Labor and Employment Law; Nonprofit and Tax Exempt Organizations

MCDONALD GROUP, THE, L.L.P.
Erie, PA .... General Practice

MCDONALD & HAYDEN
Toronto, ON, Canada .... Business Law; Family Law; Personal Injury; Real Estate Law; Securities Law; Tax Law; Trademark, Copyright and Unfair Competition

MCDONALD, HOPKINS, BURKE & HABER CO., L.P.A.
Cleveland, OH .... Appellate Practice; Business Law; Civil Trial Practice; Commercial Litigation; Employment Benefits Law; General Practice; Pension and Profit Sharing; Real Estate Law; Tax Law; Trust and Estates, Wills and Probate

MCDONALD & KANYUK, P.L.L.C.
Concord, NH .... Trust and Estates, Wills and Probate

MCDONALD KUHN
Memphis, TN .... General Practice; Insurance Defense; Product Liability Law; Workers Compensation

MCDONALD, MARYBETH, P.A.
Orlando, FL .... Insurance Defense

MCDONALD & MCDONALD
Miami, FL .... Aviation Law

MCDONALD, SAELTZER, MORRIS, CREEGGAN & WADDOCK
Sacramento, CA .... Civil Trial Practice; Insurance Defense

MCDONALD, WILLIAM H., & ASSOCIATES, P.C.
Springfield, MO .... Antitrust Law; Civil Trial Practice; Commercial Law; General Practice; Patent, Trademark, Copyright and Unfair Competition; Product Liability Law

MCDONNELL BOEHNEN HULBERT & BERGHOFF
Chicago, IL .... Intellectual Property Law; Patent, Trademark, Copyright and Unfair Competition; Trademark, Copyright and Unfair Competition

MCDONNELL TRIAL LAWYERS
Naples, FL .... Civil Trial Practice; Criminal Trial Practice; Personal Injury

MCDONOUGH, HOLLAND & ALLEN, A PROFESSIONAL CORPORATION
Sacramento, CA .... General Practice

MCDONOUGH, KORN & EICHHORN, A PROFESSIONAL CORPORATION
Springfield, NJ .... Admiralty/Maritime Law; Aviation Law; Civil Trial Practice; Criminal Trial Practice; General Practice; Insurance Defense; Medical Malpractice; Personal Injury; Product Liability Law; Professional Liability

MCDOUGALL & SELF, L.L.P.
Sumter, SC .... Family Law

MCDOWALL, COTTER, DUNN, VALE & BRACCO, A PROFESSIONAL CORPORATION
San Mateo, CA .... Civil Trial Practice; Insurance Defense

MCDOWELL & BEASON
Russellville, AL .... Corporate Law; General Practice; Insurance Defense

MCDOWELL, JOSEPH F., III, P.A.
Manchester, NH .... General Practice

MCDOWELL, WICK, DALY, GALLUP, HAUSER AND HARTLE
Bradford, PA .... General Practice

MCDUFFEE, PAUL G. II
Tampa, FL .... Personal Injury

MCELDREW & FULLAM, P.C.
Philadelphia, PA .... Civil Trial Practice; Labor and Employment Law; Medical Malpractice; Personal Injury; Product Liability Law; Professional Liability; Transportation Law

MCELROY, DEUTSCH AND MULVANEY
Morristown, NJ .... Civil Trial Practice; Commercial Law; Construction Law; Environmental Law; General Practice; Insurance Defense

MCEWAN, MARTINEZ, LUFF, DUKES & RUFFIER, P.A.
Orlando, FL .... Civil Trial Practice; Commercial Litigation; Insurance Defense; Medical Malpractice; Professional Liability

MCEWEN, SCHMITT & CO.
Vancouver, BC, Canada .... Admiralty/Maritime Law

MCFADDEN & DILLON, A PROFESSIONAL CORPORATION
Chicago, IL .... Banking Law; Civil Trial Practice; Commercial Litigation; General Practice; Labor and Employment Law

MCFARLAIN, WILEY, CASSEDY & JONES, PROFESSIONAL ASSOCIATION
Tallahassee, FL .... Administrative Law; Appellate Practice; Business Law; Civil Trial Practice; Commercial Law; Commercial Litigation; Family Law; Health Care Law; Insurance Defense; Medical Malpractice; Personal Injury; Product Liability Law; Professional Liability

MCFARLAND & HERMAN
Chicago, IL .... Transportation Law

MCGAHN, FRISS, FRANKS & TRIPICIAN
Atlantic City, NJ .... General Practice

MCGARITY & ASSOCIATES
Lawrenceville, GA .... Personal Injury

MCGARRY & LAUFENBERG
Gardena, CA .... Insurance Defense; Personal Injury; Product Liability Law

MCGAUGHEY & SPIRITO
Torrance, CA .... Family Law; Trust and Estates, Wills and Probate

MCGEE & GELMAN
Buffalo, NY .... Civil Trial Practice; General Practice; Patent, Trademark, Copyright and Unfair Competition

MCGEE & MASON, P.A.
Brooksville, FL .... General Practice

MCGEE & POWERS, P.A.
Orlando, FL .... Commercial Litigation; Insurance Defense; Product Liability Law

MCGILL, GOTSDINER, WORKMAN & LEPP, P.C.
Omaha, NE .... Banking Law; Civil Trial Practice; Commercial Litigation; Creditors Rights; General Practice; Health Care Law; International Business Law; Labor and Employment Law; Mergers and Acquisitions; Tax Law; Workers Compensation

MCGILLICUDDY, TERRENCE J., P.C.
Phoenix, AZ .... Aviation Law; Personal Injury

MCGIMPSEY & CAFFERTY
Somerset, NJ .... Communications Law; General Practice

MCGINLEY, O'DONNELL, REYNOLDS & EDWARDS, P.C.
Ogallala, NE .... General Practice

MCGINNIS, LOCHRIDGE & KILGORE, L.L.P.
Austin, TX .... General Practice
Houston, TX .... General Practice

MCGLINCHEY STAFFORD
New Orleans, LA .... Admiralty/Maritime Law; Antitrust Law; Appellate Practice; Arbitration; Aviation Law; Banking Law; Bankruptcy Law; Business Law; Civil Trial Practice; Commercial Litigation; Construction Law; Corporate Law; Employment Benefits Law; Environmental Law; Health Care Law; Immigration and Naturalization; Insurance Defense; Intellectual Property Law; International Trade Law; Labor and Employment Law; Medical Malpractice; Municipal and Zoning Law; Municipal Bond/Public Authority Financing; Pension and Profit Sharing; Product Liability Law; Professional Liability; Public Utilities Law; Real Estate Law; Securities Law; Tax Law; Toxic Torts; Trust and Estates, Wills and Probate; Workers Compensation

MCGLINN, MICHAEL D.
San Diego, CA .... Criminal Trial Practice

MCGLOTHREN, MICHAEL S., P.C.
Fairhope, AL .... Personal Injury

MCGLYNN & MCGLYNN
Belleville, IL .... Commercial Law; Personal Injury; Transportation Law
St. Louis, MO .... Personal Injury

MCGOUGAN, WRIGHT, WORLEY AND HARPER, L.L.P.
Tabor City, NC .... General Practice

MCGOVERN, CONNELLY & DAVIDSON
New Rochelle, NY .... Tax Law

MCGOVERN AND DAWSON
White Plains, NY .... Civil Trial Practice; Trust and Estates, Wills and Probate

MCGOWN, MICHAEL R.
Beaumont, TX .... Civil Trial Practice; Personal Injury; Product Liability Law

MCGRANE & NOSICH, P.A.
Miami, FL .... Insurance Defense

MCGRATH, J. NICHOLAS, P.C.
Aspen, CO .... Civil Trial Practice; General Practice; Real Estate Law

MCGRATH, NORTH, MULLIN & KRATZ, P.C.
Omaha, NE .... Antitrust Law; Civil Trial Practice; General Practice; Insurance Defense; Intellectual Property Law; Labor and Employment Law; Tax Law

MCGREGOR & ASSOCIATES, P.C.
Boston, MA .... Environmental Law

MCGUANE AND HOGAN LLP
Denver, CO .... Family Law

MCGUINESS, ROBERT D.
Oakland, CA .... Family Law

MCGUINESS NORRIS & WILLIAMS, LLP
Washington, DC .... Labor and Employment Law

MCGUINN, HILLSMAN & PALEFSKY, A PROFESSIONAL CORPORATION
San Francisco, CA .... Admiralty/Maritime Law; Labor and Employment Law; Personal Injury

MCGUIRE, KEHL & NEALON, LLP
New York, NY .... Civil Trial Practice; Education Law; Intellectual Property Law; Sports and Entertainment Law

MCGUIRE, WOOD & BISSETTE, P.A.
Asheville, NC .... Civil Trial Practice; General Practice

MCGUIRE, WOODS, BATTLE & BOOTHE LLP
Washington, DC .... General Practice
Jacksonville, FL .... General Practice
Charlottesville, VA .... General Practice
McLean, VA .... General Practice
Norfolk, VA .... General Practice
Richmond, VA .... Antitrust Law; General Practice; Labor and Employment Law; Municipal Bond/Public Authority Financing; Tax Law

MCHENRY LAW FIRM
Little Rock, AR .... Medical Malpractice

MCHIE, MYERS, MCHIE & ENSLEN
Hammond, IN .... Civil Trial Practice; General Practice

MCINNES COOPER
Fredericton, NB, Canada .... Appellate Practice; Banking Law; Bankruptcy Law; Business Law; Civil Trial Practice; Commercial Law; Commercial Litigation; Construction Law; Corporate Law; Creditors Rights; Employment Benefits Law; Energy Law; General Practice; Government Contracts; Labor and Employment Law; Medical Malpractice; Mergers and Acquisitions; Personal Injury; Product Liability Law; Professional Liability; Real Estate Law; Securities Law; Tax Law; Trust and Estates, Wills and Probate
Moncton, NB, Canada .... Administrative Law; Appellate Practice; Banking Law; Bankruptcy Law; Business Law; Civil Rights; Civil Trial Practice; Commercial Law; Commercial Litigation; Construction Law; Corporate Law; Creditors Rights; Employment Benefits Law; Environmental Law; General Practice; Insurance Defense; Medical Malpractice; Municipal and Zoning Law; Natural Resources Law; Oil and Gas Law; Personal Injury; Product Liability Law; Professional Liability; Real Estate Law; Securities Law
St. John's, NF, Canada .... Admiralty/Maritime Law; Appellate Practice; Arbitration; Aviation Law; Banking Law; Bankruptcy Law; Business Law; Civil Rights; Civil Trial Practice; Commercial Law; Commercial Litigation; Computer Law; Construction Law; Corporate Law; Creditors Rights; Criminal Trial Practice; Employment Benefits Law; Energy Law; Environmental Law; General Practice; Health Care Law; Insurance Defense; Intellectual Property Law; Labor and Employment Law; Medical Malpractice; Mergers and Acquisitions; Natural Resources Law; Oil and Gas Law; Patent, Trademark, Copyright and Unfair Competition; Personal Injury; Product Liability Law; Professional Liability; Public Utilities Law; Real Estate Law; Securities Law; Sports and Entertainment Law; Tax Law; Trademark, Copyright and Unfair Competition; Workers Compensation
Halifax, NS, Canada .... Administrative Law; Admiralty/Maritime Law; Appellate Practice; Arbitration; Aviation Law; Banking Law; Bankruptcy Law; Business Law; Civil Rights; Civil Trial Practice; Commercial Law; Commercial Litigation; Computer Law; Constitutional Law; Construction Law; Corporate Law; Creditors Rights; Employment Benefits Law; Energy Law; Environmental Law; General Practice; Government Contracts; Insurance Defense; Intellectual Property Law; International Business Law; International Trade Law; Labor and Employment Law; Land Use Law; Medical Malpractice; Mergers and Acquisitions; Municipal and Zoning Law; Municipal Bond/Public Authority Financing; Natural Resources Law; Oil and Gas Law; Pension and Profit Sharing; Personal Injury; Product Liability Law; Professional Liability; Public Utilities Law; Real Estate Law; Securities Law; Sports and Entertainment Law; Tax Law; Toxic Torts; Trademark, Copyright and Unfair Competition; Transportation Law; Trust and Estates, Wills and Probate; Workers Compensation
Charlottetown, PE, Canada .... Administrative Law; Appellate Practice; Banking Law; Bankruptcy Law; Business Law; Civil Trial Practice; Commercial Law; Commercial Litigation; Construction Law; Corporate Law; Creditors Rights; Energy Law; General Practice; Health Care Law; Immigration and Naturalization; Insurance Defense; Labor and Employment Law; Land Use Law; Medical Malpractice; Mergers and Acquisitions; Oil and Gas Law; Personal Injury; Professional Liability; Public Utilities Law; Real Estate Law; Trust and Estates, Wills and Probate

MCINTOSH & LEE
Florence, SC .... Insurance Defense

MCINTOSH, SHERARD & SULLIVAN
Anderson, SC .... General Practice

MCKAY, BYRNE & GRAHAM
Los Angeles, CA .... Civil Trial Practice; Insurance Defense; Product Liability Law

MCKAY & GUÉRARD, P.A.
Charleston, SC .... General Practice
Columbia, SC .... General Practice

MCKAY, JOHN J., JR., P.A.
Hilton Head Island, SC .... Civil Trial Practice

MCKAY & MCKAY, P.A.
Columbia, SC .... Civil Trial Practice; General Practice; Medical Malpractice; Product Liability Law

MCKENDREE, JOHN W. LAW OFFICES OF
Denver, CO .... Arbitration; Civil Rights; Civil Trial Practice; Constitutional Law; Criminal Trial Practice; Family Law; Labor and Employment Law

MCKENNA, JAMES L., P.C.
Cherry Hill, NJ .... Environmental Law; Insurance Defense

MCKENZIE, ROBERT E.
Chicago, IL .... Tax Law

MCKENZIE, MCRAE, VASSER & BARBER, PLLC
Prescott, AR .... General Practice

MCKENZIE & TAYLOR, P.A.
Pensacola, FL .... Personal Injury

MCKEOWN, FITZGERALD, ZOLLNER, BUCK, HUTCHISON & RUTTLE
Joliet, IL .... Civil Trial Practice; General Practice; Personal Injury; Trust and Estates, Wills and Probate

MCKINNEY, ANNE M., P.C.
Knoxville, TN .... Trust and Estates, Wills and Probate

MCKIRDY AND RISKIN, A PROFESSIONAL CORPORATION
Morristown, NJ .... Civil Trial Practice; Eminent Domain; Real Estate Law

MCKISSOCK & HOFFMAN, P.C.
Philadelphia, PA .... Aviation Law; Civil Trial Practice; Commercial Law; Commercial Litigation; Health Care Law; Insurance Defense; Medical Malpractice; Product Liability Law

MCKOOL SMITH, A PROFESSIONAL CORPORATION
Dallas, TX .... Civil Trial Practice

MCLAUGHLIN, LESLIE G.
Midland, TX .... Civil Trial Practice; General Practice; Insurance Defense; Personal Injury

MCLAUGHLIN AND FLORINI, LTD.
Sullivan, IL .... Trust and Estates, Wills and Probate

MCLENNAN ROSS
Calgary, AB, Canada .... Civil Trial Practice; Labor and Employment Law
Edmonton, AB, Canada .... Civil Trial Practice; General Practice; Labor and Employment Law

MCLEOD, ALEXANDER, POWEL & APFFEL, A PROFESSIONAL CORPORATION
Galveston, TX .... General Practice

MCLEOD & MOYNE, P.C.
Okemos, MI .... Intellectual Property Law; Patent, Trademark, Copyright and Unfair Competition

MCLEOD VERLANDER
Monroe, LA .... Civil Trial Practice; Family Law; Health Care Law; Medical Malpractice; Personal Injury

MCLEOD, WATKINSON & MILLER
Washington, DC .... Administrative Law

MCMAHAN, CARL A. LAW OFFICES OF
Los Angeles, CA .... Civil Trial Practice; Medical Malpractice; Personal Injury; Product Liability Law

MCMAHON, BERGER, HANNA, LINIHAN, CODY & MCCARTHY, A PROFESSIONAL CORPORATION
St. Louis, MO .... Labor and Employment Law

MCMAHON, PATRICK R., A PROF. CORP., LAW OFFICES OF
San Jose, CA .... Personal Injury

MCMAHON & SPIEGEL
Los Angeles, CA .... Oil and Gas Law

MCMAHON, TIDWELL, HANSEN, ATKINS & PEACOCK, P.C.
Odessa, TX .... General Practice

MCMANIMON & SCOTLAND, L.L.C.
Newark, NJ .... Banking Law; Commercial Law; Corporate Law; Environmental Law; General Practice; Municipal Bond/Public Authority Financing; Real Estate Law; Securities Law; Tax Law

MCMANIS, FAULKNER & MORGAN
San Jose, CA .... Antitrust Law; Appellate Practice; Civil Rights; Civil Trial Practice; Commercial Litigation; Construction Law; Criminal Trial Practice; Environmental Law; Family Law; Intellectual Property Law; Labor and Employment Law; Land Use Law; Personal Injury; Trademark, Copyright and Unfair Competition

MCMASTER, CLIFFORD F.
Fort Worth, TX .... Bankruptcy Law

MCMASTER GERVAIS
Montreal, QU, Canada .... Administrative Law; Admiralty/Maritime Law; Arbitration; Banking Law; Bankruptcy Law; Business Law; Civil Trial Practice; Commercial Law; Commercial Litigation; Computer Law; Construction Law; Corporate Law; Environmental Law; General Practice; Health Care Law; Immigration and Naturalization; Insurance Defense; Intellectual Property Law; International Business Law; Labor and Employment Law; Medical Malpractice; Municipal and Zoning Law; Municipal Bond/Public Authority Financing; Personal Injury; Product Liability Law; Professional Liability; Public Utilities Law; Real Estate Law; Securities Law; Tax Law; Trademark, Copyright and Unfair Competition; Transportation Law; Trust and Estates, Wills and Probate; Workers Compensation

MCMATH, VEHIK, DRUMMOND, HARRISON & LEDBETTER, P.A.
Little Rock, AR .... Civil Trial Practice; Medical Malpractice

MCMILLAN BINCH
Toronto, ON, Canada .... General Practice

MCMILLAN CONSTABILE, LLP
Larchmont, NY .... General Practice

MCMILLEN, REINHART & VOGHT, P.A.
Orlando, FL .... Medical Malpractice

MCMORAN & ASSOCIATES, P.C.
Iselin, NJ .... Labor and Employment Law

MCMULLEN LAW FIRM
Fort Worth, TX .... Civil Trial Practice; Commercial Litigation; Construction Law; Insurance Defense; Personal Injury

MCMURRY & LIVINGSTON
Paducah, KY .... General Practice

MCMURRY & TALBOTT
Louisville, KY .... Legal Malpractice; Medical Malpractice

MCNABB, DOUGLAS C.
Houston, TX .... Appellate Practice; Criminal Trial Practice

MCNAIR LAW FIRM, P.A.
Columbia, SC .... General Practice

MCNAMAR, FEARNOW & MCSHARAR, P.C.
Indianapolis, IN .... Administrative Law; Health Care Law; Real Estate Law

MCNAMARA, F. TIMOTHY, P.C.
Hartford, CT .... Criminal Trial Practice

MCNAMARA AND MCNAMARA
Columbus, OH .... Construction Law; Insurance Defense

MCNAMARA, TODD J., P.C.
Denver, CO .... Labor and Employment Law

MCNAUL EBEL NAWROT HELGREN & VANCE P.L.L.C.
Seattle, WA .... Civil Trial Practice; General Practice

MCNEER, HIGHLAND, MCMUNN AND VARNER, L.C.
Clarksburg, WV .... Appellate Practice; Banking Law; Bankruptcy Law; Business Law; Civil Trial Practice; Commercial Law; Commercial Litigation; Construction Law; Environmental Law; General Practice; Insurance Defense; Labor and Employment Law; Medical Malpractice; Mergers and Acquisitions; Natural Resources Law; Personal Injury; Product Liability Law; Real Estate Law; Tax Law; Trust and Estates, Wills and Probate; Workers Compensation

MCNEES, WALLACE & NURICK
Columbus, OH .... Energy Law
Harrisburg, PA .... Commercial Litigation; Construction Law; Energy Law; General Practice; Intellectual Property Law; Labor and Employment Law; Real Estate Law; Transportation Law

MCNEIL, SILVEIRA & RICE
San Rafael, CA .... Business Law

MCNEIL, SUSSON, PARRETT & TROPP, A PROFESSIONAL CORPORATION
Santa Ana, CA .... Health Care Law; Medical Malpractice

MCNICHOLAS & MCNICHOLAS, LLP
Los Angeles, CA .... Civil Trial Practice; Labor and Employment Law; Personal Injury

MCNULTY, THOMAS J. JR.
Barnstable, MA .... Trust and Estates, Wills and Probate

MCPHERSON & ROCAMORA, PLLC
Durham, NC .... Trust and Estates, Wills and Probate

MCQUADES, THE, CO., L.P.A.
Swanton, OH .... General Practice; Personal Injury; Trust and Estates, Wills and Probate

MCREYNOLDS, GREGG C., P.C.
Denver, CO .... Civil Trial Practice

MCREYNOLDS, MARY A., P.C.
Washington, DC .... Civil Trial Practice; Commercial Law

MCSHANE & BOWIE, P.L.C.
Grand Rapids, MI .... Business Law; Commercial Litigation; Corporate Law; General Practice; Real Estate Law; Securities Law; Trust and Estates, Wills and Probate

MCSHANE, DAVIS & HANCE, L.L.P.
Dallas, TX .... Family Law

MCSHEA TECCE, P.C.
Philadelphia, PA .... Civil Trial Practice

MCTAGUE LAW FIRM
Windsor, ON, Canada .... Civil Trial Practice; Commercial Law; General Practice; Insurance Defense; Labor and Employment Law; Real Estate Law

MCTIGHE, WEISS, O'ROURKE & MILNER, P.C.
Norristown, PA .... General Practice; Insurance Defense

MCTURNAN & TURNER
Indianapolis, IN .... Antitrust Law; Appellate Practice; Civil Trial Practice; Commercial Litigation; Labor and Employment Law; Securities Law

MCVAY, WILLIAM W.
Pittsburgh, PA .... Personal Injury

MCWHORTER, COBB & JOHNSON, L.L.P.
Lubbock, TX .... Civil Trial Practice; General Practice

MEAD & ASSOCIATES
Glendale, AZ .... General Practice

MEADE, BRODOVSKY, AIKEN, JACOBSEN & HINE, A LIMITED LIABILITY PARTNERSHIP
Sacramento, CA .... Personal Injury

MEAD, HECHT, CONKLIN & GALLAGHER
White Plains, NY .... General Practice

MEADOWS, ICHTER & TRIGG, P.C. A PROFESSIONAL CORPORATION
Atlanta, GA............Civil Trial Practice

MEADOWS, OWENS, COLLIER, REED, COUSINS & BLAU, L.L.P.
Dallas, TX............Corporate Law; General Practice; Mergers and Acquisitions; Real Estate Law; Securities Law; Tax Law; Trust and Estates, Wills and Probate

MEADOWS RILEY LAW FIRM
Gulfport, MS............Bankruptcy Law; Business Law; Civil Trial Practice; Corporate Law; Environmental Law; Family Law; Real Estate Law; Trust and Estates, Wills and Probate

MEAHER, AUGUSTINE, III, P.C.
Mobile, AL............Civil Trial Practice; General Practice

MEARDON, SUEPPEL, DOWNER & HAYES P.L.C.
Iowa City, IA............Civil Trial Practice; General Practice; Municipal and Zoning Law

MEARS, CHRISTOPHER B., A P.C.
Irvine, CA............Personal Injury

MEDEIROS + SANFORD INC.
Providence, RI............Antitrust Law; Business Law; Civil Trial Practice; Commercial Litigation; Labor and Employment Law; Securities Law

MEDLEN & CARROLL, LLP
San Francisco, CA............Patent, Trademark, Copyright and Unfair Competition

MEEHAN & ASSOCIATES, LAW OFFICES OF
Tucson, AZ............Commercial Litigation

MEEHAN, BOYLE & COHEN, P.C.
Boston, MA............Appellate Practice; Aviation Law; Civil Trial Practice; Medical Malpractice; Personal Injury; Product Liability Law

MEEKS, W. EDWARD JR.
Albany, GA............General Practice; Medical Malpractice; Personal Injury

MEENAN & LARIVIERE
Pasadena, CA............Civil Trial Practice; Medical Malpractice; Personal Injury; Product Liability Law

MEGANCK, ALLAN G.
Grosse Pointe Park, MI............Insurance Defense; Medical Malpractice; Product Liability Law

MEHAFFY & WEBER, A PROFESSIONAL CORPORATION
Beaumont, TX............Admiralty/Maritime Law; Civil Trial Practice; Employment Benefits Law; Environmental Law; General Practice; Insurance Defense; Medical Malpractice; Personal Injury; Product Liability Law
Houston, TX............Civil Trial Practice; Environmental Law; Insurance Defense; Personal Injury; Product Liability Law
Orange, TX............Civil Trial Practice; Environmental Law; Insurance Defense; Personal Injury

MEHLMAN & GREENBLATT, LLC
Baltimore, MD............Bankruptcy Law; Civil Trial Practice; Criminal Trial Practice; Medical Malpractice

MEHR & LAFRANCE
Freehold, NJ............General Practice

MEHRENS AND WILEMON, P.A.
Phoenix, AZ............Criminal Trial Practice

MEIER, LENGAUER, BONNER, MUSZYNSKI & DOYLE, P.A.
Orlando, FL............Civil Trial Practice; Insurance Defense; Product Liability Law

MEIGHEN DEMERS
Toronto, ON, Canada............General Practice

MEIROSE & FRISCIA, P.A.
Tampa, FL............Commercial Litigation; Construction Law; Insurance Defense

MEISLIK & LEVAVY
Montclair, NJ............Business Law; Real Estate Law

MEISNER & ASSOCIATES, P.C.
Bingham Farms, MI............Business Law; Civil Trial Practice; Real Estate Law

MEISSNER TIERNEY FISHER & NICHOLS S.C.
Milwaukee, WI............Antitrust Law; Business Law; Commercial Litigation; Elder Law; Employment Benefits Law; Environmental Law; Health Care Law; Nonprofit and Tax Exempt Organizations; Real Estate Law; Securities Law; Tax Law; Trust and Estates, Wills and Probate

MELAT, PRESSMAN, EZELL & HIGBIE, LLP
Colorado Springs, CO............Civil Trial Practice; Commercial Litigation; Personal Injury

MELEDIN, LOUISE Y.
Baltimore, MD............Tax Law

MELLEY, STEVEN M.
Rhinebeck, NY............Personal Injury

MELLI, WALKER, PEASE & RUHLY, S.C.
Madison, WI............General Practice; Labor and Employment Law

MELLON LAW FIRM, THE
Denver, CO............Civil Trial Practice; Construction Law

MELLON, WEBSTER & MELLON, A PROF. CORP., THE LAW OFFICES OF
Doylestown, PA............Personal Injury

MELTON, FLOYD M. JR.
Greenwood, MS............Trust and Estates, Wills and Probate

MELTON, WILLIAM D.
Evergreen, AL............Civil Trial Practice; Personal Injury; Product Liability Law

MELTZER, SANFORD
Syracuse, NY............Criminal Trial Practice; Family Law

MELTZER, PETER E., & ASSOCIATES, P.C., LAW OFFICES OF
Philadelphia, PA............Creditors Rights

MELVIN & MELVIN
Laurel, MS............Medical Malpractice; Personal Injury; Product Liability Law
Syracuse, NY............General Practice

MENARD, MURPHY & WALSH LLP
Boston, MA............Business Law; Civil Trial Practice; Commercial Litigation; Family Law; Labor and Employment Law; Trust and Estates, Wills and Probate

MENDELSOHN ROSENTZVEIG SHACTER
Montreal, QU, Canada............Banking Law; Bankruptcy Law; Commercial Law; Commercial Litigation; Labor and Employment Law; Patent, Trademark, Copyright and Unfair Competition; Real Estate Law; Securities Law; Tax Law

MENDES & MOUNT, LLP
New York, NY............Insurance Defense

MENES LAW CORPORATION
Los Angeles, CA............Intellectual Property Law; Sports and Entertainment Law; Trademark, Copyright and Unfair Competition

MENTZER, VUILLEMIN AND MYGRANT LTD.
Akron, OH............Bankruptcy Law; Commercial Law; Commercial Litigation; Criminal Trial Practice

MERCALDO, RONALD D., LTD.
Tucson, AZ............Medical Malpractice; Personal Injury

MERCER & MERCER
Pittsburgh, PA............Personal Injury

MERKIN, STEWART A. LAW OFFICE OF
Miami, FL............Business Law

MERKLE & MAGRI, P.A., LAW OFFICES OF
Tampa, FL............Civil Trial Practice; Commercial Litigation; Criminal Trial Practice; Personal Injury; Product Liability Law

MERLIN & HERTZ, P.A.
Coral Gables, FL............Family Law

MERLINE & THOMAS, P.A.
Greenville, SC............Mergers and Acquisitions; Pension and Profit Sharing; Tax Law; Trust and Estates, Wills and Probate

MERLO, KANOFSKY & BRINKMEIER, LTD.
Chicago, IL............Aviation Law; Insurance Defense

MERLY, LAWRENCE J.
Bridgeport, CT............Civil Trial Practice; Personal Injury

MERRILL, ABEL J., P.A.
Annapolis, MD............Trust and Estates, Wills and Probate

MERRILL & MERRILL, CHARTERED
Pocatello, ID............Appellate Practice; Business Law; Civil Trial Practice; General Practice; Health Care Law; Insurance Defense; Public Utilities Law; Real Estate Law; Trust and Estates, Wills and Probate

MERRILL, MULLINS & SPEARS, A PROFESSIONAL ASSOCIATION
Memphis, TN............Commercial Law

MERRILL, SCHULTZ & WOLDS, LIMITED
San Diego, CA............Employment Benefits Law; Labor and Employment Law

MERRILL, STONE & HAMILTON, LLC
Swainsboro, GA....................Civil Trial Practice

MERRIMAN, PATTERSON & ALLISON, L.L.P.
Longview, TX....................Insurance Defense

MERRITT & ASSOCIATES, P.C.
Oklahoma City, OK....................Medical Malpractice; Personal Injury; Product Liability Law

MERRITT, WOOTEN & JANVIER, P.A.
Raleigh, NC....................Business Law

MERRY, FARNEN & RYAN, A PROFESSIONAL CORPORATION
St. Clair Shores, MI....................Medical Malpractice; Professional Liability

MERVIS, CLARK D.
Miami, FL....................Criminal Trial Practice

MESH, GENE & ASSOCIATES
Cincinnati, OH....................Civil Trial Practice; Commercial Litigation; Securities Law

MESHBESHER & SPENCE
Minneapolis, MN....................Civil Trial Practice; Criminal Trial Practice; Medical Malpractice; Personal Injury

MESSER, HOWARD F., P.C.
Pittsburgh, PA....................Civil Trial Practice; Medical Malpractice; Personal Injury; Product Liability Law; Transportation Law

MESSINA BULZOMI
Tacoma, WA....................Personal Injury

METNICK, CHERRY & FRAZIER
Springfield, IL....................Civil Trial Practice; Criminal Trial Practice; Family Law; Personal Injury; Workers Compensation

METTE, EVANS & WOODSIDE, A PROFESSIONAL CORPORATION
Harrisburg, PA....................Administrative Law; Banking Law; Civil Trial Practice; Commercial Law; Construction Law; Environmental Law; General Practice; Municipal Bond/Public Authority Financing; Real Estate Law; Tax Law

METTLER, PETER W.
Palm Beach, FL....................Tax Law

METZGER & ASSOCIATES, LTD.
Chicago, IL....................Appellate Practice

METZGER, DIRK T., A PROFESSIONAL CORPORATION
San Diego, CA....................Commercial Litigation

METZGER, WICKERSHAM, KNAUSS & ERB, P.C.
Harrisburg, PA....................Civil Trial Practice; General Practice; Insurance Defense; Medical Malpractice; Personal Injury; Product Liability Law; Trust and Estates, Wills and Probate

MEULEMAN & MILLER, L.L.P.
Boise, ID....................Construction Law; Real Estate Law

MEYER, CAPEL, HIRSCHFELD, MUNCY, JAHN & ALDEEN, P.C.
Champaign, IL....................Business Law; Commercial Litigation; General Practice

MEYER, FLUEGGE AND TENNEY, P.S.
Yakima, WA....................General Practice

MEYER, HENDRICKS & BIVENS, P.A.
Phoenix, AZ....................Business Law; Commercial Litigation; International Business Law; Mergers and Acquisitions; Professional Liability; Securities Law

MEYER, JIM, & ASSOCIATES, P.C.
Waco, TX....................Civil Trial Practice; Family Law; Personal Injury

MEYER, KIRK, SNYDER & SAFFORD, PLLC
Bloomfield Hills, MI....................Business Law; Civil Trial Practice; Family Law; Real Estate Law; Trust and Estates, Wills and Probate
Detroit, MI....................Business Law; Civil Trial Practice; Family Law; Real Estate Law; Trust and Estates, Wills and Probate

MEYER, UNKOVIC & SCOTT LLP
Pittsburgh, PA....................General Practice

MEYERS, BILLINGSLEY, RODBELL & ROSENBAUM, P.A.
Riverdale, MD....................Bankruptcy Law; Commercial Litigation; General Practice; Municipal Bond/Public Authority Financing; Real Estate Law

MEYERS, HENTEMANN & REA CO., L.P.A.
Cleveland, OH....................Civil Trial Practice; General Practice; Insurance Defense; Product Liability Law

MEYERS, MOONEY, STANLEY & HOLLINGSWORTH
Orlando, FL....................Aviation Law; Medical Malpractice; Personal Injury; Professional Liability; Workers Compensation

MEYNER AND LANDIS
Newark, NJ....................Administrative Law; Banking Law; Bankruptcy Law; Civil Trial Practice; Commercial Law; Communications Law; Corporate Law; Creditors Rights; General Practice; Immigration and Naturalization; Land Use Law; Nonprofit and Tax Exempt Organizations; Public Utilities Law; Real Estate Law; Trust and Estates, Wills and Probate

MEZVINSKY, EDWARD M.
Narberth, PA....................General Practice; International Business Law; International Trade Law

MICHAEL, ROBERT J.
Rochester, NY....................Civil Trial Practice; Personal Injury; Product Liability Law

MICHAEL BEST & FRIEDRICH LLP
Madison, WI....................General Practice
Milwaukee, WI....................Antitrust Law; General Practice; Labor and Employment Law; Municipal Bond/Public Authority Financing; Natural Resources Law; Patent, Trademark, Copyright and Unfair Competition; Tax Law

MICHAELIS, MONTANARI & JOHNSON, A PROFESSIONAL LAW CORPORATION
Westlake Village, CA....................Insurance Defense

MICHAELS & BONNER, P.C.
Washington, DC....................Health Care Law

MICHAELS, JONES, MARTIN, PARRIS & TESSENER LAW OFFICES, PLLC
Raleigh, NC....................Medical Malpractice; Personal Injury; Product Liability Law; Workers Compensation

MICHAELS & SMOLAK, P.C.
Auburn, NY....................Civil Trial Practice

MICHAELSON, BENJAMIN, JR., P.A.
Annapolis, MD....................Real Estate Law

MICHAUD, BUSCHMANN, FOX, FERRARA & MITTELMARK, P.A.
Boca Raton, FL....................Civil Trial Practice; Construction Law; Insurance Defense; Medical Malpractice; Product Liability Law; Professional Liability; Toxic Torts; Transportation Law

MICHELI, BALDWIN, BOPELEY & NORTHRUP CO., L.P.A.
Zanesville, OH....................Civil Trial Practice; Insurance Defense; Medical Malpractice

MICHENER, LARIMORE, SWINDLE, WHITAKER, FLOWERS, SAWYER, REYNOLDS & CHALK, L.L.P.
Fort Worth, TX....................Business Law; Tax Law

MICKEY, WILSON, WEILER & RENZI, P.C.
Aurora, IL....................General Practice

MIDDENDORF, HENRY S. JR.
New York, NY....................General Practice

MIDDLEBERG, RIDDLE & GIANNA
New Orleans, LA....................Commercial Law; Insurance Defense; Real Estate Law
Dallas, TX....................Civil Trial Practice; Commercial Law; Insurance Defense; Real Estate Law

MIDDLEBROOK, KAISER & POPKA, A PROFESSIONAL CORPORATION
San Bernardino, CA....................Civil Trial Practice; Insurance Defense

MIDDLEBROOKS & SHAPIRO, P.C.
Parsippany, NJ....................Bankruptcy Law; Commercial Litigation

MIDDLETON, MATHIS, ADAMS & TATE, P.C.
Atlanta, GA....................General Practice
Milledgeville, GA....................General Practice
Savannah, GA....................General Practice

MIDDLETON & REUTLINGER, P.S.C.
Louisville, KY....................Antitrust Law; Banking Law; Bankruptcy Law; Civil Trial Practice; Environmental Law; General Practice; Insurance Defense; Patent, Trademark, Copyright and Unfair Competition; Personal Injury; Securities Law; Tax Law; Trust and Estates, Wills and Probate

MIDLEN LAW CENTER
Washington, DC....................Business Law; Communications Law; Trademark, Copyright and Unfair Competition

MIKKELBORG, BROZ, WELLS & FRYER, PLLC
Seattle, WA....................Admiralty/Maritime Law; General Practice

MIKOS, KENNETH R., P.A.
Fort Lauderdale, FL....................Civil Trial Practice; Elder Law; Trust and Estates, Wills and Probate

MIKUS LAW ASSOCIATES
Lancaster, PA....................Personal Injury; Product Liability Law

MILANO, JAY LAW OFFICES OF
Rocky River, OH....Civil Trial Practice; Criminal Trial Practice

MILBANK, TWEED, HADLEY & MCCLOY LLP
Los Angeles, CA....General Practice; Securities Law
Washington, DC....General Practice
New York, NY....Aviation Law; Banking Law; Commercial Litigation; General Practice; Securities Law; Transportation Law
Hong Kong, China....General Practice; Securities Law
London, England....General Practice; Securities Law
Tokyo, Japan....Aviation Law; General Practice; Transportation Law
Moscow, Russia....General Practice
Singapore, Singapore....General Practice

MILBERG WEISS BERSHAD HYNES & LERACH LLP
New York, NY....Antitrust Law; Civil Trial Practice

MILDE, HOFFBERG & MACKLIN, LLP
White Plains, NY....Patent, Trademark, Copyright and Unfair Competition

MILES AND MILES, A PROFESSIONAL ASSOCIATION
Plymouth, MA....Family Law

MILES, SEARS & EANNI, A PROFESSIONAL CORPORATION
Fresno, CA....Civil Trial Practice; Medical Malpractice; Personal Injury; Product Liability Law

MILIDES, GUS
Easton, PA....Family Law; General Practice; Medical Malpractice; Personal Injury; Product Liability Law

MILITELLO, ZANCK & COEN, P.C.
Crystal Lake, IL....Commercial Law; General Practice; Municipal and Zoning Law

MILLAR & AMBRETTE
Darien, CT....Family Law; General Practice; Real Estate Law; Trust and Estates, Wills and Probate

MILLAR, HODGES & BEMIS
Newport Beach, CA....Civil Trial Practice; Real Estate Law; Trust and Estates, Wills and Probate

MILLEDGE, JOHN M., P.A.
Fort Lauderdale, FL....Municipal and Zoning Law

MILLEN, WHITE, ZELANO & BRANIGAN, P.C.
Arlington, VA....Patent, Trademark, Copyright and Unfair Competition
Richmond, VA....Patent, Trademark, Copyright and Unfair Competition

MILLER, JOHN E.
Palo Alto, CA....Family Law; Trust and Estates, Wills and Probate

MILLER, ROBERT A.
Oklahoma City, OK....Oil and Gas Law

MILLER & ASSOCIATES
Destin, FL....Trust and Estates, Wills and Probate

MILLER, CANFIELD, PADDOCK AND STONE, P.L.C.
Washington, DC....Communications Law; Labor and Employment Law; Municipal Bond/Public Authority Financing
Ann Arbor, MI....Antitrust Law; Civil Rights; Civil Trial Practice; Commercial Litigation; General Practice; Health Care Law; Insurance Defense; International Business Law; Labor and Employment Law; Municipal Bond/Public Authority Financing; Real Estate Law; Securities Law
Detroit, MI....Antitrust Law; Banking Law; Bankruptcy Law; Business Law; Civil Rights; Civil Trial Practice; Commercial Litigation; Communications Law; Computer Law; Construction Law; Creditors Rights; Employment Benefits Law; Environmental Law; General Practice; Health Care Law; Intellectual Property Law; International Business Law; Labor and Employment Law; Medical Malpractice; Mergers and Acquisitions; Municipal and Zoning Law; Municipal Bond/Public Authority Financing; Patent, Trademark, Copyright and Unfair Competition; Personal Injury; Product Liability Law; Real Estate Law; Securities Law; Tax Law; Trust and Estates, Wills and Probate
Grand Rapids, MI....Antitrust Law; Business Law; Computer Law; Creditors Rights; Environmental Law; General Practice; Intellectual Property Law; International Business Law; Personal Injury; Real Estate Law; Securities Law; Tax Law; Trust and Estates, Wills and Probate
Kalamazoo, MI....Antitrust Law; Bankruptcy Law; Business Law; Civil Trial Practice; Commercial Law; Computer Law; Construction Law; Creditors Rights; Employment Benefits Law; Environmental Law; General Practice; Insurance Defense; Labor and Employment Law; Medical Malpractice; Mergers and Acquisitions; Municipal and Zoning Law; Personal Injury; Product Liability Law; Securities Law; Tax Law; Trust and Estates, Wills and Probate
Lansing, MI....Antitrust Law; Banking Law; Bankruptcy Law; Environmental Law; General Practice; Municipal Bond/Public Authority Financing; Trust and Estates, Wills and Probate
Monroe, MI....Antitrust Law; General Practice; International Business Law; Securities Law; Tax Law
Troy, MI....General Practice; Mergers and Acquisitions; Product Liability Law; Securities Law
New York, NY....Civil Trial Practice; General Practice; International Business Law

MILLER CARSON BOXBERGER & MURPHY, LLP
Bloomington, IN....Insurance Defense
Fort Wayne, IN....Banking Law; Business Law; Insurance Defense

MILLER & COHEN, P.C.
Longmont, CO....Civil Trial Practice; Creditors Rights

MILLER & COMPANY P.C.
Washington, DC....International Trade Law
Kansas City, MO....International Trade Law

MILLER, EGGLESTON & CRAMER, LTD.
Burlington, VT....Antitrust Law; Civil Trial Practice; General Practice; Health Care Law; Immigration and Naturalization; Labor and Employment Law; Public Utilities Law; Securities Law; Tax Law; Trademark, Copyright and Unfair Competition

MILLER FAIGNANT & BEHRENS, P.C.
Rutland, VT....Appellate Practice; Civil Trial Practice; General Practice; Insurance Defense; Medical Malpractice; Personal Injury; Product Liability Law; Professional Liability; Workers Compensation

MILLER, G. SPENCER, L.L.C., LAW OFFICES OF
Gladstone, MO....Medical Malpractice; Personal Injury; Professional Liability

MILLER AND HARRISON, LLC
Boulder, CO....Criminal Trial Practice; Personal Injury

MILLER, J. BRUCE, LAW GROUP
Louisville, KY....Business Law; Civil Trial Practice; General Practice

MILLER, KAGAN, RODRIGUEZ AND SILVER, PROFESSIONAL ASSOCIATION
Coral Gables, FL....Workers Compensation

MILLER, KATHLEEN ORTMAN, S.C.
Milwaukee, WI....Family Law

MILLER, KISTLER, CAMPBELL, MILLER, WILLIAMS & BENSON, INC.
Bellefonte, PA....Civil Trial Practice
State College, PA....Civil Trial Practice

MILLER LAW FIRM, A PROFESSIONAL CORPORATION
Kansas City, MO....Commercial Litigation; Construction Law

MILLER LAW GROUP
Larkspur, CA....Labor and Employment Law

MILLER LAW OFFICES, THE
Studio City, CA....Immigration and Naturalization

MILLER & MARKLE, L.L.P.
Atlanta, GA....Civil Trial Practice

MILLER & MARTIN LLP
Chattanooga, TN....General Practice

MILLER, MELVIN B., LTD.
Bala Cynwyd, PA....Business Law; Real Estate Law

MILLER, MILLER & CANBY, CHARTERED
Rockville, MD....Business Law; General Practice; Municipal and Zoning Law

MILLER MILOVE & KOB, P.C.
San Diego, CA....Business Law; Securities Law

MILLER, MORTON, CAILLAT & NEVIS
San Jose, CA....Bankruptcy Law; Business Law; Civil Trial Practice; Construction Law; General Practice; Real Estate Law; Tax Law; Trust and Estates, Wills and Probate

MILLER MULLER MENDELSON & KENNEDY
Indianapolis, IN....Business Law; Civil Trial Practice; Medical Malpractice; Personal Injury; Product Liability Law

MILLER NASH LLP
Portland, OR....Admiralty/Maritime Law; Antitrust Law; General Practice; Labor and Employment Law; Patent, Trademark, Copyright and Unfair Competition

MILLER, PEARSON, GLOE, BURNS, BEATTY & COWIE, P.C.
Decorah, IA....General Practice; Insurance Defense; Personal Injury

MILLER, PORTER & MULLER, P.C.
Princeton, NJ ....General Practice

MILLER, RICHARD F., A PROFESSIONAL CORPORATION
Pasadena, CA ....Trust and Estates, Wills and Probate

MILLER, SCHWARTZ AND MILLER, P.A.
Hollywood, FL ....General Practice

MILLER, SHINE & BRYAN, P.A.
St. Augustine, FL ....Civil Trial Practice; Family Law

MILLER, STARR & REGALIA, A PROFESSIONAL LAW CORPORATION
Menlo Park, CA ....Real Estate Law

MILLER, STRATVERT & TORGERSON, P.A.
Albuquerque, NM ....Banking Law; Civil Trial Practice; Commercial Law; General Practice; Insurance Defense; Natural Resources Law; Real Estate Law; Tax Law; Trust and Estates, Wills and Probate

MILLER THOMSON
Calgary, AB, Canada ....General Practice
Edmonton, AB, Canada ....General Practice
Markham, ON, Canada ....General Practice
Toronto, ON, Canada ....General Practice

MILLER & VAN EATON, P.L.L.C.
Washington, DC ....Communications Law

MILLER & WELCH, L.L.C.
Denver, CO ....Civil Trial Practice; Commercial Litigation; Labor and Employment Law

MILLER & WRUBEL P.C.
New York, NY ....Civil Trial Practice; Commercial Law

MILLIKEN LAW FIRM
Bowling Green, KY ....Criminal Trial Practice; Insurance Defense; Medical Malpractice

MILLING BENSON WOODWARD L.L.P.
New Orleans, LA ....Admiralty/Maritime Law; Antitrust Law; Banking Law; Commercial Litigation; Energy Law; General Practice; Health Care Law; Labor and Employment Law; Natural Resources Law; Public Utilities Law; Tax Law

MILLS, WILLIAM S.
McPherson, KS ....General Practice

MILLS LAW FIRM, THE, P.C.
Oklahoma City, OK ....Civil Rights; Civil Trial Practice; Insurance Defense; Medical Malpractice; Personal Injury; Product Liability Law

MILLS, MORAITAKIS, KUSHEL & PEARSON
Atlanta, GA ....Civil Trial Practice; Medical Malpractice; Product Liability Law

MILLS PRESBY AND ASSOCIATES, L.L.P.
Dallas, TX ....Civil Trial Practice; Criminal Trial Practice

MILLS, SHIRLEY, ECKEL & BASSETT, L.L.P.
Galveston, TX ....Insurance Defense
Houston, TX ....Insurance Defense

MILLSAP, MIKE
Lubbock, TX ....Civil Trial Practice; Medical Malpractice; Personal Injury; Product Liability Law

MILLSAP & SINGER, P.C.
St. Louis, MO ....Real Estate Law

MILLSTEIN & KNUPP
Youngwood, PA ....Appellate Practice; Business Law; Civil Trial Practice; General Practice; Real Estate Law

MILNER, LOBEL, GORANSON, SORRELS, UDASHEN & WELLS
Dallas, TX ....Criminal Trial Practice

MILODRAGOVICH, DALE, STEINBRENNER & BINNEY, P.C.
Missoula, MT ....General Practice

MILTON, LAURENCE & DIXON
Worcester, MA ....Insurance Defense; Personal Injury; Workers Compensation

MINEO & WHITTAKER
Charlotte, NC ....Patent, Trademark, Copyright and Unfair Competition
Raleigh, NC ....Aviation Law; Patent, Trademark, Copyright and Unfair Competition

MINIER, STANLEY, INC., LAW OFFICES OF
Santa Ana, CA ....Bankruptcy Law

MINK & BLAIR
Nashville, TN ....Civil Trial Practice; Insurance Defense

MINOR AND ASSOCIATES
Biloxi, MS ....Admiralty/Maritime Law; Civil Trial Practice; General Practice; Medical Malpractice; Personal Injury; Product Liability Law

MINSKY, MCCORMICK & HALLAGAN, P.C.
Chicago, IL ....Immigration and Naturalization

MINTMIRE & ASSOCIATES
Palm Beach, FL ....Business Law; Civil Trial Practice; Insurance Defense; Trust and Estates, Wills and Probate

MINTON, HARVEY S. & ASSOCIATES
Columbus, OH ....Business Law; Real Estate Law; Trust and Estates, Wills and Probate

MINTON, BURTON, FOSTER & COLLINS, A PROFESSIONAL CORPORATION
Austin, TX ....Civil Trial Practice; Criminal Trial Practice

MINTON FIRM, THE
Chicago, IL ....Family Law

MINTON, MINTON AND RAND LLP
Los Angeles, CA ....Business Law; Real Estate Law; Trust and Estates, Wills and Probate

MINTZ, LEVIN, COHN, FERRIS, GLOVSKY AND POPEO, P.C.
Washington, DC ....Antitrust Law; Communications Law; General Practice
Boston, MA ....Antitrust Law; Civil Trial Practice; Communications Law; Criminal Trial Practice; General Practice; Municipal Bond/Public Authority Financing

MINYARD AND MORRIS, LLP
Orange, CA ....Family Law

MIRES, DOUGLAS W.
Rochester Hills, MI ....Banking Law

MIRICK, O'CONNELL, DEMALLIE & LOUGEE, LLP
Worcester, MA ....General Practice

MIROFF, CROSS & KLINEMAN
Indianapolis, IN ....Family Law

MISHAN, SLOTO, GREENBERG, HELLINGER & UDOLF, P.A.
Miami, FL ....Bankruptcy Law; Commercial Litigation; Creditors Rights

MITCHELL, LINCOLN A.
Palo Alto, CA ....Family Law

MITCHELL, SHELLEY M.
Fort Lauderdale, FL ....Family Law

MITCHELL, BRISSO, DELANEY & VRIEZE
Eureka, CA ....General Practice; Insurance Defense

MITCHELL & DECLERCK, P.L.L.C.
Enid, OK ....General Practice

MITCHELL, EDDIE C., P.A.
Winston-Salem, NC ....Criminal Trial Practice

MITCHELL HURST JACOBS & DICK
Indianapolis, IN ....Business Law; Civil Trial Practice; Medical Malpractice; Personal Injury; Product Liability Law; Real Estate Law

MITCHELL, JOINER, & HARDESTY, PSC
Madisonville, KY ....Civil Trial Practice; Personal Injury

MITCHELL LAW OFFICES, A PROFESSIONAL CORPORATION
Phoenix, AZ ....Real Estate Law; Securities Law

MITCHELL, MCNUTT, THREADGILL, SMITH & SAMS, P.A.
Columbus, MS ....General Practice
Tupelo, MS ....General Practice

MITCHELL & MITCHELL, P.C.
Dalton, GA ....Civil Trial Practice; General Practice

MITCHELL, MITCHELL & BRADLEY
Marion, IL ....Commercial Litigation; General Practice; Insurance Defense

MITCHELL, MITCHELL, GRAY & GALLAGHER, A PROFESSIONAL CORPORATION
Williamsport, PA ....Aviation Law; Civil Trial Practice; Insurance Defense; Medical Malpractice; Personal Injury; Product Liability Law; Workers Compensation

MITCHELL, NEUBAUER & HANSON, P.C.
Mount Vernon, IL ....Banking Law; General Practice; Real Estate Law

MITCHELL, RALLINGS, SINGER, MCGIRT & TISSUE, PLLC
Charlotte, NC ....Bankruptcy Law; Civil Trial Practice; Commercial Law

MITCHELL, SAM C., & ASSOCIATES
West Frankfort, IL....Personal Injury; Workers Compensation

MITCHELL, SHELDON, LTD.
Phoenix, AZ....Family Law

MITCHELL, SILBERBERG & KNUPP LLP
Los Angeles, CA....Antitrust Law; Commercial Law; Environmental Law; General Practice; Intellectual Property Law; Labor and Employment Law; Patent, Trademark, Copyright and Unfair Competition; Tax Law; Trust and Estates, Wills and Probate

MITCHELL, VOGE, CORBAN AND MORRIS
Tupelo, MS....General Practice

MITHOFF & JACKS, L.L.P.
Austin, TX....Civil Trial Practice; Personal Injury

MIYAGI, NOHR & MYHRE
Honolulu, HI....Arbitration; Civil Trial Practice; Construction Law; Insurance Defense; Product Liability Law

MIZE, JAMES M.
Sacramento, CA....Family Law

MOBBS, DENNY E.
Cleveland, TN....Civil Trial Practice; General Practice; Insurance Defense

MOCKBEE HALL & DRAKE, A PROFESSIONAL ASSOCIATION
Jackson, MS....Construction Law

MODRALL, SPERLING, ROEHL, HARRIS & SISK, P.A.
Albuquerque, NM....General Practice
Las Cruces, NM....General Practice
Santa Fe, NM....General Practice

MOEN, BRUCE R.
Seattle, WA....Trust and Estates, Wills and Probate

MOEN, CAIN & O'BRIEN
Houston, TX....Appellate Practice; Criminal Trial Practice

MOEN, SHEEHAN, MEYER, LTD.
La Crosse, WI....General Practice

MOERER & BURTON, L.L.P.
Houston, TX....Corporate Law

MOFFETT & DILLON, A PROFESSIONAL CORPORATION
Birmingham, MI....Product Liability Law

MOGEL, SPEIDEL, BOBB & KERSHNER, A PROFESSIONAL CORPORATION
Reading, PA....Banking Law; Bankruptcy Law; Business Law; Commercial Law; Family Law; General Practice; Real Estate Law; Tax Law; Trust and Estates, Wills and Probate

MOGILL, KENNETH M.
Detroit, MI....Appellate Practice; Criminal Trial Practice; Professional Liability

MOHR, HACKETT, PEDERSON, BLAKLEY & RANDOLPH, P.C.
Phoenix, AZ....General Practice

MOIR & HARDMAN
Washington, DC....Communications Law

MOLDAWER & MARSHALL, P.C.
Rockville, MD....Business Law

MOLDOF, HILLIARD E., P.A.
Fort Lauderdale, FL....Criminal Trial Practice

MOLLER, ARTHUR C., P.A.
Miami, FL....Insurance Defense

MOLLICA & MURRAY
Pittsburgh, PA....Business Law; Construction Law; Insurance Defense; Municipal and Zoning Law; Real Estate Law

MOMBACH, BOYLE & HARDIN, P.A.
Fort Lauderdale, FL....Commercial Law

MONACO, MONACO & BIRDER
Gainesville, FL....Insurance Defense

MONAGHAN & GOLD, P.C.
Elkins Park, PA....Appellate Practice; Civil Trial Practice; Commercial Law; Insurance Defense; Labor and Employment Law; Medical Malpractice; Product Liability Law

MONAGHAN, LEAHY, HOCHADEL & LIBBY, LLP
Portland, ME....Banking Law; Civil Rights; Insurance Defense; Municipal and Zoning Law

MONDSCHEIN ASSOCIATES
Allentown, PA....Family Law

MONE, D'AMBROSE & HANYEN, P.C.
Brockton, MA....Civil Trial Practice

MONNET, HAYES, BULLIS, THOMPSON & EDWARDS
Oklahoma City, OK....Civil Trial Practice; General Practice; Natural Resources Law

MONTAVON, MICHAEL C., P.C.
Fairfax, VA....Commercial Litigation

MONTELEONE & MCCRORY, LLP
Los Angeles, CA....Commercial Litigation; Construction Law; General Practice

MONTERO FINIZIO VELASQUEZ WEISSING AND REYES, P.A.
Fort Lauderdale, FL....Aviation Law; International Business Law; Personal Injury

MONTFORT, HEALY, MCGUIRE & SALLEY
Garden City, NY....Appellate Practice; Civil Rights; Civil Trial Practice; Environmental Law; General Practice; Health Care Law; Insurance Defense; Medical Malpractice; Product Liability Law; Professional Liability

MONTGOMERY & ANDREWS, PROFESSIONAL ASSOCIATION
Santa Fe, NM....Administrative Law; Appellate Practice; Civil Rights; Civil Trial Practice; Environmental Law; General Practice; Insurance Defense; Labor and Employment Law; Natural Resources Law

MONTGOMERY LITTLE & MCGREW, P.C.
Denver, CO....Civil Trial Practice; Commercial Law; Commercial Litigation; Construction Law; General Practice; Health Care Law; Insurance Defense; Medical Malpractice; Product Liability Law; Professional Liability; Real Estate Law

MONTGOMERY, MCCRACKEN, WALKER & RHOADS, LLP
Philadelphia, PA....General Practice

MOODIE, MOODIE & WORTMAN
West Point, NE....General Practice

MOODY & HAYS, L.L.P.
Lubbock, TX....General Practice

MOODY, STROPLE & KLOEPPEL, INC.
Portsmouth, VA....Civil Trial Practice; Personal Injury

MOONEY, F. BENTLEY, JR., A LAW CORPORATION
North Hollywood, CA....Business Law; Trust and Estates, Wills and Probate

MOONEY LAW FIRM
Jonesboro, AR....General Practice

MOORE, JOHN R.
Selinsgrove, PA....General Practice; Trust and Estates, Wills and Probate

MOORE, R. ERIC
Christiansted, St. Croix, VI....Civil Trial Practice; Insurance Defense; Product Liability Law

MOORE, BASKIN & PARKER
Boise, ID....General Practice; Insurance Defense; Product Liability Law

MOORE & BERKOWITZ
Southampton, PA....Civil Trial Practice

MOORE & BROWN
Winston-Salem, NC....Antitrust Law
San Francisco, CA....Civil Rights; Labor and Employment Law; Personal Injury; Product Liability Law

MOORE & BRUCE, LLP
Washington, DC....Business Law; Tax Law

MOORE, BRYAN & SCHROFF, A LAW CORPORATION
Torrance, CA....Family Law; Trust and Estates, Wills and Probate

MOORE, GEORGE E., A PROFESSIONAL LAW CORPORATION
Pasadena, CA....Medical Malpractice; Personal Injury

MOORE & HANSEN
Minneapolis, MN....Patent, Trademark, Copyright and Unfair Competition

MOORE INGRAM JOHNSON & STEELE, LLP
Marietta, GA....Civil Trial Practice; Insurance Defense; Real Estate Law

MOORE, O'BRIEN, JACQUES & YELENAK
Cheshire, CT....Aviation Law; Civil Trial Practice; Medical Malpractice

MOORE, R. LAMAR, P.C.
Moultrie, GA....General Practice; Tax Law

MULVANEY, KAHAN & BARRY, A PROFESSIONAL CORPORATION
La Jolla, CA............................Antitrust Law; Banking Law; General Practice; Municipal and Zoning Law; Trust and Estates, Wills and Probate

MULVANEY, KAHAN & BARRY, A PROFESSIONAL CORPORATION
San Diego, CA........................Antitrust Law; Banking Law; General Practice; Municipal and Zoning Law; Trust and Estates, Wills and Probate

MULVANIA, WALTER L.
Rock Port, MO........................Trust and Estates, Wills and Probate

MULVEY & FLANAGAN, P.C.
Philadelphia, PA......................Civil Trial Practice; Personal Injury; Workers Compensation

MUNDAY & NATHAN, THE LAW OFFICES OF
Chicago, IL..............................Civil Trial Practice; Medical Malpractice; Personal Injury

MUNDY & GAMMAGE, P.C.
Cedartown, GA........................Civil Trial Practice; General Practice; Personal Injury

MUNDY, ROGERS & FRITH, LLP
Roanoke, VA...........................Family Law; Medical Malpractice; Personal Injury

MUNGER CHADWICK, P.L.C.
Tucson, AZ..............................Commercial Law; Real Estate Law

MUNGER, TOLLES & OLSON LLP
Los Angeles, CA......................General Practice

MUNLEY, MUNLEY & CARTWRIGHT, P.C.
Scranton, PA...........................Appellate Practice; Civil Trial Practice; Commercial Litigation; Criminal Trial Practice; Medical Malpractice; Personal Injury; Product Liability Law; Workers Compensation

MUNSILL, JOHN W.
Sacramento, CA.......................Family Law

MURAI, WALD, BIONDO & MORENO, P.A.
Miami, FL................................Civil Trial Practice; General Practice; International Business Law

MURCHISON, TAYLOR & GIBSON, L.L.P.
Wilmington, NC.......................Civil Trial Practice; Commercial Law; Real Estate Law; Tax Law

MURNAGHAN & FERGUSON, P.A.
Tampa, FL...............................Commercial Litigation; Personal Injury

MURNANE, CONLIN, WHITE & BRANDT, PROFESSIONAL ASSOCIATION
St. Paul, MN...........................General Practice

MUROV & WARD, L.L.C.
New Orleans, LA.....................Immigration and Naturalization

MURPHY, MICHAEL C.
Lawrenceville, GA...................Civil Trial Practice; Family Law; Labor and Employment Law

MURPHY, BARTOL & O'BRIEN, LLP
Mineola, NY............................Civil Trial Practice

MURPHY & DESMOND, S.C.
Madison, WI...........................General Practice

MURPHY, GILLICK, WICHT & PRACHTHAUSER
Milwaukee, WI........................Civil Trial Practice; Personal Injury

MURPHY, HESSE, TOOMEY AND LEHANE
Quincy, MA.............................Labor and Employment Law

MURPHY, HUPP, FOOTE, MIELKE AND KINNALLY
Aurora, IL...............................Civil Trial Practice; Environmental Law; General Practice; Immigration and Naturalization; Insurance Defense; Personal Injury

MURPHY, KIRKPATRICK & FAIN, P.L.L.P.
Billings, MT............................Business Law; Commercial Litigation; Real Estate Law

MURPHY, LUTEY, SCHMITT & BECK, P.L.L.C.
Kingman, AZ...........................Personal Injury
Prescott, AZ............................Civil Trial Practice; Commercial Litigation; General Practice; Personal Injury; Trust and Estates, Wills and Probate
Yuma, AZ................................Personal Injury

MURPHY AND MURPHY
Hyannis, MA...........................General Practice

MURPHY AND O'CONNOR
Philadelphia, PA.....................Civil Trial Practice

MURPHY, OLIVER, CAIOLA & GOWEN, A PROFESSIONAL LAW CORPORATION
Norristown, PA........................Business Law; Civil Trial Practice; Commercial Litigation; Elder Law; Family Law; Insurance Defense; Legal Malpractice; Medical Malpractice; Personal Injury; Product Liability Law; Toxic Torts; Trust and Estates, Wills and Probate

MURPHY, PEARSON, BRADLEY & FEENEY, A PROFESSIONAL CORPORATION
San Francisco, CA...................Appellate Practice; Banking Law; Civil Rights; Civil Trial Practice; Construction Law; Employment Benefits Law; General Practice; Insurance Defense; Medical Malpractice; Product Liability Law; Real Estate Law; Tax Law; Trademark, Copyright and Unfair Competition

MURPHY, PIAZZA & GENELLO, P.C.
Scranton, PA...........................Civil Trial Practice

MURPHY & POSNER, L.L.P.
Phoenix, AZ............................Commercial Litigation; Creditors Rights; Real Estate Law

MURPHY, POST, THOMPSON, ARNOLD & SKINNER
Batesville, AR.........................Civil Trial Practice

MURPHY, REID, PILOTTE, ORD & AUSTIN
Palm Beach, FL.......................General Practice; Real Estate Law; Tax Law; Trust and Estates, Wills and Probate

MURPHY, ROGERS & SLOSS, A PROFESSIONAL LAW CORPORATION
New Orleans, LA.....................Admiralty/Maritime Law

MURPHY, THOMAS D., P.C.
Rockville, MD..........................General Practice

MURPHY, WILLIAM T., LAW OFFICES, INC.
Providence, RI.........................Banking Law; Bankruptcy Law; Civil Trial Practice; Commercial Law; Criminal Trial Practice; Insurance Defense; Labor and Employment Law

MURRAY, DUNHAM & MURRAY
Seattle, WA............................Insurance Defense

MURRAY, JOHN A., & ASSOCIATES, LTD.
St. Paul, MN...........................Commercial Litigation; Real Estate Law; Tax Law

MURRAY LAW FIRM
New Orleans, LA.....................Personal Injury

MURRAY, PLUMB & MURRAY
Portland, ME...........................General Practice

MUSSELMAN, ROBERT M. & ASSOCIATES
Charlottesville, VA..................Bankruptcy Law; Pension and Profit Sharing; Tax Law; Trust and Estates, Wills and Probate

MUSTO & SAUNDERS, P.C.
Plymouth, PA..........................Health Care Law; Insurance Defense

MUTH, CASEBOLT, GERMAINE & DRIGGS, P.L.C.
Phoenix, AZ............................Real Estate Law

MYER, SWANSON, ADAMS & WOLF, P.C.
Denver, CO.............................Business Law; Civil Trial Practice; Commercial Law; Commercial Litigation; General Practice; Trust and Estates, Wills and Probate

MYERS, DAUGHERITY, BERRY, O'CONOR & KUZMA, LTD.
Ottawa, IL...............................Banking Law; General Practice; Insurance Defense
Streator, IL..............................General Practice

MYERS & FLEMING, LLP
Newport Beach, CA.................Construction Law; International Business Law; Natural Resources Law

MYERS & JENKINS, A PROFESSIONAL CORPORATION
Phoenix, AZ............................Bankruptcy Law; Commercial Litigation; Health Care Law; Real Estate Law

MYERS, OLIVER & PRICE, P.C.
Albuquerque, NM....................Land Use Law; Real Estate Law

MYERS, ROBERT J., & ASSOCIATES
San Antonio, TX......................Civil Trial Practice; Tax Law

MYLES AND MARTIN, LAW OFFICES OF
Tawas City, MI........................Municipal and Zoning Law; Trust and Estates, Wills and Probate

MYLOTTE, DAVID & FITZPATRICK
Philadelphia, PA.....................Civil Trial Practice; Toxic Torts

NACHSHIN & WESTON, LLP
Los Angeles, CA.....................Family Law

NAGELEY, MEREDITH & MILLER, INC.
Sacramento, CA......................Business Law; Civil Trial Practice; Construction Law; Insurance Defense; Labor and Employment Law

NAGIN GALLOP FIGUEREDO, P.A.
Miami, FL .... Antitrust Law; Environmental Law; Land Use Law; Patent, Trademark, Copyright and Unfair Competition

NAGLE, THOMAS C., A PROF. CORP., LAW OFFICES OF
Walnut Creek, CA .... Eminent Domain

NAGY & PINTÉR HOGAN & HARTSON LAW OFFICE
Budapest, Hungary .... General Practice

NAHIN, BRUCE A., A PROFESSIONAL LAW CORPORATION
Valencia, CA .... Business Law; Real Estate Law

NAKAMURA, QUINN & WALLS, LLP
Birmingham, AL .... Labor and Employment Law

NALL, MILLER, OWENS, HOCUTT & HOWARD, LLP
Atlanta, GA .... Civil Trial Practice; Commercial Litigation; Insurance Defense; Medical Malpractice; Product Liability Law

NAMAN, HOWELL, SMITH & LEE, A PROFESSIONAL CORPORATION
Austin, TX .... General Practice
Fort Worth, TX .... General Practice
Temple, TX .... General Practice
Waco, TX .... General Practice

NANCE, CACCIATORE AND HAMILTON
Melbourne, FL .... Civil Trial Practice; General Practice; Medical Malpractice; Personal Injury

NARDONI, SILVIO
Glendale, CA .... Civil Trial Practice

NARRON, O'HALE & WHITTINGTON, P.A.
Smithfield, NC .... General Practice

NASATIR, HIRSCH & PODBERESKY
Santa Monica, CA .... Criminal Trial Practice

NASH, COHENOUR, KELLEY & HUNT, P.C.
Oklahoma City, OK .... Bankruptcy Law; Commercial Law; Trust and Estates, Wills and Probate

NASH & COMPANY, A PROFESSIONAL CORPORATION
Pittsburgh, PA .... General Practice; Health Care Law

NASH & EDGERTON
Hermosa Beach, CA .... Mergers and Acquisitions

NASH, WALTER B., III, P.C.
Tucson, AZ .... Criminal Trial Practice

NASON, YEAGER, GERSON, WHITE & LIOCE, P.A.
West Palm Beach, FL .... Business Law; Civil Trial Practice; Real Estate Law

NASTASI, NICHOLAS J., A PROFESSIONAL CORPORATION
Philadelphia, PA .... Criminal Trial Practice

NATH & ASSOCIATES
Washington, DC .... Patent, Trademark, Copyright and Unfair Competition

NATHAN & NATHAN, P.C.
Southfield, MI .... Bankruptcy Law; Real Estate Law

NATHANSON & GOLDBERG, A PROFESSIONAL CORPORATION
Boston, MA .... Civil Trial Practice; Construction Law; Personal Injury; Real Estate Law

NATISS, NATISS & GORDON, P.C.
Roslyn Heights, NY .... Commercial Litigation; Corporate Law; Family Law; General Practice; Personal Injury; Real Estate Law; Trust and Estates, Wills and Probate

NAUFUL, ERNEST J., JR., P.C.
Columbia, SC .... Civil Trial Practice; General Practice; Medical Malpractice; Product Liability Law

NAVRATIL, HARDY & BOURGEOIS L.L.P.
Baton Rouge, LA .... Business Law; Insurance Defense

NAWROCKI, ROONEY & SIVERTSON, P.A.
Minneapolis, MN .... Intellectual Property Law

NEAL & ASSOCIATES
Oakland, CA .... Business Law; Trust and Estates, Wills and Probate

NEAL & DAVIS
Shelbyville, KY .... Civil Trial Practice; Personal Injury; Real Estate Law

NEARY, BRIAN J.
Hackensack, NJ .... Appellate Practice; Criminal Trial Practice

NEBEL, TOM, A PROF. CORP., LAW OFFICES OF
Nashville, TN .... Personal Injury

NEBLETT, BEARD & ARSENAULT
Alexandria, LA .... Civil Trial Practice

NEEDELL, SIEKERKA & CASTELLANI, A PROFESSIONAL CORPORATION
Trenton, NJ .... Appellate Practice; Civil Rights; Civil Trial Practice; Commercial Law; Construction Law; Employment Benefits Law; Family Law; Insurance Defense; Labor and Employment Law; Product Liability Law

NEEDHAM JOHNSON, A PROFESSIONAL CORPORATION
Dallas, TX .... Medical Malpractice

NEEF, ALLAN
Grosse Pointe Farms, MI .... Corporate Law; Tax Law; Trust and Estates, Wills and Probate

NEEL, HOOPER & KALMANS, P.C.
Houston, TX .... Labor and Employment Law

NEFF LAW FIRM, THE, LTD.
Bucyrus, OH .... Civil Trial Practice; General Practice

NEIDER & BOUCHER, S.C.
Madison, WI .... Business Law; Intellectual Property Law; Patent, Trademark, Copyright and Unfair Competition; Real Estate Law; Securities Law; Tax Law; Trademark, Copyright and Unfair Competition; Trust and Estates, Wills and Probate

NEIGHER, ALAN
Westport, CT .... Sports and Entertainment Law

NEILL GRIFFIN JEFFRIES FOWLER TIERNEY & NEILL, CHARTERED
Fort Pierce, FL .... Appellate Practice; Civil Trial Practice; Personal Injury; Real Estate Law; Trust and Estates, Wills and Probate

NEIMAN GINSBURG & MAIRANZ P.C.
New York, NY .... Administrative Law; Bankruptcy Law; Commercial Litigation; Health Care Law

NEJAME, MARK E., P.A., LAW OFFICES OF
Orlando, FL .... Criminal Trial Practice

NELSON & ASSOCIATES, P.A.
Aventura, FL .... Trust and Estates, Wills and Probate

NELSON, DRIES, CONNELL & KRAMER, S.C.
Brookfield, WI .... Civil Trial Practice; Insurance Defense; Workers Compensation

NELSON • HESSE
Sarasota, FL .... Civil Trial Practice; Commercial Law; General Practice; Product Liability Law

NELSON AND KREUGER, PROFESSIONAL CORPORATION
Grand Rapids, MI .... Commercial Litigation; Insurance Defense

NELSON, MCMAHAN & NOBLETT
Chattanooga, TN .... Environmental Law; Insurance Defense; Municipal and Zoning Law; Personal Injury

NELSON MULLINS RILEY & SCARBOROUGH, L.L.P.
Columbia, SC .... General Practice

NELSON & NELSON LLP
Bethesda, MD .... Trust and Estates, Wills and Probate

NELSON OYEN TORVIK
Montevideo, MN .... General Practice

NEMETH BURWELL, P.C.
Detroit, MI .... Labor and Employment Law

NEMETH, CABORN & BUTAUSKI
Columbus, OH .... Civil Trial Practice; Insurance Defense; Legal Malpractice; Personal Injury

NEMIER, TOLARI, LANDRY, MAZZEO & JOHNSON, P.C.
Farmington Hills, MI .... Appellate Practice; Insurance Defense; Personal Injury; Product Liability Law

NEMLAHA, BEATRICE H., P.C.
Los Angeles, CA .... Family Law

NEUBERGER, QUINN, GIELEN, RUBIN & GIBBER, P.A.
Baltimore, MD .... General Practice

NEUFELD & O'LEARY
New York, NY .... Environmental Law; Trust and Estates, Wills and Probate

NEUMEYER & BOYD, LLP
Los Angeles, CA .... Appellate Practice; Insurance Defense

NEUMILLER & BEARDSLEE, A PROFESSIONAL CORPORATION
Stockton, CA .... General Practice

NEVAS, NEVAS & CAPASSE
Westport, CT .... Business Law; Real Estate Law; Trust and Estates, Wills and Probate

NEVILLE, WILLIAM V. JR.
Eufaula, AL....General Practice; Real Estate Law

NEVILLE & KELLEY
Cambridge, MA....Insurance Defense

NEVILLE, RICHARDS, DEFRANCO & WULLER
Belleville, IL....Civil Trial Practice; Commercial Litigation; General Practice; Insurance Defense; Medical Malpractice; Professional Liability; Real Estate Law

NEVILLE SHAVER HUBBARD & MCLEAN
Stamford, CT....General Practice

NEVIN, EDWARD J.
San Francisco, CA....Civil Trial Practice

NEVIN GRUEN, LLP
Oakland, CA....Civil Trial Practice

NEVORAL, BERNARD R., AND ASSOCIATES LTD.
Chicago, IL....Civil Trial Practice; Medical Malpractice; Personal Injury; Product Liability Law; Workers Compensation

NEWBY, LEWIS, KAMINSKI & JONES
La Porte, IN....General Practice

NEWCOMB, BRIAN W.
Menlo Park, CA....Civil Trial Practice

NEWELL & MARTENS
Denver, CO....Criminal Trial Practice

NEWLAN, DOUGLAS H.
Redding, CA....Insurance Defense

NEWMAN, CRAIG
Casper, WY....Natural Resources Law

NEWMAN, DAVID, CHARTERED
La Plata, MD....Patent, Trademark, Copyright and Unfair Competition

NEWMAN FITCH ALTHEIM MYERS, P.C.
New York, NY....Civil Trial Practice; Insurance Defense

NEWMAN, FREYMAN, KLEIN & GAMACHE, P.C.
St. Louis, MO....Commercial Litigation; Family Law; Trust and Estates, Wills and Probate

NEWMAN, MATHIS, BRADY, WAKEFIELD & SPEDALE, A PROFESSIONAL LAW CORPORATION
Metairie, LA....Banking Law; Commercial Litigation

NEWMAN SCHWARTZ & GREENBERG
New York, NY....Appellate Practice; Criminal Trial Practice

NEWSOM, GRAHAM, HEDRICK & KENNON, P.A.
Durham, NC....General Practice

NEWTON AND HOFF, L.L.P.
Gulfport, MS....Business Law; Civil Trial Practice; Corporate Law; Real Estate Law; Trust and Estates, Wills and Probate

NEXSEN PRUET JACOBS & POLLARD, LLP
Columbia, SC....Commercial Litigation; Construction Law; Creditors Rights; Environmental Law; General Practice; Health Care Law; Intellectual Property Law; Labor and Employment Law; Land Use Law; Municipal Bond/Public Authority Financing; Tax Law

NG, PETER P. J.
Honolulu, HI....Real Estate Law; Tax Law; Trust and Estates, Wills and Probate

NICHOLLS & ASSOCIATES, P.C.
Denver, CO....Bankruptcy Law; Trust and Estates, Wills and Probate

NICHOLS, RICHARD L.
Jacksonville, FL....Family Law; Medical Malpractice

NICHOLS, DAVID E., P.C.
Charlotte Amalie, St. Thomas, VI....Business Law

NICHOLS, JACKSON, DILLARD, HAGER & SMITH, L.L.P.
Dallas, TX....Insurance Defense; Municipal and Zoning Law

NICHOLS, SACKS, SLANK & SWEET, A PROFESSIONAL CORPORATION
Ann Arbor, MI....Family Law

NICHOLSON, GARNER & DUGGAN
Maryville, TN....Civil Trial Practice; Commercial Litigation; Elder Law; General Practice; Personal Injury; Product Liability Law; Real Estate Law

NICKLAUS & WICKS, P.A.
Miami, FL....Insurance Defense

NICOARA & STEAGALL
Peoria, IL....Insurance Defense; Medical Malpractice; Personal Injury; Product Liability Law

NICOLETTE & PERKINS, P.A.
Hackensack, NJ....Administrative Law; Bankruptcy Law; Civil Trial Practice; Commercial Law; Corporate Law; General Practice; Trust and Estates, Wills and Probate

NICOLINI & PARADISE
Mineola, NY....Civil Trial Practice; Insurance Defense

NIKAIDO, MARMELSTEIN, MURRAY & ORAM, LLP
Washington, DC....Patent, Trademark, Copyright and Unfair Competition

NIKOLAI, MERSEREAU & DIETZ, P.A.
Minneapolis, MN....International Business Law; Patent, Trademark, Copyright and Unfair Competition

NILES, BARTON & WILMER
Baltimore, MD....Admiralty/Maritime Law; Civil Trial Practice; General Practice

NILLES, HANSEN & DAVIES, LTD.
Fargo, ND....Banking Law; Civil Trial Practice; Commercial Law; General Practice; Insurance Defense; Labor and Employment Law; Personal Injury; Real Estate Law; Tax Law; Trust and Estates, Wills and Probate

NIMS, HOWES, COLLISON, HANSEN & LACKERT
New York, NY....Intellectual Property Law; Trademark, Copyright and Unfair Competition

NIRO, SCAVONE, HALLER & NIRO
Chicago, IL....Intellectual Property Law; Patent, Trademark, Copyright and Unfair Competition

NISCHWITZ, PEMBRIDGE & CHRISZT CO., L.P.A.
Cleveland, OH....Business Law; Commercial Litigation; Family Law

NISEN & ELLIOTT
Chicago, IL....Business Law; Commercial Law; Commercial Litigation; Corporate Law; Employment Benefits Law; Mergers and Acquisitions; Tax Law; Trust and Estates, Wills and Probate

NIX, HOLTSFORD & VERCELLI, P.C.
Montgomery, AL....Business Law; Civil Trial Practice; Environmental Law; Government Contracts; Insurance Defense; Product Liability Law; Professional Liability; Workers Compensation

NIX & WINEGEART, P.C.
Sherman, TX....Bankruptcy Law; Creditors Rights

NIXON PEABODY LLP
New York, NY....General Practice
Rochester, NY....General Practice

NIXON & VANDERHYE P.C.
Arlington, VA....Patent, Trademark, Copyright and Unfair Competition

NOCE & BUCKLEY, L.L.C.
St. Louis, MO....Insurance Defense

NOEDING & MOODY, P.C.
Albuquerque, NM....Labor and Employment Law

NOKES, DAVIS & QUINN, A PROFESSIONAL CORPORATION
Laguna Beach, CA....Civil Trial Practice; Commercial Litigation; Construction Law; Family Law

NOLAN, ARMSTRONG & BARTON, LLP
Palo Alto, CA....Criminal Trial Practice

NOLAN LAW GROUP
Chicago, IL....Appellate Practice; Aviation Law; Civil Trial Practice; Medical Malpractice; Personal Injury; Product Liability Law

NOLAN, PLUMHOFF & WILLIAMS, CHARTERED
Towson, MD....Civil Trial Practice; Criminal Trial Practice; General Practice; Personal Injury; Trust and Estates, Wills and Probate

NOLAND, HAMERLY, ETIENNE & HOSS, A PROFESSIONAL CORPORATION
Salinas, CA....General Practice

NOLD, JOHN A., P.A.
Marco Island, FL....Real Estate Law; Trust and Estates, Wills and Probate

NOONAN & PROKUP
Allentown, PA....Trust and Estates, Wills and Probate

NOONAN, THOMAS J., P.C., THE LAW OFFICES OF
St. Louis, MO.......................... Insurance Defense

NORDMAN, CORMANY, HAIR & COMPTON
Oxnard, CA.......................... General Practice

NORMAN, DOWLER, SAWYER, ISRAEL, WALKER & BARTON
Ventura, CA.......................... General Practice

NORMAN, HANSON & DETROY, LLC
Portland, ME.......................... General Practice

NORMANDIN, CHENEY & O'NEIL
Laconia, NH.......................... Banking Law; Civil Trial Practice; Commercial Law; Corporate Law; Environmental Law; General Practice; Personal Injury; Product Liability Law; Real Estate Law; Trust and Estates, Wills and Probate

NORMINTON & WIITA
Beverly Hills, CA.......................... Civil Trial Practice

NORRIS, RAYMOND M. LAW OFFICES OF
Phoenix, AZ.......................... Personal Injury

NORRIS & NORRIS
Richmond, CA.......................... Civil Trial Practice

NORRIS & ROSSI LLP
San Mateo, CA.......................... Family Law

NORTH, STEVEN E., P.C.
New York, NY.......................... Medical Malpractice; Personal Injury

NORTHCUTT, CLARK, GARDNER, HRON & TATE
Ponca City, OK.......................... General Practice

NORTHEN BLUE, L.L.P.
Chapel Hill, NC.......................... Bankruptcy Law; Business Law

NORTON & CHRISTENSEN
Goshen, NY.......................... Construction Law; Environmental Law; General Practice

NORTON • LIDSTONE, LLC
Englewood, CO.......................... Civil Trial Practice; Corporate Law; Securities Law

NORTON & LUHN, P.C.
Knoxville, TN.......................... Civil Trial Practice

NORTON, MANCINI, ARGENTATI, WEILER & DEANO
Wheaton, IL.......................... Civil Trial Practice; Insurance Defense

NOTTAGE AND WARD
Chicago, IL.......................... Family Law

NOUMAIR, GEORGE J., P.C.
New York, NY.......................... Tax Law

NOVACK AND MACEY
Chicago, IL.......................... Civil Trial Practice

NOVINS, YORK & PENTONY, A PROFESSIONAL CORPORATION
Toms River, NJ.......................... Civil Trial Practice; Criminal Trial Practice; General Practice; Insurance Defense; Medical Malpractice; Personal Injury; Real Estate Law

NOVIT, SCARMINACH & WILLIAMS, P.A.
Hilton Head Island, SC.......................... Real Estate Law

NOVOSELSKY, DAVID A., & ASSOCIATES
Chicago, IL.......................... Appellate Practice

NOWELL, GEORGE W. LAW OFFICES OF
San Francisco, CA.......................... Admiralty/Maritime Law

NOWELL AMOROSO KLEIN BIERMAN, P.A.
Hackensack, NJ.......................... Civil Trial Practice; Environmental Law; Product Liability Law

NURENBERG, PLEVIN, HELLER & MCCARTHY CO., L.P.A.
Cleveland, OH.......................... Aviation Law; Civil Trial Practice; Commercial Litigation; Medical Malpractice; Personal Injury; Product Liability Law; Workers Compensation

NUSBAUM & PARRINO, P.C.
Westport, CT.......................... Family Law

NUTTALL BERMAN ATTORNEYS
Fresno, CA.......................... Criminal Trial Practice

NUTTER, MCCLENNEN & FISH, LLP
Boston, MA.......................... General Practice

NUZZO & ROBERTS, L.L.C.
Cheshire, CT.......................... Civil Trial Practice

NYEMASTER, GOODE, VOIGTS, WEST, HANSELL & O'BRIEN, A PROFESSIONAL CORPORATION
Des Moines, IA.......................... Civil Trial Practice; General Practice; Securities Law; Tax Law

OATES, KNEZEVICH & GARDENSWARTZ, P.C.
Aspen, CO.......................... Business Law; Civil Trial Practice; Family Law; General Practice; Land Use Law; Real Estate Law; Trust and Estates, Wills and Probate

O'BANION & RITCHEY LLP
Sacramento, CA.......................... Patent, Trademark, Copyright and Unfair Competition

OBENSHAIN, WILEY S., III, P.C.
Augusta, GA.......................... Civil Trial Practice; Insurance Defense; Medical Malpractice; Product Liability Law

OBERMAN & OBERMAN
Charleston, SC.......................... Civil Trial Practice; Family Law; General Practice; Real Estate Law

OBERMAYER, REBMANN, MAXWELL & HIPPEL LLP
Philadelphia, PA.......................... General Practice

OBLON, SPIVAK, MCCLELLAND, MAIER & NEUSTADT, P.C.
Arlington, VA.......................... Patent, Trademark, Copyright and Unfair Competition

O'BRIEN, WILLIAM M.
Cambridge, MA.......................... Banking Law; Commercial Law; General Practice; Real Estate Law

O'BRIEN, ANDERSON, BURGY, GARBOWICZ & BROWN, LLP
Eagle River, WI.......................... General Practice

O'BRIEN, EHRICK, WOLF, DEANER & MAUS, L.L.P.
Rochester, MN.......................... Civil Trial Practice; General Practice; Real Estate Law

O'BRIEN, TANSKI & YOUNG
Hartford, CT.......................... Health Care Law; Insurance Defense; Medical Malpractice

O'BRIEN WATTERS & DAVIS, LLP
Santa Rosa, CA.......................... General Practice

O'BRYAN, BROWN & TONER
Louisville, KY.......................... Insurance Defense; Medical Malpractice; Product Liability Law; Workers Compensation

OBUCHOWSKI LAW OFFICE
Bethel, VT.......................... Bankruptcy Law

OCHOA & SILLAS
Los Angeles, CA.......................... Administrative Law; Civil Trial Practice; Construction Law; Insurance Defense; Labor and Employment Law; Municipal Bond/Public Authority Financing

O'CONNELL AND ARONOWITZ, P.C.
Albany, NY.......................... Appellate Practice; Civil Trial Practice; Criminal Trial Practice; Health Care Law; Labor and Employment Law

O'CONNELL, BENJAMIN & COGHLAN, L.L.P.
San Antonio, TX.......................... Civil Trial Practice; Commercial Litigation; Construction Law; Insurance Defense; Labor and Employment Law; Medical Malpractice; Product Liability Law; Professional Liability; Toxic Torts

O'CONNELL, DANIEL H., P.C.
Tucson, AZ.......................... Corporate Law; Pension and Profit Sharing; Real Estate Law; Tax Law; Trust and Estates, Wills and Probate

O'CONNOR, DEGRAZIA & TAMM, P.C.
Bloomfield Hills, MI.......................... Civil Rights; Medical Malpractice; Municipal and Zoning Law

O'CONNOR & DEMAS, P.C.
Chatham, NJ.......................... Civil Trial Practice; Personal Injury

O'CONNOR, GACIOCH, POPE & TAIT, L.L.P.
Binghamton, NY.......................... Construction Law; Environmental Law; Insurance Defense; Labor and Employment Law; Medical Malpractice; Personal Injury

O'CONNOR & HANNAN, L.L.P.
Washington, DC.......................... General Practice; Tax Law

O'CONNOR, MCGUINNESS, CONTE, DOYLE & OLESON
White Plains, NY.......................... Product Liability Law; Professional Liability; Trust and Estates, Wills and Probate

O'CONNOR & MEYERS, P.A.
Miami, FL.......................... Insurance Defense

O'CONNOR, O'CONNOR, MAYBERGER & FIRST, P.C.
Albany, NY.......................... Commercial Litigation; Insurance Defense; Medical Malpractice; Product Liability Law; Toxic Torts

O'CONNOR AND RYAN, P.C.
Fitchburg, MA.......................... Civil Trial Practice; Criminal Trial Practice; Family Law; Labor and Employment Law; Personal Injury; Trust and Estates, Wills and Probate

POLLACK, DAVID S.
Port Washington, NY ....Medical Malpractice

POLLI, ROBERT P., P.A.
Tampa, FL ....Appellate Practice; Criminal Trial Practice

POLLOCK, MEYERS, EICKSTEADT & WEECH, LTD.
Marengo, IL ....General Practice

POLLOCK, VANDE SANDE & AMERNICK, R.L.L.P.
Washington, DC............Patent, Trademark, Copyright and Unfair Competition

POLSTER, LIEDER, WOODRUFF & LUCCHESI, L.C.
St. Louis, MO............Patent, Trademark, Copyright and Unfair Competition

POLSTON, DEAN & HEALY, P.A.
Tallahassee, FL ....Commercial Litigation; Computer Law; Constitutional Law; Insurance Defense; Labor and Employment Law

POMERANZ, DRAYTON & STABNICK
Glastonbury, CT ....Workers Compensation

POPE & BERGER
San Diego, CA ....Construction Law; Insurance Defense; Labor and Employment Law

POPE, MCGLAMRY, KILPATRICK & MORRISON, LLP
Atlanta, GA ....Civil Trial Practice; General Practice; Medical Malpractice; Personal Injury; Product Liability Law
Columbus, GA ....Civil Trial Practice; General Practice; Medical Malpractice; Personal Injury; Product Liability Law

POPE, MCMILLAN, KUTTEH, SIMON & BAKER, P.A.
Statesville, NC............General Practice

POPE & RODGERS
Columbia, SC............Business Law; Civil Trial Practice

POPKOFF & STERN
Los Angeles, CA ....Trust and Estates, Wills and Probate

POPPLETON, GARRETT & POLOTT, P.C.
Bethesda, MD ....Real Estate Law; Trust and Estates, Wills and Probate

PORES, JOEL MICHAEL THE LAW OFFICE OF
Laguna Hills, CA............Legal Malpractice

PORTERFIELD, HARPER & MILLS, P.A.
Birmingham, AL ....Civil Trial Practice; Insurance Defense; Medical Malpractice; Product Liability Law

PORTER, J. CHESTER, & ASSOCIATES
Shephersdville, KY............Banking Law

PORTER & PORTER
Cincinnati, OH ....Tax Law; Trust and Estates, Wills and Probate

PORTER, PORTER & HASSINGER, P.C.
Birmingham, AL ....Product Liability Law; Workers Compensation

PORTER, SCOTT, WEIBERG & DELEHANT, A PROFESSIONAL CORPORATION
Sacramento, CA ....Civil Trial Practice; Construction Law; Insurance Defense; Labor and Employment Law; Medical Malpractice; Product Liability Law; Professional Liability

PORTER WRIGHT MORRIS & ARTHUR LLP
Washington, DC............General Practice
Naples, FL............General Practice
Cincinnati, OH ....General Practice
Cleveland, OH............General Practice
Columbus, OH ....Antitrust Law; Banking Law; Bankruptcy Law; Civil Trial Practice; Environmental Law; General Practice; Labor and Employment Law; Municipal Bond/Public Authority Financing; Patent, Trademark, Copyright and Unfair Competition; Tax Law
Dayton, OH............General Practice

PORTNOY, PIDGEON & ROTH, P.C.
Bloomfield Hills, MI............Civil Trial Practice; Health Care Law; Insurance Defense; Medical Malpractice; Personal Injury

PORZIO, BROMBERG & NEWMAN, A PROFESSIONAL CORPORATION
Morristown, NJ............Environmental Law; General Practice

POSNER, POSNER & ASSOCIATES, PC
White Plains, NY............Bankruptcy Law; Commercial Law; Environmental Law; Real Estate Law; Trust and Estates, Wills and Probate

POST KIRBY NOONAN & SWEAT LLP
San Diego, CA ....Antitrust Law; Business Law; Civil Trial Practice

POST, POLAK, GOODSELL & MACNEILL, P.A.
Roseland, NJ............Business Law; Civil Trial Practice; Commercial Law; Commercial Litigation; Family Law; General Practice; Labor and Employment Law; Medical Malpractice; Real Estate Law

POST & POST
High Point, NC............General Practice

POST & SCHELL, P.C.
Philadelphia, PA ....Civil Trial Practice

POSTLEWAITE & JORDAN
Columbus, OH ....Business Law; Commercial Litigation; Construction Law

POSTNER & RUBIN
New York, NY............Civil Trial Practice; Construction Law; Environmental Law; Government Contracts; Insurance Defense; Professional Liability

POTHIER, ROSE & ASSOCIATES
Santa Ana, CA ....Real Estate Law

POTTER ANDERSON & CORROON LLP
Wilmington, DE............Banking Law; Bankruptcy Law; Civil Trial Practice; Employment Benefits Law; Environmental Law; General Practice; Municipal Bond/Public Authority Financing; Patent, Trademark, Copyright and Unfair Competition; Personal Injury; Tax Law; Trust and Estates, Wills and Probate

POULIOT, MERCURE
Montreal, QU, Canada ....Administrative Law; Banking Law; Bankruptcy Law; Business Law; Civil Trial Practice; Commercial Litigation; Environmental Law; General Practice; Intellectual Property Law; Labor and Employment Law; Mergers and Acquisitions; Municipal Bond/Public Authority Financing; Real Estate Law; Trademark, Copyright and Unfair Competition

POULSON, JON C.
Accomac, VA ....Criminal Trial Practice; Personal Injury; Real Estate Law

POULSON, ODELL & PETERSON, LLC
Denver, CO ....Arbitration; Natural Resources Law; Oil and Gas Law

POWELL, DAVID A.
Gainesville, GA............Civil Trial Practice; Criminal Trial Practice; Family Law

POWELL, RICHARD L.
Marietta, GA............Medical Malpractice; Personal Injury

POWELL, GOLDSTEIN, FRAZER & MURPHY LLP
Washington, DC............General Practice
Atlanta, GA ....General Practice; Immigration and Naturalization; Municipal Bond/Public Authority Financing

POWELL, PEEK & WEAVER
Andalusia, AL............Civil Trial Practice; General Practice; Insurance Defense; Personal Injury; Workers Compensation

POWELL, STANLEY BRUCE, P.A.
Niceville, FL............Commercial Litigation; Medical Malpractice; Personal Injury; Product Liability Law

POWER ROGERS & SMITH, P.C.
Chicago, IL............Aviation Law; Civil Trial Practice; Medical Malpractice; Personal Injury; Product Liability Law; Professional Liability

POWERS, CHAPMAN, DEAGOSTINO, MEYERS & MILIA, PROFESSIONAL CORPORATION
Troy, MI ....Business Law; Trust and Estates, Wills and Probate

POWERS, PYLES, SUTTER & VERVILLE, P.C.
Washington, DC............Administrative Law; Health Care Law

POWERS & SANTOLA
Albany, NY............Civil Trial Practice; Medical Malpractice; Personal Injury; Product Liability Law

POWERS & WILLARD, L.L.P.
Baton Rouge, LA............Banking Law; Business Law; Civil Trial Practice; Commercial Litigation; Corporate Law; General Practice; Legal Malpractice; Medical Malpractice; Product Liability Law; Toxic Torts

POZNER, LARRY, P.C.
Denver, CO ....Criminal Trial Practice

PRATHER & ASSOCIATES, P.C.
Detroit, MI............Family Law

PRATHER, JOHN G., THE FIRM OF
Somerset, KY............General Practice; Medical Malpractice

PRAY, WALKER, JACKMAN, WILLIAMSON & MARLAR, A PROFESSIONAL CORPORATION
Tulsa, OK....Civil Trial Practice; General Practice

PREEO, SILVERMAN & GREEN, P.C.
Denver, CO....Commercial Litigation; Construction Law; Corporate Law; Legal Malpractice; Real Estate Law; Trust and Estates, Wills and Probate

PREG O'DONNELL & GILLETT PLLC
Seattle, WA....Insurance Defense

PREIS, BERGERON & ATCHISON
Baton Rouge, LA....Business Law; Commercial Litigation; Mergers and Acquisitions

PREIS KRAFT & ROY, A PROFESSIONAL LAW CORPORATION
Lafayette, LA....Admiralty/Maritime Law; General Practice; Insurance Defense

PREMINGER, DANIEL M., P.C.
Philadelphia, PA....Appellate Practice; Criminal Trial Practice; Personal Injury

PRENDERGAST, RICHARD J., LTD.
Chicago, IL....Civil Trial Practice; Commercial Litigation

PRESBERG, ANDREW D., P.C., LAW OFFICES OF
Islandia, NY....Business Law; Commercial Litigation; Real Estate Law

PRESSLY & PRESSLY, P.A.
West Palm Beach, FL....Real Estate Law; Trust and Estates, Wills and Probate

PRESTHOLT, KLEEGER, FIDONE & VILLASENOR
Los Angeles, CA....Civil Trial Practice; Insurance Defense; Personal Injury

PRESTON & PRESTON, P.C.
Douglas, GA....General Practice

PRETI, FLAHERTY, BELIVEAU, PACHIOS & HALEY, LLC
Augusta, ME....General Practice
Bath, ME....General Practice
Portland, ME....Administrative Law; Bankruptcy Law; Business Law; Civil Trial Practice; Commercial Law; Communications Law; Environmental Law; General Practice; Health Care Law; Insurance Defense; Intellectual Property Law; International Business Law; Labor and Employment Law; Medical Malpractice; Municipal Bond/Public Authority Financing; Public Utilities Law; Real Estate Law; Tax Law; Trust and Estates, Wills and Probate

PRETTY, SCHROEDER & POPLAWSKI, A PROFESSIONAL CORPORATION
Los Angeles, CA....Patent, Trademark, Copyright and Unfair Competition

PREUSS WALKER & SHANAGHER LLP
San Francisco, CA....Civil Trial Practice; Commercial Litigation; Product Liability Law

PREVATT & TAYLOR
Tampa, FL....Tax Law; Trust and Estates, Wills and Probate

PREVIANT, GOLDBERG, UELMEN, GRATZ, MILLER & BRUEGGEMAN, S.C.
Milwaukee, WI....Labor and Employment Law

PREZANT & MOLLATH
Reno, NV....Land Use Law

PRICE, SMITH, HARGETT, PETHO & ANDERSON
Charlotte, NC....Personal Injury

PRICKETT, JONES & ELLIOTT, P.A.
Dover, DE....General Practice
Wilmington, DE....General Practice
Kennett Square, PA....General Practice

PRINCE, GLICK & MCFARLANE, P.A., LAW OFFICES
Fort Lauderdale, FL....Personal Injury

PRINCE & HELLINGER, P.C.
Nashville, TN....Civil Trial Practice; Insurance Defense

PRINCE, LOBEL & TYE LLP
Boston, MA....Civil Trial Practice; Criminal Trial Practice; Family Law; General Practice; Labor and Employment Law; Tax Law; Trust and Estates, Wills and Probate

PRINCE, POOLE & CROSS, P.C.
Tuscaloosa, AL....Personal Injury

PRINCE, YEATES & GELDZAHLER
Park City, UT....General Practice
Salt Lake City, UT....General Practice; Labor and Employment Law; Real Estate Law; Tax Law

PRINCE, YOUNGBLOOD & MASSAGEE
Hendersonville, NC....General Practice

PRINDLE, MALAND, SELLNER, STENNES AND KNUTSEN, CHARTERED
Montevideo, MN....General Practice

PRINGLE & PRINGLE, A PROFESSIONAL CORPORATION
Oklahoma City, OK....Banking Law; Bankruptcy Law; Commercial Litigation; General Practice; Mergers and Acquisitions

PRITCHARD, ROBERT A.
Pascagoula, MS....Personal Injury; Product Liability Law

PRITCHARD, MCCALL & JONES, L.L.C.
Birmingham, AL....Bankruptcy Law

PROFFITT, THOMAS D.
Mesa, AZ....Trust and Estates, Wills and Probate

PROLY & LAPORTE, P.A.
Port Richey, FL....Personal Injury

PROSKAUER ROSE
Paris, France....General Practice
Los Angeles, CA....General Practice
Washington, DC....General Practice
Boca Raton, FL....General Practice
New York, NY....General Practice; Labor and Employment Law

PROSPERE & RUSSELL
Dallas, TX....Criminal Trial Practice

PROTAS, MARTIN S., P.C.
Bethesda, MD....Civil Trial Practice

PROVIZER & PHILLIPS, P.C.
Bloomfield Hills, MI....Banking Law; Business Law; Civil Rights; Civil Trial Practice; Commercial Law; Commercial Litigation; Computer Law; Construction Law; Elder Law; Employment Benefits Law; Environmental Law; Health Care Law; Insurance Defense; Medical Malpractice; Personal Injury; Product Liability Law; Professional Liability; Real Estate Law; Toxic Torts; Workers Compensation

PRUITT, GUSHEE & BACHTELL
Salt Lake City, UT....Natural Resources Law

PRYOR, BARRY, SMITH, KARBER AND ALFORD P.L.C.
Fort Smith, AR....Insurance Defense

PRYOR, FLYNN, PRIEST & HARBER
Knoxville, TN....Civil Trial Practice; Criminal Trial Practice; General Practice; Medical Malpractice; Personal Injury; Product Liability Law

PRYOR & MANDELUP, L.L.P.
Westbury, NY....Bankruptcy Law; Civil Trial Practice; Commercial Litigation

PUCCINELLI & PUCCINELLI
Elko, NV....Civil Trial Practice; General Practice

PUGH AND VAN BUREN
Orlando, FL....Civil Trial Practice; Commercial Litigation; Environmental Law; Personal Injury

PULASKI, GIEGER & LABORDE, L.L.C.
New Orleans, LA....Aviation Law; Environmental Law; Insurance Defense; Natural Resources Law; Oil and Gas Law; Product Liability Law; Toxic Torts; Transportation Law

PURCELL, KRUG & HALLER
Harrisburg, PA....Bankruptcy Law

PURCELL, RIES, SHANNON, MULCAHY & O'NEILL
Bedminster, NJ....Business Law; Civil Trial Practice; Corporate Law; Environmental Law; General Practice; Insurance Defense; Labor and Employment Law; Product Liability Law; Real Estate Law

PURDY AND FLYNN, P.A.
Fort Lauderdale, FL....Commercial Litigation; Personal Injury

PURVIS, GRAY & GORDON, LLP
Boulder, CO....Civil Trial Practice; Legal Malpractice; Personal Injury
Denver, CO....Civil Trial Practice; Legal Malpractice; Personal Injury

PYNE & DERRY, P.C.
Chevy Chase, MD....Insurance Defense; Personal Injury; Trust and Estates, Wills and Probate

PYSZKA, BLACKMON, LEVY & SAVOLA, P.A.
Miami Lakes, FL....Civil Trial Practice; Insurance Defense

PYTELL & VARCHETTI, P.C.
Detroit, MI....Commercial Law; Commercial Litigation; Creditors Rights; Medical Malpractice; Personal Injury; Trust and Estates, Wills and Probate

QUACKENBUSH & QUACKENBUSH
San Mateo, CA....Labor and Employment Law

QUALE, FELDBRUEGGE, CALVELLI, THOM & CROKE, S.C.
Milwaukee, WI....Insurance Defense; Product Liability Law

QUANDT, GIFFELS & BUCK CO., L.P.A.
Cleveland, OH....Civil Trial Practice; General Practice; Insurance Defense

QUARLES & BRADY LLC
Chicago, IL....Business Law; Civil Trial Practice; General Practice; Real Estate Law; Trust and Estates, Wills and Probate

QUARLES & BRADY LLP
Phoenix, AZ....Administrative Law; Business Law; Civil Trial Practice; Commercial Law; Commercial Litigation; Environmental Law; Health Care Law; International Business Law; Labor and Employment Law; Municipal Bond/Public Authority Financing; Natural Resources Law; Patent, Trademark, Copyright and Unfair Competition; Personal Injury; Product Liability Law; Real Estate Law; Securities Law
Naples, FL....Banking Law; Business Law; Civil Trial Practice; Construction Law; General Practice; Land Use Law; Real Estate Law; Trust and Estates, Wills and Probate
West Palm Beach, FL....Bankruptcy Law; Business Law; Commercial Law; Construction Law; General Practice; Labor and Employment Law; Land Use Law; Patent, Trademark, Copyright and Unfair Competition; Real Estate Law; Trust and Estates, Wills and Probate
Madison, WI....Admiralty/Maritime Law; Antitrust Law; Business Law; Civil Trial Practice; Construction Law; Environmental Law; General Practice; Health Care Law; Municipal Bond/Public Authority Financing; Patent, Trademark, Copyright and Unfair Competition; Product Liability Law; Securities Law
Milwaukee, WI....Administrative Law; Antitrust Law; Banking Law; Bankruptcy Law; Business Law; Civil Trial Practice; Commercial Law; Construction Law; Employment Benefits Law; Environmental Law; Family Law; General Practice; Health Care Law; Immigration and Naturalization; International Business Law; Labor and Employment Law; Land Use Law; Municipal and Zoning Law; Municipal Bond/Public Authority Financing; Patent, Trademark, Copyright and Unfair Competition; Product Liability Law; Public Utilities Law; Real Estate Law; Securities Law; Tax Law; Trust and Estates, Wills and Probate

QUIGLEY, DILL & QUIGLEY
Valentine, NE....General Practice

QUINLAN & CRISHAM, LTD.
Chicago, IL....Civil Trial Practice; Commercial Litigation; Insurance Defense; Product Liability Law

QUINLIVAN & KANIEWSKI
Newport Beach, CA....Business Law; Civil Trial Practice; Trust and Estates, Wills and Probate

QUINN, PAUL G.
Denver, CO....Bankruptcy Law

QUINN, DAY & BARKER, P.L.L.C.
Belle Fourche, SD....Civil Trial Practice; Medical Malpractice; Personal Injury
Rapid City, SD....Civil Trial Practice

QUINN, JOHNSTON, HENDERSON & PRETORIUS, CHARTERED
Peoria, IL....Civil Trial Practice; General Practice

QUINN, MCGARRY & CAFFERY, P.C.
Buffalo, NY....Insurance Defense; Personal Injury

QUINN, PATTERSON & WILLARD
Columbia, SC....Business Law; Civil Trial Practice; General Practice; Real Estate Law

QUINN, RACUSIN & GAZZOLA, CHARTERED
Washington, DC....Business Law; Trust and Estates, Wills and Probate

QUIRK AND BAKALOR, P.C.
New York, NY....Appellate Practice; Civil Trial Practice; Insurance Defense

QUISUMBING TORRES
Metro Manila, Philippines....General Practice

RAAB & RAAB
Fort Lauderdale, FL....Family Law

RABBITT, PITZER & SNODGRASS, P.C.
St. Louis, MO....Civil Trial Practice; Insurance Defense

RABE, GEORGE F.
Lexington, KY....General Practice

RABIN & PECKEL LLP
New York, NY....Antitrust Law; Securities Law

RABINOVITZ & ASSOCIATES, P.C.
Tucson, AZ....Civil Trial Practice; Insurance Defense; Medical Malpractice; Personal Injury; Product Liability Law; Workers Compensation

RABINOWITZ, TRENK, LUBETKIN & TULLY, P.C.
West Orange, NJ....Bankruptcy Law; Commercial Litigation; Creditors Rights; Land Use Law; Municipal and Zoning Law

RABON, WOLF & RABON
Hugo, OK....General Practice

RACCUGLIA, ANTHONY C. & ASSOCIATES
Peru, IL....Civil Trial Practice; Medical Malpractice; Personal Injury; Product Liability Law

RACINE, OLSON, NYE, BUDGE & BAILEY, CHARTERED
Pocatello, ID....Insurance Defense

RADER, FISHMAN, GRAUER & MCGARRY PLLC
Grand Rapids, MI....Intellectual Property Law; Patent, Trademark, Copyright and Unfair Competition

RADER, FISHMAN & GRAUER PLLC
Washington, DC....Intellectual Property Law; Patent, Trademark, Copyright and Unfair Competition
Bloomfield Hills, MI....Intellectual Property Law; Patent, Trademark, Copyright and Unfair Competition

RAGGIO, CAPPEL, CHOZEN & BERNIARD
Lake Charles, LA....Civil Trial Practice; General Practice

RAGGIO AND RAGGIO, P.L.L.C.
Dallas, TX....Family Law

RAGSDALE LIGGETT, PLLC
Raleigh, NC....Business Law; Civil Trial Practice; Real Estate Law

RAICHLE, BANNING, WEISS & STEPHENS
Buffalo, NY....Business Law; Commercial Law; Corporate Law; Environmental Law; General Practice; Labor and Employment Law

RAINES, THOMAS E., P.C.
Norcross, GA....Trust and Estates, Wills and Probate

RAINS & POGREBIN, P.C.
Mineola, NY....Labor and Employment Law

RAISBECK, LARA, RODRIGUEZ & RUEDA
Bogotá, Colombia....General Practice

RAIZMAN & FRISCHMAN, P.C.
Pittsburgh, PA....Medical Malpractice

RAJALA, ERIC C.
Overland Park, KS....Bankruptcy Law

RAJKOWSKI HANSMEIER LTD.
St. Cloud, MN....Insurance Defense

RAKESTRAW & RAKESTRAW
Findlay, OH....General Practice

RALSTON, ROBERT W.
Wilmington, DE....Insurance Defense; Workers Compensation

RALSTON & POPE, LLC
Topeka, KS....Civil Trial Practice; Medical Malpractice; Personal Injury; Product Liability Law

RAMBO, ANDREW C., P.C.
Shelbyville, TN....Insurance Defense

RAMER, MOORE & GLASS
Harbor Springs, MI....Commercial Litigation; Trust and Estates, Wills and Probate

RAMEY & FLOCK, A PROFESSIONAL CORPORATION
Tyler, TX....Appellate Practice; Civil Rights; Civil Trial Practice; Commercial Law; Health Care Law; Labor and Employment Law; Medical Malpractice; Product Liability Law; Workers Compensation

RAMMELKAMP, BRADNEY, KUSTER, KEATON, FRITSCHE & LINDSAY, P.C.
Jacksonville, IL....General Practice; Insurance Defense

RAMSAY, BRIDGFORTH, HARRELSON & STARLING
Pine Bluff, AR....Civil Trial Practice; General Practice; Labor and Employment Law; Trust and Estates, Wills and Probate

RAMSEY, JOE
Sacramento, CA .... Arbitration; Civil Trial Practice; Product Liability Law

RAMSEY & MURRAY, A PROFESSIONAL CORPORATION
Houston, TX .... Appellate Practice; Arbitration; Civil Trial Practice; Environmental Law; Insurance Defense; Labor and Employment Law; Personal Injury; Product Liability Law; Toxic Torts; Workers Compensation

RAND, ALGEIER, TOSTI & WOODRUFF, A PROFESSIONAL CORPORATION
Morristown, NJ .... Civil Rights; Civil Trial Practice; Commercial Law; Construction Law; Education Law; General Practice; Labor and Employment Law; Personal Injury

RANKIN, HILL, PORTER & CLARK LLP
Cleveland, OH .... Intellectual Property Law; Patent, Trademark, Copyright and Unfair Competition

RANKIN & SULTAN
Boston, MA .... Criminal Trial Practice

RANSOME AND RAY, P.C.
Brownsville, TX .... Bankruptcy Law; Construction Law

RANSON, ARTHUR J. III
Orlando, FL .... Civil Trial Practice

RAPPORT, MEYERS, WHITBECK, SHAW & RODENHAUSEN, LLP
Hudson, NY .... General Practice

RASMUSSEN & MITCHELL
Omaha, NE .... Bankruptcy Law; Commercial Litigation; Corporate Law; Creditors Rights; Personal Injury; Real Estate Law; Trust and Estates, Wills and Probate

RASOR, C. LEWIS JR.
Greenville, SC .... Trust and Estates, Wills and Probate

RATH, YOUNG AND PIGNATELLI, PROFESSIONAL ASSOCIATION
Concord, NH .... Civil Trial Practice; Environmental Law; General Practice; Insurance Defense; Medical Malpractice; Personal Injury; Public Utilities Law; Tax Law
Nashua, NH .... General Practice; Insurance Defense; Medical Malpractice

RATHJE, WOODWARD, DYER & BURT
Wheaton, IL .... General Practice

RATTET & PASTERNAK, LLP
Harrison, NY .... Bankruptcy Law

RAUSCHER, DAVID J., P.C.
St. Louis, MO .... Personal Injury

RAVDIN & WOFFORD, A PROFESSIONAL CORPORATION
Washington, DC .... Family Law; Trust and Estates, Wills and Probate

RAVIN, GREENBERG & MARKS, A PROFESSIONAL CORPORATION
Roseland, NJ .... Bankruptcy Law

RAWLE & HENDERSON LLP
Philadelphia, PA .... Admiralty/Maritime Law; Product Liability Law

RAWLES, O'BYRNE, STANKO & KEPLEY, P.C.
Champaign, IL .... Business Law; General Practice

RAWLINGS, NIELAND, PROBASCO, KILLINGER, ELLWANGER, JACOBS & MOHRHAUSER
Sioux City, IA .... General Practice

RAWLINGS, OLSON, CANNON, GORMLEY & DESRUISSEAUX, A PROFESSIONAL CORPORATION
Las Vegas, NV .... Insurance Defense

RAWLS & DICKINSON, P.A.
Charlotte, NC .... Criminal Trial Practice; Personal Injury

RAY, CHARLES R.
Nashville, TN .... Criminal Trial Practice

RAY, MCCHRISTIAN & JEANS, A PROFESSIONAL CORPORATION
El Paso, TX .... Civil Trial Practice; Commercial Litigation; Insurance Defense; Labor and Employment Law; Medical Malpractice; Product Liability Law; Professional Liability

RAY, QUINNEY & NEBEKER, A PROFESSIONAL CORPORATION
Provo, UT .... General Practice
Salt Lake City, UT .... Antitrust Law; Banking Law; Bankruptcy Law; Civil Trial Practice; Commercial Law; General Practice; Insurance Defense; Labor and Employment Law; Natural Resources Law; Real Estate Law; Tax Law; Trust and Estates, Wills and Probate

RAY, ROBINSON, CARLE & DAVIES P.L.L.
Cleveland, OH .... Admiralty/Maritime Law; Civil Trial Practice; General Practice

RAYBURN, MOON & SMITH, P.A.
Charlotte, NC .... Business Law; Civil Trial Practice; General Practice; Securities Law

RAYBURN & PIERCE
Oxford, MS .... Civil Trial Practice

RAYMOND, GREER & SASSAMAN, P.C.
Phoenix, AZ .... Insurance Defense; Personal Injury

RAYNES, MCCARTY, BINDER, ROSS & MUNDY
Philadelphia, PA .... Personal Injury

READY, SULLIVAN & READY, L.L.P.
Monroe, MI .... General Practice

REAGER & ADLER, P.C.
Camp Hill, PA .... Civil Trial Practice; Construction Law; Municipal and Zoning Law; Real Estate Law

REAM, CHRISTOPHER
Palo Alto, CA .... Business Law; Securities Law

REARDON LAW FIRM, THE, P.C
New London, CT .... Medical Malpractice; Personal Injury; Product Liability Law

REAUD, MORGAN & QUINN
Beaumont, TX .... Commercial Law; Personal Injury; Product Liability Law

REBMAN WAGENER & LINHARES, P.C.
St. Louis, MO .... Transportation Law

RECKLESS, WALTER W.
Col...nbus, OH .... Civil Trial Practice; Personal Injury; Product Liability Law

REDDEN, MILLS & CLARK
Birmingham, AL .... Appellate Practice; Criminal Trial Practice; Family Law; Labor and Employment Law

REDFEARN & BROWN, A PROFESSIONAL CORPORATION
Kansas City, MO .... Medical Malpractice; Personal Injury; Product Liability Law

REDMAN, JAMES E.
Milwaukie, OR .... General Practice

REDMON, BOYKIN & BRASWELL, L.L.P.
Alexandria, VA .... General Practice

REDMOND, MARGARET ANN
San Jose, CA .... Immigration and Naturalization

REDMOND, BURGIN & GUTIERREZ, P.A.
Baltimore, MD .... Administrative Law; Aviation Law; Civil Rights; Criminal Trial Practice; Employment Benefits Law; Family Law; General Practice; Insurance Defense; Personal Injury; Product Liability Law; Real Estate Law

REED, ARMSTRONG, GORMAN, COFFEY, GILBERT & MUDGE, PROFESSIONAL CORPORATION
Edwardsville, IL .... Civil Trial Practice; Insurance Defense

REED, CARRERA & MCLAIN, L.L.P.
Edinburg, TX .... Appellate Practice; Civil Trial Practice

REED, ELLIOTT, CREECH & ROTH
San Jose, CA .... Business Law; Commercial Litigation; Construction Law; Energy Law; Environmental Law; Product Liability Law

REED, LUCE, TOSH, WOLFORD & DOUGLASS, A PROFESSIONAL CORPORATION
Beaver, PA .... General Practice

REED MCCLURE
Seattle, WA .... General Practice

REED, RONALD S., P.A.
Tampa, FL .... Family Law

REED SMITH HAZEL & THOMAS LLP
Falls Church, VA .... General Practice
Leesburg, VA .... General Practice
McLean, VA .... Employment Benefits Law; Labor and Employment Law
Richmond, VA .... General Practice

REED SMITH SHAW & MCCLAY LLP
Washington, DC .... Labor and Employment Law; Municipal Bond/Public Authority Financing
Newark, NJ .... Labor and Employment Law
Princeton, NJ .... Labor and Employment Law; Municipal Bond/Public Authority Financing
New York, NY .... Employment Benefits Law; Labor and Employment Law

Harrisburg, PA........................Labor and Employment Law
Philadelphia, PA......................Employment Benefits Law; Labor and Employment Law; Municipal Bond/Public Authority Financing
Pittsburgh, PA........................Employment Benefits Law; Labor and Employment Law; Municipal Bond/Public Authority Financing

REES, BROOME & DIAZ, P.C.
Vienna, VA..............................Business Law; Tax Law; Trust and Estates, Wills and Probate

REEVES, CHAVEZ, GREENFIELD & WALKER, P.A.
Las Cruces, NM......................Banking Law; Civil Trial Practice; Commercial Litigation; Health Care Law; Insurance Defense; Real Estate Law; Trust and Estates, Wills and Probate

REEVES & STEWART, P.C.
Selma, AL...............................General Practice; Insurance Defense

REGAN & CANTWELL
Charleston, SC........................Municipal and Zoning Law

REGAN, MICHAEL P., P.C., LAW OFFICES OF
Danville, VA...........................Civil Trial Practice; General Practice

REHM LAW FIRM, A PROFESSIONAL CORPORATION
Lincoln, NE............................Personal Injury; Workers Compensation

REICH, MEEKS & TREADAWAY, L.L.C.
Metairie, LA............................Admiralty/Maritime Law; Insurance Defense

REID, BURGE, PREVALLET & COLEMAN
Blytheville, AR........................Civil Trial Practice; Insurance Defense

REID, GARTH O., JR., A PROFESSIONAL LAW CORPORATION
Escondido, CA.........................Tax Law

REID AND RIEGE, P.C.
Hartford, CT...........................General Practice

REID, STRICKLAND & GILLETTE, L.L.P.
Baytown, TX...........................General Practice

REILLY LAW ASSOCIATES, INC.
Providence, RI.........................Tax Law

REILLY, PETERSEN & HANNAN, P.L.C.
Council Bluffs, IA...................Bankruptcy Law; General Practice; Personal Injury; Real Estate Law

REILLY, STUART J., P.C.
Phoenix, AZ............................Medical Malpractice; Personal Injury

REIMAN & BAYAZ, P.C.
Denver, CO.............................Antitrust Law; Appellate Practice; Civil Trial Practice; Commercial Litigation; Construction Law; Securities Law

REINER, SIMPSON & KENNEDY
Redding, CA...........................Personal Injury; Product Liability Law; Professional Liability

REINERT & ROURKE, P.C.
St. Louis, MO..........................Commercial Litigation

REINGLASS, MICHELLE A.
Laguna Hills, CA.....................Labor and Employment Law

REINHART, BOERNER, VAN DEUREN, NORRIS & RIESELBACH, S.C.
Milwaukee, WI........................General Practice

REINIS & REINIS
Los Angeles, CA.....................Business Law

REINWALD, O'CONNOR & PLAYDON
Honolulu, HI...........................Civil Trial Practice; Commercial Litigation; Tax Law; Trust and Estates, Wills and Probate

REISEMAN SHARP KELSEY & BROWN LLP
Parsippany, NJ........................Civil Trial Practice; Insurance Defense; Medical Malpractice; Personal Injury; Product Liability Law

REISER, MICHAEL J. LAW OFFICES OF
Walnut Creek, CA..................Labor and Employment Law; Legal Malpractice

REISH & LUFTMAN, A PROFESSIONAL CORPORATION
Los Angeles, CA.....................Pension and Profit Sharing

REISING, ETHINGTON, BARNES, KISSELLE, LEARMAN & MCCULLOCH, P.C.
Saginaw, MI...........................Intellectual Property Law; Patent, Trademark, Copyright and Unfair Competition
Troy, MI..................................Intellectual Property Law; Patent, Trademark, Copyright and Unfair Competition

REISMAN, GLENN M.
Shelton, CT............................Bankruptcy Law; Creditors Rights

RELIN, GOLDSTEIN AND CRANE, LLP
Rochester, NY.........................Creditors Rights

RELPH, ROBERT B.
Grand Rapids, MI...................Family Law

REMCHO, JOHANSEN AND PURCELL
San Francisco, CA..................Appellate Practice; Civil Trial Practice; Constitutional Law

REMICK MARTONE, A PROFESSIONAL CORPORATION
Philadelphia, PA.....................Insurance Defense; Sports and Entertainment Law

REMY, THOMAS AND MOOSE, LLP
Sacramento, CA......................Environmental Law; Land Use Law

RENALDO, MYERS & PALUMBO, P.C.
Buffalo, NY.............................Personal Injury

RENDLEN LAW FIRM, THE, P.C.
Hannibal, MO.........................General Practice

RENICK, SINGER AND KAMBER
Lake Worth, FL......................Family Law

RENNER CLARK BUCKWALTER & VOLTZ, P.C.
Wayne, PA..............................Business Law; Mergers and Acquisitions; Real Estate Law; Securities Law

RENNER, KENNER, GREIVE, BOBAK, TAYLOR & WEBER, A LEGAL PROFESSIONAL ASSOCIATION
Akron, OH..............................Intellectual Property Law; Patent, Trademark, Copyright and Unfair Competition
Canton, OH............................Intellectual Property Law; Patent, Trademark, Copyright and Unfair Competition

RENNER, OTTO, BOISSELLE & SKLAR, P.L.L.
Cleveland, OH.........................Intellectual Property Law; Trademark, Copyright and Unfair Competition

RESTOVICH, GEORGE F. & ASSOCIATES
Rochester, MN........................Criminal Trial Practice; Family Law; Personal Injury

RETHERFORD, MULLEN, JOHNSON & BRUCE, L.L.C.
Colorado Springs, CO............Civil Trial Practice; General Practice; Insurance Defense

RETTIG, OSBORNE, FORGETTE, O'DONNELL, ILLER & ADAMSON, LLP
Kennewick, WA......................Civil Trial Practice

REVELLE, BURLESON, LEE & REVELLE, L.L.P.
Murfreesboro, NC..................General Practice

REXON, FREEDMAN, KLEPETAR & HAMBLETON, A PROFESSIONAL CORPORATION
Los Angeles, CA.....................Labor and Employment Law

REYNOLDS & CONWAY, P.C.
Springfield, MO......................General Practice

REYNOLDS & MCARTHUR
Atlanta, GA.............................Civil Trial Practice; Medical Malpractice; Personal Injury; Product Liability Law
Macon, GA..............................Civil Trial Practice; Medical Malpractice; Personal Injury; Product Liability Law

REYNOLDS, SMITH & WINTERS, P.C.
Norfolk, VA.............................Insurance Defense

RHEES, HOPKINS & KREAMER
Phoenix, AZ............................Commercial Litigation; Construction Law; Insurance Defense

RHEINGOLD, VALET, RHEINGOLD & SHKOLNIK, P.C.
New York, NY.........................Medical Malpractice; Personal Injury; Product Liability Law

RHOADES, MCKEE, BOER, GOODRICH & TITTA
Grand Rapids, MI...................Business Law; Civil Trial Practice; Labor and Employment Law; Trust and Estates, Wills and Probate

RHOADS & SINON LLP
Harrisburg, PA........................Banking Law; Civil Trial Practice; Environmental Law; General Practice; Municipal Bond/Public Authority Financing; Tax Law

RHODA, STOUDT & BRADLEY
Reading, PA............................General Practice

RHODEN, LACY, DOWNEY & COLBERT
Jackson, MS............................Business Law; Insurance Defense; Real Estate Law

RHODES, HIERONYMUS, JONES, TUCKER & GABLE, P.L.L.C.
Tulsa, OK...............................Appellate Practice; Arbitration; Aviation Law; Bankruptcy Law; Civil Rights; Civil Trial Practice; Eminent Domain; Environmental Law; Health Care Law; Insurance Defense; Labor and Employment Law; Medical Malpractice; Personal Injury; Product Liability Law; Professional Liability; Toxic Torts; Transportation Law; Workers Compensation

RHODES & MASON, P.L.L.C.
Greensboro, NC .... Patent, Trademark, Copyright and Unfair Competition
Wilmington, NC .... Patent, Trademark, Copyright and Unfair Competition

RIBET, CLAUDIA
Los Angeles, CA .... Appellate Practice; Civil Trial Practice

RICCI, HUBBARD, LEOPOLD, FRANKEL & FARMER, P.A.
West Palm Beach, FL .... Civil Trial Practice; Personal Injury; Product Liability Law

RICCIARDI & PAUSTIAN
Las Vegas, NV .... Labor and Employment Law

RICCOLO & BAKER, P.C.
Cedar Rapids, IA .... Medical Malpractice; Personal Injury

RICE, ANDREA LYNN, LAW OFFICES OF A PROF. CORP.
Los Angeles, CA .... Professional Liability

RICE & HENDRICKSON
Harlan, KY .... Administrative Law; General Practice; Insurance Defense; Labor and Employment Law

RICHARDS, CHARLES L.
Warren, OH .... Insurance Defense; Medical Malpractice

RICHARDS & CONNOR
Tulsa, OK .... Civil Trial Practice; Insurance Defense; Medical Malpractice

RICHARDS, LAYTON & FINGER, P.A.
Wilmington, DE .... General Practice; Tax Law

RICHARDS, RALPH & SCHWAB, CHARTERED
Vernon Hills, IL .... Banking Law; Bankruptcy Law; Business Law; Commercial Litigation; Land Use Law; Real Estate Law

RICHARDS SPEARS KIBBE & ORBE
New York, NY .... Corporate Law; Securities Law

RICHARDSON, PLOWDEN, CARPENTER & ROBINSON, P.A.
Columbia, SC .... Appellate Practice; Banking Law; Business Law; Civil Trial Practice; Commercial Law; Construction Law; Environmental Law; General Practice; Health Care Law; Insurance Defense; Medical Malpractice; Personal Injury; Product Liability Law; Real Estate Law; Trust and Estates, Wills and Probate

RICHARDSON, WHITMAN, LARGE & BADGER, A PROFESSIONAL CORPORATION
Portland, ME .... Insurance Defense; Personal Injury

RICHESON, J. DAVID, & ASSOCIATES, P.A.
Fort Pierce, FL .... Labor and Employment Law
West Palm Beach, FL .... Labor and Employment Law

RICHEY, WILLIAM L., P.A.
Miami, FL .... Appellate Practice; Banking Law; Civil Trial Practice; Creditors Rights; Criminal Trial Practice

RICHILANO & RIDLEY, P.C.
Denver, CO .... Civil Trial Practice; Criminal Trial Practice

RICHMAN, GERALD M.
Ellicott City, MD .... Civil Trial Practice; Criminal Trial Practice

RICHMAN GREER WEIL BRUMBAUGH MIRABITO & CHRISTENSEN, P.A.
Miami, FL .... Civil Trial Practice

RICHMAN & JONES, P.C.
Denver, CO .... Medical Malpractice; Personal Injury

RICHMAN, LUNA, KICHAVEN & GLUSHON
Los Angeles, CA .... Natural Resources Law; Trademark, Copyright and Unfair Competition

RICKS & ANDERSON, A LAW CORPORATION
Costa Mesa, CA .... Civil Trial Practice; Labor and Employment Law

RICK, STEINER, P.C.
New York, NY .... Corporate Law; Real Estate Law

RIDBERG, PRESS & SHERBILL
Bethesda, MD .... Arbitration; Business Law; Commercial Litigation

RIDDLE & BAUMGARTNER
Houston, TX .... Personal Injury

RIDENOUR, RIDENOUR & FOX
Clinton, TN .... Personal Injury

RIDER, WEINER, FRANKEL & CALHELHA, P.C.
Newburgh, NY .... Business Law; Civil Trial Practice; Real Estate Law; Trust and Estates, Wills and Probate

RIDGWAY AND GRIFFIN, CHARTERED
Rockville, MD .... Real Estate Law

RIDOUT & MAYBEE
Ottawa, ON, Canada .... Patent, Trademark, Copyright and Unfair Competition
Toronto, ON, Canada .... Patent, Trademark, Copyright and Unfair Competition

RIEGELS CAMPOS & KENYON LLP
Sacramento, CA .... Business Law; Insurance Defense

RIEKE & SAVAGE, P.C.
Portland, OR .... Personal Injury; Professional Liability

RIESEN LAW FIRM, L.L.P.
North Charleston, SC .... Admiralty/Maritime Law; Personal Injury

RIESENBURGER & KIZNER, P.C.
Vineland, NJ .... Appellate Practice; Civil Trial Practice; Environmental Law; Real Estate Law

RIEVES & MAYTON
West Memphis, AR .... Business Law; Civil Trial Practice; General Practice; Insurance Defense; Product Liability Law; Workers Compensation

RIFKIN AND ASSOCIATES, P.A.
Miami, FL .... Immigration and Naturalization

RIGBY, THATCHER, ANDRUS, RIGBY, KAM & MOELLER, CHARTERED
Rexburg, ID .... General Practice

RIGGS & NESMITH, P.A.
Montgomery, AL .... Personal Injury; Product Liability Law

RIGHTHAND, SCOTT, P.C., LAW OFFICE OF
San Francisco, CA .... Civil Trial Practice

RIKER, DANZIG, SCHERER, HYLAND & PERRETTI LLP
Morristown, NJ .... General Practice
Trenton, NJ .... General Practice

RILEY, JOSEPH H. JR.
Tucson, AZ .... Family Law

RILEY & HARRIS, L.L.P.
Brownsville, TX .... Civil Trial Practice; Medical Malpractice; Personal Injury
Houston, TX .... Civil Trial Practice; Medical Malpractice; Personal Injury

RILEY, HURLEY & DOLENGA, P.C.
Dearborn, MI .... Civil Trial Practice; Labor and Employment Law; Sports and Entertainment Law

RILEY, MCNULTY, HEWITT & SWEITZER, A PROFESSIONAL CORPORATION
Pittsburgh, PA .... Civil Trial Practice; Commercial Law; General Practice

RILEY AND ROUMELL, P.C.
Detroit, MI .... General Practice; Labor and Employment Law

RILEY, TOM, LAW FIRM, P.L.C.
Cedar Rapids, IA .... Personal Injury

RINELLA AND RINELLA, LTD.
Chicago, IL .... Family Law

RINGO, STUBER, ENSOR & HADLOCK, P.C.
Corvallis, OR .... Personal Injury

RINGUET DANIELS & COLLIER, A PROFESSIONAL LAW CORPORATION
Lafayette, LA .... Civil Trial Practice; Commercial Law; Natural Resources Law

RINTALA, SMOOT, JAENICKE & REES
Los Angeles, CA .... Commercial Litigation; Labor and Employment Law; Trademark, Copyright and Unfair Competition

RION, RION & RION, L.P.A. INC.
Dayton, OH .... Criminal Trial Practice

RISJORD & JAMES, P.C.
Overland Park, KS .... Aviation Law; Civil Trial Practice; Personal Injury; Product Liability Law

RITCHIE & REDIKER, L.L.C.
Birmingham, AL .... Securities Law

RITER, MAYER, HOFER, WATTIER & BROWN, L.L.P.
Pierre, SD .... General Practice

RITTER EICHNER & NORRIS, PLLC
Washington, DC .... Municipal Bond/Public Authority Financing; Tax Law

RITTER AND JESPERSON
Bridgeton, NJ....................Civil Trial Practice; General Practice

RITTER, RITTER & ZARETSKY
Miami, FL....................Real Estate Law

RITTER, ROBINSON, MCCREADY & JAMES
Toledo, OH....................Civil Trial Practice; Corporate Law; General Practice; Insurance Defense; Municipal and Zoning Law; Personal Injury; Real Estate Law

RIVKIN, RADLER & KREMER LLP
Uniondale, NY....................Civil Trial Practice; General Practice

RIVKIND & PEDRAZA, P.A.
Miami, FL....................Admiralty/Maritime Law

RIVLIN, LEWIS A., P.C., LAW OFFICES OF
Washington, DC....................General Practice

ROACH, JAMES T.
Albuquerque, NM....................Personal Injury; Product Liability Law

ROACH, BROWN, MCCARTHY & GRUBER, P.C.
Buffalo, NY....................Civil Trial Practice; General Practice; Insurance Defense; Legal Malpractice; Medical Malpractice; Product Liability Law

ROACH & CARPENTER, P.C.
Boston, MA....................Bankruptcy Law; Civil Trial Practice; Commercial Litigation

ROACH LAW FIRM, THE, P.C.
Tulsa, OK....................Insurance Defense; Personal Injury; Product Liability Law

ROBBINS, STEPHEN
Sacramento, CA....................Land Use Law

ROBBINS & GREEN, A PROFESSIONAL ASSOCIATION
Phoenix, AZ....................Bankruptcy Law; Commercial Law; Commercial Litigation; Insurance Defense; Personal Injury; Real Estate Law; Trust and Estates, Wills and Probate

ROBBINS & KEEHN, A PROFESSIONAL CORPORATION
San Diego, CA....................Bankruptcy Law; Civil Trial Practice

ROBBINS & RHODES, ATTORNEYS AT LAW, A LAW CORPORATION
Honolulu, HI....................Appellate Practice; Civil Trial Practice; Health Care Law; Insurance Defense; Medical Malpractice

ROBBINS, TUNKEY, ROSS, AMSEL, RABEN & WAXMAN, P.A.
Miami, FL....................Administrative Law; Appellate Practice; Civil Rights; Constitutional Law; Criminal Trial Practice; Tax Law

ROBEIN, URANN & LURYE, A PROFESSIONAL LAW CORPORATION
Metairie, LA....................Labor and Employment Law

ROBENALT & ROBENALT
Lima, OH....................General Practice; Health Care Law

ROBERGE, WILLIAM H. JR.
Rockville, MD....................Trust and Estates, Wills and Probate

ROBERTS, FRANK H.
Reno, NV....................Insurance Defense

ROBERTS, ALLEN P., P.A.
Camden, AR....................Civil Trial Practice; General Practice; Labor and Employment Law

ROBERTS, BETZ & BLOSS, P.C.
Grand Rapids, MI....................Civil Trial Practice; Commercial Litigation; Construction Law; Environmental Law; Insurance Defense; Personal Injury

ROBERTS & ENGVALSON, P.A.
Fort Myers, FL....................Family Law; Trust and Estates, Wills and Probate

ROBERTS, LARRY K., INC.
Newport Beach, CA....................Intellectual Property Law; Patent, Trademark, Copyright and Unfair Competition

ROBERTS, MARKEL & FOLGER, L.L.P.
Houston, TX....................Admiralty/Maritime Law; Insurance Defense; Real Estate Law

ROBERTS, MARK SCOTT, AND ASSOCIATES, A PROF. LAW CORP.
Fullerton, CA....................Trust and Estates, Wills and Probate

ROBERTS, PERRYMAN, BOMKAMP & MEIVES, P.C.
St. Louis, MO....................Civil Trial Practice; Environmental Law; Insurance Defense; Product Liability Law; Workers Compensation

ROBERTS & ROWLEY, LTD.
Mesa, AZ....................Business Law; Corporate Law; Real Estate Law

ROBERTS & SALAZAR, L.L.P.
Key Biscayne, FL....................General Practice

ROBERTS & SMITH
Lexington, KY....................Criminal Trial Practice; General Practice; Insurance Defense; Personal Injury

ROBERTSON, WILLIAM DIXON III
Columbia, SC....................Construction Law

ROBERTSON & ASSOCIATES
Charleston, SC....................Construction Law

ROBERTSON, BEASLEY, COWAN & KETCHAM, PLLC
Fort Smith, AR....................Civil Trial Practice; General Practice

ROBERTSON, JAYNE JARNIGAN, P.C.
Oklahoma City, OK....................Commercial Litigation; Environmental Law

ROBERTSON, MONAGLE & EASTAUGH, A PROFESSIONAL CORPORATION
Anchorage, AK....................General Practice
Juneau, AK....................General Practice

ROBERTSON & WILLIAMS, INC.
Oklahoma City, OK....................General Practice

ROBERTSON, WILLIAMS & MCDONALD, P.A.
Orlando, FL....................Civil Trial Practice

ROBINETTE, GILBERT H.
Baltimore, MD....................Legal Malpractice; Medical Malpractice; Personal Injury

ROBINS, KAPLAN, MILLER & CIRESI L.L.P.
Minneapolis, MN....................General Practice

ROBINSON, BERT K. LAW OFFICES OF
Baton Rouge, LA....................Construction Law

ROBINSON, BRADSHAW & HINSON, P.A.
Charlotte, NC....................General Practice
Rock Hill, SC....................General Practice

ROBINSON, CALCAGNIE & ROBINSON, A PROFESSIONAL CORPORATION
Newport Beach, CA....................Civil Trial Practice; Personal Injury

ROBINSON, DIAMANT & BRILL, A PROFESSIONAL CORPORATION
Los Angeles, CA....................Bankruptcy Law

ROBINSON, DI LANDO & WHITAKER, A PROFESSIONAL LAW CORPORATION
Los Angeles, CA....................Insurance Defense; Labor and Employment Law; Product Liability Law; Professional Liability

ROBINSON DONOVAN MADDEN & BARRY, P.C.
Springfield, MA....................Banking Law; Commercial Litigation; Construction Law; Insurance Defense; Labor and Employment Law; Professional Liability; Real Estate Law; Tax Law; Trust and Estates, Wills and Probate; Workers Compensation

ROBINSON, J. RICHARD, P.C.
Okemos, MI....................Municipal and Zoning Law; Real Estate Law

ROBINSON LAW FIRM, THE
Washington, DC....................Civil Trial Practice; Commercial Litigation; Criminal Trial Practice; Medical Malpractice
Tulsa, OK....................Insurance Defense

ROBINSON, PALMER & LOGAN
Bakersfield, CA....................Civil Trial Practice; General Practice; Insurance Defense

ROBINSON SHEPPARD SHAPIRO, G.P.
Montreal, QU, Canada....................General Practice

ROBINSON & WOOD, INC.
San Jose, CA....................Civil Trial Practice; Commercial Litigation; Insurance Defense; Product Liability Law

ROBINSON WOOLSON O'CONNELL, LLP
Baltimore, MD....................Civil Trial Practice

ROBISON, BELAUSTEGUI, ROBB AND SHARP, A PROFESSIONAL CORPORATION
Reno, NV....................General Practice

ROBISON & BELSER, P.A.
Montgomery, AL....................Business Law; Civil Trial Practice; Criminal Trial Practice; Family Law; Insurance Defense; Labor and Employment Law

ROBISON & ROBISON
Denton, TX....................Labor and Employment Law; Personal Injury; Trust and Estates, Wills and Probate

ROBY & HOOD
Fort Wayne, IN....................Civil Trial Practice; Personal Injury; Product Liability Law

ROCA & SHARPE, P.A.
West Palm Beach, FL .... Civil Trial Practice; Personal Injury

ROCAP, WITCHGER & THRELKELD
Indianapolis, IN .... Commercial Litigation; General Practice; Insurance Defense

ROCHE, JOHN J. & ASSOCIATES
Cambridge, MA .... Trust and Estates, Wills and Probate

ROCHE, CARENS & DEGIACOMO, P.C.
Boston, MA .... Banking Law; Bankruptcy Law; Construction Law; Family Law; General Practice; Labor and Employment Law; Real Estate Law; Trust and Estates, Wills and Probate

ROCHE CORRIGAN MCCOY & BUSH
Albany, NY .... Civil Trial Practice; Construction Law; General Practice; Insurance Defense; Legal Malpractice; Personal Injury; Professional Liability

ROCHE AND MURPHY
Franklin, MA .... Civil Trial Practice; Land Use Law; Municipal and Zoning Law; Real Estate Law

ROCHELLE, MCCULLOCH & AULDS
Lebanon, TN .... General Practice

ROCKEY, MILNAMOW & KATZ, LTD.
Chicago, IL .... Intellectual Property Law; Patent, Trademark, Copyright and Unfair Competition

ROCKHILL, PINNICK, PEQUIGNOT, HELM, LANDIS & RIGDON
Warsaw, IN .... Business Law; Civil Trial Practice; Corporate Law; Insurance Defense; Municipal and Zoning Law

RODEHEFFER, STEPHEN C.
Portsmouth, OH .... General Practice

RODEY, DICKASON, SLOAN, AKIN & ROBB, P.A.
Albuquerque, NM .... Administrative Law; Antitrust Law; Banking Law; Bankruptcy Law; Business Law; Commercial Law; Construction Law; Criminal Trial Practice; General Practice; Health Care Law; Insurance Defense; International Business Law; Labor and Employment Law; Land Use Law; Medical Malpractice; Natural Resources Law; Personal Injury; Product Liability Law; Public Utilities Law; Real Estate Law; Securities Law; Tax Law; Trust and Estates, Wills and Probate
Santa Fe, NM .... General Practice

RODGERS, JAMES R.
Blackwell, OK .... General Practice; Trust and Estates, Wills and Probate

RODGERS AND CO., L.P.A.
Cleveland, OH .... Civil Trial Practice; Commercial Litigation; Construction Law; Insurance Defense; Product Liability Law; Real Estate Law

RODGERS, MENARD & COPPOLA, LLP
Buffalo, NY .... Civil Trial Practice

RODI, POLLOCK, PETTKER, GALBRAITH & CAHILL, A LAW CORPORATION
Los Angeles, CA .... Business Law; Civil Trial Practice; Commercial Litigation; Corporate Law; Employment Benefits Law; Environmental Law; Labor and Employment Law; Real Estate Law; Tax Law; Toxic Torts; Trust and Estates, Wills and Probate

RODRIGUEZ, CARLOS, & ASSOCIATES
Washington, DC .... Admiralty/Maritime Law; International Trade Law; Transportation Law

RODRIGUEZ, COLVIN & CHANEY, L.L.P.
Brownsville, TX .... Appellate Practice; Civil Trial Practice; Environmental Law; General Practice; Insurance Defense; Personal Injury; Product Liability Law
McAllen, TX .... Appellate Practice; Civil Trial Practice; Environmental Law; General Practice; Insurance Defense; Personal Injury; Product Liability Law

RODRIGUEZ, HORII & CHOI
Los Angeles, CA .... Tax Law

ROEDER AND ASSOCIATES, P.C.
McLean, VA .... Corporate Law; Real Estate Law

ROETZEL & ANDRESS, A LEGAL PROFESSIONAL ASSOCIATION
Akron, OH .... General Practice

ROGAN GUIDA & ORENSTEIN
White Plains, NY .... Appellate Practice; Business Law; Commercial Litigation; Corporate Law; Family Law; Insurance Defense; Personal Injury; Product Liability Law; Real Estate Law; Trust and Estates, Wills and Probate

ROGERS, BOWERS, DEMPSEY AND PALADINO
West Palm Beach, FL .... Tax Law

ROGERS & GREENBERG
Dayton, OH .... Business Law; Family Law; General Practice

ROGERS & KILLEEN
Alexandria, VA .... Intellectual Property Law; Patent, Trademark, Copyright and Unfair Competition; Trademark, Copyright and Unfair Competition

ROGERS LAW OFFICE
Toronto, ON, Canada .... Patent, Trademark, Copyright and Unfair Competition

ROGERS & SHEFFIELD, LLP
Santa Barbara, CA .... Business Law; Civil Trial Practice

ROGERS TOWNSEND & THOMAS, PC
Columbia, SC .... Aviation Law; Bankruptcy Law; Construction Law; Family Law; General Practice; Real Estate Law; Trust and Estates, Wills and Probate; Workers Compensation

ROGERS & WHALEN, P.A.
Phoenix, AZ .... Administrative Law; Labor and Employment Law

ROGIN, NASSAU, CAPLAN, LASSMAN & HIRTLE, LLC
Hartford, CT .... Business Law; Civil Trial Practice; General Practice

ROHRBACHERS, LIGHT, CRON, ZMUDA & TRIMBLE CO., L.P.A.
Toledo, OH .... Business Law; Environmental Law; Insurance Defense; Labor and Employment Law; Product Liability Law; Tax Law

ROLEWICK & GUTZKE, P.C.
Wheaton, IL .... Business Law; Commercial Litigation; Corporate Law; Trust and Estates, Wills and Probate

ROLLINGER, ROBERT S., P.C.
Bingham Farms, MI .... Real Estate Law

ROLLINS, SMALKIN, RICHARDS & MACKIE, L.L.C.
Baltimore, MD .... Civil Trial Practice; Insurance Defense; Personal Injury; Product Liability Law; Workers Compensation

ROLLS KOHN & ASSOCIATES, LLP
Buffalo, NY .... Business Law; Communications Law; Corporate Law; General Practice; Real Estate Law

ROMAIN, KUCK & EGERER, P.C.
Southfield, MI .... Insurance Defense; Personal Injury

ROOKER & GIBSON
Henderson, NV .... Antitrust Law; Business Law; Civil Trial Practice; Commercial Law; Construction Law; Corporate Law; Environmental Law; Health Care Law; Labor and Employment Law; Mergers and Acquisitions; Municipal and Zoning Law; Real Estate Law; Securities Law

ROOKS, PITTS AND POUST
Chicago, IL .... General Practice; Workers Compensation

ROOT & SCHINDLER, P.C.
Denver, CO .... Environmental Law; Natural Resources Law

ROPER & QUIGG
Chicago, IL .... Intellectual Property Law; Patent, Trademark, Copyright and Unfair Competition
Arlington, VA .... Intellectual Property Law; Patent, Trademark, Copyright and Unfair Competition

ROPERS, MAJESKI, KOHN & BENTLEY, A PROFESSIONAL CORPORATION
Los Angeles, CA .... General Practice
Redwood City, CA .... General Practice
San Francisco, CA .... General Practice
San Jose, CA .... General Practice

ROPES & GRAY
Washington, DC .... General Practice
Boston, MA .... Civil Trial Practice; General Practice; Tax Law

ROSE, MICHAEL T.
Summerville, SC .... Business Law; Civil Trial Practice

ROSE LAW FIRM, A PROFESSIONAL ASSOCIATION
Little Rock, AR .... Appellate Practice; Banking Law; Bankruptcy Law; Civil Trial Practice; Commercial Law; Communications Law; Corporate Law; Creditors Rights; Employment Benefits Law; Environmental Law; General Practice; Insurance Defense; International Business Law; Labor and Employment Law; Municipal Bond/Public Authority Financing; Patent, Trademark, Copyright and Unfair Competition; Pension and Profit Sharing; Personal Injury; Product Liability Law; Professional Liability; Public Utilities Law; Real Estate Law; Sports and Entertainment Law; Tax Law; Trust and Estates, Wills and Probate; Workers Compensation

ROSE, RAND, ORCUTT, CAULEY, BLAKE & ELLIS, P.A.
Wilson, NC..............................General Practice

ROSE & ROSE
Kenosha, WI ....Criminal Trial Practice; General Practice

ROSE, SCHMIDT, HASLEY & DISALLE, P.C.
Pittsburgh, PA ....Antitrust Law; Civil Trial Practice; General Practice; Labor and Employment Law

ROSE, SUNDSTROM & BENTLEY, LLP
Tallahassee, FL ....Administrative Law; Environmental Law; Health Care Law; Public Utilities Law; Real Estate Law

ROSEN, AVRUM J. LAW OFFICES OF
Huntington, NY.......................Bankruptcy Law

ROSEN, CHARLES A.
Roseland, NJ...........................Commercial Law; General Practice

ROSEN, BIEN & ASARO
San Francisco, CA ....Antitrust Law; Appellate Practice; Civil Trial Practice; Commercial Law; Commercial Litigation; Labor and Employment Law; Securities Law; Trademark, Copyright and Unfair Competition

ROSEN, COOK, SLEDGE, DAVIS, CADE & SHATTUCK, P.A.
Tuscaloosa, AL ....General Practice

ROSEN & DOLAN, P.C.
New Haven, CT ....Appellate Practice; Civil Rights; Civil Trial Practice; Family Law; General Practice; Labor and Employment Law; Personal Injury

ROSEN, EINBINDER & DUNN, P.C.
New York, NY.........................Civil Trial Practice; Real Estate Law

ROSEN & LOVELL, P.C.
Southfield, MI ....Construction Law; Personal Injury; Product Liability Law

ROSEN, MICHAEL J., P.A.
Miami, FL...............................Commercial Litigation; Criminal Trial Practice

ROSEN & OSBORNE, P.A.
Tampa, FL ....Workers Compensation

ROSENBAUM, RICHARD L.
Fort Lauderdale, FL................Appellate Practice; Criminal Trial Practice

ROSENBERG LAW FIRM, THE
Des Moines, IA.......................Appellate Practice; Business Law; Criminal Trial Practice; General Practice; Personal Injury

ROSENBERG, REISMAN & STEIN, LLP
Miami, FL...............................Construction Law; Real Estate Law

ROSENBERG, ROBERT MERRILL, P.A.
Minneapolis, MN.....................General Practice; Real Estate Law

ROSENBLATT, STANLEY M., PROFESSIONAL ASSOCIATION
Miami, FL...............................Civil Trial Practice

ROSENBLUM & FILAN, L.L.C.
Stamford, CT...........................Civil Trial Practice; General Practice; Health Care Law; Medical Malpractice
New York, NY.........................Medical Malpractice
White Plains, NY ....Medical Malpractice

ROSENBLUM, GOLDENHERSH, SILVERSTEIN & ZAFFT, P.C.
St. Louis, MO..........................Commercial Litigation; Corporate Law; Real Estate Law; Tax Law

ROSENBLUM & ROSENBLUM, L.L.C.
Alexandria, VA ....Bankruptcy Law; Personal Injury

ROSENBLUM, SCHWARTZ & ROGERS, L.L.C.
St. Louis, MO..........................Criminal Trial Practice

ROSENBLUM, WOLF & LLOYD, A PROFESSIONAL CORPORATION
Teaneck, NJ.............................Real Estate Law; Tax Law

ROSENFELD, WOLFF, ARONSON, KURLAND & KLEIN, A PROFESSIONAL CORPORATION
Los Angeles, CA......................Business Law; Real Estate Law; Securities Law

ROSENN, JENKINS & GREENWALD, L.L.P.
Wilkes-Barre, PA ....Bankruptcy Law; General Practice; Labor and Employment Law; Real Estate Law; Tax Law; Trust and Estates, Wills and Probate

ROSENTHAL, MARTIN R.
Boston, MA.............................Civil Trial Practice; Criminal Trial Practice

ROSENTHAL & CURRY
East Meadow, NY ....General Practice

ROSENTHAL & OSHA, L.L.P.
Houston, TX ....Intellectual Property Law; Patent, Trademark, Copyright and Unfair Competition

ROSENTHAL AND SCHANFIELD, PROFESSIONAL CORPORATION
Chicago, IL.............................Civil Trial Practice; General Practice

ROSENTHAL, SIEGEL, MUENKEL & MALONEY, LLP
Amherst, NY...........................Personal Injury
Buffalo, NY ....Medical Malpractice; Personal Injury

ROSENTHAL AND WEISBERG, P.C.
Philadelphia, PA ....Criminal Trial Practice; Health Care Law; Medical Malpractice; Personal Injury; Product Liability Law

ROSENZWEIG, JEFF
Little Rock, AR.......................Criminal Trial Practice

ROSENZWEIG, JONES & MACNABB, P.C.
Newnan, GA ....Bankruptcy Law; Civil Trial Practice; Commercial Law; Family Law; General Practice; Personal Injury; Real Estate Law; Trust and Estates, Wills and Probate

ROSEPINK & ESTES, P.L.L.C.
Scottsdale, AZ.........................Tax Law; Trust and Estates, Wills and Probate

ROSHKA HEYMAN & DEWULF, PLC
Phoenix, AZ ....Commercial Litigation; Communications Law; Public Utilities Law; Securities Law

ROSS, HARRIET
San Francisco, CA ....Criminal Trial Practice

ROSS, RICHARD M.
Sacramento, CA ....Administrative Law; Environmental Law

ROSS & ASSOCIATES
Miami, FL ....Insurance Defense

ROSS, BRITTAIN & SCHONBERG CO., L.P.A.
Cleveland, OH.........................Labor and Employment Law

ROSS & COHEN, LLP
New York, NY.........................Construction Law; Real Estate Law

ROSS, DIXON & BELL, L.L.P.
Irvine, CA...............................Civil Trial Practice
San Diego, CA ....Civil Trial Practice
Washington, DC......................Civil Trial Practice

ROSS & FERM, LLC
Ellsworth, ME.........................Personal Injury; Real Estate Law

ROSS & HARDIES
Chicago, IL.............................General Practice
New York, NY.........................General Practice

ROSS, JAMES A., JR. LAW OFFICE
Monticello, AR ....General Practice

ROSSBACHER & ASSOCIATES
Los Angeles, CA ....Commercial Litigation; Constitutional Law

ROSSI, MURNANE & HUGHES
Utica, NY...............................General Practice; Insurance Defense

ROSSIE, LUCKETT, PARKER & RIDDER, P.C.
Memphis, TN ....General Practice; Insurance Defense; Real Estate Law; Trust and Estates, Wills and Probate

ROSSMAN, BAUMBERGER & REBOSO, A PROFESSIONAL ASSOCIATION
Miami, FL...............................Civil Trial Practice

ROST & GEIGER
Wailuku, HI ....Personal Injury

ROTH, STEPHEN H.
Hackensack, NJ.......................Administrative Law; Appellate Practice; Civil Trial Practice; Commercial Law; Family Law; Real Estate Law

ROTH AND DUNCAN, P.A.
West Palm Beach, FL ....Criminal Trial Practice

ROTH FOLEY BRYANT & COOPER, PLLC
Louisville, KY ....Banking Law; Bankruptcy Law; Civil Trial Practice; Creditors Rights; Family Law; General Practice; Personal Injury; Real Estate Law; Securities Law; Tax Law; Trust and Estates, Wills and Probate

ROTHBERG & LOGAN
Fort Wayne, IN.......................Banking Law; Commercial Litigation; Family Law; General Practice

ROTHENBERG, ALLEN L., LAW FIRM OF
Philadelphia, PA ....Personal Injury

ROTHENBERG SILVERMAN & FURMAN, P.C.
Elkins Park, PA ....Labor and Employment Law

ROTHFELDER LAW OFFICES, THE
Westfield, NJ ....Communications Law; Energy Law; Public Utilities Law

ROTHSCHILD, BARRY & MYERS
Chicago, IL.............................Antitrust Law; Aviation Law; General Practice

ROTHSCHILD, MORGAN & BROWN
Columbus, GA.........................General Practice; Health Care Law; Insurance Defense; Tax Law

ROTHSCHILD, WISHEK & SANDS
Sacramento, CA......................Administrative Law; Criminal Trial Practice

ROTHSTEIN, DONATELLI, HUGHES, DAHLSTROM & SCHOENBURG, LLP
Santa Fe, NM...........................Civil Trial Practice; Criminal Trial Practice

ROTHWELL, FIGG, ERNST & KURZ, A PROFESSIONAL CORPORATION
Washington, DC.......................Intellectual Property Law

ROUDA, FEDER & TIETJEN
San Francisco, CA...................Personal Injury

ROUNTREE & SEAGLE, L.L.P.
Wilmington, NC.......................Admiralty/Maritime Law; Civil Trial Practice

ROUTMAN, MOORE, GOLDSTONE & VALENTINO
New Castle, PA........................General Practice
Sharon, PA..............................General Practice

ROVNER, GERALD C.
Boston, MA..............................Immigration and Naturalization

ROWE, GORDON H. JR.
South Fork, CO........................General Practice

ROWE, FOLTZ & MARTIN, P.C.
Atlanta, GA.............................Real Estate Law

ROWE LAW FIRM, THE, P.C.
Albuquerque, NM.....................General Practice

ROWE & ROWE
South Bend, IN........................Civil Trial Practice; General Practice; Insurance Defense; Medical Malpractice; Personal Injury; Product Liability Law

ROWLEY LAW FIRM, P.C.
Clovis, NM...............................Banking Law; General Practice

ROY, FORREST & LOPRESTO, LTD.
New Iberia, LA.........................Insurance Defense

ROY SHECTER & VOCHT
Bloomfield Hills, MI................Antitrust Law; Business Law

ROYALS, THOMAS E.
Jackson, MS.............................Civil Trial Practice; Criminal Trial Practice; General Practice

ROYCE, THOMAS L. JR.
Houston, TX.............................Criminal Trial Practice

ROYLANCE, ABRAMS, BERDO & GOODMAN, L.L.P.
Washington, DC.......................Antitrust Law; Patent, Trademark, Copyright and Unfair Competition

ROYSTON, MUELLER, MCLEAN & REID, LLP
Towson, MD.............................General Practice

ROYSTON, RAYZOR, VICKERY & WILLIAMS, L.L.P.
Brownsville, TX.......................General Practice
Corpus Christi, TX..................General Practice
Galveston, TX..........................General Practice
Houston, TX.............................Admiralty/Maritime Law; General Practice

ROZELLE AND CALL
West Palm Beach, FL...............Civil Trial Practice; Insurance Defense

RUBENSTEIN, SUSAN LAW OFFICES OF
San Francisco, CA...................Labor and Employment Law

RUBERTI, GIRVIN & FERLAZZO, P.C.
Albany, NY...............................Education Law; General Practice; Labor and Employment Law; Personal Injury

RUBIN, MILES J. LAW OFFICES OF
Los Angeles, CA......................Family Law

RUBIN & DORNBAUM
Newark, NJ...............................Immigration and Naturalization

RUBIN & HAYS
Louisville, KY.........................Municipal Bond/Public Authority Financing

RUBINBAUM LLP
New York, NY..........................General Practice

RUBNER & KUTNER, P.C.
Denver, CO..............................Bankruptcy Law

RUCCI, BURNHAM, CARTA & EDELBERG, LLP
Darien, CT...............................Banking Law; Bankruptcy Law; Business Law; Civil Trial Practice; Real Estate Law; Trust and Estates, Wills and Probate

RUDDY, BRADLEY, KOLKHORST & REGES, A PROFESSIONAL CORPORATION
Juneau, AK...............................Civil Trial Practice; Environmental Law; Natural Resources Law

RUDEN, MCCLOSKY, SMITH, SCHUSTER & RUSSELL, P.A.
Fort Lauderdale, FL.................General Practice

RUDLOFF & RUDLOFF
Bowling Green, KY..................Civil Trial Practice; Insurance Defense; Personal Injury

RUDMAN & WINCHELL, LLC
Bangor, ME..............................Business Law; Insurance Defense; Labor and Employment Law; Trust and Estates, Wills and Probate

RUDOLF & MAHER, P.A.
Chapel Hill, NC.......................Civil Trial Practice; Criminal Trial Practice

RUDOLPH, DORIAN, GOLDSTEIN, ROCHESTIE, WISNIEWSKI & TAYLOR, P.C.
Bensalem, PA...........................Commercial Litigation; Medical Malpractice; Personal Injury; Product Liability Law; Real Estate Law; Toxic Torts

RUDOLPH, FINE, PORTER & JOHNSON LLP
Evansville, IN..........................Business Law; Commercial Law; Health Care Law; Insurance Defense; Labor and Employment Law; Trust and Estates, Wills and Probate; Workers Compensation

RUFFIN, JOSEPH LUIS, P.C.
Oklahoma City, OK..................Criminal Trial Practice

RUMRELL, WAGNER & COSTABEL, LLP
Jacksonville, FL.......................Civil Trial Practice

RUNFOLA, JOHN M.
San Francisco, CA...................Criminal Trial Practice

RUNNING, WISE, FORD AND PHILLIPS, P.L.C.
Traverse City, MI.....................Corporate Law; Insurance Defense

RUNYON AND RUNYON, PLLC
Clarksville, TN........................Family Law; Personal Injury; Trust and Estates, Wills and Probate

RUS, MILIBAND & SMITH
Irvine, CA................................Bankruptcy Law; Civil Trial Practice; Commercial Litigation

RUSH MOORE CRAVEN SUTTON MORRY & BEH
Honolulu, HI............................General Practice

RUSHFORD & BONOTTO, LLP
Sacramento, CA......................Civil Trial Practice; Insurance Defense

RUSHING & GUICE
Biloxi, MS...............................Admiralty/Maritime Law; Banking Law; Business Law; Civil Trial Practice; Commercial Litigation; Product Liability Law

RUSIN PATTON MACIOROWSKI & FRIEDMAN, LTD.
Chicago, IL..............................Civil Trial Practice; Insurance Defense; Transportation Law; Workers Compensation

RUSS, AUGUST & KABAT, A PROFESSIONAL CORPORATION
Los Angeles, CA......................Trademark, Copyright and Unfair Competition

RUSSELL & BATCHELOR
Grand Rapids, MI....................Real Estate Law; Tax Law

RUSSELL, BROWN, BICKEL & BRECKENRIDGE
Nevada, MO.............................General Practice

RUSSELL LAW OFFICES, P.A.
Orlando, FL..............................Business Law; Civil Trial Practice; Commercial Litigation; Construction Law; Real Estate Law

RUSSELL, MCINTYRE, HILLIGOSS & WELKE
Kokomo, IN.............................Medical Malpractice; Personal Injury

RUSSELL & MIRKOVICH
Long Beach, CA.......................Admiralty/Maritime Law; Civil Trial Practice; Commercial Law; International Business Law; Personal Injury; Transportation Law

RUSSELL, RICHARD A., A PROFESSIONAL CORPORATION
Ocean City, NJ.........................Family Law

RUSSELL, TURNER, LAIRD & JONES, L.L.P.
Fort Worth, TX........................Civil Trial Practice; Commercial Law; Medical Malpractice; Personal Injury; Product Liability Law

RUSSO APPELLATE FIRM, P.A.
Miami, FL ..... Appellate Practice

RUSSO & HEFFERNAN, P.A.
Miami, FL ..... Civil Trial Practice; Medical Malpractice; Toxic Torts

RUST, ARMENIS, SCHWARTZ, LAMB & BILLS, A PROFESSIONAL CORPORATION
Sacramento, CA ..... Insurance Defense; Medical Malpractice
San Francisco, CA ..... Insurance Defense

RUTAN & TUCKER, LLP
Costa Mesa, CA ..... Antitrust Law; Appellate Practice; Bankruptcy Law; Business Law; Civil Rights; Civil Trial Practice; Commercial Law; Communications Law; Computer Law; Construction Law; Employment Benefits Law; Environmental Law; General Practice; Labor and Employment Law; Land Use Law; Municipal and Zoning Law; Municipal Bond/Public Authority Financing; Real Estate Law; Securities Law; Tax Law; Trademark, Copyright and Unfair Competition; Trust and Estates, Wills and Probate

RUTH & MACNEILLE, PROFESSIONAL ASSOCIATION
Hilton Head Island, SC ..... Civil Trial Practice; Corporate Law; Elder Law; Tax Law; Trust and Estates, Wills and Probate

RUTHRAUFF & ARMBRUST, P.C.
Philadelphia, PA ..... Personal Injury; Product Liability Law; Professional Liability

RUTKIN AND OLDHAM, L.L.C
Westport, CT ..... Family Law; Personal Injury

RUTLEDGE, MANION, RABAUT, TERRY & THOMAS, P.C.
Detroit, MI ..... Insurance Defense

RUTTER, ROBERT P.
Cleveland, OH ..... Personal Injury

RYAN, BROWN, MCDONNELL, BERGER GIBBONS & LAROCCA, LLP
Philadelphia, PA ..... Civil Trial Practice; Insurance Defense; Personal Injury

RYAN AND GANNON
Florham Park, NJ ..... Appellate Practice; Civil Trial Practice; Insurance Defense

RYAN, JAMIESON, MORRIS & RYAN
Kalamazoo, MI ..... Insurance Defense

RYAN KROMHOLZ & MANION, S.C.
Brookfield, WI ..... Intellectual Property Law; Patent, Trademark, Copyright and Unfair Competition

RYAN MARKS JOHNSON TODD & BRODER
Las Vegas, NV ..... Civil Trial Practice; Construction Law; Insurance Defense

RYAN & RYAN
Aitkin, MN ..... General Practice

RYAN, RYAN, JOHNSON & DELUCA, LLP
Stamford, CT ..... Civil Trial Practice; General Practice

RYAN SMITH & CARBINE, LTD.
Rutland, VT ..... General Practice

RYMER, WM. W.
Providence, RI ..... Intellectual Property Law; Patent, Trademark, Copyright and Unfair Competition

RYWANT, ALVAREZ, JONES, RUSSO & GUYTON, PROFESSIONAL ASSOCIATION
Tampa, FL ..... Civil Trial Practice; Insurance Defense; Medical Malpractice; Product Liability Law

SAALFIELD, COULSON, SHAD & JAY, P.A.
Jacksonville, FL ..... Civil Trial Practice; Insurance Defense; Medical Malpractice; Product Liability Law

SABRA & ASPDEN, PROFESSIONAL ASSOCIATION
Somerset, MA ..... Criminal Trial Practice; Personal Injury; Workers Compensation

SACCA AND SACCA
Lockport, NY ..... Corporate Law; General Practice; Trust and Estates, Wills and Probate

SACHER ZELMAN PAUL BEILEY & VAN SANT, P.A.
Miami, FL ..... Securities Law

SACHNOFF & WEAVER, LTD.
Chicago, IL ..... General Practice

SACHS, LESTER G. LAW OFFICES
San Jose, CA ..... Construction Law

SACHS, MAITLIN, FLEMING, GREENE, WILSON & MAROTTE
West Orange, NJ ..... Appellate Practice; Environmental Law; Insurance Defense; Medical Malpractice; Product Liability Law

SACHS & WERDINE, P.A.
Tampa, FL ..... Eminent Domain

SACKS MONTGOMERY, P.C.
New York, NY ..... Civil Trial Practice; Commercial Litigation; Construction Law; General Practice; Government Contracts

SACKS & SACKS, A PROFESSIONAL CORPORATION
Norfolk, VA ..... Appellate Practice; Civil Trial Practice; Criminal Trial Practice; General Practice; Personal Injury; Product Liability Law

SACKS TIERNEY P.A.
Scottsdale, AZ ..... Commercial Law; Commercial Litigation; General Practice; Health Care Law; Real Estate Law

SACOPULOS, JOHNSON, CARTER & SACOPULOS
Terre Haute, IN ..... Insurance Defense

SADOW, STEVEN H., P.C.
Atlanta, GA ..... Criminal Trial Practice

SAEGERT, ANGENEND & AUGUSTINE, P.C.
Austin, TX ..... Business Law; Civil Trial Practice; Real Estate Law

SAGASER, FRANSON & JONES, A PROFESSIONAL CORPORATION
Fresno, CA ..... Civil Trial Practice; Commercial Litigation; Environmental Law; Labor and Employment Law

SAIKLEY, GARRISON & COLOMBO, LTD.
Danville, IL ..... Commercial Law

ST. JOHN, HOWARD C. AND ASSOCIATES
Kingston, NY ..... General Practice; Real Estate Law; Trust and Estates, Wills and Probate

ST. JOHN & ST. JOHN, L.L.C.
Cullman, AL ..... Civil Trial Practice; Insurance Defense; Labor and Employment Law; Workers Compensation

ST. JOHN & WAYNE, L.L.C.
Newark, NJ ..... Banking Law; Bankruptcy Law; Civil Trial Practice; Commercial Law; Environmental Law; General Practice; Insurance Defense; Labor and Employment Law; Municipal Bond/Public Authority Financing; Tax Law

ST. MARTIN & WILLIAMS, A PROFESSIONAL LAW CORPORATION
Houma, LA ..... Personal Injury

ST. ONGE STEWARD JOHNSTON & REENS, LLC
Stamford, CT ..... Patent, Trademark, Copyright and Unfair Competition

SALADINO LAW FIRM
Paducah, KY ..... Admiralty/Maritime Law; Personal Injury; Product Liability Law

SALEH, JOHN
Lamesa, TX ..... Civil Trial Practice

SALESE & MCCARTHY, P.C.
Tucson, AZ ..... Family Law

SALES, RONALD, P.A.
West Palm Beach, FL ..... Family Law

SALITERMAN & SIEFFERMAN, P.C.
Minneapolis, MN ..... General Practice; Securities Law

SALLEY & ASSOCIATES
Metairie, LA ..... Admiralty/Maritime Law

SALLY & FITCH
Boston, MA ..... Civil Trial Practice

SALMON, LAMPERT & CLOR, PROFESSIONAL CORPORATION
Englewood, CO ..... Medical Malpractice; Personal Injury; Product Liability Law

SALSBERY & DRUCKMAN
Charleston, WV ..... Civil Trial Practice; Commercial Litigation; Criminal Trial Practice; Medical Malpractice; Personal Injury; Product Liability Law

SALTER, JAMES W., III, P.A.
Rockville, MD ..... Civil Trial Practice

SALTER, THEODORE, JR., & ASSOCIATES, P.C.
Atlanta, GA ..... Workers Compensation

SALTMAN & STEVENS, P.C.
Washington, DC ..... Business Law; Commercial Law

SALTMARSH, SARA E. LAW OFFICES OF
Austin, TX ....Family Law

SALVI & SCHOSTOK, P.C.
Waukegan, IL..........................Aviation Law; Commercial Litigation; Medical Malpractice; Personal Injury; Product Liability Law

SALVO, ALICE A.
Los Angeles, CA ....Trust and Estates, Wills and Probate

SAMEL, JEFFREY, & PARTNERS
New York, NY.........................Civil Trial Practice; General Practice; Insurance Defense; Personal Injury; Product Liability Law

SAMET, DEE-DEE, P.C.
Tucson, AZ ....Personal Injury; Workers Compensation

SAMMONS & PARKER, A PROFESSIONAL CORPORATION
Tyler, TX................................Civil Trial Practice; Insurance Defense; Real Estate Law

SAMPSON, WILLIAM A. II & ASSOCIATES
Pacific Palisades, CA ....Civil Trial Practice; Personal Injury

SAMS & LISTER, P.A.
Miami, FL ....Appellate Practice; Civil Trial Practice; General Practice; Medical Malpractice; Personal Injury; Product Liability Law

SAMUEL, RALPH D. & CO., A PROFESSIONAL CORPORATION
Philadelphia, PA ....Arbitration; Civil Trial Practice; Commercial Litigation; Constitutional Law; Medical Malpractice; Personal Injury; Product Liability Law; Workers Compensation

SAMUELS, HARVEY M.
Columbus, OH ....Family Law

SAMUELSON RIEGER & YOVINO, LLP
Garden City, NY ....Family Law

SANDALS, LANGER & TAYLOR, LLP
Philadelphia, PA ....Antitrust Law; Commercial Litigation; Employment Benefits Law

SANDENAW, CARRILLO & PIAZZA, P.C.
Las Cruces, NM......................Civil Trial Practice; Insurance Defense; Medical Malpractice

SANDERS, AUSTIN, SWOPE & FLANIGAN
Princeton, WV.........................Civil Trial Practice; Personal Injury; Product Liability Law; Workers Compensation

SANDERS, HAUGEN & SEARS, P.C.
Newnan, GA ....General Practice

SANDERS, ROBERT E., AND ASSOCIATES, P.S.C.
Covington, KY.........................Appellate Practice; Business Law; Civil Trial Practice; Criminal Trial Practice; Environmental Law; Medical Malpractice; Personal Injury; Product Liability Law

SANDLER, TRAVIS & ROSENBERG, P.A.
Miami, FL ....International Trade Law

SANDS, KENTON V. LAW OFFICE OF
Orlando, FL ....Appellate Practice; Criminal Trial Practice

SANDS & MOSKOWITZ, P.A.
Miami, FL ....Criminal Trial Practice

SANFORD HOLSHOUSER LAW FIRM PLLC, THE
Raleigh, NC............................Banking Law

SANGER & SWYSEN
Santa Barbara, CA ....Criminal Trial Practice

SANGERMAN, JAY J. & ASSOCIATES
New York, NY.........................Elder Law; Trust and Estates, Wills and Probate

SANSONE, CHARLES F.
Tampa, FL ....Civil Trial Practice; Personal Injury; Product Liability Law

SANTOS, DUTTON, LYNOTT & HENRY, P.A.
Tampa, FL ....Insurance Defense; Product Liability Law

SANTWIER, RICKARD
Pasadena, CA ....Criminal Trial Practice

SAPORITO & SLEDGE, L.L.C.
New Orleans, LA ....Insurance Defense; Product Liability Law

SAPP, SAPP & WHITE, P.C.
Austin, TX ....Administrative Law; Commercial Litigation

SARNOFF & BAYER
Miami, FL ....Admiralty/Maritime Law

SARRAIL, LYNCH & HALL
San Francisco, CA ....Insurance Defense; Product Liability Law

SARROUF, TARRICONE & FLEMMING
Boston, MA ....Aviation Law; Civil Trial Practice; Personal Injury

SASSER, CESTERO & SASSER, P.A.
West Palm Beach, FL ....Family Law; General Practice

SATHER, BYERLY & HOLLOWAY, LLP
Portland, OR ....Administrative Law; Civil Trial Practice; Insurance Defense; Labor and Employment Law; Professional Liability; Workers Compensation

SATTERFIELD, BONNIE S., P.A.
Coral Springs, FL ....Appellate Practice; Civil Trial Practice
Fort Lauderdale, FL ....Appellate Practice; Civil Trial Practice

SATZ & KIRSHON, P.C.
Poughkeepsie, NY ....Appellate Practice; Civil Trial Practice; Family Law

SAUCEDO & CORSIGLIA, A LAW CORPORATION
San Jose, CA ....Civil Trial Practice; Medical Malpractice; Personal Injury

SAUER & WAGNER LLP
Los Angeles, CA ....Civil Trial Practice

SAUL, EWING, REMICK & SAUL LLP
New York, NY.........................General Practice
Berwyn, PA ....General Practice
Philadelphia, PA ....General Practice

SAUNDERS & MONROE
Chicago, IL.............................Antitrust Law; Civil Trial Practice; Communications Law; Public Utilities Law; Securities Law

SAUNDERS & SCHMIELER
Silver Spring, MD ....Construction Law; Environmental Law; General Practice; Insurance Defense; Intellectual Property Law; Product Liability Law; Professional Liability; Toxic Torts

SAURBIER, SIEGAN & SANFIELD, P.C.
St. Clair Shores, MI ....Civil Trial Practice; Health Care Law; Insurance Defense; Medical Malpractice; Personal Injury; Product Liability Law; Transportation Law

SAVAGE, GARMER & ELLIOTT, P.S.C.
Lexington, KY ....Civil Trial Practice; Medical Malpractice; Personal Injury; Product Liability Law

SAVAGE, HERNDON & TURNER, P.C.
Savannah, GA ....Civil Trial Practice

SAVAGE, ROYALL AND SHEHEEN, L.L.P.
Camden, SC............................Civil Trial Practice; General Practice

SAVAGE & SAVAGE, P.A.
Charleston, SC ....Criminal Trial Practice; Personal Injury

SAVETT FRUTKIN PODELL & RYAN, P.C.
Philadelphia, PA ....Antitrust Law; Civil Trial Practice; Commercial Litigation; Securities Law

SAWAYA, ROSE, ROBERTS & SAWAYA, P.C.
Denver, CO ....Personal Injury

SAWYER, J. E. JR.
Enterprise, AL.........................Civil Trial Practice; General Practice

SAWYER, DAVIS, HALPERN & DEMETRI
Garden City, NY ....Civil Trial Practice; Medical Malpractice; Personal Injury

SAXON, JOHN D., P.C.
Birmingham, AL ....Civil Trial Practice; Labor and Employment Law

SAYAD & BIREN, A PROFESSIONAL CORPORATION
San Francisco, CA ....Labor and Employment Law

SAYLES & EVANS
Elmira, NY.............................Civil Trial Practice; Corporate Law

SAYLES & LIDJI, A PROFESSIONAL CORPORATION
Dallas, TX..............................Corporate Law

SAYLOR LAW FIRM, THE, LLP
Atlanta, GA ....Business Law; Tax Law; Trust and Estates, Wills and Probate

SAYRE LAW OFFICES
Seattle, WA ....General Practice

SAYRE & SAYRE, P.S.
Spokane, WA..........................Elder Law

SCADDEN, HAMILTON & RYAN
San Francisco, CA ....Appellate Practice; Civil Trial Practice; Environmental Law; Insurance Defense; Product Liability Law; Professional Liability

SCALIA, JOSEPH W. LAW OFFICES OF
Gold River, CA........................Business Law; Real Estate Law; Sports and Entertainment Law

SCALIA, JOSEPH W., LAW OFFICES OF
Sacramento, CA........................Business Law; Real Estate Law; Sports and Entertainment Law

SCALLEY & READING, A PROFESSIONAL CORPORATION
Salt Lake City, UT..................Environmental Law; Insurance Defense; Real Estate Law

SCANLAN, EDMUND J., LTD., LAW OFFICES OF
Chicago, IL..............................Civil Trial Practice; Medical Malpractice; Personal Injury

SCANLAN, ROSEN & SHAR, LLC
Baltimore, MD..........................Aviation Law; Civil Trial Practice; Commercial Litigation; Medical Malpractice; Personal Injury; Product Liability Law; Professional Liability

SCANLON & GEARINGER CO., L.P.A.
Akron, OH.................................Medical Malpractice; Personal Injury; Product Liability Law

SCANLON, HOWLEY, SCANLON & DOHERTY
Scranton, PA............................Civil Trial Practice; General Practice; Insurance Defense; Medical Malpractice; Personal Injury; Product Liability Law; Workers Compensation

SCARIANO, ELLCH, HIMES, SRAGA AND PETRARCA, CHARTERED
Chicago, IL..............................Civil Trial Practice; Employment Benefits Law; Insurance Defense; Labor and Employment Law; Municipal and Zoning Law; Municipal Bond/Public Authority Financing

SCARPELLO & ALLING, LTD. A PROFESSIONAL CORPORATION
Carson City, NV.......................General Practice
Stateline, NV...........................General Practice

SCARZAFAVA LAW OFFICE, THE
Oneonta, NY.............................Personal Injury; Product Liability Law

SCATES, J. C. TIM
Denver, CO...............................Business Law

SCHAAF & HODGES
Marietta, GA.............................Real Estate Law

SCHACHTER, KRISTOFF, ORENSTEIN & BERKOWITZ, L.L.P.
Menlo Park, CA........................Labor and Employment Law
Sacramento, CA........................Labor and Employment Law
San Francisco, CA....................Labor and Employment Law

SCHACHTER, TROMBADORE, OFFEN, STANTON & PAVICS, A PROFESSIONAL CORPORATION
Somerville, NJ..........................Appellate Practice; Bankruptcy Law; Business Law; Civil Trial Practice; Commercial Law; Commercial Litigation; Corporate Law; Criminal Trial Practice; Family Law; Land Use Law; Municipal and Zoning Law; Personal Injury; Real Estate Law; Trust and Estates, Wills and Probate

SCHADEN, KATZMAN, LAMPERT & MCCLUNE
Broomfield, CO........................Aviation Law; Civil Trial Practice; Personal Injury; Product Liability Law
Troy, MI...................................Aviation Law; Civil Trial Practice; Personal Injury; Product Liability Law

SCHAFER, GERALD S.
Greensboro, NC.......................Bankruptcy Law

SCHAFFNER & VAN DER SNICK, P.C.
Geneva, IL...............................Criminal Trial Practice; Family Law

SCHANEVILLE & BARINGER, L.L.C.
Baton Rouge, LA......................Bankruptcy Law; Tax Law

SCHANTZ, STEWART T.
Poughkeepsie, NY....................Family Law

SCHAPER, CARLOS E. LAW OFFICE
Broken Bow, NE.......................General Practice; Real Estate Law; Trust and Estates, Wills and Probate

SCHECHNER, STEPHEN H. LAW OFFICES OF
Millburn, NJ.............................Insurance Defense; Medical Malpractice; Professional Liability

SCHECHTER LAW FIRM, THE, P.C.
St. Louis, MO...........................Family Law

SCHEEHLE LAW FIRM, P.L.C.
Fountain Hills, AZ...................Tax Law

SCHEFFLER, WILLIAM L. & ASSOCIATES
Westport, CT............................Business Law; Municipal and Zoning Law; Real Estate Law

SCHELL BRAY AYCOCK ABEL & LIVINGSTON P.L.L.C.
Greensboro, NC.......................Business Law; Mergers and Acquisitions; Real Estate Law; Securities Law; Trust and Estates, Wills and Probate

SCHELLINGER & DOYLE, S.C.
Milwaukee, WI.........................Insurance Defense

SCHENCK, PRICE, SMITH & KING, LLP
Morristown, NJ.........................Civil Trial Practice; General Practice

SCHENK, BONCHER AND PRASHER, P.C.
Grand Rapids, MI.....................Commercial Litigation; Environmental Law

SCHERNER, HANSON & CORNWELL, LLC
Columbus, OH..........................Civil Trial Practice; Medical Malpractice; Personal Injury; Product Liability Law

SCHEUER, YOST & PATTERSON, A PROFESSIONAL CORPORATION
Santa Fe, NM...........................Banking Law; Civil Trial Practice; Environmental Law; General Practice; Labor and Employment Law; Real Estate Law; Trust and Estates, Wills and Probate

SCHIER, DENEWETH & PARFITT, P.C.
Troy, MI...................................Commercial Litigation; Construction Law

SCHIFF HARDIN & WAITE
Washington, DC.......................General Practice
Chicago, IL..............................General Practice

SCHIFF & HULBERT
Chicago, IL..............................Labor and Employment Law; Workers Compensation

SCHIFFRIN OLSON SCHLEMLEIN & HOPKINS, P.L.L.C.
Seattle, WA.............................Commercial Law; Construction Law

SCHILD, PETER
Boulder, CO.............................Criminal Trial Practice

SCHILLER, MARVIN
Raleigh, NC.............................Appellate Practice; Environmental Law; Labor and Employment Law; Securities Law

SCHILLER & ASSOCIATES, P.C.
New York, NY..........................Computer Law; Real Estate Law

SCHILLER, DU CANTO AND FLECK
Chicago, IL..............................Family Law
Lake Forest, IL........................Family Law

SCHINDLER AND OLSON
Mishawaka, IN.........................Personal Injury; Real Estate Law; Trust and Estates, Wills and Probate

SCHLANGER, MILLS, MAYER & SILVER, L.L.P.
Houston, TX.............................Real Estate Law

SCHLAPPRIZZI, DONALD L., P.C.
St. Louis, MO...........................Personal Injury

SCHLECHT, SHEVLIN & SHOENBERGER, A LAW CORPORATION
Palm Springs, CA.....................Business Law; Civil Trial Practice; Family Law; General Practice; Real Estate Law; Trust and Estates, Wills and Probate

SCHLICHTER, BOGARD & DENTON
St. Louis, MO...........................Personal Injury

SCHLOTHAUER & COLLINS
Los Angeles, CA......................Aviation Law; Medical Malpractice; Product Liability Law

SCHLUETER & ASSOCIATES, P.C.
Denver, CO..............................Business Law; International Business Law; Mergers and Acquisitions; Securities Law

SCHLUSSER & REIVER, P.A.
Wilmington, DE........................Tax Law; Trust and Estates, Wills and Probate

SCHMELTZER, APTAKER & SHEPARD, P.C.
Washington, DC.......................Admiralty/Maritime Law; Business Law; Civil Trial Practice; Employment Benefits Law; Health Care Law; Labor and Employment Law

SCHMIDT FIRM, THE
Dallas, TX...............................Civil Trial Practice; Medical Malpractice; Personal Injury

SCHMIDT, L. WILLIAM, JR., P.C.
Denver, CO..............................Trust and Estates, Wills and Probate

SCHMIDT, RONCA AND KRAMER, P.C.
Harrisburg, PA........................Personal Injury

SCHMIDT, SCHROYER & MORENO, P.C.
Pierre, SD...............................General Practice

SCHMITTINGER & RODRIGUEZ, PROFESSIONAL ASSOCIATION
Dover, DE....................General Practice

SCHMUKLER, MARTIN L., P.C.
New York, NY....................Criminal Trial Practice

SCHNADER HARRISON SEGAL & LEWIS LLP
Philadelphia, PA....................General Practice

SCHNAPP, ROGER H., A PROFESSIONAL CORPORATION
Newport Beach, CA....................Labor and Employment Law

SCHNEIDER, IRWIN, & ASSOCIATES, P.C.
Scranton, PA....................General Practice

SCHNEIDER, KLEINICK, WEITZ, DAMASHEK & SHOOT
New York, NY....................Civil Trial Practice; Insurance Defense; Medical Malpractice; Personal Injury; Product Liability Law

SCHNEIDER LAW FIRM
Willmar, MN....................Civil Trial Practice; Personal Injury; Product Liability Law

SCHNEIDER & MCWILLIAMS, P.C.
George West, TX....................General Practice; Natural Resources Law

SCHNEIDER, REILLY, ZABIN & COSTELLO, P.C.
Boston, MA....................Civil Trial Practice

SCHNEIDLER, JON G.
Seattle, WA....................Business Law; Real Estate Law

SCHNORF & SCHNORF CO., L.P.A., A PROFESSIONAL CORPORATION
Toledo, OH....................Civil Trial Practice; Corporate Law; General Practice; Insurance Defense; Labor and Employment Law; Personal Injury; Trust and Estates, Wills and Probate

SCHOCH & WOODRUFF, L.L.P.
Greensboro, NC....................Family Law; Tax Law
High Point, NC....................Family Law; Personal Injury; Tax Law

SCHOCHOR, FEDERICO AND STATON, P.A.
Baltimore, MD....................Civil Trial Practice; Medical Malpractice; Personal Injury; Product Liability Law

SCHOELLERMAN, JACK L.
Irvine, CA....................Business Law

SCHOEL, OGLE, LILES AND UPSHAW, LLP
Birmingham, AL....................Antitrust Law; Bankruptcy Law; Civil Trial Practice; Construction Law; General Practice

SCHOENBAUM, CURPHY & SCANLAN, P.C.
San Antonio, TX....................Business Law; Employment Benefits Law; Real Estate Law; Tax Law; Trust and Estates, Wills and Probate

SCHOFIELD & ASSOCIATES
Las Vegas, NV....................Construction Law; Eminent Domain

SCHOLZ, LOOS, PALMER, SIEBERS & DUESTERHAUS
Quincy, IL....................General Practice

SCHOONMAKER, GEORGE & COLIN, P.C.
Greenwich, CT....................Family Law

SCHOTTENSTEIN, ZOX & DUNN, A LEGAL PROFESSIONAL ASSOCIATION
Columbus, OH....................Banking Law; Bankruptcy Law; Business Law; Construction Law; Employment Benefits Law; Environmental Law; General Practice; Health Care Law; Intellectual Property Law; Labor and Employment Law; Real Estate Law; Tax Law; Trust and Estates, Wills and Probate

SCHRADER BYRD & COMPANION, PLLC
Wheeling, WV....................Banking Law; Bankruptcy Law; Civil Trial Practice; Commercial Litigation; Criminal Trial Practice; Employment Benefits Law; Family Law; General Practice; Insurance Defense; Labor and Employment Law; Medical Malpractice; Personal Injury; Real Estate Law; Tax Law

SCHRAGGER, LAVINE & NAGY
Trenton, NJ....................Business Law; Civil Trial Practice; Criminal Trial Practice; General Practice; Health Care Law; Insurance Defense; Land Use Law; Municipal and Zoning Law; Real Estate Law; Trust and Estates, Wills and Probate

SCHRAMM & PINES, L.L.C.
St. Louis, MO....................Business Law; Civil Trial Practice; Commercial Litigation; Family Law; International Business Law; Trust and Estates, Wills and Probate

SCHRECK MORRIS
Las Vegas, NV....................Appellate Practice; Bankruptcy Law; Civil Trial Practice; Commercial Law; Labor and Employment Law; Product Liability Law; Real Estate Law

SCHROEDER & LARCHE, P.A.
Boca Raton, FL....................Real Estate Law; Trust and Estates, Wills and Probate

SCHROETER, GOLDMARK & BENDER, P.S.
Seattle, WA....................Criminal Trial Practice; Employment Benefits Law; Medical Malpractice; Personal Injury; Product Liability Law

SCHROPP, BUELL & ELLIGETT, PROFESSIONAL ASSOCIATION
Tampa, FL....................Appellate Practice; Civil Trial Practice

SCHUBERT, BELLWOAR, CAHILL & QUINN, A PROFESSIONAL CORPORATION
Philadelphia, PA....................Corporate Law; Employment Benefits Law; Health Care Law; Public Utilities Law; Trust and Estates, Wills and Probate

SCHUERING ZIMMERMAN & SCULLY, LLP
Sacramento, CA....................Civil Trial Practice; Insurance Defense; Medical Malpractice; Product Liability Law

SCHULER & HALVORSON, P.A.
West Palm Beach, FL....................Medical Malpractice; Personal Injury

SCHULMAN, LEROY AND BENNETT, P.C.
Nashville, TN....................General Practice

SCHULMAN & MCMILLAN, INCORPORATED
Costa Mesa, CA....................Criminal Trial Practice

SCHULTE ROTH & ZABEL LLP
New York, NY....................Civil Trial Practice; Criminal Trial Practice; General Practice

SCHUMACHER, STEPHEN J.
Newport Beach, CA....................Tax Law

SCHWARTZ, AMITAI
San Francisco, CA....................Appellate Practice; Civil Rights

SCHWARTZ, THEODORE F.
Clayton, MO....................Commercial Litigation

SCHWARTZ, ARTHUR M., P.C.
Denver, CO....................Civil Rights; Criminal Trial Practice

SCHWARTZ & BLACKMAN
Philadelphia, PA....................Commercial Litigation; Personal Injury

SCHWARTZ, BON, WALKER & STUDER, LLC
Casper, WY....................Business Law; Commercial Litigation

SCHWARTZ, BRENDA KEEN, P.C.
Houston, TX....................Family Law

SCHWARTZ & CERA LLP
San Francisco, CA....................Civil Trial Practice

SCHWARTZ, DAVID C., P.A.
Orlando, FL....................Civil Trial Practice; Insurance Defense; Product Liability Law

SCHWARTZ & EICHELBAUM, P.C.
Austin, TX....................Civil Rights; Insurance Defense; Labor and Employment Law

SCHWARTZ AND ELLIS, LTD.
Arlington, VA....................Civil Trial Practice; Family Law; International Business Law; Medical Malpractice; Personal Injury

SCHWARTZ & JALKANEN, P.C.
Southfield, MI....................Civil Trial Practice; Family Law; Insurance Defense; Medical Malpractice; Personal Injury; Product Liability Law

SCHWARTZ, JOHN B., & ASSOCIATES
Chicago, IL....................Civil Trial Practice; Medical Malpractice; Personal Injury

SCHWARTZ JUNELL CAMPBELL & OATHOUT, L.L.P.
Houston, TX....................Admiralty/Maritime Law; Appellate Practice; Business Law; Civil Trial Practice; Commercial Law; Construction Law; Energy Law; Insurance Defense; Labor and Employment Law

SCHWARTZ KUCK & ASSOCIATES LLP
Atlanta, GA....................Immigration and Naturalization

SCHWARTZ & SCHWARTZ
Hallettsville, TX....................Personal Injury

SCHWARTZ SIMON EDELSTEIN CELSO & KESSLER
Florham Park, NJ....................Civil Trial Practice; Commercial Law; Environmental Law; Family Law; Health Care Law; Labor and Employment Law

SCHWARTZ, STEINSAPIR, DOHRMANN & SOMMERS, LLP
Los Angeles, CA....................Arbitration; Civil Trial Practice; Employment Benefits Law; Labor and Employment Law; Real Estate Law

SCHWARTZ, WISOT & WILSON, LLP
Beverly Hills, CA....................Business Law; Civil Trial Practice; Real Estate Law

SCHWARTZBERG, BARNETT & COHEN
Chicago, IL..............................Appellate Practice; Business Law; Civil Rights; Commercial Law; Construction Law; Family Law; General Practice; Health Care Law; Real Estate Law; Trust and Estates, Wills and Probate

SCHWARTZMAN, JAMES C., & ASSOCIATES, P.C.
Philadelphia, PA ....Civil Trial Practice; Commercial Litigation; Criminal Trial Practice

SCHWERIN CAMPBELL BARNARD LLP
Seattle, WA ....Labor and Employment Law

SCOBLIONKO, SCOBLIONKO, MUIR, BARTHOLOMEW & MELMAN, A PROFESSIONAL CORPORATION
Allentown, PA ....General Practice

SCOFIELD, GERARD, VERON, SINGLETARY & POHORELSKY, A PROFESSIONAL LAW CORPORATION
Lake Charles, LA.....................Civil Trial Practice; General Practice; Real Estate Law

SCOPELITIS, GARVIN, LIGHT & HANSON, P.C.
Indianapolis, IN.......................Transportation Law

SCOTT, HULSE, MARSHALL, FEUILLE, FINGER & THURMOND, P.C.
El Paso, TX.............................General Practice

SCRUDATO, PAUL A.
New York, NY..........................Civil Trial Practice; Commercial Litigation; Personal Injury; Product Liability Law; Toxic Torts

SCRUGGS, JORDAN, DODD & DODD
Fort Payne, AL.........................Civil Trial Practice; Corporate Law; General Practice; Insurance Defense; Personal Injury

SCUDDER LAW FIRM, P.C.
Lincoln, NE..............................Mergers and Acquisitions; Real Estate Law; Securities Law

SCULLY, SCOTT, MURPHY & PRESSER, A PROFESSIONAL CORPORATION
Garden City, NY ....Intellectual Property Law; Patent, Trademark, Copyright and Unfair Competition

SEALE, SMITH, ZUBER & BARNETTE
Baton Rouge, LA......................Civil Trial Practice; Commercial Litigation; Insurance Defense; Personal Injury

SEARCY DENNEY SCAROLA BARNHART & SHIPLEY, PROFESSIONAL ASSOCIATION
West Palm Beach, FL.............Aviation Law; Civil Trial Practice; Commercial Law; Commercial Litigation; General Practice; Health Care Law; Labor and Employment Law; Medical Malpractice; Personal Injury; Product Liability Law; Professional Liability; Securities Law; Sports and Entertainment Law; Toxic Torts

SEARS, M.H., THE, LAW FIRM
Washington, DC.......................Patent, Trademark, Copyright and Unfair Competition

SEBALY, SHILLITO & DYER, A LEGAL PROFESSIONAL ASSOCIATION
Dayton, OH..............................Bankruptcy Law; Business Law; Civil Trial Practice; Environmental Law; Health Care Law; Labor and Employment Law; Mergers and Acquisitions; Securities Law; Trust and Estates, Wills and Probate

SEBASTIAN, DAVID A.
Birmingham, MI.......................General Practice

SECOR, CASSIDY & MCPARTLAND, P.C.
Southbury, CT..........................General Practice
Waterbury, CT ....General Practice

SECREST, HILL & FOLLUO
Tulsa, OK.................................Insurance Defense; Medical Malpractice; Product Liability Law

SECREST, WARDLE, LYNCH, HAMPTON, TRUEX AND MORLEY
Farmington Hills, MI ....Insurance Defense

SEDER & CHANDLER
Worcester, MA.........................Bankruptcy Law; Business Law; Civil Trial Practice; Commercial Law; Tax Law; Trust and Estates, Wills and Probate

SEDGWICK, DETERT, MORAN & ARNOLD
San Francisco, CA ....General Practice

SEDIVY, WHITE AND WHITE, P.C. PROFESSIONAL CORPORATION
Bozeman, MT...........................General Practice

SEDWICK, EDWIN S. LAW OFFICE OF
Jeffersonville, IN ....Personal Injury

SEED AND BERRY LLP
Seattle, WA ....Intellectual Property Law; Patent, Trademark, Copyright and Unfair Competition

SEELEY, SAVIDGE AND EBERT, A LEGAL PROFESSIONAL ASSOCIATION
Cleveland, OH.........................Civil Trial Practice; General Practice; Insurance Defense; Labor and Employment Law; Municipal and Zoning Law; Securities Law; Trust and Estates, Wills and Probate

SEELIE, JOHN F.
Cleveland, OH.........................Family Law

SEGAL AND SHANKS
Louisville, KY ....Insurance Defense

SEGEL, GOLDMAN & MAZZOTTA, P.C.
Albany, NY.............................Business Law; Real Estate Law

SEHAM SEHAM MELTZ & PETERSEN, LLP
New York, NY.........................Labor and Employment Law; Public Utilities Law

SEIB LAW FIRM, THE, A PROFESSIONAL CORPORATION
Dallas, TX...............................Commercial Litigation; Creditors Rights

SEID, GERALD P.
Skillman, NJ............................Business Law; Corporate Law; General Practice

SEIDMAN, SILVERMAN & SEIDMAN, P.C.
New York, NY.........................Appellate Practice; Business Law; Civil Trial Practice; Criminal Trial Practice; Tax Law; Trademark, Copyright and Unfair Competition

SEIGEL & WOLFF, P.C.
St. Louis, MO..........................Commercial Litigation

SEIPP, FLICK & KISSANE, P.A.
Miami, FL...............................Product Liability Law

SEITELMAN, MARK E. LAW OFFICES
New York, NY.........................Civil Trial Practice; Personal Injury

SELDEN LAW FIRM
San Diego, CA ....Civil Trial Practice; Construction Law; Personal Injury

SELF, GIDDENS & LEES, INC.
Oklahoma City, OK................Banking Law; Bankruptcy Law; Civil Trial Practice; Commercial Law; Natural Resources Law; Real Estate Law

SELF & SELF
Florence, AL ....Civil Trial Practice; Commercial Law; Personal Injury
Tuscumbia, AL........................Civil Trial Practice; Commercial Law

SELLAR RICHARDSON, P.C.
Roseland, NJ...........................Appellate Practice; Civil Trial Practice; Insurance Defense; Product Liability Law

SELL & MELTON, L.L.P.
Macon, GA ....Banking Law; Bankruptcy Law; Business Law; Civil Trial Practice; General Practice; Health Care Law; Municipal Bond/Public Authority Financing; Personal Injury; Workers Compensation

SELMAN • BREITMAN
Los Angeles, CA.....................Civil Trial Practice; Construction Law; Insurance Defense; Personal Injury

SELTZER, JAMES JAY
Emeryville, CA........................Administrative Law; Civil Rights; Criminal Trial Practice; Health Care Law; Securities Law

SELTZER CAPLAN MCMAHON & VITEK, A PROFESSIONAL CORPORATION
San Diego, CA ....Antitrust Law; Civil Trial Practice; Criminal Trial Practice; General Practice; Tax Law

SELTZER LAW GROUP
San Francisco, CA ....Construction Law

SEMANOFF, ORMSBY & GREENBERG, LLP
Jenkintown, PA.......................Business Law; Labor and Employment Law; Real Estate Law

SEMMES, JOHN GIBSON
Potomac, MD..........................Intellectual Property Law

SEMMES, BOWEN & SEMMES, A PROFESSIONAL CORPORATION
Baltimore, MD ....General Practice

SEMPLE, MILLER & MOONEY, P.C.
Denver, CO ....Education Law; Labor and Employment Law

SENECZKO LAW OFFICES, S.C.
Milwaukee, WI ....Labor and Employment Law; Workers Compensation

SENN LEWIS & VISCIANO, P.C.
Denver, CO ....Appellate Practice; Business Law; Commercial Law; Commercial Litigation; Corporate Law; General Practice; Real Estate Law

SENNIGER, POWERS, LEAVITT & ROEDEL
St. Louis, MO....Patent, Trademark, Copyright and Unfair Competition

SENTER GOLDFARB & RICE, L.L.C.
Denver, CO....Insurance Defense

SEPARK, W. ALLEN
Marietta, GA....Business Law; Commercial Law; Tax Law; Trust and Estates, Wills and Probate

SERCHUK & ZELERMYER, LLP
White Plains, NY....Banking Law; Corporate Law

SERKO & SIMON LLP
New York, NY....International Business Law; International Trade Law; Transportation Law

SERLING, MICHAEL B., P.C.
Birmingham, MI....Personal Injury; Product Liability Law

SEROTTE, ROCKMAN & WESCOTT, P.A.
Baltimore, MD....Labor and Employment Law

SESSIONS & FISHMAN, L.L.P.
New Orleans, LA....General Practice

SESSUMS, MASON & BLACK, P.A.
Tampa, FL....Family Law

SESTRIC LAW FIRM, THE
St. Louis, MO....Appellate Practice; Civil Trial Practice

SEVIER LAW FIRM, P.C.
Memphis, TN....Family Law; General Practice; Insurance Defense

SEVILA, SAUNDERS, HUDDLESTON & WHITE, A PROFESSIONAL CORPORATION
Leesburg, VA....Civil Trial Practice; Family Law; General Practice; Land Use Law; Personal Injury

SEWARD & KISSEL LLP
Washington, DC....General Practice
New York, NY....General Practice

SEYFARTH, SHAW, FAIRWEATHER & GERALDSON
Chicago, IL....General Practice

SHACKELFORD, HONENBERGER, THOMAS, WILLIS & GREGG, P.L.C.
Orange, VA....Civil Trial Practice; Criminal Trial Practice; General Practice; Personal Injury; Real Estate Law; Trust and Estates, Wills and Probate

SHACKLEFORD, PHILLIPS, WINELAND & RATCLIFF, P.A.
El Dorado, AR....Civil Trial Practice; General Practice

SHACKLETON, HAZELTINE AND BISHOP
Ship Bottom, NJ....Admiralty/Maritime Law; Civil Trial Practice; General Practice; Insurance Defense; Medical Malpractice; Personal Injury; Product Liability Law; Real Estate Law

SHAFER, DAVIS, ASHLEY, O'LEARY & STOKER, A PROFESSIONAL CORPORATION
Odessa, TX....General Practice

SHAFER, SWICK, BAILEY, IRWIN, STACK & MILLIN
Meadville, PA....General Practice

SHAFFER, RICHARD W.
Allentown, PA....Environmental Law; Land Use Law; Trust and Estates, Wills and Probate

SHAIN, SCHAFFER & RAFANELLO, A PROFESSIONAL CORPORATION
Bernardsville, NJ....Banking Law; Business Law; Corporate Law; General Practice; Real Estate Law

SHALHOUB, ROBERT M.W., P.A., LAW OFFICES OF
West Palm Beach, FL....Family Law

SHAMBAUGH, KAST, BECK & WILLIAMS, LLP
Fort Wayne, IN....Civil Trial Practice; General Practice; Tax Law; Trust and Estates, Wills and Probate

SHAMBERG, JOHNSON & BERGMAN, CHARTERED
Overland Park, KS....Civil Trial Practice; Environmental Law; Medical Malpractice; Personal Injury; Product Liability Law

SHAMBERG MARWELL HOCHERMAN DAVIS & HOLLIS, P.C.
Mount Kisco, NY....Environmental Law; Municipal and Zoning Law

SHAMBERG, WOLF, MCDERMOTT & DEPUÉ
Grand Island, NE....General Practice

SHAMEL, C. RICHARD JR.
Deerfield Beach, FL....Trust and Estates, Wills and Probate

SHANDELL, BLITZ, BLITZ, GLASS, BOOKSON & KERN, LLP
New York, NY....Medical Malpractice; Personal Injury; Product Liability Law; Toxic Torts

SHANKLIN & MCDANIEL, L.L.P.
Wilmington, NC....Commercial Law; Real Estate Law

SHANLEY, THOMAS M.
Greenwich, CT....Family Law

SHANLEY, SWEENEY, REILLY & ALLEN, P.C.
Albany, NY....Commercial Litigation; Corporate Law; Environmental Law; General Practice; Municipal and Zoning Law; Municipal Bond/Public Authority Financing; Real Estate Law

SHANNON & FLEMING, P.C.
Phoenix, AZ....Creditors Rights

SHANNONHOUSE, JOSEPH G. IV
Oklahoma City, OK....Tax Law

SHAPIRO, LEONARD H.
Owings Mills, MD....Criminal Trial Practice

SHAPIRO, WILLIAM D. LAW OFFICES OF
San Bernardino, CA....Personal Injury

SHAPIRO & ASSOCIATES
Boston, MA....Insurance Defense; Personal Injury

SHAPIRO, COHEN
Ottawa, ON, Canada....Patent, Trademark, Copyright and Unfair Competition

SHAPIRO & CROLAND
Hackensack, NJ....Bankruptcy Law; Business Law; Civil Trial Practice; Commercial Litigation; Corporate Law; Family Law; General Practice; Real Estate Law; Tax Law

SHAPIRO & DECTOR, P.A.
Boca Raton, FL....Commercial Litigation; Real Estate Law

SHAPIRO, LIFSCHITZ AND SCHRAM, P.C.
Washington, DC....Construction Law

SHARP, CHRISTOPHER G., P.C.
Dallas, TX....Administrative Law; Health Care Law; Real Estate Law

SHARP, SMITH & HARRISON, P.A.
Tampa, FL....International Business Law; Tax Law

SHARP, TERRY, P.C., LAW OFFICE OF
Mount Vernon, IL....Bankruptcy Law; Commercial Law; Real Estate Law

SHARPE & KRUEGER
Kingsville, TX....General Practice

SHARPNACK, BIGLEY, DAVID & RUMPLE
Columbus, IN....Civil Trial Practice; Family Law; General Practice; Insurance Defense; Trust and Estates, Wills and Probate

SHARTSIS, FRIESE & GINSBURG LLP
San Francisco, CA....General Practice

SHAW LAW FIRM
Fort Smith, AR....General Practice

SHAW, LICITRA, BOHNER, ESERNIO & SCHWARTZ, P.C.
Garden City, NY....Appellate Practice; Bankruptcy Law; General Practice

SHAW, MADDOX, GRAHAM, MONK & BOLING, LLP
Rome, GA....Civil Trial Practice; General Practice

SHAWE & ROSENTHAL
Baltimore, MD....Labor and Employment Law

SHAYNE, DACHS, STANISCI, CORKER & SAUER
Mineola, NY....Insurance Defense; Medical Malpractice; Personal Injury; Professional Liability

SHEA & ASSOCIATES
Cincinnati, OH....Civil Trial Practice; Medical Malpractice; Personal Injury; Product Liability Law

SHEA & SHEA, A PROFESSIONAL LAW CORPORATION
San Jose, CA....Civil Trial Practice; Personal Injury; Product Liability Law

SHEAFFER, WILLIAM J., P.A.
Orlando, FL....Criminal Trial Practice

SHEARMAN & STERLING
San Francisco, CA....General Practice
Washington, DC....General Practice
New York, NY....General Practice
Beijing, China....General Practice
Hong Kong, China....General Practice
London, England....General Practice

Paris, France....General Practice
Düsseldorf, Germany....General Practice
Frankfurt/Main, Germany....General Practice
Tokyo, Japan....General Practice
Singapore, Singapore....General Practice
Abu Dhabi, United Arab Emirates....General Practice

SHEEHAN PHINNEY BASS + GREEN, PROFESSIONAL ASSOCIATION
Manchester, NH....Commercial Law; Environmental Law; General Practice; Insurance Defense; Labor and Employment Law; Personal Injury; Product Liability Law; Securities Law; Tax Law
Portsmouth, NH....Labor and Employment Law; Tax Law

SHEEHY, LOVELACE & MAYFIELD, P.C. A PROFESSIONAL CORPORATION
Waco, TX....Civil Trial Practice; General Practice

SHEFFER • HUTCHINSON • KINNEY
Henderson, KY....General Practice
Louisville, KY....General Practice
Owensboro, KY....General Practice
Paducah, KY....General Practice

SHEIMAN, RONALD L.
Westport, CT....Business Law; Tax Law; Trust and Estates, Wills and Probate

SHEKETOFF & HOMAN
Boston, MA....Criminal Trial Practice

SHELL, BUFORD, BUFKIN, CALLICUTT & PERRY
Jackson, MS....Civil Trial Practice; Insurance Defense

SHELL, FLEMING, DAVIS & MENGE, P.A.
Pensacola, FL....General Practice

SHELLOW, SHELLOW & GLYNN, S.C.
Milwaukee, WI....Criminal Trial Practice

SHELTON & VALADEZ, P.C.
San Antonio, TX....Civil Trial Practice; Insurance Defense

SHENKER, ARDEN E.
Portland, OR....Civil Trial Practice

SHEPARD, FILBURN & GOODBLATT, P.A.
Orlando, FL....Civil Trial Practice; Insurance Defense

SHEPHERD & CRABTREE
Chico, CA....Insurance Defense; Labor and Employment Law

SHEPHERD, GARY & MCWHORTER
Swainsboro, GA....Insurance Defense; Real Estate Law

SHEPPARD, MULLIN, RICHTER & HAMPTON LLP
Los Angeles, CA....General Practice

SHEPPARD, WHITE & THOMAS, P.A.
Jacksonville, FL....Appellate Practice; Civil Rights; Criminal Trial Practice

SHER GARNER CAHILL RICHTER KLEIN MCALISTER & HILBERT, L.L.C.
New Orleans, LA....General Practice

SHERESKY ARONSON & MAYEFSKY, LLP
New York, NY....Family Law

SHERIDAN ROSS, P.C.
Denver, CO....Intellectual Property Law; Patent, Trademark, Copyright and Unfair Competition; Trademark, Copyright and Unfair Competition

SHERIN AND LODGEN LLP
Boston, MA....Business Law; Civil Trial Practice; General Practice; Real Estate Law

SHERMAN, WILLIAM F.
Little Rock, AR....General Practice

SHERMAN & HOWARD L.L.C.
Colorado Springs, CO....General Practice
Denver, CO....Antitrust Law; Banking Law; Civil Trial Practice; General Practice; Labor and Employment Law; Municipal Bond/Public Authority Financing; Natural Resources Law; Tax Law; Trust and Estates, Wills and Probate

SHERMAN & SHALLOWAY
Alexandria, VA....Patent, Trademark, Copyright and Unfair Competition

SHERMAN, SILVERSTEIN, KOHL, ROSE & PODOLSKY, A PROFESSIONAL CORPORATION
Pennsauken, NJ....General Practice; Pension and Profit Sharing

SHERMAN, STEPHEN A., & ASSOCIATES
Oklahoma City, OK....Commercial Law; Real Estate Law

SHERMETA, CHIMKO & KILPATRICK, P.C.
Rochester Hills, MI....Bankruptcy Law; Commercial Law; Commercial Litigation

SHERRILL, CROSNOE & GOFF, A PROFESSIONAL CORPORATION
Wichita Falls, TX....General Practice

SHERRILL & ROOF, L.L.P.
Columbia, SC....Banking Law; Business Law; Elder Law; Public Utilities Law

SHERWOOD AND HARDGROVE
Los Angeles, CA....Real Estate Law

SHERWOOD, KLEIN, DUDLEY & ABRAM, P.A.
Phoenix, AZ....Commercial Litigation; Personal Injury

SHIBLEY, JEFFERY L., P.A., A LAW OFFICE OF
Tampa, FL....Civil Trial Practice; Personal Injury; Product Liability Law

SHIBLEY RIGHTON
Toronto, ON, Canada....General Practice

SHIELDS LAW OFFICE, P.A.
St. John, KS....General Practice

SHIGLEY LAW FIRM, L.L.C.
Atlanta, GA....Personal Injury; Product Liability Law

SHIMKO, TIMOTHY A., & ASSOCIATES, A LEGAL PROF. ASSN.
Cleveland, OH....Antitrust Law; Civil Trial Practice; Labor and Employment Law; Medical Malpractice; Personal Injury; Product Liability Law

SHIMMEL, HILL, BISHOP & GRUENDER, P.C.
Phoenix, AZ....Bankruptcy Law; Civil Trial Practice; Commercial Litigation; Construction Law; Creditors Rights; Employment Benefits Law; Family Law; Insurance Defense; Labor and Employment Law; Real Estate Law; Tax Law; Trust and Estates, Wills and Probate

SHINE & MASON LAW OFFICE
Kingsport, TN....General Practice; Labor and Employment Law; Workers Compensation

SHINGLES & CAPPELLI
Blue Bell, PA....Appellate Practice; Civil Trial Practice; Criminal Trial Practice; Personal Injury

SHINN, STEERMAN & SHINN
Lamar, CO....General Practice; Trust and Estates, Wills and Probate

SHIOTANI & INOUYE
Los Angeles, CA....Business Law; Real Estate Law; Tax Law; Trust and Estates, Wills and Probate

SHIPLEY & ASSOCIATES
Fort Wayne, IN....Bankruptcy Law; Commercial Law; Commercial Litigation

SHIPLEY, JENNINGS & CHAMPLIN, P.C.
Tulsa, OK....Civil Trial Practice; Environmental Law

SHIPMAN & ASSOCIATES, L.L.P.
Wilmington, NC....Construction Law; Medical Malpractice; Personal Injury

SHIPMAN & GOODWIN LLP
Hartford, CT....Environmental Law; General Practice; Labor and Employment Law; Trust and Estates, Wills and Probate
Lakeville, CT....General Practice
Stamford, CT....General Practice

SHIRINIAN & ROITMAN
Las Vegas, NV....Commercial Litigation; Construction Law; Corporate Law; Trust and Estates, Wills and Probate

SHIRK, WORK & ROBINSON, P.C.
Oklahoma City, OK....General Practice

SHIRLEY, L. MERRILL
Elba, AL....Insurance Defense; Personal Injury; Workers Compensation

SHLIMBAUM, SHLIMBAUM AND JABLONSKI
Islip, NY....Family Law; Municipal and Zoning Law; Personal Injury

SHOCKEY & ZIOBER, A PROFESSIONAL LAW CORPORATION
Baton Rouge, LA....Bankruptcy Law; Civil Trial Practice; Environmental Law; Insurance Defense; Workers Compensation

SHOECRAFT, JAMES W., P.C., ATTORNEYS' OFFICES OF
Dallas, TX....Personal Injury

SHOFI, HENNEN, GRAMOVOT & ASSOCIATES
Tampa, FL .... Insurance Defense; Professional Liability

SHOOK, HARDY & BACON L.L.P.
Kansas City, MO .... General Practice

SHOR, FRANK LAW OFFICES OF
Carrollton, TX .... Civil Trial Practice; Criminal Trial Practice

SHORALL & STEVENS, P.C.
Phoenix, AZ .... Insurance Defense

SHORT, KEVIN J.
Minneapolis, MN .... Criminal Trial Practice

SHORT & JENKINS, A PROFESSIONAL LEGAL CORPORATION
Houston, TX .... Family Law

SHOUN & BACH, P.C.
Fairfax, VA .... Family Law

SHRAGER, MCDAID, LOFTUS, FLUM & SPIVEY
Philadelphia, PA .... Medical Malpractice; Personal Injury

SHREVE, DAVID WILLIAM
Altavista, VA .... Civil Trial Practice

SHUFORD, CADDELL & FRALEY
Salisbury, NC .... General Practice

SHUGHART THOMSON & KILROY, A PROFESSIONAL CORPORATION
Overland Park, KS .... General Practice
Kansas City, MO .... Antitrust Law; Civil Trial Practice; General Practice; Labor and Employment Law

SHULLAW, WAYNE A.
Lafayette, LA .... Banking Law; Commercial Litigation

SHULMAN, CURTIN, GRUNDNER, REGAN & SNYDER, P.C.
Syracuse, NY .... Municipal and Zoning Law; Real Estate Law

SHULTZ & ROLLINS, LTD.
Tucson, AZ .... Civil Trial Practice; Medical Malpractice; Personal Injury

SHUMAKER, LOOP & KENDRICK, LLP
Columbus, OH .... Environmental Law
Toledo, OH .... Commercial Litigation; Construction Law; Environmental Law

SHUMAN, MORTON J.
Framingham, MA .... Personal Injury; Workers Compensation

SHUMAN ANNAND BAILEY WYANT & EARLES
Charleston, WV .... Appellate Practice; Business Law; Construction Law; General Practice; Insurance Defense; Medical Malpractice; Product Liability Law

SHUMARD, THOMAS J.
Phoenix, AZ .... Trust and Estates, Wills and Probate

SHUPE, REAGAN & WYNE
Santa Ana, CA .... Insurance Defense

SHUSTERMAN, CARL LAW OFFICES OF
Los Angeles, CA .... Immigration and Naturalization

SHUTTLEWORTH & INGERSOLL, P.C.
Cedar Rapids, IA .... Administrative Law; Banking Law; Civil Trial Practice; General Practice; Insurance Defense; Labor and Employment Law; Patent, Trademark, Copyright and Unfair Competition; Real Estate Law; Tax Law; Trust and Estates, Wills and Probate

SHUTTLEWORTH RULOFF & GIORDANO, P.C.
Virginia Beach, VA .... Criminal Trial Practice; Medical Malpractice; Personal Injury; Product Liability Law

SHUTTS & BOWEN LLP
Miami, FL .... Admiralty/Maritime Law; Antitrust Law; General Practice; Tax Law
Orlando, FL .... General Practice
West Palm Beach, FL .... General Practice

SIBBISON, WENDY
Greenfield, MA .... Appellate Practice

SIBLEY, THOMAS J., P.C.
Beaumont, TX .... Commercial Law

SIDKOFF, PINCUS & GREEN, P.C.
Philadelphia, PA .... Civil Trial Practice

SIDLEY & AUSTIN
Washington, DC .... General Practice
Chicago, IL .... General Practice

SIDLEY & BELL LLP
Los Angeles, CA .... Civil Trial Practice; Criminal Trial Practice

SIEBEN, GROSE, VON HOLTUM & CAREY, LTD.
Minneapolis, MN .... Medical Malpractice; Personal Injury; Workers Compensation

SIEBEN, POLK, LAVERDIERE, JONES & HAWN, A PROFESSIONAL ASSOCIATION
Hastings, MN .... Civil Trial Practice; Personal Injury

SIEGEL, BRILL, GREUPNER, DUFFY & FOSTER, P.A.
Minneapolis, MN .... Antitrust Law; Civil Trial Practice; General Practice; Land Use Law

SIEGEL, GREENFIELD, HAYES & GROSS, P.L.C.
Southfield, MI .... Corporate Law; Tax Law; Trust and Estates, Wills and Probate

SIEGFRIED, RIVERA, LERNER, DE LA TORRE & SOBEL, P.A.
Miami, FL .... Civil Trial Practice; Commercial Law; Commercial Litigation; Construction Law; Corporate Law; Real Estate Law

SIEMION, HUCKABAY, BODARY, PADILLA, MORGANTI & BOWERMAN, P.C.
Southfield, MI .... Civil Trial Practice; Insurance Defense

SIFFORD & ANDERSON, L.L.P.
Dallas, TX .... Aviation Law; Insurance Defense; Personal Injury; Product Liability Law

SIGERMAN, JON B. THE LAW OFFICES OF
San Francisco, CA .... Labor and Employment Law

SIGMON, CLARK, MACKIE, HUTTON & HANVEY, P.A.
Hickory, NC .... Civil Trial Practice; General Practice; Real Estate Law

SIKES, GRIFFIN JR.
Montgomery, AL .... Civil Trial Practice

SIKORA, FREDERICK J., P.A.
Warren, NJ .... Family Law

SILBER & VALENTE, P.A.
West Palm Beach, FL .... Aviation Law; Personal Injury

SILK, ADLER & COLVIN, A LAW CORPORATION
San Francisco, CA .... Tax Law

SILLS, NANCY M.
Albany, NY .... Tax Law; Trust and Estates, Wills and Probate

SILLS CUMMIS RADIN TISCHMAN EPSTEIN & GROSS, A PROFESSIONAL CORPORATION
Atlantic City, NJ .... General Practice
Newark, NJ .... Administrative Law; Antitrust Law; Appellate Practice; Banking Law; Bankruptcy Law; Business Law; Civil Rights; Civil Trial Practice; Commercial Law; Commercial Litigation; Communications Law; Computer Law; Construction Law; Criminal Trial Practice; Employment Benefits Law; Energy Law; Environmental Law; Family Law; General Practice; Health Care Law; Insurance Defense; International Business Law; International Trade Law; Labor and Employment Law; Land Use Law; Medical Malpractice; Municipal and Zoning Law; Municipal Bond/Public Authority Financing; Natural Resources Law; Patent, Trademark, Copyright and Unfair Competition; Personal Injury; Product Liability Law; Public Utilities Law; Real Estate Law; Securities Law; Sports and Entertainment Law; Tax Law; Transportation Law; Trust and Estates, Wills and Probate
New York, NY .... General Practice

SÍLVA, RIEDER & MAESTAS, P.C.
Albuquerque, NM .... Civil Trial Practice; Commercial Litigation; Criminal Trial Practice; Labor and Employment Law

SILVER & BROWN, A PROFESSIONAL CORPORATION
Fairfax, VA .... Commercial Litigation

SILVER, FREEDMAN & TAFF, L.L.P.
Washington, DC .... Banking Law; Mergers and Acquisitions

SILVER, GOLUB & TEITELL LLP
Stamford, CT .... Civil Trial Practice; Commercial Litigation; Criminal Trial Practice; Family Law; General Practice; Medical Malpractice; Personal Injury; Product Liability Law

SILVERMAN & DECARIA, CHARTERED
Reno, NV .... Family Law

SILVERMAN FRIMMER BERNHEIM & MCDONNELL, A PROFESSIONAL CORPORATION
Philadelphia, PA .... Banking Law; Insurance Defense

SILVERSTEIN AND MULLENS, P.L.L.C.
Washington, DC....................Tax Law

SIM, HUGHES, ASHTON & MCKAY
Toronto, ON, Canada............Computer Law; Intellectual Property Law; Patent, Trademark, Copyright and Unfair Competition

SIMKE CHODOS
Los Angeles, CA....................Civil Trial Practice; Commercial Litigation; Sports and Entertainment Law

SIMKINS & SIMKINS, P.C.
Northville, MI........................Personal Injury

SIMMONS AND DERR
Winnfield, LA........................Banking Law; Civil Trial Practice; General Practice; Real Estate Law; Trust and Estates, Wills and Probate

SIMMONS, GRIFFIN & LYDON, L.L.P.
Columbia, SC........................Environmental Law

SIMMONS, OLSEN, EDIGER, SELZER, FERGUSON & CARNEY, P.C.
Scottsbluff, NE......................General Practice

SIMMONS, WARREN, SZCZECKO & MCFEE, PROFESSIONAL ASSOCIATION
Decatur, GA..........................Business Law; Civil Trial Practice; Family Law; Real Estate Law

SIMON, FITZGERALD, COOKE, REED & WELCH
Shreveport, LA......................Bankruptcy Law; General Practice

SIMON, MCKINSEY, MILLER, ZOMMICK, SANDOR & DUNDAS, A LAW CORPORATION
Long Beach, CA.....................Trust and Estates, Wills and Probate

SIMON & SCHMIDT
Delray Beach, FL...................General Practice

SIMON AND SIMON
Kansas City, MO...................Criminal Trial Practice

SIMON, TURNBULL & MARTIN, CHARTERED
Washington, DC....................Business Law

SIMONCINI & ASSOCIATES
San Jose, CA........................Construction Law; Insurance Defense

SIMONE, ROBERTS & WEISS, P.A.
Albuquerque, NM..................Civil Trial Practice; Insurance Defense; Medical Malpractice; Personal Injury; Product Liability Law

SIMONS, CUDDY & FRIEDMAN, LLP
Santa Fe, NM........................Insurance Defense; Labor and Employment Law

SIMPSON, GARY HOWARD
Bethesda, MD........................Arbitration; Civil Rights; Civil Trial Practice; Constitutional Law; Labor and Employment Law

SIMPSON AYCOCK, P.A.
Morganton, NC......................General Practice

SIMPSON & BOYD, P.L.L.C.
Decatur, TX...........................Civil Trial Practice; Commercial Litigation; Product Liability Law

SIMPSON, KABLACK & BELL
Indiana, PA...........................General Practice

SIMPSON, KEPLER & EDWARDS, LC
Cody, WY..............................General Practice; Trust and Estates, Wills and Probate

SIMPSON, STEVEN D., P.A., LAW OFFICES OF
Raleigh, NC..........................Nonprofit and Tax Exempt Organizations

SIMPSON THACHER & BARTLETT
New York, NY.......................General Practice
Columbus, OH.......................General Practice
Hong Kong, China.................General Practice
London, England...................General Practice
Tokyo, Japan.........................General Practice
Singapore, Singapore............General Practice

SIMS, FLEMING & SPURLIN, P.C.
Tifton, GA.............................General Practice

SINCLAIR, I.B. LAW OFFICES
State College, PA..................Family Law

SINCLAIR LAW FIRM, THE
Bowie, MD............................Trust and Estates, Wills and Probate

SINDEL & SINDEL, P.C.
St. Louis, MO........................Criminal Trial Practice; Personal Injury

SINGER, ROBERT S.
Miami, FL.............................Personal Injury

SINGER FRUMENTO LLP
New York, NY.......................Securities Law

SINGLETARY LAW FIRM, P.A.
Tampa, FL.............................Personal Injury

SINGLETON & SINGLETON
Mount Kisco, NY..................General Practice; Municipal and Zoning Law; Real Estate Law

SINGLETON URQUHART
Vancouver, BC, Canada..........Construction Law; Environmental Law; General Practice; Insurance Defense; Product Liability Law; Toxic Torts

SINIARD, MCKINNEY & BRASWELL, P.C., THE LAW FIRM OF
Huntsville, AL.......................Medical Malpractice; Personal Injury; Workers Compensation

SINKELDAM, GARY P. LAW OFFICE OF
Las Vegas, NV......................Construction Law

SINKLER & BOYD, P.A.
Charleston, SC......................Admiralty/Maritime Law; Civil Trial Practice; General Practice; Municipal Bond/Public Authority Financing
Columbia, SC........................Admiralty/Maritime Law; Civil Trial Practice; General Practice; Municipal Bond/Public Authority Financing
Greenville, SC......................Municipal Bond/Public Authority Financing

SINK, POWERS, SINK & POTTER, L.L.P.
Raleigh, NC..........................General Practice

SINNOTT, DITO, MOURA & PUEBLA
Los Angeles, CA....................Commercial Litigation

SINOFF, BARRY S., P.A., LAW OFFICE OF
Jacksonville, FL.....................Family Law

SINSHEIMER, SCHIEBELHUT & BAGGETT, A PROFESSIONAL CORPORATION
San Luis Obispo, CA.............General Practice

SINTZ, CAMPBELL, DUKE & TAYLOR
Mobile, AL...........................Civil Rights; Civil Trial Practice; Constitutional Law; Corporate Law; Education Law; Insurance Defense; Labor and Employment Law; Product Liability Law; Workers Compensation

SIRKIN PINALES MEZIBOV & SCHWARTZ
Cincinnati, OH......................Civil Trial Practice; Constitutional Law; Criminal Trial Practice; Labor and Employment Law

SIROTA & SIROTA, LLP
New York, NY.......................Securities Law

SISTARE & ASSOCIATES
Fort Lauderdale, FL..............Civil Trial Practice; Insurance Defense; Medical Malpractice; Personal Injury; Professional Liability

SITLINGER, MCGLINCY, STEINER, THEILER & KAREM
Louisville, KY......................Civil Trial Practice; Insurance Defense; Medical Malpractice

SIXBEY, FRIEDMAN, LEEDOM & FERGUSON, P.C.
McLean, VA..........................Patent, Trademark, Copyright and Unfair Competition

SJOBERG & VOTTA LAW OFFICES
Warwick, RI..........................Trust and Estates, Wills and Probate

SKADDEN, ARPS, SLATE, MEAGHER & FLOM LLP
New York, NY.......................Bankruptcy Law; Criminal Trial Practice; General Practice; Labor and Employment Law

SKARECKY & HOLDER, A PROFESSIONAL ASSOCIATION
Phoenix, AZ.........................Creditors Rights

SKELDING, LABASKY & DAWS, A PROFESSIONAL ASSOCIATION
Tallahassee, FL.....................Administrative Law

SKELLEY ROTTNER P.C.
Hartford, CT.........................Insurance Defense

SKELTON, TAINTOR & ABBOTT, A PROFESSIONAL CORPORATION
Auburn, ME..........................General Practice

SKJERVEN, MORRILL, MACPHERSON, FRANKLIN & FRIEL LLP
Newport Beach, CA...............Patent, Trademark, Copyright and Unfair Competition
San Francisco, CA.................General Practice; Patent, Trademark, Copyright and Unfair Competition
San Jose, CA........................General Practice; Patent, Trademark, Copyright and Unfair Competition

SKOKOS, BEQUETTE & BILLINGSLEY, P.A.
Little Rock, AR.....................Business Law; Civil Trial Practice; Commercial Litigation

SKOLER, ABBOTT & PRESSER, P.C.
Springfield, MA........................Employment Benefits Law; Labor and Employment Law
Worcester, MA........................Employment Benefits Law; Labor and Employment Law

SKOLOFF & WOLFE, P.C.
Livingston, NJ........................Family Law; General Practice; Municipal and Zoning Law; Real Estate Law; Tax Law

SKOUSEN, SKOUSEN, GULBRANDSEN & PATIENCE, P.C.
Mesa, AZ........................Personal Injury

SKULINA, THOMAS R.
Westlake, OH........................Civil Trial Practice

SLACK & DAVIS, L.L.P.
Austin, TX........................Aviation Law; Commercial Litigation; Personal Injury; Product Liability Law

SLADE & ASSOCIATES, P.C.
New York, NY........................Commercial Litigation; Criminal Trial Practice; Labor and Employment Law; Trademark, Copyright and Unfair Competition

SLATER, MILDRED FLETCHER
Upperville, VA........................Real Estate Law

SLATER LAW FIRM, A PROFESSIONAL CORPORATION
New Orleans, LA........................Antitrust Law; Business Law; Commercial Litigation; Environmental Law; Product Liability Law; Transportation Law

SLATES, RONALD P., P.C.
Los Angeles, CA........................Bankruptcy Law; Commercial Litigation; Creditors Rights; Real Estate Law

SLAVET, ARNOLD L.
Boston, MA........................Trust and Estates, Wills and Probate

SLAVIN, FRANCIS J., P.C.
Phoenix, AZ........................Real Estate Law

SLAWSON CUNNINGHAM WHALEN & STEWART, P.L.
Palm Beach Gardens, FL........Civil Trial Practice; Personal Injury

SLAYDON, KATHLEEN AMELIA, P.C.
Houston, TX........................Commercial Litigation

SLEVIN & HART, P.C.
Washington, DC........................Employment Benefits Law

SLEWETT, ROBERT D., P.A.
North Miami Beach, FL........Trust and Estates, Wills and Probate

SLICKER, FREDERICK K.
Tulsa, OK........................Business Law

SLIVKA ROBINSON WATERS & O'DORISIO, A PROFESSIONAL CORPORATION
Denver, CO........................Banking Law; Labor and Employment Law; Mergers and Acquisitions; Real Estate Law; Tax Law

SLOAN, TODD M. LAW OFFICES OF
Malibu, CA........................Civil Trial Practice

SLOAN, RUBENS & PEEPLES
West Memphis, AR........................Banking Law; Civil Trial Practice; General Practice

SLOMSKI, RAYMOND J., P.C., LAW OFFICES OF
Phoenix, AZ........................Medical Malpractice; Personal Injury

SLOTCHIVER & SLOTCHIVER, L.L.P.
Charleston, SC........................Civil Trial Practice; Tax Law

SMALL, DANIEL W.
Nashville, TN........................Banking Law; Commercial Litigation

SMALLEY, ROBERT H., JR., P.C.
Griffin, GA........................Banking Law; Civil Trial Practice; General Practice

SMALL LARKIN, LLP
Los Angeles, CA........................Intellectual Property Law; Patent, Trademark, Copyright and Unfair Competition

SMALL, TOTH, BALDRIDGE & VAN BELKUM, P.C.
Bingham Farms, MI........................Business Law; Civil Trial Practice; Construction Law; Health Care Law; Insurance Defense; Medical Malpractice; Product Liability Law

SMALLWOOD-COOK & SCHMIEDER
Warsaw, NY........................Family Law; General Practice; Real Estate Law; Trust and Estates, Wills and Probate

SMART & BIGGAR
Vancouver, BC, Canada........................Intellectual Property Law; Patent, Trademark, Copyright and Unfair Competition; Trademark, Copyright and Unfair Competition
Ottawa, ON, Canada........................Intellectual Property Law; Patent, Trademark, Copyright and Unfair Competition; Trademark, Copyright and Unfair Competition
Toronto, ON, Canada........................Intellectual Property Law; Patent, Trademark, Copyright and Unfair Competition; Trademark, Copyright and Unfair Competition

SMITH, DANIEL T.
Denver, CO........................Criminal Trial Practice

SMITH, DAVID RANDOLPH & ASSOCIATES
Nashville, TN........................Civil Trial Practice; Medical Malpractice; Personal Injury; Product Liability Law

SMITH, E. ALFRED & ASSOCIATES
Philadelphia, PA........................Civil Trial Practice

SMITH, ROBERT B.
Jesup, GA........................Civil Trial Practice; Personal Injury

SMITH, WALTER LANDRY
Baton Rouge, LA........................Personal Injury

SMITH, A. RUSSELL
Akron, OH........................Civil Trial Practice; Medical Malpractice; Personal Injury

SMITH, ANDREWS, ROGERS & BRADY
Tampa, FL........................Workers Compensation

SMITH, BARTLETT, HEEKE, CARPENTER, LEWIS & THOMPSON
Jeffersonville, IN........................General Practice

SMITH & BEMENDERFER
Indianapolis, IN........................Insurance Defense

SMITH, BRIAN E., THE, LAW FIRM
Yuma, AZ........................Civil Trial Practice; Personal Injury; Product Liability Law

SMITH & BROOKER, P.C.
Bay City, MI........................Insurance Defense

SMITH & CASHION, PLC
Nashville, TN........................Commercial Litigation; Construction Law

SMITH, CURRIE & HANCOCK LLP
Atlanta, GA........................Construction Law; Environmental Law; Government Contracts; Labor and Employment Law

SMITH DEBNAM NARRON WYCHE STORY & MYERS, L.L.P.
Raleigh, NC........................Administrative Law; Appellate Practice; Bankruptcy Law; Civil Trial Practice; Commercial Law

SMITH & DUGGAN LLP
Boston, MA........................Commercial Litigation; Product Liability Law

SMITH ELLIOTT SMITH & GARMEY, P.A.
Saco, ME........................Civil Trial Practice; General Practice; Medical Malpractice; Personal Injury

SMITH & ELY, LLP
Birmingham, AL........................Appellate Practice; Civil Trial Practice; Commercial Litigation; Insurance Defense; Personal Injury; Product Liability Law; Professional Liability; Transportation Law; Workers Compensation

SMITH, FINKELSTEIN, LUNDBERG, ISLER AND YAKABOSKI, LLP
Riverhead, NY........................Civil Trial Practice; General Practice

SMITH, GAMBRELL & RUSSELL, LLP
Washington, DC........................Intellectual Property Law; Patent, Trademark, Copyright and Unfair Competition

SMITH, GENDLER, SHIELL, SHEFF & FORD, P.A.
Minneapolis, MN........................Real Estate Law

SMITH, GILLIAM AND WILLIAMS
Gainesville, GA........................Corporate Law; General Practice; Insurance Defense; Real Estate Law; Tax Law

SMITH, GOLDSTEIN, MAGRAM & BERENATO, A PROFESSIONAL CORPORATION
Burlington, NJ........................Civil Trial Practice; General Practice; Medical Malpractice; Personal Injury; Product Liability Law

SMITH, GRIMSLEY, BAUMAN, PINKERTON, PETERMANN & WELLS
Fort Walton Beach, FL........................General Practice

SMITH & HALE
Columbus, OH........................Municipal Bond/Public Authority Financing; Real Estate Law

SMITH AND HAMM, P.A.
Lake Alfred, FL........................Family Law

SMITH & HARRINGTON
Eastman, GA........................Civil Trial Practice

SMITH HAUGHEY RICE & ROEGGE, P.C.
East Lansing, MI........................Civil Trial Practice; General Practice; Insurance Defense; Medical Malpractice
Grand Rapids, MI........................Civil Trial Practice; General Practice; Insurance Defense; Medical Malpractice

Lansing, MI ....Civil Trial Practice; General Practice; Insurance Defense; Medical Malpractice
Traverse City, MI ....Civil Trial Practice; General Practice; Insurance Defense; Medical Malpractice

SMITH HELMS MULLISS & MOORE, L.L.P.
Charlotte, NC ....General Practice
Greensboro, NC ....General Practice
Raleigh, NC ....General Practice

SMITH, HOWARD & AJAX, LLP
Atlanta, GA ....Aviation Law; Civil Trial Practice; Construction Law; Insurance Defense; Medical Malpractice; Patent, Trademark, Copyright and Unfair Competition; Product Liability Law; Securities Law

SMITH HULSEY & BUSEY
Jacksonville, FL ....Business Law; Commercial Litigation; Environmental Law; Health Care Law; Real Estate Law; Tax Law

SMITH & JAKUBOWSKI
Abington, PA ....Trust and Estates, Wills and Probate

SMITH & JENSEN, P.C. A PROFESSIONAL CORPORATION
Richmond, VA ....Insurance Defense; Product Liability Law

SMITH & JOHNSON, ATTORNEYS, P.C.
Traverse City, MI ....Commercial Litigation; Corporate Law; Family Law; Personal Injury

SMITH, KATZENSTEIN & FURLOW LLP
Wilmington, DE ....Bankruptcy Law; Business Law; Civil Trial Practice; Commercial Law; General Practice; Insurance Defense; Labor and Employment Law; Medical Malpractice; Personal Injury; Product Liability Law; Securities Law

SMITH LARSEN & WIXOM, CHARTERED
Las Vegas, NV ....Banking Law; Commercial Litigation; Construction Law; Insurance Defense; Real Estate Law

SMITH LAW FIRM, THE, L.L.P.
Leesville, LA ....Personal Injury

SMITH, LEWIS, BECKETT, POWELL, ROARK & DURLEY, L.L.P.
Columbia, MO ....General Practice

SMITH LYONS
Toronto, ON, Canada ....General Practice

SMITH, MARSHALL, WEAVER AND VERGON
Cleveland, OH ....Civil Trial Practice; Insurance Defense; Product Liability Law

SMITH, MAURRAS, COHEN, REDD & HORAN, PLC
Fort Smith, AR ....Business Law; Commercial Litigation

SMITH MAZURE DIRECTOR WILKINS YOUNG YAGERMAN & TARALLO, P.C.
New York, NY ....Civil Trial Practice; General Practice; Insurance Defense; Toxic Torts

SMITH MCCULLOUGH, P.C.
Denver, CO ....Franchise Law

SMITH & MCELWAIN
Sioux City, IA ....Labor and Employment Law; Workers Compensation

SMITH & MOORE
Dallas, TX ....Aviation Law; Insurance Defense

SMITH, NEVILLE, LAW FIRM OF
Manchester, KY ....General Practice

SMITH AND NOWLIN
Ventura, CA ....Family Law

SMITH PETERSON LAW FIRM
Council Bluffs, IA ....Business Law; Commercial Law; Insurance Defense; Labor and Employment Law; Real Estate Law; Tax Law; Trust and Estates, Wills and Probate

SMITH, PHILLIP R., P.C.
Martinsville, IN ....General Practice

SMITH, PHILLIPS, MITCHELL, SCOTT & RUTHERFORD
Batesville, MS ....Personal Injury

SMITH, RANSCHT, CONNORS, MUTINO, NORDELL & SIRIGNANO, P.C.
White Plains, NY ....Commercial Litigation; Corporate Law; General Practice; Real Estate Law; Tax Law; Trust and Estates, Wills and Probate

SMITH, SABBATINI & MCLEARY, PLLC
Memphis, TN ....Civil Trial Practice; Commercial Litigation; General Practice; Health Care Law; Insurance Defense; Labor and Employment Law; Medical Malpractice; Personal Injury; Product Liability Law; Professional Liability; Toxic Torts; Workers Compensation

SMITH, SAUER & DEMARIA
Pensacola, FL ....General Practice

SMITH & SMITH
Vero Beach, FL ....Civil Trial Practice; General Practice; Trust and Estates, Wills and Probate

SMITH AND SMITH
Louisville, KY ....Labor and Employment Law

SMITH, SOVIK, KENDRICK & SUGNET, P.C.
Syracuse, NY ....General Practice; Medical Malpractice; Workers Compensation

SMITH, SPIRES & PEDDY, P.C.
Birmingham, AL ....Civil Trial Practice; Health Care Law; Insurance Defense; Product Liability Law; Workers Compensation

SMITH, STRATTON, WISE, HEHER & BRENNAN
Princeton, NJ ....General Practice

SMITH, UNDERWOOD & PERKINS, A PROFESSIONAL CORPORATION
Dallas, TX ....Banking Law; Business Law; Civil Trial Practice; Commercial Law; Commercial Litigation; Construction Law; Employment Benefits Law; General Practice; Insurance Defense; Intellectual Property Law; International Business Law; Labor and Employment Law; Land Use Law; Medical Malpractice; Mergers and Acquisitions; Pension and Profit Sharing; Professional Liability; Real Estate Law; Securities Law; Tax Law; Trust and Estates, Wills and Probate

SMITH & URE
Santa Ana, CA ....Personal Injury

SMITH, WELCH & BRITTAIN
McDonough, GA ....Civil Trial Practice; Family Law; General Practice; Municipal and Zoning Law; Personal Injury; Real Estate Law

SMITH & WILLIAMS
Las Vegas, NV ....Medical Malpractice; Personal Injury

SMOAK, RICHARD
Panama City, FL ....General Practice; Professional Liability

SMOCK AND WEINBERGER
Phoenix, AZ ....Antitrust Law; Commercial Litigation; Insurance Defense

SMOLEN & PLEVY P.C.
Vienna, VA ....Business Law; Family Law; Trust and Estates, Wills and Probate

SMYTH, JEFFREY A., P.S.
Seattle, WA ....Civil Trial Practice

SMYTH & LACK
Huntington, NY ....Banking Law; Corporate Law; General Practice; Real Estate Law; Trust and Estates, Wills and Probate

SNAPKA, KATHRYN
Corpus Christi, TX ....Personal Injury

SNEAD, WILLIAM O. P. III
Fairfax, VA ....Personal Injury

SNEED LANG, P.C.
Tulsa, OK ....Antitrust Law; Banking Law; Bankruptcy Law; Civil Trial Practice; Commercial Law; Commercial Litigation; Criminal Trial Practice; Energy Law; Insurance Defense; Natural Resources Law; Personal Injury; Real Estate Law; Securities Law; Trust and Estates, Wills and Probate

SNEERINGER, EUGENE M. JR.
Albany, NY ....Real Estate Law

SNELBAKER, BRENNEMAN & SPARE, P.C.
Mechanicsburg, PA ....General Practice; Municipal and Zoning Law

SNELLGROVE, LANGLEY, LOVETT & CULPEPPER
Jonesboro, AR ....General Practice; Insurance Defense

SNELLINGS, BREARD, SARTOR, INABNETT & TRASCHER, LLP
Monroe, LA ....Civil Trial Practice; General Practice

SNELL & WILMER L.L.P.
Phoenix, AZ ....Antitrust Law; Banking Law; Bankruptcy Law; Civil Trial Practice; Commercial Law; Commercial Litigation; Construction Law; Employment Benefits Law; Environmental Law; General Practice; Health Care Law; Intellectual Property Law; Labor and Employment Law; Municipal Bond/Public Authority Financing; Natural Resources Law; Product Liability Law; Real Estate Law; Sports and Entertainment Law; Tax Law; Trust and Estates, Wills and Probate

SNELL & WILMER L.L.P. — *Continued*

Tucson, AZ .... Antitrust Law; Banking Law; Bankruptcy Law; Environmental Law; Intellectual Property Law; Labor and Employment Law; Municipal Bond/Public Authority Financing; Real Estate Law; Sports and Entertainment Law; Tax Law; Trust and Estates, Wills and Probate

Irvine, CA .... Corporate Law; General Practice; Intellectual Property Law; Labor and Employment Law; Product Liability Law; Tax Law; Trust and Estates, Wills and Probate

Salt Lake City, UT .... Environmental Law; General Practice; Intellectual Property Law; Labor and Employment Law; Municipal Bond/Public Authority Financing; Natural Resources Law; Product Liability Law; Tax Law

SNOW, CHRISTENSEN & MARTINEAU, P.C.

Salt Lake City, UT .... General Practice

SNYDER, WILLIAM A.

Davie, FL .... Trust and Estates, Wills and Probate

SNYDER, MALLON A., CHARTERED

Rockville, MD .... Arbitration

SOBEL, EDWARD B.

Bradenton, FL .... Family Law

SOBEL, EDWARD B.

Sarasota, FL .... Family Law

SOBELSOHN & JOHNSON, LLP

Encino, CA .... Workers Compensation

SOBIESKI, MESSER & ASSOCIATES

Knoxville, TN .... Appellate Practice; Civil Rights; Construction Law; Family Law

SOCKRIDER, BOLIN, ANGLIN & BATTE, A PROFESSIONAL LAW CORPORATION

Shreveport, LA .... Civil Trial Practice; Family Law; Personal Injury; Trust and Estates, Wills and Probate

SOKOL, BEHOT AND FIORENZO

Hackensack, NJ .... Business Law; Civil Trial Practice; Commercial Law; Environmental Law; General Practice; Real Estate Law

SOKOLOFF, CHARLES S., INCORPORATED

Smithfield, RI .... Business Law; Commercial Litigation; Corporate Law; Franchise Law; Land Use Law; Nonprofit and Tax Exempt Organizations; Real Estate Law; Trust and Estates, Wills and Probate

SOLOMON, JEFFREY LAW OFFICE OF

Hollywood, FL .... Bankruptcy Law; Trust and Estates, Wills and Probate

SOLOMON, STEPHEN E.

Los Angeles, CA .... Tax Law

SOLOMON & BENEDICT, P.A.

Tampa, FL .... Commercial Litigation

SOLOMON, BUDMAN, STRICKER & SCHWARTZ, L.L.P.

Charleston, SC .... Civil Trial Practice; Family Law; Personal Injury; Real Estate Law; Tax Law

SOLOMON WARD SEIDENWURM & SMITH, LLP

San Diego, CA .... Civil Trial Practice; Commercial Law; Real Estate Law; Tax Law; Trust and Estates, Wills and Probate

SOLOVAY, EDLIN & EISEMAN

New York, NY .... Civil Trial Practice; Commercial Litigation; Corporate Law; General Practice; Real Estate Law; Securities Law

SOMMER & BARNARD, ATTORNEYS AT LAW, PC

Indianapolis, IN .... Administrative Law; Antitrust Law; Bankruptcy Law; Business Law; Civil Trial Practice; Commercial Law; Computer Law; Environmental Law; General Practice; Labor and Employment Law; Real Estate Law; Securities Law

SOMMERS, SCHWARTZ, SILVER & SCHWARTZ, P.C.

Southfield, MI .... Appellate Practice; Banking Law; Bankruptcy Law; Business Law; Civil Trial Practice; Commercial Law; Criminal Trial Practice; Employment Benefits Law; Environmental Law; Family Law; General Practice; Health Care Law; Insurance Defense; Labor and Employment Law; Medical Malpractice; Personal Injury; Product Liability Law; Real Estate Law; Sports and Entertainment Law; Tax Law; Trust and Estates, Wills and Probate; Workers Compensation

SONDERBY, PETER R., P.C.

Chicago, IL .... Civil Trial Practice; Commercial Litigation; Securities Law

SONNENSCHEIN NATH & ROSENTHAL

Los Angeles, CA .... General Practice

San Francisco, CA .... General Practice

Washington, DC .... General Practice

Chicago, IL .... General Practice

Kansas City, MO .... General Practice

St. Louis, MO .... General Practice

New York, NY .... General Practice

SOPUCH NOUHAN HIGGINS & ARNETT, L.L.P.

Dallas, TX .... Commercial Litigation; Construction Law

SORLING, NORTHRUP, HANNA, CULLEN AND COCHRAN, LTD.

Springfield, IL .... General Practice

SOROKIN, GROSS & HYDE, P.C.

Hartford, CT .... Administrative Law; Antitrust Law; Appellate Practice; Business Law; Civil Trial Practice; Commercial Law; Construction Law; Employment Benefits Law; Family Law; General Practice; Insurance Defense; Labor and Employment Law; Real Estate Law; Securities Law; Tax Law; Trust and Estates, Wills and Probate

SOULE, JOEL V.

Grand Rapids, MI .... Business Law

SOUTHWELL & O'ROURKE, P.S.

Spokane, WA .... Bankruptcy Law

SOWDERS, A. GLENN JR.

Kansas City, MO .... Tax Law

SOWELL, MATTHEW W., P.A.

Jacksonville, FL .... Medical Malpractice; Product Liability Law

SPAETH & MCGRATH

San Francisco, CA .... Administrative Law

SPAIN & GILLON, L.L.C.

Birmingham, AL .... Antitrust Law; Banking Law; Bankruptcy Law; Civil Trial Practice; Commercial Law; Environmental Law; General Practice; Insurance Defense; Labor and Employment Law; Medical Malpractice; Municipal Bond/Public Authority Financing; Personal Injury; Real Estate Law; Tax Law; Trust and Estates, Wills and Probate

SPANGENBERG, SHIBLEY & LIBER LLP

Cleveland, OH .... General Practice; Medical Malpractice; Personal Injury; Product Liability Law

SPANGLER, JENNINGS & DOUGHERTY, P.C.

Merrillville, IN .... Civil Trial Practice; General Practice; Insurance Defense; Personal Injury

Valparaiso, IN .... General Practice; Insurance Defense; Personal Injury; Product Liability Law

SPARBER, FERGUSON, PONDER & RYAN, A PROFESSIONAL LAW CORPORATION

San Diego, CA .... General Practice

SPARKMAN, ROBB & MASON

Miami, FL .... Civil Trial Practice; Insurance Defense

SPARKS, TEHAN & RYLEY, P.C.

Scottsdale, AZ .... Commercial Litigation; Environmental Law; Natural Resources Law; Real Estate Law; Trust and Estates, Wills and Probate

SPARLING, DENSFORD AND REYNOLDS, P.A.

Lexington Park, MD .... General Practice

SPEARS, MICHAEL E., P.A.

Spartanburg, SC .... Medical Malpractice

SPECTOR GADON & ROSEN, P.C.

Philadelphia, PA .... Business Law; Civil Trial Practice; Commercial Litigation

SPECTOR & ROSEMAN, A PROFESSIONAL CORPORATION

Philadelphia, PA .... Antitrust Law; Civil Trial Practice; Commercial Litigation; Securities Law

SPEISER KRAUSE, A PROFESSIONAL CORPORATION

Irvine, CA .... Aviation Law

Dallas, TX .... Aviation Law

Arlington, VA .... Aviation Law

New York, NY .... Aviation Law

SPEISER, LAURENCE A., LTD.

Las Vegas, NV .... Business Law

SPENCE, KOHLER, CHRISTIE & PULVER, P.A.

Baltimore, MD .... Medical Malpractice; Personal Injury

SPENCE, MORIARITY & SCHUSTER, LLC

Jackson, WY .... Civil Trial Practice; Criminal Trial Practice; General Practice; Medical Malpractice; Personal Injury; Product Liability Law

SPENCE, RICKE & THURMER, P.A.
St. Paul, MN .... Insurance Defense; Labor and Employment Law; Transportation Law

SPENCER FANE BRITT & BROWNE LLP
Kansas City, MO .... Civil Trial Practice; Environmental Law; Labor and Employment Law

SPENCER AND KLEIN, PROFESSIONAL ASSOCIATION
Miami, FL .... Civil Trial Practice; General Practice; International Business Law; Tax Law

SPENCER & SPENCER, PROFESSIONAL ASSOCIATION
Rock Hill, SC .... General Practice

SPERLING, DEAN P.
Santa Ana, CA .... Commercial Law

SPESIA, AYERS & ARDAUGH
Joliet, IL .... General Practice; Personal Injury

SPIEGEL LIAO & KAGAY
San Francisco, CA .... Antitrust Law; Appellate Practice; Commercial Litigation

SPIETH, BELL, MCCURDY & NEWELL CO., L.P.A.
Cleveland, OH .... Civil Trial Practice; General Practice; Labor and Employment Law; Real Estate Law; Tax Law; Trust and Estates, Wills and Probate

SPILMAN THOMAS & BATTLE, PLLC
Charleston, WV .... General Practice

SPITLER, VOGTSBERGER & HUFFMAN, LLP
Bowling Green, OH .... Personal Injury

SPITZ & CARR
Edmonton, AB, Canada .... Civil Trial Practice

SPITZER & FELDMAN, P.C.
New York, NY .... Civil Trial Practice; Corporate Law

SPOHRER, WILNER, MAXWELL & MATTHEWS, P.A.
Jacksonville, FL .... Aviation Law

SPRECHMAN & ASSOCIATES, P.A.
Miami, FL .... Commercial Litigation; Creditors Rights

SPRENGER & LANG, P.L.L.C.
Washington, DC .... Civil Rights; Labor and Employment Law
Minneapolis, MN .... Labor and Employment Law

SPRINGER, CASEY & DIENSTAG, P.C.
Chicago, IL .... General Practice

SPRINGER, LYLE & WATT L.L.P.
Denton, TX .... Personal Injury

SPRINGER & STEINBERG, A PROFESSIONAL CORPORATION
Denver, CO .... Criminal Trial Practice; Personal Injury

SPURRIER, RICE, WOOD & HALL
Huntsville, AL .... Civil Trial Practice; Insurance Defense

SQUIRE, SANDERS & DEMPSEY
London, England .... General Practice
Almaty, Kazakhstan .... General Practice
Moscow, Russia .... General Practice
Madrid, Spain .... General Practice
Taipei, Taiwan .... General Practice
Phoenix, AZ .... General Practice
Washington, DC .... General Practice
Jacksonville, FL .... General Practice
Miami, FL .... General Practice
New York, NY .... General Practice
Cleveland, OH .... General Practice
Columbus, OH .... General Practice
Houston, TX .... General Practice
Brussels, Belgium .... General Practice
Hong Kong, China .... General Practice
Budapest, Hungary .... General Practice
Bratislava, Slovakia .... General Practice
Kyiv (Kiev), Ukraine .... General Practice
Prague, Czech Republic .... General Practice

SREENAN, GREGORY P., P.A., LAW OFFICES OF
Miami, FL .... Aviation Law; Insurance Defense

STACEY & WALEN
Billings, MT .... General Practice; Insurance Defense

STACKHOUSE, SMITH & NEXSEN
Norfolk, VA .... Banking Law; Bankruptcy Law; Business Law; Civil Trial Practice; General Practice; Insurance Defense

STADTMAUER BAILKIN, LLP
New York, NY .... Real Estate Law

STAHANCYK, GEARING & RACKNER, P.C.
Portland, OR .... Family Law; Trust and Estates, Wills and Probate

STAITMAN SNYDER TANNENBAUM & DORENFELD, LLP
Encino, CA .... Civil Trial Practice; Insurance Defense

STALMACK, JOSEPH, & ASSOCIATES, P.C.
Hammond, IN .... Civil Trial Practice

STAMBLER, ERROL H.
Los Angeles, CA .... Criminal Trial Practice

STAMOS & TRUCCO
Chicago, IL .... Health Care Law

STAMPER, HADLEY & REASOR
Antlers, OK .... Civil Trial Practice; General Practice; Insurance Defense; Labor and Employment Law

STANISLAW ASHBAUGH, LLP
Seattle, WA .... Construction Law

STANSBURY, RICHARD T., A PROFESSIONAL ASSOCIATION
Baltimore, MD .... Business Law; Mergers and Acquisitions; Tax Law; Trust and Estates, Wills and Probate

STANTON, WILLIAM E.
Millbrook, NY .... Civil Trial Practice; Criminal Trial Practice; Medical Malpractice

STANTON & ASSOCIATES, A PROFESSIONAL CORPORATION
Washington, DC .... Bankruptcy Law

STANTON, HUGHES, DIANA, SALSBERG, CERRA & MARIANI, P.C.
Morristown, NJ .... Labor and Employment Law

STANYAR, CAROLE M.
Detroit, MI .... Appellate Practice; Criminal Trial Practice

STAPLETON & STAPLETON, A PROFESSIONAL ASSOCIATION
Tustin, CA .... Criminal Trial Practice; Family Law

STARBIRD, RUSSELL B., P.C.
Houston, TX .... Commercial Litigation

STARK DONINGER & SMITH
Indianapolis, IN .... Business Law; Environmental Law; General Practice; Real Estate Law

STARKEY, KELLY, BLANEY & WHITE
Toms River, NJ .... Civil Trial Practice; General Practice; Insurance Defense; Personal Injury; Real Estate Law; Workers Compensation

STARK & KEENAN, A PROFESSIONAL ASSOCIATION
Bel Air, MD .... Appellate Practice; Business Law; Civil Trial Practice; General Practice; Municipal and Zoning Law; Personal Injury; Real Estate Law; Trust and Estates, Wills and Probate

STARK & KNOLL CO., L.P.A.
Akron, OH .... Corporate Law; Trust and Estates, Wills and Probate

STARK, REAGAN & FINNERTY, P.C.
Troy, MI .... Business Law; Civil Trial Practice; Construction Law; Employment Benefits Law; Labor and Employment Law; Tax Law; Trust and Estates, Wills and Probate

STARK & STARK, A PROFESSIONAL CORPORATION
Princeton, NJ .... Business Law; Commercial Litigation; Family Law; Personal Injury; Product Liability Law; Real Estate Law; Securities Law; Trust and Estates, Wills and Probate; Workers Compensation

STARN, PETER, A LAW CORPORATION, LAW OFFICES OF
Honolulu, HI .... Commercial Law; Real Estate Law

STARNES & ATCHISON LLP
Birmingham, AL .... Civil Trial Practice; Construction Law; Environmental Law; Insurance Defense; Medical Malpractice; Personal Injury; Product Liability Law

STATON, PERKINSON, DOSTER, POST, SILVERMAN & ADCOCK, P.A.
Sanford, NC .... General Practice

STEAKLEY & WETSEL
Sweetwater, TX .... Oil and Gas Law

STEEFEL, LEVITT & WEISS, A PROFESSIONAL CORPORATION
San Francisco, CA .... Civil Trial Practice; General Practice

STEEG AND O'CONNOR, L.L.C.
New Orleans, LA .... Real Estate Law

STEEL, JOHN H. LAW OFFICES OF
Telluride, CO....Business Law; Civil Trial Practice

STEELE, JERRY
Phoenix, AZ....Civil Trial Practice

STEELE, STEELE, MCSOLEY & MCSOLEY
Bedford, IN....Banking Law; Civil Trial Practice; General Practice

STEEL HECTOR & DAVIS LLP
Miami, FL....General Practice

STEELMAN, BARRY L., P.A.
Baltimore, MD....Civil Trial Practice

STEEL, RUDNICK & RUBEN
Philadelphia, PA....Immigration and Naturalization

STEEN REYNOLDS & DALEHITE, LLP
Jackson, MS....Civil Trial Practice; Insurance Defense

STEIN, RICK M. LAW OFFICES OF
Palm Springs, CA....Civil Trial Practice

STEIN, FORD, SCHAAF & TOWZEY, L.L.P.
St. Petersburg, FL....Civil Trial Practice; Commercial Litigation; Labor and Employment Law; Real Estate Law; Trust and Estates, Wills and Probate

STEIN, HARVEY W., A PROFESSIONAL CORPORATION
Oakland, CA....Commercial Law

STEIN, MOORE & FAY, P.A.
St. Paul, MN....Bankruptcy Law; Real Estate Law

STEIN RISO MANTEL HASPEL & JACOBS LLP
New York, NY....Criminal Trial Practice; Family Law; Tax Law

STEIN, SCHIFINO & VAN DER WALL
Tampa, FL....Intellectual Property Law

STEIN, SPERLING, BENNETT, DE JONG, DRISCOLL, GREENFEIG & METRO, P.C.
Rockville, MD....Bankruptcy Law; Business Law; Civil Trial Practice; Commercial Law; Commercial Litigation; Corporate Law; Criminal Trial Practice; Family Law; General Practice; Labor and Employment Law; Medical Malpractice; Personal Injury; Real Estate Law; Tax Law; Trust and Estates, Wills and Probate

STEIN, STEPHEN, CHARTERED
Las Vegas, NV....Criminal Trial Practice

STEINBERG BARNESS FOSTER & FOLEY LLP
Manhattan Beach, CA....Bankruptcy Law; Business Law; Civil Trial Practice; General Practice; Real Estate Law; Trust and Estates, Wills and Probate

STEINBERG, NUTTER & BRENT, LAW CORPORATION
Santa Monica, CA....Bankruptcy Law; Civil Trial Practice; Real Estate Law

STEINBERG & RASKIN, P.C.
New York, NY....Patent, Trademark, Copyright and Unfair Competition

STEINBERG & YAFFE, P.A.
Miami Beach, FL....Trust and Estates, Wills and Probate

STEINBURG, CARWILE, HERZIK & PRIETO
Houston, TX....Personal Injury

STEINER AND STEINER
Kittanning, PA....General Practice

STEINHEIMER, RIGGIO, HAYDEL & MORDAUNT, A PROFESSIONAL LAW CORPORATION
Stockton, CA....Civil Trial Practice; General Practice

STENGER & FINNERTY
Buffalo, NY....Civil Trial Practice; Commercial Litigation; Constitutional Law; Environmental Law

STENSTROM, MCINTOSH, COLBERT, WHIGHAM & SIMMONS, P.A.
Sanford, FL....Civil Trial Practice; Family Law; General Practice; Real Estate Law; Trust and Estates, Wills and Probate

STEPHENS, BARONI, REILLY & LEWIS LLP
White Plains, NY....Civil Trial Practice; Corporate Law; Criminal Trial Practice; General Practice; Municipal and Zoning Law

STEPHENS LAW FIRM, PLLC
McLean, VA....General Practice

STEPHENS, MILLIRONS, HARRISON & GAMMONS, P.C.
Huntsville, AL....Banking Law; Bankruptcy Law; Civil Trial Practice; Corporate Law; Family Law; General Practice; Personal Injury; Real Estate Law

STEPHENSON, WORLEY, GARRATT, SCHWARTZ, GARFIELD & PRAIRIE
San Diego, CA....Employment Benefits Law; Land Use Law; Real Estate Law

STEPONOVICH & ASSOCIATES, A PROFESSIONAL LAW CORPORATION
Irvine, CA....Civil Trial Practice

STEPP & BEAUCHAMP LLP
Newport Beach, CA....Business Law; Civil Trial Practice; Corporate Law; Real Estate Law

STEPP & SULLIVAN, P.C.
Houston, TX....Admiralty/Maritime Law; Civil Trial Practice

STEPTOE & JOHNSON LLP
Phoenix, AZ....General Practice
Los Angeles, CA....General Practice
Washington, DC....General Practice

STERN & EDLIN, P.C.
Atlanta, GA....Family Law

STERN & KLEPFER, L.L.P.
Greensboro, NC....Business Law; Commercial Law; Labor and Employment Law; Real Estate Law

STERNS & WEINROTH, A PROFESSIONAL CORPORATION
Atlantic City, NJ....General Practice
Trenton, NJ....General Practice

STETINA BRUNDA GARRED & BRUCKER, A PROFESSIONAL CORPORATION
Laguna Hills, CA....Antitrust Law; Commercial Litigation; Computer Law; Patent, Trademark, Copyright and Unfair Competition

STETTNER, MILLER AND COHN, P.C.
Denver, CO....Labor and Employment Law

STEVENS, RICHARD W.
Jenkintown, PA....Trust and Estates, Wills and Probate

STEVENS, BAGLEY & STEVENS
Fayetteville, TN....General Practice

STEVENS & JOHNSON
Allentown, PA....Insurance Defense

STEVENS & KRAMER, A PROFESSIONAL CORPORATION
Irvine, CA....Arbitration; Civil Trial Practice; Elder Law; Insurance Defense; Personal Injury; Professional Liability

STEVENS LAW FIRM, P.C.
Loris, SC....Civil Trial Practice; Eminent Domain; Labor and Employment Law; Personal Injury; Product Liability Law; Real Estate Law; Workers Compensation

STEVENS, MCGHEE, MORGAN, LENNON, O'QUINN & TOLL
Wilmington, NC....Commercial Litigation; Trust and Estates, Wills and Probate

STEVENS & MINTER
Secaucus, NJ....Insurance Defense

STEVENS & O'CONNELL LLP
Sacramento, CA....Civil Trial Practice; Commercial Litigation; Criminal Trial Practice; Environmental Law

STEWART, TIMOTHY A.
Hagåtña, GU....General Practice

STEWART, COOK, CONSTANCE, STEWART & MINTON, L.L.C.
Independence, MO....General Practice

STEWART AND DE CHANT CO., L.P.A.
Cleveland, OH....Medical Malpractice; Personal Injury; Product Liability Law; Workers Compensation

STEWART, ESTES & DONNELL
Nashville, TN....Insurance Defense; Sports and Entertainment Law

STEWART, EVANS & HAFNER, P.A.
Vero Beach, FL....Health Care Law; Real Estate Law; Trust and Estates, Wills and Probate

STEWART, JAMES D., AND ASSOCIATES, INC.
San Antonio, TX....Family Law

STEWART, JOYNER & JORDAN-HOLMES, P.A.
Tampa, FL....Insurance Defense; Personal Injury; Transportation Law

STEWART MCKELVEY STIRLING SCALES
Fredericton, NB, Canada....General Practice
Moncton, NB, Canada....General Practice
Saint John, NB, Canada....General Practice
St. John's, NF, Canada....General Practice

Halifax, NS, Canada ....General Practice
Sydney, NS, Canada ....General Practice
Charlottetown, PE, Canada.....General Practice

STEWART, MELVIN & FROST, LLP
Gainesville, GA ....General Practice

STEWART, PLANT & BLUMENTHAL, LLC
Baltimore, MD ....Tax Law; Trust and Estates, Wills and Probate

STEWART AND STEWART
Washington, DC......................General Practice; International Business Law

STEWART TILGHMAN FOX & BIANCHI, P.A.
Miami, FL ....Civil Trial Practice

STICHTER, RIEDEL, BLAIN & PROSSER, P.A.
Tampa, FL ....Bankruptcy Law

STIKEMAN ELLIOTT
Vancouver, BC, Canada..........General Practice
Ottawa, ON, Canada ....General Practice
Toronto, ON, Canada.............General Practice
Montreal, QU, Canada ....General Practice
Hong Kong, China..................General Practice
London, England ....General Practice

STILES BYRUM & HORNE, L.L.P.
Charlotte, NC..........................Insurance Defense

STILES, TAYLOR & GRACE, P.A.
Boca Raton, FL ....Workers Compensation
Miami, FL ....Workers Compensation
Orlando, FL ....Workers Compensation
Tallahassee, FL ....Workers Compensation
Tampa, FL ....Workers Compensation

STILLMAN & FRIEDMAN, P.C.
New York, NY.........................Civil Trial Practice; Criminal Trial Practice

STIMMEL, STIMMEL & SMITH, A PROFESSIONAL CORPORATION
San Francisco, CA ....Business Law; Construction Law; Corporate Law; International Business Law; Trust and Estates, Wills and Probate

STINSON, JOSEPH M.
Tylertown, MS ....General Practice

STINSON, LOUIS, JR., P.A.
Miami, FL ....Admiralty/Maritime Law

STIPANOV & MEBANE, A PROFESSIONAL LAW CORPORATION
San Diego, CA ....Real Estate Law

STIRLING & KLEINTOP
Honolulu, HI..........................Family Law; Trust and Estates, Wills and Probate

STITES & HARBISON
Frankfort, KY ....General Practice
Lexington, KY ....General Practice; Natural Resources Law
Louisville, KY ....General Practice; Municipal Bond/Public Authority Financing

STITES, HOPKINS & FAIR
Kansas City, MO.....................Medical Malpractice; Personal Injury; Product Liability Law

STITES, MCELWAIN & FOWLER
Louisville, KY ....General Practice

STOCKS AND FENTIN, LLP
San Diego, CA ....Family Law

STOCKTON & SADLER
Modesto, CA ....Civil Trial Practice

STOCKWELL, SIEVERT, VICCELLIO, CLEMENTS & SHADDOCK, L.L.P.
Lake Charles, LA.....................General Practice

STOCKWOOD SPIES
Toronto, ON, Canada.............Civil Trial Practice

STOEL RIVES LLP
Portland, OR ....General Practice

STOKES, FRED
Albemarle, NC ....Criminal Trial Practice

STOKES & BARTHOLOMEW, P.A.
Nashville, TN ....General Practice

STOKES & MURPHY, P.C.
San Diego, CA ....Labor and Employment Law
Atlanta, GA ....Labor and Employment Law

STOLAR PARTNERSHIP, THE
St. Louis, MO.........................Creditors Rights; Environmental Law; Health Care Law; Mergers and Acquisitions

STOLDT, HORAN AND KOWAL, A PROFESSIONAL CORPORATION
Hackensack, NJ.......................Civil Trial Practice; Employment Benefits Law; Environmental Law; Land Use Law; Municipal and Zoning Law; Real Estate Law

STOLL, KEENON & PARK, LLP
Frankfort, KY ....General Practice
Lexington, KY ....Administrative Law; Antitrust Law; Banking Law; Bankruptcy Law; Business Law; Civil Trial Practice; Commercial Law; Communications Law; Employment Benefits Law; Environmental Law; Family Law; General Practice; Health Care Law; Insurance Defense; Labor and Employment Law; Municipal and Zoning Law; Municipal Bond/Public Authority Financing; Natural Resources Law; Patent, Trademark, Copyright and Unfair Competition; Real Estate Law; Securities Law; Tax Law; Trust and Estates, Wills and Probate
Louisville, KY ....Commercial Law; General Practice

STOLPMAN • KRISSMAN • ELBER • MANDEL & KATZMAN LLP
Long Beach, CA......................Civil Trial Practice; Personal Injury; Product Liability Law

STOLTZ, MELVIN I.
Milford, CT ....Patent, Trademark, Copyright and Unfair Competition

STOMPOLY, STROUD, GLICKSMAN & ERICKSON, P.C.
Tucson, AZ ....Civil Trial Practice; Family Law; General Practice; Medical Malpractice; Personal Injury; Product Liability Law

STONE, JACK A. LAW OFFICES OF
Evansville, IN.........................Tax Law; Trust and Estates, Wills and Probate

STONE, NANCY J.
Amarillo, TX..........................Civil Trial Practice; Commercial Litigation; Personal Injury

STONE, DOLGINER & WENZEL, A LAW CORPORATION
Los Angeles, CA ....Civil Trial Practice; Medical Malpractice; Personal Injury; Product Liability Law

STONE, EDWARD H., P.C.
Irvine, CA..............................Trust and Estates, Wills and Probate

STONE, JED, LTD., THE LAW OFFICES OF
Chicago, IL.............................Criminal Trial Practice

STONE JESSUP, P.C.
Tulsa, OK...............................Municipal Bond/Public Authority Financing

STONE, KAPLAN & CHAPMAN, P.C.
Macon, GA ....Family Law

STONE, LEYTON & GERSHMAN, A PROFESSIONAL CORPORATION
St. Louis, MO.........................Bankruptcy Law; Commercial Litigation; Real Estate Law

STONE & MOORE, CHARTERED
Chicago, IL.............................Civil Trial Practice; Commercial Litigation; Construction Law; Insurance Defense; Legal Malpractice; Product Liability Law; Professional Liability; Toxic Torts; Workers Compensation

STONE, PIGMAN, WALTHER, WITTMANN & HUTCHINSON, L.L.P.
New Orleans, LA ....General Practice

STONE & ROSENBLATT, A LAW CORPORATION
Encino, CA.............................Insurance Defense

STONEMAN, CHANDLER & MILLER LLP
Boston, MA.............................Education Law; Labor and Employment Law

STOREY & PIERONI, PLC
Phoenix, AZ ....Real Estate Law

STORM, HAWK MESA
Angel Fire, NM ....Arbitration

STOUP, ARTHUR H., & ASSOCIATES, P.C.
Kansas City, MO.....................Civil Trial Practice; Medical Malpractice; Personal Injury; Workers Compensation

STOUT, MICHAEL L. LAW OFFICES OF
Roswell, NM ....Criminal Trial Practice; Personal Injury

STRADLEY & WRIGHT
Dallas, TX..............................Insurance Defense

STRADLING YOCCA CARLSON & RAUTH, A PROFESSIONAL CORPORATION
Newport Beach, CA................General Practice

STRAIN, JAMES R. JR.
Slidell, LA ....Medical Malpractice; Personal Injury; Workers Compensation

STRAIN, DENNIS, MAYHALL & BATES, L.L.P.
Baton Rouge, LA....................Oil and Gas Law

STRAMONDO, SALVATORE F.
Lexington, MA....................Aviation Law; Civil Trial Practice

STRANG, FLETCHER, CARRIGER, WALKER, HODGE & SMITH, PLLC
Chattanooga, TN....................General Practice

STRASBURGER & PRICE, L.L.P.
Austin, TX....................General Practice
Dallas, TX....................General Practice
Houston, TX....................General Practice
Mexico, D.F., Mexico....................General Practice

STRASSER & ASSOCIATES, A PROFESSIONAL CORPORATION
Paramus, NJ....................Civil Trial Practice; Commercial Law; General Practice; Health Care Law; Real Estate Law

STRAUSS & TROY, A LEGAL PROFESSIONAL ASSOCIATION
Covington, KY....................General Practice
Cincinnati, OH....................Business Law; Civil Trial Practice; Employment Benefits Law; General Practice; Insurance Defense; Medical Malpractice; Real Estate Law; Securities Law; Tax Law

STRAUSS • URITZ, A PROFESSIONAL CORPORATION
Ventura, CA....................Business Law; Civil Trial Practice; Environmental Law; Labor and Employment Law

STREATER & MURPHY, P.A.
Winona, MN....................General Practice; Personal Injury; Product Liability Law

STRECKER & ASSOCIATES, P.C.
Tulsa, OK....................Civil Trial Practice; Labor and Employment Law

STREET, STREET, STREET, SCOTT & BOWMAN
Grundy, VA....................General Practice

STREETER, PATRICIA A.
Chicago, IL....................Civil Trial Practice
Detroit, MI....................Civil Trial Practice

STRICKLAND & STRICKLAND, P.C.
Tucson, AZ....................Environmental Law; Medical Malpractice; Natural Resources Law; Personal Injury

STRICKLAND, WILTON L., P.A.
Fort Lauderdale, FL....................Medical Malpractice; Personal Injury; Product Liability Law

STRIDE, CRADDOCK & STRIDE
Chicago, IL....................Aviation Law; Civil Trial Practice; Medical Malpractice; Personal Injury; Product Liability Law

STRIFLING, JAN S., P.A.
Columbia, SC....................Criminal Trial Practice

STRIPLING, MCMICHAEL & STRIPLING, P.A.
Gainesville, FL....................Medical Malpractice; Personal Injury

STRODEL, ROBERT C., LTD.
Peoria, IL....................Civil Trial Practice; General Practice; Medical Malpractice; Personal Injury

STROEBEL, EDWARD
Wapakoneta, OH....................Trust and Estates, Wills and Probate

STRONG & HANNI, A PROFESSIONAL CORPORATION
Salt Lake City, UT....................Business Law; General Practice; Insurance Defense; Labor and Employment Law; Medical Malpractice; Product Liability Law; Trust and Estates, Wills and Probate

STRONG LAW FIRM, THE, A PROFESSIONAL CORPORATION
Springfield, MO....................Personal Injury

STRONG, PIPKIN, NELSON, BISSELL & LEDYARD, L.L.P.
Beaumont, TX....................General Practice

STRONG & STRONG, A PROFESSIONAL CORPORATION
Maryville, MO....................Civil Trial Practice

STROOCK & STROOCK & LAVAN LLP
Los Angeles, CA....................General Practice
Washington, DC....................General Practice
Miami, FL....................General Practice
Boston, MA....................General Practice
New York, NY....................Bankruptcy Law; General Practice; Tax Law

STROUD, WILLINK & HOWARD, LLC
Madison, WI....................General Practice; Real Estate Law; Trademark, Copyright and Unfair Competition; Trust and Estates, Wills and Probate

STROUP & JONES, L.L.P.
Longview, TX....................Product Liability Law

STROUT & PAYSON, P.A.
Rockland, ME....................Civil Trial Practice; General Practice; Tax Law

STRUCKMEYER AND WILSON
Phoenix, AZ....................Insurance Defense

STRYKER, DUENSING, CASNER & DOLLISON
Charlotte Amalie, St. Thomas, VI....................General Practice

STRYKER, TAMS & DILL LLP
Newark, NJ....................General Practice

STUART, CHARLES M. JR.
Greenville, SC....................Trust and Estates, Wills and Probate

STUART & BRANIGIN
Lafayette, IN....................Appellate Practice; Banking Law; Bankruptcy Law; Business Law; Civil Trial Practice; Commercial Law; Employment Benefits Law; Environmental Law; General Practice; Health Care Law; Insurance Defense; Labor and Employment Law; Land Use Law; Medical Malpractice; Municipal Bond/Public Authority Financing; Real Estate Law; Tax Law; Trademark, Copyright and Unfair Competition; Transportation Law; Trust and Estates, Wills and Probate

STUBBS & PERDUE, P.A.
New Bern, NC....................Bankruptcy Law

STUCKERT AND YATES
Newtown, PA....................General Practice

STUDDARD & MELBY, A PROFESSIONAL CORPORATION
El Paso, TX....................General Practice

STUMP, T. DOUGLAS
Oklahoma City, OK....................Immigration and Naturalization

STUMPF CRADDOCK MASSEY & PULMAN, A PROFESSIONAL CORPORATION
Houston, TX....................Commercial Litigation; Real Estate Law

STUTMAN, TREISTER & GLATT, PROFESSIONAL CORPORATION
Los Angeles, CA....................Bankruptcy Law; Commercial Law

STUTZ, GALLAGHER, ARTIANO, SHINOFF & HOLTZ, A PROFESSIONAL CORPORATION
San Diego, CA....................Civil Trial Practice

SUAREZ & WARDELL, P.A.
Tampa, FL....................Criminal Trial Practice

SUDEKUM, ROSENBERG & CASSIDY, CHARTERED
Chicago, IL....................Insurance Defense

SUGAR, FRIEDBERG & FELSENTHAL
Chicago, IL....................Business Law; Civil Trial Practice; Commercial Litigation; Mergers and Acquisitions; Real Estate Law; Securities Law; Tax Law; Trust and Estates, Wills and Probate

SUGARMAN AND SUGARMAN, P.C.
Boston, MA....................Personal Injury

SUGARMAN, WALLACE, MANHEIM & SCHOENWALD
Buffalo, NY....................Insurance Defense
Syracuse, NY....................Appellate Practice; Civil Trial Practice; Construction Law; Insurance Defense; Legal Malpractice; Personal Injury; Professional Liability

SUGHROUE, PATRICK R., P.C.
Grand Rapids, MI....................Securities Law

SUITER & ASSOCIATES P.C.
Omaha, NE....................Intellectual Property Law; Patent, Trademark, Copyright and Unfair Competition

SUKKAR, MAZEN M., P.A.
Hollywood, FL....................Immigration and Naturalization

SULLIVAN, MIKKI ROSEMARY
San Diego, CA....................Creditors Rights

SULLIVAN & CROMWELL
Los Angeles, CA....................General Practice
Washington, DC....................General Practice
New York, NY....................Civil Trial Practice; General Practice
Melbourne, Victoria, Australia....................General Practice
Hong Kong, China....................General Practice
London, England....................General Practice
Paris, France....................General Practice
Frankfurt/Main, Germany....................General Practice
Tokyo, Japan....................General Practice
Beijing, China....................General Practice

SULLIVAN & CROWLEY, P.C.
Traverse City, MI....................Civil Trial Practice; Commercial Litigation; Environmental Law; Personal Injury

SULLIVAN, CUNNINGHAM, KEENAN, MRAZ & LEMIRE
Albany, NY....................Real Estate Law; Workers Compensation

SULLIVAN HILL LEWIN REZ & ENGEL, A PROFESSIONAL LAW CORPORATION
San Diego, CA....................Civil Trial Practice

SULLIVAN & LARGEY
Quincy, MA....................Civil Trial Practice

SULLIVAN LAW CORPORATION
Los Angeles, CA....................Aviation Law; Business Law; Civil Trial Practice; Government Contracts

SULLIVAN & LEAVITT, P.C., LAW OFFICES OF
Novi, MI....................Commercial Litigation; Corporate Law; Transportation Law

SULLIVAN, MAHONEY
Niagara Falls, ON, Canada.....General Practice
St. Catharines, ON, Canada....Business Law; General Practice

SULLIVAN & OLIVERIO
Buffalo, NY....................Appellate Practice; Civil Trial Practice; Commercial Law; Commercial Litigation; Family Law; General Practice; Real Estate Law

SULLIVAN AND SULLIVAN
Jackson, MS....................Civil Trial Practice; Commercial Litigation; Construction Law; General Practice; Medical Malpractice; Personal Injury; Product Liability Law

SULLIVAN & WARD, P.C.
Des Moines, IA....................General Practice

SULLIVAN, WARD, BONE, TYLER & ASHER, P.C.
Southfield, MI....................Insurance Defense

SULLOWAY & HOLLIS, P.L.L.C.
Concord, NH....................General Practice

SULMEYER, KUPETZ, BAUMANN & ROTHMAN, A PROFESSIONAL CORPORATION
Los Angeles, CA....................Bankruptcy Law; Commercial Law

SUMMA & RYAN, P.C.
Waterbury, CT....................Labor and Employment Law

SUMMERS, COMPTON, WELLS AND HAMBURG, PROFESSIONAL CORPORATION
St. Louis, MO....................Intellectual Property Law

SUMMERS & WYATT, P.C.
Chattanooga, TN....................Civil Trial Practice; Criminal Trial Practice; General Practice; Labor and Employment Law; Medical Malpractice; Personal Injury; Workers Compensation

SUMMIT LAW GROUP, PLLC
Seattle, WA....................Business Law; Commercial Litigation; Corporate Law; Environmental Law; Labor and Employment Law; Securities Law

SUMNER, DAVID W.
Blue Bell, PA....................Medical Malpractice

SUNDAHL, POWERS, KAPP & MARTIN, L.L.C.
Cheyenne, WY....................Administrative Law; Civil Trial Practice; Insurance Defense

SUNDERLAND, MURPHY, SPENN, JOHNSON AND LUEBCHOW
Watseka, IL....................General Practice

SUPNIK, PAUL D.
Beverly Hills, CA....................Trademark, Copyright and Unfair Competition

SUROVELL, JACKSON, COLTEN & DUGAN, P.C.
Fairfax, VA....................Family Law

SURRATT, JOHN R., P.A.
Winston-Salem, NC....................Civil Trial Practice; Commercial Law; Commercial Litigation; Real Estate Law

SURRETT & COLEMAN, P.A.
Augusta, GA....................Bankruptcy Law; Civil Trial Practice; Family Law; General Practice; Insurance Defense

SUSMAN, DUFFY & SEGALOFF, P.C.
New Haven, CT....................Business Law; Civil Trial Practice; Family Law; Real Estate Law

SUSMAN GODFREY L.L.P.
Los Angeles, CA....................Civil Trial Practice
Dallas, TX....................Civil Trial Practice
Houston, TX....................Civil Trial Practice
Seattle, WA....................Civil Trial Practice

SUTHERLAND, RICHARD T.
Wichita Falls, TX....................Family Law

SUTHERLAND ASBILL & BRENNAN LLP
Atlanta, GA....................General Practice

SUTHON, WALTER J. III
New Orleans, LA....................Trust and Estates, Wills and Probate

SUTKOWSKI & WASHKUHN LTD.
Peoria, IL....................General Practice

SUTTERFIELD & WEBB L.L.C.
New Orleans, LA....................Insurance Defense; Personal Injury; Product Liability Law

SUTTS, STROSBERG LLP
Windsor, ON, Canada....................Civil Trial Practice; Commercial Law; Criminal Trial Practice; Family Law; General Practice; Insurance Defense; Labor and Employment Law; Medical Malpractice; Personal Injury; Product Liability Law

SWADEN LAW OFFICES
Edina, MN....................Family Law

SWAIM & SCHRANDT, P.C.
Albuquerque, NM....................Tax Law; Trust and Estates, Wills and Probate

SWAINE, HARRIS, SHEEHAN & MCCLURE, P.A.
Lake Placid, FL....................General Practice
Sebring, FL....................General Practice

SWANN, HADLEY & ALVAREZ, P.A.
Winter Park, FL....................Insurance Defense

SWANSEN, SAMUEL T., P.C.
Blue Bell, PA....................Trust and Estates, Wills and Probate

SWANSON & DETTMANN
Marquette, MI....................Civil Trial Practice; Insurance Defense

SWANSON AND GIESER, A PROFESSIONAL CORPORATION
Santa Ana, CA....................Civil Trial Practice; Real Estate Law; Trust and Estates, Wills and Probate

SWANSON MIDGLEY, LLC
Kansas City, MO....................Banking Law; Business Law; Civil Trial Practice; Education Law; Franchise Law; General Practice; Intellectual Property Law; Labor and Employment Law; Real Estate Law; Tax Law; Trust and Estates, Wills and Probate

SWANSON, THOMAS & COON
Portland, OR....................Medical Malpractice; Personal Injury; Product Liability Law; Toxic Torts; Workers Compensation

SWARTZ, GERALD NEAL LAW OFFICES, THE
New York, NY....................Personal Injury; Product Liability Law

SWARTZ & REED
Washington, DC....................Medical Malpractice

SWARTZ & SWARTZ
Boston, MA....................Admiralty/Maritime Law; Civil Trial Practice; Commercial Litigation; Environmental Law; Medical Malpractice; Personal Injury; Product Liability Law

SWEDLOW, BUTLER, LEVINE, LEWIS & DYE CO., L.P.A.
Columbus, OH....................Business Law; Commercial Litigation; Mergers and Acquisitions; Real Estate Law

SWEENEY, DABAGIA, THORNE, JANES & PAGOS, L.L.P.
Michigan City, IN....................General Practice

SWENDSEID & STERN
Las Vegas, NV....................Municipal Bond/Public Authority Financing
Reno, NV....................Municipal Bond/Public Authority Financing

SWENSEN PERER & KONTOS
Pittsburgh, PA....................Civil Trial Practice; Criminal Trial Practice; Medical Malpractice; Personal Injury; Product Liability Law

SWERDLOW FLORENCE SANCHEZ & RATHBUN, A LAW CORPORATION
Beverly Hills, CA....................Labor and Employment Law

SWERGOLD, NATHANIEL M.
Cedarhurst, NY....................Civil Trial Practice

SWERLING, JACK B.
Columbia, SC....................Appellate Practice; Criminal Trial Practice

SWIFT, CURRIE, MCGHEE & HIERS
Atlanta, GA....................Commercial Litigation; Insurance Defense; Workers Compensation

SWOPE, CARDILLO, P.A.
Tampa, FL....................Personal Injury

SYKES AND COLE
Hyannis, MA....................Trust and Estates, Wills and Probate

SYLVESTER & MALEY, INC.
Burlington, VT ....Civil Trial Practice; Medical Malpractice; Personal Injury

SYNNESTVEDT & LECHNER LLP
Philadelphia, PA ....Antitrust Law; Computer Law; Intellectual Property Law; Patent, Trademark, Copyright and Unfair Competition

SZAFERMAN, LAKIND, BLUMSTEIN, WATTER & BLADER, P.C.
Lawrenceville, NJ.....................Appellate Practice; Banking Law; Business Law; Civil Trial Practice; Commercial Litigation; Environmental Law; Family Law; Labor and Employment Law; Land Use Law; Personal Injury; Professional Liability; Securities Law

TABBERT HAHN EARNEST & WEDDLE
Indianapolis, IN ....Administrative Law; Banking Law; Business Law; Civil Trial Practice; Commercial Litigation; Criminal Trial Practice; Environmental Law; Health Care Law; Insurance Defense; International Business Law; Medical Malpractice; Natural Resources Law; Real Estate Law; Tax Law; Trust and Estates, Wills and Probate

TABNER, RYAN AND KENIRY
Albany, NY..............................Business Law; Civil Trial Practice; General Practice; Medical Malpractice; Municipal and Zoning Law; Personal Injury; Real Estate Law; Trust and Estates, Wills and Probate

TAFARO & FLYNN, P.A.
New Providence, NJ ....Civil Trial Practice; Medical Malpractice; Personal Injury

TAFT & MCSALLY
Cranston, RI ....General Practice; Trust and Estates, Wills and Probate

TAFT, STETTINIUS & HOLLISTER LLP
Covington, KY..........................General Practice
Cincinnati, OH.........................General Practice
Cleveland, OH..........................General Practice
Columbus, OH ....General Practice

TAGLIA, FETTE, DUMKE, PASSARO & KAHNE, P.C.
St. Joseph, MI ....General Practice

TAIT, DONALD H. Q.C.
Windsor, ON, Canada ....Criminal Trial Practice

TAKUSHI, FUNAKI, WONG & STONE, ATTORNEYS AT LAW, A LAW CORPORATION
Honolulu, HI............................Bankruptcy Law; Business Law; Creditors Rights; Family Law; Real Estate Law; Trust and Estates, Wills and Probate

TALBOTT AND GALLAGHER, A PROFESSIONAL CORPORATION
McLean, VA..............................Business Law; Corporate Law; Real Estate Law; Securities Law

TALCOTT, LIGHTFOOT, VANDEVELDE SADOWSKY, MEDVENE & LEVINE
Los Angeles, CA.......................Civil Trial Practice; Criminal Trial Practice

TALIAFERRO, MEHLING, SHIROONI & CARRAN
Covington, KY..........................Civil Trial Practice; Criminal Trial Practice; Family Law; Labor and Employment Law; Personal Injury

TALLACKSON, JEFFREY S.
New York, NY...........................Banking Law; Commercial Law

TALLEY & SHARP, P.C.
Conyers, GA ....General Practice

TALLMAN, HUDDERS & SORRENTINO, P.C.
Allentown, PA ....Civil Trial Practice; General Practice; Trust and Estates, Wills and Probate

TAM, O'CONNOR, HENDERSON, TAIRA & YAMAUCHI, ATTORNEYS AT LAW, A LAW CORPORATION
Honolulu, HI............................Business Law; Commercial Litigation; Corporate Law; Employment Benefits Law; Insurance Defense; Labor and Employment Law; Personal Injury; Real Estate Law; Tax Law; Trust and Estates, Wills and Probate

TANENBAUM, MARK C., P.A.
Charleston, SC ....Personal Injury; Product Liability Law

TANKARD AND GORDON
Eastville, VA ....Criminal Trial Practice; General Practice; Trust and Estates, Wills and Probate

TANNER, ROD, & ASSOCIATES, P.C.
Fort Worth, TX ....Labor and Employment Law

TANSEY, JAMES J.
Washington, DC........................Commercial Litigation

TARASI LAW FIRM, THE, P.C.
Pittsburgh, PA ....Civil Trial Practice; General Practice; Medical Malpractice; Personal Injury

TARCZA & GELDERMAN, L.L.C.
New Orleans, LA......................Civil Trial Practice; Corporate Law; Trust and Estates, Wills and Probate

TARGAN, DONALD G., & ASSOCIATES, A PROF. CORP.
Atlantic City, NJ.......................Civil Trial Practice

TARLOW, BARRY, A PROF. CORP., LAW OFFICES OF
Los Angeles, CA.......................Appellate Practice; Criminal Trial Practice

TARNOW, HERMAN H.
New York, NY...........................Family Law

TARUTIS & BARRON, P.S.
Seattle, WA ....Health Care Law

TASCHNER, DANA B., P.C.
Los Angeles, CA.......................Civil Trial Practice

TATE LAW FIRM, THE
Abingdon, VA...........................Commercial Litigation; General Practice; Labor and Employment Law; Medical Malpractice; Personal Injury; Product Liability Law

TATUM & MCDOWELL
Clovis, NM...............................General Practice; Tax Law; Trust and Estates, Wills and Probate

TAUBMAN, SIMPSON, YOUNG & SULENTOR
Long Beach, CA........................Civil Trial Practice; Environmental Law; Oil and Gas Law; Real Estate Law; Tax Law

TAUNT, CHARLES J., & ASSOCIATES, P.L.L.C.
Birmingham, MI.......................Bankruptcy Law

TAVSS, FLETCHER, MAIDEN & KING, P.C.
Norfolk, VA ....Banking Law; Civil Trial Practice; General Practice; Personal Injury; Real Estate Law

TAX, ESTATE & BUSINESS LAW N.A. LLC
Albuquerque, NM....................Business Law; Tax Law; Trust and Estates, Wills and Probate

TAYLOR, LAWRENCE THE LAW OFFICES OF
Irvine, CA................................Criminal Trial Practice

TAYLOR & CAWTHORNE, LTD.
Tucson, AZ ....Trust and Estates, Wills and Probate

TAYLOR & CIRE
Houston, TX.............................Civil Trial Practice

TAYLOR, DUANE, BARTON & GILMAN, LLP
Boston, MA..............................Civil Trial Practice; General Practice; Insurance Defense

TAYLOR & FAUST, A PROFESSIONAL CORPORATION
San Francisco, CA....................Tax Law

TAYLOR, GANSON & PERRIN, L.L.P.
Boston, MA..............................Trust and Estates, Wills and Probate

TAYLOR, HARP & CALLIER
Columbus, GA..........................Civil Trial Practice; Personal Injury

TAYLOR, LAWRENCE, THE LAW OFFICES OF
Beverly Hills, CA.....................Criminal Trial Practice
Los Angeles, CA.......................Criminal Trial Practice

TAYLOR MCCORD, A LAW CORPORATION
Ventura, CA ....Appellate Practice; Civil Trial Practice; Environmental Law; Family Law; Labor and Employment Law; Personal Injury; Trust and Estates, Wills and Probate

TAYLOR, MILLER, SPROWL, HOFFNAGLE & MERLETTI
Chicago, IL..............................General Practice; Insurance Defense

TAYLOR, OLSON, ADKINS, SRALLA & ELAM, L.L.P.
Fort Worth, TX ....Municipal and Zoning Law

TAYLOR, PORTER, BROOKS & PHILLIPS, L.L.P.
Baton Rouge, LA......................General Practice

TAYLOR, STAFFORD, WOODY, CLITHERO & FITZGERALD, LLP
Springfield, MO.......................Personal Injury

TAYLOR & TAYLOR
Morehead City, NC ....General Practice

TAYLOR & WALKER, P.C.
Norfolk, VA ....Business Law; Commercial Law; Insurance Defense

TAYLOR, ZUNKA, MILNOR & CARTER, LTD.
Charlottesville, VA..................General Practice; Insurance Defense

TEAFORD, RICH, CRITES & WESP
Columbus, OH ....Personal Injury; Real Estate Law

TEAGUE, CAMPBELL, DENNIS & GORHAM, L.L.P.
Raleigh, NC....................Insurance Defense; Workers Compensation

TEAHAN & CONSTANTINO
Poughkeepsie, NY....................Tax Law; Trust and Estates, Wills and Probate

TECHMEIER & VAN GRUNSVEN, S.C.
Milwaukee, WI....................Personal Injury

TEGTMEIER LAW FIRM, P.C.
Colorado Springs, CO....................Civil Trial Practice; Criminal Trial Practice; Personal Injury

TEHIN +PARTNERS, A PROFESSIONAL CORPORATION
San Francisco, CA....................Admiralty/Maritime Law; Civil Trial Practice; Commercial Litigation; Labor and Employment Law; Medical Malpractice; Personal Injury; Product Liability Law; Professional Liability

TEICH, GROH AND FROST
Trenton, NJ....................Bankruptcy Law; Commercial Law; Family Law; General Practice

TEITLER, STANLEY A., P.C.
New York, NY....................Appellate Practice; Civil Trial Practice; Criminal Trial Practice

TEKELL, BOOK, MATTHEWS & LIMMER, L.L.P.
Houston, TX....................Civil Trial Practice; Insurance Defense; Personal Injury

TELLER, CHANEY, HASSELL & HOPSON, LLP
Vicksburg, MS....................General Practice

TELPNER, PETERSON, SMITH & RUESCH
Council Bluffs, IA....................General Practice

TEMPLE & TEMPLE
Austin, TX....................Administrative Law; Banking Law

TENENBAUM & SAAS, P.C.
Bethesda, MD....................Real Estate Law

TERAOKA & ASSOCIATES, A LAW CORPORATION
San Francisco, CA....................Business Law

TERRA LAW LLP
San Jose, CA....................Commercial Litigation; Construction Law; Creditors Rights; Land Use Law; Real Estate Law; Tax Law

TERRIBERRY, CARROLL & YANCEY, L.L.P.
New Orleans, LA....................Admiralty/Maritime Law; Corporate Law; General Practice

TERRY, EDWIN J. (TED) JR., LAW OFFICES OF
Austin, TX....................Family Law

TERRY, WILLIAM B., CHARTERED
Las Vegas, NV....................Criminal Trial Practice

TERWILLIGER, WAKEEN, PIEHLER & CONWAY, S.C.
Wausau, WI....................Insurance Defense

TESTA, HURWITZ & THIBEAULT, LLP
Boston, MA....................General Practice

TEW & ATCHISON, P.A.
Clayton, NC....................General Practice

TEW & NOWAK
Miami, FL....................Business Law; Securities Law

THAYER, BERNSTEIN & BASS, P.C.
Kansas City, MO....................Family Law

THAYER, STEVEN W., P.S.
Vancouver, WA....................Criminal Trial Practice

THE LOUDERBACK LAW FIRM
San Francisco, CA....................Civil Trial Practice; Labor and Employment Law

THELEN REID & PRIEST LLP
Los Angeles, CA....................General Practice
San Francisco, CA....................General Practice
San Jose, CA....................General Practice
Washington, DC....................General Practice
New York, NY....................General Practice

THERIAULT & JOSLIN, P.C.
Montpelier, VT....................General Practice; Insurance Defense; Medical Malpractice; Product Liability Law; Professional Liability

THEUS, GRISHAM, DAVIS & LEIGH, L.L.P.
Monroe, LA....................Insurance Defense; Tax Law; Trust and Estates, Wills and Probate

THÉVER, SHAN K., & ASSOCIATES, A PROF. CORP.
Los Angeles, CA....................Medical Malpractice

THIBODEAU, JOSEPH H., P.C., LAW OFFICES OF
Denver, CO....................Tax Law

THINNES, THOMAS A., P.A.
Phoenix, AZ....................Criminal Trial Practice

THIRKELL & CRETAN
San Mateo, CA....................Trust and Estates, Wills and Probate

THOMAN SOULE GAGE
Hamilton, ON, Canada....................Civil Trial Practice; Insurance Defense; Product Liability Law

THOMAS, ARCHIBALD J. III, LAW OFFICES OF
Jacksonville, FL....................Labor and Employment Law

THOMAS, CLAYTON H. JR.
Philadelphia, PA....................Environmental Law; Insurance Defense; Product Liability Law; Toxic Torts; Workers Compensation

THOMAS, RICHARD C.
Columbia, MO....................Civil Trial Practice; Personal Injury; Product Liability Law

THOMAS, BIRDSONG & BECKER, P.C.
Rolla, MO....................General Practice

THOMAS & CULP, L.L.P.
Dallas, TX....................Appellate Practice; Civil Trial Practice

THOMAS & ELARDO, P.C.
Phoenix, AZ....................Insurance Defense

THOMAS, FELDMAN & WILSHUSEN, L.L.P.
Dallas, TX....................Civil Trial Practice; Commercial Litigation; Construction Law

THOMAS, KAYDEN, HORSTEMEYER & RISLEY, L.L.P.
Atlanta, GA....................Patent, Trademark, Copyright and Unfair Competition

THOMAS, KENNEDY, SAMPSON & PATTERSON
Atlanta, GA....................Civil Trial Practice; Commercial Law; Insurance Defense; Medical Malpractice; Municipal Bond/Public Authority Financing; Personal Injury; Product Liability Law; Real Estate Law

THOMAS & LIBOWITZ, P.A.
Baltimore, MD....................Banking Law; Business Law; Communications Law; Corporate Law; Family Law; Franchise Law; Insurance Defense; Mergers and Acquisitions; Real Estate Law; Securities Law; Trust and Estates, Wills and Probate

THOMAS, MAMER & HAUGHEY
Champaign, IL....................General Practice

THOMAS, MEANS, GILLIS, DEVLIN, ROBINSON & SEAY, P.C.
Birmingham, AL....................Civil Rights; Civil Trial Practice; Constitutional Law; Labor and Employment Law
Montgomery, AL....................Civil Rights; Civil Trial Practice; Constitutional Law; Government Contracts; Labor and Employment Law; Personal Injury; Product Liability Law

THOMAS, SCOTT G., LAW OFFICES OF
Milwaukee, WI....................Insurance Defense

THOMAS & SELF, A PROFESSIONAL CORPORATION
Dallas, TX....................Civil Trial Practice

THOMAS, THOMAS & HAFER, LLP
Harrisburg, PA....................Civil Trial Practice; Health Care Law; Insurance Defense; Labor and Employment Law; Medical Malpractice; Workers Compensation

THOMASSON, GILBERT, COOK & MAGUIRE, L.C.
Cape Girardeau, MO....................Civil Trial Practice

THOMPSON, BETTY A., LTD.
Arlington, VA....................Family Law

THOMPSON & BOWIE
Portland, ME....................Civil Trial Practice; Construction Law; Insurance Defense; Legal Malpractice; Medical Malpractice; Personal Injury; Product Liability Law; Professional Liability; Workers Compensation

THOMPSON COBURN LLP
Washington, DC....................General Practice
Belleville, IL....................General Practice
St. Louis, MO....................Civil Trial Practice; Commercial Law; General Practice

THOMPSON, COE, COUSINS & IRONS, L.L.P.
Dallas, TX....................Administrative Law; Bankruptcy Law; Business Law; Civil Trial Practice; General Practice; Insurance Defense; Labor and Employment Law

THOMPSON, E.C., III, P.C.
Warsaw, NC....General Practice

THOMPSON, GARRETT & HINES
Brewton, AL....General Practice

THOMPSON KNIGHT BROWN PARKER & LEAHY L.L.P.
Houston, TX....Appellate Practice; Arbitration; Aviation Law; Business Law; Civil Trial Practice; Construction Law; Corporate Law; Energy Law; General Practice; Health Care Law; Insurance Defense; Intellectual Property Law; Labor and Employment Law; Legal Malpractice; Medical Malpractice; Natural Resources Law; Product Liability Law; Real Estate Law; Securities Law; Tax Law; Toxic Torts

THOMPSON & KNIGHT L.L.P.
Austin, TX....Administrative Law; Appellate Practice; Business Law; Civil Trial Practice; Corporate Law; Energy Law; Environmental Law; General Practice; Health Care Law; Insurance Defense; International Business Law; Labor and Employment Law; Medical Malpractice; Municipal and Zoning Law; Natural Resources Law; Product Liability Law; Securities Law; Tax Law; Toxic Torts; Trademark, Copyright and Unfair Competition
Dallas, TX....Administrative Law; Antitrust Law; Appellate Practice; Arbitration; Aviation Law; Banking Law; Bankruptcy Law; Business Law; Civil Trial Practice; Commercial Law; Computer Law; Construction Law; Corporate Law; Employment Benefits Law; Energy Law; Environmental Law; Franchise Law; General Practice; Health Care Law; Immigration and Naturalization; Insurance Defense; Intellectual Property Law; International Business Law; Labor and Employment Law; Legal Malpractice; Medical Malpractice; Mergers and Acquisitions; Municipal and Zoning Law; Natural Resources Law; Patent, Trademark, Copyright and Unfair Competition; Product Liability Law; Real Estate Law; Securities Law; Tax Law; Toxic Torts; Trademark, Copyright and Unfair Competition; Trust and Estates, Wills and Probate
Fort Worth, TX....Aviation Law; Banking Law; Business Law; Civil Trial Practice; Construction Law; General Practice; Health Care Law; Insurance Defense; International Business Law; Medical Malpractice; Product Liability Law; Real Estate Law; Securities Law; Tax Law; Trust and Estates, Wills and Probate
Garza Garcia, Nuevo Leon, Mexico....Business Law; General Practice; International Business Law; Securities Law

THOMPSON LAW FIRM, THE, P.A.
Conway, SC....Civil Trial Practice; Construction Law; General Practice; Insurance Defense
Myrtle Beach, SC....Civil Trial Practice; Construction Law; General Practice; Insurance Defense

THOMPSON LAW OFFICE, THE
Monterey, CA....Business Law; Civil Trial Practice; Personal Injury

THOMPSON AND LLEWELLYN, P.A.
Fort Smith, AR....Aviation Law; Commercial Litigation

THOMPSON, LYNNE R., P.A.
Melbourne, FL....Trust and Estates, Wills and Probate

THOMPSON, MARK E., A PROFESSIONAL CORPORATION
Lancaster, CA....Trust and Estates, Wills and Probate

THOMPSON, O'BRIEN, KEMP & NASUTI, P.C.
Norcross, GA....Banking Law; Commercial Litigation; Creditors Rights

THOMPSON, O'DONNELL, MARKHAM, NORTON & HANNON
Washington, DC....Civil Trial Practice; Trust and Estates, Wills and Probate

THOMPSON, O'NEIL & VANDERVEEN, P.C.
Traverse City, MI....Civil Trial Practice; Medical Malpractice; Personal Injury; Product Liability Law

THOMPSON & SMITH, P.C.
Augusta, GA....General Practice; Insurance Defense

THOMPSON, SPARKS, DEAN & MORRIS
Monroe, LA....Banking Law; Bankruptcy Law; Business Law; Commercial Law; Land Use Law; Tax Law; Trust and Estates, Wills and Probate

THOMPSON & SWEENY, P.C.
Lawrenceville, GA....General Practice

THOMPSON & THOMAS, A PROFESSIONAL CORPORATION
Lubbock, TX....Commercial Litigation; Insurance Defense

THOMPSON & WALDRON
Alexandria, VA....Construction Law

THOMS, DAVID M., & ASSOCIATES, P.C.
Detroit, MI....Business Law; Tax Law; Trust and Estates, Wills and Probate

THOMSEN AND BURKE, LLP
Washington, DC....Business Law; International Trade Law
Baltimore, MD....Business Law; International Trade Law; Tax Law; Trust and Estates, Wills and Probate

THOMSON LAW OFFICE
Edwardsville, IL....Civil Trial Practice; Insurance Defense

THOMSON & NELSON, A PROFESSIONAL LAW CORPORATION
Whittier, CA....General Practice

THOMSON, RHODES & COWIE, P.C.
Pittsburgh, PA....General Practice

THOMSON, ROGERS
Toronto, ON, Canada....General Practice

THON, BECK, VANNI, PHILLIPI & NUTT, A PROFESSIONAL CORPORATION
Pasadena, CA....Personal Injury

THORBURN, SAKOL & THRONE
Boulder, CO....Family Law

THORN AND GERSHON, LLP
Albany, NY....Medical Malpractice; Product Liability Law; Toxic Torts

THORNDAL, ARMSTRONG, DELK, BALKENBUSH & EISINGER, A PROFESSIONAL CORPORATION
Las Vegas, NV....Civil Trial Practice; Insurance Defense; Workers Compensation

THORNE, GRODNIK, RANSEL, DUNCAN, BYRON, HOSTETLER & TRIPPEL, LLP
Elkhart, IN....Bankruptcy Law; Corporate Law; Creditors Rights; Education Law; Personal Injury

THORNTON, EARLY & NAUMES LLP
Boston, MA....Civil Trial Practice; Product Liability Law

THORNTON, HEGG, REIF, DOLAN & BOWEN, P.A.
Alexandria, MN....General Practice

THORNTON, MASTRUCCI & MINKIN
Miami, FL....Medical Malpractice; Personal Injury

THORNTON & ROTHMAN, P.A.
Miami, FL....Criminal Trial Practice

THORNTON, TAYLOR, DOWNS, BECKER, TOLSON & DOHERTY
San Francisco, CA....Insurance Defense

THORP AND CLARKE
Fayetteville, NC....General Practice

THORPE, NORTH & WESTERN, L.L.P.
Sandy, UT....Computer Law; Intellectual Property Law; Patent, Trademark, Copyright and Unfair Competition

THORSNES, BARTOLOTTA, MCGUIRE & PADILLA
San Diego, CA....Business Law; Civil Trial Practice; Construction Law; Eminent Domain; Medical Malpractice; Personal Injury; Product Liability Law

THORSTEINSSONS
Vancouver, BC, Canada....Tax Law
Toronto, ON, Canada....Tax Law

THRAILKILL, HARRIS & WOOD, PLC
Brentwood, TN....Business Law; Tax Law; Trust and Estates, Wills and Probate

THRASHER, WHITLEY, HAMPTON & MORGAN, A PROFESSIONAL CORPORATION
Atlanta, GA....Business Law; International Business Law; Securities Law; Trust and Estates, Wills and Probate

THREET, MARTIN E., & ASSOCIATES
Albuquerque, NM....Appellate Practice; Civil Trial Practice; Creditors Rights; General Practice

THURBER CAPPELL, L.L.C.
Hackensack, NJ....Civil Trial Practice; Construction Law; Family Law; Labor and Employment Law; Trust and Estates, Wills and Probate

THURMAN, HOWALD, WEBER, SENKEL & NORRICK, L.L.C.
Hillsboro, MO....Civil Trial Practice; General Practice

TIERNEY & HAUGHWOUT
West Palm Beach, FL....Criminal Trial Practice

TIERNEY, ZULLO, FLAHERTY & MURPHY, P.C.
Norwalk, CT....General Practice; Real Estate Law

TIGHE, PATTON & BABBIN, P.L.L.C.
Washington, DC....Business Law

TILFORD, DOBBINS, ALEXANDER, BUCKAWAY & BLACK
Louisville, KY .... Business Law; Civil Rights; Commercial Litigation; General Practice; Insurance Defense; Real Estate Law; Trust and Estates, Wills and Probate

TILL, PETER W.
Short Hills, NJ .... Civil Rights; Civil Trial Practice; Criminal Trial Practice

TILLINGHAST LICHT & SEMONOFF LTD.
Providence, RI .... General Practice

TIMBERLAKE, SMITH, THOMAS & MOSES, P.C.
Staunton, VA .... General Practice

TIMMER, JAMO & O'LEARY
Lansing, MI .... Civil Trial Practice; General Practice; Insurance Defense; Medical Malpractice; Personal Injury

TIMMIS & INMAN L.L.P.
Detroit, MI .... Antitrust Law; Appellate Practice; Business Law; Civil Trial Practice; Commercial Law; Commercial Litigation; Corporate Law; Employment Benefits Law; Environmental Law; General Practice; Health Care Law; Insurance Defense; Intellectual Property Law; Labor and Employment Law; Mergers and Acquisitions; Pension and Profit Sharing; Personal Injury; Product Liability Law; Real Estate Law; Securities Law; Tax Law; Trust and Estates, Wills and Probate

TIMMONS & KELLY
Dallas, TX .... Intellectual Property Law; Patent, Trademark, Copyright and Unfair Competition

TINDALL & FOSTER, P.C.
Houston, TX .... Family Law; Immigration and Naturalization

TINLEY, NASTRI, RENEHAN & DOST, LLP
Waterbury, CT .... General Practice

TINSMAN & HOUSER, INC.
San Antonio, TX .... Civil Trial Practice; Commercial Law; Medical Malpractice; Personal Injury; Product Liability Law

TIROLA & HERRING
Westport, CT .... General Practice

TISHLER, NICHOLAS E.
Niskayuna, NY .... Appellate Practice

TISTAERT, LAWRENCE C.
Los Angeles, CA .... Business Law; Real Estate Law

TITUS, BRUECKNER & BERRY, P.C.
Scottsdale, AZ .... Business Law; Commercial Litigation; Real Estate Law; Securities Law

TOBIN, CRAIG D., & ASSOCIATES
Chicago, IL .... Civil Trial Practice; Criminal Trial Practice

TODD, HOLLOWAY & WARD, P.C.
Columbia, SC .... Commercial Litigation

TODD, VANDERBLOEMEN AND BRADY, P.A.
Lenoir, NC .... General Practice

TODD & WAKEFIELD
Seattle, WA .... Insurance Defense

TODD & WELD
Boston, MA .... Civil Trial Practice

TODT LAW FIRM, THE, P.C.
St. Louis, MO .... Family Law

TODTMAN, NACHAMIE, SPIZZ & JOHNS, P.C.
New York, NY .... Bankruptcy Law; Tax Law

TOGUT, SEGAL & SEGAL
New York, NY .... Bankruptcy Law

TOKYO AOYAMA LAW OFFICE
Tokyo, Japan .... General Practice

TOLLEY, VANDENBOSCH, WALTON, KOROLEWICZ & BRENGLE, P.C.
Grand Rapids, MI .... Civil Trial Practice; Construction Law; Insurance Defense; Real Estate Law

TOLLISON LAW FIRM, P.A.
Oxford, MS .... Civil Trial Practice; Personal Injury

TOMAR, SIMONOFF, ADOURIAN, O'BRIEN, KAPLAN, JACOBY & GRAZIANO, A PROFESSIONAL CORPORATION
Cherry Hill, NJ .... Labor and Employment Law; Natural Resources Law; Personal Injury
Northfield, NJ .... Environmental Law; Labor and Employment Law

TOMASETTI, DOROTHY H.
Littleton, CO .... Family Law

TOMAZIN, THOMAS J., P.C.
Englewood, CO .... Civil Trial Practice; Medical Malpractice; Personal Injury

TOMITA & SIMPSON, P.C.
Albuquerque, NM .... Trust and Estates, Wills and Probate

TOM & PETRUS
Honolulu, HI .... Civil Trial Practice; Construction Law; Insurance Defense; Product Liability Law

TOMPKINS, CLOUGH, HIRSHON & LANGER, P.A.
Portland, ME .... Admiralty/Maritime Law; Banking Law; Commercial Law

TOMPKINS, MCGUIRE, WACHENFELD & BARRY
Newark, NJ .... Banking Law; Civil Trial Practice; Criminal Trial Practice; General Practice; Insurance Defense

TOMPKINS AND MCMASTER
Columbia, SC .... Business Law; Civil Trial Practice; Criminal Trial Practice; General Practice

TONKIN & MONDL, L.C.
St. Louis, MO .... Admiralty/Maritime Law

TOOLEY & VOSS
Dallas, TX .... Appellate Practice; Civil Rights; Civil Trial Practice; Constitutional Law; Insurance Defense; Labor and Employment Law; Municipal and Zoning Law; Personal Injury; Product Liability Law

TOOMS & HOUSE
London, KY .... Civil Trial Practice; Commercial Litigation; Corporate Law; Insurance Defense

TORBERT & TORBERT, P.A.
Gadsden, AL .... Insurance Defense

TORKILDSON, KATZ, FONSECA, JAFFE, MOORE & HETHERINGTON, ATTORNEYS AT LAW, A LAW CORPORATION
Honolulu, HI .... General Practice; Health Care Law; Labor and Employment Law; Pension and Profit Sharing; Tax Law

TORSHEN, SPREYER, GARMISA & SLOBIG, LTD.
Chicago, IL .... Appellate Practice; Commercial Litigation

TORYS
New York, NY .... Business Law
Toronto, ON, Canada .... General Practice

TOWNSEND, LAWRENCE G.
San Francisco, CA .... Trademark, Copyright and Unfair Competition

TOWNSEND & BRANNON
Tampa, FL .... Bankruptcy Law; Commercial Litigation

TOWNSEND, COURTLAND K., JR., CHARTERED
Ocean City, MD .... Civil Trial Practice; Criminal Trial Practice

TOWNSEND & MONTROSS
Indianapolis, IN .... Aviation Law; Medical Malpractice; Personal Injury; Product Liability Law

TOWNSEND AND TOWNSEND AND CREW LLP
Palo Alto, CA .... Patent, Trademark, Copyright and Unfair Competition
San Francisco, CA .... Patent, Trademark, Copyright and Unfair Competition

TRACI & MARX CO., L.P.A.
Cleveland, OH .... Commercial Litigation; Medical Malpractice; Personal Injury; Product Liability Law

TRAGER, SUSAN M., A PROF. CORP., LAW OFFICES OF
Irvine, CA .... Environmental Law; Natural Resources Law

TRAGOS, GEORGE E.
Clearwater, FL .... Criminal Trial Practice

TRAINOTTI, D. MICHAEL, A PROFESSIONAL LAW CORPORATION
Long Beach, CA .... Corporate Law; Tax Law; Trust and Estates, Wills and Probate

TRALINS AND ASSOCIATES, P.A.
Miami, FL .... Commercial Litigation; General Practice

TRAPASSO, DOLAN & HOLLANDER
Newton, NJ .... Real Estate Law; Trust and Estates, Wills and Probate

TRASK, BRITT & ROSSA, A PROFESSIONAL CORPORATION
Salt Lake City, UT .... Patent, Trademark, Copyright and Unfair Competition

TRAUB, BONACQUIST & FOX LLP
New York, NY .... Bankruptcy Law; Business Law

TRAVERS & GARGAS, P.C.
Boston, MA....................Family Law

TRAVIS, WILLIAM R. LAW OFFICE OF
Austin, TX....................Family Law

TRAVIS & GOOCH
Washington, DC....................Public Utilities Law

TRAYNOR, RUTTEN & TRAYNOR
Devils Lake, ND....................General Practice

TREDENNICK, STEVEN B.
Round Rock, TX....................Business Law

TREECE, ALFREY, MUSAT & BOSWORTH, P.C.
Denver, CO....................Aviation Law; Civil Trial Practice; Commercial Litigation; Environmental Law; Medical Malpractice; Product Liability Law; Workers Compensation

TREMAYNE, PAMELA L. LAW OFFICES OF
Atlanta, GA....................Creditors Rights; Family Law

TREMBLAY & HOLSENBACK
La Jolla, CA....................Civil Trial Practice

TREMBLAY, MAURILE C., A PROF. CORP., LAW OFFICES OF
San Diego, CA....................Civil Trial Practice; Insurance Defense; Real Estate Law

TREMBLAY & SMITH, LLP
Charlottesville, VA....................Civil Trial Practice; General Practice

TRENAM, KEMKER, SCHARF, BARKIN, FRYE, O'NEILL & MULLIS, PROFESSIONAL ASSOCIATION
Tampa, FL....................General Practice

TRENCH, ROSSI E WATANABE
Brasília, Brazil....................General Practice
Rio de Janeiro, Brazil....................General Practice
São Paulo, Brazil....................General Practice

TRENTI LAW FIRM
Virginia, MN....................General Practice

TREON, STRICK, LUCIA & AGUIRRE, A PROF. ASSN. OF LAWYERS
Phoenix, AZ....................Medical Malpractice; Personal Injury

TREVETT, LENWEAVER & SALZER, P.C.
Rochester, NY....................Civil Trial Practice; Criminal Trial Practice; Insurance Defense; Labor and Employment Law; Personal Injury

TREXLER, BUSHNELL, GIANGIORGI & BLACKSTONE, LTD.
Chicago, IL....................Patent, Trademark, Copyright and Unfair Competition

TRIBLER ORPETT & CRONE, A PROFESSIONAL CORPORATION
Chicago, IL....................Civil Trial Practice; Insurance Defense

TRICHILO, BANCROFT, MCGAVIN, HORVATH & JUDKINS, P.C.
Fairfax, VA....................Civil Trial Practice; Insurance Defense

TRIMBLE, SHERINIAN, & VARANINI
Sacramento, CA....................Insurance Defense

TRINE & METCALF, P.C.
Boulder, CO....................Civil Trial Practice; Environmental Law; Medical Malpractice; Personal Injury; Product Liability Law

TRINKLE, REDMAN, SWANSON, BYRD & COTON, P.A.
Plant City, FL....................General Practice

TRIPLETT, WOOLF & GARRETSON, LLC
Wichita, KS....................Business Law; Civil Trial Practice; Commercial Law; Commercial Litigation; Construction Law; General Practice; Insurance Defense; Labor and Employment Law; Mergers and Acquisitions; Real Estate Law; Tax Law; Trust and Estates, Wills and Probate

TRIPP SCOTT
Fort Lauderdale, FL....................Environmental Law; Labor and Employment Law; Real Estate Law

TROFF, PETZKE & AMMESON
St. Joseph, MI....................Business Law; Labor and Employment Law; Personal Injury; Real Estate Law; Trust and Estates, Wills and Probate

TROMBADORE, RAYMOND R., & DAVID W., P.C.
Somerville, NJ....................Business Law; Civil Trial Practice; Commercial Law; Corporate Law; Criminal Trial Practice; General Practice; Real Estate Law

TROPE AND TROPE
Los Angeles, CA....................Family Law

TROUBH, HEISLER & PIAMPIANO, P.C.
Portland, ME....................Banking Law; Bankruptcy Law; Business Law; Civil Trial Practice; Commercial Law; General Practice; Labor and Employment Law; Personal Injury; Real Estate Law; Tax Law; Trust and Estates, Wills and Probate; Workers Compensation

TROUT & RICHARDS, P.L.L.C.
Washington, DC....................Civil Trial Practice; Criminal Trial Practice

TROUTMAN, RICHARD B., P.A.
Orlando, FL....................Medical Malpractice; Personal Injury
Winter Park, FL....................Medical Malpractice; Personal Injury

TROUTMAN, WILLIAMS, IRVIN, GREEN & HELMS, PROFESSIONAL ASSOCIATION
Winter Park, FL....................Civil Trial Practice; General Practice

TROWBRIDGE & BASINE, P.C.
Glastonbury, CT....................Construction Law; Environmental Law; Insurance Defense

TROWBRIDGE LAW FIRM, P.C.
Detroit, MI....................Corporate Law; Personal Injury

TRULY, SMITH & LATHAM
Natchez, MS....................Banking Law; Civil Trial Practice; Energy Law; Real Estate Law; Trust and Estates, Wills and Probate

TRUMAN, CRAIG L., P.C.
Denver, CO....................Criminal Trial Practice

TRYON & ASSOCIATES, P.C.
Garden City, NY....................Commercial Litigation; Construction Law

TSCHIDER & SMITH
Bismarck, ND....................Civil Trial Practice; Tax Law; Trust and Estates, Wills and Probate

TUCHOW & TRAHEY
Flat Rock, MI....................Family Law; Personal Injury; Real Estate Law; Trust and Estates, Wills and Probate

TUCKER, STEVEN L.
Santa Fe, NM....................Appellate Practice

TUCKER, HENDRYX, TAUNTON, SNYDER & SLADE, P.C.
Houston, TX....................Insurance Defense

TUCKER STROHM MILLER & TUCKER, P.C.
Phoenix, AZ....................Appellate Practice; Criminal Trial Practice; Medical Malpractice; Personal Injury; Product Liability Law; Professional Liability

TUCKER AND TUCKER, P.C.
Paoli, IN....................General Practice

TUKE YOPP & SWEENEY, PLC
Nashville, TN....................Commercial Litigation; Mergers and Acquisitions; Trademark, Copyright and Unfair Competition

TULAC, JOHN W.
Claremont, CA....................International Business Law; International Trade Law

TURBIN, RICHARD, A LAW CORPORATION, LAW OFFICES OF
Honolulu, HI....................Medical Malpractice; Personal Injury

TURK, PAUL A., JR., P.A.
Palm Beach, FL....................Civil Trial Practice; Eminent Domain

TURLEY & STUTZ, P.C.
Dallas, TX....................Medical Malpractice; Personal Injury; Product Liability Law

TURLEY, WINDLE, P.C., LAW OFFICES OF
Dallas, TX....................Aviation Law; Civil Trial Practice; Personal Injury

TURNER, BRUCE E.
Addison, TX....................Real Estate Law

TURNER, CHARLES B. LAW OFFICE OF
South Orange, NJ....................Commercial Law; General Practice

TURNER, AUBERT & FRIEDMAN, LLP
Beverly Hills, CA....................Business Law; Civil Trial Practice; General Practice; Real Estate Law

TURNER & DAVIS, A PROFESSIONAL CORPORATION
Midland, TX....................Commercial Litigation; Natural Resources Law

TURNER, JONES & BITTING
Clarinda, IA....................General Practice

TURNER, ONDERDONK, KIMBROUGH & HOWELL, P.A.
Chatom, AL....................Civil Trial Practice; Criminal Trial Practice; General Practice; Personal Injury; Product Liability Law; Workers Compensation
Mobile, AL....................General Practice

TURNER, PADGET, GRAHAM & LANEY, P.A.
Columbia, SC....................Administrative Law; Antitrust Law; Banking Law; Bankruptcy Law; Business Law; Civil Trial Practice; Commercial Law; Construction Law; Creditors Rights; Criminal Trial Practice; Environmental Law; General Practice; Government Contracts; Health Care Law; Insurance Defense; Medical Malpractice; Municipal and Zoning Law; Personal Injury; Product Liability Law; Real Estate Law; Securities Law; Trust and Estates, Wills and Probate; Workers Compensation

TURNER, REID, DUNCAN, LOOMER & PATTON, P.C.
Springfield, MO....................Civil Trial Practice

TURNER, SEABERRY & WARFORD
Eastland, TX....................General Practice

TURNER & TURNER, P.C.
Tuscaloosa, AL....................General Practice

TURNER, TURNER & TURNER, PROFESSIONAL CORPORATION
Atlanta, GA....................Family Law

TURNER, WILSON & SAWYER
Montgomery, AL....................Family Law; Real Estate Law; Trust and Estates, Wills and Probate

TUSA, MICHAEL T. JR.
Metairie, LA....................Labor and Employment Law

TUTT, CHARLES G.
Shreveport, LA....................Civil Trial Practice; Product Liability Law

TUTTLE & TAYLOR, A LAW CORPORATION
Los Angeles, CA....................General Practice

TUTTLE, TAYLOR & HERON
Washington, DC....................General Practice

TWEEDY, PENNEY & CRAWFORD, A LAW PARTNERSHIP
Sacramento, CA....................Workers Compensation

TWIGGS, ABRAMS, STRICKLAND & TREHY, P.A.
Raleigh, NC....................Civil Trial Practice; Communications Law; Medical Malpractice; Personal Injury; Product Liability Law

TWITCHELL AND RICE
Santa Maria, CA....................General Practice

TWOHIG, RAY, P.C.
Albuquerque, NM....................Civil Rights; Criminal Trial Practice

TYAN & ASSOCIES
Beirut, Lebanon....................General Practice

TYE AND TYE
Dayton, OH....................General Practice; Trust and Estates, Wills and Probate

TYLER, BARTL, BURKE AND ALBERT, P.L.C.
Alexandria, VA....................Bankruptcy Law

TYLER, CASSELL, JACKSON, PEACE & SILVER, L.L.P.
Columbia, SC....................Commercial Law; Construction Law; Real Estate Law

TYLER COOPER & ALCORN, LLP
Hartford, CT....................General Practice
New Haven, CT....................General Practice
Stamford, CT....................General Practice

TYSON, GEORGE H. JR.
Houston, TX....................Criminal Trial Practice

UDALL, SHUMWAY, BLACKHURST, ALLEN & LYONS, P.C.
Mesa, AZ....................Commercial Litigation; Education Law; Family Law; Insurance Defense; Legal Malpractice; Personal Injury; Tax Law; Trust and Estates, Wills and Probate

UFKES, JOHN H.F.
San Juan Capistrano, CA........Workers Compensation

ULMER & BERNE LLP
Cleveland, OH....................Business Law; Civil Trial Practice; General Practice; Labor and Employment Law; Tax Law

ULRICH, KESSLER & ANGER, P.C.
Phoenix, AZ....................Antitrust Law; Appellate Practice; Commercial Litigation; Health Care Law; Medical Malpractice; Municipal and Zoning Law; Natural Resources Law

UNDERBERG & KESSLER LLP
Rochester, NY....................Banking Law; Business Law; Civil Trial Practice; Environmental Law; General Practice; Health Care Law; Insurance Defense; Labor and Employment Law; Tax Law

UNDERWOOD, P. JAMES
Annapolis, MD....................Real Estate Law

UNDERWOOD KINSEY WARREN & TUCKER, P.A.
Charlotte, NC....................General Practice

UNDERWOOD LAW FIRM
Jackson, MS....................Bankruptcy Law; Real Estate Law

UNDERWOOD, WILSON, BERRY, STEIN & JOHNSON, P.C.
Amarillo, TX....................General Practice

UNGERMAN, MAYNARD I., LAW OFFICES OF
Tulsa, OK....................Family Law; Labor and Employment Law; Personal Injury

UNGLESBY, KOCH & REYNOLDS
Baton Rouge, LA....................Criminal Trial Practice; Product Liability Law; Toxic Torts

UPCHURCH, BAILEY & UPCHURCH, P.A.
St. Augustine, FL....................Civil Trial Practice; Environmental Law; General Practice; Land Use Law; Municipal and Zoning Law; Real Estate Law; Trust and Estates, Wills and Probate

UPSHAW, WILLIAMS, BIGGERS, BECKHAM & RIDDICK, LLP
Greenwood, MS....................Civil Trial Practice; Environmental Law; General Practice; Insurance Defense; Workers Compensation
Jackson, MS....................Civil Trial Practice; General Practice; Insurance Defense; Workers Compensation

URBAN, LEE D.
Portland, ME....................Real Estate Law

URBELIS, FIELDSTEEL & BAILIN, LLP
Boston, MA....................Civil Trial Practice

URICCHIO, HOWE, KRELL, JACOBSON, TOPOREK & THEOS, P.A.
Charleston, SC....................Civil Trial Practice; Criminal Trial Practice; Family Law; Workers Compensation

USSERY & PARRISH, P.A.
Albuquerque, NM....................Real Estate Law

UTZ, LITVAK, SUMMERS, POWERS & MANRING
St. Joseph, MO....................General Practice

VAAGE, ROBERT F.
San Diego, CA....................Civil Trial Practice

VAALER, ZIMNEY, FOSTER & JOHNSON, CHARTERED
Grand Forks, ND....................General Practice

VACOVEC, MAYOTTE & SINGER
Newton, MA....................International Business Law; Tax Law

VAGLICA & MEINHOLD, L.L.C.
Colorado Springs, CO............Civil Trial Practice

VAIRO, MECHLIN, TOMASI, JOHNSON & MANCHESTER
Houghton, MI....................General Practice; Insurance Defense

VAKA, LARSON & JOHNSON, P.L.
Tampa, FL....................Appellate Practice; Personal Injury

VALENTINE, ADAMS & LAMAR, L.L.P.
Nashville, NC....................General Practice

VALENTINE & ASSOCIATES, P.C.
Detroit, MI....................Civil Trial Practice; Labor and Employment Law; Personal Injury
West Bloomfield, MI....................Business Law; Civil Trial Practice; Labor and Employment Law; Personal Injury; Real Estate Law

VALENZUELA, HENRY E., P.A.
Tampa, FL....................Medical Malpractice; Personal Injury

VALLE & CRAIG, P.A.
Miami, FL....................Admiralty/Maritime Law; Civil Trial Practice; Commercial Law; Insurance Defense

VAN BLOIS & ASSOCIATES
Oakland, CA....................Aviation Law; Medical Malpractice; Personal Injury; Product Liability Law

VAN CAMP, HAYES & MEACHAM, A PROFESSIONAL ASSOCIATION
Pinehurst, NC....................General Practice

VAN COTT, BAGLEY, CORNWALL & MCCARTHY, A PROFESSIONAL CORPORATION
Ogden, UT....................General Practice
Park City, UT....................General Practice
Salt Lake City, UT....................Administrative Law; Antitrust Law; Appellate Practice; Arbitration; Banking Law; Bankruptcy Law; Business Law; Civil Trial Practice; Commercial Law; Commercial Litigation; Communications Law; Constitutional Law; Construction Law; Corporate Law; Creditors Rights; Eminent Domain; Employment Benefits Law; Energy Law; Environmental Law; Family Law; General Practice; Government Contracts; Health Care Law; Immigration and Naturalization; Insurance Defense; Intellectual Property Law; International Trade Law; Labor and Employment Law; Land Use Law; Medical Malpractice; Mergers and Acquisitions; Municipal and Zoning Law; Natural Resources Law; Oil and Gas Law; Pension and Profit Sharing; Personal Injury; Product Liability Law; Professional Liability; Public Utilities Law; Real Estate Law; Securities Law; Tax Law; Toxic Torts; Trademark, Copyright and Unfair Competition; Trust and Estates, Wills and Probate

VANDEBERG JOHNSON & GANDARA
Tacoma, WA.....General Practice

VANDEMARK, RUTH E. LAW OFFICES OF
Chicago, IL.....Appellate Practice

VANDEN BOS & CHAPMAN
Portland, OR.....Bankruptcy Law

VANDER MALE, BELLAMY, GILCHRIST, VANDE VUSSE & CAFFERTY
Detroit, MI.....Civil Trial Practice; Criminal Trial Practice; Health Care Law

VANDEVEER GARZIA, PROFESSIONAL CORPORATION
Birmingham, MI.....Insurance Defense
Detroit, MI.....Aviation Law; Civil Trial Practice; Commercial Litigation; Construction Law; Insurance Defense; Medical Malpractice; Municipal and Zoning Law; Product Liability Law

VANDEVENTER BLACK LLP
Norfolk, VA.....Admiralty/Maritime Law; Bankruptcy Law; Civil Trial Practice; Environmental Law; General Practice; Immigration and Naturalization; Labor and Employment Law; Real Estate Law; Tax Law

VAN DEWATER & VAN DEWATER
Poughkeepsie, NY.....Banking Law; Bankruptcy Law; Communications Law; Family Law; General Practice; Real Estate Law; Tax Law

VAN HOY, REUTLINGER & TAYLOR
Charlotte, NC.....Health Care Law; Labor and Employment Law

VAN MEER & BELANGER, P.A.
South Portland, ME.....Business Law; Employment Benefits Law; Health Care Law; Tax Law; Trust and Estates, Wills and Probate

VANN LAW FIRM
Camilla, GA.....General Practice

VANNAH COSTELLO CANEPA RIEDY & RUBINO
Las Vegas, NV.....Construction Law; Insurance Defense; Medical Malpractice; Personal Injury; Product Liability Law

VANNOY, COLVARD, TRIPLETT & VANNOY, P.L.L.C.
North Wilkesboro, NC.....General Practice

VAN STEENBERG, CHALOUPKA, MULLIN, HOLYOKE, PAHLKE, SMITH, SNYDER & HOFMEISTER, P.C.
Scottsbluff, NE.....Commercial Litigation

VAN SUILICHEM & ASSOCIATES, P.C.
Troy, MI.....Civil Rights; Labor and Employment Law

VAN WAGNER, ELLEN LAW OFFICES OF
Chino, CA.....Workers Compensation

VAN WERT, RONALD K., A PROFESSIONAL CORPORATION
Costa Mesa, CA.....Civil Trial Practice; Tax Law

VAN WINKLE, BUCK, WALL, STARNES AND DAVIS, P.A.
Asheville, NC.....Business Law; General Practice; Insurance Defense; Medical Malpractice

VARNADORE, M. DEWAYNE, P.C., LAW OFFICES OF
Tyler, TX.....Oil and Gas Law

VASSALLO, EDDIE, P.C., LAW OFFICES OF
Dallas, TX.....Civil Trial Practice; Eminent Domain; Personal Injury

VAUGHAN & HULL, LTD., A PROF. CORP., LAW OFFICES
Elko, NV.....General Practice

VEAL & ASSOCIATES
Birmingham, AL.....Intellectual Property Law; Patent, Trademark, Copyright and Unfair Competition

VEDDER, PRICE, KAUFMAN & KAMMHOLZ
Chicago, IL.....General Practice

VEEN, WILLIAM L., A PROFESSIONAL CORPORATION
San Francisco, CA.....Personal Injury

VELTMANN & LETO
San Diego, CA.....Family Law

VENABLE, ATTORNEYS AT LAW, VENABLE, BAETJER, HOWARD & CIVILETTI, LLP
Washington, DC.....Administrative Law; Admiralty/Maritime Law; Antitrust Law; Appellate Practice; Banking Law; Bankruptcy Law; Business Law; Civil Trial Practice; Commercial Law; Communications Law; Construction Law; Criminal Trial Practice; Employment Benefits Law; Environmental Law; General Practice; Health Care Law; Insurance Defense; Intellectual Property Law; Labor and Employment Law; Natural Resources Law; Patent, Trademark, Copyright and Unfair Competition; Product Liability Law; Real Estate Law; Securities Law; Trademark, Copyright and Unfair Competition; Transportation Law
Baltimore, MD.....Administrative Law; Admiralty/Maritime Law; Antitrust Law; Appellate Practice; Banking Law; Bankruptcy Law; Business Law; Civil Trial Practice; Commercial Law; Communications Law; Construction Law; Criminal Trial Practice; Employment Benefits Law; Environmental Law; Family Law; General Practice; Health Care Law; Immigration and Naturalization; Insurance Defense; Intellectual Property Law; Labor and Employment Law; Municipal and Zoning Law; Municipal Bond/Public Authority Financing; Natural Resources Law; Patent, Trademark, Copyright and Unfair Competition; Personal Injury; Product Liability Law; Real Estate Law; Securities Law; Tax Law; Trademark, Copyright and Unfair Competition; Transportation Law; Trust and Estates, Wills and Probate
Rockville, MD.....Administrative Law; Appellate Practice; Banking Law; Business Law; Civil Trial Practice; General Practice; Labor and Employment Law
Towson, MD.....Appellate Practice; Banking Law; Business Law; Civil Trial Practice; Commercial Law; Construction Law; General Practice; Insurance Defense; Labor and Employment Law; Municipal Bond/Public Authority Financing; Personal Injury; Product Liability Law; Real Estate Law; Trust and Estates, Wills and Probate
McLean, VA.....Appellate Practice; Banking Law; Civil Trial Practice; Commercial Law; Construction Law; General Practice; Real Estate Law

VENZIE, PHILLIPS & WARSHAWER, A PROFESSIONAL CORPORATION
Philadelphia, PA.....Arbitration; Construction Law

VEON, LESLIE L. LAW OFFICES OF
Chicago, IL.....Family Law

VERCRUYSSE METZ & MURRAY, A PROFESSIONAL CORPORATION
Bingham Farms, MI.....Labor and Employment Law

VERNER & BRUMLEY, A PROFESSIONAL CORPORATION
Dallas, TX.....Family Law

VERNER, LIIPFERT, BERNHARD, MCPHERSON AND HAND, CHARTERED
Washington, DC.....Bankruptcy Law; Commercial Law; Communications Law; Energy Law; Environmental Law; General Practice; International Business Law; Labor and Employment Law; Transportation Law

VERNER SIMON LLP
New York, NY.....Insurance Defense

VERRILL & DANA, LLP
Portland, ME.....Administrative Law; Bankruptcy Law; Business Law; Civil Trial Practice; Commercial Litigation; Construction Law; Employment Benefits Law; Environmental Law; General Practice; Health Care Law; Labor and Employment Law; Land Use Law; Real Estate Law; Trust and Estates, Wills and Probate

VERTERANO & MANOLIS
New Castle, PA.....General Practice

VETTER & WHITE, INCORPORATED
Providence, RI.....Appellate Practice; Business Law; Civil Trial Practice; Employment Benefits Law; Insurance Defense; Intellectual Property Law; Product Liability Law; Trademark, Copyright and Unfair Competition

VIAL, HAMILTON, KOCH & KNOX, L.L.P.
Dallas, TX.....General Practice

VICKERS, RIIS, MURRAY AND CURRAN, L.L.C.
Mobile, AL.....Admiralty/Maritime Law; Business Law; Commercial Law; Environmental Law; General Practice; Tax Law; Trust and Estates, Wills and Probate

VICTOR, RAYMOND M., P.C.
Norristown, PA.....Legal Malpractice; Medical Malpractice; Personal Injury; Product Liability Law

VIGORITA, LOUIS J.
Ventura, CA.....Workers Compensation

VIMONT & WILLS PLLC
Lexington, KY.....Construction Law; Family Law; Insurance Defense; Labor and Employment Law; Real Estate Law; Trust and Estates, Wills and Probate; Workers Compensation

VINAR, BENJAMIN
Garden City, NY.....Appellate Practice; Civil Trial Practice

VINSON & ELKINS
London, England.....General Practice
Washington, DC.....Civil Trial Practice; General Practice
Austin, TX.....Civil Trial Practice; General Practice
Dallas, TX.....Civil Trial Practice; General Practice

Houston, TX ....Admiralty/Maritime Law; Antitrust Law; Civil Trial Practice; Energy Law; General Practice; Labor and Employment Law; Municipal Bond/Public Authority Financing; Natural Resources Law; Patent, Trademark, Copyright and Unfair Competition; Tax Law

VINYARD & ASSOCIATES
Washington, DC............Tax Law

VIRTUE NAJJAR BARTELL MATTHEWS & BROWN P.C.
Santa Fe, NM............General Practice

VITTAL AND STERNBERG
Los Angeles, CA............Civil Trial Practice

VLADECK, WALDMAN, ELIAS & ENGELHARD, P.C.
New York, NY............Labor and Employment Law

VLASSIS & VLASSIS
Phoenix, AZ............Business Law; Immigration and Naturalization; Natural Resources Law

VOGEL, WEIR, BYE, HUNKE & MCCORMICK, LTD.
Fargo, ND............Banking Law; Bankruptcy Law; Civil Trial Practice; Commercial Law; Criminal Trial Practice; General Practice; Insurance Defense; Labor and Employment Law; Personal Injury; Real Estate Law; Tax Law; Trust and Estates, Wills and Probate

VOGL & MEREDITH
San Francisco, CA............Civil Trial Practice; Commercial Litigation; Environmental Law; Insurance Defense

VOLK LAW FIRM, THE, P.C.
Sewickley, PA............Labor and Employment Law

VOLLMER, MICHAEL V.
Newport Beach, CA............Trust and Estates, Wills and Probate

VOLLMER RULONG & KEATING, P.C.
Pittsburgh, PA............Bankruptcy Law; Civil Trial Practice; Commercial Litigation; Creditors Rights; Personal Injury

VOLPE, EDWARD L., P.C.
Denver, CO............Commercial Litigation

VOLZ, PRESTWOOD & HANAN, P.C.
Montgomery, AL............Administrative Law; Appellate Practice; Business Law; Civil Rights; Civil Trial Practice; Commercial Law; Constitutional Law; Employment Benefits Law; General Practice; Labor and Employment Law; Product Liability Law; Real Estate Law; Trust and Estates, Wills and Probate

VON MANDEL & VON MANDEL
Chicago, IL............Tax Law

VOORHEES & OUDA
Morris Plains, NJ............Civil Trial Practice; Legal Malpractice; Medical Malpractice; Professional Liability

VOORHIES & LABBÉ, A PROFESSIONAL LAW CORPORATION
Lafayette, LA............Insurance Defense; Personal Injury

VORT, ROBERT A.
Tenafly, NJ............Appellate Practice; Family Law

VORYS, SATER, SEYMOUR AND PEASE LLP
Washington, DC............General Practice
Cincinnati, OH............General Practice
Cleveland, OH............General Practice; Labor and Employment Law
Columbus, OH............Antitrust Law; Banking Law; Bankruptcy Law; General Practice; Labor and Employment Law; Municipal Bond/Public Authority Financing; Natural Resources Law; Real Estate Law; Tax Law

VOSE, BLAU & HAYES
Winter Park, FL............Commercial Litigation; Construction Law; Environmental Law; Land Use Law; Real Estate Law

VOTRE & ASSOCIATES, P.C.
New Haven, CT............Commercial Law; Health Care Law; International Business Law; Tax Law

VOUTÉ, LOHRFINK, MAGRO & COLLINS, LLP
White Plains, NY............Civil Trial Practice; General Practice; Insurance Defense; Medical Malpractice; Personal Injury; Product Liability Law

VRANESH AND RAISCH, L.L.P.
Boulder, CO............Environmental Law; Natural Resources Law
Denver, CO............Environmental Law; Natural Resources Law

WACHTEL, BIEHN & MALM
Lake Havasu City, AZ............Arbitration; Family Law; Personal Injury; Trust and Estates, Wills and Probate

WACHTEL & MASYR, LLP
New York, NY............Civil Trial Practice; Corporate Law; Tax Law

WADDICK LAW FIRM, THE, P.C.
Indianapolis, IN............Personal Injury

WADE CLARK MULCAHY
New York, NY............Civil Trial Practice; Insurance Defense; Product Liability Law

WADLEIGH, STARR & PETERS, P.L.L.C.
Manchester, NH............General Practice

WAGNER, CRAIG E.
Englewood, CO............Commercial Litigation

WAGNER & BAGOT
New Orleans, LA............Admiralty/Maritime Law; Commercial Litigation; Environmental Law; Insurance Defense; International Business Law; Labor and Employment Law; Product Liability Law

WAGNER, DAVIS & GOLD, P.C.
New York, NY............Commercial Litigation; Construction Law; General Practice; Real Estate Law; Trust and Estates, Wills and Probate

WAGNER AND GRUNDY
Tulsa, OK............Family Law

WAGNER, JOHNSON, MCAFEE & BODIK, P.A.
West Palm Beach, FL............Civil Trial Practice; Personal Injury

WAGNER LAW FIRM, THE
Fort Worth, TX............Personal Injury

WAGNER, MYERS & SANGER, A PROFESSIONAL CORPORATION
Knoxville, TN............Civil Trial Practice; General Practice; Health Care Law; Natural Resources Law; Public Utilities Law; Tax Law

WAGSTAFF, ROBERT H. LAW OFFICES OF
Anchorage, AK............Appellate Practice; Aviation Law; Insurance Defense; Medical Malpractice; Product Liability Law

WAGSTAFF, ALVIS, STUBBEMAN, SEAMSTER & LONGACRE, L.L.P.
Abilene, TX............General Practice; Insurance Defense

WAGSTAFF & CARTMELL, LLP
Kansas City, MO............Civil Trial Practice; Commercial Litigation; Medical Malpractice; Product Liability Law; Professional Liability

WAITE, SCHNEIDER, BAYLESS & CHESLEY CO., L.P.A.
Cincinnati, OH............Antitrust Law; Appellate Practice; Aviation Law; Civil Trial Practice; International Business Law; Labor and Employment Law; Personal Injury; Product Liability Law; Real Estate Law; Securities Law

WALDBAUM, CORN, KOFF AND BERGER, P.C.
Denver, CO............General Practice

WALDECK & LIND, P.A.
Minneapolis, MN............Appellate Practice; Civil Trial Practice; Insurance Defense

WALDER, SONDAK & BROGAN, A PROFESSIONAL CORPORATION
Roseland, NJ............Appellate Practice; Business Law; Civil Trial Practice; Commercial Law; Criminal Trial Practice; Environmental Law; General Practice; Insurance Defense; Tax Law

WALDRON AND FANN
Murfreesboro, TN............Personal Injury

WALKER, WOODROW W.
Arlington, VA............Creditors Rights

WALKER & BLACK
Little Rock, AR............Commercial Law; Trust and Estates, Wills and Probate

WALKER, GEORGE G., INC.
San Francisco, CA............Criminal Trial Practice

WALKER, HULBERT, GRAY & BYRD, L.L.P.
Perry, GA............General Practice

WALKER, KEELING & CARROLL, L.L.P.
Victoria, TX............Environmental Law; Insurance Defense; Labor and Employment Law

WALKER LAW FIRM, THE
Des Moines, IA............Civil Trial Practice; Personal Injury; Product Liability Law; Toxic Torts
Newport Beach, CA............Civil Trial Practice

WALKER & MCPHAIL
Monterey, CA............Trust and Estates, Wills and Probate

WALKER, SHOCK, HARP & HILL, P.L.L.C.
Fort Smith, AR........................Workers Compensation

WALKER & WALKER, P.C.
Knoxville, TN..........................Banking Law; Bankruptcy Law; Creditors Rights; General Practice

WALKER, WATTS, JACKSON & MCFARLAND
Adrian, MI..............................Banking Law; General Practice; Real Estate Law; Trust and Estates, Wills and Probate

WALKER, WILLIAM G., P.C.
Tucson, AZ..............................Civil Trial Practice; Commercial Litigation; Criminal Trial Practice

WALKUP, MELODIA, KELLY & ECHEVERRIA, A PROFESSIONAL CORPORATION
San Francisco, CA....................Employment Benefits Law; Labor and Employment Law; Medical Malpractice; Personal Injury; Product Liability Law

WALLACE & DE MAYO, P.C.
Norcross, GA...........................Bankruptcy Law; Commercial Law; Creditors Rights

WALLACE, KLOR & MANN, P.C.
Portland, OR...........................Workers Compensation

WALLACE, MORRIS & BARWICK, P.A.
Kinston, NC.............................General Practice

WALLACE, SAUNDERS, AUSTIN, BROWN & ENOCHS, CHARTERED
Overland Park, KS..................General Practice

WALLENSTEIN & WAGNER, LTD.
Chicago, IL..............................Intellectual Property Law; Patent, Trademark, Copyright and Unfair Competition

WALLER LANSDEN DORTCH & DAVIS
Columbia, TN..........................General Practice
Nashville, TN..........................General Practice

WALLER, SMITH & PALMER, P.C.
New London, CT.....................Banking Law; Business Law; Civil Trial Practice; Commercial Law; Corporate Law; General Practice; Municipal and Zoning Law; Real Estate Law; Trust and Estates, Wills and Probate
Old Lyme, CT.........................General Practice

WALLMAN, GREENBERG, GASMAN & MCKNIGHT, LLP
New York, NY.........................Corporate Law; Family Law; Real Estate Law; Trust and Estates, Wills and Probate

WALSH, MICHAEL R.
Orlando, FL.............................Family Law

WALSH, TIMOTHY J.
Mishawaka, IN........................Civil Trial Practice

WALSH, ANDERSON, BROWN, SCHULZE & ALDRIDGE, P.C.
Austin, TX...............................Civil Trial Practice; Insurance Defense

WALSH, COLUCCI, STACKHOUSE, EMRICH & LUBELEY, P.C.
Arlington, VA..........................Business Law; Civil Trial Practice; Land Use Law; Municipal and Zoning Law; Real Estate Law
Leesburg, VA..........................Real Estate Law
Woodbridge, VA......................Real Estate Law

WALSH, DANIEL R., THE LAW OFFICE OF
Carson City, NV.....................Energy Law; Environmental Law; Land Use Law

WALSH & DECLUES, LLP
Encino, CA..............................Labor and Employment Law
Santa Ana, CA........................Insurance Defense; Labor and Employment Law

WALSH & FISHER, A PROFESSIONAL ASSOCIATION
Westminster, MD....................General Practice; Real Estate Law

WALSH & KEATING, S.C.
Milwaukee, WI........................Commercial Law; Corporate Law; Real Estate Law; Tax Law; Trust and Estates, Wills and Probate

WALSH, MICHAEL P., P.A.
West Palm Beach, FL.............Family Law

WALSH, O'NEAL, & ASSOCIATES
Baton Rouge, LA....................Insurance Defense

WALSTON, WELLS, ANDERSON & BAINS, LLP
Birmingham, AL......................Civil Trial Practice; General Practice

WALSWORTH, FRANKLIN, BEVINS & MCCALL
Orange, CA.............................Environmental Law

WALTER & HAVERFIELD, P.L.L.
Cleveland, OH.........................Civil Trial Practice; Communications Law; Employment Benefits Law; Environmental Law; General Practice; Health Care Law; International Business Law; Labor and Employment Law; Mergers and Acquisitions; Municipal and Zoning Law; Pension and Profit Sharing; Real Estate Law; Tax Law; Trust and Estates, Wills and Probate

WALTERS, DAVIS & PUJADAS, P.C.
Ocilla, GA...............................Civil Trial Practice; Criminal Trial Practice; General Practice

WALTERS FRAZIER CAIETTI RUTAN & LOPEZ, LLP
San Diego, CA........................Civil Trial Practice

WALTERS & JOYCE, P.C.
Denver, CO.............................Antitrust Law; Civil Trial Practice; General Practice; Real Estate Law

WALTERS & WARD, A PROFESSIONAL CORPORATION
San Diego, CA........................Trust and Estates, Wills and Probate

WALTHER ASSOCIATES
Albuquerque, NM...................Family Law
Santa Fe, NM.........................Family Law

WALTHER, KEY, MAUPIN, OATS, COX & LEGOY, A PROFESSIONAL CORPORATION
Reno, NV.................................Arbitration; Business Law; Civil Trial Practice; Commercial Litigation; Construction Law; Corporate Law; Employment Benefits Law; Environmental Law; Health Care Law; Pension and Profit Sharing; Personal Injury; Real Estate Law; Tax Law; Trust and Estates, Wills and Probate

WALTHER LAW OFFICES, S.C.
Milwaukee, WI........................Transportation Law

WALTON LANTAFF SCHROEDER & CARSON
Fort Lauderdale, FL..............General Practice
Miami, FL...............................General Practice
West Palm Beach, FL............General Practice

WALTON, SMITH, PHILLIPS & DIXON, P.C.
Traverse City, MI..................Civil Trial Practice; Commercial Litigation; Personal Injury; Workers Compensation

WANSKER, HENRY B.
Rockingham, NC....................Personal Injury

WARBURTON, ADAMI, MCNEILL, PAISLEY & APPELL, P.C.
Alice, TX................................Banking Law; Family Law; General Practice; Trust and Estates, Wills and Probate

WARD, CRAIG B., P.A.
Orlando, FL...........................General Practice; Real Estate Law; Trust and Estates, Wills and Probate

WARD, DAMON, BEVERLY, TITTLE & POSNER, P.A.
West Palm Beach, FL............Antitrust Law; Banking Law; Bankruptcy Law; Commercial Litigation; Real Estate Law; Securities Law; Trust and Estates, Wills and Probate

WARD, KERSHAW & MINTON, A PROFESSIONAL ASSOCIATION
Baltimore, MD.......................Admiralty/Maritime Law; Antitrust Law; Civil Trial Practice; Insurance Defense

WARD NELSON, LLC
New Orleans, LA...................Commercial Litigation; Health Care Law; Insurance Defense; Medical Malpractice; Product Liability Law

WARDROP & WARDROP, P.C.
Grand Rapids, MI.................Bankruptcy Law; Commercial Law; Immigration and Naturalization; Personal Injury

WARD & WARD
Indianapolis, IN....................Civil Trial Practice; Personal Injury; Product Liability Law

WARE, DAVID A. M. & ASSOCIATES
Metairie, LA..........................Immigration and Naturalization

WARE, MICHAEL L.
Fort Worth, TX......................Criminal Trial Practice

WARE, BRYSON, WEST & KUMMER
Covington, KY......................Civil Trial Practice; General Practice; Insurance Defense; Workers Compensation

WARING COX, PLC
Memphis, TN.........................Civil Trial Practice; General Practice; Insurance Defense; Intellectual Property Law; Labor and Employment Law; Municipal Bond/Public Authority Financing; Real Estate Law; Securities Law; Tax Law

WARLICK MILSTED DOTSON & CARTER
Jacksonville, NC...................General Practice

WARLICK, TRITT & STEBBINS, L.L.P.
Augusta, GA..........................Banking Law; Bankruptcy Law; Civil Trial Practice; General Practice; Real Estate Law; Securities Law

WARNER, CHARLES G. LAW OFFICES OF
Monterey, CA........................Civil Trial Practice

WARNER ANGLE ROPER & HALLAM PLC
Phoenix, AZ .... Appellate Practice; Business Law; Commercial Litigation; Construction Law; Personal Injury; Real Estate Law; Trust and Estates, Wills and Probate

WARNER, FOX, WACKEEN, DUNGEY SEELEY, SWEET & WRIGHT, L.L.P.
Stuart, FL .... Civil Trial Practice; Commercial Litigation; Real Estate Law

WARNER, MAYOUE & BATES, P.C.
Atlanta, GA .... Family Law

WARNER NORCROSS & JUDD LLP
Grand Rapids, MI .... Antitrust Law; Banking Law; Bankruptcy Law; Business Law; Civil Trial Practice; Computer Law; Corporate Law; Employment Benefits Law; Environmental Law; Health Care Law; Immigration and Naturalization; International Business Law; Labor and Employment Law; Patent, Trademark, Copyright and Unfair Competition; Real Estate Law; Securities Law; Tax Law; Trust and Estates, Wills and Probate

WARNER, SMITH & HARRIS, PLC
Fort Smith, AR .... Civil Trial Practice; Corporate Law; Insurance Defense; Product Liability Law; Tax Law

WARNICKE & LITTLER, P.L.C.
Phoenix, AZ .... Bankruptcy Law; Commercial Litigation; Construction Law

WARREN & SINKLER, L.L.P.
Charleston, SC .... Business Law; General Practice; Real Estate Law; Securities Law; Tax Law

WARREN AND YOUNG PLL
Ashtabula, OH .... Business Law; General Practice; Insurance Defense; Labor and Employment Law

WARRICK, BENJAMIN R.
Clinton, NC .... Family Law

WARTNICK, CHABER, HAROWITZ, SMITH & TIGERMAN, A PROFESSIONAL CORPORATION
San Francisco, CA .... Business Law; Commercial Litigation; Personal Injury; Product Liability Law

WARWICK & BANISTER, P.A.
Palm Beach, FL .... Commercial Litigation; Real Estate Law; Trust and Estates, Wills and Probate

WASKA, RONALD J., A PROFESSIONAL CORPORATION
Houston, TX .... Commercial Litigation; Criminal Trial Practice

WASSER, ROSENSON & CARTER
Los Angeles, CA .... Family Law

WASSERMAN, MANCINI & CHANG
Washington, DC .... Immigration and Naturalization

WATANABE, ING & KAWASHIMA
Honolulu, HI .... Civil Trial Practice; Commercial Law; General Practice; Insurance Defense

WATERMAN, DAVID M. LAW OFFICES OF
Tucson, AZ .... Workers Compensation

WATERS, HOLT & FIELDS
Pampa, TX .... General Practice

WATERS, MCCLUSKEY & BOEHLE
Santa Monica, CA .... Civil Trial Practice; Construction Law; Insurance Defense; Personal Injury; Product Liability Law

WATERS, MCPHERSON, MCNEILL, P.C.
Secaucus, NJ .... Civil Trial Practice; General Practice

WATERS & MORSE, P.C.
Grand Rapids, MI .... Patent, Trademark, Copyright and Unfair Competition

WATERS, WARNER & HARRIS, PLLC
Clarksburg, WV .... Business Law; Civil Trial Practice; Commercial Litigation; General Practice; Insurance Defense; Mergers and Acquisitions; Natural Resources Law; Real Estate Law

WATKINS, JOHN E. JR.
White Plains, NY .... Corporate Law; Municipal and Zoning Law; Real Estate Law; Tax Law

WATKINS, BOULWARE, LUCAS, MINER, MURPHY & TAYLOR
St. Joseph, MO .... General Practice

WATKINS & EAGER
Jackson, MS .... Banking Law; Bankruptcy Law; Civil Trial Practice; Commercial Law; Commercial Litigation; Environmental Law; General Practice; Insurance Defense; Labor and Employment Law; Natural Resources Law; Personal Injury; Real Estate Law; Tax Law; Trust and Estates, Wills and Probate

WATKINSON LAIRD RUBENSTEIN LASHWAY & BALDWIN, P.C.
Eugene, OR .... General Practice; Health Care Law; Real Estate Law

WATLEY, KEVIN D.
Norman, OK .... Tax Law

WATROUS & REARDON
Albuquerque, NM .... Bankruptcy Law; Commercial Litigation; Labor and Employment Law; Real Estate Law

WATSON, TIMOTHY F. SR.
Newport, AR .... Business Law; Real Estate Law

WATSON, WILLIAM E. & ASSOCIATES
Wellsburg, WV .... General Practice

WATSON, BISHOP, LONDON, GALOW, P.C.
Austin, TX .... Civil Trial Practice; Commercial Litigation; Personal Injury

WATSON, BLANCHE, WILSON & POSNER
Baton Rouge, LA .... Commercial Litigation; Health Care Law; Medical Malpractice; Product Liability Law; Tax Law

WATSON, FARLEY & WILLIAMS
New York, NY .... Admiralty/Maritime Law; Banking Law; General Practice; Transportation Law

WATSON, HOLLOW & REEVES, P.L.C.
Knoxville, TN .... Civil Trial Practice; Communications Law; General Practice; Insurance Defense; Labor and Employment Law; Medical Malpractice; Product Liability Law

WATSON, STEVENS, FIORILLA & RUTTER, LLP
New Brunswick, NJ .... Transportation Law

WATT & SAWYIER
Chicago, IL .... Mergers and Acquisitions; Municipal Bond/Public Authority Financing; Real Estate Law; Tax Law; Trust and Estates, Wills and Probate

WATT, TIEDER, HOFFAR & FITZGERALD, L.L.P.
Washington, DC .... Commercial Law; Construction Law; Environmental Law; International Business Law; Real Estate Law
McLean, VA .... Construction Law; International Business Law; Real Estate Law

WAYCASTER, MORRIS, JOHNSON & DEAN
Dalton, GA .... Personal Injury

WAYMAN, IRVIN & MCAULEY
Pittsburgh, PA .... Insurance Defense

WEADON & ASSOCIATES
Washington, DC .... International Business Law

WEARN, JAMES MCCARTNEY, P.A.
West Palm Beach, FL .... Commercial Litigation; General Practice; Municipal and Zoning Law

WEARY, DAVIS, HENRY, STRUEBING, TROUP, KAUS & RYAN, L.C.
Junction City, KS .... General Practice

WEATHERBEE, WOODCOCK, BURLOCK & WOODCOCK
Bangor, ME .... Insurance Defense; Workers Compensation

WEBB, BURNETT, JACKSON, CORNBROOKS, WILBER, VORHIS & DOUSE, LLP
Salisbury, MD .... Business Law; Civil Trial Practice; Criminal Trial Practice

WEBB, CARLOCK, COPELAND, SEMLER & STAIR, LLP
Atlanta, GA .... Civil Trial Practice; Insurance Defense; Workers Compensation

WEBB & ELEY, P.C.
Montgomery, AL .... Commercial Litigation; Insurance Defense; Labor and Employment Law; Product Liability Law; Real Estate Law; Workers Compensation

WEBB, PATTERSON AND TAPELLA
Sacramento, CA .... Trust and Estates, Wills and Probate

WEBB, SANDERS, BALDUCCI & SMITH, P.L.L.C.
Tupelo, MS .... Civil Trial Practice; Insurance Defense

WEBB, STOKES & SPARKS
San Angelo, TX .... Personal Injury

WEBB & TIHOLIZ, LLP
Dallas, TX .... Family Law

WEBB ZIESENHEIM LOGSDON ORKIN & HANSON, P.C.
Pittsburgh, PA .... Patent, Trademark, Copyright and Unfair Competition

WEBBER, CHRISTOPHER A. JR.
Wallingford, VT .... Trust and Estates, Wills and Probate

WEBBER, JOSEPH P. LAW OFFICES OF
Austin, TX ....Civil Trial Practice; Commercial Litigation

WEBER & WEBER
Weston, WV ....Civil Trial Practice; Real Estate Law

WEBSTER, GEOFFREY E.
Columbus, OH ....Health Care Law

WEBSTER, BRANNON & BISORDI, P.A.
Shalimar, FL ....Family Law

WEBSTER, CHAMBERLAIN & BEAN
Washington, DC............................Administrative Law; Business Law; Securities Law; Tax Law

WEBSTER, FREDRICKSON & BRACKSHAW
Washington, DC............................Bankruptcy Law; Labor and Employment Law

WEEMS, SCHIMPF, HAYTER, GILSOUL & CARMOUCHE, (APLC)
Shreveport, LA............................Civil Trial Practice; Construction Law; Real Estate Law

WEGMAN, HESSLER, VANDERBURG & O'TOOLE, A LEGAL PROFESSIONAL ASSOCIATION
Cleveland, OH............................Business Law; Trust and Estates, Wills and Probate

WEGMANN, GASAWAY, STEWART, SCHNEIDER, DIEFFENBACH, TESREAU & SHERMAN, P.C.
Hillsboro, MO............................General Practice

WEHNER AND PERLMAN LLP
Los Angeles, CA............................Business Law

WEHNER & YORK
Washington, DC............................Civil Trial Practice; Criminal Trial Practice

WEICHSEL, JOHN L.
Hackensack, NJ............................Civil Trial Practice; Criminal Trial Practice

WEILER & BORST, LLP
San Ramon, CA............................Family Law

WEIL, GOTSHAL & MANGES LLP
New York, NY............................General Practice

WEIL & PETROCCHI, A PROFESSIONAL CORPORATION
Dallas, TX............................Civil Trial Practice; Commercial Litigation

WEINBERG, HOFFMAN, CASEY & ROPERS
Larkspur, CA............................Business Law; Insurance Defense; Medical Malpractice; Personal Injury; Product Liability Law

WEINBERG, MCCORMICK, CHATZINOFF AND PAUL, A PROFESSIONAL ASSOCIATION
Haddonfield, NJ............................Bankruptcy Law; Family Law

WEINBERG, WHEELER, HUDGINS, GUNN & DIAL, LLC
Atlanta, GA............................Construction Law; General Practice; Medical Malpractice; Product Liability Law; Professional Liability

WEINER & ARGO, P.A.
Ocala, FL............................Insurance Defense

WEINER, BRODSKY, SIDMAN & KIDER, P.C.
Washington, DC............................Banking Law; Transportation Law

WEINER, JEFFREY S., P.A.
Miami, FL............................Appellate Practice; Criminal Trial Practice; Environmental Law; Health Care Law

WEINER, SAMUEL B., CO., L.P.A.
Columbus, OH............................Criminal Trial Practice

WEINER, SHEAROUSE, WEITZ, GREENBERG & SHAWE, L.L.P.
Savannah, GA............................Civil Trial Practice; Real Estate Law; Trust and Estates, Wills and Probate

WEINHAUS AND DOBSON
St. Louis, MO............................Employment Benefits Law; Health Care Law

WEINSTEIN & BERGMAN LAWYERS, A PROFESSIONAL SERVICES CORP.
Seattle, WA............................Product Liability Law

WEINSTEIN, BOLDT, RACINE, HALFHIDE & CAMEL, PROFESSIONAL CORPORATION
Los Angeles, CA............................Tax Law

WEINSTEIN SNYDER, A PROFESSIONAL CORPORATION
Roseland, NJ............................Family Law

WEINSTEIN, STEPHEN S., A PROFESSIONAL CORPORATION
Morristown, NJ............................Civil Trial Practice; Commercial Litigation; Criminal Trial Practice; Insurance Defense; Medical Malpractice; Personal Injury; Product Liability Law; Professional Liability

WEINSTOCK, MANION, REISMAN, SHORE & NEUMANN, A LAW CORPORATION
Los Angeles, CA............................Tax Law; Trust and Estates, Wills and Probate

WEINTRAUB, STOCK, BENNETT, GRISHAM & UNDERWOOD, P.C.
Memphis, TN............................General Practice; Labor and Employment Law

WEIR & ALVARADO, P.C.
San Antonio, TX............................Civil Trial Practice; Criminal Trial Practice; Labor and Employment Law

WEIR & PARTNERS LLP
Philadelphia, PA............................Banking Law; Bankruptcy Law; Business Law; Civil Trial Practice; Commercial Law; Commercial Litigation; Creditors Rights; Real Estate Law

WEIR AND WALLEY
Metairie, LA............................Commercial Law; Trust and Estates, Wills and Probate

WEISFUSE & WEISFUSE
New York, NY............................Personal Injury

WEISMAN GOLDMAN BOWEN & GROSS LLP
Pittsburgh, PA............................Bankruptcy Law; Civil Trial Practice; Commercial Law; Real Estate Law

WEISS, DAVID J. LAW OFFICES OF
Santa Monica, CA............................Legal Malpractice; Medical Malpractice

WEISS & ASSOCIATES
Cleveland, OH............................Appellate Practice; Civil Trial Practice

WEISS BERRETT PETTY, L.C.
Salt Lake City, UT............................Civil Trial Practice; Criminal Trial Practice; Insurance Defense

WEISS FREDERICK WILLETT & HAYNES
Louisville, KY............................Medical Malpractice; Personal Injury; Product Liability Law

WEISS & HANDLER, P.A.
Boca Raton, FL............................Civil Trial Practice; Commercial Law; Commercial Litigation; Family Law; Personal Injury; Real Estate Law

WEISSMAN, DERVISHI, BORGO & NORDLUND, P.A.
Miami, FL............................Commercial Litigation

WEISSMAN, JOEL M., P.A.
West Palm Beach, FL............................Family Law

WEISSMANN, WOLFF, BERGMAN, COLEMAN & SILVERMAN, LLP
Beverly Hills, CA............................Sports and Entertainment Law

WEISZ & ASSOCIATES
Atlanta, GA............................Business Law; Civil Trial Practice; Commercial Law; Construction Law

WELBAUM, GUERNSEY, HINGSTON, GREENLEAF & GREGORY, L.L.P.
Miami, FL............................Civil Trial Practice; Construction Law; General Practice

WELBORN SULLIVAN MECK & TOOLEY, P.C.
Denver, CO............................Civil Trial Practice; Environmental Law; General Practice; International Business Law; Oil and Gas Law

WELCH, MICHAEL
Atlanta, GA............................Construction Law

WELCH, JONES & SMITH, P.C.
Oklahoma City, OK............................Insurance Defense

WELDON, CHARLES R.
Norwalk, CA............................Personal Injury

WELDON, E. DURWARD
Georgetown, KY............................General Practice; Real Estate Law; Tax Law; Trust and Estates, Wills and Probate

WELDON, HUSTON & KEYSER
Mansfield, OH............................Bankruptcy Law; General Practice

WELEBIR, MCCUNE & JURE, A PROFESSIONAL LAW CORPORATION
Redlands, CA............................Personal Injury; Product Liability Law

WELKER, PAUL
Clarksville, TN............................Personal Injury

WELLBORN, HOUSTON, ADKISON, MANN, SADLER & HILL, L.L.P.
Henderson, TX............................Commercial Law; Personal Injury; Product Liability Law

WELLER, GREEN, TOUPS & TERRELL, L.L.P.
Beaumont, TX............................Insurance Defense; Personal Injury

WELLES & MCGRATH
Scranton, PA............................Business Law; Commercial Law; General Practice; Real Estate Law; Trust and Estates, Wills and Probate

WELLS, ANDERSON & RACE, LLC
Denver, CO .... Aviation Law; Civil Trial Practice; Insurance Defense; Product Liability Law

WELLS, GREGORY K., & ASSOCIATES, P.A.
Largo, MD .... Civil Trial Practice; Medical Malpractice; Personal Injury

WELLS, PEYTON, GREENBERG & HUNT, L.L.P.
Beaumont, TX .... Admiralty/Maritime Law; General Practice

WELLS, PORTER, SCHMITT & JONES
Paintsville, KY .... General Practice; Insurance Defense; Workers Compensation

WELLS, PURCELL & KRAATZ
Fort Worth, TX .... Personal Injury

WELTY, JEAN L.
New Haven, CT .... Family Law

WENDEROTH, LIND & PONACK, L.L.P.
Washington, DC .... Patent, Trademark, Copyright and Unfair Competition

WENTWORTH, PAUL V.
Phoenix, AZ .... Real Estate Law

WENTWORTH, PAOLI & PURDY, LLP
Newport Beach, CA .... Personal Injury; Professional Liability

WESIERSKI & ZUREK, LLP
Irvine, CA .... Civil Trial Practice; Insurance Defense

WESNER, KEMPTON, RUSSELL AND DOMINIQUE
Jefferson City, MO .... General Practice
Sedalia, MO .... General Practice

WESSELS & PAUTSCH, P.C.
St. Charles, IL .... Labor and Employment Law

WESSELS, STOJAN & STEPHENS P.C.
Rock Island, IL .... General Practice

WEST, ROBIN PAGE
Baltimore, MD .... Civil Trial Practice; Personal Injury; Product Liability Law

WEST, GREGORY K., P.A.
Ponte Vedra Beach, FL .... Trust and Estates, Wills and Probate

WEST & ROSE
Kingsport, TN .... Aviation Law; Civil Rights; Civil Trial Practice; Insurance Defense; Medical Malpractice

WESTERMANN HAMILTON & SHEEHY
Garden City, NY .... Construction Law

WESTERVELT, JOHNSON, NICOLL & KELLER
Peoria, IL .... General Practice

WESTLING, RICHARD W., L.L.C., LAW OFFICES OF
New Orleans, LA .... Criminal Trial Practice

WESTMORELAND, VESPER & SCHWARTZ, A PROFESSIONAL CORPORATION
Atlantic City, NJ .... Banking Law; Commercial Litigation; Personal Injury; Real Estate Law

WESTON HURD FALLON PAISLEY & HOWLEY L.L.P.
Cleveland, OH .... Civil Trial Practice; Environmental Law; General Practice; Insurance Defense; Tax Law; Trademark, Copyright and Unfair Competition

WHALEN, RALPH S. JR.
New Orleans, LA .... Criminal Trial Practice; Personal Injury

WHALEN & COMPTON, A LEGAL PROFESSIONAL ASSOCIATION
Akron, OH .... Labor and Employment Law

WHAM & WHAM
Centralia, IL .... General Practice; Insurance Defense

WHARTON LEVIN EHRMANTRAUT KLEIN & NASH, A PROFESSIONAL ASSOCIATION
Annapolis, MD .... Civil Trial Practice
Baltimore, MD .... Civil Trial Practice

WHEAT, JOE F.
Houston, TX .... Real Estate Law

WHEELER, THOMPSON, PARKER & COUNTS, LLP
Easton, MD .... General Practice; Trust and Estates, Wills and Probate

WHEELER TRIGG & KENNEDY, P.C.
Denver, CO .... Civil Trial Practice; Franchise Law; Product Liability Law; Professional Liability; Toxic Torts

WHELCHEL, BROWN, READDICK & BUMGARTNER
Brunswick, GA .... Civil Trial Practice; Commercial Litigation; General Practice; Insurance Defense; Labor and Employment Law

WHELCHEL & DUNLAP, LLP
Gainesville, GA .... General Practice

WHELCHEL, WHELCHEL & CARLTON
Moultrie, GA .... General Practice

WHETSTONE LAW FIRM
Little Rock, AR .... Personal Injury

WHIPPLE AND VIELE, A PROFESSIONAL LAW CORPORATION
Ventura, CA .... Criminal Trial Practice; Family Law; Personal Injury

WHITAKER, RIDLEY M.
New York, NY .... Civil Trial Practice; Communications Law; Employment Benefits Law

WHITE, WILLIAM A. THE LAW OFFICE OF
Austin, TX .... Criminal Trial Practice

WHITE, ALLINDER & GRAHAM, L.L.C.
Independence, MO .... Business Law; Commercial Litigation; Labor and Employment Law; Medical Malpractice; Personal Injury

WHITE & CASE
Washington, DC .... General Practice
New York, NY .... Civil Trial Practice; Criminal Trial Practice; General Practice
London, England .... General Practice
Paris, France .... General Practice
Tokyo, Japan .... General Practice
Singapore, Singapore .... General Practice
Ankara, Turkey .... General Practice
Istanbul, Turkey .... General Practice
Stockholm, Sweden .... General Practice
Hong Kong, China .... General Practice

WHITE, COFFEY, GALT & FITE, P.C.
Oklahoma City, OK .... General Practice

WHITE AND CRUMPLER
Winston-Salem, NC .... Criminal Trial Practice; Family Law; Personal Injury

WHITE, CUMMINGS & LONGINO, P.C.
Phoenix, AZ .... Commercial Litigation

WHITE, DENNIS R., P.A.
Naples, FL .... Trust and Estates, Wills and Probate

WHITE & FISH, L.P.A., INC.
Columbus, OH .... Bankruptcy Law; Civil Trial Practice; Family Law; Personal Injury

WHITE, FLEISCHNER & FINO
Red Bank, NJ .... Appellate Practice; Civil Trial Practice; Insurance Defense; Intellectual Property Law; Legal Malpractice; Medical Malpractice; Product Liability Law; Professional Liability
New York, NY .... Appellate Practice; Civil Trial Practice; Commercial Litigation; Construction Law; Environmental Law; General Practice; Insurance Defense; Intellectual Property Law; Labor and Employment Law; Legal Malpractice; Medical Malpractice; Personal Injury; Product Liability Law; Professional Liability; Sports and Entertainment Law; Toxic Torts

WHITEFORD, TAYLOR & PRESTON L.L.P.
Washington, DC .... General Practice
Baltimore, MD .... General Practice; Labor and Employment Law; Municipal Bond/Public Authority Financing
Towson, MD .... General Practice

WHITEHURST, HARKNESS, OZMUN & ARCHULETA, A PROFESSIONAL CORPORATION
Austin, TX .... Aviation Law; Medical Malpractice; Personal Injury; Product Liability Law

WHITE, KOCH, KELLY & MCCARTHY, A PROFESSIONAL ASSOCIATION
Santa Fe, NM .... Commercial Law; Commercial Litigation; Criminal Trial Practice; Family Law; General Practice; Insurance Defense; Labor and Employment Law; Natural Resources Law; Oil and Gas Law; Public Utilities Law; Real Estate Law; Trust and Estates, Wills and Probate

WHITE LAW FIRM
Oklahoma City, OK .... Civil Trial Practice; Criminal Trial Practice; Personal Injury

WHITE & MCDERMOTT, P.C.
Wellesley, MA .... Corporate Law; Immigration and Naturalization; Mergers and Acquisitions; Securities Law

WHITENER & WHARTON, P.A.
Columbia, SC .... Banking Law; Corporate Law; Real Estate Law

WHITE O'CONNOR CURRY GATTI & AVANZADO LLP
Los Angeles, CA .... Civil Trial Practice; Commercial Litigation; Intellectual Property Law; Sports and Entertainment Law

WHITE & REED LLP
Los Angeles, CA .... Civil Trial Practice

WHITE, REGEN & GARTON, PLC
Dickson, TN .... General Practice

WHITE, WHITE, ASKEW & CRENSHAW
Hopkinsville, KY .... Business Law; Corporate Law

WHITFIELD & EDDY, P.L.C.
Des Moines, IA .... Banking Law; Civil Trial Practice; General Practice; Insurance Defense

WHITHAM, CURTIS & WHITHAM, PLC
Reston, VA .... Intellectual Property Law

WHITING, HAGG & HAGG
Rapid City, SD .... Banking Law; Insurance Defense; Personal Injury

WHITMAN BREED ABBOTT & MORGAN LLP
Greenwich, CT .... General Practice
New York, NY .... General Practice
London, England .... General Practice

WHITNEY & BOGRIS, LLP
Towson, MD .... Appellate Practice; Civil Trial Practice; Environmental Law; General Practice; Insurance Defense; Medical Malpractice; Personal Injury; Product Liability Law; Toxic Torts

WHITTEN, JAMES M.
Corpus Christi, TX .... Civil Trial Practice; Personal Injury

WHITTENBURG WHITTENBURG & SCHACHTER, P.C.
Amarillo, TX .... Bankruptcy Law; Civil Trial Practice; General Practice; Professional Liability
Dallas, TX .... Civil Trial Practice; General Practice; Professional Liability; Securities Law

WHITTEN, MCGUIRE, WOOD, TERRY, ROSELIUS & DITTRICH, A PROF. LTD. LIABILITY CO.
Oklahoma City, OK .... Civil Rights; Civil Trial Practice; Insurance Defense; Medical Malpractice; Personal Injury; Product Liability Law

WHITTEN & YOUNG, P.C.
Abilene, TX .... Commercial Law; Family Law; General Practice

WICKENS, HERZER & PANZA, A LEGAL PROFESSIONAL ASSOCIATION
Lorain, OH .... General Practice

WIED, C. W., PROFESSIONAL CORPORATION
San Diego, CA .... Bankruptcy Law

WIEDERHOLD, MOSES, BULFIN & RUBIN, P.A.
West Palm Beach, FL .... Civil Trial Practice; Health Care Law; Insurance Defense; Personal Injury

WIENER AND WIENER LLP
Allentown, PA .... Bankruptcy Law; Business Law; Family Law

WIEST, SAYLOR, MUOLO, NOON & SWINEHART
Sunbury, PA .... General Practice

WIGGIN & DANA
Hartford, CT .... General Practice
New Haven, CT .... Antitrust Law; Civil Trial Practice; General Practice; Health Care Law; Labor and Employment Law; Patent, Trademark, Copyright and Unfair Competition
Stamford, CT .... General Practice

WIGGIN & NOURIE, P.A.
Manchester, NH .... General Practice; Insurance Defense

WIGGINS AND MASSON, LLP
Ithaca, NY .... Civil Trial Practice; Criminal Trial Practice; Elder Law; Family Law; General Practice; Medical Malpractice; Personal Injury; Trust and Estates, Wills and Probate

WIGHT, RICHARD W.
Manasquan, NJ .... Real Estate Law

WIGODA, WILLIAM S., LTD.
Chicago, IL .... Commercial Litigation; Family Law

WILBRAHAM, LAWLER & BUBA, A PROFESSIONAL CORPORATION
Haddonfield, NJ .... Appellate Practice; Civil Trial Practice; Criminal Trial Practice; Environmental Law; Insurance Defense; Land Use Law; Product Liability Law; Toxic Torts
Philadelphia, PA .... Appellate Practice; Civil Trial Practice; Criminal Trial Practice; Environmental Law; Insurance Defense; Land Use Law; Product Liability Law; Toxic Torts

WILBURN, MASTERSON & SMILING
Tulsa, OK .... Insurance Defense; Medical Malpractice

WILCOX, ARTHUR M. JR.
San Diego, CA .... Business Law; Real Estate Law

WILCOX, GORDON W., INC. P.S.
Seattle, WA .... Family Law

WILCOX, WILCOX, ENRIGHT, HALLSTEIN, MCMAHON & ADLER, LLC
Eau Claire, WI .... Civil Trial Practice; General Practice; Insurance Defense; Real Estate Law

WILCOXEN, MONTGOMERY & HARBISON
Sacramento, CA .... Civil Trial Practice; Medical Malpractice; Personal Injury; Product Liability Law

WILDMAN, HARROLD, ALLEN & DIXON
Chicago, IL .... Antitrust Law; Appellate Practice; Aviation Law; Civil Trial Practice; Commercial Law; Commercial Litigation; Corporate Law; Creditors Rights; Criminal Trial Practice; Environmental Law; Government Contracts; Health Care Law; Insurance Defense; Intellectual Property Law; Labor and Employment Law; Medical Malpractice; Mergers and Acquisitions; Patent, Trademark, Copyright and Unfair Competition; Product Liability Law; Real Estate Law; Securities Law; Toxic Torts

WILENCHIK & BARTNESS, A PROFESSIONAL CORPORATION
Phoenix, AZ .... Civil Trial Practice; Real Estate Law

WILENTZ, GOLDMAN & SPITZER, A PROFESSIONAL CORPORATION
Eatontown, NJ .... General Practice
Perth Amboy, NJ .... General Practice
Woodbridge, NJ .... Banking Law; Civil Trial Practice; Commercial Law; Criminal Trial Practice; Environmental Law; Family Law; General Practice; Health Care Law; Labor and Employment Law; Municipal Bond/Public Authority Financing; Real Estate Law; Sports and Entertainment Law; Tax Law; Trust and Estates, Wills and Probate

WILES, BOYLE, BURKHOLDER & BRINGARDNER CO., L.P.A.
Columbus, OH .... Insurance Defense

WILES AND WILES
Marietta, GA .... Commercial Law

WILEY PRICE & RADULOVICH, LLP
Alameda, CA .... Labor and Employment Law

WILEY, REIN & FIELDING
Washington, DC .... General Practice

WILF, MERVIN M., LTD.
Cambridge, MA .... Pension and Profit Sharing; Tax Law; Trust and Estates, Wills and Probate
Philadelphia, PA .... Pension and Profit Sharing; Tax Law; Trust and Estates, Wills and Probate

WILKES, ARTIS, HEDRICK & LANE, CHARTERED
Washington, DC .... General Practice; Real Estate Law

WILKINS, TOM LAW OFFICES OF
McAllen, TX .... General Practice

WILKINS, FROHLICH, JONES, HEVIA, RUSSELL & SUTTER, P.A.
Port Charlotte, FL .... General Practice; Personal Injury

WILKINS & MADDEN, P.A.
Greenville, SC .... Civil Trial Practice; Family Law

WILKINSON, CARMODY & GILLIAM
Shreveport, LA .... Appellate Practice; Civil Trial Practice; Environmental Law; General Practice; Insurance Defense; Labor and Employment Law; Public Utilities Law; Sports and Entertainment Law; Transportation Law

WILLARD, ROBERT H.
Columbus, OH .... Insurance Defense

WILLARDSON & LIPSCOMB, LLP
Wilkesboro, NC .... General Practice; Insurance Defense

WILLCOX, PIROZZOLO AND MCCARTHY, PROFESSIONAL CORPORATION
Boston, MA .... Civil Trial Practice; General Practice; Patent, Trademark, Copyright and Unfair Competition

WILLETTE & GUERRA, L.L.P.
Brownsville, TX .... Civil Trial Practice; Insurance Defense

WILLEY & CHAMBERLAIN, L.L.P.
Grand Rapids, MI .... Criminal Trial Practice

WILLIAMS, J. SCOTT
Irvine, CA....Bankruptcy Law

WILLIAMS, PETER C.
Alexandria, VA....Banking Law; Creditors Rights

WILLIAMS & ANDERSON
Little Rock, AR....Antitrust Law; Civil Trial Practice; Commercial Law; General Practice; Municipal Bond/Public Authority Financing; Securities Law; Tax Law

WILLIAMS & ASSOCIATES, P.C.
Nashville, TN....Medical Malpractice; Personal Injury

WILLIAMS AND BALLAS
Los Angeles, CA....Tax Law; Trust and Estates, Wills and Probate

WILLIAMS, BOX, FORSHEE & BULLARD, P.C.
Oklahoma City, OK....Commercial Law; General Practice; Land Use Law; Municipal and Zoning Law; Municipal Bond/Public Authority Financing; Public Utilities Law; Real Estate Law

WILLIAMS & CONNOLLY
Washington, DC....Civil Trial Practice; Criminal Trial Practice; General Practice; Tax Law

WILLIAMS, COONEY & SHEEHY
Bridgeport, CT....Civil Trial Practice; General Practice; Insurance Defense; Medical Malpractice; Personal Injury; Product Liability Law

WILLIAMS & EOANNOU, P.C.
Bethesda, MD....Civil Trial Practice

WILLIAMS, H. DOHN, JR., P.A.
Fort Lauderdale, FL....Criminal Trial Practice

WILLIAMS, HAMMOND, MOORE, SHOCKLEY & HARRISON, P.A.
Ocean City, MD....Civil Trial Practice; Real Estate Law

WILLIAMS & HENRY, LLP
Atlanta, GA....Medical Malpractice; Personal Injury; Product Liability Law

WILLIAMS & HENRY, PROFESSIONAL ASSOCIATION
Greenville, SC....Business Law; Commercial Law; Commercial Litigation; General Practice; Real Estate Law

WILLIAMS HEWITT & ROBBINS, LLP
Greenwood, IN....Banking Law; Real Estate Law; Trust and Estates, Wills and Probate

WILLIAMS & JENSEN, A PROFESSIONAL CORPORATION
Washington, DC....Administrative Law

WILLIAMS, KATHRYN, P.A.
Greenville, SC....Workers Compensation

WILLIAMS & MCCARTHY, A PROFESSIONAL CORPORATION
Oregon, IL....Civil Trial Practice; General Practice
Rockford, IL....Civil Trial Practice; General Practice; Tax Law

WILLIAMS & MONTGOMERY LTD.
Chicago, IL....Civil Trial Practice; General Practice

WILLIAMS, MORGAN & AMERSON, P.C.
Houston, TX....Patent, Trademark, Copyright and Unfair Competition

WILLIAMS, MULLEN, CLARK & DOBBINS, A PROFESSIONAL CORPORATION
Richmond, VA....Administrative Law; Antitrust Law; Banking Law; Bankruptcy Law; Business Law; Civil Trial Practice; Commercial Law; Communications Law; Construction Law; Employment Benefits Law; Environmental Law; General Practice; Health Care Law; Immigration and Naturalization; Insurance Defense; Intellectual Property Law; International Business Law; Labor and Employment Law; Municipal and Zoning Law; Municipal Bond/Public Authority Financing; Real Estate Law; Securities Law; Tax Law; Trademark, Copyright and Unfair Competition; Trust and Estates, Wills and Probate

WILLIAMS, PARKER, HARRISON, DIETZ & GETZEN, PROFESSIONAL ASSOCIATION
Sarasota, FL....Aviation Law; Banking Law; Civil Trial Practice; General Practice; Health Care Law; International Business Law; Labor and Employment Law; Municipal Bond/Public Authority Financing; Real Estate Law; Tax Law; Trust and Estates, Wills and Probate

WILLIAMS, PATTILLO, SQUIRES & WREN, L.L.P.
Waco, TX....Civil Trial Practice

WILLIAMS, POLAN & PATTIS, LLC
New Haven, CT....Appellate Practice; Civil Rights; Civil Trial Practice; Criminal Trial Practice

WILLIAMS, PORTER, DAY & NEVILLE, P.C.
Casper, WY....Civil Trial Practice; Environmental Law; General Practice; Insurance Defense

WILLIAMS, SENNETT & SCULLY CO., L.P.A.
Twinsburg, OH....Civil Trial Practice; Insurance Defense

WILLIAMS, STROBEL, MALONE, MASON & RALPH, P.A.
Dodge City, KS....General Practice

WILLIAMS & WILLIAMS
Buffalo, NY....Civil Trial Practice; Insurance Defense; Workers Compensation

WILLIAMS, WILLIAMS AND MONTGOMERY, P.A.
Poplarville, MS....General Practice; Personal Injury

WILLIAMS, ZOGRAFOS & PECK, A PROFESSIONAL CORPORATION
Lake Oswego, OR....Labor and Employment Law

WILLIAMSON, DEAN, WILLIAMSON, PURCELL & SOJKA, L.L.P.
Laurinburg, NC....General Practice

WILLIAMSON, STEPHEN T.
Louisville, CO....Natural Resources Law

WILLIS, JOHN M.
Philadelphia, PA....Personal Injury

WILLIS & SACKETT
Perry, IA....General Practice

WILLITS, RICHARD H., P.A.
Lake Worth, FL....Civil Trial Practice; Personal Injury; Professional Liability

WILLKIE FARR & GALLAGHER
Washington, DC....General Practice
New York, NY....Civil Trial Practice; General Practice; Municipal Bond/Public Authority Financing
London, England....General Practice
Paris, France....General Practice

WILLMAN & ARNOLD, LLP
Pittsburgh, PA....Environmental Law; Insurance Defense

WILLMARTH, TANOURY, RAMAR, CORBET, GARVES & SHAW
Detroit, MI....Civil Trial Practice; Commercial Litigation; Health Care Law; Insurance Defense; Labor and Employment Law; Legal Malpractice; Medical Malpractice; Personal Injury; Product Liability Law; Professional Liability; Toxic Torts

WILLONER, CALABRESE & ROSEN, P.A.
College Park, MD....General Practice

WILLOUGHBY & HOEFER, P.A.
Columbia, SC....Communications Law; Public Utilities Law; Securities Law; Transportation Law

WILL, ROBERT P., & ASSOCIATES
Waukegan, IL....Criminal Trial Practice

WILMER, CUTLER & PICKERING
Washington, DC....Antitrust Law; Banking Law; Bankruptcy Law; Business Law; Civil Trial Practice; Communications Law; Criminal Trial Practice; Environmental Law; General Practice; Insurance Defense; International Business Law; Securities Law; Tax Law; Transportation Law
New York, NY....General Practice
Brussels, Belgium....General Practice
London, England....General Practice
Berlin, Germany....General Practice

WILNER, KLEIN & SIEGEL, A PROFESSIONAL CORPORATION
Beverly Hills, CA....Insurance Defense; Real Estate Law

WILSHIRE SCOTT & DYER, A PROFESSIONAL CORPORATION
Houston, TX....Civil Trial Practice

WILSMAN & SCHOONOVER
Cleveland, OH....Family Law

WILSON, BRUCE H.
Akron, OH....Civil Trial Practice

WILSON, FRANK M.
Montgomery, AL....Appellate Practice; Commercial Litigation; Product Liability Law

WILSON AND BARROWS, LTD.
Elko, NV....General Practice; Real Estate Law; Trust and Estates, Wills and Probate

WILSON, BAVE, CONBOY, COZZA & COUZENS, P.C.
White Plains, NY....General Practice; Insurance Defense; Medical Malpractice; Personal Injury

WILSON, BORROR, DUNN & DAVIS, LLP
San Bernardino, CA................Appellate Practice; Civil Trial Practice; General Practice; Insurance Defense; Trust and Estates, Wills and Probate

WILSON & BOWLING
New Orleans, LA................Admiralty/Maritime Law; Civil Trial Practice; Commercial Litigation; Environmental Law; Health Care Law; Medical Malpractice; Personal Injury; Product Liability Law; Workers Compensation

WILSON & CRAIG, PROFESSIONAL CORPORATION
Eldora, IA................General Practice

WILSON, CRAIG R., P.A.
North Palm Beach, FL................Criminal Trial Practice

WILSON, DECAMP & TALBOTT, P.S.C.
Lexington, KY................General Practice

WILSON, ELSER, MOSKOWITZ, EDELMAN & DICKER LLP
New York, NY................Civil Trial Practice; Insurance Defense

WILSON, ENGSTROM, CORUM & COULTER
Little Rock, AR................Civil Trial Practice; Criminal Trial Practice

WILSON GROSENHEIDER MOORE & JACOBS, L.L.P.
Austin, TX................Insurance Defense

WILSON, HALBROOK & BAYARD, PROFESSIONAL ASSOCIATION
Georgetown, DE................General Practice

WILSON, JANE P., & ASSOCIATES CO., L.P.A.
Eastlake, OH................Workers Compensation

WILSON, JOHNSON & JAFFER, P.A.
Sarasota, FL................Business Law; Computer Law; Real Estate Law; Trust and Estates, Wills and Probate

WILSON, KEHOE & WININGHAM
Indianapolis, IN................Aviation Law; Medical Malpractice; Personal Injury; Product Liability Law

WILSON, LEAVITT & SMALL, P.A.
Orlando, FL................Commercial Litigation; Eminent Domain; Environmental Law; Real Estate Law

WILSON, MCRAE, IVY, MCTYIER AND STRAIN
Memphis, TN................General Practice; Insurance Defense

WILSON & ORCUTT, P.C.
Acton, MA................Business Law; Commercial Litigation; Real Estate Law

WILSON, PETTY, KOSMO & TURNER LLP
San Diego, CA................Civil Trial Practice

WILSON SONSINI GOODRICH & ROSATI, PROFESSIONAL CORPORATION
Palo Alto, CA................General Practice

WILSON, WORLEY & GAMBLE, P.C.
Kingsport, TN................General Practice

WIMBERLY LAWSON & SEALE, PLLC
Knoxville, TN................Labor and Employment Law; Workers Compensation

WIMPFHEIMER, STEVEN
Great Neck, NY................Commercial Law; Real Estate Law

WINCKLER & HARVEY, L.L.P.
Austin, TX................Legal Malpractice; Medical Malpractice; Personal Injury

WINDELS, MARX, DAVIES & IVES
New York, NY................General Practice

WINDER & HASLAM, P.C.
Salt Lake City, UT................Business Law; Civil Trial Practice; General Practice

WINDHORST, GAUDRY, RANSON, HIGGINS & GREMILLION, L.L.C.
Gretna, LA................Business Law; Commercial Litigation; Health Care Law; Insurance Defense; Medical Malpractice; Product Liability Law

WINER MEHEULA & DEVENS
Kailua, HI................Arbitration; Civil Trial Practice; Commercial Litigation; Medical Malpractice; Personal Injury; Product Liability Law; Professional Liability

WINETSKY AND WINETSKY
Linden, NJ................General Practice; Real Estate Law

WINGERT GREBING BRUBAKER & RYAN LLP
San Diego, CA................Civil Trial Practice; Construction Law; Insurance Defense; Sports and Entertainment Law; Trust and Estates, Wills and Probate

WINGET & KANE
Peoria, IL................Civil Trial Practice; Family Law

WINIKATES & WINIKATES
Frisco, TX................Banking Law; Civil Trial Practice; Corporate Law; Insurance Defense; Trust and Estates, Wills and Probate

WINN, BEAUDRY & WINN, LLP
Dallas, TX................Trust and Estates, Wills and Probate

WINNINGHAM & STEIN
Oklahoma City, OK................Immigration and Naturalization

WINSHIP & BYRNE
Miami, FL................Intellectual Property Law

WINSTEAD SECHREST & MINICK P.C.
Austin, TX................General Practice
Dallas, TX................General Practice
Houston, TX................General Practice

WINSTEIN, KAVENSKY & WALLACE
Rock Island, IL................Civil Trial Practice; Criminal Trial Practice; Personal Injury

WINSTON, BARRY T.
Chapel Hill, NC................Civil Trial Practice; Criminal Trial Practice

WINSTON & BYRNE, LAWYERS, A PROFESSIONAL CORPORATION
Mason City, IA................Civil Trial Practice; General Practice; Trust and Estates, Wills and Probate

WINSTON & STRAWN
Washington, DC................General Practice
Chicago, IL................Antitrust Law; General Practice
New York, NY................General Practice

WINTERBAUER & DIAMOND, P.L.L.C.
Seattle, WA................Labor and Employment Law

WINTER & RHODEN
Gaffney, SC................General Practice

WINTERS, BREWSTER, CROSBY & PATCHETT
Marion, IL................General Practice

WINTERS, FEATHERSTUN, GAUMER, KENNEY, POSTLEWAIT & STOCKS
Decatur, IL................Insurance Defense

WINTERS & FORTE
Cheshire, CT................Business Law; Commercial Law; Tax Law; Trust and Estates, Wills and Probate

WINTERS, KRUG, DELBON & NASTARI
Burlingame, CA................Insurance Defense

WINTERS & MERKLE
Columbus, OH................Criminal Trial Practice

WINTHROP COUCHOT, PROFESSIONAL CORPORATION
Newport Beach, CA................Bankruptcy Law; Commercial Litigation

WINTHROP, STIMSON, PUTNAM & ROBERTS
Stamford, CT................General Practice
Washington, DC................General Practice
Palm Beach, FL................General Practice
New York, NY................Antitrust Law; Banking Law; Bankruptcy Law; Civil Trial Practice; General Practice; Tax Law
Hong Kong, China................General Practice
London, England................General Practice
Tokyo, Japan................General Practice

WINTHROP & WEINSTINE, A PROFESSIONAL ASSOCIATION
St. Paul, MN................General Practice

WIRE, R. THOMAS, A PROFESSIONAL CORPORATION
Westlake Village, CA................Personal Injury

WIRKEN GROUP, THE, A PROFESSIONAL CORPORATION
Kansas City, MO................Civil Trial Practice

WISE & MARSAC, PROFESSIONAL CORPORATION
Detroit, MI................Business Law; Civil Trial Practice

WISE, WIEZOREK, TIMMONS & WISE, A PROFESSIONAL CORPORATION
Long Beach, CA................Civil Trial Practice; Insurance Defense; Product Liability Law; Trust and Estates, Wills and Probate

WITCHER, JACK F.
Bremen, GA................Personal Injury

WITHERED CORRIGAN & SERVICE
Lafayette, IN................Civil Trial Practice; Personal Injury

WITHERS, BRANT, IGOE & MULLENNIX, P.C.
Liberty, MO................Civil Trial Practice; General Practice

WITHERSPOON, KELLEY, DAVENPORT & TOOLE, P.S.
Spokane, WA................Communications Law; General Practice

WITHEY & TOBIN, P.L.C.
Phoenix, AZ .... Land Use Law; Municipal and Zoning Law; Real Estate Law

WITMER, KARP, WARNER & THUOTTE LLP
Boston, MA .... Civil Trial Practice; Family Law

WITT, GAITHER & WHITAKER, P.C.
Chattanooga, TN .... Civil Trial Practice; Employment Benefits Law; Environmental Law; General Practice; Labor and Employment Law; Securities Law; Trust and Estates, Wills and Probate

WITTMAN & MCCORD
Colorado Springs, CO .... Insurance Defense; Oil and Gas Law; Personal Injury; Professional Liability
Denver, CO .... Insurance Defense; Personal Injury; Professional Liability

WITWER, OLDENBURG, BARRY & BEDINGFIELD, LLP
Greeley, CO .... General Practice

WITWER, POLTROCK & GIAMPIETRO
Chicago, IL .... Labor and Employment Law

WOBENSMITH, ZACHARY T. III
Valley Forge, PA .... Patent, Trademark, Copyright and Unfair Competition; Trademark, Copyright and Unfair Competition

WOFSEY, ROSEN, KWESKIN & KURIANSKY, LLP
Stamford, CT .... Banking Law; Bankruptcy Law; Business Law; Civil Trial Practice; Commercial Law; Corporate Law; Family Law; General Practice; Personal Injury; Tax Law; Trust and Estates, Wills and Probate

WOHLFORD, PAUL R.
Bristol, TN .... Family Law

WOLCOTT, RIVERS, WHEARY, BASNIGHT & KELLY, P.C.
Virginia Beach, VA .... Banking Law; Bankruptcy Law; Family Law; General Practice; Personal Injury; Real Estate Law

WOLF, WAYNE C.
Albuquerque, NM .... Civil Trial Practice

WOLF AND AKERS, A LEGAL PROFESSIONAL ASSOCIATION
Cleveland, OH .... Family Law

WOLF, ARNOLD & CARDOSO, P.C.
Washington, DC .... International Business Law; International Trade Law

WOLF, JUDITH M., P.C.
Phoenix, AZ .... Arbitration; Family Law

WOLF & RICHARDS, A LAW CORPORATION
Newport Beach, CA .... Banking Law; Bankruptcy Law; Real Estate Law

WOLF, RIFKIN & SHAPIRO, LLP
Los Angeles, CA .... Civil Trial Practice; Product Liability Law; Real Estate Law; Sports and Entertainment Law

WOLF & TIEDEKEN
Cheyenne, WY .... Criminal Trial Practice; Medical Malpractice; Personal Injury

WOLFE, JONES & BOSWELL
Huntsville, AL .... Personal Injury; Workers Compensation

WOLFE, SNOWDEN, HURD, LUERS & AHL
Lincoln, NE .... Corporate Law; Insurance Defense; Trust and Estates, Wills and Probate

WOLFF AND D'AGROSA, LAW OFFICES OF
Clayton, MO .... Criminal Trial Practice

WOLFF & SAMSON, A PROFESSIONAL CORPORATION
Roseland, NJ .... General Practice

WOLFF, WHORLEY, DE HOOGH & THOMPSON
Sheldon, IA .... General Practice

WOLFSDORF, BERNARD P., A PROFESSIONAL CORPORATION
Los Angeles, CA .... Immigration and Naturalization

WOLK & GENTER
Philadelphia, PA .... Aviation Law

WOLSKE & BLUE, A LEGAL PROFESSIONAL ASSOCIATION
Columbus, OH .... Appellate Practice; Medical Malpractice; Personal Injury

WOMACK, LANDIS, PHELPS, MCNEILL & MCDANIEL, A PROFESSIONAL ASSOCIATION
Jonesboro, AR .... General Practice; Insurance Defense

WOMACK LAW FIRM, THE
La Fayette, GA .... General Practice

WOMACK, MCCLISH & WALL, P.C.
Austin, TX .... Eminent Domain

WOMBLE CARLYLE SANDRIDGE & RICE
Charlotte, NC .... Appellate Practice; Banking Law; Business Law; Civil Trial Practice; Commercial Law; Construction Law; Employment Benefits Law; Environmental Law; General Practice; Insurance Defense; International Business Law; Labor and Employment Law; Municipal Bond/Public Authority Financing; Natural Resources Law; Real Estate Law; Securities Law; Tax Law
Raleigh, NC .... Administrative Law; Antitrust Law; Appellate Practice; Banking Law; Business Law; Civil Trial Practice; Commercial Law; Computer Law; Construction Law; Employment Benefits Law; Environmental Law; General Practice; Health Care Law; Insurance Defense; International Business Law; Labor and Employment Law; Municipal Bond/Public Authority Financing; Natural Resources Law; Patent, Trademark, Copyright and Unfair Competition; Product Liability Law; Real Estate Law; Securities Law; Tax Law
Winston-Salem, NC .... Administrative Law; Antitrust Law; Appellate Practice; Banking Law; Bankruptcy Law; Business Law; Civil Rights; Civil Trial Practice; Commercial Law; Communications Law; Computer Law; Construction Law; Employment Benefits Law; Environmental Law; Family Law; General Practice; Health Care Law; Insurance Defense; International Business Law; Labor and Employment Law; Medical Malpractice; Municipal and Zoning Law; Municipal Bond/Public Authority Financing; Natural Resources Law; Product Liability Law; Real Estate Law; Securities Law; Tax Law; Trust and Estates, Wills and Probate

WONER, GLENN, REEDER & GIRARD, P.A.
Kansas City, KS .... Bankruptcy Law; Commercial Law; Commercial Litigation
Lawrence, KS .... Bankruptcy Law; Commercial Law; Commercial Litigation
Overland Park, KS .... Bankruptcy Law; Commercial Law; Commercial Litigation
Topeka, KS .... Bankruptcy Law; Commercial Law; Commercial Litigation

WONG, MARGARET W. & ASSOCIATES
Cleveland, OH .... Immigration and Naturalization

WONG, MICHAEL J. Y.
Honolulu, HI .... Civil Trial Practice; Family Law; General Practice; Personal Injury

WONG FLEMING, P.C.
Edison, NJ .... Bankruptcy Law; Civil Rights; Commercial Litigation; General Practice; Immigration and Naturalization; Labor and Employment Law

WONG & LEOW
Singapore, Singapore .... General Practice

WOODARD, JOHN L. III
Orlando, FL .... Criminal Trial Practice

WOODARD, EMHARDT, NAUGHTON, MORIARTY & MCNETT
Indianapolis, IN .... Intellectual Property Law; Patent, Trademark, Copyright and Unfair Competition

WOOD & ASSOCIATES, P.A.
St. Petersburg, FL .... Insurance Defense; Medical Malpractice

WOODBURN AND WEDGE
Reno, NV .... Bankruptcy Law; Business Law; Civil Trial Practice; Commercial Law; Natural Resources Law; Real Estate Law; Trust and Estates, Wills and Probate

WOODBURY, DAVID P.
Prairie Village, KS .... Family Law

WOODBURY, J. WAYNE
Silver City, NM .... General Practice

WOODCOCK WASHBURN KURTZ MACKIEWICZ & NORRIS LLP
Philadelphia, PA .... Intellectual Property Law; Patent, Trademark, Copyright and Unfair Competition

WOOD CRAPO LLC
Salt Lake City, UT .... Commercial Litigation; Labor and Employment Law; Tax Law

WOODEN & MCLAUGHLIN LLP
Indianapolis, IN .... General Practice

WOOD GORDON, P.C.
Pittsburgh, PA .... Business Law

WOOD & GRANT
Atlanta, GA .... Civil Trial Practice; Medical Malpractice; Personal Injury

WOODLEY, WILLIAMS, BOUDREAU, NORMAN, BROWN & DOYLE
Lake Charles, LA....................Admiralty/Maritime Law; Commercial Law; Insurance Defense

WOOD, ODOM AND EDGE, P.A.
Newnan, GA..........................General Practice

WOOD, RIS & HAMES, PROFESSIONAL CORPORATION
Denver, CO..........................Insurance Defense

WOODRUFF, GORDON C.
Smithfield, NC.......................Bankruptcy Law; Civil Trial Practice

WOODRUFF & ASSOCIATES
Dallas, TX............................Insurance Defense

WOODRUFF, O'HAIR & POSNER, INC. A LAW CORPORATION
Sacramento, CA.......................Family Law

WOODS, BARRY A.
San Juan, PR..........................Corporate Law; General Practice; Tax Law

WOODS, RONALD G.
Houston, TX...........................Criminal Trial Practice

WOODS & BATES
Lincoln, IL............................General Practice

WOODS & PARTNERS
Montreal, QU, Canada...........Arbitration; Civil Trial Practice; Commercial Litigation; Construction Law; General Practice; Labor and Employment Law; Product Liability Law; Professional Liability; Sports and Entertainment Law

WOODSON, DANNY LAW OFFICES OF
Mount Pleasant, TX...............Family Law; Personal Injury

WOOD, THACKER & WEATHERLY, P.C.
Denton, TX............................Business Law; Civil Trial Practice; Family Law; Labor and Employment Law; Personal Injury

WOODWARD COTHRAN & HERNDON
Columbia, SC.........................Banking Law; Business Law; Civil Trial Practice; Construction Law; Personal Injury; Real Estate Law

WOODWARD, HOBSON & FULTON
Louisville, KY........................Antitrust Law; Civil Trial Practice; Environmental Law; General Practice; Health Care Law; Insurance Defense; Labor and Employment Law; Product Liability Law

WOOLFOLK, KEOUGH, DUBOSE & DEBARI, P.A.
Orlando, FL...........................Medical Malpractice; Personal Injury

WOOLLEY RUSSELL & JOHNSON
Long Beach, CA......................Admiralty/Maritime Law; Aviation Law; Civil Trial Practice; Commercial Law; Environmental Law; General Practice; International Business Law; Product Liability Law; Transportation Law

WOOTEN & HART, A PROFESSIONAL CORPORATION
Roanoke, VA..........................Banking Law; Business Law; Civil Trial Practice; Commercial Litigation; Constitutional Law; Corporate Law; Creditors Rights; Environmental Law; Family Law; Health Care Law; Insurance Defense; Medical Malpractice; Product Liability Law; Professional Liability; Trust and Estates, Wills and Probate; Workers Compensation

WOOTON, JAMES R., P.A.
Baltimore, MD.......................Bankruptcy Law

WOOTTON, RICHARD H., P.A.
Hot Springs National Park, AR..General Practice

WORDEN, THANE & HAINES, P.C.
Missoula, MT.........................General Practice

WORKER & POWER
Chicago, IL............................Civil Trial Practice; Insurance Defense

WORKMAN, NYDEGGER & SEELEY, A PROFESSIONAL CORPORATION
Salt Lake City, UT..................Intellectual Property Law

WORREL & WORREL
Fresno, CA............................Patent, Trademark, Copyright and Unfair Competition

WOTITZKY, WOTITZKY, MIZELL, ROSS & GOLDMAN, P.A.
Punta Gorda, FL.....................Personal Injury; Real Estate Law; Trust and Estates, Wills and Probate

WREN, RONALD D.
Bedford, TX...........................Appellate Practice; Civil Trial Practice

WRIGHT, CHANEY, BERRY, DANIEL, SLAUGHTER & HUGHES, P.A.
Arkadelphia, AR.....................General Practice; Product Liability Law

WRIGHT, CONSTABLE & SKEEN, LLP
Baltimore, MD.......................Admiralty/Maritime Law; Bankruptcy Law; Commercial Litigation; General Practice; Insurance Defense; Trust and Estates, Wills and Probate

WRIGHT & COON, P.A.
Portland, ME..........................Civil Trial Practice; Environmental Law; Insurance Defense; Product Liability Law; Toxic Torts

WRIGHT, DALE, JETT & CARTER
Guymon, OK..........................General Practice

WRIGHT & EVERETT, L.L.C.
Lake Charles, LA....................Real Estate Law

WRIGHT, HENSON, SOMERS, SEBELIUS, CLARK & BAKER, LLP
Topeka, KS............................Administrative Law; Banking Law; Bankruptcy Law; Civil Trial Practice; Commercial Law; Family Law; General Practice; Insurance Defense; Labor and Employment Law; Medical Malpractice; Patent, Trademark, Copyright and Unfair Competition; Personal Injury; Tax Law

WRIGHT, JUDD & WINCKLER
Las Vegas, NV........................Appellate Practice; Civil Trial Practice; Commercial Litigation; Criminal Trial Practice; Health Care Law

WRIGHT, LINDSEY & JENNINGS LLP
Little Rock, AR......................Bankruptcy Law; Commercial Litigation; Intellectual Property Law; Labor and Employment Law; Municipal Bond/Public Authority Financing; Securities Law

WRIGHT, MAX E., A PROFESSIONAL CORPORATION
Midland, TX...........................Medical Malpractice

WRIGHT & MILLS, P.A.
Skowhegan, ME......................Civil Trial Practice; Criminal Trial Practice

WRIGHT, STOUT, FITE & WILBURN
Muskogee, OK........................General Practice

WRIGHT, TOLLIVER AND GUTHALS, A PROFESSIONAL SERVICE CORPORATION
Billings, MT...........................Bankruptcy Law; Commercial Law; Family Law; Insurance Defense; Labor and Employment Law

WUERFEL & CHOLAKIAN, A PROFESSIONAL CORPORATION
San Francisco, CA..................Civil Trial Practice; Commercial Litigation; Construction Law; Insurance Defense; Labor and Employment Law

WUESTLING & JAMES, L.C.
St. Louis, MO.........................Insurance Defense; Professional Liability

WULFMEIER & OTTENWESS, PLC
Detroit, MI.............................Family Law; Insurance Defense; Labor and Employment Law; Medical Malpractice

WULFSBERG REESE & SYKES, PROFESSIONAL CORPORATION
Oakland, CA...........................Construction Law; Professional Liability

WULIGER, FADEL & BEYER
Cleveland, OH........................General Practice

WUNSCH, JOHN C., P.C.
Chicago, IL............................Aviation Law; Medical Malpractice; Personal Injury; Product Liability Law

WUSINICH AND BROGAN
Downingtown, PA...................Medical Malpractice; Personal Injury; Workers Compensation

WYATT, JAMES F. III, LAW OFFICES OF
Charlotte, NC.........................Civil Trial Practice; Criminal Trial Practice

WYATT, EARLY, HARRIS & WHEELER, L.L.P.
High Point, NC.......................Civil Trial Practice; General Practice

WYATT, TARRANT & COMBS
New Albany, IN......................General Practice
Frankfort, KY.........................General Practice
Lexington, KY........................General Practice
Louisville, KY........................Banking Law; Civil Trial Practice; Communications Law; General Practice
Nashville, TN.........................Communications Law; General Practice; Trademark, Copyright and Unfair Competition

WYLIE, PAUL R., A PROFESSIONAL CORPORATION
Bozeman, MT.........................Patent, Trademark, Copyright and Unfair Competition

WYNNE SPIEGEL ITKIN, A LAW CORPORATION
Los Angeles, CA.....................Bankruptcy Law

WYRSCH HOBBS MIRAKIAN & LEE, P.C.
Kansas City, MO.....................Appellate Practice; Civil Trial Practice; Criminal Trial Practice; General Practice

YAMAMOTO, TOSH G., A PROFESSIONAL CORPORATION
Sacramento, CA .... Trust and Estates, Wills and Probate

YANNI, PALMA R.
Washington, DC....................... Immigration and Naturalization

YARLING & ROBINSON
Indianapolis, IN .... Bankruptcy Law; Civil Trial Practice; Commercial Law; Insurance Defense; Personal Injury; Product Liability Law; Trust and Estates, Wills and Probate

YATES, MCLAMB & WEYHER, L.L.P.
Raleigh, NC............................. Civil Trial Practice; Insurance Defense; Medical Malpractice; Product Liability Law; Workers Compensation

YELTON & KEHL, LTD.
Chicago, IL.............................. Appellate Practice; Civil Trial Practice; Insurance Defense; Workers Compensation

YENGICH, RICH & XAIZ
Salt Lake City, UT.................. Criminal Trial Practice

YERRID, KNOPIK & KRIEGER, P.A.
Tampa, FL .... Commercial Litigation; Medical Malpractice; Personal Injury; Product Liability Law

YERUSHALMI & ASSOCIATES, L.L.P.
New York, NY........................ International Business Law; International Trade Law

YODER, AINLAY, ULMER & BUCKINGHAM
Goshen, IN.............................. General Practice

YORK & YORK, P.C.
Cedartown, GA........................ General Practice

YOSHA KRAHULIK & LEVY
Indianapolis, IN .... Civil Trial Practice; Medical Malpractice; Personal Injury; Product Liability Law

YOSHIDA, GERALD T.
Los Angeles, CA .... Business Law; Construction Law; Real Estate Law

YOST & TRETTA
Philadelphia, PA .... Insurance Defense

YOUNG, FRANCIS X.
White Plains, NY .... Civil Trial Practice; Personal Injury

YOUNG & ALEXANDER CO., L.P.A.
Dayton, OH.............................. Insurance Defense

YOUNG & ASSOCIATES, ATTORNEYS AT LAW, P.A.
Pensacola, FL.......................... Civil Trial Practice; Construction Law; Insurance Defense; Product Liability Law

YOUNG & ASSOCIATES, P.C.
Southfield, MI .... Antitrust Law; Civil Trial Practice; Commercial Litigation

YOUNG, BOGLE, MCCAUSLAND, WELLS & BLANCHARD, P.A.
Wichita, KS .... Civil Trial Practice; Commercial Law; Criminal Trial Practice; Environmental Law; General Practice; Insurance Defense; Natural Resources Law; Personal Injury; Product Liability Law; Real Estate Law; Trust and Estates, Wills and Probate

YOUNG CONAWAY STARGATT & TAYLOR, LLP
Georgetown, DE .... General Practice
Wilmington, DE....................... General Practice

YOUNG, GOLDMAN & VAN BEEK, A PROFESSIONAL CORPORATION
Alexandria, VA .... Business Law; Creditors Rights; Real Estate Law

YOUNG & PICKETT
Texarkana, TX .... Civil Trial Practice; Commercial Litigation; Criminal Trial Practice; General Practice

YOUNG, RICHARD W., A PROF. CORP., LAW OFFICES OF
Reno, NV .... Criminal Trial Practice; Family Law

YOUNG & THOMPSON
Arlington, VA .... Patent, Trademark, Copyright and Unfair Competition

YOUNG & VALKENET, L.L.C.
Baltimore, MD .... Business Law; Commercial Law; Construction Law; Insurance Defense

YOUNG WOOLDRIDGE, LAW OFFICES OF
Bakersfield, CA .... Civil Trial Practice; Corporate Law; General Practice; Personal Injury

YOUNKIN, JACK C.
Danville, PA............................ General Practice
Shamokin, PA .... Civil Trial Practice; General Practice

YU STROMBERG CLEVELAND, P.C.
Denver, CO .... Health Care Law

YUDES, JAMES P., A PROFESSIONAL CORPORATION
Springfield, NJ .... Family Law

YUEN, RENEE M. L., ATTORNEY AT LAW, A LAW CORPORATION
Honolulu, HI........................... Civil Trial Practice; Criminal Trial Practice; General Practice

YUKEVICH, MARCHETTI, LIEKAR & ZANGRILLI, P.C.
Pittsburgh, PA .... Banking Law; Business Law; Civil Trial Practice; Corporate Law; Oil and Gas Law

YURASKO, FRANK N.
Somerville, NJ .... General Practice

YURKO & OWENS, P.A.
Charlotte, NC.......................... Criminal Trial Practice

ZABEL, JUDITH L., P.A.
Albuquerque, NM.................... Tax Law; Trust and Estates, Wills and Probate

ZAGRANS LAW FIRM, A LEGAL PROFESSIONAL ASSOCIATION
Elyria, OH .... Antitrust Law; Appellate Practice; Civil Trial Practice; Medical Malpractice; Product Liability Law; Securities Law

ZALKIND, RODRIGUEZ, LUNT & DUNCAN
Boston, MA............................. Criminal Trial Practice

ZALK & WOOD, P.A.
Minneapolis, MN .... Family Law

ZAMANSKY PROFESSIONAL ASSOCIATION
Minneapolis, MN..................... Business Law; Real Estate Law

ZANE AND RUDOFSKY
New York, NY........................ Commercial Litigation; General Practice

ZAPPITELL & KAPRAL, P.A.
Boca Raton, FL .... Personal Injury

ZARLEY, MCKEE, THOMTE, VOORHEES & SEASE, P.L.C.
Des Moines, IA....................... Patent, Trademark, Copyright and Unfair Competition

ZARWIN, BAUM, DEVITO, KAPLAN & O'DONNELL, P.C.
Philadelphia, PA .... Civil Trial Practice; Insurance Defense

ZAVARELLO, A. WILLIAM, CO., L.P.A.
Akron, OH .... Civil Trial Practice; Medical Malpractice

ZAZZALI, ZAZZALI, FAGELLA & NOWAK, A PROFESSIONAL CORPORATION
Newark, NJ .... Administrative Law; Appellate Practice; Civil Trial Practice; Labor and Employment Law

ZDARSKY, SAWICKI & AGOSTINELLI
Buffalo, NY............................. Appellate Practice; Civil Trial Practice; Commercial Litigation; Construction Law

ZEANAH, HUST, SUMMERFORD, DAVIS, JONES & WILLIAMSON, L.L.C.
Tuscaloosa, AL .... Civil Trial Practice; General Practice; Insurance Defense; Workers Compensation

ZEFF AND ZEFF, P.C.
Detroit, MI.............................. Civil Trial Practice; Personal Injury; Product Liability Law

ZEGAS, ALAN L.
Chatham, NJ........................... Appellate Practice; Civil Trial Practice; Commercial Litigation; Criminal Trial Practice; General Practice

ZEIGER & CARPENTER
Columbus, OH .... Commercial Litigation; Communications Law; Franchise Law; Product Liability Law

ZEIGLER COHEN & KOCH
Indianapolis, IN .... Health Care Law; Insurance Defense; Medical Malpractice

ZEISLER & ZEISLER, P.C.
Bridgeport, CT .... Bankruptcy Law; Creditors Rights

ZEITLIN & ZEITLIN, P.C.
Phoenix, AZ .... Land Use Law; Real Estate Law

ZELDES, NEEDLE & COOPER, A PROFESSIONAL CORPORATION
Bridgeport, CT .... General Practice

ZELLE, HOFMANN, VOELBEL & GETTE, LLP
Minneapolis, MN .... Civil Trial Practice; General Practice

ZELLNER, KATHLEEN T. & ASSOCIATES
Naperville, IL.......................... Medical Malpractice; Personal Injury

ZEMAN, WILLIAM S.
Hartford, CT .... Labor and Employment Law

ZERMAN & MOGERMAN, L.L.C.
St. Louis, MO.......................... Family Law

ZERRENNER & ROANE
Grand Rapids, MI ....Family Law

ZEVNIK HORTON GUIBORD MCGOVERN PALMER & FOGNANI, L.L.P.
Washington, DC......................Civil Trial Practice; Environmental Law; Sports and Entertainment Law

ZICKERT, LLOYD L.
Chicago, IL..............................Intellectual Property Law

ZIDE & O'BIECUNAS
Los Angeles, CA......................Commercial Law; Commercial Litigation

ZIEMAN, SPEEGLE, JACKSON & HOFFMAN, L.L.C.
Mobile, AL..............................Business Law; Commercial Litigation; Mergers and Acquisitions

ZIEMER, STAYMAN, WEITZEL & SHOULDERS, LLP
Evansville, IN..........................Banking Law; Bankruptcy Law; Business Law; Commercial Law; Construction Law; Health Care Law; Labor and Employment Law

ZIFFREN, BRITTENHAM, BRANCA & FISCHER LLP
Los Angeles, CA......................Sports and Entertainment Law

ZIMMER KUNZ, PROFESSIONAL CORPORATION
Pittsburgh, PA ....Civil Trial Practice; General Practice; Insurance Defense

ZIMMER AND ZIMMER, L.L.P.
Wilmington, NC......................Criminal Trial Practice; Personal Injury

ZIMMERMAN, ROBERT H.
Philadelphia, PA......................Environmental Law; Real Estate Law

ZIMMERMAN, LIEBERMAN & DERENZO
Pottsville, PA ....General Practice

ZIMMERMAN, PFANNEBECKER, NUFFORT & ALBERT, LLP
Lancaster, PA..........................Civil Trial Practice; General Practice

ZIMRING, STUART D.
Los Angeles, CA......................Real Estate Law; Trust and Estates, Wills and Probate

ZINOBER & MCCREA, P.A.
Tampa, FL ....General Practice; Labor and Employment Law

ZINSER AND PATTERSON, P.L.L.C.
Nashville, TN..........................Labor and Employment Law

ZIRKLE AND HOFFMAN
Atlanta, GA ....Insurance Defense; Workers Compensation

ZISMAN AND INGRAHAM, P.C.
Denver, CO ....Tax Law; Trust and Estates, Wills and Probate

ZIZIK, LASALLE & POWERS, A PROFESSIONAL CORPORATION
Wellesley, MA.........................Civil Trial Practice; Insurance Defense

ZOLLA AND MEYER
Los Angeles, CA......................Family Law

ZUCKER, HOWARD B.
Denver, CO ....Family Law

ZUCKERMAN, SPAEDER, GOLDSTEIN, TAYLOR & KOLKER, L.L.P.
Washington, DC......................Criminal Trial Practice

ZUETEL & TOMLINSON
Pasadena, CA..........................Civil Trial Practice; Medical Malpractice

ZUGER KIRMIS & SMITH
Bismarck, ND..........................Civil Trial Practice; General Practice

ZUKOWSKI, ROGERS, FLOOD & MCARDLE
Crystal Lake, IL......................Family Law; General Practice; Municipal and Zoning Law

ZVARA, WILLIAM L., P.A.
Jacksonville, FL......................Municipal Bond/Public Authority Financing

ZWEIG, DAVID S., LAW FIRM OF
San Diego, CA ....Tax Law

PRACTICE AREAS SECTION

Volume I

Alabama–Michigan

ADMINISTRATIVE LAW

ALABAMA

*BIRMINGHAM,** Jefferson Co.

BAXLEY, DILLARD, DAUPHIN & MCKNIGHT (AV)

2008 3rd Avenue South, 35233
Telephone: 205-939-0995; 205-271-1100
Telecopier: 205-271-1108

MEMBERS OF FIRM

William J. Baxley
Joel E. Dillard
Charles A. Dauphin
Stewart D. McKnight, III
William C. Barclift
Betsy Palmer Collins
Donald R. James, Jr

ASSOCIATE

Elizabeth Louise Wood

For full biographical listings, see the Martindale-Hubbell Law Directory

*MOBILE,** Mobile Co.

ARMBRECHT, JACKSON, DEMOUY, CROWE, HOLMES & REEVES, L.L.C. (AV)

1300 Riverview Plaza, P.O. Box 290, 36601
Telephone: 334-405-1300
Facsimile: 334-432-6843; 433-3821
Email: adc@ajlaw.com

MEMBERS OF FIRM

Rae M. Crowe
E. B. Peebles III
William B. Harvey
Kirk C. Shaw
Conrad P. Armbrecht
Grover E. Asmus II
David A. Bagwell
Douglas L. Brown
Christopher I. Gruenewald
David E. Hudgens
Duane A. Graham
Broox G. Holmes, Jr.
Thomas P. Oldweiler

Representative Clients: AmSouth Bank of Alabama (Regional Counsel); Burlington Northern Santa Fe Railroad Co. (District Counsel); Loyal American Life Insurance Co.; Mobile Gas Service Corp.; Scott Paper Co.; State Pilotage Commission; Travelers Insurance Co.; WKRG-TV-Channel 5.

For Complete List of Firm Personnel, See General Section

For full biographical listings, see the Martindale-Hubbell Law Directory

*MONTGOMERY,** Montgomery Co.

BRANTLEY & WILKERSON, P.C. (AV)

405 South Hull Street, P.O. Box 830, 36101-0830
Telephone: 334-265-1500
Fax: 334-265-0319
Email: ashley@brantleywilkerson.com *URL:* http://www.brantleywilkerson.com

Paul A. Brantley
Mark D. Wilkerson

Leah Snell Stephens
R. Winston Lee

Representative Clients: MidCoast, Inc.; ALLTEL; Southeastern Cellular; TDS; Technologies Management, Inc.
Reference: SouthTrust Bank, N.A.

For full biographical listings, see the Martindale-Hubbell Law Directory

VOLZ, PRESTWOOD & HANAN, P.C. (AV)

350 Adams Avenue, P.O. Box 1910, 36102-1910
Telephone: 334-264-6401
Fax: 334-834-4954

Charles H. Volz, Jr.
Alvin T. Prestwood
Charles H. Volz, III
Ellis D. Hanan
Richard D. Lively
Judy H. Barganier

For full biographical listings, see the Martindale-Hubbell Law Directory

ARIZONA

*PHOENIX,** Maricopa Co.

CARMICHAEL & POWELL, PROFESSIONAL CORPORATION (AV)

7301 North 16th Street, Suite 103, 85020-5224
Telephone: 602-861-0777
Facsimile: 602-870-0296

Ronald W. Carmichael

(See Next Column)

Stephen Manes

Representative Clients: Home Builders Association of Central Arizona.

For full biographical listings, see the Martindale-Hubbell Law Directory

FENNEMORE CRAIG, A PROFESSIONAL CORPORATION (AV)

3003 North Central Avenue, Suite 2600, 85012-2913
Telephone: 602-916-5000
Fax: 602-916-5999
Tucson, Arizona Office: One South Church Avenue, Suite 1000, 85701-1620.
Telephone: 520-879-6800.
Fax: 520-879-6899.

C. Webb Crockett
Michael Preston Green
Timothy Berg
Norman D. James
Andrew M. Federhar
John M. Pearce

Theresa Dwyer
Jay L. Shapiro

For Complete List of Firm Personnel, See General Section

For full biographical listings, see the Martindale-Hubbell Law Directory

JOHNSTON & DODD, P.L.C. (AV)

One North First Street, Suite 700, 85004
Telephone: 602-452-0600
Facsimile: 602-716-5997
Email: johnston-doddlaw@uswest.net

Logan T. Johnston, III
Catherine M. Dodd
Anne C. Longo
Kenneth M. Rudisill, Jr.

For full biographical listings, see the Martindale-Hubbell Law Directory

LOW & CHILDERS, P.C. (AV)

2999 North 44th Street Suite 250, 85018
Telephone: 602-266-1166
Fax: 602-808-8835
Email: lowchild@doitnow.com

J. Michael Low
S. David Childers
Steven R. Henry
Christy C. Brown
Charles Bassett

For full biographical listings, see the Martindale-Hubbell Law Directory

QUARLES & BRADY LLP (AV)

One Camelback Building, One East Camelback Road, Suite 400, 85012-1649
Telephone: 602-230-5500
Fax: 602-230-5598
URL: http://www.quarles.com
Milwaukee, Wisconsin Office: 411 East Wisconsin Avenue.
Telephone: 414-277-5000.
Fax: 414-271-3552.
Madison, Wisconsin Office: First Wisconsin Plaza, One South Pinckney Street, P.O. Box 2113.
Telephone: 608-251-5000.
Fax: 608-251-9166.
West Palm Beach, Florida Office: 222 Lakeview Avenue, 4th Floor.
Telephone: 407-653-5000.
Fax: 407-653-5333.
Naples, Florida Office: Barnett Center, 4501 Tamiami Trail North, Suite 300.
Telephone: 813-262-5959.
Fax: 813-434-4999.
Chicago, Illinois Office: Quarles & Brady LLC, Citicorp Center, 500 West Madison Street, Suite 3700.
Telephone: 312-715-5000.
Fax: 312-715-5155.

MEMBER OF THE FIRM

P. Robert Fannin

For full biographical listings, see the Martindale-Hubbell Law Directory

ROGERS & WHALEN, P.A. (AV)

335 East Palm Lane, 85004
Telephone: 602-253-1500
Facsimile: 602-253-0071
Email: rogers.whalen@axtek.com

Thomas M. Rogers
Donna Hylarides Whalen

For full biographical listings, see the Martindale-Hubbell Law Directory

CALIFORNIA

*BAKERSFIELD,** Kern Co.

BORTON, PETRINI & CONRON, LLP (AV)

The Borton, Petrini & Conron Building, 1600 Truxtun Avenue, 93301
Telephone: 661-322-3051
Voice Mail: 661-395-6700
Fax: 661-322-4628
Mailing Address: P.O. Box 2026, Bakersfield, California, 93303
Email: bpcbak@bpclaw.com *URL:* http://www.bpclaw.com
Other City Locations: Fresno, Los Angeles, Modesto, Redding, Sacramento, San Bernardino, San Diego, San Francisco, San Jose, San Luis Obispo, Santa Ana and Ventura.

MEMBERS OF FIRM

George F. Martin
Paul Lafranchise
Richard E. Morton

ASSOCIATES

Stephen M. Crane
Randall Steven Joyce

For Complete List of Firm Personnel, See General Section

For full biographical listings, see the Martindale-Hubbell Law Directory

EMERYVILLE, Alameda Co.

JAMES JAY SELTZER (AV)

Watergate Towers, Tenth Floor, 2200 Powell Street, Suite 1035, 94608
Telephone: 510-596-2500
Telecopier: 510-596-2519
URL: http://www.secureadvise.com
Email: lawoffices@jjseltzer.com *URL:* http://www.lawyers.com/jamesjayseltzer

For full biographical listings, see the Martindale-Hubbell Law Directory

*LOS ANGELES,** Los Angeles Co.

BECK, DE CORSO, DALY, BARRERA & KREINDLER, A PROFESSIONAL LAW CORPORATION (AV)

601 West Fifth Street, 12th Floor, 90071-2025
Telephone: 213-688-1198
Fax: 213-489-7532
Email: beckdecorso@earthlink.net *URL:* http://www.beckdecorso.com

Mark E. Beck
Anthony A. De Corso
Bryan D. Daly
Teresa R. Barrera
Charles L. Kreindler
Suzanne E. Tracy

Peter J. Diedrich
Barbara E. Taylor
Stephen P. Jones

OF COUNSEL

Godfrey Isaac

For full biographical listings, see the Martindale-Hubbell Law Directory

DEMETRIOU, DEL GUERCIO, SPRINGER & MOYER, LLP (AV)

801 South Grand Avenue, 10th Floor, 90017
Telephone: 213-624-8407
Telecopy: 213-624-0174
Email: ddsm@juno.com

MEMBERS OF FIRM

Chris G. Demetriou (1915-1989)
Jeffrey Z. B. Springer
Craig A. Moyer
Angela Shanahan
Stephen A. Del Guercio
Michael A. Francis
Regina Liudzius Cobb
Jennifer T. Taggart
Bradley D. Pierce
Wendy M. Conole
Brian D. Langa
Silvia Saucedo

OF COUNSEL

Ronald J. Del Guercio
Richard A. Del Guercio
James P. Del Guercio
Barbara F. Stein

Reference: Bank of America, L.A. Main Office, Los Angeles, Calif.

For full biographical listings, see the Martindale-Hubbell Law Directory

KARNS & KARABIAN (AV)

Suite 530 Wilshire Grand Office Centre, 900 Wilshire Boulevard, 90017
Telephone: 213-680-9522
Fax: 213-627-3602
Email: kklawfirm@aol.com

MEMBERS OF FIRM

John Karns
Walter J. Karabian

ASSOCIATES

David E. Kenney
Jeff A. Harrison

For full biographical listings, see the Martindale-Hubbell Law Directory

OCHOA & SILLAS (AV)

444 South Flower Street, 18th Floor, 90071
Telephone: 213-362-1400
Fax: 213-622-0162
Email: sillasla@aol.com
Sacramento Office: Wells Fargo Center, 400 Capitol Mall, Suite 1850.
Telephone: 916-447-3383.
FAX: 916-447-3495. Email: OchoaSac@aol.com
Mexico City, Mexico Office: Los Cormoran No. 73, Lomas De Las Aquilas, Deleg. Alvaro Obregon, 01730, Mexico, D.F.C.F.
Telephone: 011-525-635-1145.
Fax: 011-525-53401454.

MEMBERS OF FIRM

Ralph M. Ochoa (Resident, Sacramento Office)
Herman Sillas
Jacqueline Rich Moore (Resident, Sacramento Office)
Tomás R. Lopez

ASSOCIATES

Jack T. Molodanof (Resident, Sacramento Office)
Francisco Valles Lopez (Not admitted in the United States)
Rita A. Reyes
Christopher Eric Ochoa (Resident, Sacramento Office)
Cirina A. K. Rose
M. Eric Parkan

OF COUNSEL

Daniel P. Aguilera
Cochran & Lotkin, Washington, D.C.

Representative Clients: American Golf; BKK Corp. (Toxic substance treatment); Chrysler; Department of Water and Power of Los Angeles; Sacramento Municipal Utility District; Department of Insurance; Metropolitan Water District, Los Angeles; General Motors; Hughes Aircraft; ICN Laboratories.

For full biographical listings, see the Martindale-Hubbell Law Directory

PASADENA, Los Angeles Co.

LAGERLOF, SENECAL, BRADLEY, GOSNEY & KRUSE, LLP (AV)

301 North Lake Avenue, 10th Floor, 91101-4108
Telephone: 626-793-9400
FAX: 626-793-5900
Email: mail@lagerlof.com

MEMBERS OF FIRM

Joseph J. Burris (1913-1980)
Stanley C. Lagerlof (1915-1998)
H. Jess Senecal
Jack T. Swafford
John F. Bradley
Timothy J. Gosney
William F. Kruse
Thomas S. Bunn, III
Andrew D. Turner
Rebecca J. Thyne
James D. Ciampa

ASSOCIATE

Shaun O. Kwon

Representative Clients: Gallo Glass Company; Orthopaedic Hospital; North American Chemical Company; Palmdale Water District; Public Water Agencies Group; Ventura Port District; Walnut Valley Water District; Metric Construction Co., Inc.

For full biographical listings, see the Martindale-Hubbell Law Directory

*SACRAMENTO,** Sacramento Co.

DAUER & THOMPSON (AV)

3455 American River Drive, Suite C, 95864
Telephone: 916-974-3400
Facsimile: 916-974-3405
Email: d&t@concourse.net

MEMBERS OF FIRM

Paul F. Dauer
James E. Thompson

Jennifer L. Dauer
Alan R. Barnes

For full biographical listings, see the Martindale-Hubbell Law Directory

GRATTAN & GALATI (AV)

Renaissance Tower, 801 K Street, Penthouse Suite, 95814
Telephone: 916-441-6575
Fax: 916-441-6553
Email: scarey@grattangalati.com *URL:* http://www.lawyers.com/grattan&galati

John P. Grattan, Jr.
Scott A. Galati

LEGAL SUPPORT PERSONNEL

Sandra A. Carey

For full biographical listings, see the Martindale-Hubbell Law Directory

HARMATA LAW OFFICES (AV)

2201 Q Street, 95816
Telephone: 916-442-2842
Fax: 916-442-2015
Email: harmatalaw@aol.com *URL:* http://www.lawyers.com/harmatalaw

Donald D. Harmata

(See Next Column)

HARMATA LAW OFFICES—*Continued*

LEGAL SUPPORT PERSONNEL
PARALEGAL

Debra D. Morrow

Representative Clients: Control Data Corp.; Deloitte & Touche; General Electric Co.; Myers Electric, Inc.; Syblon-Reid Co.; Systemhouse Inc.; TRW, Inc.

For full biographical listings, see the Martindale-Hubbell Law Directory

LIVINGSTON & MATTESICH, LAW CORPORATION (AV)

1201 K Street, Suite 1100, 95814
Telephone: 916-442-1111
Fax: 916-448-1709
Email: l&m@lmlaw.net *URL:* http://www.lmlaw.net

Gene Livingston
James M. Mattesich
Carol Livingston
Rebecca M. Ceniceros
Emilio E. Varanini, III
Kenneth M. Malovos
Kathleen E. Finnerty
Joanna R. Mendoza

Steven P. Belzer
Jeffrey Leacox
Randy Pollack
Alice H. Choi
Stephen Craig Hunter
Matthew J. Goldman
Joel C. Baiocchi
Baldassaro (Bill) Di Capo
John McKinsey
Timothy E. Naccarato
Craig N. Lundgren
Mary Farrell Taylor
Brian Crone
Gay L. Carroll
Steven G. Churchwell

Representative Clients: Bayer Corp.; Health Industry Manufacturers Association; Kraft Foods; Lyondell Chemical Company; Novartis Pharmaceuticals Corp.; Oxygenated Fuels Association; Reckitt & Coleman, Inc.; The Cosmetic, Toiletry and Fragrance Association; The Soap and Detergent Association.

For full biographical listings, see the Martindale-Hubbell Law Directory

RICHARD M. ROSS (AV)

400 Capitol Mall, Suite 900, 95814-4407
Telephone: 916-449-3908
Fax: 916-444-0270
Email: rross000@counsel.com

For full biographical listings, see the Martindale-Hubbell Law Directory

ROTHSCHILD, WISHEK & SANDS (AV)

901 "F" Street, Suite 200, 95814
Telephone: 916-444-9845
URL: http://www.lawyers.com/glsattylaw

MEMBERS OF FIRM

Michael Rothschild
M. Bradley Wishek

ASSOCIATES

Stacy Boulware Eurie
Jonathan C. Turner

OF COUNSEL

Michael S. Sands

For full biographical listings, see the Martindale-Hubbell Law Directory

*SAN FRANCISCO,** San Francisco Co.

SPAETH & MCGRATH (AV)

456 Montgomery Street, Suite 950, 94104
Telephone: 415-627-6770
Fax: 415-627-6789
URL: http://www.lawyers.com/spaeth&mcgrath

George A. Spaeth
Kevin J. McGrath

For full biographical listings, see the Martindale-Hubbell Law Directory

COLORADO

*DENVER,** Denver Co.

BRENMAN BROMBERG & TENENBAUM, P.C. (AV)

Mellon Financial Center Suite 1001, 1775 Sherman Street, 80203
Telephone: 303-894-0234
Fax: 303-839-1633
Email: bbt@bbtlaw.net

Albert Brenman
Thomas R. Bromberg
A. Thomas Tenenbaum
Steven W. McDonald

Sheryl A. Johnson
Judy A. Gooch

OF COUNSEL

Duane Woodard

For full biographical listings, see the Martindale-Hubbell Law Directory

BROWNSTEIN HYATT & FARBER, P.C. (AV)

Twenty-Second Floor, 410 Seventeenth Street, 80202-4437
Telephone: 303-223-1100
Telecopier: 303-223-1111
Washington, D.C. Office: 1615 L Street, N.W., Suite 450, 20036.
Telephone: 202-296-7353.
Telecopier: 202-296-7009.
Glenwood Springs, Colorado Office: Box 357, 81602.
Telephone: 970-945-5302.
Telecopier: 970-945-4921.

Norman Brownstein
Steven W. Farber
Andrew W. Loewi
Gary M. Reiff
Wayne F. Forman
Bruce A. James
Cole Finegan
Hubert A. Farbes, Jr.
William T. Brack (Resident, Washington, D.C. Office)
Mark J. Mathews

SENIOR COUNSEL

James S. Lochhead (Resident, Glenwood Springs, Colorado Office)
Thomas H. Hudson (Resident, Washington, D.C. Office)
Gale A. Norton

SPECIAL COUNSEL

Lynne M. Hufnagel

Joshua J. Widoff
Beth Doherty Quinn
Ted J. Trimpa
Andrew L. Spielman
Chad G. Asarch
David L. Bernhardt (Resident, Washington, D.C. Office)
Kurt B. Colburn

Representative Clients: Apollo Real Estate Advisors, L.P.; The Denver Broncos; The Hertz Corporation; J.D. Edwards & Company; McDonald's Corporation; Outdoor Systems Advertising; Pfizer, Inc.; Tele-Communications, Inc. (TCI); U S WEST, Inc.; United Air Lines, Inc.

For Complete List of Firm Personnel, See General Section

For full biographical listings, see the Martindale-Hubbell Law Directory

CONNECTICUT

*HARTFORD,** Hartford Co.

KILLIAN, DONOHUE & SHIPMAN, LLC (AV)

363 Main Street, 06106-1885
Telephone: 860-560-1977
Telecopier: 860-249-6638
Email: lawyers@killiandonohueshipman.com
Simsbury, Connecticut Office: 141 West Street.
Telephone: 860-658-0436.
Telecopier: 860-249-6638.

Robert K. Killian, Jr.
Thomas J. Donohue, Jr.
Mark S. Shipman
Lawrence S. Shipman

For full biographical listings, see the Martindale-Hubbell Law Directory

SOROKIN, GROSS & HYDE, P.C. (AV)

One Corporate Center, 06103
Telephone: 860-525-6645
Fax: 860-522-1781
Email: sorokin@sorokinlaw.com
Simsbury, Connecticut Office: 720 Hopmeadow Street.
Telephone: 860-651-9348.
Rocky Hill, Connecticut Office: 2360 Main Street.
Telephone: 860-563-9305.
Fax: 860-529-6931.

Lewis Rabinovitz

OF COUNSEL

Ethel Silver Sorokin

For Complete List of Firm Personnel, See General Section

For full biographical listings, see the Martindale-Hubbell Law Directory

STAMFORD, Fairfield Co.

CURTIS, BRINCKERHOFF & BARRETT, P.C. (AV)

666 Summer Street, 06901-1416
Telephone: 203-324-6777
Telecopier: 203-324-9621
Email: info@curtisbb.com

T. Ward Cleary (1916-1988)
Frederick M. Tobin
John Wayne Fox
Ward Frank Cleary
James D'Alton Murphy
Randolph T. Lovallo

OF COUNSEL

John D. Hertz
Jane F. Donovan
Richard L. Brinckerhoff
Patricia M. Gaug

(See Next Column)

CURTIS, BRINCKERHOFF & BARRETT P.C., *Stamford—Continued*

Susan L. Stratton
Derek Gilman
Michael P. Murray
John J. Louizos

Counsel for: The F. A. Bartlett Tree Expert Co.; Town of Darien; Miller Automobile Corp.; Bolliger, Inc.; Titan Sports; People's Bank, Bridgeport; Fleet Bank; Federal Deposit Insurance Co.; William Pitt Foundation; Wood Logan Associates.

For full biographical listings, see the Martindale-Hubbell Law Directory

DISTRICT OF COLUMBIA

WASHINGTON, D.C. Co.

ADDUCI, MASTRIANI & SCHAUMBERG, L.L.P. (AV)

1200 Seventeenth Street, N.W., Fifth Floor, 20036-3006
Telephone: 202-467-6300
Telefax: 202-466-2006
Email: ams@adduci.com *URL:* http://www.adduci.com

V. James Adduci, II
Louis S. Mastriani
Tom M. Schaumberg
Barbara A. Murphy
Timothy Sullivan
David A. Guth (1953-1997)
Katherine S. Nucci
Harvey B. Fox
Gregory C. Anthes

Michael L. Doane
Steven E. Adkins
Allan J. Stevenson
Alfred M. Haas
Adam F. Bobrow

A list of Representative Clients and References will be furnished upon request.

For full biographical listings, see the Martindale-Hubbell Law Directory

BAKER BOTTS L.L.P. (AV)

A Registered Limited Liability Partnership
The Warner, 1299 Pennsylvania Avenue, N.W., 20004-2400
Telephone: 202-639-7700
Fax: 202-639-7832
Email: postmaster@bakerbotts.com *URL:* http://www.bakerbotts.com
Houston, Texas Office: One Shell Plaza, 910 Louisiana.
Telephone: 713-229-1234.
Austin, Texas Office: 1600 San Jacinto Center, 98 San Jacinto Boulevard.
Telephone: 512-322-2500.
Dallas, Texas Office: 2001 Ross Avenue.
Telephone: 214-953-6500.
New York, New York Office: 599 Lexington Avenue.
Telephone: 212-705-5000.
Moscow, Russia Office: 10 ul. Bolshaya Dimitrovka (formerly Pushkinskaya), 103031.
Telephone: 7095/921-5300 (Local); 7501/929-7070 (International).
London, England Office: 45 Ludgate Hill.
Telephone: 0171-778-1400 (Local); 011-44-171-778-1400 (International).
Baku, Azerbaijan Office: 6-10 Vagif Mustafa-zadeh Street, Third Floor, Icheri Sheher, 370004.
Telephone: 994-12-97-63-88 (Local); 011-994-12-97-63-88 (International).

MEMBERS OF FIRM

Thomas J. Eastment
Steven R. Hunsicker
Bruce F. Kiely
William D. Kramer
Mark K. Lewis
Martin T. Lutz
Randolph Quaile McManus
B. Donovan Picard
Jeffrey A. Stonerock

SPECIAL COUNSEL

Debra Raggio Bolton

ASSOCIATE

Paul T. Luther

For Complete List of Firm Personnel, See General Section

For full biographical listings, see the Martindale-Hubbell Law Directory

BAKER & HOSTETLER LLP (AV)

Washington Square, Suite 1100, 1050 Connecticut Avenue, N.W., 20036-5304
Telephone: 202-861-1500
Fax: 202-861-1783
To contact an attorney on the Internet use first initial and surname followed by @baker-hostetler.com
URL: http://www.bakerlaw.com
In Cleveland, Ohio: 3200 National City Center, 1900 East Ninth Street.
Telephone: 216-621-0200.
In Cincinnati, Ohio: 312 Walnut Street, Suite 2650.
Telephone: 513-929-3400.
In Columbus, Ohio: Capitol Square, Suite 2100, 65 East State Street.
Telephone: 614-228-1541.

(See Next Column)

In Denver, Colorado: 303 East 17th Avenue, Suite 1100.
Telephone: 303-861-0600.
In Houston, Texas: 1000 Louisiana, Suite 2000.
Telephone: 713-751-1600.
In Beverly Hills, California: 9150 Wilshire Boulevard, Suite 205.
Telephone: 310-385-7500.
In Long Beach, California: 300 Oceangate, Suite 620.
Telephone: 562-432-2827.
In Los Angeles, California: 600 Wilshire Boulevard.
Telephone: 213-624-2400.
In Orlando, Florida: SunBank Center, Suite 2300, 200 South Orange Avenue.
Telephone: 407-649-4000.

PARTNERS

Frederick H. Graefe
Richard A. Hauser

OF COUNSEL

E. Mark Braden

For Complete List of Firm Personnel, See General Section

For full biographical listings, see the Martindale-Hubbell Law Directory

BERLINER, CANDON & JIMISON (AV)

1225 Nineteenth Street N.W., Suite 800, 20036
Telephone: 202-955-6067
Telecopy: 202-822-0109
Berkeley, California Office: 2560 Ninth Street, Suite 316.
Telephone: 510-549-6926.
Telecopy: 510-649-9793.
Los Angeles, California Office: 1875 Century Park East, Suite 700.
Telephone: 310-282-6848.
Telecopy: 310-282-6841.

MEMBERS OF FIRM

Roger A. Berliner
John W. Jimison
Mary Eva Candon

ASSOCIATES

Peter G. Hirst (Not admitted in DC)
Megan Grant

OF COUNSEL

Lucien Wulsin, Jr. (Not admitted in DC)
Andy Schneider

LEGISLATIVE PROFESSIONALS

Burt Margolin (Resident, Los Angeles, California Office)
Carla Kish

CONSULTANTS

R. Thomas Beach (Resident, Berkeley California Office)
Patrick G. McGuire (Resident, Berkeley, California Office)

References: Canadian Embassy; City of Vernon, California; Pacific Gas Transmission Co.; Polyisocyanurate Insulation Manufacturers Assn.; Watson Cogeneration Co.

For full biographical listings, see the Martindale-Hubbell Law Directory

BRAUDE & MARGULIES, P.C. (AV)

The Brawner Building, 888 Seventeenth Street, N.W., Suite 500, 20006
Telephone: 202-293-2993
Fax: 202-331-7916
Email: Braudemarg@aol.com

Herman M. Braude
Samuel M. Morrison, Jr.
Gerson B. Kramer

Stuart H. Sakwa
Stacie J. Broadwater

OF COUNSEL

J. Richard Margulies

For full biographical listings, see the Martindale-Hubbell Law Directory

BRUDER, GENTILE & MARCOUX, L.L.P. (AV)

1100 New York Avenue, N.W., Suite 510 East, 20005-3934
Telephone: 202-783-1350
Telecopiers: 202-737-9117; 347-2644
Email: bgmstaff@brugen.com *URL:* http://www.brugen.com

George F. Bruder (Retired)
Carmen L. Gentile
Albert R. Simonds, Jr. (Retired)
J. Michel Marcoux
David E. Goroff
Gary E. Guy
James H. McGrew
Thomas L. Blackburn

Antonia A. Frost
David Martin Connelly
Gary D. Levenson

OF COUNSEL

Peter K. Matt

For full biographical listings, see the Martindale-Hubbell Law Directory

Washington—Continued

BRUNENKANT & HASKELL, LLP (AV)

805 15th Street, N.W., Suite 1101, 20005
Telephone: 202-408-0700
Fax: 202-408-5959
Email: brunenkant@bh-law.com

Jon L. Brunenkant
Mark R. Haskell
James W. Moeller

ASSOCIATES

Cheryl J. Walker
Christie L. Richart (Not admitted in DC)
Melissa L. Lauderdale

For full biographical listings, see the Martindale-Hubbell Law Directory

COHN AND MARKS (AV)

1920 N Street, N.W., Suite 300, 20036-1622
Telephone: 202-293-3860
Fax: 202-293-4827
URL: http://www.cohnmarks.com

MEMBERS OF FIRM

Joel H. Levy
Lawrence N. Cohn
Robert B. Jacobi
Richard A. Helmick
Roy R. Russo
Wayne Coy, Jr.
Ronald A. Siegel
J. Brian De Boice
Jerold L. Jacobs

ASSOCIATES

Susan Valerie Sachs
Kevin M. Goldberg
Joseph M. Di Scipio

OF COUNSEL

Marcus Cohn
Stanley S. Neustadt
Leonard H. Marks
Richard M. Schmidt, Jr.

For full biographical listings, see the Martindale-Hubbell Law Directory

COOPER CARVIN & ROSENTHAL, PLLC (AV)

Suite 200, 1500 K Street, N.W., 20005
Telephone: 202-220-9600
Fax: 202-220-9601
URL: http://www.coopercarvin.com

PARTNERS

Charles J. Cooper
Robert J. Cynkar
Michael A. Carvin
Michael W. Kirk
Steven S. Rosenthal
Alan K. Palmer
Vincent J. Colatriano
Jeffery A. Tomasevich

ASSOCIATES

R. Ted Cruz
Craig S. Lerner
Noel John Francisco (Not admitted in DC)
David H. Thompson
Hamish P.M. Hume
Douglas A. Tucker (Not admitted in DC)

OF COUNSEL

Kenneth L. Marcus
Andrew G. McBride

For full biographical listings, see the Martindale-Hubbell Law Directory

THE CUNEO LAW GROUP, P.C. (AV)

317 Massachusetts Avenue, N.E. Suite 300, 20002
Telephone: 202-789-3960
Fax: 202-789-1813
Email: contact@cuneolaw.com *URL:* http://www.cuneolaw.com

Jonathan W. Cuneo
David W. Stanley
James J. Schweitzer
Michael G. Lenett

Arthur K. Park (Not admitted in DC)
Daniel Cohen (Not admitted in DC)

COUNSEL

Charles Tiefer

For full biographical listings, see the Martindale-Hubbell Law Directory

DUNAWAY & CROSS, A PROFESSIONAL CORPORATION (AV)

1700 K Street, N.W. Suite 800, 20006-3819
Telephone: 202-862-9700
Fax: 202-862-9710
Email: duncross@msn.com

Mac S. Dunaway
Gary E. Cross
Matthew F. Hall

COUNSEL

Raymond P. Shafer (Not admitted in DC)

For full biographical listings, see the Martindale-Hubbell Law Directory

KLEINFELD, KAPLAN AND BECKER (AV)

Suite 900, 1140 Nineteenth Street, N.W., 20036
Telephone: 202-223-5120
Telecopier: 202-223-5619
Email: kkb@kkblaw.com *URL:* http://www.kkblaw.com
San Francisco, California Office: One Market Street, Steuart Tower, Suite 1450.
Telephone: 415-538-0014.
Telecopier: 415-538-0016.

Vincent A. Kleinfeld (1907-1993)

MEMBERS OF FIRM

Alan H. Kaplan
Peter R. Mathers
Thomas O. Henteleff
Bonnie A. Beavers
Richard S. Morey
Daniel R. Dwyer
Peter O. Safir
Glenn E. Davis
Kinsey S. Reagan
Prescott M. Lassman

ASSOCIATES

Stacy L. Ehrlich
Jennifer A. Davidson

For full biographical listings, see the Martindale-Hubbell Law Directory

MCLEOD, WATKINSON & MILLER (AV)

Eighth Floor, One Massachusetts Avenue, N.W., 20001
Telephone: 202-842-2345
Telecopy: 202-408-7763
Email: mwm@mwmlaw.com *URL:* http://www.mwmlaw.com

MEMBERS OF FIRM

Michael R. McLeod
Marc Eric Miller
Wayne R. Watkinson
Richard T. Rossier

ASSOCIATES

Richard E. Pasco
Alissa Baum

LEGAL SUPPORT PERSONNEL

Laura Phelps
Stephen Frerichs
Robert Randall Green

For full biographical listings, see the Martindale-Hubbell Law Directory

POWERS, PYLES, SUTTER & VERVILLE, P.C. (AV)

Twelfth Floor, 1875 Eye Street, N.W., 20006-5409
Telephone: 202-466-6550
Fax: 202-785-1756
Email: ppsv@ppsv.com *URL:* http://www.ppsv.com

Galen D. Powers
David C. Beck
James C. Pyles
Peter W. Thomas
Ronald N. Sutter
Thomas Hylden
Richard E. Verville
Marie Catherine Infante
Mary Susan Philp
Christopher L. Keough
Mark R. Fitzgerald
Harold Damelin
Robert J. Saner, II
Joel M. Hamme
Stanley A. Freeman
Joel M. Rudnick

Marla P. Spindel
Arthur S. DiDio
Ana-Maria McKessy
Kimberly N. Brown
Karen S. Lovitch
C. Anthony Russo (Not admitted in DC)

OF COUNSEL

Rebecca L. Burke
Douglas Benson Tesdahl
Donald W. Aaronson
Edith S. Marshall

For full biographical listings, see the Martindale-Hubbell Law Directory

VENABLE ATTORNEYS AT LAW VENABLE, BAETJER, HOWARD & CIVILETTI, LLP (AV)

A Partnership including Professional Corporations
Suite 1000, 1201 New York Avenue, N.W., 20005
Telephone: 202-962-4800
Fax: 202-962-8300
URL: http://www.venable.com
Baltimore, Maryland Office: Venable, Baetjer and Howard LLP, 1800 Mercantile Bank & Trust Building, 2 Hopkins Plaza.
Telephone: 410-244-7400.
Fax: 410-244-7742.
McLean, Virginia Office: Venable, Baetjer and Howard LLP, Suite 400, 2010 Corporate Ridge.
Telephone: 703-760-1600.
Fax: 703-821-8949.
Rockville, Maryland Office: Venable, Baetjer and Howard LLP, Suite 500, One Church Street, P. O. Box 1906.
Telephone: 301-217-5600.
Fax: 301-217-5617.
Towson, Maryland Office: Venable, Baetjer and Howard LLP, 210 Allegheny Avenue, P. O. Box 5517.
Telephone: 410-494-6200.
Fax: 410-821-0147.

(See Next Column)

VENABLE ATTORNEYS AT LAW VENABLE, BAETJER, HOWARD & CIVILETTI, LLP, *Washington—Continued*

MEMBERS OF FIRM

Kenneth C. Bass, III (Also at McLean, Virginia Office)
John F. Cooney
Ronald R. Glancz
Gary M. Hnath
Jeffrey D. Knowles
Thomas J. Madden
John J. Pavlick, Jr.
Michael Schatzow (Also at Baltimore, Maryland Office)
N. Frank Wiggins

ASSOCIATE

James Nicholas Czaban

For Complete List of Firm Personnel, See General Section

For full biographical listings, see the Martindale-Hubbell Law Directory

WEBSTER, CHAMBERLAIN & BEAN (AV)

Suite 1000, 1747 Pennsylvania Avenue, N.W., 20006
Telephone: 202-785-9500
Fax: 202-835-0243

MEMBERS OF FIRM

Arthur L. Herold
Alan P. Dye
Edward D. Coleman
Frank M. Northam
John W. Hazard, Jr.
Hugh K. Webster

OF COUNSEL

Charles E. Chamberlain
J. Coleman Bean
Kent Masterson Brown (Not admitted in DC)
Burkett Van Kirk
James Bopp, Jr. (Not admitted in DC)

ASSOCIATES

Charles M. Watkins
David P. Goch
Brenley Locke Elias
Raymond Cashen, II (Not admitted in DC)

For full biographical listings, see the Martindale-Hubbell Law Directory

WILLIAMS & JENSEN, A PROFESSIONAL CORPORATION (AV)

1155 - 21st Street, N.W., Suite 300, 3 Lafayette Centre, 20036
Telephone: 202-659-8201
Facsimile: 202-659-5249
Email: fd@wms-jen.com

George D. Baker
Philip E. Bechtel
Laricke D. Blanchard (Not admitted in DC)
Barbara Wixon Bonfiglio
William B. Canfield, III
Bertram W. Carp
Winfield P. Crigler
Tracy Doherty Taylor
David E. Franasiak
Robert E. Glennon, Jr.
J. Steven Hart
Carole L. Kuebler (1948-1979)
David Michael Landers
Karen Judd Lewis
Robert J. Martinez
John J. McMackin, Jr.
George G. Olsen
Anthony J. Roda
Joseph L. Seidel
David A. Starr
Ian S. Thompson (Not admitted in DC)
Mary Lynne Whalen
J. D. Williams

OF COUNSEL

Robert E. Jensen

For full biographical listings, see the Martindale-Hubbell Law Directory

FLORIDA

BOCA RATON, Palm Beach Co.

JOSEPH HARRISON (AV)

Crystal Corporate Center, 2500 North Military Trail, Suite 275, 33431
Telephone: 561-241-9306
Fax: 561-241-9308

For full biographical listings, see the Martindale-Hubbell Law Directory

*CLEARWATER,** Pinellas Co.

KWALL, SHOWERS & COLEMAN, P.A. (AV)

133 North Fort Harrison Avenue, 33755
Telephone: 727-441-4947
Telecopier: 727-447-3158
Email: kwall@worldnet.att.net *URL:* http://www.usalaw.com/adminlaw/

Louis Kwall
Sherwood S. (Flip) Coleman

For Complete List of Firm Personnel, See General Section

For full biographical listings, see the Martindale-Hubbell Law Directory

*FORT LAUDERDALE,** Broward Co.

CUMMINGS & SNYDER, P.A. (AV)

1600 Southeast 17th Street Causeway, P.O. Box 460327, 33346-1116
Telephone: 954-761-8700
Telecopier: 954-524-6927
Email: administrator@cummingslaw.com *URL:* http://www.cummingslaw.com
Tallahassee, Florida Office: 1004 DeSoto Park Drive, P.O. Box 589, 32302-0589.
Telephone: 850-878-3700.
Telecopier: 850-656-0329.

F. Alan Cummings

Bradley S. Copenhaver
Alejandro Espino

OF COUNSEL

James E. Glass

Representative Clients: American Bridge Company; American International Group; Dillingham Construction Holdings, Inc.; Hubbard Construction Company; Odebrecht Construction, Inc.; Reliance Surety Company; Traylor Bros., Inc.; Condotte America, Inc.; Seaboard Surety Company; Alabama Department of Transportation.

For full biographical listings, see the Martindale-Hubbell Law Directory

JAMES CURRAN, P.A. (AV)

633 Southeast Third Avenue Suite 201, 33301
Telephone: 954-523-3845

James Curran

For full biographical listings, see the Martindale-Hubbell Law Directory

*MIAMI,** Dade Co.

NEIL FLAXMAN PROFESSIONAL ASSOCIATION (AV)

550 Biltmore Way, Suite 780 (Coral Gables), 33134
Telephone: 305-445-1388
Fax: 305-443-0279
URL: http://www.lawyers.com/neilflaxman

Neil Flaxman

Joseph G. Weiss, Jr.

For full biographical listings, see the Martindale-Hubbell Law Directory

HOLTZMAN, KRINZMAN, EQUELS & FURIA (AV)

2601 South Bayshore Drive, Suite 600, 33133
Telephone: 305-859-7700
Fax: 305-859-9996
Email: hkef@hkef.com *URL:* http://www.hkef.com
Orlando, Florida Office: 16 West Pine Street, 32801.
Telephone: 407-839-0095.
Fax: 407-839-2050.
Tallahassee, Florida Office: 542 East Park Avenue, 32301.
Telephone: 850-222-2900.
Fax: 850-222-2933.

Sylvan (Sonny) Holtzman
Jack L. McRay (Resident, Orlando Office)
Lisa "Li" Shearer Nelson (Resident, Tallahassee Office)

For full biographical listings, see the Martindale-Hubbell Law Directory

ROBBINS, TUNKEY, ROSS, AMSEL, RABEN & WAXMAN, P.A. (AV)

2250 Southwest Third Avenue, Fourth Floor, 33129
Telephone: Dade County 305-858-9550; Broward County 954-522-6244 (All Telephones Open 24 Hours); 1-800-226-9550
Fax: 305-858-7491
Email: RTR2250@AOL.COM *URL:* http://www.crimlawfirm.com

Frederick S. Robbins
William R. Tunkey
Alan S. Ross
Robert G. Amsel
David Raben
Benjamin S. Waxman

Mark R. Eiglarsh
Marco A. Vazquez (1968-1995)

Reference: Mellon United National Bank, Miami, Florida.

For full biographical listings, see the Martindale-Hubbell Law Directory

*ORLANDO,** Orange Co.

BROWN, WARD, SALZMAN & WEISS, P.A. (AV)

111 North Orange Avenue, Suite 875, P.O. Box 2873, 32802-2873
Telephone: 407-425-9566
Fax: 407-425-9596; Email: firm@orlandolaw.net
Email: brownu@osceola.k12.fl.us *URL:* http://www.orlandolaw.net

(See Next Column)

BROWN, WARD, SALZMAN & WEISS P.A.—*Continued*

Usher Larry Brown
John H. Ward
Gary S. Salzman
Jeffrey S. Weiss
Suzanne D'Agresta

Scott D. Danahy
James G. Vickaryous
Robert L. Butterfield, Jr.
Allison Carmine McDonald

Representative Clients: The School Board of Osceola County; The School Board of Indian River County; The School Board of Putnam County; The School Board of Flagler County; Osceola County; Orange County Comptroller; General Electric Capital Modular Space; Honeywell, Inc.

For full biographical listings, see the Martindale-Hubbell Law Directory

*TALLAHASSEE,** Leon Co.

CUMMINGS & SNYDER, P.A. (AV)

1004 DeSoto Park Drive, P.O. Box 589, 32302-0589
Telephone: 850-878-3700
Telecopier: 850-656-0329
Email: administrator@cummingslaw.com *URL:* http://www.cummingslaw.com
Fort Lauderdale, Florida Office: 1600 Southeast 17th Street Causeway, P.O. Box 460327, 33346-1116.
Telephone: 954-761-8700.
Telecopier: 954-524-6927.

F. Alan Cummings
Patricia Anne Hamilton Snyder

W. Guy McKenzie, Jr.
Daniel Te Young

Representative Clients: American Bridge Company; American International Group; Dillingham Construction Holdings, Inc.; Hubbard Construction Company; Odebrecht Construction, Inc.; Reliance Surety Company; Traylor Bros., Inc.; Condotte America, Inc.; Seaboard Surety Company; Alabama Department of Transportation.

For full biographical listings, see the Martindale-Hubbell Law Directory

KATZ, KUTTER, HAIGLER, ALDERMAN, BRYANT & YON, PROFESSIONAL ASSOCIATION (AV)

106 East College Avenue, 12th Floor, P.O. Box 1877, 32301
Telephone: 850-224-9634
Fax: 850-224-0781; 222-0103
URL: http://www.katzlaw.com
Orlando, Florida Office: 111 North Orange Avenue, Suite 900, 32801.
Telephone: 407-841-7100.
Fax: 407-648-0660.

Silvia Morell Alderman
Daniel C. Brown
Bill L. Bryant, Jr.
Gordon D. Cherr
Richard E. Coates
J. Riley Davis
Martin R. Dix
Paul R. Ezatoff, Jr.
William M. Furlow
Mitchell B. Haigler
Michael E. Ingram
Mark E. Kaplan
Allan J. Katz
Edward L. Kutter
Richard P. Lee
Ralph C. Losey (Resident, Orlando Office)
John C. Lovett
Elizabeth Waas McArthur
Miguel A. Olivella, Jr.
Joseph R. Panzl (Resident, Orlando Office)
Emery H. Rosenbluth, Jr. (Resident, Orlando Office)
Harry O. Thomas
Gary P. Timin
J. Larry Williams
David A. Yon
Paul A. Zeigler

ASSOCIATES

Coretta S. Anthony
Irene A. Bassel (Resident, Orlando Office)
Alan Harrison Brents (Resident, Orlando Office)
Junious D. Brown, III
Nancy Mason Burke
John A. Chiocca
Bert L. Combs
Katherine E. Giddings
Miles W. Hughes
Lisa M. Hurley
Brian C. Keri
Christopher B. Lunny
William Peter Martin
Travis L. Miller
Bruce D. Platt
Alexa Pleas

OF COUNSEL

O'Bannon M. Cook
Jeffrey L. Frehn
Edward S. Jaffry
Patrick F. Maroney
Michael A. Miller (Resident, Orlando Office)
John Radey

LEGAL SUPPORT PERSONNEL

Leslie Y. Dughi (Governmental Consultant)
Gerald C. Wester (Governmental Consultant)
Christine M. Klena (Special Consultant)
E. Clinton Smawley (Governmental Consultant)
Pat Griffith O'Connell (Governmental Consultant)
J. Andrew Keller, III (Executive Director)

For full biographical listings, see the Martindale-Hubbell Law Directory

MCFARLAIN, WILEY, CASSEDY & JONES, PROFESSIONAL ASSOCIATION (AV)

215 South Monroe Street, Suite 600, P.O. Box 2174, 32316-2174
Telephone: 850-222-2107
Telecopier: 850-222-8475
Email: firm@mcfarlain.com *URL:* http://www.mcfarlain.com

Richard C. McFarlain
William B. Wiley
Douglas P. Jones
Charles A. Stampelos
H. Darrell White, Jr.
Christopher Barkas
Harold R. Mardenborough, Jr.
Terrell C. Madigan

Robert A. McNeely
P. David Brannon

LEGAL SUPPORT PERSONNEL

Diane L. Doll (Office Manager)

For full biographical listings, see the Martindale-Hubbell Law Directory

ROSE, SUNDSTROM & BENTLEY, LLP (AV)

2548 Blairstone Pines Drive, P.O. Box 1567, 32301-1567
Telephone: 850-877-6555
Telecopier: 850-656-4029
URL: http://www.rsbattorneys.com

MEMBERS OF FIRM

Chris H. Bentley (P.A.)
F. Marshall Deterding
Martin S. Friedman (P.A.)
John R. Jenkins (P.A.)
William E. Sundstrom (P.A.)
Diane D. Tremor (P.A.)
John L. Wharton

Representative Clients: Aloha Utilities, Inc.; Arbor Health Care Co.; East Central Florida Services, Inc.; Florida Waterworks Assn.; Utility Board of the City of Key West.
Reference: Capital City Bank, Tallahassee.

For full biographical listings, see the Martindale-Hubbell Law Directory

SKELDING, LABASKY & DAWS, A PROFESSIONAL ASSOCIATION (AV)

The Madigan Building, 318 North Monroe Street, P.O. Box 669, 32302
Telephone: 850-222-3730
Fax: 850-224-6422

John A. Madigan, Jr. (1919-1984)
Millard F. Caldwell (1897-1984)
Jack M. Skelding, Jr.
Ronald A. Labasky
Sonya Krouskop Daws

Linda C. Cox

For full biographical listings, see the Martindale-Hubbell Law Directory

GEORGIA

*ATLANTA,** Fulton Co.

CHOREY, TAYLOR & FEIL, A PROFESSIONAL CORPORATION (AV)

Suite 1700, The Lenox Building, 3399 Peachtree Road, N.E., 30326
Telephone: 404-841-3200
Facsimile: 404-841-3221
Email: ctf@ctflegal.com

Thomas V. Chorey, Jr.
John L. Taylor, Jr.
Matthew L. Hess

For Complete List of Firm Personnel, See General Section

For full biographical listings, see the Martindale-Hubbell Law Directory

HARKLEROAD & HERMANCE, A PROFESSIONAL CORPORATION (AV)

2500 International Tower-Peachtree Center, 229 Peachtree Street, N.E., 30303
Telephone: 404-588-9211
Telecopier: 404-659-0860

Donald R. Harkleroad
James P. Hermance

For full biographical listings, see the Martindale-Hubbell Law Directory

Atlanta—Continued

LONG ALDRIDGE & NORMAN LLP (AV)

A Limited Liability Partnership including Professional Corporations
Suite 5300, 303 Peachtree Street, 30308
Telephone: 404-527-4000
Telecopier: 404-527-4198
Email: atlanta@lanlaw.com *URL:* http://www.lanlaw.com
Washington, D.C. Office: Suite 600, 701 Pennsylvania Avenue, N.W., 20004.
Telephone: 202-624-1200.
FAX: 202-624-1298.

MEMBERS OF FIRM

David L. Balser
Douglas L. Beresford (Resident, Washington, D.C. Office)
George (Buddy) Darden
L. Craig Dowdy
Albert G. Norman, Jr.
Jacolyn A. Simmons (Resident, Washington, D.C. Office)
John T. Stough, Jr. (Resident, Washington, D.C. Office)

ASSOCIATES

George F. Hobday, Jr. (Resident, Washington, D.C. Office)
Thadd A. Prisco (Resident, Washington, D.C. Office)

For Complete List of Firm Personnel, See General Section

For full biographical listings, see the Martindale-Hubbell Law Directory

*DECATUR,** De Kalb Co.

LAW OFFICES OF CHARLES L. MARTIN (AV)

123 North McDonough Street, 30030
Telephone: 404-373-3116
FAX: 404-373-4110
Email: CLMARTIN@THEOMBUDSMAN.COM *URL:* HTTP://WWW.THEOMBUDSMAN.COM/MARTIN_LAW/

Charles L. Martin
Joseph Jones

For full biographical listings, see the Martindale-Hubbell Law Directory

HAWAII

*HONOLULU,** Honolulu Co.

CARLSMITH BALL (AV)

A Partnership including Law Corporations
Suite 2200, Pacific Tower, 1001 Bishop Street, P.O. Box 656, 96809-3402
Telephone: 808-523-2500
Fax: 808-523-0842
Email: execdirector@carlsmith.com *URL:* http://www.carlsmith.com
Kapolei, Hawaii Office: Suite 318, Kapolei Building, 1001 Kamokila Boulevard, 96707.
Telephone: 808-523-2500.
Fax: 808-674-0850.
Wailuku, Maui Hawaii Office: Suite 400, One Main Plaza, 2200 Main Street, P.O. Box 1086, 96793-1086.
Telephone: 808-242-4535.
Fax: 808-244-4974.
Kailua-Kona, Hawaii Office: Suite 209, 75-1000 Henry Street, 96740.
Telephone: 808-329-6464.
Fax: 808-329-9450.
Hilo, Hawaii Office: 121 Waianuenue Avenue, P.O. Box 686, 96721-0686.
Telephone: 808-935-6644.
Fax: 808-935-7975.
Hagatna, Guam Office: Suite 401, Bank of Hawaii Building, 134 West Soledad Avenue, P.O. Box BF, 96932-5027.
Telephone: 671-472-6813.
Fax: 671-477-4375.
Telex: 721-6445 CWCMI GM.
Saipan, Commonwealth of the Northern Mariana Islands Office: Carlsmith Building, Capitol Hill, P.O. Box 5241, 96950-5241.
Telephone: 670-322-3455.
Fax: 670-322-3368.
Los Angeles, California Office: 9th Floor, 444 South Flower Street, 90071-2901.
Telephone: 213-955-1200.
Fax: 213-623-0032.
Washington, D.C. Office: Suite 300, 1201 Pennsylvania Avenue, N.W., 20004-2401.
Telephone: 202-628-2228.
Fax: 202-628-2071.
Mexico City, Mexico Office: Carlsmith Ball, Sierra Nevada 119, Lomas de Chapultepec, 11000 Mexico, D.F.
Telephone: 52-5-520-8514, 52-5-520-8757.
Fax: 52-5-540-1545.

(See Next Column)

Mexico, D.F. Office of Carlsmith Ball, S.C. (Authorized to practice as foreign legal consultants in Mexico): Sierra Nevada 119, Lomas de Chapultepec, 11000 Mexico, D.F.
Telephone: 52-5-520-8514, 52-5-520-8757.
Fax: 52-5-540-1545.

MEMBERS OF FIRM

Roger B. Baymiller (Resident at Los Angeles, California Office)
Daniel A. Bent
Randall H. Endo (Resident at Maui, Hawaii Office)
Gary G. Grimmer
Steven S. C. Lim (Resident at Hilo, Hawaii Office)
Tim Lui-Kwan
B. Martin Luna (Resident at Maui, Hawaii Office)
David R. Nevitt (Resident at Saipan Office)
Adrián Zubikarai Arriola (Resident at Mexico Office)

OF COUNSEL

Tom K. Houston (Resident at Los Angeles, California Office)

For Complete List of Firm Personnel, See General Section

For full biographical listings, see the Martindale-Hubbell Law Directory

INDIANA

*INDIANAPOLIS,** Marion Co.

HACKMAN HULETT & CRACRAFT, LLP (AV)

2400 One Indiana Square, 46204
Telephone: 317-636-5401
Facsimile: 317-686-3288

MEMBERS OF FIRM

Marvin L. Hackman
Robert S. Hulett
Michael B. Cracraft
Timothy K. Ryan
Philip B. McKiernan
Vicki L. Anderson
John D. Cochran, Jr.
Mark S. Alderfer

Marci A. Reddick
Sherri A.B. Elder
Steven W. Krohne
Ellen J. Morrison

Representative Clients: Ameritech Indiana; AT&T Technologies, Inc.; Citizens Gas & Coke Utility; Texas Eastern Products Pipeline Co.; Indiana Municipal Power Agency; Indiana Municipal Electric Assn.

For full biographical listings, see the Martindale-Hubbell Law Directory

JOHNSON SMITH PENCE & HEATH LLP (AV)

One Indiana Square Suite 1800, 46204
Telephone: 317-634-9777
Telecopier: 317-636-9061
Email: firm@jsplaw.com *URL:* http://www.jsplaw.com
Washington, D.C. Office: 555 Twelfth Street, N.W., Suite 650.
Telephone: 202-737-5410.
Fax: 202-737-5411.

MEMBERS OF FIRM

David G. Blachly
John R. Hammond, III
Robert B. Hebert
Mark A. Palmer

ASSOCIATE

Thomas A. Dickey

For Complete List of Firm Personnel, See General Section

For full biographical listings, see the Martindale-Hubbell Law Directory

MCNAMAR, FEARNOW & MCSHARAR, P.C. (AV)

Bank One Center Tower, 111 Monument Circle, Suite 4500, 46204-5145
Telephone: 317-630-4500
Fax: 317-630-4501
Email: mfm@indy.net

David F. McNamar
Randall R. Fearnow
Janet A. McSharar
Alastair J. Warr
John H. Sharpe
Paul (Rick) Rauch, III
Marianna P. Moran

For full biographical listings, see the Martindale-Hubbell Law Directory

SOMMER & BARNARD, ATTORNEYS AT LAW, PC (AV)

4000 Bank One Tower, 111 Monument Circle, 46204
Telephone: 317-630-4000
FAX: 317-236-9802
Email: sandb@sommerbarnard.com
North Office: 8900 Keystone Crossing, Suite 1150, Indianapolis, Indiana, 46240-2134.
Telephone: 317-630-4000.
FAX: 317-844-4780.

Edward W. Harris, III
Frederick M. King

Representative Clients: Comerica Bank; Federal Express; Kimball International; Monsanto; TRW, Inc.

(See Next Column)

SOMMER & BARNARD ATTORNEYS AT LAW, PC—*Continued*

For Complete List of Firm Personnel, See General Section

For full biographical listings, see the Martindale-Hubbell Law Directory

TABBERT HAHN EARNEST & WEDDLE (AV)

Suite 2100, One Indiana Square, 46204-2101
Telephone: 317-639-5444
Fax: 317-639-5232
Email: jtyrrell@tabberthahn.com *URL:* http://www.tabberthahn.com

Don A. Tabbert
Gregory F. Hahn
Lante K. Earnest
Robert G. Weddle
Mark K. Sullivan
Judy M. Tyrrell
Lara D. Engelking
William W. Mathews
Heather L. Fesko
Charles R. Whybrew

OF COUNSEL

James J. Nocon
William D. Lalley
Joseph W. Hammes
Dale E. Sporleder

For full biographical listings, see the Martindale-Hubbell Law Directory

IOWA

*CEDAR RAPIDS,** Linn Co.

SHUTTLEWORTH & INGERSOLL, P.C. (AV)

115 Third Street S.E., Suite 500, P.O. Box 2107, 52406-2107
Telephone: 319-365-9461
Fax: 319-365-8443
URL: http://www.shuttleworthlaw.com

James C. Nemmers
Michael O. McDermott
Richard S. Fry
Richard C. Garberson
Gary J. Streit
Carroll J. Reasoner
Steven J. Pace
Glenn L. Johnson
Thomas P. Peffer
Kevin H. Collins
William P. Prowell
Diane Kutzko
Mark L. Zaiger
William S. Hochstetler

COUNSEL

Joan Lipsky

Representative Clients: Amana Society; Archer-Daniels-Midland Co.; Cargill, Inc.; Firstar Bank N.A.; General Mills, Inc.; Alliant IES Utilities; MCI; McLeod USA Telecommunication Services, Inc.; PMX Industries, Inc.

For Complete List of Firm Personnel, See General Section

For full biographical listings, see the Martindale-Hubbell Law Directory

KANSAS

*TOPEKA,** Shawnee Co.

FOULSTON & SIEFKIN L.L.P. (AV)

1515 NationsBank Tower, 534 Kansas Avenue, 66603
Telephone: 785-233-3600
Fax: 785-233-1610
URL: http://www.foulston.com
Wichita, Kansas Office: 100 North Broadway, 700 NationsBank Financial Center, 67202.
Telephone: 316-267-6371.
Fax: 316-267-6345.
Dodge City, Kansas Office: 810 Frontview, P.O. Box 1147, 67801.
Telephone: 316-227-8126.
Fax: 316-227-8451.
Member: Lex Mundi, The World's Leading Association of Independent Law Firms.

SPECIAL COUNSEL

James L. Grimes, Jr.
Robert A. Fox

For full biographical listings, see the Martindale-Hubbell Law Directory

WRIGHT, HENSON, SOMERS, SEBELIUS, CLARK & BAKER, LLP (AV)

Commerce Bank Building, 100 Southeast Ninth Street, 2nd Floor, P.O. Box 3555, 66601-3555
Telephone: 785-232-2200
FAX: 785-232-3344
Email: wrighthenson@wrighthenson.com *URL:* http://www.wrighthenson.com

(See Next Column)

MEMBERS OF FIRM

Thomas E. Wright
Charles N. Henson
K. Gary Sebelius
Anne Lamborn Baker
Evelyn Zabel Wilson

ASSOCIATE

Michael M. Walker

SPECIAL COUNSEL

David P. Mudrick

OF COUNSEL

Scott S. Sumpter

For Complete List of Firm Personnel, See General Section

For full biographical listings, see the Martindale-Hubbell Law Directory

*WICHITA,** Sedgwick Co.

FOULSTON & SIEFKIN L.L.P. (AV)

700 NationsBank Financial Center, 67202
Telephone: 316-267-6371
Facsimile: 316-267-6345
URL: http://www.foulston.com
Topeka, Kansas Office: 1515 NationsBank Tower, 534 Kansas Avenue, 66603.
Telephone: 785-233-3600.
Fax: 785-233-1610.
Dodge City, Kansas Office: 810 Frontview, P.O. Box 1147, 67801.
Telephone: 316-227-8126.
Fax: 316-227-8451.
Member: Lex Mundi, The World's Leading Association of Independent Law Firms.

MEMBERS OF FIRM

Mary Kathleen Babcock
Gloria G. Farha Flentje
Douglas L. Stanley

SPECIAL COUNSEL

James L. Grimes, Jr. (Resident, Topeka Office)
Robert A. Fox (Resident, Topeka Office)

For Complete List of Firm Personnel, See General Section

For full biographical listings, see the Martindale-Hubbell Law Directory

KENTUCKY

*HARLAN,** Harlan Co.

RICE & HENDRICKSON (AV)

398 Woodland Hills, P.O. Box 980, 40831
Telephone: 606-573-3955
Fax: 606-573-3956

MEMBERS OF FIRM

William A. Rice
H. Kent Hendrickson

Representative Clients: USX Corp.; Navistar International Transportation Corp.; Bituminous Casualty Corp.; Kentucky Utilities Co.; Aetna Casualty & Surety Co.; The Hartford Insurance Group; Benham Coal, Inc.; Maytag Corporation; Harlan Cumberland Coal Co.; Pafco General Insurance.

For full biographical listings, see the Martindale-Hubbell Law Directory

*LEXINGTON,** Fayette Co.

STOLL, KEENON & PARK, LLP (AV)

201 E. Main Street, Suite 1000, 40507-1380
Telephone: 606-231-3000
Telecopier: 606-253-1093; 606-253-1027
URL: http://www.skp.com
Frankfort, Kentucky Office: 307 Washington Street, 40601.
Telephone: 502-875-6220.
Telecopier: 502-875-6235.
Henderson, Kentucky Office: 201 C North Main Street, 42420-3103.
Telephone: 270-831-1900.
Telecopier: 270-827-4060.
Louisville, Kentucky Office: 400 West Market Street, Suite 2650, 40202-3377.
Telephone: 502-568-9100.
Telecopier: 502-568-5700.

MEMBERS OF FIRM

Lindsey W. Ingram, Jr.
Robert M. Watt, III
Lizbeth Ann Tully
John Browning Park

Representative Clients: Delta Natural Gas Co.; Independent Telephone Group; Kentucky American Water Co.

For Complete List of Firm Personnel, See General Section

For full biographical listings, see the Martindale-Hubbell Law Directory

LOUISIANA

*NEW ORLEANS,** Orleans Parish

LOWE, STEIN, HOFFMAN, ALLWEISS & HAUVER, L.L.P. (AV)

One Shell Square, 701 Poydras Street Suite 3600, 70139-7735
Telephone: 504-581-2450
Telecopier: 504-581-2461

MEMBERS OF FIRM

Robert C. Lowe
Mark S. Stein
Mitchell J. Hoffman
Michael R. Allweiss
Terence L. Hauver
Ellen Widen Kessler
Max J. Cohen
Suzette Marie Smith
David M. Prados
Marynell L. Piglia

Kermit L. Roux, III
Charlton D. Hunley
Barbara H. Weiss
Paula H. Lee
Stanley Dale Broome

OF COUNSEL

Mark S. Goldstein
Alicia M. Bendana

For full biographical listings, see the Martindale-Hubbell Law Directory

*SHREVEPORT,** Caddo Parish

BARLOW AND HARDTNER L.C. (AV)

Tenth Floor, Louisiana Tower, 401 Edwards Street, 71101-3289
Telephone: 318-227-1131
Telecopier: 318-227-1141
Mailing Address: P.O. Box 8, Shreveport, Louisiana, 71161-0008

Malcolm S. Murchison
David R. Taggart
Michael B. Donald

OF COUNSEL

Jerald N. Jones

Representative Clients: Anderson Oil & Gas, Inc.; Energy Management Corporation; Central Louisiana Electric Co., Inc.; Central and South West; Franks Petroleum Inc.; Louisiana Intrastate Gas Corp.; NorAm Energy Corp. (formerly Arkla, Inc.); Panhandle Eastern Corp.; Southwestern Electric Power Company; TE Products Pipeline Company.

For Complete List of Firm Personnel, See General Section

For full biographical listings, see the Martindale-Hubbell Law Directory

MAINE

*AUGUSTA,** Kennebec Co.

DOYLE & NELSON (AV)

150 Capitol Street, 04330
Telephone: 207-622-6124
Telefax: 207-623-1358
Email: Dnlawoff@aol.com

MEMBERS OF FIRM

Jon R. Doyle
Craig H. Nelson

ASSOCIATES

Michael A. Hodgins
Stephanos Orestis

Local Counsel for: British Consulate-General; International Game Technology; Irving Oil Corp.; ITW Hi-Cone; R.J. Reynolds Tobacco Co.; West Group.
Counsel for: Central Maine Power Co.; Blue Cross/Blue Shield of Maine; Maine Association of Mental Health Services; Main Association of Substance Abuse Programs.

For full biographical listings, see the Martindale-Hubbell Law Directory

PIERCE ATWOOD (AV)

77 Winthrop Street, 04330
Telephone: 207-622-6311
Fax: 207-623-9367
Email: info@PierceAtwood.com *URL:* http://www.pierceatwood.com
Portland, Maine Office: One Monument Square.
Telephone: 207-791-1100.
Fax: 207-791-1350.
Newburyport, Massachusetts Office: 6 Harris Street.
Telephone: 978-465-9599.
Fax: 978-465-9945.

MEMBERS OF FIRM

Warren E. Winslow, Jr.
Malcolm L. Lyons
Michael D. Seitzinger
John C. Nivison

ASSOCIATES

Helen L. Edmonds
Ann M. St. Peter-Griffith

(See Next Column)

COUNSEL

Daniel J. Stevens

For full biographical listings, see the Martindale-Hubbell Law Directory

*BANGOR,** Penobscot Co.

EATON, PEABODY, BRADFORD & VEAGUE, P.A. (AV)

Fleet Center-Exchange Street, P.O. Box 1210, 04402-1210
Telephone: 207-947-0111
Telecopier: 207-942-3040
Email: eaton@eatonpeabody.com *URL:* http://www.eatonpeabody.com
Augusta, Maine Office: 77 Sewall Street, Suite 3000.
Telephone: 207-622-3747.
Telecopier: 207-622-9732.
Blue Hill, Maine Office: One East Blue Hill Road.
Telephone: 207-374-2812.
Telecopier: 207-374-2548.
Brunswick, Maine Office: 167 Park Row.
Telephone: 207-729-1144.
Telecopier: 207-729-1140.
Dover-Foxcroft, Maine Office: 30 East Main Street.
Telephone: 207-564-8378.
Telecopier: 207-564-7059.

Douglas M. Smith (Dover-Foxcroft and Augusta Offices)
Gordon H. S. Scott (Resident, Augusta Office)
William B. Devoe
P. Andrew Hamilton
Roger L. Huber

William V. Ferdinand, Jr. (Resident, Augusta Office)

For Complete List of Firm Personnel, See General Section

For full biographical listings, see the Martindale-Hubbell Law Directory

*PORTLAND,** Cumberland Co.

PIERCE ATWOOD (AV)

One Monument Square, 04101
Telephone: 207-791-1100
Fax: 207-791-1350
Email: info@PierceAtwood.com *URL:* http://www.pierceatwood.com
Augusta, Maine Office: 77 Winthrop Street.
Telephone: 207-622-6311.
Fax: 207-623-9367.
Newburyport, Massachusetts Office: 6 Harris Street.
Telephone: 978-465-9599.
Fax: 978-465-9945.

MEMBERS OF FIRM

John D. Delahanty
Thomas R. Doyle
Philip F. W. Ahrens, III
Kenneth Fairbanks Gray
William E. Taylor
Dixon P. Pike
Matthew D. Manahan

ASSOCIATES

Kate L. Geoffroy
David P. Littell
Helen L. Edmonds (Resident, Augusta Office)
Ande A. Smith

For Complete List of Firm Personnel, See General Section

For full biographical listings, see the Martindale-Hubbell Law Directory

PRETI, FLAHERTY, BELIVEAU, PACHIOS & HALEY, LLC (AV)

One City Center, P.O. Box 9546, 04112-9546
Telephone: 207-791-3000
Telecopier: 207-791-3111
Email: admin@preti.com *URL:* http://www.preti.com
Augusta, Maine Office: 45 Memorial Circle, P.O. Box 1058, 04332-1058.
Telephone: 207-623-5300.
Telefax: 207-623-2914.
Bath, Maine Office: Thirty Front Street, P.O. Box 665, 04530-0665.
Telephone: 207-443-5576.
Telefax: 207-443-6665.

MEMBERS OF FIRM

Severin M. Beliveau (Augusta Office)
Harold C. Pachios
John P. Doyle, Jr.
Bruce C. Gerrity (Augusta Office)
Anthony W. Buxton (Augusta Office)
Virginia E. Davis (Augusta Office)
Estelle A. Lavoie
Joseph G. Donahue (Augusta Office)
David B. Van Slyke
Ann R. Robinson (Augusta Office)
Charles F. Dingman (Augusta Office)
Mark B. LeDuc (Augusta Office)
Jeanne T. Cohn-Connor

ASSOCIATE

Donald J. Sipe (Augusta Office)

Representative Clients: American Insurance Assn.; Industrial Energy Consumer Group; Canadian Pacific Railroad; Bangor Hydro-Electric Co.; Maine Oil Dealers Assn.; American Express; The Hampton Group; Maine Auto Dealers Assn.; Medco Containment Services.

(See Next Column)

PRETI, FLAHERTY, BELIVEAU, PACHIOS & HALEY LLC—*Continued*

For Complete List of Firm Personnel, See General Section

For full biographical listings, see the Martindale-Hubbell Law Directory

VERRILL & DANA, LLP (AV)

One Portland Square, P.O. Box 586, 04112-0586
Telephone: 207-774-4000
Fax: 207-774-7499
Email: advice@verdan.com *URL:* http://www.verdan.com
Augusta, Maine Office: 45 Memorial Circle, P.O. Box 957.
Telephone: 207-623-3889.
Fax: 207-622-3117.
Kennebunk, Maine Office: 403-404 Lafayette Center, P.O. Box 147.
Telephone: 207-985-7193.
Fax: 207-985-3957.
Washington, D.C. Office: 400 North Capitol Street, Suite 585.
Telephone: 202-624-9733.
Fax: 202-393-5218.

OF COUNSEL

Barbara E. Merrill (Resident Of Counsel, Augusta Office)
Peter B. Bickerman (Resident Of Counsel, Augusta Office)

MEMBERS OF FIRM

Andrew M. Horton
William S. Harwood
Beth Dobson
Charles C. Soltan (Resident Partner, Augusta Office)
James I. Cohen

ASSOCIATES

Charles C. Hedrick (Resident Associate, Augusta Office)
Karin L. Larson

For Complete List of Firm Personnel, See General Section

For full biographical listings, see the Martindale-Hubbell Law Directory

MARYLAND

*BALTIMORE,** (Independent City)

FUNK & BOLTON, A PROFESSIONAL ASSOCIATION (AV)

100 Light Street, Suite 1000, 21202
Telephone: 410-659-7700
Facsimile: 410-659-7773
Email: FBLAW@FBLAW.COM
Annapolis, Maryland Office: 191 Main Street, 21401.
Telephone: 410-269-1554.
Facsimile: 410-268-0612.
Chestertown, Maryland Office: 315 High Street, Suite 202, 21620.
Telephone: 410-810-1381.
Facsimile: 410-810-1383.

David M. Funk
Bryson F. Popham (Resident, Annapolis Office)
Lindsey A. Rader
Gary C. Harriger

Ren L. Tundermann
Charles D. MacLeod (Resident, Chestertown Office)

OF COUNSEL

J. Frank Nayden
Deborah R. Rivkin (Resident, Annapolis Office)

For full biographical listings, see the Martindale-Hubbell Law Directory

KAHN, SMITH & COLLINS, P.A. (AV)

201 North Charles Street, 10th Floor, 21201
Telephone: 410-244-1010
Fax: 410-244-8001
URL: http://www.interbit.com/ksc

Andrew H. Kahn
Joel A. Smith
Francis J. Collins
David V. Diggs
Keith J. Zimmerman

Leslie A. Pladna
Sarah Pazourek Harlan
Travis M. Mastroddi
Sabrina Willis

For full biographical listings, see the Martindale-Hubbell Law Directory

REDMOND, BURGIN & GUTIERREZ, P.A. (AV)

1301, The Fidelity Building, 210 North Charles Street, 21202
Telephone: 410-752-1555
Fax: 410-752-1064
URL: http://www.RBGLAW.com
Upper Marlboro, Maryland Office: 14746 Main Street.
Telephone: 301-952-1555.

Leonard C. Redmond, III

(See Next Column)

Mark B. Martin
Joseph I. Tivvis, Jr.

For Complete List of Firm Personnel, See General Section

For full biographical listings, see the Martindale-Hubbell Law Directory

VENABLE ATTORNEYS AT LAW VENABLE, BAETJER AND HOWARD, LLP (AV)

A Partnership including Professional Corporations
1800 Mercantile Bank & Trust Building, 2 Hopkins Plaza, 21201
Telephone: 410-244-7400
Fax: 410-244-7742
URL: http://www.venable.com
Washington, D.C. Office: Venable, Baetjer, Howard & Civiletti LLP, Suite 1000, 1201 New York Avenue, N.W.
Telephone: 202-962-4800.
Fax: 202-962-8300.
McLean, Virginia Office: Suite 400, 2010 Corporate Ridge.
Telephone: 703-760-1600.
Fax: 703-821-8949.
Rockville, Maryland Office: Suite 500, One Church Street, P. O. Box 1906.
Telephone: 301-217-5600.
Fax: 301-217-5617.
Towson, Maryland Office: 210 Allegheny Avenue, P. O. Box 5517.
Telephone: 410-494-6200.
Fax: 410-821-0147.

MEMBERS OF FIRM

Thomas P. Perkins, III (P.C.)
Roger W. Titus (Resident, Rockville, Maryland Office)
Thomas J. Madden (Not admitted in MD; Resident, Washington, D.C. Office)
William L. Walsh, Jr. (P.C.) (Not admitted in MD; Resident, McLean, Virginia Office)
Ronald R. Glancz (Not admitted in MD; Resident, Washington, D.C. Office)
Kenneth C. Bass, III (Not admitted in MD; Washington, D.C. and McLean, Virginia Offices)
Paul F. Strain (P.C.)
Paul T. Glasgow (Resident, Rockville, Maryland Office)
Sondra Harans Block (Resident, Rockville, Maryland Office)
Michael Schatzow (Also at Washington, D.C. Office)
John F. Cooney (Not admitted in MD; Resident, Washington, D.C. Office)
N. Frank Wiggins (Not admitted in MD; Resident, Washington, D.C. Office)
Jeffrey D. Knowles (Not admitted in MD; Resident, Washington, D.C. Office)
John J. Pavlick, Jr. (Not admitted in MD; Resident, Washington, D.C. Office)
M. King Hill, III (Resident, Towson, Maryland Office)
Gary M. Hnath (Resident, Washington, D.C. Office)

OF COUNSEL

Emried D. Cole, Jr.
Judith A. Armold (Also at Washington, D.C. Office)

ASSOCIATES

Paul D. Barker, Jr.
Kevin B. Collins (Also at Rockville, Maryland Office)
James Nicholas Czaban (Not admitted in MD; Resident, Washington, D.C. Office)

For Complete List of Firm Personnel, See General Section

For full biographical listings, see the Martindale-Hubbell Law Directory

*ROCKVILLE,** Montgomery Co.

VENABLE ATTORNEYS AT LAW VENABLE, BAETJER AND HOWARD, LLP (AV)

A Partnership including Professional Corporations
Suite 500, One Church Street, P.O. Box 1906, 20850-4129
Telephone: 301-217-5600
Fax: 301-217-5617
URL: http://www.venable.com
Baltimore, Maryland Office: 1800 Mercantile Bank & Trust Building, 2 Hopkins Plaza.
Telephone: 410-244-7400.
Fax: 410-244-7742.
Washington, D.C. Office: Venable, Baetjer, Howard & Civiletti LLP, Suite 1000, 1201 New York Avenue, N.W.
Telephone: 202-962-4800.
Fax: 202-962-8300.
McLean, Virginia Office: Suite 400, 2010 Corporate Ridge.
Telephone: 703-760-1600.
Fax: 703-821-8949.
Towson, Maryland, Office: 210 Allegheny Avenue, P. O. Box 5517.
Telephone: 410-494-6200.
Fax: 410-821-0147.

MEMBERS OF FIRM

Roger W. Titus
Paul T. Glasgow
Sondra Harans Block

(See Next Column)

VENABLE ATTORNEYS AT LAW VENABLE, BAETJER AND HOWARD, LLP, *Rockville—Continued*

ASSOCIATE

Kevin B. Collins (Also at Baltimore, Maryland Office)

For Complete List of Firm Personnel, See General Section

For full biographical listings, see the Martindale-Hubbell Law Directory

*UPPER MARLBORO,** Prince Georges Co.

KNIGHT, MANZI, NUSSBAUM & LAPLACA, P.C. (AV)

14440 Old Mill Road, 20772
Telephone: 301-952-0100
Annapolis/Baltimore: 410-792-3786
Fax: 301-952-0221

William E. Knight
Robert A. Manzi
Ronald M. Miller
William C. Brennan, Jr.
Harry J. Trainor, Jr.
Andrew W. Nussbaum
Raymond G. LaPlaca
John F. Shay, Jr.
Sheldon L. Gnatt
Daniel A. LaPlaca
Gail Borjeson Viens
Roger C. Thomas
Monica M. Haley-Pierson
Daniel F. Lynch III
Norman D. Rivera

Robert L. Lombardo
Amy B. Glaser
Brent M. Ahalt
Terry L. Bell

Representative Clients: Hyman Bernstein and Son, Inc.; Morrison's Restuarants; First Washington REIT; Evangel Church, Inc.; Carrollton Enterprises; Washington Homes; Southland Corp.

For full biographical listings, see the Martindale-Hubbell Law Directory

MICHIGAN

BLOOMFIELD HILLS, Oakland Co.

DAVID D. PATTON & ASSOCIATES, P.C. (AV)

44 East Long Lake Road, Suite 100, P.O. Box 829, 48303-0829
Telephone: 248-258-6020
Fax: 248-258-6052
Email: litigation@aol.com *URL:* http://www.lawyers.com/dpattonlaw

David D. Patton

Ellen Bartman Jannette
Patricia C. White
Humma S. Siddiqi
Kelly P. Bekolay
David H. Patton (1912-1993)

OF COUNSEL

Lawrence J. Acker

For full biographical listings, see the Martindale-Hubbell Law Directory

*DETROIT,** Wayne Co.

BODMAN, LONGLEY & DAHLING LLP (AV)

34th Floor 100 Renaissance Center, 48243
Telephone: 313-259-7777
Fax: 313-393-7579
Email: info@bodmanlongley.com *URL:* http://www.bodmanlongley.com
Troy, Michigan Office: Suite 2020, 755 West Big Beaver Road.
Telephone: 248-362-2110.
Fax: 248-244-0780.
Ann Arbor, Michigan Office: 110 Miller, Suite 300.
Telephone: 734-761-3780.
Fax: 734-930-2494.
Northern Michigan Office: 229 Court Street, P.O. Box 405, Cheboygan.
Telephone: 231-627-4351.
Fax: 231-627-2802.

MEMBERS OF FIRM

Richard D. Rohr
Thomas A. Roach (Ann Arbor Office)
James A. Smith
James J. Walsh
Charles N. Raimi
F. Thomas Lewand
Jerold Lax (Ann Arbor Office)
Sandra L. Sorini (Ann Arbor Office)

Representative Clients: Archdiocese of Detroit; Comerica Bank; The Detroit Lions, Inc.; Ford Estates; Lear Corp.; Charles Stewart Mott Foundation; Norfolk Southern Corporation; Panhandle Eastern Corporation; State Farm Insurance Companies.

For Complete List of Firm Personnel, See General Section

For full biographical listings, see the Martindale-Hubbell Law Directory

BRADY, HATHAWAY, BRADY & BRETZ, PROFESSIONAL CORPORATION (AV)

1330 Buhl Building, 48226-3602
Telephone: 313-965-3700
Telecopier: 313-965-2830
Email: brady@bradyhathaway.com

John F. Brady
Thomas M. J. Hathaway
Thomas P. Brady
Daniel J. Bretz
Connie M. Cessante
David A. Hardesty
Paul W. Coughenour
Jeffrey A. Steele
Tracy A. Leahy

David M. Cessante

Representative Clients: Beam Stream, Inc.; Bundy Corporation; Energy Conversion Devices, Inc.; Schering Corporation; Warner-Lambert; Wolverine Technologies; ABB Environmental Services.

For full biographical listings, see the Martindale-Hubbell Law Directory

BUTZEL LONG, A PROFESSIONAL CORPORATION (AV)

Suite 900, 150 West Jefferson, 48226
Telephone: 313-225-7000
Telecopier: 313-225-7080
Email: melnick@butzel.com *URL:* http://www.butzel.com
Birmingham, Michigan Office: Suite 200, 32270 Telegraph Road.
Telephone: 810-258-1616.
Telecopier: 810-258-1439.
Okemos, Michigan Office: Suite 300, 2127 University Park Drive.
Telephone: 517-372-6622.
Telecopier: 517-372-6672.
Ann Arbor, Michigan Office: Suite 300, 350 South Main Street.
Telephone: 313-995-3110.
Telecopier: 313-995-1777.
Grosse Pointe Farms, Michigan Office: Suite 260, 21 Kercheval.
Telephone: 313-886-5446.
Telecopier: 313-886-2114.
Boca Raton, Florida Office: Suite 411, 1200 North Federal Highway.
Telephone: 561-368-2151.
Telecopier: 561-368-4668.
Palm Beach Gardens, Florida Office: Suite 227, 11382 Prosperity Farms Road.
Telephone: 561-625-4442.
Telecopier: 561-625-6901.
Naples, Florida Office: Suite 705, 801 Laurel Oak Drive.
Telephone: 941-597-4500.
Telecopier: 941-597-5623.

Robert J. Battista
John P. Hancock, Jr.
Leonard F. Charla
James C. Bruno
Carl Rashid, Jr.
Robert A. Boonin
Melvin J. Hollowell, Jr.
Taylor C. Segue, III
James J. Urban (Okemos)

SENIOR ATTORNEYS

Max R. Hoffman, Jr. (Okemos)
Thomas L. Sparks (Okemos)

Michael F. Matheson (Okemos)

Representative Clients: Bridgestone/Firestone, Inc.; The Detroit News, Inc.; Kelly Services; Merrill Lynch & Co., Inc.; Mt. Clemens General Hospital; Stroh Companies; Takata Corp.; TRW Automotive; The University of Michigan; William Beaumont Hospital.

For full biographical listings, see the Martindale-Hubbell Law Directory

CLARK HILL PLC (AV)

500 Woodward Avenue, Suite 3500, 48226-3435
Telephone: 313-965-8300
Facsimile: 313-965-8252
Email: email@clarkhill.com *URL:* http://www.clarkhill.com
Birmingham, Michigan Office: 255 S. Old Woodward Avenue, Third Floor 48009-6179.
Telephone: 248-642-9692.
Facsimile: 248-642-2174.
Okemos, Michigan Office: 2455 Woodlake Circle, 48864-5941.
Telephone: 517-381-9193.
Facsimile: 517-381-0268.

Douglas H. West (Resident, Birmingham Office)
Roderick S. Coy (Resident, Lansing Office)
Robert A. W. Strong (Resident, Birmingham Office)
Charles H. Polzin (Resident, Birmingham Office)
Dorothy Hanigan Basmaji (Resident, Birmingham Office)

OF COUNSEL

Richard C. Marsh

(See Next Column)

CLARK HILL PLC—*Continued*

Robert A. LeFevre (Resident, Lansing Office)
Haran C. Rashes (Resident, Lansing Office)

Representative Clients: Booth Communications, Inc.; LCI International Telecom Corp.; Daimler Chrysler; Ford Motor Co.; General Motors Corp.; National Steel Corp.

For Complete List of Firm Personnel, See General Section

For full biographical listings, see the Martindale-Hubbell Law Directory

---

LANSING, Ingham Co.

HOWARD & HOWARD ATTORNEYS, P.C. (AV)

The Phoenix Building, Suite 500, 222 Washington Square, North, 48933-1817
Telephone: 517-485-1483
Telecopier: 517-485-1568
Kalamazoo, Michigan Office: The Michigan Building, Suite 200, 100 Portage Street.
Telephone: 616-382-1483.
Telecopier: 616-382-1568.
Bloomfield Hills, Michigan Office: The Pinehurst Office Center, Suite 101, 1400 North Woodward Avenue.
Telephone: 248-645-1483.
Telecopier: 248-645-1568.
Peoria, Illinois Office: One Technology Plaza, Suite 600, 211 Fulton Street.
Telephone: 309-672-1483.
Telecopier: 309-672-1568.

Stewart A. Binke
Michael J. Brown

Representative Clients: National City Corp.; Kmart Corp.; DaimlerChrysler Corporation; CSX Transportation, Inc.

For Complete List of Firm Personnel, See General Section

For full biographical listings, see the Martindale-Hubbell Law Directory

---

OKEMOS, Ingham Co.

BUTZEL LONG, A PROFESSIONAL CORPORATION (AV)

Suite 300, 2127 University Park Drive, 48864-5928
Telephone: 517-372-6622
Telecopier: 517-372-6672
Email: melnick@butzel.com *URL:* http://www.butzel.com
Detroit, Michigan Office: Suite 900, 150 West Jefferson.
Telephone: 313-225-7000.
Telecopier: 313-225-7080.
Birmingham, Michigan Office: Suite 200, 32270 Telegraph Road.
Telephone: 810-258-1616.
Telecopier: 810-258-1439.
Ann Arbor, Michigan Office: Suite 300, 350 South Main Street.
Telephone: 313-995-3110.
Telecopier: 313-995-1777.
Grosse Pointe Farms, Michigan Office: Suite 260, 21 Kercheval.
Telephone: 313-886-5446.
Telecopier: 313-886-2114.
Boca Raton, Florida Office: Suite 411, 1200 North Federal Highway.
Telephone: 561-368-2151.
Telecopier: 561-368-4668.
Palm Beach Gardens, Florida Office: Suite 227, 11382 Prosperity Farms Road.
Telephone: 561-625-4442.
Telecopier: 561-625-6901.
Naples, Florida Office: Suite 705, 801 Laurel Oak Drive.
Telephone: 941-597-4500.
Telecopier: 941-597-5623.

James J. Urban

SENIOR ATTORNEYS

Max R. Hoffman, Jr.
Thomas L. Sparks

Michael F. Matheson

For full biographical listings, see the Martindale-Hubbell Law Directory

ADMIRALTY/MARITIME LAW

ALABAMA

*BIRMINGHAM,** Jefferson Co.

PITTMAN, HOOKS, DUTTON & HOLLIS, P.C. (AV)

1100 Park Place Tower, 35203
Telephone: 205-322-8880
Telecopier: 205-328-2711
Email: PHDH@4theplaintiff.com

W. Lee Pittman
Kenneth W. Hooks
Tom Dutton
L. Andrew Hollis, Jr.
Jeffrey C. Kirby
Ralph Bohanan, Jr.

Chris T. Hellums
Keith T. Belt, Jr.
Leigh King Forstman
Michael C. Bradley
Page Poerschke Liddon
Steven William Couch
J. Chris Cochran

OF COUNSEL

James H. Davis (Not admitted in AL)
Lynn A. Crosson

For full biographical listings, see the Martindale-Hubbell Law Directory

*MOBILE,** Mobile Co.

ARMBRECHT, JACKSON, DEMOUY, CROWE, HOLMES & REEVES, L.L.C. (AV)

1300 Riverview Plaza, P.O. Box 290, 36601
Telephone: 334-405-1300
Facsimile: 334-432-6843; 433-3821
Email: adc@ajlaw.com

MEMBERS OF FIRM

Rae M. Crowe
Broox G. Holmes
W. Boyd Reeves
E. B. Peebles III
Grover E. Asmus II
Douglas L. Brown
Donald C. Radcliff
Christopher I. Gruenewald
M. Kathleen Miller
Scott G. Brown

ASSOCIATES

P. Vincent Gaddy
J. Walton Jackson

Representative Clients: Cove Shipping Co.; Warrior & Gulf Navigation Co.; Cooper/T. Smith Co., Inc.; Strachan Shipping Co.; Mobile River Terminal; National Marine, Inc.; ProMar Insurance Co.; Stevedoring Services of America.

For Complete List of Firm Personnel, See General Section

For full biographical listings, see the Martindale-Hubbell Law Directory

CUNNINGHAM, BOUNDS, YANCE, CROWDER & BROWN, L.L.C. (AV)

1601 Dauphin Street, P.O. Box 66705, 36660
Telephone: 334-471-6191
Fax: 334-479-1031
Email: adm@cbycb.com

James A. Yance
John T. Crowder, Jr.
Robert T. Cunningham, Jr.
Joseph M. Brown, Jr.
Gregory B. Breedlove
Michael A. Worel
David G. Wirtes, Jr.
Toby D. Brown
Reggie Copeland, Jr.
Richard T. Dorman

J. Stephen Legg
George M. Dent, III

OF COUNSEL

Richard Bounds
Robert T. Cunningham
J. Kenyon Rainer, Sr., M.D., J.D.

References: Regions Bank; AmSouth Bank, N.A.

For full biographical listings, see the Martindale-Hubbell Law Directory

JOHNSTONE, ADAMS, BAILEY, GORDON AND HARRIS, L.L.C. (AV)

Royal St. Francis Building, 104 St. Francis Street, 8th Floor, P.O. Box 1988, 36633
Telephone: 334-432-7682
Facsimile: 334-432-0712 or 334-432-2800
Email: attorneys@JohnstoneAdams.com *URL:* http://www.JohnstoneAdams.com
Bay Minette, Alabama Office: Dahlberg Building, 107 Hand Avenue, P.O. Box 729, 36507.
Telephone: 334-937-9473.
Facsimile: 334-937-9475.

(See Next Column)

MEMBERS OF FIRM

Joseph M. Allen, Jr.
Thomas S. Rue
Alan C. Christian
E. Erich Bergdolt

For Complete List of Firm Personnel, See General Section

For full biographical listings, see the Martindale-Hubbell Law Directory

LYONS, PIPES & COOK, P.C. (AV)

2 North Royal Street, P.O. Box 2727, 36652-2727
Telephone: 334-432-4481
Cable Address: "Lysea"
Telecopier: 334-433-1820
URL: http://www.LPCLaw.com

Wesley Pipes
Marion A. Quina, Jr.
Walter M. Cook, Jr.
Allen E. Graham

General Counsel: Alabama State Docks Department (an agency of the State of Alabama); Southern Steamship Agency, Inc.
Counsel: McKenzie Tank Lines, Inc.; SCNO Barge Lines, Inc.; Scott Paper Co.; Shell Oil Corp.
Trial Counsel: Aetna Life and Casualty Co.; Chubb Group of Insurance Companies.

For Complete List of Firm Personnel, See General Section

For full biographical listings, see the Martindale-Hubbell Law Directory

PIERCE, LEDYARD, LATTA & WASDEN, P.C. (AV)

Colonial Bank Centre Suite 400, 41 North Beltline, 36608
Telephone: 334-344-5151
Facsimile: 334-344-9696
Mailing Address: P.O. Box 16046, Mobile, AL, 36616
URL: http://www.pllaw.com

Abe L. Philips, Jr.
H. William Wasden
A. Lewis Philips, III

Mark Pickett Eiland
Jeffrey U. Beaverstock

Representative Clients: American Steamship Owners Mutual Protection & Indemnity Association, Inc.; Atlantic Marine/Alabama Shipyard; Assuranceforeningen Gard; Assuranceforeningen Skuld; The Britannia Steamship Insurance Association Ltd.; The Japan Ship Owners' Mutual Protection and Indemnity Association; Liverpool and London Protection and Indemnity Association Ltd.; The Steamship Mutual Underwriting Association (Bermuda), Ltd.; The Swedish P&I Club; The United Kingdom Mutual Steam Ship Assurance Association (Bermuda) Ltd.

For full biographical listings, see the Martindale-Hubbell Law Directory

VICKERS, RIIS, MURRAY AND CURRAN, L.L.C. (AV)

8th Floor, Regions Bank Building, 106 Saint Francis Street, P.O. Box 2568, 36652
Telephone: 334-432-9772
Fax: 334-432-9781
Email: vickersriis.com

MEMBERS OF FIRM

J. Manson Murray
J. W. Goodloe, Jr.
Thomas E. Sharp, III
J. Marshall Gardner
C. Richard Wilkins

Representative Clients: Midstream Fuel Service, Inc.; Steiner Shipyard, Inc.; Marine Office of America Corp.; Murray Stevedoring Co., Inc.; Caterpillar Financial Services, Incorporated; McElroy Machine & Manufacturing Co., Inc.; Cummins Engine Company; Ocean Marine, Inc.

For Complete List of Firm Personnel, See General Section

For full biographical listings, see the Martindale-Hubbell Law Directory

CALIFORNIA

LONG BEACH, Los Angeles Co.

LAW OFFICES OF JAMES H. ACKERMAN (AV)

Suite 1440, One World Trade Center, 90831-1440
Telephone: 562-436-9911
Cable Address: "Jimack"
Telecopier: 562-436-1897

References: Farmers and Merchants Bank (Long Beach Main Office); California Bank and Trust (Long Beach Main Office).

For full biographical listings, see the Martindale-Hubbell Law Directory

Long Beach—Continued

BAKER & HOSTETLER LLP (AV)

300 Oceangate, Suite 620, 90802-6807
Telephone: 562-432-2827
FAX: 562-432-6698
To contact an attorney on the Internet use first initial and surname followed by @baker-hostetler.com
URL: http://www.bakerlaw.com
In Cleveland, Ohio: 3200 National City Center, 1900 East Ninth Street.
Telephone: 216-621-0200.
In Cincinnati, Ohio: 312 Walnut Street, Suite 2650.
Telephone: 513-929-3400.
In Columbus, Ohio: Capitol Square, Suite 2100, 65 East State Street.
Telephone: 614-228-1541.
In Denver, Colorado: 303 East 17th Avenue, Suite 1100.
Telephone: 303-861-0600.
In Houston, Texas: 1000 Louisiana, Suite 2000.
Telephone: 713-751-1600.
In Los Angeles, California: 600 Wilshire Boulevard.
Telephone: 213-624-2400.
In Orlando, Florida: SunBank Center, Suite 2300, 200 South Orange Avenue.
Telephone: 407-649-4000.
In Washington, D. C.: Washington Square, Suite 1100, 1050 Connecticut Avenue, N.W.
Telephone: 202-861-1500.

PARTNER IN CHARGE

Robert E. Coppola (Partner in Charge)

PARTNER

Christina L. Owen

For Complete List of Firm Personnel, See General Section

For full biographical listings, see the Martindale-Hubbell Law Directory

COGSWELL NAKAZAWA & CHANG (AV)

115 Pine Avenue, Suite 600, 90802-4449
Telephone: 562-951-8668
Fax: 562-951-3933
Email: cnclaw@earthlink.net

Forrest R. Cogswell

PARTNERS

Alan Nakazawa
Peiwen Chang
B. Alexander Moghaddam

ASSOCIATES

Thomas H. Van Horn
Richard J. Nikas
Thomas C. Jorgensen
Theodore W. Frank

For full biographical listings, see the Martindale-Hubbell Law Directory

FLYNN, DELICH & WISE (AV)

One World Trade Center, Suite 1800, 90831-1800
Telephone: 562-435-2626
Fax: 562-437-7555
Email: NicholasP@FDW-LAW.COM
San Francisco, California Office: One California Street, Suite 350.
Telephone: 415-693-5566.
Fax: 415-693-0410. Email: SAMD@FDW-LAW.COM

Erich P. Wise
Nicholas S. Politis
Sook H. Lee

LEGAL SUPPORT PERSONNEL

Denise C. Orr (Legal Assistant)

Representative Clients: American Hawaii Cruises; American President Lines; Through Transport Mutual Insurance Association, Ltd.; The Britannia Steam Ship Insurance Association Limited; The Steamship Mutual Underwriting Association (Bermuda) Ltd.; General Steamship Corp., Ltd.; Commodore Cruise Line, Ltd.; Interocean Steamship Corporation; Sea-Land Service, Inc.; Hatteras Yachts.

For full biographical listings, see the Martindale-Hubbell Law Directory

MOORE, RUTTER & EVANS (AV)

A Partnership including a Professional Corporation
555 East Ocean Boulevard, Suite 500, 90802-5090
Telephone: 562-435-4499
Facsimile: 562-495-4299
Email: mrelaw@gte.net *URL:* http://www.lawyers.com/moorerutter&evans
Huntington Beach, California Office: 2120 Main Street, Suite 250, 92648.
Telephone: 714-374-3333.
Fax: 714-374-9395

RESIDENT PARTNERS

Neal Moore
Mark D. Rutter
William D. Evans (P.C.)

(See Next Column)

OF COUNSEL

Michael J. Emling

For full biographical listings, see the Martindale-Hubbell Law Directory

RUSSELL & MIRKOVICH (AV)

One World Trade Center, Suite 1450, 90831-1450
Telephone: 562-436-9911
FAX: 562-436-1897
Email: counsel@russell-mirkovich.com

Carlton E. Russell
Joseph N. Mirkovich

ASSOCIATE

Margaret E. Morrow
Steven Y. Otera

For full biographical listings, see the Martindale-Hubbell Law Directory

WOOLLEY RUSSELL & JOHNSON (AV)

444 West Ocean Boulevard, Suite 1700, 90802
Telephone: 562-495-6000
Telecopier: 562-435-1359
Email: mail@transportlawyers.com *URL:* http://www.transportlawyers.com
Port Hueneme, California Office: 105 East Port Hueneme Road, 93041.
Telephone: 562-495-6000.
Fax: 562-435-1359.

MEMBERS OF FIRM

David E. R. Woolley
Thomas A. Russell
Philip L. Johnson

ASSOCIATE

Thomas G. Walsh

LEGAL SUPPORT PERSONNEL

PARALEGAL

Dawn C. Breaux

For full biographical listings, see the Martindale-Hubbell Law Directory

*LOS ANGELES,** Los Angeles Co.

BAKER & HOSTETLER LLP (AV)

600 Wilshire Boulevard, 90017-3212
Telephone: 213-624-2400
FAX: 213-975-1740
To contact an attorney on the Internet use first initial and surname followed by @baker-hostetler.com
URL: http://www.bakerlaw.com
In Cleveland, Ohio: 3200 National City Center, 1900 East Ninth Street.
Telephone: 216-621-0200.
In Cincinnati, Ohio: 312 Walnut Street, Suite 2650.
Telephone: 513-929-3400.
In Columbus, Ohio: Capitol Square, Suite 2100, 65 East State Street.
Telephone: 614-228-1541.
In Denver, Colorado: 303 East 17th Avenue, Suite 1100.
Telephone: 303-861-0600.
In Houston, Texas: 1000 Louisiana, Suite 2000.
Telephone: 713-751-1600.
In Long Beach, California: 300 Oceangate, Suite 620.
Telephone: 562-432-2827.
In Orlando, Florida: SunBank Center, Suite 2300, 200 South Orange Avenue.
Telephone: 407-649-4000.
In Washington, D. C.: Washington Square, Suite 1100, 1050 Connecticut Avenue, N.W.
Telephone: 202-861-1500.

Edward J. McCutchen (1857-1933)
Harold A. Black (1895-1970)
George Harnagel (1903-1962)
G. William Shea (1911-1986)

OFFICE MANAGING PARTNER

Peter W. James (Managing Partner, Los Angeles and Long Beach, California Offices)

PARTNERS

Angela C. Agrusa
Patrick J. Cain
Penny M. Costa
Richard A. Deeb
David A. Destino
Gary L. Gilbert
Jonathan R. Hodes
Thomas G. Roberts
Jack I. Samet
David C. Sampson
Bill E. Schroeder
Glen A. Smith
Teresa R. Tracy

ASSOCIATES

Kathleen E. Bailey
Megan E. Gray
Nigel E. Jacques
Andrew Lurie
Brian A. Ross
Wendy E. Stanford
Marcos M. Tarango
Kimberly R. Wells
Cranston J. Williams

OF COUNSEL

Lisa F. Hinchliffe

(See Next Column)

BAKER & HOSTETLER LLP—*Continued*

RETIRED PARTNERS

G. Richard Doty Howard J. Privett

For full biographical listings, see the Martindale-Hubbell Law Directory

KAYE, ROSE & PARTNERS, LLP (AV)

A Law Partnership
1801 Century Park East, #1250, 90067-2302
Telephone: 310-277-1200
Fax: 310-277-1220
Telex: 371-7740
Email: la@kayerose.com *URL:* http://www.kayerose.com
San Diego Office: Emerald Plaza, 402 West Broadway, 21st Floor.
Telephone: 619-232-6555.
Fax: 619-232-6577.
San Francisco Office: One California Street, Suite 2230
Telephone: 415-433-6555.
Fax: 415-433-6577.
Miami, Florida Office: One Biscayne Tower, 2 South Biscayne Boulevard, Suite 2300.
Telephone: 305-358-6555.
Fax: 305-374-9077.

PARTNERS

Lawrence W. Kaye Bradley M. Rose
Anita M. Eilert

ASSOCIATES

Elsa M. Ward Marva Jo Wyatt

For full biographical listings, see the Martindale-Hubbell Law Directory

OSTROVE, KRANTZ & OSTROVE, A PROFESSIONAL CORPORATION (AV)

(Successor To: Ostrove and Lancer, A Professional Corporation; David Ostrove, A Professional Corporation)
5757 Wilshire Boulevard, Suite 535, 90036-3600
Telephone: 323-939-3400
Fax: 323-939-3500
Email: OSTROVE@AOL.COM *URL:* http://www.lawyers.com/ok&olaw

David Ostrove David S. Krantz
Kenneth E. Ostrove

Reference: First Business Bank.

For full biographical listings, see the Martindale-Hubbell Law Directory

PILLSBURY MADISON & SUTRO LLP (AV)

Citicorp Plaza, 725 South Figueroa Street, Suite 1200, 90017-5443
Telephone: 213-488-7100
Fax: 213-629-1033
Email: pillsburylaw.com *URL:* http://pillsburylaw.com
Costa Mesa, California Office: 650 Town Center Drive, 7th Floor, 92626.
Telephone: 714-436-6800.
Fax: 714-436-2800.
Silicon Valley Office: 2550 Hanover Street, Palo Alto, 94034.
Telephone: 650-233-4500.
Fax: 650-233-4545.
Sacramento, California Office: 400 Capitol Mall, Suite 1700, 95814.
Telephone: 916-329-4700.
Fax: 916-441-3583.
San Diego, California Office: 101 West Broadway, Suite 1800, 92101.
Telephone: 619-234-5000.
Fax: 619-236-1995.
San Francisco, California Office: 50 Fremont Street, 94105.
Telephone: 415-983-1000.
Fax: 415-983-1200.
Washington, D.C. Office: 1100 New York Avenue, N.W., Ninth Floor, 20005.
Telephone: 202-861-3000.
Fax: 202-822-0944.
Vienna, Virginia Office: 8330 Boone Boulevard, Suite 400, 22182.
Telephone: 703-744-7600.
Fax: 703-744-7605.
New York, New York Office: 375 Park Avenue, Suite 3108, 10152.
Telephone: 212-826-1060.
Fax: 212-826-9255. One Liberty Plaza, 165 Broadway, 51st Floor.
Telephone: 212-374-1890.
Fax: 212-374-1852.
Tokyo, Japan Office: Pillsbury Madison & Sutro, Gaikokuho Jimu Bengoshi Jimusho, 5th Floor, Samon Eleven Building, 3-1, Samon-cho, Shinjuku-ku, Tokyo 160 Japan.
Telephone: 800-729-9830; 011-813-3354-3531.
Fax: 011-813-3354-3534.

MEMBER OF FIRM

Lawrence D. Bradley, Jr.

For Complete List of Firm Personnel, See General Section

For full biographical listings, see the Martindale-Hubbell Law Directory

*SAN DIEGO,** San Diego Co.

DOUGHERTY, HILDRE, DUDEK & HAKLAR (AV)

2550 Fifth Avenue, Suite 600, 92103-5624
Telephone: 619-232-9131
Telefax: 619-232-7317
Email: Douhil@aol.com

William O. Dougherty Frederick M. Dudek
Donald F. Hildre Thomas D. Haklar

For full biographical listings, see the Martindale-Hubbell Law Directory

KAYE, ROSE & PARTNERS, LLP (AV)

A Law Partnership
Emerald Plaza, 402 West Broadway, 21st Floor, 92101
Telephone: 619-232-6555
Fax: 619-232-6577
Email: sd@kayerose.com *URL:* http://www.kayerose.com
Los Angeles Office: 1801 Century Park East, Suite 1250.
Telephone: 310-277-1200.
Fax: 310-277-1220.
San Francisco Office: One California Street, Suite 2230.
Telephone: 415-433-6555.
Fax: 415-433-6577.
Miami, Florida Office: One Biscayne Tower, 2 South Biscayne Boulevard, Suite 2300.
Telephone: 305-358-6555.
Fax: 305-374-9077.

PARTNERS

Lawrence W. Kaye Anita M. Eilert
William J. Tucker

ASSOCIATES

Laurel L. Barry Lisa Marie Conner

For full biographical listings, see the Martindale-Hubbell Law Directory

PILLSBURY MADISON & SUTRO LLP (AV)

101 West Broadway, Suite 1800, 92101-8219
Telephone: 619-234-5000
FAX: 619-236-1995
Email: pillsburylaw.com *URL:* http://pillsburylaw.com
Costa Mesa, California Office: 650 Town Center Drive, 7th Floor, 92626.
Telephone: 714-436-6800.
Fax: 714-436-2800.
Los Angeles, California Office: Citicorp Plaza, 725 South Figueroa, Suite 1200, 90017.
Telephone: 213-488-7100.
Fax: 213-629-1033.
New York, New York Office: 375 Park Avenue, Suite 3108, 10152.
Telephone: 212-826-1060.
Fax: 212-826-9255.
Silicon Valley Office: 2550 Hanover Street, Palo Alto, 94034.
Telephone: 650-233-4500.
Fax: 650-233-4545.
Sacramento, California Office: 400 Capitol Mall, Suite 1700, 95814.
Telephone: 916-329-4700.
Fax: 916-441-3583.
San Francisco, California Office: 50 Fremont Street, 94105.
Telephone: 415-983-1000.
Fax: 415-983-1200.
Washington, D.C. Office: 1100 New York Avenue, N.W., Ninth Floor, 20005.
Telephone: 202-861-3000.
Fax: 202-822-0944.
Vienna, Virginia Office: 8330 Boone Boulevard, Suite 400, 22182.
Telephone: 703-744-7600.
Fax: 703-744-7605.
Tokyo, Japan Office: Pillsbury Madison & Sutro, Gaikokuho Jimu Bengoshi Jimusho, 5th Floor, Samon Eleven Building, 3-1, Samon-cho, Shinjuku-ku, Tokyo 160 Japan.
Telephone: 800-729-9830; 011-813-3354-3531.
Fax: 011-813-3354-3534.

MEMBER OF FIRM

Daniel C. Minteer

For Complete List of Firm Personnel, See General Section

For full biographical listings, see the Martindale-Hubbell Law Directory

*SAN FRANCISCO,** San Francisco Co.

PHILIP A. FANT (AV Ⓣ)

88 Kearny Street, Suite 1000, 94108-5530
Telephone: 415-982-2006
FAX: 415-393-8087
Email: pfant@inreach.com

For full biographical listings, see the Martindale-Hubbell Law Directory

San Francisco—Continued

FLYNN, DELICH & WISE (AV)

One California Street, Suite 350, 94111
Telephone: 415-693-5566
Fax: 415-693-0410
Email: SamD@fdw-law.com
Long Beach, California Office: 1 World Trade Center, Suite 1800.
Telephone: 562-435-2626.
Fax: 562-437-7555. Email: NicholasP@FDW-LAW.COM.

John A. Flynn (1945-1997)
Sam D. Delich
James B. Nebel

OF COUNSEL

Pecos Bill Field

Faye Lee Peterson
Conte C. Cicala
Jeanine S. Tede

Representative Clients: American Hawaii Cruises; American President Lines; Through Transport Mutual Insurance Association, Ltd.; The Britannia Steam Ship Insurance Association Limited; The Steamship Mutual Underwriting Association (Bermuda) Ltd.; General Steamship Corp., Ltd.; Commodore Cruise Line, Ltd.; Interocean Steamship Corporation; Sea-Land Service, Inc.; Hatteras Yachts.

For full biographical listings, see the Martindale-Hubbell Law Directory

GRAHAM & JAMES LLP (AV)

One Maritime Plaza, Suite 300, 94111
Telephone: 415-954-0200
Telecopier: 415-391-2493
Email: twoofter@gj.com *URL:* http://www.gj.com
Other offices located in: Los Angeles, Orange County, Palo Alto and Sacramento California; Seattle, Washington; Washington, D.C.; New York, New York; Milan, Italy; Beijing, China; Tokyo, Japan; London, England.
Associated Offices: Deacons Graham & James, Hong Kong, Sydney, Melbourne, Brisbane, Perth and Canberra, Australia.
Affiliated Offices: Deacons Graham & James, Hanoi and Ho Chi Minh City, Vietnam; Taipei, Taiwan and Bangkok, Thailand; In association with Dewi Soeharto & Rekan, Jakarta, Indonesia; Graham & James in affiliation with Taylor Joynson Garrett, London, England, Bucharest, Romania and Brussels, Belgium; Kau, Dusseldorf, Germany; Mishare M. Al-Ghazali & Partners, Safat, Kuwait; Law Firm of Salah Al-Hejailan, Jeddah and Riyadh, Saudi Arabia; Yeo Wee Kiong & Partners, Singapore.

Maureen Bennett
Mitsuru Claire Chino
Mark C. Dosker
Diane L. Gibson
David C. Kenny
Nathan Lane III
Michael D. Levin
David M. Lofholm
Caroline H. Mead
Michael R. Moyle
David M. Niebauer
Rodney R. Patula
Noriyuki Shimoda
Nicholas Unkovic
Thomas H. Woofter
Philip R. Zender

OF COUNSEL

Alexander D. Calhoun

ASSOCIATES

P. Craig Cardon
Priscilla J. Cortez
Melissa E. Davidson
Matthew Dickstein (Not admitted in CA)
Quoc-Huy D. Do
Darryl E. Hendrix
Achim W. Hoelzle
Caren Jenkins
Remsen M. Kinne, IV
Richard MacBride
Joseph Meckes
Catharina Yoosun Min
Ayako Onoda
Lisa Palter
Serafina Sands
Constance J. Yu

For full biographical listings, see the Martindale-Hubbell Law Directory

KAYE, ROSE & PARTNERS, LLP (AV)

A Law Partnership
One California Street, Suite 2230, 94111
Telephone: 415-433-6555
Fax: 415-433-6577
Email: sf@kayerose.com *URL:* http://www.kayerose.com
Los Angeles Office: 1801 Century Park East, Suite 1250.
Telephone: 310-277-1200.
Fax: 310-277-1220.
San Diego Office: Emerald Plaza, 402 West Broadway, 21st Floor.
Telephone: 619-232-6555.
Fax: 619-232-6577.
Miami, Florida Office: One Biscayne Tower, 2 South Biscayne Boulevard, Suite 2300.
Telephone: 305-358-6555.
Fax: 305-374-9077.

PARTNERS

James J. Tamulski
Wayne F. Emard
Eric M. Danoff
Andrew I. Port

(See Next Column)

ASSOCIATES

Louise S. Livingston
Cheryl A. Morris
Patti J. Urbanec
Robert M. Forni, Jr.
Charles Andrew Dirksen

For full biographical listings, see the Martindale-Hubbell Law Directory

MCGUINN, HILLSMAN & PALEFSKY, A PROFESSIONAL CORPORATION (AV)

535 Pacific Avenue, 94133
Telephone: 415-421-9292
Fax: 415-403-0202

John A. McGuinn
John R. Hillsman
Cliff Palefsky
Derek B. Jacobson
Keith A. Ehrman

Sharon R. Vinick

For full biographical listings, see the Martindale-Hubbell Law Directory

LAW OFFICES OF GEORGE W. NOWELL (AV)

120 Montgomery Street Suite 1900, 94104-4322
Telephone: 415-362-1333
Fax: 415-362-1344
Email: Nowelllaw@aol.com

Paul B. Arenas

For full biographical listings, see the Martindale-Hubbell Law Directory

TEHIN +PARTNERS, A PROFESSIONAL CORPORATION (AV)

Bank of America Center, 555 California Street, 33rd Floor, 94104-1609
Telephone: 415-951-8800
Fax: 415-951-8808
URL: http://www.tehin.com

Nikolai Tehin
Pamela J. Stevens
Reilly Atkinson, IV
Michael E. Brown
Bita Abdollahi

For full biographical listings, see the Martindale-Hubbell Law Directory

CONNECTICUT

STAMFORD, Fairfield Co.

HEALY & BAILLIE, LLP (AV㉦)

Stamford Harbor Park, 333 Ludlow Street, 06902-6987
Telephone: 203-961-7250
Telecopier: 203-357-7909
Email: reception@healy.com *URL:* http://www.healy.com
New York, N.Y. Office: 29 Broadway, 10006-3293.
Telephone: 212-943-3980.
Telecopier: 212-425-0131. Email: reception@healy.com.
Hong Kong Office: Healy & Baillie, Suite 1303, Dina House, Ruttonjee Centre, 11 Duddell Street, Central.
Telephone: 852-2537-8628.
Telecopier: 852-2521-9072. Email: gryu@healy.com.hk.

RESIDENT PARTNER

John W. Wall

For full biographical listings, see the Martindale-Hubbell Law Directory

STRATFORD, Fairfield Co.

LAW OFFICES OF ROBERT K. MARZIK, P.C. (AV)

1512 Main Street, 06615-7097
Telephone: 203-375-4803
Telecopier: 203-386-0136
Email: marzikr@aol.com
New York, New York Office: 120 East 41st Street.
Telephone: 212-683-2805.

Robert K. Marzik

For full biographical listings, see the Martindale-Hubbell Law Directory

DISTRICT OF COLUMBIA

WASHINGTON, D.C. Co.

BASTIANELLI, BROWN & KELLEY, CHARTERED (AV)

Two Lafayette Centre, 1133 21st Street, N.W., Suite 500, 20036
Telephone: 202-293-8815
Telecopier: 202-293-7994
Email: bbk@govconlaw.com *URL:* http://www.govconlaw.com

James A. Kelley
George W. Stiffler

Lori Ann Lange

OF COUNSEL

H. Clayton Cook, Jr.

For full biographical listings, see the Martindale-Hubbell Law Directory

H. CLAYTON COOK, JR. (AV)

Two Lafayette Centre, 1133 21st Street, N.W., Suite 500, 20036
Telephone: 202-293-8815
Facsimile: 202-293-7994
Email: PlimsollDC@aol.com
(Also Of Counsel, Bastianelli, Brown & Kelley, Chartered)

For full biographical listings, see the Martindale-Hubbell Law Directory

HOPPEL, MAYER & COLEMAN (AV)

1000 Connecticut Avenue, N.W., Suite 400, 20036
Telephone: 202-296-5460
Telecopier: 202-296-5463
URL: http://www.netcom.com/~hmcl/maritimelaw.html
Email: hmc@hmc-law.com *URL:* http://www.lawyers.com/hmc-law

MEMBERS OF FIRM

Neal Michael Mayer
Paul D. Coleman

For full biographical listings, see the Martindale-Hubbell Law Directory

CARLOS RODRIGUEZ & ASSOCIATES (AV)

1710 Rhode Island Avenue, N.W. Tenth Floor, 20036-3007
Telephone: 202-293-3300
Facsimile: 202-293-3307
Email: rodriguez@transportlaw.com
Email: cra@intr.net *URL:* http://www.tradecompass.com/rodriguez

Carlos G. Rodriguez

ASSOCIATES

Helen M. Cousineau (Not admitted in DC)
Henry P. Gonzalez (Not admitted in DC)
Robert R. Herrell (Not admitted in DC)
Daniel W. Lenehan, III

OF COUNSEL

Todd C. Fineberg

CUSTOMS AFFAIRS COUNSEL

Donald W. Lewis

LEGAL SUPPORT PERSONNEL

Ashley W. Craig

For full biographical listings, see the Martindale-Hubbell Law Directory

SCHMELTZER, APTAKER & SHEPARD, P.C. (AV)

The Watergate, Suite 1000, 2600 Virginia Avenue, N.W., 20037-1905
Telephone: 202-333-8800
Cable Address: "Ship"
Telex: 440517
Facsimile: 202-337-6065
Email: sas@saslaw.com *URL:* http://www.saspc.com
Los Angeles, California Office: 1999 Avenue of the Stars, Twenty-Seventh Floor, 90067-4095.
Telephone: 310-557-2966.
FAX: 310-286-6610.

J. Thomas Esslinger
Paul M. Heylman

COUNSEL

Edward Schmeltzer

For full biographical listings, see the Martindale-Hubbell Law Directory

VENABLE ATTORNEYS AT LAW VENABLE, BAETJER, HOWARD & CIVILETTI, LLP (AV)

A Partnership including Professional Corporations
Suite 1000, 1201 New York Avenue, N.W., 20005
Telephone: 202-962-4800
Fax: 202-962-8300
URL: http://www.venable.com
Baltimore, Maryland Office: Venable, Baetjer and Howard LLP, 1800 Mercantile Bank & Trust Building, 2 Hopkins Plaza.
Telephone: 410-244-7400.
Fax: 410-244-7742.
McLean, Virginia Office: Venable, Baetjer and Howard LLP, Suite 400, 2010 Corporate Ridge.
Telephone: 703-760-1600.
Fax: 703-821-8949.
Rockville, Maryland Office: Venable, Baetjer and Howard LLP, Suite 500, One Church Street, P. O. Box 1906.
Telephone: 301-217-5600.
Fax: 301-217-5617.
Towson, Maryland Office: Venable, Baetjer and Howard LLP, 210 Allegheny Avenue, P. O. Box 5517.
Telephone: 410-494-6200.
Fax: 410-821-0147.

MEMBERS OF FIRM

David G. Adams
Robert G. Ames (Also at Baltimore, Maryland Office)
Alan S. Anderson
James K. Archibald (Also at Baltimore, Maryland Office)
Maurice Baskin
Kenneth C. Bass, III (Also at McLean, Virginia Office)
John B. Beaty
Lawrence B. Bernard
Connie N. Bertram
Joseph G. Block
Robert J. Bolger, Jr. (Also at Baltimore, Maryland Office)
Neal D. Borden (Not admitted in DC; Also at Baltimore, Maryland Office)
James R. Burdett
Anthony M. Carey (Not admitted in DC; Also at Baltimore, Maryland Office)
Wallace E. Christner (Also at Baltimore, Maryland Office)
Arthur E. Cirulnick
Benjamin R. Civiletti (P.C.) (Also at Baltimore and Towson, Maryland Offices)
Roger A. Colaizzi
Bryson L. Cook (P.C.) (Not admitted in DC; Also at Baltimore, Maryland Office)
John F. Cooney
William D. Coston
Jeffrey A. Dunn (Also at Baltimore, Maryland Office)
Craig A. Emden
Anita J. Finkelstein
Michael R. Flyer
Andrew Fois
Robert J. Frank
Stuart M. Ginsberg
Ronald R. Glancz
Edward F. Glynn, Jr.
David W. Goewey
Michael A. Gollin
Robert Gene Gottlieb
Jan K. Guben (Not admitted in DC; Also at Baltimore, Maryland Office)
John S. Harper
Mark B. Harrison
Gregory B. Hauptman
Gary M. Hnath
Kenneth R. Hoffman (Also at Baltimore, Maryland Office)
Kenneth G. Hurwitz (Also at Baltimore, Maryland Office)
Amy Berman Jackson
Paul T. Kaplun
Lawrence A. Katz
Joshua J. Kaufman
Gabor J. Kelemen (Not admitted in DC)
Thomas J. Kelly, Jr.
Robert Kinberg
Jeffrey D. Knowles
Norman N. Kunitz
Brock R. Landry
Fernand A. Lavallee
Stephen E. Leach
Geoffrey M. Levitt
Thomas J. Madden
David M. Malone
Mary Ann Mancini
Vicki Margolis (Also at Baltimore, Maryland Office)
Charles R. "Rod" Marvin, Jr.
Lindsay Beardsworth Meyer
Daniel L. Morgan
Andrea I. O'Brien
Jerry R. O'Conor
George F. Pappas (Also at Baltimore, Maryland Office)
Thomas L. Patterson
John J. Pavlick, Jr.
Julie A. Petruzzelli
Todd H. Reuben
Tamara Schiebel Rickman
Mary Jane Saunders
Michael Schatzow (Also at Baltimore, Maryland Office)
Michael A. Schlesinger
John W. Schneller
Marina V. Schneller
James E. Scott (Not admitted in DC)
David E. Sellinger
James L. Shea (also at Baltimore, Maryland Office)
Joe A. Shull
Kenneth S. Slaughter
Herbert G. Smith, II
George H. Spencer
Judson W. Starr (Also at Baltimore and Towson, Maryland Offices)
Patrick J. Stewart (Also at Baltimore, Maryland Office)
Wayne G. Travell
Gerard Treanor
Stefan F. Tucker
Ian D. Volner
Ashley J. Wells
Judith L. Wheat
N. Frank Wiggins
Allen Wood

OF COUNSEL

Susan G. Blumenthal
Thomas J. Cooper
David G. Dickman
Susan T. Edlavitch
Gary D. Hailey
Frank Horton
Rebecca E. Pearson (Not admitted in DC)
Robert G. Rathbun (Not admitted in DC)
Janet F. Satterthwaite

(See Next Column)

VENABLE ATTORNEYS AT LAW VENABLE, BAETJER, HOWARD & CIVILETTI, LLP, *Washington—Continued*

OF COUNSEL (Continued)

Gary L. Shaffer (Not admitted in DC)
Jeffrey S. Tenenbaum
Ariel Vannier (Also at Baltimore, Maryland Office)
Barbara L. Waite

ASSOCIATES

A. Hope Adams
Theodore W. Atkinson
Marcia A. Auberger
Purvi Badiani (Not admitted in DC)
Jennifer N. Baraban (Not admitted in DC)
Nathan A. Beaver
Gregory S. Braker
Patricia Russell Brown
Fei-Fei Chao
Pier-Alysia M. Coyne (Not admitted in DC)
Carla Draluck Craft
Donald P. Creston
Kimberly A. Crowder
Peter J. Curtin (Also at Baltimore, Maryland Office)
James Nicholas Czaban
Rosemary E. Dailey
Paul A. Debolt
Kathleen S. Dolan (Not admitted in DC)
Maureen E. Donahue
Patricia A. Exposito
Catherine A. Ferguson
Andrew S. Gold (Not admitted in DC)
Rebecca L. Goldsmith (Not admitted in DC)
Kenyatta S. Green (Not admitted in DC)
Matthew B. Greiner
Keith G. Haddaway
John C. Hardwick, Jr.
Andrew M. Herzig
Linda A. Hildreth
David W. Hotes (Not admitted in DC)
Jeremy K. Huffman
Davida H. Isaacs
Jane J. Johansen (Not admitted in DC)
Matthew F. Kadish
Jordan Lee Klingsberg
Mary Ann Knoeckel
Melissa E. Lamb (Not admitted in DC)
Michael P. Leary (Not admitted in DC)
Jeanny K. Lee
Erik J. Lichter (Not admitted in DC)
Karen E. Mason (Not admitted in DC)
Heather L. McDowell
Jeannette C. Meacham (Not admitted in DC)
Emily A. Miller
John P. Moy (Not admitted in DC)
Thomas V. Mulrine
Rebecca Nassab
Chellis E. Neal
William T. Nesbitt (Not admitted in DC)
Jeanne Louise Newlon
Monica Charisse Parchment
Jill I. Prater
Andrew Douglas Price
Johana A. Reed
Martin L. Saad
Michael A. Sartori
Joshua N. Schopf (Not admitted in DC)
Sara T. Schumacher (Not admitted in DC)
Jagpreet Singh
Christine M. Sorge
Melissa Landau Steinman
Dale C. Van Demark (Not admitted in DC)
Catherine M. Voorhees
Gregory L. Waddoups (Not admitted in DC)
Robin Waugh-Farretta (Not admitted in DC)
Rita L. Wecker
Eric J. Weierstall (Not admitted in DC)
Samantha M. Williams
Kristin K. Woody
Damon W. D. Wright
George Abe Zachariah
John M. Zaremba
Scott A. Zebrak

For full biographical listings, see the Martindale-Hubbell Law Directory

FLORIDA

CORAL GABLES, Dade Co.

LANE, REESE, AULICK, SUMMERS & FIELD, P.A. (AV)

Suite 304 Douglas Centre, 2600 Douglas Road, 33134
Telephone: 305-444-4418
Fax: 305-444-5504
Email: LRASF-Miami@MSN.COM

Frank A. Lane
William S. Reese
Cecilia Aulick
William L. Summers
Paul H. Field

C. Page Lane
Lorenzo Jackson, Jr.
Luis J. Perdomo

For full biographical listings, see the Martindale-Hubbell Law Directory

*FORT LAUDERDALE,** Broward Co.

CONRAD & SCHERER (AV)

A Partnership of Professional Associations
Eighth Floor, 633 South Federal Highway, P.O. Box 14723, 33302
Telephone: 954-462-5500
Facsimile: 954-463-9244
Miami, Florida Office: 44 West Flagler Street, Suite 402, 33130.
Telephone: 305-856-9920.
Facsimile: 305-374-4408.

(See Next Column)

MEMBERS OF FIRM

William R. Scherer, Jr., (P.A.)
Gary S. Genovese (P.A.)
William V. Carcioppolo (P.A.)
Linda Rae Spaulding (P.A.)
Reid A. Cocalis (P.A.)
Willie Earl Hall (P.A.)
Ronald A. FitzGerald
James F. Carroll
Paul R. Larkin, Jr.
Dominic L. Brandy

OF COUNSEL

Rex Conrad

ASSOCIATES

Albert L. Frevola, Jr.
William R. Scherer, III
Vanessa A. Reynolds
Douglas Todd Marx
Janine Renee Kalagher
James A. Epstein
Angel Petti
Nicholas William Romanello
Shari L. McCartney
Catherine M. Rodriguez
Wendy A. Delvecchio

Local Counsel for: American Home Assurance Group; Caterpillar Tractor Co.; Division of Risk Management, State of Florida; Florida East Coast Railway; Fort Motor Co.; Liberty Mutual Insurance Co.; Ryder Truck Lines; Unigard Insurance Group.
Approved Attorneys for: Attorneys' Title Insurance Fund.
Reference: Barnett Bank of Fort Lauderdale.

For full biographical listings, see the Martindale-Hubbell Law Directory

KRUPNICK CAMPBELL MALONE ROSELLI BUSER SLAMA HANCOCK MCNELIS LIBERMAN & MCKEE, P.A. (AV)

700 Southeast 3rd Avenue, Suite 100, 33316-1186
Telephone: 954-763-8181; 877-763-8181 (Toll Free)
Fax: 954-763-8292
Email: information@krupnicklaw.com *URL:* http://www.krupnicklaw.com

Jon E. Krupnick
Walter G. Campbell, Jr.
Kevin A. Malone
Richard J. Roselli
Thomas E. Buser
Joseph J. Slama
Kelly D. Hancock
Lisa A. McNelis
Scott S. Liberman
Robert J. McKee

Carlos Acevedo (Not admitted in FL)
Louis R. Battista
Ivan F. Cabrera
Robert D. Erben
Kelley Badger Gelb
Sean J. Greene
Holly Debra Krulik
Michael J. Ryan

OF COUNSEL

Ben J. Weaver
Dianne Jay Weaver

Reference: Mellon United National Bank.

For full biographical listings, see the Martindale-Hubbell Law Directory

FORT WALTON BEACH, Okaloosa Co.

LAW OFFICES OF ARDEN J. LEA (AV Ⓣ)

29-B Miracle Strip Parkway S.W., 32548
Telephone: 850-302-0666; 850-302-0667
Telecopy: 850-302-0668
Email: AJL@Emeraldsurf.net
(Also Of Counsel to Barton, Richardson, Conseco & Whitney, New Orleans, Louisiana)

For full biographical listings, see the Martindale-Hubbell Law Directory

*JACKSONVILLE,** Duval Co.

MOSELEY, WARREN, PRICHARD & PARRISH, P.A. (AV)

501 West Bay Street, 32202
Telephone: 904-356-1306
Telecopier: 904-354-0194
Cable Address: "Ragland"
Email: firm@mwpplaw.com

Reuben Ragland (1882-1954)
Louis Kurz (1891-1965)
E. Dale Joyner (1943-1993)
James F. Moseley
Robert E. Warren
Joseph W. Prichard, Jr.
Robert B. Parrish
Andrew J. Knight II
Richard K. Jones
James F. Moseley, Jr.
Phillip A. Buhler

Stanley M. Weston
Kimberly Held Israel
Tracy A. Chesser
Michael A. Garfield
Eric Lee Hearn
Samuel Allen Maroon

OF COUNSEL

James E. Williams
Neil C. Taylor

Counsel for: CSX Transportation; Britannia Steam Ship Insurance Assn., Ltd.; The West of England Protection & Indemnity Assn. (Luxembourg); Crowley American Transport Services, Inc.; United Kingdom Mutual Steamship Assurance Assn., Ltd. (Bermuda); The London Steam-Ship Owners' Mutual Insurance Assn., Ltd.

For full biographical listings, see the Martindale-Hubbell Law Directory

*MIAMI,** Dade Co.

ABRAMSON & MAGIDSON, P.A. (AV)

Suite 904, 800 Brickell Avenue, 33131
Telephone: 305-358-4400
Fax: 305-539-0477
Email: abramson@icanect.net

John M. Abramson | David L. Magidson

For full biographical listings, see the Martindale-Hubbell Law Directory

ARMSTRONG & MEJER, P.A. (AV)

Suite 1111 Douglas Centre, 2600 Douglas Road (Coral Gables), 33134
Telephone: 305-444-3355
Fax: 305-442-4300
Email: Amesq@Aol.com

Timothy J. Armstrong | Alvaro L. Mejer

M. Emelina Mejer-Kondla

Reference: First Union National Bank.

For full biographical listings, see the Martindale-Hubbell Law Directory

CLARKE SILVERGLATE WILLIAMS & MONTGOMERY (AV)

A Partnership of Professional Corporations
100 North Biscayne Boulevard Suite 2401, 33132
Telephone: 305-377-0700
Facsimile: 305-377-3001
Chicago, Illinois Office: Williams & Montgomery Ltd., 20 North Wacker Drive, Suite 2100.
Telephone: 312-443-3200.
Telex: 206598.
Facsimile: 312-443-1323.
Waukegan, Illinois Office: Williams & Montgomery Ltd., 20 S. Utica.
Telephone: 847-360-1220.
Wheaton, Illinois Office: Williams & Montgomery Ltd., 310 S. County Farm Road.
Telephone: 630-690-3200.
Joliet, Illinois Office: Williams & Montgomery Ltd., 81 North Chicago Avenue.
Telephone: 815-727-2653.

Mercer K. Clarke | Spencer H. Silverglate

OF COUNSEL

Henry H. Bolz, III

ASSOCIATES

Kelly Anne Luther | Spencer T. Kuvin
Richard R. Cochran | Francisco Ramos, Jr.
William J. Dimmig | Edward J. Pfister
Cynthia R. Bernard | John C. Schlesinger

For full biographical listings, see the Martindale-Hubbell Law Directory

HAYDEN AND MILLIKEN, P.A. (AV)

Suite 63, 5915 Ponce de Leon Boulevard, 33146-2477
Telephone: 305-662-1523
Fax: 305-663-1358
Tampa, Florida Office: 615 De Leon Street 33606-2719.
Telephone: 813-251-1770.
Fax: 813-254-5436.
Cape Canaveral, Florida Office: 101 George King Boulevard, Suite 5, 32920,
Telephone: 407-868-0022.
Fax: 407-868-5060.

Reginald M. Hayden, Jr. | William R. Boeringer
William Barry Milliken | Timothy P. Shusta (Resident, Tampa, Florida Office)

Patrick M. Talbot

Representative Clients: Seaboard Marine, Ltd.; Tropical Shipping and Construction Co., Ltd.; Great American Insurance Co.; Marine Office of America Corp.; St. Paul Fire and Marine Insurance Co.; Britannia P & I; Newcastle P & I; Steamship Mutual; The Swedish Club.

For full biographical listings, see the Martindale-Hubbell Law Directory

HOPPE & STOKES, P.A. (AV)

2nd Floor, Concord Building, 66 West Flagler Street, 33130
Telephone: 305-358-9060
Fax: 305-374-6801
URL: http://www.hoppestokes.com
Email: pilaw@hoppestokes.com *URL:* http://www.lawyers.com/hoppestokes

Bill Hoppe | Mark L. Stokes

(See Next Column)

Jacinto J. Gonzalez | Eric Matthew Ellsley
LeAnna Vasquez

For full biographical listings, see the Martindale-Hubbell Law Directory

KAYE, ROSE & PARTNERS, LLP (AV)

One Biscayne Tower, 2 South Biscayne Boulevard, Suite 2300, 33131
Telephone: 305-358-6555
Fax: 305-374-9077
Telex: 371-7740
Email: fl@kayerose.com *URL:* http://www.kayerose.com
Los Angeles, California Office: One California Street, Suite 2230.
Telephone: 310-277-1200.
Fax: 310-277-1220.
San Diego, California Office: Emerald Plaza, 402 West Broadway, 21st Floor.
Telephone: 619-232-6555.
Fax: 619-232-6577.
San Francisco, California Office: 55 Francisco Street, Suite 610.
Telephone: 415-433-6555.
Fax: 415-433-6577.

PARTNER

Jeffrey B. Maltzman

ASSOCIATES

Carol Lynn Finklehoffe | Eduardo J. Hernandez
Darren W. Friedman | Lawrence E. Burkhalter

For full biographical listings, see the Martindale-Hubbell Law Directory

KELLER & HOUCK, A PROFESSIONAL ASSOCIATION (AV)

200 South Biscayne Boulevard Suite 3460, 33131
Telephone: 305-372-9044
Facsimile: 305-372-5044
Email: firm@KellerHouck.com *URL:* http://www.KellerHouck.com
Port Canaveral Florida Office: 101 George King Boulevard, 32920.
Telephone: 407-799-9299.
Fax: 407-799-1966.

SHAREHOLDERS

John W. Keller, III | Mark R. Houck

MEMBERS

Andrew W. Anderson | Jerry D. Hamilton
Farris J. Martin, III

ASSOCIATES

Erin E. Dardis | John M. Mitchell
David N. Gambach | Vincent O'Brien
Alexandros J. Haralambides | Jennifer P. Quildon
Edwin E. Hightower, Jr. | Julie K. Rannik
Joseph W. Janssen, III | Tara Leigh Scott
Jennifer A. Kerr | John M. Siracusa
Walter J. Mathews | Barbara Rudolph Smith
Robert Donald Tracy

For full biographical listings, see the Martindale-Hubbell Law Directory

RIVKIND & PEDRAZA, P.A. (AV)

Suite 600, 66 West Flagler Street, 33130
Telephone: 305-374-0565
Telecopier: 305-539-8341
Email: seainjury@aol.com

Brett A. Rivkind | George I. Pedraza

For full biographical listings, see the Martindale-Hubbell Law Directory

SARNOFF & BAYER (AV)

3197 Virginia Street (Coconut Grove), 33133
Telephone: 305-441-5966
Fax: 305-441-5977
Email: sarnoff@ix.netcom.com

MEMBERS OF FIRM

Neil Bayer | Marc David Sarnoff

For full biographical listings, see the Martindale-Hubbell Law Directory

SHUTTS & BOWEN LLP (AV)

A Partnership including Professional Associations
1500 Miami Center, 201 South Biscayne Boulevard, 33131
Telephone: 305-358-6300
Telefax: 305-381-9982
Email: MCONNORS@SHUTTS-LAW.COM *URL:* HTTP://WWW.SHUTTS-LAW.COM
Orlando, Florida Office: 20 North Orange Avenue, Suite 1000.
Telephone: 407-423-3200.
Fax: 407-425-8316.
West Palm Beach, Florida Office: One Clearlake Centre, 250 Australian Avenue, Suite 500.
Telephone: 561-835-8500.
Fax: 561-650-8530.

(See Next Column)

SHUTTS & BOWEN LLP, *Miami—Continued*

Tallahassee, Florida Office: 215 South Monroe Street, Suite 804.
Telephone: 850-521-0600.
Fax: 850-521-0604.
Fort Lauderdale, Florida Office: First Union Center, Suite 2000, 200 East Broward Boulevard.
Telephone: 954-524-5505.
Fax: 954-524-5506.
Amsterdam, The Netherlands Office: Shutts & Bowen, B.V., Europa Boulevard 59, 1083 AD, Amsterdam.
Telephone: (31 20) 661-0969.
Fax: (31 20) 642-1475.
London, England Office: 43 Grosvenor Street, London W1X 9PG.
Telephone: 441-71-493-4840.
Telefax: 441-71-493-4299.

MEMBER OF FIRM

Richard M. Leslie (P.A.)

Representative Clients: Paquet Cruises, Inc.; Ulysses Cruises Inc.; Dolphin Cruises Inc.; Holland America Cruises; West of England P and I Club; Lykes Bros. Steamship; United Kingdom P and I Club.

For Complete List of Firm Personnel, See General Section

For full biographical listings, see the Martindale-Hubbell Law Directory

LOUIS STINSON, JR., P.A. (AV)

Suite 305, 4675 Ponce de Leon Boulevard (Coral Gables), 33146-2113
Telephone: 305-667-7571
Fax: 305-667-0206
Email: louis@stinsonlaw.com

Louis Stinson, Jr.

OF COUNSEL

Robert J. Schaffer

For full biographical listings, see the Martindale-Hubbell Law Directory

VALLE & CRAIG, P.A. (AV)

Suite 2520 World Trade Center, 80 Southwest Eighth Street, P.O. Box 113009, 33111-3009
Telephone: 305-373-2888; 800-609-6151
Facsimile: 305-373-2889

Laurence F. Valle — Lawrance B. Craig, III
Timothy Maze Hartley

Frank J. Sioli, Jr. — Michael A. Vasquez
Michael J. Lynott — Brian M. McKell

For full biographical listings, see the Martindale-Hubbell Law Directory

*TAMPA,** Hillsborough Co.

HAYDEN AND MILLIKEN, P.A. (AV)

615 de Leon Street, 33606-2719
Telephone: 813-251-1770
Fax: 813-254-5436
Miami, Florida Office: Suite 63, 5915 Ponce de Leon Boulevard.
Telephone: 305-662-1523.
Fax: 305-663-1358.
Cape Canaveral, Florida Office: 101 George King Boulevard, Suite 5, 32920.
Telephone: 407-868-0022.
Fax: 407-868-5060.

Reginald M. Hayden, Jr. — William Barry Milliken
Timothy P. Shusta (Resident)

Matthew J. Valcourt

Representative Clients: Seaboard Marine, Ltd.; Tropical Shipping and Construction Co., Ltd.; Great American Insurance Co.; Marine Office of America Corp.; St. Paul Fire and Marine Insurance Co.; Britannia P & I; Newcastle P & I; Steamship Mutual.
Reference: Dadeland Bank.

For full biographical listings, see the Martindale-Hubbell Law Directory

*VERO BEACH,** Indian River Co.

MOSS, HENDERSON, BLANTON & LANIER, P.A. (AV)

817 Beachland Boulevard, P.O. Box 3406, 32964-3406
Telephone: 561-231-1900
Fax: 561-231-4387

OF COUNSEL

Ford J. Fegert

Representative Clients: Aetna Life & Casualty; Alcoa Florida, Inc.; Florida Power & Light Co.; Insurance Company of North America; Liberty Mutual Insurance Co.; Sears, Roebuck & Co.; Sugar Cane Growers Cooperative of Florida; Norfolk Southern Corporation/North American Van Lines, Inc.

(See Next Column)

For Complete List of Firm Personnel, See General Section

For full biographical listings, see the Martindale-Hubbell Law Directory

GEORGIA

*SAVANNAH,** Chatham Co.

BOUHAN, WILLIAMS & LEVY LLP (AV)

The Armstrong House, 447 Bull Street, P.O. Box 2139, 31402-2139
Telephone: 912-236-2491
Fax: 912-233-0811
Email: bouhan@bellsouth.net

MEMBER OF FIRM

Edwin D. Robb, Jr.

General Counsel for: Savannah Electric and Power Co.; Wachovia Bank of Georgia, N.A.; Southeastern Maritime Co.; Solomons Co.; Fiduciary Services Corp.; Peeples Industry, Inc.; Board of Education of the City of Savannah and County of Chatham; The Branigar Organization, Inc.

For Complete List of Firm Personnel, See General Section

For full biographical listings, see the Martindale-Hubbell Law Directory

HAWAII

*HONOLULU,** Honolulu Co.

CARLSMITH BALL (AV)

A Partnership including Law Corporations
Suite 2200, Pacific Tower, 1001 Bishop Street, P.O. Box 656, 96809-3402
Telephone: 808-523-2500
Fax: 808-523-0842
Email: execdirector@carlsmith.com *URL:* http://www.carlsmith.com
Kapolei, Hawaii Office: Suite 318, Kapolei Building, 1001 Kamokila Boulevard, 96707.
Telephone: 808-523-2500.
Fax: 808-674-0850.
Wailuku, Maui Hawaii Office: Suite 400, One Main Plaza, 2200 Main Street, P.O. Box 1086, 96793-1086.
Telephone: 808-242-4535.
Fax: 808-244-4974.
Kailua-Kona, Hawaii Office: Suite 209, 75-1000 Henry Street, 96740.
Telephone: 808-329-6464.
Fax: 808-329-9450.
Hilo, Hawaii Office: 121 Waianuenue Avenue, P.O. Box 686, 96721-0686.
Telephone: 808-935-6644.
Fax: 808-935-7975.
Hagatna, Guam Office: Suite 401, Bank of Hawaii Building, 134 West Soledad Avenue, P.O. Box BF, 96932-5027.
Telephone: 671-472-6813.
Fax: 671-477-4375.
Telex: 721-6445 CWCMI GM.
Saipan, Commonwealth of the Northern Mariana Islands Office: Carlsmith Building, Capitol Hill, P.O. Box 5241, 96950-5241.
Telephone: 670-322-3455.
Fax: 670-322-3368.
Los Angeles, California Office: 9th Floor, 444 South Flower Street, 90071-2901.
Telephone: 213-955-1200.
Fax: 213-623-0032.
Washington, D.C. Office: Suite 300, 1201 Pennsylvania Avenue, N.W., 20004-2401.
Telephone: 202-628-2228.
Fax: 202-628-2071.
Mexico City, Mexico Office: Carlsmith Ball, Sierra Nevada 119, Lomas de Chapultepec, 11000 Mexico, D.F.
Telephone: 52-5-520-8514, 52-5-520-8757.
Fax: 52-5-540-1545.
Mexico, D.F. Office of Carlsmith Ball, S.C. (Authorized to practice as foreign legal consultants in Mexico): Sierra Nevada 119, Lomas de Chapultepec, 11000 Mexico, D.F.
Telephone: 52-5-520-8514, 52-5-520-8757.
Fax: 52-5-540-1545.

MEMBERS OF FIRM

Steven M. Egesdal — Nenad Krek
Philip D. Isaac (Resident at Hagatna, Guam Office) — David Patrick Ledger (Resident at Hagatna, Guam Office)
Dean H. Robb

ASSOCIATE

Kevin E. Moore

For Complete List of Firm Personnel, See General Section

For full biographical listings, see the Martindale-Hubbell Law Directory

Honolulu—Continued

CRONIN, FRIED, SEKIYA, KEKINA & FAIRBANKS ATTORNEYS AT LAW, A LAW CORPORATION (AV)

1900 Davies Pacific Center, 841 Bishop Street, 96813
Telephone: 808-524-1433
Fax: 808-536-2073

Paul F. Cronin
L. Richard Fried, Jr.
Gerald Y. Sekiya
Wayne K. Kekina
David L. Fairbanks
John D. Thomas, Jr.
Stuart A. Kaneko
Bert S. Sakuda
Allen K. Williams
Keith K. H. Young

Patrick W. Border
Gregory L. Lui-Kwan
Patrick F. McTernan
Clarence S.K. Kekina
Sylvia J. Luke
Geoffrey K.S. Komeya
Frances K. Schneider

For full biographical listings, see the Martindale-Hubbell Law Directory

GOODSILL ANDERSON QUINN & STIFEL (AV)

Alii Place, Suite 1800, 1099 Alakea Street, P.O. Box 3196, 96801-3196
Telephone: 808-547-5600
FAX: 808-547-5880
Email: info@goodsill.com *URL:* http://www.goodsill.com

MEMBERS OF FIRM

John R. Lacy
Mark B. Desmarais
Corlis J. Chang
LindaLee K. Farm

ASSOCIATE

Normand R. Lezy

Representative Clients: The Britannia Steam Ship Assn., Ltd.; The Delta Queen Steamboat Co.; Fireman's Fund Marine; Matson Navigation Company, Inc.; Sunderland Marine Mutual; The Steamship Mutual Underwriting Assn., Ltd.; Transoceanic Cable Ship Co./AT&T.

For Complete List of Firm Personnel, See General Section

For full biographical listings, see the Martindale-Hubbell Law Directory

ILLINOIS

*BELLEVILLE,** St. Clair Co.

GAVIN LAW FIRM (AV)

NationsBank Building, 23 Public Square, Suite 415, 62220
Telephone: 618-236-0100
888-360-0100
Fax: 618-236-2684
Email: billg@gavinlaw.com *URL:* http://www.gavinlaw.com

William P. Gavin

For full biographical listings, see the Martindale-Hubbell Law Directory

*CHICAGO,** Cook Co.

BELGRADE AND O'DONNELL, A PROFESSIONAL CORPORATION (AV)

311 South Wacker Drive, Suite 2770, 60606
Telephone: 312-360-9500
Facsimile: 312-360-9550
Email: bodpc@aol.com

Steven B. Belgrade
John A. O'Donnell
George M. Velcich
Kim Richard Kardas

Patrick J. Cullinan
Lisa E. Nelson
James Kent Minnette
Richard P. Girzadas

For full biographical listings, see the Martindale-Hubbell Law Directory

BLATT, HAMMESFAHR & EATON (AV)

333 W. Wacker Drive, Suite 1900, 60606
Telephone: 312-849-8000
FAX: 312-357-0198
Email: BHE@BHELAW.COM *URL:* HTTP://WWW.BHELAW.COM
New York, New York Office: 45 Broadway, 12th Floor.
Telephone: 212-363-1900.
Fax: 212-363-2600. Email: bhe@bhelaw.com.

MEMBER OF FIRM

Josh M. Kantrow

ASSOCIATE

Frederic C. Goodwill, II

For full biographical listings, see the Martindale-Hubbell Law Directory

INDIANA

*EVANSVILLE,** Vanderburgh Co.

KAHN, DEES, DONOVAN & KAHN, LLP (AV)

Fifth Main Financial Plaza, Suite 305, P.O. Box 3646, 47735-3646
Telephone: 812-423-3183
Fax: 812-423-3841
Email: evvlaw@k2d2.com

MEMBERS OF FIRM

Jeffrey W. Ahlers
Christopher D. Lee

ASSOCIATE

Lee F. Baker

Representative Clients: Neare Gibbs Maritime Insurance; United States Fidelity & Guarantee; Ohio Valley Marine Service; Mulzer Crushed Stone; Mt. Vernon Barge Service.

For Complete List of Firm Personnel, See General Section

For full biographical listings, see the Martindale-Hubbell Law Directory

KENTUCKY

*PADUCAH,** McCracken Co.

DENTON & KEULER (AV)

Paducah Bank & Trust Company Building, 555 Jefferson Street, P.O. Box 929, 42001
Telephone: 502-443-8253
Fax: 502-442-6000
Email: dk@dklaw.com *URL:* http://www.dklaw.com

MEMBER OF FIRM

William E. Pinkston

LEGAL SUPPORT PERSONNEL

PARALEGALS

Douglas W. Painter
Samuel P. Watson

Reference: The Paducah Bank & Trust Co.

For Complete List of Firm Personnel, See General Section

For full biographical listings, see the Martindale-Hubbell Law Directory

SALADINO LAW FIRM (AV)

700 Clark Street, P.O. Box 1246, 42002-1246
Telephone: 502-444-0406
Fax: 502-444-0454
Email: saladino@apex.net

Charles A. Saladino

ASSOCIATES

David Vance Oakes
Kristi Saladino Schaaf
Barclay Walden Banister
Gary E. Schaaf

For full biographical listings, see the Martindale-Hubbell Law Directory

LOUISIANA

*BATON ROUGE,** East Baton Rouge Parish

DUÉ, CABALLERO, PRICE & GUIDRY, (A PROFESSIONAL ASSOCIATION) (AV)

8201 Jefferson Highway, 70809
Telephone: 225-929-7481
Fax: 225-924-4519

Paul H. Dué
Rick A. Caballero
Donald W. Price
Kirk A. Guidry

Randolph A. Piedrahita
Brandon Scott Andrews

OF COUNSEL

David W. Robertson

For full biographical listings, see the Martindale-Hubbell Law Directory

Baton Rouge—Continued

George and George, Ltd., A Professional Law Corporation (AV)

6767 Perkins Road, Suite 203, 70808
Telephone: 225-769-3064
Fax: 225-766-1591
Email: jimg@georgeandgeorge.com *URL:* http://www.georgeandgeorge.com

James A. George

LEGAL SUPPORT PERSONNEL

Cathy Richard (Administrative Assistant)

Reference: Hibernia National Bank of Baton Rouge.

For full biographical listings, see the Martindale-Hubbell Law Directory

Kean, Miller, Hawthorne, D'Armond, McCowan & Jarman, L.L.P. (AV)

22nd Floor, One American Place, 70825
Telephone: 225-387-0999
Fax: 225-388-9133
Mailing Address: P.O. Box 3513, Baton Rouge, Louisiana, 70821
URL: http://WWW.KMLAW.COM
New Orleans, Louisiana Office: Energy Centre, Suite 1560, 1100 Poydras Street, 70163.
Telephone: 504-585-3050.
Fax: 504-585-3051.
Plaquemine, Louisiana Office: Suite 10, 23425 Railroad Avenue, 70764.
Telephone: 225-687-9845.
Fax: 225-382-3445.
Lake Charles, Louisiana Office: One Lakeshore Drive, Suite 1220, 70629.
Telephone: 318-430-0350.
Fax: 318-436-5566.
Covington, Louisiana Office: 503 North New Hampshire Street, P.O. Box 3096, 70433.
Telephone: 504-875-0400.
Fax: 504-875-0500.

MEMBER OF FIRM

G. William Jarman

SPECIAL COUNSEL

Louise V. White (Resident, Covington Office)
William V. Courtney (Resident, Covington Office)
Daniel L. Daboval (Resident, New Orleans Office)

For full biographical listings, see the Martindale-Hubbell Law Directory

*HOUMA,** Terrebonne Parish

Henderson, Hanemann & Morris, A Professional Law Corporation (AV)

300 Lafayette Street, 70360
Telephone: 504-868-2081
New Orleans: 504-581-1434
Telecopier: 504-868-0080

Philip E. Henderson
Charles Hanemann
Robert L. Morris (1940-1986)
J. Mark Graham
Joseph A. Reilly, Jr.
Barry J. Boudreaux

Emilie Melancon Daye

Representative Clients: Alliance Insurance Company; Applied Hydraulic Systems, Inc.; Falcon Drilling Company, Inc.; Lafayette Insurance Company; Liverpool and London Steamship Protection and Indemnity Association Limited; Louisiana Medical Mutual Insurance Company; The Steamship Mutual Underwriter Association Limited; Gray & Co., Inc.; Union Oil Company of California; Minnesota Mining and Manufacturing Co.

For full biographical listings, see the Martindale-Hubbell Law Directory

*LAFAYETTE,** Lafayette Parish

Broussard, David & Daigle, A Professional Law Corporation (AV)

557 Jefferson Street, P.O. Drawer 3308, 70502-3308
Telephone: 318-234-7000
Fax: 318-237-0344
Email: bdandd@bdandd.com *URL:* http://www.bdandd.com

Hal J. Broussard
Susan A. Daigle
Bryan D. Scofield
Ped C. Kay, III
Todd G. Crawford

James T. Rivera
Catherine E. Hensgens

Representative Clients: Certain London Underwriters per individual approval of instructions; Lloyds of London Member Syndicates; Institute of London Underwriter Member Companies; Reliance Insurance Company of Pennsylvania; Reliance Insurance Company of Illinois; Reliance National Insurance Company; The Louisiana Insurance Guaranty Association; Louisiana Oilfield Legislative Committee, Inc. (Louisiana Association of Oilfield Casing Contractors; Association of Oilwell Servicing Contractors; Louisiana Pipeline Contractors Association; Offshore Pipeline Contractors Association; Louisiana Oilfield Contractor Association).

For full biographical listings, see the Martindale-Hubbell Law Directory

Lawrence K. Burleigh, Ltd. A Professional Law Corporation (AV)

Gordon Square, Suite 160, 100 East Vermilion Street, 70501
Telephone: 318-234-6222
Fax: 318-234-6141

Lawrence K. Burleigh, Sr.

Lawrence K. Burleigh, Jr.

For full biographical listings, see the Martindale-Hubbell Law Directory

Curtis & Lambert, A Professional Law Corporation (AV)

201 Rue Iberville, Suite 300, P.O. Box 80247, 70598-0247
Telephone: 318-235-1825
1-800-528-1825
Telefax: 318-237-0241
URL: http://www.curtis-lambertlawfirm.com

Lawrence N. Curtis
James P. Lambert

Gregory K. Klein

For full biographical listings, see the Martindale-Hubbell Law Directory

Domengeaux Wright & Roy, A Professional Law Corporation (AV)

556 Jefferson Street, Suite 500, P.O. Box 3668, 70502-3668
Telephone: 318-233-3033; 1-800-375-3106
Fax: 318-232-8213
Email: info@wrightroy.com *URL:* http://www.wrightroy.com

Bob F. Wright
James Parkerson Roy
Thomas R. Edwards
James H. Domengeaux
Gilbert Hennigan Dozier
Carla Marie Perron
Michael D. Goss

ASSOCIATE

Jamie D. Parker

OF COUNSEL

Jerome E. Domengeaux

Reference: Mid-South National Bank; Advocate Financial, L.L.C.

For full biographical listings, see the Martindale-Hubbell Law Directory

The Juneau Firm A Professional Law Corporation (AV)

The Harding Center, 1018 Harding Street Suite 202, 70503
Telephone: 318-269-0052
Facsimile: 318-269-0061
Mailing Address: P.O. Drawer 51268, Lafayette, Louisiana, 70505-1268

Patrick A. Juneau
Michael J. Juneau
Barry L. Domingue
Thomas R. Juneau
Sue Nations
John R. Whaley
Karen B. Levy

Representative Clients: American International Group; BJ Services Co.; Coastal Towing, Inc.; Duke Energy Corp.; Halliburton Co.; Kerr-McGee Corp.; M-I Drilling Fluids, Inc.; Petroleum Helicopters, Inc.; Smith International, Inc.

For full biographical listings, see the Martindale-Hubbell Law Directory

Richard R. Kennedy A Professional Law Corporation (AV)

309 Polk Street, P.O. Box 3243, 70502-3243
Telephone: 318-232-1934
Fax: 318-232-9720
Email: kennedy@net-connect.net

Richard R. Kennedy

For full biographical listings, see the Martindale-Hubbell Law Directory

Onebane, Bernard, Torian, Diaz, McNamara & Abell (AV)

Suite 600, Versailles Centre, 102 Versailles Boulevard, P.O. Box 3507, 70502
Telephone: 318-237-2660
Telecopier: 318-266-1232
Email: info@onebane.com
Monroe, Louisiana Office: 1900 N. 18th Street, Suite 420, P.O. Box 2255, 71207.
Telephone: 318-340-0220.
Fax: 318-340-0110.

(See Next Column)

ONEBANE, BERNARD, TORIAN, DIAZ, MCNAMARA & ABELL—*Continued*

Joseph Onebane (1917-1987)
John G. Torian, II (1936-1991)
James E. Diaz
Timothy J. McNamara
Edward C. Abell, Jr.
Lawrence L. Lewis, III
Robert M. Mahony
Daniel G. Fournerat
Douglas W. Truxillo
Randall C. Songy
Michael G. Durand
Greg Guidry
Joseph L. Lemoine, Jr.
Mark L. Riley
Graham N. Smith
Gordon T. Whitman
Gary P. Kraus
Richard J. Petre, Jr.
Charles J. Boudreaux, Jr.
James R. Shelton
Thomas G. Smart
Roger E. Ishee
Jennifer M. Kleinpeter
Steven C. Lanza
Joel P. Babineaux

Alison M. Brumley
Jesse D. Lambert
Brent G. Sonnier
Cary B. Bryson
Maria F. Manuel
Greg R. Mier
Jennifer L. Smith
Janice Church Reeves
Mark B. Oliver
Chanelle T. Delahoussaye
Aimee L. Williams
A.G. "Alec" Alexander, III
Terry J. Blanchard
William E. Bourgeois (Resident, Monroe, Louisiana Office)

OF COUNSEL

William E. Kellner

Representative Clients: Aries Marine Corp.; Brown & Root; Cliffs Drilling Co.; Enron Corp.; Halliburton Co.; Horizon Offshore Contractors; Marathon Oil Co.; Ocean Energy, Inc.; Pennzoil; Transocean Drilling.

For full biographical listings, see the Martindale-Hubbell Law Directory

PREIS KRAFT & ROY, A PROFESSIONAL LAW CORPORATION (AV)

Suite 400, Versailles CentrÉ, 102 Versailles Boulevard, P.O. Drawer 94-C, 70509
Telephone: 318-237-6062
Fax: 318-237-9129
Email: pkr@pkrlaw.com
NewOrleans Office: Pan American Life Center, 601 Poydras Street, Suite 1855.
Telephone: 504-581-6062.
Fax: 504-522-9129.
Houston, Texas Office: 520 Post Oak Boulevard, Suite 800.
Telephone: 713-355-6062.
Telefax: 713-572-9129.

Edwin G. Preis, Jr.
Ralph E. Kraft
L. Lane Roy
Ward F. Lafleur
F. Douglas Gatz, Jr.
Charles A. Mouton
Kay A. Theunissen
Jennifer E. Beyer
Richard J. Hymel
George Caflisch (Not admitted in LA; Resident, Houston, Texas Office)

David R. Rabalais
Marc D. Moroux
Edward King Alexander, Jr.
G. Edward Williams, Jr.
Timothy W. Basden
Larry A. Wallace, Jr.
L. Marika Steele
Jeff R. Rytlewski
Angella R. Hebert
Alison Ann Darsey
Jean Ann Billeaud

Approved Counsel for: American Gulf Group; American International Group; American Oilfield Divers, Inc.; American P & I Club; American United Life Insurance Company; Association of Diving Contractors, Inc.; Assuranceforeningen Gard; Assuranceforeningen Skuld, Automation Communication Engeneering Corporation; Cal Dive International, Inc.; CBI Industries, Inc.

For full biographical listings, see the Martindale-Hubbell Law Directory

*LAKE CHARLES,** Calcasieu Parish

BERGSTEDT & MOUNT (AV)

Second Floor, Magnolia Life Building, P.O. Drawer 3004, 70602-3004
Telephone: 318-433-3004
Facsimile: 318-433-8080

MEMBERS OF FIRM

Thomas M. Bergstedt
Benjamin W. Mount
Van C. Seneca

ASSOCIATE

Annette N. Peltier

OF COUNSEL

Charles S. Ware

Representative Clients: ARCO Chemical Company; Ashland Oil Co.; CIGNA Property & Casualty Companies; Columbia Women's & Children's Hospital; The Hartford Steam Boiler Inspection & Insurance Company; Leach Company; Olin Corporation; Occidental Chemical Corporation; Terra Corporation; R. D. Werner Company.

For full biographical listings, see the Martindale-Hubbell Law Directory

LUNDY & DAVIS, L.L.P. (AV)

Hibernia Tower, One Lakeshore Drive, Suite 1600, P.O. Box 3010, 70602
Telephone: 318-439-0707
FAX: 318-439-1029
URL: http://www.lundydavis.com
Jackson, Mississippi Office: 405 Tombigbee Street, P.O. Box 610, 39205.
Telephone: 601-948-3010.
Facsimile: 601-948-2143.
Houston, Texas Office: 777 Walker, Suite 2500, 77002.
Telephone: 713-237-0690.
Facsimile: 713-237-0999.

MEMBERS OF FIRM

Hunter W. Lundy
Clayton A. L. Davis
Matthew E. Lundy (Resident, Houston, Texas Office)
David A. Bowers (Resident, Jackson, Mississippi Office)
Samuel B. Gabb
James D. Cain, Jr.

ASSOCIATES

Jackey W. South
Michael D. Carleton
Thomas P. LeBlanc
Charles W. Peckham (Resident, Houston, Texas Office)
Andre F. Ducote (Resident, Jackson, Mississippi Office)
David H. Hanchey

OF COUNSEL

Wayne E. Ferrell, Jr. (Resident, Jackson, Mississippi Office)

For full biographical listings, see the Martindale-Hubbell Law Directory

PLAUCHÉ SMITH & NIESET, A PROFESSIONAL LAW CORPORATION (AV)

1123 Pithon Street, P.O. Drawer 1705, 70602
Telephone: 318-436-0522
Facsimile: 318-436-9637

S. W. Plauché (1889-1952)
S. W. Plauché, Jr. (1915-1966)
A. Lane Plauché
Allen L. Smith, Jr.
James R. Nieset
Frank M. Walker, Jr.
Michael J. McNulty, III
Jeffrey M. Cole
Andrew R. Johnson, IV
Charles V. Musso, Jr.
Christopher P. Ieyoub
H. David Vaughan, II
Joseph R. Pousson, Jr.
Rebecca S. Young
V. Ed McGuire, III

Representative Clients: CIGNA; CNA Insurance Cos.; Commercial Union Insurance Cos.; Crum & Forster; Reliance Insurance Cos.; Royal Insurance Group; State Farm; U.S. Insurance Group.

For full biographical listings, see the Martindale-Hubbell Law Directory

WOODLEY, WILLIAMS, BOUDREAU, NORMAN, BROWN & DOYLE (AV)

A Registered Limited Liability Company
500 Kirby Street, P.O. Box 3731, 70602-3731
Telephone: 318-433-6328
Facsimile: 318-433-7513
Email: woodley@woodleywilliams.com

MEMBERS OF FIRM

Edmund E. Woodley (1925-1989)
James E. Williams (P.C.)
Robert J. Boudreau
Rick J. Norman
Donald C. Brown
James B. Doyle
Thomas J. Solari
Darrell W. Alston
Michele S. Caballero
M. Keith Prudhomme
Matthew D. Henrich

OF COUNSEL

Milo A. Nickel

Representative Clients: Agency Management Corp.; Travelers Insurance Co.

For full biographical listings, see the Martindale-Hubbell Law Directory

METAIRIE, Jefferson Parish

HAILEY, MCNAMARA, HALL, LARMANN & PAPALE, L.L.P. (AV)

A Limited Liability Partnership including Professional Law Corporations
Suite 1400, One Galleria Boulevard, P.O. Box 8288, 70011
Telephone: 504-836-6500
Fax: 504-836-6565
URL: http://www.haileymcnamara.com

MEMBERS OF FIRM

James W. Hailey, Jr., (P.L.C.)
W. Marvin Hall (P.L.C.)
Antonio E. Papale, Jr., (P.L.C.)
Laurence E. Larmann (P.L.C.)
Michael P. Mentz
Richard T. Simmons, Jr.,(P.L.C.)
Michael J. Vondenstein
David K. Persons
Dominic J. Ovella
C. Kelly Lightfoot
John T. Culotta (P.L.C.)
John E. Unsworth, Jr.
Julie DiFulco Robles
Claude A. Greco
Valerie T. Schexnayder
W. Evan Plauche
Kurt D. Engelhardt

(See Next Column)

HAILEY, MCNAMARA, HALL, LARMANN & PAPALE L.L.P., *Metairie—Continued*

ASSOCIATES

William R. Seay, Jr.
W. Glenn Burns
James W. Hailey, III
Frederic Theodore Le Clercq
Barbara Bourdonnay O'Donnell
Kathryn T. Wiedorn
Joseph L. Spilman, III
Caroline D. Ibos
Robert D. Ford
Lynnette Hall-Lewis
Kevin O. Larmann
Tammy M. Stewart
Danny N. Bowz
Edward C. Vocke, IV
C. Angelle Goudeau
Alayne R. Corcoran
David K. Groome, Jr.
Kristen M. Baumer
Gabriel J. Veninata

OF COUNSEL

Henry D. McNamara, Jr., (P.L.C.)

Representative Clients: Diamond Offshore Drilling Inc.; The Flintkote Co.; Lockheed Martin Corporation; Rheem Manufacturing Co.; State Farm Fire & Casualty Co.; Textron, Inc; Travelers Companies; Coca-Cola Enterprises, Inc.

For full biographical listings, see the Martindale-Hubbell Law Directory

REICH, MEEKS & TREADAWAY, L.L.C. (AV)

Two Lakeway Center, Suite 1830, 3850 North Causeway Boulevard, 70002
Telephone: 504-830-3999
Fax: 504-830-3950
URL: http://www.rmtlaw.com

Robert S. Reich
S. Daniel Meeks
Randell E. Treadaway
Lawrence R. Plunkett, Jr.

Michelle L. Maraist
Jimmy Arthur Castex, Jr.
Mark S. Senter
Patricia Cowen Penton
Patrice W. Oppenheim
John B. Esnard, III

For full biographical listings, see the Martindale-Hubbell Law Directory

SALLEY & ASSOCIATES (AV)

Causeway Plaza, 3510 North Causeway Boulevard, Suite 601, 70002
Telephone: 504-846-4260
Fax: 504-846-4265
Covington, Louisiana Office: 77378 Stafford Road.
Telephone: 504-867-9761.

Fred E. Salley
Lee Morgan Peacocke

For full biographical listings, see the Martindale-Hubbell Law Directory

*NEW ORLEANS,** Orleans Parish

BENCOMO & ASSOCIATES (AV)

Suite 2110 One Poydras Plaza, 639 Loyola Avenue, 70113
Telephone: 504-529-2929
Fax: 504-529-2018

Raul R. Bencomo

OF COUNSEL

Richard E. Anderson
Helen Hairston Babin

For full biographical listings, see the Martindale-Hubbell Law Directory

BEST KOEPPEL, A PROFESSIONAL LAW CORPORATION (AV)

LL & E Tower, 909 Poydras Street Suite 2200, 70112
Telephone: 504-593-2400
Telecopier: 504-593-2401
Email: bstkpplesq@aol.com
Houston, Texas Office: 1900 West Loop South, Suite 300, 77027.
Telephone: 713-964-4072.
Telecopier: 713-963-2503.

Laurence E. Best
Peter S. Koeppel
R. Jeffrey Bridger
James H. Daigle, Jr.
M. Davis Ready
Suzanne M. Risey

LEGAL SUPPORT PERSONNEL

PARALEGAL

Debora N. Dufrene

Representative Clients: Lexington Insurance Co.; Rowan Companies, Inc.; Rowandrill, Inc.; Rowan International, Inc.; Atlantic Maritime Services, Inc.; Rowan Drilling (U.K.), Ltd.; Hartford Insurance Co.; Trinity Marine Group; Elevating Boats, Inc.; CITGO Petroleum Corp.

For full biographical listings, see the Martindale-Hubbell Law Directory

BURKE & MAYER, A PROFESSIONAL LAW CORPORATION (AV)

Twentieth Floor, Energy Centre, 1100 Poydras Street, 70163-2000
Telephone: 504-569-2900
Telefacsimile: 504-569-2099
URL: http://www. Burke-Mayer.com

(See Next Column)

Gibbons Burke (1902-1989)
James G. Burke, Jr.
Charles B. Mayer
David L. Carrigee
William B. Schwartz
Daniel E. Knowles, III
Bernard H. Ticer
Andrew C. Wilson
Wm. Daniel Wellons
Robert D. Hoffman, Jr.
Donna M. Young
Brien J. Fricke
JeanPaul P. Overton

William B. Hidalgo
Jedd S. Malish
Cindy Galpin Martin

Representative Clients: All American Marine Slip/American Marine Insurance Group; American Bureau of Shipping; AON Companies; Bender Shipbuilding & Repair Co., Inc.; Blessey Marine Services, Inc.; British Companies and Lloyds Underwriters; Carnival Cruise Lines, Inc.; CARI Corp.; Chiquita Brands Intl.; Consolidated Grain & Barge Co.

For full biographical listings, see the Martindale-Hubbell Law Directory

CAPITELLI & WICKER (AV)

2950 Energy Centre, 1100 Poydras Street, 70163-2950
Telephone: 504-582-2425
Fax: 504-582-2422
Email: cw4law@bellsouth.net

Ralph Capitelli
T. Carey Wicker, III
Paul Michael Elvir, Jr.

For full biographical listings, see the Martindale-Hubbell Law Directory

CHAFFE, MCCALL, PHILLIPS, TOLER & SARPY, L.L.P. (AV)

A Partnership including a Professional Law Corporation
2300 Energy Centre, 1100 Poydras Street, 70163-2300
Telephone: 504-585-7000
Telecopier: 504-585-7075
Cable Address: "Denegre"
Telex: (AT&T) 460122 CMPTS
Email: cmptsno%chaffe@mcimail.com *URL:* http://www.chaffe.com
Baton Rouge, Louisiana Office: 202 Two United Plaza, 8550 United Plaza Boulevard.
Telephone: 504-922-4300.
Fax: 504-922-4304.
Caracas, Venezuela Office: Edificio Exa, Piso 10, Oficina PH-10, Avenida Venezuela entre Calles EL Retiro y Alameda, El Rosal.
Telephone: 011-582-953-4136.
Fax: 011-582-953-6518.

MEMBERS OF FIRM

Robert B. Deane
J. Dwight LeBlanc, Jr.
Robert B. Fisher, Jr.
Derek Anthony Walker
Thomas D. Forbes
Daniel A. Tadros

ASSOCIATES

Keith E. Andrews
H. Michael Bush
Ivan Mauricio Rodriguez
Alexandra M. Lamothe

Representative Clients: Liverpool and London Steamship Protection and Indemnity Association, Ltd.; Nedlloyd Bulk B.V.; Newcastle Protection and Indemnity Association; The Britannia Steam Ship Insurance Association Ltd.; The Japan Ship Owners' Mutual Protection and Indemnity Association; The North of England Protecting and Indemnity Association Ltd.; The Standard Steamship Owners' Protection and Indemnity Association (Bermuda) Ltd.; The Sunderland Steamship Protecting & Indemnity Association; The United Kingdom Mutual Steamship Assurance Association (Bermuda) Ltd.; The West of England Ship Owners Mutual Insurance Association (Luxembourg).

For Complete List of Firm Personnel, See General Section

For full biographical listings, see the Martindale-Hubbell Law Directory

CHRISTOVICH AND KEARNEY, L.L.P. (AV)

Suite 2300 Pan American Life Center, 601 Poydras Street, 70130-6078
Telephone: 504-561-5700
Fax: 504-561-5743
Email: c&k@christovich.com

MEMBERS OF FIRM

Alvin R. Christovich, Jr.
William K. Christovich
J. Walter Ward, Jr.
Lawrence J. Ernst
James F. Holmes
Robert E. Peyton
C. Edgar Cloutier
Charles W. Schmidt, III
Richard K. Christovich
Terry Christovich Gay
E. Phelps Gay
J. Warren Gardner, Jr.
Kevin R. Tully
Lance R. Rydberg
Elizabeth S. Cordes
Charles M. Lanier, Jr.
Philip J. Borne
James A. Holmes

ASSOCIATES

Robert D. Peyton
Craig B. Mitchell
Joseph M. Guillot
Scott J. Sonnier
John K. Nieset
Janet L. White
Mary Beth Meyer
Kory J. Ickler

(See Next Column)

CHRISTOVICH AND KEARNEY L.L.P.—*Continued*

OF COUNSEL

John A. Stassi II

Representative Clients: Amoco Oil Co.; Liberty Mutual Insurance Co.; Atlantic Richfield Co.; Brown & Root, Inc.; Vastar Resources, Inc.; Highlands Insurance Co.; Underwriters at Lloyds; Halliburton Energy Services.

For full biographical listings, see the Martindale-Hubbell Law Directory

EMMETT, COBB, WAITS, KESSENICH & O'NEIL, A PROFESSIONAL LAW CORPORATION (AV)

Suite 1950, 1515 Poydras Street, 70112
Telephone: 504-581-1301
Telex: 58-4430
Telecopier: 504-581-6020
Email: ecwko@ecwko.com

Francis Emmett (Retired)
Randolph J. Waits
J. Fredrick Kessenich
James A. Cobb, Jr.
John F. Emmett
William E. O'Neil
Susan E. Henning
Michael G. Helm

OF COUNSEL

Terry A. McCall

Michael W. McMahon
William K. Terrill, II

Reference: First National Bank of Commerce, New Orleans.

For full biographical listings, see the Martindale-Hubbell Law Directory

FRANSEN & HARDIN, A P.L.C. (AV)

814 Howard Avenue, P.O. Box 52676, 70152-2676
Telephone: 504-522-1188
Telecopier: 504-524-8317

A. Remy Fransen, Jr.
Allain F. Hardin
P. Chris Christofferson
Christopher J. Fransen

For full biographical listings, see the Martindale-Hubbell Law Directory

FRILOT, PARTRIDGE, KOHNKE & CLEMENTS, L.C. (AV)

3600 Energy Centre, 1100 Poydras Street, 70163-3600
Telephone: 504-599-8000
Telecopier: 504-599-8100
Email: postmaster@fpkc.com *URL:* http://www.fpkc.com

Francis H. Brown, III
James H. Brown, Jr.
George E. Cain, Jr.
Michael T. Cali
Miles P. Clements
Andrew S. de Klerk
George A. Frilot, III (A Professional Law Corp.)
John J. Hainkel, III
Edward F. Kohnke, IV
Allen J. Krouse, III
J. Dwight LeBlanc, III
Douglas P. Matthews
Kenneth A. Mayeaux
Robert B. McNeal
Wayne K. McNeil
Patrick J. McShane
Joseph N. Mole
David A. Olson
Scott S. Partridge
Greg A. Pellegrini
Michael R. Phillips
James F. Shuey
James R. Silverstein
Peter E. Sperling
Patrick A. Talley (P.C.)
Patricia E. Weeks

Sidney A. Backstrom
Joel Edwin Cape (Not admitted in LA)
Nairda T. Lesa Colón
Bruce Arne Cranner
Frederick T. Greschner, Jr.
Brant David Imperatore
Stephanie Ann May
Michael B. North

For full biographical listings, see the Martindale-Hubbell Law Directory

GAINSBURGH, BENJAMIN, DAVID, MEUNIER & WARSHAUER (AV)

2800 Energy Centre, 1100 Poydras, 70163-2800
Telephone: 504-522-2304
Telecopier: 504-528-9973
Email: DPHILLIPS@GAINSBEN.COM

OF COUNSEL

Samuel C. Gainsburgh
Jack C. Benjamin

MEMBERS OF FIRM

Robert J. David
Gerald E. Meunier
Irving J. Warshauer
Stevan C. Dittman
Madeleine M. Landrieu
Darryl M. Phillips
Jeffrey A. Mitchell

ASSOCIATE

Gary B. Roth

For full biographical listings, see the Martindale-Hubbell Law Directory

GEORGE W. HEALY, IV (AV)

330 Camp Street, 70130
Telephone: 504-524-3223
Fax: 504-524-3282
Email: gwhealyiv@aol.com *URL:* http://www.healyivlaw.com

Representative Clients: Bryan Chevrolet; Gilchrist Machinery; Associated Manufacturers Agents, Inc. (AMA).

For full biographical listings, see the Martindale-Hubbell Law Directory

DARLEEN M. JACOBS A PROFESSIONAL LAW CORPORATION (AV)

823 St. Louis Street, 70112
Telephone: 504-522-3287; 522-0155
Fax: 504-522-3819
Cable Address: "Darjac."

Darleen M. Jacobs
Honorable S. Sanford Levy (1902-1989)

For full biographical listings, see the Martindale-Hubbell Law Directory

JOHNSON, JOHNSON, BARRIOS & YACOUBIAN, A PROFESSIONAL LAW CORPORATION (AV)

One Shell Square, 701 Poydras Street, Suite 4900, 70139-7701
Telephone: 504-528-3001
Facsimile: 504-528-3030
Email: jjbylaw@bellsouth.net

Ronald A. Johnson
Edward S. Johnson
Bettye A. Barrios
Alan J. Yacoubian
Salvador J. Pusateri
Rene S. Paysse, Jr.

Cindy T. Matherne
Lance E. Harwell
Salvatore A. Faso, II
Michael W. Mallory
Kevin G. Barreca
Wesley S. Alost
Thomas A. French
T. Gavin Hoppe

Representative Clients: Amoco Corporation; Aon Group, Ltd.; Burnett & Company; Commercial Union Assurance Company, PLC; Continental Underwriters, Ltd.; EEX Corporation; Genco, Inc.; Houma Industries, a Division of Lor, Inc.; Lexington Insurance Company; Offshore Logistics, Inc.

For full biographical listings, see the Martindale-Hubbell Law Directory

LEE, FUTRELL & PERLES, L.L.P. (AV)

Suite 2409, 201 St. Charles Avenue, 70170-2409
Telephone: 504-569-1725
Fax: 504-569-1726
Email: mgr@leefutrell.com *URL:* http://www.lawyers.com/lf&plaw

Gary A. Lee
John Maurice Futrell
Richard M. Perles

Representative Clients: Certain Underwriters at Lloyd's, London; Institute of London Underwriters Companies.

For full biographical listings, see the Martindale-Hubbell Law Directory

LEGER & MESTAYER (AV)

A Law Partnership including Professional Corporations
Ninth Floor, 600 Carondelet Street, 70130
Telephone: 504-588-9043
WATTS (800) 523-5787
Cable Address: "Admiralty"
Facsimile: 504-588-9980
New Iberia, Louisiana Office: 110 East Pershing Street. P.O. Box 12340.
Telephone: 318-365-8181.
Facsimile: 318-367-8811.
Cable Address: "Admiralty."
Telex: 587450.

MEMBERS OF FIRM

Walter J. Leger, Jr., (P.C.)
Michael J. Mestayer (P.C.)
Franklin G. Shaw

ASSOCIATES

Christine Reitano
Christine L. DeSue

OF COUNSEL

William S. Poole, Jr.
Stephen F. Mestayer

Representative Clients: Bergeror Marine Service, Inc.; Nautical Aviation Co., Inc.; Marine Brokers & Consultants, Inc.; Mavco, Inc.; Deep South Security, Inc.; Terremer Investment Corp.; Ryan Marine, Inc.; CBL Barge Co.; River Marine Contractors, Inc.; Cardiovascular Technological Centre, Inc.

For full biographical listings, see the Martindale-Hubbell Law Directory

LEWIS, KULLMAN & STERBCOW (AV)

2615 Pan-American Life Center, 601 Poydras Street, 70130
Telephone: 504-588-1500
Fax: 504-588-1514
Email: lewkull@bellsouth.net

(See Next Column)

LEWIS, KULLMAN & STERBCOW, *New Orleans—Continued*

MEMBERS OF FIRM

Harvey J. Lewis
Lawrence S. Kullman
Paul M. Sterbcow

ASSOCIATE

David A. Abramson

For full biographical listings, see the Martindale-Hubbell Law Directory

LUGENBUHL, BURKE, WHEATON, PECK, RANKIN & HUBBARD, A LAW CORPORATION (AV)

27th Floor, Pan-American Life Center, 601 Poydras Street, 70130-6017
Telephone: 504-568-1990
Telefax: 504-529-7418
URL: http://www.lawla.com
Gulfport, Mississippi Office: The Markham Building, 2301 14th Street, Suite 705.
Telephone: 228-865-1490.
Fax: 228-822-2170.

Charles E. Lugenbuhl
Scott R. Wheaton, Jr.
Stewart F. Peck
S. Frazer Rankin
Ralph S. Hubbard III
Stanley J. Cohn
Nathan P. Horner, Jr.
Kristopher M. Redmann
James B. Persons (Resident, Gulfport, Mississippi Office)
Claude F. Bosworth
Gordon P. Wilson
J. Clayton Davie, Jr.

Loree Peacock Leboeuf
David B. Sharpe
Mary Sprague Langston
Simeon Bernard Reimonenq, Jr.
Celeste Darmstadter Elliott
Kristopher T. Wilson

Representative Clients: Baker Hughes, Inc.; Bank of Louisiana; E.N. Bisso & Son, Inc.; Brown & Root U.S.A., Inc.; Budget Rent A Car Corp.; Budget Rent A Car Systems, Inc.; The Center Marine Managers, Inc.; Central Gulf Towing Co., Inc.; Chrysler Capital Corp.; Citrus Lands of Louisiana, Inc.

For full biographical listings, see the Martindale-Hubbell Law Directory

MAGINNIS & HURLEY, A PROFESSIONAL LAW CORPORATION (AV)

Suite 2040 Canal Place One, 365 Canal Street, 70130
Telephone: 504-524-5353
Fax: 504-524-5403
Email: maginnis+hurley@gs.net

Michael J. Maginnis
Timothy P. Hurley
José R. Cot
Sallye Goodwin Webb
Lisa D. Kothe

For full biographical listings, see the Martindale-Hubbell Law Directory

MCGLINCHEY STAFFORD (AV)

A Professional Limited Liability Company
643 Magazine Street, 70130-3477
Telephone: 504-586-1200
Fax: 504-596-2800
TDD: (504) 596-2728
Telex: 584327
Cable Address: "MACSTAC"
Mailing Address: P.O. Box 60643, New Orleans, Louisiana, 70160-0643
Email: @mcglinchey.com *URL:* http://www.mcglinchey.com
Dallas, Texas Office: 2777 Stemmons Freeway, Suite 925, 75207-2401.
Telephone: 214-860-9700.
Fax: 214-860-9750.
Houston, Texas Office: 2727 Allen Parkway, Suite 1900, 77019.
Telephone: 713-520-1900.
Fax: 713-520-1025.
Baton Rouge, Louisiana Office: Ninth Floor, One American Place, 70825-0001.
Telephone: 504-383-9000.
Fax: 504-343-3076.
Jackson, Mississippi Office: Suite 1200, SkyTel Centre, 200 South Lamar Street, 39201.
Telephone: 601-960-8400.
Fax: 601-960-8406.
Lake Providence, Louisiana Office: 405 Morgan Street, 71254-2691.
Telephone: 318-559-1200.
Fax: 318-559-0609.
Monroe, Louisiana Office: Dean ONB Tower, 130 Desiard Street, Suite 807, 71201.
Telephone: 318-651-0807.
Fax: 318-651-0809.

MEMBERS OF FIRM

Kathleen Krail Charvet
Michael J. de Blanc, Jr.
John H. Clegg
Daphne McNutt

ASSOCIATES

Daniel T. Plunkett
Sarah Suzanne Wommack Mahoney
Eric J. Simonson
Gina M. Venezia

(See Next Column)

MEMBERS OF FIRM

Michael David Ferachi (Resident, Baton Rouge Office)

For full biographical listings, see the Martindale-Hubbell Law Directory

MILLING BENSON WOODWARD L.L.P. (AV)

A Partnership including Professional Law Corporations
Suite Twenty-Three Hundred, 909 Poydras Street, 70112-1017
Telephone: 504-569-7000
Telecopier: 504-569-7001
ABA net: 15656
MCI Mail: "Milling"
Email: milling@millinglaw.com
Lafayette, Louisiana Office: 101 La Rue France, Suite 200.
Telephone: 318-232-3929.
Telecopier: 318-233-4957.
Mandeville (North Shore), Louisiana Office: 2140 8th Street.
Telephone: 504-867-9622.
Telecopier: 504-867-8364.

MEMBERS OF FIRM

Neal D. Hobson (P.C.)
Timothy T. Roniger (P.C.)
Benjamin O. Schupp (P.C.)

ASSOCIATE

Sergio J. Alarcon

See General Section for list of Representative Clients.

For Complete List of Firm Personnel, See General Section

For full biographical listings, see the Martindale-Hubbell Law Directory

MOULEDOUX, BLAND, LEGRAND & BRACKETT, LLC (AV)

Poydras Center, 650 Poydras Street, Suite 2150, 70130
Telephone: 504-595-3000
Fax: 504-522-2121
Email: admin@mblb.com *URL:* http://www.mblb.com

André J. Mouledoux
Wilton E. Bland, III
Georges M. Legrand
Alan Guy Brackett
David M. Flotte
C. William Emory
Daniel J. Hoerner
Gerard Joseph Dragna

For full biographical listings, see the Martindale-Hubbell Law Directory

MURPHY, ROGERS & SLOSS, A PROFESSIONAL LAW CORPORATION (AV)

One Shell Square, Suite 400, 701 Poydras Street, 70139
Telephone: 504-523-0400
Facsimile: 504-523-5574
Email: firm@mrsnola.com

Robert H. Murphy
E. Carroll Rogers
Peter B. Sloss
Gary J. Gambel
James M. Jacobs
Charles L. Whited, Jr.
Molly B. Halloran
John H. Musser, V
Scott E. Oliphant

Representative Clients: American Overseas Marine Corporation; The Britannia Steam Ship Insurance Association Limited; Clarendon National Insurance Company; CSX Corporation; G&B Marine, Inc.; Great Lakes Dredge & Dock Company, Inc.; Harris Transport, Inc.; Liverpool and London Steamship Protection and Indemnity Limited; National-Oilwell.

For full biographical listings, see the Martindale-Hubbell Law Directory

PHELPS DUNBAR, L.L.P. (AV)

Texaco Center, 400 Poydras Street, 70130-3245
Telephone: 504-566-1311
Telecopier: 504-568-9130, 504-568-9007
Cable Address: "Howspencer"
Telex: 584125 WU
Telex: 6821155 WUI
Email: info@phelps.com
Baton Rouge, Louisiana Office: Suite 701, 445 North Boulevard, P.O. Box 4412.
Telephone: 225-346-0285.
Telecopier: 225-381-9197.
Jackson, Mississippi Office: Suite 500, SkyTel Centre, 200 South Lamar Street, P.O. Box 23066.
Telephone: 601-352-2300.
Telecopier: 601-360-9777.
Tupelo, Mississippi Office: Seventh Floor, One Mississippi Plaza, P.O. Box 1220.
Telephone: 662-842-7907.
Telecopier: 662-842-3873.
Houston, Texas Office: Suite 900, 3040 Post Oak Boulevard.
Telephone: 713-626-1386.
Telecopier: 713-626-1388.
London, England Office: Suite 731, Level 7, Lloyd's, 1 Lime Street, London EC3M 7DQ England.
Telephone: 011-44-207-929-4765.
Telecopier: 011-44-207-929-0046.
Telex: 987321.

(See Next Column)

PHELPS DUNBAR L.L.P.—*Continued*

OF COUNSEL

George W. Healy, III
James Bradley Kemp, Jr.
John W. Sims
J. Barbee Winston

RESIDENT PARTNERS

Julia Marie Adams (Not admitted in LA; Resident, Houston, Texas Office)
Robert C. Clotworthy
Christopher O. Davis
Mark C. Dodart (Also at London, England Office)
George M. Gilly
Robert P. McCleskey, Jr. (Also at London, England Office)
Matthew R. Muth (Not admitted in LA; Resident, Houston, Texas Office)
William J. Riviere
James H. Roussel (Also at London, England Office)
Claude LeRoy Stuart, III (Not admitted in LA; Resident, Houston, Texas Office)
Brian D. Wallace
Kent E. Westmoreland (Not admitted in LA; Houston, Texas and London, England Offices)

COUNSEL

Edwin K. Legnon

RESIDENT ASSOCIATES

Jennifer M. Benson (Resident, Houston, Texas Office)
Maurice E. Bostick
Evan T. Caffrey
Stacy S. Head
Karen Klaas Milhollin (Not admitted in LA; Resident, Houston, Texas Office)
Thomas Kent Ledyard Morrison
W. Spencer Murphy
W. Sean O'Neil
Stanley T. Proctor (Not admitted in LA; Resident, Houston, Texas Office)
John L. Schouest (Resident, Houston, Texas Office)
Cynthia J. Thomas
Dawei Zhang

Representative Clients: Bludworth Bond Shipyard; The Britannia Steamship Insurance Assn., Ltd.; Edison Chouest Offshore, L.L.C.; ENSCO Offshore Company; Fairfield Industries, Inc.; Global Industries, Ltd.; Signal Mutual Indemnity Association; Standard Steamship Owners P&I Association; The Steamship Mutual Underwriting Association, Ltd.; Underwriters at Lloyd's, London.

For Complete List of Firm Personnel, See General Section

For full biographical listings, see the Martindale-Hubbell Law Directory

TERRIBERRY, CARROLL & YANCEY, L.L.P. (AV)

3100 Energy Centre, 1100 Poydras Street, 70163-3100
Telephone: 504-523-6451
Cable Address: "Terrib"
Telex: 6821224 (WUI)
Fax: 504-524-3257
Email: info@terriberry.com

Benjamin W. Yancey (1906-1991)
Walter Carroll, Jr. (Retired)

MEMBERS OF FIRM

G. Edward Merritt
John A. Bolles
Charles F. Lozes
Robert J. Barbier
Hugh Ramsay Straub
David B. Lawton
Janet Wessler Marshall
D. Kirk Boswell
Gary A. Hemphill
Laurence R. De Buys, IV
Kevin J. LaVie
Stephen E. Mattesky
Gerald M. Baca
Michael M. Butterworth
John A. Scialdone

COUNSEL

Andrew T. Martinez
Cynthia Anne Wegmann

ASSOCIATES

Evans Martin Mcleod
Kenneth J. Gelpi, Jr.

OF COUNSEL

James L. Schupp, Jr.

Representative Clients: Assuranceforeningen Gard; Assuranceforeningen Skuld; The Britannia Club; Certain Underwriters at Lloyd's; The London Steam-Ship Owners' Mutual Insurance Assn. Ltd.; New Orleans Steamship Assn.; Nordisk Skibsrederforening (Northern Shipowners Defence Club); Scandinavian Marine Claims Office, Inc.; Steamship Mutual Underwriting Assn. Ltd.; United Kingdom Mutual Steam Ship Assurance Assn. Ltd.

For full biographical listings, see the Martindale-Hubbell Law Directory

WAGNER & BAGOT (AV)

Suite 2660, Poydras Center, 650 Poydras Street, 70130-6105
Telephone: 504-525-2141
Telecopier: 504-523-1587
TWX: 5106017673
ELN: 62928850
"INCISIVE"

Thomas J. Wagner
Michael H. Bagot, Jr.

Thomas A. Rayer, Jr.
Brian P. Brancato
Thomas P. Henican
Dana A. Henderson

For full biographical listings, see the Martindale-Hubbell Law Directory

WILSON & BOWLING (AV)

A Partnership including Professional Law Corporations
Suite 2411, Bank One Center, 201 St. Charles Avenue, 70170
Telephone: 504-586-5200
Facsimile: 504-586-5201
Email: wilsbowl@gs.net
Gulfport, Mississippi Office: 715 Markham Building, 2301 14th Street, 39501.
Telephone: 228-575-6202.
Fax: 228-864-6227.

Gordon F. Wilson, Jr., (P.L.C.)
David A. Bowling (P.L.C.)

Jeanne B. Roques
Susannah Ross Cooley
John D. Acomb

For full biographical listings, see the Martindale-Hubbell Law Directory

MAINE

*PORTLAND,** Cumberland Co.

TOMPKINS, CLOUGH, HIRSHON & LANGER, P.A. (AV)

Three Canal Plaza, P.O. Box 15060, 04112-5060
Telephone: 207-874-6700
FAX: 207-874-6705

Bruce M. Tompkins
Lawrence R. Clough
David M. Hirshon
Leonard W. Langer
Marshall J. Tinkle

For full biographical listings, see the Martindale-Hubbell Law Directory

MARYLAND

*BALTIMORE,** (Independent City)

FERGUSON, SCHETELICH & HEFFERNAN, P.A. (AV)

1401 NationsBank Center, 100 South Charles Street, 21201-2725
Telephone: 410-837-2200
Fax: 410-837-1188
URL: http://www.FSHLaw.com

Robert L. Ferguson, Jr.
Thomas J. Schetelich
Christopher J. Heffernan
Craig F. Ballew
Michael N. Russo, Jr.

Peter J. Basile
Ann D. Ware
Tracey J. McLauchlin
Michele P. Zahner
Michael K. Hourigan

For full biographical listings, see the Martindale-Hubbell Law Directory

ISRAELSON, SALSBURY, CLEMENTS & BEKMAN, L.L.C. (AV)

300 West Pratt Street Suite 450, 21201
Telephone: 410-539-6633
FAX: 410-625-9554

MEMBERS OF FIRM

Stuart Marshall Salsbury
Paul D. Bekman
Daniel M. Clements
Matthew Zimmerman
Laurence A. Marder

Lauren R. Calia
Leslie Hayes Russo

COUNSEL TO THE FIRM

Max R. Israelson
Michael P. Smith

OF COUNSEL

Samuel Omar Jackson, Jr. (Semi-Retired)
Wendy Lozinsky Shiff

For full biographical listings, see the Martindale-Hubbell Law Directory

NILES, BARTON & WILMER (AV)

Suite 1400, 111 S. Calvert Street, 21202-6185
Telephone: 410-783-6300
Cable Address: "Nilwo"
Telecopier: 410-783-6363

MEMBERS OF FIRM

Robert P. O'Brien
Steven E. Leder

For Complete List of Firm Personnel, See General Section

For full biographical listings, see the Martindale-Hubbell Law Directory

Baltimore—Continued

VENABLE ATTORNEYS AT LAW VENABLE, BAETJER AND HOWARD, LLP (AV)

A Partnership including Professional Corporations
1800 Mercantile Bank & Trust Building, 2 Hopkins Plaza, 21201
Telephone: 410-244-7400
Fax: 410-244-7742
URL: http://www.venable.com
Washington, D.C. Office: Venable, Baetjer, Howard & Civiletti LLP, Suite 1000, 1201 New York Avenue, N.W.
Telephone: 202-962-4800.
Fax: 202-962-8300.
McLean, Virginia Office: Suite 400, 2010 Corporate Ridge.
Telephone: 703-760-1600.
Fax: 703-821-8949.
Rockville, Maryland Office: Suite 500, One Church Street, P. O. Box 1906.
Telephone: 301-217-5600.
Fax: 301-217-5617.
Towson, Maryland Office: 210 Allegheny Avenue, P. O. Box 5517.
Telephone: 410-494-6200.
Fax: 410-821-0147.

MEMBER OF FIRM

Lars E. Anderson (Not admitted in MD; Resident, McLean, Virginia Office)

For Complete List of Firm Personnel, See General Section

For full biographical listings, see the Martindale-Hubbell Law Directory

WARD, KERSHAW & MINTON, A PROFESSIONAL ASSOCIATION (AV)

113 West Monument Street, 21201
Telephone: 410-685-6700
Fax: 410-685-6704
Email: wkmfirm@aol.com *URL:* http://www.wkamlaw.com

John T. Ward
Robert B. Kershaw
Thomas J. Minton
April Falcon Doss
J. Dirk Schwenk

OF COUNSEL

Richard V. Falcon

For full biographical listings, see the Martindale-Hubbell Law Directory

WRIGHT, CONSTABLE & SKEEN, LLP (AV)

One Charles Center, 16th Floor, 100 N. Charles Street, 21201
Telephone: 410-659-1300
Telex: 710 234-2383 CALDAS
Fax: 410-659-1350

MEMBERS OF FIRM

James W. Constable
James D. Skeen
Stephen F. White

Representative Clients: General Ship Repair Corp.; Egan Marine Contracting Co., Inc.; Atlantic Mutual Insurance Co.; Marine Office of America Corp.; Recovery Services International; Toplis & Harding, Inc.; Firemen's Fund; Royal Insurance Co.; Gradman & Holler, Gmbh; Arkwright-Boston Insurance.

For Complete List of Firm Personnel, See General Section

For full biographical listings, see the Martindale-Hubbell Law Directory

MASSACHUSETTS

*BOSTON,** Suffolk Co.

SWARTZ & SWARTZ (AV)

10 Marshall Street, 02108
Telephone: 617-742-1900
Fax: 617-367-7193
Email: Attorney@Swartzlaw.com *URL:* http://www.Swartzlaw.com

Edward M. Swartz
Alan L. Cantor
Joseph A. Swartz
Victor A. Denaro
Joan E. Swartz
James A. Swartz
David P. Angueira
Jason Mark
Lisa V. Kaprielian

OF COUNSEL

Fredric A. Swartz

For full biographical listings, see the Martindale-Hubbell Law Directory

MICHIGAN

*DETROIT,** Wayne Co.

BRADY, HATHAWAY, BRADY & BRETZ, PROFESSIONAL CORPORATION (AV)

1330 Buhl Building, 48226-3602
Telephone: 313-965-3700
Telecopier: 313-965-2830
Email: brady@bradyhathaway.com

Thomas M. J. Hathaway
David A. Hardesty

Representative Client: Kinsman Lines.

For Complete List of Firm Personnel, See General Section

For full biographical listings, see the Martindale-Hubbell Law Directory

FOSTER, MEADOWS & BALLARD, P.C. (AV)

Shelby Congress Building, 607 Shelby, Seventh Floor, 48226
Telephone: 313-961-3234
Facsimile: 313-961-6184
Email: FosterMeadows@FosterMeadows.com *URL:* http://www.lawyers.com/fm&blaw

Sparkman D. Foster (1897-1967)
Raymond A. Ballard (1921-1996)
Charles R. Hrdlicka
Paul D. Galea
Richard A. Dietz
Robert H. Fortunate
Robert G. Lahiff
Camille A. Raffa-Dietz
Michael J. Liddane

Counsel For: Cement Transit Company; Cleveland Tankers 1991, Inc.; Great American Insurance Co.; Marine Office of America; Mutual Marine Insurance Co.; St. Paul Companies; United Kingdom Mutual Steamship Owners Protection and Indemnity Association.

For full biographical listings, see the Martindale-Hubbell Law Directory

ANTITRUST LAW

ALABAMA

*BIRMINGHAM,** Jefferson Co.

Berkowitz, Lefkovits, Isom & Kushner, A Professional Corporation (AV)

SouthTrust Tower, 420 North Twentieth Street, Suite 1600, 35203-5202
Telephone: 205-328-0480
Telecopier: 205-322-8007
URL: http://www.blik.com

B. G. Minisman, Jr.
J. Forrest Hinton
Susan S. Wagner
Richard A. Pizitz, Jr.

Ellen Elizabeth Henderson

For Complete List of Firm Personnel, See General Section

For full biographical listings, see the Martindale-Hubbell Law Directory

Bradley Arant Rose & White LLP (AV)

2001 Park Place, Suite 1400, P.O. Box 830709, 35283-0709
Telephone: 205-521-8000
Facsimile: 205-521-8800
Facsimile (SouthTrust Tower Office): 205-521-8500
URL: http://www.barw.com
Huntsville, Alabama Office: 200 Clinton Avenue West, Suite 900, 35801.
Telephone: 205-517-5100.
Facsimile: 205-533-5069.
Washington, D.C. Office: 801 Pennsylvania Avenue, NW, Suite 230, 20004.
Telephone: 202-347-8893.
Facsimile: 202-347-1684.

MEMBERS OF FIRM

James Patrick Alexander
Philip J. Carroll III
Michael S. Denniston
Linda A. Friedman
John E. Goodman
Thad Gladden Long
Joseph B. Mays Jr.
Michael D. McKibben
Michael R. Pennington
J. David Pugh
Robert K. Spotswood

ASSOCIATE

Fred M. Haston III

Counsel for: SouthTrust Bank of Alabama, National Association; Stockham Valves & Fittings, Inc.; Wolverine Tube, Inc.; Blount, Inc.; Coca-Cola Bottling Company United, Inc.; Russell Corp.; Walter Industries, Inc.

For Complete List of Firm Personnel, See General Section

For full biographical listings, see the Martindale-Hubbell Law Directory

Burr & Forman LLP (AV)

3100 SouthTrust Tower, 420 North 20th Street, P.O. Box 830719, 35283-0719
Telephone: 205-251-3000
Facsimile: 205-458-5100
URL: http://www.burr.com
Huntsville, Alabama Office: Suite 204, Regency Center, 400 Meridian Street.
Telephone: 205-551-0010.
Facsimile: 205-551-0043.
Atlanta, Georgia Office: Suite 1200, One Georgia Center, 600 West Peachtree Street, 30308.
Telephone: 404-815-3000.
Facsimile: 404-817-3244.

MEMBERS OF FIRM

John D. Clements
James Ross Forman, III
J. Patrick Logan
Gary M. London
J. Hunter Phillips, III

OF COUNSEL

A. Jackson Noble, Jr.

For Complete List of Firm Personnel, See General Section

For full biographical listings, see the Martindale-Hubbell Law Directory

Emond & Vines (AV)

2200 SouthTrust Tower, 420 North 20th Street, P.O. Box 10008, 35202-0008
Telephone: 205-324-4000
Fax: 205-324-5020
Email: EmondVines@aol.com

MEMBER OF FIRM

Lanny S. Vines

(See Next Column)

ASSOCIATES

Michael Lee Allsup
Vivian D. Vines Campbell
Frank O. Hanson, Jr.

For full biographical listings, see the Martindale-Hubbell Law Directory

Haskell Slaughter & Young, L.L.C. (AV)

1200 AmSouth/Harbert Plaza, 1901 Sixth Avenue North, 35203
Telephone: 205-251-1000
Facsimile: 205-324-1133
Email: hsy@hsy.com
Montgomery, Alabama Office: 305 South Lawrence Street, P.O. Box 4660. 36103-4660.
Telephone: 334-265-8573.
Facsimile: 334-264-7945.

James C. Huckaby, Jr.
Michael K. K. Choy

Representative Clients: The Equitable Life Assurance Society of the United States; Exxon Corporation; Rhone-Poulenc Rorer Pharmaceuticals, Inc.

For Complete List of Firm Personnel, See General Section

For full biographical listings, see the Martindale-Hubbell Law Directory

Lightfoot, Franklin & White, L.L.C. (AV)

The Clark Building, 400 20th Street North, 35203
Telephone: 205-581-0700
Facsimile: 205-581-0799
Email: LFWlaw@LFWlaw.com *URL:* http://www.lfwlaw.com

Warren B. Lightfoot
Samuel H. Franklin
John M. Johnson
E. Glenn Waldrop, Jr.

Wynn M. Shuford
Robin Hansen Graves

For full biographical listings, see the Martindale-Hubbell Law Directory

J. Vernon Patrick, Jr. & Associates, P.C. (AV)

1201 Financial Center, 505 20th Street North, 35203-4607
Telephone: 205-323-5665
Telecopier: 205-324-6221

J. Vernon Patrick, Jr.

Jeffrey Venton Havercroft

For full biographical listings, see the Martindale-Hubbell Law Directory

Schoel, Ogle, Liles and Upshaw, LLP (AV)

600 Financial Center, 505 North 20th Street, P.O. Box 1865, 35201-1865
Telephone: 205-521-7000
Telecopier: 205-521-7007
Mailing Address: Drawer 1865, Birmingham, Alabama, 35201-1865

Jerry W. Schoel
Richard F. Ogle
Paul A. Liles
David O. Upshaw
Jann J. Rice

Reference: First Alabama Bank.

For full biographical listings, see the Martindale-Hubbell Law Directory

Spain & Gillon, L.L.C. (AV)

The Zinszer Building, 2117 2nd Avenue North, 35203
Telephone: 205-328-4100
Telecopier: 205-324-8866
Email: ddh@spain-gillon.com *URL:* http://lawlinks.com:80/atty/al/sggbn.html

MEMBERS OF FIRM

Ollie L. Blan, Jr.
Alton B. Parker, Jr.
Charles D. Stewart

General Counsel for: Piggly Wiggly Alabama Distributing Co.
Counsel for: Liberty National Life Insurance Co.; Government Employees Insurance Co.; Massachusetts Mutual Life Insurance Co.

For Complete List of Firm Personnel, See General Section

For full biographical listings, see the Martindale-Hubbell Law Directory

*MOBILE,** Mobile Co.

Armbrecht, Jackson, DeMouy, Crowe, Holmes & Reeves, L.L.C. (AV)

1300 Riverview Plaza, P.O. Box 290, 36601
Telephone: 334-405-1300
Facsimile: 334-432-6843; 433-3821
Email: adc@ajlaw.com

MEMBERS OF FIRM

E. B. Peebles III
David A. Bagwell

Representative Clients: AmSouth Bank of Alabama (Regional Counsel); Loyal American Life Insurance Co.; Mobile Gas Service Corp.; Mobile Steamship Ass'n -- International Longshoremen's Pension, Welfare & Vaca-

(See Next Column)

ARMBRECHT, JACKSON, DEMOUY, CROWE, HOLMES & REEVES L.L.C., *Mobile—Continued*

tion Plans; Smith's Bakery, Inc.; Southern Pine Inspection Bureau; United Bank; WKRG-TV-Channel 5.

For Complete List of Firm Personnel, See General Section

For full biographical listings, see the Martindale-Hubbell Law Directory

JOHNSTONE, ADAMS, BAILEY, GORDON AND HARRIS, L.L.C. (AV)

Royal St. Francis Building, 104 St. Francis Street, 8th Floor, P.O. Box 1988, 36633
Telephone: 334-432-7682
Facsimile: 334-432-0712 or 334-432-2800
Email: attorneys@JohnstoneAdams.com *URL:* http://www.JohnstoneAdams.com
Bay Minette, Alabama Office: Dahlberg Building, 107 Hand Avenue, P.O. Box 729, 36507.
Telephone: 334-937-9473.
Facsimile: 334-937-9475.

MEMBERS OF FIRM

William H. Hardie, Jr. — Celia J. Collins

For Complete List of Firm Personnel, See General Section

For full biographical listings, see the Martindale-Hubbell Law Directory

ARIZONA

*PHOENIX,** Maricopa Co.

ALLEN & PRICE, P.L.C. (AV)

2850 East Camelback Road, Suite 170, 85016-4380
Telephone: 602-381-0500
Fax: 602-381-8899
Email: allen@aplaw.com
Email: price@aplaw.com
Email: schacter@aplaw.com
Email: sanders@aplaw.com

Robert E. B. Allen — Charles S. Price
Scott A. Shacter — Barry R. Sanders

For full biographical listings, see the Martindale-Hubbell Law Directory

FENNEMORE CRAIG, A PROFESSIONAL CORPORATION (AV)

3003 North Central Avenue, Suite 2600, 85012-2913
Telephone: 602-916-5000
Fax: 602-916-5999
Tucson, Arizona Office: One South Church Avenue, Suite 1000, 85701-1620.
Telephone: 520-879-6800.
Fax: 520-879-6899.

Timothy J. Burke — C. Owen Paepke

For Complete List of Firm Personnel, See General Section

For full biographical listings, see the Martindale-Hubbell Law Directory

KIMERER & LAVELLE, P.L.C. (AV)

100 W. Clarendon Suite 2100, 85013
Telephone: 602-279-5900; 800-220-6817
Fax: 602-264-5566
Email: KimLav.com

Michael J. LaVelle

For full biographical listings, see the Martindale-Hubbell Law Directory

LEWIS AND ROCA, LLP (AV)

A Limited Liability Partnership including a Professional Corporation
40 North Central Avenue, 85004-4429
Telephone: 602-262-5311
Fax: 602-262-5747
Email: clientservice@lrlaw.com *URL:* http://www.lrlaw.com
Tucson, Arizona Office: One South Church Avenue, Suite 700, 86701-1620.
Telephone: 520-622-2090.
Fax: 520-622-3088. E-Mail: clientservice@lrlaw.com.
Las Vegas, Nevada Affiliated Office: Ashcraft and Heinz LLP, 3960 Howard Hughes Parkway, 89109.
Telephone: 702-990-3570.
Fax: 702-990-3571.

(See Next Column)

MEMBERS OF FIRM

John P. Frank — George L. Paul

Representative Clients: Arizona Hospital Assn.; The Heil Co.; Rockford Corp.; Samaritan Health System.

For Complete List of Firm Personnel, See General Section

For full biographical listings, see the Martindale-Hubbell Law Directory

SMOCK AND WEINBERGER (AV)

2700 North Central Avenue Suite 1125, 85004
Telephone: 602-230-5150
Telecopier: 602-230-5155

MEMBERS OF FIRM

Timothy R. Smock — Brian A. Weinberger

ASSOCIATE

Frank W. Moskowitz

For full biographical listings, see the Martindale-Hubbell Law Directory

SNELL & WILMER L.L.P. (AV)

One Arizona Center, 85004-2202
Telephone: 602-382-6000
Fax: 602-382-6070
Email: postmaster@snellwilmer.com *URL:* http://www.swlaw.com
Tucson, Arizona Office: One South Church Avenue, Suite 1500, 85701-1612.
Telephone: 520-882-1200.
Fax: 520-884-1294.
Orange County Office: 1920 Main Street, Suite 1200, Irvine, California 92614-7230.
Telephone: 949-253-2700.
Fax: 949-955-2507.
Salt Lake City, Utah Office: 111 East Broadway, Suite 900, 84111-1004.
Telephone: 801-237-1900.
Fax: 801-237-1950.

MEMBERS OF FIRM

John J. Bouma — Daniel J. McAuliffe
Arthur P. Greenfield — Patrick G. Byrne
Patricia Lee Refo

Representative Clients: For list of Representative Clients, see end of biographical listings in the Martindale-Hubbell Law Directory.

For Complete List of Firm Personnel, See General Section

For full biographical listings, see the Martindale-Hubbell Law Directory

ULRICH, KESSLER & ANGER, P.C. (AV)

3707 North Seventh Street, Suite 250, 85014-5059
Telephone: 602-248-9465
Fax: 602-248-0165
Email: ukapc@aol.com

Paul G. Ulrich — Donn G. Kessler
William H. Anger

For full biographical listings, see the Martindale-Hubbell Law Directory

*TUCSON,** Pima Co.

SNELL & WILMER L.L.P. (AV)

One South Church Avenue, Suite 1500, 85701-1612
Telephone: 520-882-1200
Fax: 520-884-1294
URL: http://www.swlaw.com
Phoenix, Arizona Office: One Arizona Center, 85004-2202.
Telephone: 602-382-6000.
Fax: 602-382-6070.
Orange County Office: 1920 Main Street, Suite 1200, Irvine, California 92614-7230.
Telephone: 949-253-2700.
Fax: 949-955-2507.
Salt Lake City, Utah Office: 111 East Broadway, Suite 900, 84111-1004.
Telephone: 801-237-1900.
Fax: 801-237-1950.

MEMBER OF FIRM

Michael S. Milroy

Representative Clients: For list of Representative Clients, see end of biographical listings in the Martindale-Hubbell Law Directory.

For full biographical listings, see the Martindale-Hubbell Law Directory

ARKANSAS

*LITTLE ROCK,** Pulaski Co.

FRIDAY, ELDREDGE & CLARK (AV)

A Limited Liability Partnership of Individuals and Professional Associations
Formerly, Smith, Williams, Friday, Eldredge & Clark
2000 Regions Center, 400 West Capitol Avenue, 72201-3493
Telephone: 501-376-2011
Telecopier: 501-376-2147
Email: fecmh@fec.net

MEMBERS OF FIRM

James M. Simpson, Jr. (P.A.) Tony L. Wilcox (P.A.)

Counsel for: Union Pacific System; St. Paul Insurance Co.; Liberty Mutual Insurance Co.; Cigna Property & Casualty Co.; Entergy Arkansas, Inc.; Dillard's, Inc.; Browning Arms Co.; Phillips Petroleum Co.; Aetna Casualty & Surety Co.

For Complete List of Firm Personnel, See General Section

For full biographical listings, see the Martindale-Hubbell Law Directory

WILLIAMS & ANDERSON (AV)

Registered Limited Liability Partnership
Twenty-Second Floor, 111 Center Street, 72201
Telephone: 501-372-0800
Fax: 501-372-6453
Email: info@williamsanderson.com *URL:* http://www.williamsanderson.com

MEMBERS OF FIRM

Philip S. Anderson Peter G. Kumpe
J. Leon Holmes

Representative Clients: Arkansas Democrat-Gazette, Inc.; Arkansas Development Finance Authority; Entergy Corporation; Potlatch Corporation; Texaco, Inc.; Wal-Mart Stores, Inc.

For Complete List of Firm Personnel, See General Section

For full biographical listings, see the Martindale-Hubbell Law Directory

CALIFORNIA

COSTA MESA, Orange Co.

RUTAN & TUCKER, LLP (AV)

A Partnership including Professional Corporations
611 Anton Boulevard, Fourteenth Floor, P.O. Box 1950, 92626-1998
Telephone: 714-641-5100; 213-625-7586
Telecopier: 714-546-9035
Email: rutan&tucker@rutan.com *URL:* http://www.rutan.com

MEMBERS OF FIRM

Milford W. Dahl, Jr. Michael T. Hornak

OF COUNSEL

Edward D. Sybesma, Jr. (P.C.)

For Complete List of Firm Personnel, See General Section

For full biographical listings, see the Martindale-Hubbell Law Directory

LAGUNA HILLS, Orange Co.

STETINA BRUNDA GARRED & BRUCKER, A PROFESSIONAL CORPORATION (AV)

24221 Calle De La Louisa, 4th Floor, 92653-3642
Telephone: 949-855-1246
Facsimile: 949-855-6371; 949-855-8986
Email: stetinabrundagarred&brucker@stetinalaw.com

Kit M. Stetina (Mr.) Mark B. Garred
Bruce B. Brunda William J. Brucker

Matthew A. Newboles Darren S. Rimer
Thomas C. Naber (Not admitted in CA) Eric L. Tanezaki
Eric K. Proul

LEGAL SUPPORT PERSONNEL

Kristy Kay Moore

For full biographical listings, see the Martindale-Hubbell Law Directory

LA JOLLA, San Diego Co.

MULVANEY, KAHAN & BARRY, A PROFESSIONAL CORPORATION (AV)

Suite 315, 875 Prospect Street, P.O. Box 1168, 92038-1168
Telephone: 619-454-1780
Fax: 619-454-1792
San Diego, California Office: Seventeenth Floor, First National Bank Center, 401 West "A" Street.
Telephone: 619-238-1010.
Fax: 619-238-1981.
Los Angeles, California Office: Union Bank Plaza, 445 South Figueroa Street, Suite 2600.
Telephone: 213-612-7765.
Orange, California Office: The Koll Center, 500 North State College Boulevard, Suite 440.
Telephone: 714-634-7069.
Fax: 714-939-8000.

Thomas A. Henry, Jr.

For full biographical listings, see the Martindale-Hubbell Law Directory

*LOS ANGELES,** Los Angeles Co.

BELIN RAWLINGS & BADAL LLP (AV)

11601 Wilshire Boulevard, Suite 2200, 90025-1758
Telephone: 310-575-5300
Fax: 310-445-0884
Email: recption@brblaw.com

MEMBERS OF FIRM

Daniel N. Belin Henry Ben-Zvi
Douglas M. Rawlings Lawrence R. Lieberman
Robert G. Badal Ben D. Whitwell

ASSOCIATES

Peter S. Kravitz Rudolph DeFelice

OF COUNSEL

Martin S. Schwartz

SPECIAL COUNSEL

Douglas C. Emhoff

For full biographical listings, see the Martindale-Hubbell Law Directory

BLECHER & COLLINS, A PROFESSIONAL CORPORATION (AV)

611 West Sixth Street, 20th Floor, 90017
Telephone: 213-622-4222
Telecopier: 213-622-1656

Maxwell M. Blecher William C. Hsu
Harold R. Collins, Jr. Gary M. Joye
John E. Andrews James Robert Noblin
Steven J. Cannata Donald R. Pepperman
Ralph C. Hofer Alicia G. Rosenberg

For full biographical listings, see the Martindale-Hubbell Law Directory

HENNIGAN, MERCER & BENNETT (AV)

601 South Figueroa Street, Suite 3300, 90017
Telephone: 213-694-1200
Fax: 213-694-1234
Email: Silverm@hmb.com

J. Michael Hennigan James O. Johnston
Bruce Bennett Laura Lindgren
John L. Amsden Bruce R. MacLeod
Shawna L. Ballard Peter J. Most
Mary H. Chu Robert L. Palmer
Kirk D. Dillman Lee W. Potts
C. Dana Hobart Lauren A. Smith
Jeanne E. Irving Michael Swartz

ASSOCIATES

Nichole M. Auden Joshua M. Mester
Gregory K. Jones Claudia Schweikert
Linda A. Kontos Thomas Bernard Watson
Jeffrey C. Henneforth

OF COUNSEL

James W. Mercer Mark A. Albert
Kenneth A. O'Brien, Jr.

For full biographical listings, see the Martindale-Hubbell Law Directory

JONES, DAY, REAVIS & POGUE (AV)

555 West Fifth Street Suite 4600, 90013-1025
Telephone: 213-489-3939
Telecopier: 213-243-2539
Email: counsel@jonesday.com *URL:* http://www.jonesday.com
In Irvine, California: 5 Park Plaza, Suite 1100.
Telephone: 949-851-3939.
Telecopier: 949-553-7539.

(See Next Column)

JONES, DAY, REAVIS & POGUE, *Los Angeles—Continued*

In Atlanta, Georgia: 3500 SunTrust Plaza, 303 Peachtree Street.
Telephone: 404-521-3939.
Telecopier: 404-581-8330.
In Brussels, Belgium: Avenue Louise 480, 7th Floor, B-1050 Brussels.
Telephone: 32-2-645-14-11.
Telecopier: 32-2-645-14-45.
In Chicago, Illinois: 77 West Wacker.
Telephone: 312-782-3939.
Telecopier: 312-782-8585.
In Cleveland, Ohio: North Point, 901 Lakeside Avenue.
Telephone: 216-586-3939.
Telecopier: 216-579-0212.
In Columbus, Ohio: 1900 Huntington Center.
Telephone: 614-469-3939.
Telecopier: 614-461-4198.
In Dallas, Texas: 2727 North Harwood Street.
Telephone: 214-220-3939.
Telecopier: 214-969-5100.
In Frankfurt, Germany: Hochhaus am Park, Grüneburgweg 102, 60323 Frankfurt am Main.
Telephone: 49-69-9726-3939.
Telecopier: 49-69-9726-3993.
In Geneva, Switzerland: 20, rue de Candolle.
Telephone: 41-22-320-2339.
Telecopier: 41-22-320-1232.
In Hong Kong: 29th Floor, Entertainment Building, 30 Queen's Road Central.
Telephone: 852-2526-6895.
Telecopier: 852-2868-5871.
In London England: Bucklersbury House, 3 Queen Victoria Street.
Telephone: 44-20-7236-3939.
Telecopier: 44-20-7236-1113.
In New York, New York: 599 Lexington Avenue.
Telephone: 212-326-3939.
Telecopier: 212-755-7306.
In Paris, France: 120, rue du Faubourg Saint-Honoré.
Telephone: 33-1-56-59-3939.
Telecopier: 33-1-56-59-3938
In Pittsburgh, Pennsylvania: 500 Grant Street, 31st Floor.
Telephone: 412-391-3939.
Telecopier: 412-394-7959.
In Riyadh, Saudi Arabia: The International Law Firm (In Association with Jones, Day, Reavis & Pogue), Sulaymaniyah, Prince Mishari IBN, Abdulaziz Street, P.O. Box 22166.
Telephone: (966-1) 462-8866.
Telecopier: (966-1) 462-9001.
In Shanghai, China: 2805 Kerry Centre, 1515 Nanjing Road West.
Telephone: 86-21-5298-6568.
Telecopier: 86-21-5298-6569.
In Sydney, Australia: Governor Phillip Tower, Level 38, 1 Farrer Place.
Telephone: 61-2-9210-6921.
Telecopier: 61-2-9210-6926.
In Taipei, Taiwan: 8th Floor, 2 Tun Hwa South Road, Section 2.
Telephone: (886-2) 2704-6808.
Telecopier: (886-2) 2704-6791.
In Tokyo, Japan: Toranomon 45 Mori Building, 3th Floor, 1-5, Toranomon 5-Chome, Minato-ku, Tokyo 105, Japan.
Telephone: 81-3-3433-3939.
Telecopier: 81-3-5401-2725.
In Washington, D.C.: 51 Louisiana Avenue, N.W.
Telephone: 202-879-3939.
Telecopier: 202-626-1700.

MEMBERS OF FIRM IN LOS ANGELES

Gerald W. Palmer
Frederick L. McKnight
Jeffrey A. LeVee

For Complete List of Firm Personnel, See General Section

For full biographical listings, see the Martindale-Hubbell Law Directory

LOEB & LOEB LLP (AV)

A Limited Liability Partnership including Professional Corporations
Suite 1800, 1000 Wilshire Boulevard, 90017-2475
Telephone: 213-688-3400
Facsimile: 213-688-3460
Email: info@loeb.com *URL:* http://www.loeb.com
Century City, California Office: Suite 2200, 10100 Santa Monica Boulevard, Los Angeles, 90067-4164.
Telephone: 310-282-2000.
Facsimile: 310-282-2192.
New York, N.Y. Office: 345 Park Avenue, 10154-0037.
Telephone: 212-407-4000.
Facsimile: 212-407-4990.
Nashville, Tennessee Office: 45 Music Square West, 37203-3205.
Telephone: 615-749-8300;
Facsimile: 615-749-8308.
Rome, Italy Office: Piazza Digione 1, 00197.
Telephone: 011-3906-808-8456.
Facsimile: 011-3906-808-8288.

(See Next Column)

MEMBERS OF FIRM

Phillip E. Adler (A P.C.)
Robert A. Meyer
Charles H. Miller (New York City Office)

OF COUNSEL

Howard I. Friedman (A P.C.)
Robert A. Holtzman
Alfred I. Rothman

For Complete List of Firm Personnel, See General Section

For full biographical listings, see the Martindale-Hubbell Law Directory

LYON & LYON LLP (AV)

A Limited Liability Partnership including Professional Corporations
Suite 4700, 633 West Fifth Street, 90071-2066
Telephone: 213-489-1600
Fax: 213-955-0440
Email: lyon@lyonlyon.com *URL:* http://www.lyonlyon.com
Los Angeles, California Office: Suite 4700, 633 West Fifth Street, 90071-2066.
Telephone: 213-489-1600.
Irvine, California Office: Sixth Floor, 1900 Main Street, 92614.
Telephone: 949-567-2300.
Fax: 949-567-6600.
San Jose, California Office: Suite 800, 333 West San Carlos Street, 95110.
Telephone: 408-993-1555.
Fax: 408-287-2664.
La Jolla, California Office: Suite 800, 4225 Executive Square, 92037.
Telephone: 619-552-8400.
Fax: 619-552-0159.
White Plains, New York Office: Suite 1500, 1 North Lexington Avenue, 10601.
Telephone: 914-681-8851.
Fax: 914-686-4488.
Washington, D.C. Office: Suite 1040, 1701 Pennsylvania Avenue N.W., 20006.
Telephone: 202-331-3600.
Fax: 202-331-3301.

MEMBERS OF FIRM

Roland N. Smoot
Conrad R. Solum, Jr.
James W. Geriak (A Professional Corporation) (Irvine Office)
Robert M. Taylor, Jr. (Irvine Office)
Samuel B. Stone (A Professional Corporation) (Irvine Office)
Douglas E. Olson (A Professional Corporation) (La Jolla Office)
Robert E. Lyon (A Professional Corporation)
Robert C. Weiss (A Professional Corporation)
Richard E. Lyon, Jr., (A Professional Corporation)
John D. McConaghy (A Professional Corporation)
William C. Steffin (A Professional Corporation)
Coe A. Bloomberg (A Professional Corporation)
J. Donald McCarthy
Arnold Sklar
John M. Benassi (La Jolla Office)
James H. Shalek (White Plains, N.Y. Office)
Allan W. Jansen (Irvine Office)
Robert W. Dickerson
Roy L. Anderson
David B. Murphy (Irvine Office)
James C. Brooks
Jeffrey M. Olson
Steven D. Hemminger (San Jose Office)
Jerrold B. Reilly
Paul H. Meier
John A. Rafter, Jr.
Kenneth H. Ohriner
Mary S. Consalvi (La Jolla Office)
Lois M. Kwasigroch
Lawrence R. LaPorte
Robert C. Laurenson (La Jolla Office)
Carol A. Schneider
Hope E. Melville (Irvine Office)
Michael J. Wise
Richard Warburg (La Jolla Office)
Kurt T. Mulville (Irvine Office)
Theodore S. Maceiko
Bruce G. Chapman
F.T. Alexandra Mahaney (La Jolla Office)
Stephen S. Korniczky (La Jolla Office)
James P. Brogan (Irvine Office)
David A. Randall
Christopher A. Vanderlaan
James T. Carmichael (Washington D.C. Office)

ASSOCIATES

Corrine M. Freeman (Irvine Office)
David T. Burse (San Jose Office)
Charles R. Balgenorth
Jeffrey A. Miller (San Jose Office)
Armand F. Ayazi
Jessica R. Wolff (La Jolla Office)
Jeffrey William Guise (La Jolla Office)
Charles S. Berkman (La Jolla Office)
Sheryl Rubinstein Silverstein (La Jolla Office)
David E. Wang (Irvine Office)
Kenneth S. Roberts (Irvine Office)
Brent D. Sokol
John C. Kappos (Irvine Office)
Thomas J. Brindisi
Charles Calvin Fowler (Irvine Office)
Lisa C. Ward
Vicki Gee Norton (La Jolla Office)
Michael A. Tomasulo
Charles A. Kertell
Jonathan Hallman (Irvine Office)
Lynn Y. McKernan (San Jose Office)
Michael J. Bolan (Irvine Office)
Gregory R. Stephenson (White Plains, N.Y. Office)
Mary Agnes Tuck
Bernard F. Rose (San Jose Office)
Daniel M. Chambers (La Jolla Office)
Yasser M. El-Gamal
Stephen C. Beuerle (La Jolla Office)

(See Next Column)

LYON & LYON LLP—*Continued*

ASSOCIATES (Continued)

Christopher Peter Broderick
Richard San Pietro (La Jolla Office)
Kurt M. Kjelland (La Jolla Office)
Wesley B. Ames (La Jolla Office)
William Andrew English (Irvine Office)
Brian A. Schar (Irvine Office)
Carlos M. Candeloro
Peter R. Munson (La Jolla Office)
Michael S. Davidson (Irvine Office)
Todd R. Miller
Nathaniel L. Dilger (Irvine Office)
David Heskel Ben-Meir
Craig A. Neugeboren (San Jose Office)
Chad W. Miller (Irvine Office)
Manuel Federico de la Cerra (La Jolla Office)
Douglas C. Murdock (La Jolla Office)
Peter C. Mei (San Jose Office)
Alan M. Federbush (Not admitted in CA; White Plains, N.Y. Office)
Troy M. Schmelzer (La Jolla Office)
Keith Kind (La Jolla Office)
Michael D. Fabiano (La Jolla Office)
Mark A. Catan (Not admitted in CA; White Plains, N.Y. Office)
Eugene K. Hyun (Not admitted in CA; White Plains, N.Y. Office)
Mikael Havluciyan (Irvine Office)
Rahul D. Engineer (San Jose Office)
John E. Peterson (La Jolla Office)
Vincent K. Gustafson
Jon E. Maki (La Jolla Office)
Trent Edward Campione
Sarah A. Brown (Irvine Office)
Robert S. Mayer (Not admitted in CA; White Plains, N.Y. Office)
Charles M. Doyle (White Plains, N.Y. Office)
Karry W. Wang (Irvine Office)
Robert W. Prince (La Jolla Office)
Bonita L. Severy (Irvine Office)
David W. Lamb
John J. Yim (Washington D.C. Office)

OF COUNSEL

Bradford J. Duft (La Jolla Office)
Suzanne L. Biggs (La Jolla Office)
Reginald D. Greene

Representative Clients: Cedars-Sinai Medical Center; Genentech; Honda; Mag Instrument, Inc.; Mitsubishi; Panavision; Quantum Corporation; Spectra-Physics, Inc

For full biographical listings, see the Martindale-Hubbell Law Directory

---

MITCHELL, SILBERBERG & KNUPP LLP (AV)

A Partnership including Professional Corporations
11377 West Olympic Boulevard, 90064
Telephone: 310-312-2000
Fax: 310-312-3100
Email: info@msk.com *URL:* http://www.msk.com

MEMBERS OF FIRM

Thomas P. Lambert (A Professional Corporation)
Roy L. Shults (A Professional Corporation)

References: Wells Fargo Bank, N.A.; Merrill, Lynch.

For Complete List of Firm Personnel, See General Section

For full biographical listings, see the Martindale-Hubbell Law Directory

---

O'MELVENY & MYERS LLP (AV)

400 South Hope Street, 90071-2899
Telephone: 213-430-6000
Facsimile: 213-430-6407
Cable: MOMS
Telex: 674122
Email: omminfo@omm.com *URL:* http://www.omm.com
Century City, CA Office: 1999 Avenue of the Stars, Los Angeles, 90067-6035.
Telex: 674097. Tel: 310-553-6700.
Fax: 310-246-6779.
Newport Beach, CA Office: 610 Newport Center Drive, 92660-6429.
Telex: 4722088. Tel: 949-760-9600.
Fax: 949-823-6994.
San Francisco, CA Office: Embarcadero Center West, 275 Battery Street, 94111-3305. Tel: 415-984-8700.
Fax: 415-984-8701.
New York, NY Office: Citicorp Center, 153 East 53rd Street, 10022-4611.
Telex: 129165. Tel: 212-326-2000.
Fax: 212-326-2061.
Washington, DC Office: 555 13th Street, N.W., 20004-1109.
Cable: MOMSWSH.
Telex: 89622. Tel: 202-383-5300.
Fax: 202-383-5414.
London Office: O'Melveny & Myers, 3 Finsbury Square, London, EC2A 1LA, England. Tel: 44-171-256-8451. Fax 44-171-638-8205.
Tokyo Office: Akasaka Twin Tower, East 14F, 2-17-23, Akasaka, Minato-ku, Tokyo 107-0052, Japan. Tel: 03-5562-2800.
Fax: 03-5575-3840.
Hong Kong Office: O'Melveny & Myers, Suite 1905, Tower Two, Lippo Centre, 89 Queensway, Central, Hong Kong. Tel: 852-2523-8266.
Fax: 852-2522-1760.

(See Next Column)

Shanghai Office: Kerry Centre, 20F, 1515 Nanjing Road West, Shanghai, 200040 People's Republic of China. Tel: 86-21-5298-5600.
Fax: 86-21-5298-5500.

PARTNER

Henry C. Thumann

For Complete List of Firm Personnel, See General Section

For full biographical listings, see the Martindale-Hubbell Law Directory

---

PILLSBURY MADISON & SUTRO LLP (AV)

Citicorp Plaza, 725 South Figueroa Street, Suite 1200, 90017-5443
Telephone: 213-488-7100
Fax: 213-629-1033
Email: pillsburylaw.com *URL:* http://pillsburylaw.com
Costa Mesa, California Office: 650 Town Center Drive, 7th Floor, 92626.
Telephone: 714-436-6800.
Fax: 714-436-2800.
Silicon Valley Office: 2550 Hanover Street, Palo Alto, 94034.
Telephone: 650-233-4500.
Fax: 650-233-4545.
Sacramento, California Office: 400 Capitol Mall, Suite 1700, 95814.
Telephone: 916-329-4700.
Fax: 916-441-3583.
San Diego, California Office: 101 West Broadway, Suite 1800, 92101.
Telephone: 619-234-5000.
Fax: 619-236-1995.
San Francisco, California Office: 50 Fremont Street, 94105.
Telephone: 415-983-1000.
Fax: 415-983-1200.
Washington, D.C. Office: 1100 New York Avenue, N.W., Ninth Floor, 20005.
Telephone: 202-861-3000.
Fax: 202-822-0944.
Vienna, Virginia Office: 8330 Boone Boulevard, Suite 400, 22182.
Telephone: 703-744-7600.
Fax: 703-744-7605.
New York, New York Office: 375 Park Avenue, Suite 3108, 10152.
Telephone: 212-826-1060.
Fax: 212-826-9255. One Liberty Plaza, 165 Broadway, 51st Floor.
Telephone: 212-374-1890.
Fax: 212-374-1852.
Tokyo, Japan Office: Pillsbury Madison & Sutro, Gaikokuho Jimu Bengoshi Jimusho, 5th Floor, Samon Eleven Building, 3-1, Samon-cho, Shinjuku-ku, Tokyo 160 Japan.
Telephone: 800-729-9830; 011-813-3354-3531.
Fax: 011-813-3354-3534.

MEMBERS OF FIRM

Kenneth R. Chiate
Amy D. Hogue
Jennie L. La Prade
Patrick G. Rogan
Michael J. Finnegan
Sidney K. Kanazawa
Charles E. Patterson
Matthew R. Rogers
William E. Stoner

For Complete List of Firm Personnel, See General Section

For full biographical listings, see the Martindale-Hubbell Law Directory

---

PALO ALTO, Santa Clara Co.

BASIL P. FTHENAKIS (AV)

540 University Avenue, Suite 300, 94301-1912
Telephone: 650-326-1397
Fax: 650-326-3203
Email: basilp@fthenakis.com

For full biographical listings, see the Martindale-Hubbell Law Directory

---

*SAN DIEGO,** San Diego Co.

FERRIS & BRITTON, A PROFESSIONAL CORPORATION (AV)

1600 First National Bank Center, 401 West A Street, 92101
Telephone: 619-233-3131
Fax: 619-232-9316
Email: manager@ferrisbritton.com *URL:* http://www.ferrisbritton.com

Christopher Q. Britton
Michael R. Weinstein

Representative Clients: Cox Communications, Inc.; Datel Systems, Inc.; Enterprise Rent-a-Car; Exxon; Frontier Analytics, Inc.; Peninsula Bank; Structural Bioinformatics, Inc.; Teleport Communications Group; Southwest Airlines.

For Complete List of Firm Personnel, See General Section

For full biographical listings, see the Martindale-Hubbell Law Directory

San Diego—Continued

MULVANEY, KAHAN & BARRY, A PROFESSIONAL CORPORATION (AV)

Seventeenth Floor, First National Bank Center, 401 West "A" Street, 92101-7994
Telephone: 619-238-1010
Fax: 619-238-1981
Email: mkb@mkblaw.com
Los Angeles, California Office: Union Bank Plaza, 445 South Figueroa Street, Suite 2600.
Telephone: 213-612-7765.
La Jolla, California Office: Suite 315, 875 Prospect Street, P.O. Box 1168.
Telephone: 619-454-1780.
Fax: 619-454-1792.
Orange, California Office: The Koll Center, 500 North State College Boulevard, Suite 440.
Telephone: 714-634-7069.
Fax: 714-939-8000.

James F. Mulvaney
Lawrence Kahan
Everett G. Barry, Jr.
Robert A. Linn
Paula Rotenberg
Melissa A. Blackburn
Mark R. Raftery
John A. Mayers
Robin L. Cahill
Kristin L. Yokomoto
Darren John Devlin

OF COUNSEL

Rex B. Beatty
Derrick W. Samuelson (Not admitted in CA)

Representative Clients: Air Products & Chemicals, Inc.; Aoki Construction (CA) Co., Ltd.; AT&T Capital Corp.; BellSouth Communications Systems, Inc.; ITT Corp.; NationsBank; Phoenix Home Life Mutual Insurance Co.; Textron Financial Corporation; Union Bank; Wells Fargo Bank.

For full biographical listings, see the Martindale-Hubbell Law Directory

THE LAW OFFICES OF STEPHEN P. OGGEL, A P.C. (AV)

101 West Broadway, Suite 1450, 92101
Telephone: 619-696-7500
Fax: 619-232-1065

Stephen P. Oggel

For full biographical listings, see the Martindale-Hubbell Law Directory

POST KIRBY NOONAN & SWEAT LLP (AV)

A Partnership including Professional Corporations
America Plaza 600 West Broadway 11th Floor, 92101
Telephone: 619-231-8666
FAX: 619-231-9593;
619-231-4360
Email: PKNS@PKNS.com

MEMBERS OF FIRM

Gregory A. Post
Michael L. Kirby (A P.C.)
David J. Noonan
Richard W. Sweat
R. Bruce Wayne (A P.C.)
Thomas W. Bettles
David B. Oberholtzer
Charles T. Hoge
James R. Lance
Steven W. Sanchez
Theresa M. Brehl
Jeffrey P. Lendrum
Kristen T. Bruesehoff

For full biographical listings, see the Martindale-Hubbell Law Directory

SELTZER CAPLAN MCMAHON & VITEK, A PROFESSIONAL CORPORATION (AV)

2100 Symphony Towers, 750 B Street, 92101
Telephone: 619-685-3003
Fax: 619-685-3100
URL: http://www.scwm.com

Gerald L. McMahon
Reginald A. Vitek
Dennis J. Wickham

Representative Clients: Chicago Title; The Goodyear Tire & Rubber Co.; W.R. Grace & Co.—Conn.; McDonnell-Douglas Corp.; McMillin Communities; Western Financial Savings Bank.

For Complete List of Firm Personnel, See General Section

For full biographical listings, see the Martindale-Hubbell Law Directory

*SAN FRANCISCO,** San Francisco Co.

BERMAN, DEVALERIO, PEASE & TABACCO, LLP (AVⓣ)

425 California Street, 94104-2205
Telephone: 415-433-3200
Facsimile: 415-433-6382
URL: http://www.bermanesq.com
Boston, Massachusetts Office: Berman, Devalerio & Pease, One Liberty Square, 02109.
Telephone: 617-542-8300.
Facsimile: 617-542-1194.

Joseph J. Tabacco, Jr.

(See Next Column)

Christopher T. Heffelfinger, Jr.
Nicole Lavallee
Jennifer S. Abrams

OF COUNSEL

Alan Anthony Beaven

For full biographical listings, see the Martindale-Hubbell Law Directory

MICHAEL BROOKS CARROLL (AV)

180 Montgomery Street, Suite 1250, 94104
Telephone: 415-788-7600
Telecopier: 415-421-7379

For full biographical listings, see the Martindale-Hubbell Law Directory

COX & MOYER, A PROFESSIONAL CORPORATION (AV)

703 Market Street, Suite 1800, 94103
Telephone: 415-543-9464
Fax: 415-777-1828
Email: coxmoyer@aol.com

Ingemar E. Hoberg (1903-1971)
John H. Finger (1913-1991)
Phillip E. Brown (Retired)
Stephen T. Cox
David W. Moyer

Scott J. Allen

OF COUNSEL

Kenneth W. Rosenthal

For full biographical listings, see the Martindale-Hubbell Law Directory

LIEFF, CABRASER, HEIMANN & BERNSTEIN, LLP (AV)

Embarcadero Center West, 30th Floor, 275 Battery Street, 94111
Telephone: 415-956-1000
Telecopier: 415-956-1008
Email: mail@lchb.com *URL:* http://www.lchb.com
New York, N.Y. Office: 10 Rockefeller Plaza, 12th Floor, 10020-1903.
Telephone: 212-218-6600.
Fax: 212-218-6608.

Robert L. Lieff
Elizabeth J. Cabraser
Richard M. Heimann
William Bernstein
William B. Hirsch
James M. Finberg
Karen E. Karpen
Joseph R. Saveri
Donald C. Arbitblit
Steven E. Fineman (Resident, New York, N.Y. Office)
Robert J. Nelson
Jacqueline E. Mottek
Morris A. Ratner
Melanie M. Piech
Kelly M. Dermody
Jonathan D. Selbin
Richard M. Franco
Barry R. Himmelstein
Joshua P. Davis
Michael W. Sobol
Robert G. Eisler (Resident, New York, N.Y. Office)

Jennie L. Anderson
Lori E. Andrus
Caryn Becker
Joan T. Brown (Not admitted in CA)
Stephen H. Cassidy
Paulina do Amaral
Eric B. Fastiff
Hector D. Geribon (Resident, New York, N.Y. Office)
Pierce Gore
Rebecca M. Katz (Resident, New York, N.Y. Office)
Lisa J. Leebove
Karen J. Mandel (Resident, New York, N.Y. Office)
Scott P. Nealey
Erik L. Shawn (Resident, New York, N.Y. Office)
David S. Stellings (Resident, New York, N.Y. Office)
Steven M. Tindall
Fabrice N. Vincent
Jonathan M. Watkins
Heather A. Woodard
Yu-Yee Wu

For full biographical listings, see the Martindale-Hubbell Law Directory

MORGENSTEIN & JUBELIRER, LLP (AV)

One Market, Spear Street Tower, 32nd Floor, 94105
Telephone: 415-896-0666
Fax: 415-896-5592
Email: m&j@mj-sflaw.com

Marvin D. Morgenstein (Retired)
Eliot S. Jubelirer
Lee Ann Huntington
Jean L. Bertrand
Jeffrey R. Williams
James R. Balich
Rocky N. Unruh
James L. McGinnis
Charles W. LaGrave
William J. Carroll
John S. Worden
Wendi J. Berkowitz
Stephen M. Hankins
Bruce A. Wagman

(See Next Column)

MORGENSTEIN & JUBELIRER LLP—*Continued*

Lewis D. Barr
David H. Bromfield
Alexander P. Catalona
Michael "Cael" S. Davis
Roberta Nicol Dempster
Laura E. Gasser
Jill L. Gillen
Natasha L. Golding
Judith A. Holiber
Shawn D. Parrish
John J. Petry

For full biographical listings, see the Martindale-Hubbell Law Directory

ROSEN, BIEN & ASARO (AV)

Eighth Floor, 155 Montgomery Street, 94104
Telephone: 415-433-6830
Fax: 415-433-7104
Email: rba@rbalaw.com

Sanford Jay Rosen
Michael W. Bien
Andrea G. Asaro

Thomas Nolan
William H. D. Fernholz
Shana J. Margolis
Ernest J. Galvan

For full biographical listings, see the Martindale-Hubbell Law Directory

SPIEGEL LIAO & KAGAY (AV)

595 Market Street, Suite 1350, 94105-2825
Telephone: 415-956-5959
Telecopier: 415-362-1431
Email: slk@slksf@com *URL:* http://www.slksf.com

Michael I. Spiegel
Charles M. Kagay

OF COUNSEL

Bartholomew Lee
Wayne M. Liao

For full biographical listings, see the Martindale-Hubbell Law Directory

*SAN JOSE,** Santa Clara Co.

ALEXANDER, HAWES & AUDET (AV)

152 North 3rd Street, Suite 600, 95112
Telephone: 408-289-1776
Fax: 408-287-1776
URL: http://www.alexanderlaw.com
Email: access@alexanderlaw.com *URL:* http://www.lawyers.com/alexanderhawes&audet

Richard Alexander
Amanda Hawes
William M. Audet
Ann Saponara
Deborah Heller

OF COUNSEL

Michael McShane
Jana S. Stabile (Not admitted in CA)

For full biographical listings, see the Martindale-Hubbell Law Directory

MCMANIS, FAULKNER & MORGAN (AV)

160 West Santa Clara Street, 10th Floor, 95113
Telephone: 408-279-8700
Fax: 408-279-3244; 408-279-0494
Email: mfm@mfmlaw.com *URL:* http://www.mfmlaw.com

James McManis
William Faulkner
Donelle Morgan
Lisa Herrick
Michael Reedy
Erica Yew

Michelle Tidalgo
Colleen Duffy Smith
Lillian Wolf
Rebecca Hughes
Kalpana Vrudhula
Ray M. Baluyot
Catherine Bechtel
Arron Nesbitt

OF COUNSEL

Mary Arand

For full biographical listings, see the Martindale-Hubbell Law Directory

COLORADO

*DENVER,** Denver Co.

DUFFORD & BROWN, P.C. (AV)

1700 Broadway, Suite 1700, 80290-1701
Telephone: 303-861-8013
Facsimile: 303-832-3804
Colorado Springs, Colorado Office: 101 N. Tejon, Suite 410.
Telephone: 719-471-0559.
Facsimile: 719-471-0583.
Affiliated Office: Solomon, Pearl, Blum & Quinn, L.L.P., New York, NY and Denver, Colorado.

(See Next Column)

Thomas G. Brown
David W. Furgason
Craig B. Shaffer

Representative Clients: CF&I Steel, L.P.; The Colorado and Wyoming Railway Co.; PXC Denver.

For Complete List of Firm Personnel, See General Section

For full biographical listings, see the Martindale-Hubbell Law Directory

REIMAN & BAYAZ, P.C. (AV)

1600 Broadway, Suite 1340, 80202
Telephone: 303-860-1500
Fax: 303-839-4380
Email: rblaw@earthlink.net

Jeff Reiman
Marcie K. Bayaz

Debra D. Asimus

For full biographical listings, see the Martindale-Hubbell Law Directory

SHERMAN & HOWARD L.L.C. (AV)

Attorneys and Counselors at Law
633 Seventeenth Street, Suite 3000, 80202
Telephone: 303-297-2900
Telecopier: 303-298-0940
Colorado Springs, Colorado Office: Suite 1500, 90 South Cascade Avenue, 80903.
Telephone: 719-475-2440.
Las Vegas, Nevada Office: Swendseid & Stern, a member in Sherman & Howard L.L.C., 317 Sixth Street, 89101.
Telephone: 702-387-6073.
Reno, Nevada Office: Swendseid & Stern, a member in Sherman & Howard L.L.C., 50 West Liberty Street, Suite 660, 89501.
Telephone: 702-323-1980.

Paul Curtis Daw
Lawrence W. Treece

Representative Clients: BACE Industries, LLC; Flatiron Structures Co. LLC; Hanifen, Imhoff Inc.; Hathaway Corp.; J.D. Edwards & Co.; Newmont Gold Company; Public Employees' Retirement Assn.; Tele-Communications, Inc.; United Artists Theatre Circuit, Inc.; U.S. West Communications, Inc.

For Complete List of Firm Personnel, See General Section

For full biographical listings, see the Martindale-Hubbell Law Directory

WALTERS & JOYCE, P.C. (AV)

2015 York Street, 80205
Telephone: 303-322-1404
FAX: 303-377-5668

William E. Walters, III

Reference: Norwest Bank of Buckingham Square.

For Complete List of Firm Personnel, See General Section

For full biographical listings, see the Martindale-Hubbell Law Directory

CONNECTICUT

*HARTFORD,** Hartford Co.

SOROKIN, GROSS & HYDE, P.C. (AV)

One Corporate Center, 06103
Telephone: 860-525-6645
Fax: 860-522-1781
Email: sorokin@sorokinlaw.com
Simsbury, Connecticut Office: 720 Hopmeadow Street.
Telephone: 860-651-9348.
Rocky Hill, Connecticut Office: 2360 Main Street.
Telephone: 860-563-9305.
Fax: 860-529-6931.

Richard C. Robinson

For Complete List of Firm Personnel, See General Section

For full biographical listings, see the Martindale-Hubbell Law Directory

*NEW HAVEN,** New Haven Co.

WIGGIN & DANA (AV)

One Century Tower, 06508-1832
Telephone: 203-498-4400
Telefax: 203-782-2889
URL: http://www.wiggin.com
Hartford, Connecticut Office: One CityPlace.
Telephone: 203-297-3700.
Fax: 203-525-9380.

(See Next Column)

WIGGIN & DANA, *New Haven—Continued*

Stamford, Connecticut Office: Three Stamford Plaza, 301 Tresser Boulevard.
Telephone: 203-363-7600.
Telefax: 203-363-7676.

MEMBERS OF FIRM

Shaun S. Sullivan
Mark R. Kravitz
Edward Wood Dunham
William G. Millman, Jr.
Patrick J. Monahan, II (Resident, Hartford Office)
Robert M. Langer (Resident, Hartford Office)
Merton G. Gollaher

COUNSEL

Sharyn B. Zuch (Not admitted in CT; Resident, Hartford Office)

ASSOCIATE

Michelle Wilcox DeBarge (Resident, Hartford Office)

For Complete List of Firm Personnel, See General Section

For full biographical listings, see the Martindale-Hubbell Law Directory

DISTRICT OF COLUMBIA

WASHINGTON, D.C. Co.

BAKER & HOSTETLER LLP (AV)

Washington Square, Suite 1100, 1050 Connecticut Avenue, N.W., 20036-5304
Telephone: 202-861-1500
Fax: 202-861-1783
To contact an attorney on the Internet use first initial and surname followed by @baker-hostetler.com
URL: http://www.bakerlaw.com
In Cleveland, Ohio: 3200 National City Center, 1900 East Ninth Street.
Telephone: 216-621-0200.
In Cincinnati, Ohio: 312 Walnut Street, Suite 2650.
Telephone: 513-929-3400.
In Columbus, Ohio: Capitol Square, Suite 2100, 65 East State Street.
Telephone: 614-228-1541.
In Denver, Colorado: 303 East 17th Avenue, Suite 1100.
Telephone: 303-861-0600.
In Houston, Texas: 1000 Louisiana, Suite 2000.
Telephone: 713-751-1600.
In Beverly Hills, California: 9150 Wilshire Boulevard, Suite 205.
Telephone: 310-385-7500.
In Long Beach, California: 300 Oceangate, Suite 620.
Telephone: 562-432-2827.
In Los Angeles, California: 600 Wilshire Boulevard.
Telephone: 213-624-2400.
In Orlando, Florida: SunBank Center, Suite 2300, 200 South Orange Avenue.
Telephone: 407-649-4000.

PARTNERS

Gerald A. Connell
Louis R. Sernoff
Lee H. Simowitz
Alan S. Ward

OF COUNSEL

Jenifer M. Brown

For Complete List of Firm Personnel, See General Section

For full biographical listings, see the Martindale-Hubbell Law Directory

BLUMENFELD & COHEN (AV)

1625 Massachusetts Avenue, N.W., Suite 300, 20036
Telephone: 202-955-6300
Facsimile: 202-955-6460
Email: info@technologylaw.com *URL:* http://www.technologylaw.com
San Francisco, California Office: 4 Embarcadero Center, Suite 1170, 94111.
Telephone: 415-394-7500.
Facsimile: 415-394-7505.

MEMBERS OF FIRM

Jeffrey Blumenfeld
Gary M. Cohen
Glenn B. Manishin
Stephen P. Bowen (Not admitted in DC; Resident, San Francisco Office)
David M. Naseman (Not admitted in DC)
Christy C. Kunin
Elise P.W. Kiely

OF COUNSEL

Rand McQuinn

ASSOCIATE

Colin M. Alberts

For full biographical listings, see the Martindale-Hubbell Law Directory

COHEN, MILSTEIN, HAUSFELD & TOLL, P.L.L.C. (AV)

West Tower, Suite 500, 1100 New York Avenue, N.W., 20005-3964
Telephone: 202-408-4600
Facsimile: 202-408-4699
Email: lawinfo@cmht.com *URL:* http://www.CMHT.com
Seattle, Washington Office: 999 Third Avenue, Suite 3600.
Telephone: 206-521-0080.
Facsimile: 206-521-0166.

MEMBERS OF FIRM

Jerry S. Cohen (1925-1995)
Herbert E. Milstein
Michael D. Hausfeld
Steven J. Toll (Resident, Seattle, Washington Office)
Ann C. Yahner
Lisa M. Mezzetti
Andrew N. Friedman
Richard S. Lewis
Daniel S. Sommers
Daniel A. Small
Gary E. Mason
Joseph M. Sellers
Sharon A. Snyder
Mark S. Willis (Not admitted in DC)

ASSOCIATES

Lori G. Feldman (Resident, Seattle, Washington Office)
Paul T. Gallagher
Christine E. Webber
Alexander E. Barnett
Matthew James Ide (Resident, Seattle, Washington Office)
Matthew F. Pawa
Suzette M. Malveaux
Mary N. Strimel
Kristopher A. Kinkade (Resident, Seattle, Washington Office)
Agnieszka M. Fryszman
Deborah J. Vagins
Ari Karen
Charles E. Tompkins
Tamara J. Driscoll (Resident, Seattle, Washington Office)
Elizabeth Haines Cronise
Donna Solen
Lesli C. Esposito (Not admitted in DC)

OF COUNSEL

Margaret G. Farrell

For full biographical listings, see the Martindale-Hubbell Law Directory

THE CUNEO LAW GROUP, P.C. (AV)

317 Massachusetts Avenue, N.E. Suite 300, 20002
Telephone: 202-789-3960
Fax: 202-789-1813
Email: contact@cuneolaw.com *URL:* http://www.cuneolaw.com

Jonathan W. Cuneo
James J. Schweitzer
David W. Stanley
Michael G. Lenett

Arthur K. Park (Not admitted in DC)
Daniel Cohen (Not admitted in DC)

COUNSEL

Charles Tiefer

For full biographical listings, see the Martindale-Hubbell Law Directory

DOW, LOHNES & ALBERTSON, PLLC (AV)

1200 New Hampshire Avenue, N.W. Suite 800, 20036-6802
Telephone: 202-776-2000
Facsimile: 202-776-2222
Email: info@dlalaw.com *URL:* http://www.dlalaw.com
Atlanta, Georgia Office: One Ravinia Drive, Suite 1600.
Telephone: 770-901-8800.
Telecopier: 770-901-8874.

MEMBERS OF THE FIRM

Jonathan D. Hart
James A. Treanor, III

For Complete List of Firm Personnel, See General Section

For full biographical listings, see the Martindale-Hubbell Law Directory

DUNAWAY & CROSS, A PROFESSIONAL CORPORATION (AV)

1700 K Street, N.W. Suite 800, 20006-3819
Telephone: 202-862-9700
Fax: 202-862-9710
Email: duncross@msn.com

Mac S. Dunaway
Gary E. Cross
Matthew F. Hall

COUNSEL

Raymond P. Shafer (Not admitted in DC)

For full biographical listings, see the Martindale-Hubbell Law Directory

JONES, DAY, REAVIS & POGUE (AV)

51 Louisiana Avenue, N.W., 20001-2113
Telephone: 202-879-3939
Telecopier: 202-626-1700
Email: counsel@jonesday.com *URL:* http://www.jonesday.com
In Atlanta, Georgia: 3500 SunTrust Plaza, 303 Peachtree Street.
Telephone: 404-521-3939.
Telecopier: 404-581-8330.

(See Next Column)

JONES, DAY, REAVIS & POGUE—*Continued*

In Brussels, Belgium: Avenue Louise 480, 7th Floor, B-1050 Brussels.
Telephone: 32-2-645-14-11.
Telecopier: 32-2-645-14-45.
In Chicago, Illinois: 77 West Wacker.
Telephone: 312-782-3939.
Telecopier: 312-782-8585.
In Cleveland, Ohio: North Point, 901 Lakeside Avenue.
Telephone: 216-586-3939.
Telecopier: 216-579-0212.
In Columbus, Ohio: 1900 Huntington Center.
Telephone: 614-469-3939.
Telecopier: 614-461-4198.
In Dallas, Texas: 2727 North Harwood Street.
Telephone: 214-220-3939.
Telecopier: 214-969-5100.
In Frankfurt, Germany: Hochhaus am Park, Grüneburgweg 102, 60323, Frankfurt am Main.
Telephone: 49-69-9726-3939.
Telecopier: 49-69-9726-3993.
In Geneva, Switzerland: 20, rue de Candolle.
Telephone: 41-22-320-2339.
Telecopier: 41-22-320-1232.
In Hong Kong: 29th Floor, Entertainment Building, 30 Queen's Road Central.
Telephone: 852-2526-6895.
Telecopier: 852-2868-5871.
In Irvine, California: 5 Park Plaza, Suite 1100.
Telephone: 949-851-3939.
Telecopier: 949-553-7539.
In London, England: Bucklersbury House, 3 Queen Victoria Street.
Telephone: 44-171-236-3939.
Telecopier: 44-171-236-1113.
In Los Angeles, California: 555 West Fifth Street, Suite 4600.
Telephone: 213-489-3939.
Telecopier: 213-243-2539.
In New Delhi, India (Associate Office): Pathak & Associates (an associate firm of Jones, Day, Reavis & Pogue), 1st Floor, Dr. Gopal Das Bhaven, 28 Barakhamba Road.
Telephone: 91-11-373-8793.; 91-11-335-7345.
Telecopier: 91-11-335-3761.
In New York, New York: 599 Lexington Avenue.
Telephone: 212-326-3939.
Telecopier: 212-755-7306.
In Paris, France: 120, rue du Faubourg Saint-Honoré.
Telephone: 33-1-56-59-39-39.
Telecopier: 33-1-56-59-39-38
In Pittsburgh, Pennsylvania: 500 Grant Street, 31st Floor.
Telephone: 412-391-3939.
Telecopier: 412-394-7959.
In Riyadh, Saudi Arabia: The International Law Firm (In Association with Jones, Day, Reavis & Pogue), Sulaymaniyah, Prince Mishari IBN, Abdulaziz Street, P.O. Box 22166.
Telephone: (966-1) 462-8866.
Telecopier: (966-1) 462-9001.
In Shanghai, China: 2805 Kerry Centre, 1515 Nanjing Road West.
Telephone: 86-21-5298-6568.
Telecopier: 86-21-5298-6569.
In Sydney, Australia: Governor Phillip Tower, Level 38, 1 Farrer Place.
Telephone: 61-2-9210-6921.
Telecopier: 61-2-9210-6926.
In Taipei, Taiwan: 8th Floor, 2 Tun Hwa South Road, Section 2.
Telephone: (886-2) 2704-6808.
Telecopier: (886-2) 2704-6791.
In Tokyo, Japan: Toranomon MT Building, 4th Floor, 10-3, Toranomon 3-Chome, Minato-Ku, Tokyo 105, Japan.
Telephone: 81-3-3433-3939.
Telecopier: 81-3-5401-2725.

MEMBERS OF FIRM IN WASHINGTON, D.C.

Joe Sims
Tom D. Smith
Phillip A. Proger
Thomas F. Cullen, Jr.
Toby G. Singer
Kathryn M. Fenton
Kevin D. McDonald
Joseph F. Winterscheid
Charles A. James
William V. O'Reilly
Gregory G. Katsas

OF COUNSEL

William E. Swope

COUNSEL

Robert C. Jones

ASSOCIATES

Mona Lisa Flicker
Peter J. Love
Bevin M.B. Newman
Karen M. Espaldon
Leslie Overton
Brian K. Grube (Not admitted in DC)
Mia F. Cohen

For Complete List of Firm Personnel, See General Section

For full biographical listings, see the Martindale-Hubbell Law Directory

---

KING, PAGANO & HARRISON (AV)

1730 Pennsylvania Avenue, N.W., 20006
Telephone: 202-371-6800
Fax: 202-371-6770
URL: http://www.kph.com
New York, New York Office: 425 Park Avenue, 10022.
Telephone: 212-223-4000.
FAX: 212-223-4134.

MEMBERS OF FIRM

Jeffrey W. King
Jeffrey W. Pagano (Resident, New York, N.Y. Office)
Keith J. Harrison
James E. Kellett (Resident, New York, N.Y. Office)
Steven Schaars
Jeffrey L. Poston
Ira M. Saxe (Not admitted in DC; Resident, New York, N.Y. Office)

OF COUNSEL

Herbert I. Meyer (Resident, New York, N.Y. Office)

ASSOCIATES

Cheryl A. Maier
Christopher Flynn
Emily B. Zuckerman (Not admitted in DC; Resident, New York, N.Y. Office)
Thomas W. Jones, Jr.
Eric M. Carr (Not admitted in DC; Resident, New York, N.Y. Office)

Representative Clients: Brink's, Inc.; The Pittston Co.; BAX Global; Kaiser Permanente; Group Health Association of America; Capital Credit Corp; Systems Engineering Services Corp.; Noel Biscare.

For full biographical listings, see the Martindale-Hubbell Law Directory

---

MINTZ, LEVIN, COHN, FERRIS, GLOVSKY AND POPEO, P.C. (AV)

701 Pennsylvania Avenue, N.W., 20004-2608
Telephone: 202-434-7300
Fax: 202-434-7400
Internet: Each Attorney's Internet Address takes the following form: first inital, last name @mintz.com (e.g., rmintz@mintz.com)
URL: http://www.mintz.com
Boston, Massachusetts Office: One Financial Center.
Telephone: 617-542-6000.
Fax: 617-542-2241.
Reston, Virginia Office: 12021 Sunset Hills Road, Suite 310.
Telephone: 703-464-4800.
Fax: 703-464-4895.

Jerome Gotkin (Resident, Boston, Massachusetts Office)
R. Robert Popeo (Resident, Boston, Massachusetts Office)
Bruce D. Sokler
Charles Alan Samuels
Christopher J. Harvie

For Complete List of Firm Personnel, See General Section

For full biographical listings, see the Martindale-Hubbell Law Directory

---

ROYLANCE, ABRAMS, BERDO & GOODMAN, L.L.P. (AV)

1225 Connecticut Avenue, N.W., 20036-2680
Telephone: 202-659-9076
Facsimile: 202-659-9344
Email: RABG@roylance.com

D. C. Roylance (1920-1995)
David S. Abrams
Robert H. Berdo
Alfred N. Goodman
Mark S. Bicks
Richard A. Flynt
John E. Holmes
Michael T. Murphy
Garrett V. Davis
Stacey J. Longanecker (Not admitted in DC)
Thomas P. Hilliard
Joseph J. Buczynski
Robert S. Green
Wayne C. Jaeschke, Jr. (Not admitted in DC)
Antigone E. Juvelis (Not admitted in DC)

SENIOR OF COUNSEL

Frank E. Robbins (Retired)

OF COUNSEL

Susan Neuberger Weller
Lance G. Johnson

For full biographical listings, see the Martindale-Hubbell Law Directory

---

VENABLE ATTORNEYS AT LAW VENABLE, BAETJER, HOWARD & CIVILETTI, LLP (AV)

A Partnership including Professional Corporations
Suite 1000, 1201 New York Avenue, N.W., 20005
Telephone: 202-962-4800
Fax: 202-962-8300
URL: http://www.venable.com
Baltimore, Maryland Office: Venable, Baetjer and Howard LLP, 1800 Mercantile Bank & Trust Building, 2 Hopkins Plaza.
Telephone: 410-244-7400.
Fax: 410-244-7742.
McLean, Virginia Office: Venable, Baetjer and Howard LLP, Suite 400, 2010 Corporate Ridge.
Telephone: 703-760-1600.
Fax: 703-821-8949.

(See Next Column)

VENABLE ATTORNEYS AT LAW VENABLE, BAETJER, HOWARD & CIVILETTI, LLP, *Washington—Continued*

Rockville, Maryland Office: Venable, Baetjer and Howard LLP, Suite 500, One Church Street, P. O. Box 1906.
Telephone: 301-217-5600.
Fax: 301-217-5617.
Towson, Maryland Office: Venable, Baetjer and Howard LLP, 210 Allegheny Avenue, P. O. Box 5517.
Telephone: 410-494-6200.
Fax: 410-821-0147.

MEMBERS OF FIRM

James K. Archibald (Also at Baltimore, Maryland Office)
Maurice Baskin
Kenneth C. Bass, III (Also at McLean, Virginia Office)
Lawrence B. Bernard
Benjamin R. Civiletti (P.C.) (Also at Baltimore and Towson, Maryland Offices)
William D. Coston
Edward F. Glynn, Jr.
David W. Goewey
Amy Berman Jackson
Jeffrey D. Knowles
Michael Schatzow (Also at Baltimore, Maryland Office)

For Complete List of Firm Personnel, See General Section

For full biographical listings, see the Martindale-Hubbell Law Directory

WILMER, CUTLER & PICKERING (AV)

2445 M Street, N.W., 20037-1420
Telephone: 202-663-6000
Fax: 202-663-6363
Email: Law@Wilmer.Com *URL:* http://www.wilmer.com
Baltimore, Maryland Office: 100 Light Street, 21202.
Telephone: 410-986-2800.
Fax: 410-986-2828.
New York, New York Office: 520 Madison Avenue, 10022.
Telephone: 212-230-8800.
Fax: 212-230-8888.
European Offices:
4 Carlton Gardens, London, SW1Y 5AA, England. Telephone: +44 (20) 7 872 1000.
Fax: +44 (20) 7 839 3537.
Rue de la Loi 15# Wetstraat, B-1040 Brussels, Belgium. Telephone: +32 (2) 285 49 00.
Fax: +32 (2) 285 49 49.
Friedrichstrasse 95, D-10117 Berlin, Germany. Telephone: +49 (30) 20 22 64 00.
Fax: +49 (30) 20 22 65 00.

MEMBERS OF FIRM

Daniel K. Mayers
James S. Campbell
Ronald J. Greene
C. Loring Jetton, Jr.
Dieter G. F. Lange (Not admitted in DC; Resident, European Office, London, England)
William J. Kolasky, Jr.
John Rounsaville, Jr.
Matthias Wissmann (Not admitted in DC; Resident, European Office, Berlin, Germany)
James S. Venit (Not admitted in DC; Resident, European Office, Brussels, Belgium)
Dr. Andreas Weitbrecht (Not admitted in DC; Resident, European Offices, Berlin, Germany and Brussels, Belgium)
John H. Ratliff (Not admitted in DC; Resident, European Office, Brussels, Belgium)
Robert B. Bell
Thomas P. Olson
Marc C. Hansen (Not admitted in DC; Resident, European Office, Brussels, Belgium)
Thomas Mueller (Resident, European Office, Brussels, Belgium)
Christian L. Duvernoy (Resident, European Office, Brussels, Belgium)
James W. Lowe
Ali M. Stoeppelwerth

COUNSEL

John J. Kallaugher (Not admitted in DC; European Offices, London, England and Brussels, Belgium)
Leon B. Greenfield

For Complete List of Firm Personnel, See General Section

For full biographical listings, see the Martindale-Hubbell Law Directory

FLORIDA

*MIAMI,** Dade Co.

KENNY NACHWALTER SEYMOUR ARNOLD CRITCHLOW & SPECTOR, PROFESSIONAL ASSOCIATION (AV)

1100 Miami Center, 201 South Biscayne Boulevard, 33131-4327
Telephone: 305-373-1000
Facsimile: 305-372-1861
Email: admin@knsacs.com
Rogersville, Tennessee Office: 107 East Main Street, Suite 301.
Telephone: 423-272-5300.
Facsimile: 423-272-4961.

James J. Kenny
Michael Nachwalter
Richard Alan Arnold
Brian F. Spector
Kevin J. Murray
William J. Blechman
Harry R. Schafer
David H. Lichter
Scott E. Perwin

Representative Clients: Albertson's, Inc.; American Stores; A&P, Inc.; Cartier, Inc.; GTE Directories; The Kroger Co.; Nestle Food Co.; Safeway, Inc.; GTE Florida; General Motors Co.; Ford Motor Co.; Chrysler Corp.; U.S. Steel.

For Complete List of Firm Personnel, See General Section

For full biographical listings, see the Martindale-Hubbell Law Directory

NAGIN GALLOP FIGUEREDO, P.A. (AV)

3225 Aviation Avenue - Third Floor, 33133-4741
Telephone: 305-854-5353
Facsimile: 305-854-5351

Stephen E. Nagin
Earl G. Gallop
Luis R. Figueredo
Scott L. Cagan
Eve A. Boutsis
Jeffrey B. Mallory

For full biographical listings, see the Martindale-Hubbell Law Directory

SHUTTS & BOWEN LLP (AV)

A Partnership including Professional Associations
1500 Miami Center, 201 South Biscayne Boulevard, 33131
Telephone: 305-358-6300
Telefax: 305-381-9982
Email: MCONNORS@SHUTTS-LAW.COM *URL:* HTTP://WWW.SHUTTS-LAW.COM
Orlando, Florida Office: 20 North Orange Avenue, Suite 1000.
Telephone: 407-423-3200.
Fax: 407-425-8316.
West Palm Beach, Florida Office: One Clearlake Centre, 250 Australian Avenue, Suite 500.
Telephone: 561-835-8500.
Fax: 561-650-8530.
Tallahassee, Florida Office: 215 South Monroe Street, Suite 804.
Telephone: 850-521-0600.
Fax: 850-521-0604.
Fort Lauderdale, Florida Office: First Union Center, Suite 2000, 200 East Broward Boulevard.
Telephone: 954-524-5505.
Fax: 954-524-5506.
Amsterdam, The Netherlands Office: Shutts & Bowen, B.V., Europa Boulevard 59, 1083 AD, Amsterdam.
Telephone: (31 20) 661-0969.
Fax: (31 20) 642-1475.
London, England Office: 43 Grosvenor Street, London W1X 9PG.
Telephone: 441-71-493-4840.
Telefax: 441-71-493-4299.

MEMBERS OF FIRM

Jonathan Cohen
Maxine Master Long

For Complete List of Firm Personnel, See General Section

For full biographical listings, see the Martindale-Hubbell Law Directory

*ORLANDO,** Orange Co.

DEMPSEY & SASSO (AV)

Nations Bank Building, 390 North Orange Avenue, Suite 2700, P.O. Box 1980, 32802
Telephone: 407-422-5166
Telecopier: 407-422-8556
Email: demp-sas@magicnet.net

Bernard H. Dempsey, Jr.
Michael C. Sasso

Brian D. Solomon
Barbara B. Smithers
Jeffrey K. Grant
Angelia J. Sheridan

For full biographical listings, see the Martindale-Hubbell Law Directory

Orlando—Continued

HILL, REIS, ADAMS, HALL & SCHIEFFELIN, P.A. (AV)

1417 East Concord Street, 32803
Telephone: 407-896-0425
Fax: 407-896-9236
Email: mainbox@hrahs.com

G. Bruce Hill
William W. Large

Representative Clients: The Florida Hospital Trust Fund; The Florida Hospital Excess Trust Fund; Florida Hospital Workers Compensation/Self Insurance Trust Fund; Bartow Memorial Hospital; Bay Medical Center; Brooksville Regional Hospital; Cape Canaveral Hospital; Cape Coral Hospital; Desoto Memorial Hospital.

For Complete List of Firm Personnel, See General Section

For full biographical listings, see the Martindale-Hubbell Law Directory

LITCHFORD & CHRISTOPHER, PROFESSIONAL ASSOCIATION (AV)

NationsBank Center, Suite 2200, 390 North Orange Avenue, P.O. Box 1549, 32802
Telephone: 407-422-6600
Telecopier: 407-841-0325
Email: lawfirm@litchris.com *URL:* http://www.litchris.com

Hal K. Litchford
Donald E. Christopher
Mark Lang
Brian D. DeGailler
David G. Lerner
Alan B. Taylor

Scott K. Lippman
G. Steven Fender
Jill Barron Dugger
Susan E. Sewell
Joanne Reed Day

Reference: Citrus Bank.

For full biographical listings, see the Martindale-Hubbell Law Directory

*TAMPA,** Hillsborough Co.

MICHAEL C. ADDISON (AV)

Suite 1130, 220 East Madison Street, 33602
Telephone: 813-223-2000
Facsimile: 813-228-6000
Mailing Address: P.O. Box 2175, Tampa, Florida, 33601-2175
Email: michaeladdison@compuserve.com *URL:* http://www.lawyers.com/michaeladdison-law

For full biographical listings, see the Martindale-Hubbell Law Directory

*WEST PALM BEACH,** Palm Beach Co.

WARD, DAMON, BEVERLY, TITTLE & POSNER, P.A. (AV)

4420 Beacon Circle, 33407-3270
Telephone: 561-842-3000
Stuart: 561-223-5550
Fax: 561-842-3626
Email: wdbtp@wdbtp.com *URL:* http://www.wdbtp.com

James F. Cooney, Jr. (1950-1992)
Conrad Damon
Andrew Fulton, IV
Irwin R. Gilbert
Craig I. Kelley
Michael J Posner
Roger C. Stanton
James D. Tittle, Jr.
Philip H. Ward, III

OF COUNSEL

Don Beverly

For full biographical listings, see the Martindale-Hubbell Law Directory

GEORGIA

*ATLANTA,** Fulton Co.

BONDURANT, MIXSON & ELMORE, LLP (AV)

1201 W. Peachtree Street Suite 3900, 30309
Telephone: 404-881-4100
Fax: 404-881-4111
URL: http://www.bondurant-mixson.com

MEMBERS OF FIRM

Emmet J. Bondurant II
H. Lamar Mixson
M. Jerome Elmore
Edward B. Krugman
Jeffrey O. Bramlett
John E. Floyd
Michael B. Terry
P. Richard Game
Jill A. Pryor
J. Scott McClain

Representative Clients: American Dairy Queen Corp.; Avon Products, Inc.; Bottlers of Coca-Cola, U.S.A.; Blue Circle of America; Delta Air Lines, Inc.; Fina Oil and Chemical Company; Four M Corporation; Penske Motorsports; Queen Carpets, Inc.; Ticketmaster Southeast.

For full biographical listings, see the Martindale-Hubbell Law Directory

CHITWOOD & HARLEY (AV)

2900 Promenade II, 1230 Peachtree Street, N.E., 30309
Telephone: 404-873-3900
Fax: 404-876-4476
Email: mail@classlaw.com *URL:* http://www.classlaw.com

Martin D. Chitwood
Alan R. Perry, Jr.
Neal S. Berinhout
Craig G. Harley

ASSOCIATES

Nikole M. Davenport
Christi C. Mobley
John Hinton, IV
David A. Bain
Corey Daniel Holzer
Kimberly Janelle Broder

For full biographical listings, see the Martindale-Hubbell Law Directory

JONES, DAY, REAVIS & POGUE (AV)

3500 SunTrust Plaza, 303 Peachtree Street, 30308-3242
Telephone: 404-521-3939
Telecopier: 404-581-8330
Email: counsel@jonesday.com *URL:* http://www.jonesday.com
In Brussels, Belgium: Avenue Louise 480, 7th Floor, B-1050 Brussels.
Telephone: 32-2-645-14-11.
Telecopier: 32-2-645-14-45.
In Chicago, Illinois: 77 West Wacker.
Telephone: 312-782-3939.
Telecopier: 312-782-8585.
In Cleveland, Ohio: North Point. 901 Lakeside Avenue.
Telephone: 216-586-3939.
Telecopier: 216-579-0212.
In Columbus, Ohio: 1900 Huntington Center.
Telephone: 614-469-3939.
Telecopier: 614-461-4198.
In Dallas, Texas: 2727 North Harwood Street.
Telephone: 214-220-3939.
Telecopier: 214-969-5100.
In Frankfurt, Germany: Hochhaus am Park, Grüneburgweg 102, 60323 Frankfurt am Main.
Telephone: 49-69-9726-3939.
Telecopier: 49-69-9726-3993.
In Geneva, Switzerland: 20, rue de Candolle.
Telephone: 41-22-320-2339.
Telecopier: 41-22-320-1232.
In Hong Kong: 29th Floor, Entertainment Building, 30 Queen's Road Central.
Telephone: 852-2526-6895.
Telecopier: 852-2868-5871 or 852-2868-5699.
In Irvine, California: 5 Park Plaza, Suite 1100.
Telephone: 949-851-3939.
Telecopier: 949-553-7539.
In London, England: Bucklersbury House, 3 Queen Victoria Street.
Telephone: 44-171-236-3939.
Telecopier: 44-171-236-1113.
In Los Angeles, California: 555 West Fifth Street, Suite 4600.
Telephone: 213-489-3939.
Telecopier: 213-243-2539.
In New Delhi, India (Associate Office): Pathak & Associates (an associate firm of Jones, Day, Reavis & Pogue), 1st Floor, Dr. Gopal Das Bhaven, 28 Barakhamba Road.
Telephone: 91-11-373-8793; 91-11-335-7345.
Telecopier: 91-11-335-3761.
In New York, New York: 599 Lexington Avenue.
Telephone: 212-326-3939.
Telecopier: 212-755-7306.
In Paris, France: 120, rue du Faubourg Saint-Honoré.
Telephone: 33-1-56-59-39-39.
Telecopier: 33-1-56-59-39-38
In Pittsburgh, Pennsylvania: 500 Grant Street, 31st Floor.
Telephone: 412-391-3939.
Telecopier: 412-394-7959.
In Riyadh, Saudi Arabia: The International Law Firm (In Association with Jones, Day, Reavis & Pogue), Sulaymaniyah, Prince Mishari IBN, Abdulaziz Street, P.O. Box 22166.
Telephone: (966-1) 462-8866.
Telecopier: (966-1) 462-9001.
In Shanghai, China: 2805 Kerry Centre, 1515 Nanjing Road West.
Telephone: 86-21-5298-6568.
Telecopier: 86-21-5298-6569.
In Sydney, Australia: Governor Phillip Tower, Level 38, 1 Farrer Place.
Telephone: 61-2-9210-6921.
Telecopier: 61-2-9210-6926.
In Taipei, Taiwan: 8th Floor, 2 Tun Hwa South Road, Section 2.
Telephone: (886-2) 2704-6808.
Telecopier: (886-2) 2704-6791.
In Tokyo, Japan: Toranomon MT Building, 4th Floor, 10-3, Toranomon 3-Chome, Minato-ku, Tokyo 105, Japan.
Telephone: 81-3-3433-3939.
Telecopier: 81-3-5401-2725.
In Washington, D.C.: 51 Louisiana Avenue, N.W.
Telephone: 202-879-3939.
Telecopier: 202-626-1700.

(See Next Column)

JONES, DAY, REAVIS & POGUE, *Atlanta—Continued*

MEMBERS OF FIRM IN ATLANTA

Girard E. Boudreau, Jr. William B. B. Smith

COUNSEL

L. Trammell Newton, Jr.

For Complete List of Firm Personnel, See General Section

For full biographical listings, see the Martindale-Hubbell Law Directory

LONG ALDRIDGE & NORMAN LLP (AV)

A Limited Liability Partnership including Professional Corporations
Suite 5300, 303 Peachtree Street, 30308
Telephone: 404-527-4000
Telecopier: 404-527-4198
Email: atlanta@lanlaw.com *URL:* http://www.lanlaw.com
Washington, D.C. Office: Suite 600, 701 Pennsylvania Avenue, N.W., 20004.
Telephone: 202-624-1200.
FAX: 202-624-1298.

MEMBERS OF FIRM

J. James Johnson Carl W. Mullis, III

For Complete List of Firm Personnel, See General Section

For full biographical listings, see the Martindale-Hubbell Law Directory

PARKER, HUDSON, RAINER & DOBBS LLP (AV)

1500 Marquis Two Tower, 285 Peachtree Center Avenue, N.E., 30303
Telephone: 404-523-5300
Fax: 404-522-8409
Tallahassee, Florida Office: The Perkins House, 118 North Gadsden Street, 32301.
Telephone: 904-681-0191.
Fax: 904-681-9493.

MEMBER OF FIRM

J. Marbury Rainer

For full biographical listings, see the Martindale-Hubbell Law Directory

HAWAII

*HONOLULU,** Honolulu Co.

CARLSMITH BALL (AV)

A Partnership including Law Corporations
Suite 2200, Pacific Tower, 1001 Bishop Street, P.O. Box 656, 96809-3402
Telephone: 808-523-2500
Fax: 808-523-0842
Email: execdirector@carlsmith.com *URL:* http://www.carlsmith.com
Kapolei, Hawaii Office: Suite 318, Kapolei Building, 1001 Kamokila Boulevard, 96707.
Telephone: 808-523-2500.
Fax: 808-674-0850.
Wailuku, Maui Hawaii Office: Suite 400, One Main Plaza, 2200 Main Street, P.O. Box 1086, 96793-1086.
Telephone: 808-242-4535.
Fax: 808-244-4974.
Kailua-Kona, Hawaii Office: Suite 209, 75-1000 Henry Street, 96740.
Telephone: 808-329-6464.
Fax: 808-329-9450.
Hilo, Hawaii Office: 121 Waianuenue Avenue, P.O. Box 686, 96721-0686.
Telephone: 808-935-6644.
Fax: 808-935-7975.
Hagatna, Guam Office: Suite 401, Bank of Hawaii Building, 134 West Soledad Avenue, P.O. Box BF, 96932-5027.
Telephone: 671-472-6813.
Fax: 671-477-4375.
Telex: 721-6445 CWCMI GM.
Saipan, Commonwealth of the Northern Mariana Islands Office: Carlsmith Building, Capitol Hill, P.O. Box 5241, 96950-5241.
Telephone: 670-322-3455.
Fax: 670-322-3368.
Los Angeles, California Office: 9th Floor, 444 South Flower Street, 90071-2901.
Telephone: 213-955-1200.
Fax: 213-623-0032.
Washington, D.C. Office: Suite 300, 1201 Pennsylvania Avenue, N.W., 20004-2401.
Telephone: 202-628-2228.
Fax: 202-628-2071.
Mexico City, Mexico Office: Carlsmith Ball, Sierra Nevada 119, Lomas de Chapultepec, 11000 Mexico, D.F.
Telephone: 52-5-520-8514, 52-5-520-8757.
Fax: 52-5-540-1545.

(See Next Column)

Mexico, D.F. Office of Carlsmith Ball, S.C. (Authorized to practice as foreign legal consultants in Mexico): Sierra Nevada 119, Lomas de Chapultepec, 11000 Mexico, D.F.
Telephone: 52-5-520-8514, 52-5-520-8757.
Fax: 52-5-540-1545.

MEMBER OF FIRM

Gary G. Grimmer

For Complete List of Firm Personnel, See General Section

For full biographical listings, see the Martindale-Hubbell Law Directory

PITLUCK KIDO SATO & STONE (AV)

701 Bishop Street, 96813
Telephone: 808-523-5030
Telecopier: 808-545-4015
Email: pitluck@pitluck.com *URL:* http://www.pitluck.com

MEMBERS OF FIRM

Wayne Marshall Pitluck Dana Kiyomi Nalani Sato
Alan Takashi Kido James Mauliola Keaka Stone, Jr.

OF COUNSEL

John W. Reilly

Reference: Bank of Hawaii.

For full biographical listings, see the Martindale-Hubbell Law Directory

IDAHO

*BOISE,** Ada Co.

EBERLE, BERLIN, KADING, TURNBOW & MCKLVEEN, CHARTERED (AV)

Capitol Park Plaza, 300 North Sixth Street, P.O. Box 1368, 83701-1368
Telephone: 208-344-8535
Facsimile: 208-344-8542

R.M. Turnbow

Representative Clients: TJ International; Key Bank of Idaho; Agri Beef Co.

For Complete List of Firm Personnel, See General Section

For full biographical listings, see the Martindale-Hubbell Law Directory

ELAM & BURKE, A PROFESSIONAL ASSOCIATION (AV)

Key Financial Center, 702 West Idaho Street, P.O. Box 1539, 83701
Telephone: 208-343-5454
Telecopier: 208-384-5844
Email: eblaw@elamburke.com

William G. Dryden

Representative Clients: Morrison-Knudsen, Inc.; Pechiney Corp.; Sinclair Oil Company d/b/a Sun Valley Co.; Farmers Insurance Group; Healthtrust-The Hospital Co.

For Complete List of Firm Personnel, See General Section

For full biographical listings, see the Martindale-Hubbell Law Directory

ILLINOIS

*CHICAGO,** Cook Co.

FREEMAN, FREEMAN & SALZMAN, P.C. (AV)

401 North Michigan Avenue, Suite 3200, 60611-4207
Telephone: 312-222-5100
Facsimile: 312-822-0870

Lee A. Freeman (1909-1995) James T. Malysiak
Lee A. Freeman, Jr. Glynna W. Freeman
Jerrold E. Salzman Phillip L. Stern
John F. Kinney Chris C. Gair

Kevin P. Kappock Jeffrey M. Osterkamp

For full biographical listings, see the Martindale-Hubbell Law Directory

MICHAEL T. HANNAFAN & ASSOCIATES, LTD. (AV)

One East Wacker Drive, Suite 2710, 60601
Telephone: 312-527-0055
Fax: 312-527-0220
Email: mthannafan@aol.com

Michael T. Hannafan

(See Next Column)

MICHAEL T. HANNAFAN & ASSOCIATES, LTD.—*Continued*

Cory A. Johnson

Reference: The Northern Trust Co.

For full biographical listings, see the Martindale-Hubbell Law Directory

JONES, DAY, REAVIS & POGUE (AV)

77 West Wacker, 60601-1692
Telephone: 312-782-3939
Telecopier: 312-782-8585
Email: counsel@jonesday.com *URL:* http://www.jonesday.com
In Atlanta, Georgia: 3500 SunTrust Plaza, 303 Peachtree Street.
Telephone: 404-521-3939.
Telecopier: 404-581-8330. 34000 Brussels, Belgium: Avenue Louise 480, 7th Floor, B-1050 Brussels.
Telephone: 32-2-645-14-11.
Telecopier: 32-2-645-14-45.
In Cleveland, Ohio: North Point, 901 Lakeside Avenue.
Telephone: 216-586-3939.
Telecopier: 216-579-0212.
In Columbus, Ohio: 1900 Huntington Center.
Telephone: 614-469-3939.
Telecopier: 614-461-4198.
In Dallas, Texas: 2727 North Harwood Street.
Telephone: 214-220-3939.
Telecopier: 214-969-5100.
In Frankfurt, Germany: Hochhaus am Park, Grüneburgweg 102, 60323 Frankfurt am Main.
Telephone: 49-69-9726-3939.
Telecopier: 49-69-9726-3993.
In Geneva, Switzerland: 20, rue de Candolle.
Telephone: 41-22-320-2339.
Telecopier: 41-22-320-1232.
In Hong Kong: 29th Floor, Entertainment Building, 30 Queen's Road Central.
Telephone: 852-2526-6895.
Telecopier: 852-2868-5871 or 852-2868-5699.
In Irvine, California: 5 Park Plaza, Suite 1100.
Telephone: 949-851-3939.
Telecopier: 949-553-7539.
In London, England: Bucklersbury House, 3 Queen Victoria Street.
Telephone: 44-171-236-3939.
Telecopier: 44-171-236-1113.
In Los Angeles, California: 555 West Fifth Street, Suite 4600.
Telephone: 213-489-3939.
Telecopier: 213-243-2539.
In New Delhi, India (Associate Office): Pathak & Associates (an associate firm of Jones, Day, Reavis & Pogue), 1st Floor, Dr. Gopal Das Bhaven, 28 Barakhamba Road.
Telephone: 91-11-373-8793; 91-11-335-7345.
Telecopier: 91-11-335-3761.
In New York, New York: 599 Lexington Avenue.
Telephone: 212-326-3939.
Telecopier: 212-755-7306.
In Paris, France: 120, rue du Faubourg Saint-Honoré.
Telephone: 33-1-56-59-39-39.
Telecopier: 33-1-56-59-39-38
In Pittsburgh, Pennsylvania: 500 Grant Street, 31st Floor.
Telephone: 412-391-3939.
Telecopier: 412-394-7959.
In Riyadh, Saudi Arabia: The International Law Firm (In Association with Jones, Day, Reavis & Pogue), Sulaymaniyah, Prince Mishari IBN, Abdulaziz Street, P.O. Box 22166.
Telephone: (966-1) 462-8866.
Telecopier: (966-1) 462-9001.
In Shanghai, China: 2805 Kerry Centre, 1515 Nanjing Road West.
Telephone: 86-21-5298-6568.
Telecopier: 86-21-5298-6569.
In Sydney, Australia: Governor Phillip Tower, Level 38, 1 Farrer Place.
Telephone: 61-2-9210-6921.
Telecopier: 61-2-9210-6926.
In Taipei, Taiwan: 8th Floor, 2 Tun Hwa South Road, Section 2.
Telephone: (886-2) 2704-6808.
Telecopier: (886-2) 2704-6791.
In Tokyo, Japan: Toranomon MT Building, 4th Floor, 10-3, Toranomon 3-Chome, 34200o-ku, Tokyo 105, Japan.
Telephone: 81-3-3433-3939.
Telecopier: 81-3-5401-2725.
In Washington, D.C.: 51 Louisiana Avenue, N.W.
Telephone: 202-879-3939.
Telecopier: 202-626-1700.

MEMBER OF FIRM IN CHICAGO

Thomas F. Gardner

For Complete List of Firm Personnel, See General Section

For full biographical listings, see the Martindale-Hubbell Law Directory

MCBRIDE BAKER & COLES (AV)

500 West Madison Street 40th Floor, 60661-2511
Telephone: 312-715-5700
Cable Address: "Chilaw"
Telex: 270258
Telecopier: 312-993-9350
Email: lastname@mbc.com *URL:* http://www.mbc.com
Oakbrook Terrace, Illinois Office: Suite 1000, One Mid America Plaza, 60181-4710.
Telephone: 630-954-2100.
Telecopier: 630-954-2112.

MEMBERS OF FIRM

Henry S. Allen, Jr. | Robert C. Schnitz
Malcolm H. Brooks | Steven B. Varick
Clifton A. Lake | Richard R. Winter

ASSOCIATES

Naomi R. Angel | George M. Sanders
Jeffrey M. Teske

For Complete List of Firm Personnel, See General Section

For full biographical listings, see the Martindale-Hubbell Law Directory

ROTHSCHILD, BARRY & MYERS (AV)

A Partnership including Professional Corporations
Suite 3900, 55 West Monroe Street, 60603-5012
Telephone: 312-372-2345
FAX: 312-372-2350
Email: rbm01@wwa.com

MEMBERS OF FIRM

William G. Myers (P.C.) | Joseph P. Della Maria, Jr.
Melvin I. Mishkin | Christopher G. Walsh, Jr.
John J. Coffey, III | Kenneth P. Taube
Alan S. Madans

For Complete List of Firm Personnel, See General Section

For full biographical listings, see the Martindale-Hubbell Law Directory

SAUNDERS & MONROE (AV)

1600 NBC Tower, 455 North Cityfront Plaza Drive, 60611
Telephone: 312-645-6000
Fax: 312-645-9848

MEMBERS OF FIRM

George L. Saunders, Jr. | Thomas F. Bush, Jr.
Lee A. Monroe | Matthew E. Van Tine
Thomas A. Doyle

OF COUNSEL

Victoria S. Kaplan

For full biographical listings, see the Martindale-Hubbell Law Directory

WILDMAN, HARROLD, ALLEN & DIXON (AV)

225 West Wacker Drive, 30th Floor, 60606-1229
Telephone: 312-201-2000
Fax: 312-201-2555
Email: hennessy@whad.com *URL:* http://www.whad.com
Aurora, Illinois Office: 1961 W. Downer Place.
Telephone: 630-892-7021.
Fax: 630-892-7158.
Waukegan, Illinois Office: 404 West Water, P. O. Box 890.
Telephone: 847-625-5550.
Fax: 847-625-5555.
Lisle, Illinois Office: 4300 Commerce Court, Suite 320.
Telephone: 630-955-0555.
Fax: 630-955-0662
Toronto, Ontario correspondent Office: Keel Cottrelle. 36 Toronto Street, Suite 920.
Telephone: 416-367-2900.
Telefax: 416-367-2791.
Telex: 062-18660.

MEMBERS OF FIRM

Brent R. Austin | Michael Dockterman
Douglas R. Carlson | Jerald P. Esrick
Leland H. Chait | Donald Flayton
Stewart S. Dixon | Michael L. McCluggage
R. John Street

OF COUNSEL

Bernard Harrold

Kristin M. Buchholz | Dara J. Keidan

For full biographical listings, see the Martindale-Hubbell Law Directory

Chicago—Continued

WINSTON & STRAWN (AV)

35 West Wacker Drive, 60601
Telephone: 312-558-5600
Cable Address: "Winston Chicago"
Facsimile: 312-558-5700
Email: postmaster@winston.com *URL:* http://www.winston.com
Washington, D.C. Office: 1400 L Street, N.W., 20005-3502.
Telephone: 202-371-5700.
Telecopier: 202-371-5950.
Telex: 440574 INTLAW UI.
New York, N.Y. Office: 200 Park Avenue, 10166-4193.
Telephone: 212-294-6700.
Telecopier: 212-294-4700.
Cable Address: "Coledeitz, NYK".
Telex: (RCA) 232459.
Geneva, Switzerland Office: 43 Rue du Rhone, 1204.
Telephone: (4122) 7810506.
Fax: (4122) 7810361.
Paris, France Office: 21 Avenue Victor Hugo. 75116.
Telephone: 331-5364-8282.
Fax: 331-5364-8220.

MEMBERS OF FIRM

Edward L. Foote
Duane M. Kelley
R. Mark McCareins

Representative Clients: Windmere Corp.; Tropicana Products; Illinois Bell Telephone Co.; Amertech; Marmon Group.

For Complete List of Firm Personnel, See General Section

For full biographical listings, see the Martindale-Hubbell Law Directory

INDIANA

*INDIANAPOLIS,** Marion Co.

BOSE MCKINNEY & EVANS LLP (AV)

2700 First Indiana Plaza, 135 North Pennsylvania Street, 46204
Telephone: 317-684-5000
Facsimile: 317-684-5173
URL: http://www.boselaw.com
Indianapolis North Office: Suite 1500, 8888 Keystone Crossing, 46240.
Telephone: 317-574-3700.
Facsimile: 317-574-3716.

MEMBERS OF FIRM

Kendall C. Crook
Ronald E. Elberger
R. J. McConnell
Dwight L. Miller
David Williams Russell

Representative Clients: Erbrich Products Co., Inc.; First Indiana Bank; Indiana Supply Corp.; Kenra Laboratories Inc.; Lawyers Title Insurance Corp.; Muncie Power Products, Inc.; Indianapolis Life Insurance Co.; BMW Constructors, Inc.; Indiana Academy of Ophthalmology, Inc.

For Complete List of Firm Personnel, See General Section

For full biographical listings, see the Martindale-Hubbell Law Directory

ICE MILLER DONADIO & RYAN (AV)

One American Square Box 82001, 46282-0002
Telephone: 317-236-2100
Fax: 317-236-2219
Email: info@imdr.com *URL:* http://www.imdr.com
South Bend, Indiana Office: 211 West Washington Street, Suite 2420.
Telephone: 219-234-7933.
Fax: 219-234-7965. Internet E-mail: info@imdr.com. Web Site Address: http://www.imdr.com.
Chicago, Illinois Office: 135 South LaSalle Street, Suite 4100.
Telephone: 312-726-1567.
Fax: 312-641-6263. Internet E-mail: info@imdr.com. Web Site Address: http://www.imdr.com.

MEMBERS OF FIRM

Jay G. Taylor
G. Daniel Kelley, Jr.
Philip A. Whistler
Gregory L. Pemberton
Donald M. Snemis
Susan Barnhizer Rivas
Karen Ann P. Lloyd
Curtis W. McCauley
Antje C. Petersen

ASSOCIATES

A. Richard M. Blaiklock
Steven D. Stennett
Julie E. Ragsdale

Counsel for: Indianapolis Motor Speedway; Community Hospitals of Indiana; Avesta Sheffield, Inc.; Reilly Industries, Inc.; Delco Remy America; Biomet, Inc.; Irving Materials, Inc.; Eli Lilly and Co.; Magnequench International, Inc.; The University of Michigan.

For Complete List of Firm Personnel, See General Section

For full biographical listings, see the Martindale-Hubbell Law Directory

MCTURNAN & TURNER (AV)

2400 Market Tower, 10 West Market Street, 46204
Telephone: 317-464-8181
Telecopier: 317-464-8131

Lee B. McTurnan
Wayne C. Turner
Jackie M. Bennett, Jr.
Jacqueline Bowman Ponder
Steven M. Badger
John F. McCauley

For full biographical listings, see the Martindale-Hubbell Law Directory

SOMMER & BARNARD, ATTORNEYS AT LAW, PC (AV)

4000 Bank One Tower, 111 Monument Circle, 46204
Telephone: 317-630-4000
FAX: 317-236-9802
Email: sandb@sommerbarnard.com
North Office: 8900 Keystone Crossing, Suite 1150, Indianapolis, Indiana, 46240-2134.
Telephone: 317-630-4000.
FAX: 317-844-4780.

William C. Barnard
James E. Hughes
Edward W. Harris, III
Gordon L. Pittenger
Gayle A. Reindl

Representative Clients: Monsanto Co.; Comerica Bank; Federal Express; Kimball International; TRW, Inc.

For Complete List of Firm Personnel, See General Section

For full biographical listings, see the Martindale-Hubbell Law Directory

IOWA

*DES MOINES,** Polk Co.

HAWKINS & NORRIS (AV)

2501 Grand Avenue, Suite C, 50312
Telephone: 515-288-6532
Fax: 515-288-9733

MEMBERS OF FIRM

Lex Hawkins
Glenn L. Norris

ASSOCIATES

George F. Davison, Jr.
Carla Tolbert Schemmel
David N. May

Reference: West Des Moines State Bank.

For full biographical listings, see the Martindale-Hubbell Law Directory

KANSAS

*WICHITA,** Sedgwick Co.

FOULSTON & SIEFKIN L.L.P. (AV)

700 NationsBank Financial Center, 67202
Telephone: 316-267-6371
Facsimile: 316-267-6345
URL: http://www.foulston.com
Topeka, Kansas Office: 1515 NationsBank Tower, 534 Kansas Avenue, 66603.
Telephone: 785-233-3600.
Fax: 785-233-1610.
Dodge City, Kansas Office: 810 Frontview, P.O. Box 1147, 67801.
Telephone: 316-227-8126.
Fax: 316-227-8451.
Member: Lex Mundi, The World's Leading Association of Independent Law Firms.

MEMBERS OF FIRM

Robert L. Howard
James D. Oliver
Jim H. Goering

For Complete List of Firm Personnel, See General Section

For full biographical listings, see the Martindale-Hubbell Law Directory

KENTUCKY

*LEXINGTON,** Fayette Co.

STOLL, KEENON & PARK, LLP (AV)

201 E. Main Street, Suite 1000, 40507-1380
Telephone: 606-231-3000
Telecopier: 606-253-1093; 606-253-1027
URL: http://www.skp.com
Frankfort, Kentucky Office: 307 Washington Street, 40601.
Telephone: 502-875-6220.
Telecopier: 502-875-6235.
Henderson, Kentucky Office: 201 C North Main Street, 42420-3103.
Telephone: 270-831-1900.
Telecopier: 270-827-4060.
Louisville, Kentucky Office: 400 West Market Street, Suite 2650, 40202-3377.
Telephone: 502-568-9100.
Telecopier: 502-568-5700.

MEMBER OF FIRM

Samuel D. Hinkle IV

Representative Clients: C. Lee Cook; Farmers Capital Bank Corp.; Link Belt Construction Equipment Co.; General Motors Corp.; International Business Machines Corp.; Square D Co.; Jim Walter Homes, Inc.

For Complete List of Firm Personnel, See General Section

For full biographical listings, see the Martindale-Hubbell Law Directory

*LOUISVILLE,** Jefferson Co.

MIDDLETON & REUTLINGER, P.S.C. (AV)

2500 Brown and Williamson Tower, 40202-3410
Telephone: 502-584-1135
Fax: 502-561-0442
URL: http://middreut.com
Jeffersonville, Indiana Office: 530 East Court Avenue, 47130.
Telephone: 812-282-1132.
Fax: 812-282-3188.

Charles G. Middleton, III
C. Kent Hatfield
William Jay Hunter, Jr.

For Complete List of Firm Personnel, See General Section

For full biographical listings, see the Martindale-Hubbell Law Directory

WOODWARD, HOBSON & FULTON (AV)

2500 National City Tower, 101 South Fifth Street, 40202
Telephone: 502-581-8000
Fax: 502-581-8111
Email: WHF@IGLOU.COM
Lexington, Kentucky Office: PNC Bank Plaza, 200 West Vine Street, Suite 500.
Telephone: 606-244-7100.
Telecopier: 606-244-7111.

OF COUNSEL

Kenneth L. Anderson

Representative Clients: International Minerals & Chemical Corp.; Ralston Purina Co.; Sears, Roebuck & Co.; Prairie Farms Dairy, Inc.; Mid-America Dairymen, Inc.

For Complete List of Firm Personnel, See General Section

For full biographical listings, see the Martindale-Hubbell Law Directory

LOUISIANA

*BATON ROUGE,** East Baton Rouge Parish

BREAZEALE, SACHSE & WILSON, L.L.P. (AV)

Twenty-Third Floor, One American Place, P.O. Box 3197, 70821-3197
Telephone: 225-387-4000
Fax: 225-387-5397
URL: http://www.bswllp.com
New Orleans, Louisiana Office: LL&E Tower, Suite 1500, 909 Poydras Street.
Telephone: 504-584-5454.
Fax: 504-584-5452.
Covington, Louisiana Office: 2255 Highway 190 North, Suite 200.
Telephone: 504-871-9444.
Fax: 504-871-9666.

(See Next Column)

MEMBERS OF FIRM

Gordon A. Pugh
Claude F. Reynaud, Jr.
Emile C. Rolfs, III
Jude C. Bursavich
Joseph E. Friend (Resident, New Orleans Office)
James R. Chastain, Jr.
Linda Perez Clark
Luis A. Leitzelar

ASSOCIATE

Jeanne C. Comeaux

Counsel for: Allied-Signal Corp.; Reynolds Metal Co.; Illinois Central Railroad Co.

For Complete List of Firm Personnel, See General Section

For full biographical listings, see the Martindale-Hubbell Law Directory

*NEW ORLEANS,** Orleans Parish

McGLINCHEY STAFFORD (AV)

A Professional Limited Liability Company
643 Magazine Street, 70130-3477
Telephone: 504-586-1200
Fax: 504-596-2800
TDD: (504) 596-2728
Telex: 584327
Cable Address: "MACSTAC"
Mailing Address: P.O. Box 60643, New Orleans, Louisiana, 70160-0643
Email: @mcglinchey.com *URL:* http://www.mcglinchey.com
Dallas, Texas Office: 2777 Stemmons Freeway, Suite 925, 75207-2401.
Telephone: 214-860-9700.
Fax: 214-860-9750.
Houston, Texas Office: 2727 Allen Parkway, Suite 1900, 77019.
Telephone: 713-520-1900.
Fax: 713-520-1025.
Baton Rouge, Louisiana Office: Ninth Floor, One American Place, 70825-0001.
Telephone: 504-383-9000.
Fax: 504-343-3076.
Jackson, Mississippi Office: Suite 1200, SkyTel Centre, 200 South Lamar Street, 39201.
Telephone: 601-960-8400.
Fax: 601-960-8406.
Lake Providence, Louisiana Office: 405 Morgan Street, 71254-2691.
Telephone: 318-559-1200.
Fax: 318-559-0609.
Monroe, Louisiana Office: Dean ONB Tower, 130 Desiard Street, Suite 807, 71201.
Telephone: 318-651-0807.
Fax: 318-651-0809.

MEMBERS OF FIRM

Donna Guinn Klein
Craig Lewis Caesar

For full biographical listings, see the Martindale-Hubbell Law Directory

MILLING BENSON WOODWARD L.L.P. (AV)

A Partnership including Professional Law Corporations
Suite Twenty-Three Hundred, 909 Poydras Street, 70112-1017
Telephone: 504-569-7000
Telecopier: 504-569-7001
ABA net: 15656
MCI Mail: "Milling"
Email: milling@millinglaw.com
Lafayette, Louisiana Office: 101 La Rue France, Suite 200.
Telephone: 318-232-3929.
Telecopier: 318-233-4957.
Mandeville (North Shore), Louisiana Office: 2140 8th Street.
Telephone: 504-867-9622.
Telecopier: 504-867-8364.

MEMBER OF FIRM

James K. Irvin (P.C.)

See General Section for list of Representative Clients.

For Complete List of Firm Personnel, See General Section

For full biographical listings, see the Martindale-Hubbell Law Directory

SLATER LAW FIRM, A PROFESSIONAL CORPORATION (AV)

650 Poydras Street Suite 2600, 70130-6101
Telephone: 504-523-7333
Fax: 504-528-1080
URL: http://www.slaterlawfirm.com

Benjamin R. Slater, Jr.
Benjamin R. Slater, III
Mark E. Van Horn
Kevin M. Wheeler
Anne Elise Brown
Donald J. Miester, Jr.

Michael O. Waguespack
Cory Rabin Cahn
Sarah Ney
S. Joseph Welborn

(See Next Column)

SLATER LAW FIRM A PROFESSIONAL CORPORATION, *New Orleans—Continued*

SPECIAL COUNSEL

W. Malcolm Stevenson

Representative Clients: Norfolk Southern Corporation; New Orleans Steamship Association; The Quaker Oats Company; Anheuser-Busch, Incorporated; Patterson Pump Company; Diversified Foods and Seasonings, Inc.

For full biographical listings, see the Martindale-Hubbell Law Directory

MAINE

*BANGOR,** Penobscot Co.

EATON, PEABODY, BRADFORD & VEAGUE, P.A. (AV)

Fleet Center-Exchange Street, P.O. Box 1210, 04402-1210
Telephone: 207-947-0111
Telecopier: 207-942-3040
Email: eaton@eatonpeabody.com *URL:* http://www.eatonpeabody.com
Augusta, Maine Office: 77 Sewall Street, Suite 3000.
Telephone: 207-622-3747.
Telecopier: 207-622-9732.
Blue Hill, Maine Office: One East Blue Hill Road.
Telephone: 207-374-2812.
Telecopier: 207-374-2548.
Brunswick, Maine Office: 167 Park Row.
Telephone: 207-729-1144.
Telecopier: 207-729-1140.
Dover-Foxcroft, Maine Office: 30 East Main Street.
Telephone: 207-564-8378.
Telecopier: 207-564-7059.

Daniel G. McKay
Gordon H. S. Scott (Resident, Augusta Office)
Thad B. Zmistowski

For Complete List of Firm Personnel, See General Section

For full biographical listings, see the Martindale-Hubbell Law Directory

*PORTLAND,** Cumberland Co.

PIERCE ATWOOD (AV)

One Monument Square, 04101
Telephone: 207-791-1100
Fax: 207-791-1350
Email: info@PierceAtwood.com *URL:* http://www.pierceatwood.com
Augusta, Maine Office: 77 Winthrop Street.
Telephone: 207-622-6311.
Fax: 207-623-9367.
Newburyport, Massachusetts Office: 6 Harris Street.
Telephone: 978-465-9599.
Fax: 978-465-9945.

MEMBER OF FIRM

Jeffrey M. White

ASSOCIATES

William L. Worden
Margaret K. Minister

For Complete List of Firm Personnel, See General Section

For full biographical listings, see the Martindale-Hubbell Law Directory

MARYLAND

*BALTIMORE,** (Independent City)

PIPER & MARBURY L.L.P. (AV)

36 South Charles Street, 21201-3018
Telephone: 410-539-2530
FAX: 410-539-0489
Email: lawfirm@pipermar.com *URL:* http://www.pipermar.com
Washington, D.C. Office: 1200 Nineteenth Street, N.W., 20036-2430.
Telephone: 202-861-3900.
FAX: 202-223-2085.
New York, N.Y. Office: 1251 Avenue of the Americas, 10020-1104.
Telephone: 212-835-6000.
FAX: 212-835-6001.
Philadelphia, Pennsylvania Office: 3400 Two Logan Square, 18th & Arch Streets, 19103-2762.
Telephone: 215-656-3300.
FAX: 215-656-3301.
Easton, Maryland Office: 117 Bay Street, 21601-2703.
Telephone: 410-820-4460.
FAX: 410-820-4463.

(See Next Column)

Princeton, N.J. Office: 116 Village Boulevard, Suite 200, Princeton Forrestal Village, 08540.
Telephone: 609-951-2252.
FAX: 609-951-2216.
Reston, Virginia Office: 1850 Centennial Park Drive, Suite 610, Commerce Executive Park III, 20191.
Telephone: 703-391-7100.
Fax: 703-309-5299.

MEMBERS OF FIRM

Lewis A. Noonberg (Resident, Washington, D.C. Office)
Jeffrey D. Herschman
Kenneth G. Starling (Resident, Washington, D.C. Office)
Jeffrey F. Liss (Resident, Washington, D.C. Office)
Michael F. Brockmeyer
David H. Bamberger (Resident, Washington, D.C. Office)
Leonard L. Gordon (Resident, Washington, D.C. Office)

For Complete List of Firm Personnel, See General Section

For full biographical listings, see the Martindale-Hubbell Law Directory

VENABLE ATTORNEYS AT LAW VENABLE, BAETJER AND HOWARD, LLP (AV)

A Partnership including Professional Corporations
1800 Mercantile Bank & Trust Building, 2 Hopkins Plaza, 21201
Telephone: 410-244-7400
Fax: 410-244-7742
URL: http://www.venable.com
Washington, D.C. Office: Venable, Baetjer, Howard & Civiletti LLP, Suite 1000, 1201 New York Avenue, N.W.
Telephone: 202-962-4800.
Fax: 202-962-8300.
McLean, Virginia Office: Suite 400, 2010 Corporate Ridge.
Telephone: 703-760-1600.
Fax: 703-821-8949.
Rockville, Maryland Office: Suite 500, One Church Street, P. O. Box 1906.
Telephone: 301-217-5600.
Fax: 301-217-5617.
Towson, Maryland Office: 210 Allegheny Avenue, P. O. Box 5517.
Telephone: 410-494-6200.
Fax: 410-821-0147.

MEMBERS OF FIRM

Benjamin R. Civiletti (P.C.) (Also at Washington, D.C. and Towson, Maryland Offices)
John Henry Lewin, Jr. (P.C.)
Kenneth C. Bass, III (Not admitted in MD; Washington, D.C. and McLean, Virginia Offices)
Edward F. Glynn, Jr. (Resident, Washington, D.C. Office)
Michael Schatzow (Also at Washington, D.C. Office)
Lawrence B. Bernard (Resident, Washington, D.C. Office)
G. Stewart Webb, Jr.
James K. Archibald (Also at Washington, D.C. Office)
Jeffrey D. Knowles (Not admitted in MD; Resident, Washington, D.C. Office)
William D. Coston (Not admitted in MD; Resident, Washington, D.C. Office)
Maurice Baskin (Resident, Washington, D.C. Office)
Amy Berman Jackson (Not admitted in MD; Resident, Washington, D.C. Office)
Christopher R. Mellott
James A. Dunbar (Resident, Towson, Maryland Office)
David W. Goewey (Not admitted in MD; Resident, Washington, D.C. Office)
Vicki Margolis (Also at Washington, D.C. Office)

OF COUNSEL

Emried D. Cole, Jr.

ASSOCIATE

Melissa Landau Steinman (Resident, Washington, D.C. Office)

For Complete List of Firm Personnel, See General Section

For full biographical listings, see the Martindale-Hubbell Law Directory

WARD, KERSHAW & MINTON, A PROFESSIONAL ASSOCIATION (AV)

113 West Monument Street, 21201
Telephone: 410-685-6700
Fax: 410-685-6704
Email: wkmfirm@aol.com *URL:* http://www.wkamlaw.com

John T. Ward
Robert B. Kershaw
Thomas J. Minton
April Falcon Doss
J. Dirk Schwenk

OF COUNSEL

Richard V. Falcon

For full biographical listings, see the Martindale-Hubbell Law Directory

MASSACHUSETTS

*BOSTON,** Suffolk Co.

LAW OFFICES OF HAROLD BROWN & ASSOCIATES (AV)
66 Long Wharf, 02110
Telephone: 617-720-4200
Fax: 617-720-0240
Email: brownlaw@world.std.com *URL:* http://www.franchise-counsel.com

L. Michael Hankes
Linda J. Keogh
Andrea B Aptowitz
Rory A. Valas

For full biographical listings, see the Martindale-Hubbell Law Directory

CESARI AND MCKENNA, L.L.P. (AV)
30 Rowes Wharf, 02110
Telephone: 617-951-2500
Fax: 617-951-3927

Robert A. Cesari
John F. McKenna
Martin J. O'Donnell
Thomas C. O'Konski
Joseph H. Born
Patricia A. Sheehan
Michael E. Attaya
Steven J. Frank
Charles J. Barbas
William A. Loginov

Michael R. Reinemann
Rita M. Rooney
Christopher K. Gagne (Not admitted in MA)
A. Sidney Johnston (Not admitted in MA)
John H. Emilian, Jr.
Joseph Stecewycz

LEGAL SUPPORT PERSONNEL

Dora V. Dodin (Patent Engineer)
Heather B. Shapiro (Technical Specialist)

For full biographical listings, see the Martindale-Hubbell Law Directory

HANIFY & KING, PROFESSIONAL CORPORATION (AV)
One Federal Street, 02110-2007
Telephone: 617-423-0400
Telefax: 617-423-0498
URL: http://www.hanify.com

James Coyne King
John D. Hanify
Harold B. Murphy
David Lee Evans
Daniel J. Lyne
Donald F. Farrell, Jr.
Barbara W. Pfirrman
Gerard P. Richer
Timothy P. O'Neill
Terence P. McCourt

Jeffrey J. Upton
Michael R. Perry
Kathleen E. Cross
Robert E. Richards, Jr.
Joseph F. Cortellini
Andrew G. Lizotte
Donald Ethan Jeffery
Karen A. Whitley
Deena F. Christelis
Robyn J. Bartlett
Owen P. Kane
Sharon H. Patton
John C. McDonald
C. Alexander Hahn
Laurie J. Hurtt
Katherine T. Land
Brian P. McDonough
Lori A. Donovan
Brian R. Marinelli

For full biographical listings, see the Martindale-Hubbell Law Directory

MINTZ, LEVIN, COHN, FERRIS, GLOVSKY AND POPEO, P.C. (AV)
One Financial Center, 02111
Telephone: 617-542-6000
FAX: 617-542-2241
Internet: Each Attorney's Internet Address takes the following form: first initial last name @mintz.com (e.g., rmintz@mintz.com)
URL: http://www.mintz.com
Washington, D.C. Office: 701 Pennsylvania Avenue, N.W. Suite 900.
Telephone: 202-434-7300.
Fax: 202-434-7400.
Reston, Virginia Office: 12021 Sunset Hills Road, Suite 310.
Telephone: 703-464-4800.
Fax: 703-464-4895.

Jerome Gotkin
R. Robert Popeo
Bruce D. Sokler (Resident, Washington, D.C. Office)
Charles Alan Samuels (Resident, Washington, D.C. Office)
Christopher J. Harvie (Resident, Washington, D.C. Office)

For Complete List of Firm Personnel, See General Section

For full biographical listings, see the Martindale-Hubbell Law Directory

PALMER & DODGE LLP (AV)
One Beacon Street, 02108
Telephone: 617-573-0100
Facsimile: 617-227-4420
URL: http://www.palmerdodge.com

(See Next Column)

MEMBERS OF FIRM

Michael T. Gass
Kenneth W. Salinger
Thane D. Scott

For Complete List of Firm Personnel, See General Section

For full biographical listings, see the Martindale-Hubbell Law Directory

MICHIGAN

*ANN ARBOR,** Washtenaw Co.

BUTZEL LONG, A PROFESSIONAL CORPORATION (AV)
Suite 300, 350 South Main Street, 48104-2131
Telephone: 313-995-3110
Telecopier: 313-995-1777
Email: melnick@butzel.com *URL:* http://www.butzel.com
Detroit, Michigan Office: Suite 900, 150 West Jefferson.
Telephone: 313-225-7000.
Telecopier: 313-225-7080.
Birmingham, Michigan Office: Suite 200, 32270 Telegraph Road.
Telephone: 810-258-1616.
Telecopier: 810-258-1439.
Okemos, Michigan Office: Suite 300, 2127 University Park Drive.
Telephone: 517-372-6622.
Telecopier: 372-6672.
Grosse Pointe Farms, Michigan Office: Suite 260, 21 Kercheval.
Telephone: 313-886-5446.
Telecopier: 313-886-2114.
Boca Raton, Florida Office: Suite 411, 1200 North Federal Highway.
Telephone: 561-368-2151.
Telecopier: 561-368-4668.
Palm Beach Gardens, Florida Office: Suite 227, 11382 Prosperity Farms Road.
Telephone: 561-625-4442.
Telecopier: 561-625-6901.
Naples, Florida Office: Suite 705, 801 Laurel Oak Drive.
Telephone: 941-597-4500.
Telecopier: 941-597-5623.

John Henry Dudley, Jr.
James E. Stewart (Resident)
Leonard M. Niehoff (Resident)
J. Michael Huget (Resident)

John C. Blattner (Resident)
Pamela M. Zauel

For full biographical listings, see the Martindale-Hubbell Law Directory

MILLER, CANFIELD, PADDOCK AND STONE, P.L.C. (AV)
A Professional Limited Liability Company
Founded in 1852 by Sidney Davy Miller
101 North Main Street, Seventh Floor, 48104-1400
Telephone: 734-663-2445
Fax: 734-747-7147
URL: http://www.millercanfield.com
Detroit, Michigan Office: 150 West Jefferson, Suite 2500, 48226-4415.
Telephone: 313-963-6420.
Fax: 313-496-7500.
Cable Address: "Stem Detroit."
Troy, Michigan Office: 840 West Long Lake Road, Suite 200, 48098.
Telephone: 248-879-2000.
Fax: 248-879-2001.
Grand Rapids, Michigan Office: 99 Monroe, N.W., Suite 1200, 49503-2639.
Telephone: 616-454-8656.
Fax: 616-776-6322.
Howell, Michigan Office: 121 South Barnard Street, Suite 4, 48843-2305.
Telephone: 517-546-7600.
Telecopier: 517-546-6974.
Kalamazoo, Michigan Office: 444 West Michigan Avenue, 49007-3752.
Telephone: 616-381-7030.
Fax: 616-382-0244.
Lansing, Michigan Office: One Michigan Avenue, Suite 900, 48933-1609.
Telephone: 517-487-2070.
Fax: 517-374-6304.
Monroe, Michigan Office: 214 East Elm Avenue, Suite 100, 48162-2682.
Telephone: 734-243-2000.
Fax: 734-243-0901.
Washington, D.C. Office: 1900 K Street, N.W., Suite 1150. 20006.
Telephone: 202-429-5575; 785-0600.
Fax: 202-331-1118; 785-1234.
Pensacola, Florida Office: 25 West Cedar, 32501.
Telephone: 850-469-1088.
Fax: 850-432-0677.
New York, New York Office: 1450 Broadway, 41st Floor, 10018.
Telephone: 212-704-4400.
Fax: 212-704-4410.
Gdynia, Poland Office: UL. Slaska 21, 81-319.
Telephone: 011-485-831-2808.
Fax: 011-48-58-628 6411.

(See Next Column)

MILLER, CANFIELD, PADDOCK AND STONE P.L.C., *Ann Arbor—Continued*

Warsaw, Poland Office: UL. Nowogrodzkall, 5th Floor, 00-513.
Telephone: 011-4822 529 0200.
Fax: 011-4822 529 0201.
Katowice, Poland Office: UL. Francuska 35/37, 40-027.
Telephone: 011 (48-32) 757-2414.
Fax: 011 (48-32) 757-2483.

PRINCIPALS OF FIRM

Robert E. Gilbert
Gregory L. Curtner

OF COUNSEL/SENIOR COUNSEL

Edmond F. DeVine

Representative Firm Clients: Chrysler Corporation; Comerica, Incorporated; City of Detroit, Michigan; Detroit Tigers, Inc.; First of Michigan; Ford Motor Company; Ford Motor Credit Company; Great Lakes Bancorp; Henry Ford Hospital; INVETECH Company.

For Complete List of Firm Personnel, See General Section

For full biographical listings, see the Martindale-Hubbell Law Directory

BLOOMFIELD HILLS, Oakland Co.

HOWARD & HOWARD ATTORNEYS, P.C. (AV)

The Pinehurst Office Center, Suite 101, 1400 North Woodward Avenue, 48304-2855
Telephone: 248-645-1483
Telecopier: 248-645-1568
Kalamazoo, Michigan Office: The Michigan Building, Suite 200, 100 Portage Street.
Telephone: 616-382-1483.
Telecopier: 616-382-1568.
Lansing, Michigan Office: The Phoenix Building, Suite 500, 222 Washington Square, North.
Telephone: 517-485-1483.
Telecopier: 517-485-1568.
Peoria, Illinois Office: One Technology Plaza, Suite 600, 211 Fulton Street.
Telephone: 309-672-1483.
Telecopier: 309-672-1568.

Anthony P. Cho
Jon Robert Steiger
John E. Young

Representative Clients: For Representative Client list, see General Practice, Bloomfield Hills, MI.

For Complete List of Firm Personnel, See General Section

For full biographical listings, see the Martindale-Hubbell Law Directory

ROY SHECTER & VOCHT (AV)

36700 Woodward Avenue, Suite 205, 48304
Telephone: 248-540-7660
Fax: 248-540-0321
URL: http://www.lawyers.com/royshecter&vocht

MEMBERS OF FIRM

William A. Roy
Lynn H. Shecter
Michelle E. Vocht

For full biographical listings, see the Martindale-Hubbell Law Directory

*DETROIT,** Wayne Co.

BODMAN, LONGLEY & DAHLING LLP (AV)

34th Floor 100 Renaissance Center, 48243
Telephone: 313-259-7777
Fax: 313-393-7579
Email: info@bodmanlongley.com *URL:* http://www.bodmanlongley.com
Troy, Michigan Office: Suite 2020, 755 West Big Beaver Road.
Telephone: 248-362-2110.
Fax: 248-244-0780.
Ann Arbor, Michigan Office: 110 Miller, Suite 300.
Telephone: 734-761-3780.
Fax: 734-930-2494.
Northern Michigan Office: 229 Court Street, P.O. Box 405, Cheboygan.
Telephone: 231-627-4351.
Fax: 231-627-2802.

MEMBERS OF FIRM

Richard D. Rohr
Michael B. Lewiston
Herold McC. Deason
David G. Chardavoyne
Thomas J. Tallerico
Jeffrey G. Raphelson

COUNSEL

Robert A. Nitschke

Representative Clients: Archdiocese of Detroit; Comerica Bank; The Detroit Lions, Inc.; Ford Estates; Lear Corp.; Charles Stewart Mott Foundation; Norfolk Southern Corporation; Panhandle Eastern Corporation; State Farm Insurance Companies.

For Complete List of Firm Personnel, See General Section

For full biographical listings, see the Martindale-Hubbell Law Directory

BUTZEL LONG, A PROFESSIONAL CORPORATION (AV)

Suite 900, 150 West Jefferson, 48226
Telephone: 313-225-7000
Telecopier: 313-225-7080
Email: melnick@butzel.com *URL:* http://www.butzel.com
Birmingham, Michigan Office: Suite 200, 32270 Telegraph Road.
Telephone: 810-258-1616.
Telecopier: 810-258-1439.
Okemos, Michigan Office: Suite 300, 2127 University Park Drive.
Telephone: 517-372-6622.
Telecopier: 517-372-6672.
Ann Arbor, Michigan Office: Suite 300, 350 South Main Street.
Telephone: 313-995-3110.
Telecopier: 313-995-1777.
Grosse Pointe Farms, Michigan Office: Suite 260, 21 Kercheval.
Telephone: 313-886-5446.
Telecopier: 313-886-2114.
Boca Raton, Florida Office: Suite 411, 1200 North Federal Highway.
Telephone: 561-368-2151.
Telecopier: 561-368-4668.
Palm Beach Gardens, Florida Office: Suite 227, 11382 Prosperity Farms Road.
Telephone: 561-625-4442.
Telecopier: 561-625-6901.
Naples, Florida Office: Suite 705, 801 Laurel Oak Drive.
Telephone: 941-597-4500.
Telecopier: 941-597-5623.

Richard E. Rassel
Edward M. Kronk
Philip J. Kessler
Leonard M. Niehoff (Ann Arbor)

SENIOR ATTORNEY

Matthew E. Wilkins

Representative Clients: Bridgestone/Firestone, Inc.; Complete Business Solutions, Inc.; The Detroit News, Inc.; Ferndale Laboratories; Kelly Services; Merrill Lynch & Co., Inc.; Stroh Companies; Takata Corp.; TRW Automotive; The University of Michigan.

For full biographical listings, see the Martindale-Hubbell Law Directory

DYKEMA GOSSETT PLLC (AV)

400 Renaissance Center, 48243-1668
Telephone: 313-568-6800
Fax: 313-568-6545
Email: mstarrs@dykema.com *URL:* http://www.dykema.com
Ann Arbor, Michigan Office: 315 East Eisenhower Parkway, Suite 100, 48108-3306.
Telephone: 734-214-7660.
Fax: 734-214-7696.
Bloomfield Hills, Michigan Office: 1577 North Woodward Avenue, Suite 300, 48304-2820.
Telephone: 248-203-0700.
Fax: 248-203-0763.
Chicago, Illinois Office: 55 East Monroe Street, Suite 3050, 60603-5709.
Telephone: 312-551-4900.
Fax: 312-551-4919.
Grand Rapids, Michigan Office: Suite 700, 300 Ottawa Avenue, N.W., 49503-2304.
Telephone: 616-776-7500.
Fax: 616-776-7573.
Lansing, Michigan Office: 800 Michigan National Tower, 48933-1707.
Telephone: 517-374-9100.
Fax: 517-374-9191.
Washington, D.C. Office: Franklin Square, Suite 300 West, 1300 I Street, N.W., 20005-3306.
Telephone: 202-522-8600.
Fax: 202-522-8669.
Affiliated Office: Via Matconi, 3, 40122 Bologna, Italy.
Telephone: 011-39-51-228222.
Fax: 011-39-51-6593580.

MEMBERS OF FIRM

Edward A. Groobert (Not admitted in MI; Resident at Washington, D.C. Office)
Dennis M. Haffey (Member in Charge of Bloomfield Hills Office)
D. Biard MacGuineas (Not admitted in MI; Resident at Washington, D.C. Office)
Barbara Goldman Mandell (Resident at Bloomfield Hills Office)
Howard E. O'Leary, Jr. (Resident at Washington, D.C. Office)
Roger K. Timm
Fred L. Woodworth (Member in Charge of Washington, D.C. Office)

ASSOCIATES

Thomas S. Bishoff
Judy Parker Jenkins (Not admitted in MI; Resident at Washington, D.C. Office)

For Complete List of Firm Personnel, See General Section

For full biographical listings, see the Martindale-Hubbell Law Directory

Detroit—Continued

HONIGMAN MILLER SCHWARTZ AND COHN (AV)

2290 First National Building, 660 Woodward Avenue, 48226
Telephone: 313-465-7000
Telecopier: 313-465-8000
Telex: 235705
Email: mvg@honigman.com *URL:* http://law.honigman.com
Lansing, Michigan Office: Phoenix Building, 222 North Washington Square, Suite 400, 48933-1800.
Telephone: 517-484-8282.

MEMBERS OF FIRM

Gerald S. Cook
David A. Ettinger
Howard B. Iwrey

Representative Clients: Bronson Healthcare Group, Inc; Handleman Co.; Mercy Health Services.

For Complete List of Firm Personnel, See General Section

For full biographical listings, see the Martindale-Hubbell Law Directory

MILLER, CANFIELD, PADDOCK AND STONE, P.L.C. (AV)

A Professional Limited Liability Company
Founded in 1852 by Sidney Davy Miller
150 West Jefferson, Suite 2500, 48226-4415
Telephone: 313-963-6420
Fax: 313-496-7500
Cable Address: "Stem Detroit"
URL: http://www.millercanfield.com
Ann Arbor, Michigan Office: 101 North Main Street, 7th Floor, 48104-1400.
Telephone: 734-663-2445.
Fax: 734-747-7147.
Troy, Michigan Office: 840 West Long Lake Road, Suite 200, 48098.
Telephone: 248-879-2000.
Fax: 248-879-2001.
Grand Rapids, Michigan Office: 99 Monroe, N.W., Suite 1200, 49503-2639.
Telephone: 616-454-8656.
Fax: 616-776-6322.
Howell, Michigan Office: 121 South Barnard Street, Suite 4, 48843-2305.
Telephone: 517-546-7600.
Telecopier: 517-546-6974.
Kalamazoo, Michigan Office: 444 West Michigan Avenue, 49007-3752.
Telephone: 616-381-7030.
Fax: 616-382-0244.
Lansing, Michigan Office: One Michigan Avenue, Suite 900, 48933-1609.
Telephone: 517-487-2070.
Fax: 517-374-6304.
Monroe, Michigan Office: 214 East Elm Avenue, Suite 100, 48162-2682.
Telephone: 734-243-2000.
Fax: 734-243-0901.
Washington, D.C. Office: 1900 K Street, N.W., Suite 1150. 20006.
Telephone: 202-429-5575; 785-0600.
Fax: 202-331-1118; 785-1234.
Pensacola, Florida Office: 25 West Cedar, 32501.
Telephone: 850-469-1088.
Fax: 850-432-0677.
New York, New York Office: 1450 Broadway, 41st Floor, 10018.
Telephone: 212-704-4400.
Fax: 212-704-4410.
Gdynia, Poland Office: UL. Slaska 21, 81-319.
Telephone: 011-485-831-2808.
Fax: 011-48-58-628 6411.
Warsaw, Poland Office: UL. Nowogrodzkall, 5th Floor, 00-513.
Telephone: 011-4822 529 0200.
Fax: 011-4822 529 0201.
Katowice, Poland Office: UL. Francuska 35/37, 40-027.
Telephone: 011 (48-32) 757-2414.
Fax: 011 (48-32) 757-2483.

PRINCIPALS OF FIRM

Rocque E. Lipford (P.C.) (Monroe Office)
Gregory L. Curtner (Ann Arbor and New York, N.Y. Offices)
David D. Joswick (P.C.)
Larry J. Saylor
Mark T. Boonstra

OF COUNSEL/SENIOR COUNSEL

Edmond F. DeVine (Ann Arbor Office)
Richard B. Gushée
George E. Parker, III

Representative Firm Clients: Chrysler Corporation; Comerica, Incorporated; City of Detroit, Michigan; Detroit Tigers, Inc.; First of Michigan; Ford Motor Company; Ford Motor Credit Company; Great Lakes Bancorp; Henry Ford Hospital; INVETECH Company.

For Complete List of Firm Personnel, See General Section

For full biographical listings, see the Martindale-Hubbell Law Directory

TIMMIS & INMAN L.L.P. (AV)

300 Talon Centre, 48207
Telephone: 313-396-4200
Facsimile: 313-396-4228
Email: info@timmis-inman.com *URL:* http://www.timmis-inman.com

Henry J. Brennan, III
Richard M. Miettinen
Bradley J. Knickerbocker

Representative Clients: Detroit Mortgage & Realty; DMR Fiancial Services, Inc.; J. Levin Sons Co.; Green Tree Financial Servicing Corp.; Hematology-Oncology Associates East, PC; Lakeshore Ear, Nose & Throat Center, PC; Micromanagement Systems, Inc.; Phoenix Crystal Corp.; Talon Surfaces LLC; Talon Automated Equipment Company.

For Complete List of Firm Personnel, See General Section

For full biographical listings, see the Martindale-Hubbell Law Directory

*GRAND RAPIDS,** Kent Co.

MILLER, CANFIELD, PADDOCK AND STONE, P.L.C. (AV)

A Professional Limited Liability Company
Founded in 1852 by Sidney Davy Miller
99 Monroe, N.W. Suite 1200, 49503-2639
Telephone: 616-454-8656
Fax: 616-776-6322
URL: http://www.millercanfield.com
Detroit, Michigan Office: 150 West Jefferson, Suite 2500, 48226-4415.
Telephone: 313-963-6420.
Fax: 313-496-7500.
Cable Address: "Stem Detroit."
Ann Arbor, Michigan Office: 101 North Main Street, 7th Floor, 48104-1400.
Telephone: 734-663-2445.
Fax: 734-747-7147.
Troy, Michigan Office: 840 West Long Lake Road, Suite 200, 48098.
Telephone: 248-879-2000.
Fax: 248-879-2001.
Howell, Michigan Office: 121 South Barnard Street, Suite 4, 48843-2305.
Telephone: 517-546-7600.
Telecopier: 517-546-6974.
Kalamazoo, Michigan Office: 444 West Michigan Avenue, 49007-3752.
Telephone: 616-381-7030.
Fax: 616-382-0244.
Lansing, Michigan Office: One Michigan Avenue, Suite 900, 48933-1609.
Telephone: 517-487-2070.
Fax: 517-374-6304.
Monroe, Michigan Office: 214 East Elm Avenue, Suite 100, 48162-2682.
Telephone: 734-243-2000.
Fax: 734-243-0901.
Washington, D.C. Office: 1900 K Street, N.W., Suite 1150. 20006.
Telephone: 202-429-5575; 785-0600.
Fax: 202-331-1118; 785-1234.
Pensacola, Florida Office: 25 West Cedar, 32501.
Telephone: 850-469-1088.
Fax: 850-432-0677.
New York, New York Office: 1450 Broadway, 41st Floor, 10018.
Telephone: 212-704-4400.
Fax: 212-704-4410.
Gdynia, Poland Office: UL. Slaska 21, 81-319.
Telephone: 011-485-831-2808.
Fax: 011-48-58-628 6411.
Warsaw, Poland Office: UL. Nowogrodzkall, 5th Floor, 00-513.
Telephone: 011-4822 529 0200.
Fax: 011-4822 529 0201.
Katowice, Poland Office: UL. Francuska 35/37, 40-027.
Telephone: 011 (48-32) 757-2414.
Fax: 011 (48-32) 757-2483.

PRINCIPALS

Robert L. DeJong
Michael G. Campbell
Mark E. Putney
Robert E. Lee Wright
Richard A. Gaffin
Douglas W. Crim
Charles S. Mishkind
Stanley J. Stek
Vernon Bennett III

OF COUNSEL/SENIOR COUNSEL

David E. Hathaway

RESIDENT SENIOR ATTORNEYS

David J. Hasper
Stephen L. Elkins

RESIDENT ASSOCIATES

John T. Stecco
Andrew T. Blum
Vincent E. Woltjer
Robert J. Nolan

Representative Firm Clients: Chrysler Corporation; Comerica, Incorporated; City of Detroit, Michigan; Detroit Tigers, Inc.; First of Michigan; Ford Motor Company; Ford Motor Credit Company; Great Lakes Bancorp; Henry Ford Hospital; INVETECH Company.

For full biographical listings, see the Martindale-Hubbell Law Directory

Grand Rapids—Continued

WARNER NORCROSS & JUDD LLP (AV)

900 Old Kent Building, 111 Lyon Street, N.W., 49503-2489
Telephone: 616-752-2000
Fax: 616-752-2500
URL: http://www.wnj.com
Muskegon, Michigan Office: 400 Terrace Plaza, P.O. Box 900.
Telephone: 231-727-2600.
Fax: 231-727-2699.
Holland, Michigan Office: Curtis Center, Suite 300, 170 College Avenue.
Telephone: 616-396-9800.
Fax: 616-396-3656.
Southfield, Michigan Office: 1000 Town Center, Suite 650.
Telephone: 248-223-5000.
Fax: 248-223-5005.

MEMBERS OF FIRM

William K. Holmes
James H. Breay
Stephen C. Waterbury
Richard L. Bouma
Daniel R. Gravelyn
Valerie Pierre Simmons
Kevin G. Dougherty
Gordon J. Toering

ASSOCIATE

Christian E. Meyer

For full biographical listings, see the Martindale-Hubbell Law Directory

*KALAMAZOO,** Kalamazoo Co.

MILLER, CANFIELD, PADDOCK AND STONE, P.L.C. (AV)

A Professional Limited Liability Company
Founded in 1852 by Sidney Davy Miller
444 West Michigan Avenue, 49007-3752
Telephone: 616-381-7030
Fax: 616-382-0244
URL: http://www.millercanfield.com
Detroit, Michigan Office: 150 West Jefferson, Suite 2500, 48226-4415.
Telephone: 313-963-6420.
Fax: 313-496-7500.
Cable Address: "Stem Detroit."
Ann Arbor, Michigan Office: 101 North Main Street, 7th Floor, 48104-1400.
Telephone: 734-663-2445.
Fax: 734-747-7147.
Troy, Michigan Office: 840 West Long Lake Road, Suite 200, 48098.
Telephone: 248-879-2000.
Fax: 248-879-2001.
Grand Rapids, Michigan Office: 99 Monroe, N.W., Suite 1200, 49503-2639.
Telephone: 616-454-8656.
Fax: 616-776-6322.
Howell, Michigan Office: 121 South Barnard Street, Suite 4, 48843-2305.
Telephone: 517-546-7600.
Telecopier: 517-546-6974.
Lansing, Michigan Office: One Michigan Avenue, Suite 900, 48933-1609.
Telephone: 517-487-2070.
Fax: 517-374-6304.
Monroe, Michigan Office: 214 East Elm Avenue, Suite 100, 48162-2682.
Telephone: 734-243-2000.
Fax: 734-243-0901.
Washington, D.C. Office: 1900 K Street, N.W., Suite 1150. 20006.
Telephone: 202-429-5575; 785-0600.
Fax: 202-331-1118; 785-1234.
Pensacola, Florida Office: 25 West Cedar, 32501.
Telephone: 850-469-1088.
Fax: 850-432-0677.
New York, New York Office: 1450 Broadway, 41st Floor, 10018.
Telephone: 212-704-4400.
Fax: 212-704-4410.
Gdynia, Poland Office: UL. Slaska 21, 81-319.
Telephone: 011-485-831-2808.
Fax: 011-48-58-628 6411.
Warsaw, Poland Office: UL. Nowogrodzkall, 5th Floor, 00-513.
Telephone: 011-4822 529 0200.
Fax: 011-4822 529 0201.
Katowice, Poland Office: UL. Francuska 35/37, 40-027.
Telephone: 011 (48-32) 757-2414.
Fax: 011 (48-32) 757-2483.

PRINCIPALS

Eric V. Brown, Jr.
John R. Cook
James G. Vantine, Jr.

Representative Firm Clients: Chrysler Corporation; Comerica, Incorporated; City of Detroit, Michigan; Detroit Tigers, Inc.; First of Michigan; Ford Motor Company; Ford Motor Credit Company; Great Lakes Bancorp; Henry Ford Hospital; INVETECH Company.

For Complete List of Firm Personnel, See General Section

For full biographical listings, see the Martindale-Hubbell Law Directory

LANSING, Ingham Co.

MILLER, CANFIELD, PADDOCK AND STONE, P.L.C. (AV)

A Professional Limited Liability Company
Founded in 1852 by Sidney Davy Miller
Suite 900, One Michigan Avenue, 48933-1609
Telephone: 517-487-2070
Fax: 517-374-6304
URL: http://www.millercanfield.com
Detroit, Michigan Office: 150 West Jefferson, Suite 2500, 48226-4415.
Telephone: 313-963-6420.
Fax: 313-496-7500.
Cable Address: "Stem Detroit."
Ann Arbor, Michigan Office: 101 North Main Street, 7th Floor, 48104-1400.
Telephone: 734-663-2445.
Fax: 734-747-7147.
Troy, Michigan Office: 840 West Long Lake Road, Suite 200, 48098.
Telephone: 248-879-2000.
Fax: 248-879-2001.
Grand Rapids, Michigan Office: 99 Monroe, N.W., Suite 1200, 49503-2639.
Telephone: 616-454-8656.
Fax: 616-776-6322.
Howell, Michigan Office: 121 South Barnard Street, Suite 4, 48843-2305.
Telephone: 517-546-7600.
Telecopier: 517-546-6974.
Kalamazoo, Michigan Office: 444 West Michigan Avenue, 49007-3752.
Telephone: 616-381-7030.
Fax: 616-382-0244.
Monroe, Michigan Office: 214 East Elm Avenue, Suite 100, 48162-2682.
Telephone: 734-243-2000.
Fax: 734-243-0901.
Washington, D.C. Office: 1900 K Street, N.W., Suite 1150. 20006.
Telephone: 202-429-5575; 785-0600.
Fax: 202-331-1118; 785-1234.
Pensacola, Florida Office: 25 West Cedar, 32501.
Telephone: 850-469-1088.
Fax: 850-432-0677.
New York, New York Office: 1450 Broadway, 41st Floor, 10018.
Telephone: 212-704-4400.
Fax: 212-704-4410.
Gdynia, Poland Office: UL. Slaska 21, 81-319.
Telephone: 011-485-831-2808.
Fax: 011-48-58-628 6411.
Warsaw, Poland Office: UL. Nowogrodzkall, 5th Floor, 00-513.
Telephone: 011-4822 529 0200.
Fax: 011-4822 529 0201.
Katowice, Poland Office: UL. Francuska 35/37, 40-027.
Telephone: 011 (48-32) 757-2414.
Fax: 011 (48-32) 757-2483.

RESIDENT PRINCIPALS

William J. Danhof

Representative Firm Clients: Chrysler Corporation; Comerica, Incorporated; City of Detroit, Michigan; Detroit Tigers, Inc.; First of Michigan; Ford Motor Company; Ford Motor Credit Company; Great Lakes Bancorp; Henry Ford Hospital; INVETECH Company.

For Complete List of Firm Personnel, See General Section

For full biographical listings, see the Martindale-Hubbell Law Directory

*MONROE,** Monroe Co.

MILLER, CANFIELD, PADDOCK AND STONE, P.L.C. (AV)

A Professional Limited Liability Company
Founded in 1852 by Sidney Davy Miller
214 East Elm Avenue, Suite 100, 48162-2682
Telephone: 734-243-2000
Fax: 734-243-0901
URL: http://www.millercanfield.com
Detroit, Michigan Office: 150 West Jefferson, Suite 2500, 48226-4415.
Telephone: 313-963-6420.
Fax: 313-496-7500.
Cable Address: "Stem Detroit."
Ann Arbor, Michigan Office: 101 North Main Street, 7th Floor, 48104-1400.
Telephone: 734-663-2445.
Fax: 734-747-7147.
Troy, Michigan Office: 840 West Long Lake Road, Suite 200, 48098.
Telephone: 248-879-2000.
Fax: 248-879-2001.
Grand Rapids, Michigan Office: 99 Monroe, N.W., Suite 1200, 49503-2639.
Telephone: 616-454-8656.
Fax: 616-776-6322.
Howell, Michigan Office: 121 South Barnard Street, Suite 4, 48843-2305.
Telephone: 517-546-7600.
Telecopier: 517-546-6974.

(See Next Column)

MILLER, CANFIELD, PADDOCK AND STONE P.L.C.—*Continued*

Kalamazoo, Michigan Office: 444 West Michigan Avenue, 49007-3752.
Telephone: 616-381-7030.
Fax: 616-382-0244.
Lansing, Michigan Office: One Michigan Avenue, Suite 900, 48933-1609.
Telephone: 517-487-2070.
Fax: 517-374-6304.
Washington, D.C. Office: 1900 K Street, N.W., Suite 1150. 20006.
Telephone: 202-429-5575; 785-0600.
Fax: 202-331-1118; 785-1234.
Pensacola, Florida Office: 25 West Cedar, 32501.
Telephone: 850-469-1088.
Fax: 850-432-0677.
New York, New York Office: 1450 Broadway, 41st Floor, 10018.
Telephone: 212-704-4400.
Fax: 212-704-4410.
Gdynia, Poland Office: UL. Slaska 21, 81-319.
Telephone: 011-485-831-2808.
Fax: 011-48-58-628 6411.
Warsaw, Poland Office: UL. Nowogrodzkall, 5th Floor, 00-513.
Telephone: 011-4822 529 0200.
Fax: 011-4822 529 0201.
Katowice, Poland Office: UL. Francuska 35/37, 40-027.
Telephone: 011 (48-32) 757-2414.
Fax: 011 (48-32) 757-2483.

RESIDENT PRINCIPALS

Rocque E. Lipford (P.C.)

Representative Firm Clients: Chrysler Corporation; Comerica, Incorporated; City of Detroit, Michigan; Detroit Tigers, Inc.; First of Michigan; Ford Motor Company; Ford Motor Credit Company; Great Lakes Bancorp; Henry Ford Hospital; INVETECH Company.

For full biographical listings, see the Martindale-Hubbell Law Directory

SOUTHFIELD, Oakland Co.

YOUNG & ASSOCIATES, P.C. (AV)

Suite 305, Westview Office Center, 26200 American Drive, 48034
Telephone: 248-353-8620
Telecopier: 248-353-6559
Email: youngpc@aol.com

Rodger D. Young

Michael J. Fergestrom
Jeffrey M. Macy
Steven Susser
Terry Wuester Milne

For full biographical listings, see the Martindale-Hubbell Law Directory

TROY, Oakland Co.

HACKETT & MAXWELL, P.C. (AV)

City Center Building, Suite 1470, 888 West Big Beaver Road, 48084
Telephone: 810-362-2600
Fax: 810-362-3610
Email: hackmax@voyager.net

Patrick E. Hackett
Phillip B. Maxwell

Dennis W. Krakow
Mireille Leruth Phillips

For full biographical listings, see the Martindale-Hubbell Law Directory

APPELLATE PRACTICE

ALABAMA

*BIRMINGHAM,** Jefferson Co.

BRADLEY ARANT ROSE & WHITE LLP (AV)

2001 Park Place, Suite 1400, P.O. Box 830709, 35283-0709
Telephone: 205-521-8000
Facsimile: 205-521-8800
Facsimile (SouthTrust Tower Office): 205-521-8500
URL: http://www.barw.com
Huntsville, Alabama Office: 200 Clinton Avenue West, Suite 900, 35801.
Telephone: 205-517-5100.
Facsimile: 205-533-5069.
Washington, D.C. Office: 801 Pennsylvania Avenue, NW, Suite 230, 20004.
Telephone: 202-347-8893.
Facsimile: 202-347-1684.

MEMBERS OF FIRM

Philip J. Carroll III
James S. Christie Jr.
Gary C. Huckaby (Resident, Huntsville Office)
E. Cutter Hughes Jr. (Resident, Huntsville Office)
Hobart A. McWhorter Jr.
Sid J. Trant

ASSOCIATES

David M. Lawson
Kimberly B. Martin (Resident, Huntsville Office)

For Complete List of Firm Personnel, See General Section

For full biographical listings, see the Martindale-Hubbell Law Directory

LIGHTFOOT, FRANKLIN & WHITE, L.L.C. (AV)

The Clark Building, 400 20th Street North, 35203
Telephone: 205-581-0700
Facsimile: 205-581-0799
Email: LFWlaw@LFWlaw.com *URL:* http://www.lfwlaw.com

Warren B. Lightfoot
Mac M. Moorer
William H. King, III
Madeline H. Haikala

Ivan B. Cooper
Craig N. Rosler
Lisa J. Wathey

For full biographical listings, see the Martindale-Hubbell Law Directory

J. VERNON PATRICK, JR. & ASSOCIATES, P.C. (AV)

1201 Financial Center, 505 20th Street North, 35203-4607
Telephone: 205-323-5665
Telecopier: 205-324-6221

J. Vernon Patrick, Jr.

Jeffrey Venton Havercroft

For full biographical listings, see the Martindale-Hubbell Law Directory

REDDEN, MILLS & CLARK (AV)

940 Regions Bank Building, 417 North 20th Street, 35203
Telephone: 205-322-0457
Fax: 205-322-8481
URL: http://www.rmc-law.com

MEMBERS OF FIRM

L. Drew Redden
William H. Mills
William N. Clark
Gerald L. Miller
Stephen W. Shaw
Maxwell H. Pulliam, Jr.
Ronald J. Gault

References: SouthTrust Bank; Regions Bank.

For full biographical listings, see the Martindale-Hubbell Law Directory

SMITH & ELY, LLP (AV)

2000-A Southbridge Parkway Suite 405, 35209
Telephone: 205-802-2214
Fax: 205-879-4445

MEMBERS OF FIRM

Carol Ann Smith
Brenen G. Ely

ASSOCIATES

Susan Rogers
Susan Caroline Haygood
Toby Dykes

OF COUNSEL

Lisa B. Singer

For full biographical listings, see the Martindale-Hubbell Law Directory

*MOBILE,** Mobile Co.

CARR, ALFORD, CLAUSEN & McDONALD, L.L.C. (AV)

One St. Louis Centre, Suite 5000, P.O. Drawer C, 36601
Telephone: 334-432-1600
Facsimile: 334-432-1700
URL: http://www.cacm.com

Davis Carr
Helen Johnson Alford
Andrew C. Clausen
James H. McDonald, Jr.
James W. Lampkin, II
Jean M. Powers

Annette McDermott Carwie
M. Lauren Lemmon
Thomas M. Rockwell
Pamela Ann Moore
W. Ben. Broadwater
Paul V. Lagarde
Frank L. Parker, Jr.
Christina M. Adcock
Kathleen Cobb Kaufman
Joseph Anthony Zarzaur, Jr.

For full biographical listings, see the Martindale-Hubbell Law Directory

CLARK, DEEN & COPELAND, P.C. (AV)

207 Church Street, P.O. Box 2705, 36652
Telephone: 334-433-5860
Telecopier: 334-433-0703
Email: Clark003@aol.com

Robert F. Clark
T. Jefferson Deen, III
W. Lloyd Copeland

Edward C. Blount, Jr.

For full biographical listings, see the Martindale-Hubbell Law Directory

LYONS, PIPES & COOK, P.C. (AV)

2 North Royal Street, P.O. Box 2727, 36652-2727
Telephone: 334-432-4481
Cable Address: "Lysea"
Telecopier: 334-433-1820
URL: http://www.LPCLaw.com

Joseph H. Lyons (1874-1957)
Sam W. Pipes, III (1916-1982)
Walter M. Cook (1915-1988)
Wesley Pipes
Norton W. Brooker, Jr.
Cooper C. Thurber
Marion A. Quina, Jr.
Thomas F. Garth
Walter M. Cook, Jr.
W. David Johnson, Jr.
Joseph J. Minus, Jr.
Caroline C. McCarthy
William E. Shreve, Jr.
Kenneth A. Nixon
Daniel S. Cushing
Allen E. Graham
Michael C. Niemeyer
M. Warren Butler
S. Wesley Pipes, V
James D. Jeffries, Jr.
Roger E. Cole
S. Andrew Scharfenberg, Jr
Ginger L. Pierce
Philip A. Stroud

Ryan T. Northrup

General Counsel: Inchcape Shipping Services.
Counsel: The Hertz Corp.; McKenzie Tank Lines, Inc.; SCNO Barge Lines, Inc.; Scott Paper Co.; Shell Oil Corp.
Trial Counsel: Aetna Life & Casualty Co.; Chubb Group of Insurance Companies.

For full biographical listings, see the Martindale-Hubbell Law Directory

PIERCE, LEDYARD, LATTA & WASDEN, P.C. (AV)

Colonial Bank Centre Suite 400, 41 North Beltline, 36608
Telephone: 334-344-5151
Facsimile: 334-344-9696
Mailing Address: P.O. Box 16046, Mobile, AL, 36616
URL: http://www.pllaw.com

Donald F. Pierce
Forrest S. Latta
John Charles S. Pierce
W. Pemble DeLashmet

James Robert Turnipseed
Michael A. Montgomery

Representative Clients: Blue Cross and Blue Shield; Alabama Power Company; Auto Owners Insurance Company; The Business Council of Alabama; Sears, Roebuck & Co.; USF&G; Grove U.S. LLC; Terex Corporation; SGB Construction Services, Inc.

For full biographical listings, see the Martindale-Hubbell Law Directory

*MONTGOMERY,** Montgomery Co.

VOLZ, PRESTWOOD & HANAN, P.C. (AV)

350 Adams Avenue, P.O. Box 1910, 36102-1910
Telephone: 334-264-6401
Fax: 334-834-4954

(See Next Column)

VOLZ, PRESTWOOD & HANAN P.C., *Montgomery—Continued*

Charles H. Volz, Jr.
Alvin T. Prestwood
Charles H. Volz, III
Ellis D. Hanan
Richard D. Lively
Judy H. Barganier

For full biographical listings, see the Martindale-Hubbell Law Directory

FRANK M. WILSON (AV)
201 Monroe Street, 36101
Telephone: 334-263-2555
Fax: 334-263-2533
Email: fmw@zebra.net *URL:* http://www.lawyers.com/fmwilsonlaw

For full biographical listings, see the Martindale-Hubbell Law Directory

ALASKA

*ANCHORAGE,** Third Judicial District

FELDMAN & ORLANSKY (AV)
Suite 400, 500 L Street, 99501
Telephone: 907-272-3538
Telecopier: 907-274-0819
URL: http://www.frozenlaw.com

Jeffrey M. Feldman
Susan C. Orlansky

ASSOCIATE

James E. Fosler

LEGAL SUPPORT PERSONNEL

Wendy Bursiel Weber (Legal Assistant)

Reference: Key Bank of Alaska.

For full biographical listings, see the Martindale-Hubbell Law Directory

LAW OFFICES OF ROBERT H. WAGSTAFF (AV)
First National Bank Building, 425 G Street, Suite 610, 99501
Telephone: 907-277-8611
Facsimile: 907-258-7329

For full biographical listings, see the Martindale-Hubbell Law Directory

ARIZONA

*PHOENIX,** Maricopa Co.

BONN, LUSCHER, PADDEN & WILKINS, CHARTERED (AV)
805 North Second Street, 85004
Telephone: 602-254-5557
Fax: 602-254-0656
Email: firm@blpw.com

Paul V. Bonn
Jeff C. Padden
Randall D. Wilkins
John H. Cassidy
D. Michael Hall
Daniel G. Martin
James M. Barrons

OF COUNSEL

Brian A. Luscher
Marvin Kantor

Howard D. Sukenic

For full biographical listings, see the Martindale-Hubbell Law Directory

CHARLES M. BREWER, LTD. (AV)
Brewer Building, 5500 North 24th Street, P.O. Box 10720, 85064
Telephone: 602-381-8787
Fax: 602-381-1152

Charles M. Brewer

Luis Pedro Guerra
John Brian Brewer

For full biographical listings, see the Martindale-Hubbell Law Directory

BURCH & CRACCHIOLO, P.A. (AV)
702 East Osborn Road, Suite 200, 85014
Telephone: 602-274-7611
Fax: 602-234-0341
Mailing Address: P.O. Box 16882, Phoenix, AZ, 85011
Email: library@bcattorneys.com

(See Next Column)

Daniel Cracchiolo
Daryl Manhart
Daniel R. Malinski

Representative Clients: Bashas' Inc.; Farmers Insurance Group; U-Haul International, Inc.

For Complete List of Firm Personnel, See General Section

For full biographical listings, see the Martindale-Hubbell Law Directory

COPPLE, CHAMBERLIN, BOEHM & MURPHY, P.C. (AV)
Suite 300 The Brookstone, 2025 North Third Street, 85004
Telephone: 602-528-4700
Fax: 602-253-4909
Tucson, Arizona Office: 127 West Franklin.
Telephone: 520-622-8855.
Fax: 520-628-7988.

Steven D. Copple
Thomas J. Chamberlin
Scott E. Boehm
Robert S. Murphy

OF COUNSEL

Frederick O. Robertshaw

Representative Clients: National Car Rental; City of Scottsdale; City of Glendale; Northbrook Indemnity Co.; Eagle Milling Co.; Hartford; Transamerica Insurance Group; Western Golf Properties, Inc.; Aetna Casualty & Surety Co.; Verco Manufacturing Co.

For full biographical listings, see the Martindale-Hubbell Law Directory

FENNEMORE CRAIG, A PROFESSIONAL CORPORATION (AV)
3003 North Central Avenue, Suite 2600, 85012-2913
Telephone: 602-916-5000
Fax: 602-916-5999
Tucson, Arizona Office: One South Church Avenue, Suite 1000, 85701-1620.
Telephone: 520-879-6800.
Fax: 520-879-6899.

Kenneth J. Sherk
Roger T. Hargrove
Timothy Berg
Paul J. Mooney
Janice Procter-Murphy
W. T. Eggleston, Jr.
Kendis K. Muscheid

Theresa Dwyer
Mary Beth Phillips

For Complete List of Firm Personnel, See General Section

For full biographical listings, see the Martindale-Hubbell Law Directory

FOGEL, LAMBER & BRONNENKANT, PROFESSIONAL ASSOCIATION (AV)
4001 North Third Street, Suite 400, 85012
Telephone: 602-264-3330
Fax: 602-274-5117

Sherman D. Fogel
Dennis M. Lamber
Rex P. Bronnenkant

Reference: Rocky Mountain Bank.

For full biographical listings, see the Martindale-Hubbell Law Directory

GOLDSTEIN, MCGRODER & WOODS, LTD. A PROFESSIONAL CORPORATION (AV)
2200 East Camelback Road, Suite 221, 85016-3456
Telephone: 602-957-1500
Fax: 602-956-9294
Email: pmcgroder@aol.com

Philip T. Goldstein
Patrick J. McGroder, III
Grant Woods
Suzanne P. Clarke

Jane E. Evans

LEGAL SUPPORT PERSONNEL

Kevan S. DeWitt (Paralegal)
Karen Kay Rush

For full biographical listings, see the Martindale-Hubbell Law Directory

MACLEAN & JACQUES, LTD. (AV)
Suite 202, 40 East Virginia, 85004
Telephone: 602-263-5771
FAX: 602-279-5569

John H. MacLean (1932-1992)
Raoul T. Jacques

Cary T. Inabinet
Macre S. Inabinet

LEGAL SUPPORT PERSONNEL

Sharon Petterson

For full biographical listings, see the Martindale-Hubbell Law Directory

Phoenix—Continued

TUCKER STROHM MILLER & TUCKER, P.C. (AV)
1136 East Campbell, 85014
Telephone: 602-279-3660
Fax: 602-279-2162
Email: rlslaw@worldnet.att.net

Richard L. Strohm

Nedra J. Bates

For full biographical listings, see the Martindale-Hubbell Law Directory

ULRICH, KESSLER & ANGER, P.C. (AV)
3707 North Seventh Street, Suite 250, 85014-5059
Telephone: 602-248-9465
Fax: 602-248-0165
Email: ukapc@aol.com

Paul G. Ulrich
Donn G. Kessler
William H. Anger

For full biographical listings, see the Martindale-Hubbell Law Directory

WARNER ANGLE ROPER & HALLAM PLC (AV)
3550 North Central Avenue, Suite 1500, 85012
Telephone: 602-264-7101
Fax: 602-234-0419

Charles Richard Hallam
Roger K. Gilbert
John A. Buric
Jack D. Klausner

Chris R. Baniszewski
J. Brent Welker

Representative Clients: National Loan Investors; AMRESCO Management, Inc.

For full biographical listings, see the Martindale-Hubbell Law Directory

*PRESCOTT,** Yavapai Co.

FAVOUR, MOORE & WILHELMSEN, A PROFESSIONAL ASSOCIATION (AV)
1580 Plaza West Drive, P.O. Box 1391, 86302
Telephone: 520-445-2444
Fax: 520-771-0450
Email: fmw@primenet.com

John M. Favour

Representative Client: Yavapai Title Co.
Reference: Bank of America.

For Complete List of Firm Personnel, See General Section

For full biographical listings, see the Martindale-Hubbell Law Directory

ARKANSAS

*LITTLE ROCK,** Pulaski Co.

JOHN WESLEY HALL, JR. A PROFESSIONAL CORPORATION (AV)
523 West Third Street, 72201
Telephone: 501-371-9131
FAX: 501-378-0888
Email: jwh@johnwesley.com

John Wesley Hall, Jr.

For full biographical listings, see the Martindale-Hubbell Law Directory

ROSE LAW FIRM, A PROFESSIONAL ASSOCIATION (AV)
120 East Fourth Street, 72201
Telephone: 501-375-9131
Telecopy: 501-375-1309

Tim Boe
Richard T. Donovan
Amy Lee Stewart
David P. Martin
Michael G. Smith
Kathryn Bennett Perkins
Michael N. Shannon

COUNSEL

Phillip Carroll

Jennifer B. Hendren
John D. Coulter

Counsel for: ALLTEL Corporation; Aluminum Company of America; Bridgestone/Firestone, Inc.; The Equitable Life Assurance Society of The United States; General Motors Corp.; The Prudential Insurance Company of America; Stephens Group Inc.; Tyson Foods, Inc.

(See Next Column)

For Complete List of Firm Personnel, See General Section

For full biographical listings, see the Martindale-Hubbell Law Directory

CALIFORNIA

*BAKERSFIELD,** Kern Co.

BORTON, PETRINI & CONRON, LLP (AV)
The Borton, Petrini & Conron Building, 1600 Truxtun Avenue, 93301
Telephone: 661-322-3051
Voice Mail: 661-395-6700
Fax: 661-322-4628
Mailing Address: P.O. Box 2026, Bakersfield, California, 93303
Email: bpcbak@bpclaw.com *URL:* http://www.bpclaw.com
Other City Locations: Fresno, Los Angeles, Modesto, Redding, Sacramento, San Bernardino, San Diego, San Francisco, San Jose, San Luis Obispo, Santa Ana and Ventura.

MEMBERS OF FIRM

George F. Martin
Richard E. Hitchcock
John F. Petrini
Richard E. Morton

ASSOCIATE

William G. Welzenbach

OF COUNSEL

Roy J. Gargano

For Complete List of Firm Personnel, See General Section

For full biographical listings, see the Martindale-Hubbell Law Directory

BEVERLY HILLS, Los Angeles Co.

HONEY KESSLER AMADO (AV)
261 South Wetherly Drive, 90211-2515
Telephone: 310-550-8214
Fax: 310-274-7384
Email: hkaatty@earthlink.net

For full biographical listings, see the Martindale-Hubbell Law Directory

GREINES, MARTIN, STEIN & RICHLAND LLP (AV)
Suite 544, 9601 Wilshire Boulevard, 90210
Telephone: 310-859-7811
Telecopier: 310-276-5261
URL: http://www.gmsr.com

Alan G. Martin (1948-1990)

MEMBERS OF FIRM

Timothy T. Coates
Feris M. Greenberger (Ms.)
Irving H. Greines
Rex S. Heinke
Robin Meadow
Robert A. Olson
Marc J. Poster
Barbara W. Ravitz
Kent L. Richland
Martin Stein
Alison M. Turner

ASSOCIATES

Laura R. Boudreau
Alan J. Diamond
Michael D. Fitts
Dana F. Gardner
Douglas S. Irwin
Peter O. Israel
Sheila S. Kato
Jennifer L. King
Randel L. Ledesma
Carolyn Oill
Heather L. Wayland
Jessica Weisel
Barry M. Wolf
Edward Laucks Xanders

OF COUNSEL

Barbara S. Perry

Reference: City National Bank (Beverly Hills Branch).

For full biographical listings, see the Martindale-Hubbell Law Directory

COSTA MESA, Orange Co.

ALBERT, WEILAND & GOLDEN (AV)
Center Tower, 650 Town Center Drive, Suite 1350, 92626
Telephone: 714-966-1000
FAX: 714-966-1002
Email: awglawyers@aol.com

Theodor C. Albert
Michael J. Weiland
Jeffrey I. Golden

ASSOCIATES

Evan D. Smiley
Lei Lei Wang Ekvall
Philip E. Strok
Darlynn Campbell Morgan

OF COUNSEL

Marcus M. Kaufman
Jennifer Ann Golison
Steven J. Katzman

(See Next Column)

ALBERT, WEILAND & GOLDEN, *Costa Mesa—Continued*

LEGAL SUPPORT PERSONNEL

PARALEGALS

Fran L. Russell
Patricia K. Nelson
Cynthia B. Meeker
Janet Hogan
Kim Sigismondo

For full biographical listings, see the Martindale-Hubbell Law Directory

FELDHAKE, AUGUST & ROQUEMORE (AV)

Plaza Tower, Suite 1730, 600 Anton Boulevard, 92626-7124
Telephone: 714-438-3885
Fax: 714-438-3888
Email: farlaw@hqonline.com

Robert J. Feldhake
Lisa A. Roquemore
Kenneth S. August
Joshua M. Wolff

ASSOCIATES

Dimitri P. Gross
Supriya Kakkar
Katherine A. Slayton

OF COUNSEL

Arthur J. Swerdloff
Arthur M. Wilcox, Jr.

For full biographical listings, see the Martindale-Hubbell Law Directory

RUTAN & TUCKER, LLP (AV)

A Partnership including Professional Corporations
611 Anton Boulevard, Fourteenth Floor, P.O. Box 1950, 92626-1998
Telephone: 714-641-5100; 213-625-7586
Telecopier: 714-546-9035
Email: rutan&tucker@rutan.com *URL:* http://www.rutan.com

MEMBERS OF FIRM

David C. Larsen (P.C.)
M. Katherine Jenson
William W. Wynder
Duke Wahlquist
Matthew K. Ross

ASSOCIATE

Julie K. Whang

For Complete List of Firm Personnel, See General Section
For full biographical listings, see the Martindale-Hubbell Law Directory

GLENDALE, Los Angeles Co.

OTT & HOFFMAN, A PROFESSIONAL CORPORATION (AV)

700 North Central Avenue, 8th Floor, Suite 850, 91203
Telephone: 818-242-3100
Fax: 818-242-3102
Email: ohlaw@aol.com *URL:* http://www.ottlaw.com

Thomas H. Ott
Daniel E. Hoffman
Patrick Carey

For full biographical listings, see the Martindale-Hubbell Law Directory

IRVINE, Orange Co.

BORCHARD & WILLOUGHBY, A PROFESSIONAL CORPORATION (AV)

18881 Von Karman Avenue, Suite 1400, 92612
Telephone: 949-263-0424
Fax: 949-263-1913

Michael D. Borchard
Michael L. Willoughby
Mark A. Rodriguez

Stephanie A. Pittaluga

For full biographical listings, see the Martindale-Hubbell Law Directory

GAUNTLETT & ASSOCIATES (AV)

18400 Von Karman, Suite 300, 92612
Telephone: 949-553-1010
Fax: 949-553-2050
Email: info@gauntlettlaw.com *URL:* http://www.gauntlettlaw.com

David A. Gauntlett

Eileen Spadoni
Eric J. Schindler
James A. Lowe (Not admitted in CA)
Eric Robert Little
Dean H. McVay
Richard Wm. Zevnik
Raymond J. Liddy
Julia C. Weissman

For full biographical listings, see the Martindale-Hubbell Law Directory

TIMOTHY L. JOENS & ASSOCIATES A PROFESSIONAL CORPORATION (AV)

2601 Main Street, Suite 320, 92614
Telephone: 949-553-1950
Fax: 949-553-8835

Timothy L. Joens

Representative Client: Century 21 Real Estate Corp.

For full biographical listings, see the Martindale-Hubbell Law Directory

LONG BEACH, Los Angeles Co.

EDWARD P. GEORGE, JR., INC. A PROFESSIONAL CORPORATION (AV)

Suite 430, 5000 East Spring Street, 90815-1275
Telephone: 562-497-2900
Facsimile: 562-497-2904

Edward P. George, Jr.
Timothy L. O'Reilly

OF COUNSEL

Albert C. S. Ramsey

Reference: City National Bank, Long Beach.

For full biographical listings, see the Martindale-Hubbell Law Directory

LOS ANGELES, * Los Angeles Co.

BLACK, COMPEAN & HALL A LIMITED LIABILITY PARTNERSHIP (AV)

445 South Figueroa Street, Suite 2800, 90071-1632
Telephone: 213-629-9500
FAX: 213-629-4868
Email: bchinsurlaw@earthlink.com

MEMBERS OF FIRM

Robert H. Black
Michael D. Compean
Frederick G. Hall

ASSOCIATES

Vicente Valencia, Jr.
Daniel Eli
Lisa Jennifer Martin

Reference: The Pacific Bank.

For full biographical listings, see the Martindale-Hubbell Law Directory

BLECHER & COLLINS, A PROFESSIONAL CORPORATION (AV)

611 West Sixth Street, 20th Floor, 90017
Telephone: 213-622-4222
Telecopier: 213-622-1656

Maxwell M. Blecher
William C. Hsu
Harold R. Collins, Jr.
Gary M. Joye
John E. Andrews
James Robert Noblin
Steven J. Cannata
Donald R. Pepperman
Ralph C. Hofer
Alicia G. Rosenberg

For full biographical listings, see the Martindale-Hubbell Law Directory

DWYER, DALY, BROTZEN & BRUNO, LLP (AV)

550 South Hope Street, Suite 1900, 90071
Telephone: 213-627-9300
Fax: 213-624-1638
Email: DB2LAW.com

PARTNERS

Ronald A. Dwyer
Peter P. Brotzen
John A. Daly
Toni Rae Bruno

ASSOCIATES

Gregory L. Anderson
Thomas A. Kosakowski
Gregory J. Salute
James N. Fincher
Wendell F. Hall
Daniel M. Walanka
John F. Schilling
Douglas A. Schenck

For full biographical listings, see the Martindale-Hubbell Law Directory

THE FORD LAW FIRM (AV)

12400 Wilshire Boulevard, Suite 1060, 90025
Telephone: 310-826-2648
Facsimile: 310-826-2658
Email: flf@gte.com

William H. Ford, III
Claudia J. Serviss
George H. Kim

ASSOCIATE

Paul C. Cook

For full biographical listings, see the Martindale-Hubbell Law Directory

Los Angeles—Continued

Hill, Farrer & Burrill LLP (AV)

A Limited Liability Partnership including Professional Corporations
37th Floor, One California Plaza, 300 South Grand Avenue, 90071-3147
Telephone: 213-620-0460
Fax: 213-624-4840
URL: http://www.hfbllp.com

MEMBERS OF FIRM

Ronald W. Novotny (P.C.)
Dean E. Dennis (P.C.)
Jennifer L. Pancake

OF COUNSEL

Stanley E. Tobin (P.C.)
Jack R. White (P.C.)
James G. Johnson (P.C.)

For Complete List of Firm Personnel, See General Section

For full biographical listings, see the Martindale-Hubbell Law Directory

Edward J. Horowitz A Professional Corporation (AV)

Suite 1015, 11661 San Vicente Boulevard, 90049
Telephone: 310-826-6619
Fax: 310-826-8242
Email: Horowitz@appellatelaw.com

Edward J. Horowitz

Reference: Union Bank (Brentwood Branch).

For full biographical listings, see the Martindale-Hubbell Law Directory

Horvitz & Levy, LLP (AV)

A Partnership including Professional Corporations
18th Floor, 15760 Ventura Boulevard (Encino), 91436
Telephone: 818-995-0800
Fax: 818-995-3157

Ellis J. Horvitz (A P.C.)
Barry R. Levy (A P.C.)
Peter Abrahams
David M. Axelrad
Frederic D. Cohen
S. Thomas Todd
David S. Ettinger
Daniel J. Gonzalez
Mitchell C. Tilner
Christina J. Imre
Lisa Perrochet
Stephen E. Norris
Sandra J. Smith
John A. Taylor, Jr.
Julie L. Woods
Lisa R. Jaskol
H. Thomas Watson

Mary F. Dant
Holly R. Paul
Andrea M. Gauthier
Judith E. Gordon
Patricia Lofton
L. Rachel Lerman Helyar
Mary-Christine (M.C.) Sungaila
Stephanie Rae Williams
Curt Cutting
Wendy S. Albers
Robert H. Wright
Nina E. Scholtz
Orly Degani

OF COUNSEL

Jon B. Eisenberg

Reference: Bank of California (Pasadena, California Office).

For full biographical listings, see the Martindale-Hubbell Law Directory

Iverson, Yoakum, Papiano & Hatch (AV)

One Wilshire Building, 27th Floor 624 South Grand Avenue, 90017
Telephone: 213-624-7444
Telecopier: 213-629-4563

MEMBERS OF FIRM

Neil Papiano
Patrick M. Mc Adam
Arnold D. Larson
John M. Garrick

ASSOCIATES

Douglas C. Pease
Andrew K. Doty
Melissa A. Immel
Mary P. Lightfoot
Mark Pearson
Adam F. Burke
Scott A. Horton

OF COUNSEL

R. Noel Hatch

Representative Clients: Lockheed Corp.; International Paper; Bridgestone/-Firestone, Inc.
Reference: Bank of America (Los Angeles Head Office).

For Complete List of Firm Personnel, See General Section

For full biographical listings, see the Martindale-Hubbell Law Directory

Loeb & Loeb LLP (AV)

A Limited Liability Partnership including Professional Corporations
Suite 1800, 1000 Wilshire Boulevard, 90017-2475
Telephone: 213-688-3400
Facsimile: 213-688-3460
Email: info@loeb.com *URL:* http://www.loeb.com
Century City, California Office: Suite 2200, 10100 Santa Monica Boulevard, Los Angeles, 90067-4164.
Telephone: 310-282-2000.
Facsimile: 310-282-2192.
New York, N.Y. Office: 345 Park Avenue, 10154-0037.
Telephone: 212-407-4000.
Facsimile: 212-407-4990.
Nashville, Tennessee Office: 45 Music Square West, 37203-3205.
Telephone: 615-749-8300;
Facsimile: 615-749-8308.
Rome, Italy Office: Piazza Digione 1, 00197.
Telephone: 011-3906-808-8456.
Facsimile: 011-3906-808-8288.

MEMBERS OF FIRM

Andrew S. Garb (A P.C.)
Jeffrey M. Loeb
Douglas E. Mirell
Anthony Murray (A P.C.)
Robert N. Treiman

OF COUNSEL

Howard I. Friedman (A P.C.)

For Complete List of Firm Personnel, See General Section

For full biographical listings, see the Martindale-Hubbell Law Directory

Neumeyer & Boyd, LLP (AV)

2029 Century Park East, Suite 1100, 90067
Telephone: 310-553-9393
Fax: 310-553-8437

MEMBERS OF FIRM

Richard A. Neumeyer
Carol Boyd
Lydia E. Hachmeister

OF COUNSEL

Eugene R. Grace

ASSOCIATES

Katherine Tatikian
Daniel F. Sanchez
Reid L. Denham
Katy A. Nelson
Larry P. Nathenson

For full biographical listings, see the Martindale-Hubbell Law Directory

O'Melveny & Myers LLP (AV)

400 South Hope Street, 90071-2899
Telephone: 213-430-6000
Facsimile: 213-430-6407
Cable: MOMS
Telex: 674122
Email: omminfo@omm.com *URL:* http://www.omm.com
Century City, CA Office: 1999 Avenue of the Stars, Los Angeles, 90067-6035.
Telex: 674097. Tel: 310-553-6700.
Fax: 310-246-6779.
Newport Beach, CA Office: 610 Newport Center Drive, 92660-6429.
Telex: 4722088. Tel: 949-760-9600.
Fax: 949-823-6994.
San Francisco, CA Office: Embarcadero Center West, 275 Battery Street, 94111-3305. Tel: 415-984-8700.
Fax: 415-984-8701.
New York, NY Office: Citicorp Center, 153 East 53rd Street, 10022-4611.
Telex: 129165. Tel: 212-326-2000.
Fax: 212-326-2061.
Washington, DC Office: 555 13th Street, N.W., 20004-1109.
Cable: MOMSWSH.
Telex: 89622. Tel: 202-383-5300.
Fax: 202-383-5414.
London Office: O'Melveny & Myers, 3 Finsbury Square, London, EC2A 1LA, England. Tel: 44-171-256-8451. Fax 44-171-638-8205.
Tokyo Office: Akasaka Twin Tower, East 14F, 2-17-23, Akasaka, Minato-ku, Tokyo 107-0052, Japan. Tel: 03-5562-2800.
Fax: 03-5575-3840.
Hong Kong Office: O'Melveny & Myers, Suite 1905, Tower Two, Lippo Centre, 89 Queensway, Central, Hong Kong. Tel: 852-2523-8266.
Fax: 852-2522-1760.
Shanghai Office: Kerry Centre, 20F, 1515 Nanjing Road West, Shanghai, 200040 People's Republic of China. Tel: 86-21-5298-5600.
Fax: 86-21-5298-5500.

PARTNER

Charles C. Lifland

For Complete List of Firm Personnel, See General Section

For full biographical listings, see the Martindale-Hubbell Law Directory

Los Angeles—Continued

Claudia Ribet (AV)

11661 San Vicente Boulevard, Suite 1015, 90049
Telephone: 310-826-2313
FAX: 310-826-8242
Email: Ribet@appellatelaw.com

For full biographical listings, see the Martindale-Hubbell Law Directory

Law Offices of Barry Tarlow A Professional Corporation (AV)

9119 Sunset Boulevard, 90069
Telephone: 310-278-2111
Cable Address: "Habeas"
Fax: 310-550-7055
Email: lobt@earthlink.net

Mark O. Heaney — Blair Berk
Shereen J. Charlick

For full biographical listings, see the Martindale-Hubbell Law Directory

MONTEREY, Monterey Co.

Harray & Linker (AV)

80 Garden Court, Suite 260, 93940
Telephone: 831-373-3101
Fax: 831-373-6712
Email: general@harray-linker.com

Richard K. Harray — Stan L. Linker

ASSOCIATES

Christine Balbo Reed — J. Kenneth Gorman
Debra Gemgnani Tipton

For full biographical listings, see the Martindale-Hubbell Law Directory

NEWPORT BEACH, Orange Co.

Rebecca Callahan A Professional Law Corporation (AV)

5120 Campus Drive, 92660
Telephone: 949-864-5152
Facsimile: 949-864-5156
URL: http://www.lawyers.com/callahanlaw
Email: bekic@pacbell.net *URL:* http://www.rcallahan.com

Rebecca Callahan

For full biographical listings, see the Martindale-Hubbell Law Directory

NOVATO, Marin Co.

Bien & Summers LLP (AV)

23 Palomino Road, 94947
Telephone: 415-898-2900
Fax: 415-898-1922
Email: Bien@worldnet.att.net
Oakland, California Office: 3932 Reinhardt Drive.
Telephone: 510-531-3106.
Fax: 510-531-3182.
San Mateo, California Office: 7 West 41st Avenue, No. 411, 94403.
Telephone: 650-345-8653.
Fax: 650-345-9493.

Elliot L. Bien — E. Elizabeth Summers

OF COUNSEL

Dorothy K. Gustafson

For full biographical listings, see the Martindale-Hubbell Law Directory

PASADENA, Los Angeles Co.

John C. Burton (AV)

35 South Raymond Avenue, Suite 405, 91105
Telephone: 626-449-8300
Fax: 626-449-4417
Email: Johnburtonlaw@compuserve.com *URL:* http://www.lawyers.com/johnburtonlaw

For full biographical listings, see the Martindale-Hubbell Law Directory

W. Michael Mayock (AV)

The Braley Building, Fourth Floor, 35 South Raymond Avenue, 91105
Telephone: 626-405-1465; 626-405-0158
FAX: 626-405-0158
Email: mlmayock@earthlink.net *URL:* http://www.lawyers.com/mayocklaw

Reference: Union Bank.

For full biographical listings, see the Martindale-Hubbell Law Directory

*SACRAMENTO,** Sacramento Co.

Dauer & Thompson (AV)

3455 American River Drive, Suite C, 95864
Telephone: 916-974-3400
Facsimile: 916-974-3405
Email: d&t@concourse.net

MEMBERS OF FIRM

Paul F. Dauer — James E. Thompson

Jennifer L. Dauer — Alan R. Barnes

For full biographical listings, see the Martindale-Hubbell Law Directory

Eisen & Johnston (AV)

980 Ninth Street, Suite 1400, P.O. Box 111, 95812-0111
Telephone: 916-444-6171
Fax: 916-441-5810
URL: http://www.lawyers.com/e&slaw

MEMBERS OF FIRM

Jay-Allen Eisen — Marian M. Johnston

For full biographical listings, see the Martindale-Hubbell Law Directory

Livingston & Mattesich, Law Corporation (AV)

1201 K Street, Suite 1100, 95814
Telephone: 916-442-1111
Fax: 916-448-1709
Email: l&m@lmlaw.net *URL:* http://www.lmlaw.net

Gene Livingston — Emilio E. Varanini, III
James M. Mattesich — Kenneth M. Malovos
Carol Livingston — Kathleen E. Finnerty
Rebecca M. Ceniceros — Joanna R. Mendoza

Steven P. Belzer — Baldassaro (Bill) Di Capo
Jeffrey Leacox — John McKinsey
Randy Pollack — Timothy E. Naccarato
Alice H. Choi — Craig N. Lundgren
Stephen Craig Hunter — Mary Farrell Taylor
Matthew J. Goldman — Brian Crone
Joel C. Baiocchi — Gay L. Carroll
Steven G. Churchwell

Represenative Clients: California Chamber of Commerce; The Cosmetic, Toiletry and Fragrance Association.

For full biographical listings, see the Martindale-Hubbell Law Directory

Matheny Sears Linkert & Long, LLP (AV)

3638 American River Drive, P.O. Box 13711, 95853-4711
Telephone: 916-978-3434
Fax: 916-978-3430
Email: info@msll.com *URL:* http://www.msll.com

MEMBERS OF FIRM

Henry G. Matheny (1933-1984) — Kent M. Luckey
Douglas A. Sears — Matthew C. Jaime
Richard S. Linkert — Michael A. Bishop
Ernest A. Long — Robert B. Berrigan
Joann Georgallis — Ronald E. Enabnit
Eric R. Wiesel

ASSOCIATES

Andrea Croak Christensen — Paul Richard Baleria
Michael G. Jones — James F. Curran
Eric M. Bonzell — Andreas C. Rockas
Mary Elizabeth Wood — Timothy P. Chang

OF COUNSEL

James C. Damir

LEGAL SUPPORT PERSONNEL

PARALEGALS

Frances Studer — Lynell Rae Steed
Jennifer Bachman

For full biographical listings, see the Martindale-Hubbell Law Directory

*SAN BERNARDINO,** San Bernardino Co.

Wilson, Borror, Dunn & Davis, LLP (AV)

Suite 307, The Bank of California Building, 255 North D Street, 92401
Telephone: 909-884-8855
Fax: 909-884-5161

MEMBERS OF FIRM

Fred A. Wilson (1886-1973) — James R. Dunn
Wm. H. Wilson (1915-1981) — Thomas M. Davis
Sarah L. Overton

ASSOCIATES

S. Mark Strain — C. Victor Wear

(See Next Column)

WILSON, BORROR, DUNN & DAVIS LLP—*Continued*

OF COUNSEL

Caywood J. Borror

Representative Clients: Travelers Insurance Co.; Rockwell International; Westinghouse Air Brake Co.; Goodyear Tire and Rubber Co.; Home Insurance Co.; Cities of: Redlands, Chino, Colton, San Bernardino, Upland, Yucapia and Corona; Lloyd's of London; Universal Health Services, Inc.-;Lawyer's Mutual Insurance; Unified School Districts of Rialto and Fontana .

For full biographical listings, see the Martindale-Hubbell Law Directory

*SAN DIEGO,** San Diego Co.

DUKE GERSTEL SHEARER, LLP (AV)

A Registered Limited Liability Partnership
Sixth Floor, 101 West Broadway, P.O. Box 85470, 92186-5470
Telephone: 619-232-0816
800-405-0816
Fax: 619-232-4661
Email: lawyers@dgsllp.com *URL:* http://www.dgsllp.com
Costa Mesa, California Office: 3200 Park Center Drive, Suite 1000, 92626.
Telephone: 949-551-8664, 800-405-0816.
Los Angeles, California Office: 10866 Wilshire Boulevard, Suite 1400, 90024.
Telephone: 310-475-7118, 800-405-0816.
San Francisco, California Office: 744 Montgomery Street, Fifth Floor, 94111.
Telephone: 415-773-0101.
Palm Springs, California Office: 1111 East Tahquitz Canyon Way, Suite 110, 92262.
Telephone: 760-322-7846.
Phoenix, Arizona Office: One Columbus Plaza, 3636 North Central Avenue, Suite 1200, 85012.
Telephone: 602-650-2060.
Fax: 602-650-2089.
Tucson, Arizona Office: 6969 East Sunrise Drive, Suite 102, 85750.
Telephone: 520-615-8858.
Fax: 520-615-1069.
Affiliate Las Vegas, Nevada Office: Parsons & Pursiano, LLP, City Center West, Suite 108, 7201 W. Lake Mead Boulevard, 89128.
Telephone: 702-384-9900.
Facsimile: 702-384-5900.

MEMBER OF FIRM

Dawn R. Brennan

ASSOCIATE

Michelle LeRoux Burton

Reference: Bank of Commerce.

For full biographical listings, see the Martindale-Hubbell Law Directory

*SAN FRANCISCO,** San Francisco Co.

KAUFMAN & LOGAN LLP (AV)

111 Pine Street, Suite 1300, 94111
Telephone: 415-392-6677
Telecopier: 415-391-4639

MEMBERS OF FIRM

Jeffrey Kaufman
Garrett L. Cecchini
Peter J. Logan
W. Martin Tellegen
Richard A. Eggerth

ASSOCIATES

Nancy S. Coan
Paul A. Peters
Sandra L. Cross
Paulette Donsavage
Gerald F. Ellersdorfer
George D. Vanberg-Wolff

OF COUNSEL

Gerhard Stoll

LEGAL SUPPORT PERSONNEL

PARALEGALS

Karen L. Dunn, CLA
Adrienne Levin
T. Patrick Bridenstine
Paula R. Brawley

For full biographical listings, see the Martindale-Hubbell Law Directory

MURPHY, PEARSON, BRADLEY & FEENEY, A PROFESSIONAL CORPORATION (AV)

88 Kearny Street, 10th Floor, 94108
Telephone: 415-788-1900
Telecopier: 415-393-8087
Email: IndividualsFirstInitialAndLastName@mpbf.com *URL:* http://www.mpbf.com
Sacramento, California Office: 701 University Avenue, Suite 150.
Telephone: 916-565-0300.
Fax: 916-565-1636.
San Jose, California Office: 80 South Market Street, 3rd Floor.
Telephone: 408-279-5792.
Facsimile: 408-279-5785.

(See Next Column)

Los Angeles, California Office: 11400 West Olympic Boulevard, Suite 249.
Telephone: 310-312-9565.
Fax: 310-312-9566.

Mark Ellis (Resident, Sacramento Office)
Alexander J. Berline

For Complete List of Firm Personnel, See General Section

For full biographical listings, see the Martindale-Hubbell Law Directory

REMCHO, JOHANSEN AND PURCELL (AV)

Suite 800, 220 Montgomery Street, 94104
Telephone: 415-398-6230
Fax: 415-398-7256
Email: Info@RJP.Com *URL:* http://www.rjp.com
Sacramento, California Office: U.S. Bank Plaza. Suite 2140, 980 Ninth Street, 95814.
Telephone: 916-264-1818.
Fax: 916-264-1824.

MEMBERS OF FIRM

Joseph Remcho
Robin B. Johansen
Kathleen J. Purcell

James C. Harrison
Thomas A. Willis

LEGAL SUPPORT PERSONNEL

Douglas Denton (Paralegal)
Ruth Fridhandler (Legal Administrator)

For full biographical listings, see the Martindale-Hubbell Law Directory

ROSEN, BIEN & ASARO (AV)

Eighth Floor, 155 Montgomery Street, 94104
Telephone: 415-433-6830
Fax: 415-433-7104
Email: rba@rbalaw.com

Sanford Jay Rosen
Michael W. Bien
Andrea G. Asaro

Thomas Nolan
Shana J. Margolis
William H. D. Fernholz
Ernest J. Galvan

For full biographical listings, see the Martindale-Hubbell Law Directory

SCADDEN, HAMILTON & RYAN (AV)

220 Montgomery Street, 13th Floor, 94104-3410
Telephone: 415-362-5116
Telecopier: 415-362-4214
URL: http://www.shrlaw.com

James G. Scadden
Robert J. Ryan
Robert P. Hamilton
James P. Cunningham

Charles O. Thompson
Vincent C. Milani
Eileen Santana Wright
Timothy K. Killelea

LEGAL SUPPORT PERSONNEL

Edwin L. Lilley
Dennis Prime
Mary Sue Schroeder

For full biographical listings, see the Martindale-Hubbell Law Directory

AMITAI SCHWARTZ (AV)

155 Montgomery Street, Suite 800, 94104-4113
Telephone: 415-398-0922
Fax: 415-398-0978
Email: amitai@schwartzlaw.com

Monique Olivier
Elizabeth S. Letcher

For full biographical listings, see the Martindale-Hubbell Law Directory

SPIEGEL LIAO & KAGAY (AV)

595 Market Street, Suite 1350, 94105-2825
Telephone: 415-956-5959
Telecopier: 415-362-1431
Email: slk@slksf@com *URL:* http://www.slksf.com

Michael I. Spiegel
Charles M. Kagay

OF COUNSEL

Bartholomew Lee
Wayne M. Liao

For full biographical listings, see the Martindale-Hubbell Law Directory

*SAN JOSE,** Santa Clara Co.

MCMANIS, FAULKNER & MORGAN (AV)

160 West Santa Clara Street, 10th Floor, 95113
Telephone: 408-279-8700
Fax: 408-279-3244; 408-279-0494
Email: mfm@mfmlaw.com *URL:* http://www.mfmlaw.com

(See Next Column)

McMANIS, FAULKNER & MORGAN, *San Jose—Continued*

James McManis
William Faulkner
Donelle Morgan
Lisa Herrick
Michael Reedy
Erica Yew

Michelle Tidalgo
Colleen Duffy Smith
Lillian Wolf
Rebecca Hughes
Kalpana Vrudhula
Ray M. Baluyot
Catherine Bechtel
Arron Nesbitt

OF COUNSEL

Mary Arand

For full biographical listings, see the Martindale-Hubbell Law Directory

*SAN RAFAEL,** Marin Co.

JOHNS & CHRISTENSEN, A PROFESSIONAL CORPORATION (AV)

135 Paul Drive, Suite 100, 94903
Telephone: 415-459-5223
Facsimile: 415-453-2555
Email: info@johnsandchristensen.com *URL:* http://www.johnsandchristensen.com

Christopher Johns
Robert C. Christensen

David Gray Douglas
Jennifer A.D. Lehman
Farimah Faiz

OF COUNSEL

Mark J. Helmueller
Burton C. "Skip" Allyn, IV

For full biographical listings, see the Martindale-Hubbell Law Directory

*SANTA BARBARA,** Santa Barbara Co.

ANGLE, CARLSON, GOLDRICK & ROBERTS (AV)

A Partnership including a Professional Corporation
200 East Carrillo Street, Suite 310, 93101
Telephone: 805-963-7400
Fax: 805-963-7610

Robert O. Angle
Arthur W. Carlson (A P.C.)
Miles T. Goldrick
Paul A. Roberts

For full biographical listings, see the Martindale-Hubbell Law Directory

SANTA MONICA, Los Angeles Co.

HAIGHT, BROWN & BONESTEEL, L.L.P. (AV)

A Partnership including Professional Corporations
1620 26th Street, Suite 4000 North, P.O. Box 680, 90404
Telephone: 310-449-6000
Telecopier: 310-829-5117
Telex: 705837
URL: http://www.hbblaw.com
Santa Ana, California Office: Suite 900, 5 Hutton Centre Drive.
Telephone: 714-754-1100.
Telecopier: 714-754-0826.
Riverside, California Office: California Tower, 3737 Main Street, Suite 800.
Telephone: 909-341-8300.
Fax: 909-341-8309.
San Francisco, California Office: 101 Bush Street, 27th Floor.
Telephone: 415-986-7700.
Fax: 415-986-6945.
San Diego, California Office: 101 West Broadway, Suite 1000.
Telephone: 619-595-5583.
Fax: 619-595-7873.

MEMBERS OF FIRM

Roy G. Weatherup
Jules Solomon Zeman
Thomas N. Charchut
Rita Gunasekaran
Caroline E. Chan

ASSOCIATES

Jon M. Kasimov
Stephen M. Caine
Maureen Haight Gee
Stacey R. Preston
J. Alan Warfield

For full biographical listings, see the Martindale-Hubbell Law Directory

O'NEILL, LYSAGHT & SUN LLP (AV)

100 Wilshire Boulevard, Suite 700, 90401
Telephone: 310-451-5700
Telecopier: 310-399-7201

Brian O'Neill
Brian C. Lysaght
Frederick D. Friedman
Brian A. Sun
Yolanda Orozco
John M. Moscarino
Harriet Beegun Leva
Edward A. Klein
Robert L. Meylan
David E. Rosen
Paul D. Murphy

(See Next Column)

Ellyn S. Garofalo
Brian D. Hershman
Katharine A. Kates
Luan K. Phan
Kyle Y. Hoshide
Hersh Heather Elizabeth
Catherine D. Whiting

OF COUNSEL

J. Joseph Connolly

Reference: Wells Fargo Bank, Santa Monica.

For full biographical listings, see the Martindale-Hubbell Law Directory

*VENTURA,** Ventura Co.

LASCHER & LASCHER, A PROFESSIONAL CORPORATION (AV)

605 Poli Street, P.O. Box 25540, 93002
Telephone: 805-648-3228
Fax: 805-643-7692
Email: mail@lascher.com *URL:* http://www.lascher.com

Edward L. Lascher (1928-1991)
Wendy Cole Lascher

Gabriele Mezger-Lashly
Denise Abundis Brogna

Reference: Bank of Ventura.

For full biographical listings, see the Martindale-Hubbell Law Directory

TAYLOR McCORD, A LAW CORPORATION (AV)

721 East Main Street, P.O. Box 1477, 93002
Telephone: 805-648-4700
Email: vtafamlaw@aol.com

Richard L. Taylor
Robert L. McCord, Jr.
David L. Praver

Patrick Cherry
Susan D. Siple
Rebbecca F. Calderwood

LEGAL SUPPORT PERSONNEL

PARALEGALS

Stephanie Gibson
Adele Rubino (Certified Legal Assistant, California Advanced Specialist)
Diane Lovato

For full biographical listings, see the Martindale-Hubbell Law Directory

COLORADO

*ASPEN,** Pitkin Co.

AUSTIN, PEIRCE & SMITH, P.C. (AV)

Suite 205, 600 East Hopkins Avenue, 81611
Telephone: 970-925-2600
FAX: 970-925-4720
Email: aps_aspen@aol.com

Ronald D. Austin
Frederick F. Peirce
Thomas Fenton Smith

John M. Lassalette

Counsel for: Chase Manhattan of Colorado, Inc.; Clark's Market; Coates, Reid & Waldron Property Management, Inc.; Crystal Palace Corp.; Snowmass Shopping Center; Coldwell Banker The Aspen Brokers, Ltd.; William Poss & Assoc., Architects; Snowmass Village Resort Association; Aspen/-Pitkin County Housing Authority.

For full biographical listings, see the Martindale-Hubbell Law Directory

*DENVER,** Denver Co.

BERENBAUM, WEINSHIENK & EASON, P.C. (AV)

Suite 2600 Republic Plaza, 370 17th Street, 80202
Telephone: 303-825-0800
Facsimile: 303-629-7610
Email: berenbaum1@aol.com *URL:* http://www.BWELaw.com

Martin D. Buckley
M. Frances Cetrulo
Daniel S. Duggan
David R. Eason
I. H. Kaiser
Kenneth S. Kramer
Larry R. Martinez
Dean G. Panos
Edwin G. Perlmutter
Eugene M. Sprague
Robert G. Wilson, Jr.

OF COUNSEL

Richard L. Eason

(See Next Column)

BERENBAUM, WEINSHIENK & EASON P.C.—*Continued*

Carol Ann Flowers
Teri L. Lowery
Melissa Mequi

Representative Clients: Home Depot; Sprint Spectrum, L.P.; Town of Vail, Colorado; First Union Corporation; City of Englewood, Colorado; Oakwood Homes; Karman, Inc.; Wells Fargo Bank, N.A.; Berkshire Life Insurance Co.; Trinity Ventures.

For full biographical listings, see the Martindale-Hubbell Law Directory

BRENMAN BROMBERG & TENENBAUM, P.C. (AV)

Mellon Financial Center Suite 1001, 1775 Sherman Street, 80203
Telephone: 303-894-0234
Fax: 303-839-1633
Email: bbt@bbtlaw.net

Albert Brenman
A. Thomas Tenenbaum
Thomas R. Bromberg
Steven W. McDonald

Sheryl A. Johnson
Judy A. Gooch

OF COUNSEL

Duane Woodard

For full biographical listings, see the Martindale-Hubbell Law Directory

REIMAN & BAYAZ, P.C. (AV)

1600 Broadway, Suite 1340, 80202
Telephone: 303-860-1500
Fax: 303-839-4380
Email: rblaw@earthlink.net

Jeff Reiman
Marcie K. Bayaz

Debra D. Asimus

For full biographical listings, see the Martindale-Hubbell Law Directory

SENN LEWIS & VISCIANO, P.C. (AV)

1801 California Street, Suite 4300, 80202
Telephone: 303-298-1122
Facsimile: 303-296-9101

Mark A. Senn
Fredric J. Lewis
Frank W. Visciano

Luis A. Toro

For Complete List of Firm Personnel, See General Section

For full biographical listings, see the Martindale-Hubbell Law Directory

CONNECTICUT

*BRIDGEPORT,** Fairfield Co.

GERALD E. BODELL (AV)

177 State Street Suite 401, 06604
Telephone: 203-335-8955
Fax: 203-366-6812
New York, New York Office: 36 West 44th Street, Suite 303.
Telephone: 212- 398-3778.
Fax: 212-398-3779.

For full biographical listings, see the Martindale-Hubbell Law Directory

*HARTFORD,** Hartford Co.

JACKSON, O'KEEFE AND PHELAN (AV)

36 Russ Street, 06106-1571
Telephone: 860-278-4040
Fax: 860-527-2500
West Hartford, Connecticut Office: 62 LaSalle Road.
Telephone: 860-521-7500.
Fax: 860-561-5399.
Bethlehem, Connecticut Office: 423 Munger Lane. Telephone/ *Fax:* 203-266-5255.

MEMBERS OF FIRM

Jay W. Jackson
Peter K. O'Keefe
Andrew J. O'Keefe
Philip R. Dunn, Jr.
Denise Martino Phelan
Kathryn M. Cunningham
Matthew J. O'Keefe
Joseph M. Busher, Jr.
Michael E. Riley
Kristen E. Scholhamer

Representative Clients: Travelers Aetna Property Casualty Co.; ITT Hartford; Liberty Mutual Insurance Co.; Connecticut Medical Insurance Co.

For full biographical listings, see the Martindale-Hubbell Law Directory

SOROKIN, GROSS & HYDE, P.C. (AV)

One Corporate Center, 06103
Telephone: 860-525-6645
Fax: 860-522-1781
Email: sorokin@sorokinlaw.com
Simsbury, Connecticut Office: 720 Hopmeadow Street.
Telephone: 860-651-9348.
Rocky Hill, Connecticut Office: 2360 Main Street.
Telephone: 860-563-9305.
Fax: 860-529-6931.

Lisa A. Magliochetti
Lewis Rabinovitz
Richard C. Robinson

Rod W. Farrell

For Complete List of Firm Personnel, See General Section

For full biographical listings, see the Martindale-Hubbell Law Directory

*NEW HAVEN,** New Haven Co.

GALLAGHER & CALISTRO (AV)

1377 Boulevard, P.O. Box 1925, 06509
Telephone: 203-624-4165
Fax: 203-865-5598

William F. Gallagher
Barbara L. Cox
Roger B. Calistro
Kurt D. Koehler
Cynthia C. Bott
Thomas J. Airone

For full biographical listings, see the Martindale-Hubbell Law Directory

ROSEN & DOLAN, P.C. (AV)

400 Orange Street, 06511
Telephone: 203-787-3513
Fax: 203-789-1605
Email: davidrosen@snet.net
Email: sapincus@snet.net

David N. Rosen

Stephen M. Pincus

Reference: Peoples Bank.

For Complete List of Firm Personnel, See General Section

For full biographical listings, see the Martindale-Hubbell Law Directory

WILLIAMS, POLAN & PATTIS, LLC (AV)

51 Elm Street, 06510
Telephone: 203-562-9931
Fax: 203-776-9494
Email: jrw@johnrwilliams.com

John R. Williams
Diane Polan
Norman A. Pattis

Katrena Engstrom
Angelica N. Papastavros
William S. Palmieri
Rosemarie Paine

References: Webster Bank; Citizens Bank.

For full biographical listings, see the Martindale-Hubbell Law Directory

WESTPORT, Fairfield Co.

ANDREW B. BOWMAN (AV)

1804 Post Road East, 06880
Telephone: 203-259-0599
Fax: 203-255-2570
Email: andrew.bowman@snet.net

Reference: Peoples Bank.

For full biographical listings, see the Martindale-Hubbell Law Directory

DISTRICT OF COLUMBIA

WASHINGTON, D.C. Co.

MAINES & LOEB PLLC (AV)

1827 Jefferson Place, N.W., 20036
Telephone: 202-223-2817
Telecopier: 202-293-9811
URL: http://www.mainesloeb.com

(See Next Column)

MAINES & LOEB PLLC, *Washington—Continued*

Ronald D. Maines
Richard G. Wilkins
Joseph L. Hoffmann (Not admitted in DC)
Lisa K. Seilheimer (Not admitted in DC)

NON-ATTORNEY MEMBER

Don Loeb

For full biographical listings, see the Martindale-Hubbell Law Directory

VENABLE ATTORNEYS AT LAW VENABLE, BAETJER, HOWARD & CIVILETTI, LLP (AV)

A Partnership including Professional Corporations
Suite 1000, 1201 New York Avenue, N.W., 20005
Telephone: 202-962-4800
Fax: 202-962-8300
URL: http://www.venable.com
Baltimore, Maryland Office: Venable, Baetjer and Howard LLP, 1800 Mercantile Bank & Trust Building, 2 Hopkins Plaza.
Telephone: 410-244-7400.
Fax: 410-244-7742.
McLean, Virginia Office: Venable, Baetjer and Howard LLP, Suite 400, 2010 Corporate Ridge.
Telephone: 703-760-1600.
Fax: 703-821-8949.
Rockville, Maryland Office: Venable, Baetjer and Howard LLP, Suite 500, One Church Street, P. O. Box 1906.
Telephone: 301-217-5600.
Fax: 301-217-5617.
Towson, Maryland Office: Venable, Baetjer and Howard LLP, 210 Allegheny Avenue, P. O. Box 5517.
Telephone: 410-494-6200.
Fax: 410-821-0147.

MEMBERS OF FIRM

Robert G. Ames (Also at Baltimore, Maryland Office)
James K. Archibald (Also at Baltimore, Maryland Office)
Maurice Baskin
Kenneth C. Bass, III (Also at McLean, Virginia Office)
Benjamin R. Civiletti (P.C.) (Also at Baltimore and Towson, Maryland Offices)
John F. Cooney
William D. Coston
Jeffrey A. Dunn (Also at Baltimore, Maryland Office)
Ronald R. Glancz
Edward F. Glynn, Jr.
David W. Goewey
Gary M. Hnath
Amy Berman Jackson
Thomas J. Kelly, Jr.
Thomas J. Madden
George F. Pappas (Also at Baltimore, Maryland Office)
Michael Schatzow (Also at Baltimore, Maryland Office)
James L. Shea (also at Baltimore, Maryland Office)
Judson W. Starr (Also at Baltimore and Towson, Maryland Offices)
Patrick J. Stewart (Also at Baltimore, Maryland Office)
N. Frank Wiggins

ASSOCIATES

Carla Draluck Craft
Melissa Landau Steinman

For Complete List of Firm Personnel, See General Section

For full biographical listings, see the Martindale-Hubbell Law Directory

FLORIDA

CORAL GABLES, Dade Co.

JOEL HIRSCHHORN, P.A. (AV)

Douglas Centre-Penthouse One, 2600 Douglas Road, 33134
Telephone: 305-445-5320
Telefax: 305-446-1766

Joel Hirschhorn

Brian H. Bieber

Representative Clients: Former President of GDC 1B Public; Former President of Centrust 13B Bank; Former President of American Saving & Loan 10B Bank; Playboy Enterprises, Inc.; City of Miami Beach; Avis Rent-a-Car System, Inc.; International Fast Foods Corp.

For full biographical listings, see the Martindale-Hubbell Law Directory

LANE, REESE, AULICK, SUMMERS & FIELD, P.A. (AV)

Suite 304 Douglas Centre, 2600 Douglas Road, 33134
Telephone: 305-444-4418
Fax: 305-444-5504
Email: LRASF-Miami@MSN.COM

(See Next Column)

Frank A. Lane
William S. Reese
Cecilia Aulick
William L. Summers
Paul H. Field

C. Page Lane
Lorenzo Jackson, Jr.
Luis J. Perdomo

For full biographical listings, see the Martindale-Hubbell Law Directory

CORAL SPRINGS, Broward Co.

BONNIE S. SATTERFIELD, P.A. (AV)

3111 University Drive, Suite 405, 33065
Telephone: 954-341-2250
Fax: 954-345-0115
URL: http://www.bonniesatterfield.com
Email: bsatterfield@lawyers.com *URL:* http://www.lawyers.com/bonniesatterfield

Bonnie S. Satterfield

For full biographical listings, see the Martindale-Hubbell Law Directory

*FORT LAUDERDALE,** Broward Co.

CATRI, HOLTON, KESSLER & KESSLER, P.A. (AV)

The Litigation Building, 3rd Floor, 633 S. Andrews Avenue, 33302
Telephone: 954-463-8593
Fax: 954-462-1303

Charles T. Kessler (1930-1997)
Wesley L. Catri
Raymond O. Holton, Jr.
Paula C. Kessler
Andrea L. Kessler

Gerard A. Tuzzio
Edwina V. Kessler

For full biographical listings, see the Martindale-Hubbell Law Directory

HALICZER, PETTIS & WHITE, P.A. (AV)

101 Northeast Third Avenue, Sixth Floor, 33301
Telephone: 954-523-9922
Fax: 954-522-2512
Orlando, Florida Office: NationsBank Building, Suite 1275, 111 North Orange Avenue. 32801.
Telephone: 407-841-9866.
Fax: 407-841-9915.

James S. Haliczer
Eugene K. Pettis
Kenneth E. White

Amy B. Talisman
Anthony K. Goodman
Anthony V. Scalese
Debra B. Potter
William Bassett, Jr.
Frank J. Taddeo

For full biographical listings, see the Martindale-Hubbell Law Directory

RICHARD L. ROSENBAUM (AV)

Suite 1500, One East Broward Boulevard, 33301
Telephone: 954-522-7000
Facsimile: 954-522-7003
Email: rlrappeal@aol.com *URL:* http://www.lawyers.com/richardlrosenbaum

ASSOCIATE

Denise A. Bregoff

For full biographical listings, see the Martindale-Hubbell Law Directory

BONNIE S. SATTERFIELD, P.A.
(See Coral Springs)

*FORT MYERS,** Lee Co.

DEBOEST, KNUDSEN, STOCKMAN, WISEMAN, DECKER & DRYDEN, P.A. (AV)

1415 Hendry Street, P.O. Box 1470, 33902-1470
Telephone: 941-334-1381
Telecopier: 941-334-0266
Email: dkswlaw@gate.net
Naples, Florida Office: 600 Fifth Avenue South, Suite 301, 34102.
Telephone: 941-263-5040.
Fax: 941-263-6944.

Arthur K. Knudsen, Jr. (Retired)
Richard D. DeBoest
William E. Stockman
Tamela Eady Wiseman (Resident, Naples Office)
James G. Decker
Thomas M. Dryden

Representative Clients: Cobb Theatres, Inc.; WCI Communities, Inc.; Evelyn Jackman and Sons, Inc.

For full biographical listings, see the Martindale-Hubbell Law Directory

Fort Myers—Continued

GARVIN & TRIPP, A PROFESSIONAL ASSOCIATION (AV)

2532 East First Street, P.O. Drawer 2040, 33902
Telephone: 941-334-1824
FAX: 941-334-6848
Email: jgarvin@cyberstreet.com *URL:* http://www.lawyers.com/garvin&tripp

Jeffrey R. Garvin | Theodore L. Tripp, Jr.

Bruce M. Essen | Elisa S. Worthington

Reference: Northern Trust Bank, Fort Myers, Florida.

For full biographical listings, see the Martindale-Hubbell Law Directory

*FORT PIERCE,** St. Lucie Co.

BRENNAN, HAYSKAR, JEFFERSON, WALKER & SCHWERER, PROFESSIONAL ASSOCIATION (AV)

515-519 South Indian River Drive, P.O. Box 3779, 34948-3779
Telephone: 561-461-2310
Fax: 561-468-6580

John T. Brennan
Thad H. Carlton (1906-1965)
Stephen G. Hayskar
Bradford L. Jefferson
Robert V. Schwerer
James T. Walker

Garrison M. Dundas | Steven R. McCain

Representative Clients: Allstate Insurance Co.; Auto Owners Insurance Co.; Canal Insurance Co.; City of Fort Pierce; City of Stuart; First Union National Bank; First National Bank & Trust Co. of the Treasure Coast; Florida Farm Bureau Insurance Group; Kemper Insurance Group.

For full biographical listings, see the Martindale-Hubbell Law Directory

NEILL GRIFFIN JEFFRIES FOWLER TIERNEY & NEILL, CHARTERED (AV)

311 South Second Street, P.O. Box 1270, 34954
Telephone: 561-464-8200
Fax: 561-464-2566

Richard V. Neill
Michael Jeffries
J. Stephen Tierney, III
Richard V. Neill, Jr.

Local Counsel For: SunTrust Bank South Florida, N.A., (Commercial and Trust Departments); Chubb Group of Insurances Cos.
Approved Attorneys for: Attorneys' Title Insurance Fund; Commonwealth Land Title Insurance Co.
Reference: SunTrust Bank South Florida, N.A., Fort Pierce, Florida (Commercial and Trust Departments).

For full biographical listings, see the Martindale-Hubbell Law Directory

*JACKSONVILLE,** Duval Co.

SHEPPARD, WHITE & THOMAS, P.A. (AV)

215 Washington Street, 32202
Telephone: 904-356-9661
Facsimile: 904-356-9667
Email: sheppardwhitethomas@worldnet.att.com

Wm. J. Sheppard | Elizabeth L. White
D. Gray Thomas

Adam Benjamin Allen | Leslie C. Scott

For full biographical listings, see the Martindale-Hubbell Law Directory

LEESBURG, Lake Co.

AUSTIN & PEPPERMAN (AV)

Suite C, 1321 Citizens Boulevard, P.O. Drawer 490200, 34749-0200
Telephone: 352-728-1020
Fax: 352-728-0595
URL: http://www.aust-pep.com

Robert E. Austin, Jr. | Carla R. Pepperman

ASSOCIATES

Reda J. Stewart | Bradford D. Fisher

Representative Clients: Allstate Insurance Co.; American Excess Insurance Co.; American Re-Insurance Co.; Florida Rock Industries, Inc.; Goodyear Tire & Rubber Co.; Great American Insurance Co.

For full biographical listings, see the Martindale-Hubbell Law Directory

*MIAMI,** Dade Co.

BIERMAN, SHOHAT, LOEWY & KLEIN, PROFESSIONAL ASSOCIATION (AV)

Penthouse Two, 800 Brickell Avenue, 33131-2944
Telephone: 305-358-7000
Facsimile: 305-358-4010

(See Next Column)

Donald I. Bierman
Edward R. Shohat
Ira N. Loewy
Theodore Klein

Michael A. Pizzi, Jr.

Reference: United National Bank of Miami.

For full biographical listings, see the Martindale-Hubbell Law Directory

BAMBI G. BLUM, P.A. (AV)

46 Southwest First Street, Fourth Floor, 33130
Telephone: 305-371-3848
Fax: 305-358-5202
Email: bblum@interserv.com

Bambi G. Blum

For full biographical listings, see the Martindale-Hubbell Law Directory

RICHARD E. BRODSKY, P.A. (AV)

25 Southeast Second Avenue, Suite 919, 33131
Telephone: 305-755-9470
Fax: 305-381-7708
Email: reb@reblaw.com *URL:* http://www.reblaw.com

Richard E. Brodsky

For full biographical listings, see the Martindale-Hubbell Law Directory

COOPER & WOLFE, P.A. (AV)

3580 First Union Financial Center, 200 South Biscayne Boulevard, 33131-2316
Telephone: 305-371-1597
Fax: 305-374-2460

Marc Cooper | Sharon L. Wolfe (1950-1999)

Maureen E. Lefebvre | Barbara Ann Silverman
Nancy Carolyn Ciampa

For full biographical listings, see the Martindale-Hubbell Law Directory

HICKS & ANDERSON, P.A. (AV)

Suite 2402 New World Tower, 100 North Biscayne Boulevard, 33132
Telephone: 305-374-8171
Fax: 305-372-8038

Mark Hicks | Ralph O. Anderson
Jean Kneale

Gary A. Magnarini
Cindy L. Ebenfeld
Dinah S. Stein
David J. Maher
Rick A. Piccolo
Lisa Rodriguez
Kelly Gibson

OF COUNSEL

James E. Tribble | Roger L. Blackburn

For full biographical listings, see the Martindale-Hubbell Law Directory

PAUL MORRIS PROFESSIONAL ASSOCIATION (AV)

Suite 550, 999 Ponce de Leon Boulevard (Coral Gables), 33134
Telephone: 305-446-2020
Fax: 305-442-4371
Email: paulappeal@aol.com

Paul Morris

For full biographical listings, see the Martindale-Hubbell Law Directory

PODHURST, ORSECK, JOSEFSBERG, EATON, MEADOW, OLIN & PERWIN, P.A. (AV)

Suite 800 City National Bank Building, 25 West Flagler Street, 33130-1780
Telephone: 305-358-2800; Fort Lauderdale: 954-463-4346
Fax: 305-358-2382
Email: Info@podhurst.com *URL:* http://www.wwdir.com/podhurst.html

Joel D. Eaton | Joel S. Perwin

References: City National Bank of Miami; Mellon United National Bank of Miami.

For Complete List of Firm Personnel, See General Section

For full biographical listings, see the Martindale-Hubbell Law Directory

Miami—Continued

WILLIAM L. RICHEY, P.A. (AV)

One Biscayne Tower, 2 South Biscayne Boulevard, Suite 3400, 33131-1897
Telephone: 305-372-8808
Fax: 305-372-3669
Email: wlr@richeylaw.com *URL:* http://www.lawyers.com/richeylaw
Palm City, Florida Office: 5501 S.W. Sunshine Farms Way, 34990-5696.
Telephone: 561-220-0558.
Fax: 305-372-3669.

William L. Richey (Also Of Counsel to Gunster, Yoakley, Valdes-Fauli & Stewart, P.A., Miami, Florida and Stuart, Florida)

For full biographical listings, see the Martindale-Hubbell Law Directory

ROBBINS, TUNKEY, ROSS, AMSEL, RABEN & WAXMAN, P.A. (AV)

2250 Southwest Third Avenue, Fourth Floor, 33129
Telephone: Dade County 305-858-9550; Broward County 954-522-6244 (All Telephones Open 24 Hours); 1-800-226-9550
Fax: 305-858-7491
Email: RTR2250@AOL.COM *URL:* http://www.crimlawfirm.com

Frederick S. Robbins
William R. Tunkey
Alan S. Ross
Robert G. Amsel
David Raben
Benjamin S. Waxman

Mark R. Eiglarsh
Marco A. Vazquez (1968-1995)

Reference: Mellon United National Bank, Miami, Florida.

For full biographical listings, see the Martindale-Hubbell Law Directory

RUSSO APPELLATE FIRM, P.A. (AV)

Appellate Law Center, 6101 Southwest 76th Street, 33143
Telephone: 305-666-4660
Fax: 305-666-4470
Email: appeals@russoappeals.com

Elizabeth K. Russo

Stuart Barry Yanofsky
Katie G. Burnett

For full biographical listings, see the Martindale-Hubbell Law Directory

SAMS & LISTER, P.A. (AV)

73255 West 63 Avenue, Suite 201, 33143
Telephone: 305-740-5401
Fax: 305-740-5425

Murray Sams, Jr.
David P. Lister

Arthur B. Stark

For full biographical listings, see the Martindale-Hubbell Law Directory

JEFFREY S. WEINER, P.A. (AV)

Two Datran Center Nineteenth Floor, Suite 1910, 9130 South Dadeland Boulevard, 33156-7858
Telephone: 305 670-9939
Fax: 305 670-9299
Email: lawfirm@jeffweiner.com
Boca Raton, Florida Office: Mizner Park. 327 Plaza Real, Suite 215, 33432.

Jeffrey S. Weiner

Mycki L. Ratzan
Michael B. Cohen
Jason M. Wandner

LEGAL SUPPORT PERSONNEL
Duchess Weiner (Law Office Administrator)

For full biographical listings, see the Martindale-Hubbell Law Directory

NORTH MIAMI BEACH, Dade Co.

BECKHAM & BECKHAM, P.A. (AV)

1550 North East Miami Gardens Drive Suite 504, 33179
Telephone: 305-957-3900
Fax: 305-940-8706
Email: beckhamlaw@aol.com

Pamela Beckham
Eugene G. Beckham
Robert J. Beckham, Jr.

For full biographical listings, see the Martindale-Hubbell Law Directory

*ORLANDO,** Orange Co.

HILL, REIS, ADAMS, HALL & SCHIEFFELIN, P.A. (AV)

1417 East Concord Street, 32803
Telephone: 407-896-0425
Fax: 407-896-9236
Email: mainbox@hrahs.com

Gregory F. Reis
Thomas L. Schieffelin, Jr.
William W. Large
Matthew P. Bartolomei

Representative Clients: The Florida Hospital Trust Fund; The Florida Hospital Excess Trust Fund; Florida Hospital Workers Compensation/Self Insurance Trust Fund; Bartow Memorial Hospital; Bay Medical Center; Brooksville Regional Hospital; Cape Canaveral Hospital; Cape Coral Hospital; Desoto Memorial Hospital.

For Complete List of Firm Personnel, See General Section

For full biographical listings, see the Martindale-Hubbell Law Directory

LITCHFORD & CHRISTOPHER, PROFESSIONAL ASSOCIATION (AV)

NationsBank Center, Suite 2200, 390 North Orange Avenue, P.O. Box 1549, 32802
Telephone: 407-422-6600
Telecopier: 407-841-0325
Email: lawfirm@litchris.com *URL:* http://www.litchris.com

Hal K. Litchford
Donald E. Christopher
Mark Lang
Brian D. DeGailler
David G. Lerner
Alan B. Taylor

Scott K. Lippman
G. Steven Fender
Jill Barron Dugger
Susan E. Sewell
Joanne Reed Day

Reference: Citrus Bank.

For full biographical listings, see the Martindale-Hubbell Law Directory

KENNETH L. MANN, P.A. (AV)

105 East Robinson Street, Suite 540, P.O. Box 551, 32802-0551
Telephone: 407-422-0006
Fax: 407-841-9516
Email: reasonablemann@worldnet.att.net *URL:* http://www.KenMannlaw.com

Kenneth L. Mann

For full biographical listings, see the Martindale-Hubbell Law Directory

LAW OFFICE OF KENTON V. SANDS (AV)

250 North Orange Avenue, Suite 1700-Penthouse, 32801
Telephone: 407-423-3421
Fax: 407-423-4735
Email: ksands@bellsouth.net *URL:* http://www.lawyers.com/sandslaw

For full biographical listings, see the Martindale-Hubbell Law Directory

PALM BEACH GARDENS, Palm Beach Co.

MARJORIE GADARIAN GRAHAM, P.A. (AV)

Suite D 129, 11211 Prosperity Farms Road, 33410
Telephone: 561-775-1204
Fax: 561-624-4460
Email: mgg@appeal.com

Marjorie Gadarian Graham

For full biographical listings, see the Martindale-Hubbell Law Directory

*TALLAHASSEE,** Leon Co.

MCFARLAIN, WILEY, CASSEDY & JONES, PROFESSIONAL ASSOCIATION (AV)

215 South Monroe Street, Suite 600, P.O. Box 2174, 32316-2174
Telephone: 850-222-2107
Telecopier: 850-222-8475
Email: firm@mcfarlain.com *URL:* http://www.mcfarlain.com

Richard C. McFarlain
William B. Wiley
Douglas P. Jones
Charles A. Stampelos
H. Darrell White, Jr.
Christopher Barkas
Harold R. Mardenborough, Jr.
Terrell C. Madigan

Robert A. McNeely
P. David Brannon

LEGAL SUPPORT PERSONNEL
Diane L. Doll (Office Manager)

For full biographical listings, see the Martindale-Hubbell Law Directory

*TAMPA,** Hillsborough Co.

KYNES, MARKMAN & FELMAN, P.A. (AV)

P.O. Box 3396, 33601
Telephone: 813-229-1118
Facsimile: 813-221-6750

James H. Kynes (1953-1993)
Stuart C. Markman
James E. Felman
Susan H. Freemon

For full biographical listings, see the Martindale-Hubbell Law Directory

MANEY, DAMSKER & JONES, P.A. (AV)

606 Madison Street, P.O. Box 172009, 33672-0009
Telephone: 813-228-7371
Fax: 813-223-4846

David A. Maney
Lee S. Damsker
Karen Lynn Jones

Lorena L. Kiely
Patricia F. Kuhlman
Tarya A. Tribble

For full biographical listings, see the Martindale-Hubbell Law Directory

ROBERT P. POLLI, P.A. (AV)

Barnett Bank Plaza, 101 East Kennedy Boulevard, Suite 1265, 33602
Telephone: 813-222-8350
Fax: Available Upon Request

Robert P. Polli

For full biographical listings, see the Martindale-Hubbell Law Directory

SCHROPP, BUELL & ELLIGETT, PROFESSIONAL ASSOCIATION (AV)

401 East Jackson Street, Suite 2600, 33602-5226
Telephone: 813-221-2600
Fax: 813-221-1760
Email: SBELaw@aol.com

Charles P. Schropp
Mark P. Buell
Raymond T. Elligett, Jr.

Shirley Thompson Faircloth
Amy S. Farrior
Donna S. Koch

For full biographical listings, see the Martindale-Hubbell Law Directory

VAKA, LARSON & JOHNSON, P.L. (AV)

One Harbour Place, 777 South Harbour Island Blvd., Suite 300, 33602-5729
Telephone: 813-228-6688
Fax: 813-228-6699
Email: vljlaw@idnsi.net

George A. Vaka
Daniel A. Larson
Marc D. Johnson

For full biographical listings, see the Martindale-Hubbell Law Directory

*WEST PALM BEACH,** Palm Beach Co.

BEASLEY, LEACOCK & HAUSER, P.A. (AV)

Flagler Center, Suite 1400, 505 South Flagler Drive, 33401
Telephone: 561-835-0900
Fax: 561-835-0939
Email: BLH@BLHlaw.com *URL:* http://BLHlaw.com

James W. Beasley, Jr.
David Leacock
Robert J. Hauser

Ronald B. Hauser

For full biographical listings, see the Martindale-Hubbell Law Directory

CARUSO, BURLINGTON, BOHN & COMPIANI, P.A. (AV)

Suite 3A Barristers Building, 1615 Forum Place, 33401
Telephone: 561-686-8010
Fax: 561-686-8663

Edna L. Caruso
Philip M. Burlington
Russell S. Bohn
Barbara J. Compiani

For full biographical listings, see the Martindale-Hubbell Law Directory

JANE KREUSLER-WALSH, P.A. (AV)

Suite 503 Flagler Center, 501 South Flagler Drive, 33401
Telephone: 561-659-5455
Fax: 561-820-8762
Email: jkwals@worldnet.att.net

(See Next Column)

Jane Kreusler-Walsh

For full biographical listings, see the Martindale-Hubbell Law Directory

RICHARD A. KUPFER, P.A. (AV)

5725 Corporate Way, Suite 106, 33407
Telephone: 561-684-8600
Fax: 561-684-1508

Richard A. Kupfer

LEGAL SUPPORT PERSONNEL

Jan M. Setchell

For full biographical listings, see the Martindale-Hubbell Law Directory

GEORGIA

*ATLANTA,** Fulton Co.

C. MICHAEL ABBOTT, P.C. (AV)

The Grand, 75 Fourteenth Street, Suite 2500, 30309-3644
Telephone: 404-885-1994
Fax: 404-885-1677
Email: cmabbott@mindspring.com

Michael Abbott

For full biographical listings, see the Martindale-Hubbell Law Directory

JAKE ARBES (AV)

2300 Harris Tower, 233 Peachtree Street, N.E., 30303
Telephone: 404-522-1980
FAX: 404-588-0648
Email: arbesjak@avana.net

For full biographical listings, see the Martindale-Hubbell Law Directory

BONDURANT, MIXSON & ELMORE, LLP (AV)

1201 W. Peachtree Street Suite 3900, 30309
Telephone: 404-881-4100
Fax: 404-881-4111
URL: http://www.bondurant-mixson.com

MEMBERS OF FIRM

Emmet J. Bondurant II
H. Lamar Mixson
M. Jerome Elmore
Edward B. Krugman
Jeffrey O. Bramlett
John E. Floyd
Michael B. Terry
P. Richard Game
Jill A. Pryor
J. Scott McClain

Representative Clients: American Dairy Queen Corp.; Avon Products, Inc.; Bottlers of Coca-Cola, U.S.A.; Blue Circle of America; Delta Air Lines, Inc.; Fina Oil and Chemical Company; Four M Corporation; Penske Motorsports; Queen Carpets, Inc.; Ticketmaster Southeast.

For full biographical listings, see the Martindale-Hubbell Law Directory

GARLAND, SAMUEL & LOEB, P.C. (AV)

3151 Maple Drive, N.E., 30305
Telephone: 404-262-2225
Fax: 404-365-5041
Email: triallaw@atlanta.com

Edward T. M. Garland
Donald F. Samuel
Robin N. Loeb

For full biographical listings, see the Martindale-Hubbell Law Directory

LONG ALDRIDGE & NORMAN LLP (AV)

A Limited Liability Partnership including Professional Corporations
Suite 5300, 303 Peachtree Street, 30308
Telephone: 404-527-4000
Telecopier: 404-527-4198
Email: atlanta@lanlaw.com *URL:* http://www.lanlaw.com
Washington, D.C. Office: Suite 600, 701 Pennsylvania Avenue, N.W., 20004.
Telephone: 202-624-1200.
FAX: 202-624-1298.

MEMBERS OF FIRM

David L. Balser
Phillip A. Bradley
Bruce P. Brown
Deborah S. Ebel
J. James Johnson
Barbara A. McIntyre
Carl W. Mullis, III
James J. Thomas II
John L. Watkins
Terry R. Weiss

(See Next Column)

LONG ALDRIDGE & NORMAN LLP, *Atlanta—Continued*

SENIOR COUNSEL

F. T. Davis, Jr., (P.C.)

For Complete List of Firm Personnel, See General Section

For full biographical listings, see the Martindale-Hubbell Law Directory

*AUGUSTA,** Richmond Co.

GARRETT & GILLIARD (AV)

SunTrust Bank Building, 801 Broad Street, Suite 1001, 30901
Telephone: 706-724-1896
Fax: 706-724-0047
Email: g+g313@GroupZ.net *URL:* http://www.lawyers.com/g&glaw

MEMBERS OF FIRM

Michael C. Garrett
Kirk Emerson Gilliard

LEGAL SUPPORT PERSONNEL

Becky Padgett (Paralegal)

For full biographical listings, see the Martindale-Hubbell Law Directory

HAWAII

*HONOLULU,** Honolulu Co.

CARLSMITH BALL (AV)

A Partnership including Law Corporations
Suite 2200, Pacific Tower, 1001 Bishop Street, P.O. Box 656, 96809-3402
Telephone: 808-523-2500
Fax: 808-523-0842
Email: execdirector@carlsmith.com *URL:* http://www.carlsmith.com
Kapolei, Hawaii Office: Suite 318, Kapolei Building, 1001 Kamokila Boulevard, 96707.
Telephone: 808-523-2500.
Fax: 808-674-0850.
Wailuku, Maui Hawaii Office: Suite 400, One Main Plaza, 2200 Main Street, P.O. Box 1086, 96793-1086.
Telephone: 808-242-4535.
Fax: 808-244-4974.
Kailua-Kona, Hawaii Office: Suite 209, 75-1000 Henry Street, 96740.
Telephone: 808-329-6464.
Fax: 808-329-9450.
Hilo, Hawaii Office: 121 Waianuenue Avenue, P.O. Box 686, 96721-0686.
Telephone: 808-935-6644.
Fax: 808-935-7975.
Hagatna, Guam Office: Suite 401, Bank of Hawaii Building, 134 West Soledad Avenue, P.O. Box BF, 96932-5027.
Telephone: 671-472-6813.
Fax: 671-477-4375.
Telex: 721-6445 CWCMI GM.
Saipan, Commonwealth of the Northern Mariana Islands Office: Carlsmith Building, Capitol Hill, P.O. Box 5241, 96950-5241.
Telephone: 670-322-3455.
Fax: 670-322-3368.
Los Angeles, California Office: 9th Floor, 444 South Flower Street, 90071-2901.
Telephone: 213-955-1200.
Fax: 213-623-0032.
Washington, D.C. Office: Suite 300, 1201 Pennsylvania Avenue, N.W., 20004-2401.
Telephone: 202-628-2228.
Fax: 202-628-2071.
Mexico City, Mexico Office: Carlsmith Ball, Sierra Nevada 119, Lomas de Chapultepec, 11000 Mexico, D.F.
Telephone: 52-5-520-8514, 52-5-520-8757.
Fax: 52-5-540-1545.
Mexico, D.F. Office of Carlsmith Ball, S.C. (Authorized to practice as foreign legal consultants in Mexico): Sierra Nevada 119, Lomas de Chapultepec, 11000 Mexico, D.F.
Telephone: 52-5-520-8514, 52-5-520-8757.
Fax: 52-5-540-1545.

MEMBERS OF FIRM

John F. Biehl (Resident at Saipan Office)
Edward E. Case
Gary G. Grimmer

For Complete List of Firm Personnel, See General Section

For full biographical listings, see the Martindale-Hubbell Law Directory

ROBBINS & RHODES ATTORNEYS AT LAW, A LAW CORPORATION (AV)

Suite 2200 Davies Pacific Center, 841 Bishop Street, 96813
Telephone: 808-524-2355
Fax: 808-526-0290
Email: robbinsrhodes@lava.net

(See Next Column)

Kenneth S. Robbins

Representative Clients: Argonaut Insurance Co.; City and County of Honolulu; County of Maui; Guaranty National Insurance Co.; State of Hawaii; TIG Insurance Co.; Truck Insurance Exchange; Westchester Insurance Co.

For full biographical listings, see the Martindale-Hubbell Law Directory

IDAHO

*POCATELLO,** Bannock Co.

MERRILL & MERRILL, CHARTERED (AV)

Key Bank Building, P.O. Box 991, 83204
Telephone: 208-232-2286
Fax: 208-232-2499
Email: mmlaw@ida.net

Stephen S. Dunn
D. Russell Wight
David C. Nye
Kent L. Hawkins

Representative Clients: Farm Bureau Mutual Insurance Co. of Idaho; J.R. Simplot Co.; Fibreboard Corporation; Owens-Illinois, Inc.; Pittsburgh Corning Corporation; Travelers Insurance Co.; E.I. DuPont.

For Complete List of Firm Personnel, See General Section

For full biographical listings, see the Martindale-Hubbell Law Directory

ILLINOIS

*CHICAGO,** Cook Co.

ALLAN A. ACKERMAN, P.C. (AV)

2000 North Clifton Avenue, 60614-4120
Telephone: 312-332-2891; 332-2863
Fax: 773-871-3304
Email: doctrips@aol.com

Allan A. Ackerman

For full biographical listings, see the Martindale-Hubbell Law Directory

ARONBERG GOLDGEHN DAVIS & GARMISA (AV)

Suite 3000 One IBM Plaza, 60611
Telephone: 312-828-9600
Telecopier: 312-828-9635
Email: agdglaw@aol.com
Schaumberg, Illinois Office: 1901 North Roselle Road, Suite 800, 60195.
Telephone: 847-985-4060.

MEMBERS OF FIRM

Christopher J. Bannon
Mitchell S. Goldgehn
James J. Hickey
Nathan H. Lichtenstein
Marc W. O'Brien
Tami J. Reding-Brubaker
John M. Riccione
David H. Sachs
James A. Smith
Robert N. Sodikoff
Andrew S. Williams

ASSOCIATES

Lisa J. Brodsky
Howard J. Fishman
Paul A. Greenberg
William J. Serritella, Jr.

For Complete List of Firm Personnel, See General Section

For full biographical listings, see the Martindale-Hubbell Law Directory

CONNELLY & SCHROEDER (AV)

One North Franklin Street, Suite 1200, 60606-3421
Telephone: 312-251-9600
Fax: 312-251-9601
Geneva, Illinois Office: 1250 Executive Place, Suite 201.
Telephone: 630-232-6440.
FAX: 630-232-6450

MEMBERS OF FIRM

Michael P. Connelly
Raymond E. Stachnik
Mary Lisa Kamins

ASSOCIATES

Michelle L. Adams (Resident, Geneva Office)
Charina de los Reyes
Carolyn A. Schroeder (Resident, Geneva)

For full biographical listings, see the Martindale-Hubbell Law Directory

Chicago—Continued

DOWD & DOWD, LTD. (AV)

Suite 1000, 55 West Wacker Drive, 60601
Telephone: 312-704-4400
Telecopier: 312-704-4500
Lake Geneva, Wisconsin Office: P.O. Box 356.
Telephone: 414-275-0057.
Telecopier: 414-275-6786.
Des Plaines Office: 575 Lee Street.
Telephone: 847-827-5117.
Telecopier: 847-827-0076.

Joseph V. Dowd
Michael E. Dowd (1957-1996)
Kenneth Gurber
Patrick C. Dowd
Robert J. Golden
Patrick J. Ruberry
John M. McAndrews
Anthony R. Rutkowski

Daniel J. Arnett
S. Robert Depke
Beth S. Dolehide
David J. Farina
William P. Heffernan
Teri L. Meade
Matthew J Murphy
Gregory M. Norgle
Michael G. Patrizio
Michael W. Van Zalingen
Karen W. Worsek

LEGAL SUPPORT PERSONNEL

Carol Barnes

OF COUNSEL

Guenther Ahlf
Tobias G. Barry
John A. Garrity, III
Peter F. Higgins
Daniel C. McKay
Sam L. Miller
Joel S. Ostrow
Norman E. Samelson

Representative Clients: Gallagher Bassett Services, Inc.; Kemper National Insurance Companies; Schneider National Carriers; Scottsdale Insurance Company; Swift Transportation; Acceptance Insurance Companies; AI Transportation; Borg Warner Protective Services; Clarendon National Insurance Company; Landstar Inway, Inc.
Reference: American National Bank in Chicago.

For full biographical listings, see the Martindale-Hubbell Law Directory

NORMAN J. LERUM (AV)

Suite 2100, 100 West Monroe Street, 60603
Telephone: 312-782-1087
Facsimile: 312-332-6020
Email: lerum@martindalemail.com *URL:* http://www.lawyers.com/lerumlaw

For full biographical listings, see the Martindale-Hubbell Law Directory

METZGER & ASSOCIATES, LTD. (AV)

39 South La Salle Street Suite 808, 60603
Telephone: 312-782-7728
Fax: 312-782-7732
Email: dlfmetzger@mindspring.com

Donald L. F. Metzger

For full biographical listings, see the Martindale-Hubbell Law Directory

NOLAN LAW GROUP (AV)

One North La Salle Street, 35th Floor, 60602
Telephone: 312-372-5400
Toll Free: 888-372-3870
Facsimile: 312-372-0558
Email: dnolan1@ix.netcom.com

Donald J. Nolan
Albert E. Durkin, Jr.
William J. Jovan
Floyd A. Wisner
James H. Lawlor, III
Thomas P. Routh
James A. Santucci
Todd R. Mcquiston

Laura L. Ruhl

For full biographical listings, see the Martindale-Hubbell Law Directory

DAVID A. NOVOSELSKY & ASSOCIATES (AV)

120 North La Salle Street, Suite 1400, 60602-2401
Telephone: 312-346-8930
Fax: 312-346-9453
Email: mail@novoselsky.com *URL:* http://www.novoselsky.com

David A. Novoselsky

Linda A Bryceland
Kevin S. Besetzny
Eduard Adam Glavinskas

OF COUNSEL

Margarita T. Kulys

For full biographical listings, see the Martindale-Hubbell Law Directory

SCHWARTZBERG, BARNETT & COHEN (AV)

55 West Monroe Street, 2400 Xerox Centre, 60603-5040
Telephone: 312-726-3555
Fax: 312-726-6299
Cable Address: "Justice"
Email: sb&c@twty.chi.il.us

MEMBERS OF FIRM

Ralph M. Schwartzberg (1939-1975)
Mark T. Barnett (1939-1970)
Hugh J. Schwartzberg
Benjamin H. Cohen

For full biographical listings, see the Martindale-Hubbell Law Directory

TORSHEN, SPREYER, GARMISA & SLOBIG, LTD. (AV)

105 West Adams Street, Suite 3200, 60603
Telephone: 312-372-9282
Fax: 312-372-7914
Email: torshen@ais.net

Jerome H. Torshen
Abigail Kay Spreyer
James K. Genden
Zoran Dragutinovich
Steven P. Garmisa
Robert J. Slobig
Thomas J. Ramsdell
Michael P. Bregenzer

Marlaine J. McVisk

For full biographical listings, see the Martindale-Hubbell Law Directory

LAW OFFICES OF RUTH E. VANDEMARK (AV)

Suite 2200, 225 West Washington Street, 60606
Telephone: 312-419-7162
Fax: 312-419-7285
Email: revlaw@msn.com

ASSOCIATE

Ralph N. Glader

For full biographical listings, see the Martindale-Hubbell Law Directory

WILDMAN, HARROLD, ALLEN & DIXON (AV)

225 West Wacker Drive, 30th Floor, 60606-1229
Telephone: 312-201-2000
Fax: 312-201-2555
Email: hennessy@whad.com *URL:* http://www.whad.com
Aurora, Illinois Office: 1961 W. Downer Place.
Telephone: 630-892-7021.
Fax: 630-892-7158.
Waukegan, Illinois Office: 404 West Water, P. O. Box 890.
Telephone: 847-625-5550.
Fax: 847-625-5555.
Lisle, Illinois Office: 4300 Commerce Court, Suite 320.
Telephone: 630-955-0555.
Fax: 630-955-0662
Toronto, Ontario correspondent Office: Keel Cottrelle. 36 Toronto Street, Suite 920.
Telephone: 416-367-2900.
Telefax: 416-367-2791.
Telex: 062-18660.

MEMBERS OF FIRM

Ira C. Feldman
Anthony G. Hopp
Elizabeth Keiley
Thomas M. Lynch
Mark P. Miller
Richard D. Murphy Jr.
David F. Pardys (Waukegan Office)
Lisa S. Simmons
Linda E. Spring (Waukegan Office)
Robert A. Strelecky (Lisle Office)
James B. Vogts

OF COUNSEL

Thomas D. Allen

David J. Chroust (Lisle Office)
Leo P. Dombrowski
Lawrence W. Falbe
James C. James, III (Aurora Office)
Barbara M. Prohaska (Lisle Office)
Kevin B. Reid
Joleen S. Willis

For full biographical listings, see the Martindale-Hubbell Law Directory

YELTON & KEHL, LTD. (AV)

One East Wacker Drive Suite 3720, 60601
Telephone: 312-832-9255
Fax: 312-832-9277
URL: http://www.yeltonkehl.com

Robert C. Yelton III
Jeffrey Edward Kehl

Ryan J. Harrington
Karen M. Talty

OF COUNSEL

Joel S. Ostrow

For full biographical listings, see the Martindale-Hubbell Law Directory

LA SALLE, La Salle Co.

Herbolsheimer, Lannon, Henson, Duncan and Reagan, P.C. (AV)

State Bank Building, Suite 400, 654 First Street, P.O. Box 539, 61301
Telephone: 815-223-0111
Fax: 815-223-5829
Ottawa, Illinois Office: First Federal Savings Bank Building, 633 LaSalle Street, Suite 409.
Telephone: 815-434-1400.
Fax: 815-434-2423.

George L. Herbolsheimer (1911-1992)
R. James Lannon, Jr.
T. Donald Henson
John S. Duncan, III
Michael T. Reagan (Resident, Ottawa Office)
Douglas A. Gift
Gary R. Eiten

Karen C. Eiten
Michael C. Jansz (Resident, Ottawa Office)
Jill W. Klein
Lawrence M. Kaschak

Attorneys for: Aetna Insurance Group; St. Paul Fire and Marine Insurance Co.; State Farm Insurance Co.; La Salle State Bank; The Daily News Tribune Company, La Salle; Eureka Savings Bank; Illinois Valley Community Hospital; Community Hospital of Ottawa; Commonwealth Edison, Co.; United States Fidelity & Guaranty, Co.

For full biographical listings, see the Martindale-Hubbell Law Directory

INDIANA

*EVANSVILLE,** Vanderburgh Co.

Bowers, Harrison, Kent & Miller, LLP (AV)

25 N.W. Riverside Drive, P.O. Box 1287, 47706-1287
Telephone: 812-426-1231
Fax: 812-464-3676
Email: BOWERS,HARRISON,KENT&MILLER,LLP@BHKM.COM
URL: http://WWW.BHKM.COM

MEMBERS OF FIRM

F. Wesley Bowers
David V. Miller
George C. Barnett, Jr.
David E. Gray
Joseph H. Harrison, Jr.

Division Counsel in Indiana for: Southern Railway Co.
Representative Clients: Permanent Federal Savings Bank; Citizens Realty & Insurance, Inc.

For Complete List of Firm Personnel, See General Section

For full biographical listings, see the Martindale-Hubbell Law Directory

Fine & Hatfield, A Professional Corporation (AV)

520 N.W. Second Street, P.O. Box 779, 47705-0779
Telephone: 812-425-3592
Telecopier: 812-421-4269
Email: Fine@Fine-Hatfield.com *URL:* http://www.Fine-Hatfield.com

Thomas H. Bryan
Danny E. Glass
Todd I. Glass

A List of Representative Clients Furnished Upon Request.

For full biographical listings, see the Martindale-Hubbell Law Directory

*INDIANAPOLIS,** Marion Co.

McTurnan & Turner (AV)

2400 Market Tower, 10 West Market Street, 46204
Telephone: 317-464-8181
Telecopier: 317-464-8131

Lee B. McTurnan
Wayne C. Turner
Jackie M. Bennett, Jr.
Jacqueline Bowman Ponder
Steven M. Badger
John F. McCauley

For full biographical listings, see the Martindale-Hubbell Law Directory

*LAFAYETTE,** Tippecanoe Co.

Ball, Eggleston, Bumbleburg, McBride, Walkey & Stapleton, PC (AV)

810 Bank One Building, P.O. Box 1535, 47902-1535
Telephone: 765-742-9046
Fax: 765-742-1966
Email: info@ball-law.com

(See Next Column)

Cable G. Ball (1904-1981)
Owen Crook (1908-1977)
Warren N. Eggleston (1923-1991)
Joseph T. Bumbleburg
John K. McBride
Jack L. Walkey
Michael J. Stapleton
Jeffrey J. Newell
James T. Hodson
Brian Wade Walker
Cheryl M. Knodle
Randy J. Williams
Brenda Mithoefer Clapper

General Counsel for: The Lafayette Union Railway Co.
Representative Clients: Farmers Insurance Group; General Accident Fire & Life Assurance Corp.; City of Lafayette Board of Parks and Recreation; West Lafayette Community School Corp.; Travelers Insurance Co.; Trustees, West Lafayette Public Library; Town of Dayton, Indiana.

For full biographical listings, see the Martindale-Hubbell Law Directory

Stuart & Branigin (AV)

The Life Building, 300 Main Street, Suite 800, P.O. Box 1010, 47902-1010
Telephone: 765-423-1561
Telecopier: 765-742-8175
Email: sb@stuartlaw.com *URL:* http://www.stuartlaw.com
Indianapolis, Indiana Office: Suite 1401, 8888 Keystone Crossing, 46240.
Telephone: 317-574-7245.
Fax: 317-574-7050.

MEMBERS OF FIRM

Allison Ellsworth Stuart (1886-1950)
Roger D. Branigin (1902-1975)
Roger D. Branigin, Jr.
Thomas L. Ryan
Thomas R. McCully
Larry R. Fisher
Nina B. Kirkpatrick
Mark Lillianfeld
Stephen R. Pennell
Anthony S. Benton
Erik D. Spykman
William E. Emerick
John C. Duffey
Bruce McSpadden
Mark E. DeYoung
Thomas B. Parent
Laura L. Bowker
Kevin D. Nicoson
Susan K. Roberts
John M. Stuckey
Deborah B. Trice
William P. Kealey
David A. Starkweather
Geoffrey L. Blazi

SENIOR COUNSEL

Russell H. Hart

COUNSEL

John F. Bodle
James V. McGlone

ASSOCIATES

Elizabeth B. Searle
Marianne Mitten Owen
David A. Locke
Karen Orr McClure
Ann Marie Waldron
Barry L. Loftus

General Counsel for: The Lafayette Life Insurance Co.; INB National Bank, N.W.; Lafayette Home Hospital, Inc.
State Counsel for: Norfolk & Western Railway Co.
Mr. Ryan is Counsel to: The Trustees of Purdue University.
Representative Clients: Aluminum Company of America; Liberty Mutual Insurance Group.

For full biographical listings, see the Martindale-Hubbell Law Directory

MERRILLVILLE, Lake Co.

Marce Gonzalez, Jr. (AV)

Connecticut Center, 9120 Connecticut, Suite D, 46410
Telephone: 219-769-3030
FAX: 219-769-3031

For full biographical listings, see the Martindale-Hubbell Law Directory

IOWA

*DES MOINES,** Polk Co.

Finley, Alt, Smith, Scharnberg, Craig, Hilmes & Gaffney, P.C. (AV)

604 Locust Street, Fourth Floor Equitable Building, 50309
Telephone: 515-288-0145
Telecopier: 515-288-2724

Kerry A. Finley
V. Glenn Goodwin, Jr.

Representative Clients: ALAS; American Society of Composers, Authors and Publishers; Equitable Life Assurance Society of the U.S.; Federated Insurance Co.; Meredith Corp.
Iowa Attorneys for: Midwest Medical Insurance Co.
District Attorneys for: Norfolk & Southern Railroad; Soo Line Railroad Company.

For Complete List of Firm Personnel, See General Section

For full biographical listings, see the Martindale-Hubbell Law Directory

Des Moines—Continued

The Rosenberg Law Firm (AV)

1010 Insurance Exchange Building, 505 Fifth Avenue, 50309
Telephone: 515-243-7600
Email: bdr@worldnet.att.net

MEMBERS OF FIRM

Raymond Rosenberg
Dean A. Stowers
Brent D. Rosenberg

Reference: Firstar Bank, Des Moines, Iowa.

For full biographical listings, see the Martindale-Hubbell Law Directory

KANSAS

*TOPEKA,** Shawnee Co.

Fisher, Patterson, Sayler & Smith, L.L.P. (AV)

3550 S.W. 5th Street, P.O. Box 949, 66601
Telephone: 785-232-7761
Fax: 785-232-6604
Email: fpss@cjnetworks.com
Overland Park, Kansas Office: 11050 Roe Avenue, Suite 210, 66211.
Telephone: 913-339-6757.
Fax: 913-339-6187.

MEMBERS OF FIRM

Donald Patterson
Edwin Dudley Smith (Resident, Overland Park Office)
Larry G. Pepperdine
James P. Nordstrom
Justice B. King
J. Steven Pigg
Steve R. Fabert
Ronald J. Laskowski
Michael K. Seck (Resident, Overland Park Office)
David P. Madden (Resident, Overland Park Office)
Steven K. Johnson
Kristine A. Larscheid

ASSOCIATES

Billy E. Newman
David R. Cooper
Kelly A. Feyh (Resident, Overland Park Office)
Jennifer R. Rose (Resident, Overland Park Office)

OF COUNSEL

David H. Fisher

RETIRED

Charles Keith Sayler (Retired)

Representative Clients: Gage Shopping Center, Inc.; Fireman's Fund-American Insurance Cos.; United States Fidelity and Guaranty Co.; The Procter & Gamble Company; American Cyanamid Company; Commercial Union Insurance Companies; National Casualty; The Hartford; Berkshire Hathaway Companies.

For full biographical listings, see the Martindale-Hubbell Law Directory

KENTUCKY

COVINGTON, Kenton Co.

Robert E. Sanders and Associates, P.S.C. (AV)

The Charles H. Fisk House, 1017 Russell Street, 41011-3052
Telephone: 606-491-3000
Fax: 606-655-4642
Email: resanders@worldnet.att.net

Robert E. Sanders

Jeffrey M. Sanders
J. Pierre Tismo
Delana S. Pierce

LEGAL SUPPORT PERSONNEL

Shirley L. Sanders
Sandra A. Sturgeon
Sheila D. Rachal

For full biographical listings, see the Martindale-Hubbell Law Directory

*DANVILLE,** Boyle Co.

Law Offices of Kent Masterson Brown (AV)

304 West Main Street, Suite 201, 40422
Telephone: 606-238-7383
Fax: 606-238-7442
Email: kmb@usa.net

ASSOCIATE

Christopher J. Shaughnessy

For full biographical listings, see the Martindale-Hubbell Law Directory

*LEXINGTON,** Fayette Co.

Landrum & Shouse (AV)

106 West Vine Street, P.O. Box 951, 40588-0951
Telephone: 606-255-2424
Facsimile: 606-233-0308
Louisville, Kentucky Office: Suite 1900, 220 West Main Street, 40202-2119.
Telephone: 502-589-7616.
Facsimile: 502-589-2119.

MEMBERS OF FIRM

John H. Burrus
William C. Shouse
Pierce W. Hamblin
Mark L. Moseley
Leslie Patterson Vose
John R. Martin, Jr. (Resident, Louisville Office)
Larry C. Deener
Sandra Mendez Dawahare
Mark J. Hinkel
John Garry McNeill
R. Kent Westberry (Resident, Louisville Office)
Jane Durkin Samuel
Douglas L. Hoots, CPCU
Dave Whalin (Resident, Louisville Office)
Daniel E. Murner

ASSOCIATES

Stephen R. Chappell
Estill D. Banks, II
Robert Thaddeus (Thad) Keal (Resident, Louisville Office)
Sun S. Choy (Resident, Louisville Office)
Melanie Lee Straw-Boone (Resident, Louisville Office)
Carolyn C. Zerga
David W. Zahniser
Kathleen Campbell Deskins
Rheanne Dodson Falkner (Resident, Louisville Office)
Shannon M. Naish
Bradley C. Hooks
Alex L. Scutchfield

OF COUNSEL

Weldon Shouse
Thomas M. Cooper

Representative Clients: State Auto Insurance Co.; Northland Insurance Co.; Ohio Casualty Insurance; Safeco Insurance; Scottsdale Insurance Co.; Cincinnati Insurance Co.; Crawford & Co.; CSX Transportation, Inc.; Lexington-Fayette Urban County Airport; American States Insurance Co.

For full biographical listings, see the Martindale-Hubbell Law Directory

*LOUISVILLE,** Jefferson Co.

Morgan & Pottinger, P.S.C. (AV)

601 West Main Street, 40202
Telephone: 502-589-2780
Telecopier: 502-585-3498
URL: http://www.morganandpottinger.com
Lexington, Kentucky Office: 133 West Short Street.
Telephone: 606-253-1900.
Telecopier: 606-255-2038.
New Albany, Indiana Office: 120 East Market Street.
Telephone: 812-948-0008.
Telecopier: 812-944-6215.

Patrick E. Morgan
John T. McGarvey
C. Edward Hastie (Resident, Lexington Office)
M. Deane Stewart
James I. Murray (Resident, Lexington Office)
Douglas Gene Sharp
John A. Majors
Mark J. Sandlin
Scott T. Rickman (Resident, Lexington Office)
M. Thurman Senn
Hal D. Friedman

Thomas C. Fenton
Ruthanne Q. Whitt
Garret B. Hannegan (Resident, New Albany, Indiana Office)
Diane E. Bluhm (Not admitted in KY)
Laura Kincheloe (Resident, Lexington Office)
Drayer L. Bott
John Allan Combs (Resident, Lexington Office)
Jean T. Harrod

SENIOR COUNSEL

David C. Pottinger

COUNSEL

Elmer E. Morgan
J. Jeffrey Cooke

For full biographical listings, see the Martindale-Hubbell Law Directory

LOUISIANA

*LAFAYETTE,** Lafayette Parish

Richard R. Kennedy A Professional Law Corporation (AV)

309 Polk Street, P.O. Box 3243, 70502-3243
Telephone: 318-232-1934
Fax: 318-232-9720
Email: kennedy@net-connect.net

Richard R. Kennedy

For full biographical listings, see the Martindale-Hubbell Law Directory

METAIRIE, Jefferson Parish

CAMPBELL, MCCRANIE, SISTRUNK, ANZELMO & HARDY, P.C. (AV)

3445 North Causeway Boulevard, Suite 800, 70002
Telephone: 504-831-0946
Fax: 504-831-2492

Frederick R. Campbell
Burgess E. McCranie, Jr.
Michael R. Sistrunk
Thomas P. Anzelmo
Sidney J. Hardy
Lance S. Ostendorf
Roy C. Beard
Mishthi Grace Ratnesar
Charles E. Sutton, Jr.
Isidro René DeRojas
Mark Emerson Hanna
Geoffrey J. Orr

Angela M. Bowlin
Catherine M. Williams
Colin D. Sherman
James H. Hunter
Richard Andrew Houston, III
Paxton K. Stelly
Michele Butler Prokop
Marty D. Parlipiano
Peter J. Wanek
Ken D. Brown

Representative Clients: Wal-Mart Stores, Inc.; Delchamps, Inc.; Greyhound Lines, Inc.; The Dial Corporation; Transport Insurance Company; Burger King Corporation; CNA Insurance Companies; The Louisiana Motor Vehicle Commission; Insbrok; Patent Scaffolding.

For full biographical listings, see the Martindale-Hubbell Law Directory

*NEW ORLEANS,** Orleans Parish

BARHAM & ARCENEAUX, A PROFESSIONAL LAW CORPORATION (AV)

Suite 2700, Poydras Center, 650 Poydras Street, 70130-6101
Telephone: 504-525-4400
Fax: 504-525-6378
Email: barham1@bellsouth.net

Mack E. Barham
Robert E. Arceneaux
Gail N. Wise
Jerry Barfield Jordan
Travis Louis Bourgeois

Michael W. Hill

OF COUNSEL

James A. Comiskey

For full biographical listings, see the Martindale-Hubbell Law Directory

MCGLINCHEY STAFFORD (AV)

A Professional Limited Liability Company
643 Magazine Street, 70130-3477
Telephone: 504-586-1200
Fax: 504-596-2800
TDD: (504) 596-2728
Telex: 584327
Cable Address: "MACSTAC"
Mailing Address: P.O. Box 60643, New Orleans, Louisiana, 70160-0643
Email: @mcglinchey.com *URL:* http://www.mcglinchey.com
Dallas, Texas Office: 2777 Stemmons Freeway, Suite 925, 75207-2401.
Telephone: 214-860-9700.
Fax: 214-860-9750.
Houston, Texas Office: 2727 Allen Parkway, Suite 1900, 77019.
Telephone: 713-520-1900.
Fax: 713-520-1025.
Baton Rouge, Louisiana Office: Ninth Floor, One American Place, 70825-0001.
Telephone: 504-383-9000.
Fax: 504-343-3076.
Jackson, Mississippi Office: Suite 1200, SkyTel Centre, 200 South Lamar Street, 39201.
Telephone: 601-960-8400.
Fax: 601-960-8406.
Lake Providence, Louisiana Office: 405 Morgan Street, 71254-2691.
Telephone: 318-559-1200.
Fax: 318-559-0609.
Monroe, Louisiana Office: Dean ONB Tower, 130 Desiard Street, Suite 807, 71201.
Telephone: 318-651-0807.
Fax: 318-651-0809.

ASSOCIATES

Erin Fury Parkinson
Stephanie M. Sisson

OF COUNSEL

Margaret G. Diamond

For full biographical listings, see the Martindale-Hubbell Law Directory

*SHREVEPORT,** Caddo Parish

BARLOW AND HARDTNER L.C. (AV)

Tenth Floor, Louisiana Tower, 401 Edwards Street, 71101-3289
Telephone: 318-227-1131
Telecopier: 318-227-1141
Mailing Address: P.O. Box 8, Shreveport, Louisiana, 71161-0008

Malcolm S. Murchison
Joseph L. Shea, Jr.
David R. Taggart
Michael B. Donald
Jay A. Greenleaf

Representative Clients: Central and South West Corporation; Kelley Oil Corporation; Louisiana Intrastate Gas Corp.; NorAm Energy Corp. (formerly Arkla, Inc.); Southwestern Electric Power Company; Central and South West; Panhandle Eastern Corp.; Pennzoil Producing Co.

For Complete List of Firm Personnel, See General Section

For full biographical listings, see the Martindale-Hubbell Law Directory

BLANCHARD, WALKER, O'QUIN & ROBERTS, A PROFESSIONAL LAW CORPORATION (AV)

Fourteenth Floor, Premier Bank Tower, 400 Texas Street, P.O. Drawer 1126, 71101
Telephone: 318-221-6858
Fax: 318-227-2967
Email: BWOR@BWOR.com
Bossier City, Louisiana Office: 2285 Benton Road, Suite B-201.
Telephone: 318-742-9255.
Fax: 318-742-9210.

W. Michael Adams
Paul M. Adkins

OF COUNSEL

Pike Hall, Jr.

For Complete List of Firm Personnel, See General Section

For full biographical listings, see the Martindale-Hubbell Law Directory

WILKINSON, CARMODY & GILLIAM (AV)

1700 Beck Building, 400 Travis Street, P.O. Box 1707, 71166
Telephone: 318-221-4196
Telecopier: 318-221-3705
Email: wcg1895@aol.com

MEMBERS OF FIRM

John D. Wilkinson (1867-1929)
William Scott Wilkinson (1895-1985)
Arthur R. Carmody, Jr.
Bobby S. Gilliam
Mark E. Gilliam
William Allen Haynes

Representative Clients: Farmers Insurance Group; Home Federal Savings & Loan Association of Shreveport; The Kansas City Southern Railway Co.; KTAL-TV; Lincoln National Life Insurance Co.; Mobil Oil Co.; Schumpert Medical Center; Sears, Roebuck & Co.; Southern Pacific Transportation Co.; Southwestern Electric Power Co.

For full biographical listings, see the Martindale-Hubbell Law Directory

MAINE

*PORTLAND,** Cumberland Co.

PETRUCCELLI & MARTIN, LLP (AV)

50 Monument Square, P.O. Box 9733, 04104-5033
Telephone: 207-775-0200
Telecopier: 207-775-2360
Email: info@petruccellimartin.com *URL:* http://www.petruccellimartin.com

MEMBERS OF FIRM

Gerald F. Petruccelli
Joel C. Martin
James B. Haddow

Representative Clients: Associated Aviation Underwriters; Bangor Hydro-Electric Co.; Chicago Title Insurance Co.; Chubb Insurance Co.; Cumberland Farms; Maine Medical Center; Town of Jay, Maine; Union Mutual Fire Insurance Co.

For full biographical listings, see the Martindale-Hubbell Law Directory

MARYLAND

*BALTIMORE,** (Independent City)

FUNK & BOLTON, A PROFESSIONAL ASSOCIATION (AV)

100 Light Street, Suite 1000, 21202
Telephone: 410-659-7700
Facsimile: 410-659-7773
Email: FBLAW@FBLAW.COM
Annapolis, Maryland Office: 191 Main Street, 21401.
Telephone: 410-269-1554.
Facsimile: 410-268-0612.
Chestertown, Maryland Office: 315 High Street, Suite 202, 21620.
Telephone: 410-810-1381.
Facsimile: 410-810-1383.

David M. Funk
Bryan D. Bolton
Derek B. Yarmis

Michael R. McCann
James F. Taylor
Eric B. Myers

For full biographical listings, see the Martindale-Hubbell Law Directory

MCDANIEL & MARSH (AV)

118 West Mulberry Street, 21201-3606
Telephone: 410-685-3810
Telecopier: 410-685-0203

William Alden McDaniel, Jr.
Jo Bennett Marsh

For full biographical listings, see the Martindale-Hubbell Law Directory

PIERSON, PIERSON & NOLAN (AV)

Suite 2020 Redwood Tower, 217 East Redwood Street, 21202
Telephone: 410-727-7733
Fax: 410-625-0253
Email: piernol@ibm.net

MEMBERS OF FIRM

W. Michel Pierson
James J. Nolan, Jr.
Robert L. Pierson

For Complete List of Firm Personnel, See General Section

For full biographical listings, see the Martindale-Hubbell Law Directory

VENABLE ATTORNEYS AT LAW VENABLE, BAETJER AND HOWARD, LLP (AV)

A Partnership including Professional Corporations
1800 Mercantile Bank & Trust Building, 2 Hopkins Plaza, 21201
Telephone: 410-244-7400
Fax: 410-244-7742
URL: http://www.venable.com
Washington, D.C. Office: Venable, Baetjer, Howard & Civiletti LLP, Suite 1000, 1201 New York Avenue, N.W.
Telephone: 202-962-4800.
Fax: 202-962-8300.
McLean, Virginia Office: Suite 400, 2010 Corporate Ridge.
Telephone: 703-760-1600.
Fax: 703-821-8949.
Rockville, Maryland Office: Suite 500, One Church Street, P. O. Box 1906.
Telephone: 301-217-5600.
Fax: 301-217-5617.
Towson, Maryland Office: 210 Allegheny Avenue, P. O. Box 5517.
Telephone: 410-494-6200.
Fax: 410-821-0147.

MEMBERS OF FIRM

Benjamin R. Civiletti (P.C.) (Also at Washington, D.C. and Towson, Maryland Offices)
George Cochran Doub (P.C.)
John Henry Lewin, Jr. (P.C.)
Stanley Mazaroff (P.C.)
Roger W. Titus (Resident, Rockville, Maryland Office)
Thomas J. Madden (Not admitted in MD; Resident, Washington, D.C. Office)
Ronald R. Glancz (Not admitted in MD; Resident, Washington, D.C. Office)
Kenneth C. Bass, III (Not admitted in MD; Washington, D.C. and McLean, Virginia Offices)
John H. Zink, III (Resident, Towson, Maryland Office)
Paul F. Strain (P.C.)
William D. Dolan, III (P.C.) (Not admitted in MD; Resident, McLean, Virginia Office)
Paul T. Glasgow (Resident, Rockville, Maryland Office)
Joseph C. Wich, Jr. (Resident, Towson, Maryland Office)
Sondra Harans Block (Resident, Rockville, Maryland Office)
Edward F. Glynn, Jr. (Resident, Washington, D.C. Office)
Craig E. Smith
Robert G. Ames (Also at Washington, D.C. Office)
Michael Schatzow (Also at Washington, D.C. Office)
Nell B. Strachan
David G. Lane (Resident, McLean, Virginia Office)

(See Next Column)

MEMBERS OF FIRM (Continued)

N. Frank Wiggins (Not admitted in MD; Resident, Washington, D.C. Office)
G. Stewart Webb, Jr.
James K. Archibald (Also at Washington, D.C. Office)
George W. Johnston (P.C.)
Judson W. Starr (Not admitted in MD; Also at Washington, D.C. and Towson, Maryland Offices)
Jana Howard Carey (P.C.)
Jeffrey A. Dunn (Also at Washington, D.C. Office)
George F. Pappas (Also at Washington, D.C. Office)
William D. Coston (Not admitted in MD; Resident, Washington, D.C. Office)
James L. Shea (Also at Washington, D.C. Office)
Jeffrey P. Ayres (P.C.)
Elizabeth C. Honeywell
Maurice Baskin (Resident, Washington, D.C. Office)
Amy Berman Jackson (Not admitted in MD; Resident, Washington, D.C. Office)
C. Carey Deeley, Jr. (Also at Towson, Maryland Office)
Christopher R. Mellott
M. King Hill, III (Resident, Towson, Maryland Office)
James A. Dunbar (Resident, Towson, Maryland Office)
Ronald W. Taylor
Thomas J. Kelly, Jr. (Not admitted in MD; Resident, Washington, D.C. Office)
David J. Heubeck
Herbert G. Smith, II (Not admitted in MD; Resident, Washington, D.C. Office)
Patrick J. Stewart (Also at Washington, D.C. Office)
Gary M. Hnath (Resident, Washington, D.C. Office)
Mitchell Y. Mirviss
Geoffrey R. Garinther (Also at Towson, Maryland Office)
Terri L. Turner
Michael W. Robinson (Resident, McLean, Virginia Office)
Todd J. Horn
David W. Goewey (Not admitted in MD; Resident, Washington, D.C. Office)
J. Scott Hommer, III (Not admitted in MD; Resident, McLean, Virginia Office)
Gregory A. Cross
John A. McCauley
John T. Prisbe
Elizabeth Marzo Borinsky
John P. Sarbanes
Vicki Margolis (Also at Washington, D.C. Office)
Christine M. McAnney (Not admitted in MD; Resident, McLean, Virginia Office)
Maria F. Howell
Marina Lolley Sabett

OF COUNSEL

A. Samuel Cook (P.C.) (Resident, Towson, Maryland Office)

ASSOCIATES

Paul D. Barker, Jr.
Daniel William China (Resident, Towson, Maryland Office)
Patricia Gillis Cousins (Resident, Rockville, Maryland Office)
Carla Draluck Craft (Resident, Washington, D.C. Office)
E. Anne Hamel
Patricia A. Malone (Resident, Towson, Maryland Office)
Melissa Landau Steinman (Resident, Washington, D.C. Office)
Paul N. Wengert (Not admitted in MD; Resident, McLean, Virginia Office)

For Complete List of Firm Personnel, See General Section

For full biographical listings, see the Martindale-Hubbell Law Directory

*BEL AIR,** Harford Co.

STARK & KEENAN, A PROFESSIONAL ASSOCIATION (AV)

30 Office Street, 21014
Telephone: 410-838-5522
Baltimore: 410-879-2222
Fax: 410-879-0688
Email: wstarkee@aol.com
Havre de Grace Office: "The Old Ordinary" 100 St. John Street, 21078.
Telephone: 410-939-0100.

Elwood V. Stark, Jr.
Charles B. Keenan, Jr.
Edwin G. Carson
Judith Cline-Silverstein
Gregory A. Szoka
Robert S. Lynch
Paul W. Ishak

Claire Prin Blomquist
Lawrence F. Kreis, Jr.
Craig H. DeRan

For full biographical listings, see the Martindale-Hubbell Law Directory

*ROCKVILLE,** Montgomery Co.

VENABLE ATTORNEYS AT LAW VENABLE, BAETJER AND HOWARD, LLP (AV)

A Partnership including Professional Corporations
Suite 500, One Church Street, P.O. Box 1906, 20850-4129
Telephone: 301-217-5600
Fax: 301-217-5617
URL: http://www.venable.com
Baltimore, Maryland Office: 1800 Mercantile Bank & Trust Building, 2 Hopkins Plaza.
Telephone: 410-244-7400.
Fax: 410-244-7742.
Washington, D.C. Office: Venable, Baetjer, Howard & Civiletti LLP, Suite 1000, 1201 New York Avenue, N.W.
Telephone: 202-962-4800.
Fax: 202-962-8300.

(See Next Column)

VENABLE ATTORNEYS AT LAW VENABLE, BAETJER AND HOWARD, LLP, *Rockville—Continued*

McLean, Virginia Office: Suite 400, 2010 Corporate Ridge.
Telephone: 703-760-1600.
Fax: 703-821-8949.
Towson, Maryland, Office: 210 Allegheny Avenue, P. O. Box 5517.
Telephone: 410-494-6200.
Fax: 410-821-0147.

MEMBERS OF FIRM

Roger W. Titus
Paul T. Glasgow
Sondra Harans Block

ASSOCIATE

Patricia Gillis Cousins

For Complete List of Firm Personnel, See General Section

For full biographical listings, see the Martindale-Hubbell Law Directory

*TOWSON,** Baltimore Co.

VENABLE ATTORNEYS AT LAW VENABLE, BAETJER AND HOWARD, LLP (AV)

A Partnership including Professional Corporations
210 Allegheny Avenue, P.O. Box 5517, 21204
Telephone: 410-494-6200
Fax: 410-821-0147
URL: http://www.venable.com
Baltimore, Maryland Office: 1800 Mercantile Bank & Trust Building, 2 Hopkins Plaza.
Telephone: 410-244-7400.
Fax: 410-244-7742.
Washington, D.C. Office: Venable, Baetjer, Howard & Civiletti LLP, Suite 1000, 1201 New York Avenue, N.W.
Telephone: 202-962-4800.
Fax: 202-962-8300.
McLean, Virginia Office: Suite 400, 2010 Corporate Ridge.
Telephone: 703-760-1600.
Fax: 703-821-8949.
Rockville, Maryland Office: Suite 500, One Church Street, P. O. Box 1906.
Telephone: 301-217-5600.
Fax: 301-217-5617.

PARTNERS

Benjamin R. Civiletti (P.C.) (Also at Washington, D.C. and Baltimore, Maryland Offices)
John H. Zink, III
Joseph C. Wich, Jr.
C. Carey Deeley, Jr. (Also at Baltimore, Maryland Office)
M. King Hill, III

ASSOCIATE

Patricia A. Malone

For Complete List of Firm Personnel, See General Section

For full biographical listings, see the Martindale-Hubbell Law Directory

WHITNEY & BOGRIS, LLP (AV)

401 Washington Avenue, Twelfth Floor, 21204
Telephone: 410-583-8000
Fax: 410-583-8031
Email: HGWC@worldnet.att.net

MEMBERS OF FIRM

Daniel W. Whitney
George D. Bogris

ASSOCIATES

Kathleen D. Leslie
Henry Russell
Sandra A. Tofte
Michael A. Giacomazza
Arlene L. Sew
Gerald S. Gaetano (Not admitted in MD)
Scott A. McCabe (Not admitted in MD)
Jeffrey C. Shipley

OF COUNSEL

Joseph E. Dever
David L. Feldstein
Ronald V. Miller, Jr.

For full biographical listings, see the Martindale-Hubbell Law Directory

MASSACHUSETTS

*BOSTON,** Suffolk Co.

MEEHAN, BOYLE & COHEN, P.C. (AV)

2 Center Plaza Suite 600, 02108
Telephone: 617-523-8300
Fax: 617-523-0525

(See Next Column)

James F. Meehan
Leo V. Boyle
Cynthia J. Cohen
Warren F. Fitzgerald
Peter J. Black
John J. Carroll, Jr.
Michael B. Bogdanow
Karen R. Ristuben

Sherry Yee Mulloy
Samuel M. Furgang
Bradley Mead Henry
Jonathan E. Tobin

For full biographical listings, see the Martindale-Hubbell Law Directory

PACKENHAM, SCHMIDT & FEDERICO, P.C. (AV)

Four Longfellow Place, 35th Floor, 02114-2832
Telephone: 617-742-6565
Fax: 617-742-0292

Richard D. Packenham
Mary H. Schmidt
Phyllis E. Federico

Jennifer Rivera-Ulwick
Nicole R. Manny

OF COUNSEL

W. Sanford Durland III

For full biographical listings, see the Martindale-Hubbell Law Directory

PALMER & DODGE LLP (AV)

One Beacon Street, 02108
Telephone: 617-573-0100
Facsimile: 617-227-4420
URL: http://www.palmerdodge.com

MEMBER OF FIRM

Jeffrey Swope

For Complete List of Firm Personnel, See General Section

For full biographical listings, see the Martindale-Hubbell Law Directory

*GREENFIELD,** Franklin Co.

WENDY SIBBISON (AV)

158 Main Street, Suite 5, 01301
Telephone: 413-772-0329
Fax: 413-772-0009
Email: wsib@crocker.com

For full biographical listings, see the Martindale-Hubbell Law Directory

MICHIGAN

*ANN ARBOR,** Washtenaw Co.

BUTZEL LONG, A PROFESSIONAL CORPORATION (AV)

Suite 300, 350 South Main Street, 48104-2131
Telephone: 313-995-3110
Telecopier: 313-995-1777
Email: melnick@butzel.com *URL:* http://www.butzel.com
Detroit, Michigan Office: Suite 900, 150 West Jefferson.
Telephone: 313-225-7000.
Telecopier: 313-225-7080.
Birmingham, Michigan Office: Suite 200, 32270 Telegraph Road.
Telephone: 810-258-1616.
Telecopier: 810-258-1439.
Okemos, Michigan Office: Suite 300, 2127 University Park Drive.
Telephone: 517-372-6622.
Telecopier: 372-6672.
Grosse Pointe Farms, Michigan Office: Suite 260, 21 Kercheval.
Telephone: 313-886-5446.
Telecopier: 313-886-2114.
Boca Raton, Florida Office: Suite 411, 1200 North Federal Highway.
Telephone: 561-368-2151.
Telecopier: 561-368-4668.
Palm Beach Gardens, Florida Office: Suite 227, 11382 Prosperity Farms Road.
Telephone: 561-625-4442.
Telecopier: 561-625-6901.
Naples, Florida Office: Suite 705, 801 Laurel Oak Drive.
Telephone: 941-597-4500.
Telecopier: 941-597-5623.

John Henry Dudley, Jr.
James E. Stewart (Resident)
Marissa W. Pollick (Resident)
Leonard M. Niehoff (Resident)
J. Michael Huget (Resident)

John C. Blattner (Resident)
Pamela M. Zauel

For full biographical listings, see the Martindale-Hubbell Law Directory

*DETROIT,** Wayne Co.

BENDURE & THOMAS (AV)

577 East Larned, Suite 210, 48226-4392
Telephone: 313-961-1525
Fax: 313-961-1553

MEMBERS OF FIRM

Mark R. Bendure | Marc E. Thomas

ASSOCIATES

J. Christopher Caldwell | Victor S. Valenti
Kevin P. Kavanagh

OF COUNSEL

John A. Lydick | Thomas R. Present

For full biographical listings, see the Martindale-Hubbell Law Directory

BODMAN, LONGLEY & DAHLING LLP (AV)

34th Floor 100 Renaissance Center, 48243
Telephone: 313-259-7777
Fax: 313-393-7579
Email: info@bodmanlongley.com *URL:* http://www.bodmanlongley.com
Troy, Michigan Office: Suite 2020, 755 West Big Beaver Road.
Telephone: 248-362-2110.
Fax: 248-244-0780.
Ann Arbor, Michigan Office: 110 Miller, Suite 300.
Telephone: 734-761-3780.
Fax: 734-930-2494.
Northern Michigan Office: 229 Court Street, P.O. Box 405, Cheboygan.
Telephone: 231-627-4351.
Fax: 231-627-2802.

MEMBERS OF FIRM

Michael B. Lewiston
Thomas A. Roach (Ann Arbor Office)
James A. Smith
James J. Walsh
David G. Chardavoyne
Robert G. Brower
Charles N. Raimi
Lloyd C. Fell (Cheboygan Office)
Lawrence P. Hanson (Cheboygan Office)
Jerold Lax (Ann Arbor Office)
Diane L. Akers
Jeffrey G. Raphelson

For Representative Client List, See General Section

For Complete List of Firm Personnel, See General Section

For full biographical listings, see the Martindale-Hubbell Law Directory

BUTZEL LONG, A PROFESSIONAL CORPORATION (AV)

Suite 900, 150 West Jefferson, 48226
Telephone: 313-225-7000
Telecopier: 313-225-7080
Email: melnick@butzel.com *URL:* http://www.butzel.com
Birmingham, Michigan Office: Suite 200, 32270 Telegraph Road.
Telephone: 810-258-1616.
Telecopier: 810-258-1439.
Okemos, Michigan Office: Suite 300, 2127 University Park Drive.
Telephone: 517-372-6622.
Telecopier: 517-372-6672.
Ann Arbor, Michigan Office: Suite 300, 350 South Main Street.
Telephone: 313-995-3110.
Telecopier: 313-995-1777.
Grosse Pointe Farms, Michigan Office: Suite 260, 21 Kercheval.
Telephone: 313-886-5446.
Telecopier: 313-886-2114.
Boca Raton, Florida Office: Suite 411, 1200 North Federal Highway.
Telephone: 561-368-2151.
Telecopier: 561-368-4668.
Palm Beach Gardens, Florida Office: Suite 227, 11382 Prosperity Farms Road.
Telephone: 561-625-4442.
Telecopier: 561-625-6901.
Naples, Florida Office: Suite 705, 801 Laurel Oak Drive.
Telephone: 941-597-4500.
Telecopier: 941-597-5623.

William M. Saxton
John Henry Dudley, Jr.
Richard E. Rassel
Edward M. Kronk
Philip J. Kessler
Donald B. Miller
John P. Hancock, Jr.
Mark T. Nelson
Keefe A. Brooks
Lynne E. Deitch
Leonard M. Niehoff (Ann Arbor)
David H. Oermann (Birmingham)

Representative Clients: Blue Cross/Blue Shield of Michigan; Complete Business Solutions, Inc.; The Detroit News, Inc.; Indian Head Industries, Inc; Jackson National Life Insurance Co.; Kelly Services; Michigan Road Builders Assn.; Stroh Companies; Takata Corp.; The University of Michigan.

For full biographical listings, see the Martindale-Hubbell Law Directory

DAVID F. DUMOUCHEL, P.C. (AV)

150 West Jefferson, Suite 900, 48226-4430
Telephone: 313-225-7004
Email: dumouchd@butzel.com

David F. DuMouchel

For full biographical listings, see the Martindale-Hubbell Law Directory

GROSS, NEMETH & SILVERMAN, P.L.C. (AV)

535 Griswold, Suite 1850, 48226
Telephone: 313-963-8200
Fax: 313-963-9169
Email: gns_appeals@juno.com

James G. Gross | Mary T. Nemeth
Steven G. Silverman

For full biographical listings, see the Martindale-Hubbell Law Directory

KENNETH M. MOGILL (AV)

One Kennedy Square Building, Suite 1930, 719 Griswold, 48226
Telephone: 313-962-7210
Fax: 313-961-7799
(Also Member Mogill, Posner & Cohen)

For full biographical listings, see the Martindale-Hubbell Law Directory

CAROLE M. STANYAR (AV)

Suite 1938, One Kennedy Square, 48226
Telephone: 313-963-7222
Fax: 313-963-6490

For full biographical listings, see the Martindale-Hubbell Law Directory

TIMMIS & INMAN L.L.P. (AV)

300 Talon Centre, 48207
Telephone: 313-396-4200
Facsimile: 313-396-4228
Email: info@timmis-inman.com *URL:* http://www.timmis-inman.com

Michael T. Timmis
Robert E. Graziani
George A. Peck
Henry J. Brennan, III
Mark W. Peyser
Bradley J. Knickerbocker
George M. Malis

Michael F. Wais | Erich J. D'Andrea
Shannon M. Nichols

Representative Clients: Retail Resources, Inc.; Applied Process, Inc.; Insilco Corp.; Certain Underwriters at Lloyds of London; Eastpointe Radiologists, P.C.; Talon Automotive Group, Inc.; G&L Industries, Inc.; Hawthorne Metal Products Co.; Foam Rubber Products Co.; Diamond Automations, Inc.; Veltri Metal Products Co.; J&R Manufacturing, Inc.; Spiralock Corporation.

For Complete List of Firm Personnel, See General Section

For full biographical listings, see the Martindale-Hubbell Law Directory

FARMINGTON HILLS, Oakland Co.

NEMIER, TOLARI, LANDRY, MAZZEO & JOHNSON, P.C. (AV)

37000 Grand River, Suite 300, 48335
Telephone: 248-476-6900
Fax: 248-476-6564
Email: firm@ntlmj.com

Craig L. Nemier | David B. Landry
Jeffrey L. Tolari | Rik Mazzeo
Mark R. Johnson

Michelle E. Mathieu | Katharine R. Shishkovsky
Kathy Contos Nash | Carol J. Surma

OF COUNSEL

William R. Still | Terry E. Pietryga

LEGAL SUPPORT PERSONNEL

Nancy Vayda Dembinski (Paralegal)

For full biographical listings, see the Martindale-Hubbell Law Directory

SOUTHFIELD, Oakland Co.

COLLINS, EINHORN, FARRELL & ULANOFF, A PROFESSIONAL CORPORATION (AV)

4000 Town Center, Suite 909, 48075-1473
Telephone: 248-355-4141
Facsimile: 248-355-2277

(See Next Column)

McCormick & Mitchell A Professional Corporation, *San Diego—Continued*

Konrad M. Rasmussen
Deborah K. Garvin
Geoffrey E. Bishop

Reference: San Diego Trust & Savings.

For full biographical listings, see the Martindale-Hubbell Law Directory

UNIVERSAL CITY, Los Angeles Co.

Ballard, Rosenberg & Golper (AV)

10 Universal City Plaza, 16th Floor, 91608-1097
Telephone: 818-508-3700
FAX: 818-506-4827; 985-8167
Email: info@brglaw.com

MEMBERS OF FIRM

Kenneth R. Ballard
Richard S. Rosenberg
John B. Golper
Stephen R. Lueke
Jeffrey P. Fuchsman
Sherrie Lipsky Sheldon
Helene J. Wasserman
Jonathan S. Rosenberg

ASSOCIATES

John J. Manier
Matthew T. Wakefield
Stephen M. MacPhail
Douglas N. Silverstein
Alexander A. Molina
William D. Becker
Sherry B. Kampler
Erin Nemirovsky Medina
Edward L. Washington
Sandra A. Marciari

SENIOR COUNSEL

Elsa Bañuelos
Raquelle de la Rocha
Bruce A. Grossman

Reference: First Los Angeles Bank (Century City Office).

For full biographical listings, see the Martindale-Hubbell Law Directory

COLORADO

*DENVER,** Denver Co.

Harry L. Arkin & Associates, P.C. (AV)

Suite 2750 Lincoln Center, 1660 Lincoln Street, 80264
Telephone: 303-863-8400
Telefax: 303-832-4703
Email: harkin00@counsel.com
Email: hnikra@aol.com
London, England Office: Verulam Chambers, Peer House, 8-14 Verulam Street, WCIX 8LZ.
Telephone: 071 813-2400.
Fax: 071 405-3870.

Harry L. Arkin

Michael B. Levy

LEGAL SUPPORT PERSONNEL

Patricia A. Hanson
Karen R. Loveland

For full biographical listings, see the Martindale-Hubbell Law Directory

Berliner Zisser Walter & Gallegos, A Professional Corporation (AV)

One Norwest Center, 1700 Lincoln Street, Suite 4700, 80203-4547
Telephone: 303-830-1700
Facsimile: 303-830-1705
Email: bzwg@bzwg.com

Martin M. Berliner
David A. Zisser
Robert W. Walter
Larry D. Gallegos

Stacey L. Bowers

OF COUNSEL

Phillip C. Gans

For full biographical listings, see the Martindale-Hubbell Law Directory

Birge & Mayers, P.C. (AV)

1700 Broadway, Suite 1501, 80290
Telephone: 303-860-7100
Facsimile: 303-860-7338
URL: http://www.lawyers.com/birgemayerslaw
St. Louis, Missouri Office: 8000 Maryland Avenue, #250, 63105.
Telephone: 314-236-2203.
Telecopy: 314-236-2401.

Thomas D. Birge

Carla B. Minckley

(See Next Column)

SPECIAL COUNSEL

Terry L. Lister

For full biographical listings, see the Martindale-Hubbell Law Directory

Cortez Macaulay Bernhardt & Schuetze LLC (AV)

1600 Broadway, Suite 1600, 80202
Telephone: 303-864-1000
Facsimile: 303-864-1111
URL: http://www.cmblaw.com

Miles Cortez
Christopher T. Macaulay
Susan Bernhardt
Robert A. Schuetze
David H. Goldberg
Marian L. Carlson
Richard P. R. Cohn

For full biographical listings, see the Martindale-Hubbell Law Directory

Davis & Ceriani, P.C. (AV)

Suite 400, Market Center, 1350 Seventeenth Street, 80202
Telephone: 303-534-9000
Telecopier: 303-534-4618
Email: davisandceriani.com

Rick G. Davis
Gary J. Ceriani
Bruce E. Rohde
Michael P. Cillo
Charles W. Bess
John W. Himmelmann

Margaret E. Peper
Patrick John Kanouff
Mark M. Osborn
Valeri Pappas

For full biographical listings, see the Martindale-Hubbell Law Directory

Law Offices of John W. McKendree (AV)

Creswell Mansion, 1244 Grant Street, 80203
Telephone: 303-861-8906
Fax: 303-861-7773
Email: Johnwmckendree@msn.com

ASSOCIATE

Elizabeth G. McKendree

Reference: Colorado National Bank.

For full biographical listings, see the Martindale-Hubbell Law Directory

Poulson, Odell & Peterson, LLC (AV)

Suite 1400, 1775 Sherman Street, 80203
Telephone: 303-861-4400
Telecopier: 303-861-1225
Email: popllc@popllc.com

Randall M. Case
Stephen M. Thompson
Carleton L. Ekberg
Alan B. Cameron

Representative Clients: Marathon Oil Corp.; Samedan Oil Corp.

For full biographical listings, see the Martindale-Hubbell Law Directory

FLORIDA

*MIAMI,** Dade Co.

Theodore R. Bayer (AV)

9400 South Dadeland Boulevard, Suite 300, 33156
Telephone: 305-670-6300
Fax: 305-670-4847
Email: TRBLAW@AOL.COM *URL:* HTTP://WWW.LAWYERS.COM/THEODORERBAYER

For full biographical listings, see the Martindale-Hubbell Law Directory

*ORLANDO,** Orange Co.

Kenneth L. Mann, P.A. (AV)

105 East Robinson Street, Suite 540, P.O. Box 551, 32802-0551
Telephone: 407-422-0006
Fax: 407-841-9516
Email: reasonablemann@worldnet.att.net *URL:* http://www.KenMannlaw.com

Kenneth L. Mann

For full biographical listings, see the Martindale-Hubbell Law Directory

GEORGIA

*AUGUSTA,** Richmond Co.

HULL, TOWILL, NORMAN, BARRETT & SALLEY, A PROFESSIONAL CORPORATION (AV)

801 Broad Street, Suite 700, 30901
Telephone: 706-722-4481
Fax: 706-722-9779
Email: hullfirm@groupz.net *URL:* http://www.groupz.net/~advocate
Aiken, South Carolina Office: 111 Park Avenue, 29801.
Telephone: 803-648-4213.
Fax: 803-648-2601.

James M. Hull (1885-1975)
George B. Barrett (1894-1942)
Julian J. Willingham (1887-1963)
John Bell Towill (1907-1991)
Robert C. Norman (Retired, 1991)
W. Hale Barrett
Lawton Jordan, Jr.
Patrick J. Rice
Douglas D. Batchelor, Jr.
David E. Hudson
William H. Tucker (Not admitted in GA)
William F. Hammond
Mark S. Burgreen
George R. Hall
James B. Ellington
F. Michael Taylor
William J. Keogh, III
Edward J. Tarver
J. Noel Schweers, III
Susan D. Barrett
Ralph Emerson Hanna, III

James M. Holly (Not admitted in GA)
Timothy E. Moses
N. Shannon Gentry Lanier
Tara R. Simkins
Charles H. Weigle
Natalie A. Dopson
David C. Smith

OF COUNSEL

Julian B. Salley, Jr. (Not admitted in GA)

Counsel for: Morris Communications Corporation; Merry Land & Investment Company, Inc.; Castleberry/Snow's Brands, Inc.; Sun Trust Bank Augusta, N.A.; Georgia Power Co.; St. Joseph Hospital, Augusta, Georgia, Inc.; Norfolk Southern Corp.; Housing Authority of the City of Augusta; Georgia Press Association; Columbia County, Georgia.

For full biographical listings, see the Martindale-Hubbell Law Directory

HAWAII

*HONOLULU,** Honolulu Co.

CARLSMITH BALL (AV)

A Partnership including Law Corporations
Suite 2200, Pacific Tower, 1001 Bishop Street, P.O. Box 656, 96809-3402
Telephone: 808-523-2500
Fax: 808-523-0842
Email: execdirector@carlsmith.com *URL:* http://www.carlsmith.com
Kapolei, Hawaii Office: Suite 318, Kapolei Building, 1001 Kamokila Boulevard, 96707.
Telephone: 808-523-2500.
Fax: 808-674-0850.
Wailuku, Maui Hawaii Office: Suite 400, One Main Plaza, 2200 Main Street, P.O. Box 1086, 96793-1086.
Telephone: 808-242-4535.
Fax: 808-244-4974.
Kailua-Kona, Hawaii Office: Suite 209, 75-1000 Henry Street, 96740.
Telephone: 808-329-6464.
Fax: 808-329-9450.
Hilo, Hawaii Office: 121 Waianuenue Avenue, P.O. Box 686, 96721-0686.
Telephone: 808-935-6644.
Fax: 808-935-7975.
Hagatna, Guam Office: Suite 401, Bank of Hawaii Building, 134 West Soledad Avenue, P.O. Box BF, 96932-5027.
Telephone: 671-472-6813.
Fax: 671-477-4375.
Telex: 721-6445 CWCMI GM.
Saipan, Commonwealth of the Northern Mariana Islands Office: Carlsmith Building, Capitol Hill, P.O. Box 5241, 96950-5241.
Telephone: 670-322-3455.
Fax: 670-322-3368.
Los Angeles, California Office: 9th Floor, 444 South Flower Street, 90071-2901.
Telephone: 213-955-1200.
Fax: 213-623-0032.
Washington, D.C. Office: Suite 300, 1201 Pennsylvania Avenue, N.W., 20004-2401.
Telephone: 202-628-2228.
Fax: 202-628-2071.
Mexico City, Mexico Office: Carlsmith Ball, Sierra Nevada 119, Lomas de Chapultepec, 11000 Mexico, D.F.
Telephone: 52-5-520-8514, 52-5-520-8757.
Fax: 52-5-540-1545.

(See Next Column)

Mexico, D.F. Office of Carlsmith Ball, S.C. (Authorized to practice as foreign legal consultants in Mexico): Sierra Nevada 119, Lomas de Chapultepec, 11000 Mexico, D.F.
Telephone: 52-5-520-8514, 52-5-520-8757.
Fax: 52-5-540-1545.

MEMBERS OF FIRM

Edward E. Case
Gary G. Grimmer
John P. Manaut

For Complete List of Firm Personnel, See General Section

For full biographical listings, see the Martindale-Hubbell Law Directory

MIYAGI, NOHR & MYHRE (AV)

1001 Bishop Street, Suite 1200, 96813
Telephone: 808-524-2466
Fax: 808-524-2556

Melvyn M. Miyagi
Katharine M. Nohr
James V. Myhre
Michael H. Tsuchida
John E. Drotz

OF COUNSEL

Carleton B. Reid

Representative Clients: American International Group; State Farm Insurance; TIG Insurance; Crum & Forster; ITT Specialty Risk Services; Marriott International; The Hartford; USAA; Budget Rent A Car; Crawford & Company.

For full biographical listings, see the Martindale-Hubbell Law Directory

KAILUA, Honolulu Co.

WINER MEHEULA & DEVENS (AV)

970 North Kalaheo Avenue, Suite A-300, 96734
Telephone: 808-254-5855
Fax: 808-254-6872
Email: winer@pacificlaw.com *URL:* http://www.pacificlaw.com

MEMBERS OF FIRM

Andrew S. Winer
William K. Meheula
Vladimir Paul Devens

OF COUNSEL

David F. Fasi

ASSOCIATE

Blue H. Kaanehe

For full biographical listings, see the Martindale-Hubbell Law Directory

ILLINOIS

*CHICAGO,** Cook Co.

FRANCZEK SULLIVAN P.C. (AV)

Suite 3400, 300 South Wacker Drive, 60606-6785
Telephone: 312-986-0300
FAX: 312-986-9192
URL: http://www.nlfpc.com

Anthony J. Crement
J. Todd Faulkner
James C. Franczek, Jr.
Ronald J. Hein, Jr.
Lisa A. Lopatka
Bruce C. Mackey
Robert E. Mann
Paul A. Millichap
David P. Radelet
John A. Relias
Michael I. Richardson
Charles P. Rose
Sally J. Scott
William R. Sullivan, Jr.
Andrea R. Waintroob
Patricia J. Whitten
James J. Zuehl

Shelli L. Boyer
Sheila M. Conroy
Terrence T. Creamer
Erika Dillon
Edward N. Druck
Gregory D. Isbell
Thomas Koutsouvas
Darcy L. Kriha
Jeffrey M. Kropp
Jeremy C. Moritz
Alec Rubenstein
Leah D. Gidron
Jennifer L. Schilling
Michael A. Warner, Jr.
Anne Elizabeth Wilson

OF COUNSEL

Michael Z. Green
Wesley A. Wildman
John L. Wren

LEGAL SUPPORT PERSONNEL

Caty E. Kearney

For full biographical listings, see the Martindale-Hubbell Law Directory

IOWA

*DES MOINES,** Polk Co.

PEDDICORD, WHARTON, THUNE AND SPENCER, A PROFESSIONAL CORPORATION (AV)

700 Des Moines Building, 405 Sixth Avenue, P.O. Box 9130, 50306-9130
Telephone: 515-243-2100
Fax: 515-243-2132
1-800-383-2100

Roland D. Peddicord — Paul C. Thune

For full biographical listings, see the Martindale-Hubbell Law Directory

KANSAS

*TOPEKA,** Shawnee Co.

GOODELL, STRATTON, EDMONDS & PALMER, L.L.P. (AV)

515 South Kansas Avenue, 66603-3999
Telephone: 785-233-0593
Fax: 785-233-8870
Email: GSEP@CJNETWORKS.COM *URL:* http://www.cjnetworks.com/~gsep
Kansas City, Missouri Office: 10401 Holmes Road, Suite 280.
Telephone: 816-943-8577.

MEMBERS OF FIRM

Wayne T. Stratton — Arthur E. Palmer
Steve A. Schwarm

Counsel for: Columbian National Title Insurance Co.; Heartland Community Bankers Association; The Menninger Foundation; Topeka Chamber of Commerce; Washburn University of Topeka; Reser's Fine Foods; ConAgra; Monfort, Inc.

For Complete List of Firm Personnel, See General Section

For full biographical listings, see the Martindale-Hubbell Law Directory

LOUISIANA

*NEW ORLEANS,** Orleans Parish

McGLINCHEY STAFFORD (AV)

A Professional Limited Liability Company
643 Magazine Street, 70130-3477
Telephone: 504-586-1200
Fax: 504-596-2800
TDD: (504) 596-2728
Telex: 584327
Cable Address: "MACSTAC"
Mailing Address: P.O. Box 60643, New Orleans, Louisiana, 70160-0643
Email: @mcglinchey.com *URL:* http://www.mcglinchey.com
Dallas, Texas Office: 2777 Stemmons Freeway, Suite 925, 75207-2401.
Telephone: 214-860-9700.
Fax: 214-860-9750.
Houston, Texas Office: 2727 Allen Parkway, Suite 1900, 77019.
Telephone: 713-520-1900.
Fax: 713-520-1025.
Baton Rouge, Louisiana Office: Ninth Floor, One American Place, 70825-0001.
Telephone: 504-383-9000.
Fax: 504-343-3076.
Jackson, Mississippi Office: Suite 1200, SkyTel Centre, 200 South Lamar Street, 39201.
Telephone: 601-960-8400.
Fax: 601-960-8406.
Lake Providence, Louisiana Office: 405 Morgan Street, 71254-2691.
Telephone: 318-559-1200.
Fax: 318-559-0609.
Monroe, Louisiana Office: Dean ONB Tower, 130 Desiard Street, Suite 807, 71201.
Telephone: 318-651-0807.
Fax: 318-651-0809.

MEMBER OF FIRM

Anthony Rollo

OF COUNSEL

Joe Giarrusso, Jr.

For full biographical listings, see the Martindale-Hubbell Law Directory

MARYLAND

BETHESDA, Montgomery Co.

LEE F. HOLDMANN CHARTERED (AV)

9207 Old Georgetown Road, 20814
Telephone: 301-530-0900
Fax: 301-530-2852
La Plata Office: 200 Centennial Street.
Telephone: 301-934-1152.
Fax: 301-530-2852.
Annapolis Office: Glenco Building, 410 Rowe Boulevard.
Telephone: 410-268-0200.
Fax: 301-530-2852.
Leonardtown Office: Camalier Building, 22635 Washington Street.
Telephone: 301-457-2645.
Fax: 301-530-2852.

Lee F. Holdmann

Shelley R. Culhane — Charles W. Bills
Larry W. Brown — Tina B. Fernandes

LEGAL SUPPORT PERSONNEL

Sharon Lightner (Senior Paralegal)

Reference: Marriott Corporation Senior Living Services, Washington, D.C.

For full biographical listings, see the Martindale-Hubbell Law Directory

RIDBERG, PRESS & SHERBILL (AV)

Three Bethesda Metro Center, Suite 650, 20814
Telephone: 301-913-5770
FAX: 301-913-5769

MEMBERS OF FIRM

Michael D. Ridberg — Raymond J. Sherbill
Fredric A. Press — Norman L. Eule

ASSOCIATES

Stuart A. Schwager — Paul D. Smolinsky

For full biographical listings, see the Martindale-Hubbell Law Directory

GARY HOWARD SIMPSON (AV)

9505 Kingsley Avenue, 20814
Telephone: 301-493-0345
Fax: 301-493-0347
Email: ghslaw@erols.com *URL:* http://www.lawyers.com/garyhsimpson

Alane Tempchin

OF COUNSEL

Krauthamer & Stahl, Chartered, Chevy Chase, Maryland

LEGAL SUPPORT PERSONNEL

Michelle Ratcliffe (Paralegal) — Joy Simpson (Paralegal)

For full biographical listings, see the Martindale-Hubbell Law Directory

*ROCKVILLE,** Montgomery Co.

MALLON A. SNYDER CHARTERED (AV)

99 South Washington Street, 20850
Telephone: 301-762-7500
Fax: 301-762-7509
Email: mallon@erols.com *URL:* http://www.lawyers.com/marylandbusinesslaw

Mallon A. Snyder

Reference: NationsBank, Rockville Branch.

For full biographical listings, see the Martindale-Hubbell Law Directory

MASSACHUSETTS

BROCKTON, Plymouth Co.

VINCENT P. CAHALANE, P.C. (AV)

478 Torrey Street, Suite 12, 02301-4696
Telephone: 508-588-1222
Fax: 508-584-4748
URL: http://www.lawyers.com/cahalanelaw

Vincent P. Cahalane

For full biographical listings, see the Martindale-Hubbell Law Directory

MICHIGAN

BLOOMFIELD HILLS, Oakland Co.

SUE ELLEN EISENBERG, P.C. (AV)

Suite 145 33 Bloomfield Hills Parkway, 48304-2945
Telephone: 248-258-6080
Fax: 248-258-9212
Email: seepc@aol.com *URL:* http://www.lawyers.com/sueelleneisenberg

Sue Ellen Eisenberg

For full biographical listings, see the Martindale-Hubbell Law Directory

GUNSBERG & BRESKIN, P.C. (AV)

The Pinehurst Building, 1400 North Woodward Avenue, Suite 200, 48304
Telephone: 248-646-9090
Facsimile: 248-647-0638

David B. Gunsberg
Marvin Breskin

Representative Clients: Autodie International; Builders Association of S.E. Michigan; Federal Broadcasting Co.; Foamade Industries; Hercules Drawn Steel Corp.; I.S.I. Manufacturing, Inc.; McKinley Properties; Masco Industries, MascoTech; Progressive Tool; Tecumseh Products, Inc.

For full biographical listings, see the Martindale-Hubbell Law Directory

CLARKSTON, Oakland Co.

BULLARD, ANDERSON & ANDERSON, PLLC (AV)

6060 Dixie Highway, Suite H, 48346-3476
Telephone: 248-623-3888
Fax: 248-623-1883
Email: firm@baalaw.com *URL:* http://www.baalaw.com

Rockwood W. Bullard III
Rae Anne Anderson
Acie G. Anderson, III

Representative Clients: ANCAR Publications, Inc.; Audio Trends, Inc.; AVC, Inc. (Advanced Visual Concepts); Clarkston Realty, Inc.; GAC Mortgage Co.; Michaelene's Granola, Inc.; Morgan Service, Inc.; Smith Disposal, Inc.; Sunview Windows, Skylights & Doors, Ltd.
Reference: NBD Bank, NA.

For full biographical listings, see the Martindale-Hubbell Law Directory

*DETROIT,** Wayne Co.

BRADY, HATHAWAY, BRADY & BRETZ, PROFESSIONAL CORPORATION (AV)

1330 Buhl Building, 48226-3602
Telephone: 313-965-3700
Telecopier: 313-965-2830
Email: brady@bradyhathaway.com

John F. Brady
Thomas M. J. Hathaway
Thomas P. Brady
Daniel J. Bretz
Connie M. Cessante
David A. Hardesty
Paul W. Coughenour
Jeffrey A. Steele
Tracy A. Leahy

David M. Cessante

Representative Clients: Beam Stream, Inc.; Bundy Corporation; Energy Conversion Devices, Inc.; Schering Corporation; Warner-Lambert; Wolverine Technologies; ABB Environmental Services.

For full biographical listings, see the Martindale-Hubbell Law Directory

KELLER, THOMA, SCHWARZE, SCHWARZE, DUBAY & KATZ, P.C. (AV)

440 East Congress, 5th Floor, 48226
Telephone: 313-965-7610
Fax: 313-965-4480
Bingham Farms, Michigan Office: 30150 Telegraph Road, Suite 444, 48025.
Telephone: 248-642-5218.

Leonard A. Keller (1906-1970)
Thomas H. Schwarze (1943-1998)
Richard J. Thoma (Retired)
Frederick B. Schwarze
Dennis B. DuBay
James R. Miller
Stewart J. Katz
Anthony J. Heckemeyer
Thomas L. Fleury
Terrence J. Miglio
Gary P. King
Robert A. Lusk
Linda M. Foster
Bruce M. Bagdady
Carl F. Schwarze
Brian A. Kreucher
Christopher M. Murray
Mark C. Knoth
John J. Rabaut
Martha A. Proctor
Joseph R. Furton, Jr.

Karin M. Young
Richard W. Fanning, Jr.
Cara L. Brott
Jonathon A. Rabin
Priscilla L. Schwarze
Susan D. Koval

Counsel for: Livonia Public Schools; Ludington News Co., Inc.
Representative Clients: Borg-Warner Corp.; E & L Transport Co.; The Kroger Co.; Holnam, Inc.
Public Employer Clients: City of Farmington Hills; City of Flint; City of Grosse Pointe Woods; Saginaw Public Schools.

For full biographical listings, see the Martindale-Hubbell Law Directory

KAREN SMITH KIENBAUM & ASSOCIATES (AV)

440 East Congress, 4th Floor, 48226-2917
Telephone: 313-967-0700
Fax: 313-967-0244
URL: http://www.lawyers.com/ksk

ASSOCIATE

James Murphy

For full biographical listings, see the Martindale-Hubbell Law Directory

AVIATION LAW

ALABAMA

*MOBILE,** Mobile Co.

CUNNINGHAM, BOUNDS, YANCE, CROWDER & BROWN, L.L.C. (AV)

1601 Dauphin Street, P.O. Box 66705, 36660
Telephone: 334-471-6191
Fax: 334-479-1031
Email: adm@cbycb.com

James A. Yance
John T. Crowder, Jr.
Robert T. Cunningham, Jr.
Joseph M. Brown, Jr.
Gregory B. Breedlove
Michael A. Worel
David G. Wirtes, Jr.
Toby D. Brown
Reggie Copeland, Jr.
Richard T. Dorman

J. Stephen Legg
George M. Dent, III

OF COUNSEL

Richard Bounds
Robert T. Cunningham
J. Kenyon Rainer, Sr., M.D., J.D.

References: Regions Bank; AmSouth Bank, N.A.

For full biographical listings, see the Martindale-Hubbell Law Directory

HELMSING, SIMS & LEACH, P.C. (AV)

The Laclede Building, 150 Government Street, Suite 2000, P.O. Box 2767, 36652
Telephone: 334-432-5521
Telecopy: 334-432-0633

Larry U. Sims
Frederick G. Helmsing
John N. Leach, Jr.
Warren C. Herlong, Jr.
James B. Newman
Robert H. Rouse
Charles H. Dodson, Jr.
Joseph P. H. Babington
R. Alan Alexander
John J. Crowley, Jr.
Joseph D. Steadman
Todd S. Strohmeyer

William R. Lancaster
Robin Kilpatrick Fincher
John Townsend Dukes
John Casey Pipes
James Bradford Pittman, Jr.

Representative Clients: American National Property and Casualty; Associated Aviation Underwriters; Baldwin Mutual Insurance Co.; Fred S. James & Co. of Pennsylvania; INA (Aviation); Kemper Group; Liberty Mutual Insurance Co.; Mutual Assurance; Sayre & Toso, Inc.; The Canadian Indemnity Co.

For full biographical listings, see the Martindale-Hubbell Law Directory

ALASKA

*ANCHORAGE,** Third Judicial District

BLISS & WILKENS, LLC (AV)

431 West Seventh Avenue Suite 202, 99501-3583
Telephone: 907-276-2999
Facsimile: 907-276-2956

MEMBERS OF FIRM

Ronald L. Bliss
James K. Wilkens

ASSOCIATE

Alfred Clayton, Jr.

OF COUNSEL

Jean E. Kizer
Deborah K. Periman

LEGAL SUPPORT PERSONNEL

Nanette Shearer

For full biographical listings, see the Martindale-Hubbell Law Directory

LAW OFFICES OF ROBERT H. WAGSTAFF (AV)

First National Bank Building, 425 G Street, Suite 610, 99501
Telephone: 907-277-8611
Facsimile: 907-258-7329

For full biographical listings, see the Martindale-Hubbell Law Directory

ARIZONA

*PHOENIX,** Maricopa Co.

BEER & TOONE, P.C. (AV)

76 East Mitchell, 85012
Telephone: 602-263-0900
Fax: 602-263-0917
Email: law@beer-toone.com

Paul Beer
Thomas L. Toone
Michael C. Sheedy

Matthew F. Winter

LEGAL SUPPORT PERSONNEL

Adrienne D. Hogate (Legal Assistant)
Sandra Alcumbrac (Legal Assistant)

Representative Clients: AIG Aviation, Inc.; AVEMCO Insurance Company; Beech Aircraft Corporation; Cessna Aircraft Company; Loss Management Services, Inc.; Mercury Insurance Group; The Southland Corporation dba 7-Eleven Food Stores; State of Arizona; Underwriters at Lloyds, London; Thrifty Car Rental.

For full biographical listings, see the Martindale-Hubbell Law Directory

CHARLES M. BREWER, LTD. (AV)

Brewer Building, 5500 North 24th Street, P.O. Box 10720, 85064
Telephone: 602-381-8787
Fax: 602-381-1152

Charles M. Brewer

Luis Pedro Guerra
John Brian Brewer

For full biographical listings, see the Martindale-Hubbell Law Directory

TERRENCE J. McGILLICUDDY, P.C. (AV)

5090 North 40th Street, Suite 148, 85018
Telephone: 602-957-1960
800-957-1960
Fax: 602-957-7015
Email: TJMCGILLIC@AAL.COM *URL:* http://www.lawyers.com/mcgillicuddy

Terrence J. McGillicuddy

For full biographical listings, see the Martindale-Hubbell Law Directory

*TUCSON,** Pima Co.

HARALSON, MILLER, PITT & McANALLY, P.L.C. (AV)

One South Church Avenue Suite 900, 85701
Telephone: 520-792-3836
Telecopier: 520-624-5080
Email: mpmpc@azstarnet.com

Dale Haralson, P.C.

Representative Clients: Bell Atlantic Metro Mobile; Farmers Investment Co.; Forest City Enterprises; Vince Granatelli Racing; KVOA Channel 4 TV; Newmont Mining Corp.; S.L. Industries, Inc.; Tucson Unified School District; University of Arizona Foundation.

For Complete List of Firm Personnel, See General Section

For full biographical listings, see the Martindale-Hubbell Law Directory

ARKANSAS

*FORREST CITY,** St. Francis Co.

BUTLER, HICKY & LONG (AV)

A Partnership of Professional Corporations
2216 North Washington Street, P.O. Box 989, 72335
Telephone: 870-633-4611
FAX: 870-633-6848
Email: bhlfirm@IPA.NET

MEMBERS OF FIRM

Philip Hicky (Ltd.)
Fletcher Long, Jr. (P.A.)

ASSOCIATE

Rita Reed Harris

Representative Clients: First National Bank of Eastern Arkansas; Southern Farm Bureau Insurance Cos.; United States Aviation Underwriters Group; National Aviation Underwriters; Hartford Accident and Indemnity Co.; Peoples Implement Co.; Virginia Insurance Reciprocal.

For full biographical listings, see the Martindale-Hubbell Law Directory

*FORT SMITH,** Sebastian Co.

THOMPSON AND LLEWELLYN, P.A. (AV)

412 South Eighteenth Street, P.O. Box 818, 72902
Telephone: 501-785-2867
Fax: 501-782-8046

William P. Thompson | James M. Llewellyn, Jr.

Representative Clients: AIG Aviation (Texas); Loss Management Service; Fort Smith Airport Commission; Air Terminal Parking Co.

For full biographical listings, see the Martindale-Hubbell Law Directory

CALIFORNIA

CARLSBAD, San Diego Co.

GATZKE, DILLON & BALLANCE (AV)

A Partnership
Suite 200, 1921 Palomar Oaks Way, 92008
Telephone: 760-431-9501
Fax: 760-431-9512

MEMBERS OF FIRM

Michael Scott Gatzke | Mark J. Dillon
Lori D. Ballance

ASSOCIATES

Michael S. Haberkorn | Tom Deak
Stephen F. Tee | Sophia R. Ray
Jill Dian Skinner | Anne E. Bickel

For full biographical listings, see the Martindale-Hubbell Law Directory

EMERYVILLE, Alameda Co.

BISHOP, BARRY, HOWE, HANEY & RYDER, A PROFESSIONAL CORPORATION (AV)

Watergate Tower III, 2000 Powell Street, Suite 1425, 94608
Telephone: 510-596-0888
Fax: 510-596-0899
Email: FirmGeneral@BBHHR.com
San Francisco Office: 44 Montgomery Street, Suite 1300, 94104.
Telephone: 415-421-8550.

Carol L. Healey

For full biographical listings, see the Martindale-Hubbell Law Directory

IRVINE, Orange Co.

SPEISER KRAUSE, A PROFESSIONAL CORPORATION (AV)

One Park Plaza Suite 470, 92614-8520
Telephone: 949-553-1421
Fax: 949-553-1346
URL: http://www.speiserkrause.com
New York, N.Y. Office: Speiser Krause Nolan & Granito, A Professional Corporation, 34th Floor, Two Grand Central Tower, 140 East 45th Street.
Telephone: 212-661-0011.
Fax: 212-953-6483.
Arlington, Virginia Office: 2300 Clarendon Boulevard, Suite 306.
Telephone: 703-522-7500.
Fax: 703-522-7905.
Dallas, Texas Office: Founders Square, 900 Jackson Street, Suite 750.
Telephone: 214-752-4664.
Fax: 214-752-4774.
Miami, Florida Office: Miami Center, 10th Floor, 201 South Biscayne Boulevard.
Telephone: 305-375-9400.
Fax: 305-375-0337.

Juanita M. Madole (Resident) | James Teague Crouse (Resident, Arlington, Virginia Office)
John J. Veth (Resident) | Frank H. Granito, III (Resident, New York, N.Y. Office)
Gerard R. Lear (Resident, Arlington, Virginia Office) | James P. Harrison (Resident)
Kenneth P. Nolan (Resident, New York, N.Y. Office)

OF COUNSEL

Joseph T. Cook | Charles F. Krause (Not admitted in CA)
Stuart M. Speiser (Not admitted in CA)

For full biographical listings, see the Martindale-Hubbell Law Directory

LONG BEACH, Los Angeles Co.

WOOLLEY RUSSELL & JOHNSON (AV)

444 West Ocean Boulevard, Suite 1700, 90802
Telephone: 562-495-6000
Telecopier: 562-435-1359
Email: mail@transportlawyers.com *URL:* http://www.transportlawyers.com
Port Hueneme, California Office: 105 East Port Hueneme Road, 93041.
Telephone: 562-495-6000.
Fax: 562-435-1359.

MEMBERS OF FIRM

David E. R. Woolley | Thomas A. Russell
Philip L. Johnson

ASSOCIATE

Thomas G. Walsh

LEGAL SUPPORT PERSONNEL

PARALEGAL

Dawn C. Breaux

For full biographical listings, see the Martindale-Hubbell Law Directory

*LOS ANGELES,** Los Angeles Co.

BAUM, HEDLUND, ARISTEI, GUILFORD & DOWNEY, A PROFESSIONAL CORPORATION (AV)

Suite 950, 12100 Wilshire Boulevard, 90025
Telephone: 310-207-3233; 800-827-0087
Facsimile: 310-820-7444
Email: bhagd@bhagd.com *URL:* http://www.bhagd.com
Washington, D.C. Office: 1250 24th Street, N.W., Suite 300.
Telephone: 202-466-0513; 800-827-0097.
Facsimile: 202-466-0527.

Michael L. Baum | Robert E. Guilford
Paul J. Hedlund | William J. Downey III (1947-1999)
J. Clark Aristei

John A. Greaves | Robert F. Foss
Cara J. Luther (Resident, Washington, D.C. Office) | Karen A. Barth

OF COUNSEL

Goerge W. Murgatroyd III | Mary F. Schiavo (Not admitted in CA)

Reference: Union Bank.

For full biographical listings, see the Martindale-Hubbell Law Directory

BELCHER, HENZIE & BIEGENZAHN, A PROFESSIONAL CORPORATION (AV)

333 South Hope Street, Suite 3650, 90071-1479
Telephone: 213-624-8293
Telecopier: 213-576-9964

Frank B. Belcher (1891-1979) | E. Lee Horton
Leo J. Biegenzahn (1926-1996) | William T. DelHagen
David Bernard (1931-1978) | Julia Azrael
John S. Curtis | Jeffrey L. Horwith
Raymond E. Hane, III

Georgette Renata Herget | Ian C. Fusselman
John Erin McOsker | Jeffrey D. Wolf
Paul R. Flaherty | Debby Lynne Zajac

OF COUNSEL

George M. Henzie

Reference: Bank of America (Los Angeles Main Office).

For full biographical listings, see the Martindale-Hubbell Law Directory

DWYER, DALY, BROTZEN & BRUNO, LLP (AV)

550 South Hope Street, Suite 1900, 90071
Telephone: 213-627-9300
Fax: 213-624-1638
Email: DB2LAW.com

PARTNERS

Ronald A. Dwyer | Peter P. Brotzen
John A. Daly | Toni Rae Bruno

ASSOCIATES

Gregory L. Anderson | Thomas A. Kosakowski
Gregory J. Salute | James N. Fincher
Wendell F. Hall | Daniel M. Walanka
John F. Schilling | Douglas A. Schenck

For full biographical listings, see the Martindale-Hubbell Law Directory

Los Angeles—Continued

LEBOVITS & DAVID, A PROFESSIONAL CORPORATION (AV)

1880 Century Park East Suite 900, 90067
Telephone: 310-277-0200
Fax: 310-552-1028
Email: mlld@msn.com *URL:* http://www.lawyers.com/lebovits&david

Moses Lebovits Deborah A. David

Kristal M. Bowman

Reference: Imperial Bank (Main Office - Beverly Hills).

For full biographical listings, see the Martindale-Hubbell Law Directory

SCHLOTHAUER & COLLINS (AV)

11999 San Vicente Boulevard, Suite 340, 90049
Telephone: 310-472-1670
Fax: 310-472-5270
Affiliated San Jose California Office: Collins & Schlothauer, 60 South Market Street, Suite 1100, 95113-2204.
Telephone: 408-298-5161.
Fax: 408-297-5766.

PARTNER

Thomas L. Schlothauer

OF COUNSEL

Mark Scott Collins

For full biographical listings, see the Martindale-Hubbell Law Directory

SULLIVAN LAW CORPORATION (AV)

545 South Figueroa Street, Suite 1216, 90071-1599
Telephone: 213-488-9200
Telecopier: 213-362-0419
Email: flightattorney@aol.com *URL:* http://www.flightattorney.com

Michael R. Sullivan

For full biographical listings, see the Martindale-Hubbell Law Directory

MENLO PARK, San Mateo Co.

O'REILLY, COLLINS & DANKO, A PROFESSIONAL CORPORATION (AV)

2500 Sand Hill Road, Suite 201, 94025-7016
Telephone: 650-854-7700
Fax: 650-854-8350

Terry O'Reilly James P. Collins
Michael S. Danko

Rian D. Jorgensen

For full biographical listings, see the Martindale-Hubbell Law Directory

*OAKLAND,** Alameda Co.

VAN BLOIS & ASSOCIATES (AV)

Suite 2245 Ordway Building, One Kaiser Plaza, 94612
Telephone: 510-444-1906
Contra Costa County 510-947-1055
Fax: 510-444-1294
Email: rlvblaw@mindspring.com *URL:* http://www.lawyers.com/vanblois

MEMBERS OF FIRM

R. Lewis Van Blois Thomas C. Knowles

OF COUNSEL

Charles E. Farnsworth

For full biographical listings, see the Martindale-Hubbell Law Directory

*REDDING,** Shasta Co.

DUGAN BARR & ASSOCIATES (AV)

1824 Court Street, P.O. Box 994390, 96099-1648
Telephone: 530-243-8008
Fax: 530-243-1648
URL: http://www.CA-lawyer.com

Dugan Barr

ASSOCIATES

Douglas Mudford J. Michael Favor

Representative Clients: City of Redding; Mid Valley Bank; Scott Valley Bank; 3M; Enloe Hospital.
References: Scott Valley Bank, Redding Branch; Mid Valley Bank, Redding Branch.

For full biographical listings, see the Martindale-Hubbell Law Directory

*SAN DIEGO,** San Diego Co.

THE LAW OFFICES OF BIRGER GREG BACINO, APC (AV)

3033 Fifth Avenue, Suite 301, 92103
Telephone: 800-801-4878
Fax: 619-299-0086
URL: http://www.bacinolaw.com
Washington, D.C. Office: 1201 Pennsylvania Avenue, Suite 300, 20004.
Telephone: 800-801-4878.
Houston, Texas Office: 510 Bering Street, Suite 300, 77057.
Telephone: 800-801-4878.

Birger Greg Bacino Richard P. Verlasky
Philip Aman

OF COUNSEL

Patricia M. Sayre Michael B. Sayre
Anthony J. DeLellis

For full biographical listings, see the Martindale-Hubbell Law Directory

*SAN FRANCISCO,** San Francisco Co.

COX & MOYER, A PROFESSIONAL CORPORATION (AV)

703 Market Street, Suite 1800, 94103
Telephone: 415-543-9464
Fax: 415-777-1828
Email: coxmoyer@aol.com

Ingemar E. Hoberg (1903-1971) Phillip E. Brown (Retired)
John H. Finger (1913-1991) Stephen T. Cox
David W. Moyer

Scott J. Allen

OF COUNSEL

Kenneth W. Rosenthal

For full biographical listings, see the Martindale-Hubbell Law Directory

SAN MATEO, San Mateo Co.

MICHAEL L. DWORKIN AND ASSOCIATES (AV)

155 Bovet Road, Suite 455, 94402
Telephone: 650-577-1321
Fax: 650-372-1077
Email: law@avialex.com *URL:* http://www.avialex.com

ASSOCIATE

David R. Newman

For full biographical listings, see the Martindale-Hubbell Law Directory

*SANTA ANA,** Orange Co.

PHILLIP J. KOLCZYNSKI LAW CORPORATION (AV)

3 Hutton Centre, Suite 900, 92707
Telephone: 714-662-2995
Fax: 714-241-4445
Email: phil@aviationlawcorp.com *URL:* http://www.aviationlawcorp.com

Phillip J. Kolczynski

For full biographical listings, see the Martindale-Hubbell Law Directory

WALNUT CREEK, Contra Costa Co.

HINTON & ALFERT, A PROFESSIONAL CORPORATION (AV)

Suite 600, 1646 North California Boulevard, 94596-4113
Telephone: 925-932-6006
Fax: 925-932-3412
Email: ha@hintonandalfert.com *URL:* http://www.lawyers.com/hintonandalfert

Peter J. Hinton Peter W. Alfert
Scott H. Z. Sumner

Elise Sanguinetti

For full biographical listings, see the Martindale-Hubbell Law Directory

COLORADO

BROOMFIELD, Boulder Co.

SCHADEN, KATZMAN, LAMPERT & MCCLUNE (AV)

11870 Airport Way, 80021-2555
Telephone: 303-465-3663
Facsimile: 303-465-3884
Email: SCHKATZLAM@aol.com *URL:* http://www.lawyers.com/schadenlaw
Troy, Michigan Office; 100 West Big Beaver Road. Suite 130. 48084.
Telephone: 248-258-4800.
Fax: 248-258-2825.

MEMBERS OF FIRM

Richard F. Schaden
Bruce A. Lampert
David I. Katzman (Not admitted in CO)
John D. McClune (Not admitted in CO)

ASSOCIATE

Kathleen M. Schaden

OF COUNSEL

Bruce O. Wilson (Not admitted in CO)

For full biographical listings, see the Martindale-Hubbell Law Directory

*DENVER,** Denver Co.

BYRNE, KIELY & WHITE, LLP (AV)

The Chancery, Suite 1300, 1120 Lincoln Street, 80203
Telephone: 303-861-5511
Fax: 303-861-0304

MEMBERS OF FIRM

Thomas J. Byrne
Joseph A. Kiely (1944-1992)
William White

OF COUNSEL

Michael L. Poindexter

John C. Knudsen
Laynie B. Gilida

For full biographical listings, see the Martindale-Hubbell Law Directory

GRUND & BRESLAU, P.C. (AV)

303 East Seventeenth Avenue, Suite 303, 80203-1263
Telephone: 303-830-7770
Facsimile: 303-830-2313
Email: g&b@grundbreslau.com

John W. Grund
Richard R. Rardin
Brad W. Breslau
Julie J. Noonan
Della S. Nelson
Graden P. Jackson

Representative Clients: American Airlines, Inc.; Avco Corp.; Delta Air Lines, Inc.; Phoenix Aviation Managers, Inc.; Scott Aviation; United States Aviation Underwriters, Inc.

For full biographical listings, see the Martindale-Hubbell Law Directory

TREECE, ALFREY, MUSAT & BOSWORTH, P.C. (AV)

999 18th Street, Suite 1600, 80202
Telephone: 303-292-2700
Facsimile: 303-295-0414
Email: tamb@tamblaw.com *URL:* http://www.tamblaw.com

L. Richard Musat
R. Bruce Phillips

Nicholas Kemp

For full biographical listings, see the Martindale-Hubbell Law Directory

WELLS, ANDERSON & RACE, LLC (AV)

1700 Broadway, Suite 1850, 80290
Telephone: 303-830-1212
Fax: 303-830-0898

Mary A. Wells
Geoffrey S. Race
Sheryl L. Anderson
Suanne M. Dell

William Strohmeyer
L. Michael Brooks, Jr.
Nathalia S. A. Hardy

Representative Clients: Raytheon Aircraft Company; The Cessna Aircraft Company; Associated Aviation Underwriters.

For full biographical listings, see the Martindale-Hubbell Law Directory

CONNECTICUT

*BRIDGEPORT,** Fairfield Co.

KOSKOFF, KOSKOFF & BIEDER, P.C. (AV)

350 Fairfield Avenue, 06604
Telephone: 203-336-4421
Fax: 203-368-3244
Email: KKB@KOSKOFF.com
Stamford, Connecticut Office: 1172 Bedford Street.
Telephone: 203-325-3686.
Danbury, Connecticut Office: 1 Moss Avenue.
Telephone: 203-792-7100.

Michael P. Koskoff
Richard A. Bieder
Rosalind J. Koskoff

Joel Thomas Faxon

For full biographical listings, see the Martindale-Hubbell Law Directory

CHESHIRE, New Haven Co.

MOORE, O'BRIEN, JACQUES & YELENAK (AV)

700 West Johnson Avenue Suite 207, 06410
Telephone: 203-272-5881
Fax: 203-272-9273

MEMBERS OF FIRM

Garrett M. Moore
Stephen L. Jacques
Gregory E. O'Brien
William P. Yelenak

For full biographical listings, see the Martindale-Hubbell Law Directory

DISTRICT OF COLUMBIA

WASHINGTON, D.C. Co.

BARKATS & ASSOCIATES, CHARTERED, ATTORNEYS AND COUNSELORS AT LAW (AV)

1250 Eye Street, N.W., 20005
Telephone: 202-682-1396
Telecopier: 202-789-0895
URL: http://www.lawyers.com/barkatslaw
Paris, France Office: 24, Rue de Prony, 75017 Paris, France.
Telephone: 01 44 29 32 32.
Telecopier: 44 29 31 00.
Affiliated Law Firm: Robert J. Shutak, 1424 Fourth Street, Santa Monica, California 90401.
Telephone: 310-458-3343.
Telecopier: 301-451-0043.

MEMBER OF THE FIRM IN WASHINGTON, D.C.

Pierre-Philippe Barkats

ASSOCIATES

Robert Clifton Burns
Pat James Kalellis (Not admitted in DC)
Jeffrey Thomas Gutierrez (Not admitted in DC)

OF COUNSEL

Jerome K. Tankel
Jacques R. Beghain (Not admitted in the United States)

For full biographical listings, see the Martindale-Hubbell Law Directory

BAUM, HEDLUND, ARISTEI, GUILFORD & DOWNEY, A PROFESSIONAL CORPORATION (AV)

1250 24th Street, N.W., Suite 300, 20037
Telephone: 202-466-0513; 800-827-0097
Fax: 202-466-0527
Email: bhagd@bhagd.com *URL:* http://www.bhagd.com
Los Angeles, California Office: Suite 950, 12100 Wilshire Boulevard.
Telephones: 310-207-3233; 800-827-0087.
Facsimile: 310-820-7444.

Cara J. Luther

OF COUNSEL

Mary F. Schiavo

For full biographical listings, see the Martindale-Hubbell Law Directory

COALE, COOLEY, LIETZ, MCINERNY & BROADUS, A PROFESSIONAL CORPORATION (AV)

818 Connecticut Avenue, N.W., Suite 857, 20006
Telephone: 202-887-4770
Facsimile: 202-887-4778

(See Next Column)

*WEST PALM BEACH,** Palm Beach Co.

SEARCY DENNEY SCAROLA BARNHART & SHIPLEY, PROFESSIONAL ASSOCIATION (AV)
2139 Palm Beach Lakes Boulevard, P.O. Drawer 3626, 33402-3626
Telephone: 561-686-6300
800-780-8607
800-220-7006 (Spanish)
Fax: 561-478-0754
Email: CDS@SEARCYLAW.COM *URL:* http://www.searcylaw.com

Christian D. Searcy, Sr.
F. Gregory Barnhart
Christopher K. Speed

LEGAL SUPPORT PERSONNEL

David W. Gilmore (Paralegal/Investigator)
Thaddeus E. Kulesa (Paralegal/Investigator)
Kathleen Simon (Paralegal)
Steve M. Smith (Paralegal/Investigator)

For Complete List of Firm Personnel, See General Section

For full biographical listings, see the Martindale-Hubbell Law Directory

SILBER & VALENTE, P.A. (AV)
1801 South Australian Avenue, Suite 201, 33409
Telephone: 561-615-6200
Facsimile: 561-615-6206
Email: pvalente@parrot.telegraph.net

Louis M. Silber
Philip L. Valente, Jr.

For full biographical listings, see the Martindale-Hubbell Law Directory

GEORGIA

*ATLANTA,** Fulton Co.

E. ALAN ARMSTRONG (AV)
Building 5, 2900 Chamblee-Tucker Road, 30341
Telephone: 770-451-0313
Fax: 770-451-0317
Email: alanarmstrong@mindspring.com *URL:* http://alanarmstrong.home.mindspring.com

Representative Clients: ST Mobile Aerospace Engineering, Inc.; Airline Transport Professionals, Inc.; West Georgia Air Service, Inc.
References: NationsBank; Aircraft Owners and Pilots Association.

For full biographical listings, see the Martindale-Hubbell Law Directory

DAVID WM. BOONE, P.C. (AV)
3166 Mathieson Drive, 30305
Telephone: 404-239-0305
Fax: 404-239-0520

David William Boone
Simone R. Siex

For full biographical listings, see the Martindale-Hubbell Law Directory

DENNIS, CORRY & PORTER, L.L.P. (AV)
3300 One Atlanta Plaza, 950 East Paces Ferry Road, P.O. Box 18640, 30326
Telephone: 404-816-2800
Wats: 800-735-0838
Fax: 404-816-5656
URL: http://www.dcplaw.com

MEMBERS OF FIRM

James S. Strawinski
Matthew J. Jewell

ASSOCIATES

George A. Koenig
Michael Goldberg

Representative Clients: Phoenix Aviation Managers, Inc.

For Complete List of Firm Personnel, See General Section

For full biographical listings, see the Martindale-Hubbell Law Directory

GRAY & GILLILAND, P.C. (AV)
400 Perimeter Center Terrace, Suite 1050, 30346-1239
Telephone: 770-392-4800
Telecopy: 770-392-4808

John C. Gray
T. Cullen Gilliland
Charles A. Ratz
Melissa A. Garrett
T. Jeffery Lehman
Robert W. Browning

P. Steven Kratsch

(See Next Column)

OF COUNSEL

E. Reid Garrett
David S. Currie
Mark B. Bullman

For full biographical listings, see the Martindale-Hubbell Law Directory

JOHNSON & WARD (AV)
2100 The Equitable Building, 100 Peachtree Street N.W., 30303-1962
Telephone: 404-524-5626
Facsimile: 404-524-1769
Email: postmaster@johnsonward.com

MEMBERS OF FIRM

William C. Lanham
Clark H. McGehee
John C. Dabney, Jr.
William D. deGolian

For Complete List of Firm Personnel, See General Section

For full biographical listings, see the Martindale-Hubbell Law Directory

SMITH, HOWARD & AJAX, LLP (AV)
300 Atlanta Financial Center South, 3333 Peachtree Road, N.E., 30326
Telephone: 404-239-1900
Fax: 404-239-1930

MEMBERS OF FIRM

Donald R. Andersen
John A. Howard
David K. Whatley

For full biographical listings, see the Martindale-Hubbell Law Directory

HAWAII

*HONOLULU,** Honolulu Co.

CRONIN, FRIED, SEKIYA, KEKINA & FAIRBANKS ATTORNEYS AT LAW, A LAW CORPORATION (AV)
1900 Davies Pacific Center, 841 Bishop Street, 96813
Telephone: 808-524-1433
Fax: 808-536-2073

Paul F. Cronin
L. Richard Fried, Jr.
Gerald Y. Sekiya
Wayne K. Kekina
David L. Fairbanks
John D. Thomas, Jr.
Stuart A. Kaneko
Bert S. Sakuda
Allen K. Williams
Keith K. H. Young

Patrick W. Border
Gregory L. Lui-Kwan
Patrick F. McTernan
Clarence S.K. Kekina
Sylvia J. Luke
Geoffrey K.S. Komeya
Frances K. Schneider

For full biographical listings, see the Martindale-Hubbell Law Directory

ILLINOIS

*CHICAGO,** Cook Co.

CLIFFORD LAW OFFICES, P.C. (AV)
120 North La Salle Street, 31st Floor, 60602
Telephone: 312-899-9090
1-800-899-0410
Fax: 312-251-1160
Email: RACA@CliffordLaw.com *URL:* http://www.cliffordlaw.com

Robert A. Clifford
Kevin P. Durkin
Thomas K. Prindable

Richard F. Burke, Jr.

For full biographical listings, see the Martindale-Hubbell Law Directory

CONNELLY & SCHROEDER (AV)
One North Franklin Street, Suite 1200, 60606-3421
Telephone: 312-251-9600
Fax: 312-251-9601
Geneva, Illinois Office: 1250 Executive Place, Suite 201.
Telephone: 630-232-6440.
FAX: 630-232-6450

MEMBERS OF FIRM

Michael P. Connelly
John L. Schroeder (Resident, Geneva Office)
Thomas F. Tobin
Mary Lisa Kamins
Brandt R. Madsen

(See Next Column)

CONNELLY & SCHROEDER, *Chicago—Continued*

ASSOCIATE

John Michael Kelly

For full biographical listings, see the Martindale-Hubbell Law Directory

JEFFREY M. GOLDBERG & ASSOCIATES, LTD. (AV)

20 North Clark Street, Suite 3100, 60602
Telephone: 312-236-4146
Fax: 312-236-5913
Email: firm@goldberglaw.com

Jeffrey M. Goldberg

Michael H. Berman
Suzanne M. Bonds
Anthony M. Goldner
Michael B. Gunzburg
Geoffrey G. Johnson
Michael V. Marsh

For full biographical listings, see the Martindale-Hubbell Law Directory

MERLO, KANOFSKY & BRINKMEIER, LTD. (AV)

208 South La Salle Street, Suite 950, 60604
Telephone: 312-553-5500
Facsimile: 312-553-1586

Michael J. Merlo
Martin A. Kanofsky
Alan J. Brinkmeier
Michael R. Gregg
Linda J. Schneider

David G. Boyer
John D. Dalton
Sarah DiLorenzo
Michael J. Gilmartin
Molly A. Horrigan
Donald G. Machalinski
Anne M. O'Brien
Ross D. Roloff
Mark H. Shanberg
Sandra J. Weber
David R. Zeigler

For full biographical listings, see the Martindale-Hubbell Law Directory

NOLAN LAW GROUP (AV)

One North La Salle Street, 35th Floor, 60602
Telephone: 312-372-5400
Toll Free: 888-372-3870
Facsimile: 312-372-0558
Email: dnolan1@ix.netcom.com

Donald J. Nolan
Albert E. Durkin, Jr.
William J. Jovan
Floyd A. Wisner
James H. Lawlor, III
Thomas P. Routh
James A. Santucci
Todd R. Mcquiston

Laura L. Ruhl

For full biographical listings, see the Martindale-Hubbell Law Directory

PAVALON, GIFFORD, LAATSCH & MARINO (AV)

Two North La Salle Street, Suite 1600, 60602
Telephone: 312-419-7400
Fax: 312-419-7408
Email: pavgif@aol.com
Rockford, Illinois Office: 501 Seventh Street, Suite 501, 61104.
Telephone: 815-968-5100.

MEMBERS OF FIRM

Eugene I. Pavalon
Geoffrey L. Gifford
Gary K. Laatsch
Frank C. Marino
Henry Phillip Gruss

Christine Walsh Donnelly

For full biographical listings, see the Martindale-Hubbell Law Directory

POWER ROGERS & SMITH, P.C. (AV)

35 West Wacker Drive, Suite 3700, 60601
Telephone: 312-236-9381
Fax: 312-236-0920

Joseph A. Power, Jr.
Larry R. Rogers
Todd A. Smith

Thomas G. Siracusa
Paul L. Salzetta
Thomas M. Power
Larry R. Rogers, Jr.
Ruth M. Degnan
Devon C. Bruce

For full biographical listings, see the Martindale-Hubbell Law Directory

ROTHSCHILD, BARRY & MYERS (AV)

A Partnership including Professional Corporations
Suite 3900, 55 West Monroe Street, 60603-5012
Telephone: 312-372-2345
FAX: 312-372-2350
Email: rbm01@wwa.com

(See Next Column)

MEMBERS OF FIRM

Roger J. Guerin
Daniel Cummings
Alan S. Madans

ASSOCIATE

Mary T. Meegan

For Complete List of Firm Personnel, See General Section

For full biographical listings, see the Martindale-Hubbell Law Directory

STRIDE, CRADDOCK & STRIDE (AV)

111 West Washington Street, Suite 1837, 60602-2773
Telephone: 312-346-5800
Fax: 312-346-3870

Herbert F. Stride
J. Patrick Craddock
Herbert L. Stride

Nicholas C. Panos
Deborah A. Stride-Saran
Vickie Voukidis Blum
Michael J. Craddock
Arthur Z. Handelman

For full biographical listings, see the Martindale-Hubbell Law Directory

WILDMAN, HARROLD, ALLEN & DIXON (AV)

225 West Wacker Drive, 30th Floor, 60606-1229
Telephone: 312-201-2000
Fax: 312-201-2555
Email: hennessy@whad.com *URL:* http://www.whad.com
Aurora, Illinois Office: 1961 W. Downer Place.
Telephone: 630-892-7021.
Fax: 630-892-7158.
Waukegan, Illinois Office: 404 West Water, P. O. Box 890.
Telephone: 847-625-5550.
Fax: 847-625-5555.
Lisle, Illinois Office: 4300 Commerce Court, Suite 320.
Telephone: 630-955-0555.
Fax: 630-955-0662
Toronto, Ontario correspondent Office: Keel Cottrelle. 36 Toronto Street, Suite 920.
Telephone: 416-367-2900.
Telefax: 416-367-2791.
Telex: 062-18660.

MEMBERS OF FIRM

Robert E. Haley
Richard C. Palmer

OF COUNSEL

Thomas D. Allen

For full biographical listings, see the Martindale-Hubbell Law Directory

JOHN C. WUNSCH, P.C. (AV)

77 West Washington Street, Suite 1420, 60602
Telephone: 312-977-9900
Fax: 312-236-2573

John C. Wunsch

Reference: The Northern Trust Co.

For full biographical listings, see the Martindale-Hubbell Law Directory

*WAUKEGAN,** Lake Co.

SALVI & SCHOSTOK, P.C. (AV)

Established 1982 as Law Offices of Patrick A. Salvi, P.C.
218 North Utica Street, 60085
Telephone: 847-249-1227
Telefax: 847-249-0138
Email: salvilaw.com *URL:* http://www.salvilaw.com
Chicago, Illinois Office: 181 West Madison, Suite 3525, 60602.
Telephone: 312-372-1227.
Telefax: 312-372-3720.

Patrick A. Salvi
Michael P. Schostok
David J. Pritchard (Resident, Chicago Office)

John Andrew Kornak
J. Matthew Dudley
Peter M. Trobe
Ellen C. Smith
Scott E. Preusen

OF COUNSEL

Bernard E. Grysen

References: First Midwest Bank, Waukegan, Illinois; Northern Trust Bank, Lake Forest, Illinois; Commercial Litigation Clients; Anderson Consulting, LLP.; Baxter Healthcare; Brunswick Corporation, Lake Forest, Illinois.

For full biographical listings, see the Martindale-Hubbell Law Directory

INDIANA

*INDIANAPOLIS,** Marion Co.

Townsend & Montross (AV)

230 East Ohio Street, 46204
Telephone: 317-264-4444
Fax: 317-264-2080

John F. Townsend, Jr. W. Scott Montross

ASSOCIATE

John F. Townsend, III

OF COUNSEL

John F. Townsend

Reference: N.B.D. Bank, N.A.

For full biographical listings, see the Martindale-Hubbell Law Directory

Wilson, Kehoe & Winingham (AV)

2859 North Meridian, 46208
Telephone: 317-920-6400
Fax: 317-920-6405
URL: http://www.wkw.com
Richmond, Indiana Office: 2901 East Main Street, 47374.
Telephone: 765-962-9113.
Connersville, Indiana Office: 118 West 30th Street, 47331.
Telephone: 765-827-1100.
Muncie, Indiana Office: 3310 West Fox Ridge Lane, 47304.
Telephone: 765-284-2474.
Fax: 765-288-8655.

MEMBERS OF FIRM

Harry A. Wilson, Jr. D. Bruce Kehoe
William E. Winingham, Jr.

ASSOCIATES

Ralph E. Dowling Gerald A. Griffin, M.D.
William E. Lukens

OF COUNSEL

Gerald L. Lawlis

Reference: The Indiana National Bank.

For full biographical listings, see the Martindale-Hubbell Law Directory

IOWA

*DES MOINES,** Polk Co.

Peddicord, Wharton, Thune and Spencer, A Professional Corporation (AV)

700 Des Moines Building, 405 Sixth Avenue, P.O. Box 9130, 50306-9130
Telephone: 515-243-2100
Fax: 515-243-2132
1-800-383-2100

Roland D. Peddicord

For full biographical listings, see the Martindale-Hubbell Law Directory

KANSAS

OVERLAND PARK, Johnson Co.

Risjord & James, P.C. (AV)

Suite 100, 10680 Barkley, 66212
Telephone: 913-381-5151
Fax: 913-381-2569
Email: RJLaw@RisjordJames.com *URL:* http://www.risjordjames.com

Randy W. James Aaron N. Woods

Lisa C. Beckley

RETIRED

John C. Risjord

For full biographical listings, see the Martindale-Hubbell Law Directory

*WICHITA,** Sedgwick Co.

Depew and Gillen, L.L.C. (AV)

151 North Main, Suite 800, 67202-1409
Telephone: 316-262-4000
Facsimile: 316-265-3819
Email: DG@DEPEWGILLEN.COM *URL:* HTTP://WWW.DEPEWGILLEN.COM

Jack Scott McInteer

For Complete List of Firm Personnel, See General Section

For full biographical listings, see the Martindale-Hubbell Law Directory

LOUISIANA

*LAFAYETTE,** Lafayette Parish

Lawrence K. Burleigh, Ltd. A Professional Law Corporation (AV)

Gordon Square, Suite 160, 100 East Vermilion Street, 70501
Telephone: 318-234-6222
Fax: 318-234-6141

Lawrence K. Burleigh, Sr.

Lawrence K. Burleigh, Jr.

For full biographical listings, see the Martindale-Hubbell Law Directory

Davidson, Meaux, Sonnier, McElligott & Swift (AV)

810 South Buchanan Street, P.O. Drawer 2908, 70502
Telephone: 318-237-1660
Fax: 318-237-3676

MEMBERS OF FIRM

James J. Davidson, Jr. (1904-1990)
V. Farley Sonnier (1942-1988)
Richard C. Meaux, Sr.
James J. Davidson, III
John E. McElligott, Jr.
John G. Swift
Jeffrey A. Rhoades
Philip A. Fontenot
Kyle L. Gideon
Theodore G. Edwards, IV
Mark C. Andrus

ASSOCIATES

John T. Andrishok Christopher J. Piasecki
Nicholas J. Zeringue

OF COUNSEL

Jan Whitehead Swift

General Counsel: Southwest Louisiana Electric Membership Corp., Inc.; Macro Oil Co., Inc.; Dwight W. Andrus Insurance Agency; Lafayette Airport Commission.
Local Counsel: Southern Pacific Transportation Co.
Representative Clients: Highlands Insurance Co.; Wal-Mart Stores, Inc.; USAA.

For full biographical listings, see the Martindale-Hubbell Law Directory

*NEW ORLEANS,** Orleans Parish

McGlinchey Stafford (AV)

A Professional Limited Liability Company
643 Magazine Street, 70130-3477
Telephone: 504-586-1200
Fax: 504-596-2800
TDD: (504) 596-2728
Telex: 584327
Cable Address: "MACSTAC"
Mailing Address: P.O. Box 60643, New Orleans, Louisiana, 70160-0643
Email: @mcglinchey.com *URL:* http://www.mcglinchey.com
Dallas, Texas Office: 2777 Stemmons Freeway, Suite 925, 75207-2401.
Telephone: 214-860-9700.
Fax: 214-860-9750.
Houston, Texas Office: 2727 Allen Parkway, Suite 1900, 77019.
Telephone: 713-520-1900.
Fax: 713-520-1025.
Baton Rouge, Louisiana Office: Ninth Floor, One American Place, 70825-0001.
Telephone: 504-383-9000.
Fax: 504-343-3076.
Jackson, Mississippi Office: Suite 1200, SkyTel Centre, 200 South Lamar Street, 39201.
Telephone: 601-960-8400.
Fax: 601-960-8406.
Lake Providence, Louisiana Office: 405 Morgan Street, 71254-2691.
Telephone: 318-559-1200.
Fax: 318-559-0609.

(See Next Column)

McGLINCHEY STAFFORD, *New Orleans—Continued*

Monroe, Louisiana Office: Dean ONB Tower, 130 Desiard Street, Suite 807, 71201.
Telephone: 318-651-0807.
Fax: 318-651-0809.

MEMBER OF FIRM

William V. Dalferes, Jr., (P.C.)

For full biographical listings, see the Martindale-Hubbell Law Directory

PULASKI, GIEGER & LABORDE, L.L.C. (AV)

Suite 4800, One Shell Square, 701 Poydras Street, 70139
Telephone: 504-561-0400
Telecopier: 504-561-1011
Covington, Louisiana Office: 434 North Columbia Street, Suite 200, 70433.
Telephone: 504-561-0400.
Telecopier: 504-809-9677.

Marjorie Randall Brown

For full biographical listings, see the Martindale-Hubbell Law Directory

MAINE

*AUGUSTA,** Kennebec Co.

JOHNSON & WEBBERT, L.L.P. (AV)

160 Capitol Street, P.O. Box 29, 04332-0029
Telephone: 207-623-5110
Fax: 207-622-4160
Email: pjohnson@johnsonwebbert.com *URL:* http://www.lawyers.com/jwl-law

Phillip E. Johnson — David G. Webbert

Representative Clients: Air France; AIG Aviation; American Eagle Insurance Co.; AVEMCO; Cessna Aircraft Corp.; COMAV Managers; Downeast Flying Service; Loss Management Services, Inc.; MaineAir, LLC; R.L.I. Insurance Co.; USAIG.

For full biographical listings, see the Martindale-Hubbell Law Directory

MARYLAND

*ANNAPOLIS,** Anne Arundel Co.

BRASSEL & BALDWIN, P.A. (AV)

112 West Street, 21401
Telephone: 410-216-7900
DC Metro: 301-261-2199
Fax: 410-974-6019
URL: http://www.brasselbaldwin.com
Baltimore, Maryland Office: The B & O Building, Suite 920. 2 North Charles Street, 21201-3754.
Telephone: 410-974-6000.
Fax: 410-385-2939.

Rignal W. Baldwin, Jr. — Jon W. Brassel

Jonathan P. Kagan — Mary Coale Baldwin
Alexander John May

OF COUNSEL

Richard T. Stansbury (Resident, Baltimore, Maryland Office)

For full biographical listings, see the Martindale-Hubbell Law Directory

*BALTIMORE,** (Independent City)

FERGUSON, SCHETELICH & HEFFERNAN, P.A. (AV)

1401 NationsBank Center, 100 South Charles Street, 21201-2725
Telephone: 410-837-2200
Fax: 410-837-1188
URL: http://www.FSHLaw.com

Robert L. Ferguson, Jr. — Christopher J. Heffernan
Thomas J. Schetelich — Craig F. Ballew
Michael N. Russo, Jr.

Peter J. Basile — Tracey J. McLauchlin
Ann D. Ware — Michele P. Zahner
Michael K. Hourigan

For full biographical listings, see the Martindale-Hubbell Law Directory

REDMOND, BURGIN & GUTIERREZ, P.A. (AV)

1301, The Fidelity Building, 210 North Charles Street, 21202
Telephone: 410-752-1555
Fax: 410-752-1064
URL: http://www.RBGLAW.com
Upper Marlboro, Maryland Office: 14746 Main Street.
Telephone: 301-952-1555.

Leonard C. Redmond, III

For Complete List of Firm Personnel, See General Section

For full biographical listings, see the Martindale-Hubbell Law Directory

SCANLAN, ROSEN & SHAR, LLC (AV)

26 South Street, 21202-3399
Telephone: 410-244-1155
Fax: 410-244-1157
Email: lawyers@triallaw.com *URL:* http://www.triallaw.com

Alfred L. Scanlan, Jr. — Marcus Z. Shar
Marc Seldin Rosen — Michael Stuart Warshaw

Timothy Cronin Lynch — Neil E Duke
Kristofer P. Cubello

OF COUNSEL

Colleen A. Cavanaugh — Lee H. Caplan
J. Michael McWilliams

For full biographical listings, see the Martindale-Hubbell Law Directory

*ELLICOTT CITY,** Howard Co.

CHARLES M. BELL A PROFESSIONAL ASSOCIATION (AV)

Suite 215 3300 North Ridge Road, 21043
Telephone: 410-465-0445
Fax: 410-465-2183
Email: BELLAW1@AOL.COM

Charles M. Bell

For full biographical listings, see the Martindale-Hubbell Law Directory

MASSACHUSETTS

*BOSTON,** Suffolk Co.

MEEHAN, BOYLE & COHEN, P.C. (AV)

2 Center Plaza Suite 600, 02108
Telephone: 617-523-8300
Fax: 617-523-0525

James F. Meehan — Peter J. Black
Leo V. Boyle — John J. Carroll, Jr.
Cynthia J. Cohen — Michael B. Bogdanow
Warren F. Fitzgerald — Karen R. Ristuben

Sherry Yee Mulloy — Bradley Mead Henry
Samuel M. Furgang — Jonathan E. Tobin

Representative Clients: Aetna Life & Casualty Co.; United States Aviation Underwriters; Mercury Marine; A Brunswick Co.; Associated Aviation Underwriters, Inc.; Richards Medical Co.; Abbot Laboroatories, Inc.; Fireman's Fund Insurance Co.; AMICA Insurance Co.; Commercial Union Insurance Co.

For full biographical listings, see the Martindale-Hubbell Law Directory

SARROUF, TARRICONE & FLEMMING (AV)

95 Commercial Wharf, 02110
Telephone: 617-227-5800
Fax: 617-227-5470
Email: Lawyers@STFLAW.COM

Camille Francis Sarrouf — George J. Leary, Jr.
Anthony Tarricone — Daniel J. Gibson
John B. Flemming — Sheryl M. Bourbeau
Camille F. Sarrouf, Jr.

For full biographical listings, see the Martindale-Hubbell Law Directory

LEXINGTON, Middlesex Co.

SALVATORE F. STRAMONDO (AV)

3 Ballard Terrace, 02420
Telephone: 781-862-6422
Fax: Available Upon Request

For full biographical listings, see the Martindale-Hubbell Law Directory

MICHIGAN

CLARKSTON, Oakland Co.

BULLARD, ANDERSON & ANDERSON, PLLC (AV)

6060 Dixie Highway, Suite H, 48346-3476
Telephone: 248-623-3888
Fax: 248-623-1883
Email: firm@baalaw.com *URL:* http://www.baalaw.com

Rockwood W. Bullard III
Rae Anne Anderson
Acie G. Anderson, III

Representative Clients: ANCAR Publications, Inc.; Audio Trends, Inc.; AVC, Inc. (Advanced Visual Concepts); Clarkston Realty, Inc.; GAC Mortgage Co.; Michaelene's Granola, Inc.; Morgan Service, Inc.; Smith Disposal, Inc.; Sunview Windows, Skylights & Doors, Ltd.
Reference: NBD Bank, NA.

For full biographical listings, see the Martindale-Hubbell Law Directory

*DETROIT,** Wayne Co.

VANDEVEER GARZIA, PROFESSIONAL CORPORATION (AV)

Suite 1600, 333 West Fort Street, 48226
Telephone: 313-961-4880
Fax: 313-961-3822
Email: vg@voyager.net
Oakland County Office: 220 Park Street, Suite 300, Birmingham, Michigan.
Telephone: 810-645-0100.
Fax: 810-645-2430.

Fred L. Vandeveer (1879-1972)
James E. Haggerty, Sr. (1900-1966)
Leroy G. Vandeveer (1902-1981)
Buelle A. Doelle (1902-1985)
James E. Plastow, Jr.
Michael M. Hathaway
John J. Lynch, III (Resident, Oakland County Office)
Thomas M. Peters
James K. Thome
Gary Alan Miller
William L. Kiriazis
Daniel P. Steele
Shelley K. Miller (Resident, Oakland County Office)
Terrance P. Lynch
Dennis B. Cotter
Bruce E. Pearce
Hal O. Carroll
David B. Timmis (Resident, Oakland County Office)

Nancy A. Hensley
Dawn M. Twydell
Christian E. Hildebrandt (Resident, Oakland County Office)
Donald C. Brownell

Representative Clients: United States Aviation Underwriters; Delta Airlines, Inc.; American Airlines; AIG Aviation, Inc.

For full biographical listings, see the Martindale-Hubbell Law Directory

TROY, Oakland Co.

SCHADEN, KATZMAN, LAMPERT & MCCLUNE (AV Ⓣ)

100 West Big Beaver Road Suite 130, 48084
Telephone: 248-258-4800
Fax: 248-258-2825
Email: SCHKATZLAM@aol.com *URL:* http://www.lawyers.com/schadenlaw
Broomfield, Colorado Office: 11870 Airport Way.
Telephone: 303-465-3663.
Facsimile: 303-465-3884.

MEMBERS OF FIRM

Richard F. Schaden
David I. Katzman
Bruce A. Lampert
John D. McClune

ASSOCIATE

Kathleen M. Schaden

OF COUNSEL

Bruce O. Wilson

For full biographical listings, see the Martindale-Hubbell Law Directory

BANKING LAW

ALABAMA

ALBERTVILLE, Marshall Co.

GULLAHORN & HARE, P.C. (AV)

310 West Main Street, P.O. Box 1669, 35950
Telephone: 256-878-1891
Fax: 256-878-1965
Email: g-hpc@cybertyme.com

Charles R. Hare, Jr. John C. Gullahorn

Representative Clients: First Bank of Boaz; The Home Bank; Peoples Independent Bank of Boaz; AmSouth Bank; Compass Bank; Albertville Industrial Development Board; Boaz Industrial Development Board; Marshall-Dekalb Electric Cooperative; Olympia Construction, Inc.

For full biographical listings, see the Martindale-Hubbell Law Directory

*BIRMINGHAM,** Jefferson Co.

BRADLEY ARANT ROSE & WHITE LLP (AV)

2001 Park Place, Suite 1400, P.O. Box 830709, 35283-0709
Telephone: 205-521-8000
Facsimile: 205-521-8800
Facsimile (SouthTrust Tower Office): 205-521-8500
URL: http://www.barw.com
Huntsville, Alabama Office: 200 Clinton Avenue West, Suite 900, 35801.
Telephone: 205-517-5100.
Facsimile: 205-533-5069.
Washington, D.C. Office: 801 Pennsylvania Avenue, NW, Suite 230, 20004.
Telephone: 202-347-8893.
Facsimile: 202-347-1684.

MEMBERS OF FIRM

J. Paul Compton Jr.
Paige Maddox Davis
L. Susan Doss
J. David Dresher
P. Nicholas Greenwood
John E. Hagefstration Jr.
Carleta Roberts Hawley
Laurence Duncan Vinson Jr.
Meade Whitaker, Jr.
Kenneth T. Wyatt

OF COUNSEL

J. Robert Fleenor
J. Reese Murray
Edward M. Selfe
C. Larimore Whitaker

ASSOCIATES

Helena F. Barkworth
Hugh Chester Boston III
Lesley S. DeRamus
Caroline Lewis Powell
J. Keith Windle

For Complete List of Firm Personnel, See General Section

For full biographical listings, see the Martindale-Hubbell Law Directory

BURR & FORMAN LLP (AV)

3100 SouthTrust Tower, 420 North 20th Street, P.O. Box 830719, 35283-0719
Telephone: 205-251-3000
Facsimile: 205-458-5100
URL: http://www.burr.com
Huntsville, Alabama Office: Suite 204, Regency Center, 400 Meridian Street.
Telephone: 205-551-0010.
Facsimile: 205-551-0043.
Atlanta, Georgia Office: Suite 1200, One Georgia Center, 600 West Peachtree Street, 30308.
Telephone: 404-815-3000.
Facsimile: 404-817-3244.

MEMBERS OF FIRM

Jeffrey T. Baker
Eric L. Carlton
Deborah P. Fisher
Gail Livingston Mills
Dwight L. Mixson, Jr.
J. Fred Powell
Gene T. Price
Bruce A. Rawls
Joseph G. Stewart
George M. Taylor, III
A. Brand Walton

For Complete List of Firm Personnel, See General Section

For full biographical listings, see the Martindale-Hubbell Law Directory

GORDON, SILBERMAN, WIGGINS & CHILDS, P.C. (AV)

1400 SouthTrust Tower, 420 North 20th Street, 35203
Telephone: 205-328-0640
Facsimilie: 205-254-1500
Washington, D.C. Office: 1621 Connecticut Avenue, N.W., Suite 400.
Telephone: 202-238-0690.
Facsimile: 202-238-0968.

(See Next Column)

RESIDENT SHAREHOLDERS

Bruce L. Gordon
Ray D. Gibbons
Timothy D. Davis

For Complete List of Firm Personnel, See General Section

For full biographical listings, see the Martindale-Hubbell Law Directory

HASKELL SLAUGHTER & YOUNG, L.L.C. (AV)

1200 AmSouth/Harbert Plaza, 1901 Sixth Avenue North, 35203
Telephone: 205-251-1000
Facsimile: 205-324-1133
Email: hsy@hsy.com
Montgomery, Alabama Office: 305 South Lawrence Street, P.O. Box 4660. 36103-4660.
Telephone: 334-265-8573.
Facsimile: 334-264-7945.

Benjamin B. Spratling III
E. Alston Ray
James C. Huckaby, Jr.
Gwen L. Windle
Frank Hampton McFadden, Jr.

Counsel For: The Banc Corporation; The Bank; Bank of America Corporation; Covenant Bank; Heritage Bank; Federal Deposit Insurance Corporation; The Equitable Life Assurance Society of the United States (Real Estate).

For Complete List of Firm Personnel, See General Section

For full biographical listings, see the Martindale-Hubbell Law Directory

JOHNSTON BARTON PROCTOR & POWELL LLP (AV)

2900 AmSouth/Harbert Plaza, 1901 Sixth Avenue North, 35203-2618
Telephone: 205-458-9400
Telecopier: 205-458-9500
Email: Law@JBPP.com

MEMBERS OF FIRM

Don B. Long, Jr.
Gilbert E. Johnston, Jr.
Ralph H. Smith II
James C. Barton, Jr.
Thomas E. Walker
Anne P. Wheeler
William D. Jones III
Robert S. Vance, Jr.
Anthony A. Joseph
R. Marcus Givhan
James P. Pewitt
Haskins W. Jones

COUNSEL

Richard J. Brockman

OF COUNSEL

G. Burns Proctor, Jr.
Jerome K. Lanning

ASSOCIATES

Scott Wells Ford
Bradley C. Mayhew
W. Jonathan Daniel
David T. Payne
Shannon L. Barnhill
Keith Adrian Brown
Donald Eugene Hayes, Jr.
Andrew David Block

Counsel for: Bank of America, NSB; BankUnited; The Chase Manhattan Bank; The CIT Group; First American National Bank; First National Bank of Chicago; First USA Bank; New America Financial, Inc.; Resource Bancshare Mortgage Group, Inc.; SouthTrust Bank, National Assn.

For full biographical listings, see the Martindale-Hubbell Law Directory

SPAIN & GILLON, L.L.C. (AV)

The Zinszer Building, 2117 2nd Avenue North, 35203
Telephone: 205-328-4100
Telecopier: 205-324-8866
Email: ddh@spain-gillon.com *URL:* http://lawlinks.com:80/atty/al/sggbn.html

MEMBERS OF FIRM

Samuel H. Frazier
Alton B. Parker, Jr.
Glenn E. Estess, Jr.
Harold H. Goings

General Counsel for: Piggly Wiggly Alabama Distributing Co.; Alabama Insurance Guaranty Association; Alabama Life and Disability Insurance Guaranty Association; Alabama Insurance Underwriters Association.
Counsel for: Compass Bank; SouthTrust Bank; AmSouth Bank; America's First Federal Credit Union.

For Complete List of Firm Personnel, See General Section

For full biographical listings, see the Martindale-Hubbell Law Directory

*HUNTSVILLE,** Madison Co.

BURR & FORMAN LLP (AV)

Suite 204, Regency Center, 400 Meridian Street, 35801
Telephone: 205-551-0010
Facsimile: 205-551-0043
Birmingham, Alabama Office: 3100 SouthTrust Tower, 420 North 20th Street.
Telephone: 205-251-3000.
Facsimile: 205-458-5100.
Atlanta, Georgia Office: Suite 1200, One Georgia Center, 600 West Peachtree Street, 30308.
Telephone: 404-815-3000.
Facsimile: 404-817-3244.

(See Next Column)

BURR & FORMAN LLP, *Huntsville—Continued*

RESIDENT PARTNER

S. Dagnal Rowe

For full biographical listings, see the Martindale-Hubbell Law Directory

STEPHENS, MILLIRONS, HARRISON & GAMMONS, P.C. (AV)

333 Franklin Street, P.O. Box 307, 35801
Telephone: 256-533-7711
Telecopier: 256-536-9388

Arthur M. Stephens — James G. Harrison
Paul L. Millirons — Robert C. Gammons

Douglas A. Baymiller — Steven J. Shaw

Representative Clients: SouthTrust Bank, N.A.; Regions Mortgage, Inc.; Norwest Mortgage, Inc.; Chase Manhattan Mortgage Corp.; Commercial Federal Mortgage Corp.; SOUTHBank, A Federal Savings Bank.

For full biographical listings, see the Martindale-Hubbell Law Directory

*MOBILE,** Mobile Co.

ARMBRECHT, JACKSON, DEMOUY, CROWE, HOLMES & REEVES, L.L.C. (AV)

1300 Riverview Plaza, P.O. Box 290, 36601
Telephone: 334-405-1300
Facsimile: 334-432-6843; 433-3821
Email: adc@ajlaw.com

MEMBERS OF FIRM

E. B. Peebles III — David E. Hudgens
David A. Bagwell — James Dale Smith
Christopher I. Gruenewald — Thomas P. Oldweiler
Edward A. Dean — James F. Watkins

Representative Clients: AmSouth Bank of Alabama (Regional Counsel); Bay Bank; BCB Holding Co., Inc.; Evergreen Bancshares, Inc.; Guaranty National Bank of Tallahassee; Gulf Bank; Gulf Federal Bank; United Bank; United Bancorporation of Alabama, Inc.

For Complete List of Firm Personnel, See General Section

For full biographical listings, see the Martindale-Hubbell Law Directory

JOHNSTONE, ADAMS, BAILEY, GORDON AND HARRIS, L.L.C. (AV)

Royal St. Francis Building, 104 St. Francis Street, 8th Floor, P.O. Box 1988, 36633
Telephone: 334-432-7682
Facsimile: 334-432-0712 or 334-432-2800
Email: attorneys@JohnstoneAdams.com *URL:* http://www.JohnstoneAdams.com
Bay Minette, Alabama Office: Dahlberg Building, 107 Hand Avenue, P.O. Box 729, 36507.
Telephone: 334-937-9473.
Facsimile: 334-937-9475.

MEMBERS OF FIRM

Charles B. Bailey, Jr. — Alan C. Christian
William H. Hardie, Jr. — R. Gregory Watts
I. David Cherniak — William Alexander Gray, Jr.

OF COUNSEL

Brock B. Gordon

For Complete List of Firm Personnel, See General Section

For full biographical listings, see the Martindale-Hubbell Law Directory

LYONS, PIPES & COOK, P.C. (AV)

2 North Royal Street, P.O. Box 2727, 36652-2727
Telephone: 334-432-4481
Cable Address: "Lysea"
Telecopier: 334-433-1820
URL: http://www.LPCLaw.com

Wesley Pipes — W. David Johnson, Jr.

Representative Clients: Chemical Bank; First National Bank of Atmore; SouthTrust Bank of Mobile.

For Complete List of Firm Personnel, See General Section

For full biographical listings, see the Martindale-Hubbell Law Directory

PIERCE, LEDYARD, LATTA & WASDEN, P.C. (AV)

Colonial Bank Centre Suite 400, 41 North Beltline, 36608
Telephone: 334-344-5151
Facsimile: 334-344-9696
Mailing Address: P.O. Box 16046, Mobile, AL, 36616
URL: http://www.pllaw.com

(See Next Column)

Donald F. Pierce — Edward G. Isaacs Bowron
Goodman G. Ledyard — John Charles S. Pierce
H. William Wasden — W. Pemble DeLashmet
C. William Daniels, Jr.

Mark Pickett Eiland — Michael A. Montgomery

OF COUNSEL

Caroline Wells Hinds

Representative Clients: Colonial Bank; First National Bank of Atmore; First Security Savings Bank; Regions Bank; SouthTrust Bank of Alabama, NA; Liberty Mortgage Corporation; Alliance Mortgage Company; New South Federal Savings Bank; Trustmark National Bank; United Companies Lending Corp.

For full biographical listings, see the Martindale-Hubbell Law Directory

*MONTGOMERY,** Montgomery Co.

PARNELL & CRUM, P.A. (AV)

641 South Lawrence Street, P.O. Box 2189, 36102
Telephone: 334-832-4202
Telecopier: 334-832-4703
Fax: 334-293-3550
Email: cnparnell@aol.com

Charles N. Parnell, III — G. Barton Crum

Robert J. Russell, Jr. — Britt Batson Griggs
James McCauley Smith — Angie Hubbard Ingram

Reference: Colonial Bank of Montgomery.

For full biographical listings, see the Martindale-Hubbell Law Directory

*TUSCALOOSA,** Tuscaloosa Co.

HUBBARD, SMITH, MCILWAIN, BRAKEFIELD & BROWDER, P.C. (AV)

808 Lurleen Wallace Boulevard, North, P.O. Box 2427, 35403
Telephone: 205-345-6789
Telecopier: 205-759-1195

Perry Hubbard (1921-1991) — W. Marcus Brakefield
Michael D. Smith — Herbert E. "Chip" Browder
Christopher L. McIlwain — Justice D. Smyth, III

Elizabeth Faxon Colwick — Gary E. Sullivan

Counsel for: Randall Publishing Co.; United States Fidelity & Guaranty Co.; Chubb Group of Insurance Cos.; West Alabama Health Services; City of Eutaw; Kimberly-Clark Corp.; Regions Bank; City of Tuscaloosa; West Alabama Bank & Trust; Tuscaloosa County Industrial Development Authority.

For full biographical listings, see the Martindale-Hubbell Law Directory

ARIZONA

*PHOENIX,** Maricopa Co.

CRUSE, FIRETAG & BOCK, P.C. (AV)

5611 North 16th Street, 85016
Telephone: 602-279-9411
Facsimile: 602-241-1260
Email: cfbpc@cfbpc.com

Robert J. Cruse — Jules I. Firetag
Daniel A. Bock

John L. Stoss — Paul F. Dowdell

OF COUNSEL

Stephen T. Meadow (P.C.)

Reference: Norwest Bank, Arizona (Main Office).

For full biographical listings, see the Martindale-Hubbell Law Directory

FENNEMORE CRAIG, A PROFESSIONAL CORPORATION (AV)

3003 North Central Avenue, Suite 2600, 85012-2913
Telephone: 602-916-5000
Fax: 602-916-5999
Tucson, Arizona Office: One South Church Avenue, Suite 1000, 85701-1620.
Telephone: 520-879-6800.
Fax: 520-879-6899.

Robert P. Robinson — Cathy L. Reece
Robert J. Hackett — Jay S. Kramer

(See Next Column)

FENNEMORE CRAIG A PROFESSIONAL CORPORATION—*Continued*

LEGAL SUPPORT PERSONNEL

LEGAL ASSISTANTS

Donna M. Horwitz

For Complete List of Firm Personnel, See General Section

For full biographical listings, see the Martindale-Hubbell Law Directory

JENNINGS, STROUSS & SALMON, P.L.C. (AV)

A Professional Limited Liability Company
One Renaissance Square, Two North Central Avenue, 85004-2393
Telephone: 602-262-5911
Fax: 602-253-3255
Email: info@jsslaw.com *URL:* http://www.jsslaw.com
Arrowhead Office: 16150 North Arrowhead Fountains Center Drive, Suite 250, Peoria, Arizona.
Telephone: 623-878-2222.
Fax: 623-878-1333.

Lee E. Esch
I. Douglas Dunipace
Anne L. Kleindienst

ASSOCIATE

Scott M. Berg

For Complete List of Firm Personnel, See General Section

For full biographical listings, see the Martindale-Hubbell Law Directory

LEWIS AND ROCA, LLP (AV)

A Limited Liability Partnership including a Professional Corporation
40 North Central Avenue, 85004-4429
Telephone: 602-262-5311
Fax: 602-262-5747
Email: clientservice@lrlaw.com *URL:* http://www.lrlaw.com
Tucson, Arizona Office: One South Church Avenue, Suite 700, 86701-1620.
Telephone: 520-622-2090.
Fax: 520-622-3088. E-Mail: clientservice@lrlaw.com.
Las Vegas, Nevada Affiliated Office: Ashcraft and Heinz LLP, 3960 Howard Hughes Parkway, 89109.
Telephone: 702-990-3570.
Fax: 702-990-3571.

MEMBERS OF FIRM

Gerald K. Smith
Richard N. Goldsmith
Patricia K. Norris
Newman R. Porter
Brent C. Gardner
Peter D. Baird
David E. Manch
Thomas H. Campbell
Scott DeWald
Kenneth Van Winkle, Jr.
Robert H. McKirgan

Representative Clients: Bank One, Arizona, NA; Citibank; Northern Trust Bank of Arizona, N.A.; Arizona Bank Wells Fargo.

For Complete List of Firm Personnel, See General Section

For full biographical listings, see the Martindale-Hubbell Law Directory

SNELL & WILMER L.L.P. (AV)

One Arizona Center, 85004-2202
Telephone: 602-382-6000
Fax: 602-382-6070
Email: postmaster@snellwilmer.com *URL:* http://www.swlaw.com
Tucson, Arizona Office: One South Church Avenue, Suite 1500, 85701-1612.
Telephone: 520-882-1200.
Fax: 520-884-1294.
Orange County Office: 1920 Main Street, Suite 1200, Irvine, California 92614-7230.
Telephone: 949-253-2700.
Fax: 949-955-2507.
Salt Lake City, Utah Office: 111 East Broadway, Suite 900, 84111-1004.
Telephone: 801-237-1900.
Fax: 801-237-1950.

MEMBERS OF FIRM

Jon S. Cohen
Kevin J. Parker
Craig K. Williams
Nicholas J. Wood

Representative Clients: For list of Representative Clients, see end of biographical listings in the Martindale-Hubbell Law Directory.

For Complete List of Firm Personnel, See General Section

For full biographical listings, see the Martindale-Hubbell Law Directory

*TUCSON,** Pima Co.

SNELL & WILMER L.L.P. (AV)

One South Church Avenue, Suite 1500, 85701-1612
Telephone: 520-882-1200
Fax: 520-884-1294
URL: http://www.swlaw.com
Phoenix, Arizona Office: One Arizona Center, 85004-2202.
Telephone: 602-382-6000.
Fax: 602-382-6070.
Orange County Office: 1920 Main Street, Suite 1200, Irvine, California 92614-7230.
Telephone: 949-253-2700.
Fax: 949-955-2507.
Salt Lake City, Utah Office: 111 East Broadway, Suite 900, 84111-1004.
Telephone: 801-237-1900.
Fax: 801-237-1950.

MEMBER OF FIRM

Michael S. Milroy

ASSOCIATE

M. Roxanne Veliz

Representative Clients: For list of Representative Clients, see end of biographical listings in the Martindale-Hubbell Law Directory.

For full biographical listings, see the Martindale-Hubbell Law Directory

ARKANSAS

*BATESVILLE,** Independence Co.

GREGG & FARRIS (AV)

262 Boswell Street, P.O. Box 2496, 72501
Telephone: 870-793-7556
Fax: 870-793-6921

MEMBERS OF FIRM

John C. Gregg
Phillip B. Farris

For full biographical listings, see the Martindale-Hubbell Law Directory

*LITTLE ROCK,** Pulaski Co.

ALLEN LAW FIRM, A PROFESSIONAL CORPORATION (AV)

950 Centre Place, 212 Center Street, 72201
Telephone: 501-374-7100
Telecopier: 501-374-1611
Email: hwallen@cei.net *URL:* http://www.lawyers.com/allenlawfirm

H. William Allen

Representative Clients: National Bank of Commerce; Wells Fargo Bank; Union Bank & Trust Co.; Empire Funding Corporation.

For full biographical listings, see the Martindale-Hubbell Law Directory

FRIDAY, ELDREDGE & CLARK (AV)

A Limited Liability Partnership of Individuals and Professional Associations
Formerly, Smith, Williams, Friday, Eldredge & Clark
2000 Regions Center, 400 West Capitol Avenue, 72201-3493
Telephone: 501-376-2011
Telecopier: 501-376-2147
Email: fecmh@fec.net

MEMBERS OF FIRM

Paul B. Benham, III (P.A.)
Richard D. Taylor (P.A.)
Harry A. Light (P.A.)

Representative Clients: Entergy Arkansas, Inc.; Regions Bank; First National Bank of Fort Smith; First National Bank of Marianna; First National Bank of Berryville; Arvest Trust Co., N.A.; Farmers Bank & Trust Co. of Magnolia; Dillard's, Inc.; Union Pacific Railroad.

For Complete List of Firm Personnel, See General Section

For full biographical listings, see the Martindale-Hubbell Law Directory

ROSE LAW FIRM, A PROFESSIONAL ASSOCIATION (AV)

120 East Fourth Street, 72201
Telephone: 501-375-9131
Telecopy: 501-375-1309

George E. Campbell
Herbert C. Rule, III
Allen W. Bird, II
Garland J. Garrett
Charles W. Baker
Kevin R. Burns
John T. Hardin
Stephen N. Joiner
Brian Rosenthal

Representative Clients: Arkansas Bankers Association; CoreStates Bank, N.A.; Mercantile Bank of Central Arkansas; Mid-South Bancshares, Inc.; NationsBank of Arkansas, N.A.; Stephens Group Inc.; Tyson Foods, Inc.

(See Next Column)

ROSE LAW FIRM A PROFESSIONAL ASSOCIATION, *Little Rock—Continued*

For Complete List of Firm Personnel, See General Section

For full biographical listings, see the Martindale-Hubbell Law Directory

WEST MEMPHIS, Crittenden Co.

SLOAN, RUBENS & PEEPLES (AV)

An Association of Lawyers
600 North Missouri Street, P.O. Box 768, 72303
Telephone: 870-735-5500
Telecopy: 870-735-2624

Edward J. Rubens (1913-1977)
Ralph W. Sloan (1915-1996)
Kent J. Rubens
David C. Peeples
J. Michael Stephenson

OF COUNSEL

Edward B. Johnson (Not admitted in AR)

General Counsel for: Bank of West Memphis; Crittenden Publishing Co., Inc.; West Memphis School District; Razorback Concrete Company; Flash Market, Inc.
Representative Clients: Arkansas School Boards Association-Risk Management Association; Vanliner Insurance; Builder's Transport, Inc.; Citizens Bank Marion; Marion School District.

For full biographical listings, see the Martindale-Hubbell Law Directory

CALIFORNIA

*BAKERSFIELD,** Kern Co.

BORTON, PETRINI & CONRON, LLP (AV)

The Borton, Petrini & Conron Building, 1600 Truxtun Avenue, 93301
Telephone: 661-322-3051
Voice Mail: 661-395-6700
Fax: 661-322-4628
Mailing Address: P.O. Box 2026, Bakersfield, California, 93303
Email: bpcbak@bpclaw.com *URL:* http://www.bpclaw.com
Other City Locations: Fresno, Los Angeles, Modesto, Redding, Sacramento, San Bernardino, San Diego, San Francisco, San Jose, San Luis Obispo, Santa Ana and Ventura.

MEMBERS OF FIRM

George F. Martin
John F. Petrini
Steve Karcher

ASSOCIATES

Brian Jensen Stowell
Raymond G. Robinson

For Complete List of Firm Personnel, See General Section

For full biographical listings, see the Martindale-Hubbell Law Directory

COSTA MESA, Orange Co.

FELDHAKE, AUGUST & ROQUEMORE (AV)

Plaza Tower, Suite 1730, 600 Anton Boulevard, 92626-7124
Telephone: 714-438-3885
Fax: 714-438-3888
Email: farlaw@hqonline.com

Robert J. Feldhake
Kenneth S. August
Lisa A. Roquemore
Joshua M. Wolff

ASSOCIATES

Dimitri P. Gross
Supriya Kakkar
Katherine A. Slayton

OF COUNSEL

Arthur J. Swerdloff
Arthur M. Wilcox, Jr.

For full biographical listings, see the Martindale-Hubbell Law Directory

IRVINE, Orange Co.

ALDRICH & BONNEFIN, P.L.C. (AV)

18200 Von Karman Avenue, Suite 730, P.O. Box 19686, 92623
Telephone: 949-474-1944
Telecopier: 949-474-0617
Email: aldrich&bonnefin@ioc.net *URL:* http://www.aldrichandbonnefin.com

Mark E. Aldrich
Janet M. Bonnefin
Mark Alan Moore
David Bustamante
Robert K. Olsen

Eric G. Baron
Keith R. Forrester
Anne M. Sharp
Erik A. Nowacki
Bruce T. Bauer

(See Next Column)

Representative Clients: Bankers' Compliance Group; Alliance Bank; American River Bank; California Commerce Bank; California Korea Bank; State Bank of India (California); Valley Independent Bank.
References: Alliance Bank; American River Bank.

For full biographical listings, see the Martindale-Hubbell Law Directory

LA JOLLA, San Diego Co.

MULVANEY, KAHAN & BARRY, A PROFESSIONAL CORPORATION (AV)

Suite 315, 875 Prospect Street, P.O. Box 1168, 92038-1168
Telephone: 619-454-1780
Fax: 619-454-1792
San Diego, California Office: Seventeenth Floor, First National Bank Center, 401 West "A" Street.
Telephone: 619-238-1010.
Fax: 619-238-1981.
Los Angeles, California Office: Union Bank Plaza, 445 South Figueroa Street, Suite 2600.
Telephone: 213-612-7765.
Orange, California Office: The Koll Center, 500 North State College Boulevard, Suite 440.
Telephone: 714-634-7069.
Fax: 714-939-8000.

Thomas A. Henry, Jr.

For full biographical listings, see the Martindale-Hubbell Law Directory

LONG BEACH, Los Angeles Co.

CAMERON, PEARLSON & GALE (AV)

One World Trade Center, Suite 1600, 90831-1600
Telephone: 562-436-3888
Telecopier: 562-437-1967
URL: http://www.cpglawyers.com
URL: http://www.lawyers.com/cmp&glaw

MEMBERS OF FIRM

Timothy C. Cameron
Charles M. Gale
Paul R. Pearlson

ASSOCIATES

Dana K. Anderson, Jr.
Susan R. Loh

For full biographical listings, see the Martindale-Hubbell Law Directory

CAYER, KILSTOFTE & CRATON, A PROFESSIONAL LAW CORPORATION (AV)

Suite 700, 444 West Ocean Boulevard, 90802
Telephone: 562-435-6008
Fax: 562-435-3704
Email: CKCCRC@AOL.COM

John J. Cayer
Stephen R. Kilstofte
Curt R. Craton

Cortlen R. Hauge

For full biographical listings, see the Martindale-Hubbell Law Directory

*LOS ANGELES,** Los Angeles Co.

LAW OFFICES OF DAVID B. BLOOM A PROFESSIONAL CORPORATION (AV)

3325 Wilshire Boulevard, Ninth Floor, 90010
Telephone: 323-938-5248; 384-4088
Telecopier: 213-385-2009

David B. Bloom

Stephen S. Monroe (A Professional Corporation)
Raphael A. Rosemblat
James E. Adler
Roy A. Levun
Jonathan Udell
Susan Carole Jay
Edward Idell
Sandra Kamenir
Steven Wayne Lazarus
Andrew Edward Briseno
Shelley M. Gould
Ted L. Travis

For full biographical listings, see the Martindale-Hubbell Law Directory

CLARK & TREVITHICK, A PROFESSIONAL CORPORATION (AV)

800 Wilshire Boulevard, 12th Floor, 90017
Telephone: 213-629-5700
Telecopier: 213-624-9441
Email: postmaster@clarktrev.com
San Francisco, California Office: 456 Montgomery Street, 20th Floor.
Telephone: 415-288-6520.
Fax: 415-398-2820.

Philip W. Bartenetti
John A. Lapinski
Leslie R. Horowitz

(See Next Column)

CLARK & TREVITHICK A PROFESSIONAL CORPORATION—*Continued*

OF COUNSEL

Judith Ilene Bloom

For Complete List of Firm Personnel, See General Section

For full biographical listings, see the Martindale-Hubbell Law Directory

FRIED, BIRD & CRUMPACKER, A PROFESSIONAL CORPORATION (AV)

1900 Avenue of the Stars, 25th Floor, 90067-6031
Telephone: 310-551-7400
Facsimile: 310-556-4487
Email: fbclawfirm@cs.com

Jack Fried	David W. Crumpacker, Jr.
Brian James Bird	Nikki Wolontis

David K. Johnson

OF COUNSEL

Keith T. Holmes	Madge S. Beletsky

For full biographical listings, see the Martindale-Hubbell Law Directory

LOEB & LOEB LLP (AV)

A Limited Liability Partnership including Professional Corporations
Suite 1800, 1000 Wilshire Boulevard, 90017-2475
Telephone: 213-688-3400
Facsimile: 213-688-3460
Email: info@loeb.com *URL:* http://www.loeb.com
Century City, California Office: Suite 2200, 10100 Santa Monica Boulevard, Los Angeles, 90067-4164.
Telephone: 310-282-2000.
Facsimile: 310-282-2192.
New York, N.Y. Office: 345 Park Avenue, 10154-0037.
Telephone: 212-407-4000.
Facsimile: 212-407-4990.
Nashville, Tennessee Office: 45 Music Square West, 37203-3205.
Telephone: 615-749-8300;
Facsimile: 615-749-8308.
Rome, Italy Office: Piazza Digione 1, 00197.
Telephone: 011-3906-808-8456.
Facsimile: 011-3906-808-8288.

MEMBERS OF FIRM

Christopher K. Aidun (New York City Office)	Robert A. Meyer
Robert S. Barry, Jr.	Susan V. Noonoo
Michele E. Beuerlein	Thomas E. Rohlf (A P.C.)
David B. Eizenman (New York City Office)	David S. Schaefer (New York City Office)
Joseph P. Heffernan (A P.C.)	Richard P. Streicher (New York City Office)
Karen Nielsen Higgins	Ronald Weinstein
Michael A. Mayerson (Century City Office)	

For Complete List of Firm Personnel, See General Section

For full biographical listings, see the Martindale-Hubbell Law Directory

O'MELVENY & MYERS LLP (AV)

400 South Hope Street, 90071-2899
Telephone: 213-430-6000
Facsimile: 213-430-6407
Cable: MOMS
Telex: 674122
Email: omminfo@omm.com *URL:* http://www.omm.com
Century City, CA Office: 1999 Avenue of the Stars, Los Angeles, 90067-6035.
Telex: 674097. Tel: 310-553-6700.
Fax: 310-246-6779.
Newport Beach, CA Office: 610 Newport Center Drive, 92660-6429.
Telex: 4722088. Tel: 949-760-9600.
Fax: 949-823-6994.
San Francisco, CA Office: Embarcadero Center West, 275 Battery Street, 94111-3305. Tel: 415-984-8700.
Fax: 415-984-8701.
New York, NY Office: Citicorp Center, 153 East 53rd Street, 10022-4611.
Telex: 129165. Tel: 212-326-2000.
Fax: 212-326-2061.
Washington, DC Office: 555 13th Street, N.W., 20004-1109.
Cable: MOMSWSH.
Telex: 89622. Tel: 202-383-5300.
Fax: 202-383-5414.
London Office: O'Melveny & Myers, 3 Finsbury Square, London, EC2A 1LA, England. Tel: 44-171-256-8451. Fax 44-171-638-8205.
Tokyo Office: Akasaka Twin Tower, East 14F, 2-17-23, Akasaka, Minato-ku, Tokyo 107-0052, Japan. Tel: 03-5562-2800.
Fax: 03-5575-3840.
Hong Kong Office: O'Melveny & Myers, Suite 1905, Tower Two, Lippo Centre, 89 Queensway, Central, Hong Kong. Tel: 852-2523-8266.
Fax: 852-2522-1760.

(See Next Column)

Shanghai Office: Kerry Centre, 20F, 1515 Nanjing Road West, Shanghai, 200040 People's Republic of China. Tel: 86-21-5298-5600.
Fax: 86-21-5298-5500.

PARTNER

Matthew T. Kirby (Los Angeles, CA and New York, NY Offices)

For Complete List of Firm Personnel, See General Section

For full biographical listings, see the Martindale-Hubbell Law Directory

OPPENHEIMER WOLFF & DONNELLY LLP (AV)

2029 Century Park East 38th Floor, 90067
Telephone: 310-788-5000
FAX: 310-277-1297
Email: oppenheimer.com
Minneapolis, Minnesota Office: 3300 Plaza VII, 45 South Seventh Street. 55402.
Telephone: 612-607-7000.
FAX: 612-607-7100.
Amsterdam, The Netherlands Office: Keizergracht 241.
Telephone: 31-20-423-4555.
FAX: 312-20-423-4545.
Brussels, Belgium Office: Avenue Louise 240, Box 5, 1050.
Telephone: 32-2-626-0500.
FAX: 32-2-626-0510.
Geneva, Switzerland Office: Rue Gabriel Eynard, 6, 1205.
Telephone: (41/22) 311-7410.
FAX: (41/22) 311-4707.
Newport Beach, California Office: 500 Newport Center Drive, Suite 700, 92660.
Telephone: 949-823-6000.
FAX: 949-823-6100.
New York, N.Y. Office: The Chrysler East Building, 19th Floor, 666 Third Avenue, 10017.
Telephone: 212-826-5000.
FAX: 212-486-0708.
Paris, France Office: 35 Boulevard des Capucines, 75002.
Telephone: (33/1) 53 45 40 00.
FAX: (33/1) 53 45 40 10.
St. Paul, Minnesota Office: 1700 First National Bank Building, 55101.
Telephone: 651-605-2000.
FAX: 651-605-2100.
Washington, D.C. Office: Oppenheimer Wolff Donnelly & Bayh LLP, 1350 Eye Street, N.W., Suite 200, 20005.
Telephone: 202-312-8000.
FAX: 202-312-8100.
Palo Alto, California Office: 3373 Hillview Avenue, Suite 200, 94304.
Telephone: 650-320-4000.
FAX: 650-320-4100.
Chicago, Illinois Office: Oppenheimer Wolff & Donnelly (Illinois), Two Prudential Plaza, 45th Floor, 180 North Stetson Avenue, 60601.
Telephone: 312-616-1800.
Fax: 312-616-5800.

RESIDENT PARTNER

W. Mark Levinson

RESIDENT ASSOCIATE

Joon M. Khang

Reference: City National Bank (Century Plaza Office, Century City).

For full biographical listings, see the Martindale-Hubbell Law Directory

NEWPORT BEACH, Orange Co.

WOLF & RICHARDS, A LAW CORPORATION (AV)

18 Corporate Plaza Drive, 92660-7901
Telephone: 949-720-9200
Fax: 949-720-9250
Email: Alan_Wolf@wolffirm.com *URL:* http://www.wolffirm.com

Alan S. Wolf

Donna L. La Porte	David B. Lally
Steven K. Linkon	Roland P. Reynolds
Mark S. Flynn	Suzanne M. Hankins
Mark R. Beckington	Timothy M. Ryan

OF COUNSEL

Janice L. Celotti

Representative Clients: Bank of America; Chase Manhattan Mortgage Corporation; Countrywide Home Loans, Inc.; Fannie Mae; Freddie Mac; GMAC Mortgage Corporation; Meritech Mortgage Services, Inc.; Norwest Mortgage Corporation; Ocwen Federal Savings Bank; Temple Inland Mortgage Corporation.

For full biographical listings, see the Martindale-Hubbell Law Directory

*SAN DIEGO,** San Diego Co.

FERRIS & BRITTON, A PROFESSIONAL CORPORATION (AV)

1600 First National Bank Center, 401 West A Street, 92101
Telephone: 619-233-3131
Fax: 619-232-9316
Email: manager@ferrisbritton.com *URL:* http://www.ferrisbritton.com

(See Next Column)

FERRIS & BRITTON A PROFESSIONAL CORPORATION, *San Diego—Continued*

Alfred G. Ferris
Steven J. Pynes
Michael R. Weinstein

OF COUNSEL

James J. Granby

Representative Clients: Central Carolina Bank; Peninsula Bank; Valley Independent Bank.

For Complete List of Firm Personnel, See General Section

For full biographical listings, see the Martindale-Hubbell Law Directory

HIGGS, FLETCHER & MACK LLP (AV)

2000 First National Bank Building, 401 West "A" Street, Suite 2600, 92101
Telephone: 619-236-1551
Telecopier: 619-696-1410
Email: info@higgslaw.com

MEMBERS OF FIRM

Franklin T. Lloyd
Kurt L. Kicklighter

For Complete List of Firm Personnel, See General Section

For full biographical listings, see the Martindale-Hubbell Law Directory

LINDLEY, SCALES & CORBETT, A PROFESSIONAL CORPORATION (AV)

550 West C Street, Suite 1800, 92101
Telephone: 619-234-9181
Fax: 619-234-8475
Email: lsc@adnc.com

Luke R. Corbett

Representative Clients: Palomar Savings & Loan Association; Bank United.

For full biographical listings, see the Martindale-Hubbell Law Directory

LUCE, FORWARD, HAMILTON & SCRIPPS LLP (AV)

A Partnership including Professional Corporations
600 West Broadway, Suite 2600, 92101
Telephone: 619-236-1414
Fax: 619-232-8311
URL: http://www.luce.com
La Jolla, California Office: 4275 Executive Square, Suite 800, 92037.
Telephone: 858-455-6611.
Fax: 858-232-8311.
Los Angeles, California Office: 777 South Figueroa, Suite 3600, 90017.
Telephone: 213-892-4992.
Fax: 213-892-7731.
San Francisco, California Office: 121 Spear Street, Suite 200, 94105.
Telephone: 415-356-4600.
Fax: 415-356-4610.
New York, N.Y. Office: Citicorp Center, 153 East 53rd Street, 26th Floor, 10022.
Telephone: 212-754-1414.
Fax: 212-644-9727.
Chicago, Illinois Office: 180 North La Salle Street, Suite 3110, 60601.
Telephone: 312-641-0580.
Fax: 312-641-0380.

Mikel R. Bistrow
Christopher Celentino
Margaret M. Mann
John B. McNeece III
William J. A. Weir (Resident, San Francisco Office)

OF COUNSEL

Michael T. Andrew
Stephen R. Brown

ASSOCIATE

Kathryn M. S. Catherwood

For Complete List of Firm Personnel, See General Section

For full biographical listings, see the Martindale-Hubbell Law Directory

MULVANEY, KAHAN & BARRY, A PROFESSIONAL CORPORATION (AV)

Seventeenth Floor, First National Bank Center, 401 West "A" Street, 92101-7994
Telephone: 619-238-1010
Fax: 619-238-1981
Email: mkb@mkblaw.com
Los Angeles, California Office: Union Bank Plaza, 445 South Figueroa Street, Suite 2600.
Telephone: 213-612-7765.
La Jolla, California Office: Suite 315, 875 Prospect Street, P.O. Box 1168.
Telephone: 619-454-1780.
Fax: 619-454-1792.

(See Next Column)

Orange, California Office: The Koll Center, 500 North State College Boulevard, Suite 440.
Telephone: 714-634-7069.
Fax: 714-939-8000.

James F. Mulvaney
Lawrence Kahan
Everett G. Barry, Jr.
Robert A. Linn
Paula Rotenberg
Melissa A. Blackburn
Mark R. Raftery
John A. Mayers
Robin L. Cahill
Kristin L. Yokomoto
Darren John Devlin

OF COUNSEL

Rex B. Beatty
Derrick W. Samuelson (Not admitted in CA)

Representative Clients: Union Bank of California; Wells Fargo Bank; NationsBank; San Diego National Bank; Fallbrook National Bank; Rancho Santa Fe National Bank.

For full biographical listings, see the Martindale-Hubbell Law Directory

*SAN FRANCISCO,** San Francisco Co.

MURPHY, PEARSON, BRADLEY & FEENEY, A PROFESSIONAL CORPORATION (AV)

88 Kearny Street, 10th Floor, 94108
Telephone: 415-788-1900
Telecopier: 415-393-8087
Email: IndividualsFirstInitialAndLastName@mpbf.com *URL:* http://www.mpbf.com
Sacramento, California Office: 701 University Avenue, Suite 150.
Telephone: 916-565-0300.
Fax: 916-565-1636.
San Jose, California Office: 80 South Market Street, 3rd Floor.
Telephone: 408-279-5792.
Facsimile: 408-279-5785.
Los Angeles, California Office: 11400 West Olympic Boulevard, Suite 249.
Telephone: 310-312-9565.
Fax: 310-312-9566.

Timothy J. Halloran
Mark Ellis (Resident, Sacramento Office)

For Complete List of Firm Personnel, See General Section

For full biographical listings, see the Martindale-Hubbell Law Directory

*SAN JOSE,** Santa Clara Co.

MAHL REHON WALWORTH & ROBERTS, A PROFESSIONAL CORPORATION (AV)

Ten Almaden Boulevard, Suite 550, 95113
Telephone: 408-494-0900
Fax: 408-494-0909
URL: http://www.mahlrehon.com

Susan J. Mahl
Peter M. Rehon
Janet R. Walworth
Lisa C. Roberts
Rogelio M. Ruíz

Phillip E. Maroc
Chris S. Friedrich
Francis X. Ferrer

For full biographical listings, see the Martindale-Hubbell Law Directory

*SANTA ROSA,** Sonoma Co.

ABBEY, WEITZENBERG, HOFFMAN & EMERY, A PROFESSIONAL CORPORATION (AV)

1105 North Dutton Avenue, P.O. Box 1566, 95402
Telephone: 707-542-5050
Telecopier: 707-542-2589
Email: info@abbeylaw.com

Richard W. Abbey

Representative Clients: Exchange Bank of Santa Rosa; Westamerica Bank; Northwestern Title Security Co.; Geyser Peak Winery; Santa Rosa City School District; Sonoma National Bank; Arrowood Vineyards & Winery; Friedman Bros. Hardware, Inc.; Bank of Lake County; Lasercraft, Inc.

For full biographical listings, see the Martindale-Hubbell Law Directory

COLORADO

*COLORADO SPRINGS,** El Paso Co.

FLYNN MCKENNA WRIGHT & KARSH (AV)

limited liability company
Plaza of the Rockies 111 South Tejon, Suite 202, 80903-3300
Telephone: 719-578-8444
Fax: 719-578-8836

(See Next Column)

FLYNN MCKENNA WRIGHT & KARSH—*Continued*

OF COUNSEL

James T. Flynn

MEMBERS OF FIRM

R. Tim McKenna
Bruce M. Wright
Randolph M. Karsh
Brian T. Murphy
Michael C. Potarf
Karl A. Berg, Jr.

Representative Clients: Western National Bank; Chase Manhattan Mortgage Corp.; First National Bank of Canon City; Colorado Bank and Trust Company of La Junta; Merrill Lynch Credit Corporation; Bank of the Rockies, N.A.; Farmers State Bank of Calhan.

For full biographical listings, see the Martindale-Hubbell Law Directory

*DENVER,** Denver Co.

BERENBAUM, WEINSHIENK & EASON, P.C. (AV)

Suite 2600 Republic Plaza, 370 17th Street, 80202
Telephone: 303-825-0800
Facsimile: 303-629-7610
Email: berenbaum1@aol.com *URL:* http://www.BWELaw.com

Charles A. Bewley
Daniel S. Duggan
David R. Eason
H. Michael Miller
Edwin G. Perlmutter
Eugene M. Sprague
Robert G. Wilson, Jr.

OF COUNSEL

Richard L. Eason

Representative Clients: Home Depot; Sprint Spectrum, L.P.; Town of Vail, Colorado; First Union Corporation; City of Englewood, Colorado; Oakwood Homes; Karman, Inc.; Wells Fargo Bank, N.A.; Berkshire Life Insurance Co.; Trinity Ventures.

For full biographical listings, see the Martindale-Hubbell Law Directory

HOLME ROBERTS & OWEN LLP (AV)

Suite 4100, 1700 Lincoln, 80203
Telephone: 303-861-7000
Telecopier: 303-866-0200
Email: hro@hro.com *URL:* http://www.hro.com
Boulder, Colorado Office: Suite 400, 1401 Pearl Street.
Telephone: 303-444-5955.
Telecopier: 303-444-1063.
Colorado Springs, Colorado Office: Suite 1300, 90 South Cascade Avenue.
Telephone: 719-473-3800.
Telecopier: 719-633-1518.
Salt Lake City, Utah Office: Suite 1100, 111 East Broadway.
Telephone: 801-521-5800.
Telecopier: 801-521-9639.
London, England Office: Heathcoat House, 3rd Floor, 20 Savile Row.
Telephone: 011-44-171-494-5600.
Telecopier: 011-44-171-287-9344.

PARTNERS OF FIRM

Daron J. Arnold
Robert H. Bach
Phillip R. Clark
Lynn Parker Hendrix
David H. Little (Salt Lake City Office)
Martha Traudt Collins Rolle (London, England Office)

ASSOCIATES

Peter O. Hansen
William C. Holland

For Complete List of Firm Personnel, See General Section

For full biographical listings, see the Martindale-Hubbell Law Directory

OTTEN, JOHNSON, ROBINSON, NEFF & RAGONETTI, P.C. (AV)

950 Seventeenth Street, 16th Floor, 80202
Telephone: 303-825-8400
Telecopier: 303-825-6525
URL: http://www.ojrnr.com

Arthur E. Otten, Jr.
J. Thomas Macdonald
Michael Westover

Representative Clients: Aetna Life Insurance Co.; American Life and Casualty Insurance Co.; Connecticut General Life Insurance Co.; General Electric Capital Corp.; Metropolitan Life Insurance Co.; SunAmerica, Inc. and affiliates; Textron Financial Corp.; U.S. Bank National Association; U S WEST Financial Services, Inc.; Wells Fargo Bank, N.A.

For Complete List of Firm Personnel, See General Section

For full biographical listings, see the Martindale-Hubbell Law Directory

SHERMAN & HOWARD L.L.C. (AV)

Attorneys and Counselors at Law
633 Seventeenth Street, Suite 3000, 80202
Telephone: 303-297-2900
Telecopier: 303-298-0940
Colorado Springs, Colorado Office: Suite 1500, 90 South Cascade Avenue, 80903.
Telephone: 719-475-2440.

(See Next Column)

Las Vegas, Nevada Office: Swendseid & Stern, a member in Sherman & Howard L.L.C., 317 Sixth Street, 89101.
Telephone: 702-387-6073.
Reno, Nevada Office: Swendseid & Stern, a member in Sherman & Howard L.L.C., 50 West Liberty Street, Suite 660, 89501.
Telephone: 702-323-1980.

James L. Cunningham
Andrew L. Blair, Jr.
Mark L. Fulford
James F. Wood
Kenneth B. Siegel
Cynthia C. Benson
Joseph J. Bronesky
Robert L. Brown
Ronald M. Eddy

COUNSEL

John W. Low
Garth C. Grissom

Representative Clients: The Colorado State Bank of Denver; Rocky Mountain Automated Clearing House Assn., Denver; Denver Clearing House Assn.; Valley Bank (Brighton); Trust Bank of Colorado; First Trust Corp.; INVESCO Trust Co.; Resources Trust Co.

For Complete List of Firm Personnel, See General Section

For full biographical listings, see the Martindale-Hubbell Law Directory

SLIVKA ROBINSON WATERS & O'DORISIO, A PROFESSIONAL CORPORATION (AV)

Suite 2600, 1099 18th Street, 80202-1926
Telephone: 303-297-2600
Telecopier: 303-297-2750
URL: http://www.srwo.com

SHAREHOLDERS

Richard P. Slivka
Peter A. Robinson
Stephen L. Waters
John W. O'Dorisio, Jr.
Ernest J. Panasci
Chevis F. Horne, Jr.
Margaret M. McClellan
Karen Samuels Jones

Deborah A. Hogan
Kerri M. Pertcheck
Susan R. Pierson
Elizabeth E. Pinckard
Daniel A. Sweetser
Bradley S. Taylor
Jill G. VanderPloeg

SPECIAL COUNSEL

Laura J. Vogelgesang
Christine Rothe Hoth

For full biographical listings, see the Martindale-Hubbell Law Directory

VAIL, Eagle Co.

OTTO, PORTERFIELD & POST, LLC (AV)

51 Eagle Road, P.O. Box 3149, 81658-3149
Telephone: 970-949-5380
Fax: 970-845-9135
Email: wbrucep@vail.net

Frederick S. Otto
Wendell B. Porterfield, Jr.
William J. Post

References: 1st Bank of Vail; WestStar Bank.

For Complete List of Firm Personnel, See General Section

For full biographical listings, see the Martindale-Hubbell Law Directory

CONNECTICUT

DARIEN, Fairfield Co.

RUCCI, BURNHAM, CARTA & EDELBERG, LLP (AV)

800 Post Road, P.O. Box 1107, 06820
Telephone: 203-655-7695
Facsimile: 203-655-4302
URL: http://www.rbce.com
Stamford, Connecticut Office: 6 Landmark Square, Suite 470.
Telephone: 203-359-5637.

MEMBERS OF FIRM

Joseph J. Rucci, Jr.
Paul H. Burnham
Mark R. Carta
Paul B. Edelberg
William M. Carello
Robert F. Maslan, Jr.

ASSOCIATES

Colette C. Symon
Karen K. Linder
Joanna F. Bowen
David J. Rucci
Sandra J. Akoury

OF COUNSEL

Ian R. Crawford
James C. Dempsey
Lawrence H. Reilly
Alberto N. Moris (Not admitted in CT)

For full biographical listings, see the Martindale-Hubbell Law Directory

*HARTFORD,** Hartford Co.

CRANMORE, FITZGERALD & MEANEY (AV)

49 Wethersfield Avenue, 06114-1102
Telephone: 860-522-9100
Telecopier: 860-522-3379

MEMBERS OF FIRM

J. J. Cranmore
John C. FitzGerald, Jr.
Joseph V. Meaney, Jr.
John P. McHugh
Patricia D. Anderson

ASSOCIATES

Michael P. McGoldrick
Leyla F. Kimball
Wendell G. Davis, Jr. (Not admitted in CT)

For full biographical listings, see the Martindale-Hubbell Law Directory

GORDON, MUIR AND FOLEY, LLP (AV)

Hartford Square North, Ten Columbus Boulevard, 06106-5123
Telephone: 860-525-5361
Telecopier: 860-525-4849
Email: admin@gmflaw.com *URL:* http://www.gmflaw.com

MEMBERS OF FIRM

William S. Gordon, Jr. (1946-1956)
George Muir (1939-1976)
Edward J. Foley (1955-1983)
Peter C. Schwartz
John J. Reid
John H. Goodrich, Jr.
R. Bradley Wolfe
Jon Stephen Berk
William J. Gallitto
Gerald R. Swirsky
Robert J. O'Brien
Philip J. O'Connor
Kenneth G. Williams
Mary Ann Santacroce
Mary Anne Alicia Charron
Andrew J. Hern
Reneé W. Dwyer
Patty G. Swan

ASSOCIATES

Doreen West Amata
Howard A. Steinman
Erik E. Roberts
Christopher J. Casciani

Reference: People's Bank.

For full biographical listings, see the Martindale-Hubbell Law Directory

NEW LONDON, New London Co.

WALLER, SMITH & PALMER, P.C. (AV)

52 Eugene O'Neill Drive, P.O. Box 88, 06320
Telephone: 860-442-0367
Telecopier: 860-447-9915
Email: wspmain@snet.net *URL:* http://www.snetyp.com/wallersmithpalmer
Old Lyme Office: 103 Halls Road.
Telephone: 860-434-8063.
Telecopier: 860-434-9452. Email: wspol@snet.net

Tracy Waller (1862-1947)
J. Rodney Smith (1906-1979)
Birdsey G. Palmer (Retired)
William W. Miner
Robert P. Anderson, Jr.
Robert W. Marrion
Hughes Griffis
Edward B. O'Connell
Frederick B. Gahagan
Tracy M. Collins
Philip M. Johnstone
David P. Condon
Valerie Ann Votto
Charles C. Anderson

James F. Spallone

General Counsel For: Town of East Lyme.
Counsel For: Citizens Bank of Connecticut; Soneco/Northeastern, Inc.; The Nature Conservancy; Fleet Bank.
Local Counsel For: McCue Mortgage Co.; Citicorp Mortgage; U.S. Department of Housing and Urban Development.

For full biographical listings, see the Martindale-Hubbell Law Directory

STAMFORD, Fairfield Co.

WOFSEY, ROSEN, KWESKIN & KURIANSKY, LLP (AV)

600 Summer Street, 06901
Telephone: 203-327-2300
Fax: 203-967-9273

MEMBERS OF FIRM

Abraham Wofsey (1915-1944)
Michael Wofsey (1927-1951)
David M. Rosen (1926-1967)
Julius B. Kuriansky (1952-1992)
Sydney C. Kweskin (1946-1998)
Monroe Silverman
Howard C. Kaplan
Edward M. Kweskin
David M. Cohen
Marshall Goldberg
Stephen A. Finn
Judith Rosenberg
Mark H. Henderson
Steven D. Grushkin
Matthew J. Forstadt
Steven M. Frederick

OF COUNSEL

Saul Kwartin
Emanuel Margolis
Anthony R. Lorenzo

SPECIAL COUNSEL

Day R. Shields

(See Next Column)

ASSOCIATES

Joseph Brachfeld
Eric M. Higgins
William A. Harrison
Daniel M. Young
Angelo A. Ziotas

Representative Clients: Banque Paribas; Benenson Realty; Cellular Information Systems, Inc.; The Chase Manhattan Bank; First County Bank; Hartford Provision Co.; Louis Dreyfus Corp.; Norwalk Federation of Teachers; People's Bank; Ridgeway Shopping Center.

For full biographical listings, see the Martindale-Hubbell Law Directory

DELAWARE

*WILMINGTON,** New Castle Co.

POTTER ANDERSON & CORROON LLP (AV)

Hercules Plaza, 1313 N. Market Street, P.O. Box 951, 19899-0951
Telephone: 302-984-6000
Fax: 302-658-1192
URL: http://www.attys.pacdelaware.com

MEMBERS OF FIRM

Leonard S. Togman
Charles S. McDowell
David B. Brown
Harold I. Salmons, III

Representative Clients: Chase Manhattan Bank (U.S.A.) N.A.; First National Bank of Maryland; Mellon Bank (East); Mercantile Bankshares; Midatlantic Bank; Second National Federal Savings Bank; Signet Bank; Wilmington Trust Company.

For Complete List of Firm Personnel, See General Section

For full biographical listings, see the Martindale-Hubbell Law Directory

DISTRICT OF COLUMBIA

WASHINGTON, D.C. Co.

BAKER & HOSTETLER LLP (AV)

Washington Square, Suite 1100, 1050 Connecticut Avenue, N.W., 20036-5304
Telephone: 202-861-1500
Fax: 202-861-1783
To contact an attorney on the Internet use first initial and surname followed by @baker-hostetler.com
URL: http://www.bakerlaw.com
In Cleveland, Ohio: 3200 National City Center, 1900 East Ninth Street.
Telephone: 216-621-0200.
In Cincinnati, Ohio: 312 Walnut Street, Suite 2650.
Telephone: 513-929-3400.
In Columbus, Ohio: Capitol Square, Suite 2100, 65 East State Street.
Telephone: 614-228-1541.
In Denver, Colorado: 303 East 17th Avenue, Suite 1100.
Telephone: 303-861-0600.
In Houston, Texas: 1000 Louisiana, Suite 2000.
Telephone: 713-751-1600.
In Beverly Hills, California: 9150 Wilshire Boulevard, Suite 205.
Telephone: 310-385-7500.
In Long Beach, California: 300 Oceangate, Suite 620.
Telephone: 562-432-2827.
In Los Angeles, California: 600 Wilshire Boulevard.
Telephone: 213-624-2400.
In Orlando, Florida: SunBank Center, Suite 2300, 200 South Orange Avenue.
Telephone: 407-649-4000.

PARTNERS

William J. Conti
Mario V. Mirabelli

For Complete List of Firm Personnel, See General Section

For full biographical listings, see the Martindale-Hubbell Law Directory

ROSS S. DELSTON (AV)

3013 Beech Street, N.W., 20015-2203
Telephone: 202-362-2260
Fax: 202-362-2754
Email: rdelston@delston.com *URL:* http://www.delston.com

For full biographical listings, see the Martindale-Hubbell Law Directory

MULDOON, MURPHY & FAUCETTE (AV)

5101 Wisconsin Avenue, N.W., 20016
Telephone: 202-362-0840
Telecopier: 202-966-9409; 202-363-5068

(See Next Column)

MULDOON, MURPHY & FAUCETTE—*Continued*

MEMBERS OF FIRM

Joseph A. Muldoon, Jr.
George W. Murphy, Jr.
Douglas P. Faucette
John R. Hall
Thomas J. Haggerty (Not admitted in DC)
Joseph P. Daly
Lori M. Beresford
Christina M. Gattuso
Lawrence M. F. Spaccasi (Not admitted in DC)
Marc Paul Levy
Paul M. Aguggia
Eric S. Kracov
Victor L. Cangelosi
Aaron M. Kaslow
Kent M. Krudys
Thomas P. Hutton

OF COUNSEL

Leslie Ann Murphy
Sean Murphy
Arthur D. Perschetz (Not admitted in DC)

For full biographical listings, see the Martindale-Hubbell Law Directory

SILVER, FREEDMAN & TAFF, L.L.P. (AV)

A Partnership including Professional Corporations
1100 New York Avenue, N.W., Suite 700, 20005-3934
Telephone: 202-414-6100
Telecopier: 202-682-0354
URL: http://www.sftlaw.com

MEMBERS OF FIRM

Sidney J. Silver (P.C.)
Robert L. Freedman (P.C.)
Barry P. Taff (P.C.)
James S. Fleischer (P.C.)
Jeffrey M. Werthan (P.C.)
Kip A. Weissman (P.C.)
Martin L. Meyrowitz (P.C.)
Richard S. Garabedian (P.C.)
Christopher R. Kelly (P.C.)
Dave M. Muchnikoff (P.C.)
Steven M. Abramson (P.C.)
Brian L. Alpert (P.C.)
Gary A. Lax (P.C.)
Michael S. Sadow (P.C.)
Nancy M. Stiles (P.C.)
Beth A. Freedman

ASSOCIATES

Craig M. Scheer
James M. Larkins, III
Matt Allen Mullins
Song A. Pak
John F. Breyer, Jr.
Michael A. Troy (Not admitted in DC)

OF COUNSEL

Howard J. Ross (P.C.)
David B. Myatt (P.C.)
John B. Selman (Not admitted in DC)
James W. Lance (Not admitted in DC)
Martin J. O'Riordan (Not admitted in DC)
Daniel C. Holdgreiwe (Not admitted in DC)
Lawrence J. Eisenberg

For full biographical listings, see the Martindale-Hubbell Law Directory

VENABLE ATTORNEYS AT LAW VENABLE, BAETJER, HOWARD & CIVILETTI, LLP (AV)

A Partnership including Professional Corporations
Suite 1000, 1201 New York Avenue, N.W., 20005
Telephone: 202-962-4800
Fax: 202-962-8300
URL: http://www.venable.com
Baltimore, Maryland Office: Venable, Baetjer and Howard LLP, 1800 Mercantile Bank & Trust Building, 2 Hopkins Plaza.
Telephone: 410-244-7400.
Fax: 410-244-7742.
McLean, Virginia Office: Venable, Baetjer and Howard LLP, Suite 400, 2010 Corporate Ridge.
Telephone: 703-760-1600.
Fax: 703-821-8949.
Rockville, Maryland Office: Venable, Baetjer and Howard LLP, Suite 500, One Church Street, P. O. Box 1906.
Telephone: 301-217-5600.
Fax: 301-217-5617.
Towson, Maryland Office: Venable, Baetjer and Howard LLP, 210 Allegheny Avenue, P. O. Box 5517.
Telephone: 410-494-6200.
Fax: 410-821-0147.

MEMBERS OF FIRM

Kenneth C. Bass, III (Also at McLean, Virginia Office)
Benjamin R. Civiletti (P.C.) (Also at Baltimore and Towson, Maryland Offices)
Jeffrey A. Dunn (Also at Baltimore, Maryland Office)
Ronald R. Glancz
Edward F. Glynn, Jr.
George F. Pappas (Also at Baltimore, Maryland Office)
James L. Shea (also at Baltimore, Maryland Office)
Joe A. Shull

For Complete List of Firm Personnel, See General Section

For full biographical listings, see the Martindale-Hubbell Law Directory

WEINER, BRODSKY, SIDMAN & KIDER, P.C. (AV)

1350 New York Avenue, N.W., Suite 800, 20005
Telephone: 202-628-2000
Telecopier: 202-628-2011
Email: wbsk@wbsk.com

(See Next Column)

Richard J. Andreano, Jr.
James A. Brodsky
Jo A. DeRoche
Don J. Halpern
Mitchel H. Kider
Mark H. Sidman
Rugenia Silver
Harvey E. Weiner
Joseph F. Yenouskas

OF COUNSEL

Cynthia L. Gilman
Susan L. Korytkowski

Karen Ruth Gustavson (Not admitted in DC)
Michael W. Kardash (Not admitted in DC)
Sherri L. Ledner
Todd A. Newman
Howard D. Reitz, Jr.
Leah Schmulewitz (Not admitted in DC)
John D. Socknat
Michael S. Waldron
Rose-Michele Weinryb

LEGAL SUPPORT PERSONNEL

GOVERNMENT RELATIONS SPECIALISTS

Lisa M. Noel
Ann B. Shearer

COMPLIANCE SPECIALIST

Andrew E. Zirneklis

For full biographical listings, see the Martindale-Hubbell Law Directory

WILMER, CUTLER & PICKERING (AV)

2445 M Street, N.W., 20037-1420
Telephone: 202-663-6000
Fax: 202-663-6363
Email: Law@Wilmer.Com *URL:* http://www.wilmer.com
Baltimore, Maryland Office: 100 Light Street, 21202.
Telephone: 410-986-2800.
Fax: 410-986-2828.
New York, New York Office: 520 Madison Avenue, 10022.
Telephone: 212-230-8800.
Fax: 212-230-8888.
European Offices:
4 Carlton Gardens, London, SW1Y 5AA, England. Telephone: +44 (20) 7 872 1000.
Fax: +44 (20) 7 839 3537.
Rue de la Loi 15# Wetstraat, B-1040 Brussels, Belgium. Telephone: +32 (2) 285 49 00.
Fax: +32 (2) 285 49 49.
Friedrichstrasse 95, D-10117 Berlin, Germany. Telephone: +49 (30) 20 22 64 00.
Fax: +49 (30) 20 22 65 00.

MEMBERS OF FIRM

Michael R. Klein
Ronald J. Greene
Michael S. Helfer
Marianne K. Smythe
Russell J. Bruemmer
Bruce E. Coolidge
Jeremy N. Rubenstein

COUNSEL

Marcia A. Wiss

For Complete List of Firm Personnel, See General Section

For full biographical listings, see the Martindale-Hubbell Law Directory

FLORIDA

LAKELAND, Polk Co.

PETERSON & MYERS, P.A. (AV)

100 East Main Street, P.O. Box 24628, 33802-4628
Telephone: 941-683-6511; 676-6934
Telecopier: 941-682-8031
Lake Wales, Florida Office: 130 East Central Avenue, P.O. Box 1079.
Telephones: 941-676-7611; 683-8942.
Winter Haven, Florida Office: Lake Region Plaza, 141 5th Street, N.W., P.O. Drawer 7608.
Telephone: 941-294-3360.

M. David Alexander, III
Philip O. Allen
Jack P. Brandon
Kristen Marie Buzzanca
Debra Leigh Cline
J. Davis Connor
Dennis G. Corrick
Roy A. Craig, Jr.
Clinton A. Curtis
Jacob C. Dykxhoorn
Joseph A. Geary
Maria "Mia" Gerber
Jonn D. Hoppe
Dennis P. Johnson
Kevin C. Knowlton
Douglas A. Lockwood, III
Corneal B. Myers
E. Blake Paul
Robert E. Puterbaugh
Thomas B. Putnam, Jr.
Deborah A. Ruster
Stephen R. Senn
Andrea Teves Smith
Keith H. Wadsworth
Kerry M. Wilson

General Counsel for: SunTrust Bank Mid-Florida, N.A.; Lakeland Regional Medical Center, Inc.; Housing Finance Authority of Polk County.
Representative Clients: NationsBank, N.A.; First Union National Bank; Mutual Wholesale Co.; Ben Hill Griffin, Inc.; E. R. Jahna Industries, Inc.

(See Next Column)

PETERSON & MYERS P.A., *Lakeland—Continued*

Approved Attorneys for: Attorneys' Title Insurance Fund; Equitable Life Assurance Society of the United States.

For full biographical listings, see the Martindale-Hubbell Law Directory

LAKE WALES, Polk Co.

PETERSON & MYERS, P.A. (AV)

130 East Central Avenue, P.O. Box 1079, 33853
Telephone: 941-676-7611; 683-8942
Telecopier: 941-676-0643
Lakeland, Florida Office: 100 East Main Street, P.O. Box 24628.
Telephones: 941-683-6511; 676-6934.
Winter Haven, Florida Office: Lake Region Plaza, 141 5th Street, N.W., P.O. Drawer 7608.
Telephone: 941-294-3360.

M. David Alexander, III
Philip O. Allen
Jack P. Brandon
Kristen Marie Buzzanca
Debra Leigh Cline
J. Davis Connor
Dennis G. Corrick
Roy A. Craig, Jr.
Clinton A. Curtis
Jacob C. Dykxhoorn
Joseph A. Geary
Maria "Mia" Gerber
Jonn D. Hoppe
Dennis P. Johnson
Kevin C. Knowlton
Douglas A. Lockwood, III
Corneal B. Myers
E. Blake Paul
Robert E. Puterbaugh
Thomas B. Putnam, Jr.
Deborah A. Ruster
Stephen R. Senn
Andrea Teves Smith
Keith H. Wadsworth
Kerry M. Wilson

General Counsel for: SunTrust Bank Mid-Florida, N.A.; Lakeland Regional Medical Center, Inc.; Housing Finance Authority of Polk County.
Representative Clients: NationsBank, N.A.; First Union National Bank; Mutual Wholesale Co.; Ben Hill Griffin, Inc.; E. R. Jahna Industries, Inc.
Approved Attorneys for: Attorneys' Title Insurance Fund; Equitable Life Assurance Society of the United States.

For full biographical listings, see the Martindale-Hubbell Law Directory

*MIAMI,** Dade Co.

ADAMS, GALLINAR, IGLESIAS & MEYER, P.A. (AV)

Colonial Bank Center, 1200 Brickell Avenue, Ninth Floor, 33131
Telephone: 305-416-6800
Facsimile: 305-416-6811
Email: agimlaw@agimlaw.com *URL:* http://www.lawyers.com/agimlaw

Robert R. Adams
Michael D. Gallinar
Mario A. Iglesias
James M. Meyer

Marta M. Cil
Enrique N. Bascuas
Santiago Eljaiek, III

For full biographical listings, see the Martindale-Hubbell Law Directory

WILLIAM L. RICHEY, P.A. (AV)

One Biscayne Tower, 2 South Biscayne Boulevard, Suite 3400, 33131-1897
Telephone: 305-372-8808
Fax: 305-372-3669
Email: wlr@richeylaw.com *URL:* http://www.lawyers.com/richeylaw
Palm City, Florida Office: 5501 S.W. Sunshine Farms Way, 34990-5696.
Telephone: 561-220-0558.
Fax: 305-372-3669.

William L. Richey (Also Of Counsel to Gunster, Yoakley, Valdes-Fauli & Stewart, P.A., Miami, Florida and Stuart, Florida)

For full biographical listings, see the Martindale-Hubbell Law Directory

*NAPLES,** Collier Co.

QUARLES & BRADY LLP (AV)

Barnett Center, 4501 Tamiami Trail North Suite 300, 34103-3060
Telephone: 941-262-5959
Fax: 941-434-4999
URL: http://www.quarles.com
Milwaukee, Wisconsin Office: 411 East Wisconsin Avenue, 53202-4497.
Telephone: 414-277-5000.
Fax: 414-271-3552.
Madison, Wisconsin Office: Firstar Plaza, One South Pinckney Street, P.O. Box 2113, 53701-2113.
Telephone: 608-251-5000.
Fax: 608-251-9166.
West Palm Beach, Florida Office: 222 Lakeview Avenue, 4th Floor, 33401.
Telephone: 561-653-5000.
Fax: 561-653-5333.
Phoenix, Arizona Office: One Camelback Building, One East Camelback Road, Suite 400, 85012-1649.
Telephone: 602-230-5500.
Fax: 602-230-5598.

(See Next Column)

Chicago, Illinois Office: Quarles & Brady LLC, Citicorp Center, 500 West Madison Street, Suite 3700.
Telephone: 312-715-5000.
Fax: 312-715-5155.

PARTNER

F. Joseph McMackin, III

For Complete List of Firm Personnel, See General Section

For full biographical listings, see the Martindale-Hubbell Law Directory

*ORLANDO,** Orange Co.

BUTLER & HOSCH, P.A. (AV)

3185 South Conway Road, Suite E, 32812
Telephone: 407-381-5200
Fax: 407-381-5577
Email: bhatch@butlerandhosch.com

C. Victor Butler, Jr.
Robert H. Hosch, Jr.

Andrea L. Aylett-Hosch
Jane E. Bond
Michael W. Udowchenko
Estee L. Lipenholtz
Nancy A. Bishop
Christopher W. Conomos

Representative Clients: United Companies Financial Corp.; First Union Home Equity Corp.; Republic Bank for Savings; Capstead Mortgage Corp.; Rhode Island Hospital Trust; First National Bank of Boston; Countrywide Home Loans, Inc.; Norwest Mortgage, Inc.; Amresco; Associates Home Equity Corp.

For full biographical listings, see the Martindale-Hubbell Law Directory

POHL & SHORT, P.A.

(See Winter Park)

*SARASOTA,** Sarasota Co.

WILLIAMS, PARKER, HARRISON, DIETZ & GETZEN, PROFESSIONAL ASSOCIATION (AV)

200 South Orange Avenue, 34236-6749
Telephone: 941-366-4800
Telecopier: 941-366-5109
Mailing Address: P.O. Box 3258, Sarasota, Florida, 34230-3258
Email: infodesk@williamsparker.com *URL:* http://www.williamsparker.com

William T. Harrison, Jr.
James L. Ritchey
J. Michael Hartenstine
Michele B. Grimes
James L. Turner
William M. Seider
Robert W. Benjamin
Terri Salt Costa
M. Lewis Hall, III
Jeffrey A. Grebe
Susan Barrett Hecker

General Counsel for: Sarasota County Public Hospital Board; Sarasota-Manatee Airport Authority; Taylor Woodrow Homes Ltd.; FCCI Mutual Insurance Co.
Local Counsel for: Bank of America; Northern Trust Bank of Florida; SunTrust Bank, Gulfcoast.

For Complete List of Firm Personnel, See General Section

For full biographical listings, see the Martindale-Hubbell Law Directory

*STUART,** Martin Co.

MCCARTHY, SUMMERS, BOBKO, MCKEY, WOOD & SAWYER, P.A. (AV)

2081 East Ocean Boulevard, Second Floor, 34996
Telephone: 561-286-1700
Fax: 561-283-1803
URL: http://www.mcsumm.com

Terence P. McCarthy
Robert P. Summers
Noel A. Bobko
John D. McKey, Jr.
Steven J. Wood
Thomas R. Sawyer
Nicola J. Boone
Steven L. Perry

Kathryn C. Bass
Robert N. Maitland, II

Representative Clients: First National Bank and Trust Company of the Treasure Coast; Hydratech Utilities; Lost Lake at Hobe Sound; Gary Player Design Group; YMCA of Martin County; Shadow Lakes Groves, Inc.; Merrill Lynch Trust Co., (Florida); Wilmington Trust, FSB; The Huntington National Bank, N.A.; WSTU-Radio, WTCN-TV.

For full biographical listings, see the Martindale-Hubbell Law Directory

*TAMPA,** Hillsborough Co.

MORRISON & MILLS, P.A. (AV)

1200 West Platt Street Suite 100, 33606
Telephone: 813-258-3311
Telecopier: 813-258-3209
Email: mmills3@tampabay.rr.com

(See Next Column)

MORRISON & MILLS P.A.—*Continued*

Thomas K. Morrison
Frederick J. Mills

Kevin A. DiTanna
Bradley Abraham Tobin

Representative Clients: SouthTrust Bank of West Florida; SouthTrust Bank, National Association; NationsBank of Florida, N.A.; Mercantile Bank; Southern Commerce Bank; Regions Bank; CitiBank; Liberty Savings Bank.

For full biographical listings, see the Martindale-Hubbell Law Directory

*WEST PALM BEACH,** Palm Beach Co.

WARD, DAMON, BEVERLY, TITTLE & POSNER, P.A. (AV)

4420 Beacon Circle, 33407-3270
Telephone: 561-842-3000
Stuart: 561-223-5550
Fax: 561-842-3626
Email: wdbtp@wdbtp.com *URL:* http://www.wdbtp.com

James F. Cooney, Jr. (1950-1992)
Conrad Damon
Andrew Fulton, IV
Irwin R. Gilbert
Craig I. Kelley
Michael J Posner
Roger C. Stanton
James D. Tittle, Jr.
Philip H. Ward, III

OF COUNSEL

Don Beverly

For full biographical listings, see the Martindale-Hubbell Law Directory

WINTER HAVEN, Polk Co.

PETERSON & MYERS, P.A. (AV)

Lake Region Plaza, 141 5th Street N.W., P.O. Drawer 7608, 33883-7608
Telephone: 941-294-3360
Lake Wales, Florida Office: 130 East Central Avenue, P.O. Box 1079.
Telephones: 941-676-7611; 683-8942.
Lakeland, Florida Office: 100 East Main Street, P.O. Box 24628.
Telephones: 941-683-6511; 676-6934.

M. David Alexander, III
Philip O. Allen
Jack P. Brandon
Kristen Marie Buzzanca
Debra Leigh Cline
J. Davis Connor
Dennis G. Corrick
Roy A. Craig, Jr.
Clinton A. Curtis
Jacob C. Dykxhoorn
Joseph A. Geary
Maria "Mia" Gerber
Jonn D. Hoppe
Dennis P. Johnson
Kevin C. Knowlton
Douglas A. Lockwood, III
Corneal B. Myers
E. Blake Paul
Robert E. Puterbaugh
Thomas B. Putnam, Jr.
Deborah A. Ruster
Stephen R. Senn
Andrea Teves Smith
Keith H. Wadsworth
Kerry M. Wilson

General Counsel for: SunTrust Bank Mid-Florida, N.A.; Lakeland Regional Medical Center, Inc.; Housing Finance Authority of Polk County.
Representative Clients: NationsBank, N.A.; First Union National Bank; Mutual Wholesale Co.; Ben Hill Griffin, Inc.; E. R. Jahna Industries, Inc.
Approved Attorneys for: Attorneys' Title Insurance Fund; Equitable Life Assurance Society of the United States.

For full biographical listings, see the Martindale-Hubbell Law Directory

WINTER PARK, Orange Co.

POHL & SHORT, P.A. (AV)

280 West Canton Avenue, Suite 410, P.O. Box 3208, 32790
Telephone: 407-647-7645; 407-647-POHL
Telefax: 407-647-2314
Email: ps@pohlshort.com

Dwight I. Cool
Alexander S. Douglas II
Gary A. Forster
E. Givens Goodspeed
Mark A. Grimes
Robert S. Hoofman
Roger A. Kelly
Adam O. Kirwan
David J. Kohs
Frank L. Pohl
James Everett Shepherd V
Houston E. Short
John R. Simpson, Jr.

Representative Clients: American Generator Co.; Copelco Capital, Inc.; Denim U.S.A., Inc.; Ford Motor Credit Co.; Lodestar Technology, Inc.; Lutheran Brotherhood; SunTrust, N.A.; Trax, Inc.

For full biographical listings, see the Martindale-Hubbell Law Directory

GEORGIA

*ATLANTA,** Fulton Co.

HARKLEROAD & HERMANCE, A PROFESSIONAL CORPORATION (AV)

2500 International Tower-Peachtree Center, 229 Peachtree Street, N.E., 30303
Telephone: 404-588-9211
Telecopier: 404-659-0860

Donald R. Harkleroad

For full biographical listings, see the Martindale-Hubbell Law Directory

PARKER, HUDSON, RAINER & DOBBS LLP (AV)

1500 Marquis Two Tower, 285 Peachtree Center Avenue, N.E., 30303
Telephone: 404-523-5300
Fax: 404-522-8409
Tallahassee, Florida Office: The Perkins House, 118 North Gadsden Street, 32301.
Telephone: 904-681-0191.
Fax: 904-681-9493.

MEMBERS OF FIRM

C. Edward Dobbs
Mitchell M. Purvis
Robert A. Crosby
Douglas A. Nail
Bobbi Acord Gomez

For full biographical listings, see the Martindale-Hubbell Law Directory

*AUGUSTA,** Richmond Co.

WARLICK, TRITT & STEBBINS, L.L.P. (AV)

15th Floor, First Union Bank Building, 699 Broad Street, 30901-1454
Telephone: 706-722-7543
Fax: 706-722-1822
Email: wts@wts-lawfirm.com
Columbia County Office: 119 Davis Road, Martinez, Georgia 30907.
Telephone: 706-860-7595.
Fax: 706-860-7597.

MEMBERS OF FIRM

William Byrd Warlick
Roy D. Tritt (Resident, Martinez Office)
Charles C. Stebbins, III
E. L. Clark Speese
C. Gregory Bryan

OF COUNSEL

Richard E. Miley

For full biographical listings, see the Martindale-Hubbell Law Directory

*COLUMBUS,** Muscogee Co.

HATCHER, STUBBS, LAND, HOLLIS & ROTHSCHILD (AV)

A Limited Liability Partnership
Suite 500 The Corporate Center, 233 12th Street, P.O. Box 2707, 31902-2707
Telephone: 706-324-0201
Telecopier: 706-322-7747
Email: mailman@hatcherstubbs.com

MEMBERS OF FIRM

J. Barrington Vaught
George W. Mize, Jr.
John M. Tanzine, III
Alan F. Rothschild, Jr.

General Counsel for: SunTrust Bank, West Georgia, N.A.; TOM'S Foods Inc.; Muscogee County Board of Education; St. Francis Hospital, Inc.

For Complete List of Firm Personnel, See General Section

For full biographical listings, see the Martindale-Hubbell Law Directory

*GRIFFIN,** Spalding Co.

ROBERT H. SMALLEY, JR., P.C. (AV)

115 North Sixth Street, P.O. Box 907, 30224
Telephone: 770-228-2125
Telecopier: 770-228-5018

Robert H. Smalley, Jr.
Thomas E. Baynham, III

Representative Clients: Premier Bank (Local Counsel); Griffin Spalding County Development Authority.

For full biographical listings, see the Martindale-Hubbell Law Directory

*JONESBORO,** Clayton Co.

GLAZE & GLAZE, P.C. (AV)

120 North McDonough Street, 30236
Telephone: 770-478-5555
Fax: 770-478-4555
Email: glaze@mindspring.com
Stockbridge, Georgia, 205A Corporate Center Drive, 30281. Telephone: 770-474-3347.

(See Next Column)

GLAZE & GLAZE P.C., *Jonesboro—Continued*

George E. Glaze — Kirby A. Glaze

Joe M. Harris, Jr.

For full biographical listings, see the Martindale-Hubbell Law Directory

*LAWRENCEVILLE,** Gwinnett Co.

ANDERSEN, DAVIDSON & TATE, P.C. (AV)

1505 Lakes Parkway, Suite 100, P.O. Box 2000, 30043
Telephone: 770-822-0900
Telecopier: 770-822-9680
Email: a-dt@mindspring.com

Thomas J. Andersen — Jeffrey R. Mahaffey

References: Sun Trust Bank; The Bank of Gwinnett County; Embry National Bank; Chicago Title Insurance Co.; Title Insurance Company of Minnesota; Lawyers Title Insurance Co.

For Complete List of Firm Personnel, See General Section

For full biographical listings, see the Martindale-Hubbell Law Directory

*MACON,** Bibb Co.

HALL, BLOCH, GARLAND & MEYER (AV)

1500 Charter Medical Building, P.O. Box 5088, 31208-5088
Telephone: 912-745-1625
Facsimile: 912-741-8822
Email: hbgm@hbgm.com
Midtown Macon, Georgia Office: 2452 Vineville Avenue.
Telephone: 912-745-1625.
Facsimile: 912-741-3544.

OF COUNSEL

Ellsworth Hall, III

F. Kennedy Hall, Division Counsel (Georgia): Norfolk Southern Railway Company.
Counsel for: Wachovia Bank of Georgia, N.A.; Helena Chemical Corp.; Fickling & Co.; Navistar International Corporation.

For Complete List of Firm Personnel, See General Section

For full biographical listings, see the Martindale-Hubbell Law Directory

SELL & MELTON, L.L.P. (AV)

A Limited Liability Partnership including a Professional Corporation
14th Floor, 577 Mulberry Street, P.O. Box 229, 31202-0229
Telephone: 912-746-8521
Telecopier: 912-745-6426

Andrew W. McKenna (1918-1981)
John D. Comer
Mitchel P. House, Jr.
Doye E. Green
Edward S. Sell, III
John A. Draughon
R. (Chix) Miller (Managing Partner)
Russell M. Boston (P.C.)
Brian J. Passante
Jeffrey B. Hanson

OF COUNSEL

E. S. Sell, Jr. — Buckner F. Melton

Joseph W. Popper, Jr.

General Counsel for: Macon Telegraph Publishing Co. (The Macon Telegraph); Macon-Bibb County Hospital Authority; County of Bibb; Smith & Sons Foods, Inc. (S & S Cafeterias); Macon Bibb County Industrial Authority; Burgess Pigment Co.
Local Counsel For: United States Aircraft Insurance Group (USAIG); United States Aviation Underwriters, Inc. (USAU).

For Complete List of Firm Personnel, See General Section

For full biographical listings, see the Martindale-Hubbell Law Directory

*MARIETTA,** Cobb Co.

BROWNING & TANKSLEY, LLP (AV)

Suite 225, 166 Anderson Street, 30060
Telephone: 770-424-1500
Fax: 770-424-1740

MEMBERS OF FIRM

Thomas J. Browning
Jerry A. Landers, Jr.
Jeffrey G. Casurella
Michael K. Jablonski

OF COUNSEL

George T. Smith

For full biographical listings, see the Martindale-Hubbell Law Directory

NORCROSS, Gwinnett Co.

THOMPSON, O'BRIEN, KEMP & NASUTI, P.C. (AV)

4845 Jimmy Carter Boulevard, 30093-3641
Telephone: 770-925-0111
Fax: 770-925-8597
Email: tokn@tokn.com

R. Michael Thompson
J. Patrick O'Brien
Donna N. Kemp
Albert F. Nasuti
Paul J. Morochnik

Paul B. Frickey
Bret T. Thrasher
Brian L. Hansen
Ronald F. Negin

OF COUNSEL

Betty H. Morris — Scott L. Dix

For full biographical listings, see the Martindale-Hubbell Law Directory

TUCKER, De Kalb Co.

HOTZ & ASSOCIATES, P.C. (AV)

Suite 200, 1979 Lakeside Parkway, 30084
Telephone: 770-939-4861
Fax: 770-270-9749
Email: hotz@hotzlawfirm.com

Richard F. Taylor (1921-1993) — Walter H. Hotz

James H. Baskin

Representative Clients: Regional Counsel for GE Supply, a Division of General Electric Company; Atlanta Postal Credit Union; Associated & Federal Employees Credit Union; Georgia Federal Credit Union; Peachtree Federal Credit Union; Deutsche Steinindustrie A.G.; Destag of North America, Inc.; General Trailer Services, Inc.; The Network Connection, Inc.

For full biographical listings, see the Martindale-Hubbell Law Directory

HAWAII

*HONOLULU,** Honolulu Co.

CADES SCHUTTE FLEMING & WRIGHT (AV)

Formerly Smith, Wild, Beebe & Cades
Cades Schutte Fleming & Wright Building, 1000 Bishop Street, Suite 1200, P.O. Box 939, 96808
Telephone: 808-521-9200
Telecopier: 808-521-9210
Email: cades@cades.com
Kailua-Kona, Hawaii Office: Hualalai Center, Suite B-303, 75-170 Hualalai Road.
Telephone: 808-329-5811.
Telecopier: 808-326-1175.

MEMBERS OF FIRM

Robert B. Bunn
E. Gunner Schull
Donald E. Scearce
Richard A. Hicks
Bernice Littman
Nicholas C. Dreher
Mark A. Hazlett
Philip J. Leas
Larry T. Takumi
Nelson N. S. Chun
Darryl H. W. Johnston
Cary S. Matsushige
Gino L. Gabrio
Martin E. Hsia
Gail M. Tamashiro
Grace Nihei Kido
Donna Y. L. Leong
David F.E. Banks
Jeffrey D. Watts
Michele S. Loudermilk
Laurie A. Kuribayashi

ASSOCIATES

Daniel H. Devaney IV — Dean T. Yamamoto

Marc E. Rousseau

OF COUNSEL

Harold S. Wright

Counsel for: First Hawaiian Bank; The Bank of Tokyo, Ltd.; American Savings Bank, F.S.B.; The Industrial Bank of Japan, Ltd.; Bank of America, FSB; Bank of America NT&SA.

For Complete List of Firm Personnel, See General Section

For full biographical listings, see the Martindale-Hubbell Law Directory

Honolulu—Continued

CARLSMITH BALL (AV)

A Partnership including Law Corporations
Suite 2200, Pacific Tower, 1001 Bishop Street, P.O. Box 656, 96809-3402
Telephone: 808-523-2500
Fax: 808-523-0842
Email: execdirector@carlsmith.com *URL:* http://www.carlsmith.com
Kapolei, Hawaii Office: Suite 318, Kapolei Building, 1001 Kamokila Boulevard, 96707.
Telephone: 808-523-2500.
Fax: 808-674-0850.
Wailuku, Maui Hawaii Office: Suite 400, One Main Plaza, 2200 Main Street, P.O. Box 1086, 96793-1086.
Telephone: 808-242-4535.
Fax: 808-244-4974.
Kailua-Kona, Hawaii Office: Suite 209, 75-1000 Henry Street, 96740.
Telephone: 808-329-6464.
Fax: 808-329-9450.
Hilo, Hawaii Office: 121 Waianuenue Avenue, P.O. Box 686, 96721-0686.
Telephone: 808-935-6644.
Fax: 808-935-7975.
Hagatna, Guam Office: Suite 401, Bank of Hawaii Building, 134 West Soledad Avenue, P.O. Box BF, 96932-5027.
Telephone: 671-472-6813.
Fax: 671-477-4375.
Telex: 721-6445 CWCMI GM.
Saipan, Commonwealth of the Northern Mariana Islands Office: Carlsmith Building, Capitol Hill, P.O. Box 5241, 96950-5241.
Telephone: 670-322-3455.
Fax: 670-322-3368.
Los Angeles, California Office: 9th Floor, 444 South Flower Street, 90071-2901.
Telephone: 213-955-1200.
Fax: 213-623-0032.
Washington, D.C. Office: Suite 300, 1201 Pennsylvania Avenue, N.W., 20004-2401.
Telephone: 202-628-2228.
Fax: 202-628-2071.
Mexico City, Mexico Office: Carlsmith Ball, Sierra Nevada 119, Lomas de Chapultepec, 11000 Mexico, D.F.
Telephone: 52-5-520-8514, 52-5-520-8757.
Fax: 52-5-540-1545.
Mexico, D.F. Office of Carlsmith Ball, S.C. (Authorized to practice as foreign legal consultants in Mexico): Sierra Nevada 119, Lomas de Chapultepec, 11000 Mexico, D.F.
Telephone: 52-5-520-8514, 52-5-520-8757.
Fax: 52-5-540-1545.

MEMBERS OF FIRM

Ruth D. Davis (Resident at Hagatna, Guam Office)
Paul Mullin Ganley (A Law Corporation)
Michelle C. Imata
Katherine G. Leonard
Matthew M. Matsunaga
Lawrence S. Okinaga (A Law Corporation)
Tom E. Roesser
John E. Rogers (Resident at Mexico Office)
J. Thomas Van Winkle (A Law Corporation)
Jon T. Yamamura

ASSOCIATE

Keiichi Sato

For Complete List of Firm Personnel, See General Section

For full biographical listings, see the Martindale-Hubbell Law Directory

CHING, YUEN & MORIKAWA (AV)

Pacific Tower, Suite 2700, 1001 Bishop Street, 96813
Telephone: 808-524-8880
Telecopier: 808-524-7664
URL: http://www.cymlaw.com
Email: billyuen@cymlaw.com *URL:* http://www.lawyers.com/cymlaw

MEMBERS OF FIRM

Russell L. Ching
William W. L. Yuen
Randall I. Morikawa

ASSOCIATE

Chris J. Sadayasu

Representative Clients: Finance Enterprises, Ltd.; Finance Factors, Ltd.; Finance Realty, Ltd.; Goldman, Sachs & Co.; The Hertz Corporation; Kamehameha Schools Bernice Pauahi Bishop Estate; Merrill Lynch & Co.; PaineWebber Incorporated; The Sakura Bank, Ltd.; Sen Plex Corp.

For full biographical listings, see the Martindale-Hubbell Law Directory

GOODSILL ANDERSON QUINN & STIFEL (AV)

Alii Place, Suite 1800, 1099 Alakea Street, P.O. Box 3196, 96801-3196
Telephone: 808-547-5600
FAX: 808-547-5880
Email: info@goodsill.com *URL:* http://www.goodsill.com

MEMBERS OF FIRM

Lani L. Ewart
Randall K. Steverson
Ernest J. T. Loo
Vincent A. Piekarski
Leighton J. H. S. Yuen

(See Next Column)

COUNSEL

Eric H. Sonnenberg

Representative Clients: Bank of Hawaii; American Savings Bank F.S.B.; Canadian Imperial Bank of Commerce; Central Pacific Bank; The Fuji Bank, Limited; Hawaii National Bank; The Hong Kong & Shanghai Banking Corporation, Limited; Mitsui Trust & Banking Co., Ltd.; The Royal Bank of Canada; The Sumitomo Bank, Limited.

For Complete List of Firm Personnel, See General Section

For full biographical listings, see the Martindale-Hubbell Law Directory

KESSNER DUCA UMEBAYASHI BAIN & MATSUNAGA ATTORNEYS AT LAW, A LAW CORPORATION (AV)

19th Floor, Central Pacific Plaza, 220 South King Street, 96813
Telephone: 808-536-1900
Telecopier: 808-529-7177
Telex: 723 8616 OPAC IIR

Robert C. Kessner
James N. Duca
Clyde S. Umebayashi
Elton John Bain
Emma S. Matsunaga
Muriel M. Taira

Beverly S. K. Tom
Jacqueline W.S. Amai
Melanie S. Matsui
Cori Ann C. Takamiya

OF COUNSEL

Kathy K. Higham

For full biographical listings, see the Martindale-Hubbell Law Directory

IDAHO

*BOISE,** Ada Co.

ELAM & BURKE, A PROFESSIONAL ASSOCIATION (AV)

Key Financial Center, 702 West Idaho Street, P.O. Box 1539, 83701
Telephone: 208-343-5454
Telecopier: 208-384-5844
Email: eblaw@elamburke.com

Randall A. Peterman

Representative Clients: U.S. BanCorp Leasing; Wells Fargo Bank; Citizen's Community Bank; Key Bank of Idaho; U.S. Bank.

For Complete List of Firm Personnel, See General Section

For full biographical listings, see the Martindale-Hubbell Law Directory

ILLINOIS

BOLINGBROOK, Will Co.

MOSS AND BLOOMBERG, LTD. (AV)

305 West Briarcliff Road, Suite 201, P.O. Box 1158, 60440-0858
Telephone: 630-759-0800
Telecopier: 630-759-8504
Email: info@mb-lawyers.com

Barry L. Moss
Steven P. Bloomberg
George A. Marchetti
David J. Freeman
Daniel C. Shapiro

For full biographical listings, see the Martindale-Hubbell Law Directory

*CHICAGO,** Cook Co.

ARONBERG GOLDGEHN DAVIS & GARMISA (AV)

Suite 3000 One IBM Plaza, 60611
Telephone: 312-828-9600
Telecopier: 312-828-9635
Email: agdglaw@aol.com
Schaumberg, Illinois Office: 1901 North Roselle Road, Suite 800, 60195.
Telephone: 847-985-4060.

MEMBERS OF FIRM

Nathan H. Lichtenstein
Marc W. O'Brien
Ned S. Robertson
David H. Sachs
Robert N. Sodikoff
Andrew S. Williams

OF COUNSEL

Ronald J. Aronberg
Melvin A. Blum

ASSOCIATE

William J. Serritella, Jr.

For Complete List of Firm Personnel, See General Section

For full biographical listings, see the Martindale-Hubbell Law Directory

Chicago—Continued

FAGEL & HABER (AV)

140 South Dearborn Street 14th Floor, 60603
Telephone: 312-346-7500
FAX: 312-580-2201
Telex No: 754542
Cable: "NOFLAWLAW"
URL: http://www.fandh.com

MEMBERS OF FIRM

Allen J. Fagel
Howard M. Berrington
Victor A. Des Laurier

For full biographical listings, see the Martindale-Hubbell Law Directory

FIELD & GOLAN (AV)

Three First National Plaza Suite 1500, 60602-4206
Telephone: 312-263-2300
Fax: 312-263-0939

MEMBERS OF FIRM

Robert E. Field
Margaret A. Christie
Stephen L. Golan
Donna F. Hartl

ASSOCIATES

Margaret A. Gisch
Matthew J. Cozzi
Anthony R. Taglia

OF COUNSEL

Leonard W. Golan
Frank J. Dolan
Stephen Edward Smith
John E. Vranicar

For full biographical listings, see the Martindale-Hubbell Law Directory

HOLLIS AND JOHNSON (AV)

11 East Adams Street, Suite 501, 60603
Telephone: 312-427-0700
Fax: 312-427-8407
URL: http://www.digitalawyer.com/bankruptcy

Pamela S. Hollis
Donald E. Johnson

ASSOCIATE

Linda M. Kujaca

For full biographical listings, see the Martindale-Hubbell Law Directory

MCBRIDE BAKER & COLES (AV)

500 West Madison Street 40th Floor, 60661-2511
Telephone: 312-715-5700
Cable Address: "Chilaw"
Telex: 270258
Telecopier: 312-993-9350
Email: lastname@mbc.com *URL:* http://www.mbc.com
Oakbrook Terrace, Illinois Office: Suite 1000, One Mid America Plaza, 60181-4710.
Telephone: 630-954-2100.
Telecopier: 630-954-2112.

MEMBERS OF FIRM

John J. Cresto
Richard S. Lauter
Anthony L. Frink
Theodore T. Lemberis
Francis L. Keldermans
David S. Mann
Michael L. Weissman

ASSOCIATES

Michael P. Lusk
Kathleen F. O'Connor
Paul R. Simons

For Complete List of Firm Personnel, See General Section

For full biographical listings, see the Martindale-Hubbell Law Directory

MCFADDEN & DILLON, A PROFESSIONAL CORPORATION (AV)

135 South La Salle Street, Suite 2110, 60603-4402
Telephone: 312-201-8300
Facsimile: 312-201-0535
Email: mcfaddendillonlaw@ameritech.net

Roger J. McFadden
Thomas J. Dillon

Tyrrel J. Penn

For full biographical listings, see the Martindale-Hubbell Law Directory

MATTOON, Coles Co.

CRAIG & CRAIG (AV)

1807 Broadway, P.O. Box 689, 61938-0689
Telephone: 217-234-6481
Telecopier: 217-234-6486; 258-8292
Email: craiglaw@advant.com
Mount Vernon, Illinois Office: 115 North 7th Street.
Telephone: 618-244-7511.

(See Next Column)

MEMBERS OF FIRM

Craig Van Meter (1895-1981)
Stephen L. Corn
Fred H. Kelly (1894-1971)
Robert G. Grierson
Robert M. Werden (1908-1969)
Gregory C. Ray
George N. Gilkerson (1911-1985)
Paul R. Lynch (Resident, Mount Vernon Office)
John P. Ewart
Kenneth F. Werts (Resident, Mount Vernon Office)
Richard F. Record, Jr.
John L. Barger

ASSOCIATES

Kathleen M. Stockwell
Duane A. Deters
Kristine M. Tuttle
Katy C. Fain (Resident, Mount Vernon Office)
Julie A. Webb (Resident, Mount Vernon Office)
Erin E. Wisner
John M. O'Driscoll
John F. Watson

OF COUNSEL

Jack E. Horsley

Representative Clients: First Mid-Illinois Bank & Trust, Mattoon, Illinois; Okaw Building & Loan, s.b., Mattoon, Illinois.

For full biographical listings, see the Martindale-Hubbell Law Directory

*MOUNT VERNON,** Jefferson Co.

MITCHELL, NEUBAUER & HANSON, P.C. (AV)

123 South 10th Street, Mercantile Bank Building, 6th Floor, P.O. Box 1088, 62864
Telephone: 618-242-0705
Telecopier: 618-242-4820
Mailing Address: P.O. Box 1088,
Email: MNHPC@Midwest.net

A. Ben Mitchell
Timothy R. Neubauer
Leslie James Hanson

T. David Purcell
David K. Overstreet
Henry P. Villani

Attorneys for: Mercantile Bank of Southern Illinois; Mt. Vernon Grade School District #80; Stewart Brothers Oil Producers; Mt. Vernon Airport Authority; J. M. Behimer Enterprises; Marion Ford-Mercury, Inc.

For full biographical listings, see the Martindale-Hubbell Law Directory

OAKBROOK TERRACE, DuPage Co.

MCBRIDE BAKER & COLES (AV)

Suite 1000, One Mid America Plaza, 60181-4710
Telephone: 630-954-2100
Telecopier: 630-954-2112
URL: http://www.mbc.com
Chicago, Illinois Office: 500 West Madison Street, 40th Floor, 60661-2511.
Telephone: 312-715-5700.
Telecopier: 312-993-9350.

MEMBERS OF FIRM

Robert C. Aument
James A. Kohlstedt
Carl A. Neumann

ASSOCIATE

Maureen Calabrese Strauts

For Complete List of Firm Personnel, See General Section

For full biographical listings, see the Martindale-Hubbell Law Directory

*OTTAWA,** La Salle Co.

MYERS, DAUGHERITY, BERRY, O'CONOR & KUZMA, LTD. (AV)

130 East Madison Street, 61350
Telephone: 815-434-6206
Fax: 815-434-6203
Email: mdboc@TheRamp.net
Streator, Illinois Office: 7 Northpoint Drive.
Telephone: 815-672-3116.
Fax: 815-672-0738.

Eugene P. Daugherity
Richard J. Berry
Sheryl H. Kuzma

Representative Clients: Auto Owners Insurance, Co.; Union Bank; First National Bank of Ottawa, Illinois; Union Bancorp Inc.; First State Bank; First Midwest Bank; Allied Ins. Group; St. Mary's Hospital; General Casualty Insurance, Co.

For Complete List of Firm Personnel, See General Section

For full biographical listings, see the Martindale-Hubbell Law Directory

*PEORIA,** Peoria Co.

HOWARD & HOWARD ATTORNEYS, P.C. (AV)

The Creve Coeur Building, Suite 200, 321 Liberty Street, 61602-1403
Telephone: 309-672-1483
Telecopier: 309-672-1568
Kalamazoo, Michigan Office: The Michigan Building, Suite 200, 100 Portage Street.
Telephone: 616-382-1483.
Telecopier: 616-382-1568.
Bloomfield Hills, Michigan Office: The Pinehurst Office Center, Suite 101, 1400 North Woodward Avenue.
Telephone: 248-645-1483.
Telecopier: 248-645-1568.
Lansing, Michigan Office: Suite 500, The Phoenix Building, 222 Washington Square, North.
Telephone: 517-485-1483.
Telecopier: 517-485-1568.

Theodore L. Eissfeldt — Janice M. Powell
Frederick G. Hoffman — Leonard W. Sachs
Timothy J. Howard — Jeffrey G. Sorenson
Sandra M. Traicoff

Representative Clients: For Representative Client list, see General Practice, Peoria, IL.

For Complete List of Firm Personnel, See General Section

For full biographical listings, see the Martindale-Hubbell Law Directory

VERNON HILLS, Lake Co.

RICHARDS, RALPH & SCHWAB, CHARTERED (AV)

One Hawthorn Place, 175 East Hawthorn Parkway, Suite 345, 60061
Telephone: 847-367-9699
Fax: 847-367-9621
Email: dschwab@rr&s-chtd.com *URL:* http://www.lawyers.com/richardandschwab

Michael L. Ralph — Alan E. Richards
David J. Schwab

For full biographical listings, see the Martindale-Hubbell Law Directory

*WAUKEGAN,** Lake Co.

DIVER, GRACH, QUADE & MASINI (AV)

Bank of Waukegan Building, 111 North County Street, 60085
Telephone: 847-662-8611
FAX: 847-662-2960

MEMBERS OF FIRM

Clarence W. Diver (1883-1962) — David R. Quade
Thomas W. Diver — Robert J. Masini
Brian S. Grach — Sarah P. Lessman
David L. Hazan

Heidi J. Aavang — Donna-Jo Rodden Vorderstrasse
Paula Vincich Randall

A list of Representative Clients will be furnished upon request.
Reference: First Midwest Bank of Waukegan.

For full biographical listings, see the Martindale-Hubbell Law Directory

INDIANA

*BEDFORD,** Lawrence Co.

STEELE, STEELE, MCSOLEY & MCSOLEY (AV)

Bank One Building, Suite One, 1602 I Street, 47421
Telephone: 812-279-3513
Fax: 812-275-3504
URL: http://www.steele-mcsoley.com

MEMBERS OF FIRM

Byron W. Steele — Brent E. Steele

Representative Clients: Bank One, Bloomington, NA, Bedford Branch; The First National Bank of Mitchell; The Times Mail (newspaper); Ralph Rogers & Co., Inc.; Indiana Bell Telephone Co.; Texas Gas Transmission Corporation; U.S. Gypsum Company.

For Complete List of Firm Personnel, See General Section

For full biographical listings, see the Martindale-Hubbell Law Directory

*BLOOMINGTON,** Monroe Co.

BUNGER & ROBERTSON (AV)

226 South College Square, P.O. Box 910, 47402-0910
Telephone: 812-332-9295
Fax: 812-331-8808
Email: bunrob@iquest.net

MEMBERS OF FIRM

Don M Robertson — James L. Whitlatch

Representative Clients: Aetna Insurance Companies; Bloomington Hospital; Commercial Union Group; Indiana Insurance Co.; Liberty Mutual Insurance; Medical Protective Co.; Monroe County Community School Corp.; Professional Golf Car, Inc.; Prudential Insurance Company of America; State Farm Automobile Insurance Co.

For Complete List of Firm Personnel, See General Section

For full biographical listings, see the Martindale-Hubbell Law Directory

*EVANSVILLE,** Vanderburgh Co.

BOWERS, HARRISON, KENT & MILLER, LLP (AV)

25 N.W. Riverside Drive, P.O. Box 1287, 47706-1287
Telephone: 812-426-1231
Fax: 812-464-3676
Email: BOWERS,HARRISON,KENT&MILLER,LLP@BHKM.COM
URL: http://WWW.BHKM.COM

MEMBERS OF FIRM

Joseph H. Harrison — Paul E. Black
Gary R. Case

OF COUNSEL

K. Wayne Kent

Representative Clients: Permanent Federal Savings Bank; The Citizens National Bank of Evansville; First Indiana Bank; Citizens National Bank of Tell City.

For Complete List of Firm Personnel, See General Section

For full biographical listings, see the Martindale-Hubbell Law Directory

KAHN, DEES, DONOVAN & KAHN, LLP (AV)

Fifth Main Financial Plaza, Suite 305, P.O. Box 3646, 47735-3646
Telephone: 812-423-3183
Fax: 812-423-3841
Email: evvlaw@k2d2.com

MEMBERS OF FIRM

Alan N. Shovers — G. Michael Schopmeyer
Brian P. Williams — Jeffrey K. Helfrich
Marjorie J. Scharpf

ASSOCIATE

Mark S. Samila

Representative Clients: Civitas Bank; Old National Bancorp; American General Finance; Terre Haute First National Bank.

For Complete List of Firm Personnel, See General Section

For full biographical listings, see the Martindale-Hubbell Law Directory

ZIEMER, STAYMAN, WEITZEL & SHOULDERS, LLP (AV)

(Formerly Early, Arnold & Ziemer)
One Riverfront Place, 20 N.W. First Street 9th Floor, P.O. Box 916, 47706-0916
Telephone: 812-424-7575
Telecopier: 812-421-5089

MEMBERS OF FIRM

Robert F. Stayman — Marco L. DeLucio
Stephan E. Weitzel — Gregory G. Meyer

Reference: Old National Bank in Evansville.

For full biographical listings, see the Martindale-Hubbell Law Directory

*FORT WAYNE,** Allen Co.

MILLER CARSON BOXBERGER & MURPHY, LLP (AV)

1400 One Summit Square, 46802-3137
Telephone: 219-423-9411
Telecopier: 219-423-4329
Email: counsel@mcbm.com
Bloomington, Indiana Office: 3100 John Hinkle Place, Suite 106.
Telephone: 812-333-1225.
Fax: 812-333-1925. E-mail: mcbm@kiva.net.

MEMBERS OF FIRM

Milford M. Miller, Jr. — Richard P. Samek
Philip L. Carson — Phillip A. Renz
Bruce O. Boxberger — Edward J. Liptak (Resident, Bloomington, Indiana Office)
Edward L. Murphy, Jr. — Robert T. Keen, Jr.
Thomas W. Yoder — Larry L. Barnard
John J. Wernet

(See Next Column)

MILLER CARSON BOXBERGER & MURPHY LLP, *Fort Wayne—Continued*

MEMBERS OF FIRM (Continued)

Arthur E. Mandelbaum
Diana C. Bauer
James P. Buchholz
Douglas A. Hoffman (Resident, Bloomington Office)

ASSOCIATES

Karl J. Veracco
M. Randall Spencer
Stephen J. Harants
Timothy M. Pape
Calvert S. Miller
Monica S. Sandkuhler
Heidi K. Ellison
Tina M. Yordy
Jason E. Salerno (Resident, Bloomington Office)
Howard E. Green

Representative Clients: Bank One, Indiana, N.A.; National City Bank.

For full biographical listings, see the Martindale-Hubbell Law Directory

ROTHBERG & LOGAN (AV)

(Formerly, Rothberg, Gallmeyer, Fruechtenicht & Logan)
2100 National City Center, 110 West Berry Street, P.O. Box 11647, 46859-1647
Telephone: 219-422-9454
Telefax: 219-422-1622

MEMBERS OF FIRM

Thomas D. Logan
F. L. Dennis Logan
David R. Smelko
Dennis F. Dykhuizen
Gregory Martin Cole
Michael T. Deam

ASSOCIATE

J. Rickard Donovan

Counsel for: Parkview Hospital; Cameron Memorial Community Hospital; Norwest Bank Indiana, N.A.; Parkview Health System; Azar's, Incorporated; Fort Wayne-Allen County Airport Authority; Fort Wayne Public Transportation Corporation; Avis Industrial Corp.; Farm Credit Services of Mid-America, ASA; Slater Fort Wayne Federal Credit Union.

For Complete List of Firm Personnel, See General Section

For full biographical listings, see the Martindale-Hubbell Law Directory

GREENWOOD, Johnson Co.

WILLIAMS HEWITT & ROBBINS, LLP (AV)

National City Bank Building, 300 South Madison Avenue Suite 400, P.O. Box 405, 46142
Telephone: 317-888-1121
Facsimile: 317-887-4069

PARTNERS

Jon E. Williams
Brian C. Hewitt
J. Lee Robbins

ASSOCIATES

John M. White
Mark E. Need
John P. Wilkowski
Stephen K. Watson

For full biographical listings, see the Martindale-Hubbell Law Directory

*INDIANAPOLIS,** Marion Co.

BOSE MCKINNEY & EVANS LLP (AV)

2700 First Indiana Plaza, 135 North Pennsylvania Street, 46204
Telephone: 317-684-5000
Facsimile: 317-684-5173
URL: http://www.boselaw.com
Indianapolis North Office: Suite 1500, 8888 Keystone Crossing, 46240.
Telephone: 317-574-3700.
Facsimile: 317-574-3716.

MEMBERS OF FIRM

Alan W. Becker
David A. Butcher
R. J. McConnell
Dwight L. Miller
Theodore J. Nowacki
Michael A. Trentadue

ASSOCIATES

John A. Millspaugh
Mary Beth Plummer

Representative Clients: First Indiana Bank; First National Bank; Mutual Savings Bank; First State Bank; National City Bank of Indiana; Huntington National Bank of Indiana; Riddell National Bank; FCN Bank, N.A.; Monroe County Bank; State Bank of Oxford.

For Complete List of Firm Personnel, See General Section

For full biographical listings, see the Martindale-Hubbell Law Directory

ICE MILLER DONADIO & RYAN (AV)

One American Square Box 82001, 46282-0002
Telephone: 317-236-2100
Fax: 317-236-2219
Email: info@imdr.com *URL:* http://www.imdr.com
South Bend, Indiana Office: 211 West Washington Street, Suite 2420.
Telephone: 219-234-7933.
Fax: 219-234-7965. Internet E-mail: info@imdr.com. Web Site Address: http://www.imdr.com.

(See Next Column)

Chicago, Illinois Office: 135 South LaSalle Street, Suite 4100.
Telephone: 312-726-1567.
Fax: 312-641-6263. Internet E-mail: info@imdr.com. Web Site Address: http://www.imdr.com.

MEMBERS OF FIRM

Berkley W. Duck
Harry L. Gonso
Thomas H. Ristine
Philip A. Whistler
Richard J. Thrapp
Zeff A. Weiss
Stephen J. Hackman
Michael A. Wukmer
Michael J. Lewinski
Henry A. Efroymson
Dominic F. Polizzotto
Mark B. Barnes

RETIRED PARTNERS

John A. Grayson
Evan E. Steger

OF COUNSEL

Peggy J. Naile

ASSOCIATE

John M. Hakes

Counsel for: Federal Deposit Insurance Corp.; Indiana Bankers Assn.; Irwin Union Bank & Trust Co.; German American Bancorp.; Union County National Bank of Liberty; Fifth Third Bank of Central Indiana; KeyBank National Assn.; Heartland Bancshares, inc.

For Complete List of Firm Personnel, See General Section

For full biographical listings, see the Martindale-Hubbell Law Directory

JOHNSON SMITH PENCE & HEATH LLP (AV)

One Indiana Square Suite 1800, 46204
Telephone: 317-634-9777
Telecopier: 317-636-9061
Email: firm@jsplaw.com *URL:* http://www.jsplaw.com
Washington, D.C. Office: 555 Twelfth Street, N.W., Suite 650.
Telephone: 202-737-5410.
Fax: 202-737-5411.

MEMBERS OF FIRM

David R. Day
Dennis A. Johnson
Richard L. Johnson
Michael J. Kaye
John R. Kirkwood

ASSOCIATE

John B. Baxter

For Complete List of Firm Personnel, See General Section

For full biographical listings, see the Martindale-Hubbell Law Directory

LOCKE REYNOLDS LLP (AV)

1000 Capital Center South, 201 North Illinois Street, 46204-4210
Telephone: 317-237-3800
Telecopier: 317-237-3900
Email: attys@locke.com *URL:* http://www.locke.com

Michael D. Moriarty
Michael J. Schneider
Howard R. Cohen
David S. Klinestiver
Michael T. Crowley

Representative Clients: American Express Financial Services; Banc One Financial Services, Inc.; Bank One Indianapolis, N.A.; Huntington National Bank; Indiana Corporate Federal Credit Union; LaSalle National Bank.

For Complete List of Firm Personnel, See General Section

For full biographical listings, see the Martindale-Hubbell Law Directory

TABBERT HAHN EARNEST & WEDDLE (AV)

Suite 2100, One Indiana Square, 46204-2101
Telephone: 317-639-5444
Fax: 317-639-5232
Email: jtyrrell@tabberthahn.com *URL:* http://www.tabberthahn.com

Don A. Tabbert
Gregory F. Hahn
Lante K. Earnest
Robert G. Weddle
Mark K. Sullivan
Judy M. Tyrrell
Matthew W. Conner
William W. Mathews
Heather L. Fesko
Charles R. Whybrew

OF COUNSEL

James J. Nocon
William D. Lalley
Joseph W. Hammes
Dale E. Sporleder

For full biographical listings, see the Martindale-Hubbell Law Directory

*LAFAYETTE,** Tippecanoe Co.

STUART & BRANIGIN (AV)

The Life Building, 300 Main Street, Suite 800, P.O. Box 1010, 47902-1010
Telephone: 765-423-1561
Telecopier: 765-742-8175
Email: sb@stuartlaw.com *URL:* http://www.stuartlaw.com
Indianapolis, Indiana Office: Suite 1401, 8888 Keystone Crossing, 46240.
Telephone: 317-574-7245.
Fax: 317-574-7050.

(See Next Column)

STUART & BRANIGIN—*Continued*

MEMBERS OF FIRM

Allison Ellsworth Stuart (1886-1950)
Roger D. Branigin (1902-1975)
Roger D. Branigin, Jr.
Thomas L. Ryan
Thomas R. McCully
Larry R. Fisher
Nina B. Kirkpatrick
Mark Lillianfeld
Stephen R. Pennell
Anthony S. Benton
Erik D. Spykman
William E. Emerick
John C. Duffey
Bruce McSpadden
Mark E. DeYoung
Thomas B. Parent
Laura L. Bowker
Kevin D. Nicoson
Susan K. Roberts
John M. Stuckey
Deborah B. Trice
William P. Kealey
David A. Starkweather
Geoffrey L. Blazi

SENIOR COUNSEL

Russell H. Hart

COUNSEL

John F. Bodle
James V. McGlone

ASSOCIATES

Elizabeth B. Searle
Marianne Mitten Owen
David A. Locke
Karen Orr McClure
Ann Marie Waldron
Barry L. Loftus

General Counsel for: The Lafayette Life Insurance Co.; INB National Bank, N.W.; Lafayette Home Hospital, Inc.
State Counsel for: Norfolk & Western Railway Co.
Mr. Ryan is Counsel to: The Trustees of Purdue University.
Representative Clients: Aluminum Company of America; Liberty Mutual Insurance Group.

For full biographical listings, see the Martindale-Hubbell Law Directory

*TERRE HAUTE,** Vigo Co.

COX, ZWERNER, GAMBILL & SULLIVAN (AV)

511 Wabash Avenue, P.O. Box 1625, 47808-1625
Telephone: 812-232-6003
Fax: 812-232-6567

MEMBERS OF FIRM

Ernest J. Zwerner (1918-1980)
Benjamin G. Cox (1915-1988)
Gilbert W. Gambill, Jr.
James E. Sullivan
Benjamin G. Cox, Jr.
David W. Sullivan
Robert L. Gowdy
Louis F. Britton
Carroll D. Smeltzer
Jeffry A. Lind
Ronald E. Jumps
Scott Craig
Elizabeth A. Lewis

OF COUNSEL

Robert D. Hepburn

Counsel for: Terre Haute First National Bank; Farmers Insurance Group; Indiana-American Water Co.; Indiana State University; Merchants National Bank of Terre Haute; Rose-Hulman Institute of Technology; Tribune-Star Publishing Co., Inc.

For full biographical listings, see the Martindale-Hubbell Law Directory

IOWA

*CEDAR RAPIDS,** Linn Co.

SHUTTLEWORTH & INGERSOLL, P.C. (AV)

115 Third Street S.E., Suite 500, P.O. Box 2107, 52406-2107
Telephone: 319-365-9461
Fax: 319-365-8443
URL: http://www.shuttleworthlaw.com

Richard S. Fry
Gary J. Streit
Carroll J. Reasoner
Steven J. Pace
Thomas P. Peffer
Dennis J. McMenimen
William P. Prowell
Wesley B. Huisinga
Dean D. Carrington

COUNSEL

Joan Lipsky
Laurie Bergren

Representative Clients: Commercial Federal Bank; Firstar Bank N.A.; First National Bank of Cedar Rapids; Hills Bank and Trust Company.

For Complete List of Firm Personnel, See General Section

For full biographical listings, see the Martindale-Hubbell Law Directory

*DAVENPORT,** Scott Co.

GOSMA & GALLAGHER, P.L.C. (AV)

Quad City Bank Building, 4500 North Brady Street, Suite 200, 52806
Telephone: 319-388-8417
Fax: 319-388-9240
Email: lawfirm@gosma-gallagher.com
Bettendorf Office: 1989 Spruce Hills Drive.
Telephone: 319-355-5304.
Fax: 319-359-7711.

MEMBERS OF FIRM

Robert D. Wells (1904-1990)
Robert H. Gallagher
John S. Gosma
James G. Noth
Marie R. Rolling-Tarbox
David A. Millage
Robert S. Gallagher
Jane E. Zimmer

OF COUNSEL

Clay LeGrand
Nicholas W. LeGrand (Not admitted in IA)

References: American Bank and Trust Company, Rock Island; Great River Bank and Trust, Princeton.

For full biographical listings, see the Martindale-Hubbell Law Directory

*DES MOINES,** Polk Co.

DICKINSON, MACKAMAN, TYLER & HAGEN, P.C. (AV)

Suite 1600 Hub Tower, 699 Walnut Street, 50309-3986
Telephone: 515-244-2600
Telecopier: 515-246-4550
URL: http://www.dickinsonlaw.com

Howard O. Hagen
Richard A. Malm
Arthur F. Owens
Jon P. Sullivan
Paul R. Tyler
J. Marc Ward

For full biographical listings, see the Martindale-Hubbell Law Directory

FINLEY, ALT, SMITH, SCHARNBERG, CRAIG, HILMES & GAFFNEY, P.C. (AV)

604 Locust Street, Fourth Floor Equitable Building, 50309
Telephone: 515-288-0145
Telecopier: 515-288-2724

Glenn L. Smith
David C. Craig

Representative Clients: ALAS; American Society of Composers, Authors and Publishers; Equitable Life Assurance Society of the U.S.; Federated Insurance Co.; Meredith Corp.
Iowa Attorneys for: Midwest Medical Insurance Co.
District Attorneys for: Norfolk & Southern Railroad; Soo Line Railroad Company.

For Complete List of Firm Personnel, See General Section

For full biographical listings, see the Martindale-Hubbell Law Directory

WHITFIELD & EDDY, P.L.C. (AV)

317 6th Avenue, Suite 1200 Locust at 6th, 50309-4195
Telephone: 515-288-6041
Fax: 515-246-1474
Email: info@whitfieldlaw.com *URL:* http://www.whitfieldlaw.com

Benjamin B. Ullem
William L. Fairbank
Robert G. Bridges
Thomas H. Burke
George H. Frampton
Wendy L. Carlson
Gary A. Norton
Frank M. Grenard (Not admitted in IA)
Mark V. Hanson
August B. Landis

OF COUNSEL

John C. Eddy
Harley A. Whitfield

Representative Clients: Bankers Trust Co.; Brenton Bank; Iowa State Bank; Citizens Bank and Trust, Belle Plaine, Iowa; Production Credit Association of the Midlands; Citizen States Bank; Decatur County State Bank; Iowa Trust and Savings Bank; Midwest Heritage Bank.

For Complete List of Firm Personnel, See General Section

For full biographical listings, see the Martindale-Hubbell Law Directory

KANSAS

*TOPEKA,** Shawnee Co.

WRIGHT, HENSON, SOMERS, SEBELIUS, CLARK & BAKER, LLP (AV)

Commerce Bank Building, 100 Southeast Ninth Street, 2nd Floor, P.O. Box 3555, 66601-3555
Telephone: 785-232-2200
FAX: 785-232-3344
Email: wrighthenson@wrighthenson.com *URL:* http://www.wrighthenson.com

MEMBERS OF FIRM

Charles N. Henson
Dale L. Somers
Anne Lamborn Baker

Representative Clients: Kaw Valley State Bank & Trust Co.; Commerce Bank & Trust; Kansas Bankers Association.

For Complete List of Firm Personnel, See General Section

For full biographical listings, see the Martindale-Hubbell Law Directory

*WICHITA,** Sedgwick Co.

FOULSTON & SIEFKIN L.L.P. (AV)

700 NationsBank Financial Center, 67202
Telephone: 316-267-6371
Facsimile: 316-267-6345
URL: http://www.foulston.com
Topeka, Kansas Office: 1515 NationsBank Tower, 534 Kansas Avenue, 66603.
Telephone: 785-233-3600.
Fax: 785-233-1610.
Dodge City, Kansas Office: 810 Frontview, P.O. Box 1147, 67801.
Telephone: 316-227-8126.
Fax: 316-227-8451.
Member: Lex Mundi, The World's Leading Association of Independent Law Firms.

MEMBERS OF FIRM

Benjamin C. Langel
William R. Wood, II

For Complete List of Firm Personnel, See General Section

For full biographical listings, see the Martindale-Hubbell Law Directory

KENTUCKY

*BOWLING GREEN,** Warren Co.

KERRICK, GRISE & STIVERS (AV)

1025 State Street, P.O. Box 9547, 42102-9547
Telephone: 502-782-8160
Fax: 502-782-5856
Email: kgs@kgslaw.com
Elizabethtown, Kentucky Office: 2935 Dolphin Drive, Suite 102.
Telephone: 502-769-5788.
Fax: 502-737-9285.

MEMBERS OF FIRM

Thomas N. Kerrick
Gregory N. Stivers
John R. Grise
H. Brent Brennenstuhl
Laura M. Hagan

ASSOCIATES

Karl N. Crandall
Shawn Rosso Alcott
Jason B. Bell

OF COUNSEL

Jeffrey R. O'Grody

LEGAL SUPPORT PERSONNEL

Patricia Logsdon
Laura Lockhart Lico
Allison Lusk

Representative Clients: Dollar General Corp.; Columbia Greenview Regional Hospital; Hospital Corporation of America; Hardin Memorial Hospital; Fir-Star Bank; TKR Cable.

For full biographical listings, see the Martindale-Hubbell Law Directory

*LEXINGTON,** Fayette Co.

STOLL, KEENON & PARK, LLP (AV)

201 E. Main Street, Suite 1000, 40507-1380
Telephone: 606-231-3000
Telecopier: 606-253-1093; 606-253-1027
URL: http://www.skp.com
Frankfort, Kentucky Office: 307 Washington Street, 40601.
Telephone: 502-875-6220.
Telecopier: 502-875-6235.

(See Next Column)

Henderson, Kentucky Office: 201 C North Main Street, 42420-3103.
Telephone: 270-831-1900.
Telecopier: 270-827-4060.
Louisville, Kentucky Office: 400 West Market Street, Suite 2650, 40202-3377.
Telephone: 502-568-9100.
Telecopier: 502-568-5700.

MEMBERS OF FIRM

William L. Montague
J. David Smith, Jr.
R. David Lester
Dan M. Rose
Harvie B. Wilkinson
Gregory D. Pavey

Representative Clients: Farmers Capital Bank Corp.; Whitaker Bank Corporation; Fifth Third Bank of Kentucky.

For Complete List of Firm Personnel, See General Section

For full biographical listings, see the Martindale-Hubbell Law Directory

*LONDON,** Laurel Co.

FARMER, KELLEY, BROWN AND WILLIAMS (AV)

502 West Fifth Street, Drawer 490, 40741
Telephone: 606-878-7640
Fax: 606-878-2364
Email: fpfarmer@farmerlaw.com
Lexington, Kentucky Office: 1082 Griffin Gate Drive, 40511-1384.
Telephone: 606: 263-2567.
Facsimile: 606: 878-2364.

MEMBERS OF FIRM

F. Preston Farmer
Michael P. Farmer
John F. Kelley, Jr.
Martha L. Brown
Jason E. Williams

ASSOCIATES

Suzanne S. Farmer
Jennifer S. Nicholson

Representative Clients: The Aetna Casualty and Surety Co.; American States Insurance Co.; Auto-Owner's Insurance Co.; Bituminous Insurance Co.; Canadian Universal Insurance Co.; Chubb Insurance Co.; Cotton States Insurance Co.; Crum & Forster Underwriters Group; Eagle Insurance Co.; Equity Mutual Insurance Co.

For full biographical listings, see the Martindale-Hubbell Law Directory

*LOUISVILLE,** Jefferson Co.

MAPOTHER & MAPOTHER (AV)

801 West Jefferson Street, 40202
Telephone: 502-587-5400
Fax: 502-587-5444
Email: mapother@mapother-atty.com *URL:* http://www.mapother-atty.com
Lexington, Kentucky Office: 100 East Vine Street, Suite 810.
Telephone: 606-253-0003.
Fax: 606-255-3961.
Jeffersonville, Indiana Office: 505 East Seventh Street.
Telephone: 812-288-5059.
Fax: 502-587-5444.
Cincinnati, Ohio Office: Kroger Building, Suite 2220, 1014 Vine Street.
Telephone: 513-381-4888.
Fax: 513-381-3117.
Huntington, West Virginia Office: Morris Building, Suite 701, 845 Fourth Avenue.
Telephone: 304-525-1185.
Fax: 304-529-3764.
Evansville, Indiana Office: 329 Main Street, Suite 602.
Telephone: 812-421-9108.
Fax: 812-421-9109.

MEMBERS OF FIRM

William R. Mapother
Hollis L. Searcy
Thomas L. Canary, Jr.
Charles M. Friedman

Roberta S. Dunlap (Resident, Evansville, Indiana Office)
Steven B. Mulrooney
Dennis M. Ostrowski
Dean A. Langdon (Resident, Lexington, Kentucky Office)
Gerald O. Henderson, Jr. (Resident, Huntington, West Virginia Office)
Lee W. Grace
Brian E. Chapman (Resident, Cincinnati, Ohio Office)
Miles S. Apple
Joy B. Gilliam (Resident, Lexington, Kentucky Office)
T. Lawson McSwain, II
John D. Meyers (Resident, Lexington, Kentucky Office)
Vincent A. Dimasi (Not admitted in KY; Resident, Cincinnati, Ohio Office)
Lisa A. Herndon
Charlie W. Gordon
Ronda C. Gunter (Resident, Huntington, West Virginia Office)

Representative Clients: PNC Bank; NBD Bank; Fifth Third Bank; General Electric Capital Corp.; Ford Motor Credit Co.; General Motors Acceptance Corp.; Associates Commercial Corp.; Cuna Mutual Insurance Society; Chrysler Financial Corp.; Sears.

For full biographical listings, see the Martindale-Hubbell Law Directory

Louisville—Continued

MIDDLETON & REUTLINGER, P.S.C. (AV)

2500 Brown and Williamson Tower, 40202-3410
Telephone: 502-584-1135
Fax: 502-561-0442
URL: http://middreut.com
Jeffersonville, Indiana Office: 530 East Court Avenue, 47130.
Telephone: 812-282-1132.
Fax: 812-282-3188.

Charles G. Middleton, III
Charles D. Greenwell
G. Kennedy Hall, Jr.
David J. Kellerman

For Complete List of Firm Personnel, See General Section

For full biographical listings, see the Martindale-Hubbell Law Directory

MORGAN & POTTINGER, P.S.C. (AV)

601 West Main Street, 40202
Telephone: 502-589-2780
Telecopier: 502-585-3498
URL: http://www.morganandpottinger.com
Lexington, Kentucky Office: 133 West Short Street.
Telephone: 606-253-1900.
Telecopier: 606-255-2038.
New Albany, Indiana Office: 120 East Market Street.
Telephone: 812-948-0008.
Telecopier: 812-944-6215.

Patrick E. Morgan
John T. McGarvey
Douglas Gene Sharp
John A. Majors
Mark J. Sandlin
Scott T. Rickman (Resident, Lexington Office)
M. Thurman Senn

Thomas C. Fenton

For Complete List of Firm Personnel, See General Section

For full biographical listings, see the Martindale-Hubbell Law Directory

ROTH FOLEY BRYANT & COOPER, PLLC (AV)

First Trust Centre, Suite 300S, 200 South Fifth Street, 40202-3236
Telephone: 502-569-7550
Fax: 502-540-0123
Email: RFBC.com

Irvin D. Foley
David M. Roth
David H. Cooper
Lisa Koch Bryant
K. Gail Russell
Christian L. Juckett

OF COUNSEL

James E. Fahey
David W. Gray

Representative Clients: Bank One, Kentucky, NA; Commonwealth Bank and Trust Co.; Farm Credit Services of Mid-America; First Citizens Bank of Hardin Co.; Huntington National Bank; Huntington Acceptance Co.; People's State Bank; Great Financial Bank.

For full biographical listings, see the Martindale-Hubbell Law Directory

WYATT, TARRANT & COMBS (AV)

Citizens Plaza, 40202-2898
Telephone: 502-589-5235
Telecopier: 502-589-0309
URL: http://www.wyattfirm.com
Lexington, Kentucky Office: 1700 Lexington Financial Center.
Telephone: 606-233-2012.
Telecopier: 606-259-0649.
Frankfort, Kentucky Office: The Taylor-Scott Building, 311 West Main Street.
Telephone: 502-223-2104.
Telecopier: 502-227-7681.
New Albany, Indiana Office: The Elsby Building, 117 East Spring Street,
Telephone: 812-945-3561.
Telecopier: 812-949-2524.
Memphis, Tennessee Office: Crescent Center, Suite 650, 6075 Poplar Avenue.
Telephone: 901-537-1000.
Telecopier: 901-537-1010.
Nashville, Tennessee Office: 1500 Nashville City Center, 511 Union Street.
Telephone: 615-244-0020.
Telecopier: 615-256-1726.
Music Row, Nashville Office: 29 Music Square East.
Telephone: 615-255-6161.
Telecopier: 615-254-4490.
Hendersonville, Tennessee Office: 313 E. Main Street, Suite 1.
Telephone: 615-822-8822.
Telecopier: 615-824-4684.
Tri-Cities, Tennessee Office: Northeast Tennessee Business Park, 10368 Wallace Alley Street, Suite 6, Kingsport.
Telephone: 423-279-1825.
Telecopier: 423-279-9357.

(See Next Column)

MEMBER OF FIRM

Stewart E. Conner

Representative Clients: Bank One, Kentucky, NA; CBT Corp.; Cardinal Bancshares, Inc.; Citizens Bank & Trust Company and its affiliates; First Kentucky Trust Co.; PNC Bank, National Association; Republic Bank and Trust Co.; Trans Financial, Inc.; Vine Street Trust Co.

For Complete List of Firm Personnel, See General Section

For full biographical listings, see the Martindale-Hubbell Law Directory

*PADUCAH,** McCracken Co.

DENTON & KEULER (AV)

Paducah Bank & Trust Company Building, 555 Jefferson Street, P.O. Box 929, 42001
Telephone: 502-443-8253
Fax: 502-442-6000
Email: dk@dklaw.com *URL:* http://www.dklaw.com

MEMBERS OF FIRM

W. David Denton
Thomas J. Keuler

Reference: The Paducah Bank & Trust Co.

For Complete List of Firm Personnel, See General Section

For full biographical listings, see the Martindale-Hubbell Law Directory

*SHEPHERDSVILLE,** Bullitt Co.

J. CHESTER PORTER & ASSOCIATES (AV)

162 South Buckman Street, P.O. Box 159, 40165
Telephone: 502-543-2296; 955-6034
Fax: 502-543-2694
Taylorsville, Kentucky Office: 37 West Main Street, P.O. Box 509.
Telephone: 502-477-6412.
Fax: 502-477-2169.

J. Chester Porter

Ralph E. Bouvette
Phillip K. Wicker
Anne W. McAfee
Jennifer Elizabeth Porter
John F. Carroll, Jr.

For full biographical listings, see the Martindale-Hubbell Law Directory

LOUISIANA

*BATON ROUGE,** East Baton Rouge Parish

POWERS & WILLARD, L.L.P. (AV)

7967 Office Park Boulevard, P.O. Box 15948, 70895
Telephone: 225-928-1951
Fax: 225-929-9834

MEMBERS OF FIRM

John Dale Powers
William E. Willard

ASSOCIATES

Neil H. Mixon
Lindsey J. Leavoy
Edwin L. Hightower
Andrew P. Sellers, Jr.
Suzanne K. Sasser
Kyle C. Marionneaux

General Counsel for: Audubon Insurance Co.
Louisiana Counsel for: Hancock Bank & Trust Co.; Hertz Corp.; Ciba-Geigy Corp.; Utica Mutual Insurance Co.

For full biographical listings, see the Martindale-Hubbell Law Directory

*LAFAYETTE,** Lafayette Parish

WAYNE A. SHULLAW (AV)

600 Jefferson Street, Fifth Floor, Suite 502, P.O. Box 4815, 70502
Telephone: 318-266-2310
Fax: 318-266-2311

For full biographical listings, see the Martindale-Hubbell Law Directory

*LAKE CHARLES,** Calcasieu Parish

BERGSTEDT & MOUNT (AV)

Second Floor, Magnolia Life Building, P.O. Drawer 3004, 70602-3004
Telephone: 318-433-3004
Facsimile: 318-433-8080

MEMBERS OF FIRM

Thomas M. Bergstedt
Benjamin W. Mount
Van C. Seneca

ASSOCIATE

Annette N. Peltier

(See Next Column)

BERGSTEDT & MOUNT, *Lake Charles—Continued*

OF COUNSEL

Charles S. Ware

Representative Clients: ARCO Chemical Company; Ashland Oil Co.; CIGNA Property & Casualty Companies; Columbia Women's & Children's Hospital; The Hartford Steam Boiler Inspection & Insurance Company; Leach Company; Olin Corporation; Occidental Chemical Corporation; Terra Corporation; R. D. Werner Company.

For full biographical listings, see the Martindale-Hubbell Law Directory

MANDEVILLE, St. Tammany Parish

DREHER LANGER & TOMKIES L.L.P. (AV(T))

#1 Sanctuary Boulevard Suite 303, 70471
Telephone: 504-727-1664
Facsimile: 504-727-4388
Columbus, Ohio Office: 2250 Huntington Center, 41 South High Street, 43215.
Telephone: 614-628-8000.
Facsimile: 614-628-1600.

RESIDENT MEMBERS COLUMBUS, OHIO OFFICE

Darrell L. Dreher (Not admitted in LA)
Michael C. Tomkies (Not admitted in LA)
Jeffrey I. Langer (Not admitted in LA)

RESIDENT ASSOCIATES COLUMBUS, OHIO OFFICE

Elizabeth L. Anstaett (Not admitted in LA)
Judith M. Scheiderer (Not admitted in LA)
Lisa Kozakowski (Not admitted in LA)
Jean M. Schwendeman (Not admitted in LA)
Mary W. Morgan (Not admitted in LA)
Margaret M. Stolar (Not admitted in LA)

OF COUNSEL

Robin Ronquillo De Leo (Resident)
John F. Wyka (Resident)

Representative Clients: American Express Company; Associates First Capital Corporation; Banc One Corporation; BankAmerica Corp.; The Chase Manhattan Corporation; Chevron Corporation; General Electric Capital Corporation; Morgan Stanley Dean Witter & Co.; Sears, Roebuck & Co.; Transamerica Corporation.

For full biographical listings, see the Martindale-Hubbell Law Directory

METAIRIE, Jefferson Parish

NEWMAN, MATHIS, BRADY, WAKEFIELD & SPEDALE, A PROFESSIONAL LAW CORPORATION (AV)

212 Veterans Boulevard, 70005
Telephone: 504-837-9040
Telecopier: 504-834-6452
Email: newmanmath@aol.com *URL:* http://www.nmlaw.com
Baton Rouge, Louisiana Office: 3301 North Boulevard.
Telephone: 225-343-3456.
Telecopier: 225-336-9249.
New Orleans, Louisiana Office: 3723 Canal Street.
Telephone: 504-581-2552.

Ronald H. Newman (1937-1979)
Robert A. Mathis
John D. Brady (Resident, Baton Rouge Office)
Robert T. Wakefield
Charles E. Spedale (Resident, Baton Rouge Office)
Richard L. Crawford (Resident, Baton Rouge Office)
Joseph E. Fick, Jr. (Resident, New Orleans Office)
Mark C. Landry
Clay J. LeGros
Stephen J. Broussard
Gerard O. Salassi, IV

Keith M. Frey

For full biographical listings, see the Martindale-Hubbell Law Directory

*MONROE,** Ouachita Parish

THOMPSON, SPARKS, DEAN & MORRIS (AV)

A Partnership including a Professional Corporation
1401 Royal Street, P.O. Box 2867, 71207
Telephone: 318-388-1440
Fax: 318-322-0887

MEMBERS OF FIRM

M. C. Thompson (1885-1970)
James D. Sparks (1910-1987)
George B. Dean, Jr., (P.C.)
Wood T. Sparks
John C. Morris, III

ASSOCIATE

Jennifer Allen Riley

Representative Clients: South Central Bell Telephone Co.; Greater Ouachita Water Company; PHH Homequity Corp.; Commonwealth Relocation Services, Inc.; Remax, Monroe; Bell South Advertising & Publishing Corp.; Premier Mortgage Corp.; Countrywide Funding Corp.

(See Next Column)

Approved Attorneys for: BankOne; Federal Land Bank.

For full biographical listings, see the Martindale-Hubbell Law Directory

*NEW ORLEANS,** Orleans Parish

CARVER, DARDEN, KORETZKY, TESSIER, FINN, BLOSSMAN & AREAUX, L.L.C. (AV)

1100 Poydras Street, Suite 2700, 70163
Telephone: 504-585-3800
Telecopier: 504-585-3801

M. Hampton Carver
M. Taylor Darden
I. Harold Koretzky
Frank A. Tessier
William T. Finn
Roy E. Blossman
Raymond G. Areaux
John Anthony Dunlap
Leann Opotowsky Moses
David L. Browne

OF COUNSEL

John C. Christian (P.C.)
Susan Judlin Santa Cruz
Stephen Rose
Elvige Cassard Richards
Stacy Smith Brown

J. Christopher Martin
John H. Fontham
Erin M. Hart
Shawn L. Holahan
Jonathan M. Pierce
Robert J. Nichols
Ryan E. Griffitts
Linda A. Hoffman

Representative Clients: Bass Enterprises Production Co.; CXY Energy, Inc.; CanadianOxy Offshore Production; Chevron Pipe Line Company; Chevron Chemical Co.; Clovelly Oil Co., Inc.; Computerized Processes Unlimited, Inc.; Continental Land & Fur Co., Inc.; Delta Petroleum Co., Inc.

For full biographical listings, see the Martindale-Hubbell Law Directory

CORRERO FISHMAN HAYGOOD PHELPS WALMSLEY & CASTEIX, L.L.P. (AV)

Bank One Center, 46th Floor, 201 St. Charles Avenue, 70170-4600
Telephone: 504-586-5252
Fax: 504-586-5250

Anthony J. Correro, III
Louis Y. Fishman
Paul M. Haygood

Caroline B. Blitzer
Lloyd L. Drury, III

For full biographical listings, see the Martindale-Hubbell Law Directory

MCGLINCHEY STAFFORD (AV)

A Professional Limited Liability Company
643 Magazine Street, 70130-3477
Telephone: 504-586-1200
Fax: 504-596-2800
TDD: (504) 596-2728
Telex: 584327
Cable Address: "MACSTAC"
Mailing Address: P.O. Box 60643, New Orleans, Louisiana, 70160-0643
Email: @mcglinchey.com *URL:* http://www.mcglinchey.com
Dallas, Texas Office: 2777 Stemmons Freeway, Suite 925, 75207-2401.
Telephone: 214-860-9700.
Fax: 214-860-9750.
Houston, Texas Office: 2727 Allen Parkway, Suite 1900, 77019.
Telephone: 713-520-1900.
Fax: 713-520-1025.
Baton Rouge, Louisiana Office: Ninth Floor, One American Place, 70825-0001.
Telephone: 504-383-9000.
Fax: 504-343-3076.
Jackson, Mississippi Office: Suite 1200, SkyTel Centre, 200 South Lamar Street, 39201.
Telephone: 601-960-8400.
Fax: 601-960-8406.
Lake Providence, Louisiana Office: 405 Morgan Street, 71254-2691.
Telephone: 318-559-1200.
Fax: 318-559-0609.
Monroe, Louisiana Office: Dean ONB Tower, 130 Desiard Street, Suite 807, 71201.
Telephone: 318-651-0807.
Fax: 318-651-0809.

MEMBERS OF FIRM

David S. Willenzik (P.C.)
Bennet Scott Koren
Laura Hobson Brown
Joyce L. Schenewerk

ASSOCIATES

Denise Langlois Brown
John A. Marzullo

MEMBERS OF FIRM

Robert Marshall Grodner (Resident, Baton Rouge Office)
J. Scott Sheehan (Resident, Houston Office)

ASSOCIATE

Jolie S. Lenz (Resident, Houston Office)

For full biographical listings, see the Martindale-Hubbell Law Directory

New Orleans—Continued

Milling Benson Woodward L.L.P. (AV)

A Partnership including Professional Law Corporations
Suite Twenty-Three Hundred, 909 Poydras Street, 70112-1017
Telephone: 504-569-7000
Telecopier: 504-569-7001
ABA net: 15656
MCI Mail: "Milling"
Email: milling@millinglaw.com
Lafayette, Louisiana Office: 101 La Rue France, Suite 200.
Telephone: 318-232-3929.
Telecopier: 318-233-4957.
Mandeville (North Shore), Louisiana Office: 2140 8th Street.
Telephone: 504-867-9622.
Telecopier: 504-867-8364.

MEMBERS OF FIRM

David Conroy (P.C.)
Charles A. Snyder (P.C.)
Emile A. Wagner, III, (P.C.)
Jean M. Sweeney (P.C.)
J. Timothy Betbeze (P.C.)

OF COUNSEL

Guy C. Lyman, Jr., (P.C.)

ASSOCIATES

Rodrick E. Anderson
Stacie M. Hollis

See General Section for list of Representative Clients.

For Complete List of Firm Personnel, See General Section

For full biographical listings, see the Martindale-Hubbell Law Directory

Phelps Dunbar, L.L.P. (AV)

Texaco Center, 400 Poydras Street, 70130-3245
Telephone: 504-566-1311
Telecopier: 504-568-9130, 504-568-9007
Cable Address: "Howspencer"
Telex: 584125 WU
Telex: 6821155 WUI
Email: info@phelps.com
Baton Rouge, Louisiana Office: Suite 701, 445 North Boulevard, P.O. Box 4412.
Telephone: 225-346-0285.
Telecopier: 225-381-9197.
Jackson, Mississippi Office: Suite 500, SkyTel Centre, 200 South Lamar Street, P.O. Box 23066.
Telephone: 601-352-2300.
Telecopier: 601-360-9777.
Tupelo, Mississippi Office: Seventh Floor, One Mississippi Plaza, P.O. Box 1220.
Telephone: 662-842-7907.
Telecopier: 662-842-3873.
Houston, Texas Office: Suite 900, 3040 Post Oak Boulevard.
Telephone: 713-626-1386.
Telecopier: 713-626-1388.
London, England Office: Suite 731, Level 7, Lloyd's, 1 Lime Street, London EC3M 7DQ England.
Telephone: 011-44-207-929-4765.
Telecopier: 011-44-207-929-0046.
Telex: 987321.

RESIDENT PARTNERS

Lee R. Adler
Ross F. Bass, Jr. (Not admitted in LA; Resident, Jackson, Mississippi Office)
Jonathan C. Benda (Resident, Baton Rouge, Louisiana Office)
Virginia Boulet
F. M. Bush, III (Not admitted in LA; Resident, Tupelo, Mississippi Office)
Patrick J. Butler, Jr.
Philip deV. Claverie
Mark A. Fullmer
E. Clifton Hodge, Jr. (Not admitted in LA; Resident, Jackson, Mississippi Office)
Jean Magee Hogan (Not admitted in LA; Resident, Tupelo, Mississippi Office)
Stephen H. Leech, Jr. (Not admitted in LA; Resident, Jackson, Mississippi Office)
Richard E. Matheny (Resident, Baton Rouge, Louisiana Office)
James W. O'Mara (Not admitted in LA; Resident, Jackson, Mississippi Office)
Randy P. Roussel (Resident, Baton Rouge, Louisiana Office)
David P. Steiner
James A. Stuckey
Harvey D. Wagar, III
Stephen M. Wilson (Not admitted in LA; Resident, Jackson, Mississippi Office)

COUNSEL

J. Michael Cutshaw (Resident, Baton Rouge, Louisiana Office)

RESIDENT ASSOCIATES

Ashley S. Bergeron
Stratton Bull (Not admitted in LA; Resident, Jackson, Mississippi Office)
Daniel E. Davillier
Eric T. Hamer (Not admitted in LA; Resident, Jackson, Mississippi Office)
Daniel T. Pancamo
Dawn M. Rawls

(See Next Column)

Representative Clients: Bank of Mississippi; Bank One; Citicorp Real Estate, Inc.; Deposit Guaranty National Bank; Hibernia National Bank; Morgan Guaranty Trust Company of New York; NationsBank; Trustmark National Bank; Union Planters Bank; Whitney National Bank.

For Complete List of Firm Personnel, See General Section

For full biographical listings, see the Martindale-Hubbell Law Directory

*WINNFIELD,** Winn Parish

Simmons and Derr (AV)

Simmons Building, Church Street, P.O. Box 525, 71483
Telephone: 318-628-3951
Fax: 318-648-0644

MEMBERS OF FIRM

Kermit M. Simmons
Jacque D. Derr

Reference: Bank of Winnfield & Trust Co.

For full biographical listings, see the Martindale-Hubbell Law Directory

MAINE

*BANGOR,** Penobscot Co.

Eaton, Peabody, Bradford & Veague, P.A. (AV)

Fleet Center-Exchange Street, P.O. Box 1210, 04402-1210
Telephone: 207-947-0111
Telecopier: 207-942-3040
Email: eaton@eatonpeabody.com *URL:* http://www.eatonpeabody.com
Augusta, Maine Office: 77 Sewall Street, Suite 3000.
Telephone: 207-622-3747.
Telecopier: 207-622-9732.
Blue Hill, Maine Office: One East Blue Hill Road.
Telephone: 207-374-2812.
Telecopier: 207-374-2548.
Brunswick, Maine Office: 167 Park Row.
Telephone: 207-729-1144.
Telecopier: 207-729-1140.
Dover-Foxcroft, Maine Office: 30 East Main Street.
Telephone: 207-564-8378.
Telecopier: 207-564-7059.

Edward D. Leonard, III
Douglas M. Smith (Dover-Foxcroft and Augusta Offices)
Daniel G. McKay
John A. Cunningham (Resident, Brunswick Office)
Jonathan B. Huntington (Resident, Dover-Foxcroft Office)
Lorena R. Rush

For Complete List of Firm Personnel, See General Section

For full biographical listings, see the Martindale-Hubbell Law Directory

Gross, Minsky, Mogul & Singal, P.A. (AV)

Key Plaza, 23 Water Street, P.O. Box 917, 04402-0917
Telephone: 207-942-4644; 800-274-7124
Telecopier: 207-942-3699
Email: law@gmms.com

Edward I. Gross (1912-1999)
Jules L. Mogul (1930-1994)
George Z. Singal
Louis H. Kornreich
George C. Schelling
Edward W. Gould
Steven J. Mogul
James R. Wholly
Daniel A. Pileggi
Philip K. Clarke

Wayne P. Libhart (Retired)
Sandra L. Rothera
James S. Nixon

OF COUNSEL

Norman Minsky

Representative Clients: Merrill Merchants Bank; Union Trust Company of Ellsworth; Bangor Savings Bank.

For full biographical listings, see the Martindale-Hubbell Law Directory

*PORTLAND,** Cumberland Co.

Jensen Baird Gardner & Henry (AV)

Ten Free Street, P.O. Box 4510, 04112-4510
Telephone: 207-775-7271
Telecopier: 207-775-7935
Email: info@jbgh.com *URL:* http://www.jbgh.com
York County Office: 11 Main Street, Suite 4, Kennebunk, Maine, 04043.
Telephone: 207-985-4676.
Telecopier: 207-985-4932.

MEMBERS OF FIRM

Ronald A. Epstein
F. Bruce Sleeper

(See Next Column)

JENSEN BAIRD GARDNER & HENRY, *Portland—Continued*

OF COUNSEL

Merton G. Henry
John D. Bradford (Resident, York County Office)

Representative Clients: General Motors Acceptance Corp.; Key Bank; Owens Corning Fiberglass; Peoples Heritage Bank; Atlantic Bank.

For Complete List of Firm Personnel, See General Section

For full biographical listings, see the Martindale-Hubbell Law Directory

MARCUS, GRYGIEL & CLEGG, P.A. (AV)

100 Middle Street, East Tower, 04101-4102
Telephone: 207-828-8000
Fax: 207-773-3210
Email: firm@mgc-law.com

George J. Marcus
Jennie L. Clegg
Marilyn E. Mistretta
Lee H. Bals

Sean P. Joyce
Barbara G. Shaw
Michael J. Gartland
Regan M. Hornney

OF COUNSEL

Stephen G. Grygiel
Andrew Jeffrey Zulieve

For full biographical listings, see the Martindale-Hubbell Law Directory

MONAGHAN, LEAHY, HOCHADEL & LIBBY, LLP (AV)

95 Exchange Street, P.O. Box 7046, 04112-7046
Telephone: 207-774-3906
Facsimile: 207-774-3965
Email: info@mlhl.com *URL:* http://www.mlhl.com

MEMBERS OF FIRM

Thomas G. Leahy
Michael H. Hill

Representative Client: People's Heritage Bank.
Reference: Fleet Bank of Maine.

For full biographical listings, see the Martindale-Hubbell Law Directory

PIERCE ATWOOD (AV)

One Monument Square, 04101
Telephone: 207-791-1100
Fax: 207-791-1350
Email: info@PierceAtwood.com *URL:* http://www.pierceatwood.com
Augusta, Maine Office: 77 Winthrop Street.
Telephone: 207-622-6311.
Fax: 207-623-9367.
Newburyport, Massachusetts Office: 6 Harris Street.
Telephone: 978-465-9599.
Fax: 978-465-9945.

MEMBERS OF FIRM

James B. Zimpritch
Richard P. Hackett
David J. Champoux
Ryan S. Stinneford

For Complete List of Firm Personnel, See General Section

For full biographical listings, see the Martindale-Hubbell Law Directory

TOMPKINS, CLOUGH, HIRSHON & LANGER, P.A. (AV)

Three Canal Plaza, P.O. Box 15060, 04112-5060
Telephone: 207-874-6700
FAX: 207-874-6705

Bruce M. Tompkins
Lawrence R. Clough
David M. Hirshon
Leonard W. Langer
Marshall J. Tinkle

For full biographical listings, see the Martindale-Hubbell Law Directory

TROUBH, HEISLER & PIAMPIANO, P.C. (AV)

511 Congress Street, P.O. Box 9711, 04104-5011
Telephone: 207-780-6789
Fax: 207-774-2339
Email: info@thplaw.com

William B. Troubh
Edwin A. Heisler
Robert J. Piampiano
Kevin M. Gillis
Michael P. Boyd
Thomas E. Getchell
Michael Richards
William K. McKinley
Daniel F. Gilligan
Paul S. Bulger
John G. Richardson

Daniel R. Felkel
Ann Brandt
John P. Flynn, III

For full biographical listings, see the Martindale-Hubbell Law Directory

MARYLAND

*ANNAPOLIS,** Anne Arundel Co.

HYATT, PETERS & WEBER (AV)

1919 West Street, P.O. Box 6635, 21401
Telephone: 410-266-0626
Fax: 410-841-5065
Email: info@hyatt.hpwsb.com *URL:* http://www.hpwlaw.com

Alan J. Hyatt
Paula J. Peters
Paul J. Weber

ASSOCIATES

Sara H. Arthur
Sharon M. Grosfeld
Gregg M. Weinberg
Jonathan A. Hodgson
John L. Hill
Arlette K. Bright
Bruce F. Bright (Not admitted in MD)

OF COUNSEL

Steven G. Tyler

For full biographical listings, see the Martindale-Hubbell Law Directory

*BALTIMORE,** (Independent City)

BALLARD SPAHR ANDREWS & INGERSOLL, LLP (AV)

300 East Lombard Street, 19th Floor, 21202-3268
Telephone: 410-528-5600
Fax: 410-528-5650
URL: http://www.ballardspahr.com
Philadelphia, Pennsylvania Office: 1735 Market Street, 51st Floor.
Telephone: 215-665-8500.
Fax: 215-864-8999.
Voorhees, New Jersey Office: Suite 100, 1101 Laurel Oak Drive.
Telephone: 856-627-8555.
Fax: 856-627-1153.
Denver, Colorado Office: Seventeenth Street Plaza Building, Suite 2300, 1225 17th Street.
Telephone: 303-292-2400.
Fax: 303-296-3956.
Salt Lake City, Utah Office: One Utah Center, Suite 1200, 201 South Main Street.
Telephone: 801-531-3000.
Fax: 801-531-3001.
Washington, D.C. Office: Suite 1000 South, 601 13th Street, N.W.
Telephone: 202-661-2200.
Fax: 202-661-2299.
Camden, New Jersey Office: 800 Hudson Square, 5th Floor.
Telephone: 609-541-5577.
Fax: 609-541-8272.

Sophie Dagenais Goetz
S. Nelson Weeks

COUNSEL

Susan L. Spence

Teri L. Menke

For full biographical listings, see the Martindale-Hubbell Law Directory

GALLAGHER, EVELIUS & JONES, LLP (AV)

Park Charles Suite 400, 218 North Charles Street, 21201
Telephone: 410-727-7702
Facsimile: 410-468-2786
URL: http://www.gejlaw.com

MEMBERS OF FIRM

Francis X. Gallagher (1928-1972)
C. Edward Jones (1908-1999)
John C. Evelius (Retired)
Richard O. Berndt
Thomas N. Biddison, Jr.
Robert R. Kern, Jr.
Saul E. Gilstein
Thomas B. Lewis
Bonnie Abrams Travieso
Stephen A. Goldberg
Linda H. Jones
Jack C. Tranter
Leslie B. Speed
Christopher J. Fritz
David E. Raderman
Peter E. Keith
Nita L. Schultz
Michael W. Skojec
Kathryn Kelley Hoskins
Mark P. Keener
Kevin J. Davidson
Eileen M. Lunga
Lori A. Nicolle
Kenneth S. Gross
Thomas C. Dame

ASSOCIATES

Valarie K. Oulds
Margaret Stevens Jacks
Matthew W. Oakey
Rebecca A. Weaver
Michael J. Henigan
David W. Kinkopf
Paul S. Caiola
Jason W. Gaarder
M. Kirsten Andrews

LEGAL ASSISTANTS

Patricia C. Quayle
Iris T. H. Heath
Connie L. Ennis
Margaret Graff
Margo Gibson Hughes
Jonathan T. Gillis
Brenda J. Heacock
Dwayne L. Rodeheaver

(See Next Column)

GALLAGHER, EVELIUS & JONES LLP—*Continued*

Representative Clients: Mercantile-Safe Deposit and Trust Co.; GMAC Commercial Mortgage Corporation; First National Bank of Maryland; Maryland Bank & Trust Company; Municipal Mortgages and Equities, LLC.

For full biographical listings, see the Martindale-Hubbell Law Directory

THOMAS & LIBOWITZ, P.A. (AV)

100 Light Street, Suite 1100, 21202-1053
Telephone: 410-752-2468
Fax: 410-752-2046; 752-2049; 752-0979
Email: thomasandlibowitz.com *URL:* http://www.thomasandlibowitz.com

Steven Anargyros Thomas
John R. Wise
C. Wayne Davis

Representative Clients: Sinclair Broadcast Group, Inc. (Television and Radio stations); Roy Kirby & Sons, Inc. (Contractor); First Mariner Bank; Scandia Manufacturing Co. Inc. (Defense Contractor); Atlantic Automotive Corp. t/a Heritgage Automotive Group; Candy Express Franchising, Inc.; Wire Spectrum Services (Contractors-Transmission Tower Sites); Acrodyne Communications, Inc.; Alexis Logic Corporation (Software Developers); Selnic Corporation (Electronis Distributors); Liberty Mutual Insurance Company.

For full biographical listings, see the Martindale-Hubbell Law Directory

VENABLE ATTORNEYS AT LAW VENABLE, BAETJER AND HOWARD, LLP (AV)

A Partnership including Professional Corporations
1800 Mercantile Bank & Trust Building, 2 Hopkins Plaza, 21201
Telephone: 410-244-7400
Fax: 410-244-7742
URL: http://www.venable.com
Washington, D.C. Office: Venable, Baetjer, Howard & Civiletti LLP, Suite 1000, 1201 New York Avenue, N.W.
Telephone: 202-962-4800.
Fax: 202-962-8300.
McLean, Virginia Office: Suite 400, 2010 Corporate Ridge.
Telephone: 703-760-1600.
Fax: 703-821-8949.
Rockville, Maryland Office: Suite 500, One Church Street, P. O. Box 1906.
Telephone: 301-217-5600.
Fax: 301-217-5617.
Towson, Maryland Office: 210 Allegheny Avenue, P. O. Box 5517.
Telephone: 410-494-6200.
Fax: 410-821-0147.

MEMBERS OF FIRM

William J. McCarthy (P.C.)
Russell Ronald Reno, Jr. (P.C.)
James A. Cole
Benjamin R. Civiletti (P.C.) (Also at Washington, D.C. and Towson, Maryland Offices)
John Henry Lewin, Jr. (P.C.)
Lee M. Miller (P.C.)
Robert A. Shelton
Roger W. Titus (Resident, Rockville, Maryland Office)
Thomas W. W. Haines
Ronald R. Glancz (Not admitted in MD; Resident, Washington, D.C. Office)
Joe A. Shull (Resident, Washington, D.C. Office)
Kenneth C. Bass, III (Not admitted in MD; Washington, D.C. and McLean, Virginia Offices)
John H. Zink, III (Resident, Towson, Maryland Office)
Lars E. Anderson (Not admitted in MD; Resident, McLean, Virginia Office)
William D. Dolan, III (P.C.) (Not admitted in MD; Resident, McLean, Virginia Office)
Joseph C. Wich, Jr. (Resident, Towson, Maryland Office)
Edward F. Glynn, Jr. (Resident, Washington, D.C. Office)
Nell B. Strachan
Edward L. Wender (P.C.)
David M. Fleishman
Jeffrey A. Dunn (Also at Washington, D.C. Office)
Mitchell Kolkin
George F. Pappas (Also at Washington, D.C. Office)
James L. Shea (Also at Washington, D.C. Office)
Ellen F. Dyke (Not admitted in MD; Resident, McLean, Virginia Office)
Christopher R. Mellott
James A. Dunbar (Resident, Towson, Maryland Office)
Elizabeth R. Hughes
David J. Heubeck
J. Michael Brennan (Resident, Towson, Maryland Office)
Mitchell Y. Mirviss
John A. McCauley
Joseph C. Schmelter (Also at McLean, Virginia Office)
Vicki Margolis (Also at Washington, D.C. Office)

OF COUNSEL

Thomas J. Cooper (Not admitted in MD; Resident, Washington, D.C. Office)
Ariel Vannier (Also at Washington, D.C. Office)

For Complete List of Firm Personnel, See General Section

For full biographical listings, see the Martindale-Hubbell Law Directory

*ROCKVILLE,** Montgomery Co.

VENABLE ATTORNEYS AT LAW VENABLE, BAETJER AND HOWARD, LLP (AV)

A Partnership including Professional Corporations
Suite 500, One Church Street, P.O. Box 1906, 20850-4129
Telephone: 301-217-5600
Fax: 301-217-5617
URL: http://www.venable.com
Baltimore, Maryland Office: 1800 Mercantile Bank & Trust Building, 2 Hopkins Plaza.
Telephone: 410-244-7400.
Fax: 410-244-7742.
Washington, D.C. Office: Venable, Baetjer, Howard & Civiletti LLP, Suite 1000, 1201 New York Avenue, N.W.
Telephone: 202-962-4800.
Fax: 202-962-8300.
McLean, Virginia Office: Suite 400, 2010 Corporate Ridge.
Telephone: 703-760-1600.
Fax: 703-821-8949.
Towson, Maryland, Office: 210 Allegheny Avenue, P. O. Box 5517.
Telephone: 410-494-6200.
Fax: 410-821-0147.

MEMBERS OF FIRM

Paul T. Glasgow
John A. Roberts (Also at Baltimore, Maryland Office)

For Complete List of Firm Personnel, See General Section

For full biographical listings, see the Martindale-Hubbell Law Directory

*TOWSON,** Baltimore Co.

VENABLE ATTORNEYS AT LAW VENABLE, BAETJER AND HOWARD, LLP (AV)

A Partnership including Professional Corporations
210 Allegheny Avenue, P.O. Box 5517, 21204
Telephone: 410-494-6200
Fax: 410-821-0147
URL: http://www.venable.com
Baltimore, Maryland Office: 1800 Mercantile Bank & Trust Building, 2 Hopkins Plaza.
Telephone: 410-244-7400.
Fax: 410-244-7742.
Washington, D.C. Office: Venable, Baetjer, Howard & Civiletti LLP, Suite 1000, 1201 New York Avenue, N.W.
Telephone: 202-962-4800.
Fax: 202-962-8300.
McLean, Virginia Office: Suite 400, 2010 Corporate Ridge.
Telephone: 703-760-1600.
Fax: 703-821-8949.
Rockville, Maryland Office: Suite 500, One Church Street, P. O. Box 1906.
Telephone: 301-217-5600.
Fax: 301-217-5617.

PARTNERS

Benjamin R. Civiletti (P.C.) (Also at Washington, D.C. and Baltimore, Maryland Offices)
John H. Zink, III
Joseph C. Wich, Jr.
J. Michael Brennan

For Complete List of Firm Personnel, See General Section

For full biographical listings, see the Martindale-Hubbell Law Directory

*UPPER MARLBORO,** Prince Georges Co.

KNIGHT, MANZI, NUSSBAUM & LAPLACA, P.C. (AV)

14440 Old Mill Road, 20772
Telephone: 301-952-0100
Annapolis/Baltimore: 410-792-3786
Fax: 301-952-0221

William E. Knight
Robert A. Manzi
Ronald M. Miller
William C. Brennan, Jr.
Harry J. Trainor, Jr.
Andrew W. Nussbaum
Raymond G. LaPlaca
John F. Shay, Jr.
Sheldon L. Gnatt
Daniel A. LaPlaca
Gail Borjeson Viens
Roger C. Thomas
Monica M. Haley-Pierson
Daniel F. Lynch III
Norman D. Rivera

Robert L. Lombardo
Amy B. Glaser
Brent M. Ahalt
Terry L. Bell

Representative Clients: Suburban Bank; First National Bank of Maryland; Alleigience Bank.

For full biographical listings, see the Martindale-Hubbell Law Directory

MASSACHUSETTS

*BOSTON,** Suffolk Co.

BARRON & STADFELD, P.C. (AV)

50 Staniford Street, Suite 200, 02114
Telephone: 617-723-9800
Telecopier: 617-523-8359
Email: barron@barronstad.com *URL:* HTTP://WWW.BARRONSTAD.COM
Hyannis, Massachusetts Office: 258 Winter Street.
Telephone: 617-778-6622.

Thomas V. Bennett
Kevin F. Moloney
Julie Taylor Moran

OF COUNSEL

Hertz N. Henkoff

For Complete List of Firm Personnel, See General Section

For full biographical listings, see the Martindale-Hubbell Law Directory

CRAIG AND MACAULEY, PROFESSIONAL CORPORATION (AV)

Federal Reserve Plaza, 600 Atlantic Avenue, 02210-2211
Telephone: 617-367-9500
Telecopier: 617-742-1788; 617-248-0886
URL: http://prospex.com/craig-macauley/

David F. Hannon
John G. Snyder
Mary P. Brody
Christopher S. Dalton

OF COUNSEL

John C. Craig

For Complete List of Firm Personnel, See General Section

For full biographical listings, see the Martindale-Hubbell Law Directory

HINCKLEY, ALLEN & SNYDER LLP (AV)

28 State Street, 30th Floor, 02109-1775
Telephone: 617-345-9000
Email: firm@haslaw.com *URL:* http://www.haslaw.com
Providence, Rhode Island Office: 1500 Fleet Center.
Telephone: 401-274-2000.
Fax: 401-277-9600. URL: http://www.hawlaw.com.

MEMBERS OF FIRM

Paula K. Andrews
David D. Barricelli (Not admitted in MA)
E. Jerome Batty (Not admitted in MA)
Jonathan Bell
Paul Bork
Stephen J. Carlotti (Not admitted in MA)
David Barry Connolly
Joseph P. Curran (Not admitted in MA)
Michael P. DeFanti
Eric F. Eisenberg
Malcolm Farmer, III
Margaret D. Farrell (Not admitted in MA)
Hugh J. Gorman, III
Alan P. Gottlieb
William R. Grimm
Paul A. Hedstrom
Richard L. E. Jocelyn (Not admitted in MA)
Sandra Matrone Mack (Not admitted in MA)
Matthew T. Marcello, III (Not admitted in MA)
Frederick P. McClure
Elizabeth Murdock Myers
Paul F. O'Donnell, III
H. Peter Olsen (Not admitted in MA)
Julianne Palumbo
John J. Pendergast, III (Not admitted in MA)
Gerald J. Petros
James O. Reavis
Ralph J. Rivkind
David J. Rubin
Douglas F. Seaver
David R. Sullivan
Robert F. Sylvia
Howard E. Walker (Not admitted in MA)

ASSOCIATES

Mark Bianchi
Alyssa V. Boss
Andrew D. Cummings
June E. Daniel (Not admitted in MA)
Gloria Maria Gutierrez
Kelley Jordan-Price
Joseph D. Whelan (Not admitted in MA)

OF COUNSEL

Willard R. Pope
Bentley Tobin
Joachim A. Weissfeld (Not admitted in MA)

For Complete List of Firm Personnel, See General Section

For full biographical listings, see the Martindale-Hubbell Law Directory

PALMER & DODGE LLP (AV)

One Beacon Street, 02108
Telephone: 617-573-0100
Facsimile: 617-227-4420
URL: http://www.palmerdodge.com

(See Next Column)

MEMBERS OF FIRM

Matthew C. Dallett
John L. Whitlock

For Complete List of Firm Personnel, See General Section

For full biographical listings, see the Martindale-Hubbell Law Directory

ROCHE, CARENS & DEGIACOMO, P.C. (AV)

99 High Street, 02110
Telephone: 617-457-4000
Facsimile: 617-482-3868
Email: firm@rcdpc.com *URL:* http://www.rcdpc.com
Woburn, Massachusetts Office: 600 Unicorn Park Drive.
Telephone: 781-933-5505.

Michael T. Putziger
Anne Hanford

For Complete List of Firm Personnel, See General Section

For full biographical listings, see the Martindale-Hubbell Law Directory

*CAMBRIDGE,** Middlesex Co.

WILLIAM M. O'BRIEN (AV)

185 Alewife Brook Parkway, Suite 400, 02138
Telephone: 617-661-2600
Fax: 617-868-8040

For full biographical listings, see the Martindale-Hubbell Law Directory

*SPRINGFIELD,** Hampden Co.

ROBINSON DONOVAN MADDEN & BARRY, P.C. (AV)

Suite 1600, Tower Square, 1500 Main Street, 01115-5609
Telephone: 413-732-2301
Fax: 413-785-4658
Email: service@robinson-donovan.com *URL:* http://www.robinson-donovan.com

Homans Robinson (1894-1973)
Lawrence M. Sinclair (1942-1986)
Milton J. Donovan (1906-1995)

RETIRED

John H. Madden, Jr.
Edward J. Barry
Richard S. Milstein

OF COUNSEL

Victor Rosenberg

SENIOR COUNSEL

Jonathan P. Rice

Gordon H. Wentworth
James H. Tourtelotte
Ronald C. Kidd
Jeffrey W. Roberts
Jeffrey L. McCormick
James F. Martin
Robert P. Cunningham
John C. Sikorski
Nancy Frankel Pelletier
Paul S. Weinberg
Frederica H. McCarthy
Matthew J. King
Neva Kaufman Rohan
Douglas F. Boyd
James K. Bodurtha
Keith A. Minoff
Patricia M. Rapinchuk
Kimberly Davis Crear

E. Paul Amata
Lisa A. Bongiovi (Not admitted in MA)
Edward J. Carroll, III
James D. Chadwell
John E. Garber
Patrick J. Markey
Carla W. Newton
Betsy Macmillan Stevens

Representative Clients: BankBoston, N.A.; United Cooperative Bank; Fleet National Bank; CNA; Commercial Union Insurance Co.; Hanover Insurance Group.

For full biographical listings, see the Martindale-Hubbell Law Directory

*WORCESTER,** Worcester Co.

MACCARTHY, POJANI & HURLEY, LLP (AV)

Worcester Plaza, 446 Main Street, 01608
Telephone: 508-798-2480
Fax: 508-797-9561

MEMBERS OF FIRM

Dennis Pojani
John F. Hurley, Jr.

Representative Clients: Bay Finance Company, Inc.; Bay State Savings Bank; Fleet National Bank; Enrich Foods, Inc.; Family Bank, FSB; First Massachusetts Bank, N.A.

For Complete List of Firm Personnel, See General Section

For full biographical listings, see the Martindale-Hubbell Law Directory

MICHIGAN

*ADRIAN,** Lenawee Co.

WALKER, WATTS, JACKSON & MCFARLAND (AV)

160 North Winter Street, 49221
Telephone: 517-265-8138
Fax: 517-265-8286
URL: http://www.lawyers.com/wwj&m

MEMBERS OF FIRM

William H. Walker
Prosser M. Watts, Jr.
Mark A. Jackson
Michael McFarland

Attorneys for: Bank of Lenawee.

For Complete List of Firm Personnel, See General Section

For full biographical listings, see the Martindale-Hubbell Law Directory

*ANN ARBOR,** Washtenaw Co.

BRAUN KENDRICK FINKBEINER PLC (AV)

First National Building, 210 S. Main, Suite 700, 48104
Telephone: 313-995-4100
Telecopier: 313-995-4798
Email: ALBFIE@BKF-LAW.COM *URL:* http://www.bkf-law.com
Bay City, Michigan Office: 201 Phoenix Building, P.O. Box 2039.
Telephone: 517-895-8505.
Telecopier: 517-895-8437.
Saginaw, Michigan Office: 101 N. Washington, Suite 812.
Telephone: 517-753-3461.
Telecopier: 517-753-3951.
Saginaw Township, Michigan Office: 5800 Gratiot Road, Suite 107, P.O. Box 5169.
Telephone: 517-799-8692.
Fax: 517-799-4666.
Mt. Pleasant, Michigan Office: 805 North Brown.
Telephone: 517-775-7404.
Telecopier: 517-775-3764.

Barry M. Levine

Representative Clients: The Dow Chemical Co.; General Motors Corp.; Merrill, Lynch, Inc.; Saginaw General Hospital; Saginaw News; The Wickes Foundation.

For Complete List of Firm Personnel, See General Section

For full biographical listings, see the Martindale-Hubbell Law Directory

BUTZEL LONG, A PROFESSIONAL CORPORATION (AV)

Suite 300, 350 South Main Street, 48104-2131
Telephone: 313-995-3110
Telecopier: 313-995-1777
Email: melnick@butzel.com *URL:* http://www.butzel.com
Detroit, Michigan Office: Suite 900, 150 West Jefferson.
Telephone: 313-225-7000.
Telecopier: 313-225-7080.
Birmingham, Michigan Office: Suite 200, 32270 Telegraph Road.
Telephone: 810-258-1616.
Telecopier: 810-258-1439.
Okemos, Michigan Office: Suite 300, 2127 University Park Drive.
Telephone: 517-372-6622.
Telecopier: 372-6672.
Grosse Pointe Farms, Michigan Office: Suite 260, 21 Kercheval.
Telephone: 313-886-5446.
Telecopier: 313-886-2114.
Boca Raton, Florida Office: Suite 411, 1200 North Federal Highway.
Telephone: 561-368-2151.
Telecopier: 561-368-4668.
Palm Beach Gardens, Florida Office: Suite 227, 11382 Prosperity Farms Road.
Telephone: 561-625-4442.
Telecopier: 561-625-6901.
Naples, Florida Office: Suite 705, 801 Laurel Oak Drive.
Telephone: 941-597-4500.
Telecopier: 941-597-5623.

Robert B. Foster (Resident)
J. Michael Huget (Resident)

For full biographical listings, see the Martindale-Hubbell Law Directory

PEAR SPERLING EGGAN & MUSKOVITZ, P.C. (AV)

Domino's Farms, 24 Frank Lloyd Wright Drive, 48105
Telephone: 734-665-4441
Fax: 734-665-8788
Email: peare@dominos.com
Ypsilanti, Michigan Offices: 5 South Washington Street.
Telephone: 734-483-3626 and 2164 Bellevue at Washtenaw.
Telephone: 734-483-7177.

(See Next Column)

Edwin L. Pear
Andrew M. Eggan
Joel F. Graziani

Counsel For: Domino's Pizza, Inc.; Citizens Banking Corporation; The Credit Bureau of Ypsilanti.

For Complete List of Firm Personnel, See General Section

For full biographical listings, see the Martindale-Hubbell Law Directory

BATTLE CREEK, Calhoun Co.

KREIS, ENDERLE, CALLANDER & HUDGINS, A PROFESSIONAL CORPORATION (AV)

One West Michigan Avenue, 49017
Telephone: 616-966-3000
Facsimile: 616-966-3022
Email: kech@kech.com *URL:* http://www.kech.com
Kalamazoo, Michigan Office: One Moorsbridge, P.O. Box 4010, 49003-4010.
Telephone: 616-324-3000.
Fax: 616-324-3010.

Russell A. Kreis (Resident, Kalamazoo Office)
Alan G. Enderle (Resident, Kalamazoo Office)
C. Reid Hudgins III (Resident, Kalamazoo Office)
Thomas G. King (Resident, Kalamazoo Office)

For Complete List of Firm Personnel, See General Section

For full biographical listings, see the Martindale-Hubbell Law Directory

*BAY CITY,** Bay Co.

BRAUN KENDRICK FINKBEINER PLC (AV)

201 Phoenix Building, P.O. Box 2039, 48708
Telephone: 517-895-8505
Telecopier: 517-895-8437
Email: ALBFIE@BKF-LAW.COM *URL:* http://www.bkf-law.com
Saginaw, Michigan Office: 101 N. Washington, Suite 812. 8th Floor Second National Bank Building.
Telephone: 517-753-3461.
Telecopier: 517-753-3951.
Saginaw Township, Michigan Office: 5800 Gratiot Road, Suite 107, P.O. Box 5169.
Telephone: 517-799-8692.
Fax: 517-799-4666.
Ann Arbor, Michigan Office: First National Building. 201 S. Main, Suite 700.
Telephone: 313-995-4100.
Telecopier: 313-995-4798.
Mt. Pleasant, Michigan Office: 805 North Brown.
Telephone: 517-775-7404.
Telecopier: 517-775-3764.

Ralph J. Isackson
Daniel S. Opperman
Gregory T. Demers

Representative Clients: Bay Health Systems; Catholic Federal Credit Union; City of Saginaw; City of Vassar; City of Zilwaukee; Corporate Service; Cox Cable.

For Complete List of Firm Personnel, See General Section

For full biographical listings, see the Martindale-Hubbell Law Directory

BLOOMFIELD HILLS, Oakland Co.

ADKISON, NEED, GREEN & ALLEN (AV)

1533 North Woodward Avenue, Suite 210, 48304
Telephone: 248-540-7400
Fax: 248-540-7401
URL: http://www.adkisonneed.com

MEMBER OF FIRM

Paul Green

For Complete List of Firm Personnel, See General Section

For full biographical listings, see the Martindale-Hubbell Law Directory

HERTZ, SCHRAM & SARETSKY, P.C. (AV)

1760 South Telegraph Road, Suite 300, 48302
Telephone: 248-335-5000
Fax: 248-335-3346
Email: lawhss@aol.com *URL:* http://www.legalleaders.com

Bradley J. Schram
Howard Hertz
Gary M. Saretsky
Robert S. Hertzberg
Victor M. Norris
Steve J. Weiss
Robert Paul Geller
Walter J. Piszczatowski
Jeffrey A. Robbins
Mark L. Kowalsky

(See Next Column)

HERTZ, SCHRAM & SARETSKY P.C., *Bloomfield Hills—Continued*

Dana A. Donohue
Miles D. Hart
Karen A. Gould
Paul K. Villarruel
Bradford T. Yaker
Michael F. Jacobson
Michael I. Zousmer
Brian Witus
Eva T. Cantarella
Eric Andrew Michaels

COUNSEL

Richard P. Zipser
Lisa M. Kavalhuna (Not admitted in MI)
James W. Burdick

OF COUNSEL

David L. Steinberg
Albert L. Holtz
Elmer L. Roller
Robert A. Canner
Harvey D. Geller (1928-1989)

For full biographical listings, see the Martindale-Hubbell Law Directory

HOWARD & HOWARD ATTORNEYS, P.C. (AV)

The Pinehurst Office Center, Suite 101, 1400 North Woodward Avenue, 48304-2855
Telephone: 248-645-1483
Telecopier: 248-645-1568
Kalamazoo, Michigan Office: The Michigan Building, Suite 200, 100 Portage Street.
Telephone: 616-382-1483.
Telecopier: 616-382-1568.
Lansing, Michigan Office: The Phoenix Building, Suite 500, 222 Washington Square, North.
Telephone: 517-485-1483.
Telecopier: 517-485-1568.
Peoria, Illinois Office: One Technology Plaza, Suite 600, 211 Fulton Street.
Telephone: 309-672-1483.
Telecopier: 309-672-1568.

James T. Bork
Philip T. Carter
Michael G. Cruse
William H. Honaker
Robert B. Johnston
Timothy E. Kraepel
Robert D. Mollhagen
Brian J. Renaud
John E. Young
Marla Gottlieb Zwas

Representative Clients: For Representative Client list, see General Practice, Bloomfield Hills, MI.

For Complete List of Firm Personnel, See General Section

For full biographical listings, see the Martindale-Hubbell Law Directory

PROVIZER & PHILLIPS, P.C. (AV)

6785 Telegraph Road, Suite 400, 48301
Telephone: 248-642-0444
Facsimile: 248-642-6661
Toll Free: 1-800-288-9080
URL: http://www.lawyers.com/provizer&phillips

Harold M. Provizer
Randall E. Phillips

Representative Clients: Investuid Corporation; Mortgage Institute of Michigan.

For full biographical listings, see the Martindale-Hubbell Law Directory

*CHEBOYGAN,** Cheboygan Co.

BODMAN, LONGLEY & DAHLING LLP (AV)

229 Court Street, P.O. Box 405, 49721
Telephone: 231-627-4351
Fax: 231-627-2802
Email: info@bodmanlongley.com *URL:* http://www.bodmanlongley.com
Detroit, Michigan Office: 34th Floor, 100 Renaissance Center.
Telephone: 313-259-7777.
Fax: 313-393-7579.
Troy, Michigan Office: Suite 2020, 755 West Big Beaver Road.
Telephone: 248-362-2110.
Fax: 248-244-0780.
Ann Arbor, Michigan Office: 110 Miller, Suite 300.
Telephone: 734-761-3780.
Fax: 734-930-2494.

SENIOR ATTORNEY

Richard Barr West (Not admitted in MI)

For full biographical listings, see the Martindale-Hubbell Law Directory

*DETROIT,** Wayne Co.

BODMAN, LONGLEY & DAHLING LLP (AV)

34th Floor 100 Renaissance Center, 48243
Telephone: 313-259-7777
Fax: 313-393-7579
Email: info@bodmanlongley.com *URL:* http://www.bodmanlongley.com
Troy, Michigan Office: Suite 2020, 755 West Big Beaver Road.
Telephone: 248-362-2110.
Fax: 248-244-0780.

(See Next Column)

Ann Arbor, Michigan Office: 110 Miller, Suite 300.
Telephone: 734-761-3780.
Fax: 734-930-2494.
Northern Michigan Office: 229 Court Street, P.O. Box 405, Cheboygan.
Telephone: 231-627-4351.
Fax: 231-627-2802.

MEMBERS OF FIRM

Richard D. Rohr
Thomas A. Roach (Ann Arbor Office)
James T. Heimbuch
Joseph J. Kochanek
Randolph S. Perry
David W. Hipp
Larry R. Shulman
Robert J. Diehl, Jr.
Lloyd C. Fell (Cheboygan Office)
Michael A. Stack (Cheboygan Office)
Lawrence P. Hanson (Cheboygan Office)
Ralph E. McDowell
Stephen I. Greenhalgh
Kathleen O'Callaghan Hickey
Bonnie S. Sherr
Marc M. Bakst
Nicholas P. Scavone, Jr.
Sol M. Friedman

COUNSEL

James C. Conboy, Jr. (Cheboygan Office)

SENIOR ATTORNEYS

Anthony T. Finn
Richard Barr West (Cheboygan Office)

ASSOCIATES

Deanna L. Dixon
Laurie E. Phelan
Andrew Z. Spilkin
Amy J. Durant (Cheboygan Office)
Rachelle Propson Tyshka
Melissa A. Lewis
Christene M. Devitt (Cheboygan Office)
Scott P. Gyorke
Brian R. Trumbauer
Kurt M. Brauer
Erik S. Prater

For Representative Client List, See General Section

For Complete List of Firm Personnel, See General Section

For full biographical listings, see the Martindale-Hubbell Law Directory

LEWIS & MUNDAY, A PROFESSIONAL CORPORATION (AV)

(Formerly Lewis, Clay & Munday, P.C.)
1300 First National Building, 660 Woodward Avenue, 48226-3531
Telephone: 313-961-2550
Fax: 313-961-1270
Email: camille.miller@lewis-pc.com *URL:* http://www.lewis-pc.com
Washington, D.C. Office: 1120 Connecticut Avenue, Suite 280. 20036.
Telephone: 202-835-0616.
Fax: 202-833-3316.
Boston, Massachusetts Office: 101 Federal Street, Suite 1900. 02110.
Telephone: 617-478-0553.
Fax: 617-478-0543.

David Baker Lewis
Reuben A. Munday
Camille Stearns Miller
Jacqueline H. Sellers
David N. Zacks
Thomas J. Guyer
Blair A. Person
Karen Kendrick Brown (Resident, Washington, D.C. Office)
Susan D. Hoffman
Hans J. Massaquoi, Jr.

Althea Lynn Simpson
Donica Thomas Varner
Kris W. Krueger
Cylenthia LaToye Miller
Joseph N. Ejbeh
Yolanda R. Bates
Caroletta L. Edgar-Sprinkle
Derek G. McBride
Ayanna Weber
Deborah Jean Williamson
Darice Elizabeth Weber
Krystal M. Gardner
Syeda Taqi

COUNSEL

G. Allen Bass (Resident, Boston, Massachusetts Office)
Leamon R. Sowell, Jr.
Gail Pabarue Bennett
Roger M. Groves
Carol H. Rodriguez
Linda M. Bruton
Brian J. Kott

OF COUNSEL

Otis M. Smith (1922-1994)
Herbert O. Reid, Sr. (1915-1991)

Representative Clients: Aetna Life & Casualty Co.; Chrysler Motors Corp.; Chrysler Financial Corp.; MCI Communications Corp.; City of Detroit; City of Detroit Building Authority; City of Detroit Downtown Development Authority; Consolidated Rail Corp. (Conrail); Equitable Life Assurance Society of the United States.

For full biographical listings, see the Martindale-Hubbell Law Directory

Detroit—Continued

MILLER, CANFIELD, PADDOCK AND STONE, P.L.C. (AV)

A Professional Limited Liability Company
Founded in 1852 by Sidney Davy Miller
150 West Jefferson, Suite 2500, 48226-4415
Telephone: 313-963-6420
Fax: 313-496-7500
Cable Address: "Stem Detroit"
URL: http://www.millercanfield.com
Ann Arbor, Michigan Office: 101 North Main Street, 7th Floor, 48104-1400.
Telephone: 734-663-2445.
Fax: 734-747-7147.
Troy, Michigan Office: 840 West Long Lake Road, Suite 200, 48098.
Telephone: 248-879-2000.
Fax: 248-879-2001.
Grand Rapids, Michigan Office: 99 Monroe, N.W., Suite 1200, 49503-2639.
Telephone: 616-454-8656.
Fax: 616-776-6322.
Howell, Michigan Office: 121 South Barnard Street, Suite 4, 48843-2305.
Telephone: 517-546-7600.
Telecopier: 517-546-6974.
Kalamazoo, Michigan Office: 444 West Michigan Avenue, 49007-3752.
Telephone: 616-381-7030.
Fax: 616-382-0244.
Lansing, Michigan Office: One Michigan Avenue, Suite 900, 48933-1609.
Telephone: 517-487-2070.
Fax: 517-374-6304.
Monroe, Michigan Office: 214 East Elm Avenue, Suite 100, 48162-2682.
Telephone: 734-243-2000.
Fax: 734-243-0901.
Washington, D.C. Office: 1900 K Street, N.W., Suite 1150. 20006.
Telephone: 202-429-5575; 785-0600.
Fax: 202-331-1118; 785-1234.
Pensacola, Florida Office: 25 West Cedar, 32501.
Telephone: 850-469-1088.
Fax: 850-432-0677.
New York, New York Office: 1450 Broadway, 41st Floor, 10018.
Telephone: 212-704-4400.
Fax: 212-704-4410.
Gdynia, Poland Office: UL. Slaska 21, 81-319.
Telephone: 011-485-831-2808.
Fax: 011-48-58-628 6411.
Warsaw, Poland Office: UL. Nowogrodzkall, 5th Floor, 00-513.
Telephone: 011-4822 529 0200.
Fax: 011-4822 529 0201.
Katowice, Poland Office: UL. Francuska 35/37, 40-027.
Telephone: 011 (48-32) 757-2414.
Fax: 011 (48-32) 757-2483.

PRINCIPALS OF FIRM

Rocque E. Lipford (P.C.) (Monroe Office)
David D. Joswick (P.C.)
John A. Marxer (P.C.) (Troy Office)
Ronald H. Riback (Troy Office)
Thomas W. Linn
Terrence M. Crawford
J. Kevin Trimmer (Troy Office)
Brad B. Arbuckle (Bloomfield Hills Office)
Karen A. McCoy
Ronald E. Hodess (Troy Office)
Sally A. Hamby (Troy Office)

OF COUNSEL/SENIOR COUNSEL

Richard B. Gushée
George E. Parker, III
Henry R. Nolte, Jr. (Troy Office)

Representative Firm Clients: Chrysler Corporation; Comerica, Incorporated; City of Detroit, Michigan; Detroit Tigers, Inc.; First of Michigan; Ford Motor Company; Ford Motor Credit Company; Great Lakes Bancorp; Henry Ford Hospital; INVETECH Company.

For Complete List of Firm Personnel, See General Section

For full biographical listings, see the Martindale-Hubbell Law Directory

*GRAND RAPIDS,** Kent Co.

BORRE, PETERSON, FOWLER & REENS, P.C. (AV)

300 Ottawa N.W., Suite 500, P.O. Box 1767, 49501-1767
Telephone: 616-459-1971
Fax: 616-459-2393
Email: 105162.1531@compuserve.com

Mark D. Sevald
Harold E. Nelson
William R. Vander Sluis
John C. Arndts

References: NBD Bank/First Chicago Bank; The Huntington Nation Bank.

For Complete List of Firm Personnel, See General Section

For full biographical listings, see the Martindale-Hubbell Law Directory

WARNER NORCROSS & JUDD LLP (AV)

900 Old Kent Building, 111 Lyon Street, N.W., 49503-2489
Telephone: 616-752-2000
Fax: 616-752-2500
URL: http://www.wnj.com
Muskegon, Michigan Office: 400 Terrace Plaza, P.O. Box 900.
Telephone: 231-727-2600.
Fax: 231-727-2699.
Holland, Michigan Office: Curtis Center, Suite 300, 170 College Avenue.
Telephone: 616-396-9800.
Fax: 616-396-3656.
Southfield, Michigan Office: 1000 Town Center, Suite 650.
Telephone: 248-223-5000.
Fax: 248-223-5005.

MEMBERS OF FIRM

Charles E. McCallum
Jack B. Combs
James H. Breay
Ernest M. Sharpe
Gordon R. Lewis
Thomas H. Thornhill (Resident Member, Muskegon Office)
Jeffrey O. Birkhold
Timothy Hillegonds
John G. Cameron, Jr.
Rodney D. Martin
Shane B. Hansen
Jeffrey S. Battershall
Jeffrey A. Ott
Judith Lowitz Adler (Resident Member, Southfield Office)
Timothy L. Horner
R. Paul Guerre
Loren M. Andrulis

ASSOCIATES

Michael P. Lunt
Michael K. Molitor

For full biographical listings, see the Martindale-Hubbell Law Directory

HOLLAND, Ottawa Co.

CUNNINGHAM DALMAN, P.C. (AV)

321 Settlers Road, P.O. Box 1767, 49422-1767
Telephone: 616-392-1821
Fax: 616-392-4769
Email: cunndalm@crossover.net *URL:* http://www.holland-law.com

Gordon H. Cunningham
Ronald L. Dalman
Max R. Murphy
James A. Bidol
Andrew J. Mulder
Kenneth B. Breese
Jeffrey K. Helder
Ronald J. Vander Veen
David M. Zessin
Mark H. Zietlow
Randall S. Schipper
Susan E. Vroegop
Joel G. Bouwens

Gregory J. McCoy
Jason M. Milstone
Aaron Leal
Dawn J. Ward

Representative Clients: Huntington National Bank; First of America Bank-Holland, N.A.; Ameribank; City of Holland; The Title Office; Donnelly Corp.; Waste Management of Michigan.

For full biographical listings, see the Martindale-Hubbell Law Directory

*JACKSON,** Jackson Co.

MARCOUX, ALLEN, ABBOTT, SCHOMER & BOWER, P.C. (AV)

145 South Jackson Street, P.O. Box 787, 49204-0787
Telephone: 517-787-4100
Fax: 517-787-9455
Email: marcoux@jacksonmi.com

William J. Marcoux (Retired)
William O. Allen
William M. Abbott
John H. Schomer
Diane Y. Bower
William B. Nichols, Jr.
Robert T. Kendall, III
Timothy R. Allen
Richard C. Lindsey, Jr.

OF COUNSEL

Walter R. Boris
Lawrence L. Bullen
Philip M. Moilanen
Terry J. Klaasen
T. Harrison Stanton

For full biographical listings, see the Martindale-Hubbell Law Directory

*KALAMAZOO,** Kalamazoo Co.

HOWARD & HOWARD ATTORNEYS, P.C. (AV)

The Michigan Building, Suite 200, 100 Portage Street, 49007-4802
Telephone: 616-382-1483
Telecopier: 616-382-1568
Bloomfield Hills, Michigan Office: The Pinehurst Office Center, Suite 101, 1400 North Woodward Avenue.
Telephone: 248-645-1483.
Telecopier: 248-645-1568.
Lansing, Michigan Office: The Phoenix Building, Suite 500, 222 Washington Square North.
Telephone: 517-485-1483.
Telecopier: 517-485-1568.
Peoria, Illinois Office: One Technology Plaza, Suite 600, 211 Fulton Street.
Telephone: 309-672-1483.
Telecopier: 309-672-1568.

(See Next Column)

HOWARD & HOWARD ATTORNEYS P.C., *Kalamazoo—Continued*

Jeffrey P. Chalmers	James H. Geary
William A. Dornbos	Joseph B. Hemker

Representative Clients: For Representative Client list, see General Practice, Kalamazoo, MI.

For Complete List of Firm Personnel, See General Section

For full biographical listings, see the Martindale-Hubbell Law Directory

KREIS, ENDERLE, CALLANDER & HUDGINS, A PROFESSIONAL CORPORATION (AV)

One Moorsbridge, P.O. Box 4010, 49003-4010
Telephone: 616-324-3000
Facsimile: 616-324-3010
Email: kech@kech.com *URL:* http://www.kech.com
Battle Creek, Michigan Office: One West Michigan Avenue, 49017.
Telephone: 616-966-3000.
Fax: 616-966-3022.

Russell A. Kreis	C. Reid Hudgins III
Alan G. Enderle	Thomas G. King

For Complete List of Firm Personnel, See General Section

For full biographical listings, see the Martindale-Hubbell Law Directory

LANSING, Ingham Co.

FOSTER, SWIFT, COLLINS & SMITH, P.C. (AV)

313 South Washington Square, 48933-2193
Telephone: 517-371-8100
Telecopier: 517-371-8200
URL: http://www.fosterswift.com
Farmington Hills, Michigan Office: 32300 Northwestern Highway, Suite 230.
Telephone: 248-539-9900.
Fax: 248-851-7504.

Richard B. Foster (1908-1996)	Deanna Swisher
Robert J. McCullen	Michael W. Puerner
James B. Jensen, Jr.	Mark J. Burzych
James B. Croom	Scott A. Chernich
Brent A. Titus	Barbara J. Oyer

LEGAL SUPPORT PERSONNEL

LEGAL ASSISTANTS

Jeanne M. Phillips, CLA	Janice S. Underwood, CLA

For Complete List of Firm Personnel, See General Section

For full biographical listings, see the Martindale-Hubbell Law Directory

HOWARD & HOWARD ATTORNEYS, P.C. (AV)

The Phoenix Building, Suite 500, 222 Washington Square, North, 48933-1817
Telephone: 517-485-1483
Telecopier: 517-485-1568
Kalamazoo, Michigan Office: The Michigan Building, Suite 200, 100 Portage Street.
Telephone: 616-382-1483.
Telecopier: 616-382-1568.
Bloomfield Hills, Michigan Office: The Pinehurst Office Center, Suite 101, 1400 North Woodward Avenue.
Telephone: 248-645-1483.
Telecopier: 248-645-1568.
Peoria, Illinois Office: One Technology Plaza, Suite 600, 211 Fulton Street.
Telephone: 309-672-1483.
Telecopier: 309-672-1568.

Todd D. Chamberlain	C. Douglas Moran
Robert D. Mollhagen	Brad S. Rutledge

Representative Clients: For Representative Client list, see General Practice, Lansing, MI.

For Complete List of Firm Personnel, See General Section

For full biographical listings, see the Martindale-Hubbell Law Directory

MILLER, CANFIELD, PADDOCK AND STONE, P.L.C. (AV)

A Professional Limited Liability Company
Founded in 1852 by Sidney Davy Miller
Suite 900, One Michigan Avenue, 48933-1609
Telephone: 517-487-2070
Fax: 517-374-6304
URL: http://www.millercanfield.com
Detroit, Michigan Office: 150 West Jefferson, Suite 2500, 48226-4415.
Telephone: 313-963-6420.
Fax: 313-496-7500.
Cable Address: "Stem Detroit."

(See Next Column)

Ann Arbor, Michigan Office: 101 North Main Street, 7th Floor, 48104-1400.
Telephone: 734-663-2445.
Fax: 734-747-7147.
Troy, Michigan Office: 840 West Long Lake Road, Suite 200, 48098.
Telephone: 248-879-2000.
Fax: 248-879-2001.
Grand Rapids, Michigan Office: 99 Monroe, N.W., Suite 1200, 49503-2639.
Telephone: 616-454-8656.
Fax: 616-776-6322.
Howell, Michigan Office: 121 South Barnard Street, Suite 4, 48843-2305.
Telephone: 517-546-7600.
Telecopier: 517-546-6974.
Kalamazoo, Michigan Office: 444 West Michigan Avenue, 49007-3752.
Telephone: 616-381-7030.
Fax: 616-382-0244.
Monroe, Michigan Office: 214 East Elm Avenue, Suite 100, 48162-2682.
Telephone: 734-243-2000.
Fax: 734-243-0901.
Washington, D.C. Office: 1900 K Street, N.W., Suite 1150. 20006.
Telephone: 202-429-5575; 785-0600.
Fax: 202-331-1118; 785-1234.
Pensacola, Florida Office: 25 West Cedar, 32501.
Telephone: 850-469-1088.
Fax: 850-432-0677.
New York, New York Office: 1450 Broadway, 41st Floor, 10018.
Telephone: 212-704-4400.
Fax: 212-704-4410.
Gdynia, Poland Office: UL. Slaska 21, 81-319.
Telephone: 011-485-831-2808.
Fax: 011-48-58-628 6411.
Warsaw, Poland Office: UL. Nowogrodzkall, 5th Floor, 00-513.
Telephone: 011-4822 529 0200.
Fax: 011-4822 529 0201.
Katowice, Poland Office: UL. Francuska 35/37, 40-027.
Telephone: 011 (48-32) 757-2414.
Fax: 011 (48-32) 757-2483.

RESIDENT PRINCIPALS

William J. Danhof

Representative Firm Clients: Chrysler Corporation; Comerica, Incorporated; City of Detroit, Michigan; Detroit Tigers, Inc.; First of Michigan; Ford Motor Company; Ford Motor Credit Company; Great Lakes Bancorp; Henry Ford Hospital; INVETECH Company.

For Complete List of Firm Personnel, See General Section

For full biographical listings, see the Martindale-Hubbell Law Directory

*MIDLAND,** Midland Co.

CURRIE KENDALL POLASKY MEISEL, PLC (AV)

6024 Eastman Avenue, P.O. Box 2765, 48641-2765
Telephone: 517-839-0300
Fax: 517-832-0077
Saginaw, Michigan Office: 4800 Fashion Square Boulevard, Suite 100, 48603.
Telephone: 517-792-9300; 517-792-1111.
Fax: 517-792-7000; 517-793-6597.

Gilbert A. Currie (1882-1960)	Michael H. Allen (Resident, Saginaw Office)
Gilbert A. Currie (1923-1998)	Larry L. Preston (Resident, Saginaw Office)
Peter J. Kendall (1961-1999)	David J. Kolat (Resident, Saginaw Office)
William C. Collins	M. Randall Jurrens (Resident, Saginaw Office)
Ramon F. Rolf, Jr.	John E. Gannon (Resident, Saginaw Office)
Daniel J. Cline	Carolyn Pollock Cary (Resident, Saginaw Office)
Peter A. Poznak	John D. Jolley (Resident, Saginaw Office)
Julia A. Close	W. Jay Brown (Resident, Saginaw Office)
Jeffrey N. Dyer	
Jonathan E. Lauderbach	
Amy E. Wilson	
Cheryl L. Whitman	
Todd M. Gambrell	
Frank M. Polasky (Resident, Saginaw Office)	
Robert H. Meisel (Resident, Saginaw Office)	

OF COUNSEL

James A. Kendall

Counsel for: Chemical Financial Corp.; Chemical Bank & Trust Co.; Saginaw Valley State University; Northwood University; The Midland Foundation; Elsa U. Pardee Foundation; Rollin M. Gerstacker Foundation; Charles J. Strosacker Foundation.

For full biographical listings, see the Martindale-Hubbell Law Directory

ROCHESTER HILLS, Oakland Co.

DOUGLAS W. MIRES (AV)

2728 Tower Hill Lane, 48306
Telephone: 248-650-6087
Fax: 248-652-9223
Email: miresdnk@aol.com

For full biographical listings, see the Martindale-Hubbell Law Directory

*SAGINAW,** Saginaw Co.

BRAUN KENDRICK FINKBEINER PLC (AV)

101 N. Washington Suite 812, 48607-1297
Telephone: 517-753-3461
Telecopier: 517-753-3951
Email: ALBFIE@BKF-LAW.COM *URL:* http://www.bkf-law.com
Saginaw Township Office, Michigan Office: 5800 Gratiot Road, Suite 107, P.O. Box 5169. Telephone 517-799-8692.
Fax: 517-799-4666.
Bay City, Michigan Office: 201 Phoenix Building, P.O. Box 2039.
Telephone: 517-895-8505.
Telecopier: 517-895-8437.
Ann Arbor, Michigan Office: First National Building. 201 S. Main, Suite 700.
Telephone: 313-995-4100.
Telecopier: 313-995-4798.
Mt. Pleasant, Michigan Office: 805 North Brown.
Telephone: 517-775-7404.
Telecopier: 517-775-3764.

Hugo E. Braun, Jr.
Michael J. Sauer

Representative Clients: The Dow Chemical Co.; General Motors Corp.; Merrill, Lynch, Inc.; Saginaw General Hospital; Saginaw News; The Wickes Foundation.

For Complete List of Firm Personnel, See General Section

For full biographical listings, see the Martindale-Hubbell Law Directory

CURRIE KENDALL POLASKY MEISEL, PLC (AV)

4800 Fashion Square Boulevard, Suite 100, 48603
Telephone: 517-792-1111; 517-792-9300
Fax: 517-793-6597; 517-792-7000
Midland, Michigan Office: 6024 Eastman Avenue, P.O. Box, 2765.
Telephone: 517-839-0300.
Fax: 517-832-0077.

Frank M. Polasky
Robert H. Meisel
Michael H. Allen
Larry L. Preston
David J. Kolat
M. Randall Jurrens
John E. Gannon
Carolyn Pollock Cary
John D. Jolley
W. Jay Brown
William C. Collins (Resident, Midland Office)
Ramon F. Rolf, Jr. (Resident, Midland Office)
Daniel J. Cline (Resident, Midland Office)
Peter A. Poznak (Resident, Midland Office)
Julia A. Close (Resident, Midland Office)
Jeffrey N. Dyer (Resident, Midland Office)
Jonathan E. Lauderbach (Resident, Midland Office)
Amy E. Wilson (Resident, Midland Office)
Cheryl L. Whitman (Resident, Midland Office)
Todd M. Gambrell (Resident, Midland Office)

OF COUNSEL

James A. Kendall (Resident, Midland Office)

Counsel for: Chemical Financial Corp.; Chemical Bank & Trust Co.; Saginaw Valley State University; Northwood University; The Midland Foundation; Elsa U. Pardee Foundation; Rollin M. Gerstacker Foundation; Charles J. Strosacker Foundation.

For full biographical listings, see the Martindale-Hubbell Law Directory

SOUTHFIELD, Oakland Co.

MADDIN, HAUSER, WARTELL, ROTH, HELLER & PESSES, P.C. (AV)

Third Floor Essex Centre, 28400 Northwestern Highway, P.O. Box 215, 48037
Telephone: 248-354-4030, 355-5200
Telefax: 248-354-1422

Milton M. Maddin (1902-1984)
Michael W. Maddin
Mark R. Hauser
C. Robert Wartell
Richard J. Maddin
Richard F. Roth
Harvey R. Heller
Ian D. Pesses
Michael S. Leib
Robert D. Kaplow
William E. Sigler
Stewart C. W. Weiner
Charles M. Lax
Stuart M. Bordman
Steven D. Sallen
Gregory J. Gamalski
Julie Chenot Mayer
Nathaniel H. Simpson
Ronald A. Sollish
Lowell D. Salesin

Mark H. Fink
Steven M. Wolock
Lori E. Talsky
Stephen E. Handelman
Ronald M. Stern
Martin Scott Frenkel
Gary M. Remer
Jennifer S. Sternberg
George V. Cassar, Jr.
Adam J. Goldstein

OF COUNSEL

Bruce N. Goldman

Reference: Comerica Bank.

For full biographical listings, see the Martindale-Hubbell Law Directory

SOMMERS, SCHWARTZ, SILVER & SCHWARTZ, P.C. (AV)

2000 Town Center, Suite 900, 48075
Telephone: 248-355-0300
Telecopier: 248-746-4001
Plymouth, Michigan Office: 747 South Main Street.
Telephone: 313-455-4250.

Steven J. Schwartz
Gary A. Taback
Victor A. Coen
David M. Black
Joseph H. Bourgon

OF COUNSEL

Norman S. Sommers
Paul Groffsky

General Counsel for: City of Taylor; Foodland Distributors; C.A. Muer Corporation; Vlasic & Company; Midwest Health Centers, P.C.
Representative Clients: Michigan National Bank; Bank Hapoalim, B.M.; Beal Bank, S.A.

For Complete List of Firm Personnel, See General Section

For full biographical listings, see the Martindale-Hubbell Law Directory

YPSILANTI, Washtenaw Co.

PEAR SPERLING EGGAN & MUSKOVITZ, P.C. (AV)

5 South Washington Street, 48197
Telephone: 734-483-3626
Fax: 734-483-1107
Email: ameggan@ameritech.net
Ann Arbor, Michigan Office: Domino's Farms, 24 Frank Lloyd Wright Drive.
Telephone: 734-665-4441
Other Ypsilanti, Michigan Office: 2164 Bellevue at Washtenaw.
Telephone: 734-483-7177.

Lawrence W. Sperling
Andrew M. Eggan
Thomas E. Daniels

Counsel for: Domino's Pizza, Inc.; Citizens Banking Corp.; Townsend and Bottum, Inc.; The Credit Bureau of Ypsilanti; City of Ypsilanti (Labor Counsel); Michigan Municipal Worker's Compensation; Self-Insurance Fund.
Approved Attorneys for: Lawyers Title Insurance Corp.

For full biographical listings, see the Martindale-Hubbell Law Directory

BANKRUPTCY LAW

ALABAMA

*BIRMINGHAM,** Jefferson Co.

BENTON & CENTENO, L.L.P. (AV)

Landmark Center, 2100 First Avenue North, Suite 550, 35203
Telephone: 205-278-8000
Facsimile: 205-278-8008
Email: douglascen@aol.com

MEMBERS OF FIRM

Lee R. Benton — Douglas J. Centeno

For full biographical listings, see the Martindale-Hubbell Law Directory

BRADLEY ARANT ROSE & WHITE LLP (AV)

2001 Park Place, Suite 1400, P.O. Box 830709, 35283-0709
Telephone: 205-521-8000
Facsimile: 205-521-8800
Facsimile (SouthTrust Tower Office): 205-521-8500
URL: http://www.barw.com
Huntsville, Alabama Office: 200 Clinton Avenue West, Suite 900, 35801.
Telephone: 205-517-5100.
Facsimile: 205-533-5069.
Washington, D.C. Office: 801 Pennsylvania Avenue, NW, Suite 230, 20004.
Telephone: 202-347-8893.
Facsimile: 202-347-1684.

MEMBERS OF FIRM

J. Patrick Darby — Virginia Calvert Patterson
Sherri Tucker Freeman — John P. Whittington

ASSOCIATES

Jay R. Bender — James H. White

For Complete List of Firm Personnel, See General Section

For full biographical listings, see the Martindale-Hubbell Law Directory

CORLEY, MONCUS & WARD, P.C. (AV)

400 Shades Creek Parkway, Suite 100, P.O. Box 59807, 35259
Telephone: 205-879-5959
Telecopier: 205-871-4411

Ezra B. Perry, Jr.

For Complete List of Firm Personnel, See General Section

For full biographical listings, see the Martindale-Hubbell Law Directory

GORDON, SILBERMAN, WIGGINS & CHILDS, P.C. (AV)

1400 SouthTrust Tower, 420 North 20th Street, 35203
Telephone: 205-328-0640
Facsimilie: 205-254-1500
Washington, D.C. Office: 1621 Connecticut Avenue, N.W., Suite 400.
Telephone: 202-238-0690.
Facsimile: 202-238-0968.

RESIDENT SHAREHOLDERS

Wilbur G. Silberman — Harvey L. Wachsman
Mark P. Williams

For Complete List of Firm Personnel, See General Section

For full biographical listings, see the Martindale-Hubbell Law Directory

PRITCHARD, MCCALL & JONES, L.L.C. (AV)

800 Financial Center, 35203
Telephone: 205-328-9190
Fax: 205-458-0035

MEMBERS OF FIRM

William S. Pritchard (1890-1967) — Alexander W. Jones, Jr.
Alexander W. Jones (1914-1988) — F. Hilton-Green Tomlinson
William S. Pritchard, Jr. — James G. Henderson
Madison W. O'Kelley, Jr. — William S. Pritchard, III
Julian P. Hardy, Jr. — Michael L. McKerley

Representative Clients: First National Bank of Shelby County; Central State Bank of Calera; Buffalo Rock-Pepsi-Cola Bottling Co.; Gillis Advertising, Inc.; Liberty Mutual Insurance Co.; Reliance Insurance Company; SouthTrust Bank, N.A.; Bromberg & Company, Inc.; Farmers Furniture Company; First Commercial Bank.

For full biographical listings, see the Martindale-Hubbell Law Directory

SCHOEL, OGLE, LILES AND UPSHAW, LLP (AV)

600 Financial Center, 505 North 20th Street, P.O. Box 1865, 35201-1865
Telephone: 205-521-7000
Telecopier: 205-521-7007
Mailing Address: Drawer 1865, Birmingham, Alabama, 35201-1865

Jerry W. Schoel

Reference: First Alabama Bank.

For Complete List of Firm Personnel, See General Section

For full biographical listings, see the Martindale-Hubbell Law Directory

SPAIN & GILLON, L.L.C. (AV)

The Zinszer Building, 2117 2nd Avenue North, 35203
Telephone: 205-328-4100
Telecopier: 205-324-8866
Email: ddh@spain-gillon.com *URL:* http://lawlinks.com:80/atty/al/sggbn.html

MEMBERS OF FIRM

Alton B. Parker, Jr. — David S. Maxey

General Counsel for: Piggly Wiggly Alabama Distributing Co.; Alabama Insurance Guaranty Association; Alabama Life and Disability Insurance Guaranty Association; Alabama Insurance Underwriters Association; Auburn University Foundation.
Counsel for: The Minnesota Life Insurance Co.; Government Employees Insurance Co.; Massachusetts Mutual Life Insurance Co.

For Complete List of Firm Personnel, See General Section

For full biographical listings, see the Martindale-Hubbell Law Directory

*HUNTSVILLE,** Madison Co.

STEPHENS, MILLIRONS, HARRISON & GAMMONS, P.C. (AV)

333 Franklin Street, P.O. Box 307, 35801
Telephone: 256-533-7711
Telecopier: 256-536-9388

Arthur M. Stephens — Paul L. Millirons
James G. Harrison

Douglas A. Baymiller

Representative Clients: Regions Mortgage, Inc.; Norwest Mortgage, Inc.; Chase Manhattan Mortgage Corp.; Commercial Federal Mortgage Corp.

For Complete List of Firm Personnel, See General Section

For full biographical listings, see the Martindale-Hubbell Law Directory

*MOBILE,** Mobile Co.

ARMBRECHT, JACKSON, DEMOUY, CROWE, HOLMES & REEVES, L.L.C. (AV)

1300 Riverview Plaza, P.O. Box 290, 36601
Telephone: 334-405-1300
Facsimile: 334-432-6843; 433-3821
Email: adc@ajlaw.com

MEMBERS OF FIRM

E. B. Peebles III — David E. Hudgens
Christopher I. Gruenewald — Broox G. Holmes, Jr.

Representative Clients: American Security Insurance Co. (Regional Counsel); American Security Group (Regional Counsel); AmSouth Bank (Regional Counsel); Burlington Northern Railroad Co. (District Counsel); International Paper Co.; Kimberly-Clark Corp.; Loyal American Life Insurance Co.; Mutual Assurance, Inc.; Travelers Insurance Co.

For Complete List of Firm Personnel, See General Section

For full biographical listings, see the Martindale-Hubbell Law Directory

FINKBOHNER AND LAWLER, L.L.C. (AV)

169 Dauphin Street Suite 300, P.O. Box 3085, 36652
Telephone: 334-438-5871
Fax: 334-432-8052
Email: finkbohnerlawlerllc@zebra.net

MEMBERS OF FIRM

George W. Finkbohner, Jr. — George W. Finkbohner, III
John L. Lawler — Royce A. Ray, III

For full biographical listings, see the Martindale-Hubbell Law Directory

IRVIN GRODSKY, P.C. (AV)

1510 First National Bank Building, P.O. Box 3123, 36652
Telephone: 334-433-3657
Fax: 334-433-3670

Irvin Grodsky

For full biographical listings, see the Martindale-Hubbell Law Directory

Mobile—Continued

JOHNSTONE, ADAMS, BAILEY, GORDON AND HARRIS, L.L.C. (AV)

Royal St. Francis Building, 104 St. Francis Street, 8th Floor, P.O. Box 1988, 36633
Telephone: 334-432-7682
Facsimile: 334-432-0712 or 334-432-2800
Email: attorneys@JohnstoneAdams.com *URL:* http://www.JohnstoneAdams.com
Bay Minette, Alabama Office: Dahlberg Building, 107 Hand Avenue, P.O. Box 729, 36507.
Telephone: 334-937-9473.
Facsimile: 334-937-9475.

MEMBERS OF FIRM

I. David Cherniak — William Alexander Gray, Jr.

For Complete List of Firm Personnel, See General Section

For full biographical listings, see the Martindale-Hubbell Law Directory

LYONS, PIPES & COOK, P.C. (AV)

2 North Royal Street, P.O. Box 2727, 36652-2727
Telephone: 334-432-4481
Cable Address: "Lysea"
Telecopier: 334-433-1820
URL: http://www.LPCLaw.com

Wesley Pipes — W. David Johnson, Jr.

Representative Clients: Chrysler Credit Corporation; SouthTrust Bank of Mobile.

For Complete List of Firm Personnel, See General Section

For full biographical listings, see the Martindale-Hubbell Law Directory

*MONTGOMERY,** Montgomery Co.

KAUFMAN & ROTHFEDER, P.C. (AV)

2740 Zelda Road, Drawer 4540, 36103-4540
Telephone: 334-244-1111
Fax: 334-244-1969
Email: firm@krlegal.com *URL:* http://www.krlegal.com

Samuel Kaufman — George W. Thomas
Robert E. L. Gilpin — Carla Cole Gilmore
David Bowen Hughes

Counsel for: Dale Medical Center; Evergreen Medical Center; Community Health Systems, Inc.; The Russell Hospital Corporation.

For full biographical listings, see the Martindale-Hubbell Law Directory

PARNELL & CRUM, P.A. (AV)

641 South Lawrence Street, P.O. Box 2189, 36102
Telephone: 334-832-4202
Telecopier: 334-832-4703
Fax: 334-293-3550
Email: cnparnell@aol.com

Charles N. Parnell, III — G. Barton Crum

Robert J. Russell, Jr. — Britt Batson Griggs
James McCauley Smith — Angie Hubbard Ingram

Reference: Colonial Bank of Montgomery.

For full biographical listings, see the Martindale-Hubbell Law Directory

*TUSCALOOSA,** Tuscaloosa Co.

HUBBARD, SMITH, McILWAIN, BRAKEFIELD & BROWDER, P.C. (AV)

808 Lurleen Wallace Boulevard, North, P.O. Box 2427, 35403
Telephone: 205-345-6789
Telecopier: 205-759-1195

Perry Hubbard (1921-1991) — W. Marcus Brakefield
Michael D. Smith — Herbert E. "Chip" Browder
Christopher L. McIlwain — Justice D. Smyth, III

Elizabeth Faxon Colwick — Gary E. Sullivan

Counsel for: Randall Publishing Co.; United States Fidelity & Guaranty Co.; Chubb Group of Insurance Cos.; West Alabama Health Services; City of Eutaw; Kimberly-Clark Corp.; Regions Bank; City of Tuscaloosa; West Alabama Bank & Trust; Tuscaloosa County Industrial Development Authority.

For full biographical listings, see the Martindale-Hubbell Law Directory

ARIZONA

*PHOENIX,** Maricopa Co.

ATKINSON, HAMILL & BARROWCLOUGH, P.C. (AV)

3550 North Central Avenue, Suite 1150, 85012
Telephone: 602-222-4828
Facsimile: 602-222-4820

Joseph M. Atkinson — Christopher G. Hamill
Patrick R. Barrowclough

Representative Clients: Biddulph Automotive Dealerships (Oldsmobile, Honda, Pontiac, GMC, Jeep/Eagle and RV); Del Webb Corp.; Federal Deposit Insurance Corp.; Fingerhut Cos.; First American Title Insurance Company of Arizona; John Jacobs' Golf Cos.; Motorola Inc.; PACCAR Financial Corp.; Sun Automotive Group (Scottsdale Acura, Jaguar, Range Rover, Lexus, Porsche, Audi and BMW); Sentinel Real Estate Fund.

For full biographical listings, see the Martindale-Hubbell Law Directory

BONNETT, FAIRBOURN, FRIEDMAN & BALINT, P.C. (AV)

4041 North Central Avenue Suite 1100, 85012
Telephone: 602-274-1100
Fax: 602-274-1199

Jerry C. Bonnett — C. Kevin Dykstra
William G. Fairbourn — Elaine A. Ryan
Andrew S. Friedman — Tara L. Jackson
Francis J. Balint, Jr. — Wendy J. Harrison
H. Sullivan Bunch — Scott A. Erickson
Michael N. Widener — Guy A. Hanson
Robert J. Spurlock — Robert D. Ryan

Christina Bannon — Myndi M. Eakin
Jason Ebe — Barbara A. Bagdon
Andrew Quinn Everroad — David D. Weinzweig
Anthony J. Fernandez — Russell R. Yurk

OF COUNSEL

James Duke Cameron

For full biographical listings, see the Martindale-Hubbell Law Directory

JOSEPH K. BRINIG (AV)

322 West Roosevelt Street, 85003
Telephone: 602-258-1670
Fax: 602-252-2864
Email: brinig@aol.com

Reference: Bank of America.

For full biographical listings, see the Martindale-Hubbell Law Directory

BURCH & CRACCHIOLO, P.A. (AV)

702 East Osborn Road, Suite 200, 85014
Telephone: 602-274-7611
Fax: 602-234-0341
Mailing Address: P.O. Box 16882, Phoenix, AZ, 85011
Email: library@bcattorneys.com

OF COUNSEL

Howard C. Meyers

Representative Clients: Bashas' Inc.; Farmers Insurance Group; U-Haul International, Inc.

For Complete List of Firm Personnel, See General Section

For full biographical listings, see the Martindale-Hubbell Law Directory

CARMICHAEL & POWELL, PROFESSIONAL CORPORATION (AV)

7301 North 16th Street, Suite 103, 85020-5224
Telephone: 602-861-0777
Facsimile: 602-870-0296

Donald W. Powell — Sid A. Horwitz

Kim E. Hutchinson Cahill

Representative Clients: Kawasaki Motors Corp; Wendy's International, Inc.; Firstar Metropolitan Bank & Trust.

For full biographical listings, see the Martindale-Hubbell Law Directory

DAVIS & LOWE, P.C. (AV)

Suite 722, Security Building, 234 North Central Avenue, 85004
Telephone: 602-253-2882
Fax: 602-253-3088
Email: davislowe@prodigy.net

Edward E. Davis — Charles W. Lowe
Ilene J. Lashinsky

Representative Clients: Citgo Petroleum Corporation; Republic Companies; Tilden Financial Corp.; Douglas Allred Company; Fresh Quest Produce, Inc.

(See Next Column)

DAVIS & LOWE P.C.—*Continued*

Reference: Firstar Metropolitan Bank.

For full biographical listings, see the Martindale-Hubbell Law Directory

FENNEMORE CRAIG, A PROFESSIONAL CORPORATION (AV)

3003 North Central Avenue, Suite 2600, 85012-2913
Telephone: 602-916-5000
Fax: 602-916-5999
Tucson, Arizona Office: One South Church Avenue, Suite 1000, 85701-1620.
Telephone: 520-879-6800.
Fax: 520-879-6899.

Cathy L. Reece
David A. Weatherwax
Bryan A. Albue

Dewain D. Fox

LEGAL SUPPORT PERSONNEL

LEGAL ASSISTANTS

Carol Levine

For Complete List of Firm Personnel, See General Section

For full biographical listings, see the Martindale-Hubbell Law Directory

HIRSCH LAW OFFICE, P.C. (AV)

4614 East Shea Boulevard Suite D250, 85028
Telephone: 602-996-9544
Fax: 602-494-0815

Lawrence D. Hirsch
Iva S. Hirsch

For full biographical listings, see the Martindale-Hubbell Law Directory

HOLPER, WELSH & MITCHELL, LTD. (AV(T))

2415 East Camelback Road, Suite 700, 85016
Telephone: 602-508-6033
Fax: 480-483-0269
Email: rholper@aol.com *URL:* http://www.lawyers.com/holperwelsh&mitchell
Minneapolis, Minnesota Office: 4100 Multifoods Tower, 33 South Sixth Street, 55402.
Telephone: 612-317-1012.
Fax: 612-317-0947.

Richard D. Holper
Mary Ann Welsh

For full biographical listings, see the Martindale-Hubbell Law Directory

JABURG & WILK, P.C. (AV)

Great American Tower, 3200 North Central Avenue, Suite 2000, 85012
Telephone: 602-248-1000
Fax: 602-248-0522
Email: rcp@jaburglaw.com

Gary J. Jaburg
Lawrence E. Wilk
Roger L. Cohen
Randy Nussbaum
Mitchell Reichman
Beth S. Cohn
Loren Molever
Robert C. Houser, Jr.
Mervyn T. Braude
Michael E. Gottfried

Kathi Mann Sandweiss
Jeffry M. Edwards
Tracy A. Miller
Stephanie N. Monroe
George A. Tacker
Peter W. Ware, Jr.

OF COUNSEL

Richard M. Gerry

Representative Clients: Employee Solutions, Inc.; Sleep America, Inc.; Desert Schools Federal Credit Union; North Star Plumbing; Nations Bank of Texas; State of Arizona; FHLMC; Arizona Escrow & Financial Services.

For full biographical listings, see the Martindale-Hubbell Law Directory

JENNINGS, STROUSS & SALMON, P.L.C. (AV)

A Professional Limited Liability Company
One Renaissance Square, Two North Central Avenue, 85004-2393
Telephone: 602-262-5911
Fax: 602-253-3255
Email: info@jsslaw.com *URL:* http://www.jsslaw.com
Arrowhead Office: 16150 North Arrowhead Fountains Center Drive, Suite 250, Peoria, Arizona.
Telephone: 623-878-2222.
Fax: 623-878-1333.

Gary G. Keltner
Robert J. Novak
Wendy D. Woodrow
Brian N. Spector

(See Next Column)

ASSOCIATE

Herbert T. Swafford

For Complete List of Firm Personnel, See General Section

For full biographical listings, see the Martindale-Hubbell Law Directory

LEWIS AND ROCA, LLP (AV)

A Limited Liability Partnership including a Professional Corporation
40 North Central Avenue, 85004-4429
Telephone: 602-262-5311
Fax: 602-262-5747
Email: clientservice@lrlaw.com *URL:* http://www.lrlaw.com
Tucson, Arizona Office: One South Church Avenue, Suite 700, 86701-1620.
Telephone: 520-622-2090.
Fax: 520-622-3088. E-Mail: clientservice@lrlaw.com.
Las Vegas, Nevada Affiliated Office: Ashcraft and Heinz LLP, 3960 Howard Hughes Parkway, 89109.
Telephone: 702-990-3570.
Fax: 702-990-3571.

MEMBERS OF FIRM

Gerald K. Smith
Randolph J. Haines
Cathy M. Holt
Susan M. Freeman
Brent C. Gardner
Bret A. Maidman

ASSOCIATES

J. Henk Taylor
Maria E. Morales

For Complete List of Firm Personnel, See General Section

For full biographical listings, see the Martindale-Hubbell Law Directory

MARISCAL, WEEKS, MCINTYRE & FRIEDLANDER, P.A. (AV)

2901 North Central Avenue Suite 200, 85012-2705
Telephone: 602-285-5000
Fax: 602-285-5100

William Novotny

References: Northern Trust Bank of Arizona; National Bank of Arizona.

For Complete List of Firm Personnel, See General Section

For full biographical listings, see the Martindale-Hubbell Law Directory

MYERS & JENKINS, A PROFESSIONAL CORPORATION (AV)

Phoenix Corporate Center, 3003 North Central Avenue, Suite 1900, 85012
Telephone: 602-200-7900
Facsimile: 602-200-7910
Email: firm@mjlegal.com

Stephen W. Myers
William Scott Jenkins
Teresa Dawn Farrison

Gregory D. Honig

Reference: Wells Fargo Bank.

For full biographical listings, see the Martindale-Hubbell Law Directory

ROBBINS & GREEN, A PROFESSIONAL ASSOCIATION (AV)

1800 Norwest Tower, 3300 North Central Avenue, 85012-2578
Telephone: 602-248-7600
Fax: 602-266-5369
Email: @RGLaw.com

Wayne A. Smith
Jeffrey P. Boshes
Bradley J. Stevens
Peter W. Sorensen

For full biographical listings, see the Martindale-Hubbell Law Directory

SHIMMEL, HILL, BISHOP & GRUENDER, P.C. (AV)

3700 North 24th Street, 85016
Telephone: 602-224-9500
Telecopier: 602-955-6176
URL: http://www.shimmelhill.com

Joseph Wm. Kruchek
Margaret L. Steiner

Representative Clients: Farmers Insurance Cos.; Hein Werner Corp.; Arizona State Carpenters Pension Trust Funds; Operating Engineers Local 428 Pension Trust Funds; Arizona Laborers, Teamsters, Cement Masons Local 395 Pension Trust Funds; Immanuel Caring Ministries, Inc.; Wells Fargo Equipment Finance, Inc.

For full biographical listings, see the Martindale-Hubbell Law Directory

Phoenix—Continued

SNELL & WILMER L.L.P. (AV)

One Arizona Center, 85004-2202
Telephone: 602-382-6000
Fax: 602-382-6070
Email: postmaster@snellwilmer.com *URL:* http://www.swlaw.com
Tucson, Arizona Office: One South Church Avenue, Suite 1500, 85701-1612.
Telephone: 520-882-1200.
Fax: 520-884-1294.
Orange County Office: 1920 Main Street, Suite 1200, Irvine, California 92614-7230.
Telephone: 949-253-2700.
Fax: 949-955-2507.
Salt Lake City, Utah Office: 111 East Broadway, Suite 900, 84111-1004.
Telephone: 801-237-1900.
Fax: 801-237-1950.

MEMBERS OF FIRM

Peter J. Rathwell
Christopher H. Bayley
Donald L. Gaffney
Robert R. Kinas

ASSOCIATES

Steven D. Jerome
Philip Randolph Rudd
Daren W. Perkins
Lori A. Schmig

Representative Clients: For list of Representative Clients, see end of biographical listings in the Martindale-Hubbell Law Directory.

For Complete List of Firm Personnel, See General Section

For full biographical listings, see the Martindale-Hubbell Law Directory

WARNICKE & LITTLER, P.L.C. (AV)

2020 North Central Avenue, Fifth Floor, 85004-4506
Telephone: 602-256-0400
Fax: 602-256-0345
Email: wlittler@aol.com

Ronald E. Warnicke
Thomas E. Littler
Mark J. Giunta

For full biographical listings, see the Martindale-Hubbell Law Directory

SCOTTSDALE, Maricopa Co.

BREGMAN & BURT, A PROFESSIONAL ASSOCIATION (AV)

7509 East First Street, 85251-4501
Telephone: 602-945-1800
Telecopier: 602-945-9594
Email: mbregman@bregmanandburt.com

Mark A. Bregman
Sandra K. Bregman
Sandra Burt

Reference: Western Security Bank.

For full biographical listings, see the Martindale-Hubbell Law Directory

PESKIND HYMSON & GOLDSTEIN, P.C. (AV)

14595 North Scottsdale Road, Suite 14, 85254
Telephone: 602-991-9077
Fax: 602-443-8854
URL: http://www.legalcounselors.com

David B. Goldstein

Eddie A. Pantiliat

For full biographical listings, see the Martindale-Hubbell Law Directory

*TUCSON,** Pima Co.

LEONARD FELKER ALTFELD GREENBERG & BATTAILE, P.C. (AV)

250 North Meyer Avenue, P.O. Box 191, 85702-0191
Telephone: 520-622-7733
Fax: 520-622-7967

David J. Leonard
Sidney L. Felker
Jeffrey H. Greenberg
John F. Battaile III
Clifford B. Altfeld
Donna M. Aversa
R. David Sobel
Russell E. Krone
Peter B. Goldman

OF COUNSEL

Anne-Marie Brady

For full biographical listings, see the Martindale-Hubbell Law Directory

SNELL & WILMER L.L.P. (AV)

One South Church Avenue, Suite 1500, 85701-1612
Telephone: 520-882-1200
Fax: 520-884-1294
URL: http://www.swlaw.com
Phoenix, Arizona Office: One Arizona Center, 85004-2202.
Telephone: 602-382-6000.
Fax: 602-382-6070.
Orange County Office: 1920 Main Street, Suite 1200, Irvine, California 92614-7230.
Telephone: 949-253-2700.
Fax: 949-955-2507.
Salt Lake City, Utah Office: 111 East Broadway, Suite 900, 84111-1004.
Telephone: 801-237-1900.
Fax: 801-237-1950.

MEMBERS OF FIRM

Todd V. Jones
J. Matthew Derstine

OF COUNSEL

Clague A. Van Slyke

Representative Clients: For list of Representative Clients, see end of biographical listings in the Martindale-Hubbell Law Directory.

For full biographical listings, see the Martindale-Hubbell Law Directory

*YUMA,** Yuma Co.

ROBERT M. COOK (AV)

207 West Second Street, 85364
Telephone: 520-539-0959
Fax: 520-539-0960
1-800 ROBERT M
Email: robertmcook@yahoo.com

For full biographical listings, see the Martindale-Hubbell Law Directory

ARKANSAS

*FORT SMITH,** Sebastian Co.

GEAN, GEAN & GEAN (AV)

511 Garrison Avenue, 72901
Telephone: 501-783-1124
Fax: 501-783-2440

Roy Gean, Sr. (1894-1969)
Roy R. Gean, Jr.
Paul B. Gean
Roy R. Gean, III

ASSOCIATES

David C. Gean
Ellen Gean Pierce

Representative Clients: Federal Savings Bank of Rogers, Arkansas; First City Finance Corp.; First National Bank, Oklahoma; Commercial Credit Plan, Inc.; Associates, Financial Services Company of Oklahoma, Inc.; K & C Properties Real Estate Developers; Cyanede Plastics.

For full biographical listings, see the Martindale-Hubbell Law Directory

*LITTLE ROCK,** Pulaski Co.

ROSE LAW FIRM, A PROFESSIONAL ASSOCIATION (AV)

120 East Fourth Street, 72201
Telephone: 501-375-9131
Telecopy: 501-375-1309

Herbert C. Rule, III
Allen W. Bird, II
Garland J. Garrett
Charles W. Baker
John T. Hardin
Stephen N. Joiner
Brian Rosenthal

Representative Clients: Acxiom Corp.; The Equitable Life Assurance Society of the United States; Fairfield Communities, Inc.; General Electric Co.; General Motors Corp.; Mercantile Bank of Arkansas, N.A.; Bank of America, N.A.; The Prudential Insurance Company of America; Stephens Inc.; J.A. Riggs Tractor Co.

For Complete List of Firm Personnel, See General Section

For full biographical listings, see the Martindale-Hubbell Law Directory

WRIGHT, LINDSEY & JENNINGS LLP (AV)

200 West Capitol Avenue, Suite 2200, 72201
Telephone: 501-371-0808
Fax: 501-376-9442
Email: info@wlj.com *URL:* http://www.wlj.com
Fayetteville, Arkansas Office: 101 West Mountain Street, Suite 206, 72701.
Telephone: 501-575-0808.
Fax: 501-575-0999.
Russellville, Arkansas Office: 1110 West "B" Street, Suite E, 72801.
Telephone: 501-968-7995.

(See Next Column)

WRIGHT, LINDSEY & JENNINGS LLP—*Continued*

Isaac A. Scott, Jr. James J. Glover
Charles T. Coleman Judy Simmons Henry
Kimberly Wood Tucker

ASSOCIATE

Phyllis M. McKenzie

Representative Clients: Associates Commercial Corporation; NationsBank, N.A.; Oakwood Acceptance Corporation; Oakwood Mobile Homes, Inc.; Superior Federal Bank, F.S.B.

For full biographical listings, see the Martindale-Hubbell Law Directory

CALIFORNIA

*BAKERSFIELD,** Kern Co.

KLEIN, DENATALE, GOLDNER, COOPER, ROSENLIEB & KIMBALL, LLP (AV)

(Formerly Di Giorgio, Davis, Klein, Wegis, Duggan & Friedman)
ARCO Tower, 4550 California Avenue, Second Floor, 93309
Telephone: 661-395-1000
Telecopier: 661-326-0418
Mailing Address: P.O. Box 11172, Bakersfield, California, 93389-1172
Email: kleinlaw@kleinlaw.com

Anthony J. Klein (Inc.) Claude P. Kimball

Representative Clients: Bank of America; Great Western Bank; Mojave Pipeline Co.; Transamerican Title Insurance Co.; Dean Whittier Reynolds, Inc.; California Republic Bank; San Joaquin Bank; Nahama & Weagant Energy Co.; Freymiller Trucking, Inc.; Westinghouse Electric Co.

For Complete List of Firm Personnel, See General Section

For full biographical listings, see the Martindale-Hubbell Law Directory

COSTA MESA, Orange Co.

ALBERT, WEILAND & GOLDEN (AV)

Center Tower, 650 Town Center Drive, Suite 1350, 92626
Telephone: 714-966-1000
FAX: 714-966-1002
Email: awglawyers@aol.com

Theodor C. Albert Michael J. Weiland
Jeffrey I. Golden

ASSOCIATES

Evan D. Smiley Philip E. Strok
Lei Lei Wang Ekvall Darlynn Campbell Morgan

OF COUNSEL

Marcus M. Kaufman Jennifer Ann Golison
Steven J. Katzman

LEGAL SUPPORT PERSONNEL

PARALEGALS

Fran L. Russell Patricia K. Nelson
Cynthia B. Meeker Janet Hogan
Kim Sigismondo

For full biographical listings, see the Martindale-Hubbell Law Directory

FELDHAKE, AUGUST & ROQUEMORE (AV)

Plaza Tower, Suite 1730, 600 Anton Boulevard, 92626-7124
Telephone: 714-438-3885
Fax: 714-438-3888
Email: farlaw@hqonline.com

Robert J. Feldhake Lisa A. Roquemore
Kenneth S. August Joshua M. Wolff

ASSOCIATES

Dimitri P. Gross Supriya Kakkar
Katherine A. Slayton

OF COUNSEL

Arthur J. Swerdloff Arthur M. Wilcox, Jr.

For full biographical listings, see the Martindale-Hubbell Law Directory

RUTAN & TUCKER, LLP (AV)

A Partnership including Professional Corporations
611 Anton Boulevard, Fourteenth Floor, P.O. Box 1950, 92626-1998
Telephone: 714-641-5100; 213-625-7586
Telecopier: 714-546-9035
Email: rutan&tucker@rutan.com *URL:* http://www.rutan.com

MEMBERS OF FIRM

Michael F. Sitzer Lori Sarner Smith
Penelope Parmes Paul J. Sievers

(See Next Column)

SPECIAL COUNSEL

Michael K. Slattery

For Complete List of Firm Personnel, See General Section

For full biographical listings, see the Martindale-Hubbell Law Directory

*FRESNO,** Fresno Co.

DOWLING, AARON & KEELER, INCORPORATED (AV)

6051 North Fresno Street, Suite 200, 93710
Telephone: 559-432-4500
Fax: 559-432-4590
Email: dak@daklaw.com *URL:* http://www.daklaw.com
Bakersfield, California Office: 110 South Mt. Claire, Suite 203. 93309.
Telephone: 661-396-0451. Web Site: http://www.daklaw.com.

Adolfo M. Corona

Leigh W. Burnside Justin D. Harris

Reference: Wells Fargo Bank (Main).

For Complete List of Firm Personnel, See General Section

For full biographical listings, see the Martindale-Hubbell Law Directory

LANG, RICHERT & PATCH, A PROFESSIONAL CORPORATION (AV)

Fig Garden Financial Center, 5200 North Palm Avenue, 4th Floor, P.O. Box 40012, 93755
Telephone: 559-228-6700
Fax: 559-228-6727

William T. Richert (1937-1993) Charles Trudrung Taylor
Robert L. Patch, II Mark L. Creede
Val W. Saldaña Peter N. Zeitler
Douglas E. Noll Laurie L. Quigley
Michael T. Hertz Tamara L. Equals
Victoria J. Salisch Douglas E. Griffin
Rene Lastreto, II Nabil E. Zumout

Christopher B. Dorian Tracy E. Sagle
Matthew W. Quall Julie K. Hill
Michelle Oleksa

OF COUNSEL

Frank H. Lang

References: Wells Fargo Bank (Fresno Main Office).

For full biographical listings, see the Martindale-Hubbell Law Directory

IRVINE, Orange Co.

LOBEL & OPERA LLP (AV)

Suite 1100, 19800 MacArthur Boulevard, 92612-2425
Telephone: 949-476-7400
Fax: 949-476-7444
Email: webmaster@lobelopera.com *URL:* http://www.lobelopera.com

PARTNERS

William N. Lobel Pamela Zylstra Karger
Robert E. Opera Evan C. Borges
Jeffrey M. Reisner

OF COUNSEL

Curtis O. Barnes Elmer Dean Martin, III
Michael D. Good

Tavi Claire Flanagan Hamid R. Rafatjoo
Michael D. Neue

For full biographical listings, see the Martindale-Hubbell Law Directory

MARSHACK SHULMAN & HODGES LLP (AV)

8001 Irvine Center Drive, Suite 900, 92618-2921
Telephone: 949-864-0400
Facsimile: 949-864-0444
Email: marshack@marshack-law.com *URL:* http://www.marshack-law.com

Richard A. Marshack Ronald S. Hodges
Leonard M. Shulman James Charles Bastian, Jr.

TAX COUNSEL

A. Lavar Taylor

ASSOCIATES

Jon K. Alban Robert N. Ives, Jr.
Mark Bradshaw Sung H. Lee

For full biographical listings, see the Martindale-Hubbell Law Directory

Irvine—Continued

RUS, MILIBAND & SMITH (AV)

Suite 700, 2600 Michelson Drive, 92612
Telephone: 949-752-7100
Fax: 949-252-1514
Email: rmws@rmsapc.com *URL:* http://www.rmsapc.com

Ronald Rus
Joel S. Miliband
Randall A. Smith
Laurel R. Zaeske

Cathrine M. Castaldi
David Edward Hays
Leo J. Presiado
Michael B. Kushner
M. Peter Crinella

For full biographical listings, see the Martindale-Hubbell Law Directory

J. SCOTT WILLIAMS (AV)

2 Park Plaza, Suite 450, 92614
Telephone: 949-477-9070
Fax: 949-477-4127
Email: jscottw@twlfpc.com *URL:* http://www.lawyers.com/jscottwilliams

For full biographical listings, see the Martindale-Hubbell Law Directory

LONG BEACH, Los Angeles Co.

JEROME S. COHEN (AV)

400 Oceangate, Suite 800, 90802-4307
Telephone: 562-901-9970
Fax: 562-901-9972
Email: jscbklaw@earthlink.net *URL:* http://www.lawyers.com/jscohenlaw

For full biographical listings, see the Martindale-Hubbell Law Directory

*LOS ANGELES,** Los Angeles Co.

BAKER & HOSTETLER LLP (AV)

600 Wilshire Boulevard, 90017-3212
Telephone: 213-624-2400
FAX: 213-975-1740
To contact an attorney on the Internet use first initial and surname followed by @baker-hostetler.com
URL: http://www.bakerlaw.com
In Cleveland, Ohio: 3200 National City Center, 1900 East Ninth Street.
Telephone: 216-621-0200.
In Cincinnati, Ohio: 312 Walnut Street, Suite 2650.
Telephone: 513-929-3400.
In Columbus, Ohio: Capitol Square, Suite 2100, 65 East State Street.
Telephone: 614-228-1541.
In Denver, Colorado: 303 East 17th Avenue, Suite 1100.
Telephone: 303-861-0600.
In Houston, Texas: 1000 Louisiana, Suite 2000.
Telephone: 713-751-1600.
In Long Beach, California: 300 Oceangate, Suite 620.
Telephone: 562-432-2827.
In Orlando, Florida: SunBank Center, Suite 2300, 200 South Orange Avenue.
Telephone: 407-649-4000.
In Washington, D. C.: Washington Square, Suite 1100, 1050 Connecticut Avenue, N.W.
Telephone: 202-861-1500.

PARTNER

Glen A. Smith

For Complete List of Firm Personnel, See General Section

For full biographical listings, see the Martindale-Hubbell Law Directory

BAKER AND JACOBSON, A PROFESSIONAL CORPORATION (AV)

Suite 500, 11377 West Olympic Boulevard, 90064-1683
Telephone: 310-914-7990
Fax: 310-914-7913
Email: do@bakjac.com

Robert P. Baker
Lawrence M. Jacobson

For full biographical listings, see the Martindale-Hubbell Law Directory

LAW OFFICES OF DAVID B. BLOOM A PROFESSIONAL CORPORATION (AV)

3325 Wilshire Boulevard, Ninth Floor, 90010
Telephone: 323-938-5248; 384-4088
Telecopier: 213-385-2009

David B. Bloom

(See Next Column)

Stephen S. Monroe (A Professional Corporation)
Raphael A. Rosemblat
James E. Adler
Roy A. Levun
Jonathan Udell
Susan Carole Jay
Edward Idell
Sandra Kamenir
Steven Wayne Lazarus
Andrew Edward Briseno
Shelley M. Gould
Ted L. Travis

For full biographical listings, see the Martindale-Hubbell Law Directory

LAW OFFICES OF EDYTHE L. BRONSTON (AV)

10960 Wilshire Boulevard Tenth Floor, 90024
Telephone: 310-231-6422
Facsimile: 310-231-6423

For full biographical listings, see the Martindale-Hubbell Law Directory

CLARK & TREVITHICK, A PROFESSIONAL CORPORATION (AV)

800 Wilshire Boulevard, 12th Floor, 90017
Telephone: 213-629-5700
Telecopier: 213-624-9441
Email: postmaster@clarktrev.com
San Francisco, California Office: 456 Montgomery Street, 20th Floor.
Telephone: 415-288-6520.
Fax: 415-398-2820.

John A. Lapinski
Leslie R. Horowitz

OF COUNSEL

Judith Ilene Bloom

For Complete List of Firm Personnel, See General Section

For full biographical listings, see the Martindale-Hubbell Law Directory

DANNING, GILL, DIAMOND & KOLLITZ, LLP (AV)

A Limited Liability Partnership Composed of Professional Corporations
2029 Century Park East, Third Floor, 90067-2904
Telephone: 310-277-0077
Fax: 310-277-5735
Email: dgdk@dgdk.com *URL:* http://www.dgdk.com

MEMBERS OF FIRM

David A. Gill (A Professional Corporation)
Richard K. Diamond (A Professional Corporation)
Howard Kollitz (A Professional Corporation)
John J. Bingham, Jr., (A Professional Corporation)
Steven E. Smith (A Professional Corporation)
Eric P. Israel (A Professional Corporation)
David M. Poitras (A Professional Corporation)
Kathy Bazoian Phelps
George E. Schulman (A Professional Corporation)
Nancy Knupfer (A Professional Corporation)
Richard D. Burstein (A Professional Corporation)
Robert A. Hessling
Anne E. Wells

ASSOCIATES

Lauren B. Lessler
Elan S. Levey
Michael C. Abel
Gabrielle L. Albert
David B. Shemano

OF COUNSEL

Curtis B. Danning (A Professional Corporation)
James J. Joseph (A Professional Corporation)

For full biographical listings, see the Martindale-Hubbell Law Directory

DOBBERTEEN & LUNA (AV)

3540 Wilshire Boulevard Suite 417, 90010
Telephone: 213-383-1664
Fax: 213-383-1311

David A. Luna
Kenyon F. Dobberteen

For full biographical listings, see the Martindale-Hubbell Law Directory

LAW OFFICES OF RICHARD H. GIBSON A PROFESSIONAL CORPORATION (AV)

Gateway West, 1801 Avenue of the Stars, Suite 406, 90067
Telephone: 310-277-5581
Facsimile: 310-277-6035
Email: lostig@rhg-law.com

Richard H. Gibson

For full biographical listings, see the Martindale-Hubbell Law Directory

LEONARD A. GOLDMAN & ASSOCIATES (AV)

(Formerly Goldman & Gordon, L.L.P.)
1900 Avenue of the Stars, Suite 1800, 90067-4409
Telephone: 310-277-7171
FAX: 310-277-1547
Email: lagoldman@earthlink.com

(See Next Column)

LEONARD A. GOLDMAN & ASSOCIATES—*Continued*

MEMBERS OF FIRM

A. S. Goldman (1895-1966) Leonard A. Goldman

References: Bank of America, Fourth and Spring Branch, Los Angeles; Bank of America, Wilshire-San Vincente Branch, Beverly Hills.

For full biographical listings, see the Martindale-Hubbell Law Directory

HENNIGAN, MERCER & BENNETT (AV)

601 South Figueroa Street, Suite 3300, 90017
Telephone: 213-694-1200
Fax: 213-694-1234
Email: Silverm@hmb.com

J. Michael Hennigan
Bruce Bennett
John L. Amsden
Shawna L. Ballard
Mary H. Chu
Kirk D. Dillman
C. Dana Hobart
Jeanne E. Irving
James O. Johnston
Laura Lindgren
Bruce R. MacLeod
Peter J. Most
Robert L. Palmer
Lee W. Potts
Lauren A. Smith
Michael Swartz

ASSOCIATES

Nichole M. Auden
Gregory K. Jones
Linda A. Kontos
Joshua M. Mester
Claudia Schweikert
Thomas Bernard Watson
Jeffrey C. Henneforth

OF COUNSEL

James W. Mercer
Mark A. Albert
Kenneth A. O'Brien, Jr.

For full biographical listings, see the Martindale-Hubbell Law Directory

JONES, DAY, REAVIS & POGUE (AV)

555 West Fifth Street Suite 4600, 90013-1025
Telephone: 213-489-3939
Telecopier: 213-243-2539
Email: counsel@jonesday.com *URL:* http://www.jonesday.com
In Irvine, California: 5 Park Plaza, Suite 1100.
Telephone: 949-851-3939.
Telecopier: 949-553-7539.
In Atlanta, Georgia: 3500 SunTrust Plaza, 303 Peachtree Street.
Telephone: 404-521-3939.
Telecopier: 404-581-8330.
In Brussels, Belgium: Avenue Louise 480, 7th Floor, B-1050 Brussels.
Telephone: 32-2-645-14-11.
Telecopier: 32-2-645-14-45.
In Chicago, Illinois: 77 West Wacker.
Telephone: 312-782-3939.
Telecopier: 312-782-8585.
In Cleveland, Ohio: North Point, 901 Lakeside Avenue.
Telephone: 216-586-3939.
Telecopier: 216-579-0212.
In Columbus, Ohio: 1900 Huntington Center.
Telephone: 614-469-3939.
Telecopier: 614-461-4198.
In Dallas, Texas: 2727 North Harwood Street.
Telephone: 214-220-3939.
Telecopier: 214-969-5100.
In Frankfurt, Germany: Hochhaus am Park, Grüneburgweg 102, 60323 Frankfurt am Main.
Telephone: 49-69-9726-3939.
Telecopier: 49-69-9726-3993.
In Geneva, Switzerland: 20, rue de Candolle.
Telephone: 41-22-320-2339.
Telecopier: 41-22-320-1232.
In Hong Kong: 29th Floor, Entertainment Building, 30 Queen's Road Central.
Telephone: 852-2526-6895.
Telecopier: 852-2868-5871.
In London England: Bucklersbury House, 3 Queen Victoria Street.
Telephone: 44-20-7236-3939.
Telecopier: 44-20-7236-1113.
In New York, New York: 599 Lexington Avenue.
Telephone: 212-326-3939.
Telecopier: 212-755-7306.
In Paris, France: 120, rue du Faubourg Saint-Honoré.
Telephone: 33-1-56-59-3939.
Telecopier: 33-1-56-59-3938
In Pittsburgh, Pennsylvania: 500 Grant Street, 31st Floor.
Telephone: 412-391-3939.
Telecopier: 412-394-7959.
In Riyadh, Saudi Arabia: The International Law Firm (In Association with Jones, Day, Reavis & Pogue), Sulaymaniyah, Prince Mishari IBN, Abdulaziz Street, P.O. Box 22166.
Telephone: (966-1) 462-8866.
Telecopier: (966-1) 462-9001.
In Shanghai, China: 2805 Kerry Centre, 1515 Nanjing Road West.
Telephone: 86-21-5298-6568.
Telecopier: 86-21-5298-6569.

(See Next Column)

In Sydney, Australia: Governor Phillip Tower, Level 38, 1 Farrer Place.
Telephone: 61-2-9210-6921.
Telecopier: 61-2-9210-6926.
In Taipei, Taiwan: 8th Floor, 2 Tun Hwa South Road, Section 2.
Telephone: (886-2) 2704-6808.
Telecopier: (886-2) 2704-6791.
In Tokyo, Japan: Toranomon 45 Mori Building, 3th Floor, 1-5, Toranomon 5-Chome, Minato-ku, Tokyo 105, Japan.
Telephone: 81-3-3433-3939.
Telecopier: 81-3-5401-2725.
In Washington, D.C.: 51 Louisiana Avenue, N.W.
Telephone: 202-879-3939.
Telecopier: 202-626-1700.

MEMBER OF FIRM IN LOS ANGELES

William G. Wilson

ASSOCIATE

Susanne L. Meline

For Complete List of Firm Personnel, See General Section

For full biographical listings, see the Martindale-Hubbell Law Directory

LEVENE, NEALE, BENDER & RANKIN L.L.P. (AV)

1801 Avenue of the Stars, Suite 1120, 90067
Telephone: 310-229-1234
Fax: 310-229-1244
Email: (attorneys initials)@LNBLAW.COM

David W. Levene
David L. Neale
Ron Bender
Craig M. Rankin

ASSOCIATES

Monica Y. Kim
Nivin T. Youssef
N. Kemba Extavour
Elizabeth A. Duke
David B. Golubchik

Reference: 1st Business Bank.

For full biographical listings, see the Martindale-Hubbell Law Directory

LOEB & LOEB LLP (AV)

A Limited Liability Partnership including Professional Corporations
Suite 1800, 1000 Wilshire Boulevard, 90017-2475
Telephone: 213-688-3400
Facsimile: 213-688-3460
Email: info@loeb.com *URL:* http://www.loeb.com
Century City, California Office: Suite 2200, 10100 Santa Monica Boulevard, Los Angeles, 90067-4164.
Telephone: 310-282-2000.
Facsimile: 310-282-2192.
New York, N.Y. Office: 345 Park Avenue, 10154-0037.
Telephone: 212-407-4000.
Facsimile: 212-407-4990.
Nashville, Tennessee Office: 45 Music Square West, 37203-3205.
Telephone: 615-749-8300;
Facsimile: 615-749-8308.
Rome, Italy Office: Piazza Digione 1, 00197.
Telephone: 011-3906-808-8456.
Facsimile: 011-3906-808-8288.

MEMBERS OF FIRM

Andrew S. Clare (A P.C.)
David B. Eizenman (New York City Office)
Helen Gavaris (New York City Office)
Lawrence B. Gutcho
Karen Nielsen Higgins
Lance N. Jurich
David M. Satnick (New York City Office)
P. Gregory Schwed (New York City Office)

ASSOCIATES

Christian D. Carbone (New York City Office)
Paula K. Colbath (New York City Office)
Yasir Elbiali
Sonya Makunga
Todd M. Malynn
Jay D. Sanders

For Complete List of Firm Personnel, See General Section

For full biographical listings, see the Martindale-Hubbell Law Directory

O'MELVENY & MYERS LLP (AV)

400 South Hope Street, 90071-2899
Telephone: 213-430-6000
Facsimile: 213-430-6407
Cable: MOMS
Telex: 674122
Email: omminfo@omm.com *URL:* http://www.omm.com
Century City, CA Office: 1999 Avenue of the Stars, Los Angeles, 90067-6035.
Telex: 674097. Tel: 310-553-6700.
Fax: 310-246-6779.
Newport Beach, CA Office: 610 Newport Center Drive, 92660-6429.
Telex: 4722088. Tel: 949-760-9600.
Fax: 949-823-6994.
San Francisco, CA Office: Embarcadero Center West, 275 Battery Street, 94111-3305. Tel: 415-984-8700.
Fax: 415-984-8701.

(See Next Column)

O'MELVENY & MYERS LLP, *Los Angeles—Continued*

New York, NY Office: Citicorp Center, 153 East 53rd Street, 10022-4611.
Telex: 129165. Tel: 212-326-2000.
Fax: 212-326-2061.
Washington, DC Office: 555 13th Street, N.W., 20004-1109.
Cable: MOMSWSH.
Telex: 89622. Tel: 202-383-5300.
Fax: 202-383-5414.
London Office: O'Melveny & Myers, 3 Finsbury Square, London, EC2A 1LA, England. Tel: 44-171-256-8451. Fax 44-171-638-8205.
Tokyo Office: Akasaka Twin Tower, East 14F, 2-17-23, Akasaka, Minato-ku, Tokyo 107-0052, Japan. Tel: 03-5562-2800.
Fax: 03-5575-3840.
Hong Kong Office: O'Melveny & Myers, Suite 1905, Tower Two, Lippo Centre, 89 Queensway, Central, Hong Kong. Tel: 852-2523-8266.
Fax: 852-2522-1760.
Shanghai Office: Kerry Centre, 20F, 1515 Nanjing Road West, Shanghai, 200040 People's Republic of China. Tel: 86-21-5298-5600.
Fax: 86-21-5298-5500.

PARTNER

Robert J. White

For Complete List of Firm Personnel, See General Section

For full biographical listings, see the Martindale-Hubbell Law Directory

OPPENHEIMER WOLFF & DONNELLY LLP (AV)

2029 Century Park East 38th Floor, 90067
Telephone: 310-788-5000
FAX: 310-277-1297
Email: oppenheimer.com
Minneapolis, Minnesota Office: 3300 Plaza VII, 45 South Seventh Street. 55402.
Telephone: 612-607-7000.
FAX: 612-607-7100.
Amsterdam, The Netherlands Office: Keizergracht 241.
Telephone: 31-20-423-4555.
FAX: 312-20-423-4545.
Brussels, Belgium Office: Avenue Louise 240, Box 5, 1050.
Telephone: 32-2-626-0500.
FAX: 32-2-626-0510.
Geneva, Switzerland Office: Rue Gabriel Eynard, 6, 1205.
Telephone: (41/22) 311-7410.
FAX: (41/22) 311-4707.
Newport Beach, California Office: 500 Newport Center Drive, Suite 700, 92660.
Telephone: 949-823-6000.
FAX: 949-823-6100.
New York, N.Y. Office: The Chrysler East Building, 19th Floor, 666 Third Avenue, 10017.
Telephone: 212-826-5000.
FAX: 212-486-0708.
Paris, France Office: 35 Boulevard des Capucines, 75002.
Telephone: (33/1) 53 45 40 00.
FAX: (33/1) 53 45 40 10.
St. Paul, Minnesota Office: 1700 First National Bank Building, 55101.
Telephone: 651-605-2000.
FAX: 651-605-2100.
Washington, D.C. Office: Oppenheimer Wolff Donnelly & Bayh LLP, 1350 Eye Street, N.W., Suite 200, 20005.
Telephone: 202-312-8000.
FAX: 202-312-8100.
Palo Alto, California Office: 3373 Hillview Avenue, Suite 200, 94304.
Telephone: 650-320-4000.
FAX: 650-320-4100.
Chicago, Illinois Office: Oppenheimer Wolff & Donnelly (Illinois), Two Prudential Plaza, 45th Floor, 180 North Stetson Avenue, 60601.
Telephone: 312-616-1800.
Fax: 312-616-5800.

RESIDENT PARTNER

W. Mark Levinson

RESIDENT ASSOCIATE

Joon M. Khang

Reference: City National Bank (Century Plaza Office, Century City).

For full biographical listings, see the Martindale-Hubbell Law Directory

PIZER & MICHAELSON INC. (AV)

2049 Century Park East, Suite 460, 90067
Telephone: 310-843-9729
Fax: 310-843-9619
Santa Ana, California Office: 2122 North Broadway, Suite 100, 92706.
Telephone: 714-558-0535.
Telecopier: 714-550-0841.

Bradley J. Pizer

For full biographical listings, see the Martindale-Hubbell Law Directory

ROBINSON, DIAMANT & BRILL, A PROFESSIONAL CORPORATION (AV)

Suite 1500, 1888 Century Park East (Century City), 90067
Telephone: 310-277-7400
Telecopier: 310-277-7584
Email: rdblaw@earthlink.net
Irvine, California Office: 19800 MacArthur Boulevard, Suite 820, 92612.
Telephone: 949-851-1110.
Fax: 949-851-1113.

Gilbert Robinson (1927-1991)
Elliott Lisnek (1939-1992)
Lawrence A. Diamant
Martin J. Brill
Edward M. Wolkowitz
Irving M. Gross
Douglas D. Kappler
Philip A. Gasteier
Sandford L. Frey
Shawn R. Miller
Timothy J. Yoo
Robyn B. Sokol

Scott H. Yun
John N. Lee
Thomas M. LeCarner
Julie A. Page

OF COUNSEL

Michael P. Wippler

References: Fidelity & Deposit Co.; Home Savings of America (Century City Office); Imperial Bank (Los Angeles Regional Office); City National Bank (Century City Office).

For full biographical listings, see the Martindale-Hubbell Law Directory

RONALD P. SLATES, P.C. (AV)

548 South Spring Street, Suite 1012, 90013-2309
Telephone: 213-624-1515; 213-654-1461
Fax: 213-624-7536; 213-654-1463
Email: rslateslaw@aol.com *URL:* http://www.lawyers.com/slateslaw

Ronald P. Slates

Donald R. Ramenian

For full biographical listings, see the Martindale-Hubbell Law Directory

STUTMAN, TREISTER & GLATT, PROFESSIONAL CORPORATION (AV)

3699 Wilshire Boulevard, Suite 900, 90010
Telephone: 213-251-5100
FAX: 213-251-5288

John P. Schafer

For full biographical listings, see the Martindale-Hubbell Law Directory

SULMEYER, KUPETZ, BAUMANN & ROTHMAN, A PROFESSIONAL CORPORATION (AV)

300 South Grand Avenue, 14th Floor, 90071
Telephone: 213-626-2311
Fax: 213-629-4520
Email: info@skbr.com *URL:* http://www.skbr.com

Irving Sulmeyer
Arnold L. Kupetz
Richard G. Baumann
Don Rothman
Alan G. Tippie
Israel Saperstein
Victor A. Sahn
Steven R. Wainess
David S. Kupetz
Howard M. Ehrenberg
Frank Vram Zerunyan

OF COUNSEL

Wesley H. Avery
Ronald E. Gordon
Nathan H. Harris
Elissa D. Miller
Marilyn S. Scheer
Suzanne L. Weakley

Mark S. Horoupian
Stephen C. Seto
Howard N. Madris
Joon Kim

Representative Clients: General Electric Capital Corp.; Continental Insurance Co.; Litton Industries; North American Phillips Corp.; Ventura Port District; Northwest Financial; Heller Financial Inc.; Transamerica Occidental Life Insurance Co.; Transamerica Realty Services, Inc.; Body Glove International.

For full biographical listings, see the Martindale-Hubbell Law Directory

WYNNE SPIEGEL ITKIN, A LAW CORPORATION (AV)

1901 Avenue of the Stars, Suite 1600, 90067-6017
Telephone: 310-551-1015
Fax: 310-551-3059
Email: wsi@wsilaw.com *URL:* http://www.wsilaw.com

(See Next Column)

WYNNE SPIEGEL ITKIN A LAW CORPORATION—*Continued*

Richard L. Wynne
Bennett L. Spiegel
Robbin L. Itkin
Christopher W. Combs
Sharon M. Kopman
Michelle C. Campbell (Not admitted in CA)

For full biographical listings, see the Martindale-Hubbell Law Directory

MANHATTAN BEACH, Los Angeles Co.

STEINBERG BARNESS FOSTER & FOLEY LLP (AV)

1334 Park View Avenue, Suite 100, 90266
Telephone: 310-546-8160
Telecopier: 310-546-8189
Email: sbgf@ix.netcom.com

MEMBERS OF FIRM

Alex Steinberg
Daniel I. Barness
Douglas B. Foster
Shannon M. Foley

ASSOCIATES

William R. (Randy) Kirkpatrick
Jeff M. Lee
Kimberly Ann White

OF COUNSEL

Jordan G. Barness
Ronald D. Hariri (Not admitted in CA)

References: California United Bank; Wells Fargo Bank; Citizens Commerical Trust & Savings Bank; Bank of America.

For full biographical listings, see the Martindale-Hubbell Law Directory

MISSION VIEJO, Orange Co.

THE BUCKLEY FIRM, P.C. (AV)

Suite 200, 26522 La Alameda, 92691
Telephone: 949-348-8300
Facsimile: 949-348-8310
Email: TBF_law@ix.netcom.com
Email: TBFlaw@ix.netcom.com *URL:* http://www.buckleyfirm.com

Lawrence J. Buckley
John W. Klein
Paula Scotland
John R. Beisner

OF COUNSEL

Timothy D. Carlyle
Jonathan C. Cavett
Sam M. Muriella
Edgar C. Smith, III

Reference: Union Bank of California

For full biographical listings, see the Martindale-Hubbell Law Directory

NEWPORT BEACH, Orange Co.

CHRISTOPHER L. BLANK (AV)

4695 MacArthur Court, Suite 1200, 92660
Telephone: 949-250-4600
Facsimile: 949-250-4604
Email: clblank@aol.com *URL:* http://www.lawyers.com/blank

For full biographical listings, see the Martindale-Hubbell Law Directory

REBECCA CALLAHAN A PROFESSIONAL LAW CORPORATION (AV)

5120 Campus Drive, 92660
Telephone: 949-864-5152
Facsimile: 949-864-5156
URL: http://www.lawyers.com/callahanlaw
Email: bekic@pacbell.net *URL:* http://www.rcallahan.com

Rebecca Callahan

For full biographical listings, see the Martindale-Hubbell Law Directory

LAW OFFICES OF MARK A. KOMPA (AV)

20301 S.W. Acacia Street, Suite 200, 92660
Telephone: 949-250-9500
Facsimile: 949-250-9515

For full biographical listings, see the Martindale-Hubbell Law Directory

WINTHROP COUCHOT, PROFESSIONAL CORPORATION (AV)

3 Civic Plaza, Suite 280, 92660
Telephone: 949-720-4100
Fax: 949-720-4111
URL: http://www.winthropcouchot.com

OF COUNSEL

Sean A. O'Keefe

For full biographical listings, see the Martindale-Hubbell Law Directory

WOLF & RICHARDS, A LAW CORPORATION (AV)

18 Corporate Plaza Drive, 92660-7901
Telephone: 949-720-9200
Fax: 949-720-9250
Email: Alan_Wolf@wolffirm.com *URL:* http://www.wolffirm.com

(See Next Column)

Alan S. Wolf

Donna L. La Porte
Steven K. Linkon
Mark S. Flynn
Mark R. Beckington
David B. Lally
Roland P. Reynolds
Suzanne M. Hankins
Timothy M. Ryan

OF COUNSEL

Janice L. Celotti

Representative Clients: Bank of America; Chase Manhattan Mortgage Corporation; Countrywide Home Loans, Inc.; Fannie Mae; Freddie Mac; GMAC Mortgage Corporation; Meritech Mortgage Services, Inc.; Norwest Mortgage Corporation; Ocwen Federal Savings Bank; Temple Inland Mortgage Corporation.

For full biographical listings, see the Martindale-Hubbell Law Directory

PALM DESERT, Riverside Co.

CRISTE, PIPPIN & GOLDS (AV)

Suite 200, 73-550 Alessandro Drive, 92260
Telephone: 760-862-1111
Fax: 760-776-4197
Email: cpgca@aol.com

MEMBERS OF FIRM

Michael A. Criste
Robert L. Pippin
Irwin L. Golds

ASSOCIATES

Jeffrey S. Flashman
Julian S. Summers

For full biographical listings, see the Martindale-Hubbell Law Directory

PASADENA, Los Angeles Co.

LAGERLOF, SENECAL, BRADLEY, GOSNEY & KRUSE, LLP (AV)

301 North Lake Avenue, 10th Floor, 91101-4108
Telephone: 626-793-9400
FAX: 626-793-5900
Email: mail@lagerlof.com

MEMBERS OF FIRM

Joseph J. Burris (1913-1980)
Stanley C. Lagerlof (1915-1998)
H. Jess Senecal
Jack T. Swafford
John F. Bradley
Timothy J. Gosney
William F. Kruse
Thomas S. Bunn, III
Andrew D. Turner
Rebecca J. Thyne
James D. Ciampa

ASSOCIATE

Shaun O. Kwon

Representative Clients: Gallo Glass Company; Orthopaedic Hospital; North American Chemical Company; Palmdale Water District; Public Water Agencies Group; Ventura Port District; Walnut Valley Water District; Metric Construction Co., Inc.

For full biographical listings, see the Martindale-Hubbell Law Directory

*REDDING,** Shasta Co.

DENNIS K. COWAN (AV)

280 Hemsted Drive, Suite B, P.O. Box 992090, 96099-2090
Telephone: 530-221-7300
Fax: 530-221-7389
Email: dennisk@snowcrest.net *URL:* http://www.lawyers.com/cowanlaw

For full biographical listings, see the Martindale-Hubbell Law Directory

*RIVERSIDE,** Riverside Co.

HAIGHT, BROWN & BONESTEEL, L.L.P. (AV)

A Partnership including Professional Corporations
California Tower, 3737 Main Street, Suite 800, 92501
Telephone: 909-341-8300
FAX: 909-341-8309
URL: http://www.hbblaw.com
Santa Monica, California Office: 1620 26th Street, Suite 4000 North, P.O. Box 680.
Telephone: 310-449-6000.
Telecopier: 310-829-5117.
Telex: 705837.
Santa Ana, California Office: Suite 900, 5 Hutton Centre Drive.
Telephone: 714-754-1100.
Telecopier: 714-754-0826.
San Francisco, California Office: 100 Bush Street, 27th Floor.
Telephone: 415-986-7700.
Fax: 415-986-6945.
San Diego, California Office: 101 West Broadway, Suite 1000.
Telephone: 619-595-5583.
Fax: 619-595-7873.

ASSOCIATE

Jeffrey T. Gwynn

For full biographical listings, see the Martindale-Hubbell Law Directory

*SACRAMENTO,** Sacramento Co.

FELDERSTEIN WILLOUGHBY & PASCUZZI LLP (AV)

400 Capitol Mall, Suite 1450, 95814-4434
Telephone: 916-329-7400
Telecopier: 916-329-7435
Email: webmaster@fwplaw.com *URL:* http://www.fwplaw.com

MEMBERS OF FIRM

Steven H. Felderstein
Thomas A. Willoughby
Paul J. Pascuzzi

Craig R. Dandurand

OF COUNSEL

Lisa Lauritzen Ditora

Representative Clients: Union Bank of California; California Public Employees Retirement System; Columbia/HCA Healthcare Corporation; The Beverly Group; First Federal Credit Union.

For full biographical listings, see the Martindale-Hubbell Law Directory

HARDY ERICH BROWN & WILSON, A PROFESSIONAL CORPORATION (AV)

1000 G Street, 95814
Telephone: 916-449-3800
Fax: 916-449-3888
Mailing Address: P.O. Box 13530, Sacramento, California, 95853-4530
Email: hebw@hebw.com *URL:* http://www.hebw.com

L. Kent Wyatt
Michael J. Nelson

Representative Clients: Animal Protection Institute; Fireman's Fund Insurance Co.; General Motors Corp.; The Goodyear Tire & Rubber Co.; Michelin Tire Corp.; Norcal Mutual Insurance Co.; Sacramento Sierra Medical Group, Inc.

For full biographical listings, see the Martindale-Hubbell Law Directory

*SAN BERNARDINO,** San Bernardino Co.

HANOVER & SCHNITZER (AV)

665 North Arrowhead Avenue, 92401
Telephone: 909-884-2147; 683-2147
Fax: 909-889-1828
Email: hands@hanover-schnitzer.com *URL:* http://www.hanover-schnitzer.com

MEMBERS OF FIRM

Norman L. Hanover
Mark C. Schnitzer

ASSOCIATE

Roberta J. Straub

For full biographical listings, see the Martindale-Hubbell Law Directory

*SAN DIEGO,** San Diego Co.

ALHADEFF CANNON ROSE SOLAR & PARKS, LLP (AV)

550 West "C" Street, Nineteenth Floor, 92101-3540
Telephone: 619-231-8700
Facsimile: 619-231-8323
Email: ksolar@acrsp.com
Temecula, California Office: The Tower Plaza, 27555 Ynez Road, Suite 203, 92591-4677.
Telephone: 909-699-9088.
Facsimile: 909-699-9878. Email: POBERHANSLEY@ACRSP.com
Los Angeles, California Office: Olympic Center, 11150 Olympic Boulevard, Suite 860, 90064.
Telephone: 310-914-4400.
Facsimile: 310-914-0030. Email: JODONNELL@ACRSP.com
Lafayette, California Office: Lafayette Terrace, 3697 Mount Diablo Boulevard, Suite 100, 94549.
Telephone: 925-283-1599.
Facsimile: 925-283-5847. Email: GMF-CA@MSN.com

PARTNERS

Samuel C. Alhadeff
Robert D. Rose
Jerry M. Cannon
Keith R. Solar
Robert J. Parks
Philip D. Oberhansley (Resident, Temecula, California Office)
Joseph L. Marshall
Leslie C. Detwiler
Glenn M. Feeley (Resident, Lafayette, California Office)
Thomas T. Lord
Madeline Clark Cahill
John L. O'Donnell, Jr. (Resident, Los Angeles, California Office)

OF COUNSEL

Craig S. Engstrand
Robert K. Edmunds
Charles F. Gorder, Sr.

ASSOCIATES

Michael J. Barry
Richard James Bayless
Craig V. Butler
Cyril J. Dantchev
Genie Harrison
S. Douglas Kerner
Frank J. Polek
Les W. Robertson
Traci M. Selby
Marjeta Duzevic Six

(See Next Column)

For full biographical listings, see the Martindale-Hubbell Law Directory

ESTES, HOYT & HANSEN, A PROFESSIONAL CORPORATION (AV)

Suite 1300, 1010 Second Avenue, 92101
Telephone: 619-234-2111
Fax: 619-234-1509

Kevin J. Hoyt
Bernard M. Hansen

OF COUNSEL

Joel C. Estes

For full biographical listings, see the Martindale-Hubbell Law Directory

HOVEY & KIRBY, A PROFESSIONAL CORPORATION (AV)

402 West Broadway, Suite 1500, 92101
Telephone: 619-685-4000
Fax: 619-685-4004
Email: administrator@hoveylaw.com

Dean T. Kirby, Jr.
Geraldine A. Valdez

For full biographical listings, see the Martindale-Hubbell Law Directory

LUCE, FORWARD, HAMILTON & SCRIPPS LLP (AV)

A Partnership including Professional Corporations
600 West Broadway, Suite 2600, 92101
Telephone: 619-236-1414
Fax: 619-232-8311
URL: http://www.luce.com
La Jolla, California Office: 4275 Executive Square, Suite 800, 92037.
Telephone: 858-455-6611.
Fax: 858-232-8311.
Los Angeles, California Office: 777 South Figueroa, Suite 3600, 90017.
Telephone: 213-892-4992.
Fax: 213-892-7731.
San Francisco, California Office: 121 Spear Street, Suite 200, 94105.
Telephone: 415-356-4600.
Fax: 415-356-4610.
New York, N.Y. Office: Citicorp Center, 153 East 53rd Street, 26th Floor, 10022.
Telephone: 212-754-1414.
Fax: 212-644-9727.
Chicago, Illinois Office: 180 North La Salle Street, Suite 3110, 60601.
Telephone: 312-641-0580.
Fax: 312-641-0380.

Mikel R. Bistrow
Christopher Celentino
Margaret M. Mann
William J. A. Weir (Resident, San Francisco Office)

OF COUNSEL

Michael T. Andrew
Stephen R. Brown

ASSOCIATES

Dustin P. Branch
Kathryn M. S. Catherwood

For Complete List of Firm Personnel, See General Section

For full biographical listings, see the Martindale-Hubbell Law Directory

ROBBINS & KEEHN, A PROFESSIONAL CORPORATION (AV)

530 "B" Street, 24th Floor, 92101
Telephone: 619-232-1700
Telecopier: 619-544-9095

Arlington Ray Robbins
L. Scott Keehn
Michael V. Pundeff
John H. Stephens
Charles F. Robbins
Lynn Marie Beekman
Andrew J. Liska

Lisa L. Keehn

Reference: Union Bank.

For full biographical listings, see the Martindale-Hubbell Law Directory

C. W. WIED PROFESSIONAL CORPORATION (AV)

501 West Broadway, Suite 1780, 92101-3568
Telephone: 619-338-4030
Facsimile: 619-338-4022
Email: cww@cwwied.com *URL:* http://www.lawyers.com/cwwiedpc

Colin W. Wied

Sheryl S. King

For full biographical listings, see the Martindale-Hubbell Law Directory

*SAN FRANCISCO,** San Francisco Co.

BECKER LAW OFFICE (AV)

Suite 330, Robert Dollar Building, 311 California Street, 94104-2625
Telephone: 415-434-8000
Telex: 6731234 BECKER SFO
Facsimile: 415-362-7411
WUW Ca ble: BECKER, CALIF
URL: http://www.lawyers.com/beckersfo
Mailing Address: P.O. Box 192991, San Francisco, CA, 94119-2991
Email: scbecker@beckersfo.com *URL:* http://www.beckersfo.com

Stephen C. Becker

For full biographical listings, see the Martindale-Hubbell Law Directory

GOLDBERG, STINNETT, MEYERS & DAVIS, A PROFESSIONAL CORPORATION (AV)

Suite 2900, 44 Montgomery Street, 94104
Telephone: 415-362-5045
Fax: 415-362-2392

Lawrence Goldberg — Dennis D. Davis
Terrance L. Stinnett — Daniel M. Linchey
Merle C. Meyers — Katherine D. Ray

Kenneth G. DeJarnette — Eric J. Frommé
Miriam Khatiblou

Representative Clients: Alps Electric (USA) Inc.; Fremont Bank; K-Mart Corp.; Mitsubishi International Corp.; Hexcel Corp.; Finova Capital Corp.; Hambrecht & Quist; Supercuts.

For full biographical listings, see the Martindale-Hubbell Law Directory

KAUFMAN & LOGAN LLP (AV)

111 Pine Street, Suite 1300, 94111
Telephone: 415-392-6677
Telecopier: 415-391-4639

MEMBERS OF FIRM

Jeffrey Kaufman — Garrett L. Cecchini
Peter J. Logan — W. Martin Tellegen
Richard A. Eggerth

ASSOCIATES

Nancy S. Coan — Paul A. Peters
Sandra L. Cross — Paulette Donsavage
Gerald F. Ellersdorfer — George D. Vanberg-Wolff

OF COUNSEL

Gerhard Stoll

LEGAL SUPPORT PERSONNEL

PARALEGALS

Karen L. Dunn, CLA — Adrienne Levin
T. Patrick Bridenstine — Paula R. Brawley

For full biographical listings, see the Martindale-Hubbell Law Directory

MACDONALD & ASSOCIATES (AV)

Two Embarcadero Center Suite 1670, 94111-3930
Telephone: 415-362-0449
Fax: 415-394-5544
URL: http://www.macdonaldlawsf.com
Email: mac@macdonaldlawsf.com *URL:* http://www.lawyers.com/macdonaldlawsf

Iain A. Macdonald

ASSOCIATES

Kaipolani K.B. Young — Marty Kevin Courson

OF COUNSEL

Malcolm Leader-Picone

For full biographical listings, see the Martindale-Hubbell Law Directory

*SAN JOSE,** Santa Clara Co.

CAMPEAU & THOMAS, A LAW CORPORATION (AV)

Market Post Tower, 55 South Market Street, Suite 1660, 95113
Telephone: 408-295-9555
Fax: 408-295-6606
URL: http://www.campeaulaw.com

Kenneth J. Campeau — Scott L. Goodsell
Wayne H. Thomas — Kathryn J. Diemer

Marc L. Pinckney — Kathryn Infante
Judith L. Whitman

For full biographical listings, see the Martindale-Hubbell Law Directory

CHARLES E. LOGAN (AV)

95 South Market Street, Suite 570, 95113
Telephone: 408-995-0256
Fax: 408-283-1440
Email: celogan@ix.netcom.com *URL:* http://www.lawyers.com/charleselogan

ASSOCIATES

Susan B. Luce — Linda J. Littlefield

For full biographical listings, see the Martindale-Hubbell Law Directory

MILLER, MORTON, CAILLAT & NEVIS (AV)

50 West San Fernando Street, Suite 1300, 95113-2413
Telephone: 408-292-1765
Telecopier: 408-292-4484
URL: http://www.mmcn-law.com

Richard W. Morton (1916-1975) — Charles V. Caillat (1920-1990)
Harvey C. Miller (1906-1993)

MEMBERS OF FIRM

David L. Nevis — Joseph A. Scanlan, Jr.
Francis J. Hughes — Carolyn Tobiason Stuart
Peter A. Kline — William K. Hurley
Stevan C. Adelman — Peter V. Dessau

OF COUNSEL

Nancy F. Symons

ASSOCIATES

Kathryn E. Barrett — David I. Kornbluh
Katherine S. Pak — Christopher J. Hersey
Julie Neale Meyer

Representative Clients: Trammell Crow Residential; Joe Kerley Lincoln Mercury Co.; Milligan News Co.; Joseph George Distributors; Santa Clara Dental Society; Avalon Bay Communities; Hathaway-Dinwiddie Group.

For full biographical listings, see the Martindale-Hubbell Law Directory

*SAN RAFAEL,** Marin Co.

PASCOE & RAFTON (AV)

1050 Northgate Drive, Suite 356, 94903
Telephone: 415-492-1003
Fax: 415-492-3312
Email: wpascoe@lawyers.com *URL:* http://www.lawyers.com/pascoe&rafton

MEMBERS OF FIRM

William R. Pascoe — Karen A. Rafton (Retired)

OF COUNSEL

Edward J. Tredinnick

For full biographical listings, see the Martindale-Hubbell Law Directory

*SANTA ANA,** Orange Co.

BURD & NAYLOR (AV)

200 West Santa Ana Boulevard, Suite 400, 92707
Telephone: 714-708-3900
Fax: 714-708-3949

William M. Burd — Karen Sue Naylor

For full biographical listings, see the Martindale-Hubbell Law Directory

LAW OFFICES OF STANLEY MINIER, INC. (AV)

2677 North Main Street, Suite 870, 92705-6631
Telephone: 714-558-0181
Fax: 714-558-7435

Stanley W. Minier

Reference: Bank of America.

For full biographical listings, see the Martindale-Hubbell Law Directory

PIZER & MICHAELSON INC. (AV)

2122 North Broadway, Suite 100, 92706
Telephone: 714-558-0535
Telecopier: 714-550-0841
Los Angeles, California Office: 2049 Century Park East, Suite 460, 90067.
Telephone: 310-843-9729.
Fax: 310-843-9619.

Seymour S. Pizer (1930-1992) — Hugh R. Coffin
Barry S. Michaelson — Bradley J. Pizer (Resident, Los Angeles Office)

For full biographical listings, see the Martindale-Hubbell Law Directory

*SANTA BARBARA,** Santa Barbara Co.

ANGLE, CARLSON, GOLDRICK & ROBERTS (AV)

A Partnership including a Professional Corporation
200 East Carrillo Street, Suite 310, 93101
Telephone: 805-963-7400
Fax: 805-963-7610

Robert O. Angle
Miles T. Goldrick
Arthur W. Carlson (A P.C.)
Paul A. Roberts

For full biographical listings, see the Martindale-Hubbell Law Directory

SANTA MONICA, Los Angeles Co.

GILCHRIST & RUTTER, PROFESSIONAL CORPORATION (AV)

Wilshire Palisades Building, 1299 Ocean Avenue, Suite 900, 90401
Telephone: 310-393-4000
Facsimile: 310-394-4700
Email: POSTMASTER@GRLAWYERS.COM *URL:* http://www.grlawyers.com
Los Angeles, California Office: 355 South Grand Avenue, Suite 4100.
Telephone: 213-617-8000.
Facsimile: 213-534-8001.

MEMBER OF THE FIRM

Michael S. Abrams

For full biographical listings, see the Martindale-Hubbell Law Directory

HAIGHT, BROWN & BONESTEEL, L.L.P. (AV)

A Partnership including Professional Corporations
1620 26th Street, Suite 4000 North, P.O. Box 680, 90404
Telephone: 310-449-6000
Telecopier: 310-829-5117
Telex: 705837
URL: http://www.hbblaw.com
Santa Ana, California Office: Suite 900, 5 Hutton Centre Drive.
Telephone: 714-754-1100.
Telecopier: 714-754-0826.
Riverside, California Office: California Tower, 3737 Main Street, Suite 800.
Telephone: 909-341-8300.
Fax: 909-341-8309.
San Francisco, California Office: 101 Bush Street, 27th Floor.
Telephone: 415-986-7700.
Fax: 415-986-6945.
San Diego, California Office: 101 West Broadway, Suite 1000.
Telephone: 619-595-5583.
Fax: 619-595-7873.

MEMBERS OF FIRM

Douglas M. Neistat
Daniel H. Reiss

ASSOCIATES

Gary R. Wallace
Mark Bradley Aldrich

OF COUNSEL

Gerald R. Judson

For full biographical listings, see the Martindale-Hubbell Law Directory

PARIS AND PARIS, LLP (AV)

Paris Law Building, 424 Pico Boulevard, 90405-1197
Telephone: 310-392-8722
Telecopier: 310-392-1768
Email: PandP424@aol.com *URL:* http://www.ParisandParis.com
San Rafael, California Office: PMB D, 4286 Redwood Highway, 94903.

Jeffrey A. Paris
Karen M. Paris
Murray A. Zeffren

OF COUNSEL

Reynold F. Paris
Bette S. Paris
Richard E. Paris

For full biographical listings, see the Martindale-Hubbell Law Directory

STEINBERG, NUTTER & BRENT, LAW CORPORATION (AV)

501 Colorado Avenue, Suite 300, 90401
Telephone: 310-451-9714
Telecopier: 310-451-0929
Woodland Hills, California Office: 21031 Ventura Boulevard, Suite 419.
Telephone: 818-703-6204.

Peter T. Steinberg
Guy B. Nutter
Paul M. Brent

ASSOCIATE

Adam E. Chaikin

Reference: Santa Monica Bank.

For full biographical listings, see the Martindale-Hubbell Law Directory

*SANTA ROSA,** Sonoma Co.

ABBEY, WEITZENBERG, HOFFMAN & EMERY, A PROFESSIONAL CORPORATION (AV)

1105 North Dutton Avenue, P.O. Box 1566, 95402
Telephone: 707-542-5050
Telecopier: 707-542-2589
Email: info@abbeylaw.com

Richard W. Abbey
Timothy W. Hoffman

Representative Clients: Exchange Bank of Santa Rosa; Westamerica Bank; Northwestern Title Security Co.; Geyser Peak Winery; Santa Rosa City School District; Sonoma National Bank; Arrowood Vineyards & Winery; Friedman Bros. Hardware, Inc.; Bank of Lake County; Lasercraft, Inc.

For full biographical listings, see the Martindale-Hubbell Law Directory

TORRANCE, Los Angeles Co.

FINER, KIM & STEARNS (AV)

An Association of Professional Corporations
City National Bank Building, 3424 Carson Street, Suite 500, 90503
Telephone: 310-214-1477
Telecopier: 310-214-0764
Email: finerkimstearns@pobox.com *URL:* http://www.finerkimstearnslaw.com

Robert B. Parsons

OF COUNSEL

Ryan E. Stearns

For Complete List of Firm Personnel, See General Section

For full biographical listings, see the Martindale-Hubbell Law Directory

COLORADO

*BOULDER,** Boulder Co.

LIRTZMAN, NEHLS & HEPNER, A PROFESSIONAL CORPORATION (AV)

190 Arapahoe Avenue, 80302-5895
Telephone: 303-444-5141
Fax: 303-444-9253

Richard C. Nehls
Daniel A. Hepner

OF COUNSEL

Richard M. Lirtzman
Edward J. Roche, Jr.

For full biographical listings, see the Martindale-Hubbell Law Directory

*DENVER,** Denver Co.

BERENBAUM, WEINSHIENK & EASON, P.C. (AV)

Suite 2600 Republic Plaza, 370 17th Street, 80202
Telephone: 303-825-0800
Facsimile: 303-629-7610
Email: berenbaum1@aol.com *URL:* http://www.BWELaw.com

M. Frances Cetrulo
David R. Eason
Daniel S. Duggan
Edwin G. Perlmutter
Ronald I. Zall

Representative Clients: Home Depot; Sprint Spectrum, L.P.; Town of Vail, Colorado; First Union Corporation; City of Englewood, Colorado; Oakwood Homes; Karman, Inc.; Wells Fargo Bank, N.A.; Berkshire Life Insurance Co.; Trinity Ventures.

For full biographical listings, see the Martindale-Hubbell Law Directory

JON B. CLARKE, P.C. (AV)

Two DTC, Suite 150, 5290 DTC Parkway (Englewood), 80111-2721
Telephone: 303-779-0600
Fax: 303-850-7115
Email: eclarkeco@cs.com

Jon B. Clarke

For full biographical listings, see the Martindale-Hubbell Law Directory

DAVIS & CERIANI, P.C. (AV)

Suite 400, Market Center, 1350 Seventeenth Street, 80202
Telephone: 303-534-9000
Telecopier: 303-534-4618
Email: davisandceriani.com

Rick G. Davis
Michael P. Cillo
Gary J. Ceriani
Charles W. Bess
Bruce E. Rohde
John W. Himmelmann

(See Next Column)

DAVIS & CERIANI P.C.—*Continued*

Margaret E. Peper | Mark M. Osborn
Patrick John Kanouff | Valeri Pappas

For full biographical listings, see the Martindale-Hubbell Law Directory

DUFFORD & BROWN, P.C. (AV)

1700 Broadway, Suite 1700, 80290-1701
Telephone: 303-861-8013
Facsimile: 303-832-3804
Colorado Springs, Colorado Office: 101 N. Tejon, Suite 410.
Telephone: 719-471-0559.
Facsimile: 719-471-0583.
Affiliated Office: Solomon, Pearl, Blum & Quinn, L.L.P., New York, NY and Denver, Colorado.

David W. Furgason | Scott J. Mikulecky
Randall J. Feuerstein | Thomas E. J. Hazard

Terry Jo Epstein

OF COUNSEL

Morris B. Hecox, Jr.

Representative Clients: Bondholders' Committee-Wheeler Realty Company; CF&I Steel L.P.; Amdura Corporation; United Steelworkers of America; Air Line Pilots Association; Graphics Information, Inc.; IDS Life Insurance Company; Hall & Hall Mortgage Corporation; Magic Chef; Unsecured Creditor's Committee-Sargent, Inc.

For Complete List of Firm Personnel, See General Section

For full biographical listings, see the Martindale-Hubbell Law Directory

JESSOP & COMPANY, P.C. (AV)

303 East 17th Avenue, Suite 930, 80203-1264
Telephone: 303-860-7700
Facsimile: 303-860-7233
Email: jessopco@jessopco.com *URL:* http://www.jessopco.com

Douglas W. Jessop

Alice A. White | Donald D. Allen
Christopher R. Alger

For full biographical listings, see the Martindale-Hubbell Law Directory

NICHOLLS & ASSOCIATES, P.C. (AV)

1725 Gaylord Street, Suite 100, 80206-1208
Telephone: 303-329-9700, Ext. 104
Fax: 303-329-6950

Jon S. Nicholls

Stephen C. Nicholls

OF COUNSEL

Bruce R. Wyatt

Representative Clients: Little Grizzly Creek Ranch, Inc.; Clarkson Land, LLC; Lifestyle Homes, Inc.; Wheeler Realty Co., Inc; College Inn, Inc.; Dora's Mexican Restaurant, Inc.; Ramada Inn; Life Care Centers of America; First Industrial Realty.
Reference: Norwest Bank, Colorado, N.A.

For full biographical listings, see the Martindale-Hubbell Law Directory

OTTEN, JOHNSON, ROBINSON, NEFF & RAGONETTI, P.C. (AV)

950 Seventeenth Street, 16th Floor, 80202
Telephone: 303-825-8400
Telecopier: 303-825-6525
URL: http://www.ojrnr.com

A. Bruce Campbell | David T. Brennan
Darrell G. Waas | Brad W. Schacht

For Complete List of Firm Personnel, See General Section

For full biographical listings, see the Martindale-Hubbell Law Directory

PAUL G. QUINN (AV)

1725 Gaylord Street Suite 103, 80206-1208
Telephone: 303-329-9700 Ext. 103
FAX: 303-329-6950
Email: pgquinnesq@aol.com

For full biographical listings, see the Martindale-Hubbell Law Directory

RUBNER & KUTNER, P.C. (AV)

Suite 500 303 East 17th Avenue, 80203
Telephone: 303-832-2400
Fax: 303-832-1510
Email: rk@rubnerkutner.com

(See Next Column)

Paul D. Rubner | Lee M. Kutner

Thomas C. Kearns, Jr. | Deanna L. W. Zallen

OF COUNSEL

David M. Miller

For full biographical listings, see the Martindale-Hubbell Law Directory

CONNECTICUT

*BRIDGEPORT,** Fairfield Co.

ZEISLER & ZEISLER, P.C. (AV)

558 Clinton Avenue, P.O. Box 3186, 06605-0186
Telephone: 203-368-4234
Fax: 203-367-9678
Email: info@zeislaw.com *URL:* http://www.zeislaw.com
Westport Office: 25 Ford Road, Suite 2.
Telephone: 203-221-8066.
Fax: 203-222-4833.

Richard D. Zeisler | Jed Horwitt
James G. Verrillo | Matthew K. Beatman
James Berman | Dennis P. Anderson
Craig I. Lifland | Mark J. Rosen
Jeffrey Hellman

Lawrence S. Grossman | Johnpatrick O'Brien
Stephen M. Kindseth | Coleen Hurlie-Dunn
Gregory B. Schiller

OF COUNSEL

Robert M. Zeisler | Paul J. Pacifico

For full biographical listings, see the Martindale-Hubbell Law Directory

DARIEN, Fairfield Co.

RUCCI, BURNHAM, CARTA & EDELBERG, LLP (AV)

800 Post Road, P.O. Box 1107, 06820
Telephone: 203-655-7695
Facsimile: 203-655-4302
URL: http://www.rbce.com
Stamford, Connecticut Office: 6 Landmark Square, Suite 470.
Telephone: 203-359-5637.

MEMBERS OF FIRM

Joseph J. Rucci, Jr. | Paul B. Edelberg
Paul H. Burnham | William M. Carello
Mark R. Carta | Robert F. Maslan, Jr.

ASSOCIATES

Colette C. Symon | Joanna F. Bowen
Karen K. Linder | David J. Rucci
Sandra J. Akoury

OF COUNSEL

Ian R. Crawford | Lawrence H. Reilly
James C. Dempsey | Alberto N. Moris (Not admitted in CT)

For full biographical listings, see the Martindale-Hubbell Law Directory

MILFORD, New Haven Co.

HARLOW, ADAMS & FRIEDMAN, P.C. (AV)

300 Bic Drive, 06460-3508
Telephone: 203-878-0661
Fax: 203-878-9568
Email: attorney@quidproquo.com

William D. Harlow (1921-1988) | Michael P. A. Williams
George W. Adams, III | Eric R. Gaynor
Dana Eric Friedman | Joseph A. Kubic
Theodore H. Shumaker | James M. Nugent
Stephen P. Wright | James R. Winkel

For full biographical listings, see the Martindale-Hubbell Law Directory

*NEW HAVEN,** New Haven Co.

COAN, LEWENDON, ROYSTON & GULLIVER, LLC (AV)

495 Orange Street, 06511
Telephone: 203-624-4756
Fax: 203-865-3673

MEMBERS OF FIRM

Richard M. Coan | Christopher M. Royston
Whitney M. Lewendon | Carl T. Gulliver
Timothy D. Miltenberger

(See Next Column)

COAN, LEWENDON, ROYSTON & GULLIVER LLC, *New Haven—Continued*

OF COUNSEL

E. Huntington Deming

Reference: Peoples Bank.

For full biographical listings, see the Martindale-Hubbell Law Directory

SHELTON, Fairfield Co.

GLENN M. REISMAN (AV)

Two Corporate Drive, Suite 650, P.O. Box 861, 06484-0861
Telephone: 203-944-3040
Fax: 203-944-3044
URL: http://www.ReismanLaw.com
Email: Glenn.Reisman@corporate.ge.com *URL:* http://www.CreditCollectionLaw.com

J. Michelle Reisman (Not admitted in CT)

For full biographical listings, see the Martindale-Hubbell Law Directory

STAMFORD, Fairfield Co.

WOFSEY, ROSEN, KWESKIN & KURIANSKY, LLP (AV)

600 Summer Street, 06901
Telephone: 203-327-2300
Fax: 203-967-9273

MEMBERS OF FIRM

Abraham Wofsey (1915-1944)
Michael Wofsey (1927-1951)
David M. Rosen (1926-1967)
Julius B. Kuriansky (1952-1992)
Sydney C. Kweskin (1946-1998)
Monroe Silverman
Howard C. Kaplan
Edward M. Kweskin
David M. Cohen
Marshall Goldberg
Stephen A. Finn
Judith Rosenberg
Mark H. Henderson
Steven D. Grushkin
Matthew J. Forstadt
Steven M. Frederick

OF COUNSEL

Saul Kwartin
Emanuel Margolis
Anthony R. Lorenzo

SPECIAL COUNSEL

Day R. Shields

ASSOCIATES

Joseph Brachfeld
Eric M. Higgins
William A. Harrison
Daniel M. Young
Angelo A. Ziotas

Representative Clients: Banque Paribas; Benenson Realty; Cellular Information Systems, Inc.; The Chase Manhattan Bank; First County Bank; Hartford Provision Co.; Louis Dreyfus Corp.; Norwalk Federation of Teachers; People's Bank; Ridgeway Shopping Center.

For full biographical listings, see the Martindale-Hubbell Law Directory

WETHERSFIELD, Hartford Co.

CHORCHES & NOVAK, P.C. (AV)

1260 Silas Deane Highway, 06109-4331
Telephone: 860-257-1980
Telecopier: 860-257-1988

Martin Chorches
Anthony S. Novak

Teresa A. Fontaine

For full biographical listings, see the Martindale-Hubbell Law Directory

DELAWARE

*WILMINGTON,** New Castle Co.

POTTER ANDERSON & CORROON LLP (AV)

Hercules Plaza, 1313 N. Market Street, P.O. Box 951, 19899-0951
Telephone: 302-984-6000
Fax: 302-658-1192
URL: http://www.attys.pacdelaware.com

MEMBERS OF FIRM

Laurie Selber Silverstein
William R. Denny
Joanne Ceballos

ASSOCIATES

William A. Hazeltine
Elihu E. Allinson, III

Representative Clients: Meridian Oil Production, Inc.; Consolidated Rail Corporation; ConAgra, Inc.; The Chase Manhattan Bank; K-Mart Corporation; CDC Servicing, Inc.; Toyota Motor Credit Corp.; Foothill Capital Corporation.

(See Next Column)

For Complete List of Firm Personnel, See General Section

For full biographical listings, see the Martindale-Hubbell Law Directory

SMITH, KATZENSTEIN & FURLOW LLP (AV)

The Corporate Plaza, 800 Delaware Avenue, P.O. Box 410, 19899
Telephone: 302-652-8400
Fax: 302-652-8405
Email: info@skfdelaware.com *URL:* http://www.SKFDelaware.com

MEMBERS OF FIRM

Craig B. Smith
Brett D. Fallon

For Complete List of Firm Personnel, See General Section

For full biographical listings, see the Martindale-Hubbell Law Directory

DISTRICT OF COLUMBIA

WASHINGTON, D.C. Co.

STANTON & ASSOCIATES, A PROFESSIONAL CORPORATION (AV)

1000 Thomas Jefferson Street, N.W., Suite 507, 20007
Telephone: 202-342-9282
Fax: 202-298-7811

Thomas J. Stanton

For full biographical listings, see the Martindale-Hubbell Law Directory

VENABLE ATTORNEYS AT LAW VENABLE, BAETJER, HOWARD & CIVILETTI, LLP (AV)

A Partnership including Professional Corporations
Suite 1000, 1201 New York Avenue, N.W., 20005
Telephone: 202-962-4800
Fax: 202-962-8300
URL: http://www.venable.com
Baltimore, Maryland Office: Venable, Baetjer and Howard LLP, 1800 Mercantile Bank & Trust Building, 2 Hopkins Plaza.
Telephone: 410-244-7400.
Fax: 410-244-7742.
McLean, Virginia Office: Venable, Baetjer and Howard LLP, Suite 400, 2010 Corporate Ridge.
Telephone: 703-760-1600.
Fax: 703-821-8949.
Rockville, Maryland Office: Venable, Baetjer and Howard LLP, Suite 500, One Church Street, P. O. Box 1906.
Telephone: 301-217-5600.
Fax: 301-217-5617.
Towson, Maryland Office: Venable, Baetjer and Howard LLP, 210 Allegheny Avenue, P. O. Box 5517.
Telephone: 410-494-6200.
Fax: 410-821-0147.

MEMBERS OF FIRM

Kenneth C. Bass, III (Also at McLean, Virginia Office)
George F. Pappas (Also at Baltimore, Maryland Office)
Joe A. Shull

For Complete List of Firm Personnel, See General Section

For full biographical listings, see the Martindale-Hubbell Law Directory

VERNER, LIIPFERT, BERNHARD, MCPHERSON AND HAND, CHARTERED (AV)

901 15th Street, N.W., 20005-2301
Telephone: 202-371-6000
Cable Address: "Verlip"
Fax: 202-371-6279
Email: verner.com *URL:* http://www.verner.com
Houston, Texas Office: 1111 Bagby, Suite 4700, 77002.
Telephone: 713-225-7200.
Fax: 713-752-2199.
Honolulu, Hawaii Office: 745 Fort Street, Suite 600, 96813.
Telephone: 808-566-0999.
Fax: 808-566-0995.
Austin, Texas Office: Suite 1440 San Jacinto Center, 98 San Jacinto Boulevard, 78701.
Telephone: 512-703-6000.
Fax: 512-703-6003.
Las Vegas, Nevada Affiliate Office: Gary C. Moss, Hughes Center, 3960 Howard Hughes Parkway, Suite 400, 89109.
Telephone: 702-737-3433.
Fax: 702-737-1612.
Miami, Florida Office: 3100 First Union Financial Center, 200 South Biscayne Boulevard, 33131.
Telephone: 305-371-8801.
Fax: 305-371-6545.

(See Next Column)

VERNER, LIIPFERT, BERNHARD, MCPHERSON AND HAND CHARTERED—*Continued*

Patrick L. Hughes (Resident, Houston, Texas Office)
Kenric D. Kattner (Resident, Houston, Texas Office)
Kyung S. Lee (Resident, Houston, Texas Office)
John P. Melko (Resident, Houston, Texas Office)
Lenard M. Parkins (Resident, Houston, Texas Office)
John C. Shawde (Resident, Miami, Florida Office)
Keith D. Spickelmier (Resident, Houston, Texas Office)

For Complete List of Firm Personnel, See General Section

For full biographical listings, see the Martindale-Hubbell Law Directory

WEBSTER, FREDRICKSON & BRACKSHAW (AV)

Suite 300, 1819 H Street, N.W., 20006
Telephone: 202-659-8510
Telecopier: 202-659-4082
Email: firm@wf82.com

MEMBERS OF FIRM

Wendell W. Webster
Bruce A. Fredrickson
Susan L. Brackshaw
Linda M. Correia

ASSOCIATES

Jonathan C. Puth
Jeffrey E. Fallon
N. Bernard Dorsey, Jr (Not admitted in DC)

For full biographical listings, see the Martindale-Hubbell Law Directory

WILMER, CUTLER & PICKERING (AV)

2445 M Street, N.W., 20037-1420
Telephone: 202-663-6000
Fax: 202-663-6363
Email: Law@Wilmer.Com *URL:* http://www.wilmer.com
Baltimore, Maryland Office: 100 Light Street, 21202.
Telephone: 410-986-2800.
Fax: 410-986-2828.
New York, New York Office: 520 Madison Avenue, 10022.
Telephone: 212-230-8800.
Fax: 212-230-8888.
European Offices:
4 Carlton Gardens, London, SW1Y 5AA, England. Telephone: +44 (20) 7 872 1000.
Fax: +44 (20) 7 839 3537.
Rue de la Loi 15# Wetstraat, B-1040 Brussels, Belgium. Telephone: +32 (2) 285 49 00.
Fax: +32 (2) 285 49 49.
Friedrichstrasse 95, D-10117 Berlin, Germany. Telephone: +49 (30) 20 22 64 00.
Fax: +49 (30) 20 22 65 00.

MEMBERS OF FIRM

Louis R. Cohen
F. David Lake, Jr.
Stephen F. Black
Mary Carolyn Cox
William J. Perlstein
Russell J. Bruemmer
William J. Wilkins
Thomas W. White
Duane D. Morse
Philip D. Anker

For Complete List of Firm Personnel, See General Section

For full biographical listings, see the Martindale-Hubbell Law Directory

FLORIDA

BOCA RATON, Palm Beach Co.

FURR AND COHEN, P.A. (AV)

Suite 412, 1499 W. Palmetto Park Road, 33486
Telephone: 561-395-0500
Broward: 954-421-0300
Fax: 561-338-7532
Email: thefirm@furrandcohenpa.com *URL:* http://www.furrandcohenpa.com

Robert C. Furr
Charles I. Cohen

Alvin S. Goldstein
Leslie Scott Osborne
Lisa J. Chaiklin Aflalo
Bradley Scott Shraiberg

OF COUNSEL

C. William Berger

For full biographical listings, see the Martindale-Hubbell Law Directory

*FORT LAUDERDALE,** Broward Co.

BERGER DAVIS & SINGERMAN (AV)

350 East Las Olas Boulevard, Suite 1000, 33301
Telephone: 954-525-9900
Fax: 954-523-2872
Email: jberger@bdslaw.com *URL:* http://www.bdslaw.com
Miami, Florida Office: 200 South Biscayne Boulevard, Suite 2950.
Telephone: 305-755-9500.
Fax: 305-714-4340.
Tallahassee, Florida Office: 215 South Monroe Street, Suite 705, 32301.
Telephone: 850-561-3010.
Fax: 850-561-3013.

James L. Berger
Mitchell W. Berger
Franklin H. Caplan (Resident, Miami Office)
James B. Davis
Henry H. (Bucky) Fox
Van P. Geeker (Resident, Tallahassee Office)
Jordi Guso (Resident, Miami Office)
Nick Jovanovich
Robert B. Judd
Manuel Kushner
Daniel Lampert
Dawn M. Meyers
John D. C. Newton, II (Resident, Tallahassee Office)
Samuel E. Poole III
Leonard K. Samuels
Laz L. Schneider
Paul Steven Singerman (Resident, Miami Office)
Daniel H. Thompson (Resident, Tallahassee Office)

Robert W. Barron
Maria St. John Daugherty
James Harris Fierberg (Resident, Miami Office)
Ilyse Wrubel Homer (Resident, Miami Office)
Sherry A. Lambson
Lisa D. MacClugage
Brian G. Rich (Resident, Miami Office)
Holiday Hunt Russell
Jonathan C. Vair (Resident, Miami Office)
Jeffrey Scott Wertman

OF COUNSEL

James C. Cunningham, Jr.
Fred Goldberg

For full biographical listings, see the Martindale-Hubbell Law Directory

FREDRIC C. BURESH, P.A. (AV)

800 Southeast Third Avenue, Suite 400, 33316
Telephone: 954-525-2300
Fax: 954-763-4725
Email: FredBuresh@aol.com

Fredric C. Buresh

For full biographical listings, see the Martindale-Hubbell Law Directory

HOLLYWOOD, Broward Co.

JAY M. GAMBERG, P.A. (AV)

4000 Hollywood Boulevard, Suite 350 North, 33021
Telephone: Broward: 954-981-4411
Dade: 305-670-8600
Fax: 954-966-6259
Email: jmgpa@gate.net
Miami Office: 9700 South Dixie Highway, Suite 1030.

Jay M. Gamberg

OF COUNSEL

Adrienne Maidenbaum

Representative Clients: McArthur Dairy; Florida Coca-Cola Botting Co.; Casio, Inc.

For full biographical listings, see the Martindale-Hubbell Law Directory

LAW OFFICE OF JEFFREY SOLOMON (AV)

3864 Sheridan Street, 33021
Telephone: 954-967-9800
Fax: 954-963-2227
Cooper City, Florida Office: Suite 1, 10000 Stirling Road, 33024.
Telephone: 954-967-9800.

For full biographical listings, see the Martindale-Hubbell Law Directory

*JACKSONVILLE,** Duval Co.

FISCHETTE, OWEN, HELD & MCBURNEY (AV)

1301 Riverplace Blvd. Suite 1916, 32207
Telephone: 904-398-7036
Fax: 904-398-4283
Email: Attorneys@FOHMLAW.com

MEMBERS OF FIRM

James A. Fischette
Edwin W. Held Jr.
Charles W. McBurney Jr.

ASSOCIATES

R. Joseph Dill
Robert J. Perry Jr.

References: First Union National Bank of Florida; Compass Bank.

For full biographical listings, see the Martindale-Hubbell Law Directory

*MIAMI,** Dade Co.

HOLTZMAN, KRINZMAN, EQUELS & FURIA (AV)

2601 South Bayshore Drive, Suite 600, 33133
Telephone: 305-859-7700
Fax: 305-859-9996
Email: hkef@hkef.com *URL:* http://www.hkef.com
Orlando, Florida Office: 16 West Pine Street, 32801.
Telephone: 407-839-0095.
Fax: 407-839-2050.
Tallahassee, Florida Office: 542 East Park Avenue, 32301.
Telephone: 850-222-2900.
Fax: 850-222-2933.

Sylvan (Sonny) Holtzman
Richard N. Krinzman
Thomas K. Equels
Arthur J. Furia
Joseph L. Raia
R. Barbara Wien
Alan E. Krinzman
Frank P. Terzo (Resident)
Cary A. Lubetsky
Mary Kogut Equels (Resident, Orlando Office)
Charles M. Greene (Resident, Orlando Office)
Jack L. McRay (Resident, Orlando Office)
Lisa "Li" Shearer Nelson (Resident, Tallahassee Office)

Sherrie J. Cohen
Nancy M. Thevenin
Robert Quan Lee
Kevin J. Tang (Resident, Orlando Office)
Anouk M. Villegas

OF COUNSEL

Chapman L. Smith, Jr.

For full biographical listings, see the Martindale-Hubbell Law Directory

KOZYAK TROPIN & THROCKMORTON, P.A. (AV)

2800 First Union Financial Center, 200 South Biscayne Boulevard, 33131
Telephone: 305-372-1800
Telecopier: 305-372-3508
URL: http://www.kttlaw.com

John W. Kozyak
Harley S. Tropin
Charles W. Throckmorton, IV
Kenneth R. Hartmann
Paul C. Huck
Laurel M. Isicoff
David P. Milian
Corali Lopez-Castro
Gail A. McQuilkin
Jeannie M. Jontiff

Michael S. Budwick
John D. Eaton
Adam M. Moskowitz
David L. Rosendorf
Detra P. Shaw
Marilyn G. Kohn
Kerry Anne Finegan
Cheryl Elyse Glickler

OF COUNSEL

Janet L. Humphreys

For full biographical listings, see the Martindale-Hubbell Law Directory

MARKOWITZ, DAVIS, RINGEL & TRUSTY, P.A. (AV)

Two Datran Center, Suite 1225, 9130 South Dadeland Boulevard, 33156-7849
Telephone: 305-670-5000
Telecopier: 305-670-5011

Jerry M. Markowitz
Thomas M. Messana
D. Jean Ryan

Ilan Markus
Zach B. Shelomith

For full biographical listings, see the Martindale-Hubbell Law Directory

MISHAN, SLOTO, GREENBERG, HELLINGER & UDOLF, P.A. (AV)

Suite 2350, First Union Financial Center, 200 South Biscayne Boulevard, 33131
Telephone: 305-379-1792
Facsimile: 305-379-2328
Email: MishanSloto@COMPUSERVE.COM

Steven Mishan
James R. Sloto
Barry N. Greenberg
Andrew B. Hellinger
Bruce L. Udolf
Carol L. Cox
Alan M. Burger

Ana Cela Harris
Dara J. Collins
Steven J. Solomon
Coralee G. Penebad

For full biographical listings, see the Martindale-Hubbell Law Directory

*ORLANDO,** Orange Co.

BUTLER & HOSCH, P.A. (AV)

3185 South Conway Road, Suite E, 32812
Telephone: 407-381-5200
Fax: 407-381-5577
Email: bhatch@butlerandhosch.com

(See Next Column)

C. Victor Butler, Jr.
Robert H. Hosch, Jr.

Andrea L. Aylett-Hosch
Jane E. Bond
Michael W. Udowchenko
Estee L. Lipenholtz
Nancy A. Bishop
Christopher W. Conomos

Representative Clients: United Companies Financial Corp.; First Union Home Equity Corp.; Republic Bank for Savings; Capstead Mortgage Corp.; Rhode Island Hospital Trust; First National Bank of Boston; Countrywide Home Loans, Inc.; Norwest Mortgage, Inc.; Amresco; Associates Home Equity Corp.

For full biographical listings, see the Martindale-Hubbell Law Directory

NORMAN LINDER HULL, P.A. (AV)

537 North Magnolia Avenue, P.O. Box 2751, 32802
Telephone: 407-422-1235
Fax: 407-423-2842
Email: nlhull@ix.netcom.com *URL:* http://www.lawyers.com/hulllaw

Norman L. Hull

For full biographical listings, see the Martindale-Hubbell Law Directory

*TAMPA,** Hillsborough Co.

KETCHEY HORAN, P.A. (AV)

100 North Tampa Street, Suite 1900, P.O. Box 500, 33601-0500
Telephone: 813-223-9395
Fax: 813-221-1348
Email: Stephanie@KetcheyHoran.com
Sun City Center, Florida Office: 1647 Sun City Center Plaza, Suite 200.
Telephone: 813-633-1200.

SHAREHOLDERS

Michael P. Horan

ASSOCIATE

Alfred A. Colby

For full biographical listings, see the Martindale-Hubbell Law Directory

STICHTER, RIEDEL, BLAIN & PROSSER, P.A. (AV)

110 East Madison Street, Suite 200, 33602-4700
Telephone: 813-229-0144
Fax: 813-229-1811

Don M. Stichter
Harley E. Riedel, II
Russell M. Blain
Richard C. Prosser
Charles A. Postler
Scott A. Stichter
Wanda Hagan Anthony
W. Gregory Golson
Stephen R. Leslie

Luis Martinez-Monfort

For full biographical listings, see the Martindale-Hubbell Law Directory

TOWNSEND & BRANNON (AV)

608 West Horatio Street, 33606-2228
Telephone: 813-254-0088
Telecopier: 813-254-0093
URL: http://www.townsendbrannon.com

MEMBERS OF FIRM

David A. Townsend
Anita C. Brannon

For full biographical listings, see the Martindale-Hubbell Law Directory

*WEST PALM BEACH,** Palm Beach Co.

QUARLES & BRADY LLP (AV)

222 Lakeview Avenue, 4th Floor, 33401
Telephone: 561-653-5000
Fax: 561-653-5333
URL: http://www.quarles.com
Milwaukee, Wisconsin Office: 411 East Wisconsin Avenue, 53202-4497.
Telephone: 414-277-5000.
Fax: 414-271-3552.
Madison, Wisconsin Office: Firstar Plaza, One South Pinckney Street, P.O. Box 2113, 53701-2113.
Telephone: 608-251-5000.
Fax: 608-251-9166.
Naples, Florida Office: Barnett Center, 4501 Tamiami Trail North, Suite 300, 34103-3060.
Telephone: 941-262-5959.
Fax: 941-434-4999.
Phoenix, Arizona Office: One Camelback Building, One East Camelback Road, Suite 400, 85012-1649.
Telephone: 602-230-5500.
Fax: 602-230-5598.
Chicago, Illinois Office: Quarles & Brady LLC, Citicorp Center, 500 West Madison Street, Suite 3700.
Telephone: 312-715-5000.
Fax: 312-715-5155.

(See Next Column)

QUARLES & BRADY LLP—*Continued*

PARTNERS

Ned R. Nashban
Nancy Berz Colman

For Complete List of Firm Personnel, See General Section

For full biographical listings, see the Martindale-Hubbell Law Directory

WARD, DAMON, BEVERLY, TITTLE & POSNER, P.A. (AV)

4420 Beacon Circle, 33407-3270
Telephone: 561-842-3000
Stuart: 561-223-5550
Fax: 561-842-3626
Email: wdbtp@wdbtp.com *URL:* http://www.wdbtp.com

James F. Cooney, Jr. (1950-1992)
Conrad Damon
Andrew Fulton, IV
Irwin R. Gilbert
Craig I. Kelley
Michael J Posner
Roger C. Stanton
James D. Tittle, Jr.
Philip H. Ward, III

OF COUNSEL

Don Beverly

For full biographical listings, see the Martindale-Hubbell Law Directory

GEORGIA

*ATLANTA,** Fulton Co.

DAVID G. CROCKETT, P.C. (AV)

1950 Equitable Building, 100 Peachtree Street, N.W., 30303
Telephone: 404-522-4280
Telecopier: 404-589-9891
Email: CROCKLAW@BELLSOUTH.NET

David G. Crockett

Douglas L. Brooks

LEGAL SUPPORT PERSONNEL

Loraine B. Harps (Paralegal)

Approved Attorney for: Chicago Title Insurance Co.
Reference: NationsBank, N.A.

For full biographical listings, see the Martindale-Hubbell Law Directory

GRAY & GILLILAND, P.C. (AV)

400 Perimeter Center Terrace, Suite 1050, 30346-1239
Telephone: 770-392-4800
Telecopy: 770-392-4808

John C. Gray
T. Cullen Gilliland
Charles A. Ratz
Melissa A. Garrett
T. Jeffery Lehman
Robert W. Browning

P. Steven Kratsch

OF COUNSEL

E. Reid Garrett
David S. Currie
Mark B. Bullman

For full biographical listings, see the Martindale-Hubbell Law Directory

LAMBERTH, BONAPFEL, CIFELLI & STOKES, P.A. (AV)

Atlanta Financial Center, 3343 Peachtree Road, N.E. East Tower, Suite 550, 30326
Telephone: 404-262-7373
Fax: 404-262-9911

J. Michael Lamberth
James Craig Cifelli
Paul W. Bonapfel
G. Frank Nason, IV
Gregory D. Ellis

Stuart F. Clayton, Jr.
A. Alexander Teel
Laura E. Woodson

OF COUNSEL

William H. Willson, Jr.

Reference: The Riverside Bank.

For full biographical listings, see the Martindale-Hubbell Law Directory

LONG ALDRIDGE & NORMAN LLP (AV)

A Limited Liability Partnership including Professional Corporations
Suite 5300, 303 Peachtree Street, 30308
Telephone: 404-527-4000
Telecopier: 404-527-4198
Email: atlanta@lanlaw.com *URL:* http://www.lanlaw.com
Washington, D.C. Office: Suite 600, 701 Pennsylvania Avenue, N.W., 20004.
Telephone: 202-624-1200.
FAX: 202-624-1298.

MEMBERS OF FIRM

Evan Appel
Robert A. Bartlett
Charles E. Campbell
Mark S. Kaufman
J. Michael Levengood
Gary W. Marsh
Laura Fink Nix
Henry F. Sewell, Jr.
Russell A. Tolley
Charles D. Weiss

ASSOCIATES

Jeffery W. Cavender
David N. Stern
Angelyn M. Wright

For Complete List of Firm Personnel, See General Section

For full biographical listings, see the Martindale-Hubbell Law Directory

MACEY, WILENSKY, COHEN, WITTNER & KESSLER, LLP (AV)

285 Peachtree Center Avenue, Suite 600, 30303-1229
Telephone: 404-584-1200
Telecopier: 404-681-4355
Email: Lawyers@MaceyWilensky.com

MEMBERS OF FIRM

Morris W. Macey
Frank B. Wilensky
Neil C. Gordon
James R. Sacca
David B. Kurzweil

ASSOCIATES

Todd E. Hennings
Kristine M. Shryock
Louis G. McBryan

For Complete List of Firm Personnel, See General Section

For full biographical listings, see the Martindale-Hubbell Law Directory

PARKER, HUDSON, RAINER & DOBBS LLP (AV)

1500 Marquis Two Tower, 285 Peachtree Center Avenue, N.E., 30303
Telephone: 404-523-5300
Fax: 404-522-8409
Tallahassee, Florida Office: The Perkins House, 118 North Gadsden Street, 32301.
Telephone: 904-681-0191.
Fax: 904-681-9493.

MEMBERS OF FIRM

C. Edward Dobbs
Rufus Thomas Dorsey, IV

For full biographical listings, see the Martindale-Hubbell Law Directory

*AUGUSTA,** Richmond Co.

DYE, TUCKER, EVERITT, LONG & BREWTON, A PROFESSIONAL ASSOCIATION (AV)

453 Greene Street, P.O. Box 2426, 30903-2426
Telephone: 706-722-0771
Fax: 706-722-7028

A. Rowland Dye
Thomas W. Tucker
A. Zachry Everitt
John B. Long
Benjamin H. Brewton
Troy A. Lanier

OF COUNSEL

A. Montague Miller

Jon E. Ingram, Jr.

Representative Clients: State Farm Insurance Cos.; Travelers-Aetna Insurance Cos.; Georgia Power Co.; Wachovia National Bank (Augusta Division); Chubb Group; MAG Mutual Insurance Company; Augusta Board of Realtors; Canal Insurance Company; St. Paul Fire and Marine Insurance Company.

For full biographical listings, see the Martindale-Hubbell Law Directory

J. BENJAMIN KAY, III (AV)

808 First Union Bank Building, 30901
Telephone: 706-722-2008

Approved Attorney for: Lawyers Title Insurance Corp.
Reference: First Union National Bank of Georgia.
Representative Clients: American National Bank & Trust Company; Biotech Park, Inc.; Caterpillar Financial Services, Inc.; Davis-McGraw, Inc.; Ford Leasing Development Company; Ford Motor Credit Company; Gary Concrete Products, Inc.; Globe Life Insurance Company.

For full biographical listings, see the Martindale-Hubbell Law Directory

Augusta—Continued

SURRETT & COLEMAN, P.A. (AV)

901 Suntrust Bank Building, P.O. Box 1497, 30903
Telephone: 706-722-3301
Telecopier: 706-722-3318
Email: ecoleman@groupz.net

Carl J. Surrett — Edward J. Coleman, III

Representative Clients: Sears, Roebuck & Co.; American Home Assurance Co.; Great Southwest Fire Insurance Co.; Duke Buick, Inc.; American Southern Insurance Co.; Scottsdale Insurance Co.; Providence Washington Insurance Co.; Nautilus Insurance Co.

For full biographical listings, see the Martindale-Hubbell Law Directory

WARLICK, TRITT & STEBBINS, L.L.P. (AV)

15th Floor, First Union Bank Building, 699 Broad Street, 30901-1454
Telephone: 706-722-7543
Fax: 706-722-1822
Email: wts@wts-lawfirm.com
Columbia County Office: 119 Davis Road, Martinez, Georgia 30907.
Telephone: 706-860-7595.
Fax: 706-860-7597.

MEMBERS OF FIRM

William Byrd Warlick
Roy D. Tritt (Resident, Martinez Office)
Charles C. Stebbins, III
E. L. Clark Speese
C. Gregory Bryan

OF COUNSEL

Richard E. Miley

For full biographical listings, see the Martindale-Hubbell Law Directory

*COLUMBUS,** Muscogee Co.

HATCHER, STUBBS, LAND, HOLLIS & ROTHSCHILD (AV)

A Limited Liability Partnership
Suite 500 The Corporate Center, 233 12th Street, P.O. Box 2707, 31902-2707
Telephone: 706-324-0201
Telecopier: 706-322-7747
Email: mailman@hatcherstubbs.com

MEMBER OF FIRM

William C. Pound

General Counsel for: SunTrust Bank, West Georgia, N.A.; TOM'S Foods Inc.; Muscogee County Board of Education; Board of Water Commissioners of Columbus, Georgia; St. Francis Hospital, Inc.; Georgia Crown Distributing Co.; The Jordan Company.
Local Counsel for: Mercedes-Benz Credit.

For Complete List of Firm Personnel, See General Section

For full biographical listings, see the Martindale-Hubbell Law Directory

*MACON,** Bibb Co.

SELL & MELTON, L.L.P. (AV)

A Limited Liability Partnership including a Professional Corporation
14th Floor, 577 Mulberry Street, P.O. Box 229, 31202-0229
Telephone: 912-746-8521
Telecopier: 912-745-6426

Edward S. Sell, III — Brian J. Passante

General Counsel for: Macon Telegraph Publishing Co. (The Macon Telegraph); Macon-Bibb County Hospital Authority; County of Bibb; Smith & Sons Foods, Inc. (S & S Cafeterias); Macon Bibb County Industrial Authority; Burgess Pigment Co.
Local Counsel For: United States Aircraft Insurance Group (USAIG); United States Aviation Underwriters, Inc. (USAU).

For Complete List of Firm Personnel, See General Section

For full biographical listings, see the Martindale-Hubbell Law Directory

*NEWNAN,** Coweta Co.

GLOVER & DAVIS, P.A. (AV)

10 Brown Street, P.O. Box 1038, 30264
Telephone: 770-683-6000
Fax: 770-683-6010
Peachtree City, Georgia Office: Suite 130, 200 Westpark Drive.
Telephone: 770-487-5834.
Fax: 770-487-3492.

J. Littleton Glover, Jr. — Alan W. Jackson

Representative Clients: First Citizens Corporation and Banking Subsidiaries; Putnam-Greene Financial Corporation; Farmers & Merchants Bank, Eatonton, Georgia; The Farmers Bank, Union Point, Georgia; First Bank of Coastal Georgia; Peachtree National Bank; Gas, Incorporated.
Local Counsel for: West Georgia Farm Credit, ACA; First Financial Bank, FSB, Stevens Point, Wisconsin; W. S. Badcock Corp.

(See Next Column)

For Complete List of Firm Personnel, See General Section

For full biographical listings, see the Martindale-Hubbell Law Directory

ROSENZWEIG, JONES & MACNABB, P.C. (AV)

32 South Court Square, P.O. Box 220, 30264
Telephone: 770-253-3282
Fax: 770-251-7262

George C. Rosenzweig
Sidney Pope Jones, Jr.
Joseph P. MacNabb

Charles C. Witcher
Douglas L. Dreyer
Jonathan W. Hickman

Approved Attorneys for: Lawyers Title Insurance Corp.; Chicago Title Insurance Co.

For full biographical listings, see the Martindale-Hubbell Law Directory

NORCROSS, Gwinnett Co.

WALLACE & DE MAYO, P.C. (AV)

6356 Corley Road, 30071-1704
Telephone: 770-446-9996
Fax: 770-368-8331

Richard T. De Mayo — Douglas W. Wallace

Paul J. Gallo
Andrew J. Baird
Kristian Knochel

For full biographical listings, see the Martindale-Hubbell Law Directory

*SAVANNAH,** Chatham Co.

INGLESBY, FALLIGANT, HORNE, COURINGTON & NASH, A PROFESSIONAL CORPORATION (AV)

17 West McDonough Street, P.O. Box 1368, 31402-1368
Telephone: 912-232-7000
Telecopier: 912-232-7300
Email: IFHCN@aol.com

Sam P. Inglesby, Jr.
J. Daniel Falligant
Kathleen Horne
Dorothy W. Courington, II
Thomas A. Nash, Jr.
Dolly Chisholm

Amy Lee Copeland

OF COUNSEL

Robert B. Brannen, Jr.

Representative Clients: Ford Motor Credit Co.; NationsBank of Georgia, N.A.; Chase Manhattan Bank; Ameribank; National Auto; Auto Credit Clearing; United Student Aid Funds; Cometicut Student Loans Fund.

For full biographical listings, see the Martindale-Hubbell Law Directory

KARSMAN, BROOKS & CALLAWAY, P.C. (AV)

301 West Congress Street, P.O. Box 9149, 31412
Telephone: 912-238-2750
Cable Address: "Karbro"
Telecopier: 912-238-2767

Stanley M. Karsman
Charles C. Brooks
Timothy F. Callaway, III
Stanley E. Harris, Jr.
James L. Drake, Jr.
Dana F. Braun
R. Krannert Riddle
Edward M. Hughes
Timothy J. Haeussler

For full biographical listings, see the Martindale-Hubbell Law Directory

MCCALLAR AND ASSOCIATES (AV)

115 Oglethorpe Avenue West, P.O. Box 9026, 31412
Telephone: 912-234-1215
Telecopier: 912-236-7549

C. James McCallar, Jr.

Mark Bulovic

For full biographical listings, see the Martindale-Hubbell Law Directory

HAWAII

*HONOLULU,** Honolulu Co.

CARLSMITH BALL (AV)

A Partnership including Law Corporations
Suite 2200, Pacific Tower, 1001 Bishop Street, P.O. Box 656, 96809-3402
Telephone: 808-523-2500
Fax: 808-523-0842
Email: execdirector@carlsmith.com *URL:* http://www.carlsmith.com
Kapolei, Hawaii Office: Suite 318, Kapolei Building, 1001 Kamokila Boulevard, 96707.
Telephone: 808-523-2500.
Fax: 808-674-0850.
Wailuku, Maui Hawaii Office: Suite 400, One Main Plaza, 2200 Main Street, P.O. Box 1086, 96793-1086.
Telephone: 808-242-4535.
Fax: 808-244-4974.
Kailua-Kona, Hawaii Office: Suite 209, 75-1000 Henry Street, 96740.
Telephone: 808-329-6464.
Fax: 808-329-9450.
Hilo, Hawaii Office: 121 Waianuenue Avenue, P.O. Box 686, 96721-0686.
Telephone: 808-935-6644.
Fax: 808-935-7975.
Hagatna, Guam Office: Suite 401, Bank of Hawaii Building, 134 West Soledad Avenue, P.O. Box BF, 96932-5027.
Telephone: 671-472-6813.
Fax: 671-477-4375.
Telex: 721-6445 CWCMI GM.
Saipan, Commonwealth of the Northern Mariana Islands Office: Carlsmith Building, Capitol Hill, P.O. Box 5241, 96950-5241.
Telephone: 670-322-3455.
Fax: 670-322-3368.
Los Angeles, California Office: 9th Floor, 444 South Flower Street, 90071-2901.
Telephone: 213-955-1200.
Fax: 213-623-0032.
Washington, D.C. Office: Suite 300, 1201 Pennsylvania Avenue, N.W., 20004-2401.
Telephone: 202-628-2228.
Fax: 202-628-2071.
Mexico City, Mexico Office: Carlsmith Ball, Sierra Nevada 119, Lomas de Chapultepec, 11000 Mexico, D.F.
Telephone: 52-5-520-8514, 52-5-520-8757.
Fax: 52-5-540-1545.
Mexico, D.F. Office of Carlsmith Ball, S.C. (Authorized to practice as foreign legal consultants in Mexico): Sierra Nevada 119, Lomas de Chapultepec, 11000 Mexico, D.F.
Telephone: 52-5-520-8514, 52-5-520-8757.
Fax: 52-5-540-1545.

MEMBER OF FIRM

Tom E. Roesser

ASSOCIATE

David B. Rosen

For Complete List of Firm Personnel, See General Section

For full biographical listings, see the Martindale-Hubbell Law Directory

KESSNER DUCA UMEBAYASHI BAIN & MATSUNAGA ATTORNEYS AT LAW, A LAW CORPORATION (AV)

19th Floor, Central Pacific Plaza, 220 South King Street, 96813
Telephone: 808-536-1900
Telecopier: 808-529-7177
Telex: 723 8616 OPAC IIR

Robert C. Kessner
James N. Duca
Clyde S. Umebayashi
Elton John Bain
Emma S. Matsunaga
Muriel M. Taira

Beverly S. K. Tom
Jacqueline W.S. Amai
Melanie S. Matsui
Cori Ann C. Takamiya

OF COUNSEL

Kathy K. Higham

For full biographical listings, see the Martindale-Hubbell Law Directory

TAKUSHI, FUNAKI, WONG & STONE ATTORNEYS AT LAW, A LAW CORPORATION (AV)

Suite 1400 Grosvenor Center, 733 Bishop Street, 96813
Telephone: 808-543-9800
Fax: 808-543-9869
Email: tfwf@pixi.com

(See Next Column)

Roy E. Takushi
James T. Funaki
Alfred M. K. Wong
Robert M. Ehrhorn, Jr.
Dickson C. H. Lee
Peter T. Stone
James N. H. Yee
Ann L. Kurihara
Jacqueline Kong
Elizabeth A. Kane

For full biographical listings, see the Martindale-Hubbell Law Directory

IDAHO

*BOISE,** Ada Co.

ELAM & BURKE, A PROFESSIONAL ASSOCIATION (AV)

Key Financial Center, 702 West Idaho Street, P.O. Box 1539, 83701
Telephone: 208-343-5454
Telecopier: 208-384-5844
Email: eblaw@elamburke.com

Randall A. Peterman
Jeffery J. Ventrella

Geoffrey M. Baker

Representative Clients: U.S. BanCorp Leasing; Gulf USA Corporation; Pintlar Corporation; Morrison-Knudsen.

For Complete List of Firm Personnel, See General Section

For full biographical listings, see the Martindale-Hubbell Law Directory

ILLINOIS

*CHICAGO,** Cook Co.

BARNES & THORNBURG (AV)

2600 Chase Plaza, 10 South La Salle Street, 60603
Telephone: 312-357-1313
FAX: 312-759-5646
URL: http://www.btlaw.com
Indianapolis, Indiana Office: 11 South Meridian Street, 46204.
Telephone: 317-236-1313.
FAX: 317-231-7433.
Fort Wayne, Indiana Office: Suite 600, One Summit Square, 46802.
Telephone: 219-423-9440.
FAX: 219-424-8316.
South Bend, Indiana Office: 600 1st Source Bank Center, 100 North Michigan, 46601-1632.
Telephone: 219-233-1171.
FAX: 219-237-1125.
Elkhart, Indiana Office: 121 West Franklin Street, Suite 200, 46516.
Telephone: 219-293-0681.
FAX: 219-296-2535.
Washington, D.C. Office: 1401 Eye Street, N.W., Suite 500, 20005.
Telephone: 202-289-1313.
FAX: 202-289-1330.

MEMBER OF FIRM

William I. Kohn

ASSOCIATE

Kristan Quinn Laden

Representative Clients: AMPRO, Inc.; Chicago Football, LLC; Citizens Commercial Leasing Corporation; Commonwealth Edison Company; Harley-Davidson Motor Company; International Facilities Group, LLC; Marchesan Implementos E. Maquinas Agricoles Tatu SA; Ron Weber & Associates of Illinois, Inc.; Transtech Products Corporation; Whirlpool Corporation.

For Complete List of Firm Personnel, See General Section

For full biographical listings, see the Martindale-Hubbell Law Directory

EHRENBERG & FROST, P.C. (AV)

111 West Jackson Boulevard 15th Floor, 60604-3501
Telephone: 312-987-9766; 312-957-2022
Fax: 312-461-0338

Alan I. Ehrenberg
Scott C. Frost

For full biographical listings, see the Martindale-Hubbell Law Directory

FAGEL & HABER (AV)

140 South Dearborn Street 14th Floor, 60603
Telephone: 312-346-7500
FAX: 312-580-2201
Telex No: 754542
Cable: "NOFLAWLAW"
URL: http://www.fandh.com

(See Next Column)

FAGEL & HABER, *Chicago—Continued*

MEMBERS OF FIRM

Floyd Babbitt
Dennis E. Quaid
Victor A. Des Laurier

For full biographical listings, see the Martindale-Hubbell Law Directory

HOLLIS AND JOHNSON (AV)

11 East Adams Street, Suite 501, 60603
Telephone: 312-427-0700
Fax: 312-427-8407
URL: http://www.digitalawyer.com/bankruptcy

Pamela S. Hollis
Donald E. Johnson

ASSOCIATE

Linda M. Kujaca

For full biographical listings, see the Martindale-Hubbell Law Directory

*MOUNT VERNON,** Jefferson Co.

LAW OFFICE OF TERRY SHARP, P.C. (AV)

1115 Harrison Street, P.O. Box 906, 62864
Telephone: 618-242-0246
Fax: 618-242-1170
Email: TSharp.law@mvn.net
Benton, Illinois Office: 105 North Main Street.
Telephone: 618-435-5109.
FAX: 618-242-1170.

Terrell Lee Sharp

For full biographical listings, see the Martindale-Hubbell Law Directory

*SPRINGFIELD,** Sangamon Co.

GIFFIN, WINNING, COHEN & BODEWES, P.C. (AV)

1 West Old State Capitol Plaza, Suite 600 Myers Building, P.O. Box 2117, 62705
Telephone: 217-525-1571
Facsimile: 217-525-1710
Email: gifwinlaw@eosinc.com

John L. Swartz

Representative Clients: Illinois State University; Union Planters Bank; Security Bank, sb; Illinois League of Financial Institutions; Southern Illinois University School of Medicine; Central Illinois Builders of A.G.C.; Great Central Insurance Cos.

For Complete List of Firm Personnel, See General Section

For full biographical listings, see the Martindale-Hubbell Law Directory

VERNON HILLS, Lake Co.

RICHARDS, RALPH & SCHWAB, CHARTERED (AV)

One Hawthorn Place, 175 East Hawthorn Parkway, Suite 345, 60061
Telephone: 847-367-9699
Fax: 847-367-9621
Email: dschwab@rr&s-chtd.com *URL:* http://www.lawyers.com/richardandschwab

Michael L. Ralph
Alan E. Richards
David J. Schwab

For full biographical listings, see the Martindale-Hubbell Law Directory

INDIANA

ELKHART, Elkhart Co.

BARNES & THORNBURG (AV)

121 West Franklin Street, Suite 200, 46516
Telephone: 219-293-0681
FAX: 219-296-2535
URL: http://www.btlaw.com
Indianapolis, Indiana Office: 11 South Meridian Street, 46204.
Telephone: 317-236-1313.
FAX: 317-231-7433.
Fort Wayne, Indiana Office: Suite 600, One Summit Square, 46802.
Telephone: 219-423-9440.
FAX: 219-424-8316.
South Bend, Indiana Office: 600 1st Source Bank Center, 100 North Michigan, 46601-1632.
Telephone: 219-233-1171.
FAX: 219-237-1125.
Chicago, Illinois Office: 2600 Chase Plaza, 10 South La Salle Street, 60603.
Telephone: 312-357-1313.
FAX: 312-759-5646.

(See Next Column)

Washington, D.C. Office: 1401 Eye Street, N.W., Suite 500, 20005.
Telephone: 202-289-1313.
FAX: 202-289-1330.

MEMBER OF FIRM

Geoffrey K. Church

ASSOCIATE

Jennifer A. Bickley

Representative Clients: Bank One; Elkhart Community Schools; Elkhart General Hospital; Heywood Williams Group PLC; KeyBank National Association; Partners National Health Plans of Indiana, Inc.; Rieth-Riley Construction Co., Inc.; Skyline Corporation; Whirlpool Corporation.

For Complete List of Firm Personnel, See General Section

For full biographical listings, see the Martindale-Hubbell Law Directory

THORNE, GRODNIK, RANSEL, DUNCAN, BYRON, HOSTETLER & TRIPPEL, LLP (AV)

228 West High Street, 46516-3176
Telephone: 219-294-7473
FAX: 219-294-5390
Mishawaka, Indiana Office: 420 Lincoln Way West, P.O. Box 1210, 46544.
Telephone: 219-256-5660.
FAX: 219-674-6835.

MEMBERS OF FIRM

Charles H. Grodnik
J. Richard Ransel
Glenn L. Duncan
James R. Byron
Steven L. Hostetler
Michael A. Trippel

ASSOCIATES

W. Douglas Thorne
Gregg A. Hixenbaugh

OF COUNSEL

F. Richard Kramer
Joseph C. Zakas
William A. Thorne

Counsel for: Valley American Bank and Trust Co., Mishawaka, Indiana; NBD Bank.

For full biographical listings, see the Martindale-Hubbell Law Directory

*EVANSVILLE,** Vanderburgh Co.

BOWERS, HARRISON, KENT & MILLER, LLP (AV)

25 N.W. Riverside Drive, P.O. Box 1287, 47706-1287
Telephone: 812-426-1231
Fax: 812-464-3676
Email: BOWERS,HARRISON,KENT&MILLER,LLP@BHKM.COM
URL: http://WWW.BHKM.COM

MEMBERS OF FIRM

Joseph H. Harrison
Paul E. Black
Gary R. Case
Paul J. Wallace

Representative Clients: Vantage Healthcare Corporation; International Steel Company; Mellon Bank N.A.; Champion Homes, Inc.

For Complete List of Firm Personnel, See General Section

For full biographical listings, see the Martindale-Hubbell Law Directory

FINE & HATFIELD, A PROFESSIONAL CORPORATION (AV)

520 N.W. Second Street, P.O. Box 779, 47705-0779
Telephone: 812-425-3592
Telecopier: 812-421-4269
Email: Fine@Fine-Hatfield.com *URL:* http://www.Fine-Hatfield.com

James E. Marchand
Thomas H. Bryan
Danny E. Glass

Boyd A. Toler

A List of Representative Clients Furnished Upon Request.

For full biographical listings, see the Martindale-Hubbell Law Directory

ZIEMER, STAYMAN, WEITZEL & SHOULDERS, LLP (AV)

(Formerly Early, Arnold & Ziemer)
One Riverfront Place, 20 N.W. First Street 9th Floor, P.O. Box 916, 47706-0916
Telephone: 812-424-7575
Telecopier: 812-421-5089

MEMBERS OF FIRM

Robert F. Stayman
Marco L. DeLucio
Gregory G. Meyer

Reference: Old National Bank in Evansville.

For full biographical listings, see the Martindale-Hubbell Law Directory

*FORT WAYNE,** Allen Co.

BARNES & THORNBURG (AV)

Suite 600, One Summit Square, 46802
Telephone: 219-423-9440
FAX: 219-424-8316
URL: http://www.btlaw.com
Indianapolis, Indiana Office: 11 South Meridian Street, 46204.
Telephone: 317-236-1313.
FAX: 317-231-7433.
South Bend, Indiana Office: 600 1st Source Bank Center, 100 North Michigan, 46601-1632.
Telephone: 219-233-1171.
FAX: 219-237-1125.
Elkhart, Indiana Office: 121 West Franklin Street, Suite 200, 46516.
Telephone: 219-293-0681.
FAX: 219-296-2535.
Chicago, Illinois Office: 2600 Chase Plaza, 10 South La Salle Street, 60603.
Telephone: 312-357-1313.
FAX: 312-759-5646.
Washington, D.C. Office: 1401 Eye Street, N.W., Suite 500, 20005.
Telephone: 202-289-1313.
FAX: 202-289-1330.

MEMBER OF FIRM

Stephen L. Fink

ASSOCIATE

Matthew M. Hohman

Representative Clients: Demeter; Do it Best Corp.; EP Graphics, Inc.; Frick Services, Inc.; General Motors Corporation; Group Dekko International; Liberty Homes, Inc.; Lincoln National Corporation; Norwest Bank Indiana, N.A.; Zollner Pistons, L.L.C.

For Complete List of Firm Personnel, See General Section

For full biographical listings, see the Martindale-Hubbell Law Directory

BECKMAN LAWSON, LLP (AV)

800 Standard Federal Plaza, 46802
Telephone: 219-422-0800
Facsimile: 219-420-1013
Syracuse, Indiana Office: 200 West Main Street.
Telephone: 219-457-5727.
Facsimile: 219-457-2056.

MEMBERS OF FIRM

Jack W. Lawson
Frank J. Gray
Howard B. Sandler
Stephen R. Snyder
James A. Federoff
William L. Sweet, Jr.
Richard H. Blaich
John H. Brandt
Jon A. Bragalone
Brian J. T'Kindt
Douglas R. Adelsperger
Travis S. Friend
Robert L. Nicholson
David D. Cornwell
James A. Butz
Jack C. Birch
Craig R. Patterson

ASSOCIATES

John M. Ketcham
Wendy W. Davis
Jeffrey B. Harding
Martha M. Kinder
Edward J. Ormsby
Randall L. Morgan
Daniel J. Deeb
Patrick R. Hess
Georgia L. Hartman
Brian M. Simpson
James E. Rossow, Jr.
Sarah A. Hiestand
Tandra S. Johnson
Jason M. Kuchmay
Matthew J. Elliott

OF COUNSEL

Frederick A. Beckman
Neil F. Sandler
Douglas E. Miller
Loren K. Allison

Reference: National City Bank.

For full biographical listings, see the Martindale-Hubbell Law Directory

HELMKE, BEAMS, BOYER & WAGNER (AV)

300 Metro Building, Berry & Harrison Streets, 46802-2242
Telephone: 219-422-7422
Telecopier: 219-422-6764
Email: hbbwdjb@aol.com
Email: rdboyer1@fortwayne.infi.net

MEMBERS OF FIRM

Walter E. Helmke (1901-1976)
Walter P. Helmke
R. David Boyer
Robert A. Wagner
J. Timothy McCaulay
Daniel J. Borgmann
Trina Glusenkamp Gould

ASSOCIATES

Payne D. Brown
R. David Boyer, II

OF COUNSEL

Glen J. Beams
William A. Berning

Representative Clients: Aalco Distributing Co., Inc.; Brotherhood Mutual Insurance Co.; Fremont Community Schools; Air-O-Mat, Inc.; Leo Distributors, Inc.; The City of Fort Wayne, Indiana; Foellinger Foundation, Inc.

(See Next Column)

For full biographical listings, see the Martindale-Hubbell Law Directory

SHIPLEY & ASSOCIATES (AV)

230 West Main Street, Suite 100, 46802-1612
Telephone: 219-422-2700
Fax: 219-424-2960
Email: shipley@iquest.net

Grant F. Shipley

ASSOCIATE

Deborah Wiers Vincent

Representative Clients: NBD Bank, N.A.; Indiana Michigan Power Co. (AEP); Creditors Committee, Mallard Coach Co. Bankruptcy.

For full biographical listings, see the Martindale-Hubbell Law Directory

*INDIANAPOLIS,** Marion Co.

ANCEL & DUNLAP, LLP (AV)

Market Square Center, 151 North Delaware, Suite 1770, 46204-2503
Telephone: 317-634-9052
Fax: 317-263-3871
Email: ancel@netdirect.net

Steven H. Ancel
David L. Dunlap
Sorelle J. Ancel
F. Jonathan Zusy
Paul T. Deignan
Joseph L. Claypool
Edward R. Cardoza

OF COUNSEL

Bruce A. Markell

Reference: National Bank of Indianapolis.

For full biographical listings, see the Martindale-Hubbell Law Directory

BAMBERGER & FEIBLEMAN (AV)

1408 North Pennsylvania Street, 46202-2421
Telephone: 317-639-5151
FAX: 317-269-2030
Email: bandf@iquest.net

MEMBERS OF FIRM

Ralph Bamberger (1871-1947)
Isidore Feibleman (1873-1954)
Charles B. Feibleman (1916-1971)
John K. Rickles (1898-1976)
Julian Bamberger (1905-1988)
Sigmund J. Beck (1915-1991)
Willard B. Ransom (1916-1995)
D. Robert Webster

ASSOCIATE

David K. Lee

OF COUNSEL

Victor A. DeRose
Thomas D. Strodtman
Joseph H. Greenberg
Timothy E. Peterson
Neil E. Lucas

Representative Clients: C.I.T. Corp.; FFI Corporation; Kipp Brothers, Inc.; BancPlus Mortgage Corp.; Hiway Parts, Inc.; NBD, Indiana; Tube Processing Corp.; Indiana Mortgage Corp.

For full biographical listings, see the Martindale-Hubbell Law Directory

BARNES & THORNBURG (AV)

11 South Meridian Street, 46204
Telephone: 317-236-1313
FAX: 317-231-7433; 317-231-7452
URL: http://www.btlaw.com
Fort Wayne, Indiana Office: Suite 600, One Summit Square, 46802.
Telephone: 219-423-9440.
FAX: 219-424-8316.
South Bend, Indiana Office: 600 1st Source Bank Center, 100 North Michigan, 46601-1632.
Telephone: 219-233-1171.
FAX: 219-237-1125.
Elkhart, Indiana Office: 121 West Franklin Street, Suite 200, 46516.
Telephone: 219-293-0681.
FAX: 219-296-2535.
Chicago, Illinois Office: 2600 Chase Plaza, 10 South La Salle Street, 60603.
Telephone: 312-357-1313.
FAX: 312-759-5646.
Washington, D.C. Office: 1401 Eye Street, N.W., Suite 500, 20005.
Telephone: 202-289-1313.
FAX: 202-289-1330.

MEMBERS OF FIRM

David M. Powlen
Michael K. McCrory
Alan K. Mills

OF COUNSEL

Edward A. Keirn

(See Next Column)

BARNES & THORNBURG, *Indianapolis—Continued*

ASSOCIATES

Karen L. Kovalsky
Christine K. Jacobson
LaChelle D. Stepp

Representative Clients: Ameritech; DePuy Orthopaedics, Inc.; Dow Agro-Sciences; Eli Lilly and Company; Hillenbrand Industries; The Lincoln National Life Insurance Company; Purdue Research Foundation; Roche Diagnostics Corporation; Toyota Motor Corporation; Whirlpool Corporation.

For Complete List of Firm Personnel, See General Section

For full biographical listings, see the Martindale-Hubbell Law Directory

BOSE MCKINNEY & EVANS LLP (AV)

2700 First Indiana Plaza, 135 North Pennsylvania Street, 46204
Telephone: 317-684-5000
Facsimile: 317-684-5173
URL: http://www.boselaw.com
Indianapolis North Office: Suite 1500, 8888 Keystone Crossing, 46240.
Telephone: 317-574-3700.
Facsimile: 317-574-3716.

MEMBERS OF FIRM

James E. Carlberg
Theodore J. Nowacki
Michael A. Trentadue

OF COUNSEL

Rodger K. Hendershot

Representative Clients: First Indiana Bank; Indiana League of Savings Institutions, Inc.; Prudential Life Insurance Co.; Metropolitan Insurance Co.; Bank One, NA; Farm Credit Services; Fannie Mae.

For Complete List of Firm Personnel, See General Section

For full biographical listings, see the Martindale-Hubbell Law Directory

BUSCHMANN, CARR & SHANKS, PROFESSIONAL CORPORATION (AV)

1020 Market Tower, 10 West Market Street, 46204-2963
Telephone: 317-636-5511
Fax: 317-636-3661
Email: bcs@indy.net *URL:* http://www.buschmanncarr.com

John R. Carr, Jr.
Bret S. Clement
John R. Carr, III
Gary L. Dilk

Representative Clients: Archer-Daniels Midland Co.; Ball Corp.; Industrial Valley Title Insurance; Creative Risk Management, Inc.; Deflecto Corporation; Glenfed Mortgage Corp.; Gates McDonald; Merchants National Bank & Trust Company of Muncie; Monumental Life Insurance Co.; National Council on Compensation Insurance.

For full biographical listings, see the Martindale-Hubbell Law Directory

FEIWELL & HANNOY, PROFESSIONAL CORPORATION (AV)

251 North Illinois Street, Suite 1700, P.O. Box 44141, 46244-0141
Telephone: 317-237-2727
Facsimile: 317-237-2722
Email: f&h@feiwellhannoy.com *URL:* http://www.feiwellhannoy.com

Murray J. Feiwell
Douglas J. Hannoy

Michael J. Feiwell
David J. Jurkiewicz

Representative Clients: Chase Manhattan Mortgage Corp.; Countrywide Home Loans, Inc.; Fifth Third Bank; First Union Mortgage Corp.; Homecomings Financial; Ocwen Federal Bank, FSB; United Companies Lending Corp.; GMAC Mortgage Corp.; First National Bank; Norwest Mortgage, Inc.

For full biographical listings, see the Martindale-Hubbell Law Directory

HOPPER, GALLIHER & TUCKER, P.C. (AV)

Bank One Center/Circle, 111 Monument Circle, Suite 452, 46204-5170
Telephone: 317-635-5005
Facsimile: 317-634-2501

George W. Hopper
William J. Tucker
Mark R. Galliher
Ronald W. Buchmeier
Jeffrey E. Ramsey

Representative Clients: Banc One Corporation; National City Bank; Mutual Guaranty Corporation; I.T.T. Financial Services, Commercial Division; ABC Supply Co., Inc.; Sholodge, Inc.; Simon Debartolo Group, L.P.; IWC Resources Corp.; KRB Music Cos., Inc.; Whitewater Broadcasting Corp.

For full biographical listings, see the Martindale-Hubbell Law Directory

HOSTETLER & KOWALIK, P.C. (AV)

101 West Ohio Street Suite 2100, 46204
Telephone: 317-262-1001
Fax: 317-262-1010
Email: hoskow@indy.net *URL:* http://www.lawyers.com/hostetler&kowalik

(See Next Column)

Gary Lynn Hostetler
David R. Krebs
James S. Kowalik
J. Bradley Schooley
Timothy L. Black

For full biographical listings, see the Martindale-Hubbell Law Directory

ICE MILLER DONADIO & RYAN (AV)

One American Square Box 82001, 46282-0002
Telephone: 317-236-2100
Fax: 317-236-2219
Email: info@imdr.com *URL:* http://www.imdr.com
South Bend, Indiana Office: 211 West Washington Street, Suite 2420.
Telephone: 219-234-7933.
Fax: 219-234-7965. Internet E-mail: info@imdr.com. Web Site Address: http://www.imdr.com.
Chicago, Illinois Office: 135 South LaSalle Street, Suite 4100.
Telephone: 312-726-1567.
Fax: 312-641-6263. Internet E-mail: info@imdr.com. Web Site Address: http://www.imdr.com.

MEMBERS OF FIRM

Henry A. Efroymson
Dominic F. Polizzotto

OF COUNSEL

Peggy J. Naile
Susan Rogers Brooke

ASSOCIATES

John M. Hakes
Dennis H. Long

Representative Clients: National City Bank (Trust); Bank One, Indianapolis (Trust); Eastman Kodak Co.; Hewlett Packard Corp.; Indiana Bankers Assn.; Ford Motor Credit Corp.; German American Capital Corp.; The National Bank of Indianapolis; Huntington National Bank; Transamerica Insurance Finance Corp.

For Complete List of Firm Personnel, See General Section

For full biographical listings, see the Martindale-Hubbell Law Directory

JOHNSON SMITH PENCE & HEATH LLP (AV)

One Indiana Square Suite 1800, 46204
Telephone: 317-634-9777
Telecopier: 317-636-9061
Email: firm@jsplaw.com *URL:* http://www.jsplaw.com
Washington, D.C. Office: 555 Twelfth Street, N.W., Suite 650.
Telephone: 202-737-5410.
Fax: 202-737-5411.

MEMBERS OF FIRM

Michael W. Hile
Bradley C. Morris

ASSOCIATE

Kirstie D. Andersen (Not admitted in IN)

For Complete List of Firm Personnel, See General Section

For full biographical listings, see the Martindale-Hubbell Law Directory

SOMMER & BARNARD, ATTORNEYS AT LAW, PC (AV)

4000 Bank One Tower, 111 Monument Circle, 46204
Telephone: 317-630-4000
FAX: 317-236-9802
Email: sandb@sommerbarnard.com
North Office: 8900 Keystone Crossing, Suite 1150, Indianapolis, Indiana, 46240-2134.
Telephone: 317-630-4000.
FAX: 317-844-4780.

Jerald I. Ancel
Marlene Reich
Richard C. Richmond, III

Secured Creditor Representation: Bank One Bloomington, N.A.; Comerica Bank; Northwestern National Life Insurance Co.; PNC Realty Holding Corp;
Debtor Representation: Early-Daniel Company; Early-Daniel Industries; Indiana Grocery Company; Integrated Plastic Technology, Inc; Preston Safeway Foods.

For Complete List of Firm Personnel, See General Section

For full biographical listings, see the Martindale-Hubbell Law Directory

YARLING & ROBINSON (AV)

151 North Delaware, Suite 1535, P.O. Box 44128, 46204
Telephone: 317-262-8800
Fax: 317-262-3046
Email: yrhl@yarling.com *URL:* http://www.yarling.com

MEMBERS OF FIRM

Charles F. Robinson, Jr.
Douglas E. Rogers
John W. Hammel
Mark S. Gray
Linda Y. Hammel
Matthew C. Robinson

ASSOCIATE

Jeffrey R. Mitchell

(See Next Column)

YARLING & ROBINSON—*Continued*

OF COUNSEL

Richard W. Yarling

Representative Clients: Associates Financial Services; Chrysler Credit Corporation; Chrysler First Financial Services; Fleet Financenter; General Motors Acceptance Corporation; Household Finance Corporation; Indiana Telco Credit Union; Nations Credit; Norwest Financial; Security Pacific Finance Corporation.

For full biographical listings, see the Martindale-Hubbell Law Directory

*LAFAYETTE,** Tippecanoe Co.

STUART & BRANIGIN (AV)

The Life Building, 300 Main Street, Suite 800, P.O. Box 1010, 47902-1010
Telephone: 765-423-1561
Telecopier: 765-742-8175
Email: sb@stuartlaw.com *URL:* http://www.stuartlaw.com
Indianapolis, Indiana Office: Suite 1401, 8888 Keystone Crossing, 46240.
Telephone: 317-574-7245.
Fax: 317-574-7050.

MEMBERS OF FIRM

Allison Ellsworth Stuart (1886-1950)
Roger D. Branigin (1902-1975)
Roger D. Branigin, Jr.
Thomas L. Ryan
Thomas R. McCully
Larry R. Fisher
Nina B. Kirkpatrick
Mark Lillianfeld
Stephen R. Pennell
Anthony S. Benton
Erik D. Spykman
William E. Emerick
John C. Duffey
Bruce McSpadden
Mark E. DeYoung
Thomas B. Parent
Laura L. Bowker
Kevin D. Nicoson
Susan K. Roberts
John M. Stuckey
Deborah B. Trice
William P. Kealey
David A. Starkweather
Geoffrey L. Blazi

SENIOR COUNSEL

Russell H. Hart

COUNSEL

John F. Bodle
James V. McGlone

ASSOCIATES

Elizabeth B. Searle
Marianne Mitten Owen
David A. Locke
Karen Orr McClure
Ann Marie Waldron
Barry L. Loftus

General Counsel for: The Lafayette Life Insurance Co.; INB National Bank, N.W.; Lafayette Home Hospital, Inc.
State Counsel for: Norfolk & Western Railway Co.
Mr. Ryan is Counsel to: The Trustees of Purdue University.
Representative Clients: Aluminum Company of America; Liberty Mutual Insurance Group.

For full biographical listings, see the Martindale-Hubbell Law Directory

MERRILLVILLE, Lake Co.

GOUVEIA & MILLER (AV)

521 East 86th Avenue, 46410
Telephone: 219-736-6020
Fax: 219-736-2545

MEMBERS OF FIRM

Gordon E. Gouveia
Richard A. Miller

Lori D. Fisher
Mitchell A. Peters
Hilary R. Hall (Not admitted in IN; Legal Researcher)

Reference: NBD Ban, N.A.

For full biographical listings, see the Martindale-Hubbell Law Directory

*SOUTH BEND,** St. Joseph Co.

BARNES & THORNBURG (AV)

600 1st Source Bank Center, 100 North Michigan, 46601-1632
Telephone: 219-233-1171
FAX: 219-237-1125
URL: http://www.btlaw.com
Indianapolis, Indiana Office: 11 South Meridian Street, 46204.
Telephone: 317-236-1313.
FAX: 317-231-7433.
Fort Wayne, Indiana Office: Suite 600, One Summit Square, 46802.
Telephone: 219-423-9440.
FAX: 219-424-8316.
Elkhart, Indiana Office: 121 West Franklin Street, Suite 200, 46516.
Telephone: 219-293-0681.
FAX: 219-296-2535.
Chicago, Illinois Office: 2600 Chase Plaza, 10 South La Salle Street, 60603.
Telephone: 312-357-1313.
FAX: 312-759-5646.
Washington, D.C. Office: 1401 Eye Street, N.W., Suite 500, 20005.
Telephone: 202-289-1313.
FAX: 202-289-1330.

(See Next Column)

MEMBERS OF FIRM

Michael B. Watkins
Scott M. Keller
Michael D. Hardy

ASSOCIATES

Mark J. Adey
Adrianne L. Hoehner

Representative Clients: 1st Source Bank; AM General Corp.; Cadence Environmental Energy; Crowe, Chizek and Company L.L.P.; Gast Manufacturing Corporation; Memorial Hospital of South Bend; National Steel Corporation; University of Notre Dame; Whirlpool Corporation; Whiteford, Inc.

For Complete List of Firm Personnel, See General Section

For full biographical listings, see the Martindale-Hubbell Law Directory

DORAN • BLACKMOND LLP (AV)

1700 Valley American Bank Building, 211 W. Washington Street, 46601
Telephone: 219-288-1800
Fax: 219-236-4265

MEMBERS OF FIRM

M. Edward Doran (1895-1982)
John E. Doran
Don G. Blackmond

ASSOCIATES

Don Gregory Blackmond
Peter J. Van Dyke
Lynn M. Butcher

OF COUNSEL

A. Howard Williams

For full biographical listings, see the Martindale-Hubbell Law Directory

IOWA

*CEDAR RAPIDS,** Linn Co.

MOYER & BERGMAN, P.L.C. (AV)

2720 First Avenue, N.E., 52406-1943
Telephone: 319-366-7331
Telecopier: 319-366-3668
Mailing Address: P.O. Box 1943,
Email: M&B@moyerbergman.com

MEMBER OF FIRM

Eric W. Lam

Representative Clients: National Oats Co., a division of Curtice-Burns, Inc.; CRST, Inc.; SSangyong (U.S.A.), Inc.; Maquoketa State Bank; Postville State Bank; Ag Services of America, Inc.; American Family Insurance Group.

For full biographical listings, see the Martindale-Hubbell Law Directory

*COUNCIL BLUFFS,** Pottawattamie Co.

REILLY, PETERSEN & HANNAN, P.L.C. (AV)

215 South Main Street, P.O. Box 1016, 51502-1016
Telephone: 712-328-1575
Fax: 712-328-1562

C. R. Hannan
Michael G. Reilly
Deborah L. Petersen

Craig M. Dreismeier

References: Peoples National Bank of Council Bluffs.

For full biographical listings, see the Martindale-Hubbell Law Directory

*IOWA CITY,** Johnson Co.

JOHNSTON, POTTERFIELD & NATHANSON, P.C. (AV)

1902 Broadway, P.O. Box 3400, 52244
Telephone: 319-354-1712
Fax: 319-354-7265
URL: http://www.lawyers.com/johnstonlaw
Cedar Rapids Office: 129 First Avenue, S.W., P.O. Box 74210.
Telephone: 319-366-1000.
Fax: 319-366-6973.
Waterloo Office: 1506 LaPorte Road, P.O. Box 2787.
Telephone: 319-235-3000.
Fax: 319-235-2108.

Joseph C. Johnston
Amanda Potterfield
Henry E. Nathanson
Cathy L. Fitzmaurice
David Burbidge

OF COUNSEL

Carl J. Goetz, Jr.

For full biographical listings, see the Martindale-Hubbell Law Directory

KANSAS

*KANSAS CITY,** Wyandotte Co.

WONER, GLENN, REEDER & GIRARD, P.A.

(See Topeka)

*LAWRENCE,** Douglas Co.

WONER, GLENN, REEDER & GIRARD, P.A.

(See Topeka)

OVERLAND PARK, Johnson Co.

ERIC C. RAJALA (AV)

Metcalf Bank Building, Suite 341, College Boulevard at Quivira 11900 College Boulevard, 66210
Telephone: 913-339-9806
Telecopier: 913-339-6695
Email: erajala@compuserve.com

For full biographical listings, see the Martindale-Hubbell Law Directory

WONER, GLENN, REEDER & GIRARD, P.A.

(See Topeka)

*TOPEKA,** Shawnee Co.

FISHER, PATTERSON, SAYLER & SMITH, L.L.P. (AV)

3550 S.W. 5th Street, P.O. Box 949, 66601
Telephone: 785-232-7761
Fax: 785-232-6604
Email: fpss@cjnetworks.com
Overland Park, Kansas Office: 11050 Roe Avenue, Suite 210, 66211.
Telephone: 913-339-6757.
Fax: 913-339-6187.

MEMBERS OF FIRM

Donald Patterson
Edwin Dudley Smith (Resident, Overland Park Office)
Larry G. Pepperdine
James P. Nordstrom
Justice B. King
J. Steven Pigg
Steve R. Fabert
Ronald J. Laskowski
Michael K. Seck (Resident, Overland Park Office)
David P. Madden (Resident, Overland Park Office)
Steven K. Johnson
Kristine A. Larscheid

ASSOCIATES

Billy E. Newman
David R. Cooper
Kelly A. Feyh (Resident, Overland Park Office)
Jennifer R. Rose (Resident, Overland Park Office)

OF COUNSEL

David H. Fisher

RETIRED

Charles Keith Sayler (Retired)

Representative Clients: Gage Shopping Center, Inc.; Fireman's Fund-American Insurance Cos.; United States Fidelity and Guaranty Co.; The Procter & Gamble Company; Commercial Union Insurance Companies; National Casualty; The Hartford; Berkshire Hathaway Companies.

For full biographical listings, see the Martindale-Hubbell Law Directory

GOODELL, STRATTON, EDMONDS & PALMER, L.L.P. (AV)

515 South Kansas Avenue, 66603-3999
Telephone: 785-233-0593
Fax: 785-233-8870
Email: GSEP@CJNETWORKS.COM *URL:* http://www.cjnetworks.com/~gsep
Kansas City, Missouri Office: 10401 Holmes Road, Suite 280.
Telephone: 816-943-8577.

MEMBERS OF FIRM

Gerald L. Goodell
Wayne T. Stratton
Arthur E. Palmer
Charles R. Hay
John H. Stauffer, Jr.
N. Larry Bork

Representative Clients: Ford Motor Credit Company; Mazda Credit Corporation; Nebraska Student Loan Program; First National Bank, Wamego; Mercedes Credit Corporation; ECMC (Educational Credit Management Corporation; Southwestern Savings Association; Dennsion State Bank.

For Complete List of Firm Personnel, See General Section

For full biographical listings, see the Martindale-Hubbell Law Directory

WONER, GLENN, REEDER & GIRARD, P.A. (AV)

A Partnership of Professional Corporations
534 South Kansas Avenue Suite 330, 66603-3424
Telephone: 785-235-5330
Fax: 785-235-1615
URL: http://www.lawyers.com/wgr&glaw
Email: bwoner@wonerglenn.com *URL:* http://www.wonerglenn.com
Wichita, Kansas Office: 155 N. Market, Suite 708.
Telephone: 316-264-8220.
Fax: 316-264-3012.

David S. Fricke
Timothy H. Girard
Grant M. Glenn
Leon B. Graves
Patricia A. Reeder
R. Patrick Riordan
Bruce J. Woner

For full biographical listings, see the Martindale-Hubbell Law Directory

WRIGHT, HENSON, SOMERS, SEBELIUS, CLARK & BAKER, LLP (AV)

Commerce Bank Building, 100 Southeast Ninth Street, 2nd Floor, P.O. Box 3555, 66601-3555
Telephone: 785-232-2200
FAX: 785-232-3344
Email: wrighthenson@wrighthenson.com *URL:* http://www.wrighthenson.com

MEMBERS OF FIRM

Dale L. Somers
Bruce J. Clark
Anne Lamborn Baker

For Complete List of Firm Personnel, See General Section

For full biographical listings, see the Martindale-Hubbell Law Directory

*WICHITA,** Sedgwick Co.

FOULSTON & SIEFKIN L.L.P. (AV)

700 NationsBank Financial Center, 67202
Telephone: 316-267-6371
Facsimile: 316-267-6345
URL: http://www.foulston.com
Topeka, Kansas Office: 1515 NationsBank Tower, 534 Kansas Avenue, 66603.
Telephone: 785-233-3600.
Fax: 785-233-1610.
Dodge City, Kansas Office: 810 Frontview, P.O. Box 1147, 67801.
Telephone: 316-227-8126.
Fax: 316-227-8451.
Member: Lex Mundi, The World's Leading Association of Independent Law Firms.

MEMBERS OF FIRM

Terry C. Cupps
William R. Wood, II

For Complete List of Firm Personnel, See General Section

For full biographical listings, see the Martindale-Hubbell Law Directory

MORRIS, LAING, EVANS, BROCK & KENNEDY, CHARTERED (AV)

Fourth Floor, 200 West Douglas, 67202-3084
Telephone: 316-262-2671
Fax: 316-262-6226; 262-5991
Topeka, Kansas Office: 800 S.W. Jackson, Suite 914, 66612-2214.
Telephone: 913-232-2662.
Fax: 913-232-9983.

William B. Sorensen, Jr.
Robert E. Nugent
Richard F. Hayse (Resident, Topeka Office)

References: The Emprise Banks of Kansas; Mercantile Bank of Topeka; Southwest National Bank; Twin Lakes National Bank.

For Complete List of Firm Personnel, See General Section

For full biographical listings, see the Martindale-Hubbell Law Directory

KENTUCKY

*GLASGOW,** Barren Co.

GARMON & GOODMAN (AV)

139 North Public Square, P.O. Box 663, 42142-0663
Telephone: 270-651-8812
Telecopier: 270-651-8846

MEMBER OF FIRM

Charles A. Goodman III

Representative Clients: The New Farmers National Bank of Glasgow; South Central Bank of Barren County, Inc.; Taylor County Bank, Campbellsville, KY; Southern Deposit Bank, Russellville, KY.
References: The New Farmers National Bank of Glasgow, Glasgow, KY; South Central Bank of Barren County, Inc., Glasgow, KY.

(See Next Column)

GARMON & GOODMAN—*Continued*

For Complete List of Firm Personnel, See General Section

For full biographical listings, see the Martindale-Hubbell Law Directory

*LEXINGTON,** Fayette Co.

BUNCH & BROCK (AV)

271 West Short Street, Suite 805, P.O. Box 2086, 40594
Telephone: 606-254-5522
Fax: 606-233-1434

MEMBERS OF FIRM

W. Thomas Bunch
Dan D. Brock, Jr.
Gail M. Bunch
W. Thomas Bunch II
Matthew B. Bunch
Caryn L. Belobraidich

For full biographical listings, see the Martindale-Hubbell Law Directory

FOWLER, MEASLE & BELL, L.L.P. (AV)

Kincaid Towers, 300 West Vine Street, 6th Floor, 40507-1660
Telephone: 606-252-6700
Fax: 606-255-3735
Email: fmb@mis.net

MEMBERS OF FIRM

Taft A. McKinstry
John E. Hinkel, Jr.
Robert S. Ryan
Michael W. Troutman

ASSOCIATE

Cynthia J. Cutler

Representative Clients: Bank One, Lexington, N.A.; PNC Bank, Kentucky, Inc.; Citizens Union Bank of Shelbyville; National City Bank & Trust Co.; Fifth Third Leasing; Union Bank, CA.; Peoples Exchange Bank of Beattyville.

For full biographical listings, see the Martindale-Hubbell Law Directory

STOLL, KEENON & PARK, LLP (AV)

201 E. Main Street, Suite 1000, 40507-1380
Telephone: 606-231-3000
Telecopier: 606-253-1093; 606-253-1027
URL: http://www.skp.com
Frankfort, Kentucky Office: 307 Washington Street, 40601.
Telephone: 502-875-6220.
Telecopier: 502-875-6235.
Henderson, Kentucky Office: 201 C North Main Street, 42420-3103.
Telephone: 270-831-1900.
Telecopier: 270-827-4060.
Louisville, Kentucky Office: 400 West Market Street, Suite 2650, 40202-3377.
Telephone: 502-568-9100.
Telecopier: 502-568-5700.

MEMBERS OF FIRM

Harvie B. Wilkinson
Robert W. Kellerman
Gregory D. Pavey
Lea Pauley Goff
Laura Day DelCotto
William L. Montague, Jr.

ASSOCIATE

Richard B. Warne

Representative Clients: Bank One, Lexington, NA; Bank One, Kentucky, NA; Fifth Third Bank; Whitaker Bank Corporation of Kentucky.

For Complete List of Firm Personnel, See General Section

For full biographical listings, see the Martindale-Hubbell Law Directory

*LOUISVILLE,** Jefferson Co.

GOLDBERG & SIMPSON, P.S.C. (AV)

3000 National City Tower, 40202
Telephone: 502-589-4440
Telefax: 502-581-1344
Email: mail@gsatty.com *URL:* http://www.gsatty.com

Fred M. Goldberg
Jonathan D. Goldberg
Mitchell A. Charney
Steven A. Goodman
Stephen E. Smith
Mary Alice Maple
John J. McLaughlin
Charles H. Cassis
Christopher M. George
Emily L. Lawrence

Jan M. West
Sherry P. Porter
James Michael Wells
Stephanie Lynn Morgan-White
Michael F. Lawrence
Karen L. De Haan
George Hunt Rounsavall, Jr.
Stacey A. Huse

OF COUNSEL

Ronald V. Simpson
David A. Brill

Representative Clients: National City Bank; Liberty Mutual Insurance Co.; Jewish Hospital Healthcare Services, Inc.; Louisville & Jefferson County Board of Health; Providian Corp.

For full biographical listings, see the Martindale-Hubbell Law Directory

MAPOTHER & MAPOTHER (AV)

801 West Jefferson Street, 40202
Telephone: 502-587-5400
Fax: 502-587-5444
Email: mapother@mapother-atty.com *URL:* http://www.mapother-atty.com
Lexington, Kentucky Office: 100 East Vine Street, Suite 810.
Telephone: 606-253-0003.
Fax: 606-255-3961.
Jeffersonville, Indiana Office: 505 East Seventh Street.
Telephone: 812-288-5059.
Fax: 502-587-5444.
Cincinnati, Ohio Office: Kroger Building, Suite 2220, 1014 Vine Street.
Telephone: 513-381-4888.
Fax: 513-381-3117.
Huntington, West Virginia Office: Morris Building, Suite 701, 845 Fourth Avenue.
Telephone: 304-525-1185.
Fax: 304-529-3764.
Evansville, Indiana Office: 329 Main Street, Suite 602.
Telephone: 812-421-9108.
Fax: 812-421-9109.

MEMBERS OF FIRM

William R. Mapother
Thomas L. Canary, Jr.
Hollis L. Searcy
Charles M. Friedman

Roberta S. Dunlap (Resident, Evansville, Indiana Office)
Dean A. Langdon (Resident, Lexington, Kentucky Office)
Lee W. Grace
Brian E. Chapman (Resident, Cincinnati, Ohio Office)
T. Lawson McSwain, II
John D. Meyers (Resident, Lexington, Kentucky Office)
Lisa A. Herndon
Ronda C. Gunter (Resident, Huntington, West Virginia Office)
Steven B. Mulrooney
Dennis M. Ostrowski
Gerald O. Henderson, Jr. (Resident, Huntington, West Virginia Office)
Miles S. Apple
Joy B. Gilliam (Resident, Lexington, Kentucky Office)
Vincent A. Dimasi (Not admitted in KY; Resident, Cincinnati, Ohio Office)
Charlie W. Gordon

Representative Clients: Ford Motor Credit Co.; General Motors Acceptance Corp.; Associates Commercial Corp.; PNC Bank; The CIT Group/Sales Financing; NBD Bank; Fifth Third Bank; Nissan Motor Acceptance Corp.; First Merchants Acceptance Corp.; Chrysler Financial Corp.

For full biographical listings, see the Martindale-Hubbell Law Directory

MIDDLETON & REUTLINGER, P.S.C. (AV)

2500 Brown and Williamson Tower, 40202-3410
Telephone: 502-584-1135
Fax: 502-561-0442
URL: http://middreut.com
Jeffersonville, Indiana Office: 530 East Court Avenue, 47130.
Telephone: 812-282-1132.
Fax: 812-282-3188.

Charles G. Middleton, III
James R. Higgins, Jr.
Thomas W. Frentz

For Complete List of Firm Personnel, See General Section

For full biographical listings, see the Martindale-Hubbell Law Directory

MORGAN & POTTINGER, P.S.C. (AV)

601 West Main Street, 40202
Telephone: 502-589-2780
Telecopier: 502-585-3498
URL: http://www.morganandpottinger.com
Lexington, Kentucky Office: 133 West Short Street.
Telephone: 606-253-1900.
Telecopier: 606-255-2038.
New Albany, Indiana Office: 120 East Market Street.
Telephone: 812-948-0008.
Telecopier: 812-944-6215.

Patrick E. Morgan
John T. McGarvey
John A. Majors
Mark J. Sandlin
Scott T. Rickman (Resident, Lexington Office)
Hal D. Friedman

Garret B. Hannegan (Resident, New Albany, Indiana Office)
Diane E. Bluhm (Not admitted in KY)
Laura Kincheloe (Resident, Lexington Office)
Drayer L. Bott

SENIOR COUNSEL

David C. Pottinger

For Complete List of Firm Personnel, See General Section

For full biographical listings, see the Martindale-Hubbell Law Directory

Louisville—Continued

ROTH FOLEY BRYANT & COOPER, PLLC (AV)

First Trust Centre, Suite 300S, 200 South Fifth Street, 40202-3236
Telephone: 502-569-7550
Fax: 502-540-0123
Email: RFBC.com

Irvin D. Foley — Lisa Koch Bryant
David M. Roth — K. Gail Russell
David H. Cooper — Christian L. Juckett

OF COUNSEL

James E. Fahey — David W. Gray

Representative Clients: Farm Credit Services of Mid-America; Bank One, Kentucky, NA; Huntington Acceptance Co.; Huntington National Bank; Great Financial Bank; People's State Bank; Commonwealth Bank & Trust Co.; First Citizen's Bank of Hardin Co.

For full biographical listings, see the Martindale-Hubbell Law Directory

LOUISIANA

*BATON ROUGE,** East Baton Rouge Parish

KIZER, HOOD & MORGAN, L.L.P. (AV)

A Partnership including a Professional Corporation
2111 Quail Run Drive, 70808
Telephone: 225-761-0001
Fax: 225-761-0731
URL: http://www.khmllp.com

Roland C. Kizer (1899-1988) — Ralph E. Hood
Roland C. Kizer, Jr., (Ltd., A Law Corporation) — J. Donald Morgan
Walter N. O'Roark, III
Stacy G. Butler

Blake E. Rizzo

Representative Clients: Hibernia National Bank; Bank One, Louisiana, N.A.; The Dime Savings Bank of New York, FSB; G.E. Capital Asset Management Corp.; Bankers Systems, Inc.; United Companies Lending Corporation; Rabenhorst Life Insurance Co.; General Equipment, Inc. d/b/a Scott General; Old South Builders, Inc.; P.P.R., Inc.

For full biographical listings, see the Martindale-Hubbell Law Directory

SCHANEVILLE & BARINGER, L.L.C. (AV)

918 Government Street, 70802
Telephone: 225-383-9953
Fax: 225-387-3198
Email: DDSCHANE@AOL.COM

Dan D. Schaneville — Donald M. Meltzer
Dale R. Baringer — John C. Hopewell, III

Wendy E. Barberousse

OF COUNSEL

David O. Mooney

For full biographical listings, see the Martindale-Hubbell Law Directory

SHOCKEY & ZIOBER, A PROFESSIONAL LAW CORPORATION (AV)

5551 Corporate Boulevard, Suite 3-A, P.O. Box 80286, 70898-0286
Telephone: 225-929-8929
Telecopier: 225-928-7694

John David Ziober

For full biographical listings, see the Martindale-Hubbell Law Directory

*MONROE,** Ouachita Parish

THOMPSON, SPARKS, DEAN & MORRIS (AV)

A Partnership including a Professional Corporation
1401 Royal Street, P.O. Box 2867, 71207
Telephone: 318-388-1440
Fax: 318-322-0887

MEMBERS OF FIRM

M. C. Thompson (1885-1970) — George B. Dean, Jr., (P.C.)
James D. Sparks (1910-1987) — Wood T. Sparks
John C. Morris, III

ASSOCIATE

Jennifer Allen Riley

Representative Clients: South Central Bell Telephone Co.; Greater Ouachita Water Company; PHH Homequity Corp.; Commonwealth Relocation Services, Inc.; Remax, Monroe; Bell South Advertising & Publishing Corp.; Premier Mortgage Corp.; Countrywide Funding Corp.

(See Next Column)

Approved Attorneys for: BankOne; Federal Land Bank.

For full biographical listings, see the Martindale-Hubbell Law Directory

*NEW ORLEANS,** Orleans Parish

HELLER, DRAPER, HAYDEN & HORN, L.L.C. (AV)

Suite 2500, Poydras Center, 650 Poydras Street, 70130-6103
Telephone: 504-568-1888; 504-581-9595
Facsimile: 504-522-0949; 504-525-3761

Isaac S. Heller (1893-1967)

OF COUNSEL

Fred Bronfin — Sylvan J. Steinberg

MEMBERS OF FIRM

Edward M. Heller — Constant G. Marquer, III
Bernard H. Berins — Deborah Weisler Fallis
Douglas S. Draper — Warren Horn
Jan Marie Hayden — Robyn Jeana Spalter

Leslie A. Collins — Drew R. Ballina
Tristan E. Manthey

For full biographical listings, see the Martindale-Hubbell Law Directory

LANDWEHR & HOF (AV)

225 Baronne Street Suite 2116, 70112
Telephone: 504-561-8086

MEMBERS OF FIRM

Merrill T. Landwehr — Ronald J. Hof
Darryl T. Landwehr

Reference: Bank of Louisiana, New Orleans, La.

For full biographical listings, see the Martindale-Hubbell Law Directory

MCGLINCHEY STAFFORD (AV)

A Professional Limited Liability Company
643 Magazine Street, 70130-3477
Telephone: 504-586-1200
Fax: 504-596-2800
TDD: (504) 596-2728
Telex: 584327
Cable Address: "MACSTAC"
Mailing Address: P.O. Box 60643, New Orleans, Louisiana, 70160-0643
Email: @mcglinchey.com *URL:* http://www.mcglinchey.com
Dallas, Texas Office: 2777 Stemmons Freeway, Suite 925, 75207-2401.
Telephone: 214-860-9700.
Fax: 214-860-9750.
Houston, Texas Office: 2727 Allen Parkway, Suite 1900, 77019.
Telephone: 713-520-1900.
Fax: 713-520-1025.
Baton Rouge, Louisiana Office: Ninth Floor, One American Place, 70825-0001.
Telephone: 504-383-9000.
Fax: 504-343-3076.
Jackson, Mississippi Office: Suite 1200, SkyTel Centre, 200 South Lamar Street, 39201.
Telephone: 601-960-8400.
Fax: 601-960-8406.
Lake Providence, Louisiana Office: 405 Morgan Street, 71254-2691.
Telephone: 318-559-1200.
Fax: 318-559-0609.
Monroe, Louisiana Office: Dean ONB Tower, 130 Desiard Street, Suite 807, 71201.
Telephone: 318-651-0807.
Fax: 318-651-0809.

MEMBERS OF FIRM

B. Franklin Martin, III, (P.C.) — Rudy J. Cerone
Richard A. Aguilar

ASSOCIATE

David Ball

ASSOCIATE

Jon Ann H. Giblin (Resident, Baton Rouge Office)

For full biographical listings, see the Martindale-Hubbell Law Directory

*SHREVEPORT,** Caddo Parish

BLANCHARD, WALKER, O'QUIN & ROBERTS, A PROFESSIONAL LAW CORPORATION (AV)

Fourteenth Floor, Premier Bank Tower, 400 Texas Street, P.O. Drawer 1126, 71101
Telephone: 318-221-6858
Fax: 318-227-2967
Email: BWOR@BWOR.com
Bossier City, Louisiana Office: 2285 Benton Road, Suite B-201.
Telephone: 318-742-9255.
Fax: 318-742-9210.

(See Next Column)

BLANCHARD, WALKER, O'QUIN & ROBERTS A PROFESSIONAL LAW CORPORATION—*Continued*

Robert W. Johnson
Edward Keith Carter

For Complete List of Firm Personnel, See General Section

For full biographical listings, see the Martindale-Hubbell Law Directory

SIMON, FITZGERALD, COOKE, REED & WELCH (AV)

Suite 200, 4700 Line Avenue, 71106
Telephone: 318-868-2600
Telecopier: 318-868-8966

MEMBERS OF FIRM

Fred Simon (1904-1993)
Archie M. Simon (1909-1997)
Thomas P. Fitzgerald (1914-1993)
Paul M. Cooke
Chatham H. Reed
Keith M. Welch
Kevin R. Molloy

A list of Representative Clients will be furnished upon request.

For full biographical listings, see the Martindale-Hubbell Law Directory

MAINE

*AUGUSTA,** Kennebec Co.

PIERCE ATWOOD (AV)

77 Winthrop Street, 04330
Telephone: 207-622-6311
Fax: 207-623-9367
Email: info@PierceAtwood.com *URL:* http://www.pierceatwood.com
Portland, Maine Office: One Monument Square.
Telephone: 207-791-1100.
Fax: 207-791-1350.
Newburyport, Massachusetts Office: 6 Harris Street.
Telephone: 978-465-9599.
Fax: 978-465-9945.

MEMBER OF FIRM

Warren E. Winslow, Jr.

For Complete List of Firm Personnel, See General Section

For full biographical listings, see the Martindale-Hubbell Law Directory

*BANGOR,** Penobscot Co.

GROSS, MINSKY, MOGUL & SINGAL, P.A. (AV)

Key Plaza, 23 Water Street, P.O. Box 917, 04402-0917
Telephone: 207-942-4644; 800-274-7124
Telecopier: 207-942-3699
Email: law@gmms.com

Edward I. Gross (1912-1999)
Jules L. Mogul (1930-1994)
George Z. Singal
Louis H. Kornreich
George C. Schelling
Edward W. Gould
Steven J. Mogul
James R. Wholly
Daniel A. Pileggi
Philip K. Clarke

Wayne P. Libhart (Retired)
Sandra L. Rothera
James S. Nixon

OF COUNSEL

Norman Minsky

Representative Client: Dahl Chase Pathology Associates.
Local Counsel for: The St. Paul Insurance Cos.; Aetna Life & Casualty Co.; Imperial Casualty & Indemnity Co.

For full biographical listings, see the Martindale-Hubbell Law Directory

*PORTLAND,** Cumberland Co.

MARCUS, GRYGIEL & CLEGG, P.A. (AV)

100 Middle Street, East Tower, 04101-4102
Telephone: 207-828-8000
Fax: 207-773-3210
Email: firm@mgc-law.com

George J. Marcus
Jennie L. Clegg
Marilyn E. Mistretta
Lee H. Bals

Sean P. Joyce
Barbara G. Shaw
Michael J. Gartland
Regan M. Hornney

OF COUNSEL

Stephen G. Grygiel
Andrew Jeffrey Zulieve

For full biographical listings, see the Martindale-Hubbell Law Directory

PERKINS, OLSON & PRATT, P.A. (AV)

30 Milk Street, 04112
Telephone: 207-871-7159
Fax: 207-871-0521
Email: perkinspa@aol.com *URL:* http://www.lawyers.com/perkins&perkins

Donald W. Perkins
David J. Perkins
Richard P. Olson
Neal F. Pratt

For full biographical listings, see the Martindale-Hubbell Law Directory

PIERCE ATWOOD (AV)

One Monument Square, 04101
Telephone: 207-791-1100
Fax: 207-791-1350
Email: info@PierceAtwood.com *URL:* http://www.pierceatwood.com
Augusta, Maine Office: 77 Winthrop Street.
Telephone: 207-622-6311.
Fax: 207-623-9367.
Newburyport, Massachusetts Office: 6 Harris Street.
Telephone: 978-465-9599.
Fax: 978-465-9945.

MEMBER OF FIRM

Jacob A. Manheimer

ASSOCIATE

Keith J. Cunningham

For Complete List of Firm Personnel, See General Section

For full biographical listings, see the Martindale-Hubbell Law Directory

PRETI, FLAHERTY, BELIVEAU, PACHIOS & HALEY, LLC (AV)

One City Center, P.O. Box 9546, 04112-9546
Telephone: 207-791-3000
Telecopier: 207-791-3111
Email: admin@preti.com *URL:* http://www.preti.com
Augusta, Maine Office: 45 Memorial Circle, P.O. Box 1058, 04332-1058.
Telephone: 207-623-5300.
Telefax: 207-623-2914.
Bath, Maine Office: Thirty Front Street, P.O. Box 665, 04530-0665.
Telephone: 207-443-5576.
Telefax: 207-443-6665.

MEMBERS OF FIRM

Harold C. Pachios
Leonard M. Gulino
Estelle A. Lavoie
Michael Kaplan
John P. McVeigh

Representative Clients: KeyBank National Assn.; Meadowledge Associates; Southern Maine Medical Center; Colonial Supply Corp.; P.H. Chadbourne & Co.; Northern Maine General Hospital.

For Complete List of Firm Personnel, See General Section

For full biographical listings, see the Martindale-Hubbell Law Directory

TROUBH, HEISLER & PIAMPIANO, P.C. (AV)

511 Congress Street, P.O. Box 9711, 04104-5011
Telephone: 207-780-6789
Fax: 207-774-2339
Email: info@thplaw.com

William B. Troubh
Edwin A. Heisler
Robert J. Piampiano
Kevin M. Gillis
Michael P. Boyd
Thomas E. Getchell
Michael Richards
William K. McKinley
Daniel F. Gilligan
Paul S. Bulger
John G. Richardson

Daniel R. Felkel
Ann Brandt
John P. Flynn, III

For full biographical listings, see the Martindale-Hubbell Law Directory

VERRILL & DANA, LLP (AV)

One Portland Square, P.O. Box 586, 04112-0586
Telephone: 207-774-4000
Fax: 207-774-7499
Email: advice@verdan.com *URL:* http://www.verdan.com
Augusta, Maine Office: 45 Memorial Circle, P.O. Box 957.
Telephone: 207-623-3889.
Fax: 207-622-3117.
Kennebunk, Maine Office: 403-404 Lafayette Center, P.O. Box 147.
Telephone: 207-985-7193.
Fax: 207-985-3957.
Washington, D.C. Office: 400 North Capitol Street, Suite 585.
Telephone: 202-624-9733.
Fax: 202-393-5218.

MEMBER OF FIRM

Roger A. Clement, Jr.

(See Next Column)

VERRILL & DANA LLP, *Portland—Continued*

ASSOCIATE

Jonathan R. Doolittle

Counsel for: ASCAP; Bowdoin College; Fleet Bank; Hannaford Bros. Co.; Maine Blue Cross and Blue Shield; Maine Public Service Co.; Peoples Heritage Bank; Portland Water District.

For Complete List of Firm Personnel, See General Section

For full biographical listings, see the Martindale-Hubbell Law Directory

MARYLAND

*BALTIMORE,** (Independent City)

BALLARD SPAHR ANDREWS & INGERSOLL, LLP (AV)

300 East Lombard Street, 19th Floor, 21202-3268
Telephone: 410-528-5600
Fax: 410-528-5650
URL: http://www.ballardspahr.com
Philadelphia, Pennsylvania Office: 1735 Market Street, 51st Floor.
Telephone: 215-665-8500.
Fax: 215-864-8999.
Voorhees, New Jersey Office: Suite 100, 1101 Laurel Oak Drive.
Telephone: 856-627-8555.
Fax: 856-627-1153.
Denver, Colorado Office: Seventeenth Street Plaza Building, Suite 2300, 1225 17th Street.
Telephone: 303-292-2400.
Fax: 303-296-3956.
Salt Lake City, Utah Office: One Utah Center, Suite 1200, 201 South Main Street.
Telephone: 801-531-3000.
Fax: 801-531-3001.
Washington, D.C. Office: Suite 1000 South, 601 13th Street, N.W.
Telephone: 202-661-2200.
Fax: 202-661-2299.
Camden, New Jersey Office: 800 Hudson Square, 5th Floor.
Telephone: 609-541-5577.
Fax: 609-541-8272.

Nancy V. Alquist
Thomas A. Hauser

OF COUNSEL

Arthur F. Fergenson

For full biographical listings, see the Martindale-Hubbell Law Directory

LAW OFFICE OF EDWARD L. BLANTON, JR., P.A. (AV)

404 Allegheny Avenue, 21204
Telephone: 410-296-8160
Fax: 410-821-8113

Peter T. McDowell

For full biographical listings, see the Martindale-Hubbell Law Directory

ROBERT N. GROSSBART, P.A. (AV)

Suite 1902, Blaustein Building, One North Charles Street, 21201
Telephone: 410-837-0590; In MD: 1-800-286-0730
Fax: 410-837-0085
URL: http://www.lawyers.com/rngrossbart

Robert Neil Grossbart

David A. Rosenberg
David N. Portney

For full biographical listings, see the Martindale-Hubbell Law Directory

MEHLMAN & GREENBLATT, LLC (AV)

1838 Greene Tree Road, Suite 360, 21208
Telephone: 410-486-4790
Fax: 410-486-4360
URL: http://www.lawyers.com/mehlman&greenblatt

Gerson B. Mehlman
Gary R. Greenblatt
Frederic C. Heyman
Francis X. Leary
Constance M. Hare

For full biographical listings, see the Martindale-Hubbell Law Directory

VENABLE ATTORNEYS AT LAW VENABLE, BAETJER AND HOWARD, LLP (AV)

A Partnership including Professional Corporations
1800 Mercantile Bank & Trust Building, 2 Hopkins Plaza, 21201
Telephone: 410-244-7400
Fax: 410-244-7742
URL: http://www.venable.com
Washington, D.C. Office: Venable, Baetjer, Howard & Civiletti LLP, Suite 1000, 1201 New York Avenue, N.W.
Telephone: 202-962-4800.
Fax: 202-962-8300.
McLean, Virginia Office: Suite 400, 2010 Corporate Ridge.
Telephone: 703-760-1600.
Fax: 703-821-8949.
Rockville, Maryland Office: Suite 500, One Church Street, P. O. Box 1906.
Telephone: 301-217-5600.
Fax: 301-217-5617.
Towson, Maryland Office: 210 Allegheny Avenue, P. O. Box 5517.
Telephone: 410-494-6200.
Fax: 410-821-0147.

MEMBERS OF FIRM

Joe A. Shull (Resident, Washington, D.C. Office)
Kenneth C. Bass, III (Not admitted in MD; Washington, D.C. and McLean, Virginia Offices)
Paul T. Glasgow (Resident, Rockville, Maryland Office)
Joseph C. Wich, Jr. (Resident, Towson, Maryland Office)
Richard L. Wasserman (P.C.)
George F. Pappas (Also at Washington, D.C. Office)
Christopher R. Mellott
David Eugene Rice
John A. Roberts (Also at Rockville, Maryland Office)
Gregory A. Cross

ASSOCIATE

Lisa Bittle Tancredi

For Complete List of Firm Personnel, See General Section

For full biographical listings, see the Martindale-Hubbell Law Directory

JAMES R. WOOTON, P.A. (AV)

606 Baltimore Avenue, Suite 202, 21204
Telephone: 410-321-7900
Fax: 410-321-7760
URL: http://www.lawyers.com/jwooton

James R. Wooton

For full biographical listings, see the Martindale-Hubbell Law Directory

WRIGHT, CONSTABLE & SKEEN, LLP (AV)

One Charles Center, 16th Floor, 100 N. Charles Street, 21201
Telephone: 410-659-1300
Telex: 710 234-2383 CALDAS
Fax: 410-659-1350

MEMBERS OF FIRM

Wm. Pepper Constable (1882-1976)
John D. Wright (1903-1976)
George W. Constable (Retired)
Read A. McCaffrey (1913-1995)
William A. Skeen (Retired)
John Brentnall Powell, Jr.
Michael J. Abromaitis
Monte Fried
James W. Constable
David W. Skeen
James D. Skeen
Douglas G. Worrall
Kenneth F. Davies
Stephen F. White
Brian S. Goodman
Frederick L. Kobb
Paul F. Evelius
Lois A. Fenner McBride
Charles J. Morton, Jr.

ASSOCIATES

Mary Alice Smolarek
Catherine H. Bellinger
Carol J. Glover
Tracey D. King
David J. Shuster
Howard S. Stevens

COUNSEL

Francis N. Iglehart, Jr.
P. McEvoy Cromwell
C. Gordon Haines

Representative Clients: Conowingo Power Co.; Weyerhaeuser Co.; Commercial Credit Corp.; Noxell Corp.; Consolidated Rail Corp.; Murray Corp.; Atlantic Mutual Insurance Co.; Sea Containers, Ltd.; Great Atlantic & Pacific Tea Co.; Tyson Foods, Inc.

For full biographical listings, see the Martindale-Hubbell Law Directory

RIVERDALE, Prince Georges Co.

MEYERS, BILLINGSLEY, RODBELL & ROSENBAUM, P.A. (AV)

Suite 400 Berkshire Building, 6801 Kenilworth Avenue, 20737-1385
Telephone: 301-699-5800
Fax: 301-779-5746
Email: mbrrlaw@martindalemail.com
Annapolis, Maryland Office: 95 Cathedral Street, Suite 100, 21401.
Telephone: 410-267-6670.
Fax: 410-267-8222.

(See Next Column)

MEYERS, BILLINGSLEY, RODBELL & ROSENBAUM P.A.—*Continued*

William V. Meyers
Lance W. Billingsley
Paul B. Rodbell
Robert H. Rosenbaum
Russell E. Warfel
Linda C. Carter
Joseph B. Chazen
Michele LaRocca
Paul A. Turkheimer
David A. Carter

Frederick Stichnoth
Bud Stephen Tayman
M. Andree Green
Gina Marie Smith
Mindy Sue Kursban
M. Evan Meyers
Douglas C. Meister
David J. Martin

Reference: First National Bank of Maryland.

For full biographical listings, see the Martindale-Hubbell Law Directory

*ROCKVILLE,** Montgomery Co.

BARKLEY & KENNEDY, CHARTERED (AV)

Suite 1407, 51 Monroe Street, 20850
Telephone: 301-251-6600
FAX: 301-762-2606
Email: barkenlaw@erols.com *URL:* http://www.lawyers.com/barkenlaw

Brian E. Barkley
Daniel M. Kennedy, III

For full biographical listings, see the Martindale-Hubbell Law Directory

GARZA, REGAN & ROSENBLATT, P.C. (AV)

Eighteenth Floor One Metro Square 51 Monroe Street, 20850
Telephone: 301-340-8200
Fax: 301-294-6159
URL: http://www.garzanet.com
Greenbelt, Maryland Office: 6411 Ivy Lane, Suite 116.

John R. Garza
Lawrence F. Regan, Jr.
Richard B. Rosenblatt

Benjamin M. Soto
Jonathan P. Morgan
Thomas T. Andrews, Jr.
Linda M. Dorney
Edward John Kowalski
Javier M. Arroyo
Michelle R. Curtis
Dina Cannariato Johnson

Representative Clients: Capital Bank; F & M Bank Allegiance; Mego Mortgage; Nova Mortgage.

For full biographical listings, see the Martindale-Hubbell Law Directory

STEIN, SPERLING, BENNETT, DE JONG, DRISCOLL, GREENFEIG & METRO, P.C. (AV)

25 West Middle Lane, 20850-2204
Telephone: 301-340-2020; 800-435-5230
Telecopier: 301-340-8217
Email: lawfirm@steinsperling.com
Falls Church, Virginia Office: 6245 Leesburg Pike, Suite 140, 22044.
Telephone: 703-237-0500.
Telecopier: 703-534-2899.

OF COUNSEL
Alan S. Kerxton

For Complete List of Firm Personnel, See General Section

For full biographical listings, see the Martindale-Hubbell Law Directory

SILVER SPRING, Montgomery Co.

COGGINS, HARMAN & HEWITT (AV)

A Partnership of Professional Corporations
8905 Fairview Road, Suite 600, 20910
Telephone: 301-587-2880
Facsimile: 301-495-4990
Email: CHHlaw587@aol.com
Washington, D.C. Office: Suite 330, G Street Lobby, 655 15th Street, N.W.
Falls Church, Virginia Office: 254 North Washington Street.

William N. Coggins
John H. Harman
William E. Hewitt
John F. Davis

OF COUNSEL
Dale E. Duncan (Not admitted in MD)

For full biographical listings, see the Martindale-Hubbell Law Directory

LINOWES AND BLOCHER LLP (AV)

Suite 1000, 1010 Wayne Avenue, 20910-5600
Telephone: 301-588-8580
Telecopier: 301-495-9044
TTY/TDD: 301-588-3380
Email: inbox@linowes-law.com *URL:* http://www.linowes-law.com
Washington, D.C. Office: Suite 302, 1150 17th Street, N.W.
Telephone: 202-293-8510.
Telecopier: 202-293-8513.

(See Next Column)

Greenbelt, Maryland Office: Suite 202, 6411 Ivy Lane.
Telephone: 301-982-3382.
Telecopier: 301-982-0595.
Annapolis, Maryland Office: 145 Main Street.
Telephone: 410-268-0881.
Telecopier: 301-261-2603.
Frederick, Maryland Office: 228 West Patrick Street.
Telephone: 301-695-0244.
Telecopier: 301-663-6656.
Columbia, Maryland Office: Suite B215, 10015 Old Columbia Road.
Telephone: 410-312-5457.
Fax: 410-290-5285.

MEMBERS OF FIRM
Bradford F. Englander
Paul-Michael Sweeney
James A. Vidmar, Jr.

ASSOCIATE
Joel W. Ruderman

For Complete List of Firm Personnel, See General Section

For full biographical listings, see the Martindale-Hubbell Law Directory

MASSACHUSETTS

*BOSTON,** Suffolk Co.

COHN & KELAKOS LLP (AV)

101 Arch Street, 02110
Telephone: 617-951-2505
Telecopier: 617-951-0679
URL: http://www.lawyers.com/cklaw

MEMBERS OF FIRM
Daniel C. Cohn
George M. Kelakos
A. Davis Whitesell

For full biographical listings, see the Martindale-Hubbell Law Directory

CRAIG AND MACAULEY, PROFESSIONAL CORPORATION (AV)

Federal Reserve Plaza, 600 Atlantic Avenue, 02210-2211
Telephone: 617-367-9500
Telecopier: 617-742-1788; 617-248-0886
URL: http://prospex.com/craig-macauley/

William F. Macauley
Stephen Wald
William R. Moorman, Jr.
Martin P. Desmery
Christopher J. Panos

For Complete List of Firm Personnel, See General Section

For full biographical listings, see the Martindale-Hubbell Law Directory

DANIELS LAW OFFICES, P.C. (AV)

One Center Plaza, 02108-1801
Telephone: 617-227-7300
Facsimile: 617-227-9643
Email: dlopc.com *URL:* http://www.dlopc.com

Richard S. Daniels, Jr.

Peter Daukszewicz
Karen J. Wisniowski
Kenneth W. Luke
Lynn M. Flury

For full biographical listings, see the Martindale-Hubbell Law Directory

HANIFY & KING, PROFESSIONAL CORPORATION (AV)

One Federal Street, 02110-2007
Telephone: 617-423-0400
Telefax: 617-423-0498
URL: http://www.hanify.com

James Coyne King
John D. Hanify
Harold B. Murphy
David Lee Evans
Daniel J. Lyne
Donald F. Farrell, Jr.
Barbara W. Pfirrman
Gerard P. Richer
Timothy P. O'Neill
Terence P. McCourt

Jeffrey J. Upton
Michael R. Perry
Kathleen E. Cross
Robert E. Richards, Jr.
Joseph F. Cortellini
Andrew G. Lizotte
Donald Ethan Jeffery
Karen A. Whitley
Deena F. Christelis
Robyn J. Bartlett
Owen P. Kane
Sharon H. Patton
John C. McDonald
C. Alexander Hahn
Laurie J. Hurtt
Katherine T. Land
Brian P. McDonough
Lori A. Donovan
Brian R. Marinelli

For full biographical listings, see the Martindale-Hubbell Law Directory

Boston—Continued

HINCKLEY, ALLEN & SNYDER LLP (AV)

28 State Street, 30th Floor, 02109-1775
Telephone: 617-345-9000
Email: firm@haslaw.com *URL:* http://www.haslaw.com
Providence, Rhode Island Office: 1500 Fleet Center.
Telephone: 401-274-2000.
Fax: 401-277-9600. URL: http://www.hawlaw.com.

MEMBERS OF FIRM

Paula K. Andrews
Jonathan Bell
Paul Bork
Stephen J. Carlotti (Not admitted in MA)
David Barry Connolly
Joseph P. Curran (Not admitted in MA)
Michael P. DeFanti
Malcolm Farmer, III
Hugh J. Gorman, III
William R. Grimm
Paul A. Hedstrom
Joel Lewin
Sandra Matrone Mack (Not admitted in MA)
Matthew T. Marcello, III (Not admitted in MA)
Frederick P. McClure
Elizabeth Murdock Myers
Paul F. O'Donnell, III
H. Peter Olsen (Not admitted in MA)
James O. Reavis
Robert F. Sylvia

ASSOCIATES

Mark Bianchi
Alyssa V. Boss
Andrew D. Cummings
June E. Daniel (Not admitted in MA)
Gloria Maria Gutierrez

For Complete List of Firm Personnel, See General Section

For full biographical listings, see the Martindale-Hubbell Law Directory

LOONEY & GROSSMAN LLP (AV)

101 Arch Street, 02110-1112
Telephone: 617-951-2800
Fax: 617-951-2819
URL: http://www.lgllp.com

Stewart F. Grossman (P.C.)
Richard J. Grahn
Bertram E. Snyder
Robert Cushman Barber
Joseph H. Matzkin
Wesley S. Chused
Melvin S. Hoffman

SENIOR COUNSEL

William F. Looney, Jr.

OF COUNSEL

Sherman H. Starr, Jr.
Elizabeth M. Adler
Maria Galvagna Mesinger

ASSOCIATES

Adam J. Ruttenberg
Pamela A. Harbeson
Mary E. Corbett
Benjamin D. Stevenson
Edward V. Colbert, III

For full biographical listings, see the Martindale-Hubbell Law Directory

PALMER & DODGE LLP (AV)

One Beacon Street, 02108
Telephone: 617-573-0100
Facsimile: 617-227-4420
URL: http://www.palmerdodge.com

MEMBERS OF FIRM

Jeanne P. Darcey
Richard Hiersteiner
Thomas M. Spera
George Ticknor
John L. Whitlock

For Complete List of Firm Personnel, See General Section

For full biographical listings, see the Martindale-Hubbell Law Directory

ROACH & CARPENTER, P.C. (AV)

24 School Street, 02108-5513
Telephone: 617-720-1800
Telefax: 617-720-0720
Email: lawyer@rc-law.com

Christine M. Roach
M. Ellen Carpenter
Alison L. Berman
Eric A. Howard

OF COUNSEL

Scott P. Lopez

For full biographical listings, see the Martindale-Hubbell Law Directory

ROCHE, CARENS & DEGIACOMO, P.C. (AV)

99 High Street, 02110
Telephone: 617-457-4000
Facsimile: 617-482-3868
Email: firm@rcdpc.com *URL:* http://www.rcdpc.com
Woburn, Massachusetts Office: 600 Unicorn Park Drive.
Telephone: 781-933-5505.

Mark G. DeGiacomo
Thomas S. Vangel

(See Next Column)

Jacqueline F. Walsh

For Complete List of Firm Personnel, See General Section

For full biographical listings, see the Martindale-Hubbell Law Directory

*SPRINGFIELD,** Hampden Co.

KAMBERG, BERMAN, P.C. (AV)

One Financial Plaza, 1350 Main Street, 01103-1628
Telephone: 413-781-1300
Facsimile: 413-732-0860
ABA/net: KAMBERGB
Email: kamberg@kamberg.com *URL:* http://www.kamberg.com

Abraham Kamberg (1895-1981)
Eugene B. Berman
Kerry David Strayer

References: Fleet Bank of Massachusetts, N.A.; Bank Boston/Springfield.

For full biographical listings, see the Martindale-Hubbell Law Directory

*WORCESTER,** Worcester Co.

SEDER & CHANDLER (AV)

A Partnership including a Professional Corporation
Established 1918
Burnside Building, 339 Main Street, 01608
Telephone: 508-757-7721
Telecopiers: 508-798-1863; 508-831-0955

MEMBERS OF FIRM

Samuel Seder (1918-1964)
Harold Seder (1934-1988)
Burton Chandler
J. Robert Seder
Darragh K. Kasakoff
Marvin S. Silver, P.C.
Robert S. Adler
Kevin C. McGee
Kurt L. Binder

ASSOCIATES

Paul J. O'Riordan
Jeffrey P. Greenberg
Todd Rodman

OF COUNSEL

Saul A. Seder
Gerald E. Norman
Philip C. Lombardo, Jr.

Reference: First National Bank of Boston; Safety Fund National Bank; Fleet National Bank.

For full biographical listings, see the Martindale-Hubbell Law Directory

MICHIGAN

BATTLE CREEK, Calhoun Co.

KREIS, ENDERLE, CALLANDER & HUDGINS, A PROFESSIONAL CORPORATION (AV)

One West Michigan Avenue, 49017
Telephone: 616-966-3000
Facsimile: 616-966-3022
Email: kech@kech.com *URL:* http://www.kech.com
Kalamazoo, Michigan Office: One Moorsbridge, P.O. Box 4010, 49003-4010.
Telephone: 616-324-3000.
Fax: 616-324-3010.

Russell A. Kreis (Resident, Kalamazoo Office)
Robert B. Borsos (Resident, Kalamazoo Office)
Thomas G. King (Resident, Kalamazoo Office)

For Complete List of Firm Personnel, See General Section

For full biographical listings, see the Martindale-Hubbell Law Directory

*BAY CITY,** Bay Co.

BRAUN KENDRICK FINKBEINER PLC (AV)

201 Phoenix Building, P.O. Box 2039, 48708
Telephone: 517-895-8505
Telecopier: 517-895-8437
Email: ALBFIE@BKF-LAW.COM *URL:* http://www.bkf-law.com
Saginaw, Michigan Office: 101 N. Washington, Suite 812. 8th Floor Second National Bank Building.
Telephone: 517-753-3461.
Telecopier: 517-753-3951.
Saginaw Township, Michigan Office: 5800 Gratiot Road, Suite 107, P.O. Box 5169.
Telephone: 517-799-8692.
Fax: 517-799-4666.

(See Next Column)

BRAUN KENDRICK FINKBEINER PLC—*Continued*

Ann Arbor, Michigan Office: First National Building. 201 S. Main, Suite 700.
Telephone: 313-995-4100.
Telecopier: 313-995-4798.
Mt. Pleasant, Michigan Office: 805 North Brown.
Telephone: 517-775-7404.
Telecopier: 517-775-3764.

Ralph J. Isackson
Daniel S. Opperman

Representative Clients: Bay Health Systems; Catholic Federal Credit Union; City of Saginaw; City of Vassar; City of Zilwaukee; Corporate Service; Cox Cable.

For Complete List of Firm Personnel, See General Section

For full biographical listings, see the Martindale-Hubbell Law Directory

BIRMINGHAM, Oakland Co.

HYMAN LIPPITT, P.C. (AV)

185 Oakland Avenue, Suite 300, 48009
Telephone: 248-646-8292
Facsimile: 248-646-8375
Email: hymalipp@tir.com

J. Leonard Hyman
Norman L. Lippitt
Douglas A. Hyman
Brian D. O'Keefe
H. Joel Newman
Nazli G. Sater
Kenneth F. Neuman
Terry S. Givens
Paul J. Fischer
John A. Sellers
Robert H. Lippitt
Roger L. Myers
Sally A. Rutledge
Joseph Pia
John P. Gonway
Leif K. Anderson
Jennifer S. Gold
Julie Lyons Kosovec
Dawn S. Spratley
Michael T. Price

For full biographical listings, see the Martindale-Hubbell Law Directory

CHARLES J. TAUNT & ASSOCIATES, P.L.L.C. (AV)

700 East Maple Road, 48009-6359
Telephone: 248-644-7800
Direct Line: 248-647-2582
Fax: 248-647-5902

Charles J. Taunt

For full biographical listings, see the Martindale-Hubbell Law Directory

BLOOMFIELD HILLS, Oakland Co.

HERTZ, SCHRAM & SARETSKY, P.C. (AV)

1760 South Telegraph Road, Suite 300, 48302
Telephone: 248-335-5000
Fax: 248-335-3346
Email: lawhss@aol.com *URL:* http://www.legalleaders.com

Bradley J. Schram
Howard Hertz
Gary M. Saretsky
Robert S. Hertzberg
Victor M. Norris
Steve J. Weiss
Robert Paul Geller
Walter J. Piszczatowski
Jeffrey A. Robbins
Mark L. Kowalsky

Dana A. Donohue
Miles D. Hart
Karen A. Gould
Paul K. Villarruel
Bradford T. Yaker
Michael F. Jacobson
Michael I. Zousmer
Brian Witus
Eva T. Cantarella
Eric Andrew Michaels

COUNSEL

Richard P. Zipser
Lisa M. Kavalhuna (Not admitted in MI)
James W. Burdick

OF COUNSEL

David L. Steinberg
Albert L. Holtz
Elmer L. Roller
Robert A. Canner
Harvey D. Geller (1928-1989)

For full biographical listings, see the Martindale-Hubbell Law Directory

HOWARD & HOWARD ATTORNEYS, P.C. (AV)

The Pinehurst Office Center, Suite 101, 1400 North Woodward Avenue, 48304-2855
Telephone: 248-645-1483
Telecopier: 248-645-1568
Kalamazoo, Michigan Office: The Michigan Building, Suite 200, 100 Portage Street.
Telephone: 616-382-1483.
Telecopier: 616-382-1568.
Lansing, Michigan Office: The Phoenix Building, Suite 500, 222 Washington Square, North.
Telephone: 517-485-1483.
Telecopier: 517-485-1568.

(See Next Column)

Peoria, Illinois Office: One Technology Plaza, Suite 600, 211 Fulton Street.
Telephone: 309-672-1483.
Telecopier: 309-672-1568.

Philip T. Carter
Ronald R. Cook
Michael G. Cruse
Robert D. Mollhagen
John E. Young

Representative Clients: For Representative Client list, see General Practice, Bloomfield Hills, MI.

For Complete List of Firm Personnel, See General Section

For full biographical listings, see the Martindale-Hubbell Law Directory

*DETROIT,** Wayne Co.

BODMAN, LONGLEY & DAHLING LLP (AV)

34th Floor 100 Renaissance Center, 48243
Telephone: 313-259-7777
Fax: 313-393-7579
Email: info@bodmanlongley.com *URL:* http://www.bodmanlongley.com
Troy, Michigan Office: Suite 2020, 755 West Big Beaver Road.
Telephone: 248-362-2110.
Fax: 248-244-0780.
Ann Arbor, Michigan Office: 110 Miller, Suite 300.
Telephone: 734-761-3780.
Fax: 734-930-2494.
Northern Michigan Office: 229 Court Street, P.O. Box 405, Cheboygan.
Telephone: 231-627-4351.
Fax: 231-627-2802.

MEMBERS OF FIRM

Robert J. Diehl, Jr.
Lawrence P. Hanson (Cheboygan Office)
Ralph E. McDowell
Marc M. Bakst

ASSOCIATE

Brian R. Trumbauer

For Representative Client List, See General Section

For Complete List of Firm Personnel, See General Section

For full biographical listings, see the Martindale-Hubbell Law Directory

HONIGMAN MILLER SCHWARTZ AND COHN (AV)

2290 First National Building, 660 Woodward Avenue, 48226
Telephone: 313-465-7000
Telecopier: 313-465-8000
Telex: 235705
Email: mvg@honigman.com *URL:* http://law.honigman.com
Lansing, Michigan Office: Phoenix Building, 222 North Washington Square, Suite 400, 48933-1800.
Telephone: 517-484-8282.

MEMBERS OF FIRM

Donald F. Baty, Jr.
Judy B. Calton
Steven G. Howell
Theodore B. Sylwestrzak
Sheryl L. Toby
Sheldon S. Toll
Robert B. Weiss

ASSOCIATES

Peter C. Bolton
Gail A. Eynon
Frank L. Gorman
Tricia A. Sherick (Not admitted in MI)
Michelle Epstein Taigman
Scott A. Wolfson

Representative Clients: AT&T Commercial Finance Corp.; Barclays Business Credit, Inc.; First Wisconsin National Bank of Milwaukee; General Motors Corporation Legal Staff (General Motors Acceptance Corporation, General Motors Corporation); Hibernia National Bank; Hughes Aircraft Company Legal Staff; Bank One, N.A.; Security Pacific Automotive Financial Services Corp.; The Travelers Insurance Company and World Omni Leasing, Inc.

For Complete List of Firm Personnel, See General Section

For full biographical listings, see the Martindale-Hubbell Law Directory

JAFFE, RAITT, HEUER & WEISS, PROFESSIONAL CORPORATION (AV)

One Woodward Avenue, Suite 2400, 48226
Telephone: 313-961-8380
Telecopier: 313-961-8358
Cable Address: "Jafsni"
Southfield,Michigan Office: Travelers Tower, Suite 1520.
Telephone: 313-961-8380.

Thomas E. Coughlin
Jane Derse Quasarano
Louis P. Rochkind
Linda C. Scheuerman
Jay L. Welford

Stephen S. Laplante

For Complete List of Firm Personnel, See General Section

For full biographical listings, see the Martindale-Hubbell Law Directory

Detroit—Continued

MILLER, CANFIELD, PADDOCK AND STONE, P.L.C. (AV)

A Professional Limited Liability Company
Founded in 1852 by Sidney Davy Miller
150 West Jefferson, Suite 2500, 48226-4415
Telephone: 313-963-6420
Fax: 313-496-7500
Cable Address: "Stem Detroit"
URL: http://www.millercanfield.com
Ann Arbor, Michigan Office: 101 North Main Street, 7th Floor, 48104-1400.
Telephone: 734-663-2445.
Fax: 734-747-7147.
Troy, Michigan Office: 840 West Long Lake Road, Suite 200, 48098.
Telephone: 248-879-2000.
Fax: 248-879-2001.
Grand Rapids, Michigan Office: 99 Monroe, N.W., Suite 1200, 49503-2639.
Telephone: 616-454-8656.
Fax: 616-776-6322.
Howell, Michigan Office: 121 South Barnard Street, Suite 4, 48843-2305.
Telephone: 517-546-7600.
Telecopier: 517-546-6974.
Kalamazoo, Michigan Office: 444 West Michigan Avenue, 49007-3752.
Telephone: 616-381-7030.
Fax: 616-382-0244.
Lansing, Michigan Office: One Michigan Avenue, Suite 900, 48933-1609.
Telephone: 517-487-2070.
Fax: 517-374-6304.
Monroe, Michigan Office: 214 East Elm Avenue, Suite 100, 48162-2682.
Telephone: 734-243-2000.
Fax: 734-243-0901.
Washington, D.C. Office: 1900 K Street, N.W., Suite 1150. 20006.
Telephone: 202-429-5575; 785-0600.
Fax: 202-331-1118; 785-1234.
Pensacola, Florida Office: 25 West Cedar, 32501.
Telephone: 850-469-1088.
Fax: 850-432-0677.
New York, New York Office: 1450 Broadway, 41st Floor, 10018.
Telephone: 212-704-4400.
Fax: 212-704-4410.
Gdynia, Poland Office: UL. Slaska 21, 81-319.
Telephone: 011-485-831-2808.
Fax: 011-48-58-628 6411.
Warsaw, Poland Office: UL. Nowogrodzkall, 5th Floor, 00-513.
Telephone: 011-4822 529 0200.
Fax: 011-4822 529 0201.
Katowice, Poland Office: UL. Francuska 35/37, 40-027.
Telephone: 011 (48-32) 757-2414.
Fax: 011 (48-32) 757-2483.

PRINCIPALS OF FIRM

Terrence M. Crawford
Robert E. Lee Wright (Grand Rapids Offices)
Michael H. Traison
Jonathan S. Green
Donald J. Hutchinson
Lori L. Purkey (Kalamazoo Office)

ASSOCIATE

Stuart M. Heath (Kalamazoo Office)

Representative Firm Clients: Chrysler Corporation; Comerica, Incorporated; City of Detroit, Michigan; Detroit Tigers, Inc.; First of Michigan; Ford Motor Company; Ford Motor Credit Company; Great Lakes Bancorp; Henry Ford Hospital; INVETECH Company.

For Complete List of Firm Personnel, See General Section

For full biographical listings, see the Martindale-Hubbell Law Directory

FARMINGTON HILLS, Oakland Co.

COUZENS, LANSKY, FEALK, ELLIS, ROEDER & LAZAR, P.C. (AV)

39395 West 12 Mile Road, Suite 200, 48331-2913
Telephone: 248-489-8600
Facsimile: 248-489-4156
Email: info@couzens.com *URL:* http://www.couzens.com

Sheldon A. Fealk
Jerry M. Ellis
Bruce J. Lazar
Phillip L. Sternberg
Stephen Scapelliti
Mark S. Frankel

Representative Clients: Provided upon request.
Reference: Michigan National Bank.

For Complete List of Firm Personnel, See General Section

For full biographical listings, see the Martindale-Hubbell Law Directory

*GRAND RAPIDS,** Kent Co.

BORRE, PETERSON, FOWLER & REENS, P.C. (AV)

300 Ottawa N.W., Suite 500, P.O. Box 1767, 49501-1767
Telephone: 616-459-1971
Fax: 616-459-2393
Email: 105162.1531@compuserve.com

(See Next Column)

William C. Reens
Frank H. Johnson
Harold E. Nelson
John C. Arndts

References: NBD Bank/First Chicago Bank; The Huntington Bank.

For Complete List of Firm Personnel, See General Section

For full biographical listings, see the Martindale-Hubbell Law Directory

DE GROOT, KELLER, VINCENT & ALMASSIAN, P.L.C. (AV)

300 Trust Building, 40 Pearl Street, N.W., 49503
Telephone: 616-459-6251
Fax: 616-459-6352
Email: dkvkeller@aol.com

MEMBERS OF FIRM

Brian D. Vincent
James M. Keller

OF COUNSEL

Murray B. De Groot

For full biographical listings, see the Martindale-Hubbell Law Directory

WARDROP & WARDROP, P.C. (AV)

Suite 150 The Frey Building, 300 Ottawa Avenue, N.W., 49503
Telephone: 616-459-1225
Fax: 616-459-7273
Email: wardrop@wardroplaw.com

Robert F. Wardrop II
Thomas M. Wardrop

Mary Saur Cohn
Brian L. Groen

For full biographical listings, see the Martindale-Hubbell Law Directory

WARNER NORCROSS & JUDD LLP (AV)

900 Old Kent Building, 111 Lyon Street, N.W., 49503-2489
Telephone: 616-752-2000
Fax: 616-752-2500
URL: http://www.wnj.com
Muskegon, Michigan Office: 400 Terrace Plaza, P.O. Box 900.
Telephone: 231-727-2600.
Fax: 231-727-2699.
Holland, Michigan Office: Curtis Center, Suite 300, 170 College Avenue.
Telephone: 616-396-9800.
Fax: 616-396-3656.
Southfield, Michigan Office: 1000 Town Center, Suite 650.
Telephone: 248-223-5000.
Fax: 248-223-5005.

MEMBERS OF FIRM

Robert H. Skilton, III (Resident Member, Southfield Office)
Jeffrey O. Birkhold
Timothy Hillegonds
Kathleen M. Hanenburg
Stephen B. Grow
Judith Lowitz Adler (Resident Member, Southfield Office)
Gordon J. Toering

ASSOCIATE

Andrew D. Hakken

For full biographical listings, see the Martindale-Hubbell Law Directory

*KALAMAZOO,** Kalamazoo Co.

PAUL F. DAVIDOFF A PROFESSIONAL CORPORATION (AV)

405 West Michigan Avenue, Suite 130, P.O. Box 51066, 49005
Telephone: 616-388-2100
Fax: 616-388-5454
Email: pdavidoff@ameritech.net *URL:* http://www.lawyers.com/paulfdavidoff

Paul F. Davidoff

Reference: Old Kent Bank of Kalamazoo.

For full biographical listings, see the Martindale-Hubbell Law Directory

HOWARD & HOWARD ATTORNEYS, P.C. (AV)

The Michigan Building, Suite 200, 100 Portage Street, 49007-4802
Telephone: 616-382-1483
Telecopier: 616-382-1568
Bloomfield Hills, Michigan Office: The Pinehurst Office Center, Suite 101, 1400 North Woodward Avenue.
Telephone: 248-645-1483.
Telecopier: 248-645-1568.
Lansing, Michigan Office: The Phoenix Building, Suite 500, 222 Washington Square North.
Telephone: 517-485-1483.
Telecopier: 517-485-1568.
Peoria, Illinois Office: One Technology Plaza, Suite 600, 211 Fulton Street.
Telephone: 309-672-1483.
Telecopier: 309-672-1568.

Jeffrey P. Chalmers
William A. Dornbos

Representative Clients: For Representative Client list, see General Practice, Kalamazoo, MI.

(See Next Column)

HOWARD & HOWARD ATTORNEYS P.C.—*Continued*

For Complete List of Firm Personnel, See General Section

For full biographical listings, see the Martindale-Hubbell Law Directory

KREIS, ENDERLE, CALLANDER & HUDGINS, A PROFESSIONAL CORPORATION (AV)

One Moorsbridge, P.O. Box 4010, 49003-4010
Telephone: 616-324-3000
Facsimile: 616-324-3010
Email: kech@kech.com *URL:* http://www.kech.com
Battle Creek, Michigan Office: One West Michigan Avenue, 49017.
Telephone: 616-966-3000.
Fax: 616-966-3022.

Russell A. Kreis
Robert B. Borsos
Thomas G. King

For Complete List of Firm Personnel, See General Section

For full biographical listings, see the Martindale-Hubbell Law Directory

MILLER, CANFIELD, PADDOCK AND STONE, P.L.C. (AV)

A Professional Limited Liability Company
Founded in 1852 by Sidney Davy Miller
444 West Michigan Avenue, 49007-3752
Telephone: 616-381-7030
Fax: 616-382-0244
URL: http://www.millercanfield.com
Detroit, Michigan Office: 150 West Jefferson, Suite 2500, 48226-4415.
Telephone: 313-963-6420.
Fax: 313-496-7500.
Cable Address: "Stem Detroit."
Ann Arbor, Michigan Office: 101 North Main Street, 7th Floor, 48104-1400.
Telephone: 734-663-2445.
Fax: 734-747-7147.
Troy, Michigan Office: 840 West Long Lake Road, Suite 200, 48098.
Telephone: 248-879-2000.
Fax: 248-879-2001.
Grand Rapids, Michigan Office: 99 Monroe, N.W., Suite 1200, 49503-2639.
Telephone: 616-454-8656.
Fax: 616-776-6322.
Howell, Michigan Office: 121 South Barnard Street, Suite 4, 48843-2305.
Telephone: 517-546-7600.
Telecopier: 517-546-6974.
Lansing, Michigan Office: One Michigan Avenue, Suite 900, 48933-1609.
Telephone: 517-487-2070.
Fax: 517-374-6304.
Monroe, Michigan Office: 214 East Elm Avenue, Suite 100, 48162-2682.
Telephone: 734-243-2000.
Fax: 734-243-0901.
Washington, D.C. Office: 1900 K Street, N.W., Suite 1150. 20006.
Telephone: 202-429-5575; 785-0600.
Fax: 202-331-1118; 785-1234.
Pensacola, Florida Office: 25 West Cedar, 32501.
Telephone: 850-469-1088.
Fax: 850-432-0677.
New York, New York Office: 1450 Broadway, 41st Floor, 10018.
Telephone: 212-704-4400.
Fax: 212-704-4410.
Gdynia, Poland Office: UL. Slaska 21, 81-319.
Telephone: 011-485-831-2808.
Fax: 011-48-58-628 6411.
Warsaw, Poland Office: UL. Nowogrodzkall, 5th Floor, 00-513.
Telephone: 011-4822 529 0200.
Fax: 011-4822 529 0201.
Katowice, Poland Office: UL. Francuska 35/37, 40-027.
Telephone: 011 (48-32) 757-2414.
Fax: 011 (48-32) 757-2483.

PRINCIPALS

James G. Vantine, Jr.
Lori L. Purkey

RESIDENT ASSOCIATE

Stuart M. Heath

Representative Firm Clients: Chrysler Corporation; Comerica, Incorporated; City of Detroit, Michigan; Detroit Tigers, Inc.; First of Michigan; Ford Motor Company; Ford Motor Credit Company; Great Lakes Bancorp; Henry Ford Hospital; INVETECH Company.

For Complete List of Firm Personnel, See General Section

For full biographical listings, see the Martindale-Hubbell Law Directory

LANSING, Ingham Co.

MILLER, CANFIELD, PADDOCK AND STONE, P.L.C. (AV)

A Professional Limited Liability Company
Founded in 1852 by Sidney Davy Miller
Suite 900, One Michigan Avenue, 48933-1609
Telephone: 517-487-2070
Fax: 517-374-6304
URL: http://www.millercanfield.com
Detroit, Michigan Office: 150 West Jefferson, Suite 2500, 48226-4415.
Telephone: 313-963-6420.
Fax: 313-496-7500.
Cable Address: "Stem Detroit."
Ann Arbor, Michigan Office: 101 North Main Street, 7th Floor, 48104-1400.
Telephone: 734-663-2445.
Fax: 734-747-7147.
Troy, Michigan Office: 840 West Long Lake Road, Suite 200, 48098.
Telephone: 248-879-2000.
Fax: 248-879-2001.
Grand Rapids, Michigan Office: 99 Monroe, N.W., Suite 1200, 49503-2639.
Telephone: 616-454-8656.
Fax: 616-776-6322.
Howell, Michigan Office: 121 South Barnard Street, Suite 4, 48843-2305.
Telephone: 517-546-7600.
Telecopier: 517-546-6974.
Kalamazoo, Michigan Office: 444 West Michigan Avenue, 49007-3752.
Telephone: 616-381-7030.
Fax: 616-382-0244.
Monroe, Michigan Office: 214 East Elm Avenue, Suite 100, 48162-2682.
Telephone: 734-243-2000.
Fax: 734-243-0901.
Washington, D.C. Office: 1900 K Street, N.W., Suite 1150. 20006.
Telephone: 202-429-5575; 785-0600.
Fax: 202-331-1118; 785-1234.
Pensacola, Florida Office: 25 West Cedar, 32501.
Telephone: 850-469-1088.
Fax: 850-432-0677.
New York, New York Office: 1450 Broadway, 41st Floor, 10018.
Telephone: 212-704-4400.
Fax: 212-704-4410.
Gdynia, Poland Office: UL. Slaska 21, 81-319.
Telephone: 011-485-831-2808.
Fax: 011-48-58-628 6411.
Warsaw, Poland Office: UL. Nowogrodzkall, 5th Floor, 00-513.
Telephone: 011-4822 529 0200.
Fax: 011-4822 529 0201.
Katowice, Poland Office: UL. Francuska 35/37, 40-027.
Telephone: 011 (48-32) 757-2414.
Fax: 011 (48-32) 757-2483.

RESIDENT PRINCIPALS

William J. Danhof

Representative Firm Clients: Chrysler Corporation; Comerica, Incorporated; City of Detroit, Michigan; Detroit Tigers, Inc.; First of Michigan; Ford Motor Company; Ford Motor Credit Company; Great Lakes Bancorp; Henry Ford Hospital; INVETECH Company.

For Complete List of Firm Personnel, See General Section

For full biographical listings, see the Martindale-Hubbell Law Directory

ROCHESTER HILLS, Oakland Co.

SHERMETA, CHIMKO & KILPATRICK, P.C. (AV)

445 South Livernois, Suite 333, 48307
Telephone: 248-652-8200
Fax: 248-652-1292
Mailing Address: P.O. Box 5016, Rochester, Michigan, 48308
Detroit, Michigan Office: 211 West Fort Street, Suite 704, 48226.
Telephone: 313-961-4848.
Fax: 313-961-4365.
Grand Rapids, Michigan Office: 169 Louis Campau Prom., Suite 2B, 49503.
Telephone: 616-774-9258.
Fax: 616-774-9411.

Douglass H. Shermeta
Darryl J. Chimko
Richardo I. Kilpatrick
Barbara L. Adams
Henry J. Mittelstaedt III
Kelly L. Scola
Christopher E. McNeely

Robert L. Dzialo
Sheryl S. Zamplas
Lisa E. Gocha
Kevin C. Calhoun
Kristin J. Ermshler
James E. Hess
Kyle J. VonAllmen
Elizabeth M. Abood
Jessica Brown Allmand
Dina L. Centifanti
Tania A. Hricik DeVries
Sharon Denise Koerber
Heather L. Miserlian
Gregory J. Roth

(See Next Column)

SHERMETA, CHIMKO & KILPATRICK P.C., *Rochester Hills—Continued*

Larysa Sawertailo
Brent M. Lamkin
Tyra T. Brown
Charles Milne
Paul J. Smigielski

For full biographical listings, see the Martindale-Hubbell Law Directory

*SAGINAW,** Saginaw Co.

BRAUN KENDRICK FINKBEINER PLC (AV)

101 N. Washington Suite 812, 48607-1297
Telephone: 517-753-3461
Telecopier: 517-753-3951
Email: ALBFIE@BKF-LAW.COM *URL:* http://www.bkf-law.com
Saginaw Township Office, Michigan Office: 5800 Gratiot Road, Suite 107, P.O. Box 5169. Telephone 517-799-8692.
Fax: 517-799-4666.
Bay City, Michigan Office: 201 Phoenix Building, P.O. Box 2039.
Telephone: 517-895-8505.
Telecopier: 517-895-8437.
Ann Arbor, Michigan Office: First National Building. 201 S. Main, Suite 700.
Telephone: 313-995-4100.
Telecopier: 313-995-4798.
Mt. Pleasant, Michigan Office: 805 North Brown.
Telephone: 517-775-7404.
Telecopier: 517-775-3764.

Kenneth W. Kable
Timothy L Curtiss
Francis J. Keating

Representative Clients: The Dow Chemical Co.; General Motors Corp.; Merrill, Lynch, Inc.; Saginaw General Hospital; Saginaw News; The Wickes Foundation.

For Complete List of Firm Personnel, See General Section
For full biographical listings, see the Martindale-Hubbell Law Directory

SOUTHFIELD, Oakland Co.

ERMAN, TEICHER, MILLER, ZUCKER, FREEDMAN & GORDON, A PROFESSIONAL CORPORATION (AV)

100 Galleria Officentre, Suite 333, 48034
Telephone: 248-827-4100
Telecopier: 248-827-4106
URL: http://www.ermanteicher.com

Earle I. Erman
Craig E. Zucker
Julie Beth Teicher
David H. Freedman
David M. Miller
Robert D. Gordon
Richard E. Kruger

For full biographical listings, see the Martindale-Hubbell Law Directory

GOLD LANGE & MAJOROS, P.C. (AV)

24901 Northwestern Highway, Suite 444, 48075
Telephone: 248-350-8220
Fax: 248-350-0519
Email: goldbricks@aol.com *URL:* http://www.lawyers.com/glm

Stuart A. Gold
John C. Lange
Elias Themistocles Majoros

Marilyn R. Somers
Deborah S. Rubin
Ronna Stevens Gold
Scott A. Gies

For full biographical listings, see the Martindale-Hubbell Law Directory

NATHAN & NATHAN, P.C. (AV)

Suite 260, Franklin Center, 29100 Northwestern Highway, 48034
Telephone: 248-351-0099
Fax: 248-351-0487
Email: rnathan@nathannathan.com

Robert B. Nathan
Kenneth A. Nathan

Robert N. Bassel

For full biographical listings, see the Martindale-Hubbell Law Directory

SOMMERS, SCHWARTZ, SILVER & SCHWARTZ, P.C. (AV)

2000 Town Center, Suite 900, 48075
Telephone: 248-355-0300
Telecopier: 248-746-4001
Plymouth, Michigan Office: 747 South Main Street.
Telephone: 313-455-4250.

James J. Vlasic
David M. Black

Jennifer M. Grieco

General Counsel for: City of Taylor; Foodland Distributors; C.A. Muer Corporation; Vlasic & Company; Nederlander Corporation; Midwest Health Centers, P.C.

Representative Clients: Michigan National Bank; Universal Underwriters Insurance Co.; Rite-Aid of Michigan.

For Complete List of Firm Personnel, See General Section
For full biographical listings, see the Martindale-Hubbell Law Directory

TROY, Oakland Co.

AUSTIN HIRSCHHORN, P.C. (AV)

Suite 710 Columbia Center, 201 West Big Beaver Road, 48084-4152
Telephone: 248-680-1660
Fax: 248-680-1671
Email: austinh@ix.netcom.com

Austin Hirschhorn

For full biographical listings, see the Martindale-Hubbell Law Directory

BUSINESS LAW

ALABAMA

*BAY MINETTE,** Baldwin Co.

JOHNSTONE, ADAMS, BAILEY, GORDON AND HARRIS, L.L.C. (AV)

Dahlberg Building, 104 Hand Avenue, P.O. Box 729, 36507
Telephone: 334-937-9473
Facsimile: 334-937-9475
Email: attorneys@JohnstoneAdams.com *URL:* http://www.JohnstoneAdams.com
Mobile, Alabama Office: Royal St. Francis Building, 104 St. Francis Street, P.O. Box 1988, 36633.
Telephone: 334-432-7682.
Facsimile: 334-432-2800; 432-0712.

MEMBER OF FIRM

Charles C. Simpson, III (Resident)

For full biographical listings, see the Martindale-Hubbell Law Directory

*BIRMINGHAM,** Jefferson Co.

BERKOWITZ, LEFKOVITS, ISOM & KUSHNER, A PROFESSIONAL CORPORATION (AV)

SouthTrust Tower, 420 North Twentieth Street, Suite 1600, 35203-5202
Telephone: 205-328-0480
Telecopier: 205-322-8007
URL: http://www.blik.com

Arnold K. Lefkovits
Chervis Isom
Harold B. Kushner
B. G. Minisman, Jr.
Edward P. Meyerson
David A. Larsen
Barry S. Marks
D. J. Simonetti
Steven B. Corenblum
Denise W. Killebrew
Thomas J. Mahoney, Jr.
Thomas O. Kolb
Lana K. Hawkins (Not admitted in AL)
Richard A. Pizitz, Jr.
Walton E. Williams III
Nancy C. Hughes

Hewes T. Hull
Matthew W. Barnes
Alane A. Phillips
Andrew R. Chambless
Robert Buchanan Phillips, II

For Complete List of Firm Personnel, See General Section

For full biographical listings, see the Martindale-Hubbell Law Directory

BRADLEY ARANT ROSE & WHITE LLP (AV)

2001 Park Place, Suite 1400, P.O. Box 830709, 35283-0709
Telephone: 205-521-8000
Facsimile: 205-521-8800
Facsimile (SouthTrust Tower Office): 205-521-8500
URL: http://www.barw.com
Huntsville, Alabama Office: 200 Clinton Avenue West, Suite 900, 35801.
Telephone: 205-517-5100.
Facsimile: 205-533-5069.
Washington, D.C. Office: 801 Pennsylvania Avenue, NW, Suite 230, 20004.
Telephone: 202-347-8893.
Facsimile: 202-347-1684.

MEMBERS OF FIRM

Hall B. Bryant III (Resident, Huntsville Office)
Thomas Neely Carruthers Jr.
J. Paul Compton Jr.
Deane K. Corliss
L. Susan Doss
J. David Dresher
Denson Nauls Franklin III
Stuart Joseph Frentz
M. Williams Goodwyn Jr.
John B. Grenier (Resident, Huntsville Office)
John E. Hagefstration Jr.
John G. Harrell
George Bryan Harris
Carleta Roberts Hawley
Kevin J. Henderson
William L. Hinds Jr.
T. Barr Linton (Not admitted in AL)
Scott E. Ludwig (Resident, Huntsville Office)
John K. Molen
Virginia Calvert Patterson
James E. Rotch
Charles R. Smith Jr. (Resident, Huntsville Office)
Paul S. Ware
Meade Whitaker, Jr.

OF COUNSEL

S. Revelle Gwyn (Resident, Huntsville Office)
Edward M. Selfe
C. Larimore Whitaker
John N. Wrinkle

ASSOCIATES

Helena F. Barkworth
Hugh Chester Boston III
James W. Childs, Jr.
Thomas M. Goodrich
K. Wood Herren
Erika Jenke-Huber (Resident, Huntsville Office)
Jennifer Byers McLeod (Resident, Huntsville Office)
Dorothy D. Pak

(See Next Column)

ASSOCIATES (Continued)

David E. Roth
Frederic L. Smith, Jr.
Joseph E. Smith
Tracy M. Thompson
Laura P. Washburn (Not admitted in AL)
James H. White

For Complete List of Firm Personnel, See General Section

For full biographical listings, see the Martindale-Hubbell Law Directory

BURR & FORMAN LLP (AV)

3100 SouthTrust Tower, 420 North 20th Street, P.O. Box 830719, 35283-0719
Telephone: 205-251-3000
Facsimile: 205-458-5100
URL: http://www.burr.com
Huntsville, Alabama Office: Suite 204, Regency Center, 400 Meridian Street.
Telephone: 205-551-0010.
Facsimile: 205-551-0043.
Atlanta, Georgia Office: Suite 1200, One Georgia Center, 600 West Peachtree Street, 30308.
Telephone: 404-815-3000.
Facsimile: 404-817-3244.

MEMBERS OF FIRM

Louis H. Anders, Jr.
Jeffrey T. Baker
Henry Graham Beene
Eric L. Carlton
Deborah P. Fisher
Gail Livingston Mills
Dwight L. Mixson, Jr.
Samuel W. Oliver, Jr.
Marvin Glenn Perry, Jr.
J. Fred Powell
Gene T. Price
Bruce A. Rawls
Jack P. Stephenson, Jr.
Joseph G. Stewart
George M. Taylor, III
A. Brand Walton

For Complete List of Firm Personnel, See General Section

For full biographical listings, see the Martindale-Hubbell Law Directory

GORDON, SILBERMAN, WIGGINS & CHILDS, P.C. (AV)

1400 SouthTrust Tower, 420 North 20th Street, 35203
Telephone: 205-328-0640
Facsimilie: 205-254-1500
Washington, D.C. Office: 1621 Connecticut Avenue, N.W., Suite 400.
Telephone: 202-238-0690.
Facsimile: 202-238-0968.

RESIDENT SHAREHOLDERS

Bruce L. Gordon
Ray D. Gibbons
Timothy D. Davis
Joseph H. Calvin, III
Linda J. Peacock

RESIDENT ASSOCIATE

Karen Gurley Kolaczek

For Complete List of Firm Personnel, See General Section

For full biographical listings, see the Martindale-Hubbell Law Directory

GORHAM & WALDREP, P.C. (AV)

2101 6th Avenue North, Suite 700, 35203
Telephone: 205-254-3216; 251-9166
Telecopier: 205-324-3802
Email: info@gorham-waldrep.com *URL:* http://www.gorham-waldrep.com
Montgomery, Alabama Office: 250 Commerce Street, P.O. Box 4837, 36103-4837.
Telephone: 334-262-0777.
Telecopier: 334-262-0742.

Thomas L. Stewart
Michael G. Kendrick
John T. Natter

Leslie Miller Klasing

Representative Clients: Jefferson County Personnel Board; Birmingham-Jefferson Civic Center Authority; The Water Works and Sewer Board of the City of Birmingham; City of Homewood; American Federation of Government Employees Local #1945; City of Pelham; Town of Kimberly; Alabama Tire Dealers Assn.; Southern States Body Shop Assn.

For Complete List of Firm Personnel, See General Section

For full biographical listings, see the Martindale-Hubbell Law Directory

HASKELL SLAUGHTER & YOUNG, L.L.C. (AV)

1200 AmSouth/Harbert Plaza, 1901 Sixth Avenue North, 35203
Telephone: 205-251-1000
Facsimile: 205-324-1133
Email: hsy@hsy.com
Montgomery, Alabama Office: 305 South Lawrence Street, P.O. Box 4660. 36103-4660.
Telephone: 334-265-8573.
Facsimile: 334-264-7945.

(See Next Column)

HASKELL SLAUGHTER & YOUNG L.L.C., *Birmingham—Continued*

Robert E. Lee Garner
Benjamin B. Spratling III
Robert D. Shattuck, Jr.
Mark Edward Ezell
Ross N. Cohen
Gwen L. Windle
Frank Hampton McFadden, Jr.

OF COUNSEL

Donald T. Locke (Not admitted in AL)

Lynn Reynolds
Kimberly L. Hager
Matthew T. Franklin
S. Jason Nabors

Representative Clients: The Banc Corporation; The Bank; Electronic Health-care Systems, Inc.; HEALTHSOUTH Corporation/HEALTHSOUTH Medical Centers; Marshall Durbin Companies.

For Complete List of Firm Personnel, See General Section

For full biographical listings, see the Martindale-Hubbell Law Directory

*DOTHAN,** Houston Co.

DOW T. HUSKEY (AV)

112 West Adams Street P.O. Drawer 550, 36302
Telephone: 334-794-3366
Telecopier: 334-794-7292

Representative Clients: Troy State University; Northside Mall; CNA Insurance Cos.; Employers Reinsurance; Tudor Insurance Co.; Rail Management; Wilmington Terminal Railway; Atlantic & Western Railway; S & S Imports.

For full biographical listings, see the Martindale-Hubbell Law Directory

*HUNTSVILLE,** Madison Co.

BURR & FORMAN LLP (AV)

Suite 204, Regency Center, 400 Meridian Street, 35801
Telephone: 205-551-0010
Facsimile: 205-551-0043
Birmingham, Alabama Office: 3100 SouthTrust Tower, 420 North 20th Street.
Telephone: 205-251-3000.
Facsimile: 205-458-5100.
Atlanta, Georgia Office: Suite 1200, One Georgia Center, 600 West Peachtree Street, 30308.
Telephone: 404-815-3000.
Facsimile: 404-817-3244.

RESIDENT PARTNER

S. Dagnal Rowe

For full biographical listings, see the Martindale-Hubbell Law Directory

*MOBILE,** Mobile Co.

ARMBRECHT, JACKSON, DEMOUY, CROWE, HOLMES & REEVES, L.L.C. (AV)

1300 Riverview Plaza, P.O. Box 290, 36601
Telephone: 334-405-1300
Facsimile: 334-432-6843; 433-3821
Email: adc@ajlaw.com

MEMBERS OF FIRM

E. B. Peebles III
William B. Harvey
David A. Bagwell
Christopher I. Gruenewald
David E. Hudgens
James Dale Smith
Duane A. Graham
Thomas P. Oldweiler
James F. Watkins

ASSOCIATE

Leah P. Ladd

Representative Clients: AmSouth Bank of Alabama (Regional Counsel); Dean Witter Reynolds, Inc.; General Electric Credit Corp.; Gulf Electric of Mobile, Inc.; Loyal American Life Insurance Co.; Mobile Gas Service Corp.; Southern Pine Inspection Bureau; United Bank; WKRG-TV-Channel 5.

For Complete List of Firm Personnel, See General Section

For full biographical listings, see the Martindale-Hubbell Law Directory

ATCHISON, CROSBY, SAAD & BEEBE, P.C. (AV)

3030 Knollwood Drive, 36693
Telephone: 334-665-7200
Fax: 334-665-7250
URL: http://www.acsblaw.com

James E. Atchison
James H. Crosby
Elias J. Saad
Donald G. Beebe

Mona Ann Vivar
Jacqueline M. McConaha
Daryl A. Atchison

Representative Clients: City of Mobile; Alabama State Docks; Mobile Area Water and Sewer Board; Owens Corning, Inc.; Pilot Catastrophe Services, Inc.; Shell Oil Co.; Premdor,Inc.; Melvin Pierce Paint Co.; Commonwealth National Bank; Fiberglass Canada,Inc.

(See Next Column)

For full biographical listings, see the Martindale-Hubbell Law Directory

JOHNSTONE, ADAMS, BAILEY, GORDON AND HARRIS, L.L.C. (AV)

Royal St. Francis Building, 104 St. Francis Street, 8th Floor, P.O. Box 1988, 36633
Telephone: 334-432-7682
Facsimile: 334-432-0712 or 334-432-2800
Email: attorneys@JohnstoneAdams.com *URL:* http://www.JohnstoneAdams.com
Bay Minette, Alabama Office: Dahlberg Building, 107 Hand Avenue, P.O. Box 729, 36507.
Telephone: 334-937-9473.
Facsimile: 334-937-9475.

MEMBERS OF FIRM

Charles B. Bailey, Jr.
Ben H. Harris, Jr.
William H. Hardie, Jr.
Joseph M. Allen, Jr.
I. David Cherniak
Wade B. Perry, Jr.
R. Gregory Watts

ASSOCIATE

Scott Alton Browning

For Complete List of Firm Personnel, See General Section

For full biographical listings, see the Martindale-Hubbell Law Directory

PIERCE, LEDYARD, LATTA & WASDEN, P.C. (AV)

Colonial Bank Centre Suite 400, 41 North Beltline, 36608
Telephone: 334-344-5151
Facsimile: 334-344-9696
Mailing Address: P.O. Box 16046, Mobile, AL, 36616
URL: http://www.pllaw.com

Donald F. Pierce
Goodman G. Ledyard
Forrest S. Latta
H. William Wasden
Edward G. Isaacs Bowron
John Charles S. Pierce
W. Pemble DeLashmet
C. William Daniels, Jr.

Mark Pickett Eiland
James Robert Turnipseed
Michael A. Montgomery

OF COUNSEL

Caroline Wells Hinds

Representative Clients: First National Bank of Atmore; Terra International, Inc.; Magnolia Mortgage Company, Inc.; The Mitchell Company; Colonial Bank; Blue Cross and Blue Shield; Grove U.S. LLC; SouthTrust Bank of Alabama, NA; Trustmark National Bank; United Companies Lending Corp.

For full biographical listings, see the Martindale-Hubbell Law Directory

VICKERS, RIIS, MURRAY AND CURRAN, L.L.C. (AV)

8th Floor, Regions Bank Building, 106 Saint Francis Street, P.O. Box 2568, 36652
Telephone: 334-432-9772
Fax: 334-432-9781
Email: vickersriis.com

MEMBERS OF FIRM

J. Manson Murray
Edwin J. Curran, Jr.
Zebulon M. P. Inge, Jr.
Ronald P. Davis

Representative Clients: Mobile Forest Products, Inc.; Azalea Aviation, Inc.; Midstream Fuel Services; McPhillips Manufacturing Co., Inc.; Spring Hill College; Steiner Shipyard, Inc.; Marine Office of America Corp.; Cummins Alabama, Inc.; Ben M. Radcliff Contractor, Inc.; Gulf Distributing Co., Inc.

For Complete List of Firm Personnel, See General Section

For full biographical listings, see the Martindale-Hubbell Law Directory

ZIEMAN, SPEEGLE, JACKSON & HOFFMAN, L.L.C. (AV)

107 St. Francis Street, Suite 3200, P.O. Box 11, 36601
Telephone: 334-694-1700
Facsimile: 334-694-1998

MEMBERS OF THE FIRM

Thomas Troy Zieman, Jr.
Jerome E. Speegle
Robert G. Jackson, Jr.
Anthony Michael Hoffman
Ben H. Harris, III

For full biographical listings, see the Martindale-Hubbell Law Directory

*MONTGOMERY,** Montgomery Co.

BRANTLEY & WILKERSON, P.C. (AV)

405 South Hull Street, P.O. Box 830, 36101-0830
Telephone: 334-265-1500
Fax: 334-265-0319
Email: ashley@brantleywilkerson.com *URL:* http://www.brantleywilkerson.com

Paul A. Brantley
Mark D. Wilkerson

(See Next Column)

BRANTLEY & WILKERSON P.C.—*Continued*

Leah Snell Stephens

Representative Clients: MidCoast, Inc.; ALLTEL; Southeastern Cellular; TDS.
Reference: SouthTrust Bank, N.A.

For full biographical listings, see the Martindale-Hubbell Law Directory

KAUFMAN & ROTHFEDER, P.C. (AV)
2740 Zelda Road, Drawer 4540, 36103-4540
Telephone: 334-244-1111
Fax: 334-244-1969
Email: firm@krlegal.com *URL:* http://www.krlegal.com

Alan E. Rothfeder
Richardson B. McKenzie III
Robert E. L. Gilpin
John Ward Weiss
Robert M. Ritchey
William B. Sellers
J. Scott Pierce
Mark Monroe Gibson
Jo Claudia Mitchum
Eric Lloyd Pruitt

Counsel for: Dale Medical Center; Evergreen Medical Center; Community Health Systems, Inc.; The Russell Hospital Corporation.

For full biographical listings, see the Martindale-Hubbell Law Directory

NIX, HOLTSFORD & VERCELLI, P.C. (AV)
300 A Water Street, Suite 300, P.O. Box 4128, 36103
Telephone: 334-262-2006
Fax: 334-834-3616
Email: NHV@JUNO.COM

H. E. Nix, Jr.
Alex L. Holtsford, Jr.
Charles E. Vercelli, Jr.
Floyd R. Gilliland, Jr.
T. Randall Lyons
Steven A. Higgins
Kenneth A. Hitson, Jr.

David P. Stevens
Todd E. Hughes
Rick A. Howard
Stacy Anne Linn
Jay S. Tuley

LEGAL SUPPORT PERSONNEL

Richard M. Seibert (Firm Manager)
Ashley Collins (Paralegal)
Monica E. Jayroe (Paralegal)
Suzanne H. Long (Legal Assistant)
Kelley S. Tracy (Paralegal)

For full biographical listings, see the Martindale-Hubbell Law Directory

ROBISON & BELSER, P.A. (AV)
200 Coosa Street, 36104
Telephone: 334-834-7000
Telecopier: 334-834-7011
Mailing Address: Drawer 1470, Montgomery, AL, 36102
Email: tsides@mont.mindspring.com

James R. Seale

General Counsel for: Montgomery County Board of Education.
Representative Clients: Union Bank & Trust Co.; Liberty National Life Insurance Co.; State Farm Mutual Fire & Casualty Co.

For full biographical listings, see the Martindale-Hubbell Law Directory

VOLZ, PRESTWOOD & HANAN, P.C. (AV)
350 Adams Avenue, P.O. Box 1910, 36102-1910
Telephone: 334-264-6401
Fax: 334-834-4954

Charles H. Volz, Jr.
Alvin T. Prestwood
Charles H. Volz, III
Ellis D. Hanan
Richard D. Lively
Judy H. Barganier

For full biographical listings, see the Martindale-Hubbell Law Directory

*TUSCALOOSA,** Tuscaloosa Co.

HUBBARD, SMITH, MCILWAIN, BRAKEFIELD & BROWDER, P.C. (AV)
808 Lurleen Wallace Boulevard, North, P.O. Box 2427, 35403
Telephone: 205-345-6789
Telecopier: 205-759-1195

Perry Hubbard (1921-1991)
Michael D. Smith
Christopher L. McIlwain
W. Marcus Brakefield
Herbert E. "Chip" Browder
Justice D. Smyth, III

Elizabeth Faxon Colwick
Gary E. Sullivan

Counsel for: Randall Publishing Co.; United States Fidelity & Guaranty Co.; Chubb Group of Insurance Cos.; West Alabama Health Services; City of Eutaw; Kimberly-Clark Corp.; Regions Bank; City of Tuscaloosa; West Alabama Bank & Trust; Tuscaloosa County Industrial Development Authority.

For full biographical listings, see the Martindale-Hubbell Law Directory

PHELPS, JENKINS, GIBSON & FOWLER, L.L.P. (AV)
1201 Greensboro Avenue, P.O. Box 020848, 35402-0848
Telephone: 205-345-5100
Fax: 205-758-4394
Fax: 205-391-6658
Fax: 205-391-6663

MEMBERS OF FIRM

Sam M. Phelps
James J. Jenkins
Johnson Russell Gibson, III
Randolph M. Fowler
C. Barton Adcox
Farley A. Poellnitz
A. Courtney Crowder

ASSOCIATES

Karen C. Welborn
Stephen E. Snow
W. David Ryan
Bryan Patrick Winter
John M. Compton
Charles T. Grimes
Jenny B. Compton (Not admitted in AL)
Laura C. Karns

LEGAL SUPPORT PERSONNEL

Christine Holt (Paralegal)
Lori R. Woodard (Paralegal)
Melissa D. Harvey (Paralegal)

Representative Clients: Accuchek, Inc.; Alabama Reassurance Corp.; Anderson/GEMCO News Company; Credit Bureau Systems, Inc.; Peco Foods, Inc.; Witness Wear; Vulcan Oil Company, Inc.; Cahaba Pressure Treated Forest Products, Inc.; Affiliated Paper Companies, Inc.; Ox Bodies, Inc.

For full biographical listings, see the Martindale-Hubbell Law Directory

ALASKA

*ANCHORAGE,** Third Judicial District

DELISIO MORAN GERAGHTY & ZOBEL, P.C. (AV)
943 West Sixth Avenue, 99501-2033
Telephone: 907-279-9574
Facsimile: 907-276-4231
Email: delisiomoran@dmgz.com

Joseph M. Moran
Patricia L. Zobel
Gregory L. Youngmun
David D. Floerchinger

Kevin J. Anderson

Representative Clients: Arctic Slope Regional Corporation; National Bank of Alaska.

For full biographical listings, see the Martindale-Hubbell Law Directory

ARIZONA

*FLAGSTAFF,** Coconino Co.

MANGUM, WALL, STOOPS & WARDEN, P.L.L.C. (AV)
100 North Elden, P.O. Box 10, 86002
Telephone: 520-779-6951
Fax: 520-773-1312

H. Karl Mangum (1908-1993)

OF COUNSEL

Douglas J. Wall
Robert W. Warden
Daniel J. Stoops

MEMBERS OF FIRM

A. Dean Pickett
Stephen K. Smith
Melinda L. Garrahan
Michael H. Hinson

ASSOCIATES

Annette Star Lustgarten
Rebecca Smith Currey
R. Scott Currey
Melinda K. Jacquez
Franklin Hoover

Representative Clients: Northern Arizona University; Flagstaff Unified School District; Museum of Northern Arizona; Arizona School Board Association.
Local Counsel for: Bank of America-Arizona; Arizona Public Service; U.S.A.A.; State Farm Fire & Casualty Insurance Co.; Property Development Co.

For Complete List of Firm Personnel, See General Section

For full biographical listings, see the Martindale-Hubbell Law Directory

MESA, Maricopa Co.

JACKSON WHITE GARDNER WEECH & WALKER, P.C. (AV)

40 North Center Street, Suite 200, 85201
Telephone: 480-464-1111
Fax: 480-464-5692
Statewide: 800-243-1160
Email: firm@azmesalaw.com *URL:* http://www.azmesalaw.com
Payson, Arizona Office: 708 East Highway 260, Suite C1-E.
Telephone: 520-472-8878.

Wayne L. Gardner
Eric M. Jackson
Michael R. Pruitt
J. Grant Walker
Bradley D. Weech
Richard A. White
David L. Weed
Roger R. Foote
Otto S. Shill, III

Eric K. Macdonald
Kelly G. Black
Melody K. Seal
Patricia A. Mancabelli
Bobbie J. Rasmusson
Maureen P. Kane
James L. Tanner

For full biographical listings, see the Martindale-Hubbell Law Directory

ROBERTS & ROWLEY, LTD. (AV)

63 East Main Street, Suite 501, 85201-7423
Telephone: 480-833-1113
Fax: 480-833-1114
URL: http://www.azlegal.com

Richard Roberts
Paul S. Rowley

Brian D. Strong
Kevin J. Chapman
Jessica Carpenter
Sean M. Sabo

For full biographical listings, see the Martindale-Hubbell Law Directory

*PHOENIX,** Maricopa Co.

BONN, LUSCHER, PADDEN & WILKINS, CHARTERED (AV)

805 North Second Street, 85004
Telephone: 602-254-5557
Fax: 602-254-0656
Email: firm@blpw.com

Paul V. Bonn
Jeff C. Padden
Randall D. Wilkins
John H. Cassidy
D. Michael Hall
Daniel G. Martin
James M. Barrons

OF COUNSEL

Brian A. Luscher
Marvin Kantor
Howard D. Sukenic

For full biographical listings, see the Martindale-Hubbell Law Directory

FENNEMORE CRAIG, A PROFESSIONAL CORPORATION (AV)

3003 North Central Avenue, Suite 2600, 85012-2913
Telephone: 602-916-5000
Fax: 602-916-5999
Tucson, Arizona Office: One South Church Avenue, Suite 1000, 85701-1620.
Telephone: 520-879-6800.
Fax: 520-879-6899.

Arthur D. Ehrenreich
C. Webb Crockett
Robert P. Robinson
Jay S. Ruffner
Ronald L. Ballard
Stephen M. Savage
Don J. Miner
Gregg Hanks
Karen Ciupak McConnell
J. Barry Shelley
W. T. Eggleston, Jr.
Stephen A. Good

Jeffrey S. Pitcher
Thomas F. O'Malley, III
Susan M. Wissink
Paul A. Krulisky

LEGAL SUPPORT PERSONNEL

LEGAL ASSISTANTS

Vicki Montei

For Complete List of Firm Personnel, See General Section

For full biographical listings, see the Martindale-Hubbell Law Directory

FOGEL, LAMBER & BRONNENKANT, PROFESSIONAL ASSOCIATION (AV)

4001 North Third Street, Suite 400, 85012
Telephone: 602-264-3330
Fax: 602-274-5117

(See Next Column)

Sherman D. Fogel
Dennis M. Lamber
Rex P. Bronnenkant

Reference: Rocky Mountain Bank.

For full biographical listings, see the Martindale-Hubbell Law Directory

GOODSON, MANLEY & DURFEE, P.L.C. (AV)

The Brookstone Building, 2025 North 3rd Street, Suite 200, 85004-1471
Telephone: 602-252-5110
Fax: 602-257-1883
URL: http://www.gmdlaw.com
Email: gmdlaw@primenet.com *URL:* http://www.lawyers.com/goodson_manley_durfee

John F. Goodson
Colleen C. Manley
Richard E. Durfee, Jr.
Benjamin D. Benedict

A list of Representative Clients will be furnished upon request.
Reference: Pacific Century Bank.

For full biographical listings, see the Martindale-Hubbell Law Directory

JOHN D. HARRIS, P.C. (AV)

1 East Camelback Road, Suite 630, 85012-1651
Telephone: 602-340-1234
Telecopier: 602-277-6678
Email: jdharris@doitnow.com

John Duke Harris

J. Scott Conlon

For full biographical listings, see the Martindale-Hubbell Law Directory

HOLPER, WELSH & MITCHELL, LTD. (AV Ⓣ)

2415 East Camelback Road, Suite 700, 85016
Telephone: 602-508-6033
Fax: 480-483-0269
Email: rholper@aol.com *URL:* http://www.lawyers.com/holperwelsh&mitchell
Minneapolis, Minnesota Office: 4100 Multifoods Tower, 33 South Sixth Street, 55402.
Telephone: 612-317-1012.
Fax: 612-317-0947.

Richard D. Holper
Mary Ann Welsh

For full biographical listings, see the Martindale-Hubbell Law Directory

JABURG & WILK, P.C. (AV)

Great American Tower, 3200 North Central Avenue, Suite 2000, 85012
Telephone: 602-248-1000
Fax: 602-248-0522
Email: rcp@jaburglaw.com

Gary J. Jaburg
Lawrence E. Wilk
Roger L. Cohen
Randy Nussbaum
Mitchell Reichman
Beth S. Cohn
Loren Molever
Robert C. Houser, Jr.
Mervyn T. Braude
Michael E. Gottfried

Kathi Mann Sandweiss
Jeffry M. Edwards
Tracy A. Miller
Stephanie N. Monroe
George A. Tacker
Peter W. Ware, Jr.

OF COUNSEL

Richard M. Gerry

Representative Clients: Employee Solutions, Inc.; Sleep America, Inc.; Desert Schools Federal Credit Union; North Star Plumbing; Nations Bank of Texas; State of Arizona; FHLMC; Arizona Escrow & Financial Services.

For full biographical listings, see the Martindale-Hubbell Law Directory

JENNINGS, HAUG & CUNNINGHAM, L.L.P. (AV)

2800 North Central Avenue Suite Eighteen Hundred, 85004-1049
Telephone: 602-234-7800
Fax: 602-277-5595
Email: main@jhc-law.com

MEMBERS OF FIRM

Curtis A. Jennings
John G. Sinodis

For full biographical listings, see the Martindale-Hubbell Law Directory

LANE & EHRLICH, LTD. (AV)

Fairmount Place, Suite 400, 4001 North Third Street, 85012
Telephone: 602-264-4442
Telecopier: 602-264-5006
Email: azcorplaw@aol.com

Robert L. Lane
Gerald F. Ehrlich

(See Next Column)

LANE & EHRLICH LTD.—*Continued*

LEGAL SUPPORT PERSONNEL

LEGAL ASSISTANTS

Sherrie L. Lane
Janice K. Hull
Kathy S. Watkins

References: Bank One Arizona; Harris Trust & Savings Bank; The Northern Trust Bank Arizona.

For full biographical listings, see the Martindale-Hubbell Law Directory

LEWIS AND ROCA, LLP (AV)

A Limited Liability Partnership including a Professional Corporation
40 North Central Avenue, 85004-4429
Telephone: 602-262-5311
Fax: 602-262-5747
Email: clientservice@lrlaw.com *URL:* http://www.lrlaw.com
Tucson, Arizona Office: One South Church Avenue, Suite 700, 86701-1620.
Telephone: 520-622-2090.
Fax: 520-622-3088. E-Mail: clientservice@lrlaw.com.
Las Vegas, Nevada Affiliated Office: Ashcraft and Heinz LLP, 3960 Howard Hughes Parkway, 89109.
Telephone: 702-990-3570.
Fax: 702-990-3571.

MEMBERS OF FIRM

Gerald K. Smith
Douglas R. Chandler
Richard N. Goldsmith
Susan M. Freeman
David E. Manch
Randolph J. Haines
Patrick Derdenger
Amy R. Porter
Scott DeWald
Rosemarie Christofolo
Bryant D. Barber
Kenneth Van Winkle, Jr.
Hope Leibsohn
Kevin G. Hunter
Glenn D. Forcucci
Anderson L. Carper

OF COUNSEL

Barbara Anstey Hoerner
Julie M. Arvo MacKenzie

Representative Clients: Arizona Hospital Assn.; Blood Systems, Inc.; The Dial Corp; The Industrial Development Authority of the City of Phoenix; MarkAir; Phoenix Memorial Hospital; Rockford Corp.; Samaritan Health System; Skymall, Inc.

For Complete List of Firm Personnel, See General Section

For full biographical listings, see the Martindale-Hubbell Law Directory

MEYER, HENDRICKS & BIVENS, P.A. (AV)

3003 North Central Avenue Suite 1200, 85012-2915
Telephone: 602-604-2200
Facsimile: (24 Hrs.) 602-263-5333
Mailing Address: P.O. Box 2199, 85001-2199

Rand Haddock
Robert K. Rogers
Scott M. Theobald

Randall Lindsey
Salmeh K. Fodor

Reference: Northern Trust Bank of Arizona.

For full biographical listings, see the Martindale-Hubbell Law Directory

QUARLES & BRADY LLP (AV)

One Camelback Building, One East Camelback Road, Suite 400, 85012-1649
Telephone: 602-230-5500
Fax: 602-230-5598
URL: http://www.quarles.com
Milwaukee, Wisconsin Office: 411 East Wisconsin Avenue.
Telephone: 414-277-5000.
Fax: 414-271-3552.
Madison, Wisconsin Office: First Wisconsin Plaza, One South Pinckney Street, P.O. Box 2113.
Telephone: 608-251-5000.
Fax: 608-251-9166.
West Palm Beach, Florida Office: 222 Lakeview Avenue, 4th Floor.
Telephone: 407-653-5000.
Fax: 407-653-5333.
Naples, Florida Office: Barnett Center, 4501 Tamiami Trail North, Suite 300.
Telephone: 813-262-5959.
Fax: 813-434-4999.
Chicago, Illinois Office: Quarles & Brady LLC, Citicorp Center, 500 West Madison Street, Suite 3700.
Telephone: 312-715-5000.
Fax: 312-715-5155.

MEMBERS OF THE FIRM

P. Robert Fannin
Jon E. Pettibone
Charles W. Herf
Roger K. Spencer
P. Robert Moya
Peter A. Terry
William M. Shattuck
Glenn Spencer Bacal
James D. Vieregg
David G. Beauchamp
Robert T. Bailes
Daniel L. Muchow

(See Next Column)

MEMBERS OF THE FIRM (Continued)

David A. Selden
Robert S. Bornhoft
Gerald L. Shelley
Benjamin R. Norris
Colleen A. Scherkenbach

ASSOCIATES

Michael G. Galloway
Douglas P. Martin (Not admitted in AZ)
Wendy Gerlach Briggs
Sherry W. Schumm
David T. Barton
Gregory J. Stanton
David G. Bray
C. Christine Burns
Sean D. Garrison
Alicia M. Dagosta (Not admitted in AZ)
Mary Beth Miller Orson
Leezie Kim
Julie A. Pace
Sean D. Johnson
Mark K. Briggs
Mireya Castillo Martin (Not admitted in AZ)
Kevin M. Duddlesten (Not admitted in AZ)
Allen J. Moss
Maureen Henry
Mark A. Torre
Jeffrey A. Sandquist
David J. Wood
Nicole E. Dorsey

For full biographical listings, see the Martindale-Hubbell Law Directory

VLASSIS & VLASSIS (AV)

1545 West Thomas Road, 85015
Telephone: 602-248-8811
Fax: 602-274-8983
Email: vlassis@compuserve.com *URL:* http://www.lawyers.com/vlassis&vlassis

George P. Vlassis
Elizabeth D. Vlassis

References: Bank One; First Star Metropolitan Bank & Trust.

For full biographical listings, see the Martindale-Hubbell Law Directory

WARNER ANGLE ROPER & HALLAM PLC (AV)

3550 North Central Avenue, Suite 1500, 85012
Telephone: 602-264-7101
Fax: 602-234-0419

Jerry L. Angle
Stephen E. Jackson
Ted F. Warner
Larry C. Schafer
Edward (Ted) L. Roper
Dean J. Formanek
Charles Richard Hallam
Jerome K. Elwell
Peter D. Ambelang
John A. Buric
Jack D. Klausner

Chris R. Baniszewski
Bryan C. Moody

Representative Clients: Raytheon Aircraft Credit Corp.; Miller Brands of Pheonix, L.L.C.; Budget Rent-A-Car of Arizona; Coldwell Banker Sucess Realty; Data Systems of Arizona; Pinnacle Mfg. Co., Inc.; Discount Car and Truck Rentals; U.S. Airweld Inc.; Service Resource Corporation.

For full biographical listings, see the Martindale-Hubbell Law Directory

*PRESCOTT,** Yavapai Co.

FAVOUR, MOORE & WILHELMSEN, A PROFESSIONAL ASSOCIATION (AV)

1580 Plaza West Drive, P.O. Box 1391, 86302
Telephone: 520-445-2444
Fax: 520-771-0450
Email: fmw@primenet.com

John M. Favour
Mark M. Moore
David K. Wilhelmsen

Representative Client: Yavapai Title Co.
Reference: Bank of America.

For Complete List of Firm Personnel, See General Section

For full biographical listings, see the Martindale-Hubbell Law Directory

SCOTTSDALE, Maricopa Co.

BENNETT, CARMICHAEL & KENNEDY, L.L.P. (AV)

6991 East Camelback Road, Suite B-111, 85251
Telephone: 602-990-1133; 602-947-8303
Fax: 602-945-2149

MEMBERS OF FIRM

William F. Bennett
David H. Carmichael
Robert T. Kennedy

For full biographical listings, see the Martindale-Hubbell Law Directory

PAUL J. BUSER (AV Ⓣ)

7633 East Acoma Drive, Suite 106, 85260-3486
Telephone: 480-951-1222
Fax: 480-951-2568
Email: pjbazlit@worldnet.att.net *URL:* http://www.lawyers.com/paulbusercactuslaw

For full biographical listings, see the Martindale-Hubbell Law Directory

Scottsdale—Continued

PESKIND HYMSON & GOLDSTEIN, P.C. (AV)

14595 North Scottsdale Road, Suite 14, 85254
Telephone: 602-991-9077
Fax: 602-443-8854
URL: http://www.legalcounselors.com

E. J. Peskind
Irving Hymson
Marilee Miller Clarke
Jeffrey A. Leyton

For full biographical listings, see the Martindale-Hubbell Law Directory

TITUS, BRUECKNER & BERRY, P.C. (AV)

Scottsdale Centre Suite B-252, 7373 North Scottsdale Road, 85253-3527
Telephone: 602-483-9600
Fax: 602-483-3215
Email: TBandB@aol.com

Jon A. Titus
Kurt M. Brueckner
Charles R. Berry
Garry S. O'Rafferty
David R. Jordan

Marc D. Blonstein
Todd Michael Johnson
Matthew B. Levine
Christopher D. Lonn
Robin C. Martindale

OF COUNSEL

John R. Tellier
Timothy G. Burns

LEGAL SUPPORT PERSONNEL

Kellie E. Dicarlo
Belle Taylor

Representative Clients: Arizona Department of Insurance, Receivership Division; Beazer Homes; Cigna; Equipment Leasing Corp.; Hancock Communities; Harvard Investments; Heritage West Securities; Joseph Charles & Associates, Inc.; Peacock, Hislop, Staley Given, Inc.; Woodside Homes.

For full biographical listings, see the Martindale-Hubbell Law Directory

*TUCSON,** Pima Co.

ERNEST ALLEN COHEN (AV)

6426 Calle de Los Seris, P.O. Box 37273, 85740
Telephone: 520-297-4100
Fax: 520-297-4105

Representative Clients: International Organization of Masters, Mates & Pilots, ILA, AFL-CIO; Lawyers Mediation Service Corp.; Coast Guard Legal Aid Counsel; Masters, Mates & Pilots Health & Benefit Plan; Co-Counsel, Officers Union of International Seamen; Arizona Airlines, Inc.

For full biographical listings, see the Martindale-Hubbell Law Directory

ARKANSAS

*FAYETTEVILLE,** Washington Co.

BALL & MOURTON, LTD., PLLC (AV)

A Professional Limited Liability Company
Suite 700, E.J. Ball Plaza, P.O. Box 1948, 72702
Telephone: 501-442-6213
Fax: 501-442-6233
Email: contact@ballandmourton.com *URL:* http://www.BallandMourton.com
Siloam Springs, Arkansas Office: 106 South Broadway. P.O. Box 1348, 72761.
Telephone: 501-524-2337.
Fax: 501-524-3693.

E. J. Ball
Kenneth R. Mourton
John T. Lee
Rayburn W. Green

David G. Bercaw
J. Michael Threet
Joseph D. Reece
Shannon L. Poore

OF COUNSEL

Neal R. Pendergraft

Representative Clients: Arkansas Western Gas Co.; Coors of Western Arkansas, Inc.; Rebel Enterprises, Inc.; Southwestern Energy Co.; Stephens Production Co.; Ohlendorf Investment Co.; Central Health Corporation; McIlroy Bank & Trust.

For full biographical listings, see the Martindale-Hubbell Law Directory

*FORT SMITH,** Sebastian Co.

SMITH, MAURRAS, COHEN, REDD & HORAN, PLC (AV)

510 North Greenwood Avenue, P.O. Box 10205, 72917
Telephone: 501-782-1001
Telefax: 501-782-1279

(See Next Column)

R. A. Young, Jr. (1908-1973)
Don A. Smith
S. Walton Maurras
Robert Y. Cohen, II
Michael K. Redd
Matthew Horan

Lee M. Kirner

Counsel for: Arkansas Best Corp.; ABF Freight System, Inc.; Riverside Furniture Corp.; The City National Bank of Fort Smith; O.K. Industries, Inc.

For full biographical listings, see the Martindale-Hubbell Law Directory

*LITTLE ROCK,** Pulaski Co.

PERRONI AND JAMES (AV)

Stewart Building, 801 West Third Street, 72201
Telephone: 501-372-6555
Fax: 501-372-6333
Email: sperroni@aol.com *URL:* http://www.lawyers.com/perroniandjames

Samuel A. Perroni
Patrick R. James (P.A.)

JaNan Arnold Davis (P.A.)
Susan L. Keller (P.A.)

LEGAL SUPPORT PERSONNEL

Sherry Joyce, CLA

References: Regions Bank, Little Rock, Ark.; Bank of Little Rock, Ark.

For full biographical listings, see the Martindale-Hubbell Law Directory

SKOKOS, BEQUETTE & BILLINGSLEY, P.A. (AV)

3200 TCBY Tower, 425 West Capitol Avenue, 72201-3439
Telephone: 501-374-1107
Facsimile: 501-374-5092

Theodore C. Skokos
George J. Bequette, Jr.
Keith I. Billingsley

For full biographical listings, see the Martindale-Hubbell Law Directory

*NEWPORT,** Jackson Co.

TIMOTHY F. WATSON, SR. (AV)

209 Walnut Street, P.O. Box 988, 72112
Telephone: 870-523-8420
Fax: 870-523-4639
Email: timow1@swbell.net

For full biographical listings, see the Martindale-Hubbell Law Directory

WEST MEMPHIS, Crittenden Co.

RIEVES & MAYTON (AV)

304 East Broadway, P.O. Box 1359, 72303
Telephone: 870-735-3420
Telecopier: 870-735-4678
Email: rieves.mayton@worldnet.att.net
Little Rock, Arkansas Office: Suite 1719, First Commercial Building, 400 West Capitol.
Telephone: 501-376-0504.
Telecopier: 501-372-3482.

MEMBERS OF FIRM

Elton A. Rieves, Jr. (1909-1984)
Elton A. Rieves, III
Michael R. Mayton
Elton A. Rieves, IV

ASSOCIATES

David S. Wilson, III
Eric Newkirk

For full biographical listings, see the Martindale-Hubbell Law Directory

CALIFORNIA

*BAKERSFIELD,** Kern Co.

BORTON, PETRINI & CONRON, LLP (AV)

The Borton, Petrini & Conron Building, 1600 Truxtun Avenue, 93301
Telephone: 661-322-3051
Voice Mail: 661-395-6700
Fax: 661-322-4628
Mailing Address: P.O. Box 2026, Bakersfield, California, 93303
Email: bpcbak@bpclaw.com *URL:* http://www.bpclaw.com
Other City Locations: Fresno, Los Angeles, Modesto, Redding, Sacramento, San Bernardino, San Diego, San Francisco, San Jose, San Luis Obispo, Santa Ana and Ventura.

MEMBERS OF FIRM

George F. Martin
John F. Petrini
Stephen M. Dake
Richard E. Morton
Steve Karcher

(See Next Column)

BORTON, PETRINI & CONRON LLP—*Continued*

ASSOCIATES

William G. Welzenbach
Stephen M. Crane
Raymond G. Robinson
Michael S. Abril

For Complete List of Firm Personnel, See General Section

For full biographical listings, see the Martindale-Hubbell Law Directory

ELDON R. HUGIE (AV)

3403 Stockdale Highway, 93309
Telephone: 805-396-0100
Fax: 805-396-0400
Email: ERH@Lightspeed.net

Representative Clients: Tri-Fanucchi Farms, Inc.; Kern College Land Co.; Lake Boulevard Shopping Center; Madison Group USA, Inc.
References: West America Bank (Bakersfield Main Branch); Bank of America (Riverlakes Branch).

For full biographical listings, see the Martindale-Hubbell Law Directory

KLEIN, DENATALE, GOLDNER, COOPER, ROSENLIEB & KIMBALL, LLP (AV)

(Formerly Di Giorgio, Davis, Klein, Wegis, Duggan & Friedman)
ARCO Tower, 4550 California Avenue, Second Floor, 93309
Telephone: 661-395-1000
Telecopier: 661-326-0418
Mailing Address: P.O. Box 11172, Bakersfield, California, 93389-1172
Email: kleinlaw@kleinlaw.com

Thomas R. Davis (1920-1990)
Anthony J. Klein (Inc.)
Thomas V. DeNatale, Jr.
Barry L. Goldner
Jay L. Rosenlieb
David J. Cooper
Claude P. Kimball
William A. Bruce
Leonard K. Welsh
Christopher P. Burger
Ned E. Dunphy
Melvin L. Ehrlich
Kevin C. Findley
Krystyna L. Jamieson

T. Scott Belden
Catherine E. Bennett
David D. Blaine
Nicole M. Misner
Timothy G. Scanlon

OF COUNSEL

Bruce F. Bunker
Thomas C. Fallgatter
Craig D. Braun

Representative Clients: Bank of America; Great Western Bank; Mojave Pipeline Co.; Transamerican Title Insurance Co.; Dean Whittier Reynolds, Inc.; California Republic Bank; San Joaquin Bank; Nahama & Weagant Energy Co.; Freymiller Trucking, Inc.; Westinghouse Electric Co.

For full biographical listings, see the Martindale-Hubbell Law Directory

BEVERLY HILLS, Los Angeles Co.

HERZOG, FISHER, GRAYSON & WOLFE, A LAW CORPORATION (AV)

9460 Wilshire Boulevard Fifth Floor, 90212
Telephone: 310-278-4300
Fax: 310-278-5430

James P. Herzog
David R. Fisher
Michael A. Grayson
Herbert N. Wolfe

Doreen W. Shenfeld
Jerry R. Sparks
Bree Arlyn-Pessin

OF COUNSEL

Todd I. Grayson

For full biographical listings, see the Martindale-Hubbell Law Directory

HOCHMAN, SALKIN, RETTIG, TOSCHER & PEREZ, A PROFESSIONAL CORPORATION (AV)

9150 Wilshire Boulevard Suite 300, 90212-3414
Telephone: 310-281-3200; 273-1181
Fax: 310-859-1430
URL: http://www.taxlitigator.com

Bruce I. Hochman
Avram Salkin
Charles P. Rettig
Dennis Perez
Steven R. Toscher

OF COUNSEL

George DeRoy
Nathan Joseph Hochman

Stuart A. Simon
Steven D. Blanc
Michel R. Stein

Reference: Union Bank of California.

For full biographical listings, see the Martindale-Hubbell Law Directory

KIRSHMAN, HARRIS & BRANTON, A PROFESSIONAL CORPORATION (AV)

315 South Beverly Drive, Suite 315, 90212
Telephone: 310-277-2323
Telecopier: 310-277-6701
Las Vegas, Nevada Office: 411 E. Bonneville Avenue, Suite 300.
Telephone: 702-384-3877.
Telecopier: 702-384-7057.

Norman H. Kirshman
Michael S. Harris
Gary G. Branton
Roger L. Grandgenett, II

Mary F. Chapman (Not admitted in CA)

For full biographical listings, see the Martindale-Hubbell Law Directory

SCHWARTZ, WISOT & WILSON, LLP (AV)

315 South Beverly Drive, Suite 315, 90212
Telephone: 310-277-2323
Fax: 310-556-2308
Email: swwllp@aol.com *URL:* http://www.lawyers.com/swwllp

Bruce Edward Schwartz
Valerie Wisot
John D. Wilson

Kathleen A. Calaway-McLean

OF COUNSEL

Paula Reddish Zinnemann

Reference: City National Bank, Beverly Hills, California.

For full biographical listings, see the Martindale-Hubbell Law Directory

TURNER, AUBERT & FRIEDMAN, LLP (AV)

Formerly Turner, Gerstenfeld, Wilk & Tigerman
Suite 510, 8383 Wilshire Boulevard, 90211
Telephone: 323-653-3900
Facsimile: 323-653-3021

MEMBERS OF FIRM

Rubin M. Turner
Ronald D. Aubert
Edward Friedman
Michael J. Hanna

ASSOCIATES

Dortha Larene Pyles
Diane H. Pappas

OF COUNSEL

Yelena Yeruhim

For Complete List of Firm Personnel, See General Section

For full biographical listings, see the Martindale-Hubbell Law Directory

BURBANK, Los Angeles Co.

ALVIN N. LOSKAMP A LAW CORPORATION (AV)

290 East Verdugo Avenue, Suite 103, 91502-1331
Telephone: 818-846-9000
Fax: 818-843-1441
URL: http://www.loskamp.com
Email: aloskamp@hotmail.com *URL:* http://www.lawyers.com/loskamplaw

Alvin N. Loskamp

References: Wells Fargo Bank, Business Branch, Burbank.

For full biographical listings, see the Martindale-Hubbell Law Directory

CORONA, Riverside Co.

CLAYSON, MANN, YAEGER & HANSEN, A PROFESSIONAL LAW CORPORATION (AV)

Clayson Law Building, 601 South Main Street, P.O. Box 1447, 92878-1447
Telephone: 909-737-1910
Riverside: 909-689-7241
Fax: 909-737-4384

Walter S. Clayson (1887-1972)
E. Spurgeon Rothrock (1918-1979)
Roy H. Mann
Derrill E. Yaeger
Gary K. Rosenzweig
Kent A. Hansen
Roland C. Bainer
David R. Saunders
Sallie Barnett
Barry M. Walker

Counsel for: Lee Lake Municipal Water District; Palo Verde Irrigation District; Loma Linda University.
Local Counsel: Minnesota Mining & Manufacturing Co.; U.S.A. Waste.

For full biographical listings, see the Martindale-Hubbell Law Directory

COSTA MESA, Orange Co.

FELDHAKE, AUGUST & ROQUEMORE (AV)

Plaza Tower, Suite 1730, 600 Anton Boulevard, 92626-7124
Telephone: 714-438-3885
Fax: 714-438-3888
Email: farlaw@hqonline.com

Robert J. Feldhake | Lisa A. Roquemore
Kenneth S. August | Joshua M. Wolff

ASSOCIATES

Dimitri P. Gross | Supriya Kakkar
Katherine A. Slayton

OF COUNSEL

Arthur J. Swerdloff | Arthur M. Wilcox, Jr.

For full biographical listings, see the Martindale-Hubbell Law Directory

RUTAN & TUCKER, LLP (AV)

A Partnership including Professional Corporations
611 Anton Boulevard, Fourteenth Floor, P.O. Box 1950, 92626-1998
Telephone: 714-641-5100; 213-625-7586
Telecopier: 714-546-9035
Email: rutan&tucker@rutan.com *URL:* http://www.rutan.com

MEMBERS OF FIRM

Gilbert N. Kruger | Evridiki (Vicki) Dallas
Joseph D. Carruth | Thomas J. Crane
James B. O'Neal | Kim D. Thompson
Marcia A. Forsyth | Larry A. Cerutti
Steven A. Nichols | David H. Hochner
Thomas G. Brockington | Kraig C. Kilger

SPECIAL COUNSEL

Debra Dunn Steel

ASSOCIATES

Kent M. Clayton | Natalie Sibbald Dundas
Steven John Goon | Alison M. Barbarosh
Cristy Lomenzo Parker | W. Andrew Moore
Natasha L. Pavia

OF COUNSEL

Edward D. Sybesma, Jr. (P.C.)

For Complete List of Firm Personnel, See General Section

For full biographical listings, see the Martindale-Hubbell Law Directory

DANVILLE, Contra Costa Co.

CRADDICK, CANDLAND & CONTI, PROFESSIONAL CORPORATION (AV)

Danville-San Ramon Medical Center, 915 San Ramon Valley Boulevard, Suite 260, 94526-0810
Telephone: 925-838-1100
Fax: 925-743-0729

Marrs A. Craddick (1928-1996) | W. David Walker
D. Stuart Candland | Andrew S. Miller
Richard J. Conti | Thomas G. Manning
Robert W. Hodges | Steven L. Brown, Jr.

Jean Louise Perry | Matthew C. Mani
Kristine Keala Meredith | Emily C. Millar
Michael E. Gatto

Representative Clients: Kaiser Foundation Hospitals; Medical Insurance Exchange of California; The Doctor's Co.; County of Contra Costa; Farmers Insurance Group (Truck Insurance Exchange); Professional Risk Management of California, Inc.; Claremont Liability Insurance Company; Program Beta.

For full biographical listings, see the Martindale-Hubbell Law Directory

*FRESNO,** Fresno Co.

BOLEN, FRANSEN & BOOSTROM LLP (AV)

Suite 430, East Tower Guarantee Financial Center, 1322 East Shaw Avenue, 93710
Telephone: 559-226-8177
Fax: 559-227-4971
Email: firm@bolenfransen.com *URL:* http://www.bolenfransen.com
Clovis, California Office: 414 Pollasky Avenue.
Telephone: 559-297-6250.
Fax: 559-322-6778.

PARTNERS

Hal H. Bolen II | Jeffrey A. Russell
Kenneth J. Fransen | Virginia Miller Pedreira

ASSOCIATE

Kim Marie Herold

(See Next Column)

OF COUNSEL

Donna Boostrom

For full biographical listings, see the Martindale-Hubbell Law Directory

DOWLING, AARON & KEELER, INCORPORATED (AV)

6051 North Fresno Street, Suite 200, 93710
Telephone: 559-432-4500
Fax: 559-432-4590
Email: dak@daklaw.com *URL:* http://www.daklaw.com
Bakersfield, California Office: 110 South Mt. Claire, Suite 203. 93309.
Telephone: 661-396-0451. Web Site: http://www.daklaw.com.

Michael D. Dowling | Philip David Kopp
Richard M. Aaron | John C. Ganahl
Bruce S. Fraser | Dale Ikeda
Christopher A. Brown

Larry B. Lindenau | Michael P. Dowling
Justin D. Harris

Reference: Wells Fargo Bank (Main).

For Complete List of Firm Personnel, See General Section

For full biographical listings, see the Martindale-Hubbell Law Directory

MARDEROSIAN, OREN & PABOOJIAN, A PROFESSIONAL CORPORATION (AV)

1260 Fulton Mall, 93721-1783
Telephone: 559-441-7991
Facsimilie: 559-441-8170

C. Sam Titus (1957-1990) | Warren R. Paboojian
Michael G. Marderosian | Brett L. Runyon
Eric P. Oren | Alan M. Simpson
Sue Ann Cercone

Michael E. Lehman | Lance E. Armo
David J. Frankenberger, Jr. | Stephen T. Knudsen

For full biographical listings, see the Martindale-Hubbell Law Directory

GLENDALE, Los Angeles Co.

BRIGHT AND BROWN (AV)

550 North Brand Boulevard, Suite 2100, 91203
Telephone: 818-243-2121; 213-489-1414
Facsimile: 818-243-3225
Email: attorneys@brightandbrown.com

James S. Bright | Maureen J. Bright
Gregory C. Brown | John Quirk
Brian L. Becker

ASSOCIATES

PhillipaL. Altmann | Kristin L. Gamble

For full biographical listings, see the Martindale-Hubbell Law Directory

GILL AND BALDWIN (AV)

130 North Brand Boulevard Fourth Floor, 91203
Telephone: 818-500-7755; 323-245-3131
Fax: 818-242-4305
URL: http://www.lawyers.com/g&blaw
Email: gillandbal@aol.com *URL:* http://www.gillandbaldwin.com

MEMBERS OF FIRM

John M. Carmack | Kirk S. MacDonald

Representative Clients: Morrison-Knudsen Corp.; Bireley Foundation.
Reference: Bank of Los Angeles.

For full biographical listings, see the Martindale-Hubbell Law Directory

GREENWALD, HOFFMAN, MEYER & MONTES, L.L.P. (AV)

500 North Brand Boulevard, Suite 920, 91203-1923
Telephone: 818-507-8100; 213-381-1131
Fax: 818-507-8484

MEMBERS OF FIRM

Guy Preston Greenwald, Jr. (1914-1984) | Donald M. Hoffman
Lawrence F. Meyer
Raul M. Montes

References: Bank of America (Los Angeles and Pasadena Trust Offices); Northern Trust of California (Headquarters Office); Bank of America (Glendale Main Branch).

For full biographical listings, see the Martindale-Hubbell Law Directory

O'ROURKE, ALLAN & FONG, LLP (AV)

100 West Broadway, Suite 1250, P.O. Box 10220, 91210
Telephone: 818-247-4303
Fax: 818-247-1451
Email: OAFLAW@aol.com

(See Next Column)

O'ROURKE, ALLAN & FONG LLP—*Continued*

MEMBERS OF FIRM

Denis M. O'Rourke
Joan H. Allan
Roderick D. Fong

ASSOCIATES

Denise Michelle O'Rourke
Marina Manoukian
Toshiko Kobayashi

References: Verdugo Banking Co. (Glendale, California); Community Bank (Glendale, California).

For full biographical listings, see the Martindale-Hubbell Law Directory

GOLD RIVER, Sacramento Co.

LAW OFFICES OF JOSEPH W. SCALIA (AV)

11335 Gold Express, Suite 105, 95670-4491
Telephone: 916-858-2286
Fax: 916-852-5777
Email: jscalia@ix.netcom.com

Representative Clients: California Capital Small Business Development Corp.; Chorro Communications, Inc.; Excel Trade Group, Inc.; GEC Alsthom Schilling Robotic Systems, Inc.; Green Tree Financial Corp.; Capitol City Health Clubs; Phoenix Pacific Development Co.; McKim Homes, Inc.; Phoenix Chiropratic, Inc.; Interactive Entertainment Corp.

For full biographical listings, see the Martindale-Hubbell Law Directory

IRVINE, Orange Co.

LAW OFFICES OF HUGH BRECKENRIDGE (AV)

4199 Campus Drive, Suite 700, 92612
Telephone: 949-854-2520
FAX: 949-854-4897
URL: http://pages.prodigy.net/hughbreck
Email: Hughbreck@prodigy.net *URL:* http://www.lawyers.com/hughbreckenridge

For full biographical listings, see the Martindale-Hubbell Law Directory

GALFIN & PASSON, LLP (AV)

18101 Von Karman Avenue, Suite 1400, 92612-1043
Telephone: 949-752-2444
Facsimile: 949-833-8256
Email: galpas@aol.com
Santa Ana, California Office: 2122 North Broadway, Suite 100.
Telephone: 949-752-2444.

MEMBERS OF FIRM

Ted A. Galfin
Kenneth D. Passon
Lorraine Kay Smyth
Michael R. Adams
Marcelle Suzanne Strauss
Adam M. Greely

For full biographical listings, see the Martindale-Hubbell Law Directory

GEORGE & SHIELDS, LLP (AV)

30 Corporate Park, Suite 300, 92606-5133
Telephone: 949-263-1085
Fax: 949-263-0585
Email: toplaw@george-shields.com *URL:* http://www.george-shields.com

MEMBERS OF FIRM

Robert K. George
Timothy F. Shields
David W. Sparks

For full biographical listings, see the Martindale-Hubbell Law Directory

GRECO, MOLLIS & O'HARA, A PROFESSIONAL CORPORATION (AV)

18400 Von Karman, Suite 500, 92612-1514
Telephone: 949-263-0600
Fax: 949-263-1513

Thomas A. Greco
Ronald A. Mollis
Kevin O'Hara
Charles A. Mollis

For full biographical listings, see the Martindale-Hubbell Law Directory

TIMOTHY L. JOENS & ASSOCIATES A PROFESSIONAL CORPORATION (AV)

2601 Main Street, Suite 320, 92614
Telephone: 949-553-1950
Fax: 949-553-8835

Timothy L. Joens

Representative Client: Century 21 Real Estate Corp.

For full biographical listings, see the Martindale-Hubbell Law Directory

LAW OFFICES OF C. WILLIAM KIRCHER, JR. A PROFESSIONAL CORPORATION (AV)

2603 Main Street Suite 1050, 92614
Telephone: 949-720-9753
Fax: 949-720-8752
Email: cwklo@aol.com

C. William Kircher, Jr., (Professional Corporation)

Reference: California State Bank (Corona Del Mar Branch).

For full biographical listings, see the Martindale-Hubbell Law Directory

LEE, GODDARD & DUFFY LLP (AV)

A Limited Liability Partnership
18500 Von Karman Avenue, Suite 700, 92612
Telephone: 949-253-0500
Facsimile: 949-253-0505

Raymond A. Lee
William A. Goddard, IV
Anthony C. Duffy
Sherman O. Halstead, Jr.
Thomas B. Griffen
Bradley A. Patterson
Douglas L. Collins

Loren A. Deters
Lauren M. Seng
Jeffrey A. Coste (Not admitted in CA)

For full biographical listings, see the Martindale-Hubbell Law Directory

JACK L. SCHOELLERMAN (AV)

2030 Main Street, Suite 1600, 92614
Telephone: 949-660-7000
Fax: 949-660-6096

For full biographical listings, see the Martindale-Hubbell Law Directory

LARKSPUR, Marin Co.

WEINBERG, HOFFMAN, CASEY & ROPERS (AV)

A Partnership including a Professional Corporation
900 Larkspur Landing Circle, Suite 155, 94939
Telephone: 415-461-9666
Fax: 415-461-9681

Ivan Weinberg
Joseph Hoffman
A. Michael Casey
Mark Ropers

For full biographical listings, see the Martindale-Hubbell Law Directory

*LOS ANGELES,** Los Angeles Co.

ALVARADO, SMITH & SANCHEZ, A PROFESSIONAL CORPORATION (AV)

611 West Sixth Street, Suite 2650, 90017
Telephone: 213-229-2400
Facsimile: 213-229-2499
URL: http://www.alvarado-smith.com
Irvine, California Office: 4 Park Plaza, Suite 1200, 92614.
Telephone: 949-955-6800.
Fax: 949-955-6899.

Raymond G. Alvarado
Ruben A. Smith
Maurice Sanchez
John M. Sorich
Raúl F. Salinas
Frances Q. Jett
Theresa Eileen Antonucci
Diane C. Barrio
Rosario M. Tobias

OF COUNSEL

Martin N. Burton

For full biographical listings, see the Martindale-Hubbell Law Directory

BACON & MILLS, LLP (AV)

800 Wilshire Boulevard, Suite 950, 90017
Telephone: 213-486-6500
Fax: 213-486-6552
Email: baconmills@earthlink.net *URL:* http://www.baconmills.com
Brea, California Office: Three Pointe Drive, Suite 308.
Telephone: 714-257-2100.
Fax: 714-257-2101.

Robert Parker Mills
Robert L. Bacon (Resident, Brea Office)
Theodore E. Bacon (Resident, Brea Office)
John F. Norris (Resident, Brea Office)
James W. Colfer
Patrick A. Connolly, III
Jill L. Johnson
Melissa Lee Mello

Representative Clients: Lucas Varity, PLC; Lucas Industries, Inc.; Columbia Showcase & Cabinet Co.; Cannon Fabrication, Inc.; Singer, Lewak, Greenbaum and Goldstein, LLP; Optical Components, Inc.; Femino Foundation; Coleman Foundation; Laguna Clay Co.

For full biographical listings, see the Martindale-Hubbell Law Directory

Los Angeles—Continued

BARBOSA GARCIA LLP (AV)

A Partnership including a Professional Corporation
801 South Grand Avenue Suite 300, 90017-4621
Telephone: 213-612-0800
Fax: 213-612-8085

Henry S. Barbosa (P.C.)
Lorie A. Campos
Kenneth T. Fong
Bonifacio Bonny Garcia (P.C.)
Michael L. Kadish
John F. Lagle
Peter E. Langsfeld
Benjamin D. Nieberg
Gary W. Park
Roberta R. Sistos
Jonathan B. Stone
Rajeev M. Talwani
Sylvia J. Trujillo
Thuy-Whien Vuong
John G. Yslas

OF COUNSEL

Albert A. Erkel, Jr.

SPECIAL COUNSEL

Adrienne D. Konigar
Joyce E. Paul
Melvin D. Peters

LEGAL SUPPORT PERSONNEL

Victor M. Estrada (Paralegal)
Janice H. Minamoto (Paralegal)

For full biographical listings, see the Martindale-Hubbell Law Directory

PAUL L. BASILE, JR. (AV)

11400 West Olympic Boulevard, Suite 350, 90064-1558
Telephone: 310-478-2114
Toll Free: 800-511-2114
Fax: 310-478-0229
Email: pbasile@basile-law.com *URL:* http://www.basile-law.com

For full biographical listings, see the Martindale-Hubbell Law Directory

BECK, DE CORSO, DALY, BARRERA & KREINDLER, A PROFESSIONAL LAW CORPORATION (AV)

601 West Fifth Street, 12th Floor, 90071-2025
Telephone: 213-688-1198
Fax: 213-489-7532
Email: beckdecorso@earthlink.net *URL:* http://www.beckdecorso.com

Mark E. Beck
Anthony A. De Corso
Bryan D. Daly
Teresa R. Barrera
Charles L. Kreindler
Suzanne E. Tracy

Peter J. Diedrich
Barbara E. Taylor
Stephen P. Jones

OF COUNSEL

Godfrey Isaac

For full biographical listings, see the Martindale-Hubbell Law Directory

BELIN RAWLINGS & BADAL LLP (AV)

11601 Wilshire Boulevard, Suite 2200, 90025-1758
Telephone: 310-575-5300
Fax: 310-445-0884
Email: recption@brblaw.com

MEMBERS OF FIRM

Daniel N. Belin
Douglas M. Rawlings
Robert G. Badal
Henry Ben-Zvi
Lawrence R. Lieberman
Ben D. Whitwell

ASSOCIATES

Peter S. Kravitz
Rudolph DeFelice

OF COUNSEL

Martin S. Schwartz

SPECIAL COUNSEL

Douglas C. Emhoff

For full biographical listings, see the Martindale-Hubbell Law Directory

BERGMAN, WEDNER & DACEY, INC. (AV)

Suite 900, 10880 Wilshire Boulevard, 90024
Telephone: 310-470-6110
Fax: 310-474-0931
Email: ofc@bergman-wedner.com *URL:* http://www.bergman-wedner.com

Gregory M. Bergman
Gregory A. Wedner
John P. Dacey
Alan Harvey Mittelman
Robert M. Mason III
Kristi Anne Sjoholm-Sierchio
John V. Tamborelli

Lisa S. Newnan
Daphne M. Humphreys
Michele M. Goldsmith
Denise G. Godfrey
William Daryl Strickland
Pamela R. Fleming
Matthew R. Hicks
Jorge J. Luna
Paul V. Rayburn
Mark W. Waterman

(See Next Column)

OF COUNSEL

Lloyd A. Bergman (1923-1994)
Jacob A. Wedner
Marvin Goldsmith
Mark K. Kitabayashi

SPECIAL COUNSEL

Richard V. Godino

For full biographical listings, see the Martindale-Hubbell Law Directory

BLANC WILLIAMS JOHNSTON & KRONSTADT, LLP (AV)

A Partnership including Professional Corporations
Suite 1700, 1900 Avenue of the Stars, 90067
Telephone: 310-552-2500
Telecopier: 310-552-1191
Email: bwjk@bwjk.com

MEMBERS OF FIRM

Ronald L. Blanc (P.C.)
Harley J. Williams (P.C.)
Ronald L. Johnston (P.C.)
John A. Kronstadt
James R. Farrand
Richard T. McCoy III
Regina A. Stagg
John C. Rawls III
Daniel M. Grigsby
Suzanne V. Wilson
Dawn Weekes Glenn

James S. Blackburn
Vivian W. Yang
Allison Binder
Jennifer M. Lloyd
Mark S. Dancsecs

OF COUNSEL

Sol Rosenthal

Reference: Santa Monica Bank (Beverly Hills Office).

For full biographical listings, see the Martindale-Hubbell Law Directory

BLECHER & COLLINS, A PROFESSIONAL CORPORATION (AV)

611 West Sixth Street, 20th Floor, 90017
Telephone: 213-622-4222
Telecopier: 213-622-1656

Maxwell M. Blecher
Harold R. Collins, Jr.
John E. Andrews
Steven J. Cannata
Ralph C. Hofer
William C. Hsu
Gary M. Joye
James Robert Noblin
Donald R. Pepperman
Alicia G. Rosenberg

For full biographical listings, see the Martindale-Hubbell Law Directory

LAW OFFICES OF DAVID B. BLOOM A PROFESSIONAL CORPORATION (AV)

3325 Wilshire Boulevard, Ninth Floor, 90010
Telephone: 323-938-5248; 384-4088
Telecopier: 213-385-2009

David B. Bloom

Stephen S. Monroe (A Professional Corporation)
Raphael A. Rosemblat
James E. Adler
Roy A. Levun
Jonathan Udell
Susan Carole Jay
Edward Idell
Sandra Kamenir
Steven Wayne Lazarus
Andrew Edward Briseno
Shelley M. Gould
Ted L. Travis

For full biographical listings, see the Martindale-Hubbell Law Directory

CLARK & TREVITHICK, A PROFESSIONAL CORPORATION (AV)

800 Wilshire Boulevard, 12th Floor, 90017
Telephone: 213-629-5700
Telecopier: 213-624-9441
Email: postmaster@clarktrev.com
San Francisco, California Office: 456 Montgomery Street, 20th Floor.
Telephone: 415-288-6520.
Fax: 415-398-2820.

Donald P. Clark
Alexander C. McGilvray, Jr.
Kevin P. Fiore
Dean I. Friedman
Robert F. DeMeter
Michael K. Wofford
Brent A. Reinke
James S. Arico
Robert W. Renken

For Complete List of Firm Personnel, See General Section

For full biographical listings, see the Martindale-Hubbell Law Directory

DARLING, HALL & RAE, LLP (AV)

520 South Grand Avenue, 7th Floor, 90071
Telephone: 213-627-8104
Fax: 213-627-7795
Email: darlinghallrae@compuserve.com

(See Next Column)

DARLING, HALL & RAE LLP—*Continued*

MEMBERS OF FIRM

Hugh W. Darling (1901-1986)
Edward S. Shattuck (1901-1965)
George Gaylord Gute (1922-1981)
Donald Keith Hall (1918-1984)
Matthew S. Rae, Jr.
Richard L. Stack
Edwin Freston

OF COUNSEL

Edward F. Pearson

Reference: City National Bank (Pershing Square Office, Los Angeles, California).

For full biographical listings, see the Martindale-Hubbell Law Directory

DAVIS & FOX (AV)

1901 Avenue of the Stars, Suite 400, 90067
Telephone: 310-286-2915
Fax: 310-286-2916

Calvin E. Davis
Steven A. Fox
Elizabeth A. Kooyman
John J. Stumreiter
Amy L. Freisleben
Barbara Kekich
Gregory M. Sinderbrand

For full biographical listings, see the Martindale-Hubbell Law Directory

DEMETRIOU, DEL GUERCIO, SPRINGER & MOYER, LLP (AV)

801 South Grand Avenue, 10th Floor, 90017
Telephone: 213-624-8407
Telecopy: 213-624-0174
Email: ddsm@juno.com

MEMBERS OF FIRM

Angela Shanahan
Stephen A. Del Guercio
Michael A. Francis

OF COUNSEL

Ronald J. Del Guercio
James P. Del Guercio

Reference: Bank of America, L.A. Main Office, Los Angeles, Calif.

For full biographical listings, see the Martindale-Hubbell Law Directory

DONAHUE MESEREAU & LEIDS L.L.P. (AV)

A Limited Liability Partnership including Professional Corporations
1900 Avenue of the Stars Suite 2700, 90067
Telephone: 310-277-1441
Facsimile: 310-277-2888

Michael D. Donahue (A Professional Corporation)
Asher M. Leids
Dave Lenny
Kirsten L. Anderson
Jacqueline L. Shulman
Amy S. Novicoff (Not admitted in CA)
Julia A. Longjohn

OF COUNSEL

Thomas A. Mesereau, Jr. (A Professional Corporation)

For full biographical listings, see the Martindale-Hubbell Law Directory

GRAY, YORK & DUFFY LLP (AV)

15760 Ventura Boulevard, 16th Floor (Encino), 91436
Telephone: 818-907-4000; 310-553-0445
Fax: 818-783-4551
Email: gydlaw@pacbell.net
Redwood City, California Office: 702 Marshall Street, Suite 500, 94063.
Telephone: 650-365-7343.
Fax: 650-365-6225.
San Francisco, California Office: 660 Market Street, Suite 490, 94105.
Telephone: 415-908-1300.
Fax: 415-974-6199.

MEMBERS OF FIRM

Gary S. Gray
James R. York
John J. Duffy
Arlene A. Colman
Barry D. Brown
William F. Flahavan
Jeffrey S. Stern

ASSOCIATES

Amalia L. Taylor
Kenneth A. Hearn
Gabriel H. Wainfeld
Frank J. Ozello, Jr.
Debra Hartman Warfel
Jeanine M. St. Pierre-Kumar

Reference: Marathon National Bank, Los Angeles, California.

For full biographical listings, see the Martindale-Hubbell Law Directory

IVERSON, YOAKUM, PAPIANO & HATCH (AV)

One Wilshire Building, 27th Floor 624 South Grand Avenue, 90017
Telephone: 213-624-7444
Telecopier: 213-629-4563

Paul E. Iverson (1907-1975)
Frank B. Yoakum, Jr. (1906-1991)

(See Next Column)

MEMBERS OF FIRM

Neil Papiano
Dennis A. Page
Patrick M. Mc Adam
Arnold D. Larson
John M. Garrick

ASSOCIATES

Douglas C. Pease
Andrew K. Doty
Melissa A. Immel
Mary P. Lightfoot
Mark Pearson
Gioia M. Fasi
Adam F. Burke
Scott A. Horton

OF COUNSEL

R. Noel Hatch

Representative Clients: Lockheed Corp.; International Paper; Bridgestone/-Firestone, Inc.
Reference: Bank of America (Los Angeles Head Office).

For full biographical listings, see the Martindale-Hubbell Law Directory

H. ROY JEPPSON A PROFESSIONAL CORPORATION (AV)

11900 W. Olympic Boulevard Sixth Floor, 90064
Telephone: 310-826-5566
Fax: 310-826-5350
URL: http://www.lawyers.com/jeppsonlaw
Oxnard, California Office: 300 Esplanade Drive, Suite 1810.
Telephone: 805-604-1100.
Fax: 805-604-1600.

H. Roy Jeppson

Robyn F. Stalk

For full biographical listings, see the Martindale-Hubbell Law Directory

KNOPFLER & ROBERTSON, LLP (AV)

Suite 500, 21650 Oxnard Street (Woodland Hills), 91367
Telephone: 818-227-0770; 213-624-1111
Telefax: 818-227-0777
Irvine, California Office: 19800 MacArthur Boulevard, Suite 270, 92612.
Telephone: 714-261-6191.
Pleasanton, California Office: 400 Main Street, Suite 204, 94566.
Telephone: 510-425-7250.
Las Vegas, Nevada Office: Knopfler & Robertson in Association with Broom & Vaisbort, LLP, 3753 Howard Hughes Parkway, Suite 200, 89109.
Telephone: 702-792-2413.
Camarillo, California Office: 1200 Paseo, Suite 170, 93010.
Telephone: 805-482-1903; 800-CONDOLAW.
Fax: 805-484-5917.

George Knopfler
Alexander Robertson, IV
Deborah Broom
Richard A. Capella
Jonathan S. Vick
Edward D. Vaisbort
William G. Kelsberg

OF COUNSEL

Scott C. Haith
James P. Lingl (Resident, Camarillo Office)
Christina S. Robertson

Janice M. Michaels
James M. Pazos
Mark Rohrer
Craig Smith
Robert Nation
William S. Dunlevy (Resident, Camarillo Office)
Scott A. Hunter

For full biographical listings, see the Martindale-Hubbell Law Directory

LEVINE & ASSOCIATES (AV)

Suite 710, 2049 Century Park East, 90067
Telephone: 310-553-8400
Fax: 310-553-8455
Email: lalaw310@aol.com
Seattle, Washington Office: 999 Third Avenue, Suite 3210, 98104.
Telephone: 206-626-5310.
Fax: 206-626-5313.

Jerome L. Levine

ASSOCIATES

Mary L. Prevost (Resident, Seattle, Washington Office)
Erin M. Copeland
Frank R. Lawrence
Wendy T. Parnell

For full biographical listings, see the Martindale-Hubbell Law Directory

MATTHIAS & BERG LLP (AV)

1990 South Bundy Drive, Suite 790, 90025-5244
Telephone: 310-820-0083
Facsimile: 310-820-8313
Email: info@matthiasberg.com

MEMBERS OF FIRM

Michael R. Matthias
Jeffrey P. Berg

(See Next Column)

MATTHIAS & BERG LLP, *Los Angeles—Continued*

ASSOCIATES

Kenneth M. H. Hoff
Ari Lorin Markow

OF COUNSEL

Stuart R. Singer

Representative Clients: Am Tec, Inc.; Chatsworth Products, Inc.; Columbia Capital Corp.; Greater China Corp.; National Quality Care, Inc.; Network Holdings International, Inc.; Private Investors Equity Group; Residential Resources, Inc.; Anthony Advisors.

For full biographical listings, see the Martindale-Hubbell Law Directory

MINTON, MINTON AND RAND LLP (AV)

510 West Sixth Street, 90014
Telephone: 213-624-9394
Fax: 213-624-9323

MEMBERS OF FIRM

Carl W. Minton (1902-1974)
Carl Minton
David E. Rand

Reference: Bank of America National Trust & Savings Assn. (Seventh & Flower Office, Los Angeles, Calif.).

For full biographical listings, see the Martindale-Hubbell Law Directory

O'MELVENY & MYERS LLP (AV)

400 South Hope Street, 90071-2899
Telephone: 213-430-6000
Facsimile: 213-430-6407
Cable: MOMS
Telex: 674122
Email: omminfo@omm.com *URL:* http://www.omm.com
Century City, CA Office: 1999 Avenue of the Stars, Los Angeles, 90067-6035.
Telex: 674097. Tel: 310-553-6700.
Fax: 310-246-6779.
Newport Beach, CA Office: 610 Newport Center Drive, 92660-6429.
Telex: 4722088. Tel: 949-760-9600.
Fax: 949-823-6994.
San Francisco, CA Office: Embarcadero Center West, 275 Battery Street, 94111-3305. Tel: 415-984-8700.
Fax: 415-984-8701.
New York, NY Office: Citicorp Center, 153 East 53rd Street, 10022-4611.
Telex: 129165. Tel: 212-326-2000.
Fax: 212-326-2061.
Washington, DC Office: 555 13th Street, N.W., 20004-1109.
Cable: MOMSWSH.
Telex: 89622. Tel: 202-383-5300.
Fax: 202-383-5414.
London Office: O'Melveny & Myers, 3 Finsbury Square, London, EC2A 1LA, England. Tel: 44-171-256-8451. Fax 44-171-638-8205.
Tokyo Office: Akasaka Twin Tower, East 14F, 2-17-23, Akasaka, Minato-ku, Tokyo 107-0052, Japan. Tel: 03-5562-2800.
Fax: 03-5575-3840.
Hong Kong Office: O'Melveny & Myers, Suite 1905, Tower Two, Lippo Centre, 89 Queensway, Central, Hong Kong. Tel: 852-2523-8266.
Fax: 852-2522-1760.
Shanghai Office: Kerry Centre, 20F, 1515 Nanjing Road West, Shanghai, 200040 People's Republic of China. Tel: 86-21-5298-5600.
Fax: 86-21-5298-5500.

PARTNER

Frederick B. McLane

For Complete List of Firm Personnel, See General Section

For full biographical listings, see the Martindale-Hubbell Law Directory

REINIS & REINIS (AV)

550 South Hope Street, 20th Floor, 90071
Telephone: 213-624-4246
Facsimile: 213-624-4709

MEMBERS OF FIRM

Mitchell N. Reinis
Richard G. Reinis

ASSOCIATES

Laura P. Worsinger
Gregory N. Weisman
Steven M. Harrison
Richard A. Fisher

For full biographical listings, see the Martindale-Hubbell Law Directory

RODI, POLLOCK, PETTKER, GALBRAITH & CAHILL, A LAW CORPORATION (AV)

444 South Flower Street, Suite 1700, 90071-2901
Telephone: 213-895-4900
Telecopiers: 213-895-4921; 895-4922; 895-4750
URL: http://www.rodipollock.com

(See Next Column)

Karl B. Rodi (1908-1982)
Allan E. Ceran
John D. Cahill
Elizabeth B. Blakely
John D. Pettker
Robert C. Norton
Daniel C. Bond (1942-1977)
Tim G. Ceperley
William R. Christian
Coralie Kupfer
Henry P. Pramov, Jr.
Cris K. O'Neall
John F. Cermak, Jr.
Scott E. Adamson
Margaret Rosenthal

Sonja A. Inglin
Donna Yamini
Michael A. Abraham
Wade E. Norwood
Kenneth A. Franklin
Deepak Nanda
Richard Nessary
David J. Elbaz

OF COUNSEL

John P. Pollock
James M. Galbraith

For full biographical listings, see the Martindale-Hubbell Law Directory

ROSENFELD, WOLFF, ARONSON, KURLAND & KLEIN, A PROFESSIONAL CORPORATION (AV)

2049 Century Park East, Suite 3090, 90067
Telephone: 310-556-1221
Fax: 310-556-0401

Morton M. Rosenfeld
Alan D. Aronson
Steven G. Wolff
Marta T. Kurland
David C. Klein

Paul R. Rosenbaum
Debra E. Best

For full biographical listings, see the Martindale-Hubbell Law Directory

SHIOTANI & INOUYE (AV)

1901 Avenue of the Stars Suite 1010, 90067
Telephone: 310-712-0100
Telecopier: 310-712-0110
Email: silaw@earthlink.net *URL:* http://www.lawyers.com/shiotani&inouye

MEMBERS OF FIRM

Barney B. Shiotani
Lawrence G. Inouye

ASSOCIATE

Nicole Grattan Pearson

References: First Los Angeles Bank (Airport Office); Bank of California.

For full biographical listings, see the Martindale-Hubbell Law Directory

SULLIVAN LAW CORPORATION (AV)

545 South Figueroa Street, Suite 1216, 90071-1599
Telephone: 213-488-9200
Telecopier: 213-362-0419
Email: flightattorney@aol.com *URL:* http://www.flightattorney.com

Michael R. Sullivan

For full biographical listings, see the Martindale-Hubbell Law Directory

LAWRENCE C. TISTAERT (AV)

11766 Wilshire Boulevard, Suite 770, 90025-6537
Telephone: 310-312-0874
Fax: 310-312-1034
Email: lctist@ix.netcom.com

Representative Clients: Bell Foundry Co.; Brendan Tours; Franklin Telecommunications Corp.; Munro Properties; United States Tour Operators Association.
Reference: Bank of America.

For full biographical listings, see the Martindale-Hubbell Law Directory

WEHNER AND PERLMAN LLP (AV)

A Partnership of Professional Corporations
12121 Wilshire Boulevard Suite 1120, 90025-1123
Telephone: 310-478-3131
Facsimile: 310-312-0078
Email: wehnerandp@aol.com

MEMBERS OF FIRM

Charles C. Wehner (P.C.)
Rodney M. Perlman (P.C.)

ASSOCIATES

David Eum
Stephen T. Hodge
James D. Henderson, Jr.

For full biographical listings, see the Martindale-Hubbell Law Directory

Los Angeles—Continued

GERALD T. YOSHIDA (AV)

12400 Wilshire Boulevard, Suite 400, 90025-1023
Telephone: 310-571-2756
Fax: 310-207-0954

Representative Clients: Vido Artukovich & Sons Construction; McKean Construction; Spiess Construction; Gierlich-Mitchell, Inc.; Hill Crane Service, Inc.; ACI General Engineering Contractors; A.A. Portanova & Sons, Inc.; Rough Terrain, Inc.; Altfillisch Construction; Ameron.

For full biographical listings, see the Martindale-Hubbell Law Directory

MANHATTAN BEACH, Los Angeles Co.

STEINBERG BARNESS FOSTER & FOLEY LLP (AV)

1334 Park View Avenue, Suite 100, 90266
Telephone: 310-546-8160
Telecopier: 310-546-8189
Email: sbgf@ix.netcom.com

MEMBERS OF FIRM

Alex Steinberg
Daniel I. Barness
Douglas B. Foster
Shannon M. Foley

ASSOCIATES

William R. (Randy) Kirkpatrick
Jeff M. Lee
Kimberly Ann White

OF COUNSEL

Jordan G. Barness
Ronald D. Hariri (Not admitted in CA)

References: California United Bank; Wells Fargo Bank; Citizens Commerical Trust & Savings Bank; Bank of America.

For full biographical listings, see the Martindale-Hubbell Law Directory

*MODESTO,** Stanislaus Co.

RICHARD DOUGLAS BREW A PROFESSIONAL LAW CORPORATION (AV)

Suite 350 / Judge Frank C. Damrell Building, 1601 I Street, 95354-1135
Telephone: 209-572-3157
Telefax: 209-572-4641
Email: rdbplc@interleg.com

Richard Douglas Brew

For full biographical listings, see the Martindale-Hubbell Law Directory

GIANELLI & FORES, A PROFESSIONAL LAW CORPORATION (AV)

1014 16th Street, P.O. Box 3212, 95353
Telephone: 209-521-6260
Telecopier: 209-521-5971
Email: gianelli@ainet.com *URL:* http://www.gianelli-fores.com

Louis F. Gianelli
Michael L. Gianelli
Robert P. Fores
David L. Gianelli
Brett L. Dickerson
Terry L. Campbell

For full biographical listings, see the Martindale-Hubbell Law Directory

MONTEREY, Monterey Co.

THE THOMPSON LAW OFFICE (AV)

580 Calle Principal, First Floor, 93940-2818
Telephone: 831-646-1224
Fax: 831-646-1225
URL: http://www.lawyers.com/justice-4-you
Email: rwt111@justice-4-you.com *URL:* http://www.justice-4-you.com

Ralph W. Thompson III

For full biographical listings, see the Martindale-Hubbell Law Directory

*NAPA,** Napa Co.

GAW, VAN MALE, SMITH, MYERS & MIROGLIO, A PROFESSIONAL LAW CORPORATION (AV)

944 Main Street, 94559-3045
Telephone: 707-252-9000
Telecopier: 707-252-0792
URL: http://www.gvmsmm.com
Fairfield, California Office: Corporate Plaza. 1261 Travis Boulevard, Suite 350, 94533-4801.
Telephone: 707-425-1250.
Fax: 707-425-1255.
Redlands, California Office: 300 E. State Street, Suite 101, 92372-5200.
Telephone: 909-798-3190.
Fax: 909-798-3092.

Wyman G. Smith, III
Bruce A. Myers
S. Scott Reynolds

(See Next Column)

Michael A. Rubin
Kathleen M. Bock

Reference: The Vintage Bank.

For full biographical listings, see the Martindale-Hubbell Law Directory

NEWPORT BEACH, Orange Co.

BIDNA & KEYS, A PROFESSIONAL LAW CORPORATION (AV)

5120 Campus Drive, 92660
Telephone: 949-752-7030
Telecopier: 949-752-8770
URL: http://www.bidnakeys.com

Howard M. Bidna
Richard D. Keys
Harvey M. Moore
Jon A. Longerbone

Reference: Union Bank of California (Orange County Airport Branch).

For full biographical listings, see the Martindale-Hubbell Law Directory

CHRISTOPHER L. BLANK (AV)

4695 MacArthur Court, Suite 1200, 92660
Telephone: 949-250-4600
Facsimile: 949-250-4604
Email: clblank@aol.com *URL:* http://www.lawyers.com/blank

For full biographical listings, see the Martindale-Hubbell Law Directory

CAPRETZ & ASSOCIATES (AV)

5000 Birch Street, West Tower Suite 2500, 92660-2139
Telephone: 949-724-3000
Fax: 949-757-2635
URL: http://www.lawyers.com/capretzradcliffe
Email: crlawl@ix.netcom.com *URL:* http://www.CAPRETZ.com

MEMBER OF FIRM

James T. Capretz

OF COUNSEL

William B. Lawless (Not admitted in CA)

LEGAL SUPPORT PERSONNEL

Sandra L. Koop (Law Clerk)

For full biographical listings, see the Martindale-Hubbell Law Directory

DAVIS, PUNELLI & KEATHLEY LLP (AV)

610 Newport Center Drive, Suite 1000, P.O. Box 7920, 92658-7920
Telephone: 949-640-0700
Telecopier: 949-640-0714
URL: http://www.lawyers.com/dpkllp

MEMBERS OF FIRM

S. Eric Davis
Frank Punelli, Jr.
H. James Keathley
Katherine D. Keathley

OF COUNSEL

Lewis K. Uhler

For full biographical listings, see the Martindale-Hubbell Law Directory

THEODORE M. HANKIN (AV)

1301 Dove Street, Suite 900, 92660
Telephone: 949-752-8840
FAX: 949-752-2710
URL: http://www.lawyers.com/hankinlaw

For full biographical listings, see the Martindale-Hubbell Law Directory

LAUTSCH LAW CORPORATION (AV)

1200 Quail Street, Suite 140, 92660
Telephone: 949-955-9095
Telefax: 949-955-2978
Email: jlautsch@ibm.net

John C. Lautsch

For full biographical listings, see the Martindale-Hubbell Law Directory

JEFFREY R. MATSEN & ASSOCIATES (AV)

5001 Birch Street, 92660
Telephone: 949-442-9191
Fax: 949-442-9199
Email: jmatsen@urjet.net *URL:* http://www.lawyers.com/jeffreyrmatsen

For full biographical listings, see the Martindale-Hubbell Law Directory

MCCAULEY & ASSOCIATES ALC (AV)

610 Newport Center Drive, Suite 1010, 92660
Telephone: 949-644-2922
Fax: 949-644-9627
Email: info@mccauleylaw.com

MEMBER OF FIRM

John J. McCauley

(See Next Column)

McCauley & Associates ALC, *Newport Beach—Continued*

Linda McCauley
Sue S. Okuda

For full biographical listings, see the Martindale-Hubbell Law Directory

Quinlivan & Kaniewski (AV)

1401 Dove Street, Suite 580, 92660
Telephone: 714-851-7788
Fax: 714-851-3842
URL: http://www.lawyers.com/quinlivan-kaniewski
Email: Quikanlaw@aol.com *URL:* http://qklaw.wld.com

MEMBERS OF FIRM

Patrick C. Quinlivan
John A. Kaniewski

ASSOCIATES

Danniel J. Wexler
Pamela Jean Richardson
Paige F. Rubinfeld

For full biographical listings, see the Martindale-Hubbell Law Directory

Stepp & Beauchamp LLP (AV)

A Limited Liability Partnership of Professional Corporations
1301 Dove Street, Suite 460, 92660-2422
Telephone: 949-660-9700
Fax: 949-660-9010
Email: ndh@stepp-beauchamp.com *URL:* http://www.lawyers.com/stepp&beauchampllp

Thomas E. Stepp, Jr.
Robert B. Beauchamp
Mynette D. Beauchamp
Deron Matthew Colby
Michael J. Muellerleile

For full biographical listings, see the Martindale-Hubbell Law Directory

NORTH HOLLYWOOD, Los Angeles Co.

F. Bentley Mooney, Jr. A Law Corporation (AV)

4605 Lankershim Boulevard, Suite 718, 91602
Telephone: 818-769-4221
Fax: 818-769-5002
Email: fbmooney@pacbell.net *URL:* http://www.1bc.com/fbmoney

F. Bentley Mooney, Jr.

For full biographical listings, see the Martindale-Hubbell Law Directory

*OAKLAND,** Alameda Co.

Neal & Associates (AV)

Montclair Village, 6200 Antioch Street, Suite 202, 94611
Telephone: 510-339-0233
FAX: 510-339-6672
Mailing Address: P.O. Box 13314, 500, 94661-0314
Email: hdn@nealaw.com *URL:* http://www.nealaw.com

Howard D. Neal

Steven S. Miyake
Barbara E. Scramstad

For full biographical listings, see the Martindale-Hubbell Law Directory

ORINDA, Contra Costa Co.

Perez & McNabb, A Professional Corporation (AV)

140 Brookwood Road, Suite 200, 94563
Telephone: 925-254-6100
Fax: 925-254-0653
Email: perezmcnabb@attmail.com *URL:* http://www.perezmcnabb.com

Richard L. Perez
Jeffrey A. Miller
Sandra J. McNabb
Richard G. Thomas
Marjorie A. Wallace

Representative Clients: Actuate Software Corp.; Any Mountain Ltd.; AT&T Corporation; Beal Bank; Cygna Development Inc.; NCR Corp.; U.S. West Communications, Inc.

For full biographical listings, see the Martindale-Hubbell Law Directory

OXNARD, Ventura Co.

England, Whitfield, Schröeder & Tredway, L.L.P. (AV)

300 Esplanade Drive, 6th Floor, 93030
Telephone: 805-485-9627
Ventura: 647-8237
Southern California Toll Free: 800-255-3485
Fax: 805-983-0297
URL: http://www.tsurf.com/ewst/

(See Next Column)

Theodore J. England
Mitchel B. Kahn
Anson M. Whitfield
Mark A. Nelson
Robert W. Schröeder
Eric J. Kananen
David W. Tredway
Mary E. Schröeder
Robert A. McSorley
Oscar C. Gonzalez
Stuart A. Comis
Madison M. Christian
Kurt Edward Kananen

Melissa E. Cohen
Kevin L. Dorhout
Linda Kathryn Ash
Anthony M. Ramos
Mark T. Barney
Gregory J. Ramirez

Representative Clients: Dah Chong Hong (automobile dealerships); Steve thomas BMW; Vreeland Cadillac, Inc.; Willamette Industries; The Port of Hueneme; Viola, Inc. (General Contracting); Santa Clara Chemical Co.; Nakamura Berry Growers; John Taft Electric Co.; Rodgers Mortgage Co.

For full biographical listings, see the Martindale-Hubbell Law Directory

H. Roy Jeppson A Professional Corporation (AV)

300 Esplanade Drive, Suite 1810, 93030
Telephone: 805-604-1100
Fax: 805-604-1600
URL: http://www.lawyers.com/jeppsonlaw
Los Angeles, California Office: 11900 West Olympic Boulevard. Sixth Floor. 90064.
Telephone: 310-826-5566.
Fax: 310-826-5350.

H. Roy Jeppson

Robyn F. Stalk

For full biographical listings, see the Martindale-Hubbell Law Directory

PALM DESERT, Riverside Co.

Criste, Pippin & Golds (AV)

Suite 200, 73-550 Alessandro Drive, 92260
Telephone: 760-862-1111
Fax: 760-776-4197
Email: cpgca@aol.com

MEMBERS OF FIRM

Michael A. Criste
Robert L. Pippin
Irwin L. Golds

ASSOCIATES

Jeffrey S. Flashman
Julian S. Summers

For full biographical listings, see the Martindale-Hubbell Law Directory

PALM SPRINGS, Riverside Co.

Schlecht, Shevlin & Shoenberger, A Law Corporation (AV)

801 East Tahquitz Canyon Way, Suite 100, P.O. Box 2744, 92263-2744
Telephone: 760-320-7161
Facsimile: 760-323-1758
Email: ssslaw@gte.net *URL:* http://www.ssslaw.com

James M. Schlecht
Jon A. Shoenberger
John C. Shevlin
Daniel T. Johnson

David Darrin

Representative Clients: Outdoor Resorts of America; The Escrow Connection; Palm Hills Land Corp.; Shadowrock; Palm Springs Marquis.

For full biographical listings, see the Martindale-Hubbell Law Directory

PALO ALTO, Santa Clara Co.

Flicker & Kerin (AV)

Suite 460, 285 Hamilton, P.O. Box 840, 94302
Telephone: 650-321-0947
Fax: 650-326-9722

MEMBERS OF FIRM

Michael R. Flicker
Anthony J. Kerin, III
Rhesa C. Rubin

ASSOCIATES

Cheri A. Bell
Eleni Adams

For full biographical listings, see the Martindale-Hubbell Law Directory

Christopher Ream (AV)

1755 Embarcadero Road, Suite 200, 94303
Telephone: 650-424-0821
Facsimile: 650-493-7912
Email: ream@aya.yale.edu

For full biographical listings, see the Martindale-Hubbell Law Directory

PLEASANTON, Alameda Co.

JG, P.C. BUSINESS & CORPORATE LAW (AV)

5000 Hopyard Road, Suite 400, 94588
Telephone: 925-463-9600
Facsimile: 925-463-9644
Email: jgulseth@jgpc.com *URL:* http://www.jgpc.com

James H. Gulseth | Robert L. Taylor

LEGAL SUPPORT PERSONNEL

Jennifer Gray (Paralegal)

For full biographical listings, see the Martindale-Hubbell Law Directory

RANCHO SANTA FE, San Diego Co.

LAW OFFICES OF ROBERT S. KILBORNE IV (AV)

7872 Rio Senda, P.O. Box 7288, 92067
Telephone: 619-759-9050
Fax: 619-759-8020
Email: triallawyer@kilborne.com *URL:* http://www.kilborne.com

ASSOCIATE

Albert E. Cressey, III

OF COUNSEL

Russell B. Wagner

For full biographical listings, see the Martindale-Hubbell Law Directory

*SACRAMENTO,** Sacramento Co.

BOUTIN, DENTINO, GIBSON DI GIUSTO, HODELL & WEST, A PROFESSIONAL CORPORATION (AV)

455 Capitol Mall, Suite 300, 95814-4406
Telephone: 916-321-4444
Telecopier: 916-441-7597
URL: http://www.boutindentino.com
Tucson, Arizona Office: 405 West Franklin Street, 85718.
Telephone: 520-882-2944.

Stephen F. Boutin
William Dentino
Chris Gibson
John E. Di Giusto
Douglas M. Hodell
R. Michael West
Robert D. Swanson
Ned M. Gelhaar

Kimberly L. Jackson
Mark W. Owens
James R. Moore
Michael T. Sparks
Sallie-Carol Orbas
Jeffrey B. Slaton

OF COUNSEL

Robert G. West | Thomas G. Manolakas

For full biographical listings, see the Martindale-Hubbell Law Directory

DROBNY LAW OFFICES (AV)

2485 Natomas Park Drive, Suite 500, 95833
Telephone: 916-641-0526
FAX: 916-441-2352
Stockton, California Office: 7510 Shoreline Drive, Suite B-1, 95219.
Telephone: 209-464-3408.
Fax: 916-441-2352.

Mark S. Drobny

Leland J. Ellison
Todd R. Robie
Chris B. Knepshield
Leslie Ann Arnal
Lori A. Adasiewicz
Quinn Michael Jalli

For full biographical listings, see the Martindale-Hubbell Law Directory

HUNTER RICHEY DI BENEDETTO & BREWER, LLP (AV)

A Limited Liability Partnership
Renaissance Tower, 801 K Street, 23rd Floor, 95814-3525
Telephone: 916-491-3000
Facsimile: 916-491-3080
Email: hrdb@hrdb.com *URL:* http://www.hrdb.com

MEMBERS OF FIRM

William S. Hunter
Win R. Richey
Florence L. Di Benedetto
Roy E. Brewer
Anne E. Ferguson
James F. Geary
Janet C. Eisenbeis
Stephen C. Ruehmann
Sharon K. Sandeen
Jack V. Lovell
Patricia J. Hartman

OF COUNSEL

Laurie E. Davis

(See Next Column)

LEGAL SUPPORT PERSONNEL

Lori J. Moody (Paralegal)
Deborah M. Johnson (Paralegal)
Linda Jane Hall (Executive Assistant)
Jennifer E. Mueller (Legal Assistant)
Michele L. Nickell (Legal Assistant)
Lynetta G. Goodwin

For full biographical listings, see the Martindale-Hubbell Law Directory

LIVINGSTON & MATTESICH, LAW CORPORATION (AV)

1201 K Street, Suite 1100, 95814
Telephone: 916-442-1111
Fax: 916-448-1709
Email: l&m@lmlaw.net *URL:* http://www.lmlaw.net

Gene Livingston
James M. Mattesich
Carol Livingston
Rebecca M. Ceniceros
Emilio E. Varanini, III
Kenneth M. Malovos
Kathleen E. Finnerty
Joanna R. Mendoza

Steven P. Belzer
Jeffrey Leacox
Randy Pollack
Alice H. Choi
Stephen Craig Hunter
Matthew J. Goldman
Joel C. Baiocchi
Baldassaro (Bill) Di Capo
John McKinsey
Timothy E. Naccarato
Craig N. Lundgren
Mary Farrell Taylor
Brian Crone
Gay L. Carroll
Steven G. Churchwell

Representative Clients: 3M Company; Combe, Inc.; Guaranty Federal Bank, F.S.B.; Mid-America Dairymen, Inc.; Trans Union.

For full biographical listings, see the Martindale-Hubbell Law Directory

MATHENY SEARS LINKERT & LONG, LLP (AV)

3638 American River Drive, P.O. Box 13711, 95853-4711
Telephone: 916-978-3434
Fax: 916-978-3430
Email: info@msll.com *URL:* http://www.msll.com

MEMBERS OF FIRM

Henry G. Matheny (1933-1984)
Douglas A. Sears
Richard S. Linkert
Ernest A. Long
Joann Georgallis
Kent M. Luckey
Matthew C. Jaime
Michael A. Bishop
Robert B. Berrigan
Ronald E. Enabnit
Eric R. Wiesel

ASSOCIATES

Andrea Croak Christensen
Michael G. Jones
Eric M. Bonzell
Mary Elizabeth Wood
Paul Richard Baleria
James F. Curran
Andreas C. Rockas
Timothy P. Chang

OF COUNSEL

James C. Damir

LEGAL SUPPORT PERSONNEL

PARALEGALS

Frances Studer
Lynell Rae Steed
Jennifer Bachman

For full biographical listings, see the Martindale-Hubbell Law Directory

NAGELEY, MEREDITH & MILLER, INC. (AV)

8001 Folsom Boulevard, Suite 100, 95826
Telephone: 916-386-8282
Fax: 916-386-8952
Email: mail@mnlawfirm.com

Sam R. Nageley
Gregory A. Meredith
Andrea M. Miller
Lawrence N. Hensley
Craig S. MacGlashan
Janet M. Meredith
Carole Hansen Sharples
L. Alan Warwick
Drew M. Johnson
James C. Keowen
Duane S. Oliveira

For full biographical listings, see the Martindale-Hubbell Law Directory

RIEGELS CAMPOS & KENYON LLP (AV)

2500 Venture Oaks Way, Suite 220, 95833-4222
Telephone: 916-779-7100
Fax: 916-779-7120
Email: rckrecpt@rcklaw.com *URL:* http://www.rcklaw.com

MEMBERS OF FIRM

Dennis M. Campos
John E. Fischer
Cyrus A. Johnson
Charity Kenyon
Jeffery Owensby
David A. Riegels
Sue Ellen Wooldridge

Representative Clients: Chevron Oil Company; EDS Corporation; Eldorado Bank; McClatchy Newspapers, Inc.; Minolta Corporation; Raleys, Inc.; Regents of the University of California; Sinclair Broadcasting.

For full biographical listings, see the Martindale-Hubbell Law Directory

Sacramento—Continued

LAW OFFICES OF JOSEPH W. SCALIA

(See Gold River)

*SAN DIEGO,** San Diego Co.

ALHADEFF CANNON ROSE SOLAR & PARKS, LLP (AV)

550 West "C" Street, Nineteenth Floor, 92101-3540
Telephone: 619-231-8700
Facsimile: 619-231-8323
Email: ksolar@acrsp.com
Temecula, California Office: The Tower Plaza, 27555 Ynez Road, Suite 203, 92591-4677.
Telephone: 909-699-9088.
Facsimile: 909-699-9878. Email: POBERHANSLEY@ACRSP.com
Los Angeles, California Office: Olympic Center, 11150 Olympic Boulevard, Suite 860, 90064.
Telephone: 310-914-4400.
Facsimile: 310-914-0030. Email: JODONNELL@ACRSP.com
Lafayette, California Office: Lafayette Terrace, 3697 Mount Diablo Boulevard, Suite 100, 94549.
Telephone: 925-283-1599.
Facsimile: 925-283-5847. Email: GMF-CA@MSN.com

PARTNERS

Samuel C. Alhadeff
Robert D. Rose
Jerry M. Cannon
Keith R. Solar
Robert J. Parks
Philip D. Oberhansley (Resident, Temecula, California Office)
Joseph L. Marshall
Leslie C. Detwiler
Glenn M. Feeley (Resident, Lafayette, California Office)
Thomas T. Lord
Madeline Clark Cahill
John L. O'Donnell, Jr. (Resident, Los Angeles, California Office)

OF COUNSEL

Craig S. Engstrand
Robert K. Edmunds
Charles F. Gorder, Sr.

ASSOCIATES

Michael J. Barry
Richard James Bayless
Craig V. Butler
Cyril J. Dantchev
Genie Harrison
S. Douglas Kerner
Frank J. Polek
Les W. Robertson
Traci M. Selby
Marjeta Duzevic Six

For full biographical listings, see the Martindale-Hubbell Law Directory

CASEY, GERRY, REED & SCHENK (AV)

110 Laurel Street, 92101
Telephone: 619-238-1811
Fax: 619-544-9232
Email: cglaw@cglaw.com *URL:* http://www.CGlaw.com

MEMBERS OF FIRM

David S. Casey
Richard F. Gerry
Scott C. Cummins
David S. Casey, Jr.
Richard D. Westbrook, Jr. (1944-1982)
T. Michael Reed
Frederick Schenk
Robert J. Francavilla
Gayle Meryl Blatt
Thomas D. Penfield
Michael P. Montgomery
Suzanne C. Etpison
Bonnie E. Kane
Thomas Luneau

Reference: San Diego National Bank.

For full biographical listings, see the Martindale-Hubbell Law Directory

CHAPIN SHEA MCNITT & CARTER, A PROFESSIONAL CORPORATION (AV)

Library, 501 West Broadway, 15th Floor, 92101
Telephone: 619-232-4261
Telefax: 619-232-4840
Email: info@chapinlaw.com *URL:* http://www.chapinlaw.com
Los Angeles, California Office: 12424 Wilshire Boulevard, 9th Floor, 90025.
Telephone: 310-826-0133.
Telefax: 310-207-4236.

Dave Carothers
Edward D. Chapin
Shirley A. Gauvin
Aaron H. Katz
Andrew G. Loeb
Earl H. Maas III
Roger L. McNitt
Steven A. Micheli
Maria C. Roberts
Lawrence W. Shea, II
Nancy L. Vaughan
Peter C. Ward

COUNSEL

Daniel P. Groszkruger
Arthur W. Jones
Thomas P. Redick

Brian A. Barnhorst
Christina A. Bernstein
Kelli Jean Brooks
Jeffery L. Caufield
Daniel W. Coffey
Amy K. Cressey-Yates
Daniel J. Curran
Glen F. Dorgan

(See Next Column)

Natasha L. Drew
Jeffrey S. Eddington
Patrick M. Howe
Bruno W. Katz
Brian Maienschein
Peter B. Maretz
Carmen M. Mosier McCormick
Jeffrey K. Miyamoto
Leticia Olivarez
Mark T. Petersen
James H. Prenton
Amanda M. Rowe
Patricia L. Sullivan
Brandy Thompson-Cody
Heather K. Van Blarcom

LOS ANGELES OFFICE

Craig H. Bell
John J. Calvagna
Richard D. Carter
Robert Ehrenreich
Leslie J. Eng
Tina Fisher
Ronald F. Gari
Neil R. Gunny
Daniel S. Imber
Shaun Dabby Jacobs
Robin James
Dana Marie Lawson
Jeffrey J. Leist
David A. Myers
Charles F. Peterson
Steven J. Renshaw
Mark Schaeffer
Mark M. Senior
Erin C. Slape
Howard J. Smith
Jeffrey C. Stodel
Stephen Z. Vegh
Irwin Waldman (A P.C.)

For full biographical listings, see the Martindale-Hubbell Law Directory

DOSTART CLAPP & COVENEY, LLP (AV)

4370 La Jolla Village Drive, Suite 970, 92122
Telephone: 619-623-4200
Facsimile: 619-623-4299
URL: http://www.sdlaw.com

PARTNERS

Paul J. Dostart
James F. Clapp
Kenneth G. Coveney

ASSOCIATES

Kevin P. Gordon
Jonathan A. Grissom

For full biographical listings, see the Martindale-Hubbell Law Directory

DUKE GERSTEL SHEARER, LLP (AV)

A Registered Limited Liability Partnership
Sixth Floor, 101 West Broadway, P.O. Box 85470, 92186-5470
Telephone: 619-232-0816
800-405-0816
Fax: 619-232-4661
Email: lawyers@dgsllp.com *URL:* http://www.dgsllp.com
Costa Mesa, California Office: 3200 Park Center Drive, Suite 1000, 92626.
Telephone: 949-551-8664, 800-405-0816.
Los Angeles, California Office: 10866 Wilshire Boulevard, Suite 1400, 90024.
Telephone: 310-475-7118, 800-405-0816.
San Francisco, California Office: 744 Montgomery Street, Fifth Floor, 94111.
Telephone: 415-773-0101.
Palm Springs, California Office: 1111 East Tahquitz Canyon Way, Suite 110, 92262.
Telephone: 760-322-7846.
Phoenix, Arizona Office: One Columbus Plaza, 3636 North Central Avenue, Suite 1200, 85012.
Telephone: 602-650-2060.
Fax: 602-650-2089.
Tucson, Arizona Office: 6969 East Sunrise Drive, Suite 102, 85750.
Telephone: 520-615-8858.
Fax: 520-615-1069.
Affiliate Las Vegas, Nevada Office: Parsons & Pursiano, LLP, City Center West, Suite 108, 7201 W. Lake Mead Boulevard, 89128.
Telephone: 702-384-9900.
Facsimile: 702-384-5900.

MEMBERS OF FIRM

Stephen V. Rupp (A Professional Corporation)
Eric W. Sachrison

ASSOCIATE

William E. Mayer

Reference: Bank of Commerce.

For full biographical listings, see the Martindale-Hubbell Law Directory

FERRIS & BRITTON, A PROFESSIONAL CORPORATION (AV)

1600 First National Bank Center, 401 West A Street, 92101
Telephone: 619-233-3131
Fax: 619-232-9316
Email: manager@ferrisbritton.com *URL:* http://www.ferrisbritton.com

Alfred G. Ferris
Tamara K. Fogg
Gary T. Moyer
Margaret Prodanov

Representative Clients: Air Support Facilities, Inc.; Cox Communications, Inc.; Datel Systems, Inc.; Enterprise Rent-a-Car; Exxon; Frontier Analytics, Inc.; Peninsula Bank; Teleport Communications Group; Southwest Airlines; ZyGam, Inc.

For Complete List of Firm Personnel, See General Section

For full biographical listings, see the Martindale-Hubbell Law Directory

San Diego—Continued

FISCH, SPIEGLER, GINSBURG, LADNER & ATTARIAN, A PROFESSIONAL LAW CORPORATION (AV)

1551 Fourth Avenue, Suite 300, 92101-3184
Telephone: 619-234-1551
Telecopier: 619-234-1568
Email: FSGLA@AOL.com

Joseph J. Fisch
Mark A. Spiegler
Phillip L. Ginsburg
Karen M. Ladner
Peter J. Attarian, Jr.

For full biographical listings, see the Martindale-Hubbell Law Directory

HECHT, SOLBERG, ROBINSON & GOLDBERG, LLP (AV)

One America Plaza, 600 West Broadway, Eighth Floor, 92101
Telephone: 619-239-3444
Telecopier: 619-232-6828
Email: mail@hsrg.com

MEMBERS OF FIRM

Alan John Hecht (A Professional Corporation)
Darryl O. Solberg (A Professional Corporation)
Jerold H. Goldberg (A Professional Corporation)
Paul E. Robinson (A Professional Corporation)
David W. Bagley, II (A Professional Corporation)
Michael J. Maher
R. Martin Bohl
Anton Dimitroff
Susan Lee Daly

SENIOR ATTORNEYS

Richard A. Schulman
Michael A. Van Horne
Peter K. Solecki
Kenneth C. Jones

ASSOCIATES

Tricia L. Greenlee
Erik Olav Valderhaug
Nataki A. Finch

For full biographical listings, see the Martindale-Hubbell Law Directory

HOVEY & KIRBY, A PROFESSIONAL CORPORATION (AV)

402 West Broadway, Suite 1500, 92101
Telephone: 619-685-4000
Fax: 619-685-4004
Email: administrator@hoveylaw.com

Gregg B. Hovey
Dean T. Kirby, Jr.

For full biographical listings, see the Martindale-Hubbell Law Directory

KENNERSON SCHWARTZ SEMERDJIAN & HAILE LLP (AV)

A Limited Liability Partnership
101 West Broadway, Suite 810, 92101
Telephone: 619-236-8821
Facsimile: 619-236-8827
URL: http://www.lawyers.com/ksshlaw

OF COUNSEL

Paul R. Kennerson

MEMBERS OF FIRM

Ross J. Schwartz
Dick A. Semerdjian
Jeffrey A. Haile

James R. Ballard
John K. Grant

For full biographical listings, see the Martindale-Hubbell Law Directory

LAW OFFICES OF CHARLES P. LEBEAU (AV)

Historic Hayward-Patterson Building, 1887, 2148 Broadway, 92102
Telephone: 858-456-1100
Fax: 858-455-5024
Email: lebeaulaw@worldnet.att.net *URL:* http://www.lebeaulaw.com

LEGAL SUPPORT PERSONNEL

Rebecca Cisinsky (Paralegal/Secretary)
Jill Gisondo (Secretary)

For full biographical listings, see the Martindale-Hubbell Law Directory

LINDLEY, SCALES & CORBETT, A PROFESSIONAL CORPORATION (AV)

550 West C Street, Suite 1800, 92101
Telephone: 619-234-9181
Fax: 619-234-8475
Email: lsc@adnc.com

Luke R. Corbett
Robert M. McLeod

Representative Clients: McGraw-Hill Broadcasting Co.; DYK, Incorporated; AKW Medical, Inc.; Hydroscape Products, Inc.; Keith's Restaurant, Inc.; West & Associates, PAC; Fillipi's Pizza Grotto.

For full biographical listings, see the Martindale-Hubbell Law Directory

LUCE, FORWARD, HAMILTON & SCRIPPS LLP (AV)

A Partnership including Professional Corporations
600 West Broadway, Suite 2600, 92101
Telephone: 619-236-1414
Fax: 619-232-8311
URL: http://www.luce.com
La Jolla, California Office: 4275 Executive Square, Suite 800, 92037.
Telephone: 858-455-6611.
Fax: 858-232-8311.
Los Angeles, California Office: 777 South Figueroa, Suite 3600, 90017.
Telephone: 213-892-4992.
Fax: 213-892-7731.
San Francisco, California Office: 121 Spear Street, Suite 200, 94105.
Telephone: 415-356-4600.
Fax: 415-356-4610.
New York, N.Y. Office: Citicorp Center, 153 East 53rd Street, 26th Floor, 10022.
Telephone: 212-754-1414.
Fax: 212-644-9727.
Chicago, Illinois Office: 180 North La Salle Street, Suite 3110, 60601.
Telephone: 312-641-0580.
Fax: 312-641-0380.

G. Edward Arledge
Terrence L. Bingman
Charles A. Bird
John W. Brooks
Kevin A. Cahill
Sean L. Collin
Robert G. Copeland
Dennis J. Doucette
Jeffrey L. Fillerup (Resident, San Francisco Office)
Peter K. Hahn
Mark W. Hansen
Christopher J. Healey
Charles L. Hellerich
James B. Hicks (Resident, Los Angeles Office)
Valentine S. Hoy, VIII
Phillip L. Jelsma
Kathy A. Jorrie (Resident, Los Angeles Office)
Mark L. Mann
John B. McNeece III
Cary W. Miller
Otto E. Sorensen
Richard R. Spirra
Robert G. Steiner
Darryl Steinhause
Robert L. Young

OF COUNSEL

Gregory D. Roper

SPECIAL COUNSEL

Karla R. Kelly

ASSOCIATES

John T. Brooks
Thomas A. Butler
Guillermo Cabrera
David M. Clark
John P. Cooley
Steven J. Davis
Jana Ford-Harder
Michael G. Fraunces
Russell A. Gold
James A. Goniea (Resident, San Francisco Office)
Jeanne M. Malitz
Carrie G. Pratt (Resident, San Francisco Office)
Edward H. Sikorski (Not admitted in CA)
John D. Vaughn

For Complete List of Firm Personnel, See General Section

For full biographical listings, see the Martindale-Hubbell Law Directory

MILLER MILOVE & KOB, P.C. (AV)

The Koll Center, 501 West Broadway, Suite 720, 92101
Telephone: 619-696-5200
Facsimile: 619-696-5393
Email: mmandkob@ix.netcom.com *URL:* http://www.lawyers.com/millermilove&kob

Brian D. Miller
Bradd L. Milove
Jeffrey S. Kob
Cynthia M. Schleindl

Beth A. Saurer

Representative Clients: Broadcort Capital Corporation; First Wall Street; Bank of Commerce; Personal Computers Products, Inc.; IDS Financial Services; Iowa Grain Company; JB Oxford & Company; Sentra Securities; Spelman & Co.; Vanguard Capital.

For full biographical listings, see the Martindale-Hubbell Law Directory

THE LAW OFFICES OF STEPHEN P. OGGEL, A P.C. (AV)

101 West Broadway, Suite 1450, 92101
Telephone: 619-696-7500
Fax: 619-232-1065

Stephen P. Oggel

For full biographical listings, see the Martindale-Hubbell Law Directory

San Diego—Continued

POST KIRBY NOONAN & SWEAT LLP (AV)

A Partnership including Professional Corporations
America Plaza 600 West Broadway 11th Floor, 92101
Telephone: 619-231-8666
FAX: 619-231-9593;
619-231-4360
Email: PKNS@PKNS.com

MEMBERS OF FIRM

Gregory A. Post
Michael L. Kirby (A P.C.)
David J. Noonan
Richard W. Sweat
R. Bruce Wayne (A P.C.)
Thomas W. Bettles
David B. Oberholtzer
Charles T. Hoge
James R. Lance
Steven W. Sanchez
Theresa M. Brehl
Jeffrey P. Lendrum
Kristen T. Bruesehoff

For full biographical listings, see the Martindale-Hubbell Law Directory

THORSNES, BARTOLOTTA, MCGUIRE & PADILLA (AV)

A Partnership including Professional Corporations
Fifth Avenue Financial Center, 11th Floor, 2550 Fifth Avenue, 92103
Telephone: 619-236-9363
Fax: 619-236-9653
Email: TBMPmail@TBMP.com *URL:* http://www.tbmp.com

Michael T. Thorsnes (A.P.C., P.C.)
Vincent J. Bartolotta, Jr., (P.C.)
John F. McGuire (P.C.)
Kevin F. Quinn (P.C.)
C. Brant Noziska (P.C.)
Mitchell S. Golub (P.C.)
Palma Cesar Hooper (P.C.)
Neal H. Rockwood (P.C.)
Daral B. Mazzarella (P.C.)
R. Christian Hulburt (P.C.)

ASSOCIATES

Catherine A. Richardson
Jodi L. Hautaluoma
Douglas J. Billings
Scott A. Kennedy
Dori K. Rybacki
James T. Atkins
Leo Bartolotta
Jill E. Cleary
James B. Drimmer
Timothy J. Tatro

OF COUNSEL

Robert S. Kennedy

For full biographical listings, see the Martindale-Hubbell Law Directory

ARTHUR M. WILCOX, JR. (AV)

Koll Center, 501 West Broadway, Suite 750, 92101
Telephone: 619-696-6788
Fax: 619-696-8685
Email: amwilcox@ix.netcom.com *URL:* http://www.lawyers.com/wilcoxlaw

For full biographical listings, see the Martindale-Hubbell Law Directory

*SAN FRANCISCO,** San Francisco Co.

RAYMOND N. STELLA ERLACH (AV)

One Maritime Plaza, Fourth Floor, 94111
Telephone: 415-788-3322
Fax: 415-788-8613

OF COUNSEL

Gregory J. Erlach
Stephen Peter U. Erlach

Reference: Bank of America Private Banking, San Francisco, California.

For full biographical listings, see the Martindale-Hubbell Law Directory

LAW OFFICES OF KEVIN W. FINCK (AV)

Two Embarcadero Center, Suite 1670, 94111
Telephone: 415-296-9100
Facsimile: 415-394-6446
Email: kfinck@flash.net

OF COUNSEL

Marla Raucher Osborn

For full biographical listings, see the Martindale-Hubbell Law Directory

LAW OFFICES OF ROGER JUSTICE FLEISCHMANN (AV)

One Maritime Plaza, Fourth Floor, 94111
Telephone: 415-981-0140
Fax: 415-788-6234
Email: rjf@rjflawoffices.com

Representative Clients: Toshiba Corp.; Toshiba International Corp.; Toshiba Ceramics Co., Ltd. and its U.S. subsidiary, Toshiba Ceramics America Inc.; Toshiba America, Inc.; Ishikawajima-Harima Heavy Industries Co. Ltd.; IHI Inc.; Ebara Corp.; Komatsu Electronic Metals Co., Ltd.; Marubeni America Corp.; GN Comtext, Inc. and GN Comtext Ltd., subsidiaries of Great Nordic Company.

For full biographical listings, see the Martindale-Hubbell Law Directory

KAY & MERKLE (AV)

100 The Embarcadero Penthouse, 94105
Telephone: 415-357-1200
Facsimile: 415-512-9277
Email: kmlaw100@kmlaw100.com

MEMBERS OF FIRM

Steven Kay
Walter F. Merkle, Jr.
W. Bruce Bercovich
John W. Merkle
Alan J. Silver
Douglas A. Marshall
Douglas A Hutchinson

OF COUNSEL

Lionel T. Aiken

For full biographical listings, see the Martindale-Hubbell Law Directory

MACINNIS, DONNER & KOPLOWITZ (AV)

Suite 222, 465 California Street, 94104
Telephone: 415-434-2400
FAX: 415-433-1917

MEMBERS OF FIRM

James Martin MacInnis (1914-1979)
Conrad Donner
Edward A. Koplowitz

For full biographical listings, see the Martindale-Hubbell Law Directory

MANWELL & MILTON (AV)

20 California Street, Third Floor, 94111
Telephone: 415-362-2375
Telecopier: 415-362-1010
URL: http://www.MMLAWOFFICES.COM

Edmund R. Manwell
Denise B. Milton

OF COUNSEL

Maria A. Chanco

ASSOCIATES

Ian R. Schwartz
Katayoon M. Cotto
Lissa G. Maldonado

For full biographical listings, see the Martindale-Hubbell Law Directory

STIMMEL, STIMMEL & SMITH, A PROFESSIONAL CORPORATION (AV)

100 Bush Street, Suite 850, 94104
Telephone: 415-392-2018
Fax: 415-391-2124
Email: stimmelpc@stimmel-law.com *URL:* http://www.stimmel-law.com

Norman S. Stimmel (1914-1991)
Lee D. Stimmel
Andrine K. Smith

OF COUNSEL

Jeffrey S. Rosen
Joanne M. Reming
Susan B. Jordan
Darrick T. Chase

For full biographical listings, see the Martindale-Hubbell Law Directory

TERAOKA & ASSOCIATES, A LAW CORPORATION (AV)

One Embarcadero Center, Suite 1020, 94111
Telephone: 415-981-3100
Telecopier: 415-981-0222
Email: teraokalaw@aol.com

Steven G. Teraoka

Catherine M. Gormley
Tatsuji T. Shimazaki

OF COUNSEL

Scott R. Keene
Joseph L. Strabala

Representative Clients: Kikkoman International Inc.; JFC International Inc.; Sega of America, Inc.; CSK International Headquarters, Inc.; Japan Travel Bureau International; Viz Communications, Inc. (Shogakukan, Inc.); Goldilocks Bake Shops (Philippines); Inabata America Corporation; United Charter Services, Inc.; Samsung Heavy Industries, Inc. (Korea).

For full biographical listings, see the Martindale-Hubbell Law Directory

WARTNICK, CHABER, HAROWITZ, SMITH & TIGERMAN, A PROFESSIONAL CORPORATION (AV)

101 California Street, Suite 2200, 94111-5802
Telephone: 415-986-5566
Fax: 415-986-5896
Email: postoffice@wartnicklaw.com *URL:* http://www.wartnicklaw.com

Harry F. Wartnick
Madelyn J. Chaber
Steven M. Harowitz
Stephen M. Tigerman

(See Next Column)

WARTNICK, CHABER, HAROWITZ, SMITH & TIGERMAN A PROFESSIONAL CORPORATION—*Continued*

Phillip Scott Chan
Christopher C. Lamerdin
Garry Cohen
Cheryl L. White
Gregory M. Sheffer
Martha A. H. Berman
Courtney S. Lui
Diana M. Garcia
Richard A. Brody
Leslie Shawn Kerth
Marileni (Mia) Mattis
Max Jiro Kimura
Mark L. Nissenbaum
Tod Manning
Charlene A. Jimenez

OF COUNSEL

Audrey A. Smith
Robert Brown

For full biographical listings, see the Martindale-Hubbell Law Directory

*SAN JOSE,** Santa Clara Co.

LAW OFFICES OF THOMAS R. HOGAN (AV)

10 Almaden Boulevard, Suite 535, 95113-2258
Telephone: 408-292-7600
Facsimile: 408-292-7611
URL: http://www.lawyers.com/thomasrhogan
Email: trh@hoganlaw.com *URL:* http://www.hoganlaw.com

ASSOCIATE

Leslie Holmes

For full biographical listings, see the Martindale-Hubbell Law Directory

MILLER, MORTON, CAILLAT & NEVIS (AV)

50 West San Fernando Street, Suite 1300, 95113-2413
Telephone: 408-292-1765
Telecopier: 408-292-4484
URL: http://www.mmcn-law.com

Richard W. Morton (1916-1975)
Charles V. Caillat (1920-1990)
Harvey C. Miller (1906-1993)

MEMBERS OF FIRM

David L. Nevis
Francis J. Hughes
Peter A. Kline
Stevan C. Adelman
Joseph A. Scanlan, Jr.
Carolyn Tobiason Stuart
William K. Hurley
Peter V. Dessau

OF COUNSEL

Nancy F. Symons

ASSOCIATES

Kathryn E. Barrett
Katherine S. Pak
David I. Kornbluh
Christopher J. Hersey
Julie Neale Meyer

Representative Clients: Trammell Crow Residential; Joe Kerley Lincoln Mercury Co.; Milligan News Co.; Joseph George Distributors; Santa Clara Dental Society; Avalon Bay Communities; Bershire Life Insurance Co; Hathaway-Dinwiddie Group; South Bay Circuits; John Alden Life Insurance Co.

For full biographical listings, see the Martindale-Hubbell Law Directory

REED, ELLIOTT, CREECH & ROTH (AV)

99 Almaden Boulevard, Eighth Floor, 95113
Telephone: 408-993-9911
Fax: 408-993-1335
URL: http://www.sjlegal.com

MEMBERS OF FIRM

John W. Elliott
Randall C. Creech
Thomas A. Elliott
Jeffrey S. Lawson
Peter A. Liebow
Raymond A. Brinson

ASSOCIATES

Lauren Berger
Nancy L. Mathis
Edward A. Kraus
Betty Chen
Bonnie L. Portis

OF COUNSEL

Steven J. Roth
Charles R. Reed
Thomas G. Perkins

Reference: Union Bank of California.

For full biographical listings, see the Martindale-Hubbell Law Directory

*SAN LUIS OBISPO,** San Luis Obispo Co.

ANDRE, MORRIS & BUTTERY, A PROFESSIONAL LAW CORPORATION (AV)

1102 Laurel Lane, P.O. Box 730, 93406-0730
Telephone: 805-543-4171
Fax: 805-543-0752
Email: amb@amblaw.com *URL:* http://www.amblaw.com

Michael J. Morris
James C. Buttery
Dennis D. Law
J. Todd Mirolla
Scott W. Wall

(See Next Column)

Kevin D. Morris
William V. Douglass
Timothy L. Hodge

References: Bank of America National Trust and Savings Assn. (San Luis Obispo Main Branch); Mid-State Bank (San Luis Obispo).

For full biographical listings, see the Martindale-Hubbell Law Directory

SAN MATEO, San Mateo Co.

G. A. LASTER (AV)

630 North San Mateo Drive, P.O. Box 152, 94401-2328
Telephone: 650-342-3523
Telecopier: 650-342-6392
Email: galaster@aol.com

Gerald A. Laster

Representative Clients: Coastside Preservation and Recreation, Inc.; Midcoast Park Lands; Half Moon Bay Open Space Trust. Financing for: The French Co.; CFS Continental, Inc.; Ameritec; Selecta Switch, Inc.; Sensortronics, Inc.; Sumitomo Metal Mining California Corp.; Cashman, Ltd.

For full biographical listings, see the Martindale-Hubbell Law Directory

*SAN RAFAEL,** Marin Co.

MCNEIL, SILVEIRA & RICE (AV)

An Association of Professional Corporations
55 Professional Center Parkway, Suite A, 94903
Telephone: 415-472-3434
Telecopier: 415-472-1298

Patrick J. McNeil (A Professional Corporation)
Ronald A. Silveira (A Professional Corporation)
Mark J. Rice (A Professional Corporation)

For full biographical listings, see the Martindale-Hubbell Law Directory

PASCOE & RAFTON (AV)

1050 Northgate Drive, Suite 356, 94903
Telephone: 415-492-1003
Fax: 415-492-3312
Email: wpascoe@lawyers.com *URL:* http://www.lawyers.com/pascoe&rafton

MEMBERS OF FIRM

William R. Pascoe
Karen A. Rafton (Retired)

OF COUNSEL

Edward J. Tredinnick

For full biographical listings, see the Martindale-Hubbell Law Directory

*SANTA ANA,** Orange Co.

CALLAHAN & BLAINE, A PROFESSIONAL LAW CORPORATION (AV)

3 Hutton Centre Drive, Suite 900, 92707
Telephone: 714-241-4444
Fax: 714-241-4445
Email: info@callahan-law.com *URL:* http://www.callahan-law.com

Daniel J. Callahan
Stephen E. Blaine

Jim P. Mahacek
Michael J. Sachs
Edward Susolik
Kathleen L. Dunham
Robyn Dimino
Reed N. Archambault
Nicki N. Eke
David Kam Ng
Douglas W. Schroeder

OF COUNSEL

Shelley M. Liberto
Walt D. Mahaffa

For full biographical listings, see the Martindale-Hubbell Law Directory

FERRUZZO & FERRUZZO (AV)

A Partnership of Professional Corporations
2114 North Broadway, 92706
Telephone: 714-834-9322
Facsimile: 714-834-9358
URL: http://www.ferruzzo.com

MEMBERS OF FIRM

Thomas G. Ferruzzo (A Professional Corporation)
James J. Ferruzzo (A Professional Corporation)
James K. Leese (A Professional Corporation)

(See Next Column)

FERRUZZO & FERRUZZO, *Santa Ana—Continued*

ASSOCIATES

John R. Pelle
Dirk E. Petchul
Gregory J. Ferruzzo
M. Susan Watson
Sherry D. Graybehl
Linda J. Berberian
Steven T. Myers
William Nichols Villard
Jason D. Cohn

For full biographical listings, see the Martindale-Hubbell Law Directory

MARLIN & SALTZMAN, A PROFESSIONAL LAW CORPORATION (AV)

203 North Golden Circle Drive, Suite 310, 92705
Telephone: 714-560-9300
Fax: 714-560-9313
URL: http://www.marlinandsaltzman.com
Woodland Hills, California Office: Westhills Plaza, 20700 Ventura Boulevard, Suite 227, 91364.
Telephone: 818-702-0600.
Fax: 818-702-6555.

Louis M. Marlin
Stanley D. Saltzman

Thomas F. Hozduk
Stephen P. O'Dell
Sven D. Buncher
Alan S. Lazar

For full biographical listings, see the Martindale-Hubbell Law Directory

PIZER & MICHAELSON INC. (AV)

2122 North Broadway, Suite 100, 92706
Telephone: 714-558-0535
Telecopier: 714-550-0841
Los Angeles, California Office: 2049 Century Park East, Suite 460, 90067.
Telephone: 310-843-9729.
Fax: 310-843-9619.

Seymour S. Pizer (1930-1992)
Barry S. Michaelson
Hugh R. Coffin
Bradley J. Pizer
(Resident, Los Angeles Office)

For full biographical listings, see the Martindale-Hubbell Law Directory

*SANTA BARBARA,** Santa Barbara Co.

HOLLISTER & BRACE, A PROFESSIONAL CORPORATION (AV)

1126 Santa Barbara Street, P.O. Box 630, 93101
Telephone: 805-963-6711
Fax: 805-965-0329
Email: hblaw@hbsb.com

William A. Brace (Retired)
J. James Hollister, III (Retired)
John S. Poucher
Richard C. Monk
George A. Rempe, III
Steven Evans Kirby
Bradford F. Ginder
John G. Busby
Susan H. McCollum
Robert L. Brace
Marcus Scott Bird
Charles W. Willey (P.C.)
Alexis W. Willey
Peter L. Candy

Attorneys For: Chandlery, Inc.; First American Title Insurance Co.; Gainey Vineyards; The Harbor of Santa Barbara, Inc.; Marborg Disposal, Inc.; R.J. Carroll & Sons, Inc.; Santa Barbara Trust for Historic Preservation; Vetronix Corp.; Yardi Systems, Inc.; Starbuck, Tisdale & Assoc.

For full biographical listings, see the Martindale-Hubbell Law Directory

ROGERS & SHEFFIELD, LLP (AV)

427 East Carrillo Street, P.O. Box 22257, 93121-2257
Telephone: 805-963-9721
Fax: 805-966-3715
Email: rs@rogerssheffield.com

MEMBERS OF FIRM

Homer G. Sheffield, Jr.
William K. Rogers
Philip I. Moncharsh
Scott B. Campbell

OF COUNSEL

B. Keith Martin
Richard G. Kravetz
Marlea F. Jarrette

Representative Clients: Fibreoptics Development Systems, Inc.; First Fidelity Thrift and Loan; Great Days Publishing Inc.; Gainey Ranch; Hendry Mechanical Works; Santa Barbara Community College District; Santa Barbara Symphony; Wil-Co Distributors; Wyatt Technology Corp.; Santa Barbara Metropolitan Transit District.

For full biographical listings, see the Martindale-Hubbell Law Directory

SANTA MONICA, Los Angeles Co.

GILCHRIST & RUTTER, PROFESSIONAL CORPORATION (AV)

Wilshire Palisades Building, 1299 Ocean Avenue, Suite 900, 90401
Telephone: 310-393-4000
Facsimile: 310-394-4700
Email: POSTMASTER@GRLAWYERS.COM *URL:* http://www.grlawyers.com
Los Angeles, California Office: 355 South Grand Avenue, Suite 4100.
Telephone: 213-617-8000.
Facsimile: 213-534-8001.

MEMBERS OF THE FIRM

Frank Gooch, III
Jonathan S. Gross
Paul S. Rutter
James R. Andrews
Susan Fowler McNally
James M. Jimenez
Richard H. Close
Ellen K. Wolf
Michael S. Abrams

ASSOCIATES

Steven P. Heller
Cynthia L. Masters

For full biographical listings, see the Martindale-Hubbell Law Directory

*SANTA ROSA,** Sonoma Co.

ABBEY, WEITZENBERG, HOFFMAN & EMERY, A PROFESSIONAL CORPORATION (AV)

1105 North Dutton Avenue, P.O. Box 1566, 95402
Telephone: 707-542-5050
Telecopier: 707-542-2589
Email: info@abbeylaw.com

Richard W. Abbey
Lewis R. Warren

Representative Clients: Exchange Bank of Santa Rosa; Westamerica Bank; Northwestern Title Security Co.; Geyser Peak Winery; Santa Rosa City School District; Sonoma National Bank; Arrowood Vineyards & Winery; Friedman Bros. Hardware, Inc.; Bank of Lake County; Lasercraft, Inc.

For full biographical listings, see the Martindale-Hubbell Law Directory

ANDERSON, ZEIGLER, DISHAROON, GALLAGHER & GRAY, PROFESSIONAL CORPORATION (AV)

50 Old Courthouse Square, 5th Floor, P.O. Box 1498, 95404
Telephone: 707-545-4910
Fax: 707-544-0260
Other Santa Rosa, California Office: 6641 Oakmont Drive, 95409.
Telephone: 707-539-3880.
Petaluma, California Office: 17 Keller Street, 94952.
Telephone: 707-763-0937.

Edwin C. Anderson, Jr.
Kirt F. Zeigler
Robert Disharoon
Barbara Detrich Gallagher
Margaret M. Elliott
David G. Bjornstrom
Robert S. Rutherfurd
Christopher M. Mazzia
Tricia A. Shindledecker
Jeremy L. Olsan

Wendy D. Whitson
Daniel E. Post
Mary Catherine Doherty
Lisa Yoshida
Matthew E. Hannum

OF COUNSEL

John J. King, Jr.

LEGAL SUPPORT PERSONNEL

Edward J. Gibson
Daniel B. Flock
(Director of Information)

For full biographical listings, see the Martindale-Hubbell Law Directory

BABIN, SEEGER, CROW & MANWELL, LLP (AV)

100 Stony Point Road, Suite 125, 95401
Telephone: 707-526-7370
Fax: 707-526-0307

MEMBERS OF FIRM

Norbert C. Babin
Martin L. Seeger, IV
Debra Crow
Malcolm T. Manwell
Susan H. Rapp

ASSOCIATES

Constance F. Morrison
Frank E. Preston
Max R. Breall

For full biographical listings, see the Martindale-Hubbell Law Directory

*STOCKTON,** San Joaquin Co.

ASKEW & ARCHBOLD, A PROFESSIONAL CORPORATION (AV)

1776 West March Lane Suite 350, 95207-6450
Telephone: 209-955-2260
FAX: 209-955-2270
Email: ASKARCH@AOL.COM

(See Next Column)

ASKEW & ARCHBOLD A PROFESSIONAL CORPORATION—*Continued*

James A. Askew Richard M. Archbold

For full biographical listings, see the Martindale-Hubbell Law Directory

THOUSAND OAKS, Ventura Co.

COHEN, ALEXANDER & CLAYTON, A PROFESSIONAL CORPORATION (AV)

One Boardwalk, Suite 102, 91360-5799
Telephone: 805-497-0802
Fax: 805-373-6082
Email: lawcac@ix.netcom.com

Charles W. Cohen
Leonard Alexander
Raymond C. Clayton
Ruth D. Morrow
Marguerite A. Wilson

Thomas S. Cohen

Representative Clients: Comsat General Corp.; Conejo Valley Chamber of Commerce; South Coast Area Transit.

For full biographical listings, see the Martindale-Hubbell Law Directory

TORRANCE, Los Angeles Co.

FINER, KIM & STEARNS (AV)

An Association of Professional Corporations
City National Bank Building, 3424 Carson Street, Suite 500, 90503
Telephone: 310-214-1477
Telecopier: 310-214-0764
Email: finerkimstearns@pobox.com *URL:* http://www.finerkimstearnslaw.com

Harry J. Kim (A Professional Corporation)
W. A. Finer (A Professional Corporation)
Robert David Ciaccio
Robert B. Parsons

OF COUNSEL

Bennett A. Rheingold Ryan E. Stearns

LEGAL SUPPORT PERSONNEL

Marcia E. Talbert

For Complete List of Firm Personnel, See General Section

For full biographical listings, see the Martindale-Hubbell Law Directory

UPLAND, San Bernardino Co.

ALTHOUSE & McDONOUGH (AV)

Second Floor, Metro Commerce Bank Building, 188 North Euclid Avenue, P.O. Box 698, 91785
Telephone: 909-985-9828
Telecopier: 909-985-3282
Email: AltandMcD@aol.com *URL:* http://www.Alt-McD.com

Charles S. Althouse Elizabeth A. McDonough

References: Metro Commerce Bank, Upland, California; Upland Bank, Upland, California.

For Complete List of Firm Personnel, See General Section

For full biographical listings, see the Martindale-Hubbell Law Directory

VALENCIA, Los Angeles Co.

BRUCE A. NAHIN A PROFESSIONAL LAW CORPORATION (AV)

24510 Town Center Drive, 91355-1322
Telephone: 661-287-3610
Fax: 661-287-3612
Email: nu64@earthlink.net
Los Angeles, California Office: 6500 Wilshire Boulevard, Suite 17th Floor.
Telephone: 323-651-0170.
Telecopier: 323-651-0158.

Bruce A. Nahin

For full biographical listings, see the Martindale-Hubbell Law Directory

*VENTURA,** Ventura Co.

STRAUSS • URITZ A PROFESSIONAL CORPORATION (AV)

290 Maple Court, Suite 200, 93003
Telephone: 805-644-7458
Fax: 805-644-4325
Email: mail@venturalaw.com *URL:* http://www.venturalaw.com

Anthony R. Strauss Curt W. Uritz

For full biographical listings, see the Martindale-Hubbell Law Directory

WOODLAND HILLS, Los Angeles Co.

DIAMOND & SCHARNBERGER (AV)

5303 Comercio Way, 91364
Telephone: 818-999-2144
Fax: 818-999-6845
Email: staff@lawcase.com *URL:* http://www.staff@lawcase.com

Robert L. Diamond
Laurence M. Scharnberger
Kenneth D. Zwicker

For full biographical listings, see the Martindale-Hubbell Law Directory

COLORADO

*ASPEN,** Pitkin Co.

OATES, KNEZEVICH & GARDENSWARTZ, P.C. (AV)

Aspen Plaza Building, 3rd Floor, 533 East Hopkins Avenue, 81611
Telephone: 970-920-1700
Fax: 970-920-1121
Email: ohkg@rof.net

Leonard M. Oates
Richard A. Knezevich
Ted D. Gardenswartz
David B. Kelly

David B. Mueller

OF COUNSEL

John Thomas Kelly Michael Feigenbaum

For full biographical listings, see the Martindale-Hubbell Law Directory

*BOULDER,** Boulder Co.

DOTY & SHAPIRO, P.C. (AV)

1720 Fourteenth Street, Suite 100, 80302-6353
Telephone: 303-443-3234
Telecopier: 303-443-3438

H. McGregor Doty, II Mark R. Shapiro

For full biographical listings, see the Martindale-Hubbell Law Directory

*COLORADO SPRINGS,** El Paso Co.

BELTZ, EDWARDS & SABO, L.L.P. (AV)

128 South Tejon, Suite 310, 80903
Telephone: 719-634-6620
Fax: 719-634-3142
Email: BES_LLP@aol.com *URL:* http://www.lawyers.com/beslaw
Other Colorado Springs, Colorado Office: 729 South Cascade, 80903.
Telephone: 719-473-4444.
Fax: 719-444-0186.

Daniel P. Edwards
W. Thomas Beltz
John W. Sabo, III

ASSOCIATE

Daniel A. West

Representative Clients: AMI Industries, Inc.; Analytical Surveys, Inc.; A.C. Israel Enterprises, Inc.; Boddington Lumber Co., Inc.; Cardiovascular Surgeons of Colorado Springs, P.C.; Colorado Springs Radiologists, P.C.; Digital, Inc.; Music Semiconductors, Inc.; Schlage Lock Co.; Texas Instruments.

For full biographical listings, see the Martindale-Hubbell Law Directory

*DENVER,** Denver Co.

HARRY L. ARKIN & ASSOCIATES, P.C. (AV)

Suite 2750 Lincoln Center, 1660 Lincoln Street, 80264
Telephone: 303-863-8400
Telefax: 303-832-4703
Email: harkin00@counsel.com
Email: hnikra@aol.com
London, England Office: Verulam Chambers, Peer House, 8-14 Verulam Street, WCIX 8LZ.
Telephone: 071 813-2400.
Fax: 071 405-3870.

Harry L. Arkin

Michael B. Levy

LEGAL SUPPORT PERSONNEL

Patricia A. Hanson Karen R. Loveland

For full biographical listings, see the Martindale-Hubbell Law Directory

Denver—Continued

BERENBAUM, WEINSHIENK & EASON, P.C. (AV)

Suite 2600 Republic Plaza, 370 17th Street, 80202
Telephone: 303-825-0800
Facsimile: 303-629-7610
Email: berenbaum1@aol.com *URL:* http://www.BWELaw.com

Joseph Berenbaum
Charles A. Bewley
Joseph S. Borus
Daniel S. Duggan
Amy L. Durfee
Steven C. Hoth
James A. Jacobson
James L. Kurtz-Phelan
Charles P. Leder
Dan A. Sciullo
John B. Wills
Ronald I. Zall

OF COUNSEL

Richard L. Eason

Michael James Cook
Heather Scheel Hagemann

Representative Clients: Home Depot; Sprint Spectrum, L.P.; Town of Vail, Colorado; First Union Corporation; City of Englewood, Colorado; Oakwood Homes; Karman, Inc.; Wells Fargo Bank, N.A.; Berkshire Life Insurance Co.; Trinity Ventures.

For full biographical listings, see the Martindale-Hubbell Law Directory

BRENMAN BROMBERG & TENENBAUM, P.C. (AV)

Mellon Financial Center Suite 1001, 1775 Sherman Street, 80203
Telephone: 303-894-0234
Fax: 303-839-1633
Email: bbt@bbtlaw.net

Albert Brenman
Thomas R. Bromberg
A. Thomas Tenenbaum
Steven W. McDonald

Sheryl A. Johnson
Judy A. Gooch

OF COUNSEL

Duane Woodard

For full biographical listings, see the Martindale-Hubbell Law Directory

JAMES E. BROWN & ASSOCIATES, P.C. (AV)

1350 Seventeenth Street, Suite 306, 80202
Telephone: 303-825-1818
Fax: 303-825-2828
Email: wy0j@aol.com

James E. Brown

OF COUNSEL

Michael B. Levy

For full biographical listings, see the Martindale-Hubbell Law Directory

BROWNSTEIN HYATT & FARBER, P.C. (AV)

Twenty-Second Floor, 410 Seventeenth Street, 80202-4437
Telephone: 303-223-1100
Telecopier: 303-223-1111
Washington, D.C. Office: 1615 L Street, N.W., Suite 450, 20036.
Telephone: 202-296-7353.
Telecopier: 202-296-7009.
Glenwood Springs, Colorado Office: Box 357, 81602.
Telephone: 970-945-5302.
Telecopier: 970-945-4921.

Norman Brownstein
Steven W. Farber
Edward N. Barad
John R. Call
Steven M. Sommers
Ronald B. Merrill
Lynda A. McNeive
Laura Jean Christman
Wayne H. Hykan
Michael J. Sternick
Gary M. Reiff
Michael R. McGinnis
Bruce A. James
Thomas J. Mancuso
Jeffrey M. Knetsch
Hubert A. Farbes, Jr.
Steven S. Siegel
John L. Ruppert
Gregory W. Berger
Robert Kaufmann
Steven C. Demby
Brent T. Slosky
Jay F. Kamlet
Ana Lazo Tenzer

SENIOR COUNSEL

John R. Garrett

OF COUNSEL

Jack N. Hyatt
Ann B. Riley
Jacquelyn Kilmer
Lawrence Bass

Howard J. Pollack
Ellen O. Kauffmann
Joshua J. Widoff
Kent C. Veio
Lea Ann T. Groesser
Robert M. Fogler
Christopher D. Reiss
Tad S. Rogers
Adam J. Agron
Jeffrey J. Schroeder

Representative Clients: American Medical Response; Atlantic Gulf Communities Corporation; Boston Chicken, Inc.; Brothers Gourmet Coffees, Inc.; Capital Associates, Inc.; Donaldson Lufkin & Jenrette Securities Corporation; Kohlberg & Co.; The Prudential Insurance Company of America; SunAmerica Inc.; Thoma Cressey Equity Partners.

(See Next Column)

For Complete List of Firm Personnel, See General Section

For full biographical listings, see the Martindale-Hubbell Law Directory

CORTEZ MACAULAY BERNHARDT & SCHUETZE LLC (AV)

1600 Broadway, Suite 1600, 80202
Telephone: 303-864-1000
Facsimile: 303-864-1111
URL: http://www.cmblaw.com

Miles Cortez
Christopher T. Macaulay
Susan Bernhardt
Robert A. Schuetze
David H. Goldberg
Marian L. Carlson
Richard P. R. Cohn

For full biographical listings, see the Martindale-Hubbell Law Directory

DUFFORD & BROWN, P.C. (AV)

1700 Broadway, Suite 1700, 80290-1701
Telephone: 303-861-8013
Facsimile: 303-832-3804
Colorado Springs, Colorado Office: 101 N. Tejon, Suite 410.
Telephone: 719-471-0559.
Facsimile: 719-471-0583.
Affiliated Office: Solomon, Pearl, Blum & Quinn, L.L.P., New York, NY and Denver, Colorado.

Thomas G. Brown
Randall J. Feuerstein

Michael Roch

Representative Clients: CF&I Steel, L.P.; Colorado Permanente Medical Group, Inc.; Equilease Corporation; General Electric Company; Hall and Hall Mortgage Corporation; Metallurgy International Inc.; Hewlett-Packard Co.; Hong Kong & Shanghai Banking Corporation; The Lincoln National Life Insurance Company; G.T. Colorado, Inc.

For Complete List of Firm Personnel, See General Section

For full biographical listings, see the Martindale-Hubbell Law Directory

GORSUCH KIRGIS LLP (AV)

Tower 1, Suite 1000, 1515 Arapahoe Street, 80202
Telephone: 303-376-5000
Fax: 303-376-5001

PARTNERS

S. Lee Terry, Jr.
Cynthia Smith Cain

ASSOCIATES

Pantea M. Garroussi
Anastasia G. Khokhryakova

LEGAL SUPPORT PERSONNEL

Lansing Wallace
Veronica Ehrenzeller

For full biographical listings, see the Martindale-Hubbell Law Directory

HAMILTON AND FAATZ, A PROFESSIONAL CORPORATION (AV)

Suite 500 Colorado State Bank Building, 1600 Broadway, 80202-4905
Telephone: 303-830-0500
Facsimile: 303-860-7855
Email: HandF@HandF.com

Pierpont Fuller (1906-1983)
John M. Evans (1911-1984)
Dwight Alan Hamilton
Clyde A. Faatz, Jr.
John T. Willson
Michael E. Gurley
James H. Marlow
Jan E. Montgomery
Gregory W. Smith

Christopher J.W. Forrest
Cynthia Treadwell-Miller
Tal Diamant

OF COUNSEL

Kenneth W. Caughey

Representative Clients: Arapahoe County Public Airport Authority; Colorado Baptist General Convention; First Industrial Realty Trust; Masonic Temple Association of Denver; Meridian Investment Management Corp.; Public Employees' Retirement Association of Colorado; Randall and Blake, Inc.; Rocky Mountain Clothing Co.; South Denver Cardiology Associates, P.C.; Unisource Worldwide, Inc.

For full biographical listings, see the Martindale-Hubbell Law Directory

KATZ, LOOK & MOISON, PROFESSIONAL CORPORATION (AV)

1120 Lincoln Street, Suite 1100, 80203
Telephone: 303-832-1900
Fax: 303-863-0412

Michael M. Katz
Harley K. Look, Jr.
Peter R. Moison
Kathryn A. Reeves

(See Next Column)

KATZ, LOOK & MOISON PROFESSIONAL CORPORATION—*Continued*

Brian E. Onorato
Melisa A. Vogel
Arthur T. DiMeo
Delwyn G. Haroldson
Barbara J. Stauch

SPECIAL COUNSEL

Ogborn, Summerlin & Ogborn, L.L.C., Denver, Colorado

For full biographical listings, see the Martindale-Hubbell Law Directory

LAFF STEIN CAMPBELL TUCKER & DELANEY, LLP (AV)

A Partnership including Professional Corporations
7730 East Belleview Avenue, Suite 204 (Englewood), 80111-2616
Telephone: 303-740-7200
Telecopier: 303-740-7300

Alan D. Laff (Member of Laff Campbell & Delaney, P.C.)
Alan L. Stein (Member of Alan L. Stein, P.C.)
Darrel L. Campbell (Member of Laff Campbell & Delaney, P.C.)
Ronald C. Tucker
Stacia Bank Delaney (Member of Laff Campbell & Delaney, P.C.)

LOHF, SHAIMAN & JACOBS, P.C. (AV)

950 South Cherry Street, Suite 900, 80246-2666
Telephone: 303-753-9000
Telecopier: 303-753-9997

Neil E. Ayervais
Charles H. Jacobs
Moshe Luber
Robert Shaiman

Reference: Vectra Bank Colorado.

For full biographical listings, see the Martindale-Hubbell Law Directory

MYER, SWANSON, ADAMS & WOLF, P.C. (AV)

The Colorado State Bank Building, 1600 Broadway, Suite 1480, 80202-4915
Telephone: 303-866-9800
Facsimile: 303-866-9818

Fred E. Neef (1910-1986)
Rendle Myer (1929-1999)
Allan B. Adams
Thomas J. Wolf

John M. Anderson
Karen S. Proc

OF COUNSEL

Robert Swanson

Representative Clients: The Oppenheimer Funds; Panorama Series Fund; The Centennial Trusts; Mile High Chapter of American Red Cross; Master Lease; Heartland Management Co.; Kan-Build of Colorado, Inc.
Reference: The Colorado State Bank and Trust of Denver.

For full biographical listings, see the Martindale-Hubbell Law Directory

OTTEN, JOHNSON, ROBINSON, NEFF & RAGONETTI, P.C. (AV)

950 Seventeenth Street, 16th Floor, 80202
Telephone: 303-825-8400
Telecopier: 303-825-6525
URL: http://www.ojrnr.com

A. Bruce Campbell
William R. Neff
Neil M. Goff
Blair L. Lockwood
Douglas R. Wright
Michael Westover
Randall G. Alt
Daniel M. Minzer
Kevin A. Gliwa
Karen L. Barsch
John R. Marcil
Michael C. Villano
James D. Leonard
Paul D. Zier
Michael C. Matheson
C. Ander Smith
Jeffrey A. Sherman

OF COUNSEL

Barbara J. Kelley

Representative Clients: Amstar Group, Ltd.; Coram Healthcare Corp.; Frontier Airlines; General Electric Capital Corp.; GeriMed of America, Inc.; Koala Corp.; OmniTRAX, Inc.; Rocky Mountain Broadcasting Network, Inc.; Silver Oak Winery; Simpson Housing Limited Partnership; StarTek, Inc.; TIC Holdings, Inc.; Trinidad/Benham Corp.; United General Financial Services, Inc.; U.S. Bank National Association.

For Complete List of Firm Personnel, See General Section

For full biographical listings, see the Martindale-Hubbell Law Directory

J. C. TIM SCATES (AV)

4101 South Quebec Street, 80237
Telephone: 303-779-4441
Telecopier: 303-741-6122
Email: scateslaw@aol.com

For full biographical listings, see the Martindale-Hubbell Law Directory

SCHLUETER & ASSOCIATES, P.C. (AV)

1050 Seventeenth Street, Suite 1700, 80265
Telephone: 303-292-3883
Facsimile: 303-296-8880
Email: 76304.3546@compuserve.com

Henry F. Schlueter

Celia Velletri

For full biographical listings, see the Martindale-Hubbell Law Directory

SENN LEWIS & VISCIANO, P.C. (AV)

1801 California Street, Suite 4300, 80202
Telephone: 303-298-1122
Facsimile: 303-296-9101

Mark A. Senn
Fredric J. Lewis
Frank W. Visciano
Stephen W. Arent
Ellen Kirschenbaum

Rosemarie E. Delmonte
Mark A. Redmiles
Luis A. Toro
Margie J. Titus

OF COUNSEL

Lawrence A. Atler
Brenda Jansen

For Complete List of Firm Personnel, See General Section

For full biographical listings, see the Martindale-Hubbell Law Directory

*GREELEY,** Weld Co.

BREGA & WINTERS P.C. (AV)

1100 Tenth Street, Suite 402, 80631
Telephone: 970-352-4805
Fax: 970-352-6547
Denver, Colorado Office: One Norwest Center, 1700 Lincoln Street, Suite 2222.
Telephone: 303-866-9400.
Fax: 303-861-9109.

Jerry D. Winters
Pamela A. Shaddock
William W. Hughes

Julie Scroggins Frantz
Bradley D. Laue

For full biographical listings, see the Martindale-Hubbell Law Directory

*TELLURIDE,** San Miguel Co.

LAW OFFICES OF JOHN H. STEEL (AV Ⓣ)

126 West Colorado Avenue, P.O. Box 2784, 81435
Telephone: 970-728-1300
Fax: 970-728-1021
Email: justice@rmi.net *URL:* http://www.lawyers.com/steel

For full biographical listings, see the Martindale-Hubbell Law Directory

CONNECTICUT

*BRIDGEPORT,** Fairfield Co.

ELSTEIN AND ELSTEIN, P.C. (AV)

Suite 400 1087 Broad Street, 06604-4231
Telephone: 203-367-4421
Telecopier: 203-366-8615

Henry Elstein
Bruce L. Elstein

For full biographical listings, see the Martindale-Hubbell Law Directory

CHESHIRE, New Haven Co.

WINTERS & FORTE (AV)

Waverly Professional Park, 315 Highland Avenue, Suite 102, P.O. Box 844, 06410
Telephone: 203-272-2927
Fax: 203-271-1222
Email: david.wayne.winters@snet.net *URL:* http://www.snetyp.com/wintersforte

MEMBERS OF FIRM

David Wayne Winters
Michael C. Forte

ASSOCIATE

Anthony R. DePaolo

A List of Representative Clients will be furnished upon request.
References: Bank of Boston, Connecticut; LaFayette American Bank & Trust Co.

For full biographical listings, see the Martindale-Hubbell Law Directory

DARIEN, Fairfield Co.

RUCCI, BURNHAM, CARTA & EDELBERG, LLP (AV)

800 Post Road, P.O. Box 1107, 06820
Telephone: 203-655-7695
Facsimile: 203-655-4302
URL: http://www.rbce.com
Stamford, Connecticut Office: 6 Landmark Square, Suite 470.
Telephone: 203-359-5637.

MEMBERS OF FIRM

Joseph J. Rucci, Jr.
Paul H. Burnham
Mark R. Carta
Paul B. Edelberg
William M. Carello
Robert F. Maslan, Jr.

ASSOCIATES

Colette C. Symon
Karen K. Linder
Joanna F. Bowen
David J. Rucci
Sandra J. Akoury

OF COUNSEL

Ian R. Crawford
James C. Dempsey
Lawrence H. Reilly
Alberto N. Moris (Not admitted in CT)

For full biographical listings, see the Martindale-Hubbell Law Directory

GREENWICH, Fairfield Co.

ALBERT, WARD & JOHNSON, P.C. (AV)

125 Mason Street, P.O. Box 1668, 06836
Telephone: 203-661-8600
Telecopier: 203-661-8051

Tom S. Ward, Jr.
Scott R. Johnson
Jane D. Hogeman
Howard R. Wolfe
Christopher A. Kristoff
Vicki K. Comberiati

OF COUNSEL

David Albert
C. Robton Perelli-Minetti

For full biographical listings, see the Martindale-Hubbell Law Directory

FOGARTY COHEN SELBY & NEMIROFF LLC (AV)

88 Field Point Road, P.O. Box 2508, 06836-2508
Telephone: 203-661-1000
Telefax: 203-629-7300

MEMBERS OF FIRM

James R. Fogarty
Bruce F. Cohen
Leland C. Selby
Andrew P. Nemiroff
Steven W. Russo

COUNSEL

Robert A. Epstein
Everett Fisher
Jennifer N. Boyd

ASSOCIATES

William Bradford Smith, Jr.
Carolyn Alexander Collins
Lawrence F. Reilly
Anne M. Piedade
Eric R. Posmantier

For full biographical listings, see the Martindale-Hubbell Law Directory

HOLLAND KAUFMANN & BARTELS, LLC (AV)

289 Greenwich Avenue, 06830-6595
Telephone: 203-869-5600
Fax: 203-869-4648

Alexander J. Holland
Charles B. Kaufmann, III
Philip H. Bartels
Harold R. Burke
Jean Mills Aranha
Lori E. Romano
John C. Fusco

OF COUNSEL

Beth K. Hansson

For full biographical listings, see the Martindale-Hubbell Law Directory

*HARTFORD,** Hartford Co.

GOULD, KILLIAN & WYNNE (AV)

280 Trumbull Street, 25th Floor, 06103-3595
Telephone: 860-278-1270
Telecopier: 860-244-9290

MEMBERS OF FIRM

Samuel Gould (1905-1994)
Robert K. Killian
Francis J. Wynne
Martin A. Gould
Mark W. Baronas
William F. Healey
Nancy E. Gould
Robert O. Wynne

For full biographical listings, see the Martindale-Hubbell Law Directory

ROGIN, NASSAU, CAPLAN, LASSMAN & HIRTLE, LLC (AV)

CityPlace I, 22nd Floor, 185 Asylum Street, 06103-3460
Telephone: 860-278-7480
Fax: 860-278-2179

(See Next Column)

MEMBERS OF FIRM

Robert L. Hirtle
Steven D. Bartelstone
David M. Call
Paul B. Zolan
David J. Heinlein
Lewis K. Wise
Joan G. Engel
Thomas M. Divine
Mark A. Rosenblum
Barry S. Feigenbaum
Donald G. Gaudreau
Peter S. Sorokin
Iris June Brown
Benjamin Engel
Lawrence G. Rosenthal

ASSOCIATES

Clara A. Porcello
Mark J. Lassman
Brendan T. Flynn
Elizabeth R. Houde
Jonathan M. Starble
Monique R. Polidoro
Lisa M. Anderson

OF COUNSEL

Jerome E. Caplan
Edwin A. Lassman

RETIRED

Edward S. Rogin (Retired)
Louis E. Nassau (Retired)

For full biographical listings, see the Martindale-Hubbell Law Directory

SOROKIN, GROSS & HYDE, P.C. (AV)

One Corporate Center, 06103
Telephone: 860-525-6645
Fax: 860-522-1781
Email: sorokin@sorokinlaw.com
Simsbury, Connecticut Office: 720 Hopmeadow Street.
Telephone: 860-651-9348.
Rocky Hill, Connecticut Office: 2360 Main Street.
Telephone: 860-563-9305.
Fax: 860-529-6931.

Morris W. Banks
Sharon Kowal Freilich
Andrew C. Glassman
Barry D. Greene
Keith D. Robbins

Rod W. Farrell
Margaret M. Murphy
Gwen P. Weisberg

OF COUNSEL

Charles R. Moore, Jr.

For Complete List of Firm Personnel, See General Section

For full biographical listings, see the Martindale-Hubbell Law Directory

*NEW HAVEN,** New Haven Co.

SUSMAN, DUFFY & SEGALOFF, P.C. (AV)

55 Whitney Avenue, 06510-1300
Telephone: 203-624-9830
Fax: 203-562-8430
Mailing Address: P.O. Box 1684, New Haven, Connecticut, 06507-1684

Allen H. Duffy (1931-1986)
Michael Susman
James H. Segaloff
Joseph E. Faughnan
Susan W. Wolfson
Laura M. Sklaver
Andrew R. Lubin
James J. Perito
Matthew C. Susman
Thomas E. Katon

Jennifer L. Schancupp
Peter G. Kruzynski
Vincent J. Candelora
Karen Baldwin Kravetz

OF COUNSEL

Diana C. Ballard
David P. Hambleton

For full biographical listings, see the Martindale-Hubbell Law Directory

NEW LONDON, New London Co.

DUPONT AND RADLAUER, L.L.P. (AV)

Captain's Walk, 165 State Street, Suite 502, P.O. Box 710, 06320-0710
Telephone: 860-447-0090
Fax: 860-437-7442
Email: radlaw@snet.net *URL:*
http://www.lawyers.com/dupontandradlauer

MEMBERS OF FIRM

Ralph P. Dupont
Barbara J. Radlauer

For full biographical listings, see the Martindale-Hubbell Law Directory

WALLER, SMITH & PALMER, P.C. (AV)

52 Eugene O'Neill Drive, P.O. Box 88, 06320
Telephone: 860-442-0367
Telecopier: 860-447-9915
Email: wspmain@snet.net *URL:*
http://www.snetyp.com/wallersmithpalmer
Old Lyme Office: 103 Halls Road.
Telephone: 860-434-8063.
Telecopier: 860-434-9452. Email: wspol@snet.net

(See Next Column)

WALLER, SMITH & PALMER P.C.—*Continued*

Tracy Waller (1862-1947)
J. Rodney Smith (1906-1979)
Birdsey G. Palmer (Retired)
William W. Miner
Robert P. Anderson, Jr.
Robert W. Marrion
Hughes Griffis
Edward B. O'Connell
Frederick B. Gahagan
Tracy M. Collins
Philip M. Johnstone
David P. Condon
Valerie Ann Votto
Charles C. Anderson

James F. Spallone

General Counsel For: Town of East Lyme.
Counsel For: Citizens Bank of Connecticut; Soneco/Northeastern, Inc.; The Nature Conservancy; Fleet Bank.
Local Counsel For: McCue Mortgage Co.; Citicorp Mortgage; U.S. Department of Housing and Urban Development.

For full biographical listings, see the Martindale-Hubbell Law Directory

SOUTHPORT, Fairfield Co.

BRODY, WILKINSON AND OBER, P.C. (AV)

2507 Post Road, 06490
Telephone: 203-319-7100
Fax: 203-254-1772

Seth O. L. Brody
Peter Wilkinson
Frank Fritz Ober
S. Giles Payne
James E. Rice
William J. Britt
Barbara S. Miller
Robert L. Teicher
Ronald B. Noren
Peter T. Mott
Thomas J. Walsh, Jr.
Diane F. Martucci
Seth L. Cooper
Douglas R. Brown
Charles S. Brody (1894-1976)

OF COUNSEL

Bruce E. Dillingham
Roy W. Moore, III

For full biographical listings, see the Martindale-Hubbell Law Directory

STAMFORD, Fairfield Co.

CACACE, TUSCH & SANTAGATA (AV)

777 Summer Street, P.O. Box 15859, 06901-0859
Telephone: 203-327-2000
Telecopier: 203-353-3392
Email: lawcts@aol.com

MEMBERS OF FIRM

Michael J. Cacace
Mark P. Santagata
Paul T. Tusch
Richard S. Fisher

OF COUNSEL

Kenneth A. DellaRocco
Eric D. Grayson

ASSOCIATES

Edward F. Nemchek
Alice Ann Fitzpatrick
Ronald E. Kowalski II
Aamina Ahmad
Demaris Page Hetrick
Patrick L. Poeschl

LEGAL SUPPORT PERSONNEL

Eva L. Chan
Cynthia L. Mammone

For full biographical listings, see the Martindale-Hubbell Law Directory

CURTIS, BRINCKERHOFF & BARRETT, P.C. (AV)

666 Summer Street, 06901-1416
Telephone: 203-324-6777
Telecopier: 203-324-9621
Email: info@curtisbb.com

T. Ward Cleary (1916-1988)
Frederick M. Tobin
John Wayne Fox
Ward Frank Cleary
James D'Alton Murphy
Randolph T. Lovallo

OF COUNSEL

John D. Hertz
Jane F. Donovan
Richard L. Brinckerhoff
Patricia M. Gaug

Susan L. Stratton
Derek Gilman
Michael P. Murray
John J. Louizos

Counsel for: The F. A. Bartlett Tree Expert Co.; Town of Darien; Miller Automobile Corp.; Bolliger, Inc.; Titan Sports; People's Bank, Bridgeport; Fleet Bank; Federal Deposit Insurance Co.; William Pitt Foundation; Wood Logan Associates.

For full biographical listings, see the Martindale-Hubbell Law Directory

LAW OFFICES OF DONALD A. HERNER (AV)

One Landmark Square, 4th Floor, 06901
Telephone: 203-351-1020
Fax: 203-351-1029
Email: herner@erols.com *URL:* http://www.lawyers.com/donaldaherner

(See Next Column)

OF COUNSEL

Barbara J. Beghin (Not admitted in CT)

For full biographical listings, see the Martindale-Hubbell Law Directory

PHELAN & MITRI (AV)

One Atlantic Street, 06901
Telephone: 203-967-4140
Fax: 203-325-3056
Email: pmchart@pmchart.com *URL:* http://www.pmchart.com

MEMBERS OF FIRM

William J. Phelan
Michael F. Mitri

ASSOCIATE

Edmund J. Cienava

For full biographical listings, see the Martindale-Hubbell Law Directory

WOFSEY, ROSEN, KWESKIN & KURIANSKY, LLP (AV)

600 Summer Street, 06901
Telephone: 203-327-2300
Fax: 203-967-9273

MEMBERS OF FIRM

Abraham Wofsey (1915-1944)
Michael Wofsey (1927-1951)
David M. Rosen (1926-1967)
Julius B. Kuriansky (1952-1992)
Sydney C. Kweskin (1946-1998)
Monroe Silverman
Howard C. Kaplan
Edward M. Kweskin
David M. Cohen
Marshall Goldberg
Stephen A. Finn
Judith Rosenberg
Mark H. Henderson
Steven D. Grushkin
Matthew J. Forstadt
Steven M. Frederick

OF COUNSEL

Saul Kwartin
Emanuel Margolis
Anthony R. Lorenzo

SPECIAL COUNSEL

Day R. Shields

ASSOCIATES

Joseph Brachfeld
Eric M. Higgins
William A. Harrison
Daniel M. Young
Angelo A. Ziotas

Representative Clients: Banque Paribas; Benenson Realty; Cellular Information Systems, Inc.; The Chase Manhattan Bank; First County Bank; Hartford Provision Co.; Louis Dreyfus Corp.; Norwalk Federation of Teachers; People's Bank; Ridgeway Shopping Center.

For full biographical listings, see the Martindale-Hubbell Law Directory

WESTPORT, Fairfield Co.

LEVETT ROCKWOOD P.C. (AV)

33 Riverside Avenue, P.O. Box 5116, 06881
Telephone: 203-222-0885
Telecopier: 203-226-8025

Suzanne B. Albani
Robert O. Barberi
Edward B. Chansky
Madeleine F. Grossman
Dorit Schutzengel Heimer
Cheryl L. Johnson
Marc J. Kurzman
David R. Levett
Judy A. Rabkin
Sharon M. Schweitzer
Steven M. Siegelaub
Peter H. Struzzi
Barbara A. Young

OF COUNSEL

William O. Rockwood, Jr.

Debra R. Cardinali
Stephen M. Cowherd
Christopher M. Graham
Robin K. Higgins
Douglas R. Sansted
Rodger F. Smith, Jr.
Patricia D. Weitzman

Representative Clients: Cannondale Corp.; Caradon, Inc.; DataViz, Inc.; Dooney & Bourke, Inc.; GAF Corporation; Heyman Properties; Hospital of Saint Raphael; Marketing Corporation of America; Olin Corporation; St. Vincent's Medical Center.

For full biographical listings, see the Martindale-Hubbell Law Directory

NEVAS, NEVAS & CAPASSE (AV)

246 Post Road East, P.O. Box 791, 06881
Telephone: 203-226-1211
Fax: 203-454-3419
Email: law@nevascapasse.com

Bernard A. Nevas (1900-1942)
Leo Nevas
Edward J. Capasse
Jamie Kay Gerard
Andrew B. Nevas

OF COUNSEL

Stephen Tate
Stephen E. Nevas

For full biographical listings, see the Martindale-Hubbell Law Directory

Westport—Continued

WILLIAM L. SCHEFFLER & ASSOCIATES (AV Ⓣ)

P.O. Box 2773, 06880-0773
Telephone: 203-226-6600; 1-800-429-4480
Telecopier: 203-227-1873
Email: scheff@optonline.net

For full biographical listings, see the Martindale-Hubbell Law Directory

RONALD L. SHEIMAN (AV)

1804 Post Road East, 06880
Telephone: 203-259-0599
Telecopier: 203-255-2570

For full biographical listings, see the Martindale-Hubbell Law Directory

DELAWARE

*WILMINGTON,** New Castle Co.

CONNOLLY BOVE LODGE & HUTZ LLP (AV)

1220 Market Street, P.O. Box 2207, 19899-2207
Telephone: 302-658-9141
Telecopier: 302-658-5614
Email: cblhlaw@cblhlaw.com *URL:* http://www.cblhlaw.com

James M. Mulligan, Jr.
Arthur G. Connolly, Jr.
Stanley C. Macel, III
Henry E. Gallagher, Jr.
Richard David Levin
Jeffrey B. Bove
Collins J. Seitz, Jr.
Charles J. Durante
Arthur G. Connolly, III
James D. Heisman
Jeffrey C. Wisler
M. Edward Danberg
Anne Love Barnett
Matthew F. Boyer
Karen C. Bifferato
Samuel D. Brickley II
Thomas A. Stevens

For Complete List of Firm Personnel, See General Section

For full biographical listings, see the Martindale-Hubbell Law Directory

SMITH, KATZENSTEIN & FURLOW LLP (AV)

The Corporate Plaza, 800 Delaware Avenue, P.O. Box 410, 19899
Telephone: 302-652-8400
Fax: 302-652-8405
Email: info@skfdelaware.com *URL:* http://www.SKFDelaware.com

MEMBERS OF FIRM

Craig B. Smith
Robert J. Katzenstein
David A. Jenkins
Brett D. Fallon
Charles E. Butler

For Complete List of Firm Personnel, See General Section

For full biographical listings, see the Martindale-Hubbell Law Directory

DISTRICT OF COLUMBIA

WASHINGTON, D.C. Co.

BAKER BOTTS L.L.P. (AV)

A Registered Limited Liability Partnership
The Warner, 1299 Pennsylvania Avenue, N.W., 20004-2400
Telephone: 202-639-7700
Fax: 202-639-7832
Email: postmaster@bakerbotts.com *URL:* http://www.bakerbotts.com
Houston, Texas Office: One Shell Plaza, 910 Louisiana.
Telephone: 713-229-1234.
Austin, Texas Office: 1600 San Jacinto Center, 98 San Jacinto Boulevard.
Telephone: 512-322-2500.
Dallas, Texas Office: 2001 Ross Avenue.
Telephone: 214-953-6500.
New York, New York Office: 599 Lexington Avenue.
Telephone: 212-705-5000.
Moscow, Russia Office: 10 ul. Bolshaya Dimitrovka (formerly Pushkinskaya), 103031.
Telephone: 7095/921-5300 (Local); 7501/929-7070 (International).
London, England Office: 45 Ludgate Hill.
Telephone: 0171-778-1400 (Local); 011-44-171-778-1400 (International).
Baku, Azerbaijan Office: 6-10 Vagif Mustafa-zadeh Street, Third Floor, Icheri Sheher, 370004.
Telephone: 994-12-97-63-88 (Local); 011-994-12-97-63-88 (International).

MEMBERS OF FIRM

Kevin B. Dent
James R. Doty
Leslie Anne Freiman
Nancy M. Persechino
David N. Powers

(See Next Column)

SPECIAL COUNSEL

Robert J. Bohme (Not admitted in DC)

ASSOCIATES

Michael A. Gold
Jon B. Jordan
Jane Boland Keough
Nikesh R. Patel
Tamar C. Stanley
Jennifer J. Yi
Susan Aldrich Zoch

For Complete List of Firm Personnel, See General Section

For full biographical listings, see the Martindale-Hubbell Law Directory

CAPLIN & DRYSDALE, CHARTERED (AV)

One Thomas Circle, N.W., 20005
Telephone: 202-862-5000
Cable Address: "Capdale"
Telex: 904001 CAPL UR WSH
Fax: 202-429-3301
URL: http://www.caplindrysdale.com
New York, N.Y. Office: 399 Park Avenue, 36th Floor.
Telephone: 212-319-7125.
Fax: 212-644-6755.

Mortimer M. Caplin
Thomas A. Troyer
David N. Webster
H. David Rosenbloom
Peter Van N. Lockwood
Richard W. Skillman
Patricia G. Lewis
Bernard S. Bailor
Albert G. Lauber, Jr.
Julie W. Davis
Trevor W. Swett III
James E. Salles
Craig A. Sharon
Catherine E. Livingston
Seth M. Green
Douglas D. Drysdale
Ralph A. Muoio
Elihu Inselbuch
(Resident, New York Office)
Cono R. Namorato
Daniel B. Rosenbaum
Richard E. Timbie
Stafford Smiley
Scott D. Michel
Kent A. Mason
Robert A. Boisture
Milton Cerny
Matthew W. Frank
Jessica L. Katz
Christopher S. Rizek

Nathan D. Finch
Douglas N. Varley
Neal M. Kochman
Jason K. Bortz
(Not admitted in DC)
April J. Adams
(Not admitted in DC)
Elizabeth M. Sellers
Lloyd H. Mayer
Rita C. Tobin
(Resident, New York Office)
H. Carter Hood
(Not admitted in DC)

OF COUNSEL

Robert H. Elliott, Jr.
Myron C. Baum
Ann C. McMillan

For full biographical listings, see the Martindale-Hubbell Law Directory

COLE, RAYWID & BRAVERMAN, L.L.P. (AV)

1919 Pennsylvania Avenue, N.W., 20006
Telephone: 202-659-9750
Cable Address: "Crab"
Telecopier: 202-452-0067
URL: http://www.crblaw.com

John P. Cole, Jr.
Alan Raywid (1930-1991)
Burt A. Braverman
Robert L. James
John D. Seiver
Wesley R. Heppler
Paul Glist
David M. Silverman
James F. Ireland, III
Maurita K. Coley
Steven Jay Horvitz
Christopher W. Savage
Ann E. Flowers
Robert G. Scott, Jr.
Susan Whelan Westfall
Theresa A. Zeterberg
Karlyn D. Stanley
John Davidson Thomas
John Dodge

Frederick W. Giroux
Geoffrey C. Cook
Maria T. Browne
Donna Carrie Rattley
T. Scott Thompson
Adam S. Caldwell
Sandra G. Gibbs
Mark S. Kristiansen
Christin S. McMeley
(Not admitted in DC)
Sara J. Kiernan
(Not admitted in DC)
Heather M. Wilson
David N. Tobenkin

OF COUNSEL

Frances J. Chetwynd
Ellen S. Deutsch

For full biographical listings, see the Martindale-Hubbell Law Directory

DE MARTINO FINKELSTEIN ROSEN & VIRGA (AV)

Suite 400, 1818 N Street, N.W., 20036
Telephone: 202-659-0494
Telecopier: 202-659-1290
Email: BUSLAW@mail.dfrv.com
New York, N.Y. Office: Suite 1700, 90 Broad Street.
Telephone: 212-363-2500.
Telecopier: 212-363-2723. Email: DFRV90Brd@aol.com

(See Next Column)

DE MARTINO FINKELSTEIN ROSEN & VIRGA—*Continued*

MEMBERS OF FIRM

Ralph V. De Martino (Resident)
Steven R. Finkelstein (Not admitted in DC; Resident, New York, N.Y. Office)
Jeffrey S. Rosen (Resident)
Gerard A. Virga (Not admitted in DC; Resident, New York, N.Y. Office)

Keith H. Peterson (Not admitted in DC; Resident, New York, N.Y. Office)
Caroline George
Bertin Henry Pérez

OF COUNSEL

Neil R.E. Carr (Resident)
Paula A. Argento

LEGAL SUPPORT PERSONNEL

J. Keoni Robinson (Legal Assistant)

For full biographical listings, see the Martindale-Hubbell Law Directory

---

THE FEINBERG GROUP, LLP (AV)

1120 20th Street, N.W. Suite 740 South, 20036-3437
Telephone: 202-371-1110
Fax: 202-962-9290
Email: kfeinberg@thefeinberggroup.com *URL:* http://www.krfassociates.com
New York, N.Y. Office: 780 3rd Avenue, Suite 2202.
Telephone: 212-527-9600.
Fax: 212-527-9611. Email: kfeinberg@thefeinberggroup.com.

PARTNERS

Kenneth R. Feinberg
Deborah E. Greenspan
Michael K. Rozen (Resident, New York Office)
Peter H. Woodin (Resident, New York Office)

ASSOCIATE

Fredric M. Brooks (Not admitted in DC)

SENIOR COUNSEL

Jacqueline E. Zins

For full biographical listings, see the Martindale-Hubbell Law Directory

---

FELDESMAN, TUCKER, LEIFER, FIDELL & BANK LLP (AV)

2001 L Street, N.W., 2nd Floor, 20036
Telephone: 202-466-8960
Telefax: 202-293-8103
Rockville, Maryland Office: One Church Street, Suite 800.
Telephone: 301-279-6770.
Falls Church, Virginia Office: 5661 Columbia Pike, Suite 200.
Telephone: 703-671-5800.

Margaret H. Long (1940-1990)

MEMBERS OF FIRM

James L. Feldesman
Marna S. Tucker
Jacqueline C. Leifer
Eugene R. Fidell
Rita M. Bank
Pamela B. Forbes
Mary S. Pence
Jonathan M. Dana
Beth Goodman
Edward T. Waters
Roger A. Schwartz
Michael B. Glomb
Tanya A. Harvey
Richard C. Shadyac, Jr.
David P. Sheldon
Bruce F. Hoffmeister
M. Toni Waldman

ASSOCIATES

Robin A. Clark
Jennifer P. Rosenberg
Garrett L. Lee
Marcie H. Zakheim
Kathy S. Ghiladi
Daniel L. Gray
Mary Price
Savalle C. Sims
Alice J. Gallin-Dwyer
Elizabeth A. Greczek
Jennifer L. Dziedzic
Alan J. Van Luven

For full biographical listings, see the Martindale-Hubbell Law Directory

---

MIDLEN LAW CENTER (AV)

3238 Prospect Street, N.W., 20007-3214
Telephone: 202-333-1500
Facsimile: 202-333-6852
Email: john@midlen.com *URL:* http://www.midlen.com

John H. Midlen, Jr.
John H. Midlen (1910-1978)

For full biographical listings, see the Martindale-Hubbell Law Directory

---

MOORE & BRUCE, LLP (AV)

1072 Thomas Jefferson Street, N.W., 20007
Telephone: 202-965-5300
Facsimile: 202-965-7745
URL: http://www.lawyers.com/moore&brucellp

Charles M. Bruce
Jonathon R. Moore

(See Next Column)

OF COUNSEL

Mark A. Cohen
Michael C. Durney
William Morris

For full biographical listings, see the Martindale-Hubbell Law Directory

---

QUINN, RACUSIN & GAZZOLA, CHARTERED (AV)

1400 K Street, N.W. Suite 1010, 20005-2403
Telephone: 202-842-9300
Facsimile: 202-682-0148
URL: http://www.qrg-law.com
Email: qrg@qrg-law.com *URL:* http://www.lawyers.com/quinnracusin&gazzola

Aaron J. Racusin (1915-1998)
John H. Quinn, Jr.
Robert A. Gazzola
Susan Yoder Torres

Robin Duncan Culbertson

LEGAL SUPPORT PERSONNEL

Kevin Srivastava (Paralegal)
Francesca West Watson (Paralegal)

For full biographical listings, see the Martindale-Hubbell Law Directory

---

SALTMAN & STEVENS, P.C. (AV)

1801 K Street, N.W. Suite M-110, 20006
Telephone: 202-452-2140
Fax: 202-775-8217

Alan I. Saltman
Gary G. Stevens
Ruth G. Tiger
Kevin Garden

Richard W. Goeken

For full biographical listings, see the Martindale-Hubbell Law Directory

---

SCHMELTZER, APTAKER & SHEPARD, P.C. (AV)

The Watergate, Suite 1000, 2600 Virginia Avenue, N.W., 20037-1905
Telephone: 202-333-8800
Cable Address: "Ship"
Telex: 440517
Facsimile: 202-337-6065
Email: sas@saslaw.com *URL:* http://www.saspc.com
Los Angeles, California Office: 1999 Avenue of the Stars, Twenty-Seventh Floor, 90067-4095.
Telephone: 310-557-2966.
FAX: 310-286-6610.

J. Thomas Esslinger
Mark I. Gruhin
J. Anthony Smith

Suzanne Langford Sanford
Carlos M. Paz-Soldan

For full biographical listings, see the Martindale-Hubbell Law Directory

---

SIMON, TURNBULL & MARTIN, CHARTERED (AV)

2000 Pennsylvania Avenue, N.W., Suite 4600, 20006-1812
Telephone: 202-785-2202
Fax: 202-785-2273
Email: info@stmlaw.com

William D. Simon
Lowell D. Turnbull
Jeffrey L. Squires

John A. Knab

OF COUNSEL

Robert Martin
Michael B. Sheppard

For full biographical listings, see the Martindale-Hubbell Law Directory

---

THOMSEN AND BURKE, LLP (AV)

Suite 500, 1225 Eye Street, N.W., 20005
Telephone: 202-682-4741
Fax: 202-547-3713
URL: http://www.t-b.com
Baltimore, Maryland Office: Suite 400, One North Charles Street, 21201.
Telephone: 410-539-2595.
FAX: 410-783-0710.

Roszel C. Thomsen, II

Antoinette D. Paytas

For full biographical listings, see the Martindale-Hubbell Law Directory

Washington—Continued

TIGHE, PATTON & BABBIN, P.L.L.C. (AV)

A Professional Limited Liability Company
1747 Pennsylvania Avenue, N.W. Suite 300, 20006
Telephone: 202-293-0398
Telecopier: 202-393-0363
Email: TOMTPTB@AOL.COM

Kevin P. Tighe (P.C.)
Thomas Earl Patton
Jed L. Babbin
Paul N. Murphy
Walter G. Birkel
Brent S. Franzel
John M. Wyser-Pratte (Not admitted in DC; 1936-1998)
Carol Elder Bruce
Kermit A. Rosenberg
John B. Montgomery
Richard H. Gordin

Brian C. Quinn (Not admitted in DC)

OF COUNSEL

Edward B. MacMahon, Jr.
Alan H. Kent
Marc Edward Chafetz
Leslie A. Stout-Tabackman
Sharon L. Babbin

For full biographical listings, see the Martindale-Hubbell Law Directory

VENABLE ATTORNEYS AT LAW VENABLE, BAETJER, HOWARD & CIVILETTI, LLP (AV)

A Partnership including Professional Corporations
Suite 1000, 1201 New York Avenue, N.W., 20005
Telephone: 202-962-4800
Fax: 202-962-8300
URL: http://www.venable.com
Baltimore, Maryland Office: Venable, Baetjer and Howard LLP, 1800 Mercantile Bank & Trust Building, 2 Hopkins Plaza.
Telephone: 410-244-7400.
Fax: 410-244-7742.
McLean, Virginia Office: Venable, Baetjer and Howard LLP, Suite 400, 2010 Corporate Ridge.
Telephone: 703-760-1600.
Fax: 703-821-8949.
Rockville, Maryland Office: Venable, Baetjer and Howard LLP, Suite 500, One Church Street, P. O. Box 1906.
Telephone: 301-217-5600.
Fax: 301-217-5617.
Towson, Maryland Office: Venable, Baetjer and Howard LLP, 210 Allegheny Avenue, P. O. Box 5517.
Telephone: 410-494-6200.
Fax: 410-821-0147.

MEMBERS OF FIRM

Maurice Baskin
Kenneth C. Bass, III (Also at McLean, Virginia Office)
Joseph G. Block
Robert J. Bolger, Jr. (Also at Baltimore, Maryland Office)
Neal D. Borden (Not admitted in DC; Also at Baltimore, Maryland Office)
Anthony M. Carey (Not admitted in DC; Also at Baltimore, Maryland Office)
Benjamin R. Civiletti (P.C.) (Also at Baltimore and Towson, Maryland Offices)
Bryson L. Cook (P.C.) (Not admitted in DC; Also at Baltimore, Maryland Office)
William D. Coston
Jan K. Guben (Not admitted in DC; Also at Baltimore, Maryland Office)
Jeffrey D. Knowles
Fernand A. Lavallee
Joe A. Shull

ASSOCIATE

Donald P. Creston

For Complete List of Firm Personnel, See General Section

For full biographical listings, see the Martindale-Hubbell Law Directory

WEBSTER, CHAMBERLAIN & BEAN (AV)

Suite 1000, 1747 Pennsylvania Avenue, N.W., 20006
Telephone: 202-785-9500
Fax: 202-835-0243

MEMBERS OF FIRM

Arthur L. Herold
Alan P. Dye
Edward D. Coleman
Frank M. Northam
John W. Hazard, Jr.
Hugh K. Webster

OF COUNSEL

Charles E. Chamberlain
J. Coleman Bean
Kent Masterson Brown (Not admitted in DC)
Burkett Van Kirk
James Bopp, Jr. (Not admitted in DC)

ASSOCIATES

Charles M. Watkins
David P. Goch
Brenley Locke Elias
Raymond Cashen, II (Not admitted in DC)

For full biographical listings, see the Martindale-Hubbell Law Directory

WILMER, CUTLER & PICKERING (AV)

2445 M Street, N.W., 20037-1420
Telephone: 202-663-6000
Fax: 202-663-6363
Email: Law@Wilmer.Com *URL:* http://www.wilmer.com
Baltimore, Maryland Office: 100 Light Street, 21202.
Telephone: 410-986-2800.
Fax: 410-986-2828.
New York, New York Office: 520 Madison Avenue, 10022.
Telephone: 212-230-8800.
Fax: 212-230-8888.
European Offices:
4 Carlton Gardens, London, SW1Y 5AA, England. Telephone: +44 (20) 7 872 1000.
Fax: +44 (20) 7 839 3537.
Rue de la Loi 15# Wetstraat, B-1040 Brussels, Belgium. Telephone: +32 (2) 285 49 00.
Fax: +32 (2) 285 49 49.
Friedrichstrasse 95, D-10117 Berlin, Germany. Telephone: +49 (30) 20 22 64 00.
Fax: +49 (30) 20 22 65 00.

MEMBERS OF FIRM

Louis R. Cohen
Michael R. Klein
William T. Lake
Dieter G. F. Lange (Not admitted in DC; Resident, European Office, London, England)
Richard W. Cass
Mark Pollak (Not admitted in DC; Resident, Baltimore, Maryland Office)
Roberto Dañino
Mary Carolyn Cox
William J. Perlstein
Stephen P. Doyle
George P. Stamas
Russell J. Bruemmer
Robert M. Kimmitt
Thomas W. White
Duane D. Morse
W. Scott Blackmer
John B. Watkins V
Philip D. Anker
Meredith B. Cross
Paul A. von Hehn (Not admitted in DC; Resident, European Office, Brussels, Belgium)
Marc C. Hansen (Not admitted in DC; Resident, European Office, Brussels, Belgium)
Andrew K. Parnell (Not admitted in DC; Resident, European Office, London, England)
Eric R. Markus
Jorge E. Alers
Mark A. Dewire
Paul S. Dwyer Jr.
R. Scott Kilgore
Thomas E.D. Millspaugh (Not admitted in DC; Resident, Baltimore, Maryland Office)
Dr. Natalie Lübben (Not admitted in DC; Resident, European Office, Berlin, Germany)
Michael R. Holter (Not admitted in DC; Resident, European Office, London, England)
Thomas Mueller (Resident, European Office, Brussels, Belgium)
Gregorio B. Cater
Dr. Roland Steinmeyer (Not admitted in DC; Resident, European Office, Berlin, Germany)

COUNSEL

William J. Flanagan
Marcia A. Wiss
Roger J. Patterson
Joanne F. Catanese (Not admitted in DC; Resident, Baltimore, Maryland Office)
Glynn D. Key

For Complete List of Firm Personnel, See General Section

For full biographical listings, see the Martindale-Hubbell Law Directory

FLORIDA

BOCA RATON, Palm Beach Co.

HARVEY G. KOPELOWITZ (AV)

7251 West Palmetto Park Road, Suite 201
Telephone: 561-392-4115
Fax: 561-392-0351

For full biographical listings, see the Martindale-Hubbell Law Directory

*CLEARWATER,** Pinellas Co.

ELIHU H. BERMAN, P.A. (AV)

509 South Greenwood Avenue, 33756
Telephone: 727-465-1977
Fax: 727-465-9593
Email: elihu@gte.net

Elihu H. Berman

OF COUNSEL

Marc A. B. Silverman

References: First Union Bank; South Trust Bank; AmSouth Bank.

For full biographical listings, see the Martindale-Hubbell Law Directory

Clearwater—Continued

KWALL, SHOWERS & COLEMAN, P.A. (AV)

133 North Fort Harrison Avenue, 33755
Telephone: 727-441-4947
Telecopier: 727-447-3158
Email: kwall@worldnet.att.net *URL:* http://www.usalaw.com/adminlaw/

Elizabeth M. Gannon

For Complete List of Firm Personnel, See General Section

For full biographical listings, see the Martindale-Hubbell Law Directory

*FORT LAUDERDALE,** Broward Co.

BERGER DAVIS & SINGERMAN (AV)

350 East Las Olas Boulevard, Suite 1000, 33301
Telephone: 954-525-9900
Fax: 954-523-2872
Email: jberger@bdslaw.com *URL:* http://www.bdslaw.com
Miami, Florida Office: 200 South Biscayne Boulevard, Suite 2950.
Telephone: 305-755-9500.
Fax: 305-714-4340.
Tallahassee, Florida Office: 215 South Monroe Street, Suite 705, 32301.
Telephone: 850-561-3010.
Fax: 850-561-3013.

James L. Berger
Mitchell W. Berger
Franklin H. Caplan (Resident, Miami Office)
James B. Davis
Henry H. (Bucky) Fox
Van P. Geeker (Resident, Tallahassee Office)
Jordi Guso (Resident, Miami Office)
Nick Jovanovich
Robert B. Judd
Manuel Kushner
Daniel Lampert
Dawn M. Meyers
John D. C. Newton, II (Resident, Tallahassee Office)
Samuel E. Poole III
Leonard K. Samuels
Laz L. Schneider
Paul Steven Singerman (Resident, Miami Office)
Daniel H. Thompson (Resident, Tallahassee Office)

Robert W. Barron
Maria St. John Daugherty
James Harris Fierberg (Resident, Miami Office)
Ilyse Wrubel Homer (Resident, Miami Office)
Sherry A. Lambson
Lisa D. MacClugage
Brian G. Rich (Resident, Miami Office)
Holiday Hunt Russell
Jonathan C. Vair (Resident, Miami Office)
Jeffrey Scott Wertman

OF COUNSEL

James C. Cunningham, Jr.
Fred Goldberg

For full biographical listings, see the Martindale-Hubbell Law Directory

BRINKLEY, MCNERNEY, MORGAN, SOLOMON & TATUM, LLP (AV)

Suite 1800, New River Center, 200 East Las Olas Boulevard, P.O. Box 522, 33301-2209
Telephone: 954-522-2200
Facsimile: 954-522-9123
Email: lawfirm@brinkleymcnerney.com *URL:* http://www.brinkleymcnerney.com

W. Michael Brinkley
Michael J. McNerney
Philip J. Morgan
Harris K. Solomon
Thomas R. Tatum
Kenneth E. Keechl
Stephen L. Ziegler
Donald J. Lunny, Jr.
Roberta G. Stanley
Christopher M. Trapani
Kevin P. Crosby

Kenneth J. Joyce
Thomas J. Ansbro
David F. Hanley
Sean L. Wilson
Jonathan M. Streisfeld
W. Michael Brinkley, Jr.
Lindsey A. Payne
Marc K. Swickle
Kenneth A. Gordon
Juliette E. Lippman
Dawn M. Heisey
Veronica Vilarchao

OF COUNSEL

Amy R. Reeck

Approved Attorneys for: Attorneys' Title Insurance Fund; Chicago Title Insurance Co.; First American Title Insurance Co.

For full biographical listings, see the Martindale-Hubbell Law Directory

FREDRIC C. BURESH, P.A. (AV)

800 Southeast Third Avenue, Suite 400, 33316
Telephone: 954-525-2300
Fax: 954-763-4725
Email: FredBuresh@aol.com

Fredric C. Buresh

For full biographical listings, see the Martindale-Hubbell Law Directory

ESLER & LINDIE, P.A. (AV)

Suite 300 The Advocate Building, 315 S.E. Seventh Street, 33301
Telephone: 954-764-5400
FAX: 954-764-5408
Email: eslerandlindie@martindalemail.com *URL:* http://www.lawyers.com/esler&lindie

Gary A. Esler
Beth G. Lindie

Representative Clients: The Chubb Group of Insurance Cos.; Fireman's Fund Insurance Co.; State of Florida-Department of Risk Management; Marriott Corp.; Mobile America Insurance Group, Inc.; Ohio Casualty Insurance Co.
Reference: Capital Bank.

For full biographical listings, see the Martindale-Hubbell Law Directory

MASTRIANA & CHRISTIANSEN, PROFESSIONAL ASSOCIATION (AV)

1500 North Federal Highway, Suite 200, 33304
Telephone: Broward: 954-566-1234
Dade: 305-949-1234
URL: http://www.lawyers.com/m&cpa

Frank A. Mastriana (1916-1991)
F. Ronald Mastriana
Michael Eric Christiansen
Stephen Vincent Hoffman
Jon M. Henning

Representative Clients: Dadeland Mall; Family Center, Inc. (A & P); Leonard L. Farber Corp.; Parkson Corp.

For full biographical listings, see the Martindale-Hubbell Law Directory

*FORT MYERS,** Lee Co.

DEBOEST, KNUDSEN, STOCKMAN, WISEMAN, DECKER & DRYDEN, P.A. (AV)

1415 Hendry Street, P.O. Box 1470, 33902-1470
Telephone: 941-334-1381
Telecopier: 941-334-0266
Email: dkswlaw@gate.net
Naples, Florida Office: 600 Fifth Avenue South, Suite 301, 34102.
Telephone: 941-263-5040.
Fax: 941-263-6944.

Arthur K. Knudsen, Jr. (Retired)
Richard D. DeBoest
William E. Stockman
Tamela Eady Wiseman (Resident, Naples Office)
James G. Decker
Thomas M. Dryden

Representative Clients: Cobb Theatres, Inc.; WCI Communities, Inc.; Evelyn Jackman and Sons, Inc.

For full biographical listings, see the Martindale-Hubbell Law Directory

HENDERSON, FRANKLIN, STARNES & HOLT, PROFESSIONAL ASSOCIATION (AV)

1715 Monroe Street, P.O. Box 280, 33902-0280
Telephone: 941-334-4121
Telecopier: 941-332-4494

Albert M. Frierson
Ernest H. Hatch, Jr.
Stephen L. Helgemo
Ronald W. Smalley
John A. Noland
William N. Horowitz
Gerald W. Pierce
J. Terrence Porter
Michael J. Corso
Vicki L. Sproat
Denis H. Noah
John W. Lewis
Craig Ferrante
James L. Nulman
Harold N. Hume, Jr.
Bruce M. Stanley Sr.
Daniel W. Sheppard
Russell P. Schropp
Chad J. Motes
Guy E. Whitesman
Steven G. Koeppel
Douglas B. Szabo
Charles J. Basinait
Randal H. Thomas
Robert C. Shearman
Andrew L. Ringers, Jr.
John F. Potanovic, Jr.
Thomas H. Gunderson
David K. Fowler
Paula F. Kelley
Jeffrey D. Kottkamp
J. Eric Stiffler
Thomas P. Clark
Theresa M. Kolish
Tricia A. Spivey
Cora Cisneros Molloy
Keith R. Kyle
Joseph M. Madden, Jr.
Danni Lynn Germano
Carlos A. Kelly
Elizabeth Wolt
Alane C. Laboda
Grace Gutierrez
Laurie Hannan-Anton
Neil R. Jetter

Representative Clients: CIGNA Group; CSX Transportation, Inc.; Fireman's Fund Insurance Cos.; The Hartford Insurance Group; Huntington National Bank, N.A.; NationsBank, N.A.; Travelers/Aetna Insurance Group; Sprint-Florida, Inc.

For full biographical listings, see the Martindale-Hubbell Law Directory

*JACKSONVILLE,** Duval Co.

ALLEN, BRINTON, SIMMONS & MCCARTHY, P.A. (AV)

One Independent Drive, Suite 3200, 32202
Telephone: 904-353-8800
Fax: 904-353-8770

(See Next Column)

ALLEN, BRINTON, SIMMONS & MCCARTHY P.A., *Jacksonville—Continued*

A. Graham Allen
William D. Brinton
Sidney S. Simmons, II
Edward McCarthy, III

Joelle Jackson Dillard

Representative Clients: Anheuser-Busch Companies, Inc.; Adventure Landing, Inc.; Avis Rent A Car System, Inc.; M.I.T. Marine Electric Corp.; The Haskell Co.; Johnson & Johnson; Masthead Industries, Inc.; U-Haul Co.

For full biographical listings, see the Martindale-Hubbell Law Directory

SAMUEL L. LEPRELL (AV)

1930 San Marco Boulevard Suite 201, St. Mark's Place, 32207-3256
Telephone: 904-390-2705
Fax: 904-390-2711
Email: juvandyleprellaw@worldnet.att.net *URL:* http://www.lawyers.com/leprellaw

For full biographical listings, see the Martindale-Hubbell Law Directory

LOBRANO & KINCAID, P.L. (AV)

Suite 1650 Independent Life Building, 1 Independent Drive, 32202
Telephone: 904-359-2100
Facsimile: 904-353-1332

Stephen D. Lobrano
Wade McK. Hampton

OF COUNSEL

W. Douglas Smith (Not admitted in FL)

For full biographical listings, see the Martindale-Hubbell Law Directory

SMITH HULSEY & BUSEY (AV)

1800 First Union National Bank Tower, 225 Water Street, P.O. Box 53315, 32201-3315
Telephone: 904-359-7700
Facsimile: 904-359-7708; 353-9908
Email: vsharp@smithhulsey.com

Lloyd Smith (1915-1987)

MEMBERS OF FIRM

Stephen D. Busey
Earl E. Googe, Jr.
Jeanne E. Helton
Cynthia C. Jackson
G. Preston Keyes
Richard E. Klein
William E. Kuntz
Lauren P. Langham
M. Richard Lewis, Jr.
John F. MacLennan
Raymond R. Magley
E. Owen McCuller, Jr.
James H. Post
Bryan L. Putnal
E. Lanny Russell
Joel Settembrini, Jr.
Tim E. Sleeth
John R. Smith, Jr.
Harry M. Wilson, III

Brandon L. Ayscue
Brannon B. Belcastro
James A. Bolling, Jr.
Charmaine T.M. Chiu
Ryan C. Curtis
Michael R. Freed
Reynold N. Hoover
Michael J. Ivan, Jr.
Tonya L. Janney
Charles H. Keller
Bradley R. Markey
R. Leanne McKnight
Bert J. Millis
Stephen D. Moore, Jr.
Jon L. Swergold

OF COUNSEL

Mark Hulsey
John E. Thrasher

Representative Clients: ATP Tour, Inc; Baptist/St. Vincent's Health System, Inc.; Browning-Ferris Industries, Inc.; First Union National Bank of Florida; Florida Rock Industries, Inc.; PGA Tour, Inc.; KPMG Peat Marwick; The Regency Group, Inc.; The Ritz-Carlton Hotel Co.; University of Florida.

For full biographical listings, see the Martindale-Hubbell Law Directory

*MIAMI,** Dade Co.

ARMSTRONG & MEJER, P.A. (AV)

Suite 1111 Douglas Centre, 2600 Douglas Road (Coral Gables), 33134
Telephone: 305-444-3355
Fax: 305-442-4300
Email: Amesq@Aol.com

Timothy J. Armstrong
Alvaro L. Mejer

M. Emelina Mejer-Kondla

Reference: First Union National Bank.

For full biographical listings, see the Martindale-Hubbell Law Directory

WARREN P. GAMMILL (AV)

Suite 1700 BIV Tower, 1101 Brickell Avenue, 33131
Telephone: 305-579-9014; 305-579-0000
Fax: 305-371-6927
Email: w.p.gammill-miami@worldnet.att.net *URL:* http://www.lawyers.com/wpglaw

For full biographical listings, see the Martindale-Hubbell Law Directory

HAYDEN AND MILLIKEN, P.A. (AV)

Suite 63, 5915 Ponce de Leon Boulevard, 33146-2477
Telephone: 305-662-1523
Fax: 305-663-1358
Tampa, Florida Office: 615 De Leon Street 33606-2719.
Telephone: 813-251-1770.
Fax: 813-254-5436.
Cape Canaveral, Florida Office: 101 George King Boulevard, Suite 5, 32920,
Telephone: 407-868-0022.
Fax: 407-868-5060.

Reginald M. Hayden, Jr.
William Barry Milliken
William R. Boeringer
Timothy P. Shusta (Resident, Tampa, Florida Office)

Patrick M. Talbot

Representative Clients: Seaboard Marine, Ltd.; Tropical Shipping and Construction Co., Ltd.; Great American Insurance Co.; Marine Office of America Corp.; St. Paul Fire and Marine Insurance Co.; Britannia P & I; Newcastle P & I; Steamship Mutual; The Swedish Club.

For full biographical listings, see the Martindale-Hubbell Law Directory

HOFFMAN & HERTZIG, P.A. (AV)

Suite 900, 241 Sevilla Avenue (Coral Gables), 33134
Telephone: 305-445-3100
Fax: 305-444-5656

Carl H. Hoffman
David Hertzig

Howard Kraft Pita

References: City National Bank of Miami, Coral Gables.

For full biographical listings, see the Martindale-Hubbell Law Directory

LAW OFFICE OF STEWART A. MERKIN (AV)

Rivergate Plaza, Suite 300, 444 Brickell Avenue, 33131
Telephone: 305-358-5800
Fax: 305-358-2490
Email: merkmia@aol.com *URL:* http://www.lawyers.com/merkin

For full biographical listings, see the Martindale-Hubbell Law Directory

TEW & NOWAK (AV)

A Partnership including Professional Corporations
Miami Center, Suite 340, 201 South Biscayne Boulevard, 33131
Telephone: 305-577-3900
1-800-577-3906
Fax: 305-577-9911
Email: tewandnowak@lawyers.com *URL:* http://www.lawyers.com/tew&nowak

Jeffrey Tew
Dennis A. Nowak

ASSOCIATE

Karen Levine

For full biographical listings, see the Martindale-Hubbell Law Directory

*NAPLES,** Collier Co.

QUARLES & BRADY LLP (AV)

Barnett Center, 4501 Tamiami Trail North Suite 300, 34103-3060
Telephone: 941-262-5959
Fax: 941-434-4999
URL: http://www.quarles.com
Milwaukee, Wisconsin Office: 411 East Wisconsin Avenue, 53202-4497.
Telephone: 414-277-5000.
Fax: 414-271-3552.
Madison, Wisconsin Office: Firstar Plaza, One South Pinckney Street, P.O. Box 2113, 53701-2113.
Telephone: 608-251-5000.
Fax: 608-251-9166.
West Palm Beach, Florida Office: 222 Lakeview Avenue, 4th Floor, 33401.
Telephone: 561-653-5000.
Fax: 561-653-5333.
Phoenix, Arizona Office: One Camelback Building, One East Camelback Road, Suite 400, 85012-1649.
Telephone: 602-230-5500.
Fax: 602-230-5598.

(See Next Column)

QUARLES & BRADY LLP—*Continued*

Chicago, Illinois Office: Quarles & Brady LLC, Citicorp Center, 500 West Madison Street, Suite 3700.
Telephone: 312-715-5000.
Fax: 312-715-5155.

PARTNERS

Thomas E. Maloney
David L. Petersen
F. Joseph McMackin, III
Timothy G. Hains
Robert E. Doyle, Jr.
Leo J. Salvatori
Kimberly Leach Johnson
John D. Humphreville

ASSOCIATES

Samara S. Holland
Mark Hubert Muller
Lisa Carozza Lottes
James T. Demarest
Susan Kubar
Edmond E. Koester
C. Lane Wood

For Complete List of Firm Personnel, See General Section

For full biographical listings, see the Martindale-Hubbell Law Directory

*ORLANDO,** Orange Co.

BROWN, WARD, SALZMAN & WEISS, P.A. (AV)

111 North Orange Avenue, Suite 875, P.O. Box 2873, 32802-2873
Telephone: 407-425-9566
Fax: 407-425-9596; Email: firm@orlandolaw.net
Email: brownu@osceola.k12.fl.us *URL:* http://www.orlandolaw.net

Usher Larry Brown
John H. Ward
Gary S. Salzman
Jeffrey S. Weiss
Suzanne D'Agresta

Scott D. Danahy
James G. Vickaryous
Robert L. Butterfield, Jr.
Allison Carmine McDonald

Representative Clients: The School Board of Osceola County; The School Board of Indian River County; Osceola County; Osceola Sheriff (Osceola County Investigative Bureau); Orange County Comptroller; General Electric Capital Modular Space; Honeywell, Inc.; Massachusetts Mutual Life Ins. Co.; Fleetwood Enterprises, Inc.; Central Brevard Anesthesiologists, P.A.

For full biographical listings, see the Martindale-Hubbell Law Directory

DECUBELLIS & MEEKS, P.A. (AV)

Suite 801, Citrus Center, 255 South Orange Avenue, P.O. Box 4976, 32802-4976
Telephone: 407-872-2200
Telecopier: 407-423-1038

Daniel L. DeCubellis
Mary B. Meeks
John A. Shughart, Jr.
Jennifer C. Carter
Brett M. Wendt

Representative Clients: Design Professional Insurance Corp.; Florida Lawyers Mutual Insurance Corp.; International Game Technology, Inc.; Jennings Environmental Services, Inc.; Mader Southeast, Inc.; Orange County; PGA Tour, Inc.; SouthTrust Bank, N.A.

For full biographical listings, see the Martindale-Hubbell Law Directory

NORMAN LINDER HULL, P.A. (AV)

537 North Magnolia Avenue, P.O. Box 2751, 32802
Telephone: 407-422-1235
Fax: 407-423-2842
Email: nlhull@ix.netcom.com *URL:* http://www.lawyers.com/hulllaw

Norman L. Hull

For full biographical listings, see the Martindale-Hubbell Law Directory

MORGAN COLLING & GILBERT, A PROFESSIONAL ASSOCIATION (AV)

20 North Orange Avenue, 16th Floor, Suite 1607, P.O. Box 4979, 32802-4979
Telephone: 407-420-1414
Fax: 407-425-8171
URL: http://www.morgancollinggilbert.com
Tampa, Florida Office: 101 East Kennedy Boulevard, Suite 1790, 33602.
Telephone: 813-223-5505.
Fax: 813-223-5402.

Ultima Degnan Morgan

Reference: Sun Bank.

For full biographical listings, see the Martindale-Hubbell Law Directory

POHL & SHORT, P.A.

(See Winter Park)

RUSSELL LAW OFFICES, P.A. (AV)

537 North Magnolia Avenue, P.O. Box 886, 32802
Telephone: 407-422-1234
Telecopier: 407-423-2842
Email: RussLaw@compuserve.com *URL:* http://www.lawyers.com/russlaw

Rodney Laird Russell

For full biographical listings, see the Martindale-Hubbell Law Directory

PALM BEACH, Palm Beach Co.

LAW OFFICES OF HARRISON K. CHAUNCEY, JR., P.A. (AV)

241 Bradley Place, 33480
Telephone: 561-833-3001
Fax: 561-833-9060
Email: hchauncey@chainceylaw.com

Harrison K. Chauncey Jr.
Mark R. Brown

For full biographical listings, see the Martindale-Hubbell Law Directory

MINTMIRE & ASSOCIATES (AV)

265 Sunrise Avenue, Suite 204, 33480
Telephone: 561-832-5696
Fax: 561-659-5371
Email: MintmireFL@aol.com

Donald F. Mintmire
Jeffrey A. Shaffer
Mercedes Travis (Mrs.)
Bradley F. Rothenberg

OF COUNSEL

Paul Safran, Jr.

LEGAL SUPPORT PERSONNEL

Thomas V. Flynn (Legal Intern)

For full biographical listings, see the Martindale-Hubbell Law Directory

*PENSACOLA,** Escambia Co.

PHILIP A. BATES (AV)

25 West Cedar Street, Suite 304, 32501
Telephone: 850-470-0091
Fax: 850-470-0441

For full biographical listings, see the Martindale-Hubbell Law Directory

*SARASOTA,** Sarasota Co.

WILSON, JOHNSON & JAFFER, P.A. (AV)

27 South Orange Avenue, 34236-5822
Telephone: 941-955-5800
Fax: 941-955-7353
Email: wilson@lawsites.com *URL:* http://www.lawsites.com

Clyde H. Wilson (1908-1994)
Robert M. Johnson
Clyde H. Wilson, Jr.
John S. Jaffer

For full biographical listings, see the Martindale-Hubbell Law Directory

*TALLAHASSEE,** Leon Co.

GENE D. BROWN (AV)

3848 Killearn Court, 32308
Telephone: 850-668-6103
FAX: 850-668-0441
Email: gbrown@istal.com

For full biographical listings, see the Martindale-Hubbell Law Directory

MCFARLAIN, WILEY, CASSEDY & JONES, PROFESSIONAL ASSOCIATION (AV)

215 South Monroe Street, Suite 600, P.O. Box 2174, 32316-2174
Telephone: 850-222-2107
Telecopier: 850-222-8475
Email: firm@mcfarlain.com *URL:* http://www.mcfarlain.com

Richard C. McFarlain
William B. Wiley
Douglas P. Jones
Charles A. Stampelos
H. Darrell White, Jr.
Christopher Barkas
Harold R. Mardenborough, Jr.
Terrell C. Madigan

Robert A. McNeely
P. David Brannon

LEGAL SUPPORT PERSONNEL

Diane L. Doll (Office Manager)

For full biographical listings, see the Martindale-Hubbell Law Directory

*TAMPA,** Hillsborough Co.

GATLIN & BIRCH, P.A. (AV)

620 Twiggs Street, 33602
Telephone: 813-229-8561
FAX: 813-229-0422

(See Next Column)

GATLIN & BIRCH P.A., *Tampa—Continued*

C. Elmon Gatlin Dean W. Birch

For full biographical listings, see the Martindale-Hubbell Law Directory

HAYDEN AND MILLIKEN, P.A. (AV)

615 de Leon Street, 33606-2719
Telephone: 813-251-1770
Fax: 813-254-5436
Miami, Florida Office: Suite 63, 5915 Ponce de Leon Boulevard.
Telephone: 305-662-1523.
Fax: 305-663-1358.
Cape Canaveral, Florida Office: 101 George King Boulevard, Suite 5, 32920.
Telephone: 407-868-0022.
Fax: 407-868-5060.

Reginald M. Hayden, Jr. William Barry Milliken
Timothy P. Shusta (Resident)

Matthew J. Valcourt

Representative Clients: Seaboard Marine, Ltd.; Tropical Shipping and Construction Co., Ltd.; Great American Insurance Co.; Marine Office of America Corp.; St. Paul Fire and Marine Insurance Co.; Britannia P & I; Newcastle P & I; Steamship Mutual.
Reference: Dadeland Bank.

For full biographical listings, see the Martindale-Hubbell Law Directory

KETCHEY HORAN, P.A. (AV)

100 North Tampa Street, Suite 1900, P.O. Box 500, 33601-0500
Telephone: 813-223-9395
Fax: 813-221-1348
Email: Stephanie@KetcheyHoran.com
Sun City Center, Florida Office: 1647 Sun City Center Plaza, Suite 200.
Telephone: 813-633-1200.

SHAREHOLDERS

Michael P. Horan Charles F. Ketchey, Jr.
John B. Neukamm

ASSOCIATES

Alfred A. Colby Christopher Charles Nash

For full biographical listings, see the Martindale-Hubbell Law Directory

MORRISON & MILLS, P.A. (AV)

1200 West Platt Street Suite 100, 33606
Telephone: 813-258-3311
Telecopier: 813-258-3209
Email: mmills3@tampabay.rr.com

Thomas K. Morrison Frederick J. Mills

Kevin A. DiTanna Bradley Abraham Tobin

Representative Clients: SouthTrust Bank of West Florida; SouthTrust Bank, National Association; NationsBank of Florida, N.A., Mercantile Bank; Southern Commerce Bank; Regions Bank; Hillsborough County Industrial Development Authority; Medical Data Management, Inc.; Floors, Inc.; Logan Lumber Company.

For full biographical listings, see the Martindale-Hubbell Law Directory

*VERO BEACH,** Indian River Co.

MOSS, HENDERSON, BLANTON & LANIER, P.A. (AV)

817 Beachland Boulevard, P.O. Box 3406, 32964-3406
Telephone: 561-231-1900
Fax: 561-231-4387

George H. Moss, II Steve L. Henderson
Fred L. Kretschmer, Jr.

Representative Clients: Aetna Life & Casualty; Alcoa Florida, Inc.; Florida Power & Light Co.; Insurance Company of North America; Liberty Mutual Insurance Co.; Sears, Roebuck & Co.; Sugar Cane Growers Cooperative of Florida; Norfolk Southern Corporation/North American Van Lines, Inc.

For Complete List of Firm Personnel, See General Section

For full biographical listings, see the Martindale-Hubbell Law Directory

*WEST PALM BEACH,** Palm Beach Co.

ACKERMAN, LINK & SARTORY, P.A. (AV)

222 Lakeview Avenue, Suite 1250, Esperante, 33401
Telephone: 561-838-4100
Fax: 561-838-5305
Email: alslaw@alslaw.com *URL:* http://www.alslaw.com

David P. Ackerman Scott J. Link
Wendy Sartory Link

(See Next Column)

Lawrence J. Diamond Gregory J. Newcomm
John C. Kelly Amy B. Nunziella

For full biographical listings, see the Martindale-Hubbell Law Directory

BEASLEY, LEACOCK & HAUSER, P.A. (AV)

Flagler Center, Suite 1400, 505 South Flagler Drive, 33401
Telephone: 561-835-0900
Fax: 561-835-0939
Email: BLH@BLHlaw.com *URL:* http://BLHlaw.com

James W. Beasley, Jr. David Leacock
Robert J. Hauser

Ronald B. Hauser

For full biographical listings, see the Martindale-Hubbell Law Directory

NASON, YEAGER, GERSON, WHITE & LIOCE, P.A. (AV)

Mellon United National Bank Tower, Suite 1200, 1645 Palm Beach Lakes Boulevard, 33401
Telephone: 561-686-3307
Fax: 561-686-5442

Thomas J. Yeager Nathan E. Nason
Gary N. Gerson Gregory L. Scott
John White, II Charles W. Edgar, III
Domenick R. Lioce Joseph A. Caccamo
Alan I. Armour, II Manuel Farach
Mark A. Pachman George E. Harding
Elaine Johnson James Amanda Parks Schlechter

William J. Romanos, III Bruce E. Sands

LEGAL SUPPORT PERSONNEL

Sandra R. Gronek (Principal Administrator) Elsie T. Pollak (Litigation/Probate Paralegal)
L. Ann Jaeckin (Corporate Paralegal) Georgina J. Popham (Corporate/Securities Paralegal)
Kathleen S. Loviska (Real Estate Paralegal) Coral R. St. Pierre (Real Estate/Corporate Paralegal)
Lisa M. Mroczko (Litigation/Probate Paralegal)

For full biographical listings, see the Martindale-Hubbell Law Directory

QUARLES & BRADY LLP (AV)

222 Lakeview Avenue, 4th Floor, 33401
Telephone: 561-653-5000
Fax: 561-653-5333
URL: http://www.quarles.com
Milwaukee, Wisconsin Office: 411 East Wisconsin Avenue, 53202-4497.
Telephone: 414-277-5000.
Fax: 414-271-3552.
Madison, Wisconsin Office: Firstar Plaza, One South Pinckney Street, P.O. Box 2113, 53701-2113.
Telephone: 608-251-5000.
Fax: 608-251-9166.
Naples, Florida Office: Barnett Center, 4501 Tamiami Trail North, Suite 300, 34103-3060.
Telephone: 941-262-5959.
Fax: 941-434-4999.
Phoenix, Arizona Office: One Camelback Building, One East Camelback Road, Suite 400, 85012-1649.
Telephone: 602-230-5500.
Fax: 602-230-5598.
Chicago, Illinois Office: Quarles & Brady LLC, Citicorp Center, 500 West Madison Street, Suite 3700.
Telephone: 312-715-5000.
Fax: 312-715-5155.

PARTNERS

J. Rodman Steele, Jr. Nancy Berz Colman
Ned R. Nashban Joseph W. Bain
Gregory A. Nelson Robert J. Sacco

OF COUNSEL

John S. Sammond

ASSOCIATES

Stanley A. Kim Scott D. Paul

For Complete List of Firm Personnel, See General Section

For full biographical listings, see the Martindale-Hubbell Law Directory

WINTER PARK, Orange Co.

HADDOCK PROFESSIONAL ASSOCIATION (AV)

3260 University Boulevard, Suite 210, 32792
Telephone: 407-679-6171
Fax: 407-679-8810
Email: ehaddock@fullsail.com
Mailing Address: P.O. Box 5148, Winter Park, FL, 32793-5148
Email: edhaddock@aol.com

Edward E. Haddock, Jr.

Approved Attorneys For: American Pioneer Title Insurance Co.
Reference: Colonial Bank, Orlando, Florida.

For full biographical listings, see the Martindale-Hubbell Law Directory

POHL & SHORT, P.A. (AV)

280 West Canton Avenue, Suite 410, P.O. Box 3208, 32790
Telephone: 407-647-7645; 407-647-POHL
Telefax: 407-647-2314
Email: ps@pohlshort.com

Dwight I. Cool
Alexander S. Douglas II
Gary A. Forster
E. Givens Goodspeed
Mark A. Grimes
Robert S. Hoofman
Roger A. Kelly
Adam O. Kirwan
David J. Kohs
Frank L. Pohl
James Everett Shepherd V
Houston E. Short
John R. Simpson, Jr.

Representative Clients: American Generator Co.; Copelco Capital, Inc.; Denim U.S.A., Inc.; Ford Motor Credit Co.; Lodestar Technology, Inc.; Lutheran Brotherhood; SunTrust, N.A.; Trax, Inc.

For full biographical listings, see the Martindale-Hubbell Law Directory

GEORGIA

*ATLANTA,** Fulton Co.

BOVIS, KYLE & BURCH, LLC (AV)

A Limited Liability Corporation including Professional Corporations
Third Floor, 53 Perimeter Center East, 30346
Telephone: 770-391-9100
Telecopier: 770-668-0878
Email: bkb@boviskyle.com *URL:* http://www.boviskyle.com

John M. Bovis (P.C.)
C. Sam Thomas (P.C.)
J. Wesley Skinner

John David Etheriedge

For Complete List of Firm Personnel, See General Section
For full biographical listings, see the Martindale-Hubbell Law Directory

CUSHING, MORRIS, ARMBRUSTER & JONES, LLP (AV)

2110 Peachtree Center International Tower, 229 Peachtree Street, N.E., 30303
Telephone: 404-521-2323
Fax: 404-658-9865; 404-522-0607

MEMBERS OF FIRM

W. Hampton Morris
Charles M. Cushing, Jr.
Kevin R. Armbruster
Roy M. Jones
William M. Ellard
Jeffrey F. Montgomery

ASSOCIATES

Shawn R. Holtzclaw
Leticia D. Alfonso
J. Parker Gilbert

For full biographical listings, see the Martindale-Hubbell Law Directory

HARKLEROAD & HERMANCE, A PROFESSIONAL CORPORATION (AV)

2500 International Tower-Peachtree Center, 229 Peachtree Street, N.E., 30303
Telephone: 404-588-9211
Telecopier: 404-659-0860

Donald R. Harkleroad
James P. Hermance

For full biographical listings, see the Martindale-Hubbell Law Directory

HARMAN, OWEN, SAUNDERS & SWEENEY, A PROFESSIONAL CORPORATION (AV)

1900 Peachtree Center Tower, 230 Peachtree Street, N.W., 30303
Telephone: 404-688-2600
Telecopier: 404-525-4347

(See Next Column)

H. Andrew Owen
Frederick F. Saunders, Jr.
Timothy J. Sweeney
Perry A. Phillips
David C. Will

For full biographical listings, see the Martindale-Hubbell Law Directory

THE HISHON FIRM, LLC (AV)

999 Peachtree Street N.E. Suite 1900, 30309
Telephone: 404-817-7791
Fax: 404-817-2486

Elizabeth Anderson Hishon (1944-1999)
Robert H. Hishon

Nancy R. Daspit

For full biographical listings, see the Martindale-Hubbell Law Directory

HOFFMAN & FOWLER, LLP (AV)

A Partnership of Professional Corporations
5040 Roswell Road, N.E. Suite 250, 30342
Telephone: 404-256-6464
Fax: 404-256-1422

MEMBERS OF FIRM

Clifford G. Hoffman (P.C.)
Michael C. Fowler (P.C.)

For full biographical listings, see the Martindale-Hubbell Law Directory

HOLT NEY ZATCOFF & WASSERMAN, LLP (AV)

A Partnership including Professional Corporations
100 Galleria Parkway, Suite 600, 30339
Telephone: 770-956-9600
Facsimile: 770-956-1490
Email: mthomas@hnzw.com

MEMBERS OF FIRM

Robert G. Holt (P.C.)
James M. Ney (P.C.)
Sanford H. Zatcoff (P.C.)
Michael G. Wasserman (P.C.)
Richard P. Vornholt
Brian P. Cain
Jay Frank Castle

OF COUNSEL

Penni A. Dudley

ASSOCIATES

Gregory A. Randall (Not admitted in GA)
Thomas K. Anderson

Representative Clients: American Realty Trust, Inc.; Citicorp Real Estate, Inc.; Cobb County Chamber of Commerce, Inc.; Cummins South, Inc.; Gables Residential Trust; Primavera Financial Services; Roberts Realty Investors, Inc.; Sterling Trust; Trammell Crow Residential; The University Financing Foundation, Inc.

For Complete List of Firm Personnel, See General Section
For full biographical listings, see the Martindale-Hubbell Law Directory

JOHNSON & WARD (AV)

2100 The Equitable Building, 100 Peachtree Street N.W., 30303-1962
Telephone: 404-524-5626
Facsimile: 404-524-1769
Email: postmaster@johnsonward.com

MEMBERS OF FIRM

John C. Dabney, Jr.
Baxter P. Jones
William D. deGolian

For Complete List of Firm Personnel, See General Section
For full biographical listings, see the Martindale-Hubbell Law Directory

DOUGLAS W. KESSLER, P.C. (AV)

600 West Peachtree Street, Suite 800, 30308
Telephone: 404-876-3100

Douglas W. Kessler

For full biographical listings, see the Martindale-Hubbell Law Directory

KREVOLIN & HORST, LLC (AV)

Suite 2150, 100 Colony Square, 1175 Peachtree Street, N.E., 30361
Telephone: 404-888-9700
Fax: 404-888-9577

Douglas P. Krevolin
Jeffrey D. Horst

Michael G. Regas II
Michael D. Flint

For full biographical listings, see the Martindale-Hubbell Law Directory

Atlanta—Continued

LAMBERTH, BONAPFEL, CIFELLI & STOKES, P.A. (AV)

Atlanta Financial Center, 3343 Peachtree Road, N.E. East Tower, Suite 550, 30326
Telephone: 404-262-7373
Fax: 404-262-9911

J. Michael Lamberth
James Craig Cifelli
Paul W. Bonapfel
Gary D. Stokes
Carter L. Stout
G. Frank Nason, IV
Gregory D. Ellis

Stuart F. Clayton, Jr.
A. Alexander Teel
Laura E. Woodson

OF COUNSEL

William H. Willson, Jr.

Reference: The Riverside Bank.

For full biographical listings, see the Martindale-Hubbell Law Directory

LONG ALDRIDGE & NORMAN LLP (AV)

A Limited Liability Partnership including Professional Corporations
Suite 5300, 303 Peachtree Street, 30308
Telephone: 404-527-4000
Telecopier: 404-527-4198
Email: atlanta@lanlaw.com *URL:* http://www.lanlaw.com
Washington, D.C. Office: Suite 600, 701 Pennsylvania Avenue, N.W., 20004.
Telephone: 202-624-1200.
FAX: 202-624-1298.

MEMBERS OF FIRM

Robert A. Bartlett
Steven K. Bender
Wayne N. Bradley
Charles E. Campbell
J. David Dantzler, Jr.
Jeffrey K. Haidet
Edward D. Hirsch
David M. Ivey
H. Franklin Layson
J. Michael Levengood
Clay C. Long
Maurice Ted Maloof
Henry F. Sewell, Jr.
Jesse J. Spikes
Briggs L. Tobin
Robert E. Tritt
Lisa W. Wannamaker
Charles E. Wilson, III

SENIOR COUNSEL

F. T. Davis, Jr., (P.C.)
Robert E. Hicks
W. Stell Huie

ASSOCIATES

Claire Alison Addlestone
Karl J. Forrest
Terri Annette Herron
Ann-Marie M. McGaughey
Julie Sonenshine Porter
G. Scott Rafshoon
Melissa A. Schnell
Johnathan H. Short
Richard R. Willis

For Complete List of Firm Personnel, See General Section

For full biographical listings, see the Martindale-Hubbell Law Directory

MCCULLOUGH SHERRILL, LLP (AV)

1409 Peachtree Street, N.E., 30309
Telephone: 404-885-1500
Telecopier: 404-892-1801
Email: info@mslegal.com *URL:* http://www.mslegal.com

MEMBERS OF FIRM

William M. Joseph
James W. King
Chester G. Rosenberg
Jerry A. Shaifer
W. Clayton Sparrow, Jr.
Bradley J. Taylor

ASSOCIATES

Susan T. Craighead
Loren E. Kalish
Joseph V. Myers, III

For Complete List of Firm Personnel, See General Section

For full biographical listings, see the Martindale-Hubbell Law Directory

PARKER, HUDSON, RAINER & DOBBS LLP (AV)

1500 Marquis Two Tower, 285 Peachtree Center Avenue, N.E., 30303
Telephone: 404-523-5300
Fax: 404-522-8409
Tallahassee, Florida Office: The Perkins House, 118 North Gadsden Street, 32301.
Telephone: 904-681-0191.
Fax: 904-681-9493.

MEMBERS OF FIRM

Paul L. Hudson, Jr.
Mitchell M. Purvis

For full biographical listings, see the Martindale-Hubbell Law Directory

THE SAYLOR LAW FIRM, LLP (AV)

100 Colony Square, Suite 1224, 1175 Peachtree Street, N.E., 30361
Telephone: 404-892-4400
Telecopier: 404-892-2400
Email: SAYLOR_ATLANTA@PRODIGY.COM

(See Next Column)

C. Murray Saylor, Jr.
Jacquelyn Harmon Saylor

ASSOCIATE

Stephen C. Beeler

For full biographical listings, see the Martindale-Hubbell Law Directory

THRASHER, WHITLEY, HAMPTON & MORGAN, A PROFESSIONAL CORPORATION (AV)

Suite 2150, Five Concourse Parkway, 30328
Telephone: 770-804-8000
Telecopier: 770-804-5555
Email: law@twhm.com
Email: main@twhm.com

H. Grady Thrasher, III
Robert E. Whitley
Robert T. Morgan

Representative Clients: First Southeastern Securities Group, Inc.; Georgia Dental Assn.; Middle Bay Oil Company, Inc.; Perry & Co.; Smallwood, Reynolds, Stewart, Stewart & Assoc., Inc.; Sunchase Holdings, Ltd.; Touch Industries, Inc.

For full biographical listings, see the Martindale-Hubbell Law Directory

WEISZ & ASSOCIATES (AV)

Suite 900 Live Oak Center, 3475 Lenox Road, N.E., 30326-1232
Telephone: 404-233-7888
Facsimile: 404-261-1925
Email: prw1@bellsouth.net

Peter R. Weisz

ASSOCIATE

Cathy R. Nash

Representative Clients: L.M. Scofield Co.; S. Champion Constr. Co.; Deerfield Construction Co.; Cee Klein Accessories, LTD.
Reference: First Union National Bank.

For full biographical listings, see the Martindale-Hubbell Law Directory

*AUGUSTA,** Richmond Co.

DYE, TUCKER, EVERITT, LONG & BREWTON, A PROFESSIONAL ASSOCIATION (AV)

453 Greene Street, P.O. Box 2426, 30903-2426
Telephone: 706-722-0771
Fax: 706-722-7028

A. Rowland Dye
Thomas W. Tucker
A. Zachry Everitt
John B. Long
Benjamin H. Brewton
Troy A. Lanier

OF COUNSEL

A. Montague Miller

Jon E. Ingram, Jr.

Representative Clients: State Farm Insurance Cos.; Travelers-Aetna Insurance Cos.; Georgia Power Co.; Wachovia National Bank (Augusta Division); Chubb Group; MAG Mutual Insurance Company; Augusta Board of Realtors; Canal Insurance Company; St. Paul Fire and Marine Insurance Company.

For full biographical listings, see the Martindale-Hubbell Law Directory

HALL & MULLINS, P.C. (AV)

1202 First Union Bank Building, 699 Broad Street, 30901
Telephone: 706-722-7062
Fax: 706-722-7201
URL: http://www.lawyers.com/hall&mullins

J. Randal Hall

For full biographical listings, see the Martindale-Hubbell Law Directory

HULL, TOWILL, NORMAN, BARRETT & SALLEY, A PROFESSIONAL CORPORATION (AV)

801 Broad Street, Suite 700, 30901
Telephone: 706-722-4481
Fax: 706-722-9779
Email: hullfirm@groupz.net *URL:* http://www.groupz.net/~advocate
Aiken, South Carolina Office: 111 Park Avenue, 29801.
Telephone: 803-648-4213.
Fax: 803-648-2601.

James M. Hull (1885-1975)
George B. Barrett (1894-1942)
Julian J. Willingham (1887-1963)
John Bell Towill (1907-1991)
Robert C. Norman (Retired, 1991)
W. Hale Barrett
Lawton Jordan, Jr.
Patrick J. Rice
Douglas D. Batchelor, Jr.
David E. Hudson
William H. Tucker (Not admitted in GA)
William F. Hammond
Mark S. Burgreen
George R. Hall

(See Next Column)

HULL, TOWILL, NORMAN, BARRETT & SALLEY A PROFESSIONAL CORPORATION—*Continued*

James B. Ellington
F. Michael Taylor
William J. Keogh, III
Edward J. Tarver
J. Noel Schweers, III
Susan D. Barrett
Ralph Emerson Hanna, III

James M. Holly (Not admitted in GA)
Timothy E. Moses
N. Shannon Gentry Lanier
Tara R. Simkins
Charles H. Weigle
Natalie A. Dopson
David C. Smith

OF COUNSEL

Julian B. Salley, Jr. (Not admitted in GA)

Counsel for: Morris Communications Corporation; Merry Land & Investment Company, Inc.; Castleberry/Snow's Brands, Inc.; Chipman-Union, Inc.; Augusta National, Inc.; Sun Trust Bank Augusta, N.A.; Georgia Power Co.; St. Joseph Hospital, Augusta, Georgia, Inc.; Norfolk Southern Corp.; Housing Authority of the City of Augusta.

For full biographical listings, see the Martindale-Hubbell Law Directory

*DECATUR,** De Kalb Co.

SIMMONS, WARREN, SZCZECKO & MCFEE, PROFESSIONAL ASSOCIATION (AV)

315 West Ponce de Leon Avenue, Suite 850, 30030
Telephone: 404-378-1711
Fax: 404-377-6101

M. T. Simmons, Jr.
Joseph Szczecko
William C. McFee, Jr.

Representative Clients: Julian LeCraw & Company (Real Estate); Intown Suites, Inc.; Preferred Lodging Systems, Inc.; Royal Oldsmobile,; Cotter & Co.; Atlanta Neurosurgical Associates, P.A.; Troncalli Motors, Inc.

For full biographical listings, see the Martindale-Hubbell Law Directory

*GRIFFIN,** Spalding Co.

JOHN M. COGBURN, JR. (AV)

115 North Sixth Street, P.O. Box 907, 30224
Telephone: 770-228-2148
Telecopier: 770-228-5018
Email: JMCOGBURN@AOL.COM *URL:* http://www.lawyers.com/cogburnlaw

Representative Clients: Griffin-Spalding County Hospital Authority; Spalding Health Care Trust (Nonprofit Community Health Care Organization); Allstar Knitwear Co., Inc. (Textiles); Dender Distributing Co. (Wholesale Beer Distributor); The Mouchet Corp. (Textile By-Products); Industrial Refrigeration Enterprises, Inc. (Refrigeration Engineers and Contractors); Cronic Chevrolet, Pontiac, Nissan (Automobile Dealership); Atlanta Tees, Inc. (Sportswear Distribution); Hi-Tech Rentals, Inc. (Computerized Audio-Visual Equipment for Trade Shows).

For full biographical listings, see the Martindale-Hubbell Law Directory

*LAWRENCEVILLE,** Gwinnett Co.

ANDERSEN, DAVIDSON & TATE, P.C. (AV)

1505 Lakes Parkway, Suite 100, P.O. Box 2000, 30043
Telephone: 770-822-0900
Telecopier: 770-822-9680
Email: a-dt@mindspring.com

Thomas J. Andersen
Thomas T. Tate
Jeffrey R. Mahaffey
William M. Ray, II

References: Sun Trust Bank; The Bank of Gwinnett County; Chicago Title Insurance Co.; Title Insurance Company of Minnesota.

For Complete List of Firm Personnel, See General Section

For full biographical listings, see the Martindale-Hubbell Law Directory

*LOUISVILLE,** Jefferson Co.

ABBOT, MURPHY AND HARVEY, P.C. (AV)

190 East 7th Street, P.O. Box 31, 30434
Telephone: 912-625-7281
Facsimile: 912-625-8200

W. Wright Abbot (1892-1969)
James C. Abbot (1926-1997)
John R. Murphy, III
Fred K. Harvey, Jr.

Representative Clients: First National Bank & Trust Co., Louisville, Georgia; City of Louisville; J.M. Huber Corp.; Jefferson E.M.C.; Town of Bartow; Bank of Wadley; Forstmann and Company, Inc.; Fulghum Industries, Inc.; Hospital Authority of Jefferson County; Allied Business Systems.

For full biographical listings, see the Martindale-Hubbell Law Directory

*MACON,** Bibb Co.

HALL, BLOCH, GARLAND & MEYER (AV)

1500 Charter Medical Building, P.O. Box 5088, 31208-5088
Telephone: 912-745-1625
Facsimile: 912-741-8822
Email: hbgm@hbgm.com
Midtown Macon, Georgia Office: 2452 Vineville Avenue.
Telephone: 912-745-1625.
Facsimile: 912-741-3544.

MEMBERS OF FIRM

Benjamin M. Garland
J. Patrick Meyer, Jr.
J. Steven Stewart
Duncan D. Walker, III
Mark E. Toth
John Flanders Kennedy
Todd C. Brooks

ASSOCIATE

Kimberly Cofer Harris

Counsel for: Wachovia Bank of Georgia, N.A.; BellSouth Mobility, Inc.; Helena Chemical Corp.; Navistar International Corporation.

For Complete List of Firm Personnel, See General Section

For full biographical listings, see the Martindale-Hubbell Law Directory

SELL & MELTON, L.L.P. (AV)

A Limited Liability Partnership including a Professional Corporation
14th Floor, 577 Mulberry Street, P.O. Box 229, 31202-0229
Telephone: 912-746-8521
Telecopier: 912-745-6426

Brian J. Passante

OF COUNSEL

E. S. Sell, Jr.
Buckner F. Melton
Joseph W. Popper, Jr.

General Counsel for: Macon Telegraph Publishing Co. (The Macon Telegraph); Macon-Bibb County Hospital Authority; County of Bibb; Smith & Sons Foods, Inc. (S & S Cafeterias); Macon Bibb County Industrial Authority; Burgess Pigment Co.
Local Counsel For: United States Aircraft Insurance Group (USAIG); United States Aviation Underwriters, Inc. (USAU).

For Complete List of Firm Personnel, See General Section

For full biographical listings, see the Martindale-Hubbell Law Directory

*MARIETTA,** Cobb Co.

W. ALLEN SEPARK (AV)

250 Church Street, Second Floor, P.O. Box 3475, 30061-3475
Telephone: 770-422-3200
Fax: 770-514-1148

Representative Clients: Martin's Restaurant Systems, Inc.; Snowden Enterprises, Inc.; Sparkles Roller Rinks; Bearden & Smith, P.C.; The Halifax Group, Inc. formerly Oak Hill Farms, Inc.; Southern Polytechnic State University Foundation, Inc.; Metro North Youth Soccer Association, Inc.; Wellstar Foundation, Inc. formerly PROMINA Northwest Health Foundation, Inc.; The Georgia Ballet, Inc.

For full biographical listings, see the Martindale-Hubbell Law Directory

*NEWNAN,** Coweta Co.

GLOVER & DAVIS, P.A. (AV)

10 Brown Street, P.O. Box 1038, 30264
Telephone: 770-683-6000
Fax: 770-683-6010
Peachtree City, Georgia Office: Suite 130, 200 Westpark Drive.
Telephone: 770-487-5834.
Fax: 770-487-3492.

J. Littleton Glover, Jr.
Alan W. Jackson

Peter A. Durham

Representative Clients: Batson-Cook Company, General Corporate and Construction Divisions; J. Smith Lanier & Company and Insurance Subsidiaries; Durand-Wayland, Inc.; Gas, Inc.; Gas, Incorporated and Subsidiaries; Book Warehouse of Georgia, Inc.; First Citizens Corporation and Banking Subsidiaries; Putnam-Greene Financial Corporation and Banking Subsidiaries; Peachtree National Bank.
Local Counsel for: International Platex Corp.

For Complete List of Firm Personnel, See General Section

For full biographical listings, see the Martindale-Hubbell Law Directory

*ROME,** Floyd Co.

Brinson, Askew, Berry, Seigler, Richardson & Davis, LLP (AV)

Omberg House, 615 West First Street, P.O. Box 5513, 30162-5513
Telephone: 706-291-8853;
Atlanta: 404-521-0908
Telecopier: 706-234-3574
Email: law@brinson-askew.com *URL:* http://www.brinson-askew.com

MEMBERS OF FIRM

Robert M. Brinson (P.C.)
C. King Askew (P.C.)
Robert L. Berry
Joseph M. Seigler, Jr.
Thomas D. Richardson
J. Anderson Davis
Hendrick L. Cromartie, III
Wright W. Smith
Mark M. J. Webb
Joseph B. Atkins
I. Stewart Duggan

ASSOCIATES

James Daniel Blitch, IV
Stephen B. Moseley

Representative Clients: Georgia Power Co.; General Electric Company; Unilever; News Publishing Company (Rome News Tribune); Oglethorpe Power Corp.; AmSouth Bank; ConAgra, Inc.; Browning-Ferris Industries (BFI); Shaw Industries, Inc.; City of Rome.

For full biographical listings, see the Martindale-Hubbell Law Directory

*SAVANNAH,** Chatham Co.

Bouhan, Williams & Levy LLP (AV)

The Armstrong House, 447 Bull Street, P.O. Box 2139, 31402-2139
Telephone: 912-236-2491
Fax: 912-233-0811
Email: bouhan@bellsouth.net

MEMBER OF FIRM

Walter C. Hartridge

General Counsel for: Savannah Electric and Power Co.; Wachovia Bank of Georgia, N.A.; Southeastern Maritime Co.; Solomons Co.; Fiduciary Services Corp.; Peeples Industry, Inc.; Board of Education of the City of Savannah and County of Chatham; The Branigar Organization, Inc.

For Complete List of Firm Personnel, See General Section

For full biographical listings, see the Martindale-Hubbell Law Directory

Hunter, Maclean, Exley & Dunn, P.C. (AV)

200 East St. Julian Street, P.O. Box 9848, 31412
Telephone: 912-236-0261
Cable Address: "Ancan"
Telecopier: 912-236-4936
Telex: 54-6483
Email: hmed.com *URL:* http://www.bobbs@hmed.com
Atlanta, Georgia Office: The Peachtree, 1355 Peachtree Street, N.E., Suite 640.
Telephone: 404-876-3611.
Fax: 404-870-2025.

Henry M. Dunn, Jr.
John M. Tatum
John M. Hewson, III
J. Reid Williamson, III
Michael Jonas Thomerson
Thomas Sean Cullen
Michael D. Robl

OF COUNSEL

Don L. Waters

Representative Clients: SunTrust Bank, Savannah, N.A.; Great Dane Trailers; Atlantic Wood Industries, Inc.; Carson Products Co.; Brasseler, U.S.A., Inc.; Prudential Insurance Company of America; Historic Savannah Foundation, Inc.; John Hancock Mutual Life Insurance Co.; Norfolk Southern Corp.

For Complete List of Firm Personnel, See General Section

For full biographical listings, see the Martindale-Hubbell Law Directory

Karsman, Brooks & Callaway, P.C. (AV)

301 West Congress Street, P.O. Box 9149, 31412
Telephone: 912-238-2750
Cable Address: "Karbro"
Telecopier: 912-238-2767

Stanley M. Karsman
Charles C. Brooks
Timothy F. Callaway, III
Stanley E. Harris, Jr.
James L. Drake, Jr.
Dana F. Braun
R. Krannert Riddle
Edward M. Hughes
Timothy J. Haeussler

For full biographical listings, see the Martindale-Hubbell Law Directory

Lee, Black, Scheer & Hart, P.C. (AV)

10th Floor, 24 Drayton Street, P.O. Box 8205, 31412
Telephone: 912-233-1271
Telecopier: 912-232-7344
Other Savannah Office: 6555 Abercorn Street, Suite 121, P.O. Box 14477.
Telephone: 912-355-1131.

(See Next Column)

Edward H. Lee
W. Jerrold Black
Steven E. Scheer
R. Jonathan Hart

Christopher L. Rouse
John D. Lange

For full biographical listings, see the Martindale-Hubbell Law Directory

HAWAII

*HONOLULU,** Honolulu Co.

Carlsmith Ball (AV)

A Partnership including Law Corporations
Suite 2200, Pacific Tower, 1001 Bishop Street, P.O. Box 656, 96809-3402
Telephone: 808-523-2500
Fax: 808-523-0842
Email: execdirector@carlsmith.com *URL:* http://www.carlsmith.com
Kapolei, Hawaii Office: Suite 318, Kapolei Building, 1001 Kamokila Boulevard, 96707.
Telephone: 808-523-2500.
Fax: 808-674-0850.
Wailuku, Maui Hawaii Office: Suite 400, One Main Plaza, 2200 Main Street, P.O. Box 1086, 96793-1086.
Telephone: 808-242-4535.
Fax: 808-244-4974.
Kailua-Kona, Hawaii Office: Suite 209, 75-1000 Henry Street, 96740.
Telephone: 808-329-6464.
Fax: 808-329-9450.
Hilo, Hawaii Office: 121 Waianuenue Avenue, P.O. Box 686, 96721-0686.
Telephone: 808-935-6644.
Fax: 808-935-7975.
Hagatna, Guam Office: Suite 401, Bank of Hawaii Building, 134 West Soledad Avenue, P.O. Box BF, 96932-5027.
Telephone: 671-472-6813.
Fax: 671-477-4375.
Telex: 721-6445 CWCMI GM.
Saipan, Commonwealth of the Northern Mariana Islands Office: Carlsmith Building, Capitol Hill, P.O. Box 5241, 96950-5241.
Telephone: 670-322-3455.
Fax: 670-322-3368.
Los Angeles, California Office: 9th Floor, 444 South Flower Street, 90071-2901.
Telephone: 213-955-1200.
Fax: 213-623-0032.
Washington, D.C. Office: Suite 300, 1201 Pennsylvania Avenue, N.W., 20004-2401.
Telephone: 202-628-2228.
Fax: 202-628-2071.
Mexico City, Mexico Office: Carlsmith Ball, Sierra Nevada 119, Lomas de Chapultepec, 11000 Mexico, D.F.
Telephone: 52-5-520-8514, 52-5-520-8757.
Fax: 52-5-540-1545.
Mexico, D.F. Office of Carlsmith Ball, S.C. (Authorized to practice as foreign legal consultants in Mexico): Sierra Nevada 119, Lomas de Chapultepec, 11000 Mexico, D.F.
Telephone: 52-5-520-8514, 52-5-520-8757.
Fax: 52-5-540-1545.

MEMBERS OF FIRM

Annie Kun Baker (Partner, Resident at Los Angeles, California Office)
Roger B. Baymiller (Resident at Los Angeles, California Office)
Michael I. Blaylock (Not admitted in HI; Resident at Los Angeles, California Office)
Stephen L. Bradford (Resident at Los Angeles, California Office)
Edward E. Case
James H. Case (A Law Corporation)
Albert H. Ebright (Resident at Los Angeles, California Office)
Steven M. Egesdal
Terrence A. Everett (Resident at Los Angeles, California Office)
Alfonso García Cacho (Resident at Mexico Office)
Karl K. Kobayashi
Tom C. Leuteneker (Resident at Maui, Hawaii Office)
Tim Lui-Kwan
John P. Manaut
Matthew M. Matsunaga
Randolph G. Muhlestein (Resident at Los Angeles, California Office)
Harry Y. Oda
Lawrence S. Okinaga (A Law Corporation)
David S. Olson (Resident at Los Angeles, California Office)
John D. Osborn (Resident at Saipan Office)
James Polish (Resident at Los Angeles, California Office)
Dean H. Robb
Tom E. Roesser
John E. Rogers (Resident at Mexico Office)
Marcia K. Schultz (Resident at Saipan Office)
Jonathan L. Smoller (Resident at Los Angeles, California Office)
Robert E. Strand
Lance F. Taniguchi
Sinforoso M. Tolentino (Resident at Hagatna, Guam Office)
Robert D. Triantos (Resident at Kailua-Kona, Hawaii Office)
J. Thomas Van Winkle (A Law Corporation)
Donald C. Williams (Resident at Los Angeles, California Office)

(See Next Column)

CARLSMITH BALL—*Continued*

MEMBERS OF FIRM (Continued)

William C. Williams, Jr. (Not admitted in HI)
Jon T. Yamamura
Adrián Zubikarai Arriola (Resident at Mexico Office)

ASSOCIATES

Francisco A. Gil-Elorduy (Resident at Mexico Office)
Joanne L. Grimes
Dana A. Gutierrez (Resident at Hagatna, Guam Office)
Kevin E. Moore
David B. Rosen

OF COUNSEL

Herbert G. Baerwitz (Resident at Los Angeles, California Office)
Robert N. Katayama

For Complete List of Firm Personnel, See General Section

For full biographical listings, see the Martindale-Hubbell Law Directory

KOBAYASHI, SUGITA & GODA (AV)

A Partnership including Professional Corporations
999 Bishop Street, Suite 2600, 96813
Telephone: 808-539-8700
Telecopier: 808-539-8799
Telex: 6502396585 MCI
MCI Mail: 23 96585
ABA/Net: ABA2281
Email: ksg@aloha.net

OF COUNSEL

Bert T. Kobayashi, Sr.
Michael J. McGivern (Not admitted in HI)

Reference: First Hawaiian Bank.

For Complete List of Firm Personnel, See General Section

For full biographical listings, see the Martindale-Hubbell Law Directory

MCCORRISTON MIHO MILLER MUKAI (AV)

Five Waterfront Plaza, 4th Floor, 500 Ala Moana Boulevard, 96813
Telephone: 808-529-7300
Facsimile: 808-524-8293
Cable: Attorneys, Honolulu
Mailing Address: P.O. Box 2800, Honolulu, Hawaii, 96803-2800
Email: info@m4Law.com

PARTNERS

Clifford J. Miller
Franklin K. Mukai
Stanley Y. Mukai
D. Scott MacKinnon
Kenneth B. Marcus
Kenneth G. K. Hoo
Patrick K. Lau
Brian T. Hirai
David N. Kuriyama
Michael J. O'Malley
Eric T. Kawatani
Michael Rosenthal
Sharon H. Nishi
Randall F. Sakumoto
Andrew W. Char
Alexander R. Jampel
Peter J. Hamasaki

COUNSEL

Charles E. Pear, Jr.

ASSOCIATE

Stewart Pressman

Representative Clients: The Neiman Marcus Group; Seven-Eleven Hawaii, Inc.; Toshiba Hawaii, Inc.; Daewoo Hawaii Corporation; Hawaii Dental Service; Pacific Basin Economic Council; Gallo Winery; Oahu Gas Service; Oji Paper Co., Ltd.; Marubeni Corporation.

For Complete List of Firm Personnel, See General Section

For full biographical listings, see the Martindale-Hubbell Law Directory

PITLUCK KIDO SATO & STONE (AV)

701 Bishop Street, 96813
Telephone: 808-523-5030
Telecopier: 808-545-4015
Email: pitluck@pitluck.com *URL:* http://www.pitluck.com

MEMBERS OF FIRM

Wayne Marshall Pitluck
Alan Takashi Kido
Dana Kiyomi Nalani Sato
James Mauliola Keaka Stone, Jr.

OF COUNSEL

John W. Reilly

Reference: Bank of Hawaii.

For full biographical listings, see the Martindale-Hubbell Law Directory

TAKUSHI, FUNAKI, WONG & STONE ATTORNEYS AT LAW, A LAW CORPORATION (AV)

Suite 1400 Grosvenor Center, 733 Bishop Street, 96813
Telephone: 808-543-9800
Fax: 808-543-9869
Email: tfwf@pixi.com

(See Next Column)

Roy E. Takushi
James T. Funaki
Alfred M. K. Wong
Robert M. Ehrhorn, Jr.
Dickson C. H. Lee
Peter T. Stone
James N. H. Yee
Ann L. Kurihara
Jacqueline Kong
Elizabeth A. Kane

For full biographical listings, see the Martindale-Hubbell Law Directory

TAM, O'CONNOR, HENDERSON, TAIRA & YAMAUCHI ATTORNEYS AT LAW, A LAW CORPORATION (AV)

20th Floor, Central Pacific Plaza, 220 South King Street, 96813
Telephone: 808-545-3030
Fax: 808-523-8051
Fax: 808-537-6782
Email: lawyers@50thstatelaw.com

James K. Tam
Michael F. O'Connor
Harvey E. Henderson, Jr.
Lissa H. Andrews
Robert M. Yamauchi
Darryl M. Taira
Stuart M. Kodish

Wesley H. Ikeda
Russ S. Awakuni
Kevin W. Herring
Fred I. Waki

OF COUNSEL

Paul M. Dold

Representative Clients: Chubb/Pacific Indemnity Group; Alexander & Baldwin, Inc.; Castle Medical Center; International Savings & Loan; United States Services Automobile Assn.; Fringe Benefit Trust Funds for Plumbing Industry; Electrical Industry, Operationg Engineers Industry, Cable Television Industry, Carpet & Soft Tile Industry.

For full biographical listings, see the Martindale-Hubbell Law Directory

IDAHO

*BOISE,** Ada Co.

ELAM & BURKE, A PROFESSIONAL ASSOCIATION (AV)

Key Financial Center, 702 West Idaho Street, P.O. Box 1539, 83701
Telephone: 208-343-5454
Telecopier: 208-384-5844
Email: eblaw@elamburke.com

Carl P. Burke
David B. Lincoln
Sandra L. Clapp

Jayne Tracy Davis

Representative Clients: Morrison-Knudsen; J.R. Simplot Co.; U.S. BanCorp Leasing; Sinclair Oil d/b/a Sun Valley Co.; Micron Construction, Inc.; United Heritage Life Insurance Co.; Idaho Life and Health Guaranty Association.

For Complete List of Firm Personnel, See General Section

For full biographical listings, see the Martindale-Hubbell Law Directory

*POCATELLO,** Bannock Co.

MERRILL & MERRILL, CHARTERED (AV)

Key Bank Building, P.O. Box 991, 83204
Telephone: 208-232-2286
Fax: 208-232-2499
Email: mmlaw@ida.net

Dave R. Gallafent
D. Russell Wight
Kent L. Hawkins

Representative Clients: West One Bank of Idaho; J.R. Simplot Co.; School District #25, Bannock County, Idaho; First American Title Insurance Co.; Pocatello Dental Group, P.L.L.C.; Jackson State Bank; Eastern Idaho Development Corp.; BankAmerica.

For Complete List of Firm Personnel, See General Section

For full biographical listings, see the Martindale-Hubbell Law Directory

ILLINOIS

CHAMPAIGN, Champaign Co.

MEYER, CAPEL, HIRSCHFELD, MUNCY, JAHN & ALDEEN, P.C. (AV)

306 West Church Street, P.O. Box 6750, 61826-6750
Telephone: 217-352-1800
Telecopier: 217-352-1083
Email: attorneys@meyercapel.com *URL:* http://www.meyercapel.com

(See Next Column)

MEYER, CAPEL, HIRSCHFELD, MUNCY, JAHN & ALDEEN P.C., *Champaign—Continued*

James L. Capel, Jr. (1933-1991)
John C. Hirschfeld
Dennis K. Muncy
Francis J. Jahn
Donald R. Aldeen
John H. Elder
David B. Sholem
Mark D. Lipton
Tracy J. Nugent
Richard T. West
Rusty W. Freeland
Lorna K. Geiler
Patrick T. Fitzgerald
Todd J. Black
Joseph D. Murphy
Neil R. Rafferty
James M. Mullady
William B. Moore
Evan D. Coobs
John J. Powers
Rochelle A. Funderburg

Matt C. Deering
Jeffrey M. Davis
Marjorie A. Harris
Gregory T. Mizen
Brian C. Lawlyes

OF COUNSEL

August C. Meyer, Jr.
Richard J. Winkel, Jr.
John H. McCord

Representative Clients: BankIllinois in Champaign; Bell Foods, Inc.; Christie Clinic; Illini Cablevision, Inc.; Kuck & Associates, Inc.; Midwest Television, Inc.; Parkland College.

For full biographical listings, see the Martindale-Hubbell Law Directory

RAWLES, O'BYRNE, STANKO & KEPLEY, P.C. (AV)
501 West Church Street, P.O. Box 800, 61824-0800
Telephone: 217-352-7661
Telecopier: 217-352-2169
URL: http://www.roskiaw.com

Donald M. Reno (1906-1987)
J. Michael O'Byrne
Vance I. Kepley (Retired)
Edward H. Rawles
Stephen M. O'Byrne
Glenn A. Stanko
Brett A. Kepley
Timothy S. Jefferson

LEGAL SUPPORT PERSONNEL

Rose M. Lanter (Legal Assistant)
Karen B. Judd (Legal Assistant)

Local Counsel for: Bank One of Champaign, Urbana; Covenant Medical Center; Gibson Community Hospital; Frances Nelson Health Center; University of Illinois; Pekin Insurance Company; Union Insurance Group; New Hampshire Insurance Group; Construction Industry Welfare Fund of Central Illinois; Terra International Inc.

For full biographical listings, see the Martindale-Hubbell Law Directory

*CHICAGO,** Cook Co.

ALBERT, WHITEHEAD & McGAUGH, P.C. (AV)
One South Wacker Drive, Suite 1990, 60606
Telephone: 312-357-6300
Fax: 312-357-6219

Charles G. Albert
Victor P. Henderson
Laurie D. Jaffe
Robert Kinchen
Raymond S. McGaugh
Gregory C. Whitehead

Angela E.L. Barnes
Trasha D. Embry
Stephanie S. Green
Robin D. Shoffner
Allison L. Wood

OF COUNSEL

Rory Dean Smith

For full biographical listings, see the Martindale-Hubbell Law Directory

BECKER & KAPLAN LLC (AV)
19 South La Salle Street Suite 1500, 60603
Telephone: 312-621-9500
Fax: 312-621-9011
Email: firm@beckerkaplan.com *URL:* http://www.beckerkaplan.com

Theodore M. Becker
Daniel S. Kaplan

Edward R. White
Michael J. Boxerman

For full biographical listings, see the Martindale-Hubbell Law Directory

FIELD & GOLAN (AV)
Three First National Plaza Suite 1500, 60602-4206
Telephone: 312-263-2300
Fax: 312-263-0939

MEMBERS OF FIRM

Robert E. Field
Stephen L. Golan
Margaret A. Christie
Donna F. Hartl

ASSOCIATES

Margaret A. Gisch
Matthew J. Cozzi
Anthony R. Taglia

(See Next Column)

OF COUNSEL

Leonard W. Golan
Stephen Edward Smith
Frank J. Dolan
John E. Vranicar

For full biographical listings, see the Martindale-Hubbell Law Directory

GORDON & EINSTEIN, LTD. (AV)
224 East Ontario, 60611
Telephone: 312-280-7766
Telecopier: 312-280-9599
URL: http://www.gordon-einstein.com

Raymond P. Gordon
Jean M. Einstein

LEGAL SUPPORT PERSONNEL

Laura A. Kozicki

For full biographical listings, see the Martindale-Hubbell Law Directory

HOLLIS AND JOHNSON (AV)
11 East Adams Street, Suite 501, 60603
Telephone: 312-427-0700
Fax: 312-427-8407
URL: http://www.digitalawyer.com/bankruptcy

Pamela S. Hollis
Donald E. Johnson

ASSOCIATE

Linda M. Kujaca

For full biographical listings, see the Martindale-Hubbell Law Directory

HOWARD GORDON KAPLAN, LTD. (AV)
180 North La Salle Street, 28th Floor, 60601
Telephone: 312-641-2555
Facsimile No.: 312-641-6265
Email: howie641@aol.com

Howard Gordon Kaplan
Leonard J. Brenner
Rhonda D. Kaplan-Katz

For full biographical listings, see the Martindale-Hubbell Law Directory

THE LAW OFFICES OF MARC J. LANE A PROFESSIONAL CORPORATION (AV)
Suite 2100 180 North La Salle Street, 60601-2701
Telephone: 312-372-1040
800-372-1040
Fax: 312-346-1040
Email: success@marcjlane.com *URL:* http://www.lawyers.com/marcjlane

Marc J. Lane

Gregory A. Papiernik
Scott E. Galbreath
Robert Graham Harles

For full biographical listings, see the Martindale-Hubbell Law Directory

McBRIDE BAKER & COLES (AV)
500 West Madison Street 40th Floor, 60661-2511
Telephone: 312-715-5700
Cable Address: "Chilaw"
Telex: 270258
Telecopier: 312-993-9350
Email: lastname@mbc.com *URL:* http://www.mbc.com
Oakbrook Terrace, Illinois Office: Suite 1000, One Mid America Plaza, 60181-4710.
Telephone: 630-954-2100.
Telecopier: 630-954-2112.

MEMBERS OF FIRM

David Ackerman
Michael J. Boland
Martin J. Campanella
Nina J. Fain
Lola Miranda Hale
Kenneth A. Jenero
Thomas J. Kinasz
David S. Mann
Anne Hamblin Schiave
Robert I. Schwimmer
Michael L. Weissman
Larry M. Zanger

SENIOR COUNSEL

Lawrence A. Coles, Jr.

OF COUNSEL

Robert O. Case
William J. Cooney
Evan M. Kjellenberg
G. Gale Roberson, Jr.

ASSOCIATES

Jerald Holisky
Todd J. Schneider

For Complete List of Firm Personnel, See General Section

For full biographical listings, see the Martindale-Hubbell Law Directory

NISEN & ELLIOTT (AV)
200 West Adams Street, Suite 2500, 60606
Telephone: 312-346-7800
Telecopier: 312-346-9316

(See Next Column)

NISEN & ELLIOTT—*Continued*

MEMBERS OF FIRM

Paul F. Gerbosi
Robert O. Middleton
Edward B. Mueller
William G. Daluga, Jr.
Anthony Packard
Kenneth J. Rojc
Mark F. Zaenger
Thomas V. McCauley
Michael J. Daley
Helen M. Jensen
John Foster Lesch
William A. Walker
John K. Kneafsey
Daniel P. Dawson
Michael H. Moirano
Michael J. Pavlicek

Robert Christie
Brian C. Kelly
Donald F. Froehlke
Mary Rose C. Manczak
Thomas K. Juffernbruch
Bradley S. McCann
Brendan J. Kelly
Brian D. Proctor

OF COUNSEL

Charles M. Nisen
Donald C. Shine

For full biographical listings, see the Martindale-Hubbell Law Directory

QUARLES & BRADY LLC (AV)

Citicorp Center, 500 West Madison Street, Suite 3700, 60661-2511
Telephone: 312-715-5000
Fax: 312-715-5155
URL: http://www.quarles.com
Milwaukee, Wisconsin Office: Quarles & Brady LLP, 411 East Wisconsin Avenue, 53202-4497.
Telephone: 414-277-5000.
Fax: 414-271-3552.
Madison, Wisconsin Office: Quarles & Brady LLP, Firstar Plaza, One South Pinckney Street, P.O. Box 2113, 53701-2113.
Telephone: 608-251-5000.
Fax: 608-251-9166.
West Palm Beach, Florida Office: Quarles & Brady LLP, 222 Lakeview Avenue, 4th Floor, 33401.
Telephone: 561-653-5000.
Fax: 561-653-5333.
Naples, Florida Office: Quarles & Brady LLP, Barnett Center, 4501 Tamiami Trail North, Suite 300, 34103-3060.
Telephone: 941-262-5959.
Fax: 941-434-4999.
Phoenix, Arizona Office: Quarles & Brady LLP, One Camelback Building, One East Camelback Road, Suite 400, 85012-1649.
Telephone: 602-230-5500.
Fax: 602-230-5598.

Richard L. Horn
Thomas J. Magill
Gary H. Kline
Alexander Terras
Kendall R. Meyer
John P. Vail
Thomas A. Polachek
Douglas R. Hoffman
Thomas E. Chomicz
Stephanie B. Shellenback
Robert F. Forrer
Sarah M. Linsley
James J. Gatziolis
Richard P. Blessen
Peter A. Sarasek
Marie K. Eitrheim
Leonard S. Shifflett
Timothy S. Harris
Janice E. Rodgers
Todd A. Rowden
Patrick J. Bitterman

David B. Altman
Joel A. Brodsky
Kurt T. Temple
Jason N. Kaplan
Jessamyn L. Bagley

For Complete List of Firm Personnel, See General Section

For full biographical listings, see the Martindale-Hubbell Law Directory

SCHWARTZBERG, BARNETT & COHEN (AV)

55 West Monroe Street, 2400 Xerox Centre, 60603-5040
Telephone: 312-726-3555
Fax: 312-726-6299
Cable Address: "Justice"
Email: sb&c@twty.chi.il.us

MEMBERS OF FIRM

Ralph M. Schwartzberg (1939-1975)
Mark T. Barnett (1939-1970)
Hugh J. Schwartzberg
Benjamin H. Cohen

For full biographical listings, see the Martindale-Hubbell Law Directory

SUGAR, FRIEDBERG & FELSENTHAL (AV)

30 North La Salle Street, Suite 2600, 60602
Telephone: 312-704-9400
Telecopier: 312-372-7951
Cable: "SUGARFREE"

(See Next Column)

MEMBERS OF FIRM

Richard A. Sugar
Jonathan L. Mills
Michael R. Friedberg
Etahn M. Cohen
Steven A. Felsenthal
Howard M. Helsinger
Andrew B. David
Robert F. Simon
Leslie J. Weiss
Martin M. Weinstein
Ira S. Neiman
Charles H. Braun
Kathryn A. Erickson

ASSOCIATES

Aron L. Bornstein
Norman J. Ginsparg
Annette L. Brands
William F. McGuinn
Kathryn T. Cha
Suzanne J. Massel
Deanne Elizabeth Clarke

For full biographical listings, see the Martindale-Hubbell Law Directory

MATTOON, Coles Co.

CRAIG & CRAIG (AV)

1807 Broadway, P.O. Box 689, 61938-0689
Telephone: 217-234-6481
Telecopier: 217-234-6486; 258-8292
Email: craiglaw@advant.com
Mount Vernon, Illinois Office: 115 North 7th Street.
Telephone: 618-244-7511.

MEMBERS OF FIRM

Craig Van Meter (1895-1981)
Stephen L. Corn
Fred H. Kelly (1894-1971)
Robert G. Grierson
Robert M. Werden (1908-1969)
Gregory C. Ray
George N. Gilkerson (1911-1985)
Paul R. Lynch (Resident, Mount Vernon Office)
John P. Ewart
Kenneth F. Werts (Resident, Mount Vernon Office)
Richard F. Record, Jr.
John L. Barger

ASSOCIATES

Kathleen M. Stockwell
Duane A. Deters
Kristine M. Tuttle
Katy C. Fain (Resident, Mount Vernon Office)
Julie A. Webb (Resident, Mount Vernon Office)
Erin E. Wisner
John M. O'Driscoll
John F. Watson

OF COUNSEL

Jack E. Horsley

Representative Clients: Marathon Oil Co.; Natural Gas Pipeline; Illinois Central R.R.; Okaw Building & Loan, s.b., Mattoon, Illinois; Consolidated Communications, Inc.; Kal-Kan; D-CO, Inc.; Mattoon Enterprise Park, L.L.C.; Lake Land College.

For full biographical listings, see the Martindale-Hubbell Law Directory

OAKBROOK TERRACE, DuPage Co.

BISHOP, ROSSI & SCARLATI, LTD. (AV)

Two TransAm Plaza, Suite 200, 60181
Telephone: 630-916-0123
Telecopier: 630-916-0567
Email: mmccawley@zootsplace.com

Raymond E. Rossi
Frank S. Scarlati Jr.
Robert A. Hall

George F. LaForte, Jr.

OF COUNSEL

Leslie R. Bishop (1928-1997)
Lucy M. Bishop (Retired)

For full biographical listings, see the Martindale-Hubbell Law Directory

MCBRIDE BAKER & COLES (AV)

Suite 1000, One Mid America Plaza, 60181-4710
Telephone: 630-954-2100
Telecopier: 630-954-2112
URL: http://www.mbc.com
Chicago, Illinois Office: 500 West Madison Street, 40th Floor, 60661-2511.
Telephone: 312-715-5700.
Telecopier: 312-993-9350.

MEMBERS OF FIRM

Robert C. Aument
Carl A. Neumann
David H. Hight
Jacqueline W. Vlaming
James A. Kohlstedt
David E. Zajicek

OF COUNSEL

John T. Huntington

ASSOCIATE

Robert E. Harig

For Complete List of Firm Personnel, See General Section

For full biographical listings, see the Martindale-Hubbell Law Directory

OAK PARK, Cook Co.

GOEDERT, HUNTINGTON & DEBOER (AV)

1011 Lake Street Suite 303, 60301-1138
Telephone: 708-848-6066
Fax: 708-848-6067
Email: mdeboer@csi.com *URL:* http://www.lawyers.com/gh&dlaw

MEMBERS OF FIRM

John P. Goedert
Robert A. Huntington
Michael J. DeBoer

For full biographical listings, see the Martindale-Hubbell Law Directory

*PEKIN,** Tazewell Co.

ELLIFF, KEYSER, OBERLE & DANCEY, P.C. (AV)

109 South Fourth Street, P.O. Box 873, 61554
Telephone: 309-346-4148
Fax: 309-346-0633

John T. Elliff (1872-1960)
Patrick E. Oberle
Nathan T. Elliff (1905-1993)
Burt L. Dancey
William P. Streeter

OF COUNSEL

Ronald L. Keyser

Representative Clients: City of Pekin Central Illinois Dock.
Local Counsel for: The Prudential Insurance Company of America.

For full biographical listings, see the Martindale-Hubbell Law Directory

*PEORIA,** Peoria Co.

HOWARD & HOWARD ATTORNEYS, P.C. (AV)

The Creve Coeur Building, Suite 200, 321 Liberty Street, 61602-1403
Telephone: 309-672-1483
Telecopier: 309-672-1568
Kalamazoo, Michigan Office: The Michigan Building, Suite 200, 100 Portage Street.
Telephone: 616-382-1483.
Telecopier: 616-382-1568.
Bloomfield Hills, Michigan Office: The Pinehurst Office Center, Suite 101, 1400 North Woodward Avenue.
Telephone: 248-645-1483.
Telecopier: 248-645-1568.
Lansing, Michigan Office: Suite 500, The Phoenix Building, 222 Washington Square, North.
Telephone: 517-485-1483.
Telecopier: 517-485-1568.

Theodore L. Eissfeldt
Timothy J. Howard
Frederick G. Hoffman
Michael R. Lied

Representative Clients: For Representative Client list, see General Practice, Peoria, IL.

For Complete List of Firm Personnel, See General Section

For full biographical listings, see the Martindale-Hubbell Law Directory

*SPRINGFIELD,** Sangamon Co.

BROWN, HAY & STEPHENS (AV)

700 Mercantile Bank Building, P.O. Box 2459, 62701-1489
Telephone: 217-544-8491
Fax: 217-544-9609

MEMBERS OF FIRM

Harvey B. Stephens
Almon A. Manson, Jr.
Edward J. Cunningham
Dwight H. O'Keefe, III
Robert A. Stuart, Jr.
Donald R. Tracy
J. Patrick Joyce, Jr.
Emmet A. Fairfield
Eric L. Grenzebach
Denise M. Druhot
Jeffery M. Wilday
Harvey M. Stephens
William F. Trapp
John E. Childress
Paul Bown
James W. Bruner
Lorilea Buerkett

COUNSEL

Elizabeth W. Anderson

ASSOCIATES

Michael J. Drake
Ronald J. Giacone, II
Catherine A. DeGenova-Carter
Rudolph M. Braud, Jr.

OF COUNSEL

Norman P. Jones
Simon L. Friedman
Ben L. DeBoice
Robert M. Magill

For full biographical listings, see the Martindale-Hubbell Law Directory

VERNON HILLS, Lake Co.

RICHARDS, RALPH & SCHWAB, CHARTERED (AV)

One Hawthorn Place, 175 East Hawthorn Parkway, Suite 345, 60061
Telephone: 847-367-9699
Fax: 847-367-9621
Email: dschwab@rr&s-chtd.com *URL:* http://www.lawyers.com/richardandschwab

Michael L. Ralph
Alan E. Richards
David J. Schwab

For full biographical listings, see the Martindale-Hubbell Law Directory

*WHEATON,** DuPage Co.

ROLEWICK & GUTZKE, P.C. (AV)

Danada West Professional Center, 1776 South Naperville Road, Suite 104A, 60187-8133
Telephone: 630-653-1577
Fax: 630-653-1579
Email: rgpclaw@aol.com *URL:* http://www.lawyers.com/rolewickandgutzke

David F. Rolewick
Karen Johnson Guilde
John D. Gutzke
Christopher L. Cook

For full biographical listings, see the Martindale-Hubbell Law Directory

INDIANA

*BLOOMINGTON,** Monroe Co.

BUNGER & ROBERTSON (AV)

226 South College Square, P.O. Box 910, 47402-0910
Telephone: 812-332-9295
Fax: 812-331-8808
Email: bunrob@iquest.net

MEMBERS OF FIRM

Don M Robertson
Samuel R. Ardery
Joseph D. O'Connor
Margaret M. Frisbie
James L. Whitlatch
William J. Beggs

ASSOCIATE

Stephen G. Miller

Representative Clients: Aetna Insurance Companies; Bloomington Hospital; Commercial Union Group; Indiana Insurance Co.; Liberty Mutual Insurance; Medical Protective Co.; Monroe County Community School Corp.; Professional Golf Car, Inc.; Prudential Insurance Company of America; State Farm Automobile Insurance Co.

For Complete List of Firm Personnel, See General Section

For full biographical listings, see the Martindale-Hubbell Law Directory

JONES, MCGLASSON & BENCKART, P.C. (AV)

205 South Walnut Street, P.O. Box 279, 47402
Telephone: 812-332-4431
Fax: 812-332-0554
Email: jmbattys@bloomington.in.us *URL:* http://www.Bloomington.in.us/jmbattys

Robert Delano Jones
Judith Corcoran Benckart
Thomas M. McGlasson
Gregory Scott Lauer

OF COUNSEL

David Rogers

Representative Clients: Woolery Stone Co., Inc. Rogers Group Investments; Blackwell Construction; Stone Belt Freight Lines, Inc.; Wendy's of Bloomington, Inc.; Carpetland U.S.A.; Bloomington Bagel Co.; Independent Limestone Co.
Reference: Monroe County Bank.

For full biographical listings, see the Martindale-Hubbell Law Directory

CARMEL, Hamilton Co.

KNOWLES & ASSOCIATES, LLC (AV)

811 South Range Line Road, 46032
Telephone: 317-848-4360
Telecopier: 317-848-4363
Email: knowlesassociates@worldnet.att.net *URL:* http://www.lawyers.com/knowles

William W. Knowles

D. Brandon Johnston

For full biographical listings, see the Martindale-Hubbell Law Directory

*EVANSVILLE,** Vanderburgh Co.

Bowers, Harrison, Kent & Miller, LLP (AV)

25 N.W. Riverside Drive, P.O. Box 1287, 47706-1287
Telephone: 812-426-1231
Fax: 812-464-3676
Email: BOWERS,HARRISON,KENT&MILLER,LLP@BHKM.COM
URL: http://WWW.BHKM.COM

MEMBERS OF FIRM

David V. Miller
George C. Barnett, Jr.

Division Counsel in Indiana for: Southern Railway Co.
Representative Clients: Permanent Federal Savings Bank; Citizens Realty & Insurance, Inc.

For Complete List of Firm Personnel, See General Section

For full biographical listings, see the Martindale-Hubbell Law Directory

Law Offices of Randall K. Craig (AV)

5000 East Virginia, Suite 1, 47715
Telephone: 812-477-3337
Telefax: 812-477-3658
Email: rkcraig@dynasty.net

For full biographical listings, see the Martindale-Hubbell Law Directory

Fine & Hatfield, A Professional Corporation (AV)

520 N.W. Second Street, P.O. Box 779, 47705-0779
Telephone: 812-425-3592
Telecopier: 812-421-4269
Email: Fine@Fine-Hatfield.com *URL:* http://www.Fine-Hatfield.com

James E. Marchand
Leslie C. Shively
Todd I. Glass
Thomas R. Fitzsimmons

Maria T. Worthington
David D. Sanders

A List of Representative Clients Furnished Upon Request.

For full biographical listings, see the Martindale-Hubbell Law Directory

Rudolph, Fine, Porter & Johnson LLP (AV)

221 N.W. Fifth Street, Second Floor, P.O. Box 1507, 47706
Telephone: 812-422-9444
Fax: 812-421-7459
URL: http://www.rfpj@rfpj.com

MEMBERS OF FIRM

Marc D. Fine
L. Montgomery Porter
James D. Johnson
Scott S. Stone
Krista B. Lockyear

ASSOCIATES

Keith A. Sermersheim
Jeffrey D. Thompson

Reference: National City Bank of Evansville.

For full biographical listings, see the Martindale-Hubbell Law Directory

Ziemer, Stayman, Weitzel & Shoulders, LLP (AV)

(Formerly Early, Arnold & Ziemer)
One Riverfront Place, 20 N.W. First Street 9th Floor, P.O. Box 916, 47706-0916
Telephone: 812-424-7575
Telecopier: 812-421-5089

MEMBERS OF FIRM

Ted C. Ziemer, Jr.
Stephan E. Weitzel
Marco L. DeLucio
Gregory G. Meyer

ASSOCIATE

Charles A. Compton

Reference: Old National Bank in Evansville.

For full biographical listings, see the Martindale-Hubbell Law Directory

*FORT WAYNE,** Allen Co.

Miller Carson Boxberger & Murphy, LLP (AV)

1400 One Summit Square, 46802-3137
Telephone: 219-423-9411
Telecopier: 219-423-4329
Email: counsel@mcbm.com
Bloomington, Indiana Office: 3100 John Hinkle Place, Suite 106.
Telephone: 812-333-1225.
Fax: 812-333-1925. E-mail: mcbm@kiva.net.

MEMBERS OF FIRM

Milford M. Miller, Jr.
Philip L. Carson
Bruce O. Boxberger
Edward L. Murphy, Jr.
Thomas W. Yoder
John J. Wernet
Richard P. Samek
Phillip A. Renz
Edward J. Liptak (Resident, Bloomington, Indiana Office)
Robert T. Keen, Jr.
Larry L. Barnard

(See Next Column)

MEMBERS OF FIRM (Continued)

Arthur E. Mandelbaum
Diana C. Bauer
James P. Buchholz
Douglas A. Hoffman (Resident, Bloomington Office)

ASSOCIATES

Karl J. Veracco
M. Randall Spencer
Stephen J. Harants
Timothy M. Pape
Calvert S. Miller
Monica S. Sandkuhler
Heidi K. Ellison
Tina M. Yordy
Jason E. Salerno (Resident, Bloomington Office)
Howard E. Green

Representative Clients: Advanced Machine & Tool Corporation; American Electric Power Company; Bank One, Indiana, N.A.; Corporate Staffing Resources; Indiana Medical Associates; Irmscher, Inc.; Perfection Bakeries, Inc.; Sweetwater Sound, Inc.; Three Rivers Ambulance Authority; Wal-Mart Inc.

For full biographical listings, see the Martindale-Hubbell Law Directory

*INDIANAPOLIS,** Marion Co.

Backer & Backer, A Professional Corporation (AV)

8710 North Meridian Street, 46260
Telephone: 317-571-0500
Telecopier: 317-571-0700
Email: sabacker@ameritech.net

Herbert J. Backer (1914-1995)
Stephen A. Backer

Reference: Bank One, Indianapolis.

For full biographical listings, see the Martindale-Hubbell Law Directory

Cohen, Garelick & Glazier, A Professional Corporation (AV)

Suite 800, Keystone Crossing Plaza, 8888 Keystone Crossing Boulevard, 46240
Telephone: 317-573-8888
Telecopier: 317-574-3855
Email: chuckindy@aol.com *URL:* http://www.indianapolislawyers.com

Samuel J. Mantel (1893-1978)
Thomas D. Mantel (Retired)
Charles A. Cohen
Robert A. Garelick
Steven J. Glazier
Sandra Lazarus Rothbaum
Steven M. Crell
Bradley H. Cohen
Jill Elizabeth Goldenberg

Bryan S. Redding

OF COUNSEL

Joseph J. Reiswerg
Richard L. Darst

Reference: NBD Bank.

For full biographical listings, see the Martindale-Hubbell Law Directory

Hall & Brogden, P.C. (AV)

9200 Keystone Crossing, Suite 230, 46240-2167
Telephone: 317-580-4959
Fax: 317-580-4960
Email: hallbrog@indy.net

Richard M. Hall
Annette T. Brogden

Douglas S. Byrum
Pamela K. Koehler

For full biographical listings, see the Martindale-Hubbell Law Directory

Miller Muller Mendelson & Kennedy (AV)

8900 Keystone Crossing Suite 1250, 46240
Telephone: 317-574-4500
1-800-394-3094
Fax: 317-574-4501
Email: mmmk@iquest.net

MEMBERS OF FIRM

Michael S. Miller
John Muller
Tilden Mendelson
Timothy J. Kennedy

ASSOCIATE

Catherine A. Kling

For full biographical listings, see the Martindale-Hubbell Law Directory

Mitchell Hurst Jacobs & Dick (AV)

152 East Washington Street, 46204
Telephone: 317-636-0808
1-800-636-0808
Fax: 317-633-7680
URL: http://www.mhjd.com

MEMBERS OF FIRM

Marvin H. Mitchell
Richard J. Dick

(See Next Column)

MITCHELL HURST JACOBS & DICK, *Indianapolis—Continued*

ASSOCIATE

Michael T. McNelis

General Counsel For: Dr. Tavel's Vision Center; Calderon Bros. Vending Machines, Inc.; Grocers Supply Co., Inc.; Power Train Services, Inc.; Frank E. Irish, Inc.; Bedding Liquidators; Galyan's Trading Co.; Harcourt Management Co., Inc.; Kosene & Kosene Mgt. & Dev. Co., Inc.; Hasten Bankcorp.

For full biographical listings, see the Martindale-Hubbell Law Directory

SOMMER & BARNARD, ATTORNEYS AT LAW, PC (AV)

4000 Bank One Tower, 111 Monument Circle, 46204
Telephone: 317-630-4000
FAX: 317-236-9802
Email: sandb@sommerbarnard.com
North Office: 8900 Keystone Crossing, Suite 1150, Indianapolis, Indiana, 46240-2134.
Telephone: 317-630-4000.
FAX: 317-844-4780.

James K. Sommer
Dan G. Sterner
Jerald I. Ancel
James A. Strain
Eric R. Johnson
Julianne S. Lis-Milam
Philip L. McCool

OF COUNSEL

Charles E. Valliere

Representative Clients: Comerica Bank; Federal Express; Kimball International; Monsanto; TRW, Inc.

For Complete List of Firm Personnel, See General Section

For full biographical listings, see the Martindale-Hubbell Law Directory

STARK DONINGER & SMITH (AV)

Suite 700, 50 South Meridian Street, 46204
Telephone: 317-638-2400
Fax: 317-633-6618; 633-6619

MEMBERS OF FIRM

John C. Stark
Bruce E. Smith
John W. Van Buskirk
Richard W. Dyar
Patricia Seasor Bailey
Brian J. Tuohy
Mark A. Bailey
Lewis E. Willis, Jr.
Thomas A. Brodnik

ASSOCIATES

Richard B. Kaufman
Paul T. Belch
John J. Moore
Dennis R. Tyler

COUNSEL

Clarence H. Doninger
Gregory S. Fehribach
Robert D. Maas
William K. Byrum

Reference: National Bank of Indianapolis.

For full biographical listings, see the Martindale-Hubbell Law Directory

TABBERT HAHN EARNEST & WEDDLE (AV)

Suite 2100, One Indiana Square, 46204-2101
Telephone: 317-639-5444
Fax: 317-639-5232
Email: jtyrrell@tabberthahn.com *URL:* http://www.tabberthahn.com

Don A. Tabbert
Gregory F. Hahn
Lante K. Earnest
Robert G. Weddle
Mark K. Sullivan
Judy M. Tyrrell
Lara D. Engelking
Matthew W. Conner
William W. Mathews
Heather L. Fesko
Charles R. Whybrew

OF COUNSEL

James J. Nocon
William D. Lalley
Joseph W. Hammes
Dale E. Sporleder

For full biographical listings, see the Martindale-Hubbell Law Directory

*LAFAYETTE,** Tippecanoe Co.

STUART & BRANIGIN (AV)

The Life Building, 300 Main Street, Suite 800, P.O. Box 1010, 47902-1010
Telephone: 765-423-1561
Telecopier: 765-742-8175
Email: sb@stuartlaw.com *URL:* http://www.stuartlaw.com
Indianapolis, Indiana Office: Suite 1401, 8888 Keystone Crossing, 46240.
Telephone: 317-574-7245.
Fax: 317-574-7050.

MEMBERS OF FIRM

Allison Ellsworth Stuart (1886-1950)
Roger D. Branigin (1902-1975)
Roger D. Branigin, Jr.
Thomas L. Ryan
Thomas R. McCully
Larry R. Fisher
Nina B. Kirkpatrick
Mark Lillianfeld
Stephen R. Pennell
Anthony S. Benton
Erik D. Spykman

(See Next Column)

MEMBERS OF FIRM (Continued)

William E. Emerick
John C. Duffey
Bruce McSpadden
Mark E. DeYoung
Thomas B. Parent
Laura L. Bowker
Kevin D. Nicoson
Susan K. Roberts
John M. Stuckey
Deborah B. Trice
William P. Kealey
David A. Starkweather
Geoffrey L. Blazi

SENIOR COUNSEL

Russell H. Hart

COUNSEL

John F. Bodle
James V. McGlone

ASSOCIATES

Elizabeth B. Searle
Marianne Mitten Owen
David A. Locke
Karen Orr McClure
Ann Marie Waldron
Barry L. Loftus

General Counsel for: The Lafayette Life Insurance Co.; INB National Bank, N.W.; Lafayette Home Hospital, Inc.
State Counsel for: Norfolk & Western Railway Co.
Mr. Ryan is Counsel to: The Trustees of Purdue University.
Representative Clients: Aluminum Company of America; Liberty Mutual Insurance Group.

For full biographical listings, see the Martindale-Hubbell Law Directory

*WARSAW,** Kosciusko Co.

ROCKHILL, PINNICK, PEQUIGNOT, HELM, LANDIS & RIGDON (AV)

105 East Main Street, 46580-2742
Telephone: 219-267-6116
Telecopier: 219-269-9264
Email: rockhill@kconline.com

MEMBERS OF FIRM

Brooks C. Pinnick
Stanley E. Pequignot
Richard K. Helm
Vern K. Landis
Jay A. Rigdon
Jamelyn E. Freeman

ASSOCIATE

Dana Leon

Representative Clients: Warsaw Times-Union Newspaper; State Farm Insurance Cos.; Farmers State Bank; C & D Foods, Inc.; Maple Leaf Farms, Inc.; Othy, Inc.; Phend & Brown, Inc.

For full biographical listings, see the Martindale-Hubbell Law Directory

IOWA

*COUNCIL BLUFFS,** Pottawattamie Co.

SMITH PETERSON LAW FIRM (AV)

35 Main Place, Suite 300, P.O. Box 249, 51502
Telephone: 712-328-1833
Fax: 712-328-8320
Email: email@smithpeterson.com
Omaha, Nebraska Office: 9290 West Dodge Road, Suite 205.
Telephone: 402-397-8500.
Fax: 402-397-5519.

MEMBERS OF FIRM

Raymond A. Smith (1892-1977)
John LeRoy Peterson (1895-1969)
Harold T. Beckman
Robert J. Laubenthal
Richard A. Heininger
Lawrence J. Beckman
Gregory G. Barntsen
W. Curtis Hewett
Steven H. Krohn
Randy R. Ewing
Joseph D. Thornton
T. J. Pattermann

ASSOCIATES

Daniel L. Fretheim
Paul M. Shotkoski

Representative Clients: Redland Insurance Group; Iowa Western Community College; Farm Credit Service of The Midlands; Demma Fruit Co.; Peoples National Bank; Council Bluffs Board of Water Works Trustee.

For full biographical listings, see the Martindale-Hubbell Law Directory

*DAVENPORT,** Scott Co.

GOSMA & GALLAGHER, P.L.C. (AV)

Quad City Bank Building, 4500 North Brady Street, Suite 200, 52806
Telephone: 319-388-8417
Fax: 319-388-9240
Email: lawfirm@gosma-gallagher.com
Bettendorf Office: 1989 Spruce Hills Drive.
Telephone: 319-355-5304.
Fax: 319-359-7711.

(See Next Column)

GOSMA & GALLAGHER P.L.C.—*Continued*

MEMBERS OF FIRM

Robert D. Wells (1904-1990)
Robert H. Gallagher
John S. Gosma
James G. Noth
Marie R. Rolling-Tarbox
David A. Millage
Robert S. Gallagher
Jane E. Zimmer

OF COUNSEL

Clay LeGrand
Nicholas W. LeGrand (Not admitted in IA)

References: American Bank and Trust Company, Rock Island; Great River Bank and Trust, Princeton.

For full biographical listings, see the Martindale-Hubbell Law Directory

*DES MOINES,** Polk Co.

FINLEY, ALT, SMITH, SCHARNBERG, CRAIG, HILMES & GAFFNEY, P.C. (AV)

604 Locust Street, Fourth Floor Equitable Building, 50309
Telephone: 515-288-0145
Telecopier: 515-288-2724

Glenn L. Smith
David C. Craig

Representative Clients: ALAS; American Society of Composers, Authors and Publishers; Equitable Life Assurance Society of the U.S.; Federated Insurance Co.; Meredith Corp.
Iowa Attorneys for: Midwest Medical Insurance Co.
District Attorneys for: Norfolk & Southern Railroad; Soo Line Railroad Company.

For Complete List of Firm Personnel, See General Section

For full biographical listings, see the Martindale-Hubbell Law Directory

HAWKINS & NORRIS (AV)

2501 Grand Avenue, Suite C, 50312
Telephone: 515-288-6532
Fax: 515-288-9733

MEMBERS OF FIRM

Lex Hawkins
Glenn L. Norris

ASSOCIATES

George F. Davison, Jr.
Carla Tolbert Schemmel
David N. May

Reference: West Des Moines State Bank.

For full biographical listings, see the Martindale-Hubbell Law Directory

THE ROSENBERG LAW FIRM (AV)

1010 Insurance Exchange Building, 505 Fifth Avenue, 50309
Telephone: 515-243-7600
Email: bdr@worldnet.att.net

MEMBERS OF FIRM

Raymond Rosenberg
Dean A. Stowers
Brent D. Rosenberg

Reference: Firstar Bank, Des Moines, Iowa.

For full biographical listings, see the Martindale-Hubbell Law Directory

KANSAS

*DODGE CITY,** Ford Co.

FOULSTON & SIEFKIN L.L.P. (AV)

810 Frontview, P.O. Box 1147, 67801
Telephone: 316-227-8126
Fax: 316-227-8451
URL: http://www.foulston.com
Wichita, Kansas Office: 100 North Broadway, 700 NationsBank Financial Center, 67202.
Telephone: 316-267-6371.
FAX: 316-267-6345.
Topeka, Kansas Office: 1515 NationsBank Tower, 534 Kansas Avenue, 66603.
Telephone: 785-233-3600.
FAX: 785-233-1610.
Member: Lex Mundi, The World's Leading Association of Independent Law Firms.

MEMBERS OF FIRM

William P. Trenkle, Jr.
David J. Rebein
Thomas W. Young

For Complete List of Firm Personnel, See General Section

For full biographical listings, see the Martindale-Hubbell Law Directory

*TOPEKA,** Shawnee Co.

FOULSTON & SIEFKIN L.L.P. (AV)

1515 NationsBank Tower, 534 Kansas Avenue, 66603
Telephone: 785-233-3600
Fax: 785-233-1610
URL: http://www.foulston.com
Wichita, Kansas Office: 100 North Broadway, 700 NationsBank Financial Center, 67202.
Telephone: 316-267-6371.
Fax: 316-267-6345.
Dodge City, Kansas Office: 810 Frontview, P.O. Box 1147, 67801.
Telephone: 316-227-8126.
Fax: 316-227-8451.
Member: Lex Mundi, The World's Leading Association of Independent Law Firms.

MEMBERS OF FIRM

James D. Oliver
James P. Rankin

SPECIAL COUNSEL

James L. Grimes, Jr.

For full biographical listings, see the Martindale-Hubbell Law Directory

*WICHITA,** Sedgwick Co.

DEPEW AND GILLEN, L.L.C. (AV)

151 North Main, Suite 800, 67202-1409
Telephone: 316-262-4000
Facsimile: 316-265-3819
Email: DG@DEPEWGILLEN.COM *URL:* HTTP://WWW.DEPEWGILLEN.COM

Spencer L. Depew
Jack Scott McInteer

For Complete List of Firm Personnel, See General Section

For full biographical listings, see the Martindale-Hubbell Law Directory

FOULSTON & SIEFKIN L.L.P. (AV)

700 NationsBank Financial Center, 67202
Telephone: 316-267-6371
Facsimile: 316-267-6345
URL: http://www.foulston.com
Topeka, Kansas Office: 1515 NationsBank Tower, 534 Kansas Avenue, 66603.
Telephone: 785-233-3600.
Fax: 785-233-1610.
Dodge City, Kansas Office: 810 Frontview, P.O. Box 1147, 67801.
Telephone: 316-227-8126.
Fax: 316-227-8451.
Member: Lex Mundi, The World's Leading Association of Independent Law Firms.

MEMBERS OF FIRM

Benjamin C. Langel
Stanley G. Andeel
Harvey R. Sorensen
James D. Oliver
Larry G. Rapp
Gary E. Knight
William R. Wood, II

For Complete List of Firm Personnel, See General Section

For full biographical listings, see the Martindale-Hubbell Law Directory

KAHRS, NELSON, FANNING, HITE & KELLOGG L.L.P. (AV)

200 W. Douglas, Suite 600, 67202
Telephone: 316-265-7761
Telecopier: 316-267-7803
URL: http://www.kahrsnelson.com

MEMBERS OF FIRM

Richard C. Hite
Clark R. Nelson
Steven D. Gough
Linda S. Parks
Forrest James Robinson, Jr.
John G. Pike
Dennis V. Lacey
Donald N. Peterson, II

ASSOCIATE

Scott R. Schillings

OF COUNSEL

H. W. Fanning

Representative Clients: Advance Chemical Dist., Inc.; Amoco Production Co.; Business Systems, Inc.; Central Detroit Diesel Allison, Inc.; Coastal Oil & Gas Corp.; Professional Engineering Consultants, P.A.; Vornado Air Circulation Systems, Inc.; Wichita Greyhound Park.

For Complete List of Firm Personnel, See General Section

For full biographical listings, see the Martindale-Hubbell Law Directory

TRIPLETT, WOOLF & GARRETSON, LLC (AV)

2959 North Rock Road, Suite 300, 67226
Telephone: 316-630-8100
Fax: 316-630-8101
Email: twg@twgfirm.com

(See Next Column)

TRIPLETT, WOOLF & GARRETSON LLC, *Wichita—Continued*

MEMBERS OF FIRM

Thomas C. Triplett
John P. Woolf
Thomas P. Garretson
James A. Walker
Timothy E. McKee
Theron E. Fry
Eric B. Metz
Ron H. Harnden
Lee Thompson
Eric S. Strickler
Tad Patton
Bradley A. Stout
Rachael K. Pirner
Jeffrey D. Leonard

ASSOCIATES

Jeffery C. Dahlgren
Jeffrey E. Goering
Jerald W. Rogers
Christopher C. Swyers
Kent G. Voth

Representative Clients: Anheuser-Busch Companies, Inc.; Brite Voice Systems, Inc.; Coleman Company, Inc.; Dow Chemical Co.; Friends University; KPMG Peat Marwick; National Plastics Color, Inc.; Total Petroleum, Inc.; Travelers Insurance Co.; Willis Corroon of Kansas, Inc.

For full biographical listings, see the Martindale-Hubbell Law Directory

KENTUCKY

*BOWLING GREEN,** Warren Co.

HARNED, BACHERT & DENTON (AV)

324 East 10th Avenue, P.O. Box 1270, 42102-1270
Telephone: 502-782-3938
Telecopier: 502-781-4737

MEMBERS OF FIRM

Norman E. Harned
Scott A. Bachert

For full biographical listings, see the Martindale-Hubbell Law Directory

KERRICK, GRISE & STIVERS (AV)

1025 State Street, P.O. Box 9547, 42102-9547
Telephone: 502-782-8160
Fax: 502-782-5856
Email: kgs@kgslaw.com
Elizabethtown, Kentucky Office: 2935 Dolphin Drive, Suite 102.
Telephone: 502-769-5788.
Fax: 502-737-9285.

MEMBERS OF FIRM

Thomas N. Kerrick
John R. Grise
Gregory N. Stivers
H. Brent Brennenstuhl
Laura M. Hagan

ASSOCIATES

Karl N. Crandall
Shawn Rosso Alcott
Jason B. Bell

OF COUNSEL

Jeffrey R. O'Grody

LEGAL SUPPORT PERSONNEL

Patricia Logsdon
Laura Lockhart Lico
Allison Lusk

Representative Clients: Dollar General Corp.; Columbia Greenview Regional Hospital; Hospital Corporation of America; Hardin Memorial Hospital; FirStar Bank; TKR Cable.

For full biographical listings, see the Martindale-Hubbell Law Directory

COVINGTON, Kenton Co.

ROBERT E. SANDERS AND ASSOCIATES, P.S.C. (AV)

The Charles H. Fisk House, 1017 Russell Street, 41011-3052
Telephone: 606-491-3000
Fax: 606-655-4642
Email: resanders@worldnet.att.net

Robert E. Sanders

Jeffrey M. Sanders
J. Pierre Tismo
Delana S. Pierce

LEGAL SUPPORT PERSONNEL

Shirley L. Sanders
Sandra A. Sturgeon
Sheila D. Rachal

For full biographical listings, see the Martindale-Hubbell Law Directory

*HOPKINSVILLE,** Christian Co.

WHITE, WHITE, ASKEW & CRENSHAW (AV)

707 South Main Street, P.O. Box 2, 42241
Telephone: 502-885-5377
Fax: 502-885-5383

(See Next Column)

MEMBERS OF FIRM

Pollard White
Lee T. White
Logan B. Askew
Julia T. Crenshaw

ASSOCIATE

Scott P. Kasierski

Counsel for: First City Bank & Trust Co.; Jennie Stuart Medical Center; Hopkinsville Milling Co., Inc.; White Hydraulics, Inc.; Plymouth Tube Co.; City of Hopkinsville.
Representative Clients: Farm Credit Services; The Equitable Life Assurance Society; Government Employees Insurance Co.; Seay Oil Co., Inc.

For full biographical listings, see the Martindale-Hubbell Law Directory

*LEXINGTON,** Fayette Co.

STOLL, KEENON & PARK, LLP (AV)

201 E. Main Street, Suite 1000, 40507-1380
Telephone: 606-231-3000
Telecopier: 606-253-1093; 606-253-1027
URL: http://www.skp.com
Frankfort, Kentucky Office: 307 Washington Street, 40601.
Telephone: 502-875-6220.
Telecopier: 502-875-6235.
Henderson, Kentucky Office: 201 C North Main Street, 42420-3103.
Telephone: 270-831-1900.
Telecopier: 270-827-4060.
Louisville, Kentucky Office: 400 West Market Street, Suite 2650, 40202-3377.
Telephone: 502-568-9100.
Telecopier: 502-568-5700.

MEMBERS OF FIRM

William L. Montague
William T. Bishop, III
Robert M. Watt, III
Samuel D. Hinkle IV
R. David Lester
Robert W. Kellerman
J. David Smith, Jr.
Dan M. Rose
J. Mel Camenisch, Jr.
Culver V. Halliday
Richard A. Nunnelley
William L. Montague, Jr.

ASSOCIATES

Mary Beth Griffith
Richard B. Warne

Representative Clients: Bank One, Lexington, NA; Delta Natural Gas Co.; Farmers Capital Bank Corp.; Keeneland Association, Inc.; Kentucky American Water Co.; Kentucky Utilities Co.; Link Belt Construction Equipment Co.; General Motors Corp.; International Business Machines Corp.; Lexmark International, Inc.

For Complete List of Firm Personnel, See General Section

For full biographical listings, see the Martindale-Hubbell Law Directory

*LOUISVILLE,** Jefferson Co.

FORE, MILLER & SCHWARTZ (AV)

First Trust Centre, Suite 700 North, 200 South Fifth Street, 40202
Telephone: 502-589-5250
Fax: 502-589-1637

MEMBERS OF FIRM

F. Larkin Fore
Dan T. Schwartz
Stephen H. Miller
Bryan J. Dillon
Donald J. LaDuke

ASSOCIATES

Louis I. Waterman
Joseph C. Spalding

OF COUNSEL

Karl M. Walz

References: American States Insurance Co.; Crawford & Company; Paragon Group, Inc.; Queens Group; Southeastern Dairies, Inc.; Ticor Title Co.; First National Bank of Louisville; Stockyards Bank; Arrow Electric Co.

For full biographical listings, see the Martindale-Hubbell Law Directory

J. BRUCE MILLER LAW GROUP (AV)

One Riverfront Plaza, Suite 1800, 40202-2927
Telephone: 502-587-0900
Telecopier: 502-587-9008
Email: jbm@jbmlg.com *URL:* http://www.jbmlg.com

J. Bruce Miller
Norma C. Miller
Katherine G. Kitchen
Angela Lee Summers
David Scott Dupps
Ashley N. Blacketer
Jason A. Kron
Nicholas Garrett Hawkins

OF COUNSEL

Michael J. Kitchen
Denis B. Fleming, Jr.

Representative Clients: Advance Machinery Co., Inc.; Anson Machine Mfg. Co.; Biddinger Investment Capital Corp. (Indiana); Carneal Enterprises, Inc. (Kentucky/Florida); MPD Inc. (Owensboro, Kentucky); Motion Picture Association of America; Packaging Unlimited Group (Kentucky/North Carolina); Paducah Medical Supply, Inc. (Kentucky/Tennessee/Florida); Sun Group Broadcasting, Inc. (Indiana/Tennessee); Louisville Gas & Electric Co.

For full biographical listings, see the Martindale-Hubbell Law Directory

Louisville—Continued

TILFORD, DOBBINS, ALEXANDER, BUCKAWAY & BLACK (AV)

Suite 1400, One Riverfront Plaza, 40202
Telephone: 502-584-6137
Fax: 502-584-2318

MEMBERS OF FIRM

Charles W. Dobbins (1916-1992)
Henry J. Tilford (1880-1968)
George S. Wetherby (1905-1954)
Lawrence W. Wetherby (1908-1994)
John T. Metcalf (1890-1974)
Stuart E. Alexander
William A. Buckaway, Jr.
Charles W. Dobbins, Jr.
Terrell L. Black
Mark Wesley Dobbins
Stuart E. Alexander, III
John M. Nader

ASSOCIATES

John A. Wilmes
Sandra F. Keene
Patrick T. Schmidt
Thomas J.B. Hurst
H. Kevin Eddins
William J. Walsh, IV
Dana M. Taylor

OF COUNSEL

Randolph Noe
Carolyn K. Balleisen
Michael G. Karem

For full biographical listings, see the Martindale-Hubbell Law Directory

LOUISIANA

*ALEXANDRIA,** Rapides Parish

CROWELL AND OWENS, L.L.C. (AV)

Hibernia National Bank Building Sixth Floor, P.O. Box 330, 71309-0330
Telephone: 318-445-1488
Fax: 318-445-9098

MEMBERS OF FIRM

Richard L. Crowell (1916-1994)
Richard B. Crowell
William B. Owens
W. Brent Pearson

ASSOCIATES

W. Alan Pesnell
Jeff J. Horn, Jr.

Counsel For: Coushatta Empire, Inc.; Hixson Brothers Funeral Home; L,H. Bossier, Inc.; Louisiana College; Provine School Pictures; Southern Chevrolet-Geo; Ratcliff Construction Company.
References: Rapides Bank and Trust Company, Alexandria, La.; Whitney National Bank, New Orleans, La.; Hibernia National Bank, Alexandria, La.

For full biographical listings, see the Martindale-Hubbell Law Directory

*BATON ROUGE,** East Baton Rouge Parish

NAVRATIL, HARDY & BOURGEOIS L.L.P. (AV)

445 North Boulevard, Suite 800, P.O. Box 3551, 70821-3551
Telephone: 225-379-7300
Fax: 225-379-7316

MEMBERS OF FIRM

Boris F. Navratil
David H. Hardy
André G. Bourgeois

ASSOCIATE

Alan P. McGlynn

OF COUNSEL

Robert L. Boese
Johnnie L. Matthews

For full biographical listings, see the Martindale-Hubbell Law Directory

POWERS & WILLARD, L.L.P. (AV)

7967 Office Park Boulevard, P.O. Box 15948, 70895
Telephone: 225-928-1951
Fax: 225-929-9834

MEMBERS OF FIRM

John Dale Powers
William E. Willard

ASSOCIATES

Neil H. Mixon
Lindsey J. Leavoy
Edwin L. Hightower
Andrew P. Sellers, Jr.
Suzanne K. Sasser
Kyle C. Marionneaux

General Counsel for: Audubon Insurance Co.
Louisiana Counsel for: Hancock Bank & Trust Co.; Hertz Corp.; Ciba-Geigy Corp.; Utica Mutual Insurance Co.

For full biographical listings, see the Martindale-Hubbell Law Directory

PREIS, BERGERON & ATCHISON (AV)

450 Laurel Street, Suite 1000, P.O. Box 2786, 70821-2786
Telephone: 225-387-0707
Facsimile: 225-344-0510
Email: preisber@aol.com

(See Next Column)

Phillip W. Preis
Kirk A. Bergeron
Ashley C. Atchison
Charles M. Gordon, Jr.

For full biographical listings, see the Martindale-Hubbell Law Directory

*GRETNA,** Jefferson Parish

WINDHORST, GAUDRY, RANSON, HIGGINS & GREMILLION, L.L.C. (AV)

Oakwood Corporate Center, 401 Whitney Avenue Suite 500, P.O. Box 1910, 70056
Telephone: 504-362-2466; 367-9247
Telcopier: 504-362-5938
Email: wgrhg@gs.verio.net

Thomas L. Gaudry, Jr.
Daniel A. Ranson
Daryl A. Higgins
Gregory G. Gremillion
Wade A. Langlois, III
Michael D. Peytavin

OF COUNSEL

Fritz H. Windhorst (Retired)

Steven Dow Oliver
Thomas W. Darling
David J. Dowell, Jr.
John A Leslie
Walter Patrick Maestri
B. Wesley Pitts

Reference: Hibernia National Bank.

For full biographical listings, see the Martindale-Hubbell Law Directory

*LAFAYETTE,** Lafayette Parish

DAVIDSON, MEAUX, SONNIER, MCELLIGOTT & SWIFT (AV)

810 South Buchanan Street, P.O. Drawer 2908, 70502
Telephone: 318-237-1660
Fax: 318-237-3676

MEMBERS OF FIRM

James J. Davidson, Jr. (1904-1990)
V. Farley Sonnier (1942-1988)
Richard C. Meaux, Sr.
James J. Davidson, III
John E. McElligott, Jr.
John G. Swift
Jeffrey A. Rhoades
Philip A. Fontenot
Kyle L. Gideon
Theodore G. Edwards, IV
Mark C. Andrus

ASSOCIATES

John T. Andrishok
Christopher J. Piasecki
Nicholas J. Zeringue

OF COUNSEL

Jan Whitehead Swift

General Counsel: Southwest Louisiana Electric Membership Corp., Inc.; Macro Oil Co., Inc.; Dwight W. Andrus Insurance Agency; Lafayette Airport Commission.
Local Counsel: Southern Pacific Transportation Co.
Representative Clients: Highlands Insurance Co.; Wal-Mart Stores, Inc.; USAA.

For full biographical listings, see the Martindale-Hubbell Law Directory

ONEBANE, BERNARD, TORIAN, DIAZ, MCNAMARA & ABELL (AV)

Suite 600, Versailles Centre, 102 Versailles Boulevard, P.O. Box 3507, 70502
Telephone: 318-237-2660
Telecopier: 318-266-1232
Email: info@onebane.com
Monroe, Louisiana Office: 1900 N. 18th Street, Suite 420, P.O. Box 2255, 71207.
Telephone: 318-340-0220.
Fax: 318-340-0110.

Joseph Onebane (1917-1987)
John G. Torian, II (1936-1991)
James E. Diaz
Timothy J. McNamara
Edward C. Abell, Jr.
Lawrence L. Lewis, III
Robert M. Mahony
Daniel G. Fournerat
Douglas W. Truxillo
Randall C. Songy
Michael G. Durand
Greg Guidry
Joseph L. Lemoine, Jr.
Mark L. Riley
Graham N. Smith
Gordon T. Whitman
Gary P. Kraus
Richard J. Petre, Jr.
Charles J. Boudreaux, Jr.
James R. Shelton
Thomas G. Smart
Roger E. Ishee
Jennifer M. Kleinpeter
Steven C. Lanza
Joel P. Babineaux

Alison M. Brumley
Jesse D. Lambert
Brent G. Sonnier
Cary B. Bryson
Maria F. Manuel
Greg R. Mier
Jennifer L. Smith
Janice Church Reeves
Mark B. Oliver
Chanelle T. Delahoussaye
Aimee L. Williams
A.G. "Alec" Alexander, III
Terry J. Blanchard
William E. Bourgeois (Resident, Monroe, Louisiana Office)

(See Next Column)

ONEBANE, BERNARD, TORIAN, DIAZ, MCNAMARA & ABELL, *Lafayette—Continued*

OF COUNSEL

William E. Kellner

Representative Clients: Bruce Foods Corp.; First National Bank of Lafayette; Greywolf Drilling Co.; Hibernia National Bank; MidSouth National Bank; Stuller Settings, Inc.; Sunland Construction; Whitney National Bank.

For full biographical listings, see the Martindale-Hubbell Law Directory

*MINDEN,** Webster Parish

JAMES M. JOHNSON (AV)

105 Pearl Street, P.O. Box 1015, 71058-1015
Telephone: 318-377-4978
Toll Free: 877-827-4294
Fax: 318-377-9026

For full biographical listings, see the Martindale-Hubbell Law Directory

*MONROE,** Ouachita Parish

THOMPSON, SPARKS, DEAN & MORRIS (AV)

A Partnership including a Professional Corporation
1401 Royal Street, P.O. Box 2867, 71207
Telephone: 318-388-1440
Fax: 318-322-0887

MEMBERS OF FIRM

M. C. Thompson (1885-1970)
George B. Dean, Jr., (P.C.)
James D. Sparks (1910-1987)
Wood T. Sparks
John C. Morris, III

ASSOCIATE

Jennifer Allen Riley

Representative Clients: South Central Bell Telephone Co.; Greater Ouachita Water Company; PHH Homequity Corp.; Commonwealth Relocation Services, Inc.; Remax, Monroe; Bell South Advertising & Publishing Corp.; Premier Mortgage Corp.; Countrywide Funding Corp.
Approved Attorneys for: BankOne; Federal Land Bank.

For full biographical listings, see the Martindale-Hubbell Law Directory

*NEW ORLEANS,** Orleans Parish

BALDWIN & HASPEL, L.L.C. (AV)

Energy Centre, Suite 2200, 1100 Poydras Street, 70163-2200
Telephone: 504-585-7711
Fax: 504-585-7751
URL: http://www.baldwinhaspel.com

MEMBERS OF FIRM

Cuthbert S. Baldwin (1891-1969)
Leon H. Rittenberg, Jr.
Edward Haspel (1889-1983)
John A. Rouchell
Conrad Meyer, III
Jeannie Morris Randazzo
Jerome J. Reso, Jr.
James P. Magee
Joel A. Mendler
Dennis M. LaBorde
Conrad Meyer, IV
Beverly Klundt Baudouin
Malcolm A. Meyer
Karl J. Zimmermann
Monica Tufano Surprenant
Lance J. Arnold

OF COUNSEL

A. B. Kupperman
Frederick W. "Fritz" Veters

Leon H. Rittenberg, III
Thomas M. Long

Representative Clients: Bean Dredging Corp.; Hibernia National Bank; Alfa-Laval, Inc.

For full biographical listings, see the Martindale-Hubbell Law Directory

CORRERO FISHMAN HAYGOOD PHELPS WALMSLEY & CASTEIX, L.L.P. (AV)

Bank One Center, 46th Floor, 201 St. Charles Avenue, 70170-4600
Telephone: 504-586-5252
Fax: 504-586-5250

Anthony J. Correro, III
Robert M. Walmsley, Jr.
Louis Y. Fishman
Michael J. Casteix
Paul M. Haygood
Sterling Scott Willis

John D. Werner
Lloyd L. Drury, III
Caroline B. Blitzer
Loretta G. Mince

For full biographical listings, see the Martindale-Hubbell Law Directory

MICHAEL L. ECKSTEIN ATTORNEY AT LAW A PROFESSIONAL CORPORATION (AV)

1515 Poydras Street, Suite 2195, 70112
Telephone: 504-527-0701
Telecopier: 504-566-0040
VMX: 504-889-8876
Email: eck@eck-law.com

(See Next Column)

Michael L. Eckstein
David Coleman Raphael, Jr.

Representative Clients: Anserphone of New Orleans, Inc.; Dixie Web Graphic Corporation; Kencoil, Inc.; Life Point Systems, Inc.; Meeks Petroleum Company; Dan-Gulf Shipping, Inc.; Axonn Corporation; Action Ink, Inc.; TCB Industries, Inc.

For full biographical listings, see the Martindale-Hubbell Law Directory

LOWE, STEIN, HOFFMAN, ALLWEISS & HAUVER, L.L.P. (AV)

One Shell Square, 701 Poydras Street Suite 3600, 70139-7735
Telephone: 504-581-2450
Telecopier: 504-581-2461

MEMBERS OF FIRM

Mark S. Stein
Mitchell J. Hoffman

Charlton D. Hunley
Barbara H. Weiss

OF COUNSEL

Mark S. Goldstein
Alicia M. Bendana

For Complete List of Firm Personnel, See General Section

For full biographical listings, see the Martindale-Hubbell Law Directory

MCGLINCHEY STAFFORD (AV)

A Professional Limited Liability Company
643 Magazine Street, 70130-3477
Telephone: 504-586-1200
Fax: 504-596-2800
TDD: (504) 596-2728
Telex: 584327
Cable Address: "MACSTAC"
Mailing Address: P.O. Box 60643, New Orleans, Louisiana, 70160-0643
Email: @mcglinchey.com *URL:* http://www.mcglinchey.com
Dallas, Texas Office: 2777 Stemmons Freeway, Suite 925, 75207-2401.
Telephone: 214-860-9700.
Fax: 214-860-9750.
Houston, Texas Office: 2727 Allen Parkway, Suite 1900, 77019.
Telephone: 713-520-1900.
Fax: 713-520-1025.
Baton Rouge, Louisiana Office: Ninth Floor, One American Place, 70825-0001.
Telephone: 504-383-9000.
Fax: 504-343-3076.
Jackson, Mississippi Office: Suite 1200, SkyTel Centre, 200 South Lamar Street, 39201.
Telephone: 601-960-8400.
Fax: 601-960-8406.
Lake Providence, Louisiana Office: 405 Morgan Street, 71254-2691.
Telephone: 318-559-1200.
Fax: 318-559-0609.
Monroe, Louisiana Office: Dean ONB Tower, 130 Desiard Street, Suite 807, 71201.
Telephone: 318-651-0807.
Fax: 318-651-0809.

MEMBERS OF FIRM

B. Franklin Martin, III, (P.C.)
James M. Fantaci

MEMBERS OF FIRM

Michael David Ferachi (Resident, Baton Rouge Office)
Wilton J. Johnson, III (Resident, Jackson Office)
Rodolfo J. Aguilar, Jr. (Resident, Baton Rouge Office)
William S. Mendenhall (Resident, Jackson Office)
Samuel E. Scott (Resident, Jackson Office)

ASSOCIATES

Jon Ann H. Giblin (Resident, Baton Rouge Office)
Amy Kebert Elder (Resident, Jackson Office)
Derrick B. Carson (Resident, Houston Office)
Pamela L. Hancock (Resident, Jackson Office)
Kathleen H. Eiler (Resident, Jackson Office)
Jean-Paul Perrault (Resident, Baton Rouge Office)

For full biographical listings, see the Martindale-Hubbell Law Directory

SLATER LAW FIRM, A PROFESSIONAL CORPORATION (AV)

650 Poydras Street Suite 2600, 70130-6101
Telephone: 504-523-7333
Fax: 504-528-1080
URL: http://www.slaterlawfirm.com

Benjamin R. Slater, Jr.
Kevin M. Wheeler
Benjamin R. Slater, III
Anne Elise Brown
Mark E. Van Horn
Donald J. Miester, Jr.

Michael O. Waguespack
Sarah Ney
Cory Rabin Cahn
S. Joseph Welborn

(See Next Column)

SLATER LAW FIRM A PROFESSIONAL CORPORATION—*Continued*

SPECIAL COUNSEL

W. Malcolm Stevenson

Representative Clients: Norfolk Southern Corporation; New Orleans Steamship Association; Anheuser-Busch, Incorporated; The Quaker Oats Company; Tulane University; Copeland's of New Orleans, Inc.; New Orleans Publishing Group.

For full biographical listings, see the Martindale-Hubbell Law Directory

*SHREVEPORT,** Caddo Parish

BARLOW AND HARDTNER L.C. (AV)

Tenth Floor, Louisiana Tower, 401 Edwards Street, 71101-3289
Telephone: 318-227-1131
Telecopier: 318-227-1141
Mailing Address: P.O. Box 8, Shreveport, Louisiana, 71161-0008

Quintin T. Hardtner, III
Malcolm S. Murchison
Joseph L. Shea, Jr.
David R. Taggart
Michael B. Donald
Jay A. Greenleaf

OF COUNSEL

Cecil E. Ramey, Jr.

Representative Clients: Kelley Oil Corporation; NorAm Energy Corp. (formerly Arkla, Inc.); Central and South West Corporation; Panhandle Eastern Corp.; Pennzoil Producing Co.; Ashland Oil, Inc.; Southwestern Electric Power Company; The Centex Construction Group; The Brinkmann Corporation; TSE International, Inc.

For Complete List of Firm Personnel, See General Section

For full biographical listings, see the Martindale-Hubbell Law Directory

DAVIDSON, NIX & JONES, A PROFESSIONAL LAW CORPORATION (AV)

509 Market Street, Suite 800, 71101
Telephone: 318-424-4342
Fax: 318-226-0168

Randall S. Davidson
Ernest L. Nix, Jr.
Allison A. Jones
John S. Hodge

Grant E. Summers

For full biographical listings, see the Martindale-Hubbell Law Directory

ROBERT U. GOODMAN, P.L.C. (AV)

Mid South Towers, 416 Travis Street, Suite 1105, 71101-5514
Telephone: 318-221-1601
Fax: 318-221-1749
Email: goodman@prysm.net

Robert U. Goodman

Representative Clients: Aeropres Corp.; Dealers Truck & Equipment Co.; Housing Authority of the City of Shreveport; Specht Newspapers, Inc.; Graham Brothers Entertainment, Inc.; Integrated Exploration, Inc.

For full biographical listings, see the Martindale-Hubbell Law Directory

MAINE

*BANGOR,** Penobscot Co.

EATON, PEABODY, BRADFORD & VEAGUE, P.A. (AV)

Fleet Center-Exchange Street, P.O. Box 1210, 04402-1210
Telephone: 207-947-0111
Telecopier: 207-942-3040
Email: eaton@eatonpeabody.com *URL:* http://www.eatonpeabody.com
Augusta, Maine Office: 77 Sewall Street, Suite 3000.
Telephone: 207-622-3747.
Telecopier: 207-622-9732.
Blue Hill, Maine Office: One East Blue Hill Road.
Telephone: 207-374-2812.
Telecopier: 207-374-2548.
Brunswick, Maine Office: 167 Park Row.
Telephone: 207-729-1144.
Telecopier: 207-729-1140.
Dover-Foxcroft, Maine Office: 30 East Main Street.
Telephone: 207-564-8378.
Telecopier: 207-564-7059.

Malcolm E. Morrell, Jr.
Daniel G. McKay
Michael B. Trainor
Judy A.S. Metcalf (Resident, Brunswick Office)

For Complete List of Firm Personnel, See General Section

For full biographical listings, see the Martindale-Hubbell Law Directory

RUDMAN & WINCHELL, LLC (AV)

84 Harlow Street, P.O. Box 1401, 04402-1401
Telephone: 207-947-4501
Telecopy: 207-941-9715
URL: http://www.rudman-winchell.com

MEMBERS OF FIRM

Abraham M. Rudman (1896-1970)
Albert H. Winchell, Jr. (1924-1992)
Gerald E. Rudman
Phillip D. Buckley
Michael P. Friedman
Winfred A. Stevens
Robert E. Sutcliffe
Paul W. Chaiken
David C. King
John W. McCarthy
Frank T. McGuire
Bruce C. Mallonee
Paul H. Sighinolfi
William H. Hanson
George F. Eaton, II
Edith A. Richardson
Michael M. McAleer
Brett D. Baber
Barbara A. Cardone
Robert E. Murray, Jr.
Edmond J. Bearor
Curtis E. Kimball
Brent A. Singer

ASSOCIATES

Jane E. Skelton
Leigh Stephens McCarthy
Virginia Kozak Putnam
Ajaz S. Fiazzuddin
Anne-Marie Storey Hamer
Hans S. Peterson
Christopher J. Austin

Counsel for: Penobscot Shoe Co.; Sherman Lumber Co.; Webber Oil Co.; Fleet Bank of Maine; Key Bank of Maine; McCain Foods, Inc.
Local Counsel for: Commercial Union York Insurance Cos.; Hanover Insurance Company; Liberty Mutual Insurance Co.

For full biographical listings, see the Martindale-Hubbell Law Directory

*PORTLAND,** Cumberland Co.

BENNETT BENNETT AND TROIANO, P.A. (AV)

Suite 300, 121 Middle Street, P.O. Box 7799, 04112-7799
Telephone: 207-773-4775
Telecopier: 207-774-2366
Email: lawyers@bennettlegal.com *URL:* http://www.bennettlegal.com

Herbert H. Bennett (1928-1992)
Peter Bennett
Jeffrey Bennett
Joseph A. Troiano
Frederick B. Finberg

Julie A. Boesky

OF COUNSEL

Jonathan M. Dunitz

Counsel for: Associated Grocers of New England; General Star Indemnity Company; Coca Cola Bottling Company of Northern New England, Inc.; Northern Utilities/Bay State Gas; Pratt & Whitney (Division of United Technologies); Primerica Financial Services (Citigroup); Sprague Energy (C.H. Sprague & Son); Perrier Group of America, Inc.; Lepage Bakeries, Inc. (Country Kitchen); Texaco, Inc.

For full biographical listings, see the Martindale-Hubbell Law Directory

BURNS RAY & DELANO, PROFESSIONAL ASSOCIATION (AV)

193 Middle Street, 04101-4062
Telephone: 207-775-3581
Facsimile: 207-775-3814
Email: mailcenter@brdlaw.com

George F. Burns
David P. Ray
Arnold C. Macdonald
Mary DeLano
Elizabeth A. Burns
Carrie A. Green

OF COUNSEL

Joanne F. Cole

Representative Clients: Maine Yankee Atomic Power Company; Tractebel Power, Inc.; Hancock Lumber Co., Inc.; Jackson Laboratory; Hague International (engineering); Aetna Life & Casualty Co.; The Hartford; Great American Insurance Co.; Wausau Insurance Co.

For full biographical listings, see the Martindale-Hubbell Law Directory

MARCUS, GRYGIEL & CLEGG, P.A. (AV)

100 Middle Street, East Tower, 04101-4102
Telephone: 207-828-8000
Fax: 207-773-3210
Email: firm@mgc-law.com

George J. Marcus
Jennie L. Clegg
Marilyn E. Mistretta
Lee H. Bals

Sean P. Joyce
Barbara G. Shaw
Michael J. Gartland
Regan M. Hornney

OF COUNSEL

Stephen G. Grygiel
Andrew Jeffrey Zulieve

For full biographical listings, see the Martindale-Hubbell Law Directory

Portland—Continued

PIERCE ATWOOD (AV)

One Monument Square, 04101
Telephone: 207-791-1100
Fax: 207-791-1350
Email: info@PierceAtwood.com *URL:* http://www.pierceatwood.com
Augusta, Maine Office: 77 Winthrop Street.
Telephone: 207-622-6311.
Fax: 207-623-9367.
Newburyport, Massachusetts Office: 6 Harris Street.
Telephone: 978-465-9599.
Fax: 978-465-9945.

MEMBERS OF FIRM

Bruce A. Coggeshall
James B. Zimpritch
Richard P. Hackett
David J. Champoux
Gloria A. Pinza
Robert B. Ravenelle
Ryan S. Stinneford
Elizabeth R. Butler

OF COUNSEL

Jeremiah D. Newbury

ASSOCIATES

James M. Saffian
Jonathan A. Block
William L. Worden
Keith J. Cunningham
Daniel H. Roberts
Thomas A. Loureiro
Steven J. Scott

For Complete List of Firm Personnel, See General Section

For full biographical listings, see the Martindale-Hubbell Law Directory

PRETI, FLAHERTY, BELIVEAU, PACHIOS & HALEY, LLC (AV)

One City Center, P.O. Box 9546, 04112-9546
Telephone: 207-791-3000
Telecopier: 207-791-3111
Email: admin@preti.com *URL:* http://www.preti.com
Augusta, Maine Office: 45 Memorial Circle, P.O. Box 1058, 04332-1058.
Telephone: 207-623-5300.
Telefax: 207-623-2914.
Bath, Maine Office: Thirty Front Street, P.O. Box 665, 04530-0665.
Telephone: 207-443-5576.
Telefax: 207-443-6665.

MEMBERS OF FIRM

Harold C. Pachios
Mark L. Haley (Bath Office)
Michael J. Gentile (Augusta Office)
Eric P. Stauffer
Jonathan S. Piper
Randall B. Weill
James C. Pitney, Jr. (Augusta Office)
Leonard M. Gulino
Dennis C. Sbrega
Estelle A. Lavoie
Susan E. LoGiudice
Michael Kaplan
Michael L. Sheehan
John P. McVeigh
Jeanne T. Cohn-Connor
Timothy J. Bryant

COUNSEL

Naomi Sakamoto

ASSOCIATES

James E. Phipps
Bonnie L. Martinolich
Elizabeth A. Campbell

Representative Clients: KeyBank National Assn.; Blethen-Maine Newspapers, Inc.; Hussey Seating Co.; The Woodlands Club; P.H. Chadbourne & Co.; Community Service Telephone Co.; Goldman, Sachs & Co.; Maine Turnpike Authority; Bangor Hydro-Electric Co.; Unitel, Inc.

For Complete List of Firm Personnel, See General Section

For full biographical listings, see the Martindale-Hubbell Law Directory

TROUBH, HEISLER & PIAMPIANO, P.C. (AV)

511 Congress Street, P.O. Box 9711, 04104-5011
Telephone: 207-780-6789
Fax: 207-774-2339
Email: info@thplaw.com

William B. Troubh
Edwin A. Heisler
Robert J. Piampiano
Kevin M. Gillis
Michael P. Boyd
Thomas E. Getchell
Michael Richards
William K. McKinley
Daniel F. Gilligan
Paul S. Bulger
John G. Richardson

Daniel R. Felkel
Ann Brandt
John P. Flynn, III

For full biographical listings, see the Martindale-Hubbell Law Directory

VERRILL & DANA, LLP (AV)

One Portland Square, P.O. Box 586, 04112-0586
Telephone: 207-774-4000
Fax: 207-774-7499
Email: advice@verdan.com *URL:* http://www.verdan.com
Augusta, Maine Office: 45 Memorial Circle, P.O. Box 957.
Telephone: 207-623-3889.
Fax: 207-622-3117.
Kennebunk, Maine Office: 403-404 Lafayette Center, P.O. Box 147.
Telephone: 207-985-7193.
Fax: 207-985-3957.
Washington, D.C. Office: 400 North Capitol Street, Suite 585.
Telephone: 202-624-9733.
Fax: 202-393-5218.

MEMBERS OF FIRM

Peter B. Webster
Gregory S. Fryer
David E. Warren
Keith C. Jones
Alan D. MacEwan
Charles P. Bacall

ASSOCIATE

Stephen C. Jordan

Counsel for: ASCAP; Bowdoin College; Fleet Bank; Hannaford Bros. Co.; Maine Blue Cross and Blue Shield; Maine Public Service Co.; Peoples Heritage Bank; Portland Water District.

For Complete List of Firm Personnel, See General Section

For full biographical listings, see the Martindale-Hubbell Law Directory

SOUTH PORTLAND, Cumberland Co.

VAN MEER & BELANGER, P.A. (AV)

25 Long Creek Drive, 04106
Telephone: 207-871-7500
Fax: 207-871-7505
Email: VBLAW@GWI.NET

Thomas J. Van Meer
Norman R. Belanger
D. Kelley Young
Richard N. Bryant

Betts J. Gorsky
Mary McQuillen

For full biographical listings, see the Martindale-Hubbell Law Directory

MARYLAND

*ANNAPOLIS,** Anne Arundel Co.

ALEXANDER & CLEAVER, P.A. (AV)

54 State Circle, 21401
Telephone: 410-974-9000; Toll free: 1-800-292-LAWS
Cable: "ALEXLAW"
Fax: 410-974-9002
Waldorf, MD, Fort Washington, MD & Alexandria, VA
Email: ac@alexander-cleaver.com
Ft. Washington, Maryland Office: 11414 Livingston Road.
Telephone: 301-292-3300.
Alexandria, Virginia Office: 1513 King Street.
Telephone: 703-548-7777.
Waldorf, Maryland Office: Hamilton Centre, 3200 Highway 301.
Telephone: 301-870-8080.

Gary R. Alexander
James A. Cleaver

Gerald F. Keipert
Todd K. Pounds
Denise M. Bowman
Thomas W. Kinnane
Joseph P. Hart
Jason A. Deloach
Chantel Renee Ornstein

For full biographical listings, see the Martindale-Hubbell Law Directory

COUNCIL, BARADEL, KOSMERL & NOLAN, P.A. (AV)

125 West Street, Fourth Floor, P.O. Box 2289, 21404-2289
Telephone: 410-268-6600
Baltimore: 410-269-6190
Washington, D.C.: 301-261-2247
FAX: 410-269-8409
Email: cbkn@cbknlaw.com

Ronald E. Council
Ronald A. Baradel
Wayne T. Kosmerl
James P. Nolan
William F. Flood, III
Kevin M. Schaeffer
Donna McCabe Schaeffer
Frederick C. Sussman

John Naumann Strange
Susan T. Ford
Edwin H. Staples, II
Susan Stobbart Shapiro

(See Next Column)

COUNCIL, BARADEL, KOSMERL & NOLAN P.A.—*Continued*

OF COUNSEL

George N. Manis | Nicholas Goldsborough

Representative Clients: Anne Arundel County; Annapolis Bank and Trust; Bank of Maryland; State Farm Mutual Automobile Insurance Co.; Annapolis Yacht Club; Annapolis Yacht Sales, Inc.

For full biographical listings, see the Martindale-Hubbell Law Directory

*BALTIMORE,** (Independent City)

FUNK & BOLTON, A PROFESSIONAL ASSOCIATION (AV)

100 Light Street, Suite 1000, 21202
Telephone: 410-659-7700
Facsimile: 410-659-7773
Email: FBLAW@FBLAW.COM
Annapolis, Maryland Office: 191 Main Street, 21401.
Telephone: 410-269-1554.
Facsimile: 410-268-0612.
Chestertown, Maryland Office: 315 High Street, Suite 202, 21620.
Telephone: 410-810-1381.
Facsimile: 410-810-1383.

Bryson F. Popham (Resident, Annapolis Office)
Lindsey A. Rader

Ren L. Tundermann
Charles D. MacLeod (Resident, Chestertown Office)

For full biographical listings, see the Martindale-Hubbell Law Directory

GALLAGHER, EVELIUS & JONES, LLP (AV)

Park Charles Suite 400, 218 North Charles Street, 21201
Telephone: 410-727-7702
Facsimile: 410-468-2786
URL: http://www.gejlaw.com

MEMBERS OF FIRM

Francis X. Gallagher (1928-1972)
C. Edward Jones (1908-1999)
John C. Evelius (Retired)
Richard O. Berndt
Thomas N. Biddison, Jr.
Robert R. Kern, Jr.
Saul E. Gilstein
Thomas B. Lewis
Bonnie Abrams Travieso
Stephen A. Goldberg
Linda H. Jones
Jack C. Tranter
Leslie B. Speed
Christopher J. Fritz
David E. Raderman
Peter E. Keith
Nita L. Schultz
Michael W. Skojec
Kathryn Kelley Hoskins
Mark P. Keener
Kevin J. Davidson
Eileen M. Lunga
Lori A. Nicolle
Kenneth S. Gross
Thomas C. Dame

ASSOCIATES

Valarie K. Oulds
Margaret Stevens Jacks
Matthew W. Oakey
Rebecca A. Weaver
Michael J. Henigan
David W. Kinkopf
Paul S. Caiola
Jason W. Gaarder
M. Kirsten Andrews

LEGAL ASSISTANTS

Patricia C. Quayle
Iris T. H. Heath
Connie L. Ennis
Margaret Graff
Margo Gibson Hughes
Jonathan T. Gillis
Brenda J. Heacock
Dwayne L. Rodeheaver

Representative Clients: Roman Catholic Archdiocese of Baltimore; The Shelter Group; Alban Tractor Company; Municipal Mortgage and Equities, LLC; The Humphries Companies.

For full biographical listings, see the Martindale-Hubbell Law Directory

KOLLMAN & SHEEHAN, P.A. (AV)

Sun Life Building, 20 South Charles Street, 21201-3225
Telephone: 410-727-4300
Telecopier: 410-727-4391
URL: http://www.kollman-sheehan.com

Frank L. Kollman
David M. Sheehan
Peter S. Saucier
Francis R. Laws
Darrell R. VanDeusen
Clifford B. Geiger

Bruce M. Luchansky
Richard P. Rieman, Jr.
Randi Klein Hyatt
Desmond Terrell McIlwain
Joseph R. Salko
Tracy L. Knight
Jeffrey A. Trueman

For full biographical listings, see the Martindale-Hubbell Law Directory

RICHARD T. STANSBURY A PROFESSIONAL ASSOCIATION (AV)

Suite 920, The B & O Building, Two North Charles Street, 21201-3754
Telephone: 410-727-6200
Facsimile: 410-385-2939
Email: rts1law@aol.com *URL:* http://www.lawyers.com/richardstansburylaw
Annapolis, Maryland Office: 112 West Street, 21401.
Telephone: 410-974-6000.
Facsimile: 410-974-6019.

Richard T. Stansbury

For full biographical listings, see the Martindale-Hubbell Law Directory

THOMAS & LIBOWITZ, P.A. (AV)

100 Light Street, Suite 1100, 21202-1053
Telephone: 410-752-2468
Fax: 410-752-2046; 752-2049; 752-0979
Email: thomasandlibowitz.com *URL:* http://www.thomasandlibowitz.com

Steven Anargyros Thomas
Clinton R. Black, IV
C. Wayne Davis
James E. Myers

Representative Clients: Sinclair Broadcast Group, Inc. (Television and Radio stations); Roy Kirby & Sons, Inc. (Contractor); First Mariner Bank; Scandia Manufacturing Co. Inc. (Defense Contractor); Atlantic Automotive Corp. t/a Heritgage Automotive Group; Candy Express Franchising, Inc.; Wire Spectrum Services (Contractors-Transmission Tower Sites); Acrodyne Communications, Inc.; Alexis Logic Corporation (Software Developers); Selnic Corporation (Electronis Distributors); Liberty Mutual Insurance Company.

For full biographical listings, see the Martindale-Hubbell Law Directory

THOMSEN AND BURKE, LLP (AV)

Suite 400, One North Charles Street, 21201
Telephone: 410-539-2595
Fax: 410-783-0710
URL: http://www.T-B.com
Washington, D.C. Office: Suite 500, 1225 Eye Street, N.W.
Telephone: 202-682-4741.
Fax: 202-547-3713.

MEMBERS OF FIRM

George E. Thomsen
Paul E. Burke, Jr.
Roszel C. Thomsen, II
John B. Ward, Jr.

ASSOCIATES

Hedley A. Clark
Robin McDaniel Hough
Antoinette D. Paytas

References: NationsBank; Mercantile-Safe Deposit & Trust Co.; Carroll County Bank and Trust Co.

For full biographical listings, see the Martindale-Hubbell Law Directory

VENABLE ATTORNEYS AT LAW VENABLE, BAETJER AND HOWARD, LLP (AV)

A Partnership including Professional Corporations
1800 Mercantile Bank & Trust Building, 2 Hopkins Plaza, 21201
Telephone: 410-244-7400
Fax: 410-244-7742
URL: http://www.venable.com
Washington, D.C. Office: Venable, Baetjer, Howard & Civiletti LLP, Suite 1000, 1201 New York Avenue, N.W.
Telephone: 202-962-4800.
Fax: 202-962-8300.
McLean, Virginia Office: Suite 400, 2010 Corporate Ridge.
Telephone: 703-760-1600.
Fax: 703-821-8949.
Rockville, Maryland Office: Suite 500, One Church Street, P. O. Box 1906.
Telephone: 301-217-5600.
Fax: 301-217-5617.
Towson, Maryland Office: 210 Allegheny Avenue, P. O. Box 5517.
Telephone: 410-494-6200.
Fax: 410-821-0147.

MEMBERS OF FIRM

Jacques T. Schlenger (P.C.)
William J. McCarthy (P.C.)
Thomas P. Perkins, III (P.C.)
Benjamin R. Civiletti (P.C.) (Also at Washington, D.C. and Towson, Maryland Offices)
John B. Howard (Resident, Towson, Maryland Office)
Anthony M. Carey (Also at Washington, D.C. Office)
Lee M. Miller (P.C.)
Neal D. Borden (Also at Washington, D.C. Office)
Robert A. Shelton
Roger W. Titus (Resident, Rockville, Maryland Office)
Jan K. Guben (Also at Washington, D. C Office)
Joe A. Shull (Resident, Washington, D.C. Office)
Kenneth C. Bass, III (Not admitted in MD; Washington, D.C. and McLean, Virginia Offices)
John H. Zink, III (Resident, Towson, Maryland Office)
Paul T. Glasgow (Resident, Rockville, Maryland Office)
Joseph G. Block (Not admitted in MD; Resident, Washington, D.C. Office)
Sondra Harans Block (Resident, Rockville, Maryland Office)
Bryson L. Cook (P.C.) (Also at Washington, D.C. Office)
David M. Fleishman
Jana Howard Carey (P.C.)

(See Next Column)

VENABLE ATTORNEYS AT LAW VENABLE, BAETJER AND HOWARD, LLP, *Baltimore—Continued*

MEMBERS OF FIRM (Continued)

Jeffrey D. Knowles (Not admitted in MD; Resident, Washington, D.C. Office)
William D. Coston (Not admitted in MD; Resident, Washington, D.C. Office)
Maurice Baskin (Resident, Washington, D.C. Office)
Robert Zinkham
Elizabeth R. Hughes
Robert J. Bolger, Jr. (Also at Washington, D.C. Office)
J. Michael Brennan (Resident, Towson, Maryland Office)
Newton B. Fowler, III
Michael J. Baader
Davis V. R. Sherman
Wallace E. Christner (Also at Washington, D.C. Office)
Jeffrey K. Gonya
John A. McCauley
Joseph C. Schmelter (Also at McLean, Virginia Office)
Robert H. Geis, Jr.
Fernand A. Lavallee (Not admitted in MD; Resident, Washington, D. C. Office)

OF COUNSEL

Arthur W. Machen, Jr. (P.C.)
Emried D. Cole, Jr.
Ariel Vannier (Also at Washington, D.C. Office)
Robin L. Zimelman

ASSOCIATES

Kevin B. Collins (Also at Rockville, Maryland Office)
Michael W. Conron
Donald P. Creston (Not admitted in MD; Resident, Washington, D.C. Office)
John P. Edgar
Neal H. Strum

For Complete List of Firm Personnel, See General Section

For full biographical listings, see the Martindale-Hubbell Law Directory

YOUNG & VALKENET, L.L.C. (AV)

Suite 707 The Susquehanna Building, 29 West Susquehanna Avenue, 21204
Telephone: 410-583-2414
Telefax: 410-583-2418

Thomas G. Young, III
Thomas C. Valkenet

For full biographical listings, see the Martindale-Hubbell Law Directory

*BEL AIR,** Harford Co.

STARK & KEENAN, A PROFESSIONAL ASSOCIATION (AV)

30 Office Street, 21014
Telephone: 410-838-5522
Baltimore: 410-879-2222
Fax: 410-879-0688
Email: wstarkee@aol.com
Havre de Grace Office: "The Old Ordinary" 100 St. John Street, 21078.
Telephone: 410-939-0100.

Elwood V. Stark, Jr.
Charles B. Keenan, Jr.
Edwin G. Carson
Judith Cline-Silverstein
Gregory A. Szoka
Robert S. Lynch
Paul W. Ishak

Claire Prin Blomquist
Lawrence F. Kreis, Jr.
Craig H. DeRan

For full biographical listings, see the Martindale-Hubbell Law Directory

BETHESDA, Montgomery Co.

EIG AND SCHWARTZ, CHARTERED (AV)

7475 Wisconsin Avenue, Suite 500, 20814
Telephone: 301-654-4884
Telecopier: 301-654-0165

Linda D. Schwartz
Wayne D. Eig
Katherine Palumbo
Paul G. Marcotte, Jr.
Arnold B. Sherman

For full biographical listings, see the Martindale-Hubbell Law Directory

K.K.M., P.A. (AV)

5225 Pooks Hill Road, Suite 1121 South, 20814
Telephone: 301-493-9335
Fax: 301-493-6025
Email: kkm@erols.com

K. (Teya) Moore

For full biographical listings, see the Martindale-Hubbell Law Directory

RIDBERG, PRESS & SHERBILL (AV)

Three Bethesda Metro Center, Suite 650, 20814
Telephone: 301-913-5770
FAX: 301-913-5769

(See Next Column)

MEMBERS OF FIRM

Michael D. Ridberg
Fredric A. Press
Raymond J. Sherbill
Norman L. Eule

ASSOCIATES

Stuart A. Schwager
Paul D. Smolinsky

For full biographical listings, see the Martindale-Hubbell Law Directory

COLUMBIA, Howard Co.

GUY B. MASERITZ (AV)

Hobbit's Glen, 5040 Rushlight Path, 21044
Telephone: 410-997-9400
Fax: 410-997-3116
Email: consult@maseritzlaw.com *URL:* http://www.maseritzlaw.com

Reference: First National Bank of Maryland.

*ROCKVILLE,** Montgomery Co.

BRAULT, GRAHAM, SCOTT & BRAULT, LLC (AV)

101 South Washington Street, 20850
Telephone: 301-424-1060
Fax: 301-424-7991
Email: bgsb@earthlink.net
Washington, D.C. Office: Brault, Graham, Scott & Brault, PLLC, 1140 Connecticut Avenue, N.W., Suite 250.
Telephone: 202-785-1200.
FAX: 202-785-4301.
Fairfax, Virginia Office: Suite 500, 11350 Random Hills Road, Fair Oaks Plaza, 22030-7429.
Telephone: 202-785-1200.

OF COUNSEL

Laurence T. Scott
James Robert Miller

MEMBERS OF FIRM

Denver H. Graham (1922-1987)
Albert E. Brault (Retired)
Albert D. Brault (Resident)
Leo A. Roth, Jr.
James S. Wilson (Resident)
Ronald G. Guziak
Daniel L. Shea (Resident)
M. Kathleen Parker (Resident)
David G. Mulquin (Resident)
James M. Brault (Resident)
Regina Ann Casey (Resident)

ASSOCIATES

Rhonda Ann Hurwitz (Resident)
Joan F. Brault (Resident)

Representative Clients: American Oil Co.; Crum & Forster Group; Fireman's Fund American Insurance Cos.; Kemper Group; Reliance Insurance Cos.; Safeco Group; Government Employees Insurance Co.; Medical Mutual Insurance Society of Maryland; Legal Mutual Liability Insurance Society of Maryland.

For full biographical listings, see the Martindale-Hubbell Law Directory

STEVEN M. KATZ, P.A. (AV)

Suite 208 401 East Jefferson Street, 20850
Telephone: 301-738-8441
Fax: 301-294-9484
Email: smkatz@intr.net *URL:* http://www.lawyers.com/stevenkatz

Steven M. Katz

Jeffrey D. Katz

For full biographical listings, see the Martindale-Hubbell Law Directory

MILLER, MILLER & CANBY, CHARTERED (AV)

200-B Monroe Street, 20850
Telephone: 301-762-5212
Fax: 301-762-6044

William M. Canby (1930-1994)
Patrick C. McKeever
James L. Thompson
Lewis R. Schumann
Joel S. Kline
Joseph P. Suntum
Maury S. Epner

OF COUNSEL

Robert L. Burchett
James R. Miller, Jr.

Ellen S. Walker
Susan W. Carter
Suzanne Levant Rotbert
Michael Gert Campbell
Robert E. Gough

Representative Clients: Asbury Methodist Home Inc.; Sandy Spring National Bank of Maryland.

For full biographical listings, see the Martindale-Hubbell Law Directory

MOLDAWER & MARSHALL, P.C. (AV)

30 Courthouse Square, 20850-2302
Telephone: 301-340-3200; 800-776-8653
Fax: 301-340-7309
Email: AMOLDLAW@AOL.COM

(See Next Column)

MOLDAWER & MARSHALL P.C.—*Continued*

Alan B. Moldawer | John Marshall

Eric J. Pelletier

Representative Clients: Barwood Transportation, Inc.; Yellow Transportation, Inc. (Baltimore); Washington Shuttle, Inc. (Super Shuttle); National Con-Serv, Inc.; Quanta Systems Corporation.
Approved Attorneys for: Security Title Guarantee Corp.
References: NationsBank; Montgomery County Bar Association.

For full biographical listings, see the Martindale-Hubbell Law Directory

STEIN, SPERLING, BENNETT, DE JONG, DRISCOLL, GREENFEIG & METRO, P.C. (AV)

25 West Middle Lane, 20850-2204
Telephone: 301-340-2020; 800-435-5230
Telecopier: 301-340-8217
Email: lawfirm@steinsperling.com
Falls Church, Virginia Office: 6245 Leesburg Pike, Suite 140, 22044.
Telephone: 703-237-0500.
Telecopier: 703-534-2899.

Millard S. Bennett
David S. De Jong
A. Howard Metro
Jeffrey M. Schwaber
Donald N. Sperling

Karen Plave Goldstein
Edward D. McGuire, Jr.

For Complete List of Firm Personnel, See General Section

For full biographical listings, see the Martindale-Hubbell Law Directory

VENABLE ATTORNEYS AT LAW VENABLE, BAETJER AND HOWARD, LLP (AV)

A Partnership including Professional Corporations
Suite 500, One Church Street, P.O. Box 1906, 20850-4129
Telephone: 301-217-5600
Fax: 301-217-5617
URL: http://www.venable.com
Baltimore, Maryland Office: 1800 Mercantile Bank & Trust Building, 2 Hopkins Plaza.
Telephone: 410-244-7400.
Fax: 410-244-7742.
Washington, D.C. Office: Venable, Baetjer, Howard & Civiletti LLP, Suite 1000, 1201 New York Avenue, N.W.
Telephone: 202-962-4800.
Fax: 202-962-8300.
McLean, Virginia Office: Suite 400, 2010 Corporate Ridge.
Telephone: 703-760-1600.
Fax: 703-821-8949.
Towson, Maryland, Office: 210 Allegheny Avenue, P. O. Box 5517.
Telephone: 410-494-6200.
Fax: 410-821-0147.

MEMBERS OF FIRM

Roger W. Titus | Paul T. Glasgow

For Complete List of Firm Personnel, See General Section

For full biographical listings, see the Martindale-Hubbell Law Directory

*SALISBURY,** Wicomico Co.

WEBB, BURNETT, JACKSON, CORNBROOKS, WILBER, VORHIS & DOUSE, LLP (AV)

115 Broad Street, P.O. Box 910, 21801
Telephone: 410-742-3176
Fax: 410-742-0438
Email: webnett@shore.intercom.net

MEMBERS OF FIRM

Frederick W. C. Webb (1889-1956)
John W. T. Webb (1918-1990)
K. King Burnett
W. Newton Jackson, 3rd
Ernest I. Cornbrooks, III
Paul D. Wilber
David A. Vorhis
David B. Douse

ASSOCIATE

Chris Schiller Mason

Counsel for: First National Bank of Maryland (Salisbury branch); K & L Microwave, Inc.; Peninsula General Hospital Medical Center.
Local Attorneys for: State Farm Insurance Cos.; Nationwide Insurance Cos.; Travelers Insurance Co.; United States Fidelity & Guaranty Co.; Aetna Casualty & Surety Co.; Insurance Company of North America.

For full biographical listings, see the Martindale-Hubbell Law Directory

SILVER SPRING, Montgomery Co.

LINOWES AND BLOCHER LLP (AV)

Suite 1000, 1010 Wayne Avenue, 20910-5600
Telephone: 301-588-8580
Telecopier: 301-495-9044
TTY/TDD: 301-588-3380
Email: inbox@linowes-law.com *URL:* http://www.linowes-law.com
Washington, D.C. Office: Suite 302, 1150 17th Street, N.W.
Telephone: 202-293-8510.
Telecopier: 202-293-8513.
Greenbelt, Maryland Office: Suite 202, 6411 Ivy Lane.
Telephone: 301-982-3382.
Telecopier: 301-982-0595.
Annapolis, Maryland Office: 145 Main Street.
Telephone: 410-268-0881.
Telecopier: 301-261-2603.
Frederick, Maryland Office: 228 West Patrick Street.
Telephone: 301-695-0244.
Telecopier: 301-663-6656.
Columbia, Maryland Office: Suite B215, 10015 Old Columbia Road.
Telephone: 410-312-5457.
Fax: 410-290-5285.

MEMBERS OF FIRM

David M. Cohen
Maurice J. Montaldi (Not admitted in MD)
John R. Orrick, Jr.
Midgett S. Parker, Jr. (Resident Partner, Greenbelt, Maryland office)

For Complete List of Firm Personnel, See General Section

For full biographical listings, see the Martindale-Hubbell Law Directory

*TOWSON,** Baltimore Co.

VENABLE ATTORNEYS AT LAW VENABLE, BAETJER AND HOWARD, LLP (AV)

A Partnership including Professional Corporations
210 Allegheny Avenue, P.O. Box 5517, 21204
Telephone: 410-494-6200
Fax: 410-821-0147
URL: http://www.venable.com
Baltimore, Maryland Office: 1800 Mercantile Bank & Trust Building, 2 Hopkins Plaza.
Telephone: 410-244-7400.
Fax: 410-244-7742.
Washington, D.C. Office: Venable, Baetjer, Howard & Civiletti LLP, Suite 1000, 1201 New York Avenue, N.W.
Telephone: 202-962-4800.
Fax: 202-962-8300.
McLean, Virginia Office: Suite 400, 2010 Corporate Ridge.
Telephone: 703-760-1600.
Fax: 703-821-8949.
Rockville, Maryland Office: Suite 500, One Church Street, P. O. Box 1906.
Telephone: 301-217-5600.
Fax: 301-217-5617.

PARTNERS

Benjamin R. Civiletti (P.C.) (Also at Washington, D.C. and Baltimore, Maryland Offices)
John B. Howard
John H. Zink, III
J. Michael Brennan

For Complete List of Firm Personnel, See General Section

For full biographical listings, see the Martindale-Hubbell Law Directory

*UPPER MARLBORO,** Prince Georges Co.

KNIGHT, MANZI, NUSSBAUM & LAPLACA, P.C. (AV)

14440 Old Mill Road, 20772
Telephone: 301-952-0100
Annapolis/Baltimore: 410-792-3786
Fax: 301-952-0221

William E. Knight
Robert A. Manzi
Ronald M. Miller
William C. Brennan, Jr.
Harry J. Trainor, Jr.
Andrew W. Nussbaum
Raymond G. LaPlaca
John F. Shay, Jr.
Sheldon L. Gnatt
Daniel A. LaPlaca
Gail Borjeson Viens
Roger C. Thomas
Monica M. Haley-Pierson
Daniel F. Lynch III
Norman D. Rivera

Robert L. Lombardo
Amy B. Glaser
Brent M. Ahalt
Terry L. Bell

Representative Clients: Hyman Bernstein and Son, Inc.; Morrison's Restuarants; First Washington REIT; Evangel Church, Inc.; Carrollton Enterprises; Washington Homes; Southland Corp.

For full biographical listings, see the Martindale-Hubbell Law Directory

MASSACHUSETTS

ACTON, Middlesex Co.

Wilson & Orcutt, P.C. (AV)

201 Great Road, 01720
Telephone: 978-264-4770
Telecopier: 978-263-7142
Email: wilcutt@wilsonorcutt.com *URL:* http://www.wilsonorcutt.com

MEMBERS OF FIRM

Daniel B. Greenberg
Jacob C. Diemert

For full biographical listings, see the Martindale-Hubbell Law Directory

AMESBURY, Essex Co.

The Hamel Law Firm (AV)

Five Market Square, P.O. Box 198, 01913-0398
Telephone: 978-388-3558
Telecopier: 978-388-0441
Email: hamellaw@excelr8.net
Email: hamellaw@lawyers.com *URL:* http://www.lawyers.com/hamellaw

MEMBER OF FIRM

Richard P. Hamel

ASSOCIATE

Peter R. Ayer, Jr.

Representative Clients: First and Ocean National Bank, Newburyport, MA.
Approved Attorneys for: Chicago Title Insurance; Old Republic Title Insurance Co.

For Complete List of Firm Personnel, See General Section

For full biographical listings, see the Martindale-Hubbell Law Directory

*BOSTON,** Suffolk Co.

Barron & Stadfeld, P.C. (AV)

50 Staniford Street, Suite 200, 02114
Telephone: 617-723-9800
Telecopier: 617-523-8359
Email: barron@barronstad.com *URL:* HTTP://WWW.BARRONSTAD.COM
Hyannis, Massachusetts Office: 258 Winter Street.
Telephone: 617-778-6622.

Bernard A. Dwork
Enid M. Starr
Thomas V. Bennett
Edward E. Kelly
Kevin F. Moloney
David P. Dwork
Julie Taylor Moran
Robert J. Hoffer
Joseph G. Butler
Denise L. Page
Rosemary Purtell
John K. Britt

Roger T. Manwaring
Shawn P. O'Rourke
Kevin P. Scanlon
Kathleen M. Morrissey
Edward J. Fallman

OF COUNSEL

Hertz N. Henkoff

For Complete List of Firm Personnel, See General Section

For full biographical listings, see the Martindale-Hubbell Law Directory

Bernkopf, Goodman & Baseman LLP (AV)

125 Summer Street, 02110-1621
Telephone: 617-790-3000
Telecopier: 617-790-3300
URL: http://www.bgblaw.com

MEMBERS OF FIRM

Abraham K. Cohen (1891-1957)
Max E. Bernkopf (1919-1967)
Sylvan A. Goodman (1935-1981)
Kenneth M. Goldberg
Alan J. Grace
Marvin N. Geller
Neil R. Markson
Gary P. Lilienthal
James B. Fox
Peter B. McGlynn
Sheryl C. Starr
Richard B. Michaud
Lydia G. Chesnick
Martin C. Pomeroy
Eric R. Allon
David L. Doyle
John B. Harkavy
James D. Friedman

OF COUNSEL

Harris I. Baseman

ASSOCIATES

Bruce D. Levin
Richard P. Bennett
Michael J. Radin
John F. Farraher, Jr.
Todd D. Goldberg
Jason A. Manekas
Elizabeth A. Long
Richard D. Vetstein

For full biographical listings, see the Martindale-Hubbell Law Directory

Bromberg & Sunstein LLP (AV)

125 Summer Street, 11th Floor, 02110
Telephone: 617-443-9292
Fax: 617-443-0004
Email: IPLAW@bromsun.com *URL:* http://www.bromsun.com

MEMBERS OF FIRM

Bruce D. Sunstein
Lee Carl Bromberg
Kerry L. Timbers
Joel R. Leeman
Thomas C. Carey
Edward J. Dailey

ASSOCIATES

Lisa M. Fleming
Theodore E. MacVeagh
Julia Huston

For full biographical listings, see the Martindale-Hubbell Law Directory

Burns & Levinson LLP (AV)

125 Summer Street, 02110-1624
Telephone: 617-345-3000
Telecopier: 617-345-3299
URL: http://www.burnslevinson.com
Hingham, Massachusetts Office: 175 Derby Street.
Telephone: 781-749-3810.
Telecopier: 781-749-3980.
Wellesley, Massachusetts Office: 60 Walnut Street.
Telephone: 781-235-1034.
Telecopier: 781-235-5975.

Paul G. Boylan
William H. Clancy
Dennis J. Kelly
Kevin G. Kenneally
Jeffrey R. Martin
Darrell Mook
Robert J. O'Regan
Maria-Eugenia Recalde
Gary W. Smith
Paul E. Stanzler
Michael G. Tracy
Mark Ventola
Richard L. Wulsin

ASSOCIATES

Andrew P. Botti
Michael P. Giunta
Renee Inomata
John Joseph Kenney, Jr.
David M. Losier
Paul R. Mastrocola
YeWon Min
Mark F. Murphy
Virginia L. Wondolowski

For Complete List of Firm Personnel, See General Section

For full biographical listings, see the Martindale-Hubbell Law Directory

Casner & Edwards, LLP (AV)

1 Federal Street, 27th Floor, 02110-2003
Telephone: 617-426-5900
Telecopier: 617-426-8810
Email: ce@thecia.net

MEMBERS OF FIRM

Thomas D. Edwards (1931-1987)
Andrew J. Casner, Jr. (1931-1999)
Haskell A. Kassler
Walter H. Mayo, III
Martin E. Greenblatt
Charles M. Hamann
Robert A. Murphy
Robert E. Cowden, III
John H. Ashby
Douglas K. Mansfield
Andrew M. Higgins
Terrance J. Hamilton
Robert S. Kutner
David J. Chavolla
Stephen M. Perry
Gary L. Hoff
Anita W. Robboy
Peter A. Caro
Gregg S. Blackburn
Linda A. Ouellette
Joan M. Griffin

ASSOCIATES

Donna Brewer MacKenna
Gary L. Kemp
Matthew T. Murphy
Mark W. Williamson
William F. McSweeny, III
Elizabeth L. Desmond
Martha A. Coravos

For full biographical listings, see the Martindale-Hubbell Law Directory

Cherwin, Glickman & Theise, LLP (AV)

A Limited Liability Partnership including Professional Corporations
One International Place, 02110-2622
Telephone: 617-330-1625
Fax: 617-330-1642
Email: cgandt@cgandt.com

Joel I. Cherwin (P.C.)
Jay F. Theise
Marshall D. Stein
David K. Wanger
William O. Rizzo
Lisa Lee Foster
Julie A. Koshgarian

LEGAL SUPPORT PERSONNEL

Beverly Twomey (Administrator)

For full biographical listings, see the Martindale-Hubbell Law Directory

Boston—Continued

CRAIG AND MACAULEY, PROFESSIONAL CORPORATION (AV)

Federal Reserve Plaza, 600 Atlantic Avenue, 02210-2211
Telephone: 617-367-9500
Telecopier: 617-742-1788; 617-248-0886
URL: http://prospex.com/craig-macauley/

William F. Macauley
David F. Hannon
Mary P. Brody
A. Van C. Lanckton
John G. Snyder
Christopher J. Panos
Christopher S. Dalton

OF COUNSEL

John C. Craig

For Complete List of Firm Personnel, See General Section

For full biographical listings, see the Martindale-Hubbell Law Directory

DIONNE & GASS (AV)

73 Tremont Street, 02108
Telephone: 617-723-3300
Fax: 617-723-4151

Richard D. Dionne
Richard D. Gass

OF COUNSEL

Maria Tilaro Higgins
Toni Ann Motta
Michael S. Sher

For full biographical listings, see the Martindale-Hubbell Law Directory

HEMENWAY & BARNES (AV)

60 State Street, 02109
Telephone: 617-227-7940
Fax: 617-227-0781

MEMBERS OF FIRM

Alfred Hemenway (1863-1927)
Charles B. Barnes (1893-1956)
Roy A. Hammer
Lawrence T. Perera
John J. Madden
George T. Shaw
Timothy F. Fidgeon
Michael B. Elefante
Michael J. Puzo
Thomas L. Guidi
Edward Notis-McConarty
Diane C. Tillotson
Stephen W. Kidder
Susan Hughes Banning
Frederic J. Marx
Deborah J. Hall
Kurt F. Somerville
Teresa A. Belmonte
Brian C. Broderick
Charles Fayerweather

ASSOCIATES

Andrea H. Maislen
Maureen E. Curran
Joseph L. Bierwirth, Jr.
J. David Gibbs
Kendra Chencus

OF COUNSEL

George H. Kidder
David H. Morse

For Complete List of Firm Personnel, See General Section

For full biographical listings, see the Martindale-Hubbell Law Directory

HINCKLEY, ALLEN & SNYDER LLP (AV)

28 State Street, 30th Floor, 02109-1775
Telephone: 617-345-9000
Email: firm@haslaw.com *URL:* http://www.haslaw.com
Providence, Rhode Island Office: 1500 Fleet Center.
Telephone: 401-274-2000.
Fax: 401-277-9600. URL: http://www.hawlaw.com.

MEMBERS OF FIRM

Paula K. Andrews
David D. Barricelli (Not admitted in MA)
E. Jerome Batty (Not admitted in MA)
Jonathan Bell
Paul Bork
Stephen J. Carlotti (Not admitted in MA)
David Barry Connolly
Joseph P. Curran (Not admitted in MA)
Michael P. DeFanti
Eric F. Eisenberg
Malcolm Farmer, III
Margaret D. Farrell (Not admitted in MA)
Pasco Gasbarro Jr.
Bruce G. Goodman
Hugh J. Gorman, III
Alan P. Gottlieb
Gerard R. Goulet
William R. Grimm
Paul A. Hedstrom
Richard L. E. Jocelyn (Not admitted in MA)
Michael J. Kelly
Joel Lewin
Sandra Matrone Mack (Not admitted in MA)
Matthew T. Marcello, III (Not admitted in MA)
Frederick P. McClure
Elizabeth Murdock Myers
Paul F. O'Donnell, III
H. Peter Olsen (Not admitted in MA)
Julianne Palumbo
John J. Pendergast, III (Not admitted in MA)
Gerald J. Petros
James O. Reavis
Jeremy Ritzenberg
Ralph J. Rivkind
David J. Rubin
Charles E. Schaub, Jr.
Douglas F. Seaver
Scott E. Sheridan

(See Next Column)

MEMBERS OF FIRM (Continued)

Paul A. Silver
Herman Snyder
David R. Sullivan
Robert F. Sylvia
Howard E. Walker (Not admitted in MA)
Richard D. Wayne

ASSOCIATES

Jessica M. Bettencourt (Not admitted in MA)
Mark Bianchi
Alyssa V. Boss
Alexandra K. Callam
Jane E. Cohen
Andrew D. Cummings
June E. Daniel (Not admitted in MA)
Kim Herman Goslant
Gloria Maria Gutierrez
Kelley Jordan-Price
Catherine S. Kim
Christopher W. Morog
Elena B. Olson
Lawrence W. Vernaglia
Joseph D. Whelan (Not admitted in MA)

OF COUNSEL

Willard R. Pope
Bentley Tobin
Joachim A. Weissfeld (Not admitted in MA)

For Complete List of Firm Personnel, See General Section

For full biographical listings, see the Martindale-Hubbell Law Directory

LOONEY & GROSSMAN LLP (AV)

101 Arch Street, 02110-1112
Telephone: 617-951-2800
Fax: 617-951-2819
URL: http://www.lgllp.com

Stewart F. Grossman (P.C.)
Richard J. Grahn
Bertram E. Snyder
Robert Cushman Barber
Joseph H. Matzkin
Wesley S. Chused
Melvin S. Hoffman

SENIOR COUNSEL

William F. Looney, Jr.

OF COUNSEL

Sherman H. Starr, Jr.
Elizabeth M. Adler
Maria Galvagna Mesinger

ASSOCIATES

Adam J. Ruttenberg
Pamela A. Harbeson
Mary E. Corbett
Benjamin D. Stevenson
Edward V. Colbert, III

For full biographical listings, see the Martindale-Hubbell Law Directory

MENARD, MURPHY & WALSH LLP (AV)

One Financial Center, 02111
Telephone: 617-832-2500
Telecopier: 617-832-2550
Email: mmw@mmwlaw.com
Washington, D.C. Office: Farragut Park, 910 17th Street, NW, Suite 800, 20006.
Telephone: 202-293-3500.
Telecopier: 202-293-3596.

Arthur P. Menard
Paul J. Murphy
Joseph H. Walsh
John E. Coyne
John S. Leonard

COUNSEL

Theodore E. Daiber

ASSOCIATES

Kevin G. Mahoney
Kevin P. Sweeney
Robert S. Steinberg

For full biographical listings, see the Martindale-Hubbell Law Directory

PALMER & DODGE LLP (AV)

One Beacon Street, 02108
Telephone: 617-573-0100
Facsimile: 617-227-4420
URL: http://www.palmerdodge.com

MEMBERS OF FIRM

F. Andrew Anderson
James T. Barrett
Matthew C. Dallett
Jeanne P. Darcey
Lynnette C. Fallon
Steven N. Farber
Mark A. Fischer
Christopher M. Flanagan
Nathaniel S. Gardiner
Richard Hiersteiner
Malcolm E. Hindin
Stanley Keller
Michael Lytton
Maureen P. Manning
Steven L. Paul
David R. Pokross, Jr.
John A. Rissman (Not admitted in MA)
Marc A. Rubenstein
Yvonne E. Schlaeppi (Not admitted in MA)
Thomas M. Spera
George Ticknor
John L. Whitlock
John Taylor Williams

For Complete List of Firm Personnel, See General Section

For full biographical listings, see the Martindale-Hubbell Law Directory

Boston—Continued

SHERIN AND LODGEN LLP (AV)

100 Summer Street, 02110
Telephone: 617-426-5720
Fax: 617-542-5186
Email: lawyers@sherin.com *URL:* http://www.sherin.com
Los Angeles, California Office: 11300 W. Olympic Boulevard, Suite 700.
Telephone: 310-914-7891.
Fax: 310-552-5327.

MEMBERS OF FIRM

Arthur L. Sherin (1946-1964)
George E. Lodgen (1946-1971)
Morton B. Brown
George Waldstein
John M. Reed
Robert J. Muldoon, Jr.
Alette E. Reed
Edward M. Bloom
Joshua M. Alper
Gary M. Markoff
Bryan G. Killian
David A. Guberman
Frank J. Bailey
Kenneth J. Mickiewicz
Craig M. Brown
Thomas A. Hippler
Ronald W. Ruth
Mark A. Nowak
Thomas P. Gorman
Steven D. Eimert
Andrew Royce
John J. Slater III
John C. La Liberte
C. Forbes Sargent III
David A. Brown
Michael S. Strauss
Christopher A. Kenney

ASSOCIATES

Robert M. Carney
Caroline Woodward
Michael S. Bloom
Kenneth D. Small
Margaret H. Paget
Michael J. Ostroskey
James M. Wodarski
Jessica R. Yaffie
William P. Keefe
Amy D. Porter
Thomas F. Dunn
Brian G. Luneau
Michael P. Sams
Erin M. McNamara
James W. Matthews
Thomas S. Dean

OF COUNSEL

Janet E. Bostwick
Kurt A. James

For full biographical listings, see the Martindale-Hubbell Law Directory

*CAMBRIDGE,** Middlesex Co.

BARRETT & ASSOCIATES (AV)

One Kendall Square, Suite 2200, 02139
Telephone: 617-621-1579
Fax: 617-621-1556
Email: barrettd@earthlink.net

Donal B. Barrett

For full biographical listings, see the Martindale-Hubbell Law Directory

HOLYOKE, Hampden Co.

LYON, FERRITER & FITZPATRICK, LLP (AV)

Whitney Place, 14 Bobala Road, 01040
Telephone: 413-536-4000
Fax: 413-536-3773
Email: lyonferr@aol.com

MEMBERS OF FIRM

Maurice J. Ferriter
Clarke S. Lyon
William D. Fitzpatrick
James F. Donnelly
Peter C. Connor
John J. Ferriter
Priscilla Fifield Chesky
Robert C. Sacco

ASSOCIATE

Robyn Andrea Porter

OF COUNSEL

William E. Begley

Representative Clients: Mount Holyoke College; Newspapers of New England, Inc.; Loomis House Retirement Community; Atlas Copco Compressors Inc.; Hazen Paper Company.

For full biographical listings, see the Martindale-Hubbell Law Directory

LOWELL, Middlesex Co.

DONAHUE & DONAHUE, ATTORNEYS, P.C. (AV)

21 George Street, 01852
Telephone: 978-458-6887
Fax: 978-458-3424

Daniel J. Donahue (1860-1939)
Joseph P. Donahue (1889-1973)
Charles A. Donahue (1891-1964)
Richard K. Donahue
Joseph P. Donahue, Jr.
Joseph D. Regan
Michael W. Gallagher
Richard K. Donahue, Jr.
Andrea S. Barisano
Matthew C. Donahue
Richard E. Cavanaugh
Kelly R. Spencer
Alicia A. Donahue

(See Next Column)

Kelly M. Quigley

Representative Clients: The Travelers Insurance Co.; Ciro's Restaurants; Black & Decker; Jim Witt Automotive Group; Demoulas Super Markets, Inc.

For full biographical listings, see the Martindale-Hubbell Law Directory

GOLDMAN & CURTIS, P.C. (AV)

Lowell Place, 144 Merrimack Street, 01852
Telephone: 978-454-8804; 729-2625
Fax: 978-459-2730

Frank Goldman (1890-1965)
Robert H. Goldman (1918-1991)
James T. Curtis
Cornelia C. Adams
Gregory T. Curtis
Carolyn L. Greenberg
James T. Curtis, Jr.

OF COUNSEL

Efthemios J. Bentas
Matthew P. Demaras

For full biographical listings, see the Martindale-Hubbell Law Directory

*WORCESTER,** Worcester Co.

SEDER & CHANDLER (AV)

A Partnership including a Professional Corporation
Established 1918
Burnside Building, 339 Main Street, 01608
Telephone: 508-757-7721
Telecopiers: 508-798-1863; 508-831-0955

MEMBERS OF FIRM

Samuel Seder (1918-1964)
Harold Seder (1934-1988)
Burton Chandler
J. Robert Seder
Darragh K. Kasakoff
Marvin S. Silver, P.C.
Robert S. Adler
Kevin C. McGee
Kurt L. Binder

ASSOCIATES

Paul J. O'Riordan
Jeffrey P. Greenberg
Todd Rodman

OF COUNSEL

Saul A. Seder
Gerald E. Norman
Philip C. Lombardo, Jr.

Reference: First National Bank of Boston; Safety Fund National Bank; Fleet National Bank.

For full biographical listings, see the Martindale-Hubbell Law Directory

MICHIGAN

*ANN ARBOR,** Washtenaw Co.

HOOPER, HATHAWAY, PRICE, BEUCHE & WALLACE (AV)

126 South Main Street, 48104
Telephone: 313-662-4426
Fax: 313-662-9559
Email: hhpbw@voyager.net

James R. Beuche
Charles W. Borgsdorf
Kurtis R. Dumaw

Representative Clients: Avfuel Corporation; Bank of Ann Arbor; Castrol North America; Chem-Trend Incorporated; Ervin Industries, Inc.; First Martin Corporation; Glacier Hills, Inc.; Prestolite Electric, Inc.; Southern States Cooperative; E.B. Eddy Forest Products, Ltd.

For Complete List of Firm Personnel, See General Section

For full biographical listings, see the Martindale-Hubbell Law Directory

PEAR SPERLING EGGAN & MUSKOVITZ, P.C. (AV)

Domino's Farms, 24 Frank Lloyd Wright Drive, 48105
Telephone: 734-665-4441
Fax: 734-665-8788
Email: peare@dominos.com
Ypsilanti, Michigan Offices: 5 South Washington Street.
Telephone: 734-483-3626 and 2164 Bellevue at Washtenaw.
Telephone: 734-483-7177.

Edwin L. Pear
Lawrence W. Sperling
Andrew M. Eggan
Melvin J. Muskovitz
Thomas E. Daniels
Joel F. Graziani
Paul R. Fransway
Francyne Stacey
Karl V. Fink
Scott H. Mandel
David E. Kempner
Jeffrey P. Thennisch

Counsel for: Domino's Pizza, Inc.; Townsend and Bottum, Inc.; Cleary College; Victory Lane Quick Oil Change Inc.; Citizens Banking Corp.; Washtenaw News Co., Inc.; Ann Arbor Transportation Authority; Meadowbrook Insurance Group; Michigan Municipal Liability & Property Pool.

(See Next Column)

PEAR SPERLING EGGAN & MUSKOVITZ P.C.—*Continued*

Approved Attorneys for: Lawyers Title Insurance Corp.

For full biographical listings, see the Martindale-Hubbell Law Directory

BATTLE CREEK, Calhoun Co.

KREIS, ENDERLE, CALLANDER & HUDGINS, A PROFESSIONAL CORPORATION (AV)

One West Michigan Avenue, 49017
Telephone: 616-966-3000
Facsimile: 616-966-3022
Email: kech@kech.com *URL:* http://www.kech.com
Kalamazoo, Michigan Office: One Moorsbridge, P.O. Box 4010, 49003-4010.
Telephone: 616-324-3000.
Fax: 616-324-3010.

Russell A. Kreis (Resident, Kalamazoo Office)
C. Reid Hudgins III (Resident, Kalamazoo Office)
Robert B. Borsos (Resident, Kalamazoo Office)
Jeffrey C. O'Brien (Resident, Kalamazoo Office)
Stephen J. Hessen (Resident, Kalamazoo Office)
Thomas G. King (Resident, Kalamazoo Office)
Stephen L. Simons
Mark E. Kreter
Daniel P. McGlinn (Resident, Kalamazoo Office)
Janice Roark Peters (Resident, Kalamazoo Office)
Matthew S. DePerno (Resident, Kalamazoo Office)
Peter F. Davis (Resident, Kalamazoo Office)
Manuel R. Rupe (Resident, Kalamazoo Office)

For Complete List of Firm Personnel, See General Section

For full biographical listings, see the Martindale-Hubbell Law Directory

BINGHAM FARMS, Oakland Co.

MEISNER & ASSOCIATES, P.C. (AV)

Suite 467, 30200 Telegraph Road, 48025-4506
Telephone: 248-644-4433
Fax: 248-644-2941
Email: bmeisner@mich.com *URL:* http://www.meisner-law.com

Robert M. Meisner

Robert R. Maxwell
Richard M. Delonis

For full biographical listings, see the Martindale-Hubbell Law Directory

SMALL, TOTH, BALDRIDGE & VAN BELKUM, P.C. (AV)

30100 Telegraph Road Suite 250, 48025-4516
Telephone: 248-647-9595
Facsimile: 248-647-9599

Richard L. Small
John M. Toth
David M. Baldridge
Thomas G. Van Belkum
Keith P. Felty

Stephanie A. Griz-Kochkodan
Kristin Allen

Representative Clients: Michigan Society of Oral and Maxillofacial Surgeons; Michigan Association of Orthodontists; Michigan Association of Endodontists; Illinois Society of Oral and Maxillofacial Surgeons; California Association of Oral and Maxillofacial Surgeons; New York Society of Oral and Maxillofacial Surgeons.

For full biographical listings, see the Martindale-Hubbell Law Directory

BIRMINGHAM, Oakland Co.

HYMAN LIPPITT, P.C. (AV)

185 Oakland Avenue, Suite 300, 48009
Telephone: 248-646-8292
Facsimile: 248-646-8375
Email: hymalipp@tir.com

J. Leonard Hyman
Norman L. Lippitt
Douglas A. Hyman
Brian D. O'Keefe
H. Joel Newman
Nazli G. Sater
Kenneth F. Neuman
Terry S. Givens
Paul J. Fischer
John A. Sellers
Robert H. Lippitt
Roger L. Myers
Sally A. Rutledge
Joseph Pia
John P. Gonway
Leif K. Anderson
Jennifer S. Gold
Julie Lyons Kosovec
Dawn S. Spratley
Michael T. Price

For full biographical listings, see the Martindale-Hubbell Law Directory

BLOOMFIELD HILLS, Oakland Co.

ADKISON, NEED, GREEN & ALLEN (AV)

1533 North Woodward Avenue, Suite 210, 48304
Telephone: 248-540-7400
Fax: 248-540-7401
URL: http://www.adkisonneed.com

MEMBERS OF FIRM

Phillip G. Adkison
Gregory K. Need
Paul Green
Kelly A. Allen

For Complete List of Firm Personnel, See General Section

For full biographical listings, see the Martindale-Hubbell Law Directory

COLOMBO AND COLOMBO, P.C. (AV)

1701 N. Woodward Avenue Suite 50, P.O. Box 2028, 48303-2028
Telephone: 248-645-9300
Facsimile: 248-645-5418
Email: C&C@Colombopc.com

Louis J. Colombo
Louis J. Colombo, Jr. (1911-1979)
Frederick Colombo
Charles A. LeFevre
John P. Hartwig
Lawrence F. Raniszeski
Robert Y. Weller, II
Michael J. O'Shaughnessy

Patrick J. Ennis
Michael J. Weikert

OF COUNSEL

Russell E. Knister
David J. Wellman
James H. Hudnut
Peter Leto (P.C.)

For full biographical listings, see the Martindale-Hubbell Law Directory

DAWDA, MANN, MULCAHY & SADLER, P.L.C. (AV)

1533 North Woodward Avenue Suite 200, 48304-2815
Telephone: 248-642-3700
Fax: 248-642-7791
Email: EMail@DMMS.Com

Michael D. Mulcahy
Edward C. Dawda
Curtis J. Mann
Paul A. Bringer
Glenn G. Ross
William L. Rosin
Todd A. Schafer

Daniel M. Halprin
Paul C. Apap
Daniel M. Israel
Wayne S. Segal
Vincent J. Wilk
Richard S. Bailey

Representative Clients: AEGON USA Realty Advisors, Inc.; BASF Corp.; Cardell Corp.; Cargill, Inc.; City Management; Ford Motor Company; Ladbroke Racing Corp.; La-Z-Boy, Inc.; The Sherwin-Williams Company.

For full biographical listings, see the Martindale-Hubbell Law Directory

DROLET, FREEMAN, COTTON & NORRIS, P.C. (AV)

33 Bloomfield Hills Parkway, Suite 100, 48304
Telephone: 248-642-2255
Fax: 248-642-6460
Email: droletfreeman@voyager.net

David G. Barnett (1915-1989)
H. William Freeman
J. Kingsley Cotton, III
Matthew C. Norris

Brian P. Henry
Suzanne S. Reynolds
Lauren D. Honet
David M. Blau

Representative Clients: Angelo Iafrate Construction Co.; ASC, Incorporated; Cadillac Asphalt Paving Co.; Carroll Packaging, Inc.; Choice Hotels International; Clawson Concrete Co.; Commerica Bank; Corrosion Control Engineering; Emcor; Farmington Public Schools.

For full biographical listings, see the Martindale-Hubbell Law Directory

HARDIG PARSONS PEDERSEN & STOUT, PLLC (AV)

74 West Long Lake Road, Suite 203, 48304
Telephone: 248-642-3500
Facsimile: 248-645-1128
URL: http://www.hpplaw.com
Charlevoix, Michigan Office: 212 Bridge Street. 49720.
Telephone: 616-547-1200.
Pawleys Island, South Caroline Office: 216 Highway 17. P.O. Box 1607. 29585.
Telephone: 803-237-9121.
West Palm Beach, Florida Office: 1450 North Bridge Tower. 515 North Flagler. 33401.
Telephone: 561-833-1622.

(See Next Column)

HARDIG PARSONS PEDERSEN & STOUT PLLC, *Bloomfield Hills—Continued*

MEMBERS OF FIRM

Joseph L. Hardig, Jr.
Donald H. Parsons (Resident, Charlevoix Office)
Joseph L. Hardig, III
Edward C. Pedersen
Bradley S. Stout
John C. Benso (Not admitted in MI; Resident, Pawleys Island, South Carolina Office)

OF COUNSEL

John W. Henke
Patrick T. Barone
Gordon A. Snavely
Robert J. Cucco
Edward K. Pedersen, Jr.

For full biographical listings, see the Martindale-Hubbell Law Directory

HERTZ, SCHRAM & SARETSKY, P.C. (AV)

1760 South Telegraph Road, Suite 300, 48302
Telephone: 248-335-5000
Fax: 248-335-3346
Email: lawhss@aol.com *URL:* http://www.legalleaders.com

Bradley J. Schram
Howard Hertz
Gary M. Saretsky
Robert S. Hertzberg
Victor M. Norris
Steve J. Weiss
Robert Paul Geller
Walter J. Piszczatowski
Jeffrey A. Robbins
Mark L. Kowalsky

Dana A. Donohue
Miles D. Hart
Karen A. Gould
Paul K. Villarruel
Bradford T. Yaker
Michael F. Jacobson
Michael I. Zousmer
Brian Witus
Eva T. Cantarella
Eric Andrew Michaels

COUNSEL

Richard P. Zipser
Lisa M. Kavalhuna (Not admitted in MI)
James W. Burdick

OF COUNSEL

David L. Steinberg
Albert L. Holtz
Elmer L. Roller
Robert A. Canner
Harvey D. Geller (1928-1989)

For full biographical listings, see the Martindale-Hubbell Law Directory

HOWARD & HOWARD ATTORNEYS, P.C. (AV)

The Pinehurst Office Center, Suite 101, 1400 North Woodward Avenue, 48304-2855
Telephone: 248-645-1483
Telecopier: 248-645-1568
Kalamazoo, Michigan Office: The Michigan Building, Suite 200, 100 Portage Street.
Telephone: 616-382-1483.
Telecopier: 616-382-1568.
Lansing, Michigan Office: The Phoenix Building, Suite 500, 222 Washington Square, North.
Telephone: 517-485-1483.
Telecopier: 517-485-1568.
Peoria, Illinois Office: One Technology Plaza, Suite 600, 211 Fulton Street.
Telephone: 309-672-1483.
Telecopier: 309-672-1568.

Brian R. Balow
James T. Bork
Mark A. Davis
Christopher R. Herter
Robert B. Johnston
Douglas R. Kelly
Timothy E. Kraepel
David B. Lipski
Lee A. Sartori
Robert L. Schwartz
Jon Robert Steiger
Donald F. Tucker
James C. Wickens
Timothy M. Wittebort
John E. Young

Representative Clients: For Representative Client list, see General Practice, Bloomfield Hills, MI.

For Complete List of Firm Personnel, See General Section

For full biographical listings, see the Martindale-Hubbell Law Directory

MEYER, KIRK, SNYDER & SAFFORD, PLLC (AV)

Suite 100, 100 West Long Lake Road, 48304
Telephone: 248-647-5111
Telecopier: 248-647-6079
Email: mkss@michbar.org
Detroit, Michigan Office: 1400 Ford Building, 615 Griswold, 48226.
Telephone: 313-961-1261.

George H. Meyer
John M. Kirk
Donald H. Baker, Jr.

Michelle R. Puricelli

Representative Clients: Available Upon Request.

For full biographical listings, see the Martindale-Hubbell Law Directory

DAVID D. PATTON & ASSOCIATES, P.C. (AV)

44 East Long Lake Road, Suite 100, P.O. Box 829, 48303-0829
Telephone: 248-258-6020
Fax: 248-258-6052
Email: litigation@aol.com *URL:* http://www.lawyers.com/dpattonlaw

David D. Patton

Ellen Bartman Jannette
Patricia C. White
Humma S. Siddiqi
Kelly P. Bekolay
David H. Patton (1912-1993)

OF COUNSEL

Lawrence J. Acker

For full biographical listings, see the Martindale-Hubbell Law Directory

PROVIZER & PHILLIPS, P.C. (AV)

6785 Telegraph Road, Suite 400, 48301
Telephone: 248-642-0444
Facsimile: 248-642-6661
Toll Free: 1-800-288-9080
URL: http://www.lawyers.com/provizer&phillips

Harold M. Provizer
Randall E. Phillips
Marilyn A. Madorsky
Noel F. Beck
Mark S. Baumkel

Constance S. Hall
Ellen C. Busch
Donald J. Parthum, Jr.

Representative Clients: Investaid Corp.; Leo, Frank & Sims; Mortgage Institute of Michigan; Norm's Jewelry & Loan.

For full biographical listings, see the Martindale-Hubbell Law Directory

ROY SHECTER & VOCHT (AV)

36700 Woodward Avenue, Suite 205, 48304
Telephone: 248-540-7660
Fax: 248-540-0321
URL: http://www.lawyers.com/royshecter&vocht

MEMBERS OF FIRM

William A. Roy
Lynn H. Shecter
Michelle E. Vocht

For full biographical listings, see the Martindale-Hubbell Law Directory

CLARKSTON, Oakland Co.

BULLARD, ANDERSON & ANDERSON, PLLC (AV)

6060 Dixie Highway, Suite H, 48346-3476
Telephone: 248-623-3888
Fax: 248-623-1883
Email: firm@baalaw.com *URL:* http://www.baalaw.com

Rockwood W. Bullard III
Rae Anne Anderson
Acie G. Anderson, III

Representative Clients: ANCAR Publications, Inc.; Audio Trends, Inc.; AVC, Inc. (Advanced Visual Concepts); Clarkston Realty, Inc.; GAC Mortgage Co.; Michaelene's Granola, Inc.; Morgan Service, Inc.; Smith Disposal, Inc.; Sunview Windows, Skylights & Doors, Ltd.
Reference: NBD Bank, NA.

For full biographical listings, see the Martindale-Hubbell Law Directory

*DETROIT,** Wayne Co.

ABBOTT, NICHOLSON, QUILTER, ESSHAKI & YOUNGBLOOD, P.C. (AV)

300 River Place, Suite 3000, 48207-4225
Telephone: 313-566-2500
Telecopier: 313-566-2502
Email: anqey@anqey.com *URL:* http://www.anqey.com

C. Richard Abbott
John R. Nicholson
Thomas R. Quilter III
Gene J. Esshaki
John F. Youngblood
James B. Perry
Carl F. Jarboe
Jay A. Kennedy
Timothy A. Stoepker
Timothy J. Kramer
Norbert T. Madison, Jr.
William D. Gilbride, Jr.
Mary P. Nelson
Michael R. Blum
Anne Warren Bagno
Thomas J. Giachino

Eric J. Girdler
Jill A. Bankey
Daniel G. Kielczewski
George P. Butler III
Christopher P. Baker
Faith M. Gaudaen

OF COUNSEL

Thomas C. Shumaker
Lisa R. Gorman

For full biographical listings, see the Martindale-Hubbell Law Directory

Detroit—Continued

BODMAN, LONGLEY & DAHLING LLP (AV)

34th Floor 100 Renaissance Center, 48243
Telephone: 313-259-7777
Fax: 313-393-7579
Email: info@bodmanlongley.com *URL:* http://www.bodmanlongley.com
Troy, Michigan Office: Suite 2020, 755 West Big Beaver Road.
Telephone: 248-362-2110.
Fax: 248-244-0780.
Ann Arbor, Michigan Office: 110 Miller, Suite 300.
Telephone: 734-761-3780.
Fax: 734-930-2494.
Northern Michigan Office: 229 Court Street, P.O. Box 405, Cheboygan.
Telephone: 231-627-4351.
Fax: 231-627-2802.

MEMBERS OF FIRM

Richard D. Rohr
Walter O. Koch (Troy Office)
Michael B. Lewiston
George D. Miller, Jr.
Mark W. Griffin (Ann Arbor Office)
Thomas A. Roach (Ann Arbor Office)
Kenneth R. Lango (Troy Office)
James T. Heimbuch
Herold McC. Deason
James R. Buschmann
Joseph J. Kochanek
David G. Chardavoyne
Terrence B. Larkin (Troy Office)
Robert J. Diehl, Jr.
Harvey W. Berman (Ann Arbor Office)
Barbara A. Bowman
Sandra L. Sorini (Ann Arbor Office)

COUNSEL

Lewis A. Rockwell

ASSOCIATES

Deanna L. Dixon
Timothy R. Damschroder (Ann Arbor Office)
Rachelle Propson Tyshka
Gene P. Bowen (Troy Office)
Forrest O. Dillon
Ursula A. Petrozzi

For Representative Client List, See General Section.

For Complete List of Firm Personnel, See General Section

For full biographical listings, see the Martindale-Hubbell Law Directory

BUTZEL LONG, A PROFESSIONAL CORPORATION (AV)

Suite 900, 150 West Jefferson, 48226
Telephone: 313-225-7000
Telecopier: 313-225-7080
Email: melnick@butzel.com *URL:* http://www.butzel.com
Birmingham, Michigan Office: Suite 200, 32270 Telegraph Road.
Telephone: 810-258-1616.
Telecopier: 810-258-1439.
Okemos, Michigan Office: Suite 300, 2127 University Park Drive.
Telephone: 517-372-6622.
Telecopier: 517-372-6672.
Ann Arbor, Michigan Office: Suite 300, 350 South Main Street.
Telephone: 313-995-3110.
Telecopier: 313-995-1777.
Grosse Pointe Farms, Michigan Office: Suite 260, 21 Kercheval.
Telephone: 313-886-5446.
Telecopier: 313-886-2114.
Boca Raton, Florida Office: Suite 411, 1200 North Federal Highway.
Telephone: 561-368-2151.
Telecopier: 561-368-4668.
Palm Beach Gardens, Florida Office: Suite 227, 11382 Prosperity Farms Road.
Telephone: 561-625-4442.
Telecopier: 561-625-6901.
Naples, Florida Office: Suite 705, 801 Laurel Oak Drive.
Telephone: 941-597-4500.
Telecopier: 941-597-5623.

Frank B. Vecchio (Birmingham)
C. Peter Theut
Robert B. Foster (Ann Arbor)
Paul L. Triemstra (Birmingham)
James C. Bruno
John J. Raymond, Jr. (Boca Raton, Naples and Palm Beach Gardens, Florida and Birmingham)
Carl Rashid, Jr.
Justin G. Klimko
Michael F. Golab (Birmingham)
James L. Hughes
Arthur Dudley II
Gordon W. Didier (Birmingham)
Terry O. Lang
James Y. Stewart (Birmingham)
Melvin J. Hollowell, Jr.
Nicholas J. Stasevich

SENIOR ATTORNEYS

Matthew E. Wilkins
Eric R. Wapnick
Gustaf R. Andreasen

Michael F. Matheson (Okemos)

Representative Clients: American Tape Co.; Complete Business Solutions, Inc.; The Detroit News, Inc.; Dunham's Athleisure, Inc.; Harvard Industries; Jackson National Life Insurance Co.; Ricardo Companies; Stroh Companies; Takata, Inc.; William Beaumont Hospital.

For full biographical listings, see the Martindale-Hubbell Law Directory

JAFFE, RAITT, HEUER & WEISS, PROFESSIONAL CORPORATION (AV)

One Woodward Avenue, Suite 2400, 48226
Telephone: 313-961-8380
Telecopier: 313-961-8358
Cable Address: "Jafsni"
Southfield,Michigan Office: Travelers Tower, Suite 1520.
Telephone: 313-961-8380.

Derek S. Adolf
Wallace H. Glendening
Robert J. Gordon
Jeffrey G. Heuer
Blair B. Hysni
Ira J. Jaffe
Robin H. Krueger
Mark P. Krysinski
Joel J. Morris
Stephen G. Schafer
Elliot A. Spoon
David D. Warner
Arthur A. Weiss
Jeffrey M. Weiss
Richard A. Zussman

Carla Mecoli Kamp

Representative Clients: Durr Industries; Edgemere Enterprises; McClain Industries, Inc.; New England Mutual Life Insurance Co.

For Complete List of Firm Personnel, See General Section

For full biographical listings, see the Martindale-Hubbell Law Directory

LEWIS & MUNDAY, A PROFESSIONAL CORPORATION (AV)

(Formerly Lewis, Clay & Munday, P.C.)
1300 First National Building, 660 Woodward Avenue, 48226-3531
Telephone: 313-961-2550
Fax: 313-961-1270
Email: camille.miller@lewis-pc.com *URL:* http://www.lewis-pc.com
Washington, D.C. Office: 1120 Connecticut Avenue, Suite 280. 20036.
Telephone: 202-835-0616.
Fax: 202-833-3316.
Boston, Massachusetts Office: 101 Federal Street, Suite 1900. 02110.
Telephone: 617-478-0553.
Fax: 617-478-0543.

David Baker Lewis
Reuben A. Munday
Camille Stearns Miller
Jacqueline H. Sellers
David N. Zacks
Thomas J. Guyer
Blair A. Person
Karen Kendrick Brown (Resident, Washington, D.C. Office)
Susan D. Hoffman
Hans J. Massaquoi, Jr.

Althea Lynn Simpson
Donica Thomas Varner
Kris W. Krueger
Cylenthia LaToye Miller
Joseph N. Ejbeh
Yolanda R. Bates
Caroletta L. Edgar-Sprinkle
Derek G. McBride
Ayanna Weber
Deborah Jean Williamson
Darice Elizabeth Weber
Krystal M. Gardner
Syeda Taqi

COUNSEL

G. Allen Bass (Resident, Boston, Massachusetts Office)
Leamon R. Sowell, Jr.
Gail Pabarue Bennett
Roger M. Groves
Carol H. Rodriguez
Linda M. Bruton
Brian J. Kott

OF COUNSEL

Otis M. Smith (1922-1994)
Herbert O. Reid, Sr. (1915-1991)

Representative Clients: Aetna Life & Casualty Co.; Chrysler Motors Corp.; Chrysler Financial Corp.; MCI Communications Corp.; City of Detroit; City of Detroit Building Authority; City of Detroit Downtown Development Authority; Consolidated Rail Corp. (Conrail); Equitable Life Assurance Society of the United States.

For full biographical listings, see the Martindale-Hubbell Law Directory

MEYER, KIRK, SNYDER & SAFFORD, PLLC (AV)

1400 Ford Building, 615 Griswold, 48226
Telephone: 313-961-1261
Fax: 248-647-6079
Bloomfield Hills, Michigan Office: Suite 100, 100 West Long Lake Road.
Telephone: 248-647-5111.
Telecopier: 248-647-6079.

George H. Meyer
John M. Kirk
Donald H. Baker, Jr.

Michelle R. Puricelli

Representative Clients: Available Upon Request.

For full biographical listings, see the Martindale-Hubbell Law Directory

Detroit—Continued

MILLER, CANFIELD, PADDOCK AND STONE, P.L.C. (AV)

A Professional Limited Liability Company
Founded in 1852 by Sidney Davy Miller
150 West Jefferson, Suite 2500, 48226-4415
Telephone: 313-963-6420
Fax: 313-496-7500
Cable Address: "Stem Detroit"
URL: http://www.millercanfield.com
Ann Arbor, Michigan Office: 101 North Main Street, 7th Floor, 48104-1400.
Telephone: 734-663-2445.
Fax: 734-747-7147.
Troy, Michigan Office: 840 West Long Lake Road, Suite 200, 48098.
Telephone: 248-879-2000.
Fax: 248-879-2001.
Grand Rapids, Michigan Office: 99 Monroe, N.W., Suite 1200, 49503-2639.
Telephone: 616-454-8656.
Fax: 616-776-6322.
Howell, Michigan Office: 121 South Barnard Street, Suite 4, 48843-2305.
Telephone: 517-546-7600.
Telecopier: 517-546-6974.
Kalamazoo, Michigan Office: 444 West Michigan Avenue, 49007-3752.
Telephone: 616-381-7030.
Fax: 616-382-0244.
Lansing, Michigan Office: One Michigan Avenue, Suite 900, 48933-1609.
Telephone: 517-487-2070.
Fax: 517-374-6304.
Monroe, Michigan Office: 214 East Elm Avenue, Suite 100, 48162-2682.
Telephone: 734-243-2000.
Fax: 734-243-0901.
Washington, D.C. Office: 1900 K Street, N.W., Suite 1150. 20006.
Telephone: 202-429-5575; 785-0600.
Fax: 202-331-1118; 785-1234.
Pensacola, Florida Office: 25 West Cedar, 32501.
Telephone: 850-469-1088.
Fax: 850-432-0677.
New York, New York Office: 1450 Broadway, 41st Floor, 10018.
Telephone: 212-704-4400.
Fax: 212-704-4410.
Gdynia, Poland Office: UL. Slaska 21, 81-319.
Telephone: 011-485-831-2808.
Fax: 011-48-58-628 6411.
Warsaw, Poland Office: UL. Nowogrodzkall, 5th Floor, 00-513.
Telephone: 011-4822 529 0200.
Fax: 011-4822 529 0201.
Katowice, Poland Office: UL. Francuska 35/37, 40-027.
Telephone: 011 (48-32) 757-2414.
Fax: 011 (48-32) 757-2483.

PRINCIPALS OF FIRM

Eric V. Brown, Jr. (Kalamazoo Office)
Bruce D. Birgbauer
Erik H. Serr (Ann Arbor Office)
John A. Campbell (Kalamazoo Office)
David D. Joswick (P.C.)
Kent E. Shafer
John R. Cook (Kalamazoo Office)
Mark E. Putney (Grand Rapids Office)
Terrence M. Crawford
Thomas H. Van Dis (Kalamazoo Office)
Karen A. McCoy
Steven M. Stankewicz (Kalamazoo Office)
J. David Reck (Ann Arbor and Howell Offices)

OF COUNSEL/SENIOR COUNSEL

Eric V. Brown, Sr. (Kalamazoo Office)

Representative Firm Clients: Chrysler Corporation; Comerica, Incorporated; City of Detroit, Michigan; Detroit Tigers, Inc.; First of Michigan; Ford Motor Company; Ford Motor Credit Company; Great Lakes Bancorp; Henry Ford Hospital; INVETECH Company.

For Complete List of Firm Personnel, See General Section

For full biographical listings, see the Martindale-Hubbell Law Directory

DAVID M. THOMS & ASSOCIATES, P.C. (AV)

400 Renaissance Center, Suite 950, 48243
Telephone: 313-259-6333
Facsimile: 313-259-7037
Email: Thoms@ameritech.net *URL:* http://www.lawyers.com/thoms&associates

David M. Thoms

Audrey R. Holley
Danielle M. Spehar
Joseph A. Durocher

Representative Clients: Avion Concepts, Inc.; Gibbs World Wide Wines, Inc.; deBary Voyage, Inc.; North Management, Inc.; R.G. & G.R. Harris Funeral Home, Inc.; St. Jude Children's Research Hospital; The Salvation Army.
References: Comerica Bank-Detroit; National Bank of Detroit.

For full biographical listings, see the Martindale-Hubbell Law Directory

TIMMIS & INMAN L.L.P. (AV)

300 Talon Centre, 48207
Telephone: 313-396-4200
Facsimile: 313-396-4228
Email: info@timmis-inman.com *URL:* http://www.timmis-inman.com

Michael T. Timmis
Robert E. Graziani
George A. Peck
Henry J. Brennan, III
Mark W. Peyser
Richard M. Miettinen
Bradley J. Knickerbocker
George M. Malis

Michael F. Wais
Erich J. D'Andrea
Shannon M. Nichols
Alex N. Saleh

OF COUNSEL

William B. Fitzgerald
David E. Costa

LEGAL SUPPORT PERSONNEL

PARALEGALS

Linda M. Bierl

Representative Clients: Detroit Mortgage & Realty; DMR Fiancial Services, Inc.; J. Levin Sons Co.; Green Tree Financial Servicing Corp.; Hematology-Oncology Associates East, PC; Lakeshore Ear, Nose & Throat Center, PC; Micromanagement Systems, Inc.; Phoenix Crystal Corp.; Talon Surfaces LLC; Talon Automated Equipment Company.

For Complete List of Firm Personnel, See General Section

For full biographical listings, see the Martindale-Hubbell Law Directory

WISE & MARSAC, PROFESSIONAL CORPORATION (AV)

11th Floor Buhl Building, 48226-3681
Telephone: 313-962-0643
Telecopier: 313-962-0688
URL: http://www.wisemarsac.com
Ann Arbor, Michigan Office: 300 North Fifth Avenue, Suite 230.
Telephone: 734-213-2700.
Birmingham, Michigan Office: 255 East Brown Street, Suite 210.
Telephone: 248-642-4345.
Affiliate Offices: Williams Mullen Christian & Dobbins, Richmond, Virginia/Washington, D.C.; Giles & Associates, London, England.

Stephen M. Fleming (1951-1998)
John A. Wise
Robert A. Marsac
Eric H. Lipsitt
Edward V. Keelean
Daniel F. Berry
Lisa A. Robinson
Richard P. Manczak
Thomas E. Dew (Resident, Ann Arbor Office)
Guy P. Hoadley
Gary A. Kendra
Jeannine F. Gleeson-Smith (Resident, Birmingham Office)
Mark T. Butler
Scott A. Steinhoff (Resident, Birmingham Office)

OF COUNSEL

Louis J. Burnett (Resident, Birmingham Office)
Robert E. Day
Julious P. Smith, Jr. (Not admitted in MI)

SENIOR COUNSEL

Albert L. Lieberman
William D. Maroney (Not admitted in MI)
Elijah Poxson

Gayle L. Landrum
John F. Brent
Mark V. Heusel (Resident, Ann Arbor Office)
J. Benjamin Dolan
Sean M. Walsh
Deborah H. Boshaw
Michael A. Sneyd
Reema Dow
Clint J. Gage
L. Pahl Zinn
Kimberly M. Huston

Representative Clients: Camp, Dresser & McKee, Inc.; The Detroit Edison Co.; The Dow Chemical Co.; HomeTown Communications Network, Inc.; HomeTown Newspapers, Inc.; Observer & Eccentric Newspapers, Inc.; Seaboard Surety Co.; Texaco, Inc.; Union Carbide Corp.

For full biographical listings, see the Martindale-Hubbell Law Directory

FARMINGTON HILLS, Oakland Co.

COUZENS, LANSKY, FEALK, ELLIS, ROEDER & LAZAR, P.C. (AV)

39395 West 12 Mile Road, Suite 200, 48331-2913
Telephone: 248-489-8600
Facsimile: 248-489-4156
Email: info@couzens.com *URL:* http://www.couzens.com

Sheldon A. Fealk
Jack S. Couzens, II
Jerry M. Ellis
Donald M. Lansky
Bruce J. Lazar
Alan C. Roeder
Renard J. Kolasa
Kathryn Gilson Sussman
Jeffrey A. Levine
Phillip L. Sternberg
Marc L. Prey
Lisa J. Walters
Stephen Scapelliti
Donald A. Wagner

(See Next Column)

COUZENS, LANSKY, FEALK, ELLIS, ROEDER & LAZAR P.C.—*Continued*

Michael P. Witzke
Cyrus Raamin Kashef
Gregg A. Nathanson
David B. Deutsch
Mark S. Frankel

Roger E. Winkelman
Alisa A. Kwang
Turkia Awada Mullin
Raoul K. Maitra

Representative Clients: Provided upon request.
Reference: Michigan National Bank.

For full biographical listings, see the Martindale-Hubbell Law Directory

HALIW SICILIANO AND MYCHALOWYCH (AV)

37000 Grand River, Suite 350, 48335
Telephone: 248-442-0510
Fax: 248-442-0518
Email: hsmfirm@aol.com

MEMBERS OF FIRM

Andrew J. Haliw III
Joseph A. Siciliano
Andrew W. Mychalowych
Nanette Lynn Korpi
Raymond L. Feul
John N. Kaspers
David A. Monroe
Scott A. Decius
Katherine A. Jarred
Mark Gerard Chiesa

OF COUNSEL

Frank C. Kerr
Alphonse Tabaka
David Loeffler
William W. Decker, Jr.

For full biographical listings, see the Martindale-Hubbell Law Directory

*FLINT,** Genesee Co.

GAULT DAVISON A PROFESSIONAL SERVICE CORPORATION (AV)

Tenth Floor, Northbank Center, 432 North Saginaw Street, 48502-2032
Telephone: 810-234-3633
Fax: 810-233-3387
Email: gltdav@tir.com *URL:* http://www.gaultdavison.com

Russell E. Bowers
Bernard L. McAra

Christine A. Waun

Representative Clients: Al Serra Automobile Cos.; Milburn Peat Co.; Eldon L. Auker Associates; BankOne; Citizens Commercial & Savings Bank; Howard Delivery Service, Inc.; Millburn Peat Co.

For full biographical listings, see the Martindale-Hubbell Law Directory

*GRAND RAPIDS,** Kent Co.

BORRE, PETERSON, FOWLER & REENS, P.C. (AV)

300 Ottawa N.W., Suite 500, P.O. Box 1767, 49501-1767
Telephone: 616-459-1971
Fax: 616-459-2393
Email: 105162.1531@compuserve.com

Glen V. Borre
James B. Peterson
Ben A. Fowler
William C. Reens
Frank H. Johnson
Mark D. Sevald
Harold E. Nelson
William R. Vander Sluis
William G. Krupar
John C. Arndts

Michelle H. Anthes

References: Old Kent Bank; NBD Bank/First Chicago Bank; The Huntington Bank.

For full biographical listings, see the Martindale-Hubbell Law Directory

DAMON, OOSTERHOUSE & WITTE, L.L.P. (AV)

220 Lyon Street, N.W., Suite 525, 49503-2210
Telephone: 616-459-8357
Facsimile: 616-459-3462
Email: cdamon300@aol.com

MEMBERS OF FIRM

John E. Damon
Charles E. Damon
Donald F. Oosterhouse
Curtis R. Witte

MCSHANE & BOWIE, P.L.C. (AV)

1100 Campau Square Plaza, 99 Monroe Avenue, N.W., P.O. Box 360, 49501-0360
Telephone: 616-732-5000
Fax: 616-732-5099

MEMBERS OF FIRM

William H. Bowie
Keith P. Walker
John F. Shape
Wayne P. Bryan
Richard A. Durell
Steven E. Bratschie

(See Next Column)

ASSOCIATES

Michael D. DeVries
Laura J. Luyendyk

Representative Clients: Old Kent Bank; Amway Hotel Corp.; Randers Engineering, Inc.; BETA Design Group, Inc.; Wolverine Gas & Oil Co., Inc.; M. W. VanderVeen Co.; Betten Imports, Inc.; Adac Plastics, Inc.; Toefco Engineering, Inc.; Mountain Ridge Development Corp.

For Complete List of Firm Personnel, See General Section

For full biographical listings, see the Martindale-Hubbell Law Directory

MILLER, CANFIELD, PADDOCK AND STONE, P.L.C. (AV)

A Professional Limited Liability Company
Founded in 1852 by Sidney Davy Miller
99 Monroe, N.W. Suite 1200, 49503-2639
Telephone: 616-454-8656
Fax: 616-776-6322
URL: http://www.millercanfield.com
Detroit, Michigan Office: 150 West Jefferson, Suite 2500, 48226-4415.
Telephone: 313-963-6420.
Fax: 313-496-7500.
Cable Address: "Stem Detroit."
Ann Arbor, Michigan Office: 101 North Main Street, 7th Floor, 48104-1400.
Telephone: 734-663-2445.
Fax: 734-747-7147.
Troy, Michigan Office: 840 West Long Lake Road, Suite 200, 48098.
Telephone: 248-879-2000.
Fax: 248-879-2001.
Howell, Michigan Office: 121 South Barnard Street, Suite 4, 48843-2305.
Telephone: 517-546-7600.
Telecopier: 517-546-6974.
Kalamazoo, Michigan Office: 444 West Michigan Avenue, 49007-3752.
Telephone: 616-381-7030.
Fax: 616-382-0244.
Lansing, Michigan Office: One Michigan Avenue, Suite 900, 48933-1609.
Telephone: 517-487-2070.
Fax: 517-374-6304.
Monroe, Michigan Office: 214 East Elm Avenue, Suite 100, 48162-2682.
Telephone: 734-243-2000.
Fax: 734-243-0901.
Washington, D.C. Office: 1900 K Street, N.W., Suite 1150. 20006.
Telephone: 202-429-5575; 785-0600.
Fax: 202-331-1118; 785-1234.
Pensacola, Florida Office: 25 West Cedar, 32501.
Telephone: 850-469-1088.
Fax: 850-432-0677.
New York, New York Office: 1450 Broadway, 41st Floor, 10018.
Telephone: 212-704-4400.
Fax: 212-704-4410.
Gdynia, Poland Office: UL. Slaska 21, 81-319.
Telephone: 011-485-831-2808.
Fax: 011-48-58-628 6411.
Warsaw, Poland Office: UL. Nowogrodzkall, 5th Floor, 00-513.
Telephone: 011-4822 529 0200.
Fax: 011-4822 529 0201.
Katowice, Poland Office: UL. Francuska 35/37, 40-027.
Telephone: 011 (48-32) 757-2414.
Fax: 011 (48-32) 757-2483.

PRINCIPALS

Mark E. Putney
Michael G. Campbell

OF COUNSEL/SENIOR COUNSEL

David E. Hathaway

RESIDENT SENIOR ATTORNEY

David J. Hasper

RESIDENT ASSOCIATE

Robert J. Nolan

Representative Firm Clients: Chrysler Corporation; Comerica, Incorporated; City of Detroit, Michigan; Detroit Tigers, Inc.; First of Michigan; Ford Motor Company; Ford Motor Credit Company; Great Lakes Bancorp; Henry Ford Hospital; INVETECH Company.

For Complete List of Firm Personnel, See General Section

For full biographical listings, see the Martindale-Hubbell Law Directory

RHOADES, MCKEE, BOER, GOODRICH & TITTA (AV)

600 Waters Building, 161 Ottawa Avenue NW, 49503-2793
Telephone: 616-235-3500
Fax: 616-235-1639
Email: webmaster@grlaw.com *URL:* http://www.grlaw.com

(See Next Column)

RHOADES, MCKEE, BOER, GOODRICH & TITTA, *Grand Rapids—Continued*

Edward B. Goodrich
Peter A. Titta
Arthur C. Spalding
Robert J. Dugan
Terrence L. Groesser
Thomas P. Hogan
James M. Flaggert
Mary Ann Cartwright
James L. Schipper
Stephen A. Hilger
Gregory G. Timmer
Mary Lynette Williams
Scott J. Steiner
Robert C. Shaver
John M. Lichtenberg

Todd Allen Hendricks
Kenneth M. Horjus
Randy J. Kolar
Peter J. Lozicki

Reference: First Michigan Bank.

For full biographical listings, see the Martindale-Hubbell Law Directory

JOEL V. SOULE (AV)

161 Ottawa Northwest, Suite 411 South, 49503
Telephone: 616-774-8215
Fax: 616-774-0326

For full biographical listings, see the Martindale-Hubbell Law Directory

WARNER NORCROSS & JUDD LLP (AV)

900 Old Kent Building, 111 Lyon Street, N.W., 49503-2489
Telephone: 616-752-2000
Fax: 616-752-2500
URL: http://www.wnj.com
Muskegon, Michigan Office: 400 Terrace Plaza, P.O. Box 900.
Telephone: 231-727-2600.
Fax: 231-727-2699.
Holland, Michigan Office: Curtis Center, Suite 300, 170 College Avenue.
Telephone: 616-396-9800.
Fax: 616-396-3656.
Southfield, Michigan Office: 1000 Town Center, Suite 650.
Telephone: 248-223-5000.
Fax: 248-223-5005.

MEMBERS OF FIRM

George L. Whitfield
Charles E. McCallum
Jerome M. Smith
William K. Holmes
I. John Snider, II (Resident Member, Muskegon Office)
John R. Marquis (Resident Member, Holland Office)
James H. Breay
Robert H. Skilton, III (Resident Member, Southfield Office)
Ernest M. Sharpe
Vernon P. Saper
Hugh H. Makens
Gordon R. Lewis
Robert J. Chovanec
J. A. Cragwall, Jr.
Stephen R. Kretschman
W. Michael Van Haren
Michael L. Robinson
Eugene E. Smary
Thomas H. Thornhill (Resident Member, Muskegon Office)
Timothy Hillegonds
John G. Cameron, Jr.
John H. McKendry, Jr. (Resident Member, Muskegon Office)
Carl W. Dufendach
Stephen C. Waterbury
Rodney D. Martin
Richard E. Cassard
Alex J. DeYonker
John D. Dunn
William W. Hall
Bruce C. Young
Shane B. Hansen
Paul R. Jackson (Resident Member, Muskegon Office)
Janet Percy Knaus
Kathleen M. Hanenburg
Tracy T. Larsen
Sue O. Conway
Cameron S. DeLong
Jeffrey B. Power
Richard L. Bouma
Robert J. Jonker
Devin S. Schindler
Michael H. Schubert (Resident Member, Muskegon Office)
James Moskal
Mark K. Harder (Resident Member, Holland Office)
Jeffrey S. Battershall
Jeffrey A. Ott
Judith Lowitz Adler (Resident Member, Southfield Office)
Melvin G. Moseley, Jr.
Timothy L. Horner
R. Paul Guerre
Loren M. Andrulis
Susan Gell Meyers
Gordon J. Toering

ASSOCIATES

Mark J. Wassink
Andrew D. Hakken
Michael P. Lunt
Michael K. Molitor
Melissa Nestico Collar
Tashia L. Rivard
John E. Kessler (Resident, Holland Office)
Steven D. Johnson (Resident, Muskegon Office)
Jonathan J. Siebers
Gregory E. Schmidt
Jaron J. Nyhof (Resident, Holland Office)

OF COUNSEL

Conrad A. Bradshaw
R. Malcolm Cumming
Roger H. Oetting

COUNSEL

Jerry D. Hanscum (Resident Member, Southfield Office)
Joseph M. Sweeney

For full biographical listings, see the Martindale-Hubbell Law Directory

GROSSE POINTE FARMS, Wayne Co.

JOHNSON & MCPHERSON, P.L.C. (AV)

81 Kercheval, 48236
Telephone: 313-885-4700
Fax: 313-888-5872

Edward C. Johnson
Dale T. McPherson

RETIRED

Jarvis J. Schmidt

For full biographical listings, see the Martindale-Hubbell Law Directory

HOLLAND, Ottawa Co.

CUNNINGHAM DALMAN, P.C. (AV)

321 Settlers Road, P.O. Box 1767, 49422-1767
Telephone: 616-392-1821
Fax: 616-392-4769
Email: cunndalm@crossover.net *URL:* http://www.holland-law.com

Gordon H. Cunningham
Ronald L. Dalman
Max R. Murphy
James A. Bidol
Andrew J. Mulder
Kenneth B. Breese
Jeffrey K. Helder
Ronald J. Vander Veen
David M. Zessin
Mark H. Zietlow
Randall S. Schipper
Susan E. Vroegop
Joel G. Bouwens

Gregory J. McCoy
Jason M. Milstone
Aaron Leal
Dawn J. Ward

Representative Clients: Huntington National Bank; First of America Bank-Holland, N.A.; Ameribank; City of Holland; Auto Club Insurance Assn. (AAA); American States Insurance Co.; Holland Economic Development Corp.; Hope College; Western Theological Seminary.
Reference: Huntington National Bank.

For full biographical listings, see the Martindale-Hubbell Law Directory

*KALAMAZOO,** Kalamazoo Co.

EARLY, LENNON, PETERS & CROCKER, P.C. (AV)

900 Comerica Building, 49007-4752
Telephone: 616-381-8844
Fax: 616-349-8525
Email: elpc@michbar.org

George H. Lennon, III
Lawrence M. Brenton
Gordon C. Miller
Robert M. Taylor
Andrew J. Vorbrich

Attorneys for: Aetna Insurance: Kemper Group; Medical Protective Co.; Zurich Insurance; Liberty Mutual; Home Insurance.

For Complete List of Firm Personnel, See General Section

For full biographical listings, see the Martindale-Hubbell Law Directory

HOWARD & HOWARD ATTORNEYS, P.C. (AV)

The Michigan Building, Suite 200, 100 Portage Street, 49007-4802
Telephone: 616-382-1483
Telecopier: 616-382-1568
Bloomfield Hills, Michigan Office: The Pinehurst Office Center, Suite 101, 1400 North Woodward Avenue.
Telephone: 248-645-1483.
Telecopier: 248-645-1568.
Lansing, Michigan Office: The Phoenix Building, Suite 500, 222 Washington Square North.
Telephone: 517-485-1483.
Telecopier: 517-485-1568.
Peoria, Illinois Office: One Technology Plaza, Suite 600, 211 Fulton Street.
Telephone: 309-672-1483.
Telecopier: 309-672-1568.

Jeffrey P. Chalmers
Richard M. Clark
William A. Dornbos

Representative Clients: For Representative Client list, see General Practice, Kalamazoo, MI.

For Complete List of Firm Personnel, See General Section

For full biographical listings, see the Martindale-Hubbell Law Directory

KREIS, ENDERLE, CALLANDER & HUDGINS, A PROFESSIONAL CORPORATION (AV)

One Moorsbridge, P.O. Box 4010, 49003-4010
Telephone: 616-324-3000
Facsimile: 616-324-3010
Email: kech@kech.com *URL:* http://www.kech.com
Battle Creek, Michigan Office: One West Michigan Avenue, 49017.
Telephone: 616-966-3000.
Fax: 616-966-3022.

(See Next Column)

KREIS, ENDERLE, CALLANDER & HUDGINS A PROFESSIONAL CORPORATION—*Continued*

Russell A. Kreis
C. Reid Hudgins III
Robert B. Borsos
Jeffrey C. O'Brien
Stephen J. Hessen
Thomas G. King
Stephen L. Simons (Resident, Battle Creek Office)
Mark E. Kreter (Resident, Battle Creek Office)
Daniel P. McGlinn
Janice Roark Peters
Matthew S. DePerno
Peter F. Davis
Manuel R. Rupe

For Complete List of Firm Personnel, See General Section

For full biographical listings, see the Martindale-Hubbell Law Directory

LEWIS & ALLEN, P.C. (AV)

Old Kent Bank Building, Suite 800, 136 East Michigan Avenue, 49007-3946
Telephone: 616-388-7600
Fax: 616-349-3831

Dean S. Lewis
W. Fred Allen, Jr.
Barry R. Smith
William A. Redmond
Stephen M. Denenfeld
Anne McGregor Fries
Gregory G. St. Arnauld
James M. Marquardt
Christopher T. Haenicke
Winfield J. Hollander (1906-1996)

LEGAL SUPPORT PERSONNEL

Dorothy B. Kelly

For full biographical listings, see the Martindale-Hubbell Law Directory

MILLER, CANFIELD, PADDOCK AND STONE, P.L.C. (AV)

A Professional Limited Liability Company
Founded in 1852 by Sidney Davy Miller
444 West Michigan Avenue, 49007-3752
Telephone: 616-381-7030
Fax: 616-382-0244
URL: http://www.millercanfield.com
Detroit, Michigan Office: 150 West Jefferson, Suite 2500, 48226-4415.
Telephone: 313-963-6420.
Fax: 313-496-7500.
Cable Address: "Stem Detroit."
Ann Arbor, Michigan Office: 101 North Main Street, 7th Floor, 48104-1400.
Telephone: 734-663-2445.
Fax: 734-747-7147.
Troy, Michigan Office: 840 West Long Lake Road, Suite 200, 48098.
Telephone: 248-879-2000.
Fax: 248-879-2001.
Grand Rapids, Michigan Office: 99 Monroe, N.W., Suite 1200, 49503-2639.
Telephone: 616-454-8656.
Fax: 616-776-6322.
Howell, Michigan Office: 121 South Barnard Street, Suite 4, 48843-2305.
Telephone: 517-546-7600.
Telecopier: 517-546-6974.
Lansing, Michigan Office: One Michigan Avenue, Suite 900, 48933-1609.
Telephone: 517-487-2070.
Fax: 517-374-6304.
Monroe, Michigan Office: 214 East Elm Avenue, Suite 100, 48162-2682.
Telephone: 734-243-2000.
Fax: 734-243-0901.
Washington, D.C. Office: 1900 K Street, N.W., Suite 1150. 20006.
Telephone: 202-429-5575; 785-0600.
Fax: 202-331-1118; 785-1234.
Pensacola, Florida Office: 25 West Cedar, 32501.
Telephone: 850-469-1088.
Fax: 850-432-0677.
New York, New York Office: 1450 Broadway, 41st Floor, 10018.
Telephone: 212-704-4400.
Fax: 212-704-4410.
Gdynia, Poland Office: UL. Slaska 21, 81-319.
Telephone: 011-485-831-2808.
Fax: 011-48-58-628 6411.
Warsaw, Poland Office: UL. Nowogrodzkall, 5th Floor, 00-513.
Telephone: 011-4822 529 0200.
Fax: 011-4822 529 0201.
Katowice, Poland Office: UL. Francuska 35/37, 40-027.
Telephone: 011 (48-32) 757-2414.
Fax: 011 (48-32) 757-2483.

PRINCIPALS

Eric V. Brown, Jr.
John A. Campbell
John R. Cook
Thomas H. Van Dis
Steven M. Stankewicz

OF COUNSEL/SENIOR COUNSEL

Eric V. Brown, Sr.

Representative Firm Clients: Chrysler Corporation; Comerica, Incorporated; City of Detroit, Michigan; Detroit Tigers, Inc.; First of Michigan; Ford Motor Company; Ford Motor Credit Company; Great Lakes Bancorp; Henry Ford Hospital; INVETECH Company.

(See Next Column)

For Complete List of Firm Personnel, See General Section

For full biographical listings, see the Martindale-Hubbell Law Directory

LANSING, Ingham Co.

HOWARD & HOWARD ATTORNEYS, P.C. (AV)

The Phoenix Building, Suite 500, 222 Washington Square, North, 48933-1817
Telephone: 517-485-1483
Telecopier: 517-485-1568
Kalamazoo, Michigan Office: The Michigan Building, Suite 200, 100 Portage Street.
Telephone: 616-382-1483.
Telecopier: 616-382-1568.
Bloomfield Hills, Michigan Office: The Pinehurst Office Center, Suite 101, 1400 North Woodward Avenue.
Telephone: 248-645-1483.
Telecopier: 248-645-1568.
Peoria, Illinois Office: One Technology Plaza, Suite 600, 211 Fulton Street.
Telephone: 309-672-1483.
Telecopier: 309-672-1568.

Stewart A. Binke
Michael J. Brown
Todd D. Chamberlain
Michele LaForest Halloran
Gina M. Torielli

Representative Clients: For Representative Client list, see General Practice, Lansing, MI.

For Complete List of Firm Personnel, See General Section

For full biographical listings, see the Martindale-Hubbell Law Directory

*MONROE,** Monroe Co.

BRAUNLICH, RUSSOW & BRAUNLICH, A PROFESSIONAL CORPORATION (AV)

111 South Macomb Street, 48161
Telephone: 734-241-8300
Fax: 734-241-7715

William J. Braunlich, Jr. (1924-1992)
Thomas P. Russow
William H. Braunlich

Philip A. Costello
Ann L. Nickel
Jeffrey A. Dulany, P.C.

LEGAL SUPPORT PERSONNEL

Ruth G. Flint

Representative Clients: State Farm Mutual Insurance Co.; Auto Club Insurance Assn.; Board of Road Commissioners, Monroe County; Port of Monroe; Monroe County Community College; City of Luna Pier; City of Petersburg; Auto-Owners Insurance Co.; Fremont Mutual Insurance Co.; Citizens Insurance Co. of America.

For full biographical listings, see the Martindale-Hubbell Law Directory

*MUSKEGON,** Muskegon Co.

CULVER, SHERIDAN, KNOWLTON, EVEN & FRANKS, P.C. (AV)

250 Terrace Plaza, P.O. Box 629, 49443
Telephone: 231-724-4320
Telecopier: 231-724-4330
Email: cskef@novagate.com

Fred C. Culver, Jr.
James M. Sheridan
Michael M. Knowlton
Kevin B. Even
Eugene A. Franks

David E. Waterstradt
Foster D. Potter
Douglas Poland
Scott Knowlton
Joseph S. Bush

Representative Clients: SPX Corp.; National City Bank of Michigan/Illinois; Old Kent Bank of Grand Haven; Comerica Bank; NBD Bank; East Shore Chemical Company; Muskegon County Association of Realtors; Midland Groceries.

For full biographical listings, see the Martindale-Hubbell Law Directory

LAGUE, NEWMAN & IRISH, A PROFESSIONAL CORPORATION (AV)

600 Terrace Plaza, P.O. Box 389, 49443
Telephone: 231-725-8148
Telecopier: 231-726-3404
Email: firm@lnilaw.com

Todd L. Helle
Richard C. Lague
William M. Newman
Michael J. Philbrick
J. Scott Timmer
Alvin D. Treado

General Counsel: Hackley Hospital & Medical Center; Kaydon Corp.; Cole's Quality Foods; Kurdziel Industries.
Local Counsel: SPX Corp.; Booth Newspapers Inc.; National City Bank; Neway Anchorlok International.

(See Next Column)

LAGUE, NEWMAN & IRISH A PROFESSIONAL CORPORATION, *Muskegon—Continued*

For Complete List of Firm Personnel, See General Section

For full biographical listings, see the Martindale-Hubbell Law Directory

PLYMOUTH, Wayne Co.

DRAUGELIS & ASHTON, L.L.P. (AV)

843 Penniman Avenue, 48170-1690
Telephone: 734-453-4044
Fax: 734-453-2011
Clawson, Michigan Office: 380 North Main Street.
Telephone: 248-588-7704.

MEMBERS OF FIRM

Edward F. Draugelis
John A. Ashton
Donald S. Scully
Richard T. Haynes
Lamberto DiStefano
David T. Rogers
Joseph R. Conte
Steven O. Ashton

ASSOCIATES

Floyd C. Virant
Taras P. Jarema
Timothy M. McKercher
Joel B. Ashton
Donald E. Walker
Heather A. Jefferson
Roger D. Ajluni
Margaret L. Browning

Representative Client: State Farm Mutual Automobile Insurance Co.
Reference: National Bank of Detroit, Plymouth Branch.

For full biographical listings, see the Martindale-Hubbell Law Directory

*ST. JOSEPH,** Berrien Co.

TROFF, PETZKE & AMMESON (AV)

Law and Title Building, 811 Ship Street, P.O. Box 67, 49085
Telephone: 616-983-0161
Facsimile: 616-983-0166
Email: pnalaw@qtm.net

MEMBERS OF FIRM

Roger A. Petzke
Charles F. Ammeson

For full biographical listings, see the Martindale-Hubbell Law Directory

SOUTHFIELD, Oakland Co.

DE VINE & KOHN, PLLC (AV)

29800 Telegraph Road, 48034
Telephone: 248-353-6500
Fax: 248-353-2514

Clifford J. De Vine
Sheldon B. Kohn

For full biographical listings, see the Martindale-Hubbell Law Directory

ROBERT B. LABE, P.C. (AV)

2000 Town Center, Suite 1780, 48075
Telephone: 248-354-3100
Telecopier: 248-354-3926

Robert B. Labe

Cecile Kohl

References: Comerica Bank, N.A.; Morgan Stanley Dean Witter.

For full biographical listings, see the Martindale-Hubbell Law Directory

MADDIN, HAUSER, WARTELL, ROTH, HELLER & PESSES, P.C. (AV)

Third Floor Essex Centre, 28400 Northwestern Highway, P.O. Box 215, 48037
Telephone: 248-354-4030, 355-5200
Telefax: 248-354-1422

Milton M. Maddin (1902-1984)
Michael W. Maddin
Mark R. Hauser
C. Robert Wartell
Richard J. Maddin
Richard F. Roth
Harvey R. Heller
Ian D. Pesses
Michael S. Leib
Robert D. Kaplow
William E. Sigler
Stewart C. W. Weiner
Charles M. Lax
Stuart M. Bordman
Steven D. Sallen
Gregory J. Gamalski
Julie Chenot Mayer
Nathaniel H. Simpson
Ronald A. Sollish
Lowell D. Salesin

Mark H. Fink
Steven M. Wolock
Lori E. Talsky
Stephen E. Handelman
Ronald M. Stern
Martin Scott Frenkel
Gary M. Remer
Jennifer S. Sternberg
George V. Cassar, Jr.
Adam J. Goldstein

(See Next Column)

OF COUNSEL

Bruce N. Goldman

Reference: Comerica Bank.

For full biographical listings, see the Martindale-Hubbell Law Directory

MORGANROTH & MORGANROTH (AV)

3000 Town Center, Suite 1500, 48075
Telephone: 248-355-3084
Fax: 248-355-3017
URL: http://www.lawyers.com/morganrothlawfirm
New York, N.Y. Office: 156 W. 56th Street, Suite 1101. 10019.
Telephone: 212-586-5905.
Fax: 212-586-7302.

MEMBERS OF FIRM

Mayer Morganroth
Jeffrey B. Morganroth
Cherie Morganroth
Jason Ross Hirsch

Representative Clients: APCOA,Inc.; ; Mayor Coleman Young (Detroit); John Z. DeLorean; Realtek Industries, Inc.; Dr. Jack Kevorkian; Carolyn Warmus; Edward J. Holland, Jr.; Lyndon LaRouche; Thomas Warmus; Walter Keating.

For full biographical listings, see the Martindale-Hubbell Law Directory

SOMMERS, SCHWARTZ, SILVER & SCHWARTZ, P.C. (AV)

2000 Town Center, Suite 900, 48075
Telephone: 248-355-0300
Telecopier: 248-746-4001
Plymouth, Michigan Office: 747 South Main Street.
Telephone: 313-455-4250.

Steven J. Schwartz
Patrick B. McCauley
Gary A. Taback
James J. Vlasic
Leon M. Schurgin
Joseph H. Bourgon

Lena Agree

OF COUNSEL

Paul Groffsky
Donald R. Epstein

General Counsel For: City of Taylor; Foodland Distributors; C.A. Muer Corporation; Vlasic & Company; Nederlander Corporation; Midwest Health Centers, P.C.
Representative Clients: Michigan National Bank; Rite-Aid of Michigan, Inc.; Universal Underwriters Insurance Co.; Don Lee Distributor.

For Complete List of Firm Personnel, See General Section

For full biographical listings, see the Martindale-Hubbell Law Directory

*TRAVERSE CITY,** Grand Traverse Co.

BISHOP & HEINTZ, P.C. (AV)

440 W. Front at Oak Street, P.O. Box 707, 49685
Telephone: 616-946-4100
Fax: 616-946-8543
Email: info@bishop-heintztc.com *URL:* http://www.lawyers.com/bishopheintzlaw

Douglas S. Bishop
Patrick E. Heintz
David A. Cvengros

OF COUNSEL

Arthur R. Curtis

Representative Clients: Old Kent Bank-Grand Traverse; Old Kent Bank & Trust Co.; NBD Bank, N.A.; Ball Aircraft, Inc.; Power Play International Inc.; National Cherry Festival; PDM Industries, Inc.; Bolthouse Machine Corp.; Corrections Management, Inc.; Buck Wilder, Inc.

For full biographical listings, see the Martindale-Hubbell Law Directory

DINGEMAN, DANCER & CHRISTOPHERSON, P.L.C. (AV)

100 Park Street, 49684
Telephone: 231-929-0500
Fax: 231-929-0504
Email: dingeman@dingemandancer.com *URL:* http://www.Dingemandancer.com

Daniel J. Dingeman
Mark R. Dancer
James A. Christopherson

Representative Clients: Black Forest Motors-Mercedes Benz; WWTV/WWUP TV 9 & 10; Heritage Broadcasting; Acme Township; Northern Physicians Organization, Inc.; Northern Physicians Company, Ltd.; The Homestead Resort; Texas Instrument, Inc.

For full biographical listings, see the Martindale-Hubbell Law Directory

TROY, Oakland Co.

BARLOW & DERBY (AV)

1450 West Long Lake Road Suite 365, 48098
Telephone: 248-641-3300
Facsimile: 248-641-3305
Email: barlowlan@aol.com

(See Next Column)

BARLOW & DERBY—*Continued*

Thomas W. H. Barlow
Matthew S. Derby

ASSOCIATES

Holly Christine Beatty
Christine R. Essique

For full biographical listings, see the Martindale-Hubbell Law Directory

CAMPBELL, O'BRIEN & MISTELE, P.C. (AV)

850 Stephenson Highway Suite 410, 48083-1163
Telephone: 248-588-5800
Fax: 248-588-6669; 1-888-647-8353
Email: COMLAW@ADVDATA.NET *URL:* http://www.lawyers.com/comlaw

Edwin G. O'Brien (1907-1983)
Dale C. Campbell
Henry E. Mistele
Paul W. Loock
Robert J. Figa
Curtis H. Mistele

References: First Federal of Michigan; Comerica Bank.

For full biographical listings, see the Martindale-Hubbell Law Directory

DRIGGERS, SCHULTZ & HERBST, A PROFESSIONAL CORPORATION (AV)

2600 West Big Beaver Road, Suite 550, 48084
Telephone: 248-649-6000
Telecopier: 248-649-6442

Nathan B. Driggers (1929-1996)
Laurence S. Schultz
Jay A. Herbst
Richard B. Tomlinson
Daniel R. Boynton
Joseph W. Thomas
Raymond J. Sterling
William C. Schaefer

Edward S. Toth
Mark E. Mueller
Ronald Edwin Beier, II
Christopher P. Mansur
Andrew R. Biscoglia
Daniel G. Heller

OF COUNSEL

Laura D. Mason

Representative Clients: Applied Dynamics International, Inc.; Automotive Industries, Inc.; Autotek Sealants; Peter A. Basile Sons, Inc.; C & I Mechanical Contractors; Dunn Blue Print Co.;
Reference: NBD Bank.

For full biographical listings, see the Martindale-Hubbell Law Directory

HACKETT & MAXWELL, P.C. (AV)

City Center Building, Suite 1470, 888 West Big Beaver Road, 48084
Telephone: 810-362-2600
Fax: 810-362-3610
Email: hackmax@voyager.net

Patrick E. Hackett
Phillip B. Maxwell

Dennis W. Krakow
Mireille Leruth Phillips

For full biographical listings, see the Martindale-Hubbell Law Directory

HAINER & BERMAN, P.C. (AV)

888 West Big Beaver, Suite 1400, 48084
Telephone: 248-244-8424
Fax: 248-244-8455

Michael J. Hainer
Leonard K. Berman
Kay E. Malaney

Drew S. Norton
Paul S. Miller

OF COUNSEL

Michael A. Kus
Robert F. Riley
Mark S. Demorest

Representative Clients: American Empire Surplus Lines Insurance Co.; Biomass Energy Systems, Inc.; Bridgestone/Firestone, Inc.; Central Distributors of Beer, Inc.; Champion Enterprises, Inc.; City Management Corp.; Clarklift of Detroit, Inc.; Federal Reserve Bank of Chicago; Hotel Investment Services, Inc.; M&O Marketing, Inc.

For full biographical listings, see the Martindale-Hubbell Law Directory

AUSTIN HIRSCHHORN, P.C. (AV)

Suite 710 Columbia Center, 201 West Big Beaver Road, 48084-4152
Telephone: 248-680-1660
Fax: 248-680-1671
Email: austinh@ix.netcom.com

Austin Hirschhorn

For full biographical listings, see the Martindale-Hubbell Law Directory

POLING, MCGAW & POLING, P.C. (AV)

Suite 275, 5435 Corporate Drive, 48098
Telephone: 248-641-0500
Telecopier: 248-641-0506
URL: http://www.lawyers.com/polingmcgaw&poling

Benson T. Buck (1926-1989)
Richard B. Poling
D. Douglas McGaw
Richard B. Poling, Jr.
Gregory C. Hamilton
Veronica B. O'Hara
James R. Parker
Shannon M. Acton

OF COUNSEL

Ralph S. Moore

Representative Clients: City of Troy; United States Fidelity & Guaranty Co.; Sentry Insurance Co.; Admiral Insurance; DeMaria Construction Co.; Leo Corporation; Aetna Casualty and Surety Co.; Concord Design; Pneumo-Abex.

For full biographical listings, see the Martindale-Hubbell Law Directory

POWERS, CHAPMAN, DEAGOSTINO, MEYERS & MILIA, PROFESSIONAL CORPORATION (AV)

Suite 704, 3001 West Big Beaver Road, 48084
Telephone: 248-643-6500
Telecopier: 248-643-0280

Conrad D. Chapman
L. Gene DeAgostino
Allen M. Meyers
Richard A. Novak, Jr.
Robert P. Milia
Joseph M. McGlynn
Nelson B. Stieper
Richard T. Chapman
Randy J. Ordway

Michael S. Holmes
Ronald T. Charlebois
Connie Skinner McNealy
Craig Tarpinian
David A. Perez, II
Kevin A Casey
Robert M. Yonkers

OF COUNSEL

Ward D. Powers
John R. Brown

General Counsel for: Davis Industries, Inc.; Fuller Tool Co.; Charles Dalgleish Cadillac, Inc.
Reference: Huntington National Bank.

For full biographical listings, see the Martindale-Hubbell Law Directory

STARK, REAGAN & FINNERTY, P.C. (AV)

Suite 202, 1111 West Long Lake Road, P.O. Box 7037, 48007-7037
Telephone: 248-641-9955
Facsimile: 248-641-9921
Email: @SRFPC.COM
Boca Raton, Florida Office: Suite 307B, 4800 North Federal Highway.
Telephone: 561-994-2266.
Traverse City, Michigan Office: 475 Eastwood Shores.
Telephone: 231-943-8230.
Facsimile: 231-943-8711.

Michael H. Whiting
Kenneth M. Boyer
Thomas H. Finnerty
R. Keith Stark
Joseph C. Bird
Joseph A. Ahern
Christopher E. LeVasseur
Daniel E. Chapman
William D. Girardot
James R. Waldvogel
Jeffrey J. Fleury
Michael D. FitzPatrick

OF COUNSEL

Harry S. Stark (Resident Of Counsel, Traverse City Office)
Willard M. Reagan
James E. Beall

For full biographical listings, see the Martindale-Hubbell Law Directory

WEST BLOOMFIELD, Oakland Co.

VALENTINE & ASSOCIATES, P.C. (AV)

5767 West Maple Road, Suite 400, 48322
Telephone: 248-851-3010
Fax: 248-851-1553
Email: vallaw@umich.edu

Stephen K. Valentine, Jr.

For full biographical listings, see the Martindale-Hubbell Law Directory

WESTLAND, Wayne Co.

ASKER, CHAPP & CLOS, P.C. (AV)

35551 Ford Road, Suite 100, 48185
Telephone: 734-326-2101
Fax: 734-595-9771
URL: http://www.lawyers.com/michigan
Torrance, California Office: 615 Hawaii Avenue, 90503.
Telephone: 310-320-5766.

(See Next Column)

ASKER, CHAPP & CLOS P.C., *Westland—Continued*

Paul P. Asker	Gary E. Perlmuter
Sandra J. Chapp	Brian J. Considine
Charles E. Clos	J. Matthew Catchick, Jr.

For full biographical listings, see the Martindale-Hubbell Law Directory

CIVIL RIGHTS

ALABAMA

*BIRMINGHAM,** Jefferson Co.

BRADLEY ARANT ROSE & WHITE LLP (AV)

2001 Park Place, Suite 1400, P.O. Box 830709, 35283-0709
Telephone: 205-521-8000
Facsimile: 205-521-8800
Facsimile (SouthTrust Tower Office): 205-521-8500
URL: http://www.barw.com
Huntsville, Alabama Office: 200 Clinton Avenue West, Suite 900, 35801.
Telephone: 205-517-5100.
Facsimile: 205-533-5069.
Washington, D.C. Office: 801 Pennsylvania Avenue, NW, Suite 230, 20004.
Telephone: 202-347-8893.
Facsimile: 202-347-1684.

ASSOCIATES

Abdul K. Kallon
T. Matthew Miller
Arnold W. Umbach III

For Complete List of Firm Personnel, See General Section

For full biographical listings, see the Martindale-Hubbell Law Directory

GORDON, SILBERMAN, WIGGINS & CHILDS, P.C. (AV)

1400 SouthTrust Tower, 420 North 20th Street, 35203
Telephone: 205-328-0640
Facsimilie: 205-254-1500
Washington, D.C. Office: 1621 Connecticut Avenue, N.W., Suite 400.
Telephone: 202-238-0690.
Facsimile: 202-238-0968.

RESIDENT SHAREHOLDERS

Bruce L. Gordon
James Mendelsohn
Ann K. Wiggins

RESIDENT ASSOCIATES

Gregory O. Wiggins
Rocco Calamusa, Jr.

For Complete List of Firm Personnel, See General Section

For full biographical listings, see the Martindale-Hubbell Law Directory

GORHAM & WALDREP, P.C. (AV)

2101 6th Avenue North, Suite 700, 35203
Telephone: 205-254-3216; 251-9166
Telecopier: 205-324-3802
Email: info@gorham-waldrep.com *URL:* http://www.gorham-waldrep.com
Montgomery, Alabama Office: 250 Commerce Street, P.O. Box 4837, 36103-4837.
Telephone: 334-262-0777.
Telecopier: 334-262-0742.

Thomas L. Stewart
Michael G. Kendrick
LaVeeda Morgan Battle

Victoria Franklin-Sisson

Representative Clients: Jefferson County Personnel Board; Birmingham-Jefferson Civic Center Authority; The Water Works and Sewer Board of the City of Birmingham; City of Homewood; American Federation of Government Employees Local #1945; City of Pelham; Town of Kimberly; Alabama Tire Dealers Assn.; Southern States Body Shop Assn.

For Complete List of Firm Personnel, See General Section

For full biographical listings, see the Martindale-Hubbell Law Directory

THOMAS, MEANS, GILLIS, DEVLIN, ROBINSON & SEAY, P.C. (AV)

1035 Financial Center, 505 20th Street North, 35203-2605
Telephone: 205-328-7915
Fax: 205-214-6160
Mailing Address: P.O. Box 370497, Birmingham, AL, 35237-0447
Email: tmgpc.lawfirm@tmgpc.com *URL:* http://www.tmgpc.com
Montgomery, Alabama Office: 3121 Zelda Court, P.O. Drawer 5058, 36103-5058.
Telephone: 334-270-1033.
Fax: 334-260-9396. E-mail: tmgpc.lawfirm@tmgpc.com. URL: http://www.tmgpc.com
Atlanta, Georgia Office: The Chandler Building, Suite 300, 127 Peachtree Street N.E., 30303.
Telephone: 404-222-8400.
Fax: 404-222-0080. E-Mail: tmgpc.lawfir@tmgpc.com. URL: http://www.tmgpc.com

Kenneth L. Thomas (Resident)

(See Next Column)

James L. Richey (Resident)
Lisa F. Brown (Resident)
Wendell J. Chambliss (Resident)
Valerie L. Acoff (Resident)
Edward J. Berry (Resident)

For full biographical listings, see the Martindale-Hubbell Law Directory

*MOBILE,** Mobile Co.

SINTZ, CAMPBELL, DUKE & TAYLOR (AV)

3763 Professional Parkway, 36609
Telephone: 334-344-7241
Fax: 334-344-7400

MEMBERS OF FIRM

Peter V. Sintz (1940-1997)
Frank G. Taylor
Robert C. Campbell, III
Steven L. Terry

ASSOCIATES

Wm. Kyle Morris
Kathryn W. Petersen
Barry C. Prine

OF COUNSEL

Leon G. Duke

LEGAL SUPPORT PERSONEL

James A. Koblas

Representative Clients: Aetna C & S Insurance Co.; Mobile County School Board; Auto-Owners Insurance Co.; Argonaut Insurance Co.; Mostellar Medical Clinic; Scottsdale Insurance Co.; American International Group; Alabama School of Math and Science; Mobile County Sheriff's Office.

For full biographical listings, see the Martindale-Hubbell Law Directory

*MONTGOMERY,** Montgomery Co.

THOMAS, MEANS, GILLIS, DEVLIN, ROBINSON & SEAY, P.C. (AV)

3121 Zelda Court, P.O. Drawer 5058, 36103-5058
Telephone: 334-270-1033
Fax: 334-260-9396
Email: tmgpc.lawfirm@tmgpc.com *URL:* http://www.tmgpc.com
Birmingham, Alabama Office: 1035 Financial Center, 505 20th Street North, 35203. Mailing Address: P.O. Box 370447, Birmingham, AL., 35237-0447.
Telephone: 205-328-7915.
Fax: 205-214-6160. E-mail: tmgpc.lawfirm@tmgpc.com. URL: http://www.tmgpc.com
Atlanta, Georgia Office: The Chandler Building, Suite 300, 127 Peachtree Street, N.E., 30303.
Telephone: 404-222-8400.
Fax: 404-222-0080. E-Mail: tmgpc.lawfirm@tmgpc.com. URL: http://www.tmgpc.com

Kenneth L. Thomas (Resident, Birmingham, Alabama Office)
Tyrone C. Means
H. Lewis Gillis
Marvin A. Devlin (Resident, Atlanta, Georgia Office)
Mark E. Robinson (Resident, Atlanta, Georgia Office)
Quinton S. Seay (Resident, Atlanta, Georgia Office)

James L. Richey (Resident, Birmingham, Alabama Office)
Wendell J. Chambliss (Resident, Birmingham Office)
Lisa F. Brown (Resident, Birmingham, Alabama Office)
Valerie L. Acoff (Resident, Birmingham, Alabama Office)
John W. Adams, Jr.
Paul C. Williams
Jennifer D. Odom (Resident, Atlanta, Georgia Office)
Darnell D. Coley
Edward J. Berry (Resident, Birmingham, Alabama Office)
Thaddeus L. Hamilton (Resident, Birmingham, Alabama Office)

LEGAL SUPPORT PERSONNEL

Joyce L. Lehmann
Tonya White
Bryan Palmer
Felicia Kolley
John Baker (Office Administrator)
Cathy Allen
Lakesha Baker
Larry Holmes
Linda Steele
Mary Duncan
Pamela Watkins
Paula Mosely
Rodney Barganier
Tamara Venice
Linda Stoudemier

For full biographical listings, see the Martindale-Hubbell Law Directory

VOLZ, PRESTWOOD & HANAN, P.C. (AV)

350 Adams Avenue, P.O. Box 1910, 36102-1910
Telephone: 334-264-6401
Fax: 334-834-4954

Charles H. Volz, Jr.
Alvin T. Prestwood
Charles H. Volz, III
Ellis D. Hanan
Richard D. Lively
Judy H. Barganier

For full biographical listings, see the Martindale-Hubbell Law Directory

CALIFORNIA

COSTA MESA, Orange Co.

RUTAN & TUCKER, LLP (AV)

A Partnership including Professional Corporations
611 Anton Boulevard, Fourteenth Floor, P.O. Box 1950, 92626-1998
Telephone: 714-641-5100; 213-625-7586
Telecopier: 714-546-9035
Email: rutan&tucker@rutan.com *URL:* http://www.rutan.com

MEMBERS OF FIRM

Leonard A. Hampel, Jr.
David C. Larsen (P.C.)
Robert S. Bower
Philip D. Kohn
William W. Wynder
M. Katherine Jenson
Hans Van Ligten
Jeffrey Wertheimer
Jeffrey A. Goldfarb

ASSOCIATE

Todd O. Litfin

For Complete List of Firm Personnel, See General Section

For full biographical listings, see the Martindale-Hubbell Law Directory

EMERYVILLE, Alameda Co.

JAMES JAY SELTZER (AV)

Watergate Towers, Tenth Floor, 2200 Powell Street, Suite 1035, 94608
Telephone: 510-596-2500
Telecopier: 510-596-2519
URL: http://www.secureadvise.com
Email: lawoffices@jjseltzer.com *URL:* http://www.lawyers.com/jamesjayseltzer

For full biographical listings, see the Martindale-Hubbell Law Directory

PASADENA, Los Angeles Co.

JOHN C. BURTON (AV)

35 South Raymond Avenue, Suite 405, 91105
Telephone: 626-449-8300
Fax: 626-449-4417
Email: Johnburtonlaw@compuserve.com *URL:* http://www.lawyers.com/johnburtonlaw

For full biographical listings, see the Martindale-Hubbell Law Directory

*SACRAMENTO,** Sacramento Co.

ANGELO, KILDAY & KILDUFF (AV)

601 University Avenue, Suite 150, 95825
Telephone: 916-564-6100
Telecopier: 916-564-6263

MEMBERS OF FIRM

Laurence L. Angelo
Bruce A. Kilday
Carolee Kilduff
Christine Green Sanfilippo
J. Scott Smith
Jeffrey S. Stone
Amy H. Ruggles
Ronald J. Scholar

LEGAL SUPPORT PERSONNEL

Susan M. Jarboe (Paralegal-Law Librarian)

For full biographical listings, see the Martindale-Hubbell Law Directory

*SAN FRANCISCO,** San Francisco Co.

MOORE & BROWNING (AV)

100 Bush Street, Suite 225, 94104
Telephone: 415-956-6500
Fax: 415-956-6580

Michael B. Moore
Charles A. Browning

LEGAL SUPPORT PERSONNEL

Pat Medina (Paralegal)

For full biographical listings, see the Martindale-Hubbell Law Directory

MURPHY, PEARSON, BRADLEY & FEENEY, A PROFESSIONAL CORPORATION (AV)

88 Kearny Street, 10th Floor, 94108
Telephone: 415-788-1900
Telecopier: 415-393-8087
Email: IndividualsFirstInitialAndLastName@mpbf.com *URL:* http://www.mpbf.com
Sacramento, California Office: 701 University Avenue, Suite 150.
Telephone: 916-565-0300.
Fax: 916-565-1636.
San Jose, California Office: 80 South Market Street, 3rd Floor.
Telephone: 408-279-5792.
Facsimile: 408-279-5785.

(See Next Column)

Los Angeles, California Office: 11400 West Olympic Boulevard, Suite 249.
Telephone: 310-312-9565.
Fax: 310-312-9566.

John H. Feeney

For Complete List of Firm Personnel, See General Section

For full biographical listings, see the Martindale-Hubbell Law Directory

AMITAI SCHWARTZ (AV)

155 Montgomery Street, Suite 800, 94104-4113
Telephone: 415-398-0922
Fax: 415-398-0978
Email: amitai@schwartzlaw.com

Monique Olivier
Elizabeth S. Letcher

For full biographical listings, see the Martindale-Hubbell Law Directory

*SAN JOSE,** Santa Clara Co.

McMANIS, FAULKNER & MORGAN (AV)

160 West Santa Clara Street, 10th Floor, 95113
Telephone: 408-279-8700
Fax: 408-279-3244; 408-279-0494
Email: mfm@mfmlaw.com *URL:* http://www.mfmlaw.com

James McManis
William Faulkner
Donelle Morgan
Lisa Herrick
Michael Reedy
Erica Yew

Michelle Tidalgo
Colleen Duffy Smith
Lillian Wolf
Rebecca Hughes
Kalpana Vrudhula
Ray M. Baluyot
Catherine Bechtel
Arron Nesbitt

OF COUNSEL

Mary Arand

For full biographical listings, see the Martindale-Hubbell Law Directory

COLORADO

*DENVER,** Denver Co.

LAW OFFICES OF JOHN W. McKENDREE (AV)

Creswell Mansion, 1244 Grant Street, 80203
Telephone: 303-861-8906
Fax: 303-861-7773
Email: Johnwmckendree@msn.com

ASSOCIATE

Elizabeth G. McKendree

Reference: Colorado National Bank.

For full biographical listings, see the Martindale-Hubbell Law Directory

ARTHUR M. SCHWARTZ, P.C. (AV)

Suite 420 1630 Welton Street, 80202
Telephone: 303-893-2500
Fax: 303-893-3349
Email: amspc1@aol.com *URL:* http://www.lawyers.com/arthurschwartz

Arthur M. Schwartz

Michael W. Gross
Cindy D. Schwartz
Gary M. Kramer

Reference: Wells Fargo Bank of Denver.

For full biographical listings, see the Martindale-Hubbell Law Directory

CONNECTICUT

*BRIDGEPORT,** Fairfield Co.

GERALD E. BODELL (AV)

177 State Street Suite 401, 06604
Telephone: 203-335-8955
Fax: 203-366-6812
New York, New York Office: 36 West 44th Street, Suite 303.
Telephone: 212- 398-3778.
Fax: 212-398-3779.

For full biographical listings, see the Martindale-Hubbell Law Directory

Bridgeport—Continued

KOSKOFF, KOSKOFF & BIEDER, P.C. (AV)

350 Fairfield Avenue, 06604
Telephone: 203-336-4421
Fax: 203-368-3244
Email: KKB@KOSKOFF.com
Stamford, Connecticut Office: 1172 Bedford Street.
Telephone: 203-325-3686.
Danbury, Connecticut Office: 1 Moss Avenue.
Telephone: 203-792-7100.

Michael P. Koskoff
Richard A. Bieder
Vincent M. Musto

Joel Thomas Faxon

For full biographical listings, see the Martindale-Hubbell Law Directory

*NEW HAVEN,** New Haven Co.

ROSEN & DOLAN, P.C. (AV)

400 Orange Street, 06511
Telephone: 203-787-3513
Fax: 203-789-1605
Email: davidrosen@snet.net
Email: sapincus@snet.net

David N. Rosen

Stephen M. Pincus

Reference: Peoples Bank.

For Complete List of Firm Personnel, See General Section

For full biographical listings, see the Martindale-Hubbell Law Directory

WILLIAMS, POLAN & PATTIS, LLC (AV)

51 Elm Street, 06510
Telephone: 203-562-9931
Fax: 203-776-9494
Email: jrw@johnrwilliams.com

John R. Williams
Diane Polan
Norman A. Pattis

Katrena Engstrom
Angelica N. Papastavros
William S. Palmieri
Rosemarie Paine

References: Webster Bank; Citizens Bank.

For full biographical listings, see the Martindale-Hubbell Law Directory

DISTRICT OF COLUMBIA

WASHINGTON, D.C. Co.

COHEN, MILSTEIN, HAUSFELD & TOLL, P.L.L.C. (AV)

West Tower, Suite 500, 1100 New York Avenue, N.W., 20005-3964
Telephone: 202-408-4600
Facsimile: 202-408-4699
Email: lawinfo@cmht.com *URL:* http://www.CMHT.com
Seattle, Washington Office: 999 Third Avenue, Suite 3600.
Telephone: 206-521-0080.
Facsimile: 206-521-0166.

MEMBERS OF FIRM

Jerry S. Cohen (1925-1995)
Herbert E. Milstein
Michael D. Hausfeld
Steven J. Toll (Resident, Seattle, Washington Office)
Ann C. Yahner
Lisa M. Mezzetti
Andrew N. Friedman
Richard S. Lewis
Daniel S. Sommers
Daniel A. Small
Gary E. Mason
Joseph M. Sellers
Sharon A. Snyder
Mark S. Willis (Not admitted in DC)

ASSOCIATES

Lori G. Feldman (Resident, Seattle, Washington Office)
Paul T. Gallagher
Christine E. Webber
Alexander E. Barnett
Matthew James Ide (Resident, Seattle, Washington Office)
Matthew F. Pawa
Suzette M. Malveaux
Mary N. Strimel
Kristopher A. Kinkade (Resident, Seattle, Washington Office)
Agnieszka M. Fryszman
Deborah J. Vagins
Ari Karen
Charles E. Tompkins
Tamara J. Driscoll (Resident, Seattle, Washington Office)
Elizabeth Haines Cronise
Donna Solen
Lesli C. Esposito (Not admitted in DC)

(See Next Column)

OF COUNSEL

Margaret G. Farrell

For full biographical listings, see the Martindale-Hubbell Law Directory

JOSEPH D. GEBHARDT, P.C. (AV)

1101 17th Street N.W., Suite 607, 20036
Telephone: 202-496-0400
Fax: 202-496-0404

Joseph D. Gebhardt

Charles Williamson Day, Jr.

For full biographical listings, see the Martindale-Hubbell Law Directory

SPRENGER & LANG, P.L.L.C. (AV)

1614 Twentieth Street, N.W., 20009
Telephone: 202-265-8010
Fax: 202-332-6652
Minneapolis, Minnesota Office: Sprenger & Lang, P.L.L.C., 325 Ridgewood Avenue.
Telephone: 612-871-8910.
Fax: 612-871-9270.

MEMBERS OF FIRM

Paul C. Sprenger (Resident)
Jane Lang (Resident)
Michael D. Lieder (Resident)
Lawrence P. Schaefer (Not admitted in DC; Resident, Minneapolis, Minnesota Office)
James R. Behrenbrinker (Not admitted in DC; Resident, Minneapolis, Minnesota Office)
Eli Gottesdiener (Resident)
Susan E. Stokes (Not admitted in DC; Resident, Minneapolis, Minnesota Office)
Maia R. Caplan (Resident)

Lisa C. Stratton (Resident, Minneapolis, Minnesota Office)

OF COUNSEL

Jean M. Boler (Not admitted in DC; Resident, Minneapolis, Minnesota Office)
Mara R. Thompson (Not admitted in DC; Resident, Minneapolis, Minnesota Office)

For full biographical listings, see the Martindale-Hubbell Law Directory

FLORIDA

*CLEARWATER,** Pinellas Co.

KWALL, SHOWERS & COLEMAN, P.A. (AV)

133 North Fort Harrison Avenue, 33755
Telephone: 727-441-4947
Telecopier: 727-447-3158
Email: kwall@worldnet.att.net *URL:* http://www.usalaw.com/adminlaw/

Louis Kwall
Sherwood S. (Flip) Coleman

For Complete List of Firm Personnel, See General Section

For full biographical listings, see the Martindale-Hubbell Law Directory

*FORT MYERS,** Lee Co.

PATRICK E. GERAGHTY A PROFESSIONAL ASSOCIATION (AV)

The Courtney Building, Suite 100, 2069 First Street, P.O. Box 1605, 33902-1605
Telephone: 941-334-9500
Fax: 941-334-8930
URL: http://www.lawyers.com/pgeraghty

Patrick E. Geraghty
Thomas M. Dougherty

For full biographical listings, see the Martindale-Hubbell Law Directory

*JACKSONVILLE,** Duval Co.

BROWN, TERRELL, HOGAN, ELLIS, McCLAMMA & YEGELWEL, P.A. (AV)

Suite 804 Blackstone Building, 233 East Bay Street, 32202-3417
Telephone: 904-632-2424
Fax: 904-632-2027
Email: mail@bthemy-law.com *URL:* http://www.bthemy-law.com

(See Next Column)

BROWN, TERRELL, HOGAN, ELLIS, MCCLAMMA & YEGELWEL P.A., *Jacksonville—Continued*

Thomas R. Brown
James T. Terrell
Wayne Hogan
Timothy D. Ellis
T. Edward McClamma
Evan J. Yegelwel
Thomas E. Duffy, Jr.
Christopher G. Burns
Anita Pryor
Alan M. Pickert

Carroll Cayer
Michael S. Sharrit
Theodore Samuel Pina, Jr.
Mark E. Calvin
Leslie A. Goller
Patricia M. Dodson
Jennifer Kolinski Millis

Reference: NCNB.

For full biographical listings, see the Martindale-Hubbell Law Directory

SHEPPARD, WHITE & THOMAS, P.A. (AV)

215 Washington Street, 32202
Telephone: 904-356-9661
Facsimile: 904-356-9667
Email: sheppardwhitethomas@worldnet.att.com

Wm. J. Sheppard
Elizabeth L. White
D. Gray Thomas

Adam Benjamin Allen
Leslie C. Scott

For full biographical listings, see the Martindale-Hubbell Law Directory

*MIAMI,** Dade Co.

ANDREW J. ANTHONY, P.A. (AV)

999 Ponce de Leon Boulevard (Coral Gables) Suite 1035, 33134-5822
Telephone: 305-444-8927
Fax: 305-529-1072

Andrew J. Anthony

Bradley Allan Silverman

OF COUNSEL

Neal Gary Rosensweig

For full biographical listings, see the Martindale-Hubbell Law Directory

ROBBINS, TUNKEY, ROSS, AMSEL, RABEN & WAXMAN, P.A. (AV)

2250 Southwest Third Avenue, Fourth Floor, 33129
Telephone: Dade County 305-858-9550; Broward County 954-522-6244 (All Telephones Open 24 Hours); 1-800-226-9550
Fax: 305-858-7491
Email: RTR2250@AOL.COM *URL:* http://www.crimlawfirm.com

Frederick S. Robbins
William R. Tunkey
Alan S. Ross
Robert G. Amsel
David Raben
Benjamin S. Waxman

Mark R. Eiglarsh
Marco A. Vazquez (1968-1995)

Reference: Mellon United National Bank, Miami, Florida.

For full biographical listings, see the Martindale-Hubbell Law Directory

*ORLANDO,** Orange Co.

PARKER, LANDERMAN & PARKER, P.A. (AV)

108 East Hillcrest Street, P.O. Box 2867, 32802
Telephone: 407-425-4910
Facsimile: 407-423-3140
Email: parkerpa@digital.net

E. Clay Parker
Alan J. Landerman
Henry Clay Parker, IV

For full biographical listings, see the Martindale-Hubbell Law Directory

*TAMPA,** Hillsborough Co.

FECHTER & DICKSON, P.A. (AV)

1201 Swann Avenue, 33606
Telephone: 813-254-2404
Facsimile: 813-254-7750

Adrienne Fechter
Thomas W. Dickson
Luis Cabassa

For full biographical listings, see the Martindale-Hubbell Law Directory

GEORGIA

*ATLANTA,** Fulton Co.

FREEMAN MATHIS & GARY, LLP (AV)

100 Galleria Parkway, 16th Floor, 30339-5959
Telephone: 770-818-0000
Fax: 770-937-9960
URL: http://www.fmglaw.com

MEMBERS

Theodore Freeman
Benton J. Mathis, Jr.
Christopher E. Parker
Philip Wade Savrin
Maureen M. Middleton
Matthew P. Stone

ASSOCIATES

Mary Anne Ackourey
Dana Kristin Maine
Jennifer E. Moore
Robert W. Stanley
William H. Buechner, Jr.
Robert W. Capobianco

Representative Clients: Association of County Commissioners of Georgia; Cherokee County, Georgia; Cobb County, Georgia; Coregis Insurance Company; DeKalb County, Georgia; Douglas County, Georgia; General Star Indemnity; Scottsdale Insurance; Safeco Insurance Co.; The St. Paul Companies.

For full biographical listings, see the Martindale-Hubbell Law Directory

HAWKINS & PARNELL, LLP (AV)

4000 SunTrust Plaza, 303 Peachtree Street, N.E., 30308-3243
Telephone: 404-614-7400
Fax: 404-614-7500
Email: relliott@hplegal.com *URL:* http://www.hawkinsparnell.com

MEMBERS OF FIRM

Michael J. Goldman
H. Lane Young, II
Frank C. Bedinger, III
T. Ryan Mock, Jr.
Robert U. Wright
Kimberly Houston
Charles R. Beans
Cullen Christie Wilkerson, Jr.
Kristine Berry Morain
Thomas G. Tidwell

ASSOCIATES

Allen L. Broughton
Debra E. LeVorse
Anita Wallace Thomas
Robert S. Thompson
Carl H. Anderson, Jr.
Alycen G. Adams

Representative Clients: ACCG-IRMA; GIRMA; Willis Corroon Corporation of Georgia; Titan Insurance Co.; American International Group; Gallagher Bassett Services, Inc.

For Complete List of Firm Personnel, See General Section

For full biographical listings, see the Martindale-Hubbell Law Directory

THOMAS E. MADDOX, JR., P.C. (AV)

3521 Habersham at Northlake (Tucker), 30084-4001
Telephone: 770-414-8055
Telecopier: 770-414-8755
Email: tommylaw@worldnet.att.net

Thomas E. Maddox, Jr.

LEGAL SUPPORT PERSONNEL

Matthew K. Johnson, Jr.

For full biographical listings, see the Martindale-Hubbell Law Directory

*ROME,** Floyd Co.

BRINSON, ASKEW, BERRY, SEIGLER, RICHARDSON & DAVIS, LLP (AV)

Omberg House, 615 West First Street, P.O. Box 5513, 30162-5513
Telephone: 706-291-8853;
Atlanta: 404-521-0908
Telecopier: 706-234-3574
Email: law@brinson-askew.com *URL:* http://www.brinson-askew.com

MEMBERS OF FIRM

Robert M. Brinson (P.C.)
C. King Askew (P.C.)
Robert L. Berry
Joseph M. Seigler, Jr.
Thomas D. Richardson
J. Anderson Davis
Hendrick L. Cromartie, III
Wright W. Smith
Mark M. J. Webb
Joseph B. Atkins
I. Stewart Duggan

ASSOCIATES

James Daniel Blitch, IV
Stephen B. Moseley

Representative Clients: City of Rome; State of Georgia; City of Gainesville. Ga.; Georgia Power Co.; News Publishing Company (Rome News Tribune); Columbia Redmond Regional Medical Center; Georgia Interlocal Risk Management Assn. (GIRMA); Scottsdale Insurance Co.; Housing Authority of Rome; First Mercury Syndicate, Inc.

For full biographical listings, see the Martindale-Hubbell Law Directory

ILLINOIS

*CHICAGO,** Cook Co.

GESSLER, HUGHES & SOCOL, LTD. (AV)

Three First National Plaza, Suite 2200, 60602
Telephone: 312-580-0100
Telecopy: 312-580-1994

Benjamin P. Beringer
Anjali Dayal
Mark S. Dym
George W. Gessler
John K. Hughes
Joshua Karsh
Peter M. Katsaros
Kimberley Marsh
Alex W. Miller
Terence J. Moran
Matthew J. Piers
Kalman D. Resnick
Frederick S. Rhine
Jonathan A. Rothstein
Michael P. Simkus
Donna Kaner Socol

Gary Chodorow
Ruth M. Dunning
S. Todd Neal
Mark A. Pellegrino
Steven C. Steinback
Dana H. Sukenik
J. Eric Vander Arend
Mark B. Weiner
Charles H. Wintersteen

OF COUNSEL

Darius S. Francescatti, M.D.
Susan R. Gzesh

For full biographical listings, see the Martindale-Hubbell Law Directory

SCHWARTZBERG, BARNETT & COHEN (AV)

55 West Monroe Street, 2400 Xerox Centre, 60603-5040
Telephone: 312-726-3555
Fax: 312-726-6299
Cable Address: "Justice"
Email: sb&c@twty.chi.il.us

MEMBERS OF FIRM

Ralph M. Schwartzberg (1939-1975)
Mark T. Barnett (1939-1970)
Hugh J. Schwartzberg
Benjamin H. Cohen

For full biographical listings, see the Martindale-Hubbell Law Directory

INDIANA

*INDIANAPOLIS,** Marion Co.

BAMBERGER & FEIBLEMAN (AV)

1408 North Pennsylvania Street, 46202-2421
Telephone: 317-639-5151
FAX: 317-269-2030
Email: bandf@iquest.net

MEMBERS OF FIRM

Ralph Bamberger (1871-1947)
Isidore Feibleman (1873-1954)
Charles B. Feibleman (1916-1971)
John K. Rickles (1898-1976)
Julian Bamberger (1905-1988)
Sigmund J. Beck (1915-1991)
Willard B. Ransom (1916-1995)
D. Robert Webster

ASSOCIATE

David K. Lee

OF COUNSEL

Victor A. DeRose
Thomas D. Strodtman
Joseph H. Greenberg
Timothy E. Peterson
Neil E. Lucas

Representative Clients: C.I.T. Corp.; FFI Corporation; Kipp Brothers, Inc.; BancPlus Mortgage Corp.; Hiway Parts, Inc.; NBD, Indiana; Tube Processing Corp.; Indiana Mortgage Corp.

For full biographical listings, see the Martindale-Hubbell Law Directory

IOWA

*DES MOINES,** Polk Co.

ROXANNE B. CONLIN AND ASSOCIATES, P.C. (AV)

The Plaza, 300 Walnut Street - Suite 5, 50309-2239
Telephone: 515-282-3329
Fax: 515-282-0318

Roxanne B. Conlin

(See Next Column)

Thomas J. Duff
Melinda Kaye Ellwanger
Tiffany B. Klosener

For full biographical listings, see the Martindale-Hubbell Law Directory

KANSAS

OVERLAND PARK, Johnson Co.

FISHER, PATTERSON, SAYLER & SMITH, L.L.P. (AV)

11050 Roe Avenue, Suite 210, 66211
Telephone: 913-339-6757
FAX: 913-339-6187
Email: fpss@worldnet.att.net
Topeka, Kansas Office: 3550 S.W. 5th Street, P.O. Box 949, 66601.
Telephone: 785-232-7761.
Fax: 785-232-6604.

MEMBERS OF FIRM

Edwin Dudley Smith (Resident)
Michael K. Seck (Resident)
David P. Madden (Resident)

ASSOCIATES

Kelly A. Feyh (Resident)
Jennifer R. Rose (Resident)

For full biographical listings, see the Martindale-Hubbell Law Directory

*TOPEKA,** Shawnee Co.

FISHER, PATTERSON, SAYLER & SMITH, L.L.P. (AV)

3550 S.W. 5th Street, P.O. Box 949, 66601
Telephone: 785-232-7761
Fax: 785-232-6604
Email: fpss@cjnetworks.com
Overland Park, Kansas Office: 11050 Roe Avenue, Suite 210, 66211.
Telephone: 913-339-6757.
Fax: 913-339-6187.

MEMBERS OF FIRM

Donald Patterson
Edwin Dudley Smith (Resident, Overland Park Office)
Larry G. Pepperdine
James P. Nordstrom
Justice B. King
J. Steven Pigg
Steve R. Fabert
Ronald J. Laskowski
Michael K. Seck (Resident, Overland Park Office)
David P. Madden (Resident, Overland Park Office)
Steven K. Johnson
Kristine A. Larscheid

ASSOCIATES

Billy E. Newman
David R. Cooper
Kelly A. Feyh (Resident, Overland Park Office)
Jennifer R. Rose (Resident, Overland Park Office)

OF COUNSEL

David H. Fisher

RETIRED

Charles Keith Sayler (Retired)

Representative Clients: Gage Shopping Center, Inc.; Fireman's Fund-American Insurance Cos.; United States Fidelity and Guaranty Co.; The Procter & Gamble Company; Commercial Union Insurance Companies; National Casualty; The Hartford; Berkshire Hathaway Companies; National Casualty Scottsdale Insurance Co.

For full biographical listings, see the Martindale-Hubbell Law Directory

KENTUCKY

*LOUISVILLE,** Jefferson Co.

LANDRUM & SHOUSE (AV)

Suite 1900 220 West Main Street, 40202-1395
Telephone: 502-589-7616
Facsimile: 502-589-2119
Lexington, Kentucky Office: 106 West Vine Street, P.O. Box 951.
Telephone: 606-255-2424.
Facsimile: 606-233-0308.

RESIDENT MEMBER OF THE FIRM

Dave Whalin

RESIDENT ASSOCIATES

Melanie Lee Straw-Boone
Robert Thaddeus (Thad) Keal
Sun S. Choy

For full biographical listings, see the Martindale-Hubbell Law Directory

Louisville—Continued

TILFORD, DOBBINS, ALEXANDER, BUCKAWAY & BLACK (AV)

Suite 1400, One Riverfront Plaza, 40202
Telephone: 502-584-6137
Fax: 502-584-2318

MEMBERS OF FIRM

Charles W. Dobbins (1916-1992)
Henry J. Tilford (1880-1968)
George S. Wetherby (1905-1954)
Lawrence W. Wetherby (1908-1994)
John T. Metcalf (1890-1974)
Stuart E. Alexander
William A. Buckaway, Jr.
Charles W. Dobbins, Jr.
Terrell L. Black
Mark Wesley Dobbins
Stuart E. Alexander, III
John M. Nader

ASSOCIATES

John A. Wilmes
Sandra F. Keene
Patrick T. Schmidt
Thomas J.B. Hurst
H. Kevin Eddins
William J. Walsh, IV
Dana M. Taylor

OF COUNSEL

Randolph Noe
Carolyn K. Balleisen
Michael G. Karem

For full biographical listings, see the Martindale-Hubbell Law Directory

MAINE

*PORTLAND,** Cumberland Co.

MONAGHAN, LEAHY, HOCHADEL & LIBBY, LLP (AV)

95 Exchange Street, P.O. Box 7046, 04112-7046
Telephone: 207-774-3906
Facsimile: 207-774-3965
Email: info@mlhl.com *URL:* http://www.mlhl.com

MEMBERS OF FIRM

Thomas F. Monaghan
Thomas G. Leahy
Joseph M. Hochadel
Kevin G. Libby
Christopher C. Dinan
Matthew J. Monaghan
Michael H. Hill

ASSOCIATES

Cornelia Fuchs Fisher
John J. Wall, III
Noah D. Wuesthoff
Ivy L. Frignoca
Carol G. Ford

For full biographical listings, see the Martindale-Hubbell Law Directory

MARYLAND

*BALTIMORE,** (Independent City)

ALLEN, JOHNSON, ALEXANDER & KARP, P.A. (AV)

Suite 1540, 100 East Pratt Street, 21202
Telephone: 410-727-5000
Fax: 410-727-0861
Email: ajakmd@aol.com
Washington, D.C. Office: 1707 L Street, N.W., Suite 1050.
Telephone: 202-828-4141.

Daniel Karp

Representative Clients: Scottsdale Insurance Co.; Nautilus Insurance Co.; Jefferson Insurance Co.; Liberty Mutual Insurance Co.; Avis Rent-A-Car; Otis Elevator Co.; Montgomery Elevator Co.; Admiral Insurance Co.; Local Government Insurance Trust; Penn National Insurance Co.

For Complete List of Firm Personnel, See General Section

For full biographical listings, see the Martindale-Hubbell Law Directory

GEORGE E. GOLOMB (AV)

Suite 2700, 111 South Calvert Street, 21202
Telephone: 410-752-3866
Telefax: 410-385-5201
Email: goegle@erols.com

For full biographical listings, see the Martindale-Hubbell Law Directory

REDMOND, BURGIN & GUTIERREZ, P.A. (AV)

1301, The Fidelity Building, 210 North Charles Street, 21202
Telephone: 410-752-1555
Fax: 410-752-1064
URL: http://www.RBGLAW.com
Upper Marlboro, Maryland Office: 14746 Main Street.
Telephone: 301-952-1555.

Leonard C. Redmond, III

(See Next Column)

Mark B. Martin

For Complete List of Firm Personnel, See General Section

For full biographical listings, see the Martindale-Hubbell Law Directory

BETHESDA, Montgomery Co.

GARY HOWARD SIMPSON (AV)

9505 Kingsley Avenue, 20814
Telephone: 301-493-0345
Fax: 301-493-0347
Email: ghslaw@erols.com *URL:* http://www.lawyers.com/garyhsimpson

Alane Tempchin

OF COUNSEL

Krauthamer & Stahl, Chartered, Chevy Chase, Maryland

LEGAL SUPPORT PERSONNEL

Michelle Ratcliffe (Paralegal)
Joy Simpson (Paralegal)

For full biographical listings, see the Martindale-Hubbell Law Directory

MICHIGAN

*ANN ARBOR,** Washtenaw Co.

MILLER, CANFIELD, PADDOCK AND STONE, P.L.C. (AV)

A Professional Limited Liability Company
Founded in 1852 by Sidney Davy Miller
101 North Main Street, Seventh Floor, 48104-1400
Telephone: 734-663-2445
Fax: 734-747-7147
URL: http://www.millercanfield.com
Detroit, Michigan Office: 150 West Jefferson, Suite 2500, 48226-4415.
Telephone: 313-963-6420.
Fax: 313-496-7500.
Cable Address: "Stem Detroit."
Troy, Michigan Office: 840 West Long Lake Road, Suite 200, 48098.
Telephone: 248-879-2000.
Fax: 248-879-2001.
Grand Rapids, Michigan Office: 99 Monroe, N.W., Suite 1200, 49503-2639.
Telephone: 616-454-8656.
Fax: 616-776-6322.
Howell, Michigan Office: 121 South Barnard Street, Suite 4, 48843-2305.
Telephone: 517-546-7600.
Telecopier: 517-546-6974.
Kalamazoo, Michigan Office: 444 West Michigan Avenue, 49007-3752.
Telephone: 616-381-7030.
Fax: 616-382-0244.
Lansing, Michigan Office: One Michigan Avenue, Suite 900, 48933-1609.
Telephone: 517-487-2070.
Fax: 517-374-6304.
Monroe, Michigan Office: 214 East Elm Avenue, Suite 100, 48162-2682.
Telephone: 734-243-2000.
Fax: 734-243-0901.
Washington, D.C. Office: 1900 K Street, N.W., Suite 1150. 20006.
Telephone: 202-429-5575; 785-0600.
Fax: 202-331-1118; 785-1234.
Pensacola, Florida Office: 25 West Cedar, 32501.
Telephone: 850-469-1088.
Fax: 850-432-0677.
New York, New York Office: 1450 Broadway, 41st Floor, 10018.
Telephone: 212-704-4400.
Fax: 212-704-4410.
Gdynia, Poland Office: UL. Slaska 21, 81-319.
Telephone: 011-485-831-2808.
Fax: 011-48-58-628 6411.
Warsaw, Poland Office: UL. Nowogrodzkall, 5th Floor, 00-513.
Telephone: 011-4822 529 0200.
Fax: 011-4822 529 0201.
Katowice, Poland Office: UL. Francuska 35/37, 40-027.
Telephone: 011 (48-32) 757-2414.
Fax: 011 (48-32) 757-2483.

PRINCIPALS OF FIRM

Robert E. Gilbert
Gregory L. Curtner

Representative Firm Clients: Chrysler Corporation; Comerica, Incorporated; City of Detroit, Michigan; Detroit Tigers, Inc.; First of Michigan; Ford Motor Company; Ford Motor Credit Company; Great Lakes Bancorp; Henry Ford Hospital; INVETECH Company.

For Complete List of Firm Personnel, See General Section

For full biographical listings, see the Martindale-Hubbell Law Directory

BLOOMFIELD HILLS, Oakland Co.

GUNSBERG & BRESKIN, P.C. (AV)

The Pinehurst Building, 1400 North Woodward Avenue, Suite 200, 48304
Telephone: 248-646-9090
Facsimile: 248-647-0638

David B. Gunsberg
Marvin Breskin

Representative Clients: Autodie International; Builders Association of S.E. Michigan; Federal Broadcasting Co.; Foamade Industries; Hercules Drawn Steel Corp.; I.S.I. Manufacturing, Inc.; McKinley Properties; Masco Industries, MascoTech; Progressive Tool; Tecumseh Products, Inc.

For full biographical listings, see the Martindale-Hubbell Law Directory

O'CONNOR, DEGRAZIA & TAMM, P.C. (AV)

4111 Andover Road East, 48302
Telephone: 248-433-2000
Fax: 248-433-2001
Email: odtlaw@ameritech.net

Richard M. O'Connor
James I. DeGrazia
James E. Tamm
Julie McCann O'Connor
Audrey J. Forbush

Thomas H. Schram
Timothy Mulligan
Lauri Beth Stewart
Christopher P. Kohler

Representative Clients: Regents of the University of Michigan; William Beaumont Hospital; Mutual Ins. Corp. of America; Botsford General Hospital; Michigan Municipal League; Michigan Municipal Liability and Property Pool; St. Paul Insurance Cos.; Meadowbrook Inc. Co.; National Chiropractic Mutual.

For full biographical listings, see the Martindale-Hubbell Law Directory

PROVIZER & PHILLIPS, P.C. (AV)

6785 Telegraph Road, Suite 400, 48301
Telephone: 248-642-0444
Facsimile: 248-642-6661
Toll Free: 1-800-288-9080
URL: http://www.lawyers.com/provizer&phillips

Randall E. Phillips
Marilyn A. Madorsky

Representative Clients: Jefferson Ins. Co.; Protective National Ins. Co.; City of Inkster.

For full biographical listings, see the Martindale-Hubbell Law Directory

*DETROIT,** Wayne Co.

CHARFOOS, REITER, PETERSON, HOLMQUIST & PILCHAK, P.C. (AV)

476 State of Michigan Plaza Building, 1200 Sixth Street, 48226
Telephone: 313-961-7011
Email: CRPHP@crphp.com
Farmington Hills, Michigan Office: 30500 Northwestern Highway, Suite 400.
Telephone: 248-626-7300.
Fax: 248-626-7305.

Myron B. Charfoos
James A. Reiter
Daniel Peterson
C. John Holmquist, Jr.
William E. Pilchak
Daniel G. Cohen

Kenneth E. Jones
Deborah S. Dorland
Danial J. Hébert
Robert C. Tice
Nedra D. Campbell

For full biographical listings, see the Martindale-Hubbell Law Directory

MILLER, CANFIELD, PADDOCK AND STONE, P.L.C. (AV)

A Professional Limited Liability Company
Founded in 1852 by Sidney Davy Miller
150 West Jefferson, Suite 2500, 48226-4415
Telephone: 313-963-6420
Fax: 313-496-7500
Cable Address: "Stem Detroit"
URL: http://www.millercanfield.com
Ann Arbor, Michigan Office: 101 North Main Street, 7th Floor, 48104-1400.
Telephone: 734-663-2445.
Fax: 734-747-7147.
Troy, Michigan Office: 840 West Long Lake Road, Suite 200, 48098.
Telephone: 248-879-2000.
Fax: 248-879-2001.
Grand Rapids, Michigan Office: 99 Monroe, N.W., Suite 1200, 49503-2639.
Telephone: 616-454-8656.
Fax: 616-776-6322.

(See Next Column)

Howell, Michigan Office: 121 South Barnard Street, Suite 4, 48843-2305.
Telephone: 517-546-7600.
Telecopier: 517-546-6974.
Kalamazoo, Michigan Office: 444 West Michigan Avenue, 49007-3752.
Telephone: 616-381-7030.
Fax: 616-382-0244.
Lansing, Michigan Office: One Michigan Avenue, Suite 900, 48933-1609.
Telephone: 517-487-2070.
Fax: 517-374-6304.
Monroe, Michigan Office: 214 East Elm Avenue, Suite 100, 48162-2682.
Telephone: 734-243-2000.
Fax: 734-243-0901.
Washington, D.C. Office: 1900 K Street, N.W., Suite 1150. 20006.
Telephone: 202-429-5575; 785-0600.
Fax: 202-331-1118; 785-1234.
Pensacola, Florida Office: 25 West Cedar, 32501.
Telephone: 850-469-1088.
Fax: 850-432-0677.
New York, New York Office: 1450 Broadway, 41st Floor, 10018.
Telephone: 212-704-4400.
Fax: 212-704-4410.
Gdynia, Poland Office: UL. Slaska 21, 81-319.
Telephone: 011-485-831-2808.
Fax: 011-48-58-628 6411.
Warsaw, Poland Office: UL. Nowogrodzkall, 5th Floor, 00-513.
Telephone: 011-4822 529 0200.
Fax: 011-4822 529 0201.
Katowice, Poland Office: UL. Francuska 35/37, 40-027.
Telephone: 011 (48-32) 757-2414.
Fax: 011 (48-32) 757-2483.

PRINCIPALS OF FIRM

Gregory L. Curtner (Ann Arbor and New York, N.Y. Offices)
Donna J. Donati

Representative Firm Clients: Chrysler Corporation; Comerica, Incorporated; City of Detroit, Michigan; Detroit Tigers, Inc.; First of Michigan; Ford Motor Company; Ford Motor Credit Company; Great Lakes Bancorp; Henry Ford Hospital; INVETECH Company.

For Complete List of Firm Personnel, See General Section

For full biographical listings, see the Martindale-Hubbell Law Directory

FARMINGTON HILLS, Oakland Co.

CHARFOOS, REITER, PETERSON, HOLMQUIST & PILCHAK, P.C. (AV)

30500 Northwestern Highway, Suite 400, 48334-3179
Telephone: 248-626-7300
Facsimile: 248-626-7305
Email: CRPHP@crphp.com
Detroit, Michigan Office: 1200 Sixth Street.
Telephone: 313-961-7011.

Myron B. Charfoos
James A. Reiter
Daniel Peterson
C. John Holmquist, Jr.
William E. Pilchak
Daniel G. Cohen

Kenneth E. Jones
Deborah S. Dorland
Danial J. Hébert
Robert C. Tice
Nedra D. Campbell

For full biographical listings, see the Martindale-Hubbell Law Directory

*GRAND RAPIDS,** Kent Co.

DREW, COOPER & ANDING (AV)

Ledyard Building, Suite 300, 125 Ottawa Avenue, N.W., 49503-2898
Telephone: 616-454-8300
Fax: 616-454-0036
Email: DCADVOCATE@AOL.COM

Stephen R. Drew
John E. Anding
Ann M. Cooper
Christopher G. Hastings
Bridget C. Kehoe
Brian K. Lawson

For full biographical listings, see the Martindale-Hubbell Law Directory

TROY, Oakland Co.

BROWN SCHWARTZ PATTERSON & ANKERS, P.C. (AV)

2301 West Big Beaver Road, Suite 212, 48084
Telephone: 248-816-6100
Fax: 248-816-6370

Malcolm D. Brown
Craig S. Schwartz
Scott T. Patterson
Gary C. Ankers

Jeffrey T. Harrison

For full biographical listings, see the Martindale-Hubbell Law Directory

Troy—Continued

POLING, MCGAW & POLING, P.C. (AV)

Suite 275, 5435 Corporate Drive, 48098
Telephone: 248-641-0500
Telecopier: 248-641-0506
URL: http://www.lawyers.com/polingmcgaw&poling

Benson T. Buck (1926-1989)	Gregory C. Hamilton
Richard B. Poling	Veronica B. O'Hara
D. Douglas McGaw	James R. Parker
Richard B. Poling, Jr.	Shannon M. Acton

OF COUNSEL

Ralph S. Moore

Representative Clients: City of Troy; United States Fidelity & Guaranty Co.; Sentry Insurance Co.; Admiral Insurance; DeMaria Construction Co.; Leo Corporation; Aetna Casualty and Surety Co.; Concord Design; Pneumo-Abex.

For full biographical listings, see the Martindale-Hubbell Law Directory

VAN SUILICHEM & ASSOCIATES, P.C. (AV)

2301 West Big Beaver Road, Suite 212, 48084
Telephone: 248-816-2000
Fax: 248-816-2014

Donald A. Van Suilichem	Christina M. Brookshire

Randal Ray Cole

For full biographical listings, see the Martindale-Hubbell Law Directory

CIVIL TRIAL PRACTICE

ALABAMA

ALBERTVILLE, Marshall Co.

GULLAHORN & HARE, P.C. (AV)

310 West Main Street, P.O. Box 1669, 35950
Telephone: 256-878-1891
Fax: 256-878-1965
Email: g-hpc@cybertyme.com

Charles R. Hare, Jr. | John C. Gullahorn

Representative Clients: First Bank of Boaz; The Home Bank; Peoples Independent Bank of Boaz; AmSouth Bank; Compass Bank; Albertville Industrial Development Board; Boaz Industrial Development Board; Marshall-Dekalb Electric Cooperative; Olympia Construction, Inc.

For full biographical listings, see the Martindale-Hubbell Law Directory

ALEXANDER CITY, Tallapoosa Co.

MORRIS, HAYNES & HORNSBY (AV)

131 Main Street, P.O. Box 1660, 35011-1660
Telephone: 256-329-2000
Fax: 256-329-2015
Email: morrishayn@webshoppe.net

Larry W. Morris
Randall Stark Haynes
Clay Hornsby
Nancy L. Eady

OF COUNSEL

John F. Dillon, IV (1930-1998)
Jennie Lee Kelley

Representative Clients: Aliant Bank; City of Alexander City; Town of Wadley.
Approved Attorneys for: Lawyers Title Insurance Corp.; Mississippi Valley Title Insurance Co.

For full biographical listings, see the Martindale-Hubbell Law Directory

*ANDALUSIA,** Covington Co.

ALBRITTONS, CLIFTON, ALVERSON & MOODY, P.C. (AV)

(Powell, Albritton & Albritton)
(Albrittons & Rankin)
(Albrittons, Givhan, Clifton & Alverson)
(Albrittons & Givhan)
109 Opp Avenue, P.O. Box 880, 36420
Telephone: 334-222-3177
Telecopier: 334-222-2696

Ed. T. Albritton (1857-1925)
Wm. Harold Albritton, Sr. (1881-1929)
Dempsey M. Powell (1863-1949)
Albert L. Rankin (1909-1970)
Robert Bynum Albritton (1905-1983)
William H. Albritton, Jr. (1907-1983)
James Marvin Albritton (1915-1987)
James R. Clifton
William Harold Albritton, IV
William B. Alverson, Jr.
Thomas B. Albritton
Julie S. Moody

Benjamin M. Bowden

General Counsel for: Coca-Cola Bottling Co. of Andalusia; Opp-Micolas Cotton Mills.
Attorneys for: First Alabama Bank; Alabama Power Co.; The Travelers; Liberty Mutual Ins. Co; Kemper Insurance; Crum & Forster Insurance Cos; CSX Transporation.

For full biographical listings, see the Martindale-Hubbell Law Directory

POWELL, PEEK & WEAVER (AV)

201 East Troy Street, Drawer 969, 36420
Telephone: 334-222-4103
Facsimile: 334-222-4105
Email: ppw@alaweb.com

MEMBERS OF FIRM

Abner R. Powell (1875-1940)
Abner R. Powell, Jr. (1916-1987)
Abner R. Powell, III
John M. Peek
Gary L. Weaver
Abner Riley Powell, IV

Representative Clients: State Farm Insurance Group; ALFA Insurance Companies; U.S.F.& G. Co.; CNA Insurance; Auto Owners Insurance Co.; Southern Guaranty Co.; Covington County Bank; Colonial Bank of Opp, Alabama.

For full biographical listings, see the Martindale-Hubbell Law Directory

*BAY MINETTE,** Baldwin Co.

JOHNSTONE, ADAMS, BAILEY, GORDON AND HARRIS, L.L.C. (AV)

Dahlberg Building, 104 Hand Avenue, P.O. Box 729, 36507
Telephone: 334-937-9473
Facsimile: 334-937-9475
Email: attorneys@JohnstoneAdams.com *URL:* http://www.JohnstoneAdams.com
Mobile, Alabama Office: Royal St. Francis Building, 104 St. Francis Street, P.O. Box 1988, 36633.
Telephone: 334-432-7682.
Facsimile: 334-432-2800; 432-0712.

MEMBER OF FIRM

Charles C. Simpson, III (Resident)

For full biographical listings, see the Martindale-Hubbell Law Directory

*BIRMINGHAM,** Jefferson Co.

BERKOWITZ, LEFKOVITS, ISOM & KUSHNER, A PROFESSIONAL CORPORATION (AV)

SouthTrust Tower, 420 North Twentieth Street, Suite 1600, 35203-5202
Telephone: 205-328-0480
Telecopier: 205-322-8007
URL: http://www.blik.com

Henry I Frohsin
Edward P. Meyerson
J. Forrest Hinton
Susan S. Wagner
Frank S. James III
Patricia Clotfelter
Wesley C. Redmond
Michael R. Silberman

N. Andrew Rotenstreich
Ellen Elizabeth Henderson
Stanley W. Logan
Lee T. Clanton

For Complete List of Firm Personnel, See General Section

For full biographical listings, see the Martindale-Hubbell Law Directory

BRADLEY ARANT ROSE & WHITE LLP (AV)

2001 Park Place, Suite 1400, P.O. Box 830709, 35283-0709
Telephone: 205-521-8000
Facsimile: 205-521-8800
Facsimile (SouthTrust Tower Office): 205-521-8500
URL: http://www.barw.com
Huntsville, Alabama Office: 200 Clinton Avenue West, Suite 900, 35801.
Telephone: 205-517-5100.
Facsimile: 205-533-5069.
Washington, D.C. Office: 801 Pennsylvania Avenue, NW, Suite 230, 20004.
Telephone: 202-347-8893.
Facsimile: 202-347-1684.

MEMBERS OF FIRM

Joseph S. Bird III
T. Michael Brown
Philip J. Carroll III
G. Edward Cassady III
James S. Christie Jr.
Brittin Turner Coleman
Forrest K. Covington
Stewart M. Cox
J. Patrick Darby
A. H. Gaede Jr.
James W. Gewin
John E. Goodman
Patrick H. Graves Jr. (Resident, Huntsville Office)
George Bryan Harris
Warne S. Heath (Resident, Huntsville Office)
Gary C. Huckaby (Resident, Huntsville Office)
David Glenn Hymer
Norman Jetmundsen Jr.
Matthew H. Lembke
Thad Gladden Long
Joseph B. Mays Jr.
Michael D. McKibben
Hobart A. McWhorter Jr.
Richard H. Monk III
John H. Morrow
Andrew J. Noble III
Michael R. Pennington
E. Mabry Rogers
Walter J. Sears III
Robert K. Spotswood
Jay D. St. Clair
Sid J. Trant
John D. Watson III

OF COUNSEL

Stanley D. Bynum
Macbeth Wagnon Jr. (Retired)

COUNSEL

Amy K. Myers

ASSOCIATES

James F. Archibald III
Denise Avery Dodson
Douglas E. Eckert
Julie S. Elmer
Fred M. Haston III
David M. Lawson
Justin T. McDonald
T. Matthew Miller
Kenneth M. Perry
John W. Smith T

Representative Clients: Ford Motor Co.; Volkswagen of America; Chrysler Corp.; The Firestone Tire & Rubber Co.; The Goodyear Tire & Rubber Co.; Torchmark Corp.; Lincoln National Life Insurance Co.; J. I. Case Co.; Monsanto Co.; A. H. Robins Co.

For Complete List of Firm Personnel, See General Section

For full biographical listings, see the Martindale-Hubbell Law Directory

Birmingham—Continued

BURR & FORMAN LLP (AV)

3100 SouthTrust Tower, 420 North 20th Street, P.O. Box 830719, 35283-0719
Telephone: 205-251-3000
Facsimile: 205-458-5100
URL: http://www.burr.com
Huntsville, Alabama Office: Suite 204, Regency Center, 400 Meridian Street.
Telephone: 205-551-0010.
Facsimile: 205-551-0043.
Atlanta, Georgia Office: Suite 1200, One Georgia Center, 600 West Peachtree Street, 30308.
Telephone: 404-815-3000.
Facsimile: 404-817-3244.

MEMBERS OF FIRM

Henry Graham Beene
Paul P. Bolus
"Ginger" M. Busby
John D. Clements
D. Frank Davis
John F. DeBuys, Jr.
David A. Elliott
James Ross Forman, III
Gerald P. Gillespy
Robert S. W. Given
Victor L. Hayslip
J. Fredric Ingram
William C. Knight, Jr.
Mark McCarroll Lawson
Joseph W. Letzer
J. Patrick Logan
Gary M. London
E. Clayton Lowe, Jr.
Michael L. Lucas
Timothy M. Lupinacci
John C. Morrow
Dent M. Morton
William F. Murray, Jr.
J. Hunter Phillips, III
James J. Robinson
Robert H. Rutherford, Jr.
Carol H. Stewart

OF COUNSEL

A. Jackson Noble, Jr.
C. V. Stelzenmuller
Robert G. Tate

For Complete List of Firm Personnel, See General Section

For full biographical listings, see the Martindale-Hubbell Law Directory

CABANISS, JOHNSTON, GARDNER, DUMAS & O'NEAL (AV)

Park Place Tower, 2001 Park Place North, Suite 700, P.O. Box 830612, 35283-0612
Telephone: 205-716-5200
Fax: 205-716-5389
Email: bgm@cabaniss.com *URL:* http://www.cabaniss.com
Mobile, Alabama Office: 700 Riverview Plaza, P.O. Box 2906.
Telephone: 334-433-6961.
Fax: 334-415-7350.

MEMBERS OF FIRM

William F. Gardner
Crawford S. McGivaren, Jr.
Sydney F. Frazier, Jr.
William K. Thomas
R. Carlton Smyly
Steve A. Tucker
R. Taylor Abbot, Jr.
Richard Eldon Davis
Melanie Merkle Bass
John M. Graham

COUNSEL

L. Murray Alley

ASSOCIATES

Joseph V. Musso
Annette Lanning Kinderman
Michael E. Turner
Stephen Andrew Walsh

Counsel for: Schuler Industries, Inc.; Carraway Methodist Health Systems; Doster Construction Co., Inc.; Liberty Mutual Insurance Co.; MacMillan Bloedel Packaging, Inc.; Norfolk Southern Corp.; O'Neal Steel, Inc.

For Complete List of Firm Personnel, See General Section

For full biographical listings, see the Martindale-Hubbell Law Directory

CARR, ALLISON, PUGH, HOWARD, OLIVER & SISSON, P.C. (AV)

400 Vestavia Parkway, Suite 400, 35216
Telephone: 205-822-2006
Fax: 205-822-2057
Email: CFC@caphos.com
Florence, Alabama Office: 212 South Cedar Street, 35630.
Telephone: 256-718-6040.
Fax: 256-718-2150.
Mobile, Alabama Office: P.O. Box 781,36601-0781.
Telephone: 334-621-4340.
Fax: 334-626-8928.

Charles F. Carr (Resident, Daphne Office)
Russell Q. Allison
Bennett L. Pugh
David K. Howard (Resident, Florence Office)
Thomas L. Oliver, II
William H. Sisson (Resident, Daphne Office)
Glenn E. Ireland
Thomas C. Logan
Donald B. Kirkpatrick, II
Sarah J. Carlisle
Craig W. Goolsby (Resident, Daphne Office)

(See Next Column)

Gregg L. Smith
Joseph H. Driver
Brett A. Ross
Thomas S. Thornton, III
W. Bradford Kittrell
Jeffrey B. Carr
Joseph H. Hilley
Jeremy N. Trousdale
Ryan G. Brake
Caroline T. Pryor (Resident, Daphne Office)

For full biographical listings, see the Martindale-Hubbell Law Directory

CLARK & SCOTT, P.C. (AV)

3500 Blue Lake Drive, Suite 350, P.O. Box 380548, 35238-0548
Telephone: 205-967-9675
Telecopier: 205-967-7563
WATS: 800-955-8678
Mobile, Alabama Office: Clark, Scott & Sullivan, P.C., 10th Floor, Regions Bank Building, 56 St. Joseph Street, P.O. Box 1034.
Telephone: 205-433-1346.
Telecopier: 205-433-1086. WATS: 800-239-6733.
Jackson, Mississippi Office: Clark, Scott & Streetman, P.A., 447 Northpark Drive, Ridgeland, 39157.
Telephone: 601-977-0102.
Telecopier: 601-957-0690.

William A. Scott, Jr.
John W. Clark, Jr.
G. Steven Henry
Anthony N. Fox
Judith E. Dolan
Wayne Morse
James C. Ayers, Jr.
Kelly W. Otto
David Whittington McDowell
Joseph E. Stott
Shane M. Oncale

Cynthia A. Martin
Tommy C. Ritter, Jr.
J. Craig Lewis
Rosemary Sizemore Moore
Freddie N. Harrington, Jr.

Representative Clients: American International Group; ITT Hartford; Fireman's Fund Insurance Company; American Medical Systems, Inc.; Crum & Forster Companies; MEDMARC Insurance Company; Parke Davis/Warner Lambert Co.; Pfizer, Inc.; GAINSCO; Southern Heritage Insurance Company.

For full biographical listings, see the Martindale-Hubbell Law Directory

DOMINICK, FLETCHER, YEILDING, WOOD & LLOYD, P.A. (AV)

2121 Highland Avenue, 35209
Telephone: 205-939-0033
URL: http://members.aol.com/dfywandl/lawyer.htm

J. Fred Wood, Jr.

Christopher A. Bottcher

Counsel for: Citizens Federal Savings Bank; St. Vincent's Hospital; Birmingham-Southern College; Castle Mortgage Corporation.

For Complete List of Firm Personnel, See General Section

For full biographical listings, see the Martindale-Hubbell Law Directory

GORDON, SILBERMAN, WIGGINS & CHILDS, P.C. (AV)

1400 SouthTrust Tower, 420 North 20th Street, 35203
Telephone: 205-328-0640
Facsimilie: 205-254-1500
Washington, D.C. Office: 1621 Connecticut Avenue, N.W., Suite 400.
Telephone: 202-238-0690.
Facsimile: 202-238-0968.

RESIDENT SHAREHOLDERS

Bruce L. Gordon
Robert L. Wiggins, Jr.
Robert F. Childs, Jr.
Dennis George Pantazis
James Mendelsohn
Richard J. Ebbinghouse
Samuel Fisher
Ann C. Robertson
Mark P. Williams
Joseph H. Calvin, III

RESIDENT ASSOCIATES

Timothy C. Gann
Rocco Calamusa, Jr.
Brian M. Clark
Craig L. Lowell
Nicole L. Gordon
Edward McFarland Johnson

For Complete List of Firm Personnel, See General Section

For full biographical listings, see the Martindale-Hubbell Law Directory

GORHAM & WALDREP, P.C. (AV)

2101 6th Avenue North, Suite 700, 35203
Telephone: 205-254-3216; 251-9166
Telecopier: 205-324-3802
Email: info@gorham-waldrep.com *URL:* http://www.gorham-waldrep.com
Montgomery, Alabama Office: 250 Commerce Street, P.O. Box 4837, 36103-4837.
Telephone: 334-262-0777.
Telecopier: 334-262-0742.

(See Next Column)

GORHAM & WALDREP P.C.—*Continued*

Charlie D. Waldrep
Thomas L. Stewart
Michael G. Kendrick
John T. Natter
Frank G. Alfano
Kay L. McNabb Cason

Representative Clients: Jefferson County Personnel Board; Birmingham-Jefferson Civic Center Authority; The Water Works and Sewer Board of the City of Birmingham; City of Homewood; American Federation of Government Employees Local #1945; City of Pelham; Town of Kimberly; Alabama Tire Dealers Assn.; Southern States Body Shop Assn.

For Complete List of Firm Personnel, See General Section

For full biographical listings, see the Martindale-Hubbell Law Directory

HARE, WYNN, NEWELL AND NEWTON (AV)

A Partnership including Professional Corporations
Suite 800 Massey Building, 290 21st Street North, 35203
Telephone: 205-328-5330
Fax: 205-324-2165

MEMBERS OF FIRM

Francis H. Hare (1904-1983)
Carlton T. Wynn
Neal C. Newell
Alex W. Newton
C. Terrell Wynn, Jr.
James J. Thompson, Jr.
Alva C. Caine
Ray O. (Ronnie) Noojin, Jr. (1945-1996)
John W. Haley (P.C.)
D. Leon Ashford (P.C.)
Scott A. Powell
James R. Pratt, III
S. Shay Samples
Bruce J. McKee
Michael D. Ermert
Nolan Edward Awbrey
James B. Gunther, Jr.
Don McKenna
Martin E. Burke

COUNSEL

Francis H. Hare, Jr., (P.C.)
James O. Haley
James K. Baker

References: AmSouth Bank of Birmingham; First Commercial Bank of Birmingham.

For full biographical listings, see the Martindale-Hubbell Law Directory

HARRIS, CLECKLER & HOLLIS (AV)

Historic 2007 Building, 2007 Third Avenue North, 35203-2366
Telephone: 205-328-2366
Telecopier: 205-328-0013
Email: hcbr@mindspring.com *URL:* http://www.harriscleckler.com

Lyman H. Harris
Michael H. Cleckler
Jeffrey K. Hollis

ASSOCIATE

Jason A. Shamblin

For full biographical listings, see the Martindale-Hubbell Law Directory

HASKELL SLAUGHTER & YOUNG, L.L.C. (AV)

1200 AmSouth/Harbert Plaza, 1901 Sixth Avenue North, 35203
Telephone: 205-251-1000
Facsimile: 205-324-1133
Email: hsy@hsy.com
Montgomery, Alabama Office: 305 South Lawrence Street, P.O. Box 4660. 36103-4660.
Telephone: 334-265-8573.
Facsimile: 334-264-7945.

William M. Slaughter
Frank M. Young, III
Thomas T. Gallion, III (Resident, Montgomery Office)
James C. Huckaby, Jr.
Stephen L. Poer
Beverly P. Baker
Constance C. Walker (Resident, Montgomery Office)
Richard H. Walston
Michael K. K. Choy
Carter H. Dukes
John W. Scott
R. Scott Williams

Georgia Sullivan Roberson
James A. Patton, Jr.
Joseph N. Harden

Representative Clients: CNA Insurance Co.; The Equitable Life Assurance Society of the United States; Executive Risk; Fireman's Fund Insurance Companies; Jefferson County Racing Association; Marshall Durbin Companies; Montgomery County, Alabama; Raytheon Aircraft Company; Rhone-Poulenc Rorer Pharmaceuticals, Inc.;

For Complete List of Firm Personnel, See General Section

For full biographical listings, see the Martindale-Hubbell Law Directory

HOGAN, SMITH & ALSPAUGH, P.C. (AV)

2323 Second Avenue, North, 35203
Telephone: 205-324-5635
Telecopier: 205-324-5637
Email: Chris@Hogan-Smith.com *URL:* http://www.hsa-pc.com

(See Next Column)

William W. Smith
M. Clay Alspaugh
R. Benjamin Hogan, III
Ronald R. Crook
Richard D. Stratton
Jack Lee Roberts, Jr.
Benjamin E. Baker, Jr.

Maxwell D. Carter

Reference: Regions Bank.

For full biographical listings, see the Martindale-Hubbell Law Directory

HUIE, FERNAMBUCQ AND STEWART, LLP (AV)

Suite 800, Regions Bank Building, 417 N. 20th Street, 35203
Telephone: 205-251-1193
Telecopy: 205-251-1256

MEMBERS OF FIRM

Thomas B. Huie (1915-1990)
William B. Fernambucq (1922-1997)
Charles A. Stewart, Jr. (1923-1983)
Eugene D. Martenson
Stanley A. Cash
James R. Shaw
Robert M. Girardeau
John S. Civils, Jr.
Frank E. Lankford, Jr.
M. Keith Gann
Charles H. Clark, Jr.
John D. Herndon
J. Allen Sydnor, Jr.
D. Alan Thomas
William G. Gantt
T. Kelly May
Christopher S. Rodgers
Walter J. Price, III
H. Lanier Brown, II

ASSOCIATES

Robert V. Rodgers
Gregory L. Schuck
Paul F. Malek
Jennifer Devereaux Segers
Philip R. Collins
Brandy Murphy Lee
Thomas E. Bazemore, III
R. Gordon Sproule, Jr.
Martha Leach Thompson
Patrick O. Gray
James W. Moss
H. Cannon Lawley
Anna Katherine Graves

Representative Clients: Allstate Insurance; CNA Insurance Co.; Crawford & Company; Kemper Group; TM Claims; Zurich-American Insurance Co.; Capital Alliance Insurance; First Real Estate Corp.; Insbrok; Direct Insurance.

For full biographical listings, see the Martindale-Hubbell Law Directory

LAMAR, BURGESS, HALE, MILLER, NORRIS & FELDMAN, P.C. (AV)

1600 Financial Center, 505 20th Street, North, 35203
Telephone: 205-326-0000
Fax: 205-323-2945
Email: boblamar@worldnet.att.net

Robert S. Lamar, Jr.
J. Thomas Burgess
Thomas S. Hale
Paul A. Miller
Rick D. Norris, Jr.
Daniel B. Feldman

Lynn B. Randall
William Marsh Acker, III
James A. Haggerty, Jr.
Murray H. Gibson, Jr.
Ethan R. Dettling
J. Stuart McAtee
Van Douglas McMahan
L. Jonathan Goldstein

For full biographical listings, see the Martindale-Hubbell Law Directory

LIGHTFOOT, FRANKLIN & WHITE, L.L.C. (AV)

The Clark Building, 400 20th Street North, 35203
Telephone: 205-581-0700
Facsimile: 205-581-0799
Email: LFWlaw@LFWlaw.com *URL:* http://www.lfwlaw.com

Warren B. Lightfoot
Samuel H. Franklin
Jere F. White, Jr.
Mac M. Moorer
John M. Johnson
M. Christian King
E. Glenn Waldrop, Jr.
Adam K. Peck
Harlan I. Prater, IV
Michael L. Bell
William S. Cox, III
William H. King, III
Sara Anne Ford
Madeline H. Haikala
William H. Brooks
J. Banks Sewell, III
Lee M. Hollis
Jackson R. Sharman, III

Wynn M. Shuford
John Q. Somerville
Suzanne Alldredge
Stephanie Keller Womack
Melody L. Hurdle
Robin Hansen Graves
J. Bradley Powell
William H. Morrow
Anne Sikes Hornsby
Stephen Jackson Rowe
Ivan B. Cooper
Craig N. Rosler
Lisa J. Wathey
Marjorie P. Slaughter
William Larkin Radney, IV
James F. Hughey, III

Representative Clients: AT&T; Ford Motor Company; Emerson Electric Co.; Monsanto Company; Chrysler Corporation; General Motors Corporation; The Upjohn Company; Bristol-Myers Squibb Company; The Goodyear Tire & Rubber Company; Mitsubishi Motor Sales of America, Inc.

For full biographical listings, see the Martindale-Hubbell Law Directory

Birmingham—Continued

LLOYD, SCHREIBER & GRAY, P.C. (AV)

Two Perimeter Park South Suite 100, 35243
Telephone: 205-967-8822
Telecopier: 205-967-2380
Email: lsgpc@aol.com

James S. Lloyd
Joseph Allen Schreiber
James C. Gray, III
Mark C. Peterson
Gerald Alan Templeton
Stephen Errol Whitehead

Legrand H. Amberson, Jr.
Thomas J. Skinner, IV
Laura C. Nettles
Howard Yeilding Downey
E. Britton Monroe
Ashley T. Robinson
Brock G. Murphy
Jennifer A. McCammon
Kathy R. Davis
Heidi Wells
Michael J. Clemmer

For full biographical listings, see the Martindale-Hubbell Law Directory

LUSK, FRALEY, MCALISTER & SIMMS, P.C. (AV)

Suite 1700 AmSouth/Harbert Plaza, 1901 Sixth Avenue North, 35203
Telephone: 205-323-7100
Fax: 205-323-7050
Email: Lusk-Fraley.com

Donald D. Lusk
John M. Fraley
David L. McAlister
Keri Donald Simms
Kenneth A. Dowdy
David Lawrence Dean
David Thurston White, III
Susan Gilman McAlister
Payton Caldwell Lusk
Leslie Ann Caldwell

For full biographical listings, see the Martindale-Hubbell Law Directory

J. VERNON PATRICK, JR. & ASSOCIATES, P.C. (AV)

1201 Financial Center, 505 20th Street North, 35203-4607
Telephone: 205-323-5665
Telecopier: 205-324-6221

J. Vernon Patrick, Jr.

Jeffrey Venton Havercroft

For full biographical listings, see the Martindale-Hubbell Law Directory

PORTERFIELD, HARPER & MILLS, P.A. (AV)

22 Inverness Center Parkway, Suite 600, P.O. Box 530790, 35242-4821
Telephone: 205-980-5000
Fax: 205-980-5001

Jack B. Porterfield, Jr.
Larry W. Harper
William T. Mills, II
William Dudley Motlow, Jr.
H. C. "Trey" Ireland, III
Keith J. Pflaum
Michael L. Haggard
Stephen Douglas Christie
Don L. Hall
Mark E. King

Timothy W. Knight
Karen Walker Casey
Kristin Daniels Horn
W. Perry Webb
Eric Daniel Hoaglund
Michael Robert Lunsford
Neal D. Moore, III
J. Paul Sizemore
C. Jeffery Ash

Representative Clients: CIGNA; St. Paul Insurance Co.; The Travelers; Figgie International; White Consolidated Industries; Terex Corp.; Wausau Insurance; Baptist Health Systems, Inc.; Bruno's, Inc.; Harley Davidson, Inc.

For full biographical listings, see the Martindale-Hubbell Law Directory

JOHN D. SAXON, P.C. (AV)

1000 Financial Center, 505 North 20th Street, 35203
Telephone: 205-324-0223
Facsimile: 205-323-1583

John D. Saxon

Tammy Cecile Murphy Woolley

LEGAL SUPPORT PERSONNEL

Delilah Cole

For full biographical listings, see the Martindale-Hubbell Law Directory

SCHOEL, OGLE, LILES AND UPSHAW, LLP (AV)

600 Financial Center, 505 North 20th Street, P.O. Box 1865, 35201-1865
Telephone: 205-521-7000
Telecopier: 205-521-7007
Mailing Address: Drawer 1865, Birmingham, Alabama, 35201-1865

Jerry W. Schoel
Richard F. Ogle
Paul A. Liles
David O. Upshaw
Jann J. Rice

(See Next Column)

Reference: First Alabama Bank.

For full biographical listings, see the Martindale-Hubbell Law Directory

SMITH & ELY, LLP (AV)

2000-A Southbridge Parkway Suite 405, 35209
Telephone: 205-802-2214
Fax: 205-879-4445

MEMBERS OF FIRM

Carol Ann Smith
Brenen G. Ely

ASSOCIATES

Susan Rogers
Susan Caroline Haygood
Toby Dykes

OF COUNSEL

Lisa B. Singer

For full biographical listings, see the Martindale-Hubbell Law Directory

SMITH, SPIRES & PEDDY, P.C. (AV)

2015 Second Avenue North Suite 200, 35203
Telephone: 205-251-5885
Fax: 205-251-8642

Paul G. Smith
Thomas S. Spires
A. Joe Peddy
Todd Hamilton
Thomas Coleman, Jr.

B. Scott Tyra
James L. Sanders, II
Julie L. Jenkins
Matthew C. Williams
Clarence "Chip" Rivers, IV
Jason M. Langley
R. Timothy Estes

Representative Clients: Racetrac Petroleum Inc.; Birmingham Steel Erectors; Brasfield & Gorrie Construction; Old Dominion Freight Line, Inc.; Winn Dixie, Inc.; Huddle House, Inc.; Picadilly Cafeterias Inc.; John Deere; Circuit City, Inc.; Ervin Cable Construction.

For full biographical listings, see the Martindale-Hubbell Law Directory

SPAIN & GILLON, L.L.C. (AV)

The Zinszer Building, 2117 2nd Avenue North, 35203
Telephone: 205-328-4100
Telecopier: 205-324-8866
Email: ddh@spain-gillon.com *URL:* http://lawlinks.com:80/atty/al/sggbn.html

MEMBERS OF FIRM

Ollie L. Blan, Jr.
Eugene P. Stutts
Alton B. Parker, Jr.
Charles D. Stewart
Elizabeth Ann McMahan
Paul L. Sotherland
Robert L. Williams
Gary A. Parker
David S. Maxey
W. Gregory Smith
Steve R. Burford
Earl H. Lawson, Jr.
James P. Rea

General Counsel for: Alabama Insurance Guaranty Association; Alabama Insurance Underwriters Association; Auburn University Foundation.
Counsel for: The Minnesota Life Insurance Co.; Government Employees Insurance Co.; Massachusetts Mutual Life Insurance Co.

For Complete List of Firm Personnel, See General Section

For full biographical listings, see the Martindale-Hubbell Law Directory

STARNES & ATCHISON LLP (AV)

100 Brookwood Place, 35209
Telephone: 205-868-6000
Telecopier: 205-868-6099
Mailing Address: P.O. Box 598512, 35259-8512
Email: information@starneslaw.com
Mobile, Alabama Office: Riverview Plaza, Suite 1106, 63 South Royal Street, 36602.
Telephone: 334-433-6049.

MEMBERS OF FIRM

W. Stancil Starnes
W. Michael Atchison
William Anthony Davis, III
Michael A. Florie
John P. Scott, Jr.
L. Graves Stiff, III
Chris N. Galanos
Randal H. Sellers
J. Bentley Owens, III
Walter William Bates
Michael K. Wright
Robert P. Mackenzie, III
Allan R. Wheeler
Laura Howard Peck
Thomas Lawson Selden
Mark Christopher Eagan
Sybil Vogtle Abbot

ASSOCIATES

Sharon A. Woodard
Joseph S. Miller
Scott M. Salter
Jeannie Bugg Walston
Ashley E. Watkins
Anthony Cameron Harlow
Rik S. Tozzi
Philip G. Piggott
Reed R. Bates
Bryan Oxford Balogh
Elise Beth May
Blake D. Andrews
W. Christian Hines, III
Joseph L. Reese, Jr.

(See Next Column)

STARNES & ATCHISON LLP—*Continued*

ASSOCIATES (Continued)

Geoffrey S. Bald
James M. Terrell
L. Jackson Young, Jr.
Alfred H. Perkins, Jr.

Representative Clients: MAIC Holdings Inc.; Drummond Co., Inc.; Protective, Inc.; Mutual of Omaha; American Honda; Synthes (USA); American Heritage Insurance Co.; Rheem Manufacturing Co.; Glaxo Wellcome, Inc.; Brookwood Medical Center.

For full biographical listings, see the Martindale-Hubbell Law Directory

THOMAS, MEANS, GILLIS, DEVLIN, ROBINSON & SEAY, P.C. (AV)

1035 Financial Center, 505 20th Street North, 35203-2605
Telephone: 205-328-7915
Fax: 205-214-6160
Mailing Address: P.O. Box 370497, Birmingham, AL, 35237-0447
Email: tmgpc.lawfirm@tmgpc.com *URL:* http://www.tmgpc.com
Montgomery, Alabama Office: 3121 Zelda Court, P.O. Drawer 5058, 36103-5058.
Telephone: 334-270-1033.
Fax: 334-260-9396. E-mail: tmgpc.lawfirm@tmgpc.com. URL: http://www.tmgpc.com
Atlanta, Georgia Office: The Chandler Building, Suite 300, 127 Peachtree Street N.E., 30303.
Telephone: 404-222-8400.
Fax: 404-222-0080. E-Mail: tmgpc.lawfir@tmgpc.com. URL: http://www.tmgpc.com

Kenneth L. Thomas (Resident)

James L. Richey (Resident)
Wendell J. Chambliss (Resident)
Lisa F. Brown (Resident)
Valerie L. Acoff (Resident)
Edward J. Berry (Resident)

For full biographical listings, see the Martindale-Hubbell Law Directory

WALSTON, WELLS, ANDERSON & BAINS, LLP (AV)

Suite 500 Financial Center, 505 20th Street North, 35203
Telephone: 205-251-9600
Telecopier: 205-251-0700
Mailing Address: P.O. Box 830642, Birmingham, AL, 35283-0642

Robert H. Walston (Retired)
Frank C. Galloway, Jr.
Lawrence Dumas, III
C. Henry Marston
Vernon L. Wells, II
James L. Birchall
Michael C. Quillen
David B. Anderson
Larry B. Childs
William R. Sylvester
Kay K. Bains
Heyward C. Hosch III
Ronald A. Levitt
Elizabeth Champlin Bishop
C. Ellis Brazeal, III
David B. Walston
Anne Stone Sumblin
Emily Sides Bonds
Julia Boaz Cooper

OF COUNSEL

Edward J. Ashton
Jerry Dean Hillman

ASSOCIATES

Randall D. Quarles
N. Christian Glenos
Barry A. Brock
Dawn Helms Sharff
Elizabeth M. Davis
David B. Ringelstein, II
J. David Moore
Erin O. Brooks
Alan Michael Warfield
Benjamin Earl Waller
Tracy H. Beauchamp

For full biographical listings, see the Martindale-Hubbell Law Directory

*CHATOM,** Washington Co.

TURNER, ONDERDONK, KIMBROUGH & HOWELL, P.A. (AV)

1021 Central Avenue, P.O. Drawer 1389, 36518
Telephone: 334-847-2237
Fax: 334-847-3115
Email: firm@tokh.com *URL:* http://www.tokh.com
Mobile, Alabama Office: 1359 Dauphin Street.
Telephone: 334-432-2855.
Fax: 334-432-2863.

Edward P. Turner, Jr.
A. Michael Onderdonk
William A. Kimbrough, Jr. (Resident, Mobile Office)
Gordon K. Howell
Marc E. Bradley (Resident, Mobile Office)
Halron W. Turner
Frank Woodson (Resident, Mobile Office)
David M. Huggins (Resident, Mobile Office)
E. Tatum Turner

LEGAL SUPPORT PERSONNEL

Thomas E. Fuller

For full biographical listings, see the Martindale-Hubbell Law Directory

*CULLMAN,** Cullman Co.

ST. JOHN & ST. JOHN, L.L.C. (AV)

108 Third Street South East, P.O. Drawer K, 35056-3542
Telephone: 256-734-3542
Fax: 256-734-3544

MEMBERS OF FIRM

F. E. St. John (1874-1943)
Finis E. St. John (1909-1984)
Finis E. St. John, III (1933-1984)
Finis E. St. John, IV
Gaynor L. St. John

ASSOCIATE

Rita P. Farris

OF COUNSEL

Juliet G. St. John

Attorneys for: U.S. Fidelity & Guaranty Co.; Travelers Insurance Co.; Liberty Mutual Insurance Co.; ALFA Mutual Insurance Co.; First Federal Savings & Loan; The Atlanta Casualty Companies; Auto-Owners Insurance Co.; Golden-Rod Broilers, Inc.; Cullman Products, Inc.; McGriff Industries, Inc.

For full biographical listings, see the Martindale-Hubbell Law Directory

*DECATUR,** Morgan Co.

HARRIS, CADDELL & SHANKS, P.C. (AV)

214 Johnston Street, S.E., P.O. Box 2688, 35602-2688
Telephone: 256-340-8000
Telecopier: 256-340-8040
Email: hcs@ala-net.com

Julian Harris (1904-1994)
Norman W. Harris (1907-1998)
Philip T. Shanks (Retired)
Charles L. Murphree (Retired)
John A. Caddell
Robert H. Harris
Jon H. Moores
Thomas A. Caddell
William E. Shinn, Jr.
Gary A. Phillips
Dow M. Perry, Jr.
Barnes F. Lovelace, Jr.
Jeffrey S. Brown
David W. Langston
Huel Harris

Attorneys for: First American Bank, Decatur, Alabama; SouthTrust Bank of Alabama N.A. (Morgan County); Morgan County Commission; The Industrial Development Board of the City of Decatur, Alabama; The Boeing Company; Amoco Chemical Co.; BellSouth Inc.; Auto-Owners Insurance Co.; ALFA Insurance Cos.; U.S.F. & G. Co.

For full biographical listings, see the Martindale-Hubbell Law Directory

*DOTHAN,** Houston Co.

COBB & SHEALY, P.A. (AV)

206 North Lena Street, P.O. Box 6346, 36302
Telephone: 334-794-8526
Fax: 334-677-0030
URL: http://www.cobb-shealy.com

Herman W. Cobb
Steadman S. Shealy, Jr.
Raymond Todd Derrick
Richard Elder Crum
James H. Pike
Joseph A. Morris
Brian T. Mosholder
Joseph D. Talmadge, Jr.

Representative Clients: Travelers Insurance; Nationwide Insurance; Auto-Owners Insurance; Employers Casualty of Texas; Safeco Insurance; Federated Insurance; Universal Underwriters; National Security Insurance; Great Central Insurance.
Approved Title Attorneys for: Mississippi Valley Title Ins. Co.

For full biographical listings, see the Martindale-Hubbell Law Directory

HARDWICK, HAUSE & SEGREST (AV)

212 North Lena Street, P.O. Box 1469, 36302
Telephone: 334-794-4144
Fax: 334-671-9330
URL: http://www.lawyers.com/hhslawfirm

W. G. Hardwick (1910-1993)
William G. Hause (Retired)

MEMBERS OF FIRM

Jere C. Segrest
Kevin Walding
Tina Whitehead Stamps

Counsel for: Dothan City Board of Education; American General; Alabama Power Co.; General Motors Acceptance Corp.; Liberty National Life Ins. Co.

For full biographical listings, see the Martindale-Hubbell Law Directory

LEE & MCINISH (AV)

238 West Main Street, P.O. Box 1665, 36302
Telephone: 334-792-4156
Facsimile: 334-794-8342
Email: leemc@graceba.net

(*See Next Column*)

LEE & MCINISH, *Dothan—Continued*

MEMBERS OF FIRM

W. L. Lee (1873-1944) Alan C. Livingston
Alto V. Lee, III (1915-1987) William C. Carn, III
William L. Lee, III Peter A. McInish
Jerry M. White

ASSOCIATES

William L. Lee, IV William W. Nichols
William C. White, II

OF COUNSEL

H. Dwight McInish

Counsel for: Seaboard Coast Line Railroad Co.; Atlanta & St. Andrews Bay Railroad Co.; ALFA; U. S. F. & G. Co.; Maryland Casualty Co.; Continental Insurance Cos.; Royal-Globe Group; Slocomb National Bank; GTE South.

For full biographical listings, see the Martindale-Hubbell Law Directory

ENTERPRISE, Coffee Co.

CASSADY, FULLER & MARSH, LLP (AV)

203 East Lee Avenue, P.O. Box 310910, 36331
Telephone: 334-347-2626
Telecopier: 334-393-1396

MEMBERS OF FIRM

Joe C. Cassady M. Dale Marsh
Kenneth T. Fuller Joe C. Cassady, Jr.
R. Rainer Cotter, III

Representative Clients: RegionsBank; Enterprise Health Care Authority; Sessions Co., Inc.; Allstate; State Farm Mutual Insurance Co.; Community Bank & Trust Co.; Conagra, Inc.
Approved Attorneys for: First American Title Insurance Co.

For full biographical listings, see the Martindale-Hubbell Law Directory

J. E. SAWYER, JR. (AV)

203 South Edwards Street, 36330
Telephone: 334-347-6447
Fax: 334-347-8217
Email: sawyer@entercomp.com

ASSOCIATE

Stanley P. Walker

For full biographical listings, see the Martindale-Hubbell Law Directory

*EVERGREEN,** Conecuh Co.

WILLIAM D. MELTON (AV)

Melton Building, 100 Liberty Hill Drive, Drawer 800, 36401-0800
Telephone: 334-578-2423
Fax: 334-578-2427

References: Bank of Evergreen, Evergreen, Alabama; First National Bank of Brewton, Alabama.

For full biographical listings, see the Martindale-Hubbell Law Directory

*FLORENCE,** Lauderdale Co.

SELF & SELF (AV)

408 West Dr. Hicks Boulevard, P.O. Box 1062, 35631
Telephone: 256-767-2570; 1-800-336-2574
Fax: 256-767-2632

MEMBERS OF FIRM

Henry (Hank) H. Self, Jr. Gilbert P. Self

ASSOCIATE

Missy Homan Hibbett

Reference: Bank Independent; AmSouth Bank; Compass Bank.

For full biographical listings, see the Martindale-Hubbell Law Directory

*FORT PAYNE,** De Kalb Co.

SCRUGGS, JORDAN, DODD & DODD (AV)

207 Alabama Avenue, South, P.O. Box 681109, 35967
Telephone: 256-845-5932
Fax: 256-845-4325
Email: scruggs@peop.tdsnet.com *URL:* http://www.lawyers.com/scruggsjordandodd&dodd

William D. Scruggs, Jr. J. David Dodd
Robert K. Jordan E. Allen Dodd, Jr.
Holly Hendrickson

Representative Clients: State Farm Insurance Company; Allstate Insurance Co., Inc.; USF&G Insurance Co.; Nucor, Inc.; Ladd Engineering, Inc.; ALABAMA Band; First Federal Bank; Fritz Structural Steel, Inc.; Williamson Oil Co., Inc.

For full biographical listings, see the Martindale-Hubbell Law Directory

*GADSDEN,** Etowah Co.

FORD AND HOWARD, P.C. (AV)

(Formerly Ford & Associates)
The Lancaster Building, 645 Walnut Street, Suite 5, P.O. Box 388, 35902
Telephone: 256-546-5432
Fax: 256-546-5435
Email: fordfirm@aol.com

George P. Ford H. Edgar Howard

Bradley Williams Cornett Vann Allan Spray

OF COUNSEL

Elizabeth R. Howard

Reference: AmSouth Bank, N.A.

For full biographical listings, see the Martindale-Hubbell Law Directory

INZER, HANEY, JOHNSON & MCWHORTER, P.A. (AV)

(Inzer, Suttle, Swann & Stivender)
Second Floor, Compass Bank Building, 601 Broad Street, P.O. Drawer 287, 35902-0287
Telephone: 256-546-1656
Telecopier: 256-546-1093
Email: inzerlaw@cybrtyme.com

W. Roscoe Johnson, III Robert D. McWhorter, Jr.
James C. Inzer, III James W. McGlaughn
F. Michael Haney Elizabeth Golson McGlaughn

Assistant Division Counsel for: Southern Railway System.
Attorneys for: L & N Railroad; General Motors Corp.; Gulf States Steel; Goodyear Tire & Rubber Corp.; Alabama Power Co.; Insurance Company of North America; Allstate Insurance Co.; Travelers Insurance Co.; Cincinnati Insurance Co.

For Complete List of Firm Personnel, See General Section

For full biographical listings, see the Martindale-Hubbell Law Directory

*HUNTSVILLE,** Madison Co.

BRADLEY ARANT ROSE & WHITE LLP (AV)

200 Clinton Avenue West, Suite 900, 35801
Telephone: 205-517-5100
Facsimile: 205-517-5200
URL: http://www.barw.com
Birmingham, Alabama Office: 2001 Park Place, Suite 1400, P.O. Box 830709.
Telephone: 205-521-8000.
Facsimile: 205-521-8800. Facsimile (SouthTrust Tower Office): 205-521-8500.
Washington, D.C. Office: 801 Pennsylvania Avenue, NW, Suite 230, 20004.
Telephone: 202-347-8893.
Facsimile: 202-347-1684.

RESIDENT PARTNERS

Patrick H Graves Jr. Gary C. Huckaby
Warne S. Heath E. Cutter Hughes Jr.

RESIDENT ASSOCIATE

Kimberly B. Martin

For Complete List of Firm Personnel, See General Section

For full biographical listings, see the Martindale-Hubbell Law Directory

HORNSBY, WATSON & MEGINNISS (AV)

1110 Gleneagles Drive, 35801
Telephone: 256-650-5500
Fax: 256-650-5504
Email: rwhj@mindspring.com

Ralph W. Hornsby, Sr. Ralph W. Hornsby, Jr.
S. A. "Bud" Watson, Jr. Jeffrey G. Blackwell

OF COUNSEL

David H. Meginniss

For full biographical listings, see the Martindale-Hubbell Law Directory

MORRIS, CLOUD AND CONCHIN, P.C. (AV)

521 Madison Street, P.O. Box 248, 35804
Telephone: 256-534-0065
Fax: 256-539-0741

Harvey B. Morris (P.C.) Joseph M. Cloud
Gary V. Conchin

Maureen "Mike" K. Cooper Daniel B. Banks, Jr.

For full biographical listings, see the Martindale-Hubbell Law Directory

Huntsville—Continued

SPURRIER, RICE, WOOD & HALL (AV)

3226 Bob Wallace Avenue, 35805
Telephone: 256-533-5015
Fax: 256-536-0105
Email: srwhlaw@hiwaay.net

MEMBERS OF FIRM

Donald N. Spurrier
Robert V. Wood, Jr.
Benjamin R. Rice
Ruth Ann Hall

ASSOCIATES

Earl Thomas Forbes
Jonathan B. Medlock
Deborah S. Hensley
Richard L. Morris
Craig A. Bardell

Representative Clients: Alfa Mutual Insurance Co.; Allstate Insurance Co.; American Indemnity Group; Harleyville Insurance Co.; State Farm Insurance Cos.; Risk Co.; CNA Maryland Casualty Co.; Farmers Insurance Group; Guidant Insurance Co.

For full biographical listings, see the Martindale-Hubbell Law Directory

STEPHENS, MILLIRONS, HARRISON & GAMMONS, P.C. (AV)

333 Franklin Street, P.O. Box 307, 35801
Telephone: 256-533-7711
Telecopier: 256-536-9388

Arthur M. Stephens
James G. Harrison
Paul L. Millirons
Robert C. Gammons

Douglas A. Baymiller
Steven J. Shaw

Representative Clients: SouthTrust Bank, N.A.,; Regions Mortgage, Inc.; Chase Manhattan Mortgage Corp.; Amiras, Inc. (d/b/a/ Buy-Wise Drugs); Huntsville Ford Tractor; Brookhill Management Group.

For full biographical listings, see the Martindale-Hubbell Law Directory

*MOBILE,** Mobile Co.

ARMBRECHT, JACKSON, DEMOUY, CROWE, HOLMES & REEVES, L.L.C. (AV)

1300 Riverview Plaza, P.O. Box 290, 36601
Telephone: 334-405-1300
Facsimile: 334-432-6843; 433-3821
Email: adc@ajlaw.com

MEMBERS OF FIRM

Rae M. Crowe
M. Kathleen Miller
Broox G. Holmes
Edward A. Dean
W. Boyd Reeves
David E. Hudgens
Kirk C. Shaw
Wm. Steele Holman II
Norman E. Waldrop, Jr.
Broox G. Holmes, Jr.
Conrad P. Armbrecht
James E. Robertson, Jr.
Grover E. Asmus II
Scott G. Brown
David A. Bagwell
Clifford C. Brady
Douglas L. Brown
Richard W. Franklin
Donald C. Radcliff
Rodney R. Cate

ASSOCIATES

P. Vincent Gaddy
A. Edwin Stuardi, III
Timothy D. Ryan
J. Walton Jackson
Sam David Knight

Representative Clients: Airgas, Inc.; American Security Insurance Co.; American Security Group (Regional Counsel); AmSouth Bank of Alabama (Regional Counsel); Burlington Northern Santa Fe Railroad Co. (District Counsel); International Paper Co.; Kimberly-Clark Corp.; Loyal American Life Insurance Co.; Mutual Assurance, Inc.; New York Life Insurance Co.; Travelers Insurance Co.

For Complete List of Firm Personnel, See General Section

For full biographical listings, see the Martindale-Hubbell Law Directory

ATCHISON, CROSBY, SAAD & BEEBE, P.C. (AV)

3030 Knollwood Drive, 36693
Telephone: 334-665-7200
Fax: 334-665-7250
URL: http://www.acsblaw.com

James E. Atchison
Elias J. Saad
James H. Crosby
Donald G. Beebe

Mona Ann Vivar
Jacqueline M. McConaha
Daryl A. Atchison

Representative Clients: City of Mobile; Alabama State Docks; Mobile Area Water and Sewer Board; Owens Corning, Inc.; Pilot Catastrophe Services, Inc.; Shell Oil Co.; Premdor,Inc.; Melvin Pierce Paint Co.; Commonwealth National Bank; Fiberglass Canada,Inc.

For full biographical listings, see the Martindale-Hubbell Law Directory

BRISKMAN & BINION, P.C. (AV)

205 Church Street, P.O. Box 43, 36601
Telephone: 334-433-7600
Fax: 334-433-4485
Email: briskman@zebra.net

Donald M. Briskman
Christ N. Coumanis
Mack B. Binion
Kimberly C. Hodgson

A List of Representative Clients will be furnished upon request.
References: Regions Bank; AmSouth Bank, N.A.; Southtrust Bank of Mobile.

For full biographical listings, see the Martindale-Hubbell Law Directory

DAVID P. BROOME (AV)

AmSouth Bank Building, 107 St. Francis Street Suite 1408, 36633
Telephone: 334-432-9933
Fax: 334-432-9706
Mailing Address: P.O. Box 1944, Mobile, Alabama, 36633-1944
Email: broomelaw@aol.com

LEGAL SUPPORT PERSONNEL

Heidi Marie Fundinger

References: AmSouth Bank, NA; The Bank of Mobile.

For full biographical listings, see the Martindale-Hubbell Law Directory

CABANISS, JOHNSTON, GARDNER, DUMAS & O'NEAL (AV)

700 Riverview Plaza, P.O. Box 2906, 36652
Telephone: 334-433-6961
Fax: 334-415-7350
Email: bgm@cabaniss.com *URL:* http://www.cabaniss.com
Birmingham, Alabama Office: Park Place Tower. 2001 Park Place North, Suite 700. P.O. Box 830612.
Telephone: 205-716-5200.
Fax: 205-716-5389.

MEMBERS OF FIRM

Benjamen T. Rowe (Resident)
William K. Thomas
William A. Robinson (Resident)
David L. Kane (Resident)
Patrick H. Sims (Resident)
R. Boyd Miller (Resident)
Donald J. Stewart (Resident)
Sandy G. Robinson (Resident)

ASSOCIATES

Rebecca D. Parks (Resident)
Ian D. Rosenthal (Resident)
Jarrod J. White (Resident)

Representative Clients: Liberty Mutual Insurance Co.; Liberty National Life Insurance Co.; Rohr Aeroservices; International Paper Company; Boise Cascade Corporation; Employers Reinsurance Co.; Montgomery Kone, Inc.; UOP; Vanity Fair Intimates, Inc.

For full biographical listings, see the Martindale-Hubbell Law Directory

CARR, ALFORD, CLAUSEN & MCDONALD, L.L.C. (AV)

One St. Louis Centre, Suite 5000, P.O. Drawer C, 36601
Telephone: 334-432-1600
Facsimile: 334-432-1700
URL: http://www.cacm.com

Davis Carr
James H. McDonald, Jr.
Helen Johnson Alford
James W. Lampkin, II
Andrew C. Clausen
Jean M. Powers

Annette McDermott Carwie
Paul V. Lagarde
M. Lauren Lemmon
Frank L. Parker, Jr.
Thomas M. Rockwell
Christina M. Adcock
Pamela Ann Moore
Kathleen Cobb Kaufman
W. Ben. Broadwater
Joseph Anthony Zarzaur, Jr.

For full biographical listings, see the Martindale-Hubbell Law Directory

CLARK, SCOTT & SULLIVAN, P.C. (AV)

10th Floor, Regions Bank Building, 56 St. Joseph Street, P.O. Box 1034, 36602
Telephone: 334-433-1346
Telecopier: 334-433-1086
WATS: 800-239-6733
Email: clarssull@aol.com
Birmingham, Alabama Office: Clark & Scott, P.C., 3500 Blue Lake Drive, Suite 350, P.O. Box 380548.
Telephone: 205-967-9675.
Telecopier: 205-967-7563. WATS: 800-955-8678.
Jackson, Mississippi Office: Clark, Scott & Streetman, P.A., 447 Northpark Drive, Ridgeland, 39157.
Telephone: 601-977-0102.
Telecopier: 601-957-0690.

(See Next Column)

CLARK, SCOTT & SULLIVAN P.C., *Mobile—Continued*

Carroll Sullivan (Resident)
George M. Zoghby (Resident)
William E. Pipkin, Jr. (Resident)
Jannea S. Rogers (Resident)
Geoffrey DeWitt Lavies Alexander (Resident)
Margaret Molette Deakle

For full biographical listings, see the Martindale-Hubbell Law Directory

CUNNINGHAM, BOUNDS, YANCE, CROWDER & BROWN, L.L.C. (AV)

1601 Dauphin Street, P.O. Box 66705, 36660
Telephone: 334-471-6191
Fax: 334-479-1031
Email: adm@cbycb.com

James A. Yance
John T. Crowder, Jr.
Robert T. Cunningham, Jr.
Joseph M. Brown, Jr.
Gregory B. Breedlove
Michael A. Worel
David G. Wirtes, Jr.
Toby D. Brown
Reggie Copeland, Jr.
Richard T. Dorman

J. Stephen Legg
George M. Dent, III

OF COUNSEL

Richard Bounds
Robert T. Cunningham
J. Kenyon Rainer, Sr., M.D., J.D.

References: Regions Bank; AmSouth Bank, N.A.

For full biographical listings, see the Martindale-Hubbell Law Directory

FINKBOHNER AND LAWLER, L.L.C. (AV)

169 Dauphin Street Suite 300, P.O. Box 3085, 36652
Telephone: 334-438-5871
Fax: 334-432-8052
Email: finkbohnerlawlerllc@zebra.net

MEMBERS OF FIRM

George W. Finkbohner, Jr.
John L. Lawler
George W. Finkbohner, III
Royce A. Ray, III

For full biographical listings, see the Martindale-Hubbell Law Directory

FRAZER, GREENE, UPCHURCH & BAKER, L.L.C. (AV)

First National Bank Building, Suite 2206 107 Saint Francis Street, 36602
Telephone: 334-431-6020
Facsimile: 334-431-6030
URL: http://www.frazergreene.com

MEMBERS OF FIRM

A. Danner Frazer, Jr.
Edward C. Greene
Michael E. Upchurch
D. Brent Baker

Bruce M. Westbrook
W. Austin Mulherin, III
Marcus Edward McDowell

For full biographical listings, see the Martindale-Hubbell Law Directory

HELMSING, SIMS & LEACH, P.C. (AV)

The Laclede Building, 150 Government Street, Suite 2000, P.O. Box 2767, 36652
Telephone: 334-432-5521
Telecopy: 334-432-0633

Larry U. Sims
Frederick G. Helmsing
John N. Leach, Jr.
Warren C. Herlong, Jr.
James B. Newman
Robert H. Rouse
Charles H. Dodson, Jr.
Joseph P. H. Babington
R. Alan Alexander
John J. Crowley, Jr.
Joseph D. Steadman
Todd S. Strohmeyer

William R. Lancaster
Robin Kilpatrick Fincher
John Townsend Dukes
John Casey Pipes
James Bradford Pittman, Jr.

For full biographical listings, see the Martindale-Hubbell Law Directory

INGE, TWITTY & DUFFY (AV)

1410 Regions Bank Building, 56 St. Joseph Street, P.O. Box 1109, 36633
Telephone: 334-433-3200
Facsimile: 334-433-3444

MEMBERS OF FIRM

James J. Duffy, Jr.
James J. Duffy, III

Francis H. Inge (1902-1959)
Thos. E. Twitty (1901-1975)
Richard H. Inge (1912-1980)

For full biographical listings, see the Martindale-Hubbell Law Directory

JOHNSTONE, ADAMS, BAILEY, GORDON AND HARRIS, L.L.C. (AV)

Royal St. Francis Building, 104 St. Francis Street, 8th Floor, P.O. Box 1988, 36633
Telephone: 334-432-7682
Facsimile: 334-432-0712 or 334-432-2800
Email: attorneys@JohnstoneAdams.com *URL:* http://www.JohnstoneAdams.com
Bay Minette, Alabama Office: Dahlberg Building, 107 Hand Avenue, P.O. Box 729, 36507.
Telephone: 334-937-9473.
Facsimile: 334-937-9475.

MEMBERS OF FIRM

Ben H. Harris, Jr.
William H. Hardie, Jr.
Joseph M. Allen, Jr.
I. David Cherniak
David C. Hannan
Wade B. Perry, Jr.
Thomas S. Rue
Alan C. Christian
Celia J. Collins
Tracy P. Turner
E. Erich Bergdolt

ASSOCIATES

E. Russell March, III
Scott Alton Browning
Craig Bryant Morris

OF COUNSEL

Brock B. Gordon

For Complete List of Firm Personnel, See General Section

For full biographical listings, see the Martindale-Hubbell Law Directory

LYONS, PIPES & COOK, P.C. (AV)

2 North Royal Street, P.O. Box 2727, 36652-2727
Telephone: 334-432-4481
Cable Address: "Lysea"
Telecopier: 334-433-1820
URL: http://www.LPCLaw.com

Wesley Pipes
Norton W. Brooker, Jr.
Cooper C. Thurber
Marion A. Quina, Jr.
Walter M. Cook, Jr.
Joseph J. Minus, Jr.
Caroline C. McCarthy
William E. Shreve, Jr.
Kenneth A. Nixon
Daniel S. Cushing
Allen E. Graham
Michael C. Niemeyer
M. Warren Butler
S. Wesley Pipes, V
James D. Jeffries, Jr.

General Counsel: Alabama State Docks Department (an agency of the State of Alabama).
Counsel: McKenzie Tank Lines, Inc.; SCNO Barge Lines, Inc.; Scott Paper Co.; Shell Oil Corp.
Trial Counsel: Aetna Life & Casualty Co.; Chubb Group of Insurance Companies.

For Complete List of Firm Personnel, See General Section

For full biographical listings, see the Martindale-Hubbell Law Directory

AUGUSTINE MEAHER, III, P.C. (AV)

107 St. Francis Street, Suite 2118, 36602-3321
Telephone: 334-432-9971
Fax: 334-432-9978

Augustine Meaher, III

References: Bank of Mobile, Mobile, Alabama; AmSouth Bank, Mobile, Alabama.

For full biographical listings, see the Martindale-Hubbell Law Directory

PIERCE, LEDYARD, LATTA & WASDEN, P.C. (AV)

Colonial Bank Centre Suite 400, 41 North Beltline, 36608
Telephone: 334-344-5151
Facsimile: 334-344-9696
Mailing Address: P.O. Box 16046, Mobile, AL, 36616
URL: http://www.pllaw.com

Donald F. Pierce
Abe L. Philips, Jr.
Goodman G. Ledyard
Forrest S. Latta
H. William Wasden
Edward G. Isaacs Bowron
John Charles S. Pierce
W. Pemble DeLashmet
C. William Daniels, Jr.

Mark Pickett Eiland
James Robert Turnipseed
Michael A. Montgomery

Representative Clients: Grove U.S. LLC; Beloit Corp.; Koehring Cranes & Excavators; Winnebago; Blue Cross and Blue Shield; Connecticut Mutual Life Insurance Co.; Harnischfeger Industries; Terex Corporation; Hubbell Incorporated; Genuine Parts Company.

For full biographical listings, see the Martindale-Hubbell Law Directory

Mobile—Continued

SINTZ, CAMPBELL, DUKE & TAYLOR (AV)

3763 Professional Parkway, 36609
Telephone: 334-344-7241
Fax: 334-344-7400

MEMBERS OF FIRM

Peter V. Sintz (1940-1997)
Robert C. Campbell, III
Frank G. Taylor
Steven L. Terry

ASSOCIATES

Wm. Kyle Morris
Kathryn W. Petersen
Barry C. Prine

OF COUNSEL

Leon G. Duke

LEGAL SUPPORT PERSONEL

James A. Koblas

Representative Clients: Aetna C & S Insurance Co.; Mobile County School Board; Auto-Owners Insurance Co.; Argonaut Insurance Co.; Mostellar Medical Clinic; Scottsdale Insurance Co.; American International Group; Alabama School of Math and Science; Mobile County Sheriff's Office.

For full biographical listings, see the Martindale-Hubbell Law Directory

*MONTGOMERY,** Montgomery Co.

BALL, BALL, MATTHEWS & NOVAK, P.A. (AV)

2000 Interstate Park Drive, Suite 204, 36109
Telephone: 334-387-7680
Fax: 334-387-3222
Email: Firm@Ball-Ball.com

Fred S. Ball (1866-1942)
Charles A. Ball (1904-1969)
Fred S. Ball, Jr. (1896-1974)
Richard A. Ball (1906-1983)
John R. Matthews, Jr.
Richard A. Ball, Jr.
Tabor R. Novak, Jr.
Clyde C. Owen, Jr.
C. Winston Sheehan, Jr.
William H. Brittain II
E. Hamilton Wilson, Jr.
Richard E. Broughton
T. Cowin Knowles
Gerald C. Swann, Jr.
Mark T. Davis
James A. Rives

Fred B. Matthews
Allison L. Alford
Michael L. White
Emily C. Marks
Brandy A. Adkins
George R. Parker

LEGAL SUPPORT PERSONNEL

Lon Worley (Office Manager)

Counsel for: Beech Aircraft Corporation; Bell Helicopter Co.; John Deere Co.; Government Employees Insurance Co.; Chubb & Son; Cigna Co.; Chrysler Corp.; Associated Aviation Underwriters.

For full biographical listings, see the Martindale-Hubbell Law Directory

HASKELL SLAUGHTER YOUNG & GALLION, L.L.C. (AV)

305 South Lawrence Street, P.O. Box 4660, 36103-4660
Telephone: 334-265-8573
Facsimile: 334-264-7945
Email: hsymont@actworld.net
Birmingham, Alabama Office: 1200 AmSouth/Harbert Plaza, 1901 Sixth Avenue North. 35203
Telephone: 205-251-1000.
Facsimile: 205-324-1133.

Thomas T. Gallion, III
Constance C. Walker

Representative Clients: The Equitable Life Assurance Society of the United States; Federal Deposit Insurance Corporation; Fireman's Fund Insurance Companies; Marshall Durbin Companies; Montgomery County, Alabama; Raytheon Aircraft Company.

For full biographical listings, see the Martindale-Hubbell Law Directory

HILL, HILL, CARTER, FRANCO, COLE & BLACK, P.C. (AV)

425 South Perry Street, P.O. Box 116, 36101-0116
Telephone: 334-834-7600
Fax: 334-263-5969

Thomas B. Hill, Jr. (1903-1984)
Wm. Inge Hill (1911-1995)
James T. Stovall (1905-1972)
James J. Carter (1913-1985)
William A. Oldacre (1932-1973)
Ralph A. Franco
T. Bowen Hill, III
Harry Cole
Robert C. Black, Sr.
William I. Hill, II
John M. Milling, Jr.
William Inge Hill, Jr.
Gerald W. Hartley
Randall Morgan
Robert W. Bradford, Jr.
David E. Allred
Laura L. Crum
Mark A. Franco
Joana S. Ellis
John R. Bradwell
William C. McGowin
Robert C. Black, Jr.
Thomas C. Tankersley

(See Next Column)

Pamela Pelekis Swan
Elizabeth Brannen Carter
Doy Leale McCall, III
Erika Perrone Tatum

Representative Clients: The Aetna Group; The State Farm Group; ALFA; General Electric Co.; General Motors Corp; Blue Cross and Blue Shield of Alabama; Allstate Insurance Co.; Winn-Dixie Stores, Inc.; Scottsdale Insurance Co.; National Casualty Co.

For full biographical listings, see the Martindale-Hubbell Law Directory

NIX, HOLTSFORD & VERCELLI, P.C. (AV)

300 A Water Street, Suite 300, P.O. Box 4128, 36103
Telephone: 334-262-2006
Fax: 334-834-3616
Email: NHV@JUNO.COM

H. E. Nix, Jr.
Alex L. Holtsford, Jr.
Charles E. Vercelli, Jr.
Floyd R. Gilliland, Jr.
T. Randall Lyons
Steven A. Higgins
Kenneth A. Hitson, Jr.

David P. Stevens
Todd E. Hughes
Rick A. Howard
Stacy Anne Linn
Jay S. Tuley

LEGAL SUPPORT PERSONNEL

Richard M. Seibert (Firm Manager)
Ashley Collins (Paralegal)
Monica E. Jayroe (Paralegal)
Suzanne H. Long (Legal Assistant)
Kelley S. Tracy (Paralegal)

For full biographical listings, see the Martindale-Hubbell Law Directory

ROBISON & BELSER, P.A. (AV)

200 Coosa Street, 36104
Telephone: 334-834-7000
Telecopier: 334-834-7011
Mailing Address: Drawer 1470, Montgomery, AL, 36102
Email: tsides@mont.mindspring.com

Vaughan H. Robison (1918-1995)
Richard C. Belser (1927-1991)
Philip H. Butler
David B. Byrne, Jr.
James R. Seale
John M. Bolton, III
Robert F. Northcutt
Martha Ann Miller
Terry A. Sides
Charles B. Haigler, III

General Counsel for: Montgomery County Board of Education.
Representative Clients: Union Bank & Trust Co.; Liberty National Life Insurance Co.; State Farm Mutual Fire & Casualty Co.

For full biographical listings, see the Martindale-Hubbell Law Directory

GRIFFIN SIKES, JR. (AV)

644 South Perry Street, P.O. Box 4446, 36103
Telephone: 334-269-0033
Telefax: 334-264-2658

For full biographical listings, see the Martindale-Hubbell Law Directory

THOMAS, MEANS, GILLIS, DEVLIN, ROBINSON & SEAY, P.C. (AV)

3121 Zelda Court, P.O. Drawer 5058, 36103-5058
Telephone: 334-270-1033
Fax: 334-260-9396
Email: tmgpc.lawfirm@tmgpc.com *URL:* http://www.tmgpc.com
Birmingham, Alabama Office: 1035 Financial Center, 505 20th Street North, 35203. Mailing Address: P.O. Box 370447, Birmingham, AL., 35237-0447.
Telephone: 205-328-7915.
Fax: 205-214-6160. E-mail: tmgpc.lawfirm@tmgpc.com. URL: http://www.tmgpc.com
Atlanta, Georgia Office: The Chandler Building, Suite 300, 127 Peachtree Street, N.E., 30303.
Telephone: 404-222-8400.
Fax: 404-222-0080. E-Mail: tmgpc.lawfirm@tmgpc.com. URL: http://www.tmgpc.com

Kenneth L. Thomas (Resident, Birmingham, Alabama Office)
Tyrone C. Means
H. Lewis Gillis
Marvin A. Devlin (Resident, Atlanta, Georgia Office)
Mark E. Robinson (Resident, Atlanta, Georgia Office)
Quinton S. Seay (Resident, Atlanta, Georgia Office)

James L. Richey (Resident, Birmingham, Alabama Office)
Wendell J. Chambliss (Resident, Birmingham Office)
Lisa F. Brown (Resident, Birmingham, Alabama Office)
Valerie L. Acoff (Resident, Birmingham, Alabama Office)
John W. Adams, Jr.
Paul C. Williams
Jennifer D. Odom (Resident, Atlanta, Georgia Office)

(See Next Column)

THOMAS, MEANS, GILLIS, DEVLIN, ROBINSON & SEAY P.C., *Montgomery—Continued*

Darnell D. Coley
Edward J. Berry (Resident, Birmingham, Alabama Office)
Thaddeus L. Hamilton (Resident, Birmingham, Alabama Office)

LEGAL SUPPORT PERSONNEL

Joyce L. Lehmann
Tonya White
Bryan Palmer
Felicia Kolley
John Baker (Office Administrator)
Cathy Allen
Lakesha Baker
Larry Holmes
Linda Steele
Mary Duncan
Pamela Watkins
Paula Mosely
Rodney Barganier
Tamara Venice
Linda Stoudemier

For full biographical listings, see the Martindale-Hubbell Law Directory

VOLZ, PRESTWOOD & HANAN, P.C. (AV)

350 Adams Avenue, P.O. Box 1910, 36102-1910
Telephone: 334-264-6401
Fax: 334-834-4954

Charles H. Volz, Jr.
Alvin T. Prestwood
Charles H. Volz, III
Ellis D. Hanan
Richard D. Lively
Judy H. Barganier

For full biographical listings, see the Martindale-Hubbell Law Directory

PELL CITY, St. Clair Co.

BLAIR AND PARSONS (AV)

St. Clair Land Title Building, 1711 Cogswell Avenue, 35125
Telephone: 205-884-3440
Fax: 205-884-3442

MEMBERS OF FIRM

A. Dwight Blair
Elizabeth S. Parsons

Representative Clients: Colonial Bank; Metro Bank; Am South Bank; State Farm Mutual Insurance Cos; ALFA Mutual Insurance Co.; Allstate Insurance Co.; St. Paul Insurance Cos.; Auto Owners Insurance Co.; Reliance Insurance Cos.; National Bank of Commerce.

For full biographical listings, see the Martindale-Hubbell Law Directory

*TROY,** Pike Co.

CALHOUN, FAULK, WATKINS & FAIRCLOTH, L.L.C. (AV)

78 South Court Square, P.O. Box 489, 36081
Telephone: 334-566-7200
Fax: 334-566-7584

Richard F. Calhoun
Joseph E. Faulk
William Keith Watkins
Robert Curry Faircloth
James G. Clower (Retired)

General Counsel for: City of Troy; City of Brundidge; Regions Bank, Troy; First National Bank of Brundidge; Troy City Board of Education; Pike County Board of Education; South Alabama Electric Cooperative, Inc.; Airtek Engineering, Inc.

For full biographical listings, see the Martindale-Hubbell Law Directory

*TUSCALOOSA,** Tuscaloosa Co.

DAVIDSON, WIGGINS, JONES & COLEMAN, P.C. (AV)

2625 Eighth Street, P.O. Box 1939, 35403
Telephone: 205-759-5771
Fax: 205-752-8259
Email: wiggins@dbtech.net
Email: tj@dbtech.net

G. Stephen Wiggins
Thomas R. Jones, Jr.
Charles M. Coleman

Randal Kevin Davis
J. Paul Zimmerman
Roman Ashley Shaul

OF COUNSEL

M. McCoy Davidson

Representative Clients: Peco Foods, Inc.; St. Paul Companies, Inc.; Illinois-Central Railroad Co.; The Travelers Group; Mutual Assurance, Inc.; Cigna Insurance Companies; Zenith Insurance Company; Industrial Development Board of the City of Tuscaloosa, Alabama; Nationwide Insurance Company; Blue Cross and Blue Shield of Alabama.

For full biographical listings, see the Martindale-Hubbell Law Directory

HUBBARD, SMITH, MCILWAIN, BRAKEFIELD & BROWDER, P.C. (AV)

808 Lurleen Wallace Boulevard, North, P.O. Box 2427, 35403
Telephone: 205-345-6789
Telecopier: 205-759-1195

(See Next Column)

Perry Hubbard (1921-1991)
Michael D. Smith
Christopher L. McIlwain
W. Marcus Brakefield
Herbert E. "Chip" Browder
Justice D. Smyth, III

Elizabeth Faxon Colwick
Gary E. Sullivan

Counsel for: Randall Publishing Co.; United States Fidelity & Guaranty Co.; Chubb Group of Insurance Cos.; West Alabama Health Services; City of Eutaw; Kimberly-Clark Corp.; Regions Bank; City of Tuscaloosa; West Alabama Bank & Trust; Tuscaloosa County Industrial Development Authority.

For full biographical listings, see the Martindale-Hubbell Law Directory

OWENS & ALMOND, LLP (AV)

2606 8th Street, P.O. Box 2487, 35403-2487
Telephone: 205-750-0750
Facsimile: 205-750-0355
Email: owensalm@dbtech.net

John A. Owens
M. Bradley Almond
Apsilah Owens Millsaps

Anna Northington Hutcheson

For full biographical listings, see the Martindale-Hubbell Law Directory

PHELPS, JENKINS, GIBSON & FOWLER, L.L.P. (AV)

1201 Greensboro Avenue, P.O. Box 020848, 35402-0848
Telephone: 205-345-5100
Fax: 205-758-4394
Fax: 205-391-6658
Fax: 205-391-6663

MEMBERS OF FIRM

Sam M. Phelps
James J. Jenkins
Johnson Russell Gibson, III
Randolph M. Fowler
C. Barton Adcox
Farley A. Poellnitz
A. Courtney Crowder

ASSOCIATES

Karen C. Welborn
Stephen E. Snow
W. David Ryan
Bryan Patrick Winter
John M. Compton
Charles T. Grimes
Jenny B. Compton (Not admitted in AL)
Laura C. Karns

LEGAL SUPPORT PERSONNEL

Christine Holt (Paralegal)
Lori R. Woodard (Paralegal)
Melissa D. Harvey (Paralegal)

Attorneys for: Aetna Insurance Co.; Allstate Insurance Co.; Carolina Casualty Insurance Co.; Continental Insurance Cos.; Fireman's Fund-American Insurance Cos.; Great American Insurance Co.; Hanover Insurance Co.

For full biographical listings, see the Martindale-Hubbell Law Directory

ZEANAH, HUST, SUMMERFORD, DAVIS, JONES & WILLIAMSON, L.L.C. (AV)

Seventh Floor, AmSouth Bank Building, P.O. Box 1310, 35403
Telephone: 205-349-1383
Fax: 205-391-1319
Email: ZHSDJ@mail.dbtech.net

MEMBERS OF FIRM

Olin W. Zeanah (1922-1987)
Wilbor J. Hust, Jr.
E. Clark Summerford
Kenneth D. Davis
Christopher H. Jones
Beverly Smith Williamson

OF COUNSEL

Marvin T. Ormond

Representative Clients: Alfa Insurance Cos.; Hartford Insurance Group; Home Insurance Co.; Nationwide Insurance Co.; Alabama Power Co.; Liberty Mutual Insurance Co.; The Uniroyal Goodrich Tire Co.

For full biographical listings, see the Martindale-Hubbell Law Directory

*TUSCUMBIA,** Colbert Co.

ASHE, TANNER, WRIGHT & KELLEY, P.C. (AV)

105 West Second Street, P.O. Box 899, 35674
Telephone: 256-383-6357
Telecopier: 256-381-4612

Braxton W. Ashe
J. Michael Tanner
Grant A. Wright
Charles J. Kelley (Resident)

Nickolas J. Steles

For full biographical listings, see the Martindale-Hubbell Law Directory

SELF & SELF

(See Florence)

ALASKA

*ANCHORAGE,** Third Judicial District

BLISS & WILKENS, LLC (AV)

431 West Seventh Avenue Suite 202, 99501-3583
Telephone: 907-276-2999
Facsimile: 907-276-2956

MEMBERS OF FIRM

Ronald L. Bliss
James K. Wilkens

ASSOCIATE

Alfred Clayton, Jr.

OF COUNSEL

Jean E. Kizer
Deborah K. Periman

LEGAL SUPPORT PERSONNEL

Nanette Shearer

For full biographical listings, see the Martindale-Hubbell Law Directory

DELISIO MORAN GERAGHTY & ZOBEL, P.C. (AV)

943 West Sixth Avenue, 99501-2033
Telephone: 907-279-9574
Facsimile: 907-276-4231
Email: delisiomoran@dmgz.com

Michael C. Geraghty
Patricia L. Zobel
Gregory L. Youngmun
David D. Floerchinger
Deirdre D. Ford

John D. Harjehausen

For full biographical listings, see the Martindale-Hubbell Law Directory

FELDMAN & ORLANSKY (AV)

Suite 400, 500 L Street, 99501
Telephone: 907-272-3538
Telecopier: 907-274-0819
URL: http://www.frozenlaw.com

Jeffrey M. Feldman
Susan C. Orlansky

ASSOCIATE

James E. Fosler

LEGAL SUPPORT PERSONNEL

Wendy Bursiel Weber (Legal Assistant)

Reference: Key Bank of Alaska.

For full biographical listings, see the Martindale-Hubbell Law Directory

HEDLAND, BRENNAN, HEIDEMAN & COOKE, A PROFESSIONAL CORPORATION (AV)

Suite 300, 1227 West 9th Avenue, 99501
Telephone: 907-279-5528, 279-5529, 279-5520
Telefax: 907-278-0877
Email: hbhc@alaska.net
Bethel, Alaska Office: 251 Seventh Avenue, P.O. Box 555.
Telephone: 907-543-2744. E-mail: cookelaw@unicom-alaska.com.

John S. Hedland
James T. Brennan
Christopher R. Cooke (Resident, Bethel Office)
Sara E. Heideman
Amy L. Vaudreuil
Jim Valcarce (Resident, Bethel Office)
Patrick Michael Anderson

Reference: National Bank of Alaska.

For full biographical listings, see the Martindale-Hubbell Law Directory

*JUNEAU,** First Judicial District

RUDDY, BRADLEY, KOLKHORST & REGES, A PROFESSIONAL CORPORATION (AV)

Jordan Creek Center, 8800 Glacier Highway, Suite 223, P.O. Box 34338, 99801
Telephone: 907-789-0047
Fax: 907-789-0783
Email: rbklaw@alaska.net *URL:* http://www.alaska.net/~rbklaw/

J. B. Bradley (1932-1997)
William G. Ruddy
Kathryn Kolkhorst
Robert K. Reges, Jr.

For full biographical listings, see the Martindale-Hubbell Law Directory

ARIZONA

*FLAGSTAFF,** Coconino Co.

MANGUM, WALL, STOOPS & WARDEN, P.L.L.C. (AV)

100 North Elden, P.O. Box 10, 86002
Telephone: 520-779-6951
Fax: 520-773-1312

H. Karl Mangum (1908-1993)

OF COUNSEL

Douglas J. Wall
Robert W. Warden
Daniel J. Stoops

MEMBERS OF FIRM

A. Dean Pickett
Stephen K. Smith
Melinda L. Garrahan
Michael H. Hinson

ASSOCIATES

Annette Star Lustgarten
Rebecca Smith Currey
R. Scott Currey
Melinda K. Jacquez
Franklin Hoover

Representative Clients: United States Automobile Assn.; Federated Insurance; Hartford Insurance Co.; State Farm Fire & Casualty Insurance Co.; Cincinnati Insurance Co.; Canal Insurance Co.; Economy Fire & Casualty Co.; Guaranty National Insurance Co.; Progressive Insurance Co.; Transamerica Insurance Co.

For Complete List of Firm Personnel, See General Section

For full biographical listings, see the Martindale-Hubbell Law Directory

*PHOENIX,** Maricopa Co.

ALLEN & PRICE, P.L.C. (AV)

2850 East Camelback Road, Suite 170, 85016-4380
Telephone: 602-381-0500
Fax: 602-381-8899
Email: allen@aplaw.com
Email: price@aplaw.com
Email: schacter@aplaw.com
Email: sanders@aplaw.com

Robert E. B. Allen
Charles S. Price

Scott A. Shacter
Barry R. Sanders

For full biographical listings, see the Martindale-Hubbell Law Directory

BEGAM, LEWIS, MARKS & WOLFE (AV)

A Professional Association of Lawyers
111 West Monroe Street, Suite 1400, 85003-1787
Telephone: 602-254-6071; 1-800-285-0481
Fax: 602-252-0042
Email: blmw@aol.com

Robert G. Begam
Frank Lewis
Stanley J. Marks
Elliot G. Wolfe
Kelly J. McDonald
Daniel J. Adelman
Lisa Kurtz
Dena Rosen Epstein
Steven M. Friedman
Richard P. Traulsen
Serena C. Montague

Reference: National Bank of Arizona.

For full biographical listings, see the Martindale-Hubbell Law Directory

BESS KUNZ, A PROFESSIONAL CORPORATION (AV)

7210 North 16th Street, 85020-5201
Telephone: 602-331-4600
Telecopier: 602-331-8600

Leon D. Bess
Donald R. Kunz
Timothy R. Hyland
William M. Demlong
Matthew D. Kleifield

Thomas P. Liddy
Connie Totorica Gould
Elliot H. Wernick
Beth H. Schneider

Representative Clients: John Alden Life Insurance Co.; John Hancock Mutual Insurance Co.; Lincoln National Life Insurance Co.; MassMutual; Metropolitan Life Insurance Co.; New York Life Insurance Co.; President Companies, Inc.; Safeco Insurance Company of America; The Equitable Life Assurance Society of the United States; The Travelers Insurance.

For full biographical listings, see the Martindale-Hubbell Law Directory

BONN, LUSCHER, PADDEN & WILKINS, CHARTERED (AV)

805 North Second Street, 85004
Telephone: 602-254-5557
Fax: 602-254-0656
Email: firm@blpw.com

(See Next Column)

BONN, LUSCHER, PADDEN & WILKINS CHARTERED, *Phoenix—Continued*

Paul V. Bonn
Randall D. Wilkins
John H. Cassidy
D. Michael Hall

OF COUNSEL

Brian A. Luscher

For full biographical listings, see the Martindale-Hubbell Law Directory

BONNETT, FAIRBOURN, FRIEDMAN & BALINT, P.C. (AV)

4041 North Central Avenue Suite 1100, 85012
Telephone: 602-274-1100
Fax: 602-274-1199

Jerry C. Bonnett
William G. Fairbourn
Andrew S. Friedman
Francis J. Balint, Jr.
H. Sullivan Bunch
Robert J. Spurlock
C. Kevin Dykstra
Elaine A. Ryan
Tara L. Jackson
Wendy J. Harrison
Scott A. Erickson
Robert D. Ryan

For full biographical listings, see the Martindale-Hubbell Law Directory

CHARLES M. BREWER, LTD. (AV)

Brewer Building, 5500 North 24th Street, P.O. Box 10720, 85064
Telephone: 602-381-8787
Fax: 602-381-1152

Charles M. Brewer

Luis Pedro Guerra
John Brian Brewer

For full biographical listings, see the Martindale-Hubbell Law Directory

BURCH & CRACCHIOLO, P.A. (AV)

702 East Osborn Road, Suite 200, 85014
Telephone: 602-274-7611
Fax: 602-234-0341
Mailing Address: P.O. Box 16882, Phoenix, AZ, 85011
Email: library@bcattorneys.com

Daniel Cracchiolo
Stephen E. Silver
Brian Kaven
Daryl Manhart
Ian Neale
Andrew Abraham
Donald W. Lindholm
F. Michael Carroll
Daniel R. Malinski
Edwin D. Fleming
Ralph D. Harris
David M. Villadolid

Theodore (Todd) Julian
Thomas A. Longfellow
Mitchell J. Resnick
Steven M. Serrano

Representative Clients: Bashas' Inc.; Farmers Insurance Group; U-Haul International, Inc.

For Complete List of Firm Personnel, See General Section

For full biographical listings, see the Martindale-Hubbell Law Directory

COHEN KENNEDY DOWD & QUIGLEY, P.C. (AV)

The Esplanade, 2425 East Camelback Road, Suite 1100, 85016
Telephone: 602-252-8400
Fax: 602-252-5339
Email: cklaw@cohenkennedylaw.com

Ronald Jay Cohen
Laura H. Kennedy
Daniel G. Dowd
Daniel P. Quigley

Raymond K. Ramella
Eva C. Miller
J. Christopher Gooch
Ann Thompson Uglietta
David D. Burkhead
Rebecca Lee van Doren

SPECIAL COUNSEL

Paula M. DeMore

Representative Clients: Pricewaterhouse Coopers, LLP; Del Webb Corp.; Phelps Dodge Corp.; Inter-Tel; Kabuto Arizona Properties; Exxon Company USA; Park Electrochemical Corp.; Integrated Information Systems, Inc.; Arizona State University; Grubb & Ellis Realty Co.

For full biographical listings, see the Martindale-Hubbell Law Directory

CROWE & SCOTT, P.A. (AV)

1100 East Washington Suite 200, 85034-1090
Telephone: 602-252-2570
Fax: 602-252-1939
URL: http://www.lawyers.com/crowe&scott

Tom Crowe
Michael B. Scott (1945-1997)

Ginette M. Chinichian

For full biographical listings, see the Martindale-Hubbell Law Directory

WILLIAM J. DOWNEY, P.C. (AV)

3636 North Central Avenue, Suite 1150, 85012
Telephone: 602-222-4350
Facsimile: 602-222-4353
Email: downey@primenet.com *URL:* http://www.lawyers.com/williamjdowney

William J. Downey

Dane London Wood
Patrick B. Sigl
Elan Shai Mizrahi

For full biographical listings, see the Martindale-Hubbell Law Directory

DUSHOFF & MCCALL, A PROFESSIONAL CORPORATION (AV)

Two Renaissance Square, Suite 1000, 40 North Central, 85004
Telephone: 602-254-3800
Fax: 602-258-2551
URL: http://www.dushoff@neta.com

Jay Dushoff
Jack E. McCall (1942-1995)
Michael Riikola
Leonard M. Bell

Patrick J. McGill
Robert H. Kreutzer

LEGAL SUPPORT PERSONNEL

Thomas M. Flynn

For full biographical listings, see the Martindale-Hubbell Law Directory

FENNEMORE CRAIG, A PROFESSIONAL CORPORATION (AV)

3003 North Central Avenue, Suite 2600, 85012-2913
Telephone: 602-916-5000
Fax: 602-916-5999
Tucson, Arizona Office: One South Church Avenue, Suite 1000, 85701-1620.
Telephone: 520-879-6800.
Fax: 520-879-6899.

Calvin H. Udall
James Powers
Kenneth J. Sherk
John D. Everroad
Donald R. Gilbert
Roger T. Hargrove
David T. Maddox
William L. Thorpe
David A. Weatherwax
Graeme Hancock
Scott M. Finical
Andrew M. Federhar
Christopher L. Callahan
Christopher P. Staring
Janet W. Lord
James J. Trimble
Keith L. Hendricks
Douglas C. Northup
Marc H. Lamber

Mark H. Brain
James D. Burgess
Scott L. Altes
Mary Beth Phillips
Erin E. Flaharty
David M. Call
Vera E. Munoz
Sal J. Rivera
Joel B. Shapiro
Michelle G. Marshall
Joseph Sciarrotta, Jr.
William S. Gates
Rosa Mroz

LEGAL SUPPORT PERSONNEL

LEGAL ASSISTANTS

Beverly Cooper
Nancy E. Esser
Jane Friedman

For Complete List of Firm Personnel, See General Section

For full biographical listings, see the Martindale-Hubbell Law Directory

FOGEL, LAMBER & BRONNENKANT, PROFESSIONAL ASSOCIATION (AV)

4001 North Third Street, Suite 400, 85012
Telephone: 602-264-3330
Fax: 602-274-5117

Sherman D. Fogel
Dennis M. Lamber
Rex P. Bronnenkant

Reference: Rocky Mountain Bank.

For full biographical listings, see the Martindale-Hubbell Law Directory

AMY J. GITTLER, PLC (AV)

2633 East Indian School Road, Suite 300, 85016-6759
Telephone: 602-224-6300
Facsimile: 602-224-6020
Email: amy@cgson.com *URL:* http://www.lawyers.com/gittlerlaw

Amy J. Gittler

Tricia Brown

For full biographical listings, see the Martindale-Hubbell Law Directory

Phoenix—Continued

GOLDSTEIN, MCGRODER & WOODS, LTD. A PROFESSIONAL CORPORATION (AV)

2200 East Camelback Road, Suite 221, 85016-3456
Telephone: 602-957-1500
Fax: 602-956-9294
Email: pmcgroder@aol.com

Philip T. Goldstein
Patrick J. McGroder, III
Grant Woods
Suzanne P. Clarke

Jane E. Evans

LEGAL SUPPORT PERSONNEL

Kevan S. DeWitt (Paralegal)
Karen Kay Rush

For full biographical listings, see the Martindale-Hubbell Law Directory

DAVID F. GOMEZ A PROFESSIONAL CORPORATION (AV)

2525 East Camelback Road Suite 860, 85016
Telephone: 602-957-8686
Telecopier: 602-956-9854
Email: DFGPC@aol.com

David F. Gomez
Michael J. Petitti, Jr.

For full biographical listings, see the Martindale-Hubbell Law Directory

RICHARD J. HERTZBERG (AV)

16 Luhrs Arcade 11 West Jefferson, 85003
Telephone: 602-253-1781
Fax: 602-253-0928

For full biographical listings, see the Martindale-Hubbell Law Directory

HORNE, BISTROW & DULBERG, P.C. (AV)

Renaissance Two, 40 North Central, Suite 2800, 85004
Telephone: 602-253-9700
Fax: 602-258-4805
Email: kcorson@azlitigation.com *URL:* http://www.azlitigation.com

Thomas C. Horne
Eric J. Bistrow
Michael S. Dulberg

Joel E. Sannes

For full biographical listings, see the Martindale-Hubbell Law Directory

JENNINGS, HAUG & CUNNINGHAM, L.L.P. (AV)

2800 North Central Avenue Suite Eighteen Hundred, 85004-1049
Telephone: 602-234-7800
Fax: 602-277-5595
Email: main@jhc-law.com

MEMBERS OF FIRM

Curtis A. Jennings
William F. Haug
Jack R. Cunningham
Dean Kim Lough
Chad L. Schexnayder
Mark E. Barker
John G. Sinodis
James L. Csontos
Larry J. Crown
Jeff R. Wilhelm
Edward Rubacha
Laurence R. Sharlot
Dean M. Dinner
Jorge Franco, Jr.

ASSOCIATES

K. Alan Holcomb
Lisa A. Shannon
Stephen J. Anthony

OF COUNSEL

James W. Washington (Not admitted in AZ)

For full biographical listings, see the Martindale-Hubbell Law Directory

JENNINGS, STROUSS & SALMON, P.L.C. (AV)

A Professional Limited Liability Company
One Renaissance Square, Two North Central Avenue, 85004-2393
Telephone: 602-262-5911
Fax: 602-253-3255
Email: info@jsslaw.com *URL:* http://www.jsslaw.com
Arrowhead Office: 16150 North Arrowhead Fountains Center Drive, Suite 250, Peoria, Arizona.
Telephone: 623-878-2222.
Fax: 623-878-1333.

Gary G. Keltner
T. Patrick Flood
W. Michael Flood
Douglas G. Zimmerman
Gerald W. Alston
Michael G. Helms
John G. Sestak, Jr.
Kenneth C. Sundlof, Jr.
Douglas F. Behm
Rita A. Meiser
Joseph W. Mott
Gary L. Lassen
Richard N. Morrison
David Brnilovich
John C. West
Jay A. Fradkin
Michael R. Palumbo
David W. Kash

(See Next Column)

Glenn J. Carter
H. Christian Bode
James M. Ackerman
Ernest Calderón
Wendy D. Woodrow
Michael V. Perry
Dean C. Robertson
Brian N. Spector
Michael J. O'Connor
John J. Egbert
Michael J. Farrell
Robert D. Haws
Jennifer M. Bligh
Kim D. Steinmetz
Cody M. Hall
David B. Earl
Lydia A. Jones

OF COUNSEL

Gary L. Stuart

ASSOCIATES

Cynthia A. Coates
Gordon Lewis
Andrew B. Turk
Bryan S. VanMeveren
Stacey A. Dowdell
Scott Rhodes
John P. Robertson, II
Johnny J. Sorenson
Jeffrey C. Whitley
C. David Martinez
Kimberly J. Cilke
Anoma T. Nolan
Kevin R. Robling

For Complete List of Firm Personnel, See General Section

For full biographical listings, see the Martindale-Hubbell Law Directory

JOHNSTON & DODD, P.L.C. (AV)

One North First Street, Suite 700, 85004
Telephone: 602-452-0600
Facsimile: 602-716-5997
Email: johnston-doddlaw@uswest.net

Logan T. Johnston, III
Catherine M. Dodd
Anne C. Longo
Kenneth M. Rudisill, Jr.

For full biographical listings, see the Martindale-Hubbell Law Directory

KIMERER & LAVELLE, P.L.C. (AV)

100 W. Clarendon Suite 2100, 85013
Telephone: 602-279-5900; 800-220-6817
Fax: 602-264-5566
Email: KimLav.com

Michael J. LaVelle
Lori L. Voepel

Representative Clients: The National Basketball Association; Aetna Insurance Co.; Kaibab Industries; Centric Jones Constructors; B & B Masonry; Western Block.

For full biographical listings, see the Martindale-Hubbell Law Directory

LEWIS AND ROCA, LLP (AV)

A Limited Liability Partnership including a Professional Corporation
40 North Central Avenue, 85004-4429
Telephone: 602-262-5311
Fax: 602-262-5747
Email: clientservice@lrlaw.com *URL:* http://www.lrlaw.com
Tucson, Arizona Office: One South Church Avenue, Suite 700, 86701-1620.
Telephone: 520-622-2090.
Fax: 520-622-3088. E-Mail: clientservice@lrlaw.com.
Las Vegas, Nevada Affiliated Office: Ashcraft and Heinz LLP, 3960 Howard Hughes Parkway, 89109.
Telephone: 702-990-3570.
Fax: 702-990-3571.

MEMBERS OF FIRM

John P. Frank
Peter D. Baird
Merton E. Marks (P.C.)
Richard S. Cohen
José A. Cárdenas
Foster Robberson
Michael J. Holden
Sheila Carmody
Thomas G. Ryan
Jesse B. Simpson
Robert F. Roos
James T. Acuff, Jr.
Carl F. Mariano
Robert H. McKirgan
Pamela B. Petersen
Jane E. Reddin
Richard A. Halloran
Joseph E. McGarry
Douglas L. Irish
R. Kent Klein
Patricia K. Norris
Dale A. Danneman
Thomas H. Campbell
Newman R. Porter
George L. Paul
Stephen M. Bressler
James K. Kloss
Mary Ellen Simonson
Steven J. Hulsman
Christopher J. Brelje
Steven J. Burr
L. Keith Beauchamp
Greg S. Como
Janell M. Adams

ASSOCIATES

Dawn M. Bergin
Todd E. Hale
W. Todd Coleman
Randy Papetti
Bruce E. Samuels
Daniel A. Goldfried
Jon Weiss

OF COUNSEL

Jeremy E. Butler
James L. Hohnbaum
Barbara Anstey Hoerner

Representative Clients: Blood Systems, Inc.; Bristol-Myers Squibb Co.; Del Webb Corp.; The Dial Corp; E.I. du Pont de Nemours and Co.; MCI Communications Corp.; The Prudential Insurance Company of America; Southwest Risk Services; Target Stores; Zurich Insurance Co.

(See Next Column)

LEWIS AND ROCA LLP, *Phoenix—Continued*

For Complete List of Firm Personnel, See General Section

For full biographical listings, see the Martindale-Hubbell Law Directory

MUCHMORE & WALLWORK, A PROFESSIONAL CORPORATION (AV)

2700 North Central Avenue, Suite 1225, 85004-1165
Telephone: 602-240-6699
Data: 602-240-6698
Facsimile: 602-240-6697
Email: muchwork@mmww.com *URL:* http://www.mmww.com

Charles J. Muchmore
Nicholas J. Wallwork
Fredric D. Bellamy

SENIOR COUNSEL

Steve Owens

COUNSEL

Bridget S. Bade

Christopher D. Payne
Margaret Benny Hurst
Carolina L. Carver
Mindy K. Brinker

OF COUNSEL

Leslie Kyman Cooper
George H. King

LEGAL SUPPORT PERSONNEL

Gloria A. Torres (Administrator)
Gale James (Finance Manager)
James R. Potts (Systems Administrator and Litigation Support Manager)

Representative Clients: AgrEvo USA Company; BHP Copper, Inc.; Chevron U.S.A., Inc.; Cyprus Amax Minerals Company; Homes by Dave Brown, Inc.; National Indemnity Insurance Company; Standard Insurance Company; Washington Mills Electro Minerals Corporation; Cadbury Beverages, Inc.; Eisenberg Company.

For full biographical listings, see the Martindale-Hubbell Law Directory

QUARLES & BRADY LLP (AV)

One Camelback Building, One East Camelback Road, Suite 400, 85012-1649
Telephone: 602-230-5500
Fax: 602-230-5598
URL: http://www.quarles.com
Milwaukee, Wisconsin Office: 411 East Wisconsin Avenue.
Telephone: 414-277-5000.
Fax: 414-271-3552.
Madison, Wisconsin Office: First Wisconsin Plaza, One South Pinckney Street, P.O. Box 2113.
Telephone: 608-251-5000.
Fax: 608-251-9166.
West Palm Beach, Florida Office: 222 Lakeview Avenue, 4th Floor.
Telephone: 407-653-5000.
Fax: 407-653-5333.
Naples, Florida Office: Barnett Center, 4501 Tamiami Trail North, Suite 300.
Telephone: 813-262-5959.
Fax: 813-434-4999.
Chicago, Illinois Office: Quarles & Brady LLC, Citicorp Center, 500 West Madison Street, Suite 3700.
Telephone: 312-715-5000.
Fax: 312-715-5155.

MEMBER OF THE FIRM

Glenn Spencer Bacal

ASSOCIATES

David T. Barton
C. Christine Burns

For full biographical listings, see the Martindale-Hubbell Law Directory

SHIMMEL, HILL, BISHOP & GRUENDER, P.C. (AV)

3700 North 24th Street, 85016
Telephone: 602-224-9500
Telecopier: 602-955-6176
URL: http://www.shimmelhill.com

Daniel F. Gruender
Margaret L. Steiner
Keith F. Overholt
Susan M. Swick
Scott J. Richardson
S. Gregory Jones
Joseph Wm. Kruchek
Glenn B. Hotchkiss
John W. Moody

OF COUNSEL

Charles A. Finch

Representative Clients: The Ashton Cos.; Associated General Contractors; Bashas' Stores; Black Mesa Pipeline Co.; CC Shops dba Cost Cutters Hairsetters; Christiania Bank; Citizen Auto Stage Line; Connecticut General Life Insurance Co.; Delta Airlines; Dunn Del Re Steel, Inc.

For full biographical listings, see the Martindale-Hubbell Law Directory

SNELL & WILMER L.L.P. (AV)

One Arizona Center, 85004-2202
Telephone: 602-382-6000
Fax: 602-382-6070
Email: postmaster@snellwilmer.com *URL:* http://www.swlaw.com
Tucson, Arizona Office: One South Church Avenue, Suite 1500, 85701-1612.
Telephone: 520-882-1200.
Fax: 520-884-1294.
Orange County Office: 1920 Main Street, Suite 1200, Irvine, California 92614-7230.
Telephone: 949-253-2700.
Fax: 949-955-2507.
Salt Lake City, Utah Office: 111 East Broadway, Suite 900, 84111-1004.
Telephone: 801-237-1900.
Fax: 801-237-1950.

MEMBERS OF FIRM

John J. Bouma
Warren E. Platt
George H. Lyons
Peter J. Rathwell
Daniel J. McAuliffe
Douglas W. Seitz
Robert B. Hoffman
Barry D. Halpern
Joel P. Hoxie
James R. Condo
Lonnie J. Williams, Jr.
Vaughn A. Crawford
Arthur P. Greenfield
Suzanne McCann
Donald L. Gaffney
Arthur T. Anderson
Richard W. Shapiro
Timothy G. O'Neill
Heidi McNeil Staudenmaier
E. Jeffrey Walsh
Martha E. Gibbs
Katherine M. Harmeyer
James J. Sienicki
George J. Coleman, III
Janet E. Barton
Kevin J. Parker
Donald H. Smith
Steven S. Guy
Christopher H. Bayley
Robert R. Kinas
Charles P. Keller
Patrick X. Fowler
Barbara J. Dawson
Brian J. Foster
Bob J. McCullough
Patrick G. Byrne
Prithviraj S. Sivananthan
Patricia Lee Refo
GinaMarie Rossano
Timothy J. Casey
Jeffrey Webb Crockett
Lisa M. Coulter

Representative Clients: For list of Representative Clients, see end of biographical listings in the Martindale-Hubbell Law Directory.

For Complete List of Firm Personnel, See General Section

For full biographical listings, see the Martindale-Hubbell Law Directory

JERRY STEELE (AV)

Building C, Suite 201, 4131 North 24th Street, 85016
Telephone: 602-956-8336
Fax: 602-955-6445
Email: jlsteele@sprynet.com

WILENCHIK & BARTNESS, A PROFESSIONAL CORPORATION (AV)

The Wilenchik & Bartness Building, 2810 North Third Street, 85004
Telephone: 602-606-2810
Facsimile: 602-606-2811
Email: diw@wb-law.com *URL:* http://www.wb-law.com/wb-law

Dennis I. Wilenchik
George H. Foster, Jr.
Becky Ann Bartness
Adam P. Weber

Matthew H. Sloan
Aryeh David Schwartz
Wade J. Skalsky

Representative Clients: Richmond American Homes; Saddleback Homes; C.B. Richard Ellis; Blanford Homes; Monterey Homes; Chicago Title; Chase Bank; Columbia Communities; The State of Arizona; Southwest Risk Management.

For full biographical listings, see the Martindale-Hubbell Law Directory

*PRESCOTT,** Yavapai Co.

FAVOUR, MOORE & WILHELMSEN, A PROFESSIONAL ASSOCIATION (AV)

1580 Plaza West Drive, P.O. Box 1391, 86302
Telephone: 520-445-2444
Fax: 520-771-0450
Email: fmw@primenet.com

John M. Favour
Mark M. Moore
David K. Wilhelmsen

Representative Clients: Yavapai Regional Medical Center; Yavapai Title Co.; Father Wasson's Orphans; Hidden Valley Ranch; Bank of America; Employers Mutual Co.; Lawyers Title Insurance Co.; Farmers Insurance Group; Inter-Cal Corp.; Arroyo Seco Development.

For Complete List of Firm Personnel, See General Section

For full biographical listings, see the Martindale-Hubbell Law Directory

Prescott—Continued

MURPHY, LUTEY, SCHMITT & BECK, P.L.L.C. (AV)

Elks Building, 117 East Gurley Street, 86301
Telephone: 520-445-6860
Fax: 520-445-6488
Email: MLSB@GOODNET.COM
Yuma, Arizona Office: Valley Professional Plaza, 1763 West Twenty-Fourth Street, Suite 200.
Telephone: 520-726-0314.
Fax: 520-341-1079.
Kingman, Arizona Office: 2601 Stockton Hill Road, Suite H8.
Telephone: 520-718-0888; 1-800-281-0822.

MEMBERS OF FIRM

Thelton D. Beck
Michael R. Murphy
Selmer D. Lutey
Robert E. Schmitt
Dan A. Wilson
Alex B. Vakula

Scott K. Risley

Counsel for: State Farm Mutual Automobile Insurance Co.; Allstate Insurance Co.; Farmers Insurance; Western Agricultural Insurance Co.;
Local Counsel for: Bank One Arizona, NA; The Stockmen's Bank.
Representative Clients: Prescott College; Galpin Ford, Inc.; Sedona-Oak Creek Airport Authority; Yavapai County Fair Association (Prescott Downs).

For full biographical listings, see the Martindale-Hubbell Law Directory

SCOTTSDALE, Maricopa Co.

BENNETT, CARMICHAEL & KENNEDY, L.L.P. (AV)

6991 East Camelback Road, Suite B-111, 85251
Telephone: 602-990-1133; 602-947-8303
Fax: 602-945-2149

MEMBERS OF FIRM

William F. Bennett
David H. Carmichael
Robert T. Kennedy

For full biographical listings, see the Martindale-Hubbell Law Directory

JOHN H. COTTON & ASSOCIATES, LTD. (AV)

6900 East Camelback Road, Suite 320, 85251
Telephone: 480-423-2034
Fax: 480-423-2035
Email: jhcotton1@aol.com
Las Vegas, Nevada Office: 2300 West Sahara, Suite 420, 89102.
Telephone: 702-367-9993.
Fax: 702-367-9977.

John H. Cotton

Bart J. Patterson (Resident)
Scott F. Frerichs (Resident)
Melanie Beth Bernstein (Not admitted in AZ)
Richard S. Johnson (Not admitted in AZ)
Edward R. Miley (Not admitted in AZ)

Representative Clients: American Continental/MMI Companies; Carpenter Industries; DLR Group, Inc.; KPMG Peat Marwick; Law Society of British Columbia; Opthalmic Mutual Insurance Company; The St. Paul Companies; Simula, Inc.; Tenet Health Care; The Doctors' Company.

For full biographical listings, see the Martindale-Hubbell Law Directory

HERMAN, GOLDSTEIN & FORSYTH, P.C. (AV)

(Formerly Grossman, Goldstein & Forsyth, P.C.)
5040 East Shea Boulevard Suite 168, 85254
Telephone: 602-948-9424
Fax: 602-948-9425

Jill A. Herman
Evan S. Goldstein
Keith B. Forsyth

Pari K. Scroggin
Sanford K. Gerber

For full biographical listings, see the Martindale-Hubbell Law Directory

PESKIND HYMSON & GOLDSTEIN, P.C. (AV)

14595 North Scottsdale Road, Suite 14, 85254
Telephone: 602-991-9077
Fax: 602-443-8854
URL: http://www.legalcounselors.com

E. J. Peskind
David B. Goldstein
Marilee Miller Clarke
Jeffrey A. Leyton
Pamela L. Kingsley

Eddie A. Pantiliat

For full biographical listings, see the Martindale-Hubbell Law Directory

*TUCSON,** Pima Co.

CHANDLER, TULLAR, UDALL & REDHAIR, L.L.P. (AV)

1700 Bank of America Plaza, 33 North Stone Avenue, 85701-1415
Telephone: 520-623-4353
Telefax: 520-792-3426

MEMBERS OF FIRM

Thomas Chandler
D. B. Udall
Jack Redhair
Steven Weatherspoon
Edwin M. Gaines, Jr.
Dwight M. Whitley, Jr.
E. Hardy Smith
John J. Brady
Charles V. Harrington
Kurt Kroese

ASSOCIATES

Lori A. Petersen
Elizabeth D. Bushell
Christopher R. Pennison
Charles Alexander Davis
Michael Scott Redhair
Sue Ann Welch
Stephen L. Wetherell
Edward Moomjian, II

Representative Clients: Arizona Electric Power Cooperative, Inc.; Atlantic & Richfield Co.; Northwestern Mutual Life Insurance Co.; Rex Broadcasting Co.; Citizen Auto Stage Company; Grayline Tours; Winnebago Industries; Starr Pass; Echo Trucking Co.

For full biographical listings, see the Martindale-Hubbell Law Directory

GABROY, ROLLMAN & BOSSÉ, P.C. (AV)

3507 North Campbell Avenue, Suite 111, 85719
Telephone: 520-320-1300
Telefax: 520-320-0717
Email: admin@gabroylaw.com

Richard M. Rollman
John Gabroy
Ronald M. Lehman
Lyle D. Aldridge
Ronna L. Fickbohm

Richard A. Brown
Nicole Gabroy-Ayaz

For Complete List of Firm Personnel, See General Section

For full biographical listings, see the Martindale-Hubbell Law Directory

GOERING, ROBERTS, BERKMAN, RUBIN & BROGNA, P.C. (AV)

Suite 302, 1840 East River Road, 85718
Telephone: 520-577-9300
Fax: 520-577-0848
Email: grbrb@aol.com

Scott Goering
Howard T. Roberts, Jr.
David L. Berkman
William L. Rubin
Carmine A. Brogna
Christopher L. Enos

Representative Clients: Fireman's Fund Insurance; Safeco Insurance; Royal Insurance; Sentry Insurance; American International Group; Farmers Insurance Co.; USAA; Country Companies; Cigna; Arizona Municipal Risk Retention Pool.
Reference: Bank One.

For full biographical listings, see the Martindale-Hubbell Law Directory

HARALSON, MILLER, PITT & MCANALLY, P.L.C. (AV)

One South Church Avenue Suite 900, 85701
Telephone: 520-792-3836
Telecopier: 520-624-5080
Email: mpmpc@azstarnet.com

Barry N. Akin (1939-1988)
Dale Haralson, P.C.
G. Eugene Isaak
Gerald Maltz
Janice A. Wezelman
Philip J. Hall
Grace McIlvain
Thomas G. Cotter
Lindsay E. Brew
Armando Rivera
Gus Aragón, Jr.
Carole A. Summers
Bradley P. Miller

OF COUNSEL

Richard L. McAnally

Representative Clients: Bell Atlantic Metro Mobile; Evergreen International Aviation; Farmers Investment Co.; Forest City Enterprises; Vince Granatelli Racing; KVOA Channel 4 TV; Newmont Mining Corp.; S.L. Industries, Inc.; Tucson Unified School District; University of Arizona Foundation.

For Complete List of Firm Personnel, See General Section

For full biographical listings, see the Martindale-Hubbell Law Directory

EDWARD HARRIS LABER, LTD. (AV)

33 North Tucson Boulevard, 85716
Telephone: 520-624-3000
Fax: 520-624-3332
Email: laber@azstarnet.com

Edward Harris Laber

For full biographical listings, see the Martindale-Hubbell Law Directory

Tucson—Continued

LEONARD FELKER ALTFELD GREENBERG & BATTAILE, P.C. (AV)

250 North Meyer Avenue, P.O. Box 191, 85702-0191
Telephone: 520-622-7733
Fax: 520-622-7967

David J. Leonard
Clifford B. Altfeld
Sidney L. Felker
Donna M. Aversa
Jeffrey H. Greenberg
R. David Sobel
John F. Battaile III
Russell E. Krone
Peter B. Goldman

OF COUNSEL

Anne-Marie Brady

For full biographical listings, see the Martindale-Hubbell Law Directory

CARTER MOREY, P.C. (AV)

Formerly Haralson, Kinerk & Morey (1978)
82 South Stone Avenue "The Citizen Building", 85701
Telephone: 520-792-4330
Fax: 520-623-9568

Carter Morey

Gregory G. Wasley
Linda S. Sherrill

For full biographical listings, see the Martindale-Hubbell Law Directory

RABINOVITZ & ASSOCIATES, P.C. (AV)

721 North 4th Avenue, P.O. Box 41600, 85717
Telephone: 520-624-5526
Toll Free: 1-800-365-0821
Fax: 520-622-3776

Bernard I. Rabinovitz

John D. Ellis

LEGAL SUPPORT PERSONNEL

Michael Nielson (Paralegal)
Lisa Busciglio (Paralegal)
Ruth Polizzi (Paralegal)

Representative Client: Firemans Fund Insurance Co.

For full biographical listings, see the Martindale-Hubbell Law Directory

SHULTZ & ROLLINS, LTD. (AV)

St. Philip's Plaza, 4280 North Campbell Avenue, Suite 214, 85718-6580
Telephone: 520-577-7777

Silas H. Shultz
Michael F. Rollins

James E. Marner

For full biographical listings, see the Martindale-Hubbell Law Directory

STOMPOLY, STROUD, GLICKSMAN & ERICKSON, P.C. (AV)

1820 Norwest Tower, One South Church Avenue, 85702
Telephone: 520-628-8300
Telefax: 520-628-9948
Mailing Address: P.O. Box 190, Tucson, AZ, 85702-0190

John G. Stompoly
Elliot A. Glicksman
James L. Stroud
George Erickson

For full biographical listings, see the Martindale-Hubbell Law Directory

WILLIAM G. WALKER, P.C. (AV)

145 South Sixth Avenue, 85701
Telephone: 520-622-3330
Fax: 520-882-6833

William G. Walker

For full biographical listings, see the Martindale-Hubbell Law Directory

*YUMA,** Yuma Co.

ROBERT M. COOK (AV)

207 West Second Street, 85364
Telephone: 520-539-0959
Fax: 520-539-0960
1-800 ROBERT M
Email: robertmcook@yahoo.com

For full biographical listings, see the Martindale-Hubbell Law Directory

THE BRIAN E. SMITH LAW FIRM (AV)

The Brian Smith Building, 301 South 2nd Avenue, 85364
Telephone: 520-783-8811
Fax: 520-782-2018

(See Next Column)

Brian E. Smith
William J. Kerekes
Frank A. Fila

LEGAL SUPPORT PERSONNEL

Briget M. Marquez

Reference: Bank of America.

For full biographical listings, see the Martindale-Hubbell Law Directory

ARKANSAS

*BATESVILLE,** Independence Co.

MURPHY, POST, THOMPSON, ARNOLD & SKINNER (AV)

1141 East Main Street Suite 301, P.O. Box 2595, 72501
Telephone: 870-793-3821
Fax: 870-793-3815

W. D. Murphy, Jr. (1912-1987)

MEMBERS OF FIRM

Jerry Post
Blair Arnold
Tom Thompson
J. T. Skinner

References will be supplied on request.

For full biographical listings, see the Martindale-Hubbell Law Directory

*BENTON,** Saline Co.

BAXTER, JENSEN, PAYNE, YOUNG & SMITH (AV)

A Partnership including a Professional Association
310 West Conway Street, P.O. Drawer 1038, 72018-1038
Telephone: 501-315-0600
Fax: 501-315-0088
URL: http://www.baxterlaw.com

MEMBERS OF FIRM

Ray Baxter (P.A.)
John Payne
Terence C. Jensen
Perry Y. Young
David E. Smith

LEGAL SUPPORT PERSONNEL

Meleah Carter

Representative CLients: Lumberman's Underwriting Alliance; Union Bank of Benton; American States Insurance Co.; Farm Bureau Insurance; General Accident Insurance Co.; Arkansas School Board Assn. (self-insurance program); Harleysville Insurance Co.; Nationwide Insurance Co.; Travelers Insurance Co.
Reference: Union Bank of Benton.

For full biographical listings, see the Martindale-Hubbell Law Directory

ELLIS LAW FIRM (AV)

126 North Main Street, P.O. Box 1259, 72018
Telephone: 501-315-1000
Fax: 501-315-4222
Email: gdellis@aristotle.net

MEMBER OF FIRM

George D. Ellis

LEGAL SUPPORT PERSONNEL

Rhonda Beck Malone (Paralegal)

References: The Union Bank of Benton; Benton State Bank.

For full biographical listings, see the Martindale-Hubbell Law Directory

*BLYTHEVILLE,** Mississippi Co.

REID, BURGE, PREVALLET & COLEMAN (AV)

417 North Broadway, P.O. Box 107, 72316-0107
Telephone: 870-763-4586
Fax: 870-763-4642
URL: http://www.lawyers.com/rbpclaw

MEMBERS OF FIRM

Max B. Reid (1895-1959)
Richard A. Reid
Dan M. Burge
Donald E. Prevallet
Robert Lynn Coleman

Counsel for: Farmers Bank and Trust Co.; Arkansas Power & Light Co.; Bush Canning Co.; Allstate Insurance Cos.; Farmers Insurance Group; Wausau Insurance Cos.; United States Fidelity & Guaranty Co.; State Farm Cos.; Hartford Group.

For full biographical listings, see the Martindale-Hubbell Law Directory

*CAMDEN,** Ouachita Co.

ALLEN P. ROBERTS, P.A. (AV)

325 Jefferson Street, S.W., P.O. Box 280, 71711-0280
Telephone: 870-836-5310
FAX: 870-836-9662
Email: aroberts@cei.net

Allen P. Roberts

Representative Clients: International Paper Co.; Camden Fairview School District; The City of Camden; Byars Oil Co.; American Fuel Cell & Coated Fabrics Co.; Star City School District; Highland Resources, Inc.; Circle B Logging Co.; First National Bank, Magnolia, Arkansas.

For full biographical listings, see the Martindale-Hubbell Law Directory

*EL DORADO,** Union Co.

SHACKLEFORD, PHILLIPS, WINELAND & RATCLIFF, P.A. (AV)

100 East Church Street, P.O. Box 1718, 71731-1718
Telephone: 870-862-5523
FAX: 870-862-9443
Email: SPWR@IPA.NET

John M. Shackleford (1896-1968)
Dennis L. Shackleford
Norwood Phillips
Teresa Wineland
Brian H. Ratcliff
Michelle H. Cauley

OF COUNSEL

John M. Shackleford, Jr.

Representative Insurance Clients: American Interstate Insurance Co.; CIGNA Cos.; CNA Insurance Co.; Commercial Union Insurance Co.; Fireman's Fund Insurance Co.; General Accident Insurance Co.; Liberty Mutual Insurance Co.; Medical Protective Insurance Co.; The St. Paul Cos.; Zurich Insurance Co.

For full biographical listings, see the Martindale-Hubbell Law Directory

*FAYETTEVILLE,** Washington Co.

BASSETT LAW FIRM (AV)

221 North College Avenue, P.O. Box 3618, 72702-3618
Telephone: 501-521-9996
Fax: 501-521-9600
Email: places212@aol.com

MEMBERS OF FIRM

Woodson W. Bassett, Jr.
Woodson W. Bassett, III
Tod C. Bassett
Wm. Robert Still, Jr.
Walker Dale Garrett
Curtis L. Nebben
Earl Buddy Chadick, Jr.
Angela M. Doss
Gary V. Weeks
J. David Wall
Vincent O. Chadick
James M. Graves
Scott Edward Wray
Shannon L. Fant

Representative Clients: Hartford Insurance Group; Tyson Foods, Inc.; Scottsdale Insurance Co.; St. Paul Fire and Marine Insurance Co.; AIG Aviation Ins. Co.; WAUSAU; USAA; Baldor Corp.; Wal-Mart Stores, Inc.

For full biographical listings, see the Martindale-Hubbell Law Directory

CONNER & WINTERS, P.L.L.C. (AV)

100 West Center Street, Suite 200, 72701-6081
Telephone: 501-582-5711
Facsimile: 501-587-1426
Email: postmaster@cwlaw.com
Tulsa, Oklahoma Office: Conner & Winters, A Professional Corporation, 3700 First Place Tower, 15 East 5th Street, 74103-4344.
Telephone: 918-586-5711.
Facsimile: 918-586-8982.
Oklahoma City, Oklahoma Office: Conner & Winters, A Professional Corporation, One Leadership Square, 211 North Robinson, Suite 1700, 73102-7101.
Telephone: 405-272-5711.
Facsimile: 405-232-2695.
Washington, D.C. Office: Conner & Winters, A Professional Corporation, 1101 Seventeenth Street, N.W., Suite 606, 20036-4704.
Telephone: 202-783-5711.
Facsimile: 202-783-5720.

John R. Elrod
Ruth Ann Wisener

For Complete List of Firm Personnel, See General Section

For full biographical listings, see the Martindale-Hubbell Law Directory

DAVIS, COX & WRIGHT, PLC (AV)

19 East Mountain Street, P.O. Drawer 1688, 72702-1688
Telephone: 501-521-7600
Fax: 501-521-7661
Email: daviscoxwright@dcw-plc.com *URL:* http://www.dcw-plc.com

(See Next Column)

Sidney P. Davis, Jr.
Walter B. Cox
Tilden P. Wright, III
Constance G. Clark
William Jackson Butt, II
Kelly P. Carithers
Don A. Taylor
Paul H. Taylor
John G. Trice
Laura J. Andress

Mark W. Dossett
S. Lance Cox
Robin Miller

Representative Clients: Arkansas Farm Bureau Insurance Cos.; Fireman's Fund Insurance Group; St. Paul Insurance Cos; Chrysler Motors Corp.; Kemper Insurance Group; Kawasaki Motors Corp.; CIGNA; The Medical Protective Company; Employers Mutual Companies; CNA Ins. Cos.

For full biographical listings, see the Martindale-Hubbell Law Directory

ODOM & ELLIOTT (AV)

No. 1 East Mountain Street, P.O. Drawer 1868, 72702
Telephone: 501-442-7575
FAX: 501-442-9008
Email: rzrbk63@aol.com *URL:* http://www.odomelliott.com

MEMBERS OF FIRM

Bobby Lee Odom
Don R. Elliott, Jr.
Russell B. Winburn
J. Timothy Smith
Conrad T. Odom
Jennifer Wheeler Haskins

Reference: Bank of Fayetteville, Fayetteville, Arkansas.

For full biographical listings, see the Martindale-Hubbell Law Directory

*FORREST CITY,** St. Francis Co.

BUTLER, HICKY & LONG (AV)

A Partnership of Professional Corporations
2216 North Washington Street, P.O. Box 989, 72335
Telephone: 870-633-4611
FAX: 870-633-6848
Email: bhlfirm@IPA.NET

MEMBERS OF FIRM

Philip Hicky (Ltd.)
Fletcher Long, Jr. (P.A.)

ASSOCIATE

Rita Reed Harris

Representative Clients: First National Bank of Eastern Arkansas; Southern Farm Bureau Insurance Cos.; United States Aviation Underwriters Group; National Aviation Underwriters; Hartford Accident and Indemnity Co.; Peoples Implement Co.; Virginia Insurance Reciprocal.

For full biographical listings, see the Martindale-Hubbell Law Directory

W. FRANK MORLEDGE, P.A. (AV)

205 North Washington, P.O. Box 912, 72335
Telephone: 870-633-9531
Fax: 870-633-2219

W. Frank Morledge

Representative Clients: Union Planters National Bank; Hughes Grain Corp.; Don Edmondson Foods, Inc.; Forrest City Ready Mix Concrete Co.; Thomas International; Japan Forest Industries; Wynne Progress Publishing, Inc.; East Arkansas Community College.

For full biographical listings, see the Martindale-Hubbell Law Directory

*FORT SMITH,** Sebastian Co.

DAILY & WOODS, P.L.L.C. (AV)

Stephens Office Building, 623 Garrison Avenue, P.O. Box 1446, 72902
Telephone: 501-782-0361
Fax: 501-782-6160
Email: DailyWoods@aol.com

MEMBERS OF FIRM

Ben Core
Jerry L. Canfield
Thomas A. Daily
Wyman R. Wade, Jr.
Stanley A. Leasure
Douglas M. Carson

ASSOCIATES

Todd Patrick Lewis
Barry D. Neal
Leigh M. Chiles

OF COUNSEL

James E. West

Counsel for: Claims Management, Inc. (Wal-Mart); Arkla, Inc.; City of Fort Smith; Commercial Union Insurance Cos.; Pennzoil Exploration and Production Co.; Silvey Cos., Inc.; Metropolitan Life Insurance Co.; Chevron U.S.A., Inc.

For full biographical listings, see the Martindale-Hubbell Law Directory

JONES, JACKSON & MOLL, PLC (AV)

401 North Seventh Street, P.O. Box 2023, 72902-2023
Telephone: 501-782-7203
Fax: 501-782-9460
Email: jjmlaw@aol.com

(See Next Column)

JONES, JACKSON & MOLL PLC, *Fort Smith—Continued*

MEMBERS OF FIRM

Robert L. Jones, Jr.
Randolph C. Jackson
Mark A. Moll
J. Scott Hardin

M. Chad Trammell
Jay William Kutchka

Insurance Counsel for: Farmers Insurance Group; State Farm Insurance Cos.; Maryland Insurance Cos.; Shelter Insurance Cos.; Travelers Insurance Co.; CNA Insurance Co.; Automobile Club Insurance Cos.
Counsel for: Merchants National Bank, Fort Smith, Arkansas; Beverly Enterprises, Inc.; Austin Powder Co.

For full biographical listings, see the Martindale-Hubbell Law Directory

ROBERTSON, BEASLEY, COWAN & KETCHAM, PLLC (AV)

615 North B Street, P.O. Box 23, 72902
Telephone: 501-782-7911
Fax: 501-782-7964
Email: RBCK@CEI.NET
Waldron, Arkansas Office: 205 South Main Street, 72958.
Telephone: 501-637-1197.
Fax: 501-782-7964.

MEMBERS OF FIRM

Donald P. Callaway (1935-1984)
Thomas E. Robertson, Jr.
John R. Beasley
Kenneth W. Cowan
Matthew J. Ketcham

Representative Clients: The Aetna Casualty & Surety Co.; James River - Dixie Cup; Arkansas-Oklahoma Gas Corp.; Beverage Products Corp. (Pepsi-Cola); The Prudential Insurance Company of America; Sentry - Dairyland Insurance Co; General Tire and Rubber; Quanex Corp.; The Fort Smith Municipal Airport Commission; Southern Steel & Wire Co.

For full biographical listings, see the Martindale-Hubbell Law Directory

WARNER, SMITH & HARRIS, PLC (AV)

214 North Sixth Street, P.O. Box 1626, 72901
Telephone: 501-782-6041
Fax: 501-782-0841

Harry Preston Warner (1885-1969)
Cecil Randolph Warner (1890-1955)
Thomas G. Graves (1939-1971)
Douglas O. Smith, Jr.
C. Wayne Harris
Gerald L. DeLung
Patrick Neill Moore
Lillard Cody Hayes
G. Alan Wooten
James Melvin Dunn
John Alan Lewis
Joel D. Johnson
J. Randall McGinnis
Kathryn Stocks Campbell
R. Gregory Aclin

Jason Trevor Browning
Matthew C. Carter

OF COUNSEL

C. R. Warner, Jr.

District Attorneys for: Burlington Northern Railroad Co.
Local Counsel for: Planters Division, Nabisco Brands, Inc.; Gerber Products Co.; Aetna Group; Fireman's Fund-American Insurance Cos.; Hiram Walker & Sons, Inc.; Continental National American Group.

For full biographical listings, see the Martindale-Hubbell Law Directory

*JONESBORO,** Craighead Co.

BARRETT & DEACON, A PROFESSIONAL ASSOCIATION (AV)

Union Planters Bank Building, 300 South Church Street, P.O. Box 1700, 72403
Telephone: 870-931-1700
Fax: 870-931-1800

Joe C. Barrett (1897-1980)
John C. Deacon
J. Barry Deacon
Ralph W. Waddell
Paul D. Waddell
D. Price Marshall, Jr.
James D. Bradbury

Kevin W. Cole
Robert S. Jones
Jennifer S. Cameron
James F. Gramling, Jr

For full biographical listings, see the Martindale-Hubbell Law Directory

*LITTLE ROCK,** Pulaski Co.

THE BAKER LAW FIRM (AV)

8 Shackleford Plaza, Suite 207, P.O. Box 21220, 72221
Telephone: 501-224-3904
Fax: 501-224-3768
Email: dbaker@cei.net

Darryl E. (Chip) Baker

For full biographical listings, see the Martindale-Hubbell Law Directory

CEARLEY LAW FIRM, P.A. (AV)

Centre Place, Second Floor, 212 Center Street, 72201
Telephone: 501-372-5600
Fax: 501-374-3463
Email: bcearley@CearleyLawFirm.com *URL:* http://www.CearleyLawFirm.com

Robert M. Cearley, Jr.

Counsel for: Arkansas Bankers Association; Greyhound Lines, Inc.; Arkansas State Medical Board.

For full biographical listings, see the Martindale-Hubbell Law Directory

CHISENHALL, NESTRUD & JULIAN, P.A. (AV)

400 West Capitol, Suite 2840, 72201
Telephone: 501-372-5800
Telecopier: 501-372-4941
Email: cnjlaw@cnjlaw.com

Lawrence E. Chisenhall, Jr.
Charles R. Nestrud
Jim L. Julian
Ann P. Faitz
Michael T. Jackson

For full biographical listings, see the Martindale-Hubbell Law Directory

DUNCAN & RAINWATER TRIAL LAWYERS A PROFESSIONAL ASSOCIATION (AV)

6315 Ranch Drive, 72221-5938
Telephone: 501-228-7600
Fax: 501-228-7664
URL: http://www.lawyers.com/duncanandrainwater
Email: duncanlaw@aristotle.net *URL:* http://www.duncan-rainwater.com

Phillip J. Duncan (P.A.)
Michael R. Rainwater
Neil Ray Chamberlin
Michelle Banks Odum
J. Stephen Holt

For full biographical listings, see the Martindale-Hubbell Law Directory

FRIDAY, ELDREDGE & CLARK (AV)

A Limited Liability Partnership of Individuals and Professional Associations
Formerly, Smith, Williams, Friday, Eldredge & Clark
2000 Regions Center, 400 West Capitol Avenue, 72201-3493
Telephone: 501-376-2011
Telecopier: 501-376-2147
Email: fecmh@fec.net

MEMBERS OF FIRM

William H. Sutton (P.A.)
John Dewey Watson (P.A.)
Paul B. Benham, III (P.A.)
Larry W. Burks (P.A.)
James M. Simpson, Jr. (P.A.)
Elizabeth Robben Murray (P.A.)
Kevin A. Crass (P.A.)
William A. Waddell, Jr. (P.A.)
Tonia P. Jones (P.A.)
David D. Wilson (P.A.)
Jeffrey H. Moore (P.A.)
R. Christopher Lawson (P.A.)
Tony L. Wilcox (P.A.)

ASSOCIATES

Clifford W. Plunkett
Ellen M. Owens
Susan N. Childers
Christopher A. Averitt
Joseph P. McKay

Counsel for: Union Pacific System; St. Paul Insurance Co.; Liberty Mutual Insurance Co.; Cigna Property & Casualty Co.; Entergy Arkansas, Inc.; Dillard's, Inc.; Browning Arms Co.; Phillips Petroleum Co.; Aetna Casualty & Surety Co.

For Complete List of Firm Personnel, See General Section

For full biographical listings, see the Martindale-Hubbell Law Directory

HILBURN, CALHOON, HARPER, PRUNISKI & CALHOUN, LTD. (AV)

P.O. Box 1256, 72203-1256
Telephone: 501-372-0110
Fax: 501-372-2029
Email: hilburn@aristotle.net
North Little Rock, Arkansas Office: Eighth Floor, Mercantile Bank Building, One Riverfront Place, P.O. Box 5551, 72119.
Telephone: 501-372-0110.
Fax: 501-372-2029.

Sam Hilburn
John E. Pruniski, III
John C. Calhoun, Jr.
David M. Fuqua
James M. McHaney, Jr.
Phil Campbell
J. Maurice Rogers
Scott Thomas Vaughn
James D. Lawson

Pamela Moseley Roberts
Randy L. Grice
Traci Harris LaCerra

Representative Clients: Mercantile Bank of Arkansas, N.A.; Merrill Lynch Pierce Fenner & Smith, Inc.; Allstate Insurance Company; Central Arkansas Risk Management Association; Salomon Smith Barney, Inc.; Deere & Co.; Case Corp.; Vanliner Insurance Company.

(See Next Column)

HILBURN, CALHOON, HARPER, PRUNISKI & CALHOUN LTD.—*Continued*

For Complete List of Firm Personnel, See General Section

For full biographical listings, see the Martindale-Hubbell Law Directory

HUCKABAY, MUNSON, ROWLETT & TILLEY, P.A. (AV)

Regions Center, Suite 1900, 400 West Capitol, 72201
Telephone: 501-374-6535
Fax: 501-374-5906

Mike Huckabay
Bruce E. Munson
Beverly A. Rowlett
James W. Tilley
John E. Moore
Tim Boone
Rick Runnells
Sarah Ann Presson
D. Michael Huckabay, Jr.
Carol Lockard Worley
Mark S. Breeding

Elizabeth Fletcher Rogers
Julia L. Busfield
Jane M. Yocum
Terry D. Dugger

Representative Clients: Allstate Insurance Company; American International Group; Farmers Insurance Group; General Electric Company; Nationwide Insurance Company; Safeco Insurance Company; State Farm Mutual Automobile Insurance Company; State Farm Fire and Casualty Company; Tenet Healthcare Corp.

For full biographical listings, see the Martindale-Hubbell Law Directory

LASER, WILSON, BUFFORD & WATTS, P.A. (AV)

101 South Spring Street, Suite 300, 72201-2488
Telephone: 501-376-2981
Telecopier: 501-376-2417
Email: laser@laserlaw.com

Sam Laser
Dan F. Bufford
Richard N. Watts
J. Kendal "Ken" Cook
Alfred F. Angulo, Jr.
David M. Donovan
Kevin J. Staten

Brian A. Brown
Karen J. Hughes
Thomas J. Diaz
Keith Martin McPherson
Deborah S. Denton
Andy L. Turner
Donna L. Gay
Sara A. Farris

Representative Clients: Allstate Insurance Co.; American International Insurance Group; Continental Insurance Cos.; Farm Bureau Insurance Cos. (Casualty & Fire); Farmers Insurance Group; GAB Business Services, Inc.; St. Paul Insurance Cos.; Scottsdale Insurance Co.; State Farm Auto (Fire) Insurance Cos.

For Complete List of Firm Personnel, See General Section

For full biographical listings, see the Martindale-Hubbell Law Directory

MCMATH, VEHIK, DRUMMOND, HARRISON & LEDBETTER, P.A. (AV)

711 West Third Street, 72201
Telephone: 501-396-5400
Fax: 501-374-5118
Email: jbmcmath@aristotle.net *URL:* http://www.mvdhpa.com

Phillip H. McMath
James Bruce McMath
Mart Vehik
Winslow Drummond
Paul E. Harrison
Samuel E. Ledbetter
Sandra L. Sanders
Joseph Henry (Hank) Bates
Eileen Harrison

OF COUNSEL

Sidney S. McMath
Leland F. Leatherman

For full biographical listings, see the Martindale-Hubbell Law Directory

WILLIAM L. OWEN (AV)

917 West Markham Street, P.O. Box 989, 72203
Telephone: 501-372-1655
Fax: 501-372-7884
Email: wlowen@aristotle.net *URL:* http://www.lawyers.com/wlowen_law

For full biographical listings, see the Martindale-Hubbell Law Directory

ROSE LAW FIRM, A PROFESSIONAL ASSOCIATION (AV)

120 East Fourth Street, 72201
Telephone: 501-375-9131
Telecopy: 501-375-1309

David L. Williams
Richard T. Donovan
Amy Lee Stewart
David P. Martin
Michael G. Smith
Kathryn Bennett Perkins
Michael N. Shannon

COUNSEL

Phillip Carroll

(See Next Column)

John D. Coulter

Representative Clients: Acxiom Corporation; Aluminum Company of America; The Equitable Life Assurance Society of the United States; Bridgestone/-Firestone, Inc.; CIGNA Companies; General Motors Corp.; Kemper Insurance Group; NationsBank of Arkansas, N.A.; New York Life Insurance Co.; The Prudential Insurance Company of America.

For Complete List of Firm Personnel, See General Section

For full biographical listings, see the Martindale-Hubbell Law Directory

SKOKOS, BEQUETTE & BILLINGSLEY, P.A. (AV)

3200 TCBY Tower, 425 West Capitol Avenue, 72201-3439
Telephone: 501-374-1107
Facsimile: 501-374-5092

Theodore C. Skokos
George J. Bequette, Jr.
Keith I. Billingsley

For full biographical listings, see the Martindale-Hubbell Law Directory

WILLIAMS & ANDERSON (AV)

Registered Limited Liability Partnership
Twenty-Second Floor, 111 Center Street, 72201
Telephone: 501-372-0800
Fax: 501-372-6453
Email: info@williamsanderson.com *URL:* http://www.williamsanderson.com

MEMBERS OF FIRM

W. Jackson Williams
Philip S. Anderson
Peter G. Kumpe
David F. Menz
Steven W. Quattlebaum
John E. Tull, III
J. Leon Holmes
James E. Hathaway III
Thomas G. Williams
Patrick A. Burrow

Edie R. Ervin
Stephen B. Niswanger
Kristine Gerhard Baker
Robert F. Thompson III

Representative Clients: Arkansas Democrat-Gazette, Inc.; Arkansas Development Finance Authority; Baldor Electric Co.; Coca-Cola Enterprises, Inc.; Entergy Corporation; Lennox International, Inc.; Mercedes-Benz of North America, Inc.; Potlatch Corporation; Texaco, Inc.; Wal-Mart Stores, Inc.

For Complete List of Firm Personnel, See General Section

For full biographical listings, see the Martindale-Hubbell Law Directory

WILSON, ENGSTROM, CORUM & COULTER (AV)

809 West Third Street, P.O. Box 71, 72203
Telephone: 501-375-6453
FAX: 501-375-5914

MEMBERS OF FIRM

Roxanne Wilson (1947-1992)
Stephen Engstrom
Gary D. Corum
Nate Coulter

For full biographical listings, see the Martindale-Hubbell Law Directory

*PINE BLUFF,** Jefferson Co.

RAMSAY, BRIDGFORTH, HARRELSON & STARLING (AV)

11th Floor, Simmons First National Building, P.O. Drawer 8509, 71611
Telephone: 870-535-9000
Fax: 870-535-8544

MEMBERS OF FIRM

William Franklin Coleman (1870-1956)
Nicholas J. Gantt, Jr. (1879-1975)
Marion J. Starling, Jr. (1941-1990)
William C. Bridgforth
F. Daniel Harrelson
Spencer F. Robinson
Phillip A. Raley
Rosalind M. Mouser
William M. Bridgforth
David R. Bridgforth
Christopher C. May
Anthony A. Hilliard

OF COUNSEL

Louis L. Ramsay, Jr.

Representative Clients: Simmons First National Bank; Pine Bluff Sand & Gravel Co.; Stant, Inc.; McGeorge Contracting Co., Inc.; Television Station KATV.

For full biographical listings, see the Martindale-Hubbell Law Directory

*TEXARKANA,** Miller Co.

DUNN, NUTTER, MORGAN & SHAW (AV)

State Line Plaza, 6th Floor, P.O. Box 8030, 71854-5945
Telephone: 870-773-5651
Texas Telephone: 903-793-5651
Telecopier: 870-772-2037
Email: lawfirm@dnms.com *URL:* http://www.dnms.com

(See Next Column)

DUNN, NUTTER, MORGAN & SHAW, *Texarkana—Continued*

MEMBERS OF FIRM

Winford L. Dunn, Jr. Nelson V. Shaw
R. Gary Nutter R. David Freeze
W. David Carter

ASSOCIATES

Jeff M. Addison Adam O. Fellows

OF COUNSEL

Hayes C. McClerkin

LEGAL SUPPORT PERSONNEL

LEGAL ASSISTANTS

Myra Conaway Wells Sonja L. Oliver

Representative Clients: Regions Bank; CNA Insurance Cos.; First Federal Savings & Loan Assn.; Christus St. Michael Health System; Shelter Insurance Cos.; CIGNA Insurance Cos.; Sentry Insurance; State Auto Insurance Co.; Kemper Insurance Co.; Georgia-Pacific Corp.

For Complete List of Firm Personnel, See General Section

For full biographical listings, see the Martindale-Hubbell Law Directory

WEST MEMPHIS, Crittenden Co.

HALE, FOGLEMAN & ROGERS (AV)

108 Dover Road, P.O. Box 1666, 72301
Telephone: 870-735-1900
Fax: 870-735-1662

MEMBERS OF FIRM

Julian B. Fogleman Joe M. Rogers

ASSOCIATES

Timothy A. Ginn Gerald Dickinson, Jr.

General Counsel for: Drainage Districts # 2, 3 and 8 of Crittenden County; Edmondson Hotel Service, Inc.; Heath & House Construction Co.; Crittenden County, Arkansas.
Local Counsel for: Southern Farm Bureau Casualty Insurance Co.; Shelby Mutual Insurance Co.; Greyhound Lines, Inc.; American Justice Insurance Reciprocal; Graward General Companies.

For full biographical listings, see the Martindale-Hubbell Law Directory

RIEVES & MAYTON (AV)

304 East Broadway, P.O. Box 1359, 72303
Telephone: 870-735-3420
Telecopier: 870-735-4678
Email: rieves.mayton@worldnet.att.net
Little Rock, Arkansas Office: Suite 1719, First Commercial Building, 400 West Capitol.
Telephone: 501-376-0504.
Telecopier: 501-372-3482.

MEMBERS OF FIRM

Elton A. Rieves, Jr. (1909-1984) Michael R. Mayton
Elton A. Rieves, III Elton A. Rieves, IV

ASSOCIATES

David S. Wilson, III Eric Newkirk

For full biographical listings, see the Martindale-Hubbell Law Directory

SLOAN, RUBENS & PEEPLES (AV)

An Association of Lawyers
600 North Missouri Street, P.O. Box 768, 72303
Telephone: 870-735-5500
Telecopy: 870-735-2624

Edward J. Rubens (1913-1977) Kent J. Rubens
Ralph W. Sloan (1915-1996) David C. Peeples
J. Michael Stephenson

OF COUNSEL

Edward B. Johnson (Not admitted in AR)

General Counsel for: Bank of West Memphis; Crittenden Publishing Co., Inc.; West Memphis School District; Razorback Concrete Company; Flash Market, Inc.
Representative Clients: Arkansas School Boards Association-Risk Management Association; Vanliner Insurance; Builder's Transport, Inc.; Citizens Bank Marion; Marion School District.

For full biographical listings, see the Martindale-Hubbell Law Directory

CALIFORNIA

*BAKERSFIELD,** Kern Co.

KLEIN, DENATALE, GOLDNER, COOPER, ROSENLIEB & KIMBALL, LLP (AV)

(Formerly Di Giorgio, Davis, Klein, Wegis, Duggan & Friedman)
ARCO Tower, 4550 California Avenue, Second Floor, 93309
Telephone: 661-395-1000
Telecopier: 661-326-0418
Mailing Address: P.O. Box 11172, Bakersfield, California, 93389-1172
Email: kleinlaw@kleinlaw.com

Anthony J. Klein (Inc.) Jay L. Rosenlieb
Thomas V. DeNatale, Jr. David J. Cooper
Barry L. Goldner William A. Bruce

Representative Clients: Bank of America; Great Western Bank; Mojave Pipeline Co.; Transamerican Title Insurance Co.; Dean Whittier Reynolds, Inc.; California Republic Bank; San Joaquin Bank; Nahama & Weagant Energy Co.; Freymiller Trucking, Inc.; Westinghouse Electric Co.

For Complete List of Firm Personnel, See General Section

For full biographical listings, see the Martindale-Hubbell Law Directory

ROBINSON, PALMER & LOGAN (AV)

Suite 150, 3434 Truxtun Avenue, 93301
Telephone: 805-323-8277
Fax: 805-323-4205
Email: RPLLAW@AOL.COM

MEMBERS OF FIRM

Oliver U. Robinson William D. Palmer
Gary L. Logan

For Complete List of Firm Personnel, See General Section

For full biographical listings, see the Martindale-Hubbell Law Directory

LAW OFFICES OF YOUNG WOOLDRIDGE (AV)

1800 30th Street, Fourth Floor, 93301
Telephone: 661-327-9661
Facsimile: 661-327-1087
Email: youngwooldridge@lightspeed.net *URL:* http://www.young.wooldridge.com

MEMBERS OF FIRM

G. Neil Farr Larry R. Cox
Steve W. Nichols Scott K. Kuney
Scott D. Howry

ASSOCIATE

Christopher Finberg

Representative Clients: Arvin-Edison Water Storage District; Motor City Truck Sales and Service.
References: Wells Fargo Bank; First Interstate Bank; California Republic Bank.

For Complete List of Firm Personnel, See General Section

For full biographical listings, see the Martindale-Hubbell Law Directory

BEVERLY HILLS, Los Angeles Co.

NORMINTON & WIITA (AV)

A Partnership of Professional Corporations
433 North Camden Drive Suite 1111, 90210
Telephone: 310-288-5900
Facsimile: 310-288-5901
Email: norminton@earthlink.net

Thomas M. Norminton (P.C.) Douglas P. Wiita (P.C.)
Kathleen Dority Fuster (P.C.).

For full biographical listings, see the Martindale-Hubbell Law Directory

SCHWARTZ, WISOT & WILSON, LLP (AV)

315 South Beverly Drive, Suite 315, 90212
Telephone: 310-277-2323
Fax: 310-556-2308
Email: swwllp@aol.com *URL:* http://www.lawyers.com/swwllp

Bruce Edward Schwartz Valerie Wisot
John D. Wilson

Kathleen A. Calaway-McLean

OF COUNSEL

Paula Reddish Zinnemann

Reference: City National Bank, Beverly Hills, California.

For full biographical listings, see the Martindale-Hubbell Law Directory

Beverly Hills—Continued

TURNER, AUBERT & FRIEDMAN, LLP (AV)

Formerly Turner, Gerstenfeld, Wilk & Tigerman
Suite 510, 8383 Wilshire Boulevard, 90211
Telephone: 323-653-3900
Facsimile: 323-653-3021

MEMBER OF FIRM
Edward Friedman
ASSOCIATES
Dortha Larene Pyles
Steven A. Morris

For Complete List of Firm Personnel, See General Section

For full biographical listings, see the Martindale-Hubbell Law Directory

CARLSBAD, San Diego Co.

GATZKE, DILLON & BALLANCE (AV)

A Partnership
Suite 200, 1921 Palomar Oaks Way, 92008
Telephone: 760-431-9501
Fax: 760-431-9512

MEMBERS OF FIRM
Michael Scott Gatzke
Mark J. Dillon
Lori D. Ballance
ASSOCIATES
Michael S. Haberkorn
Tom Deak
Stephen F. Tee
Sophia R. Ray
Jill Dian Skinner
Anne E. Bickel

For full biographical listings, see the Martindale-Hubbell Law Directory

CLAREMONT, Los Angeles Co.

JOHN C. McCARTHY (AV)

401 Harvard Avenue, 91711
Telephone: 909-621-4984
Telecopier: 909-621-5757
(Also Member, Morrisons, McCarthy & Baraban, Claremont, California and Whitefish, Montana)

For full biographical listings, see the Martindale-Hubbell Law Directory

COSTA MESA, Orange Co.

ALBERT, WEILAND & GOLDEN (AV)

Center Tower, 650 Town Center Drive, Suite 1350, 92626
Telephone: 714-966-1000
FAX: 714-966-1002
Email: awglawyers@aol.com

Theodor C. Albert
Michael J. Weiland
Jeffrey I. Golden
ASSOCIATES
Evan D. Smiley
Philip E. Strok
Lei Lei Wang Ekvall
Darlynn Campbell Morgan
OF COUNSEL
Marcus M. Kaufman
Jennifer Ann Golison
Steven J. Katzman
LEGAL SUPPORT PERSONNEL
PARALEGALS
Fran L. Russell
Patricia K. Nelson
Cynthia B. Meeker
Janet Hogan
Kim Sigismondo

For full biographical listings, see the Martindale-Hubbell Law Directory

THE COULOMBE LAW FIRM A PROFESSIONAL CORPORATION (AV)

3200 Park Center Drive, Suite 1000, 92626
Telephone: 714-540-1234
Fax: 714-754-0808
Email: rbc@coulombe.com

Ronald B. Coulombe

For full biographical listings, see the Martindale-Hubbell Law Directory

FELDHAKE, AUGUST & ROQUEMORE (AV)

Plaza Tower, Suite 1730, 600 Anton Boulevard, 92626-7124
Telephone: 714-438-3885
Fax: 714-438-3888
Email: farlaw@hqonline.com

Robert J. Feldhake
Lisa A. Roquemore
Kenneth S. August
Joshua M. Wolff
ASSOCIATES
Dimitri P. Gross
Supriya Kakkar
Katherine A. Slayton

(See Next Column)

OF COUNSEL
Arthur J. Swerdloff
Arthur M. Wilcox, Jr.

For full biographical listings, see the Martindale-Hubbell Law Directory

McCORMICK, KIDMAN & BEHRENS, LLP (AV)

A Partnership of Professional Corporations
Imperial Bank Building, 695 Town Center Drive Suite 1400, 92626-7187
Telephone: 714-755-3100
Fax: 714-755-3110; 1-800-755-3125
Email: mkb1@ix.netcom.com
Sacramento, California Office: 980 Ninth Street. 16th Floor. 95814-2736.
Telephone: 916-449-9533.
Fax: 916-446-7104.
Effective April 1, 1999 the new address will be: Imperial Bank Building, 695 Town Center Drive, Suite 400.

MEMBERS OF FIRM
Homer L. (Mike) McCormick, Jr., (P.C.)
Russell G. Behrens (P.C.)
Suzanne M. Tague (P.C.)
Arthur G. Kidman (P.C.)
Janet R. Morningstar (P.C.)
Keith E. McCullough (P.C.)
ASSOCIATES
David D. Boyer
Gary D. Grant
Paeter E. Garcia
Edward L. Bertrand

For full biographical listings, see the Martindale-Hubbell Law Directory

RICKS & ANDERSON, A LAW CORPORATION (AV)

3200 Park Center Drive, Suite 1155, 92626-7163
Telephone: 714-966-9190

Cecil E. Ricks, Jr.
Annette L. Anderson

For full biographical listings, see the Martindale-Hubbell Law Directory

RUTAN & TUCKER, LLP (AV)

A Partnership including Professional Corporations
611 Anton Boulevard, Fourteenth Floor, P.O. Box 1950, 92626-1998
Telephone: 714-641-5100; 213-625-7586
Telecopier: 714-546-9035
Email: rutan&tucker@rutan.com *URL:* http://www.rutan.com

MEMBERS OF FIRM
Leonard A. Hampel, Jr.
Joel D. Kuperberg
John B. Hurlbut, Jr.
William W. Wynder
Milford W. Dahl, Jr.
Michael F. Sitzer
Theodore I. Wallace, Jr. (P.C.)
Penelope Parmes
Robert C. Braun
Duke Wahlquist
Thomas S. Salinger (P.C.)
Jayne Taylor Kacer
Clifford E. Frieden
Stephen A. Ellis
Michael D. Rubin
Matthew K. Ross
Ira G. Rivin (P.C.)
Layne H. Melzer
Robert S. Bower
Richard K. Howell
William M. Marticorena
David H. Hochner
William J. Caplan
A. Patrick Muñoz
Michael T. Hornak
S. Daniel Harbottle
Paul J. Sievers
SPECIAL COUNSEL
Debra Dunn Steel
ASSOCIATES
Steven John Goon
Terence J. Gallagher
Sean P. Farrell
Julie K. Whang
John W. Hamilton, Jr.
Charles A. Davenport, III
B. Lynn Loschin
Richard D. Arko
Philip J. Blanchard
Mark M. Malovos
OF COUNSEL
Edward D. Sybesma, Jr. (P.C.)

For Complete List of Firm Personnel, See General Section

For full biographical listings, see the Martindale-Hubbell Law Directory

RONALD K. VAN WERT A PROFESSIONAL CORPORATION (AV)

3200 Park Center Drive Suite 1110, 92626
Telephone: 714-546-2400
Fax: 714-546-5008

Ronald K. Van Wert

For full biographical listings, see the Martindale-Hubbell Law Directory

DANVILLE, Contra Costa Co.

CRADDICK, CANDLAND & CONTI, PROFESSIONAL CORPORATION (AV)

Danville-San Ramon Medical Center, 915 San Ramon Valley Boulevard, Suite 260, 94526-0810
Telephone: 925-838-1100
Fax: 925-743-0729

(See Next Column)

CRADDICK, CANDLAND & CONTI PROFESSIONAL CORPORATION, *Danville—Continued*

Marrs A. Craddick (1928-1996)
D. Stuart Candland
Richard J. Conti
Robert W. Hodges
W. David Walker
Andrew S. Miller
Thomas G. Manning
Steven L. Brown, Jr.

Jean Louise Perry
Kristine Keala Meredith
Matthew C. Mani
Emily C. Millar
Michael E. Gatto

Representative Clients: Kaiser Foundation Hospitals; Medical Insurance Exchange of California; The Doctor's Co.; County of Contra Costa; Farmers Insurance Group (Truck Insurance Exchange); Professional Risk Management of California, Inc.; Claremont Liability Insurance Company; Program Beta.

For full biographical listings, see the Martindale-Hubbell Law Directory

EMERYVILLE, Alameda Co.

BISHOP, BARRY, HOWE, HANEY & RYDER, A PROFESSIONAL CORPORATION (AV)

Watergate Tower III, 2000 Powell Street, Suite 1425, 94608
Telephone: 510-596-0888
Fax: 510-596-0899
Email: FirmGeneral@BBHHR.com
San Francisco Office: 44 Montgomery Street, Suite 1300, 94104.
Telephone: 415-421-8550.

Ross R. Ryder (1940-1989)
Nelson C. Barry
Drayton F. Howe, Jr.
Jeffrey N. Haney
Thomas O. Haran
Rebecca B. Aherne
Michael W. Bolechowski
Mark C. Raskoff
Patricia S. Lakner
Gregory R. de la Peña

J. Scott Wood
Mitchell J. Alward
Marco R. Sumarriva
Jane E. Carey
Carol L. Healey
Mary Margaret Ryan
Thomas Edward Foran
John F. Cooke
Jean H. Hurricane
Daniel M. O'Connell
Lisa S. Wiggins
Edward M. Lai

OF COUNSEL

Lawrence S. Molton
David P. Osako

Representative Clients: Agricultural Excess & Surplus Ins. Co.; Carolina Casualty Co.; Federated Department Stores, Inc.; The Gap, Inc. Group of Companies.
Reference: Golden Gate Bank.

For full biographical listings, see the Martindale-Hubbell Law Directory

LEGAL STRATEGIES GROUP (AV)

5905 Christie Avenue, 94608
Telephone: 510-450-9600
Fax: 510-450-9601
URL: http://www.lsglaw.com

SHAREHOLDERS

Ralph C. Alldredge
Timothy R. Cahn
Joshua R. Floum
Karen S. Frank
Gregory S. Gilchrist
Peter H. Goldsmith
Vincent L. Johnson
Leigh A. Kirmssé
Louise E. Ma
Maureen A. Sheehy
Heather A. Young

OF COUNSEL

Robert J. Vizas

ASSOCIATE

Jeffrey N. Hyman

AFFILIATE COUNSEL

Christine A. Amatruda
Gia L. Cincone
R. Dennis Claessens (Not admitted in CA)
Gregory P. Farnham
Ariela Freed
Jennifer Connors Hayes
Daniel J. Kroll
Jonathan P. Marvin
Paul J. Neibergs
Margaret R. O'Donnell
William Michael Quinn, Jr.
Nancy Lee Tang

For full biographical listings, see the Martindale-Hubbell Law Directory

ENCINO, Los Angeles Co.

STAITMAN SNYDER TANNENBAUM & DORENFELD, LLP (AV)

Suite 1401, 16633 Ventura Boulevard, 91436-1840
Telephone: 818-981-5300; 213-872-3530
FAX: 818-981-7104

Bradley A. Snyder
Jack J. Tannenbaum
David K. Dorenfeld

(See Next Column)

Rodger S. Greiner
Deborah K. Galer
Peter A. Mittenthal

For full biographical listings, see the Martindale-Hubbell Law Directory

FOLSOM, Sacramento Co.

THE BLEIER LAW FIRM (AV)

110 Blue Ravine Road, Suite 201, 95630
Telephone: 916-454-2100
Fax: 916-454-2121
Email: tblf@bleier.com *URL:* http://www.bleier.com

Brenton A. Bleier

ASSOCIATE

Bradford A. Bleier

For full biographical listings, see the Martindale-Hubbell Law Directory

*FRESNO,** Fresno Co.

DOWLING, AARON & KEELER, INCORPORATED (AV)

6051 North Fresno Street, Suite 200, 93710
Telephone: 559-432-4500
Fax: 559-432-4590
Email: dak@daklaw.com *URL:* http://www.daklaw.com
Bakersfield, California Office: 110 South Mt. Claire, Suite 203. 93309.
Telephone: 661-396-0451. Web Site: http://www.daklaw.com.

William J. Keeler, Jr.
Stephen M. Blumberg
Philip David Kopp
Dale Ikeda
Adolfo M. Corona
Gary M. Fachin
Francine Marie Kanne
James C. Sherwood
David J. Weiland

Leigh W. Burnside

Reference: Wells Fargo Bank (Main).

For Complete List of Firm Personnel, See General Section

For full biographical listings, see the Martindale-Hubbell Law Directory

JORY, PETERSON, WATKINS & SMITH (AV)

555 West Shaw, Suite C-1, P.O. Box 5394, 93755
Telephone: 559-225-6700
Telecopier: 559-225-3416
Email: jpws@jpws.com

MEMBERS OF FIRM

Jay V. Jory
John E. Peterson
Cal B. Watkins, Jr.
Michael Jens F. Smith
Marcia A. Ross
William M. Woolman
Jeffrey T. Hammerschmidt

ASSOCIATES

Carla M. McCormack
Shannon R. McFarland
Patti L. Williams
Annette A. Ballatore-Williamson

Reference: Wells Fargo Bank.

For full biographical listings, see the Martindale-Hubbell Law Directory

LANG, RICHERT & PATCH, A PROFESSIONAL CORPORATION (AV)

Fig Garden Financial Center, 5200 North Palm Avenue, 4th Floor, P.O. Box 40012, 93755
Telephone: 559-228-6700
Fax: 559-228-6727

William T. Richert (1937-1993)
Robert L. Patch, II
Val W. Saldaña
Douglas E. Noll
Michael T. Hertz
Victoria J. Salisch
Rene Lastreto, II
Charles Trudrung Taylor
Mark L. Creede
Peter N. Zeitler
Laurie L. Quigley
Tamara L. Equals
Douglas E. Griffin
Nabil E. Zumout

Christopher B. Dorian
Matthew W. Quall
Tracy E. Sagle
Julie K. Hill
Michelle Oleksa

OF COUNSEL

Frank H. Lang

References: Wells Fargo Bank (Fresno Main Office).

For full biographical listings, see the Martindale-Hubbell Law Directory

MILES, SEARS & EANNI, A PROFESSIONAL CORPORATION (AV)

2844 Fresno Street, P.O. Box 1432, 93716
Telephone: 559-486-5200
Fax: 559-486-5240
Email: mse@good.attitude.com

(See Next Column)

MILES, SEARS & EANNI A PROFESSIONAL CORPORATION—*Continued*

Wm. M. Miles (1909-1991)
Robert E. Sears (1918-1992)
Carmen A. Eanni
Richard C. Watters
William J. Seiler
Douglas L. Gordon

For full biographical listings, see the Martindale-Hubbell Law Directory

SAGASER, FRANSON & JONES, A PROFESSIONAL CORPORATION (AV)

2445 Capitol Street, Second Floor, P.O. Box 1632, 93717-1632
Telephone: 559-233-4800
Fax: 559-233-9330

Howard A. Sagaser
Eric K. Hansen (1952-1996)
Donald R. Franson, Jr.
Timothy Jones
Kristi R. Culver Kapetan
Elise M. Shebelut Krause
Nancy A. Maler
W. Allen Bennett
Mark D. Kruthers
Michael S. Helsley
Jamie Katzman

For full biographical listings, see the Martindale-Hubbell Law Directory

GLENDALE, Los Angeles Co.

GILL AND BALDWIN (AV)

130 North Brand Boulevard Fourth Floor, 91203
Telephone: 818-500-7755; 323-245-3131
Fax: 818-242-4305
URL: http://www.lawyers.com/g&blaw
Email: gillandbal@aol.com *URL:* http://www.gillandbaldwin.com

MEMBERS OF FIRM

John M. Carmack
Kirk S. MacDonald

Representative Clients: Morrison-Knudsen Corp.; Bireley Foundation.
Reference: Bank of Los Angeles.

For full biographical listings, see the Martindale-Hubbell Law Directory

SILVIO NARDONI (AV)

206 North Jackson Street Suite 100, 91206
Telephone: 818-550-1800
Fax: 818-550-1850
URL: http://www.lawyers.com/nardonilaw
Email: s.nardoni@worldnet.att.net *URL:* http://www.LABankruptcy.com

For full biographical listings, see the Martindale-Hubbell Law Directory

O'ROURKE, ALLAN & FONG, LLP (AV)

100 West Broadway, Suite 1250, P.O. Box 10220, 91210
Telephone: 818-247-4303
Fax: 818-247-1451
Email: OAFLAW@aol.com

MEMBERS OF FIRM

Denis M. O'Rourke
Joan H. Allan
Roderick D. Fong

ASSOCIATES

Denise Michelle O'Rourke
Marina Manoukian
Toshiko Kobayashi

References: Verdugo Banking Co. (Glendale, California); Community Bank (Glendale, California).

For full biographical listings, see the Martindale-Hubbell Law Directory

OTT & HOFFMAN, A PROFESSIONAL CORPORATION (AV)

700 North Central Avenue, 8th Floor, Suite 850, 91203
Telephone: 818-242-3100
Fax: 818-242-3102
Email: ohlaw@aol.com *URL:* http://www.ottlaw.com

Thomas H. Ott
Daniel E. Hoffman

Patrick Carey

Representative Clients: Alhambra Unified School District; Calif. Credit Union League; Cuna Mutual Ins. Group; Hughes Aircraft Corp.; Lockheed Federal Credit Union.

For full biographical listings, see the Martindale-Hubbell Law Directory

IRVINE, Orange Co.

BARNES, CROSBY, FITZGERALD & ZEMAN LLP (AV)

2030 Main Street, Suite 1050, 92614
Telephone: 949-852-1100
Fax: 949-852-1501

MEMBERS OF FIRM

Robert Samuel Barnes
William M. Crosby
Michael J. FitzGerald
Larry S. Zeman
Mark H. Cheung
Matthew R. Seifen

(See Next Column)

OF COUNSEL

Frederick J. Stemmler
Morland C. Fischer

For full biographical listings, see the Martindale-Hubbell Law Directory

CHAIREZ & ASSOCIATES (AV)

Jamboree Center, 4 Park Plaza, Suite 1230, 92614
Telephone: 949-794-9225
Facsimile: 949-794-9220
Email: jlchaz@aol.com

Joseph L. Chairez

For full biographical listings, see the Martindale-Hubbell Law Directory

THE ENTERPRISE COUNSEL GROUP (AV)

5 Park Plaza, 92614
Telephone: 949-553-2404
Fax: 949-553-2434
URL: http://www.enterprisecounsel.com

David A. Robinson
Corey E. Taylor
Susan M. Masson
Jeffrey Lewis

For full biographical listings, see the Martindale-Hubbell Law Directory

GEORGE & SHIELDS, LLP (AV)

30 Corporate Park, Suite 300, 92606-5133
Telephone: 949-263-1085
Fax: 949-263-0585
Email: toplaw@george-shields.com *URL:* http://www.george-shields.com

MEMBERS OF FIRM

Robert K. George
Timothy F. Shields
David W. Sparks

For full biographical listings, see the Martindale-Hubbell Law Directory

TIMOTHY L. JOENS & ASSOCIATES A PROFESSIONAL CORPORATION (AV)

2601 Main Street, Suite 320, 92614
Telephone: 949-553-1950
Fax: 949-553-8835

Timothy L. Joens

Representative Client: Century 21 Real Estate Corp.

For full biographical listings, see the Martindale-Hubbell Law Directory

JONES, DAY, REAVIS & POGUE (AV)

5 Park Plaza, Suite 1100, 92614
Telephone: 949-851-3939
Telecopier: 949-553-7539
Email: counsel@jonesday.com *URL:* http://www.jonesday.com
In Los Angeles, California: 555 West Fifth Street, Suite 4600.
Telephone: 213-489-3939.
Telecopier: 213-243-2539.
In Atlanta, Georgia: 3500 SunTrust Plaza, 303 Peachtree Street.
Telephone: 404-521-3939.
Telecopier: 404-581-8330.
In Brussels, Belgium: Avenue Louise 480, 7th Floor, B-1050 Brussels.
Telephone: 32-2-645-14-11.
Telecopier: 32-2-645-14-45.
In Chicago, Illinois: 77 West Wacker.
Telephone: 312-782-3939.
Telecopier: 312-782-8585.
In Cleveland, Ohio: North Point, 901 Lakeside Avenue.
Telephone: 216-586-3939.
Telecopier: 216-579-0212.
In Columbus, Ohio: 1900 Huntington Center.
Telephone: 614-469-3939.
Telecopier: 614-461-4198.
In Dallas, Texas: 2727 North Harwood Street.
Telephone: 214-220-3939.
Telecopier: 214-969-5100.
In Frankfurt, Germany: Hochhaus am Park, Grüneburgweg 102, 60323 Frankfurt am Main.
Telephone: 49-69-9726-3939.
Telecopier: 49-69-9726-3993.
In Geneva, Switzerland: 20, rue de Candolle.
Telephone: 41-22-320-2339.
Telecopier: 41-22-320-1232.
In Hong Kong: 29th Floor, Entertainment Building, 30 Queen's Road Central.
Telephone: 852-2526-6895.
Telecopier: 852-2868-5871.
In London, England: Bucklersbury House, 3 Queen Victoria Street.
Telephone: 44-20-7236-3939.
Telecopier: 44-20-7236-1113.
In New York, New York: 599 Lexington Avenue.
Telephone: 212-326-3939.
Telecopier: 212-755-7306.

(See Next Column)

JONES, DAY, REAVIS & POGUE, *Irvine—Continued*

In Paris, France: 120, rue du Faubourg Saint-Honoré.
Telephone: 33-1-56-59-3939.
Telecopier: 33-1-56-59-3938
In Pittsburgh, Pennsylvania: 500 Grant Street, 31st Floor.
Telephone: 412-391-3939.
Telecopier: 412-394-7959.
In Riyadh, Saudi Arabia: The International Law Firm (In Association with Jones, Day, Reavis & Pogue), Sulaymaniyah, Prince Mishari IBN, Abdulaziz Street, P.O. Box 22166.
Telephone: (966-1) 462-8866.
Telecopier: (966-1) 462-9001.
In Shanghai, China: 2805 Kerry Centre, 1515 Nanjing Road West.
Telephone: 86-21-5298-6568.
Telecopier: 86-21-5298-6569.
In Sydney, Australia: Governor Phillip Tower, Level 38, 1 Farrer Place.
Telephone: 61-2-9210-6921.
Telecopier: 61-2-9210-6926.
In Taipei, Taiwan: 8th Floor, 2 Tun Hwa South Road, Section 2.
Telephone: (886-2) 2704-6808.
Telecopier: (886-2) 2704-6791.
In Tokyo, Japan: Toranomon 45 Mori Building, 3th Floor, 1-5, Toranomon 5-Chome, Minato-ku, Tokyo 105, Japan.
Telephone: 81-3-3433-3939.
Telecopier: 81-3-5401-2725.
In Washington, D.C.: 51 Louisiana Avenue, N.W.
Telephone: 202-879-3939.
Telecopier: 202-626-1700.

MEMBER OF FIRM IN IRVINE

Thomas R. Malcolm

For Complete List of Firm Personnel, See General Section

For full biographical listings, see the Martindale-Hubbell Law Directory

LEE, GODDARD & DUFFY LLP (AV)

A Limited Liability Partnership
18500 Von Karman Avenue, Suite 700, 92612
Telephone: 949-253-0500
Facsimile: 949-253-0505

Raymond A. Lee — Sherman O. Halstead, Jr.
William A. Goddard, IV — Thomas B. Griffen
Anthony C. Duffy — Bradley A. Patterson
Douglas L. Collins

Loren A. Deters — Jeffrey A. Coste (Not admitted in CA)
Lauren M. Seng

For full biographical listings, see the Martindale-Hubbell Law Directory

MOWER, KOELLER, NEBEKER, CARLSON & HALUCK, LLP (AV)

108 Pacifica, P.O. Box 19799, 92623-9799
Telephone: 714-753-1229
Fax: 714-753-1413
Email: infoir@mknch.com *URL:* http://www.mknch.com
San Bernardino, California Office: 412 West Hospitality Lane, Suite 300, 92408.
Telephone: 909-381-3334.
Fax: 909-889-2007.
San Diego, California Office: 225 Broadway, 21st Floor.
Telephone: 619-233-1600.
Fax: 619-236-0527.
Yuma, Arizona Office: P.O. Box 10969, 85366.
Telephone: 520-782-2531.
Phoenix, Arizona Office: 3200 North Central Avenue, Suite 2300, 85012-2443.
Telephone: 602-256-0000.
Fax: 602-256-2488.

MEMBERS OF FIRM

Jon R. Mower — Joseph J. Cullen
Keith D. Koeller — Patrick A. Carreon
William L. Haluck — Edward W. Schmitt
Ellen E. Hunter

Mark D. Newcomb — Aashish Y. Desai
Terrence J. Giannone — Daniel Gavin
Eric W. Smith — Erik R. Musurlian
John R. Armstrong

For full biographical listings, see the Martindale-Hubbell Law Directory

PAONE CALLAHAN MCHOLM & WINTON, LLP (AV)

Eighth Floor, 19100 Von Karman Avenue, P.O. Box 19613, 92623-9613
Telephone: 949-955-2900
Facsimile: 949-955-9009
Email: info@paone.com *URL:* http://www.paone.com

(See Next Column)

MEMBERS OF FIRM

Robert E. Callahan — Kenneth S. Kramer
Richard J. Foster — Steven A. McHolm
Susan K. Hori — Tim Paone
Alan Jules Kessel — Martin J. Stein
Daniel K. Winton

OF COUNSEL

Roger A. Grable — Kathleen Carothers Paone
William P. Tanner, III

Clay Shevlin — L. Elizabeth Strahlstrom

For full biographical listings, see the Martindale-Hubbell Law Directory

ROSS, DIXON & BELL, L.L.P. (AV)

5 Park Plaza, Suite 1200, 92614-8529
Telephone: 949-622-2700
Fax: 949-622-2739
Email: info@rdblaw.com *URL:* http://www.rdblaw.com
Washington, D.C. Office: 601 Pennsylvania Avenue, N.W., North Building, 20004-2688.
Telephone: 202-662-2000.
Fax: 202-662-2190.
San Diego, California Office: 550 West B Street, Suite 400, 92101-3538.
Telephone: 619-235-4040.
Fax: 619-231-8796.

PARTNERS

Alec M. Barinholtz — Gilbert D. Jensen
Roy Morrow Bell — Terrence R. McInnis
Timothy P. Irving — Robert M. Pozin

ASSOCIATES

J. Kirk Donnelly — Michele L. Lynch
Kevin J. Kieffer — Jennifer Mathis
Kim S. Orbeck

For full biographical listings, see the Martindale-Hubbell Law Directory

RUS, MILIBAND & SMITH (AV)

Suite 700, 2600 Michelson Drive, 92612
Telephone: 949-752-7100
Fax: 949-252-1514
Email: rmws@rmsapc.com *URL:* http://www.rmsapc.com

Ronald Rus — Randall A. Smith
Joel S. Miliband — Laurel R. Zaeske

Cathrine M. Castaldi — Leo J. Presiado
David Edward Hays — Michael B. Kushner
M. Peter Crinella

For full biographical listings, see the Martindale-Hubbell Law Directory

STEPONOVICH & ASSOCIATES, A PROFESSIONAL LAW CORPORATION (AV)

Koll Center Irvine, 18201 Von Karman Avenue, Suite 650, 92612-1005
Telephone: 949-852-1073
Fax: 949-852-1276
Email: STEPOLAW@aol.com

Michael J. Steponovich, Jr.

STEVENS & KRAMER, A PROFESSIONAL CORPORATION (AV)

18022 Cowan, Suite 200D, 92614-6808
Telephone: 949-253-9553
Fax: 949-253-9643
Agoura Hills, California Office: 30401 W. Agoura Road, Suite 102.
Telephone: 818-879-1699.
Fax: 818-879-1673.

Carl R. Stevens

Lee E. Burrows — Javier H. Van Oordt

For full biographical listings, see the Martindale-Hubbell Law Directory

WESIERSKI & ZUREK, LLP (AV)

One Corporate Park Drive Second Floor, 92606
Telephone: 949-975-1000
Telecopier: 949-756-0517
Email: Lawyers@wzllp.com
Los Angeles, California Office: 777 South Figueroa, Suite 850, 90017.
Telephone: 213-627-2300.
Telecopier: 213-629-2725.

PARTNERS

Christopher P. Wesierski — Terence P. Carney
Ronald Zurek (Resident, Los Angeles Office) — Thomas G. Wianecki

JUNIOR PARTNER

Paul J. Lipman (Resident, Los Angeles Office)

(See Next Column)

WESIERSKI & ZUREK LLP—*Continued*

Mark J. Giannamore (Resident, Los Angeles Office)
Bruce Vail Rorty
Regina A. Leago (Resident, Los Angeles Office)
Thomas E. Martin
G. Brent Sims
Lisa M. Dale
Kevin T. Meade
Jonyson Allen Pierce
Raymond E. Brown
Brett G. Hampton (Resident, Los Angeles Office)
Jeffrey N. Gesell

OF COUNSEL

Daniel J. Ford, Jr.

For full biographical listings, see the Martindale-Hubbell Law Directory

LAGUNA BEACH, Orange Co.

NOKES, DAVIS & QUINN, A PROFESSIONAL CORPORATION (AV)

450 Ocean Avenue, 92651
Telephone: 949-376-3055
FAX: 949-376-3070
Email: ndqlaw@gte.net

Laurence P. Nokes
Thomas P. Davis
Thomas P. Quinn, Jr.

OF COUNSEL

Paul W. Davis

For full biographical listings, see the Martindale-Hubbell Law Directory

LA JOLLA, San Diego Co.

DARVY MACK COHAN (AV)

1200 Prospect Street, Suite 550, 92037
Telephone: 858-459-4432
Fax: 858-454-3548
Email: cohanlaw@worldnet.att.net *URL:* http://www.cohanlaw.com

For full biographical listings, see the Martindale-Hubbell Law Directory

MAURER LAW FIRM (AV)

7825 Fay Avenue, Suite 200, 92037
Telephone: 619-456-5570
Fax: 619-551-8919
Email: maurerlawfirm@msn.com *URL:* http://www.lawyers.com/maurerlawfirm

Charles D. Maurer, Jr.

For full biographical listings, see the Martindale-Hubbell Law Directory

TREMBLAY & HOLSENBACK (AV)

La Jolla Eastgate Building, 9404 Genesee Avenue, Suite 300, 92037-1355
Telephone: 619-546-8583
Facsimile: 619-546-8808
Email: don@tremblayandholsenback.com *URL:* http://www.tremblayandholsenback.com

Donald P. Tremblay
J. Daniel Holsenback
Jonathan R. Flora
Peter Q. Schluederberg
Tanya R. Tice

Representative Clients: Bumper Development Corporation, Ltd.; Genfoot America, Inc.; DuFFS; IBSC Insurance Services, Inc.; Rhino Linings USA, Inc.

LONG BEACH, Los Angeles Co.

CAMERON, PEARLSON & GALE (AV)

One World Trade Center, Suite 1600, 90831-1600
Telephone: 562-436-3888
Telecopier: 562-437-1967
URL: http://www.cpglawyers.com
URL: http://www.lawyers.com/cmp&glaw

MEMBERS OF FIRM

Timothy C. Cameron
Charles M. Gale
Paul R. Pearlson

ASSOCIATES

Dana K. Anderson, Jr.
Susan R. Loh

For full biographical listings, see the Martindale-Hubbell Law Directory

CAYER, KILSTOFTE & CRATON, A PROFESSIONAL LAW CORPORATION (AV)

Suite 700, 444 West Ocean Boulevard, 90802
Telephone: 562-435-6008
Fax: 562-435-3704
Email: CKCCRC@AOL.COM

John J. Cayer
Stephen R. Kilstofte
Curt R. Craton

(See Next Column)

Cortlen R. Hauge

For full biographical listings, see the Martindale-Hubbell Law Directory

FLYNN, DELICH & WISE (AV)

One World Trade Center, Suite 1800, 90831-1800
Telephone: 562-435-2626
Fax: 562-437-7555
Email: NicholasP@FDW-LAW.COM
San Francisco, California Office: One California Street, Suite 350.
Telephone: 415-693-5566.
Fax: 415-693-0410. Email: SAMD@FDW-LAW.COM

Erich P. Wise
Nicholas S. Politis

Sook H. Lee

LEGAL SUPPORT PERSONNEL

Denise C. Orr (Legal Assistant)

Representative Clients: American Hawaii Cruises; American President Lines; Through Transport Mutual Insurance Association, Ltd.; The Britannia Steam Ship Insurance Association Limited; The Steamship Mutual Underwriting Association (Bermuda) Ltd.; General Steamship Corp., Ltd.; Commodore Cruise Line, Ltd.; Interocean Steamship Corporation; Sea-Land Service, Inc.; Hatteras Yachts.

For full biographical listings, see the Martindale-Hubbell Law Directory

FORD, WALKER, HAGGERTY & BEHAR, PROFESSIONAL LAW CORPORATION (AV)

One World Trade Center, Twenty Seventh Floor, 90831
Telephone: 562-983-2500
Telecopier: 562-983-2555
Email: FWHB@FWHB.COM

G. Richard Ford
Timothy L. Walker
William C. Haggerty
Jeffrey S. Behar
Mark Steven Hennings
Donna Rogers Kirby
Tina Ivankovic Mangarpan
Joseph A. Heath
Robert J. Chavez
James D. Savage
Patrick J. Gibbs
Robert Reisinger

Arthur W. Schultz
Jon T. Moseley
Maxine J. Lebowitz
Timothy P. McDonald
K. Michele Williams
Stephen Ward Moore
James O. Miller
Stanley L. Scarlett
Scott A. Ritsema
Colleen A. Deziel
Thomas L. Gourdé
Patrick J. Stark
Shayne L. Wulterin
Charles J. Schmitt
John A. Haughton
Kristen C. Vine
Joel E. D. Odou
Christopher L. Mass
Robert Montes, Jr.
Alison S. Mathews
Tatia M. Tokunaga
Mark F. Wendorff
Anneke Joan Stewart
Pamela J. Paluga

OF COUNSEL

Theodore P. Shield, P.L.C.

For full biographical listings, see the Martindale-Hubbell Law Directory

EDWARD P. GEORGE, JR., INC. A PROFESSIONAL CORPORATION (AV)

Suite 430, 5000 East Spring Street, 90815-1275
Telephone: 562-497-2900
Facsimile: 562-497-2904

Edward P. George, Jr.
Timothy L. O'Reilly

OF COUNSEL

Albert C. S. Ramsey

Reference: City National Bank, Long Beach.

For full biographical listings, see the Martindale-Hubbell Law Directory

MOORE, RUTTER & EVANS (AV)

A Partnership including a Professional Corporation
555 East Ocean Boulevard, Suite 500, 90802-5090
Telephone: 562-435-4499
Facsimile: 562-495-4299
Email: mrelaw@gte.net *URL:* http://www.lawyers.com/moorerutter&evans
Huntington Beach, California Office: 2120 Main Street, Suite 250, 92648.
Telephone: 714-374-3333.
Fax: 714-374-9395

RESIDENT PARTNERS

Neal Moore
Mark D. Rutter
William D. Evans (P.C.)

OF COUNSEL

Michael J. Emling

For full biographical listings, see the Martindale-Hubbell Law Directory

Long Beach—Continued

PERONA, LANGER, BECK & LALLANDE, A PROFESSIONAL CORPORATION (AV)

300 East San Antonio, 90807
Telephone: 562-426-6155
Facsimile: 562-490-9823
Los Angeles, California Office: 9255 Sunset Boulevard, Suite 920.
Telephone: 562-426-6155.

James T. Perona
Major A. Langer
Ronald Beck
M. Lawrence Lallande
Ellen R. Serbin
E. Todd Trumper
Robert M. Zavidow

Michel F. Mills
Eric A. Hoerchner
Cathy A. Muller
Lupe G. Morales
David L. Scott
Arnold Eisenberg

For full biographical listings, see the Martindale-Hubbell Law Directory

RUSSELL & MIRKOVICH (AV)

One World Trade Center, Suite 1450, 90831-1450
Telephone: 562-436-9911
FAX: 562-436-1897
Email: counsel@russell-mirkovich.com

Carlton E. Russell
Joseph N. Mirkovich

ASSOCIATE

Margaret E. Morrow
Steven Y. Otera

For full biographical listings, see the Martindale-Hubbell Law Directory

STOLPMAN • KRISSMAN • ELBER • MANDEL & KATZMAN LLP (AV)

A Limited Liability Partnership
Nineteenth Floor, 111 West Ocean Boulevard, 90802-4649
Telephone: 562-435-8300
Telecopier: 562-435-8304
Email: stolpman@ix.netcom.com
Los Angeles (Westwood), California Office: Suite 1800, 10880 Wilshire Boulevard.

MEMBERS OF FIRM

Thomas G. Stolpman
Leonard H. Mandel
Bernard Katzman (Inc.)
Joel Krissman
Mary Nielsen Abbott
Donna Silver
Dennis M. Elber

ASSOCIATES

Edwin Silver
Elaine Mandel
Michael L. Luboviski

For full biographical listings, see the Martindale-Hubbell Law Directory

TAUBMAN, SIMPSON, YOUNG & SULENTOR (AV)

249 East Ocean Boulevard, Suite 700, P.O. Box 22670, 90801-5670
Telephone: 562-436-9201
FAX: 562-590-9695
Email: thefirm@tsyslaw.com

E. C. Denio (1864-1952)
Geo. A. Hart (1881-1967)
Geo. P. Taubman, Jr. (1897-1970)
Matthew C. Simpson (1900-1988)
Roger W. Young
William J. Sulentor
Peter M. Williams
Maria M. Rohaidy
Stuart C. Talley

Attorneys for: Bixby Land Co.; Renick Cadillac, Inc.; Oil Operators Inc.
Local Counsel: Crown Cork & Seal Co., Inc.

For full biographical listings, see the Martindale-Hubbell Law Directory

WISE, WIEZOREK, TIMMONS & WISE, A PROFESSIONAL CORPORATION (AV)

3700 Santa Fe Avenue, Suite 300, P.O. Box 2190, 90801-2190
Telephone: 310-834-5028; 562-595-5318
Fax: 310-834-8018
URL: http://www.wwtw.com
Redding, California Office: 292 Hemsted Drive, Suite 101.
Telephone: 530-221-7632.
Fax: 530-221-8832.

George E. Wise
Duane H. Timmons
Anthony F. Wiezorek
Susan E. Anderson Wise
Michael J. Pearce
Mark C. Allen, III
Richard P. Dieffenbach
Steven C. Rice
Stephen M. Smith
Thomas J. Yocis
James M. Cox
Mathew J. Vande Wydeven

Susan Graham

For full biographical listings, see the Martindale-Hubbell Law Directory

WOOLLEY RUSSELL & JOHNSON (AV)

444 West Ocean Boulevard, Suite 1700, 90802
Telephone: 562-495-6000
Telecopier: 562-435-1359
Email: mail@transportlawyers.com *URL:* http://www.transportlawyers.com
Port Hueneme, California Office: 105 East Port Hueneme Road, 93041.
Telephone: 562-495-6000.
Fax: 562-435-1359.

MEMBERS OF FIRM

David E. R. Woolley
Thomas A. Russell
Philip L. Johnson

ASSOCIATE

Thomas G. Walsh

LEGAL SUPPORT PERSONNEL

PARALEGAL

Dawn C. Breaux

For full biographical listings, see the Martindale-Hubbell Law Directory

*LOS ANGELES,** Los Angeles Co.

AGAPAY, LEVYN & HALLING, A PROFESSIONAL CORPORATION (AV)

Fourth Floor, 10801 National Boulevard, 90064
Telephone: 310-470-1700
Fax: 310-470-2602
URL: http://www.AGAPAY.COM
Orange, California Office: One City Boulevard West, Suite 1030, 92868.
Telephone: 714-634-1744.
Fax: 714-634-0417.

Joe M. Agapay, Jr.
Thomas S. Levyn
Chris W. Halling

Glen R. Segal (Resident Member, Orange Office)
Peter J. Krupinsky
Steven A. Sokol
Nanci E. Murdock
David S. Olson
Pablo De Leon, Jr.

OF COUNSEL

Alan B. Grass
Glen Dresser

For full biographical listings, see the Martindale-Hubbell Law Directory

ALVARADO, SMITH & SANCHEZ, A PROFESSIONAL CORPORATION (AV)

611 West Sixth Street, Suite 2650, 90017
Telephone: 213-229-2400
Facsimile: 213-229-2499
URL: http://www.alvarado-smith.com
Irvine, California Office: 4 Park Plaza, Suite 1200, 92614.
Telephone: 949-955-6800.
Fax: 949-955-6899.

Raymond G. Alvarado
Ruben A. Smith
Maurice Sanchez
John M. Sorich
Raúl F. Salinas
Frances Q. Jett
Theresa Eileen Antonucci
Diane C. Barrio
Rosario M. Tobias

OF COUNSEL

Martin N. Burton

For full biographical listings, see the Martindale-Hubbell Law Directory

BAKER & HOSTETLER LLP (AV)

600 Wilshire Boulevard, 90017-3212
Telephone: 213-624-2400
FAX: 213-975-1740
To contact an attorney on the Internet use first initial and surname followed by @baker-hostetler.com
URL: http://www.bakerlaw.com
In Cleveland, Ohio: 3200 National City Center, 1900 East Ninth Street.
Telephone: 216-621-0200.
In Cincinnati, Ohio: 312 Walnut Street, Suite 2650.
Telephone: 513-929-3400.
In Columbus, Ohio: Capitol Square, Suite 2100, 65 East State Street.
Telephone: 614-228-1541.
In Denver, Colorado: 303 East 17th Avenue, Suite 1100.
Telephone: 303-861-0600.
In Houston, Texas: 1000 Louisiana, Suite 2000.
Telephone: 713-751-1600.
In Long Beach, California: 300 Oceangate, Suite 620.
Telephone: 562-432-2827.
In Orlando, Florida: SunBank Center, Suite 2300, 200 South Orange Avenue.
Telephone: 407-649-4000.
In Washington, D. C.: Washington Square, Suite 1100, 1050 Connecticut Avenue, N.W.
Telephone: 202-861-1500.

(See Next Column)

BAKER & HOSTETLER LLP—*Continued*

PARTNERS

Angela C. Agrusa
Penny M. Costa
David A. Destino
Patrick J. Cain
Richard A. Deeb
Bill E. Schroeder

For Complete List of Firm Personnel, See General Section

For full biographical listings, see the Martindale-Hubbell Law Directory

BAKER AND JACOBSON, A PROFESSIONAL CORPORATION (AV)
Suite 500, 11377 West Olympic Boulevard, 90064-1683
Telephone: 310-914-7990
Fax: 310-914-7913
Email: do@bakjac.com

Robert P. Baker
Lawrence M. Jacobson

For full biographical listings, see the Martindale-Hubbell Law Directory

BARTON, KLUGMAN & OETTING LLP (AV)
333 South Grand Avenue, Suite 3700, 90071-1599
Telephone: 213-621-4000
Telecopier: 213-625-1832

Robert M. Barton (Retired)
Richard F. Oetting (Retired)

COUNSEL TO FIRM

Robert H. Klugman *

MEMBERS OF FIRM

David F. Morgan *
William D. Herz *
Charles J. Schufreider *
Robert Louis Fisher *
David J. Cartano *
Martin J. Spear
Thomas E. McCurnin
Tod V. Beebe *
Ronald R. St. John
Jeffrey B. Harris *
Mark A. Newton *

ASSOCIATES

Barbara W. G. Crowley
Sharon K. Brown

References: Union Bank of California (Southern California Headquarters); Wells Fargo Bank, N.A. (Wells Fargo Center, Los Angeles).
*Denotes a lawyer whose Professional Corporation is a member of the partnership or is Counsel to the Firm

For full biographical listings, see the Martindale-Hubbell Law Directory

BECK, DE CORSO, DALY, BARRERA & KREINDLER, A PROFESSIONAL LAW CORPORATION (AV)
601 West Fifth Street, 12th Floor, 90071-2025
Telephone: 213-688-1198
Fax: 213-489-7532
Email: beckdecorso@earthlink.net *URL:* http://www.beckdecorso.com

Mark E. Beck
Anthony A. De Corso
Bryan D. Daly
Teresa R. Barrera
Charles L. Kreindler
Suzanne E. Tracy

Peter J. Diedrich
Barbara E. Taylor
Stephen P. Jones

OF COUNSEL

Godfrey Isaac

For full biographical listings, see the Martindale-Hubbell Law Directory

BERGMAN, WEDNER & DACEY, INC. (AV)
Suite 900, 10880 Wilshire Boulevard, 90024
Telephone: 310-470-6110
Fax: 310-474-0931
Email: ofc@bergman-wedner.com *URL:* http://www.bergman-wedner.com

Gregory M. Bergman
Gregory A. Wedner
John P. Dacey
Alan Harvey Mittelman
Robert M. Mason III
Kristi Anne Sjoholm-Sierchio
John V. Tamborelli

Lisa S. Newnan
Daphne M. Humphreys
Michele M. Goldsmith
Denise G. Godfrey
William Daryl Strickland
Pamela R. Fleming
Matthew R. Hicks
Jorge J. Luna
Paul V. Rayburn
Mark W. Waterman

OF COUNSEL

Lloyd A. Bergman (1923-1994)
Jacob A. Wedner
Marvin Goldsmith
Mark K. Kitabayashi

SPECIAL COUNSEL

Richard V. Godino

For full biographical listings, see the Martindale-Hubbell Law Directory

BLACK, COMPEAN & HALL A LIMITED LIABILITY PARTNERSHIP (AV)
445 South Figueroa Street, Suite 2800, 90071-1632
Telephone: 213-629-9500
FAX: 213-629-4868
Email: bchinsurlaw@earthlink.com

MEMBERS OF FIRM

Robert H. Black
Michael D. Compean
Frederick G. Hall

ASSOCIATES

Vicente Valencia, Jr.
Daniel Eli
Lisa Jennifer Martin

Reference: The Pacific Bank.

For full biographical listings, see the Martindale-Hubbell Law Directory

BLECHER & COLLINS, A PROFESSIONAL CORPORATION (AV)
611 West Sixth Street, 20th Floor, 90017
Telephone: 213-622-4222
Telecopier: 213-622-1656

Maxwell M. Blecher
Harold R. Collins, Jr.
John E. Andrews
Steven J. Cannata
Ralph C. Hofer
William C. Hsu
Gary M. Joye
James Robert Noblin
Donald R. Pepperman
Alicia G. Rosenberg

For full biographical listings, see the Martindale-Hubbell Law Directory

LAW OFFICES OF DAVID B. BLOOM A PROFESSIONAL CORPORATION (AV)
3325 Wilshire Boulevard, Ninth Floor, 90010
Telephone: 323-938-5248; 384-4088
Telecopier: 213-385-2009

David B. Bloom

Stephen S. Monroe (A Professional Corporation)
Raphael A. Rosemblat
James E. Adler
Roy A. Levun
Jonathan Udell
Susan Carole Jay
Edward Idell
Sandra Kamenir
Steven Wayne Lazarus
Andrew Edward Briseno
Shelley M. Gould
Ted L. Travis

For full biographical listings, see the Martindale-Hubbell Law Directory

CLARK & TREVITHICK, A PROFESSIONAL CORPORATION (AV)
800 Wilshire Boulevard, 12th Floor, 90017
Telephone: 213-629-5700
Telecopier: 213-624-9441
Email: postmaster@clarktrev.com
San Francisco, California Office: 456 Montgomery Street, 20th Floor.
Telephone: 415-288-6520.
Fax: 415-398-2820.

Philip W. Bartenetti
Vincent Tricarico
Leonard Brazil
Leslie R. Horowitz
Arturo Santana Jr.

OF COUNSEL

Dolores Cordell
Judith Ilene Bloom
Raimund Freihube

For Complete List of Firm Personnel, See General Section

For full biographical listings, see the Martindale-Hubbell Law Directory

DAPEER, ROSENBLIT & LITVAK, LLP (AV)
11500 West Olympic Boulevard, Suite 550, 90064-1524
Telephone: 310-203-8200
Fax: 310-203-8213

William Litvak
Steven H. Rosenblit
Kenneth B. Dapeer

For full biographical listings, see the Martindale-Hubbell Law Directory

DARLING, HALL & RAE, LLP (AV)
520 South Grand Avenue, 7th Floor, 90071
Telephone: 213-627-8104
Fax: 213-627-7795
Email: darlinghallrae@compuserve.com

MEMBERS OF FIRM

Hugh W. Darling (1901-1986)
Edward S. Shattuck (1901-1965)
George Gaylord Gute (1922-1981)
Donald Keith Hall (1918-1984)
Matthew S. Rae, Jr.
Richard L. Stack
Edwin Freston

(See Next Column)

DARLING, HALL & RAE LLP, *Los Angeles—Continued*

OF COUNSEL

Edward F. Pearson

Reference: City National Bank (Pershing Square Office, Los Angeles, California).

For full biographical listings, see the Martindale-Hubbell Law Directory

DAVIS & FOX (AV)

1901 Avenue of the Stars, Suite 400, 90067
Telephone: 310-286-2915
Fax: 310-286-2916

Calvin E. Davis
Steven A. Fox
Elizabeth A. Kooyman
John J. Stumreiter
Amy L. Freisleben
Barbara Kekich
Gregory M. Sinderbrand

For full biographical listings, see the Martindale-Hubbell Law Directory

DECAROLIS, SAENZ & TROPE, LLP (AV)

1801 Century Park East 26th Floor, 90067
Telephone: 310-552-2444
Facsimile: 310-552-0441
Email: pdecarolis@mindspring.com *URL:* http://www.lawyers.com/decarsape

Patrick DeCarolis, Jr.
Edgar A. Saenz
Michael L. Trope

For full biographical listings, see the Martindale-Hubbell Law Directory

DEMETRIOU, DEL GUERCIO, SPRINGER & MOYER, LLP (AV)

801 South Grand Avenue, 10th Floor, 90017
Telephone: 213-624-8407
Telecopy: 213-624-0174
Email: ddsm@juno.com

MEMBERS OF FIRM

Chris G. Demetriou (1915-1989)
Jeffrey Z. B. Springer
Craig A. Moyer
Angela Shanahan
Stephen A. Del Guercio
Michael A. Francis
Regina Liudzius Cobb
Jennifer T. Taggart
Bradley D. Pierce
Wendy M. Conole
Brian D. Langa
Silvia Saucedo

OF COUNSEL

Ronald J. Del Guercio
Richard A. Del Guercio
James P. Del Guercio
Barbara F. Stein

Reference: Bank of America, L.A. Main Office, Los Angeles, Calif.

For full biographical listings, see the Martindale-Hubbell Law Directory

DWYER, DALY, BROTZEN & BRUNO, LLP (AV)

550 South Hope Street, Suite 1900, 90071
Telephone: 213-627-9300
Fax: 213-624-1638
Email: DB2LAW.com

PARTNERS

Ronald A. Dwyer
John A. Daly
Peter P. Brotzen
Toni Rae Bruno

ASSOCIATES

Gregory L. Anderson
Gregory J. Salute
Wendell F. Hall
John F. Schilling
Thomas A. Kosakowski
James N. Fincher
Daniel M. Walanka
Douglas A. Schenck

For full biographical listings, see the Martindale-Hubbell Law Directory

LAW OFFICES OF ROBERT W. EISFELDER, P.C. (AV)

11755 Wilshire Boulevard, Suite 2150, 90025-1543
Telephone: 310-820-4500
Facsimile: 310-826-0683

Robert W. Eisfelder

John Thayer Clark

For full biographical listings, see the Martindale-Hubbell Law Directory

FAGELBAUM & HELLER LLP (AV)

2049 Century Park East, Suite 2050, 90067
Telephone: 310-286-7666
Fax: 310-286-7086
Email: bestlawyers@worldnet.att.net

MEMBERS OF FIRM

Jerold Fagelbaum
Philip Heller

For full biographical listings, see the Martindale-Hubbell Law Directory

THE FORD LAW FIRM (AV)

12400 Wilshire Boulevard, Suite 1060, 90025
Telephone: 310-826-2648
Facsimile: 310-826-2658
Email: flf@gte.com

William H. Ford, III
Claudia J. Serviss
George H. Kim

ASSOCIATE

Paul C. Cook

For full biographical listings, see the Martindale-Hubbell Law Directory

GALTON & HELM LLP (AV)

500 South Grand Avenue Suite 1200, 90071
Telephone: 213-629-8800
Telecopier: 213-629-0037
Email: GaltonHelm@GaltonHelm.usa.com
Palm Desert, California Office: 73-929 Larrea.
Telephone: 760-776-5600.
Fax: 760-776-5602.

MEMBERS OF FIRM

Stephen H. Galton
Hugh H. Helm
Michael F. Bell
Daniel W. Maguire (Resident at Palm Desert)
David A. Lingenbrink
Robert F. Keehn

ASSOCIATES

Melissa M. Cowan
Joanna M. Todd
Michael B. Bernacchi
David J. Weinman
Nicole Blohm Pomerantz
Jennifer L. Kurzon
Eduardo A. Brito
Deanna E. McCray
Ann C. Schneider
Edith S. Shea

LEGAL SUPPORT PERSONNEL

Lana Banks (Paralegal)
Mardi Walsh (Paralegal)
Lynne M. Koss (Paralegal)
Toni Quigley (Paralegal)

For full biographical listings, see the Martindale-Hubbell Law Directory

LAW OFFICES OF RICHARD H. GIBSON A PROFESSIONAL CORPORATION (AV)

Gateway West, 1801 Avenue of the Stars, Suite 406, 90067
Telephone: 310-277-5581
Facsimile: 310-277-6035
Email: lostig@rhg-law.com

Richard H. Gibson

For full biographical listings, see the Martindale-Hubbell Law Directory

GIRARDI AND KEESE (AV)

1126 Wilshire Boulevard, 90017-1904
Telephone: 213-977-0211
FAX: 213-481-1554
San Bernardino, California Office: 155 West Hospitality Lane, Suite 260.
Telephone: 909-381-1551.
FAX: 909-381-2566.

MEMBERS OF FIRM

Thomas V. Girardi
Robert M. Keese
John A. Girardi
James B. Kropff
Robert W. Finnerty
James G. O'Callahan
V. Andre Rekte (Resident, San Bernardino Office)
John K. Courtney
Amy Fisch Solomon
Thomas C. Morgan
David N. Bigelow
Carrie J. Rognlien
David R. Lira
John Alan Roberts
Shane M. Emerson Coons
Amanda L. McClintock

ASSOCIATE

Jennifer M. Ingram

References: Wells Fargo Bank (Los Angeles Head Office); Comerica Bank.

For full biographical listings, see the Martindale-Hubbell Law Directory

LEONARD A. GOLDMAN & ASSOCIATES (AV)

(Formerly Goldman & Gordon, L.L.P.)
1900 Avenue of the Stars, Suite 1800, 90067-4409
Telephone: 310-277-7171
FAX: 310-277-1547
Email: lagoldman@earthlink.com

MEMBERS OF FIRM

A. S. Goldman (1895-1966)
Leonard A. Goldman

References: Bank of America, Fourth and Spring Branch, Los Angeles; Bank of America, Wilshire-San Vincente Branch, Beverly Hills.

For full biographical listings, see the Martindale-Hubbell Law Directory

Los Angeles—Continued

GRAY, YORK & DUFFY LLP (AV)

15760 Ventura Boulevard, 16th Floor (Encino), 91436
Telephone: 818-907-4000; 310-553-0445
Fax: 818-783-4551
Email: gydlaw@pacbell.net
Redwood City, California Office: 702 Marshall Street, Suite 500, 94063.
Telephone: 650-365-7343.
Fax: 650-365-6225.
San Francisco, California Office: 660 Market Street, Suite 490, 94105.
Telephone: 415-908-1300.
Fax: 415-974-6199.

MEMBERS OF FIRM

Gary S. Gray
James R. York
John J. Duffy
Arlene A. Colman
Barry D. Brown
William F. Flahavan
Jeffrey S. Stern

ASSOCIATES

Amalia L. Taylor
Kenneth A. Hearn
Gabriel H. Wainfeld
Frank J. Ozello, Jr.
J. Scott McNamara (Resident, San Francisco Office)
Jeffrey D. Livingston (Resident, Redwood City Office)

Reference: Marathon National Bank, Los Angeles, California.

For full biographical listings, see the Martindale-Hubbell Law Directory

HAWKINS, SCHNABEL, LINDAHL & BECK, LLP (AV)

660 South Figueroa Street, Suite 1500, 90017
Telephone: 213-488-3900
Telecopier: 213-486-9883
Email: hslb@hslblaw.com

MEMBERS OF FIRM

Roger E. Hawkins
Laurence H. Schnabel
George M. Lindahl
Kelley K. Beck
Jon P. Kardassakis
William E. Keitel
Rena Denton Stone
Timothy A. Gonzales
Ram F. Cogan
Kurt G. Gresenz
David C. Moore

For full biographical listings, see the Martindale-Hubbell Law Directory

HENNIGAN, MERCER & BENNETT (AV)

601 South Figueroa Street, Suite 3300, 90017
Telephone: 213-694-1200
Fax: 213-694-1234
Email: Silverm@hmb.com

J. Michael Hennigan
Bruce Bennett
John L. Amsden
Shawna L. Ballard
Mary H. Chu
Kirk D. Dillman
C. Dana Hobart
Jeanne E. Irving
James O. Johnston
Laura Lindgren
Bruce R. MacLeod
Peter J. Most
Robert L. Palmer
Lee W. Potts
Lauren A. Smith
Michael Swartz

ASSOCIATES

Nichole M. Auden
Gregory K. Jones
Linda A. Kontos
Joshua M. Mester
Claudia Schweikert
Thomas Bernard Watson
Jeffrey C. Henneforth

OF COUNSEL

James W. Mercer
Mark A. Albert
Kenneth A. O'Brien, Jr.

For full biographical listings, see the Martindale-Hubbell Law Directory

HILL, FARRER & BURRILL LLP (AV)

A Limited Liability Partnership including Professional Corporations
37th Floor, One California Plaza, 300 South Grand Avenue, 90071-3147
Telephone: 213-620-0460
Fax: 213-624-4840
URL: http://www.hfbllp.com

MEMBERS OF FIRM

William M. Bitting (P.C.)
Steven W. Bacon (P.C.)
Arthur B. Cook, II, (P.C.)
Scott L. Gilmore (P.C.)
Kevin H. Brogan (P.C.)
Neil D. Martin (P.C.)
Daniel J. McCarthy (P.C.)
Ronald W. Novotny (P.C.)
Benjamin B. Salvaty (P.C.)
James R. Evans, Jr., (P.C.)
G. Cresswell Templeton III, (P.C.)
Michael S. Turner (P.C.)
Ian M. Green (P.C.)
Jennifer L. Pancake
Byron T. Ball
Paul M. Porter

OF COUNSEL

Stanley E. Tobin (P.C.)
James G. Johnson (P.C.)

ASSOCIATES

Dean A. Reeves
Arnold D. Woo
Karen S. Seigel

For Complete List of Firm Personnel, See General Section

For full biographical listings, see the Martindale-Hubbell Law Directory

HORNBERGER, GHAZARIANS & BREWER (AV)

444 South Flower, 31st Floor, 90071
Telephone: 213-488-1655
Facsimile: 213-488-1255

MEMBERS OF FIRM

Nicholas W. Hornberger
Ann M. Ghazarians
Michael A. Brewer

ASSOCIATES

James M. Slominski
Michael C. Denlinger
Michael D. Hirsch
Michael G. Robinson

For full biographical listings, see the Martindale-Hubbell Law Directory

IVERSON, YOAKUM, PAPIANO & HATCH (AV)

One Wilshire Building, 27th Floor 624 South Grand Avenue, 90017
Telephone: 213-624-7444
Telecopier: 213-629-4563

MEMBERS OF FIRM

Neil Papiano
Patrick M. Mc Adam
Arnold D. Larson
John M. Garrick

ASSOCIATES

Douglas C. Pease
Andrew K. Doty
Melissa A. Immel
Mary P. Lightfoot
Mark Pearson
Adam F. Burke
Scott A. Horton

OF COUNSEL

R. Noel Hatch

Representative Clients: Lockheed Corp.; International Paper; Bridgestone/-Firestone, Inc.
Reference: Bank of America (Los Angeles Head Office).

For Complete List of Firm Personnel, See General Section

For full biographical listings, see the Martindale-Hubbell Law Directory

JONES, DAY, REAVIS & POGUE (AV)

555 West Fifth Street Suite 4600, 90013-1025
Telephone: 213-489-3939
Telecopier: 213-243-2539
Email: counsel@jonesday.com *URL:* http://www.jonesday.com
In Irvine, California: 5 Park Plaza, Suite 1100.
Telephone: 949-851-3939.
Telecopier: 949-553-7539.
In Atlanta, Georgia: 3500 SunTrust Plaza, 303 Peachtree Street.
Telephone: 404-521-3939.
Telecopier: 404-581-8330.
In Brussels, Belgium: Avenue Louise 480, 7th Floor, B-1050 Brussels.
Telephone: 32-2-645-14-11.
Telecopier: 32-2-645-14-45.
In Chicago, Illinois: 77 West Wacker.
Telephone: 312-782-3939.
Telecopier: 312-782-8585.
In Cleveland, Ohio: North Point, 901 Lakeside Avenue.
Telephone: 216-586-3939.
Telecopier: 216-579-0212.
In Columbus, Ohio: 1900 Huntington Center.
Telephone: 614-469-3939.
Telecopier: 614-461-4198.
In Dallas, Texas: 2727 North Harwood Street.
Telephone: 214-220-3939.
Telecopier: 214-969-5100.
In Frankfurt, Germany: Hochhaus am Park, Grüneburgweg 102, 60323 Frankfurt am Main.
Telephone: 49-69-9726-3939.
Telecopier: 49-69-9726-3993.
In Geneva, Switzerland: 20, rue de Candolle.
Telephone: 41-22-320-2339.
Telecopier: 41-22-320-1232.
In Hong Kong: 29th Floor, Entertainment Building, 30 Queen's Road Central.
Telephone: 852-2526-6895.
Telecopier: 852-2868-5871.
In London England: Bucklersbury House, 3 Queen Victoria Street.
Telephone: 44-20-7236-3939.
Telecopier: 44-20-7236-1113.
In New York, New York: 599 Lexington Avenue.
Telephone: 212-326-3939.
Telecopier: 212-755-7306.
In Paris, France: 120, rue du Faubourg Saint-Honoré.
Telephone: 33-1-56-59-3939.
Telecopier: 33-1-56-59-3938

(See Next Column)

JONES, DAY, REAVIS & POGUE, *Los Angeles—Continued*

In Pittsburgh, Pennsylvania: 500 Grant Street, 31st Floor.
Telephone: 412-391-3939.
Telecopier: 412-394-7959.
In Riyadh, Saudi Arabia: The International Law Firm (In Association with Jones, Day, Reavis & Pogue), Sulaymaniyah, Prince Mishari IBN, Abdulaziz Street, P.O. Box 22166.
Telephone: (966-1) 462-8866.
Telecopier: (966-1) 462-9001.
In Shanghai, China: 2805 Kerry Centre, 1515 Nanjing Road West.
Telephone: 86-21-5298-6568.
Telecopier: 86-21-5298-6569.
In Sydney, Australia: Governor Phillip Tower, Level 38, 1 Farrer Place.
Telephone: 61-2-9210-6921.
Telecopier: 61-2-9210-6926.
In Taipei, Taiwan: 8th Floor, 2 Tun Hwa South Road, Section 2.
Telephone: (886-2) 2704-6808.
Telecopier: (886-2) 2704-6791.
In Tokyo, Japan: Toranomon 45 Mori Building, 3th Floor, 1-5, Toranomon 5-Chome, Minato-ku, Tokyo 105, Japan.
Telephone: 81-3-3433-3939.
Telecopier: 81-3-5401-2725.
In Washington, D.C.: 51 Louisiana Avenue, N.W.
Telephone: 202-879-3939.
Telecopier: 202-626-1700.

MEMBERS OF FIRM IN LOS ANGELES

Gerald W. Palmer
Elwood Lui
Frederick L. McKnight

For Complete List of Firm Personnel, See General Section

For full biographical listings, see the Martindale-Hubbell Law Directory

LAW OFFICES OF STEVEN S. KARIC A PROFESSIONAL CORPORATION (AV)

800 Wilshire Boulevard, Suite 1050, 90017-2614
Telephone: 213-955-0100
Fax: 213-955-0111
Email: sskaric@kariclaw.com *URL:* http://www.kariclaw.com

Steven S. Karic

Nora Tu-Willis

For full biographical listings, see the Martindale-Hubbell Law Directory

KERN & GONZALEZ, A PROFESSIONAL CORPORATION (AV)

601 West 5th Street, Suite 1100, 90071
Telephone: 213-629-8100
Facsimile: 213-627-8765
URL: http://www.kernlaw.net

René J. Kern, Jr.
Michael D. Gonzalez
Tina L. Gentile

Christina L. Young
Angela J. Armitage
Michele Marsh
Cynthia L. Filla
David G. Hoiles, Jr.
Michele Sherer Ancheta
Sue S. Kim
Gail S. Taningco

Representative Clients: Bridgestone/Firestone, Inc.; Makita Corporation; Merrill Lynch; TrizecHahn Centers, Inc.; United States Fidelity and Guaranty Company.

For full biographical listings, see the Martindale-Hubbell Law Directory

LAGERLOF, SENECAL, BRADLEY, GOSNEY & KRUSE, LLP

(See Pasadena)

JOSÉ Y. LAUCHENGCO, JR. (AV)

3545 Wilshire Boulevard, Suite 247, 90010
Telephone: 213-380-9897

For full biographical listings, see the Martindale-Hubbell Law Directory

LEBOVITS & DAVID, A PROFESSIONAL CORPORATION (AV)

1880 Century Park East Suite 900, 90067
Telephone: 310-277-0200
Fax: 310-552-1028
Email: mlld@msn.com *URL:* http://www.lawyers.com/lebovits&david

Moses Lebovits
Deborah A. David

Kristal M. Bowman

Reference: Imperial Bank (Main Office - Beverly Hills).

For full biographical listings, see the Martindale-Hubbell Law Directory

LEOPOLD, PETRICH & SMITH, A PROFESSIONAL CORPORATION (AV)

(Formerly Youngman, Hungate & Leopold)
Suite 3110, 2049 Century Park East (Century City), 90067-3274
Telephone: 310-277-3333
Telecopier: 310-277-7444
URL: http://www.lpsla.com

Gordon E. Youngman (1903-1983)
A. Fredric Leopold
Louis P. Petrich
Joel McCabe Smith
Edward A. Ruttenberg
Vincent Cox
Donald R. Gordon
Walter R. Sadler
Daniel M. Mayeda
David Aronoff
Robert S. Gutierrez

Paul M. Krekorian
Lincoln D. Bandlow

OF COUNSEL

Richard Hungate

For full biographical listings, see the Martindale-Hubbell Law Directory

LIM, RUGER & KIM, LLP (AV)

Suite 2800, 1055 West 7th Street, 90017
Telephone: 213-955-9500
Telecopier: 213-955-9511

MEMBERS OF FIRM

Christopher Kim
Richard M. Ruger
John S. C. Lim
Bryan King Sheldon
Pio S. Kim

OF COUNSEL

S. Deborah Lim
Esther Y. Kim

ASSOCIATES

Marc J. Manason
Brian M. McDonald
Steve R. Segura
Christine M. Chang
James T. Lim

For full biographical listings, see the Martindale-Hubbell Law Directory

LOEB & LOEB LLP (AV)

A Limited Liability Partnership including Professional Corporations
Suite 1800, 1000 Wilshire Boulevard, 90017-2475
Telephone: 213-688-3400
Facsimile: 213-688-3460
Email: info@loeb.com *URL:* http://www.loeb.com
Century City, California Office: Suite 2200, 10100 Santa Monica Boulevard, Los Angeles, 90067-4164.
Telephone: 310-282-2000.
Facsimile: 310-282-2192.
New York, N.Y. Office: 345 Park Avenue, 10154-0037.
Telephone: 212-407-4000.
Facsimile: 212-407-4990.
Nashville, Tennessee Office: 45 Music Square West, 37203-3205.
Telephone: 615-749-8300;
Facsimile: 615-749-8308.
Rome, Italy Office: Piazza Digione 1, 00197.
Telephone: 011-3906-808-8456.
Facsimile: 011-3906-808-8288.

MEMBERS OF FIRM

Brant H. Dveirin
David B. Eizenman (New York City Office)
Helen Gavaris (New York City Office)
John F. Lang (New York City Office)
Robert A. Meyer
Stephen R. Mick (Century City Office)
Charles H. Miller (New York City Office)
Douglas E. Mirell
Daniel G. Murphy
Anthony Murray (A P.C.)
Diane B. Paul
Martin R. Pollner (New York City Office)
Victor A. Rodgers
David M. Satnick (New York City Office)
P. Gregory Schwed (New York City Office)
Peter S. Selvin
Brian R. Socolow (New York City Office)
Adam F. Streisand
Robert N. Treiman
Alan W. Wilken
Michael P. Zweig (New York City Office)

OF COUNSEL

Howard I. Friedman (A P.C.)
Robert A. Holtzman
Alfred I. Rothman

ASSOCIATES

Christian D. Carbone (New York City Office)
Paula K. Colbath (New York City Office)
Shanda W. Connolly
Daniel J. Friedman
Patrick P. Gunn
Lisa L. Horlick
Vivek K. Malhotra
Thu Minh Nguyen
Philippa J. Smith (New York City Office)
Maria L. Zanfini (New York City Office)

For Complete List of Firm Personnel, See General Section

For full biographical listings, see the Martindale-Hubbell Law Directory

Los Angeles—Continued

LYNBERG & WATKINS, A PROFESSIONAL CORPORATION (AV)

Sixteenth Floor International Tower Plaza, 888 South Figueroa Street, 90017-5465
Telephone: 213-624-8700
Fax: 213-892-2763
Santa Ana, California Office: Suite 101, 2020 E. 1st Street.
Telephone: 714-973-1220.
Fax: 714-973-1002.

Charles A. Lynberg
Judith Gold
Norman J. Watkins
R. Jeff Carlisle
Dana J. McCune
Michael J. Larin
Randall J. Peters
Ric C. Ottaiano **
Dana A. Fox
Stephen M. Harber
Ruth Segal
Catherine L. Ferro
Hellar-Ann C. Hancock
Louis E. Marino, Jr.
Douglas G. MacKay
Peggy Kolkey
Wendy E. Schultz

Michael C. Kellar
William F. Bernard **
Thomas G. Oesterreich
Jerome P. Doctors
Guy N. Webster
Jamie L. Vels
Timothy F. Rivers
Barry L. Bookbinder
Kristine J. Exton
Kenton E. Moore
Kathy M. Gandara
Michael J. Pepek
Todd Harrison Stitt
Timothy Hix
Laura E. Michelman
Jerid R. Maybaum
Melinda N. Muir
Bianca E. Putters
Marlon C. Wadlington **
Matthew J. Saly

LEGAL SUPPORT PERSONNEL

Murray E. Heltzer

OF COUNSEL

Patrick L. Hanrahan
Martin D. Kaplan

Representative Clients: The American International Group of Companies (AIG); Universal Underwriters; National Home Life Insurance Co.; Gallagher-Bassett, Keenan & Associates (Third Party Administrators).
**Santa Ana Office

For full biographical listings, see the Martindale-Hubbell Law Directory

GERALD C. MACRAE (AV)

601 West 5th Street, 8th Floor, 90071-2004
Telephone: 213-627-6146
Fax: 213-627-1739
Email: gcmlaw@earthlink.net

For full biographical listings, see the Martindale-Hubbell Law Directory

LAW OFFICES OF JEFFREY A. MATZ (AV)

12400 Wilshire Boulevard, Suite 1300, 90025-1030
Telephone: 310-820-2822
FAX: 310-820-4544

For full biographical listings, see the Martindale-Hubbell Law Directory

MCKAY, BYRNE & GRAHAM (AV)

3250 Wilshire Boulevard, Suite 603, 90010
Telephone: 213-386-6900
Fax: 213-381-1762
Email: mbg@mbglaw.com

John P. McKay
Michael A. Byrne
Robert L. Graham
Mark G. Cunningham
Paul A. de Lorimier

Jeffrey Cabot Myers
Debra Ellwood Meppen
Dawn M. Flores-Oster
April Paradise
Gabriela Escudero Goldberg
Nancy A. Ramsey

OF COUNSEL

Gail D. Solo (A Professional Corporation)

For full biographical listings, see the Martindale-Hubbell Law Directory

LAW OFFICES OF CARL A. MCMAHAN (AV)

827 Moraga Drive (Bel Air), 90049
Telephone: 310-472-8078
Fax: 310-472-7014
Email: camcmahan@earthlink.net *URL:* http://www.lawyers.com/mcmahan

OF COUNSEL

Peter J. McNulty

Reference: City National Bank, Beverly Hills, California.

For full biographical listings, see the Martindale-Hubbell Law Directory

MCNICHOLAS & MCNICHOLAS, LLP (AV)

10866 Wilshire Boulevard, Suite 1400, 90024
Telephone: 310-474-1582
FAX: 310-475-7871
URL: http://www.mcnicholaslaw.com

MEMBERS OF FIRM

John P. McNicholas
Patrick McNicholas
David M. Ring

ASSOCIATES

Eric A. Gowey
Matthew S. McNicholas
Steven G. Mehta

For full biographical listings, see the Martindale-Hubbell Law Directory

MOSTEN & TUFFIAS (AV)

11601 Wilshire Boulevard, Suite 1840, 90025-1754
Telephone: 310-473-7611
Facsimile: 310-473-7422
Email: mosten@mediate.com *URL:* http://www.mediate.com/mosten

MEMBERS OF FIRM

Forrest S. Mosten
Heidi S. Tuffias

For full biographical listings, see the Martindale-Hubbell Law Directory

OCHOA & SILLAS (AV)

444 South Flower Street, 18th Floor, 90071
Telephone: 213-362-1400
Fax: 213-622-0162
Email: sillasla@aol.com
Sacramento Office: Wells Fargo Center, 400 Capitol Mall, Suite 1850.
Telephone: 916-447-3383.
FAX: 916-447-3495. Email: OchoaSac@aol.com
Mexico City, Mexico Office: Los Cormoran No. 73, Lomas De Las Aquilas, Deleg. Alvaro Obregon, 01730, Mexico, D.F.C.F.
Telephone: 011-525-635-1145.
Fax: 011-525-53401454.

MEMBERS OF FIRM

Ralph M. Ochoa (Resident, Sacramento Office)
Herman Sillas
Jacqueline Rich Moore (Resident, Sacramento Office)
Tomás R. Lopez

ASSOCIATES

Jack T. Molodanof (Resident, Sacramento Office)
Francisco Valles Lopez (Not admitted in the United States)
Rita A. Reyes
Christopher Eric Ochoa (Resident, Sacramento Office)
Cirina A. K. Rose
M. Eric Parkan

OF COUNSEL

Daniel P. Aguilera
Cochran & Lotkin, Washington, D.C.

Representative Clients: American Golf; BKK Corp. (Toxic substance treatment); Chrysler; Department of Water and Power of Los Angeles; Sacramento Municipal Utility District; Department of Insurance; Metropolitan Water District, Los Angeles; General Motors; Hughes Aircraft; ICN Laboratories.

For full biographical listings, see the Martindale-Hubbell Law Directory

O'MELVENY & MYERS LLP (AV)

400 South Hope Street, 90071-2899
Telephone: 213-430-6000
Facsimile: 213-430-6407
Cable: MOMS
Telex: 674122
Email: omminfo@omm.com *URL:* http://www.omm.com
Century City, CA Office: 1999 Avenue of the Stars, Los Angeles, 90067-6035.
Telex: 674097. Tel: 310-553-6700.
Fax: 310-246-6779.
Newport Beach, CA Office: 610 Newport Center Drive, 92660-6429.
Telex: 4722088. Tel: 949-760-9600.
Fax: 949-823-6994.
San Francisco, CA Office: Embarcadero Center West, 275 Battery Street, 94111-3305. Tel: 415-984-8700.
Fax: 415-984-8701.
New York, NY Office: Citicorp Center, 153 East 53rd Street, 10022-4611.
Telex: 129165. Tel: 212-326-2000.
Fax: 212-326-2061.
Washington, DC Office: 555 13th Street, N.W., 20004-1109.
Cable: MOMSWSH.
Telex: 89622. Tel: 202-383-5300.
Fax: 202-383-5414.
London Office: O'Melveny & Myers, 3 Finsbury Square, London, EC2A 1LA, England. Tel: 44-171-256-8451. Fax 44-171-638-8205.
Tokyo Office: Akasaka Twin Tower, East 14F, 2-17-23, Akasaka, Minato-ku, Tokyo 107-0052, Japan. Tel: 03-5562-2800.
Fax: 03-5575-3840.
Hong Kong Office: O'Melveny & Myers, Suite 1905, Tower Two, Lippo Centre, 89 Queensway, Central, Hong Kong. Tel: 852-2523-8266.
Fax: 852-2522-1760.

(See Next Column)

O'MELVENY & MYERS LLP, *Los Angeles—Continued*

Shanghai Office: Kerry Centre, 20F, 1515 Nanjing Road West, Shanghai, 200040 People's Republic of China. Tel: 86-21-5298-5600.
Fax: 86-21-5298-5500.

PARTNER

Henry C. Thumann

For Complete List of Firm Personnel, See General Section

For full biographical listings, see the Martindale-Hubbell Law Directory

PILLSBURY MADISON & SUTRO LLP (AV)

Citicorp Plaza, 725 South Figueroa Street, Suite 1200, 90017-5443
Telephone: 213-488-7100
Fax: 213-629-1033
Email: pillsburylaw.com *URL:* http://pillsburylaw.com
Costa Mesa, California Office: 650 Town Center Drive, 7th Floor, 92626.
Telephone: 714-436-6800.
Fax: 714-436-2800.
Silicon Valley Office: 2550 Hanover Street, Palo Alto, 94034.
Telephone: 650-233-4500.
Fax: 650-233-4545.
Sacramento, California Office: 400 Capitol Mall, Suite 1700, 95814.
Telephone: 916-329-4700.
Fax: 916-441-3583.
San Diego, California Office: 101 West Broadway, Suite 1800, 92101.
Telephone: 619-234-5000.
Fax: 619-236-1995.
San Francisco, California Office: 50 Fremont Street, 94105.
Telephone: 415-983-1000.
Fax: 415-983-1200.
Washington, D.C. Office: 1100 New York Avenue, N.W., Ninth Floor, 20005.
Telephone: 202-861-3000.
Fax: 202-822-0944.
Vienna, Virginia Office: 8330 Boone Boulevard, Suite 400, 22182.
Telephone: 703-744-7600.
Fax: 703-744-7605.
New York, New York Office: 375 Park Avenue, Suite 3108, 10152.
Telephone: 212-826-1060.
Fax: 212-826-9255. One Liberty Plaza, 165 Broadway, 51st Floor.
Telephone: 212-374-1890.
Fax: 212-374-1852.
Tokyo, Japan Office: Pillsbury Madison & Sutro, Gaikokuho Jimu Bengoshi Jimusho, 5th Floor, Samon Eleven Building, 3-1, Samon-cho, Shinjuku-ku, Tokyo 160 Japan.
Telephone: 800-729-9830; 011-813-3354-3531.
Fax: 011-813-3354-3534.

MEMBERS OF FIRM

Lawrence D. Bradley, Jr.
Kent B. Goss
Sidney K. Kanazawa
Kenneth R. Chiate
Amy D. Hogue
Catherine D. Meyer
William E. Stoner

For Complete List of Firm Personnel, See General Section

For full biographical listings, see the Martindale-Hubbell Law Directory

PIZER & MICHAELSON INC. (AV)

2049 Century Park East, Suite 460, 90067
Telephone: 310-843-9729
Fax: 310-843-9619
Santa Ana, California Office: 2122 North Broadway, Suite 100, 92706.
Telephone: 714-558-0535.
Telecopier: 714-550-0841.

Bradley J. Pizer

For full biographical listings, see the Martindale-Hubbell Law Directory

PRESTHOLT, KLEEGER, FIDONE & VILLASENOR (AV)

Suite 1600, 1055 West 7th Street, 90017
Telephone: 213-895-4811
FAX: 213-895-4817
San Francisco, California Office: 989 Market Street, 6th Floor.
Telephone: 415-267-6362.
Fax: 415-267-6275.

MEMBERS OF FIRM

David A. Prestholt
Gary P. Fidone
Lisa A. Villasenor
Brian D. Holmberg
David Crawford, III
Archie Chin
Avigal Horrow
Marjorie E. Motooka

For full biographical listings, see the Martindale-Hubbell Law Directory

CLAUDIA RIBET (AV)

11661 San Vicente Boulevard, Suite 1015, 90049
Telephone: 310-826-2313
FAX: 310-826-8242
Email: Ribet@appellatelaw.com

For full biographical listings, see the Martindale-Hubbell Law Directory

RODI, POLLOCK, PETTKER, GALBRAITH & CAHILL, A LAW CORPORATION (AV)

444 South Flower Street, Suite 1700, 90071-2901
Telephone: 213-895-4900
Telecopiers: 213-895-4921; 895-4922; 895-4750
URL: http://www.rodipollock.com

Karl B. Rodi (1908-1982)
John D. Cahill
John D. Pettker
Daniel C. Bond (1942-1977)
William R. Christian
Henry P. Pramov, Jr.
John F. Cermak, Jr.
Allan E. Ceran
Elizabeth B. Blakely
Robert C. Norton
Tim G. Ceperley
Coralie Kupfer
Cris K. O'Neall
Scott E. Adamson
Margaret Rosenthal

Sonja A. Inglin
Michael A. Abraham
Kenneth A. Franklin
Richard Nessary
Donna Yamini
Wade E. Norwood
Deepak Nanda
David J. Elbaz

OF COUNSEL

John P. Pollock
James M. Galbraith

For full biographical listings, see the Martindale-Hubbell Law Directory

SAUER & WAGNER LLP (AV)

1801 Century Park East, Suite 520, 90067
Telephone: 310-712-8100
Fax: 310-712-8108
Email: sauwag@swattys.com *URL:* http://www.swattys.com

Gerald L. Sauer
Eve H. Wagner

For full biographical listings, see the Martindale-Hubbell Law Directory

SCHWARTZ, STEINSAPIR, DOHRMANN & SOMMERS, LLP (AV)

6300 Wilshire Boulevard, Suite 2000, 90048
Telephone: 323-655-4700
Fax: 323-655-4488
Pittsburgh, Pennsylvania Office: 1007 Mt. Royal Boulevard, 15223.
Telephone: 412-492-8797.
Fax: 412-492-8978.

MEMBERS OF FIRM

Laurence D. Steinsapir
Robert M. Dohrmann
Richard D. Sommers
Stuart Libicki
Michael R. Feinberg
Michael D. Four
Margo A. Feinberg
Henry M. Willis
D. William Heine, Jr.
Claude Cazzulino
Dolly M. Gee

ASSOCIATE

Erika A. Zucker

For full biographical listings, see the Martindale-Hubbell Law Directory

SELMAN • BREITMAN (AV)

11766 Wilshire Boulevard, Sixth Floor, 90025-6538
Telephone: 310-445-0800
Fax: 310-473-2525
San Diego, California Office: Wyndham Emerald Plaza, 402 W. Broadway, Suite 400, 92101.
Telephone: 619-595-4880.
Facsimile: 619-595-4890.
San Francisco, California Office: Citicorp Center, One Sansome Street, Suite 1900, 94104.
Telephone: 415-951-4646.
Fax: 415-951-4676.
Santa Ana, California Office: 450 4th Street, Suite 250, 92701.
Telephone: 714-647-9700.
Fax: 714-647-9200.

MEMBERS OF FIRM

Sterling Tao (1961-1998)
Neil Selman
Craig R. Breitman
Robert A. Steller
Alan B. Yuter
Nancy W. Shokohi
Jeffrey C. Segal
A. Scott Goldberg
Elaine K. Fresch
Nicholas Banko (Partner, San Francisco Office)
Brad D. Bleichner
Monica Cruz Thornton
John S. Knowlton
Jerry C. Popovich (Partner, Santa Ana Office)

OF COUNSEL

Jan Long Pocaterra
Jacqueline F. Stein (Resident, San Diego Office)
Paul Edmond Stephan (Resident, San Francisco Office)

Lynette Klawon
Anthony L. Cione
Sheryl W. Leichenger
Lisa H. Kahn
David H. Oken
Pauline A. New
Eldon S. Edson
Sarah F. Burke (Resident, San Francisco Office)
Linda Wendell Hsu (Resident, San Francisco Office)
Jack M. Zakariaie

(See Next Column)

SELMAN • BREITMAN—*Continued*

Jean Dettmann Fisher (Resident, San Diego Office)
Lincoln V. Horton
Nichelle D. Frelix
Albert T. Liou (Resident, Santa Ana Office)
Viiu Spangler
Meka Moore
Richard T. Breen
Christopher R. Aker (Resident, San Francisco Office)
Mindi C. Grant
Ben M. Llaneta (Resident, San Diego Office)
Richard Scott
Craig R. Maki
Jennifer J. Capabianco (Resident, San Francisco Office)
Michelle L. Koskella (Resident, San Francisco Office)
Kelly M. Lynch
Kimberly S. Poese (Resident, Santa Ana Office)
Veronica E. Aitken
Roger G. Honey
Shereef Moharram
Kiera Berkley
Gregory J. Newman
Tamara Madenlian
Michelle E. Davis
Josh I. Keane
Michael Robert Hoffman
Natalie A. Barbanell
Kirk J. Retz
Paul A. Herp (Resident, San Francisco Office)
Greg M. Whaling (Resident, San Francisco Office)

Reference: City National Bank (Beverly Hills Branch).

For full biographical listings, see the Martindale-Hubbell Law Directory

SIDLEY & BELL LLP (AV)

2940 Westwood Boulevard, Second Floor, 90064
Telephone: 310-229-8940
Fax: 310- 474-2541
Email: westlalaw@aol.com

Michael I. Sidley
Anthony E. Bell

For full biographical listings, see the Martindale-Hubbell Law Directory

SIMKE CHODOS (AV)

A Partnership of Professional Corporations
Suite 1511, 1880 Century Park East, 90067-1615
Telephone: 310-203-3888
Fax: 310-203-3866
Email: sclawltd@aol.com

Stuart A. Simke
David M. Chodos

Richard A. Fond

OF COUNSEL

James L. Keane
Ellen Resinski Rosen

Reference: City National Bank (Wilshire-La Cienega Branch).

For full biographical listings, see the Martindale-Hubbell Law Directory

STONE, DOLGINER & WENZEL, A LAW CORPORATION (AV)

6500 Wilshire Boulevard Suite 2060, 90048
Telephone: 323-653-2244
Fax: 323-658-1155
Email: sdwlaw@aol.com *URL:* http://www.lawyers.com/sdwfirm

Robert N. Stone
Charles I. Dolginer
Mark D. Wenzel

Henry N. Seligsohn

OF COUNSEL

A. J. Connick Doran

Reference: Union Bank (Head Office, 900 South Main Street, Los Angeles).

For full biographical listings, see the Martindale-Hubbell Law Directory

SULLIVAN LAW CORPORATION (AV)

545 South Figueroa Street, Suite 1216, 90071-1599
Telephone: 213-488-9200
Telecopier: 213-362-0419
Email: flightattorney@aol.com *URL:* http://www.flightattorney.com

Michael R. Sullivan

For full biographical listings, see the Martindale-Hubbell Law Directory

SUSMAN GODFREY L.L.P. (AV)

A Registered Limited Liability Partnership including Professional Corporations
Suite 950 1880 Century Park East, 90067-1606
Telephone: 310-789-3100
Fax: 310-789-3150
URL: http://www.susmangodfrey
Houston, Texas Office: Suite 5100, 1000 Louisiana.
Telephone: 713-651-9366.
Telecopy: 713- 0653-7897.

(See Next Column)

Dallas, Texas Office: Suite 1400, 2323 Bryan Street.
Telephone: 214-754-1900.
Fax: 214-754-1933. New address effective March, 2000: Suite 4100, 901 Main Street, 75202.
Seattle, Washington Office: Suite 3090, 1201 Third Avenue.
Telephone: 206-516-3880.
Telecopy: 206-516-3883.

MEMBER OF FIRM

Marc M. Seltzer (Resident)

ASSOCIATES

David H. Boren (Resident)
Corey C. Watson (Not admitted in CA; Resident)

Reference: Laredo National Bank, Houston.

For full biographical listings, see the Martindale-Hubbell Law Directory

TALCOTT, LIGHTFOOT, VANDEVELDE SADOWSKY, MEDVENE & LEVINE (AV)

Thirteenth Floor 655 South Hope Street, 90017
Telephone: 213-622-4750
Fax: 213-622-2690
Email: law@talcottlightfoot.com *URL:* http://www.talcottlightfoot.com

John S. Crouchley
Janet I. Levine
Michael J. Lightfoot
James H. Locklin
John P. Martin
Edward M. Medvene
Stephen B. Sadowsky
Robert M. Talcott
John D. Vandevelde
Melissa N. Widdifield
David K. Willingham

Reference: Sterling Bank, Los Angeles, California.

For full biographical listings, see the Martindale-Hubbell Law Directory

DANA B. TASCHNER, P.C. (AV Ⓣ)

2122 Century Park Lane, Suite 407, 90067
Telephone: 310-552-4800
Fax: 310-552-4885
Email: dbtaschner@aol.com *URL:* http://www.ContingencyLaw.com
Newport Beach Office: 620 Newport Centre Drive, 11th Floor.
Telephone: 800-448-5800.

Dana B. Taschner

For full biographical listings, see the Martindale-Hubbell Law Directory

VITTAL AND STERNBERG (AV)

1900 Avenue of the Stars, 25th Floor, 90067-4506
Telephone: 310-551-0900
Facsimile: 310-551-2710
Email: javittal@ix.netcom.com
Woodland Hills, California Office: 21700 Oxnard Street. Suite 1640. 91367-3670.
Telephone: 818-710-7801.
Facsimile: 818-593-6192.

J. Anthony Vittal (Resident)
Terence M. Sternberg (Resident, Woodland Hills Office)

For full biographical listings, see the Martindale-Hubbell Law Directory

WHITE O'CONNOR CURRY GATTI & AVANZADO LLP (AV)

10100 Santa Monica Boulevard Suite 300, 90067
Telephone: 310-712-6100
Fax: 310-712-6199

Andrew M. White
Michael J. O'Connor
James E. Curry
Melvin N.A. Avanzado
John M. Gatti

OF COUNSEL

Jonathan D. Avila
Frederick F. Mumm

Jonathan H. Anschell
David E. Fink
James W. Irey
Holly J. Sadlon
Lee S. Brenner
Katherine J. Kunberger
Sydney Arfin
Edward Muir Anderson
Marci D. Friedman
Meredith C. Hightower
J Rudy Freeman, II

For full biographical listings, see the Martindale-Hubbell Law Directory

WHITE & REED LLP (AV)

2029 Century Park East, Suite 2050, 90067
Telephone: 310-843-9065
Fax: 310-843-9064
Email: mrwhitelaw@earthlink.net
Email: jsreedlaw@earthlink.net *URL:* http://www.lawyers.com/whitereedlaw

(See Next Column)

WHITE & REED LLP, *Los Angeles—Continued*

Michael R. White
James S. Reed

For full biographical listings, see the Martindale-Hubbell Law Directory

WOLF, RIFKIN & SHAPIRO, LLP (AV)

A Partnership including a Professional Corporation
11400 West Olympic Boulevard Ninth Floor, 90064-1565
Telephone: 310-478-4100
Fax: 310-479-1422
Email: wrs@wrslawyers.com
Las Vegas, Nevada Office: Schulman & Grode, LLP, 2255-A Renaissance Drive 89119.
Telephone: 702-341-5200.
Fax: 702-341-5300.

MEMBERS OF FIRM

Michael Wolf (A Professional Corporation)
Daniel C. Shapiro
Roy G. Rifkin
Michael T. Schulman
Leslie Steven Marks
Mindy Sheps
Norman S. Wisnicki
Barry T. Mitidiere (A Professional Corporation)
Marc E. Rohatiner
Michael W. Rabkin
Andrew S. Gelb
Matthew L. Grode
Richard S. Grant
S. Michael Leventhal

ASSOCIATES

Douglas A. Lusson
Mark J. Rosenbaum
Kelly Allegra Weil
Matthew J. Hafey
Whitney B. Wilds
Keli N. Osaki
Laura S. Withrow
Lisa A. Makarem
Joseph A. Petro
Elsa M. Horowitz

OF COUNSEL

Steven A. Silver
Eric J. Feig
Jeff W. Lane
Jeffrey R. Liebster
Denise M. Parga
Simon Aron

For full biographical listings, see the Martindale-Hubbell Law Directory

MALIBU, Los Angeles Co.

LAW OFFICES OF TODD M. SLOAN (AV)

22601 Pacific Coast Highway, Suite 240, 90265
Telephone: 310-456-7900
Facsimile: 310-317-6266

ASSOCIATE

Julia L. Birkel

For full biographical listings, see the Martindale-Hubbell Law Directory

MANHATTAN BEACH, Los Angeles Co.

STEINBERG BARNESS FOSTER & FOLEY LLP (AV)

1334 Park View Avenue, Suite 100, 90266
Telephone: 310-546-8160
Telecopier: 310-546-8189
Email: sbgf@ix.netcom.com

MEMBERS OF FIRM

Alex Steinberg
Daniel I. Barness
Douglas B. Foster
Shannon M. Foley

ASSOCIATES

William R. (Randy) Kirkpatrick
Jeff M. Lee
Kimberly Ann White

OF COUNSEL

Jordan G. Barness
Ronald D. Hariri (Not admitted in CA)

References: California United Bank; Wells Fargo Bank; Citizens Commerical Trust & Savings Bank; Bank of America.

For full biographical listings, see the Martindale-Hubbell Law Directory

MENLO PARK, San Mateo Co.

DYER & WHITE LLP (AV)

Suite 200, 800 Oak Grove Avenue, 94025
Telephone: 650-325-7000
Fax: 650-325-3116
Email: cdyer@dyer-white.com

MEMBERS OF FIRM

Charles A. Dyer
Rand N. White

For full biographical listings, see the Martindale-Hubbell Law Directory

BRIAN W. NEWCOMB (AV)

770 Menlo Avenue, Suite 101, 94025
Telephone: 650-322-7780
Telefax: 650-327-0619
Email: BNewc322@aol.com

For full biographical listings, see the Martindale-Hubbell Law Directory

O'REILLY, COLLINS & DANKO, A PROFESSIONAL CORPORATION (AV)

2500 Sand Hill Road, Suite 201, 94025-7016
Telephone: 650-854-7700
Fax: 650-854-8350

Terry O'Reilly
James P. Collins
Michael S. Danko

Rian D. Jorgensen

For full biographical listings, see the Martindale-Hubbell Law Directory

*MERCED,** Merced Co.

ALLEN, POLGAR, PROIETTI & FAGALDE (AV)

1640 "N" Street, Suite 200, P.O. Box 2184, 95344
Telephone: 209-723-4372
Fax: 209-723-7397
URL: http://www.mercedlaw.com
Mariposa, California Office: 5079 Highway 140. P.O. Box 1907.
Telephone: 209-966-3007.
Fax: 209-742-6353.

MEMBERS OF FIRM

Terry L. Allen
Gary B. Polgar
Donald J. Proietti
Michael A. Fagalde
Jeffrey S. Kaufman
F. Dana Walton (Resident, Mariposa Office)
Brian L. McCabe
Paul C. Lo
Susan L. Albertoni
Karen R. Spinardi

LEGAL SUPPORT PERSONNEL

Timothy J. Kolb (Paralegal)
Conrad J. Kranz (Paralegal)
Bethanne Dowlan (Paralegal)
Karen E. Kaufman (Paralegal)

For full biographical listings, see the Martindale-Hubbell Law Directory

MISSION VIEJO, Orange Co.

THE BUCKLEY FIRM, P.C. (AV)

Suite 200, 26522 La Alameda, 92691
Telephone: 949-348-8300
Facsimile: 949-348-8310
Email: TBF_law@ix.netcom.com
Email: TBFlaw@ix.netcom.com *URL:* http://www.buckleyfirm.com

Lawrence J. Buckley
John W. Klein
Paula Scotland
John R. Beisner

OF COUNSEL

Timothy D. Carlyle
Jonathan C. Cavett
Sam M. Muriella
Edgar C. Smith, III

Reference: Union Bank of California

For full biographical listings, see the Martindale-Hubbell Law Directory

*MODESTO,** Stanislaus Co.

BRUNN & FLYNN, A PROFESSIONAL CORPORATION (AV)

928 12th Street, P.O. Box 3366, 95353
Telephone: 209-521-2133
Fax: 209-521-7584
Email: brunnfly@ix.netcom.com

Charles K. Brunn
Timothy T. Flynn
Gerald E. Brunn
Roger S. Matzkind

Michael G. Donovan
Andrew N. Eshoo

Representative Clients: ACWA-Joint Powers Insurance Authority; Basic Resources, Inc.; Boudreau Corp.; Donco Carriers, Inc.; Duarte Nurseries, Inc.; George Reed, Inc.; Independent Tractor Rental; International Paper Co.; Kmart Corp.; May Company Department Stores, Inc.

For full biographical listings, see the Martindale-Hubbell Law Directory

DAMRELL, NELSON, SCHRIMP, PALLIOS & LADINE, A PROFESSIONAL CORPORATION (AV)

1601 I Street, Fifth Floor, 95354
Telephone: 209-526-3500
Fax: 209-526-3534
Email: general@dnspl.com
Oakdale, California Office: 703 West "F" Street, P.O. Drawer C.
Telephone: 209-848-3500.
Fax: 209-848-3400.

Frank C. Damrell (1898-1988)
Duane L. Nelson
Roger M. Schrimp
Steven G. Pallios
Wray F. Ladine
Matthew O. Pacher
Fred A. Silva

(See Next Column)

DAMRELL, NELSON, SCHRIMP, PALLIOS & LADINE A PROFESSIONAL CORPORATION—*Continued*

James F. Lewis	Stephen V. Imburg
Michelle Burke McKenzie	Curtis M. Fiorini
Clinton P. Walker	Gerry Preciado
Shana A. Bagley	Lisa W. Chao
Amy Elliott Neumann	Khanh T. Tran

Representative Clients: American Honda Motor Co., Inc.; Bronco Wine Co.; E. & J. Gallo Winery; Gallo Glass Co.; Norfolk Southern Corp.; Pep Boys of California, Inc.; W. R. Grace & Co.; United Rentals, Inc.; Tenet Healthcare Corporation.

For full biographical listings, see the Martindale-Hubbell Law Directory

STOCKTON & SADLER (AV)

1034 Twelfth Street, P.O. Box 3153, 95353
Telephone: 209-523-6416
Fax: 209-523-2315

MEMBERS OF FIRM

Cleveland J. Stockton — James L. Sadler

ASSOCIATE

Karen Tall Sadler

Representative Clients: Dan Mellis Liquors; American Lumber Co.; Paul's Rexall Drug Stores; Tro-Pic-Kal Mfg. Co.; Pete Pappas Broadcasting Co.; Sanders Construction Co.; Goldrush Broadcasting, Inc.; Paul M. Zagaris Realtor, Inc.

For full biographical listings, see the Martindale-Hubbell Law Directory

MONTEREY, Monterey Co.

HARRAY & LINKER (AV)

80 Garden Court, Suite 260, 93940
Telephone: 831-373-3101
Fax: 831-373-6712
Email: general@harray-linker.com

Richard K. Harray — Stan L. Linker

ASSOCIATES

Christine Balbo Reed — J. Kenneth Gorman
Debra Gemgnani Tipton

Representative Clients: The Travelers Insurance Co.; OPTIMA HEALTH-CARE/CHIC; State Farm; Beta Healthcare; CNA/RSKCE; DPIC; Sequoia Insurance Co.; Midstate Insurance Co.; County of Monterey; Cities of Monterey, Pacific Grove and Seaside; Community Hospital of Monterey Peninsula; Kmart; Salinas Valley Memorial Hospital; John Deere Co.

For full biographical listings, see the Martindale-Hubbell Law Directory

THE THOMPSON LAW OFFICE (AV)

580 Calle Principal, First Floor, 93940-2818
Telephone: 831-646-1224
Fax: 831-646-1225
URL: http://www.lawyers.com/justice-4-you
Email: rwt111@justice-4-you.com *URL:* http://www.justice-4-you.com

Ralph W. Thompson III

For full biographical listings, see the Martindale-Hubbell Law Directory

LAW OFFICES OF CHARLES G. WARNER (AV)

2340 Garden Road, Suite 208, 93940
Telephone: 831-375-0203
San Francisco: 415-984-0203
Facsimile: 831-375-4159
URL: http://www.warnerlaw.com

For full biographical listings, see the Martindale-Hubbell Law Directory

*NAPA,** Napa Co.

GAW, VAN MALE, SMITH, MYERS & MIROGLIO, A PROFESSIONAL LAW CORPORATION (AV)

944 Main Street, 94559-3045
Telephone: 707-252-9000
Telecopier: 707-252-0792
URL: http://www.gvmsmm.com
Fairfield, California Office: Corporate Plaza. 1261 Travis Boulevard, Suite 350, 94533-4801.
Telephone: 707-425-1250.
Fax: 707-425-1255.
Redlands, California Office: 300 E. State Street, Suite 101, 92372-5200.
Telephone: 909-798-3190.
Fax: 909-798-3092.

Nicholas R. Van Male — Bruce A. Miroglio

(See Next Column)

Rhonda L. Savitch	David G. Knitter
Teresa A. Cunningham	Young S. Lee

Reference: The Vintage Bank.

For full biographical listings, see the Martindale-Hubbell Law Directory

NEWPORT BEACH, Orange Co.

REBECCA CALLAHAN A PROFESSIONAL LAW CORPORATION (AV)

5120 Campus Drive, 92660
Telephone: 949-864-5152
Facsimile: 949-864-5156
URL: http://www.lawyers.com/callahanlaw
Email: bekic@pacbell.net *URL:* http://www.rcallahan.com

Rebecca Callahan

For full biographical listings, see the Martindale-Hubbell Law Directory

CAPRETZ & ASSOCIATES (AV)

5000 Birch Street, West Tower Suite 2500, 92660-2139
Telephone: 949-724-3000
Fax: 949-757-2635
URL: http://www.lawyers.com/capretzradcliffe
Email: crlawl@ix.netcom.com *URL:* http://www.CAPRETZ.com

MEMBER OF FIRM

James T. Capretz

OF COUNSEL

William B. Lawless (Not admitted in CA)

LEGAL SUPPORT PERSONNEL

Sandra L. Koop (Law Clerk)

For full biographical listings, see the Martindale-Hubbell Law Directory

DAVIS, PUNELLI & KEATHLEY LLP (AV)

610 Newport Center Drive, Suite 1000, P.O. Box 7920, 92658-7920
Telephone: 949-640-0700
Telecopier: 949-640-0714
URL: http://www.lawyers.com/dpkllp

MEMBERS OF FIRM

S. Eric Davis	H. James Keathley
Frank Punelli, Jr.	Katherine D. Keathley

OF COUNSEL

Lewis K. Uhler

For full biographical listings, see the Martindale-Hubbell Law Directory

LOPEZ, HODES, RESTAINO, MILMAN & SKIKOS, A LAW CORPORATION (AV)

450 Newport Center Drive, 2nd Floor, 92660
Telephone: 949-640-8222
Fax: 949-640-8294
San Francisco, California Office: 625 Market Street, Fifteenth Floor, 94105.
Telephone: 415-956-5257.
Fax: 415-956-4416.

Ramon Rossi Lopez	Jeffrey A. Milman
Daniel M. Hodes	Peter John Polos
John M. Restaino, Jr.	Steven J. Skikos (Resident)

Christina A. Lopez Fountain	Thomas A. Schultz
Steven B. Eggleston (Resident, San Francisco Office)	Mark G. Crawford
Gregory T. Skikos (Resident, San Francisco Office)	Hilary Poulsen Gilles

OF COUNSEL

David L. Suggs (Not admitted in CA)	Jane E. Joseph (Not admitted in CA)

For full biographical listings, see the Martindale-Hubbell Law Directory

MARIO W. MAINERO, JR., INC. (AV)

Suite 201, 5160 Birch Street, 92660
Telephone: 714-851-7763
FAX: 714-851-8188 (7765)
Email: mwmlaw@aol.com

Mario W. Mainero, Jr. — Jan A. Zemanek

LEGAL SUPPORT PERSONNEL

Louis W. Tully (Paralegal)

Reference: Bank of America.

For full biographical listings, see the Martindale-Hubbell Law Directory

Newport Beach—Continued

McCauley & Associates ALC (AV)

610 Newport Center Drive, Suite 1010, 92660
Telephone: 949-644-2922
Fax: 949-644-9627
Email: info@mccauleylaw.com

MEMBER OF FIRM

John J. McCauley

Linda McCauley · Sue S. Okuda

For full biographical listings, see the Martindale-Hubbell Law Directory

Millar, Hodges & Bemis (AV)

One Newport Place, Suite 900, 1301 Dove Street, 92660-2448
Telephone: 949-752-7722
Fax: 949-752-6131

MEMBERS OF FIRM

Richard W. Millar, Jr. · Kenneth R. Hodges
Larry R. Bemis

ASSOCIATE

David A. St. Clair

Reference: Manufacturers Bank, Newport Beach, California.

For full biographical listings, see the Martindale-Hubbell Law Directory

Mozingo & Price, LLP (AV)

One Newport Place, 1301 Dove Street, Suite 900, 92660
Telephone: 949-752-2255
Facsimile: 949-752-6636
Sacramento, California Office: US Bank Plaza, 980 Ninth Street, Suite 2120, 95814.
Telephone: 916-492-0525.
Facsimile: 916-492-0635.

MEMBERS OF FIRM

Glen R. Mozingo · Don G. Price
Jeffrey W. Fohrman

Representative Clients: Salomon Smith Barney-Charles Schwab; Keller, Collins, Hakopian & Leisure (Investment Advisors); American River Fire District; Merchants National Bank; Good & Roberts Construction, Inc.; Essex Insurance Co.; Integrated Environmental, Inc.; International Gateway Insurance Brokers; Coastal Pacific Funding Corp.

Quinlivan & Kaniewski (AV)

1401 Dove Street, Suite 580, 92660
Telephone: 714-851-7788
Fax: 714-851-3842
URL: http://www.lawyers.com/quinlivan-kaniewski
Email: Quikanlaw@aol.com *URL:* http://qklaw.wld.com

MEMBERS OF FIRM

Patrick C. Quinlivan · John A. Kaniewski

ASSOCIATES

Danniel J. Wexler · Pamela Jean Richardson
Paige F. Rubinfeld

For full biographical listings, see the Martindale-Hubbell Law Directory

Robinson, Calcagnie & Robinson, A Professional Corporation (AV)

Incorporated 1986
620 Newport Center Drive 7th Floor, 92660
Telephone: 949-720-1288
Fax: 949-720-1292
Email: rpc@robinson-pilaw.com
San Diego, California Office: 110 Laurel Street.
Telephone: 619-338-4060.
Fax: 619-338-0423.

Mark P. Robinson, Jr. · Jeoffrey L. Robinson
Kevin F. Calcagnie · Allan F. Davis
Joseph L. Dunn

Carlos A. Prietto, III · Stephanie M. Smith

LEGAL SUPPORT PERSONNEL

Lin Moen · Francine Teer
Donna Hosea · Linda Baker
Darleen Perkins · Erin Walker

For full biographical listings, see the Martindale-Hubbell Law Directory

Stepp & Beauchamp LLP (AV)

A Limited Liability Partnership of Professional Corporations
1301 Dove Street, Suite 460, 92660-2422
Telephone: 949-660-9700
Fax: 949-660-9010
Email: ndh@stepp-beauchamp.com *URL:* http://www.lawyers.com/stepp&beauchampllp

Thomas E. Stepp, Jr. · Robert B. Beauchamp
Mynette D. Beauchamp · Deron Matthew Colby
Michael J. Muellerleile

For full biographical listings, see the Martindale-Hubbell Law Directory

The Walker Law Firm A Professional Corporation (AV)

Suite 450, 1301 Dove Street, 92660-2464
Telephone: 949-752-2522
Telecopier: 949-752-0439
Email: JWALKER208@AOL.COM *URL:* http://www.thewalkerlawfirm.com

Joseph A. Walker

Karyn S. Neue

OF COUNSEL

Duff S. McEvers · David T. Sanford
Michael B. Moad

Reference: Marine National Bank.

For full biographical listings, see the Martindale-Hubbell Law Directory

NORTH HOLLYWOOD, Los Angeles Co.

Maurice Harwick (AV)

7401 Laurel Canyon Boulevard Suite 22, 91606
Telephone: 818-255-0077
Fax: 818-255-0070

*OAKLAND,** Alameda Co.

Anthony & Carlson, LLP (AV)

1999 Harrison Street, Suite 2000, 94612-3517
Telephone: 510-835-8400
Fax: 510-835-5566

MEMBERS OF FIRM

Steven R. Anthony · Richard H. Carlson

Felicia C. Strankman

OF COUNSEL

Jane L. Trigero

For full biographical listings, see the Martindale-Hubbell Law Directory

Bennett, Samuelsen, Reynolds and Allard, A Professional Corporation (AV)

1951 Webster Street, Suite 200, 94612-2909
Telephone: 510-444-7688; 510-987-8001
Fax: 510-444-5849
Email: BSRALIT@AOL.COM

Bryant M. Bennett (Retired) · Richard L. Reynolds
David J. Samuelsen · Anthony J. Allard
John G. Cowperthwaite

Roger Blake Hohnsbeen · Candace Dabney-Smith
Thomas S. Gelini · David L. Dees
Frederick W. Gatt · Roderick D. Hill

Representative Clients: Allstate Insurance Co.; California State Automobile Assn.; The Continental Insurance Cos.; County of Alameda.

For full biographical listings, see the Martindale-Hubbell Law Directory

Berry & Berry, A Professional Corporation (AV)

1300 Clay Street, Ninth Floor, P.O. Box 70250, 94612-0250
Telephone: 510-835-8330
Fax: 510-835-5117
Email: phillipberry@berryandberry.com

Phillip S. Berry · Peter R. Gilbert
Leonardo J. Vacchina · Lynne P. Blair

Evanthia Spanos · Laura Przetak
Sheila Flanagan

Representative Clients: Parke-Davis; Warner-Lambert; Farmers Insurance Co.; Fireman's Fund Insurance Co.; American International Underwriters; American Optical; Hyatt, Inc.; Osram-Sylvania.

For full biographical listings, see the Martindale-Hubbell Law Directory

Oakland—Continued

FILICE, BROWN, EASSA & MCLEOD, LLP (AV)
1999 Harrison Street, 18th Floor, 94612
Telephone: 510-444-3131
Fax: 510-839-7940

Gennaro A. Filice III
Eugene Brown, Jr.
Robert D. Eassa
Bruce E. McLeod
Raymond J. Bergez
Nicholas D. Kayhan
John A. De Pasquale
Peter A. Strotz
Richard V. Normington III
Amee A. Mikacich
Stephen J. Valen

Jennifer Walker O'Sullivan
Jason J. Curliano
Kristin Ashurst Hughes
Lisa M. Brown
Jennifer K. Pearce
Constance J. McNeil
Michael H. Kim
Carla M. Nakata
Katrina C. Decker

OF COUNSEL

Barrie Engel
Paul R. Johnson

Representative Clients: AstraZeneca, Inc.; Chevron Corp.; Dow Chemical Co.; Ford Motor Co.; ICI Americas, Inc.; Long's Drug Stores California; PPG Industries, Inc.; Rhodia, Inc.; Tosco Refining Co.; Unocal Corp.

For full biographical listings, see the Martindale-Hubbell Law Directory

HAIMS, MACGOWAN, VALENTINO & PEEBLES, L.L.P. (AV)
490 Grand Avenue, 94610
Telephone: 510-835-0500
Facsimile: 510-835-2833

MEMBERS OF FIRM

Arnold B. Haims
Clyde L. MacGowan
Caroline N. Valentino
Dianne D. Peebles

For full biographical listings, see the Martindale-Hubbell Law Directory

KAZAN, MCCLAIN, EDISES, SIMON & ABRAMS, A PROFESSIONAL LAW CORPORATION (AV)
171 Twelfth Street, Suite 300, 94607
Telephone: 510-465-7728; 893-7211
TDD: (510) 763-8808
Fax: 510-835-4913
Email: postmaster@kmesa.com *URL:* http://www.KMESA.COM

Steven Kazan
David M. McClain
Aaron H. Simon
Denise Abrams
Francis E. Fernandez
Dianna J. Lyons
Simona A. Farrise

Anne Michelle Burr
Frances C. Schreiberg
Susan S. Ochi
Terry Gross
Cyrus Wadia
Gordon D. Greenwood
James L. Oberman
Andrea C. Huston
Diana Esquivel
Anthony D. Prince

OF COUNSEL

Philip A. Harley

LEGAL SUPPORT PERSONNEL

Elizabeth C. Johnson (Director of Administration and Finance)

Reference: Union Bank (Oakland Main Branch).

For full biographical listings, see the Martindale-Hubbell Law Directory

LOMBARDI, LOPER & CONANT, LLP (AV)
1999 Harrison Street, Suite 1950, 94612
Telephone: 510-433-2600
Fax: 510-433-2699

Ralph A. Lombardi
Bruce P. Loper
Matthew S. Conant
Chris P. Lavdiotis
Peter O. Glaessner
Timothy J. McCaffery
GayLynn Renee Kirn

Jeffrey D Hosking
Joseph Blaise Adams
Paul S. Lecky

OF COUNSEL

George S. Peyton, Jr.
Linda C. Roodhouse
Lori A. Sebransky

For full biographical listings, see the Martindale-Hubbell Law Directory

NEVIN GRUEN LLP (AV)
180 Grand Avenue, Suite 950, 94612
Telephone: 510-873-8600
Fax: 510-873-8601
Email: jnevin@nevinlaw.com *URL:* http://www.info@nevinlaw.com
San Francisco, California Office: 507 Polk Street, Suite 300.
Telephone: 415-834-1777.
Fax: 415-834-1774.

(See Next Column)

Sacramento, California Office: 555 Capital Mall, Suite 645.
Telephone: 916-447-2306.
Fax: 916-447-2307.

Jeffrey G. Nevin
Jan A. Gruen

David M. Miller
Kelly Catherine Levy
Karen Brown Kepler

For full biographical listings, see the Martindale-Hubbell Law Directory

ONTARIO, San Bernardino Co.

COVINGTON & CROWE LLP (AV)
1131 West Sixth Street, P.O. Box 1515, 91762
Telephone: 909-983-9393
Fax: 909-391-6762
URL: http://www.covcrowe.com

MEMBERS OF FIRM

Maurice G. Covington (1908-1997)
Harold A. Bailin (1930-1988)
Samuel P. Crowe
George W. Porter
Robert E. Dougherty
Donald G. Haslam
Robert F. Schauer
Jette R. Anderson
Audrey A. Perri
Tracy L. Tibbals
Melanie Fisch
R. Douglas Donesky
Tammy S. Jager
Katrina West

ASSOCIATES

J. Michael Kaler
Eric S. Vail
Khymberli S. Apaloo

OF COUNSEL

Edward A. Hopson

For full biographical listings, see the Martindale-Hubbell Law Directory

ORINDA, Contra Costa Co.

GILLIN, JACOBSON, ELLIS & LARSEN (AV)
2 Theatre Square Suite 230, 94563
Telephone: 925-253-5800
Fax: 925-253-5858
Email: lawfirm@gjeld.com
San Francisco, California Office: 44 Montgomery Street, Suite 500, 94101.
Telephone: 415-986-4777.

Andrew R. Gillin
Ralph L. Jacobson
Luke Ellis
James Paul Larsen
Kristin Lucey

For full biographical listings, see the Martindale-Hubbell Law Directory

PACIFIC PALISADES, Los Angeles Co.

WILLIAM A. SAMPSON II & ASSOCIATES (AV)
15332 Antioch Street, Suite 525, 90272-3628
Telephone: 310-472-1839
Fax: 310-472-8670

For full biographical listings, see the Martindale-Hubbell Law Directory

PALM DESERT, Riverside Co.

CRISTE, PIPPIN & GOLDS (AV)
Suite 200, 73-550 Alessandro Drive, 92260
Telephone: 760-862-1111
Fax: 760-776-4197
Email: cpgca@aol.com

MEMBERS OF FIRM

Michael A. Criste
Robert L. Pippin
Irwin L. Golds

ASSOCIATES

Jeffrey S. Flashman
Julian S. Summers

For full biographical listings, see the Martindale-Hubbell Law Directory

PALM SPRINGS, Riverside Co.

SCHLECHT, SHEVLIN & SHOENBERGER, A LAW CORPORATION (AV)
801 East Tahquitz Canyon Way, Suite 100, P.O. Box 2744, 92263-2744
Telephone: 760-320-7161
Facsimile: 760-323-1758
Email: ssslaw@gte.net *URL:* http://www.ssslaw.com

John C. Shevlin
Jon A. Shoenberger

David Darrin

Representative Clients: Outdoor Resorts of America; The Escrow Connection; Palm Hills Land Corp.; Shadowrock; Palm Springs Marquis.

For Complete List of Firm Personnel, See General Section

For full biographical listings, see the Martindale-Hubbell Law Directory

Palm Springs—Continued

LAW OFFICES OF RICK M. STEIN (AV)

400 South Farrell Drive Suite B-203, 92262
Telephone: 760-325-5990
Facsimile: 760-325-6265
Email: rsteinboy@aol.com

For full biographical listings, see the Martindale-Hubbell Law Directory

PALO ALTO, Santa Clara Co.

BASIL P. FTHENAKIS (AV)

540 University Avenue, Suite 300, 94301-1912
Telephone: 650-326-1397
Fax: 650-326-3203
Email: basilp@fthenakis.com

For full biographical listings, see the Martindale-Hubbell Law Directory

PASADENA, Los Angeles Co.

JOHN C. BURTON (AV)

35 South Raymond Avenue, Suite 405, 91105
Telephone: 626-449-8300
Fax: 626-449-4417
Email: Johnburtonlaw@compuserve.com *URL:* http://www.lawyers.com/johnburtonlaw

For full biographical listings, see the Martindale-Hubbell Law Directory

COLLINS, COLLINS, MUIR & TRAVER LLP (AV)

Successor to Collins & Collins
Suite 300, 265 North Euclid, 91101
Telephone: 626-793-1163
FAX: 626-793-5982
Newport Beach, California Office: 333 Bayside Drive, 92660.
Telephone: 949-723-7700.
Fax: 949-723-7701.
Affiliated Offices: Drage, Olson & Tiet, LLP, 810 S. Casino Center Boulevard, Las Vegas, Nevada, 89101.
Telephone: 702-384-1600.
Fax: 702-384-1664.

MEMBERS OF FIRM

James E. Collins (1910-1987)
Robert J. Traver (Retired)
Paul L. Rupard (Retired)
John J. Collins
Samuel J. Muir
Frank J. D'Oro
Brian K. Stewart

ASSOCIATES

Robert H. Stellwagen, Jr.
Tomas A. Guterres
Christine E. Drage
Stephen W. Olson
Peter L. Stacy
Kien C. Tiet
Martha L. Cazeneuve
Howard Franco, Jr.
Jeffrey M. Hall
Michael M. Bergfeld
Jennifer M. Gregg

For full biographical listings, see the Martindale-Hubbell Law Directory

FREEBURG, JUDY & NETTELS (AV)

600 South Lake Avenue, Suite 500, 91106
Telephone: 626-585-4150
Fax: 626-585-0718
Tustin, California Office: 440 West First Street, Suite 102, 92780-3047.
Telephone: 714-508-1800.
Facsimile: 714-508-1809.

Steven J. Freeburg
J. Lawrence Judy
Charles F. Nettels

ASSOCIATES

Ingall W. Bull, Jr.
Richard B. Castle
Cynthia B. Schaldenbrand (Resident, Tustin Office)
Holly A. McNulty
Karen S. Freeburg
Jennifer D. Helsel
Carla Lynn Crochet (Resident, Tustin Office)
Edward William Burns

For full biographical listings, see the Martindale-Hubbell Law Directory

LAGERLOF, SENECAL, BRADLEY, GOSNEY & KRUSE, LLP (AV)

301 North Lake Avenue, 10th Floor, 91101-4108
Telephone: 626-793-9400
FAX: 626-793-5900
Email: mail@lagerlof.com

MEMBERS OF FIRM

Joseph J. Burris (1913-1980)
Stanley C. Lagerlof (1915-1998)
H. Jess Senecal
Jack T. Swafford
John F. Bradley
Timothy J. Gosney
William F. Kruse
Thomas S. Bunn, III
Andrew D. Turner
Rebecca J. Thyne
James D. Ciampa

(See Next Column)

ASSOCIATE

Shaun O. Kwon

Representative Clients: Gallo Glass Company; Orthopaedic Hospital; North American Chemical Company; Palmdale Water District; Public Water Agencies Group; Ventura Port District; Walnut Valley Water District; Metric Construction Co., Inc.

For full biographical listings, see the Martindale-Hubbell Law Directory

MEENAN & LARIVIERE (AV)

790 East Colorado Boulevard Ninth Floor Penthouse, 91101-2113
Telephone: 626-398-0000
Fax: 626-585-0999
Email: meenlaw@msn.com *URL:* http://www.lawyers.com/meenlaw

Kevin Meenan
Denise L. Lariviere

For full biographical listings, see the Martindale-Hubbell Law Directory

ZUETEL & TOMLINSON (AV)

215 North Marengo Avenue, Suite 195, 91101
Telephone: 626-577-3499
Fax: 323-684-1275

MEMBERS OF FIRM

Kenneth R. Zuetel, Jr.
Rodney G. Tomlinson

ASSOCIATE

Victoria K. Torigian

For full biographical listings, see the Martindale-Hubbell Law Directory

RANCHO SANTA FE, San Diego Co.

LAW OFFICES OF ROBERT S. KILBORNE IV (AV)

7872 Rio Senda, P.O. Box 7288, 92067
Telephone: 619-759-9050
Fax: 619-759-8020
Email: triallawyer@kilborne.com *URL:* http://www.kilborne.com

ASSOCIATE

Albert E. Cressey, III

OF COUNSEL

Russell B. Wagner

For full biographical listings, see the Martindale-Hubbell Law Directory

CHARLES S. LIMANDRI (AV)

Building 3, 16236 San Dieguito Road, Suite 3-15, P.O. Box 9120, 92067
Telephone: 619-759-9930
Fax: 619-759-9938
Email: climandri@limandri.com *URL:* http://www.limandri.com

ASSOCIATES

Mark A. Ginella
G. Patrick Connors, III
Michael S. Dea
Mark T. Dea

Representative Clients: The Standard Steamship Owners Protection and Indemnity Association, Ltd. (London); Caribbean Marine Service Co., Inc. (San Diego); Century National Insurance.
Reference: Wells Fargo Bank.

For full biographical listings, see the Martindale-Hubbell Law Directory

*REDDING,** Shasta Co.

DUGAN BARR & ASSOCIATES (AV)

1824 Court Street, P.O. Box 994390, 96099-1648
Telephone: 530-243-8008
Fax: 530-243-1648
URL: http://www.CA-lawyer.com

Dugan Barr

ASSOCIATES

Douglas Mudford
J. Michael Favor

Representative Clients: City of Redding; Mid Valley Bank; Scott Valley Bank; 3M; Enloe Hospital.
References: Scott Valley Bank, Redding Branch; Mid Valley Bank, Redding Branch.

For full biographical listings, see the Martindale-Hubbell Law Directory

CARR, KENNEDY, PETERSON & FROST, A LAW CORPORATION (AV)

420 Redcliff Drive, P.O. Box 492396, 96049
Telephone: 530-222-2100
Fax: 530-222-0504
Email: info@ckpf.com

(See Next Column)

CARR, KENNEDY, PETERSON & FROST A LAW CORPORATION—*Continued*

Francis Carr (1875-1944)
Lawrence J. Kennedy, Sr. (1883-1975)
Laurence J. Kennedy, Jr. (1918-1986)
Laurence W. Carr (1912-1991)
R. Russ Peterson
Daniel S. Frost
Robert M. Harding
Evan L. Delgado
Stephen H. Baker
Michael P. Ashby
Randall C. Nelson
Robert A. West

Representative Clients: Catholic Health Care West; Chicago Title Insurance Co.; CH2M Hill California, Inc.; Design Professional Insurance Co.; Fruit Growers Supply Co.; Louisiana-Pacific Corp.; PacifiCorp; Rayonier, Inc.; Roseburg Lumber Co.; Stewart Title Insurance Co.

For full biographical listings, see the Martindale-Hubbell Law Directory

MOSS & ENOCHIAN, A LAW CORPORATION (AV)

2701 Park Marina Drive, P.O. Box 994608, 96099-4608
Telephone: 530-225-8990
Fax: 530-241-5734
Email: postmaster@mossenochian.com *URL:* http://www.mossenochian.com

Steven R. Enochian
Larry B. Moss
Todd E. Slaughter
John S. Kenny
Robert A. Spano

Sandra L. Johnson
Mark D. Norcross
David S. Perrine
Rich Dalrymple
Adam B. Ryan
Andreas Mittry
Brigham P. Jones

Reference: Tri Counties Bank.

For full biographical listings, see the Martindale-Hubbell Law Directory

*REDWOOD CITY,** San Mateo Co.

CODDINGTON, HICKS & DANFORTH, A PROFESSIONAL CORPORATION (AV)

Suite 300, 555 Twin Dolphin Drive, Paragon Center, Redwood Shores, 94065
Telephone: 650-592-5400
Facsimile: 650-592-5027
Email: CHDLawyers@aol.com

Clinton H. Coddington
Randolph S. Hicks
Lee J. Danforth
David M. King
Richard G. Grotch
David W. Wessel
R. Wardell Loveland
Pamela A. Bower

Edward A. Heinlein
Troy B. Overton
Richard S. Baum
Laura Elizabeth Read

OF COUNSEL

William G. Tucker
Arnold I Bennigson

For full biographical listings, see the Martindale-Hubbell Law Directory

HANNIG LAW FIRM LLP (AV)

2991 El Camino Real, Suite 100, 94061
Telephone: 650-482-3040
Facsimile: 650-482-2820
Email: tjh@hanniglaw.com *URL:* http://www.hanniglaw.com

Ted J. Hannig
H. Ann Liroff
David M. Rose

OF COUNSEL

John Antonakos
Michael D. Barry

For full biographical listings, see the Martindale-Hubbell Law Directory

HOWARD ROME MARTIN & RIDLEY LLP (AV)

643 Bair Island Road, Suite 400, P.O. Box 2189, 94064-2189
Telephone: 650-365-7715
Facsimile: 650-364-5297

MEMBERS OF FIRM

Joseph C. Howard, Jr.
Henry D. Rome
Glenn D. Martin
Shawn M. Ridley

Beth Clare Hopwood
Scott L. Johnson
James M. Harrington

OF COUNSEL

Kristi L. Curtis

Representative Clients: Ryobi North America, Inc.; Association of Bay Area Governments PLAN; Pacific Gas & Electric Company; YMCA; San Carlos; Cities of: Redwood City, South San Francisco, Sunnyvale, Pacifica, Palo Alto.

For full biographical listings, see the Martindale-Hubbell Law Directory

RICHMOND, Contra Costa Co.

NORRIS & NORRIS (AV)

3260 Blume Drive, Suite 400, 94806
Telephone: 510-222-2100
Facsimile: 510-222-5992
Email: rnorris@norrislaw.com
Walnut Creek, California Office: 1850 Mt. Diablo Boulevard, Suite 530, 94596.
Telephone: 925-934-8181.
Facsimile: 925-934-3665.

MEMBERS OF FIRM

Richard E. Norris
Douglas C. Straus
Cy Epstein
Colin J. Coffey
Edward L. Shaffer
Sharon Moody Iversen

ASSOCIATES

Michael B. Peterson
Paula L. Baca
Noël M. Caughman
Michael A. Sweet
Daniel D. Purnell

For full biographical listings, see the Martindale-Hubbell Law Directory

*RIVERSIDE,** Riverside Co.

LAW OFFICES OF TERRY BRIDGES (AV)

Mission Square Plaza, 3750 University Avenue, Suite 240, 92501-3313
Telephone: 909-682-2760
Facsimile: 909-682-8626
Email: Terry@TBridges.com

ASSOCIATE

Alan J. Leahy

For full biographical listings, see the Martindale-Hubbell Law Directory

HAIGHT, BROWN & BONESTEEL, L.L.P. (AV)

A Partnership including Professional Corporations
California Tower, 3737 Main Street, Suite 800, 92501
Telephone: 909-341-8300
FAX: 909-341-8309
URL: http://www.hbblaw.com
Santa Monica, California Office: 1620 26th Street, Suite 4000 North, P.O. Box 680.
Telephone: 310-449-6000.
Telecopier: 310-829-5117.
Telex: 705837.
Santa Ana, California Office: Suite 900, 5 Hutton Centre Drive.
Telephone: 714-754-1100.
Telecopier: 714-754-0826.
San Francisco, California Office: 100 Bush Street, 27th Floor.
Telephone: 415-986-7700.
Fax: 415-986-6945.
San Diego, California Office: 101 West Broadway, Suite 1000.
Telephone: 619-595-5583.
Fax: 619-595-7873.

RESIDENT MEMBERS

Mark S. Lester
Kevin M. Osterberg

ASSOCIATES

Bonnie B. Bailey-Jones
John W. Short
Jeffrey T. Gwynn

For full biographical listings, see the Martindale-Hubbell Law Directory

*SACRAMENTO,** Sacramento Co.

ABBOTT & NOLEN (AV)

350 University Avenue, Suite 280, 95825
Telephone: 916-564-9990
Fax: 916-564-9991
Email: abbott_nolen@compuserve.com *URL:* http://www.lawyers.com/abbottandnolen

David W. Abbott
Rhudolph Nolen, Jr.

ASSOCIATE

Bruce M. Timm

Representative Clients: National Chiropractic Mutual Ins. Co.; Pi Omega Delta Ins. Co.; Travelers Ins. Co.

For full biographical listings, see the Martindale-Hubbell Law Directory

BOUTIN, DENTINO, GIBSON DI GIUSTO, HODELL & WEST, A PROFESSIONAL CORPORATION (AV)

455 Capitol Mall, Suite 300, 95814-4406
Telephone: 916-321-4444
Telecopier: 916-441-7597
URL: http://www.boutindentino.com
Tucson, Arizona Office: 405 West Franklin Street, 85718.
Telephone: 520-882-2944.

(See Next Column)

BOUTIN, DENTINO, GIBSON DI GIUSTO, HODELL & WEST A PROFESSIONAL CORPORATION, *Sacramento—Continued*

Stephen F. Boutin
William Dentino
Chris Gibson
John E. Di Giusto
Douglas M. Hodell
R. Michael West
Robert D. Swanson
Ned M. Gelhaar

Kimberly L. Jackson
Mark W. Owens
James R. Moore
Michael T. Sparks
Sallie-Carol Orbas
Jeffrey B. Slaton

OF COUNSEL

Robert G. West
Thomas G. Manolakas

For full biographical listings, see the Martindale-Hubbell Law Directory

CALLAHAN & DEACON (AV)

A Partnership including a Corporation
77 Cadillac Drive, Suite 240, 95825
Telephone: 916-929-1999
Fax: 916-929-1090
Email: gbc8esd@calweb.com *URL:* http://www.lawyers.com/callahan&deacon

Gary B. Callahan (Inc.)
Edward S. Deacon

For full biographical listings, see the Martindale-Hubbell Law Directory

DONAHUE, WOOD, LOVING & VOGEL (AV)

83 Scripps Drive, Suite 200, 95825
Telephone: 916-648-7444
Fax: 916-648-7447

MEMBERS OF FIRM

James E. Donahue
Gerrit W. Wood
Walter H. Loving, III
Barry Vogel
William K. Blakemore
Stephen J. Mackey
Mark A. Bates
Thomas P. Connolly III

Douglas P. Winter
Aleshia M. White
Luke A. Foster
Judith Clark Martin
Brian J. O'Connor
Catherine L. Manske

For full biographical listings, see the Martindale-Hubbell Law Directory

GREVE, CLIFFORD, WENGEL & PARAS, LLP (AV)

980 Ninth Street, Suite 1900, 95814-2739
Telephone: 916-443-2011
Telecopier: 916-441-7457
Email: greveclifford.com *URL:* http://www.greveclifford.com

MEMBERS OF FIRM

Edward T. Clifford
Lawrence A. Wengel
Gary L. Vinson
Bradley R. Larson
William L. Baker
Robert L. Collins
Scott E. Cofer
William J. Barcellona
Bradley W. Kragel
Craig L. Scott

ASSOCIATES

John D. Broghammer
Terry A. German

OF COUNSEL

Irving H. Perluss

RETIRED

Claire H. Greve
George E. Paras

PARALEGALS

Claudia Cross
H. Gregory Vitaich

Representative Clients: Allstate Insurance Co.; Atlantic Richfield, Corp.; Commercial Union Insurance Co.; Design Professionals Insurance Co.; E & O Professionals; Great American Insurance Cos.; State of California; Union Oil Co.; United Pacific/Reliance Insurance Cos.

For full biographical listings, see the Martindale-Hubbell Law Directory

HARDY ERICH BROWN & WILSON, A PROFESSIONAL CORPORATION (AV)

1000 G Street, 95814
Telephone: 916-449-3800
Fax: 916-449-3888
Mailing Address: P.O. Box 13530, Sacramento, California, 95853-4530
Email: hebw@hebw.com *URL:* http://www.hebw.com

John Quincy Brown, Jr.
Anthony D. Osmundson
Thomas C. Richards
L. Thomas Wagner
David L. Perrault
Sara A. Clark
John Quincy Brown, III
David S. Worthington
L. Kent Wyatt
Bruce E. Salenko
Brian H. Charter
Richard L. Alley
Glenda N. Reager
Whitney A. Davis
John C. Miller, Jr.
Michael J. Nelson

(See Next Column)

OF COUNSEL

Cavan Hardy
Norwood R. Erich
William A. Wilson
Richard M. Cunha

Kelly F. Watson
Kristine E. Balogh
Karin G. Shine
Reginald A. Dunn
Lisa L. Palombo

Representative Clients: Continental General Tire; The Dexter Corporation; The Dial Corporation; Foamex International, Inc.; GenCorp; The Goodyear Tire & Rubber Company; Kmart Corporation; La Z Boy, Inc.; United Way California Capital Region; VIAD Corporation.

For full biographical listings, see the Martindale-Hubbell Law Directory

HUNTER RICHEY DI BENEDETTO & BREWER, LLP (AV)

A Limited Liability Partnership
Renaissance Tower, 801 K Street, 23rd Floor, 95814-3525
Telephone: 916-491-3000
Facsimile: 916-491-3080
Email: hrdb@hrdb.com *URL:* http://www.hrdb.com

MEMBERS OF FIRM

William S. Hunter
Win R. Richey
Florence L. Di Benedetto
Roy E. Brewer
Anne E. Ferguson
James F. Geary
Janet C. Eisenbeis
Stephen C. Ruehmann
Sharon K. Sandeen
Jack V. Lovell
Patricia J. Hartman

OF COUNSEL

Laurie E. Davis

LEGAL SUPPORT PERSONNEL

Lori J. Moody (Paralegal)
Deborah M. Johnson (Paralegal)
Linda Jane Hall (Executive Assistant)
Jennifer E. Mueller (Legal Assistant)
Michele L. Nickell (Legal Assistant)
Lynetta G. Goodwin

For full biographical listings, see the Martindale-Hubbell Law Directory

JOHNSON, SCHACHTER & COLLINS, A PROFESSIONAL CORPORATION (AV)

California Plaza, 2180 Harvard Street, #560, 95815
Telephone: 916-921-5800
Telecopier: 916-921-0247
Email: law@jscattorneys.com

Robert H. Johnson
Alesa M. Schachter
Kim H. Collins
George W. Holt
Kellie M. Murphy
Alvin Gittisriboongul

Susan E. Slager

OF COUNSEL

Ford R. Smith
Carolyn M. Wood
Susanne M. Shelley

Representative Clients: CAMICO; Chicago Insurance; Fireman's Fund Insurance Cos.; Insurance Company of the West; Interstate National; NAVISTAR; Sears, Roebuck and Co.; Shand Morahan; Westport Insurance Corp.
Reference: U.S. Bank, Sacramento.

For full biographical listings, see the Martindale-Hubbell Law Directory

JOHN B. LEWIS (AV)

1006 Fourth Street, 10th Floor, 95814
Telephone: 916-443-2051
Fax: 916-443-2651

For full biographical listings, see the Martindale-Hubbell Law Directory

LIVINGSTON & MATTESICH, LAW CORPORATION (AV)

1201 K Street, Suite 1100, 95814
Telephone: 916-442-1111
Fax: 916-448-1709
Email: l&m@lmlaw.net *URL:* http://www.lmlaw.net

Gene Livingston
James M. Mattesich
Carol Livingston
Rebecca M. Ceniceros
Emilio E. Varanini, III
Kenneth M. Malovos
Kathleen E. Finnerty
Joanna R. Mendoza

Steven P. Belzer
Jeffrey Leacox
Randy Pollack
Alice H. Choi
Stephen Craig Hunter
Matthew J. Goldman
Joel C. Baiocchi
Baldassaro (Bill) Di Capo
John McKinsey
Timothy E. Naccarato
Craig N. Lundgren
Mary Farrell Taylor
Brian Crone
Gay L. Carroll
Steven G. Churchwell

(See Next Column)

LIVINGSTON & MATTESICH LAW CORPORATION—*Continued*

Representative Clients: Agra Foundations, Inc.; Colgate-Palmolive; Guaranty Federal Bank, F.S.B.; H.J. Heinz Company; Hansen Information Technologies, Inc.; Hertz Equipment Rental Corp.; Johnson & Johnson; Stonesfair Financial Corporation; Unilever United States, Inc.

For full biographical listings, see the Martindale-Hubbell Law Directory

THOMAS F. LYTLE (AV)

1220 25th Street, 95816-5005
Telephone: 916-442-0701
Fax: 916-442-0786
Email: tomlytle@msn.com

For full biographical listings, see the Martindale-Hubbell Law Directory

MASON & THOMAS (AV)

2151 River Plaza Drive, Suite 100, 95833
Telephone: 916-567-8211
Fax: 916-567-8212
Email: M&T@MasonThomas.com

MEMBERS OF FIRM

Stephen A. Mason
Bradley S. Thomas

ASSOCIATES

Douglas W. Brown
Robert G. Kruse
David S. Yost
Patrick J. Hehir
Kevin L. Elder
Michele Raley

For full biographical listings, see the Martindale-Hubbell Law Directory

MATHENY SEARS LINKERT & LONG, LLP (AV)

3638 American River Drive, P.O. Box 13711, 95853-4711
Telephone: 916-978-3434
Fax: 916-978-3430
Email: info@msll.com *URL:* http://www.msll.com

MEMBERS OF FIRM

Henry G. Matheny (1933-1984)
Douglas A. Sears
Richard S. Linkert
Ernest A. Long
Joann Georgallis
Kent M. Luckey
Matthew C. Jaime
Michael A. Bishop
Robert B. Berrigan
Ronald E. Enabnit
Eric R. Wiesel

ASSOCIATES

Andrea Croak Christensen
Michael G. Jones
Eric M. Bonzell
Mary Elizabeth Wood
Paul Richard Baleria
James F. Curran
Andreas C. Rockas
Timothy P. Chang

OF COUNSEL

James C. Damir

LEGAL SUPPORT PERSONNEL

PARALEGALS

Frances Studer
Lynell Rae Steed
Jennifer Bachman

For full biographical listings, see the Martindale-Hubbell Law Directory

MCDONALD, SAELTZER, MORRIS, CREEGGAN & WADDOCK (AV)

555 Capitol Mall, Suite 700, 95814
Telephone: 916-444-5706
Fax: 916-444-8529

MEMBERS OF FIRM

Richard C. Creeggan
Thomas P. Waddock
Gregory R. Madsen

ASSOCIATES

Jennifer Hammond-Carroll
Patricia M. Keegan
Lance J Curtis
Greg T. Mino

OF COUNSEL

William O. Morris

Reference: Wells Fargo Bank.

For full biographical listings, see the Martindale-Hubbell Law Directory

NAGELEY, MEREDITH & MILLER, INC. (AV)

8001 Folsom Boulevard, Suite 100, 95826
Telephone: 916-386-8282
Fax: 916-386-8952
Email: mail@mnlawfirm.com

Sam R. Nageley
Gregory A. Meredith
Andrea M. Miller
Lawrence N. Hensley
Craig S. MacGlashan
Janet M. Meredith
Carole Hansen Sharples
L. Alan Warwick
Drew M. Johnson
James C. Keowen
Duane S. Oliveira

For full biographical listings, see the Martindale-Hubbell Law Directory

PORTER, SCOTT, WEIBERG & DELEHANT, A PROFESSIONAL CORPORATION (AV)

350 University Avenue, Suite 200, 95825
Telephone: 916-929-1481
Fax: 916-927-3706
Email: pswdlaw@aol.com

Russell G. Porter
A. Irving Scott, Jr.
Edwin T. Weiberg
John W. Delehant
Anthony S. Warburg
Ned P. Telford
James K. Mirabell
Craig A. Caldwell
Terence J. Cassidy
Tom H. Bailey
Carl J. Calnero
Russ J. Wunderli
Nancy J. Sheehan
Norman V. Prior
Timothy M. Blaine
Stephen E. Horan
Carl L. Fessenden

Elisa Ungerman
Michael J. Baytosh
David A. Melton
Jennifer E. Duggan
Vanessa W. Whang
Dennis C. Huie
Michael W. Pott
Kellianne Akbar
Daniel M. Steinberg
Jack Woodside
Jonathan A. Corr
Kristina M. Hall
Alden J. Parker
Avery E. Dority
Robin Weideman
Denise A. Carnaroli
Lara S. Hilley
Sean Allen
Ralph R. Nevis
Darrin M. Menezes
Shane Singh

For full biographical listings, see the Martindale-Hubbell Law Directory

JOE RAMSEY (AV)

1001 G Street, Suite 201, 95814
Telephone: 916-448-5353
Facsimile: 916-443-7372
Email: ojr@sna.com

For full biographical listings, see the Martindale-Hubbell Law Directory

RUSHFORD & BONOTTO, LLP (AV)

2277 Fair Oaks Boulevard, Suite 495, 95825
Telephone: 916-565-0590
Facsimile: 916-565-0599
Mailing Address: P.O. Box 255689, Sacramento, CA, 95865
Email: Rushford-BonottoLLP@worldnet.att.net

MEMBERS OF FIRM

James W. Rushford
Phillip R. Bonotto
Brett Rosenthal
Curtis W. Cable

Jennifer R. Porter

Representative Clients: Allstate Insurance Company; Bayer Corporation (formerly Miles, Inc.); California Builders Supply; Dravo Corporation; Federated Insurance Company; Federated Department Stores; GLC Carbon Corporation; General Mills, Inc.; Government Employees Insurance Company (GEICO); Grange Insurance Group; Liberty Mutual Insurance Company; Hopeman Brothers, Inc.

For full biographical listings, see the Martindale-Hubbell Law Directory

SCHUERING ZIMMERMAN & SCULLY, LLP (AV)

400 University Avenue, 95825
Telephone: 916-567-0400
Fax: 916-568-0400
Email: szs@szs.com

MEMBERS OF FIRM

Steven T. Scully (1948-1994)
Leo H. Schuering, Jr.
Robert H. Zimmerman
Thomas J. Doyle
Lawrence S. Giardina
Anthony D. Lauria
Keith D. Chidlaw
John J. Sillis
Scott A. Linn
Donna W. Low
Raymond R. Gates

Christian Koster
Michael W. McCall
Dominique A. Pollara
Theodore D. Poppinga
John P. Rhode
Stephen L. Ramazzini
Jonathan A. Saul
Jeffrey J. Whitelaw

For full biographical listings, see the Martindale-Hubbell Law Directory

STEVENS & O'CONNELL LLP (AV)

400 Capitol Mall, Suite 1400, 95814-4412
Telephone: 916-329-9111
Facsimile: 916-329-9110

(See Next Column)

STEVENS & O'CONNELL LLP, *Sacramento—Continued*

Charles J. Stevens
George L. O'Connell
Richard Pachter
David A. Cheit
Craig C. Allison
Bradley A. Benbrook
Todd M. Noonan
Timothy P. Grieve

For full biographical listings, see the Martindale-Hubbell Law Directory

WILCOXEN, MONTGOMERY & HARBISON (AV)

A Partnership including a Professional Corporation
2114 K Street, 95816
Telephone: 916-442-2777
Email: wmh@wilcoxenlaw.com *URL:* http://www.wilcoxenlaw.com

Daniel E. Wilcoxen (Inc.)
James R. Montgomery
Joseph F. Harbison, III

Patrick L. Hinrichsen
David E. Smith
Steven H. Schultz
Michelle C. Jenni

References: SierraWest Bank; Wells Fargo Bank.

For full biographical listings, see the Martindale-Hubbell Law Directory

*SAN BERNARDINO,** San Bernardino Co.

MIDDLEBROOK, KAISER & POPKA, A PROFESSIONAL CORPORATION (AV)

1411 North "D" Street, P.O. Box 1319, 92402-1319
Telephone: 909-888-5751
Fax: 909-888-7360
Email: MKPSB2@PacBell.net
Palm Springs Office: 3001 East Tahquitz Canyon Way, Suite 109.
Telephone: 619-322-0806.
Fax: 619-322-8979.

Greg C. Middlebrook
Michael R. Kaiser (Resident, Palm Springs Office)
Dennis G. Popka

Jeffrey Mark Yoss (Resident, Palm Springs Office)
Sandra A. Shoupe-Gorga (Resident, Palm Springs Office)
Dennis R. Stout
Julie A. Sohnlein
Daren E. Hengesbach

OF COUNSEL

John W. Furness

Reference: Wells Fargo Bank.

For full biographical listings, see the Martindale-Hubbell Law Directory

WILSON, BORROR, DUNN & DAVIS, LLP (AV)

Suite 307, The Bank of California Building, 255 North D Street, 92401
Telephone: 909-884-8855
Fax: 909-884-5161

MEMBERS OF FIRM

Fred A. Wilson (1886-1973)
Wm. H. Wilson (1915-1981)
James R. Dunn
Thomas M. Davis
Sarah L. Overton

ASSOCIATES

S. Mark Strain
C. Victor Wear

OF COUNSEL

Caywood J. Borror

Representative Clients: Travelers Insurance Co.; Rockwell International; Westinghouse Air Brake Co.; Goodyear Tire and Rubber Co.; Home Insurance Co.; Cities of: Redlands, Chino, Colton, San Bernardino, Upland, Yucapia and Corona; Lloyd's of London; Universal Health Services, Inc.-;Lawyer's Mutual Insurance; Unified School Districts of Rialto and Fontana .

For full biographical listings, see the Martindale-Hubbell Law Directory

*SAN DIEGO,** San Diego Co.

ALHADEFF CANNON ROSE SOLAR & PARKS, LLP (AV)

550 West "C" Street, Nineteenth Floor, 92101-3540
Telephone: 619-231-8700
Facsimile: 619-231-8323
Email: ksolar@acrsp.com
Temecula, California Office: The Tower Plaza, 27555 Ynez Road, Suite 203, 92591-4677.
Telephone: 909-699-9088.
Facsimile: 909-699-9878. Email: POBERHANSLEY@ACRSP.com
Los Angeles, California Office: Olympic Center, 11150 Olympic Boulevard, Suite 860, 90064.
Telephone: 310-914-4400.
Facsimile: 310-914-0030. Email: JODONNELL@ACRSP.com

(See Next Column)

Lafayette, California Office: Lafayette Terrace, 3697 Mount Diablo Boulevard, Suite 100, 94549.
Telephone: 925-283-1599.
Facsimile: 925-283-5847. Email: GMF-CA@MSN.com

PARTNERS

Samuel C. Alhadeff
Robert D. Rose
Jerry M. Cannon
Keith R. Solar
Robert J. Parks
Philip D. Oberhansley (Resident, Temecula, California Office)
Joseph L. Marshall
Leslie C. Detwiler
Glenn M. Feeley (Resident, Lafayette, California Office)
Thomas T. Lord
Madeline Clark Cahill
John L. O'Donnell, Jr. (Resident, Los Angeles, California Office)

OF COUNSEL

Craig S. Engstrand
Robert K. Edmunds
Charles F. Gorder, Sr.

ASSOCIATES

Michael J. Barry
Richard James Bayless
Craig V. Butler
Cyril J. Dantchev
Genie Harrison
S. Douglas Kerner
Frank J. Polek
Les W. Robertson
Traci M. Selby
Marjeta Duzevic Six

For full biographical listings, see the Martindale-Hubbell Law Directory

BACALSKI, BYRNE & KOSKA (AV)

A Partnership including a Professional Corporation
24th Floor, Emerald Plaza 402 West Broadway, 92101
Telephone: 619-239-4340
Fax: 619-239-0116
Email: lawbbk@lawbbk.com

A. Daniel Bacalski Jr. (A Professional Corporation)
Margaret M. Byrne
William K. Koska
Richard R. Roy
David P. Ramirez
Andrew J. Marton
Susie J. Kater

Kerry F. Kawamura
Christopher John Workman
David B. Monks
Matthew J. Evans
Wendy L. Tucker
Christopher S. Trunzo
Stephen M. Lerner

Representative Clients: California State University System; AIG; Unigard Insurance Company; Ward North American, Inc.; Wassau/Nationwide Insurance Companies; Peninsula Beverly Hills; Medline; Southern California Water Company; Sunbeam Household Products; Ranger Insurance.

For full biographical listings, see the Martindale-Hubbell Law Directory

JOSEPH J. BARR, JR. A PROFESSIONAL CORPORATION (AV)

501 West Broadway, Suite 2080, 92101
Telephone: 619-235-0444
Facsimile: 619-235-0650

Joseph J. Barr, Jr.
Gary L. Ritchie
Dennis S. O'Neill

For full biographical listings, see the Martindale-Hubbell Law Directory

BUTZ DUNN DESANTIS & BINGHAM, A PROFESSIONAL CORPORATION (AV)

101 West Broadway, Suite 1700, 92101
Telephone: 619-233-4777
Fax: 619-231-0341
URL: http://www.butzdunn.com
Irvine (Orange County) California Office: 19800 MacArthur Boulevard, Suite 300, 92612.
Telephone: 949-757-4135.
Fax: 949-724-4566.

Douglas M. Butz
K. Elizabeth Dunn
Kevin V. DeSantis
Roger P. Bingham

Alan D. Leeth
Jerri Ryan Kent
Steven C. Uribe
Brett M. Weaver

OF COUNSEL

J. Lawrence Irving

For full biographical listings, see the Martindale-Hubbell Law Directory

CASEY, GERRY, REED & SCHENK (AV)

110 Laurel Street, 92101
Telephone: 619-238-1811
Fax: 619-544-9232
Email: cglaw@cglaw.com *URL:* http://www.CGlaw.com

(See Next Column)

CASEY, GERRY, REED & SCHENK—*Continued*

MEMBERS OF FIRM

David S. Casey
Richard F. Gerry
Scott C. Cummins
David S. Casey, Jr.
T. Michael Reed
Frederick Schenk
Robert J. Francavilla
Gayle Meryl Blatt
Thomas D. Penfield
Michael P. Montgomery
Suzanne C. Etpison
Bonnie E. Kane
Thomas Luneau

Reference: San Diego National Bank.

For full biographical listings, see the Martindale-Hubbell Law Directory

CHAPIN SHEA MCNITT & CARTER, A PROFESSIONAL CORPORATION (AV)

Library, 501 West Broadway, 15th Floor, 92101
Telephone: 619-232-4261
Telefax: 619-232-4840
Email: info@chapinlaw.com *URL:* http://www.chapinlaw.com
Los Angeles, California Office: 12424 Wilshire Boulevard, 9th Floor, 90025.
Telephone: 310-826-0133.
Telefax: 310-207-4236.

Dave Carothers
Edward D. Chapin
Shirley A. Gauvin
Aaron H. Katz
Andrew G. Loeb
Earl H. Maas III
Roger L. McNitt
Steven A. Micheli
Maria C. Roberts
Lawrence W. Shea, II
Nancy L. Vaughan
Peter C. Ward

COUNSEL

Daniel P. Groszkruger
Arthur W. Jones
Thomas P. Redick

Brian A. Barnhorst
Christina A. Bernstein
Kelli Jean Brooks
Jeffery L. Caufield
Daniel W. Coffey
Amy K. Cressey-Yates
Daniel J. Curran
Glen F. Dorgan
Natasha L. Drew
Jeffrey S. Eddington
Patrick M. Howe
Bruno W. Katz
Brian Maienschein
Peter B. Maretz
Carmen M. Mosier McCormick
Jeffrey K. Miyamoto
Leticia Olivarez
Mark T. Petersen
James H. Prenton
Amanda M. Rowe
Patricia L. Sullivan
Brandy Thompson-Cody
Heather K. Van Blarcom

LOS ANGELES OFFICE

Craig H. Bell
John J. Calvagna
Richard D. Carter
Robert Ehrenreich
Leslie J. Eng
Tina Fisher
Ronald F. Gari
Neil R. Gunny
Daniel S. Imber
Shaun Dabby Jacobs
Robin James
Dana Marie Lawson
Jeffrey J. Leist
David A. Myers
Charles F. Peterson
Steven J. Renshaw
Mark Schaeffer
Mark M. Senior
Erin C. Slape
Howard J. Smith
Jeffrey C. Stodel
Stephen Z. Vegh
Irwin Waldman (A P.C.)

For full biographical listings, see the Martindale-Hubbell Law Directory

DETISCH & CHRISTENSEN (AV)

444 West C Street, Suite 200, 92101
Telephone: 619-236-9343
Fax: 619-236-8307
Email: dclaw@adnc.com

MEMBERS OF FIRM

Charles B. Christensen
Donald W. Detisch

ASSOCIATES

Sean D. Schwerdtfeger
Carl E. Sizemore
John Frederick Smith

OF COUNSEL

Harold O. Valderhaug

For full biographical listings, see the Martindale-Hubbell Law Directory

DUCKOR SPRADLING & METZGER, A LAW CORPORATION (AV)

401 West A Street, Suite 2400, 92101-7909
Telephone: 619-231-3666
Telecopier: 619-231-6629
Email: dsm@dsm-law.com *URL:* http://www.dsm-law.com

(See Next Column)

Michael J. Duckor
Gary J. Spradling
Scott L. Metzger
John C. Wynne
John W. Cutchin
Robert L. Kenny
Li-An C. Leonard
Stephen A. Bond
R. Anthony Mahavier
Robin Assaf Wofford
K. Jill Osmars
Stephen A. Colley
Kevin M. Bagley
Robert J. Solis
John J. Freni

Jamie M. Ryan
Pamela LaBruyere
James B. Ryan
Gregory P. Olson
Robert M. Shaughnessy
Michael W. Vivoli
Matthew O. Osborne
Scott R. Omohundro
Michael A. Reed

Representative Clients: E & J Gallo Wineries; McMillen Communities; Sedgwick James International; Siemens Credit Corp.; Transamerica Financial Services; Van Camp Seafood Co.; Western Energy Management; Watt Industries; City of San Diego; Chicago Title Ins. Co.

For full biographical listings, see the Martindale-Hubbell Law Directory

EDWARDS, SOOY & BYRON, A PROFESSIONAL CORPORATION (AV)

101 West Broadway, Ninth Floor, 92101
Telephone: 619-231-1500
Fax: 619-231-1588
URL: http://www.esb-legal.com
Las Vegas, Nevada Office: 3960 Howard Hughes Parkway, Fifth Floor, 89109.
Telephone: 702-474-6677.
Fax: 702-474-4538.

Michael M. Edwards
Richard R. Sooy
Thomas W. Byron
Glen M. Rasmussen
William P. Harris, III

Michael M. Edwards, Jr.
Alfred Paul Centofanti, III
Napoleon L.D. Taylor
Valerie L. McLaughlin
Jeffrey T. Brei
Douglas J. Suits
Jesse J.M. Blyth
Demetri D. Lahanas
Kathryn M. Loock
David A. Rentto
Scott B. Hilberg
Bart M. Blechschmidt
John K. Schlichting
J. Scott Schaller

OF COUNSEL

Stanley J. Wezelman

For full biographical listings, see the Martindale-Hubbell Law Directory

ESTES, HOYT & HANSEN, A PROFESSIONAL CORPORATION (AV)

Suite 1300, 1010 Second Avenue, 92101
Telephone: 619-234-2111
Fax: 619-234-1509

Kevin J. Hoyt
Bernard M. Hansen

OF COUNSEL

Joel C. Estes

For full biographical listings, see the Martindale-Hubbell Law Directory

FERRIS & BRITTON, A PROFESSIONAL CORPORATION (AV)

1600 First National Bank Center, 401 West A Street, 92101
Telephone: 619-233-3131
Fax: 619-232-9316
Email: manager@ferrisbritton.com *URL:* http://www.ferrisbritton.com

Christopher Q. Britton
Steven J. Pynes
Michael R. Weinstein

Representative Clients: Agouron Pharmaceuticals, Inc.; Allstate Insurance Co.; Cox Communications, Inc.; Datel, Inc.; Enterprise Rent-a-Car; Exxon; Frontier Analytics, Inc.; Peninsula Bank; Teleport Communications Group; Southwest Airlines.

For Complete List of Firm Personnel, See General Section

For full biographical listings, see the Martindale-Hubbell Law Directory

FISCH, SPIEGLER, GINSBURG, LADNER & ATTARIAN, A PROFESSIONAL LAW CORPORATION (AV)

1551 Fourth Avenue, Suite 300, 92101-3184
Telephone: 619-234-1551
Telecopier: 619-234-1568
Email: FSGLA@AOL.com

Joseph J. Fisch
Mark A. Spiegler
Phillip L. Ginsburg
Karen M. Ladner
Peter J. Attarian, Jr.

For full biographical listings, see the Martindale-Hubbell Law Directory

San Diego—Continued

HAASIS & GOODIN (AV)

101 West Broadway, Suite 1700, 92101
Telephone: 619-236-9933
Fax: 619-236-8961
Email: njgoodin@home.com *URL:* http://www.lawyers.com/haasis&goodin

Steven R. Haasis

OF COUNSEL

Nelson J. Goodin

For full biographical listings, see the Martindale-Hubbell Law Directory

HAIGHT, BROWN & BONESTEEL, L.L.P. (AV)

A Partnership including Professional Corporations
101 West Broadway, Suite 1000, 92101-3544
Telephone: 619-595-5583
Telecopier: 619-595-7873
URL: http://www.hbblaw.com
Santa Monica, California Office: 1620 26th Street, Suite 4000 North, P.O. Box 680.
Telephone: 310-449-6000.
Telecopier: 310-829-5117.
Telex: 705837.
Santa Ana, California Office: Suite 900, 5 Hutton Centre Drive.
Telephone: 714-754-1100.
Telecopier: 714-754-0826.
Riverside, California Office: California Tower, 3737 Main Street, Suite 800.
Telephone: 909-341-8300.
Fax: 909-341-8309.
San Francisco, California Office: 101 Bush Street, 27th Floor.
Telephone: 415-986-7700.
Fax: 415-986-6945.

RESIDENT MEMBERS

Robert V. Closson
George R. Gonzalez
Terrell A. Quealy
DeAnn M. Salcido
Richard R. Castillo

RESIDENT ASSOCIATES

Scott M. Bonesteel
Siobhan A. Cullen
Jodi E. Lambert

OF COUNSEL

David E. Lundin

For full biographical listings, see the Martindale-Hubbell Law Directory

HIGGS, FLETCHER & MACK LLP (AV)

2000 First National Bank Building, 401 West "A" Street, Suite 2600, 92101
Telephone: 619-236-1551
Telecopier: 619-696-1410
Email: info@higgslaw.com

MEMBERS OF FIRM

Henry Pitts Mack (1909-1974)
Joe N. Turner
Craig D. Higgs
Harry L. Carter
Michael F. Boyle
John Morris
John L. Morrell
David R. Clark
M. Cory Brown
Patricia P. Hollenbeck
James M. Peterson
Susan Moriarty Hack
Peter S. Doody
Daniel C. Herbert
Phillip C. Samouris

OF COUNSEL

Ferdinand T. Fletcher

SPECIAL COUNSEL

James E. Fox

ASSOCIATES

Liong Lie Gan Penfield
Michael T. Quinn

For Complete List of Firm Personnel, See General Section

For full biographical listings, see the Martindale-Hubbell Law Directory

HOVEY & KIRBY, A PROFESSIONAL CORPORATION (AV)

402 West Broadway, Suite 1500, 92101
Telephone: 619-685-4000
Fax: 619-685-4004
Email: administrator@hoveylaw.com

Gregg B. Hovey
Dean T. Kirby, Jr.
Geraldine A. Valdez

For full biographical listings, see the Martindale-Hubbell Law Directory

JOHNSON & EDWARDS LLP (AV)

A Registered Limited Liability Partnership including a Professional Corporation
402 W. Broadway, Suite 1140, 92101-8513
Telephone: 619-696-6211
Fax: 619-696-7516
Sacramento, California Office: 1006 4th Street, 6th Floor, 95814.
Telephone: 916-492-0435.
Fax: 916-492-0530.

MEMBERS OF FIRM

Kevin K. Johnson (A Professional Law Corporation)
John E. Edwards

ASSOCIATES

David D. Cross
Jared P. Hanson
Heidi E. Brown
Jeanne L. MacKinnon

OF COUNSEL

Daniel B. McCarthy

For full biographical listings, see the Martindale-Hubbell Law Directory

KENNERSON SCHWARTZ SEMERDJIAN & HAILE LLP (AV)

A Limited Liability Partnership
101 West Broadway, Suite 810, 92101
Telephone: 619-236-8821
Facsimile: 619-236-8827
URL: http://www.lawyers.com/ksshlaw

OF COUNSEL

Paul R. Kennerson

MEMBERS OF FIRM

Ross J. Schwartz
Dick A. Semerdjian
Jeffrey A. Haile

James R. Ballard
John K. Grant

For full biographical listings, see the Martindale-Hubbell Law Directory

KLINEDINST, FLIEHMAN & MCKILLOP, A PROFESSIONAL CORPORATION (AV)

The Koll Center, 501 West Broadway, Suite 600, 92101-3584
Telephone: 619-239-8131
Fax: 619-238-8707
URL: http://www.kfmlaw.com
Orange County Office: Civic Center Law Building, 611 Civic Center Drive, Suite 250, Santa Ana, California, 92701.
Telephone: 714-542-1800.
Los Angeles, California Office: Wells Fargo Center, 333 South Grand Avenue, 33rd Floor, 90071.
Telephone: 213-625-8100.

SHAREHOLDERS

John D. Klinedinst
Donald R. McKillop, Sr.
G. William (Bill) Van De Weghe, Jr.
Thomas S. Ingrassia
Douglas A. Pettit
Gregory A. Garbacz
Arthur S. Moreau, III

Kendra J. Hall
Andrew N. Kohn
M. Shawn Payment
Kurt U. Campbell
G. Dale Britton
Susan S. Kohn
Heather L. Rosing
Debora A. Cappucci
Dayna Lyn Chmelka
Jennifer N. Lehman
Dennis C. Crovella
Carey L. Cooper
Kevin J. Gramling

PARALEGALS

Mary Ann Murphy-Brown
Cam B. Picano

Reference: Bank of America.

For full biographical listings, see the Martindale-Hubbell Law Directory

LEVINE, STEINBERG & MILLER (AV)

550 West C Street, Suite 1810, 92101-8596
Telephone: 619-231-9449
Telecopier: 619-231-8638

MEMBERS OF FIRM

Harvey R. Levine
Harris I. Steinberg
Craig A. Miller
Jordan M. Cohen
Richard A. Huver

For full biographical listings, see the Martindale-Hubbell Law Directory

LINDLEY, SCALES & CORBETT, A PROFESSIONAL CORPORATION (AV)

550 West C Street, Suite 1800, 92101
Telephone: 619-234-9181
Fax: 619-234-8475
Email: lsc@adnc.com

(See Next Column)

LINDLEY, SCALES & CORBETT A PROFESSIONAL CORPORATION—*Continued*

Luke R. Corbett
Robert M. McLeod

Representative Clients: Palomar Savings & Loan Association; Chicago Title Insurance Company.

For full biographical listings, see the Martindale-Hubbell Law Directory

MCCLELLAN & BROWN, A PROFESSIONAL CORPORATION (AV)

1144 State Street, 92101
Telephone: 619-231-0505
Fax: 619-544-0540
Email: mcclellan9@aol.com *URL:* http://www.lawyers.com/mcclellan&brown

Craig R. McClellan
LaMar B. Brown

For full biographical listings, see the Martindale-Hubbell Law Directory

MOWER, KOELLER, NEBEKER, CARLSON & HALUCK, LLP (AV)

225 Broadway, 21st Floor, 92101
Telephone: 619-233-1600
Fax: 619-236-0527
Email: infoir@mknch.com
Irvine, California Office: 108 Pacifica, P.O. Box 19799.
Telephone: 714-753-1229.
Fax: 714-753-1413.
San Bernardino, California Office: 412 West Hospitality Lane, Suite 300, 92408.
Telephone: 909-381-3334.
Fax: 909-889-2007.
Yuma, Arizona Office: P.O. Box 10969, 85366.
Telephone: 520-782-2531.
Phoenix, Arizona Office: 3200 North Central Avenue, Suite 2300, 85012-2443.
Telephone: 602-256-0000.
Fax: 602-256-2488.

MEMBERS OF FIRM

Robert C. Carlson (Resident)
Christopher J. Hallman
Megan K. Dorsey

Michael J. Kielty
Martha J. Dorsey
Robert N. Clark
Laura Ellen Barton
Anna Tomalino Amundson
Sharon A. Huerta
Jay M. Bulger

For full biographical listings, see the Martindale-Hubbell Law Directory

OLINS, FOERSTER & HAYES (AV)

A Legal Liability Partnership including A Professional Corporation
2214 Second Avenue, 92101
Telephone: 619-238-1601
Fax: 619-238-1613
URL: http://www.ofh.com
Santa Ana, California Office: 1314 West Fifth Street, Suite C, 92703.
Telephone: 714-836-9777.
Fax: 714-954-1156.

MEMBERS OF FIRM

Douglas F. Olins
Barrett J. Foerster (A P.C.)
Dennis J. Hayes

ASSOCIATES

Laura H. Miller
Barbara J. Ginsberg
John C. Zucconi
(Resident, Santa Ana Office)

Representative Clients: Association of Orange County Deputy Sheriffs; Riverside Sheriffs' Assn.; Sacramento County Deputy Sheriffs' Assn.; United Food & Commercial Workers International Union, AFL-CIO; United Food & Commercial Workers, Local 1428; Santa Ana Firemen's Benevolent Assn.; Chula Vista Firefighters Assn.; American Postal Workers Union.

For full biographical listings, see the Martindale-Hubbell Law Directory

THE PAGE FIRM, A P.C. (AV)

401 B Street, Suite 2100, 92101-4244
Telephone: 619-231-1822
Fax: 619-231-1877
URL: http://www.lawyers.com/pagefirm

Richard W. Page

For full biographical listings, see the Martindale-Hubbell Law Directory

POST KIRBY NOONAN & SWEAT LLP (AV)

A Partnership including Professional Corporations
America Plaza 600 West Broadway 11th Floor, 92101
Telephone: 619-231-8666
FAX: 619-231-9593;
619-231-4360
Email: PKNS@PKNS.com

(See Next Column)

MEMBERS OF FIRM

Gregory A. Post
David B. Oberholtzer
Michael L. Kirby (A P.C.)
Charles T. Hoge
David J. Noonan
James R. Lance
Richard W. Sweat
Steven W. Sanchez
R. Bruce Wayne (A P.C.)
Theresa M. Brehl
Thomas W. Bettles
Jeffrey P. Lendrum
Kristen T. Bruesehoff

For full biographical listings, see the Martindale-Hubbell Law Directory

ROBBINS & KEEHN, A PROFESSIONAL CORPORATION (AV)

530 "B" Street, 24th Floor, 92101
Telephone: 619-232-1700
Telecopier: 619-544-9095

Arlington Ray Robbins
John H. Stephens
L. Scott Keehn
Charles F. Robbins
Michael V. Pundeff
Lynn Marie Beekman
Andrew J. Liska

Lisa L. Keehn

Reference: Union Bank.

For full biographical listings, see the Martindale-Hubbell Law Directory

ROSS, DIXON & BELL, L.L.P. (AV)

Suite 400, 550 West "B" Street, 92101-3599
Telephone: 619-235-4040
Fax: 619-231-8796
Email: info@rdblaw.com *URL:* http://www.rdblaw.com
Washington, D.C. Office: 601 Pennsylvania Avenue, N.W., North Building, 20004-2688.
Telephone: 202-662-2000.
Fax: 202-662-2190.
Irvine, California Office: 5 Park Plaza, Suite 1200, 92614.
Telephone: 949-622-2700.
Fax: 949-622-2739.

PARTNERS

Roy Morrow Bell
Terrence R. McInnis
Van E. Haynie
Fletcher W. Paddison
Timothy P. Irving
Robert M. Pozin
Sharon T. Maier
Van A. Tengberg

ASSOCIATES

Christopher P. "Hawk" Barry
Glenn Fuller
James J. Dalessio
James W. Stubblefield
Rexford P. Edwards
Michael J. Whitton
Tina M. Fryar
Carol L. Young
(Not admitted in CA)

OF COUNSEL

James T. Waring

For full biographical listings, see the Martindale-Hubbell Law Directory

SELDEN LAW FIRM (AV)

1230 Columbia Street, Suite 1060, 92101
Telephone: 619-515-1111
Facsimile: 619-515-1114
Email: lseldenii@aol.com
Las Vegas, Nevada Office: Selden, Lynch & Hopper, 501 South Rancho Drive, Suite C-12, 89106.
Telephone: 702-315-1115.
Facsimile: 702-315-1114.

Lynde Selden, II

For full biographical listings, see the Martindale-Hubbell Law Directory

SELTZER CAPLAN MCMAHON & VITEK, A PROFESSIONAL CORPORATION (AV)

2100 Symphony Towers, 750 B Street, 92101
Telephone: 619-685-3003
Fax: 619-685-3100
URL: http://www.scwm.com

Gerald L. McMahon
Neal P. Panish
Reginald A. Vitek
Vera P. Pardee
Julie P. Dubick
Michael R. Seyle
Joyce A. McCoy
David J. Zubkoff
Dennis J. Wickham
John D. Hershberger
James P. Delphey
Gregory E. Flynn
Craig E. Courter
Michael A. Leone
Michael G. Nardi
Daniel A. Andrist
J. Scott Scheper

(See Next Column)

SELTZER CAPLAN MCMAHON & VITEK A PROFESSIONAL CORPORATION, *San Diego—Continued*

Elisa A. Brandes
Kelly Rae Waggonner
Lee E. Hejmanowski
Christine M. Dabrowski
Christopher J. Weaver
Laura H. Roppe
Scott W. Sigman
Daniel E. Eaton
Jennifer L. Hardy
Marnie S. Skeen
Romy A. Selati
David M. Greeley
Troy A. Kingshaven
Charles B. Witham
William K. Browning

STAFF ATTORNEY

John M. Toscano (Not admitted in CA)

OF COUNSEL

Julie Genthner Lopez
Patricia Garcia
Kathleen Furness

Representative Clients: Chicago Title; The Goodyear Tire & Rubber Co.; W.R. Grace & Co.—Conn.; McDonnell-Douglas Corp.; McMillin Communities; Western Financial Savings Bank.

For Complete List of Firm Personnel, See General Section

For full biographical listings, see the Martindale-Hubbell Law Directory

SOLOMON WARD SEIDENWURM & SMITH, LLP (AV)

1200 Wells Fargo Plaza, 401 B Street, 92101
Telephone: 619-231-0303
Telecopier: 619-231-4755
Email: mvafi@swsslaw.com *URL:* http://www.swsslaw.com

PARTNERS OF FIRM

Michael D. Breslauer
Cynthia L. Eldred
Lawrence J. Kaplan (P.C.)
Richard E. McCarthy
Edward J. McIntyre
Paul S. Metsch
Alison L. Pivonka
Harry J. Proctor (P.C.)
Jeffrey A. Schneider
Richard L. Seidenwurm (P.C.)
Jeffrey H. Silberman
Miguel A. Smith
Norman L. Smith
Herbert J. Solomon

ASSOCIATES

Daniel E. Gardenswartz
David T. Gluck
Amy Perkins Melden
Karl A. Sandoval
Kurt E. Scheuerman
Elizabeth A. Trevino

OF COUNSEL

Robert F. La Scala
William O. Ward, III (Retired)

For full biographical listings, see the Martindale-Hubbell Law Directory

STUTZ, GALLAGHER, ARTIANO, SHINOFF & HOLTZ, A PROFESSIONAL CORPORATION (AV)

15th Floor, First National Bank Building, 401 West "A" Street, 92101-7906
Telephone: 619-232-3122
Fax: 619-232-3264
Email: info@stutzlawfirm.com
Temecula, California Office: 41593 Winchester Road Suite 101, 92590-3611.
Telephone: 909-699-1231.
Fax: 909-699-1261.
Los Angeles, California Office: 660 South Figueroa Street, Suite 2129, 90017-3442.
Telephone: 213-489-1131.
Fax: 213-489-5620.
Irvine, California Office: 19800 MacArthur Boulevard, Suite 514, 92612.
Telephone: 949-757-4174.
Fax: 949-757-4176.

Robert E. Gallagher, Jr.
Ray J. Artiano
Daniel R. Shinoff
James F. Holtz
Lesa Wilson
Robert R. Templeton, Jr. (Resident, Irvine Office)
Christopher J. Welsh
Robert B. Titus
Jack M. Sleeth, Jr.
Jeffery A. Morris
Bret W. Eubank (Resident, Temecula Office)

Mary Ellen M. Nosel (Resident, Temecula Office)
Thomas R. Kelleher
James P. Thompson (Resident, Los Angeles Office)
Ian G. Williamson
Paul V. Carelli, IV
Gil Abed
Matthew W. Nelson (Resident, Temecula Office)
Hashem Karoum
Christopher K. Teng (Resident, Temecula Office)
William J. Collier

OF COUNSEL

Sidney A. Stutz

For full biographical listings, see the Martindale-Hubbell Law Directory

SULLIVAN HILL LEWIN REZ & ENGEL, A PROFESSIONAL LAW CORPORATION (AV)

550 West C Street, Suite 1500, 92101-3540
Telephone: 619-233-4100
Rapifax: 619-231-4372
Email: shlaw@shlaw.com *URL:* http://www.shlaw.com/shlaw/

James P. Hill
Jeffrey D. Lewin
Donald G. Rez
John R. Engel
Brian L. Burchett
Robert J. Brown
Candace M. Carroll
Russell S. Schwartzman

OF COUNSEL

Jim Sullivan
Keith E. McWilliams
John R. Heisner

K. Todd Curry
Cynthia A. Fissel
Kit J. Gardner
Barton L. Jacka
Raul Cadena
Rosemarie Coakley
Sylvia L. Depta (Not admitted in CA)
Robert D. Richley (Not admitted in CA)

For full biographical listings, see the Martindale-Hubbell Law Directory

THORSNES, BARTOLOTTA, MCGUIRE & PADILLA (AV)

A Partnership including Professional Corporations
Fifth Avenue Financial Center, 11th Floor, 2550 Fifth Avenue, 92103
Telephone: 619-236-9363
Fax: 619-236-9653
Email: TBMPmail@TBMP.com *URL:* http://www.tbmp.com

Michael T. Thorsnes (A.P.C., P.C.)
Vincent J. Bartolotta, Jr., (P.C.)
John F. McGuire (P.C.)
Kevin F. Quinn (P.C.)
C. Brant Noziska (P.C.)
Mitchell S. Golub (P.C.)
Palma Cesar Hooper (P.C.)
Neal H. Rockwood (P.C.)
Daral B. Mazzarella (P.C.)
R. Christian Hulburt (P.C.)

ASSOCIATES

Catherine A. Richardson
Jodi L. Hautaluoma
Douglas J. Billings
Scott A. Kennedy
Dori K. Rybacki
James T. Atkins
Leo Bartolotta
Jill E. Cleary
James B. Drimmer
Timothy J. Tatro

OF COUNSEL

Robert S. Kennedy

For full biographical listings, see the Martindale-Hubbell Law Directory

LAW OFFICES OF MAURILE C. TREMBLAY A PROFESSIONAL CORPORATION (AV)

4370 La Jolla Village Drive, Suite 675, 92122-1252
Telephone: 858-558-3030
Fax: 858-558-2502
Email: lawmct@aol.com *URL:* http://www.lawyers.com/mauriletremblay

Maurile C. Tremblay

Lana Hanisko-Greenberg

For full biographical listings, see the Martindale-Hubbell Law Directory

ROBERT F. VAAGE (AV)

110 West "C" Street, Suite 2105, 92101
Telephone: 619-338-0505
Fax: 619-338-0588
Email: rfvaage@aol.com *URL:* http://www.lawyers.com/vaagelaw

ASSOCIATE

Debra A. Morse

For full biographical listings, see the Martindale-Hubbell Law Directory

WALTERS FRAZIER CAIETTI RUTAN & LOPEZ, LLP (AV)

701 B Street, Suite 300, 92101
Telephone: 619-233-6600
Fax: 619-544-7477
Email: sflop@aol.com

MEMBERS OF FIRM

Carolyn M. Caietti (Emme)
Ronald F. Frazier
Stephen F. Lopez
Kenneth A. Rutan
Douglas F. Walters
Karen D. Wood

Lauren L. Derstine
Susan D. Gauthier

For full biographical listings, see the Martindale-Hubbell Law Directory

San Diego—Continued

WILSON, PETTY, KOSMO & TURNER LLP (AV)

Attorneys At Law
550 West "C" Street, Suite 1050, 92101-3532
Telephone: 619-236-9600
Facsimile: 619-236-9669
Email: wpkt@wpkt.com

Claudette G. Wilson
Regina A. Petty
Vickie E. Turner
Frederick W. Kosmo, Jr.
Lois M. Kosch

ASSOCIATES

Thomas W. Tierney
Michael S. Kalt
Meryl C. Maneker
Aaron A. Buckley
Robert Shields

OF COUNSEL

Theresa Osterman Stevenson

Representative Clients: Blockbuster Inc.; Ericsson, Inc.; Ford Motor Company; Johnson & Johnson; Mail Boxes Etc. USA, Inc.; Sun Microsystems; Toyota Motor Sales, U.S.A., Inc.; Union Bank of California; University of California Board of Regents; The Vons Companies, Inc.

For full biographical listings, see the Martindale-Hubbell Law Directory

WINGERT GREBING BRUBAKER & RYAN LLP (AV)

A Limited Liability Partnership including Professional Corporations
One America Plaza, Seventh Floor, 600 West Broadway, 92101
Telephone: 619-232-8151
Facsimile: 619-232-4665
URL: http://www.wgbrlaw.com
Las Vegas, Nevada Office: Ryan Marks Johnson & Todd, 1120 Town Center Drive, Suite 200, 89144.
Telephone: 702-341-7870.
Fax: 702-341-8049.

MEMBERS OF FIRM

Charles R. Grebing (A Professional Corporation)
Alan K. Brubaker (A Professional Corporation)
Norman A. Ryan
James Goodwin
Shawn D. Morris
Robert M. Juskie
Dan H. Deuprey
Robert M. Caietti
Eileen Mulligan Marks
Christopher W. Todd
Robert L. Johnson
John S. Addams
Michael Sullivan
James J. Brown, Jr.
Terie M. Theis
Craig Gross

ASSOCIATES

Stephen C. Grebing
Brian P. Worthington
Marco B. Mercaldo
Solveig Store Deuprey
Kimberly Diane Howatt
Jay A. Kenyon
T. Steven Gregor
Jana M. Beck
Brad Lovelace

OF COUNSEL

William L. Todd, Jr.
John R. Wingert (A Professional Corporation)

LEGAL SUPPORT PERSONNEL

Carol C. Berry

Representative Clients: Angelic Entertainment; Becton Dickinson; Brookfield Homes Pacific Inc.; California Casualty; Columbia/HCI; Cooper. of Amer. Physicians; Concan Davidson Homes; Discover R. Insurance; Farmers Insurance; Guaranty National.

For full biographical listings, see the Martindale-Hubbell Law Directory

*SAN FRANCISCO,** San Francisco Co.

ALDEN ARONOVSKY & SAX LLP (AV)

235 Montgomery Street, 28th Floor, 94104-2902
Telephone: 415-732-5820
Facsimile: 415-732-5840
Email: law@aaslaw.com

MEMBERS OF FIRM

David W. Alden
Ronald G. Aronovsky
Brian M. Sax (1945-1997)

ASSOCIATES

Jeffrey S. Koppelmaa
Sherry A. Glassman

For full biographical listings, see the Martindale-Hubbell Law Directory

ALPER & McCULLOCH (AV)

425 California Street, 18th Floor, 94104-2203
Telephone: 415-434-8744
Facsimile: 415-434-3450
Email: alpermc@pacbell.net *URL:* http://www.lawyers.com/a&mlaw

Dean A. Alper

OF COUNSEL

Tracy Beggs McCulloch

For full biographical listings, see the Martindale-Hubbell Law Directory

BARTKO, ZANKEL, TARRANT & MILLER, PROFESSIONAL CORPORATION (AV)

900 Front Street, Suite 300, 94111-1427
Telephone: 415-956-1900
Fax: 415-956-1152
Email: bztm@bztm.com *URL:* http://www.bztm.com

John J. Bartko
Martin I. Zankel
Richard T. Tarrant
Charles G. Miller
Robert H. Bunzel
Michael D. Welch
Michael D. Abraham
M. Manuel Fishman
Christopher J. Hunt
John S. Lottier
Theani Christine Louskos
Howard L. Pearlman
C. Griffith Towle
Glenn P. Zwang
Christopher D. Sullivan

Thomas E. Cooper
Gail E. Kavanagh
Brenda M. Lillington
Tyler Roberts Meade
Rosanna S. Russell
Carissa Shubb
Russell G. Young

COUNSEL

Thomas A. Lee, Jr.
Darryl A. Hart

For full biographical listings, see the Martindale-Hubbell Law Directory

BIANCO & MURPHY (AV)

500 Sansome Street, 8th Floor, 94111
Telephone: 415-362-3344
Telecopier: 415-986-5271
Email: LAWRLB@AOL.COM

MEMBERS OF FIRM

Robert L. Bianco
Stephen M. Murphy

ASSOCIATES

Gregory O. Bianco
Christopher M. Windle

For full biographical listings, see the Martindale-Hubbell Law Directory

ROBERT D. CARROW (AV)

One Embarcadero Center, Suite 880, 94111
Telephone: 415-981-1691
Telecopier: 415-492-8419
Telex: 470562 LAW UI
Cable Address: "JURIS"
Email: robert@carrow.com *URL:* http://www.carrow.com/
London, England Chambers: 33 Bedford Row, WC1.
Telephone: +0171 242-6476.
Telecopier: +0171 831-6065.
San Rafael, California Office: 7 Mount Lassen Drive, Suite C134. 94903.
Telephone: 415-492-1225.
Telecopier: 415-492-8419.
(Also of Counsel to Goldstein & Musto, A Professional Corporation)

For full biographical listings, see the Martindale-Hubbell Law Directory

COX & MOYER, A PROFESSIONAL CORPORATION (AV)

703 Market Street, Suite 1800, 94103
Telephone: 415-543-9464
Fax: 415-777-1828
Email: coxmoyer@aol.com

Ingemar E. Hoberg (1903-1971)
John H. Finger (1913-1991)
Phillip E. Brown (Retired)
Stephen T. Cox
David W. Moyer

Scott J. Allen

OF COUNSEL

Kenneth W. Rosenthal

For full biographical listings, see the Martindale-Hubbell Law Directory

CYRIL & CROWLEY LLP (AV)

17th Floor, 456 Montgomery Street, 94104-1233
Telephone: 415-989-1100
Facsimile: 415-421-6651
Email: candc@ix.netcom.com

MEMBERS OF FIRM

John W. Crowley
Robert B. Stringer
Michael W. Field
Carol P. Rohwer
Wendy J. Hannum

OF COUNSEL

Paul H. Cyril (A Professional Corporation)

Mark D. Fenske
Jason T. Shafron

For full biographical listings, see the Martindale-Hubbell Law Directory

San Francisco—Continued

DRATH, CLIFFORD, MURPHY, WENNERHOLM & HAGEN, A PROFESSIONAL CORPORATION (AV)

44 Montgomery Street, Suite 1500, 94104
Telephone: 415-392-3006
Telefax: 415-391-3348
Email: dcmwh@msn.com
San Diego, California Office: 600 B Street, Suite 1550.
Telephone: 619-595-3060.
Fax: 619-595-3066.

John M. Drath
Rick J. Murphy
Traci E. Wennerholm
David F. Beach
Laura M. Sagmeister
Ilene M. Isert-Kott
Gretchen W. Latimer
Dennis E. Raglin
Alan E. Lacy

OF COUNSEL

Frederick Mahan

For full biographical listings, see the Martindale-Hubbell Law Directory

ELLMAN, BURKE, HOFFMAN & JOHNSON, A PROFESSIONAL CORPORATION (AV)

One Ecker, Suite 200, 94105
Telephone: 415-777-2727
Fax: 415-495-7587
Email: managingdirector@ellman-burke.com *URL:* http://www.ellman-burke.com

Howard N. Ellman
Michael J. Burke
Kenneth N. Burns
John D. Hoffman
Jeffrey W. Johnson
Thomas Paine
Jay L. Paxton
Thomas M. Sherwood
Leslie M. Browne
Jodi Billehus Fedor

JoAnne L. Dunec
Sarah Richards Gansa
Christina W. Chi

For full biographical listings, see the Martindale-Hubbell Law Directory

RAYMOND N. STELLA ERLACH (AV)

One Maritime Plaza, Fourth Floor, 94111
Telephone: 415-788-3322
Fax: 415-788-8613

OF COUNSEL

Gregory J. Erlach
Stephen Peter U. Erlach

Reference: Bank of America Private Banking, San Francisco, California.

For full biographical listings, see the Martindale-Hubbell Law Directory

FLYNN, DELICH & WISE (AV)

One California Street, Suite 350, 94111
Telephone: 415-693-5566
Fax: 415-693-0410
Email: SamD@fdw-law.com
Long Beach, California Office: 1 World Trade Center, Suite 1800.
Telephone: 562-435-2626.
Fax: 562-437-7555. Email: NicholasP@FDW-LAW.COM.

John A. Flynn (1945-1997)
Sam D. Delich
James B. Nebel

OF COUNSEL

Pecos Bill Field

Faye Lee Peterson
Conte C. Cicala
Jeanine S. Tede

Representative Clients: American Hawaii Cruises; American President Lines; Through Transport Mutual Insurance Association, Ltd.; The Britannia Steam Ship Insurance Association Limited; The Steamship Mutual Underwriting Association (Bermuda) Ltd.; General Steamship Corp., Ltd.; Commodore Cruise Line, Ltd.; Interocean Steamship Corporation; Sea-Land Service, Inc.; Hatteras Yachts.

For full biographical listings, see the Martindale-Hubbell Law Directory

GOLDSTEIN & MUSTO, A PROFESSIONAL CORPORATION (AV)

One Embarcadero Center, Eighth Floor, 94111
Telephone: 415-981-8855
Telecopier: 415-981-0196
Email: gmlaw@goldstein-musto.com *URL:* http://www.lawyers.com/gmlaw

Alvin H. Goldstein, Jr.
Mark L. Musto

OF COUNSEL

Robert D. Carrow
Peter W. Fisher

For full biographical listings, see the Martindale-Hubbell Law Directory

JOHN N. GULICK, JR. (AV)

369 Broadway, Suite 110, 94133-4512
Telephone: 415-782-1330
Fax: 415-421-2544
Email: jgulick@gulicklaw.com *URL:* http://www.lawyers.com/johngulick

For full biographical listings, see the Martindale-Hubbell Law Directory

HAIGHT, BROWN & BONESTEEL, L.L.P. (AV)

A Partnership including Professional Corporations
100 Bush Street, 27th Floor, 94104-3902
Telephone: 415-986-7700
Telecopier: 415-986-6945
URL: http://www.hbblaw.com
Santa Monica, California Office: 1620 26th Street, Suite 4000 North, P.O. Box 680.
Telephone: 310-449-6000.
Telecopier: 310-829-5117.
Telex: 705837.
Santa Ana, California Office: Suite 900, 5 Hutton Centre Drive.
Telephone: 714-754-1100.
Telecopier: 714-754-0826.
Riverside, California Office: California Tower, 3737 Main Street, Suite 800.
Telephone: 909-341-8300.
Fax: 909-341-8309.
San Diego, California Office: 101 West Broadway, Suite 1000.
Telephone: 619-595-5583.
Fax: 619-595-7873.

RESIDENT MEMBERS

Amor A. Esteban
Lisa L. Oberg
David W. Evans
Patricia H. Perry
Daniel J. Kelly

ASSOCIATES

Helene Emilie Swanson
Felicia Y. Feng
Arlene Mendoza
Laura Lea Allen
Russell J. Smith

For full biographical listings, see the Martindale-Hubbell Law Directory

HARDIMAN & CARROLL, A LAW PARTNERSHIP (AV)

160 Pine Street, Suite 700, 94111
Telephone: 415-248-3930
Fax: 415-248-3933
Email: postmaster@hc.sflawfirm.com

Michael F. Hardiman
Gerald K. Carroll

ASSOCIATES

Dolores Bastian-Dalton
Lynn Diringer McCabe
Deirdre J. Cox
Melissa R. Meyers
Cheryl Castrogiovanni
John P. Cogger
Shaana Rahman

For full biographical listings, see the Martindale-Hubbell Law Directory

LAW OFFICES OF JOHN E. HILL (AV)

747 Leavenworth Street, 94109
Telephone: 415-398-2434
Facsimile: 415-392-2809
Email: johnhill-law@msn.com
Oakland, California Office: 8105 Edgewater Drive, Suite 100, 94621-2017.
Telephone: 510-729-6330.
Facsimile: 510-729-6333.

Daniel A. Stenson
LeRoy F. Vadney
James E. Keller
Michael P. Guta
Ian M. Cooper
Dylan R. Lawrence
T. William Hyndman
Mark J. Shostak
Natasha B. Oden
George Clinton Stafford
Robert J. Douglas

For full biographical listings, see the Martindale-Hubbell Law Directory

KAUFMAN & LOGAN LLP (AV)

111 Pine Street, Suite 1300, 94111
Telephone: 415-392-6677
Telecopier: 415-391-4639

MEMBERS OF FIRM

Jeffrey Kaufman
Peter J. Logan
Garrett L. Cecchini
W. Martin Tellegen
Richard A. Eggerth

ASSOCIATES

Nancy S. Coan
Sandra L. Cross
Gerald F. Ellersdorfer
Paul A. Peters
Paulette Donsavage
George D. Vanberg-Wolff

OF COUNSEL

Gerhard Stoll

(See Next Column)

KAUFMAN & LOGAN LLP—*Continued*

LEGAL SUPPORT PERSONNEL

PARALEGALS

Karen L. Dunn, CLA
Adrienne Levin
T. Patrick Bridenstine
Paula R. Brawley

For full biographical listings, see the Martindale-Hubbell Law Directory

KEKER & VAN NEST, L.L.P. (AV)

710 Sansome Street, 94111-1704
Telephone: 415-391-5400
Fax: 415-397-7188

MEMBERS OF FIRM

John W. Keker
Elliot R. Peters
Robert A. Van Nest
Jon B. Streeter
Jeffrey R. Chanin
Stuart L. Gasner
Henry C. Bunsow
James M. Emery
Gary M. Cohen
Jon S. Tigar
Susan J. Harriman
Daralyn Jeannine Durie
Jan Nielsen Little
Ragesh K. Tangri
Karin Kramer
Michael H. Page
Christopher C. Kearney
Brian L. Ferrall

OF COUNSEL

Steven A. Hirsch

ASSOCIATES

Wendy J. Thurm
E. Stewart Moritz
Elizabeth A. Egan
Rebecca Kathleen Sullivan
Leo L. Lam
Amy M. McNamer
Christa M. Anderson
Cassandra Knight
Kara M. Andersen
Stacey L. Wexler
Marc D. Katz
Sheila Mary Cuthbert
David J. Silbert
Elizabeth E. Launer
Ethan Atticus Balogh
Christopher D. Nelson
Rachael E. Meny
Daniel E. Purcell
G. Whitney Leigh
Robert Andres Bonta
Lloyd Farnham

For full biographical listings, see the Martindale-Hubbell Law Directory

LASKY, HAAS & COHLER, PROFESSIONAL CORPORATION (AV)

Two Transamerica Center, 505 Sansome Street, 12th Floor, 94111-3183
Telephone: 415-788-2700
Facsimile: 415-981-4025

Charles B. Cohler
Kevin C. McCann
William A. Logan, Jr.
Jeffrey F. Silverman
Christopher S. Yates

Jason Bergmann
Natasha Sankovitch

OF COUNSEL

Moses Lasky

For full biographical listings, see the Martindale-Hubbell Law Directory

LIEFF, CABRASER, HEIMANN & BERNSTEIN, LLP (AV)

Embarcadero Center West, 30th Floor, 275 Battery Street, 94111
Telephone: 415-956-1000
Telecopier: 415-956-1008
Email: mail@lchb.com *URL:* http://www.lchb.com
New York, N.Y. Office: 10 Rockefeller Plaza, 12th Floor, 10020-1903.
Telephone: 212-218-6600.
Fax: 212-218-6608.

Robert L. Lieff
Robert J. Nelson
Elizabeth J. Cabraser
Jacqueline E. Mottek
Richard M. Heimann
Morris A. Ratner
William Bernstein
Melanie M. Piech
William B. Hirsch
Kelly M. Dermody
James M. Finberg
Jonathan D. Selbin
Karen E. Karpen
Richard M. Franco
Joseph R. Saveri
Barry R. Himmelstein
Donald C. Arbitblit
Joshua P. Davis
Steven E. Fineman (Resident, New York, N.Y. Office)
Michael W. Sobol
Robert G. Eisler (Resident, New York, N.Y. Office)

Jennie L. Anderson
Rebecca M. Katz (Resident, New York, N.Y. Office)
Lori E. Andrus
Lisa J. Leebove
Caryn Becker
Karen J. Mandel (Resident, New York, N.Y. Office)
Joan T. Brown (Not admitted in CA)
Scott P. Nealey
Stephen H. Cassidy
Erik L. Shawn (Resident, New York, N.Y. Office)
Paulina do Amaral
Eric B. Fastiff
David S. Stellings (Resident, New York, N.Y. Office)
Hector D. Geribon (Resident, New York, N.Y. Office)
Pierce Gore
Steven M. Tindall

(See Next Column)

Fabrice N. Vincent
Heather A. Woodard
Jonathan M. Watkins
Yu-Yee Wu

For full biographical listings, see the Martindale-Hubbell Law Directory

THE LUCAS LAW FIRM (AV)

1700 California Street, Suite 340, 94109
Telephone: 415-434-3100
FAX: 415-434-0300
Email: lucaslaw@aol.com

Kathleen M. Lucas

For full biographical listings, see the Martindale-Hubbell Law Directory

MORGENSTEIN & JUBELIRER, LLP (AV)

One Market, Spear Street Tower, 32nd Floor, 94105
Telephone: 415-896-0666
Fax: 415-896-5592
Email: m&j@mj-sflaw.com

Marvin D. Morgenstein (Retired)
Rocky N. Unruh
Eliot S. Jubelirer
James L. McGinnis
Lee Ann Huntington
Charles W. LaGrave
Jean L. Bertrand
William J. Carroll
Jeffrey R. Williams
John S. Worden
James R. Balich
Wendi J. Berkowitz
Stephen M. Hankins
Bruce A. Wagman

Lewis D. Barr
Laura E. Gasser
David H. Bromfield
Jill L. Gillen
Alexander P. Catalona
Natasha L. Golding
Michael "Cael" S. Davis
Judith A. Holiber
Roberta Nicol Dempster
Shawn D. Parrish
John J. Petry

For full biographical listings, see the Martindale-Hubbell Law Directory

MURPHY, PEARSON, BRADLEY & FEENEY, A PROFESSIONAL CORPORATION (AV)

88 Kearny Street, 10th Floor, 94108
Telephone: 415-788-1900
Telecopier: 415-393-8087
Email: IndividualsFirstInitialAndLastName@mpbf.com *URL:* http://www.mpbf.com
Sacramento, California Office: 701 University Avenue, Suite 150.
Telephone: 916-565-0300.
Fax: 916-565-1636.
San Jose, California Office: 80 South Market Street, 3rd Floor.
Telephone: 408-279-5792.
Facsimile: 408-279-5785.
Los Angeles, California Office: 11400 West Olympic Boulevard, Suite 249.
Telephone: 310-312-9565.
Fax: 310-312-9566.

James A. Murphy
Michael P. Bradley

For Complete List of Firm Personnel, See General Section

For full biographical listings, see the Martindale-Hubbell Law Directory

EDWARD J. NEVIN (AV)

22 Battery Street, Suite 333, 94111
Telephone: 415-392-5040
Fax: 415-392-3729
Email: ednevin@creative.net

For full biographical listings, see the Martindale-Hubbell Law Directory

HERMAN D. PAPA (AV)

Suite 333, 22 Battery Street, 94111
Telephone: 415-391-4903
Fax: 415-788-4122

For full biographical listings, see the Martindale-Hubbell Law Directory

J. MICHAEL PHELPS (AV)

One Maritime Plaza, Suite 1600, 94111
Telephone: 415-433-3733
Voicemail: 415-433-3739
Fax: 415-781-1034

Representative Clients: Heinz, U.S.A.; Continental Insurance Cos.; Farmers Insurance Group; Travelers Insurance Co.

For full biographical listings, see the Martindale-Hubbell Law Directory

PREUSS WALKER & SHANAGHER LLP (AV)

225 Bush Street, 15th Floor, 94104
Telephone: 415-397-1730
Facsimile: 415-397-1735
Email: pws@pwsllp.com *URL:* http://www.pwsllp.com

(See Next Column)

PREUSS WALKER & SHANAGHER LLP, *San Francisco—Continued*

MEMBERS OF FIRM

Charles F. Preuss
Gary T. Walker
Denis F. Shanagher
Vernon I. Zvoleff
Kenneth J. Philpot
Donald F. Zimmer, Jr.
Sheila Doyle Kelley
Thomas W. Pulliam, Jr.
Alan J. Lazarus
Michael J. Stortz
John J. Powers
Kenneth P. Conour
Catherine M. Leon

Elizabeth Ewert Pilchik
Jonathan M. Rolbin
Jessica L. Grant
Brian M. Collins
Christopher L. Lebsock
Michelle A. Childers
Matthew Lepore
Edward P. Joy
Kristy Wheeler Bonagofsky
Karene I. Alvarado
Andrew Thornborrow
Katherine A. Woodward

Representative Clients: ACE USA; AirTouch Communications; Ford Motor Company; Johnson & Johnson; Mallinckrodt-Baker, Inc.; Nissan North America, Inc.; SmithKline Beecham; Sun Microsystems; Toyota Motor Sales, USA, Inc.; Varian Associates, Inc.

For full biographical listings, see the Martindale-Hubbell Law Directory

---

REMCHO, JOHANSEN AND PURCELL (AV)

Suite 800, 220 Montgomery Street, 94104
Telephone: 415-398-6230
Fax: 415-398-7256
Email: Info@RJP.Com *URL:* http://www.rjp.com
Sacramento, California Office: U.S. Bank Plaza. Suite 2140, 980 Ninth Street, 95814.
Telephone: 916-264-1818.
Fax: 916-264-1824.

MEMBERS OF FIRM

Joseph Remcho
Robin B. Johansen
Kathleen J. Purcell

James C. Harrison
Thomas A. Willis

LEGAL SUPPORT PERSONNEL

Douglas Denton (Paralegal)
Ruth Fridhandler (Legal Administrator)

For full biographical listings, see the Martindale-Hubbell Law Directory

---

LAW OFFICE OF SCOTT RIGHTHAND, P.C. (AV)

100 Spear Street, Suite 700, 94105
Telephone: 415-544-0115
Fax: 415-957-9080
Email: righthand.law@slip.net *URL:* http://www.lawyers.com/righthandlaw

Scott D. Righthand

For full biographical listings, see the Martindale-Hubbell Law Directory

---

ROSEN, BIEN & ASARO (AV)

Eighth Floor, 155 Montgomery Street, 94104
Telephone: 415-433-6830
Fax: 415-433-7104
Email: rba@rbalaw.com

Sanford Jay Rosen
Michael W. Bien
Andrea G. Asaro

Thomas Nolan
William H. D. Fernholz
Shana J. Margolis
Ernest J. Galvan

For full biographical listings, see the Martindale-Hubbell Law Directory

---

SCADDEN, HAMILTON & RYAN (AV)

220 Montgomery Street, 13th Floor, 94104-3410
Telephone: 415-362-5116
Telecopier: 415-362-4214
URL: http://www.shrlaw.com

James G. Scadden
Robert P. Hamilton
Robert J. Ryan
James P. Cunningham

Charles O. Thompson
Eileen Santana Wright
Vincent C. Milani
Timothy K. Killelea

LEGAL SUPPORT PERSONNEL

Edwin L. Lilley
Dennis Prime
Mary Sue Schroeder

For full biographical listings, see the Martindale-Hubbell Law Directory

SCHWARTZ & CERA LLP (AV)

555 Montgomery Street, Suite 720, 94111
Telephone: 415-956-2600
Fax: 415-438-2655
Boston, Massachusetts Office: 7 Wells Avenue. (Newton, Massachusetts). 02459.
Telephone: 617-965-8400.
Fax: 617-965-1194.

MEMBERS OF FIRM

Douglas R. Schwartz
Kenneth B. Cera

Charlene M. (Walker) Drummer
Petra M. Reinecke
Frank J. Gilbert

OF COUNSEL

Tia Welch Maerz

For full biographical listings, see the Martindale-Hubbell Law Directory

---

STEEFEL, LEVITT & WEISS, A PROFESSIONAL CORPORATION (AV)

30th Floor, One Embarcadero Center, 94111
Telephone: 415-788-0900
Fax: 415-788-2019
Email: slw@steefel.com
Stamford, Connecticut Office: Six Landmark Square, Fourth Floor, 06901-2792.
Telephone: 203-359-5605.
Fax: 203-359-5805.

Lenard G. Weiss
Michael J. Lawson
Michael D. Early
Barry W. Lee
Daryl S. Landy
Mark Fogelman

For Complete List of Firm Personnel, See General Section

For full biographical listings, see the Martindale-Hubbell Law Directory

---

TEHIN +PARTNERS, A PROFESSIONAL CORPORATION (AV)

Bank of America Center, 555 California Street, 33rd Floor, 94104-1609
Telephone: 415-951-8800
Fax: 415-951-8808
URL: http://www.tehin.com

Nikolai Tehin
Pamela J. Stevens
Reilly Atkinson, IV
Michael E. Brown
Bita Abdollahi

For full biographical listings, see the Martindale-Hubbell Law Directory

---

THE LOUDERBACK LAW FIRM (AV)

115 Sansome Street, Suite 1005, 94104
Telephone: 415-398-7860
Fax: 415-398-7863
Email: clouderback@louderback.org *URL:* http://www.louderback.org

Charles M. Louderback

ASSOCIATES

Elizabeth M. McQuillan
Jesse L. Miller
Stephen R. Raab

LEGAL SUPPORT PERSONNEL

Bradly M. Hamilton (Firm Administrator)
Eliza Alvarez (Secretary)

For full biographical listings, see the Martindale-Hubbell Law Directory

---

VOGL & MEREDITH (AV)

456 Montgomery Street, 20th Floor, 94104
Telephone: 415-398-0200
Facsimile: 415-398-2820

Samuel E. Meredith
David R. Vogl
John P. Walovich
Jean N. Yeh
Thomas S. Clifton

Nicole L. Meredith
Dennis Gildea
Michael S. Burke
Martin Ross Sances
Joshua A. Ridless
David G. Valdez

For full biographical listings, see the Martindale-Hubbell Law Directory

---

WUERFEL & CHOLAKIAN, A PROFESSIONAL CORPORATION (AV)

555 Montgomery Street, Ninth Floor, 94111
Telephone: 415-398-1551; 800-992-5990
FAX: 415-398-3301
Email: sos@sflaw.net *URL:* http://www.sflaw.net
Santa Rosa, California Office: 131-A Stony Circle, Suite 515, 95401.
Telephones: 415-398-1551; 800-992-5990.
FAX: 415-398-1551.
Costa Mesa, California Office: Avenue of the Arts.
Telephone: 714-825-3590; 800-992-5990.

(See Next Column)

WUERFEL & CHOLAKIAN A PROFESSIONAL CORPORATION—*Continued*

Mark D. Wuerfel
Kevin K. Cholakian
Julian J. Pardini
Nan R. Hooven
Sherri K. McElroy

SPECIAL COUNSEL

Dean C. Burnick
Charlene P. Rosack
Jonathan Gross
Michael A. Topp

Aaron D. Bigby
D. Clark Burton
Anthony J. Calero
Elizabeth A. Doyle
Linda L. Duiven
Jay E. Framson
Stephen D. Geist
Andrew A. Goode
David J. Heilman
Timothy S. Kirk
Stephen J. Liberatore
Anne Marie Master
Thomas A. Moore
Julianne Pinter

LEGAL SUPPORT PERSONNEL

Marla J. Kuresa (Legal Administrator)

For full biographical listings, see the Martindale-Hubbell Law Directory

*SAN JOSE,** Santa Clara Co.

ALEXANDER, HAWES & AUDET (AV)

152 North 3rd Street, Suite 600, 95112
Telephone: 408-289-1776
Fax: 408-287-1776
URL: http://www.alexanderlaw.com
Email: access@alexanderlaw.com *URL:* http://www.lawyers.com/alexanderhawes&audet

Richard Alexander
Amanda Hawes
William M. Audet
Ann Saponara
Deborah Heller

OF COUNSEL

Michael McShane
Jana S. Stabile (Not admitted in CA)

For full biographical listings, see the Martindale-Hubbell Law Directory

BERGESON & ELIOPOULOS, LLP (AV)

55 Almaden Boulevard, Suite 400, 95113
Telephone: 408-291-6200
Fax: 408-297-6000
URL: http://www.beglaw.com
Washington, D.C. Affiliate Office: Bergeson & Campbell, P.C., 1300 Eye Street, NW, Suite 100 West, 20005.
Telephone: (202)-962-8585.
Fax: (202)-962-8599. URL: www.bclaw.com.

Daniel J. Bergeson
William T. Eliopoulos
Mary Anne Rodgers
John L. Antracoli
Donald P. Gagliardi
Ina Stangenes
Marily P. Lerner

OF COUNSEL

Anthony M. Glassman

ASSOCIATES

Marc G. Van Niekerk
Eunhae Park
Mark E. Waite
Evelyn A. Peyton
William A. Hodkowski

For full biographical listings, see the Martindale-Hubbell Law Directory

CAMPEAU & THOMAS, A LAW CORPORATION (AV)

Market Post Tower, 55 South Market Street, Suite 1660, 95113
Telephone: 408-295-9555
Fax: 408-295-6606
URL: http://www.campeaulaw.com

Kenneth J. Campeau
Wayne H. Thomas
Scott L. Goodsell
Kathryn J. Diemer

Marc L. Pinckney
Kathryn Infante
Judith L. Whitman

For full biographical listings, see the Martindale-Hubbell Law Directory

JAN CHAMPION (AV)

Ten Almaden Boulevard, Suite 1250, 95113-2233
Telephone: 408-286-5550
Fax: 408-270-6777
URL: http://www.lawyers.com/jchampionlaw
Email: jan@championlaw.com

For full biographical listings, see the Martindale-Hubbell Law Directory

COLLINS & SCHLOTHAUER (AV)

60 South Market Street, Suite 1100, 95113-2369
Telephone: 408-298-5161
Fax: 408-297-5766
Email: msc@cslawfirm.com
Los Angeles, California Office, Schlothauer & Collins: 11999 San Vicente Boulevard, Suite 340, 90049.
Telephone: 310-472-1670.
Fax: 310-472-5270.

Mark Scott Collins (Inc.)
David N. Poll
Jovita P. Tamor

OF COUNSEL

Thomas L. Schlothauer

For full biographical listings, see the Martindale-Hubbell Law Directory

HAWKINS • BLICK (AV)

96 North Third Street, Suite 300, 95112
Telephone: 408-280-7111
Fax: 408-292-7868
URL: http://www.hawkins-law.com

MEMBERS OF FIRM

Charles F. Hawkins
Stephen L. Blick

ASSOCIATE

Richard E. Eichenbaum

For full biographical listings, see the Martindale-Hubbell Law Directory

LAW OFFICES OF THOMAS R. HOGAN (AV)

10 Almaden Boulevard, Suite 535, 95113-2258
Telephone: 408-292-7600
Facsimile: 408-292-7611
URL: http://www.lawyers.com/thomasrhogan
Email: trh@hoganlaw.com *URL:* http://www.hoganlaw.com

ASSOCIATE

Leslie Holmes

For full biographical listings, see the Martindale-Hubbell Law Directory

DAVID MALNICK A PROFESSIONAL CORPORATION (AV)

Ten Almaden Boulevard, Suite 500, 95113-2226
Telephone: 408-292-5900
Fax: 408-292-5995
Email: verdict@malnicklaw.com

David E. Malnick

For full biographical listings, see the Martindale-Hubbell Law Directory

MCMANIS, FAULKNER & MORGAN (AV)

160 West Santa Clara Street, 10th Floor, 95113
Telephone: 408-279-8700
Fax: 408-279-3244; 408-279-0494
Email: mfm@mfmlaw.com *URL:* http://www.mfmlaw.com

James McManis
William Faulkner
Donelle Morgan
Lisa Herrick
Michael Reedy
Erica Yew

Michelle Tidalgo
Colleen Duffy Smith
Lillian Wolf
Rebecca Hughes
Kalpana Vrudhula
Ray M. Baluyot
Catherine Bechtel
Arron Nesbitt

OF COUNSEL

Mary Arand

For full biographical listings, see the Martindale-Hubbell Law Directory

MILLER, MORTON, CAILLAT & NEVIS (AV)

50 West San Fernando Street, Suite 1300, 95113-2413
Telephone: 408-292-1765
Telecopier: 408-292-4484
URL: http://www.mmcn-law.com

Richard W. Morton (1916-1975)
Charles V. Caillat (1920-1990)
Harvey C. Miller (1906-1993)

MEMBERS OF FIRM

David L. Nevis
Francis J. Hughes
Peter A. Kline
Stevan C. Adelman
Joseph A. Scanlan, Jr.
Carolyn Tobiason Stuart
William K. Hurley
Peter V. Dessau

OF COUNSEL

Nancy F. Symons

ASSOCIATES

Kathryn E. Barrett
Katherine S. Pak
David I. Kornbluh
Christopher J. Hersey
Julie Neale Meyer

(See Next Column)

MILLER, MORTON, CAILLAT & NEVIS, *San Jose—Continued*

Representative Clients: Trammell Crow Residential; Joe Kerley Lincoln Mercury Co.; Milligan News Co.; Joseph George Distributors; Santa Clara Dental Society; Avalon Bay Communities; Hathaway-Dinwiddie Group.

For full biographical listings, see the Martindale-Hubbell Law Directory

ROBINSON & WOOD, INC. (AV)

227 North First Street, 95113
Telephone: 408-298-7120
Fax: 408-298-0477
Email: rw@r-winc.com

Archie S. Robinson
Weldon S. Wood
Thomas R. Fellows
David S. Henningsen
Hugh F. Lennon
Jesse F. Ruiz
Christian B. Nielsen
Jonathan L. Lee
Jon B. Zimmerman
Mark B. Schellerup
Andrew W. Olsson
Arthur J. Casey
Joseph C. Balestrieri
John L. Winchester, III
Robert A. Nakamae

Rebecca L. Moon
Ann A. Nguyen
Kenneth I. Schumaker
Anne C. Bailey
Stephen D. Bays
Jill K. Ernst
Colin G. McCarthy
Bonnie M. Ross
Mario Alvarado
Christopher K. Karic
Alison M. Hershberger
Camille L. Acayan
Valerie M. Drogus
Jennifer L. Bautista

For full biographical listings, see the Martindale-Hubbell Law Directory

SAUCEDO & CORSIGLIA, A LAW CORPORATION (AV)

50 West San Fernando Street, Suite 425, 95113
Telephone: 408-289-1417
Fax: 408-289-8127
Email: saucor@compuserve.com

Norman W. Saucedo
Bradley M. Corsiglia

For full biographical listings, see the Martindale-Hubbell Law Directory

SHEA & SHEA, A PROFESSIONAL LAW CORPORATION (AV)

The James Square Building, 255 North Market Street, Suite 190, 95110
Telephone: 408-292-2434
Facsimile: 408-292-1264
Email: shea-shea@worldnet.att.net *URL:* http://www.shea-shea.com

Michael M. Shea
Michael M. Shea, Jr.

For full biographical listings, see the Martindale-Hubbell Law Directory

*SAN LUIS OBISPO,** San Luis Obispo Co.

ANDRE, MORRIS & BUTTERY, A PROFESSIONAL LAW CORPORATION (AV)

1102 Laurel Lane, P.O. Box 730, 93406-0730
Telephone: 805-543-4171
Fax: 805-543-0752
Email: amb@amblaw.com *URL:* http://www.amblaw.com

James C. Buttery
Dennis D. Law

Mary E. McAlister
Kathryn M. Eppright
Kevin D. Morris

References: Bank of America National Trust and Savings Assn. (San Luis Obispo Main Branch); Mid-State Bank (San Luis Obispo).

For full biographical listings, see the Martindale-Hubbell Law Directory

SAN MATEO, San Mateo Co.

McDOWALL, COTTER, DUNN, VALE & BRACCO, A PROFESSIONAL CORPORATION (AV)

2070 Pioneer Court, P.O. Box 937, 94403
Telephone: 650-572-7933
Fax: 650-572-0834
Email: lawyers@mcdowalllaw.com
Palo Alto, California Office: 425 Sherman Avenue, Suite 100.
Telephone: 408-244-8755; Other Areas: 415-326-8410.
Fax: 415-326-3911.

William D. McDowall
Bernard T. Cotter
Thomas G. Dunn
Robert D. Vale
Michael A. Bracco
Richard M. Kelly

Representative Clients: State Farm Mutual Automobile Insurance Co.; State Farm Fire & Casualty Co.; California State Automobile Assn.; Allegiance Insurance Co.; Argonaut Insurance Cos.

For full biographical listings, see the Martindale-Hubbell Law Directory

DAVID JAY MORGAN A PROFESSIONAL CORPORATION (AV)

1900 O'Farrell Street, Suite 190, 94403
Telephone: 650-286-1212
Fax: 650-286-1216

David Jay Morgan

Batya F. Smernoff

For full biographical listings, see the Martindale-Hubbell Law Directory

*SAN RAFAEL,** Marin Co.

JOHNS & CHRISTENSEN, A PROFESSIONAL CORPORATION (AV)

135 Paul Drive, Suite 100, 94903
Telephone: 415-459-5223
Facsimile: 415-453-2555
Email: info@johnsandchristensen.com *URL:* http://www.johnsandchristensen.com

Christopher Johns
Robert C. Christensen

David Gray Douglas
Jennifer A.D. Lehman
Farimah Faiz

OF COUNSEL

Mark J. Helmueller
Burton C. "Skip" Allyn, IV

For full biographical listings, see the Martindale-Hubbell Law Directory

*SANTA ANA,** Orange Co.

CASSIDY, WARNER, LANE & WINSTEAD, A PROFESSIONAL CORPORATION (AV)

600 West Santa Ana Boulevard, Suite 700, 92701
Telephone: 714-835-9431
Fax: 714-835-5264
Email: cdaly@cassidywarner.com

B. Kent Warner
Timothy X. Lane
Bruce A. Winstead

David C. Olson
Glen A. Stebens

OF COUNSEL

Alvin M. Cassidy

For full biographical listings, see the Martindale-Hubbell Law Directory

THOMAS A. CULBERTSON (AV)

2677 North Main Street Suite 200, 92705-6625
Telephone: 714-541-4454; 310-379-7298
Fax: 714-564-0748; 310-379-7298

For full biographical listings, see the Martindale-Hubbell Law Directory

HAIGHT, BROWN & BONESTEEL, L.L.P. (AV)

A Partnership including Professional Corporations
Suite 900, 5 Hutton Centre Drive, 92707
Telephone: 714-754-1100
Telecopier: 714-754-0826
URL: http://www.hbblaw.com
Santa Monica, California Office: 1620 26th Street, Suite 4000 North, P.O. Box 680.
Telephone: 310-449-6000.
Telecopier: 310-829-5117.
Telex: 705837.
Riverside, California Office: California Tower, 3737 Maine Street, Suite 800.
Telephone: 909-341-8300.
Fax: 909-341-8309.
San Francisco, California Office: 100 Bush Street, 27th Floor.
Telephone: 415-986-7700.
Fax: 415-986-6945.
San Diego, California Office: 101 West Broadway, Suite 1000.
Telephone: 619-595-5583.
Fax: 619-595-7873.

RESIDENT MEMBERS

Bruce L. Cleeland
Mark R. VonderHaar
Jeffrey S. Gerardo
Richard O. Knapp
Pamela G. Lacey
Edwin J. Richards

ASSOCIATES

Laura M. Knox
Jeffrey D. Farrow
Wendy J. Schmitt
Steven M. Dailey
S. Ann Salisbury
Antoinette P. Hewitt
D. Chad Anderton

Counsel for: Orange County: Aetna Casualty and Surety Co.; Zurich-American Insurance Cos.; Industrial Indemnity Co.; Professional Liability Claims Managers; Maryland Casualty Insurance Co.; Royal Insurance Company of America.

For full biographical listings, see the Martindale-Hubbell Law Directory

Santa Ana—Continued

MARTIN, WILSON & MACDOWELL, A PROFESSIONAL CORPORATION (AV)

6 Hutton Centre Drive, Suite 500, 92707-5762
Telephone: 714-972-1200
Facsimile: 714-972-1283
Email: mwmlaw@msn.com

Scott A. Martin
Thomas L. Wilson
John R. MacDowell

Vivienne J. Alston
Steven S. Wang
Mark E. Matheson

For full biographical listings, see the Martindale-Hubbell Law Directory

PIZER & MICHAELSON INC. (AV)

2122 North Broadway, Suite 100, 92706
Telephone: 714-558-0535
Telecopier: 714-550-0841
Los Angeles, California Office: 2049 Century Park East, Suite 460, 90067.
Telephone: 310-843-9729.
Fax: 310-843-9619.

Seymour S. Pizer (1930-1992)
Hugh R. Coffin
Barry S. Michaelson
Bradley J. Pizer (Resident, Los Angeles Office)

For full biographical listings, see the Martindale-Hubbell Law Directory

SWANSON AND GIESER, A PROFESSIONAL CORPORATION (AV)

4 Hutton Centre Drive, Suite 200, 92707-5770
Telephone: 714-755-3500
Fax: 714-755-3505
URL: http://www.lawyers.com/swansongieserlaw
San Diego, California Office: 600 B Street, Suite 2120, 92101.
Telephone: 619-686-6100.
Fax: 619-686-6105.

C. Brent Swanson (1941-1998)
Thomas M. Gieser

Elaine B. Alston

For full biographical listings, see the Martindale-Hubbell Law Directory

*SANTA BARBARA,** Santa Barbara Co.

HOLLISTER & BRACE, A PROFESSIONAL CORPORATION (AV)

1126 Santa Barbara Street, P.O. Box 630, 93101
Telephone: 805-963-6711
Fax: 805-965-0329
Email: hblaw@hbsb.com

William A. Brace (Retired)
John G. Busby
J. James Hollister, III (Retired)
Susan H. McCollum
John S. Poucher
Robert L. Brace
Richard C. Monk
Marcus Scott Bird
George A. Rempe, III
Charles W. Willey (P.C.)
Steven Evans Kirby
Alexis W. Willey
Bradford F. Ginder
Peter L. Candy

For full biographical listings, see the Martindale-Hubbell Law Directory

MULLEN & HENZELL, L.L.P. (AV)

A California registered limited liability partnership
112 East Victoria Street, Post Office Drawer 789, 93102-0789
Telephone: 805-966-1501
FAX: 805-966-9204
Email: mh@mullenlaw.com

MEMBERS OF FIRM

Thomas M. Mullen (1915-1991)
Edward C. Thoits
Arthur A. Henzell (Retired)
William E. Degen

OF COUNSEL

Charles S. Bargiel

ASSOCIATE

Paul K. Wilcox

Representative Clients: California State Auto Association (No. Calif. Auto Club); Interinsurance Exchange of the Automobile Club of Southern California; Fireman's Fund Insurance Co.; State Farm Fire & Casualty Co.; State Farm Mutual Automobile Insurance Co.

For full biographical listings, see the Martindale-Hubbell Law Directory

ROGERS & SHEFFIELD, LLP (AV)

427 East Carrillo Street, P.O. Box 22257, 93121-2257
Telephone: 805-963-9721
Fax: 805-966-3715
Email: rs@rogerssheffield.com

(See Next Column)

MEMBERS OF FIRM

Homer G. Sheffield, Jr.
Philip I. Moncharsh
William K. Rogers
Scott B. Campbell

OF COUNSEL

B. Keith Martin
Richard G. Kravetz
Marlea F. Jarrette

Representative Clients: Applied Silicone Corp.; Brenner Foods; Lumitron; Multiplex Broadband Technologies; Santa Barbara Graduate School (Pacifica Institute); Santa Barbara Healthcare Inc.; Santa Barbara Metropolitan Transit District; Sima Corp.; Santa Barbara Company Retirement System.

For full biographical listings, see the Martindale-Hubbell Law Directory

SANTA MONICA, Los Angeles Co.

BIENSTOCK & CLARK (AV)

A Partnership of Professional Corporations
3250 Ocean Park Boulevard, Suite 350, 90405
Telephone: 310-314-8660
Facsimile: 310-314-8662
Miami, Florida Office: First Union Financial Center, 200 South Biscayne Boulevard, Suite 3160.
Telephone: 305-373-1100.
Facsimile: 305-358-1226.
Chicago, Illinois Office: 311 South Wacker Drive, Suite 4550.
Telephone: 312-697-4965.
Facsimile: 312-697-4966.
Kalamazoo, Michigan Office: 5360 Holiday Terrace.
Telephone: 616-353-3900.
Facsimile: 616-353-3906.

Terry S. Bienstock (P.A.) (Resident Partner, Miami, Florida)
Christopher C. Cinnamon (Resident Partner, Chicago, Illinois)
Eric E. Breisach (Resident Partner, Kalamazoo, Michigan)
Roger W. Clark
Robert D. Goldberg

For full biographical listings, see the Martindale-Hubbell Law Directory

FOGEL, FELDMAN, OSTROV, RINGLER & KLEVENS, A LAW CORPORATION (AV)

1620 26th Street, Suite 100 South, 90404-4040
Telephone: 310-453-6711
Fax: 310-828-2191

Daniel Fogel (1923-1991)
Joel N. Klevens
Lester G. Ostrov
Robert M. Turner
Larry R. Feldman
Jerome L. Ringler
Richard L. Rosett

Thomas H. Peters
Sandra L. Lepson
David Bricker
Lawrence C. Jones
Stephanie Chase
Stacie L. Feldman
Jan Greenberg Levine
John T. Fogarty

OF COUNSEL

Carol S. May

Reference: Republic Bank of California, Beverly Hills, California.

For full biographical listings, see the Martindale-Hubbell Law Directory

HAIGHT, BROWN & BONESTEEL, L.L.P. (AV)

A Partnership including Professional Corporations
1620 26th Street, Suite 4000 North, P.O. Box 680, 90404
Telephone: 310-449-6000
Telecopier: 310-829-5117
Telex: 705837
URL: http://www.hbblaw.com
Santa Ana, California Office: Suite 900, 5 Hutton Centre Drive.
Telephone: 714-754-1100.
Telecopier: 714-754-0826.
Riverside, California Office: California Tower, 3737 Main Street, Suite 800.
Telephone: 909-341-8300.
Fax: 909-341-8309.
San Francisco, California Office: 101 Bush Street, 27th Floor.
Telephone: 415-986-7700.
Fax: 415-986-6945.
San Diego, California Office: 101 West Broadway, Suite 1000.
Telephone: 619-595-5583.
Fax: 619-595-7873.

MEMBERS OF FIRM

Michael J. Bonesteel (A Professional Corporation)
Steven L. Hoch (A Professional Corporation)
Gary C. Ottoson (A Professional Corporation)
John W. Sheller (A Professional Corporation)
Roy G. Weatherup
William G. Baumgaertner (A Professional Corporation)
Peter Q. Ezzell (A Professional Corporation)
Bruce A. Armstrong (A Professional Corporation)
Dennis K. Wheeler (A Professional Corporation)
Morton Rosen

(See Next Column)

HAIGHT, BROWN & BONESTEEL L.L.P., *Santa Monica—Continued*

MEMBERS OF FIRM (Continued)

Peter A. Dubrawski
Michael J. Leahy
Lori R. Behar
Robert L. Kaufman
William J. Sayers
Barry Z. Brodsky
Kevin R. Crisp
Lee Marshall
George Christensen
Desmond J. Hinds, Jr.
Neil G. McNiece
Thomas M. Moore
Kenneth G. Anderson
Victor Anderson III
William O. Martin, Jr.
Jennifer K. Saunders
Theresa M. Marchlewski
William E. Ireland
Valerie A. Moore
David C. McGovern
Jeffrey B. Margulies
S. Christian Stouder
Cary D. Glassner
Michael H. Gottschlich
Farah Sohaili Nicol

ASSOCIATES

Jon M. Kasimov
Holly M. Teel
Sean E. Judge
Kristine W. Samuels

OF COUNSEL

William M. Fitzhugh
R. Roy Finkle
Gerald R. Judson
Caroline Kelley Moore

For full biographical listings, see the Martindale-Hubbell Law Directory

O'NEILL, LYSAGHT & SUN LLP (AV)

100 Wilshire Boulevard, Suite 700, 90401
Telephone: 310-451-5700
Telecopier: 310-399-7201

Brian O'Neill
Brian C. Lysaght
Frederick D. Friedman
Brian A. Sun
Yolanda Orozco
John M. Moscarino
Harriet Beegun Leva
Edward A. Klein
Robert L. Meylan
David E. Rosen
Paul D. Murphy

Ellyn S. Garofalo
Brian D. Hershman
Katharine A. Kates
Luan K. Phan
Kyle Y. Hoshide
Hersh Heather Elizabeth
Catherine D. Whiting

OF COUNSEL

J. Joseph Connolly

Reference: Wells Fargo Bank, Santa Monica.

For full biographical listings, see the Martindale-Hubbell Law Directory

PAUL & JANOFSKY (AV)

1401 Ocean Avenue, Suite 200, 90401-1701
Telephone: 310-458-7900
Facsimile: 310-458-6823

MEMBERS OF FIRM

Gary M. Paul
John S. Janofsky

ASSOCIATE

Daniel Amos
Michael B. Gurien

OF COUNSEL

Michael L. Goldberg

For full biographical listings, see the Martindale-Hubbell Law Directory

STEINBERG, NUTTER & BRENT, LAW CORPORATION (AV)

501 Colorado Avenue, Suite 300, 90401
Telephone: 310-451-9714
Telecopier: 310-451-0929
Woodland Hills, California Office: 21031 Ventura Boulevard, Suite 419.
Telephone: 818-703-6204.

Peter T. Steinberg
Guy B. Nutter
Paul M. Brent

ASSOCIATE

Adam E. Chaikin

Reference: Santa Monica Bank.

For full biographical listings, see the Martindale-Hubbell Law Directory

WATERS, MCCLUSKEY & BOEHLE (AV)

3250 Ocean Park Boulevard, Suite 300, 90405-3220
Telephone: 310-396-3411
Facsimile: 310-450-0925
Email: wmb@wmboehle.com
Santa Ana, California Office: Suite 1000, 200 West Santa Ana Boulevard.
Telephone: 714-953-4407.
Facsimile: 714-953-2118.

(See Next Column)

MEMBERS OF FIRM

William W. Waters (1898-1979)
Laurence R. Corcoran (1927-1987)
Fritz B. Hax
Wayne J. Boehle
Richard A. Wall (Resident, Santa Ana Office)
Timothy R. Lee
Gregg W. Brugger
Kevin G. McCluskey
Stacey B. Spurlock (Resident, Santa Ana Office)
Michael T. Montgomery

ASSOCIATES

Quyen H. Khuong (Resident, Santa Ana)
Christine Y. Chien (Resident, Santa Ana Office)
Portasha R. Moore
Julie C. Chang-Lee (Resident, Santa Ana Office)
Joseph C. Graven
Kirk Michael Olson (Resident, Santa Ana Office)
Brett C. Drouet

References: Bank of America; Santa Monica Business Park, Santa Monica; California National Bank, Los Angeles; First Republic, Los Angeles.

For full biographical listings, see the Martindale-Hubbell Law Directory

*SANTA ROSA,** Sonoma Co.

ABBEY, WEITZENBERG, HOFFMAN & EMERY, A PROFESSIONAL CORPORATION (AV)

1105 North Dutton Avenue, P.O. Box 1566, 95402
Telephone: 707-542-5050
Telecopier: 707-542-2589
Email: info@abbeylaw.com

W. Barton Weitzenberg
Patrick W. Emery
Lewis R. Warren

Representative Clients: Exchange Bank of Santa Rosa; Westamerica Bank; Northwestern Title Security Co.; Geyser Peak Winery; Santa Rosa City School District; Sonoma National Bank; Arrowood Vineyards & Winery; Friedman Bros. Hardware, Inc.; Bank of Lake County; Lasercraft, Inc.

For full biographical listings, see the Martindale-Hubbell Law Directory

*STOCKTON,** San Joaquin Co.

PARISH & NELSON, A PROFESSIONAL CORPORATION (AV)

1919 Grand Canal Boulevard, Suite A-5, 95207-8114
Telephone: 209-952-1992
Fax: 209-952-0250
Email: pnlaw@parishnelson.com *URL:* http://www.parishnelson.com

William H. Parish
Robert D. Nelson
Arthur Atwell Small II

Representative Clients: Bank of Stockton; Bank of Lodi; Granite Construction Co.; Pacific State Bank; Kirk State Bank; The Money Store; Lewis Mechanical; McDonald-Glenn Co.; E.I. DuPont deNemours & Co.; Silverado Broadcasting Co.

For full biographical listings, see the Martindale-Hubbell Law Directory

STEINHEIMER, RIGGIO, HAYDEL & MORDAUNT, A PROFESSIONAL LAW CORPORATION (AV)

400 East Main Street, Suite 600, 95290-0600
Telephone: 209-464-8732
Fax: 209-464-9165
Sonora, California Office: 38 North Washington Street, Suite A.
Telephone: 209-532-1424.
Fax: 209-532-4233.
Affiliated Office: Law Offices of M. Max Steinheimer, 301 Flint Street, Reno, Nevada 89505-3295.
Telephone: 702-322-2240.

M. Max Steinheimer
Donald M. Riggio
Douglas A. Haydel
Michael R. Mordaunt
Peter J. Kelly
Mark F. Ornellas
William D. Johnson
Kate Powell Segerstrom (Resident, Sonora Office)
Kevin M. Seibert
Elizabeth R. Bogart
Frank R. Perrott

Corinne K. Reynolds
Neal C. Lutterman
Daniel C. Cederborg
Rachelle C. Sanchez
Robert T. Waters
Nicole E. Bader
Amy Plomteaux
James Mark Mylles

Counsel for: Pacific Gas and Electric Co.; Kleinfelder Inc.; Turlock Irrigation District.
Insurance Clients: Allied Insurance Group; Design Professional Insurance Co.; The Doctors Co.; Kemper Insurance Co.; Norcal Mutual Insurance Co.; The Travelers.

For full biographical listings, see the Martindale-Hubbell Law Directory

TORRANCE, Los Angeles Co.

AGNEW & BRUSAVICH (AV)

20355 Hawthorne Boulevard, 90503
Telephone: 310-793-1400
Facsimile: 310-793-1499
Email: agnewbru@ix.netcom.com *URL:* http://www.agnew-brusavich.com

Gerald E. Agnew, Jr. Bruce M. Brusavich

ASSOCIATES

Susan E. Hargrove Christopher A. Kall

For full biographical listings, see the Martindale-Hubbell Law Directory

FINER, KIM & STEARNS (AV)

An Association of Professional Corporations
City National Bank Building, 3424 Carson Street, Suite 500, 90503
Telephone: 310-214-1477
Telecopier: 310-214-0764
Email: finerkimstearns@pobox.com *URL:* http://www.finerkimstearnslaw.com

Harry J. Kim (A Professional Corporation)
W. A. Finer (A Professional Corporation)
Robert David Ciaccio
Robert B. Parsons

OF COUNSEL

Bennett A. Rheingold Ryan E. Stearns

LEGAL SUPPORT PERSONNEL

Marcia E. Talbert

For Complete List of Firm Personnel, See General Section

For full biographical listings, see the Martindale-Hubbell Law Directory

UPLAND, San Bernardino Co.

ALTHOUSE & McDONOUGH (AV)

Second Floor, Metro Commerce Bank Building, 188 North Euclid Avenue, P.O. Box 698, 91785
Telephone: 909-985-9828
Telecopier: 909-985-3282
Email: AltandMcD@aol.com *URL:* http://www.Alt-McD.com

Charles S. Althouse Elizabeth A. McDonough

References: Metro Commerce Bank, Upland, California; Upland Bank, Upland, California.

For Complete List of Firm Personnel, See General Section

For full biographical listings, see the Martindale-Hubbell Law Directory

VAN NUYS, Los Angeles Co.

DAVID I. KARP (AV)

13818 Cumpston Street, 91401
Telephone: 818-781-1458
Fax: 818-781-7733
URL: http://members.aol.com/DavidIKarp

For full biographical listings, see the Martindale-Hubbell Law Directory

*VENTURA,** Ventura Co.

FERGUSON, CASE, ORR, PATERSON & CUNNINGHAM LLP (AV)

1050 South Kimball Road, 93004
Telephone: 805-659-6800
Telecopier: 805-659-6818
Email: info@fcopc.com *URL:* http://www.fcopc.com

Thomas R. Ferguson
Michael W. Case
John C. Orr
William E. Paterson
David L. Cunningham
Lou Carpiac
Joseph L. Strohman, Jr.
Robert L. Gallaway
Sandra M. Robertson
David L. Shain
William B. Smith
Gisele Goetz
Ramon L. Guizar
Gregory W. Herring
Douglas E. Kulper
David B. Shea

James Q. McDermott

Representative Clients: First American Title Insurance Company; Wells Fargo Bank; Area Housing Authority of the County of Ventura; Citibank; AT&T Wireless Services of California, Inc.; Catholic Health Care West, Central Coast; Autologic Information International, Inc.; GTE of California; County of Ventura; Calleguas Municipal Water District.

For full biographical listings, see the Martindale-Hubbell Law Directory

JOHN H. HOWARD (AV)

3585 Maple Street, Suite 220, 93003
Telephone: 805-644-5894; 656-2300
Fax: 805-644-6482
Email: 1111Sooakland@msn.com

ASSOCIATE

James Edward Doles

For full biographical listings, see the Martindale-Hubbell Law Directory

STRAUSS • URITZ A PROFESSIONAL CORPORATION (AV)

290 Maple Court, Suite 200, 93003
Telephone: 805-644-7458
Fax: 805-644-4325
Email: mail@venturalaw.com *URL:* http://www.venturalaw.com

Anthony R. Strauss Curt W. Uritz

Bruce P. Crary Mikael W. Via

For full biographical listings, see the Martindale-Hubbell Law Directory

TAYLOR McCORD, A LAW CORPORATION (AV)

721 East Main Street, P.O. Box 1477, 93002
Telephone: 805-648-4700
Email: vtafamlaw@aol.com

Richard L. Taylor Robert L. McCord, Jr.
David L. Praver

Patrick Cherry Susan D. Siple
Rebbecca F. Calderwood

LEGAL SUPPORT PERSONNEL

PARALEGALS

Stephanie Gibson
Adele Rubino (Certified Legal Assistant, California Advanced Specialist)
Diane Lovato

For full biographical listings, see the Martindale-Hubbell Law Directory

WALNUT CREEK, Contra Costa Co.

ANDERSON, GALLOWAY & LUCCHESE, A PROFESSIONAL CORPORATION (AV)

1676 North California Boulevard Suite 500, 94596-4183
Telephone: 925-943-6383
Facsimile: 925-943-7542

Robert L. Anderson
George Patrick Galloway
David R. Lucchese
Martin J. Everson
Thomas J. Donnelly
Ralph J. Smith
James M. Nelson
Scott E. Murray
David A. Depolo
Karen A. Sparks
Stephen J. Brooks
Joseph S. Picchi
Erin Ruddy Sabey
Lea K. Baldacci
Michael E. Brewer
Sonja M. Dahl
Patricia A. Timm
Jeffrey S. Mitchell

Martha J. James
Shelton L. Smith
Steven M. McKinley
William L. Brelsford, Jr.

For full biographical listings, see the Martindale-Hubbell Law Directory

HINTON & ALFERT, A PROFESSIONAL CORPORATION (AV)

Suite 600, 1646 North California Boulevard, 94596-4113
Telephone: 925-932-6006
Fax: 925-932-3412
Email: ha@hintonandalfert.com *URL:* http://www.lawyers.com/hintonandalfert

Peter J. Hinton Peter W. Alfert
Scott H. Z. Sumner

Elise Sanguinetti

For full biographical listings, see the Martindale-Hubbell Law Directory

COLORADO

*ASPEN,** Pitkin Co.

AUSTIN, PEIRCE & SMITH, P.C. (AV)

Suite 205, 600 East Hopkins Avenue, 81611
Telephone: 970-925-2600
FAX: 970-925-4720
Email: aps_aspen@aol.com

(See Next Column)

AUSTIN, PEIRCE & SMITH P.C., *Aspen—Continued*

Ronald D. Austin
Frederick F. Peirce
Thomas Fenton Smith

John M. Lassalette

Counsel for: Chase Manhattan of Colorado, Inc.; Clark's Market; Coates, Reid & Waldron Property Management, Inc.; Crystal Palace Corp.; Snowmass Shopping Center; Coldwell Banker The Aspen Brokers, Ltd.; William Poss & Assoc., Architects; Snowmass Village Resort Association; Aspen/-Pitkin County Housing Authority.

For full biographical listings, see the Martindale-Hubbell Law Directory

J. NICHOLAS MCGRATH, P.C. (AV)

Suite 203, 600 East Hopkins Avenue, 81611
Telephone: 970-925-2612
Telecopier: 970-925-4402
Email: jnm@jnmpc.com *URL:* http://www.jnmpc.com

J. Nicholas McGrath

Representative Clients: Alpine Banks (litigation); Aspen Center for Physics; Aspen Chamber Resort Association.; The Gant Condominium Association; Aspen Alps Condominium Assn.; Gerald D. Hines; Steak Pit, Inc.

For full biographical listings, see the Martindale-Hubbell Law Directory

OATES, KNEZEVICH & GARDENSWARTZ, P.C. (AV)

Aspen Plaza Building, 3rd Floor, 533 East Hopkins Avenue, 81611
Telephone: 970-920-1700
Fax: 970-920-1121
Email: ohkg@rof.net

Leonard M. Oates
Ted D. Gardenswartz
Richard A. Knezevich
David B. Kelly

David B. Mueller

OF COUNSEL

John Thomas Kelly
Michael Feigenbaum

For full biographical listings, see the Martindale-Hubbell Law Directory

*BOULDER,** Boulder Co.

HOWARD BITTMAN (AV)

1406 Pearl Street, Suite 200, 80302
Telephone: 303-443-2281
Fax: 303-443-2862
Email: bittmanh@aol.com *URL:* http://www.lawyers.com/howardbittman

For full biographical listings, see the Martindale-Hubbell Law Directory

COOK & LEE, P.C. (AV)

5390 Manhattan Circle, 2nd Floor, 80303
Telephone: 303-543-1000
Fax: 303-543-8582
Email: cookleepc@bewellnet.com

Stephen H. Cook
Larry D. Lee

Robert K. Reimann

For full biographical listings, see the Martindale-Hubbell Law Directory

JOSEPH ADAMS COPE (AV)

4750 Table Mesa Drive, 80303-5575
Telephone: 303-494-3000
Fax: 303-494-6309
Email: jay@Frascona.com *URL:* http://www.Frascona.com
(Also Of Counsel to Frascona, Joiner and Goodman)

For full biographical listings, see the Martindale-Hubbell Law Directory

ENWALL & GRANT, L.L.C. (AV)

720 Pearl Street, 80302
Telephone: 303-449-3891
Fax: 303-449-3992
Email: enwall@nilenet.com

Michael R. Enwall
Barbara K. Grant

For full biographical listings, see the Martindale-Hubbell Law Directory

FRENCH & STONE, P.C. (AV)

720 Pearl Street, 80302
Telephone: 303-449-3891
Fax: 303-449-3992

(See Next Column)

Joseph C. French
David M. Haynes
Robert W. Stone
Mark M. Haynes

Reference: Bank of Boulder.

For full biographical listings, see the Martindale-Hubbell Law Directory

PURVIS, GRAY & GORDON, LLP (AV)

The Exeter Building, Suite 501, 1050 Walnut Street, 80302
Telephone: 303-442-3366
Fax: 303-440-3688
Email: info@pgglaw.com *URL:*
http://www.lawyers.com/purvisgrayschuetze&gordon
Denver, Colorado Office: 303 East 17th Avenue, Suite 700.
Telephone: 303-860-1888.

MEMBERS OF FIRM

William R. Gray
John A. Purvis
Glen F. Gordon

For full biographical listings, see the Martindale-Hubbell Law Directory

TRINE & METCALF, P.C. (AV)

1435 Arapahoe Avenue, 80302-6390
Telephone: 303-442-0173
Fax: 303-443-7677
Email: firm@trine-metcalf.com *URL:* http://www.trine-metcalf.com

William A. Trine
J. Conard Metcalf

T. Michael Kennedy

Reference: Norwest Bank of Boulder.

For full biographical listings, see the Martindale-Hubbell Law Directory

BROOMFIELD, Boulder Co.

SCHADEN, KATZMAN, LAMPERT & MCCLUNE (AV)

11870 Airport Way, 80021-2555
Telephone: 303-465-3663
Facsimile: 303-465-3884
Email: SCHKATZLAM@aol.com *URL:*
http://www.lawyers.com/schadenlaw
Troy, Michigan Office; 100 West Big Beaver Road. Suite 130. 48084.
Telephone: 248-258-4800.
Fax: 248-258-2825.

MEMBERS OF FIRM

Richard F. Schaden
Bruce A. Lampert
David I. Katzman (Not admitted in CO)
John D. McClune (Not admitted in CO)

ASSOCIATE

Kathleen M. Schaden

OF COUNSEL

Bruce O. Wilson (Not admitted in CO)

For full biographical listings, see the Martindale-Hubbell Law Directory

*COLORADO SPRINGS,** El Paso Co.

BELTZ, EDWARDS & SABO, L.L.P. (AV)

128 South Tejon, Suite 310, 80903
Telephone: 719-634-6620
Fax: 719-634-3142
Email: BES__LLP@aol.com *URL:* http://www.lawyers.com/beslaw
Other Colorado Springs, Colorado Office: 729 South Cascade, 80903.
Telephone: 719-473-4444.
Fax: 719-444-0186.

Daniel P. Edwards
W. Thomas Beltz
John W. Sabo, III

ASSOCIATE

Daniel A. West

Representative Clients: A.M.I. Industries, Inc.; Analytical Surveys, Inc.; A.C. Israel Enterprises, Inc.; Boddington Lumber Co., Inc.; Cardiovascular Surgeons of Colorado Springs, P.C.; Colorado Springs Radiologists, P.C.; Digital, Inc.; Music Semi-Conductors, Inc.; Schlage Lock Co.; Texas Instruments.

For full biographical listings, see the Martindale-Hubbell Law Directory

KANE, DONLEY & JOHNSON, P.C. (AV)

90 South Cascade Avenue, Suite 830, 80903
Telephone: 719-471-1650
Fax: 719-471-1663
Mailing Address: P.O. Box 1119, Colorado Springs, CO, 80901
Email: kdandjpc@earthlink.net

Jerry A. Donley
Jack E. Donley
Mark H. Kane
David M. Johnson
Hayden W. Kane, II

(See Next Column)

KANE, DONLEY & JOHNSON P.C.—*Continued*

William A. Palmer
Katherine L. Hays

OF COUNSEL

Hayden W. Kane

Representative Clients: American International Companies; Shelter Insurance Co.; Metropolitan Insurance Co.
Reference: State Bank & Trust and Bank One.

For full biographical listings, see the Martindale-Hubbell Law Directory

MELAT, PRESSMAN, EZELL & HIGBIE, LLP (AV)

711 South Tejon Street, 80903-4054
Telephone: 719-475-0304
Fax: 719-475-0242
Email: mpeh4@aol.com

MEMBERS OF FIRM

Justin R. Melat
Glenn S. Pressman
E. Steven Ezell
Alanson Higbie

ASSOCIATES

Rebecca A. Lorenz
Judith K. Funderburg

References: U.S. Bank; Colorado Bank-Exchange.

For full biographical listings, see the Martindale-Hubbell Law Directory

RETHERFORD, MULLEN, JOHNSON & BRUCE, L.L.C. (AV)

415 South Sahwatch, P.O. Box 1580, 80901
Telephone: 719-475-2014
Toll Free: 1-800-281-2014
Fax: 719-630-1267
Email: info@rmjblaw.com

MEMBERS OF FIRM

Jerry A. Retherford
J. Stephen Mullen
Anthony A. Johnson
Neil C. Bruce
Patrick R. Salt
Lori M. Moore

ASSOCIATES

Timothy E. Reilly
Debra P. DeRee

OF COUNSEL

Marilyn Brock Doig
Patricia L. Peterson

Representative Clients: Albertson's, Inc.; Boulder Community Hospital (Boulder); City of Colorado Springs Memorial Hospital; Parkview Episcopal Hospital (Pueblo); Rhone-Poulenc Agricultural Company; Southwest Memorial Hospital (Cortez); Vail Valley Medical Center (Vail).

For full biographical listings, see the Martindale-Hubbell Law Directory

TEGTMEIER LAW FIRM, P.C. (AV)

518 North Nevada, Suite 200, 80903
Telephone: 719-473-5757
Telefax: 719-473-6767
Email: richard@worldclasslaw.com

Richard L. Tegtmeier

OF COUNSEL

Stephen A. Brunette

For full biographical listings, see the Martindale-Hubbell Law Directory

VAGLICA & MEINHOLD, L.L.C. (AV)

105 East Moreno, Suite 100, 80903
Telephone: 719-634-5724
Telefax: 719-634-8592
Englewood, Colorado Office: 9200 East Mineral Avenue, Suite 350.

Phillip A. Vaglica
Don H. Meinhold
Su-Lyn Combs

OF COUNSEL

Deborah S. Youngblood

For full biographical listings, see the Martindale-Hubbell Law Directory

*DENVER,** Denver Co.

BAKER & HOSTETLER LLP (AV)

303 East 17th Avenue, Suite 1100, 80203-1264
Telephone: 303-861-0600
FAX: 303-861-7805
To contact an attorney on the Internet use first initial and surname followed by @baker-hostetler.com
URL: http://www.bakerlaw.com
In Cleveland, Ohio: 3200 National City Center, 1900 East Ninth Street.
Telephone: 216-621-0200.
In Cincinnati, Ohio: 312 Walnut Street, Suite 2650.
Telephone: 513-929-3400.
In Columbus, Ohio: Capitol Square, Suite 2100, 65 East State Street.
Telephone: 614-228-1541.
In Houston, Texas: 1000 Louisiana, Suite 2000.
Telephone: 713-751-1600.

(See Next Column)

In Beverly Hills, California: 9150 Wilshire Boulevard, Suite 205.
Telephone: 310-385-7500.
In Long Beach, California: 300 Oceangate, Suite 620.
Telephone: 562-432-2827.
In Los Angeles, California: 600 Wilshire Boulevard.
Telephone: 213-624-2400.
In Orlando, Florida: SunBank Center, Suite 2300, 200 South Orange Avenue.
Telephone: 407-649-4000.
In Washington, D. C.: Washington Square, Suite 1100, 1050 Connecticut Avenue, N.W.
Telephone: 202-861-1500.

PARTNERS

Timothy R. Beyer
Mary Price Birk
James A. Clark
Marc D. Flink
Peter J. Korneffel, Jr.
Michael G. Martin
John B. Moorhead
Michael J. Roche

For Complete List of Firm Personnel, See General Section

For full biographical listings, see the Martindale-Hubbell Law Directory

BALLARD SPAHR ANDREWS & INGERSOLL, LLP (AV)

Seventeenth Street Plaza Building, Suite 2300, 1225 17th Street, 80202-5596
Telephone: 303-292-2400
Fax: 303-296-3956
URL: http://www.ballardspahr.com
Baltimore, Maryland Office: 300 East Lombard Street. 19th Floor.
Telephone: 410-528-5600.
Fax: 410-528-5650.
Camden, New Jersey Office: 800 Hudson Square, 5th Floor.
Telephone: 856-541-5577.
Fax: 856-541-8272.
Philadelphia, Pennsylvania Office: 1735 Market Street, 51st Floor.
Telephone: 215-665-8500.
Fax: 215-864-8999.
Salt Lake City, Utah Office: One Utah Center, Suite 1200, 201 South Main Street.
Telephone: 801-531-3000.
Fax: 801-531-3001.
Voorhees, New Jersey Office: Suite 100, 1101 Laurel Oak Drive.
Telephone: 856-627-8555.
Fax: 856-627-1153.
Washington, D.C. Office: Suite 1000 South, 601 13th Street, N.W.
Telephone: 202-661-2200.
Fax: 202-661-2299.

Leslie A. Eaton
Kevin Michael Shea
Roger P. Thomasch

OF COUNSEL

Denise S. Maes

William T. Slamkowski

For Complete List of Firm Personnel, See General Section

For full biographical listings, see the Martindale-Hubbell Law Directory

BEEM & MANN, PROFESSIONAL CORPORATION (AV)

One Norwest Center, Suite 3901, 1700 Lincoln Street, 80203
Telephone: 303-894-8100
Fax: 303-832-5010
Email: BeemMann@aol.com

Clifford L. Beem
Stuart Mann

OF COUNSEL

Virginia Elaine Kellogg
Patrick F. Kenney

A. Mark Isley

References: Norwest Bank Denver, N.A.; The Bank of Cherry Creek

For full biographical listings, see the Martindale-Hubbell Law Directory

BERENBAUM, WEINSHIENK & EASON, P.C. (AV)

Suite 2600 Republic Plaza, 370 17th Street, 80202
Telephone: 303-825-0800
Facsimile: 303-629-7610
Email: berenbaum1@aol.com *URL:* http://www.BWELaw.com

Martin D. Buckley
M. Frances Cetrulo
Daniel S. Duggan
David R. Eason
I. H. Kaiser
Kenneth S. Kramer
Larry R. Martinez
Dean G. Panos
Edwin G. Perlmutter
Eugene M. Sprague

OF COUNSEL

Richard L. Eason

(See Next Column)

BERENBAUM, WEINSHIENK & EASON P.C., *Denver—Continued*

Carol Ann Flowers Teri L. Lowery
Melissa Mequi

Representative Clients: Home Depot; Sprint Spectrum, L.P.; Town of Vail, Colorado; First Union Corporation; City of Englewood, Colorado; Oakwood Homes; Karman, Inc.; Wells Fargo Bank, N.A.; Berkshire Life Insurance Co.; Trinity Ventures.

For full biographical listings, see the Martindale-Hubbell Law Directory

BREGA & WINTERS P.C. (AV)

One Norwest Center, 1700 Lincoln Street, Suite 2222, 80203
Telephone: 303-866-9400
Fax: 303-861-9109
Greeley, Colorado Office: 1100 Tenth Street, Suite 402, 80631.
Telephone: 303-352-4805.
Fax: 303-352-6547.

James W. Bain
Stuart N. Bennett
Charles F. Brega
Robert R. Dormer
Wesley B. Howard, Jr.
William W. Hughes (Resident, Greeley Office)
Robert C. Kaufman
Ronald S. Loser
Brian A. Magoon
Loren L. Mall
Glenn W. Merrick
Pamela A. Shaddock (Resident, Greeley Office)
Jay John Schnell
Jerry D. Winters (Resident, Greeley Office)

Jennifer S. Fox
Julie Scroggins Frantz (Resident, Greeley Office)
Brent W. Houston
S. Scott Lasher
Bradley D. Laue (Resident, Greeley Office)
Eric B. Liebman
Kevin C. Massaro
Scott T. Rodgers

For full biographical listings, see the Martindale-Hubbell Law Directory

BRENMAN BROMBERG & TENENBAUM, P.C. (AV)

Mellon Financial Center Suite 1001, 1775 Sherman Street, 80203
Telephone: 303-894-0234
Fax: 303-839-1633
Email: bbt@bbtlaw.net

Albert Brenman
Thomas R. Bromberg
A. Thomas Tenenbaum
Steven W. McDonald

Sheryl A. Johnson Judy A. Gooch

OF COUNSEL
Duane Woodard

For full biographical listings, see the Martindale-Hubbell Law Directory

JAMES E. BROWN & ASSOCIATES, P.C. (AV)

1350 Seventeenth Street, Suite 306, 80202
Telephone: 303-825-1818
Fax: 303-825-2828
Email: wy0j@aol.com

James E. Brown
OF COUNSEL
Michael B. Levy

For full biographical listings, see the Martindale-Hubbell Law Directory

BROWNSTEIN HYATT & FARBER, P.C. (AV)

Twenty-Second Floor, 410 Seventeenth Street, 80202-4437
Telephone: 303-223-1100
Telecopier: 303-223-1111
Washington, D.C. Office: 1615 L Street, N.W., Suite 450, 20036.
Telephone: 202-296-7353.
Telecopier: 202-296-7009.
Glenwood Springs, Colorado Office: Box 357, 81602.
Telephone: 970-945-5302.
Telecopier: 970-945-4921.

Mark F. Leonard
Andrew W. Loewi
Stanley L. Garnett
Lisa Hogan
Wayne F. Forman
Hubert A. Farbes, Jr.
Terence C. Gill
Mark J. Mathews

SPECIAL COUNSEL

Lynne M. Hufnagel Richard P. Barkley

Joshua J. Widoff
Beth Doherty Quinn
David S. Chipman
Jeanine M. Anderson
James D. Sloan
A.W. Victoria Jacobs
Jennifer C. Robinson
Meghan W. Martinez

Representative Clients: Amrion, Inc.; Citicorp North America, Inc.; Coeur d'Alene Mines Corporation; Columbia/HCA Healthcare Corporation; Franklin Haney Company; Med-Alliance, Inc.; Metro Taxi, Inc.; PCL Construction Services, Inc.; Trammell Crow Company; United Air Lines, Inc.

(See Next Column)

For Complete List of Firm Personnel, See General Section

For full biographical listings, see the Martindale-Hubbell Law Directory

CANGES, IWASHKO & BETHKE, A PROFESSIONAL CORPORATION (AV)

303 East 17th Avenue Suite 400, 80203-1257
Telephone: 303-860-1900
Fax: 303-860-1665
URL: http://www.lawyers.com/ciblaw

E. Michael Canges
Nina A. Iwashko
Erich L. Bethke
James S. Bailey

Michelle L. Lukowicz

Reference: Norwest Bank Denver.

For full biographical listings, see the Martindale-Hubbell Law Directory

CORTEZ MACAULAY BERNHARDT & SCHUETZE LLC (AV)

1600 Broadway, Suite 1600, 80202
Telephone: 303-864-1000
Facsimile: 303-864-1111
URL: http://www.cmblaw.com

Miles Cortez
Christopher T. Macaulay
Susan Bernhardt
Robert A. Schuetze
David H. Goldberg
Marian L. Carlson
Richard P. R. Cohn

For full biographical listings, see the Martindale-Hubbell Law Directory

DAVIS & CERIANI, P.C. (AV)

Suite 400, Market Center, 1350 Seventeenth Street, 80202
Telephone: 303-534-9000
Telecopier: 303-534-4618
Email: davisandceriani.com

Rick G. Davis
Gary J. Ceriani
Bruce E. Rohde
Michael P. Cillo
Charles W. Bess
John W. Himmelmann

Margaret E. Peper
Patrick John Kanouff
Mark M. Osborn
Valeri Pappas

For full biographical listings, see the Martindale-Hubbell Law Directory

FRIEDLOB SANDERSON RASKIN PAULSON & TOURTILLOTT, LLC (AV)

1400 Glenarm Place, 80202-5099
Telephone: 303-571-1400
Fax: 303-595-3159; 303-595-3970; 303-615-5472
Englewood, Colorado Office: 8400 East Prentice Avenue, 80111-2918.
Telephone: 303-571-1400.
Santa Cruz, California Office: 519 Seabright Avenue, Suite 208, 95062-3482.
Telephone: 813-460-3966.
Fax: 813-460-3968.

Richard H. Goldberg
SPECIAL COUNSEL
John H. Tatlock

For full biographical listings, see the Martindale-Hubbell Law Directory

GODFREY & ASSOCIATES, PROFESSIONAL CORPORATION (AV)

4643 S. Ulster, Suite 920, 80237
Telephone: 303-592-5980
FAX: 303-592-5985
Email: Brett_Godfrey@msn.com

Brett Marshall Godfrey Paul B. Godfrey (1927-1998)

Michelle A. Pinkowski James A. Johnson

For full biographical listings, see the Martindale-Hubbell Law Directory

HALABY CROSS & SCHLUTER (AV)

Suite 1400, 1873 South Bellaire Street, 80222
Telephone: 303-691-5300
Fax: 303-691-5307

Theodore S. Halaby Jonathan A. Cross
Leslie L. Schluter

ASSOCIATES

Andrew J. Carafelli
E. James Wilder, IV
Matthew A. Samuelson
Sue Ann Haskell
Marc C. Diamant

For full biographical listings, see the Martindale-Hubbell Law Directory

Denver—Continued

HAMILTON AND FAATZ, A PROFESSIONAL CORPORATION (AV)

Suite 500 Colorado State Bank Building, 1600 Broadway, 80202-4905
Telephone: 303-830-0500
Facsimile: 303-860-7855
Email: HandF@HandF.com

Pierpont Fuller (1906-1983)
John M. Evans (1911-1984)
Dwight Alan Hamilton
Clyde A. Faatz, Jr.
John T. Willson
Michael E. Gurley
James H. Marlow
Jan E. Montgomery
Gregory W. Smith

Christopher J.W. Forrest
Cynthia Treadwell-Miller
Tal Diamant

OF COUNSEL

Kenneth W. Caughey

Representative Clients: Arapahoe County Public Airport Authority; Colorado Baptist General Convention; First Industrial Realty Trust; Masonic Temple Association of Denver; Meridian Investment Management Corp.; Public Employees' Retirement Association of Colorado; Randall and Blake, Inc.; Rocky Mountain Clothing Co.; South Denver Cardiology Associates, P.C.; Unisource Worldwide, Inc.

For full biographical listings, see the Martindale-Hubbell Law Directory

---

HOLME ROBERTS & OWEN LLP (AV)

Suite 4100, 1700 Lincoln, 80203
Telephone: 303-861-7000
Telecopier: 303-866-0200
Email: hro@hro.com *URL:* http://www.hro.com
Boulder, Colorado Office: Suite 400, 1401 Pearl Street.
Telephone: 303-444-5955.
Telecopier: 303-444-1063.
Colorado Springs, Colorado Office: Suite 1300, 90 South Cascade Avenue.
Telephone: 719-473-3800.
Telecopier: 719-633-1518.
Salt Lake City, Utah Office: Suite 1100, 111 East Broadway.
Telephone: 801-521-5800.
Telecopier: 801-521-9639.
London, England Office: Heathcoat House, 3rd Floor, 20 Savile Row.
Telephone: 011-44-171-494-5600.
Telecopier: 011-44-171-287-9344.

PARTNERS OF FIRM

Dennis L. Arfmann
Donald K. Bain
Duncan E. Barber
Blaine J. Benard (Salt Lake City Office)
Bruce F. Black
Boyd N. Boland
Elizabeth E. Brown
Linnea Brown
Charles B. Bruce, Jr.
Susan E. Duffey Campbell (Colorado Springs Office)
Spencer T. Denison
Daniel J. Dunn
Elizabeth T. Dunning (Salt Lake City Office)
Adam R. Eaton
Richard L. Gabriel
Nancy J. Gegenheimer
George M. Haley, III (Salt Lake City Office)
Colin G. Harris
Henry W. Ipsen
Eric E. Johnson
Sherri Heckel Kuhlmann
Lawrence L. Levin
Martin D. Litt
Kenneth W. Lund
George G. Matava
John D. McCarthy
John V. McDermott
Richard L. Nagl (Colorado Springs Office)
Charlotte Louise Neitzel
K. Preston Oade, Jr.
Katherine Jean Peck
Brent E. Rychener (Colorado Springs Office)
Greggory J. Savage (Salt Lake City Office)
David S. Steefel
Robert L. Stolebarger (Salt Lake City Office)
Mary Hurley Stuart
Patricia C. Tisdale
Robert Tuchman
John R. Webb
David B. Wilson
Richard R. Young (Managing Partner, Colorado Springs Office)

OF COUNSEL

Frank E. Moss (Salt Lake City Office)
Richard L. Schrepferman

SPECIAL COUNSEL

Carolyn Cox (Salt Lake City Office)

SENIOR COUNSEL

A. Edgar Benton
Lawrence M. Zavadil

ASSOCIATES

Mark A. Adams
Kelly M. Condon
Matthew N. Evans (Salt Lake City Office)
Elizabeth K. Flaagan
Elizabeth A. González
Michael J. Hofmann
Ashley Warren Jordaan (Colorado Springs Office)
Donald I. J. Kelso
Tonya Feit Lark (Colorado Springs Office)
Matt A. Mayer
Deborah S. Menkins (Colorado Springs Office)
Jennifer Nelson (Salt Lake City Office)
Roxane J. Perruso
J. Daniel Phelan

(See Next Column)

ASSOCIATES (Continued)

Kevin Joseph Simon (Salt Lake City Office)
Philip C. Zimmerman

For Complete List of Firm Personnel, See General Section

For full biographical listings, see the Martindale-Hubbell Law Directory

---

THE LAW FIRM OF EDWIN A. HOWE, P.C. (AV)

950 South Cherry Street, Suite 1502, 80246
Telephone: 303-756-5060
Fax: 303-756-5114
URL: http://www.lawyers.com/howelaw

Edwin A. Howe, II

LEGAL SUPPORT PERSONNEL

Julie Rotenberg (Office Administrator)

For full biographical listings, see the Martindale-Hubbell Law Directory

---

KATZ, LOOK & MOISON, PROFESSIONAL CORPORATION (AV)

1120 Lincoln Street, Suite 1100, 80203
Telephone: 303-832-1900
Fax: 303-863-0412

Michael M. Katz
Harley K. Look, Jr.
Peter R. Moison
Kathryn A. Reeves

Brian E. Onorato
Melisa A. Vogel
Arthur T. DiMeo
Delwyn G. Haroldson
Barbara J. Stauch

SPECIAL COUNSEL

Ogborn, Summerlin & Ogborn, L.L.C., Denver, Colorado

For full biographical listings, see the Martindale-Hubbell Law Directory

---

KENNEDY & CHRISTOPHER, P.C. (AV)

1660 Wynkoop Street, Suite 900, 80202
Telephone: 303-825-2700
Fax: 303-825-0434
Email: admn@Kennedy-Christopher.com

Frank R. Kennedy
Daniel R. Christopher
Kim B. Childs
Elizabeth A. Starrs
Mark A. Fogg
Michael T. Mihm
Charles R. Ledbetter
Lisa B. Heintz
Ronald H. Nemirow
Barbara H. Glogiewicz
Dawn E. Mitzner
John R. Mann
Daniel R. McCune
Dean A. McConnell
Edward D. Bronfin

OF COUNSEL

Paul E. Scott

Christopher K. Miller
Carolyn Sprinthall Knaut
David B. Gelman
Kevin P. Perez
Steven H. Weigler
Garrison W. Kaufman
Leslie C. Dolan
Susan Michelle Englert
Chad K. Gillam
Benjamin Alexander Kahn
Steven A. Michalek
Jeremy A. Sitcoff
Renee E. Christian
Laura M. Wassmuth

Representative Clients: American Medical International; Blue Cross/Blue Shield of Colorado; COPIC; The Doctors Co.; Hartford Insurance Co.; Home Insurance Co.; St. Paul Fire and Marine Insurance Co.; PRMS, Colorado Insurance Guaranty Association.

For full biographical listings, see the Martindale-Hubbell Law Directory

---

KONCILJA & ASSOCIATES, P.C. (AV)

Suite 300, 800 Eighteenth Street, 80202
Telephone: 303-675-0900
Facsimile: 303-675-0401
Email: koncilja@ix.netcom.com *URL:* http://www.Koncilja-associates.com

Frances A. Koncilja

OF COUNSEL

David V. Millard

For full biographical listings, see the Martindale-Hubbell Law Directory

---

THE LEVENTHAL LAW FIRM, P.C. (AV)

950 South Cherry Street, Suite 600, 80246
Telephone: 303-759-9945
Fax: 303-759-9692
Email: office@leventhal-law.com

Jim Leventhal
Natalie Brown
Beth L. Krulewitch

(See Next Column)

THE LEVENTHAL LAW FIRM, P.C., *Denver—Continued*

James E. Puga — Timothy G. Buxton

Reference: Vectra Bank.

For full biographical listings, see the Martindale-Hubbell Law Directory

LEVY & LAMBDIN, P.C. (AV)

Plaza Tower One, Suite 900, 6400 South Fiddlers Green Circle (Englewood), 80111
Telephone: 303-796-2900
Telecopier: 303-796-2081

Marc R. Levy — Stuart D. Morse
Suzanne J. Lambdin — Karen Hannah Wheeler

Martha C. Ferris — Stephanie Ann Montague
Gerald D. Pratt — Brian J. Waters
Michael S. Power — Ivan A. Sarkissian
Janet S. Bouffard — Lelia Kathleen Chaney
Jane E. Hershey

For full biographical listings, see the Martindale-Hubbell Law Directory

LONG & JAUDON, P.C. (AV)

The Bailey Mansion, 1600 Ogden Street, 80218-1414
Telephone: 303-832-1122
FAX: 303-832-1348

Lawrence A. Long (1908-1992) — Michael T. McConnell
Joseph C. Jaudon, Jr. — Stephen P. Hopkins
David B. Higgins — Alan D. Avery
Frederick W. Long — Cecelia A. Fleischner
Gary B. Blum — Walter N. Houghtaling
Christine Anne Craigmile

Sheri Hood Roswell — David H. Yun

Representative Clients: St. Joseph Hospital, Inc.; King Soopers, Inc.; Travelers Property Casualty Company; COPIC; The Doctors Co.; Home Insurance Company; Montgomery Wards.

For Complete List of Firm Personnel, See General Section

For full biographical listings, see the Martindale-Hubbell Law Directory

MARKUSSON, GREEN & JARVIS, P.C. (AV)

Suite 2300, 1050 Seventeenth Street, 80265
Telephone: 303-572-4200
Fax: 303-595-3780

James K. Green — Dennis H. Markusson
H. Keith Jarvis — Thomas E. Napp

Kirstin G. Lindberg — William B. Stanton
Jason L. Romero — William T. Webb
Ashley E. Moller

Representative Clients: Albertson's; CGU; Sherwin-Williams; Travelers Insurance Cos.; Reliance Insurance Co.; Republic Insurance; Electric Mutual Insurance; Ohio Casualty Insurance Co.; Dow Agro Sciences Co.; The Terracon Companies.

For full biographical listings, see the Martindale-Hubbell Law Directory

LAW OFFICES OF JOHN W. MCKENDREE (AV)

Creswell Mansion, 1244 Grant Street, 80203
Telephone: 303-861-8906
Fax: 303-861-7773
Email: Johnwmckendree@msn.com

ASSOCIATE

Elizabeth G. McKendree

Reference: Colorado National Bank.

For full biographical listings, see the Martindale-Hubbell Law Directory

GREGG C. MCREYNOLDS, P.C. (AV)

Financial Plaza, Suite 200 7720 East Belleview Avenue (Englewood), 80111-2614
Telephone: 303-694-1800
Fax: 303-694-2443
Email: gmcr@aol.com *URL:* http://www.lawyers.com/mcreynoldslaw

Gregg C. McReynolds

For full biographical listings, see the Martindale-Hubbell Law Directory

THE MELLON LAW FIRM (AV)

2255 East Eighteenth Avenue Smith Mansion - Carriage House, 80206
Telephone: 303-320-5800
Facsimilie: 303-399-8038

(See Next Column)

MEMBERS OF FIRM

Joseph J. Mellon — Mary F. Mellon

For full biographical listings, see the Martindale-Hubbell Law Directory

MILLER & WELCH, L.L.C. (AV)

730 - 17th Street, Suite 925, 80202-3503
Telephone: 303-623-6005
Facsimile: 303-623-0311

James Rollin Miller, Jr. — Carol M. Welch
Paul R. Wood

Candace M. Dunley — Joycelyn Crucillo
Matthew D. Macy

For full biographical listings, see the Martindale-Hubbell Law Directory

MONTGOMERY LITTLE & MCGREW, P.C. (AV)

The Quadrant, 5445 DTC Parkway, Suite 800 (Englewood), 80111
Telephone: 303-773-8100
Telecopier: 303-220-0412
URL: http://www.mlmpc.com

Roy E. Montgomery (1907-1986) — Daniel P. Murphy
Robert R. Montgomery — Robert N. Spencer
David C. Little — John R. Riley
Richard L. Murray, Jr. — Christopher B. Little
Kevin J. Kuhn — Karen B. Best
Robert J. Beattie — Timothy M. Schulte
William H. Knapp — Carole Salamaha
Patrick T. O'Rourke
Julie J. Collett

OF COUNSEL

J. Bayard Young

Representative Clients: BP Amoco; Bristol-Myers Squibb; Colorado Physicians Insurance; The St. Paul Insurance Cos.; University of Colorado Health Sciences Center; HealthOne; Westport Insurance Corp.; CNA; Design Professionals Insurance Corp.; Teva Pharmaceuticals.

For Complete List of Firm Personnel, See General Section

For full biographical listings, see the Martindale-Hubbell Law Directory

MYER, SWANSON, ADAMS & WOLF, P.C. (AV)

The Colorado State Bank Building, 1600 Broadway, Suite 1480, 80202-4915
Telephone: 303-866-9800
Facsimile: 303-866-9818

Fred E. Neef (1910-1986) — Rendle Myer (1929-1999)
Thomas J. Wolf

John M. Anderson

OF COUNSEL

Robert Swanson

Representative Clients: The Oppenheimer Funds; Panorama Series Fund; The Centennial Trusts; Mile High Chapter of American Red Cross; Master Lease; Heartland Management Co.; Kan-Build of Colorado, Inc.
Reference: The Colorado State Bank and Trust of Denver.

For Complete List of Firm Personnel, See General Section

For full biographical listings, see the Martindale-Hubbell Law Directory

OGBORN, SUMMERLIN & OGBORN, L.L.C. (AV)

1120 Lincoln Street, Suite 1100, 80203
Telephone: 303-861-7472
Fax: 303-830-8516
Email: mike@osolaw.com
Lincoln, Nebraska Office: 330 South Tenth Street, Suite 210, 68508.
Telephone: 402-434-8040.
Fax: 402-434-8044.

Murray Ogborn — Michael J. Ogborn
V. Gene Summerlin (Resident, Lincoln, Nebraska)

Krista L. Kester (Resident, Lincoln, Nebraska) — David A. Laird

Representative Clients: The American Simmental Association; Black & Decker, (U.S.) Inc.; Braunvich Association of America; National Pedigreed Livestock Council; Nucor Corporation; Cyprus Amax; Concrete Management, Inc.; L & S Electric, Inc.; Welsheimer Construction Co., Inc.; Omnitrax R.R.

For full biographical listings, see the Martindale-Hubbell Law Directory

Denver—Continued

PENDLETON, FRIEDBERG, WILSON & HENNESSEY, P.C. (AV)
Seventeenth & Grant Building, Suite 1000, 303 East 17th Avenue, 80203
Telephone: 303-839-1204
Telecopier: 303-831-0786

Brian Pendleton
Alan C. Friedberg
Robert F. Wilson
Richard F. Hennessey
F. Stephen Collins
Michael E. Romero
Susan M. Hargleroad
Joel W. Cantrick
Nancy R. Crow
William S. Martin
Stephen J. Ismert

Noriko K. Nakamura
John Christopher Haas
Timothy M. Kratz
Kathryn A. Wingard
John E. Horneck

SPECIAL COUNSEL

Paul G. Bursiek
Jeffrey R. Fiske

Reference: Norwest Bank of Denver.

For full biographical listings, see the Martindale-Hubbell Law Directory

PURVIS, GRAY & GORDON, LLP (AV)
303 East 17th Avenue, Suite 700, 80203
Telephone: 303-860-1888
Email: info@pgglaw.com *URL:* http://www.lawyers.com/purvisgrayschuetze&gordon
Boulder, Colorado Office: The Exeter Building, Suite 501, 1050 Walnut Street.
Telephone: 303-442-3366.
Fax: 303-440-3688.

MEMBERS OF FIRM

William R. Gray
John A. Purvis
Glen F. Gordon

For full biographical listings, see the Martindale-Hubbell Law Directory

REIMAN & BAYAZ, P.C. (AV)
1600 Broadway, Suite 1340, 80202
Telephone: 303-860-1500
Fax: 303-839-4380
Email: rblaw@earthlink.net

Jeff Reiman
Marcie K. Bayaz

Debra D. Asimus

For full biographical listings, see the Martindale-Hubbell Law Directory

RICHILANO & RIDLEY, P.C. (AV)
1800 15th Street, Suite 101, 80202-1185
Telephone: 303-893-8000
Telecopier: 303-893-8055
Email: patridley@aol.com
Email: richilano@lawyernet.com

John M. Richilano
Patrick L. Ridley

For full biographical listings, see the Martindale-Hubbell Law Directory

SHERMAN & HOWARD L.L.C. (AV)
Attorneys and Counselors at Law
633 Seventeenth Street, Suite 3000, 80202
Telephone: 303-297-2900
Telecopier: 303-298-0940
Colorado Springs, Colorado Office: Suite 1500, 90 South Cascade Avenue, 80903.
Telephone: 719-475-2440.
Las Vegas, Nevada Office: Swendseid & Stern, a member in Sherman & Howard L.L.C., 317 Sixth Street, 89101.
Telephone: 702-387-6073.
Reno, Nevada Office: Swendseid & Stern, a member in Sherman & Howard L.L.C., 50 West Liberty Street, Suite 660, 89501.
Telephone: 702-323-1980.

Christopher Lane
Mark L. Fulford
Kenneth B. Siegel
Joseph J. Bronesky
Richard N. Baer
Leanne B. DeVos
Stefan D. Stein
Lawrence W. Treece
Hugh J. McClearn
Milton L. "Skip" Smith, III (Colorado Springs Office)
John W. Mill

Christopher R. Mosley
Jeffrey S. Lyons
Peter A. Cal
Cherry J. Hearn
Kurt L. Gottschall
Noel M. Franklin
Dawn A. Leporati

Representative Clients: BACE Industries, LLC; Flatiron Structures Co. LLC; Hanifen, Imhoff Inc.; Hathaway Corp.; J.D. Edwards & Co.; Newmont Gold Company; Public Employees' Retirement Assn.; Tele-Communications, Inc.; United Artists Theatre Circuit, Inc.; U.S. West Communications, Inc.

(See Next Column)

For Complete List of Firm Personnel, See General Section

For full biographical listings, see the Martindale-Hubbell Law Directory

TREECE, ALFREY, MUSAT & BOSWORTH, P.C. (AV)
999 18th Street, Suite 1600, 80202
Telephone: 303-292-2700
Facsimile: 303-295-0414
Email: tamb@tamblaw.com *URL:* http://www.tamblaw.com

Robert S. Treece
Thomas N. Alfrey
L. Richard Musat
Arthur H. Bosworth, II
June Baker Laird
Paul E. Collins
Michael L. Hutchinson
Timothy J. Judson
R. Bruce Phillips
David C. von Gunten

Nicholas Kemp

For full biographical listings, see the Martindale-Hubbell Law Directory

WALTERS & JOYCE, P.C. (AV)
2015 York Street, 80205
Telephone: 303-322-1404
FAX: 303-377-5668

Craig D. Joyce

Anne Baudino Holton

OF COUNSEL

Julia T. Waggener

Reference: Norwest Bank of Buckingham Square; Mountain States Bank.

For Complete List of Firm Personnel, See General Section

For full biographical listings, see the Martindale-Hubbell Law Directory

WELBORN SULLIVAN MECK & TOOLEY, P.C. (AV)
1775 Sherman Street, Suite 1800, 80203-4318
Telephone: 303-376-4490
Facsimile: 303-376-4495
Email: wsmt@aol.com

Keith D. Tooley
Brian S. Tooley
Scott L. Sells
Mary V. Laitos
William R. Rapson
Danielle V. Smith

SPECIAL COUNSEL

Norman S. Early, Jr.

Representative Clients: BP Amoco Corporation; Evergreen Resources, Inc.; Falcon Creek Resources, Inc.; HS Resources, Inc.; Inland Resources, Inc.; J-W Operating Company; KCS Mountain Resources, Inc.; Texaco Exploration & Production, Inc.; Union Pacific Resources Company; Whiting Petroleum Company.

For Complete List of Firm Personnel, See General Section

For full biographical listings, see the Martindale-Hubbell Law Directory

WELLS, ANDERSON & RACE, LLC (AV)
1700 Broadway, Suite 1850, 80290
Telephone: 303-830-1212
Fax: 303-830-0898

Mary A. Wells
Sheryl L. Anderson
Geoffrey S. Race
Suanne M. Dell

William Strohmeyer
L. Michael Brooks, Jr.
Nathalia S. A. Hardy

Representative Clients: Associated Aviation Underwriters; Baxter Healthcare Corporation; The Cessna Aircraft Co.; Raytheon Aircraft Company; State Farm Mutual Auto. Ins. Co.; State Farm Fire & Casualty Co.; Royal Insurance Co.; Great American Insurance Cos.; United Fire and Casualty Co.; 3M; Mentor Corporation.

For full biographical listings, see the Martindale-Hubbell Law Directory

WHEELER TRIGG & KENNEDY, P.C. (AV)
Suite 3600, 1801 California Street, 80202
Telephone: 303-292-2525
Telecopier: 303-294-1879
Email: info@wtklaw.com *URL:* http://www.wtklaw.com
Roslyn, New York Office: 1800 Northern Boulevard, Suite 208, 11576.
Telephone: 516-484-9701.
Fax: 516-484-6362.

(See Next Column)

WHEELER TRIGG & KENNEDY P.C., *Denver—Continued*

Malcolm E. Wheeler
John R. Trigg
Mark F. Kennedy
Paul F. Hultin
Michael L. O'Donnell
Robert B. Hunter
Gwen J. Young
Christopher J. Meyer
Lori L. Roberts
Habib Nasrullah
Edward C. Stewart
James E. Hooper, Jr.

OF COUNSEL

Joseph B. Valentine (Not admitted in CO)
Andrew J. Mihalick (Not admitted in CO)

Sean D. Baker
Mark T. Clouatre
Bryan D. Cross
Wendy A. Harvey
David A. Lamb
Lee A. Mickus
Amy L. Padden
Kimberly A. Stout (Not admitted in CO)

For full biographical listings, see the Martindale-Hubbell Law Directory

ENGLEWOOD, Arapahoe Co.

BANTA, HOYT, EVERALL & FARRINGTON, L.L.C. (AV)

Suite 240E, 5690 DTC Boulevard, 80111-3232
Telephone: 303-220-8000
Fax: 303-220-0153

Richard J. Banta
Stephen G. Everall

Representative Clients: Cherry Creek School District No. 5; Colorado School District Self Insurance Pool; Copper Mountain Consolidated Metropolitan District; Kiewit Western Co.; Littleton Public Schools; National Union Fire Insurance Co. (local); South Arapahoe Santation District.

For Complete List of Firm Personnel, See General Section

For full biographical listings, see the Martindale-Hubbell Law Directory

BURG SIMPSON ELDREDGE & HERSH, P.C. (AV)

40 Inverness Drive East, 80112
Telephone: 303-792-5595
Fax: 303-708-0527
URL: http://www.burgsimpson.com
Cody, Wyoming Office: 1135 14th Street.
Telephone: 307-527-7891.
Fax: 307-527-7897.
Sterling, Colorado Office: 131 Hamilton Street.
Telephone: 970-521-1010.

Michael S. Burg
Peter W. Burg
Alan K. Simpson (Not admitted in CO)
Scott J. Eldredge
David P. Hersh
Thomas W. Henderson
Matthew R. Giacomini
Kerry N. Jardine
William L. Simpson (Not admitted in CO)
Colin M. Simpson (Not admitted in CO)

Kieth Van Doren
Matthew S. McElhiney
Rosemary Orsini
Robb A. Nelson
Holly S. Baer
Diane Vaksdal Smith
Joseph M. Kiple
Douglas J. Kotarek
David K. Te Selle
Tiffanie D. Stasiak

OF COUNSEL

Dale J. Coplan

Reference: Norwest Colorado, Inc.

For full biographical listings, see the Martindale-Hubbell Law Directory

KING • PETERSON • DYMOND LLP (AV)

The Edward Building, 8400 E. Prentice Avenue, Suite 1040, 80111
Telephone: 303-793-3400
Facsimile: 303-793-3678
Email: mail@kpdlaw.com *URL:* Http://www.kpdlaw.com

MEMBERS OF FIRM

Richard G. Peterson
Lewis W. Dymond, Jr.
Michael W. Reagor

ASSOCIATE

Michael S. Deen

OF COUNSEL

Charles E. King

For full biographical listings, see the Martindale-Hubbell Law Directory

NORTON • LIDSTONE, LLC (AV)

The Quadrant, 5445 DTC Parkway, Suite 850, 80111
Telephone: 303-221-5552
Fax: 303-221-5553
URL: http://www.lawyers.com/norton_lidstone_law

(See Next Column)

Michael J. Norton
Herrick K. Lidstone, Jr.

For full biographical listings, see the Martindale-Hubbell Law Directory

THOMAS J. TOMAZIN, P.C. (AV)

Suite 200, 5655 South Yosemite, 80111
Telephone: 303-771-1900
FAX: 303-793-0923

Thomas J. Tomazin

Representative Clients: Design Drywall Specialities; Elm Contracting; Kumpf Lincoln Mercury, Inc.; Omni Business Brokers, Inc.; Contract Design Services, Inc.; American Natural Gas Corp.; Sonex Enterprises, Inc.; Am West Energy, Inc.; Mountain States Asphalt Paving, Inc.
Reference: Guaranty Bank & Trust Co.

For full biographical listings, see the Martindale-Hubbell Law Directory

*GOLDEN,** Jefferson Co.

HOLLEY, ALBERTSON & POLK, P.C. (AV)

Suite 100, 1667 Cole Boulevard, 80401-3295
Telephone: 303-233-7838
Fax: 303-233-2860

George Alan Holley
Scott D. Albertson
Dennis B. Polk
Eric E. Torgersen
Howard R. Stone

Heather M. Davis

Reference: First Bank of Wheat Ridge.

For full biographical listings, see the Martindale-Hubbell Law Directory

*GREELEY,** Weld Co.

BREGA & WINTERS P.C. (AV)

1100 Tenth Street, Suite 402, 80631
Telephone: 970-352-4805
Fax: 970-352-6547
Denver, Colorado Office: One Norwest Center, 1700 Lincoln Street, Suite 2222.
Telephone: 303-866-9400.
Fax: 303-861-9109.

Jerry D. Winters
Pamela A. Shaddock
William W. Hughes

Julie Scroggins Frantz
Bradley D. Laue

For full biographical listings, see the Martindale-Hubbell Law Directory

GREENWOOD VILLAGE, Arapahoe Co.

ICENOGLE, NORTON & SETER, A PROFESSIONAL CORPORATION (AV)

5690 DTC Boulevard Suite 300, 80111
Telephone: 303-773-1666
Fax: 303-773-1883
Email: INS@inspc.com

Charles E. Norton
Kim J. Seter
Edward J. Blieszner

Alan D. Pogue

Representative Clients: Bromley Park Metropolitan District; City of Cherry Hills Village, Colorado; E-470 Public Highway Authority; Educational Development Corp., d/b/a Denver Technical College; City of Lone Tree, Colorado; U.S. Home Corporation.

For full biographical listings, see the Martindale-Hubbell Law Directory

*LAMAR,** Prowers Co.

JOHN GEHLHAUSEN, P.C. (AV)

200 South Fifth Street, Drawer 1079, 81052
Telephone: 719-336-9071
Fax: 719-336-9617
URL: http://www.tractorlaw.com

John Gehlhausen

Curtis L. Fleming

For full biographical listings, see the Martindale-Hubbell Law Directory

LONGMONT, Boulder Co.

MILLER & COHEN, P.C. (AV)

344 Main Street, P.O. Box 1259, 80502-1259
Telephone: 303-772-0165
Nationally: 800-606-0165
Fax: 303-772-6450
Email: info@creditorsrights.com *URL:* http://www.creditorsrights.com

John Wayne Miller
Arlene Cohen Miller

Kathy Hix

For full biographical listings, see the Martindale-Hubbell Law Directory

*MONTROSE,** Montrose Co.

EDWARD D. DURHAM (AV)

543 South Second Street, P.O. Box 1721, 81402
Telephone: 970-249-2274
Fax: 970-249-6482; 970-249-6592

Reference: Norwest Bank of Montrose.

For full biographical listings, see the Martindale-Hubbell Law Directory

*TELLURIDE,** San Miguel Co.

LAW OFFICES OF JOHN H. STEEL (AV(T))

126 West Colorado Avenue, P.O. Box 2784, 81435
Telephone: 970-728-1300
Fax: 970-728-1021
Email: justice@rmi.net *URL:* http://www.lawyers.com/steel

For full biographical listings, see the Martindale-Hubbell Law Directory

VAIL, Eagle Co.

DUNN, ABPLANALP & MAURIELLO, P.C. (AV)

Suite 300 Weststar Bank Building, 108 South Frontage Road West, 81657-5087
Telephone: 970-476-0300
Telecopier: 970-476-4765
Email: vaillaw@vail.net *URL:* http://www.lawyers.com/vaillaw

John W. Dunn
Diane Herman Mauriello
Carrie A. Hendon

OF COUNSEL

Jerry W. Hannah

For Complete List of Firm Personnel, See General Section

For full biographical listings, see the Martindale-Hubbell Law Directory

WESTMINSTER, Adams Co.

CIANCIO & JONSEN, P.C. (AV)

12000 North Pecos Street Suite 200, 80234-2079
Telephone: 303-451-0300
Fax: 303-280-0614
Email: ciancio@csn.net
Email: jonsen@csn.net

Gene A. Ciancio
Eric R. Jonsen

Cynthia M. Ciancio

For full biographical listings, see the Martindale-Hubbell Law Directory

CONNECTICUT

*BRIDGEPORT,** Fairfield Co.

BAI, POLLOCK AND COYNE, P.C. (AV)

Park City Plaza, 10 Middle Street, P.O. Box 1978, 06604
Telephone: 203-366-7991
Fax: 203-366-4723
Email: bpc@snet.net

Arnold J. Bai (1931-1992)
Paul E. Pollock
James E. Coyne
Jeffrey A. Blueweiss
Garie J. Mulcahey
Raymond J. Plouffe, Jr.
Philip F. von Kuhn
Madonna A. Sacco
Michael S. Lynch
David J. Robertson
Edward P. Brady III

(See Next Column)

Gaileen A. Kaufman
Kevin S. Coyne
Colleen D. Fries
Neal P. Rogan
Louis A. Annecchino
Robert J. Weber, III
Heidi Marie Priwall
Anthony D. Sutton
Kevin J. Curseaden

For full biographical listings, see the Martindale-Hubbell Law Directory

GERALD E. BODELL (AV)

177 State Street Suite 401, 06604
Telephone: 203-335-8955
Fax: 203-366-6812
New York, New York Office: 36 West 44th Street, Suite 303.
Telephone: 212- 398-3778.
Fax: 212-398-3779.

For full biographical listings, see the Martindale-Hubbell Law Directory

LESSER & SOBEL, P.C. (AV)

1000 Lafayette Boulevard, 06604
Telephone: 203-336-1811
Facsimile: 203-334-8069

Robert K. Lesser
Stanton H. Lesser
Paul A. Sobel
Neil A. Lieberthal

For full biographical listings, see the Martindale-Hubbell Law Directory

LAWRENCE J. MERLY (AV)

76 Lyon Terrace, 06604
Telephone: 203-333-1353
Fax: 203-332-7984

Reference: Peoples Savings Bank.

For full biographical listings, see the Martindale-Hubbell Law Directory

WILLIAMS, COONEY & SHEEHY (AV)

One Lafayette Circle, 06604
Telephone: 203-331-0888
Telecopier: 203-331-0896
Email: wilcooshee@aol.com

MEMBERS OF FIRM

Ronald D. Williams
Robert J. Cooney
Edward Maum Sheehy
Dion W. Moore
Ronald D. Williams, Jr.
Francis A. Smith, Jr. (1951-1989)

Suzannah Kim Nigro
Michael Richard Brandt

Representative Clients: Connecticut Medical Insurance Co.; Zimmer Manufacturing Co.; Textron-Lycoming; The Stop & Shop Companies, Inc.; Fleet Bank; Podiatry Insurance Company of America; Town of Easton, Conn.

For full biographical listings, see the Martindale-Hubbell Law Directory

CHESHIRE, New Haven Co.

MOORE, O'BRIEN, JACQUES & YELENAK (AV)

700 West Johnson Avenue Suite 207, 06410
Telephone: 203-272-5881
Fax: 203-272-9273

MEMBERS OF FIRM

Garrett M. Moore
Gregory E. O'Brien
Stephen L. Jacques
William P. Yelenak

For full biographical listings, see the Martindale-Hubbell Law Directory

NUZZO & ROBERTS, L.L.C. (AV)

One Town Center, P.O. Box 747, 06410
Telephone: 203-250-2000
Fax: 203-250-3131
Email: NUZZO-ROBERTS.COM

Anthony Nuzzo, Jr.
Richard A. Roberts
Thomas H. Winslow
Frederick L. Murolo
David J. Weil
Karen T. Gerber

Jane E. Stoddard
Brad N. Mondschein
Marc J. Ubaldi
James D. Slavin, III
Robert J. Chomiak, Jr.
Jason M. Lipsky
Nicole C. Dabekis
Kathleen B. Garner
Michele C. Camerota
Olga E. Zargos
Erich H. Gaston

For full biographical listings, see the Martindale-Hubbell Law Directory

DANBURY, Fairfield Co.

DRISCOLL, TALARICO, FRIZZELL, OLIVO & DRISCOLL (AV)

142 Deer Hill Avenue, 06810-7727
Telephone: 203-792-8333
Facsimile: 203-778-9570
Email: driscoll@javanet.com
Bethel, Connecticut Office: 235 Greenwood Avenue, 06801-2186.
Telephone: 203-744-5000; 743-5556.
Facsimile: 203-798-7790.
Southbury, Connecticut Office: Three Pomperaug Office Park, Suite 203, P.O. Box 252, 06488-0252.
Telephone: 203-264-9650.
Facsimile: 203-798-2175.

Julius J. Bielizna (1914-1988)
Kenneth H. Murray (1905-1984)
Herbert B. Wanderer (1902-1979)
James C. Driscoll, Jr. (Resident, Southbury Office)
Robert N. Talarico
Thomas A. Frizzell
Steven M. Olivo
James C. Driscoll, III (Resident, Bethel Office)
Jerome A. Mayer
Richard W. Hanna
D. Joseph Lane, Jr.
George S. Papazoglou

For full biographical listings, see the Martindale-Hubbell Law Directory

PINNEY, PAYNE, VAN LENTEN, BURRELL, WOLFE & DILLMAN, P.C. (AV)

Lee Farm Corporate Park, 83 Wooster Heights, P.O. Box 3499, 06813-3499
Telephone: 203-743-2721
Fax: 203-792-4759
URL: http://www.ppvlaw.com

Thomas W. Van Lenten
Hugh A. Burrell
Robert J. Wolfe
John M. Dillman
Martin A. Rader, Jr.
William S. Steele, Jr.
Sheldon A. Rosenbaum
Jackie Chan
Richard D. Arconti
Ted D. Backer
Joseph Dimyan
Daniel E. Casagrande
Kim E. Nolan
Wendy A. Grispin

Robin Edwards Otto
John H. Van Lenten

OF COUNSEL

A. Searle Pinney
Bobby S. Payne

Representative Clients: Savings Bank of Danbury.

For full biographical listings, see the Martindale-Hubbell Law Directory

DARIEN, Fairfield Co.

RUCCI, BURNHAM, CARTA & EDELBERG, LLP (AV)

800 Post Road, P.O. Box 1107, 06820
Telephone: 203-655-7695
Facsimile: 203-655-4302
URL: http://www.rbce.com
Stamford, Connecticut Office: 6 Landmark Square, Suite 470.
Telephone: 203-359-5637.

MEMBERS OF FIRM

Joseph J. Rucci, Jr.
Paul H. Burnham
Mark R. Carta
Paul B. Edelberg
William M. Carello
Robert F. Maslan, Jr.

ASSOCIATES

Colette C. Symon
Karen K. Linder
Joanna F. Bowen
David J. Rucci
Sandra J. Akoury

OF COUNSEL

Ian R. Crawford
James C. Dempsey
Lawrence H. Reilly
Alberto N. Moris (Not admitted in CT)

For full biographical listings, see the Martindale-Hubbell Law Directory

FAIRFIELD, Fairfield Co.

HOLAHAN, GUMPPER & DOWLING (AV)

1375 Kings Highway East, P.O. Box 320177, 06432-0177
Telephone: 203-384-1385
Fax: 203-335-3594
Email: hgd.law@snet.net

MEMBERS OF FIRM

Edward J. Holahan, Jr.
Kevin J. Gumpper
Michael A. Dowling

ASSOCIATES

John M. Rowan
John E. McCain

OF COUNSEL

William P. Gumpper

For full biographical listings, see the Martindale-Hubbell Law Directory

GREENWICH, Fairfield Co.

ALBERT, WARD & JOHNSON, P.C. (AV)

125 Mason Street, P.O. Box 1668, 06836
Telephone: 203-661-8600
Telecopier: 203-661-8051

Tom S. Ward, Jr.
Scott R. Johnson
Jane D. Hogeman
Howard R. Wolfe
Christopher A. Kristoff
Vicki K. Comberiati

OF COUNSEL

David Albert
C. Robton Perelli-Minetti

For full biographical listings, see the Martindale-Hubbell Law Directory

FOGARTY COHEN SELBY & NEMIROFF LLC (AV)

88 Field Point Road, P.O. Box 2508, 06836-2508
Telephone: 203-661-1000
Telefax: 203-629-7300

MEMBERS OF FIRM

James R. Fogarty
Bruce F. Cohen
Leland C. Selby
Andrew P. Nemiroff
Steven W. Russo

COUNSEL

Robert A. Epstein
Everett Fisher
Jennifer N. Boyd

ASSOCIATES

William Bradford Smith, Jr.
Carolyn Alexander Collins
Lawrence F. Reilly
Anne M. Piedade
Eric R. Posmantier

For full biographical listings, see the Martindale-Hubbell Law Directory

HOLLAND KAUFMANN & BARTELS, LLC (AV)

289 Greenwich Avenue, 06830-6595
Telephone: 203-869-5600
Fax: 203-869-4648

Alexander J. Holland
Charles B. Kaufmann, III
Philip H. Bartels
Harold R. Burke
Jean Mills Aranha
Lori E. Romano
John C. Fusco

OF COUNSEL

Beth K. Hansson

For full biographical listings, see the Martindale-Hubbell Law Directory

*HARTFORD,** Hartford Co.

CRANMORE, FITZGERALD & MEANEY (AV)

49 Wethersfield Avenue, 06114-1102
Telephone: 860-522-9100
Telecopier: 860-522-3379

MEMBERS OF FIRM

J. J. Cranmore
John C. FitzGerald, Jr.
Joseph V. Meaney, Jr.
John P. McHugh
Patricia D. Anderson

ASSOCIATES

Michael P. McGoldrick
Leyla F. Kimball
Wendell G. Davis, Jr. (Not admitted in CT)

For full biographical listings, see the Martindale-Hubbell Law Directory

GORDON, MUIR AND FOLEY, LLP (AV)

Hartford Square North, Ten Columbus Boulevard, 06106-5123
Telephone: 860-525-5361
Telecopier: 860-525-4849
Email: admin@gmflaw.com *URL:* http://www.gmflaw.com

MEMBERS OF FIRM

William S. Gordon, Jr. (1946-1956)
George Muir (1939-1976)
Edward J. Foley (1955-1983)
Peter C. Schwartz
John J. Reid
John H. Goodrich, Jr.
R. Bradley Wolfe
Jon Stephen Berk
William J. Gallitto
Gerald R. Swirsky
Robert J. O'Brien
Philip J. O'Connor
Kenneth G. Williams
Mary Ann Santacroce
Mary Anne Alicia Charron
Andrew J. Hern
Reneé W. Dwyer
Patty G. Swan

ASSOCIATES

Doreen West Amata
Howard A. Steinman
Erik E. Roberts
Christopher J. Casciani

Reference: People's Bank.

For full biographical listings, see the Martindale-Hubbell Law Directory

Hartford—Continued

JACKSON, O'KEEFE AND PHELAN (AV)

36 Russ Street, 06106-1571
Telephone: 860-278-4040
Fax: 860-527-2500
West Hartford, Connecticut Office: 62 LaSalle Road.
Telephone: 860-521-7500.
Fax: 860-561-5399.
Bethlehem, Connecticut Office: 423 Munger Lane. Telephone/
Fax: 203-266-5255.

MEMBERS OF FIRM

Jay W. Jackson
Andrew J. O'Keefe
Denise Martino Phelan
Matthew J. O'Keefe
Michael E. Riley
Peter K. O'Keefe
Philip R. Dunn, Jr.
Kathryn M. Cunningham
Joseph M. Busher, Jr.
Kristen E. Scholhamer

Representative Clients: Travelers Aetna Property Casualty Co.; ITT Hartford; Liberty Mutual Insurance Co.; Connecticut Medical Insurance Co.

For full biographical listings, see the Martindale-Hubbell Law Directory

ROGIN, NASSAU, CAPLAN, LASSMAN & HIRTLE, LLC (AV)

CityPlace I, 22nd Floor, 185 Asylum Street, 06103-3460
Telephone: 860-278-7480
Fax: 860-278-2179

MEMBERS OF FIRM

Robert L. Hirtle
Steven D. Bartelstone
David M. Call
Paul B. Zolan
David J. Heinlein
Lewis K. Wise
Joan G. Engel
Thomas M. Divine
Mark A. Rosenblum
Barry S. Feigenbaum
Donald G. Gaudreau
Peter S. Sorokin
Iris June Brown
Benjamin Engel
Lawrence G. Rosenthal

ASSOCIATES

Clara A. Porcello
Mark J. Lassman
Brendan T. Flynn
Elizabeth R. Houde
Jonathan M. Starble
Monique R. Polidoro
Lisa M. Anderson

OF COUNSEL

Jerome E. Caplan
Edwin A. Lassman

RETIRED

Edward S. Rogin (Retired)
Louis E. Nassau (Retired)

For full biographical listings, see the Martindale-Hubbell Law Directory

SOROKIN, GROSS & HYDE, P.C. (AV)

One Corporate Center, 06103
Telephone: 860-525-6645
Fax: 860-522-1781
Email: sorokin@sorokinlaw.com
Simsbury, Connecticut Office: 720 Hopmeadow Street.
Telephone: 860-651-9348.
Rocky Hill, Connecticut Office: 2360 Main Street.
Telephone: 860-563-9305.
Fax: 860-529-6931.

Jeffery P. Apuzzo
Lisa A. Magliochetti
Jeffrey R. Martin
Lewis Rabinovitz
Richard C. Robinson

Rod W. Farrell
Jeffrey R. Neidle
Gwen P. Weisberg

For Complete List of Firm Personnel, See General Section

For full biographical listings, see the Martindale-Hubbell Law Directory

*NEW HAVEN,** New Haven Co.

WILLIAM H. CLENDENEN, JR. A PROFESSIONAL CORPORATION (AV)

400 Orange Street, P.O. Box 301, 06502-0301
Telephone: 203-787-1183
Fax: 203-787-2847

William H. Clendenen, Jr.

James E. Clifford
Nancy L. Walker
Thomas C. Pellegrino

For full biographical listings, see the Martindale-Hubbell Law Directory

DEL SOLE & DEL SOLE, L.L.P. (AV)

27 Elm Street, 06510
Telephone: 203-785-8500
Fax: 203-777-4485
Email: delsole@delsoledelsole.com
Wallingford, Connecticut Office: 46 South Whittlesey Avenue, 06492.
Telephone: 203-284-8000.
Fax: 203-284-9800.

MEMBERS OF FIRM

Stephen P. Del Sole
Michael P. Del Sole
Denise Del Sole-Kennedy (Resident, Wallingford Office)

ASSOCIATES

Edward F. Piazza
Michael J. Cartier
Alfred P. Bruno
Ellen M. Costello

OF COUNSEL

Dominic P. Del Sole

For full biographical listings, see the Martindale-Hubbell Law Directory

GALLAGHER & CALISTRO (AV)

1377 Boulevard, P.O. Box 1925, 06509
Telephone: 203-624-4165
Fax: 203-865-5598

William F. Gallagher
Roger B. Calistro
Cynthia C. Bott
Barbara L. Cox
Kurt D. Koehler
Thomas J. Airone

For full biographical listings, see the Martindale-Hubbell Law Directory

JACOBS, GRUDBERG, BELT & DOW, P.C. (AV)

350 Orange Street, P.O. Box 606, 06503
Telephone: 203-772-3100
Fax: 203-772-1691
Email: jacobslaw@jacobslaw.com *URL:* http://www.jacobslaw.com

Israel J. Jacobs (1918-1963)
Howard A. Jacobs
Ira B. Grudberg
David L. Belt
William F. Dow, III
Jonathan Katz
Susan H. Bartholomew
Charles B. Price, Jr.
William M. Bloss
Shirley V. Hoogstra
David T. Grudberg
David A. Leff

Steven J. DeFrank
Alinor C. Sterling
Phillip A. Escoriaza
Marybeth C. Gauthier
Bernard C. Christianson

For full biographical listings, see the Martindale-Hubbell Law Directory

JACOBS & JACOBS (AV)

Granite Square, 700 State Street, 3rd Floor, 06511
Telephone: 203-777-2300
Fax: 203-787-5628
Email: JACOBSLAW1@AOL.com

MEMBERS OF FIRM

Israel J. Jacobs (1918-1963)
Stanley A. Jacobs
Bruce D. Jacobs
Carol Wolven
Irene Prosky Jacobs
Charles R. Douthat

Kevin Ryder

Reference: BankBoston.

For full biographical listings, see the Martindale-Hubbell Law Directory

KENNEDY, JOHNSON, D'ELIA & GILLOOLY (AV)

Long Wharf Maritime Center, 545 Long Wharf Drive, 06511
Telephone: 203-865-8430
Fax: 203-865-5345
Email: kennedyjoh@aol.com

MEMBERS OF FIRM

David H. Johnson
John J. Kennedy, Jr.
John J. D'Elia
Dennis Gillooly

ASSOCIATES

Robert L. Schwab
Stephanie Z. Roberge

Reference: Bank of Boston - Connecticut.

For full biographical listings, see the Martindale-Hubbell Law Directory

PARRETT, PORTO, PARESE & COLWELL, P.C. (AV)

357 Whitney Avenue, 06511
Telephone: 203-772-0300
Fax: 203-776-0401
North Haven, Connecticut Office: 13 Peck Street.
Telephone: 203-239-1111.

(See Next Column)

PARRETT, PORTO, PARESE & COLWELL P.C., *New Haven—Continued*

Richard J. Parrett
Carl M. Porto
John A. Parese
William S. Colwell
Gregory P. Kinsella
Michael Dean Amato
Kenneth J. Papa
Louis M. Federici
Anthony M. Solomine
Carl M. Porto II
Joseph M. Porto
John H. Krick

Michelle L. Daley
William M. Raccio

Reference: The Bank of New Haven.

For full biographical listings, see the Martindale-Hubbell Law Directory

ROSEN & DOLAN, P.C. (AV)

400 Orange Street, 06511
Telephone: 203-787-3513
Fax: 203-789-1605
Email: davidrosen@snet.net
Email: sapincus@snet.net

David N. Rosen

Stephen M. Pincus

Reference: Peoples Bank.

For Complete List of Firm Personnel, See General Section

For full biographical listings, see the Martindale-Hubbell Law Directory

SUSMAN, DUFFY & SEGALOFF, P.C. (AV)

55 Whitney Avenue, 06510-1300
Telephone: 203-624-9830
Fax: 203-562-8430
Mailing Address: P.O. Box 1684, New Haven, Connecticut, 06507-1684

Allen H. Duffy (1931-1986)
Michael Susman
James H. Segaloff
Joseph E. Faughnan
Susan W. Wolfson
Laura M. Sklaver
Andrew R. Lubin
James J. Perito
Matthew C. Susman
Thomas E. Katon

Jennifer L. Schancupp
Peter G. Kruzynski
Vincent J. Candelora
Karen Baldwin Kravetz

OF COUNSEL

Diana C. Ballard
David P. Hambleton

For full biographical listings, see the Martindale-Hubbell Law Directory

WIGGIN & DANA (AV)

One Century Tower, 06508-1832
Telephone: 203-498-4400
Telefax: 203-782-2889
URL: http://www.wiggin.com
Hartford, Connecticut Office: One CityPlace.
Telephone: 203-297-3700.
Fax: 203-525-9380.
Stamford, Connecticut Office: Three Stamford Plaza, 301 Tresser Boulevard.
Telephone: 203-363-7600.
Telefax: 203-363-7676.

MEMBERS OF FIRM

William J. Doyle
Shaun S. Sullivan
Jeremy G. Zimmermann
William H. Prout, Jr.
Mark R. Kravitz
Edward Wood Dunham
Alan G. Schwartz
Patrick J. Monahan, II (Resident, Hartford Office)
Robert M. Langer (Resident, Hartford Office)
John F. Conway
Jeffrey R. Babbin
Ian E. Bjorkman
David B. Fein (Resident, Stamford Office)
Stephen B. Harris (Resident, Hartford Office)
Phyllis M. Pari
Kevin M. Kennedy
William J. Speranza (Resident, Stamford Office)

SENIOR COUNSEL

S. Robert Jelley

COUNSEL

Penny Quinn Seaman
Sharyn B. Zuch (Not admitted in CT; Resident, Hartford Office)

ASSOCIATES

Eileen Reynolds Becker
Penelope I. Bellamy
James H. Bicks (Not admitted in CT; Resident, Stamford Office)
Isabel E. Chenoweth
Lori R. Clark (Resident, Hartford Office)
Patrick J. Corcoran
James O. Craven
Michelle Wilcox DeBarge (Resident, Hartford Office)

(See Next Column)

ASSOCIATES (Continued)

Timothy A. Diemand
Jonathan W. Haray
Lisa Page Heslin
Stuart C. Johnson
Daniel J. Klau (Resident, Hartford Office)
Tracey M. Lane
Kenneth W. Lord (Not admitted in CT; Resident, Stamford Office)
Nicholas J. Maglio (Resident, Hartford Office)
Richard F. Nace, Jr.
Stewart E. Newman
David J. O'Callaghan
Suzanne E. Wachsstock (Resident, Stamford Office)

For Complete List of Firm Personnel, See General Section

For full biographical listings, see the Martindale-Hubbell Law Directory

WILLIAMS, POLAN & PATTIS, LLC (AV)

51 Elm Street, 06510
Telephone: 203-562-9931
Fax: 203-776-9494
Email: jrw@johnrwilliams.com

John R. Williams
Diane Polan
Norman A. Pattis

Katrena Engstrom
William S. Palmieri
Angelica N. Papastavros
Rosemarie Paine

References: Webster Bank; Citizens Bank.

For full biographical listings, see the Martindale-Hubbell Law Directory

NEW LONDON, New London Co.

DUPONT AND RADLAUER, L.L.P. (AV)

Captain's Walk, 165 State Street, Suite 502, P.O. Box 710, 06320-0710
Telephone: 860-447-0090
Fax: 860-437-7442
Email: radlaw@snet.net *URL:* http://www.lawyers.com/dupontandradlauer

MEMBERS OF FIRM

Ralph P. Dupont
Barbara J. Radlauer

For full biographical listings, see the Martindale-Hubbell Law Directory

WALLER, SMITH & PALMER, P.C. (AV)

52 Eugene O'Neill Drive, P.O. Box 88, 06320
Telephone: 860-442-0367
Telecopier: 860-447-9915
Email: wspmain@snet.net *URL:* http://www.snetyp.com/wallersmithpalmer
Old Lyme Office: 103 Halls Road.
Telephone: 860-434-8063.
Telecopier: 860-434-9452. Email: wspol@snet.net

Edward B. O'Connell
Tracy M. Collins

General Counsel For: Town of East Lyme.
Counsel For: Citizens Bank of Connecticut; Soneco/Northeastern, Inc.; The Nature Conservancy; Fleet Bank.
Local Counsel For: McCue Mortgage Co.; Citicorp Mortgage; U.S. Department of Housing and Urban Development.

For Complete List of Firm Personnel, See General Section

For full biographical listings, see the Martindale-Hubbell Law Directory

SOUTHPORT, Fairfield Co.

BRODY, WILKINSON AND OBER, P.C. (AV)

2507 Post Road, 06490
Telephone: 203-319-7100
Fax: 203-254-1772

Seth O. L. Brody
Peter Wilkinson
Frank Fritz Ober
S. Giles Payne
James E. Rice
William J. Britt
Barbara S. Miller
Robert L. Teicher
Ronald B. Noren
Peter T. Mott
Thomas J. Walsh, Jr.
Diane F. Martucci
Seth L. Cooper
Douglas R. Brown
Charles S. Brody (1894-1976)

OF COUNSEL

Bruce E. Dillingham
Roy W. Moore, III

For full biographical listings, see the Martindale-Hubbell Law Directory

STAMFORD, Fairfield Co.

CACACE, TUSCH & SANTAGATA (AV)

777 Summer Street, P.O. Box 15859, 06901-0859
Telephone: 203-327-2000
Telecopier: 203-353-3392
Email: lawcts@aol.com

(See Next Column)

CACACE, TUSCH & SANTAGATA—*Continued*

MEMBERS OF FIRM

Michael J. Cacace
Paul T. Tusch
Mark P. Santagata
Richard S. Fisher

OF COUNSEL

Kenneth A. DellaRocco
Eric D. Grayson

ASSOCIATES

Edward F. Nemchek
Aamina Ahmad
Alice Ann Fitzpatrick
Demaris Page Hetrick
Ronald E. Kowalski II
Patrick L. Poeschl

LEGAL SUPPORT PERSONNEL

Eva L. Chan
Cynthia L. Mammone

For full biographical listings, see the Martindale-Hubbell Law Directory

CASPER & DE TOLEDO LLC (AV)

1111 Summer Street, 06905
Telephone: 203-325-8600
Fax: 203-323-5970
Email: casperdetoledo.com *URL:* http://www.casperdetoledo.com

Stewart M. Casper
Victoria de Toledo

Gwendolyn Field Noto
Anastasios T. Savvaides

For full biographical listings, see the Martindale-Hubbell Law Directory

LAW OFFICES OF MICHAEL GENE CLEAR (AV)

184 Atlantic Street, P.O. Box 3292, 06905
Telephone: 203-973-0240
Facsimile: 203-973-0244
Email: MCLEAR9948@aol.com

For full biographical listings, see the Martindale-Hubbell Law Directory

CURTIS, BRINCKERHOFF & BARRETT, P.C. (AV)

666 Summer Street, 06901-1416
Telephone: 203-324-6777
Telecopier: 203-324-9621
Email: info@curtisbb.com

T. Ward Cleary (1916-1988)
Ward Frank Cleary
Frederick M. Tobin
James D'Alton Murphy
John Wayne Fox
Randolph T. Lovallo

OF COUNSEL

John D. Hertz
Richard L. Brinckerhoff
Jane F. Donovan
Patricia M. Gaug

Susan L. Stratton
Michael P. Murray
Derek Gilman
John J. Louizos

Counsel for: The F. A. Bartlett Tree Expert Co.; Town of Darien; Miller Automobile Corp.; Bolliger, Inc.; Titan Sports; People's Bank, Bridgeport; Fleet Bank; Federal Deposit Insurance Co.; William Pitt Foundation; Wood Logan Associates.

For full biographical listings, see the Martindale-Hubbell Law Directory

PIAZZA & PICKEL (AV)

112 Prospect Street, P.O. Box 15390, 06901
Telephone: 203-348-2465
Fax: 203-964-9509
Email: aap@piazza-pickel.com *URL:* http://www.piazza-pickel.com

Anthony A. Piazza
Alan Scott Pickel

ASSOCIATES

Tara C.F. Ryan
Michelle M. Napoli

For full biographical listings, see the Martindale-Hubbell Law Directory

ROSENBLUM & FILAN, L.L.C. (AV Ⓣ)

One Landmark Square, 06901
Telephone: 203-358-9200
Fax: 203-358-0687
Email: counsel@rosenblumfilan.com *URL:* http://www.rosenblumfilan.com
White Plains, New York Office: 50 Main Street.
Telephone: 914-686-6100.
Fax: 914-686-6140.
New York, New York Office: 400 Madison Avenue.
Telephone: 212-888-8001.
Fax: 212-888-3331.

MEMBERS OF FIRM

Patrick J. Filan
Alan S. Rubenstein
James B. Rosenblum
Samuel Tannenbaum
James S. Newfield

James F. Biondo
James A. Mahar

(See Next Column)

OF COUNSEL

Theodore J. Greene

For full biographical listings, see the Martindale-Hubbell Law Directory

RYAN, RYAN, JOHNSON & DELUCA, LLP (AV)

80 Fourth Street, P.O. Box 3057, 06905
Telephone: 203-357-9200
FAX: 203-357-7915
Email: ryanlaw@rrjmd.com
New York, New York Office: Park Avenue Atrium, 237 Park Avenue.
Telephone: 212-551-1430.

MEMBERS OF FIRM

Daniel E. Ryan, Jr.
Daniel E. Ryan, III
W. Patrick Ryan
Michael T. Ryan
J. Paul Johnson
Kevin M. Tepas
Charles A. Deluca
Robert C.E. Laney
John F. Leydon, Jr.

OF COUNSEL

Charles M. McCaghey

ASSOCIATES

Beverly J. Hunt
Robert O. Hickey
Darren P. Renner
Danielle DiBerardini-Albrecht
Catherine S. Nietzel
Joseph N. DeFilippo
Janine M. Kelly
Jennifer R. Mazzella
Robert R. Statchen
Brock T. Dubin

For full biographical listings, see the Martindale-Hubbell Law Directory

SILVER, GOLUB & TEITELL LLP (AV)

184 Atlantic Street, P.O. Box 389, 06904
Telephone: 203-325-4491
Fax: 203-325-3769
Email: silvergolubteitell.com *URL:* http://www.sgtlaw.com

MEMBERS OF FIRM

Richard A. Silver
Elaine T. Silver
David S. Golub
John D. Josel
Ernest F. Teitell
Mario DiNatale
Patricia M. Haugh (1942-1988)
Jonathan M. Levine

Marilyn J. Ramos
Kathleen L. Brandt
Richard H. Greenwood
Paul A. Slager
Mary G. Curry
(Not admitted in CT)
Brad C. Gustafson

For full biographical listings, see the Martindale-Hubbell Law Directory

WOFSEY, ROSEN, KWESKIN & KURIANSKY, LLP (AV)

600 Summer Street, 06901
Telephone: 203-327-2300
Fax: 203-967-9273

MEMBERS OF FIRM

Abraham Wofsey (1915-1944)
David M. Cohen
Michael Wofsey (1927-1951)
Marshall Goldberg
David M. Rosen (1926-1967)
Stephen A. Finn
Julius B. Kuriansky (1952-1992)
Judith Rosenberg
Sydney C. Kweskin (1946-1998)
Mark H. Henderson
Monroe Silverman
Steven D. Grushkin
Howard C. Kaplan
Matthew J. Forstadt
Edward M. Kweskin
Steven M. Frederick

OF COUNSEL

Saul Kwartin
Emanuel Margolis
Anthony R. Lorenzo

SPECIAL COUNSEL

Day R. Shields

ASSOCIATES

Joseph Brachfeld
William A. Harrison
Eric M. Higgins
Daniel M. Young
Angelo A. Ziotas

Representative Clients: Banque Paribas; Benenson Realty; Cellular Information Systems, Inc.; The Chase Manhattan Bank; First County Bank; Hartford Provision Co.; Louis Dreyfus Corp.; Norwalk Federation of Teachers; People's Bank; Ridgeway Shopping Center.

For full biographical listings, see the Martindale-Hubbell Law Directory

*VERNON,** Tolland Co.

FLAHERTY, MEISLER & COURTNEY (AV)

30 Lafayette Square, Suite 116, 06066-4554
Telephone: 860-872-7200
Fax: 860-875-6594
Email: FMACATTY@aol.com

MEMBERS OF FIRM

Leo B. Flaherty Jr. (1923-1998)
Arthur P. Meisler
Joseph D. Courtney

(See Next Column)

FLAHERTY, MEISLER & COURTNEY, *Vernon—Continued*

ASSOCIATE

Elizabeth C. Foran

Reference: Savings Bank of Rockville.

For full biographical listings, see the Martindale-Hubbell Law Directory

WEST HARTFORD, Hartford Co.

BERMAN, BOURNS & CURRIE, LLC (AV)

970 Farmington Avenue, P.O. Box 271837, 06127-1837
Telephone: 860-232-4471
Fax: 860-523-4605

John A. Berman
Courtney B. Bourns

Mary Beth Anderson
Steven R. Dembo
Annemarie Burnham

OF COUNSEL

John K. Currie

For full biographical listings, see the Martindale-Hubbell Law Directory

WESTPORT, Fairfield Co.

ANDREW B. BOWMAN (AV)

1804 Post Road East, 06880
Telephone: 203-259-0599
Fax: 203-255-2570
Email: andrew.bowman@snet.net

Reference: Peoples Bank.

For full biographical listings, see the Martindale-Hubbell Law Directory

LAW OFFICES OF PAUL J. PACIFICO (AV)

25 Ford Road, Suite 2, 06880
Telephone: 203-221-8066
Fax: 203-222-4833

For full biographical listings, see the Martindale-Hubbell Law Directory

DELAWARE

*WILMINGTON,** New Castle Co.

ASHBY & GEDDES (AV)

One Rodney Square, P.O. Box 1150, 19899
Telephone: 302-654-1888
Fax: 302-654-2067

MEMBERS OF FIRM

Lawrence C. Ashby
James McC. Geddes
Stephen E. Jenkins
Randall E. Robbins
Steven J. Balick
Regina A. Iorii
William P. Bowden
Richard D. Heins
Philip Trainer, Jr.

ASSOCIATES

Amy Arnott Quinlan
Steven T. Margolin
Christopher S. Sontchi
Richard I.G. Jones, Jr.
Aaron A. Garber
(Not admitted in DE)

For full biographical listings, see the Martindale-Hubbell Law Directory

BIGGS AND BATTAGLIA (AV)

1800 Mellon Bank Center, P.O. Box 1489, 19899-1489
Telephone: 302-655-9677
Email: B-B@DOL.NET

MEMBERS OF FIRM

Victor F. Battaglia
Robert D. Goldberg
Robert K. Beste, Jr.
Philip B. Bartoshesky
Victor F. Battaglia, Jr.
Linda F. Shopland
Nancy E. Whinnery

OF COUNSEL

John Biggs, III
Gerard P. Kavanaugh, Sr.
S. Bernard Ableman

For full biographical listings, see the Martindale-Hubbell Law Directory

CASARINO, CHRISTMAN & SHALK (AV)

Suite 1220, 222 Delaware Avenue, P.O. Box 1276, 19899
Telephone: 302-594-4500
Telecopier: 302-594-4509
URL: http://www.casarino.com

(See Next Column)

MEMBERS OF FIRM

Stephen P. Casarino
Colin M. Shalk
Beth H. Christman
Donald M. Ransom

Kenneth M. Doss
Diane M. Willette
Stacey L. Cummings
Thomas P. Leff

For full biographical listings, see the Martindale-Hubbell Law Directory

MORRIS, JAMES, HITCHENS & WILLIAMS, LLP (AV)

222 Delaware Avenue, P.O. Box 2306, 19899-2306
Telephone: 302-888-6800
Telecopier: 302-571-1750
URL: http://www.morrisjames.com
Dover, Delaware Office: Suite 202, 32 West Loockerman Street, 19904-7356.
Telephone: 302-678-8815.
Telecopier: 302-678-9063.
Newark, Delaware Office: 22 Polly Drummond Hill Road, 19711-5703.
Telephone: 302-368-4200.
Fax: 302-368-6259.

MEMBERS OF FIRM

Henry N. Herndon, Jr.
George C. Hering, III
Grover C. Brown
William R. Hitchens, Jr.
Richard P. Beck
Glenn E. Hitchens
(Resident at Dover)
Edward M. McNally
Norris P. Wright
James W. Semple
David H. Williams
P. Clarkson Collins, Jr.
Richard Galperin
Steven R. Director
Richard D. Kirk
Lewis H. Lazarus
Michael M. Ledyard
Francis J. Jones, Jr. (Resident, Newark, Delaware Office)
Daniel P. McCollom
Barbara MacDonald
Robert L. Symonds, Jr.
Stephen M. Miller
John D. Demmy
Mary M. Culley
Joseph R. Slights, III
Sherry C. McReynolds
Neal C. Belgam
Laura Sunstein Murphy
Kevin G. Healy (Resident, Newark, Delaware Office)
Nicholas J. Caggiano, Jr.
Michael J. Maimone
Lewis C. Ledyard, III
Joseph C. Schoell

ASSOCIATES

Gretchen Ann Bender
Norman M. Powell
Eileen K. Andersen
Gretchen S. Knight
Ellen Marie Cooper
John T. Meli, Jr.
Matthew J. O'Toole
Francis J. Schanne
Michael A. Weidinger
Mary L. Sutherland
(Resident at Dover)
Stephanie M. Tarabicos
Nancy W. Law
Roger D. Anderson
James E. Drnec
Ricardo Palacio

For full biographical listings, see the Martindale-Hubbell Law Directory

POTTER ANDERSON & CORROON LLP (AV)

Hercules Plaza, 1313 N. Market Street, P.O. Box 951, 19899-0951
Telephone: 302-984-6000
Fax: 302-658-1192
URL: http://www.attys.pacdelaware.com

MEMBERS OF FIRM

Charles S. Crompton, Jr.
Robert K. Payson
Richard E. Poole
Michael D. Goldman
James F. Burnett
Daniel F. Wolcott, Jr.
David B. Brown
Somers S. Price, Jr.
Donald J. Wolfe, Jr.
Gregory A. Inskip
David J. Baldwin
John E. James
W. Harding Drane, Jr.
Richard L. Horwitz
Kathleen Furey McDonough
Laurie Selber Silverstein
Peter J. Walsh, Jr.
Stephen C. Norman
Arthur L. Dent
William R. Denny
Philip A. Rovner
Jennifer Gimler Brady
Joanne Ceballos

ASSOCIATES

Wendy K. Voss
Kevin R. Shannon
Todd L. Goodman
Michael A. Pittenger
William A. Hazeltine
Eileen M. Filliben
Emilie R. Ninan
Deborah A. Cuoco
Gregory M. Johnson
John J. Quinn, III

Representative Clients: Monsanto Company; Philips Electronics North America Corporation; KAO Corporation; Conectiv, Inc.; General Motors Corporation; Chrysler Corporation; Delaware Trust Capital Management, Inc.; University of Delaware; Conrail; Hercules, Inc.; E.I. duPont de Nemours & Company, Inc.

For Complete List of Firm Personnel, See General Section

For full biographical listings, see the Martindale-Hubbell Law Directory

Wilmington—Continued

SMITH, KATZENSTEIN & FURLOW LLP (AV)

The Corporate Plaza, 800 Delaware Avenue, P.O. Box 410, 19899
Telephone: 302-652-8400
Fax: 302-652-8405
Email: info@skfdelaware.com *URL:* http://www.SKFDelaware.com

MEMBERS OF FIRM

Craig B. Smith
Robert J. Katzenstein
David A. Jenkins
Laurence V. Cronin
Brett D. Fallon
Charles E. Butler

Michele C. Gott
Kathleen M. Miller

For Complete List of Firm Personnel, See General Section

For full biographical listings, see the Martindale-Hubbell Law Directory

DISTRICT OF COLUMBIA

WASHINGTON, D.C. Co.

ALLEN, JOHNSON, ALEXANDER & KARP, P.A. (AV)

1707 L Street, N.W., Suite 1050, 20036
Telephone: 202-828-4141
Fax: 202-429-8798
Email: ajakdc@aol.com
Baltimore, Maryland Office: Suite 1540, 100 East Pratt Street.
Telephone: 410-727-5000.

D'Ana E. Johnson

Representative Clients: Scottsdale Insurance Co.; Nautilus Insurance Co.; Jefferson Insurance Co.; Liberty Mutual Insurance Co.; Avis Rent-A-Car; Otis Elevator Co.; Montgomery Elevator Co.; Admiral Insurance Co.; Local Government Insurance Trust; Penn National Insurance Co.

For Complete List of Firm Personnel, See General Section

For full biographical listings, see the Martindale-Hubbell Law Directory

ANDERSON KILL & OLICK, L.L.P. (AV)

2000 Pennsylvania Avenue, N.W. Suite 7500, 20006
Telephone: 202-728-3100
Fax: 202-728-3199
Email: akodc@andersonkill.com *URL:* http://www.andersonkill.com
New York, N.Y. Office: Anderson Kill & Olick, P.C., 1251 Avenue of the Americas.
Telephone: 212-278-1000.
Fax: 212-278-1733
Philadelphia, Pennsylvania Office: Anderson Kill & Olick, P.C., 1600 Market Street.
Telephone: 215-568-4202.
Fax: 215-568-4573.
Newark, New Jersey Office: Anderson Kill & Olick, P.C. One Gateway Center, Suite 901.
Telephone: 973-642-5858.
Fax: 973-621-6361.
Chicago, Illinois Office: Anderson Kill & Olick, 227 West Monroe Street, Mezzanine Level.
Telephone: 312-857-2500.
Fax: 312-857-0122.

Paula M. Bresnan Gibson (Not admitted in DC)
Steven J. Dolmanisth (Not admitted in DC)
Michele A. Gallagher
Lorelie S. Masters
Rhonda D. Orin
Lia B. Royle (Not admitted in DC)
Koorosh Talieh

For full biographical listings, see the Martindale-Hubbell Law Directory

ASBILL, JUNKIN & MOFFITT, CHTD. (AV)

1615 New Hampshire Avenue, N.W., Suite 200, 20009
Telephone: 202-234-9000
Facsimile: 202-332-6480
Email: ajmchtd@erols.com *URL:* http://www.lawyers.com/asbill

Henry W. Asbill
Timothy deForest Junkin
William B. Moffitt (Not admitted in DC)

OF COUNSEL

Oscar I. Dodek, Jr.
Matthew L. Myers
W. Louis Hennessy

For full biographical listings, see the Martindale-Hubbell Law Directory

BAKER BOTTS L.L.P. (AV)

A Registered Limited Liability Partnership
The Warner, 1299 Pennsylvania Avenue, N.W., 20004-2400
Telephone: 202-639-7700
Fax: 202-639-7832
Email: postmaster@bakerbotts.com *URL:* http://www.bakerbotts.com
Houston, Texas Office: One Shell Plaza, 910 Louisiana.
Telephone: 713-229-1234.
Austin, Texas Office: 1600 San Jacinto Center, 98 San Jacinto Boulevard.
Telephone: 512-322-2500.
Dallas, Texas Office: 2001 Ross Avenue.
Telephone: 214-953-6500.
New York, New York Office: 599 Lexington Avenue.
Telephone: 212-705-5000.
Moscow, Russia Office: 10 ul. Bolshaya Dimitrovka (formerly Pushkinskaya), 103031.
Telephone: 7095/921-5300 (Local); 7501/929-7070 (International).
London, England Office: 45 Ludgate Hill.
Telephone: 0171-778-1400 (Local); 011-44-171-778-1400 (International).
Baku, Azerbaijan Office: 6-10 Vagif Mustafa-zadeh Street, Third Floor, Icheri Sheher, 370004.
Telephone: 994-12-97-63-88 (Local); 011-994-12-97-63-88 (International).

MEMBERS OF FIRM

Thomas J. Eastment
Steven R. Hunsicker
Bruce F. Kiely
Mark K. Lewis
Randolph Quaile McManus
David A. Super
Kirk K. Van Tine

ASSOCIATES

Wendy L. Cox
Kelly Riley Donovan
Martin Schaefermeier
James F. H. Scott (Not admitted in DC)

For Complete List of Firm Personnel, See General Section

For full biographical listings, see the Martindale-Hubbell Law Directory

BAKER & HOSTETLER LLP (AV)

Washington Square, Suite 1100, 1050 Connecticut Avenue, N.W., 20036-5304
Telephone: 202-861-1500
Fax: 202-861-1783
To contact an attorney on the Internet use first initial and surname followed by @baker-hostetler.com
URL: http://www.bakerlaw.com
In Cleveland, Ohio: 3200 National City Center, 1900 East Ninth Street.
Telephone: 216-621-0200.
In Cincinnati, Ohio: 312 Walnut Street, Suite 2650.
Telephone: 513-929-3400.
In Columbus, Ohio: Capitol Square, Suite 2100, 65 East State Street.
Telephone: 614-228-1541.
In Denver, Colorado: 303 East 17th Avenue, Suite 1100.
Telephone: 303-861-0600.
In Houston, Texas: 1000 Louisiana, Suite 2000.
Telephone: 713-751-1600.
In Beverly Hills, California: 9150 Wilshire Boulevard, Suite 205.
Telephone: 310-385-7500.
In Long Beach, California: 300 Oceangate, Suite 620.
Telephone: 562-432-2827.
In Los Angeles, California: 600 Wilshire Boulevard.
Telephone: 213-624-2400.
In Orlando, Florida: SunBank Center, Suite 2300, 200 South Orange Avenue.
Telephone: 407-649-4000.

OFFICE MANAGING PARTNER

William H. Schweitzer (Managing Partner, Washington, D.C. Office)

PARTNERS

Ralph G. Blasey, III
Frederick W. Chockley, III
Mark A. Cymrot
Lee T. Ellis, Jr.
Leonard C. Greenebaum
Robert D. Lystad
Bruce W. Sanford
Belinda Jayne Scrimenti

For Complete List of Firm Personnel, See General Section

For full biographical listings, see the Martindale-Hubbell Law Directory

BRAUDE & MARGULIES, P.C. (AV)

The Brawner Building, 888 Seventeenth Street, N.W., Suite 500, 20006
Telephone: 202-293-2993
Fax: 202-331-7916
Email: Braudemarg@aol.com

Herman M. Braude
Samuel M. Morrison, Jr.
Gerson B. Kramer

Stuart H. Sakwa
Stacie J. Broadwater

(See Next Column)

BRAUDE & MARGULIES P.C., *Washington—Continued*

OF COUNSEL

J. Richard Margulies

For full biographical listings, see the Martindale-Hubbell Law Directory

CAPLIN & DRYSDALE, CHARTERED (AV)

One Thomas Circle, N.W., 20005
Telephone: 202-862-5000
Cable Address: "Capdale"
Telex: 904001 CAPL UR WSH
Fax: 202-429-3301
URL: http://www.caplindrysdale.com
New York, N.Y. Office: 399 Park Avenue, 36th Floor.
Telephone: 212-319-7125.
Fax: 212-644-6755.

Mortimer M. Caplin
Thomas A. Troyer
David N. Webster
H. David Rosenbloom
Peter Van N. Lockwood
Richard W. Skillman
Patricia G. Lewis
Bernard S. Bailor
Albert G. Lauber, Jr.
Julie W. Davis
Trevor W. Swett III
James E. Salles
Craig A. Sharon
Catherine E. Livingston
Seth M. Green
Douglas D. Drysdale
Ralph A. Muoio
Elihu Inselbuch (Resident, New York Office)
Cono R. Namorato
Daniel B. Rosenbaum
Richard E. Timbie
Stafford Smiley
Scott D. Michel
Kent A. Mason
Robert A. Boisture
Milton Cerny
Matthew W. Frank
Jessica L. Katz
Christopher S. Rizek

Nathan D. Finch
Douglas N. Varley
Neal M. Kochman
Jason K. Bortz (Not admitted in DC)
April J. Adams (Not admitted in DC)
Elizabeth M. Sellers
Lloyd H. Mayer
Rita C. Tobin (Resident, New York Office)
H. Carter Hood (Not admitted in DC)

OF COUNSEL

Robert H. Elliott, Jr.
Myron C. Baum
Ann C. McMillan

For full biographical listings, see the Martindale-Hubbell Law Directory

COALE, COOLEY, LIETZ, MCINERNY & BROADUS, A PROFESSIONAL CORPORATION (AV)

818 Connecticut Avenue, N.W., Suite 857, 20006
Telephone: 202-887-4770
Facsimile: 202-887-4778

John P. Coale (A Professional Corporation)
Diane E. Cooley
David K. Lietz
Julia Wernett McInerny
Charlsa (Sandy) Broadus

Deborah St. Jean
Joseph Coale (Not admitted in DC)

For full biographical listings, see the Martindale-Hubbell Law Directory

THE FEINBERG GROUP, LLP (AV)

1120 20th Street, N.W. Suite 740 South, 20036-3437
Telephone: 202-371-1110
Fax: 202-962-9290
Email: kfeinberg@thefeinberggroup.com *URL:* http://www.krfassociates.com
New York, N.Y. Office: 780 3rd Avenue, Suite 2202.
Telephone: 212-527-9600.
Fax: 212-527-9611. Email: kfeinberg@thefeinberggroup.com.

PARTNERS

Kenneth R. Feinberg
Deborah E. Greenspan
Michael K. Rozen (Resident, New York Office)
Peter H. Woodin (Resident, New York Office)

ASSOCIATE

Fredric M. Brooks (Not admitted in DC)

SENIOR COUNSEL

Jacqueline E. Zins

For full biographical listings, see the Martindale-Hubbell Law Directory

IFSHIN & FRIEDMAN, P.L.L.C. (AV)

888 16th Street N.W., Suite 400, 20006
Telephone: 202-835-7466
Fax: 202-296-8791
Email: clsactn@aol.com

(See Next Column)

MEMBERS OF FIRM

David M. Ifshin (1948-1996)
Philip S. Friedman

For full biographical listings, see the Martindale-Hubbell Law Directory

JONES, DAY, REAVIS & POGUE (AV)

51 Louisiana Avenue, N.W., 20001-2113
Telephone: 202-879-3939
Telecopier: 202-626-1700
Email: counsel@jonesday.com *URL:* http://www.jonesday.com
In Atlanta, Georgia: 3500 SunTrust Plaza, 303 Peachtree Street.
Telephone: 404-521-3939.
Telecopier: 404-581-8330.
In Brussels, Belgium: Avenue Louise 480, 7th Floor, B-1050 Brussels.
Telephone: 32-2-645-14-11.
Telecopier: 32-2-645-14-45.
In Chicago, Illinois: 77 West Wacker.
Telephone: 312-782-3939.
Telecopier: 312-782-8585.
In Cleveland, Ohio: North Point, 901 Lakeside Avenue.
Telephone: 216-586-3939.
Telecopier: 216-579-0212.
In Columbus, Ohio: 1900 Huntington Center.
Telephone: 614-469-3939.
Telecopier: 614-461-4198.
In Dallas, Texas: 2727 North Harwood Street.
Telephone: 214-220-3939.
Telecopier: 214-969-5100.
In Frankfurt, Germany: Hochhaus am Park, Grüneburgweg 102, 60323, Frankfurt am Main.
Telephone: 49-69-9726-3939.
Telecopier: 49-69-9726-3993.
In Geneva, Switzerland: 20, rue de Candolle.
Telephone: 41-22-320-2339.
Telecopier: 41-22-320-1232.
In Hong Kong: 29th Floor, Entertainment Building, 30 Queen's Road Central.
Telephone: 852-2526-6895.
Telecopier: 852-2868-5871.
In Irvine, California: 5 Park Plaza, Suite 1100.
Telephone: 949-851-3939.
Telecopier: 949-553-7539.
In London, England: Bucklersbury House, 3 Queen Victoria Street.
Telephone: 44-171-236-3939.
Telecopier: 44-171-236-1113.
In Los Angeles, California: 555 West Fifth Street, Suite 4600.
Telephone: 213-489-3939.
Telecopier: 213-243-2539.
In New Delhi, India (Associate Office): Pathak & Associates (an associate firm of Jones, Day, Reavis & Pogue), 1st Floor, Dr. Gopal Das Bhaven, 28 Barakhamba Road.
Telephone: 91-11-373-8793.; 91-11-335-7345.
Telecopier: 91-11-335-3761.
In New York, New York: 599 Lexington Avenue.
Telephone: 212-326-3939.
Telecopier: 212-755-7306.
In Paris, France: 120, rue du Faubourg Saint-Honoré.
Telephone: 33-1-56-59-39-39.
Telecopier: 33-1-56-59-39-38
In Pittsburgh, Pennsylvania: 500 Grant Street, 31st Floor.
Telephone: 412-391-3939.
Telecopier: 412-394-7959.
In Riyadh, Saudi Arabia: The International Law Firm (In Association with Jones, Day, Reavis & Pogue), Sulaymaniyah, Prince Mishari IBN, Abdulaziz Street, P.O. Box 22166.
Telephone: (966-1) 462-8866.
Telecopier: (966-1) 462-9001.
In Shanghai, China: 2805 Kerry Centre, 1515 Nanjing Road West.
Telephone: 86-21-5298-6568.
Telecopier: 86-21-5298-6569.
In Sydney, Australia: Governor Phillip Tower, Level 38, 1 Farrer Place.
Telephone: 61-2-9210-6921.
Telecopier: 61-2-9210-6926.
In Taipei, Taiwan: 8th Floor, 2 Tun Hwa South Road, Section 2.
Telephone: (886-2) 2704-6808.
Telecopier: (886-2) 2704-6791.
In Tokyo, Japan: Toranomon MT Building, 4th Floor, 10-3, Toranomon 3-Chome, Minato-Ku, Tokyo 105, Japan.
Telephone: 81-3-3433-3939.
Telecopier: 81-3-5401-2725.

MEMBERS OF FIRM IN WASHINGTON, D.C.

Thomas F. Cullen, Jr.
Stephen J. Brogan
Glen D. Nager

For Complete List of Firm Personnel, See General Section

For full biographical listings, see the Martindale-Hubbell Law Directory

Washington—Continued

KING, PAGANO & HARRISON (AV)

1730 Pennsylvania Avenue, N.W., 20006
Telephone: 202-371-6800
Fax: 202-371-6770
URL: http://www.kph.com
New York, New York Office: 425 Park Avenue, 10022.
Telephone: 212-223-4000.
FAX: 212-223-4134.

MEMBERS OF FIRM

Jeffrey W. King
Jeffrey W. Pagano (Resident, New York, N.Y. Office)
Keith J. Harrison
James E. Kellett (Resident, New York, N.Y. Office)
Steven Schaars
Jeffrey L. Poston
Ira M. Saxe (Not admitted in DC; Resident, New York, N.Y. Office)

OF COUNSEL

Herbert I. Meyer (Resident, New York, N.Y. Office)

ASSOCIATES

Cheryl A. Maier
Christopher Flynn
Emily B. Zuckerman (Not admitted in DC; Resident, New York, N.Y. Office)
Thomas W. Jones, Jr.
Eric M. Carr (Not admitted in DC; Resident, New York, N.Y. Office)

Representative Clients: Brink's, Inc.; The Pittston Co.; BAX Global; GEO Logistics; Air Transport International, L.L.C.; G.A.B. Robbins, Inc.; SGS Control Services, Inc.; Kaiser Permanente; American Association of Health Plans; Weichert Realtors.

For full biographical listings, see the Martindale-Hubbell Law Directory

MACLEAY, LYNCH, GREGG & LYNCH, P.C. (AV)

Suite 1150, 1629 K Street, N.W., 20006
Telephone: 202-785-0123
FAX: 202-393-3390
Email: maclmac@aol.com

Donald Macleay (1908-1994)
Hugh Lynch, Jr. (1913-1994)
John C. Lynch
Michael Maloney
Robert P. Lynch
Robert G. McGinley
James C. Gregg

Jack David Lapidus
David C. Numrych

For full biographical listings, see the Martindale-Hubbell Law Directory

MARY A. MCREYNOLDS, P.C. (AV)

Suite 400, 888 Sixteenth Street, N.W., 20006
Telephone: 202-835-7455
Telecopier: 202-296-8791
URL: http://www.lawyers.com/maryamcreynolds

Mary A. McReynolds

For full biographical listings, see the Martindale-Hubbell Law Directory

PAULSON & NACE (AV)

1814 N Street, N.W., 20036
Telephone: 202-463-1999
Fax: 202-223-6824
Email: p&n@lawtort.com *URL:* http://www.lawyers.com/lawtort
Martinsburg, West Virginia Office: 1444 Edwin Miller Boulevard, P.O. Box 1938, 25402.
Telephone: 888-529-2628.

MEMBERS OF FIRM

Richard S. Paulson (1928-1986)
Barry J. Nace

ASSOCIATE

James A. Ferguson

OF COUNSEL

Irving R. M. Panzer

For full biographical listings, see the Martindale-Hubbell Law Directory

THE ROBINSON LAW FIRM (AV)

Market Square, 717 D Street, N.W., 4th Floor, 20004
Telephone: 202-347-6100
Fax: 202-347-0081
URL: http://www.lawyers.com/robinsonlaw

MEMBER OF FIRM

Kenneth Michael Robinson

ASSOCIATES

Cameron Robinson Kourtesis (Not admitted in DC)
Nikolaos Panagiotis Kourtesis (Not admitted in DC)

For full biographical listings, see the Martindale-Hubbell Law Directory

ROSS, DIXON & BELL, L.L.P. (AV)

601 Pennsylvania Avenue, N.W., North Building, 20004-2688
Telephone: 202-662-2000
Fax: 202-662-2190
Email: info@rdblaw.com *URL:* http://www.rdblaw.com
Irvine, California Office: 5 Park Plaza, Suite 1200, 92614.
Telephone: 949-622-2700.
Fax: 949-622-2739.
San Diego, California Office: 550 West B Street, Suite 400, 92101-3538.
Telephone: 619-235-4040.
Fax: 619-231-8796.

PARTNERS

Leslie S. Ahari
Alec M. Barinholtz (Resident, Irvine, California)
Roy Morrow Bell (Irvine and San Diego, California)
Charles T. Blair
William H. Briggs, Jr.
Wallace A. Christensen
Gary V. Dixon
John W. Duchelle
David R. Dwares
Barbara E. Etkind
Elizabeth Sarah Gere
John R. Gerstein
David M. Gische
Garrick P. Grobler
Charles I. Hadden
Sean M. Hanifin
Van E. Haynie (Resident, San Diego, California)
Merril Jay Hirsh
William D. Hopkins
Timothy P. Irving (Irvine and San Diego, California)
Gilbert D. Jensen (Resident, Irvine, California)
Thomas T. Locke
Lewis K. Loss
Sharon T. Maier (Resident, San Diego, California)
Terrence R. McInnis (Irvine and San Diego, California)
Fletcher W. Paddison (Resident, San Diego, California)
David L. Perry
Robert M. Pozin (Irvine and San Diego, California)
Richard J. Pratt
Rebecca L. Ross
Stuart Philip Ross
Cathy Ann Simon
Richard A. Simpson
Van A. Tengberg (Resident, San Diego, California)
Peter G. Thompson
Solomon Louis Wisenberg (Not admitted in DC)

ASSOCIATES

Daniel Aronowitz
Vicki E. Bajefsky
Christopher P. "Hawk" Barry (Resident, San Diego, California)
Tara Boland (Not admitted in DC)
Jodi L. Cleesattle
Jill Robin Coogan
Jacqueline K. Cuncannan (Not admitted in DC)
James J. Dalessio (Resident, San Diego, California)
J. Kirk Donnelly (Resident, Irvine, California)
Rexford P. Edwards (Resident, San Diego, California)
Stacey E. Engelbrecht (Not admitted in DC)
Tina M. Fryar (Resident, San Diego, California)
Glenn Fuller (Resident, San Diego, California)
Julie P. Glass
Jason Hadges (Not admitted in DC)
Sam R. Hananel
David A. Harrington
Carol Schanno Johnson (Not admitted in DC)
Charles A. Jones
Thomas J. Judge
Kevin J. Kieffer (Resident, Irvine, California)
Amy E. Ledoux
Michele L. Lynch (Resident, Irvine, California)
Jena Martin
Jennifer Mathis (Resident, Irvine, California)
Stacey L. McGraw
Kim S. Orbeck (Resident, Irvine, California)
Cynthia Mather Pratt
Susan Prolman (Not admitted in DC)
Gabriela A. Richeimer
Stephanie T. Schmelz
Richard C. Seavey
Pragna Soni
James W. Stubblefield (Resident, San Diego, California)
Andrea R. Tebbets
Paul C. Vitrano (Not admitted in DC)
Jeffrey J. Ward
Michael J. Whitton (Resident, San Diego, California)
Carol L. Young (Not admitted in DC; Resident, San Diego, California)

STAFF ATTORNEYS

Sharon Lynn Gibson
Marcus B. Holladay
Scott H. Moskol (Not admitted in DC)
Jeannine M. Smith

OF COUNSEL

Karen Hahn Ventrell (Not admitted in DC)
Harold E. Masback, III
James T. Waring (Resident, San Diego, California)

For full biographical listings, see the Martindale-Hubbell Law Directory

SCHMELTZER, APTAKER & SHEPARD, P.C. (AV)

The Watergate, Suite 1000, 2600 Virginia Avenue, N.W., 20037-1905
Telephone: 202-333-8800
Cable Address: "Ship"
Telex: 440517
Facsimile: 202-337-6065
Email: sas@saslaw.com *URL:* http://www.saspc.com
Los Angeles, California Office: 1999 Avenue of the Stars, Twenty-Seventh Floor, 90067-4095.
Telephone: 310-557-2966.
FAX: 310-286-6610.

(See Next Column)

SCHMELTZER, APTAKER & SHEPARD P.C., *Washington—Continued*

J. Thomas Esslinger
Ralph H. Johnson
Robert L. Zisk
Leon B. Taranto
Lynn K. McKay
Thomas P. Carroll

David Worthen
Steven A. Browne (Not admitted in DC)
Thomas M. Finan
Richard L. Creech

COUNSEL

Stephen Horn
Michael C. White (Not admitted in DC)
Larry H. Mitchell
Neal M. Sher

For full biographical listings, see the Martindale-Hubbell Law Directory

THOMPSON, O'DONNELL, MARKHAM, NORTON & HANNON (AV)

The Southern Building, 805 Fifteenth Street, N.W., Suite 705, 20005
Telephone: 202-289-1133
Facsimile: 202-289-0275
Email: Jude@mtolympus.ari.net

John Jude O'Donnell
Julian E. Markham, Jr.
Randell Hunt Norton
James W. Greene
J. Michael Hannon
Kenneth G. Stallard

ASSOCIATES

Brooke A. Pinkerton
Matthew W. Carlson
Michele L. Bulger

OF COUNSEL

James F. Bromley

Representative Clients: CNA Insurance Companies; Washington Mutual Investors Fund; FMB Trust Company, N.A.; Bernard F. Locraft, Civil Engineers, Washington, D. C.
References: Franklin National Bank; The First National Bank of Maryland; NationsBank.

For full biographical listings, see the Martindale-Hubbell Law Directory

TROUT & RICHARDS, P.L.L.C. (AV)

1742 N Street, N.W., 4th Floor, 20036
Telephone: 202-463-1920
Fax: 202-463-1925
Email: trlaw@troutrichards.com *URL:* http://www.troutrichards.com
Alexandria, Virginia Office: 301 North Pitt Street, 22314.
Telephone: 703-519-8840.

Robert P. Trout
John Thorpe Richards, Jr.

For full biographical listings, see the Martindale-Hubbell Law Directory

VENABLE ATTORNEYS AT LAW VENABLE, BAETJER, HOWARD & CIVILETTI, LLP (AV)

A Partnership including Professional Corporations
Suite 1000, 1201 New York Avenue, N.W., 20005
Telephone: 202-962-4800
Fax: 202-962-8300
URL: http://www.venable.com
Baltimore, Maryland Office: Venable, Baetjer and Howard LLP, 1800 Mercantile Bank & Trust Building, 2 Hopkins Plaza.
Telephone: 410-244-7400.
Fax: 410-244-7742.
McLean, Virginia Office: Venable, Baetjer and Howard LLP, Suite 400, 2010 Corporate Ridge.
Telephone: 703-760-1600.
Fax: 703-821-8949.
Rockville, Maryland Office: Venable, Baetjer and Howard LLP, Suite 500, One Church Street, P. O. Box 1906.
Telephone: 301-217-5600.
Fax: 301-217-5617.
Towson, Maryland Office: Venable, Baetjer and Howard LLP, 210 Allegheny Avenue, P. O. Box 5517.
Telephone: 410-494-6200.
Fax: 410-821-0147.

MEMBERS OF FIRM

Robert G. Ames (Also at Baltimore, Maryland Office)
James K. Archibald (Also at Baltimore, Maryland Office)
Maurice Baskin
Kenneth C. Bass, III (Also at McLean, Virginia Office)
Benjamin R. Civiletti (P.C.) (Also at Baltimore and Towson, Maryland Offices)
William D. Coston
Jeffrey A. Dunn (Also at Baltimore, Maryland Office)
Ronald R. Glancz
Edward F. Glynn, Jr.
David W. Goewey
Gary M. Hnath
Amy Berman Jackson
Thomas J. Kelly, Jr.
Thomas J. Madden
George F. Pappas (Also at Baltimore, Maryland Office)
Michael Schatzow (Also at Baltimore, Maryland Office)
James L. Shea (also at Baltimore, Maryland Office)

(See Next Column)

MEMBERS OF FIRM (Continued)

Judson W. Starr (Also at Baltimore and Towson, Maryland Offices)
Patrick J. Stewart (Also at Baltimore, Maryland Office)
N. Frank Wiggins

ASSOCIATES

Carla Draluck Craft
Melissa Landau Steinman

For Complete List of Firm Personnel, See General Section

For full biographical listings, see the Martindale-Hubbell Law Directory

VINSON & ELKINS L.L.P. (AV)

A Registered Limited Liability Partnership
The Willard Office Building, 1455 Pennsylvania Avenue, N.W., 20004-1008
Telephone: 202-639-6500
Fax: 202-639-6604
URL: http://www.velaw.com
Austin, Texas Office: One American Center Suite 2700, 600 Congress Avenue, Austin, Texas, 78701-3200.
Telephone: 512-495-8400.
Fax: 512-495-8612.
Beijing, China Office: 20/F, Beijing Silver Tower, No. 2, Dong San Huan Bei Lu, Chaoyang District, 100027.
Telephone: +86-10-6410-6300.
Fax: +86-10-6410-6360.
Dallas, Texas Office: 3700 Trammell Crow Center, 2001 Ross Avenue, Dallas, Texas, 75201-2975.
Telephone: 214-220-7700.
Fax: 214-220-7716.
Houston, Texas Office: 2300 First City Tower, 1001 Fannin, Houston, Texas, 77002-6760.
Telephone: 713-758-2222.
Fax: 713-758-2346.
London, England Office: Regis House, 8th Floor, 45 King William Street, London, EC4R 9AN, England.
Telephone: (44-171) 618-6000.
Fax: (44-171) 618-6001.
Moscow, Russia Office: 16 Ulitsa Spiridonovka, Second Floor, 103001 Moscow, Russia.
Telephone: (7-095) 956-1995. Local
Fax: (7-095) 956-1996. U.S. Satellite
Fax: (212) 803-0142.
New York, N.Y. Office: 1325 Avenue of the Americas, 17th Floor, New York, N.Y., 10019.
Telephone: 917-206-8000.
Fax: 917-206-8100.
Singapore Office: 6 Battery Road, #39-01, Singapore, 049909.
Telephone: (65) 536-8300.
Fax: (65) 536-8311. Avenue, N.W., Washington, D.C., 20004-1008.

RESIDENT PARTNERS

Alden L. Atkins
C. Michael Buxton
Michael R. Charness
Ky P. Ewing, Jr.
Michael J. Henke
Neil W. Imus
David R. Johnson
Cathy A. Lewis
Kathleen C. Little
John D. Taurman
Charles D. Tetrault
Mark H. Tuohey, III
Paul L. Yde

RESIDENT OF COUNSEL

Tegan M. Flynn
William E. Lawler, III

RESIDENT ASSOCIATES

Virginia Navarrete Brooks
Vanessa Y. Chandler (Not admitted in DC)
James R. Farnsworth
John M. Faust
Robert S. Field (Not admitted in DC)
Joseph E. Hunsader (Not admitted in DC)
Bruce C. McCulloch (Not admitted in DC)
Philip A. Nickles
Daniel A. Petalas (Not admitted in DC)
Suzanne D. Reifman
Robert J. Rothwell (Not admitted in DC)
Jerome A. Swindell

For Complete List of Firm Personnel, See General Section

For full biographical listings, see the Martindale-Hubbell Law Directory

WEHNER & YORK (AV)

1029 Vermont Avenue, N.W. Suite 300, 20005
Telephone: 202-543-2700
Facsimile: 202-543-2023
Email: litigation@wehner-york-law.com *URL:* http://www.lawyers.com/w&ylaw
Bridgeport, West Virginia Office: Grande Meadows, Saltwell Road and Route 73, Suite 230.
Telephone: 304-592-3400. E-Mail: litigation@wehner-york-law.com.

MEMBERS OF FIRM

Stephen V. Wehner
Michael M. York

ASSOCIATES

Gregory M. Kline (Not admitted in DC)
Charles Hildebrandt (Not admitted in DC)
Damien V. Alexander

(See Next Column)

WEHNER & YORK—*Continued*

LEGAL SUPPORT PERSONNEL

Charleen Hamrick (Legal Assistant)

For full biographical listings, see the Martindale-Hubbell Law Directory

WILLIAMS & CONNOLLY (AV)

725 Twelfth Street, N.W., 20005-5901
Telephone: 202-434-5000
Fax: 202-434-5029

MEMBERS OF FIRM

Jeremiah C. Collins
David Povich
Steven M. Umin
John W. Vardaman
Paul Martin Wolff
J. Alan Galbraith
John G. Kester
William E. McDaniels
Brendan V. Sullivan, Jr.
Aubrey M. Daniel, III
Richard M. Cooper
Gerald A. Feffer
Robert P. Watkins
Jerry L. Shulman
Lawrence Lucchino
Lewis H. Ferguson, III
Robert B. Barnett
David E. Kendall
Gregory B. Craig
John J. Buckley, Jr.
Terrence O'Donnell
John K. Villa
Barry S. Simon
Kevin T. Baine
Stephen L. Urbanczyk
Philip J. Ward
James A. Bruton, III
Peter J. Kahn
Lon S. Babby
Michael S. Sundermeyer
James T. Fuller, III
David D. Aufhauser
Bruce R. Genderson
Carolyn H. Williams
Frank Lane Heard III
Steven R. Kuney
Gerson A. Zweifach
Paul Mogin
Howard W. Gutman
Nancy F. Lesser
Richard S. Hoffman
Steven A. Steinbach
Mark S. Levinstein
Mary Greer Clark
Victoria Radd Rollins
Daniel Franklin Katz
Nicole K. Seligman
Robert M. Krasne
Kathleen L. Beggs
William R. Murray, Jr.
Eva Petko Esber
Stephen D. Raber
David C. Kiernan
Lon E. Musslewhite
Robin E. Jacobsohn
Charles A. Sweet
Heidi K. Hubbard
Glenn J. Pfadenhauer
George A. Borden
Robert J. Shaughnessy
Jonathan P. Graham
Allen P. Waxman
David S. Blatt
Ari S. Zymelman
Joseph D. Piorkowski, Jr.
Regina G. Maloney
Dane H. Butswinkas
Laurie S. Fulton

OF COUNSEL

Vincent J. Fuller
Raymond W. Bergan
Lyman G. Friedman

COUNSEL

Eric M. Braun

For Complete List of Firm Personnel, See General Section

For full biographical listings, see the Martindale-Hubbell Law Directory

WILMER, CUTLER & PICKERING (AV)

2445 M Street, N.W., 20037-1420
Telephone: 202-663-6000
Fax: 202-663-6363
Email: Law@Wilmer.Com *URL:* http://www.wilmer.com
Baltimore, Maryland Office: 100 Light Street, 21202.
Telephone: 410-986-2800.
Fax: 410-986-2828.
New York, New York Office: 520 Madison Avenue, 10022.
Telephone: 212-230-8800.
Fax: 212-230-8888.
European Offices:
4 Carlton Gardens, London, SW1Y 5AA, England. Telephone: +44 (20) 7 872 1000.
Fax: +44 (20) 7 839 3537.
Rue de la Loi 15# Wetstraat, B-1040 Brussels, Belgium. Telephone: +32 (2) 285 49 00.
Fax: +32 (2) 285 49 49.
Friedrichstrasse 95, D-10117 Berlin, Germany. Telephone: +49 (30) 20 22 64 00.
Fax: +49 (30) 20 22 65 00.

MEMBERS OF FIRM

Daniel K. Mayers
Stephen H. Sachs
Dennis M. Flannery
Louis R. Cohen
Michael R. Klein
Paul J. Mode, Jr.
Stephen F. Black
Gary D. Wilson
Michael L. Burack
William J. Kolasky, Jr.
A. Stephen Hut, Jr.
John Rounsaville, Jr.
Roger M. Witten
William J. Perlstein
Andrew B. Weissman
Lynn Bregman
Bruce E. Coolidge
Juanita A. Crowley
John Payton
Bruce M. Berman
Thomas F. Connell
Charles E. Davidow
Daniel H. Squire
Gary B. Born (European Offices, London, England and Berlin, Germany)
Philip D. Anker
Joseph K. Brenner

(See Next Column)

MEMBERS OF FIRM (Continued)

Carol Clayton
Thomas P. Olson
Patrick J. Carome
Jane C. Sherburne
Sheila C. Cheston
David P. Donovan
Howard M. Shapiro
Roger W. Yoerges
Laura B. Ahearn
Mark D. Cahn
Eric J. Mogilnicki
Lewis J. Liman (Not admitted in DC; Resident, New York, New York Office)
Steven F. Cherry
Susan P. Crawford
Steven M. Dunne
Denise Esposito

SENIOR COUNSEL

John H. Pickering

COUNSEL

Max O. Truitt, Jr.
Carol H. Fishman
Joseph E. Killory, Jr.
Brent J. Gurney
Nancy L. Manzer

For Complete List of Firm Personnel, See General Section

For full biographical listings, see the Martindale-Hubbell Law Directory

ZEVNIK HORTON GUIBORD MCGOVERN PALMER & FOGNANI, L.L.P. (AV)

The Warner Building, 1299 Pennsylvania Avenue, N.W. Ninth Floor, 20004
Telephone: 202-824-0950
Facsimile: 202-824-0955
Email: law@dc.zhgm.com *URL:* http://www.zevnik.com
Boston, Massachusetts Office: One International Place, Fourteenth Floor.
Telephone: 617-790-2970.
Facsimile: 617-790-2910.
San Francisco, California Office: 225 Bush Street, Seventeenth Floor.
Telephone: 415-364-6300.
Facsimile: 415-364-6333.
Los Angeles, California Office: 333 South Grande Avenue, Twenty First Floor.
Telephone: 213-437-5200.
Facsimile: 213-437-5222.
New York, New York Office: 1330 Avenue of the Americas, Eleventh Floor.
Telephone: 212-407-0600.
Facsimile: 212-407-0606.
Chicago, Illinois Office: 77 West Wacker Drive, Thirty Third Floor.
Telephone: 312-977-2500.
Facsimile: 312-977-2560.
London, England Office: 4 Kings Bench Walk, Temple, London EC4Y 7DL.
Telephone: 171-822-8822.
Facsimile: 171-822-8844.
San Diego, California Office: 101 West Broadway, Seventeenth Floor.
Telephone: 619-515-9600.
Facsimile: 619-515-9628.
Denver, Colorado Office: 555 Seventeenth Street, Twenty Sixth Floor.
Telephone: 303-382-6200.
Facsimile: 303-382-6210.
Woodcliff Lake, New Jersey Office: 50 Tice Boulevard, First Floor.
Telephone: 201-476-9600.
Facsimile: 201-476-9666.
Philadelphia, Pennsylvania Office: 620 Chestnut Street, Tenth Floor.
Telephone: 215-440-8450.
Facsimile: 215-440-8459.

Paul Anton Zevnik
Michel Yves Horton (Resident, Los Angeles, California Office)
Barbara B. Guibord (Resident, Chicago, Illinois Office)
Patrick Michael McGovern (Resident, New York, New York Office)
David G. Palmer (Resident, Denver, Colorado Office)
John D. Fognani (Resident, Denver, Colorado Office)
Joseph G. Homsy (Resident, Chicago, Illinois Office)
John K. Crossman (Resident, New York, New York Office)
Jonathan L. Osborne
John W. Roberts (Resident, Chicago, Illinois Office)
Steven E. Knott (Resident, Los Angeles, California Office)
Kenneth D. Polin (Resident, San Diego, California Office)
Steven G. Rowles (Resident, San Diego, California Office)
Charles J. Malaret (Resident, Los Angeles, California Office)
Michael John Miguel (Resident, Boston, Massachusetts Office)
Lea Leadbeater (Not admitted in DC; Resident, Chicago, Illinois Office)

Michael J. Wilson
Gregory M. Cork (Not admitted in DC)
Yolanda C. Griffin
Dolores R. Lyons (Not admitted in DC)

For full biographical listings, see the Martindale-Hubbell Law Directory

FLORIDA

*BARTOW,** Polk Co.

FROST & SAUNDERS, P.A. (AV)

395 South Central Avenue, P.O. Box 2188, 33830
Telephone: 941-533-0314; 800-533-0967
Telecopier: 941-533-8985
Email: jfrost1985@aol.com

John W. Frost, II
Thomas C. Saunders
Richard E. "Rick" Dantzler
John Marc Tamayo
Mark A. Sessums
Robert J. Aranda
Peter W. Van den Boom
Nicholas D. Zorn, Jr.

Reference: Community National Bank, Bartow.

For full biographical listings, see the Martindale-Hubbell Law Directory

PANSLER & MOODY, P.A. (AV)

575 North Broadway, P.O. Box 246, 33830
Telephone: 941-533-5300
Telecopier: 941-534-1001
Email: kpdm@gte.net

Karl F. Pansler
Daniel D. Moody
Beth Billing

References: Citrus and Chemical Bank, Bartow, FL; Community National Bank, Bartow, FL; Sun Trust Bank, Bartow, FL; First Union Bank, Bartow, FL.

For full biographical listings, see the Martindale-Hubbell Law Directory

BOCA RATON, Palm Beach Co.

LAW OFFICES OF CARTER & THOMAS LLP (AV)

1200 North Federal Highway, Suite 312, 33432
Telephone: 561-368-9900
Broward 954-427-0933
Fax: 561-368-0293
Email: carterboca@aol.com

John E. Carter
Donald Joseph Thomas

Colleen M. Stiger

For full biographical listings, see the Martindale-Hubbell Law Directory

MICHAUD, BUSCHMANN, FOX, FERRARA & MITTELMARK, P.A. (AV)

33 Southeast 8th Street, 33432
Telephone: 561-392-0540
Fax: 561-392-0582
Email: Bocalaw@MBFFM.com *URL:* http://www.MBFFM.com

Scott H. Michaud
Paul Buschmann
Brian S. Fox
James T. Ferrara
Michael K. Mittelmark
Marc T. Millian

Marcy G. Blitz
Linda A. McCullough
Kimberly M. Hall

For full biographical listings, see the Martindale-Hubbell Law Directory

WEISS & HANDLER, P.A. (AV)

Suite 218A, One Boca Place, 2255 Glades Road, 33431-7313
Telephone: 561-997-9995
Broward: 954-421-5101
Palm Beach: 561-734-8008
Telecopier: 561-997-5280
Email: weisshand@aol.com
West Palm Beach, Florida Office: 505 South Flagler Drive, Suite 1331, 33401.
Telephone: 561-655-3433.
New York, NY Office: 45 Rockefeller Plaza, Suite 1501.
Telephone: 212-332-2900.

Howard I. Weiss
Henry B. Handler

Manuel R. Comras
Donald Feldman
William M. Franz
David K. Friedman
Carol A. Kartagener
Allison L. Kay
Bruce A. Harris
Howard M. Rudolph (Resident, West Palm Beach Office)
Stacy E. Welt

OF COUNSEL

Malcolm L. Stein (Not admitted in FL)
Harry Winderman

For full biographical listings, see the Martindale-Hubbell Law Directory

*BRADENTON,** Manatee Co.

GRIMES GOEBEL GRIMES HAWKINS & GLADFELTER, P.A. (AV)

The Professional Building, 1023 Manatee Avenue West, P.O. Box 1550, 34206
Telephone: 941-748-0151
Fax: 941-748-0158
Email: ggghg@gte.net
Tampa, Florida Office: Old Hyde Park Village, 1509 West Swann Avenue, Suite 275.
Telephone: 813-258-2557.
Fax: 813-258-2327.

Caleb J. Grimes
John D. Hawkins
William S. Galvano
Douglas A. Peebles

For full biographical listings, see the Martindale-Hubbell Law Directory

*CLEARWATER,** Pinellas Co.

ELIHU H. BERMAN, P.A. (AV)

509 South Greenwood Avenue, 33756
Telephone: 727-465-1977
Fax: 727-465-9593
Email: elihu@gte.net

Elihu H. Berman

OF COUNSEL

Marc A. B. Silverman

References: First Union Bank; South Trust Bank; AmSouth Bank.

For full biographical listings, see the Martindale-Hubbell Law Directory

CORAL GABLES, Dade Co.

LANE, REESE, AULICK, SUMMERS & FIELD, P.A. (AV)

Suite 304 Douglas Centre, 2600 Douglas Road, 33134
Telephone: 305-444-4418
Fax: 305-444-5504
Email: LRASF-Miami@MSN.COM

Frank A. Lane
William S. Reese
Cecilia Aulick
William L. Summers
Paul H. Field

C. Page Lane
Lorenzo Jackson, Jr.
Luis J. Perdomo

For full biographical listings, see the Martindale-Hubbell Law Directory

CORAL SPRINGS, Broward Co.

BONNIE S. SATTERFIELD, P.A. (AV)

3111 University Drive, Suite 405, 33065
Telephone: 954-341-2250
Fax: 954-345-0115
URL: http://www.bonniesatterfield.com
Email: bsatterfield@lawyers.com *URL:* http://www.lawyers.com/bonniesatterfield

Bonnie S. Satterfield

For full biographical listings, see the Martindale-Hubbell Law Directory

CRYSTAL RIVER, Citrus Co.

BEST & ANDERSON, P.A. (AV)

Executive Center Condos, 7655 West Gulf to Lake Highway, Suite 6, 34429
Telephone: 352-795-1107
Orlando, Florida Office: 1201 East Robinson Street, 32801.
Telephone: 407-425-2985.
Melbourne, Florida Office: Healthsouth Marina Towers, 709 South Harbor City Boulevard, Suite 270, 32901.
Telephone: 407-727-9923.

David R. Best
George H. "Dutch" Anderson, III

Angela O'Neil
James William Nuebel
Lora L. Wilson
Louis Allen DeFreitas, Jr.

For full biographical listings, see the Martindale-Hubbell Law Directory

*FORT LAUDERDALE,** Broward Co.

BERGER DAVIS & SINGERMAN (AV)

350 East Las Olas Boulevard, Suite 1000, 33301
Telephone: 954-525-9900
Fax: 954-523-2872
Email: jberger@bdslaw.com *URL:* http://www.bdslaw.com
Miami, Florida Office: 200 South Biscayne Boulevard, Suite 2950.
Telephone: 305-755-9500.
Fax: 305-714-4340.

(See Next Column)

BERGER DAVIS & SINGERMAN—*Continued*

Tallahassee, Florida Office: 215 South Monroe Street, Suite 705, 32301.
Telephone: 850-561-3010.
Fax: 850-561-3013.

James L. Berger
Mitchell W. Berger
Franklin H. Caplan (Resident, Miami Office)
James B. Davis
Henry H. (Bucky) Fox
Van P. Geeker (Resident, Tallahassee Office)
Jordi Guso (Resident, Miami Office)
Nick Jovanovich
Robert B. Judd
Manuel Kushner
Daniel Lampert
Dawn M. Meyers
John D. C. Newton, II (Resident, Tallahassee Office)
Samuel E. Poole III
Leonard K. Samuels
Laz L. Schneider
Paul Steven Singerman (Resident, Miami Office)
Daniel H. Thompson (Resident, Tallahassee Office)

Robert W. Barron
Maria St. John Daugherty
James Harris Fierberg (Resident, Miami Office)
Ilyse Wrubel Homer (Resident, Miami Office)
Sherry A. Lambson
Lisa D. MacClugage
Brian G. Rich (Resident, Miami Office)
Holiday Hunt Russell
Jonathan C. Vair (Resident, Miami Office)
Jeffrey Scott Wertman

OF COUNSEL

James C. Cunningham, Jr.
Fred Goldberg

For full biographical listings, see the Martindale-Hubbell Law Directory

CATRI, HOLTON, KESSLER & KESSLER, P.A. (AV)

The Litigation Building, 3rd Floor, 633 S. Andrews Avenue, 33302
Telephone: 954-463-8593
Fax: 954-462-1303

Charles T. Kessler (1930-1997)
Wesley L. Catri
Raymond O. Holton, Jr.
Paula C. Kessler
Andrea L. Kessler

Gerard A. Tuzzio
Edwina V. Kessler

For full biographical listings, see the Martindale-Hubbell Law Directory

CONRAD & SCHERER (AV)

A Partnership of Professional Associations
Eighth Floor, 633 South Federal Highway, P.O. Box 14723, 33302
Telephone: 954-462-5500
Facsimile: 954-463-9244
Miami, Florida Office: 44 West Flagler Street, Suite 402, 33130.
Telephone: 305-856-9920.
Facsimile: 305-374-4408.

MEMBERS OF FIRM

William R. Scherer, Jr., (P.A.)
Gary S. Genovese (P.A.)
William V. Carcioppolo (P.A.)
Linda Rae Spaulding (P.A.)
Reid A. Cocalis (P.A.)

OF COUNSEL

Rex Conrad

ASSOCIATE

Albert L. Frevola, Jr.

Local Counsel for: American Home Assurance Group; Caterpillar Tractor Co.; Division of Risk Management, State of Florida; Florida East Coast Railway; Fort Motor Co.; Liberty Mutual Insurance Co.; Ryder Truck Lines; Unigard Insurance Group.
Approved Attorneys for: Attorneys' Title Insurance Fund.
Reference: Barnett Bank of Fort Lauderdale.

For Complete List of Firm Personnel, See General Section

For full biographical listings, see the Martindale-Hubbell Law Directory

DONAHOE, PECARO & VOLLENDER, P.A. (AV)

Trial Lawyers Building, 633 Southeast 3rd Avenue, Suite 301, 33301-3151
Telephone: 954-761-3800
1-800-761-3801
FAX: 954-761-1855
Email: donpecvol@aol.com

John E. Donahoe
Paul R. Pecaro
Donald W. Vollender

Representative Clients: Allstate Insurance Co.

For full biographical listings, see the Martindale-Hubbell Law Directory

ESLER & LINDIE, P.A. (AV)

Suite 300 The Advocate Building, 315 S.E. Seventh Street, 33301
Telephone: 954-764-5400
FAX: 954-764-5408
Email: eslerandlindie@martindalemail.com *URL:* http://www.lawyers.com/esler&lindie

(See Next Column)

Gary A. Esler
Beth G. Lindie

Representative Clients: The Chubb Group of Insurance Cos.; Fireman's Fund Insurance Co.; State of Florida-Department of Risk Management; Marriott Corp.; Mobile America Insurance Group, Inc.; Ohio Casualty Insurance Co.
Reference: Capital Bank.

For full biographical listings, see the Martindale-Hubbell Law Directory

GILLESPIE, GOLDMAN & KRONENGOLD (AV)

Port Royale Financial Center, 6550 North Federal Highway, 33308
Telephone: 954-771-0908
Facsimile: 954-771-9880
Email: mail@ggklaw.com *URL:* http://www.lawyers.com/ggklaw

MEMBERS OF FIRM

John R. Gillespie, Jr.
Peter R. Goldman
Jeffrey L. Kronengold

ASSOCIATE

Gary M. Farmer, Jr.

For full biographical listings, see the Martindale-Hubbell Law Directory

HALICZER, PETTIS & WHITE, P.A. (AV)

101 Northeast Third Avenue, Sixth Floor, 33301
Telephone: 954-523-9922
Fax: 954-522-2512
Orlando, Florida Office: NationsBank Building, Suite 1275, 111 North Orange Avenue. 32801.
Telephone: 407-841-9866.
Fax: 407-841-9915.

James S. Haliczer
Eugene K. Pettis
Kenneth E. White

Amy B. Talisman
Anthony K. Goodman
Anthony V. Scalese
Debra B. Potter
William Bassett, Jr.
Frank J. Taddeo

For full biographical listings, see the Martindale-Hubbell Law Directory

WILLIAM W. HAURY, JR. (AV)

SouthTrust Bank Building, 10th Floor, 4875 North Federal Highway, 33308
Telephone: 954-491-2431; 800-741-2431
Fax: 954-491-4409
Email: bhaury@gate.net *URL:* http://www.lawyers.com/williamhaury

For full biographical listings, see the Martindale-Hubbell Law Directory

HEINRICH GORDON HARGROVE WEIHE & JAMES, P.A. (AV)

500 East Broward Boulevard, Suite 1000, 33394-3092
Telephone: 954-527-2800
Facsimile: 954-524-9481
Email: talexander@heinrichgordon.com *URL:* http://www.heinrichgordon.com
Orlando, Florida Office: 201 South Orange Avenue, Suite 1015.
Telephone: 407-317-9117.
Facsimile: 407-317-9114.

Elicia D. Blackwell
Mark R. Boyd
William Kent Brown
Bruce A. Chaimowitz
Richard G. Gordon
Thomas A. Groendyke
John R. Hargrove
Eugene L. Heinrich
Gordon James, III
Scott A. Markowitz
Moises Melendez
Jeffrey A. O'Keefe
Cristina M. Pierson
Valerie Shea
Gilbert E. Theissen
Kenneth W. Waterway
Bruce A. Weihe

Representative Clients: Allstate Insurance Company; Amerisure Companies; Amoco Oil Company; The BellSouth Companies; Carrier Corporation; First Union National Bank of Florida; Schindler Elevator Corporation; Tribune Company/Sun Sentinel.

For Complete List of Firm Personnel, See General Section

For full biographical listings, see the Martindale-Hubbell Law Directory

KLUGER, PERETZ, KAPLAN & BERLIN, P.A. (AV)

1100 Sun Trust Tower, One East Broward Boulevard, 33301
Telephone: Broward: 305-761-1100 Dade: 305-379-9000
Facsimile: Broward: 954-761-1138 Dade: 305-379-3428
Miami
Email: tmeyers@@kpkb.com *URL:* http://www.kpkb.com
Miami, Florida Office: Miami Center - 17th Floor, 201 South Biscayne Boulevard, 33131.
Telephone: Dade: 305-379-9000, Broward: 954-728-8100.
Fax: 305-379-3428.

Andrew P. Gold

Seth A. Honowitz
Todd A. Levine
Jason Marks
Jason S. Oletsky

(See Next Column)

KLUGER, PERETZ, KAPLAN & BERLIN P.A., *Fort Lauderdale—Continued*

OF COUNSEL

Michael Wrubel

LEGAL SUPPORT PERSONNEL

Cathie J. Recca

For full biographical listings, see the Martindale-Hubbell Law Directory

KRUPNICK CAMPBELL MALONE ROSELLI BUSER SLAMA HANCOCK McNELIS LIBERMAN & McKEE, P.A. (AV)

700 Southeast 3rd Avenue, Suite 100, 33316-1186
Telephone: 954-763-8181; 877-763-8181 (Toll Free)
Fax: 954-763-8292
Email: information@krupnicklaw.com *URL:* http://www.krupnicklaw.com

Jon E. Krupnick
Walter G. Campbell, Jr.
Kevin A. Malone
Richard J. Roselli
Thomas E. Buser
Joseph J. Slama
Kelly D. Hancock
Lisa A. McNelis
Scott S. Liberman
Robert J. McKee

Carlos Acevedo (Not admitted in FL)
Louis R. Battista
Ivan F. Cabrera
Robert D. Erben
Kelley Badger Gelb
Sean J. Greene
Holly Debra Krulik
Michael J. Ryan

OF COUNSEL

Ben J. Weaver
Dianne Jay Weaver

Reference: Mellon United National Bank.

For full biographical listings, see the Martindale-Hubbell Law Directory

KENNETH R. MIKOS, P.A. (AV)

2780 East Oakland Park Boulevard, 33306
Telephone: 954-566-7200
Facsimile: 954-566-1568

Kenneth R. Mikos

Douglas F. Hoffman

Special Counsel to: Fort Lauderdale Civil Service Board.

For full biographical listings, see the Martindale-Hubbell Law Directory

PHILLIPS P. O'SHAUGHNESSY, P.A. (AV Ⓣ)

One East Broward Boulevard, Suite 700, 33301
Telephone: 800-882-3133
Email: phil.osh@worldnet.att.net *URL:* http://oshaughnessy.wld.com
Baltimore, Maryland Main Office: 1102 Terrace Glen, 21210.
Telephone: 410-532-0300.
Fax: 410-532-2220.

Phillips P. O'Shaughnessy

For full biographical listings, see the Martindale-Hubbell Law Directory

BONNIE S. SATTERFIELD, P.A.

(See Coral Springs)

SISTARE & ASSOCIATES (AV)

600 South Andrews Avenue, Suite 600, 33301
Telephone: 954-522-2320
Fax: 954-522-2223
Email: sistare@gate.net *URL:* http://www.sistare.com

MEMBER OF FIRM

Susan P. Sistare

ASSOCIATE

Jahna Y. (Jay) Hoyte

For full biographical listings, see the Martindale-Hubbell Law Directory

*FORT MYERS,** Lee Co.

DEBOEST, KNUDSEN, STOCKMAN, WISEMAN, DECKER & DRYDEN, P.A. (AV)

1415 Hendry Street, P.O. Box 1470, 33902-1470
Telephone: 941-334-1381
Telecopier: 941-334-0266
Email: dkswlaw@gate.net
Naples, Florida Office: 600 Fifth Avenue South, Suite 301, 34102.
Telephone: 941-263-5040.
Fax: 941-263-6944.

(See Next Column)

Arthur K. Knudsen, Jr. (Retired)
Richard D. DeBoest
William E. Stockman
Tamela Eady Wiseman (Resident, Naples Office)
James G. Decker
Thomas M. Dryden

Representative Clients: Cobb Theatres, Inc.; WCI Communities, Inc.; Evelyn Jackman and Sons, Inc.

For full biographical listings, see the Martindale-Hubbell Law Directory

PATRICK E. GERAGHTY A PROFESSIONAL ASSOCIATION (AV)

The Courtney Building, Suite 100, 2069 First Street, P.O. Box 1605, 33902-1605
Telephone: 941-334-9500
Fax: 941-334-8930
URL: http://www.lawyers.com/pgeraghty

Patrick E. Geraghty
Thomas M. Dougherty

For full biographical listings, see the Martindale-Hubbell Law Directory

HENDERSON, FRANKLIN, STARNES & HOLT, PROFESSIONAL ASSOCIATION (AV)

1715 Monroe Street, P.O. Box 280, 33902-0280
Telephone: 941-334-4121
Telecopier: 941-332-4494

Stephen L. Helgemo
John A. Noland
Gerald W. Pierce
J. Terrence Porter
Michael J. Corso
Vicki L. Sproat
John W. Lewis
Craig Ferrante
James L. Nulman
Harold N. Hume, Jr.
Bruce M. Stanley Sr.
Daniel W. Sheppard
Steven G. Koeppel
Douglas B. Szabo
Robert C. Shearman
Andrew L. Ringers, Jr.
John F. Potanovic, Jr.
Jeffrey D. Kottkamp
Keith R. Kyle
Carlos A. Kelly
Alane C. Laboda

Representative Clients: CIGNA Group; CSX Transportation, Inc.; Fireman's Fund Insurance Cos.; The Hartford Insurance Group; Huntington National Bank, N.A.; NationsBank, N.A.; Travelers/Aetna Insurance Group; Sprint-Florida, Inc.

For Complete List of Firm Personnel, See General Section

For full biographical listings, see the Martindale-Hubbell Law Directory

*FORT PIERCE,** St. Lucie Co.

BRENNAN, HAYSKAR, JEFFERSON, WALKER & SCHWERER, PROFESSIONAL ASSOCIATION (AV)

515-519 South Indian River Drive, P.O. Box 3779, 34948-3779
Telephone: 561-461-2310
Fax: 561-468-6580

John T. Brennan
Thad H. Carlton (1906-1965)
Stephen G. Hayskar
Bradford L. Jefferson
Robert V. Schwerer
James T. Walker

Garrison M. Dundas
Steven R. McCain

Representative Clients: Allstate Insurance Co.; Auto Owners Insurance Co.; Canal Insurance Co.; Florida Farm Bureau Insurance Group; Kemper Insurance Group; First Union National Bank of Fla.; Scottsdale Insurance Group; USF&G; Gallagher Bassett.

For full biographical listings, see the Martindale-Hubbell Law Directory

NEILL GRIFFIN JEFFRIES FOWLER TIERNEY & NEILL, CHARTERED (AV)

311 South Second Street, P.O. Box 1270, 34954
Telephone: 561-464-8200
Fax: 561-464-2566

Richard V. Neill
Michael Jeffries
J. Stephen Tierney, III
Richard V. Neill, Jr.

Local Counsel For: SunTrust Bank South Florida, N.A., (Commercial and Trust Departments); Chubb Group of Insurances Cos.
Approved Attorneys for: Attorneys' Title Insurance Fund; Commonwealth Land Title Insurance Co.
Reference: SunTrust Bank South Florida, N.A., Fort Pierce, Florida (Commercial and Trust Departments).

For full biographical listings, see the Martindale-Hubbell Law Directory

HOLLYWOOD, Broward Co.

STEVEN A. MASON, P.A. (AV)

3363 Sheridan Street, Suite 201, 33021
Telephone: 954-963-5900
Fax: 954-985-9811
Email: passat902@aol.com *URL:* http://www.lawyers.com/stevenmasonpa

(See Next Column)

STEVEN A. MASON, P.A.—*Continued*

Steven A. Mason

Representative Clients: T.S.I., Inc.; Southern Security Bank; Dental Centers of America.

For full biographical listings, see the Martindale-Hubbell Law Directory

JACKSONVILLE, * Duval Co.

ALLEN, BRINTON, SIMMONS & MCCARTHY, P.A. (AV)

One Independent Drive, Suite 3200, 32202
Telephone: 904-353-8800
Fax: 904-353-8770

A. Graham Allen
William D. Brinton
Sidney S. Simmons, II
Edward McCarthy, III

Joelle Jackson Dillard

Representative Clients: Anheuser-Busch Companies, Inc.; Avis Rent A Car System, Inc.; Bridgestone/Firestone, Inc.; Jacksonville Transportation Authority; The Haskell Co.; Johnson & Johnson; Masthead Industries, Inc.; U-Haul Co.

For full biographical listings, see the Martindale-Hubbell Law Directory

GLENN K. ALLEN A PROFESSIONAL ASSOCIATION (AV)

The Plaza Building, 353 East Forsyth Street, 32202-2822
Telephone: 904-355-7506
Facsimile: 904-353-8814
URL: http://www.glennallenpa.com
Email: GKA@glennallenpa.com *URL:* http://www.lawyers.com/glennallen

Glenn K. Allen

Jennifer Workinger Fites

For full biographical listings, see the Martindale-Hubbell Law Directory

BLEDSOE, SCHMIDT, LIPPES, MOONLY & ROBERSON, P.A. (AV)

1301 Riverplace Boulevard, Suite 1818, 32207
Telephone: 904-398-1818
Fax: 904-398-7073

James A. Bledsoe, Jr.
Terrance E. Schmidt
Harold S. Lippes
Stephen K. Moonly
Cheryl A. Roberson

For full biographical listings, see the Martindale-Hubbell Law Directory

BULLOCK, CHILDS, PENDLEY, REED, HERZFELD & RUBIN (AV)

711 Blackstone Building, 233 East Bay Street, 32202
Telephone: 904-354-0286; 800-940-5299
Fax: 904-354-2778
Email: dchilds@bellsouth.net

Bruce S. Bullock
W. Douglas Childs
Michael C. Pendley
Ronald E. Reed

ASSOCIATE

Tyler F. Tygart

Representative Clients: A List of Representative Clients will be furnished upon request.
Reference: First Union National Bank.

For full biographical listings, see the Martindale-Hubbell Law Directory

GENTRY, PHILLIPS AND HODAK, P.A. (AV)

Suite 400, 6 East Bay Street, 32202
Telephone: 904-356-4100
Fax: 904-358-1895

William C. Gentry
Mary Kleyla Phillips
Corinne C. Hodak

Angelo M. Patacca, Jr.

For full biographical listings, see the Martindale-Hubbell Law Directory

HEDRICK, DEWBERRY & REGAN, P.A. (AV)

50 North Laura Street, Suite 2225, 32202
Telephone: 904-356-1300
Fax: 904-356-8050

Michael J. Dewberry
Alexandra Krueger Hedrick
Jeffrey C. Regan

Clinton Allen Wright III

For full biographical listings, see the Martindale-Hubbell Law Directory

LILES, GAVIN & COSTANTINO (AV)

One Enterprise Center, Suite 1500, 225 Water Street, 32202
Telephone: 904-634-1100
Fax: 904-634-1234
Email: triallaw@bellsouth.net

Rutledge R. Liles
R. Kyle Gavin
R. Scott Costantino

ASSOCIATES

Niels P. Murphy
Robert Bruce George

For full biographical listings, see the Martindale-Hubbell Law Directory

RUMRELL, WAGNER & COSTABEL, LLP (AV)

Suite 250, Building 100, 10151 Deerwood Park Boulevard, P.O. Box 550668, 32256
Telephone: 904-996-1100
Facsimile: 904-996-1120
Email: firm@rumrelllaw.com *URL:* http://www.RumrellLaw.com
Miami, Florida Office: 14 N.E. First Avenue, Suite 1105-1. 33132.
Telephone: 305-371-2618.
Facsimile: 305-371-4643.
Orlando, Florida Office: 2400 Maitland Center Parkway, Suite 225, P.O. Box 540537. 32854-0537.
Telephone: 407-875-0922.
Facsimile: 407-875-1303.
Alachua (Gainesville), Florida Office: P.O. Box 999, 14528 N.W. 154th Terrace. 32616.
Telephone: 904-462-0833.
Facsimile: 904-462-0836.

Richard G. Rumrell
Lynn E. Wagner (Resident, Orlando Office)
Attilio M. Costabel (Resident, Miami Office)

Lindsey C. Brock III

OF COUNSEL

Michael E. Hanrahan (1919-1998)

RESIDENT ATTORNEY
ORLANDO, FLORIDA OFFICE

Richard A. Solomon

RESIDENT ATTORNEY
ALCHUA, FLORIDA OFFICE

Alfred C. Warrington, V, (P.A.)

For full biographical listings, see the Martindale-Hubbell Law Directory

SAALFIELD, COULSON, SHAD & JAY, P.A. (AV)

225 Water Street, Suite 1000, 32202-4458
Telephone: 904-355-4401
Fax: 904-355-3503
Email: SCJ4401@BellSouth.net

John R. Saalfield
Michael I. Coulson
Charles Thomas Shad
Harvey L. Jay, III
Joseph B. Stokes, III

Gail A Stafford
Brett Q. Lucas
Carl Scott Schuler

Representative Clients: American Continental Ins. Co.; Baptist/St. Vincent's Health System; Century Products; CNA Ins. Co.; Cosco, Inc.; Crawford & Co.; Dependable Protective Mutual; Dillard Dept. Stores, Inc.; First Floridian Ins. Co.; Florida Podiatrist Trust.

For full biographical listings, see the Martindale-Hubbell Law Directory

KISSIMMEE, * Osceola Co.

A. CLIFTON BLACK (AV)

903 West Emmett Street, 34741
Telephone: 407-932-1115
Fax: 407-932-1097
Email: blacklaw@gdi.com

Representative Clients: American Polymers, Inc.; Banc One Leasing Corp.; Maury L. Carter & Associates, Inc.; Douglass Fertilizer & Chemical, Inc.

For full biographical listings, see the Martindale-Hubbell Law Directory

POHL & SHORT, P.A.

(See Winter Park)

LAKELAND, Polk Co.

LANE, TROHN, BERTRAND & VREELAND, P.A. (AV)

One Lake Morton Drive, P.O. Box 3, 33802-0003
Telephone: 941-284-2200
Telecopier: 941-688-0310
URL: http://www.lanetrohn.com

(See Next Column)

LANE, TROHN, BERTRAND & VREELAND P.A., *Lakeland—Continued*

A. H. Lane (Retired)
Robert L. Trohn
Robert J. Bertrand
John K. Vreeland
Christopher M. Fear
Gary S. Rabin
Robert M. Brush
Kingswood Sprott, Jr.
Hank B. Campbell
Patrick J. Murphy
Mitchell D. Franks
Janet M. Stuart
Robert G. Stokes
Mark N. Miller
Jonathan B. Trohn
T. W. Weeks, III
Neil A. Roddenbery

Stephen B. French
Jack P. James, III
E. Alexander Pujol
David D. Hallock, Jr.
Louise Wilkinson Spivey
Mark G. Capron
Connie C. Durrence

Counsel for: Ewell Industries, Inc.
Local Counsel for: Auto Owners Insurance Co.; Liberty Mutual Insurance Co.; St. Paul Fire & Marine Insurance Cos.; State Farm Insurance Cos.
Approved Attorneys for: Attorneys' Title Insurance Fund.

For full biographical listings, see the Martindale-Hubbell Law Directory

PETERSON & MYERS, P.A. (AV)

100 East Main Street, P.O. Box 24628, 33802-4628
Telephone: 941-683-6511; 676-6934
Telecopier: 941-682-8031
Lake Wales, Florida Office: 130 East Central Avenue, P.O. Box 1079.
Telephones: 941-676-7611; 683-8942.
Winter Haven, Florida Office: Lake Region Plaza, 141 5th Street, N.W., P.O. Drawer 7608.
Telephone: 941-294-3360.

M. David Alexander, III
Philip O. Allen
Jack P. Brandon
Kristen Marie Buzzanca
Debra Leigh Cline
J. Davis Connor
Dennis G. Corrick
Roy A. Craig, Jr.
Clinton A. Curtis
Jacob C. Dykxhoorn
Joseph A. Geary
Maria "Mia" Gerber
Jonn D. Hoppe
Dennis P. Johnson
Kevin C. Knowlton
Douglas A. Lockwood, III
Corneal B. Myers
E. Blake Paul
Robert E. Puterbaugh
Thomas B. Putnam, Jr.
Deborah A. Ruster
Stephen R. Senn
Andrea Teves Smith
Keith H. Wadsworth
Kerry M. Wilson

General Counsel for: SunTrust Bank Mid-Florida, N.A.; Lakeland Regional Medical Center, Inc.; Housing Finance Authority of Polk County.
Representative Clients: NationsBank, N.A.; First Union National Bank; Mutual Wholesale Co.; Ben Hill Griffin, Inc.; E. R. Jahna Industries, Inc.
Approved Attorneys for: Attorneys' Title Insurance Fund; Equitable Life Assurance Society of the United States.

For full biographical listings, see the Martindale-Hubbell Law Directory

LAKE WALES, Polk Co.

PETERSON & MYERS, P.A. (AV)

130 East Central Avenue, P.O. Box 1079, 33853
Telephone: 941-676-7611; 683-8942
Telecopier: 941-676-0643
Lakeland, Florida Office: 100 East Main Street, P.O. Box 24628.
Telephones: 941-683-6511; 676-6934.
Winter Haven, Florida Office: Lake Region Plaza, 141 5th Street, N.W., P.O. Drawer 7608.
Telephone: 941-294-3360.

M. David Alexander, III
Philip O. Allen
Jack P. Brandon
Kristen Marie Buzzanca
Debra Leigh Cline
J. Davis Connor
Dennis G. Corrick
Roy A. Craig, Jr.
Clinton A. Curtis
Jacob C. Dykxhoorn
Joseph A. Geary
Maria "Mia" Gerber
Jonn D. Hoppe
Dennis P. Johnson
Kevin C. Knowlton
Douglas A. Lockwood, III
Corneal B. Myers
E. Blake Paul
Robert E. Puterbaugh
Thomas B. Putnam, Jr.
Deborah A. Ruster
Stephen R. Senn
Andrea Teves Smith
Keith H. Wadsworth
Kerry M. Wilson

General Counsel for: SunTrust Bank Mid-Florida, N.A.; Lakeland Regional Medical Center, Inc.; Housing Finance Authority of Polk County.
Representative Clients: NationsBank, N.A.; First Union National Bank; Mutual Wholesale Co.; Ben Hill Griffin, Inc.; E. R. Jahna Industries, Inc.
Approved Attorneys for: Attorneys' Title Insurance Fund; Equitable Life Assurance Society of the United States.

For full biographical listings, see the Martindale-Hubbell Law Directory

LAKE WORTH, Palm Beach Co.

RICHARD H. WILLITS, P.A. (AV)

2290 10th Avenue North Suite 404, 33461
Telephone: 1-800-870-0573
561-582-7600
Fax: 561-588-8819
URL: http://www.lawyers.com/willitslaw

Richard H. Willits

For full biographical listings, see the Martindale-Hubbell Law Directory

LEESBURG, Lake Co.

AUSTIN & PEPPERMAN (AV)

Suite C, 1321 Citizens Boulevard, P.O. Drawer 490200, 34749-0200
Telephone: 352-728-1020
Fax: 352-728-0595
URL: http://www.aust-pep.com

Robert E. Austin, Jr.
Carla R. Pepperman

ASSOCIATES

Reda J. Stewart
Bradford D. Fisher

Representative Clients: Allstate Insurance Co.; American Excess Insurance Co.; American Re-Insurance Co.; Florida Rock Industries, Inc.; Goodyear Tire & Rubber Co.; Great American Insurance Co.

For full biographical listings, see the Martindale-Hubbell Law Directory

LONGWOOD, Seminole Co.

JAMES B. BYRNE, JR., P.A. (AV)

Crown Oak Centre, 370 Crown Oak Centre Drive, 32750
Telephone: 407-831-0450
Fax: 407-339-0542
Email: JBBPA@aol.com *URL:* http://www.lawyers.com/jimbyrne

James B. Byrne, Jr.

For full biographical listings, see the Martindale-Hubbell Law Directory

MELBOURNE, Brevard Co.

BEST & ANDERSON, P.A. (AV)

Healthsouth Marina Towers, 709 South Harbor City Boulevard, Suite 270, 32901
Telephone: 407-727-9923
Orlando, Florida Office: 1201 East Robinson Street, 32801.
Telephone: 407-425-2985.
Crystal River, Florida Office: Executive Center Condos, 7655 West Gulf to Lake Highway, Suite 6, 34429.
Telephone: 352-795-1107.

David R. Best
George H. "Dutch" Anderson, III

Angela O'Neil
James William Nuebel
Lora L. Wilson
Louis Allen DeFreitas, Jr.

For full biographical listings, see the Martindale-Hubbell Law Directory

NANCE, CACCIATORE AND HAMILTON (AV)

525 North Harbor City Boulevard, 32935
Telephone: 321-254-8416
Fax: 321-259-8243
Email: nancacc@iu.net

MEMBERS OF FIRM

James H. Nance
S. Sammy Cacciatore
John N. Hamilton
Charles G. Barger, Jr.
James N. Nance
Sammy M. Cacciatore

Reference: The Bank.

For full biographical listings, see the Martindale-Hubbell Law Directory

*MIAMI,** Dade Co.

ADAMS & ADAMS (AV)

5th Floor, Concord Building, 66 West Flagler Street, 33130
Telephone: 305-371-3333
Broward: 954-728-8770
Telecopier: 305-372-3987

Richard B. Adams (1926-1983)
Richard B. Adams, Jr.
R. Wade Adams

ASSOCIATES

Andrew D. Stone
Peter G. Walsh

LEGAL SUPPORT PERSONNEL

Sonia Torres

For full biographical listings, see the Martindale-Hubbell Law Directory

Miami—Continued

ANGONES, HUNTER, MCCLURE, LYNCH & WILLIAMS, P.A. (AV)

Ninth Floor-Concord Building, 66 West Flagler Street, 33130-1805
Telephone: 305-371-5000
Fort Lauderdale: 954-728-9112
Fax: 305-371-3948
Fort Lauderdale, Florida Office: Suite 203N Justice Building, 524 South Andrews Avenue.
Telephone: 954-779-3456.
Fax: 954-832-0037.

Frank R. Angones
Steven Kent Hunter
John McClure
Christopher J. Lynch
Stewart D. Williams
B. Scott Hunter
Leopoldo Garcia, Jr.

Thomas W. Paradise (Resident, Fort Lauderdale Office)
Donna Joy Hunter
Lourdes Alfonsin Ruiz
Kara D. Phinney
C. David Durkee

Insurance Clients: Allstate Insurance Co.; Prudential Property & Casualty Insurance Co.; Travelers Insurance Co.; Rollins Hudig Hall Healthcare Risk, Inc.

For Complete List of Firm Personnel, See General Section

For full biographical listings, see the Martindale-Hubbell Law Directory

ARMSTRONG & MEJER, P.A. (AV)

Suite 1111 Douglas Centre, 2600 Douglas Road (Coral Gables), 33134
Telephone: 305-444-3355
Fax: 305-442-4300
Email: Amesq@Aol.com

Timothy J. Armstrong
Alvaro L. Mejer

M. Emelina Mejer-Kondla

Reference: First Union National Bank.

For full biographical listings, see the Martindale-Hubbell Law Directory

BURD MAGATHAN LOZANO & ZACHERL, L.L.P. (AV)

601 Brickell Key Drive Suite 500, 33131
Telephone: 305-374-3100
Facsimile: 305-374-3161
Email: (Initial & Last Name)@BDMLAW.COM

MEMBERS OF FIRM

William G. Burd
Madelyn Simon Lozano
Francis A. Zacherl III

ASSOCIATES

John Scott McPhee
Colleen A. Hoey
David Alan Seiler
Michael A. Hession (Not admitted in FL)

For full biographical listings, see the Martindale-Hubbell Law Directory

DEUTSCH & BLUMBERG, P.A. (AV)

Suite 2802 New World Tower, 100 North Biscayne Boulevard, 33132
Telephone: 305-358-6329
Fax: 305-358-9304

Steven K. Deutsch
Edward R. Blumberg
James C. Blecke
Louis Thaler

For full biographical listings, see the Martindale-Hubbell Law Directory

FERRARO & ASSOCIATES, P.A. (AV)

First Union Financial Center, 200 S. Biscayne Boulevard Suite 3800, 33131-2310
Telephone: 305-375-0111
Telefax: 305-379-6222
URL: http://www.ferrarolaw.com

James L. Ferraro

Ana M. Rivero
Dino G. Galardi
Valerie A. Conzo
O. Oliver Wragg
Kerry A. Raleigh

For full biographical listings, see the Martindale-Hubbell Law Directory

FERRELL SCHULTZ CARTER & FERTEL, P.A. (AV)

201 South Biscayne Boulevard Miami Center, 34th Floor, 33131-4325
Telephone: 305-371-8585
Telecopier: 305-371-5732
Email: receptionist@ferrellscf.com *URL:* http://www.ferrellscf.com

(See Next Column)

Milton M. Ferrell, Jr.
Alan K. Fertel

Reference: City National Bank of Florida.

For full biographical listings, see the Martindale-Hubbell Law Directory

HAGGARD, PARKS & STONE, P.A. (AV)

330 Alhambra Circle (Coral Gables), 33134
Telephone: 305-446-5700
Fax: 305-446-1154
Email: mail@haggardparksstone.com *URL:* http://www.lawyers.com/haggardparksstone

Wm. Andrew Haggard
Robert L. Parks
Mark D. Stone

Jeannete Lewis Bologna
Michael Andrew Haggard

Reference: Sun Bank of Coral Gables.

For full biographical listings, see the Martindale-Hubbell Law Directory

HALL, DAVID AND JOSEPH, P.A. (AV)

Penthouse 1428 Brickell Avenue, P.O. Box 019113, 33131-9113
Telephone: 305-374-5030
Fax: 305-374-5033

Andrew C. Hall
Christopher M. David
Allan A. Joseph

Adam S. Hall
Michael L Cotzen
Ilene Schnall
Santiago A. Cueto
Kimberly S. Rogers

For full biographical listings, see the Martindale-Hubbell Law Directory

HARDY, BISSETT & TEICHNER, P.A. (AV)

501 Northeast First Avenue, 33132
Telephone: 305-358-6200
Broward: 954-462-6377
Fax: 305-577-8230

G. Jack Hardy
G. William Bissett
Lee Philip Teichner

Lyle E. Shapiro

Representative Clients: International Paper Co.; Bridgestone/Firestone, Inc.; American International Underwriters; American International Group, Inc.; Crown Equipment Corp.; The Budd Company; Loewen Group International, Inc.; St. Paul Insurance Company; Titan International, Inc.; Sunstate Manufactured Homes of Georgia, Inc. d/b/a Peach State Homes, Inc.

For full biographical listings, see the Martindale-Hubbell Law Directory

HEISE MARKARIAN P.A. (AV)

2937 Southwest 27th Avenue, Suite 104, 33133
Telephone: 305-530-8888
Fax: 305-530-8004
Email: markarianlaw@bellsouth.net

Mark J. Heise
David K. Markarian

Reginald A. Mathis

For full biographical listings, see the Martindale-Hubbell Law Directory

HIGH, STACK, LAZENBY, PALAHACH & FEILER (AV)

A Partnership including Professional Associations
3929 Ponce de Leon Boulevard (Coral Gables), 33134
Telephone: 305-443-3329
Fax: 305-443-0850
Email: Highstack@aol.com
Melbourne, Florida Office: High, Stack, Lazenby, Maxwell & Platt, 525 Strawbridge Avenue.
Telephone: 407-725-5525.
FAX: 407-984-2411.

MEMBERS OF FIRM

Robert King High (1924-1967)
Charles R. Stack (P.A.)
Michael Palahach, III, (P.A.)
Michael B. Feiler

ASSOCIATES

Carlos Cruanes
Kimberly B. Bonder (Resident at Melborne Office)

OF COUNSEL

Fernando M. Palacios
Christopher M. Rundle, P.A.
Reed C. Cary
Irving J. Whitman

For full biographical listings, see the Martindale-Hubbell Law Directory

Miami—Continued

HOFFMAN & HERTZIG, P.A. (AV)

Suite 900, 241 Sevilla Avenue (Coral Gables), 33134
Telephone: 305-445-3100
Fax: 305-444-5656

Carl H. Hoffman
David Hertzig

Howard Kraft Pita

References: City National Bank of Miami, Coral Gables.

For full biographical listings, see the Martindale-Hubbell Law Directory

HOLTZMAN, KRINZMAN, EQUELS & FURIA (AV)

2601 South Bayshore Drive, Suite 600, 33133
Telephone: 305-859-7700
Fax: 305-859-9996
Email: hkef@hkef.com *URL:* http://www.hkef.com
Orlando, Florida Office: 16 West Pine Street, 32801.
Telephone: 407-839-0095.
Fax: 407-839-2050.
Tallahassee, Florida Office: 542 East Park Avenue, 32301.
Telephone: 850-222-2900.
Fax: 850-222-2933.

Thomas K. Equels
Joseph L. Raia
R. Barbara Wien
Cary A. Lubetsky
Mary Kogut Equels (Resident, Orlando Office)
Charles M. Greene (Resident, Orlando Office)

Sherrie J. Cohen
Nancy M. Thevenin
Kevin J. Tang (Resident, Orlando Office)

OF COUNSEL

Chapman L. Smith, Jr.

For full biographical listings, see the Martindale-Hubbell Law Directory

JOSEPHS, JACK & GAEBE, P.A. (AV)

Grove Professional Building, 2950 S.W. 27th Avenue, Suite 100, 33133-3765
Telephone: Dade County: 305-445-3800
Telecopier: 305-448-5800
Email: TheFirm@FloridaAttorneys.com *URL:* http://www.Florida-Attorneys.com

Michael R. Josephs
Lewis N. Jack, Jr.
John S. Gaebe

Elisabeth M. Allen
Helen Leen Miranda
Scott A. Cole
Stephanie E. Demos
Scott T. McCullough
Tamara D. McKeown
Christopher T. Lemos

Representative Clients: U-Haul Corporation; ITT Sheraton; Zurich-American Insurance Company; Republic Claims Service Company; Southern Fire Insurance Adjusters.

For full biographical listings, see the Martindale-Hubbell Law Directory

KENNY NACHWALTER SEYMOUR ARNOLD CRITCHLOW & SPECTOR, PROFESSIONAL ASSOCIATION (AV)

1100 Miami Center, 201 South Biscayne Boulevard, 33131-4327
Telephone: 305-373-1000
Facsimile: 305-372-1861
Email: admin@knsacs.com
Rogersville, Tennessee Office: 107 East Main Street, Suite 301.
Telephone: 423-272-5300.
Facsimile: 423-272-4961.

James J. Kenny
Michael Nachwalter
Thomas H. Seymour
Richard Alan Arnold
Richard H. Critchlow
Brian F. Spector
Kevin J. Murray
William J. Blechman
Harry R. Schafer
Deborah Sampieri Corbishley
David H. Lichter
Scott E. Perwin
Jeffrey T. Foreman
Pamela I. Perry
Lauren C. Ravkind
Katherine Clark Silverglate
Amanda M. McGovern
Paul C. Huck, Jr.
Robert D.W. Landon, III
Maria J. Beguiristain

Representative Clients: Albertson's, Inc.; American Bankers Insurance Group; Cartier, Inc.; Ethan Allen, Inc.; Federated Department Stores, Inc.; The Florida Bar; GTE Directories Corp.; Siemens Credit Corp.; GTE Florida; Columbia HCA.

For full biographical listings, see the Martindale-Hubbell Law Directory

KLUGER, PERETZ, KAPLAN & BERLIN, P.A. (AV)

Miami Center - 17th Floor, 201 South Biscayne Boulevard, 33131
Telephone: Dade: 305-379-9000
Broward: 305-761-1100
Fax: 305-379-3428
Broward: 954-761-1138
Email: tmeyers@kpkb.com *URL:* http://www.kpkb.com
Fort Lauderdale, Florida Office: 1100 SunTrust Tower, One East Broward Boulevard, 33301.
Telephone: 954-761-1100.
Fax: 954-761-1138.

Alan J. Kluger
Abbey L. Kaplan
Steven I. Peretz
Howard J. Berlin
Steve I. Silverman
Bruce A. Katzen
Andrew P. Gold (Resident, Fort Lauderdale Office)
Jon C. Chassen
Michael B. Chesal
Eliot C. Abbott
Gregory P. Borgognoni
Michael D. Ehrenstein

D. Fernando Bobadilla
Eugenia Chu
Stephen M. Gaffigan
Ronny J. Halperin
Seth A. Honowitz (Resident, Fort Lauderdale Office)
Todd A. Levine (Resident, Fort Lauderdale Office)
Jason Marks (Resident, Fort Lauderdale Office)
Terri Meyers
Jason S. Oletsky (Resident, Fort Lauderdale Office)
Michael S. Perse
Jena E. Rissman
C. Mark Robson
Michael D. Seese
Deborah Berlin Talenfeld
Michael Tanner

OF COUNSEL

Richard A. Sharpstein
Michael Wrubel (Resident, Fort Lauderdale Office)
Andrew V. Tramont (Also Practicing Individually)

LEGAL SUPPORT PERSONNEL

PARALEGALS

Vernia Contreras
Kristine H. Kadlac
Diana M. Payne
Maria A. Tucci
Katherine L. Hoyt
Cathie J. Recca (Resident, Fort Lauderdale Office)

For full biographical listings, see the Martindale-Hubbell Law Directory

KUTNER, RUBINOFF, BUSH & LERNER (AV)

501 N.E. 1st Avenue, P.O. Box 9700, 33101
Telephone: 305-358-6200; Broward: 954-462-6377
Fax: 305-577-8230
Email: Kutner@KRBL.com

MEMBERS OF FIRM

Arno Kutner
Edward G. Rubinoff
Kenneth J. Bush
Susan Scrivani Lerner

For Complete List of Firm Personnel, See General Section

For full biographical listings, see the Martindale-Hubbell Law Directory

LEESFIELD, LEIGHTON, RUBIO & MAHFOOD, P.A. (AV)

2350 South Dixie Highway, 33133
Telephone: 305-854-4900; 800-836-6400 (toll free)
Fax: 305-854-8266
Email: LEESFIELD@AOL.COM *URL:* http://www.LLRM.com
Key West, Florida Office: 615 1/2 Whitehead Street.
Telephone: 305-296-1342.
Fax: 305-294-1793.

Ira H. Leesfield
John Elliott Leighton
Maria L. Rubio
George G. Mahfood

Robert B. Boyers
Patricia M. Kennedy (P.A.)

For full biographical listings, see the Martindale-Hubbell Law Directory

MURAI, WALD, BIONDO & MORENO, P.A. (AV)

9th Floor Ingraham Building, 25 Southeast 2nd Avenue, 33131
Telephone: 305-358-5900
Fax: 305-358-9490
Email: mwbm@gate.net

Rene V. Murai
Gerald B. Wald
Gerald J. Biondo
M. Cristina Moreno
Cristina Echarte Brochin

Antonio Arzola
Maria Victoria Currais
Lynette Ebeoglu McGuinness

Reference: Union Planters Bank.

For full biographical listings, see the Martindale-Hubbell Law Directory

Miami—Continued

PAYTON & CARLSON, P.A. (AV)

SunTrust International Center, Suite 1200, One Southeast Third Avenue, 33131
Telephone: 305-372-3500
Fax: 305-577-4895
Email: hapayton@bellsouth.net

Harry A. Payton — Curtis Carlson

Ronald J. Lewittes — Julie Anne Moxley

OF COUNSEL

Mara Beth Sommers

For full biographical listings, see the Martindale-Hubbell Law Directory

PODHURST, ORSECK, JOSEFSBERG, EATON, MEADOW, OLIN & PERWIN, P.A. (AV)

Suite 800 City National Bank Building, 25 West Flagler Street, 33130-1780
Telephone: 305-358-2800; Fort Lauderdale: 954-463-4346
Fax: 305-358-2382
Email: Info@podhurst.com *URL:* http://www.wwdir.com/podhurst.html

Aaron Podhurst
Robert Orseck (1934-1978)
Robert C. Josefsberg
Joel D. Eaton
Barry L. Meadow
Michael S. Olin
Joel S. Perwin
Steven C. Marks
Victor M. Diaz, Jr.
Katherine W. Ezell

Xavier Martínez

OF COUNSEL

Walter H. Beckham, Jr. — Karen Podhurst Dern

Representative Clients: Burger King Corp.; Ryder System, Inc.; Ernst & Young; Lennar Corporation; The Continental Companies.
Reference: Mellon United National Bank of Miami; City National Bank of Miami.

For full biographical listings, see the Martindale-Hubbell Law Directory

WILLIAM L. RICHEY, P.A. (AV)

One Biscayne Tower, 2 South Biscayne Boulevard, Suite 3400, 33131-1897
Telephone: 305-372-8808
Fax: 305-372-3669
Email: wlr@richeylaw.com *URL:* http://www.lawyers.com/richeylaw
Palm City, Florida Office: 5501 S.W. Sunshine Farms Way, 34990-5696.
Telephone: 561-220-0558.
Fax: 305-372-3669.

William L. Richey (Also Of Counsel to Gunster, Yoakley, Valdes-Fauli & Stewart, P.A., Miami, Florida and Stuart, Florida)

For full biographical listings, see the Martindale-Hubbell Law Directory

RICHMAN GREER WEIL BRUMBAUGH MIRABITO & CHRISTENSEN, P.A. (AV)

Miami Center, Tenth Floor, 201 South Biscayne Boulevard, 33131
Telephone: 305-373-4000
Fax: 305-373-4099
Email: info@richmangreer.com *URL:* http://www.richmangreer.com
West Palm Beach, Florida Office: Phillips Point East, Suite 1100, 777 South Flagler Drive, 33401.
Telephone: 561-803-3500.
Fax: 561-820-1608.

Gerald F. Richman
Alan G. Greer
Kenneth J. Weil
John M. Brumbaugh
Andrew J. Mirabito
Bruce A. Christensen
Charles H. Johnson
Gary S. Betensky
Diane Wagner Katzen
Manuel A. Garcia-Linares

Mark A. Romance
Steven M. Brady
Lawrence H. Kunin
Kenneth L. Dobkin
Joseph F. Hession
Carol M. Brewer

OF COUNSEL

Robert L. Floyd — Ray H. Pearson

Representative Clients: Motorola, Inc.; Minnesota Mining and Manufacturing Co.; Republic of Panama; Hallmark; Microsoft Corporation; Direct TV; Gemstar.

For full biographical listings, see the Martindale-Hubbell Law Directory

STANLEY M. ROSENBLATT PROFESSIONAL ASSOCIATION (AV)

12th Floor, Concord Building, 66 West Flagler Street, 33130
Telephone: 305-374-6131
Fax: 305-381-8818

Stanley M. Rosenblatt

(See Next Column)

Susan Rosenblatt
Mary Margaret Schneider
John A Hoag
Maureen G. Markwith

For full biographical listings, see the Martindale-Hubbell Law Directory

ROSSMAN, BAUMBERGER & REBOSO, A PROFESSIONAL ASSOCIATION (AV)

23rd Floor, Courthouse Tower, 44 West Flagler Street, 33130
Telephone: 305-373-0708
Fax: 305-577-4370
Email: trial-law@rbrlaw.com *URL:* http://www.rbrlaw.com

Charles H. Baumberger — Stephen F. Rossman
Manuel A. Reboso

Howard A. Spier — Lincoln J. Connolly

Reference: United National Bank of Miami.

For full biographical listings, see the Martindale-Hubbell Law Directory

RUSSO & HEFFERNAN, P.A. (AV)

7990 Red Road, 33143
Telephone: 305-665-7171
Fax: 305-665-7146
Email: lawyers@rhpa.com *URL:* http://www.lawyers.com/russo&heffernan

Don Russo — David R. Heffernan

For full biographical listings, see the Martindale-Hubbell Law Directory

SAMS & LISTER, P.A. (AV)

73255 West 63 Avenue, Suite 201, 33143
Telephone: 305-740-5401
Fax: 305-740-5425

Murray Sams, Jr. — David P. Lister

Arthur B. Stark

For full biographical listings, see the Martindale-Hubbell Law Directory

SIEGFRIED, RIVERA, LERNER, DE LA TORRE & SOBEL, P.A. (AV)

Suite 1102, 201 Alhambra Circle (Coral Gables), 33134
Telephone: 305-442-3334
Fax: 305-443-3292
URL: http://www.siegfriedlaw.com

Steven M. Siegfried
Oscar R. Rivera
Lisa A. Lerner
Helio De La Torre
Peter H. Edwards
Stuart H. Sobel
Maria Victoria Arias
James F. Harrington
Elisabeth D. Kozlow

Gary Louis Brown
David B. Israel
Laura Michelle Manning
Fern F. Musselwhite
Grissel C. Picot
Marc C. Pugliese

OF COUNSEL

H. Hugh Mc Connell

For full biographical listings, see the Martindale-Hubbell Law Directory

SPARKMAN, ROBB & MASON (AV)

Suite 1003 Biscayne Building, 19 West Flagler Street, 33130
Telephone: 305-374-0033
Broward: 954-522-0045
Fax: 305-539-0767
Fort Lauderdale, Florida Office: Suite 402, 200 S.E. Sixth Street.
Telephones: 305-463-3590; Dade: 305-945-4461.

MEMBERS OF FIRM

James T. Sparkman — Michael A. Robb
Donald Edward Mason

ASSOCIATE

John William Gautier

For full biographical listings, see the Martindale-Hubbell Law Directory

SPENCER AND KLEIN, PROFESSIONAL ASSOCIATION (AV)

Suite 1901, 801 Brickell Avenue, 33131
Telephone: 305-374-7700
Telecopier: 305-374-4890
Email: SandK@primenet.com

Thomas R. Spencer, Jr.

(See Next Column)

SPENCER AND KLEIN PROFESSIONAL ASSOCIATION, *Miami—Continued*

Paul D. Breitner
David M. Tarlow
Kevin Spencer
Edelberto Farres

Representative Clients: America Publishing Group; American Association of Physicians and Surgeons; Chrysler Corporation; Coldwell Banker; Editorial Televisa; Grupo Anaya, S.A.; Independent Living Care, Inc.; Managed Care of America, Inc.; New Times, Inc.; Winn-Dixie Stores.

For Complete List of Firm Personnel, See General Section

For full biographical listings, see the Martindale-Hubbell Law Directory

STEWART TILGHMAN FOX & BIANCHI, P.A. (AV)

One Southeast Third Avenue Suite 3000, 33131-1764
Telephone: 305-358-6644
Fax: 305-358-4707

Larry S. Stewart
James B. Tilghman, Jr.
Gary D. Fox
David W. Bianchi
Stuart N. Ratzan

Jeremy W. Alters

For full biographical listings, see the Martindale-Hubbell Law Directory

VALLE & CRAIG, P.A. (AV)

Suite 2520 World Trade Center, 80 Southwest Eighth Street, P.O. Box 113009, 33111-3009
Telephone: 305-373-2888; 800-609-6151
Facsimile: 305-373-2889

Laurence F. Valle
Lawrance B. Craig, III
Timothy Maze Hartley

Frank J. Sioli, Jr.
Michael J. Lynott
Michael A. Vasquez
Brian M. McKell

For full biographical listings, see the Martindale-Hubbell Law Directory

WELBAUM, GUERNSEY, HINGSTON, GREENLEAF & GREGORY, L.L.P. (AV)

Penthouse Suite, 901 Ponce de Leon Boulevard (Coral Gables), 33134-3009
Telephone: 305-441-8900
Fax: 305-441-2255
Email: wghgglaw@bellsouth.net

MEMBERS OF FIRM

R. Earl Welbaum
Dan B. Guernsey
Robert A. Hingston
W. Frank Greenleaf
John H. Gregory

ASSOCIATES

Michael Yates
Michael Jay Rune, II

OF COUNSEL

René Sacasas

For full biographical listings, see the Martindale-Hubbell Law Directory

MIAMI LAKES, Dade Co.

PYSZKA, BLACKMON, LEVY & SAVOLA, P.A. (AV)

14750 Northwest 77th Court, Suite 300, 33016
Telephone: 305-512-3737
Fax: 305-512-1237
Email: Pyszka_Douberley@compuserve.com

Gerard E. Pyszka
Phillip D. Blackmon, Jr.
Benjamin D. Levy
L.H. Steven Savola

Cindy J. Mishcon

For full biographical listings, see the Martindale-Hubbell Law Directory

*NAPLES,** Collier Co.

MCDONNELL TRIAL LAWYERS (AV)

1165 Eighth Street South, 34102
Telephone: 941-434-7711; 1-800-873-8060
Fax: 941-434-5629
Email: attyfirstname@mcdonnelltriallawyers. com
URL: http://www.lawyers.com/mtl

Michael McDonnell

ASSOCIATE

Gary Layne Green

For full biographical listings, see the Martindale-Hubbell Law Directory

QUARLES & BRADY LLP (AV)

Barnett Center, 4501 Tamiami Trail North Suite 300, 34103-3060
Telephone: 941-262-5959
Fax: 941-434-4999
URL: http://www.quarles.com
Milwaukee, Wisconsin Office: 411 East Wisconsin Avenue, 53202-4497.
Telephone: 414-277-5000.
Fax: 414-271-3552.
Madison, Wisconsin Office: Firstar Plaza, One South Pinckney Street, P.O. Box 2113, 53701-2113.
Telephone: 608-251-5000.
Fax: 608-251-9166.
West Palm Beach, Florida Office: 222 Lakeview Avenue, 4th Floor, 33401.
Telephone: 561-653-5000.
Fax: 561-653-5333.
Phoenix, Arizona Office: One Camelback Building, One East Camelback Road, Suite 400, 85012-1649.
Telephone: 602-230-5500.
Fax: 602-230-5598.
Chicago, Illinois Office: Quarles & Brady LLC, Citicorp Center, 500 West Madison Street, Suite 3700.
Telephone: 312-715-5000.
Fax: 312-715-5155.

PARTNERS

F. Joseph McMackin, III
Robert E. Doyle, Jr.

ASSOCIATES

Mark Hubert Muller
Lisa Carozza Lottes
James T. Demarest
Edmond E. Koester
C. Lane Wood

For Complete List of Firm Personnel, See General Section

For full biographical listings, see the Martindale-Hubbell Law Directory

NORTH PALM BEACH, Palm Beach Co.

LAW OFFICES OF PATRICK C. MASSA, P.A. (AV)

Crystal Tree Office Centre, 1201 U.S. Highway One, Suite 400, 33408
Telephone: 561-694-1800
Facsimile: 561-694-1833
Email: pmassalaw@aol.com

Patrick C. Massa

For full biographical listings, see the Martindale-Hubbell Law Directory

*ORLANDO,** Orange Co.

W. RILEY ALLEN, P.A. (AV)

Lake Copeland Historic District, 228 Annie Street, 32806
Telephone: 407-423-8822
Fax: 407-425-1755
Email: wra@iag.net *URL:* http://www.floridatriallawyer.com

W. Riley Allen

Daniel Riveiro Jr.
Kim Michael Cullen

OF COUNSEL

James R. Hooper

For full biographical listings, see the Martindale-Hubbell Law Directory

BAKER & HOSTETLER LLP (AV)

SunBank Center, Suite 2300, 200 South Orange Avenue, 32802-3432
Telephone: 407-649-4000
Fax: 407-841-0168
To contact an attorney on the Internet use first initial and surname followed by @baker-hostetler.com
URL: http://www.bakerlaw.com
In Cleveland, Ohio: 3200 National City Center, 1900 East Ninth Street.
Telephone: 216-621-0200.
In Cincinnati, Ohio: 312 Walnut Street, Suite 2650.
Telephone: 513-929-3400.
In Columbus, Ohio: Capitol Square, Suite 2100, 65 East State Street.
Telephone: 614-228-1541.
In Denver, Colorado: 303 East 17th Avenue, Suite 1100.
Telephone: 303-861-0600.
In Houston, Texas: 1000 Louisiana, Suite 2000.
Telephone: 713-751-1600.
In Long Beach, California: 300 Oceangate, Suite 620.
Telephone: 362-432-2827.
In Los Angeles, California: 600 Wilshire Boulevard.
Telephone: 213-624-2400.
In Washington, D. C.: Washington Square, Suite 1100, 1050 Connecticut Avenue, N.W.
Telephone: 202-861-1500.

PARTNERS

John W. Foster, Sr.
Jerry R. Linscott

For Complete List of Firm Personnel, See General Section

For full biographical listings, see the Martindale-Hubbell Law Directory

Orlando—Continued

BEST & ANDERSON, P.A. (AV)

1201 East Robinson Street, 32801
Telephone: 407-425-2985
Email: cab@bestandanderson.com *URL:* http://www.bestandanderson.com
Crystal River, Florida Office: Executive Center Condos, 7655 West Gulf to Lake Highway, Suite 6, 34429.
Telephone: 352-795-1107.
Melbourne, Florida Office: Healthsouth Marina Towers, 709 South Harbor City Boulevard, Suite 270, 32901.
Telephone: 407-727-9923.

David R. Best
George H. "Dutch" Anderson, III

Angela O'Neil
James William Nuebel
Lora L. Wilson
Louis Allen DeFreitas, Jr.

For full biographical listings, see the Martindale-Hubbell Law Directory

BROWN, WARD, SALZMAN & WEISS, P.A. (AV)

111 North Orange Avenue, Suite 875, P.O. Box 2873, 32802-2873
Telephone: 407-425-9566
Fax: 407-425-9596; Email: firm@orlandolaw.net
Email: brownu@osceola.k12.fl.us *URL:* http://www.orlandolaw.net

Usher Larry Brown
John H. Ward
Gary S. Salzman
Jeffrey S. Weiss
Suzanne D'Agresta

Scott D. Danahy
James G. Vickaryous
Robert L. Butterfield, Jr.
Allison Carmine McDonald

Representative Clients: The Walt Disney Company; Walt Disney World Co.; Walt Disney World Hospitality & Recreation Corp.; Reedy Creek Energy Services; The School Board of Osceola County; Osceola County; Orange County Comptroller; General Electric Capital Modular Space; Honeywell, Inc.

For full biographical listings, see the Martindale-Hubbell Law Directory

CABANISS, McDONALD, SMITH & WIGGINS, P.A. (AV)

390 N. Orange Avenue, Suite 1600, P.O. Box 2513, 32802-2513
Telephone: 407-246-1800
Facsimile: 407-246-1895
URL: http://www.cmsw.com
Atlanta, Georgia Office: 5555 Glenridge Connector, Suite 200, 30342.
Telephone: 404-531-5080.
Facsimile: 404-531-5081.

Ronald E. Cabaniss
Francis M. McDonald, Jr.
Larry D. Smith
Michael J. Wiggins
M. Gary Toole

David E. Cannella
Earnest DeLoach, Jr.
Sarah A. Long
Michelle M. Perez-Sotolongo
Douglas J. Petro
John R. Reid, Jr.
Scott A. Richman
F. Rand Wallis

For full biographical listings, see the Martindale-Hubbell Law Directory

CAMERON, MARRIOTT, WALSH, HODGES & COLEMAN, P.A. (AV)

15 West Church Street, Suite 301, 32801
Telephone: 407-841-5030
Fax: 407-843-1727
Email: cammariott@aol.com
Daytona Beach, Florida Office: 432 South Beach Street.
Telephone: 904-257-1755.
Fax: 904-252-5601.
Ocala, Florida Office: 25 East Silver Springs Boulevard.
Telephone: 904-351-1119.
Fax: 904-351-0151.

A. Craig Cameron
E. Peyton Hodges

Douglas J. LaPointe
Louis D. Kaye
Brian R. Pink
G. Yates Rumbley
Martin J. Jaffe
Richard M. Adams
Frank M. Costanzo

Representative Clients: Albertson's; AIG; All-State; Auto Owners; American Family Insurance Group; American Fire and Casualty Insurance Co.; AT&T; Automobile Club Insurance Co.; Avis; Black & Decker.

For full biographical listings, see the Martindale-Hubbell Law Directory

DECUBELLIS & MEEKS, P.A. (AV)

Suite 801, Citrus Center, 255 South Orange Avenue, P.O. Box 4976, 32802-4976
Telephone: 407-872-2200
Telecopier: 407-423-1038

(See Next Column)

Daniel L. DeCubellis
Mary B. Meeks
John A. Shughart, Jr.
Jennifer C. Carter
Brett M. Wendt

Representative Clients: Design Professional Insurance Corp.; Florida Lawyers Mutual Insurance Corp.; International Game Technology, Inc.; Jennings Environmental Services, Inc.; Mader Southeast, Inc.; Orange County; PGA Tour, Inc.; SouthTrust Bank, N.A.

For full biographical listings, see the Martindale-Hubbell Law Directory

DEMPSEY & SASSO (AV)

Nations Bank Building, 390 North Orange Avenue, Suite 2700, P.O. Box 1980, 32802
Telephone: 407-422-5166
Telecopier: 407-422-8556
Email: demp-sas@magicnet.net

Bernard H. Dempsey, Jr.
Michael C. Sasso

Brian D. Solomon
Barbara B. Smithers
Jeffrey K. Grant
Angelia J. Sheridan

For full biographical listings, see the Martindale-Hubbell Law Directory

DRAGE, DE BEAUBIEN, KNIGHT, SIMMONS, MANTZARIS & NEAL (AV)

332 North Magnolia Avenue, P.O. Box 87, 32802-0087
Telephone: 407-422-2454
Fax: 407-849-1845

Thomas B. Drage, Jr.
Hugo H. de Beaubien
T. Kevin Knight
David H. Simmons
Thomas F. Neal
Daniel F. Mantzaris
Julie Hions O'Kane
D. John Morgeson, Jr.

Dale T. Gobel
Patrick C. Howell
Kenneth P. Hazouri
Yvette Rodriguez Brown
Jennifer C. Frank
Blair Thomas Jackson
Elizabeth A. Lanham-Patrie
P. Hayden Haskins, Jr.
Stephen James Jacobs
Rachael McMorris Crag-Chaderton
Julie Fink Kaufman
Daniel J. O'Malley
Ben Rossi, Jr.
Darlene Duggan Beneke
Julian Gonzalez
Nicola A. Boothe-Perry
Maria B. Vazquez
Daniel P. Osterndorf
Aliette-Marie Charles
Elmer Sanchez
Kenneth E. Andrews
Nancy J. Abernathy
Eduardo Rodriguez
Megan Lubozynski
Sean Conway

For full biographical listings, see the Martindale-Hubbell Law Directory

EUBANKS, HILYARD & BOGAN, P.A. (AV)

Suite 600 First Union Building, 20 North Orange Avenue, P.O. Box 4973, 32802-4973
Telephone: 407-425-4251
Telecopier: 407-841-8431

Ernest H. Eubanks
Rodney G. Ross (1934-1982)
Sutton G. Hilyard, Jr.
Bruce R. Bogan

Bobby G. Palmer, Jr.
W. Gregory Lockeby

Representative Clients: AIG Aviation, Inc.; AVEMCO Insurance Co.; Phoenix Aviation Managers, Inc.; Ranger Insurance Co.; Old Republic Insurance Co.; Signal Aviation Underwriters; Underwriters at Lloyds; Orange County Sheriff's Office; United Technologies Corp.; Reliance Insurance Co.

For full biographical listings, see the Martindale-Hubbell Law Directory

GURNEY & HANDLEY, P.A. (AV)

225 East Robinson Street, Suite 450, 32801
Telephone: 407-843-9500
Facsimile: 407-649-4941
Email: gurney-handley@worldnet.att.net

Leon H. Handley
John L. Sewell
Robert S. Green
W. Marvin Hardy, III
Ronald L. Harrop
Francis E. Pierce, III
Peter N. Smith
Richard E. Dunegan
David Brian Falstad

Steven H. Preston
Paul D. Rang

OF COUNSEL

Richard W. Lassiter
David W. Roquemore, Jr.
Ley H. Smith

Representative Clients: Government Employees Insurance Co.; John Hancock Mutual Life Insurance Co.; University of Florida; Liberty National Life Insurance Company; Empire Fire & Marine Insurance Company; Crown Bank, FSB.

For full biographical listings, see the Martindale-Hubbell Law Directory

Orlando—Continued

HARTLEY, WALL & NORMAN (AV)

200 South Orange Avenue, Suite 2810, P.O. Box 2168, 32802
Telephone: 407-422-7992
Fax: 407-425-2182

MEMBERS OF FIRM

Carl W. Hartley, Jr.
Todd K. Norman
Richard F. Wall
Terrance L. Ashanta-Barker

Reference: SunTrust Bank, Central Florida, N.A.

For full biographical listings, see the Martindale-Hubbell Law Directory

HILL AND PONTON, PROFESSIONAL ASSOCIATION (AV)

Suite 500, 605 East Robinson Street, P.O. Box 2673, 32802
Telephone: 407-422-4665
URL: http://www.hillponton.com

Brian D. Hill
Carol J. Ponton

Maria D. Santana (Not admitted in FL)
Silvia R. Sanders
Jeffrey D. Starker

For full biographical listings, see the Martindale-Hubbell Law Directory

HILL, REIS, ADAMS, HALL & SCHIEFFELIN, P.A. (AV)

1417 East Concord Street, 32803
Telephone: 407-896-0425
Fax: 407-896-9236
Email: mainbox@hrahs.com

G. Bruce Hill
Larry D. Hall
Gregory F. Reis
Thomas L. Schieffelin, Jr.
Janet W. Adams
William W. Large
Matthew P. Bartolomei

David O Doyle, Jr
Andrew Vlahos
Heidi Jo Haycook

Representative Clients: The Florida Hospital Trust Fund; The Florida Hospital Excess Trust Fund; Florida Hospital Workers Compensation/Self Insurance Trust Fund; Bartow Memorial Hospital; Bay Medical Center; Brooksville Regional Hospital; Cape Canaveral Hospital; Cape Coral Hospital; Desoto Memorial Hospital.

For full biographical listings, see the Martindale-Hubbell Law Directory

NORMAN LINDER HULL, P.A. (AV)

537 North Magnolia Avenue, P.O. Box 2751, 32802
Telephone: 407-422-1235
Fax: 407-423-2842
Email: nlhull@ix.netcom.com *URL:* http://www.lawyers.com/hulllaw

Norman L. Hull

For full biographical listings, see the Martindale-Hubbell Law Directory

KING, BLACKWELL & DOWNS, P.A. (AV)

25 East Pine Street, P.O. Box 1631, 32802-1631
Telephone: 407-422-2472
Fax: 407-648-0161
Email: kbdfirm@mindspring.com *URL:* http://www.kbdlaw.com

David B. King
Bruce B. Blackwell
Mayanne Downs

John F. Tannian
Thomas A. Zehnder

For full biographical listings, see the Martindale-Hubbell Law Directory

LITCHFORD & CHRISTOPHER, PROFESSIONAL ASSOCIATION (AV)

NationsBank Center, Suite 2200, 390 North Orange Avenue, P.O. Box 1549, 32802
Telephone: 407-422-6600
Telecopier: 407-841-0325
Email: lawfirm@litchris.com *URL:* http://www.litchris.com

Hal K. Litchford
Brian D. DeGailler
Donald E. Christopher
David G. Lerner
Mark Lang
Alan B. Taylor

Scott K. Lippman
Jill Barron Dugger
G. Steven Fender
Susan E. Sewell
Joanne Reed Day

Reference: Citrus Bank.

For full biographical listings, see the Martindale-Hubbell Law Directory

KENNETH L. MANN, P.A. (AV)

105 East Robinson Street, Suite 540, P.O. Box 551, 32802-0551
Telephone: 407-422-0006
Fax: 407-841-9516
Email: reasonablemann@worldnet.att.net *URL:* http://www.KenMannlaw.com

Kenneth L. Mann

For full biographical listings, see the Martindale-Hubbell Law Directory

TERRY L. MCCOLLOUGH, P.A. (AV)

400 North Ferncreek Avenue, 32803
Telephone: 407-894-8600
Fax: 407-894-8685
Email: terry131@aol.com

Terry L. McCollough

LEGAL SUPPORT PERSONNEL

Jacqueline G. Kinker (Paralegal)
Colby D. Griffin (Paralegal)

For full biographical listings, see the Martindale-Hubbell Law Directory

MCEWAN, MARTINEZ, LUFF, DUKES & RUFFIER, P.A. (AV)

108 East Central Boulevard, P.O. Box 753, 32801
Telephone: 407-423-8571
Fax: 407-423-8637

Wilson Sanders (1911-1981)
Rafael E. "Ralph" Martinez
O. Beverley McEwan (1913-1995)
H. David Luff
Thomas E. Dukes, III
John S. McEwan, II
William E. Ruffier
Tyler S. McClay

Juan A. Ruiz
Ruth C. Osborne
Susan D. Kennedy

Representative Clients: Bridgestone/Firestone, Inc.; City Cab of Orlando, Inc.; CNA Insurance Company; Dependable Protective Mutual; Florida Physicians Insurance Co.; Gulf Atlantic Insurance Co.; Marine Office of America; M.C.I. Telecommunications Corporation.

For full biographical listings, see the Martindale-Hubbell Law Directory

MEIER, LENGAUER, BONNER, MUSZYNSKI & DOYLE, P.A. (AV)

37 North Orange Avenue, Suite 1100, 32801
Telephone: 407-872-7774
Facsimile: 407-872-7997

George A. Meier III
Alexander Muszynski III
Steven F. Lengauer
Donna Canina Doyle
Robert E. Bonner
Donald L. O'Dell

Ernest J. Myers
Mercedes R. Wechsler
Veronica Lee Harvey
Mary Catherine Wellman
Melinda G. Baum
Melodie Brosious Jaffe

Representative Clients: AIG Aviation, Inc.; Auto Owners Insurance Company; Chubb & Son; City of Orlando; Federal Express Corp.; Gallagher-Bassett Insurance Service; Phoenix Avaition, Inc.; Westfield Companies; Zurich Insurance Co.; Crum and Forster Insurance.

For full biographical listings, see the Martindale-Hubbell Law Directory

MORAN & SHAMS, P.A. (AV)

111 North Orange Avenue, Suite 1200, P.O. Box 472, 32802-0472
Telephone: 407-841-4141
Fax: 407-841-4148
Email: moran-shams@moran-shams.com

Kelly T. Blystone
Christopher C. Skambis
Brian J. Moran
Sidney H. Shams

Jennifer S. Eden
Cristina Arechaga

Representative Clients: Adventist Health System Sunbelt Healthcare Corporation; Florida Hospital; All Florida Resorts Management; Dayron; Gencor Industries Inc.; Insurance Office of America, Inc.; MEDai, Inc.; Photo Chemical Systems of Florida, Inc.; Vermont American Corporation.

For full biographical listings, see the Martindale-Hubbell Law Directory

O'NEILL, CHAPIN, LIEBMAN & COOPER (AV)

A Partnership including Professional Associations
865 Eola Park Center, 200 East Robinson Street, 32801
Telephone: 407-425-2751
Telex: 407-423-1192

Bernard C. O'Neill, Jr. (P.A.)
John B. Liebman (P.A.)
Mark O. Cooper (P.A.)

ASSOCIATE

Rod C. Lundy

(See Next Column)

O'NEILL, CHAPIN, LIEBMAN & COOPER—*Continued*

OF COUNSEL

Bruce E. Chapin (P.A.)

Reference: First Union National Bank.

For full biographical listings, see the Martindale-Hubbell Law Directory

WILLIAM G. OSBORNE, P.A. (AV)

538 East Washington Street, 32801-1996
Telephone: 407-422-5385
Fax: 407-422-5381

William G. Osborne

LEGAL SUPPORT PERSONNEL

Elizabeth I. Dunnigan (Office Manager)
Catherine C. Braungart (Legal Assistant)

For full biographical listings, see the Martindale-Hubbell Law Directory

PARKER, LANDERMAN & PARKER, P.A. (AV)

108 East Hillcrest Street, P.O. Box 2867, 32802
Telephone: 407-425-4910
Facsimile: 407-423-3140
Email: parkerpa@digital.net

E. Clay Parker
Alan J. Landerman
Henry Clay Parker, IV

For full biographical listings, see the Martindale-Hubbell Law Directory

POHL & SHORT, P.A.

(See Winter Park)

PUGH AND VAN BUREN (AV)

218 Annie Street, 32806
Telephone: 407-843-5840
Email: igpugh@aol.com *URL:* http://www.lawyers.com/pvblaw

Irby G. Pugh
Tye W. Van Buren

For full biographical listings, see the Martindale-Hubbell Law Directory

ARTHUR J. RANSON, III (AV)

401 W. Colonial Drive, Suite 2, 32804-6855
Telephone: 407-839-3443
Facsimile: 407-839-8821

For full biographical listings, see the Martindale-Hubbell Law Directory

ROBERTSON, WILLIAMS & McDONALD, P.A. (AV)

538 East Washington Street, 32801
Telephone: 407-425-1606
Fax: 407-425-6195

John M. Robertson (1935-1997)
Hubert W. Williams (1937-1986)
J. Stephen McDonald

LEGAL SUPPORT PERSONNEL

Leslie Morgan-Christman, C.L.A. (Legal Assistant)
Kim J. Stroupe (Office Manager)

For full biographical listings, see the Martindale-Hubbell Law Directory

RUSSELL LAW OFFICES, P.A. (AV)

537 North Magnolia Avenue, P.O. Box 886, 32802
Telephone: 407-422-1234
Telecopier: 407-423-2842
Email: RussLaw@compuserve.com *URL:* http://www.lawyers.com/russlaw

Rodney Laird Russell

Representative Clients: BMW Financial Services, N.A., Inc.; BellSouth Communications Systems, Inc; Consumer Portfolio Services, Inc.; Federal Express Corp.; Graybar Electric Co., Inc.; Grunau Company, Inc.; McClain Leasing Corp.; PacJets Financial, Ltd.; Turner Construction Co.; Vistana Resort Development, Inc.

For full biographical listings, see the Martindale-Hubbell Law Directory

DAVID C. SCHWARTZ, P.A. (AV)

201 East Pine Street, Suite 700, 32801
Telephone: 407-481-8500
Fax: 407-481-9010
Email: dcschwartz@prodigy.net

David C. Schwartz

For full biographical listings, see the Martindale-Hubbell Law Directory

SHEPARD, FILBURN & GOODBLATT, P.A. (AV)

221 Northeast Ivanhoe Boulevard Suite 205, 32804
Telephone: 407-206-2020
Fax: 407-206-2021
Email: sfglaw@sfg-law.com

Clifford B. Shepard, III
Mark C. Filburn
Amy E. Goodblatt

Nicole J. Ferrara
Dani S. Theobald

Representative Clients: Sovereign Bank; Cintas Corporation; Intercargo Insurance Company; Trade Insurance Services, Inc.; Heilig-Myers Furniture Co.; Danella Construction Company; Adventist Health Systems, Inc.; Hersh National Painting & Roofing Company; Home Depot U.S.A., Inc.

For full biographical listings, see the Martindale-Hubbell Law Directory

PALM BEACH, Palm Beach Co.

MINTMIRE & ASSOCIATES (AV)

265 Sunrise Avenue, Suite 204, 33480
Telephone: 561-832-5696
Fax: 561-659-5371
Email: MintmireFL@aol.com

Donald F. Mintmire
Jeffrey A. Shaffer
Bradley F. Rothenberg

OF COUNSEL

Paul Safran, Jr.

For full biographical listings, see the Martindale-Hubbell Law Directory

PAUL A. TURK, JR., P.A. (AV)

324 Royal Palm Way, Suite 303, 33480
Telephone: 561-655-5807
Fax: 561-655-3775

Paul A. Turk, Jr.

For full biographical listings, see the Martindale-Hubbell Law Directory

PALM BEACH GARDENS, Palm Beach Co.

MICHAEL C. KNECHT & ASSOCIATES, P.A. (AV)

Suite 101 11380 Prosperity Farms Road, 33410
Telephone: 561-625-4110
Fax: 561-625-4115

Michael C. Knecht

SLAWSON CUNNINGHAM WHALEN & STEWART, P.L. (AV)

Harbour Financial Center, 2401 PGA Boulevard, Suite 140, 33410
Telephone: 561-625-6260
Facsimile: 561-625-6269

Richard W. Slawson (P.A.)
Jeanmarie Whalen (P.A.)
Fred A. Cunningham (P.A.)
Todd S. Stewart (P.A.)

For full biographical listings, see the Martindale-Hubbell Law Directory

*PENSACOLA,** Escambia Co.

BOZEMAN, JENKINS & MATTHEWS, P.A. (AV)

SunTrust Tower, 220 West Garden Street, Suite 801, P.O. Box 13105, 32501
Telephone: 850-434-6223
Fax: 850-434-5242
Email: bojema@pen.net *URL:* http://www.bojema.pen.net
Fort Walton Beach Office: 151 Mary Esther Boulevard, Suite 401.
Telephone: 850-651-2151.
Fax: 850-434-5242.
Panama City Office: 475 Harrison Avenue, Suite 203A.
Telephone: 850-872-0110.
Fax: 850-434-5242.

Frank C. Bozeman, Jr.
Larry A. Matthews
Thomas R. Jenkins
Janice K. Skievaski
Frank C. Bozeman, III

Robert T. Bleach
Raymond F. Higgins, III
John B. Fricke, Jr.
Jeremiah J. Talbott
J. Andrew Talbert
Sidney M. McCrackin

For full biographical listings, see the Martindale-Hubbell Law Directory

EMMANUEL, SHEPPARD & CONDON (AV)

30 South Spring, 32501
Telephone: 850-433-6581
800-433-6581
Fax: 850-434-5856
URL: http://www.esclaw.com
Navarre, Florida Office: 9466 Navarre Parkway, Suite E.
Telephone: 850-939-0037.
Fax: 850-936-0307.

(See Next Column)

EMMANUEL, SHEPPARD & CONDON, *Pensacola—Continued*

A. G. Condon, Jr.
Erick M. Drlicka
Robert A. Emmanuel
Wm. Douglas Marsh
Gerald McKenzie
Wanda W. Radcliffe
Crystal Collins Spencer
Warren R. Todd

For full biographical listings, see the Martindale-Hubbell Law Directory

FULLER, JOHNSON & FARRELL, P.A. (AV)

Quayside Quarters, 700 South Palafox, Suite 170, P.O. Box 12219, 32581
Telephone: 850-434-8845
Fax: 850-432-6667
Tallahassee, Florida Office: 111 North Calhoun Street, P.O. Box 1739, 32302-1739.
Telephone: 850-224-4663.
Fax: 850-561-8839.

Michael W. Kehoe
Alan R. Horky

Jason W. Peterson (Resident)

Representative Clients: Aetna Life & Casualty; Amoco Oil Co.; Anesthesiologists' Professional Assurance Trust; CIGNA; Crum & Forster Insurance Cos.; Fireman's Fund; Florida Physicians Insurance Reciprocal; GEICO; Toyota Motor Corp.

For full biographical listings, see the Martindale-Hubbell Law Directory

KERRIGAN, ESTESS, RANKIN & McLEOD (AV)

400 East Government Street, 32501
Telephone: 850-444-4444
Watts No.: 1-800-444-4404
FAX: 850-444-4495
Email: lawfirm@kerrigan.com *URL:* http://www.kerrigan.com
Fort Walton Beach, Florida Office: 212 SE Eglin Parkway, Suite C.
Telephone: 850-244-1111.
Panama City, Florida Office: 836 Jenks Avenue.
Telephone: 850-871-5000.
FAX: 850-872-2148.

MEMBERS OF FIRM

Robert G. Kerrigan
George W. Estess
William Rankin
T. Michael McLeod
Randle D. Thompson
Marcus J. Michles II
Mary Ann Patti

LEGAL SUPPORT PERSONNEL

James Michael Kerrigan, Ph.D.

Reference: 1st American Bank of Pensacola.

For full biographical listings, see the Martindale-Hubbell Law Directory

YOUNG & ASSOCIATES, ATTORNEYS AT LAW, P.A. (AV)

Seville Tower, Seventh Floor, 226 South Palafox Place, 32501
Telephone: 850-432-2222
Fax: 850-432-1444
Tampa, Florida Office: 1517 Seventh Avenue, Suite C, 33605.
Telephone: 813-242-6262.
Fax: 813-342-6363.

B. Richard Young

Michael T. Bill
David A. Fugett
Peter S. Roumbos
B. B. Boles, III
Ricardo J. Diaz
James R. Barnes

For full biographical listings, see the Martindale-Hubbell Law Directory

POMPANO BEACH, Broward Co.

HARRY D. DENNIS, JR. (AV)

1401 East Atlantic Boulevard, 33060
Telephone: 954-946-0360
Fax: 954-946-9382
Email: HDDJan@worldnet.att.net

For full biographical listings, see the Martindale-Hubbell Law Directory

PORT ORANGE, Volusia Co.

CLIFF B. GOSNEY, JR. (AV)

P.O. Box 291850, 32129-1850
Telephone: 904-767-5573
Fax: 904-322-7904
Email: gosney@bellsouth.net

For full biographical listings, see the Martindale-Hubbell Law Directory

*ST. AUGUSTINE,** St. Johns Co.

MILLER, SHINE & BRYAN, P.A. (AV)

97 Orange Street, P.O. Box 3376, 32085-3376
Telephone: 904-824-0484
Email: msbpa@aol.com

(See Next Column)

Joe C. Miller, II
Judith G. Shine
Linda Logan Bryan

For full biographical listings, see the Martindale-Hubbell Law Directory

UPCHURCH, BAILEY & UPCHURCH, P.A. (AV)

780 North Ponce de Leon Boulevard, P.O. Drawer 3007, 32085-3007
Telephone: 904-829-9066
Facsimile: 904-825-4862
Email: info@ubulaw.com

Frank D. Upchurch, III
Katherine Gaertner Jones
Stephen A. Faustini

General Counsel for: Flagler College; Flagler Hospital, Inc.; Prosperity Bank; St. Johns County School Board.
Representative Clients: Aero Sport, Inc.; American Culinary Federation, Inc.; Penney Retirement Community, Inc.; St. Augustine Alligator Farm, Inc.; St. Augustine-St. Johns County Board of Realtors, Inc.

For Complete List of Firm Personnel, See General Section

For full biographical listings, see the Martindale-Hubbell Law Directory

ST. PETERSBURG, Pinellas Co.

KALEEL & KALEEL, P.A. (AV)

3819 Central Avenue, P.O. Box 15697, 33733-5697
Telephone: 727-321-0744

Wm. C. Kaleel, Sr. (1903-1976)
William C. Kaleel, Jr.
H. Shelton Philips
Robert L. Kaleel

Representative Clients: State Farm Mutual Automobile Insurance Co.; Auto Owners Insurance Co.; Allstate Insurance Co.
Reference: First Union National Bank of Florida.

For full biographical listings, see the Martindale-Hubbell Law Directory

KEANE, REESE & VESELY, P.A. (AV)

North Trust Bank Building, 100 Second Avenue, South Suite 1201, P.O. Box 57, 33701
Telephone: 727-823-5000
Fax: 727-894-1023
Palm Harbor, Florida Office: 36426 U.S. 19 North, 34684.
Telephone: 727-787-1355.
Fax: 727-789-0821.

Michael J. Keane
Michael K. Reese
Shirin Mohammadbhoy Vesely

Richard Scott Maselli
Brandon S. Vesely

LEGAL SUPPORT PERSONNEL

Kenneth P. Malcolm

For full biographical listings, see the Martindale-Hubbell Law Directory

STEIN, FORD, SCHAAF & TOWZEY, L.L.P. (AV)

501 First Avenue North, Suite 1000, 33701
Telephone: 727-894-4333
Fax: 727-894-0175

Henry A. Stein
Harvey A. Ford
Paul A. Nelson
Gary M. Schaaf
Phyllis J. Towzey
Sarah E. Williams

For full biographical listings, see the Martindale-Hubbell Law Directory

*SANFORD,** Seminole Co.

STENSTROM, McINTOSH, COLBERT, WHIGHAM & SIMMONS, P.A. (AV)

200 West First, Suite 22, P.O. Box 4848, 32772-4848
Telephone: 407-322-2171
Fax: 407-330-2379
Orlando/Winterpark Telephone: 407-834-5119
DeLand/DeBary Telephone: 407-668-1479
URL: http://www.stenstrom.com

Thomas E. Whigham (1952-1988)
Douglas Stenstrom (Retired)
William L. Colbert
Franklin C. Whigham
Clayton D. Simmons
Robert K. McIntosh
Donna L. Surratt-McIntosh
William E. Reischmann, Jr.

Catherine D. Reischmann
James J. Partlow
Dawn M. Harrison

OF COUNSEL

Kenneth W. McIntosh
S. Kirby Moncrief

Representative Clients: City of Sanford; City of Oviedo; City of Casselberry; Seminole Community College; City of Lake Mary; Sanford Housing Authority; City of DeBary; Seminole Soccer Club, Inc.; Tuskawilla Homeowners' Association; South Seminole-North Orange Wastewater Transmission Authority.

(See Next Column)

STENSTROM, MCINTOSH, COLBERT, WHIGHAM & SIMMONS P.A.—*Continued*

For full biographical listings, see the Martindale-Hubbell Law Directory

*SARASOTA,** Sarasota Co.

DICKINSON & GIBBONS, P.A. (AV)
1750 Ringling Boulevard, P.O. Box 3979, 34230
Telephone: 941-366-4680
FAX: 941-953-3136
URL: http://dglawyers.com

Gary H. Larsen
Camden T. French
Ralph L. Marchbank, Jr.
A. James Rolfes
Burwell J. Jones
Richard R. Garland
Stephen G. Brannan
Deborah J. Blue
Jeffrey D. Peairs
David S. Preston
S. Mathew Whyte

OF COUNSEL

Patrick H. Dickinson
G. Hunter Gibbons
Ward E. Dahlgren

Representative Clients: Allstate Insurance Co.; Liberty Mutual; Nationwide Insurance Co.; St. Paul Fire & Marine Insurance Co.; Cincinnati Insurance Co.; Ohio Casualty Insurance Co.; Florida Physicians Insurance Co.; Travelers Insurance Co.; Prudential Insurance Co.; State Farm Insurance Company.

For Complete List of Firm Personnel, See General Section

For full biographical listings, see the Martindale-Hubbell Law Directory

NELSON • HESSE (AV)
2070 Ringling Boulevard, P.O. Box 2524, 34230
Telephone: 941-366-7550
Fax: 941-955-3708

MEMBERS OF FIRM

Richard E. Nelson
Ronald Alexander Cyril (1938-1988)
Richard L. Smith
F. Steven Herb
Omer S. Causey
William A. Dooley
Michael S. Drews
Frederick J. Elbrecht
Gary W. Peal

ASSOCIATES

J. Neal Mobley
J. Corey Feist
Alison Hosmer

General Counsel for: Provident Bank; Dooley Mack Construction Co.
Representative Clients: Wellcraft Marine; American Marine Holdings; Vanliner Insurance; Time Warner Cable; SMH Radiology, Inc.; The Carlton Ranch, Inc.
References: Southtrust Bank; Provident Bank.

For full biographical listings, see the Martindale-Hubbell Law Directory

WILLIAMS, PARKER, HARRISON, DIETZ & GETZEN, PROFESSIONAL ASSOCIATION (AV)
200 South Orange Avenue, 34236-6749
Telephone: 941-366-4800
Telecopier: 941-366-5109
Mailing Address: P.O. Box 3258, Sarasota, Florida, 34230-3258
Email: infodesk@williamsparker.com *URL:* http://www.williamsparker.com

John V. Cannon, III
Frank Strelec
David A. Wallace
Mark A. Schwartz
M. Lewis Hall, III
Morgan R. Bentley
Elvin W. Phillips
Carol Ann Kalish
Kimberly Page Walker

General Counsel for: Sarasota County Public Hospital Board; Sarasota-Manatee Airport Authority; Taylor Woodrow Homes Ltd.; FCCI Mutual Insurance Co.
Local Counsel for: Bank of America; Northern Trust Bank of Florida; SunTrust Bank, Gulfcoast.

For Complete List of Firm Personnel, See General Section

For full biographical listings, see the Martindale-Hubbell Law Directory

*STUART,** Martin Co.

COHEN, CONWAY, COPELAND & PAIVA, P.A. (AV)
10 Central Parkway, Suite 400, 34994
Telephone: 561-221-0999
Fax: 561-221-0996
Email: C3PLAW@AOL.COM *URL:* http://www.COHENCONWAY.COM

Marc B. Cohen
James A. Conway
John K. Copeland
Chad S. Paiva

Representative Clients: First Union National Bank; First National Bank and Trust of the Treasure Coast, N.A.; SunTrust Bankcard, N.A.; Universal Bank; Riverside National Bank of Florida; Indian River National Bank; Stuart Jet Center; Lentine Marine; Ludlum Construction Co.; Eutro Group Holding, Inc.

For full biographical listings, see the Martindale-Hubbell Law Directory

MCCARTHY, SUMMERS, BOBKO, MCKEY, WOOD & SAWYER, P.A. (AV)
2081 East Ocean Boulevard, Second Floor, 34996
Telephone: 561-286-1700
Fax: 561-283-1803
URL: http://www.mcsumm.com

Terence P. McCarthy
Robert P. Summers
Noel A. Bobko
John D. McKey, Jr.
Steven J. Wood
Thomas R. Sawyer
Nicola J. Boone
Steven L. Perry

Kathryn C. Bass
Robert N. Maitland, II

Representative Clients: First National Bank and Trust Company of the Treasure Coast; Hydratech Utilities; Lost Lake at Hobe Sound; Gary Player Design Group; YMCA of Martin County; Shadow Lakes Groves, Inc.; Merrill Lynch Trust Co., (Florida); Wilmington Trust, FSB; The Huntington National Bank, N.A.; WSTU-Radio, WTCN-TV.

For full biographical listings, see the Martindale-Hubbell Law Directory

WARNER, FOX, WACKEEN, DUNGEY SEELEY, SWEET & WRIGHT, L.L.P. (AV)
1100 South Federal Highway, P.O. Drawer 6, 34995-0006
Telephone: 561-287-4444
Fax: 561-220-1489
Email: wfsds@gate.net

Thomas E. Warner
M. Lanning Fox
W. Thomas Wackeen
Richard J. Dungey
Gary L. Sweet
Tim B. Wright
Deborah Bigham Beard

Louis E. Lozeau, Jr.
William Raymond Ponsoldt, Jr.
Anthony L. Conticello
Susann Ward
Michael J. McCluskey
Shawn C. Gray

OF COUNSEL

Robert L. Seeley
Aaron A. Foosaner

Approved Attorneys for: Attorneys' Title Insurance Fund; Commonwealth Land Title Insurance Co.

For full biographical listings, see the Martindale-Hubbell Law Directory

*TALLAHASSEE,** Leon Co.

COOPER, COPPINS & MONROE, P.A. (AV)
1319 Thomaswood Drive P.O. Drawer 14447, 32317-4447
Telephone: 850-422-2420
Facsimile: 850-422-2730
Email: info@law-ccm.com

John C. Cooper
Michael F. Coppins
D. Lloyd Monroe IV
Gwendolyn P. Adkins

Floy M. Busby
David B. Switalski
Holly Ashby Dincman
Henry J. Graham
Dorothy Moseley Ridgway

Reference: Sun Trust Bank of Tallahassee.

For full biographical listings, see the Martindale-Hubbell Law Directory

FULLER, JOHNSON & FARRELL, P.A. (AV)
111 North Calhoun Street, P.O. Box 1739, 32302-1739
Telephone: 850-224-4663
Fax: 850-561-8839
Pensacola, Florida Office: Quayside Quarters, 700 South Palafox, Suite 170, P.O. Box 12219, 32581.
Telephone: 850-434-8845.
FAX: 850-432-6667.

Ben A. Andrews
Jeannette M. Andrews
Wm. Stephen Black, II
Robert C. Crabtree
Patrick J. Farrell, Jr.
S. William Fuller, Jr.
Alan R. Horky (Resident, Pensacola Office)
Fred M. Johnson
Michael W. Kehoe (Resident, Pensacola Office)
J. Craig Knox
William R. Mabile, III
P. Scott Mitchell
Steven Michael Puritz
Beverly H. Smith
Michael J. Thomas

(See Next Column)

FULLER, JOHNSON & FARRELL P.A., *Tallahassee—Continued*

Gregory K. Rettig
Jason W. Peterson
(Resident, Pensacola Office)
Scot B. Copeland

Representative Clients: Aetna Life & Casualty; CIGNA Companies; Cotton States Insurance; Crum & Forster Insurance Companies; Ford Motor Company; Gallagher Bassett Services, Inc.; MMI Companies; The St. Paul Insurance Companies, Inc.; Toyota Motor Sales, U.S.A., Inc.

For full biographical listings, see the Martindale-Hubbell Law Directory

HENRY, BUCHANAN, HUDSON, SUBER & CARTER, P.A. (AV)

117 South Gadsden Street P.O. Drawer 1049, 32302
Telephone: 850-222-2920
Telecopier: 850-224-0034
Affiliated with Henry, Buchanan, Hudson, Suber, Carter & Kaywell, L.C., 201 West Marion Avenue, Suite 207, Punta Gorda, Florida, 33950.
Telephone: 941-639-4343.
Fax: 941-639-7121.

Bryan W. Henry (1925-1986)
John D. Buchanan, Jr.
Edwin R. Hudson
Jesse F. Suber
J. Steven Carter
Laura Beth Faragasso

SPECIAL COUNSEL

James W. Kaywell

Reference: Barnett Bank of Tallahassee, Inc.

For full biographical listings, see the Martindale-Hubbell Law Directory

KITCHEN, JUDKINS, SIMPSON & HIGH (AV)

1102 North Gadsden Street, 32303
Telephone: 850-222-6040
Telecopier: 850-561-1471

E. C. Deeno Kitchen
James P. Judkins
Larry D. Simpson
Robert King High, Jr.

ASSOCIATE

Paul M. Villeneuve
Thomas J. Schulte, Jr.

OF COUNSEL

John R. Overchuck

For full biographical listings, see the Martindale-Hubbell Law Directory

McCONNAUGHHAY, DUFFY, COONROD, POPE & WEAVER, P.A. (AV)

Suite 900, 101 North Monroe Street, P.O. Drawer 229, 32302-0229
Telephone: 850-222-8121
Telecopier: 850-222-4359
Pensacola, Florida Office: 316 South Baylen Street, Suite 500.
Telephone: 850-434-7122.
Telecopier: 850-435-0924.
Panama City, Florida Office: 306 E. 19th Street.
Telephone: 850-784-2599.
Telecopier: 850-769-5461.
Jacksonville, Florida Office: 8381 Dix Ellis Trail, Suite 100.
Telephone: 904-363-1950.
Telecopier: 904-363-1510.
Sarasota, Florida Office: 1800 Second Street, Suite 954.
Telephone: 941-955-6141.
Telecopier: 941-955-6244.
Ocala, Florida Office: Building 600, Laurel Run Professional Center, 2100 S.E. 17th Street.
Telephone: 352-840-0330.
Fax: 352-401-9518.
Gainesville, Florida Office: 5024 N.W. 27th Court.
Telephone: 352-378-4422.
Fax: 352-378-7826.

James N. McConnaughhay
Brian S. Duffy
R. Stephen Coonrod
Robert D. Pope
(Resident at Jacksonville)
Patrick E. Weaver
(Resident at Panama City)
E. Louis Stern
(Resident at Sarasota)
Michael J. Rudicell
(Resident at Pensacola)
Mary Lalley Wakeman
Michael C. Crumpler
(Resident at Jacksonville)
M. Kemmerly Thomas
Elizabeth F. Campo
(Resident at Gainesville)
Betty D. Marion
(Resident at Ocala)
Holly A. Davis
(Resident at Ocala)
Robert A. Keeter
(Resident at Gainesville)

Mary Ellen Ingley
Jana E. McConnaughhay
Sarah M. Stokes
Tracey J. Hyde
(Resident at Panama City)
Jacqueline L. Blanton
(Resident at Sarasota)
Susan L. Fara
(Resident at Sarasota)

(See Next Column)

Susan N. Marks
(Resident at Pensacola)
Kyle Lee Redfearn
William Jemison Mims, Jr.
(Resident at Pensacola)
Renee M. Armbruster
(Resident at Sarasota)
Wallace W. Hardy
Kathryn L. Johnson
Jeffrey R. Richardson
Eric D. Schurger
(Resident at Pensacola)
Monett B. Kent
(Resident at Jacksonville)
Timothy R. Whitney
(Resident at Panama City)
Dale J. Stone
(Resident at Jacksonville)
Teri A. Bussey
Joe G. Durrett
W. Scott Van Ness
(Resident at Sarasota)
H. Lee Futch
Nicole D. Lindsey
(Resident at Ocala)
Mark A. Massey
(Resident at Ocala)
Sharon Neil Ruth
(Resident at Gainesville)
Gary S. Weisman
Gregory Carter Harrell
Sean S. O'Connor
(Resident at Ocala)
Iris M. DuBois
(Resident at Sarasota)

For full biographical listings, see the Martindale-Hubbell Law Directory

McFARLAIN, WILEY, CASSEDY & JONES, PROFESSIONAL ASSOCIATION (AV)

215 South Monroe Street, Suite 600, P.O. Box 2174, 32316-2174
Telephone: 850-222-2107
Telecopier: 850-222-8475
Email: firm@mcfarlain.com *URL:* http://www.mcfarlain.com

Richard C. McFarlain
William B. Wiley
Douglas P. Jones
Charles A. Stampelos
H. Darrell White, Jr.
Christopher Barkas
Harold R. Mardenborough, Jr.
Terrell C. Madigan

Robert A. McNeely
P. David Brannon

LEGAL SUPPORT PERSONNEL

Diane L. Doll (Office Manager)

For full biographical listings, see the Martindale-Hubbell Law Directory

*TAMPA,** Hillsborough Co.

MICHAEL C. ADDISON (AV)

Suite 1130, 220 East Madison Street, 33602
Telephone: 813-223-2000
Facsimile: 813-228-6000
Mailing Address: P.O. Box 2175, Tampa, Florida, 33601-2175
Email: michaeladdison@compuserve.com *URL:* http://www.lawyers.com/michaeladdison-law

For full biographical listings, see the Martindale-Hubbell Law Directory

ALLEN, DELL, FRANK & TRINKLE, P.A. (AV)

1240 Barnett Plaza, 101 East Kennedy Boulevard, P.O. Box 2111, 33601
Telephone: 813-223-5351
Telecopier: 813-229-6682

Stewart C. Eggert
Joseph G. Heyck, Jr.
Michael N. Brown
Marian P. McCulloch
Robert A. Mora
Benjamin G. Morris
A. Christopher Kasten, II
Richard A. Harrison
James S. Eggert
Donald W. Stanley, Jr.
John W. Wilcox
M. David Linton
Tabatha A. Liebert

OF COUNSEL

Ralph C. Dell

Representative Clients: Tampa International Airport; Bank of Tampa; Seminole Electric Cooperative Inc.; Tampa General Healthcare; Tampa Greyhound Track; Tampa Bay Water, A Regional Water Supply Authority.

For Complete List of Firm Personnel, See General Section

For full biographical listings, see the Martindale-Hubbell Law Directory

ALPERT, BARKER & RODEMS, P.A. (AV)

First Union Center, Suite 2000, 100 South Ashley Drive (33602), P.O. Box 3270, 33601-3270
Telephone: 813-223-4131
Fax: 813-228-9612
Email: Alpertfirm@Aol.com

Jonathan L. Alpert
Chris A. Barker
Ryan Christopher Rodems
David D. Ferrentino
William J. Cook

Scott J. Flint
Natalie Pedregal

For full biographical listings, see the Martindale-Hubbell Law Directory

Tampa—Continued

Timothy G. Anderson, P.A. (AV)

213 South Brevard Avenue, 33606
Telephone: 813-251-0072
1-800-848-3024

Timothy G. Anderson

Leslie Longshore

For full biographical listings, see the Martindale-Hubbell Law Directory

Barr, Murman, Tonelli, Herzfeld & Rubin (AV)

Suite 1750, 201 East Kennedy Boulevard, P.O. Box 172669, 33672-0669
Telephone: 813-223-3951
Fax: 813-229-2254
URL: http://www.hrfirm.com
New Port Richey, Florida Office: 7613 Little Road, 34654.
Telephone: 727-846-8646;
Fax: 727-846-8913.

James A. Murman
Michael A. Tonelli
Daniel H. Sleet
T. Gregory Slother
John W. Boult
Gregory G. Frazier
Joseph S. Silver
Clifford L. Somers

ASSOCIATES

John J. Kozak
Morris D. Purcell, Jr.
Robert J. Scanlan
Pamela A. Walton
Edward D. Friscia
James R. Wilson
Jerry A. Setchel

OF COUNSEL

Billy R. Barr

Representative Clients: School Board of Hillsborough County, Florida; Werner, Co.; The Hertz Corporation; Federal Express Corp.; CIGNA Insurance Co.; Allstate Insurance Co.; Royal Insurance Co.; Enterprise Leasing; Risk Management (Kash 'N Karry/Food Lion); Kenan Transport.

For full biographical listings, see the Martindale-Hubbell Law Directory

Ray Calafell, Jr., P.A. (AV)

105 South Armenia Avenue, 33609
Telephone: 813-871-3890
Fax: Available upon Request

Ray Calafell

For full biographical listings, see the Martindale-Hubbell Law Directory

Clark, Charlton, Martino & Borders, P.A. (AV)

3407 W. Kennedy Boulevard, 33609-2905
Telephone: 813-879-0700
Fax: 813-879-5498
URL: http://www.ccmb.net
Email: mail@ccmb.net *URL:* http://www.lawyers.com/ccm&b-law

Scott T. Borders
Scott Charlton
James W. Clark
Anthony T. Martino
Deborah A. Fleming

Reference: Southtrust Bank of Tampa.

For full biographical listings, see the Martindale-Hubbell Law Directory

The Law Firm of Cohen, Jayson & Foster, P.A. (AV)

First of America Plaza, Suite 1700, 201 East Kennedy Boulevard, P.O. Box 172538, 33672-0538
Telephone: 813-225-1655
Fax: 813-225-1921
URL: http://www.cjfslawfirm.com

Barry A. Cohen
Christopher P. Jayson
Todd Foster
Mark H. Wright

E. Patrick Buntz
Michael A. Gold

For full biographical listings, see the Martindale-Hubbell Law Directory

Cunningham, Clark & Greiwe, P.A. (AV)

100 Ashley Drive, South, Suite 100, 33602
Telephone: 813-228-0505
Telefax: 813-229-7982

Anthony W. Cunningham
Donald G. Greiwe
James D. Clark
D. Frank Winkles

For full biographical listings, see the Martindale-Hubbell Law Directory

Patrick H. Dekle, P.A. (AV)

808 Landmark Building, 412 Madison Street, 33602-4640
Telephone: 813-223-2300
Fax: 813-223-2659

(See Next Column)

Patrick H. Dekle

For full biographical listings, see the Martindale-Hubbell Law Directory

Ford & Harrison LLP (AV)

101 E. Kennedy Boulevard Suite 900, 33602
Telephone: 813-261-7800
Fax: 813-261-7899
Email: firm@fordharrison.com *URL:* http://www.fordharrison.com
Atlanta, Georgia Office: 600 Peachtree at the Circle Building, 1275 Peachtree Street, N.E. 30309.
Telephone: 404-888-3800.
Fax: 404-888-3863.
Los Angeles, California Office: 333 South Grand Avenue, Suite 3680. 90071.
Telephone: 213-680-3410.
Fax: 213-680-4161.
Memphis, Tennessee Office: 6750 Poplar Avenue, Suite 600, P.O. Box 171375. 38187-1375.
Telephone: 901-756-1550.
Telecopier: 901-756-1016.
Jacksonville, Florida Office: 121 West Forsyth Street, Suite 1000. 32203.
Telephone: 904-356-8073.
Fax: 904-358-2319.
Miami, Florida Office: 516 Ingraham Building, 25 S.E. 2nd Avenue. 33131.
Telephone: 305-379-3811.
Fax: 305-358-5933.
Washington, D.C. Office: 1920 N Street, N.W., Suite 200. 20036.
Telephone: 202-463-6633.
Fax: 202-466-5705.

MEMBERS OF FIRM

Granville M. Alley, Jr. (1929-1976)
John-Edward Alley
Joseph Z. Fleming
Robert D. Hall, Jr. (Resident)
Tony B. Griffin (Resident)
James M. Craig (Resident)
Edmund J. McKenna (Resident)

ASSOCIATES

Todd Sidney Aidman (Resident)
Youndy C. Cook (Resident)
Peter H. Harutunian (Resident)
David S. Harvey, Jr (Resident)
Tracey Karen Jaensch (Resident)
Amy Wright Littrell (Resident)
Jennifer M. Monrose (Resident)
Melanie C. Parrish (Resident)
Tammie L. Rattray (Resident)
Dawn Siler-Nixon (Resident)

Representative Clients: TCI Cablevision; K-Mart Corp.; Pasco County School Board; Pinellas County, Florida; Publix Super Markets, Inc.; Southern Bakeries, Inc.; Sysco Corp.; The Wackenhut Corp. and subsidiaries; TJX Cos. (T.J. Maxx).

For full biographical listings, see the Martindale-Hubbell Law Directory

Levine, Hirsch, Segall & Brennan, P.A. (AV)

First Union Center, 100 South Ashley Drive, Suite 1600, P.O. Box 3429, 33601-3429
Telephone: 813-229-6585
Telecopier: 813-229-7210
Email: lhsb@lhsblaw.com

Arnold D. Levine
Richard A. Hirsch
Stephen L. Segall
Edward M. Brennan

For full biographical listings, see the Martindale-Hubbell Law Directory

Maney, Damsker & Jones, P.A. (AV)

606 Madison Street, P.O. Box 172009, 33672-0009
Telephone: 813-228-7371
Fax: 813-223-4846

David A. Maney
Lee S. Damsker

Lorena L. Kiely
Patricia F. Kuhlman

For full biographical listings, see the Martindale-Hubbell Law Directory

Law Offices of Merkle & Magri, P.A. (AV)

5510 West LaSalle Street, 33607
Telephone: 813-281-9000; Clearwater, 727-441-2699
Fax: 813-281-2223

Robert W. Merkle
Joseph D. Magri
Ward A. Meythaler
David J. Plante
Gerard J. Roble

For full biographical listings, see the Martindale-Hubbell Law Directory

Morrison & Mills, P.A. (AV)

1200 West Platt Street Suite 100, 33606
Telephone: 813-258-3311
Telecopier: 813-258-3209
Email: mmills3@tampabay.rr.com

Thomas K. Morrison
Frederick J. Mills

(See Next Column)

MORRISON & MILLS P.A., *Tampa—Continued*

Kevin A. DiTanna
Bradley Abraham Tobin

Representative Clients: SouthTrust Bank of West Florida; SouthTrust Bank, National Association; NationsBank of Florida, N.A.; Mercantile Bank; Southern Commerce Bank; Regions Bank; Hillsborough County Industrial Development Authority; Medical Data Management, Inc.

For full biographical listings, see the Martindale-Hubbell Law Directory

RYWANT, ALVAREZ, JONES, RUSSO & GUYTON, PROFESSIONAL ASSOCIATION (AV)

Suite 500 Perry Paint & Glass Building, 109 North Brush Street, P.O. Box 3283, 33601
Telephone: 813-229-7007
Fax: 813-223-6544
Ocala, Florida Office: 3300 S.W. 34th Avenue, Suite 124C, 32674.
Telephone: 904-237-8810.
FAX: 904-237-2022.

Carmen Alpizar
Manuel J. Alvarez
Matthew R. Danahy
Matthew D. Emerson
Lisa A. Griffin
John A.C. Guyton, III
M.C. Collins Guyton
Gregory D. Jones
Burke G. Lopez
Andrew F. Russo
Michael S. Rywant

LEGAL SUPPORT PERSONNEL

Bradley Hugh Holt

Representative Clients: Peerless Insurance Co.; Gulf Insurance Group; Employers Casualty Co.; Landmark Insurance Co.

For full biographical listings, see the Martindale-Hubbell Law Directory

CHARLES F. SANSONE (AV)

P.O. Box 18306, 33679-8306
Telephone: 813-223-9282
Fax: 813-229-0595
Email: cfsansone@aol.com

For full biographical listings, see the Martindale-Hubbell Law Directory

SCHROPP, BUELL & ELLIGETT, PROFESSIONAL ASSOCIATION (AV)

401 East Jackson Street, Suite 2600, 33602-5226
Telephone: 813-221-2600
Fax: 813-221-1760
Email: SBELaw@aol.com

Charles P. Schropp
Mark P. Buell
Raymond T. Elligett, Jr.

Shirley Thompson Faircloth
Amy S. Farrior
Donna S. Koch

For full biographical listings, see the Martindale-Hubbell Law Directory

A LAW OFFICE OF JEFFERY L. SHIBLEY, P.A. (AV)

13902 North Dale Mabry Highway, Suite 102, 33618
Telephone: 813-264-7200
Fax: 813-960-2755
Email: tortsjd@aol.com *URL:* http://www.lawyers.com/jefferyshibley

Jeffery L. Shibley

For full biographical listings, see the Martindale-Hubbell Law Directory

*VERO BEACH,** Indian River Co.

CLEM, POLACKWICH & VOCELLE (AV)

A Partnership including Professional Associations
3333 20th Street, 32960-2469
Telephone: 561-562-8111
Fax: 561-562-2870
Email: bvocelle@cpvlaw.com *URL:* http://www.cpvlaw.com

MEMBERS OF FIRM

Chester Clem (P.A.)
Alan S. Polackwich, Sr. (P.A.)
Louis B. Vocelle, Jr., (P.A.)
Paul Richard Berg

ASSOCIATE

Janet M. Carney

OF COUNSEL

Robert Golden

References: Barnett Bank of The Treasure Coast; Northern Trust Bank of Vero Beach; Indian River National Bank; Riverside National Bank of Florida.

For full biographical listings, see the Martindale-Hubbell Law Directory

COLLINS, BROWN, CALDWELL, BARKETT & GARAVAGLIA, CHARTERED (AV)

756 Beachland Boulevard, P.O. Box 3686, 32964
Telephone: 561-231-4343
FAX: 561-234-5213
Email: cbc@verolaw.com

George G. Collins, Jr.
Calvin B. Brown
William W. Caldwell
Bruce D. Barkett
Michael J. Garavaglia
Lisa N. Thompson
Susan A. Calistri

Reference: First Union Bank of Indian River County, Vero Beach, Florida.

For full biographical listings, see the Martindale-Hubbell Law Directory

GOULD, COOKSEY, FENNELL, O'NEILL, MARINE & CARTER, PROFESSIONAL ASSOCIATION (AV)

979 Beachland Boulevard, 32963
Telephone: 561-231-1100
Fax: 561-231-2020

John R. Gould (1921-1988)
Byron T. Cooksey
Darrell Fennell
Eugene J. O'Neill
Christopher H. Marine
David M. Carter
Todd W. Fennell
Susan L. Chenault
Elsbeth T. Peshel
(Not admitted in FL)

Counsel for: Indian River National Bank; Island Hopper Boats International, Inc.; Northern Trust Bank of Florida.
Approved Attorneys for: Attorneys' Title Insurance Fund; Commonwealth Land Title Insurance Company.

For full biographical listings, see the Martindale-Hubbell Law Directory

MOSS, HENDERSON, BLANTON & LANIER, P.A. (AV)

817 Beachland Boulevard, P.O. Box 3406, 32964-3406
Telephone: 561-231-1900
Fax: 561-231-4387

George H. Moss, II
Robin A. Blanton
Clinton W. Lanier
Fred L. Kretschmer, Jr.
Lewis W. Murphy, Jr.

Casey Walker
Jennifer J. Huber

Representative Clients: Aetna Life & Casualty; Alcoa Florida, Inc.; Florida Power & Light Co.; Insurance Company of North America; Liberty Mutual Insurance Co.; Sears, Roebuck & Co.; Sugar Cane Growers Cooperative of Florida.

For Complete List of Firm Personnel, See General Section

For full biographical listings, see the Martindale-Hubbell Law Directory

SMITH & SMITH (AV)

Citrus Financial Center, Suite 301, 1717 Indian River Boulevard, 32960
Telephone: 561-567-4351
Fax: 561-567-4298

MEMBERS OF FIRM

Sherman N. Smith, Jr. (1914-1998)
Sherman N. Smith, III
Anthony T. Golden

References: Citrus Bank, N.A.; Northern Trust Bank of Vero Beach.

For full biographical listings, see the Martindale-Hubbell Law Directory

*WEST PALM BEACH,** Palm Beach Co.

ADAMS, COOGLER, WATSON & MERKEL, P.A. (AV)

Suite 1600, 1555 Palm Beach Lakes Boulevard, P.O. Box 2069, 33402
Telephone: 561-478-4500
Fax: 561-684-7346
Email: ACWMLAW@AOL.COM

Samuel H. Adams (1913-1981)
Roy R. Watson
Robert G. Merkel
James C. Barry
Reed W. Kellner
Catherine Lynn Kasten
Scott S. Warburton
Peter A. Cooke
Patricia A. Judge
Kathryn L. Tignor

Alexander D. Barker
Jodi G. Barrett
Stephanie Brown
James W. Flanagan
Paul L. Harwood
Thomas Hodas
Catherine M. Paris

OF COUNSEL

L. C. Shepard, Jr.

For full biographical listings, see the Martindale-Hubbell Law Directory

West Palm Beach—Continued

FARISH, FARISH & ROMANI (AV)

316 Banyan Boulevard, P.O. Box 4118, 33402
Telephone: 561-659-3500
1-800-401-4LAW
Fax: 561-655-3158
Email: farish@bellsouth.net

MEMBERS OF FIRM

Joseph D. Farish (1892-1977) Joseph D. Farish, Jr.
Robert V. Romani

ASSOCIATES

S. Emory Rogers Peter M. Bassaline

LEGAL SUPPORT PERSONNEL

Ken P. Beelner

References: 1st Union Bank.

For full biographical listings, see the Martindale-Hubbell Law Directory

HICKS, BRAMS & SCHER (AV)

United National Bank Tower, Suite 1050, 1645 Palm Beach Lakes Boulevard, 33401
Telephone: 561-683-2300
Fax: 561-697-3852
Email: lawdogs@gate.net *URL:* http://www.lawyers.com/hicks-brams-scher

James H. Hicks Daniel J. Brams
Brian T. Scher

William Hoffman Pincus Michael A. Motto

For full biographical listings, see the Martindale-Hubbell Law Directory

LEWIS KAPNER, P.A. (AV)

Suite 1402, One Clearlake Centre, 250 Australian Avenue South, P.O. Box 1428, 33402
Telephone: 561-655-3000
Delray/Ft. Lauderdale: 305-930-9191
Fax: 561-655-8899
Email: KAPNER1@aol.com
Boca Raton Office: 621 Northwest 53rd Street.
Telephone: 305-930-9191.

Lewis Kapner Victoria A. Calebrese
Michael C. Spain

For full biographical listings, see the Martindale-Hubbell Law Directory

THOMAS E. KINGCADE PROFESSIONAL ASSOCIATION (AV)

209 South Olive Avenue, 33401
Telephone: 561-659-7300; 800-869-9409
Fax: 561-655-1593
Email: tekingcade@aol.com *URL:* http://www.lawyers.com/kingcade

Thomas E. Kingcade

William W. Booth

For full biographical listings, see the Martindale-Hubbell Law Directory

LIGGIO, BENRUBI & WILLIAMS, P.A. (AV)

1615 Forum Place, Suite 3B, 33401
Telephone: 561-616-3333
Fax: 561-616-3266
Email: liggio@aol.com *URL:* http://www.lawyers.com/liggiolaw

Jeffrey M. Liggio Richard M. Benrubi
Jene P. Williams

LEGAL SUPPORT PERSONNEL

Yara B. Vega (Paralegal) Kathy G. Harmon (Paralegal)
Sharon Lynn (Paralegal)

For full biographical listings, see the Martindale-Hubbell Law Directory

NASON, YEAGER, GERSON, WHITE & LIOCE, P.A. (AV)

Mellon United National Bank Tower, Suite 1200, 1645 Palm Beach Lakes Boulevard, 33401
Telephone: 561-686-3307
Fax: 561-686-5442

Thomas J. Yeager
Gary N. Gerson
John White, II
Domenick R. Lioce
Alan I. Armour, II
Mark A. Pachman
Elaine Johnson James
Nathan E. Nason
Gregory L. Scott
Charles W. Edgar, III
Joseph A. Caccamo
Manuel Farach
George E. Harding
Amanda Parks Schlechter

William J. Romanos, III Bruce E. Sands

(See Next Column)

LEGAL SUPPORT PERSONNEL

Sandra R. Gronek (Principal Administrator)
L. Ann Jaeckin (Corporate Paralegal)
Kathleen S. Loviska (Real Estate Paralegal)
Lisa M. Mroczko (Litigation/Probate Paralegal)
Elsie T. Pollak (Litigation/Probate Paralegal)
Georgina J. Popham (Corporate/Securities Paralegal)
Coral R. St. Pierre (Real Estate/Corporate Paralegal)

For full biographical listings, see the Martindale-Hubbell Law Directory

KEITH H. PARK, P.A. (AV)

Suite 200, 2240 Palm Beach Lakes Boulevard, P.O. Box 3563, 33402
Telephone: 561-686-7711
Fax: 561-686-8021
Email: kparkpa@unidial.com

Keith H. Park

For full biographical listings, see the Martindale-Hubbell Law Directory

PAXTON, CROW, BRAGG, SMITH & NELSON, P.A. (AV)

Barristers Building, Suite 500, 1615 Forum Place, 33401
Telephone: 561-684-2121
Fax: 561-684-6855
Email: cus@flinet.com *URL:* http://flinet.com/~pcbsn

Ralph B. Paxton (Retired)
David F. Crow
Morgan S. Bragg (Retired)
Clark W. Smith
Michele I. Nelson
Michael B. Davis
Sandra Bosso-Pardo

Kenneth M. Curtin
Pamela Jean Hennig
Thomas Brown Miller
Fay E. Ryan

OF COUNSEL

Stephen C. McAliley Douglas N. Yeargin

For full biographical listings, see the Martindale-Hubbell Law Directory

RICCI, HUBBARD, LEOPOLD, FRANKEL & FARMER, P.A. (AV)

1645 Palm Beach Lakes Boulevard, Suite 250, P.O. Box 2946, 33402
Telephone: 561-684-6500
Fax: 561-697-2383
Email: Ricci@bellsouth.net *URL:* http://www.riccihubbard.com

Edward M. Ricci
James R. Hubbard
Theodore J. Leopold
Lois J. Frankel
Duncan J. Farmer
Scott C. Murray
Steven G. Dell
Marina F. Parrish
Andrea D. McMillan

For full biographical listings, see the Martindale-Hubbell Law Directory

ROCA & SHARPE, P.A. (AV)

707 North Flagler Drive, 33401
Telephone: 561-659-3433
Fax: 561-659-3390
Email: rocasharpe@aol.com *URL:* http://www.roca-sharpe.com

Rafael J. Roca (P.A.) Tracy R. Sharpe (P.A.)

For full biographical listings, see the Martindale-Hubbell Law Directory

ROZELLE AND CALL (AV)

470 Columbia Drive Suite E-100, 33409
Telephone: 561-689-1050
Fax: 561-689-6147

MEMBERS OF FIRM

Douglas D. Rozelle, Jr. John S. Call, Jr.

ASSOCIATE

Glenn T. Williams

Representative Clients: Wal-Mart Stores, Inc.; Motors Insurance Corp.; American Contractors Insurance Group, Inc.; The Equitable Life Assurance Society; Connecticut General Life Insurance Co.; Safeco Insurance Co.; Phar-Mor of Florida, Inc.; World Wide Insurance Group; Chrysler Insurance Co.; United Service Automobile Association; The Hartford Insurance Company.

For full biographical listings, see the Martindale-Hubbell Law Directory

SEARCY DENNEY SCAROLA BARNHART & SHIPLEY, PROFESSIONAL ASSOCIATION (AV)

2139 Palm Beach Lakes Boulevard, P.O. Drawer 3626, 33402-3626
Telephone: 561-686-6300
800-780-8607
800-220-7006 (Spanish)
Fax: 561-478-0754
Email: CDS@SEARCYLAW.COM *URL:* http://www.searcylaw.com

(See Next Column)

SEARCY DENNEY SCAROLA BARNHART & SHIPLEY PROFESSIONAL ASSOCIATION, *West Palm Beach—Continued*

Christian D. Searcy, Sr.
Earl L. Denney, Jr.
John Scarola
F. Gregory Barnhart
John A. Shipley
David K. Kelley, Jr.
Lance J. Block, Jr.
C. Calvin Warriner, III
William A. Norton
David J. Sales
Christopher K. Speed
William B. King
David J. White

Karen E. Terry
Sean C. Domnick
Harry A. Shevin
Patrick E. Quinlan
Darryl L. Lewis
Ellen F. Brandt

LEGAL SUPPORT PERSONNEL

Laurie J. Briggs (Paralegal)
Deane L. Cady (Paralegal/Investigator)
Daniel J. Calloway (Paralegal/Investigator)
Emilio Diamantis (Paralegal/Investigator)
David W. Gilmore (Paralegal/Investigator)
John C. Hopkins (Paralegal/Investigator)
Thaddeus E. Kulesa (Paralegal/Investigator)
J. Peter Love (Paralegal/Investigator)
William H. Seabold (Paralegal/Investigator)
Kathleen Simon (Paralegal)
Steve M. Smith (Paralegal/Investigator)
Kevin J. Walsh (Paralegal/Investigator)
Judson Whitehorn (Paralegal/Investigator)
Samantha M. Johansen (Paralegal/Investigator)

For full biographical listings, see the Martindale-Hubbell Law Directory

WAGNER, JOHNSON, MCAFEE & BODIK, P.A. (AV)

Commerce Pointe, Suite 450, 1818 South Australian Avenue, 33409
Telephone: 561-686-5200
Fax: 561-686-6710
Email: macwjm@icanect.net

Ward Wagner, Jr.
Robert R. Johnson
Helen Wagner McAfee
William J. McAfee
Michael G. Bodik

References: SunTrust Bank, South Florida, N.A.; Fidelity Federal Savings & Loan Association of West Palm Beach.

For full biographical listings, see the Martindale-Hubbell Law Directory

WIEDERHOLD, MOSES, BULFIN & RUBIN, P.A. (AV)

Northbridge Centre, Suite 800, 515 North Flagler Drive, P.O. Box 3918, 33402
Telephone: 561-659-2296;
Broward: 954-763-5630
Fax: 561-659-2865
Email: bobmoses@bellsouth.net

John P. Wiederhold
Robert D. Moses
John J. Bulfin
Kenneth M. Rubin

Lawrence I. Bass
Kay Seeber Hoff
Bruce R. Katzell

LEGAL SUPPORT PERSONNEL

Gina Truzzolino (Paralegal/Investigator)

Reference: Bank of America.

For full biographical listings, see the Martindale-Hubbell Law Directory

WINTER HAVEN, Polk Co.

PETERSON & MYERS, P.A. (AV)

Lake Region Plaza, 141 5th Street N.W., P.O. Drawer 7608, 33883-7608
Telephone: 941-294-3360
Lake Wales, Florida Office: 130 East Central Avenue, P.O. Box 1079.
Telephones: 941-676-7611; 683-8942.
Lakeland, Florida Office: 100 East Main Street, P.O. Box 24628.
Telephones: 941-683-6511; 676-6934.

M. David Alexander, III
Philip O. Allen
Jack P. Brandon
Kristen Marie Buzzanca
Debra Leigh Cline
J. Davis Connor
Dennis G. Corrick
Roy A. Craig, Jr.
Clinton A. Curtis
Jacob C. Dykxhoorn
Joseph A. Geary
Maria "Mia" Gerber
Jonn D. Hoppe
Dennis P. Johnson
Kevin C. Knowlton
Douglas A. Lockwood, III
Corneal B. Myers
E. Blake Paul
Robert E. Puterbaugh
Thomas B. Putnam, Jr.
Deborah A. Ruster
Stephen R. Senn
Andrea Teves Smith
Keith H. Wadsworth
Kerry M. Wilson

General Counsel for: SunTrust Bank Mid-Florida, N.A.; Lakeland Regional Medical Center, Inc.; Housing Finance Authority of Polk County.
Representative Clients: NationsBank, N.A.; First Union National Bank; Mutual Wholesale Co.; Ben Hill Griffin, Inc.; E. R. Jahna Industries, Inc.

(See Next Column)

Approved Attorneys for: Attorneys' Title Insurance Fund; Equitable Life Assurance Society of the United States.

For full biographical listings, see the Martindale-Hubbell Law Directory

WINTER PARK, Orange Co.

GRAHAM, CLARK, JONES, BUILDER, PRATT & MARKS (AV)

Third Floor, NationsBank Building, 369 North New York Avenue, P.O. Drawer 1690, 32790
Telephone: 407-647-4455
Telefax: 407-740-7063
URL: http://www.grahamclark.com

MEMBERS OF FIRM

Jesse E. Graham
Scott D. Clark
Frederick W. Jones
J. Lindsay Builder, Jr.
James R. Pratt
Howard S. Marks

Geoffrey D. Withers
Jesse E. Graham, Jr.
Samuel M. Nelson
Jessica K. Hew
Jeffrey L. Kaplan
Douglas K. Gartenlaub
William A. Davis, Jr.

Approved Attorneys for: Chicago Title Insurance Co.
Reference: NationsBank of Florida.

For full biographical listings, see the Martindale-Hubbell Law Directory

POHL & SHORT, P.A. (AV)

280 West Canton Avenue, Suite 410, P.O. Box 3208, 32790
Telephone: 407-647-7645; 407-647-POHL
Telefax: 407-647-2314
Email: ps@pohlshort.com

Dwight I. Cool
Alexander S. Douglas II
Gary A. Forster
E. Givens Goodspeed
Mark A. Grimes
Robert S. Hoofman
Roger A. Kelly
Adam O. Kirwan
David J. Kohs
Frank L. Pohl
James Everett Shepherd V
Houston E. Short
John R. Simpson, Jr.

Representative Clients: American Generator Co.; Copelco Capital, Inc.; Denim U.S.A., Inc.; Ford Motor Credit Co.; Lodestar Technology, Inc.; Lutheran Brotherhood; SunTrust, N.A.; Trax, Inc.

For full biographical listings, see the Martindale-Hubbell Law Directory

TROUTMAN, WILLIAMS, IRVIN, GREEN & HELMS, PROFESSIONAL ASSOCIATION (AV)

311 West Fairbanks Avenue, 32789-5001
Telephone: 407-647-2277
Toll Free: 1-800-432-5106
Telefax: 407-628-2986
Oviedo, Florida Office: 1757 West Broadway Street, Suite 4, 32765.
Telephone: 407-359-7848.
Fax: 407-358-7849.

Russell Troutman
Joseph H. Williams
Paul B. Irvin
Robert F. Green
Roger D. Helms
Joseph J. Polich, Jr.

Robert N. Hemphill

For full biographical listings, see the Martindale-Hubbell Law Directory

GEORGIA

*ALBANY,** Dougherty Co.

CANNON, MEYER VON BREMEN & GOSS, LLP (AV)

2417 Westgate Drive, P.O. Box 70909, 31708-0909
Telephone: 912-435-1470
Telefax: 912-888-2156
Email: cmvblaw@cmvb.com

MEMBERS OF FIRM

William E. Cannon, Jr.
Michael S. Meyer von Bremen
Stephen S. Goss

ASSOCIATES

Timothy O. Davis
Toysha M. Flowers
William H. Gregory, II

For full biographical listings, see the Martindale-Hubbell Law Directory

*ATHENS,** Clarke Co.

BLASINGAME, BURCH, GARRARD, BRYANT & ASHLEY, P.C. (AV)

440 College Avenue North, P.O. Box 832, 30603
Telephone: 706-354-4000
Telecopier: 706-353-0673
Greensboro, Georgia Office: 122 N. Main Street, P.O. Box 67, 30642.
Telephone: 706-453-7139.
Fax: 706-453-7842.

J. Ralph Beaird
Gary B. Blasingame
E. Davison Burch
Henry G. Garrard, III
Everett Clay Bryant
W. Seaborn Ashley, Jr.
M. Steven Heath
Andrew J. Hill, III
Michael A. Morris
Thomas H. Rogers, Jr.
William D. Harvard
Rikard L. Bridges
Ivan A. Gustafson
David S. Thomson
Richard W. Schmidt

Matthew N. Padgett
Christopher G. Conley
Pamela Lohr Hendrix
Amy Lou Reynolds
Sean P. Dolan
Carter A. Lawson
Matthew Allen Moseley
Molly K. O'Steen
Josh B. Wages

Representative Clients: NationsBank; Georgia Power Co.; Atlanta Gas Light Company; Pittsburgh Corning Corp.; Downtown Athens Development Authority; Fowler Products Co., Inc.; Athens Newspapers, Inc.; First National Bank of Commerce; Athens First Bank & Trust Co.; Reynolds Plantation.

For full biographical listings, see the Martindale-Hubbell Law Directory

*ATLANTA,** Fulton Co.

STEVEN D. BARNHART & ASSOCIATES, P.C. (AV)

One Georgia Center, Suite 2450, 600 West Peachtree Street, N.W., 30308-3605
Telephone: 404-874-2660
Facsimile: 404-874-2357

Steven D. Barnhart

Ken E. Jarrard
Regina T. Stamps
Michelle P. Badaruddin
Jami E. Philpott
Lara G. Cullinane

For full biographical listings, see the Martindale-Hubbell Law Directory

WILLIAM Q. BIRD AND ASSOCIATES, P.C. (AV)

14 Seventeenth Street, Suite 5, P.O. Box 7009, 30357
Telephone: 404-873-4696
Fax: 404-872-3745
Email: info@williamqbird.com *URL:* http://www.williamqbird.com

William Q. Bird

John G. Mabrey
Karin Middleton Allen

For full biographical listings, see the Martindale-Hubbell Law Directory

BONDURANT, MIXSON & ELMORE, LLP (AV)

1201 W. Peachtree Street Suite 3900, 30309
Telephone: 404-881-4100
Fax: 404-881-4111
URL: http://www.bondurant-mixson.com

MEMBERS OF FIRM

Emmet J. Bondurant II
H. Lamar Mixson
M. Jerome Elmore
Edward B. Krugman
Jeffrey O. Bramlett
John E. Floyd
Michael B. Terry
P. Richard Game
Jill A. Pryor
J. Scott McClain

Representative Clients: American Dairy Queen Corp.; Avon Products, Inc.; Bottlers of Coca-Cola, U.S.A.; Blue Circle of America; Delta Air Lines, Inc.; Fina Oil and Chemical Company; Four M Corporation; Penske Motorsports; Queen Carpets, Inc.; Ticketmaster Southeast.

For full biographical listings, see the Martindale-Hubbell Law Directory

DAVID WM. BOONE, P.C. (AV)

3166 Mathieson Drive, 30305
Telephone: 404-239-0305
Fax: 404-239-0520

David William Boone
Simone R. Siex

For full biographical listings, see the Martindale-Hubbell Law Directory

BUTLER, WOOTEN, OVERBY, FRYHOFER, DAUGHTERY & SULLIVAN (AV)

2719 Buford Highway, 30324
Telephone: 404-321-1700
WATS 1-800-242-2962
Fax: 404-321-1713
Columbus, Georgia Office: 1500 Second Avenue, P.O. Box 2766.
Telephone: 706-322-1990; National Wats: 1-800-233-4086.
Fax: 706-323-2962.

MEMBERS OF FIRM

James E. Butler, Jr.
Joel O. Wooten, Jr.
C. Frederick Overby
George W. Fryhofer III
Peter J. Daughtery
Lee Tarte Wallace
Terrance C. Sullivan

ASSOCIATES

Jason L. Crawford
Keith A. Pittman
Joshua Sacks
Teresa Thomas Abell
Cale H. Conley

Reference: Columbus Bank and Trust, Columbus, Ga.

For full biographical listings, see the Martindale-Hubbell Law Directory

CARR, TABB & POPE (AV)

1355 Peachtree Street, N.E. Suite 2000, 30309
Telephone: 404-876-7790
Fax: 404-873-4683
URL: http://www.net-sales.com/carrtabbandpope

W. Pitts Carr
Judy N. Tabb
David H. Pope
J. Reneé Kastanakis
Render Crayton Freeman
Richard M. Bayus, II
Eric Noyes Van De Water

For full biographical listings, see the Martindale-Hubbell Law Directory

CHOREY, TAYLOR & FEIL, A PROFESSIONAL CORPORATION (AV)

Suite 1700, The Lenox Building, 3399 Peachtree Road, N.E., 30326
Telephone: 404-841-3200
Facsimile: 404-841-3221
Email: ctf@ctflegal.com

John L. Taylor, Jr.
Otto F. Feil III
Celeste McCollough
Matthew L. Hess

For Complete List of Firm Personnel, See General Section

For full biographical listings, see the Martindale-Hubbell Law Directory

DAVID G. CROCKETT, P.C. (AV)

1950 Equitable Building, 100 Peachtree Street, N.W., 30303
Telephone: 404-522-4280
Telecopier: 404-589-9891
Email: CROCKLAW@BELLSOUTH.NET

David G. Crockett

Douglas L. Brooks

LEGAL SUPPORT PERSONNEL

Loraine B. Harps (Paralegal)

Approved Attorney for: Chicago Title Insurance Co.
Reference: NationsBank, N.A.

For full biographical listings, see the Martindale-Hubbell Law Directory

DENNIS, CORRY & PORTER, L.L.P. (AV)

3300 One Atlanta Plaza, 950 East Paces Ferry Road, P.O. Box 18640, 30326
Telephone: 404-816-2800
Wats: 800-735-0838
Fax: 404-816-5656
URL: http://www.dcplaw.com

MEMBERS OF FIRM

Robert E. Corry, Jr.
R. Clay Porter
James S. Strawinski
Grant B. Smith
Matthew J. Jewell
Raymond J. Kurey
Ronald Ray Coleman, Jr.
Scott W. McMickle

OF COUNSEL

Douglas Dennis

ASSOCIATES

Thomas D. Trask
Christopher D. Pixley
John D. Dixon
Stephanie F. Goff
Kerry A. Quinn
George A. Koenig
Michael Goldberg
Michael F. Coogan
Todd M. Yates
Nicole L. Wolfe
Alisa W. Terry
Stephanie Collings Patel
Michael A. Prieto

Representative Clients: Schneider National, Inc.; Roadway Express, Inc.; Caliber System, Inc.

(See Next Column)

DENNIS, CORRY & PORTER L.L.P., *Atlanta—Continued*

For full biographical listings, see the Martindale-Hubbell Law Directory

DOFFERMYRE, SHIELDS, CANFIELD, KNOWLES & DEVINE (AV)

Suite 1600, 1355 Peachtree Street, 30309
Telephone: 404-881-8900
Fax: 404-881-3007

Foy R. Devine
Robert E. Shields
Everette L. Doffermyre
Kenneth S. Canfield
Ralph I. Knowles, Jr.
Leslie J. Bryan
Georgiana Rizk
Samuel W. Wethern
David S. Hagy
Bonnie L. Keith

For full biographical listings, see the Martindale-Hubbell Law Directory

EIDSON & ASSOCIATES, P.C. (AV)

Suite 300, 600 South Central Avenue (Hapeville), 30354
Telephone: 404-763-3401
Fax: 404-763-3404

James A. Eidson

Timothy R. Brennan

Reference: Regions Bank of Atlanta.

For full biographical listings, see the Martindale-Hubbell Law Directory

FAIN, MAJOR, WILEY & BRENNAN, P.C. (AV)

100 Glenridge Point Parkway Suite 500, 30342-1440
Telephone: 404-688-6633
Telecopier: 404-420-1544

Gene A. Major
Charles A. Wiley, Jr.
Thomas E. Brennan
John K. Miles, Jr.
Darryl G. Haynes

Brian Alligood
Kim Monroe Jackson

Representative Clients: Allstate Insurance Co.; Budget Rent-A-Car; Arkansas Best Corp.; Chrysler Insurance Co.; Georgia Farm Bureau Mutual Insurance Co.; Hertz Corp.; Universal Underwriters Insurance Co.; Westfield Insurance Co.; Winn-Dixie Stores, Inc.

For Complete List of Firm Personnel, See General Section

For full biographical listings, see the Martindale-Hubbell Law Directory

FREEMAN, WRIGHT & HERMAN (AV)

3060 Peachtree Road, N.W. Suite 720, 30305-2240
Telephone: 404-262-2962
Fax: 404-237-1926
Email: bhi@bellsouth.net

MEMBERS OF FIRM

Joe C. Freeman, Jr.
Arnold Wright, Jr.
Robert L. Herman

For full biographical listings, see the Martindale-Hubbell Law Directory

GAMBRELL & STOLZ, L.L.P. (AV)

SunTrust Plaza, 303 Peachtree Street Suite 4300, 30308
Telephone: 404-577-6000
FAX: 404-221-6501
Email: lawfirm@gambrell.com *URL:* http://www.gambrell.com
Northpark Office: Suite 1230, Northpark 400 Tower, 1000 Abernathy Road, N.E., Atlanta, 30328.
Telephone: 404-577-6000.
FAX: 404-589-3400.

David H. Gambrell
Irwin W. Stolz, Jr.
Bryan M. Cavan
James R. McGuone
Nedom A. Haley
Robert G. Brazier
Tobin N. Watt
George M. Bobo
Henry B. Levi
Leo J. Fogarty
Linda A. Klein
Gary A. Barnes
Nancy E. Gordon
Michael M. Smith
Andrew H. Prussack
Robert E. DeWitt
Jennifer Grandoff Cooper

ASSOCIATES

Seaton D. Purdom
Michelle Kenyon
Allison P. Coplein
Adam L. Smith
Daniel M. Epstein
Gregory G. Schultz
Jessica A. Ryan
Joshua Tropper
(Not admitted in GA)
Steven G. Hall

For full biographical listings, see the Martindale-Hubbell Law Directory

GARLAND, SAMUEL & LOEB, P.C. (AV)

3151 Maple Drive, N.E., 30305
Telephone: 404-262-2225
Fax: 404-365-5041
Email: triallaw@atlanta.com

Edward T. M. Garland
Donald F. Samuel
Robin N. Loeb

For full biographical listings, see the Martindale-Hubbell Law Directory

GOLDNER, SOMMERS, SCRUDDER & BASS (AV)

900 Circle 75 Parkway Suite 850, 30339
Telephone: 770-612-9200
Facsimile: 770-612-9201

MEMBERS OF FIRM

Stephen L. Goldner
Susan V. Sommers
Henry E. Scrudder, Jr.
Glenn S. Bass

For Complete List of Firm Personnel, See General Section

For full biographical listings, see the Martindale-Hubbell Law Directory

GOODMAN, MCGUFFEY, AUST & LINDSEY, LLP (AV)

2100 Tower Place, 3340 Peachtree Road, N.E., 30326-1084
Telephone: 404-264-1500
Fax: 404-264-1737
Email: gmal@atlanta.com

MEMBERS OF FIRM

William S. Goodman
C. Wade McGuffey, Jr.
Judy Farrington Aust
Edward H. Lindsey, Jr.
Joe David Jackson
Kathryn A. Cater
Debra L. Dalton
Lisa A. Wade

Michael A. Dalton
Danielle F. Forte

For full biographical listings, see the Martindale-Hubbell Law Directory

GRAY & GILLILAND, P.C. (AV)

400 Perimeter Center Terrace, Suite 1050, 30346-1239
Telephone: 770-392-4800
Telecopy: 770-392-4808

John C. Gray
T. Cullen Gilliland
Charles A. Ratz
Melissa A. Garrett
T. Jeffery Lehman
Robert W. Browning

P. Steven Kratsch

OF COUNSEL

E. Reid Garrett
David S. Currie
Mark B. Bullman

For full biographical listings, see the Martindale-Hubbell Law Directory

HALL, BOOTH, SMITH & SLOVER, A PROFESSIONAL CORPORATION (AV)

230 Peachtree Street, N.W., Suite 2500, 30303-1515
Telephone: 404-954-5000
Fax: 404-954-5020
Email: mail@hbss.net

John E. Hall, Jr.
Alexander H. Booth
Rush S. Smith, Jr.
Jack G. Slover, Jr.
Timothy H. Bendin
Michael A. Pannier
Roger S. Sumrall
Robert L. Shannon, Jr.
Michael G. Frick
T. Andrew Graham
Phillip E. Friduss

Karl M. Braun
Heather C. McGrotty
Deborah L. Stevenson
Sharon Davis King
Jonathan Marigliano
Roger G. Martin
Steven D. Prelutsky
Fred L. Hubbs Jr.
Steven J. Zaloudek
Ashley D. Phillips
Rob S. Register
Noel Langston Hurley
L. Clint Crosby
Cheveda D. Grier
Rebecca T. Christian
Wendy A. Weber
(Not admitted in GA)

Reference: Wachovia Bank of Georgia.

For full biographical listings, see the Martindale-Hubbell Law Directory

HAWKINS & PARNELL, LLP (AV)

4000 SunTrust Plaza, 303 Peachtree Street, N.E., 30308-3243
Telephone: 404-614-7400
Fax: 404-614-7500
Email: relliott@hplegal.com *URL:* http://www.hawkinsparnell.com

(See Next Column)

HAWKINS & PARNELL LLP—*Continued*

MEMBERS OF FIRM

Paul M. Hawkins
J. Bruce Welch
Albert H. Parnell
A. Timothy Jones
Alan F. Herman
Michael J. Goldman
H. Lane Young, II
Frank C. Bedinger, III
William H. Major, III
T. Ryan Mock, Jr.
Jack N. Sibley
Warner S. Fox
Robert U. Wright
Michael E. Hutchins
Ollie M. Harton
Kimberly Houston
Kevin J. Bahr
Charles R. Beans
Cullen Christie Wilkerson, Jr.
Peter R. York
Kristine Berry Morain
Roger M. Goode
Dennis J. Manganiello
Blanche Rose Miller
Thomas G. Tidwell

ASSOCIATES

Andrew A. Davenport
Stephen Michael Bowers
Robert S. Thompson
Matthew F. Barr
Michael J. Crist
Alycen G. Adams

Representative Clients: The Coca-Cola Company; Ashland Oil Company; American International Group; Tenneco Oil Co.; The Goodyear Tire & Rubber Co.; Georgia-Pacific Corp.; Monsanto Corporation; Center for Claims Resolution; Celanese, Ltd.

For Complete List of Firm Personnel, See General Section

For full biographical listings, see the Martindale-Hubbell Law Directory

THE HISHON FIRM, LLC (AV)

999 Peachtree Street N.E. Suite 1900, 30309
Telephone: 404-817-7791
Fax: 404-817-2486

Robert H. Hishon

Nancy R. Daspit

For Complete List of Firm Personnel, See General Section

For full biographical listings, see the Martindale-Hubbell Law Directory

HOFFMAN & FOWLER, LLP (AV)

A Partnership of Professional Corporations
5040 Roswell Road, N.E. Suite 250, 30342
Telephone: 404-256-6464
Fax: 404-256-1422

MEMBERS OF FIRM

Clifford G. Hoffman (P.C.)
Michael C. Fowler (P.C.)

LEGAL SUPPORT PERSONNEL

Penny J. Farr (Paralegal)

For full biographical listings, see the Martindale-Hubbell Law Directory

HOLT NEY ZATCOFF & WASSERMAN, LLP (AV)

A Partnership including Professional Corporations
100 Galleria Parkway, Suite 600, 30339
Telephone: 770-956-9600
Facsimile: 770-956-1490
Email: mthomas@hnzw.com

MEMBERS OF FIRM

J. Scott Jacobson
Stephen C. Greenberg
Jay Frank Castle

ASSOCIATE

Scott E. Morris

Representative Clients: American Stair Corporation; Cummins South, Inc.; Gables Residential Trust; Highwoods Properties, Inc.; Lincoln Property Co.; Northpark Associates, L.L.L.P.; Safety-Kleen Corp.; Trammell Crow Residential Cos.; John Wieland Homes, Inc.; Childress Klein Properties.

For Complete List of Firm Personnel, See General Section

For full biographical listings, see the Martindale-Hubbell Law Directory

JOHNSON & WARD (AV)

2100 The Equitable Building, 100 Peachtree Street N.W., 30303-1962
Telephone: 404-524-5626
Facsimile: 404-524-1769
Email: postmaster@johnsonward.com

MEMBERS OF FIRM

William C. Lanham
Clark H. McGehee
John C. Dabney, Jr.
Baxter P. Jones
William D. deGolian
Bruce A. Maxwell

For Complete List of Firm Personnel, See General Section

For full biographical listings, see the Martindale-Hubbell Law Directory

JONES, DAY, REAVIS & POGUE (AV)

3500 SunTrust Plaza, 303 Peachtree Street, 30308-3242
Telephone: 404-521-3939
Telecopier: 404-581-8330
Email: counsel@jonesday.com *URL:* http://www.jonesday.com
In Brussels, Belgium: Avenue Louise 480, 7th Floor, B-1050 Brussels.
Telephone: 32-2-645-14-11.
Telecopier: 32-2-645-14-45.
In Chicago, Illinois: 77 West Wacker.
Telephone: 312-782-3939.
Telecopier: 312-782-8585.
In Cleveland, Ohio: North Point. 901 Lakeside Avenue.
Telephone: 216-586-3939.
Telecopier: 216-579-0212.
In Columbus, Ohio: 1900 Huntington Center.
Telephone: 614-469-3939.
Telecopier: 614-461-4198.
In Dallas, Texas: 2727 North Harwood Street.
Telephone: 214-220-3939.
Telecopier: 214-969-5100.
In Frankfurt, Germany: Hochhaus am Park, Grüneburgweg 102, 60323 Frankfurt am Main.
Telephone: 49-69-9726-3939.
Telecopier: 49-69-9726-3993.
In Geneva, Switzerland: 20, rue de Candolle.
Telephone: 41-22-320-2339.
Telecopier: 41-22-320-1232.
In Hong Kong: 29th Floor, Entertainment Building, 30 Queen's Road Central.
Telephone: 852-2526-6895.
Telecopier: 852-2868-5871 or 852-2868-5699.
In Irvine, California: 5 Park Plaza, Suite 1100.
Telephone: 949-851-3939.
Telecopier: 949-553-7539.
In London, England: Bucklersbury House, 3 Queen Victoria Street.
Telephone: 44-171-236-3939.
Telecopier: 44-171-236-1113.
In Los Angeles, California: 555 West Fifth Street, Suite 4600.
Telephone: 213-489-3939.
Telecopier: 213-243-2539.
In New Delhi, India (Associate Office): Pathak & Associates (an associate firm of Jones, Day, Reavis & Pogue), 1st Floor, Dr. Gopal Das Bhaven, 28 Barakhamba Road.
Telephone: 91-11-373-8793; 91-11-335-7345.
Telecopier: 91-11-335-3761.
In New York, New York: 599 Lexington Avenue.
Telephone: 212-326-3939.
Telecopier: 212-755-7306.
In Paris, France: 120, rue du Faubourg Saint-Honoré.
Telephone: 33-1-56-59-39-39.
Telecopier: 33-1-56-59-39-38
In Pittsburgh, Pennsylvania: 500 Grant Street, 31st Floor.
Telephone: 412-391-3939.
Telecopier: 412-394-7959.
In Riyadh, Saudi Arabia: The International Law Firm (In Association with Jones, Day, Reavis & Pogue), Sulaymaniyah, Prince Mishari IBN, Abdulaziz Street, P.O. Box 22166.
Telephone: (966-1) 462-8866.
Telecopier: (966-1) 462-9001.
In Shanghai, China: 2805 Kerry Centre, 1515 Nanjing Road West.
Telephone: 86-21-5298-6568.
Telecopier: 86-21-5298-6569.
In Sydney, Australia: Governor Phillip Tower, Level 38, 1 Farrer Place.
Telephone: 61-2-9210-6921.
Telecopier: 61-2-9210-6926.
In Taipei, Taiwan: 8th Floor, 2 Tun Hwa South Road, Section 2.
Telephone: (886-2) 2704-6808.
Telecopier: (886-2) 2704-6791.
In Tokyo, Japan: Toranomon MT Building, 4th Floor, 10-3, Toranomon 3-Chome, Minato-ku, Tokyo 105, Japan.
Telephone: 81-3-3433-3939.
Telecopier: 81-3-5401-2725.
In Washington, D.C.: 51 Louisiana Avenue, N.W.
Telephone: 202-879-3939.
Telecopier: 202-626-1700.

MEMBERS OF FIRM IN ATLANTA

Girard E. Boudreau, Jr.
G. Lee Garrett, Jr.
J. Lawrence Manning, Jr. (Not admitted in GA)

For Complete List of Firm Personnel, See General Section

For full biographical listings, see the Martindale-Hubbell Law Directory

KREVOLIN & HORST, LLC (AV)

Suite 2150, 100 Colony Square, 1175 Peachtree Street, N.E., 30361
Telephone: 404-888-9700
Fax: 404-888-9577

Douglas P. Krevolin
Jeffrey D. Horst

Michael G. Regas II
Michael D. Flint

For full biographical listings, see the Martindale-Hubbell Law Directory

Atlanta—Continued

LIPSHUTZ, GREENBLATT & KING (AV)

2300 Harris Tower-Peachtree Center, 233 Peachtree Street, N.E., 30303
Telephone: 404-688-2300
Fax: 404-588-0648
Email: rmllgk@aol.com

MEMBERS OF FIRM

Robert J. Lipshutz
Randall M. Lipshutz
Edward L. Greenblatt
James V. Zito

OF COUNSEL

William R. King
Tito Mazzetta

ASSOCIATE

Paula B. Smith
Mindy C. Waitsman

For full biographical listings, see the Martindale-Hubbell Law Directory

LONG ALDRIDGE & NORMAN LLP (AV)

A Limited Liability Partnership including Professional Corporations
Suite 5300, 303 Peachtree Street, 30308
Telephone: 404-527-4000
Telecopier: 404-527-4198
Email: atlanta@lanlaw.com *URL:* http://www.lanlaw.com
Washington, D.C. Office: Suite 600, 701 Pennsylvania Avenue, N.W., 20004.
Telephone: 202-624-1200.
FAX: 202-624-1298.

MEMBERS OF FIRM

David L. Balser
Phillip A. Bradley
Bruce P. Brown
Deborah S. Ebel
J. James Johnson
Barbara A. McIntyre
Carl W. Mullis, III
James J. Thomas II
John L. Watkins
Terry R. Weiss

ASSOCIATES

Barry J. Armstrong
R. Daniel Beale
Karen L. Bernstein
Gregory S. Brow
Jennifer Froneberger
Sheryl McCalla
Russell J. Rogers
Lawrence A. Slovensky
Steven Paul Smith

OF COUNSEL

J. Michell Philpott

For Complete List of Firm Personnel, See General Section

For full biographical listings, see the Martindale-Hubbell Law Directory

MACEY, WILENSKY, COHEN, WITTNER & KESSLER, LLP (AV)

285 Peachtree Center Avenue, Suite 600, 30303-1229
Telephone: 404-584-1200
Telecopier: 404-681-4355
Email: Lawyers@MaceyWilensky.com

MEMBERS OF FIRM

Morris W. Macey
Frank B. Wilensky
H. William Cohen
Richard P. Kessler, Jr.
Neil C. Gordon
Susan L. Howick
M. Todd Westfall
James R. Sacca
David B. Kurzweil
Robert A. Winter
Richard C. Litwin

ASSOCIATES

Pamela Gronauer Hill
Rachel Anderson Snider
Michael C. Kaplan
Michael R. Wing

For Complete List of Firm Personnel, See General Section

For full biographical listings, see the Martindale-Hubbell Law Directory

MARX & MARX (AV(T))

400 Perimeter Center Terrace, N.E. Suite 900, 30346
Telephone: 404-261-9559
Email: lawmarx@aol.com
New York, New York Office: 575 Madison Avenue, 10022.
Telephone: 212-689-8516.

MEMBERS OF FIRM

Robert N. Marx
Jean Simonoff Marx (Resident)

For full biographical listings, see the Martindale-Hubbell Law Directory

MATTHEWS & STEEL (AV)

462 East Paces Ferry Road, 30305
Telephone: 404-264-1292
800-776-0098
Fax: 404-264-0161
Email: postmaster@matthewssteellaw.com

(See Next Column)

MEMBERS OF FIRM

James B. Matthews, III
John B. Briggs
John D. Steel
H. Craig Stafford

For full biographical listings, see the Martindale-Hubbell Law Directory

McCULLOUGH SHERRILL, LLP (AV)

1409 Peachtree Street, N.E., 30309
Telephone: 404-885-1500
Telecopier: 404-892-1801
Email: info@mslegal.com *URL:* http://www.mslegal.com

MEMBERS OF FIRM

John A. Sherrill
C. Walker Ingraham
Michael D. Crisp
George L. Murphy, Jr.
Kathryn M. Zickert

ASSOCIATES

Jana L. Evans
Steven M. Staes

For Complete List of Firm Personnel, See General Section

For full biographical listings, see the Martindale-Hubbell Law Directory

MEADOWS, ICHTER & TRIGG, P.C. A PROFESSIONAL CORPORATION (AV)

Eight Piedmont Center, Suite 300, 3525 Piedmont Road, N.E., 30305
Telephone: 404-261-6020
Facsimile: 404-261-3656
Email: firm@mitlaw.com *URL:* http://www.mitlaw.com

James Dartlin (Dart) Meadows
Cary Ichter
Mark G. Trigg
Lauren Slepin Antonino
Betsy Vance Peterzell
Karen R. Cashion

OF COUNSEL

Michael J. Bowers

Steven M. Kushner
David A. Hooker
T. Joshua R. Archer
Matthew B. Ames
Celia P. Quillian
Lorna McGilvray Norton
Margie M. Eget
Christopher S. Anulewicz
Merrick D. Bernstein

Representative Clients: Adventist Health System Sunbelt; Baskin-Robbins; Black & Decker; BMW; Delta Air Lines; Dunkin Donuts; Prison Health Services; SCMI.
Reference: SunTrust Bank.

For full biographical listings, see the Martindale-Hubbell Law Directory

MILLER & MARKLE, L.L.P. (AV)

23 Lenox Pointe, N.E., 30324
Telephone: 404-262-1955
Fax: 404-848-9181
Email: edm@bellsouth.net

Eric D. Miller
D. Todd Markle

Representative Clients: CNA Insurance Companies; Dobbs RAM Co.; Ohio Casualty Co.; Auto-Owners Insurance Co.; Bio-Tek Industries, Inc.

For full biographical listings, see the Martindale-Hubbell Law Directory

MILLS, MORAITAKIS, KUSHEL & PEARSON (AV)

Suite 425 3445 Peachtree Road, Northeast, 30326-1276
Telephone: 404-261-0016
Facsimile: 404-261-0024

Roger Mills
Nicholas C. Moraitakis
Glenn E. Kushel
Albert M. Pearson, III

ASSOCIATE

Martha D. Turner

For full biographical listings, see the Martindale-Hubbell Law Directory

NALL, MILLER, OWENS, HOCUTT & HOWARD, LLP (AV)

Suite 200 Peachtree & Broad Building, 66 Luckie Street, 30303
Telephone: 404-522-2200
Fax: 404-522-2208

MEMBERS OF FIRM

James S. Owens, Jr.
Robert B. Hocutt
James R. Howard
George Robert Neuhauser
Robert L. Goldstucker
Kenneth P. McDuffie
Michael D. Hostetter

COUNSEL

Samuel A. Miller

ASSOCIATES

Charles Richard Carson
Paul Jay Pontrelli
Mary Anne Palma

(See Next Column)

NALL, MILLER, OWENS, HOCUTT & HOWARD LLP—*Continued*

LEGAL SUPPORT PERSONNEL

W. Gary Bush (Registered Nurse, Legal Assistant)
Michelle Henderson McGhee (Paralegal)
Natalie D. Summers (Paralegal)
Janice F. Clark (Paralegal)

Approved Attorneys for: Lawyers Title Insurance Corp.; Commonwealth Land Title Insurance Co.

For full biographical listings, see the Martindale-Hubbell Law Directory

PIERCE & YOUNG (AV)

Building 1700, 2255 Cumberland Parkway Northwest, 30339-4575
Telephone: 770-435-0500
Telecopier: 770-435-0362

MEMBERS OF FIRM

J. Wayne Pierce
Richard M. Young
Christy A. Dunkelberger

For full biographical listings, see the Martindale-Hubbell Law Directory

POPE, MCGLAMRY, KILPATRICK & MORRISON, LLP (AV)

A Partnership including Professional Corporations
The Pinnacle, 3455 Peachtree Road, N.E., 30326-3243
Telephone: 404-523-7706
Fax: 404-524-1648
Phenix City, Alabama: 334-298-7354
Mailing Address: P.O. Box 191625, Atlanta, GA, 31119-1625
Email: pmkm@pmkm.com
Columbus, Georgia Office: 318 11th Street, 2nd Floor, P.O. Box 2128, 31902-2128.
Telephone: 706-324-0050.
Fax: 706-327-1536.

MEMBERS OF FIRM

C. Neal Pope (P.C.)
Max R. McGlamry (P.C.) (Resident, Columbus, Georgia Office)
Paul V. Kilpatrick, Jr. (Resident, Columbus, Georgia Office)
R. Timothy Morrison
Michael L. McGlamry
Earle F. Lasseter
William Usher Norwood, III
Jay F. Hirsch
Wade H. Tomlinson, III
Teresa Pike Tomlinson

RESIDENT ASSOCIATE

C. Elizabeth Pope

Reference: Columbus Bank & Trust Co.

For full biographical listings, see the Martindale-Hubbell Law Directory

REYNOLDS & MCARTHUR (AV)

A Partnership including a Professional Corporation
Overlook II, Suite 270, 2839 Paces Ferry Rd., N.W., 30339
Telephone: 770-438-8997; 770-438-9062
Fax: 770-438-8536
Macon, Georgia Office: 850 Walnut Street, 31201.
Telephone: 912-741-6000.
Fax: 912-742-0750. Email: firm@rmtriallaw.com

MEMBERS OF FIRM

W. Carl Reynolds (P.C.)
Katherine L. McArthur
Charles M. Cork, III
O. Wendell Horne, III
Bradley J. Survant

For full biographical listings, see the Martindale-Hubbell Law Directory

SMITH, HOWARD & AJAX, LLP (AV)

300 Atlanta Financial Center South, 3333 Peachtree Road, N.E., 30326
Telephone: 404-239-1900
Fax: 404-239-1930

MEMBERS OF FIRM

Fred W. Ajax, Jr.
Donald R. Andersen
Bruce H. Beerman
James T. Brieske
Susan Teale Couvillon
Harvey S. Gray
John A. Howard
Matthew G. Moffett
Michael J. Rust
Marion Smith, II
Michael D. St. Amand
David K. Whatley

ASSOCIATES

Mark D. Gropp
Joseph P. Hewes
Matthew L. Hilt
Meredith H. Ragains
LaXavier Patrice Reddick-Hood

OF COUNSEL

T. Michael Hurley, Jr.
Larry S. McReynolds

For full biographical listings, see the Martindale-Hubbell Law Directory

THOMAS, KENNEDY, SAMPSON & PATTERSON (AV)

3355 Main Street, 30337
Telephone: 404-688-4503
Telecopier: 404-681-2950; Litigation Dept.
Telecopier: 404-684-9515
URL: http://www.tksp.com

MEMBERS OF FIRM

R. E. Thomas, Jr. (1911-1996)
John Loren Kennedy (1942-1994)
Thomas G. Sampson
P. Andrew Patterson
Jeffrey E. Tompkins

ASSOCIATES

Thomas G. Sampson, II
Ceasar C. Mitchell, II.
Erika Nicole Jackson

LEGAL SUPPORT PERSONNEL

Gwendolyn C.H. Dixon
Elbetha (Beth) Martin (Paralegal)
Nancy Allen-Haskell
Yvonne Torrence
Shyril E. Beck
Constance Harris (Paralegal)
Lisa Russell Johnson

For full biographical listings, see the Martindale-Hubbell Law Directory

WEBB, CARLOCK, COPELAND, SEMLER & STAIR, LLP (AV)

A Partnership including Professional Corporations
2600 Marquis Two Tower, 285 Peachtree Center Avenue, P.O. Box 56887, 30343-0887
Telephone: 404-522-8220
Fax: 404-523-2345; 404-222-9482

MEMBERS OF FIRM

Dennis J. Webb (P.C.)
Thomas S. Carlock (P.C.)
Wade K. Copeland (P.C.)
Robert C. Semler (P.C.)
Kent T. Stair (P.C.)
Douglas W. Smith
David F. Root
William E. Zschunke
Wayne D. McGrew, III
Douglas A. Wilde
E. Alan Miller
Frederick M. Valz, III
Johannes S. Kingma
Dennis G. Lovell, Jr.
Brian R. Neary
Marvin D. Dikeman
Adam L. Appel
R. Michael Ethridge
Daniel J. Huff
Scott D. Huray
Gregory H. Wheeler
Christopher A. Whitlock

ASSOCIATES

Mary Katherine Greene
Leslie B. Zacks
James R. Doyle, II
Kimberly K. Nagy
Melissa C. Duffey
Charles E. Rogers
Chad D. Graddy
Lisa Shaw Estes
Jessica D. McKinney
Jonathon A. Fligg
Lynn B. Olmert
Jerry B. McNally
Jerry W. Cain, Jr.
Austin E. Carter
Brian J. Amero
John C. Patton
James S. V. Weston
Erika K. Kohler
Katherine K. Bone
Amy H. Ferguson
James A. Collura, Jr.
Kimberly P. Murphy
Ashley E. Sexton

For full biographical listings, see the Martindale-Hubbell Law Directory

WEISZ & ASSOCIATES (AV)

Suite 900 Live Oak Center, 3475 Lenox Road, N.E., 30326-1232
Telephone: 404-233-7888
Facsimile: 404-261-1925
Email: prw1@bellsouth.net

Peter R. Weisz

ASSOCIATE

Cathy R. Nash

Representative Clients: L.M. Scofield Co.; S. Champion Constr. Co.; Deerfield Construction Co.; Cee Klein Accessories, LTD.
Reference: First Union National Bank.

For full biographical listings, see the Martindale-Hubbell Law Directory

WOOD & GRANT (AV)

The Equitable Building Suite 2140, 100 Peachtree Street, 30303
Telephone: 404-522-1713
Fax: 404-522-1716

MEMBERS OF FIRM

L. Lin Wood
Wayne Grant

ASSOCIATE

Kimberly W. Rabren

For full biographical listings, see the Martindale-Hubbell Law Directory

*AUGUSTA,** Richmond Co.

RICHARD E. ALLEN (AV)

440 Greene Street, 30901
Telephone: 706-724-4466
Fax: 706-722-1677
Email: RALLENLAW@AOL.COM

For full biographical listings, see the Martindale-Hubbell Law Directory

BURNSIDE, WALL, DANIEL, ELLISON & REVELL (AV)

A Partnership including Professional Corporations
454 Greene Street, P.O. Box 2125, 30903
Telephone: 706-722-0768
Fax: 706-722-5984

MEMBERS OF FIRM

Robert C. Daniel, Jr. (1943-1993)
Thomas R. Burnside, Jr. (P.C.)
James B. Wall (P.C.)
James W. Ellison
Harry D. Revell
Thomas R. Burnside, III

Representative Clients: Augusta-Richmond County Commission; National Science Center Foundation, Inc.; CSRA Regional Development Center; City of Harlem, Georgia; Liquid Carbonic Corp.; Southeastern Equipment Co.; SECO Aviation, Inc.; SECO Parts & Equipment, Inc.

For full biographical listings, see the Martindale-Hubbell Law Directory

DYE, TUCKER, EVERITT, LONG & BREWTON, A PROFESSIONAL ASSOCIATION (AV)

453 Greene Street, P.O. Box 2426, 30903-2426
Telephone: 706-722-0771
Fax: 706-722-7028

A. Rowland Dye
Thomas W. Tucker
A. Zachry Everitt
John B. Long
Benjamin H. Brewton
Troy A. Lanier

OF COUNSEL

A. Montague Miller

Jon E. Ingram, Jr.

Representative Clients: State Farm Insurance Cos.; Travelers-Aetna Insurance Cos.; Georgia Power Co.; Wachovia National Bank (Augusta Division); Chubb Group; MAG Mutual Insurance Company; Augusta Board of Realtors; Canal Insurance Company; St. Paul Fire and Marine Insurance Company.

For full biographical listings, see the Martindale-Hubbell Law Directory

HULL, TOWILL, NORMAN, BARRETT & SALLEY, A PROFESSIONAL CORPORATION (AV)

801 Broad Street, Suite 700, 30901
Telephone: 706-722-4481
Fax: 706-722-9779
Email: hullfirm@groupz.net *URL:* http://www.groupz.net/~advocate
Aiken, South Carolina Office: 111 Park Avenue, 29801.
Telephone: 803-648-4213.
Fax: 803-648-2601.

James M. Hull (1885-1975)
George B. Barrett (1894-1942)
Julian J. Willingham (1887-1963)
John Bell Towill (1907-1991)
Robert C. Norman (Retired, 1991)
W. Hale Barrett
Lawton Jordan, Jr.
Patrick J. Rice
Douglas D. Batchelor, Jr.
David E. Hudson
William H. Tucker (Not admitted in GA)
William F. Hammond
Mark S. Burgreen
George R. Hall
James B. Ellington
F. Michael Taylor
William J. Keogh, III
Edward J. Tarver
J. Noel Schweers, III
Susan D. Barrett
Ralph Emerson Hanna, III

James M. Holly (Not admitted in GA)
Timothy E. Moses
N. Shannon Gentry Lanier
Tara R. Simkins
Charles H. Weigle
Natalie A. Dopson
David C. Smith

OF COUNSEL

Julian B. Salley, Jr. (Not admitted in GA)

Counsel for: Morris Communications Corporation; Merry Land & Investment Company, Inc.; Sun Trust Bank Augusta, N.A.; Georgia Power Co.; St. Joseph Hospital, Augusta, Georgia, Inc.; Norfolk Southern Corp.; Housing Authority of the City of Augusta; Georgia Press Association; Columbia County, Georgia; Nationwide Insurance Co.

For full biographical listings, see the Martindale-Hubbell Law Directory

WILEY S. OBENSHAIN, III, P.C. (AV)

511 Court House Lane, 30904
Telephone: 706-722-1789
Fax: 706-722-3934

Wiley S. Obenshain, III

For full biographical listings, see the Martindale-Hubbell Law Directory

SURRETT & COLEMAN, P.A. (AV)

901 Suntrust Bank Building, P.O. Box 1497, 30903
Telephone: 706-722-3301
Telecopier: 706-722-3318
Email: ecoleman@groupz.net

Carl J. Surrett
Edward J. Coleman, III

Representative Clients: Sears, Roebuck & Co.; American Home Assurance Co.; Great Southwest Fire Insurance Co.; Duke Buick, Inc.; American Southern Insurance Co.; Scottsdale Insurance Co.; Providence Washington Insurance Co.; Nautilus Insurance Co.

For full biographical listings, see the Martindale-Hubbell Law Directory

WARLICK, TRITT & STEBBINS, L.L.P. (AV)

15th Floor, First Union Bank Building, 699 Broad Street, 30901-1454
Telephone: 706-722-7543
Fax: 706-722-1822
Email: wts@wts-lawfirm.com
Columbia County Office: 119 Davis Road, Martinez, Georgia 30907.
Telephone: 706-860-7595.
Fax: 706-860-7597.

MEMBERS OF FIRM

William Byrd Warlick
Roy D. Tritt (Resident, Martinez Office)
Charles C. Stebbins, III
E. L. Clark Speese
C. Gregory Bryan

OF COUNSEL

Richard E. Miley

For full biographical listings, see the Martindale-Hubbell Law Directory

*BRUNSWICK,** Glynn Co.

AUSTIN E. CATTS (AV)

1529 1/2 Reynolds Street, 31520
Telephone: 912-261-8448
Fax: 912-261-7919
Email: aecatts@compuserve.com *URL:* http://www.lawyers.com/austincattslaw

For full biographical listings, see the Martindale-Hubbell Law Directory

FENDIG, MCLEMORE, TAYLOR, WHITWORTH & DURHAM, P.C. (AV)

Suite 200 Suntrust Bank Building, P.O. Box 1996, 31521
Telephone: 912-264-4126
Telecopier: 912-264-0591

Albert Fendig, Jr.
Gilbert C. McLemore, Jr.
Philip R. Taylor
David T. Whitworth
James B. Durham
Donna L. Crossland
Beth M. Duncan

For full biographical listings, see the Martindale-Hubbell Law Directory

GILBERT, HARRELL, GILBERT, SUMERFORD & MARTIN, P.C. (AV)

Suite 200 NationsBank Plaza, 31521
Telephone: 912-265-6700
Fax: 912-264-3917
Email: gilbharr@gate.net

Wallace E. Harrell
James B. Gilbert, Jr.
Rees M. Sumerford
M. Fleming Martin, III
Jameson L. Gregg
Wallace E. Harrell, III
Charles G. Spalding
Lisa Godbey Wood
Mark D. Johnson
J. Benedict Hartman
Carlton A. DeVooght
Kathryn Hackney Smith

OF COUNSEL

James B. Gilbert
Joseph A. Whittle
H. Hall Ware, III

Attorneys for: Sea Island Co.; Georgia-Pacific Corp.; Atlanta Gas Light Co.; Sea Harvest Packing Co.; Zurich General Accident & Liability Insurance Co.; Lumbermens Mutual Casualty Co.
Counsel for: Hercules Inc.

For full biographical listings, see the Martindale-Hubbell Law Directory

WHELCHEL, BROWN, READDICK & BUMGARTNER (AV)

5 Glynn Avenue, P.O. Box 220, 31521-0220
Telephone: 912-264-8544
Telecopier: 912-264-9667

(See Next Column)

WHELCHEL, BROWN, READDICK & BUMGARTNER—*Continued*

MEMBERS OF FIRM

J. Thomas Whelchel
Richard A. Brown, Jr.
Terry L. Readdick
John E. Bumgartner
B. Kaye Katz

ASSOCIATES

G. Todd Carter
Richard K. Strickland
Bradley J. Watkins

Representative Clients: Georgia Power Co.; Sears, Roebuck & Co.; Allstate Insurance Co.; Commercial Union Insurance Co.; Georgia Farm Bureau Mutual Insurance Co.; Government Employees Insurance Co.; Nationwide Insurance Co.; State Farm Insurance Cos.; Wausau Insurance Cos.

For full biographical listings, see the Martindale-Hubbell Law Directory

*CARTERSVILLE,** Bartow Co.

DAVID G. ARCHER, P.C. (AV)

336 South Tennessee Street, P.O. Box 1024, 30120
Telephone: 770-386-1116
Fax: 770-382-7484
Email: dgapc@innerx.net

David G. Archer

E. Keith Lovell
M. Faye McCord

For full biographical listings, see the Martindale-Hubbell Law Directory

*CEDARTOWN,** Polk Co.

MUNDY & GAMMAGE, P.C. (AV)

216 Main Street, P.O. Box 930, 30125-0930
Telephone: 770-748-3870
Fax: 770-748-2489
Rome, Georgia Office: The Carnegie Building, 607 Broad Street.
Telephone: 706-290-5180.

Emil Lamar Gammage, Jr.
William D. Sparks
Miles L. Gammage
John S. Husser
B. Jean Crane
G. Brian McWhorter

For full biographical listings, see the Martindale-Hubbell Law Directory

*COLUMBUS,** Muscogee Co.

BUTLER, WOOTEN, OVERBY, FRYHOFER, DAUGHTERY & SULLIVAN (AV)

1500 Second Avenue, P.O. Box 2766, 31902
Telephone: 706-322-1990;
National Wats: 1-800-233-4086
Fax: 706-323-2962
Atlanta, Georgia Office: 2719 Buford Highway, 30324.
Telephone: 404-321-1700.
Fax: 404-321-1713. Wats Line: 1-800-242-2962.

MEMBERS OF FIRM

James E. Butler, Jr.
Joel O. Wooten, Jr.
C. Frederick Overby
George W. Fryhofer III
Peter J. Daughtery
Lee Tarte Wallace
Terrance C. Sullivan

ASSOCIATES

Jason L. Crawford
Keith A. Pittman
Joshua Sacks
Teresa Thomas Abell
Cale H. Conley

Reference: Columbus Bank and Trust, Columbus, Ga.

For full biographical listings, see the Martindale-Hubbell Law Directory

POPE, MCGLAMRY, KILPATRICK & MORRISON, LLP (AV)

A Partnership including Professional Corporations
318 11th Street, 2nd Floor, P.O. Box 2128, 31902-2128
Telephone: 706-324-0050
Phenix City, Alabama: 334-298-7354
Fax: 706-327-1536
Email: pmkm@pmkm.com
Atlanta, Georgia Office: The Pinnacle, 3455 Peachtree Road, N.E. (30326-3243), P.O. Box 191625 (31119-1625).
Telephone: 404-523-7706.
Fax: 404-524-1648.

MEMBERS OF FIRM

C. Neal Pope (P.C.)
Max R. McGlamry (P.C.) (Resident)
Paul V. Kilpatrick, Jr. (Resident)
R. Timothy Morrison
Michael L. McGlamry
Earle F. Lasseter
William Usher Norwood, III (Resident, Atlanta Office)
Jay F. Hirsch
Wade H. Tomlinson, III
Teresa Pike Tomlinson

(See Next Column)

RESIDENT ASSOCIATE

Matthew N. Pope

Reference: Columbus Bank & Trust Co.

For full biographical listings, see the Martindale-Hubbell Law Directory

TAYLOR, HARP & CALLIER (AV)

Suite 900 The Corporate Center, P.O. Box 2645, 31902-2645
Telephone: 706-323-7711
National WATS: 1-800-422-3352
Fax: 706-323-7544
Email: TandH@aol.com *URL:* http://www.lawyers.com/taylorharp&callier

MEMBERS OF FIRM

J. Sherrod Taylor
J. Anderson Harp
Jefferson C. Callier

LEGAL SUPPORT PERSONNEL

Ann W. Watson (Office Manager)
Ethel M. Britton (Legal Assistant)
Charlotte McLendon (Legal Assistant)
Tracy A. Lowry (Secretary)

For full biographical listings, see the Martindale-Hubbell Law Directory

*CORDELE,** Crisp Co.

GREGORY, CHRISTY & MANIKLAL (AV)

708 East Sixteenth Avenue, P.O. Drawer 5230, 31015
Telephone: 912-273-7150
Fax: 912-273-7578
Email: mail@gcmfirm.com *URL:* http://www.gcmfirm.com

MEMBERS OF FIRM

Hardy Gregory, Jr.
Gary C. Christy
Preyesh K. Maniklal

For full biographical listings, see the Martindale-Hubbell Law Directory

CORNELIA, Habersham Co.

CATHEY & STRAIN (AV)

6 Irvin Street, P.O. Box 689, 30531
Telephone: 706-778-2601
Fax: 706-776-2899

MEMBERS OF FIRM

Dennis T. Cathey
Edward E. Strain, III
J. Edward Staples
David A. Sleppy

For full biographical listings, see the Martindale-Hubbell Law Directory

*DALTON,** Whitfield Co.

MITCHELL & MITCHELL, P.C. (AV)

101 North Thornton Avenue, 30722
Telephone: 706-278-2040
Fax: 706-278-3040
Email: mandm@ocsonline.com

D. Wright Mitchell (1895-1970)
Douglas W. Mitchell (1921-1984)
Erwin Mitchell
Neil Wester
Terry L. Miller
William J. Kimsey
G. Gargandi Vaughn

Counsel for: The City of Dalton, Georgia; First Bank of Dalton, Inc.
Local Counsel for: NationsBank of Dalton, Georgia.
Reference: Nations Bank of Dalton, Georgia; First Bank of Dalton, Inc.

For full biographical listings, see the Martindale-Hubbell Law Directory

*DECATUR,** De Kalb Co.

SIMMONS, WARREN, SZCZECKO & MCFEE, PROFESSIONAL ASSOCIATION (AV)

315 West Ponce de Leon Avenue, Suite 850, 30030
Telephone: 404-378-1711
Fax: 404-377-6101

Joseph Szczecko
William C. McFee, Jr.

Representative Clients: Julian LeCraw & Company (Real Estate); Intown Suites, Inc.; Preferred Lodging Systems, Inc.; Royal Oldsmobile,; Cotter & Co.; Atlanta Neurosurgical Associates, P.A.; Troncalli Motors, Inc.

For full biographical listings, see the Martindale-Hubbell Law Directory

*EASTMAN,** Dodge Co.

SMITH & HARRINGTON (AV)

505 Anson Avenue, P.O. Drawer 130, 31023
Telephone: 912-374-3488
Fax: 912-374-6317
Email: paliden@accucomm.net *URL:* http://www.lawyers.com/smith&harrington

(See Next Column)

SMITH & HARRINGTON, *Eastman—Continued*

MEMBERS OF FIRM

Will Ed Smith (1906-1990) Wilton D. Harrington
John P. Harrington

For full biographical listings, see the Martindale-Hubbell Law Directory

GAINESVILLE, Hall Co.*

DAVID A. POWELL (AV)

604 Green Street, N.E., Suite 3, 30501
Telephone: 770-287-1300
Fax: 770-287-0033
Email: dapowell@earthlink.net

For full biographical listings, see the Martindale-Hubbell Law Directory

GRIFFIN, Spalding Co.*

ROBERT H. SMALLEY, JR., P.C. (AV)

115 North Sixth Street, P.O. Box 907, 30224
Telephone: 770-228-2125
Telecopier: 770-228-5018

Robert H. Smalley, Jr. Thomas E. Baynham, III

Representative Clients: Premier Bank (Local Counsel); Griffin Spalding County Development Authority.

For full biographical listings, see the Martindale-Hubbell Law Directory

HAHIRA, Harris Co.

ODOM & DES ROCHES, LLP (AV Ⓣ)

A Partnership including Professional Corporations
217 West Main Street, P.O. Box 523, 31632
Telephone: 912-794-3412
Fax: 912-794-3544
Email: jodom@surfsouth.com
New Orleans, Louisiana Office: 35th Floor, Bank One Center, 201 Saint Charles Avenue, 70170-3500.
Telephone: 504-522-0077.
Fax: 504-522-0078.

John Gregory Odom, PLC

OF COUNSEL

Randall S. Acree (Resident)

For full biographical listings, see the Martindale-Hubbell Law Directory

HARTWELL, Hart Co.*

THE GORDON LAW FIRM (AV)

Gordon Building, P.O. Box 870, 30643
Telephone: 706-376-5418
Fax: 706-376-5416
Email: wgordon@hartcom.net

Walter James Gordon

Kimberly A. Wilkerson

References: NationsBank of Georgia, N.A.; The Bank of Hartwell; Athens First Bank & Trust Company.

For full biographical listings, see the Martindale-Hubbell Law Directory

JESUP, Wayne Co.*

ROBERT B. SMITH (AV)

356 East Cherry Street, P.O. Box 285, 31598
Telephone: 912-427-4779; 427-4629
Fax: 912-427-9203

References: Trust Company Bank of Southeast Georgia; Wayne National Bank; Baxley Federal Savings Bank; The Patterson Bank.

For full biographical listings, see the Martindale-Hubbell Law Directory

JONESBORO, Clayton Co.*

OLIVER, DUCKWORTH, SPARGER & WINKLE, P.C. (AV)

146 N. McDonough Street, P.O. Box 37, 30236
Telephone: 770-478-8883
Fax: 770-473-0872
Email: ODSWPC@AOL.COM

G. Robert Oliver Kevin W. Sparger
David P. Winkle

Kathy Brown Valencia Jason E. Bring

(See Next Column)

OF COUNSEL

William H. Duckworth, Jr.

Local Counsel for: Atlanta Gas Light Co.
Representative Clients: Clayton County Hospital Authority; Southern Regional Medical Center; Clayton College and State University Foundation, Inc.; Clayton County Development Authority; Low Temp Industries, Inc.; City of Fayetteville.

For full biographical listings, see the Martindale-Hubbell Law Directory

KINGSLAND, Camden Co.

JOHN J. OSSICK, JR., P.C. (AV)

P.O. Box 1087 230 South Lee Street, 31548
Telephone: 912-729-5864
Fax: 912-729-2230
Email: ossick@gate.net

John J. Ossick, Jr.

Representative Clients: City of Kingsland Downtown Development Authority; Cumberland Transport, Inc.; Southeastern Bank.

For full biographical listings, see the Martindale-Hubbell Law Directory

LAWRENCEVILLE, Gwinnett Co.*

ANDERSEN, DAVIDSON & TATE, P.C. (AV)

1505 Lakes Parkway, Suite 100, P.O. Box 2000, 30043
Telephone: 770-822-0900
Telecopier: 770-822-9680
Email: a-dt@mindspring.com

Gerald Davidson, Jr. Thomas T. Tate
William M. Ray, II

Stephen J. Tyde, Jr.

References: Sun Trust Bank; The Bank of Gwinnett County; Commercial Bank of Georgia; Madison Ventures, Ltd.; Gwinnett Hospital System, Inc.; AT&T Wireless.

For Complete List of Firm Personnel, See General Section

For full biographical listings, see the Martindale-Hubbell Law Directory

MICHAEL C. MURPHY (AV)

390 West Crogan Street Suite 301, 30045
Telephone: 770-682-5952
Fax: 770-682-5113
Email: michaelcmurphy@worldnet.att.net

For full biographical listings, see the Martindale-Hubbell Law Directory

MACON, Bibb Co.*

HALL, BLOCH, GARLAND & MEYER (AV)

1500 Charter Medical Building, P.O. Box 5088, 31208-5088
Telephone: 912-745-1625
Facsimile: 912-741-8822
Email: hbgm@hbgm.com
Midtown Macon, Georgia Office: 2452 Vineville Avenue.
Telephone: 912-745-1625.
Facsimile: 912-741-3544.

MEMBERS OF FIRM

F. Kennedy Hall Mark E. Toth
Benjamin M. Garland John Flanders Kennedy
J. Steven Stewart Todd C. Brooks

ASSOCIATES

Kimberly Cofer Harris J. Ellsworth Hall, IV

F. Kennedy Hall, Division Counsel (Georgia): Norfolk Southern Railway Company.
Counsel for: Wachovia Bank of Georgia, N.A.; BellSouth Mobility, Inc.; United States Fidelity and Guaranty Company; Helena Chemical Corporation; The ENT Center of Central Georgia, P.C.; Fickling & Co.

For Complete List of Firm Personnel, See General Section

For full biographical listings, see the Martindale-Hubbell Law Directory

REYNOLDS & McARTHUR (AV)

A Partnership including a Professional Corporation
850 Walnut Street, 31201
Telephone: 912-741-6000
Fax: 912-742-0750
Email: firm@rmtriallaw.com
Atlanta, Georgia Office: Overlook II, Suite 270, 2839 Paces Ferry Road, N.W., 30339.
Telephone: 770-438-8997; 770-438-9062.
Fax: 770-438-8536.

(See Next Column)

REYNOLDS & MCARTHUR—*Continued*

MEMBERS OF FIRM

W. Carl Reynolds (P.C.)
Katherine L. McArthur
Charles M. Cork, III
O. Wendell Horne, III
Bradley J. Survant

For full biographical listings, see the Martindale-Hubbell Law Directory

SELL & MELTON, L.L.P. (AV)

A Limited Liability Partnership including a Professional Corporation
14th Floor, 577 Mulberry Street, P.O. Box 229, 31202-0229
Telephone: 912-746-8521
Telecopier: 912-745-6426

Andrew W. McKenna (1918-1981)
John D. Comer
Mitchel P. House, Jr.
Doye E. Green
Edward S. Sell, III
John A. Draughon
R. (Chix) Miller (Managing Partner)
Russell M. Boston (P.C.)
Brian J. Passante
Jeffrey B. Hanson
Robert D. McCullers

ASSOCIATE

David M. Cusson

OF COUNSEL

E. S. Sell, Jr.
Buckner F. Melton
Joseph W. Popper, Jr.

General Counsel for: Macon Telegraph Publishing Co. (The Macon Telegraph); Macon-Bibb County Hospital Authority; County of Bibb; Smith & Sons Foods, Inc. (S & S Cafeterias); Macon Bibb County Industrial Authority; Burgess Pigment Co.
Local Counsel For: United States Aircraft Insurance Group (USAIG); United States Aviation Underwriters, Inc. (USAU).

For Complete List of Firm Personnel, See General Section

For full biographical listings, see the Martindale-Hubbell Law Directory

*MARIETTA,** Cobb Co.

D. ROBERT AUTREY, JR., P.C. (AV)

331 Washington Avenue, N.E., 30060
Telephone: 770-424-7500
Fax: 770-424-7509
Email: dra7500@aol.com

D. Robert Autrey, Jr.

For full biographical listings, see the Martindale-Hubbell Law Directory

BROWNING & TANKSLEY, LLP (AV)

Suite 225, 166 Anderson Street, 30060
Telephone: 770-424-1500
Fax: 770-424-1740

MEMBERS OF FIRM

Thomas J. Browning
Charles B. Tanksley
Thomas J. Casurella (1956-1989)
Jerry A. Landers, Jr.
Jeffrey G. Casurella
Benny C. Priest
Michael K. Jablonski

OF COUNSEL

George T. Smith

For full biographical listings, see the Martindale-Hubbell Law Directory

DOWNEY & CLEVELAND, LLP (AV)

288 Washington Avenue, 30060
Telephone: 770-422-3233
Fax: 770-423-4199
Email: downey-cleveland@email.msn.com

OF COUNSEL

Lynn A. Downey

MEMBERS OF FIRM

Robert H. Cleveland (1940-1989)
Joseph C. Parker
Y. Kevin Williams
Russell B. Davis
G. Lee Welborn
Rodney S. Shockley
W. Curtis Anderson

ASSOCIATES

Richard A. Griggs
Tara Waller Scullion
Robert A. De Metz, Jr.
Kevin Salisbury
Sean L. Hynes

Representative Clients: Allstate Insurance Co.; St. Paul Insurance Cos.; Georgia Farm Bureau Mutual Insurance Co.; State Farm Insurance Cos.; Cotton States Mutual Insurance Co.; Colonial Insurance Co. of California; Progressive Insurance Company; Auto Owners Insurance Company; Deep South Surplus, Inc.; Ed Voyles Oldsmobile, Honda and Chrysler-Plymouth.

For full biographical listings, see the Martindale-Hubbell Law Directory

MOORE INGRAM JOHNSON & STEELE, LLP (AV)

A Limited Liability Company
192 Anderson Street, P.O. Box 3305, 30060-8604
Telephone: 770-429-1499
Telecopier: 770-429-8631

MEMBERS OF FIRM

John H. Moore
Stephen C. Steele
William R. Johnson
Robert D. Ingram
G. Phillip Beggs
Eldon L. Basham

ASSOCIATES

Diane Matassino Busch
David Ian Matthews
Jere C. Smith
Kevin B. Carlock
Alexander T. Galloway, III
J. Kevin Moore

Representative Client: C.W. Matthews Contracting Co., Inc.
Approved Attorneys for: Chicago Title Insurance Co.
References: Charter Bank and Trust Co.; First Alliance Bank.

For full biographical listings, see the Martindale-Hubbell Law Directory

*MCDONOUGH,** Henry Co.

SMITH, WELCH & BRITTAIN (AV)

200 The Commerce Building, 235 Keys Ferry Street, P.O. Box 31, 30253
Telephone: 770-957-3937
Fax: 770-957-9165
Stockbridge, Georgia Office: 1239 Eagle's Landing Parkway.
Telephone: 770-389-4864.
Fax: 770-389-5157.

MEMBERS OF FIRM

Ernest M. Smith (1911-1992)
A. J. Welch, Jr.
J. Mark Brittain (Resident, Stockbridge Office)
E. Gilmore Maxwell

ASSOCIATES

Thomas Bruce McFarland
John P. Webb (Resident, Stockbridge Office)
Katharyne Clark Johnson
Tricia B. Smith
Bruce R. Vail

Representative Clients: Atlanta Motor Speedway, Inc.; Bellamy-Strickland Chevrolet, Inc.; Columbia/HCA Healthcare Corp.; Ceramic and Metal Coatings Corp.; Cities of Hampton, Locust Grove and Stockbridge; Georgia Farm Bureau Mutual Insurance; Killearn Properties, Inc. of Georgia; RSKCO, Inc.

For full biographical listings, see the Martindale-Hubbell Law Directory

*NEWNAN,** Coweta Co.

GLOVER & DAVIS, P.A. (AV)

10 Brown Street, P.O. Box 1038, 30264
Telephone: 770-683-6000
Fax: 770-683-6010
Peachtree City, Georgia Office: Suite 130, 200 Westpark Drive.
Telephone: 770-487-5834.
Fax: 770-487-3492.

J. Littleton Glover, Jr.
Asa M. Powell, Jr.
Jerry Ann Conner

Peter A. Durham

Representative Clients: First Citizens Corporation and Banking Subsidiaries; Putnam-Greene Financial Corporation and Banking Subsidiaries; Peachtree National Bank; Coweta County, Georgia; Batson-Cook Company; General Corporate and Construction Divisions; Pyramid Masonry, Inc.
Local Counsel for: West Georgia Farm Credit, ACA; International Playtex Corp.

For Complete List of Firm Personnel, See General Section

For full biographical listings, see the Martindale-Hubbell Law Directory

ROSENZWEIG, JONES & MACNABB, P.C. (AV)

32 South Court Square, P.O. Box 220, 30264
Telephone: 770-253-3282
Fax: 770-251-7262

George C. Rosenzweig
Sidney Pope Jones, Jr.
Joseph P. MacNabb

Douglas L. Dreyer
Jonathan W. Hickman

Approved Attorneys for: Lawyers Title Insurance Corp.; Chicago Title Insurance Co.

For Complete List of Firm Personnel, See General Section

For full biographical listings, see the Martindale-Hubbell Law Directory

NORCROSS, Gwinnett Co.

DEMING, PARKER, HOFFMAN, GREEN & CAMPBELL, P.C. (AV)

4851 Jimmy Carter Boulevard, 30093
Telephone: 770-564-2600
Fax: 770-564-2267
Covington, Georgia Office: Suite 11, 3236 Highway 278.
Telephone: 770-787-2600.
Fax: 770-564-2267.
Cumming, Georgia Office: 425 Tribble Gap Road, Suite 398, 30130.
Telephone: 770-889-2600.
Fax: 770-564-2267.

Michael D. Deming
Franklin E. Parker
Paul M. Hoffman
Jim R. Green, Jr.
Richard A. Campbell
Stephen R. Williams

OF COUNSEL

Robert E. Born
Richard K. Valldejuli, Jr.
Robert M.N. Shaker

Mark L. Wells
Christopher W. T. Daly
E. Nicole Harrison
Suzanne M. Boykin
Jeffrey C. Renz
David Black
Robert A. Leonard
Joan S. Pepe
Nadiyah Muhammad

For full biographical listings, see the Martindale-Hubbell Law Directory

*OCILLA,** Irwin Co.

WALTERS, DAVIS & PUJADAS, P.C. (AV)

South Cherry Street, P.O. Box 247, 31774
Telephone: 912-468-7472; 468-9433
Fax: 912-468-9022

W. Emory Walters
J. Harvey Davis
Thomas E. Pujadas
C. Vinson Walters, II

Attorneys for: Irwin County Board of Education; First State Bank of Ocilla; Irwin County; Wilcox County.
Local Counsel for: Georgia Farm Bureau Mutual Insurance Co.
Approved Attorneys for: Kaiser Aluminum & Chemical Sales, Inc.; Lawyers Title Insurance Corp.; Ticor Title Insurance Co.; Farmers Home Administration; Federal Land Bank of Columbia.

For Complete List of Firm Personnel, See General Section

For full biographical listings, see the Martindale-Hubbell Law Directory

*ROME,** Floyd Co.

BRINSON, ASKEW, BERRY, SEIGLER, RICHARDSON & DAVIS, LLP (AV)

Omberg House, 615 West First Street, P.O. Box 5513, 30162-5513
Telephone: 706-291-8853;
Atlanta: 404-521-0908
Telecopier: 706-234-3574
Email: law@brinson-askew.com *URL:* http://www.brinson-askew.com

MEMBERS OF FIRM

Robert M. Brinson (P.C.)
C. King Askew (P.C.)
Robert L. Berry
Joseph M. Seigler, Jr.
Thomas D. Richardson
J. Anderson Davis
Hendrick L. Cromartie, III
Wright W. Smith
Mark M. J. Webb
Joseph B. Atkins
I. Stewart Duggan

ASSOCIATES

James Daniel Blitch, IV
Stephen B. Moseley

Representative Clients: City of Rome; Georgia Power Co.; Unilever; General Electric Company; News Publishing Company (Rome News Tribune); Columbia Redmond Regional Medical Center; Oglethorpe Power Corp.; Suhner Manufacturing, Inc.; United States Fidelity & Guaranty Co; Shaw Industries, Inc.

For full biographical listings, see the Martindale-Hubbell Law Directory

MAGRUDER & SUMNER (AV)

701 Broad Street, P.O. Drawer 5187, 30162-5187
Telephone: 706-291-7050
Telefax: 706-291-9881

MEMBERS OF FIRM

J. Clinton Sumner, Jr.
Karl M. Kothe
Clay M. White

ASSOCIATES

Kay Ann Atha
John Rexford Weech
J. Andrew Owens

(See Next Column)

OF COUNSEL

Dudley B. Magruder, Jr. (1914-1995)
Jack Rogers (1908-1998)
Wade C. Hoyt, Jr. (1913-1997)

Counsel for: State Farm Insurance Cos.; Atlanta Gas Light Co.; Best Manufacturing Co.; Georgia Power Co.; West Point-Stevens. Inc.; BellSouth Telecommunications, Inc.; Liberty Mutual Insurance Co.

For full biographical listings, see the Martindale-Hubbell Law Directory

SHAW, MADDOX, GRAHAM, MONK & BOLING, LLP (AV)

SunTrust Bank Building, P.O. Box 29, 30162-0029
Telephone: 706-291-6223
Toll Free: 888-291-6223
Telecopier: 706-291-7429
Email: law@shawmaddox.com *URL:* http://www.shawmaddox.com
Cedartown, Georgia Office: 223 South College Street, 30125.
Telephone: 770-749-6723.
Telecopier: 770-749-6729.

MEMBERS OF FIRM

Charles C. Shaw
John M. Graham, III
C. Wade Monk
William H. Boling, Jr.
Jo H. Stegall, III
David F. Guldenschuh
Daniel M. Roper
Jule W. Peek, Jr.
Virginia B. Harman
Scott M. Smith
Thomas H. Manning
Mather D. Graham

ASSOCIATE

Preston W. Smith

OF COUNSEL

Oscar M. Smith
James D. Maddox

LEGAL SUPPORT PERSONNEL

Christopher S. Rainwater (Senior Paralegal)
Debra A. Thwaites

Representative Clients: SunTrust Bank, Northwest Georgia N.A.; Inland Paperboard and Packaging, Inc.; Norfolk Southern Railway Co.; Aetna Casualty & Surety Co.; American Mutual Liability Insurance; Commercial Union Insurance Cos.; Hartford Accident & Indemnity Co.; St. Paul Insurance Cos.; Zurich-American Insurance Co.

For full biographical listings, see the Martindale-Hubbell Law Directory

*SAVANNAH,** Chatham Co.

HUNTER, MACLEAN, EXLEY & DUNN, P.C. (AV)

200 East St. Julian Street, P.O. Box 9848, 31412
Telephone: 912-236-0261
Cable Address: "Ancan"
Telecopier: 912-236-4936
Telex: 54-6483
Email: hmed.com *URL:* http://www.bobbs@hmed.com
Atlanta, Georgia Office: The Peachtree, 1355 Peachtree Street, N.E., Suite 640.
Telephone: 404-876-3611.
Fax: 404-870-2025.

Malcolm R. Maclean
John B. Miller
John M. Tatum
Arnold C. Young
Robert S. Glenn, Jr.
J. Reid Williamson, III
William E. Dillard, III
Christopher Weis Phillips
Robert Alvin Lewallen, Jr.
Kirby Gould Mason
Halsey G. Knapp, Jr. (Resident, Atlanta Office)

Representative Clients: SunTrust Bank, Savannah, N.A.; Memorial Medical Center, Inc.; Prudential Insurance Company of America; Historic Savannah Foundation, Inc.; John Hancock Mutual Life Insurance Co.; Norfolk Southern Corp.

For Complete List of Firm Personnel, See General Section

For full biographical listings, see the Martindale-Hubbell Law Directory

KARSMAN, BROOKS & CALLAWAY, P.C. (AV)

301 West Congress Street, P.O. Box 9149, 31412
Telephone: 912-238-2750
Cable Address: "Karbro"
Telecopier: 912-238-2767

Stanley M. Karsman
Charles C. Brooks
Timothy F. Callaway, III
Stanley E. Harris, Jr.
James L. Drake, Jr.
Dana F. Braun
R. Krannert Riddle
Edward M. Hughes
Timothy J. Haeussler

For full biographical listings, see the Martindale-Hubbell Law Directory

KENT, WORSHAM & SMART (AV)

18 East Bay Street, P.O. Box 9117, 31412
Telephone: 912-238-1500
FAX: 912-238-5515

(See Next Column)

KENT, WORSHAM & SMART—*Continued*

MEMBERS OF FIRM

Martin Kent
Hugh M. Worsham, Jr.
Don Smart
Joseph Y. Rahimi, II

References: The Coastal Bank of Georgia.

For full biographical listings, see the Martindale-Hubbell Law Directory

LEE, BLACK, SCHEER & HART, P.C. (AV)

10th Floor, 24 Drayton Street, P.O. Box 8205, 31412
Telephone: 912-233-1271
Telecopier: 912-232-7344
Other Savannah Office: 6555 Abercorn Street, Suite 121, P.O. Box 14477.
Telephone: 912-355-1131.

Edward H. Lee
W. Jerrold Black
Steven E. Scheer
R. Jonathan Hart

Christopher L. Rouse
John D. Lange

For full biographical listings, see the Martindale-Hubbell Law Directory

McCALLAR AND ASSOCIATES (AV)

115 Oglethorpe Avenue West, P.O. Box 9026, 31412
Telephone: 912-234-1215
Telecopier: 912-236-7549

C. James McCallar, Jr.

Mark Bulovic

For full biographical listings, see the Martindale-Hubbell Law Directory

SAVAGE, HERNDON & TURNER, P.C. (AV)

304 East Bay Street, P.O. Box 8969, 31412-8969
Telephone: 912-231-1140
Fax: 912-232-4212
Email: eastbay@aol.com

Brent J. Savage
Thomas R. Herndon
Robert B. Turner

R. Scot Kraeuter
Ivanna Marie Livingstone
Christopher Dorian Britt

For full biographical listings, see the Martindale-Hubbell Law Directory

WEINER, SHEAROUSE, WEITZ, GREENBERG & SHAWE, L.L.P. (AV)

14 East State Street, P.O. Box 10105, 31412-0305
Telephone: 912-233-2251
Telecopier: 912-235-5464
Email: WSWGS@Sysconn.com

MEMBERS OF FIRM

Nelson Haslam (1926-1974)
Aron G. Weiner
William W. Shearouse, Jr.
N. Harvey Weitz
Stephen F. Greenberg
Mark T. Shawe
Malcolm Mackenzie, III
Edwin R. Byck

Christine Tambakis McDonnell

For full biographical listings, see the Martindale-Hubbell Law Directory

*SUMMERVILLE,** Chattooga Co.

COOK & CONNELLY (AV)

128 South Commerce Street, P.O. Box 370, 30747
Telephone: 706-857-3421
Fax: 706-857-1520

MEMBERS OF FIRM

Bobby Lee Cook
A. Cecil Palmour (1913-1980)
Bobby Lee Cook, Jr. (1950-1995)
L. Branch S. Connelly

For full biographical listings, see the Martindale-Hubbell Law Directory

*SWAINSBORO,** Emanuel Co.

MERRILL, STONE & HAMILTON, LLC (AV)

2nd Floor, 101 South Main Street, P.O. Box 129, 30401
Telephone: 912-237-7029
Fax: 912-237-9211
Statesboro, Georgia Office: 201 South Zetterower, 30458.
Telephone: 912-764-3897.

MEMBER OF FIRM

Chas. Brett Merrill, Jr.

References: First Liberty Bank; The Spivey State Bank.

For full biographical listings, see the Martindale-Hubbell Law Directory

TUCKER, De Kalb Co.

HOTZ & ASSOCIATES, P.C. (AV)

Suite 200, 1979 Lakeside Parkway, 30084
Telephone: 770-939-4861
Fax: 770-270-9749
Email: hotz@hotzlawfirm.com

Richard F. Taylor (1921-1993)
Walter H. Hotz

James H. Baskin

Representative Clients: Regional Counsel for GE Supply, a Division of General Electric Company; Atlanta Postal Credit Union; Associated & Federal Employees Credit Union; Georgia Federal Credit Union; Peachtree Federal Credit Union; Deutsche Steinindustrie A.G.; Destag of North America, Inc.; General Trailer Services, Inc.; The Network Connection, Inc.

For full biographical listings, see the Martindale-Hubbell Law Directory

*VALDOSTA,** Lowndes Co.

COLEMAN, TALLEY, NEWBERN, KURRIE, PRESTON & HOLLAND, LLP (AV)

910 North Patterson Street, P.O. Box 5437, 31603-5437
Telephone: 912-242-7562
Fax: 912-333-0885
Email: clf@datasys.net

Henry T. Brice (1925-1976)
B. Lamar Tillman (1912-1990)

MEMBERS OF FIRM

Wade H. Coleman
George T. Talley
C. George Newbern
Thompson Kurrie, Jr.
Richard L. Coleman
Edward F. Preston
William E. Holland
R. Clay Powell
Gregory T. Talley

Russell D. Henry

OF COUNSEL

John T. McTier

Attorneys for: Bank of America; Georgia Power Company; Atlanta Gas Company; Griffin Agricultural Chemicals Group; Sears; The Park Avenue Bank; Liberty Mutual Insurance Company; USF&G Company; MAG Mutual Insurance Company.

For full biographical listings, see the Martindale-Hubbell Law Directory

DODD AND DENNIS, P.C. (AV)

613 N. Patterson Street, P.O. Box 1066, 31603-1066
Telephone: 912-242-4470
Telefax: 912-245-7731
URL: http://www.lawyers.com/dodd&dennis
Email: doddlaw@mail.datasys.net *URL:* http://www.doddlaw.com

Roger J. Dodd
Sam D. Dennis

References: First Union Bank; First State Bank and Trust Co.; Park Avenue Bank.

For full biographical listings, see the Martindale-Hubbell Law Directory

ELLIOTT & BLACKBURN (AV)

First Liberty Bank Building, 509 North Patterson Street Suite 201, P.O. Box 579, 31603-0579
Telephone: 912-247-0800
912-242-3333
Telecopier: 912-242-0696
Email: eblaw@surfsouth.com

W. Gus Elliott
Oris D. Blackburn, Jr.
Walter G. Elliott, II
James L. Elliott

Representative Clients: Hospital Authority of Valdosta and Lowndes County d/b/a South Georgia Medical Center; Lowndes County; The Valdosta Daily Times; Bell South Telecommunications, Inc.; Sears, Roebuck & Company; Levi Strauss & Co.; John Deere & Co.; E. I. DuPont de Nemours & Company; BP Exploration & Oil, Inc.; National Indemnity Company.

For full biographical listings, see the Martindale-Hubbell Law Directory

HAWAII

*HONOLULU,** Honolulu Co.

LAW OFFICE OF SHERRY P. BRODER A LAW CORPORATION (AV)

Davies Pacific Center, 841 Bishop Street, Suite 800, 96813
Telephone: 808-531-1411; 808-944-1139
Facsimile: 808-531-8411
Email: broder@lava.net

Sherry P. Broder

Reference: Bank of Honolulu.

For full biographical listings, see the Martindale-Hubbell Law Directory

CADES SCHUTTE FLEMING & WRIGHT (AV)

Formerly Smith, Wild, Beebe & Cades
Cades Schutte Fleming & Wright Building, 1000 Bishop Street, Suite 1200, P.O. Box 939, 96808
Telephone: 808-521-9200
Telecopier: 808-521-9210
Email: cades@cades.com
Kailua-Kona, Hawaii Office: Hualalai Center, Suite B-303, 75-170 Hualalai Road.
Telephone: 808-329-5811.
Telecopier: 808-326-1175.

MEMBERS OF FIRM

Jeffrey S. Portnoy
Philip J. Leas
William A. Cardwell
C. Michael Hare
Richard R. Clifton
Roy A. Vitousek, III (Resident Partner, Kona Office)
David Schulmeister
Milton M. Yasunaga
Colin O. Miwa
Peter W. Olson
Patricia J. McHenry
K. James Steiner, Jr.
James H. Ashford
Dennis W. Chong Kee
Catherine Carey

ASSOCIATES

Kelly G. LaPorte
Kimberly A. Jackson (Resident, Kona Office)
Alexander Woody
Jodi Shin Yamamoto

Counsel for: First Hawaiian Bank; Alexander & Baldwin, Inc.; Theo. H. Davies & Co., Ltd.; C. Brewer & Company, Ltd.; Bank of America, FSB; The Bank of Tokyo, Ltd.; Haseko (Hawaii), Inc.; The Industrial Bank of Japan, Ltd.; Hawaii Association of Physicians for Indemnification (HAPI); Tamarack American Insurance Co.

For Complete List of Firm Personnel, See General Section

For full biographical listings, see the Martindale-Hubbell Law Directory

CARLSMITH BALL (AV)

A Partnership including Law Corporations
Suite 2200, Pacific Tower, 1001 Bishop Street, P.O. Box 656, 96809-3402
Telephone: 808-523-2500
Fax: 808-523-0842
Email: execdirector@carlsmith.com *URL:* http://www.carlsmith.com
Kapolei, Hawaii Office: Suite 318, Kapolei Building, 1001 Kamokila Boulevard, 96707.
Telephone: 808-523-2500.
Fax: 808-674-0850.
Wailuku, Maui Hawaii Office: Suite 400, One Main Plaza, 2200 Main Street, P.O. Box 1086, 96793-1086.
Telephone: 808-242-4535.
Fax: 808-244-4974.
Kailua-Kona, Hawaii Office: Suite 209, 75-1000 Henry Street, 96740.
Telephone: 808-329-6464.
Fax: 808-329-9450.
Hilo, Hawaii Office: 121 Waianuenue Avenue, P.O. Box 686, 96721-0686.
Telephone: 808-935-6644.
Fax: 808-935-7975.
Hagatna, Guam Office: Suite 401, Bank of Hawaii Building, 134 West Soledad Avenue, P.O. Box BF, 96932-5027.
Telephone: 671-472-6813.
Fax: 671-477-4375.
Telex: 721-6445 CWCMI GM.
Saipan, Commonwealth of the Northern Mariana Islands Office: Carlsmith Building, Capitol Hill, P.O. Box 5241, 96950-5241.
Telephone: 670-322-3455.
Fax: 670-322-3368.
Los Angeles, California Office: 9th Floor, 444 South Flower Street, 90071-2901.
Telephone: 213-955-1200.
Fax: 213-623-0032.
Washington, D.C. Office: Suite 300, 1201 Pennsylvania Avenue, N.W., 20004-2401.
Telephone: 202-628-2228.
Fax: 202-628-2071.

(See Next Column)

Mexico City, Mexico Office: Carlsmith Ball, Sierra Nevada 119, Lomas de Chapultepec, 11000 Mexico, D.F.
Telephone: 52-5-520-8514, 52-5-520-8757.
Fax: 52-5-540-1545.
Mexico, D.F. Office of Carlsmith Ball, S.C. (Authorized to practice as foreign legal consultants in Mexico): Sierra Nevada 119, Lomas de Chapultepec, 11000 Mexico, D.F.
Telephone: 52-5-520-8514, 52-5-520-8757.
Fax: 52-5-540-1545.

MEMBERS OF FIRM

Joseph A. Ball (Resident at Los Angeles, California Office)
Gary G. Grimmer
John P. Manaut
John D. Osborn (Resident at Saipan Office)
Thomas R. Sylvester

ASSOCIATES

Deborah Elise Barack (Resident at Los Angeles, California Office)
Leopoldo Galvan Mendez (Resident at Mexico Office)
Edmund W.K. Haitsuka (Resident at Kailua-Kona, Hawaii Office)
Carol A. Uyeno

OF COUNSEL

Susan Lloyd Harrison Evans (Resident at Kailua-Kona, Hawaii Office)
John R. McDonough (Resident at Los Angeles, California Office)

For Complete List of Firm Personnel, See General Section

For full biographical listings, see the Martindale-Hubbell Law Directory

CHAR SAKAMOTO ISHII LUM & CHING (AV)

Suite 850, 841 Bishop Street, 96813
Telephone: 808-522-5133
Facsimile: 808-522-5144
Email: law_csil@aol.com

MEMBERS OF FIRM

Vernon F. L. Char
Earl M. Ching
Steven L. Ching
Carolyn E. Hayashi
Elizabeth Ann Ishii
David M. K. Lum
Ronald R. Sakamoto
Michael K. Tanigawa

Keith S. Agena
Jacqueline H. Furuta
Carolyn M. Oshiro
Melissa T. Pavlicek

For full biographical listings, see the Martindale-Hubbell Law Directory

FUJIYAMA, DUFFY & FUJIYAMA ATTORNEYS AT LAW, A LAW CORPORATION (AV)

2700 Pauahi Tower, Bishop Square, 1001 Bishop Street, 96813
Telephone: 808-536-0802
Telecopier: 808-536-5117

Wallace S. Fujiyama (1925-1994)
James E. Duffy, Jr.
Rodney M. Fujiyama
Archie T. Ikehara

Lee T. Nakamura
Ward F. N. Fujimoto
Gregg M. Ushiroda
Danielle Noel Degele-Mathews
Deborah S. Jackson
Duane R. Miyashiro

OF COUNSEL

Davis D. Higa
Robert P. Richards (A Law Corporation)
Michele-Lynn E. Luke

Representative Clients: The Dow Chemical Company; Johnson & Johnson; Harley-Davidson; Wyeth-Ayerst Laboratories; Tokio Marine & Fire Insurance Co., Ltd.; Clark Material Handling Company; State of Hawaii Office of Hawaiian Affairs; Smithkline Beecham Corporation; Merck & Co.; Sears Roebuck.

For full biographical listings, see the Martindale-Hubbell Law Directory

FUKUNAGA MATAYOSHI HERSHEY & CHING (AV)

A Partnership including a Law Corporation
841 Bishop Street, Suite 1200, 96813
Telephone: 808-533-4300
Fax: 808-531-7585

PARTNERS

Kenneth K. Fukunaga
Jerold T. Matayoshi (A Law Corporation)
James H. Hershey
Wesley H. H. Ching
Patricia Kehau Wall

ASSOCIATES

Lois H. Yamaguchi
Robert R. Sadaoka
Celia A. Urion
Sheree Kon-Herrera

OF COUNSEL

Leighton K. Chong
Kathleen M. Douglas

For full biographical listings, see the Martindale-Hubbell Law Directory

Honolulu—Continued

GOODSILL ANDERSON QUINN & STIFEL (AV)

Alii Place, Suite 1800, 1099 Alakea Street, P.O. Box 3196, 96801-3196
Telephone: 808-547-5600
FAX: 808-547-5880
Email: info@goodsill.com *URL:* http://www.goodsill.com

MEMBERS OF FIRM

Martin Anderson
David J. Dezzani
John R. Lacy
Thomas W. Williams, Jr.
William S. Miller
Jacqueline L. S. Earle
Gary M. Slovin
Lisa Woods Munger
Bruce L. Lamon
Mark B. Desmarais
Corlis J. Chang
Barbara A. Petrus
Patricia Mathias NaPier
Mark F. Ito
Wayne H. Muraoka
Walter C. Davison
LindaLee K. Farm
Margaret Jenkins Leong
Carol Ann Eblen
Roy John Tjioe
A. Richard Philpott
Lennes N. Omuro
Derek R. Kobayashi

ASSOCIATES

Thomas L. Benedict
Edmund K. Saffery
Lisa A. Bail
Carolyn K. Gugelyk
Normand R. Lezy
Darcy L. Endo-Omoto
Kathleen A. Kelly
Tonya C. Kong
J. Denice von Gnechten
Teresa R. Favilla
M. Elizabeth Raxter
Anne T. Horiuchi

Representative Clients: CNA Insurance Co.; E. I. du Pont de Nemours & Company; Hawaiian Electric Industries, Inc.; Lorillard Tobacco Company; MEDMARC; Sears Roebuck & Co.; State Farm Insurance Companies; United States Aviation Underwriters, Inc.

For Complete List of Firm Personnel, See General Section

For full biographical listings, see the Martindale-Hubbell Law Directory

DAVID W. HALL ATTORNEY AT LAW, A LAW CORPORATION (AV)

Dillingham Transportation Building, Suite 236, 735 Bishop Street, 96813
Telephone: 808-526-0402
Fax: 808-526-0404
URL: http://www.lawyers.com/hall_firm

David W. Hall

For full biographical listings, see the Martindale-Hubbell Law Directory

KAWACHIKA & OSAKI (AV)

Grosvenor Center, Mauka Tower, 737 Bishop Street, Suite 2750, 96813
Telephone: 808-537-3939
Facsimile: 808-537-4349
Email: jak@hawaii.rr.com

James A. Kawachika
Carl H. Osaki

For full biographical listings, see the Martindale-Hubbell Law Directory

JAMES KRUEGER ATTORNEY AT LAW, A LAW CORPORATION

(See Wailuku)

LYONS, BRANDT, COOK & HIRAMATSU (AV)

841 Bishop Street, Suite 1800, 96813
Telephone: 808-524-7030
Facsimile: 808-533-3011
Email: lbch@hits.net

MEMBERS OF FIRM

Samuel A. B. Lyons
George W. Brandt
Thomas E. Cook
Beverly Lynne K. Hiramatsu
Jeffrey A. Griswold
Bradford F. K. Bliss
Steven Y. Otaguro
Stefan M. Reinke
Paul R. Grable
Edquon Lee
Bonnie L. Moore

OF COUNSEL

Birney Baxter Bervar

For full biographical listings, see the Martindale-Hubbell Law Directory

MCCORRISTON MIHO MILLER MUKAI (AV)

Five Waterfront Plaza, 4th Floor, 500 Ala Moana Boulevard, 96813
Telephone: 808-529-7300
Facsimile: 808-524-8293
Cable: Attorneys, Honolulu
Mailing Address: P.O. Box 2800, Honolulu, Hawaii, 96803-2800
Email: info@m4Law.com

(See Next Column)

PARTNERS

William C. McCorriston
Kenneth G. K. Hoo
Mark J. Bennett
Nadine Y. Ando
Darolyn Hatsuko Lendio
Randall K. Schmitt
John Y. Yamano
Edward T. Schorr
David J. Minkin
Lisa M. Ginoza
Kimberly Rae McCorkle
Carrie K. S. Okinaga
Christopher J. Cole

COUNSEL

R. John Seibert

ASSOCIATES

Trisha M. Kimura
Reese R. Nakamura
Maria B. Mazzeo
Jonathan H. Steiner
Stacey M. Robinson
Kevin A. Souza
Kenneth J. Mansfield
Deborah L. P. Mueller
Daniel James Kunkel
Kara B. Moran

Representative Clients: City & County of Hawaii; County of Kauai; Hawaii County and Shared Medical Systems Corporation.

For Complete List of Firm Personnel, See General Section

For full biographical listings, see the Martindale-Hubbell Law Directory

MIYAGI, NOHR & MYHRE (AV)

1001 Bishop Street, Suite 1200, 96813
Telephone: 808-524-2466
Fax: 808-524-2556

Melvyn M. Miyagi
Katharine M. Nohr
James V. Myhre
Michael H. Tsuchida
John E. Drotz

OF COUNSEL

Carleton B. Reid

Representative Clients: American International Group; State Farm Insurance; TIG Insurance; Crum & Forster; ITT Specialty Risk Services; Marriott International; The Hartford; USAA; Budget Rent A Car; Crawford & Company.

For full biographical listings, see the Martindale-Hubbell Law Directory

PERKIN & HOSODA (AV)

2440 Mauka Tower, Grosvenor Center, 737 Bishop Street, 96813
Telephone: 808-523-2300
Fax: 808-531-8898

MEMBERS OF FIRM

John Francis Perkin
Lyle S. Hosoda

For full biographical listings, see the Martindale-Hubbell Law Directory

REINWALD, O'CONNOR & PLAYDON (AV)

(Formerly Anthony, Hoddick, Reinwald & O'Connor)
2400 Makai Tower, Grosvenor Center, P.O. Box 3199, 96801-3199
Telephone: 808-524-8350
Telecopier: 808-531-8628
Email: info@roplaw.com *URL:* http://www.roplaw.com

MEMBERS OF FIRM

Dennis E. W. O'Connor
George W. Playdon, Jr.
W. Thomas Fagan
Michael J. McGuigan
Cid H. Inouye
Kelvin H. Kaneshiro

For full biographical listings, see the Martindale-Hubbell Law Directory

ROBBINS & RHODES ATTORNEYS AT LAW, A LAW CORPORATION (AV)

Suite 2200 Davies Pacific Center, 841 Bishop Street, 96813
Telephone: 808-524-2355
Fax: 808-526-0290
Email: robbinsrhodes@lava.net

Kenneth S. Robbins
Vincent A. Rhodes

Representative Clients: City and County of Honolulu; Coldwell Banker Pacific Properties; County of Maui; Farmers Insurance Group; Kapiolani Health Care Systems, Inc.; Lloyd's of London; State of Hawaii; Textron, Inc.; Westin Hotel Company, Inc.

For full biographical listings, see the Martindale-Hubbell Law Directory

TOM & PETRUS (AV)

212 Merchant Street Suite 200, 96813
Telephone: 808-522-0800
Fax: 808-522-0809

MEMBERS OF FIRM

Michael D. Tom
Brad S. Petrus
Richard B. Miller

ASSOCIATES

Leslie H. Kondo
Stephen M. Teves
David R. Harada-Stone
Lauren K. Rauschenburg

(See Next Column)

TOM & PETRUS, *Honolulu—Continued*

COUNSEL

Lyle Minoru Ishida

Representative Clients: Dillingham Construction Pacific, Ltd.; JDH Construction Ltd.; Scottsdale Insurance Company; Dames & Moore; Delta Construction Corporation; Kapi'olani Health (Medical Center for Women and Children and Kapi'olani Medical Center at Pali Momi); St. Francis Health System (St. Francis Medical Center and St. Francis Medical Center West); Applied Technology Corporation; Nordic/PCL (HawaiiConvention Center); Travelers Property Casualty; Gilbarco Inc.

For full biographical listings, see the Martindale-Hubbell Law Directory

WATANABE, ING & KAWASHIMA (AV)

A Partnership including Professional Corporations
First Hawaiian Center, 999 Bishop Street, 23rd Floor, 96813
Telephone: 808-544-8300
Facsimile: 808-544-8399
Email: allwik@wik.com

MEMBERS OF FIRM

Jeffrey N. Watanabe (Atty. At Law, A Law Corp.)
James Kawashima (Atty. At Law, A Law Corp.)
J. Douglas Ing (Atty. At Law, A Law Corp.)
Wray H. Kondo (Atty. At Law, A Law Corp.)
John T. Komeiji (Atty. At Law, A Law Corp.)
Ronald Y. K. Leong (Atty. At Law, A Law Corp.)
Robert T. Takamatsu (Atty. At Law, A Law Corp.)
Cynthia Winegar (Atty. at Law, A Law Corp.)
Randall Y. Yamamoto (Atty. At Law, A Law Corp.)
Lyle Y. Harada (Atty. At Law, A Law Corp.)
Michael A. Lorusso (Atty. At Law, A Law Corp.)
Pamela J. Larson (Atty. At Law, A Law Corp.)
John R. Aube (Atty. At Law, A Law Corp.)
Jan M.L.Y. Amii (Atty. at Law, A Law Corp.)
Seth M. Reiss (Atty. At Law, A Law Corp.)
Curtis C. Kim
Lani Narikiyo (Atty. at Law, A Law Corp.)

ASSOCIATES

Donna Y. Kanemaru
Peter L. Fritz
Beth K. Fujimoto
Patsy H. Kirio
Kevin H. Oda
Michael C. Bird
Brian Y. Hiyane
Dennis J. Hwang
Teri Y. Kondo

ASIA PACIFIC CONSULTANTS

George R. Ariyoshi
Victor Hao Li (Not admitted in HI)

LEGAL SUPPORT PERSONNEL

GOVERNMENT AFFAIRS ADVISORS

Millicent M. Y. H. Kim
Lori Ann C. Lum

References: First Hawaiian Bank; American Savings Bank.

For Complete List of Firm Personnel, See General Section

For full biographical listings, see the Martindale-Hubbell Law Directory

MICHAEL J. Y. WONG (AV)

2222 Central Pacific Plaza, 220 South King Street, 96813
Telephone: 808-536-1855
Fax: 808-536-1857

For full biographical listings, see the Martindale-Hubbell Law Directory

RENEE M. L. YUEN ATTORNEY AT LAW, A LAW CORPORATION (AV)

Haseko Center, 820 Mililani Street, Suite 702A, 96813-2937
Telephone: 808-523-0125
Facsimile: 808-523-0127
Email: yuenlaw@hawaii.rr.com

Renee M. L. Yuen

For full biographical listings, see the Martindale-Hubbell Law Directory

KAILUA, Honolulu Co.

WINER MEHEULA & DEVENS (AV)

970 North Kalaheo Avenue, Suite A-300, 96734
Telephone: 808-254-5855
Fax: 808-254-6872
Email: winer@pacificlaw.com *URL:* http://www.pacificlaw.com

MEMBERS OF FIRM

Andrew S. Winer
William K. Meheula
Vladimir Paul Devens

OF COUNSEL

David F. Fasi

(See Next Column)

ASSOCIATE

Blue H. Kaanehe

For full biographical listings, see the Martindale-Hubbell Law Directory

KAILUA-KONA, Hawaii Co.

CADES SCHUTTE FLEMING & WRIGHT (AV)

Hualalai Center, Suite B-303, 75-170 Hualalai Road, 96740
Telephone: 808-329-5811
Telecopier: 808-326-1175
Email: cades@cades.com
Honolulu, Hawaii Office: Cades Schutte Fleming & Wright Building, 1000 Bishop Street, Suite 1200, P. O. Box 939.
Telephone: 808-521-9200.

RESIDENT PARTNER

Roy A. Vitousek, III

RESIDENT ASSOCIATE

Kimberly A. Jackson

For Complete List of Firm Personnel, See General Section

For full biographical listings, see the Martindale-Hubbell Law Directory

*LIHUE,** Kauai Co.

JAMES KRUEGER ATTORNEY AT LAW, A LAW CORPORATION

(See Wailuku)

*WAILUKU,** Maui Co.

JAMES KRUEGER ATTORNEY AT LAW, A LAW CORPORATION (AV)

2065 Main Street, 96793
Telephone: 808-244-7444; Honolulu: 536-7474
Facsimile: 808-244-4177
Email: maulaw@maui.net *URL:* http://www.kruegerlaw-hawaii.org

James Krueger

Eve M. Green
Cynthia Kanoholani Wong

A List of Representative Clients and References will be furnished upon request.

For full biographical listings, see the Martindale-Hubbell Law Directory

IDAHO

*BOISE,** Ada Co.

EBERLE, BERLIN, KADING, TURNBOW & MCKLVEEN, CHARTERED (AV)

Capitol Park Plaza, 300 North Sixth Street, P.O. Box 1368, 83701-1368
Telephone: 208-344-8535
Facsimile: 208-344-8542

R.B. Kading, Jr.
Warren Eugene Jones
Mark S. Geston

Representative Clients: Key Bank of Idaho; Cessna Aircraft Co.

For Complete List of Firm Personnel, See General Section

For full biographical listings, see the Martindale-Hubbell Law Directory

ELAM & BURKE, A PROFESSIONAL ASSOCIATION (AV)

Key Financial Center, 702 West Idaho Street, P.O. Box 1539, 83701
Telephone: 208-343-5454
Telecopier: 208-384-5844
Email: eblaw@elamburke.com

Carl P. Burke
M. Allyn Dingel, Jr.
John Magel
James D. LaRue
William G. Dryden
Trudy Hanson Fouser

Rebecca A. Broadbent

Representative Clients: Morrison-Knudsen, Inc.; Prudential Securities, Inc.; Pechiney Corp.; Dow Corning Corporation; State Farm Insurance Cos.; Sinclair Oil Co. d/b/a Sun Valley Co.; Farmers Insurance Group.

For Complete List of Firm Personnel, See General Section

For full biographical listings, see the Martindale-Hubbell Law Directory

GREEN LAW OFFICES (AV)

P.O. Box 2597, 83701-2597
Telephone: 208-342-8915
Fax: 208-342-2718
Email: cumergreen@aol.com *URL:* http://www.greenedlaw.com

(See Next Column)

GREEN LAW OFFICES—*Continued*

Cumer L. Green

ASSOCIATE

Debra A. Silk

LEGAL SUPPORT PERSONNEL

Gary W. Shaw (Chief, Legal Support Group)

Representative Clients: Idaho School Boards Association, Inc.; Potlatch Corporation; Bell Helmets, Inc.; R.C. Bigelow, Inc.; Fleetwood Enterprises, Inc.; United Airlines; Pacific Crown Timber; Croman Corp.; Ida-West Energy Co.; LJD Holdings, Inc.; Ram International; VFP VC Ltd.; Developers Diversified Realty Corporation; Dakota Company, Inc.

For full biographical listings, see the Martindale-Hubbell Law Directory

*POCATELLO,** Bannock Co.

MERRILL & MERRILL, CHARTERED (AV)

Key Bank Building, P.O. Box 991, 83204
Telephone: 208-232-2286
Fax: 208-232-2499
Email: mmlaw@ida.net

Dave R. Gallafent
Stephen S. Dunn
D. Russell Wight
David C. Nye
Kent L. Hawkins
Thomas W. Clark
Thomas J. Lyons

Representative Clients: Western States Equipment Co.; J. R. Simplot Co.

For Complete List of Firm Personnel, See General Section

For full biographical listings, see the Martindale-Hubbell Law Directory

ILLINOIS

AURORA, Kane Co.

MURPHY, HUPP, FOOTE, MIELKE AND KINNALLY (AV)

North Island Center, P.O. Box 5030, 60507
Telephone: 630-844-0056
Fax: 630-844-1905
Email: mhfmk@insnet.com

MEMBERS OF FIRM

William C. Murphy
Robert B. Hupp
Robert M. Foote
Craig S. Mielke
Patrick M. Kinnally
Paul G. Krentz
Joseph C. Loran
Gerald K. Hodge

Timothy D. O'Neil
Matthew J. Herman

Representative Clients: American Telephone & Telegraph Co.; Fox Valley Park District; Lyon Metal Products; Kane County Forest Preserve District; Hollywood Casino; Employers Mutual Insurance Co.; Forty-Eight Insulations, Inc.; UNR Asbestos Disease Trust; Richards-Wilcox Co.; National Bank & Trust Company of Syracuse.

For full biographical listings, see the Martindale-Hubbell Law Directory

*BELLEVILLE,** St. Clair Co.

DUNHAM, BOMAN & LESKERA (AV)

208 N. High, 62220
Telephone: 618-235-7222
Telecopier: 618-236-2800; 618-236-1899
Collinsville Office: 300 West Clay Street.
Telephone: 618-344-7734.
Telecopier: 618-344-3853.

M.F. Oehmke (1887-1963)
Wm. C. Dunham (1893-1975)
Howard Boman (1917-1985)
John W. Leskera
William L. Berry
Eric C. Young
Robert D. Francis
John L. Bitzer

Attorneys for: Collinsville School District #10; Hanover Insurance Co.; Hartford Insurance Group; State Farm Insurance Cos.; Transamerica Insurance Group; The Travelers Indemnity Co.; Wausau Insurance Cos.; Nationwide Insurance Co.; RLI Insurance Group.

For full biographical listings, see the Martindale-Hubbell Law Directory

NEVILLE, RICHARDS, DEFRANCO & WULLER (AV)

5 Park Place, 62226
Telephone: 618-277-0900
Facsimile: 618-277-0970
Email: nrdw@nrdw-law.com *URL:* http://www.nrdw-law.com

MEMBERS OF FIRM

James E. Neville
Timothy S. Richards
James E. DeFranco
Robert G. Wuller, Jr.

(See Next Column)

ASSOCIATES

Shari M. Brunton
Ellen M. Edmonds
Daniel L. Bradley
Matthew Charles Zittel

For full biographical listings, see the Martindale-Hubbell Law Directory

*BENTON,** Franklin Co.

HART AND HART (AV)

602 West Public Square, P.O. Box 937, 62812-0937
Telephone: 618-435-8123
Telecopier: 618-435-2962
URL: http://news2.intrnet.net/~hart/index.html

Richard O. Hart
Murphy C. Hart
A. Courtney Cox
Pamela Sue Lacey

ASSOCIATE

Jeffrey M. Feltman

Representative Clients: NationsBank; Illinois Central Railroad; State Bankof Whittington; Healthcare Revenue Management, Inc.; Credit Bureau Systems, Inc.; Lloyd's of London, England; Hospital & Physician Publishing, Inc.; Players International, Inc.; Laidlaw Corporation; Walgreen Distribution Centers.

For Complete List of Firm Personnel, See General Section

For full biographical listings, see the Martindale-Hubbell Law Directory

*CARLINVILLE,** Macoupin Co.

PHELPS, KASTEN, RUYLE, BURNS, CARMODY & SIMS (AV)

130 East Main Street, P.O. Box 587, 62626
Telephone: 217-854-3283
FAX: 217-854-9527
Email: pkrb@accunet.net

MEMBERS OF FIRM

Edward R. Phelps (1904-1985)
John W. Russell (Retired)
Carl E. Kasten
Nancy L. Ruyle
Thomas P. Burns
Stephen R. Carmody
Byron J. Sims

Representative Clients: Carlinville National Bank; Blackburn University; Area Diesel Service, Inc.; H & H Construction Services, Inc.

For full biographical listings, see the Martindale-Hubbell Law Directory

*CHICAGO,** Cook Co.

ABRAMSON & FOX (AV)

One East Wacker Drive, 60601
Telephone: 312-644-8500
Fax: 644-0798
Email: AandF1@aol.com
Evergreen, Colorado Office: 1202 Highway 74.
Telephone: 303-674-1328.
Fax: 303-674-0437.

MEMBERS OF FIRM

Floyd H. Abramson
Donald P. Colleton
John K. Eggers (1936-1991)
Joseph C. Grayson
Richard S. Hartford
Anthony P. Janik

OF COUNSEL

John J. Alioto
Robert J. Amedeo (Resident, Evergreen, Colorado Office)
Renato L. Amponin
James L. Fox
Jacob N. Gross (Ltd.)
Richard Hirschtritt
Anthony R. Hofeld
Malcolm S. Kamin
Juris Kins
Marc R. Kromelow

For full biographical listings, see the Martindale-Hubbell Law Directory

ALBERT, WHITEHEAD & MCGAUGH, P.C. (AV)

One South Wacker Drive, Suite 1990, 60606
Telephone: 312-357-6300
Fax: 312-357-6219

Charles G. Albert
Laurie D. Jaffe
Robert Kinchen

Allison L. Wood

For full biographical listings, see the Martindale-Hubbell Law Directory

ANESI, OZMON, RODIN, NOVAK & KOHEN, LTD. (AV)

161 North Clark Street, 21st Floor, 60601
Telephone: 312-372-3822
Fax: 312-372-3833

Nat P. Ozmon
Curt N. Rodin
Mark Novak
Bruce M. Kohen
Douglas A. Colby
Joseph J. Miroballi
Marc A. Taxman
Daniel V. O'Connor

(See Next Column)

ANESI, OZMON, RODIN, NOVAK & KOHEN LTD., *Chicago—Continued*

David J. Comeau
Alain Leval
Scott H. Rudin
John A. Salzeider
Telly C. Nakos
Martin J. Lucas
John M. Popelka
Edward D. D'Arcy, Jr.
Paul W. Pasche
Mark Murnane
Samantha Kavathas
Bruce D. Ogron
James G. McCarthy
Steven A. Berman
Peter J. Stavropoulos
George G. Argionis
Steven W. Burrows
Andrew M. DeLuca
Bradley Michael Arnold
Michael P. Hellman

OF COUNSEL

Noel C. Lindenmuth
Irving D. Fasman
Charles E. Anesi (1912-1995)
Richard A. Lewin (1925-1985)

For full biographical listings, see the Martindale-Hubbell Law Directory

ARONBERG GOLDGEHN DAVIS & GARMISA (AV)

Suite 3000 One IBM Plaza, 60611
Telephone: 312-828-9600
Telecopier: 312-828-9635
Email: agdglaw@aol.com
Schaumberg, Illinois Office: 1901 North Roselle Road, Suite 800, 60195.
Telephone: 847-985-4060.

MEMBERS OF FIRM

Christopher J. Bannon
Jay A. Frank
Mitchell S. Goldgehn
James J. Hickey
Nathan H. Lichtenstein
Marc W. O'Brien
Tami J. Reding-Brubaker
John M. Riccione
David H. Sachs
James A. Smith

ASSOCIATES

Lisa J. Brodsky
Howard J. Fishman
Paul A. Greenberg
Elizabeth Olen Lazzara
William J. Serritella, Jr.

For Complete List of Firm Personnel, See General Section
For full biographical listings, see the Martindale-Hubbell Law Directory

BATES MECKLER BULGER & TILSON (AV)

8300 Sears Tower, 233 South Wacker, 60606
Telephone: 312-474-7900
Facsimile: 312-474-7898
URL: http://www.bmbt.com

MEMBER OF FIRM

Brian J Williams

ASSOCIATES

Dawn M. Gonzalez
J. Robert Hall
Eric E. Newman
Joseph P. Pozen
(Not admitted in IL)

OF COUNSEL

Matthew M. Murphy

For full biographical listings, see the Martindale-Hubbell Law Directory

BECKER & KAPLAN LLC (AV)

19 South La Salle Street Suite 1500, 60603
Telephone: 312-621-9500
Fax: 312-621-9011
Email: firm@beckerkaplan.com *URL:* http://www.beckerkaplan.com

Theodore M. Becker
Daniel S. Kaplan

Edward R. White
Michael J. Boxerman

For full biographical listings, see the Martindale-Hubbell Law Directory

BLATT, HAMMESFAHR & EATON (AV)

333 W. Wacker Drive, Suite 1900, 60606
Telephone: 312-849-8000
FAX: 312-357-0198
Email: BHE@BHELAW.COM *URL:* HTTP://WWW.BHELAW.COM
New York, New York Office: 45 Broadway, 12th Floor.
Telephone: 212-363-1900.
Fax: 212-363-2600. Email: bhe@bhelaw.com.

MEMBERS OF FIRM

Richard L. Blatt
Joan S. Callan
Zacarias R. Chacon
Hugo Chaviano
Larry R. Eaton
Robert W. Hammesfahr
Gregory D. Hopp
Josh M. Kantrow
Kathleen A. McQueeny
Catherine A. T. Nelson
Lori S. Nugent
Matthew T. Walsh

(See Next Column)

ASSOCIATES

Kristy L. Allen
Mary I. Babbo
Jennifer L. Barron
Lesley A. Dable
Keith B. Daniels, Jr.
Robin Christine Dusek
Eli A. Franks
Peggy A. Glenn
Frederic C. Goodwill, II
Ryan M. Henderson
John A. Leja
Bruce M. Lichtcsien
Joseph G. Lyons
Marc A. Polansky
Leena Soni

For full biographical listings, see the Martindale-Hubbell Law Directory

CARPONELLI & KRUG (AV)

Suite 2350, 55 West Monroe Street, 60603
Telephone: 312-372-2707
Fax: 312-641-6174
Email: eastonlaw@aol.com *URL:* http://www.lawyers.com/carponellikrug

Stephen P. Carponelli
Robert F. Krug, Jr.

Gregory J. Chinlund
Don F. Taylor

For full biographical listings, see the Martindale-Hubbell Law Directory

CLARK & DEGRAND (AV)

One South Wacker Drive, Suite 1495, 60606-4616
Telephone: 312-425-0500
Fax: 312-425-0501
Email: CandDeG@aol.com

MEMBERS OF FIRM

Donald C. Clark, Jr.
Luke DeGrand
Jennifer S. Holloway

ASSOCIATE

Tracey L. Wolfe

For full biographical listings, see the Martindale-Hubbell Law Directory

CLIFFORD LAW OFFICES, P.C. (AV)

120 North La Salle Street, 31st Floor, 60602
Telephone: 312-899-9090
1-800-899-0410
Fax: 312-251-1160
Email: RACA@CliffordLaw.com *URL:* http://www.cliffordlaw.com

Robert A. Clifford
Keith A. Hebeisen
Kevin P. Durkin
Thomas K. Prindable

Robert P. Walsh, Jr.
Susan A. Capra
Jeffrey J. Kroll
Richard F. Burke, Jr.
Matthew I. Baker
Timothy P. Rhatigan
Isobel S. Thomas
Michael S. Krzak
Timothy S. Tomasik
Brian Thomas Nash
Donald James Storino III
Sheri L. Tarr

OF COUNSEL

Robert P. Sheridan

For full biographical listings, see the Martindale-Hubbell Law Directory

CONNELLY & SCHROEDER (AV)

One North Franklin Street, Suite 1200, 60606-3421
Telephone: 312-251-9600
Fax: 312-251-9601
Geneva, Illinois Office: 1250 Executive Place, Suite 201.
Telephone: 630-232-6440.
FAX: 630-232-6450

MEMBERS OF FIRM

Michael P. Connelly
John L. Schroeder
(Resident, Geneva Office)
Thomas F. Tobin
Raymond E. Stachnik
Daniel F. Konicek
(Also at Geneva Office)
Eugene S. Kraus
Mary Lisa Kamins
Brandt R. Madsen
Robert J. Kartholl, Jr.

ASSOCIATES

Michelle L. Adams
(Resident, Geneva Office)
Matthew Patrick Connelly
Thomas W. Dillon
(Resident, Geneva Office)
John Michael Kelly
Colleen Konicek
Charina de los Reyes
Carolyn A. Schroeder
(Resident, Geneva)
Martha Swatek
(Resident, Geneva Office)

For full biographical listings, see the Martindale-Hubbell Law Directory

CORBOY & DEMETRIO, P.C. (AV)

33 North Dearborn Street 21st Floor, 60602
Telephone: 312-346-3191
FAX: 312-346-5562
TDD: 312-236-3191
Email: phc9@corboydemetrio.com *URL:* http://www.corboydemetrio.com

(See Next Column)

CORBOY & DEMETRIO P.C.—*Continued*

Philip H. Corboy
Thomas A. Demetrio
Philip Harnett Corboy, Jr.

Robert J. Bingle
Francis Patrick Murphy
Susan J. Schwartz
Michael K. Demetrio
Kevin G. Burke
Michael G. Mahoney

Thomas F. Boleky
Barry R. Chafetz
G. Grant Dixon III
Shawn S. Kasserman
Tilden Katz
Thomas A. Killoren, Jr.
Daniel S. Kirschner
Daniel M. Kotin
Kenneth T. Lumb
Cyril J. McIlhargie
Michelle Elyse Meklir
Michael K. Muldoon
Margaret M. Power
Linda Marie Roeback
Edward G. Willer
David C. Wise

Reference: The American National Bank & Trust Company, Chicago, Illinois.

For full biographical listings, see the Martindale-Hubbell Law Directory

JAMES E. DAHL & ASSOCIATES (AV)

Suite 1125, 225 West Washington Street, 60606
Telephone: 312-641-3245
Fax: 312-641-1662
Email: dahlfirm@aol.com

ASSOCIATES

Paul N. Bonadies
Brian Michael Nach
Michael J. Lynch

OF COUNSEL

Walter P. Dahl

For full biographical listings, see the Martindale-Hubbell Law Directory

FIGLIULO & SILVERMAN, P.C. (AV)

10 South La Salle Street, Suite 3600, 60603
Telephone: 312-251-4600
Fax: 312-251-4610

James R. Figliulo
Peter A. Silverman
Carl A. Gigante
Brian P. Liston
Marc S. Porter
James H. Bowhay

James J. Sipchen, Jr.
Adam E. Bossov
Michael K. Desmond

For full biographical listings, see the Martindale-Hubbell Law Directory

FORAN & SCHULTZ (AV)

Suite 3000, 30 North La Salle Street, 60602
Telephone: 312-368-8330
Fax: 312-580-2600
Email: law@foran.com *URL:* http://www.Foran.com

MEMBERS OF FIRM

Thomas A. Foran
Richard G. Schultz
Stephen A. Gorman
Jeff D. Harris
Jack J. Carriglio
Steven H. Gistenson
Brooke R. Whitted
Jeffrey C. Blumenthal
Teresa F. Frisbie

ASSOCIATES

Daniel D. Kasten
Paul A. Henmueller
Jessica D. Klein
Robert B. Slocum
Charles M. Baum
George K. Katsoudas
John R. Flynn
Lara A. Cleary

OF COUNSEL

Harry G. Comerford
Robert J. Weber
Lauren B. Schreeder

References: American National Bank and Trust Co. of Chicago; Amalgamated Trust and Savings Bank.

For full biographical listings, see the Martindale-Hubbell Law Directory

FRANCZEK SULLIVAN P.C. (AV)

Suite 3400, 300 South Wacker Drive, 60606-6785
Telephone: 312-986-0300
FAX: 312-986-9192
URL: http://www.nlfpc.com

Anthony J. Crement
J. Todd Faulkner
James C. Franczek, Jr.
Ronald J. Hein, Jr.
Lisa A. Lopatka
Bruce C. Mackey
Robert E. Mann
Paul A. Millichap
David P. Radelet
John A. Relias
Michael I. Richardson
Charles P. Rose

(*See Next Column*)

Sally J. Scott
William R. Sullivan, Jr.
Andrea R. Waintroob
Patricia J. Whitten
James J. Zuehl

Shelli L. Boyer
Sheila M. Conroy
Terrence T. Creamer
Erika Dillon
Edward N. Druck
Gregory D. Isbell
Thomas Koutsouvas
Darcy L. Kriha
Jeffrey M. Kropp
Jeremy C. Moritz
Alec Rubenstein
Leah D. Gidron
Jennifer L. Schilling
Michael A. Warner, Jr.
Anne Elizabeth Wilson

OF COUNSEL

Michael Z. Green
Wesley A. Wildman
John L. Wren

LEGAL SUPPORT PERSONNEL

Caty E. Kearney

For full biographical listings, see the Martindale-Hubbell Law Directory

GESSLER, HUGHES & SOCOL, LTD. (AV)

Three First National Plaza, Suite 2200, 60602
Telephone: 312-580-0100
Telecopy: 312-580-1994

Benjamin P. Beringer
Anjali Dayal
Mark S. Dym
George W. Gessler
John K. Hughes
Joshua Karsh
Peter M. Katsaros
Kimberley Marsh
Alex W. Miller
Terence J. Moran
Matthew J. Piers
Kalman D. Resnick
Frederick S. Rhine
Jonathan A. Rothstein
Michael P. Simkus
Donna Kaner Socol

Gary Chodorow
Ruth M. Dunning
S. Todd Neal
Mark A. Pellegrino
Steven C. Steinback
Dana H. Sukenik
J. Eric Vander Arend
Mark B. Weiner
Charles H. Wintersteen

OF COUNSEL

Darius S. Francescatti, M.D.
Susan R. Gzesh

For full biographical listings, see the Martindale-Hubbell Law Directory

MICHAEL T. HANNAFAN & ASSOCIATES, LTD. (AV)

One East Wacker Drive, Suite 2710, 60601
Telephone: 312-527-0055
Fax: 312-527-0220
Email: mthannafan@aol.com

Michael T. Hannafan

Cory A. Johnson

Reference: The Northern Trust Co.

For full biographical listings, see the Martindale-Hubbell Law Directory

HARRINGTON, THOMPSON, ACKER & HARRINGTON, LTD. (AV)

310 South Michigan Avenue, Suite 2000, 60604
Telephone: 312-922-8833

Robert E. Harrington, Jr.
Robert B. Thompson
Laurence C. Acker
Patrick J. Harrington
Kenneth J. Sophie, Jr.
Monica A. Coscia
Christy L. LeVan
James K. Schultz
Vincent B. Browne
John B. Corso
Christopher S. Crawford

Reference: American National Bank and Trust Co., Chicago, Illinois.

For full biographical listings, see the Martindale-Hubbell Law Directory

WILLIAM J. HARTE, LTD. (AV)

Suite 1100, 111 West Washington Street, 60602
Telephone: 312-726-5015
Fax: 312-641-1288

William J. Harte

Sylvia A. Sotiras
Erik D. Gruber
Stephen L. Garcia
Joan M. Mannix

OF COUNSEL

Daniel K. Schlorf
David J. Walker
P. A. Sorrentino
Robert L. Tucker

For full biographical listings, see the Martindale-Hubbell Law Directory

Chicago—Continued

HASKELL & PERRIN (AV)

200 West Adams, Suite 2600, 60606
Telephone: 312-781-9393
Fax: 312-781-9178
Email: hasper@haskellperrin.com

MEMBERS OF FIRM

James Kirk Perrin
John J. Lynch
Mary Elizabeth Denefe

OF COUNSEL

Donald M. Haskell

ASSOCIATE

Nancy J. Robinson

For full biographical listings, see the Martindale-Hubbell Law Directory

JOHNSON & BELL, LTD. (AV)

Suite 2200, 222 North La Salle Street, 60601
Telephone: 312-372-0770
Facsimile: 312-372-9818
Waukegan, Illinois Office: Nine North County Street, Suite G-1, 60085.
Telephone: 847-662-7458.
Facsimile: 847-662-7366.
Highland, Indiana Office: 900 Indianapolis Boulevard, Suite A, 46322.
Telephone: 219-923-5250.
Facsimile: 219-923-6170.

William V. Johnson
John W. Bell
Jack T. Riley, Jr.
Brian C. Fetzer
Thomas H. Fegan
Thomas J. Andrews
William G. Beatty
John A. Childers
Margaret A. Unger
Howard Patrick Morris
Scott W. Hoyne
James S. Stickles, Jr.
Frederick S. Mueller
Joseph R. Marconi
Robert M. Burke
Kurt C. Meihofer
Glenn F. Fencl
Cornelius J. Harrington, III
David J. Loughnane
Michael P. Siavelis
William A. Geiser
Kevin G. Owens
Dennis C. Cusack
Charles P. Rantis
Robert J. Comfort
Alan Jay Goldstein
Steven B. Novy
Daniel C. Murray
William K. McVisk
Joseph F. Spitzzeri
Joseph B. Carini, III
Kathryn K. Loft
Gregory D. Conforti
Frank P. Nowicki
Frank S. Gildea
Joseph J. McNerney
Gregory E. Schiller
Howard W. Foster
William J. Anaya
Robert R. McNamara
Marilyn McCabe Reidy
William B. Bower

W. Gregory Aimonette
Michael J. Burns
Timothy R. Couture
Patrick T. Garvey
Laura B. Glaser
Stefanie R. Glover
Guy Halpern
Susan W. Horn
Mark D. Johnson
Matthew L. Johnson
Mindy L. Kallus
Mary Kenney
Andrew J. Kovarik
Richard P. Long
David M. Macksey
Steven A. Marderosian
Julie M. McClelland
Laura J. McGrath
Victor Michel
Susan V. Nordheim
Michael A. Pauletto
Lynn M. Reid
Joseph D. Ryan
Todd M. Saranecki
Charlene M. Sheridan
Ann M. Smith
Robert Spitkovsky, Jr.
Terry Takash
Kendra A. Thramann
Kelly N. Warnick
Steven D. Welhouse
David A. Wilford
David A. Wilson (Resident, Highland, Indiana Office)
Steven F. Wittman
Jennifer D. Yoder (Resident, Highland, Indiana Office)

References available upon request.

For full biographical listings, see the Martindale-Hubbell Law Directory

JONES, DAY, REAVIS & POGUE (AV)

77 West Wacker, 60601-1692
Telephone: 312-782-3939
Telecopier: 312-782-8585
Email: counsel@jonesday.com *URL:* http://www.jonesday.com
In Atlanta, Georgia: 3500 SunTrust Plaza, 303 Peachtree Street.
Telephone: 404-521-3939.
Telecopier: 404-581-8330. 34000 Brussels, Belgium: Avenue Louise 480, 7th Floor, B-1050 Brussels.
Telephone: 32-2-645-14-11.
Telecopier: 32-2-645-14-45.
In Cleveland, Ohio: North Point, 901 Lakeside Avenue.
Telephone: 216-586-3939.
Telecopier: 216-579-0212.
In Columbus, Ohio: 1900 Huntington Center.
Telephone: 614-469-3939.
Telecopier: 614-461-4198.

(See Next Column)

In Dallas, Texas: 2727 North Harwood Street.
Telephone: 214-220-3939.
Telecopier: 214-969-5100.
In Frankfurt, Germany: Hochhaus am Park, Grüneburgweg 102, 60323 Frankfurt am Main.
Telephone: 49-69-9726-3939.
Telecopier: 49-69-9726-3993.
In Geneva, Switzerland: 20, rue de Candolle.
Telephone: 41-22-320-2339.
Telecopier: 41-22-320-1232.
In Hong Kong: 29th Floor, Entertainment Building, 30 Queen's Road Central.
Telephone: 852-2526-6895.
Telecopier: 852-2868-5871 or 852-2868-5699.
In Irvine, California: 5 Park Plaza, Suite 1100.
Telephone: 949-851-3939.
Telecopier: 949-553-7539.
In London, England: Bucklersbury House, 3 Queen Victoria Street.
Telephone: 44-171-236-3939.
Telecopier: 44-171-236-1113.
In Los Angeles, California: 555 West Fifth Street, Suite 4600.
Telephone: 213-489-3939.
Telecopier: 213-243-2539.
In New Delhi, India (Associate Office): Pathak & Associates (an associate firm of Jones, Day, Reavis & Pogue), 1st Floor, Dr. Gopal Das Bhaven, 28 Barakhamba Road.
Telephone: 91-11-373-8793; 91-11-335-7345.
Telecopier: 91-11-335-3761.
In New York, New York: 599 Lexington Avenue.
Telephone: 212-326-3939.
Telecopier: 212-755-7306.
In Paris, France: 120, rue du Faubourg Saint-Honoré.
Telephone: 33-1-56-59-39-39.
Telecopier: 33-1-56-59-39-38
In Pittsburgh, Pennsylvania: 500 Grant Street, 31st Floor.
Telephone: 412-391-3939.
Telecopier: 412-394-7959.
In Riyadh, Saudi Arabia: The International Law Firm (In Association with Jones, Day, Reavis & Pogue), Sulaymaniyah, Prince Mishari IBN, Abdulaziz Street, P.O. Box 22166.
Telephone: (966-1) 462-8866.
Telecopier: (966-1) 462-9001.
In Shanghai, China: 2805 Kerry Centre, 1515 Nanjing Road West.
Telephone: 86-21-5298-6568.
Telecopier: 86-21-5298-6569.
In Sydney, Australia: Governor Phillip Tower, Level 38, 1 Farrer Place.
Telephone: 61-2-9210-6921.
Telecopier: 61-2-9210-6926.
In Taipei, Taiwan: 8th Floor, 2 Tun Hwa South Road, Section 2.
Telephone: (886-2) 2704-6808.
Telecopier: (886-2) 2704-6791.
In Tokyo, Japan: Toranomon MT Building, 4th Floor, 10-3, Toranomon 3-Chome, 34200o-ku, Tokyo 105, Japan.
Telephone: 81-3-3433-3939.
Telecopier: 81-3-5401-2725.
In Washington, D.C.: 51 Louisiana Avenue, N.W.
Telephone: 202-879-3939.
Telecopier: 202-626-1700.

MEMBERS OF FIRM IN CHICAGO

Thomas F. Gardner
David L. Carden

For Complete List of Firm Personnel, See General Section

For full biographical listings, see the Martindale-Hubbell Law Directory

KIESLER & BERMAN (AV)

Suite 1300, 188 West Randolph Street, 60601
Telephone: 312-332-2840
FAX: 312-332-4547
Email: info@thekillerbees.com *URL:* http://www.kieslerberman.com
Wheaton Office: 2100 Manchester, Suite 605.
Telephone: 630-752-8247.
Fax: 630-752-9587.
Joliet Office: 57 West Jefferson Street.
Telephone: 815-723-2755.
Fax: 815-723-2763.
Waukegan Office: 216 Madison Street.
Telephone: 847-244-5805.
Fax: 847-244-3996.

FOUNDERS

Marvin D. Berman
Robert L. Kiesler

MEMBERS OF FIRM

Stephen B. Frew (Managing Partner)
Clinton J. Feil
Alan P. Miller
John R. Garofalo
Dale L. Schlafer
Lyle F. Koester
Mark S. Vilimek
Rory D. Cassidy
Patti Olson Deuel
David J. Kiesler
Jeffrey S. Pavlovich
John J. Piegore
Pamela K. Harman

SENIOR TRIAL COUNSEL

Edward L. Cooper

(See Next Column)

KIESLER & BERMAN—*Continued*

ASSOCIATES

Donna D. Ciancio
Donald E. Elder
Mary E. Haeger
Shari J. Kalik
Thomas J. Kanyock
Bryan W. Luce
William P. McElligott
Peter R. Mennella
Shannon F. O'Shea
John P. Palumbo
Jeanne M. Zeiger

SENIOR COUNSEL

Frank N. Rago

For full biographical listings, see the Martindale-Hubbell Law Directory

LAWRENCE, KAMIN, SAUNDERS & UHLENHOP (AV)

208 South La Salle Street, Suite 1750, 60604-1188
Telephone: 312-372-1947
Telecopier: 312-372-2389
Email: LKSU@LKSU.com

MEMBERS OF FIRM

Paul B. Uhlenhop
Kent Lawrence
David E. Muschler
Charles J. Risch
Lawrence A. Rosen
Michael Wise
David L. Reich

ASSOCIATES

Peter E. Cooper
John S. Monical
Paul M. Weltlich

OF COUNSEL

Robert J. Lawrence

For full biographical listings, see the Martindale-Hubbell Law Directory

NORMAN J. LERUM (AV)

Suite 2100, 100 West Monroe Street, 60603
Telephone: 312-782-1087
Facsimile: 312-332-6020
Email: lerum@martindalemail.com *URL:* http://www.lawyers.com/lerumlaw

For full biographical listings, see the Martindale-Hubbell Law Directory

SUSAN E. LOGGANS & ASSOCIATES, P.C. (AV)

Suite 2850, 200 West Madison Street, 60606
Telephone: 312-201-8600
Telecopier: 312-201-1180
Email: loggans@logganslaw.com *URL:* http://www.logganslaw.com

Susan E. Loggans

James G. McConnell
Gregg E. Strellis
John T. Ferjak
Patrick D. Flanagan
Norman L. Rubenstein

For full biographical listings, see the Martindale-Hubbell Law Directory

MACCABE & MCGUIRE (AV)

Suite 3333, 77 West Wacker Drive, 60601
Telephone: 312-357-2600
Fax: 312-357-0317
Email: MacMcLaw77@aol.com

MEMBERS OF FIRM

Edward H. MacCabe
Maureen A. McGuire

ASSOCIATES

Timothy J. Murphy
Diedre S. Dunn
Margaret T. Conway

OF COUNSEL

Brian J. Mulhern

For full biographical listings, see the Martindale-Hubbell Law Directory

MANDEL, LIPTON AND STEVENSON LIMITED (AV)

Suite 2900, 120 North La Salle Street, 60602
Telephone: 312-236-7080
Facsimile: 312-236-0781

Alfred R. Lipton
Leonard M. Malkin
R. Peter Carey
Henry A. Waller
Kathleen Roseborough
Richard A. Lifshitz
Terry Yale Feiertag
Uve R. Jerzy
Carolyn E. Winter
Leo G. Aubel

Andrés J. Gallegos
Jennifer R. Shapiro
Joan Comiskey

OF COUNSEL

Richard L. Mandel
Nicholas Stevenson

(See Next Column)

LEGAL SUPPORT PERSONNEL

Jacqueline Steffens (Paralegal)

References: Northern Trust Co.; American National Bank of Chicago; La Salle Bank FSB.

For full biographical listings, see the Martindale-Hubbell Law Directory

MCFADDEN & DILLON, A PROFESSIONAL CORPORATION (AV)

135 South La Salle Street, Suite 2110, 60603-4402
Telephone: 312-201-8300
Facsimile: 312-201-0535
Email: mcfaddendillonlaw@ameritech.net

Roger J. McFadden
Thomas J. Dillon

Tyrrel J. Penn

For full biographical listings, see the Martindale-Hubbell Law Directory

THE LAW OFFICES OF MUNDAY & NATHAN (AV)

33 North Dearborn Street, Suite 2220, 60602
Telephone: 312-346-5678
Fax: 312-346-8394

John J. Munday
Thomas J. Nathan

Edward G. Proctor, Jr.
Jeffrey A. Schulkin

For full biographical listings, see the Martindale-Hubbell Law Directory

BERNARD R. NEVORAL AND ASSOCIATES LTD. (AV)

150 North Wacker Drive, Suite 2450, 60606
Telephone: 312 263-7058
FAX: 312-263-4566

Bernard R. Nevoral

Jeremy Michael West
Daniel M. Extrom
David F Szczecin

For full biographical listings, see the Martindale-Hubbell Law Directory

NOLAN LAW GROUP (AV)

One North La Salle Street, 35th Floor, 60602
Telephone: 312-372-5400
Toll Free: 888-372-3870
Facsimile: 312-372-0558
Email: dnolan1@ix.netcom.com

Donald J. Nolan
Albert E. Durkin, Jr.
William J. Jovan
Floyd A. Wisner
James H. Lawlor, III
Thomas P. Routh
James A. Santucci
Todd R. Mcquiston

Laura L. Ruhl

For full biographical listings, see the Martindale-Hubbell Law Directory

NOVACK AND MACEY (AV)

303 West Madison Street, Suite 1500, 60606
Telephone: 312-419-6900
Fax: 312-419-6928
URL: http://www.novackandmacey.com

MEMBERS OF FIRM

Bruce E. Braverman
P. Andrew Fleming
Karen Levine
Eric N. Macey
Mitchell L. Marinello
Timothy J. Miller
Stephen Novack
Stephen J. Siegel
Donald A. Tarkington
Michael A. Weinberg

ASSOCIATES

Peter T. Berk
Gillian Dworsky Madsen
R. Peter Nessen
Michael D. Paley
Joel S. Schreier
Peter D. Zarov
Shelby L. Zweig

For full biographical listings, see the Martindale-Hubbell Law Directory

STEPHEN M. PASSEN, LTD. (AV)

Suite 2525 One IBM Plaza, 60611
Telephone: 312-527-4500
Facsimile: 312-527-4435
Email: spassen@IBM.net *URL:* http://www.lawyers.com/passenlaw

Stephen M. Passen

John J. Driscoll

For full biographical listings, see the Martindale-Hubbell Law Directory

Chicago—Continued

PAVALON, GIFFORD, LAATSCH & MARINO (AV)
Two North La Salle Street, Suite 1600, 60602
Telephone: 312-419-7400
Fax: 312-419-7408
Email: pavgif@aol.com
Rockford, Illinois Office: 501 Seventh Street, Suite 501, 61104.
Telephone: 815-968-5100.

MEMBERS OF FIRM

Eugene I. Pavalon
Geoffrey L. Gifford
Gary K. Laatsch
Frank C. Marino
Henry Phillip Gruss

Christine Walsh Donnelly

For full biographical listings, see the Martindale-Hubbell Law Directory

POWER ROGERS & SMITH, P.C. (AV)
35 West Wacker Drive, Suite 3700, 60601
Telephone: 312-236-9381
Fax: 312-236-0920

Joseph A. Power, Jr.
Larry R. Rogers
Todd A. Smith

Thomas G. Siracusa
Paul L. Salzetta
Thomas M. Power
Larry R. Rogers, Jr.
Ruth M. Degnan
Devon C. Bruce

For full biographical listings, see the Martindale-Hubbell Law Directory

RICHARD J. PRENDERGAST, LTD. (AV)
111 West Washington-Suite 1100, 60602-2768
Telephone: 312-641-0881
Fax: 312-641-3562
Email: rprendergastltd@msn.com *URL:* http://www.lawyers.com/prendergast

Richard J. Prendergast
James Prendergast

Ellen M. Murphy
Michael T. Layden
Deirdre Ann Close

For full biographical listings, see the Martindale-Hubbell Law Directory

QUARLES & BRADY LLC (AV)
Citicorp Center, 500 West Madison Street, Suite 3700, 60661-2511
Telephone: 312-715-5000
Fax: 312-715-5155
URL: http://www.quarles.com
Milwaukee, Wisconsin Office: Quarles & Brady LLP, 411 East Wisconsin Avenue, 53202-4497.
Telephone: 414-277-5000.
Fax: 414-271-3552.
Madison, Wisconsin Office: Quarles & Brady LLP, Firstar Plaza, One South Pinckney Street, P.O. Box 2113, 53701-2113.
Telephone: 608-251-5000.
Fax: 608-251-9166.
West Palm Beach, Florida Office: Quarles & Brady LLP, 222 Lakeview Avenue, 4th Floor, 33401.
Telephone: 561-653-5000.
Fax: 561-653-5333.
Naples, Florida Office: Quarles & Brady LLP, Barnett Center, 4501 Tamiami Trail North, Suite 300, 34103-3060.
Telephone: 941-262-5959.
Fax: 941-434-4999.
Phoenix, Arizona Office: Quarles & Brady LLP, One Camelback Building, One East Camelback Road, Suite 400, 85012-1649.
Telephone: 602-230-5500.
Fax: 602-230-5598.

Richard L. Horn
Kendall R. Meyer
Robert F. Forrer
Leonard S. Shifflett
Thomas J. Magill
Alexander Terras
Timothy S. Harris
Todd A. Rowden

David B. Altman
Kurt T. Temple
Joel A. Brodsky

For Complete List of Firm Personnel, See General Section

For full biographical listings, see the Martindale-Hubbell Law Directory

QUINLAN & CRISHAM, LTD. (AV)
30 North La Salle Street, Suite 2900, 60602
Telephone: 312-263-0900
Telecopier: 312-263-5013

(See Next Column)

William R. Quinlan
Thomas M. Crisham
Thomas C. Hynes
Gino L. DiVito
Mary Patricia Benz
Michael C. Bruck
James R. Carroll
Thomas C. Hofbauer
John F. Kennedy
Jeffrey T. Kubes
Eugene E. Murphy, Jr.
Michael I Rothstein
Caesar A. Tabet
Cheryl I. Niro

Frank M. Adams, Jr.
Brian J. Alesia
Michael T. Beirne
Catherine J. Casey
Jasmine De La Torre
Karina H. DeHayes
Edward Fitzsimmons Dunne
Lisa M. Hegedus
Erin Bolan Hines
John N. Hourihane, Jr.
David M. Jenkins
J. Christopher Madden
Michelle A. Michalik
James A. Niewiara
Martin J. O'Hara
John P. O'Malley
J. Jeffrey Patton
Jean M. Prendergast
Melissa M. Riahei
John H. Scheid
Daniel L. Stanner
Michael A. Steigmann

For full biographical listings, see the Martindale-Hubbell Law Directory

ROSENTHAL AND SCHANFIELD, PROFESSIONAL CORPORATION (AV)
Suite 4620, 55 East Monroe Street, 60603
Telephone: 312-236-5622
Telecopier: 312-236-7274

Cheryl J. Colston
James M. Dash
James A. Field
Barbara A. Gimbel
Jay Russell Goldberg
David A. Golin
Meanith Huon
William H. Kelly, Jr.
Stephen P. Kikoler
Ira M. Levin
David Manjarres
Gregory R. Meeder
Howard L. Mocerf
Gerald B. Mullin
Joseph R. Podlewski, Jr.
Mark L. Shapiro

OF COUNSEL

Monte Viner

For Complete List of Firm Personnel, See General Section

For full biographical listings, see the Martindale-Hubbell Law Directory

RUSIN PATTON MACIOROWSKI & FRIEDMAN, LTD. (AV)
Suite 1530 10 South Riverside Plaza, 60606
Telephone: 312-454-5110
Fax: 312-454-6166
Urbana, Illinois Office: 301 West Green Street, P.O. Box 985, 61803-0985.
Telephone: 217-328-7091.
Fax: 217-328-7093.

Michael E. Rusin
Stephen J. Friedman
John W. Patton Jr.
John A. Maciorowski
Kenneth N. Marshall
Gregory G. Vacala
Daniel Arkin
Randall R. Stark

Anuradha Y Boyapati
Todd A. Bresney
Luke A. Casson
R. Mark Cosimini (Resident, Urbana Office)
Daniel R. Egan
Frederick Scott Glassman
William J. Harrington
Daniel P. Johnston
David M. Lewin
Theodore James Powers
Gregory A. Rode
Mark P. Rusin
David F. Ryan
Douglas Sullivan
Edward R. Tomkowiak
Cynthia M. Wallach
Catherine A. Zaryczny

For full biographical listings, see the Martindale-Hubbell Law Directory

SAUNDERS & MONROE (AV)
1600 NBC Tower, 455 North Cityfront Plaza Drive, 60611
Telephone: 312-645-6000
Fax: 312-645-9848

MEMBERS OF FIRM

George L. Saunders, Jr.
Lee A. Monroe
Thomas F. Bush, Jr.
Matthew E. Van Tine
Thomas A. Doyle

OF COUNSEL

Victoria S. Kaplan

For full biographical listings, see the Martindale-Hubbell Law Directory

LAW OFFICES OF EDMUND J. SCANLAN, LTD. (AV)
134 North La Salle Street, Suite 1700, 60602
Telephone: 312-372-0020
Fax: 312-372-1211
URL: http://www.lawyers.com/edmundjscanlanltd

Edmund J. Scanlan

(See Next Column)

LAW OFFICES OF EDMUND J. SCANLAN, LTD.—*Continued*

Mario C. Palermo

For full biographical listings, see the Martindale-Hubbell Law Directory

SCARIANO, ELLCH, HIMES, SRAGA AND PETRARCA, CHARTERED (AV)

Two Prudential Plaza 180 North Stetson Suite 3100, 60601-6224
Telephone: 312-565-3100
Facsimile: 312-565-0000
Chicago Heights, Illinois Office: 1450 Aberdeen, 60411.
Telephone: 708-755-1900.
Facsimile: 708-755-0000.

Anthony G. Scariano
Robert H. Ellch
A. Lynn Himes
Alan T. Sraga
Justino D. Petrarca
Lawrence Jay Weiner
John M. Izzo
Raymond A. Hauser
Kathleen Roche Hirsman
Daniel M. Boyle
Teri E. Engler
Rosanne Ciambrone

Kelly A. Hayden
Todd K. Hayden
Christopher L. Petrarca
Sarah E. Joyce
Joel R. DeTella
Susan H. Walter (Resident)
Brian J. Fahey
David A. Harley
Bradley C. Coleman
Christina Sepiol
Alan M. Mullins
John E. Fester
Michael Alan DeBartolo

OF COUNSEL

John Kralovec

For full biographical listings, see the Martindale-Hubbell Law Directory

JOHN B. SCHWARTZ & ASSOCIATES (AV)

Suite 408, Thirty-Nine South La Salle Street, 60603
Telephone: 312-332-1586
Fax: 312-332-7009
Email: JSCHW888@aol.com

John B. Schwartz

ASSOCIATE

David J. Spira

OF COUNSEL

Thomas W. Duda

For full biographical listings, see the Martindale-Hubbell Law Directory

PETER R. SONDERBY, P.C. (AV)

135 South La Salle Street Suite 1424, 60603
Telephone: 312-201-0999
Fax: 312-201-0749; 201-4559
Email: Psond@starnetinc.com

Peter R. Sonderby

For full biographical listings, see the Martindale-Hubbell Law Directory

STONE & MOORE, CHARTERED (AV)

30 North La Salle Street, Suite 4300, 60602
Telephone: 312-332-5656
Fax: 312-332-5858
URL: http://www.stonemoore.com
Merrillville, Indiana Office: 500 E. 86th Avenue, 46410.
Telephone: 219-736-5959.
Fax: 219-736-5858.
Wheaton, Illinois Office: 600 W. Roosevelt Road, Suite 1A, 60187.
Telephone: 630-221-9292.
Fax: 630-221-9393.

William G. Stone
Robert Charles Moore (Also at Wheaton, Illinois Office)
Raymond R. Pesavento
Rosario Cibella
Richard M. Johnson, Jr.
J. Murray Pinkston, III
Julie Osswald Hooven

Christian D. Ambler
Jeffrey W. Henning
Erica Lewis Battaglia
Kevin Kemp Lyons
Kristin E. Rooney
Daniel S. Schulz
Matthew B. Stephens
A. Christine Svenson
Douglas W. Walker

For full biographical listings, see the Martindale-Hubbell Law Directory

PATRICIA A. STREETER (AV Ⓣ)

111 West Washington, Suite 1611, 60602-2710
Telephone: 312-372-4410
Fax: 312-372-4412
Email: PatStreeter@prodigy.net
Detroit, Michigan Office: 1817 Penobscot Building, 48226.
Telephone: 313-962-1177.
Fax: 313-962-0199.

For full biographical listings, see the Martindale-Hubbell Law Directory

STRIDE, CRADDOCK & STRIDE (AV)

111 West Washington Street, Suite 1837, 60602-2773
Telephone: 312-346-5800
Fax: 312-346-3870

Herbert F. Stride
J. Patrick Craddock
Herbert L. Stride

Nicholas C. Panos
Deborah A. Stride-Saran
Vickie Voukidis Blum
Michael J. Craddock
Arthur Z. Handelman

For full biographical listings, see the Martindale-Hubbell Law Directory

SUGAR, FRIEDBERG & FELSENTHAL (AV)

30 North La Salle Street, Suite 2600, 60602
Telephone: 312-704-9400
Telecopier: 312-372-7951
Cable: "SUGARFREE"

MEMBERS OF FIRM

Richard A. Sugar
Michael R. Friedberg
Steven A. Felsenthal
Andrew B. David
Leslie J. Weiss
Ira S. Neiman
Jonathan L. Mills
Etahn M. Cohen
Howard M. Helsinger
Robert F. Simon
Martin M. Weinstein
Charles H. Braun
Kathryn A. Erickson

ASSOCIATES

Aron L. Bornstein
Annette L. Brands
Kathryn T. Cha
Norman J. Ginsparg
William F. McGuinn
Suzanne J. Massel
Deanne Elizabeth Clarke

For full biographical listings, see the Martindale-Hubbell Law Directory

CRAIG D. TOBIN & ASSOCIATES (AV)

Three First National Plaza, Suite 535, 60602
Telephone: 312-641-1321
Fax: 312-641-5220
Email: ctobin@barristers.com

Craig D. Tobin

For full biographical listings, see the Martindale-Hubbell Law Directory

TRIBLER ORPETT & CRONE, A PROFESSIONAL CORPORATION (AV)

30 North La Salle Street, Suite 2200, 60602
Telephone: 312-201-6400
Fax: 312-201-6401
Email: to&c@tribler.com *URL:* http://www.tribler.com

John W. Carver
Douglas C. Crone
Steven R. McMannon
Michael J. Meyer
Mitchell A. Orpett
H. Wesley Sunu
Panos T. Topalis
Willis R. Tribler

Angela Coumas
Michael W. Donaubauer
David R. Edsey
Ana M. McNamara
Kevin A. Titus
William Yu

OF COUNSEL

Daniel D. Drew

For full biographical listings, see the Martindale-Hubbell Law Directory

WILDMAN, HARROLD, ALLEN & DIXON (AV)

225 West Wacker Drive, 30th Floor, 60606-1229
Telephone: 312-201-2000
Fax: 312-201-2555
Email: hennessy@whad.com *URL:* http://www.whad.com
Aurora, Illinois Office: 1961 W. Downer Place.
Telephone: 630-892-7021.
Fax: 630-892-7158.
Waukegan, Illinois Office: 404 West Water, P. O. Box 890.
Telephone: 847-625-5550.
Fax: 847-625-5555.
Lisle, Illinois Office: 4300 Commerce Court, Suite 320.
Telephone: 630-955-0555.
Fax: 630-955-0662

(See Next Column)

WILDMAN, HARROLD, ALLEN & DIXON, *Chicago—Continued*

Toronto, Ontario correspondent Office: Keel Cottrelle. 36 Toronto Street, Suite 920.
Telephone: 416-367-2900.
Telefax: 416-367-2791.
Telex: 062-18660.

MEMBERS OF FIRM

Richard C. Bartelt
James A. Christman
Steven E. Danekas
Robert E. Haley
Helaine Wachs Heydemann
Anthony G. Hopp
David A. Kanter
Steven L. Larson (Waukegan Office)
Donald R. McGarrah
Mark P. Miller
Timothy G. Nickels
Sarah L. Olson
Richard C. Palmer
David F. Pardys (Waukegan Office)
Douglas L. Prochnow
Robert A. Strelecky (Lisle Office)
James B. Vogts
Dale G. Wills

OF COUNSEL

Thomas D. Allen

Helen A. Contos (Lisle Office)
Lawrence W. Falbe
Michone J. Kuhlman (Waukegan Office)
Heather Huthwaite Martin
Martha D. Owens
Barbara M. Prohaska (Lisle Office)
Kevin B. Reid
John A. Terselic (Waukegan Office)

For full biographical listings, see the Martindale-Hubbell Law Directory

WILLIAMS & MONTGOMERY LTD. (AV)

20 North Wacker Drive Suite 2100, 60606
Telephone: 312-443-3200
Facsimile: 312-443-1323
Email: SERVICES@WILLMONT.COM
Waukegan, Illinois Office: 20 S. Utica.
Telephone: 847-360-1220.
Wheaton, Illinois Office: 310 S. County Farm Road.
Telephone: 630-690-3200.
Joliet, Illinois Office: 81 North Chicago Avenue.
Telephone: 815-727-2653.
Miami, Florida Office: Clarke, Silverglate, Williams and Montgomery, 100 North Biscayne Boulevard.
Telephone: 305-377-0700.
Facsimile: 305-377-3001.

Lloyd E. Williams, Jr.
C. Barry Montgomery
Thomas H. Neuckranz
Barry L. Kroll
Anthony P. Katauskas
David E. Morgans
Edward J. Murphy
Alton C. Haynes
Patrick F. Klunder
David E. Stevenson
Lawrence K. Rynning
Jeffrey H. Lipe
Lawrence A. Szymanski
Gregory J. Bird
Hall Adams, III
Mary Anne Sliwinski
Thomas J. Pontikis
Mark R. Misiorowski
Brigid E. Kennedy
Douglas A. Miller
Edward O. Pacer
Gregory W. Beihl

David E. Neumeister
Shimon B. Kahan
Brian J. Hunt
Bradley C. Nahrstadt

Representative Clients: Black & Decker; Columbus-Cabrini Medical Center; Federal Express; Fisher-Price; Ford Motor Company; General Electric; Goodyear Tire and Rubber; Kimberly-Clark Corp.; Waste Management; Zenith Electronics.

For Complete List of Firm Personnel, See General Section

For full biographical listings, see the Martindale-Hubbell Law Directory

WORKER & POWER (AV)

55 East Monroe Suite 4550, 60603
Telephone: 312-345-1718
Fax: 312-345-1778
Email: worker@starnetusa.com *URL:* http://www.workerandpower.com

Danny L. Worker
John M. Power
Kevin J. Glenn
Mary F. Sitko
Kimberly A. Wilkins
Miguel A. Ruiz

ASSOCIATES

Nancy S. Miller
Laura A. Caldwell
Matthew J. Ligda
Margaret M. O'Connell
Jennifer L. Green

OF COUNSEL

Gary W. Leydig
J. Timothy Lovett

For full biographical listings, see the Martindale-Hubbell Law Directory

YELTON & KEHL, LTD. (AV)

One East Wacker Drive Suite 3720, 60601
Telephone: 312-832-9255
Fax: 312-832-9277
URL: http://www.yeltonkehl.com

Robert C. Yelton III
Jeffrey Edward Kehl

Ryan J. Harrington
Karen M. Talty

OF COUNSEL

Joel S. Ostrow

For full biographical listings, see the Martindale-Hubbell Law Directory

COLLINSVILLE, Madison Co.

DUNHAM, BOMAN & LESKERA (AV)

300 West Clay Street, 62234
Telephone: 618-344-7734
Telecopier: 618-344-3853
Belleville Office: 208 N. High.
Telephone: 618-235-7222.
Telecopier: 618-236-2800; 618-236-1899.

John W. Leskera
William L. Berry
Eric C. Young
Robert D. Francis
John L. Bitzer

Attorneys for: Collinsville School District #10; Hanover Insurance Co.; Hartford Insurance Group; State Farm Insurance Cos.; Transamerica Insurance Group; The Travelers Indemnity Co.; Wausau Insurance Cos.; Nationwide Insurance Co.

For full biographical listings, see the Martindale-Hubbell Law Directory

*DANVILLE,** Vermilion Co.

HUTTON, LAURY, YOUNG & LIETZ (AV)

16 West Madison Street, P.O. Box 1128, 61832
Telephone: 217-446-9436
FAX: 217-446-9462

MEMBERS OF FIRM

Everett L. Laury
Frank R. Young
Gregory G. Lietz

Representative Clients: Employers Reinsurance Corporation; Pro National Insurance Company; Kentucky National Insurance Company; Pekin Insurance Company; Illinois State Medical Insurance Services, Inc.; Sentry Insurance; Rockford Mutual Insurance Company; Frankenmuth Mutual Insurance Company; Cumis Insurance Society; The Equitable Life Assurance Society.

For Complete List of Firm Personnel, See General Section

For full biographical listings, see the Martindale-Hubbell Law Directory

*EDWARDSVILLE,** Madison Co.

BURROUGHS, HEPLER, BROOM, MACDONALD & HEBRANK (AV)

Two Mark Twain Plaza, Suite 300, 103 West Vandalia Street, P.O. Box 510, 62025-0510
Telephone: 618-656-0184
Telecopier: 618-656-1364
Email: firm@ilmolaw.com *URL:* http://www.ilmolaw.com

MEMBERS OF FIRM

George D. Burroughs (1873-1977)
William G. Burroughs (1872-1952)
Mallory L. Burroughs (1884-1965)
Jesse L. Simpson (1884-1973)
David L. Simpson (Retired)
G. Gordon Burroughs (Of Counsel)
Larry E. Hepler
Gordon R. Broom
Theodore J. MacDonald, Jr.
Jeffrey S. Hebrank
Gary E. True
Paul W. Johnson
William J. Knapp
Lisa K. Franke

ASSOCIATES

Jack H. Humes, Jr.
L. David Green
Kathryn A. Klein
J. Todd Hayes
Daniel W. Farroll
Donald J. Ohl
Gary A. Meadows
Thomas Scott Stewart
Amy C. Gunn
Troy A. Bozarth
Robert H. Sands
Elizabeth A. Bradley
Robert J. Evola
Veronica Felton Armouti
Christine E. Duden
James M. Watson
Kristen Lynn Dieterich
Michael A. Powell

Representative Clients: Ameritech; Travelers Insurance Co.; Fireman's Fund-American Insurance Group; CILCO; Employers Union Insurance Co.; The Hartford; Illinois Power Co.; W.R. Grace; Mark Twain Bank; Prairie Farms.

For full biographical listings, see the Martindale-Hubbell Law Directory

Edwardsville—Continued

LUCCO BROWN & MUDGE (AV)

224 St. Louis Street, P.O. Box 539, 62025
Telephone: 618-656-2321
Fax: 618-656-2363
Email: lbm@plantnet.com

Dick H. Mudge, Jr. (1919-1978)
J. William Lucco
Joseph R. Brown, Jr.
William A. Mudge

ASSOCIATES

Michael Shaheen
Billie L. Johnson

Reference: Bank of Edwardsville, Edwardsville, Illinois.

For full biographical listings, see the Martindale-Hubbell Law Directory

REED, ARMSTRONG, GORMAN, COFFEY, GILBERT & MUDGE, PROFESSIONAL CORPORATION (AV)

One Mark Twain Plaza, Suite 300, P.O. Box 368, 62025
Telephone: 618-656-0257
Facsimile: 618-692-4416
Email: reed@ezl.com
Other Edwardsville Office: 125 North Buchanan, P.O. Box 247.
Telephone: 618-656-2244.
Fax: 618-658-1307.

Harry C. Armstrong
James E. Gorman
Stephen C. Mudge
Martin K. Morrissey
Michael J. Bedesky
David Laurent

Bryan L. Skelton
Ronald D. Robinson
Katherine M. Smith
Tara Inlow English

Representative Clients: State Farm Insurance Cos; Country Companies; Standard Mutual Casualty Co.; General Casualty Co. Of Wisconsin; Lloyds of London; Hawkeye Security Insurance Co.; Shelter Insurance Companies; Pekin Insurance Cos.; American International Adjusting Co.; Employers Reinsurance Corp.

For full biographical listings, see the Martindale-Hubbell Law Directory

THOMSON LAW OFFICE (AV)

A Professional Corporation
1 Sunset Hill Professional Centre Suite B, P.O. Box 538, 62025
Telephone: 618-692-0028
Telecopier: 618-692-0269
Email: firminfo@thomsonlaw.com
Springfield, Illinois Office: 1920 South Spring Street, 62703.
Telephone: 217-522-3620.
Facsimile: 217-525-6557.

Stephen W. Thomson

Danya L. Johnson
Brian L. Gifford

For full biographical listings, see the Martindale-Hubbell Law Directory

*HARRISBURG,** Saline Co.

JELLIFFE, FERRELL, MORRIS, DOERGE & FOSTER (AV)

108 East Walnut Street, P.O. Box 406, 62946
Telephone: 618-253-7153; 253-7647
Telecopier: 618-252-1843

OF COUNSEL

Charles R. Jelliffe

MEMBERS OF FIRM

DeWitt Twente (1904-1976)
Donald V. Ferrell
Walden E. Morris
Michal Doerge
Thomas J. Foster

Representative Clients: Auto-Owners Insurance; Country Cos; Metropolitan Life Insurance; Ohio Casualty Group; Standard Mutual Insurance Co.; State Farm Cos.; Aetna Casualty & Surety Co.; Sahara Coal Co.

For full biographical listings, see the Martindale-Hubbell Law Directory

*JOLIET,** Will Co.

MCKEOWN, FITZGERALD, ZOLLNER, BUCK, HUTCHISON & RUTTLE (AV)

2455 Glenwood Avenue, 60435
Telephone: 815-729-4800
Fax: 815-729-4711
Frankfort Office: 28 Kansas Street.
Telephone: 815-469-2176.
FAX: 815-469-0295.

MEMBERS OF FIRM

Charles J. McKeown (1908-1985)
Paul O. McKeown (1913-1982)
Richard T. Buck (1936-1992)
Douglas P. Hutchison (1939-1998)
Joseph C. Fitzgerald (Retired)
Max E. Zollner

(See Next Column)

MEMBERS OF FIRM (Continued)

David L. Ruttle
Theodore J. Jarz
Douglas J. McKeown
James B. Harvey
Kenneth A. Grey
Michael R. Lucas
Christopher N. Wise
Gary S. Mueller
John C. Roth
Arthur J. Wilhelmi
Thomas M. Carney

ASSOCIATE

Christopher S. Ward (Resident)

OF COUNSEL

George E. Sangmeister
Stewart C. Hutchison

Representative Clients: First Midwest Bank, N.A.; Silver Cross Hospital; Villages of Plainfield and Mokena; Southwest Agency for Risk Management; Joliet Junior College; Kipling Development, Inc.; Cat Scales Co.; Joliet Valves, Inc.; Nicor Inc.

For full biographical listings, see the Martindale-Hubbell Law Directory

*KANKAKEE,** Kankakee Co.

ACKMAN, MAREK & BOYD, LTD. (AV)

Suite 400, One Dearborn Square, 60901
Telephone: 815-933-6681
Email: marek1@netcom.net
Watseka, Illinois Office: 223 East Mulberry Street.
Telephone: 815-432-5215.

Richard L. Ackman
J. Dennis Marek
Robert W. Boyd
John J. Boyd

James A. Devine
Dana M. Meyer

Representative Clients: American States Insurance Co.; Auto Owners Insurance Co.; Consumers Illinois Water Co.; Country Mutual Insurance Co.; EMCASCO; Farmers Insurance Group; Grinnell Mutual Insurance Co.; Martin Boyer Co. Inc.; Medical Protective Co.; Economy Fire & Casualty Co.; Union Insurance Co.; Western States Insurance Co.

For full biographical listings, see the Martindale-Hubbell Law Directory

LA SALLE, La Salle Co.

HERBOLSHEIMER, LANNON, HENSON, DUNCAN AND REAGAN, P.C. (AV)

State Bank Building, Suite 400, 654 First Street, P.O. Box 539, 61301
Telephone: 815-223-0111
Fax: 815-223-5829
Ottawa, Illinois Office: First Federal Savings Bank Building, 633 LaSalle Street, Suite 409.
Telephone: 815-434-1400.
Fax: 815-434-2423.

George L. Herbolsheimer (1911-1992)
R. James Lannon, Jr.
T. Donald Henson
John S. Duncan, III
Michael T. Reagan (Resident, Ottawa Office)
Douglas A. Gift
Gary R. Eiten

Karen C. Eiten
Michael C. Jansz (Resident, Ottawa Office)
Jill W. Klein
Lawrence M. Kaschak

Attorneys for: Aetna Insurance Group; St. Paul Fire and Marine Insurance Co.; State Farm Insurance Co.; La Salle State Bank; The Daily News Tribune Company, La Salle; Eureka Savings Bank; Illinois Valley Community Hospital; Community Hospital of Ottawa; Commonwealth Edison, Co.; United States Fidelity & Guaranty, Co.

For full biographical listings, see the Martindale-Hubbell Law Directory

MATTOON, Coles Co.

CRAIG & CRAIG (AV)

1807 Broadway, P.O. Box 689, 61938-0689
Telephone: 217-234-6481
Telecopier: 217-234-6486; 258-8292
Email: craiglaw@advant.com
Mount Vernon, Illinois Office: 115 North 7th Street.
Telephone: 618-244-7511.

MEMBERS OF FIRM

John P. Ewart
Richard F. Record, Jr.
Stephen L. Corn
Robert G. Grierson
Gregory C. Ray
Paul R. Lynch (Resident, Mount Vernon Office)
Kenneth F. Werts (Resident, Mount Vernon Office)
John L. Barger

ASSOCIATE

Kathleen M. Stockwell

(See Next Column)

CRAIG & CRAIG, *Mattoon—Continued*

OF COUNSEL

Jack E. Horsley

Representative Clients: Marathon Oil Co.; Illinois Central R.R. Co.; Consolidated Communications Inc.; Illinois Municipal League Risk Management Association; The Medical Protective Co.; Illinois State Medical Inter-Insurance Exchange; St. Paul Insurance Co.; Cincinnati Insurance Co.

For Complete List of Firm Personnel, See General Section

For full biographical listings, see the Martindale-Hubbell Law Directory

*MOUNT VERNON,** Jefferson Co.

CAMPBELL, BLACK, CARNINE, HEDIN, BALLARD & MCDONALD, P.C. (AV)

P.O. Drawer C, 62864
Telephone: 618-242-3310
Fax: 618-242-3735
Email: cbch@midwest.net *URL:* http://www.cbch.com

David A. Campbell
Terry R. Black
Roy L. Carnine
Craig R. Hedin
Mark J. Ballard
Jerome E. McDonald
Howard W. Campbell (1911-1980)
John E. Jacobsen (1922-1985)
Glenn E. Moore (1911-1991)
David E. Furnall (1905-1993)

Fred R. Mann
Charles L.P. Flynn
Matthew K. Wollin
Aaron S. Carnine

Representative Clients: Kerr-McGee Coal Corp.; Good Samaritan Hospital; Country Mutual Insurance Co.; Southern Illinois Stone Co; Rend Lake Conservancy District; Consolidation Coal Co.; Illinois State Medical Insurance Services; State Farm Automobile Insurance Co.; John Hancock Mutual Life Insurance Co.

For full biographical listings, see the Martindale-Hubbell Law Directory

NAPERVILLE, DuPage Co.

STEVEN B. LEVY, LTD. (AV)

40 Shuman Boulevard Suite 151, 60563
Telephone: 630-416-6300
Telefax: 630-416-6564
URL: http://www.lawyers.com/stevenblevy
Email: SBLEVYLTD@aol.com *URL:* http://www.sblevyltdlaw.com

Steven B. Levy

For full biographical listings, see the Martindale-Hubbell Law Directory

*OREGON,** Ogle Co.

WILLIAMS & MCCARTHY, A PROFESSIONAL CORPORATION (AV)

607 Washington Street, P.O. Box 339, 61061
Telephone: 815-732-2101
Fax: 815-732-2289
Rockford, Illinois Office: 321 West State Street, P.O. Box 219.
Telephone: 815-987-8900.
Fax: 815-968-0019.

Clayton L. Lindsey
Kari A. Vanderzyl

Representative Clients: Aircraft Gear Corp.; Anderson Industries, Inc.; Gallagher Bassett Insurance Co.; Liberty Mutual Insurance Co.; Atwood Industries, Inc.; The Travelers; American Mutual Insurance Co.; Rockford Health Systems; Chrysler Corp.; USF&G, West Bend.

For Complete List of Firm Personnel, See General Section

For full biographical listings, see the Martindale-Hubbell Law Directory

*PEORIA,** Peoria Co.

CASSIDY & MUELLER (AV)

323 Commerce Bank Building, 416 Main Street, 61602
Telephone: 309-676-0591
Fax: 309-676-8036

MEMBERS OF FIRM

John E. Cassidy (1896-1984)
John E. Cassidy, Jr.
David B. Mueller
John E. Cassidy, III
Timothy J. Cassidy
Andrew D. Cassidy
Christopher F. Cassidy
Timothy J. Cusack
Michael W. Powell
John D. Moses
Robert M. McBride

Representative Clients: Aetna Casualty & Surety Co.; Chicago Motor Club Ins. Co.; Dow Corning, Inc.; E.I. DuPont-DeNemours & Company; Economy Fire & Casualty Co.; Hartford Insurance Group; Lake State Insurance Company; Liberty Mutual Insurance Co.; Meridian Insurance Co.; Nationwide Insurance Co.

For full biographical listings, see the Martindale-Hubbell Law Directory

KAVANAGH, SCULLY, SUDOW, WHITE & FREDERICK, P.C. (AV)

301 S.W. Adams Street, Suite 700, 61602
Telephone: 309-676-1381
FAX: 309-676-0324
Email: KSSWF@aol.com
East Peoria, Illinois Office: 111 West Washington Street, Suite 206B.
Telephone: 309-694-3707.
Fax: 309-676-0324.

Julian E. Cannell
Charles G. Roth
David J. Dubicki
Phillip B. Lenzini
James W. Springer

Counsel for: First of America Bank - Illinois, N.A.; AgriBank, FCB; Construction Equipment Federal Credit Union; Travelers Insurance Co.; Phoenix Mutual Life Insurance Co.; United States Fidelity & Guaranty Co.; Equitable Life Assurance Society of the U.S.; Board of Education of the City of Peoria School District, 150; Anderson State Bank.

For Complete List of Firm Personnel, See General Section

For full biographical listings, see the Martindale-Hubbell Law Directory

KINGERY DURREE WAKEMAN & RYAN, ASSOC. (AV)

Commerce Bank Building, 416 Main Street, Suite 915, 61602
Telephone: 309-676-3612
FAX: 309-676-1329
Email: KDWRyan@aol.com

Arthur R. Kingery
Edward R. Durree
Steven A. Wakeman
Christopher P. Ryan
Philip M. O'Donnell
James P. Lawson
Michael S. McKinley

Reference: Commerce Bank of Peoria.

For full biographical listings, see the Martindale-Hubbell Law Directory

QUINN, JOHNSTON, HENDERSON & PRETORIUS, CHARTERED (AV)

(Formerly McConnell, Kennedy, Quinn & Johnston)
227 N. E. Jefferson Street, 61602
Telephone: 309-674-1133
Telecopier: 309-674-6503
Email: quinnlaw@qjhp.com *URL:* http://www.qjhp.com
Springfield, Illinois Office: Three North, Old State Capitol Plaza, 62701.
Telephone: 217-753-1133.

R. Michael Henderson
Murvel Pretorius, Jr.
Bradley W. Dunham
Robert H. Jennetten
Gregory A. Cerulo
Paul P. Gilfillan
Mary W. McDade
Stanley L. Morris (Resident, Springfield Office)
James Andrew Borland (Resident, Springfield Office)
Julie A. Ward
David Blair Collins
John F. Kamin
Michael J. Holt (Resident, Springfield Office)
Matthew B. Smith
Laura Marie Donahue
Peter R. Jennetten
Jo Tewes Wetherill
Laura A. Sallmann
Jonathan A. Stump

OF COUNSEL

Richard E. Quinn
W. Thomas Johnston

Representative Clients: Allstate Insurance Co.; American International Insurance Co.; Bituminous Casualty Corp.; General Motors; Illinois State Medical Insurance Services, Inc.; Pekin Insurance; Peoria Journal Star, Inc.; St. Paul Insurance Co.

For Complete List of Firm Personnel, See General Section

For full biographical listings, see the Martindale-Hubbell Law Directory

ROBERT C. STRODEL, LTD. (AV)

927 Commerce Bank Building, 61602
Telephone: 309-676-4500
Fax: 309-676-4566

Robert C. Strodel

For full biographical listings, see the Martindale-Hubbell Law Directory

WINGET & KANE (AV)

Commerce Bank Building, 416 Main Street, Suite 807, 61602
Telephone: 309-674-2310
Fax: 309-674-9722

MEMBERS OF FIRM

Walter W. Winget
James F. Kane

ASSOCIATE

Nicole V. Nemec

Representative Client: Davison-Fulton Ltd.
References: Commerce Bank.

For full biographical listings, see the Martindale-Hubbell Law Directory

PERU, La Salle Co.

ANTHONY C. RACCUGLIA & ASSOCIATES (AV)

1200 Maple Drive, 61354
Telephone: 815-223-0230
Ottawa, Illinois Office: 633 La Salle Street.
Telephone: 815-434-2003.

ASSOCIATES

James A. McPhedran
Louis L. Bertrand

References: La Salle National Bank; Citizens First National Bank of Peru, Illinois.

For full biographical listings, see the Martindale-Hubbell Law Directory

*ROCKFORD,** Winnebago Co.

WILLIAMS & McCARTHY, A PROFESSIONAL CORPORATION (AV)

321 West State Street, P.O. Box 219, 61105-0219
Telephone: 815-987-8900
Fax: 815-968-0019
Email: mail@wilmac.com *URL:* http://www.wilmac.com
Oregon, Illinois Office: 607 Washington Street. P.O. Box 339.
Telephone: 815-732-2101.
Fax: 815-732-2289.

Thomas S. Johnson (President, Williams & McCarthy)
Edward R. Telling, III
Russell D. Anderson
John E. Pfau
Richard A. Berman
John L. Shepherd
Terry D. Anderson
Kim D. Krahenbuhl (Resident Partner, Oregon, Illinois Office)
Scott C. Sullivan
Carol N. Bailey
James P. Devine
John J. Holevas
Timothy J. Rollins
Clayton L. Lindsey (Resident Partner, Oregon, Illinois Office)
Stephen E. Balogh
Marc C. Gravino
Thomas P. Sandquist
Carl A. Ecklund

Wendy S. Howarter (Resident, Oregon, Illinois Office)
Michael T. Cyrs
Troy E. Haggestad
Kari A. Vanderzyl (Resident, Oregon, Illinois Office)
Brendan A. Maher
Daniel Andrew Dunn, Jr

Representative Clients: Aircraft Gear Corp.; Anderson Industries, Inc.; Gallagher Bassett Insurance Co.; Liberty Mutual Insurance Co.; Atwood Industries, Inc.; The Travelers; American Mutual Insurance Co.; Rockford Health Systems; Chrysler Corp.; USF&G, West Bend.

For full biographical listings, see the Martindale-Hubbell Law Directory

*ROCK ISLAND,** Rock Island Co.

WINSTEIN, KAVENSKY & WALLACE (AV)

4th Floor, Rock Island Bank Building, 224 18th Street, P.O. Box 4298, 61201
Telephone: 309-794-1515; 800-747-1527
Fax: 309-794-9929

MEMBERS OF FIRM

Stewart R. Winstein
Harrison H. Kavensky
Franklin S. Wallace
Craig L. Kavensky
Arthur R. Winstein
David L. Cunningham

John Allan Hartsock
Robert Kelly Leyshon
Barbara K. Wallace

Local Regional Counsel for: United Auto Workers.
Reference: First National Bank of Quad Cities.

For full biographical listings, see the Martindale-Hubbell Law Directory

*SPRINGFIELD,** Sangamon Co.

GIFFIN, WINNING, COHEN & BODEWES, P.C. (AV)

1 West Old State Capitol Plaza, Suite 600 Myers Building, P.O. Box 2117, 62705
Telephone: 217-525-1571
Facsimile: 217-525-1710
Email: gifwinlaw@eosinc.com

Carol Hansen Posegate
R. Mark Mifflin
Thomas P. Schanzle-Haskins, III
Gregory K. Harris

Representative Clients: Illinois State University Board of Trustees; Auto Owners Insurance Co.; Grinnell Mutual Reinsurance Company; Horace Mann Insurance Company; Great Central Insurance Cos.; Standard Mutual Insurance Co.; Transamerica Insurance Company; Associated Beer Distributors of Illinois Risk Management Association.

For Complete List of Firm Personnel, See General Section

For full biographical listings, see the Martindale-Hubbell Law Directory

METNICK, CHERRY & FRAZIER (AV)

Second Floor, Myers Building, 1 West Old State Capitol Plaza, P.O. Box 12140, 62791
Telephone: 217-753-4242
Telefax: 217-753-4642
Email: SPRINGLAW@AOL.COM

MEMBERS OF FIRM

Michael B. Metnick
Diana N. Cherry
Richard D. Frazier

ASSOCIATES

Kathryn Saltmarsh
Scott A. Sabin

For full biographical listings, see the Martindale-Hubbell Law Directory

*WAUKEGAN,** Lake Co.

DIVER, GRACH, QUADE & MASINI (AV)

Bank of Waukegan Building, 111 North County Street, 60085
Telephone: 847-662-8611
FAX: 847-662-2960

MEMBERS OF FIRM

Clarence W. Diver (1883-1962)
Thomas W. Diver
Brian S. Grach
David R. Quade
Robert J. Masini
Sarah P. Lessman
David L. Hazan

Heidi J. Aavang
Donna-Jo Rodden Vorderstrasse
Paula Vincich Randall

A list of Representative Clients will be furnished upon request.
Reference: First Midwest Bank of Waukegan.

For full biographical listings, see the Martindale-Hubbell Law Directory

*WHEATON,** DuPage Co.

DONOVAN AND ROBERTS, P.C. (AV)

104 East Roosevelt Road, Suite 202, 60187
Telephone: 630-668-4211
Fax: 630-668-2076

Keith E. Roberts, Sr.
Keith E. (Chuck) Roberts, Jr.
Henry B. Vess, III

Marie F. Leach
Robert S. Marcott
Eric A. Burgeson
Kevin H. Saville

For full biographical listings, see the Martindale-Hubbell Law Directory

STEVEN B. LEVY, LTD.

(See Naperville)

NORTON, MANCINI, ARGENTATI, WEILER & DEANO (AV)

109 North Hale Street, P.O. Box 846, 60189-0846
Telephone: 630-668-9440
Fax: 630-668-9489
Chicago, Illinois Office: 111 West Washington Street, Suite 835.
Telephone: 312-807-4999.
Fax: 312-807-4998.

John E. Norton
Lorenzo A. Mancini
Patricia L. Argentati
Thomas R. Weiler
James L. DeAno
Thomas J. Long

Denis K. Sheehan
W. Mark Sickles
Dawn C. Didier
W. Anthony Andrews
Christopher J. May
Scott D. Braun
Melissa M. Tomaska
Paul E. Brady

OF COUNSEL

Adrianna K. Liber

Representative Clients: Aetna Life & Casualty; Allstate Insurance Company; Chicago Motor Club Insurance Company; County of DuPage; Frontier Insurance Co.; CNA Insurance Company; Hartford Insurance Company; Illinois State Medical Insurance Services, Inc.; St. Paul Insurance Company; Wausau Insurance Companies.

For full biographical listings, see the Martindale-Hubbell Law Directory

*WOODSTOCK,** McHenry Co.

CALDWELL, BERNER & CALDWELL (AV)

100 1/2 Cass Street, P.O. Box 1289, 60098
Telephone: 815-338-3300
Fax: 815-338-0015

MEMBERS OF FIRM

William I. Caldwell (1908-1971)
James E. Berner
William I. Caldwell, Jr.
Jeffrey A. Rouhandeh

(See Next Column)

CALDWELL, BERNER & CALDWELL, *Woodstock—Continued*

OF COUNSEL

Louis A. Bianchi

Representative Clients: Amcore Bank N.A., Woodstock; Allstate Insurance Co.; American States Insurance Co.; Capitol Indemnity Corp.; Maryland Casualty Co.; Kemper Insurance Group; Northwestern National Insurance Group; C.N.A. Group; Universal Underwriters Insurance Co.; American Home Group.

For full biographical listings, see the Martindale-Hubbell Law Directory

LAW OFFICE OF THEODORE A.E. POEHLMANN, P.C. (AV)

202 West South Street, P.O. Box 271, 60098-0271
Telephone: 815-337-3337
Fax: 815-337-3340

Theodore A. E. Poehlmann

Stephen J. Tasch
Mia Lucas (Not admitted in IL)

For full biographical listings, see the Martindale-Hubbell Law Directory

INDIANA

*BEDFORD,** Lawrence Co.

STEELE, STEELE, MCSOLEY & MCSOLEY (AV)

Bank One Building, Suite One, 1602 I Street, 47421
Telephone: 812-279-3513
Fax: 812-275-3504
URL: http://www.steele-mcsoley.com

MEMBERS OF FIRM

Ruel W. Steele (1908-1992)
Byron W. Steele
Brent E. Steele
Patrick S. McSoley
Darlene Steele McSoley

Representative Clients: The First National Bank of Mitchell; The Times Mail (newspaper); Indiana Bell Telephone Co.; Texas Gas Transmission Corporation; U.S. Gypsum Company. Bank One Mortgage Corp. Hoosier Hills Credit Union W.F. Meyers, Inc.; Tri Star Engineering, Inc.; Stone City Products, Inc.; Crowders Drug Stores, Inc.; Whitney Tool. Co.; Ritter Tool & Die Corp.; Adventure Media,Inc.

For full biographical listings, see the Martindale-Hubbell Law Directory

*BLOOMINGTON,** Monroe Co.

THOMAS A. BERRY & ASSOCIATES (AV)

701 North Walnut Street, 47404
Telephone: 812-336-8300
Fax: 812-336-2343
Email: lawyer@tomberry.com

ASSOCIATE

Michelle Berry Domer

For full biographical listings, see the Martindale-Hubbell Law Directory

BUNGER & ROBERTSON (AV)

226 South College Square, P.O. Box 910, 47402-0910
Telephone: 812-332-9295
Fax: 812-331-8808
Email: bunrob@iquest.net

MEMBERS OF FIRM

Don M Robertson
Joseph D. O'Connor
James L. Whitlatch
Samuel R. Ardery
William J. Beggs
John W. Richards

Representative Clients: Aetna Insurance Companies; Bloomington Hospital; Commercial Union Group; Indiana Insurance Co.; Liberty Mutual Insurance; Medical Protective Co.; Monroe County Community School Corp.; Professional Golf Car, Inc.; Prudential Insurance Company of America; State Farm Automobile Insurance Co.

For Complete List of Firm Personnel, See General Section

For full biographical listings, see the Martindale-Hubbell Law Directory

KELLEY, BELCHER & BROWN, A PROFESSIONAL CORPORATION (AV)

301 West Seventh Street, P.O. Box 3250, 47402-3250
Telephone: 812-336-9963
Telecopier: 812-336-4588

William H. Kelley
Thomas J. Belcher
Darla Sue Brown

(See Next Column)

Shannon L. Robinson
Kyle M. Baker
Michael W. Phelps

For full biographical listings, see the Martindale-Hubbell Law Directory

CARMEL, Hamilton Co.

KNOWLES & ASSOCIATES, LLC (AV)

811 South Range Line Road, 46032
Telephone: 317-848-4360
Telecopier: 317-848-4363
Email: knowlesassociates@worldnet.att.net *URL:* http://www.lawyers.com/knowles

William W. Knowles

D. Brandon Johnston

For full biographical listings, see the Martindale-Hubbell Law Directory

*COLUMBUS,** Bartholomew Co.

SHARPNACK, BIGLEY, DAVID & RUMPLE (AV)

321 Washington Street, P.O. Box 310, 47202-0310
Telephone: 812-372-1553
Fax: 812-372-1567
Email: sbdr@hsonline.net

MEMBERS OF FIRM

Thomas C. Bigley, Jr.
Timothy J. Vrana
John A. Stroh
Joan Tupin Crites

Representative Clients: Irwin Union Bank and Trust Co.; Ameritech; State Farm Mutual Insurance Cos.; Home News Enterprises; Centra Credit Union.

For Complete List of Firm Personnel, See General Section

For full biographical listings, see the Martindale-Hubbell Law Directory

*CROWN POINT,** Lake Co.

EDWARD P. GRIMMER (AV)

603 N. Main Street, 46307-3233
Telephone: 219-662-1661
Fax: 219-663-4151
Email: Grimmerlaw@msn.com

Representative Clients: Furnished Upon Request.

For full biographical listings, see the Martindale-Hubbell Law Directory

ELKHART, Elkhart Co.

DANIELS, SANDERS, PIANOWSKI, TODD & THOMAS (AV)

401 West High Street, 46516
Telephone: 219-294-1499
Fax: 219-294-7277

MEMBERS OF FIRM

Philip E. Byron, Jr. (1911-1977)
Robert C. Daniels (1928-1995)
Robert T. Sanders, III
Michael A. Pianowski
James L. Todd
David G. Thomas
Matthew A. Yeakey
P. Shawn Lewis

ASSOCIATE

Jason G. Ward

Representative Clients: KeyBank Corp.; Commercial Union Insurance Cos.; Aetna Casualty and Surety Co.; Ohio Casualty Insurance Co.; Yoder Oil Co., Inc.; Double Eagle Industries, Inc.; WKJG-TV; Tri-State Coach Lines, Inc.; Tom Naquin Chevrolet, Inc.

For full biographical listings, see the Martindale-Hubbell Law Directory

*EVANSVILLE,** Vanderburgh Co.

BERGER AND BERGER (AV)

313 Main Street, 47708-1485
Telephone: 812-425-8101
Outside Indiana: 800-327-0182
Fax: 812-421-5909
Email: berger@bergerlaw.com *URL:* http://www.bergerlaw.com

MEMBERS OF FIRM

Sydney L. Berger (1917-1988)
Charles L. Berger
Sheila M. Corcoran
Mark W. Rietman
David L. Clark

References: Citizens National Bank of Evansville; Old National Bank in Evansville.

For full biographical listings, see the Martindale-Hubbell Law Directory

Evansville—Continued

BOWERS, HARRISON, KENT & MILLER, LLP (AV)

25 N.W. Riverside Drive, P.O. Box 1287, 47706-1287
Telephone: 812-426-1231
Fax: 812-464-3676
Email: BOWERS,HARRISON,KENT&MILLER,LLP@BHKM.COM
URL: http://WWW.BHKM.COM

MEMBERS OF FIRM

F. Wesley Bowers
David V. Miller
Paul E. Black
Arthur D. Rutkowski
George C. Barnett, Jr.
Terry Noffsinger
Thomas A. Massey
Greg A. Granger
Joseph H. Harrison, Jr.
Lawrence L. Grimes

Representative Clients: Ameritech Publishing, Inc.; Southern Railway Company; Bootz Manufacturing Company; Indiana Bell Telephone: Company; Black Beauty Resources, Inc.

For Complete List of Firm Personnel, See General Section

For full biographical listings, see the Martindale-Hubbell Law Directory

FINE & HATFIELD, A PROFESSIONAL CORPORATION (AV)

520 N.W. Second Street, P.O. Box 779, 47705-0779
Telephone: 812-425-3592
Telecopier: 812-421-4269
Email: Fine@Fine-Hatfield.com *URL:* http://www.Fine-Hatfield.com

Ronald R. Allen
Thomas H. Bryan
Leslie C. Shively
Danny E. Glass
Elaine Brown Elliott

H. Linwood Shannon, III
Boyd A. Toler
Laura L. Pamplin

A List of Representative Clients Furnished Upon Request.

For full biographical listings, see the Martindale-Hubbell Law Directory

KAHN, DEES, DONOVAN & KAHN, LLP (AV)

Fifth Main Financial Plaza, Suite 305, P.O. Box 3646, 47735-3646
Telephone: 812-423-3183
Fax: 812-423-3841
Email: evvlaw@k2d2.com

MEMBERS OF FIRM

Alan N. Shovers
Thomas O. Magan
Jon D. Goldman
Brian P. Williams
Jeffrey W. Ahlers
Christopher D. Lee

ASSOCIATES

Mark A. McAnulty
Robert F. "Ted" Barron II
Steven S. Hoar
Jason H. Guthrie
Scott F. Hill
Todd C. Barsumian
Lee F. Baker

Representative Clients: University of Southern Indiana; Cresline Plastic Pipe Co., Inc.; Deaconess Hospital, Inc.; Kaiser Aluminum Chemical Corporation; MallincKrodt Group; Combustion Engineering, Inc.; Wright Motors; Schmitt Refrigeration; Toyota Motor Manufacturing of Indiana, Inc.; D-Patrick, Inc.

For Complete List of Firm Personnel, See General Section

For full biographical listings, see the Martindale-Hubbell Law Directory

*FORT WAYNE,** Allen Co.

HELMKE, BEAMS, BOYER & WAGNER (AV)

300 Metro Building, Berry & Harrison Streets, 46802-2242
Telephone: 219-422-7422
Telecopier: 219-422-6764
Email: hbbwdjb@aol.com
Email: rdboyer1@fortwayne.infi.net

MEMBERS OF FIRM

Walter E. Helmke (1901-1976)
Walter P. Helmke
R. David Boyer
Robert A. Wagner
J. Timothy McCaulay
Daniel J. Borgmann
Trina Glusenkamp Gould

ASSOCIATES

Payne D. Brown
R. David Boyer, II

OF COUNSEL

Glen J. Beams
William A. Berning

Representative Clients: Aalco Distributing Co., Inc.; Brotherhood Mutual Insurance Co.; Fremont Community Schools; Air-O-Mat, Inc.; Leo Distributors, Inc.; The City of Fort Wayne, Indiana; Foellinger Foundation, Inc.

For full biographical listings, see the Martindale-Hubbell Law Directory

ROBY & HOOD (AV)

Standard Federal Plaza, 200 East Main Street, Suite 520, 46802
Telephone: 219-423-3366
Fax: 219-423-3367
Anderson, Indiana Office: One Citizens Plaza, 305 Key Bank, 46016.
Telephone: 765-642-2402.
Marion, Indiana Office: 1315 West Gillespie Street, 46952.
Telephone: 765-651-0677.

MEMBERS OF FIRM

Daniel A. Roby
G. Stanley Hood
Thomas A. Manges
David Joseph Stach

References: Norwest Bank; Bank One.

For full biographical listings, see the Martindale-Hubbell Law Directory

SHAMBAUGH, KAST, BECK & WILLIAMS, LLP (AV)

600 Standard Federal Plaza, 46802-2405
Telephone: 219-423-1430
Fax: 219-422-9038
Email: skbwlawyers@skbw.com *URL:* http://www.skbw.com

MEMBERS OF FIRM

Willard Shambaugh (1897-1976)
Michael H. Kast
Edward E. Beck
Stephen J. Williams
Daniel E. Serban
John B. Powell
Ronald D. Felger
James D. Streit
Paul R. Sturm

Counsel for: Hagerman Construction Corp.; Rogers Markets, Inc.; K & H Realty Corp.; Olive B. Cole Foundation; M. E. Raker Foundation, Inc.; Associates Financial Services Co., of Indiana, Inc.; Professional Federal Credit Union; Fort Wayne Education Association; CBT Credit Services, Inc.; Ian & Miriam Rolland Foundation, Inc.

For Complete List of Firm Personnel, See General Section

For full biographical listings, see the Martindale-Hubbell Law Directory

HAMMOND, Lake Co.

ABRAHAMSON, REED & ADLEY (AV)

200 Russell Street, 46320
Telephone: 219-937-1500
Fax: 219-937-3174

MEMBERS OF FIRM

Harold Abrahamson
Kenneth D. Reed
Michael C. Adley

ASSOCIATES

Scott R. Bilse
John P. Reed

References: Calumet National Bank, Hammond; Mercantile National Bank, Hammond.

For full biographical listings, see the Martindale-Hubbell Law Directory

MCHIE, MYERS, MCHIE & ENSLEN (AV)

53 Muenich Court, 46320
Telephone: 219-931-1707
Telecopier: 219-932-2417

MEMBERS OF FIRM

G. Edward McHie
Charles A. Myers
James E. McHie
Charles Endicott Enslen
Carol M. Green

Representative Clients: USX Corporation; Ronwal Transportation, Inc.; Hammond Redevelopment Commission; Hammond Economic Development Commission; Hammond Redevelopment Authority; Highland Redevelopment Commission; Whiting Redevelopment Commission; Raytrans, Inc.; La Salle Steel Co.; Emro Marketing Co., A Division of Marathon Oil; Combined Transport Systems, Inc.; Smith Motors, Inc. of Hammond d/b/a/ Smith Cheverolet; Smith Ford of Lowell, Inc.

For full biographical listings, see the Martindale-Hubbell Law Directory

JOSEPH STALMACK & ASSOCIATES, P.C. (AV)

5253 Hohman Avenue, 46320
Telephone: 219-937-3700
Toll Free: 800-552-6860
Telecopier: 219-931-1677
ABA NET: 1051
Chicago, Illinois Office: Suite 2238, 221 North LaSalle Street.
Telephone: 773-978-6200.

Joseph Stalmack

Stephen Duane Bannwart

OF COUNSEL

Nanette K. Raduenz

Representative Clients: General Electric Co.; General Motors Corporation; Liberty Mutual Insurance Company; Royal Insurance Companies.

For full biographical listings, see the Martindale-Hubbell Law Directory

INDIANAPOLIS, Marion Co.*

BOSE MCKINNEY & EVANS LLP (AV)

2700 First Indiana Plaza, 135 North Pennsylvania Street, 46204
Telephone: 317-684-5000
Facsimile: 317-684-5173
URL: http://www.boselaw.com
Indianapolis North Office: Suite 1500, 8888 Keystone Crossing, 46240.
Telephone: 317-574-3700.
Facsimile: 317-574-3716.

MEMBERS OF FIRM

Debra Linn Burns
Robert B. Clemens
Ronald E. Elberger
Daniel C. Emerson
Amy Rankin Kennelly
V. Samuel Laurin III
Theodore J. Nowacki
George Thomas Patton, Jr.
George E. Purdy
Steven G. Rudolf
C. Joseph Russell
Michael A. Trentadue

ASSOCIATES

Cathy Elliott
Stephanie Franco Holtzlander
Bernie W. Keller
Andrew M. McNeil
Kevin S. Smith
Alan S. Townsend
Monique C. Winkler

Representative Clients: Chicago Title Insurance Co.; Duke Construction and Development Cos.; Emmis Communications Corp.; First Indiana Bank; Metropolitan Life Insurance Co.; The Travelers Insurance Co.; Indianapolis Colts, Inc.; United Parcel Service, Inc.; WorldCom Network Services, Inc.; Royal Indemnity.

For Complete List of Firm Personnel, See General Section

For full biographical listings, see the Martindale-Hubbell Law Directory

BRATTAIN & MINNIX (AV)

151 North Delaware Street Suite 760, 46204
Telephone: 317-231-1750
Facsimile: 317-231-1760

Bruce D. Brattain
Larry A. Minnix

For full biographical listings, see the Martindale-Hubbell Law Directory

BUSCHMANN, CARR & SHANKS, PROFESSIONAL CORPORATION (AV)

1020 Market Tower, 10 West Market Street, 46204-2963
Telephone: 317-636-5511
Fax: 317-636-3661
Email: bcs@indy.net *URL:* http://www.buschmanncarr.com

John R. Carr, III
Stephen R. Buschmann

Representative Clients: Archer-Daniels Midland Co.; Ball Corp.; Industrial Valley Title Insurance; Creative Risk Management, Inc.; Deflecto Corporation; Glenfed Mortgage Corp.; Gates McDonald; Merchants National Bank & Trust Company of Muncie; Monumental Life Insurance Co.; National Council on Compensation Insurance.

For full biographical listings, see the Martindale-Hubbell Law Directory

CHRISTOPHER & TAYLOR (AV)

1219 North Delaware Street, P.O. Box 2850, 46206-2850
Telephone: 317-635-9000
Telecopier: 317-686-2200
Fowler Office: 306 East Fifth Street, P.O. Box 72.
Telephone: 317-884-0810.

Rodney V. Taylor
Michael C. Peek
David J. Theising
Randall D. Smith
John D. Connor
Michael A. Beason

OF COUNSEL

Richard L. Christopher (Resident, Fowler Office)

For full biographical listings, see the Martindale-Hubbell Law Directory

COHEN & MALAD, P.C. (AV)

136 North Delaware Street, P.O. Box 627, 46206-0627
Telephone: 317-636-6481
Fax: 317-636-2593
Fishers, Indiana Office: 7444 East 116th Street, Suite 200.
Telephone: 317-595-9000.
Fax: 317-841-1443.

Louis F. Cohen (1936-1992)
Richard M. Malad
Irwin B. Levin
Richard N. Bell
Eric C. Redman
John E. Bator
Paul D. Ludwig
Jarrell B. Hammond
KC Cohen (Resident, Fishers Office)
Gerald L. Williams
David J. Cutshaw

Teresa E. Dearing
Gregory L. Laker
Thomas L. Blackburn
Marilyn Ann Moores
Samuel Hodson
Deetta H. Steinmetz
John L. Stewart
Richard E. Shevitz

(See Next Column)

Richard L. Ford
Penny L. Carey
Heather V. Kimmons
Amy L. McCabe
Lisa K. Pitner Caterine
Laura S. Cohen
John M. Hauber
Maureen T. Keefe
John P. Gulyas
Mary E. Baird
Keith E. Gifford
Brian K. Zoeller
Robert E. Shive

OF COUNSEL

Stephen M. Sellmer (Resident, Fishers Office)

Reference: Bank One, Indianapolis, N.A.

For full biographical listings, see the Martindale-Hubbell Law Directory

CONOUR • DOEHRMAN • STARKEY (AV)

III Meridian Plaza, Suite 100, 10333 N. Meridian Street, 46290
Telephone: 317-705-4444
Fax: 317-705-4455
Toll Free: 800-269-3443
URL: http://www.indianalaw.com

MEMBERS OF FIRM

William F. Conour
Thomas C. Doehrman
Martha T. Starkey
Daniel S. Chamberlain

ASSOCIATE

Amber D. Kennedy

For full biographical listings, see the Martindale-Hubbell Law Directory

ICE MILLER DONADIO & RYAN (AV)

One American Square Box 82001, 46282-0002
Telephone: 317-236-2100
Fax: 317-236-2219
Email: info@imdr.com *URL:* http://www.imdr.com
South Bend, Indiana Office: 211 West Washington Street, Suite 2420.
Telephone: 219-234-7933.
Fax: 219-234-7965. Internet E-mail: info@imdr.com. Web Site Address: http://www.imdr.com.
Chicago, Illinois Office: 135 South LaSalle Street, Suite 4100.
Telephone: 312-726-1567.
Fax: 312-641-6263. Internet E-mail: info@imdr.com. Web Site Address: http://www.imdr.com.

MEMBERS OF FIRM

Jim A. O'Neal
Ralph A. Cohen
Arthur P. Kalleres
Jay G. Taylor
G. Daniel Kelley, Jr.
David M. Mattingly
James R. Fisher
Cory Brundage
David J. Mallon, Jr.
Phillip R. Scaletta, III
James L. Petersen
Gary J. Dankert
Philip A. Whistler
John F. Prescott, Jr.
Mary Nold Larimore
Richard A. Smikle
L. Alan Whaley
Bonnie L. Gallivan
Debra Hanley Miller
Michael A. Wukmer
Michael J. Lewinski
Michael D. Marine
Terri Ann Czajka
Donald M. Snemis
Michael A. Wilkins
Sherry A. Fabina-Abney
Alan H. Goldstein
Judy Starobin Okenfuss
Curtis W. McCauley

RETIRED PARTNER

Evan E. Steger

SENIOR COUNSEL

Bradley L. Williams

OF COUNSEL

Nancy Menard Riddle
John T. Murphy
Kathleen K. Shortridge
Diana L. Wann
Kelly Bauman Pitcher
Susan Rogers Brooke
Laure V. Flaniken
Edward P. Steegmann

STAFF ATTORNEY

Nathan B. Maudlin

ASSOCIATES

Robert A. Anderson
John J. Morse
Thomas E. Mixdorf
Adam Arceneaux
Tara L. Schulstad
Rebecca J. Seamands
Christopher S. Sears
Franklin E. Breckenridge, Jr.
Lisa Erb Harrison

Counsel for: American Cyanamid Co.; Chrysler Corp.; Community Hospitals of Indiana, Inc.; Cummins Engine Co., Inc.; Ford Motor Company; Howard Needles, Tammen & Bergendoff; Indiana Department of Insurance; Parke-Davis; Proctor & Gamble Co.

For Complete List of Firm Personnel, See General Section

For full biographical listings, see the Martindale-Hubbell Law Directory

Indianapolis—Continued

JOHNSON SMITH PENCE & HEATH LLP (AV)

One Indiana Square Suite 1800, 46204
Telephone: 317-634-9777
Telecopier: 317-636-9061
Email: firm@jsplaw.com *URL:* http://www.jsplaw.com
Washington, D.C. Office: 555 Twelfth Street, N.W., Suite 650.
Telephone: 202-737-5410.
Fax: 202-737-5411.

MEMBERS OF FIRM

Wayne O Adams, III
Thomas A. Barnard
David G. Blachly
David J. Carr
Sean Michael Clapp
David R. Day
Mark W. Ford
G. Ronald Heath
Robert B. Hebert
John David Hoover
Andrew W. Hull
Bradley C. Morris
Linda L. Pence
David D. Robinson
Sally Franklin Zweig

ASSOCIATES

Julie Meredith Conrad
John C. Erickson, III
James Scott Fanzini
Jane Ann Himsel
Alice McKenzie Morical
Steven J. Moss
Michael D. Ramsey
Ronald G. Sentman
William C. Wagner
Jill S. Walschlager
Sean T. White

For Complete List of Firm Personnel, See General Section

For full biographical listings, see the Martindale-Hubbell Law Directory

LOCKE REYNOLDS LLP (AV)

1000 Capital Center South, 201 North Illinois Street, 46204-4210
Telephone: 317-237-3800
Telecopier: 317-237-3900
Email: attys@locke.com *URL:* http://www.locke.com

Hugh E. Reynolds, Jr.
Lloyd H. Milliken, Jr.
William V. Hutchens
David S. Allen
David M. Haskett
Michael A. Bergin
David T. Kasper
Steven J. Strawbridge
Thomas L. Davis
Robert A. Fanning
Randall R. Riggs
Alan S. Brown
Mark J. Roberts
Kevin Charles Murray
Julia Blackwell Gelinas
Kim F. Ebert
Terrence L. Brookie
Richard A. Huser
Thomas J. Campbell
Diane Parsons Emswiller
Charles B. Baldwin
Thomas W. Farlow
Jeffrey R. Gaither
Karl M. Koons, III
James Dimos
Kristen K. Rollison
Thomas R. Schultz
Todd J. Kaiser
Eric A. Riegner
Kevin C. Schiferl
Ariane Schallwig Johnson
Peter H. Pogue
John H. Daerr
John K. McDavid
Jeffrey J. Mortier
Nicholas C. Pappas
Brian L. McDermott

Stephen L. Vaughan
Deanna A. Dean-Webster
Kenneth B. Siepman
Jon M. Pinnick
Mary A. Schopper
Susan E. Cline
Bruce J. Alvarado
Mary Margaret Ruth Feldhake
Nelson D. Alexander
Donald B. Kite, Sr.
Thomas F. Bedsole
David A. Sorensen
Shannon Stewart
Derek S. Burrell
Dean R. Brackenridge
T. Joseph Wendt
Michelle Davis Carmichael
John D. Papageorge
Heather L. Wilson
Vincent J. Wong
Daniel G. Foote
Dionne Carroll McCoy
Kristin B. Keltner
Carol M. Wyatt
Joel E. Tragesser
Tricia L. Thompson
Allison Southgate Avery (Not admitted in IN)

OF COUNSEL

William H. Vobach
Robert C. Riddell

Representative Clients: American Honda Motor Co., Inc; Center for Claims Resolution; Citizens Insurance Company of America; CNA Insurance Cos.; General Motors Corp.; PEPSICO, Inc.; PSI Energy, Inc.; St. Francis Hospital; U.S. Aircraft Insurance Group; Wal-Mart Stores, Inc.

For Complete List of Firm Personnel, See General Section

For full biographical listings, see the Martindale-Hubbell Law Directory

MCTURNAN & TURNER (AV)

2400 Market Tower, 10 West Market Street, 46204
Telephone: 317-464-8181
Telecopier: 317-464-8131

Lee B. McTurnan
Wayne C. Turner
Jackie M. Bennett, Jr.
Jacqueline Bowman Ponder
Steven M. Badger
John F. McCauley

(See Next Column)

Representative Clients: Ameritech Indiana; Ameritech Services, Inc.; PricewaterhouseCoopers, LLP; Prudential Securities Incorporated; Western Newspaper Publishing Company; Associates Financial Services Co., Inc.; McGraw-Hill Broadcasting Co., Inc., (WRTV-6); IPALCO Enterprises, Inc.; Eli Lilly and Company.

For full biographical listings, see the Martindale-Hubbell Law Directory

MILLER MULLER MENDELSON & KENNEDY (AV)

8900 Keystone Crossing Suite 1250, 46240
Telephone: 317-574-4500
1-800-394-3094
Fax: 317-574-4501
Email: mmmk@iquest.net

MEMBERS OF FIRM

Michael S. Miller
John Muller
Tilden Mendelson
Timothy J. Kennedy

ASSOCIATE

Catherine A. Kling

For full biographical listings, see the Martindale-Hubbell Law Directory

MITCHELL HURST JACOBS & DICK (AV)

152 East Washington Street, 46204
Telephone: 317-636-0808
1-800-636-0808
Fax: 317-633-7680
URL: http://www.mhjd.com

MEMBERS OF FIRM

Marvin H. Mitchell
William W. Hurst
Samuel L. Jacobs
Richard J. Dick
Marshall S. Hanley
Robert W. Strohmeyer, Jr.

ASSOCIATES

Danielle A. Takla
Michael T. McNelis
Jennifer Levin Sinder
Todd R. Ryden

General Counsel For: Dr. Tavel's Vision Center; Calderon Bros. Vending Machines, Inc.; Grocers Supply Co., Inc.; Power Train Services, Inc.; Frank E. Irish, Inc.; Bedding Liquidators; Galyan's Trading Co.; Harcourt Management Co., Inc.; Kosene & Kosene Mgt. & Dev. Co., Inc.; Hasten Bancorp.

For full biographical listings, see the Martindale-Hubbell Law Directory

SOMMER & BARNARD, ATTORNEYS AT LAW, PC (AV)

4000 Bank One Tower, 111 Monument Circle, 46204
Telephone: 317-630-4000
FAX: 317-236-9802
Email: sandb@sommerbarnard.com
North Office: 8900 Keystone Crossing, Suite 1150, Indianapolis, Indiana, 46240-2134.
Telephone: 317-630-4000.
FAX: 317-844-4780.

William C. Barnard
James E. Hughes
Edward W. Harris, III
Gordon L. Pittenger
Michael C. Terrell
Richard C. Richmond, III
Steven C. Shockley
Gayle A. Reindl

OF COUNSEL

Debra McVicker Lynch

Representative Clients: Comerica Bank; Federal Express; Kimball International; TRW, Inc.

For Complete List of Firm Personnel, See General Section

For full biographical listings, see the Martindale-Hubbell Law Directory

TABBERT HAHN EARNEST & WEDDLE (AV)

Suite 2100, One Indiana Square, 46204-2101
Telephone: 317-639-5444
Fax: 317-639-5232
Email: jtyrrell@tabberthahn.com *URL:* http://www.tabberthahn.com

Don A. Tabbert
Gregory F. Hahn
Lante K. Earnest
Robert G. Weddle
Mark K. Sullivan
Judy M. Tyrrell
Lara D. Engelking
Matthew W. Conner
William W. Mathews
Heather L. Fesko
Charles R. Whybrew

OF COUNSEL

James J. Nocon
William D. Lalley
Joseph W. Hammes
Dale E. Sporleder

For full biographical listings, see the Martindale-Hubbell Law Directory

WARD & WARD (AV)

1014 Circle Tower Building, 55 Monument Circle, 46204
Telephone: 317-639-9501
Fax: 317-637-1919
Email: cpw@wardlawfirm.com

(See Next Column)

WARD & WARD, *Indianapolis—Continued*

MEMBERS OF FIRM

Donald W. Ward
Charles P. Ward

For full biographical listings, see the Martindale-Hubbell Law Directory

YARLING & ROBINSON (AV)

151 North Delaware, Suite 1535, P.O. Box 44128, 46204
Telephone: 317-262-8800
Fax: 317-262-3046
Email: yrhl@yarling.com *URL:* http://www.yarling.com

MEMBERS OF FIRM

Charles F. Robinson, Jr.
John W. Hammel
Linda Y. Hammel
Douglas E. Rogers
Mark S. Gray
Matthew C. Robinson

ASSOCIATE

Jeffrey R. Mitchell

OF COUNSEL

Richard W. Yarling

Representative Clients: Allstate Insurance Co.; American Family Mutual Insurance Company; General Motors Acceptance Corporation; Monroe Guaranty Insurance Company; Northbrook Property & Casualty Company; Pafco General Insurance Company; Progressive Insurance Companies; USFG/St. Paul Insurance Company; Wausau Insurance Companies.

For full biographical listings, see the Martindale-Hubbell Law Directory

YOSHA KRAHULIK & LEVY (AV)

Pyramid II, First Floor, 3500 West DePauw Boulevard, Suite 2015, P.O. Box 68979, 46268
Telephone: 317-334-9200
Toll Free: 800-875-5759
Fax: 317-228-3355
URL: http://www.yoshalaw.com

MEMBERS OF FIRM

Louis Buddy Yosha
William Levy
Jon D. Krahulik

ASSOCIATES

David C. Krahulik
Jeff D. Oliphant
Julie C. Welp
Janice D. Heidt

Reference: National Bank of Indianapolis.

For full biographical listings, see the Martindale-Hubbell Law Directory

*LAFAYETTE,** Tippecanoe Co.

BALL, EGGLESTON, BUMBLEBURG, MCBRIDE, WALKEY & STAPLETON, PC (AV)

810 Bank One Building, P.O. Box 1535, 47902-1535
Telephone: 765-742-9046
Fax: 765-742-1966
Email: info@ball-law.com

Cable G. Ball (1904-1981)
Owen Crook (1908-1977)
Warren N. Eggleston (1923-1991)
Joseph T. Bumbleburg
John K. McBride
Jack L. Walkey
Michael J. Stapleton
Jeffrey J. Newell
James T. Hodson
Brian Wade Walker
Cheryl M. Knodle
Randy J. Williams
Brenda Mithoefer Clapper

General Counsel for: The Lafayette Union Railway Co.
Representative Clients: Farmers Insurance Group; General Accident Fire & Life Assurance Corp.; City of Lafayette Board of Parks and Recreation; West Lafayette Community School Corp.; Travelers Insurance Co.; Trustees, West Lafayette Public Library; Town of Dayton, Indiana.

For full biographical listings, see the Martindale-Hubbell Law Directory

LAYDEN & LAYDEN (AV)

Suite 712, Bank One Building, 201 Main Street, P.O. Box 909, 47902-0909
Telephone: 765-742-7646
Fax: 765-742-0983
Email: cmlayden@iquest.net

MEMBERS OF FIRM

Charles Max Layden
Lynn M. Layden

For full biographical listings, see the Martindale-Hubbell Law Directory

STUART & BRANIGIN (AV)

The Life Building, 300 Main Street, Suite 800, P.O. Box 1010, 47902-1010
Telephone: 765-423-1561
Telecopier: 765-742-8175
Email: sb@stuartlaw.com *URL:* http://www.stuartlaw.com
Indianapolis, Indiana Office: Suite 1401, 8888 Keystone Crossing, 46240.
Telephone: 317-574-7245.
Fax: 317-574-7050.

(See Next Column)

MEMBERS OF FIRM

Allison Ellsworth Stuart (1886-1950)
Roger D. Branigin (1902-1975)
Larry R. Fisher
Stephen R. Pennell
Anthony S. Benton
William E. Emerick
John C. Duffey
Thomas B. Parent
Laura L. Bowker
Kevin D. Nicoson
Susan K. Roberts
John M. Stuckey
Deborah B. Trice
William P. Kealey
David A. Starkweather
Geoffrey L. Blazi

SENIOR COUNSEL

Russell H. Hart

COUNSEL

James V. McGlone

General Counsel for: The Lafayette Life Insurance Co.; INB National Bank, N.W.; Lafayette Home Hospital, Inc.
State Counsel for: Norfolk & Western Railway Co.
Mr. Ryan is Counsel to: The Trustees of Purdue University.
Representative Clients: Aluminum Company of America; Liberty Mutual Insurance Group.

For Complete List of Firm Personnel, See General Section

For full biographical listings, see the Martindale-Hubbell Law Directory

WITHERED CORRIGAN & SERVICE (AV)

8 North Third Street, Suite 401, P.O. Box 499, 47902-0499
Telephone: 765-742-1988
Fax: 765-742-8774
Email: info@witheredlaw.com

Jerome L. Withered
Christopher D. Corrigan
Angela M. Service

ASSOCIATE

Michael H. Dowler

For full biographical listings, see the Martindale-Hubbell Law Directory

MERRILLVILLE, Lake Co.

HODGES & DAVIS, P.C. (AV)

8700 Broadway, 46410
Telephone: 219-641-8700
Fax: 219-641-8710
URL: http://www.hodgesdavis.com
Portage, Indiana Office: 6082 Lute Road. P.O. Box 1037.
Telephone: 219-762-9129.
Fax: 219-762-2826.

Clyde D. Compton
William B. Davis
Earle F. Hites
R. Lawrence Steele
Gregory A. Sobkowski
Bonnie C. Coleman
Jill M. Madajczyk
Laura B. Frost
David H. Kreider
Jeanne B. Blumenthal

OF COUNSEL

Edward J. Hussey

Representative Clients: Dominick's Finer Foods, Inc.; Merrillville Community School Corporation; The Methodist Hospitals, Inc.; Nielsen Buick Jeep Eagle; Northwest Indiana Water Company; City of Portage; Portage Township Schools; The Prudential Insurance Company; Shaver Motors, Inc.

For Complete List of Firm Personnel, See General Section

For full biographical listings, see the Martindale-Hubbell Law Directory

SPANGLER, JENNINGS & DOUGHERTY, P.C. (AV)

8396 Mississippi Street, 46410-6398
Telephone: 219-769-2323
Facsimile: 219-769-5007
Email: spangler@sjdlaw.com
Valparaiso, Indiana Office: 150 Lincolnway, Suite 3001.
Telephone: 219-462-6151.
FAX: 219-477-4935.

Harry J. Jennings
Richard A. Mayer
Jay A. Charon
John P. McQuillan
Samuel J. Bernardi, Jr. (Valparaiso Office)
Jon F. Schmoll
Robert D. Hawk
Peter G. Koransky
David J. Hanson
Robert P. Kennedy
Allen B. Zaremba
James T. McNiece
Daniel A. Gioia
James D. McQuillan
David L. Abel, II
Harold G. Hagberg
Lawrence A. Kalina
Robert P. Stoner (Valparaiso Office)
Gregory J. Tonner
Kathleen M. Maicher
Paul B. Poracky
Robert D. Brown
Robert J. Dignam

(See Next Column)

SPANGLER, JENNINGS & DOUGHERTY P.C.—*Continued*

ASSOCIATES

Anthony F. Tavitas
Lloyd P. Mullen
Kisti Good Risse
Mark D. Geheb
Greg A. Bouwer
James M. Portelli
Edward W. Hearn (Valparaiso Office)
Robert D. Hawk, Jr.
Ricardo A. Hall
Sharon L. Stanzione

OF COUNSEL

Patrick J. Dougherty (Valparaiso Office)

Representative Clients: Allstate Insurance Company; Civitas Bank; CNA Insurance: Farmers Insurance Group; Ford Motor Credit Co.; Inland Steel Co.; School Town of Munster; St. Paul Insurance Cos.; State Farm Cos.

For Complete List of Firm Personnel, See General Section

For full biographical listings, see the Martindale-Hubbell Law Directory

MISHAWAKA, St. Joseph Co.

TIMOTHY J. WALSH (AV)

Edison Centre, Suite 250, 245 West Edison Road, 46545
Telephone: 219-258-6090
Fax: 219-258-6091
Email: tjwalsh@netnitco.net
Email: tjwalsh@tjwalshatty.com *URL:* http://www.tjwalshatty.com

For full biographical listings, see the Martindale-Hubbell Law Directory

MUNSTER, Lake Co.

LAW OFFICES OF EUGENE M. FEINGOLD (AV)

625 Ridge Road, Suite A, 46321
Telephone: 219-836-8800
Fax: 219-836-8944

ASSOCIATE

Steven P. Kennedy

For full biographical listings, see the Martindale-Hubbell Law Directory

LAW OFFICES OF TIMOTHY F. KELLY (AV)

Suite 2A, 9250 Columbia Avenue, 46321
Telephone: 219-836-4062
Telecopier: 219-836-0167
Email: tfklaw@tfklaw.net

MEMBERS OF FIRM

Timothy F. Kelly
Karl K. Vanzo

ASSOCIATE

Steven J. Sersic

For Complete List of Firm Personnel, See General Section

For full biographical listings, see the Martindale-Hubbell Law Directory

PORTAGE, Porter Co.

HODGES & DAVIS, P.C. (AV)

6082 Lute Road, P.O. Box 1037, 46368
Telephone: 219-762-9129
Fax: 219-762-2826
URL: http://www.hodgesdavis.com
Merrillville, Indiana Office: 8700 Broadway.
Telephone: 219-641-8700.
Fax: 219-641-8710.

Clyde D. Compton
Earle F. Hites
R. Lawrence Steele
Gregory A. Sobkowski
Bonnie C. Coleman
Laura B. Frost

Representative Clients: Dominick's Finer Foods, Inc.; Merrillville Community School Corporation; The Methodist Hospitals, Inc.; Nielsen Buick Jeep Eagle; Northwest Indiana Water Company; City of Portage; Portage Township Schools; The Prudential Insurance Company; Shaver Motors, Inc.

For full biographical listings, see the Martindale-Hubbell Law Directory

*SOUTH BEND,** St. Joseph Co.

DORAN • BLACKMOND LLP (AV)

1700 Valley American Bank Building, 211 W. Washington Street, 46601
Telephone: 219-288-1800
Fax: 219-236-4265

MEMBERS OF FIRM

M. Edward Doran (1895-1982)
John E. Doran
Don G. Blackmond

ASSOCIATES

Don Gregory Blackmond
Peter J. Van Dyke
Lynn M. Butcher

(See Next Column)

OF COUNSEL

A. Howard Williams

For full biographical listings, see the Martindale-Hubbell Law Directory

ROWE & ROWE (AV)

Suite 900 Keybank Building, 46601
Telephone: 219-233-8200
Fax: 219-234-5987

R. Kent Rowe
R. Kent Rowe, III

ASSOCIATES

Robert D. Truitt
Gregory J. Haines
Marie Anne Hendrie

For full biographical listings, see the Martindale-Hubbell Law Directory

*TERRE HAUTE,** Vigo Co.

COX, ZWERNER, GAMBILL & SULLIVAN (AV)

511 Wabash Avenue, P.O. Box 1625, 47808-1625
Telephone: 812-232-6003
Fax: 812-232-6567

MEMBERS OF FIRM

Ernest J. Zwerner (1918-1980)
Benjamin G. Cox (1915-1988)
Gilbert W. Gambill, Jr.
James E. Sullivan
Benjamin G. Cox, Jr.
David W. Sullivan
Robert L. Gowdy
Louis F. Britton
Carroll D. Smeltzer
Jeffry A. Lind
Ronald E. Jumps
Scott Craig
Elizabeth A. Lewis

OF COUNSEL

Robert D. Hepburn

Counsel for: Terre Haute First National Bank; Farmers Insurance Group; Indiana-American Water Co.; Indiana State University; Merchants National Bank of Terre Haute; Rose-Hulman Institute of Technology; Tribune-Star Publishing Co., Inc.; Equitable Life Assurance Society of U.S.; Federated Mutual Insurance Co.; Fireman's Fund; General Accident Group; Guaranty National Insurance; Milwaukee Mutual Insurance Co.; Ohio Casualty Insurance Co.; Hartford Insurance; The Travelers Co.; United Services Auto Assn.; Vernon Insurance Co.

For full biographical listings, see the Martindale-Hubbell Law Directory

MANN LAW FIRM (AV)

33 South Sixth Street, P.O. Box 1643, 47808-1643
Telephone: 812-232-0107
FAX: 812-232-3414
Email: mannlawfirm.com *URL:* http://www.mannlawfirm.com

MEMBERS OF FIRM

Hansford C. Mann (1911-1998)
Max E. Goodwin
Stephen L. Williams
Bruce D. Aukerman
John T. Roach III

References: Terre Haute First National Bank; Indiana State Bank.

For full biographical listings, see the Martindale-Hubbell Law Directory

*VALPARAISO,** Porter Co.

BLACHLY, TABOR, BOZIK & HARTMAN (AV)

56 South Washington Street Suite 401, 46383
Telephone: 219-464-1041
Fax: 219-464-0927
Fort Wayne, Indiana Office: 4656 West Jefferson. Suite 120. 46804.

MEMBERS OF FIRM

James S. Bozik
Duane W. Hartman
David L. Hollenbeck
Thomas F. Macke
Randall J. Zromkoski
Richard J. Rupcich
Craig R. Van Schouwen

OF COUNSEL

Glenn J. Tabor

Reference: First National Bank.

For Complete List of Firm Personnel, See General Section

For full biographical listings, see the Martindale-Hubbell Law Directory

*WARSAW,** Kosciusko Co.

LEMON, ARMEY, HEARN & LEININGER (AV)

210 North Buffalo Street, P.O. Box 770, 46581-0770
Telephone: 219-268-9111
Telecopier: 219-267-8647

MEMBERS OF FIRM

Robert L. Rasor (1922-1997)
Thomas R. Lemon
Michael E. Armey
R. Steven Hearn
Daniel K. Leininger
Jane L. Kauffman

(See Next Column)

LEMON, ARMEY, HEARN & LEININGER, *Warsaw—Continued*

ASSOCIATES

Millard P. Plumlee, III
W. Douglas Lemon
Mark C. Sherer

Representative Clients: Lake City Bank; The Dalton Foundries, Inc.; Grace Schools, Inc.

For full biographical listings, see the Martindale-Hubbell Law Directory

ROCKHILL, PINNICK, PEQUIGNOT, HELM, LANDIS & RIGDON (AV)

105 East Main Street, 46580-2742
Telephone: 219-267-6116
Telecopier: 219-269-9264
Email: rockhill@kconline.com

MEMBERS OF FIRM

Brooks C. Pinnick
Stanley E. Pequignot
Richard K. Helm
Vern K. Landis
Jay A. Rigdon
Jamelyn E. Freeman

ASSOCIATE

Dana Leon

Representative Clients: Warsaw Times-Union Newspaper; State Farm Insurance Cos.; Farmers State Bank; C & D Foods, Inc.; Maple Leaf Farms, Inc.; Othy, Inc.; Phend & Brown, Inc.; Freeman Builders, Inc.

For full biographical listings, see the Martindale-Hubbell Law Directory

IOWA

*CEDAR RAPIDS,** Linn Co.

LYNCH, DALLAS, SMITH & HARMAN, P.C. (AV)

526 Second Avenue SE, P.O. Box 2457, 52406-2457
Telephone: 319-365-9101
Facsimile: 319-365-9512
Email: attorneys@lynchdallas.com

Donald G. Ribble
Scott E. McLeod
Robert R. Rush
Wilford H. Stone
Sean W. McPartland
Matthew J. Nagle

Representative Clients: American States Insurance Co.; Connecticut General Life Insurance Company; Deere & Co.; Rockwell International Corp.; State Farm Insurance Cos.; The Travelers Insurance Cos.

For Complete List of Firm Personnel, See General Section

For full biographical listings, see the Martindale-Hubbell Law Directory

PICKENS, BARNES & ABERNATHY (AV)

Tenth Floor American Building, P.O. Box 74170, 52407-4170
Telephone: 319-366-7621
Fax: 319-366-3158
Email: PBAbernath@AOL.com

MEMBERS OF FIRM

Terry J. Abernathy
Matthew G. Novak

ASSOCIATES

Thad J. Collins
Stephanie L. Hinz

RETIRED

James F. Pickens
Minor Barnes

A list of Representative Clients furnished upon request.

For full biographical listings, see the Martindale-Hubbell Law Directory

SHUTTLEWORTH & INGERSOLL, P.C. (AV)

115 Third Street S.E., Suite 500, P.O. Box 2107, 52406-2107
Telephone: 319-365-9461
Fax: 319-365-8443
URL: http://www.shuttleworthlaw.com

John M. Bickel
Robert D. Houghton
Richard S. Fry
Richard C. Garberson
Steven J. Pace
Glenn L. Johnson
Thomas P. Peffer
Kevin H. Collins
Diane Kutzko
Mark L. Zaiger
Douglas R. Oelschlaeger
Constance M. Alt
Kurt L. Kratovil

Nancy J. Penner
Kevin J. Caster
Theresa C. Davis
Sarah J. Gayer
Jennifer Rinden Clark

Representative Clients: Archer-Daniels-Midland Co.; Cargill, Inc.; CIGNA Companies; CNA Insurance Companies; Fireman's Fund Insurance Companies; Firstar Bank N.A.; General Casualty Company of Wisconsin; General Motors Corp.; Grinnell Mutual Insurance Company.

(See Next Column)

For Complete List of Firm Personnel, See General Section

For full biographical listings, see the Martindale-Hubbell Law Directory

*DES MOINES,** Polk Co.

BELIN LAMSON MCCORMICK ZUMBACH FLYNN, A PROFESSIONAL CORPORATION (AV)

The Financial Center, 666 Walnut Street, Suite 2000, 50309-3989
Telephone: 515-243-7100
Fax: 515-282-7615

Mark McCormick
Roger T. Stetson
David L. Charles
Quentin R. Boyken
Charles F. Becker
Mark E. Weinhardt
Dennis P. Ogden
Edward M. Mansfield
Margaret C. Callahan
Robert D. Sharp
Michael R. Reck
Jennifer J. Lucas (Not admitted in IA)
David K. Basler

Danielle Marie Shelton

For Complete List of Firm Personnel, See General Section

For full biographical listings, see the Martindale-Hubbell Law Directory

FINLEY, ALT, SMITH, SCHARNBERG, CRAIG, HILMES & GAFFNEY, P.C. (AV)

604 Locust Street, Fourth Floor Equitable Building, 50309
Telephone: 515-288-0145
Telecopier: 515-288-2724

Thomas A. Finley
Steven K. Scharnberg
John D. (Jack) Hilmes
R. Todd Gaffney
Kerry A. Finley
Pamela J. Prager
Kevin J. Driscoll
V. Glenn Goodwin, Jr.

Representative Clients: ALAS; American Society of Composers, Authors and Publishers; Equitable Life Assurance Society of the U.S.; Federated Insurance Co.; Meredith Corp.
Iowa Attorneys for: Midwest Medical Insurance Co.
District Attorneys for: Norfolk & Southern Railroad; Soo Line Railroad Company.

For Complete List of Firm Personnel, See General Section

For full biographical listings, see the Martindale-Hubbell Law Directory

GREFE & SIDNEY, P.L.C. (AV)

2222 Grand Avenue, P.O. Box 10434, 50306
Telephone: 515-245-4300
Fax: 515-245-4452
Email: grandfirm@aol.com
Pella, Iowa Office: 725 Franklin Street, 50219.
Telephone: 515-628-9343.
Fax: 515-628-7252.

Henry A. Harmon
Claude H. Freeman
Stephen D. Hardy
John Werner
Patrick J. McNulty
Mark W. Thomas
Guy R. Cook
Andrew D. Hall

Stephanie Glenn Techau
Mark A. Schultheis
Marcy A. O'Brien
Donna R. Miller
Marc D. McKay

OF COUNSEL

Ross H. Sidney

Representative Clients: Capitol Communications; Easter Enterprises, Inc.; Freeman Decorating Co.; Koehring Co.; Liberty Mutual Insurance Co.; Otis Elevator Company; Pella Corp.; State Farm Mutual Insurance Companies; The St. Paul Companies; Zurich-American Insurance Group.

For Complete List of Firm Personnel, See General Section

For full biographical listings, see the Martindale-Hubbell Law Directory

HANSEN, MCCLINTOCK & RILEY (AV)

Eighth Floor - Fleming Building, 218 Sixth Avenue, 50309
Telephone: 515-244-2141
Fax: 515-244-2931
Email: hmrlaw@aol.com

MEMBERS OF FIRM

Haemer Wheatcraft (1904-1983)
J. Rudolph Hansen (1904-1995)
John A. McClintock
Ronald A. Riley
Chester C. Woodburn, III
William D. Scherle
David L. Brown
John E. Swanson

ASSOCIATES

James M. Ballard
Aaron T. Oliver

Representative Clients: The St. Paul Companies; Bituminous Insurance Companies; Northwestern National Insurance Co.; The Travelers Insurance Companies; United States Aviation Insurance Group; American International

(See Next Column)

HANSEN, MCCLINTOCK & RILEY—*Continued*

Companies; Iowa Credit Union League; The McAninch Corp.; R. J. Reynolds Tobacco Co.; Brown Bros., Inc. Electrical Contractors.

For full biographical listings, see the Martindale-Hubbell Law Directory

HAWKINS & NORRIS (AV)

2501 Grand Avenue, Suite C, 50312
Telephone: 515-288-6532
Fax: 515-288-9733

MEMBERS OF FIRM

Lex Hawkins
Glenn L. Norris

ASSOCIATES

George F. Davison, Jr.
Carla Tolbert Schemmel
David N. May

Reference: West Des Moines State Bank.

For full biographical listings, see the Martindale-Hubbell Law Directory

HUBER, BOOK, CORTESE, HAPPE & BROWN, P.L.C. (AV)

317 Sixth Avenue, Suite 200, 50309-4127
Telephone: 515-243-4148
Fax: 515-243-5481
Email: huber@desmoineslaw.com

MEMBERS OF FIRM

James C. Huber
Richard G. Book
Joseph S. Cortese II
Joseph A. Happe
Patrick D. Smith

Representative Clients: Atlantic Mutual Cos.; CNA Insurance Cos.; Fireman's Fund American Insurance Companies; Great West Casualty Co.; Liberty Mutual Insurance Co.; Maryland Insurance Group; Prudential Property and Casualty Insurance Co.; USF&G Company.
Reference: Bank of America.

For full biographical listings, see the Martindale-Hubbell Law Directory

NYEMASTER, GOODE, VOIGTS, WEST, HANSELL & O'BRIEN, A PROFESSIONAL CORPORATION (AV)

700 Walnut, Suite 1600, 50309
Telephone: 515-283-3100
Telecopier: 515-283-3108
Ames, Iowa Office: 1416 Buckeye Avenue, Ames, Iowa 50010.
Telephone: 515-233-3000.
Telecopier: 515-232-3846.

LeRoy R. Voigts
James B. West
Edgar F. Hansell
W. Don Brittin, Jr.
Don Muyskens
R. Craig Shives
Roger L. Ferris
Lawrence E. Myers
Keith E. Luchtel
Gerald J. Newbrough
Robert A. VanOrsdel
Richard J. Sapp
G. R. Neumann
Russell E. Schrage
Carlton T. King
Gregory P. Page
Randall G. Horstmann
Jay Eaton
Bradford L. Austin
Burns Mossman
Phyllis E. Pearson
Hayward L. Draper
Sara J. Sersland
James E. Gritzner
Michael W. Thrall
Mark C. Dickinson
Gregory B. Wilcox
John F. Lorentzen
Rod Kubat
Steven J. Roy
Frank B. Harty
James C. Wine
Bruce W. Baker
Thomas W. Foley
Steven H. Lytle
Terry C. Hancock
Anthony A. Longnecker
Wade H. Schut
Mark D. Aljets
G. Thomas Sullivan
Joseph A. Quinn
Joan Fletcher
Thomas H. Walton
Willard L. Boyd III
Lisette Sell
Jeffrey William Courter
Hallie E. Still-Caris
Brian J. Humke
Deborah S. Krauth

Paula S. Dierenfeld
John B. Tuffnell
Jill M. Stevenson
Angel West
Kathryn Atkinson Overberg
Angela L. Watson
Jennifer L. Vergilii
Debra L. Dalton
Amy L. VanDuyn
Neal K. Westin
John T. Clendenin
Stephanie L. Marett

OF COUNSEL

Samuel G. O'Brien
John J. McLaughlin
Drew R. Tillotson
Frank B. Comfort
Luther L. Hill, Jr.
Barry Nadler

Representative Clients: Burlington Northern and Santa Fe Railway Company; East Des Moines National Bank; Northwestern Bell Telephone Co.; Amoco Oil Co.; Inter-State Assurance Co.; Central Life Assurance Co.; Montgomery Ward; Deere & Co.

For full biographical listings, see the Martindale-Hubbell Law Directory

PATTERSON, LORENTZEN, DUFFIELD, TIMMONS, IRISH, BECKER & ORDWAY, L.L.P. (AV)

729 Insurance Exchange Building, 50309
Telephone: 515-283-2147
Fax: 515-283-1002
Email: mail@pattersonfirm.com *URL:* http://www.pattersonfirm.com

MEMBERS OF FIRM

G. O. Patterson (1914-1982)
James A. Lorentzen (Retired)
Theodore T. Duffield
William E. Timmons (Retired)
Roy M. Irish
F. H. Becker (Retired)
Gary D. Ordway
Robin L. Hermann
Harry Perkins, III
Michael F. Lacey, Jr.
Gregory J. Wilson
Jeffrey A. Boehlert
Douglas A. Haag
Charles E. Cutler
Michael D. Huppert
Martin C. Sprock
William A. Wickett
Frederick M. Haskins
Jeffrey A. Baker
Janice M. Herfkens
Coreen K. Bezdicek
Patrick V. Waldron

ASSOCIATE

Michael S. Jones

General Counsel for: Iowa Insurance Institute.
Representative Clients: Allied Mutual Insurance Company; CNA Insurance Company; Chubb Insurance Group; Continental Western Insurance Co.; Farmers Insurance Group; Farmland Insurance Company; Grinnell Mutual Reinsurance Company; Hawkeye Security Insurance Company; Iowa Insurance Institute, St. Paul Fire & Marine Insurance Company.

For full biographical listings, see the Martindale-Hubbell Law Directory

THE WALKER LAW FIRM (AV)

2501 Grand Avenue, Suite E, 50312
Telephone: 515-281-1488
Fax: 515-281-1489
Email: ERWJK@aol.com

E. Ralph Walker
David J. Darrell
Joseph W. Fernandez

OF COUNSEL

Fred E. Rizk (Not admitted in IA)

For full biographical listings, see the Martindale-Hubbell Law Directory

WHITFIELD & EDDY, P.L.C. (AV)

317 6th Avenue, Suite 1200 Locust at 6th, 50309-4195
Telephone: 515-288-6041
Fax: 515-246-1474
Email: info@whitfieldlaw.com *URL:* http://www.whitfieldlaw.com

Timothy J. Walker
David L. Phipps
Benjamin B. Ullem
Robert L. Fanter
Bernard L. "Jerry" Spaeth
William L. Fairbank
Robert G. Bridges
Jaki K. Samuelson
Kevin M. Reynolds
Thomas H. Burke
Thomas Henderson
George H. Frampton
Megan Manning Antenucci
Wendy L. Carlson
Gary A. Norton
Frank M. Grenard (Not admitted in IA)
Mark V. Hanson
Maureen Roach Tobin
August B. Landis
Richard J. Kirschman
John F. Fatino

Jason M. Casini
Roscoe A. Ries, Jr.
Lisa A. Nelson
J. Campbell Helton
Anjela A. Shutts
Danette L. Kennedy
Stephen E. Doohen
Sean A. Pelletier
Matthew C. Ahmann

General Counsel for: Hawkeye-Security Insurance Co.; United Security Insurance Co.
Representative Clients: Allied Mutual Insurance Co.; Clark Equipment Co.; General Motors Corp.; Marriott International, Inc.; Old Republic Surety; Royal Insurance Co.; Tudor Insurance Co.; Western World Insurance Co.

For Complete List of Firm Personnel, See General Section
For full biographical listings, see the Martindale-Hubbell Law Directory

*HAMPTON,** Franklin Co.

HOBSON, CADY & CADY (AV)

9 First Street S.W., P.O. Box 456, 50441
Telephone: 515-456-2555
Fax: 515-456-3315
Email: cadyart@rconnect.com

MEMBERS OF FIRM

A. J. Hobson (1903-1972)
G. Arthur Cady
G. A. Cady, III

General Counsel for: Ag Services of America, Inc.
A list of Representative Clients will be furnished upon request.
References: First National Bank of Hampton.

For full biographical listings, see the Martindale-Hubbell Law Directory

*IOWA CITY,** Johnson Co.

JOHNSTON, POTTERFIELD & NATHANSON, P.C. (AV)
1902 Broadway, P.O. Box 3400, 52244
Telephone: 319-354-1712
Fax: 319-354-7265
URL: http://www.lawyers.com/johnstonlaw
Cedar Rapids Office: 129 First Avenue, S.W., P.O. Box 74210.
Telephone: 319-366-1000.
Fax: 319-366-6973.
Waterloo Office: 1506 LaPorte Road, P.O. Box 2787.
Telephone: 319-235-3000.
Fax: 319-235-2108.

Joseph C. Johnston
Amanda Potterfield
Henry E. Nathanson
Cathy L. Fitzmaurice
David Burbidge

OF COUNSEL

Carl J. Goetz, Jr.

For full biographical listings, see the Martindale-Hubbell Law Directory

MEARDON, SUEPPEL, DOWNER & HAYES P.L.C. (AV)
122 South Linn Street, 52240
Telephone: 319-338-9222
Fax: 319-338-7250

William L. Meardon (1919-1997)
James D. McCarragher
Thomas D. Hobart
Charles A. Meardon

Representative Clients: United Technologies-Automotive; Perpetual Savings Bank; Economy Advertising Company; Metro Pavers, Inc.; League of Iowa Municipalities; Hills Bank and Trust Co.; J.M. Swank Co.; City of Muscatine; McComas-Lacina Construction Co., Inc.; Diamond Dave's Taco Company, Inc.

For Complete List of Firm Personnel, See General Section

For full biographical listings, see the Martindale-Hubbell Law Directory

PITTON LAW OFFICES, P.A. (AV Ⓣ)
503 Iowa State Bank Building, 102 South Clinton Street, 52240
Telephone: 319-338-2508
Fax: 319-338-3334
WATS: 800-488-4430
Email: pittonlaw@iowacity.net
Minneapolis, Minnesota Office: 110 Southdale Place, 3400 West 66th Street, 55435.
Telephone: 612-925-6900.

Michael J. Pitton

For full biographical listings, see the Martindale-Hubbell Law Directory

*MASON CITY,** Cerro Gordo Co.

WINSTON & BYRNE, LAWYERS, A PROFESSIONAL CORPORATION (AV)
119 Second Street, N.W., 50401
Telephone: 515-423-1913
Fax: 515-423-8998
Email: winston.byrne@mach3ww.com

Harold R. Winston
Michael G. Byrne
Patrick B. Byrne

Representative Clients: Woodharbor Molding & Millworks, Inc.; Winkleman Farms, Inc.; Sparboe Iowa Corporation; Schmidt Family Farms, Inc.; First Citizen's National Bank of Mason City; Norwest Bank Iowa, N.A.

For full biographical listings, see the Martindale-Hubbell Law Directory

*SIOUX CITY,** Woodbury Co.

HEIDMAN, REDMOND, FREDREGILL, PATTERSON, PLAZA & DYKSTRA, L.L.P. (AV)
A Registered Limited Liability Partnership including Professional Corporations
701 Pierce Street, Suite 200, P.O. Box 3086, 51102
Telephone: 712-255-8838
Fax: 712-258-6714
Email: lawyers@pionet.net

MEMBERS OF FIRM

Marvin F. Heidman
James W. Redmond
Alan E. Fredregill (P.C.)
Charles T. Patterson
Thomas M. Plaza
Daniel D. Dykstra
Lance D. Ehmcke
Margaret M. Prahl
Gregg E. Williams
Cynthia C. Moser
Judith A. Higgs
John C. Gray
Daniel B. Shuck
Rita C. Grimm
Edward C."Ted" Poulsen
Patrick L. Sealey

ASSOCIATES

Jeff W. Wright
Sarah J. Kuehl

(See Next Column)

OF COUNSEL

John W. Gleysteen (Retired)
Robert R. Eidsmoe (Retired)
Jacob C. Gleysteen (1883-1943)
H. Clifford Harper (1891-1959)

Representative Clients: Mercy Medical Center; Allied Insurance Group; Irving F. Jensen, Co.; Terra International, Inc.; P.I.C. International Group, P.L.C.; Grinnell Mutual Reinsurance Co.; Travelers Insurance Co.; United Fire & Casualty; Kemper Insurance Group; American Family Insurance.

For Complete List of Firm Personnel, See General Section

For full biographical listings, see the Martindale-Hubbell Law Directory

MAYNE & MAYNE (AV)
400 Pioneer Bank Building, 701 Pierce Street, P.O. Box 5049, 51102-5049
Telephone: 712-252-3220
Fax: 712-252-1535
Email: maynelaw@aol.com

OF COUNSEL

Wiley Mayne

MEMBERS OF FIRM

John D. Mayne
Robert J. Pierson

Representative Clients: American Telephone & Telegraph Co.; Amoco Oil Company; Central United Life Insurance Company of America; Credit Bureau of Sioux City; Design Professionals Financial Corp.; Ford Motor Credit Company; Metz Baking Company; Podiatry Insurance Company of America; Shell Chemical Company; U.S. West Communications Company.

For full biographical listings, see the Martindale-Hubbell Law Directory

WEST DES MOINES, Polk Co.

LAMARCA & LANDRY, P.C. (AV)
1300 50th Street, 50266
Telephone: 515-225-2600
Fax: 515-225-8581
Islamorada, Florida Office: 202 Biscayne Boulevard, 33036.
Telephone: 305-664-8527.

George A. LaMarca
Gregory W. Landry

Gary G. Mattson
Justin E. LaVan

OF COUNSEL

Martin R. Anderson
Samuel S. Duffey

For full biographical listings, see the Martindale-Hubbell Law Directory

KANSAS

*DODGE CITY,** Ford Co.

FOULSTON & SIEFKIN L.L.P. (AV)
810 Frontview, P.O. Box 1147, 67801
Telephone: 316-227-8126
Fax: 316-227-8451
URL: http://www.foulston.com
Wichita, Kansas Office: 100 North Broadway, 700 NationsBank Financial Center, 67202.
Telephone: 316-267-6371.
FAX: 316-267-6345.
Topeka, Kansas Office: 1515 NationsBank Tower, 534 Kansas Avenue, 66603.
Telephone: 785-233-3600.
FAX: 785-233-1610.
Member: Lex Mundi, The World's Leading Association of Independent Law Firms.

MEMBERS OF FIRM

David J. Rebein
Thomas W. Young

For Complete List of Firm Personnel, See General Section

For full biographical listings, see the Martindale-Hubbell Law Directory

*HUTCHINSON,** Reno Co.

GILLILAND & HAYES, P.A. A PROFESSIONAL ASSOCIATION (AV)
20 West 2nd Avenue, 2nd Floor, P.O. Box 2977, 67504-2977
Telephone: 316-662-0537
Facsimile: 316-669-9426
URL: http://www.gillilandhayes.com
Wichita, Kansas Office: The Orpheum Centre, Suite 300, 200 North Broadway, P.O. Box 49406.
Telephone: 316-262-2266.
Facsimile: 316-263-2202.
Kansas City, Missouri Office: 12th Floor, 3100 Broadway.
Telephone: 816-753-3100.
Facsimile: 816-753-2271.

(See Next Column)

GILLILAND & HAYES P.A. A PROFESSIONAL ASSOCIATION—*Continued*

Robert J. Gilliland
John F. Hayes
James R. Gilliland
John S. Schmidt
Bruce B. Waugh (Not admitted in KS; Resident, Kansas City, Missouri Office)
Michael R. O'Neal
Bradley D. Dillon
Gerald L. Green
David N. Zimmerman (Not admitted in KS; Resident, Kansas City, Missouri Office)
Scott J. Mann
Carol Z. Smith (Resident, Kansas City, Missouri Office)
Kathleen A. Hardee (Resident, Kansas City, Missouri Office)
Kendall R. Cunningham (Resident, Wichita Office)
Mark R. Maloney (Resident, Wichita Office)

Thomas A. Dower
Tracy Applegate Cole
Laura A. Hederstedt
Terri Roberts Munsell (Resident, Kansas City, Missouri Office)
Lisa M. Ward
Kimberly Breda Bushek (Resident, Kansas City, Missouri Office)
E. Thomas Pyle, III
Tara L. Bragg

OF COUNSEL

Robert P. Reams (Not admitted in KS; Resident, Kansas City, Missouri Office)

Representative Clients: Allied Group; CNA Insurance; Dillon Companies; Farm Bureau Mutual Insurance Co.; Fidelity Deposit Co. of Maryland; Kansas Medical Mutual Insurance Co.; St. Paul Fire and Marine Insurance Co.; St. Paul/USF&G; Travelers Insurance Companies; U.S. Fidelity Corp.

For full biographical listings, see the Martindale-Hubbell Law Directory

---

*JUNCTION CITY,** Geary Co.

HARPER, HORNBAKER, ALTENHOFEN & OPAT, CHARTERED (AV)

715 North Washington Street, P.O. Box 168, 66441
Telephone: 913-762-2100
Fax: 913-762-2291
Email: harphorn@nqks.com *URL:* http://www.harphorn.com

Howard W. Harper (1912-1988)
Lee Hornbaker
Steven Hornbaker
Charles W. Harper, II
Craig Altenhofen
Steven L. Opat
Dan Mitchell McCulley

Representative Clients: Commercial Union Insurance Co.; Dodson Group; State Farm Insurance Cos.; Reliance Insurance Co.; Employers Mutual; U.S.F.&G.
Approved Attorneys for: Chicago Title & Trust; Columbian Title & Trust.

For full biographical listings, see the Martindale-Hubbell Law Directory

---

*KANSAS CITY,** Wyandotte Co.

HOLBROOK, HEAVEN & OSBORN, P.A. (AV)

757 Armstrong, P.O. Box 171927, 66117
Telephone: 913-342-2500
Fax: 913-342-0603
Merriam, Kansas Office: 6700 Antioch Street.
Telephone: 913-677-1717.
Fax: 913-677-0403.

Reid F. Holbrook
Lewis A. Heaven, Jr. (Resident, Merriam Office)
Thomas E. Osborn
Robert L. Kennedy
Janet M. Simpson
John D. Tongier (Resident, Merriam Office)
Thomas M. Sutherland
Thomas S. Busch (Resident, Merriam Office)
Kurt S. Brack (Resident, Merriam Office)
Douglas G. Peterson
Daniel W. Peters

For Complete List of Firm Personnel, See General Section

For full biographical listings, see the Martindale-Hubbell Law Directory

---

OVERLAND PARK, Johnson Co.

FISHER, PATTERSON, SAYLER & SMITH, L.L.P. (AV)

11050 Roe Avenue, Suite 210, 66211
Telephone: 913-339-6757
FAX: 913-339-6187
Email: fpss@worldnet.att.net
Topeka, Kansas Office: 3550 S.W. 5th Street, P.O. Box 949, 66601.
Telephone: 785-232-7761.
Fax: 785-232-6604.

MEMBERS OF FIRM

Edwin Dudley Smith (Resident)
Michael K. Seck (Resident)
David P. Madden (Resident)

ASSOCIATES

Kelly A. Feyh (Resident)
Jennifer R. Rose (Resident)

For full biographical listings, see the Martindale-Hubbell Law Directory

KLAMANN & HUBBARD, P.A. (AV)

7101 College Boulevard, Suite 120, 66210
Telephone: 913-327-7600
Fax: 913-327-7800
Email: klamann@sprintmail.com *URL:* http://look-on.com/sherlaw/

John M. Klamann
Dirk L. Hubbard

For full biographical listings, see the Martindale-Hubbell Law Directory

---

RISJORD & JAMES, P.C. (AV)

Suite 100, 10680 Barkley, 66212
Telephone: 913-381-5151
Fax: 913-381-2569
Email: RJLaw@RisjordJames.com *URL:* http://www.risjordjames.com

Randy W. James
Aaron N. Woods

Lisa C. Beckley

RETIRED

John C. Risjord

For full biographical listings, see the Martindale-Hubbell Law Directory

---

SHAMBERG, JOHNSON & BERGMAN, CHARTERED (AV)

Suite 355, 4551 West 107th Street, 66207
Telephone: 913-642-0600
Fax: 913-642-9629
Email: mail@sjblaw.com *URL:* http://www.sjblaw.com
Kansas City, Kansas Office: Suite M-4, One Security Plaza.
Telephone: 913-281-1900.
Kansas City, Missouri Office: Suite 205, Scarritt Arcade Building, 819 Walnut.
Telephone: 816-556-9431.

Lynn R. Johnson
Victor A. Bergman
John M. Parisi

Steven G. Brown
Steve N. Six

OF COUNSEL

John E. Shamberg

For full biographical listings, see the Martindale-Hubbell Law Directory

---

*TOPEKA,** Shawnee Co.

FISHER, PATTERSON, SAYLER & SMITH, L.L.P. (AV)

3550 S.W. 5th Street, P.O. Box 949, 66601
Telephone: 785-232-7761
Fax: 785-232-6604
Email: fpss@cjnetworks.com
Overland Park, Kansas Office: 11050 Roe Avenue, Suite 210, 66211.
Telephone: 913-339-6757.
Fax: 913-339-6187.

MEMBERS OF FIRM

Donald Patterson
Edwin Dudley Smith (Resident, Overland Park Office)
Larry G. Pepperdine
James P. Nordstrom
Justice B. King
J. Steven Pigg
Steve R. Fabert
Ronald J. Laskowski
Michael K. Seck (Resident, Overland Park Office)
David P. Madden (Resident, Overland Park Office)
Steven K. Johnson
Kristine A. Larscheid

ASSOCIATES

Billy E. Newman
David R. Cooper
Kelly A. Feyh (Resident, Overland Park Office)
Jennifer R. Rose (Resident, Overland Park Office)

OF COUNSEL

David H. Fisher

RETIRED

Charles Keith Sayler (Retired)

Representative Clients: Gage Shopping Center, Inc.; Fireman's Fund-American Insurance Cos.; United States Fidelity and Guaranty Co.; The Procter & Gamble Company; Commercial Union Insurance Companies; National Casualty; The Hartford; Berkshire Hathaway Companies.

For full biographical listings, see the Martindale-Hubbell Law Directory

---

GOODELL, STRATTON, EDMONDS & PALMER, L.L.P. (AV)

515 South Kansas Avenue, 66603-3999
Telephone: 785-233-0593
Fax: 785-233-8870
Email: GSEP@CJNETWORKS.COM *URL:* http://www.cjnetworks.com/~gsep
Kansas City, Missouri Office: 10401 Holmes Road, Suite 280.
Telephone: 816-943-8577.

(See Next Column)

GOODELL, STRATTON, EDMONDS & PALMER L.L.P., *Topeka—Continued*

MEMBERS OF FIRM

Gerald L. Goodell
Wayne T. Stratton
Arthur E. Palmer
Harold S. Youngentob
Charles R. Hay
Patrick M. Salsbury
Les E. Diehl
David E. Bruns
N. Larry Bork
Catherine M. Walberg
Steve A. Schwarm

ASSOCIATE

Anne M. Kindling

SPECIAL COUNSEL

Marta Fisher Linenberger
Curtis J. Waugh

Counsel for: Farm Bureau Mutual Insurance Co.; Metropolitan Life Insurance Co.; St. Paul Fire & Marine Insurance Co.; American Home Life Insurance Co.; Columbian National Title Insurance Co.; The Menninger Foundation; Ford Motor Credit Co.; Kansas Medical Mutual Insurance Co.; National Farmers Union Property and Casualty Co.

For Complete List of Firm Personnel, See General Section

For full biographical listings, see the Martindale-Hubbell Law Directory

RALSTON & POPE, LLC (AV)

2913 Southwest Maupin Lane, 66614-4139
Telephone: 913-273-8002; 888-913-2783
FAX: 913-273-0744
Email: ERalston@AOL.Com

Eugene B. Ralston
Kevin L. Diehl
Ronald P. Pope

LEGAL SUPPORT PERSONNEL

PARALEGALS

Barbara Cobuluis
Corri Wecker
Colleen Wright
Ashanti Smith

For full biographical listings, see the Martindale-Hubbell Law Directory

WRIGHT, HENSON, SOMERS, SEBELIUS, CLARK & BAKER, LLP (AV)

Commerce Bank Building, 100 Southeast Ninth Street, 2nd Floor, P.O. Box 3555, 66601-3555
Telephone: 785-232-2200
FAX: 785-232-3344
Email: wrighthenson@wrighthenson.com *URL:* http://www.wrighthenson.com

MEMBERS OF FIRM

Thomas E. Wright
K. Gary Sebelius
Bruce J. Clark
Anne Lamborn Baker
Evelyn Zabel Wilson

ASSOCIATE

Michael M. Walker

SPECIAL COUNSEL

David P. Mudrick

Representative Clients: Continental Insurance Companies; American Family Insurance Companies; Shelter Insurance Companies; Newtek, Inc.; Phico Group; Insurance Co.; Kansas Bankers Association; Western Resources, Inc.; KPL/Gas Service Co.; Payless ShoeSource, Inc.

For Complete List of Firm Personnel, See General Section

For full biographical listings, see the Martindale-Hubbell Law Directory

*WICHITA,** Sedgwick Co.

DEPEW AND GILLEN, L.L.C. (AV)

151 North Main, Suite 800, 67202-1409
Telephone: 316-262-4000
Facsimile: 316-265-3819
Email: DG@DEPEWGILLEN.COM *URL:* HTTP://WWW.DEPEWGILLEN.COM

Dennis L. Gillen
Randall K. Rathbun
Nicholas S. Daily
Charles C. Steincamp

For Complete List of Firm Personnel, See General Section

For full biographical listings, see the Martindale-Hubbell Law Directory

FOULSTON & SIEFKIN L.L.P. (AV)

700 NationsBank Financial Center, 67202
Telephone: 316-267-6371
Facsimile: 316-267-6345
URL: http://www.foulston.com
Topeka, Kansas Office: 1515 NationsBank Tower, 534 Kansas Avenue, 66603.
Telephone: 785-233-3600.
Fax: 785-233-1610.
Dodge City, Kansas Office: 810 Frontview, P.O. Box 1147, 67801.
Telephone: 316-227-8126.
Fax: 316-227-8451.

(See Next Column)

Member: Lex Mundi, The World's Leading Association of Independent Law Firms.

MEMBERS OF FIRM

Robert L. Howard
Mikel L. Stout
Richard D. Ewy
Darrell L. Warta
James M. Armstrong
Mary Kathleen Babcock
Gary L. Ayers
Jay F. Fowler
Wyatt M. Wright
Amy S. Lemley
J. Steven Massoni
Jeffery A. Jordan
Trisha A. Thelen
Craig W. West
Carol A. Beier

For Complete List of Firm Personnel, See General Section

For full biographical listings, see the Martindale-Hubbell Law Directory

GRACE, UNRUH & PRATT, L.C. (AV)

Suite 501, 155 North Market Street, 67202-1816
Telephone: 316-269-2006
FAX: 316-269-0437
Email: litigation@fn.net

Brian G. Grace
Terry L. Unruh
Corlin J. Pratt
Gilbert L. Guthrie
Sharon A. Werner
Kevin A. Grace

For full biographical listings, see the Martindale-Hubbell Law Directory

KAHRS, NELSON, FANNING, HITE & KELLOGG L.L.P. (AV)

200 W. Douglas, Suite 600, 67202
Telephone: 316-265-7761
Telecopier: 316-267-7803
URL: http://www.kahrsnelson.com

MEMBERS OF FIRM

Richard C. Hite
Richard L. Honeyman
Larry A. Withers
Steven D. Gough
Randy Troutt
Arthur S. Chalmers
Forrest James Robinson, Jr.
Alan R. Pfaff
Lisa Adrian McPherson

ASSOCIATES

Jerry D. Hawkins
Richard D. Crowder

OF COUNSEL

H. W. Fanning
Vince P. Wheeler

Representative Clients: ABF Freight System, Inc.; American Telephone & Telegraph Co.; Amoco Production Co.; General Motors Corp.; Michelin Tire Corp.; St. Paul Insurance Co.; United States Fidelity and Guaranty Co.; Walmart Stores, Inc.

For Complete List of Firm Personnel, See General Section

For full biographical listings, see the Martindale-Hubbell Law Directory

MORRIS, LAING, EVANS, BROCK & KENNEDY, CHARTERED (AV)

Fourth Floor, 200 West Douglas, 67202-3084
Telephone: 316-262-2671
Fax: 316-262-6226; 262-5991
Topeka, Kansas Office: 800 S.W. Jackson, Suite 914, 66612-2214.
Telephone: 913-232-2662.
Fax: 913-232-9983.

Joseph W. Kennedy
Ken M. Peterson
Richard D. Greene
Dennis M. Feeney
Jeffery L. Carmichael
Robert W. Coykendall
Susan R. Schrag
Robert E. Nugent
Michael Lennen
Jana Deines Abbott
Richard F. Hayse (Resident, Topeka Office)
Thomas R. Docking
Diane S. Worth
Tim J. Moore

References: The Emprise Banks of Kansas; Mercantile Bank of Topeka; Southwest National Bank; Twin Lakes National Bank.

For Complete List of Firm Personnel, See General Section

For full biographical listings, see the Martindale-Hubbell Law Directory

TRIPLETT, WOOLF & GARRETSON, LLC (AV)

2959 North Rock Road, Suite 300, 67226
Telephone: 316-630-8100
Fax: 316-630-8101
Email: twg@twgfirm.com

MEMBERS OF FIRM

John P. Woolf
James A. Walker
Timothy E. McKee
Eric B. Metz
Lee Thompson
Eric S. Strickler
Bradley A. Stout
Rachael K. Pirner
Jeffrey D. Leonard

(See Next Column)

TRIPLETT, WOOLF & GARRETSON LLC—*Continued*

ASSOCIATES

Jeffrey E. Goering
Jerald W. Rogers
Christopher C. Swyers

Representative Clients: Anheuser-Busch Companies, Inc.; Brite Voice Systems, Inc.; Coleman Company, Inc.; Dow Chemical Co.; Friends University; KPMG Peat Marwick; National Plastics Color, Inc.; Total Petroleum, Inc.; Travelers Insurance Co.; Willis Corroon of Kansas, Inc.

For Complete List of Firm Personnel, See General Section

For full biographical listings, see the Martindale-Hubbell Law Directory

YOUNG, BOGLE, MCCAUSLAND, WELLS & BLANCHARD, P.A. (AV)

106 West Douglas, Suite 923, 67202
Telephone: 316-265-7841
Facsimile: 316-265-3956
Email: ybmwblaw@aol.com

Glenn D. Young, Jr.
Jerry D. Bogle
Paul S. McCausland
William A. Wells
Patrick C. Blanchard

J. Michael Peters

OF COUNSEL

Orlin L. Wagner

Representative Clients: Bridgestone/Firestone, Inc.; Deere & Co.; GAF Corp.; Sears Roebuck & Co.; Deere Credit Services, Inc.; Horace Mann Insurance, Co.; Lida Advertising.

For Complete List of Firm Personnel, See General Section

For full biographical listings, see the Martindale-Hubbell Law Directory

KENTUCKY

ASHLAND, Boyd Co.

MARTIN, JUSTICE & VINCENT (AV)

431 Sixteenth Street, P.O. Box 2528, 41105-2528
Telephone: 606-329-8338
Fax: 606-325-8199
Email: mjvlaw@zoomnet.net

Richard W. Martin
David Justice
John F. Vincent
Thomas Wade Lavender, II

ASSOCIATE

Charles D. Oppenheimer

Representative Clients: City of Ashland; FIVCO Area Development District; Boyd County Sanitation District No. 2.
Insurance Counsel for: State Farm Mutual Automobile Insurance Co.; State Farm Fire and Casualty Co.; Travelers Insurance Co.; Grange Mutual Insurance Co.; Great American Insurance Co.

For full biographical listings, see the Martindale-Hubbell Law Directory

*BOWLING GREEN,** Warren Co.

COLE, MOORE & BAKER (AV)

921 College Street-Phoenix Place, P.O. Box 10240, 42102-7240
Telephone: 270-782-6666
FAX: 270-782-8666
Email: CMB@Premiernet.net

MEMBERS OF FIRM

John David Cole
Frank Hampton Moore, Jr.
Matthew J. Baker
Dov Moore

ASSOCIATES

John David Cole, Jr.
Stefan R. Hughes
Matthew P. Cook

OF COUNSEL

Frank R. Goad

Counsel for: Western Kentucky Cola-Cola Bottling Co.; Clark Distributing Co., Inc.; Scotty's Contracting & Stone Co.
Local Counsel for: General Electric Co.; Bucyrus-Erie Company; Wal-Mart Stores, Inc.; Kroger/Country Oven.
Representative Insurance Clients: Liberty Mutual Insurance Co.; Travelers Insurance Co.; Wausau Insurance Co.

For full biographical listings, see the Martindale-Hubbell Law Directory

HARLIN, PARKER, ALCOTT & CHAUDOIN, P.S.C. (AV)

519 East Tenth Street, P.O. Box 390, 42102-0390
Telephone: 502-842-5611
Telefax: 502-842-2607
Email: hpac@premiernet.net *URL:* http://www.lawyers.com/hp

(See Next Column)

William Jerry Parker
James David Bryant
Mark D. Alcott
Robert C. Chaudoin

Robert Shannon Morgan

Representative Clients: General Motors Corp.; Ford Motor Co.; The Goodyear Tire and Rubber Co.; CSX Transportation, Inc.; BellSouth Communications, Inc.; CNA Insurance Cos.; Maryland Casualty Co.; American International Group; Holley Performance Products, Inc.

For Complete List of Firm Personnel, See General Section

For full biographical listings, see the Martindale-Hubbell Law Directory

HARNED, BACHERT & DENTON (AV)

324 East 10th Avenue, P.O. Box 1270, 42102-1270
Telephone: 502-782-3938
Telecopier: 502-781-4737

MEMBERS OF FIRM

Norman E. Harned
Scott A. Bachert
Joy D. Denton

For full biographical listings, see the Martindale-Hubbell Law Directory

KERRICK, GRISE & STIVERS (AV)

1025 State Street, P.O. Box 9547, 42102-9547
Telephone: 502-782-8160
Fax: 502-782-5856
Email: kgs@kgslaw.com
Elizabethtown, Kentucky Office: 2935 Dolphin Drive, Suite 102.
Telephone: 502-769-5788.
Fax: 502-737-9285.

MEMBERS OF FIRM

Thomas N. Kerrick
John R. Grise
Gregory N. Stivers
H. Brent Brennenstuhl
Laura M. Hagan

ASSOCIATES

Karl N. Crandall
Shawn Rosso Alcott
Jason B. Bell

OF COUNSEL

Jeffrey R. O'Grody

LEGAL SUPPORT PERSONNEL

Patricia Logsdon
Laura Lockhart Lico
Allison Lusk

Representative Clients: Dollar General Corp.; Columbia Greenview Regional Hospital; Hospital Corporation of America; Western Kentucky University; Cincinnati Insurance Co.; Kentucky Hospital Association Trust; Kentucky Medical Insurance Co.; Nationwide Insurance Co.; Anthem Casualty Insurance Group.

For full biographical listings, see the Martindale-Hubbell Law Directory

RUDLOFF & RUDLOFF (AV)

553 East Main Street, 42101
Telephone: 270-781-7754
Fax: 270-843-0473

MEMBERS OF FIRM

William J. Rudloff
Daniel B. Rudloff

For full biographical listings, see the Martindale-Hubbell Law Directory

COVINGTON, Kenton Co.

ROBERT C. CETRULO, P.S.C. (AV)

The Cetrulo Building, 620 Washington Street, 41011
Telephone: 606-491-6200
FAX: 606-491-6201

Robert C. Cetrulo

Representative Clients: Atlanta Casualty Insurance Co.; Celina Insurance Group; Commercial Union Assurance Cos.; Fireman's Fund; Dairyland Insurance Co.; Gates Rubber Co.; Greyhound Lines, Inc.; Kentucky Insurance Guaranty Assn.; Universal Underwriters Insurance Co.; Zurich-American Insurance Cos.

For full biographical listings, see the Martindale-Hubbell Law Directory

ROBERT E. SANDERS AND ASSOCIATES, P.S.C. (AV)

The Charles H. Fisk House, 1017 Russell Street, 41011-3052
Telephone: 606-491-3000
Fax: 606-655-4642
Email: resanders@worldnet.att.net

Robert E. Sanders

Jeffrey M. Sanders
J. Pierre Tismo
Delana S. Pierce

(See Next Column)

ROBERT E. SANDERS AND ASSOCIATES, P.S.C., *Covington—Continued*

LEGAL SUPPORT PERSONNEL

Shirley L. Sanders
Sandra A. Sturgeon
Sheila D. Rachal

For full biographical listings, see the Martindale-Hubbell Law Directory

TALIAFERRO, MEHLING, SHIROONI & CARRAN (AV)

1005 Madison Avenue, P.O. Box 468, 41012-0468
Telephone: 606-291-9900
Fax: 606-291-3014

MEMBERS OF FIRM

Philip Taliaferro, III
Christopher J. Mehling
Lucinda C. Shirooni
Robert W. Carran

ASSOCIATES

Howard L. Tankersley
Alice G. Keys
Jerome N. Epping, Jr.
Michelle Snodgrass-Deimling

OF COUNSEL

Norbert J. Bischoff
F. Edward Worland, Jr.

For full biographical listings, see the Martindale-Hubbell Law Directory

WARE, BRYSON, WEST & KUMMER (AV)

157 Barnwood Drive, 41017
Telephone: 606-341-0255
Fax: 606-341-1876

MEMBERS OF FIRM

Rodney S. Bryson
Larry C. West
John R. Kummer
Mark W. Howard
Greg D. Voss
Robert B. Cetrulo
Susanne M. Cetrulo
David W. Martin

ASSOCIATE

James M. West
Orie S. Ware (1882-1974)
William O. Ware (1908-1961)
James C. Ware (1913-1991)

Attorneys For: First National Bank of Northern Ky.; State Farm Insurance Co.; Reliance Insurance Group; Maryland Casualty Insurance Co.; Kemper Insurance Co.; State Farm Fire & Casualty Insurance Co.; Shelby Mutual Insurance Co.; Cincinnati Insurance Co.; Travelers/Aetna Group; Allstate Ins. Cos.

For full biographical listings, see the Martindale-Hubbell Law Directory

*DANVILLE,** Boyle Co.

LAW OFFICES OF KENT MASTERSON BROWN (AV)

304 West Main Street, Suite 201, 40422
Telephone: 606-238-7383
Fax: 606-238-7442
Email: kmb@usa.net

ASSOCIATE

Christopher J. Shaughnessy

For full biographical listings, see the Martindale-Hubbell Law Directory

*GLASGOW,** Barren Co.

HERBERT & HERBERT (AV)

135 North Public Square, P.O. Box 1000, 42141
Telephone: 502-651-9000
Fax: 502-651-3317
Email: h&hlaw@glasgow-ky.com

MEMBERS OF FIRM

H. Jefferson Herbert, Jr.
Betty Reece Herbert

ASSOCIATES

Brian K. Pack
Wesley W. Stephens

Representative Clients: Eaton Corp.; Fireman's Fund Insurance Companies; Glasgow Foods, Inc.; Alliance Corp. (Construction); Indiana Insurance Co.; Kentucky Hospital Association Trust; Wininger Oil Co.; Supreme Mills, Inc.; T.J. Samson Community Hospital, Inc.; Travelers Insurance Co.

For full biographical listings, see the Martindale-Hubbell Law Directory

*HAZARD,** Perry Co.

GULLETT, COMBS, REED & BOWLING (AV)

109 Broadway, Second Floor, P.O. Box 1039, 41702-1039
Telephone: 606-439-1373; 1-800-949-8812
Fax: 606-439-4450
Email: apgullet@mis.net
Email: 1234rong@tgtel.com

MEMBERS OF FIRM

Asa P. Gullett, III
Ronald G. Combs
Teresa G. Combs Reed
Matthew Lawton Bowling

ASSOCIATE

Jameson D. Combs

(See Next Column)

LEGAL SUPPORT PERSONNEL

Jacqueline E. Goodin
Jimmie Lynn Jones

Reference: Peoples Bank and Trust Co.

For full biographical listings, see the Martindale-Hubbell Law Directory

*HENDERSON,** Henderson Co.

DEEP & WOMACK (AV)

790 Bob Posey Street, P.O. Box 50, 42419-0050
Telephone: 502-827-2522
Fax: 502-826-2870
Email: deep@henderson.net
Louisville, Kentucky Office: 1228 Starks Building, 455 South Fourth Avenue. P.O. Box 70033, 40270-0033.
Telephone: 502-589-2530.
Fax: 502-589-9297. E-Mail: Deep__Womack@msn.com

MEMBERS OF FIRM

Charles David Deep
Zack N. Womack

ASSOCIATES

Toni Cline Renfro (Resident, Louisville Office)
Carol Schureck Petitt (Resident, Louisville Office)
Jacqueline Chauvin (Resident, Louisville Office)

For full biographical listings, see the Martindale-Hubbell Law Directory

*LEXINGTON,** Fayette Co.

BOEHL STOPHER & GRAVES (AV)

444 West Second Street, 40508
Telephone: 606-252-6721
FAX: 606-253-1445
Louisville, Kentucky Office: Suite 2300, Aegon Center, 400 West Market Street.
Telephone: 502-589-5980.
Fax: 502-561-9400.
Paducah, Kentucky Office: Suite 340 Executive Inn Riverfront, One Executive Boulevard.
Telephone: 270-442-4369.
Fax: 270-442-4689.
Prestonsburg, Kentucky Office: 105 West Court Street.
Telephone: 606-886-8004.
Fax: 606-886-9579.
New Albany, Indiana Office: Elsby East, Suite 204, 400 Pearl Street.
Telephone: 812-948-5053.
Fax: 812-948-9233.

RESIDENT PARTNERS

W. T. Adkins
Nolan Carter, Jr.
Ronald L. Green
Kim Martin Wilkie
Guillermo A. Carlos
James B. Cooper
Steven R. Armstrong

RESIDENT ASSOCIATES

Brennen C. Ragone
William E. Brown, II
Ronald E. Thornsberry

Counsel for: Ford Motor Co.; Texas Eastern Transmission Corp.; Coca-Cola Bottling Co.; National Collegiate Athletic Assn.; Hartford Accident and Indemnity Co.; Continental Insurance Group; St. Paul Fire & Marine Insurance Co.; Lloyds of London; Old Republic Insurance Co.

For full biographical listings, see the Martindale-Hubbell Law Directory

GALLION, BAKER & BRAY, P.S.C. (AV)

200 West Vine Street, Suite 710, 40507-1620
Telephone: 606-255-6885; 800-897-0837
Telecopier: 606-253-9709
Email: gbbatty@lex.infi.net

William J. Gallion
Michael H. Baker
Pamela W. Bray
Barbara A. Kriz
Christopher R. Jenkins
James R. Carpenter

H. Caywood Prewitt, Jr.
David C. Jones
James M. Kennedy
Bruce D. Gehle
David L. Helmers
Elizabeth R. Overton

For full biographical listings, see the Martindale-Hubbell Law Directory

McCOY & WEST (AV)

309 North Broadway, 40507
Telephone: 606-254-6363
FAX: 606-233-4234

MEMBERS OF FIRM

R. Burl McCoy, Jr.
John Kevin West

Charles E. Beal, II
Tonya S. Conner

For full biographical listings, see the Martindale-Hubbell Law Directory

Lexington—Continued

PETER PERLMAN LAW OFFICES, P.S.C. (AV)

388 South Broadway, 40508
Telephone: 606-253-3919
Fax: 606-259-0493

Peter Perlman

Bryce D. Franklin, Jr.

OF COUNSEL

Thomas R. Hays

For full biographical listings, see the Martindale-Hubbell Law Directory

PIPER, WELLMAN & BOWERS (AV)

200 North Upper Street, 40507
Telephone: 606-231-1012
Fax: 606-231-1015
Email: pwb200@uky.campus.mci.net

MEMBERS OF FIRM

George C. Piper
Dean T. Wellman
Barbara J. Bowers

ASSOCIATE

Johann F. Herklotz

Representative Clients: The Virginia Insurance Reciprocal; Woodford Hospital; Clark Regional Medical Center; Garrard Memorial Hospital; Century American Insurance Co.; Equity Residential Properties Trust; Nazareth Health, Inc. d/b/a/ St. Josephs Hospital, a division of Sisters of Charity of Nazareth Health Corp.; Kentucky River Medical Center; Appalachian Regional Healthcare, Inc.; Central Kentucky Physicians, Inc. (CKPI).

For full biographical listings, see the Martindale-Hubbell Law Directory

SAVAGE, GARMER & ELLIOTT, P.S.C. (AV)

Opera House Office Building, 141 North Broadway, 40507
Telephone: 606-254-9351
Fax: 606-233-9769

Joe C. Savage
William R. Garmer
Robert L. Elliott

For full biographical listings, see the Martindale-Hubbell Law Directory

STOLL, KEENON & PARK, LLP (AV)

201 E. Main Street, Suite 1000, 40507-1380
Telephone: 606-231-3000
Telecopier: 606-253-1093; 606-253-1027
URL: http://www.skp.com
Frankfort, Kentucky Office: 307 Washington Street, 40601.
Telephone: 502-875-6220.
Telecopier: 502-875-6235.
Henderson, Kentucky Office: 201 C North Main Street, 42420-3103.
Telephone: 270-831-1900.
Telecopier: 270-827-4060.
Louisville, Kentucky Office: 400 West Market Street, Suite 2650, 40202-3377.
Telephone: 502-568-9100.
Telecopier: 502-568-5700.

MEMBERS OF FIRM

Leslie W. Morris II
Lindsey W. Ingram, Jr.
Bennett Clark
Charles E. Shivel, Jr.
Robert M. Watt, III
J. Peter Cassidy, Jr.
Samuel D. Hinkle IV
Robert F. Houlihan, Jr.
William M. Lear, Jr.
Donald P. Wagner
Robert W. Kellerman
Lizbeth Ann Tully
Eileen M. O'Brien
David C. Schwetschenau
Anita M. Britton
Denise Kirk Ash
Bonnie Hoskins
Diane M. Carlton
Larry A. Sykes
P. Douglas Barr
Perry M. Bentley
Dan M. Rose
Gregory D. Pavey
J. Mel Camenisch, Jr.
David E. Fleenor
Lea Pauley Goff
Laura Day DelCotto
Palmer G. Vance, II
William L. Montague, Jr.

ASSOCIATES

Susan Beverly Jones
Todd S. Page
Patricia Kirkwood Burgess
Steven B. Loy
Jeffery T. Barnett
Crystal Lynn Osborne

Representative Clients: Ashland, Inc.; Bank One, NA; Caterpillar, Inc.; General Motors; International Business Machines Corp.; Keeneland Assn.; Kentucky-American Water Co.; Kentucky Utilities Co.; Lexington Herald-Leader Inc.; Lexmark International, Inc.

For Complete List of Firm Personnel, See General Section

For full biographical listings, see the Martindale-Hubbell Law Directory

*LONDON,** Laurel Co.

FARMER, KELLEY, BROWN AND WILLIAMS (AV)

502 West Fifth Street, Drawer 490, 40741
Telephone: 606-878-7640
Fax: 606-878-2364
Email: fpfarmer@farmerlaw.com
Lexington, Kentucky Office: 1082 Griffin Gate Drive, 40511-1384.
Telephone: 606: 263-2567.
Facsimile: 606: 878-2364.

MEMBERS OF FIRM

F. Preston Farmer
John F. Kelley, Jr.
Michael P. Farmer
Martha L. Brown
Jason E. Williams

ASSOCIATES

Suzanne S. Farmer
Jennifer S. Nicholson

Representative Clients: Wal-Mart Stores; Bituminous Insurance Co.; State Farm Fire & Casualty Insurance; Geico; Kentucky National Insurance Co.; Sentry Claims; Shelter Insurance Co.; Crum & Forester Underwriters Group; Omni.

For full biographical listings, see the Martindale-Hubbell Law Directory

TOOMS & HOUSE (AV)

310 West Fifth Street, P.O. Box 520, 40743-0520
Telephone: 606-864-4145
FAX: 606-864-4279

MEMBERS OF FIRM

Murray L. Brown (1894-1980)
Roy E. Tooms (1917-1986)
R. William Tooms
Brian C. House

ASSOCIATE

Roy G. Collins

Representative Clients: State Auto Mutual Insurance Co.; Grange Mutual Casualty Co.; Kentucky Farm Bureau Mutual Insurance Co.

For full biographical listings, see the Martindale-Hubbell Law Directory

*LOUISVILLE,** Jefferson Co.

BOEHL STOPHER & GRAVES (AV)

Suite 2300 Aegon Center, 400 West Market Street, 40202-3354
Telephone: 502-589-5980
FAX: 502-561-9400
Lexington, Kentucky Office: 444 West Second Street.
Telephone: 606-252-6721.
Fax: 606-253-1445.
Paducah, Kentucky Office: Suite 340 Executive Inn Riverfront, One Executive Boulevard.
Telephone: 270-442-4369.
Fax: 270-442-4689.
Prestonsburg, Kentucky Office: 105 West Court Street.
Telephone: 606-886-8004.
Fax: 606-886-9579.
New Albany, Indiana Office: Elsby East, Suite 204, 400 Pearl Street.
Telephone: 812-948-5053.
Fax: 812-948-9233.

OF COUNSEL

Joseph E. Stopher
George R. Effinger (Resident at Paducah)
Galen J. White, Jr.

MEMBERS OF FIRM

Herbert F. Boehl (1894-1986)
Arthur J. Deindoerfer (1907-1990)
Raymond O. Harmon (1918-1990)
James M. Graves (1912-1994)
William M. Newman, Jr. (1949-1995)
William O. Guethlein
Larry L. Johnson
W. T. Adkins (Resident at Lexington)
Edward H. Stopher
Nolan Carter, Jr. (Resident at Lexington)
Jefferson K. Streepey
Wesley G. Gatlin
George R. Carter
Robert E. Stopher
Philip J. Reverman, Jr.
Peter J. Glauber
Raymond G. Smith
Walter E. Harding
Robert M. Brooks
Ronald L. Green (Resident at Lexington)
Richard L. Walter (Resident at Paducah)
Douglas A. U'Sellis
Kim Martin Wilkie (Resident at Lexington)
John Harlan Callis, III (Resident at Prestonsburg)
Charles D. Walter (Resident at Paducah)
Janie McKenzie Wells (Resident at Prestonsburg)
Guillermo A. Carlos (Resident at Lexington)
Jeffrey L. Hansford (Resident at New Albany, Indiana)
Matthew Hunter Jones (Resident at New Albany, Indiana)
James B. Cooper (Resident at Lexington)
Martin H. Kinney, Jr.
Bayard V. Collier (Resident at Prestonsburg)
Richard W. Edwards
David T. Klapheke
Daniel S. Stratemeyer (Resident at Paducah)
Steven R. Armstrong (Resident at Lexington)

(See Next Column)

BOEHL STOPHER & GRAVES, *Louisville—Continued*

ASSOCIATES

Mary Ann Kiwala
Bruce D. Atherton
William J. Crowe
Denise Basford Askin
Deron L. Johnson (Resident at Prestonsburg)
Brennen C. Ragone (Resident at Lexington)
Gretchen Nunn Gullett (Resident at Prestonsburg)
C. Tom Anderson (Resident at Prestonsburg)
Timothy L. Gray
Richard Vernon Evans
George T. T. Kitchen III
Elizabeth A. Schott (Resident at New Albany, Indiana)
James L. Fischer, Jr. (Resident at Albany, Indiana)
Ronald E. Thornsberry (Resident at Lexington)
Scott A. Davidson
Kurt A. Scharfenberger
P. Kevin Moore

Counsel for: Ford Motor Co.; Texas Eastern Transmission Corp.; Coca-Cola Bottling Co.; Hartford Accident and Indemnity Co.; Continental Insurance Group; St. Paul Fire & Marine Insurance Co.; Lloyds of London; Old Republic Insurance Co.

For full biographical listings, see the Martindale-Hubbell Law Directory

FRANKLIN AND HANCE, P.S.C. (AV)

The Speed House, 505 West Ormsby Avenue, 40203
Telephone: 502-637-6000
Fax: 502-637-1413
Email: golfatty@aol.com *URL:* http://www.lawyers.com/fhlaw

Larry B. Franklin
Michael R. Hance

David B. Gray
Hope Fitzpatrick Brooks

Reference: First National Bank.

For full biographical listings, see the Martindale-Hubbell Law Directory

GOLDBERG & SIMPSON, P.S.C. (AV)

3000 National City Tower, 40202
Telephone: 502-589-4440
Telefax: 502-581-1344
Email: mail@gsatty.com *URL:* http://www.gsatty.com

Fred M. Goldberg
Jonathan D. Goldberg
Mitchell A. Charney
Steven A. Goodman
Stephen E. Smith
Mary Alice Maple
John J. McLaughlin
Charles H. Cassis
Christopher M. George
Emily L. Lawrence

Jan M. West
Sherry P. Porter
James Michael Wells
Stephanie Lynn Morgan-White
Michael F. Lawrence
Karen L. De Haan
George Hunt Rounsavall, Jr.
Stacey A. Huse

OF COUNSEL

Ronald V. Simpson
David A. Brill

Representative Clients: National City Bank; Liberty Mutual Insurance Co.; Jewish Hospital Healthcare Services, Inc.; Louisville & Jefferson County Board of Health; Providian Corp.

For full biographical listings, see the Martindale-Hubbell Law Directory

FRANK P. HILLIARD (AV)

The Starks Building, Suite 380, 455 South 4th Avenue, 40202
Telephone: 502-583-0380
Fax: 502-583-9089
Email: fphil380@bellsouth.net

ASSOCIATE

Charles Edward Monarch

For full biographical listings, see the Martindale-Hubbell Law Directory

LANDRUM & SHOUSE (AV)

Suite 1900 220 West Main Street, 40202-1395
Telephone: 502-589-7616
Facsimile: 502-589-2119
Lexington, Kentucky Office: 106 West Vine Street, P.O. Box 951.
Telephone: 606-255-2424.
Facsimile: 606-233-0308.

RESIDENT MEMBERS OF THE FIRM

John R. Martin, Jr.
R. Kent Westberry
Dave Whalin

RESIDENT ASSOCIATES

Melanie Lee Straw-Boone
Robert Thaddeus (Thad) Keal
Sun S. Choy
Rheanne Dodson Falkner

For full biographical listings, see the Martindale-Hubbell Law Directory

MIDDLETON & REUTLINGER, P.S.C. (AV)

2500 Brown and Williamson Tower, 40202-3410
Telephone: 502-584-1135
Fax: 502-561-0442
URL: http://middreut.com
Jeffersonville, Indiana Office: 530 East Court Avenue, 47130.
Telephone: 812-282-1132.
Fax: 812-282-3188.

O. Grant Bruton
Kenneth S. Handmaker
James N. Williams, Jr.
Charles G. Middleton, III
Charles D. Greenwell
John W. Bilby
D. Randall Gibson
G. Kennedy Hall, Jr.
Mark S. Fenzel
Kathiejane Oehler
William Jay Hunter, Jr.
James E. Milliman
David J. Kellerman
Dennis D. Murrell
Henry S. Alford

Augustus S. Herbert
Thomas P. O'Brien III
Nancy J. Schook
Scot A. Duvall
Jason P. K. Underwood

For Complete List of Firm Personnel, See General Section

For full biographical listings, see the Martindale-Hubbell Law Directory

J. BRUCE MILLER LAW GROUP (AV)

One Riverfront Plaza, Suite 1800, 40202-2927
Telephone: 502-587-0900
Telecopier: 502-587-9008
Email: jbm@jbmlg.com *URL:* http://www.jbmlg.com

J. Bruce Miller
Norma C. Miller
Katherine G. Kitchen
Angela Lee Summers
David Scott Dupps
Ashley N. Blacketer
Jason A. Kron
Nicholas Garrett Hawkins

OF COUNSEL

Michael J. Kitchen
Denis B. Fleming, Jr.

Representative Clients: Advance Machinery Co., Inc.; Anson Machine Mfg. Co.; Biddinger Investment Capital Corp. (Indiana); Carneal Enterprises, Inc. (Kentucky/Florida); MPD Inc. (Owensboro, Kentucky); Motion Picture Association of America; Packaging Unlimited Group (Kentucky/North Carolina); Paducah Medical Supply, Inc. (Kentucky/Tennessee/Florida); Sun Group Broadcasting, Inc. (Indiana/Tennessee); Louisville Gas & Electric Co.

For full biographical listings, see the Martindale-Hubbell Law Directory

PEDLEY ZIELKE GORDINIER OLT & PENCE, PLLC (AV)

1150 Starks Building, 455 South Fourth Avenue, 40202
Telephone: 502-589-4600
Fax: 502-584-0422
Email: pzgop@undial.com

MEMBERS OF FIRM

Lawrence L. Pedley
Laurence J. Zielke
John K. Gordinier
Joseph M. Whittle
William W. Stodghill
Stephen B. Pence
Ronald L. Gaffney
John H. Dwyer, Jr.
Ilam E. Smith

OF COUNSEL

Schuyler J. Olt
Linda Shearer Speed

Caroline George Meena
Randal K. Perkins
Michael D. Ekman
Benjamin S. Schecter
Robert Bruce Bonar
Janice M. Theriot

Representative Clients: Kentucky Independent Community Bankers Assoc.; Louisville and Jefferson County Metropolitan Sewer District; Storer Communications of Jefferson County; Gannet Co.; Hitachi Consumer Products of America; Service Painting Co.; Irwin H. Whitehouse & Sons, Inc.; American Marine Service Barge Lines; Aetna Life & Casualty Co; Travelmax International.

For full biographical listings, see the Martindale-Hubbell Law Directory

ROTH FOLEY BRYANT & COOPER, PLLC (AV)

First Trust Centre, Suite 300S, 200 South Fifth Street, 40202-3236
Telephone: 502-569-7550
Fax: 502-540-0123
Email: RFBC.com

Irvin D. Foley
David M. Roth
David H. Cooper
Lisa Koch Bryant
K. Gail Russell
Christian L. Juckett

OF COUNSEL

James E. Fahey
David W. Gray

Representative Clients: Bank One, Kentucky, N.A.; Huntington National Bank; Commonwealth Bank & Trust Co.; Farm Credit Services of Mid-America; Century Indemnity Co.; Travelers Casualty and Insurance Co.

For full biographical listings, see the Martindale-Hubbell Law Directory

Louisville—Continued

SITLINGER, MCGLINCY, STEINER, THEILER & KAREM (AV)

Suite 370, Starks Building, 455 South Fourth Street, 40202-2508
Telephone: 502-589-2627
Fax: 502-583-3415

MEMBERS OF FIRM

Lee E. Sitlinger
Dennis R. McGlincy
Jack W. Steiner, Jr.
Charles E. Theiler, II
Edmund Pete Karem
Curt Sitlinger
Scott Edmund Karem
Tammy C. Snyder

LEGAL SUPPORT PERSONNEL

Lynn Wockenfuss

Representative Clients: State Farm Mutual Automobile Insurance Co.; State Farm Fire & Casualty Co.; American International Insurance Co.; Walgreen Company.
Reference: Commonwealth Bank & Trust Co.

For full biographical listings, see the Martindale-Hubbell Law Directory

WOODWARD, HOBSON & FULTON (AV)

2500 National City Tower, 101 South Fifth Street, 40202
Telephone: 502-581-8000
Fax: 502-581-8111
Email: WHF@IGLOU.COM
Lexington, Kentucky Office: PNC Bank Plaza, 200 West Vine Street, Suite 500.
Telephone: 606-244-7100.
Telecopier: 606-244-7111.

MEMBERS OF FIRM

William D. Grubbs
Lionel A. Hawse (Resident, Lexington, Kentucky Office)
Harry K. Herren
Glen S. Bagby (Resident, Lexington, Kentucky Office)
David R. Monohan
Will H. Fulton
Robert L. Hallenberg
Richard H. C. Clay
Thomas A. Hoy
John F. Gleason
J. Robert Lyons, Jr. (Resident, Lexington, Kentucky Office)
J. Michael Dalton
Elizabeth Ullmer Mendel
Michael A. Luvisi
Alice Barns Herrington
Jann B. Logsdon
Linsey W. West (Resident, Lexington, Kentucky Office)
David T. Schaefer
Patrick Michael
D. Craig York
Donna King Perry

OF COUNSEL

Kenneth L. Anderson

Representative Clients: CSX Transportation; General Motors Corp.; Ralston Purina Co.; Brown-Forman Corp.; Toyota Motor Company; Nissan Motor Company, Ltd.; American Home Products; Navistar International Transportation Company.

For Complete List of Firm Personnel, See General Section

For full biographical listings, see the Martindale-Hubbell Law Directory

WYATT, TARRANT & COMBS (AV)

Citizens Plaza, 40202-2898
Telephone: 502-589-5235
Telecopier: 502-589-0309
URL: http://www.wyattfirm.com
Lexington, Kentucky Office: 1700 Lexington Financial Center.
Telephone: 606-233-2012.
Telecopier: 606-259-0649.
Frankfort, Kentucky Office: The Taylor-Scott Building, 311 West Main Street.
Telephone: 502-223-2104.
Telecopier: 502-227-7681.
New Albany, Indiana Office: The Elsby Building, 117 East Spring Street,
Telephone: 812-945-3561.
Telecopier: 812-949-2524.
Memphis, Tennessee Office: Crescent Center, Suite 650, 6075 Poplar Avenue.
Telephone: 901-537-1000.
Telecopier: 901-537-1010.
Nashville, Tennessee Office: 1500 Nashville City Center, 511 Union Street.
Telephone: 615-244-0020.
Telecopier: 615-256-1726.
Music Row, Nashville Office: 29 Music Square East.
Telephone: 615-255-6161.
Telecopier: 615-254-4490.
Hendersonville, Tennessee Office: 313 E. Main Street, Suite 1.
Telephone: 615-822-8822.
Telecopier: 615-824-4684.
Tri-Cities, Tennessee Office: Northeast Tennessee Business Park, 10368 Wallace Alley Street, Suite 6, Kingsport.
Telephone: 423-279-1825.
Telecopier: 423-279-9357.

(See Next Column)

MEMBERS OF FIRM

Edgar A. Zingman
Richard W. Iler
Robert C. Ewald
Samuel G. Bridge, Jr.
Robert I. Cusick
John P. Reisz
K. Gregory Haynes
M. Stephen Pitt
Walter M. Jones
Frank F. Chuppe, Jr.
Merrill S. Schell
Virginia Hamilton Snell
Byron E. Leet

Representative Clients: Ashland Inc.; Churchill Downs, Inc.; E.I. du Pont de Nemours and Company; Ford Motor Co.; General Electric Co.; Kentucky Hospital Assn.; Metropolitan Life Insurance Co.; PNC Bank, National Association.

For Complete List of Firm Personnel, See General Section

For full biographical listings, see the Martindale-Hubbell Law Directory

*MADISONVILLE,** Hopkins Co.

MITCHELL, JOINER, & HARDESTY, PSC (AV)

113 East Center Street, Drawer 659, 42431-0659
Telephone: 270-825-4455
Telefax: 270-825-9600

Thomas A. Mitchell
Richard M. Joiner
Randall L. Hardesty

For full biographical listings, see the Martindale-Hubbell Law Directory

*PADUCAH,** McCracken Co.

BOEHL STOPHER & GRAVES (AV)

Suite 340 Executive Inn Riverfront, One Executive Boulevard, 42001
Telephone: 270-442-4369
FAX: 270-442-4689
Louisville, Kentucky Office: Aegon Center, Suite 2300, 400 West Market Street.
Telephone: 502-589-5980.
Fax: 502-561-9400.
Lexington, Kentucky Office: 444 West Second Street.
Telephone: 606-252-6721.
Fax: 606-253-1445.
Prestonsburg, Kentucky Office: 105 West Court Street.
Telephone: 606-886-8004.
Fax: 606-886-9579.
New Albany, Indiana Office: Elsby East, Suite 204, 400 Pearl Street.
Telephone: 812-948-5053.
Fax: 812-948-9233.

RESIDENT PARTNERS

Richard L. Walter
Charles D. Walter
Daniel S. Stratemeyer

Counsel for: Ford Motor Co.; Texas Eastern Transmission Corp.; Coca-Cola Bottling Co.; National Collegiate Athletic Assn.; Hartford Accident and Indemnity Co.; Continental Insurance Group; St. Paul Fire & Marine Insurance Co.; Lloyds of London; Old Republic Insurance Co.

For Complete List of Firm Personnel, See General Section

For full biographical listings, see the Martindale-Hubbell Law Directory

BOSWELL & SIMS (AV)

425 South 6th Street, 42003
Telephone: 270-442-9237
Fax: 270-442-9411
Mailing Address: P.O. Box 1265, 42002-1265
Email: BoswelSims@counsel.com

MEMBERS OF FIRM

J. David Boswell
Van F. Sims

ASSOCIATES

R. Brent Vasseur
Kara L. Daniel

LEGAL SUPPORT PERSONNEL

Marla J. Douglas (Legal Assistant)

Local Counsel for: Kentucky School Board Insurance Trust.
Insurance Clients: Kemper Group; Indiana Insurance Cos.; State Automobile Insurance Co.; Farmers Insurance Group; American States Insurance Co.; Kentucky Hospital Trust Association; Farmland Insurance Co.; Canal Insurance Co.; Employers Reinsurance Corp.; Westfield Cos.

For full biographical listings, see the Martindale-Hubbell Law Directory

*SHELBYVILLE,** Shelby Co.

NEAL & DAVIS (AV)

931 Main Street, P.O. Box 40, 40066-0040
Telephone: 502-633-6002;
Louisville: 502-589-9888
Email: tdavis@neal-davis.com
URL: http://www.neal-davis.com

(See Next Column)

NEAL & DAVIS, *Shelbyville—Continued*

Gregg Y. Neal | Thomas Todd Davis

Reference: Republic Bank and Trust Co.

For full biographical listings, see the Martindale-Hubbell Law Directory

LOUISIANA

*ALEXANDRIA,** Rapides Parish

NEBLETT, BEARD & ARSENAULT (AV)

A Registered Limited Liability Partnership including Law Corporations
2220 Bonaventure Court, P.O. Box 1190, 71301
Telephone: 318-487-9874; 1-800-256-1050
Fax: 318-561-2591

Robert B. Neblett (1927-1991)
Richard W. Beard (1955-1988)
Richard J. Arsenault (Law Corporation)
C. Michael Bollinger
David O. Walker (Law Corporation)
Paul J. Tellarico
William S. Neblett
Michael S. Koch
Wesley J. Gralapp

ASSOCIATE

Gary J. Arsenault

Reference: Hibernia National Bank.

For full biographical listings, see the Martindale-Hubbell Law Directory

*BATON ROUGE,** East Baton Rouge Parish

BREAZEALE, SACHSE & WILSON, L.L.P. (AV)

Twenty-Third Floor, One American Place, P.O. Box 3197, 70821-3197
Telephone: 225-387-4000
Fax: 225-387-5397
URL: http://www.bswllp.com
New Orleans, Louisiana Office: LL&E Tower, Suite 1500, 909 Poydras Street.
Telephone: 504-584-5454.
Fax: 504-584-5452.
Covington, Louisiana Office: 2255 Highway 190 North, Suite 200.
Telephone: 504-871-9444.
Fax: 504-871-9666.

MEMBERS OF FIRM

Gordon A. Pugh
Paul M. Hebert, Jr.
Claude F. Reynaud, Jr.
Christine Lipsey
David R. Kelly
Robert L. Atkinson
Douglas K. Williams
John E. Heinrich
Michael R. Hubbell
John W. Barton, Jr.
Jude C. Bursavich
James R. Chastain, Jr.
Linda Perez Clark

ASSOCIATES

Jeanne C. Comeaux
W. Brett Mason
Scott N. Hensgens

OF COUNSEL

Victor A. Sachse, III

Counsel for: Allied-Signal Corp.; Reynolds Metal Co.; Illinois Central Railroad Co.

For Complete List of Firm Personnel, See General Section

For full biographical listings, see the Martindale-Hubbell Law Directory

KANTROW, SPAHT, WEAVER & BLITZER, A PROFESSIONAL LAW CORPORATION (AV)

Suite 300, City Plaza, 445 North Boulevard, P.O. Box 2997, 70821-2997
Telephone: 225-383-4703
Fax: 225-343-0630; 343-0637

Byron R. Kantrow (1909-1997)
Carlos G. Spaht
Geraldine B. Weaver
Sidney M. Blitzer, Jr.
Paul H. Spaht
Lee C. Kantrow
John C. Miller
Vincent P. Fornias
David S. Rubin
Diane L. Crochet
Richard F. Zimmerman, Jr.
Bob D. Tucker
Martin E. Golden
J. Michael Robinson, Jr.
Connell L. Archey
Randal J. Robert

C. William Belsom, Jr.
Linda Orlansky Posner

Representative Clients: CNA Insurance Cos.; Federal Deposit Insurance Corp.; Hartford Insurance Group; Air Products and Chemicals, Inc.; CF Industries, Inc.; AT&T; United Companies Financial Corp.

For full biographical listings, see the Martindale-Hubbell Law Directory

KEAN, MILLER, HAWTHORNE, D'ARMOND, MCCOWAN & JARMAN, L.L.P. (AV)

22nd Floor, One American Place, 70825
Telephone: 225-387-0999
Fax: 225-388-9133
Mailing Address: P.O. Box 3513, Baton Rouge, Louisiana, 70821
URL: http://WWW.KMLAW.COM
New Orleans, Louisiana Office: Energy Centre, Suite 1560, 1100 Poydras Street, 70163.
Telephone: 504-585-3050.
Fax: 504-585-3051.
Plaquemine, Louisiana Office: Suite 10, 23425 Railroad Avenue, 70764.
Telephone: 225-687-9845.
Fax: 225-382-3445.
Lake Charles, Louisiana Office: One Lakeshore Drive, Suite 1220, 70629.
Telephone: 318-430-0350.
Fax: 318-436-5566.
Covington, Louisiana Office: 503 North New Hampshire Street, P.O. Box 3096, 70433.
Telephone: 504-875-0400.
Fax: 504-875-0500.

MEMBERS OF FIRM

William R. D'Armond
Charles S. McCowan, Jr.
G. William Jarman
Leonard L. Kilgore III
Gary A. Bezet
Michael C. Garrard
Vance A. Gibbs
James R. Lackie
David K. Nelson
J. Carter Wilkinson
Sandra L. Edwards
Bradley C. Myers
Melanie M. Hartmann
Linda Sarradet Akchin
James P. Doré
Erich P. Rapp
Charles L. Patin, Jr.
Mathile W. Abramson
Cynthia M. Chemay
Gregg R. Kronenberger
Charles S. McCowan III
Gayla M. Moncla
Jay M. Jalenak, Jr.
Linda G. Rodrigue
Glenn M. Farnet
Esteban Herrera, Jr.
Barrye Panepinto Miyagi
Yul D. Lorio (Resident, Lake Charles Office)

Theresa R. Hagen
Robert E. Dille
Gordon D. Polozola
Lana Davis Crump
Gregory M. Anding
Troy J. Charpentier
Amy deGeneres Berret
J. Jeffery Raborn
Scott D. Johnson
Pamela Roman Mascari
Yuxian Wang
Jennifer G. Gary (Resident, Lake Charles Office)
Shannan Sweeney Rieger
Craig M. Freeman
Jason R. Cashio

Representative Clients: BASF Corporation, Parsippany, NJ; CONDEA Vista Company; DSI Tansports, Inc.; Exxon Company, U.S.A., Baton Rouge, LA; Fair Grounds Corporation; Georgia-Pacific Corporation, Atlanta, GA; Insurance Corporation of America, Houston, TX; Joslyn Corporation; Louisiana Medical Mutual Insurance Company, Metairie, LA; Metropolitan Life Insurance Company, New York, NY.

For full biographical listings, see the Martindale-Hubbell Law Directory

KLEINPETER & KLEINPETER (AV)

1680 South Lobdell Avenue, Suite E, P.O. Box 66443, 70896
Telephone: 225-926-5093
Telecopier: 225-926-5318

MEMBERS OF FIRM

Robert L. Kleinpeter | R. Loren Kleinpeter

Representative Clients: Argonaut Insurance Co.; American Indemnity Co.; Allstate Insurance Co.; Consolidated American Inc. Co.; South Carolina Insurance Co.; TransAmerica Insurance Group; St. Paul Fire & Marine Insurance Co.; Scottsdale Insurance Co.; Fireman's Fund Insurance Co.; Western Heritage Insurance Co.

For full biographical listings, see the Martindale-Hubbell Law Directory

PHELPS DUNBAR, L.L.P. (AV)

Suite 701, 445 North Boulevard, P.O. Box 4412, 70821-4412
Telephone: 225-346-0285
Telecopier: 225-381-9197
Email: info@phelps.com
New Orleans, Louisiana Office: Texaco Center, 400 Poydras Street.
Telephone 504-566-1311.
Telecopier: 504-568-9130; 504-568-9007.
Cable Address: "Howspencer."
Telex: 584125 WU.
Telex: 6821155 WUI.
Jackson, Mississippi Office: Suite 500, SkyTel Centre, 200 South Lamar Street, P.O. Box 23066.
Telephone: 601-352-2300.
Telecopier: 601-360-9777.
Tupelo, Mississippi Office: Seventh Floor, One Mississippi Plaza, P.O. Box 1220.
Telephone: 662-842-7907.
Telecopier: 662-842-3873.
Houston, Texas Office: Suite 900, 3040 Post Oak Boulevard.
Telephone: 713-626-1386.
Telecopier: 713-626-1388.

(See Next Column)

PHELPS DUNBAR L.L.P.—*Continued*

London, England Office: Suite 731, Level 7, Lloyd's, 1 Lime Street, London EC3M 7DQ England.
Telephone: 011-44-207-929-4765.
Telecopier: 011-44-207-929-0046.
Telex: 987321.

RESIDENT PARTNERS

Allen D. Darden
Susan W. Furr
Michael D. Hunt
H. Alston Johnson, III
F. Scott Kaiser
Thomas H. Kiggans
Steven J. Levine
Freddie Pitcher, Jr.
Marshall M. Redmon (Also at London, England Office)

COUNSEL

Jane A. Robert

RESIDENT ASSOCIATES

Jane H. Barney
Rebecca Bellows Crawford
Christine S. Goldberg
Gwen P. Harmon
Kimberly L. Hood
Clinton D. Howie
Karleen Joseph
Kelsey B. Kornick
Patrick O'Hara
Clinton Ryan Stuart
Virginia Yoder Trainor

Representative Clients: Bank One; Great Southern Life Insurance Company; Hibernia National Bank; Louisiana Companies; Louisiana Farm Bureau Casualty Company; Louisiana Lottery Corporation; Louisiana Public Facilities Authority; Louisiana Workers' Compensation Corporation; Union Pacific Railroad Company; Uniroyal Chemical Company.

For Complete List of Firm Personnel, See General Section

For full biographical listings, see the Martindale-Hubbell Law Directory

POWERS & WILLARD, L.L.P. (AV)

7967 Office Park Boulevard, P.O. Box 15948, 70895
Telephone: 225-928-1951
Fax: 225-929-9834

MEMBERS OF FIRM

John Dale Powers
William E. Willard

ASSOCIATES

Neil H. Mixon
Lindsey J. Leavoy
Edwin L. Hightower
Andrew P. Sellers, Jr.
Suzanne K. Sasser
Kyle C. Marionneaux

General Counsel for: Audubon Insurance Co.
Louisiana Counsel for: Hancock Bank & Trust Co.; Hertz Corp.; Ciba-Geigy Corp.; Utica Mutual Insurance Co.

For full biographical listings, see the Martindale-Hubbell Law Directory

SEALE, SMITH, ZUBER & BARNETTE (AV)

Two United Plaza, Suite 200, 8550 United Plaza Boulevard, 70809
Telephone: 225-924-1600
Telecopier: 225-924-6100
Email: SSZB@WORLDNET.ATT.NET

Armbrust Gordon Seale (1913-1989)
Robert W. Smith (1922-1989)
Donald S. Zuber
Kenneth E. Barnette
William C. Kaufman III
John W. L. Swanner
James H. Morgan III
Ronald A. Seale
Charles K. Watts
Brent E. Kinchen
Myron A. Walker, Jr.
Daniel A. Reed
Lawrence R. Anderson, Jr.
Catherine S. Nobile
Anthony J. Russo, Jr.
Richard T. Reed

ASSOCIATE

Michael P. Bienvenu

OF COUNSEL

William H. Brown

Representative Clients: Farmers Insurance Group; St. Paul Fire and Marine Insurance Company; United Services Automobile Association.
Reference: Bank One, Louisiana, N.A., Baton Rouge, Louisiana.

For full biographical listings, see the Martindale-Hubbell Law Directory

SHOCKEY & ZIOBER, A PROFESSIONAL LAW CORPORATION (AV)

5551 Corporate Boulevard, Suite 3-A, P.O. Box 80286, 70898-0286
Telephone: 225-929-8929
Telecopier: 225-928-7694

John David Ziober
William C. Shockey

Douglas J. Cochran
James E. Moore, Jr.

For full biographical listings, see the Martindale-Hubbell Law Directory

*CROWLEY,** Acadia Parish

BAROUSSE & CRATON (AV)

211 North Parkerson Avenue, P.O. Drawer 1305, 70527-1305
Telephone: 318-785-1000
Facsimile: 318-785-2000
Email: barcra@juno.com

MEMBERS OF FIRM

Homer Ed Barousse, Jr.
John F. Craton

Representative Clients: First Bank, N.A. of Crowley and Lake Charles; Francis Drilling Fluids, Ltd.; Farm Credit Bank of Texas; First South Production Credit Association; J.I. Case Credit Corporation; Louisiana Sheriffs' Association; Broussard Rice Mill, Inc.; Mermentau River Harbor and Terminal District; Farm Service Agency.

For full biographical listings, see the Martindale-Hubbell Law Directory

*LAFAYETTE,** Lafayette Parish

BROUSSARD, DAVID & DAIGLE, A PROFESSIONAL LAW CORPORATION (AV)

557 Jefferson Street, P.O. Drawer 3308, 70502-3308
Telephone: 318-234-7000
Fax: 318-237-0344
Email: bdandd@bdandd.com *URL:* http://www.bdandd.com

Hal J. Broussard
Susan A. Daigle
Bryan D. Scofield
Ped C. Kay, III
Todd G. Crawford

James T. Rivera
Catherine E. Hensgens

Representative Clients: Certain London Underwriters per individual approval of instructions; Lloyds of London Member Syndicates; Institute of London Underwriter Member Companies; Reliance Insurance Company of Pennsylvania; Reliance Insurance Company of Illinois; Reliance National Insurance Company; The Louisiana Insurance Guaranty Association; Louisiana Oilfield Legislative Committee, Inc. (Louisiana Association of Oilfield Casing Contractors; Association of Oilwell Servicing Contractors; Louisiana Pipeline Contractors Association; Offshore Pipeline Contractors Association; Louisiana Oilfield Contractor Association).

For full biographical listings, see the Martindale-Hubbell Law Directory

DAVIDSON, MEAUX, SONNIER, MCELLIGOTT & SWIFT (AV)

810 South Buchanan Street, P.O. Drawer 2908, 70502
Telephone: 318-237-1660
Fax: 318-237-3676

MEMBERS OF FIRM

James J. Davidson, Jr. (1904-1990)
V. Farley Sonnier (1942-1988)
Richard C. Meaux, Sr.
James J. Davidson, III
John E. McElligott, Jr.
John G. Swift
Jeffrey A. Rhoades
Philip A. Fontenot
Kyle L. Gideon
Theodore G. Edwards, IV
Mark C. Andrus

ASSOCIATES

John T. Andrishok
Christopher J. Piasecki
Nicholas J. Zeringue

OF COUNSEL

Jan Whitehead Swift

Representative Clients: Southern Pacific Transportation Co., Wal-Mart Stores, Inc.; Power Rig Drilling Co., Inc.; Southwest Louisiana Electric Membership Corp.; Macro Oil Company; Highlands Insurance Company; United Services Automobile Association; Sears, Roebuck & Company; Lawyers Title Insurance Corporation; Wal-Mart Stores, Inc.; USAA.

For full biographical listings, see the Martindale-Hubbell Law Directory

DOMENGEAUX WRIGHT & ROY, A PROFESSIONAL LAW CORPORATION (AV)

556 Jefferson Street, Suite 500, P.O. Box 3668, 70502-3668
Telephone: 318-233-3033; 1-800-375-3106
Fax: 318-232-8213
Email: info@wrightroy.com *URL:* http://www.wrightroy.com

Bob F. Wright
James Parkerson Roy
Thomas R. Edwards
James H. Domengeaux
Gilbert Hennigan Dozier
Carla Marie Perron
Michael D. Goss

ASSOCIATE

Jamie D. Parker

OF COUNSEL

Jerome E. Domengeaux

Reference: Mid-South National Bank; Advocate Financial, L.L.C.

For full biographical listings, see the Martindale-Hubbell Law Directory

Lafayette—Continued

JEANSONNE & REMONDET, L.L.C. (AV)

200 West Congress Street, Suite 1100, P.O. Box 91530, 70509
Telephone: 318-237-4370
Facsimile: 318-235-2011
New Orleans, Louisiana Office: 1 Canal Place, 365 Canal Street, Suite 2300.
Telephone: 504-524-7333.
Fax: 504-524-3339.
Shreveport, Louisiana Office: Harry Patterson Tower, 6007 Financial Plaza, Suite 708.
Telephone: 318-671-8102.
Fax: 318-671-8103.

John A. Jeansonne, Jr.
Michael J. Remondet, Jr.

G. Andrew Veazey
Donald W. Washington
Dona K. Renegar
Jason B. Boudreaux
Thomas H. Huval
James T. McManus
Joseph S. Cage, Jr.
Pride J. Doran
R. Royal Alexander
Mary Katherine Paine

LEGAL SUPPORT PERSONNEL

Monica L. Abshire (Paralegal, Office Manager and Notary Public)
Nancy M. Fruge (Paralegal)
Christi A. Guidry
S. Dianne Thibodeaux (Paralegal)

For full biographical listings, see the Martindale-Hubbell Law Directory

RICHARD R. KENNEDY A PROFESSIONAL LAW CORPORATION (AV)

309 Polk Street, P.O. Box 3243, 70502-3243
Telephone: 318-232-1934
Fax: 318-232-9720
Email: kennedy@net-connect.net

Richard R. Kennedy

For full biographical listings, see the Martindale-Hubbell Law Directory

ONEBANE, BERNARD, TORIAN, DIAZ, MCNAMARA & ABELL (AV)

Suite 600, Versailles Centre, 102 Versailles Boulevard, P.O. Box 3507, 70502
Telephone: 318-237-2660
Telecopier: 318-266-1232
Email: info@onebane.com
Monroe, Louisiana Office: 1900 N. 18th Street, Suite 420, P.O. Box 2255, 71207.
Telephone: 318-340-0220.
Fax: 318-340-0110.

Joseph Onebane (1917-1987)
John G. Torian, II (1936-1991)
James E. Diaz
Timothy J. McNamara
Edward C. Abell, Jr.
Lawrence L. Lewis, III
Robert M. Mahony
Daniel G. Fournerat
Douglas W. Truxillo
Randall C. Songy
Michael G. Durand
Greg Guidry
Joseph L. Lemoine, Jr.
Mark L. Riley
Graham N. Smith
Gordon T. Whitman
Gary P. Kraus
Richard J. Petre, Jr.
Charles J. Boudreaux, Jr.
James R. Shelton
Thomas G. Smart
Roger E. Ishee
Jennifer M. Kleinpeter
Steven C. Lanza
Joel P. Babineaux

Alison M. Brumley
Jesse D. Lambert
Brent G. Sonnier
Cary B. Bryson
Maria F. Manuel
Greg R. Mier
Jennifer L. Smith
Janice Church Reeves
Mark B. Oliver
Chanelle T. Delahoussaye
Aimee L. Williams
A.G. "Alec" Alexander, III
Terry J. Blanchard
William E. Bourgeois (Resident, Monroe, Louisiana Office)

OF COUNSEL

William E. Kellner

Representative Clients: Commercial Union Insurance Co.; Enron Corp.; First National Bank of Lafayette; Highlands Insurance Co.; Marathon Oil Co.; Ocean Energy, Inc.; Pizza Hut, Inc.; Schering-Plough Corp.; Tenneco, Inc.; Whitney National Bank.

For full biographical listings, see the Martindale-Hubbell Law Directory

RINGUET DANIELS & COLLIER, A PROFESSIONAL LAW CORPORATION (AV)

302 Rue France, Suite 201, P.O. Box 52647, 70505-2647
Telephone: 318-232-0002
Fax: 318-232-3410
Email: ringuet@earthlink.net
Jennings, Louisiana Office: 227 North Main Street, 70546.
Telephone: 318-824-2000.

Reginald J. Ringuet
James L. Daniels
William H. Collier

Representative Clients: Acadiana Medical Laboratories, Ltd.; Carrollton Resources Corporation; Dependable Insurance Company; Forest Oil Corp.; Goodrich Operating Company, Inc.; Ron Guidry Enterprises, Inc.

For full biographical listings, see the Martindale-Hubbell Law Directory

*LAKE CHARLES,** Calcasieu Parish

BERGSTEDT & MOUNT (AV)

Second Floor, Magnolia Life Building, P.O. Drawer 3004, 70602-3004
Telephone: 318-433-3004
Facsimile: 318-433-8080

MEMBERS OF FIRM

Thomas M. Bergstedt
Benjamin W. Mount
Van C. Seneca

ASSOCIATE

Annette N. Peltier

OF COUNSEL

Charles S. Ware

Representative Clients: ARCO Chemical Company; Ashland Oil Co.; CIGNA Property & Casualty Companies; Columbia Women's & Children's Hospital; The Hartford Steam Boiler Inspection & Insurance Company; Leach Company; Olin Corporation; Occidental Chemical Corporation; Terra Corporation; R. D. Werner Company.

For full biographical listings, see the Martindale-Hubbell Law Directory

PLAUCHÉ SMITH & NIESET, A PROFESSIONAL LAW CORPORATION (AV)

1123 Pithon Street, P.O. Drawer 1705, 70602
Telephone: 318-436-0522
Facsimile: 318-436-9637

S. W. Plauché (1889-1952)
S. W. Plauché, Jr. (1915-1966)
A. Lane Plauché
Allen L. Smith, Jr.
James R. Nieset
Frank M. Walker, Jr.
Michael J. McNulty, III
Jeffrey M. Cole
Andrew R. Johnson, IV
Charles V. Musso, Jr.
Christopher P. Ieyoub
H. David Vaughan, II
Joseph R. Pousson, Jr.
Rebecca S. Young
V. Ed McGuire, III

Representative Clients: CIGNA; CNA Insurance Cos.; Commercial Union Insurance Cos.; Crum & Forster; Reliance Insurance Cos.; Royal Insurance Group; State Farm; U.S. Insurance Group.

For full biographical listings, see the Martindale-Hubbell Law Directory

RAGGIO, CAPPEL, CHOZEN & BERNIARD (AV)

500 Magnolia Life Building, P.O. Box 820, 70601
Telephone: 318-436-9481
Fax: 318-436-9499
Email: RCCB@RaggioCappel.com

MEMBERS OF FIRM

Thomas L. Raggio (Retired)
Richard B. Cappel
Frederick L. Cappel
Richard A. Chozen
Stephen A. Berniard, Jr.
Christopher M. Trahan
L. Paul Foreman
Kevin J. Koenig

Counsel for: Aetna Casualty & Surety Co.; Allstate Insurance Co.; United States Fidelity and Guaranty Co.; E. I. duPont de Nemours & Co., Inc.; ABB Lummus Global, Inc.; The St. Paul Companies; Windsor Insurance Group; Coregis Insurance Co.; Government Employees Insurance Co.; Calcasieu Parish Police Jury.

For Complete List of Firm Personnel, See General Section

For full biographical listings, see the Martindale-Hubbell Law Directory

SCOFIELD, GERARD, VERON, SINGLETARY & POHORELSKY, A PROFESSIONAL LAW CORPORATION (AV)

1114 Ryan Street, P.O. Drawer 3028, 70601
Telephone: 318-433-9436
Telefax: 318-436-0306
URL: http://www.sgvsp.com

(See Next Column)

SCOFIELD, GERARD, VERON, SINGLETARY & POHORELSKY A PROFESSIONAL LAW CORPORATION—*Continued*

John B. Scofield
Richard E. Gerard, Jr.
J. Michael Veron
C. Eston Singletary
John R. Pohorelsky
Scott J. Scofield
Patrick D. Gallaugher, Jr.
Robert E. Landry
Russell J. Stutes, Jr.
W. Todd Fontenot
David W. Clark

Representative Clients: Admiral Insurance Co.; Amoco Production Co.; Banc One; Browning-Ferris Industries, Inc.; Brown & Root Construction Co.; Cosmos Broadcasting Corp.; Dresser Industries, Inc.; Kansas City Southern Railway Co.; Mobil Oil Corp.; Phillips Petroleum Co.

For full biographical listings, see the Martindale-Hubbell Law Directory

METAIRIE, Jefferson Parish

CAMPBELL, MCCRANIE, SISTRUNK, ANZELMO & HARDY, P.C. (AV)

3445 North Causeway Boulevard, Suite 800, 70002
Telephone: 504-831-0946
Fax: 504-831-2492

Frederick R. Campbell
Burgess E. McCranie, Jr.
Michael R. Sistrunk
Thomas P. Anzelmo
Sidney J. Hardy
Lance S. Ostendorf
Roy C. Beard
Mishthi Grace Ratnesar
Charles E. Sutton, Jr.
Isidro René DeRojas
Mark Emerson Hanna
Geoffrey J. Orr

Angela M. Bowlin
Catherine M. Williams
Colin D. Sherman
James H. Hunter
Richard Andrew Houston, III
Paxton K. Stelly
Michele Butler Prokop
Marty D. Parlipiano
Peter J. Wanek
Ken D. Brown

Representative Clients: Wal-Mart Stores, Inc.; Delchamps, Inc.; Greyhound Lines, Inc.; The Dial Corporation; Transport Insurance Company; Burger King Corporation; CNA Insurance Companies; The Louisiana Motor Vehicle Commission; Insbrok; Patent Scaffolding.

For full biographical listings, see the Martindale-Hubbell Law Directory

DUPLASS, ZWAIN & BOURGEOIS, A PROFESSIONAL LAW CORPORATION (AV)

Three Lakeway Center, 3838 N. Causeway Boulevard, Suite 2900, 70002
Telephone: 504-832-3700
Fax: 504-837-3119

Lawrence J. Duplass
Gary M. Zwain
David J. Bourgeois
C. Michael Pfister, Jr.
Gregory O. Currier
Andrew D. Weinstock
Joseph B. Morton, III
Geoffrey P. Clement
Danna E. Schwab
Guyton H. Valdin, Jr.
Roy E. Sasser

Bernard J. Williams
Kathleen C. Marksbury
Kelly Cambre Bogart
Claire E. Breaux
Christian B. Bogart
Joseph G. Glass
Dana Anderson-Carson
Louis O. Oubre
Darrell R. Sims

OF COUNSEL

Kenneth J. Berke
Lesli S. Bolner
Richard K. Ingolia

For full biographical listings, see the Martindale-Hubbell Law Directory

*MINDEN,** Webster Parish

JAMES M. JOHNSON (AV)

105 Pearl Street, P.O. Box 1015, 71058-1015
Telephone: 318-377-4978
Toll Free: 877-827-4294
Fax: 318-377-9026

For full biographical listings, see the Martindale-Hubbell Law Directory

*MONROE,** Ouachita Parish

HAYES, HARKEY, SMITH & CASCIO, L.L.P. (AV)

2811 Kilpatrick Boulevard, P.O. Box 8032, 71211-8032
Telephone: 318-387-2422
FAX: 318-388-5809

Thomas M. Hayes, Jr. (1915-1994)
Louis D. Smith (Retired)
Joseph D. Cascio, Jr.
Charles S. Smith
Thomas M. Hayes, III
Bruce McKamy Mintz
C. Joseph Roberts, III
John B. Saye

OF COUNSEL

Haynes L. Harkey, Jr.

(See Next Column)

Karen L. Hayes
Harry McClellan Moffett, IV

Representative Clients: Cigna; CNA Insurance Group; St. Francis Medical Center, Inc.; St. Paul Insurance Group; Cooper Industries, Inc.; State Farm Insurance Cos.; Riverwood International Corp.; Scott Truck and Tractor Co.; Northeast Louisiana Cancer Institute.

For full biographical listings, see the Martindale-Hubbell Law Directory

MCLEOD VERLANDER (AV)

A Partnership including Professional Law Corporations
1900 North 18th Street, Suite 610, P.O. Box 2270, 71207-2270
Telephone: 318-325-7000
Telecopier: 318-324-0580
Email: mv@mv-law.com *URL:* http://www.lawyers.com/mvlaw

MEMBERS OF FIRM

Robert P. McLeod (P.L.C.)
David E. Verlander, III (P.L.C.)

Rick W. Duplissey
Donald C. Douglas, Jr.
Laurie J. Burkett

For full biographical listings, see the Martindale-Hubbell Law Directory

SNELLINGS, BREARD, SARTOR, INABNETT & TRASCHER, LLP (AV)

1503 North 19th Street, P.O. Box 2055, 71207-2055
Telephone: 318-387-8000
Fax: 318-387-8200
Email: sbsit@bayou.com *URL:* http://www.bayou.com/sbsit

MEMBERS OF FIRM

George M. Snellings, Jr. (1910-1984)
Daniel Ryan Sartor, Jr.
Carrick R. Inabnett
Charles C. Trascher, III
L. Kent Breard, Jr.
Clara Moss Sartor
William Brooks Watson
David C. McMillin
Jon Keith Guice

ASSOCIATES

Wendy E. W. Giovingo
William Michael Street

OF COUNSEL

Kent Breard

Representative Clients: Bank One; Cross Keys Bank; Delta Air Lines, Inc.; Federal Deposit Insurance Co.; Glenwood Regional Medical Center; John Hancock Mutual Life Insurance Company; Kemper Insurance Group; Horace Mann Insurance Cos.; Louisiana Association of Educators; Midland Mortgage Company.

For full biographical listings, see the Martindale-Hubbell Law Directory

*NEW ORLEANS,** Orleans Parish

ADAMS AND JOHNSTON, A PROFESSIONAL LAW CORPORATION (AV)

Suite 2490, Pan American Life Center, 601 Poydras Street, 70130
Telephone: 504-581-2606
Fax: 504-525-1488
Email: a&j@aj-law.com

Jesse R. Adams, Jr.
Robert M. Johnston
D. Russell Holwadel
Bruce R. Hoefer, Jr. (P.C.)
Thomas S. Morse
Anne Derbes Keller
Shannon Howard-Duhon
Scott A. Cannon

Representative Clients: Allianz Insurance Company; Amana Refrigeration, Inc.; Associated Risk Services Inc.; Beech Aircraft Corporation; Fairgrounds Corporation; Fireman's Fund Insurance Companies; Interstate Insurance Group; Trinity Universal Ins. Companies.

For full biographical listings, see the Martindale-Hubbell Law Directory

BARHAM & ARCENEAUX, A PROFESSIONAL LAW CORPORATION (AV)

Suite 2700, Poydras Center, 650 Poydras Street, 70130-6101
Telephone: 504-525-4400
Fax: 504-525-6378
Email: barham1@bellsouth.net

Mack E. Barham
Robert E. Arceneaux
Gail N. Wise
Jerry Barfield Jordan
Travis Louis Bourgeois

Michael W. Hill

OF COUNSEL

James A. Comiskey

For full biographical listings, see the Martindale-Hubbell Law Directory

New Orleans—Continued

BUCKLEY & HAYES, L.L.P. (AV)

A Partnership including a Professional Corporation
1555 Poydras Street Suite 1700, 70112
Telephone: 504-523-5100
Fax: 504-523-5698
Covington, Louisiana Office: 2301 North HIghway 190, Suite 3, 70433.
Telephone: 504-871-7005.
Fax: 504-871-7051.

MEMBERS OF FIRM

Lloyd W. Hayes
E. Ross Buckley, Jr., (A Professional Law Corp.)
Marianne S. Pensa
William H. Voigt

ASSOCIATES

Michele D. Ahlers
Ernest Philip Legier, Jr.
Elton A. Foster

OF COUNSEL

Harold A. Thomas

For full biographical listings, see the Martindale-Hubbell Law Directory

CAPITELLI & WICKER (AV)

2950 Energy Centre, 1100 Poydras Street, 70163-2950
Telephone: 504-582-2425
Fax: 504-582-2422
Email: cw4law@bellsouth.net

Ralph Capitelli
T. Carey Wicker, III
Paul Michael Elvir, Jr.

For full biographical listings, see the Martindale-Hubbell Law Directory

FAVRET, DEMAREST, RUSSO & LUTKEWITTE, A PROFESSIONAL LAW CORPORATION (AV)

Suite 1400, 1515 Poydras Building, 1515 Poydras Street, 70112
Telephone: 504-561-1006
Telecopier: 504-523-0699
Email: favret@bellsouth.net

Clarence F. Favret, Sr. (1896-1988)
Marshall J. Favret
J. Paul Demarest
Anthony J. Russo
Thomas J. Lutkewitte
Clarence F. Favret, III

Angela C. Imbornone
Dean Joseph Favret
Michael W. Boleware
Seth H. Schaumburg

Reference: Hibernia National Bank.

For full biographical listings, see the Martindale-Hubbell Law Directory

THE GODFREY FIRM A PROFESSIONAL LAW CORPORATION (AV)

2500 Energy Centre, 1100 Poydras Street, 70163-2500
Telephone: 504-585-7538
Fax: 504-585-7535
Email: godfryfirm@aol.com

Jarrell E. Godfrey, Jr.
Cloyd F. Van Hook
Patrick M. Files
Elizabeth Earnest

For full biographical listings, see the Martindale-Hubbell Law Directory

HERMAN, HERMAN, KATZ & COTLAR, L.L.P. (AV)

A Partnership including Professional Law Corporations
Formerly Herman & Herman
820 O'Keefe Avenue, 70113
Telephone: 504-581-4892
Telecopier: 504-561-6024
Email: HHKC@HHKC.COM

Harry Herman (1914-1987)
Russ M. Herman (A Professional Law Corporation)
Maury A. Herman (A Professional Law Corporation)
Morton H. Katz (A Professional Law Corporation)
Sidney A. Cotlar (A Professional Law Corporation)
Steven J. Lane
Leonard A. Davis (A Professional Law Corporation)
James C. Klick

Steve Herman
Brian D. Katz
Richard E. King
David K. Fox

OF COUNSEL

Joseph A. Kott
Warren A. Goldstein

For full biographical listings, see the Martindale-Hubbell Law Directory

HOUSE, KINGSMILL & RIESS, L.L.C. (AV)

201 St. Charles Avenue, Suite 3300, 70170
Telephone: 504-581-3300
Fax: 504-581-3310
Email: hkrs3300@aol.com
Houston, Texas Office: Chase Tower, Suite 6950, 600 Travis Street, 77002.
Telephone: 713-222-6950.
Fax: 713-222-6955.

MEMBERS OF FIRM

W. Richard House, Jr.
Marguerite K. Kingsmill
Michael R.C. Riess
Jeffrey E. Combes
Barbara G. Haynie
William B. Underwood, III (Resident, Houston, Texas Office)

OF COUNSEL

Robert B. Evans, Jr.

ASSOCIATES

Charles B. Colvin
Randal R. Cangelosi
Robert B. Evans, III
Shannon S. Peters (Not admitted in LA; Resident, Houston, Texas Office)
Laura H. Spalding (Not admitted in LA)
Churita H. Hansell
Rebecca M. Goforth

For full biographical listings, see the Martindale-Hubbell Law Directory

LEAKE, ANDERSSON & MANN, L.L.P. (AV)

1700 Energy Centre, 1100 Poydras Street, 70163-1701
Telephone: 504-585-7500
Facsimile: 504-585-7775

W. Paul Andersson
Lawrence A. Mann
Kevin Cramer O'Bryon
George D. Fagan
Donald E. McKay, Jr.
Stanton E. Shuler, Jr.
Guy D. Perrier

OF COUNSEL

Robert E. Leake, Jr.

ASSOCIATES

J. Ronald Ward, Jr.
Louis P. Bonnaffons
Ellen Heidingsfelder Manning
Dean M. Arruebarrena
Craig M. Cousins
Charles R. Daniel, II

Representative Clients: Government Employees Insurance Co.; National Food Processors, Inc.; National Union Fire Insurance Co.; Nationwide Insurance Co.; Professional Construction Services, Inc.; Invacare Corp.; Med Marc.

For full biographical listings, see the Martindale-Hubbell Law Directory

LEE, FUTRELL & PERLES, L.L.P. (AV)

Suite 2409, 201 St. Charles Avenue, 70170-2409
Telephone: 504-569-1725
Fax: 504-569-1726
Email: mgr@leefutrell.com *URL:* http://www.lawyers.com/lf&plaw

Gary A. Lee
John Maurice Futrell
Richard M. Perles

Representative Clients: Certain Underwriters at Lloyd's, London; Institute of London Underwriters Companies.

For full biographical listings, see the Martindale-Hubbell Law Directory

LOWE, STEIN, HOFFMAN, ALLWEISS & HAUVER, L.L.P. (AV)

One Shell Square, 701 Poydras Street Suite 3600, 70139-7735
Telephone: 504-581-2450
Telecopier: 504-581-2461

MEMBERS OF FIRM

Robert C. Lowe
Mark S. Stein
Mitchell J. Hoffman
Michael R. Allweiss
Terence L. Hauver
Ellen Widen Kessler
Max J. Cohen
Suzette Marie Smith
David M. Prados
Marynell L. Piglia

Kermit L. Roux, III
Charlton D. Hunley
Barbara H. Weiss
Paula H. Lee
Stanley Dale Broome

OF COUNSEL

Mark S. Goldstein
Alicia M. Bendana

For full biographical listings, see the Martindale-Hubbell Law Directory

New Orleans—Continued

McGlinchey Stafford (AV)

A Professional Limited Liability Company
643 Magazine Street, 70130-3477
Telephone: 504-586-1200
Fax: 504-596-2800
TDD: (504) 596-2728
Telex: 584327
Cable Address: "MACSTAC"
Mailing Address: P.O. Box 60643, New Orleans, Louisiana, 70160-0643
Email: @mcglinchey.com *URL:* http://www.mcglinchey.com
Dallas, Texas Office: 2777 Stemmons Freeway, Suite 925, 75207-2401.
Telephone: 214-860-9700.
Fax: 214-860-9750.
Houston, Texas Office: 2727 Allen Parkway, Suite 1900, 77019.
Telephone: 713-520-1900.
Fax: 713-520-1025.
Baton Rouge, Louisiana Office: Ninth Floor, One American Place, 70825-0001.
Telephone: 504-383-9000.
Fax: 504-343-3076.
Jackson, Mississippi Office: Suite 1200, SkyTel Centre, 200 South Lamar Street, 39201.
Telephone: 601-960-8400.
Fax: 601-960-8406.
Lake Providence, Louisiana Office: 405 Morgan Street, 71254-2691.
Telephone: 318-559-1200.
Fax: 318-559-0609.
Monroe, Louisiana Office: Dean ONB Tower, 130 Desiard Street, Suite 807, 71201.
Telephone: 318-651-0807.
Fax: 318-651-0809.

MEMBERS OF FIRM

William V. Dalferes, Jr., (P.C.)
Stephen P. Beiser

For full biographical listings, see the Martindale-Hubbell Law Directory

---

Moseley & Associates, A Professional Law Corporation (AV)

866 Camp Street, 70130
Telephone: 504-523-5220
Fax: 504-523-5225
Email: rockslaw@aol.com

Rockne L. Moseley
Janet M. Ahern

For full biographical listings, see the Martindale-Hubbell Law Directory

---

Odom & Des Roches, LLP (AV)

A Partnership including Professional Corporations
35th Floor, Bank One Center, 201 Saint Charles Avenue, 70170-3500
Telephone: 504-522-0077
Fax: 504-522-0078
Hahira, Georgia Office: 217 West Main Street, P.O. Box 523, 31632.
Telephone: 912-794-3412.
Fax: 912-794-3544.

John Gregory Odom, PLC
Stuart E. Des Roches

OF COUNSEL

Randall S. Acree (Resident, Hahira, Georgia Office)

For full biographical listings, see the Martindale-Hubbell Law Directory

---

Phelps Dunbar, L.L.P. (AV)

Texaco Center, 400 Poydras Street, 70130-3245
Telephone: 504-566-1311
Telecopier: 504-568-9130, 504-568-9007
Cable Address: "Howspencer"
Telex: 584125 WU
Telex: 6821155 WUI
Email: info@phelps.com
Baton Rouge, Louisiana Office: Suite 701, 445 North Boulevard, P.O. Box 4412.
Telephone: 225-346-0285.
Telecopier: 225-381-9197.
Jackson, Mississippi Office: Suite 500, SkyTel Centre, 200 South Lamar Street, P.O. Box 23066.
Telephone: 601-352-2300.
Telecopier: 601-360-9777.
Tupelo, Mississippi Office: Seventh Floor, One Mississippi Plaza, P.O. Box 1220.
Telephone: 662-842-7907.
Telecopier: 662-842-3873.
Houston, Texas Office: Suite 900, 3040 Post Oak Boulevard.
Telephone: 713-626-1386.
Telecopier: 713-626-1388.
London, England Office: Suite 731, Level 7, Lloyd's, 1 Lime Street, London EC3M 7DQ England.
Telephone: 011-44-207-929-4765.
Telecopier: 011-44-207-929-0046.
Telex: 987321.

(See Next Column)

RESIDENT PARTNERS

Brent B. Barriere
Gerardo R. Barrios
Roy C. Cheatwood
Nancy Scott Degan
Sessions Ault Hootsell III
John P. Manard, Jr.
Paul L. Peyronnin
Harry Rosenberg
Mary Ellen Roy
Bruce V. Schewe
Danny G. Shaw

RESIDENT ASSOCIATES

Thomas M. Beh
Peggy Eileen Bordelon
Jennifer L. Burrows
Lawrence W. DaGate
Katherine Miller Determan
Caroline McS. Dolan
Hansel M. Harlan
Christopher L. Hewitt (Not admitted in LA)
M. David Kurtz
Kent A. Lambert
Mark L. McNamara
Sheryl A. Odems (Not admitted in LA)
David L. Patrón
Owen Bennett St. Amant
Eric M. Schroeder
Tania Tetlow

Representative Clients: Bank One; Entergy Enterprises, Inc.; Fidelity Investments; Hibernia National Bank; Hilton Hotels Corp.; Lawyers Title Insurance Company; MCI Communications Corporation; Pulitzer Broadcasting Corp.; Texas Gas Transmission Corp.; The Travelers Insurance Company.

For Complete List of Firm Personnel, See General Section

For full biographical listings, see the Martindale-Hubbell Law Directory

---

Tarcza & Gelderman, L.L.C. (AV)

Thirteen Ten Whitney Building, Two Twenty Eight St. Charles Avenue, 70130
Telephone: 504-525-6696
Fax: 504-525-6701

Robert E. Tarcza
G. Anthony Gelderman, III

ASSOCIATE

Juliet Puissegur Bland

For full biographical listings, see the Martindale-Hubbell Law Directory

---

Wilson & Bowling (AV)

A Partnership including Professional Law Corporations
Suite 2411, Bank One Center, 201 St. Charles Avenue, 70170
Telephone: 504-586-5200
Facsimile: 504-586-5201
Email: wilsbowl@gs.net
Gulfport, Mississippi Office: 715 Markham Building, 2301 14th Street, 39501.
Telephone: 228-575-6202.
Fax: 228-864-6227.

Gordon F. Wilson, Jr., (P.L.C.)
David A. Bowling (P.L.C.)

Jeanne B. Roques
Susannah Ross Cooley
John D. Acomb

For full biographical listings, see the Martindale-Hubbell Law Directory

---

*SHREVEPORT,** Caddo Parish

Troy E. Bain (AV)

1540 Irving Place, 71101
Telephone: 318-221-0076
Fax: 318-227-8290

Reference: Commercial National Bank of Shreveport.

For full biographical listings, see the Martindale-Hubbell Law Directory

---

Barlow and Hardtner L.C. (AV)

Tenth Floor, Louisiana Tower, 401 Edwards Street, 71101-3289
Telephone: 318-227-1131
Telecopier: 318-227-1141
Mailing Address: P.O. Box 8, Shreveport, Louisiana, 71161-0008

Malcolm S. Murchison
Kay Cowden Medlin
Joseph L. Shea, Jr.
David R. Taggart
Michael B. Donald
Jay A. Greenleaf

Representative Clients: Anderson Oil & Gas, Inc.; Kelley Oil Corporation; NorAm Energy Corp. (formerly Arkla, Inc.); Panhandle Eastern Corp.; Southwestern Electric Power Company; Central and South West Corporation; Pennzoil Producing Co.; First Family Financial Services, Inc.

For Complete List of Firm Personnel, See General Section

For full biographical listings, see the Martindale-Hubbell Law Directory

Shreveport—Continued

Blanchard, Walker, O'Quin & Roberts, A Professional Law Corporation (AV)

Fourteenth Floor, Premier Bank Tower, 400 Texas Street, P.O. Drawer 1126, 71101
Telephone: 318-221-6858
Fax: 318-227-2967
Email: BWOR@BWOR.com
Bossier City, Louisiana Office: 2285 Benton Road, Suite B-201.
Telephone: 318-742-9255.
Fax: 318-742-9210.

John T. Cox, Jr.
W. Michael Adams
Robert W. Johnson
Edward Keith Carter
Paul M. Adkins
A. M. Stroud, III
Pamela G. Nathan

For Complete List of Firm Personnel, See General Section

For full biographical listings, see the Martindale-Hubbell Law Directory

Robert U. Goodman, P.L.C. (AV)

Mid South Towers, 416 Travis Street, Suite 1105, 71101-5514
Telephone: 318-221-1601
Fax: 318-221-1749
Email: goodman@prysm.net

Robert U. Goodman

Representative Clients: Aeropres Corp.; Dealers Truck & Equipment Co.; Housing Authority of the City of Shreveport; Specht Newspapers, Inc.; Graham Brothers Entertainment, Inc.; Integrated Exploration, Inc.

For full biographical listings, see the Martindale-Hubbell Law Directory

Hargrove, Pesnell & Wyatt, A P.L.C. (AV)

505 Travis Street Suite 300, 71101
Telephone: 318-429-7200
Fax: 318-429-7201
Mailing Address: P.O. Box 59, Shreveport, Louisiana, 71161-0059
Email: hpwlaw@prysm.net

Thomas James Wyatt (1942-1996)
Billy R. Pesnell
Joseph L. Hargrove, Jr.
David L. Smelley
A. L. Wedgeworth, III
Paul A. Strickland
Scott C. Sinclair

ASSOCIATE

W. Brooks May

For full biographical listings, see the Martindale-Hubbell Law Directory

Mayer, Smith & Roberts, L.L.P. (AV)

1550 Creswell, 71101
Telephone: 318-222-2135, 222-2268
Fax: 318-222-6420
Email: (Attorney's First Name)@MSRLAW.COM

MEMBERS OF FIRM

Caldwell Roberts
Walter O. Hunter, Jr.
Mark A. Goodwin
Ben Marshall, Jr.
Alexander S. Lyons
Kim Purdy Thomas
David Butterfield
Henry N. Bellamy
John C. Turnage
Paul R. Mayer, Jr.
Steven E. Soileau
Deborah Shea Baukman
Caldwell Roberts, Jr.
Frank K. Carroll
Dalton Roberts Ross

OF COUNSEL

Paul R. Mayer

Representative Clients: CNA Insurance Companies; Liberty Mutual Insurance Company; United States Fidelity and Guaranty Company; Schumpert Medical Center; Travelers Insurance Company; Great American Insurance Company; Insurance Corporation of America; Highlands Insurance Company.

For full biographical listings, see the Martindale-Hubbell Law Directory

Sockrider, Bolin, Anglin & Batte, A Professional Law Corporation (AV)

327 Crockett Street, 71101
Telephone: 318-221-5503
Fax: 318-221-3849

John R. Pleasant (1905-1983)
H. F. Sockrider, Jr.
James E. Bolin, Jr.
D. Rex Anglin
Gregory H. Batte

For full biographical listings, see the Martindale-Hubbell Law Directory

Charles G. Tutt (AV)

900 Pierremont Road, Suite 206, 71106
Telephone: 318-868-6633
Fax: 318-868-5006
Email: cgtutt@softdisk.com *URL:* http://www.lawyers.com/charlestutt

(See Next Column)

ASSOCIATE

Thomas A. Bordelon

Representative Clients: Albany Insurance Co.; Bituminous Insurance Cos.; Dana Corporation; General Agents Insurance Co.; ITT Hartford; Louisiana Insurance Guaranty Assn.; Lazy Boy, Inc.; Louisiana Medical Mutual Insurance Co.; Medical Protective Insurance Company; The Millers Group.

For full biographical listings, see the Martindale-Hubbell Law Directory

Weems, Schimpf, Hayter, Gilsoul & Carmouche, (APLC) (AV)

912 Kings Highway, 71104
Telephone: 318-222-2100
Facsimile: 318-226-5100
URL: http://www.weems-law.com

Carey T. Schimpf
John O. Hayter, III
Paul J. Carmouche
Brian D. Landry

Representative Clients: Royal Insurance Co.; Patterson Ins. Co.; Louisiana Insurance Guaranty Association; State of Louisiana; Louisiana State University Medical Center; Hibernia National Bank; St. Paul Fire & Marine Insurance Company; Clarendon National Insurance; Commercial Union Insurance Co.; Penn/American Insurance; Davison Insurance Co.; Davison Transport, Inc.; Stephenson Trucking; Harvest Foods Inc.

For full biographical listings, see the Martindale-Hubbell Law Directory

Wilkinson, Carmody & Gilliam (AV)

1700 Beck Building, 400 Travis Street, P.O. Box 1707, 71166
Telephone: 318-221-4196
Telecopier: 318-221-3705
Email: wcg1895@aol.com

MEMBERS OF FIRM

John D. Wilkinson (1867-1929)
William Scott Wilkinson (1895-1985)
Arthur R. Carmody, Jr.
Bobby S. Gilliam
Mark E. Gilliam
William Allen Haynes

Representative Clients: Farmers Insurance Group; Home Federal Savings & Loan Association of Shreveport; The Kansas City Southern Railway Co.; KTAL-TV; Lincoln National Life Insurance Co.; Mobil Oil Co.; Schumpert Medical Center; Sears, Roebuck & Co.; Southern Pacific Transportation Co.; Southwestern Electric Power Co.

For full biographical listings, see the Martindale-Hubbell Law Directory

*WINNFIELD,** Winn Parish

Simmons and Derr (AV)

Simmons Building, Church Street, P.O. Box 525, 71483
Telephone: 318-628-3951
Fax: 318-648-0644

MEMBERS OF FIRM

Kermit M. Simmons
Jacque D. Derr

Reference: Bank of Winnfield & Trust Co.

For full biographical listings, see the Martindale-Hubbell Law Directory

MAINE

*AUGUSTA,** Kennebec Co.

Lipman & Katz, P.A. (AV)

227 Water Street, P.O. Box 1051, 04332-1051
Telephone: 207-622-3711
Telecopier: 207-622-7415
Email: lipmankatz@ibm.net

Sumner H. Lipman
David M. Lipman
Roger J. Katz
Robert J. Stolt
Keith R. Varner
Ronald E. Colby, III
Walter F. McKee

Karen E. Lipman
Tracie L. Adamson
Gregg D. Bernstein

OF COUNSEL

Joseph B. Campbell

For full biographical listings, see the Martindale-Hubbell Law Directory

Augusta—Continued

PIERCE ATWOOD (AV)

77 Winthrop Street, 04330
Telephone: 207-622-6311
Fax: 207-623-9367
Email: info@PierceAtwood.com *URL:* http://www.pierceatwood.com
Portland, Maine Office: One Monument Square.
Telephone: 207-791-1100.
Fax: 207-791-1350.
Newburyport, Massachusetts Office: 6 Harris Street.
Telephone: 978-465-9599.
Fax: 978-465-9945.

MEMBERS OF FIRM

Malcolm L. Lyons
Michael D. Seitzinger
John C. Nivison

ASSOCIATE

Ann M. St. Peter-Griffith

COUNSEL

Daniel J. Stevens

For Complete List of Firm Personnel, See General Section

For full biographical listings, see the Martindale-Hubbell Law Directory

---

*BANGOR,** Penobscot Co.

EATON, PEABODY, BRADFORD & VEAGUE, P.A. (AV)

Fleet Center-Exchange Street, P.O. Box 1210, 04402-1210
Telephone: 207-947-0111
Telecopier: 207-942-3040
Email: eaton@eatonpeabody.com *URL:* http://www.eatonpeabody.com
Augusta, Maine Office: 77 Sewall Street, Suite 3000.
Telephone: 207-622-3747.
Telecopier: 207-622-9732.
Blue Hill, Maine Office: One East Blue Hill Road.
Telephone: 207-374-2812.
Telecopier: 207-374-2548.
Brunswick, Maine Office: 167 Park Row.
Telephone: 207-729-1144.
Telecopier: 207-729-1140.
Dover-Foxcroft, Maine Office: 30 East Main Street.
Telephone: 207-564-8378.
Telecopier: 207-564-7059.

Thomas M. Brown
Bernard J. Kubetz
Stephen G. Morrell (Resident, Brunswick Office)
Glen L. Porter
Gordon H. S. Scott (Resident, Augusta Office)
William B. Devoe
Laurie A. Dart
Judy A.S. Metcalf (Resident, Brunswick Office)
Jonathan B. Huntington (Resident, Dover-Foxcroft Office)
Thad B. Zmistowski

OF COUNSEL

Martin L. Wilk (Resident, Brunswick Office)

For Complete List of Firm Personnel, See General Section

For full biographical listings, see the Martindale-Hubbell Law Directory

GROSS, MINSKY, MOGUL & SINGAL, P.A. (AV)

Key Plaza, 23 Water Street, P.O. Box 917, 04402-0917
Telephone: 207-942-4644; 800-274-7124
Telecopier: 207-942-3699
Email: law@gmms.com

Edward I. Gross (1912-1999)
Jules L. Mogul (1930-1994)
George Z. Singal
Louis H. Kornreich
George C. Schelling
Edward W. Gould
Steven J. Mogul
James R. Wholly
Daniel A. Pileggi
Philip K. Clarke

Wayne P. Libhart (Retired)
Sandra L. Rothera
James S. Nixon

OF COUNSEL

Norman Minsky

Representative Client: Dahl Chase Pathology Associates.
Local Counsel for: The St. Paul Insurance Cos.; Aetna Life & Casualty Co.; Imperial Casualty & Indemnity Co.

For full biographical listings, see the Martindale-Hubbell Law Directory

---

BAR HARBOR, Hancock Co.

FENTON, CHAPMAN, FENTON, SMITH & KANE, P.A. (AV)

109 Main Street, P.O. Box B, 04609
Telephone: 207-288-3331
Fax: 207-288-9326
Email: fentonlawfirm@acadia.net *URL:* http://www.lawyers.com/fcfs&klaw

(See Next Column)

William Fenton
Douglas B. Chapman
Nathaniel R. Fenton
Chadbourn H. Smith

Margaret T. Jeffery

Reference: Bar Harbor Banking and Trust Co.

For Complete List of Firm Personnel, See General Section

For full biographical listings, see the Martindale-Hubbell Law Directory

---

*ELLSWORTH,** Hancock Co.

HALE & HAMLIN (AV)

10 State Street, P.O. Box 729, 04605
Telephone: 207-667-2561
Telefax: 207-667-8790
Email: barry@halehamlin.com *URL:* http://www.halehamlin.com

MEMBER OF FIRM

Barry K. Mills

Approved Attorneys for: Lawyers Title Insurance Corp.

For full biographical listings, see the Martindale-Hubbell Law Directory

---

*PORTLAND,** Cumberland Co.

BENNETT BENNETT AND TROIANO, P.A. (AV)

Suite 300, 121 Middle Street, P.O. Box 7799, 04112-7799
Telephone: 207-773-4775
Telecopier: 207-774-2366
Email: lawyers@bennettlegal.com *URL:* http://www.bennettlegal.com

Herbert H. Bennett (1928-1992)
Peter Bennett
Jeffrey Bennett
Joseph A. Troiano
Frederick B. Finberg

Julie A. Boesky

OF COUNSEL

Jonathan M. Dunitz

Counsel for: Associated Grocers of New England; Coca Cola Bottling Company of Northern New England, Inc.; General Star Indemnity Company; Northern Utilities/Bay State Gas; Pratt & Whitney (Division of United Technologies); Primerica Financial Services (Citigroup); Sprague Energy (C.H. Sprague & Son); Perrier Group of America, Inc.; Lepage Bakeries, Inc. (Country Kitchen); Texaco, Inc.

For full biographical listings, see the Martindale-Hubbell Law Directory

FRIEDMAN BABCOCK & GAYTHWAITE (AV)

Suite 400, Six City Center, P.O. Box 4726, 04112-4726
Telephone: 207-761-0900
Telecopier: 207-761-0186
Email: info@fbg-law.com *URL:* http://www.fbg-law.com

MEMBERS OF FIRM

Harold J. Friedman
Ernest J. Babcock
Martha C. Gaythwaite
Karen Frink Wolf
Jennifer S. Riggle
Laurence H. Leavitt
Elizabeth A. Germani
Michelle Allott
Tracy D. Hill

ASSOCIATES

Susan J. Guerette
L. John Topchik
Sally A. Morris
Catherine C. Miller
Kieran N. Shields
Evan Smith

For full biographical listings, see the Martindale-Hubbell Law Directory

JENSEN BAIRD GARDNER & HENRY (AV)

Ten Free Street, P.O. Box 4510, 04112-4510
Telephone: 207-775-7271
Telecopier: 207-775-7935
Email: info@jbgh.com *URL:* http://www.jbgh.com
York County Office: 11 Main Street, Suite 4, Kennebunk, Maine, 04043.
Telephone: 207-985-4676.
Telecopier: 207-985-4932.

MEMBERS OF FIRM

Michael A. Nelson
Joseph H. Groff III
Deborah M. Mann

OF COUNSEL

James E. Kaplan

ASSOCIATE

Brendan P. Rielly

Representative Clients: General Motors Acceptance Corp.; Shaw's Supermarkets; American Petroleum Institute; Lorillard; CTC Communications Corp.; St. Lawrence & Atlantic Railway Co.; Maryland Insurance Group; Outboard Marine Corp.; Mercury Marine; Arbella Mutual Insurance Co.

For Complete List of Firm Personnel, See General Section

For full biographical listings, see the Martindale-Hubbell Law Directory

Portland—Continued

PERKINS, THOMPSON, HINCKLEY & KEDDY, P.A. (AV)

One Canal Plaza, P.O. Box 426, 04112-0426
Telephone: 207-774-2635
Fax: 207-871-8026
Email: admin@pthklaw.com *URL:* http://www.pthklaw.com

Thomas Schulten
Bruce E. Leddy
Douglas S. Carr
Andrew A. Cadot
Philip C. Hunt
John S. Upton
Peggy L. McGehee
Melissa Hanley Murphy
John H. Rich III
John A. Ciraldo
John A. Hobson
Timothy P. Benoit
Fred W. Bopp III
Craig N. Denekas
Mark P. Snow
William J. Sheils

OF COUNSEL

Owen W. Wells

For Complete List of Firm Personnel, See General Section

For full biographical listings, see the Martindale-Hubbell Law Directory

PETRUCCELLI & MARTIN, LLP (AV)

50 Monument Square, P.O. Box 9733, 04104-5033
Telephone: 207-775-0200
Telecopier: 207-775-2360
Email: info@petruccellimartin.com *URL:* http://www.petruccellimartin.com

MEMBERS OF FIRM

Gerald F. Petruccelli
Joel C. Martin
Michael K. Martin
James B. Haddow
Linda C. Russell

Thomas C. Bradley

Representative Clients: Associated Aviation Underwriters; Bombardier, Inc.; Chicago Title Insurance Co.; Chubb Insurance Co.; Coopers & Lybrand; Cumberland Farms; Granger Northern Construction Co.; Maine Medical Center; Union Mutual Fire Insurance Co.; Vermont Mutual Insurance Co.

For full biographical listings, see the Martindale-Hubbell Law Directory

PIERCE ATWOOD (AV)

One Monument Square, 04101
Telephone: 207-791-1100
Fax: 207-791-1350
Email: info@PierceAtwood.com *URL:* http://www.pierceatwood.com
Augusta, Maine Office: 77 Winthrop Street.
Telephone: 207-622-6311.
Fax: 207-623-9367.
Newburyport, Massachusetts Office: 6 Harris Street.
Telephone: 978-465-9599.
Fax: 978-465-9945.

MEMBERS OF FIRM

Ralph I. Lancaster, Jr.
Jotham D. Pierce, Jr.
Malcolm L. Lyons (Resident, Augusta Office)
Peter W. Culley
Jeffrey M. White
Louise K. Thomas
Michael D. Seitzinger (Resident, Augusta Office)
Daniel M. Snow
William J. Kayatta, Jr.
James R. Erwin
Robert H. Stier, Jr.
John C. Nivison (Resident, Augusta Office)
John J. Aromando
Catherine R. Connors
David E. Barry

OF COUNSEL

Vincent L. McKusick

ASSOCIATES

Jared S. des Rosiers
Debra L. Brown
Geraldine G. Sanchez
K. Douglas Erdmann
Byrne J. Decker
Christopher T. Roach
Margaret K. Minister
Nathan V. Gemmiti
Ann M. St. Peter-Griffith (Resident, Augusta Office)
Peter S. Black

COUNSEL

Daniel J. Stevens (Resident, Augusta Office)

For Complete List of Firm Personnel, See General Section

For full biographical listings, see the Martindale-Hubbell Law Directory

PRETI, FLAHERTY, BELIVEAU, PACHIOS & HALEY, LLC (AV)

One City Center, P.O. Box 9546, 04112-9546
Telephone: 207-791-3000
Telecopier: 207-791-3111
Email: admin@preti.com *URL:* http://www.preti.com
Augusta, Maine Office: 45 Memorial Circle, P.O. Box 1058, 04332-1058.
Telephone: 207-623-5300.
Telefax: 207-623-2914.

(See Next Column)

Bath, Maine Office: Thirty Front Street, P.O. Box 665, 04530-0665.
Telephone: 207-443-5576.
Telefax: 207-443-6665.

MEMBERS OF FIRM

Severin M. Beliveau (Augusta Office)
Mark L. Haley (Bath Office)
Christopher D. Nyhan
Jonathan S. Piper
Daniel Rapaport
Bruce C. Gerrity (Augusta Office)
Jeffrey T. Edwards
Michael G. Messerschmidt
Randall B. Weill
Evan M. Hansen
Geoffrey K. Cummings
Michael Kaplan
Stephen E. F. Langsdorf (Augusta Office)
John P. McVeigh
Elizabeth A. Olivier
Nelson J Larkins
Robert O. Newton
Timothy J. Bryant
Brian L. Champion (Bath Office)

COUNSEL

Albert J. Beliveau, Jr.
Gregory P. Hansel

ASSOCIATES

Kevin J. Beal
Tracey G. Burton (Bath Office)
Elizabeth A. Campbell
Jon A. Fitzgerald (Bath Office)
Jeffrey W. Peters (Bath Office)
Matthew J. LaMourie

Representative Clients: American Home Products; Compania Chilena de Fosforos, S.A. (Chile); Blethen-Maine Newspapers, Inc.; KeyBank National Assn.; National Semiconductor Corp.; Sumitomo Marine & Fire Insurance Co., Ltd.; St. Paul Companies; Wal-Mart Stores, Inc.

For Complete List of Firm Personnel, See General Section

For full biographical listings, see the Martindale-Hubbell Law Directory

THOMPSON & BOWIE (AV)

Three Canal Plaza, P.O. Box 4630, 04112
Telephone: 207-774-2500
Telecopier: 207-774-3591
Email: law@thompsonbowie.com

MEMBERS OF FIRM

Roy E. Thompson, Jr.
James M. Bowie
Daniel R. Mawhinney
Rebecca H. Farnum
Glenn H. Robinson
Frank W. DeLong, III
Michael E. Saucier
Mark V. Franco
Edward R. Benjamin, Jr.
Cathy S. Roberts
Paul C. Catsos

ASSOCIATES

Elizabeth Knox Peck
Thomas G. Diebold
Michael R. Bosse
Lisa M. Fitzgibbon

For full biographical listings, see the Martindale-Hubbell Law Directory

TROUBH, HEISLER & PIAMPIANO, P.C. (AV)

511 Congress Street, P.O. Box 9711, 04104-5011
Telephone: 207-780-6789
Fax: 207-774-2339
Email: info@thplaw.com

William B. Troubh
Edwin A. Heisler
Robert J. Piampiano
Kevin M. Gillis
Michael P. Boyd
Thomas E. Getchell
Michael Richards
William K. McKinley
Daniel F. Gilligan
Paul S. Bulger
John G. Richardson

Daniel R. Felkel
Ann Brandt
John P. Flynn, III

For full biographical listings, see the Martindale-Hubbell Law Directory

VERRILL & DANA, LLP (AV)

One Portland Square, P.O. Box 586, 04112-0586
Telephone: 207-774-4000
Fax: 207-774-7499
Email: advice@verdan.com *URL:* http://www.verdan.com
Augusta, Maine Office: 45 Memorial Circle, P.O. Box 957.
Telephone: 207-623-3889.
Fax: 207-622-3117.
Kennebunk, Maine Office: 403-404 Lafayette Center, P.O. Box 147.
Telephone: 207-985-7193.
Fax: 207-985-3957.
Washington, D.C. Office: 400 North Capitol Street, Suite 585.
Telephone: 202-624-9733.
Fax: 202-393-5218.

OF COUNSEL

Roger A. Putnam
Linda A. Monica

MEMBERS OF FIRM

Michael T. Healy
Andrew M. Horton
James G. Goggin
William C. Knowles
Gene R. Libby (Resident Partner, Kennebunk Office)
Michael J. Donlan (Resident Partner, Kennebunk Office)
Seth W. Brewster

(See Next Column)

VERRILL & DANA LLP—*Continued*

ASSOCIATES

Hope K. Creal
Janet P. Judge
Christopher B. McLaughlin
Jacqueline W. Rider
Daniel L. Rosenthal

Counsel for: ASCAP; Bowdoin College; Fleet Bank; Hannaford Bros. Co.; Maine Blue Cross and Blue Shield; Maine Public Service Co.; Peoples Heritage Bank; Portland Water District.

For Complete List of Firm Personnel, See General Section

For full biographical listings, see the Martindale-Hubbell Law Directory

WRIGHT & COON, P.A. (AV)

Four Canal Plaza, P.O. Box 7526, 04112
Telephone: 207-775-7722
Fax: 207-772-7045
Email: lexfori@lexfori.com

Steven F. Wright
John R. Coon
Brita J. Forssberg

For full biographical listings, see the Martindale-Hubbell Law Directory

*ROCKLAND,** Knox Co.

STROUT & PAYSON, P.A. (AV)

10 Masonic Street, P.O. Box 248, 04841-0248
Telephone: 207-594-8400
Fax: 207-594-2724
Email: splaw@midcoast.com

Arthur E. Strout
Joseph B. Pellicani (1936-1988)
Robert J. Levine
Esther R. Barnhart
Carol Ann Lundquist
Randal E. Watkinson
Elizabeth E. Biddle
James Davidson

OF COUNSEL

Curtis M. Payson
John Knight

Approved Attorneys for: First American Title Insurance Co.; Chicago Title Insurance Co.

For full biographical listings, see the Martindale-Hubbell Law Directory

SACO, York Co.

SMITH ELLIOTT SMITH & GARMEY, P.A. (AV)

199 Main Street, P.O. Box 1179, 04072
Telephone: 207-774-3199
Telefax: 207-774-2235
Email: info@sesgattorneys.com *URL:* http://www.sesgattorneys.com

Randall E. Smith
Charles W. Smith, Jr.
Terrence D. Garmey
Peter W. Schroeter
Richard P. Romeo
Robert H. Furbish
John H. O'Neil, Jr.
Harry B. Center, II
David S. Abramson

Representative Clients: City of Biddeford; Saco and Biddeford Savings Institution; Ocean Communities Federal Credit Union.
Local Counsel for: East Guard Insurance Co.
Reference: Saco & Biddeford Savings Institution.

For Complete List of Firm Personnel, See General Section

For full biographical listings, see the Martindale-Hubbell Law Directory

*SKOWHEGAN,** Somerset Co.

WRIGHT & MILLS, P.A. (AV)

218 Water Street, P.O. Box 9, 04976-0009
Telephone: 207-474-3324
Telefax: 207-474-3609
Email: millslaw@somtel.com

Carl R. Wright
S. Peter Mills
Paul P. Sumberg
Janet T. Mills
Kenneth A. Lexier
Robert H. Conkling

Representative Clients: Design Professionals Insurance Co., New Jersey; Solon Manufacturing Co., Solon, Maine; Kleinschmidt Associates-Engineers, Pittsfield, Maine; Acheron Engineering, Newport, Maine; E.W. Littlefield-Contractors, Hartland, Maine; WBRC-Architects, Bangor, Maine; Town of Skowhegan; Town of Norridgewock.

For full biographical listings, see the Martindale-Hubbell Law Directory

MARYLAND

*ANNAPOLIS,** Anne Arundel Co.

COUNCIL, BARADEL, KOSMERL & NOLAN, P.A. (AV)

125 West Street, Fourth Floor, P.O. Box 2289, 21404-2289
Telephone: 410-268-6600
Baltimore: 410-269-6190
Washington, D.C.: 301-261-2247
FAX: 410-269-8409
Email: cbkn@cbknlaw.com

Ronald E. Council
Ronald A. Baradel
Wayne T. Kosmerl
James P. Nolan
William F. Flood, III
Kevin M. Schaeffer
Donna McCabe Schaeffer
Frederick C. Sussman

John Naumann Strange
Susan T. Ford
Edwin H. Staples, II
Susan Stobbart Shapiro

OF COUNSEL

George N. Manis
Nicholas Goldsborough

Representative Clients: Anne Arundel County; Annapolis Bank and Trust; Bank of Maryland; State Farm Mutual Automobile Insurance Co.; Annapolis Yacht Club; Annapolis Yacht Sales, Inc.

For full biographical listings, see the Martindale-Hubbell Law Directory

DALNEKOFF & MASON, P.A. (AV)

Suite 301 West Court Building, 2448 Holly Avenue, 21401-3177
Telephone: 410-841-6500; 266-0544
D.C.: 301-261-8671
Fax: 410-224-4135
Email: info@dalnekoffmason.com *URL:* http://www.dalnekoffmason.com
Affiliated with: Morgan and Hendrick, 317 Whitehead Street, Key West, Florida.
Telephone: 305-296-5676.

Carol S. Craig
Barry J. Dalnekoff
Mark E. Mason
Royal G. Shannonhouse, III
Nelson R. Stewart
Thomas J. Voigt

Erin D. Gable

OF COUNSEL

Leonard E. Moodispaw
Matthew S. Evans, Jr.

Reference: NationsBank, Annapolis, Maryland.

For full biographical listings, see the Martindale-Hubbell Law Directory

HYATT, PETERS & WEBER (AV)

1919 West Street, P.O. Box 6635, 21401
Telephone: 410-266-0626
Fax: 410-841-5065
Email: info@hyatt.hpwsb.com *URL:* http://www.hpwlaw.com

Alan J. Hyatt
Paula J. Peters
Paul J. Weber

ASSOCIATES

Sara H. Arthur
Sharon M. Grosfeld
Gregg M. Weinberg
Jonathan A. Hodgson
John L. Hill
Arlette K. Bright
Bruce F. Bright (Not admitted in MD)

OF COUNSEL

Steven G. Tyler

For full biographical listings, see the Martindale-Hubbell Law Directory

WHARTON LEVIN EHRMANTRAUT KLEIN & NASH, A PROFESSIONAL ASSOCIATION (AV)

104 West Street, P.O. Box 551, 21404-0551
Telephone: 800-322-1984; 410-263-5900
Facsimile: 410-280-2230; 410-263-1562
Baltimore, Maryland Office: 400 East Pratt Street.
Telephone: 410-269-7529.

James T. Wharton
David A. Levin
Robert Dale Klein
Brian J. Nash
A. Gwynn Bowie, Jr.
Jack L. Harvey
Michael T. Wharton
Andrew E. Vernick
D. Lee Rutland
David A. Roling
Daniel C. Costello
Christian A. Lodowski
Stuart N. Herschfeld
Linda G. Wales

OF COUNSEL

William A. Ehrmantraut

(See Next Column)

WHARTON LEVIN EHRMANTRAUT KLEIN & NASH A PROFESSIONAL ASSOCIATION, *Annapolis—Continued*

Douglas K. Schrader
Leonard William Dooren, III
Marian L. Hogan
Mary C. Rice
Michael Kevin Wiggins
Thomas C. Marriner
Victoria H. Wink
Julia Renee Arfaa

For full biographical listings, see the Martindale-Hubbell Law Directory

*BALTIMORE,** (Independent City)

ALBRIGHT BROWN & GOERTEMILLER, LLC (AV)

120 East Baltimore Street, Suite 2150, 21202
Telephone: 410-244-0350
Facsimile: 410-244-0356
Elkton, Maryland Office: 205 East Main Street. 21921.
Telephone: 410-398-3850.
Fax: 410-398-0666.

David F. Albright
C. Thomas Brown
Benjamin R. Goertemiller

For full biographical listings, see the Martindale-Hubbell Law Directory

ALLEN, JOHNSON, ALEXANDER & KARP, P.A. (AV)

Suite 1540, 100 East Pratt Street, 21202
Telephone: 410-727-5000
Fax: 410-727-0861
Email: ajakmd@aol.com
Washington, D.C. Office: 1707 L Street, N.W., Suite 1050.
Telephone: 202-828-4141.

Daniel Karp
Yvette M. Bryant

Representative Clients: Scottsdale Insurance Co.; Nautilus Insurance Co.; Jefferson Insurance Co.; Liberty Mutual Insurance Co.; Avis Rent-A-Car; Otis Elevator Co.; Montgomery Elevator Co.; Admiral Insurance Co.; Local Government Insurance Trust; Penn National Insurance Co.

For Complete List of Firm Personnel, See General Section

For full biographical listings, see the Martindale-Hubbell Law Directory

ANDERSON, COE & KING, L.L.P. (AV)

201 North Charles Street, Suite 2000, 21201-4135
Telephone: 410-752-1630
Cable Address: ABKO
Fax: 410-752 0085
Ocean City, Maryland Office: 12934 Kelly Bridge Lane, P.O. Box 535.
Telephone: 410-213-2681.
Fax: 410-213-2685.

COUNSEL

G. C. A. Anderson (1898-1985)
Ward B. Coe, Jr. (1913-1996)

OF COUNSEL

Frank J. Vecella
John F. King

MEMBERS OF FIRM

Robert H. Bouse, Jr.
E. Dale Adkins, III
James A. Rothschild
M. Bradley Hallwig
J. Michael Sloneker
E. Philip Franke, III
Philip C. Jacobson
Lynne B. Malone
Gregory L. VanGeison
Barbara McC. Stanley
Matthew T. Angotti
Hugh Cropper, IV (Resident, Ocean City Office)
James S. Aist

ASSOCIATES

Charles Ian Joseph
Neil R. Lebowitz
Alison J. McGriff
Stacie Free Farley
Harris Patrick Murphy
Allison Epstein Rubin
Brian P. Wyatt

Representative Clients: Hartford Accident & Indemnity Co.; The St. Paul Insurance Cos.; Medical Mutual Liability Society of Maryland; Chrysler Corp.; Provident Life and Accident Insurance Co.; Emerson Electric Co.; Pennsylvania Hospital Insurance Co.; Maryland Association of Boards of Education Group Insurance Pool; Pittsburgh Corning Corp.

For full biographical listings, see the Martindale-Hubbell Law Directory

BAKER, BAKER & TWOMEY, P.A. (AV)

409 Washington Avenue, Suite 1000, 21204-4905
Telephone: 410-823-8500
Facsimile: 410-823-8509

George W. Baker
William P. Baker
Daniel M. Twomey

H. Scott Jones

Representative Clients: John Deere Construction Equipment Co.; John Deere Insurance Co.; Munich American Reinsurance Co.; Planet Insurance Co.; Commonwealth Mortgage Assurance Co.; Shakey's Inc.; Balcon, Inc.; Durrett- Sheppard Steel Co., Inc.; Shenandoah Brick Corporation;

(See Next Column)

Reference: Nations Bank, Baltimore, Maryland.

For full biographical listings, see the Martindale-Hubbell Law Directory

BALLARD SPAHR ANDREWS & INGERSOLL, LLP (AV)

300 East Lombard Street, 19th Floor, 21202-3268
Telephone: 410-528-5600
Fax: 410-528-5650
URL: http://www.ballardspahr.com
Philadelphia, Pennsylvania Office: 1735 Market Street, 51st Floor.
Telephone: 215-665-8500.
Fax: 215-864-8999.
Voorhees, New Jersey Office: Suite 100, 1101 Laurel Oak Drive.
Telephone: 856-627-8555.
Fax: 856-627-1153.
Denver, Colorado Office: Seventeenth Street Plaza Building, Suite 2300, 1225 17th Street.
Telephone: 303-292-2400.
Fax: 303-296-3956.
Salt Lake City, Utah Office: One Utah Center, Suite 1200, 201 South Main Street.
Telephone: 801-531-3000.
Fax: 801-531-3001.
Washington, D.C. Office: Suite 1000 South, 601 13th Street, N.W.
Telephone: 202-661-2200.
Fax: 202-661-2299.
Camden, New Jersey Office: 800 Hudson Square, 5th Floor.
Telephone: 609-541-5577.
Fax: 609-541-8272.

Nancy V. Alquist
Charles S. Hirsch
David G. Mandelbaum
Glenn L. Unterberger

OF COUNSEL

Arthur F. Fergenson

Robert A. Scott
Jennifer Conway Sharkey

For full biographical listings, see the Martindale-Hubbell Law Directory

LAW OFFICE OF EDWARD L. BLANTON, JR., P.A. (AV)

404 Allegheny Avenue, 21204
Telephone: 410-296-8160
Fax: 410-821-8113

Peter T. McDowell

For full biographical listings, see the Martindale-Hubbell Law Directory

BOULAND & BRUSH, L.L.C. (AV)

Suite 2400 201 North Charles Street, 21201-4105
Telephone: 410-752-6000
Washington D.C. Area: 301-585-1249
Fax: 410-625-3859

H. Dean Bouland
Edward J. Brush
Catherine Chen Hester
Paul D. Raschke
Richard C. Afrookteh
Leslie J. Williams
Robert H. Burrow

ASSOCIATES

Lori B. Kisch
Kimberly S. Keith

OF COUNSEL

Alan A. Abramowitz

For full biographical listings, see the Martindale-Hubbell Law Directory

ELLIN AND BAKER (AV)

Second Floor, 1101 St. Paul Street, 21202
Telephone: 410-727-1787
Fax: 410-547-1787
1-800-237-1787
Email: Ellinlaw@aol.com

MEMBER OF FIRM

Marvin Ellin

For full biographical listings, see the Martindale-Hubbell Law Directory

FERGUSON, SCHETELICH & HEFFERNAN, P.A. (AV)

1401 NationsBank Center, 100 South Charles Street, 21201-2725
Telephone: 410-837-2200
Fax: 410-837-1188
URL: http://www.FSHLaw.com

Robert L. Ferguson, Jr.
Thomas J. Schetelich
Christopher J. Heffernan
Craig F. Ballew
Michael N. Russo, Jr.

(See Next Column)

FERGUSON, SCHETELICH & HEFFERNAN P.A.—*Continued*

Peter J. Basile
Ann D. Ware
Tracey J. McLauchlin
Michele P. Zahner
Michael K. Hourigan

For full biographical listings, see the Martindale-Hubbell Law Directory

DAVID E. FINK (AV)

10 North Calvert Street, Suite 750, 21202
Telephone: 410-547-0480
Fax: 410-547-7206

For full biographical listings, see the Martindale-Hubbell Law Directory

FREISHTAT & SANDLER (AV)

Suite 1500, One Calvert Plaza, 201 E. Baltimore Street, 21202
Telephone: 410-727-7740
FAX: 410-727-7356

MEMBERS OF FIRM

David Freishtat
Paul Mark Sandler
Raymond F. Altman
Raymond Daniel Burke
William Michael Mullen
Lloyd J. Snow
Stacie F. Dubnow

Roderick R. Barnes
Jeffrey S. Rosenfeld
Thomas K. Harris

OF COUNSEL

Lynn Weinberg

For full biographical listings, see the Martindale-Hubbell Law Directory

GALLAGHER, EVELIUS & JONES, LLP (AV)

Park Charles Suite 400, 218 North Charles Street, 21201
Telephone: 410-727-7702
Facsimile: 410-468-2786
URL: http://www.gejlaw.com

MEMBERS OF FIRM

Francis X. Gallagher (1928-1972)
C. Edward Jones (1908-1999)
John C. Evelius (Retired)
Richard O. Berndt
Thomas N. Biddison, Jr.
Robert R. Kern, Jr.
Saul E. Gilstein
Thomas B. Lewis
Bonnie Abrams Travieso
Stephen A. Goldberg
Linda H. Jones
Jack C. Tranter
Leslie B. Speed
Christopher J. Fritz
David E. Raderman
Peter E. Keith
Nita L. Schultz
Michael W. Skojec
Kathryn Kelley Hoskins
Mark P. Keener
Kevin J. Davidson
Eileen M. Lunga
Lori A. Nicolle
Kenneth S. Gross
Thomas C. Dame

ASSOCIATES

Valarie K. Oulds
Margaret Stevens Jacks
Matthew W. Oakey
Rebecca A. Weaver
Michael J. Henigan
David W. Kinkopf
Paul S. Caiola
Jason W. Gaarder
M. Kirsten Andrews

LEGAL ASSISTANTS

Patricia C. Quayle
Iris T. H. Heath
Connie L. Ennis
Margaret Graff
Margo Gibson Hughes
Jonathan T. Gillis
Brenda J. Heacock
Dwayne L. Rodeheaver

Representative Clients: Roman Catholic Archdiocese of Baltimore; Mercy Medical Center, Inc.; Caronia Corporation; P. Flanigan; Baltimore Equitable Society; Fannie Mae.

For full biographical listings, see the Martindale-Hubbell Law Directory

HAROLD I. GLASER (AV)

Suite 1717, 201 North Charles Street, 21201
Telephone: 410-244-8822
Fax: 410-625-1028
Email: HIGlaser@aol.com

MEMBER OF FIRM

Michael S. Glushakow

For full biographical listings, see the Martindale-Hubbell Law Directory

GORDON & HENESON, P.A. (AV)

Suite 1900, Blaustein Building, One North Charles Street, 21201
Telephone: 410-539-0666
Fax: 410-547-8453
Email: GORHEN@AOL.COM

Michael I. Gordon
Allan Heneson

Stephen R. Robinson

(See Next Column)

LEGAL SUPPORT PERSONNEL

Shelly Abrams (Administrator)

For full biographical listings, see the Martindale-Hubbell Law Directory

ISRAELSON, SALSBURY, CLEMENTS & BEKMAN, L.L.C. (AV)

300 West Pratt Street Suite 450, 21201
Telephone: 410-539-6633
FAX: 410-625-9554

MEMBERS OF FIRM

Stuart Marshall Salsbury
Paul D. Bekman
Daniel M. Clements
Matthew Zimmerman
Laurence A. Marder

Lauren R. Calia
Leslie Hayes Russo

COUNSEL TO THE FIRM

Max R. Israelson
Michael P. Smith

OF COUNSEL

Samuel Omar Jackson, Jr. (Semi-Retired)
Wendy Lozinsky Shiff

For full biographical listings, see the Martindale-Hubbell Law Directory

KERR McDONALD, LLP (AV)

31 Light Street, Suite 400, 21202
Telephone: 410-539-2900
Fax: 410-539-2956
Email: KrMcd@aol.com *URL:* http://www.lawyers.com/kerrmcdonald

Charles M. Kerr
Kathleen Morris McDonald

ASSOCIATE

Carrie L. Blackburn

OF COUNSEL

Robert G. Cassilly

For full biographical listings, see the Martindale-Hubbell Law Directory

MARTIN, SNYDER & BERNSTEIN, P.A. (AV)

Redwood Tower, Suite 2000, 217 East Redwood Street, 21202
Telephone: 410-547-7163
Facsimile: 410-547-1605

Gerard P. Martin
David L. Snyder
Gregg L. Bernstein

Kimberly Dunn Spelman
Caroline DeLisle Ciraolo
Steven F. Wrobel
Denis J. Charlesworth

OF COUNSEL

Steven J. Sibel

LEGAL SUPPORT PERSONNEL

Joanna L. Trela (Administrator)
D'Ann Auty (Paralegal)

For full biographical listings, see the Martindale-Hubbell Law Directory

McDANIEL & MARSH (AV)

118 West Mulberry Street, 21201-3606
Telephone: 410-685-3810
Telecopier: 410-685-0203

William Alden McDaniel, Jr.
Jo Bennett Marsh

For full biographical listings, see the Martindale-Hubbell Law Directory

MEHLMAN & GREENBLATT, LLC (AV)

1838 Greene Tree Road, Suite 360, 21208
Telephone: 410-486-4790
Fax: 410-486-4360
URL: http://www.lawyers.com/mehlman&greenblatt

Gerson B. Mehlman
Gary R. Greenblatt
Frederic C. Heyman
Francis X. Leary
Constance M. Hare

For full biographical listings, see the Martindale-Hubbell Law Directory

NILES, BARTON & WILMER (AV)

Suite 1400, 111 S. Calvert Street, 21202-6185
Telephone: 410-783-6300
Cable Address: "Nilwo"
Telecopier: 410-783-6363

MEMBERS OF FIRM

Larry J. Albert
V. Timothy Bambrick
Robert P. O'Brien
John L. Wood
Steven E. Leder
R. Wayne Pierce
David D. Gilliss
Paul McDermott Finamore
George E. Reede, Jr.
Jeffrey A. Wothers
Craig D. Roswell

(See Next Column)

NILES, BARTON & WILMER, *Baltimore—Continued*

ASSOCIATES

Kevin J. Willging
Jason C. Brino
Donald L. Speidel
Joel P. Williams
Eric A. Frechtel
Brian L. Moffet
Matthew G. Hjortsberg
Bambi L. Wilson
Thomas P. Turgeon
Julie A. Furst
Ronald E. Council, Jr
Ranji Martelli Garrett
Ann M. Grillo
Susan S. Muller
Robert S. Reverski, Jr.

For Complete List of Firm Personnel, See General Section

For full biographical listings, see the Martindale-Hubbell Law Directory

PHILLIPS P. O'SHAUGHNESSY, P.A. (AV)

1102 Terrace Glen, 21210
Telephone: 410-532-0300
FAX: 410-532-2220
URL: http://www.oshaughnessy.wld.com
Ft. Lauderdale, Florida Office: One East Broward Boulevard, Suite 700, 33301.
Telephone: 800-882-3133.

Phillips P. O'Shaughnessy
Robin Frazier Kandel

For full biographical listings, see the Martindale-Hubbell Law Directory

PIERSON, PIERSON & NOLAN (AV)

Suite 2020 Redwood Tower, 217 East Redwood Street, 21202
Telephone: 410-727-7733
Fax: 410-625-0253
Email: piernol@ibm.net

MEMBERS OF FIRM

W. Michel Pierson
James J. Nolan, Jr.
Robert L. Pierson

For Complete List of Firm Personnel, See General Section

For full biographical listings, see the Martindale-Hubbell Law Directory

ROBINSON WOOLSON O'CONNELL, LLP (AV)

Redwood Tower Suite 1500, 217 East Redwood Street, 21202
Telephone: 410-625-0000
Fax: 410-625-0201
Email: robinsonwoolson@juno.com
Elgin, Illinois Office: 217 North McLean Boulevard, Suite 2-C, 60123.
Telephone: 847-741-4603.

Deborah L. Robinson
Peter A. Woolson
Daniel J. O'Connell (Not admitted in MD)

Jill E. O'Donnell

For full biographical listings, see the Martindale-Hubbell Law Directory

ROLLINS, SMALKIN, RICHARDS & MACKIE, L.L.C. (AV)

401 North Charles Street, 21201
Telephone: 410-727-2443
Fax: 410-727-8390
URL: http://www.rsrm.com

MEMBERS OF FIRM

H. Beale Rollins (1898-1985)
Samuel S. Smalkin (1906-1982)
Edward C. Mackie
John F. Linsenmeyer
Thomas C. Gentner
Glenn W. Trimmer
Patrick G. Cullen
James P. O'Meara
Paul G. Donoghue
Ralph E. Wilson III

ASSOCIATES

Kenneth G. Macleay
Donna Lynn Kolakowski-Hollen
Meg Bantley Whiteford
J. James Roos
Jessica R. Di Cicco

OF COUNSEL

Raymond A. Richards (Retired)

LEGAL SUPPORT PERSONNEL

Guy M. Craig

For full biographical listings, see the Martindale-Hubbell Law Directory

SCANLAN, ROSEN & SHAR, LLC (AV)

26 South Street, 21202-3399
Telephone: 410-244-1155
Fax: 410-244-1157
Email: lawyers@triallaw.com *URL:* http://www.triallaw.com

Alfred L. Scanlan, Jr.
Marc Seldin Rosen
Marcus Z. Shar
Michael Stuart Warshaw

Timothy Cronin Lynch
Neil E Duke
Kristofer P. Cubello

(See Next Column)

OF COUNSEL

Colleen A. Cavanaugh
Lee H. Caplan
J. Michael McWilliams

For full biographical listings, see the Martindale-Hubbell Law Directory

SCHOCHOR, FEDERICO AND STATON, P.A. (AV)

The Paulton, 1211 St. Paul Street, 21202
Telephone: 410-234-1000
Toll Free: 888-234-0001
Facsimile: 410-234-1010
URL: http://www.sfspa.com
Washington D.C. Office: 10 G Street, N.E., Suite 650.
Telephone: 202-408-3300.

Jonathan Schochor
Philip C. Federico
Kerry D. Staton

Christopher P. Kennedy
Robert J. Farley
Bonnie Ardinger Winders

For full biographical listings, see the Martindale-Hubbell Law Directory

BARRY L. STEELMAN, P.A. (AV)

305 W. Chesapeake Avenue, Suite 300, 21204
Telephone: 410-321-4740
Fax: 410-321-4746
Email: steelmanlaw@erols.com *URL:* http://www.lawyers.com/steelmanlaw

Barry L. Steelman

Mark S. Dachille

For full biographical listings, see the Martindale-Hubbell Law Directory

VENABLE ATTORNEYS AT LAW VENABLE, BAETJER AND HOWARD, LLP (AV)

A Partnership including Professional Corporations
1800 Mercantile Bank & Trust Building, 2 Hopkins Plaza, 21201
Telephone: 410-244-7400
Fax: 410-244-7742
URL: http://www.venable.com
Washington, D.C. Office: Venable, Baetjer, Howard & Civiletti LLP, Suite 1000, 1201 New York Avenue, N.W.
Telephone: 202-962-4800.
Fax: 202-962-8300.
McLean, Virginia Office: Suite 400, 2010 Corporate Ridge.
Telephone: 703-760-1600.
Fax: 703-821-8949.
Rockville, Maryland Office: Suite 500, One Church Street, P. O. Box 1906.
Telephone: 301-217-5600.
Fax: 301-217-5617.
Towson, Maryland Office: 210 Allegheny Avenue, P. O. Box 5517.
Telephone: 410-494-6200.
Fax: 410-821-0147.

MEMBERS OF FIRM

Benjamin R. Civiletti (P.C.) (Also at Washington, D.C. and Towson, Maryland Offices)
George Cochran Doub (P.C.)
John Henry Lewin, Jr. (P.C.)
Stanley Mazaroff (P.C.)
Roger W. Titus (Resident, Rockville, Maryland Office)
Thomas J. Madden (Not admitted in MD; Resident, Washington, D.C. Office)
Ronald R. Glancz (Not admitted in MD; Resident, Washington, D.C. Office)
Kenneth C. Bass, III (Not admitted in MD; Washington, D.C. and McLean, Virginia Offices)
John H. Zink, III (Resident, Towson, Maryland Office)
Paul F. Strain (P.C.)
William D. Dolan, III (P.C.) (Not admitted in MD; Resident, McLean, Virginia Office)
Paul T. Glasgow (Resident, Rockville, Maryland Office)
Joseph C. Wich, Jr. (Resident, Towson, Maryland Office)
Sondra Harans Block (Resident, Rockville, Maryland Office)
Edward F. Glynn, Jr. (Resident, Washington, D.C. Office)
Craig E. Smith
Robert G. Ames (Also at Washington, D.C. Office)
Michael Schatzow (Also at Washington, D.C. Office)
Nell B. Strachan
David G. Lane (Resident, McLean, Virginia Office)
N. Frank Wiggins (Not admitted in MD; Resident, Washington, D.C. Office)
G. Stewart Webb, Jr.
James K. Archibald (Also at Washington, D.C. Office)
George W. Johnston (P.C.)
Judson W. Starr (Not admitted in MD; Also at Washington, D.C. and Towson, Maryland Offices)
Jana Howard Carey (P.C.)
Jeffrey A. Dunn (Also at Washington, D.C. Office)
George F. Pappas (Also at Washington, D.C. Office)
William D. Coston (Not admitted in MD; Resident, Washington, D.C. Office)
James L. Shea (Also at Washington, D.C. Office)
Jeffrey P. Ayres (P.C.)
Elizabeth C. Honeywell
Maurice Baskin (Resident, Washington, D.C. Office)

(See Next Column)

VENABLE ATTORNEYS AT LAW VENABLE, BAETJER AND HOWARD, LLP—*Continued*

MEMBERS OF FIRM (Continued)

Amy Berman Jackson (Not admitted in MD; Resident, Washington, D.C. Office)
C. Carey Deeley, Jr. (Also at Towson, Maryland Office)
Christopher R. Mellott
M. King Hill, III (Resident, Towson, Maryland Office)
James A. Dunbar (Resident, Towson, Maryland Office)
Ronald W. Taylor
Thomas J. Kelly, Jr. (Not admitted in MD; Resident, Washington, D.C. Office)
David J. Heubeck
Herbert G. Smith, II (Not admitted in MD; Resident, Washington, D.C. Office)
Patrick J. Stewart (Also at Washington, D.C. Office)
Gary M. Hnath (Resident, Washington, D.C. Office)
Mitchell Y. Mirviss
Geoffrey R. Garinther (Also at Towson, Maryland Office)
Terri L. Turner
Michael W. Robinson (Resident, McLean, Virginia Office)
Todd J. Horn
David W. Goewey (Not admitted in MD; Resident, Washington, D.C. Office)
J. Scott Hommer, III (Not admitted in MD; Resident, McLean, Virginia Office)
Gregory A. Cross
John A. McCauley
John T. Prisbe
Elizabeth Marzo Borinsky
John P. Sarbanes
Vicki Margolis (Also at Washington, D.C. Office)
Christine M. McAnney (Not admitted in MD; Resident, McLean, Virginia Office)
Maria F. Howell
Marina Lolley Sabett

OF COUNSEL

A. Samuel Cook (P.C.) (Resident, Towson, Maryland Office)

ASSOCIATES

Paul D. Barker, Jr.
Daniel William China (Resident, Towson, Maryland Office)
Patricia Gillis Cousins (Resident, Rockville, Maryland Office)
Carla Draluck Craft (Resident, Washington, D.C. Office)
E. Anne Hamel
Patricia A. Malone (Resident, Towson, Maryland Office)
Daniel P. Moylan (Resident, Towson, Maryland Office)
Melissa Landau Steinman (Resident, Washington, D.C. Office)
Paul N. Wengert (Not admitted in MD; Resident, McLean, Virginia Office)

For Complete List of Firm Personnel, See General Section

For full biographical listings, see the Martindale-Hubbell Law Directory

---

WARD, KERSHAW & MINTON, A PROFESSIONAL ASSOCIATION (AV)

113 West Monument Street, 21201
Telephone: 410-685-6700
Fax: 410-685-6704
Email: wkmfirm@aol.com *URL:* http://www.wkamlaw.com

John T. Ward
Robert B. Kershaw
Thomas J. Minton
April Falcon Doss
J. Dirk Schwenk

OF COUNSEL

Richard V. Falcon

For full biographical listings, see the Martindale-Hubbell Law Directory

---

ROBIN PAGE WEST (AV)

20 South Charles Street, Suite 703, 21201-3291
Telephone: 410-244-0400
Fax: 410-244-0402
Email: rwestn01@erols.com *URL:* http://www.lawyers.com/qui_tam

For full biographical listings, see the Martindale-Hubbell Law Directory

---

WHARTON LEVIN EHRMANTRAUT KLEIN & NASH, A PROFESSIONAL ASSOCIATION (AV)

400 East Pratt Street, 21202
Telephone: 800-322-1984; 410-269-7529
Annapolis, Maryland Office: 104 West Street, P.O. Box 551, Annapolis.
Telephone: 800-322-1984; 410-263-5900.
Facsimile: 410-280-2230; 410-263-1562.

James T. Wharton
David A. Levin
Robert Dale Klein
Brian J. Nash
A. Gwynn Bowie, Jr.
Jack L. Harvey
Michael T. Wharton
Andrew E. Vernick
D. Lee Rutland
David A. Roling
Daniel C. Costello
Christian A. Lodowski
Stuart N. Herschfeld
Linda G. Wales

OF COUNSEL

William A. Ehrmantraut

(See Next Column)

Douglas K. Schrader
Leonard William Dooren, III
Marian L. Hogan
Mary C. Rice
Michael Kevin Wiggins
Thomas C. Marriner
Victoria H. Wink
Julia Renee Arfaa

For full biographical listings, see the Martindale-Hubbell Law Directory

---

*BEL AIR,** Harford Co.

BROWN, BROWN & BROWN, A PROFESSIONAL ASSOCIATION (AV)

200 South Main Street, 21014
Telephone: 410-838-5500
Baltimore: 410-879-2220
Fax: 410-893-0402

A. Freeborn Brown (1915-1998)
T. Carroll Brown
Augustus F. Brown
Albert J. A. Young

Harold Douglas Norton
Christopher R. vanRoden
David E. Carey

Attorneys for: Baltimore Gas & Electric Co.; Chesapeake & Potomac Telephone Co.; Aberdeen Proving Ground Federal Credit Union; First National Bank of Maryland; Bell Atlantic Mobile Systems; First Harbor Securities; Maryland Portable Concrete, Inc.
Approved Counsel for: The Chicago Title Insurance Co. of Maryland, Inc.

For full biographical listings, see the Martindale-Hubbell Law Directory

---

STARK & KEENAN, A PROFESSIONAL ASSOCIATION (AV)

30 Office Street, 21014
Telephone: 410-838-5522
Baltimore: 410-879-2222
Fax: 410-879-0688
Email: wstarkee@aol.com
Havre de Grace Office: "The Old Ordinary" 100 St. John Street, 21078.
Telephone: 410-939-0100.

Elwood V. Stark, Jr.
Charles B. Keenan, Jr.
Edwin G. Carson
Judith Cline-Silverstein
Gregory A. Szoka
Robert S. Lynch
Paul W. Ishak

Claire Prin Blomquist
Lawrence F. Kreis, Jr.
Craig H. DeRan

For full biographical listings, see the Martindale-Hubbell Law Directory

---

BETHESDA, Montgomery Co.

MOSS, STRICKLER & SACHITANO, P.A. (AV)

Suite 700 N, 4550 Montgomery Avenue, 20814
Telephone: 301-657-8805
Facsimile: 301-657-8815
Email: mss@mss-law.com

Stephen E. Moss
Scott Michael Strickler
Nancy A. Sachitano

Hadrian N. Hatfield
Jonathan J. Biedron
Aubrey L. Moss

LEGAL ASSISTANTS

Tri Bostelman
Beverly Feldman
Marcie Laderman

For full biographical listings, see the Martindale-Hubbell Law Directory

---

MARTIN S. PROTAS, P.C. (AV Ⓣ)

6707 Democracy Boulevard, Suite 400, 20817-1129
Telephone: 301-897-2700
Fax: 301-897-5001
Email: Mprotas@aol.com *URL:* http://www.lawyers.com/mprotaslaw

Martin S. Protas

Jennifer R. Fantuz

For full biographical listings, see the Martindale-Hubbell Law Directory

---

GARY HOWARD SIMPSON (AV)

9505 Kingsley Avenue, 20814
Telephone: 301-493-0345
Fax: 301-493-0347
Email: ghslaw@erols.com *URL:* http://www.lawyers.com/garyhsimpson

---

Alane Tempchin

OF COUNSEL

Krauthamer & Stahl, Chartered, Chevy Chase, Maryland

(See Next Column)

GARY HOWARD SIMPSON, *Bethesda—Continued*

LEGAL SUPPORT PERSONNEL

Michelle Ratcliffe (Paralegal)
Joy Simpson (Paralegal)

For full biographical listings, see the Martindale-Hubbell Law Directory

WILLIAMS & EOANNOU, P.C. (AV)

7315 Wisconsin Avenue, Suite 630 North Tower, 20814
Telephone: 301-469-3940
Fax: 301-469-3943
Email: dhw4law@erols.com *URL:* http://ourworld.compuserve.com/homepages/dhwilliams
Washington, D.C. Office: 202 G Street, Northeast.
Telephone: 202-659-1360.

David Huntington Williams
Carol L. Eoannou (Not admitted in MD)
David J. Federbush

OF COUNSEL

Ian Goldsworthy, Q.C.
Linda Lucille Murphy

For full biographical listings, see the Martindale-Hubbell Law Directory

CHEVY CHASE, Montgomery Co.

KIVITZ & LIPTZ, LLC (AV)

650 Barlow Building, 5454 Wisconsin Avenue, 20815-6901
Telephone: 301-951-3400
Facsimile: 301-951-3646
Email: lkoenick@erols.com *URL:* http://www.lawyers.com/kivitz

Murray A. Kivitz
Irwin H. Liptz
Leonard J. Koenick
Harlan L. Weiss

For full biographical listings, see the Martindale-Hubbell Law Directory

COLUMBIA, Howard Co.

GUIDA & EAGAN, P.A. (AV)

Suite 600, Merrill Lynch Building, 10320 Little Patuxent Parkway, 21044
Telephone: 410-992-4545
FAX: 410-992-1605
Email: info@lakeviewtitle.com

Vincent M. Guida
James K. Eagan, III

Elizabeth J. Case

Reference: Taneytown Bank & Trust Co.

For full biographical listings, see the Martindale-Hubbell Law Directory

*EASTON,** Talbot Co.

EWING, DIETZ, TURNER & KEHOE, PROFESSIONAL ASSOCIATION (AV)

16 South Washington Street, P.O. Box 1146, 21601
Telephone: 410-822-1988
Fax: 410-820-5053
URL: http://www.edtklaw.com

L. Clark Ewing (1919-1998)
Philip E. L. Dietz, Jr.
Christopher B. Kehoe
John F. Hall
Karen M. Kaludis
Stephen H. Kehoe

Sharon M. Shilling

OF COUNSEL

Henry P. Turner

References: The Talbot Bank of Easton, Maryland; St. Michaels Bank.

For full biographical listings, see the Martindale-Hubbell Law Directory

*ELLICOTT CITY,** Howard Co.

GERALD M. RICHMAN (AV)

Suite 204, 3454 Ellicott Center Drive, 21043-4128
Telephone: 410-465-6666
FAX: 410-465-8964
Email: GMRPALAW@AOL.COM *URL:* http://www.lawyers.com/gmrichmanlaw

For full biographical listings, see the Martindale-Hubbell Law Directory

GAITHERSBURG, Montgomery Co.

CONROY, BALLMAN & DAMERON, CHARTERED (AV)

Six Montgomery Village Avenue, Suite 402, 20879
Telephone: 301-921-1900
FAX: 301-948-9020
Email: conroylaw@aol.com *URL:* http://www.conroylaw.com
Bowie, Maryland Office: 4201 Northview Drive.
Telephone: 301-805-1400.
Fax: 301-805-0952.

(See Next Column)

John M. Conroy (1916-1986)
B. George Ballman
J. Michael Conroy, Jr.
Thomas D. Gibbons
Stephen J. Orens
Glenn C. Etelson
Robert H. Haslinger (Resident)
Wendy D. Pullano
Eileen T. Basaman
Lynn R. Kromminga (Resident, Bowie Office)
Benjamin C. Winn, Jr. (Not admitted in MD)
Maureen Devine D'Souza
Deborah L. Moran
Jon A. Frank
Maury L. DeFreitas
Edward P. Henneberry

Representative Clients: NationsBank; U.S. Home Corp.; The Ryland Group, Inc.; Greater Capitol Area Association of REALTORS, Inc.; Citibank (Md.) N.A.; NVHomes; Elm Street Development, Inc.

For full biographical listings, see the Martindale-Hubbell Law Directory

GREENBELT, Prince Georges Co.

FOSSETT & BRUGGER, CHARTERED (AV)

6404 Ivy Lane, Suite 720, 20770
Telephone: 301-486-1900
Telecopier: 301-486-0999
La Plata, Maryland Office: 105 LaGrange Avenue, P.O. Box F.
Telephone: 301-934-4200.

George A. Brugger
Clarence L. Fossett
Nancy L. Slepicka
William M. Shipp
John C. Fredrickson
Mary A. Zambri
Eric M. Elmore
Mark S. Petrauskas

John A. Giannetti, Jr.

LEGAL SUPPORT PERSONNEL

Dean Armstrong (Consulting Land Planner)

Representative Clients: Cafritz Companies; Citicorp Real Estate, Inc.; Coscan Brookfield Homes; Crestar Bank; The Driggs Corp.; Kettler Brothers; Kiplinger Washington Editors; The Mutual Life Insurance Company of New York; Richmond-American Homes; The Simon DeBartolo Group.

For full biographical listings, see the Martindale-Hubbell Law Directory

STANLEY S. PICKETT (AV)

Suite 414 Capital Office Park, 6411 Ivy Lane, 20770
Telephone: 301-513-0613
Fax: 301-513-0618
Email: lossp@intr.net

Stanley Sinclair Pickett

ASSOCIATES

Gordon J. Brumback
Stacy S. Pickett Trimble

LEGAL SUPPORT PERSONNEL

Vivian A. Wolfe (Paralegal)

Representative Clients: B.F. Saul Co.; McDonald and Eudy Printers, Inc.; Condominium Management, Inc.; Long & Foster Realtors; Mitron Systems Corp.; Glenanden Housing Authority; Community Associations, Inc.; Hagmer Management, Inc.; Quantum Management, Inc.

For full biographical listings, see the Martindale-Hubbell Law Directory

LARGO, Prince Georges Co.

GREGORY K. WELLS & ASSOCIATES, P.A. (AV)

1801 McCormick Drive Suite 160, 20774
Telephone: 301-925-2000
Fax: 301-925-2006
Email: gkw.associates@erols.com *URL:* http://www.lawyers.com/gregorykwells

Gregory K. Wells

Edward J. Maginnis

OF COUNSEL

Robert C. Maynard

LEGAL SUPPORT PERSONNEL

Juernine M. Wright

For full biographical listings, see the Martindale-Hubbell Law Directory

OCEAN CITY, Worcester Co.

AYRES, JENKINS, GORDY & ALMAND, P.A. (AV)

5200-B Coastal Highway, 21842
Telephone: 410-723-1400
Fax: 410-723-1861
Email: ajga@beachin.net
Berlin, Maryland Office: 11047 Race Track Road (Ocean Pines).
Telephone: 410-641-5033.
Fax: 410-641-6926.

Guy R. Ayres, III
M. Dean Jenkins
Harold B. Gordy, Jr. (Resident, Berlin Office)
James W. Almand
William E. Esham, III
Mark Spencer Cropper

(See Next Column)

AYRES, JENKINS, GORDY & ALMAND P.A.—*Continued*

Paul Timmons Haskell

References: Calvin B. Taylor Banking Co.; Peninsula Bank.

For full biographical listings, see the Martindale-Hubbell Law Directory

COURTLAND K. TOWNSEND, JR. CHARTERED (AV)

The Executive Building, Suite 101, 7200 Coastal Highway, 21842
Telephone: 410-524-4300
FAX: 410-524-4953

Courtland K. Townsend, Jr.

For full biographical listings, see the Martindale-Hubbell Law Directory

WILLIAMS, HAMMOND, MOORE, SHOCKLEY & HARRISON, P.A. (AV)

3509 Coastal Highway, P.O. Box 739, 21842
Telephone: 410-289-3553
Fax: 410-289-4157
Email: whmsh@shore.intercom.net
Berlin, Maryland Office: 11070 Cathell Road, Suite 19.
Telephone: 410-641-8080.
Fax: 410-641-8282.

Marcus J. Williams (1923-1995)
Edward H. Hammond, Jr.
Joseph E. Moore
Raymond C. Shockley
Joseph G. Harrison, Jr.

J. Richard Collins
Regan James Reno Smith
Jeffrey A. Pilchard
Brian D. Shockley
Olivia Harrison Phillips

For full biographical listings, see the Martindale-Hubbell Law Directory

*ROCKVILLE,** Montgomery Co.

ANDERSON & QUINN (AV)

The Adams Law Center, 25 Wood Lane, 20850
Telephone: 301-762-3303
Fax: 301-762-3776
Email: rscanlon@andersonquinn.com

MEMBERS OF FIRM

Charles C. Collins (1900-1973)
Robert E. Anderson (Retired)
Francis X. Quinn
Donald P. Maiberger
Robert P. Scanlon
John A. Rego
Alice Kelley Scanlon

ASSOCIATES

Kerry S. McGeever
Timothy J. Mulreany
Todd P. Maiberger
Jennifer D. Burke
Marc N. Steren

Representative Clients: C & P Telephone; Allstate Insurance Co.; State Farm Mutual Automobile Insurance Co.; Liberty Mutual Insurance Co.; American International Adjustment Co.; Marriott Corp.

For full biographical listings, see the Martindale-Hubbell Law Directory

ARMSTRONG, DONOHUE, CEPPOS & VAUGHAN, CHARTERED (AV)

Suite 101, 204 Monroe Street, 20850
Telephone: 301-251-0440
Telecopier: 301-279-5929

Larry A. Ceppos
H. Patrick Donohue
John C. Monahan
H. Kenneth Armstrong
Benjamin S. Vaughan
Pamela Barrow Kincheloe

Sharon A. Marcial
J. Eric Rhoades
Richard S. Schrager
Andrew J. Marter
Susan E. Mikorski

For full biographical listings, see the Martindale-Hubbell Law Directory

BRAULT, GRAHAM, SCOTT & BRAULT, LLC (AV)

101 South Washington Street, 20850
Telephone: 301-424-1060
Fax: 301-424-7991
Email: bgsb@earthlink.net
Washington, D.C. Office: Brault, Graham, Scott & Brault, PLLC, 1140 Connecticut Avenue, N.W., Suite 250.
Telephone: 202-785-1200.
FAX: 202-785-4301.
Fairfax, Virginia Office: Suite 500, 11350 Random Hills Road, Fair Oaks Plaza, 22030-7429.
Telephone: 202-785-1200.

OF COUNSEL

Laurence T. Scott
James Robert Miller

(See Next Column)

MEMBERS OF FIRM

Denver H. Graham (1922-1987)
Albert E. Brault (Retired)
Albert D. Brault (Resident)
Leo A. Roth, Jr.
James S. Wilson (Resident)
Ronald G. Guziak
Daniel L. Shea (Resident)
M. Kathleen Parker (Resident)
David G. Mulquin (Resident)
James M. Brault (Resident)
Regina Ann Casey (Resident)

ASSOCIATES

Rhonda Ann Hurwitz (Resident)
Joan F. Brault (Resident)

Representative Clients: American Oil Co.; Crum & Forster Group; Fireman's Fund American Insurance Cos.; Kemper Group; Reliance Insurance Cos.; Safeco Group; Government Employees Insurance Co.; Medical Mutual Insurance Society of Maryland; Legal Mutual Liability Insurance Society of Maryland.

For full biographical listings, see the Martindale-Hubbell Law Directory

CATTERTON, KEMP & GREENBERG, P.A. (AV)

Suite 215, 200 A Monroe Street, 20850
Telephone: 301-294-0460
FAX: 301-294-4568
Email: PFKemp@aol.com

Judith R. Catterton
Paul F. Kemp
Robert A. Greenberg

Linda M. Schaefer

OF COUNSEL

Jane Macht

For full biographical listings, see the Martindale-Hubbell Law Directory

MICHAEL S. MORGENSTERN & ASSOCIATES, P.C. (AV)

51 Monroe Street, Suite 1604, 20850
Telephone: 301-217-9500
Fax: 301-217-9579
Toll Free: 1-888-888-0005
Mailing Address: P.O. Box 4690, Rockville, MD, 20850
Email: MSMlaw@erols.com
Washington, D.C. Office: 601 Pennsylvania Avenue, N.W. 20004.
Telephone: 202-393-2500.
Frederick, Maryland Office: 228 West Patrick Street. 21701.
Telephone: 301-620-7900.

Michael S. Morgenstern
Carl Morgenstern (Not admitted in MD)
Barbara L. Morgenstern (Not admitted in MD)

OF COUNSEL

W. David Allen

For full biographical listings, see the Martindale-Hubbell Law Directory

JAMES W. SALTER, III, P.A. (AV)

Suite 105, Old Town Center, 17 West Jefferson Street, 20850
Telephone: 301-762-8011
Fax: 301-762-4740

James F. Tomes (1952-1976)
James W. Salter (1941-1973)
James W. Salter, III

For full biographical listings, see the Martindale-Hubbell Law Directory

STEIN, SPERLING, BENNETT, DE JONG, DRISCOLL, GREENFEIG & METRO, P.C. (AV)

25 West Middle Lane, 20850-2204
Telephone: 301-340-2020; 800-435-5230
Telecopier: 301-340-8217
Email: lawfirm@steinsperling.com
Falls Church, Virginia Office: 6245 Leesburg Pike, Suite 140, 22044.
Telephone: 703-237-0500.
Telecopier: 703-534-2899.

Millard S. Bennett
David C. Driscoll, Jr.
Stuart S. Greenfeig
Jeffrey M. Schwaber
Paul T. Stein

Jeffrey D. Goldstein
David W. Lease
Darcy A. Shoop
Debra Sue Grimes

For Complete List of Firm Personnel, See General Section

For full biographical listings, see the Martindale-Hubbell Law Directory

Rockville—Continued

VENABLE ATTORNEYS AT LAW VENABLE, BAETJER AND HOWARD, LLP (AV)

A Partnership including Professional Corporations
Suite 500, One Church Street, P.O. Box 1906, 20850-4129
Telephone: 301-217-5600
Fax: 301-217-5617
URL: http://www.venable.com
Baltimore, Maryland Office: 1800 Mercantile Bank & Trust Building, 2 Hopkins Plaza.
Telephone: 410-244-7400.
Fax: 410-244-7742.
Washington, D.C. Office: Venable, Baetjer, Howard & Civiletti LLP, Suite 1000, 1201 New York Avenue, N.W.
Telephone: 202-962-4800.
Fax: 202-962-8300.
McLean, Virginia Office: Suite 400, 2010 Corporate Ridge.
Telephone: 703-760-1600.
Fax: 703-821-8949.
Towson, Maryland, Office: 210 Allegheny Avenue, P. O. Box 5517.
Telephone: 410-494-6200.
Fax: 410-821-0147.

MEMBERS OF FIRM

Roger W. Titus
Sondra Harans Block

ASSOCIATE

Patricia Gillis Cousins

For Complete List of Firm Personnel, See General Section

For full biographical listings, see the Martindale-Hubbell Law Directory

*SALISBURY,** Wicomico Co.

ADKINS, POTTS & SMETHURST, L.L.P. (AV)

Suite 600, One Plaza East, P.O. Box 4247, 21803-4247
Telephone: 410-749-0161
Fax: 410-749-5021

MEMBER OF FIRM

Raymond Stevens Smethurst, Jr.

Representative Clients: Bell Atlantic NYNEX Mobile; Campbell Soup Company; Delmarva Power & Light Co.; Lawyers' Title Insurance Corp.; PNC Bank; Peninsula Roofing Co.; Rogers Refrigeration Co.; Shopco Group; Shore Sheet Metal, Inc.; WBOC-TV.

For full biographical listings, see the Martindale-Hubbell Law Directory

ANTHENELLI & OTWAY (AV)

108 The Plaza, P.O. Box 4096, 21801
Telephone: 410-749-3900
Fax: 410-749-8577

MEMBERS OF FIRM

James V. Anthenelli
James L. Otway

ASSOCIATE

John K. Phoebus

For full biographical listings, see the Martindale-Hubbell Law Directory

DUVALL & DUVALL, L.L.P. (AV)

108 East Market Street, P.O. Box 4077, 21803-4077
Telephone: 410-548-1010
Fax: 410-548-1045
Email: billduva@shore.intercom.net

MEMBERS OF FIRM

William G. Duvall
Richard M. Duvall

Reference: Nations Bank.

For full biographical listings, see the Martindale-Hubbell Law Directory

WEBB, BURNETT, JACKSON, CORNBROOKS, WILBER, VORHIS & DOUSE, LLP (AV)

115 Broad Street, P.O. Box 910, 21801
Telephone: 410-742-3176
Fax: 410-742-0438
Email: webnett@shore.intercom.net

MEMBERS OF FIRM

Frederick W. C. Webb (1889-1956)
John W. T. Webb (1918-1990)
K. King Burnett
W. Newton Jackson, 3rd
Ernest I. Cornbrooks, III
Paul D. Wilber
David A. Vorhis
David B. Douse

ASSOCIATE

Chris Schiller Mason

Counsel for: First National Bank of Maryland (Salisbury branch); K & L Microwave, Inc.; Peninsula General Hospital Medical Center.
Local Attorneys for: State Farm Insurance Cos.; Nationwide Insurance Cos.; Travelers Insurance Co.; United States Fidelity & Guaranty Co.; Aetna Casualty & Surety Co.; Insurance Company of North America.

(See Next Column)

For full biographical listings, see the Martindale-Hubbell Law Directory

SILVER SPRING, Montgomery Co.

COGGINS, HARMAN & HEWITT (AV)

A Partnership of Professional Corporations
8905 Fairview Road, Suite 600, 20910
Telephone: 301-587-2880
Facsimile: 301-495-4990
Email: CHHlaw587@aol.com
Washington, D.C. Office: Suite 330, G Street Lobby, 655 15th Street, N.W.
Falls Church, Virginia Office: 254 North Washington Street.

William N. Coggins
John H. Harman
William E. Hewitt
John F. Davis

OF COUNSEL

Dale E. Duncan (Not admitted in MD)

For full biographical listings, see the Martindale-Hubbell Law Directory

*TOWSON,** Baltimore Co.

FREEMAN, WOLFE & GREENBAUM, P.A. (AV)

409 Washington Avenue Suite 300, 21204
Telephone: 410-321-8400
Fax: 410-321-8407
Email: Lawyers@fwglaw.com

Steven R. Freeman
Thomas D. Wolfe
David A. Greenbaum

LEGAL SUPPORT PERSONNEL

Mary E. Stielper
Joan M. Johnson (Office Administrator)

For full biographical listings, see the Martindale-Hubbell Law Directory

NOLAN, PLUMHOFF & WILLIAMS, CHARTERED (AV)

Suite 700, Nottingham Centre, 502 Washington Avenue, 21204-4528
Telephone: 410-823-7800
Fax: 410-296-2765
Email: npw@nolanplumhoff.com

William P. Englehart, Jr.
Stephen J. Nolan
Robert L. Hanley, Jr.
Robert E. Cahill, Jr.
C. William Clark

Representative Clients: Anne Arundel County, Maryland; Baltimore County, Maryland; Board of Education of Anne Arundel County; Board of Education of Baltimore County (Special Counsel in Environmental Cost Recovery Litigation); Bituminous Insurance Companies; Carolina Freight Carriers Corporation; First Fidelity Bank; Humane Society of Baltimore County, Inc.; Keystone Insurance Company; Maryland Automobile Insurance Fund.

For Complete List of Firm Personnel, See General Section

For full biographical listings, see the Martindale-Hubbell Law Directory

VENABLE ATTORNEYS AT LAW VENABLE, BAETJER AND HOWARD, LLP (AV)

A Partnership including Professional Corporations
210 Allegheny Avenue, P.O. Box 5517, 21204
Telephone: 410-494-6200
Fax: 410-821-0147
URL: http://www.venable.com
Baltimore, Maryland Office: 1800 Mercantile Bank & Trust Building, 2 Hopkins Plaza.
Telephone: 410-244-7400.
Fax: 410-244-7742.
Washington, D.C. Office: Venable, Baetjer, Howard & Civiletti LLP, Suite 1000, 1201 New York Avenue, N.W.
Telephone: 202-962-4800.
Fax: 202-962-8300.
McLean, Virginia Office: Suite 400, 2010 Corporate Ridge.
Telephone: 703-760-1600.
Fax: 703-821-8949.
Rockville, Maryland Office: Suite 500, One Church Street, P. O. Box 1906.
Telephone: 301-217-5600.
Fax: 301-217-5617.

PARTNERS

Benjamin R. Civiletti (P.C.) (Also at Washington, D.C. and Baltimore, Maryland Offices)
John H. Zink, III
Joseph C. Wich, Jr.
C. Carey Deeley, Jr. (Also at Baltimore, Maryland Office)
M. King Hill, III

ASSOCIATES

Patricia A. Malone
Daniel P. Moylan

For Complete List of Firm Personnel, See General Section

For full biographical listings, see the Martindale-Hubbell Law Directory

Towson—Continued

WHITNEY & BOGRIS, LLP (AV)

401 Washington Avenue, Twelfth Floor, 21204
Telephone: 410-583-8000
Fax: 410-583-8031
Email: HGWC@worldnet.att.net

MEMBERS OF FIRM

Daniel W. Whitney
George D. Bogris

ASSOCIATES

Kathleen D. Leslie
Henry Russell
Sandra A. Tofte
Michael A. Giacomazza
Arlene L. Sew
Gerald S. Gaetano (Not admitted in MD)
Scott A. McCabe (Not admitted in MD)
Jeffrey C. Shipley

OF COUNSEL

Joseph E. Dever
David L. Feldstein
Ronald V. Miller, Jr.

For full biographical listings, see the Martindale-Hubbell Law Directory

*UPPER MARLBORO,** Prince Georges Co.

KNIGHT, MANZI, NUSSBAUM & LAPLACA, P.C. (AV)

14440 Old Mill Road, 20772
Telephone: 301-952-0100
Annapolis/Baltimore: 410-792-3786
Fax: 301-952-0221

William E. Knight
Robert A. Manzi
Ronald M. Miller
William C. Brennan, Jr.
Harry J. Trainor, Jr.
Andrew W. Nussbaum
Raymond G. LaPlaca
John F. Shay, Jr.
Sheldon L. Gnatt
Daniel A. LaPlaca
Gail Borjeson Viens
Roger C. Thomas
Monica M. Haley-Pierson
Daniel F. Lynch III
Norman D. Rivera

Robert L. Lombardo
Amy B. Glaser
Brent M. Ahalt
Terry L. Bell

For full biographical listings, see the Martindale-Hubbell Law Directory

MASSACHUSETTS

*BOSTON,** Suffolk Co.

ANDERSON, ADLER, COHEN & HARVEY LLP (AV)

230 Congress Street, 02110
Telephone: 617-423-6674
Telefax: 617-423-7152
Email: aach@aachlaw.com *URL:* http://www.aachlaw.com

MEMBERS OF FIRM

James H. Anderson
Sidney W. Adler
Ellen Epstein Cohen
Alexandra B. Harvey
George E. Wakeman, Jr.
A. Bernard Guekguezian

ASSOCIATES

Laura Berg Susich
Charles M. Waters
Emily Haycock Fournier
Shelley A. McNamee
Windy L. Rosebush
Michael F. Conway
J. Yasmin Tayyab
Ethan I. Davis

For full biographical listings, see the Martindale-Hubbell Law Directory

ATWOOD & CHERNY (AV)

Dexter House, 393 Commonwealth Avenue, 02115-1802
Telephone: 617-262-6400
Telecopier: 617-421-9482

Jacob M. Atwood
David E. Cherny

OF COUNSEL

Margaret F. McGovern

For full biographical listings, see the Martindale-Hubbell Law Directory

BARRON & STADFELD, P.C. (AV)

50 Staniford Street, Suite 200, 02114
Telephone: 617-723-9800
Telecopier: 617-523-8359
Email: barron@barronstad.com *URL:* HTTP://WWW.BARRONSTAD.COM
Hyannis, Massachusetts Office: 258 Winter Street.
Telephone: 617-778-6622.

(See Next Column)

Bernard A. Dwork
Enid M. Starr
Thomas V. Bennett
Edward E. Kelly
Kevin F. Moloney
David P. Dwork
Julie Taylor Moran
Robert J. Hoffer
Joseph G. Butler
Denise L. Page
Rosemary Purtell
John K. Britt

Roger T. Manwaring
Shawn P. O'Rourke
Kevin P. Scanlon
Kathleen M. Morrissey
Edward J. Fallman

OF COUNSEL

Hertz N. Henkoff

For Complete List of Firm Personnel, See General Section

For full biographical listings, see the Martindale-Hubbell Law Directory

BLOOM & BUELL (AV)

1340 Soldiers Field Road, 02135-1020
Telephone: 617-254-4400; 800-354-6004
Telecopier: 617-254-7610
Email: office@bloombuell.com *URL:* http://www.bloombuell.com

MEMBERS OF FIRM

Laurence J. Bloom
Barbara Hayes Buell
William J. Davenport
Marc J. Gervais
Richard M. Haley

ASSOCIATES

Barry T. Putterman
Barbara D. Weninger

For full biographical listings, see the Martindale-Hubbell Law Directory

BROMBERG & SUNSTEIN LLP (AV)

125 Summer Street, 11th Floor, 02110
Telephone: 617-443-9292
Fax: 617-443-0004
Email: IPLAW@bromsun.com *URL:* http://www.bromsun.com

MEMBERS OF FIRM

Bruce D. Sunstein
Lee Carl Bromberg
Robert L. Kann
Timothy M. Murphy
Kerry L. Timbers
Joel R. Leeman
Robert M. Asher
Thomas C. Carey
Edward J. Dailey

ASSOCIATES

Judith R.S. Stern
Lisa M. Fleming
Erik P. Belt
Theodore E. MacVeagh
Julia Huston
Jennifer G. Cramer
Steven G. Saunders
Samuel J. Petuchowski
Lisa M. Tittemore
John J. Stickevers (Not admitted in MA)
Karen L. Peterson
A. Damien Puller
Herbert Alan Newborn
R.J. Sims Preston
Jeffrey T. Klayman
Christopher D. Engebretson
Jay Sandvos
Jean M. Tibbetts

LEGAL SUPPORT PERSONNEL

Harriet Strimpel, Ph.D. (Patent Agent)
Sonia K. Guterman, Technology Specialist

For full biographical listings, see the Martindale-Hubbell Law Directory

CARR & LISTON (AV)

294 Washington Street, Suite 506, 02108-4608
Telephone: 617-482-6355
Fax: 617-482-7197
Email: ecarr@socialaw.com *URL:* http://www.lawyers.com/carrliston

MEMBERS OF FIRM

Edwin J. Carr
Michael J. Liston

For full biographical listings, see the Martindale-Hubbell Law Directory

CASNER & EDWARDS, LLP (AV)

1 Federal Street, 27th Floor, 02110-2003
Telephone: 617-426-5900
Telecopier: 617-426-8810
Email: ce@thecia.net

MEMBERS OF FIRM

Thomas D. Edwards (1931-1987)
Andrew J. Casner, Jr. (1931-1999)
Haskell A. Kassler
Walter H. Mayo, III
Martin E. Greenblatt
Charles M. Hamann
Robert A. Murphy
Robert E. Cowden, III
John H. Ashby
Douglas K. Mansfield
Andrew M. Higgins
Terrance J. Hamilton
Robert S. Kutner
David J. Chavolla
Stephen M. Perry
Gary L. Hoff
Anita W. Robboy
Peter A. Caro
Gregg S. Blackburn
Linda A. Ouellette
Joan M. Griffin

(See Next Column)

CASNER & EDWARDS LLP, *Boston—Continued*

ASSOCIATES

Donna Brewer MacKenna
Gary L. Kemp
Matthew T. Murphy
Mark W. Williamson
William F. McSweeny, III
Elizabeth L. Desmond
Martha A. Coravos

For full biographical listings, see the Martindale-Hubbell Law Directory

COGAVIN AND WAYSTACK (AV)

2 Center Plaza, 02108
Telephone: 617-742-3340
Telecopier: 617-723-7563
Email: law@cogway.com *URL:* http://cogway.com

MEMBERS OF FIRM

John J. Cogavin
Edward W. Waystack
John P. Fitzgerald
Gerard A. Butler
Kevin J. McGinty

ASSOCIATES

David T. Donnelly
John J. Jarosak
Thomas M. Franco
Mark A. Darling
Owen Roe O'Neill
Audrey Lewchik Bradley
Daniel S. McInnis
William P. Hurley
Denis P. Bergin
Mark R. Freitas
Kevin M. Tierney

For full biographical listings, see the Martindale-Hubbell Law Directory

CORNELL & GOLLUB (AV)

75 Federal Street, 02110
Telephone: 617-482-8100
Telecopier: 617-482-3917
Email: CornellGollub@worldnet.att.net
Wakefield, Rhode Island Office: 146 Main Street, 02879.
Telephone: 401-782-2072.
Telecopier: 401-782-4941.

MEMBERS OF FIRM

Robert W. Cornell (1910-1988)
Karl L. Gollub (1934-1985)
David H. Sempert
Peter M. Durney
Paul F. Lynch
Jane Treen Brand
Janet J. Bobit
David W. McGough

ASSOCIATES

Thomas A. Pursley
Susan Donaldson Novins
Marie Chadeayne Chafe
Kelly L. Wilkins
James P. Kerr
Patricia A. Hartnett
David G. Braithwaite
Jennifer L. Davis
Matthew J. Ginsburg
Kenneth M. Robbins

OF COUNSEL

Philip J. Foley

For full biographical listings, see the Martindale-Hubbell Law Directory

CURLEY & CURLEY, P.C. (AV)

27 School Street, 02108-4391
Telephone: 617-523-2990
Fax: 617-523-7602

Robert A. Curley
Robert A. Curley, Jr.
Eugene F. Nowell
David D. Dowd
Martin J. Rooney
Lisabeth Ryan Kundert
Stephen J. Gill
Charles Mark Furcolo
Joni Katz Mackler

For full biographical listings, see the Martindale-Hubbell Law Directory

DENNIS J. CURRAN (AV)

Historic City Hall, 45 School Street, 2nd Floor, 02108-3204
Telephone: 617-742-3010
Fax: 617-742-1799
URL: http://www.lawyers.com/personalinj

For full biographical listings, see the Martindale-Hubbell Law Directory

CURTIN, MURPHY & O'REILLY, P.C. (AV)

55 Summer Street, 02110
Telephone: 617-574-1700
Facsimile: 617-574-1710

William H. Murphy
Thomas P. O'Reilly
Richard N. Curtin
Linda C. Scarano
Scott E. Richardson
Linda D. Oliveira
Paul M. Moretti
Jeffrey C. McLucas

Kevin P. Jones
Chrisann Leal
Christine Lynn DeRosa

OF COUNSEL

Richard T. Corbett
Dori P. Kelly

For full biographical listings, see the Martindale-Hubbell Law Directory

DEUTSCH WILLIAMS BROOKS DERENSIS HOLLAND & DRACHMAN, P.C. (AV)

99 Summer Street, 02110-1235
Telephone: 617-951-2300
Fax: 617-951-2323
Email: dwbdhd@ix.netcom.com
Nantucket, Massachusetts Office: 5 Gladlands Avenue.
Telephone: 508-228-8725.
Fax: 508-325-5860.

Burton L. Williams
Steven J. Brooks
Paul R. DeRensis
Robert E. Holland
Allan W. Drachman
Roland Gray, III
Richard D. Bickelman
Valerie Swett
John Foskett
Barry L. Mintzer
Daniel R. Deutsch
Janet L. Maloof
Randy J. Kaplan
Rodney G. Hoffman
Peter J. Berry
Lawrence R. Holland
Richard S. Blank
Robert D. Hillman
Susan A. Moniz
Regina M. Hurley

Laurie W. Engdahl
Frank J. Weiner
Catherine Skahan Reidy
Andrea T. Beaudry
Elizabeth B. Valerio
Scott C Merrill
Tammy L. Richardson
Kimberly M. Saillant
Berin Sultan
William Studzinski, Jr.
Jennifer Smith Mitchelson
Anthony M. D'Imperio
David M. Forman
Kathryn Palmer

OF COUNSEL

Jack Green (P.C.)
A. Theodore Welburn
Gerald A. Berlin
Matthew A. Berlin

For full biographical listings, see the Martindale-Hubbell Law Directory

ELLIS & RAPACKI (AV)

85 Merrimac Street Suite 300, 02114
Telephone: 617-523-4800
Facsimile: 617-523-6901
Email: rellis4174@aol.com

Fredric L. Ellis
Edward D. Rapacki
Edward A. Broderick

For full biographical listings, see the Martindale-Hubbell Law Directory

ESDAILE, BARRETT & ESDAILE (AV)

75 Federal Street, 02110
Telephone: 617-482-0333
Fax: 617-426-2978
Email: Esdaile@AOL.COM

MEMBERS OF FIRM

J. Newton Esdaile
Charles W. Barrett, Jr.
James N. Esdaile, Jr.
Norman I. Jacobs
Michael E. Mone
Patricia L. Kelly
Robert J. Rutecki

ASSOCIATES

Shaun Spencer Forsyth
Rhonda Traver Maloney
Steven J. Ryan
C. William Barrett
Mary Moynihan Conneely
Jon M. Jacobs
Kathryn E. Hand

OF COUNSEL

Charles J. Murray

For full biographical listings, see the Martindale-Hubbell Law Directory

FRIEDMAN & ATHERTON (AV)

(Formerly Friedman, Atherton, King & Turner)
(Formerly Friedman, Atherton, Sisson & Kozol)
Exchange Place, 53 State Street, 02109-2803
Telephone: 617-227-5540
Telecopier: 617-523-1559

Lee M. Friedman (1897-1957)
Percy A. Atherton (1903-1940)
Frank L. Kozol (1927-1993)
Robert D. Kozol (1938-1999)

OF COUNSEL

Frank H. Shapiro

MEMBERS OF FIRM

Joel A. Kozol
Lee H. Kozol
William I. Cowin
Richard M. Zinner
Matthew S. Kozol
David M. Kozol

ASSOCIATES

Christine P. Deshler
Angela M. Kalivas
Janet Kenton-Walker
Olive E. Larson
David A. Rich
Meredith Anne Rosenthal
Herbert Weinberg

(See Next Column)

FRIEDMAN & ATHERTON—*Continued*

COUNSEL

Paul S. Alpert
Thomas C. Bailey
Michael P. Morizio

For full biographical listings, see the Martindale-Hubbell Law Directory

GADSBY & HANNAH LLP (AV)

225 Franklin Street, 02110-2811
Telephone: 617-345-7000
Telefax: 617-345-7050
Email: gadsby@ghlaw.com *URL:* http://www.ghlaw.com
Washington, D.C. Office: 1747 Pennsylvania Avenue, N.W.
Telephone: 202-429-9600.

PARTNERS

Richard K. Allen
Ronald G. Busconi
Peter M. Coppinger
Allan R. Curhan
Charles A. Dale, III
John R. Hallal
Robert J. Kaler
Daniel J. Kelly
Stanley A. Martin
John M. McKelway, Jr.
James J. Myers
Michael N. Sheetz
Evan Slavitt
William A. Zucker

ASSOCIATES

M. Carolina Avellaneda
Joseph A. Barra
Michael B. Donahue
Paul Marshall Harris
Daniel C. Hohler
Andrew A. Honegger
Edward W. Little, Jr.
Susan J. Matthew
Lisa T. McElroy
Elizabeth R. Sahatjian
Risa G. Sorkin
David M. Watson

WASHINGTON, D.C. OFFICE
RESIDENT PARTNERS

Michael A. Hordell
Paul F. Kilmer (Not admitted in MA)
Carol L. B. Matthews (Not admitted in MA)
Lawrence G. Meyer (Not admitted in MA)

RESIDENT ASSOCIATES

Thomas W. Brooke (Not admitted in MA)
Laura L. Hoffman (Not admitted in MA)
Stephen J. Jeffries (Not admitted in MA)

For Complete List of Firm Personnel, See General Section

For full biographical listings, see the Martindale-Hubbell Law Directory

GELB & GELB LLP (AV)

20 Custom House Street, 02110
Telephone: 617-345-0010
Facsimile: 617-345-0009
Email: g&g@gelbgelb.com *URL:* http://www.gelbgelb.com

MEMBERS OF FIRM

Richard M. Gelb
Gail Kleven Gelb

Aaron J. Bullwinkel
Brian G. Cafferty

For full biographical listings, see the Martindale-Hubbell Law Directory

GOVERNO AND KAVANAGH LLP (AV)

99 High Street, 02110
Telephone: 617-423-4500
Fax: 617-423-4505
Email: dgoverno@counsel.com *URL:* http://www.governoandkavanagh.com

David M. Governo
Eileen P. Kavanagh

ASSOCIATES

Ann M. Collins
Lisa A. Hack
Michael D. Riseberg
Cynthia J. Stephens
Adam A. Larson

OF COUNSEL

Gregory J. Wenger
Timothy J. Dodd (Not admitted in MA)

For full biographical listings, see the Martindale-Hubbell Law Directory

HANIFY & KING, PROFESSIONAL CORPORATION (AV)

One Federal Street, 02110-2007
Telephone: 617-423-0400
Telefax: 617-423-0498
URL: http://www.hanify.com

James Coyne King
John D. Hanify
Harold B. Murphy
David Lee Evans
Daniel J. Lyne
Donald F. Farrell, Jr.
Barbara W. Pfirrman
Gerard P. Richer
Timothy P. O'Neill
Terence P. McCourt

(See Next Column)

Jeffrey J. Upton
Michael R. Perry
Kathleen E. Cross
Robert E. Richards, Jr.
Joseph F. Cortellini
Andrew G. Lizotte
Donald Ethan Jeffery
Karen A. Whitley
Deena F. Christelis
Robyn J. Bartlett
Owen P. Kane
Sharon H. Patton
John C. McDonald
C. Alexander Hahn
Laurie J. Hurtt
Katherine T. Land
Brian P. McDonough
Lori A. Donovan
Brian R. Marinelli

For full biographical listings, see the Martindale-Hubbell Law Directory

KOPELMAN AND PAIGE, P.C. (AV)

Park Square Building, 31 St. James Avenue, 7th Floor, 02116
Telephone: 617-556-0007
Fax: 617-654-1735

Leonard Kopelman
Donald G. Paige
Elizabeth A. Lane
Joyce F. Frank
John W. Giorgio
Barbara J. Saint Andre
Joel B. Bard
Everett Joseph Marder
Patrick J. Costello
Anne-Marie M. Hyland
Deborah Eliason
Richard Bowen

William Hewig, III
Judith Chanoux Cutler
Brian W. Riley
Thomas P. Lane, Jr.

For Complete List of Firm Personnel, See General Section

For full biographical listings, see the Martindale-Hubbell Law Directory

LANGAN, DEMPSEY AND BRODIGAN (AV)

40 Broad Street Suite 220, 02109
Telephone: 617-542-1871
Telecopier: 617-482-1871

James M. Langan (1907-1998)
Daniel J. Dempsey (1945-1970)
Joseph J. Brodigan
James M. Langan, Jr.

William D. Gardiner
Joseph J. Brodigan, Jr.
Michael Brodigan

For full biographical listings, see the Martindale-Hubbell Law Directory

ARTHUR F. LICATA, P.C. (AV)

Federal Reserve Plaza, 600 Atlantic Avenue, 27th Floor, 02210
Telephone: 617-523-9977
Fax: 617-523-7443
Email: Licata@worldnet.att.net *URL:* http://www.ALicata.com

Arthur F. Licata

For full biographical listings, see the Martindale-Hubbell Law Directory

LOONEY & GROSSMAN LLP (AV)

101 Arch Street, 02110-1112
Telephone: 617-951-2800
Fax: 617-951-2819
URL: http://www.lgllp.com

Stewart F. Grossman (P.C.)
Richard J. Grahn
Bertram E. Snyder
Robert Cushman Barber
Joseph H. Matzkin
Wesley S. Chused
Melvin S. Hoffman

SENIOR COUNSEL

William F. Looney, Jr.

OF COUNSEL

Sherman H. Starr, Jr.
Elizabeth M. Adler
Maria Galvagna Mesinger

ASSOCIATES

Adam J. Ruttenberg
Pamela A. Harbeson
Mary E. Corbett
Benjamin D. Stevenson
Edward V. Colbert, III

For full biographical listings, see the Martindale-Hubbell Law Directory

LAW OFFICE OF SCOTT P. LOPEZ (AV)

24 School Street, 8th Floor, 02108
Telephone: 617-742-5700
Fax: 617-742-5715
Email: lopez@lopezlaw.com *URL:* http://www.lopezlaw.com
(Also Of Counsel, Roach & Carpenter, P.C.)

For full biographical listings, see the Martindale-Hubbell Law Directory

Boston—Continued

McCormack & Epstein (AV)

One International Place, 02110
Telephone: 617-951-2929
Telecopier: 617-951-2672
New York, N.Y. Office: The Empire State Building, 350 Fifth Avenue, 60th Floor, 10118-6098.
Telephone: 212-935-0881.

MEMBERS OF FIRM

Robert D. Epstein
Michael J. McCormack
Mark E. Cohen
Joseph H. Aronson

Brian C. Duffey
George X. Pucci
Marc L. LaCasse
Amy M. Soisson
Stephen D. Rosenberg
Lisa M. Solomon (Not admitted in MA)
Nicole M. Arangio
Ara J. Balikian
Anil Adyanthaya
John A. Krebs

Representative Clients: First State Insurance Co.; Crum & Forster Commercial Insurance; Liberty Mutual Insurance Co.; Massachusetts Bay Transportation Authority; Technical Aid Corporation.

For full biographical listings, see the Martindale-Hubbell Law Directory

Meehan, Boyle & Cohen, P.C. (AV)

2 Center Plaza Suite 600, 02108
Telephone: 617-523-8300
Fax: 617-523-0525

James F. Meehan
Leo V. Boyle
Cynthia J. Cohen
Warren F. Fitzgerald
Peter J. Black
John J. Carroll, Jr.
Michael B. Bogdanow
Karen R. Ristuben

Sherry Yee Mulloy
Samuel M. Furgang
Bradley Mead Henry
Jonathan E. Tobin

For full biographical listings, see the Martindale-Hubbell Law Directory

Menard, Murphy & Walsh LLP (AV)

One Financial Center, 02111
Telephone: 617-832-2500
Telecopier: 617-832-2550
Email: mmw@mmwlaw.com
Washington, D.C. Office: Farragut Park, 910 17th Street, NW, Suite 800, 20006.
Telephone: 202-293-3500.
Telecopier: 202-293-3596.

Arthur P. Menard
Paul J. Murphy
Joseph H. Walsh
John E. Coyne
John S. Leonard

COUNSEL

Theodore E. Daiber

ASSOCIATES

Kevin G. Mahoney
Kevin P. Sweeney
Robert S. Steinberg

For full biographical listings, see the Martindale-Hubbell Law Directory

Mintz, Levin, Cohn, Ferris, Glovsky and Popeo, P.C. (AV)

One Financial Center, 02111
Telephone: 617-542-6000
FAX: 617-542-2241
Internet: Each Attorney's Internet Address takes the following form: first initial last name @mintz.com (e.g., rmintz@mintz.com)
URL: http://www.mintz.com
Washington, D.C. Office: 701 Pennsylvania Avenue, N.W. Suite 900.
Telephone: 202-434-7300.
Fax: 202-434-7400.
Reston, Virginia Office: 12021 Sunset Hills Road, Suite 310.
Telephone: 703-464-4800.
Fax: 703-464-4895.

R. Robert Popeo
Peter M. Saparoff
Thomas R. Murtagh
Stephen M. Leonard
Robert M. Gault
Martha J. Koster
John K. Markey
Michael S. Gardener
Cameron F. Kerry
Patrick J. Sharkey
Elizabeth B. Burnett
Kenneth M. Bello
Peter A. Biagetti
H. Joseph Hameline
Paul D. Wilson
Joseph G. Blute
Samuel M. Starr
Timothy J. Langella
Henry A. Sullivan
Kim V. Marrkand
William M. Hill
Tracy A. Miner
Rosemary M. Allen
Michael F. Connolly
Beth I. Z. Boland
John F. Sylvia

(See Next Column)

OF COUNSEL

Francis X. Bellotti

For Complete List of Firm Personnel, See General Section

For full biographical listings, see the Martindale-Hubbell Law Directory

Nathanson & Goldberg, A Professional Corporation (AV)

Two Oliver Street, 8th Floor, 02109-4901
Telephone: 617-210-4800
Fax: 617-210-4824
Email: natgolaw@earthlink.net *URL:* http://www.natgolaw.com

Alvin S. Nathanson
Arthur Goldberg
Shannon M. Fitzpatrick
José Centeio
Stuart J. Frank

For full biographical listings, see the Martindale-Hubbell Law Directory

Palmer & Dodge LLP (AV)

One Beacon Street, 02108
Telephone: 617-573-0100
Facsimile: 617-227-4420
URL: http://www.palmerdodge.com

MEMBERS OF FIRM

Michael T. Gass
Laurie S. Gill
Jeffrey F. Jones
Michael J. Lacek
William L. Lahey
Daryl J. Lapp
Scott P. Lewis
Francis C. Lynch
Kenneth W. Salinger
Steven L. Schreckinger
Thane D. Scott
Craig E. Stewart
Russell B. Swapp
Jeffrey Swope
Peter S. Terris
Tamara S. Wolfson

For Complete List of Firm Personnel, See General Section

For full biographical listings, see the Martindale-Hubbell Law Directory

Curtis C. Pfunder (AV)

92 State Street, 02109
Telephone: 617-248-0200
Fax: 617-248-0331

For full biographical listings, see the Martindale-Hubbell Law Directory

Prince, Lobel & Tye LLP (AV)

585 Commercial Street, 02109-1024
Telephone: 617-367-2202
Fax: 617-523-0977

MEMBERS OF FIRM

Elliot D. Lobel, P.C.
Walter B. Prince
William A. Worth

ASSOCIATES

Nancy A. Dolberg
Thomas A. Bockhorst
Laurie F. Rubin
Angela L. Lackard

OF COUNSEL

Richard C. Heidlage

For Complete List of Firm Personnel, See General Section

For full biographical listings, see the Martindale-Hubbell Law Directory

Roach & Carpenter, P.C. (AV)

24 School Street, 02108-5513
Telephone: 617-720-1800
Telefax: 617-720-0720
Email: lawyer@rc-law.com

Christine M. Roach
M. Ellen Carpenter
Alison L. Berman
Eric A. Howard

OF COUNSEL

Scott P. Lopez

For full biographical listings, see the Martindale-Hubbell Law Directory

Ropes & Gray (AV)

One International Place, 02110
Telephone: 617-951-7000
Fax: 617-951-7050
Email: postmaster@ropesgray.com *URL:* http://www.ropesgray.com
Washington, D.C. Office: One Franklin Square, 1301 K Street, NW, Suite 800 East.
Telephone: 202-626-3900.
Telecopy: 202-626-3961.
Providence, Rhode Island Office: 30 Kennedy Plaza.
Telephone: 401-455-4400.
Telecopy: 401-455-4401.

(See Next Column)

ROPES & GRAY—*Continued*

MEMBERS OF FIRM

Thomas G. Dignan, Jr. | James L. Sigel
Paul B. Galvani | Thomas H. Hannigan, Jr.
William G. Meserve | John C. Bartenstein
G. Marshall Moriarty | Douglas H. Meal
William L. Patton | John D. Donovan, Jr.
John C. Kane, Jr. | Steven A. Kaufman
Robert K. Gad, III | Michael K. Fee
Kenneth W. Erickson | Martin J. Newhouse
John T. Montgomery | Mark P. Szpak
Harvey J. Wolkoff | Randall W. Bodner
Jeffrey B. Storer | Lee Rubin-Collins
Lisa M. Ropple

COUNSEL

Clayton S. Marsh

ASSOCIATES

Richard D. Batchelder, Jr. | Colleen M. Granahan
Matthew M. Burke | Michael P. Allen
David R. Baron

OF COUNSEL

George C. Caner, Jr. | George H. Lewald
Jerome M. Leonard | A. Lane McGovern
George T. Finnegan

For Complete List of Firm Personnel, See General Section

For full biographical listings, see the Martindale-Hubbell Law Directory

---

MARTIN R. ROSENTHAL (AV)

65A Atlantic Avenue, 02110
Telephone: 617-742-0606
Fax: 617-367-1407
Email: martyros@world.std.com

For full biographical listings, see the Martindale-Hubbell Law Directory

---

SALLY & FITCH (AV)

225 Franklin Street, 02110-2804
Telephone: 617-542-5542
Telecopy: 617-542-1542
URL: http://www.sally-fitch.com
Providence, Rhode Island Office: 56 Pine Street, 02903.
Telephone: 401-521-6500.
Fax: 401-274-2780.

MEMBERS OF FIRM

Francis J. Sally | Thomas P. Billings
Jonathan W. Fitch | Andrea Peraner-Sweet
James B. Re | Paul M. McDermott
Donn A. Randall

COUNSEL

Robert J. Hallisey | Stephen G. Doucette
Suzanne Sheldon

ASSOCIATES

Stephen C. Reilly | Karen W. Salon
Suzanne Q. Feldman | Gretchen Althoff
Carter D. Morse, Jr.

For full biographical listings, see the Martindale-Hubbell Law Directory

---

SARROUF, TARRICONE & FLEMMING (AV)

95 Commercial Wharf, 02110
Telephone: 617-227-5800
Fax: 617-227-5470
Email: Lawyers@STFLAW.COM

Camille Francis Sarrouf | George J. Leary, Jr.
Anthony Tarricone | Daniel J. Gibson
John B. Flemming | Sheryl M. Bourbeau
Camille F. Sarrouf, Jr.

For full biographical listings, see the Martindale-Hubbell Law Directory

---

SCHNEIDER, REILLY, ZABIN & COSTELLO, P.C. (AV)

Three Center Plaza, Suite 430, 02108
Telephone: 617-227-7500
Facsimile: 617-722-0286
Email: rcostello@prodigy.net

Joseph Schneider (1924-1985) | E. L. Schneider (1931-1973)
Joseph E. Reilly (1930-1951) | Joanne D'Alcomo
Albert P. Zabin | Marcia J. Allar
Robert V. Costello | Robert C. Zaffrann

For full biographical listings, see the Martindale-Hubbell Law Directory

---

SHERIN AND LODGEN LLP (AV)

100 Summer Street, 02110
Telephone: 617-426-5720
Fax: 617-542-5186
Email: lawyers@sherin.com *URL:* http://www.sherin.com
Los Angeles, California Office: 11300 W. Olympic Boulevard, Suite 700.
Telephone: 310-914-7891.
Fax: 310-552-5327.

MEMBERS OF FIRM

Arthur L. Sherin (1946-1964) | Kenneth J. Mickiewicz
George E. Lodgen (1946-1971) | Craig M. Brown
Morton B. Brown | Thomas A. Hippler
George Waldstein | Ronald W. Ruth
John M. Reed | Mark A. Nowak
Robert J. Muldoon, Jr. | Thomas P. Gorman
Alette E. Reed | Steven D. Eimert
Edward M. Bloom | Andrew Royce
Joshua M. Alper | John J. Slater III
Gary M. Markoff | John C. La Liberte
Bryan G. Killian | C. Forbes Sargent III
David A. Guberman | David A. Brown
Frank J. Bailey | Michael S. Strauss
Christopher A. Kenney

ASSOCIATES

Robert M. Carney | William P. Keefe
Caroline Woodward | Amy D. Porter
Michael S. Bloom | Thomas F. Dunn
Kenneth D. Small | Brian G. Luneau
Margaret H. Paget | Michael P. Sams
Michael J. Ostroskey | Erin M. McNamara
James M. Wodarski | James W. Matthews
Jessica R. Yaffie | Thomas S. Dean

OF COUNSEL

Janet E. Bostwick | Kurt A. James

For full biographical listings, see the Martindale-Hubbell Law Directory

---

SWARTZ & SWARTZ (AV)

10 Marshall Street, 02108
Telephone: 617-742-1900
Fax: 617-367-7193
Email: Attorney@Swartzlaw.com *URL:* http://www.Swartzlaw.com

Edward M. Swartz | Joan E. Swartz
Alan L. Cantor | James A. Swartz
Joseph A. Swartz | David P. Angueira
Victor A. Denaro | Jason Mark
Lisa V. Kaprielian

OF COUNSEL

Fredric A. Swartz

For full biographical listings, see the Martindale-Hubbell Law Directory

---

TAYLOR, DUANE, BARTON & GILMAN, LLP (AV)

111 Devonshire Street, 02109
Telephone: 617-654-8200
Fax: 617-482-5350
Providence, Rhode Island Office: 10 Dorrance Street, Suite 700, 02903.
Telephone: 401-273-7171.
Fax: 401-273-2904.

MEMBERS OF FIRM

Allan E. Taylor | Edward D. Shoulkin
James J. Duane, III | Jennifer Ellis Burke
John J. Barton | Francis A. Connor, III
Pamela Slater Gilman | Gina Witalec Verdi

ASSOCIATES

Robert C. Shindell | Sheri L. Pizzi
Craig R. Waksler | Tryntje I. Houghton
Stephen Adams | Robert M. Elmer
Christine A. Kelly | Tamara J. Smith
Andria Coletta | Jennifer L. Buckley

For full biographical listings, see the Martindale-Hubbell Law Directory

---

THORNTON, EARLY & NAUMES LLP (AV)

100 Summer Street, 30th Floor, 02110
Telephone: 617-720-1333; 800-431-4600
Fax: 617-720-2445
Email: tenlaw@socialaw.com *URL:* http://www.tenlaw.com

MEMBERS OF FIRM

Michael P. Thornton | Edwin L. Wallace
John T. Barrett | Robert M. Byrne, Jr.
Robert T. Naumes | David C. Strouss
Neil T. Leifer | Joseph R. Donohue
David J. McMorris | Patricia M. Flannery

OF COUNSEL

James F. Early (Not admitted in MA) | Robert P. Malone

(See Next Column)

THORNTON, EARLY & NAUMES LLP, *Boston—Continued*

ASSOCIATES

Andrew S. Wainwright
Celina Gerbic
Michael A. Lesser
Marilyn T. McGoldrick
Garrett J. Bradley
Brad J. Mitchell

For full biographical listings, see the Martindale-Hubbell Law Directory

TODD & WELD (AV)

28 State Street, 02109
Telephone: 617-720-2626
Fax: 617-227-5777
Email: info@toddweld.com

MEMBERS OF FIRM

J. Owen Todd
Christopher Weld, Jr.
Lisa G. Arrowood
Ian Crawford
Howard M. Cooper
Elaine M. Epstein
Christopher R. O'Hara
Kevin T. Peters

ASSOCIATES

James A. Schuh
Gary Owen Todd
Juliet A. Davison
Kurt S. Kusiak
Thomas A. Reed
Nicholas B. Carter
Edward Foye
Kathleen M. Genova
Karen Katz
Madonna E. Cournoyer
Bret A. Cohen
Jeffrey N. Catalano
Anthony M. Mansfield
David H. Rich
John Grady Cayer
Charlene A. Caldeira

For full biographical listings, see the Martindale-Hubbell Law Directory

URBELIS, FIELDSTEEL & BAILIN, LLP (AV)

155 Federal Street, 02110-1727
Telephone: 617-338-2200
Telecopier: 617-338-0122
Andover, Massachusetts Office: 26 Chestnut Street, 01810-3600.
Telephone: 978-475-4552.

Thomas J. Urbelis
John W. Fieldsteel
Devra G. Bailin

OF COUNSEL

Thomas G. Fiore
George M. Dallas
Jacqueline Lillard Allen
Dale Ann Kaiser

For full biographical listings, see the Martindale-Hubbell Law Directory

WILLCOX, PIROZZOLO AND MCCARTHY, PROFESSIONAL CORPORATION (AV)

50 Federal Street, 02110
Telephone: 617-482-5470
Telecopier: 617-423-1572

Harold M. Willcox (1925-1975)
Jack R. Pirozzolo
Richard F. McCarthy

Richard L. Binder
Richard E. Bennett
Judith Seplowitz Ziss
Christopher R. Goddu
Katherine L. Young

OF COUNSEL

Richard P. Crowley

For full biographical listings, see the Martindale-Hubbell Law Directory

WITMER, KARP, WARNER & THUOTTE LLP (AV)

28 State Street, 02109
Telephone: 617-248-0550
Telefax: 617-248-0607
Email: wkwt@28state.com

Ronald A. Witmer
Eric H. Karp
Mark J. Warner
Robert W. Thuotte

ASSOCIATES

Elisabeth A. Pelletier
Daniel J. Dwyer
Melanie B. Jacobs
Laura W. Gal

For full biographical listings, see the Martindale-Hubbell Law Directory

BROCKTON, Plymouth Co.

VINCENT P. CAHALANE, P.C. (AV)

478 Torrey Street, Suite 12, 02301-4696
Telephone: 508-588-1222
Fax: 508-584-4748
URL: http://www.lawyers.com/cahalanelaw

Vincent P. Cahalane
Robert J. Zullas
Julie A. Cahalane Cahill
Andrew H. P. Norton
Kristopher S. Stefani

Representative Clients: Quincy Mutual Fire Insurance Co.; Admiral Insurance Co.

(See Next Column)

For full biographical listings, see the Martindale-Hubbell Law Directory

MONE, D'AMBROSE & HANYEN, P.C. (AV)

529 Pearl Street, 02401
Telephone: 508-583-7010
Fax: 508-583-7062

Francis D. Mone (1930-1962)
William K. Mone (1949-1979)
James J. D'Ambrose
Clyde K. Hanyen, Jr.
Brian J. Mone
Robert E. Langway, Jr.
J. Gary Bennett

LEGAL ADMINISTRATOR

Judith B. Sypek

Representative Clients: Commercial Union Insurance Cos.; Southeastern Regional Vocational School Committee; Providence-Washington Insurance Co.
Reference: People's Savings Bank.

For full biographical listings, see the Martindale-Hubbell Law Directory

*DEDHAM,** Norfolk Co.

GELERMAN, CASHMAN & DONAHUE (AV)

270 Bridge Street, 02026-1764
Telephone: 617-329-8300
Telecopier: 781-329-0387
URL: http://www.lawyers.com/gelerman_cashman_donahue

MEMBERS OF FIRM

Michael C. Donahue
Daniel F. Cashman
Richard A. Gelerman
Gail M. Buschmann
John M. Lovely
Robert Nichols
M. Christine Breslin
Michael C. Bainum

OF COUNSEL

Richard A. Feigenbaum

For full biographical listings, see the Martindale-Hubbell Law Directory

FITCHBURG, Worcester Co.

O'CONNOR AND RYAN, P.C. (AV)

61 Academy Street, 01420
Telephone: 978-345-4166
Fax: 978-343-8416

John M. O'Connor
Edward P. Ryan, Jr.

Eugene P. O'Donnell, Jr.

For full biographical listings, see the Martindale-Hubbell Law Directory

FRAMINGHAM, Middlesex Co.

DOMESTICO & BARRY (AV)

The Meadows, 161 Worcester Road, 01701
Telephone: 508-626-9000
Fax: 508-626-9001
Email: DandBLaw@aol.com

MEMBERS OF FIRM

Charles J. Domestico
Susan Moran-Barry
James A. Kobe

For full biographical listings, see the Martindale-Hubbell Law Directory

FRANKLIN, Norfolk Co.

ROCHE AND MURPHY (AV)

Franklin Office Park West, 38 Pond Street, Suite 308, P.O. Box 267, 02038
Telephone: 508-528-8300
FAX: 508-528-8889
Email: jroche@ncounty.net

MEMBERS OF FIRM

Neil J. Roche
Paul G. Murphy

ASSOCIATE

John J. Roche

For full biographical listings, see the Martindale-Hubbell Law Directory

LEXINGTON, Middlesex Co.

SALVATORE F. STRAMONDO (AV)

3 Ballard Terrace, 02420
Telephone: 781-862-6422
Fax: Available Upon Request

For full biographical listings, see the Martindale-Hubbell Law Directory

LYNN, Essex Co.

DEMAKIS LAW OFFICES, P.C. (AV)

56 Central Avenue, 01901
Telephone: 781-595-3311
FAX: 781-592-4990

Thomas C. Demakis
Gregory C. Demakis
Sandor Rabkin

OF COUNSEL

Charles Demakis

Reference: Fleet Bank.

For full biographical listings, see the Martindale-Hubbell Law Directory

MEDFORD, Middlesex Co.

DAVID BERMAN (AV)

100 George P. Hassett Drive, 02155
Telephone: 781-395-7520
Fax: 781-396-8250

Reference: US Trust.

For full biographical listings, see the Martindale-Hubbell Law Directory

MILFORD, Worcester Co.

GREENWALD, GREENWALD, POWERS & WINSOR LLP (AV)

409 Fortune Boulevard Granite Park, 01757-1746
Telephone: 508-478-8611
Fax: 508-634-3959; 478-5937
Email: ggp@ggplaw@.com *URL:* http://www.ggplaw.com

John D. Powers

For full biographical listings, see the Martindale-Hubbell Law Directory

*NANTUCKET,** Nantucket Co.

DEUTSCH WILLIAMS BROOKS DERENSIS HOLLAND & DRACHMAN, P.C. (AV)

5 Gladlands Avenue, 02554
Telephone: 508-228-8725
Fax: 508-325-5860
Email: pderensis@dwboston.com
Boston, Massachusetts Office: 99 Summer Street.
Telephone: 617-951-2300.
Fax: 617-951-2323.

Paul R. DeRensis

For full biographical listings, see the Martindale-Hubbell Law Directory

QUINCY, Norfolk Co.

SULLIVAN & LARGEY (AV)

277 Newport Avenue, 02170
Telephone: 617-328-6900
FAX: 617-328-6655
Email: sullnd@errols.com *URL:* http://www.lawyers.com/sullivanlargey&barone

MEMBERS OF FIRM

William F. Sullivan
Thomas L. Largey
Joseph F. Killion

For full biographical listings, see the Martindale-Hubbell Law Directory

WALTHAM, Middlesex Co.

HARNISH, JENNEY, MITCHELL AND RESH (AV)

564 Main Street, 02154
Telephone: 781-894-0000
Telecopier: 781-893-8357

MEMBERS OF FIRM

Francis E. Jenney
David L. Mitchell
Harvey J. Resh
Joseph Melone
Robert C. Mann
Margaret Manzon Skinner

ASSOCIATE

Rhonda B. Fogel

For full biographical listings, see the Martindale-Hubbell Law Directory

WELLESLEY, Norfolk Co.

ZIZIK, LASALLE & POWERS, A PROFESSIONAL CORPORATION (AV)

One Hollis Street, Suite 400, 02482
Telephone: 781-431-8777
Fax: 781-431-8749
Email: ZLPLAW@aol.com
Providence, Rhode Island Office: 40 Westminister Street, Suite 201, 02903.
Telephone: 401-421-7110.
Fax: 401-421-7111.
Boston, Massachusetts Office: 101 Federal Street, Suite 1900, 02110.
Telephone: 781-431-8777.
Fax: 781-431-8749.
Cape Cod, Massachusetts Office: 49 Locust Street, Falmouth, 02540.
Telephone: 508-540-1113.
Fax: 508-540-1144.

David W. Zizik
Richard E. Powers
Faith A. LaSalle
Brian A. O'Connell
Cathryn Spaulding
Donna M. LaMontagne
Karen M. Connors
William J. Fidurko
Scott A. Bell
Kimberly K. Ryan

For full biographical listings, see the Martindale-Hubbell Law Directory

*WORCESTER,** Worcester Co.

MACCARTHY, POJANI & HURLEY, LLP (AV)

Worcester Plaza, 446 Main Street, 01608
Telephone: 508-798-2480
Fax: 508-797-9561

RETIRED PARTNER

Philip J. MacCarthy

MEMBERS OF FIRM

John F. Hurley, Jr.
William J. Ritter

Representative Clients: American Polymers, Inc.; Commerce Insurance Company; E.J. Cross, Inc.; Fleet National Bank; Health Plans, Inc.; Liberty Mutual Insurance Company; Marane Oil Heat, Inc.; The Talbots, Inc.; Western World Insurance Co.; Worcester Insurance Co..

For Complete List of Firm Personnel, See General Section

For full biographical listings, see the Martindale-Hubbell Law Directory

SEDER & CHANDLER (AV)

A Partnership including a Professional Corporation
Established 1918
Burnside Building, 339 Main Street, 01608
Telephone: 508-757-7721
Telecopiers: 508-798-1863; 508-831-0955

MEMBERS OF FIRM

Samuel Seder (1918-1964)
Harold Seder (1934-1988)
Burton Chandler
J. Robert Seder
Darragh K. Kasakoff
Marvin S. Silver, P.C.
Robert S. Adler
Kevin C. McGee
Kurt L. Binder

ASSOCIATES

Paul J. O'Riordan
Jeffrey P. Greenberg
Todd Rodman

OF COUNSEL

Saul A. Seder
Gerald E. Norman
Philip C. Lombardo, Jr.

Reference: First National Bank of Boston; Safety Fund National Bank; Fleet National Bank.

For full biographical listings, see the Martindale-Hubbell Law Directory

MICHIGAN

*ANN ARBOR,** Washtenaw Co.

GARAN, LUCOW, MILLER & SEWARD, P.C. (AV)

101 North Main Street, Suite 460, 48104-1400
Telephone: 734-930-5600
Fax: 734-930-0043
URL: http://www.garanlucow.com
Detroit, Michigan Office: 1000 Woodbridge Place.
Telephone: 313-446-1530.
Fax: 313-259-0450.
Port Huron, Michigan Office: Port Huron Office Center, 511 Fort Street, Suite 505.
Telephone: 810-985-4400.
Fax: 810-985-4107.

(See Next Column)

GARAN, LUCOW, MILLER & SEWARD P.C., *Ann Arbor—Continued*

Grand Blanc, Michigan Office: 8332 Office Park Drive.
Telephone: 810-695-3700.
Fax: 810-695-6488.
Troy, Michigan Office: 1111 West Long Lake Road, Suite 300.
Telephone: 248-641-7600.
Fax: 248-641-0222.
Mount Clemens, Michigan Office: Towne Square Development, 10 South Main Street, Suite 307.
Telephone: 810-954-3800:
Fax: 810-954-3803.
Grand Rapids, Michigan Office: First of America Center, 171 Monroe Avenue, N.W., Suite 950.
Telephone: 616-742-5500.
Fax: 616-742-5566.
Lansing, Michigan Office: 530 Creyts Road, Suite A.
Telephone: 517-327-0300.
Fax: 517-327-0309.
Traverse City, Michigan Office: 1131 East Eighth Street, P.O. Box 3150.
Telephone: 231-941-1611.
Fax: 231-941-4420.
Marquette, Michigan Office: 228 West Washington Street, Suite 4,
Telephone: 906-228-7772.
Fax: 906-228-5999.

Judith A. Moskus (Resident) John W. Whitman

John J. Koselka Suzanne R. Fanning

For full biographical listings, see the Martindale-Hubbell Law Directory

HOOPER, HATHAWAY, PRICE, BEUCHE & WALLACE (AV)

126 South Main Street, 48104
Telephone: 313-662-4426
Fax: 313-662-9559
Email: hhpbw@voyager.net

Bruce T. Wallace Mark R. Daane
Charles W. Borgsdorf William J. Stapleton
Anthony P. Patti

Representative Clients: Avfuel Corporation; Bank of Ann Arbor; Castrol North America; Chem-Trend Incorporated; Ervin Industries, Inc.; First Martin Corporation; Glacier Hills, Inc.; Prestolite Electric, Inc.; Southern States Cooperative; E.B. Eddy Forest Products, Ltd.

For Complete List of Firm Personnel, See General Section

For full biographical listings, see the Martindale-Hubbell Law Directory

MILLER, CANFIELD, PADDOCK AND STONE, P.L.C. (AV)

A Professional Limited Liability Company
Founded in 1852 by Sidney Davy Miller
101 North Main Street, Seventh Floor, 48104-1400
Telephone: 734-663-2445
Fax: 734-747-7147
URL: http://www.millercanfield.com
Detroit, Michigan Office: 150 West Jefferson, Suite 2500, 48226-4415.
Telephone: 313-963-6420.
Fax: 313-496-7500.
Cable Address: "Stem Detroit."
Troy, Michigan Office: 840 West Long Lake Road, Suite 200, 48098.
Telephone: 248-879-2000.
Fax: 248-879-2001.
Grand Rapids, Michigan Office: 99 Monroe, N.W., Suite 1200, 49503-2639.
Telephone: 616-454-8656.
Fax: 616-776-6322.
Howell, Michigan Office: 121 South Barnard Street, Suite 4, 48843-2305.
Telephone: 517-546-7600.
Telecopier: 517-546-6974.
Kalamazoo, Michigan Office: 444 West Michigan Avenue, 49007-3752.
Telephone: 616-381-7030.
Fax: 616-382-0244.
Lansing, Michigan Office: One Michigan Avenue, Suite 900, 48933-1609.
Telephone: 517-487-2070.
Fax: 517-374-6304.
Monroe, Michigan Office: 214 East Elm Avenue, Suite 100, 48162-2682.
Telephone: 734-243-2000.
Fax: 734-243-0901.
Washington, D.C. Office: 1900 K Street, N.W., Suite 1150. 20006.
Telephone: 202-429-5575; 785-0600.
Fax: 202-331-1118; 785-1234.
Pensacola, Florida Office: 25 West Cedar, 32501.
Telephone: 850-469-1088.
Fax: 850-432-0677.
New York, New York Office: 1450 Broadway, 41st Floor, 10018.
Telephone: 212-704-4400.
Fax: 212-704-4410.
Gdynia, Poland Office: UL. Slaska 21, 81-319.
Telephone: 011-485-831-2808.
Fax: 011-48-58-628 6411.

(See Next Column)

Warsaw, Poland Office: UL. Nowogrodzkall, 5th Floor, 00-513.
Telephone: 011-4822 529 0200.
Fax: 011-4822 529 0201.
Katowice, Poland Office: UL. Francuska 35/37, 40-027.
Telephone: 011 (48-32) 757-2414.
Fax: 011 (48-32) 757-2483.

PRINCIPALS OF FIRM

Robert E. Gilbert David A. French
Allyn D. Kantor Marta A. Manildi

Representative Firm Clients: Chrysler Corporation; Comerica, Incorporated; City of Detroit, Michigan; Detroit Tigers, Inc.; First of Michigan; Ford Motor Company; Ford Motor Credit Company; Great Lakes Bancorp; Henry Ford Hospital; INVETECH Company.

For Complete List of Firm Personnel, See General Section

For full biographical listings, see the Martindale-Hubbell Law Directory

PEAR SPERLING EGGAN & MUSKOVITZ, P.C. (AV)

Domino's Farms, 24 Frank Lloyd Wright Drive, 48105
Telephone: 734-665-4441
Fax: 734-665-8788
Email: peare@dominos.com
Ypsilanti, Michigan Offices: 5 South Washington Street.
Telephone: 734-483-3626 and 2164 Bellevue at Washtenaw.
Telephone: 734-483-7177.

Edwin L. Pear Joel F. Graziani
Lawrence W. Sperling Paul R. Fransway
Andrew M. Eggan Francyne Stacey
Melvin J. Muskovitz Scott H. Mandel
Thomas E. Daniels David E. Kempner

Counsel for: Domino's Pizza, Inc.; Technical Engineering Consultants, Inc.; Victory Lane Quick Oil Change, Inc.; Citizens Banking Corporation; The Credit Bureau of Ypsilanti; Meadowbrook Insurance Group; Michigan Municipal Liability & Property Pool.

For Complete List of Firm Personnel, See General Section

For full biographical listings, see the Martindale-Hubbell Law Directory

BATTLE CREEK, Calhoun Co.

KREIS, ENDERLE, CALLANDER & HUDGINS, A PROFESSIONAL CORPORATION (AV)

One West Michigan Avenue, 49017
Telephone: 616-966-3000
Facsimile: 616-966-3022
Email: kech@kech.com *URL:* http://www.kech.com
Kalamazoo, Michigan Office: One Moorsbridge, P.O. Box 4010, 49003-4010.
Telephone: 616-324-3000.
Fax: 616-324-3010.

Douglas L. Callander (Resident, Kalamazoo Office)
Raymond C. Schultz (Resident, Kalamazoo Office)
Jeffrey C. O'Brien (Resident, Kalamazoo Office)
James C. Boerigter (Resident, Kalamazoo Office)
Stephen J. Hessen (Resident, Kalamazoo Office)
John F. Koryto (Resident, Kalamazoo Office)
Jeffery S. Rubel (Resident, Kalamazoo Office)
Annette D. Nickel (Resident, Kalamazoo Office)
Thomas G. King (Resident, Kalamazoo Office)
Peter F. Davis (Resident, Kalamazoo Office)
Mark E. Kreter
Floyd E. Gates, Jr.

For Complete List of Firm Personnel, See General Section

For full biographical listings, see the Martindale-Hubbell Law Directory

BINGHAM FARMS, Oakland Co.

MEISNER & ASSOCIATES, P.C. (AV)

Suite 467, 30200 Telegraph Road, 48025-4506
Telephone: 248-644-4433
Fax: 248-644-2941
Email: bmeisner@mich.com *URL:* http://www.meisner-law.com

Robert M. Meisner

Robert R. Maxwell Richard M. Delonis

For full biographical listings, see the Martindale-Hubbell Law Directory

SMALL, TOTH, BALDRIDGE & VAN BELKUM, P.C. (AV)

30100 Telegraph Road Suite 250, 48025-4516
Telephone: 248-647-9595
Facsimile: 248-647-9599

Richard L. Small David M. Baldridge
John M. Toth Thomas G. Van Belkum
Keith P. Felty

(See Next Column)

SMALL, TOTH, BALDRIDGE & VAN BELKUM P.C.—*Continued*

Stephanie A. Griz-Kochkodan | Kristin Allen

Representative Clients: The Medical Protective Co.; Michigan Physicians Mutual Liability Insurance Co.; Physicians Insurance Company of Michigan; Kemper Insurance Group; AAMOS National; CNA Insurance Group; Anthem Insurance Co.; Oakwood United Hospitals; The Detroit Medical Center Affiliated Hospital; Hastings Mutual Insurance Co.

For full biographical listings, see the Martindale-Hubbell Law Directory

BIRMINGHAM, Oakland Co.

BINKLEY & ASSOCIATES (AV)

219 Elm Street, 48009
Telephone: 248-540-2299
Facsimile: 248-540-9522
URL: http://www.binkleylaw.com

David A. Binkley | Howard B. Smith

For full biographical listings, see the Martindale-Hubbell Law Directory

HYMAN LIPPITT, P.C. (AV)

185 Oakland Avenue, Suite 300, 48009
Telephone: 248-646-8292
Facsimile: 248-646-8375
Email: hymalipp@tir.com

J. Leonard Hyman
Norman L. Lippitt
Douglas A. Hyman
Brian D. O'Keefe
H. Joel Newman
Nazli G. Sater
Kenneth F. Neuman
Terry S. Givens
Paul J. Fischer
John A. Sellers
Robert H. Lippitt
Roger L. Myers
Sally A. Rutledge
Joseph Pia
John P. Gonway
Leif K. Anderson
Jennifer S. Gold
Julie Lyons Kosovec
Dawn S. Spratley
Michael T. Price

For full biographical listings, see the Martindale-Hubbell Law Directory

LACEY & JONES, LLP (AV)

600 South Adams Road, Suite 300, 48009-6827
Telephone: 248-433-1414
Fax: 248-433-1241
URL: http://www.laceyjones.com
Ann Arbor, Michigan Office: Suite 525, 220 East Huron, 48104.
Telephone: 734-761-8358.
Fax: 734-761-3134.
Detroit, Michigan Office: Suite 3250, Penobscot Building, 645 Griswold, 48226.
Telephone: 313-961-6474.
Fax: 313-961-5688.
Grand Rapids, Michigan Office: Suite 430, Ledyard Building, 125 Ottawa Avenue, N.W., 49503.
Telephone: 616-776-3641.
Fax: 616-776-3516.
Jackson, Michigan Office: 740 West Michigan Avenue, 49201.
Telephone: 517-782-2000.
Fax: 517-782-3917.

Ralph B. Lacey (1885-1966)
William J. Jones (1908-1991)
Robert B. Lacey (1912-1976)
John A. Hilgendorf (Retired)
Theodore A. Lughezzani (Retired)
Steve N. Yardley (Retired)

MEMBERS OF FIRM

Brian S. Ahearn (Resident, Detroit)
Kathleen McNichol Behn
Larry P. Beidelman
Mary F. Clinton (Resident, Ann Arbor)
William A. Day
David J. Duthie (Resident, Grand Rapids)
T. F. Felker, Jr.
John Hayes
Charles J. Hurbis (Resident, Ann Arbor)
Lawrence G. Kozaruk
Richard N. Lovernick (Resident, Ann Arbor)
Charles E. Mann
Gerald M. Marcinkoski
J. Patrick O'Neill
Sean J. Powers
Michael T. Reinholm
Bruce C. Roberts
Peter M. Roggenbaum
Thomas J. Sullivan (Resident, Jackson)
Dennis E. Zacharski

Carrie G. Barrett
John C. Dickinson
Dawn M. Drobnich
Timothy D. Finegan
Timothy M. McAree (Resident, Grand Rapids)
D. Michael McCann
Dallas G. Moon
Robert H. Orlowski, Jr.
Johnnie B. Rambus
Kenneth S. Wilson

OF COUNSEL

Robert L. Beardslee
Georgette E. David (Resident, Ann Arbor)
Robert G. Lewandowski
William G. Sinn

(See Next Column)

Representative Clients: Alexsis, Inc.; Ameritech; Chrysler Corporation; CIGNA; Liberty Mutual Insurance Company; Meijer, Inc.; Metropolitan Prop. & Casualty; Michigan Hospital Association; Travelers Insurance Company; University of Michigan.

For full biographical listings, see the Martindale-Hubbell Law Directory

BLOOMFIELD HILLS, Oakland Co.

DAWDA, MANN, MULCAHY & SADLER, P.L.C. (AV)

1533 North Woodward Avenue Suite 200, 48304-2815
Telephone: 248-642-3700
Fax: 248-642-7791
Email: EMail@DMMS.Com

Suanne Tiberio Trimmer
Susan J. Sadler
Tyler D. Tennent
Sherwin E. Zamler
John Mucha, III
Keith James

Maureen B. Connaughton | John Gerald Gleeson, Jr.

Representative Clients: Bally's Total Fitness Corp.; BASF Corp.; Cargill, Inc.; City Management; Home Depot U.S.A., Inc.; Ladbroke Racing Corp.; Pep Boys; The Sherwin-Williams Company; Trammell Crow Company; Wal-Mart Stores, Inc.

For full biographical listings, see the Martindale-Hubbell Law Directory

FEDERLEIN & KERANEN, P.C. (AV)

6895 Telegraph Road, 48301
Telephone: 248-647-9653
Fax: 248-647-9683
Email: firm@fk-law.com *URL:* http://www.fk-law.com
Detroit, Michigan Office: 407 East Fort, Suite 350.
Telephone: 313-965-6090.
Marquette, Michigan Office: 122 West Spring Street.
Telephone: 906-225-1770.
Fax: 906-225-1764.
Sault Ste. Marie, Michigan Office: 204 East Spruce Street.
Telephone: 906-635-6286.
Fax: 906-635-5390.

Walter J. Federlein | Thomas M. Keranen

Frederick F. Butters
Maria J. Bernard (Resident, Detroit Office)
Peter J. Cavanaugh
J. Christian Hauser (Resident, Detroit Office)
Gary Quesada
Jeffrey Michael Gallant

For full biographical listings, see the Martindale-Hubbell Law Directory

FEENEY KELLETT WIENNER & BUSH, PROFESSIONAL CORPORATION (AV)

35980 Woodward Avenue Second Floor, 48304-0394
Telephone: 248-258-1580
Fax: 248-258-0421

James P. Feeney
S. Thomas Wienner
Peter M. Kellett
Cheryl A. Bush
Thomas J. Manganello
Seth D. Gould
Patrick G. Seyferth

James J. Majernik
G. Gregory Schuetz
Erin L. Dougherty
Michael A. Tesner
Clay A. Guise
Sarah A. McLaren
Lennox Emmanuel
Kathleen M. Horchler
Helen Melia Hammond

OF COUNSEL

Jerry L. Johnson

For full biographical listings, see the Martindale-Hubbell Law Directory

GUNSBERG & BRESKIN, P.C. (AV)

The Pinehurst Building, 1400 North Woodward Avenue, Suite 200, 48304
Telephone: 248-646-9090
Facsimile: 248-647-0638

David B. Gunsberg | Marvin Breskin

Representative Clients: Autodie International; Builders Association of S.E. Michigan; Federal Broadcasting Co.; Foamade Industries; Hercules Drawn Steel Corp.; I.S.I. Manufacturing, Inc.; McKinley Properties; Masco Industries, MascoTech; Progressive Tool; Tecumseh Products, Inc.

For full biographical listings, see the Martindale-Hubbell Law Directory

HARDIG PARSONS PEDERSEN & STOUT, PLLC (AV)

74 West Long Lake Road, Suite 203, 48304
Telephone: 248-642-3500
Facsimile: 248-645-1128
URL: http://www.hpplaw.com
Charlevoix, Michigan Office: 212 Bridge Street. 49720.
Telephone: 616-547-1200.

(See Next Column)

HARDIG PARSONS PEDERSEN & STOUT PLLC, *Bloomfield Hills—Continued*

Pawleys Island, South Caroline Office: 216 Highway 17. P.O. Box 1607. 29585.
Telephone: 803-237-9121.
West Palm Beach, Florida Office: 1450 North Bridge Tower. 515 North Flagler. 33401.
Telephone: 561-833-1622.

MEMBERS OF FIRM

Joseph L. Hardig, Jr.
Edward C. Pedersen
Donald H. Parsons (Resident, Charlevoix Office)
Bradley S. Stout
John C. Benso (Not admitted in MI; Resident, Pawleys Island, South Carolina Office)
Joseph L. Hardig, III

OF COUNSEL

John W. Henke
Gordon A. Snavely
Patrick T. Barone
Robert J. Cucco
Edward K. Pedersen, Jr.

For full biographical listings, see the Martindale-Hubbell Law Directory

ROBERT HARRISON & ASSOCIATES (AV)

Bloomfield Office Pavilion, 2550 Telegraph Road, Suite 275, 48302
Telephone: 248-253-1800
Fax: 248-253-9446
URL: http://www.lawyers.com/harrison&associates

Robert S. Harrison

ASSOCIATES

Michael J. Rex
Michael James Harrison

References: Comerica Bank, Southfield; Huntington Banks of Michigan, W. Bloomfield.

For full biographical listings, see the Martindale-Hubbell Law Directory

LISS AND ASSOCIATES, P.C. (AV)

The Pinehurst Building, 1400 North Woodward Avenue, Suite 200, 48304
Telephone: 248-647-9700
Facsimile: 248-647-5477; 248-647-0638

Arthur Y. Liss
Christine S. Reiner
Ronald S. Smith

Karen E. Seder

For full biographical listings, see the Martindale-Hubbell Law Directory

MEYER, KIRK, SNYDER & SAFFORD, PLLC (AV)

Suite 100, 100 West Long Lake Road, 48304
Telephone: 248-647-5111
Telecopier: 248-647-6079
Email: mkss@michbar.org
Detroit, Michigan Office: 1400 Ford Building, 615 Griswold, 48226.
Telephone: 313-961-1261.

George E. Snyder
Patrick K. Rode
Ralph R. Safford
Boyd C. Farnam

Debra S. Meier

Representative Clients: Available Upon Request.

For full biographical listings, see the Martindale-Hubbell Law Directory

DAVID D. PATTON & ASSOCIATES, P.C. (AV)

44 East Long Lake Road, Suite 100, P.O. Box 829, 48303-0829
Telephone: 248-258-6020
Fax: 248-258-6052
Email: litigation@aol.com *URL:* http://www.lawyers.com/dpattonlaw

David D. Patton

Ellen Bartman Jannette
Humma S. Siddiqi
Patricia C. White
Kelly P. Bekolay
David H. Patton (1912-1993)

OF COUNSEL

Lawrence J. Acker

For full biographical listings, see the Martindale-Hubbell Law Directory

PORTNOY, PIDGEON & ROTH, P.C. (AV)

3883 Telegraph, Suite 103, 48302
Telephone: 248-647-4242
Fax: 248-647-8251
Email: DWINNIE103@AOL.COM *URL:* http://www.lawyers.com/portnoypidgeon&roth

(See Next Column)

Bernard N. Portnoy (Retired)
Sheila Connor-Heath
James M. Pidgeon
Anne Loridas Randall
Robert P. Roth
Joseph M. LaBella
Marc S. Berlin
Melinda A. Davis

Representative Clients: North Oakland Medical Center, Pontiac General Hospital Division; Hurley Medical Center, Flint, Michigan; McLaren Regional Medical Center, Flint, Michigan; William Beaumont Hospital, Royal Oak, Michigan; Riverside Osteopathic Hospital; Lapeer Regional Hospital.

For full biographical listings, see the Martindale-Hubbell Law Directory

PROVIZER & PHILLIPS, P.C. (AV)

6785 Telegraph Road, Suite 400, 48301
Telephone: 248-642-0444
Facsimile: 248-642-6661
Toll Free: 1-800-288-9080
URL: http://www.lawyers.com/provizer&phillips

Harold M. Provizer
Marilyn A. Madorsky
Randall E. Phillips
Noel F. Beck
Mark S. Baumkel

Donald J. Parthum, Jr.
Gregory A. Nave

Representative Clients: Reliance National Ins. Co.; Jefferson Ins. Co.; Jefferson Ins. Group; Blackmoor Group.

For full biographical listings, see the Martindale-Hubbell Law Directory

CLARKSTON, Oakland Co.

BULLARD, ANDERSON & ANDERSON, PLLC (AV)

6060 Dixie Highway, Suite H, 48346-3476
Telephone: 248-623-3888
Fax: 248-623-1883
Email: firm@baalaw.com *URL:* http://www.baalaw.com

Rockwood W. Bullard III
Rae Anne Anderson
Acie G. Anderson, III

Representative Clients: ANCAR Publications, Inc.; Audio Trends, Inc.; AVC, Inc. (Advanced Visual Concepts); Clarkston Realty, Inc.; GAC Mortgage Co.; Michaelene's Granola, Inc.; Morgan Service, Inc.; Smith Disposal, Inc.; Sunview Windows, Skylights & Doors, Ltd.
Reference: NBD Bank, NA.

For full biographical listings, see the Martindale-Hubbell Law Directory

DEARBORN, Wayne Co.

RILEY, HURLEY & DOLENGA, P.C. (AV)

19853 West Outer Drive, Suite 300, 48124
Telephone: 313-565-1330
Facsimile: 313-565-1318
Email: rfrpc@pop.net

Robert F. Riley
William C. Hurley
Michael D. Dolenga

Judy L. Burgard

OF COUNSEL

Mark S. Demorest
Michael J. Hainer
Leonard K. Berman

For full biographical listings, see the Martindale-Hubbell Law Directory

*DETROIT,** Wayne Co.

ABBOTT, NICHOLSON, QUILTER, ESSHAKI & YOUNGBLOOD, P.C. (AV)

300 River Place, Suite 3000, 48207-4225
Telephone: 313-566-2500
Telecopier: 313-566-2502
Email: anqey@anqey.com *URL:* http://www.anqey.com

C. Richard Abbott
Timothy A. Stoepker
John R. Nicholson
Timothy J. Kramer
Thomas R. Quilter III
Norbert T. Madison, Jr.
Gene J. Esshaki
William D. Gilbride, Jr.
John F. Youngblood
Mary P. Nelson
James B. Perry
Michael R. Blum
Carl F. Jarboe
Anne Warren Bagno
Jay A. Kennedy
Thomas J. Giachino

Eric J. Girdler
Christopher P. Baker
Jill A. Bankey
Faith M. Gaudaen
Daniel G. Kielczewski
Kim A. Linthorst Homan
George P. Butler III
Christopher T. Koch

OF COUNSEL

Thomas C. Shumaker
Lisa R. Gorman

For full biographical listings, see the Martindale-Hubbell Law Directory

Detroit—Continued

BARRIS, SOTT, DENN & DRIKER, P.L.L.C. (AV)

211 West Fort Street, Fifteenth Floor, 48226-3281
Telephone: 313-965-9725
Telecopier: 313-965-2493
313-965-5398

Donald E. Barris	John A. Libby
Herbert Sott	James S. Fontichiaro
David L. Denn	Robert E. Epstein
Eugene Driker	Daniel J. LaCombe
William G. Barris	Dennis M. Barnes
Sharon M. Woods	Matthew J. Boettcher
Stephen E. Glazek	Thomas F. Cavalier
Robert E. Kass	Michael J. Reynolds
Daniel M. Share	C. David Bargamian
Elaine Fieldman	Eric S. Rosenthal
Morley Witus	Todd R. Mendel

COUNSEL
Leon S. Cohan
OF COUNSEL
Stanley M. Weingarden

Elizabeth A. Carrie	Timothy D. Batdorf
Monique K. Cirelli	Laura Cadarette Ragold
Claudia D. Orr	Cynthia I. Brody
Ronni Tischler	James D. VandeWyngearde

Representative Clients: Avis Rent A Car System, Inc.; Borman's, Inc.; Consumers Power Co.; County of Wayne, Michigan; Ford Motor Co.; The Great Atlantic & Pacific Tea Company, Inc.; Henry Ford Health System; Michigan Consolidated Gas Co.; NBD Bank, N.A.; Textron, Inc.

For full biographical listings, see the Martindale-Hubbell Law Directory

BENDURE & THOMAS (AV)

577 East Larned, Suite 210, 48226-4392
Telephone: 313-961-1525
Fax: 313-961-1553

MEMBERS OF FIRM

Mark R. Bendure	Marc E. Thomas

ASSOCIATES

J. Christopher Caldwell	Victor S. Valenti

Kevin P. Kavanagh

OF COUNSEL

John A. Lydick	Thomas R. Present

For full biographical listings, see the Martindale-Hubbell Law Directory

BODMAN, LONGLEY & DAHLING LLP (AV)

34th Floor 100 Renaissance Center, 48243
Telephone: 313-259-7777
Fax: 313-393-7579
Email: info@bodmanlongley.com *URL:* http://www.bodmanlongley.com
Troy, Michigan Office: Suite 2020, 755 West Big Beaver Road.
Telephone: 248-362-2110.
Fax: 248-244-0780.
Ann Arbor, Michigan Office: 110 Miller, Suite 300.
Telephone: 734-761-3780.
Fax: 734-930-2494.
Northern Michigan Office: 229 Court Street, P.O. Box 405, Cheboygan.
Telephone: 231-627-4351.
Fax: 231-627-2802.

MEMBERS OF FIRM

James A. Smith	Harvey W. Berman (Ann Arbor Office)
George G. Kemsley	Lawrence P. Hanson (Cheboygan Office)
James J. Walsh	Diane L. Akers
Robert G. Brower	Thomas J. Tallerico
Charles N. Raimi	Dennis J. Levasseur
Thomas Van Dusen (Troy Office)	Stephen K. Postema (Ann Arbor Office)
John C. Cashen (Troy Office)	Jeffrey G. Raphelson
Lloyd C. Fell (Cheboygan Office)	

ASSOCIATES

Sarah Heisler Gidley	Thomas G. Cecil
Michael J. Laramie (Troy Office)	Charles S. Hegarty
David L. Kasper (Troy Office)	Kimberley R. Crouch
Amy J. Durant (Cheboygan Office)	

For Representative Client List, See General Section

For Complete List of Firm Personnel, See General Section

For full biographical listings, see the Martindale-Hubbell Law Directory

BOOTHMAN, HEBERT & ELLER, P.C. (AV)

Marquette Building, 243 West Congress, Suite 950, 48226
Telephone: 313-964-0150
Fax: 313-964-2226
Email: boothman@mail.mich.com

Dale L. Hebert	Richard C. Boothman

Gary S. Eller

Edward C. Reynolds, Jr.	Marta J. Hoffman

Representative Clients: University of Michigan; Mutual Insurance Corporation of America; Emergency Physicians Medical Group; Pronational; HCR Manor Care, Inc.
Reference: Comerica Bank-Detroit.

For full biographical listings, see the Martindale-Hubbell Law Directory

BRADY, HATHAWAY, BRADY & BRETZ, PROFESSIONAL CORPORATION (AV)

1330 Buhl Building, 48226-3602
Telephone: 313-965-3700
Telecopier: 313-965-2830
Email: brady@bradyhathaway.com

John F. Brady	Connie M. Cessante
Thomas M. J. Hathaway	David A. Hardesty
Thomas P. Brady	Paul W. Coughenour
Daniel J. Bretz	Jeffrey A. Steele

Tracy A. Leahy

David M. Cessante

Representative Clients: Beam Stream, Inc.; Bundy Corporation; Energy Conversion Devices, Inc.; Schering Corporation; Warner-Lambert; Wolverine Technologies; ABB Environmental Services.

For full biographical listings, see the Martindale-Hubbell Law Directory

BUTZEL LONG, A PROFESSIONAL CORPORATION (AV)

Suite 900, 150 West Jefferson, 48226
Telephone: 313-225-7000
Telecopier: 313-225-7080
Email: melnick@butzel.com *URL:* http://www.butzel.com
Birmingham, Michigan Office: Suite 200, 32270 Telegraph Road.
Telephone: 810-258-1616.
Telecopier: 810-258-1439.
Okemos, Michigan Office: Suite 300, 2127 University Park Drive.
Telephone: 517-372-6622.
Telecopier: 517-372-6672.
Ann Arbor, Michigan Office: Suite 300, 350 South Main Street.
Telephone: 313-995-3110.
Telecopier: 313-995-1777.
Grosse Pointe Farms, Michigan Office: Suite 260, 21 Kercheval.
Telephone: 313-886-5446.
Telecopier: 313-886-2114.
Boca Raton, Florida Office: Suite 411, 1200 North Federal Highway.
Telephone: 561-368-2151.
Telecopier: 561-368-4668.
Palm Beach Gardens, Florida Office: Suite 227, 11382 Prosperity Farms Road.
Telephone: 561-625-4442.
Telecopier: 561-625-6901.
Naples, Florida Office: Suite 705, 801 Laurel Oak Drive.
Telephone: 941-597-4500.
Telecopier: 941-597-5623.

John Henry Dudley, Jr.	Gordon J. Walker (Birmingham)
Richard E. Rassel	E. William S. Shipman
Abba I. Friedman (Ann Arbor)	Gordon W. Didier (Birmingham)
Edward D. Gold (Birmingham)	Bruce L. Sendek
Jack D. Shumate (Birmingham)	Lynne E. Deitch
Edward M. Kronk	Daniel B. Tukel
Philip J. Kessler	Alan S. Levine (Birmingham)
Donald B. Miller	Leonard M. Niehoff (Ann Arbor)
John P. Hancock, Jr.	Carey A. DeWitt
Frederick G. Buesser, III (Birmingham)	David H. Oermann (Birmingham)
T. Gordon Scupholm II (Birmingham)	James Y. Stewart (Birmingham)
Thomas B. Radom (Birmingham)	Eric J. Flessland (Birmingham)
David W. Berry (Birmingham)	Lynn Abraham Sheehy
Carl Rashid, Jr.	Robert A. Boonin
D. Stewart Green (Birmingham)	Andrea Roumell Dickson
Dennis B. Schultz	J. Michael Huget (Ann Arbor)
Mark T. Nelson	Anthony J. Saulino, Jr. (Birmingham)
Daniel P. Malone	James S. Rosenfeld
Keefe A. Brooks	Ronald E. Reynolds (Birmingham)
James E. Wynne	Kenneth H. Adamczyk
Michael J. Lavoie	

Representative Clients: Bridgestone/Firestone, Inc.; Complete Business Solutions, Inc.; The Detroit News, Inc.; Kelly Services; Merrill Lynch; Stroh Companies; Takata Corp.; TRW Automotive; The University of Michigan.

(See Next Column)

BUTZEL LONG A PROFESSIONAL CORPORATION, *Detroit—Continued*

For full biographical listings, see the Martindale-Hubbell Law Directory

DICKINSON WRIGHT PLLC (AV)

500 Woodward Avenue, Suite 4000, 48226-3425
Telephone: 313-223-3500
Facsimile: 313-223-3598
URL: http://www.dickinson-wright.com
Bloomfield Hills, Michigan Office: 525 North Woodward Avenue, Suite 2000.
Telephone: 248-433-7200.
Facsimile: 248-433-7274.
Grand Rapids, Michigan Office: 200 Ottawa Avenue, N.W., Suite 900.
Telephone: 616-458-1300.
Facsimile: 616-458-6753.
Lansing, Michigan Office: Suite 200, 215 South Washington Square.
Telephone: 517-371-1730.
Facsimile: 517-487-4700.
Washington, D.C. Office: Suite 800, 1901 L Street, N.W.
Telephone: 202-457-0160.
Facsimile: 202-659-1559.

Selden S. Dickinson (1892-1964)
Edward P. Wright (1894-1962)
Richard C. Van Dusen (1925-1991)

MEMBERS OF FIRM

Harolyn D. Beverly
Richard M. Bolton
Andrew S. Boyce
Richard L. Braun, II
William T. Burgess
Lawrence G. Campbell
James N. Candler, Jr.
Margaret A. Coughlin
Julia Donovan Darlow
Bernadette M. Dennehy
Mark Alan Densmore
David R. Deromedi
Terence M. Donnelly
Barbara Hughes Erard
John A. Everhardus
K. Scott Hamilton
Michael C. Hammer
Thomas D. Hammerschmidt, Jr.
Craig W. Hammond
Verne C. Hampton, II
Mark R. High
Steven H. Hilfinger
Edgar C. Howbert
Timothy H. Howlett
Maurice G. Jenkins
W. Anthony Jenkins
Robert S. Krause
Monica J. Labe
Kathleen A. Lang
John K. Lawrence
Keith J. Lerminiaux
Joseph C. Marshall, III
Kenneth J. McIntyre
Thomas G. McNeill
David L. Morrow (Not admitted in MI)
Sharon R. Newlon
Francis R. Ortiz
James A. Plemmons
Claudia Rast
Mark K. Riashi
Douglas D. Roche
Jeffrey S. Ruprich
James A. Samborn
Jerome M. Schwartz
John E. S. Scott
Colleen M. Shevnock
William P. Shield, Jr.
Herbert G. Sparrow, III
Bruce C. Thelen
Louis Theros
Michelle V. Thurber
Michael Gary Vartanian
Richard A. Wilhelm
J. Bryan Williams
Paul M. Wyzgoski
Thomas V. Yates

CONSULTING MEMBERS

Fred W. Freeman
Charles R. Kinnaird
Patrick J. Ledwidge
Russell A. McNair, Jr.
Charles R. Moon

OF COUNSEL

Thomas G. Peck

ASSOCIATES

Patricia M. Adler
Brian M. Akkashian
Paul R. Bernard
Robert F. Boesiger
Shari M. Borsini
Michael G. Brady
Bruce R. Byrd
Dawn R. Copley
Ann-Jeannine Foeller
Rick A. Haberman
Matthew F. Hiser
Scott A. MacGriff
Leah H. Maguire
Brian Martinuzzi
Amy E. Metz
Jodi M. Schebel
Scott T. Seabolt
Rachele L. Szot
Andrew J. Tavi
Joseph P. Tocco
David F. Viviano
Peter H. Webster
Rhonda D. Welburn
Kathryn S. Wood

LEGAL SUPPORT PERSONNEL

CHIEF INFORMATION OFFICER

Michael W. Harnish

JAPANESE CLIENT SUPPORT

Yukiko Sato (Director, Japanese Business) (Bloomfield Hills Office)

For Representative Client list, see General Section.

For full biographical listings, see the Martindale-Hubbell Law Directory

DYKEMA GOSSETT PLLC (AV)

400 Renaissance Center, 48243-1668
Telephone: 313-568-6800
Fax: 313-568-6545
Email: mstarrs@dykema.com *URL:* http://www.dykema.com
Ann Arbor, Michigan Office: 315 East Eisenhower Parkway, Suite 100, 48108-3306.
Telephone: 734-214-7660.
Fax: 734-214-7696.
Bloomfield Hills, Michigan Office: 1577 North Woodward Avenue, Suite 300, 48304-2820.
Telephone: 248-203-0700.
Fax: 248-203-0763.
Chicago, Illinois Office: 55 East Monroe Street, Suite 3050, 60603-5709.
Telephone: 312-551-4900.
Fax: 312-551-4919.
Grand Rapids, Michigan Office: Suite 700, 300 Ottawa Avenue, N.W., 49503-2304.
Telephone: 616-776-7500.
Fax: 616-776-7573.
Lansing, Michigan Office: 800 Michigan National Tower, 48933-1707.
Telephone: 517-374-9100.
Fax: 517-374-9191.
Washington, D.C. Office: Franklin Square, Suite 300 West, 1300 I Street, N.W., 20005-3306.
Telephone: 202-522-8600.
Fax: 202-522-8669.
Affiliated Office: Via Matconi, 3, 40122 Bologna, Italy.
Telephone: 011-39-51-228222.
Fax: 011-39-51-6593580.

MEMBERS OF FIRM

Ted T. Amsden
Susan Artinian
James M. Cameron, Jr. (Resident at Ann Arbor Office)
Laurence D. Connor
Michael P. Cooney
Margaret A. Costello
Joseph K. Erhardt
Robert J. Franzinger
Alan M. Greene (Resident at Bloomfield Hills Office)
Dennis M. Haffey (Member in Charge of Bloomfield Hills Office)
Mark E. Hauck
Joseph H. Hickey (Resident at Bloomfield Hills Office)
E. Edward Hood (Member in Charge of Ann Arbor Office)
Kathryn J. Humphrey
Craig L. John (Resident at Bloomfield Hills Office)
Zora E. Johnson
Sharon M. Kelly (Resident at Ann Arbor Office)
Gregory M. Kopacz (Resident at Bloomfield Hills Office)
Richard J. Landau (Resident at Ann Arbor Office)
Kathleen McCree Lewis
Barbara Goldman Mandell (Resident at Bloomfield Hills Office)
Bonnie L. Mayfield
Richard J. McClear
Andrew J. McGuinness (Resident at Ann Arbor Office)
Derek I. Meier
Stephen S. Muhich (Resident at Grand Rapids Office)
Howard E. O'Leary, Jr. (Resident at Washington, D.C. Office)
Marilyn A. Peters (Resident at Bloomfield Hills Office)
Suzanne Sahakian
Lori M. Silsbury (Resident at Lansing Office)
Daniel J. Stephenson (Resident at Ann Arbor Office)
Mark H. Sutton (Resident at Bloomfield Hills Office)
Roger K. Timm
Ronald J. Torbert
Jill M. Wheaton
Daniel G. Wyllie
Donald S. Young

ASSOCIATES

Kimberly A. Bickersteth (Resident at Bloomfield Hills Office)
Thomas S. Bishoff
Cheryl Anne Fletcher
Douglas J. Fryer (Resident at Bloomfield Hills Office)
Kevin P. Fularczyk
David G. Hagens (Resident at Grand Rapids Office)
Robert M. Horwitz
Bradley L. Smith (Resident at Ann Arbor Office)
Steven A. Susswein (Resident at Ann Arbor Office)
Andrea L. Szymanski
Mark David van der Laan (Resident at Grand Rapids Office)
Katherine M. White
Marvin Douglas Wilder
Tiffany N. Wilder
Kevin M. Zielke

For Complete List of Firm Personnel, See General Section

For full biographical listings, see the Martindale-Hubbell Law Directory

FILDEW HINKS, P.L.L.C. (AV)

3600 Penobscot Building, 645 Griswold Street, 48226-4291
Telephone: 313-961-9700
Facsimile: 313-961-0754

MEMBERS OF FIRM

Stanley L. Fildew (1896-1978)
Frank T. Hinks (1887-1974)
Richard E. Hinks (1916-1990)
John H. Fildew
Alan C. Miller
Randall S. Wangen
Mary Jane Ruffley
Robert D. Welchli
William P. Thorpe
Colleen A. Kramer
Stephen J. Pokoj
Charles S. Kennedy III

(See Next Column)

FILDEW HINKS P.L.L.C.—*Continued*

ASSOCIATE

Walter B. Fisher Jr.

References: First of America Bank-Detroit, N.A.; Comerica Bank-Detroit; National Bank of Detroit.

For full biographical listings, see the Martindale-Hubbell Law Directory

GARAN, LUCOW, MILLER & SEWARD, P.C. (AV)

1000 Woodbridge Place, 48207-3192
Telephone: 313-446-1530
Fax: 313-259-0450
URL: http://www.garanlucow.com
Grand Blanc, Michigan Office: 8332 Office Park Drive.
Telephone: 810-695-3700.
Fax: 810-695-6488.
Port Huron, Michigan Office: Port Huron Office Center, 511 Fort Street, Suite 505.
Telephone: 810-985-4400.
Fax: 810-985-4107.
Ann Arbor, Michigan Office: 101 North Main Street, Suite 460.
Telephone: 734-930-5600.
Fax: 734-930-0043.
Troy, Michigan Office: 1111 West Long Lake Road, Suite 300.
Telephone: 248-641-7600.
Fax: 248-641-0222.
Mount Clemens, Michigan Office: Towne Square Development, 10 S. Main Street, Suite 307.
Telephone: 810-954-3800.
Fax: 810-954-3803.
Grand Rapids, Michigan Office: First of America Center, 171 Monroe Avenue, N.W., Suite 950.
Telephone: 616-742-5500.
Fax: 616-742-5566.
Lansing, Michigan Office: 530 Creyts Road, Suite A.
Telephone: 517-327-0300.
Fax: 517-327-0309.
Traverse City, Michigan Office: 1131 East Eighth Street, P.O. Box 3150.
Telephone: 231-941-1611.
Fax: 231-941-4420.
Marquette, Michigan Office: 228 West Washington Street, Suite 4,
Telephone: 906-228-7772.
Fax: 906-228-5999.

Daniel L. Garan (1922-1997)
Thomas F. Myers
Dennis P. Partridge
John E. McSorley
Lamont E. Buffington
Thomas L. Misuraca
Rosalind Rochkind
James J. Hayes, Jr.
Thomas W. Emery
Boyd E. Chapin, Jr.
Frederick B. Plumb
James S. Goulding
John J. Gillooly
Robert D. Goldstein
Michael J. DePolo
Thomas R. Paxton
Daniel S. Saylor
David M. Shafer
C. David Miller, II
Robert A. Obringer

Lynn E. Geist
Mark T. Rajt
Jami E. Leach
Allison L. Hoff
Charles A. Harrison, III
Erik Stamell
David M. Saperstein
Clare M. Cylkowski
Timothy James Jordan
David Allan Couch
Stacey Lynn King
Stephen Hudak

OF COUNSEL

Milton Lucow
Albert A. Miller
Matthew A. Seward
Jon P. Desenberg
Nancy J. Bourget

Counsel for: Allstate Insurance Co.; Sears, Roebuck & Co.; Liberty Mutual Insurance Co.; Continental Insurance Companies.

For Complete List of Firm Personnel, See General Section

For full biographical listings, see the Martindale-Hubbell Law Directory

DAVID GRIEM (AV)

One Woodward Avenue, Suite 2400, 48226
Telephone: 313-961-8380
Email: dgriem@jafferaitt.com *URL:* http://www.jafferaitt.com
Mount Clemens, Michigan Office: 14 First Street, 48043.
Telephone: 313-465-4900.

For full biographical listings, see the Martindale-Hubbell Law Directory

HAYDUK, ANDREWS & HYPNAR, P.C. (AV)

1700 Buhl Building, 535 Griswold, 48226
Telephone: 313-962-4500
Fax: 313-964-6577
Email: hahpc3@aol.com

Mark S. Hayduk
Robin K. Andrews
Mark A. Hypnar

(See Next Column)

Sean Angus McPhillips
Francis J. Lagrou

Representative Clients: Farmers Insurance Group; Admiral Insurance Co.; Heritage Insurance; Meijer, Inc.; Alexis Condon & Forsyth; Pinkerton's Inc.; Vik Brothers Ins.; American Modern Home Ins.

For full biographical listings, see the Martindale-Hubbell Law Directory

HONIGMAN MILLER SCHWARTZ AND COHN (AV)

2290 First National Building, 660 Woodward Avenue, 48226
Telephone: 313-465-7000
Telecopier: 313-465-8000
Telex: 235705
Email: mvg@honigman.com *URL:* http://law.honigman.com
Lansing, Michigan Office: Phoenix Building, 222 North Washington Square, Suite 400, 48933-1800.
Telephone: 517-484-8282.

MEMBERS OF FIRM

Peter M. Alter
Ann L. Andrews (Lansing, Michigan Office)
Norman C. Ankers
Frederick M. Baker, Jr. (Lansing, Michigan Office)
Richard Bisio
Cameron J. Evans
Herschel P. Fink
William F. Frey
Mark A. Goldsmith
Andrea Hansen (Lansing, Michigan Office)
Daniel G. Helton
Raymond W. Henney
Norman Hyman
Robert M. Jackson
Sandra L. Jasinski (Lansing, Michigan Office)
John S. Kane (Lansing, Michigan Office)
Timothy Sawyer Knowlton (Lansing, Michigan Office)
Ronald S. Longhofer
Lawrence J. Murphy
John D. Pirich (Lansing, Michigan Office)
William D. Sargent
Mark A. Stern
Stuart H. Teger
Cynthia G. Thomas
Mark R. Werder
I. W. Winsten
Ruth E. Zimmerman (Lansing, Michigan Office)
Richard E. Zuckerman

ASSOCIATES

Jason Schian Conti
Andrew S. Doctoroff
Amy B. Folbe
Richard T. Karcher
Richard W. Paige
Daniel L. Stanley (Lansing, Michigan Office)
Jennifer S. Zbytowski

OF COUNSEL

Milton J. Miller

Representative Clients: Ameritech Michigan; Consumers Power Co.; The Detroit Edison Co.; The Detroit Free Press; Ford Motor Co.; General Motors Corporation, Legal Staff (General Motors Corporation and General Motors Acceptance Corporation); Michigan Hospital Association; The Taubman Company, Inc.; ThornApple Valley, Inc.; Walbridge Aldinger Co.

For Complete List of Firm Personnel, See General Section

For full biographical listings, see the Martindale-Hubbell Law Directory

JAFFE, RAITT, HEUER & WEISS, PROFESSIONAL CORPORATION (AV)

One Woodward Avenue, Suite 2400, 48226
Telephone: 313-961-8380
Telecopier: 313-961-8358
Cable Address: "Jafsni"
Southfield,Michigan Office: Travelers Tower, Suite 1520.
Telephone: 313-961-8380.

Christopher A. Andreoff
R. Christopher Cataldo
Wallace H. Glendening
Jeffrey G. Heuer
Sharon J. LaDuke
Melanie LaFave
Susan S. Lichterman
Eric A. Linden
Michael A. Rajt
Brian G. Shannon
Joseph J. Shannon
Lawrence R. Shoffner
George A. Sumnik
Jeffrey D. Weisserman
Thomas H. Williams

Thomas L. Shaevsky

Representative Clients: Genova Products, Inc.; Honey Baked Ham Co.; Masco Tech, Inc.; McClain Industries, Inc.

For Complete List of Firm Personnel, See General Section

For full biographical listings, see the Martindale-Hubbell Law Directory

KELLER, THOMA, SCHWARZE, SCHWARZE, DUBAY & KATZ, P.C. (AV)

440 East Congress, 5th Floor, 48226
Telephone: 313-965-7610
Fax: 313-965-4480
Bingham Farms, Michigan Office: 30150 Telegraph Road, Suite 444, 48025.
Telephone: 248-642-5218.

(See Next Column)

KELLER, THOMA, SCHWARZE, SCHWARZE, DUBAY & KATZ P.C., *Detroit—Continued*

Thomas L. Fleury	Carl F. Schwarze
Terrence J. Miglio	Brian A. Kreucher
Robert A. Lusk	Christopher M. Murray
Linda M. Foster	Mark C. Knoth
Bruce M. Bagdady	Joseph R. Furton, Jr.

Karin M. Young	Cara L. Brott
Richard W. Fanning, Jr.	Jonathon A. Rabin

Susan D. Koval

Counsel For: H & H Tube & Manufacturing; Howard Plating Industries, Inc.; Livonia Public Schools; Ludington News Company, Inc.; Northville Public Schools; Ryco Engineering, Inc.; Sign of the Beefcarver, Inc.
Representative Clients: General: Baxter Healthcare Corp.; Borg-Warner Corp.; Detrex Industries, Inc.

For Complete List of Firm Personnel, See General Section

For full biographical listings, see the Martindale-Hubbell Law Directory

KITCH DRUTCHAS WAGNER DENARDIS & VALITUTTI, A PROFESSIONAL CORPORATION (AV)

One Woodward, Tenth Floor, 48226-3499
Telephone: 313-965-7900
Fax: 313-965-7403
URL: http://www.kitch.com
Lansing, Michigan Office: 120 Washington Square, North, Suite 280, One Michigan Avenue, 48933-1609.
Telephone: 517-372-6430.
Fax: 517-372-0441.
Macomb County Office: Towne Square Development, 10 South Main Street, Suite 301, Mount Clemens, 48043-7903.
Telephone: 810-463-9770.
Fax: 810-463-8994.
Toledo, Ohio Office: 405 Madison Avenue, Suite 1500, 43604-1235.
Telephone: 419-243-4006.
Fax: 419-243-7333.
Marquette, Michigan Office: Old City Hall, 220 West Washington, Suite 500, 49855-4344.
Telephone: 906-228-0001.
Fax: 906-228-0003.
Ann Arbor, Michigan Office: 303 Detroit Street, Suite 400, P.O. Box 8610, 48107-8610.
Telephone: 734-994-7600.
Fax: 734-994-7626.
Grand Rapids, Michigan Office: 300 Ottawa, NW, Suite 210, 49503.
Telephone: 616-456-8384.
Fax: 616-456-8795.

FIRM PRINCIPALS

Richard A. Kitch	Richard S. Baron
Ronald E. Wagner (Managing Principal)	Susan Healy Zitterman
Ralph F. Valitutti, Jr.	John S. Wasung (Principal, Toledo, Ohio Office)
Richard R. DeNardis	William W. Vertes
Mona K. Majzoub	Karen Bernard Berkery
Harry J. Sherbrook	R. Michael O'Boyle
Anthony G. Arnone	Daniel R. Shirey
Charles W. Fisher	John M. Sier
Clyde M. Metzger, III (Principal, Ann Arbor Office)	Richard T. Counsman
	Steven M. Waclawski
Thomas J. Foley	Stephen R. Brzezinski
Victor J. Abela	Thomas R. Shimmel
James H. Hughesian	Carole S. Empey (Ann Arbor)
John P. Ryan (Principal, Lansing Office)	Michael J. Watza
	Sara Mae Gerbitz
William D. Chaklos	Linda M. Garbarino
Steve N. Cheolas (Principal, Macomb County Office)	Susan Marie Beutel
	Mark A. Wisniewski

FIRM ASSOCIATE PRINCIPALS

Susan M. Ramage (Grand Rapids Office)	Barbara A. Martin
	Cheryl A. Cardelli
Daniel J. Niemann (Ann Arbor Office)	Paula M. Burgess (Toledo, Ohio Office)
Sharon A. DeWaele	Lauri A. Read
Kenneth M. Essad	Cullen B. McKinney
Kim J. Sveska	Anthony J. Nellis
Dean A. Etsios	Jeffrey T. Gorcyca

FIRM SENIOR ASSOCIATES

Antonio Mauti	Laura L. Selzer
Joseph P. McGill	R. Lisa Panah
Sheley L. DeGraw	Christina A. Ginter

For Complete List of Firm Personnel, See General Section

For full biographical listings, see the Martindale-Hubbell Law Directory

LEWIS & MUNDAY, A PROFESSIONAL CORPORATION (AV)

(Formerly Lewis, Clay & Munday, P.C.)
1300 First National Building, 660 Woodward Avenue, 48226-3531
Telephone: 313-961-2550
Fax: 313-961-1270
Email: camille.miller@lewis-pc.com *URL:* http://www.lewis-pc.com
Washington, D.C. Office: 1120 Connecticut Avenue, Suite 280. 20036.
Telephone: 202-835-0616.
Fax: 202-833-3316.
Boston, Massachusetts Office: 101 Federal Street, Suite 1900. 02110.
Telephone: 617-478-0553.
Fax: 617-478-0543.

David Baker Lewis	Blair A. Person
Reuben A. Munday	Karen Kendrick Brown (Resident, Washington, D.C. Office)
Camille Stearns Miller	
Jacqueline H. Sellers	
David N. Zacks	Susan D. Hoffman
Thomas J. Guyer	Hans J. Massaquoi, Jr.

Althea Lynn Simpson	Caroletta L. Edgar-Sprinkle
Donica Thomas Varner	Derek G. McBride
Kris W. Krueger	Ayanna Weber
Cylenthia LaToye Miller	Deborah Jean Williamson
Joseph N. Ejbeh	Darice Elizabeth Weber
Yolanda R. Bates	Krystal M. Gardner

Syeda Taqi

COUNSEL

G. Allen Bass (Resident, Boston, Massachusetts Office)	Roger M. Groves
	Carol H. Rodriguez
Leamon R. Sowell, Jr.	Linda M. Bruton
Gail Pabarue Bennett	Brian J. Kott

OF COUNSEL

Otis M. Smith (1922-1994)	Herbert O. Reid, Sr. (1915-1991)

Representative Clients: Aetna Life & Casualty Co.; Chrysler Motors Corp.; Chrysler Financial Corp.; MCI Communications Corp.; City of Detroit; City of Detroit Building Authority; City of Detroit Downtown Development Authority; Consolidated Rail Corp. (Conrail); Equitable Life Assurance Society of the United States.

For full biographical listings, see the Martindale-Hubbell Law Directory

MEYER, KIRK, SNYDER & SAFFORD, PLLC (AV)

1400 Ford Building, 615 Griswold, 48226
Telephone: 313-961-1261
Fax: 248-647-6079
Bloomfield Hills, Michigan Office: Suite 100, 100 West Long Lake Road.
Telephone: 248-647-5111.
Telecopier: 248-647-6079.

George E. Snyder	Patrick K. Rode
Ralph R. Safford	Boyd C. Farnam

Debra S. Meier

Representative Clients: Available Upon Request.

For full biographical listings, see the Martindale-Hubbell Law Directory

MILLER, CANFIELD, PADDOCK AND STONE, P.L.C. (AV)

A Professional Limited Liability Company
Founded in 1852 by Sidney Davy Miller
150 West Jefferson, Suite 2500, 48226-4415
Telephone: 313-963-6420
Fax: 313-496-7500
Cable Address: "Stem Detroit"
URL: http://www.millercanfield.com
Ann Arbor, Michigan Office: 101 North Main Street, 7th Floor, 48104-1400.
Telephone: 734-663-2445.
Fax: 734-747-7147.
Troy, Michigan Office: 840 West Long Lake Road, Suite 200, 48098.
Telephone: 248-879-2000.
Fax: 248-879-2001.
Grand Rapids, Michigan Office: 99 Monroe, N.W., Suite 1200, 49503-2639.
Telephone: 616-454-8656.
Fax: 616-776-6322.
Howell, Michigan Office: 121 South Barnard Street, Suite 4, 48843-2305.
Telephone: 517-546-7600.
Telecopier: 517-546-6974.
Kalamazoo, Michigan Office: 444 West Michigan Avenue, 49007-3752.
Telephone: 616-381-7030.
Fax: 616-382-0244.
Lansing, Michigan Office: One Michigan Avenue, Suite 900, 48933-1609.
Telephone: 517-487-2070.
Fax: 517-374-6304.
Monroe, Michigan Office: 214 East Elm Avenue, Suite 100, 48162-2682.
Telephone: 734-243-2000.
Fax: 734-243-0901.

(See Next Column)

MILLER, CANFIELD, PADDOCK AND STONE P.L.C.—*Continued*

Washington, D.C. Office: 1900 K Street, N.W., Suite 1150. 20006.
Telephone: 202-429-5575; 785-0600.
Fax: 202-331-1118; 785-1234.
Pensacola, Florida Office: 25 West Cedar, 32501.
Telephone: 850-469-1088.
Fax: 850-432-0677.
New York, New York Office: 1450 Broadway, 41st Floor, 10018.
Telephone: 212-704-4400.
Fax: 212-704-4410.
Gdynia, Poland Office: UL. Slaska 21, 81-319.
Telephone: 011-485-831-2808.
Fax: 011-48-58-628 6411.
Warsaw, Poland Office: UL. Nowogrodzkall, 5th Floor, 00-513.
Telephone: 011-4822 529 0200.
Fax: 011-4822 529 0201.
Katowice, Poland Office: UL. Francuska 35/37, 40-027.
Telephone: 011 (48-32) 757-2414.
Fax: 011 (48-32) 757-2483.

PRINCIPALS OF FIRM

Carl H. von Ende
Allyn D. Kantor (Ann Arbor Office)
Charles E. Ritter (Kalamazoo Office)
Gregory L. Curtner (Ann Arbor and New York, N.Y. Offices)
Joseph F. Galvin
Clarence L. Pozza, Jr.
Michael W. Hartmann
Larry J. Saylor
James G. Vantine, Jr. (Kalamazoo Office)
Marjory G. Basile
Michael P. Coakley
James E. Spurr (Kalamazoo Office)
Mark T. Boonstra
David A. French (Ann Arbor Office)
Le Roy L. Asher, Jr.
Richard T. Urbis
Steven A. Roach
Lawrence M. Dudek
Marta A. Manildi (Ann Arbor Office)
Ballard Jay Yelton III (Kalamazoo Office)
Thomas R. Cox
Frederick A. Acomb

OF COUNSEL/SENIOR COUNSEL

Gilbert E. Gove
George E. Bushnell, Jr.

ASSOCIATES

A. Michael Palizzi
Kurt P. McCamman (Kalamazoo Office)
Scott R. Sikkenga (Kalamazoo Office)

Representative Firm Clients: Chrysler Corporation; Comerica, Incorporated; City of Detroit, Michigan; Detroit Tigers, Inc.; First of Michigan; Ford Motor Company; Ford Motor Credit Company; Great Lakes Bancorp; Henry Ford Hospital; INVETECH Company.

For Complete List of Firm Personnel, See General Section

For full biographical listings, see the Martindale-Hubbell Law Directory

PATTERSON, PHIFER & PHILLIPS, P.C. (AV)

L.B. King Building, 1274 Library Street, Suite 500, 48226
Telephone: 313-964-2360
Fax: 313-964-6870
URL: http://www.lawyers.com/p3

Michael D. Patterson
Randolph D. Phifer
Dwight W. Phillips
Joseph M. White

Marvin Allen Cooke

Representative Clients: Detroit Board of Education; Fireman's Fund Insurance Co.; General Motors Corp.; Liberty Mutual Insurance Co.; Metropolitan Life Insurance Co.; Michigan Basic Property Insurance Assn.; New York Life Insurance Co.; Wayne State University.
Reference: First of American Bank-Detroit, N.A.

For full biographical listings, see the Martindale-Hubbell Law Directory

PATRICIA A. STREETER (AV)

1817 Penobscot Building, 48226
Telephone: 313-962-1177
Fax: 313-962-0199
Email: PatStreeter@prodigy.net
Chicago, Illinois Office: 111 West Washington, Suite 1611, 60602-2710.
Telephone: 312-372-4410.
Fax: 312-372-4412.

TIMMIS & INMAN L.L.P. (AV)

300 Talon Centre, 48207
Telephone: 313-396-4200
Facsimile: 313-396-4228
Email: info@timmis-inman.com *URL:* http://www.timmis-inman.com

Robert E. Graziani
George A. Peck
Mark W. Peyser
George M. Malis

(See Next Column)

Michael F. Wais
Anthony J. Long
Michael J. Sheehan
John E.F. Gerlach

Representative Clients: Wash/Blount; International Talon, L.L.C.; Certain Underwriters at Lloyds of London; TIG Insurance Co.; CNA Insurance Companies; AIG Technical Services, Inc.

For Complete List of Firm Personnel, See General Section

For full biographical listings, see the Martindale-Hubbell Law Directory

VALENTINE & ASSOCIATES, P.C.

(See West Bloomfield)

VANDER MALE, BELLAMY, GILCHRIST, VANDE VUSSE & CAFFERTY (AV)

333 West Fort, Suite 1100, 48226
Telephone: 313-964-3070
Fax: 313-628-4701
Email: HEALTHLAWYERS@wwnet.net

MEMBERS OF FIRM

Frederick B. Bellamy
Alan G. Gilchrist
Bruce A. Vande Vusse
Michael S. Cafferty
Keith J. Soltis

ASSOCIATES

Joseph E. Kozely, Jr.
Michael P. Risko
Lawrence David Rosenstock

For full biographical listings, see the Martindale-Hubbell Law Directory

VANDEVEER GARZIA, PROFESSIONAL CORPORATION (AV)

Suite 1600, 333 West Fort Street, 48226
Telephone: 313-961-4880
Fax: 313-961-3822
Email: vg@voyager.net
Oakland County Office: 220 Park Street, Suite 300, Birmingham, Michigan.
Telephone: 810-645-0100.
Fax: 810-645-2430.

Fred L. Vandeveer (1879-1972)
James E. Haggerty, Sr. (1900-1966)
Leroy G. Vandeveer (1902-1981)
Buelle A. Doelle (1902-1985)
James E. Plastow, Jr.
Michael M. Hathaway
John J. Lynch, III (Resident, Oakland County Office)
Thomas M. Peters
James K. Thome
Gary Alan Miller
William L. Kiriazis
Daniel P. Steele
Shelley K. Miller (Resident, Oakland County Office)
Terrance P. Lynch
Dennis B. Cotter
Bruce E. Pearce
Hal O. Carroll
David B. Timmis (Resident, Oakland County Office)

Nancy A. Hensley
Dawn M. Twydell
Christian E. Hildebrandt (Resident, Oakland County Office)
Donald C. Brownell

Representative Clients: Bic Corp.; CNA Insurance Group; Travelers Insurance Co.; United States Aviation Underwriters; Goodyear Tire & Rubber Co.

For full biographical listings, see the Martindale-Hubbell Law Directory

WILLMARTH, TANOURY, RAMAR, CORBET, GARVES & SHAW (AV)

535 Griswold, Suite 1730, 48226-3602
Telephone: 313-964-6300
Fax: 313-964-6310
Email: mdwillth@home.net

MEMBERS OF FIRM

Daniel R. Corbet
Brian R. Garves
David R. Nauts
Anthony J. Paradiso
John M. Perrin
John J. Ramar
Bruce R. Shaw
William A. Tanoury
Mark D. Willmarth

ASSOCIATES

Marie C. Kennedy
Wayne Walker
Elizabeth L. Sokol
Robert S. Silverman
Carmine G. Paterra
Joseph J. Ceglarek, II
Derek Steven Wilczynski
Frank Hamidi
Kristen E. Skaff
Steven J. Bonasso
Colleen P. O'Connor
Lara R. Stutz
Eric G. Tucciarone
Michael P. Robach

For full biographical listings, see the Martindale-Hubbell Law Directory

Detroit—Continued

WISE & MARSAC, PROFESSIONAL CORPORATION (AV)

11th Floor Buhl Building, 48226-3681
Telephone: 313-962-0643
Telecopier: 313-962-0688
URL: http://www.wisemarsac.com
Ann Arbor, Michigan Office: 300 North Fifth Avenue, Suite 230.
Telephone: 734-213-2700.
Birmingham, Michigan Office: 255 East Brown Street, Suite 210.
Telephone: 248-642-4345.
Affiliate Offices: Williams Mullen Christian & Dobbins, Richmond, Virginia/Washington, D.C.; Giles & Associates, London, England.

Stephen M. Fleming (1951-1998)
John A. Wise
Robert A. Marsac
Eric H. Lipsitt
Edward V. Keelean
Daniel F. Berry
Lisa A. Robinson
Richard P. Manczak
Thomas E. Dew (Resident, Ann Arbor Office)
Guy P. Hoadley
Gary A. Kendra
Jeannine F. Gleeson-Smith (Resident, Birmingham Office)
Mark T. Butler
Scott A. Steinhoff (Resident, Birmingham Office)

OF COUNSEL

Louis J. Burnett (Resident, Birmingham Office)
Robert E. Day
Julious P. Smith, Jr. (Not admitted in MI)

SENIOR COUNSEL

Albert L. Lieberman
William D. Maroney (Not admitted in MI)
Elijah Poxson

Gayle L. Landrum
John F. Brent
Mark V. Heusel (Resident, Ann Arbor Office)
J. Benjamin Dolan
Sean M. Walsh
Deborah H. Boshaw
Michael A. Sneyd
Reema Dow
Clint J. Gage
L. Pahl Zinn
Kimberly M. Huston

Representative Clients: Camp, Dresser & McKee, Inc.; The Detroit Edison Co.; The Dow Chemical Co.; HomeTown Communications Network, Inc.; HomeTown Newspapers, Inc.; Observer & Eccentric Newspapers, Inc.; Seaboard Surety Co.; Texaco, Inc.; Union Carbide Corp.

For full biographical listings, see the Martindale-Hubbell Law Directory

ZEFF AND ZEFF, P.C. (AV)

The Buhl Building, 535 Griswold, Suite 1630, 48226
Telephone: 313-962-3825
Fax: 313-962-6007
URL: http://www.lawyers.com/zeffzefflaw

Louis Zeff (1896-1966)
A. Robert Zeff

Sheryl L. Berenbaum
Paul W. Broschay

For full biographical listings, see the Martindale-Hubbell Law Directory

EAST LANSING, Ingham Co.

RAYMOND JOSEPH & ASSOCIATES (AV)

713 Applegate Lane, 48823-2109
Telephone: 517-351-5540
Fax: 517-351-8343

OF COUNSEL

George R. Sidwell (1899-1983)
Michael Bowman
Bruce C. Blanton
Mary E. Low

Representative Clients: Ashland Oil, Inc.; Complete Auto Transit, Inc.; Employers Insurance of Wausau; Evans Products Co.; Grain Dealers Mutl.; Harbor Insurance Co.; Interstate Motor Freight System; Lansing Symphony Assn., Inc.; Prudential LMI Insurance Co.

For full biographical listings, see the Martindale-Hubbell Law Directory

SMITH HAUGHEY RICE & ROEGGE, P.C. (AV)

1400 Abbott Road, Suite 410, 48823-1902
Telephone: 517-332-3030
Facsimile: 517-332-3468
Grand Rapids, Michigan Office: 200 Calder Plaza Building, 250 Monroe Avenue, N.W., 49503-2251.
Telephone: 616-774-8000.
Facsimile: 616-774-2461.
Traverse City, Michigan Office: City Centre Plaza, Suite 100, 202 East State Street, P.O. Box 848, 49685-0848.
Telephone: 231-929-4878.
Facsimile: 231-929-4182.

Douglas G. Powe
Richard C. Kraus

(See Next Column)

Veronica A. Marsich
Mary K. Robbins-Kralapp
Brian E. Madar
Margaret A. Chamberlain

Representative Clients: Chevron; Cincinnati Insurance Co.; General Motors Corp.; Kemper Insurance Group; Michigan Hospital Assn.; Navistar International; St. Paul Insurance Cos.; Steelcase, Inc.; Dow Elanco.

For full biographical listings, see the Martindale-Hubbell Law Directory

FARMINGTON HILLS, Oakland Co.

COUZENS, LANSKY, FEALK, ELLIS, ROEDER & LAZAR, P.C. (AV)

39395 West 12 Mile Road, Suite 200, 48331-2913
Telephone: 248-489-8600
Facsimile: 248-489-4156
Email: info@couzens.com *URL:* http://www.couzens.com

Sheldon A. Fealk
Jerry M. Ellis
Bruce J. Lazar
Phillip L. Sternberg
Stephen Scapelliti
Mark S. Frankel

Representative Clients: Provided upon request.
Reference: Michigan National Bank.

For Complete List of Firm Personnel, See General Section

For full biographical listings, see the Martindale-Hubbell Law Directory

MICHAEL H. GOLOB (AV)

30300 Northwestern Highway, Suite 300, 48334
Telephone: 248-855-2626
Fax: 248-932-4009

For full biographical listings, see the Martindale-Hubbell Law Directory

*FLINT,** Genesee Co.

CLINE, CLINE & GRIFFIN (AV)

1000 Mott Foundation Building, 48502
Telephone: 810-232-3141
Fax: 810-232-1079
Email: Admin@ccglawyers.com *URL:* http://www.ccglawyers.com
Grand Blanc, Michigan Office: G-8469 Saginaw Road.
Telephone: 810-695-5104.
Fax: 810-695-6244.

MEMBERS OF FIRM

Earl J. Cline
Howard D. Cline, Jr.
Walter P. Griffin
Timothy H. Knecht
José Tomas Brown

ASSOCIATES

Glenn M. Simmington
J. Brian MacDonald
Robert H S. Schaffer
Jonathan M. Hartman

For full biographical listings, see the Martindale-Hubbell Law Directory

GAULT DAVISON A PROFESSIONAL SERVICE CORPORATION (AV)

Tenth Floor, Northbank Center, 432 North Saginaw Street, 48502-2032
Telephone: 810-234-3633
Fax: 810-233-3387
Email: gltdav@tir.com *URL:* http://www.gaultdavison.com

F. Robert Schmelzer
Frederick L. Schmoll, III
Edward B. Davison
Richard C. Hohenstein

John R. Moynihan
Christopher A. Hajek
Michael W. Edmunds

Representative Clients: Automobile Club Insurance Assn.; State Farm Insurance Companies; Farm Bureau Insurance Group; Al Serra Automobile Cos.; Harley-Davidson Inc.; Shoney's, Inc.; City of Flint.

For full biographical listings, see the Martindale-Hubbell Law Directory

*GAYLORD,** Otsego Co.

BENSINGER, COTANT, MENKES & AARDEMA, P.C. (AV)

308 West Main Street, P.O. Box 1000, 49735
Telephone: 517-732-7536
Fax: 517-732-4922
URL: http://www.bcma.net
Grand Rapids, Michigan Office: 983 Spaulding Avenue, S.E.
Telephone: 616-949-7963.
Fax: 616-949-5264.
Marquette, Michigan Office: 122 West Bluff.
Telephone: 906-225-1000.
Fax: 906-225-0818.

(See Next Column)

BENSINGER, COTANT, MENKES & AARDEMA P.C.—*Continued*

Richard G. Bensinger
James C. Cotant
Michael E. Menkes
Robert Bryan Aardema (Resident, Grand Rapids Office)
Patrick J. Michaels
Kerr L. Moyer (Resident, Grand Rapids)
Dale L. Arndt (Resident, Grand Rapids)
Gregory A. Elzinga (Resident, Marquette)
William J. Maynard (Resident, Marquette)
Glenn W. Smith (Resident, Marquette)
Daniel Joseph Bebble
Michael G. Summers (Resident, Marquette Office)
Lynn A. Moon (Resident, Marquette Office)
Roger W. Zappa (Resident, Marquette Office)
Scott R. Eckhold
Frank S. Spies (Resident, Grand Rapids Office)
William M. Fury

Representative Clients: Accident Fund of Michigan; Auto-Owner Insurance Co.; Citizens/Hanover Insurance Co.; Farm Bureau Mutual Insurance Co.; Employers Reinsurance Co,; Lake State Mutual Insurance Co.; Michigan Hospital Association; Michigan Licensed Beverage Association; Physicians Insurance Co. of Michigan; State Farm Mutual Insurance Co.

For full biographical listings, see the Martindale-Hubbell Law Directory

GRAND BLANC, Genesee Co.

GARAN, LUCOW, MILLER & SEWARD, P.C. (AV)

8332 Office Park Drive, 48439
Telephone: 810-695-3700
Fax: 810-695-6488
URL: http://www.garanlucow.com
Detroit, Michigan Office: 1000 Woodbridge Place.
Telephone: 313-446-1530.
Fax: 313-259-0450.
Port Huron, Michigan Office: Port Huron Office Center, 511 Fort Street, Suite 505.
Telephone: 810-985-4400.
Fax: 810-985-4187.
Ann Arbor, Michigan Office: 101 North Main Street, Suite 460.
Telephone: 734-930-5600.
Fax: 734-930-0043.
Troy, Michigan Office: 1111 West Long Lake Road, Suite 300.
Telephone: 248-641-7600.
Fax: 248-641-0222.
Mount Clemens, Michigan Office: Towne Square Development, 10 S. Main Street, Suite 307.
Telephone: 810-954-3800.
Fax: 810-954-3803.
Grand Rapids, Michigan Office: First of America Center, 171 Monroe Avenue, N.W., Suite 950.
Telephone: 616-742-5500.
Fax: 616-742-5566.
Lansing, Michigan Office: 530 Creyts Road, Suite A.
Telephone: 517-327-0300.
Fax: 517-327-0309.
Traverse City, Michigan Office: 1131 East Eighth Street, P.O. Box 3150.
Telephone: 231-941-1611.
Fax: 231-941-4420.
Marquette, Michigan Office: 228 West Washington Street, Suite 4,
Telephone: 906-228-7772.
Fax: 906-228-5999.

Joseph Kochis (Resident)
William J. Brickley (Resident)

Peter L. Diesel
John B. Farrell
Robert H. Shannon

For full biographical listings, see the Martindale-Hubbell Law Directory

*GRAND RAPIDS,** Kent Co.

BORRE, PETERSON, FOWLER & REENS, P.C. (AV)

300 Ottawa N.W., Suite 500, P.O. Box 1767, 49501-1767
Telephone: 616-459-1971
Fax: 616-459-2393
Email: 105162.1531@compuserve.com

William C. Reens
Frank H. Johnson

References: Old Kent Bank; NBD Bank/First Chicago Bank.

For Complete List of Firm Personnel, See General Section

For full biographical listings, see the Martindale-Hubbell Law Directory

BOS & GLAZIER, P.L.C. (AV)

300 Ottawa N.W., Suite 800, 49503
Telephone: 616-458-6814
Fax: 616-458-0608
Email: bglazier@bosglazier.com *URL:* http://www.bosglazier.com

Carole D. Bos
Bradley K. Glazier
Susan Wilson Keener

(See Next Column)

ASSOCIATES

Gwen E. Buday
Thomas S. Olsson

For full biographical listings, see the Martindale-Hubbell Law Directory

BRANSDORFER & BRANSDORFER, P.C. (AV)

Suite 305, Ledyard Building, 125 Ottawa Avenue, N.W., 49503
Telephone: 616-458-4004
Fax: 616-458-4422

Stephen C. Bransdorfer
Mark S. Bransdorfer
David C. Bransdorfer
George L. McCargar, III

For full biographical listings, see the Martindale-Hubbell Law Directory

BUCHANAN, SILVER & BECKERING, P.L.C. (AV)

300 Ottawa N.W., Suite 800, 49503
Telephone: 616-458-2464
Fax: 616-458-0608
URL: http://www.bsblaw.com
Email: rbuchanan@bsblaw.com *URL:* http://www.lawyers.com/bsblaw

MEMBERS OF FIRM

John C. Buchanan
Lee T. Silver
Robert J. Buchanan
Jane M. Beckering

LEGAL SUPPORT PERSONNEL

Raymond E. Beckering, Jr., M.D. (Medical Consultant)

Representative Clients: Blimpie International, Inc.; Melroe Ingersoll-Rand; T.W. Hager Lumber Co.; Montgomery Kone; Wendy's West Michigan, Inc.

For full biographical listings, see the Martindale-Hubbell Law Directory

DE GROOT, KELLER, VINCENT & ALMASSIAN, P.L.C. (AV)

300 Trust Building, 40 Pearl Street, N.W., 49503
Telephone: 616-459-6251
Fax: 616-459-6352
Email: dkvkeller@aol.com

MEMBER OF FIRM

Brian D. Vincent

OF COUNSEL

Murray B. De Groot

For full biographical listings, see the Martindale-Hubbell Law Directory

DREW, COOPER & ANDING (AV)

Ledyard Building, Suite 300, 125 Ottawa Avenue, N.W., 49503-2898
Telephone: 616-454-8300
Fax: 616-454-0036
Email: DCADVOCATE@AOL.COM

Stephen R. Drew
John E. Anding
Ann M. Cooper
Christopher G. Hastings
Bridget C. Kehoe
Brian K. Lawson

For full biographical listings, see the Martindale-Hubbell Law Directory

GARAN, LUCOW, MILLER & SEWARD, P.C. (AV)

First of America Center, 171 Monroe Avenue, N.W., Suite 950, 49503
Telephone: 616-742-5500
Fax: 616-742-5566
URL: http://www.garanlucow.com
Detroit, Michigan Office: 10000 Woodbridge Place.
Telephone: 313-446-1530.
Fax: 313-259-0450.
Grand Blanc, Michigan Office: 8332 Office Park Drive.
Telephone: 810-695-3700.
Fax: 810-695-6488.
Port Huron, Michigan Office: Port Huron Office Center, 511 Fort Street, Suite 505.
Telephone: 810-985-4400.
Fax: 810-985-4107.
Ann Arbor, Michigan Office: 101 North Main Street, Suite 460.
Telephone: 734-930-5600.
Fax: 734-930-0043.
Troy, Michigan Office: 1111 West Long Lake Road, Suite 300.
Telephone: 248-641-7600.
Fax: 248-641-0222.
Mount Clemens, Michigan Office: Towne Square Development, 10 S. Main Street, Suite 307.
Telephone: 810-954-3800.
Fax: 810-954-3803.
Lansing, Michigan Office: 530 Creyts Road, Suite A.
Telephone: 517-327-0300.
Fax: 517-327-0309.
Traverse City, Michigan Office: 1131 East Eighth Street, P.O. Box 3150.
Telephone: 231-941-1611.
Fax: 231-941-4420.
Marquette, Michigan Office: 228 West Washington Street, Suite 4,
Telephone: 906-228-7772.
Fax: 906-228-5999.

(See Next Column)

GARAN, LUCOW, MILLER & SEWARD P.C., *Grand Rapids—Continued*

David N. Campos
Richard E. Holmes, Jr.

Thomas R. TerMaat
Matthew P. Venema
Michael D. Wade
Lori A. Ittner
Jill S Mulder

Counsel for: Allstate Insurance Co.; Sears, Roebuck & Co.; Liberty Mutual Insurance Co.; Continental Insurance Companies.

For full biographical listings, see the Martindale-Hubbell Law Directory

GRUEL, MILLS, NIMS AND PYLMAN (AV)

50 Monroe Place, Suite 700 West, 49503
Telephone: 616-235-5500
Fax: 616-235-5550

MEMBERS OF FIRM

Grant J. Gruel
William F. Mills
J. Clarke Nims
Norman H. Pylman, II
Scott R. Melton
Brion J. Brooks
Thomas R. Behm
J. Paul Janes

Representative Clients: Aquinas College; Bell Helmet Co.; Blodgett Memorial Medical Center; Chem Central, Inc.; Cook Pump Co.; Grove, Inc.; NBDC; Heim Corp.

For full biographical listings, see the Martindale-Hubbell Law Directory

RHOADES, MCKEE, BOER, GOODRICH & TITTA (AV)

600 Waters Building, 161 Ottawa Avenue NW, 49503-2793
Telephone: 616-235-3500
Fax: 616-235-1639
Email: webmaster@grlaw.com *URL:* http://www.grlaw.com

Roger W. Boer
Peter A. Titta
Richard G. Leonard
Arthur C. Spalding
Bruce W. Neckers
Robert J. Dugan
Terrence L. Groesser
Mary Ann Cartwright
Daniel L. Elve
Thomas L. Saxe
James L. Schipper
Laurie M. Strong
Gregory G. Timmer
Mary Lynette Williams
Scott J. Steiner
Douglas P. Vanden Berge

Paul A. McCarthy
Kenneth M. Horjus

Reference: First Michigan Bank.

For full biographical listings, see the Martindale-Hubbell Law Directory

ROBERTS, BETZ & BLOSS, P.C. (AV)

5005 Cascade Road SE, 49546-3724
Telephone: 616-285-8899
Telecopier: 616-285-0045

Michael J. Roberts
Michael W. Betz
David J. Bloss
Gregory A. Block
Michael T. Small
Ralph M. Reisinger
Henry S. Emrich

Marshall W. Grate
Connie R. Thacker

For full biographical listings, see the Martindale-Hubbell Law Directory

SMITH HAUGHEY RICE & ROEGGE, P.C. (AV)

200 Calder Plaza Building, 250 Monroe Avenue, N.W., 49503-2251
Telephone: 616-774-8000
Facsimile: 616-774-2461
East Lansing, Michigan Office: 1400 Abbott Rd., Suite 410, 48823-1902.
Telephone: 517-332-3030.
Facsimile: 517-332-3468.
Traverse City, Michigan Office: City Centre Plaza, Suite 100, 202 East State Street, P.O. Box 848, 49685-0848.
Telephone: 231-929-4878.
Facsimile: 231-929-4182.

Clifford A. Mitts (1902-1962)
Laurence D. Smith (1913-1980)
Robert V.V. Rice (1899-1982)
Michael S. Barnes (1944-1989)
L. Roland Roegge
Thomas F. Blackwell
P. Laurence Mulvihill
Lawrence P. Mulligan
Thomas R. Tasker
Paul H. Reinhardt
Lance R. Mather
Charles F. Behler
John R. Sparks
Gary A. Rowe
William W. Jack, Jr.
William J. Hondorp
Thomas M. Weibel
James G. Black
E. Thomas Mc Carthy, Jr.
Glenn W. House, Jr.
Craig R. Noland
Paul M. Oleniczak
Craig S. Neckers
John C. O'Loughlin
Anthony J. Quarto
John M. Kruis
Paul Van Oostenburg
Dale Ann Iverson
William R. Jewell
Jon D. Vander Ploeg
Patrick F. Geary
Terence J. Ackert
Brian J. Kilbane
Robert C. Stone

(See Next Column)

Albert J. Engel, III
Phillip K. Mowers
Carol D. Carlson
Christopher R. Genther
Marilyn S. Nickell Tyree
Beth Suzanne Kromer
Robert M. Kruse
Aileen M. Leipprandt
David J. DeGraw
Matthew L. Meyer

Martha P. Forman
Karl Werner Butterer, Jr.
Garrett J. Tenhave-Chapman
J. Joseph Rossi
Stacie R. Seitz
William A. Sikkel IV
James J. Rosloniec
Angela T. Ross

OF COUNSEL

A. B. Smith, Jr.
David O. Haughey

Representative Clients: Chevron; Cincinnati Insurance Co.; General Motors Corp.; Kemper Insurance Group; Michigan Hospital Assn.; Navistar International; St. Paul Insurance Cos.; Steelcase, Inc.; Sears Roebuck & Co.; Dow Elanco.

For full biographical listings, see the Martindale-Hubbell Law Directory

TOLLEY, VANDENBOSCH, WALTON, KOROLEWICZ & BRENGLE, P.C. (AV)

1700 East Beltline, N.E., Suite 200, 49525-4512
Telephone: 616-447-1800
Fax: 616-447-1881

Peter R. Tolley
Lynwood P. VandenBosch
Michael C. Walton
Lawrence Korolewicz
Todd R. Dickinson
James B. Doezema
Richard J. Durden
Robert C. Greene
Miles J. Postema
James K. Schepers
Scott H. Hogan
Susan Jasper Stein
Mark J. Colon

Representative Clients: Brunswick Corp.; Citadel Corp.; Erb Lumber Company; Gordon Food Service; First Michigan Bank; State Farm Insurance Co.; Sentry Insurance Co.; Fremont Mutual Insurance Co.; Nationwide Insurance Co.; Auto Owners Insurance Co.

For full biographical listings, see the Martindale-Hubbell Law Directory

WARNER NORCROSS & JUDD LLP (AV)

900 Old Kent Building, 111 Lyon Street, N.W., 49503-2489
Telephone: 616-752-2000
Fax: 616-752-2500
URL: http://www.wnj.com
Muskegon, Michigan Office: 400 Terrace Plaza, P.O. Box 900.
Telephone: 231-727-2600.
Fax: 231-727-2699.
Holland, Michigan Office: Curtis Center, Suite 300, 170 College Avenue.
Telephone: 616-396-9800.
Fax: 616-396-3656.
Southfield, Michigan Office: 1000 Town Center, Suite 650.
Telephone: 248-223-5000.
Fax: 248-223-5005.

MEMBERS OF FIRM

Wallson G. Knack
John D. Tully
William K. Holmes
Roger M. Clark
John H. Logie
Jack B. Combs
Hugh H. Makens
Robert J. Chovanec
Peter L. Gustafson
J. A. Cragwall, Jr.
Eugene E. Smary
Douglas E. Wagner
Jeffrey O. Birkhold
Paul T. Sorensen
Rodney D. Martin
F. William McKee
Louis C. Rabaut
Douglas A. Dozeman
Stephen B. Grow
Daniel R. Gravelyn
Robert J. Jonker
Devin S. Schindler
Valerie Pierre Simmons
James Moskal
Martha Walters Atwater
Rodrick W. Lewis
Kevin G. Dougherty
Melvin G. Moseley, Jr.
Gordon J. Toering

ASSOCIATES

Kenneth W. Vermeulen
Mark E. Brouwer
Norbert F. Kugele
Andrea J. Bernard
Lori L. Gibson
Gerardyne M. Drozdowski
Edward J. Bardelli
Daniel P. Ettinger
John E. Kessler (Resident, Holland Office)
Christopher J. Predko
Christian E. Meyer
Dean F. Pacific
Jonathan J. Siebers

For full biographical listings, see the Martindale-Hubbell Law Directory

GROSSE POINTE WOODS, Wayne Co.

LAW OFFICES ALAN H. BROAD, P.C. (AV)

19251 Mack Avenue Suite 550 Pointe Plaza, 48236
Telephone: 313-884-3110
Fax: 313-882-4860

Alan Hugh Broad

For full biographical listings, see the Martindale-Hubbell Law Directory

HOLLAND, Ottawa Co.

CUNNINGHAM DALMAN, P.C. (AV)

321 Settlers Road, P.O. Box 1767, 49422-1767
Telephone: 616-392-1821
Fax: 616-392-4769
Email: cunndalm@crossover.net *URL:* http://www.holland-law.com

Gordon H. Cunningham
Ronald L. Dalman
Max R. Murphy
James A. Bidol
Andrew J. Mulder
Kenneth B. Breese
Jeffrey K. Helder
Ronald J. Vander Veen
David M. Zessin
Mark H. Zietlow
Randall S. Schipper
Susan E. Vroegop
Joel G. Bouwens

Gregory J. McCoy
Jason M. Milstone
Aaron Leal
Dawn J. Ward

Representative Clients: Huntington National Bank; Auto Club Insurance Assn. (AAA); American States Insurance Co.; Board of County Road Commissioners; Hope College; Western Theological Seminary; Elzinga & Volkers, Inc.; USF Holland Motor Express, Inc.; Gra-Bell Truck Lines.

For full biographical listings, see the Martindale-Hubbell Law Directory

*JACKSON,** Jackson Co.

MARCOUX, ALLEN, ABBOTT, SCHOMER & BOWER, P.C. (AV)

145 South Jackson Street, P.O. Box 787, 49204-0787
Telephone: 517-787-4100
Fax: 517-787-9455
Email: marcoux@jacksonmi.com

William J. Marcoux (Retired)
William O. Allen
William M. Abbott
John H. Schomer
Diane Y. Bower
William B. Nichols, Jr.
Robert T. Kendall, III
Timothy R. Allen
Richard C. Lindsey, Jr.

OF COUNSEL

Walter R. Boris
Lawrence L. Bullen
Philip M. Moilanen
Terry J. Klaasen
T. Harrison Stanton

For full biographical listings, see the Martindale-Hubbell Law Directory

*KALAMAZOO,** Kalamazoo Co.

KREIS, ENDERLE, CALLANDER & HUDGINS, A PROFESSIONAL CORPORATION (AV)

One Moorsbridge, P.O. Box 4010, 49003-4010
Telephone: 616-324-3000
Facsimile: 616-324-3010
Email: kech@kech.com *URL:* http://www.kech.com
Battle Creek, Michigan Office: One West Michigan Avenue, 49017.
Telephone: 616-966-3000.
Fax: 616-966-3022.

Douglas L. Callander
Jeffrey C. O'Brien
Stephen J. Hessen
Jeffery S. Rubel
Thomas G. King
Mark E. Kreter (Resident, Battle Creek Office)
Raymond C. Schultz
James C. Boerigter
John F. Koryto
Annette D. Nickel
Peter F. Davis
Floyd E. Gates, Jr. (Resident, Battle Creek Office)

For Complete List of Firm Personnel, See General Section

For full biographical listings, see the Martindale-Hubbell Law Directory

MILLER, CANFIELD, PADDOCK AND STONE, P.L.C. (AV)

A Professional Limited Liability Company
Founded in 1852 by Sidney Davy Miller
444 West Michigan Avenue, 49007-3752
Telephone: 616-381-7030
Fax: 616-382-0244
URL: http://www.millercanfield.com
Detroit, Michigan Office: 150 West Jefferson, Suite 2500, 48226-4415.
Telephone: 313-963-6420.
Fax: 313-496-7500.
Cable Address: "Stem Detroit."
Ann Arbor, Michigan Office: 101 North Main Street, 7th Floor, 48104-1400.
Telephone: 734-663-2445.
Fax: 734-747-7147.
Troy, Michigan Office: 840 West Long Lake Road, Suite 200, 48098.
Telephone: 248-879-2000.
Fax: 248-879-2001.
Grand Rapids, Michigan Office: 99 Monroe, N.W., Suite 1200, 49503-2639.
Telephone: 616-454-8656.
Fax: 616-776-6322.

(See Next Column)

Howell, Michigan Office: 121 South Barnard Street, Suite 4, 48843-2305.
Telephone: 517-546-7600.
Telecopier: 517-546-6974.
Lansing, Michigan Office: One Michigan Avenue, Suite 900, 48933-1609.
Telephone: 517-487-2070.
Fax: 517-374-6304.
Monroe, Michigan Office: 214 East Elm Avenue, Suite 100, 48162-2682.
Telephone: 734-243-2000.
Fax: 734-243-0901.
Washington, D.C. Office: 1900 K Street, N.W., Suite 1150. 20006.
Telephone: 202-429-5575; 785-0600.
Fax: 202-331-1118; 785-1234.
Pensacola, Florida Office: 25 West Cedar, 32501.
Telephone: 850-469-1088.
Fax: 850-432-0677.
New York, New York Office: 1450 Broadway, 41st Floor, 10018.
Telephone: 212-704-4400.
Fax: 212-704-4410.
Gdynia, Poland Office: UL. Slaska 21, 81-319.
Telephone: 011-485-831-2808.
Fax: 011-48-58-628 6411.
Warsaw, Poland Office: UL. Nowogrodzkall, 5th Floor, 00-513.
Telephone: 011-4822 529 0200.
Fax: 011-4822 529 0201.
Katowice, Poland Office: UL. Francuska 35/37, 40-027.
Telephone: 011 (48-32) 757-2414.
Fax: 011 (48-32) 757-2483.

PRINCIPALS

Charles E. Ritter
James G. Vantine, Jr.
Ronald E. Baylor
James E. Spurr
Ballard Jay Yelton, III

RESIDENT ASSOCIATES

Kurt P. McCamman
Scott R. Sikkenga

Representative Firm Clients: Chrysler Corporation; Comerica, Incorporated; City of Detroit, Michigan; Detroit Tigers, Inc.; First of Michigan; Ford Motor Company; Ford Motor Credit Company; Great Lakes Bancorp; Henry Ford Hospital; INVETECH Company.

For Complete List of Firm Personnel, See General Section

For full biographical listings, see the Martindale-Hubbell Law Directory

LANSING, Ingham Co.

FOSTER, SWIFT, COLLINS & SMITH, P.C. (AV)

313 South Washington Square, 48933-2193
Telephone: 517-371-8100
Telecopier: 517-371-8200
URL: http://www.fosterswift.com
Farmington Hills, Michigan Office: 32300 Northwestern Highway, Suite 230.
Telephone: 248-539-9900.
Fax: 248-851-7504.

John L. Collins
William K. Fahey
Stephen O. Schultz
William R. Schulz
David H. Aldrich
Scott A. Storey
Charles E. Barbieri
James B. Jensen, Jr.
Scott L. Mandel
James B. Croom
Michael D. Sanders
David J. Houston
Kenneth T. Brooks
Kevin T. McGraw
Michael J. Bommarito
Brian G. Goodenough

LEGAL SUPPORT PERSONNEL

LEGAL ASSISTANTS

Marsha M. Pullen
Carole M. Schneider
Theresa G. Solberg

For Complete List of Firm Personnel, See General Section

For full biographical listings, see the Martindale-Hubbell Law Directory

FRASER TREBILCOCK DAVIS & FOSTER, P.C. (AV)

1000 Michigan National Tower, 48933
Telephone: 517-482-5800
Fax: 517-482-0887
URL: http://WWW.FTDF.COM
Detroit, Michigan Office: One Woodward Avenue, Suite 1550.
Telephone: 313-237-7300.
Fax: 313-961-1651.

Ronald R. Pentecost
Peter L. Dunlap
Michael E. Cavanaugh
C. Mark Hoover
Brett J. Bean
Gary C. Rogers
Mark A. Bush
Michael H. Perry
Mark R. Fox
Michael C. Levine

Counsel for: Auto Club Insurance Assn. (A.C.I.A); Auto Owners Insurance Co.; Farm Bureau, Inc.; State Farm Insurance Companies; Michigan State University; Crystal Mountain Resort; Michigan Lawyers Mutual Insurance Co.; Green Tree Financial Servicing Corporation; ProNational Insurance Corp.; Mutual Insurance Corporation of America.

For full biographical listings, see the Martindale-Hubbell Law Directory

Lansing—Continued

GARAN, LUCOW, MILLER & SEWARD, P.C. (AV)

Office Park West, 530 Creyts Road, Suite A, 48917
Telephone: 517-327-0300
Fax: 517-327-0309
URL: http://www.garanlucow.com
Detroit, Michigan Office: 1000 Woodbridge Place.
Telephone: 313-446-1530.
Fax: 313-259-0450.
Port Huron, Michigan Office: Port Huron Office Center, 511 Fort Street, Suite 505.
Telephone: 810-985-4400.
Fax: 810-985-4187.
Ann Arbor, Michigan Office: 101 North Main Street, Suite 460.
Telephone: 734-930-5600.
Fax: 734-930-0043.
Troy, Michigan Office: 1111 West Long Lake Road, Suite 300.
Telephone: 248-641-7600.
Fax: 248-641-0222.
Mount Clemens, Michigan Office: Towne Square Development, 10 S. Main Street, Suite 307.
Telephone: 810-954-3800.
Fax: 810-954-3803.
Grand Rapids, Michigan Office: First of America Center, 171 Monroe Avenue, N.W., Suite 950.
Telephone: 616-742-5500.
Fax: 616-742-5566.
Grand Blanc, Michigan Office: 8332 Office Park Drive.
Telephone: 810-695-3700.
Fax: 810-695-6488.
Traverse City, Michigan Office: 1131 East Eighth Street, P.O. Box 3150.
Telephone: 231-941-1611.
Fax: 231-941-4420.
Marquette, Michigan Office: 228 West Washington Street, Suite 4,
Telephone: 906-228-7772.
Fax: 906-228-5999.

Kenneth V. Klaus (Resident)

Paul E. Tower (Resident)

For full biographical listings, see the Martindale-Hubbell Law Directory

HONIGMAN MILLER SCHWARTZ AND COHN (AV)

A Partnership including Professional Corporations
222 North Washington Square, Suite 400, 48933-1800
Telephone: 517-484-8282
Telecopier: 517-484-8286
Email: mvg@honigman.com *URL:* http://law.honigman.com
Detroit, Michigan Office: 2290 First National Building, 660 Woodward Avenue, 48226.
Telephone: 313-465-7000.

MEMBERS

Richard J. Aaron
Ann L. Andrews
Frederick M. Baker, Jr.
Andrea Hansen
Sandra L. Jasinski
Timothy Sawyer Knowlton
John D. Pirich
Ruth E. Zimmerman

ASSOCIATES

Andrew J. Gerdes
Alison M. Stanley
Daniel L. Stanley

Representative Clients: Ameritech Michigan; American Society of Composers, Authors and Publishers (ASCAP); Greater Detroit Resource Recovery Authority; Michigan Gas Utilities, a division of UtiliCorp United, Inc.; Michigan Health and Hospital Association.

For Complete List of Firm Personnel, See General Section

For full biographical listings, see the Martindale-Hubbell Law Directory

SMITH HAUGHEY RICE & ROEGGE, P.C.

(See East Lansing)

TIMMER, JAMO & O'LEARY (AV)

521 Seymour Avenue, 48933
Telephone: 517-371-3500
Fax: 517-371-4514
Email: TIMJAMOLOP@MICHBAR.ORG

MEMBERS OF FIRM

James A. Timmer
James S. Jamo
James S. O'Leary
Kathleen A. Lopilato

Representative Clients: Auto-Owners Insurance Co.; National Indemnity Insurance Co.; Pennsylvania Insurance Co.; Travelers Insurance Co.; Ohio Farmers Insurance Co.; Bankers Life & Casualty Co.; Western Casualty & Surety Co.; Indiana Insurance Group; Western Surety Co.; United States Aviation Underwriters, Inc.

For full biographical listings, see the Martindale-Hubbell Law Directory

*MANISTEE,** Manistee Co.

GOCKERMAN, WILSON, SAYLOR & HESSLIN, P.C. (AV)

414 Water Street, P.O. Box 537, 49660-1531
Telephone: 231-723-8333
Fax: 231-723-3888
Toll Free: 1-800-748-0534
Email: gwsh@gwsh.com *URL:* http://www.gwsh.com
Grand Rapids, Michigan Office: 124 East Fulton Street. .
Telephone: 616-458-3994.
Beulah, Michigan Office: 425 N. U.S. 31,
Telephone: 231-882-7130.

Bruce C. Gockerman
Richard M. Wilson, Jr.
George V. Saylor, III
Daniel D. Hesslin
Lisa Martinuzzi
James B. Flickinger
David J. Bedells (Resident, Beulah Office)

For full biographical listings, see the Martindale-Hubbell Law Directory

*MARQUETTE,** Marquette Co.

SWANSON & DETTMANN (AV)

Marquette Professional Building, 148 West Washington Street, 49855
Telephone: 906-228-7355
Fax: 906-228-7357

MEMBERS OF FIRM

Keith E. Swanson
Darrell R. Dettmann

LEGAL SUPPORT PERSONNEL

Susan Frances Valenti

Representative Clients: Kemper Insurance Cos.; USF&G Insurance Co.; SETSEG, Inc.; Gallagher Bassett Insurance Service; North Pointe Insurance Co.; Auto Owners Insurance Co.; CoreSource, Inc.; USAA; Upper Peninsula Health Education Corp.; Travelers Insurance Co.
Reference: First of America Bank-Marquette, N.A.

For full biographical listings, see the Martindale-Hubbell Law Directory

*MIDLAND,** Midland Co.

CURRIE KENDALL POLASKY MEISEL, PLC (AV)

6024 Eastman Avenue, P.O. Box 2765, 48641-2765
Telephone: 517-839-0300
Fax: 517-832-0077
Saginaw, Michigan Office: 4800 Fashion Square Boulevard, Suite 100, 48603.
Telephone: 517-792-9300; 517-792-1111.
Fax: 517-792-7000; 517-793-6597.

Gilbert A. Currie (1882-1960)
Gilbert A. Currie (1923-1998)
Peter J. Kendall (1961-1999)
William C. Collins
Ramon F. Rolf, Jr.
Daniel J. Cline
Peter A. Poznak
Julia A. Close
Jeffrey N. Dyer
Jonathan E. Lauderbach
Amy E. Wilson
Cheryl L. Whitman
Todd M. Gambrell
Frank M. Polasky (Resident, Saginaw Office)
Robert H. Meisel (Resident, Saginaw Office)
Michael H. Allen (Resident, Saginaw Office)
Larry L. Preston (Resident, Saginaw Office)
David J. Kolat (Resident, Saginaw Office)
M. Randall Jurrens (Resident, Saginaw Office)
John E. Gannon (Resident, Saginaw Office)
Carolyn Pollock Cary (Resident, Saginaw Office)
John D. Jolley (Resident, Saginaw Office)
W. Jay Brown (Resident, Saginaw Office)

OF COUNSEL

James A. Kendall

Counsel for: Chemical Financial Corp.; Chemical Bank & Trust Co.; Saginaw Valley State University; Northwood University; The Midland Foundation; Elsa U. Pardee Foundation; Rollin M. Gerstacker Foundation; Charles J. Strosacker Foundation.

For full biographical listings, see the Martindale-Hubbell Law Directory

*MOUNT CLEMENS,** Macomb Co.

GARAN, LUCOW, MILLER & SEWARD, P.C. (AV)

Towne Square Development, 10 S. Main Street Suite 307, 48043-2370
Telephone: 810-954-3800
Fax: 810-954-3803
URL: http://www.garanlucow.com
Detroit, Michigan Office: 1000 Woodbridge Place.
Telephone: 313-446-1530.
Fax: 313-259-0450.
Grand Blanc, Michigan Office: 8332 Office Park Drive.
Telephone: 810-695-3700.
Fax: 810-695-6488.
Ann Arbor, Michigan Office: 101 North Main Street, Suite 460.
Telephone: 734-930-5600.
Fax: 734-930-0043.

(See Next Column)

GARAN, LUCOW, MILLER & SEWARD P.C.—*Continued*

Troy, Michigan Office: 1111 West Long Lake Road, Suite 300.
Telephone: 248-641-7600.
Fax: 248-641-0222.
Port Huron, Michigan Office: Port Huron Office Center, 511 Fort Street, Suite 505.
Telephone: 810-985-4400.
Fax: 810-985-4107.
Grand Rapids, Michigan Office: First of America Center, 171 Monroe Avenue, N.W., Suite 950.
Telephone: 616-742-5500.
Fax: 616-742-5566.
Lansing, Michigan Office: 530 Creyts Road, Suite A.
Telephone: 517-327-0300.
Fax: 517-327-0309.
Traverse City, Michigan Office: 1131 East Eighth Street, P.O. Box 3150.
Telephone: 231-941-1611.
Fax: 231-941-4420.
Marquette, Michigan Office: 228 West Washington Street, Suite 4,
Telephone: 906-228-7772.
Fax: 906-228-5999.

Richard E. Eaton (Resident) Robert F. MacAlpine

For full biographical listings, see the Martindale-Hubbell Law Directory

DAVID GRIEM (AV)

14 First Street, 48043
Telephone: 810-465-4900
Email: dgriem@jafferaitt.com *URL:* http://www.jafferaitt.com
Detroit, Michigan Office: One Woodward Avenue, Suite 2400, 48226.
Telephone: 313-961-8380.

For full biographical listings, see the Martindale-Hubbell Law Directory

MARTIN, BACON & MARTIN, P.C. (AV)

44 First Street, 48043
Telephone: 810-979-6500
Fax: 810-468-7016
URL: http://www.lawyers.com/martin

James N. Martin
Jonathan E. Martin
Paul R. VanTol
Michael R. Janes
Kevin L. Moffatt
John W. Crimando
Victor T. Van Camp

Patrick D. Ball
Amy M. Johnston
Sean S. Cleland

Reference: Community Central Bank - Mt. Clemens.

For full biographical listings, see the Martindale-Hubbell Law Directory

*MUSKEGON,** Muskegon Co.

LAGUE, NEWMAN & IRISH, A PROFESSIONAL CORPORATION (AV)

600 Terrace Plaza, P.O. Box 389, 49443
Telephone: 231-725-8148
Telecopier: 231-726-3404
Email: firm@lnilaw.com

Eric R. Gielow
Charyn K. Hain
William M. Newman
Bruce P. Rissi
Alvin D. Treado

LEGAL SUPPORT PERSONNEL

Rebecca A. McCroskey

General Counsel: Hackley Hospital & Medical Center; Kaydon Corp.; Cole's Quality Foods; Kurdziel Industries.
Local Counsel: SPX Corp.; Booth Newspapers Inc.; National City Bank.

For Complete List of Firm Personnel, See General Section

For full biographical listings, see the Martindale-Hubbell Law Directory

PLYMOUTH, Wayne Co.

DRAUGELIS & ASHTON, L.L.P. (AV)

843 Penniman Avenue, 48170-1690
Telephone: 734-453-4044
Fax: 734-453-2011
Clawson, Michigan Office: 380 North Main Street.
Telephone: 248-588-7704.

MEMBERS OF FIRM

Edward F. Draugelis
John A. Ashton
Donald S. Scully
Richard T. Haynes
Lamberto DiStefano
David T. Rogers
Joseph R. Conte
Steven O. Ashton

ASSOCIATES

Floyd C. Virant
Taras P. Jarema
Timothy M. McKercher
Joel B. Ashton
Donald E. Walker
Heather A. Jefferson
Roger D. Ajluni
Margaret L. Browning

(See Next Column)

Representative Clients: State Farm Mutual Automobile Insurance Co.; State Farm Fire and Casualty Co.; Secura Insurance Co.; United States Fidelity and Guaranty Co.; RLI Insurance Co.; United States Automobile Association; Michigan Automobile Insurance Placement Facility; Northville Downs.

For full biographical listings, see the Martindale-Hubbell Law Directory

*PORT HURON,** St. Clair Co.

GARAN, LUCOW, MILLER & SEWARD, P.C. (AV)

Port Huron Office Center, 511 Fort Street, Suite 505, 48060-3922
Telephone: 810-985-4400
Fax: 810-985-4107
URL: http://www.garanlucow.com
Detroit, Michigan Office: 1000 Woodbridge Place.
Telephone: 313-446-1530.
Fax: 313-259-0450.
Grand Blanc, Michigan Office: 8332 Office Park Drive.
Telephone: 810-695-3700.
Fax: 810-695-6488.
Ann Arbor, Michigan Office: 101 North Main Street, Suite 460.
Telephone: 734-930-5600.
Fax: 734-930-0043.
Troy, Michigan Office: 1111 West Long Lake Road, Suite 300.
Telephone: 248-641-7600.
Fax: 248-641-0222.
Mount Clemens, Michigan Office: Towne Square Development, 10 S. Main Street, Suite 307.
Telephone: 810-954-3800.
Fax: 810-954-3803.
Grand Rapids, Michigan Office: First of America Center, 171 Monroe Avenue, N.W., Suite 950.
Telephone: 616-742-5500.
Fax: 616-742-5566.
Lansing, Michigan Office: 530 Creyts Road, Suite A.
Telephone: 517-327-0300.
Fax: 517-327-0309.
Traverse City, Michigan Office: 1131 East Eighth Street, P.O. Box 3150.
Telephone: 231-941-1611.
Fax: 231-941-4420.
Marquette, Michigan Office: 228 West Washington Street, Suite 4,
Telephone: 906-228-7772.
Fax: 906-228-5999.

Randolph J. Martinek

Robert L. Goldenbogen
Meghan A. McGlynn

For full biographical listings, see the Martindale-Hubbell Law Directory

*SAGINAW,** Saginaw Co.

CURRIE KENDALL POLASKY MEISEL, PLC (AV)

4800 Fashion Square Boulevard, Suite 100, 48603
Telephone: 517-792-1111; 517-792-9300
Fax: 517-793-6597; 517-792-7000
Midland, Michigan Office: 6024 Eastman Avenue, P.O. Box, 2765.
Telephone: 517-839-0300.
Fax: 517-832-0077.

Frank M. Polasky
Robert H. Meisel
Michael H. Allen
Larry L. Preston
David J. Kolat
M. Randall Jurrens
John E. Gannon
Carolyn Pollock Cary
John D. Jolley
W. Jay Brown
William C. Collins (Resident, Midland Office)
Ramon F. Rolf, Jr. (Resident, Midland Office)
Daniel J. Cline (Resident, Midland Office)
Peter A. Poznak (Resident, Midland Office)
Julia A. Close (Resident, Midland Office)
Jeffrey N. Dyer (Resident, Midland Office)
Jonathan E. Lauderbach (Resident, Midland Office)
Amy E. Wilson (Resident, Midland Office)
Cheryl L. Whitman (Resident, Midland Office)
Todd M. Gambrell (Resident, Midland Office)

OF COUNSEL

James A. Kendall (Resident, Midland Office)

Counsel for: Chemical Financial Corp.; Chemical Bank & Trust Co.; Saginaw Valley State University; Northwood University; The Midland Foundation; Elsa U. Pardee Foundation; Rollin M. Gerstacker Foundation; Charles J. Strosacker Foundation.

For full biographical listings, see the Martindale-Hubbell Law Directory

ST. CLAIR SHORES, Macomb Co.

SAURBIER, SIEGAN & SANFIELD, P.C. (AV)

Suite 402, 400 Maple Park Boulevard, 48081
Telephone: 810-447-3700
Fax: 810-447-3755
Email: scott@saurbier.com
Detroit Office: 1028 Buhl Building.
Telephone: 313-965-2220.

(See Next Column)

SAURBIER, SIEGAN & SANFIELD P.C., *St. Clair Shores—Continued*

SHAREHOLDERS

Scott A. Saurbier
Renée S. Siegan
Joel A. Sanfield

Marc D. Saurbier
Sara B. Keough
Lawrence T. Garcia
David C. Wiegel
John C. Valenti
Matthew J. Nagaj
Valerie Henning Mock

For full biographical listings, see the Martindale-Hubbell Law Directory

SOUTHFIELD, Oakland Co.

COLLINS, EINHORN, FARRELL & ULANOFF, A PROFESSIONAL CORPORATION (AV)

4000 Town Center, Suite 909, 48075-1473
Telephone: 248-355-4141
Facsimile: 248-355-2277

Morton H. Collins
Kenneth C. Merritt
Brian D. Einhorn
Noreen L. Slank
Clayton F. Farrell
Michael J. Sullivan
Stuart A. Ulanoff
Janice G. Hildenbrand
Dale J. McLellan
Neil W. MacCallum

Theresa M. Asoklis
Kevin P. Moloughney
Karen C. Liddle
Susan P. Saltzman
Deborah A. Lujan
Daniel E. Collins
Shannon M. Kos
J. Mark Cooney
David C. Anderson

For full biographical listings, see the Martindale-Hubbell Law Directory

MADDIN, HAUSER, WARTELL, ROTH, HELLER & PESSES, P.C. (AV)

Third Floor Essex Centre, 28400 Northwestern Highway, P.O. Box 215, 48037
Telephone: 248-354-4030, 355-5200
Telefax: 248-354-1422

Milton M. Maddin (1902-1984)
William E. Sigler
Michael W. Maddin
Stewart C. W. Weiner
Mark R. Hauser
Charles M. Lax
C. Robert Wartell
Stuart M. Bordman
Richard J. Maddin
Steven D. Sallen
Richard F. Roth
Gregory J. Gamalski
Harvey R. Heller
Julie Chenot Mayer
Ian D. Pesses
Nathaniel H. Simpson
Michael S. Leib
Ronald A. Sollish
Robert D. Kaplow
Lowell D. Salesin

Mark H. Fink
Martin Scott Frenkel
Steven M. Wolock
Gary M. Remer
Lori E. Talsky
Jennifer S. Sternberg
Stephen E. Handelman
George V. Cassar, Jr.
Ronald M. Stern
Adam J. Goldstein

OF COUNSEL

Bruce N. Goldman

Reference: Comerica Bank.

For full biographical listings, see the Martindale-Hubbell Law Directory

MORGANROTH & MORGANROTH (AV)

3000 Town Center, Suite 1500, 48075
Telephone: 248-355-3084
Fax: 248-355-3017
URL: http://www.lawyers.com/morganrothlawfirm
New York, N.Y. Office: 156 W. 56th Street, Suite 1101. 10019.
Telephone: 212-586-5905.
Fax: 212-586-7302.

MEMBERS OF FIRM

Mayer Morganroth
Cherie Morganroth
Jeffrey B. Morganroth
Jason Ross Hirsch

Representative Clients: APCOA,Inc.; ; Mayor Coleman Young (Detroit); John Z. DeLorean; Realtek Industries, Inc.; Dr. Jack Kevorkian; Carolyn Warmus; Edward J. Holland, Jr.; Lyndon LaRouche; Thomas Warmus; Walter Keating.

For full biographical listings, see the Martindale-Hubbell Law Directory

SCHWARTZ & JALKANEN, P.C. (AV)

24400 Northwestern Highway, Suite 200, 48075-6821
Telephone: 248-352-2555
Facsimile: 248-352-5963

Melvin R. Schwartz
Arthur W. Jalkanen
Karl Eric Hannum

(See Next Column)

Gregory A. Light
David C. Dixon

For full biographical listings, see the Martindale-Hubbell Law Directory

SIEMION, HUCKABAY, BODARY, PADILLA, MORGANTI & BOWERMAN, P.C. (AV)

One Towne Square Suite 1400, P.O. Box 5068, 48086-5068
Telephone: 248-357-1400
Fax: 248-357-3343
Email: siemhuck@michbar.org

Robert P. Siemion
Michael J. Rinkel
Charles A. Huckabay
Mark A. Roberts
James W. Bodary
Arnold J. Matusz
Gerald V. Padilla
Steven B. Sinkoff
Raymond W. Morganti
Eugene Kelly Cullen
Cathy Rogers Bowerman
Karen M. Leonetti
Thomas M. Caplis

Donna Montano Severyn
Rita V. Countegan

For full biographical listings, see the Martindale-Hubbell Law Directory

SOMMERS, SCHWARTZ, SILVER & SCHWARTZ, P.C. (AV)

2000 Town Center, Suite 900, 48075
Telephone: 248-355-0300
Telecopier: 248-746-4001
Plymouth, Michigan Office: 747 South Main Street.
Telephone: 313-455-4250.

Stanley S. Schwartz
Joseph A. Golden
Leonard B. Schwartz
Richard D. Fox
Lawrence Warren
Frank Mafrice
Jeffrey N. Shillman
James J. Vlasic
David R. Getto
Richard L. Groffsky
Robert H. Darling
David J. Winter
Paul W. Hines
David M. Black
Donald J. Gasiorek
Daniel D. Swanson
Patrick B. McCauley
David A. Kotzian
Justin C. Ravitz
Patricia A. Stamler
David L. Nelson
Andrew Kochanowski

Gerald D. Keller
Jennifer M. Grieco
Randall M. Blau
Cameron R. Getto
Marc C. Tucker
Matthew A. Fraiberg

OF COUNSEL

Jeremy L. Winer

General Counsel for: City of Taylor; Foodland Distributors; C.A. Muer Corporation; Vlasic & Company; Nederlander Corporation; Midwest Health Centers, P.C.
Representative Clients: Michigan National Bank; Universal Underwriters Insurance Co.; Don Lee Distributor; Rite-Aid of Michigan.

For Complete List of Firm Personnel, See General Section

For full biographical listings, see the Martindale-Hubbell Law Directory

YOUNG & ASSOCIATES, P.C. (AV)

Suite 305, Westview Office Center, 26200 American Drive, 48034
Telephone: 248-353-8620
Telecopier: 248-353-6559
Email: youngpc@aol.com

Rodger D. Young

Michael J. Fergestrom
Jeffrey M. Macy
Steven Susser
Terry Wuester Milne

For full biographical listings, see the Martindale-Hubbell Law Directory

*TRAVERSE CITY,** Grand Traverse Co.

DINGEMAN, DANCER & CHRISTOPHERSON, P.L.C. (AV)

100 Park Street, 49684
Telephone: 231-929-0500
Fax: 231-929-0504
Email: dingeman@dingemandancer.com *URL:* http://www.Dingemandancer.com

Mark R. Dancer
James A. Christopherson

ASSOCIATES

Brian L. Johnson
Michael J. Daray
John J. Rizzo, III

Representative Clients: Texas Instruments, Inc.; Georgia-Pacific Corporation; Martin Marietta Magesia Specialitiews, Inc.; Elf Atochem North America, Inc.; Busch Oil Company; Lachine Oil Company; Charmilles Technologoes Corporation; Glawe Corporations; Stomberg Carlson Products, Inc.; L'DaRu Lakeside Resort.

For full biographical listings, see the Martindale-Hubbell Law Directory

Traverse City—Continued

GARAN, LUCOW, MILLER & SEWARD, P.C. (AV)

1131 East Eighth Street, P.O. Box 3150, 49685-3150
Telephone: 231-941-1611
Fax: 231-941-4420
URL: http://www.garanlucow.com
Detroit, Michigan Office: 1000 Woodbridge Place.
Telephone: 313-446-1530.
Fax: 313-259-0450.
Port Huron, Michigan Office: Port Huron Office Center, 511 Fort Street, Suite 505.
Telephone: 810-985-4400.
Fax: 810-985-4187.
Ann Arbor, Michigan Office: 101 North Main Street, Suite 460.
Telephone: 734-930-5600.
Fax: 734-930-0043.
Troy, Michigan Office: 1111 West Long Lake Road, Suite 300.
Telephone: 248-641-7600.
Fax: 248-641-0222.
Mount Clemens, Michigan Office: Towne Square Development, 10 S. Main Street, Suite 307.
Telephone: 810-954-3800.
Fax: 810-954-3803.
Grand Rapids, Michigan Office: First of America Center, 171 Monroe Avenue, N.W., Suite 950.
Telephone: 616-742-5500.
Fax: 616-742-5566.
Grand Blanc, Michigan Office: 8332 Office Park Drive.
Telephone: 810-695-3700.
Fax: 810-695-6488.
Lansing, Michigan Office: 530 Creyts Road, Suite A.
Telephone: 517-327-0300.
Fax: 517-327-0309.
Marquette, Michigan Office: 228 West Washington Street, Suite 4,
Telephone: 906-228-7772.
Fax: 906-228-5999.

Peter B. Worden, Jr.
Douglas J. Read
John W. Sharp
Michael J. Swogger

Linda Marsh-Raetz

For full biographical listings, see the Martindale-Hubbell Law Directory

OLSON, NOONAN & BZDOK, P.C. (AV)

420 East Front Street, P.O. Box 2358, 49685-2358
Telephone: 616-946-0044
Fax: 616-946-4807

James M. Olson
John D. Noonan
Christopher M. Bzdok
Karen L. Ferguson
Scott W. Howard

For full biographical listings, see the Martindale-Hubbell Law Directory

SMITH HAUGHEY RICE & ROEGGE, P.C. (AV)

City Centre Plaza, Suite 100, 202 East State Street, P.O. Box 848, 49685-0848
Telephone: 231-929-4878
Facsimile: 231-929-4182
Grand Rapids, Michigan Office: 200 Calder Plaza Building, 250 Monroe Avenue, N.W., 49503-2251.
Telephone: 616-774-8000.
Facsimile: 616-774-2461.
East Lansing, Michigan Office: 1400 Abbott Rd., Suite 410, 48823-1902.
Telephone: 517-332-3030.
Facsimile: 517-332-3468.

George Frederick Bearup
Mark P. Bickel
R. Jay Hardin
Charles B. Judson
Robert W. Tubbs
Jeffrey R. Wonacott
Robert W. Parker
Paul T. Jarboe
Jeffrey E. Gwillim

Todd W. Millar
Erin Eileen Gerrity
Peter J. Boyles
Rachel Y. Brochert
Eric W. Phelps

Representative Clients: Chevron; Cincinnati Insurance Co.; General Motors Corp.; Kemper Insurance Group; Michigan Hospital Assn.; Navistar International; St. Paul Insurance Cos.; Steelcase, Inc.; Dow Elanco.

For full biographical listings, see the Martindale-Hubbell Law Directory

SULLIVAN & CROWLEY, P.C. (AV)

735 South Garfield, Suite 202, 49686
Telephone: 616-922-1888
Fax: 616-922-2221
Email: sullcro@GTII.com *URL:* http://www.lawyers.com/sullivancrowleylaw

(See Next Column)

James I. Sullivan
Philip J. Crowley
Jeffrey J. Noorman

For full biographical listings, see the Martindale-Hubbell Law Directory

THOMPSON, O'NEIL & VANDERVEEN (AV)

309 East Front Street, P.O. Box 429, 49685
Telephone: 231-929-9700; 1-800-678-1307
Fax: 231-929-7262
Email: tov@traverse.com *URL:* http://www.lawyers.com/tovtraverse

George R. Thompson
Daniel P. O'Neil
John R. VanderVeen

Jessica G. Rickard

For full biographical listings, see the Martindale-Hubbell Law Directory

WALTON, SMITH, PHILLIPS & DIXON, P.C. (AV)

216 Cass Street, P.O. Box 549, 49685
Telephone: 616-947-7410
Fax: 616-947-5112

Geoff G. Smith
L. Kent Walton
Thomas L. Phillips

Representative Clients: The Travelers Insurance Cos.; Farm Bureau Insurance Group; TIG Insurance.
Reference: Huntington National Bank.

For full biographical listings, see the Martindale-Hubbell Law Directory

TROY, Oakland Co.

GARAN, LUCOW, MILLER & SEWARD, P.C. (AV)

1111 West Long Lake Road, Suite 300, 48098-6333
Telephone: 248-641-7600
Fax: 248-641-0222
URL: http://www.garanlucow.com
Detroit, Michigan Office: 10000 Woodbridge Place.
Telephone: 313-446-1530.
Fax: 313-259-0450.
Grand Blanc, Michigan Office: 8332 Office Park Drive.
Telephone: 810-695-3700.
Fax: 810-695-6488.
Port Huron, Michigan Office: Port Huron Office Center, 511 Fort Street, Suite 505.
Telephone: 810-985-4400.
Fax: 810-985-4107.
Ann Arbor, Michigan Office: 101 North Main Street, Suite 460.
Telephone: 734-930-5600.
Fax: 734-930-0043.
Mount Clemens, Michigan Office: Suite 307, Towne Square Development, 10 South Main Street.
Telephone: 810-954-3800.
Fax: 810-954-3803.
Grand Rapids, Michigan Office: First of America Center, 171 Monroe Avenue, N.W., Suite 950.
Telephone: 616-742-5500.
Fax: 616-742-5566.
Lansing, Michigan Office: 530 Creyts Road, Suite A.
Telephone: 517-327-0300.
Fax: 517-327-0309.
Traverse City, Michigan Office: 1131 East Eighth Street, P.O. Box 3150.
Telephone: 231-941-1611.
Fax: 231-941-4420.
Marquette, Michigan Office: 228 West Washington Street, Suite 4,
Telephone: 906-228-7772.
Fax: 906-228-5999.

James L. Borin
Roger A. Smith
Mark Shreve
John P. Seyfried (Resident)
Edward M. Freeland
Steven A. Matta
Ian C. Simpson
Susan M. Williams

David J. Lankford
Brian E. Etzel
Dawn M. Patterson
Kristin Stiles Smolek
Monia (Monica) C. Gregor
Beth A. Andrews
Darryl Keenan Segars
Adam K. Gordon

Counsel For: Aetna Life & Casualty Co.; Allstate Insurance Co.; American Home Insurance Co.; American International Adjustment Co.; American States Insurance Co.; Amerisure-Insurance Co.; Amsted Industries; Auto Club Insurance Assn.; Auto-Owners Insurance Co.; Buckeye Union Insurance Co.

For full biographical listings, see the Martindale-Hubbell Law Directory

HACKETT & MAXWELL, P.C. (AV)

City Center Building, Suite 1470, 888 West Big Beaver Road, 48084
Telephone: 810-362-2600
Fax: 810-362-3610
Email: hackmax@voyager.net

(See Next Column)

HACKETT & MAXWELL P.C., *Troy—Continued*

Patrick E. Hackett Phillip B. Maxwell

Dennis W. Krakow Mireille Leruth Phillips

For full biographical listings, see the Martindale-Hubbell Law Directory

HAINER & BERMAN, P.C. (AV)

888 West Big Beaver, Suite 1400, 48084
Telephone: 248-244-8424
Fax: 248-244-8455

Michael J. Hainer Leonard K. Berman
Kay E. Malaney

Drew S. Norton Paul S. Miller

OF COUNSEL

Michael A. Kus Robert F. Riley
Mark S. Demorest

Representative Clients: American Empire Surplus Lines Insurance Co.; Biomass Energy Systems, Inc.; Bridgestone/Firestone, Inc.; Central Distributors of Beer, Inc.; Champion Enterprises, Inc.; City Management Corp.; Clarklift of Detroit, Inc.; Federal Reserve Bank of Chicago; Hotel Investment Services, Inc.; M&O Marketing, Inc.

For full biographical listings, see the Martindale-Hubbell Law Directory

AUSTIN HIRSCHHORN, P.C. (AV)

Suite 710 Columbia Center, 201 West Big Beaver Road, 48084-4152
Telephone: 248-680-1660
Fax: 248-680-1671
Email: austinh@ix.netcom.com

Austin Hirschhorn

For full biographical listings, see the Martindale-Hubbell Law Directory

HOLAHAN, MALLOY, MAYBAUGH, MONNICH & DELIE (AV)

Suite 100, 2690 Crooks Road, 48084-4700
Telephone: 248-362-4747
Fax: 248-362-4779
East Tawas, Michigan Office: 910 East Bay Street.
Telephone: 517-362-4747.
Fax: 517-362-7331.

MEMBERS OF FIRM

J. Michael Malloy, III John R. Monnich
James D. Maybaugh David L. Delie, Jr.

OF COUNSEL

Thomas H. O'Connor Maureen Holahan (Retired; Resident, East Tawas Office)

Representative Clients: Johnson & Higgens; Employers Reinsurance; Chubb Companies; American States Insurance Co.; Travelers Insurance; Pontiac Osteopathic Hospital; Michigan Health Care Corporation.

For full biographical listings, see the Martindale-Hubbell Law Directory

POLING, MCGAW & POLING, P.C. (AV)

Suite 275, 5435 Corporate Drive, 48098
Telephone: 248-641-0500
Telecopier: 248-641-0506
URL: http://www.lawyers.com/polingmcgaw&poling

Benson T. Buck (1926-1989) Gregory C. Hamilton
Richard B. Poling Veronica B. O'Hara
D. Douglas McGaw James R. Parker
Richard B. Poling, Jr. Shannon M. Acton

OF COUNSEL

Ralph S. Moore

Representative Clients: City of Troy; United States Fidelity & Guaranty Co.; Sentry Insurance Co.; Admiral Insurance; DeMaria Construction Co.; Leo Corporation; Aetna Casualty and Surety Co.; Concord Design; Pneumo-Abex.

For full biographical listings, see the Martindale-Hubbell Law Directory

SCHADEN, KATZMAN, LAMPERT & MCCLUNE (AV Ⓣ)

100 West Big Beaver Road Suite 130, 48084
Telephone: 248-258-4800
Fax: 248-258-2825
Email: SCHKATZLAM@aol.com *URL:* http://www.lawyers.com/schadenlaw
Broomfield, Colorado Office: 11870 Airport Way.
Telephone: 303-465-3663.
Facsimile: 303-465-3884.

MEMBERS OF FIRM

Richard F. Schaden Bruce A. Lampert
David I. Katzman John D. McClune

ASSOCIATE

Kathleen M. Schaden

OF COUNSEL

Bruce O. Wilson

For full biographical listings, see the Martindale-Hubbell Law Directory

STARK, REAGAN & FINNERTY, P.C. (AV)

Suite 202, 1111 West Long Lake Road, P.O. Box 7037, 48007-7037
Telephone: 248-641-9955
Facsimile: 248-641-9921
Email: @SRFPC.COM
Boca Raton, Florida Office: Suite 307B, 4800 North Federal Highway.
Telephone: 561-994-2266.
Traverse City, Michigan Office: 475 Eastwood Shores.
Telephone: 231-943-8230.
Facsimile: 231-943-8711.

Michael H. Whiting Christopher E. LeVasseur
Kenneth M. Boyer Daniel E. Chapman
Thomas H. Finnerty William D. Girardot
R. Keith Stark James R. Waldvogel
Joseph C. Bird Jeffrey J. Fleury
Joseph A. Ahern Michael D. FitzPatrick

OF COUNSEL

Harry S. Stark (Resident Of Counsel, Traverse City Office) Willard M. Reagan
James E. Beall

For full biographical listings, see the Martindale-Hubbell Law Directory

WEST BLOOMFIELD, Oakland Co.

CHEATHAM, ESTES & HOLLMAN, P.C. (AV)

5777 West Maple Road, Suite 130, P.O. Box 255002, 48325-5002
Telephone: 248-932-2000
Fax: 248-932-2008

Charles C. Cheatham Lee Estes
Mary E. Hollman

Christopher P. Jelinek

COUNSEL

Lynn L. Lower

For full biographical listings, see the Martindale-Hubbell Law Directory

VALENTINE & ASSOCIATES, P.C. (AV)

5767 West Maple Road, Suite 400, 48322
Telephone: 248-851-3010
Fax: 248-851-1553
Email: vallaw@umich.edu

Stephen K. Valentine, Jr.

For full biographical listings, see the Martindale-Hubbell Law Directory

YPSILANTI, Washtenaw Co.

PEAR SPERLING EGGAN & MUSKOVITZ, P.C. (AV)

5 South Washington Street, 48197
Telephone: 734-483-3626
Fax: 734-483-1107
Email: ameggan@ameritech.net
Ann Arbor, Michigan Office: Domino's Farms, 24 Frank Lloyd Wright Drive.
Telephone: 734-665-4441
Other Ypsilanti, Michigan Office: 2164 Bellevue at Washtenaw.
Telephone: 734-483-7177.

Lawrence W. Sperling Andrew M. Eggan
Thomas E. Daniels

Counsel for: Domino's Pizza, Inc.; Citizens Banking Corp.; Townsend and Bottum, Inc.; The Credit Bureau of Ypsilanti; City of Ypsilanti (Labor Counsel); Michigan Municipal Worker's Compensation; Self-Insurance Fund.
Approved Attorneys for: Lawyers Title Insurance Corp.

For full biographical listings, see the Martindale-Hubbell Law Directory

COMMERCIAL LAW

ALABAMA

*BIRMINGHAM,** Jefferson Co.

BRADLEY ARANT ROSE & WHITE LLP (AV)

2001 Park Place, Suite 1400, P.O. Box 830709, 35283-0709
Telephone: 205-521-8000
Facsimile: 205-521-8800
Facsimile (SouthTrust Tower Office): 205-521-8500
URL: http://www.barw.com
Huntsville, Alabama Office: 200 Clinton Avenue West, Suite 900, 35801.
Telephone: 205-517-5100.
Facsimile: 205-533-5069.
Washington, D.C. Office: 801 Pennsylvania Avenue, NW, Suite 230, 20004.
Telephone: 202-347-8893.
Facsimile: 202-347-1684.

MEMBERS OF FIRM

T. Michael Brown
Stewart M. Cox
J. Patrick Darby
Patrick H. Graves Jr. (Resident, Huntsville Office)
George Bryan Harris
Carleta Roberts Hawley
Michael R. Pennington
Sid J. Trant
Bobby C. Underwood
Laurence Duncan Vinson Jr.
Paul S. Ware
John D. Watson III
Kenneth T. Wyatt

ASSOCIATES

Helena F. Barkworth
Abdul K. Kallon

For Complete List of Firm Personnel, See General Section

For full biographical listings, see the Martindale-Hubbell Law Directory

GORDON, SILBERMAN, WIGGINS & CHILDS, P.C. (AV)

1400 SouthTrust Tower, 420 North 20th Street, 35203
Telephone: 205-328-0640
Facsimilie: 205-254-1500
Washington, D.C. Office: 1621 Connecticut Avenue, N.W., Suite 400.
Telephone: 202-238-0690.
Facsimile: 202-238-0968.

RESIDENT SHAREHOLDERS

Wilbur G. Silberman
Bruce L. Gordon
Augustus J. Beck, Jr.
Ray D. Gibbons
Timothy D. Davis

RESIDENT ASSOCIATES

Paul H. Webb
Timothy C. Gann
Brian M. Clark

For Complete List of Firm Personnel, See General Section

For full biographical listings, see the Martindale-Hubbell Law Directory

HASKELL SLAUGHTER & YOUNG, L.L.C. (AV)

1200 AmSouth/Harbert Plaza, 1901 Sixth Avenue North, 35203
Telephone: 205-251-1000
Facsimile: 205-324-1133
Email: hsy@hsy.com
Montgomery, Alabama Office: 305 South Lawrence Street, P.O. Box 4660. 36103-4660.
Telephone: 334-265-8573.
Facsimile: 334-264-7945.

E. Alston Ray
Thomas E. Reynolds
Gwen L. Windle
R. Scott Williams

Lynn Reynolds
Kimberly L. Hager
Matthew T. Franklin

Representative Clients: The Banc Corporation; The Bank; The Equitable Life Assurance Society of the United States; Federal Deposit Insurance Corporation; First National Bank of Chicago; NationsCredit Financial Services Corporation.

For Complete List of Firm Personnel, See General Section

For full biographical listings, see the Martindale-Hubbell Law Directory

SPAIN & GILLON, L.L.C. (AV)

The Zinszer Building, 2117 2nd Avenue North, 35203
Telephone: 205-328-4100
Telecopier: 205-324-8866
Email: ddh@spain-gillon.com *URL:* http://lawlinks.com:80/atty/al/sggbn.html

(See Next Column)

MEMBERS OF FIRM

Eugene P. Stutts
Samuel H. Frazier
Alton B. Parker, Jr.
David S. Maxey

General Counsel for: Piggly Wiggly Alabama Distributing Co.
Counsel for: America's First Federal Credit Union; Compass Bank; AmSouth Bank; SouthTrust Bank; The City of Birmingham.

For Complete List of Firm Personnel, See General Section

For full biographical listings, see the Martindale-Hubbell Law Directory

*FLORENCE,** Lauderdale Co.

SELF & SELF (AV)

408 West Dr. Hicks Boulevard, P.O. Box 1062, 35631
Telephone: 256-767-2570; 1-800-336-2574
Fax: 256-767-2632

MEMBERS OF FIRM

Henry (Hank) H. Self, Jr.
Gilbert P. Self

ASSOCIATE

Missy Homan Hibbett

Reference: Bank Independent; AmSouth Bank; Compass Bank.

For full biographical listings, see the Martindale-Hubbell Law Directory

*MOBILE,** Mobile Co.

BURNS, CUNNINGHAM & MACKEY, P.C. (AV)

50 St. Emanuel Street, P.O. Box 1583, 36633
Telephone: 334-432-0612
Fax: 334-432-0625
URL: http://www.bcmlawyers.com

Peter F. Burns
William M. Cunningham, Jr.
Peter S. Mackey
Gary W. Fillingim

For full biographical listings, see the Martindale-Hubbell Law Directory

FINKBOHNER AND LAWLER, L.L.C. (AV)

169 Dauphin Street Suite 300, P.O. Box 3085, 36652
Telephone: 334-438-5871
Fax: 334-432-8052
Email: finkbohnerlawlerllc@zebra.net

MEMBERS OF FIRM

George W. Finkbohner, Jr.
John L. Lawler
George W. Finkbohner, III
Royce A. Ray, III

For full biographical listings, see the Martindale-Hubbell Law Directory

HELMSING, SIMS & LEACH, P.C. (AV)

The Laclede Building, 150 Government Street, Suite 2000, P.O. Box 2767, 36652
Telephone: 334-432-5521
Telecopy: 334-432-0633

Larry U. Sims
Frederick G. Helmsing
John N. Leach, Jr.
Warren C. Herlong, Jr.
James B. Newman
Robert H. Rouse
Charles H. Dodson, Jr.
Joseph P. H. Babington
R. Alan Alexander
John J. Crowley, Jr.
Joseph D. Steadman
Todd S. Strohmeyer

William R. Lancaster
Robin Kilpatrick Fincher
John Townsend Dukes
John Casey Pipes
James Bradford Pittman, Jr.

Representative Clients: American National Property and Casualty; Associated Aviation Underwriters; Baldwin Mutual Insurance Co.; Fred S. James & Co. of Pennsylvania; INA (Aviation); Kemper Group; Liberty Mutual Insurance Co.; Mutual Assurance; Sayre & Toso, Inc.; The Canadian Indemnity Co.

For full biographical listings, see the Martindale-Hubbell Law Directory

LYONS, PIPES & COOK, P.C. (AV)

2 North Royal Street, P.O. Box 2727, 36652-2727
Telephone: 334-432-4481
Cable Address: "Lysea"
Telecopier: 334-433-1820
URL: http://www.LPCLaw.com

Marion A. Quina, Jr.
Thomas F. Garth
W. David Johnson, Jr.
Allen E. Graham
Michael C. Niemeyer

Representative Clients: Aetna Life & Casualty Company; Alabama Insurance Guaranty Association; American Family Life Insurance Company; Carrier's Container Council, Inc.; Champion Incorporation; Chubb; Crawford & Company; Crum & Forster Commercial Insurance; Maryland Casualty Company; Massachusetts Mutual Life Insurance Co.

For Complete List of Firm Personnel, See General Section

For full biographical listings, see the Martindale-Hubbell Law Directory

Mobile—Continued

VICKERS, RIIS, MURRAY AND CURRAN, L.L.C. (AV)

8th Floor, Regions Bank Building, 106 Saint Francis Street, P.O. Box 2568, 36652
Telephone: 334-432-9772
Fax: 334-432-9781
Email: vickersriis.com

MEMBERS OF FIRM

Erling Riis, Jr.
J. Manson Murray
J. W. Goodloe, Jr.
Ronald P. Davis
M. Kathryn Knight

Representative Clients: Mobile Forest Products, Inc.; Azalea Aviation, Inc.; Midstream Fuel Services; McPhillips Manufacturing Co., Inc.; Spring Hill College; Steiner Shipyard, Inc.; Marine Office of America Corp.; Cummins Alabama, Inc.; Ben M. Radcliff Contractor, Inc.; Grady Buick Company, Inc.

For Complete List of Firm Personnel, See General Section

For full biographical listings, see the Martindale-Hubbell Law Directory

*MONTGOMERY,** Montgomery Co.

KAUFMAN & ROTHFEDER, P.C. (AV)

2740 Zelda Road, Drawer 4540, 36103-4540
Telephone: 334-244-1111
Fax: 334-244-1969
Email: firm@krlegal.com *URL:* http://www.krlegal.com

Samuel Kaufman
Alan E. Rothfeder
Thomas R. DeBray
Richardson B. McKenzie III
Robert E. L. Gilpin
George W. Thomas
Robert M. Ritchey
William B. Sellers
J. Scott Pierce

Counsel for: Dale Medical Center; Evergreen Medical Center; Community Health Systems, Inc.; The Russell Hospital Corporation.

For full biographical listings, see the Martindale-Hubbell Law Directory

PARNELL & CRUM, P.A. (AV)

641 South Lawrence Street, P.O. Box 2189, 36102
Telephone: 334-832-4202
Telecopier: 334-832-4703
Fax: 334-293-3550
Email: cnparnell@aol.com

Charles N. Parnell, III
G. Barton Crum

Robert J. Russell, Jr.
James McCauley Smith
Britt Batson Griggs
Angie Hubbard Ingram

Reference: Colonial Bank of Montgomery.

For full biographical listings, see the Martindale-Hubbell Law Directory

VOLZ, PRESTWOOD & HANAN, P.C. (AV)

350 Adams Avenue, P.O. Box 1910, 36102-1910
Telephone: 334-264-6401
Fax: 334-834-4954

Charles H. Volz, Jr.
Alvin T. Prestwood
Charles H. Volz, III
Ellis D. Hanan
Richard D. Lively
Judy H. Barganier

For full biographical listings, see the Martindale-Hubbell Law Directory

*TUSCUMBIA,** Colbert Co.

SELF & SELF

(See Florence)

ALASKA

*ANCHORAGE,** Third Judicial District

OWENS & TURNER, A PROFESSIONAL CORPORATION (AV)

1500 West 33rd Avenue, Suite 200, 99503-3502
Telephone: 907-276-3963
Facsimile: 907-277-3695
Email: mail@owensturner.com *URL:* http://www.owensturner.com

Thomas P. Owens, Jr.
Terrance A. Turner
William F. Mede
Scott J. Nordstrand

Erin Rose
Patrick J McCabe
Kimberly K. Geariety
Dennis J. Efta

(See Next Column)

LEGAL SUPPORT PERSONNEL

Susan M. Lamb

Representative Clients: Alaska Finance & Insurance Co., Inc.; Alaska Railroad Corporation; Alaska Science & Technology Foundation; Baugh Construction & Engineering Company; Bethel Utilities Corporation; Dynamic Capital Management, Inc.; Merrill Lynch Pierce Fenner & Smith, Inc.; Ounalashka Corporation; Tanadgusix Corporation; Watterson Construction Company.

For full biographical listings, see the Martindale-Hubbell Law Directory

ARIZONA

*FLAGSTAFF,** Coconino Co.

HUFFORD, HORSTMAN, MONGINI, PARNELL & MCCARTHY, P.C. (AV)

323 North Leroux Street, P.O. Box B, 86002-0808
Telephone: 520-774-1453
Fax: 520-779-3621

C. Benson Hufford
Patrice M. Horstman
Michael E.J. Mongini
Eve A. Parnell
Philip (Jay) McCarthy, Jr.

E. Duane Weston

LEGAL SUPPORT PERSONNEL

R. Gehl Tucker (Legal Assistant)
Doris Utzinger (Legal Assistant)
Vickie Belman (Legal Assistant)
Jan Blackman (Paralegal)
Dawn L. Karsten (Paralegal)

Reference: Norwest Bank Arizona, N.A.

For full biographical listings, see the Martindale-Hubbell Law Directory

MANGUM, WALL, STOOPS & WARDEN, P.L.L.C. (AV)

100 North Elden, P.O. Box 10, 86002
Telephone: 520-779-6951
Fax: 520-773-1312

H. Karl Mangum (1908-1993)

OF COUNSEL

Douglas J. Wall
Robert W. Warden
Daniel J. Stoops

MEMBERS OF FIRM

A. Dean Pickett
Stephen K. Smith
Melinda L. Garrahan
Michael H. Hinson

ASSOCIATES

Annette Star Lustgarten
Rebecca Smith Currey
R. Scott Currey
Melinda K. Jacquez
Franklin Hoover

Representative Clients: Northern Arizona University; Flagstaff Unified School District; Museum of Northern Arizona; Arizona School Board Association.
Local Counsel for: Bank of America-Arizona; Arizona Public Service; U.S.A.; State Farm Fire & Casualty Insurance Co.; Property Development Co.

For Complete List of Firm Personnel, See General Section

For full biographical listings, see the Martindale-Hubbell Law Directory

*PHOENIX,** Maricopa Co.

BURCH & CRACCHIOLO, P.A. (AV)

702 East Osborn Road, Suite 200, 85014
Telephone: 602-274-7611
Fax: 602-234-0341
Mailing Address: P.O. Box 16882, Phoenix, AZ, 85011
Email: library@bcattorneys.com

Stephen E. Silver
Daryl Manhart
Edwin C. Bull
Bryan F. Murphy
Donald W. Lindholm
F. Michael Carroll
Daniel R. Malinski
Edwin D. Fleming
Ralph D. Harris
David M. Villadolid

Amy DeLaplace Howland
Steven J. Lippman
Thomas A. Longfellow
Steven M. Serrano

Representative Clients: Bashas' Inc.; Farmers Insurance Group; U-Haul International, Inc.

For Complete List of Firm Personnel, See General Section

For full biographical listings, see the Martindale-Hubbell Law Directory

Phoenix—Continued

CRUSE, FIRETAG & BOCK, P.C. (AV)

5611 North 16th Street, 85016
Telephone: 602-279-9411
Facsimile: 602-241-1260
Email: cfbpc@cfbpc.com

Robert J. Cruse
Jules I. Firetag
Daniel A. Bock

John L. Stoss
Paul F. Dowdell

OF COUNSEL
Stephen T. Meadow (P.C.)

Reference: Norwest Bank, Arizona (Main Office).

For full biographical listings, see the Martindale-Hubbell Law Directory

FENNEMORE CRAIG, A PROFESSIONAL CORPORATION (AV)

3003 North Central Avenue, Suite 2600, 85012-2913
Telephone: 602-916-5000
Fax: 602-916-5999
Tucson, Arizona Office: One South Church Avenue, Suite 1000, 85701-1620.
Telephone: 520-879-6800.
Fax: 520-879-6899.

Robert P. Robinson
Robert J. Hackett
Jay S. Ruffner
Ronald L. Ballard
Stephen M. Savage
Mark A. Nesvig
George T. Cole
Charles M. King
Michael V. Mulchay
Don J. Miner
Margaret R. Gallogly
Jay S. Kramer
David E. Vieweg
W. T. Eggleston, Jr.
M. Virginia Perry

Elizabeth M. Behnke
Jeffrey S. Pitcher
Thomas F. O'Malley, III
Susan M. Wissink
Theodore D. Setzer
Paul A. Krulisky

LEGAL SUPPORT PERSONNEL
LEGAL ASSISTANTS

Vicki Montei
Nancy E. Esser
Julie Hodges
Charlene Sarich

For Complete List of Firm Personnel, See General Section

For full biographical listings, see the Martindale-Hubbell Law Directory

LEWIS AND ROCA, LLP (AV)

A Limited Liability Partnership including a Professional Corporation
40 North Central Avenue, 85004-4429
Telephone: 602-262-5311
Fax: 602-262-5747
Email: clientservice@lrlaw.com *URL:* http://www.lrlaw.com
Tucson, Arizona Office: One South Church Avenue, Suite 700, 86701-1620.
Telephone: 520-622-2090.
Fax: 520-622-3088. E-Mail: clientservice@lrlaw.com.
Las Vegas, Nevada Affiliated Office: Ashcraft and Heinz LLP, 3960 Howard Hughes Parkway, 89109.
Telephone: 702-990-3570.
Fax: 702-990-3571.

MEMBERS OF FIRM

John P. Frank
Peter D. Baird
Richard N. Goldsmith
Randolph J. Haines
José A. Cárdenas
Foster Robberson
Newman R. Porter
Thomas G. Ryan
Brent C. Gardner
Cathy M. Holt
Christopher J. Brelje
Pamela B. Petersen
Gerald K. Smith
Douglas L. Irish
Susan M. Freeman
Patricia K. Norris
Dale A. Danneman
Thomas H. Campbell
George L. Paul
Jesse B. Simpson
Mary Ellen Simonson
James T. Acuff, Jr.
Robert H. McKirgan
L. Keith Beauchamp
Richard A. Halloran

ASSOCIATES

Dawn M. Bergin
Randy Papetti

OF COUNSEL
Jeremy E. Butler

Representative Clients: Associates Financial Services; Citibank; The Dial Corp; Digital Equipment Corp.; MCI Communications Corp.; Prudential Securities.

For Complete List of Firm Personnel, See General Section

For full biographical listings, see the Martindale-Hubbell Law Directory

MACLEAN & JACQUES, LTD. (AV)

Suite 202, 40 East Virginia, 85004
Telephone: 602-263-5771
FAX: 602-279-5569

John H. MacLean (1932-1992)
Raoul T. Jacques

Cary T. Inabinet
Macre S. Inabinet

LEGAL SUPPORT PERSONNEL
Sharon Petterson

For full biographical listings, see the Martindale-Hubbell Law Directory

QUARLES & BRADY LLP (AV)

One Camelback Building, One East Camelback Road, Suite 400, 85012-1649
Telephone: 602-230-5500
Fax: 602-230-5598
URL: http://www.quarles.com
Milwaukee, Wisconsin Office: 411 East Wisconsin Avenue.
Telephone: 414-277-5000.
Fax: 414-271-3552.
Madison, Wisconsin Office: First Wisconsin Plaza, One South Pinckney Street, P.O. Box 2113.
Telephone: 608-251-5000.
Fax: 608-251-9166.
West Palm Beach, Florida Office: 222 Lakeview Avenue, 4th Floor.
Telephone: 407-653-5000.
Fax: 407-653-5333.
Naples, Florida Office: Barnett Center, 4501 Tamiami Trail North, Suite 300.
Telephone: 813-262-5959.
Fax: 813-434-4999.
Chicago, Illinois Office: Quarles & Brady LLC, Citicorp Center, 500 West Madison Street, Suite 3700.
Telephone: 312-715-5000.
Fax: 312-715-5155.

MEMBERS OF THE FIRM

Gerald L. Shelley
Benjamin R. Norris

ASSOCIATE
Maureen Henry

For full biographical listings, see the Martindale-Hubbell Law Directory

ROBBINS & GREEN, A PROFESSIONAL ASSOCIATION (AV)

1800 Norwest Tower, 3300 North Central Avenue, 85012-2578
Telephone: 602-248-7600
Fax: 602-266-5369
Email: @RGLaw.com

Philip A. Robbins
William H. Sandweg III
Jeffrey P. Boshes
Brian Imbornoni
Janet B. Hutchison
Alfred W. Ricciardi

For full biographical listings, see the Martindale-Hubbell Law Directory

SNELL & WILMER L.L.P. (AV)

One Arizona Center, 85004-2202
Telephone: 602-382-6000
Fax: 602-382-6070
Email: postmaster@snellwilmer.com *URL:* http://www.swlaw.com
Tucson, Arizona Office: One South Church Avenue, Suite 1500, 85701-1612.
Telephone: 520-882-1200.
Fax: 520-884-1294.
Orange County Office: 1920 Main Street, Suite 1200, Irvine, California 92614-7230.
Telephone: 949-253-2700.
Fax: 949-955-2507.
Salt Lake City, Utah Office: 111 East Broadway, Suite 900, 84111-1004.
Telephone: 801-237-1900.
Fax: 801-237-1950.

MEMBERS OF FIRM

Jon S. Cohen
Terry Morris Roman
Nicholas J. Wood

Representative Clients: For list of Representative Clients, see end of biographical listings in the Martindale-Hubbell Law Directory.

For Complete List of Firm Personnel, See General Section

For full biographical listings, see the Martindale-Hubbell Law Directory

*PRESCOTT,** Yavapai Co.

FAVOUR, MOORE & WILHELMSEN, A PROFESSIONAL ASSOCIATION (AV)

1580 Plaza West Drive, P.O. Box 1391, 86302
Telephone: 520-445-2444
Fax: 520-771-0450
Email: fmw@primenet.com

(See Next Column)

FAVOUR, MOORE & WILHELMSEN A PROFESSIONAL ASSOCIATION, *Prescott—Continued*

John M. Favour
Mark M. Moore
David K. Wilhelmsen

Representative Client: Yavapai Title Co.
Reference: Bank of America.

For Complete List of Firm Personnel, See General Section

For full biographical listings, see the Martindale-Hubbell Law Directory

SCOTTSDALE, Maricopa Co.

PESKIND HYMSON & GOLDSTEIN, P.C. (AV)

14595 North Scottsdale Road, Suite 14, 85254
Telephone: 602-991-9077
Fax: 602-443-8854
URL: http://www.legalcounselors.com

E. J. Peskind
Irving Hymson
David B. Goldstein
Marilee Miller Clarke
Pamela L. Kingsley

Eddie A. Pantiliat

For full biographical listings, see the Martindale-Hubbell Law Directory

SACKS TIERNEY P.A. (AV)

4250 North Civic Center Boulevard, 85251
Telephone: 480-425-2600
Facsimile: 480-970-4610
Email: ST@sackstierney.com
Phoenix, Arizona Office: Two North Central Avenue, Suite 1960. 85004.
Telephone: 480-435-2600.
Fax: 480-970-4610.

Seymour Sacks
Marvin S. Cohen
David C. Tierney
Stephen Aron Benson
Michael R. Rooney
Robert G. Kimball
Stephen P. Linzer
Marcia J. Busching
Randall S. Yavitz
Sharon Brook Shively
James W. Armstrong
Steven M. Goldstein
Judith M. Dworkin
Robert J. Lord
Sharon S. Moyer
Candess J. Hunter
Lori R. Miller
Brian E. Ditsch

Sharyl Poulson Speaker
Steven W. Bienstock
Andrew Lane de Mars
Scott B. Cohen
Mark D. Dillon
John L. Habib
W. Kevin Bell
Isabel M. Humphrey
Julie A. Inderlied
Laura G. Meyer
Stephen A. Wolf

Reference: M&I Thunderbird Bank.

For full biographical listings, see the Martindale-Hubbell Law Directory

*TUCSON,** Pima Co.

CHANDLER, TULLAR, UDALL & REDHAIR, L.L.P. (AV)

1700 Bank of America Plaza, 33 North Stone Avenue, 85701-1415
Telephone: 520-623-4353
Telefax: 520-792-3426

MEMBERS OF FIRM

Dwight M. Whitley, Jr.
E. Hardy Smith
John J. Brady
Kurt Kroese

ASSOCIATES

Elizabeth D. Bushell
Charles Alexander Davis
Edward Moomjian, II

Representative Clients: Arizona Electric Power Cooperative, Inc.; Atlantic Richfield Co.; CNA Insurance; Farmers Insurance Exchange; MICA; Chubb Insurance Group; State Farm Mutual Insurance Companies; LaFrontera Center; Starpass Properties.
Reference: Arizona Bank.

For Complete List of Firm Personnel, See General Section

For full biographical listings, see the Martindale-Hubbell Law Directory

MUNGER CHADWICK, P.L.C. (AV)

333 North Wilmot, Suite 300, 85711
Telephone: 520-721-1900
Fax: 520-747-1550
Email: m-c@mungerchadwick.com *URL:* http://www.mungerchadwick.com
Phoenix Appointment Office: 5225 N. Central, Suite 235, 85012-1452.
Telephone: 602-230-1850.

(See Next Column)

John F. Munger

Representative Clients: Jones Intercable; Mountain Telecommunications, Inc.; Tucson Greyhound Park; Tucson Realty and Trust; Southwest Gas Corporation; Pacific Gas & Electric; Whetstone Homes; Lawley Motors; Mexicana Food & Spirits, LLC; The Winters Co.

For full biographical listings, see the Martindale-Hubbell Law Directory

*YUMA,** Yuma Co.

ROBERT M. COOK (AV)

207 West Second Street, 85364
Telephone: 520-539-0959
Fax: 520-539-0960
1-800 ROBERT M
Email: robertmcook@yahoo.com

For full biographical listings, see the Martindale-Hubbell Law Directory

ARKANSAS

*FAYETTEVILLE,** Washington Co.

DAVIS, COX & WRIGHT, PLC (AV)

19 East Mountain Street, P.O. Drawer 1688, 72702-1688
Telephone: 501-521-7600
Fax: 501-521-7661
Email: daviscoxwright@dcw-plc.com *URL:* http://www.dcw-plc.com

Sidney P. Davis, Jr.
Walter B. Cox
Tilden P. Wright, III
Constance G. Clark
William Jackson Butt, II
Kelly P. Carithers
Don A. Taylor
Paul H. Taylor
John G. Trice
Laura J. Andress

Mark W. Dossett
S. Lance Cox
Robin Miller

Representative Clients: USA Waste; J.V. Manufacturing; Wal Mart Stores, Inc.; Arvest Bank Group; Associates Commercial Corp.; Mercedes Benz Credit Corp.; Farm Credit Services of Western Arkansas.

For full biographical listings, see the Martindale-Hubbell Law Directory

*LITTLE ROCK,** Pulaski Co.

BARBER, McCASKILL, JONES & HALE, P.A. (AV)

2700 Regions Center, 400 West Capitol Avenue, 72201-3414
Telephone: 501-372-6175
Telecopier: 501-375-2802

Azro L. Barber (1885-1979)
Elbert A. Henry (1889-1966)
John B. Thurman (1912-1971)
Austin McCaskill, Sr.
Glenn W. Jones
Michael E. Hale
John S. Cherry, Jr.
Robert L. Henry, III
Micheal L. Alexander
William H. Edwards, Jr.
G. Spence Fricke
Gail Ponder Gaines
Michael J. Emerson
R. Kenny McCulloch
Tim A. Cheatham
Joseph F. Kolb
Scott Michael Strauss
Baucum Fulk
D. Keith Fortner
Wendy Scholtens Wood
Morris L. Williams, III
Michelle Bass Miller

Attorneys for: CNA Insurance Companies; Fireman's Fund Insurance Co.; First Counsel Bank; General Motors Corp.; General Motors Acceptance Corp.; Hanover Insurance Co.; Royal Insurance; United States Fidelity & Guaranty Co.; Universal Underwriters Insurance Co.

For full biographical listings, see the Martindale-Hubbell Law Directory

HOPKINS LAW FIRM, A PROFESSIONAL ASSOCIATION (AV)

1000 West Second Street, 72201
Telephone: 501-375-1517
Facsimile: 501-375-0231
URL: http://www.hopkinslawfirm.com
Email: HopkinsLaw@hopkinslawfirm.com *URL:* http://www.lawyers.com/hopkinslawfirm

Gregory M. Hopkins

William P. Allison

Representative Client: PPG Industries, Inc.

For full biographical listings, see the Martindale-Hubbell Law Directory

ROSE LAW FIRM, A PROFESSIONAL ASSOCIATION (AV)

120 East Fourth Street, 72201
Telephone: 501-375-9131
Telecopy: 501-375-1309

(See Next Column)

ROSE LAW FIRM A PROFESSIONAL ASSOCIATION—*Continued*

Herbert C. Rule, III
Allen W. Bird, II
Garland J. Garrett
Charles W. Baker
John T. Hardin
Brian Rosenthal

Representative Clients: Arkansas Capital Corp.; The Equitable Life Assurance Society of America; John Hancock Mutual Life Insurance Co.; International Paper Co.; Mercantile Bank of Central Arkansas; The Prudential Insurance Company of America; Stephens Group Inc.; Trammell Crow Cos.

For Complete List of Firm Personnel, See General Section

For full biographical listings, see the Martindale-Hubbell Law Directory

WALKER & BLACK (AV)

1000 West Third Street, P.O. Box 3780, 72203-3780
Telephone: 501-376-2382
Fax: 501-376-3352

MEMBERS OF FIRM

W. J. Walker
Kendell R. Black

ASSOCIATE

Phillip M. Hendry

Reference: Central Bank & Trust.

For full biographical listings, see the Martindale-Hubbell Law Directory

WILLIAMS & ANDERSON (AV)

Registered Limited Liability Partnership
Twenty-Second Floor, 111 Center Street, 72201
Telephone: 501-372-0800
Fax: 501-372-6453
Email: info@williamsanderson.com *URL:* http://www.williamsanderson.com

MEMBERS OF FIRM

Philip S. Anderson
Peter G. Kumpe
Steven W. Quattlebaum
John E. Tull, III
Timothy W. Grooms
Thomas G. Williams
Patrick A. Burrow

Edie R. Ervin
Stephen B. Niswanger
Kristine Gerhard Baker
Robert F. Thompson III

Representative Clients: Arkansas Democrat-Gazette, Inc.; Arkansas Development Finance Authority; Arkansas Realtors Association; Camden News Publishing Company; Coca-Cola Enterprises, Inc.; Entergy Corporation; Potlatch Corporation; Texaco Inc.; Roman Catholic Diocese of Little Rock; Wal-Mart Stores, Inc.

For Complete List of Firm Personnel, See General Section

For full biographical listings, see the Martindale-Hubbell Law Directory

CALIFORNIA

*BAKERSFIELD,** Kern Co.

KLEIN, DENATALE, GOLDNER, COOPER, ROSENLIEB & KIMBALL, LLP (AV)

(Formerly Di Giorgio, Davis, Klein, Wegis, Duggan & Friedman)
ARCO Tower, 4550 California Avenue, Second Floor, 93309
Telephone: 661-395-1000
Telecopier: 661-326-0418
Mailing Address: P.O. Box 11172, Bakersfield, California, 93389-1172
Email: kleinlaw@kleinlaw.com

Anthony J. Klein (Inc.)
Thomas V. DeNatale, Jr.
Barry L. Goldner
Jay L. Rosenlieb
David J. Cooper

Representative Clients: Bank of America; California Republic Bank; San Joaquin Bank.

For Complete List of Firm Personnel, See General Section

For full biographical listings, see the Martindale-Hubbell Law Directory

COSTA MESA, Orange Co.

FELDHAKE, AUGUST & ROQUEMORE (AV)

Plaza Tower, Suite 1730, 600 Anton Boulevard, 92626-7124
Telephone: 714-438-3885
Fax: 714-438-3888
Email: farlaw@hqonline.com

Robert J. Feldhake
Kenneth S. August
Lisa A. Roquemore
Joshua M. Wolff

(See Next Column)

ASSOCIATES

Dimitri P. Gross
Supriya Kakkar
Katherine A. Slayton

OF COUNSEL

Arthur J. Swerdloff
Arthur M. Wilcox, Jr.

For full biographical listings, see the Martindale-Hubbell Law Directory

RUTAN & TUCKER, LLP (AV)

A Partnership including Professional Corporations
611 Anton Boulevard, Fourteenth Floor, P.O. Box 1950, 92626-1998
Telephone: 714-641-5100; 213-625-7586
Telecopier: 714-546-9035
Email: rutan&tucker@rutan.com *URL:* http://www.rutan.com

MEMBERS OF FIRM

John B. Hurlbut, Jr.
Clifford E. Frieden
Ira G. Rivin (P.C.)
Marcia A. Forsyth
Michael F. Sitzer
Thomas J. Crane
Penelope Parmes
Richard K. Howell
Paul J. Sievers

SPECIAL COUNSEL

Michael K. Slattery

ASSOCIATES

Treg A. Julander
John W. Hamilton, Jr.
Philip J. Blanchard
Julie K. Whang
Richard D. Arko
Mark M. Malovos

For Complete List of Firm Personnel, See General Section

For full biographical listings, see the Martindale-Hubbell Law Directory

*FRESNO,** Fresno Co.

DOWLING, AARON & KEELER, INCORPORATED (AV)

6051 North Fresno Street, Suite 200, 93710
Telephone: 559-432-4500
Fax: 559-432-4590
Email: dak@daklaw.com *URL:* http://www.daklaw.com
Bakersfield, California Office: 110 South Mt. Claire, Suite 203. 93309.
Telephone: 661-396-0451. Web Site: http://www.daklaw.com.

Michael D. Dowling
Richard M. Aaron
Bruce S. Fraser
John C. Ganahl
Gary M. Fachin
Christopher A. Brown
James C. Sherwood

Larry B. Lindenau
Michael P. Dowling
Leigh W. Burnside
Justin D. Harris

OF COUNSEL

Morris M. Sherr

Reference: Wells Fargo Bank (Main).

For Complete List of Firm Personnel, See General Section

For full biographical listings, see the Martindale-Hubbell Law Directory

IRVINE, Orange Co.

LOBEL & OPERA LLP (AV)

Suite 1100, 19800 MacArthur Boulevard, 92612-2425
Telephone: 949-476-7400
Fax: 949-476-7444
Email: webmaster@lobelopera.com *URL:* http://www.lobelopera.com

PARTNERS

William N. Lobel
Robert E. Opera
Pamela Zylstra Karger
Evan C. Borges
Jeffrey M. Reisner

OF COUNSEL

Curtis O. Barnes
Elmer Dean Martin, III
Michael D. Good

Tavi Claire Flanagan
Hamid R. Rafatjoo
Michael D. Neue

For full biographical listings, see the Martindale-Hubbell Law Directory

LONG BEACH, Los Angeles Co.

RUSSELL & MIRKOVICH (AV)

One World Trade Center, Suite 1450, 90831-1450
Telephone: 562-436-9911
FAX: 562-436-1897
Email: counsel@russell-mirkovich.com

Carlton E. Russell
Joseph N. Mirkovich

ASSOCIATE

Margaret E. Morrow
Steven Y. Otera

For full biographical listings, see the Martindale-Hubbell Law Directory

Long Beach—Continued

WOOLLEY RUSSELL & JOHNSON (AV)

444 West Ocean Boulevard, Suite 1700, 90802
Telephone: 562-495-6000
Telecopier: 562-435-1359
Email: mail@transportlawyers.com *URL:* http://www.transportlawyers.com
Port Hueneme, California Office: 105 East Port Hueneme Road, 93041.
Telephone: 562-495-6000.
Fax: 562-435-1359.

MEMBERS OF FIRM

David E. R. Woolley
Thomas A. Russell
Philip L. Johnson

ASSOCIATE

Thomas G. Walsh

LEGAL SUPPORT PERSONNEL

PARALEGAL

Dawn C. Breaux

For full biographical listings, see the Martindale-Hubbell Law Directory

*LOS ANGELES,** Los Angeles Co.

LAW OFFICES OF DAVID B. BLOOM A PROFESSIONAL CORPORATION (AV)

3325 Wilshire Boulevard, Ninth Floor, 90010
Telephone: 323-938-5248; 384-4088
Telecopier: 213-385-2009

David B. Bloom

Stephen S. Monroe (A Professional Corporation)
Raphael A. Rosemblat
James E. Adler
Roy A. Levun
Jonathan Udell
Susan Carole Jay
Edward Idell
Sandra Kamenir
Steven Wayne Lazarus
Andrew Edward Briseno
Shelley M. Gould
Ted L. Travis

For full biographical listings, see the Martindale-Hubbell Law Directory

CLARK & TREVITHICK, A PROFESSIONAL CORPORATION (AV)

800 Wilshire Boulevard, 12th Floor, 90017
Telephone: 213-629-5700
Telecopier: 213-624-9441
Email: postmaster@clarktrev.com
San Francisco, California Office: 456 Montgomery Street, 20th Floor.
Telephone: 415-288-6520.
Fax: 415-398-2820.

Philip W. Bartenetti
Vincent Tricarico
Leonard Brazil
Leslie R. Horowitz
Arturo Santana Jr.

OF COUNSEL

Dolores Cordell
Judith Ilene Bloom
Raimund Freihube

For Complete List of Firm Personnel, See General Section

For full biographical listings, see the Martindale-Hubbell Law Directory

DEMETRIOU, DEL GUERCIO, SPRINGER & MOYER, LLP (AV)

801 South Grand Avenue, 10th Floor, 90017
Telephone: 213-624-8407
Telecopy: 213-624-0174
Email: ddsm@juno.com

MEMBERS OF FIRM

Chris G. Demetriou (1915-1989)
Jeffrey Z. B. Springer
Craig A. Moyer
Angela Shanahan
Stephen A. Del Guercio
Michael A. Francis
Regina Liudzius Cobb
Jennifer T. Taggart
Bradley D. Pierce
Wendy M. Conole
Brian D. Langa
Silvia Saucedo

OF COUNSEL

Ronald J. Del Guercio
Richard A. Del Guercio
James P. Del Guercio
Barbara F. Stein

Reference: Bank of America, L.A. Main Office, Los Angeles, Calif.

For full biographical listings, see the Martindale-Hubbell Law Directory

LEONARD A. GOLDMAN & ASSOCIATES (AV)

(Formerly Goldman & Gordon, L.L.P.)
1900 Avenue of the Stars, Suite 1800, 90067-4409
Telephone: 310-277-7171
FAX: 310-277-1547
Email: lagoldman@earthlink.com

(See Next Column)

MEMBERS OF FIRM

A. S. Goldman (1895-1966)
Leonard A. Goldman

References: Bank of America, Fourth and Spring Branch, Los Angeles; Bank of America, Wilshire-San Vincente Branch, Beverly Hills.

For full biographical listings, see the Martindale-Hubbell Law Directory

MITCHELL, SILBERBERG & KNUPP LLP (AV)

A Partnership including Professional Corporations
11377 West Olympic Boulevard, 90064
Telephone: 310-312-2000
Fax: 310-312-3100
Email: info@msk.com *URL:* http://www.msk.com

MEMBERS OF FIRM

Anthony A. Adler (A Professional Corporation)
Lessing E. Gold (A Professional Corporation)
Ron R. Goldie (A Professional Corporation)
John E. Hatherley (A Professional Corporation)
Andrew E. Katz (A Professional Corporation)
David J. Katz (A Professional Corporation)
John M. Kuechle (A Professional Corporation)
Chester I. Lappen (A Professional Corporation)
Marvin Leon (A Professional Corporation)
Mark R. Moskowitz (A Professional Corporation)
Alan L. Pepper (A Professional Corporation)

OF COUNSEL

Richard E. Ackerknecht
Daniel M. Freedman
H. Wayne Taylor

ASSOCIATES

Celine M. Guillou
Jocelyn M. Gutiérrez
Carolyn Hoff
Gamze Onur
Michael J. Zerman

References: Wells Fargo Bank, N.A.; Merrill, Lynch.

For Complete List of Firm Personnel, See General Section

For full biographical listings, see the Martindale-Hubbell Law Directory

O'MELVENY & MYERS LLP (AV)

400 South Hope Street, 90071-2899
Telephone: 213-430-6000
Facsimile: 213-430-6407
Cable: MOMS
Telex: 674122
Email: omminfo@omm.com *URL:* http://www.omm.com
Century City, CA Office: 1999 Avenue of the Stars, Los Angeles, 90067-6035.
Telex: 674097. Tel: 310-553-6700.
Fax: 310-246-6779.
Newport Beach, CA Office: 610 Newport Center Drive, 92660-6429.
Telex: 4722088. Tel: 949-760-9600.
Fax: 949-823-6994.
San Francisco, CA Office: Embarcadero Center West, 275 Battery Street, 94111-3305. Tel: 415-984-8700.
Fax: 415-984-8701.
New York, NY Office: Citicorp Center, 153 East 53rd Street, 10022-4611.
Telex: 129165. Tel: 212-326-2000.
Fax: 212-326-2061.
Washington, DC Office: 555 13th Street, N.W., 20004-1109.
Cable: MOMSWSH.
Telex: 89622. Tel: 202-383-5300.
Fax: 202-383-5414.
London Office: O'Melveny & Myers, 3 Finsbury Square, London, EC2A 1LA, England. Tel: 44-171-256-8451. Fax 44-171-638-8205.
Tokyo Office: Akasaka Twin Tower, East 14F, 2-17-23, Akasaka, Minato-ku, Tokyo 107-0052, Japan. Tel: 03-5562-2800.
Fax: 03-5575-3840.
Hong Kong Office: O'Melveny & Myers, Suite 1905, Tower Two, Lippo Centre, 89 Queensway, Central, Hong Kong. Tel: 852-2523-8266.
Fax: 852-2522-1760.
Shanghai Office: Kerry Centre, 20F, 1515 Nanjing Road West, Shanghai, 200040 People's Republic of China. Tel: 86-21-5298-5600.
Fax: 86-21-5298-5500.

PARTNER

Frederick B. McLane

For Complete List of Firm Personnel, See General Section

For full biographical listings, see the Martindale-Hubbell Law Directory

OSTROVE, KRANTZ & OSTROVE, A PROFESSIONAL CORPORATION (AV)

(Successor To: Ostrove and Lancer, A Professional Corporation; David Ostrove, A Professional Corporation)
5757 Wilshire Boulevard, Suite 535, 90036-3600
Telephone: 323-939-3400
Fax: 323-939-3500
Email: OSTROVE@AOL.COM *URL:* http://www.lawyers.com/ok&olaw

(See Next Column)

OSTROVE, KRANTZ & OSTROVE A PROFESSIONAL CORPORATION—*Continued*

David Ostrove
David S. Krantz
Kenneth E. Ostrove

Reference: First Business Bank.

For full biographical listings, see the Martindale-Hubbell Law Directory

STUTMAN, TREISTER & GLATT, PROFESSIONAL CORPORATION (AV)

3699 Wilshire Boulevard, Suite 900, 90010
Telephone: 213-251-5100
FAX: 213-251-5288

John P. Schafer

For full biographical listings, see the Martindale-Hubbell Law Directory

SULMEYER, KUPETZ, BAUMANN & ROTHMAN, A PROFESSIONAL CORPORATION (AV)

300 South Grand Avenue, 14th Floor, 90071
Telephone: 213-626-2311
Fax: 213-629-4520
Email: info@skbr.com *URL:* http://www.skbr.com

Irving Sulmeyer
Arnold L. Kupetz
Richard G. Baumann
Don Rothman
Alan G. Tippie
Israel Saperstein
Victor A. Sahn
Steven R. Wainess
David S. Kupetz
Howard M. Ehrenberg
Frank Vram Zerunyan

OF COUNSEL

Wesley H. Avery
Ronald E. Gordon
Nathan H. Harris
Elissa D. Miller
Marilyn S. Scheer
Suzanne L. Weakley

Mark S. Horoupian
Stephen C. Seto
Howard N. Madris
Joon Kim

Representative Clients: General Electric Capital Corp.; Continental Insurance Co.; Litton Industries; North American Phillips Corp.; Ventura Port District; Northwest Financial; Heller Financial Inc.; Transamerica Occidental Life Insurance Co.; Transamerica Realty Services, Inc.; Body Glove International.

For full biographical listings, see the Martindale-Hubbell Law Directory

ZIDE & O'BIECUNAS (AV)

Suite 403, 1300 West Olympic Boulevard, 90015
Telephone: 213-487-7550
Fax: 213-382-6095
Mailing Address: P.O. Box 15363, Del Valle Station,
Email: leoatzano@aol.com *URL:* http://www.zolaw.com
Ventura, California Office: 101 South Victoria Avenue.
Telephone: 805-642-8426.
Fax: 805-642-8881. Email: zanoven@aol.com.

Thomas Zide
Leo G. O'Biecunas, Jr.

OF COUNSEL

Douglas M. Kaye

ASSOCIATE

Marcella C. Oka

For full biographical listings, see the Martindale-Hubbell Law Directory

NEWPORT BEACH, Orange Co.

CAPRETZ & ASSOCIATES (AV)

5000 Birch Street, West Tower Suite 2500, 92660-2139
Telephone: 949-724-3000
Fax: 949-757-2635
URL: http://www.lawyers.com/capretzradcliffe
Email: crlawl@ix.netcom.com *URL:* http://www.CAPRETZ.com

MEMBER OF FIRM

James T. Capretz

OF COUNSEL

William B. Lawless (Not admitted in CA)

LEGAL SUPPORT PERSONNEL

Sandra L. Koop (Law Clerk)

For full biographical listings, see the Martindale-Hubbell Law Directory

*OAKLAND,** Alameda Co.

EDWARD L. BLUM (AV)

201 19th Street, Suite 200, 94612
Telephone: 510-452-4400
Fax: 510-452-4406
Email: edblum@blumlaw.com

For full biographical listings, see the Martindale-Hubbell Law Directory

HARVEY W. STEIN A PROFESSIONAL CORPORATION (AV)

Suite 210 Oakland City Center, 499 Fourteenth Street, 94612
Telephone: 510-763-6233
Fax: 510-832-1717
Email: advocado@pipeline.com

Harvey W. Stein

For full biographical listings, see the Martindale-Hubbell Law Directory

*RIVERSIDE,** Riverside Co.

HAIGHT, BROWN & BONESTEEL, L.L.P. (AV)

A Partnership including Professional Corporations
California Tower, 3737 Main Street, Suite 800, 92501
Telephone: 909-341-8300
FAX: 909-341-8309
URL: http://www.hbblaw.com
Santa Monica, California Office: 1620 26th Street, Suite 4000 North, P.O. Box 680.
Telephone: 310-449-6000.
Telecopier: 310-829-5117.
Telex: 705837.
Santa Ana, California Office: Suite 900, 5 Hutton Centre Drive.
Telephone: 714-754-1100.
Telecopier: 714-754-0826.
San Francisco, California Office: 100 Bush Street, 27th Floor.
Telephone: 415-986-7700.
Fax: 415-986-6945.
San Diego, California Office: 101 West Broadway, Suite 1000.
Telephone: 619-595-5583.
Fax: 619-595-7873.

RESIDENT MEMBER

Mark S. Lester

For full biographical listings, see the Martindale-Hubbell Law Directory

*SAN DIEGO,** San Diego Co.

CHAPIN SHEA MCNITT & CARTER, A PROFESSIONAL CORPORATION (AV)

Library, 501 West Broadway, 15th Floor, 92101
Telephone: 619-232-4261
Telefax: 619-232-4840
Email: info@chapinlaw.com *URL:* http://www.chapinlaw.com
Los Angeles, California Office: 12424 Wilshire Boulevard, 9th Floor, 90025.
Telephone: 310-826-0133.
Telefax: 310-207-4236.

Dave Carothers
Edward D. Chapin
Shirley A. Gauvin
Aaron H. Katz
Andrew G. Loeb
Earl H. Maas III
Roger L. McNitt
Steven A. Micheli
Maria C. Roberts
Lawrence W. Shea, II
Nancy L. Vaughan
Peter C. Ward

COUNSEL

Daniel P. Groszkruger
Arthur W. Jones
Thomas P. Redick

Brian A. Barnhorst
Christina A. Bernstein
Kelli Jean Brooks
Jeffery L. Caufield
Daniel W. Coffey
Amy K. Cressey-Yates
Daniel J. Curran
Glen F. Dorgan
Natasha L. Drew
Jeffrey S. Eddington
Patrick M. Howe
Bruno W. Katz
Brian Maienschein
Peter B. Maretz
Carmen M. Mosier McCormick
Jeffrey K. Miyamoto
Leticia Olivarez
Mark T. Petersen
James H. Prenton
Amanda M. Rowe
Patricia L. Sullivan
Brandy Thompson-Cody
Heather K. Van Blarcom

LOS ANGELES OFFICE

Craig H. Bell
John J. Calvagna
Richard D. Carter
Robert Ehrenreich
Leslie J. Eng
Tina Fisher
Ronald F. Gari
Neil R. Gunny
Daniel S. Imber
Shaun Dabby Jacobs
Robin James
Dana Marie Lawson

(See Next Column)

CHAPIN SHEA MCNITT & CARTER A PROFESSIONAL CORPORATION, *San Diego—Continued*

LOS ANGELES OFFICE (Continued)

Jeffrey J. Leist
David A. Myers
Charles F. Peterson
Steven J. Renshaw
Mark Schaeffer
Mark M. Senior
Erin C. Slape
Howard J. Smith
Jeffrey C. Stodel
Stephen Z. Vegh
Irwin Waldman (A P.C.)

For full biographical listings, see the Martindale-Hubbell Law Directory

DUCKOR SPRADLING & METZGER, A LAW CORPORATION (AV)

401 West A Street, Suite 2400, 92101-7909
Telephone: 619-231-3666
Telecopier: 619-231-6629
Email: dsm@dsm-law.com *URL:* http://www.dsm-law.com

Michael J. Duckor
Gary J. Spradling
Scott L. Metzger
John C. Wynne
John W. Cutchin
Robert L. Kenny
Li-An C. Leonard
Stephen A. Bond
R. Anthony Mahavier
Robin Assaf Wofford
K. Jill Osmars
Stephen A. Colley
Kevin M. Bagley
Robert J. Solis
John J. Freni

Jamie M. Ryan
Pamela LaBruyere
James B. Ryan
Gregory P. Olson
Robert M. Shaughnessy
Michael W. Vivoli
Matthew O. Osborne
Scott R. Omohundro
Michael A. Reed

Representative Clients: Computer Sciences Corp.; E & J Gallo Wineries; General Electric Capital Corp.; Great Western Bank; Pathology Medical Laboratories; Princess Resorts; Sedgwick James International; Siemens Credit Corp.; Transamerica Financial Services; Chicago Title Ins. Co.

For full biographical listings, see the Martindale-Hubbell Law Directory

FERRIS & BRITTON, A PROFESSIONAL CORPORATION (AV)

1600 First National Bank Center, 401 West A Street, 92101
Telephone: 619-233-3131
Fax: 619-232-9316
Email: manager@ferrisbritton.com *URL:* http://www.ferrisbritton.com

Alfred G. Ferris
Tamara K. Fogg
Gary T. Moyer
Margaret Prodanov

Representative Clients: Cox Communications, Inc.; Datel, Inc.; Enterprise Rent-a-Car; Exxon; Frontier Analytics, Inc.; Peninsula Bank; Teleport Communications Group; Southwest Airlines; Terminix International, Co.; ZyGam, Inc.

For Complete List of Firm Personnel, See General Section

For full biographical listings, see the Martindale-Hubbell Law Directory

HOVEY & KIRBY, A PROFESSIONAL CORPORATION (AV)

402 West Broadway, Suite 1500, 92101
Telephone: 619-685-4000
Fax: 619-685-4004
Email: administrator@hoveylaw.com

Dean T. Kirby, Jr.
M. Leslie Hovey
Geraldine A. Valdez

For full biographical listings, see the Martindale-Hubbell Law Directory

KENNERSON SCHWARTZ SEMERDJIAN & HAILE LLP (AV)

A Limited Liability Partnership
101 West Broadway, Suite 810, 92101
Telephone: 619-236-8821
Facsimile: 619-236-8827
URL: http://www.lawyers.com/ksshlaw

OF COUNSEL

Paul R. Kennerson

MEMBERS OF FIRM

Ross J. Schwartz
Dick A. Semerdjian
Jeffrey A. Haile

James R. Ballard
John K. Grant

For full biographical listings, see the Martindale-Hubbell Law Directory

LINDLEY, SCALES & CORBETT, A PROFESSIONAL CORPORATION (AV)

550 West C Street, Suite 1800, 92101
Telephone: 619-234-9181
Fax: 619-234-8475
Email: lsc@adnc.com

(See Next Column)

Luke R. Corbett

Representative Clients: Palomar Savings & Loan Assn.; Northern Trust Bank of California, N.A.; Bank United.

For full biographical listings, see the Martindale-Hubbell Law Directory

SOLOMON WARD SEIDENWURM & SMITH, LLP (AV)

1200 Wells Fargo Plaza, 401 B Street, 92101
Telephone: 619-231-0303
Telecopier: 619-231-4755
Email: mvafi@swsslaw.com *URL:* http://www.swsslaw.com

PARTNERS OF FIRM

Michael D. Breslauer
Cynthia L. Eldred
Lawrence J. Kaplan (P.C.)
Richard E. McCarthy
Edward J. McIntyre
Paul S. Metsch
Alison L. Pivonka
Harry J. Proctor (P.C.)
Jeffrey A. Schneider
Richard L. Seidenwurm (P.C.)
Jeffrey H. Silberman
Miguel A. Smith
Norman L. Smith
Herbert J. Solomon

ASSOCIATES

Daniel E. Gardenswartz
David T. Gluck
Amy Perkins Melden
Karl A. Sandoval
Kurt E. Scheuerman
Elizabeth A. Trevino

OF COUNSEL

Robert F. La Scala
William O. Ward, III (Retired)

For full biographical listings, see the Martindale-Hubbell Law Directory

*SAN FRANCISCO,** San Francisco Co.

LAW OFFICES OF KEVIN W. FINCK (AV)

Two Embarcadero Center, Suite 1670, 94111
Telephone: 415-296-9100
Facsimile: 415-394-6446
Email: kfinck@flash.net

OF COUNSEL

Marla Raucher Osborn

For full biographical listings, see the Martindale-Hubbell Law Directory

JENKINS, GOODMAN & NEUMAN (AV)

417 Montgomery Street, 10th Floor, 94104
Telephone: 415-705-0400
FAX: 415-705-0411
URL: http://www.jgn.com

MEMBERS OF FIRM

Charles D. Jenkins
Joshua S. Goodman
Farley J. Neuman

ASSOCIATES

Pavan L. Rosati
Helen P. Bequette
Charles E. Perkins
Anjali Talwar
John S. Throckmorton
Paul P. DeAngelis
Jan C. Morimoto
Charles H. Taylor

For full biographical listings, see the Martindale-Hubbell Law Directory

ROSEN, BIEN & ASARO (AV)

Eighth Floor, 155 Montgomery Street, 94104
Telephone: 415-433-6830
Fax: 415-433-7104
Email: rba@rbalaw.com

Sanford Jay Rosen
Michael W. Bien
Andrea G. Asaro

Thomas Nolan
William H. D. Fernholz
Shana J. Margolis
Ernest J. Galvan

For full biographical listings, see the Martindale-Hubbell Law Directory

*SAN JOSE,** Santa Clara Co.

CAMPEAU & THOMAS, A LAW CORPORATION (AV)

Market Post Tower, 55 South Market Street, Suite 1660, 95113
Telephone: 408-295-9555
Fax: 408-295-6606
URL: http://www.campeaulaw.com

Kenneth J. Campeau
Wayne H. Thomas
Scott L. Goodsell
Kathryn J. Diemer

Marc L. Pinckney
Kathryn Infante
Judith L. Whitman

For full biographical listings, see the Martindale-Hubbell Law Directory

San Jose—Continued

Hopkins & Carley, A Law Corporation (AV)

Sixth Floor, 2 West Santa Clara Street, 95113-1824
Telephone: 408-286-9800
Facsimile: 408-998-4790
Mailing Address: P.O. Box 1469, San Jose, CA, 95109-1469
URL: http://www.hopkinscarley.com

Garth E. Pickett
Arthur V. Plank
Stephen J. Kottmeier
Jon Michaelson
Ross G. Adler
Jeffrey E. Essner
William S. Klein
Robert O. Whyte
Jay M. Ross
Linda Larson Usoz

John W. Easterbrook
Mark R. Figueiredo
Phillip K. Wang
Denise Y. Yamamoto

For Complete List of Firm Personnel, See General Section

For full biographical listings, see the Martindale-Hubbell Law Directory

*SANTA ANA,** Orange Co.

Dean P. Sperling (AV)

201 East Sandpointe, Suite 470, 92707-5742
Telephone: 714-438-8090
Facsimile: 714-438-8088
Email: dsperling@sperlinglaw.com *URL:* http://www.sperlinglaw.com

For full biographical listings, see the Martindale-Hubbell Law Directory

SANTA MONICA, Los Angeles Co.

O'Neill, Lysaght & Sun LLP (AV)

100 Wilshire Boulevard, Suite 700, 90401
Telephone: 310-451-5700
Telecopier: 310-399-7201

Brian O'Neill
Brian C. Lysaght
Frederick D. Friedman
Brian A. Sun
Yolanda Orozco
John M. Moscarino
Harriet Beegun Leva
Edward A. Klein
Robert L. Meylan
David E. Rosen
Paul D. Murphy

Ellyn S. Garofalo
Brian D. Hershman
Katharine A. Kates
Luan K. Phan
Kyle Y. Hoshide
Hersh Heather Elizabeth
Catherine D. Whiting

OF COUNSEL
J. Joseph Connolly

Reference: Wells Fargo Bank, Santa Monica.

For full biographical listings, see the Martindale-Hubbell Law Directory

TORRANCE, Los Angeles Co.

Ronald D. Ellis (AV)

4302 Mesa Street, 90505
Telephone: 310-387-4533
Fax: 310-375-5997
URL: http://www.lawyers.com/rdellislaw

For full biographical listings, see the Martindale-Hubbell Law Directory

COLORADO

*BOULDER,** Boulder Co.

French & Stone, P.C. (AV)

720 Pearl Street, 80302
Telephone: 303-449-3891
Fax: 303-449-3992

Joseph C. French
Robert W. Stone
Gary S. Mallo
David M. Haynes
Mark M. Haynes

Reference: Bank of Boulder.

For full biographical listings, see the Martindale-Hubbell Law Directory

*COLORADO SPRINGS,** El Paso Co.

Flynn McKenna Wright & Karsh (AV)

limited liability company
Plaza of the Rockies 111 South Tejon, Suite 202, 80903-3300
Telephone: 719-578-8444
Fax: 719-578-8836

(See Next Column)

OF COUNSEL
James T. Flynn

MEMBERS OF FIRM
R. Tim McKenna
Bruce M. Wright
Randolph M. Karsh
Brian T. Murphy
Michael C. Potarf
Karl A. Berg, Jr.

Representative Clients: Western National Bank; Tour Ice National, Inc.; Chase Manhattan Mortgage Corp.; Colorado Bank and Trust Company of La Junta; Merrill Lynch Credit Corporation; Community Health Centers; JNC Enterprises; Daniels Motors; Colorado Springs Health Partners.

For full biographical listings, see the Martindale-Hubbell Law Directory

*DENVER,** Denver Co.

Ballard Spahr Andrews & Ingersoll, LLP (AV)

Seventeenth Street Plaza Building, Suite 2300, 1225 17th Street, 80202-5596
Telephone: 303-292-2400
Fax: 303-296-3956
URL: http://www.ballardspahr.com
Baltimore, Maryland Office: 300 East Lombard Street. 19th Floor.
Telephone: 410-528-5600.
Fax: 410-528-5650.
Camden, New Jersey Office: 800 Hudson Square, 5th Floor.
Telephone: 856-541-5577.
Fax: 856-541-8272.
Philadelphia, Pennsylvania Office: 1735 Market Street, 51st Floor.
Telephone: 215-665-8500.
Fax: 215-864-8999.
Salt Lake City, Utah Office: One Utah Center, Suite 1200, 201 South Main Street.
Telephone: 801-531-3000.
Fax: 801-531-3001.
Voorhees, New Jersey Office: Suite 100, 1101 Laurel Oak Drive.
Telephone: 856-627-8555.
Fax: 856-627-1153.
Washington, D.C. Office: Suite 1000 South, 601 13th Street, N.W.
Telephone: 202-661-2200.
Fax: 202-661-2299.

Thomas H. Duncan

For Complete List of Firm Personnel, See General Section

For full biographical listings, see the Martindale-Hubbell Law Directory

Birge & Mayers, P.C. (AV)

1700 Broadway, Suite 1501, 80290
Telephone: 303-860-7100
Facsimile: 303-860-7338
URL: http://www.lawyers.com/birgemayerslaw
St. Louis, Missouri Office: 8000 Maryland Avenue, #250, 63105.
Telephone: 314-236-2203.
Telecopy: 314-236-2401.

Thomas D. Birge

Carla B. Minckley

SPECIAL COUNSEL
Terry L. Lister

For full biographical listings, see the Martindale-Hubbell Law Directory

Carpenter & Klatskin, P.C. (AV)

1500 Denver Club Building, 518 Seventeenth Street, 80202
Telephone: 303-534-6315
Telecopier: 303-534-0514

Willis V. Carpenter
Andrew S. Klatskin

Judith C. McNerny

OF COUNSEL
Robert R. Marshall, Jr.

LEGAL SUPPORT PERSONNEL
PARALEGAL
Holly S. Hoxeng

Reference: Colorado State Bank and Trust.

For full biographical listings, see the Martindale-Hubbell Law Directory

Dufford & Brown, P.C. (AV)

1700 Broadway, Suite 1700, 80290-1701
Telephone: 303-861-8013
Facsimile: 303-832-3804
Colorado Springs, Colorado Office: 101 N. Tejon, Suite 410.
Telephone: 719-471-0559.
Facsimile: 719-471-0583.
Affiliated Office: Solomon, Pearl, Blum & Quinn, L.L.P., New York, NY and Denver, Colorado.

(See Next Column)

DUFFORD & BROWN P.C., *Denver—Continued*

Thomas G. Brown
Richard L. Fanyo
Randall J. Feuerstein
S. Kirk Ingebretsen

Michael Roch

OF COUNSEL

Morris B. Hecox, Jr.

Representative Clients: CF&I Steel, L.P.; The Colorado and Wyoming Railway Co.; GT Land Colorado Inc.; Hall and Hall Mortgage Corporation; Hewlett Packard Co.

For Complete List of Firm Personnel, See General Section

For full biographical listings, see the Martindale-Hubbell Law Directory

GRUND & BRESLAU, P.C. (AV)

303 East Seventeenth Avenue, Suite 303, 80203-1263
Telephone: 303-830-7770
Facsimile: 303-830-2313
Email: g&b@grundbreslau.com

Brad W. Breslau
Della S. Nelson
Julie J. Noonan
Graden P. Jackson

Representative Clients: Amoco Production Co.; Basic Capital Management, Inc.; Chevron U.S.A. Production Co.; Citywide Banks; Colorado Farm Bureau Mutual Insurance Co.; Gallagher, Bassett Services, Inc.; McKesson Corp.; Scott Aviation.

For full biographical listings, see the Martindale-Hubbell Law Directory

MONTGOMERY LITTLE & MCGREW, P.C. (AV)

The Quadrant, 5445 DTC Parkway, Suite 800 (Englewood), 80111
Telephone: 303-773-8100
Telecopier: 303-220-0412
URL: http://www.mlmpc.com

James J. Soran, III
Debra Piazza
Michael H. Smith
Rebecca B. Givens

Joel A. Mayo

OF COUNSEL

Thomas C. Deline
David M. Treadwell

Representative Clients: BP Amoco; Bristol-Myers Squibb; Colorado Medical Society; Cyprus Minerals; Dillon Cos., Inc., d/b/a King Soopers; The St. Paul Insurance Cos.; University of Colorado Health Sciences Center; HealthOne; Regency Realty Corp.; Koch Industries.

For Complete List of Firm Personnel, See General Section

For full biographical listings, see the Martindale-Hubbell Law Directory

MYER, SWANSON, ADAMS & WOLF, P.C. (AV)

The Colorado State Bank Building, 1600 Broadway, Suite 1480, 80202-4915
Telephone: 303-866-9800
Facsimile: 303-866-9818

Fred E. Neef (1910-1986)
Rendle Myer (1929-1999)
Allan B. Adams
Thomas J. Wolf

John M. Anderson
Karen S. Proc

OF COUNSEL

Robert Swanson

Representative Clients: The Oppenheimer Funds; Panorama Series Fund; The Centennial Trusts; Mile High Chapter of American Red Cross; Master Lease; Heartland Management Co.; Kan-Build of Colorado, Inc.
Reference: The Colorado State Bank and Trust of Denver.

For full biographical listings, see the Martindale-Hubbell Law Directory

SENN LEWIS & VISCIANO, P.C. (AV)

1801 California Street, Suite 4300, 80202
Telephone: 303-298-1122
Facsimile: 303-296-9101

Mark A. Senn
Fredric J. Lewis
Frank W. Visciano
Stephen W. Arent

Ellen Kirschenbaum

Rosemarie E. Delmonte
Luis A. Toro
Margie J. Titus
Vivian Lee Perla

OF COUNSEL

Lawrence A. Atler
Brenda Jansen

For Complete List of Firm Personnel, See General Section

For full biographical listings, see the Martindale-Hubbell Law Directory

*DURANGO,** La Plata Co.

FRANK J. ANESI (AV)

Suite 220, 835 East Second Avenue, P.O. Box 2185, 81302
Telephone: 970-247-9246
Fax: 970-259-2793
Email: fjanesi@frontier.net

References: First National Bank of Durango; Burns Bank, Durango.

For full biographical listings, see the Martindale-Hubbell Law Directory

ENGLEWOOD, Arapahoe Co.

BURG SIMPSON ELDREDGE & HERSH, P.C. (AV)

40 Inverness Drive East, 80112
Telephone: 303-792-5595
Fax: 303-708-0527
URL: http://www.burgsimpson.com
Cody, Wyoming Office: 1135 14th Street.
Telephone: 307-527-7891.
Fax: 307-527-7897.
Sterling, Colorado Office: 131 Hamilton Street.
Telephone: 970-521-1010.

Michael S. Burg
Peter W. Burg
Alan K. Simpson (Not admitted in CO)
Scott J. Eldredge
David P. Hersh
Thomas W. Henderson
Matthew R. Giacomini
Kerry N. Jardine
William L. Simpson (Not admitted in CO)
Colin M. Simpson (Not admitted in CO)

Kieth Van Doren
Matthew S. McElhiney
Rosemary Orsini
Robb A. Nelson
Holly S. Baer
Diane Vaksdal Smith
Joseph M. Kiple
Douglas J. Kotarek
David K. Te Selle
Tiffanie D. Stasiak

OF COUNSEL

Dale J. Coplan

Representative Clients: AT&T; Budget Rent-A-Car; Communications World International, Inc.; Coors Brewing Co.; CWE, Inc.; Del Webb Commercial Properties Corp.; Douglas Toyota; First Interstate Bank of Denver, N.A.; Independence Funding Company, LLC.; Safeway, Inc.

For full biographical listings, see the Martindale-Hubbell Law Directory

KING • PETERSON • DYMOND LLP (AV)

The Edward Building, 8400 E. Prentice Avenue, Suite 1040, 80111
Telephone: 303-793-3400
Facsimile: 303-793-3678
Email: mail@kpdlaw.com *URL:* Http://www.kpdlaw.com

MEMBERS OF FIRM

Richard G. Peterson
Lewis W. Dymond, Jr.

Michael W. Reagor

ASSOCIATE

Michael S. Deen

OF COUNSEL

Charles E. King

For full biographical listings, see the Martindale-Hubbell Law Directory

CONNECTICUT

CHESHIRE, New Haven Co.

WINTERS & FORTE (AV)

Waverly Professional Park, 315 Highland Avenue, Suite 102, P.O. Box 844, 06410
Telephone: 203-272-2927
Fax: 203-271-1222
Email: david.wayne.winters@snet.net *URL:* http://www.snetyp.com/wintersforte

MEMBERS OF FIRM

David Wayne Winters
Michael C. Forte

ASSOCIATE

Anthony R. DePaolo

A List of Representative Clients will be furnished upon request.
References: Bank of Boston, Connecticut; LaFayette American Bank & Trust Co.

For full biographical listings, see the Martindale-Hubbell Law Directory

DANBURY, Fairfield Co.

DRISCOLL, TALARICO, FRIZZELL, OLIVO & DRISCOLL (AV)

142 Deer Hill Avenue, 06810-7727
Telephone: 203-792-8333
Facsimile: 203-778-9570
Email: driscoll@javanet.com
Bethel, Connecticut Office: 235 Greenwood Avenue, 06801-2186.
Telephone: 203-744-5000; 743-5556.
Facsimile: 203-798-7790.
Southbury, Connecticut Office: Three Pomperaug Office Park, Suite 203, P.O. Box 252, 06488-0252.
Telephone: 203-264-9650.
Facsimile: 203-798-2175.

Julius J. Bielizna (1914-1988)
Kenneth H. Murray (1905-1984)
Herbert B. Wanderer (1902-1979)
James C. Driscoll, Jr. (Resident, Southbury Office)
Robert N. Talarico
Thomas A. Frizzell
Steven M. Olivo
James C. Driscoll, III (Resident, Bethel Office)
Jerome A. Mayer
Richard W. Hanna
D. Joseph Lane, Jr.
George S. Papazoglou

For full biographical listings, see the Martindale-Hubbell Law Directory

*HARTFORD,** Hartford Co.

GORDON, MUIR AND FOLEY, LLP (AV)

Hartford Square North, Ten Columbus Boulevard, 06106-5123
Telephone: 860-525-5361
Telecopier: 860-525-4849
Email: admin@gmflaw.com *URL:* http://www.gmflaw.com

MEMBERS OF FIRM

William S. Gordon, Jr. (1946-1956)
George Muir (1939-1976)
Edward J. Foley (1955-1983)
Peter C. Schwartz
John J. Reid
John H. Goodrich, Jr.
R. Bradley Wolfe
Jon Stephen Berk
William J. Gallitto
Gerald R. Swirsky
Robert J. O'Brien
Philip J. O'Connor
Kenneth G. Williams
Mary Ann Santacroce
Mary Anne Alicia Charron
Andrew J. Hern
Reneé W. Dwyer
Patty G. Swan

ASSOCIATES

Doreen West Amata
Howard A. Steinman
Erik E. Roberts
Christopher J. Casciani

Reference: People's Bank.

For full biographical listings, see the Martindale-Hubbell Law Directory

SOROKIN, GROSS & HYDE, P.C. (AV)

One Corporate Center, 06103
Telephone: 860-525-6645
Fax: 860-522-1781
Email: sorokin@sorokinlaw.com
Simsbury, Connecticut Office: 720 Hopmeadow Street.
Telephone: 860-651-9348.
Rocky Hill, Connecticut Office: 2360 Main Street.
Telephone: 860-563-9305.
Fax: 860-529-6931.

Jeffery P. Apuzzo
Andrew C. Glassman
Barry D. Greene
John J. Kindl
Keith D. Robbins

Rod W. Farrell
Jeffrey R. Neidle
Gwen P. Weisberg

OF COUNSEL

Joseph D. Hurwitz
Paula G. Pressman

For Complete List of Firm Personnel, See General Section

For full biographical listings, see the Martindale-Hubbell Law Directory

MILFORD, New Haven Co.

BERCHEM, MOSES & DEVLIN, A PROFESSIONAL CORPORATION (AV)

75 Broad Street, 06460-3363
Telephone: 203-783-1200
Facsimile: 203-878-2235; 203-877-8422
URL: http://www.bmd-law.com

Robert L. Berchem
Marsha Belman Moses
Michael P. Devlin
Stephen W. Studer
Richard J. Buturla
Floyd J. Dugas
Kenneth R. Plumb
Lawrence B. Pellegrino

(See Next Column)

Brian A. Lema
Warren L. Holcomb
Michelle C. Laubin
Jonathan David Berchem
Dean R. Singewald

For full biographical listings, see the Martindale-Hubbell Law Directory

*NEW HAVEN,** New Haven Co.

VOTRE & ASSOCIATES, P.C. (AV)

105 Court Street, Suite 302, 06511-6957
Telephone: 203-498-0065
Fax: 203-821-3595
URL: http://www.lawyers.com/votre&associates

Kenneth A. Votre

John-Henry M. Steele

OF COUNSEL

Neil K. Rutter

For full biographical listings, see the Martindale-Hubbell Law Directory

NEW LONDON, New London Co.

WALLER, SMITH & PALMER, P.C. (AV)

52 Eugene O'Neill Drive, P.O. Box 88, 06320
Telephone: 860-442-0367
Telecopier: 860-447-9915
Email: wspmain@snet.net *URL:* http://www.snetyp.com/wallersmithpalmer
Old Lyme Office: 103 Halls Road.
Telephone: 860-434-8063.
Telecopier: 860-434-9452. Email: wspol@snet.net

Robert W. Marrion
Edward B. O'Connell
Frederick B. Gahagan
Tracy M. Collins
Philip M. Johnstone
David P. Condon
Valerie Ann Votto
Charles C. Anderson

General Counsel For: Town of East Lyme.
Counsel For: Citizens Bank of Connecticut; Soneco/Northeastern, Inc.; The Nature Conservancy; Fleet Bank.
Local Counsel For: McCue Mortgage Co.; Citicorp Mortgage; U.S. Department of Housing and Urban Development.

For Complete List of Firm Personnel, See General Section

For full biographical listings, see the Martindale-Hubbell Law Directory

STAMFORD, Fairfield Co.

CURTIS, BRINCKERHOFF & BARRETT, P.C. (AV)

666 Summer Street, 06901-1416
Telephone: 203-324-6777
Telecopier: 203-324-9621
Email: info@curtisbb.com

T. Ward Cleary (1916-1988)
Frederick M. Tobin
John Wayne Fox
Ward Frank Cleary
James D'Alton Murphy
Randolph T. Lovallo

OF COUNSEL

John D. Hertz
Jane F. Donovan
Richard L. Brinckerhoff
Patricia M. Gaug

Susan L. Stratton
Derek Gilman
Michael P. Murray
John J. Louizos

Counsel for: The F. A. Bartlett Tree Expert Co.; Town of Darien; Miller Automobile Corp.; Bolliger, Inc.; Titan Sports; People's Bank, Bridgeport; Fleet Bank; Federal Deposit Insurance Co.; William Pitt Foundation; Wood Logan Associates.

For full biographical listings, see the Martindale-Hubbell Law Directory

WOFSEY, ROSEN, KWESKIN & KURIANSKY, LLP (AV)

600 Summer Street, 06901
Telephone: 203-327-2300
Fax: 203-967-9273

MEMBERS OF FIRM

Abraham Wofsey (1915-1944)
Michael Wofsey (1927-1951)
David M. Rosen (1926-1967)
Julius B. Kuriansky (1952-1992)
Sydney C. Kweskin (1946-1998)
Monroe Silverman
Howard C. Kaplan
Edward M. Kweskin
David M. Cohen
Marshall Goldberg
Stephen A. Finn
Judith Rosenberg
Mark H. Henderson
Steven D. Grushkin
Matthew J. Forstadt
Steven M. Frederick

OF COUNSEL

Saul Kwartin
Emanuel Margolis
Anthony R. Lorenzo

SPECIAL COUNSEL

Day R. Shields

(See Next Column)

WOFSEY, ROSEN, KWESKIN & KURIANSKY LLP, *Stamford—Continued*

ASSOCIATES

Joseph Brachfeld
Eric M. Higgins
William A. Harrison
Daniel M. Young
Angelo A. Ziotas

Representative Clients: Banque Paribas; Benenson Realty; Cellular Information Systems, Inc.; The Chase Manhattan Bank; First County Bank; Hartford Provision Co.; Louis Dreyfus Corp.; Norwalk Federation of Teachers; People's Bank; Ridgeway Shopping Center.

For full biographical listings, see the Martindale-Hubbell Law Directory

DELAWARE

*WILMINGTON,** New Castle Co.

CONNOLLY BOVE LODGE & HUTZ LLP (AV)

1220 Market Street, P.O. Box 2207, 19899-2207
Telephone: 302-658-9141
Telecopier: 302-658-5614
Email: cblhlaw@cblhlaw.com *URL:* http://www.cblhlaw.com

James M. Mulligan, Jr.
Arthur G. Connolly, Jr.
Stanley C. Macel, III
Henry E. Gallagher, Jr.
Richard David Levin
Jeffrey B. Bove
Collins J. Seitz, Jr.
Charles J. Durante
Arthur G. Connolly, III
James D. Heisman
Jeffrey C. Wisler
M. Edward Danberg
Anne Love Barnett
Matthew F. Boyer
Karen C. Bifferato
Samuel D. Brickley II
Thomas A. Stevens

For Complete List of Firm Personnel, See General Section

For full biographical listings, see the Martindale-Hubbell Law Directory

SMITH, KATZENSTEIN & FURLOW LLP (AV)

The Corporate Plaza, 800 Delaware Avenue, P.O. Box 410, 19899
Telephone: 302-652-8400
Fax: 302-652-8405
Email: info@skfdelaware.com *URL:* http://www.SKFDelaware.com

MEMBER OF FIRM

Craig B. Smith

For Complete List of Firm Personnel, See General Section

For full biographical listings, see the Martindale-Hubbell Law Directory

DISTRICT OF COLUMBIA

WASHINGTON, D.C. Co.

BAKER BOTTS L.L.P. (AV)

A Registered Limited Liability Partnership
The Warner, 1299 Pennsylvania Avenue, N.W., 20004-2400
Telephone: 202-639-7700
Fax: 202-639-7832
Email: postmaster@bakerbotts.com *URL:* http://www.bakerbotts.com
Houston, Texas Office: One Shell Plaza, 910 Louisiana.
Telephone: 713-229-1234.
Austin, Texas Office: 1600 San Jacinto Center, 98 San Jacinto Boulevard.
Telephone: 512-322-2500.
Dallas, Texas Office: 2001 Ross Avenue.
Telephone: 214-953-6500.
New York, New York Office: 599 Lexington Avenue.
Telephone: 212-705-5000.
Moscow, Russia Office: 10 ul. Bolshaya Dimitrovka (formerly Pushkinskaya), 103031.
Telephone: 7095/921-5300 (Local); 7501/929-7070 (International).
London, England Office: 45 Ludgate Hill.
Telephone: 0171-778-1400 (Local); 011-44-171-778-1400 (International).
Baku, Azerbaijan Office: 6-10 Vagif Mustafa-zadeh Street, Third Floor, Icheri Sheher, 370004.
Telephone: 994-12-97-63-88 (Local); 011-994-12-97-63-88 (International).

MEMBERS OF FIRM

Kevin B. Dent
James R. Doty
Leslie Anne Freiman
David N. Powers

ASSOCIATES

Michael A. Gold
Jon B. Jordan
Nikesh R. Patel

For Complete List of Firm Personnel, See General Section

For full biographical listings, see the Martindale-Hubbell Law Directory

THE FEINBERG GROUP, LLP (AV)

1120 20th Street, N.W. Suite 740 South, 20036-3437
Telephone: 202-371-1110
Fax: 202-962-9290
Email: kfeinberg@thefeinberggroup.com *URL:* http://www.krfassociates.com
New York, N.Y. Office: 780 3rd Avenue, Suite 2202.
Telephone: 212-527-9600.
Fax: 212-527-9611. Email: kfeinberg@thefeinberggroup.com.

PARTNERS

Kenneth R. Feinberg
Deborah E. Greenspan
Michael K. Rozen
(Resident, New York Office)
Peter H. Woodin
(Resident, New York Office)

ASSOCIATE

Fredric M. Brooks (Not admitted in DC)

SENIOR COUNSEL

Jacqueline E. Zins

For full biographical listings, see the Martindale-Hubbell Law Directory

MARY A. MCREYNOLDS, P.C. (AV)

Suite 400, 888 Sixteenth Street, N.W., 20006
Telephone: 202-835-7455
Telecopier: 202-296-8791
URL: http://www.lawyers.com/maryamcreynolds

Mary A. McReynolds

For full biographical listings, see the Martindale-Hubbell Law Directory

SALTMAN & STEVENS, P.C. (AV)

1801 K Street, N.W. Suite M-110, 20006
Telephone: 202-452-2140
Fax: 202-775-8217

Alan I. Saltman
Gary G. Stevens
Ruth G. Tiger
Kevin Garden

Richard W. Goeken

For full biographical listings, see the Martindale-Hubbell Law Directory

VENABLE ATTORNEYS AT LAW VENABLE, BAETJER, HOWARD & CIVILETTI, LLP (AV)

A Partnership including Professional Corporations
Suite 1000, 1201 New York Avenue, N.W., 20005
Telephone: 202-962-4800
Fax: 202-962-8300
URL: http://www.venable.com
Baltimore, Maryland Office: Venable, Baetjer and Howard LLP, 1800 Mercantile Bank & Trust Building, 2 Hopkins Plaza.
Telephone: 410-244-7400.
Fax: 410-244-7742.
McLean, Virginia Office: Venable, Baetjer and Howard LLP, Suite 400, 2010 Corporate Ridge.
Telephone: 703-760-1600.
Fax: 703-821-8949.
Rockville, Maryland Office: Venable, Baetjer and Howard LLP, Suite 500, One Church Street, P. O. Box 1906.
Telephone: 301-217-5600.
Fax: 301-217-5617.
Towson, Maryland Office: Venable, Baetjer and Howard LLP, 210 Allegheny Avenue, P. O. Box 5517.
Telephone: 410-494-6200.
Fax: 410-821-0147.

MEMBERS OF FIRM

James K. Archibald (Also at Baltimore, Maryland Office)
Kenneth C. Bass, III (Also at McLean, Virginia Office)
Robert J. Bolger, Jr. (Also at Baltimore, Maryland Office)
Neal D. Borden (Not admitted in DC; Also at Baltimore, Maryland Office)
Benjamin R. Civiletti (P.C.) (Also at Baltimore and Towson, Maryland Offices)
Bryson L. Cook (P.C.) (Not admitted in DC; Also at Baltimore, Maryland Office)
William D. Coston
Jeffrey A. Dunn (Also at Baltimore, Maryland Office)
Edward F. Glynn, Jr.
David W. Goewey
Gary M. Hnath
Amy Berman Jackson
Fernand A. Lavallee
Vicki Margolis (Also at Baltimore, Maryland Office)
Charles R. "Rod" Marvin, Jr.
George F. Pappas (Also at Baltimore, Maryland Office)
Michael Schatzow (Also at Baltimore, Maryland Office)
James L. Shea (also at Baltimore, Maryland Office)
Joe A. Shull
Kenneth S. Slaughter

For Complete List of Firm Personnel, See General Section

For full biographical listings, see the Martindale-Hubbell Law Directory

Washington—Continued

VERNER, LIIPFERT, BERNHARD, MCPHERSON AND HAND, CHARTERED (AV)

901 15th Street, N.W., 20005-2301
Telephone: 202-371-6000
Cable Address: "Verlip"
Fax: 202-371-6279
Email: verner.com *URL:* http://www.verner.com
Houston, Texas Office: 1111 Bagby, Suite 4700, 77002.
Telephone: 713-225-7200.
Fax: 713-752-2199.
Honolulu, Hawaii Office: 745 Fort Street, Suite 600, 96813.
Telephone: 808-566-0999.
Fax: 808-566-0995.
Austin, Texas Office: Suite 1440 San Jacinto Center, 98 San Jacinto Boulevard, 78701.
Telephone: 512-703-6000.
Fax: 512-703-6003.
Las Vegas, Nevada Affiliate Office: Gary C. Moss, Hughes Center, 3960 Howard Hughes Parkway, Suite 400, 89109.
Telephone: 702-737-3433.
Fax: 702-737-1612.
Miami, Florida Office: 3100 First Union Financial Center, 200 South Biscayne Boulevard, 33131.
Telephone: 305-371-8801.
Fax: 305-371-6545.

Berl Bernhard
Steven A. Buxbaum (Resident, Houston, Texas Office)
Hopewell H. Darneille, III
Harold I. Freilich
Lloyd N. Hand
Thomas M. Ingoldsby
Lawrence E. Levinson (Not admitted in DC)
Martin Mendelsohn
Lenard M. Parkins (Resident, Houston, Texas Office)
Susan O'Hearn Temkin
John D. Waihee, III (Resident, Honolulu, Hawaii Office)

SPECIAL COUNSEL

Robert J. Dole (Not admitted in DC)
George J. Mitchell

SENIOR COUNSEL

Alvaro Cifuentes de Castro

SENIOR ADVISOR

Ann W. Richards (Resident, Austin, Texas Office)

OF COUNSEL

Howell E. Begle, Jr.
Philip R. Hochberg
John R. Hohlt (Resident, Houston, Texas Office)
James K. Jackson
Frederick J. McConville
Mikol S. B. Neilson
Renton L. K. Nip (Resident, Honolulu, Hawaii Office)
Gene Schleppenbach

For Complete List of Firm Personnel, See General Section

For full biographical listings, see the Martindale-Hubbell Law Directory

WATT, TIEDER, HOFFAR & FITZGERALD, L.L.P. (AV)

601 Pennsylvania Avenue, N.W., Suite 900, 20004
Telephone: 703-749-1000
Telecopier: 703-893-8029
Email: contactus@wthf.com *URL:* http://www.wthf.com
McLean Virginia Office: 7929 Westpark Drive, Suite 400,
Telephone: 703-749-1000.
Telecopier: 703-893-8029.
Irvine California Office: 3 Park Plaza, Suite 1500.
Telephone: 949-852-6700.

MEMBERS OF FIRM

John B. Tieder, Jr.
Robert K. Cox

For full biographical listings, see the Martindale-Hubbell Law Directory

FLORIDA

BOCA RATON, Palm Beach Co.

WEISS & HANDLER, P.A. (AV)

Suite 218A, One Boca Place, 2255 Glades Road, 33431-7313
Telephone: 561-997-9995
Broward: 954-421-5101
Palm Beach: 561-734-8008
Telecopier: 561-997-5280
Email: weisshand@aol.com
West Palm Beach, Florida Office: 505 South Flagler Drive, Suite 1331, 33401.
Telephone: 561-655-3433.
New York, NY Office: 45 Rockefeller Plaza, Suite 1501.
Telephone: 212-332-2900.

Howard I. Weiss
Henry B. Handler

(See Next Column)

Manuel R. Comras
Donald Feldman
William M. Franz
David K. Friedman
Carol A. Kartagener
Allison L. Kay
Bruce A. Harris
Howard M. Rudolph (Resident, West Palm Beach Office)
Stacy E. Welt

OF COUNSEL

Malcolm L. Stein (Not admitted in FL)
Harry Winderman

For full biographical listings, see the Martindale-Hubbell Law Directory

*FORT LAUDERDALE,** Broward Co.

BRIAN C. DEUSCHLE CHARTERED (AV)

800 Southeast Third Avenue Suite 400, 33316
Telephone: 954-763-7200
Facsimile: 954-522-7728
Email: B.C.D.Chartered@worldnet.att.net

Brian C. Deuschle

Christopher D. Hale

Representative Clients: Drexel Investments, Inc.; Seabulk Tankers, Ltd.; Seabulk Chemical Carriers, Inc.; Hvide Marine, Inc.; Eller & Co.; American National Bank.
Approved Attorneys for: Attorneys' Title Insurance Fund; American National Bank; Norwest Mortgage, Inc.

For full biographical listings, see the Martindale-Hubbell Law Directory

MOMBACH, BOYLE & HARDIN, P.A. (AV)

Suite 1950 Broward Financial Centre, 500 East Broward Boulevard, 33394-3079
Telephone: 954-467-2200
Telecopier: 954-467-2210

Geoffrey S. Mombach
Conrad J. Boyle
David C. Hardin
Gary S. Singer

Mark R. Wysocki
John D. Olivier
Douglas L. Roberts
Scott J. Reit
Lawrence B. Steinberg

Representative Clients: BankAtlantic; Citibank, F.S.B.; Shenandoah Life; National Bank of Canada; NationsBank N.A., (South); Keenan Development Group; Net Realty Holding Trust; Original Pancake House Restaurants; Cat Cay Yacht Club.

For full biographical listings, see the Martindale-Hubbell Law Directory

*FORT MYERS,** Lee Co.

PATRICK E. GERAGHTY A PROFESSIONAL ASSOCIATION (AV)

The Courtney Building, Suite 100, 2069 First Street, P.O. Box 1605, 33902-1605
Telephone: 941-334-9500
Fax: 941-334-8930
URL: http://www.lawyers.com/pgeraghty

Patrick E. Geraghty
Thomas M. Dougherty

For full biographical listings, see the Martindale-Hubbell Law Directory

GOLDSTEIN, BUCKLEY, CECHMAN, RICE & PURTZ, P.A. (AV)

1515 Broadway, P.O. Box 2366, 33902-2366
Telephone: 941-334-1146
Fax: 941-334-3039
Email: info@gbclaw.com *URL:* http://www.GBClaw.com
Port Charlotte, Florida Office: Emerald Square, Suite 1, 2852 Tamiami Trail, 33952.
Telephone: 941-624-2393.
Fax: 941-624-2155.
Cape Coral, Florida Office: 1603 Hancock Bridge Parkway, 33990.
Telephone: 941-574-5575.
Fax: 941-574-9213.
Lehigh Acres, Florida Office: 1458 Lee Boulevard, Lee Boulevard Shopping Center, 33936.
Telephone: 941-368-6101.
Fax: 941-368-2461.
Naples, Florida Office: 4947 North Tamiami Trail, Suite 101, 34103.
Telephone: 941-262-4888.
Fax: 941-262-8716.

Stephen W. Buckley
J. Jeffrey Rice

Approved Attorneys for: Attorneys' Title Insurance Fund.

For Complete List of Firm Personnel, See General Section

For full biographical listings, see the Martindale-Hubbell Law Directory

*MIAMI,** Dade Co.

CLARKE SILVERGLATE WILLIAMS & MONTGOMERY (AV)

A Partnership of Professional Corporations
100 North Biscayne Boulevard Suite 2401, 33132
Telephone: 305-377-0700
Facsimile: 305-377-3001
Chicago, Illinois Office: Williams & Montgomery Ltd., 20 North Wacker Drive, Suite 2100.
Telephone: 312-443-3200.
Telex: 206598.
Facsimile: 312-443-1323.
Waukegan, Illinois Office: Williams & Montgomery Ltd., 20 S. Utica.
Telephone: 847-360-1220.
Wheaton, Illinois Office: Williams & Montgomery Ltd., 310 S. County Farm Road.
Telephone: 630-690-3200.
Joliet, Illinois Office: Williams & Montgomery Ltd., 81 North Chicago Avenue.
Telephone: 815-727-2653.

Mercer K. Clarke — Spencer H. Silverglate

OF COUNSEL

Henry H. Bolz, III

ASSOCIATES

Kelly Anne Luther — Spencer T. Kuvin
Richard R. Cochran — Francisco Ramos, Jr.
William J. Dimmig — Edward J. Pfister
Cynthia R. Bernard — John C. Schlesinger

For full biographical listings, see the Martindale-Hubbell Law Directory

COLSON, HICKS, EIDSON, COLSON, MATTHEWS, MARTINEZ & MENDOZA (AV)

Floor 47 First Union Financial Center, 200 South Biscayne Boulevard, 33131-2351
Telephone: 305-373-5400
Fax: 305-374-4796
URL: http://www.colson.com/

MEMBERS OF FIRM

William M. Hicks (1928-1996) — Roberto Martinez
Bill Colson — Enid Duany Mendoza
Mike Eidson — Julie Braman Kane
Dean C. Colson — Robert H. Fernandez
Joseph M. Matthews — Joseph J. Kalbac, Jr.
Daniel Uhlfelder

Reference: Northern Trust Bank of Florida.

For full biographical listings, see the Martindale-Hubbell Law Directory

KAREN EVANS LITIGATION RESOLUTION, INC. (AV)

169 East Flagler Street, Suite 1200, 33131
Telephone: 305-371-3250
Facsimile: 305-371-3341
Email: LitResInc@aol.com

Karen Evans

For full biographical listings, see the Martindale-Hubbell Law Directory

HALL, DAVID AND JOSEPH, P.A. (AV)

Penthouse 1428 Brickell Avenue, P.O. Box 019113, 33131-9113
Telephone: 305-374-5030
Fax: 305-374-5033

Andrew C. Hall — Christopher M. David
Allan A. Joseph

Adam S. Hall — Ilene Schnall
Michael L Cotzen — Santiago A. Cueto
Kimberly S. Rogers

For full biographical listings, see the Martindale-Hubbell Law Directory

LIGMAN, MARTIN & EVANS, P.L. (AV)

230 Catalonia Avenue, 33134-6705
Telephone: 305-445-2682
Fax: 305-445-6571
Email: lmepl@gateway.net
Pompano Beach Office: 1280 S.W. 36th Avenue, Suite 303.
Telephone: (954) 9689922.
Fax: (954) 968-9933.
South Dade Office: Dadeland Towers North, 9200 S. Dadeland Boulevard, Suite 700, Miami Florida, 33156.
Telephone: 305-670-6000.
Fax: 305-670-6068.
West Palm Beach Office: 201 Arkana Court, West Palm Beach, Florida, 33401.
Telephone: 561-835-9809.

(See Next Column)

Michael G. Martin (1935-1981) — James M. Redmond
Daniel V. Ligman (P.A.) — Donald F. Harrington
Gordon J. Evans (P.A.) — D. Brent Davis
Joseph W. Ligman (P.A.) — Richard Giardino
John J. Phillips, Jr. — George A. David
Gregory J Prusak — Michael R. Seward

For full biographical listings, see the Martindale-Hubbell Law Directory

SIEGFRIED, RIVERA, LERNER, DE LA TORRE & SOBEL, P.A. (AV)

Suite 1102, 201 Alhambra Circle (Coral Gables), 33134
Telephone: 305-442-3334
Fax: 305-443-3292
URL: http://www.siegfriedlaw.com

Steven M. Siegfried — Peter H. Edwards
Oscar R. Rivera — Stuart H. Sobel
Lisa A. Lerner — Maria Victoria Arias
Helio De La Torre — James F. Harrington
Elisabeth D. Kozlow

Gary Louis Brown — Fern F. Musselwhite
David B. Israel — Grissel C. Picot
Laura Michelle Manning — Marc C. Pugliese

OF COUNSEL

H. Hugh Mc Connell

For full biographical listings, see the Martindale-Hubbell Law Directory

VALLE & CRAIG, P.A. (AV)

Suite 2520 World Trade Center, 80 Southwest Eighth Street, P.O. Box 113009, 33111-3009
Telephone: 305-373-2888; 800-609-6151
Facsimile: 305-373-2889

Laurence F. Valle — Lawrance B. Craig, III
Timothy Maze Hartley

Frank J. Sioli, Jr. — Michael A. Vasquez
Michael J. Lynott — Brian M. McKell

For full biographical listings, see the Martindale-Hubbell Law Directory

*ORLANDO,** Orange Co.

MORAN & SHAMS, P.A. (AV)

111 North Orange Avenue, Suite 1200, P.O. Box 472, 32802-0472
Telephone: 407-841-4141
Fax: 407-841-4148
Email: moran-shams@moran-shams.com

Thomas P. Moran — Robert S. MacDonald
Maurice Shams — Christopher C. Skambis

Jennifer S. Eden — Lawrence H. Haber

Representative Clients: Adventist Health System Sunbelt Healthcare Corporation; China Group, Inc.; Cruises Only, LLC; Gencor Industries Inc.; Hartman & Associates, Inc.; Manpower of Cedar Rapids and Central Florida; MEDai, Inc.; Presbyterian Retirement Communities, Inc.; Travel Services International, Inc.; Vermont American Corporation.

For full biographical listings, see the Martindale-Hubbell Law Directory

O'NEILL, CHAPIN, LIEBMAN & COOPER (AV)

A Partnership including Professional Associations
865 Eola Park Center, 200 East Robinson Street, 32801
Telephone: 407-425-2751
Telex: 407-423-1192

Bernard C. O'Neill, Jr. (P.A.) — John B. Liebman (P.A.)
Mark O. Cooper (P.A.)

ASSOCIATE

Rod C. Lundy

OF COUNSEL

Bruce E. Chapin (P.A.)

Reference: First Union National Bank.

For full biographical listings, see the Martindale-Hubbell Law Directory

POHL & SHORT, P.A.

(See Winter Park)

*SARASOTA,** Sarasota Co.

NELSON • HESSE (AV)

2070 Ringling Boulevard, P.O. Box 2524, 34230
Telephone: 941-366-7550
Fax: 941-955-3708

(See Next Column)

NELSON • HESSE—*Continued*

MEMBERS OF FIRM

Richard E. Nelson
Ronald Alexander Cyril (1938-1988)
Richard L. Smith
F. Steven Herb
Omer S. Causey
William A. Dooley
Michael S. Drews
Frederick J. Elbrecht
Gary W. Peal

ASSOCIATES

J. Neal Mobley
J. Corey Feist
Alison Hosmer

General Counsel for: Provident Bank; Dooley Mack Construction Co.
Representative Clients: Wellcraft Marine; American Marine Holdings; Vanliner Insurance; Time Warner Cable; SMH Radiology, Inc.; The Carlton Ranch, Inc.
References: Southtrust Bank; Provident Bank.

For full biographical listings, see the Martindale-Hubbell Law Directory

*STUART,** Martin Co.

MCCARTHY, SUMMERS, BOBKO, MCKEY, WOOD & SAWYER, P.A. (AV)

2081 East Ocean Boulevard, Second Floor, 34996
Telephone: 561-286-1700
Fax: 561-283-1803
URL: http://www.mcsumm.com

Terence P. McCarthy
Robert P. Summers
Noel A. Bobko
John D. McKey, Jr.
Steven J. Wood
Thomas R. Sawyer
Nicola J. Boone
Steven L. Perry

Kathryn C. Bass
Robert N. Maitland, II

Representative Clients: First National Bank and Trust Company of the Treasure Coast; Hydratech Utilities; Lost Lake at Hobe Sound; Gary Player Design Group; YMCA of Martin County; Shadow Lakes Groves, Inc.; Merrill Lynch Trust Co., (Florida); Wilmington Trust, FSB; The Huntington National Bank, N.A.; WSTU-Radio, WTCN-TV.

For full biographical listings, see the Martindale-Hubbell Law Directory

*TALLAHASSEE,** Leon Co.

MCFARLAIN, WILEY, CASSEDY & JONES, PROFESSIONAL ASSOCIATION (AV)

215 South Monroe Street, Suite 600, P.O. Box 2174, 32316-2174
Telephone: 850-222-2107
Telecopier: 850-222-8475
Email: firm@mcfarlain.com *URL:* http://www.mcfarlain.com

Richard C. McFarlain
William B. Wiley
Douglas P. Jones
Charles A. Stampelos
H. Darrell White, Jr.
Christopher Barkas
Harold R. Mardenborough, Jr.
Terrell C. Madigan

Robert A. McNeely
P. David Brannon

LEGAL SUPPORT PERSONNEL

Diane L. Doll (Office Manager)

For full biographical listings, see the Martindale-Hubbell Law Directory

*WEST PALM BEACH,** Palm Beach Co.

QUARLES & BRADY LLP (AV)

222 Lakeview Avenue, 4th Floor, 33401
Telephone: 561-653-5000
Fax: 561-653-5333
URL: http://www.quarles.com
Milwaukee, Wisconsin Office: 411 East Wisconsin Avenue, 53202-4497.
Telephone: 414-277-5000.
Fax: 414-271-3552.
Madison, Wisconsin Office: Firstar Plaza, One South Pinckney Street, P.O. Box 2113, 53701-2113.
Telephone: 608-251-5000.
Fax: 608-251-9166.
Naples, Florida Office: Barnett Center, 4501 Tamiami Trail North, Suite 300, 34103-3060.
Telephone: 941-262-5959.
Fax: 941-434-4999.
Phoenix, Arizona Office: One Camelback Building, One East Camelback Road, Suite 400, 85012-1649.
Telephone: 602-230-5500.
Fax: 602-230-5598.
Chicago, Illinois Office: Quarles & Brady LLC, Citicorp Center, 500 West Madison Street, Suite 3700.
Telephone: 312-715-5000.
Fax: 312-715-5155.

(See Next Column)

PARTNERS

Ned R. Nashban
Nancy Berz Colman

For Complete List of Firm Personnel, See General Section

For full biographical listings, see the Martindale-Hubbell Law Directory

SEARCY DENNEY SCAROLA BARNHART & SHIPLEY, PROFESSIONAL ASSOCIATION (AV)

2139 Palm Beach Lakes Boulevard, P.O. Drawer 3626, 33402-3626
Telephone: 561-686-6300
800-780-8607
800-220-7006 (Spanish)
Fax: 561-478-0754
Email: CDS@SEARCYLAW.COM *URL:* http://www.searcylaw.com

John Scarola
F. Gregory Barnhart
C. Calvin Warriner, III
William A. Norton
David J. Sales
William B. King
David J. White

Sean C. Domnick
Ellen F. Brandt

LEGAL SUPPORT PERSONNEL

Emilio Diamantis (Paralegal/Investigator)
John C. Hopkins (Paralegal/Investigator)
J. Peter Love (Paralegal/Investigator)
Kevin J. Walsh (Paralegal/Investigator)

For Complete List of Firm Personnel, See General Section

For full biographical listings, see the Martindale-Hubbell Law Directory

WINTER PARK, Orange Co.

LYON KIRWIN, P.A. (AV Ⓣ)

338 Morse Boulevard, Suite 150, 32789
Telephone: 407-740-6600
Facsimile: 407-740-6363

V. Frederic Lyon
Brian P. Kirwin
Bruce Alan Norris
Brian W. Bennett

James C. Washburn
Michelle B. Kane
Michael D. Chiumento, III

Representative Clients: American Express; Centex-Rooney; City of St. Petersburg; Clancy & Theys Construction Co.; Duke Engineering & Services; Florida Power Corp.; Sea World of Florida; Seminole County, Florida; Seminole County Public Schools; South Florida Water Management District; U.S. Steel.

For full biographical listings, see the Martindale-Hubbell Law Directory

POHL & SHORT, P.A. (AV)

280 West Canton Avenue, Suite 410, P.O. Box 3208, 32790
Telephone: 407-647-7645; 407-647-POHL
Telefax: 407-647-2314
Email: ps@pohlshort.com

Dwight I. Cool
Alexander S. Douglas II
Gary A. Forster
E. Givens Goodspeed
Mark A. Grimes
Robert S. Hoofman
Roger A. Kelly
Adam O. Kirwan
David J. Kohs
Frank L. Pohl
James Everett Shepherd V
Houston E. Short
John R. Simpson, Jr.

Representative Clients: American Generator Co.; Copelco Capital, Inc.; Denim U.S.A., Inc.; Ford Motor Credit Co.; Lodestar Technology, Inc.; Lutheran Brotherhood; SunTrust, N.A.; Trax, Inc.

For full biographical listings, see the Martindale-Hubbell Law Directory

GEORGIA

*ATLANTA,** Fulton Co.

MICHAEL L. CHAPMAN (AV)

Two Midtown Plaza, Suite 1100, 1349 West Peachtree Street, N.E., 30309
Telephone: 404-685-9600
FAX: 404-875-0666
URL: http://www.chapmanfirm.com

For full biographical listings, see the Martindale-Hubbell Law Directory

DAVID G. CROCKETT, P.C. (AV)

1950 Equitable Building, 100 Peachtree Street, N.W., 30303
Telephone: 404-522-4280
Telecopier: 404-589-9891
Email: CROCKLAW@BELLSOUTH.NET

(See Next Column)

DAVID G. CROCKETT, P.C., *Atlanta—Continued*

David G. Crockett

Douglas L. Brooks

LEGAL SUPPORT PERSONNEL

Loraine B. Harps (Paralegal)

Approved Attorney for: Chicago Title Insurance Co.
Reference: NationsBank, N.A.

For full biographical listings, see the Martindale-Hubbell Law Directory

GOLDNER, SOMMERS, SCRUDDER & BASS (AV)

900 Circle 75 Parkway Suite 850, 30339
Telephone: 770-612-9200
Facsimile: 770-612-9201

MEMBERS OF FIRM

Henry E. Scrudder, Jr.
Glenn S. Bass

For Complete List of Firm Personnel, See General Section

For full biographical listings, see the Martindale-Hubbell Law Directory

HAWKINS & PARNELL, LLP (AV)

4000 SunTrust Plaza, 303 Peachtree Street, N.E., 30308-3243
Telephone: 404-614-7400
Fax: 404-614-7500
Email: relliott@hplegal.com *URL:* http://www.hawkinsparnell.com

MEMBERS OF FIRM

Jack N. Sibley
Cullen Christie Wilkerson, Jr.
Christine Lupo Mast
Thomas G. Tidwell

ASSOCIATES

Robert S. Thompson
Michael J. Crist
Carl H. Anderson, Jr.

Representative Clients: Figgie Acceptance Corp.; Figgie Leasing Corp.; Motel 6; Johnson & Higgins; The Breckenridge Group, Inc.; Warren Sewell Clothing Company; Bremen Bowden Investment Company; Sequa Corporation; Trust Company Bank; Quantum Chemical.

For Complete List of Firm Personnel, See General Section

For full biographical listings, see the Martindale-Hubbell Law Directory

HOLT NEY ZATCOFF & WASSERMAN, LLP (AV)

A Partnership including Professional Corporations
100 Galleria Parkway, Suite 600, 30339
Telephone: 770-956-9600
Facsimile: 770-956-1490
Email: mthomas@hnzw.com

MEMBERS OF FIRM

Robert G. Holt (P.C.)
Michael G. Wasserman (P.C.)
Richard P. Vornholt
Brian P. Cain

OF COUNSEL

Penni A. Dudley

ASSOCIATE

Thomas K. Anderson

Representative Clients: First Union National Bank of Georgia; NationsBank, N.A.; Citibank, N.A.; Primavera Financial Services; The University Financing Foundation, Inc.

For Complete List of Firm Personnel, See General Section

For full biographical listings, see the Martindale-Hubbell Law Directory

PIERCE & YOUNG (AV)

Building 1700, 2255 Cumberland Parkway Northwest, 30339-4575
Telephone: 770-435-0500
Telecopier: 770-435-0362

MEMBERS OF FIRM

J. Wayne Pierce
Richard M. Young

For full biographical listings, see the Martindale-Hubbell Law Directory

THOMAS, KENNEDY, SAMPSON & PATTERSON (AV)

3355 Main Street, 30337
Telephone: 404-688-4503
Telecopier: 404-681-2950; Litigation Dept.
Telecopier: 404-684-9515
URL: http://www.tksp.com

MEMBERS OF FIRM

R. E. Thomas, Jr. (1911-1996)
John Loren Kennedy (1942-1994)
Thomas G. Sampson
P. Andrew Patterson
Jeffrey E. Tompkins

ASSOCIATES

Thomas G. Sampson, II
Ceasar C. Mitchell, II.
Erika Nicole Jackson

(See Next Column)

LEGAL SUPPORT PERSONNEL

Gwendolyn C.H. Dixon
Elbetha (Beth) Martin (Paralegal)
Nancy Allen-Haskell
Yvonne Torrence
Shyril E. Beck
Constance Harris (Paralegal)
Lisa Russell Johnson

For full biographical listings, see the Martindale-Hubbell Law Directory

WEISZ & ASSOCIATES (AV)

Suite 900 Live Oak Center, 3475 Lenox Road, N.E., 30326-1232
Telephone: 404-233-7888
Facsimile: 404-261-1925
Email: prw1@bellsouth.net

Peter R. Weisz

ASSOCIATE

Cathy R. Nash

Representative Clients: L.M. Scofield Co.; S. Champion Constr. Co.; Deerfield Construction Co.; Cee Klein Accessories, LTD.
Reference: First Union National Bank.

For full biographical listings, see the Martindale-Hubbell Law Directory

*COLUMBUS,** Muscogee Co.

JACOB BEIL (AV)

Heritage Tower, Suite 301, 18 - 9th Street, P.O. Box 1126, 31902
Telephone: 706-596-9912
Fax: 706-576-5583

Reference: First Union National Bank of Georgia.

For full biographical listings, see the Martindale-Hubbell Law Directory

HATCHER, STUBBS, LAND, HOLLIS & ROTHSCHILD (AV)

A Limited Liability Partnership
Suite 500 The Corporate Center, 233 12th Street, P.O. Box 2707, 31902-2707
Telephone: 706-324-0201
Telecopier: 706-322-7747
Email: mailman@hatcherstubbs.com

MEMBERS OF FIRM

Alan F. Rothschild
Morton A. Harris
J. Barrington Vaught
Charles T. Staples
Joseph L. Waldrep
George W. Mize, Jr.
John M. Tanzine, III
Alan F. Rothschild, Jr.
William C. Pound

General Counsel for: SunTrust Bank, West Georgia, N.A.; TOM'S Foods Inc.; Georgia Crown Distributing Co.; Bill Heard Enterprises, Inc.; Rehabilitation Services; Spectrum Stores Inc.; Flournoy Development Company; The Jordan Company.
Local Counsel for: AFLAC, Inc.

For Complete List of Firm Personnel, See General Section

For full biographical listings, see the Martindale-Hubbell Law Directory

*MARIETTA,** Cobb Co.

W. ALLEN SEPARK (AV)

250 Church Street, Second Floor, P.O. Box 3475, 30061-3475
Telephone: 770-422-3200
Fax: 770-514-1148

Representative Clients: Martin's Restaurant Systems, Inc.; Snowden Enterprises, Inc.; Sparkles Roller Rinks; Bearden & Smith, P.C.; The Halifax Group, Inc. formerly Oak Hill Farms, Inc.; Southern Polytechnic State University Foundation, Inc.; Metro North Youth Soccer Association, Inc.; Wellstar Foundation, Inc. formerly PROMINA Northwest Health Foundation, Inc.; The Georgia Ballet, Inc.

For full biographical listings, see the Martindale-Hubbell Law Directory

WILES AND WILES (AV)

Suite 800, 1850 Parkway Place, 30067-8260
Telephone: 770-426-4619
Fax: 770-426-4846
Email: wiles@evict.net

MEMBERS OF FIRM

John J. Wiles
Janet Hughes Wiles
N. Jackson Cotney, Jr.

ASSOCIATE

Susann Deborah Estroff

Representative Clients: The Equitable Life Assurance Society of the United States; John Portman Properties; Carter & Associates; Principle Mutual Life Insurance Company; Regency Realty; Trammell Crow; Cousins Properties, Inc.; CB Richard Ellis.

For full biographical listings, see the Martindale-Hubbell Law Directory

*NEWNAN,** Coweta Co.

ROSENZWEIG, JONES & MACNABB, P.C. (AV)

32 South Court Square, P.O. Box 220, 30264
Telephone: 770-253-3282
Fax: 770-251-7262

George C. Rosenzweig
Sidney Pope Jones, Jr.
Joseph P. MacNabb

Charles C. Witcher
Douglas L. Dreyer
Jonathan W. Hickman

Approved Attorneys for: Lawyers Title Insurance Corp.; Chicago Title Insurance Co.

For full biographical listings, see the Martindale-Hubbell Law Directory

NORCROSS, Gwinnett Co.

WALLACE & DE MAYO, P.C. (AV)

6356 Corley Road, 30071-1704
Telephone: 770-446-9996
Fax: 770-368-8331

Richard T. De Mayo

For full biographical listings, see the Martindale-Hubbell Law Directory

*SAVANNAH,** Chatham Co.

KARSMAN, BROOKS & CALLAWAY, P.C. (AV)

301 West Congress Street, P.O. Box 9149, 31412
Telephone: 912-238-2750
Cable Address: "Karbro"
Telecopier: 912-238-2767

Stanley M. Karsman
Charles C. Brooks
Timothy F. Callaway, III
Stanley E. Harris, Jr.
James L. Drake, Jr.
Dana F. Braun
R. Krannert Riddle
Edward M. Hughes
Timothy J. Haeussler

For full biographical listings, see the Martindale-Hubbell Law Directory

HAWAII

*HONOLULU,** Honolulu Co.

BAYS, DEAVER, HIATT, LUNG & ROSE (AV)

A Partnership including Professional Corporations
16th Floor, Alii Place, 1099 Alakea Street, P.O. Box 1760, 96806
Telephone: 808-523-9000
Telecopier: 808-533-4184
Telex: RCA 7238976
Email: bdhlr@aloha.net *URL:* http://www.bdhlr.com
Kamuela, Hawaii Office: Suite 204 Parker Square, 65-1279 Kawaihae Road.
Telephone: 808-885-3400.
Telecopier: 808-885-6765.

MEMBERS OF FIRM

A. Bernard Bays (A Law Corporation)
Phillip L. Deaver (A Law Corporation)
Jerry Michael Hiatt (A Law Corporation)
Harvey J. Lung (A Law Corporation)
Crystal K. Rose (A Law Corporation)
Jason N. Baba (A Law Corporation)
Michael W. Thomas
Karin L. Holma

ASSOCIATES

Mahilani E.K. Hiatt
Wendy J. Utsumi
Bruce Voss
Edward J. Corwin
Craig P. Wagnild
Rafael G. del Castillo
Kim A. Tomey
Liane L. Brown
Elizabeth A.C. Thompson

For full biographical listings, see the Martindale-Hubbell Law Directory

CARLSMITH BALL (AV)

A Partnership including Law Corporations
Suite 2200, Pacific Tower, 1001 Bishop Street, P.O. Box 656, 96809-3402
Telephone: 808-523-2500
Fax: 808-523-0842
Email: execdirector@carlsmith.com *URL:* http://www.carlsmith.com
Kapolei, Hawaii Office: Suite 318, Kapolei Building, 1001 Kamokila Boulevard, 96707.
Telephone: 808-523-2500.
Fax: 808-674-0850.

(See Next Column)

Wailuku, Maui Hawaii Office: Suite 400, One Main Plaza, 2200 Main Street, P.O. Box 1086, 96793-1086.
Telephone: 808-242-4535.
Fax: 808-244-4974.
Kailua-Kona, Hawaii Office: Suite 209, 75-1000 Henry Street, 96740.
Telephone: 808-329-6464.
Fax: 808-329-9450.
Hilo, Hawaii Office: 121 Waianuenue Avenue, P.O. Box 686, 96721-0686.
Telephone: 808-935-6644.
Fax: 808-935-7975.
Hagatna, Guam Office: Suite 401, Bank of Hawaii Building, 134 West Soledad Avenue, P.O. Box BF, 96932-5027.
Telephone: 671-472-6813.
Fax: 671-477-4375.
Telex: 721-6445 CWCMI GM.
Saipan, Commonwealth of the Northern Mariana Islands Office: Carlsmith Building, Capitol Hill, P.O. Box 5241, 96950-5241.
Telephone: 670-322-3455.
Fax: 670-322-3368.
Los Angeles, California Office: 9th Floor, 444 South Flower Street, 90071-2901.
Telephone: 213-955-1200.
Fax: 213-623-0032.
Washington, D.C. Office: Suite 300, 1201 Pennsylvania Avenue, N.W., 20004-2401.
Telephone: 202-628-2228.
Fax: 202-628-2071.
Mexico City, Mexico Office: Carlsmith Ball, Sierra Nevada 119, Lomas de Chapultepec, 11000 Mexico, D.F.
Telephone: 52-5-520-8514, 52-5-520-8757.
Fax: 52-5-540-1545.
Mexico, D.F. Office of Carlsmith Ball, S.C. (Authorized to practice as foreign legal consultants in Mexico): Sierra Nevada 119, Lomas de Chapultepec, 11000 Mexico, D.F.
Telephone: 52-5-520-8514, 52-5-520-8757.
Fax: 52-5-540-1545.

MEMBERS OF FIRM

Annie Kun Baker (Partner, Resident at Los Angeles, California Office)
Daniel A. Bent
John F. Biehl (Resident at Saipan Office)
Stephen L. Bradford (Resident at Los Angeles, California Office)
Edward E. Case
James H. Case (A Law Corporation)
Ruth D. Davis (Resident at Hagatna, Guam Office)
Albert H. Ebright (Resident at Los Angeles, California Office)
Steven M. Egesdal
Terrence A. Everett (Resident at Los Angeles, California Office)
Alfonso García Cacho (Resident at Mexico Office)
Eric A. James
Richard Kiefer
Karl K. Kobayashi
Tim Lui-Kwan
Randolph G. Muhlestein (Resident at Los Angeles, California Office)
Lawrence S. Okinaga (A Law Corporation)
David S. Olson (Resident at Los Angeles, California Office)
Dean H. Robb
Tom E. Roesser
John E. Rogers (Resident at Mexico Office)
Marcia K. Schultz (Resident at Saipan Office)
Robert E. Strand
Lance F. Taniguchi
Sinforoso M. Tolentino (Resident at Hagatna, Guam Office)
Robert D. Triantos (Resident at Kailua-Kona, Hawaii Office)
J. Thomas Van Winkle (A Law Corporation)
Donald C. Williams (Resident at Los Angeles, California Office)
William C. Williams, Jr. (Not admitted in HI)
Jon T. Yamamura
Adrián Zubikarai Arriola (Resident at Mexico Office)

ASSOCIATES

Bruce A. Bradley (Not admitted in HI; Resident at Hagatna, Guam Office)
Francisco A. Gil-Elorduy (Resident at Mexico Office)
Kevin E. Moore
Brent K. Yamashita

OF COUNSEL

Donn W. Carlsmith
Robert N. Katayama
Robert R. Thornton (Resident at Los Angeles, California Office)

For Complete List of Firm Personnel, See General Section

For full biographical listings, see the Martindale-Hubbell Law Directory

EDMUNDS MAKI VERGA & THORN (AV)

Suite 2104, Davies Pacific Center, 841 Bishop Street, 96813
Telephone: 808-524-2000
Telecopier: 808-528-3585

John S. Edmunds
Paul Maki
Ronald J. Verga
Elise Owens Thorn
Joy S. Omonaka
Wesley D. Shimazu

Reference: Bank of Hawaii.

For full biographical listings, see the Martindale-Hubbell Law Directory

Honolulu—Continued

KOBAYASHI, SUGITA & GODA (AV)

A Partnership including Professional Corporations
999 Bishop Street, Suite 2600, 96813
Telephone: 808-539-8700
Telecopier: 808-539-8799
Telex: 6502396585 MCI
MCI Mail: 23 96585
ABA/Net: ABA2281
Email: ksg@aloha.net

MEMBERS OF FIRM

Bert T. Kobayashi, Jr., (Atty. At Law, A Law Corp.)
Kenneth Y. Sugita (Atty. At Law, A Law Corp.)
Alan M. Goda (Atty. At Law, A Law Corp.)
Dale W. Lee (Atty. At Law, A Law Corp.)
Lex R. Smith (Atty. At Law, A Law Corp.)
David L. Monroy (Atty. At Law, A Law Corp.)
Wendell H. Fuji (Atty. At Law, A Law Corp.)
Robert K. Ichikawa (Atty. At Law, A Law Corp.)
Janeen-Ann A. Olds (Atty. At Law, A Law Corp.)
Clifford K. Higa (Atty. At Law, A Law Corp.)
Charles W. Gall (Atty. At Law, A Law Corp.)
John F. Lezak (Atty. At Law, A Law Corp.)
Larry L. Myers (Atty. At Law, A Law Corp.)
Ernest H. Nomura (Atty. At Law, A Law Corp.)
Craig K. Shikuma (Atty. At Law, A Law Corp.)
Rod S. Aoki (Atty. At Law, A Law Corp.)

ASSOCIATES

Burt T. Lau
Christopher T. Kobayashi
Nathan H. Yoshimoto
Jonathan A. Kobayashi
Bruce A. Nakamura
Gary K. Nakata
Ruth K. Oh
David B. Tongg
Matthew H. Kobayashi
Vivian Tsoi
Ronald T. Ogomori
Elena J. Onaga
Curtis Saiki
William S. Bailey
Paul S. Kawai
Kenneth M. Nakasone
Duane C. Seabolt

OF COUNSEL

Bert T. Kobayashi, Sr.
Michael J. McGivern (Not admitted in HI)

Reference: First Hawaiian Bank.

For full biographical listings, see the Martindale-Hubbell Law Directory

LAW OFFICES OF PETER STARN A LAW CORPORATION (AV)

Suite 1740 Grosvenor Center Mauka Tower, 737 Bishop Street, 96813
Telephone: 808-537-6100
Fax: 808-537-5434
Email: landlaw@poi.net

Peter Starn
Duane R. Fisher
Sharon Valentine Lovejoy

Todd K. Apo

For full biographical listings, see the Martindale-Hubbell Law Directory

WATANABE, ING & KAWASHIMA (AV)

A Partnership including Professional Corporations
First Hawaiian Center, 999 Bishop Street, 23rd Floor, 96813
Telephone: 808-544-8300
Facsimile: 808-544-8399
Email: allwik@wik.com

MEMBERS OF FIRM

Jeffrey N. Watanabe (Atty. At Law, A Law Corp.)
James Kawashima (Atty. At Law, A Law Corp.)
J. Douglas Ing (Atty. At Law, A Law Corp.)
Wray H. Kondo (Atty. At Law, A Law Corp.)
John T. Komeiji (Atty. At Law, A Law Corp.)
Ronald Y. K. Leong (Atty. At Law, A Law Corp.)
Robert T. Takamatsu (Atty. At Law, A Law Corp.)
Cynthia Winegar (Atty. at Law, A Law Corp.)
Randall Y. Yamamoto (Atty. At Law, A Law Corp.)
Lyle Y. Harada (Atty. At Law, A Law Corp.)
Michael A. Lorusso (Atty. At Law, A Law Corp.)
Pamela J. Larson (Atty. At Law, A Law Corp.)
John R. Aube (Atty. At Law, A Law Corp.)
Jan M.L.Y. Amii (Atty. at Law, A Law Corp.)
Edward B. Rogin (Atty. at Law, A Law Corp.)
Seth M. Reiss (Atty. At Law, A Law Corp.)
Curtis C. Kim
Lani Narikiyo (Atty. at Law, A Law Corp.)

(See Next Column)

ASSOCIATES

Donna Y. Kanemaru
Peter L. Fritz
Beth K. Fujimoto
Patsy H. Kirio
Kevin H. Oda
Michael C. Bird
Brian Y. Hiyane
Dennis J. Hwang
Teri Y. Kondo
Gregory Y.P. Tom
Peter A. Horovitz
Diane F. Imamura
Brandon Davidson
R. Scott Simon

ASIA PACIFIC CONSULTANTS

George R. Ariyoshi
Victor Hao Li (Not admitted in HI)

LEGAL SUPPORT PERSONNEL

GOVERNMENT AFFAIRS ADVISORS

Millicent M. Y. H. Kim
Lori Ann C. Lum

References: First Hawaiian Bank; American Savings Bank.

For Complete List of Firm Personnel, See General Section

For full biographical listings, see the Martindale-Hubbell Law Directory

IDAHO

*BOISE,** Ada Co.

ELAM & BURKE, A PROFESSIONAL ASSOCIATION (AV)

Key Financial Center, 702 West Idaho Street, P.O. Box 1539, 83701
Telephone: 208-343-5454
Telecopier: 208-384-5844
Email: eblaw@elamburke.com

M. Allyn Dingel, Jr.
David B. Lincoln
Randall A. Peterman
William G. Dryden
Jeffery J. Ventrella
Jeffrey A. Thomson

J. Ray Durtschi

Representative Clients: Morrison-Knudsen, Inc.; Prudential Securities, Inc.; Pechiney Corp.; United Heritage & Mutual Life Insurance Co.; Sinclair Oil Co. d/b/a Sun Valley Co.; Micron Construction.

For Complete List of Firm Personnel, See General Section

For full biographical listings, see the Martindale-Hubbell Law Directory

ILLINOIS

*BELLEVILLE,** St. Clair Co.

MCGLYNN & MCGLYNN (AV)

65 South 65th Street, 62223
Telephone: 618-398-5112; 314-381-5112
Telecopier: 618-398-5189

MEMBERS OF FIRM

Robert E. McGlynn
James McGlynn (Retired)
Michael L. McGlynn
Stephen P. McGlynn

For full biographical listings, see the Martindale-Hubbell Law Directory

*CHICAGO,** Cook Co.

BATES MECKLER BULGER & TILSON (AV)

8300 Sears Tower, 233 South Wacker, 60606
Telephone: 312-474-7900
Facsimile: 312-474-7898
URL: http://www.bmbt.com

MEMBERS OF FIRM

Robert J. Bates, Jr.
Brian W. Bulger
Catherine M. Crisham
Janet R. Davis
Maria G. Enriquez
J. Stuart Garbutt
Paul R. Garry
Brent J. Graber
Maryann C. Hayes
Robert C. Heist
Kathleen H. Jensen
James H. Kallianis, Jr.
Philip R. King
Mari Henry Leigh
Michael I. Leonard
Mary F. Licari
Michael M. Marick
Bruce R. Meckler
Steven D. Pearson
John E. Rodewald
Scott M. Seaman
Mark G. Sheridan
Joseph E. Tilson
Brian J Williams
Timothy A. Wolfe

(See Next Column)

BATES MECKLER BULGER & TILSON—*Continued*

ASSOCIATES

Dina L. Brantman
John F. Curley (Not admitted in IL)
John K. Daly
Robin I. Edelstein
Mary E. Gootjes
Christopher E. Kentra
Lisa A. Miller
F. Allan Storning
Monica T. Sullivan

OF COUNSEL

Eileen King Bower
Brett D. Heinrich
Darlene M. Jarzyna-Price
Matthew M. Murphy
Joseph D. O'Brien, Jr.
Thomas J. O'Brien

For full biographical listings, see the Martindale-Hubbell Law Directory

HAMMAN & BENN (AV)

Suite 3300, 10 South La Salle Street, 60603-1002
Telephone: 312-372-2920
Facsimile: 312-372-7762

George W. Hamman
Marvin N. Benn
Dawn M. Cassie
Richard J. Superfine
Stephen J. Cassin
Jeanne M. Hoffmann
Jack Shore

OF COUNSEL

Jeffrey M. Carey
Ronald Olbrysh
Mitchell H. Saranow

For full biographical listings, see the Martindale-Hubbell Law Directory

WILLIAM J. HARTE, LTD. (AV)

Suite 1100, 111 West Washington Street, 60602
Telephone: 312-726-5015
Fax: 312-641-1288

William J. Harte

Sylvia A. Sotiras
Erik D. Gruber
Stephen L. Garcia
Joan M. Mannix

OF COUNSEL

Daniel K. Schlorf
David J. Walker
P. A. Sorrentino
Robert L. Tucker

For full biographical listings, see the Martindale-Hubbell Law Directory

HOLLIS AND JOHNSON (AV)

11 East Adams Street, Suite 501, 60603
Telephone: 312-427-0700
Fax: 312-427-8407
URL: http://www.digitalawyer.com/bankruptcy

Pamela S. Hollis
Donald E. Johnson

ASSOCIATE

Linda M. Kujaca

For full biographical listings, see the Martindale-Hubbell Law Directory

NISEN & ELLIOTT (AV)

200 West Adams Street, Suite 2500, 60606
Telephone: 312-346-7800
Telecopier: 312-346-9316

MEMBERS OF FIRM

Paul F. Gerbosi
Edward B. Mueller
Anthony Packard
Mark F. Zaenger
Michael J. Daley
John Foster Lesch
John K. Kneafsey
Michael H. Moirano
Robert O. Middleton
William G. Daluga, Jr.
Kenneth J. Rojc
Thomas V. McCauley
Helen M. Jensen
William A. Walker
Daniel P. Dawson
Michael J. Pavlicek

Robert Christie
Donald F. Froehlke
Thomas K. Juffernbruch
Brendan J. Kelly
Brian C. Kelly
Mary Rose C. Manczak
Bradley S. McCann
Brian D. Proctor

OF COUNSEL

Charles M. Nisen
Donald C. Shine

For full biographical listings, see the Martindale-Hubbell Law Directory

SCHWARTZBERG, BARNETT & COHEN (AV)

55 West Monroe Street, 2400 Xerox Centre, 60603-5040
Telephone: 312-726-3555
Fax: 312-726-6299
Cable Address: "Justice"
Email: sb&c@twty.chi.il.us

(See Next Column)

MEMBERS OF FIRM

Ralph M. Schwartzberg (1939-1975)
Mark T. Barnett (1939-1970)
Hugh J. Schwartzberg
Benjamin H. Cohen

For full biographical listings, see the Martindale-Hubbell Law Directory

WILDMAN, HARROLD, ALLEN & DIXON (AV)

225 West Wacker Drive, 30th Floor, 60606-1229
Telephone: 312-201-2000
Fax: 312-201-2555
Email: hennessy@whad.com *URL:* http://www.whad.com
Aurora, Illinois Office: 1961 W. Downer Place.
Telephone: 630-892-7021.
Fax: 630-892-7158.
Waukegan, Illinois Office: 404 West Water, P. O. Box 890.
Telephone: 847-625-5550.
Fax: 847-625-5555.
Lisle, Illinois Office: 4300 Commerce Court, Suite 320.
Telephone: 630-955-0555.
Fax: 630-955-0662
Toronto, Ontario correspondent Office: Keel Cottrelle. 36 Toronto Street, Suite 920.
Telephone: 416-367-2900.
Telefax: 416-367-2791.
Telex: 062-18660.

James C. James, III (Aurora Office)
Ian J. McPheron

For full biographical listings, see the Martindale-Hubbell Law Directory

CRYSTAL LAKE, McHenry Co.

MILITELLO, ZANCK & COEN, P.C. (AV)

40 Brink Street, 60014
Telephone: 815-459-8800
FAX: 815-459-8429

James G. Militello
Thomas C. Zanck
Patrick D. Coen
James L. Wright

Mark S. Saladin
James G. Militello, III
Barbara H. Switzer
D. Chad Mihevc
Nancy A. Stingle
David G. Phoenix

OF COUNSEL

Michael A. Ungvarsky, Jr.

References: Home State Bank of Crystal Lake; First National Bank of Crystal Lake; McHenry State Bank; Amcore Bank N.A., Woodstock.

For full biographical listings, see the Martindale-Hubbell Law Directory

*DANVILLE,** Vermilion Co.

SAIKLEY, GARRISON & COLOMBO, LTD. (AV)

208 West North Street, P.O. Box 6, 61834-0006
Telephone: 217-442-0244
FAX: 217-442-0582

Albert Saikley (1912-1987)
William L. Garrison
Gilbert H. Saikley
Kevin M. Colombo

References: First Midwest Bank; Palmer American National Bank.

For full biographical listings, see the Martindale-Hubbell Law Directory

*KANKAKEE,** Kankakee Co.

BARMANN, KRAMER & BOHLEN, P.C. (AV)

Suite 502, 200 East Court Street, P.O. Box 1787, 60901
Telephone: 815-939-1133
Fax: 815-939-0994

Glen R. Barmann
Christopher W. Bohlen
Michael D. Kramer

For Complete List of Firm Personnel, See General Section

For full biographical listings, see the Martindale-Hubbell Law Directory

MATTOON, Coles Co.

CRAIG & CRAIG (AV)

1807 Broadway, P.O. Box 689, 61938-0689
Telephone: 217-234-6481
Telecopier: 217-234-6486; 258-8292
Email: craiglaw@advant.com
Mount Vernon, Illinois Office: 115 North 7th Street.
Telephone: 618-244-7511.

(See Next Column)

CRAIG & CRAIG, *Mattoon—Continued*

MEMBERS OF FIRM

Craig Van Meter (1895-1981)
Fred H. Kelly (1894-1971)
Robert M. Werden (1908-1969)
George N. Gilkerson (1911-1985)
John P. Ewart
Richard F. Record, Jr.
Stephen L. Corn
Robert G. Grierson
Gregory C. Ray
Paul R. Lynch (Resident, Mount Vernon Office)
Kenneth F. Werts (Resident, Mount Vernon Office)
John L. Barger

ASSOCIATES

Kathleen M. Stockwell
Kristine M. Tuttle
Julie A. Webb (Resident, Mount Vernon Office)
John M. O'Driscoll
Duane A. Deters
Katy C. Fain (Resident, Mount Vernon Office)
Erin E. Wisner
John F. Watson

OF COUNSEL

Jack E. Horsley

Representative Clients: Marathon Oil Co.; Illinois Central R.R.; Okaw Building & Loan, s.b., Mattoon, Illinois; Howell Paving, Inc.; Consolidated Communications, Inc.; D-CO, Inc.; Mattoon Enterprise Park, L.L.C.; Lake Land College.

For full biographical listings, see the Martindale-Hubbell Law Directory

*MOUNT VERNON,** Jefferson Co.

LAW OFFICE OF TERRY SHARP, P.C. (AV)

1115 Harrison Street, P.O. Box 906, 62864
Telephone: 618-242-0246
Fax: 618-242-1170
Email: TSharp.law@mvn.net
Benton, Illinois Office: 105 North Main Street.
Telephone: 618-435-5109.
FAX: 618-242-1170.

Terrell Lee Sharp

For full biographical listings, see the Martindale-Hubbell Law Directory

INDIANA

*EVANSVILLE,** Vanderburgh Co.

BOWERS, HARRISON, KENT & MILLER, LLP (AV)

25 N.W. Riverside Drive, P.O. Box 1287, 47706-1287
Telephone: 812-426-1231
Fax: 812-464-3676
Email: BOWERS,HARRISON,KENT&MILLER,LLP@BHKM.COM
URL: http://WWW.BHKM.COM

MEMBERS OF FIRM

David V. Miller
Paul E. Black
Gary R. Case
Timothy J. Hubert
Thomas A. Massey
Greg A. Granger
Joseph H. Harrison, Jr.

Division Counsel in Indiana for: Southern Railway Co.
Representative Clients: Permanent Federal Savings Bank; Citizens Realty & Insurance, Inc.

For Complete List of Firm Personnel, See General Section

For full biographical listings, see the Martindale-Hubbell Law Directory

RUDOLPH, FINE, PORTER & JOHNSON LLP (AV)

221 N.W. Fifth Street, Second Floor, P.O. Box 1507, 47706
Telephone: 812-422-9444
Fax: 812-421-7459
URL: http://www.rfpj@rfpj.com

MEMBERS OF FIRM

Ross E. Rudolph
James D. Johnson

ASSOCIATES

Jennifer L. Johnson
James A. Edgar

Reference: National City Bank of Evansville.

For full biographical listings, see the Martindale-Hubbell Law Directory

ZIEMER, STAYMAN, WEITZEL & SHOULDERS, LLP (AV)

(Formerly Early, Arnold & Ziemer)
One Riverfront Place, 20 N.W. First Street 9th Floor, P.O. Box 916, 47706-0916
Telephone: 812-424-7575
Telecopier: 812-421-5089

MEMBERS OF FIRM

Robert F. Stayman
Stephan E. Weitzel
Marco L. DeLucio
Gregory G. Meyer

(See Next Column)

ASSOCIATE

Charles A. Compton

Reference: Old National Bank in Evansville.

For full biographical listings, see the Martindale-Hubbell Law Directory

*FORT WAYNE,** Allen Co.

SHIPLEY & ASSOCIATES (AV)

230 West Main Street, Suite 100, 46802-1612
Telephone: 219-422-2700
Fax: 219-424-2960
Email: shipley@iquest.net

Grant F. Shipley

ASSOCIATE

Deborah Wiers Vincent

Representative Clients: NBD Bank, N.A.; Petroleum Traders Corp.; Fleet Capital Corp.

For full biographical listings, see the Martindale-Hubbell Law Directory

*INDIANAPOLIS,** Marion Co.

BACKER & BACKER, A PROFESSIONAL CORPORATION (AV)

8710 North Meridian Street, 46260
Telephone: 317-571-0500
Telecopier: 317-571-0700
Email: sabacker@ameritech.net

Herbert J. Backer (1914-1995)
Stephen A. Backer

Reference: Bank One, Indianapolis.

For full biographical listings, see the Martindale-Hubbell Law Directory

BAMBERGER & FEIBLEMAN (AV)

1408 North Pennsylvania Street, 46202-2421
Telephone: 317-639-5151
FAX: 317-269-2030
Email: bandf@iquest.net

MEMBERS OF FIRM

Ralph Bamberger (1871-1947)
Isidore Feibleman (1873-1954)
Charles B. Feibleman (1916-1971)
John K. Rickles (1898-1976)
Julian Bamberger (1905-1988)
Sigmund J. Beck (1915-1991)
Willard B. Ransom (1916-1995)
D. Robert Webster

ASSOCIATE

David K. Lee

OF COUNSEL

Victor A. DeRose
Thomas D. Strodtman
Joseph H. Greenberg
Timothy E. Peterson
Neil E. Lucas

Representative Clients: C.I.T. Corp.; FFI Corporation; Kipp Brothers, Inc.; BancPlus Mortgage Corp.; Hiway Parts, Inc.; NBD, Indiana; Tube Processing Corp.; Indiana Mortgage Corp.

For full biographical listings, see the Martindale-Hubbell Law Directory

BUSCHMANN, CARR & SHANKS, PROFESSIONAL CORPORATION (AV)

1020 Market Tower, 10 West Market Street, 46204-2963
Telephone: 317-636-5511
Fax: 317-636-3661
Email: bcs@indy.net *URL:* http://www.buschmanncarr.com

John R. Carr, III
Stephen R. Buschmann
Gary L. Dilk

Representative Clients: Archer-Daniels Midland Co.; Ball Corp.; Industrial Valley Title Insurance; Creative Risk Management, Inc.; Deflecto Corporation; Glenfed Mortgage Corp.; Gates McDonald; Merchants National Bank & Trust Company of Muncie; Monumental Life Insurance Co.; National Council on Compensation Insurance.

For full biographical listings, see the Martindale-Hubbell Law Directory

FEIWELL & HANNOY, PROFESSIONAL CORPORATION (AV)

251 North Illinois Street, Suite 1700, P.O. Box 44141, 46244-0141
Telephone: 317-237-2727
Facsimile: 317-237-2722
Email: f&h@feiwellhannoy.com *URL:* http://www.feiwellhannoy.com

Murray J. Feiwell
Douglas J. Hannoy

Michael J. Feiwell
David J. Jurkiewicz

Representative Clients: Fifth Third Bank; Revel & Underwood, LLC; F & C Real Estate Services, Inc.; American Credit Indemnity; Browning Investments, Inc.; Jewelers Board of Trade; Stanley Tulchin Associates; First National Bank; Metro Realty Ltd. Partnership.

For full biographical listings, see the Martindale-Hubbell Law Directory

Indianapolis—Continued

Hoffman Drewry Hancock & Simmons (AV)

9100 Keystone Crossing, Suite 350, 46240
Telephone: 317-580-4848
Telecopier: 317-580-4855

Robert J. Hoffman
Michael F. Drewry
William J. Hancock
David L. Simmons
Richard S. Pitts
David B. Vornehm
Joseph M. Leone
Richard W. McMinn

OF COUNSEL

S. Douglas Trolson

For full biographical listings, see the Martindale-Hubbell Law Directory

Hostetler & Kowalik, P.C. (AV)

101 West Ohio Street Suite 2100, 46204
Telephone: 317-262-1001
Fax: 317-262-1010
Email: hoskow@indy.net *URL:* http://www.lawyers.com/hostetler&kowalik

Gary Lynn Hostetler
James S. Kowalik
David R. Krebs
J. Bradley Schooley
Timothy L. Black

For full biographical listings, see the Martindale-Hubbell Law Directory

Ice Miller Donadio & Ryan (AV)

One American Square Box 82001, 46282-0002
Telephone: 317-236-2100
Fax: 317-236-2219
Email: info@imdr.com *URL:* http://www.imdr.com
South Bend, Indiana Office: 211 West Washington Street, Suite 2420.
Telephone: 219-234-7933.
Fax: 219-234-7965. Internet E-mail: info@imdr.com. Web Site Address: http://www.imdr.com.
Chicago, Illinois Office: 135 South LaSalle Street, Suite 4100.
Telephone: 312-726-1567.
Fax: 312-641-6263. Internet E-mail: info@imdr.com. Web Site Address: http://www.imdr.com.

MEMBERS OF FIRM

Berkley W. Duck
Harry L. Gonso
Thomas H. Ristine
John R. Thornburgh
Richard J. Thrapp
Henry A. Efroymson
Dominic F. Polizzotto

OF COUNSEL

Peggy J. Naile
Susan Rogers Brooke

ASSOCIATES

John M. Hakes
Dennis H. Long

Representative Clients: Amax Coal, Inc.; Bank One, Indianapolis, N.S.; Clark Equipment Co.; Ford Motor Credit Co.; National City Bank (Trust); Indiana Bankers Assn.; Stoops Freightliner Quality Trailers, Inc.; The National Bank of Indianapolis; Huntington National Bank; Transamerica Insurance Finance Corp.

For Complete List of Firm Personnel, See General Section

For full biographical listings, see the Martindale-Hubbell Law Directory

Johnson Smith Pence & Heath LLP (AV)

One Indiana Square Suite 1800, 46204
Telephone: 317-634-9777
Telecopier: 317-636-9061
Email: firm@jsplaw.com *URL:* http://www.jsplaw.com
Washington, D.C. Office: 555 Twelfth Street, N.W., Suite 650.
Telephone: 202-737-5410.
Fax: 202-737-5411.

MEMBERS OF FIRM

David G. Blachly
David R. Day
Michael W. Hile
Dennis A. Johnson
Richard L. Johnson
Michael J. Kaye
John R. Kirkwood

For Complete List of Firm Personnel, See General Section

For full biographical listings, see the Martindale-Hubbell Law Directory

Sommer & Barnard, Attorneys at Law, PC (AV)

4000 Bank One Tower, 111 Monument Circle, 46204
Telephone: 317-630-4000
FAX: 317-236-9802
Email: sandb@sommerbarnard.com
North Office: 8900 Keystone Crossing, Suite 1150, Indianapolis, Indiana, 46240-2134.
Telephone: 317-630-4000.
FAX: 317-844-4780.

(See Next Column)

James K. Sommer
William C. Barnard
James E. Hughes
Edward W. Harris, III
Jerald I. Ancel
Eric R. Johnson
Gordon L. Pittenger
Marlene Reich
Richard C. Richmond, III
Julianne S. Lis-Milam

Representative Clients: Comerica Bank; Federal Express; Kimball International; Monsanto; TRW, Inc.

For Complete List of Firm Personnel, See General Section

For full biographical listings, see the Martindale-Hubbell Law Directory

Yarling & Robinson (AV)

151 North Delaware, Suite 1535, P.O. Box 44128, 46204
Telephone: 317-262-8800
Fax: 317-262-3046
Email: yrhl@yarling.com *URL:* http://www.yarling.com

MEMBERS OF FIRM

Charles F. Robinson, Jr.
John W. Hammel
Linda Y. Hammel
Douglas E. Rogers
Mark S. Gray
Matthew C. Robinson

ASSOCIATE

Jeffrey R. Mitchell

OF COUNSEL

Richard W. Yarling

Representative Clients: Associates Financial Services; Chrysler Credit Corporation; Chrysler First Financial Services; Fleet Financenter; General Motors Acceptance Corporation; Household Finance Corporation; Indiana Telco Credit Union; Nations Credit; Norwest Financial; Security Pacific Finance Corporation.

For full biographical listings, see the Martindale-Hubbell Law Directory

*LAFAYETTE,** Tippecanoe Co.

Stuart & Branigin (AV)

The Life Building, 300 Main Street, Suite 800, P.O. Box 1010, 47902-1010
Telephone: 765-423-1561
Telecopier: 765-742-8175
Email: sb@stuartlaw.com *URL:* http://www.stuartlaw.com
Indianapolis, Indiana Office: Suite 1401, 8888 Keystone Crossing, 46240.
Telephone: 317-574-7245.
Fax: 317-574-7050.

MEMBERS OF FIRM

Allison Ellsworth Stuart (1886-1950)
Roger D. Branigin (1902-1975)
Roger D. Branigin, Jr.
Thomas L. Ryan
Thomas R. McCully
Larry R. Fisher
Nina B. Kirkpatrick
Mark Lillianfeld
Stephen R. Pennell
Anthony S. Benton
Erik D. Spykman
William E. Emerick
John C. Duffey
Bruce McSpadden
Mark E. DeYoung
Thomas B. Parent
Laura L. Bowker
Kevin D. Nicoson
Susan K. Roberts
John M. Stuckey
Deborah B. Trice
William P. Kealey
David A. Starkweather
Geoffrey L. Blazi

SENIOR COUNSEL

Russell H. Hart

COUNSEL

John F. Bodle
James V. McGlone

ASSOCIATES

Elizabeth B. Searle
Marianne Mitten Owen
David A. Locke
Karen Orr McClure
Ann Marie Waldron
Barry L. Loftus

General Counsel for: The Lafayette Life Insurance Co.; INB National Bank, N.W.; Lafayette Home Hospital, Inc.
State Counsel for: Norfolk & Western Railway Co.
Mr. Ryan is Counsel to: The Trustees of Purdue University.
Representative Clients: Aluminum Company of America; Liberty Mutual Insurance Group.

For full biographical listings, see the Martindale-Hubbell Law Directory

MERRILLVILLE, Lake Co.

Hodges & Davis, P.C. (AV)

8700 Broadway, 46410
Telephone: 219-641-8700
Fax: 219-641-8710
URL: http://www.hodgesdavis.com
Portage, Indiana Office: 6082 Lute Road. P.O. Box 1037.
Telephone: 219-762-9129.
Fax: 219-762-2826.

(See Next Column)

HODGES & DAVIS P.C., *Merrillville—Continued*

Clyde D. Compton
William B. Davis
Earle F. Hites
R. Lawrence Steele
Gregory A. Sobkowski
Bonnie C. Coleman
Jill M. Madajczyk
Laura B. Frost
David H. Kreider
Jeanne B. Blumenthal

OF COUNSEL

Edward J. Hussey

Representative Clients: Lake Mortgage Co., Inc.; Nielsen Buick Jeep Eagle; Pine Chevrolet, Inc.; McDonald's Corporation; Northwest Indiana Water Co.

For Complete List of Firm Personnel, See General Section

For full biographical listings, see the Martindale-Hubbell Law Directory

PORTAGE, Porter Co.

HODGES & DAVIS, P.C. (AV)

6082 Lute Road, P.O. Box 1037, 46368
Telephone: 219-762-9129
Fax: 219-762-2826
URL: http://www.hodgesdavis.com
Merrillville, Indiana Office: 8700 Broadway.
Telephone: 219-641-8700.
Fax: 219-641-8710.

Clyde D. Compton
Earle F. Hites
R. Lawrence Steele
Gregory A. Sobkowski
Bonnie C. Coleman
Laura B. Frost

Representative Clients: Lake Mortgage Co., Inc.; Nielson Buick Jeep Eagle; Pine Chevrolet, Inc.; McDonald's Corporation; Northwest Indiana Water Company.

For full biographical listings, see the Martindale-Hubbell Law Directory

*SOUTH BEND,** St. Joseph Co.

DORAN • BLACKMOND LLP (AV)

1700 Valley American Bank Building, 211 W. Washington Street, 46601
Telephone: 219-288-1800
Fax: 219-236-4265

MEMBERS OF FIRM

M. Edward Doran (1895-1982)
John E. Doran
Don G. Blackmond

ASSOCIATES

Don Gregory Blackmond
Peter J. Van Dyke
Lynn M. Butcher

OF COUNSEL

A. Howard Williams

For full biographical listings, see the Martindale-Hubbell Law Directory

IOWA

*COUNCIL BLUFFS,** Pottawattamie Co.

SMITH PETERSON LAW FIRM (AV)

35 Main Place, Suite 300, P.O. Box 249, 51502
Telephone: 712-328-1833
Fax: 712-328-8320
Email: email@smithpeterson.com
Omaha, Nebraska Office: 9290 West Dodge Road, Suite 205.
Telephone: 402-397-8500.
Fax: 402-397-5519.

MEMBERS OF FIRM

Raymond A. Smith (1892-1977)
John LeRoy Peterson (1895-1969)
Harold T. Beckman
Robert J. Laubenthal
Richard A. Heininger
Lawrence J. Beckman
Gregory G. Barntsen
W. Curtis Hewett
Steven H. Krohn
Randy R. Ewing
Joseph D. Thornton
T. J. Pattermann

ASSOCIATES

Daniel L. Fretheim
Paul M. Shotkoski

Representative Clients: Redland Insurance Group; Iowa Western Community College; Farm Credit Service of The Midlands; Demma Fruit Co.; Peoples National Bank; Council Bluffs Board of Water Works Trustee.

For full biographical listings, see the Martindale-Hubbell Law Directory

*DES MOINES,** Polk Co.

PINGEL & TEMPLER, P.C. (AV)

Suite 437 3737 Woodland Avenue (West Des Moines), P.O. Box 1991, 50309
Telephone: 515-225-3737
Fax: 515-225-9510

Ronni F. Begleiter
Thomas M. Cunningham
Jeffrey L. Goodman
John R. Perkins
G. Brian Pingel
Jeffrey D. Stone
John A. Templer, Jr.

For Complete List of Firm Personnel, See General Section

For full biographical listings, see the Martindale-Hubbell Law Directory

*IOWA CITY,** Johnson Co.

JOHNSTON, POTTERFIELD & NATHANSON, P.C. (AV)

1902 Broadway, P.O. Box 3400, 52244
Telephone: 319-354-1712
Fax: 319-354-7265
URL: http://www.lawyers.com/johnstonlaw
Cedar Rapids Office: 129 First Avenue, S.W., P.O. Box 74210.
Telephone: 319-366-1000.
Fax: 319-366-6973.
Waterloo Office: 1506 LaPorte Road, P.O. Box 2787.
Telephone: 319-235-3000.
Fax: 319-235-2108.

Joseph C. Johnston
Amanda Potterfield
Henry E. Nathanson
Cathy L. Fitzmaurice
David Burbidge

OF COUNSEL

Carl J. Goetz, Jr.

For full biographical listings, see the Martindale-Hubbell Law Directory

WEST DES MOINES, Polk Co.

LAMARCA & LANDRY, P.C. (AV)

1300 50th Street, 50266
Telephone: 515-225-2600
Fax: 515-225-8581
Islamorada, Florida Office: 202 Biscayne Boulevard, 33036.
Telephone: 305-664-8527.

George A. LaMarca
Gregory W. Landry

Gary G. Mattson
Justin E. LaVan

OF COUNSEL

Martin R. Anderson
Samuel S. Duffey

For full biographical listings, see the Martindale-Hubbell Law Directory

KANSAS

*KANSAS CITY,** Wyandotte Co.

WONER, GLENN, REEDER & GIRARD, P.A.

(See Topeka)

*LAWRENCE,** Douglas Co.

WONER, GLENN, REEDER & GIRARD, P.A.

(See Topeka)

OVERLAND PARK, Johnson Co.

FISHER, PATTERSON, SAYLER & SMITH, L.L.P. (AV)

11050 Roe Avenue, Suite 210, 66211
Telephone: 913-339-6757
FAX: 913-339-6187
Email: fpss@worldnet.att.net
Topeka, Kansas Office: 3550 S.W. 5th Street, P.O. Box 949, 66601.
Telephone: 785-232-7761.
Fax: 785-232-6604.

MEMBERS OF FIRM

Edwin Dudley Smith (Resident)
Michael K. Seck (Resident)
David P. Madden (Resident)

ASSOCIATES

Kelly A. Feyh (Resident)
Jennifer R. Rose (Resident)

For full biographical listings, see the Martindale-Hubbell Law Directory

Overland Park—Continued

WONER, GLENN, REEDER & GIRARD, P.A.

(See Topeka)

*TOPEKA,** Shawnee Co.

FISHER, PATTERSON, SAYLER & SMITH, L.L.P. (AV)

3550 S.W. 5th Street, P.O. Box 949, 66601
Telephone: 785-232-7761
Fax: 785-232-6604
Email: fpss@cjnetworks.com
Overland Park, Kansas Office: 11050 Roe Avenue, Suite 210, 66211.
Telephone: 913-339-6757.
Fax: 913-339-6187.

MEMBERS OF FIRM

Donald Patterson
Edwin Dudley Smith (Resident, Overland Park Office)
Larry G. Pepperdine
James P. Nordstrom
Justice B. King
J. Steven Pigg
Steve R. Fabert
Ronald J. Laskowski
Michael K. Seck (Resident, Overland Park Office)
David P. Madden (Resident, Overland Park Office)
Steven K. Johnson
Kristine A. Larscheid

ASSOCIATES

Billy E. Newman
David R. Cooper
Kelly A. Feyh (Resident, Overland Park Office)
Jennifer R. Rose (Resident, Overland Park Office)

OF COUNSEL

David H. Fisher

RETIRED

Charles Keith Sayler (Retired)

Representative Clients: Gage Shopping Center, Inc.; Fireman's Fund-American Insurance Cos.; United States Fidelity and Guaranty Co.; The Procter & Gamble Company; Commercial Union Insurance Companies; National Casualty; The Hartford; Berkshire Hathaway Companies.

For full biographical listings, see the Martindale-Hubbell Law Directory

WONER, GLENN, REEDER & GIRARD, P.A. (AV)

A Partnership of Professional Corporations
534 South Kansas Avenue Suite 330, 66603-3424
Telephone: 785-235-5330
Fax: 785-235-1615
URL: http://www.lawyers.com/wgr&glaw
Email: bwoner@wonerglenn.com *URL:* http://www.wonerglenn.com
Wichita, Kansas Office: 155 N. Market, Suite 708.
Telephone: 316-264-8220.
Fax: 316-264-3012.

David S. Fricke
Timothy H. Girard
Grant M. Glenn
Leon B. Graves
Patricia A. Reeder
R. Patrick Riordan
Bruce J. Woner

For full biographical listings, see the Martindale-Hubbell Law Directory

WRIGHT, HENSON, SOMERS, SEBELIUS, CLARK & BAKER, LLP (AV)

Commerce Bank Building, 100 Southeast Ninth Street, 2nd Floor, P.O. Box 3555, 66601-3555
Telephone: 785-232-2200
FAX: 785-232-3344
Email: wrighthenson@wrighthenson.com *URL:* http://www.wrighthenson.com

MEMBERS OF FIRM

Thomas E. Wright
Charles N. Henson
Dale L. Somers
Bruce J. Clark
Anne Lamborn Baker

ASSOCIATE

John H. Hutton

For Complete List of Firm Personnel, See General Section

For full biographical listings, see the Martindale-Hubbell Law Directory

*WICHITA,** Sedgwick Co.

FOULSTON & SIEFKIN L.L.P. (AV)

700 NationsBank Financial Center, 67202
Telephone: 316-267-6371
Facsimile: 316-267-6345
URL: http://www.foulston.com
Topeka, Kansas Office: 1515 NationsBank Tower, 534 Kansas Avenue, 66603.
Telephone: 785-233-3600.
Fax: 785-233-1610.

(See Next Column)

Dodge City, Kansas Office: 810 Frontview, P.O. Box 1147, 67801.
Telephone: 316-227-8126.
Fax: 316-227-8451.
Member: Lex Mundi, The World's Leading Association of Independent Law Firms.

MEMBERS OF FIRM

Benjamin C. Langel
James D. Oliver
Larry G. Rapp
Gary E. Knight
Terry C. Cupps
William R. Wood, II

For Complete List of Firm Personnel, See General Section

For full biographical listings, see the Martindale-Hubbell Law Directory

TRIPLETT, WOOLF & GARRETSON, LLC (AV)

2959 North Rock Road, Suite 300, 67226
Telephone: 316-630-8100
Fax: 316-630-8101
Email: twg@twgfirm.com

MEMBERS OF FIRM

Thomas C. Triplett
John P. Woolf
Thomas P. Garretson
James A. Walker
Timothy E. McKee
Theron E. Fry
Eric B. Metz
Ron H. Harnden
Lee Thompson
Eric S. Strickler
Tad Patton
Bradley A. Stout
Rachael K. Pirner
Jeffrey D. Leonard

ASSOCIATES

Jeffery C. Dahlgren
Jeffrey E. Goering
Jerald W. Rogers
Christopher C. Swyers
Kent G. Voth

Representative Clients: Anheuser-Busch Companies, Inc.; Brite Voice Systems, Inc.; Coleman Company, Inc.; Dow Chemical Co.; Friends University; KPMG Peat Marwick; National Plastics Color, Inc.; Total Petroleum, Inc.; Travelers Insurance Co.; Willis Corroon of Kansas, Inc.

For full biographical listings, see the Martindale-Hubbell Law Directory

YOUNG, BOGLE, MCCAUSLAND, WELLS & BLANCHARD, P.A. (AV)

106 West Douglas, Suite 923, 67202
Telephone: 316-265-7841
Facsimile: 316-265-3956
Email: ybmwblaw@aol.com

Jerry D. Bogle
Paul S. McCausland
William A. Wells
Patrick C. Blanchard

J. Michael Peters

OF COUNSEL

Orlin L. Wagner

Representative Clients: Deere Credit Services, Inc.; Agricredit Acceptance Corp.; Equitable Agri-Business, Inc.; General Mills, Inc.

For Complete List of Firm Personnel, See General Section

For full biographical listings, see the Martindale-Hubbell Law Directory

KENTUCKY

*BOWLING GREEN,** Warren Co.

KERRICK, GRISE & STIVERS (AV)

1025 State Street, P.O. Box 9547, 42102-9547
Telephone: 502-782-8160
Fax: 502-782-5856
Email: kgs@kgslaw.com
Elizabethtown, Kentucky Office: 2935 Dolphin Drive, Suite 102.
Telephone: 502-769-5788.
Fax: 502-737-9285.

MEMBERS OF FIRM

Thomas N. Kerrick
John R. Grise
Gregory N. Stivers
H. Brent Brennenstuhl
Laura M. Hagan

ASSOCIATES

Karl N. Crandall
Shawn Rosso Alcott
Jason B. Bell

OF COUNSEL

Jeffrey R. O'Grody

LEGAL SUPPORT PERSONNEL

Patricia Logsdon
Laura Lockhart Lico
Allison Lusk

Representative Clients: Dollar General Corp.; Columbia Greenview Regional Hospital; Hospital Corporation of America; Hardin Memorial Hospital; Fir-Star Bank; TKR Cable.

(See Next Column)

KERRICK, GRISE & STIVERS, *Bowling Green—Continued*

For full biographical listings, see the Martindale-Hubbell Law Directory

*LEXINGTON,** Fayette Co.

STOLL, KEENON & PARK, LLP (AV)

201 E. Main Street, Suite 1000, 40507-1380
Telephone: 606-231-3000
Telecopier: 606-253-1093; 606-253-1027
URL: http://www.skp.com
Frankfort, Kentucky Office: 307 Washington Street, 40601.
Telephone: 502-875-6220.
Telecopier: 502-875-6235.
Henderson, Kentucky Office: 201 C North Main Street, 42420-3103.
Telephone: 270-831-1900.
Telecopier: 270-827-4060.
Louisville, Kentucky Office: 400 West Market Street, Suite 2650, 40202-3377.
Telephone: 502-568-9100.
Telecopier: 502-568-5700.

MEMBERS OF FIRM

Samuel D. Hinkle IV
R. David Lester
Harvie B. Wilkinson
Robert W. Kellerman
Dan M. Rose
Gregory D. Pavey
Lea Pauley Goff
Laura Day DelCotto
Culver V. Halliday
William L. Montague, Jr.

ASSOCIATE

Richard B. Warne

Representative Clients: Bank One, Lexington, NA; Bank One, Kentucky, NA; Fifth Third Bank; Whitaker Bank Corporation of Kentucky.

For Complete List of Firm Personnel, See General Section

For full biographical listings, see the Martindale-Hubbell Law Directory

*LOUISVILLE,** Jefferson Co.

FORE, MILLER & SCHWARTZ (AV)

First Trust Centre, Suite 700 North, 200 South Fifth Street, 40202
Telephone: 502-589-5250
Fax: 502-589-1637

MEMBERS OF FIRM

F. Larkin Fore
Dan T. Schwartz
Stephen H. Miller
Bryan J. Dillon
Donald J. LaDuke

ASSOCIATES

Louis I. Waterman
Joseph C. Spalding

OF COUNSEL

Karl M. Walz

References: American States Insurance Co.; Crawford & Company; Paragon Group, Inc.; Queens Group; Southeastern Dairies, Inc.; Ticor Title Co.; First National Bank of Louisville; Stockyards Bank; Arrow Electric Co.

For full biographical listings, see the Martindale-Hubbell Law Directory

STOLL, KEENON & PARK, LLP (AV)

400 West Market Street Suite 2650, 40202-3377
Telephone: 502-568-9100
Telecopier: 502-568-5700
URL: http://www.skp.com
Frankfort, Kentucky Office: 307 Washington Street, 40601.
Telephone: 502-875-6220.
Telecopier: 502-875-6235.
Henderson, Kentucky Office: 201 C North Main Street, 42420-3103.
Telephone: 270-831-1900.
Telecopier: 270-827-4060.
Lexington, Kentucky Office: 210 E. Main Street, Suite 1000, 40507-1380.
Telephone: 606-231-3000.
Telecopier: 606-253-1093; 606-253-1380.

MEMBER OF FIRM

Samuel D. Hinkle, IV

For Complete List of Firm Personnel, See General Section

For full biographical listings, see the Martindale-Hubbell Law Directory

*PIKEVILLE,** Pike Co.

GARY C. JOHNSON, P.S.C. (AV)

104 Caroline Avenue, P.O. Box 231, 41502
Telephone: 606-437-4002
Telecopier: 606-437-0021
Hazard, Kentucky Office: 941 Memorial Drive, P.O. Box 509, 41702.
Telephone: 606-436-6059.
Fax: 606-436-4599.
Lexington, Kentucky Office: 101 Prosperous Place, Suite 100, 40509.
Telephone: 606-263-4002.
Fax: 606-263-9651.

(See Next Column)

Richmond, Kentucky Office: 128 North Second Street, 40475.
Telephone: 606-624-0505.
Fax: 606-624-5393.

Gary C. Johnson

Anita Johnson
Roy J. Downey
Julie A. Butcher (Resident, Lexington Office)
Jeffrey R. Morgan (Resident, Hazard Office)
Jeremy R. Morgan (Resident, Hazard Office)
Masten Childers, II (Resident, Richmond Office)
Rhonda Jennings Blackburn
Angela Pergrem Owens (Resident, Richmond Office)
William R. Johnson
Bryan K. Sergent

For full biographical listings, see the Martindale-Hubbell Law Directory

LOUISIANA

*BATON ROUGE,** East Baton Rouge Parish

KANTROW, SPAHT, WEAVER & BLITZER, A PROFESSIONAL LAW CORPORATION (AV)

Suite 300, City Plaza, 445 North Boulevard, P.O. Box 2997, 70821-2997
Telephone: 225-383-4703
Fax: 225-343-0630; 343-0637

Byron R. Kantrow (1909-1997)
Carlos G. Spaht
Geraldine B. Weaver
Sidney M. Blitzer, Jr.
Paul H. Spaht
Lee C. Kantrow
John C. Miller
Vincent P. Fornias
David S. Rubin
Diane L. Crochet
Richard F. Zimmerman, Jr.
Bob D. Tucker
Martin E. Golden
J. Michael Robinson, Jr.
Connell L. Archey
Randal J. Robert

C. William Belsom, Jr.
Linda Orlansky Posner

Representative Clients: CNA Insurance Cos.; Federal Deposit Insurance Corp.; Hartford Insurance Group; Air Products and Chemicals, Inc.; CF Industries, Inc.; AT&T; United Companies Financial Corp.

For full biographical listings, see the Martindale-Hubbell Law Directory

KEAN, MILLER, HAWTHORNE, D'ARMOND, MCCOWAN & JARMAN, L.L.P. (AV)

22nd Floor, One American Place, 70825
Telephone: 225-387-0999
Fax: 225-388-9133
Mailing Address: P.O. Box 3513, Baton Rouge, Louisiana, 70821
URL: http://WWW.KMLAW.COM
New Orleans, Louisiana Office: Energy Centre, Suite 1560, 1100 Poydras Street, 70163.
Telephone: 504-585-3050.
Fax: 504-585-3051.
Plaquemine, Louisiana Office: Suite 10, 23425 Railroad Avenue, 70764.
Telephone: 225-687-9845.
Fax: 225-382-3445.
Lake Charles, Louisiana Office: One Lakeshore Drive, Suite 1220, 70629.
Telephone: 318-430-0350.
Fax: 318-436-5566.
Covington, Louisiana Office: 503 North New Hampshire Street, P.O. Box 3096, 70433.
Telephone: 504-875-0400.
Fax: 504-875-0500.

MEMBERS OF FIRM

Ben R. Miller, Jr.
Carey J. Messina
Isaac M. Gregorie, Jr.
G. Blane Clark, Jr.
James R. Lackie
Todd A. Rossi
Dean Paul Cazenave

Mark D. Mese
Aileen Johnson
Charles R. Elkins, II
Brett N. Brinson

Representative Clients: Amco Industries, Inc., Baton Rouge, LA; Associated Grocers, Inc., Baton Rouge, LA; Exxon Chemical Americas and Exxon Corporation, Baton Rouge, LA; Hancock Bank, Baton Rouge, LA; Lamar Advertising Co., Baton Rouge, LA; Mobil Oil Corporation, Fairfax, VA; Piccadilly Cafeterias, Inc.; Pipeline Technologies, Houston, TX; Union Planters Bank, NA, Baton Rouge, LA; Whitney Bank, New Orleans, LA.

For full biographical listings, see the Martindale-Hubbell Law Directory

*COVINGTON,** St. Tammany Parish

LAW OFFICES OF WILLIAM J. DUTEL (AV)

325 North New Hampshire Street, 70433
Telephone: 504-892-6474
Fax: 504-892-7307
Email: bdutel@fastband.com
New Orleans, Louisiana Office: 2960 Energy Centre, 1100 Poydras Street.
Telephone: 504-582-2429.

William J. Dutel

OF COUNSEL

Kimberly Kammler Dutel

For full biographical listings, see the Martindale-Hubbell Law Directory

*LAFAYETTE,** Lafayette Parish

RINGUET DANIELS & COLLIER, A PROFESSIONAL LAW CORPORATION (AV)

302 Rue France, Suite 201, P.O. Box 52647, 70505-2647
Telephone: 318-232-0002
Fax: 318-232-3410
Email: ringuet@earthlink.net
Jennings, Louisiana Office: 227 North Main Street, 70546.
Telephone: 318-824-2000.

Reginald J. Ringuet
James L. Daniels
William H. Collier

Representative Clients: Acadiana Medical Laboratories, Ltd.; Carrollton Resources Corporation; Chevron U.S.A., Inc.; Dependable Insurance Company; Forest Oil Corp.; Goodrich Operating Company, Inc.; Ron Guidry Enterprises, Inc.

For full biographical listings, see the Martindale-Hubbell Law Directory

*LAKE CHARLES,** Calcasieu Parish

WOODLEY, WILLIAMS, BOUDREAU, NORMAN, BROWN & DOYLE (AV)

A Registered Limited Liability Company
500 Kirby Street, P.O. Box 3731, 70602-3731
Telephone: 318-433-6328
Facsimile: 318-433-7513
Email: woodley@woodleywilliams.com

MEMBERS OF FIRM

Edmund E. Woodley (1925-1989)
James E. Williams (P.C.)
Robert J. Boudreau
Rick J. Norman
Donald C. Brown
James B. Doyle
Thomas J. Solari
Darrell W. Alston
Michele S. Caballero
M. Keith Prudhomme
Matthew D. Henrich

OF COUNSEL

Milo A. Nickel

Representative Clients: Agency Management Corp.; Travelers Insurance Co.

For full biographical listings, see the Martindale-Hubbell Law Directory

METAIRIE, Jefferson Parish

CAMPBELL, MCCRANIE, SISTRUNK, ANZELMO & HARDY, P.C. (AV)

3445 North Causeway Boulevard, Suite 800, 70002
Telephone: 504-831-0946
Fax: 504-831-2492

Frederick R. Campbell
Burgess E. McCranie, Jr.
Michael R. Sistrunk
Thomas P. Anzelmo
Sidney J. Hardy
Lance S. Ostendorf
Roy C. Beard
Mishthi Grace Ratnesar
Charles E. Sutton, Jr.
Isidro René DeRojas
Mark Emerson Hanna
Geoffrey J. Orr

Angela M. Bowlin
Catherine M. Williams
Colin D. Sherman
James H. Hunter
Richard Andrew Houston, III
Paxton K. Stelly
Michele Butler Prokop
Marty D. Parlipiano
Peter J. Wanek
Ken D. Brown

Representative Clients: Wal-Mart Stores, Inc.; Delchamps, Inc.; Greyhound Lines, Inc.; The Dial Corporation; Transport Insurance Company; Burger King Corporation; CNA Insurance Companies; The Louisiana Motor Vehicle Commission; Insbrok; Patent Scaffolding.

For full biographical listings, see the Martindale-Hubbell Law Directory

WEIR AND WALLEY (AV)

2721 Division Street, 70002-7084
Telephone: 504-455-7264
Fax: 504-455-7266
Email: weirwall@iamerica.net *URL:* http://www.weirandwalley.com

(See Next Column)

Andrew M. Weir
James M. Walley

ASSOCIATES

Mark Needham
Lisa A. Colby
Kenneth S. Moran

References: The Whitney National Bank; Omni Bank.

For full biographical listings, see the Martindale-Hubbell Law Directory

*MONROE,** Ouachita Parish

THOMPSON, SPARKS, DEAN & MORRIS (AV)

A Partnership including a Professional Corporation
1401 Royal Street, P.O. Box 2867, 71207
Telephone: 318-388-1440
Fax: 318-322-0887

MEMBERS OF FIRM

M. C. Thompson (1885-1970)
James D. Sparks (1910-1987)
George B. Dean, Jr., (P.C.)
Wood T. Sparks
John C. Morris, III

ASSOCIATE

Jennifer Allen Riley

Representative Clients: South Central Bell Telephone Co.; Greater Ouachita Water Company; PHH Homequity Corp.; Commonwealth Relocation Services, Inc.; Remax, Monroe; Bell South Advertising & Publishing Corp.; Premier Mortgage Corp.; Countrywide Funding Corp.
Approved Attorneys for: BankOne; Federal Land Bank.

For full biographical listings, see the Martindale-Hubbell Law Directory

*NEW ORLEANS,** Orleans Parish

LEAKE, ANDERSSON & MANN, L.L.P. (AV)

1700 Energy Centre, 1100 Poydras Street, 70163-1701
Telephone: 504-585-7500
Facsimile: 504-585-7775

W. Paul Andersson
Lawrence A. Mann
Kevin Cramer O'Bryon
George D. Fagan
Guy D. Perrier

OF COUNSEL

Robert E. Leake, Jr.

Representative Clients: Trailer Train; KFC; The Kroger Co.; Amway Corporation; Safelite Glass Co.; Wilsonart International; Montgomery KONE, Inc.; Newton & Assoc. Inc.

For Complete List of Firm Personnel, See General Section

For full biographical listings, see the Martindale-Hubbell Law Directory

LOWE, STEIN, HOFFMAN, ALLWEISS & HAUVER, L.L.P. (AV)

One Shell Square, 701 Poydras Street Suite 3600, 70139-7735
Telephone: 504-581-2450
Telecopier: 504-581-2461

MEMBERS OF FIRM

Mark S. Stein
Mitchell J. Hoffman
Michael R. Allweiss

For Complete List of Firm Personnel, See General Section

For full biographical listings, see the Martindale-Hubbell Law Directory

MIDDLEBERG, RIDDLE & GIANNA (AV)

201 St. Charles Avenue Suite 3100, 70170-3100
Telephone: 504-525-7200
Telecopier: 504-581-5983
Dallas, Texas Office: 2323 Bryan Street, Suite 1600.
Telephone: 214-220-6300;
Telecopier: 214-220-2785.
Austin, Texas Office: 1300 South Mopac Expressway, First Floor.
Telephone: 512-434-8334.
Houston, Texas Office: 7676 Woodway, Suite 325.
Telephone: 713-430-5000.
Telecopier: 713-430-5090.

MEMBERS OF FIRM

Ira Joel Middleberg
Michael Lee Riddle (Not admitted in LA)
Dominic J. Gianna

Paul J. Mirabile
John D. Person
Alan Dean Weinberger
L. Marlene Quarles
Edward T. Suffern, Jr.
Barry H. Grodsky
E. Ralph Lupin
A.J. Herbert, III
Marshall J. Simien, Jr.
Wade P. Webster
Rebecca J. King
Alvin Moon
Ernestine L. Anderson-Trahan

For full biographical listings, see the Martindale-Hubbell Law Directory

*SHREVEPORT,** Caddo Parish

BARLOW AND HARDTNER L.C. (AV)

Tenth Floor, Louisiana Tower, 401 Edwards Street, 71101-3289
Telephone: 318-227-1131
Telecopier: 318-227-1141
Mailing Address: P.O. Box 8, Shreveport, Louisiana, 71161-0008

Quintin T. Hardtner, III
David R. Taggart

Representative Clients: Kelley Oil Corporation; NorAm Energy Corp. (formerly Arkla, Inc.); Central and South West Corporation; Central Louisiana Electric Company; Panhandle Eastern Corp.; Pennzoil Producing Co.; Ashland Oil, Inc.; Southwestern Electric Power Company; General Electric Co.

For Complete List of Firm Personnel, See General Section

For full biographical listings, see the Martindale-Hubbell Law Directory

BLANCHARD, WALKER, O'QUIN & ROBERTS, A PROFESSIONAL LAW CORPORATION (AV)

Fourteenth Floor, Premier Bank Tower, 400 Texas Street, P.O. Drawer 1126, 71101
Telephone: 318-221-6858
Fax: 318-227-2967
Email: BWOR@BWOR.com
Bossier City, Louisiana Office: 2285 Benton Road, Suite B-201.
Telephone: 318-742-9255.
Fax: 318-742-9210.

John T. Cox, Jr.
Robert W. Johnson
Edward Keith Carter
Gary H. Love

For Complete List of Firm Personnel, See General Section

For full biographical listings, see the Martindale-Hubbell Law Directory

ROBERT U. GOODMAN, P.L.C. (AV)

Mid South Towers, 416 Travis Street, Suite 1105, 71101-5514
Telephone: 318-221-1601
Fax: 318-221-1749
Email: goodman@prysm.net

Robert U. Goodman

Representative Clients: Aeropres Corp.; Dealers Truck & Equipment Co.; Housing Authority of the City of Shreveport; Specht Newspapers, Inc.; Graham Brothers Entertainment, Inc.; Integrated Exploration, Inc.

For full biographical listings, see the Martindale-Hubbell Law Directory

MAINE

*PORTLAND,** Cumberland Co.

MARCUS, GRYGIEL & CLEGG, P.A. (AV)

100 Middle Street, East Tower, 04101-4102
Telephone: 207-828-8000
Fax: 207-773-3210
Email: firm@mgc-law.com

George J. Marcus
Jennie L. Clegg
Marilyn E. Mistretta
Lee H. Bals

Sean P. Joyce
Barbara G. Shaw
Michael J. Gartland
Regan M. Hornney

OF COUNSEL

Stephen G. Grygiel
Andrew Jeffrey Zulieve

For full biographical listings, see the Martindale-Hubbell Law Directory

PIERCE ATWOOD (AV)

One Monument Square, 04101
Telephone: 207-791-1100
Fax: 207-791-1350
Email: info@PierceAtwood.com *URL:* http://www.pierceatwood.com
Augusta, Maine Office: 77 Winthrop Street.
Telephone: 207-622-6311.
Fax: 207-623-9367.
Newburyport, Massachusetts Office: 6 Harris Street.
Telephone: 978-465-9599.
Fax: 978-465-9945.

MEMBERS OF FIRM

Bruce A. Coggeshall
James B. Zimpritch
Richard P. Hackett
David J. Champoux
Gloria A. Pinza
Ryan S. Stinneford

OF COUNSEL

Jeremiah D. Newbury

(See Next Column)

ASSOCIATES

James M. Saffian
William L. Worden
Keith J. Cunningham
Steven J. Scott

For Complete List of Firm Personnel, See General Section

For full biographical listings, see the Martindale-Hubbell Law Directory

PRETI, FLAHERTY, BELIVEAU, PACHIOS & HALEY, LLC (AV)

One City Center, P.O. Box 9546, 04112-9546
Telephone: 207-791-3000
Telecopier: 207-791-3111
Email: admin@preti.com *URL:* http://www.preti.com
Augusta, Maine Office: 45 Memorial Circle, P.O. Box 1058, 04332-1058.
Telephone: 207-623-5300.
Telefax: 207-623-2914.
Bath, Maine Office: Thirty Front Street, P.O. Box 665, 04530-0665.
Telephone: 207-443-5576.
Telefax: 207-443-6665.

MEMBERS OF FIRM

Harold C. Pachios
Michael J. Gentile (Augusta Office)
Eric P. Stauffer
Jonathan S. Piper
Randall B. Weill
James C. Pitney, Jr. (Augusta Office)
Leonard M. Gulino
Dennis C. Sbrega
Estelle A. Lavoie
Susan E. LoGiudice
Michael Kaplan
Michael L. Sheehan
John P. McVeigh
Jeanne T. Cohn-Connor
Timothy J. Bryant

COUNSEL

Gregory P. Hansel

ASSOCIATES

James E. Phipps
Bonnie L. Martinolich
Roy T. Pierce
Elizabeth A. Campbell

Representative Clients: KeyBank National Assn.; Blethen-Maine Newspapers, Inc.; Hussey Seating Co.; The Woodlands Club; P.H. Chadbourne & Co.; Rain Forest Aquaculture Products Inc.; Hannaford Brothers Co.

For Complete List of Firm Personnel, See General Section

For full biographical listings, see the Martindale-Hubbell Law Directory

TOMPKINS, CLOUGH, HIRSHON & LANGER, P.A. (AV)

Three Canal Plaza, P.O. Box 15060, 04112-5060
Telephone: 207-874-6700
FAX: 207-874-6705

Bruce M. Tompkins
Lawrence R. Clough
David M. Hirshon
Leonard W. Langer
Marshall J. Tinkle

For full biographical listings, see the Martindale-Hubbell Law Directory

TROUBH, HEISLER & PIAMPIANO, P.C. (AV)

511 Congress Street, P.O. Box 9711, 04104-5011
Telephone: 207-780-6789
Fax: 207-774-2339
Email: info@thplaw.com

William B. Troubh
Edwin A. Heisler
Robert J. Piampiano
Kevin M. Gillis
Michael P. Boyd
Thomas E. Getchell
Michael Richards
William K. McKinley
Daniel F. Gilligan
Paul S. Bulger
John G. Richardson

Daniel R. Felkel
Ann Brandt
John P. Flynn, III

For full biographical listings, see the Martindale-Hubbell Law Directory

MARYLAND

*ANNAPOLIS,** Anne Arundel Co.

ALEXANDER & CLEAVER, P.A. (AV)

54 State Circle, 21401
Telephone: 410-974-9000; Toll free: 1-800-292-LAWS
Cable: "ALEXLAW"
Fax: 410-974-9002
Waldorf, MD, Fort Washington, MD & Alexandria, VA
Email: ac@alexander-cleaver.com
Ft. Washington, Maryland Office: 11414 Livingston Road.
Telephone: 301-292-3300.
Alexandria, Virginia Office: 1513 King Street.
Telephone: 703-548-7777.
Waldorf, Maryland Office: Hamilton Centre, 3200 Highway 301.
Telephone: 301-870-8080.

(See Next Column)

ALEXANDER & CLEAVER P.A.—*Continued*

Gary R. Alexander
James A. Cleaver

Gerald F. Keipert
Thomas W. Kinnane
Todd K. Pounds
Joseph P. Hart
Denise M. Bowman
Jason A. Deloach
Chantel Renee Ornstein

For full biographical listings, see the Martindale-Hubbell Law Directory

HYATT, PETERS & WEBER (AV)

1919 West Street, P.O. Box 6635, 21401
Telephone: 410-266-0626
Fax: 410-841-5065
Email: info@hyatt.hpwsb.com *URL:* http://www.hpwlaw.com

Alan J. Hyatt
Paula J. Peters
Paul J. Weber

ASSOCIATES

Sara H. Arthur
John L. Hill
Sharon M. Grosfeld
Arlette K. Bright
Gregg M. Weinberg
Bruce F. Bright (Not admitted in MD)
Jonathan A. Hodgson

OF COUNSEL

Steven G. Tyler

For full biographical listings, see the Martindale-Hubbell Law Directory

*BALTIMORE,** (Independent City)

BALLARD SPAHR ANDREWS & INGERSOLL, LLP (AV)

300 East Lombard Street, 19th Floor, 21202-3268
Telephone: 410-528-5600
Fax: 410-528-5650
URL: http://www.ballardspahr.com
Philadelphia, Pennsylvania Office: 1735 Market Street, 51st Floor.
Telephone: 215-665-8500.
Fax: 215-864-8999.
Voorhees, New Jersey Office: Suite 100, 1101 Laurel Oak Drive.
Telephone: 856-627-8555.
Fax: 856-627-1153.
Denver, Colorado Office: Seventeenth Street Plaza Building, Suite 2300, 1225 17th Street.
Telephone: 303-292-2400.
Fax: 303-296-3956.
Salt Lake City, Utah Office: One Utah Center, Suite 1200, 201 South Main Street.
Telephone: 801-531-3000.
Fax: 801-531-3001.
Washington, D.C. Office: Suite 1000 South, 601 13th Street, N.W.
Telephone: 202-661-2200.
Fax: 202-661-2299.
Camden, New Jersey Office: 800 Hudson Square, 5th Floor.
Telephone: 609-541-5577.
Fax: 609-541-8272.

Tracy A. Bacigalupo
James J. Hanks, Jr.
Douglas M. Fox
Charles R. Moran
Sophie Dagenais Goetz
S. Nelson Weeks

For full biographical listings, see the Martindale-Hubbell Law Directory

GALLAGHER, EVELIUS & JONES, LLP (AV)

Park Charles Suite 400, 218 North Charles Street, 21201
Telephone: 410-727-7702
Facsimile: 410-468-2786
URL: http://www.gejlaw.com

MEMBERS OF FIRM

Francis X. Gallagher (1928-1972)
Leslie B. Speed
C. Edward Jones (1908-1999)
Christopher J. Fritz
John C. Evelius (Retired)
David E. Raderman
Richard O. Berndt
Peter E. Keith
Thomas N. Biddison, Jr.
Nita L. Schultz
Robert R. Kern, Jr.
Michael W. Skojec
Saul E. Gilstein
Kathryn Kelley Hoskins
Thomas B. Lewis
Mark P. Keener
Bonnie Abrams Travieso
Kevin J. Davidson
Stephen A. Goldberg
Eileen M. Lunga
Linda H. Jones
Lori A. Nicolle
Jack C. Tranter
Kenneth S. Gross
Thomas C. Dame

ASSOCIATES

Valarie K. Oulds
Michael J. Henigan
Margaret Stevens Jacks
David W. Kinkopf
Matthew W. Oakey
Paul S. Caiola
Rebecca A. Weaver
Jason W. Gaarder
M. Kirsten Andrews

(See Next Column)

LEGAL ASSISTANTS

Patricia C. Quayle
Margo Gibson Hughes
Iris T. H. Heath
Jonathan T. Gillis
Connie L. Ennis
Brenda J. Heacock
Margaret Graff
Dwayne L. Rodeheaver

Representative Clients: The Shelter Group; Mercantile-Safe Deposit and Trust Co.; The Enterprise Social Investment Corp.; GMAC Commercial Mortgage Corporation; Municipal Mortgages & Equities, LLC.

For full biographical listings, see the Martindale-Hubbell Law Directory

KOLLMAN & SHEEHAN, P.A. (AV)

Sun Life Building, 20 South Charles Street, 21201-3225
Telephone: 410-727-4300
Telecopier: 410-727-4391
URL: http://www.kollman-sheehan.com

Frank L. Kollman
Francis R. Laws
David M. Sheehan
Darrell R. VanDeusen
Peter S. Saucier
Clifford B. Geiger

Bruce M. Luchansky
Desmond Terrell McIlwain
Richard P. Rieman, Jr.
Joseph R. Salko
Randi Klein Hyatt
Tracy L. Knight
Jeffrey A. Trueman

For full biographical listings, see the Martindale-Hubbell Law Directory

VENABLE ATTORNEYS AT LAW VENABLE, BAETJER AND HOWARD, LLP (AV)

A Partnership including Professional Corporations
1800 Mercantile Bank & Trust Building, 2 Hopkins Plaza, 21201
Telephone: 410-244-7400
Fax: 410-244-7742
URL: http://www.venable.com
Washington, D.C. Office: Venable, Baetjer, Howard & Civiletti LLP, Suite 1000, 1201 New York Avenue, N.W.
Telephone: 202-962-4800.
Fax: 202-962-8300.
McLean, Virginia Office: Suite 400, 2010 Corporate Ridge.
Telephone: 703-760-1600.
Fax: 703-821-8949.
Rockville, Maryland Office: Suite 500, One Church Street, P. O. Box 1906.
Telephone: 301-217-5600.
Fax: 301-217-5617.
Towson, Maryland Office: 210 Allegheny Avenue, P. O. Box 5517.
Telephone: 410-494-6200.
Fax: 410-821-0147.

MEMBERS OF FIRM

Thomas P. Perkins, III (P.C.)
David M. Fleishman
Benjamin R. Civiletti (P.C.) (Also at Washington, D.C. and Towson, Maryland Offices)
Jeffrey A. Dunn (Also at Washington, D.C. Office)
Mitchell Kolkin
George F. Pappas (Also at Washington, D.C. Office)
John Henry Lewin, Jr. (P.C.)
Neal D. Borden (Also at Washington, D.C. Office)
William D. Coston (Not admitted in MD; Resident, Washington, D.C. Office)
Robert A. Shelton
Roger W. Titus (Resident, Rockville, Maryland Office)
Kenneth S. Slaughter (Not admitted in MD; Resident, Washington, D.C. Office)
James D. Wright (P.C.)
Joe A. Shull (Resident, Washington, D.C. Office)
James L. Shea (Also at Washington, D.C. Office)
Kenneth C. Bass, III (Not admitted in MD; Washington, D.C. and McLean, Virginia Offices)
Jeffrey P. Ayres (P.C.)
Amy Berman Jackson (Not admitted in MD; Resident, Washington, D.C. Office)
John H. Zink, III (Resident, Towson, Maryland Office)
C. Carey Deeley, Jr. (Also at Towson, Maryland Office)
Paul F. Strain (P.C.)
Christopher R. Mellott
William D. Dolan, III (P.C.) (Not admitted in MD; Resident, McLean, Virginia Office)
M. King Hill, III (Resident, Towson, Maryland Office)
James A. Dunbar (Resident, Towson, Maryland Office)
Paul T. Glasgow (Resident, Rockville, Maryland Office)
John A. Roberts (Also at Rockville, Maryland Office)
Joseph C. Wich, Jr. (Resident, Towson, Maryland Office)
Robert J. Bolger, Jr. (Also at Washington, D.C. Office)
Edward F. Glynn, Jr. (Resident, Washington, D.C. Office)
Charles R. "Rod" Marvin, Jr. (Not admitted in MD; Resident, Washington, D.C. Office)
Michael Schatzow (Also at Washington, D.C. Office)
Bryson L. Cook (P.C.) (Also at Washington, D.C. Office)
David J. Heubeck
J. Michael Brennan (Resident, Towson, Maryland Office)
Nell B. Strachan
David G. Lane (Resident, McLean, Virginia Office)
Herbert G. Smith, II (Not admitted in MD; Resident, Washington, D.C. Office)
G. Stewart Webb, Jr.
James K. Archibald (Also at Washington, D.C. Office)
David C. Mancini (Resident, McLean, Virginia Office)
Edward L. Wender (P.C.)

(See Next Column)

VENABLE ATTORNEYS AT LAW VENABLE, BAETJER AND HOWARD, LLP, *Baltimore—Continued*

MEMBERS OF FIRM (Continued)

Gary M. Hnath (Resident, Washington, D.C. Office)
Kevin L. Shepherd
Newton B. Fowler, III
Michael J. Baader
Mitchell Y. Mirviss
Wallace E. Christner (Also at Washington, D.C. Office)
Michael W. Robinson (Resident, McLean, Virginia Office)
David W. Goewey (Not admitted in MD; Resident, Washington, D.C. Office)
John A. McCauley
John T. Prisbe
Elizabeth Marzo Borinsky
Robert H. Geis, Jr.
Fernand A. Lavallee (Not admitted in MD; Resident, Washington, D. C. Office)
Vicki Margolis (Also at Washington, D.C. Office)
Maria F. Howell

OF COUNSEL

Emried D. Cole, Jr.
Robin L. Zimelman

ASSOCIATES

Paul D. Barker, Jr.
Daniel William China (Resident, Towson, Maryland Office)
Charles W. Durant (Not admitted in MD; Resident, McLean, Virginia Office)
Neal H. Strum

For Complete List of Firm Personnel, See General Section

For full biographical listings, see the Martindale-Hubbell Law Directory

YOUNG & VALKENET, L.L.C. (AV)

Suite 707 The Susquehanna Building, 29 West Susquehanna Avenue, 21204
Telephone: 410-583-2414
Telefax: 410-583-2418

Thomas G. Young, III
Thomas C. Valkenet

For full biographical listings, see the Martindale-Hubbell Law Directory

*ROCKVILLE,** Montgomery Co.

BRAULT, GRAHAM, SCOTT & BRAULT, LLC (AV)

101 South Washington Street, 20850
Telephone: 301-424-1060
Fax: 301-424-7991
Email: bgsb@earthlink.net
Washington, D.C. Office: Brault, Graham, Scott & Brault, PLLC, 1140 Connecticut Avenue, N.W., Suite 250.
Telephone: 202-785-1200.
FAX: 202-785-4301.
Fairfax, Virginia Office: Suite 500, 11350 Random Hills Road, Fair Oaks Plaza, 22030-7429.
Telephone: 202-785-1200.

OF COUNSEL

Laurence T. Scott
James Robert Miller

MEMBERS OF FIRM

Denver H. Graham (1922-1987)
Albert E. Brault (Retired)
Albert D. Brault (Resident)
Leo A. Roth, Jr.
James S. Wilson (Resident)
Ronald G. Guziak
Daniel L. Shea (Resident)
M. Kathleen Parker (Resident)
David G. Mulquin (Resident)
James M. Brault (Resident)
Regina Ann Casey (Resident)

ASSOCIATES

Rhonda Ann Hurwitz (Resident)
Joan F. Brault (Resident)

Representative Clients: American Oil Co.; Crum & Forster Group; Fireman's Fund American Insurance Cos.; Kemper Group; Reliance Insurance Cos.; Safeco Group; Government Employees Insurance Co.; Medical Mutual Insurance Society of Maryland; Legal Mutual Liability Insurance Society of Maryland.

For full biographical listings, see the Martindale-Hubbell Law Directory

STEIN, SPERLING, BENNETT, DE JONG, DRISCOLL, GREENFEIG & METRO, P.C. (AV)

25 West Middle Lane, 20850-2204
Telephone: 301-340-2020; 800-435-5230
Telecopier: 301-340-8217
Email: lawfirm@steinsperling.com
Falls Church, Virginia Office: 6245 Leesburg Pike, Suite 140, 22044.
Telephone: 703-237-0500.
Telecopier: 703-534-2899.

Millard S. Bennett
A. Howard Metro
Jeffrey M. Schwaber
Donald N. Sperling

Jeffrey D. Goldstein
Karen Plave Goldstein
David W. Lease

For Complete List of Firm Personnel, See General Section

For full biographical listings, see the Martindale-Hubbell Law Directory

*TOWSON,** Baltimore Co.

VENABLE ATTORNEYS AT LAW VENABLE, BAETJER AND HOWARD, LLP (AV)

A Partnership including Professional Corporations
210 Allegheny Avenue, P.O. Box 5517, 21204
Telephone: 410-494-6200
Fax: 410-821-0147
URL: http://www.venable.com
Baltimore, Maryland Office: 1800 Mercantile Bank & Trust Building, 2 Hopkins Plaza.
Telephone: 410-244-7400.
Fax: 410-244-7742.
Washington, D.C. Office: Venable, Baetjer, Howard & Civiletti LLP, Suite 1000, 1201 New York Avenue, N.W.
Telephone: 202-962-4800.
Fax: 202-962-8300.
McLean, Virginia Office: Suite 400, 2010 Corporate Ridge.
Telephone: 703-760-1600.
Fax: 703-821-8949.
Rockville, Maryland Office: Suite 500, One Church Street, P. O. Box 1906.
Telephone: 301-217-5600.
Fax: 301-217-5617.

PARTNERS

Benjamin R. Civiletti (P.C.) (Also at Washington, D.C. and Baltimore, Maryland Offices)
John H. Zink, III
Joseph C. Wich, Jr.
C. Carey Deeley, Jr. (Also at Baltimore, Maryland Office)
M. King Hill, III
J. Michael Brennan

For Complete List of Firm Personnel, See General Section

For full biographical listings, see the Martindale-Hubbell Law Directory

*UPPER MARLBORO,** Prince Georges Co.

KNIGHT, MANZI, NUSSBAUM & LAPLACA, P.C. (AV)

14440 Old Mill Road, 20772
Telephone: 301-952-0100
Annapolis/Baltimore: 410-792-3786
Fax: 301-952-0221

William E. Knight
Robert A. Manzi
Ronald M. Miller
William C. Brennan, Jr.
Harry J. Trainor, Jr.
Andrew W. Nussbaum
Raymond G. LaPlaca
John F. Shay, Jr.
Sheldon L. Gnatt
Daniel A. LaPlaca
Gail Borjeson Viens
Roger C. Thomas
Monica M. Haley-Pierson
Daniel F. Lynch III
Norman D. Rivera

Robert L. Lombardo
Amy B. Glaser
Brent M. Ahalt
Terry L. Bell

Representative Clients: Doctors Community Hospital of Maryland; The Fairways Group; AMOCO Oil Co., Southland Corp.

For full biographical listings, see the Martindale-Hubbell Law Directory

MASSACHUSETTS

AMESBURY, Essex Co.

THE HAMEL LAW FIRM (AV)

Five Market Square, P.O. Box 198, 01913-0398
Telephone: 978-388-3558
Telecopier: 978-388-0441
Email: hamellaw@excelr8.net
Email: hamellaw@lawyers.com *URL:* http://www.lawyers.com/hamellaw

MEMBER OF FIRM

Richard P. Hamel

ASSOCIATES

H. Scott Haskell
Peter R. Ayer, Jr.
Roger D. Turgeon

Representative Clients: First and Ocean National Bank, Newburyport, MA.
Approved Attorneys for: Chicago Title Insurance; Old Republic Title Insurance Co.

For full biographical listings, see the Martindale-Hubbell Law Directory

*BOSTON,** Suffolk Co.

BADGER, DOLAN, PARKER & COHEN (AV)

Formerly Badger, Sullivan, Kelley & Cole
2 Oliver Street, 02109
Telephone: 617-482-3030
Fax: 617-482-6919
Email: badger@badgerlaw.com *URL:* http://www.badgerlaw.com

(See Next Column)

BADGER, DOLAN, PARKER & COHEN—*Continued*

MEMBERS OF FIRM

Walter I. Badger (1885-1926)
John J. Sullivan (1926-1979)
David W. Kelley (1935-1986)
George F. Parker, III
James B. Dolan, Jr.
Lawrence J. Cohen

ASSOCIATE

R. Christopher Green

OF COUNSEL

G. Mitchell Eckel, III
Dorothy M. Bickford

For full biographical listings, see the Martindale-Hubbell Law Directory

CHERWIN, GLICKMAN & THEISE, LLP (AV)

A Limited Liability Partnership including Professional Corporations
One International Place, 02110-2622
Telephone: 617-330-1625
Fax: 617-330-1642
Email: cgandt@cgandt.com

Joel I. Cherwin (P.C.)
Jay F. Theise
Marshall D. Stein
David K. Wanger
William O. Rizzo
Lisa Lee Foster
Julie A. Koshgarian

For Complete List of Firm Personnel, See General Section

For full biographical listings, see the Martindale-Hubbell Law Directory

HANIFY & KING, PROFESSIONAL CORPORATION (AV)

One Federal Street, 02110-2007
Telephone: 617-423-0400
Telefax: 617-423-0498
URL: http://www.hanify.com

James Coyne King
John D. Hanify
Harold B. Murphy
David Lee Evans
Daniel J. Lyne
Donald F. Farrell, Jr.
Barbara W. Pfirrman
Gerard P. Richer
Timothy P. O'Neill
Terence P. McCourt

Jeffrey J. Upton
Michael R. Perry
Kathleen E. Cross
Robert E. Richards, Jr.
Joseph F. Cortellini
Andrew G. Lizotte
Donald Ethan Jeffery
Karen A. Whitley
Deena F. Christelis
Robyn J. Bartlett
Owen P. Kane
Sharon H. Patton
John C. McDonald
C. Alexander Hahn
Laurie J. Hurtt
Katherine T. Land
Brian P. McDonough
Lori A. Donovan
Brian R. Marinelli

For full biographical listings, see the Martindale-Hubbell Law Directory

HASSENFELD & LEDERMAN (AV)

An Association including a Professional Corporation
62 Commercial Wharf, 02110
Telephone: 617-367-6400
Fax: 617-367-0280

Merrill I. Hassenfeld, P.C.
Maury E. Lederman

For full biographical listings, see the Martindale-Hubbell Law Directory

HINCKLEY, ALLEN & SNYDER LLP (AV)

28 State Street, 30th Floor, 02109-1775
Telephone: 617-345-9000
Email: firm@haslaw.com *URL:* http://www.haslaw.com
Providence, Rhode Island Office: 1500 Fleet Center.
Telephone: 401-274-2000.
Fax: 401-277-9600. URL: http://www.hawlaw.com.

MEMBERS OF FIRM

Paula K. Andrews
David D. Barricelli
(Not admitted in MA)
E. Jerome Batty
(Not admitted in MA)
Jonathan Bell
Paul Bork
Stephen J. Carlotti
(Not admitted in MA)
David Barry Connolly
Joseph P. Curran
(Not admitted in MA)
Michael P. DeFanti
Eric F. Eisenberg
Malcolm Farmer, III
Margaret D. Farrell
(Not admitted in MA)
Pasco Gasbarro Jr.
Bruce G. Goodman
Hugh J. Gorman, III
Alan P. Gottlieb
Gerard R. Goulet
William R. Grimm
Paul A. Hedstrom
Richard L. E. Jocelyn
(Not admitted in MA)
Michael J. Kelly
Joel Lewin
Sandra Matrone Mack
(Not admitted in MA)
Matthew T. Marcello, III
(Not admitted in MA)
Frederick P. McClure
Elizabeth Murdock Myers
Paul F. O'Donnell, III
H. Peter Olsen
(Not admitted in MA)
Julianne Palumbo
John J. Pendergast, III
(Not admitted in MA)

(See Next Column)

MEMBERS OF FIRM (Continued)

Gerald J. Petros
James O. Reavis
Jeremy Ritzenberg
Ralph J. Rivkind
David J. Rubin
Charles E. Schaub, Jr.
Douglas F. Seaver
Scott E. Sheridan
Herman Snyder
David R. Sullivan
Robert F. Sylvia
Howard E. Walker
(Not admitted in MA)
Richard D. Wayne

ASSOCIATES

Jessica M. Bettencourt
(Not admitted in MA)
Mark Bianchi
Alyssa V. Boss
Alexandra K. Callam
Jane E. Cohen
Andrew D. Cummings
June E. Daniel
(Not admitted in MA)
Kim Herman Goslant
Gloria Maria Gutierrez
Kelley Jordan-Price
Catherine S. Kim
Christopher W. Morog
Elena B. Olson
Lawrence W. Vernaglia
Joseph D. Whelan
(Not admitted in MA)

OF COUNSEL

Willard R. Pope
Bentley Tobin
Joachim A. Weissfeld
(Not admitted in MA)

For Complete List of Firm Personnel, See General Section

For full biographical listings, see the Martindale-Hubbell Law Directory

*CAMBRIDGE,** Middlesex Co.

WILLIAM M. O'BRIEN (AV)

185 Alewife Brook Parkway, Suite 400, 02138
Telephone: 617-661-2600
Fax: 617-868-8040

For full biographical listings, see the Martindale-Hubbell Law Directory

LYNN, Essex Co.

DEMAKIS LAW OFFICES, P.C. (AV)

56 Central Avenue, 01901
Telephone: 781-595-3311
FAX: 781-592-4990

Thomas C. Demakis
Gregory C. Demakis
Sandor Rabkin

OF COUNSEL

Charles Demakis

Reference: Fleet Bank.

For full biographical listings, see the Martindale-Hubbell Law Directory

*SPRINGFIELD,** Hampden Co.

KAMBERG, BERMAN, P.C. (AV)

One Financial Plaza, 1350 Main Street, 01103-1628
Telephone: 413-781-1300
Facsimile: 413-732-0860
ABA/net: KAMBERGB
Email: kamberg@kamberg.com *URL:* http://www.kamberg.com

Abraham Kamberg (1895-1981)
Eugene B. Berman
Kerry David Strayer

References: Fleet Bank of Massachusetts, N.A.; Bank Boston/Springfield.

For full biographical listings, see the Martindale-Hubbell Law Directory

*WORCESTER,** Worcester Co.

SEDER & CHANDLER (AV)

A Partnership including a Professional Corporation
Established 1918
Burnside Building, 339 Main Street, 01608
Telephone: 508-757-7721
Telecopiers: 508-798-1863; 508-831-0955

MEMBERS OF FIRM

Samuel Seder (1918-1964)
Harold Seder (1934-1988)
Burton Chandler
J. Robert Seder
Darragh K. Kasakoff
Marvin S. Silver, P.C.
Robert S. Adler
Kevin C. McGee
Kurt L. Binder

ASSOCIATES

Paul J. O'Riordan
Jeffrey P. Greenberg
Todd Rodman

OF COUNSEL

Saul A. Seder
Gerald E. Norman
Philip C. Lombardo, Jr.

Reference: First National Bank of Boston; Safety Fund National Bank; Fleet National Bank.

For full biographical listings, see the Martindale-Hubbell Law Directory

MICHIGAN

*ANN ARBOR,** Washtenaw Co.

BRAUN KENDRICK FINKBEINER PLC (AV)

First National Building, 210 S. Main, Suite 700, 48104
Telephone: 313-995-4100
Telecopier: 313-995-4798
Email: ALBFIE@BKF-LAW.COM *URL:* http://www.bkf-law.com
Bay City, Michigan Office: 201 Phoenix Building, P.O. Box 2039.
Telephone: 517-895-8505.
Telecopier: 517-895-8437.
Saginaw, Michigan Office: 101 N. Washington, Suite 812.
Telephone: 517-753-3461.
Telecopier: 517-753-3951.
Saginaw Township, Michigan Office: 5800 Gratiot Road, Suite 107, P.O. Box 5169.
Telephone: 517-799-8692.
Fax: 517-799-4666.
Mt. Pleasant, Michigan Office: 805 North Brown.
Telephone: 517-775-7404.
Telecopier: 517-775-3764.

Barry M. Levine

Representative Clients: APV Chemical Machinery, Inc.; Bay Health Systems; Berger & Co.; Catholic Federal Credit Union; City of Saginaw; City of Vassar; City of Zilwaukee; Corporate Service; Cox Cable.

For Complete List of Firm Personnel, See General Section

For full biographical listings, see the Martindale-Hubbell Law Directory

BATTLE CREEK, Calhoun Co.

KREIS, ENDERLE, CALLANDER & HUDGINS, A PROFESSIONAL CORPORATION (AV)

One West Michigan Avenue, 49017
Telephone: 616-966-3000
Facsimile: 616-966-3022
Email: kech@kech.com *URL:* http://www.kech.com
Kalamazoo, Michigan Office: One Moorsbridge, P.O. Box 4010, 49003-4010.
Telephone: 616-324-3000.
Fax: 616-324-3010.

Russell A. Kreis (Resident, Kalamazoo Office)
C. Reid Hudgins III (Resident, Kalamazoo Office)
Robert B. Borsos (Resident, Kalamazoo Office)
Jeffrey C. O'Brien (Resident, Kalamazoo Office)
Stephen J. Hessen (Resident, Kalamazoo Office)
Thomas G. King (Resident, Kalamazoo Office)
Daniel P. McGlinn (Resident, Kalamazoo Office)
Janice Roark Peters (Resident, Kalamazoo Office)
Matthew S. DePerno (Resident, Kalamazoo Office)
Manuel R. Rupe (Resident, Kalamazoo Office)

For Complete List of Firm Personnel, See General Section

For full biographical listings, see the Martindale-Hubbell Law Directory

*BAY CITY,** Bay Co.

BRAUN KENDRICK FINKBEINER PLC (AV)

201 Phoenix Building, P.O. Box 2039, 48708
Telephone: 517-895-8505
Telecopier: 517-895-8437
Email: ALBFIE@BKF-LAW.COM *URL:* http://www.bkf-law.com
Saginaw, Michigan Office: 101 N. Washington, Suite 812. 8th Floor Second National Bank Building.
Telephone: 517-753-3461.
Telecopier: 517-753-3951.
Saginaw Township, Michigan Office: 5800 Gratiot Road, Suite 107, P.O. Box 5169.
Telephone: 517-799-8692.
Fax: 517-799-4666.
Ann Arbor, Michigan Office: First National Building. 201 S. Main, Suite 700.
Telephone: 313-995-4100.
Telecopier: 313-995-4798.
Mt. Pleasant, Michigan Office: 805 North Brown.
Telephone: 517-775-7404.
Telecopier: 517-775-3764.

Ralph J. Isackson
Daniel S. Opperman
Gregory T. Demers

Representative Clients: Bay Health Systems; Catholic Federal Credit Union; City of Saginaw; City of Vassar; City of Zilwaukee; Corporate Service; Cox Cable.

For Complete List of Firm Personnel, See General Section

For full biographical listings, see the Martindale-Hubbell Law Directory

BIRMINGHAM, Oakland Co.

HYMAN LIPPITT, P.C. (AV)

185 Oakland Avenue, Suite 300, 48009
Telephone: 248-646-8292
Facsimile: 248-646-8375
Email: hymalipp@tir.com

J. Leonard Hyman
Norman L. Lippitt
Douglas A. Hyman
Brian D. O'Keefe
H. Joel Newman
Nazli G. Sater
Kenneth F. Neuman
Terry S. Givens
Paul J. Fischer
John A. Sellers
Robert H. Lippitt
Roger L. Myers
Sally A. Rutledge
Joseph Pia
John P. Gonway
Leif K. Anderson
Jennifer S. Gold
Julie Lyons Kosovec
Dawn S. Spratley
Michael T. Price

For full biographical listings, see the Martindale-Hubbell Law Directory

BLOOMFIELD HILLS, Oakland Co.

JON H. BERKEY, P.C. (AV)

1700 North Woodward Avenue, Suite 101, 48304-2249
Telephone: 248-593-6460
Fax: 248-593-6470
URL: http://www.lawyers.com/jonberkeylaw

Jon H. Berkey

Anthony A. Yezbick

OF COUNSEL

Kenneth J. Wrobel, Jr.

For full biographical listings, see the Martindale-Hubbell Law Directory

FEENEY KELLETT WIENNER & BUSH, PROFESSIONAL CORPORATION (AV)

35980 Woodward Avenue Second Floor, 48304-0394
Telephone: 248-258-1580
Fax: 248-258-0421

James P. Feeney
S. Thomas Wienner
Peter M. Kellett
Cheryl A. Bush
Thomas J. Manganello
Seth D. Gould
Patrick G. Seyferth

James J. Majernik
G. Gregory Schuetz
Erin L. Dougherty
Michael A. Tesner
Clay A. Guise
Sarah A. McLaren
Lennox Emmanuel
Kathleen M. Horchler
Helen Melia Hammond

OF COUNSEL

Jerry L. Johnson

For full biographical listings, see the Martindale-Hubbell Law Directory

HERTZ, SCHRAM & SARETSKY, P.C. (AV)

1760 South Telegraph Road, Suite 300, 48302
Telephone: 248-335-5000
Fax: 248-335-3346
Email: lawhss@aol.com *URL:* http://www.legalleaders.com

Bradley J. Schram
Howard Hertz
Gary M. Saretsky
Robert S. Hertzberg
Victor M. Norris
Steve J. Weiss
Robert Paul Geller
Walter J. Piszczatowski
Jeffrey A. Robbins
Mark L. Kowalsky

Dana A. Donohue
Miles D. Hart
Karen A. Gould
Paul K. Villarruel
Bradford T. Yaker
Michael F. Jacobson
Michael I. Zousmer
Brian Witus
Eva T. Cantarella
Eric Andrew Michaels

COUNSEL

Richard P. Zipser
Lisa M. Kavalhuna (Not admitted in MI)
James W. Burdick

OF COUNSEL

David L. Steinberg
Albert L. Holtz
Elmer L. Roller
Robert A. Canner
Harvey D. Geller (1928-1989)

For full biographical listings, see the Martindale-Hubbell Law Directory

LISS AND ASSOCIATES, P.C. (AV)

The Pinehurst Building, 1400 North Woodward Avenue, Suite 200, 48304
Telephone: 248-647-9700
Facsimile: 248-647-5477; 248-647-0638

(See Next Column)

LISS AND ASSOCIATES P.C.—*Continued*

Arthur Y. Liss
Christine S. Reiner
Ronald S. Smith

Karen E. Seder

For full biographical listings, see the Martindale-Hubbell Law Directory

---

PROVIZER & PHILLIPS, P.C. (AV)

6785 Telegraph Road, Suite 400, 48301
Telephone: 248-642-0444
Facsimile: 248-642-6661
Toll Free: 1-800-288-9080
URL: http://www.lawyers.com/provizer&phillips

Harold M. Provizer
Randall E. Phillips
Marilyn A. Madorsky
Noel F. Beck
Mark S. Baumkel

Constance S. Hall

Representative Clients: Investuid Corporation; Mortgage Institute of Michigan.

For full biographical listings, see the Martindale-Hubbell Law Directory

---

*DETROIT,** Wayne Co.

BODMAN, LONGLEY & DAHLING LLP (AV)

34th Floor 100 Renaissance Center, 48243
Telephone: 313-259-7777
Fax: 313-393-7579
Email: info@bodmanlongley.com *URL:* http://www.bodmanlongley.com
Troy, Michigan Office: Suite 2020, 755 West Big Beaver Road.
Telephone: 248-362-2110.
Fax: 248-244-0780.
Ann Arbor, Michigan Office: 110 Miller, Suite 300.
Telephone: 734-761-3780.
Fax: 734-930-2494.
Northern Michigan Office: 229 Court Street, P.O. Box 405, Cheboygan.
Telephone: 231-627-4351.
Fax: 231-627-2802.

MEMBERS OF FIRM

Richard D. Rohr
Walter O. Koch (Troy Office)
Thomas A. Roach (Ann Arbor Office)
Kenneth R. Lango (Troy Office)
Herold McC. Deason
James R. Buschmann
Joseph J. Kochanek
Larry R. Shulman
Terrence B. Larkin (Troy Office)
Robert J. Diehl, Jr.
Barbara A. Bowman
Lawrence P. Hanson (Cheboygan Office)

COUNSEL

Alfred C. Wortley, Jr.
Lewis A. Rockwell
James C. Conboy, Jr. (Cheboygan Office)

For Representative Client List, See General Section

For Complete List of Firm Personnel, See General Section

For full biographical listings, see the Martindale-Hubbell Law Directory

---

PYTELL & VARCHETTI, P.C. (AV)

18580 Mack Avenue, 48236
Telephone: 313-343-9200; 1-888-292-4LAW
Fax: 313-343-0207
Email: PROBATE@compuserve.com *URL:* http://www.MIprobate.com

Robert H. Pytell
Henry C. Pytell (1903-1988)
Paul E. Varchetti

For full biographical listings, see the Martindale-Hubbell Law Directory

---

TIMMIS & INMAN L.L.P. (AV)

300 Talon Centre, 48207
Telephone: 313-396-4200
Facsimile: 313-396-4228
Email: info@timmis-inman.com *URL:* http://www.timmis-inman.com

Henry J. Brennan, III
Richard M. Miettinen
Bradley J. Knickerbocker

Erich J. D'Andrea
Anthony J. Long
Alex N. Saleh
Michael J. Sheehan

OF COUNSEL

David E. Costa

Representative Clients: Detroit Mortgage & Realty; DMR Fiancial Services, Inc.; J. Levin Sons Co.; Green Tree Financial Servicing Corp.; Hematology-Oncology Associates East, PC; Lakeshore Ear, Nose & Throat Center, PC; Micromanagement Systems, Inc.; Phoenix Crystal Corp.; Talon Surfaces LLC; Talon Automated Equipment Company.

(See Next Column)

For Complete List of Firm Personnel, See General Section

For full biographical listings, see the Martindale-Hubbell Law Directory

---

FARMINGTON HILLS, Oakland Co.

COUZENS, LANSKY, FEALK, ELLIS, ROEDER & LAZAR, P.C. (AV)

39395 West 12 Mile Road, Suite 200, 48331-2913
Telephone: 248-489-8600
Facsimile: 248-489-4156
Email: info@couzens.com *URL:* http://www.couzens.com

Sheldon A. Fealk
Jack S. Couzens, II
Jerry M. Ellis
Donald M. Lansky
Bruce J. Lazar
Alan C. Roeder
Renard J. Kolasa
Kathryn Gilson Sussman
Jeffrey A. Levine
Phillip L. Sternberg
Marc L. Prey
Lisa J. Walters
Stephen Scapelliti
Donald A. Wagner
Michael P. Witzke
Cyrus Raamin Kashef
Gregg A. Nathanson
David B. Deutsch
Mark S. Frankel

Roger E. Winkelman
Alisa A. Kwang
Turkia Awada Mullin
Raoul K. Maitra

Representative Clients: Provided upon request.
Reference: Michigan National Bank.

For full biographical listings, see the Martindale-Hubbell Law Directory

---

MICHAEL H. GOLOB (AV)

30300 Northwestern Highway, Suite 300, 48334
Telephone: 248-855-2626
Fax: 248-932-4009

For full biographical listings, see the Martindale-Hubbell Law Directory

---

*FLINT,** Genesee Co.

GAULT DAVISON A PROFESSIONAL SERVICE CORPORATION (AV)

Tenth Floor, Northbank Center, 432 North Saginaw Street, 48502-2032
Telephone: 810-234-3633
Fax: 810-233-3387
Email: gltdav@tir.com *URL:* http://www.gaultdavison.com

F. Robert Schmelzer
Richard C. Hohenstein

John R. Moynihan
Christopher A. Hajek

Representative Clients: Al Serra Automobile Co.; Harley-Davidson, Inc.; Harley Owners Group; Shoney's, Inc.; City of Flint; Vic Canever Chevrolet Co.

For full biographical listings, see the Martindale-Hubbell Law Directory

---

*GRAND RAPIDS,** Kent Co.

BORRE, PETERSON, FOWLER & REENS, P.C. (AV)

300 Ottawa N.W., Suite 500, P.O. Box 1767, 49501-1767
Telephone: 616-459-1971
Fax: 616-459-2393
Email: 105162.1531@compuserve.com

Glen V. Borre
James B. Peterson
Ben A. Fowler
William C. Reens
Frank H. Johnson
Mark D. Sevald
Harold E. Nelson
William R. Vander Sluis
John C. Arndts

Michelle H. Anthes

References: Old Kent Bank; NBD Bank/First Chicago Bank; The Huntington Bank.

For Complete List of Firm Personnel, See General Section

For full biographical listings, see the Martindale-Hubbell Law Directory

---

DE GROOT, KELLER, VINCENT & ALMASSIAN, P.L.C. (AV)

300 Trust Building, 40 Pearl Street, N.W., 49503
Telephone: 616-459-6251
Fax: 616-459-6352
Email: dkvkeller@aol.com

MEMBER OF FIRM

Brian D. Vincent

OF COUNSEL

Murray B. De Groot

For full biographical listings, see the Martindale-Hubbell Law Directory

Grand Rapids—Continued

GRUEL, MILLS, NIMS AND PYLMAN (AV)

50 Monroe Place, Suite 700 West, 49503
Telephone: 616-235-5500
Fax: 616-235-5550

MEMBERS OF FIRM

Grant J. Gruel
William F. Mills
J. Clarke Nims
Norman H. Pylman, II
Scott R. Melton
Brion J. Brooks
Thomas R. Behm
J. Paul Janes

Representative Clients: Aquinas College; Bell Helmet Co.; Blodgett Memorial Medical Center; Chem Central, Inc.; Cook Pump Co.; Grove, Inc.; NBDC; Heim Corp.

For full biographical listings, see the Martindale-Hubbell Law Directory

WARDROP & WARDROP, P.C. (AV)

Suite 150 The Frey Building, 300 Ottawa Avenue, N.W., 49503
Telephone: 616-459-1225
Fax: 616-459-7273
Email: wardrop@wardroplaw.com

Robert F. Wardrop II
Thomas M. Wardrop

Mary Saur Cohn
Brian L. Groen

For full biographical listings, see the Martindale-Hubbell Law Directory

*KALAMAZOO,** Kalamazoo Co.

KREIS, ENDERLE, CALLANDER & HUDGINS, A PROFESSIONAL CORPORATION (AV)

One Moorsbridge, P.O. Box 4010, 49003-4010
Telephone: 616-324-3000
Facsimile: 616-324-3010
Email: kech@kech.com *URL:* http://www.kech.com
Battle Creek, Michigan Office: One West Michigan Avenue, 49017.
Telephone: 616-966-3000.
Fax: 616-966-3022.

Russell A. Kreis
C. Reid Hudgins III
Robert B. Borsos
Jeffrey C. O'Brien
Stephen J. Hessen
Thomas G. King
Daniel P. McGlinn
Janice Roark Peters
Matthew S. DePerno
Manuel R. Rupe

For Complete List of Firm Personnel, See General Section

For full biographical listings, see the Martindale-Hubbell Law Directory

LEWIS & ALLEN, P.C. (AV)

Old Kent Bank Building, Suite 800, 136 East Michigan Avenue, 49007-3946
Telephone: 616-388-7600
Fax: 616-349-3831

Dean S. Lewis
W. Fred Allen, Jr.
Barry R. Smith
William A. Redmond
Stephen M. Denenfeld
Anne McGregor Fries
Gregory G. St. Arnauld
James M. Marquardt
Christopher T. Haenicke
Winfield J. Hollander (1906-1996)

LEGAL SUPPORT PERSONNEL

Dorothy B. Kelly

For full biographical listings, see the Martindale-Hubbell Law Directory

MILLER, CANFIELD, PADDOCK AND STONE, P.L.C. (AV)

A Professional Limited Liability Company
Founded in 1852 by Sidney Davy Miller
444 West Michigan Avenue, 49007-3752
Telephone: 616-381-7030
Fax: 616-382-0244
URL: http://www.millercanfield.com
Detroit, Michigan Office: 150 West Jefferson, Suite 2500, 48226-4415.
Telephone: 313-963-6420.
Fax: 313-496-7500.
Cable Address: "Stem Detroit."
Ann Arbor, Michigan Office: 101 North Main Street, 7th Floor, 48104-1400.
Telephone: 734-663-2445.
Fax: 734-747-7147.
Troy, Michigan Office: 840 West Long Lake Road, Suite 200, 48098.
Telephone: 248-879-2000.
Fax: 248-879-2001.
Grand Rapids, Michigan Office: 99 Monroe, N.W., Suite 1200, 49503-2639.
Telephone: 616-454-8656.
Fax: 616-776-6322.

(See Next Column)

Howell, Michigan Office: 121 South Barnard Street, Suite 4, 48843-2305.
Telephone: 517-546-7600.
Telecopier: 517-546-6974.
Lansing, Michigan Office: One Michigan Avenue, Suite 900, 48933-1609.
Telephone: 517-487-2070.
Fax: 517-374-6304.
Monroe, Michigan Office: 214 East Elm Avenue, Suite 100, 48162-2682.
Telephone: 734-243-2000.
Fax: 734-243-0901.
Washington, D.C. Office: 1900 K Street, N.W., Suite 1150. 20006.
Telephone: 202-429-5575; 785-0600.
Fax: 202-331-1118; 785-1234.
Pensacola, Florida Office: 25 West Cedar, 32501.
Telephone: 850-469-1088.
Fax: 850-432-0677.
New York, New York Office: 1450 Broadway, 41st Floor, 10018.
Telephone: 212-704-4400.
Fax: 212-704-4410.
Gdynia, Poland Office: UL. Slaska 21, 81-319.
Telephone: 011-485-831-2808.
Fax: 011-48-58-628 6411.
Warsaw, Poland Office: UL. Nowogrodzkall, 5th Floor, 00-513.
Telephone: 011-4822 529 0200.
Fax: 011-4822 529 0201.
Katowice, Poland Office: UL. Francuska 35/37, 40-027.
Telephone: 011 (48-32) 757-2414.
Fax: 011 (48-32) 757-2483.

PRINCIPALS

Eric V. Brown, Jr.
John R. Cook
Thomas H. Van Dis
James E. Spurr
Steven M. Stankewicz
Ballard Jay Yelton, III
Lori L. Purkey

Representative Firm Clients: Chrysler Corporation; Comerica, Incorporated; City of Detroit, Michigan; Detroit Tigers, Inc.; First of Michigan; Ford Motor Company; Ford Motor Credit Company; Great Lakes Bancorp; Henry Ford Hospital; INVETECH Company.

For Complete List of Firm Personnel, See General Section

For full biographical listings, see the Martindale-Hubbell Law Directory

LANSING, Ingham Co.

McCLELLAND & ANDERSON, L.L.P. (AV)

1305 South Washington, 48933
Telephone: 517-482-4890
Fax: 517-482-4875
URL: http://www.mcclelland-anderson.com

Gregory L. McClelland
Gail A. Anderson
David E. Pierson
Melissa A. Hagen
Kelly A. Myers

Marc D. Matlock
Jason W. Johnson

For full biographical listings, see the Martindale-Hubbell Law Directory

ROCHESTER HILLS, Oakland Co.

SHERMETA, CHIMKO & KILPATRICK, P.C. (AV)

445 South Livernois, Suite 333, 48307
Telephone: 248-652-8200
Fax: 248-652-1292
Mailing Address: P.O. Box 5016, Rochester, Michigan, 48308
Detroit, Michigan Office: 211 West Fort Street, Suite 704, 48226.
Telephone: 313-961-4848.
Fax: 313-961-4365.
Grand Rapids, Michigan Office: 169 Louis Campau Prom., Suite 2B, 49503.
Telephone: 616-774-9258.
Fax: 616-774-9411.

Douglass H. Shermeta
Darryl J. Chimko
Richardo I. Kilpatrick
Barbara L. Adams
Henry J. Mittelstaedt III
Kelly L. Scola
Christopher E. McNeely

Robert L. Dzialo
Sheryl S. Zamplas
Lisa E. Gocha
Kevin C. Calhoun
Kristin J. Ermshler
James E. Hess
Kyle J. VonAllmen
Elizabeth M. Abood
Jessica Brown Allmand
Dina L. Centifanti
Tania A. Hricik DeVries
Sharon Denise Koerber
Heather L. Miserlian
Gregory J. Roth
Larysa Sawertailo
Tyra T. Brown
Brent M. Lamkin
Charles Milne
Paul J. Smigielski

For full biographical listings, see the Martindale-Hubbell Law Directory

ROYAL OAK, Oakland Co.

CARDELLI HEBERT, P.C. (AV)

322 West Lincoln, 48067
Telephone: 248-544-1100
Toll Free 1-800-411-7774
Telecopier: 248-544-1191
Email: cardelli.hebert@worldnet.att.net

Thomas G. Cardelli — Deborah A. Hebert

Mary Ann J. O'Neil
Nicholas S. Andrews
John L. Weston
R. Carl Lanfear, Jr.
Robert J. Lantzy
Catherine Dritsas
Mark G. Cooper
Timothy R. Noonan

Representative Clients: Dana Corporation; General Motors Corporation; Otis Elevator Company; Raymond Corporation.

For full biographical listings, see the Martindale-Hubbell Law Directory

*SAGINAW,** Saginaw Co.

BRAUN KENDRICK FINKBEINER PLC (AV)

101 N. Washington Suite 812, 48607-1297
Telephone: 517-753-3461
Telecopier: 517-753-3951
Email: ALBFIE@BKF-LAW.COM *URL:* http://www.bkf-law.com
Saginaw Township Office, Michigan Office: 5800 Gratiot Road, Suite 107, P.O. Box 5169. Telephone 517-799-8692.
Fax: 517-799-4666.
Bay City, Michigan Office: 201 Phoenix Building, P.O. Box 2039.
Telephone: 517-895-8505.
Telecopier: 517-895-8437.
Ann Arbor, Michigan Office: First National Building. 201 S. Main, Suite 700.
Telephone: 313-995-4100.
Telecopier: 313-995-4798.
Mt. Pleasant, Michigan Office: 805 North Brown.
Telephone: 517-775-7404.
Telecopier: 517-775-3764.

Michael J. Sauer
Timothy L Curtiss
Francis J. Keating

Representative Clients: APV Chemical Machinery, Inc.; Bay Health Systems; Berger & Co.; Catholic Federal Credit Union; City of Saginaw; City of Vassar; City of Zilwaukee; Corporate Service; Cox Cable.

For Complete List of Firm Personnel, See General Section

For full biographical listings, see the Martindale-Hubbell Law Directory

SOUTHFIELD, Oakland Co.

COLLINS, EINHORN, FARRELL & ULANOFF, A PROFESSIONAL CORPORATION (AV)

4000 Town Center, Suite 909, 48075-1473
Telephone: 248-355-4141
Facsimile: 248-355-2277

Morton H. Collins
Brian D. Einhorn
Clayton F. Farrell
Stuart A. Ulanoff
Dale J. McLellan
Kenneth C. Merritt
Noreen L. Slank
Michael J. Sullivan
Janice G. Hildenbrand
Neil W. MacCallum

Theresa M. Asoklis
Karen C. Liddle
Deborah A. Lujan
Shannon M. Kos
Kevin P. Moloughney
Susan P. Saltzman
Daniel E. Collins
J. Mark Cooney
David C. Anderson

For full biographical listings, see the Martindale-Hubbell Law Directory

MASON STEINHARDT JACOBS PERLMAN & PESICK, PROFESSIONAL CORPORATION (AV)

Suite 1500, 4000 Town Center, 48075-1415
Telephone: 248-358-2090
Fax: 248-358-3599
Email: admin@msjp.com *URL:* http://www.msjp.com

John E. Jacobs
Michael B. Perlman
Jerome P. Pesick
Neil S. Silver
L. Jeffrey Zauberman
H. Adam Cohen
Diane Flagg Goldstein

Representative Clients: Citibank, N.A.; City of Dearborn; DeMattia Development Co.; Forest City Enterprises; Michigan Wholesale Drug Assn.; Mortgage Bankers Association of Michigan; Nationwide Insurance Co.; City of Taylor; Union Labor Life Insurance Co.; Yellow Freight Systems, Inc.

For Complete List of Firm Personnel, See General Section

For full biographical listings, see the Martindale-Hubbell Law Directory

MORGANROTH & MORGANROTH (AV)

3000 Town Center, Suite 1500, 48075
Telephone: 248-355-3084
Fax: 248-355-3017
URL: http://www.lawyers.com/morganrothlawfirm
New York, N.Y. Office: 156 W. 56th Street, Suite 1101. 10019.
Telephone: 212-586-5905.
Fax: 212-586-7302.

MEMBERS OF FIRM

Mayer Morganroth
Jeffrey B. Morganroth
Cherie Morganroth
Jason Ross Hirsch

Representative Clients: APCOA,Inc.; ; Mayor Coleman Young (Detroit); John Z. DeLorean; Realtek Industries, Inc.; Dr. Jack Kevorkian; Carolyn Warmus; Edward J. Holland, Jr.; Lyndon LaRouche; Thomas Warmus; Walter Keating.

For full biographical listings, see the Martindale-Hubbell Law Directory

SOMMERS, SCHWARTZ, SILVER & SCHWARTZ, P.C. (AV)

2000 Town Center, Suite 900, 48075
Telephone: 248-355-0300
Telecopier: 248-746-4001
Plymouth, Michigan Office: 747 South Main Street.
Telephone: 313-455-4250.

Steven J. Schwartz
Gary A. Taback
James J. Vlasic
David M. Black
Joseph H. Bourgon

David J. Szymanski
Jennifer M. Grieco
Matthew A. Fraiberg

OF COUNSEL

Charles S. Farmer

Representative Clients: Foodland Distributors; C.A. Muer Corporation; Vlasic & Company; Nederlander Corporation; Midwest Health Centers, P.C.; Vesco Oil Corporation.
Representative Clients: Michigan National Bank; Don Lee Distibutors; Rite-Aid of Michigan.

For Complete List of Firm Personnel, See General Section

For full biographical listings, see the Martindale-Hubbell Law Directory

TROY, Oakland Co.

BOWEN, RADABAUGH, MILTON & BROWN, P.C. (AV)

4967 Crooks Road, Suite 150, 48098
Telephone: 248-641-8000
Fax: 248-641-8219
Email: brmb@brmb.com *URL:* http://www.brmb.com

Thomas R. Bowen
James M. Radabaugh
Lisa T. Milton
Susan Leigh Brown

Geoffrey D. Marshall
Mark P. Dunn

OF COUNSEL

Meri Craver Borin

For full biographical listings, see the Martindale-Hubbell Law Directory

AUSTIN HIRSCHHORN, P.C. (AV)

Suite 710 Columbia Center, 201 West Big Beaver Road, 48084-4152
Telephone: 248-680-1660
Fax: 248-680-1671
Email: austinh@ix.netcom.com

Austin Hirschhorn

For full biographical listings, see the Martindale-Hubbell Law Directory

POLING, MCGAW & POLING, P.C. (AV)

Suite 275, 5435 Corporate Drive, 48098
Telephone: 248-641-0500
Telecopier: 248-641-0506
URL: http://www.lawyers.com/polingmcgaw&poling

Benson T. Buck (1926-1989)
Richard B. Poling
D. Douglas McGaw
Richard B. Poling, Jr.
Gregory C. Hamilton
Veronica B. O'Hara
James R. Parker
Shannon M. Acton

OF COUNSEL

Ralph S. Moore

Representative Clients: City of Troy; United States Fidelity & Guaranty Co.; Sentry Insurance Co.; Admiral Insurance; DeMaria Construction Co.; Leo Corporation; Aetna Casualty and Surety Co.; Concord Design; Pneumo-Abex; Ryko Manufacturing, Inc.

For full biographical listings, see the Martindale-Hubbell Law Directory

COMMERCIAL LITIGATION

ALABAMA

*BIRMINGHAM,** Jefferson Co.

BENTON & CENTENO, L.L.P. (AV)
Landmark Center, 2100 First Avenue North, Suite 550, 35203
Telephone: 205-278-8000
Facsimile: 205-278-8008
Email: douglascen@aol.com

MEMBERS OF FIRM

Lee R. Benton
Douglas J. Centeno

For full biographical listings, see the Martindale-Hubbell Law Directory

CAMPBELL, WALLER & MCCALLUM, L.L.C. (AV)
Suite 330, 2000-A Southbridge Parkway, 35209
Telephone: 205-803-0051
Fax: 205-803-0053

MEMBERS OF FIRM

Andrew P. Campbell
Jonathan H. Waller
Charles A. McCallum, III
David M. Loper
Martha Reeves Cook
Elizabeth Barger Anthony

For full biographical listings, see the Martindale-Hubbell Law Directory

EMOND & VINES (AV)
2200 SouthTrust Tower, 420 North 20th Street, P.O. Box 10008, 35202-0008
Telephone: 205-324-4000
Fax: 205-324-5020
Email: EmondVines@aol.com

MEMBER OF FIRM

Lanny S. Vines

ASSOCIATES

Michael Lee Allsup
Vivian D. Vines Campbell
Frank O. Hanson, Jr.

For full biographical listings, see the Martindale-Hubbell Law Directory

JOHNSTON BARTON PROCTOR & POWELL LLP (AV)
2900 AmSouth/Harbert Plaza, 1901 Sixth Avenue North, 35203-2618
Telephone: 205-458-9400
Telecopier: 205-458-9500
Email: Law@JBPP.com

MEMBERS OF FIRM

Don B. Long, Jr.
Charles L. Robinson
J. William Rose, Jr.
Gilbert E. Johnston, Jr.
James C. Barton, Jr.
Thomas E. Walker
Anne P. Wheeler
Hollinger F. Barnard
William D. Jones III
David W. Proctor
Oscar M. Price III
Robert S. Vance, Jr.
Anthony A. Joseph
R. Marcus Givhan
James P. Pewitt
David M. Hunt
Lee M. Pope

ASSOCIATES

Scott Wells Ford
Helen Kathryn Downs
David T. Payne
Anna R. Minor
Keith Adrian Brown
Andrew David Block

Counsel for: Bank of America, NSB; The Chase Manhattan Bank; The CIT Group/Equipment Financing, Inc.; Equifax, Inc.; General Motors Acceptance Corp.; Goldome Credit Corp.; Green Tree Acceptance, Inc.; Hyundai Motor Finance Co.; Mercedes-Benz Credit Corp.; Newcourt Financial USA, Inc.

For full biographical listings, see the Martindale-Hubbell Law Directory

LIGHTFOOT, FRANKLIN & WHITE, L.L.C. (AV)
The Clark Building, 400 20th Street North, 35203
Telephone: 205-581-0700
Facsimile: 205-581-0799
Email: LFWlaw@LFWlaw.com *URL:* http://www.lfwlaw.com

Warren B. Lightfoot
Samuel H. Franklin
Jere F. White, Jr.
Mac M. Moorer
John M. Johnson
M. Christian King
Adam K. Peck
Harlan I. Prater, IV
Michael L. Bell
William S. Cox, III
William H. King, III
Sara Anne Ford
William H. Brooks
Lee M. Hollis

(See Next Column)

Wynn M. Shuford
John Q. Somerville
Stephanie Keller Womack
Melody L. Hurdle
Robin Hansen Graves
J. Bradley Powell

For full biographical listings, see the Martindale-Hubbell Law Directory

LUSK, FRALEY, MCALISTER & SIMMS, P.C. (AV)
Suite 1700 AmSouth/Harbert Plaza, 1901 Sixth Avenue North, 35203
Telephone: 205-323-7100
Fax: 205-323-7050
Email: Lusk-Fraley.com

Donald D. Lusk
John M. Fraley
David L. McAlister
Keri Donald Simms
Kenneth A. Dowdy
David Lawrence Dean
David Thurston White, III
Susan Gilman McAlister
Payton Caldwell Lusk
Leslie Ann Caldwell

For full biographical listings, see the Martindale-Hubbell Law Directory

SMITH & ELY, LLP (AV)
2000-A Southbridge Parkway Suite 405, 35209
Telephone: 205-802-2214
Fax: 205-879-4445

MEMBERS OF FIRM

Carol Ann Smith
Brenen G. Ely

ASSOCIATES

Susan Rogers
Susan Caroline Haygood
Toby Dykes

OF COUNSEL

Lisa B. Singer

For full biographical listings, see the Martindale-Hubbell Law Directory

*DOTHAN,** Houston Co.

FARMER, PRICE, HORNSBY & WEATHERFORD, L.L.P. (AV)
115 West Adams Street, Drawer 2228, 36302
Telephone: 334-793-2424
Fax: 334-793-6624
Email: ehornsby@ala.net; eglasgow@ala.net
Email: eprice@ala.net

MEMBERS OF FIRM

J. Hubert Farmer (1896-1976)
Edward M. Price, Jr.
Ernest H. Hornsby
Joel W. Weatherford
D. Lewis Terry, Jr.
Elizabeth B. Glasgow
J. Vincent Edge

Representative Clients: AmSouth Bank, N.A.; Pea River Electric Cooperative; Hollis & Spann, Inc.; Faulkner Construction Co., Inc.; Burnham Shoes, Inc.; Quality Inn Carousel; Sheraton Inn; Holiday Inn-Ozark; Holiday Inn-Crestview; Inn South-Montgomery.

For full biographical listings, see the Martindale-Hubbell Law Directory

*MOBILE,** Mobile Co.

ARMBRECHT, JACKSON, DEMOUY, CROWE, HOLMES & REEVES, L.L.C. (AV)
1300 Riverview Plaza, P.O. Box 290, 36601
Telephone: 334-405-1300
Facsimile: 334-432-6843; 433-3821
Email: adc@ajlaw.com

MEMBERS OF FIRM

Rae M. Crowe
Broox G. Holmes
E. B. Peebles III
Kirk C. Shaw
Norman E. Waldrop, Jr.
Conrad P. Armbrecht
Grover E. Asmus II
David A. Bagwell
Douglas L. Brown
M. Kathleen Miller
Edward A. Dean
David E. Hudgens
Duane A. Graham
Wm. Steele Holman II
Broox G. Holmes, Jr.
James E. Robertson, Jr.
Clifford C. Brady

ASSOCIATES

Leah P. Ladd
J. Walton Jackson

Representative Clients: American Security Insurance Co. (Regional Counsel); American Security Group (Regional Counsel); AmSouth Bank (Regional Counsel); Burlington Northern Railroad Co. (District Counsel); International Paper Co.; Kimberly-Clark Corp.; Loyal American Life Insurance Co.; Mutual Assurance, Inc.; Travelers Insurance Co.

For Complete List of Firm Personnel, See General Section

For full biographical listings, see the Martindale-Hubbell Law Directory

Mobile—Continued

DAVID P. BROOME (AV)

AmSouth Bank Building, 107 St. Francis Street Suite 1408, 36633
Telephone: 334-432-9933
Fax: 334-432-9706
Mailing Address: P.O. Box 1944, Mobile, Alabama, 36633-1944
Email: broomelaw@aol.com

LEGAL SUPPORT PERSONNEL
Heidi Marie Fundinger

References: AmSouth Bank, NA; The Bank of Mobile.

For full biographical listings, see the Martindale-Hubbell Law Directory

FRAZER, GREENE, UPCHURCH & BAKER, L.L.C. (AV)

First National Bank Building, Suite 2206 107 Saint Francis Street, 36602
Telephone: 334-431-6020
Facsimile: 334-431-6030
URL: http://www.frazergreene.com

MEMBERS OF FIRM

A. Danner Frazer, Jr.
Edward C. Greene
Michael E. Upchurch
D. Brent Baker

Bruce M. Westbrook
W. Austin Mulherin, III
Marcus Edward McDowell

For full biographical listings, see the Martindale-Hubbell Law Directory

IRVIN GRODSKY, P.C. (AV)

1510 First National Bank Building, P.O. Box 3123, 36652
Telephone: 334-433-3657
Fax: 334-433-3670

Irvin Grodsky

For full biographical listings, see the Martindale-Hubbell Law Directory

HELMSING, SIMS & LEACH, P.C. (AV)

The Laclede Building, 150 Government Street, Suite 2000, P.O. Box 2767, 36652
Telephone: 334-432-5521
Telecopy: 334-432-0633

Larry U. Sims
Frederick G. Helmsing
John N. Leach, Jr.
Warren C. Herlong, Jr.
James B. Newman
Robert H. Rouse
Charles H. Dodson, Jr.
Joseph P. H. Babington
R. Alan Alexander
John J. Crowley, Jr.
Joseph D. Steadman
Todd S. Strohmeyer

William R. Lancaster
Robin Kilpatrick Fincher
John Townsend Dukes
John Casey Pipes
James Bradford Pittman, Jr.

For full biographical listings, see the Martindale-Hubbell Law Directory

ZIEMAN, SPEEGLE, JACKSON & HOFFMAN, L.L.C. (AV)

107 St. Francis Street, Suite 3200, P.O. Box 11, 36601
Telephone: 334-694-1700
Facsimile: 334-694-1998

MEMBERS OF THE FIRM

Thomas Troy Zieman, Jr.
Jerome E. Speegle
Robert G. Jackson, Jr.
Anthony Michael Hoffman
Ben H. Harris, III

For full biographical listings, see the Martindale-Hubbell Law Directory

*MONTGOMERY,** Montgomery Co.

BEASLEY, ALLEN, CROW, METHVIN, PORTIS & MILES, P.C. (AV)

218 Commerce Street, P.O. Box 4160, 36104
Telephone: 334-269-2343
Fax: 334-269-2371
Mailing Address: P.O. Box 4160, 36103-4160
Email: lisa@bwamc.com

James W. Traeger (1953-1987)
Jere Locke Beasley
Thomas J. Methvin
R. Graham Esdale, Jr.
L. Landis Sexton
Rhon E. Jones
Stephen W. Drinkard

Andy D. Birchfield, Jr.
Joseph H. Jay Aughtman
Delacie C. Hester
J. Mark Englehart
Scott T. McArdle
Clinton C. Carter
Tiernan W. Luck, III
Karen L. Mastin

(See Next Column)

LEGAL SUPPORT PERSONNEL
Lisa Harris (Office Manager)
Sidney Garcia (Information Technology Director)

For full biographical listings, see the Martindale-Hubbell Law Directory

BRANTLEY & WILKERSON, P.C. (AV)

405 South Hull Street, P.O. Box 830, 36101-0830
Telephone: 334-265-1500
Fax: 334-265-0319
Email: ashley@brantleywilkerson.com *URL:* http://www.brantleywilkerson.com

Paul A. Brantley
Mark D. Wilkerson

Amanda C. Carter

Representative Clients: MidCoast, Inc.; ALLTEL; Southeastern Cellular; TDS.
Reference: SouthTrust Bank, N.A.

For full biographical listings, see the Martindale-Hubbell Law Directory

KAUFMAN & ROTHFEDER, P.C. (AV)

2740 Zelda Road, Drawer 4540, 36103-4540
Telephone: 334-244-1111
Fax: 334-244-1969
Email: firm@krlegal.com *URL:* http://www.krlegal.com

Alan E. Rothfeder
Thomas R. DeBray
George W. Thomas
Simeon F. Penton
Carla Cole Gilmore

Counsel for: Dale Medical Center; Evergreen Medical Center; Community Health Systems, Inc.; The Russell Hospital Corporation.

For full biographical listings, see the Martindale-Hubbell Law Directory

PARNELL & CRUM, P.A. (AV)

641 South Lawrence Street, P.O. Box 2189, 36102
Telephone: 334-832-4202
Telecopier: 334-832-4703
Fax: 334-293-3550
Email: cnparnell@aol.com

Charles N. Parnell, III
G. Barton Crum

Robert J. Russell, Jr.
James McCauley Smith
Britt Batson Griggs
Angie Hubbard Ingram

Reference: Colonial Bank of Montgomery.

For full biographical listings, see the Martindale-Hubbell Law Directory

WEBB & ELEY, P.C. (AV)

166 Commerce Street, Suite 300, P.O. Box 238, 36101-0238
Telephone: 334-262-1850
Fax: 334-262-1772
Email: webbeley1@mindspring.com

James W. Webb
Michael M. Eley
Kendrick E. Webb
Craig S. Dillard
Bart Harmon
William R. Chandler

Frank E. Bankston, Jr.
Pamela Robinson Higgins
Shawn Junkins Cole
Michael J. Cohan
Lisa D. Van Wagner

LEGAL SUPPORT PERSONNEL
Janice B. Miller (Business Manager)

Reference: Regions Bank.

For full biographical listings, see the Martindale-Hubbell Law Directory

FRANK M. WILSON (AV)

201 Monroe Street, 36101
Telephone: 334-263-2555
Fax: 334-263-2533
Email: fmw@zebra.net *URL:* http://www.lawyers.com/fmwilsonlaw

For full biographical listings, see the Martindale-Hubbell Law Directory

*TUSCALOOSA,** Tuscaloosa Co.

PHELPS, JENKINS, GIBSON & FOWLER, L.L.P. (AV)

1201 Greensboro Avenue, P.O. Box 020848, 35402-0848
Telephone: 205-345-5100
Fax: 205-758-4394
Fax: 205-391-6658
Fax: 205-391-6663

(See Next Column)

PHELPS, JENKINS, GIBSON & FOWLER L.L.P.—*Continued*

MEMBERS OF FIRM

Sam M. Phelps
James J. Jenkins
Johnson Russell Gibson, III
Randolph M. Fowler
C. Barton Adcox
Farley A. Poellnitz
A. Courtney Crowder

ASSOCIATES

Karen C. Welborn
Stephen E. Snow
W. David Ryan
Bryan Patrick Winter
John M. Compton
Charles T. Grimes
Jenny B. Compton
(Not admitted in AL)
Laura C. Karns

LEGAL SUPPORT PERSONNEL

Christine Holt (Paralegal)
Lori R. Woodard (Paralegal)
Melissa D. Harvey (Paralegal)

Attorneys for: Aetna Insurance Co.; Allstate Insurance Co.; Carolina Casualty Insurance Co.; Continental Insurance Cos.; Fireman's Fund-American Insurance Cos.; Great American Insurance Co.; Hanover Insurance Co.

For full biographical listings, see the Martindale-Hubbell Law Directory

ARIZONA

MESA, Maricopa Co.

CHARLES HULTSTRAND, P.C. (AV)

151 North Country Club Drive, 85201-6521
Telephone: 480-461-9000
Facsimile: 480-461-8543

Charles Hultstrand

For full biographical listings, see the Martindale-Hubbell Law Directory

JACKSON WHITE GARDNER WEECH & WALKER, P.C. (AV)

40 North Center Street, Suite 200, 85201
Telephone: 480-464-1111
Fax: 480-464-5692
Statewide: 800-243-1160
Email: firm@azmesalaw.com *URL:* http://www.azmesalaw.com
Payson, Arizona Office: 708 East Highway 260, Suite C1-E.
Telephone: 520-472-8878.

Wayne L. Gardner
Eric M. Jackson
Michael R. Pruitt
J. Grant Walker
Bradley D. Weech
Richard A. White
David L. Weed
Roger R. Foote
Otto S. Shill, III

Eric K. Macdonald
Kelly G. Black
Melody K. Seal
Patricia A. Mancabelli
Bobbie J. Rasmusson
Maureen P. Kane
James L. Tanner

For full biographical listings, see the Martindale-Hubbell Law Directory

UDALL, SHUMWAY, BLACKHURST, ALLEN & LYONS, P.C. (AV)

30 West First Street, 85201-1446
Telephone: 480-461-5300
Facsimile: 480-461-5398
Email: usbalsea@vtc.net
Willcox, Arizona Office: 135 East Maley.
Telephone: 602-384-3389.
Fax: 602-384-2280.

David K. Udall
Dale R. Shumway
Dennis P. Blackhurst
John H. Lyons
Barry C. Dickerson
Steven H. Everts
Clark R. Richter
Roger C. Decker
Peter W. Taylor
Denise Lowell-Britt
Stephen L. West

David R. Schwartz
Robert M. Jarrett, Jr.
(Resident, Willcox Office)
Brian T. Allen
Curtis M. Chipman
April A. Speelmon

Representative Clients: Mesa Public Schools; Ticor Title; University of Arizona; Wal-Mart Stores, Inc.; Church of Jesus Christ of Latter Day Saints.

For full biographical listings, see the Martindale-Hubbell Law Directory

*PHOENIX,** Maricopa Co.

ATKINSON, HAMILL & BARROWCLOUGH, P.C. (AV)

3550 North Central Avenue, Suite 1150, 85012
Telephone: 602-222-4828
Facsimile: 602-222-4820

(See Next Column)

Joseph M. Atkinson
Christopher G. Hamill
Patrick R. Barrowclough

Representative Clients: Biddulph Automotive Dealerships (Oldsmobile, Honda, Pontiac, GMC, Jeep/Eagle and RV); Del Webb Corp.; Federal Deposit Insurance Corp.; Fingerhut Cos.; First American Title Insurance Company of Arizona; John Jacobs' Golf Cos.; Motorola Inc.; PACCAR Financial Corp.; Sun Automotive Group (Scottsdale Acura, Jaguar, Range Rover, Lexus, Porsche, Audi and BMW); Sentinel Real Estate Fund.

For full biographical listings, see the Martindale-Hubbell Law Directory

BAIRD, WILLIAMS, DAVIS & SMITH (AV)

340 East Palm Lane Suite 150, 85004-4530
Telephone: 602-256-9400
Fax: 602-271-9308
Email: bwds@primenet.com *URL:* http://www.lawyers.com/bwds

MEMBERS OF FIRM

J. Ernest Baird
Daryl M. Williams
Patrick J. Davis
David Earl Smith

ASSOCIATE

Russell R. Rea

For full biographical listings, see the Martindale-Hubbell Law Directory

BEUS, GILBERT & DEVITT, P.L.L.C. (AV)

Suite 1000, Great American Tower, 3200 North Central Avenue, 85012-2417
Telephone: 602-274-8229
Fax: 602-234-5893

John V. Berry
Leo R. Beus
Laurie B. Craig
Michael R. Devitt
Nicholas J. DiCarlo
Paul E. Gilbert
Scott D. Larmore
Anthony H. Misseldine
Paul L. Mueller
Quinton F. Seamons
(Not admitted in AZ)
Richard R. Thomas
Gordon M. Wasson

Jeffrey R. Adams
Diana Archer
Christopher A. Caserta
Craig D. Henley
Richard X. Herrera
J. Ridge Hicks
Christine N. Jones
Timothy G. Kasparek
Alan C. Kuffner
Malcolm Loeb
Michele L. Lorenzen
Daniel D. Maddy
Christopher E. Martin
Robert T. Mills
Jason Barclay Morris
Marc F. Pappalardo
Joseph B. Pierce
Wendy M. Rector

Representative Clients: Albertsons; Bonneville Pacific Corp.; Cardon; Carioca Oil Co.; Dillards Department Stores; Hard Rock America; J.R. Norton Co.; John C. Lincoln Hospital Foundation; Mayo Clinic Scottsdale; McDonalds Corp.

For full biographical listings, see the Martindale-Hubbell Law Directory

BONN, LUSCHER, PADDEN & WILKINS, CHARTERED (AV)

805 North Second Street, 85004
Telephone: 602-254-5557
Fax: 602-254-0656
Email: firm@blpw.com

Paul V. Bonn
Jeff C. Padden
Randall D. Wilkins
John H. Cassidy
D. Michael Hall
Daniel G. Martin
James M. Barrons

OF COUNSEL

Brian A. Luscher
Marvin Kantor

Howard D. Sukenic

For full biographical listings, see the Martindale-Hubbell Law Directory

BONNETT, FAIRBOURN, FRIEDMAN & BALINT, P.C. (AV)

4041 North Central Avenue Suite 1100, 85012
Telephone: 602-274-1100
Fax: 602-274-1199

Jerry C. Bonnett
William G. Fairbourn
Andrew S. Friedman
Francis J. Balint, Jr.
H. Sullivan Bunch
Michael N. Widener
Robert J. Spurlock
C. Kevin Dykstra
Elaine A. Ryan
Tara L. Jackson
Wendy J. Harrison
Scott A. Erickson
Guy A. Hanson
Robert D. Ryan

Christina Bannon
Jason Ebe
Andrew Quinn Everroad
Anthony J. Fernandez
Myndi M. Eakin
Barbara A. Bagdon
David D. Weinzweig
Russell R. Yurk

(See Next Column)

BONNETT, FAIRBOURN, FRIEDMAN & BALINT P.C., *Phoenix—Continued*

OF COUNSEL

James Duke Cameron

For full biographical listings, see the Martindale-Hubbell Law Directory

LAW OFFICES OF JAMES BUSH, P.C. (AV)

322 West Roosevelt Street, 85003-1325
Telephone: 602-256-2874
Fax: 602-252-2864
Email: attybush@primenet.com

James A. Bush

For full biographical listings, see the Martindale-Hubbell Law Directory

COHEN KENNEDY DOWD & QUIGLEY, P.C. (AV)

The Esplanade, 2425 East Camelback Road, Suite 1100, 85016
Telephone: 602-252-8400
Fax: 602-252-5339
Email: cklaw@cohenkennedylaw.com

Ronald Jay Cohen
Laura H. Kennedy
Daniel G. Dowd
Daniel P. Quigley

Raymond K. Ramella
Eva C. Miller
J. Christopher Gooch
Ann Thompson Uglietta
David D. Burkhead
Rebecca Lee van Doren

SPECIAL COUNSEL

Paula M. DeMore

Representative Clients: Pricewaterhouse Coopers, LLP; Del Webb Corp.; Phelps Dodge Corp.; Inter-Tel; Kabuto Arizona Properties; Exxon Company USA; Park Electrochemical Corp.; Integrated Information Systems, Inc.; Arizona State University; Grubb & Ellis Realty Co.

For full biographical listings, see the Martindale-Hubbell Law Directory

DUSHOFF & MCCALL, A PROFESSIONAL CORPORATION (AV)

Two Renaissance Square, Suite 1000, 40 North Central, 85004
Telephone: 602-254-3800
Fax: 602-258-2551
URL: http://www.dushoff@neta.com

Jay Dushoff
Jack E. McCall (1942-1995)
Michael Riikola
Leonard M. Bell

Patrick J. McGill
Robert H. Kreutzer

LEGAL SUPPORT PERSONNEL

Thomas M. Flynn

For full biographical listings, see the Martindale-Hubbell Law Directory

FENNEMORE CRAIG, A PROFESSIONAL CORPORATION (AV)

3003 North Central Avenue, Suite 2600, 85012-2913
Telephone: 602-916-5000
Fax: 602-916-5999
Tucson, Arizona Office: One South Church Avenue, Suite 1000, 85701-1620.
Telephone: 520-879-6800.
Fax: 520-879-6899.

Jordan Green
Donald R. Gilbert
Timothy J. Burke
Ronald J. Stolkin
Roger T. Hargrove
David T. Maddox
C. Owen Paepke
William L. Thorpe
David A. Weatherwax
Ray K. Harris
Andrew M. Federhar
Christopher L. Callahan
Janet W. Lord
John J. Balitis, Jr.
James J. Trimble
Keith L. Hendricks
Douglas C. Northup

Mark H. Brain
Dewain D. Fox
Jay L. Shapiro
James D. Burgess
Scott L. Altes
Mary Beth Phillips
Erin E. Flaharty
Vera E. Munoz
Sal J. Rivera
Barney M. Holtzman
Joseph Sciarrotta, Jr.
Rosa Mroz

LEGAL SUPPORT PERSONNEL

LEGAL ASSISTANTS

Claudia E. Anderson
Beverly Cooper
Nancy E. Esser
Ann V. Kooi

For Complete List of Firm Personnel, See General Section

For full biographical listings, see the Martindale-Hubbell Law Directory

FOGEL, LAMBER & BRONNENKANT, PROFESSIONAL ASSOCIATION (AV)

4001 North Third Street, Suite 400, 85012
Telephone: 602-264-3330
Fax: 602-274-5117

Sherman D. Fogel
Dennis M. Lamber
Rex P. Bronnenkant

For full biographical listings, see the Martindale-Hubbell Law Directory

AMY J. GITTLER, PLC (AV)

2633 East Indian School Road, Suite 300, 85016-6759
Telephone: 602-224-6300
Facsimile: 602-224-6020
Email: amy@cgson.com *URL:* http://www.lawyers.com/gittlerlaw

Amy J. Gittler

Tricia Brown

For full biographical listings, see the Martindale-Hubbell Law Directory

GLOVER & VAN COTT, A PROFESSIONAL ASSOCIATION (AV)

Suite 260, The Brookstone, 2025 North Third Street, 85004-1487
Telephone: 602-257-9160
Telecopier: 602-257-9180

Michael R. Glover
Joyce N. Van Cott
Dari S. Hing

Ryan J. Talamante
Mary Grace McNear
Darrien O. Shuquem

Representative Clients: American Bonding Company; Arizona Department of Insurance; FitzGibbons, Tharp and Associates, Inc.; Farm and Home Life Insurance Company; Legacy Life Insurance Company; Pentad Securities; American Way Enterprises; The Raymond Co.; Abacus Inn Restaurant; Carefree Pool & Patio, Inc.

For full biographical listings, see the Martindale-Hubbell Law Directory

JOHN D. HARRIS, P.C. (AV)

1 East Camelback Road, Suite 630, 85012-1651
Telephone: 602-340-1234
Telecopier: 602-277-6678
Email: jdharris@doitnow.com

John Duke Harris

J. Scott Conlon

For full biographical listings, see the Martindale-Hubbell Law Directory

HOLPER, WELSH & MITCHELL, LTD. (AV Ⓣ)

2415 East Camelback Road, Suite 700, 85016
Telephone: 602-508-6033
Fax: 480-483-0269
Email: rholper@aol.com *URL:* http://www.lawyers.com/holperwelsh&mitchell
Minneapolis, Minnesota Office: 4100 Multifoods Tower, 33 South Sixth Street, 55402.
Telephone: 612-317-1012.
Fax: 612-317-0947.

Richard D. Holper
Mary Ann Welsh

For full biographical listings, see the Martindale-Hubbell Law Directory

HORNE, BISTROW & DULBERG, P.C. (AV)

Renaissance Two, 40 North Central, Suite 2800, 85004
Telephone: 602-253-9700
Fax: 602-258-4805
Email: kcorson@azlitigation.com *URL:* http://www.azlitigation.com

Thomas C. Horne
Eric J. Bistrow
Michael S. Dulberg

Joel E. Sannes

For full biographical listings, see the Martindale-Hubbell Law Directory

JABURG & WILK, P.C. (AV)

Great American Tower, 3200 North Central Avenue, Suite 2000, 85012
Telephone: 602-248-1000
Fax: 602-248-0522
Email: rcp@jaburglaw.com

(See Next Column)

JABURG & WILK P.C.—*Continued*

Gary J. Jaburg
Lawrence E. Wilk
Roger L. Cohen
Randy Nussbaum
Mitchell Reichman
Beth S. Cohn
Loren Molever
Robert C. Houser, Jr.
Mervyn T. Braude
Michael E. Gottfried

Kathi Mann Sandweiss
Jeffry M. Edwards
Tracy A. Miller
Stephanie N. Monroe
George A. Tacker
Peter W. Ware, Jr.

OF COUNSEL

Richard M. Gerry

Representative Clients: Employee Solutions, Inc.; Sleep America, Inc.; Desert Schools Federal Credit Union; North Star Plumbing; Nations Bank of Texas; State of Arizona; FHLMC; Arizona Escrow & Financial Services.

For full biographical listings, see the Martindale-Hubbell Law Directory

KIMERER & LAVELLE, P.L.C. (AV)

100 W. Clarendon Suite 2100, 85013
Telephone: 602-279-5900; 800-220-6817
Fax: 602-264-5566
Email: KimLav.com

Michael D. Kimerer
Michael J. LaVelle
Clark L. Derrick

Teri Dyan McCall

Representative Clients: The National Basketball Association; Aetna Insurance Co.; Kaibab Industries; Centric Jones Constructors; B & B Masonry; Western Block.

For full biographical listings, see the Martindale-Hubbell Law Directory

LIEBERMAN, DODGE, SENDROW & GERDING, LTD. (AV)

Phoenix Corporate Center 18th Floor, 3003 North Central Avenue, 85012
Telephone: 602-277-3000
Fax: 602-277-7478
URL: http://www.azlawyers.com

Robert G. Anderson
David D. Dodge
David N. Farren
Paul S. Gerding
Karen L. Kothe
Marc R. Lieberman
Susan G. Sendrow

Paul S. Gerding, Jr.

SPECIAL COUNSEL

Michael J. Fuller
Connie J. Mableson
Lawrence J. Buckley

Representative Clients: Arizona Education Association; Public Safety Personnel Retirement System; Wells Fargo Bank and Credit Corp.; Regency Savings Bank; Baxter Healthcare Corporation; Aetna Life Insurance Company; Fairbanks Capital Corp.

For full biographical listings, see the Martindale-Hubbell Law Directory

MARISCAL, WEEKS, MCINTYRE & FRIEDLANDER, P.A. (AV)

2901 North Central Avenue Suite 200, 85012-2705
Telephone: 602-285-5000
Fax: 602-285-5100

Richard A. Friedlander
Michael S. Rubin
Gary L. Birnbaum
Robert A. Shull
Michael R. Scheurich
Andrew L. Pringle
Brian M. Mueller
P. Bruce Converse
Leonce A. Richard
Scott A. Holcomb
David J. Ouimette
D. Samuel Coffman
Scot L. Claus
David D. Rodgers
Valerie Costa-Sheedy
Allison R. Shiff

References: Northern Trust Bank of Arizona; National Bank of Arizona.

For Complete List of Firm Personnel, See General Section

For full biographical listings, see the Martindale-Hubbell Law Directory

MCCABE O'DONNELL, A PROFESSIONAL ASSOCIATION (AV)

3101 North Central Avenue Suite 700, P.O. Box 33457, 85012
Telephone: 602-264-0800
Facsimile: 602-274-0146
URL: http://www.lawyers.com/mccabephx.com

Joseph I. McCabe
Alan L. Tipton
Clifford J. Roth

A List of Representative Clients will be Furnished upon Request.

For full biographical listings, see the Martindale-Hubbell Law Directory

MEYER, HENDRICKS & BIVENS, P.A. (AV)

3003 North Central Avenue Suite 1200, 85012-2915
Telephone: 602-604-2200
Facsimile: (24 Hrs.) 602-263-5333
Mailing Address: P.O. Box 2199, 85001-2199

Don Bivens
Tom Galbraith
Ed Hendricks
Jennifer P. Nore

Michael F. Barry
Viet V. Le
Nona M. Lee
Paul L. Stoller
Michael R. Ross
Ed Hendricks, Jr.
Gerald F. Giordano, Jr.

Reference: Northern Trust Bank of Arizona.

For full biographical listings, see the Martindale-Hubbell Law Directory

MUCHMORE & WALLWORK, A PROFESSIONAL CORPORATION (AV)

2700 North Central Avenue, Suite 1225, 85004-1165
Telephone: 602-240-6699
Data: 602-240-6698
Facsimile: 602-240-6697
Email: muchwork@mmww.com *URL:* http://www.mmww.com

Charles J. Muchmore
Nicholas J. Wallwork
Fredric D. Bellamy

SENIOR COUNSEL

Steve Owens

COUNSEL

Bridget S. Bade

Christopher D. Payne
Carolina L. Carver
Margaret Benny Hurst
Mindy K. Brinker

OF COUNSEL

Leslie Kyman Cooper
George H. King

LEGAL SUPPORT PERSONNEL

Gloria A. Torres (Administrator)
James R. Potts (Systems Administrator and Litigation Support Manager)
Gale James (Finance Manager)

Representative Clients: AgrEvo USA Company; BHP Copper, Inc.; Chevron U.S.A., Inc.; Cyprus Amax Minerals Company; Homes by Dave Brown, Inc.; National Indemnity Insurance Company; Standard Insurance Company; Washington Mills Electro Minerals Corporation; Cadbury Beverages, Inc.; Eisenberg Company.

For full biographical listings, see the Martindale-Hubbell Law Directory

MURPHY & POSNER, L.L.P. (AV)

3200 East Camelback Road, Suite 300, 85018
Telephone: 602-224-5900
Telecopier: 602-224-5754
Email: lawfirm@murphy-posner.com *URL:* http://www.murphy-posner.com

Terry L. Rakow
Don A. Davis
K. Bellamy Brown
Earl E. Berg

ASSOCIATE

Don C. Fletcher

OF COUNSEL

John A. Murphy, Jr.

Representative Clients: The Westcor Companies; Westcor Partners; Amerimar Enterprises, Inc.; Spieker Properties; Irwin Mortgage Corporation.

For full biographical listings, see the Martindale-Hubbell Law Directory

MYERS & JENKINS, A PROFESSIONAL CORPORATION (AV)

Phoenix Corporate Center, 3003 North Central Avenue, Suite 1900, 85012
Telephone: 602-200-7900
Facsimile: 602-200-7910
Email: firm@mjlegal.com

Stephen W. Myers
William Scott Jenkins
Teresa Dawn Farrison

Gregory D. Honig

Reference: Wells Fargo Bank.

For full biographical listings, see the Martindale-Hubbell Law Directory

Phoenix—Continued

QUARLES & BRADY LLP (AV)

One Camelback Building, One East Camelback Road, Suite 400, 85012-1649
Telephone: 602-230-5500
Fax: 602-230-5598
URL: http://www.quarles.com
Milwaukee, Wisconsin Office: 411 East Wisconsin Avenue.
Telephone: 414-277-5000.
Fax: 414-271-3552.
Madison, Wisconsin Office: First Wisconsin Plaza, One South Pinckney Street, P.O. Box 2113.
Telephone: 608-251-5000.
Fax: 608-251-9166.
West Palm Beach, Florida Office: 222 Lakeview Avenue, 4th Floor.
Telephone: 407-653-5000.
Fax: 407-653-5333.
Naples, Florida Office: Barnett Center, 4501 Tamiami Trail North, Suite 300.
Telephone: 813-262-5959.
Fax: 813-434-4999.
Chicago, Illinois Office: Quarles & Brady LLC, Citicorp Center, 500 West Madison Street, Suite 3700.
Telephone: 312-715-5000.
Fax: 312-715-5155.

MEMBERS OF THE FIRM

William M. Shattuck
Benjamin R. Norris
Colleen A. Scherkenbach

ASSOCIATE

David J. Wood

For full biographical listings, see the Martindale-Hubbell Law Directory

RHEES, HOPKINS & KREAMER (AV)

100 West Clarendon Suite 700, 85013
Telephone: 602-263-6010
Fax: 602-263-6016
Email: rhk@primenet.com

MEMBERS OF FIRM

Michael L. Rhees
Stephen M. Hopkins
Joseph C. Kreamer
Kelly Brown

For full biographical listings, see the Martindale-Hubbell Law Directory

ROBBINS & GREEN, A PROFESSIONAL ASSOCIATION (AV)

1800 Norwest Tower, 3300 North Central Avenue, 85012-2578
Telephone: 602-248-7600
Fax: 602-266-5369
Email: @RGLaw.com

Philip A. Robbins
William H. Sandweg III
Jeffrey P. Boshes
Brian Imbornoni
Dwayne Ross
Alfred W. Ricciardi
Peter W. Sorensen
Bruce M. Phillips
James O. Ehinger

For full biographical listings, see the Martindale-Hubbell Law Directory

ROSHKA HEYMAN & DEWULF, PLC (AV)

Two Arizona Center, 400 North 5th Street, Suite 1000, 85004
Telephone: 602-256-6100
Facsimile: 602-256-6800
Email: rheyman@rhd-law.com

Paul J. Roshka, Jr.
Raymond S. Heyman
John E. DeWulf
Darlene M. Wauro

Alan S. Baskin
Randall H. Warner
Linda D. Skon

For full biographical listings, see the Martindale-Hubbell Law Directory

SHERWOOD, KLEIN, DUDLEY & ABRAM, P.A. (AV)

201 North Central Avenue Suite 2400, 85073
Telephone: 602-254-7041
Fax: 602-254-7540
Email: lawyers@sherwoodklein.com

Andrew R. Sherwood
Andrew G. Klein
Gordon E. Dudley
Thomas L. Abram
Gregory J. Meell

For full biographical listings, see the Martindale-Hubbell Law Directory

SHIMMEL, HILL, BISHOP & GRUENDER, P.C. (AV)

3700 North 24th Street, 85016
Telephone: 602-224-9500
Telecopier: 602-955-6176
URL: http://www.shimmelhill.com

(See Next Column)

Daniel F. Gruender
Keith F. Overholt
Scott J. Richardson
Joseph Wm. Kruchek
Susan M. Swick
S. Gregory Jones
Glenn B. Hotchkiss
John W. Moody

OF COUNSEL

Charles A. Finch

Representative Clients: American Airlines; Associated General Contractors of America, Inc., Arizona Chapter; Delta Airlines; Harkins Amusement Enterprises, Inc.; Farmers Insurance Group; The Original Apartment Movers, Inc.; Rastra Technologies, Inc.; State of Arizona Property and Casualty Guarantee Fund; Wells Fargo Equipment Finance, Inc.

For full biographical listings, see the Martindale-Hubbell Law Directory

SMOCK AND WEINBERGER (AV)

2700 North Central Avenue Suite 1125, 85004
Telephone: 602-230-5150
Telecopier: 602-230-5155

MEMBERS OF FIRM

Timothy R. Smock
Brian A. Weinberger

ASSOCIATE

Frank W. Moskowitz

For full biographical listings, see the Martindale-Hubbell Law Directory

SNELL & WILMER L.L.P. (AV)

One Arizona Center, 85004-2202
Telephone: 602-382-6000
Fax: 602-382-6070
Email: postmaster@snellwilmer.com *URL:* http://www.swlaw.com
Tucson, Arizona Office: One South Church Avenue, Suite 1500, 85701-1612.
Telephone: 520-882-1200.
Fax: 520-884-1294.
Orange County Office: 1920 Main Street, Suite 1200, Irvine, California 92614-7230.
Telephone: 949-253-2700.
Fax: 949-955-2507.
Salt Lake City, Utah Office: 111 East Broadway, Suite 900, 84111-1004.
Telephone: 801-237-1900.
Fax: 801-237-1950.

MEMBERS OF FIRM

John J. Bouma
George H. Lyons
Daniel J. McAuliffe
James R. Condo
Vaughn A. Crawford
E. Jeffrey Walsh
James J. Sienicki
Janet E. Barton
Steven S. Guy
Brian J. Foster
Patrick G. Byrne
Warren E. Platt
Peter J. Rathwell
Joel P. Hoxie
Lonnie J. Williams, Jr.
Heidi McNeil Staudenmaier
Katherine M. Harmeyer
George J. Coleman, III
Kevin J. Parker
Barbara J. Dawson
Bob J. McCullough
Patricia Lee Refo

ASSOCIATES

Andrew S. Ashworth
Stephanie R. Derby
Robert M. Kort
David E. Rauch
Terri N.A. Buccino
Andrew Foster Halaby
Craig A. Marquiz
Donald Zavala

Representative Clients: For list of Representative Clients, see end of biographical listings in the Martindale-Hubbell Law Directory.

For Complete List of Firm Personnel, See General Section

For full biographical listings, see the Martindale-Hubbell Law Directory

ULRICH, KESSLER & ANGER, P.C. (AV)

3707 North Seventh Street, Suite 250, 85014-5059
Telephone: 602-248-9465
Fax: 602-248-0165
Email: ukapc@aol.com

Paul G. Ulrich
Donn G. Kessler
William H. Anger

For full biographical listings, see the Martindale-Hubbell Law Directory

WARNER ANGLE ROPER & HALLAM PLC (AV)

3550 North Central Avenue, Suite 1500, 85012
Telephone: 602-264-7101
Fax: 602-234-0419

Jerry L. Angle
Ted F. Warner
Edward (Ted) L. Roper
Charles Richard Hallam
Roger K. Gilbert
Stephen E. Jackson
Clark W. Watkin, Jr.
Jerome K. Elwell
John A. Buric
Jack D. Klausner

(See Next Column)

WARNER ANGLE ROPER & HALLAM PLC—*Continued*

Chris R. Baniszewski
Alison K. Shea
J. Brent Welker

Representative Clients: Data Systems of Arizona; D.L. Withers Construction, Inc.; Coreslab Structures; Pete King Construction Co.; Butte Construction Co.; Beech Acceptance Corp., Inc.; Coldwell Banker Success Realty; Raytheon Aircraft Credit Corp.

For full biographical listings, see the Martindale-Hubbell Law Directory

WARNICKE & LITTLER, P.L.C. (AV)

2020 North Central Avenue, Fifth Floor, 85004-4506
Telephone: 602-256-0400
Fax: 602-256-0345
Email: wlittler@aol.com

Ronald E. Warnicke
Thomas E. Littler
Mark J. Giunta
Blake D. Gunn

For full biographical listings, see the Martindale-Hubbell Law Directory

WHITE, CUMMINGS & LONGINO, P.C. (AV)

2920 East Camelback Road Suite 150, 85016
Telephone: 602-553-8188
Fax: 602-553-0911
Email: wcllaw@aol.com

David L. White
Preston H. Longino, Jr.
Frederick M. Cummings

Robert W. Blesch
Gary Beren

For full biographical listings, see the Martindale-Hubbell Law Directory

*PRESCOTT,** Yavapai Co.

MURPHY, LUTEY, SCHMITT & BECK, P.L.L.C. (AV)

Elks Building, 117 East Gurley Street, 86301
Telephone: 520-445-6860
Fax: 520-445-6488
Email: MLSB@GOODNET.COM
Yuma, Arizona Office: Valley Professional Plaza, 1763 West Twenty-Fourth Street, Suite 200.
Telephone: 520-726-0314.
Fax: 520-341-1079.
Kingman, Arizona Office: 2601 Stockton Hill Road, Suite H8.
Telephone: 520-718-0888; 1-800-281-0822.

MEMBERS OF FIRM

Thelton D. Beck
Michael R. Murphy
Selmer D. Lutey
Robert E. Schmitt
Dan A. Wilson
Alex B. Vakula

Scott K. Risley

Counsel for: State Farm Mutual Automobile Insurance Co.; Allstate Insurance Co.; Farmers Insurance; Western Agricultural Insurance Co.;
Local Counsel for: Bank One Arizona, NA; The Stockmen's Bank.
Representative Clients: Prescott College; Galpin Ford, Inc.; Sedona-Oak Creek Airport Authority; Yavapai County Fair Association (Prescott Downs).

For full biographical listings, see the Martindale-Hubbell Law Directory

SCOTTSDALE, Maricopa Co.

CAMPANA, VIEH, SHORE, OWENS & LOEB (AV)

4422 North Civic Center Plaza, Suite 101, 85251
Telephone: 480-707-5000
Fax: 480-707-5005

Richard V. Campana
James E. Vieh
William F. Shore, III
Bernard C. Owens
Donald O. Loeb

LEGAL SUPPORT PERSONNEL

Lois V. Johnson (Legal Assistant)

For full biographical listings, see the Martindale-Hubbell Law Directory

BRENT E. CORWIN, P.C. (AV)

5665 North Scottsdale Road Suite F-110, 85250-5959
Telephone: 480-949-0520
Fax: 480-949-2650
Email: brent.corwin@scottsdalelaw.com *URL:* http://www.scottsdalelaw.com

Brent E. Corwin

For full biographical listings, see the Martindale-Hubbell Law Directory

JOHN H. COTTON & ASSOCIATES, LTD. (AV)

6900 East Camelback Road, Suite 320, 85251
Telephone: 480-423-2034
Fax: 480-423-2035
Email: jhcotton1@aol.com
Las Vegas, Nevada Office: 2300 West Sahara, Suite 420, 89102.
Telephone: 702-367-9993.
Fax: 702-367-9977.

John H. Cotton

Bart J. Patterson (Resident)
Scott F. Frerichs (Resident)
Melanie Beth Bernstein (Not admitted in AZ)
Richard S. Johnson (Not admitted in AZ)
Edward R. Miley (Not admitted in AZ)

Representative Clients: American Continental/MMI Companies; Carpenter Industries; DLR Group, Inc.; KPMG Peat Marwick; Law Society of British Columbia; Opthalmic Mutual Insurance Company; The St. Paul Companies; Simula, Inc.; Tenet Health Care; The Doctors' Company.

For full biographical listings, see the Martindale-Hubbell Law Directory

SACKS TIERNEY P.A. (AV)

4250 North Civic Center Boulevard, 85251
Telephone: 480-425-2600
Facsimile: 480-970-4610
Email: ST@sackstierney.com
Phoenix, Arizona Office: Two North Central Avenue, Suite 1960. 85004.
Telephone: 480-435-2600.
Fax: 480-970-4610.

Seymour Sacks
Marvin S. Cohen
David C. Tierney
Stephen Aron Benson
Michael R. Rooney
Robert G. Kimball
Stephen P. Linzer
Marcia J. Busching
Randall S. Yavitz
Sharon Brook Shively
James W. Armstrong
Steven M. Goldstein
Judith M. Dworkin
Robert J. Lord
Sharon S. Moyer
Candess J. Hunter
Lori R. Miller
Brian E. Ditsch

Sharyl Poulson Speaker
Steven W. Bienstock
Andrew Lane de Mars
Scott B. Cohen
Mark D. Dillon
John L. Habib
W. Kevin Bell
Isabel M. Humphrey
Julie A. Inderlied
Laura G. Meyer
Stephen A. Wolf

Reference: M&I Thunderbird Bank.

For full biographical listings, see the Martindale-Hubbell Law Directory

SPARKS, TEHAN & RYLEY, P.C. (AV)

7503 First Street, 85251-4573
Telephone: 480-949-1339
Fax: 480-949-7587

Joe P. Sparks
Kevin T. Tehan
John H. Ryley

LEGAL SUPPORT PERSONNEL

Pamela L. Sparks
Joshua Morgan Sparks
Catherine L. McComb

References: Bank One, Arizona, Trust Department; Northern Trust Bank of Arizona, N.A.; Wells Fargo Bank of Arizona.

For full biographical listings, see the Martindale-Hubbell Law Directory

TITUS, BRUECKNER & BERRY, P.C. (AV)

Scottsdale Centre Suite B-252, 7373 North Scottsdale Road, 85253-3527
Telephone: 602-483-9600
Fax: 602-483-3215
Email: TBandB@aol.com

Jon A. Titus
Kurt M. Brueckner
Charles R. Berry
Garry S. O'Rafferty
David R. Jordan

Marc D. Blonstein
Todd Michael Johnson
Matthew B. Levine
Christopher D. Lonn
Robin C. Martindale

OF COUNSEL

John R. Tellier
Timothy G. Burns

LEGAL SUPPORT PERSONNEL

Kellie E. Dicarlo
Belle Taylor

Representative Clients: Arizona Department of Insurance, Receivership Division; Beazer Homes; Cigna; Equipment Leasing Corp.; Hancock Communities; Harvard Investments; Heritage West Securities; Joseph Charles & Associates, Inc.; Peacock, Hislop, Staley Given, Inc.; Woodside Homes.

For full biographical listings, see the Martindale-Hubbell Law Directory

*TUCSON,** Pima Co.

MARK L. COLLINS (AV)

The Davis House, 262 North Main, 85701
Telephone: 520-884-0024
Fax: 520-624-7034
URL: http://www.lawyers.com/markcollins

Representative Clients: Savers Property & Casualty Insurance Company; Metropolitan Mortgage.

For full biographical listings, see the Martindale-Hubbell Law Directory

LEONARD FELKER ALTFELD GREENBERG & BATTAILE, P.C. (AV)

250 North Meyer Avenue, P.O. Box 191, 85702-0191
Telephone: 520-622-7733
Fax: 520-622-7967

David J. Leonard
Sidney L. Felker
Jeffrey H. Greenberg
John F. Battaile III
Clifford B. Altfeld
Donna M. Aversa
R. David Sobel
Russell E. Krone
Peter B. Goldman

OF COUNSEL

Anne-Marie Brady

For full biographical listings, see the Martindale-Hubbell Law Directory

LAW OFFICES OF MEEHAN & ASSOCIATES (AV)

33 North Stone, Suite 830, P.O. Box 1671, 85702-1671
Telephone: 520-882-4188
Fax: 520-882-4487
Email: MJM@MMEEHAN.com *URL:* http://www.lawyers.com/meehan&associates

Michael J. Meehan

ASSOCIATE

Mark E. Yonan

For full biographical listings, see the Martindale-Hubbell Law Directory

WILLIAM G. WALKER, P.C. (AV)

145 South Sixth Avenue, 85701
Telephone: 520-622-3330
Fax: 520-882-6833

William G. Walker

For full biographical listings, see the Martindale-Hubbell Law Directory

*YUMA,** Yuma Co.

CLARK AND ASSOCIATES (AV)

256 South Second Avenue, 85364
Telephone: 520-783-6233
Fax: 520-783-0533
Email: jasclark@yahoo.com *URL:* http://www.lawyers.com/j_clark&assoc

MEMBER OF FIRM

A. James Clark

ASSOCIATE

Heather D. Moore

Representative Clients: Fresh Express; Bruce Church Inc.; Western Farm Service; KB Media, Inc.; Ryder Dedicated Logistics, Inc.; Skyview Cooling Co.; Desert Mix Cooling Co.; Yuma Mesa Irrigation and Drainage District.

For full biographical listings, see the Martindale-Hubbell Law Directory

ARKANSAS

*BATESVILLE,** Independence Co.

GREGG & FARRIS (AV)

262 Boswell Street, P.O. Box 2496, 72501
Telephone: 870-793-7556
Fax: 870-793-6921

MEMBERS OF FIRM

John C. Gregg
Phillip B. Farris

For full biographical listings, see the Martindale-Hubbell Law Directory

*FAYETTEVILLE,** Washington Co.

DAVIS, COX & WRIGHT, PLC (AV)

19 East Mountain Street, P.O. Drawer 1688, 72702-1688
Telephone: 501-521-7600
Fax: 501-521-7661
Email: daviscoxwright@dcw-plc.com *URL:* http://www.dcw-plc.com

Sidney P. Davis, Jr.
Walter B. Cox
Tilden P. Wright, III
Constance G. Clark
William Jackson Butt, II
Kelly P. Carithers
Don A. Taylor
Paul H. Taylor
John G. Trice
Laura J. Andress
Mark W. Dossett
S. Lance Cox
Robin Miller

Representative Clients: Arkansas Farm Bureau Insurance Cos.; Fireman's Fund Insurance Group; St. Paul Insurance Cos; Chrysler Motors Corp.; Kemper Insurance Group; Kawasaki Motors Corp.; CIGNA; CNA Insurance Companies; USA Waste; Wal-Mart Stores, Inc.

For full biographical listings, see the Martindale-Hubbell Law Directory

*FORT SMITH,** Sebastian Co.

SMITH, MAURRAS, COHEN, REDD & HORAN, PLC (AV)

510 North Greenwood Avenue, P.O. Box 10205, 72917
Telephone: 501-782-1001
Telefax: 501-782-1279

R. A. Young, Jr. (1908-1973)
Don A. Smith
S. Walton Maurras
Robert Y. Cohen, II
Michael K. Redd
Matthew Horan

Lee M. Kirner

Counsel for: Arkansas Best Corp.; ABF Freight System, Inc.; Riverside Furniture Corp.; The City National Bank of Fort Smith; O.K. Industries, Inc.

For full biographical listings, see the Martindale-Hubbell Law Directory

THOMPSON AND LLEWELLYN, P.A. (AV)

412 South Eighteenth Street, P.O. Box 818, 72902
Telephone: 501-785-2867
Fax: 501-782-8046

William P. Thompson
James M. Llewellyn, Jr.

Representative Clients: Whirlpool Corp.; Otis Elevator Co.; Parts Industries Corp.; GKN, plc; National Home Centers, Inc.; Shipley Baking Co.; Outboard Marine Corp.; KNP Air Lease, Inc.; Chase Manhattan Leasing Co.; Federal Signal Corp.

For full biographical listings, see the Martindale-Hubbell Law Directory

*LITTLE ROCK,** Pulaski Co.

ALLEN LAW FIRM, A PROFESSIONAL CORPORATION (AV)

950 Centre Place, 212 Center Street, 72201
Telephone: 501-374-7100
Telecopier: 501-374-1611
Email: hwallen@cei.net *URL:* http://www.lawyers.com/allenlawfirm

H. William Allen

Representative Clients: Wells Fargo Bank; Comcast; Arkansas Electric Cooperative Corporation; Empire Funding Corporation.

For full biographical listings, see the Martindale-Hubbell Law Directory

SKOKOS, BEQUETTE & BILLINGSLEY, P.A. (AV)

3200 TCBY Tower, 425 West Capitol Avenue, 72201-3439
Telephone: 501-374-1107
Facsimile: 501-374-5092

Theodore C. Skokos
George J. Bequette, Jr.
Keith I. Billingsley

For full biographical listings, see the Martindale-Hubbell Law Directory

WRIGHT, LINDSEY & JENNINGS LLP (AV)

200 West Capitol Avenue, Suite 2200, 72201
Telephone: 501-371-0808
Fax: 501-376-9442
Email: info@wlj.com *URL:* http://www.wlj.com
Fayetteville, Arkansas Office: 101 West Mountain Street, Suite 206, 72701.
Telephone: 501-575-0808.
Fax: 501-575-0999.
Russellville, Arkansas Office: 1110 West "B" Street, Suite E, 72801.
Telephone: 501-968-7995.

(See Next Column)

WRIGHT, LINDSEY & JENNINGS LLP—*Continued*

John G. Lile
David M. Powell
M. Samuel Jones, III
H. Keith Morrison
(Resident, Fayetteville Office)
Roger D. Rowe
Claire Shows Hancock
Stephen R. Lancaster

ASSOCIATES

Elisa Masterson White
Robert W. George
(Resident, Fayetteville Office)

Representative Clients: General Electric Capital Corp.; Helena Chemical Co.; Murphy Oil U.S.A., Inc.; NationsBank, N.A.

For full biographical listings, see the Martindale-Hubbell Law Directory

SPRINGDALE, Washington Co.

CYPERT, CROUCH, CLARK & HARWELL (AV)

111 Holcomb Street, P.O. Box 1400, 72765-4496
Telephone: 501-751-5222
Fax: 501-751-5777
Email: nwark.com

Courtney C. Crouch (1912-1975)
James E. Crouch
William M. Clark, Jr.
Charles L. Harwell

ASSOCIATES

R. Jeffrey Reynerson
Marcus W. Van Pelt

SENIOR COUNSEL

James D. Cypert

OF COUNSEL

Stanley W. Ludwig

General Counsel for: First National Bank of Springdale; Northwest Health Systems; Springdale School District.
Representative Clients: Purina Mills, Inc.; Swift-Eckrich, Inc.; Arkansas and Missouri RRCO.
Insurance Clients: American National Property and Casualty Co.; Liberty Mutual; Fireman's Fund; Chicago Title.

For full biographical listings, see the Martindale-Hubbell Law Directory

*TEXARKANA,** Miller Co.

DUNN, NUTTER, MORGAN & SHAW (AV)

State Line Plaza, 6th Floor, P.O. Box 8030, 71854-5945
Telephone: 870-773-5651
Texas Telephone: 903-793-5651
Telecopier: 870-772-2037
Email: lawfirm@dnms.com *URL:* http://www.dnms.com

MEMBERS OF FIRM

R. Gary Nutter
R. David Freeze
W. David Carter

ASSOCIATES

Jeff M. Addison
Adam O. Fellows

LEGAL SUPPORT PERSONNEL

LEGAL ASSISTANTS

Myra Conaway Wells
Sonja L. Oliver

Representative Clients: Georgia-Pacific Corp.; FNB Lewisville; S.W. Arkansas Electric Corp.; Southern Greyhound Lines; Reliant Energy, Incorporated; Tyson Foods, Inc.; Milway Federal Credit Union; Hill & Knowlton.

For Complete List of Firm Personnel, See General Section

For full biographical listings, see the Martindale-Hubbell Law Directory

CALIFORNIA

*BAKERSFIELD,** Kern Co.

BORTON, PETRINI & CONRON, LLP (AV)

The Borton, Petrini & Conron Building, 1600 Truxtun Avenue, 93301
Telephone: 661-322-3051
Voice Mail: 661-395-6700
Fax: 661-322-4628
Mailing Address: P.O. Box 2026, Bakersfield, California, 93303
Email: bpcbak@bpclaw.com *URL:* http://www.bpclaw.com
Other City Locations: Fresno, Los Angeles, Modesto, Redding, Sacramento, San Bernardino, San Diego, San Francisco, San Jose, San Luis Obispo, Santa Ana and Ventura.

MEMBERS OF FIRM

George F. Martin
Richard E. Hitchcock
John F. Petrini
Richard E. Morton

ASSOCIATES

Brian Jensen Stowell
Richard D. Brown
Raymond G. Robinson
Michael S. Abril
Timothy B. Liebaert

(See Next Column)

For Complete List of Firm Personnel, See General Section

For full biographical listings, see the Martindale-Hubbell Law Directory

BEVERLY HILLS, Los Angeles Co.

HERZOG, FISHER, GRAYSON & WOLFE, A LAW CORPORATION (AV)

9460 Wilshire Boulevard Fifth Floor, 90212
Telephone: 310-278-4300
Fax: 310-278-5430

James P. Herzog
David R. Fisher
Michael A. Grayson
Herbert N. Wolfe

Doreen W. Shenfeld
Jerry R. Sparks
Bree Arlyn-Pessin

OF COUNSEL

Todd I. Grayson

For full biographical listings, see the Martindale-Hubbell Law Directory

COSTA MESA, Orange Co.

ALBERT, WEILAND & GOLDEN (AV)

Center Tower, 650 Town Center Drive, Suite 1350, 92626
Telephone: 714-966-1000
FAX: 714-966-1002
Email: awglawyers@aol.com

Theodor C. Albert
Michael J. Weiland
Jeffrey I. Golden

ASSOCIATES

Evan D. Smiley
Lei Lei Wang Ekvall
Philip E. Strok
Darlynn Campbell Morgan

OF COUNSEL

Marcus M. Kaufman
Jennifer Ann Golison
Steven J. Katzman

LEGAL SUPPORT PERSONNEL

PARALEGALS

Fran L. Russell
Cynthia B. Meeker
Patricia K. Nelson
Janet Hogan
Kim Sigismondo

For full biographical listings, see the Martindale-Hubbell Law Directory

FELDHAKE, AUGUST & ROQUEMORE (AV)

Plaza Tower, Suite 1730, 600 Anton Boulevard, 92626-7124
Telephone: 714-438-3885
Fax: 714-438-3888
Email: farlaw@hqonline.com

Robert J. Feldhake
Kenneth S. August
Lisa A. Roquemore
Joshua M. Wolff

ASSOCIATES

Dimitri P. Gross
Supriya Kakkar
Katherine A. Slayton

OF COUNSEL

Arthur J. Swerdloff
Arthur M. Wilcox, Jr.

For full biographical listings, see the Martindale-Hubbell Law Directory

EMERYVILLE, Alameda Co.

CHILVERS & TAYLOR, PC (AV)

Baybridge Office Plaza, 5801 Christie Avenue, Suite 590, 94608
Telephone: 510-923-6230
Fax: 510-923-6236
Email: counsel@chilvers-taylor.com *URL:* http://www.chilvers-taylor.com

Robert M. Chilvers
William "Zak" Taylor

Leila Clark-Riddell
Aviva Cuyler

OF COUNSEL

Kathy L. Hensley

Representative Clients: Omni Healthcare, Inc.; San Francisco IPA; Saatchi & Saatchi Advertising, N.A., Inc.; United Broadcasting Co.any.

For full biographical listings, see the Martindale-Hubbell Law Directory

FOLSOM, Sacramento Co.

THE BLEIER LAW FIRM (AV)

110 Blue Ravine Road, Suite 201, 95630
Telephone: 916-454-2100
Fax: 916-454-2121
Email: tblf@bleier.com *URL:* http://www.bleier.com

Brenton A. Bleier

(See Next Column)

THE BLEIER LAW FIRM, *Folsom—Continued*

ASSOCIATE

Bradford A. Bleier

For full biographical listings, see the Martindale-Hubbell Law Directory

*FRESNO,** Fresno Co.

DIETRICH, GLASRUD, MALLEK & AUNE (AV)

An Association of Attorneys including Law Corporations
5250 North Palm Avenue, Suite 402, 93704
Telephone: 559-435-5250
Facsimile: 559-435-8776
Email: info@dgmalaw.com

Richard W. Dietrich (Inc.) (1930-1999)
Donald H. Glasrud (Inc.)
Robert A. Mallek Jr. (Inc.)
Richard E. Aune (Inc.)
Bruce A. Owdom
Thomas W. Isaac

Douglas D. Schorling
Leslie G. Miessner
Daniel J. Tekunoff

OF COUNSEL

Timothy J. Buchanan

Representative Clients: Fresno Surgery and Recovery Care Center; Helm Fertilizer, Inc.; Gragnani Farms; Wathen-Castanos, Inc.; Chicago Title Company; ABC, Inc.; The McClatchy Company; Monsanto Company; Armstrong World Industries, Inc.; Stewart Title Guaranty Company.

For full biographical listings, see the Martindale-Hubbell Law Directory

SAGASER, FRANSON & JONES, A PROFESSIONAL CORPORATION (AV)

2445 Capitol Street, Second Floor, P.O. Box 1632, 93717-1632
Telephone: 559-233-4800
Fax: 559-233-9330

Howard A. Sagaser
Eric K. Hansen (1952-1996)
Donald R. Franson, Jr.
Timothy Jones
Kristi R. Culver Kapetan
Elise M. Shebelut Krause
Nancy A. Maler
W. Allen Bennett
Mark D. Kruthers
Michael S. Helsley
Jamie Katzman

For full biographical listings, see the Martindale-Hubbell Law Directory

GOLD RIVER, Sacramento Co.

HACKARD, HOLT & HELLER (AV)

11335 Gold Express Drive, Suite 155, 95670
Telephone: 916-853-3000
Facsimile: 916-853-3010
Email: tholt@hackardlaw.com *URL:* http://www.hackardlaw.com

MEMBERS OF FIRM

Michael A. Hackard
Theodore J. Holt

OF COUNSEL

Steven M. Heller
Paige M. Hibbert

ASSOCIATES

David R. Zarka
Jenny M. Fickel
Eric L. Graves
Gregory W. Bayless

For full biographical listings, see the Martindale-Hubbell Law Directory

IRVINE, Orange Co.

EISENBERG & FINK LLP (AV)

100 Pacifica, Suite 200, 92618
Telephone: 949-753-1500
Fax: 949-753-1516
Email: ef@ef-law.com *URL:* http://www.lawyers.com/ef-law

Lawrence S. Eisenberg
Steven A. Fink

Michael G. Mattern
Judith F. Zuckert

For full biographical listings, see the Martindale-Hubbell Law Directory

GALFIN & PASSON, LLP (AV)

18101 Von Karman Avenue, Suite 1400, 92612-1043
Telephone: 949-752-2444
Facsimile: 949-833-8256
Email: galpas@aol.com
Santa Ana, California Office: 2122 North Broadway, Suite 100.
Telephone: 949-752-2444.

MEMBERS OF FIRM

Ted A. Galfin
Kenneth D. Passon
Lorraine Kay Smyth
Michael R. Adams
Marcelle Suzanne Strauss
Adam M. Greely

For full biographical listings, see the Martindale-Hubbell Law Directory

LOBEL & OPERA LLP (AV)

Suite 1100, 19800 MacArthur Boulevard, 92612-2425
Telephone: 949-476-7400
Fax: 949-476-7444
Email: webmaster@lobelopera.com *URL:* http://www.lobelopera.com

PARTNERS

William N. Lobel
Robert E. Opera
Pamela Zylstra Karger
Evan C. Borges
Jeffrey M. Reisner

OF COUNSEL

Curtis O. Barnes
Elmer Dean Martin, III
Michael D. Good

Tavi Claire Flanagan
Hamid R. Rafatjoo
Michael D. Neue

For full biographical listings, see the Martindale-Hubbell Law Directory

MARSHACK SHULMAN & HODGES LLP (AV)

8001 Irvine Center Drive, Suite 900, 92618-2921
Telephone: 949-864-0400
Facsimile: 949-864-0444
Email: marshack@marshack-law.com *URL:* http://www.marshack-law.com

Richard A. Marshack
Leonard M. Shulman
Ronald S. Hodges
James Charles Bastian, Jr.

TAX COUNSEL

A. Lavar Taylor

ASSOCIATES

Jon K. Alban
Mark Bradshaw
Robert N. Ives, Jr.
Sung H. Lee

For full biographical listings, see the Martindale-Hubbell Law Directory

RUS, MILIBAND & SMITH (AV)

Suite 700, 2600 Michelson Drive, 92612
Telephone: 949-752-7100
Fax: 949-252-1514
Email: rmws@rmsapc.com *URL:* http://www.rmsapc.com

Ronald Rus
Joel S. Miliband
Randall A. Smith
Laurel R. Zaeske

Cathrine M. Castaldi
David Edward Hays
Leo J. Presiado
Michael B. Kushner
M. Peter Crinella

For full biographical listings, see the Martindale-Hubbell Law Directory

LAGUNA BEACH, Orange Co.

NOKES, DAVIS & QUINN, A PROFESSIONAL CORPORATION (AV)

450 Ocean Avenue, 92651
Telephone: 949-376-3055
FAX: 949-376-3070
Email: ndqlaw@gte.net

Laurence P. Nokes
Thomas P. Davis
Thomas P. Quinn, Jr.

OF COUNSEL

Paul W. Davis

For full biographical listings, see the Martindale-Hubbell Law Directory

LAGUNA HILLS, Orange Co.

STETINA BRUNDA GARRED & BRUCKER, A PROFESSIONAL CORPORATION (AV)

24221 Calle De La Louisa, 4th Floor, 92653-3642
Telephone: 949-855-1246
Facsimile: 949-855-6371; 949-855-8986
Email: stetinabrundagarred&brucker@stetinalaw.com

Kit M. Stetina (Mr.)
Bruce B. Brunda
Mark B. Garred
William J. Brucker

Matthew A. Newboles
Thomas C. Naber (Not admitted in CA)
Darren S. Rimer
Eric L. Tanezaki
Eric K. Proul

LEGAL SUPPORT PERSONNEL

Kristy Kay Moore

For full biographical listings, see the Martindale-Hubbell Law Directory

LONG BEACH, Los Angeles Co.

FORD, WALKER, HAGGERTY & BEHAR, PROFESSIONAL LAW CORPORATION (AV)

One World Trade Center, Twenty Seventh Floor, 90831
Telephone: 562-983-2500
Telecopier: 562-983-2555
Email: FWHB@FWHB.COM

G. Richard Ford
Timothy L. Walker
William C. Haggerty
Jeffrey S. Behar
Mark Steven Hennings
Donna Rogers Kirby
Tina Ivankovic Mangarpan
Joseph A. Heath
Robert J. Chavez
James D. Savage
Patrick J. Gibbs
Robert Reisinger

Arthur W. Schultz
Jon T. Moseley
Maxine J. Lebowitz
Timothy P. McDonald
K. Michele Williams
Stephen Ward Moore
James O. Miller
Stanley L. Scarlett
Scott A. Ritsema
Colleen A. Deziel
Thomas L. Gourdé
Patrick J. Stark
Shayne L. Wulterin
Charles J. Schmitt
John A. Haughton
Kristen C. Vine
Joel E. D. Odou
Christopher L. Mass
Robert Montes, Jr.
Alison S. Mathews
Tatia M. Tokunaga
Mark F. Wendorff
Anneke Joan Stewart
Pamela J. Paluga

OF COUNSEL

Theodore P. Shield, P.L.C.

For full biographical listings, see the Martindale-Hubbell Law Directory

*LOS ANGELES,** Los Angeles Co.

ALVARADO, SMITH & SANCHEZ, A PROFESSIONAL CORPORATION (AV)

611 West Sixth Street, Suite 2650, 90017
Telephone: 213-229-2400
Facsimile: 213-229-2499
URL: http://www.alvarado-smith.com
Irvine, California Office: 4 Park Plaza, Suite 1200, 92614.
Telephone: 949-955-6800.
Fax: 949-955-6899.

Raymond G. Alvarado
Ruben A. Smith
Maurice Sanchez
John M. Sorich
Raúl F. Salinas
Frances Q. Jett
Theresa Eileen Antonucci
Diane C. Barrio
Rosario M. Tobias

OF COUNSEL

Martin N. Burton

For full biographical listings, see the Martindale-Hubbell Law Directory

ANDERSON, ABLON, LEWIS & GALE, LLP (AV)

Suite 2000 Equitable Plaza Building, 3435 Wilshire Boulevard, 90010-2006
Telephone: 213-388-3385
Fax: 213-388-8432
URL: http://www.aalg.com
San Juan Capistrano, California Office: 30240 Rancho Viejo Road, Suite F, 92675.
Telephone: 949-248-8040.
Fax: 949-248-8044.
Thousand Oaks, California Office: 220-H Briarwood Building, 299 West Hillcrest Drive, 91360.
Telephone: 805-373-5273.
Fax: 805-495-1456.

MEMBERS OF FIRM

Robert E. Lewis
Jerald E. Gale
Harris D. Bass

OF COUNSEL

Lawrence Jay Poteet
Charles R. Anderson
Herman Ablon

ASSOCIATES

Farhad Kazemzadeh
Candace Connart Bleifer
Ronald A. Gorrie
Michael D. Anderson

For full biographical listings, see the Martindale-Hubbell Law Directory

BARBOSA GARCIA LLP (AV)

A Partnership including a Professional Corporation
801 South Grand Avenue Suite 300, 90017-4621
Telephone: 213-612-0800
Fax: 213-612-8085

(See Next Column)

Henry S. Barbosa (P.C.)
Lorie A. Campos
Kenneth T. Fong
Bonifacio Bonny Garcia (P.C.)
Michael L. Kadish
John F. Lagle
Peter E. Langsfeld
Benjamin D. Nieberg
Gary W. Park
Roberta R. Sistos
Jonathan B. Stone
Rajeev M. Talwani
Sylvia J. Trujillo
Thuy-Whien Vuong
John G. Yslas

OF COUNSEL

Albert A. Erkel, Jr.

SPECIAL COUNSEL

Adrienne D. Konigar
Joyce E. Paul
Melvin D. Peters

LEGAL SUPPORT PERSONNEL

Victor M. Estrada (Paralegal)
Janice H. Minamoto (Paralegal)

For full biographical listings, see the Martindale-Hubbell Law Directory

BELIN RAWLINGS & BADAL LLP (AV)

11601 Wilshire Boulevard, Suite 2200, 90025-1758
Telephone: 310-575-5300
Fax: 310-445-0884
Email: recption@brblaw.com

MEMBERS OF FIRM

Daniel N. Belin
Douglas M. Rawlings
Robert G. Badal
Henry Ben-Zvi
Lawrence R. Lieberman
Ben D. Whitwell

ASSOCIATES

Peter S. Kravitz
Rudolph DeFelice

OF COUNSEL

Martin S. Schwartz

SPECIAL COUNSEL

Douglas C. Emhoff

For full biographical listings, see the Martindale-Hubbell Law Directory

BLANC WILLIAMS JOHNSTON & KRONSTADT, LLP (AV)

A Partnership including Professional Corporations
Suite 1700, 1900 Avenue of the Stars, 90067
Telephone: 310-552-2500
Telecopier: 310-552-1191
Email: bwjk@bwjk.com

MEMBERS OF FIRM

Ronald L. Blanc (P.C.)
Harley J. Williams (P.C.)
Ronald L. Johnston (P.C.)
John A. Kronstadt
James R. Farrand
Richard T. McCoy III
Regina A. Stagg
John C. Rawls III
Daniel M. Grigsby
Suzanne V. Wilson
Dawn Weekes Glenn

James S. Blackburn
Vivian W. Yang
Allison Binder
Jennifer M. Lloyd
Mark S. Dancsecs

OF COUNSEL

Sol Rosenthal

Reference: Santa Monica Bank (Beverly Hills Office).

For full biographical listings, see the Martindale-Hubbell Law Directory

CLARK & TREVITHICK, A PROFESSIONAL CORPORATION (AV)

800 Wilshire Boulevard, 12th Floor, 90017
Telephone: 213-629-5700
Telecopier: 213-624-9441
Email: postmaster@clarktrev.com
San Francisco, California Office: 456 Montgomery Street, 20th Floor.
Telephone: 415-288-6520.
Fax: 415-398-2820.

Philip W. Bartenetti
Vincent Tricarico
Leonard Brazil
Arturo Santana Jr.

OF COUNSEL

Dolores Cordell
Judith Ilene Bloom
Raimund Freihube

For Complete List of Firm Personnel, See General Section

For full biographical listings, see the Martindale-Hubbell Law Directory

PAUL F. COHEN (AV)

4929 Wilshire, Suite 410, 90010-3818
Telephone: 323-937-7105
Fax: 323-937-0958
Email: paulfred@aol.com

For full biographical listings, see the Martindale-Hubbell Law Directory

Los Angeles—Continued

FAGELBAUM & HELLER LLP (AV)

2049 Century Park East, Suite 2050, 90067
Telephone: 310-286-7666
Fax: 310-286-7086
Email: bestlawyers@worldnet.att.net

MEMBERS OF FIRM

Jerold Fagelbaum
Philip Heller

For full biographical listings, see the Martindale-Hubbell Law Directory

FRIED, BIRD & CRUMPACKER, A PROFESSIONAL CORPORATION (AV)

1900 Avenue of the Stars, 25th Floor, 90067-6031
Telephone: 310-551-7400
Facsimile: 310-556-4487
Email: fbclawfirm@cs.com

Jack Fried
Brian James Bird
David W. Crumpacker, Jr.
Nikki Wolontis
Diane J. Crumpacker

David K. Johnson

OF COUNSEL

Keith T. Holmes
Madge S. Beletsky

For full biographical listings, see the Martindale-Hubbell Law Directory

GIRARDI AND KEESE (AV)

1126 Wilshire Boulevard, 90017-1904
Telephone: 213-977-0211
FAX: 213-481-1554
San Bernardino, California Office: 155 West Hospitality Lane, Suite 260.
Telephone: 909-381-1551.
FAX: 909-381-2566.

MEMBERS OF FIRM

Thomas V. Girardi
Robert M. Keese
John A. Girardi
James B. Kropff
Robert W. Finnerty
James G. O'Callahan
V. Andre Rekte (Resident, San Bernardino Office)
John K. Courtney
Amy Fisch Solomon
Thomas C. Morgan
David N. Bigelow
Carrie J. Rognlien
David R. Lira
John Alan Roberts
Shane M. Emerson Coons
Amanda L. McClintock

ASSOCIATE

Jennifer M. Ingram

References: Wells Fargo Bank (Los Angeles Head Office); Comerica Bank.

For full biographical listings, see the Martindale-Hubbell Law Directory

HENNIGAN, MERCER & BENNETT (AV)

601 South Figueroa Street, Suite 3300, 90017
Telephone: 213-694-1200
Fax: 213-694-1234
Email: Silverm@hmb.com

J. Michael Hennigan
Bruce Bennett
John L. Amsden
Shawna L. Ballard
Mary H. Chu
Kirk D. Dillman
C. Dana Hobart
Jeanne E. Irving
James O. Johnston
Laura Lindgren
Bruce R. MacLeod
Peter J. Most
Robert L. Palmer
Lee W. Potts
Lauren A. Smith
Michael Swartz

ASSOCIATES

Nichole M. Auden
Gregory K. Jones
Linda A. Kontos
Joshua M. Mester
Claudia Schweikert
Thomas Bernard Watson
Jeffrey C. Henneforth

OF COUNSEL

James W. Mercer
Mark A. Albert
Kenneth A. O'Brien, Jr.

For full biographical listings, see the Martindale-Hubbell Law Directory

HORVITZ & LEVY, LLP (AV)

A Partnership including Professional Corporations
18th Floor, 15760 Ventura Boulevard (Encino), 91436
Telephone: 818-995-0800
Fax: 818-995-3157

Ellis J. Horvitz (A P.C.)
Barry R. Levy (A P.C.)
Peter Abrahams
David M. Axelrad
Frederic D. Cohen
S. Thomas Todd
David S. Ettinger
Daniel J. Gonzalez
Mitchell C. Tilner
Christina J. Imre

(See Next Column)

Lisa Perrochet
Stephen E. Norris
Sandra J. Smith
John A. Taylor, Jr.
Julie L. Woods
Lisa R. Jaskol
H. Thomas Watson

Mary F. Dant
Holly R. Paul
Andrea M. Gauthier
Judith E. Gordon
Patricia Lofton
L. Rachel Lerman Helyar
Mary-Christine (M.C.) Sungaila
Stephanie Rae Williams
Curt Cutting
Wendy S. Albers
Robert H. Wright
Nina E. Scholtz
Orly Degani

OF COUNSEL

Jon B. Eisenberg

Reference: Bank of California (Los Angeles, California Office).

For full biographical listings, see the Martindale-Hubbell Law Directory

HUANG & MITCHELL, A PROFESSIONAL LAW CORPORATION (AV)

3250 Wilshire Boulevard Suite 1600, 90010
Telephone: 213-251-8188
Fax: 213-251-8199
URL: http://www.huangandmitchell.com

Patrick K. Huang
Judith M. Mitchell

Gail Sanes

Reference: Union Bank, Beverly Hills.

For full biographical listings, see the Martindale-Hubbell Law Directory

H. ROY JEPPSON A PROFESSIONAL CORPORATION (AV)

11900 W. Olympic Boulevard Sixth Floor, 90064
Telephone: 310-826-5566
Fax: 310-826-5350
URL: http://www.lawyers.com/jeppsonlaw
Oxnard, California Office: 300 Esplanade Drive, Suite 1810.
Telephone: 805-604-1100.
Fax: 805-604-1600.

H. Roy Jeppson

Robyn F. Stalk

For full biographical listings, see the Martindale-Hubbell Law Directory

LAW OFFICES OF STEVEN S. KARIC A PROFESSIONAL CORPORATION (AV)

800 Wilshire Boulevard, Suite 1050, 90017-2614
Telephone: 213-955-0100
Fax: 213-955-0111
Email: sskaric@kariclaw.com *URL:* http://www.kariclaw.com

Steven S. Karic

Nora Tu-Willis

For full biographical listings, see the Martindale-Hubbell Law Directory

KESSLER & KESSLER, A LAW CORPORATION (AV)

2029 Century Park East, Suite 1520, 90067
Telephone: 310-552-9800
Fax: 310-552-0442
Email: kkalawcorp@aol.com

Warren J. Kessler
Joan B. Kessler
Lisa C. Alexander
Lisa K. Skaist

For full biographical listings, see the Martindale-Hubbell Law Directory

MATTHIAS & BERG LLP (AV)

1990 South Bundy Drive, Suite 790, 90025-5244
Telephone: 310-820-0083
Facsimile: 310-820-8313
Email: info@matthiasberg.com

MEMBERS OF FIRM

Michael R. Matthias
Jeffrey P. Berg

ASSOCIATES

Kenneth M. H. Hoff
Ari Lorin Markow

OF COUNSEL

Stuart R. Singer

Representative Clients: Am Tec, Inc.; Chatsworth Products, Inc.; Columbia Capital Corp.; Greater China Corp.; Maxitile, Inc.; National Quality Care, Inc.; Network Holdings International, Inc.; Private Investors Equity Group; Residential Resources, Inc.; Anthony Advisors.

For full biographical listings, see the Martindale-Hubbell Law Directory

Los Angeles—Continued

MONTELEONE & MCCRORY, LLP (AV)

A Limited Liability Partnership including Professional Corporations
725 South Figueroa Street Suite 3750, 90017-5402
Telephone: 213-612-9900
FAX: 213-612-9930
Email: montmcc@pacbell.net
Santa Ana, California Office: Suite 750, 1551 North Tustin Avenue, 92705.
Telephone: 714-565-3170.
Fax: 714-565-3184.

Stephen Monteleone (1886-1962)
Darrell P. McCrory (Retired)
G. Robert Hale (P.C.)
Patrick J. Duffy, III (P.C.)
Michael F. Minchella (P.C.)
Thomas P. McGuire (P.C.)
Philip C. Putnam (P.C.)
Joseph A. Miller (P.C.)
Donald J. Shields
David C. Romyn

Andrew W. Hawthorne
Jeffrey S. Hurst
William R. Baerg
Steven B. Copeland
Dennis C. Tulsiak
Scott R. Lane
Matthew S. Rork
Keith E. Davis
Sandra S. Fujiyama
Nilay A. Shah
Cha-Hee Nagashima Lee
William J. Ingalsbe (P.C.) (Resident, Santa Ana Office)
Diana M. Dron (Resident, Santa Ana Office)
Barry J. Jensen (Resident, Santa Ana Office)
Gerald W. Mouzis (Resident, Santa Ana Office)

OF COUNSEL

Joseph C. Malpasuto

For full biographical listings, see the Martindale-Hubbell Law Directory

OPPENHEIMER WOLFF & DONNELLY LLP (AV)

2029 Century Park East 38th Floor, 90067
Telephone: 310-788-5000
FAX: 310-277-1297
Email: oppenheimer.com
Minneapolis, Minnesota Office: 3300 Plaza VII, 45 South Seventh Street. 55402.
Telephone: 612-607-7000.
FAX: 612-607-7100.
Amsterdam, The Netherlands Office: Keizergracht 241.
Telephone: 31-20-423-4555.
FAX: 312-20-423-4545.
Brussels, Belgium Office: Avenue Louise 240, Box 5, 1050.
Telephone: 32-2-626-0500.
FAX: 32-2-626-0510.
Geneva, Switzerland Office: Rue Gabriel Eynard, 6, 1205.
Telephone: (41/22) 311-7410.
FAX: (41/22) 311-4707.
Newport Beach, California Office: 500 Newport Center Drive, Suite 700, 92660.
Telephone: 949-823-6000.
FAX: 949-823-6100.
New York, N.Y. Office: The Chrysler East Building, 19th Floor, 666 Third Avenue, 10017.
Telephone: 212-826-5000.
FAX: 212-486-0708.
Paris, France Office: 35 Boulevard des Capucines, 75002.
Telephone: (33/1) 53 45 40 00.
FAX: (33/1) 53 45 40 10.
St. Paul, Minnesota Office: 1700 First National Bank Building, 55101.
Telephone: 651-605-2000.
FAX: 651-605-2100.
Washington, D.C. Office: Oppenheimer Wolff Donnelly & Bayh LLP, 1350 Eye Street, N.W., Suite 200, 20005.
Telephone: 202-312-8000.
FAX: 202-312-8100.
Palo Alto, California Office: 3373 Hillview Avenue, Suite 200, 94304.
Telephone: 650-320-4000.
FAX: 650-320-4100.
Chicago, Illinois Office: Oppenheimer Wolff & Donnelly (Illinois), Two Prudential Plaza, 45th Floor, 180 North Stetson Avenue, 60601.
Telephone: 312-616-1800.
Fax: 312-616-5800.

RESIDENT PARTNERS

William Poms
Guy Porter Smith
Gary E. Lande
Michael D. Harris
Mark P. Wine
Gregory B. Wood
Christopher Darrow
David J. Oldenkamp
Marc E. Brown
J. Patrick Weir
Charles Rosenberg
Mark L. Jubelt
Alan P. Block
Scott R. Hansen

RESIDENT ASSOCIATES

Cynthia A. Lock
Joel D. Voelzke
George L. Fountain

Reference: City National Bank (Century Plaza Office, Century City).

For full biographical listings, see the Martindale-Hubbell Law Directory

PARKER MILLS & PATEL LLP (AV)

865 South Figueroa Street, Suite 850, 90017
Telephone: 213-622-4441
Fax: 213-622-1444
Email: pmp@pmplaw.com *URL:* http://www.pmplaw.com

David B. Parker
William K. Mills
Jayesh Patel
Danny T. Morin

ASSOCIATES

Rina J. Pakula
Angeli Cuesta-Aragon
Alicia J. Gonzales

For full biographical listings, see the Martindale-Hubbell Law Directory

RINTALA, SMOOT, JAENICKE & REES (AV)

10351 Santa Monica Boulevard, Suite 400, 90025-6937
Telephone: 310-203-0935
Facsimile: 310-556-8921
Email: RSJ&R@RSJR.com

MEMBERS OF FIRM

William T. Rintala
Peter C. Smoot
J. Larson Jaenicke
Robert A. Rees
Melodie K. Larsen
Frank E. Melton
Robert W. Hodges
G. Howden Fraser

ASSOCIATES

Michael B. Garfinkel
Emily Peters
Jeffrey H. Thaler
Jaclyn A. Hoekstra

Representative Clients: William Morris Agency, Inc.; Broadcast Music, Inc.; Eaton Corp.
Reference: Santa Monica Bank.

For full biographical listings, see the Martindale-Hubbell Law Directory

RODI, POLLOCK, PETTKER, GALBRAITH & CAHILL, A LAW CORPORATION (AV)

444 South Flower Street, Suite 1700, 90071-2901
Telephone: 213-895-4900
Telecopiers: 213-895-4921; 895-4922; 895-4750
URL: http://www.rodipollock.com

Karl B. Rodi (1908-1982)
John D. Cahill
John D. Pettker
Daniel C. Bond (1942-1977)
William R. Christian
Henry P. Pramov, Jr.
John F. Cermak, Jr.
Allan E. Ceran
Elizabeth B. Blakely
Robert C. Norton
Tim G. Ceperley
Coralie Kupfer
Cris K. O'Neall
Scott E. Adamson
Margaret Rosenthal

Sonja A. Inglin
Michael A. Abraham
Kenneth A. Franklin
Richard Nessary
Donna Yamini
Wade E. Norwood
Deepak Nanda
David J. Elbaz

OF COUNSEL

John P. Pollock
James M. Galbraith

For full biographical listings, see the Martindale-Hubbell Law Directory

ROSSBACHER & ASSOCIATES (AV)

444 South Flower Street, Suite 2100, 90071-2922
Telephone: 213-895-6500
Fax: 213-895-6161
Email: rossbach@soca.com *URL:* http://www.rossbacher.com

MEMBER OF FIRM

Henry H. Rossbacher

ASSOCIATES

James S. Cahill
Nanci E. Nishimura
Clara I. Duran Reed
My T. Huynh

LEGAL SUPPORT PERSONNEL

Linda Connell (Legal Administrator)
Martha E. Guilmette (Paralegal)

For full biographical listings, see the Martindale-Hubbell Law Directory

SIMKE CHODOS (AV)

A Partnership of Professional Corporations
Suite 1511, 1880 Century Park East, 90067-1615
Telephone: 310-203-3888
Fax: 310-203-3866
Email: sclawltd@aol.com

Stuart A. Simke
David M. Chodos

Richard A. Fond

(See Next Column)

SIMKE CHODOS, *Los Angeles—Continued*

OF COUNSEL

James L. Keane
Ellen Resinski Rosen

Reference: City National Bank (Wilshire-La Cienega Branch).

For full biographical listings, see the Martindale-Hubbell Law Directory

SINNOTT, DITO, MOURA & PUEBLA (AV)

660 South Figueroa Street Suite 2300, 90017
Telephone: 213-996-4200
Fax: 213-892-8322
San Francisco, California Office: Two Embarcadero, Suite 2330, 94111-3910.
Telephone: 415-352-6200.
Fax: 415-352-6224.

MEMBERS OF FIRM

Randolph P. Sinnott
John A. Dito
John J. Moura
Debra R. Puebla
Suzanne M. Rufflo
David M. Harris

ASSOCIATES

Gail L. Orr
Winnie C. Louie
Joette Marea Gonzalez

For full biographical listings, see the Martindale-Hubbell Law Directory

RONALD P. SLATES, P.C. (AV)

548 South Spring Street, Suite 1012, 90013-2309
Telephone: 213-624-1515; 213-654-1461
Fax: 213-624-7536; 213-654-1463
Email: rslateslaw@aol.com *URL:* http://www.lawyers.com/slateslaw

Ronald P. Slates

Donald R. Ramenian

For full biographical listings, see the Martindale-Hubbell Law Directory

WHITE O'CONNOR CURRY GATTI & AVANZADO LLP (AV)

10100 Santa Monica Boulevard Suite 300, 90067
Telephone: 310-712-6100
Fax: 310-712-6199

Andrew M. White
Michael J. O'Connor
James E. Curry
Melvin N.A. Avanzado
John M. Gatti

OF COUNSEL

Jonathan D. Avila
Frederick F. Mumm

Jonathan H. Anschell
David E. Fink
James W. Irey
Holly J. Sadlon
Lee S. Brenner
Katherine J. Kunberger
Sydney Arfin
Edward Muir Anderson
Marci D. Friedman
Meredith C. Hightower
J Rudy Freeman, II

For full biographical listings, see the Martindale-Hubbell Law Directory

ZIDE & O'BIECUNAS (AV)

Suite 403, 1300 West Olympic Boulevard, 90015
Telephone: 213-487-7550
Fax: 213-382-6095
Mailing Address: P.O. Box 15363, Del Valle Station,
Email: leoatzano@aol.com *URL:* http://www.zolaw.com
Ventura, California Office: 101 South Victoria Avenue.
Telephone: 805-642-8426.
Fax: 805-642-8881. Email: zanoven@aol.com.

Thomas Zide
Leo G. O'Biecunas, Jr.

OF COUNSEL

Douglas M. Kaye

ASSOCIATE

Marcella C. Oka

For full biographical listings, see the Martindale-Hubbell Law Directory

*MODESTO,** Stanislaus Co.

GIANELLI & FORES, A PROFESSIONAL LAW CORPORATION (AV)

1014 16th Street, P.O. Box 3212, 95353
Telephone: 209-521-6260
Telecopier: 209-521-5971
Email: gianelli@ainet.com *URL:* http://www.gianelli-fores.com

Louis F. Gianelli
Michael L. Gianelli
Robert P. Fores
David L. Gianelli
Brett L. Dickerson
Terry L. Campbell

For full biographical listings, see the Martindale-Hubbell Law Directory

NEWPORT BEACH, Orange Co.

REBECCA CALLAHAN A PROFESSIONAL LAW CORPORATION (AV)

5120 Campus Drive, 92660
Telephone: 949-864-5152
Facsimile: 949-864-5156
URL: http://www.lawyers.com/callahanlaw
Email: bekic@pacbell.net *URL:* http://www.rcallahan.com

Rebecca Callahan

For full biographical listings, see the Martindale-Hubbell Law Directory

CAPRETZ & ASSOCIATES (AV)

5000 Birch Street, West Tower Suite 2500, 92660-2139
Telephone: 949-724-3000
Fax: 949-757-2635
URL: http://www.lawyers.com/capretzradcliffe
Email: crlawl@ix.netcom.com *URL:* http://www.CAPRETZ.com

MEMBER OF FIRM

James T. Capretz

OF COUNSEL

William B. Lawless (Not admitted in CA)

LEGAL SUPPORT PERSONNEL

Sandra L. Koop (Law Clerk)

For full biographical listings, see the Martindale-Hubbell Law Directory

OPPENHEIMER WOLFF & DONNELLY LLP (AV)

500 Newport Center Drive, Suite 700, 92660
Telephone: 949-823-6000
FAX: 949-823-6100
Email: info@oppenheimer.com *URL:* http://www.oppenheimer.com
Minneapolis, Minnesota Office: 3300 Plaza VII, 45 South Seventh Street. 55402.
Telephone: 612-607-7000.
FAX: 612-607-7100.
Amsterdam, The Netherlands Office: Keizergracht 241.
Telephone: 31-20-423-4555.
FAX: 312-20-423-4545.
Brussels, Belgium Office: Avenue Louise 240, Box 5, 1050.
Telephone: 32-2-626-0500.
FAX: 32-2-626-0510.
Geneva, Switzerland Office: Rue Gabriel Eynard, 6, 1205.
Telephone: (41/22) 311-7410.
FAX: (41/22) 311-4707.
New York, N.Y. Office: The Chrysler East Building, 19th Floor, 666 Third Avenue, 10017.
Telephone: 212-826-5000.
FAX: 212-486-0708.
Paris, France Office: 35 Boulevard des Capucines, 75002.
Telephone: (33/1) 53 45 40 00.
FAX: (33/1) 53 45 40 10.
St. Paul, Minnesota Office: 1700 First National Bank Building, 55101.
Telephone: 651-605-2000.
FAX: 651-605-2100.
Washington, D.C. Office: Oppenheimer Wolff Donnelly & Bayh LLP, 1350 Eye Street, N.W., Suite 200, 20005.
Telephone: 202-312-8000.
FAX: 202-312-8100.
Los Angeles, California Office: 2029 Century Park East, 38th Floor, 90067.
Telephone: 310-788-5000.
FAX: 310-277-1297.
Palo Alto, California Office: 3373 Hillview Avenue, Suite 200, 94304.
Telephone: 650-320-4000.
FAX: 650-320-4100.
Chicago, Illinois Office: Oppenheimer Wolff & Donnelly (Illinois), Two Prudential Plaza, 45th Floor, 180 North Stetson Avenue, 60601.
Telephone: 312-616-1800.
Fax: 312-616-5800.

RESIDENT PARTNERS

Edward F. O'Connor
Paul C. Nyquist

RESIDENT ASSOCIATES

Kevin W. Kirsch
Thomas C. Bacon

Reference: City National Bank (Century Plaza Office, Century City).

For full biographical listings, see the Martindale-Hubbell Law Directory

WINTHROP COUCHOT, PROFESSIONAL CORPORATION (AV)

3 Civic Plaza, Suite 280, 92660
Telephone: 949-720-4100
Fax: 949-720-4111
URL: http://www.winthropcouchot.com

OF COUNSEL

Sean A. O'Keefe

For full biographical listings, see the Martindale-Hubbell Law Directory

ORINDA, Contra Costa Co.

GILLIN, JACOBSON, ELLIS & LARSEN (AV)

2 Theatre Square Suite 230, 94563
Telephone: 925-253-5800
Fax: 925-253-5858
Email: lawfirm@gjeld.com
San Francisco, California Office: 44 Montgomery Street, Suite 500, 94101.
Telephone: 415-986-4777.

Andrew R. Gillin
Ralph L. Jacobson
Luke Ellis
James Paul Larsen
Kristin Lucey

For full biographical listings, see the Martindale-Hubbell Law Directory

OXNARD, Ventura Co.

H. ROY JEPPSON A PROFESSIONAL CORPORATION (AV)

300 Esplanade Drive, Suite 1810, 93030
Telephone: 805-604-1100
Fax: 805-604-1600
URL: http://www.lawyers.com/jeppsonlaw
Los Angeles, California Office: 11900 West Olympic Boulevard. Sixth Floor. 90064.
Telephone: 310-826-5566.
Fax: 310-826-5350.

H. Roy Jeppson

Robyn F. Stalk

For full biographical listings, see the Martindale-Hubbell Law Directory

PALO ALTO, Santa Clara Co.

OPPENHEIMER WOLFF & DONNELLY LLP (AV)

3373 Hillview Avenue, Suite 200, 94304
Telephone: 650-320-4000
FAX: 650-320-4100
Email: oppenheimer.com
Minneapolis, Minnesota Office: 3300 Plaza VII, 45 South Seventh Street. 55402.
Telephone: 612-607-7000.
FAX: 612-607-7100.
Amsterdam, The Netherlands Office: Keizergracht 241.
Telephone: 31-20-423-4555.
FAX: 312-20-423-4545.
Brussels, Belgium Office: Avenue Louise 240, Box 5, 1050.
Telephone: 32-2-626-0500.
FAX: 32-2-626-0510.
Geneva, Switzerland Office: Rue Gabriel Eynard, 6, 1205.
Telephone: (41/22) 311-7410.
FAX: (41/22) 311-4707.
Newport Beach, California Office: 500 Newport Center Drive, Suite 700, 92660.
Telephone: 949-823-6000.
FAX: 949-823-6100.
New York, N.Y. Office: The Chrysler East Building, 19th Floor, 666 Third Avenue, 10017.
Telephone: 212-826-5000.
FAX: 212-486-0708.
Paris, France Office: 35 Boulevard des Capucines, 75002.
Telephone: (33/1) 53 45 40 00.
FAX: (33/1) 53 45 40 10.
St. Paul, Minnesota Office: 1700 First National Bank Building, 55101.
Telephone: 651-605-2000.
FAX: 651-605-2100.
Washington, D.C. Office: Oppenheimer Wolff Donnelly & Bayh LLP, 1350 Eye Street, N.W., Suite 200, 20005.
Telephone: 202-312-8000.
FAX: 202-312-8100.
Los Angeles, California Office: 2029 Century Park East, 38th Floor, 90067.
Telephone: 310-788-5000.
FAX: 310-277-1297.
Chicago, Illinois Office: Oppenheimer Wolff & Donnelly (Illinois), Two Prudential Plaza, 45th Floor, 180 North Stetson Avenue, 60601.
Telephone: 312-616-1800.
Fax: 312-616-5800.

RESIDENT PARTNERS

Michael H. Kalkstein
Claude A. S. Hamrick
Robert O. Guillot
Chris S. Graham
E. Patrick Ellisen
Chien (Chris) W. Chou

RESIDENT ASSOCIATES

Esther H. La
Lisa K. Roberts
Valerie M. Wagner
Michael N. Edelman
Justin F. Boyce
David B. Moyer

Reference: City National Bank (Century Plaza Office, Century City).

For full biographical listings, see the Martindale-Hubbell Law Directory

*SACRAMENTO,** Sacramento Co.

GREBEN & ASSOCIATES (AV)

Wells Fargo Center, 400 Capitol Mall, Suite 1100, 95814
Telephone: 916-558-6148
Fax: 916-447-2414
Email: jgreben@pacbell.net *URL:* http://www.lawyers.com/greben&associates

Jan Adam Greben

ASSOCIATE

Daniel Chester

For full biographical listings, see the Martindale-Hubbell Law Directory

LIVINGSTON & MATTESICH, LAW CORPORATION (AV)

1201 K Street, Suite 1100, 95814
Telephone: 916-442-1111
Fax: 916-448-1709
Email: l&m@lmlaw.net *URL:* http://www.lmlaw.net

Gene Livingston
James M. Mattesich
Carol Livingston
Rebecca M. Ceniceros
Emilio E. Varanini, III
Kenneth M. Malovos
Kathleen E. Finnerty
Joanna R. Mendoza

Steven P. Belzer
Jeffrey Leacox
Randy Pollack
Alice H. Choi
Stephen Craig Hunter
Matthew J. Goldman
Joel C. Baiocchi
Baldassaro (Bill) Di Capo
John McKinsey
Timothy E. Naccarato
Craig N. Lundgren
Mary Farrell Taylor
Brian Crone
Gay L. Carroll
Steven G. Churchwell

Representative Clients: Agra Foundations, Inc.; California Department of Corrections; California Department of Water Resources; Comstock Mortgage; Guaranty Federal Bank, F.S.B.; HPT Research, Inc.; Hygiea Biological Laboratories, Inc.; National Mortgage; R Systems, Inc.; Stonesfair Financial Corporation.

For full biographical listings, see the Martindale-Hubbell Law Directory

STEVENS & O'CONNELL LLP (AV)

400 Capitol Mall, Suite 1400, 95814-4412
Telephone: 916-329-9111
Facsimile: 916-329-9110

Charles J. Stevens
George L. O'Connell
Richard Pachter
David A. Cheit
Craig C. Allison
Bradley A. Benbrook
Todd M. Noonan
Timothy P. Grieve

For full biographical listings, see the Martindale-Hubbell Law Directory

*SAN DIEGO,** San Diego Co.

BARKER THOMAS & WALTERS, A PROFESSIONAL LAW CORPORATION (AV)

1455 Frazee Road, Suite 800, 92108
Telephone: 619-682-4040
Facsimile: 619-220-7056
Email: info@btwlaw.com *URL:* http://www.btwlaw.com

Douglas H. Barker
Anastasia E. Thomas

Catherine Petrecca
Marc A. Geffen
Lori L. Krupa

For full biographical listings, see the Martindale-Hubbell Law Directory

HAIGHT, BROWN & BONESTEEL, L.L.P. (AV)

A Partnership including Professional Corporations
101 West Broadway, Suite 1000, 92101-3544
Telephone: 619-595-5583
Telecopier: 619-595-7873
URL: http://www.hbblaw.com
Santa Monica, California Office: 1620 26th Street, Suite 4000 North, P.O. Box 680.
Telephone: 310-449-6000.
Telecopier: 310-829-5117.
Telex: 705837.
Santa Ana, California Office: Suite 900, 5 Hutton Centre Drive.
Telephone: 714-754-1100.
Telecopier: 714-754-0826.
Riverside, California Office: California Tower, 3737 Main Street, Suite 800.
Telephone: 909-341-8300.
Fax: 909-341-8309.
San Francisco, California Office: 101 Bush Street, 27th Floor.
Telephone: 415-986-7700.
Fax: 415-986-6945.

(See Next Column)

HAIGHT, BROWN & BONESTEEL L.L.P., *San Diego—Continued*

RESIDENT MEMBER

DeAnn M. Salcido

RESIDENT ASSOCIATE

Jeffrey A. Ruzicka

For full biographical listings, see the Martindale-Hubbell Law Directory

KLINEDINST, FLIEHMAN & MCKILLOP, A PROFESSIONAL CORPORATION (AV)

The Koll Center, 501 West Broadway, Suite 600, 92101-3584
Telephone: 619-239-8131
Fax: 619-238-8707
URL: http://www.kfmlaw.com
Orange County Office: Civic Center Law Building, 611 Civic Center Drive, Suite 250, Santa Ana, California, 92701.
Telephone: 714-542-1800.
Los Angeles, California Office: Wells Fargo Center, 333 South Grand Avenue, 33rd Floor, 90071.
Telephone: 213-625-8100.

SHAREHOLDERS

John D. Klinedinst
Donald R. McKillop, Sr.
G. William (Bill) Van De Weghe, Jr.
Thomas S. Ingrassia
Douglas A. Pettit
Gregory A. Garbacz
Arthur S. Moreau, III

Kendra J. Hall
Andrew N. Kohn
M. Shawn Payment
Kurt U. Campbell
G. Dale Britton
Susan S. Kohn
Heather L. Rosing
Debora A. Cappucci
Dayna Lyn Chmelka
Jennifer N. Lehman
Dennis C. Crovella
Carey L. Cooper
Kevin J. Gramling

PARALEGALS

Mary Ann Murphy-Brown
Cam B. Picano

Reference: Bank of America.

For full biographical listings, see the Martindale-Hubbell Law Directory

LINDLEY, SCALES & CORBETT, A PROFESSIONAL CORPORATION (AV)

550 West C Street, Suite 1800, 92101
Telephone: 619-234-9181
Fax: 619-234-8475
Email: lsc@adnc.com

Luke R. Corbett
Robert M. McLeod

Representative Clients: Palomar Savings & Loan Assn.; McGraw-Hill Broadcasting Co.; Chicago Title Insurance Co.; San Diego Hospital Assn.; Bank United.

For full biographical listings, see the Martindale-Hubbell Law Directory

DIRK T. METZGER A PROFESSIONAL CORPORATION (AV)

Wells Fargo Bank Building, 101 West Broadway, Suite 1450, 92101
Telephone: 619-557-8331
FAX: 619-557-2718
Email: dtmetzger@msn.com

Dirk T. Metzger

For full biographical listings, see the Martindale-Hubbell Law Directory

SAN FRANCISCO, * San Francisco Co.

ALDEN ARONOVSKY & SAX LLP (AV)

235 Montgomery Street, 28th Floor, 94104-2902
Telephone: 415-732-5820
Facsimile: 415-732-5840
Email: law@aaslaw.com

MEMBERS OF FIRM

David W. Alden
Ronald G. Aronovsky
Brian M. Sax (1945-1997)

ASSOCIATES

Jeffrey S. Koppelmaa
Sherry A. Glassman

For full biographical listings, see the Martindale-Hubbell Law Directory

ALPER & MCCULLOCH (AV)

425 California Street, 18th Floor, 94104-2203
Telephone: 415-434-8744
Facsimile: 415-434-3450
Email: alpermc@pacbell.net *URL:* http://www.lawyers.com/a&mlaw

Dean A. Alper

OF COUNSEL

Tracy Beggs McCulloch

For full biographical listings, see the Martindale-Hubbell Law Directory

BARTKO, ZANKEL, TARRANT & MILLER, PROFESSIONAL CORPORATION (AV)

900 Front Street, Suite 300, 94111-1427
Telephone: 415-956-1900
Fax: 415-956-1152
Email: bztm@bztm.com *URL:* http://www.bztm.com

John J. Bartko
Martin I. Zankel
Richard T. Tarrant
Charles G. Miller
Robert H. Bunzel
Michael D. Welch
Michael D. Abraham
M. Manuel Fishman
Christopher J. Hunt
John S. Lottier
Theani Christine Louskos
Howard L. Pearlman
C. Griffith Towle
Glenn P. Zwang
Christopher D. Sullivan

Thomas E. Cooper
Gail E. Kavanagh
Brenda M. Lillington
Tyler Roberts Meade
Rosanna S. Russell
Carissa Shubb
Russell G. Young

COUNSEL

Thomas A. Lee, Jr.
Darryl A. Hart

For full biographical listings, see the Martindale-Hubbell Law Directory

LAW OFFICES OF PHILIP BOROWSKY A PROFESSIONAL CORPORATION (AV)

Steuart Street Tower, Suite 2600, One Market Plaza, 94105-1417
Telephone: 415-896-6800
Facsimile: 415-896-0600
Email: info@borowsky.com *URL:* http://www.borowsky.com
Los Angeles, California Office: 2049 Century Park East, Suite 900, 90067-3111.
Telephone: 310-551-6960.
Fax: 310-553-7237.

Philip Borowsky

Christopher J. Hayes

For full biographical listings, see the Martindale-Hubbell Law Directory

ANTHONY P. DAVID A PROFESSIONAL CORPORATION (AV)

One Embarcadero Center, Suite 880, 94111
Telephone: 415-981-0166
Fax: 415-981-0196
URL: http://www.lawyers.com/davidlaw

Anthony P. David

For full biographical listings, see the Martindale-Hubbell Law Directory

MICHAEL Q. EAGAN (AV)

Three Embarcadero Center, 8th Floor, 94111
Telephone: 415-765-4600
FAX: 415-765-4659
Email: lomqe@aol.com

For full biographical listings, see the Martindale-Hubbell Law Directory

HAIGHT, BROWN & BONESTEEL, L.L.P. (AV)

A Partnership including Professional Corporations
100 Bush Street, 27th Floor, 94104-3902
Telephone: 415-986-7700
Telecopier: 415-986-6945
URL: http://www.hbblaw.com
Santa Monica, California Office: 1620 26th Street, Suite 4000 North, P.O. Box 680.
Telephone: 310-449-6000.
Telecopier: 310-829-5117.
Telex: 705837.
Santa Ana, California Office: Suite 900, 5 Hutton Centre Drive.
Telephone: 714-754-1100.
Telecopier: 714-754-0826.
Riverside, California Office: California Tower, 3737 Main Street, Suite 800.
Telephone: 909-341-8300.
Fax: 909-341-8309.
San Diego, California Office: 101 West Broadway, Suite 1000.
Telephone: 619-595-5583.
Fax: 619-595-7873.

RESIDENT MEMBERS

Amor A. Esteban
Lisa L. Oberg
David W. Evans
Daniel J. Kelly

ASSOCIATES

Helene Emilie Swanson
Felicia Y. Feng
Russell J. Smith

For full biographical listings, see the Martindale-Hubbell Law Directory

San Francisco—Continued

KAUFMAN & LOGAN LLP (AV)
111 Pine Street, Suite 1300, 94111
Telephone: 415-392-6677
Telecopier: 415-391-4639

MEMBERS OF FIRM

Jeffrey Kaufman
Peter J. Logan
Garrett L. Cecchini
W. Martin Tellegen
Richard A. Eggerth

ASSOCIATES

Nancy S. Coan
Sandra L. Cross
Gerald F. Ellersdorfer
Paul A. Peters
Paulette Donsavage
George D. Vanberg-Wolff

OF COUNSEL

Gerhard Stoll

LEGAL SUPPORT PERSONNEL

PARALEGALS

Karen L. Dunn, CLA
T. Patrick Bridenstine
Adrienne Levin
Paula R. Brawley

For full biographical listings, see the Martindale-Hubbell Law Directory

---

MORGENSTEIN & JUBELIRER, LLP (AV)
One Market, Spear Street Tower, 32nd Floor, 94105
Telephone: 415-896-0666
Fax: 415-896-5592
Email: m&j@mj-sflaw.com

Marvin D. Morgenstein (Retired)
Eliot S. Jubelirer
Lee Ann Huntington
Jean L. Bertrand
Jeffrey R. Williams
James R. Balich
Rocky N. Unruh
James L. McGinnis
Charles W. LaGrave
William J. Carroll
John S. Worden
Wendi J. Berkowitz
Stephen M. Hankins
Bruce A. Wagman

Lewis D. Barr
David H. Bromfield
Alexander P. Catalona
Michael "Cael" S. Davis
Roberta Nicol Dempster
Laura E. Gasser
Jill L. Gillen
Natasha L. Golding
Judith A. Holiber
Shawn D. Parrish
John J. Petry

For full biographical listings, see the Martindale-Hubbell Law Directory

PREUSS WALKER & SHANAGHER LLP (AV)
225 Bush Street, 15th Floor, 94104
Telephone: 415-397-1730
Facsimile: 415-397-1735
Email: pws@pwsllp.com *URL:* http://www.pwsllp.com

MEMBERS OF FIRM

Charles F. Preuss
Gary T. Walker
Denis F. Shanagher
Vernon I. Zvoleff
Kenneth J. Philpot
Donald F. Zimmer, Jr.
Sheila Doyle Kelley
Thomas W. Pulliam, Jr.
Alan J. Lazarus
Michael J. Stortz
John J. Powers
Kenneth P. Conour
Catherine M. Leon

Elizabeth Ewert Pilchik
Jonathan M. Rolbin
Jessica L. Grant
Brian M. Collins
Christopher L. Lebsock
Michelle A. Childers
Matthew Lepore
Edward P. Joy
Kristy Wheeler Bonagofsky
Karene I. Alvarado
Andrew Thornborrow
Katherine A. Woodward

Representative Clients: Cargill Incorporated; County of Sonoma; Federal Deposit Insurance Corporation; Franklin Resources; First Colonial Insurance Company; Grubb & Ellis Co.; Hamilton Resources Corporation; Marsh & McLennan Companies; Reliance National Insurance Company; Sun Microsystems.

For full biographical listings, see the Martindale-Hubbell Law Directory

---

ROSEN, BIEN & ASARO (AV)
Eighth Floor, 155 Montgomery Street, 94104
Telephone: 415-433-6830
Fax: 415-433-7104
Email: rba@rbalaw.com

Sanford Jay Rosen
Michael W. Bien
Andrea G. Asaro

Thomas Nolan
William H. D. Fernholz
Shana J. Margolis
Ernest J. Galvan

For full biographical listings, see the Martindale-Hubbell Law Directory

SPIEGEL LIAO & KAGAY (AV)
595 Market Street, Suite 1350, 94105-2825
Telephone: 415-956-5959
Telecopier: 415-362-1431
Email: slk@slksf@com *URL:* http://www.slksf.com

Michael I. Spiegel
Charles M. Kagay

OF COUNSEL

Bartholomew Lee
Wayne M. Liao

For full biographical listings, see the Martindale-Hubbell Law Directory

---

TEHIN +PARTNERS, A PROFESSIONAL CORPORATION (AV)
Bank of America Center, 555 California Street, 33rd Floor, 94104-1609
Telephone: 415-951-8800
Fax: 415-951-8808
URL: http://www.tehin.com

Nikolai Tehin
Pamela J. Stevens
Reilly Atkinson, IV
Michael E. Brown
Bita Abdollahi

For full biographical listings, see the Martindale-Hubbell Law Directory

---

VOGL & MEREDITH (AV)
456 Montgomery Street, 20th Floor, 94104
Telephone: 415-398-0200
Facsimile: 415-398-2820

Samuel E. Meredith
David R. Vogl
John P. Walovich
Jean N. Yeh
Thomas S. Clifton

Nicole L. Meredith
Dennis Gildea
Michael S. Burke
Martin Ross Sances
Joshua A. Ridless
David G. Valdez

For full biographical listings, see the Martindale-Hubbell Law Directory

---

WARTNICK, CHABER, HAROWITZ, SMITH & TIGERMAN, A PROFESSIONAL CORPORATION (AV)
101 California Street, Suite 2200, 94111-5802
Telephone: 415-986-5566
Fax: 415-986-5896
Email: postoffice@wartnicklaw.com *URL:* http://www.wartnicklaw.com

Harry F. Wartnick
Madelyn J. Chaber
Steven M. Harowitz
Stephen M. Tigerman

Phillip Scott Chan
Christopher C. Lamerdin
Garry Cohen
Cheryl L. White
Gregory M. Sheffer
Martha A. H. Berman
Courtney S. Lui
Diana M. Garcia
Richard A. Brody
Leslie Shawn Kerth
Marileni (Mia) Mattis
Max Jiro Kimura
Mark L. Nissenbaum
Tod Manning
Charlene A. Jimenez

OF COUNSEL

Audrey A. Smith
Robert Brown

For full biographical listings, see the Martindale-Hubbell Law Directory

---

WUERFEL & CHOLAKIAN, A PROFESSIONAL CORPORATION (AV)
555 Montgomery Street, Ninth Floor, 94111
Telephone: 415-398-1551; 800-992-5990
FAX: 415-398-3301
Email: sos@sflaw.net *URL:* http://www.sflaw.net
Santa Rosa, California Office: 131-A Stony Circle, Suite 515, 95401.
Telephones: 415-398-1551; 800-992-5990.
FAX: 415-398-1551.
Costa Mesa, California Office: Avenue of the Arts.
Telephone: 714-825-3590; 800-992-5990.

Mark D. Wuerfel
Kevin K. Cholakian
Julian J. Pardini
Nan R. Hooven
Sherri K. McElroy

SPECIAL COUNSEL

Dean C. Burnick
Charlene P. Rosack
Jonathan Gross
Michael A. Topp

Aaron D. Bigby
D. Clark Burton
Anthony J. Calero
Elizabeth A. Doyle
Linda L. Duiven
Jay E. Framson
Stephen D. Geist
Andrew A. Goode
David J. Heilman
Timothy S. Kirk
Stephen J. Liberatore
Anne Marie Master
Thomas A. Moore
Julianne Pinter

LEGAL SUPPORT PERSONNEL

Marla J. Kuresa (Legal Administrator)

For full biographical listings, see the Martindale-Hubbell Law Directory

SAN JOSE, * Santa Clara Co.

BERGESON & ELIOPOULOS, LLP (AV)

55 Almaden Boulevard, Suite 400, 95113
Telephone: 408-291-6200
Fax: 408-297-6000
URL: http://www.beglaw.com
Washington, D.C. Affiliate Office: Bergeson & Campbell, P.C., 1300 Eye Street, NW, Suite 100 West, 20005.
Telephone: (202)-962-8585.
Fax: (202)-962-8599. URL: www.bclaw.com.

Daniel J. Bergeson
William T. Eliopoulos
Mary Anne Rodgers
John L. Antracoli
Donald P. Gagliardi
Ina Stangenes
Marily P. Lerner

OF COUNSEL

Anthony M. Glassman

ASSOCIATES

Marc G. Van Niekerk
Eunhae Park
Mark E. Waite
Evelyn A. Peyton
William A. Hodkowski

For full biographical listings, see the Martindale-Hubbell Law Directory

MAHL REHON WALWORTH & ROBERTS, A PROFESSIONAL CORPORATION (AV)

Ten Almaden Boulevard, Suite 550, 95113
Telephone: 408-494-0900
Fax: 408-494-0909
URL: http://www.mahlrehon.com

Susan J. Mahl
Peter M. Rehon
Janet R. Walworth
Lisa C. Roberts
Rogelio M. Ruíz

Phillip E. Maroc
Chris S. Friedrich
Francis X. Ferrer

For full biographical listings, see the Martindale-Hubbell Law Directory

MCMANIS, FAULKNER & MORGAN (AV)

160 West Santa Clara Street, 10th Floor, 95113
Telephone: 408-279-8700
Fax: 408-279-3244; 408-279-0494
Email: mfm@mfmlaw.com *URL:* http://www.mfmlaw.com

James McManis
William Faulkner
Donelle Morgan
Lisa Herrick
Michael Reedy
Erica Yew

Michelle Tidalgo
Colleen Duffy Smith
Lillian Wolf
Rebecca Hughes
Kalpana Vrudhula
Ray M. Baluyot
Catherine Bechtel
Arron Nesbitt

OF COUNSEL

Mary Arand

For full biographical listings, see the Martindale-Hubbell Law Directory

REED, ELLIOTT, CREECH & ROTH (AV)

99 Almaden Boulevard, Eighth Floor, 95113
Telephone: 408-993-9911
Fax: 408-993-1335
URL: http://www.sjlegal.com

MEMBERS OF FIRM

John W. Elliott
Randall C. Creech
Thomas A. Elliott
Jeffrey S. Lawson
Peter A. Liebow
Raymond A. Brinson

ASSOCIATES

Lauren Berger
Nancy L. Mathis
Edward A. Kraus
Betty Chen
Bonnie L. Portis

OF COUNSEL

Steven J. Roth
Charles R. Reed
Thomas G. Perkins

Reference: Union Bank of California.

For full biographical listings, see the Martindale-Hubbell Law Directory

ROBINSON & WOOD, INC. (AV)

227 North First Street, 95113
Telephone: 408-298-7120
Fax: 408-298-0477
Email: rw@r-winc.com

(See Next Column)

Archie S. Robinson
Weldon S. Wood
Thomas R. Fellows
David S. Henningsen
Hugh F. Lennon
Jesse F. Ruiz
Christian B. Nielsen
Jonathan L. Lee
Jon B. Zimmerman
Mark B. Schellerup
Andrew W. Olsson
Arthur J. Casey
Joseph C. Balestrieri
John L. Winchester, III
Robert A. Nakamae

Rebecca L. Moon
Ann A. Nguyen
Kenneth I. Schumaker
Anne C. Bailey
Stephen D. Bays
Jill K. Ernst
Colin G. McCarthy
Bonnie M. Ross
Mario Alvarado
Christopher K. Karic
Alison M. Hershberger
Camille L. Acayan
Valerie M. Drogus
Jennifer L. Bautista

For full biographical listings, see the Martindale-Hubbell Law Directory

TERRA LAW LLP (AV)

60 South Market Street, Suite 200, 95113
Telephone: 408-288-7325
Fax: 408-998-4895
Burlingame, California Office: 1350 Old Bayshore Highway, Suite 760, 94010.
Telephone: 650-685-7325.
Fax: 650-685-4895.

George H. Cole, Jr.
D. D. Hughmanick
R. Prescott Jaunich
Richard O. McDonald
Breck E. Milde
William L. Myers
Jane P. Relyea
Jason R. Biggs
Joan Paul
Ronald I. Rainey

Katharine L. Hardt-Mason
Thomas E. Rossmeissl

For full biographical listings, see the Martindale-Hubbell Law Directory

SAN MATEO, San Mateo Co.

ANDERLINI, FINKELSTEIN & EMERICK, A PROFESSIONAL CORPORATION (AV)

400 South El Camino Real, Suite 700, 94402
Telephone: 650-348-0102
Fax: 650-348-0962
Email: info@afelaw.com *URL:* http://www.afelaw.com

P. Terry Anderlini
John J. Guheen (1944-1995)
David G. Finkelstein
Merrill G. Emerick
Joern-Eric W. Brugger

Paul J. Smoot
Anne Kristen Brauer

OF COUNSEL

Daniel J. Monaco
Robert M. Desky
Bruce M. Lubarsky

A list of Representative Clients will be furnished upon request.

For full biographical listings, see the Martindale-Hubbell Law Directory

SAN RAFAEL, * Marin Co.

JOHNS & CHRISTENSEN, A PROFESSIONAL CORPORATION (AV)

135 Paul Drive, Suite 100, 94903
Telephone: 415-459-5223
Facsimile: 415-453-2555
Email: info@johnsandchristensen.com *URL:* http://www.johnsandchristensen.com

Christopher Johns
Robert C. Christensen

David Gray Douglas
Jennifer A.D. Lehman
Farimah Faiz

OF COUNSEL

Mark J. Helmueller
Burton C. "Skip" Allyn, IV

For full biographical listings, see the Martindale-Hubbell Law Directory

SANTA ANA, * Orange Co.

CALLAHAN & BLAINE, A PROFESSIONAL LAW CORPORATION (AV)

3 Hutton Centre Drive, Suite 900, 92707
Telephone: 714-241-4444
Fax: 714-241-4445
Email: info@callahan-law.com *URL:* http://www.callahan-law.com

Daniel J. Callahan
Stephen E. Blaine

(See Next Column)

Callahan & Blaine A Professional Law Corporation—*Continued*

Jim P. Mahacek
Michael J. Sachs
Edward Susolik
Kathleen L. Dunham
Robyn Dimino
Reed N. Archambault
Nicki N. Eke
David Kam Ng
Douglas W. Schroeder

OF COUNSEL

Shelley M. Liberto
Walt D. Mahaffa

For full biographical listings, see the Martindale-Hubbell Law Directory

---

Haight, Brown & Bonesteel, L.L.P. (AV)

A Partnership including Professional Corporations
Suite 900, 5 Hutton Centre Drive, 92707
Telephone: 714-754-1100
Telecopier: 714-754-0826
URL: http://www.hbblaw.com
Santa Monica, California Office: 1620 26th Street, Suite 4000 North, P.O. Box 680.
Telephone: 310-449-6000.
Telecopier: 310-829-5117.
Telex: 705837.
Riverside, California Office: California Tower, 3737 Maine Street, Suite 800.
Telephone: 909-341-8300.
Fax: 909-341-8309.
San Francisco, California Office: 100 Bush Street, 27th Floor.
Telephone: 415-986-7700.
Fax: 415-986-6945.
San Diego, California Office: 101 West Broadway, Suite 1000.
Telephone: 619-595-5583.
Fax: 619-595-7873.

RESIDENT MEMBERS

Bruce L. Cleeland
Edwin J. Richards

ASSOCIATE

Jeffrey D. Farrow

Counsel for: Orange County: Aetna Casualty and Surety Co.; Zurich-American Insurance Cos.; Industrial Indemnity Co.; Professional Liability Claims Managers; Maryland Casualty Insurance Co.; Royal Insurance Company of America.

For full biographical listings, see the Martindale-Hubbell Law Directory

---

*SANTA BARBARA,** Santa Barbara Co.

Angle, Carlson, Goldrick & Roberts (AV)

A Partnership including a Professional Corporation
200 East Carrillo Street, Suite 310, 93101
Telephone: 805-963-7400
Fax: 805-963-7610

Robert O. Angle
Arthur W. Carlson (A P.C.)
Miles T. Goldrick
Paul A. Roberts

For full biographical listings, see the Martindale-Hubbell Law Directory

---

SANTA MONICA, Los Angeles Co.

Baker, Keener & Nahra, LLP (AV)

2850 Ocean Park Boulevard, Suite 300, 90405-2936
Telephone: 310-399-0900
Fax: 310-399-1644
Email: general@bknlawyers.com *URL:* http://www.bknlawyers.com

MEMBERS OF FIRM

Robert C. Baker
Karl A. Keener
John P. Nahra
Michael H. Bailey
Steven T. Adams
Melissa S. Fink
Jeffrey P. Nolan
Constance A. Endelicato

Brenda K. Benson
Mitchell F. Mulbarger
James D. Hepworth
Phillip A. Baker
George P. Hawley
Thomas M. Mills
R. Jeffrey Neer
Wendy Wen Yun Chang

OF COUNSEL

Daniel P. Leonard

Reference: Wells Fargo Bank (Los Angeles Head Office).

For full biographical listings, see the Martindale-Hubbell Law Directory

Haight, Brown & Bonesteel, L.L.P. (AV)

A Partnership including Professional Corporations
1620 26th Street, Suite 4000 North, P.O. Box 680, 90404
Telephone: 310-449-6000
Telecopier: 310-829-5117
Telex: 705837
URL: http://www.hbblaw.com
Santa Ana, California Office: Suite 900, 5 Hutton Centre Drive.
Telephone: 714-754-1100.
Telecopier: 714-754-0826.
Riverside, California Office: California Tower, 3737 Main Street, Suite 800.
Telephone: 909-341-8300.
Fax: 909-341-8309.
San Francisco, California Office: 101 Bush Street, 27th Floor.
Telephone: 415-986-7700.
Fax: 415-986-6945.
San Diego, California Office: 101 West Broadway, Suite 1000.
Telephone: 619-595-5583.
Fax: 619-595-7873.

MEMBERS OF FIRM

Gary C. Ottoson (A Professional Corporation)
Bruce A. Armstrong (A Professional Corporation)
Morton Rosen
Theresa M. Marchlewski
William E. Ireland
Christopher I. Ritter

ASSOCIATES

Gary R. Wallace
Chanmaly Kendie Chung

OF COUNSEL

R. Roy Finkle
Gerald R. Judson

For full biographical listings, see the Martindale-Hubbell Law Directory

---

WALNUT CREEK, Contra Costa Co.

Gumbiner & Eskridge LLP (AV)

2121 North California Boulevard Suite 320, 94596
Telephone: 925-933-5800
Fax: 925-933-5837
URL: http://www.insuredlaw.com
URL: http://www.lawyers.com/g&elaw

Joel P. Gumbiner
Jack D. Eskridge

OF COUNSEL

David W. Rudy

For full biographical listings, see the Martindale-Hubbell Law Directory

Hinton & Alfert, A Professional Corporation (AV)

Suite 600, 1646 North California Boulevard, 94596-4113
Telephone: 925-932-6006
Fax: 925-932-3412
Email: ha@hintonandalfert.com *URL:* http://www.lawyers.com/hintonandalfert

Peter J. Hinton
Peter W. Alfert
Scott H. Z. Sumner

Elise Sanguinetti

For full biographical listings, see the Martindale-Hubbell Law Directory

---

COLORADO

*COLORADO SPRINGS,** El Paso Co.

Flynn McKenna Wright & Karsh (AV)

limited liability company
Plaza of the Rockies 111 South Tejon, Suite 202, 80903-3300
Telephone: 719-578-8444
Fax: 719-578-8836

OF COUNSEL

James T. Flynn

MEMBERS OF FIRM

R. Tim McKenna
Bruce M. Wright
Randolph M. Karsh
Brian T. Murphy
Michael C. Potarf
Karl A. Berg, Jr.

For full biographical listings, see the Martindale-Hubbell Law Directory

---

Melat, Pressman, Ezell & Higbie, LLP (AV)

711 South Tejon Street, 80903-4054
Telephone: 719-475-0304
Fax: 719-475-0242
Email: mpeh4@aol.com

MEMBERS OF FIRM

Justin R. Melat
Glenn S. Pressman
E. Steven Ezell
Alanson Higbie

(See Next Column)

MELAT, PRESSMAN, EZELL & HIGBIE LLP, *Colorado Springs—Continued*

ASSOCIATES

Rebecca A. Lorenz
Judith K. Funderburg

References: U.S. Bank; Colorado Bank-Exchange.

For full biographical listings, see the Martindale-Hubbell Law Directory

*DENVER,** Denver Co.

BEEM & MANN, PROFESSIONAL CORPORATION (AV)

One Norwest Center, Suite 3901, 1700 Lincoln Street, 80203
Telephone: 303-894-8100
Fax: 303-832-5010
Email: BeemMann@aol.com

Clifford L. Beem
Stuart Mann

OF COUNSEL

Virginia Elaine Kellogg
Patrick F. Kenney

A. Mark Isley

References: Norwest Bank Denver, N.A.; The Bank of Cherry Creek

For full biographical listings, see the Martindale-Hubbell Law Directory

JAMES R. BENSON, JR. (AV)

303 East Seventeenth Avenue, Suite 800, P.O. Box 18948, 80218
Telephone: 303-832-5931
Fax: 303-832-2337
Email: jrobertb@ix.netcom.com *URL:* http://www.lawyers.com/benson

For full biographical listings, see the Martindale-Hubbell Law Directory

BRENMAN BROMBERG & TENENBAUM, P.C. (AV)

Mellon Financial Center Suite 1001, 1775 Sherman Street, 80203
Telephone: 303-894-0234
Fax: 303-839-1633
Email: bbt@bbtlaw.net

Albert Brenman
Thomas R. Bromberg
A. Thomas Tenenbaum
Steven W. McDonald

Sheryl A. Johnson
Judy A. Gooch

OF COUNSEL

Duane Woodard

For full biographical listings, see the Martindale-Hubbell Law Directory

BROWNSTEIN HYATT & FARBER, P.C. (AV)

Twenty-Second Floor, 410 Seventeenth Street, 80202-4437
Telephone: 303-223-1100
Telecopier: 303-223-1111
Washington, D.C. Office: 1615 L Street, N.W., Suite 450, 20036.
Telephone: 202-296-7353.
Telecopier: 202-296-7009.
Glenwood Springs, Colorado Office: Box 357, 81602.
Telephone: 970-945-5302.
Telecopier: 970-945-4921.

Mark F. Leonard
Andrew W. Loewi
Stanley L. Garnett
Lisa Hogan
Wayne F. Forman
Hubert A. Farbes, Jr.
Terence C. Gill
Mark J. Mathews

OF COUNSEL

Lawrence Bass

SPECIAL COUNSEL

Lynne M. Hufnagel
Richard P. Barkley

Beth Doherty Quinn
David S. Chipman
Jeanine M. Anderson
James D. Sloan
Andrew L. Spielman
A.W. Victoria Jacobs
Chad G. Asarch
Jennifer C. Robinson
Meghan W. Martinez

Representative Clients: Couer d'Alene Mines Corporation; Columbia/HCA Healthcare Corp.; Delgratia Mining Corp.; John Elway Dealerships; Melody Homes, Inc.; Teletech Teleservices, Inc.; Trammell Crow Company; United Air Lines, Inc.; U S WEST, Inc.; Western Wireless Corp.

For Complete List of Firm Personnel, See General Section

For full biographical listings, see the Martindale-Hubbell Law Directory

CANGES, IWASHKO & BETHKE, A PROFESSIONAL CORPORATION (AV)

303 East 17th Avenue Suite 400, 80203-1257
Telephone: 303-860-1900
Fax: 303-860-1665
URL: http://www.lawyers.com/ciblaw

(See Next Column)

E. Michael Canges
Nina A. Iwashko
Erich L. Bethke
James S. Bailey

Michelle L. Lukowicz

Reference: Norwest Bank Denver.

For full biographical listings, see the Martindale-Hubbell Law Directory

CORTEZ MACAULAY BERNHARDT & SCHUETZE LLC (AV)

1600 Broadway, Suite 1600, 80202
Telephone: 303-864-1000
Facsimile: 303-864-1111
URL: http://www.cmblaw.com

Miles Cortez
Christopher T. Macaulay
Susan Bernhardt
Robert A. Schuetze
David H. Goldberg
Marian L. Carlson
Richard P. R. Cohn

For full biographical listings, see the Martindale-Hubbell Law Directory

COX PADMORE SKOLNIK & SHAKARCHY (AV)

Suite 2550, 1775 Sherman Street, 80203
Telephone: 303-839-9191
Fax: 303-839-9318
Email: cpss@aol.com
Palo Alto, California Office: 755 Page Mill Road, Suite A280.
Telephone: 650-424-0600.
Fax: 650-493-9408.
New York, New York Office: 630 Third Avenue.
Telephone: 212-953-6633.
Fax: 212-949-6943.

Gerald Padmore
Theresa M. Moore

OF COUNSEL

Charlotte R. Robinson

Reference: Norwest Bank.

For full biographical listings, see the Martindale-Hubbell Law Directory

DAVIS & CERIANI, P.C. (AV)

Suite 400, Market Center, 1350 Seventeenth Street, 80202
Telephone: 303-534-9000
Telecopier: 303-534-4618
Email: davisandceriani.com

Rick G. Davis
Gary J. Ceriani
Bruce E. Rohde
Michael P. Cillo
Charles W. Bess
John W. Himmelmann

Margaret E. Peper
Patrick John Kanouff
Mark M. Osborn
Valeri Pappas

For full biographical listings, see the Martindale-Hubbell Law Directory

DODSON AND ASSOCIATES, P.C. (AV)

410 Seventeenth Street, Suite 1300, 80202
Telephone: 303-892-0900
Fax: 303-446-0803
Email: rdodson@attymail.com *URL:* http://www.lawyers.com/dodson

Rocco A. Dodson

For full biographical listings, see the Martindale-Hubbell Law Directory

FEATHERSTONE DESISTO LLP (AV)

600 17th Street, Suite 2400, 80202
Telephone: 303-626-7100
Facsimile: 303-626-7101
Email: public@featherstonelaw.com

Bruce A. Featherstone
John A. DeSisto

William L. Gagnon
Gregory W. LePage
Martha Charepoo Alai
Timothy R. Pitner

For full biographical listings, see the Martindale-Hubbell Law Directory

GORSUCH KIRGIS LLP (AV)

Tower 1, Suite 1000, 1515 Arapahoe Street, 80202
Telephone: 303-376-5000
Fax: 303-376-5001

PARTNERS

James A. Jablonski
Dudley P. Spiller
Timothy J. Parsons
David B. Seserman
Dean C. Heizer

(See Next Column)

GORSUCH KIRGIS LLP—*Continued*

ASSOCIATES

Morgan Word
Heather Anne Hawker
Julie Leamon Rosen

For full biographical listings, see the Martindale-Hubbell Law Directory

THE HUSTEAD LAW FIRM A PROFESSIONAL CORPORATION (AV)

Regency Plaza One, 4643 South Ulster Street, Suite 1250, 80237
Telephone: 303-721-5000
Facsimile: 303-721-5001
URL: http://www.thlf.com

Patrick Q. Hustead

Stephen C. Larson
Duane E. Bolin
Benton J. Barton (Not admitted in CO)
Janlynn R. Fleener

Representative Clients: Acceptance Group Insurance Companies; Amwest Insurance Company; Colorado Western Insurance Company; Connecticut Surety; Contractors Bonding and Insurance Company; Insurance Company of the West; Merchants Bonding Company; Underwriters at Lloyd's London; Odyessy Re London; The St. Paul Surety Group.

For full biographical listings, see the Martindale-Hubbell Law Directory

KATZ, LOOK & MOISON, PROFESSIONAL CORPORATION (AV)

1120 Lincoln Street, Suite 1100, 80203
Telephone: 303-832-1900
Fax: 303-863-0412

Michael M. Katz
Harley K. Look, Jr.
Peter R. Moison
Kathryn A. Reeves

Brian E. Onorato
Melisa A. Vogel
Arthur T. DiMeo
Delwyn G. Haroldson
Barbara J. Stauch

SPECIAL COUNSEL

Ogborn, Summerlin & Ogborn, L.L.C., Denver, Colorado

For full biographical listings, see the Martindale-Hubbell Law Directory

KONCILJA & ASSOCIATES, P.C. (AV)

Suite 300, 800 Eighteenth Street, 80202
Telephone: 303-675-0900
Facsimile: 303-675-0401
Email: koncilja@ix.netcom.com *URL:* http://www.Koncilja-associates.com

Frances A. Koncilja

OF COUNSEL

David V. Millard

For full biographical listings, see the Martindale-Hubbell Law Directory

LAPUYADE, WASHINGTON & MOLK, LLC (AV)

4100 East Mississippi Avenue, Suite 600, 80246
Telephone: 303-759-3535
Facsimile: 303-758-2246
URL: http://www.lawyers.com/lapuyadewash&moik

Keith Dale Lapuyade
Alan G. Molk

For full biographical listings, see the Martindale-Hubbell Law Directory

LEVY & LAMBDIN, P.C. (AV)

Plaza Tower One, Suite 900, 6400 South Fiddlers Green Circle (Englewood), 80111
Telephone: 303-796-2900
Telecopier: 303-796-2081

Marc R. Levy
Suzanne J. Lambdin
Stuart D. Morse
Karen Hannah Wheeler

Martha C. Ferris
Gerald D. Pratt
Michael S. Power
Janet S. Bouffard
Stephanie Ann Montague
Brian J. Waters
Ivan A. Sarkissian
Lelia Kathleen Chaney
Jane E. Hershey

For full biographical listings, see the Martindale-Hubbell Law Directory

MILLER & WELCH, L.L.C. (AV)

730 - 17th Street, Suite 925, 80202-3503
Telephone: 303-623-6005
Facsimile: 303-623-0311

James Rollin Miller, Jr.
Carol M. Welch
Paul R. Wood

(See Next Column)

Candace M. Dunley
Joycelyn Crucillo
Matthew D. Macy

For full biographical listings, see the Martindale-Hubbell Law Directory

MONTGOMERY LITTLE & MCGREW, P.C. (AV)

The Quadrant, 5445 DTC Parkway, Suite 800 (Englewood), 80111
Telephone: 303-773-8100
Telecopier: 303-220-0412
URL: http://www.mlmpc.com

Robert R. Montgomery
David C. Little
Richard L. Murray, Jr.
Kevin J. Kuhn
William H. Knapp
Daniel P. Murphy
Christopher B. Little

Representative Clients: BP Amoco; Bristol-Myers Squibb; Cyprus Minerals; Dillon Cos., Inc., d/b/a King Soopers; The St. Paul Insurance Cos.; University of Colorado Health Services Center; Graebel Van Lines; Koch Industries; Teva Pharmaceuticals USA.

For Complete List of Firm Personnel, See General Section

For full biographical listings, see the Martindale-Hubbell Law Directory

MYER, SWANSON, ADAMS & WOLF, P.C. (AV)

The Colorado State Bank Building, 1600 Broadway, Suite 1480, 80202-4915
Telephone: 303-866-9800
Facsimile: 303-866-9818

Fred E. Neef (1910-1986)
Rendle Myer (1929-1999)
Thomas J. Wolf

John M. Anderson

OF COUNSEL

Robert Swanson

Representative Clients: The Oppenheimer Funds; Panorama Series Fund; The Centennial Trusts; Mile High Chapter of American Red Cross; Master Lease; Heartland Management Co.; Kan-Build of Colorado, Inc.
Reference: The Colorado State Bank and Trust of Denver.

For Complete List of Firm Personnel, See General Section

For full biographical listings, see the Martindale-Hubbell Law Directory

OTTEN, JOHNSON, ROBINSON, NEFF & RAGONETTI, P.C. (AV)

950 Seventeenth Street, 16th Floor, 80202
Telephone: 303-825-8400
Telecopier: 303-825-6525
URL: http://www.ojrnr.com

William F. Schoeberlein
David W. Stark
Lawrence W. Marquess
Darrell G. Waas
Hugh Q. Gottschalk
J. Thomas Macdonald
P. Kathleen Lower
David T. Brennan
Terence M. Ridley
Kenneth K. Skogg
Brad W. Schacht
David P. Hutchinson
Todd A. Fredrickson
Darin Mackender
Patricia C. Campbell
Karen L. Brody
Patricia A. Thatcher
Heidi G. Duston
Nancy L. Lipson
Carolyn J. Fairless
Katherine L. Ruff

Representative Clients: Conoco, Inc.; FMC Corp.; Information Handling Services Group, Inc.; Pulte Homes Corp.; QualMed, Inc.; Terex Cranes, Inc.; Tom Brown, Inc.; TrizecHahn Centers, Inc.; U.S. Fire Insurance Co.

For Complete List of Firm Personnel, See General Section

For full biographical listings, see the Martindale-Hubbell Law Directory

PHILIP E. PANKOFF, P.C. (AV)

1625 Broadway, Suite 1830, 80202
Telephone: 303-573-7524
Fax: 303-573-3823
Email: ppankoff@aol.com *URL:* http://www.lawyers.com/pankofflaw

Philip E. Pankoff

Representative Clients: Kirkwood Oil and Gas; Cannon Energy, Inc.; Tellis Gold Mining Company; Technology Trading Systems, Inc.; Foothill Technical Management Consultants, Inc.
Reference: Norwest Bank Denver, N.A.

For full biographical listings, see the Martindale-Hubbell Law Directory

PREEO, SILVERMAN & GREEN, P.C. (AV)

1401 17th Street, Suite 800, 80202
Telephone: 303-296-4440
Fax: 303-296-3330

(See Next Column)

PREEO, SILVERMAN & GREEN P.C., *Denver—Continued*

Robert L. Preeo
Eldon E. Silverman
Jersey M. Green
Martin J. Green
Gilbert R. Egle
Marilyn W. McWilliams
Timothy Kyle Jordan
Brandon S Culter

For full biographical listings, see the Martindale-Hubbell Law Directory

REIMAN & BAYAZ, P.C. (AV)

1600 Broadway, Suite 1340, 80202
Telephone: 303-860-1500
Fax: 303-839-4380
Email: rblaw@earthlink.net

Jeff Reiman
Marcie K. Bayaz

Debra D. Asimus

For full biographical listings, see the Martindale-Hubbell Law Directory

SENN LEWIS & VISCIANO, P.C. (AV)

1801 California Street, Suite 4300, 80202
Telephone: 303-298-1122
Facsimile: 303-296-9101

Frank W. Visciano

Mark A. Redmiles
Luis A. Toro
Margie J. Titus

For Complete List of Firm Personnel, See General Section

For full biographical listings, see the Martindale-Hubbell Law Directory

TREECE, ALFREY, MUSAT & BOSWORTH, P.C. (AV)

999 18th Street, Suite 1600, 80202
Telephone: 303-292-2700
Facsimile: 303-295-0414
Email: tamb@tamblaw.com *URL:* http://www.tamblaw.com

Robert S. Treece
Thomas N. Alfrey
L. Richard Musat
Arthur H. Bosworth, II
Timothy J. Judson

Nicholas Kemp

For full biographical listings, see the Martindale-Hubbell Law Directory

EDWARD L. VOLPE, P.C. (AV)

1660 Lincoln, Suite 2800, 80264
Telephone: 303-861-7800
Fax: 303-831-1181

Edward L. Volpe

For full biographical listings, see the Martindale-Hubbell Law Directory

ENGLEWOOD, Arapahoe Co.

CRAIG E. WAGNER (AV)

5690 DTC Boulevard, Suite 240 East, 80111-3232
Telephone: 303-220-8000
Fax: 303-220-0153
Email: craig@wagner2law.com *URL:* http://wagner2law.com

Reference: Norwest Bank - Arapahoe and Denver.

For full biographical listings, see the Martindale-Hubbell Law Directory

CONNECTICUT

*BRIDGEPORT,** Fairfield Co.

KOSKOFF, KOSKOFF & BIEDER, P.C. (AV)

350 Fairfield Avenue, 06604
Telephone: 203-336-4421
Fax: 203-368-3244
Email: KKB@KOSKOFF.com
Stamford, Connecticut Office: 1172 Bedford Street.
Telephone: 203-325-3686.
Danbury, Connecticut Office: 1 Moss Avenue.
Telephone: 203-792-7100.

Richard A. Bieder
Michael A. Stratton

Joel Thomas Faxon

For full biographical listings, see the Martindale-Hubbell Law Directory

DANBURY, Fairfield Co.

PINNEY, PAYNE, VAN LENTEN, BURRELL, WOLFE & DILLMAN, P.C. (AV)

Lee Farm Corporate Park, 83 Wooster Heights, P.O. Box 3499, 06813-3499
Telephone: 203-743-2721
Fax: 203-792-4759
URL: http://www.ppvlaw.com

Thomas W. Van Lenten
Hugh A. Burrell
Robert J. Wolfe
John M. Dillman
Martin A. Rader, Jr.
William S. Steele, Jr.
Sheldon A. Rosenbaum
Jackie Chan
Richard D. Arconti
Ted D. Backer
Joseph Dimyan
Daniel E. Casagrande
Kim E. Nolan
Wendy A. Grispin

Robin Edwards Otto
John H. Van Lenten

OF COUNSEL

A. Searle Pinney
Bobby S. Payne

Representative Clients: Savings Bank of Danbury.

For full biographical listings, see the Martindale-Hubbell Law Directory

GREENWICH, Fairfield Co.

HOLLAND KAUFMANN & BARTELS, LLC (AV)

289 Greenwich Avenue, 06830-6595
Telephone: 203-869-5600
Fax: 203-869-4648

Alexander J. Holland
Charles B. Kaufmann, III
Philip H. Bartels
Harold R. Burke
Jean Mills Aranha
Lori E. Romano
John C. Fusco

OF COUNSEL

Beth K. Hansson

For full biographical listings, see the Martindale-Hubbell Law Directory

STAMFORD, Fairfield Co.

CACACE, TUSCH & SANTAGATA (AV)

777 Summer Street, P.O. Box 15859, 06901-0859
Telephone: 203-327-2000
Telecopier: 203-353-3392
Email: lawcts@aol.com

MEMBERS OF FIRM

Michael J. Cacace
Mark P. Santagata
Paul T. Tusch
Richard S. Fisher

OF COUNSEL

Kenneth A. DellaRocco
Eric D. Grayson

ASSOCIATES

Edward F. Nemchek
Alice Ann Fitzpatrick
Ronald E. Kowalski II
Aamina Ahmad
Demaris Page Hetrick
Patrick L. Poeschl

LEGAL SUPPORT PERSONNEL

Eva L. Chan
Cynthia L. Mammone

For full biographical listings, see the Martindale-Hubbell Law Directory

CURTIS, BRINCKERHOFF & BARRETT, P.C. (AV)

666 Summer Street, 06901-1416
Telephone: 203-324-6777
Telecopier: 203-324-9621
Email: info@curtisbb.com

T. Ward Cleary (1916-1988)
Frederick M. Tobin
John Wayne Fox
Ward Frank Cleary
James D'Alton Murphy
Randolph T. Lovallo

OF COUNSEL

John D. Hertz
Jane F. Donovan
Richard L. Brinckerhoff
Patricia M. Gaug

Susan L. Stratton
Derek Gilman
Michael P. Murray
John J. Louizos

Counsel for: The F. A. Bartlett Tree Expert Co.; Town of Darien; Miller Automobile Corp.; Bolliger, Inc.; Titan Sports; People's Bank, Bridgeport; Fleet Bank; Federal Deposit Insurance Co.; William Pitt Foundation; Wood Logan Associates.

For full biographical listings, see the Martindale-Hubbell Law Directory

Stamford—Continued

SILVER, GOLUB & TEITELL LLP (AV)

184 Atlantic Street, P.O. Box 389, 06904
Telephone: 203-325-4491
Fax: 203-325-3769
Email: silvergolubteitell.com *URL:* http://www.sgtlaw.com

MEMBERS OF FIRM

Richard A. Silver
David S. Golub
Ernest F. Teitell
Patricia M. Haugh (1942-1988)
Elaine T. Silver
John D. Josel
Mario DiNatale
Jonathan M. Levine

Marilyn J. Ramos
Richard H. Greenwood
Mary G. Curry
Kathleen L. Brandt
Paul A. Slager (Not admitted in CT)
Brad C. Gustafson

For full biographical listings, see the Martindale-Hubbell Law Directory

WATERBURY, New Haven Co.

DRUBNER, HARTLEY, O'CONNOR & MENGACCI (AV)

500 Chase Parkway, 06708
Telephone: 203-753-9291
FAX: 203-753-6373
Email: drubner@dhom.com

MEMBERS OF FIRM

Norman S. Drubner
James E. Hartley, Jr.
Gary B. O'Connor
Joseph A. Mengacci
Gary D. Jones

ASSOCIATES

Linda T. Wihbey
Jayne Elser Welch

For full biographical listings, see the Martindale-Hubbell Law Directory

DISTRICT OF COLUMBIA

WASHINGTON, D.C. Co.

CHARAPP, DEESE & WEISS, LLP (AV)

1901 Pennsylvania Avenue, N.W., Suite 1001, 20006
Telephone: 202-463-9100
Fax: 202-463-2091
Vienna, Virginia Office: 8300 Boone Boulevard, Suite 500, 22182. Telephone 703-714-9576.
Bethesda, Maryland Office: 3 Bethesda Metro Center, Suite 700, 20814. *Telephone:* 301-657-6258.
Richmond, Virginia Office: 2201 West Broad Street, Suite 201, 23220. *Telephone:* 804-358-8680. *Fax:* 804-358-3889.

Michael G. Charapp
C. Michael Deese
Brad D. Weiss

William T. Lehner (Resident, Richmond, Virginia Office)
John J. Delaney
Sarah Daly Jackowski
Brenda Houck Harbison (Resident, Richmond, Virginia Office)
Michael C. Gartner (Not admitted in DC)
James B. St. John, III (Not admitted in DC)

OF COUNSEL

Edward H. Kim

For full biographical listings, see the Martindale-Hubbell Law Directory

COHEN, MILSTEIN, HAUSFELD & TOLL, P.L.L.C. (AV)

West Tower, Suite 500, 1100 New York Avenue, N.W., 20005-3964
Telephone: 202-408-4600
Facsimile: 202-408-4699
Email: lawinfo@cmht.com *URL:* http://www.CMHT.com
Seattle, Washington Office: 999 Third Avenue, Suite 3600. *Telephone:* 206-521-0080. *Facsimile:* 206-521-0166.

MEMBERS OF FIRM

Jerry S. Cohen (1925-1995)
Herbert E. Milstein
Michael D. Hausfeld
Steven J. Toll (Resident, Seattle, Washington Office)
Ann C. Yahner
Lisa M. Mezzetti
Andrew N. Friedman
Richard S. Lewis
Daniel S. Sommers
Daniel A. Small
Gary E. Mason
Joseph M. Sellers
Sharon A. Snyder
Mark S. Willis (Not admitted in DC)

(See Next Column)

ASSOCIATES

Lori G. Feldman (Resident, Seattle, Washington Office)
Paul T. Gallagher
Christine E. Webber
Alexander E. Barnett
Matthew James Ide (Resident, Seattle, Washington Office)
Matthew F. Pawa
Suzette M. Malveaux
Mary N. Strimel
Kristopher A. Kinkade (Resident, Seattle, Washington Office)
Agnieszka M. Fryszman
Deborah J. Vagins
Ari Karen
Charles E. Tompkins
Tamara J. Driscoll (Resident, Seattle, Washington Office)
Elizabeth Haines Cronise
Donna Solen
Lesli C. Esposito (Not admitted in DC)

OF COUNSEL

Margaret G. Farrell

For full biographical listings, see the Martindale-Hubbell Law Directory

COLE, RAYWID & BRAVERMAN, L.L.P. (AV)

1919 Pennsylvania Avenue, N.W., 20006
Telephone: 202-659-9750
Cable Address: "Crab"
Telecopier: 202-452-0067
URL: http://www.crblaw.com

John P. Cole, Jr.
Alan Raywid (1930-1991)
Burt A. Braverman
Robert L. James
John D. Seiver
Wesley R. Heppler
Paul Glist
David M. Silverman
James F. Ireland, III
Maurita K. Coley
Steven Jay Horvitz
Christopher W. Savage
Ann E. Flowers
Robert G. Scott, Jr.
Susan Whelan Westfall
Theresa A. Zeterberg
Karlyn D. Stanley
John Davidson Thomas
John Dodge

Frederick W. Giroux
Geoffrey C. Cook
Maria T. Browne
Donna Carrie Rattley
T. Scott Thompson
Adam S. Caldwell
Sandra G. Gibbs
Mark S. Kristiansen
Christin S. McMeley (Not admitted in DC)
Sara J. Kiernan (Not admitted in DC)
Heather M. Wilson
David N. Tobenkin

OF COUNSEL

Frances J. Chetwynd
Ellen S. Deutsch

For full biographical listings, see the Martindale-Hubbell Law Directory

THE CUNEO LAW GROUP, P.C. (AV)

317 Massachusetts Avenue, N.E. Suite 300, 20002
Telephone: 202-789-3960
Fax: 202-789-1813
Email: contact@cuneolaw.com *URL:* http://www.cuneolaw.com

Jonathan W. Cuneo
James J. Schweitzer
David W. Stanley
Michael G. Lenett

Arthur K. Park (Not admitted in DC)
Daniel Cohen (Not admitted in DC)

COUNSEL

Charles Tiefer

For full biographical listings, see the Martindale-Hubbell Law Directory

OPPENHEIMER WOLFF DONNELLY & BAYH LLP (AV)

1350 Eye Street, N.W. Suite 200, 20005
Telephone: 202-312-8000
FAX: 202-312-8100
URL: http://www.owdlaw.com
Oppenheimer Wolff & Donnelly LLP
Minneapolis, Minnesota Office: 3300 Plaza VII, 45 South Seventh Street. 55402. *Telephone:* 612-607-7000. *FAX:* 612-607-7100.
Amsterdam, The Netherlands Office: Keizergracht 241. *Telephone:* 31-20-423-4555. *FAX:* 31-20-423-4545.
Brussels, Belgium Office: Avenue Louise 240, Box 5, 1050. *Telephone:* 32-2-626-0500. *FAX:* 32-2-626-0510.
Geneva, Switzerland Office: Rue Gabriel Eynard, 6, 1206. *Telephone:* (41/22) 311-7410. *FAX:* (41/22) 311-7407.
New York, N.Y. Office: Citicorp Center, 153 East 53rd Street, 10022. *Telephone:* 212-826-5000. *FAX:* 212-486-0708.
Newport Beach, California Office: 500 Newport Center Drive, Suite 700, 92660. *Telephone:* 949-719-6000. *FAX:* 949-719-6020.

(See Next Column)

OPPENHEIMER WOLFF DONNELLY & BAYH LLP, *Washington—Continued*

Paris, France Office: 53 Avenue Montaigne, 75008.
Telephone: (33/1) 44 95 03 50.
FAX: (33/1) 44 95 03 40.
St. Paul, Minnesota Office: 1700 First National Bank Building, 55101.
Telephone: 651-605-2000.
FAX: 651-605-2100.
Los Angeles, California Office: 2029 Century Park East, 38th Floor, 90067.
Telephone: 310-788-5000.
FAX: 310-277-1297.
Palo Alto, California Office: 3373 Hillview Avenue, Suite 200, 94304.
Telephone: 650-320-4000.
FAX: 650-320-4100.
Chicago, Illinois Office: Oppenheimer Wolff & Donnelly (Illinois), Two Prudential Plaza, 45th Floor, 180 North Stetson Avenue, 60601.
Telephone: 312-616-1800.
Fax: 312-616-5800.

RESIDENT PARTNERS

Harry W. Cladouhos
Courtenay Ellis
John H. Korns
Paul M. Laurenza
Margaret N. Strand
Carole Stern
Thomas Lawrence, III (Not admitted in DC)
Karen M. Hansen (Not admitted in DC)

RESIDENT ASSOCIATES

Lynn A. Bulan
Robin A. Williams (Not admitted in DC)
Edward J. Fishman

For full biographical listings, see the Martindale-Hubbell Law Directory

PIERSON & BURNETT, L.L.P. (AV)

1667 K Street, N.W., Suite 801, 20006
Telephone: 202-466-3044
Fax: 202-466-3055
URL: http://www.comspacelaw.com

W. Theodore Pierson, Jr.
Dennis J. Burnett

David L. Lihani

For full biographical listings, see the Martindale-Hubbell Law Directory

THE ROBINSON LAW FIRM (AV)

Market Square, 717 D Street, N.W., 4th Floor, 20004
Telephone: 202-347-6100
Fax: 202-347-0081
URL: http://www.lawyers.com/robinsonlaw

MEMBER OF FIRM

Kenneth Michael Robinson

ASSOCIATES

Cameron Robinson Kourtesis (Not admitted in DC)
Nikolaos Panagiotis Kourtesis (Not admitted in DC)

For full biographical listings, see the Martindale-Hubbell Law Directory

JAMES J. TANSEY (AV)

2823 29th Street, N.W., 20008
Telephone: 202-232-8557
Fax: 202-232-8549

For full biographical listings, see the Martindale-Hubbell Law Directory

FLORIDA

AVENTURA, Dade Co.

BEDZOW, KORN, BROWN, MILLER & ZEMEL, P.A. (AV)

The Aventura Corporate Center, 20803 Biscayne Boulevard Suite 200, 33180
Telephone: 305-935-6888
Outside Dade County: 1-800-935-6889
FAX: 305-936-9502

Alan J. Kan (1947-1994)
Michael Bedzow
Gary A. Korn
Gary L. Brown
Robert B. Miller
Franklin L. Zemel

Jennifer Levin
Teri L. Di Giulian
Robin I. Willner
Oscar Grisales-Racini
N. Fraser Schuh, III
Robert S. Covitz
Matthew H. Mandel
Nishan C. Mahendran
Brian W. Chaiken
Jessica Garcia
John M. Cooney

References: NationsBank, N.A.; Commonwealth Land Title Insurance Co.

For full biographical listings, see the Martindale-Hubbell Law Directory

*BARTOW,** Polk Co.

FROST & SAUNDERS, P.A. (AV)

395 South Central Avenue, P.O. Box 2188, 33830
Telephone: 941-533-0314; 800-533-0967
Telecopier: 941-533-8985
Email: jfrost1985@aol.com

John W. Frost, II
Thomas C. Saunders
Richard E. "Rick" Dantzler
John Marc Tamayo
Mark A. Sessums
Robert J. Aranda
Peter W. Van den Boom
Nicholas D. Zorn, Jr.

Reference: Community National Bank, Bartow.

For full biographical listings, see the Martindale-Hubbell Law Directory

BOCA RATON, Palm Beach Co.

HARVEY G. KOPELOWITZ (AV)

7251 West Palmetto Park Road, Suite 201
Telephone: 561-392-4115
Fax: 561-392-0351

For full biographical listings, see the Martindale-Hubbell Law Directory

SHAPIRO & DECTOR, P.A. (AV)

7777 Glades Road, Suite 200, 33434
Telephone: 561-477-7800
Facsimile: 561-477-7722
Email: ShapDec@aol.com

Michael B. Shapiro
Andrew M. Dector
Vincent J. Piazza

OF COUNSEL

Michael D. Mopsick
Steven J. Asarch
Wayne Kaplan

For full biographical listings, see the Martindale-Hubbell Law Directory

WEISS & HANDLER, P.A. (AV)

Suite 218A, One Boca Place, 2255 Glades Road, 33431-7313
Telephone: 561-997-9995
Broward: 954-421-5101
Palm Beach: 561-734-8008
Telecopier: 561-997-5280
Email: weisshand@aol.com
West Palm Beach, Florida Office: 505 South Flagler Drive, Suite 1331, 33401.
Telephone: 561-655-3433.
New York, NY Office: 45 Rockefeller Plaza, Suite 1501.
Telephone: 212-332-2900.

Howard I. Weiss
Henry B. Handler

Manuel R. Comras
Donald Feldman
William M. Franz
David K. Friedman
Carol A. Kartagener
Allison L. Kay
Bruce A. Harris
Howard M. Rudolph (Resident, West Palm Beach Office)
Stacy E. Welt

OF COUNSEL

Malcolm L. Stein (Not admitted in FL)
Harry Winderman

For full biographical listings, see the Martindale-Hubbell Law Directory

*CLEARWATER,** Pinellas Co.

KWALL, SHOWERS & COLEMAN, P.A. (AV)

133 North Fort Harrison Avenue, 33755
Telephone: 727-441-4947
Telecopier: 727-447-3158
Email: kwall@worldnet.att.net *URL:* http://www.usalaw.com/adminlaw/

Elizabeth M. Gannon

For Complete List of Firm Personnel, See General Section

For full biographical listings, see the Martindale-Hubbell Law Directory

*FORT LAUDERDALE,** Broward Co.

CONRAD & SCHERER (AV)

A Partnership of Professional Associations
Eighth Floor, 633 South Federal Highway, P.O. Box 14723, 33302
Telephone: 954-462-5500
Facsimile: 954-463-9244
Miami, Florida Office: 44 West Flagler Street, Suite 402, 33130.
Telephone: 305-856-9920.
Facsimile: 305-374-4408.

(See Next Column)

CONRAD & SCHERER—*Continued*

MEMBERS OF FIRM

William R. Scherer, Jr., (P.A.)
Gary S. Genovese (P.A.)
William V. Carcioppolo (P.A.)
Linda Rae Spaulding (P.A.)
Reid A. Cocalis (P.A.)
Willie Earl Hall (P.A.)
Ronald A. FitzGerald
James F. Carroll
Paul R. Larkin, Jr.
Dominic L. Brandy

OF COUNSEL

Rex Conrad

ASSOCIATES

Albert L. Frevola, Jr.
William R. Scherer, III
Vanessa A. Reynolds
Douglas Todd Marx
Janine Renee Kalagher
James A. Epstein
Angel Petti
Nicholas William Romanello
Shari L. McCartney
Catherine M. Rodriguez
Wendy A. Delvecchio

Local Counsel for: American Home Assurance Group; Caterpillar Tractor Co.; Division of Risk Management, State of Florida; Florida East Coast Railway; Fort Motor Co.; Liberty Mutual Insurance Co.; Ryder Truck Lines; Unigard Insurance Group.
Approved Attorneys for: Attorneys' Title Insurance Fund.
Reference: Barnett Bank of Fort Lauderdale.

For full biographical listings, see the Martindale-Hubbell Law Directory

KENNETH D. COOPER, P.A. (AV)

400 S.E. Eighth Street, 33316
Telephone: 954-522-7177
Fax: 954-764-5874
URL: http://www.lawyers.com/cooperlaw

Kenneth D. Cooper

For full biographical listings, see the Martindale-Hubbell Law Directory

BRIAN C. DEUSCHLE CHARTERED (AV)

800 Southeast Third Avenue Suite 400, 33316
Telephone: 954-763-7200
Facsimile: 954-522-7728
Email: B.C.D.Chartered@worldnet.att.net

Brian C. Deuschle

Christopher D. Hale

Representative Clients: Drexel Investments, Inc.; Seabulk Tankers, Ltd.; Seabulk Chemical Carriers, Inc.; Hvide Marine, Inc.; Eller & Co.; American National Bank.
Approved Attorneys for: Attorneys' Title Insurance Fund; American National Bank; Norwest Mortgage, Inc.

For full biographical listings, see the Martindale-Hubbell Law Directory

ESLER & LINDIE, P.A. (AV)

Suite 300 The Advocate Building, 315 S.E. Seventh Street, 33301
Telephone: 954-764-5400
FAX: 954-764-5408
Email: eslerandlindie@martindalemail.com *URL:* http://www.lawyers.com/esler&lindie

Gary A. Esler
Beth G. Lindie

Representative Clients: The Chubb Group of Insurance Cos.; Fireman's Fund Insurance Co.; State of Florida-Department of Risk Management; Marriott Corp.; Mobile America Insurance Group, Inc.; Ohio Casualty Insurance Co.
Reference: Capital Bank.

For full biographical listings, see the Martindale-Hubbell Law Directory

GILLESPIE, GOLDMAN & KRONENGOLD (AV)

Port Royale Financial Center, 6550 North Federal Highway, 33308
Telephone: 954-771-0908
Facsimile: 954-771-9880
Email: mail@ggklaw.com *URL:* http://www.lawyers.com/ggklaw

MEMBERS OF FIRM

John R. Gillespie, Jr.
Peter R. Goldman
Jeffrey L. Kronengold

ASSOCIATE

Gary M. Farmer, Jr.

For full biographical listings, see the Martindale-Hubbell Law Directory

WILLIAM W. HAURY, JR. (AV)

SouthTrust Bank Building, 10th Floor, 4875 North Federal Highway, 33308
Telephone: 954-491-2431; 800-741-2431
Fax: 954-491-4409
Email: bhaury@gate.net *URL:* http://www.lawyers.com/williamhaury

For full biographical listings, see the Martindale-Hubbell Law Directory

KIPNIS TESCHER LIPPMAN & VALINSKY (AV)

100 Northeast Third Avenue, Suite 610, 33301
Telephone: 954-467-1964
Fax: 954-467-2264

MEMBERS OF FIRM

Alan G. Kipnis
Howard A. Tescher
Steven N. Lippman
Jay L. Valinsky

ASSOCIATES

Richard B. Storfer
Patricia Fox-Butler
Michelle L. LaRue

For full biographical listings, see the Martindale-Hubbell Law Directory

OPPENHEIM & PILELSKY, P.A. (AV)

1290 Weston Road, Suite 300, 33326
Telephone: 954-384-6114
Toll Free: 888-384-6114
Fax: 954-384-6115
Email: Info@oppenheimlaw.com *URL:* http://www.oppenheimlaw.com

Roy D. Oppenheim
Ellen B. Pilelsky

Representative Clients: Stuart Supply, Inc.; World Office Products Manufacturing, Inc.; Danro Homes, Inc.; Intelihomes Development, Inc.; Danal Homes Development, Inc.; Landmark Building & Design, Inc.; Ambry Homes, Ltd.; Delcourt Homes, Inc.; Weston Title & Escrow, Inc.

For full biographical listings, see the Martindale-Hubbell Law Directory

PURDY AND FLYNN, P.A. (AV)

1107 Southeast Fourth Avenue, 33316
Telephone: 954-356-0008
Fax: 954-356-0017
Email: purdyflynn@worldnet.att.net *URL:* http://www.purdyflynn.com

H. Mark Purdy
Rose Ann Flynn

Craig Joseph Trocino

OF COUNSEL

Michael S. Insler

For full biographical listings, see the Martindale-Hubbell Law Directory

*FORT MYERS,** Lee Co.

GARVIN & TRIPP, A PROFESSIONAL ASSOCIATION (AV)

2532 East First Street, P.O. Drawer 2040, 33902
Telephone: 941-334-1824
FAX: 941-334-6848
Email: jgarvin@cyberstreet.com *URL:* http://www.lawyers.com/garvin&tripp

Jeffrey R. Garvin
Theodore L. Tripp, Jr.

Bruce M. Essen
Elisa S. Worthington

Reference: Northern Trust Bank, Fort Myers, Florida.

For full biographical listings, see the Martindale-Hubbell Law Directory

HOLLYWOOD, Broward Co.

STEVEN A. MASON, P.A. (AV)

3363 Sheridan Street, Suite 201, 33021
Telephone: 954-963-5900
Fax: 954-985-9811
Email: passat902@aol.com *URL:* http://www.lawyers.com/stevenmasonpa

Steven A. Mason

Representative Clients: T.S.I., Inc.; Southern Security Bank; Dental Centers of America.

For full biographical listings, see the Martindale-Hubbell Law Directory

*JACKSONVILLE,** Duval Co.

ALLEN, BRINTON, SIMMONS & MCCARTHY, P.A. (AV)

One Independent Drive, Suite 3200, 32202
Telephone: 904-353-8800
Fax: 904-353-8770

A. Graham Allen
William D. Brinton
Sidney S. Simmons, II
Edward McCarthy, III

Joelle Jackson Dillard

Representative Clients: Anheuser-Busch Companies, Inc.; Avis Rent A Car System, Inc.; Bridgestone/Firestone, Inc.; Jacksonville Transportation Authority; The Haskell Co.; Johnson & Johnson; Masthead Industries, Inc.; U-Haul Co.

For full biographical listings, see the Martindale-Hubbell Law Directory

Jacksonville—Continued

JOHN F. CALLENDER (AV)

1301 River Place Boulevard Suite 2105, 32207
Telephone: 904-398-8833
Fax: 904-396-4457
URL: http://www.willcontestfla.com

Reference: First Union National Bank.

For full biographical listings, see the Martindale-Hubbell Law Directory

FISCHETTE, OWEN, HELD & MCBURNEY (AV)

1301 Riverplace Blvd. Suite 1916, 32207
Telephone: 904-398-7036
Fax: 904-398-4283
Email: Attorneys@FOHMLAW.com

MEMBERS OF FIRM

James A. Fischette
Edwin W. Held Jr.
Charles W. McBurney Jr.

ASSOCIATES

R. Joseph Dill
Robert J. Perry Jr.

References: First Union National Bank of Florida; Compass Bank; SunTrust Bank.

For full biographical listings, see the Martindale-Hubbell Law Directory

HEDRICK, DEWBERRY & REGAN, P.A. (AV)

50 North Laura Street, Suite 2225, 32202
Telephone: 904-356-1300
Fax: 904-356-8050

Michael J. Dewberry
Alexandra Krueger Hedrick
Jeffrey C. Regan

Clinton Allen Wright III

For full biographical listings, see the Martindale-Hubbell Law Directory

LILES, GAVIN & COSTANTINO (AV)

One Enterprise Center, Suite 1500, 225 Water Street, 32202
Telephone: 904-634-1100
Fax: 904-634-1234
Email: triallaw@bellsouth.net

Rutledge R. Liles
R. Kyle Gavin
R. Scott Costantino

ASSOCIATES

Niels P. Murphy
Robert Bruce George

For full biographical listings, see the Martindale-Hubbell Law Directory

LOBRANO & KINCAID, P.L. (AV)

Suite 1650 Independent Life Building, 1 Independent Drive, 32202
Telephone: 904-359-2100
Facsimile: 904-353-1332

Stephen D. Lobrano
Wade McK. Hampton

OF COUNSEL

W. Douglas Smith (Not admitted in FL)

For full biographical listings, see the Martindale-Hubbell Law Directory

SMITH HULSEY & BUSEY (AV)

1800 First Union National Bank Tower, 225 Water Street, P.O. Box 53315, 32201-3315
Telephone: 904-359-7700
Facsimile: 904-359-7708; 353-9908
Email: vsharp@smithhulsey.com

Lloyd Smith (1915-1987)

MEMBERS OF FIRM

Stephen D. Busey
Earl E. Googe, Jr.
Jeanne E. Helton
Cynthia C. Jackson
G. Preston Keyes
Richard E. Klein
William E. Kuntz
Lauren P. Langham
M. Richard Lewis, Jr.
John F. MacLennan
Raymond R. Magley
E. Owen McCuller, Jr.
James H. Post
Bryan L. Putnal
E. Lanny Russell
Joel Settembrini, Jr.
Tim E. Sleeth
John R. Smith, Jr.
Harry M. Wilson, III

(See Next Column)

Brandon L. Ayscue
Brannon B. Belcastro
James A. Bolling, Jr.
Charmaine T.M. Chiu
Ryan C. Curtis
Michael R. Freed
Reynold N. Hoover
Michael J. Ivan, Jr.
Tonya L. Janney
Charles H. Keller
Bradley R. Markey
R. Leanne McKnight
Bert J. Millis
Stephen D. Moore, Jr.
Jon L. Swergold

OF COUNSEL

Mark Hulsey
John E. Thrasher

Representative Clients: ATP Tour, Inc; Baptist/St. Vincent's Health System, Inc.; Browning-Ferris Industries, Inc.; First Union National Bank of Florida; Florida Rock Industries, Inc.; PGA Tour, Inc.; KPMG Peat Marwick; The Regency Group, Inc.; The Ritz-Carlton Hotel Co.; University of Florida.

For full biographical listings, see the Martindale-Hubbell Law Directory

LAKELAND, Polk Co.

HAHN, MCCLURG, WATSON, GRIFFITH & BUSH, P.A. (AV)

101 South Florida Avenue, 33801-4619
Telephone: 941-688-7747
Telecopier: 941-683-4582
Mailing Address: P.O. Box 38, 33802-0038
Email: lawfirm@hahnmcclurg.com *URL:* http://www.hmwgb@gte.net

James P. Hahn
E.V. McClurg
Stephen C. Watson
John R. Griffith
Philip H. Bush
James M. Craig, II

General Counsel: Huntington National Bank, Lakeland, Florida; Florida-First Bank, Lakeland, Florida; Publix Super Markets, Inc.
Approved Attorneys For: Attorneys' Title Insurance Fund; American Title Insurance Co.; Title & Trust Company of Florida; Federal Land Bank of Columbia, Columbia, S.C.
Reference: Huntington National Bank, Lakeland, Florida.

For full biographical listings, see the Martindale-Hubbell Law Directory

*MIAMI,** Dade Co.

ARAGON, BURLINGTON, WEIL & CROCKETT, P.A. (AV)

Office in the Grove - Penthouse, 2699 South Bayshore Drive, 33133
Telephone: 305-858-2900
Telefax: 305-858-5261
Email: info@abwc.com

Rudolph F. Aragon
Robert K. Burlington
Jeffrey B. Crockett
Ronald P. Weil
Paul J. Schwiep
Kevin C. Kaplan
Daniel F. Blonsky
Ava Borrasso
Sean R. Santini

For full biographical listings, see the Martindale-Hubbell Law Directory

BERMAN WOLFE RENNERT VOGEL & MANDLER, P.A. (AV)

35th Floor, International Place, 100 Southeast Second Street, 33131-2130
Telephone: 305-577-4177
Fax: 305-373-6036
Email: administrator@bwr-law.com *URL:* http://www.bwr-law.com
Boca Raton, Florida Office: Boca Corporate Center, 2101 NW Corporate Boulevard, Suite 107, 33431.
Telephone: 561-995-2232.
Fax: 561-995-1668.

Neil J. Berman
Leon J. Wolfe
Charles J. Rennert
Howard J. Vogel
Jeffrey L. Mandler
Jill Nexon Berman

Jonathan L. Gaines
Miriam Cruz-Bustillo
Claire P. Menard
Shamira Klein
Julie M. Schwartz

OF COUNSEL

Anthony A. Rolle

For full biographical listings, see the Martindale-Hubbell Law Directory

BUSTO & JENNINGS, PROFESSIONAL ASSOCIATION (AV)

370 Minorca Avenue (Coral Gables), 33134-4311
Telephone: 305-443-2444
Fax: 305-443-8578

Mercedes Busto
William G. Jennings, III

For full biographical listings, see the Martindale-Hubbell Law Directory

CARUANA AND LORENZEN, P.A. (AV)

1000 Courthouse Tower, 44 West Flagler Street, 33130
Telephone: 305-371-7972
Fax: 305-358-6907

(See Next Column)

CARUANA AND LORENZEN P.A.—*Continued*

Albert G. Caruana
Dirk Lorenzen

Georg H. Ketelhohn
Lisa Mullins

For full biographical listings, see the Martindale-Hubbell Law Directory

DUNWODY WHITE & LANDON, P.A. (AV)

550 Biltmore Way, Suite 810 (Coral Gables), 33134
Telephone: 305-529-1500
Fax: 305-529-8855
Email: dwl-law.com
Naples Office: 4001 Tamiami Trail North, Suite 200.
Telephone: 941-263-5885.
Fax: 941-262-1442.
Palm Beach Office: 239 South County Road, Suite 300, P.O. Box 3165.
Telephone: 561-655-2120.
Fax: 561-655-2168.

Atwood Dunwody (1912-1996)
Jonna S. Brown
Jackson M. Bruce, Jr. (Resident, Naples Office)
Neil R. Chrystal
Jack A. Falk, Jr.
John J. Grundhauser
Robert D. W. Landon, II
Thomas J. Matkov
William T. Muir
Mitchell E. Silverstein
Robert A. White

Patrick J. Lannon

For full biographical listings, see the Martindale-Hubbell Law Directory

FELDMAN GALE & WEBER, P.A. (AV)

201 South Biscayne Boulevard, 19th Floor, 33131-4329
Telephone: 305-358-5001
Fax: 305-358-3309
Email: fgwlaw@fgwlaw.com
Suffield, Connecticut Office: 40 Crane Hill Road, 06078.
Telephone: 860-668-0226.
Fax: 860-668-0696. Email: WCNEALON@FGWLAW.COM; WCNEALON@AOL.COM.

Jeffrey D. Feldman
James A. Gale
Michael J. Weber

Sean N. R. Wells
John C. Carey
Jennifer Johnson Watkins
Ozzie A. Farres
Nancy J. Flint
Greg Tung Nguyen

OF COUNSEL

William C. Nealon (Not admitted in FL)

For full biographical listings, see the Martindale-Hubbell Law Directory

HECTOR & HARKE LLP (AV)

Miami Center, Suite 1050, 201 South Biscayne Boulevard, 33131
Telephone: 305-536-8220
Fax: 305-536-8229
Email: hectorharke@hectorharke.com

Alice G. Hector (P.A.)
Lance A. Harke

Sarah Becket Clasby
Emilia A. Quesada
Franklin G. Cosmen, Jr.
Jeffrey A. Sudduth
Alba Varela
Eileen L. Parsons

For full biographical listings, see the Martindale-Hubbell Law Directory

HOLTZMAN, KRINZMAN, EQUELS & FURIA (AV)

2601 South Bayshore Drive, Suite 600, 33133
Telephone: 305-859-7700
Fax: 305-859-9996
Email: hkef@hkef.com *URL:* http://www.hkef.com
Orlando, Florida Office: 16 West Pine Street, 32801.
Telephone: 407-839-0095.
Fax: 407-839-2050.
Tallahassee, Florida Office: 542 East Park Avenue, 32301.
Telephone: 850-222-2900.
Fax: 850-222-2933.

Thomas K. Equels
Joseph L. Raia
R. Barbara Wien
Cary A. Lubetsky
Mary Kogut Equels (Resident, Orlando Office)
Charles M. Greene (Resident, Orlando Office)

Sherrie J. Cohen
Nancy M. Thevenin
Kevin J. Tang (Resident, Orlando Office)

OF COUNSEL

Chapman L. Smith, Jr.

For full biographical listings, see the Martindale-Hubbell Law Directory

JOSEPHS, JACK & GAEBE, P.A. (AV)

Grove Professional Building, 2950 S.W. 27th Avenue, Suite 100, 33133-3765
Telephone: Dade County: 305-445-3800
Telecopier: 305-448-5800
Email: TheFirm@FloridaAttorneys.com *URL:* http://www.Florida-Attorneys.com

Michael R. Josephs
Lewis N. Jack, Jr.
John S. Gaebe

Elisabeth M. Allen
Helen Leen Miranda
Scott A. Cole
Stephanie E. Demos
Scott T. McCullough
Tamara D. McKeown
Christopher T. Lemos

Representative Clients: U-Haul Corporation; ITT Sheraton; Zurich-American Insurance Company; Republic Claims Service Company; Southern Fire Insurance Adjusters.

For full biographical listings, see the Martindale-Hubbell Law Directory

KATZ, BARRON, SQUITERO, FAUST & BERMAN, P.A. (AV)

Seventh Floor, 2699 South Bayshore Drive, 33133-5408
Telephone: 305-856-2444; North Broward/Boca Raton: 954-781-4720; *Broward:* 954-522-3636; North Broward: 954-781-0637
Facsimile: 305-285-9227
URL: http://www.kbsfb.com
Fort Lauderdale, Florida Office: 100 Northeast 3rd Avenue, Suite 280, 33301.
Telephone: 305-860-2599.
Fax: 954-522-5119.

Michael D. Katz
Ronald M. Barron (1945-1994)
John R. Squitero
Marc L. Faust
Richard E. Berman
Anthony H. Pelle
Howard L. Friedberg
Robert C. Grady
Erica L. English
William D. Rohrer
Richard B. Ivans
Bernard Allen
W. Todd Boyd
David S. Drobner
Charles D. Robbins
Charles D. Brecker

OF COUNSEL

William A. Zeiher
Roger S. Goldman
Richard Morton

Michael I. Kean
Michele L. McNichol
Adam J. Lamb
William R. Trueba
Alex Espenkotter
Jill D. Levy
Jose R. Riguera
Monica A. Rey-Moran
Mathai Jacob

For full biographical listings, see the Martindale-Hubbell Law Directory

LASH & GOLDBERG LLP (AV)

NationsBank Tower Suite 1200, 100 Southeast Second Street, 33131
Telephone: 305-347-4040
Fax: 305-347-4050
Email: lglaw@lashgoldberg.com *URL:* http://www.lashgoldberg.com

Alan D. Lash
Martin B. Goldberg

Alice Jacobson Lash
Stacey Schauer Dawes
Kathryn M. Fried
Jessica Lima Leyva

Representative Clients: Arthur Andersen LLP; Coopers & Lybrand Limited; Yankee Clipper Enterprises, Inc. (Joe DiMaggio); Tenet Healthcare Corporation; Boston Water & Sewer Commission; Lennar Partners, Inc.; Sound Advice, Inc.; Family Golf Centers, Inc.; Jardine Insurance Brokers, Inc.; Response Oncology, Inc.

For full biographical listings, see the Martindale-Hubbell Law Directory

LEVINE & PARTNERS, P.A. (AV)

1110 Brickell Avenue, 7th Floor, 33131
Telephone: Dade: 305-372-1350
Telefax: 305-372-1352
URL: http://www.levinelawfirm.com

I. Stanley Levine
Robert J. Levine
Suzan Jon Jacobs
Alan W. Levine
Allan S. Reiss
Judith L. Gelber

For full biographical listings, see the Martindale-Hubbell Law Directory

THE LAW OFFICES OF RONALD S. LOWY (AV)

5615 Lagorce Drive Penthouse, 33140
Telephone: 305-673-5699
Telecopier: 305-865-1809
Email: rlowyesq@bellsouth.net

Representative Clients: Tate Enterprises; British Airways, PLC; Alleghany Mutual Co.; SunTrust of Miami; Crescent Heights Companies.

For full biographical listings, see the Martindale-Hubbell Law Directory

Miami—Continued

MARKOWITZ, DAVIS, RINGEL & TRUSTY, P.A. (AV)

Two Datran Center, Suite 1225, 9130 South Dadeland Boulevard, 33156-7849
Telephone: 305-670-5000
Telecopier: 305-670-5011

Joseph I. Davis, Jr.

Jonathan S. Leiderman
Ilan Markus
Mark A. Gatica
Darrel T. King

For full biographical listings, see the Martindale-Hubbell Law Directory

MARTENS DUNAJ MARLOWE DAVIS & MARLOWE (AV)

Miami Center, Suite 880, 201 South Biscayne Boulevard, 33131
Telephone: 305-373-9977
Fax: 305-373-8877
Email: postmaster@miamilaw.net *URL:* http://www.miamilaw.net
New Port Richey, Florida Office: 8726 Old County Road 54, Suite E.
Telephone: 727-376-9599.
Fax: 727-376-3146. Email: postmaster@miamilaw.net. URL: http://www.miamilaw.net.

Sherryll Martens Dunaj
Ronald J. Marlowe
Gary L. Davis
Russell G. Marlowe
Linda G. McLoughlin
John L. Urban

For full biographical listings, see the Martindale-Hubbell Law Directory

MISHAN, SLOTO, GREENBERG, HELLINGER & UDOLF, P.A. (AV)

Suite 2350, First Union Financial Center, 200 South Biscayne Boulevard, 33131
Telephone: 305-379-1792
Facsimile: 305-379-2328
Email: MishanSloto@COMPUSERVE.COM

Steven Mishan
James R. Sloto
Barry N. Greenberg
Andrew B. Hellinger
Bruce L. Udolf
Carol L. Cox
Alan M. Burger

Ana Cela Harris
Dara J. Collins
Steven J. Solomon
Coralee G. Penebad

For full biographical listings, see the Martindale-Hubbell Law Directory

MOSCOWITZ STARKMAN & MAGOLNICK (AV)

100 Southeast 2nd Street Suite 3700, 33131
Telephone: 305-379-8300
Facsimile: 305-379-4404
Email: law@msmmiami.com *URL:* http://www.lawyers.com/msm-law

MEMBERS OF FIRM

Joel S. Magolnick
Jane Wollner Moscowitz
Norman A. Moscowitz
Jay Starkman

ASSOCIATES

Jennifer B. Glinsky
Mitchell R. Katz
Farah J. Korn
Lizbeth M. Michel

OF COUNSEL

Bradley L. Mirkin

For full biographical listings, see the Martindale-Hubbell Law Directory

PAYTON & CARLSON, P.A. (AV)

SunTrust International Center, Suite 1200, One Southeast Third Avenue, 33131
Telephone: 305-372-3500
Fax: 305-577-4895
Email: hapayton@bellsouth.net

Harry A. Payton
Curtis Carlson

Ronald J. Lewittes
Julie Anne Moxley

OF COUNSEL

Mara Beth Sommers

For full biographical listings, see the Martindale-Hubbell Law Directory

PODHURST, ORSECK, JOSEFSBERG, EATON, MEADOW, OLIN & PERWIN, P.A. (AV)

Suite 800 City National Bank Building, 25 West Flagler Street, 33130-1780
Telephone: 305-358-2800; Fort Lauderdale: 954-463-4346
Fax: 305-358-2382
Email: Info@podhurst.com *URL:* http://www.wwdir.com/podhurst.html

(See Next Column)

Aaron Podhurst
Robert Orseck (1934-1978)
Robert C. Josefsberg
Joel D. Eaton
Barry L. Meadow
Michael S. Olin
Joel S. Perwin
Steven C. Marks
Victor M. Diaz, Jr.
Katherine W. Ezell

Xavier Martínez

OF COUNSEL

Walter H. Beckham, Jr.
Karen Podhurst Dern

References: City National Bank of Miami; Mellon United National Bank of Miami.

For full biographical listings, see the Martindale-Hubbell Law Directory

MICHAEL J. ROSEN, P.A. (AV)

2400 South Dixie Highway Suite 105, 33133-3141
Telephone: 305-858-9700
Fax: 305-858-7299
Email: MJRPALAW@aol.com *URL:* http://www.lawyers.com/mjrpalaw

Michael J. Rosen

For full biographical listings, see the Martindale-Hubbell Law Directory

SIEGFRIED, RIVERA, LERNER, DE LA TORRE & SOBEL, P.A. (AV)

Suite 1102, 201 Alhambra Circle (Coral Gables), 33134
Telephone: 305-442-3334
Fax: 305-443-3292
URL: http://www.siegfriedlaw.com

Steven M. Siegfried
Oscar R. Rivera
Lisa A. Lerner
Helio De La Torre
Peter H. Edwards
Stuart H. Sobel
Maria Victoria Arias
James F. Harrington
Elisabeth D. Kozlow

Gary Louis Brown
David B. Israel
Laura Michelle Manning
Fern F. Musselwhite
Grissel C. Picot
Marc C. Pugliese

OF COUNSEL

H. Hugh Mc Connell

For full biographical listings, see the Martindale-Hubbell Law Directory

SPRECHMAN & ASSOCIATES, P.A. (AV)

Nationsbank Building, 18305 Biscayne Boulevard, Suite 213, 33160-2172
Telephone: 305-931-0100
Facsimile: 305-936-0200
Email: sprechman@aol.com *URL:* http://www.sprechmanlaw.com

Steven B. Sprechman

Stacey S. Fisher
Scott E. Modlin
George J. Batarseh

For full biographical listings, see the Martindale-Hubbell Law Directory

TRALINS AND ASSOCIATES, P.A. (AV)

Suite 3310 2 South Biscayne Boulevard, 33131
Telephone: 305-374-3300
Telefax: 305-374-4933

Myles J. Tralins

For full biographical listings, see the Martindale-Hubbell Law Directory

WEISSMAN, DERVISHI, BORGO & NORDLUND, P.A. (AV)

100 Southeast 2nd Street, Suite 2610, 33131
Telephone: 305-347-4070
Fax: 305-347-4077
Fort Lauderdale Office: Emerald Lake Corporate Park, Suite 101, 3109 Stirling Road, 33312.
Telephone: 954-981-7400.
Fax: 954-989-8068.

John R. Borgo
Brian S. Dervishi
Randall Nordlund
Maria H. Ruiz
Jeffrey M. Weissman

For full biographical listings, see the Martindale-Hubbell Law Directory

NICEVILLE, Okaloosa Co.

STANLEY BRUCE POWELL, P.A. (AV)

107 North Partin Drive, P.O. Box 400, 32588-0400
Telephone: 850-678-2118
Fax: 850-678-8336
Email: BPOWELLPA@AOL.COM

(See Next Column)

STANLEY BRUCE POWELL, P.A.—*Continued*

Stanley Bruce Powell
David R. Swanick III

Representative Clients: Peoples National Bank of Niceville; Destin Bank; Big Kahuna's, Inc.
References: Peoples National Bank of Niceville; Destin Bank; Vanguard Bank and Trust Co.

For full biographical listings, see the Martindale-Hubbell Law Directory

---

*ORLANDO,** Orange Co.

ALLEN, DYER, DOPPELT, MILBRATH & GILCHRIST (AV)

255 South Orange Avenue, Suite 1401, P.O. Box 3791, 32802-3791
Telephone: 407-841-2330
Fax: 407-841-2343
Email: info@addmg.com

Herbert L. Allen
Robert Dyer
Ava K. Doppelt
Stephen D. Milbrath
Brian R. Gilchrist
Christopher F. Regan
Jeffrey S. Whittle
David L. Sigalow
Richard K. Warther
Michael W. Taylor (Not admitted in FL)
Enrique G. Estevez

LEGAL SUPPORT PERSONNEL
PATENT AGENTS

Carl M. Napolitano, Ph.D.
Jacqueline E. Hartt, Ph.D.

For full biographical listings, see the Martindale-Hubbell Law Directory

BROWN, WARD, SALZMAN & WEISS, P.A. (AV)

111 North Orange Avenue, Suite 875, P.O. Box 2873, 32802-2873
Telephone: 407-425-9566
Fax: 407-425-9596; Email: firm@orlandolaw.net
Email: brownu@osceola.k12.fl.us *URL:* http://www.orlandolaw.net

Usher Larry Brown
John H. Ward
Gary S. Salzman
Jeffrey S. Weiss
Suzanne D'Agresta

Scott D. Danahy
James G. Vickaryous
Robert L. Butterfield, Jr.
Allison Carmine McDonald

Representative Clients: The School Board of Osceola County; The School Board of Indian River County; Osceola County; Orange County Comptroller; General Electric Capital Modular Space; Honeywell, Inc.; Central Brevard Anesthesiologists, P.A.

For full biographical listings, see the Martindale-Hubbell Law Directory

---

THOMAS F. EGAN, P.A. (AV)

204 Park Lake Street, 32803
Telephone: 407-849-1055
Fax: 407-849-1094
Email: eganatty@aol.com

Thomas F. Egan

For full biographical listings, see the Martindale-Hubbell Law Directory

---

HARTLEY, WALL & NORMAN (AV)

200 South Orange Avenue, Suite 2810, P.O. Box 2168, 32802
Telephone: 407-422-7992
Fax: 407-425-2182

MEMBERS OF FIRM

Carl W. Hartley, Jr.
Richard F. Wall
Todd K. Norman
Terrance L. Ashanta-Barker

Reference: SunTrust Bank, Central Florida, N.A.

For full biographical listings, see the Martindale-Hubbell Law Directory

---

NORMAN LINDER HULL, P.A. (AV)

537 North Magnolia Avenue, P.O. Box 2751, 32802
Telephone: 407-422-1235
Fax: 407-423-2842
Email: nlhull@ix.netcom.com *URL:* http://www.lawyers.com/hulllaw

Norman L. Hull

For full biographical listings, see the Martindale-Hubbell Law Directory

---

KING, BLACKWELL & DOWNS, P.A. (AV)

25 East Pine Street, P.O. Box 1631, 32802-1631
Telephone: 407-422-2472
Fax: 407-648-0161
Email: kbdfirm@mindspring.com *URL:* http://www.kbdlaw.com

David B. King
Bruce B. Blackwell
Mayanne Downs

(See Next Column)

John F. Tannian
Thomas A. Zehnder

For full biographical listings, see the Martindale-Hubbell Law Directory

LITCHFORD & CHRISTOPHER, PROFESSIONAL ASSOCIATION (AV)

NationsBank Center, Suite 2200, 390 North Orange Avenue, P.O. Box 1549, 32802
Telephone: 407-422-6600
Telecopier: 407-841-0325
Email: lawfirm@litchris.com *URL:* http://www.litchris.com

Hal K. Litchford
Donald E. Christopher
Mark Lang
Brian D. DeGailler
David G. Lerner
Alan B. Taylor

Scott K. Lippman
G. Steven Fender
Jill Barron Dugger
Susan E. Sewell
Joanne Reed Day

Reference: Citrus Bank.

For full biographical listings, see the Martindale-Hubbell Law Directory

---

KENNETH L. MANN, P.A. (AV)

105 East Robinson Street, Suite 540, P.O. Box 551, 32802-0551
Telephone: 407-422-0006
Fax: 407-841-9516
Email: reasonablemann@worldnet.att.net *URL:* http://www.KenMannlaw.com

Kenneth L. Mann

For full biographical listings, see the Martindale-Hubbell Law Directory

---

TERRY L. McCOLLOUGH, P.A. (AV)

400 North Ferncreek Avenue, 32803
Telephone: 407-894-8600
Fax: 407-894-8685
Email: terry131@aol.com

Terry L. McCollough

LEGAL SUPPORT PERSONNEL

Jacqueline G. Kinker (Paralegal)
Colby D. Griffin (Paralegal)

For full biographical listings, see the Martindale-Hubbell Law Directory

---

McEWAN, MARTINEZ, LUFF, DUKES & RUFFIER, P.A. (AV)

108 East Central Boulevard, P.O. Box 753, 32801
Telephone: 407-423-8571
Fax: 407-423-8637

Wilson Sanders (1911-1981)
O. Beverley McEwan (1913-1995)
John S. McEwan, II
Rafael E. "Ralph" Martinez
H. David Luff
Thomas E. Dukes, III
William E. Ruffier
Tyler S. McClay

Juan A. Ruiz
Ruth C. Osborne
Susan D. Kennedy

Representative Clients: Bridgestone/Firestone, Inc.; City Cab of Orlando, Inc.; CNA Insurance Company; Dependable Protective Mutual; Florida Physicians Insurance Co.; Gulf Atlantic Insurance Co.; Marine Office of America; M.C.I. Telecommunications Corporation.

For full biographical listings, see the Martindale-Hubbell Law Directory

---

McGEE & POWERS, P.A. (AV)

201 East Pine Street, Suite 700, P.O. Box 3589, 32801
Telephone: 407-422-5742
Telecopy: 407-423-1377

Patrick A. McGee
James K. Powers
Brenda J. Newman
Donna C. Valin

For full biographical listings, see the Martindale-Hubbell Law Directory

---

MORAN & SHAMS, P.A. (AV)

111 North Orange Avenue, Suite 1200, P.O. Box 472, 32802-0472
Telephone: 407-841-4141
Fax: 407-841-4148
Email: moran-shams@moran-shams.com

Kelly T. Blystone
Brian J. Moran
Christopher C. Skambis
Sidney H. Shams

Jennifer S. Eden
Cristina Arechaga

Representative Clients: Adventist Health System Sunbelt Healthcare Corporation; Florida Hospital; All Florida Resorts Management; Dayron; Gencor Industries Inc.; Insurance Office of America, Inc.; MEDai, Inc.; Photo Chemical Systems of Florida, Inc.; Vermont American Corporation.

For full biographical listings, see the Martindale-Hubbell Law Directory

Orlando—Continued

KENNETH D. MORSE A PROFESSIONAL ASSOCIATION (AV)

390 North Orange Avenue, Suite 2100, 32801
Telephone: 407-422-2411
Fax: 407-422-2451
URL: http://www.morselaw.com
URL: http://www.lawyers.com/morselaw

Kenneth D. Morse

For full biographical listings, see the Martindale-Hubbell Law Directory

O'NEILL, CHAPIN, LIEBMAN & COOPER (AV)

A Partnership including Professional Associations
865 Eola Park Center, 200 East Robinson Street, 32801
Telephone: 407-425-2751
Telex: 407-423-1192

Bernard C. O'Neill, Jr. (P.A.) John B. Liebman (P.A.)
Mark O. Cooper (P.A.)

ASSOCIATE

Rod C. Lundy

OF COUNSEL

Bruce E. Chapin (P.A.)

Reference: First Union National Bank.

For full biographical listings, see the Martindale-Hubbell Law Directory

WILLIAM G. OSBORNE, P.A. (AV)

538 East Washington Street, 32801-1996
Telephone: 407-422-5385
Fax: 407-422-5381

William G. Osborne

LEGAL SUPPORT PERSONNEL

Elizabeth I. Dunnigan (Office Manager) Catherine C. Braungart (Legal Assistant)

For full biographical listings, see the Martindale-Hubbell Law Directory

PUGH AND VAN BUREN (AV)

218 Annie Street, 32806
Telephone: 407-843-5840
Email: igpugh@aol.com *URL:* http://www.lawyers.com/pvblaw

Irby G. Pugh Tye W. Van Buren

For full biographical listings, see the Martindale-Hubbell Law Directory

RUSSELL LAW OFFICES, P.A. (AV)

537 North Magnolia Avenue, P.O. Box 886, 32802
Telephone: 407-422-1234
Telecopier: 407-423-2842
Email: RussLaw@compuserve.com *URL:* http://www.lawyers.com/russlaw

Rodney Laird Russell

For full biographical listings, see the Martindale-Hubbell Law Directory

WILSON, LEAVITT & SMALL, P.A. (AV)

437 North Magnolia Avenue, 32801-1524
Telephone: 407-843-4321
Fax: 407-423-1505
Email: wlspa@aol.com *URL:* http://www.lawyers.com/eminentdomain

J. Christy Wilson, III Jay W. Small
Mark R. Leavitt Kurt H. Garber

Representative Clients: Circle K; Cumberland Farms; Hardee's Food Systems; Mobil Oil; Public Storage; Southland Corp.; U.S.F.& G.; Oerther Foods; Seventh Day Adventists; McDonald's Corporation.

For full biographical listings, see the Martindale-Hubbell Law Directory

PALM BEACH, Palm Beach Co.

AVIS & AVIS, P.A. (AV)

125 Worth Avenue, Suite 221, 33480
Telephone: 561-659-0200
Fax: 561-659-0942
Email: info@avislaw.com *URL:* http://www.avislaw.com

Warren E. Avis, Jr. Deborah K. Avis

OF COUNSEL

Jill E. Kaufman Richard D. Grow

Representative Clients: Florida Apple, Inc.; K-Rain Manufacturing Corp.; Sentry Paint Technology, Inc.; Palm Beach Precision Molding Co.; Arena Brands, Inc.; Wellington Industries, Inc.; Enterprise National Bank; Avis Enterprises; PAR Microsystems; Den-mat Corp.

(See Next Column)

For full biographical listings, see the Martindale-Hubbell Law Directory

WARWICK & BANISTER, P.A. (AV)

140 Royal Palm Way, Suite 205, 33480
Telephone: 561-655-7776
Telecopier: 561-655-2271
Email: johnban140@aol.com *URL:* http://www.lawyers.com/palmbeachlaw

Charles H. Warwick, Jr. (1894-1967) Charles H. Warwick, III
John R. Banister

For full biographical listings, see the Martindale-Hubbell Law Directory

*PENSACOLA,** Escambia Co.

PHILIP A. BATES (AV)

25 West Cedar Street, Suite 304, 32501
Telephone: 850-470-0091
Fax: 850-470-0441

For full biographical listings, see the Martindale-Hubbell Law Directory

BOZEMAN, JENKINS & MATTHEWS, P.A. (AV)

SunTrust Tower, 220 West Garden Street, Suite 801, P.O. Box 13105, 32501
Telephone: 850-434-6223
Fax: 850-434-5242
Email: bojema@pen.net *URL:* http://www.bojema.pen.net
Fort Walton Beach Office: 151 Mary Esther Boulevard, Suite 401.
Telephone: 850-651-2151.
Fax: 850-434-5242.
Panama City Office: 475 Harrison Avenue, Suite 203A.
Telephone: 850-872-0110.
Fax: 850-434-5242.

Frank C. Bozeman, Jr. Larry A. Matthews
Thomas R. Jenkins Janice K. Skievaski
Frank C. Bozeman, III

Robert T. Bleach Raymond F. Higgins, III
John B. Fricke, Jr. Jeremiah J. Talbott
J. Andrew Talbert Sidney M. McCrackin

For full biographical listings, see the Martindale-Hubbell Law Directory

*ST. AUGUSTINE,** St. Johns Co.

DOBSON & BROWN, P.A. (AV)

66 Cuna Street, Suite A, 32084
Telephone: 904-824-9032
Fax: 904-824-9236
Email: dblaw@aug.com *URL:* http://www.lawdb.com

Geoffrey B. Dobson Ronald W Brown

For full biographical listings, see the Martindale-Hubbell Law Directory

ST. PETERSBURG, Pinellas Co.

RALEIGH —LEE— GREENE III (AV)

401 Fourth Street North, 33701
Telephone: 727-821-2900
Fax: 727-822-7686

Raleigh "Lee" Greene III

STEIN, FORD, SCHAAF & TOWZEY, L.L.P. (AV)

501 First Avenue North, Suite 1000, 33701
Telephone: 727-894-4333
Fax: 727-894-0175

Henry A. Stein Gary M. Schaaf
Harvey A. Ford Phyllis J. Towzey
Paul A. Nelson Sarah E. Williams

For full biographical listings, see the Martindale-Hubbell Law Directory

*SARASOTA,** Sarasota Co.

BROWN CLARK, A PROFESSIONAL ASSOCIATION (AV)

Suite 500, Sarasota City Center, 1819 Main Street, 34236
Telephone: 941-957-3800
Telefax: 941-957-3888
Email: brownclark@mindspring.com *URL:* http://www.brownclark.com

Daryl J. Brown Jennifer G. Maglio
William G. Christopher Michael L. Morgan
Donald D. Clark Robin S. Trupp

For full biographical listings, see the Martindale-Hubbell Law Directory

*STUART,** Martin Co.

WESLEY R. HARVIN, P.A. (AV)

900 East Ocean Boulevard, Suite 210-B, 34994
Telephone: 561-286-3630
Fax: 561-286-6166
Email: WRH@gate.NET

Wesley R. Harvin

For full biographical listings, see the Martindale-Hubbell Law Directory

MCCARTHY, SUMMERS, BOBKO, MCKEY, WOOD & SAWYER, P.A. (AV)

2081 East Ocean Boulevard, Second Floor, 34996
Telephone: 561-286-1700
Fax: 561-283-1803
URL: http://www.mcsumm.com

Terence P. McCarthy
Robert P. Summers
Noel A. Bobko
John D. McKey, Jr.
Steven J. Wood
Thomas R. Sawyer
Nicola J. Boone
Steven L. Perry

Kathryn C. Bass
Robert N. Maitland, II

Representative Clients: First National Bank and Trust Company of the Treasure Coast; Hydratech Utilities; Lost Lake at Hobe Sound; Gary Player Design Group; YMCA of Martin County; Shadow Lakes Groves, Inc.; Merrill Lynch Trust Co., (Florida); Wilmington Trust, FSB; The Huntington National Bank, N.A.; WSTU-Radio, WTCN-TV.

For full biographical listings, see the Martindale-Hubbell Law Directory

WARNER, FOX, WACKEEN, DUNGEY SEELEY, SWEET & WRIGHT, L.L.P. (AV)

1100 South Federal Highway, P.O. Drawer 6, 34995-0006
Telephone: 561-287-4444
Fax: 561-220-1489
Email: wfsds@gate.net

Thomas E. Warner
M. Lanning Fox
W. Thomas Wackeen
Richard J. Dungey
Gary L. Sweet
Tim B. Wright
Deborah Bigham Beard

Louis E. Lozeau, Jr.
William Raymond Ponsoldt, Jr.
Anthony L. Conticello
Susann Ward
Michael J. McCluskey
Shawn C. Gray

OF COUNSEL

Robert L. Seeley
Aaron A. Foosaner

Approved Attorneys for: Attorneys' Title Insurance Fund; Commonwealth Land Title Insurance Co.

For full biographical listings, see the Martindale-Hubbell Law Directory

*TALLAHASSEE,** Leon Co.

KITCHEN, JUDKINS, SIMPSON & HIGH (AV)

1102 North Gadsden Street, 32303
Telephone: 850-222-6040
Telecopier: 850-561-1471

E. C. Deeno Kitchen
James P. Judkins
Larry D. Simpson
Robert King High, Jr.

ASSOCIATE

Paul M. Villeneuve
Thomas J. Schulte, Jr.

OF COUNSEL

John R. Overchuck

For full biographical listings, see the Martindale-Hubbell Law Directory

MCFARLAIN, WILEY, CASSEDY & JONES, PROFESSIONAL ASSOCIATION (AV)

215 South Monroe Street, Suite 600, P.O. Box 2174, 32316-2174
Telephone: 850-222-2107
Telecopier: 850-222-8475
Email: firm@mcfarlain.com *URL:* http://www.mcfarlain.com

Richard C. McFarlain
William B. Wiley
Douglas P. Jones
Charles A. Stampelos
H. Darrell White, Jr.
Christopher Barkas
Harold R. Mardenborough, Jr.
Terrell C. Madigan

Robert A. McNeely
P. David Brannon

LEGAL SUPPORT PERSONNEL

Diane L. Doll (Office Manager)

For full biographical listings, see the Martindale-Hubbell Law Directory

POLSTON, DEAN & HEALY, P.A. (AV)

Suite 900, Highpoint Center, 106 East College Avenue (32301), P.O. Box 1836, 32302-1836
Telephone: 850-513-0404
Fax: 850-681-0506
Email: polston@polstonlaw.com *URL:* http://www.lawyers.com/polstonlaw

Ricky L. Polston
James J. Dean
David P. Healy

For full biographical listings, see the Martindale-Hubbell Law Directory

*TAMPA,** Hillsborough Co.

ALPERT, BARKER & RODEMS, P.A. (AV)

First Union Center, Suite 2000, 100 South Ashley Drive (33602), P.O. Box 3270, 33601-3270
Telephone: 813-223-4131
Fax: 813-228-9612
Email: Alpertfirm@Aol.com

Jonathan L. Alpert
Chris A. Barker
Ryan Christopher Rodems
David D. Ferrentino
William J. Cook

Scott J. Flint
Natalie Pedregal

For full biographical listings, see the Martindale-Hubbell Law Directory

JOHN W. BAKAS, JR. (AV)

201 East Kennedy Boulevard, Suite 400, 33602-5823
Telephone: 813-228-8015
Fax: 813-228-8208
Email: jbakas@aol.com *URL:* http://www.bakas.com

For full biographical listings, see the Martindale-Hubbell Law Directory

BARR, MURMAN, TONELLI, HERZFELD & RUBIN (AV)

Suite 1750, 201 East Kennedy Boulevard, P.O. Box 172669, 33672-0669
Telephone: 813-223-3951
Fax: 813-229-2254
URL: http://www.hrfirm.com
New Port Richey, Florida Office: 7613 Little Road, 34654.
Telephone: 727-846-8646;
Fax: 727-846-8913.

James A. Murman
Michael A. Tonelli
Daniel H. Sleet
T. Gregory Slother
John W. Boult
Gregory G. Frazier
Joseph S. Silver
Clifford L. Somers

ASSOCIATES

John J. Kozak
Morris D. Purcell, Jr.
Robert J. Scanlan
Pamela A. Walton
Edward D. Friscia
James R. Wilson
Jerry A. Setchel

OF COUNSEL

Billy R. Barr

Representative Clients: Thomasson Lumber Co.; Osmose Wood Preserving, Inc.

For full biographical listings, see the Martindale-Hubbell Law Directory

BAVOL, BUSH & SISCO, P.L.L.C. (AV)

100 South Ashley, Suite 2100, P.O. Box 3423, 33601-3423
Telephone: 813-228-7000
Telefax: 813-273-0091

Charles D. Bavol
Ronald E. Bush
Dale R. Sisco
Jack E. Fernandez, Jr.
Dominick J. Graziano

Robert W. Bleakley
William R. Daniel
Kevin M. Gilhool
Andrew L. Rosenkranz (On Leave)
Jay P. Dinan
Jaret J. Fuente
Kerry C. McGuinn, Jr.
Pegi Money McCabe

For full biographical listings, see the Martindale-Hubbell Law Directory

BURTON & MURPHY (AV)

101 East Kennedy Boulevard Suite 1165, 33602
Telephone: 813-226-8500
Fax: 813-226-4266
Mailing Address: P.O. Box 172069, Tampa, Florida, 33672
Email: Attorneys@BurtonMurphy.com *URL:* http://www.BurtonMurphy.com

Steven G. Burton
Jeffrey D. Murphy
Charles G. Geitner

(See Next Column)

BURTON & MURPHY, *Tampa—Continued*

Beatriz M. Carta Wagman

For full biographical listings, see the Martindale-Hubbell Law Directory

CAREY, O'MALLEY, WHITAKER & MANSON, P.A. (AV)

712 South Oregon Avenue, 33606
Telephone: 813-250-0577
Telecopier: 813-250-9898
Email: cowmpa@aol.com

Michael R. Carey
Andrew M. O'Malley
Daniel D. Whitaker
Douglas P. Manson
Randall P. Mueller

For full biographical listings, see the Martindale-Hubbell Law Directory

DE LA PARTE, GILBERT & BALES, PROFESSIONAL ASSOCIATION (AV)

101 East Kennedy, Suite 3400, P.O. Box 2350, 33601-2350
Telephone: 813-229-2775
FAX: 813-229-2712

Louis A. de la Parte (Founder, Retired)
Richard A. Gilbert
Edward P. de la Parte, Jr.
John Calhoun Bales
L. David de la Parte
Patrick J. McNamara
Michael A. Skelton
David M. Caldevilla
David Dallas Dickey

Ronald Anthony Christaldi
Charles Robert Fletcher
Charles W. Crabtree, Jr
Michael S. Dorris

For full biographical listings, see the Martindale-Hubbell Law Directory

FULLER HOLSONBACK & BIVINS, P.A. (AV)

100 North Tampa Street, Suite 2650, 33602
Telephone: 813-229-9119
Fax: Available Upon Request
Email: jfuller521@aol.com

Jeffery M. Fuller
John P. Holsonback
Robert W. Bivins
Christina C. Young
Steven F. Thompson
William D. Mercer, Jr

For full biographical listings, see the Martindale-Hubbell Law Directory

GATLIN & BIRCH, P.A. (AV)

620 Twiggs Street, 33602
Telephone: 813-229-8561
FAX: 813-229-0422

C. Elmon Gatlin
Dean W. Birch

For full biographical listings, see the Martindale-Hubbell Law Directory

KETCHEY HORAN, P.A. (AV)

100 North Tampa Street, Suite 1900, P.O. Box 500, 33601-0500
Telephone: 813-223-9395
Fax: 813-221-1348
Email: Stephanie@KetcheyHoran.com
Sun City Center, Florida Office: 1647 Sun City Center Plaza, Suite 200.
Telephone: 813-633-1200.

SHAREHOLDERS

Charles F. Ketchey, Jr.

ASSOCIATES

Alfred A. Colby
Sarah H. Dennis

For full biographical listings, see the Martindale-Hubbell Law Directory

JOHN F. LAURO, P.A. (AV)

Barnett Plaza, 101 East Kennedy Boulevard, Suite 3950, 33602
Telephone: 813-222-8990
FAX: 813-222-8991

John F. Lauro

For full biographical listings, see the Martindale-Hubbell Law Directory

MANEY, DAMSKER & JONES, P.A. (AV)

606 Madison Street, P.O. Box 172009, 33672-0009
Telephone: 813-228-7371
Fax: 813-223-4846

David A. Maney
Lee S. Damsker
Karen Lynn Jones

Lorena L. Kiely
Patricia F. Kuhlman
Tarya A. Tribble

For full biographical listings, see the Martindale-Hubbell Law Directory

MEIROSE & FRISCIA, P.A. (AV)

500 North Westshore Boulevard, Suite 635, 33609
Telephone: 813-289-8800
Fax: 813-281-2005
Email: mftampa@worldnet.att.net

Leo H. Meirose, Jr.
Francis E. Friscia

Gregory Scott R. Haney

For full biographical listings, see the Martindale-Hubbell Law Directory

LAW OFFICES OF MERKLE & MAGRI, P.A. (AV)

5510 West LaSalle Street, 33607
Telephone: 813-281-9000; Clearwater, 727-441-2699
Fax: 813-281-2223

Robert W. Merkle
Joseph D. Magri
Ward A. Meythaler
David J. Plante
Gerard J. Roble

For full biographical listings, see the Martindale-Hubbell Law Directory

MURNAGHAN & FERGUSON, P.A. (AV)

Suite 2600, 100 North Tampa Street, P.O. Box 2937, 33601-2937
Telephone: 813-222-0123
Fax: 813-222-0124

Dennis R. Ferguson
Peter P. Murnaghan

Representative Clients: Amerada Hess Corporation; Ashland, Inc.; APAC, Inc.; Berry-Sprint Publishing, Inc.; Catalina Marketing Corporation; Golden Rule Insurance Company; Lincare Inc.; Sprint Publishing and Advertising, Inc.; Sprint Communications Company, L.P.; United Telephone Company of Florida, Inc.

For full biographical listings, see the Martindale-Hubbell Law Directory

SOLOMON & BENEDICT, P.A. (AV)

3000 NationsBank Plaza, 400 North Ashley Drive, 33602
Telephone: 813-225-1818
Telecopier: 813-225-1050
URL: http://www.solomonlaw.com

Stanford R. Solomon (Founder and President)
Betsy McCoy Benedict

Melody E. Altman
Hallie Smith Evans
F. Lorraine Jahn
Heather A. Pigman
Matthew E. Thatcher

For full biographical listings, see the Martindale-Hubbell Law Directory

TOWNSEND & BRANNON (AV)

608 West Horatio Street, 33606-2228
Telephone: 813-254-0088
Telecopier: 813-254-0093
URL: http://www.townsendbrannon.com

MEMBERS OF FIRM

David A. Townsend
Anita C. Brannon

For full biographical listings, see the Martindale-Hubbell Law Directory

YERRID, KNOPIK & KRIEGER, P.A. (AV)

Barnett Plaza, Suite 2160, 101 East Kennedy Boulevard, 33602
Telephone: 813-222-8222
Fax: 813-222-8224
URL: http://www.yerridknopik.com

C. Steven Yerrid
Christopher S. Knopik
Edwin P. Krieger

Ralph L. Gonzalez
Richard C. Alvarez
Claire D. Hancock

For full biographical listings, see the Martindale-Hubbell Law Directory

*VERO BEACH,** Indian River Co.

MOSS, HENDERSON, BLANTON & LANIER, P.A. (AV)

817 Beachland Boulevard, P.O. Box 3406, 32964-3406
Telephone: 561-231-1900
Fax: 561-231-4387

Steve L. Henderson
Clinton W. Lanier
Fred L. Kretschmer, Jr.
Lewis W. Murphy, Jr.

Representative Clients: Aetna Life & Casualty; Alcoa Florida, Inc.; Florida Power & Light Co.; Insurance Company of North America; Liberty Mutual Insurance Co.; Sears, Roebuck & Co.; Sugar Cane Growers Cooperative of Florida; Norfolk Southern Corporation/North American Van Lines, Inc.

(See Next Column)

MOSS, HENDERSON, BLANTON & LANIER P.A.—*Continued*

For Complete List of Firm Personnel, See General Section

For full biographical listings, see the Martindale-Hubbell Law Directory

*WEST PALM BEACH,** Palm Beach Co.

ADAMS, COOGLER, WATSON & MERKEL, P.A. (AV)

Suite 1600, 1555 Palm Beach Lakes Boulevard, P.O. Box 2069, 33402
Telephone: 561-478-4500
Fax: 561-684-7346
Email: ACWMLAW@AOL.COM

Samuel H. Adams (1913-1981)
Roy R. Watson
Robert G. Merkel
James C. Barry
Reed W. Kellner
Catherine Lynn Kasten
Scott S. Warburton
Peter A. Cooke
Patricia A. Judge
Kathryn L. Tignor

Alexander D. Barker
Jodi G. Barrett
Stephanie Brown
James W. Flanagan
Paul L. Harwood
Thomas Hodas
Catherine M. Paris

OF COUNSEL

L. C. Shepard, Jr.

For full biographical listings, see the Martindale-Hubbell Law Directory

BEASLEY, LEACOCK & HAUSER, P.A. (AV)

Flagler Center, Suite 1400, 505 South Flagler Drive, 33401
Telephone: 561-835-0900
Fax: 561-835-0939
Email: BLH@BLHlaw.com *URL:* http://BLHlaw.com

James W. Beasley, Jr.
David Leacock
Robert J. Hauser

Ronald B. Hauser

For full biographical listings, see the Martindale-Hubbell Law Directory

THE LAW OFFICE OF TERRENCE F. DYTRYCH, P.A. (AV)

2023 North Flagler Drive, 33407
Telephone: 561-655-7808
Telecopier: 561-659-0685
Email: dytrycht@bellsouth.net

Terrence F. Dytrych

For full biographical listings, see the Martindale-Hubbell Law Directory

JONAS & LASORTE (AV)

Suite 1000, United National Bank Tower, 1645 Palm Beach Lakes Boulevard, 33401
Telephone: 561-684-3000
FAX: 561-684-3004
Email: alasorte@worldnet.att.net

Michael N. Jonas
Alfred A. LaSorte, Jr.

ASSOCIATE

Jane M. Gordon

For full biographical listings, see the Martindale-Hubbell Law Directory

THOMAS E. KINGCADE PROFESSIONAL ASSOCIATION (AV)

209 South Olive Avenue, 33401
Telephone: 561-659-7300; 800-869-9409
Fax: 561-655-1593
Email: tekingcade@aol.com *URL:* http://www.lawyers.com/kingcade

Thomas E. Kingcade

William W. Booth

For full biographical listings, see the Martindale-Hubbell Law Directory

PATRICK M. O'HARA, P.A. (AV)

Commerce Center, Suite 100, 324 Datura Street, 33401
Telephone: 561-659-3771
Fax: 561-659-4224

Patrick M. O'Hara

For full biographical listings, see the Martindale-Hubbell Law Directory

SEARCY DENNEY SCAROLA BARNHART & SHIPLEY, PROFESSIONAL ASSOCIATION (AV)

2139 Palm Beach Lakes Boulevard, P.O. Drawer 3626, 33402-3626
Telephone: 561-686-6300
800-780-8607
800-220-7006 (Spanish)
Fax: 561-478-0754
Email: CDS@SEARCYLAW.COM *URL:* http://www.searcylaw.com

John Scarola
F. Gregory Barnhart
C. Calvin Warriner, III
William A. Norton
David J. Sales
William B. King
David J. White

Sean C. Domnick
Ellen F. Brandt

LEGAL SUPPORT PERSONNEL

Daniel J. Calloway (Paralegal/Investigator)
Emilio Diamantis (Paralegal/Investigator)
John C. Hopkins (Paralegal/Investigator)
J. Peter Love (Paralegal/Investigator)
Kevin J. Walsh (Paralegal/Investigator)

For Complete List of Firm Personnel, See General Section

For full biographical listings, see the Martindale-Hubbell Law Directory

WARD, DAMON, BEVERLY, TITTLE & POSNER, P.A. (AV)

4420 Beacon Circle, 33407-3270
Telephone: 561-842-3000
Stuart: 561-223-5550
Fax: 561-842-3626
Email: wdbtp@wdbtp.com *URL:* http://www.wdbtp.com

James F. Cooney, Jr. (1950-1992)
Conrad Damon
Andrew Fulton, IV
Irwin R. Gilbert
Craig I. Kelley
Michael J Posner
Roger C. Stanton
James D. Tittle, Jr.
Philip H. Ward, III

OF COUNSEL

Don Beverly

For full biographical listings, see the Martindale-Hubbell Law Directory

JAMES MCCARTNEY WEARN, P.A. (AV)

2023 North Flagler Drive, 33407
Telephone: 561-659-0655
Fax: 561-659-0685

James McCartney Wearn

For full biographical listings, see the Martindale-Hubbell Law Directory

WINTER PARK, Orange Co.

WENDY L. AIKIN, P.A. (AV)

288 Park Avenue North, 32789
Telephone: 407-644-4040
Fax: 407-644-4414
Email: aikinlaw@aol.com *URL:* http://www.lawyers.com/wendyaikin

Wendy L. Aikin

OF COUNSEL

Donald N. Crowell
Brenda Lee London

For full biographical listings, see the Martindale-Hubbell Law Directory

LYON KIRWIN, P.A. (AV(T))

338 Morse Boulevard, Suite 150, 32789
Telephone: 407-740-6600
Facsimile: 407-740-6363

V. Frederic Lyon
Brian P. Kirwin
Bruce Alan Norris
Brian W. Bennett

James C. Washburn
Michelle B. Kane
Michael D. Chiumento, III

Representative Clients: American Express; Centex-Rooney; City of St. Petersburg; Clancy & Theys Construction Co.; Duke Engineering & Services; Florida Power Corp.; Sea World of Florida; Seminole County, Florida; Seminole County Public Schools; South Florida Water Management District; U.S. Steel.

For full biographical listings, see the Martindale-Hubbell Law Directory

VOSE, BLAU & HAYES (AV)

2705 West Fairbanks Avenue, 32789
Telephone: 407-645-3735
Fax: 407-628-5670
Email: bvose@vbh-law.com *URL:* http://www.vbh-law.com

(See Next Column)

VOSE, BLAU & HAYES, *Winter Park—Continued*

Gretchen R. H. Vose
Leslie A. Blau
Rosemary H. Hayes

ASSOCIATES

Carolyn S. Crichton
Christina M. Page
Peter J. Meadows
Aubrey Harry Ducker, Jr.

For full biographical listings, see the Martindale-Hubbell Law Directory

GEORGIA

*ATLANTA,** Fulton Co.

BONDURANT, MIXSON & ELMORE, LLP (AV)

1201 W. Peachtree Street Suite 3900, 30309
Telephone: 404-881-4100
Fax: 404-881-4111
URL: http://www.bondurant-mixson.com

MEMBERS OF FIRM

Emmet J. Bondurant II
H. Lamar Mixson
M. Jerome Elmore
Edward B. Krugman
Jeffrey O. Bramlett
John E. Floyd
Michael B. Terry
P. Richard Game
Jill A. Pryor
J. Scott McClain

Representative Clients: American Dairy Queen Corp.; Avon Products, Inc.; Bottlers of Coca-Cola, U.S.A.; Blue Circle of America; Delta Air Lines, Inc.; Fina Oil and Chemical Company; Four M Corporation; Penske Motorsports; Queen Carpets, Inc.; Ticketmaster Southeast.

For full biographical listings, see the Martindale-Hubbell Law Directory

BOVIS, KYLE & BURCH, LLC (AV)

A Limited Liability Corporation including Professional Corporations
Third Floor, 53 Perimeter Center East, 30346
Telephone: 770-391-9100
Telecopier: 770-668-0878
Email: bkb@boviskyle.com *URL:* http://www.boviskyle.com

John M. Bovis (P.C.)
Steven J. Kyle (P.C.)
John V. Burch (P.C.)
C. Sam Thomas (P.C.)
James E. Singer
J. Wesley Skinner
Gregory R. Veal
Timothy J. Burson
Charles M. Medlin
John H. Peavy Jr.

J.S. Scott Busby
Christina A. Craddock
Timothy A. Hickey, Jr.
Jana B. Tabor
Carl A. Hassler
John David Etheriedge
Everett A. Kliphouse

For full biographical listings, see the Martindale-Hubbell Law Directory

FINESTONE & MORRIS (AV)

2500 Tower Place, Suite 2540, 3340 Peachtree Road, N.E., 30326
Telephone: 404-262-2500
Telecopier: 404-231-1930
Email: administrator@fmattorneys.com *URL:* http://www.lawyers.com/f&mlaw

MEMBER OF FIRM

Stuart Finestone

Reference: NationsBank.

For full biographical listings, see the Martindale-Hubbell Law Directory

KREVOLIN & HORST, LLC (AV)

Suite 2150, 100 Colony Square, 1175 Peachtree Street, N.E., 30361
Telephone: 404-888-9700
Fax: 404-888-9577

Douglas P. Krevolin
Jeffrey D. Horst

Michael G. Regas II
Michael D. Flint

For full biographical listings, see the Martindale-Hubbell Law Directory

MATTHEWS & STEEL (AV)

462 East Paces Ferry Road, 30305
Telephone: 404-264-1292
800-776-0098
Fax: 404-264-0161
Email: postmaster@matthewssteellaw.com

MEMBERS OF FIRM

James B. Matthews, III
John D. Steel
John B. Briggs
H. Craig Stafford

For full biographical listings, see the Martindale-Hubbell Law Directory

NALL, MILLER, OWENS, HOCUTT & HOWARD, LLP (AV)

Suite 200 Peachtree & Broad Building, 66 Luckie Street, 30303
Telephone: 404-522-2200
Fax: 404-522-2208

MEMBERS OF FIRM

James S. Owens, Jr.
Robert B. Hocutt
James R. Howard
George Robert Neuhauser
Robert L. Goldstucker
Kenneth P. McDuffie
Michael D. Hostetter

COUNSEL

Samuel A. Miller

ASSOCIATES

Charles Richard Carson
Paul Jay Pontrelli
Mary Anne Palma

LEGAL SUPPORT PERSONNEL

W. Gary Bush (Registered Nurse, Legal Assistant)
Michelle Henderson McGhee (Paralegal)
Natalie D. Summers (Paralegal)
Janice F. Clark (Paralegal)

Approved Attorneys for: Lawyers Title Insurance Corp.; Commonwealth Land Title Insurance Co.

For full biographical listings, see the Martindale-Hubbell Law Directory

PARKER, HUDSON, RAINER & DOBBS LLP (AV)

1500 Marquis Two Tower, 285 Peachtree Center Avenue, N.E., 30303
Telephone: 404-523-5300
Fax: 404-522-8409
Tallahassee, Florida Office: The Perkins House, 118 North Gadsden Street, 32301.
Telephone: 904-681-0191.
Fax: 904-681-9493.

MEMBERS OF FIRM

David G. Russell
G. Wayne Hillis, Jr.
William J. Holley, II

For full biographical listings, see the Martindale-Hubbell Law Directory

ROBERT K. PICKER, JR. (AV)

4360 Georgetown Square Suite 820, 30338
Telephone: 770-454-7009
FAX: 770-457-0103
Email: kinpicker@mindspring.com

LEGAL ASSISTANT

Rebecca A. Stowers

For full biographical listings, see the Martindale-Hubbell Law Directory

SWIFT, CURRIE, MCGHEE & HIERS (AV)

1355 Peachtree Street, N.E., 30309-3238
Telephone: 404-874-8800
Telecopier: 404-888-6199
Email: scmhlaw.com

MEMBERS OF FIRM

James T. McDonald, Jr.
John F. Sacha
Michael H. Schroder
Stephen L. Cotter
Robert R. Potter
Douglas A. Bennett
Mark T. Dietrichs
Lynn M. Roberson
Mark J. Goodman
Joseph A. Munger
R. Briggs Peery
Thomas D. Martin
Bradley S. Wolff
Frederick Owen Ferrand
John W. Campbell
Stephen M. Schatz
Richard H. Sapp, III
Charles M. McDaniel, Jr.
Michael Ryder
Susan A. Dewberry

OF COUNSEL

Frank M. Swift
Warner S. Currie
Glover McGhee
James B. Hiers, Jr.

ASSOCIATES

Michael H. Friedman
Debra Dawn Chambers
Micheal D. Watson
Thomas E. Best
Richard A. Watts
Peggy R. Goodnight
Kenneth B. Still
Michael C. Kendall
Timothy C. Lemke
Bright Kinnett Wright
Douglas W. Brown, Jr.
Christopher D. Balch
Joan Perkins Shaker
David Charles King
Willie C. Adams
W. Wright Mitchell
H. Lee Pruett
Thomas J. Mazziotti
Robert E. Jones
Kristine J. Moschella
Megan W. Grout
Kenneth A. David
J. Michael Parsons
Lloyd N. Bell
Erik S. Rodriguez
James D. Johnson
Cabell D. Townsend
Scott M. Williamson
Sharon Leah Neal
John F. Blount
Casey W. Stevens
Amy Greenstein

(See Next Column)

SWIFT, CURRIE, MCGHEE & HIERS—*Continued*

Representative Clients: Chubb Insurance Group; Cagle's Inc.; Gold Kist, Inc.; Kemper Insurance Group; Maryland Casualty Cos.; PHH Homequity; Sedgwick James; State Farm Fire & Casualty Co.; The Travelers Cos.; Super Valu.

For full biographical listings, see the Martindale-Hubbell Law Directory

*AUGUSTA,** Richmond Co.

BURNSIDE, WALL, DANIEL, ELLISON & REVELL (AV)

A Partnership including Professional Corporations
454 Greene Street, P.O. Box 2125, 30903
Telephone: 706-722-0768
Fax: 706-722-5984

MEMBERS OF FIRM

Robert C. Daniel, Jr. (1943-1993)
Thomas R. Burnside, Jr. (P.C.)
James B. Wall (P.C.)
James W. Ellison
Harry D. Revell
Thomas R. Burnside, III

Representative Clients: Augusta-Richmond County Commission; National Science Center Foundation, Inc.; CSRA Regional Development Center; City of Harlem, Georgia; Liquid Carbonic Corp.; Southeastern Equipment Co.; SECO Aviation, Inc.; SECO Parts & Equipment, Inc.

For full biographical listings, see the Martindale-Hubbell Law Directory

*BRUNSWICK,** Glynn Co.

WHELCHEL, BROWN, READDICK & BUMGARTNER (AV)

5 Glynn Avenue, P.O. Box 220, 31521-0220
Telephone: 912-264-8544
Telecopier: 912-264-9667

MEMBERS OF FIRM

J. Thomas Whelchel
Richard A. Brown, Jr.
Terry L. Readdick
John E. Bumgartner
B. Kaye Katz

ASSOCIATES

G. Todd Carter
Richard K. Strickland
Bradley J. Watkins

Representative Clients: Georgia Power Co.; Sears, Roebuck & Co.; Allstate Insurance Co.; Commercial Union Insurance Co.; Georgia Farm Bureau Mutual Insurance Co.; Government Employees Insurance Co.; Nationwide Insurance Co.; State Farm Insurance Cos.; Wausau Insurance Cos.

For full biographical listings, see the Martindale-Hubbell Law Directory

*JONESBORO,** Clayton Co.

GLAZE & GLAZE, P.C. (AV)

120 North McDonough Street, 30236
Telephone: 770-478-5555
Fax: 770-478-4555
Email: glaze@mindspring.com
Stockbridge, Georgia, 205A Corporate Center Drive, 30281. Telephone: 770-474-3347.

George E. Glaze
Kirby A. Glaze

Joe M. Harris, Jr.

For full biographical listings, see the Martindale-Hubbell Law Directory

NORCROSS, Gwinnett Co.

THOMPSON, O'BRIEN, KEMP & NASUTI, P.C. (AV)

4845 Jimmy Carter Boulevard, 30093-3641
Telephone: 770-925-0111
Fax: 770-925-8597
Email: tokn@tokn.com

R. Michael Thompson
J. Patrick O'Brien
Donna N. Kemp
Albert F. Nasuti
Paul J. Morochnik

Paul B. Frickey
Bret T. Thrasher
Brian L. Hansen
Ronald F. Negin

OF COUNSEL

Betty H. Morris
Scott L. Dix

For full biographical listings, see the Martindale-Hubbell Law Directory

*SAVANNAH,** Chatham Co.

MCCALLAR AND ASSOCIATES (AV)

115 Oglethorpe Avenue West, P.O. Box 9026, 31412
Telephone: 912-234-1215
Telecopier: 912-236-7549

C. James McCallar, Jr.

(See Next Column)

Mark Bulovic

For full biographical listings, see the Martindale-Hubbell Law Directory

HAWAII

*HONOLULU,** Honolulu Co.

CARLSMITH BALL (AV)

A Partnership including Law Corporations
Suite 2200, Pacific Tower, 1001 Bishop Street, P.O. Box 656, 96809-3402
Telephone: 808-523-2500
Fax: 808-523-0842
Email: execdirector@carlsmith.com *URL:* http://www.carlsmith.com
Kapolei, Hawaii Office: Suite 318, Kapolei Building, 1001 Kamokila Boulevard, 96707.
Telephone: 808-523-2500.
Fax: 808-674-0850.
Wailuku, Maui Hawaii Office: Suite 400, One Main Plaza, 2200 Main Street, P.O. Box 1086, 96793-1086.
Telephone: 808-242-4535.
Fax: 808-244-4974.
Kailua-Kona, Hawaii Office: Suite 209, 75-1000 Henry Street, 96740.
Telephone: 808-329-6464.
Fax: 808-329-9450.
Hilo, Hawaii Office: 121 Waianuenue Avenue, P.O. Box 686, 96721-0686.
Telephone: 808-935-6644.
Fax: 808-935-7975.
Hagatna, Guam Office: Suite 401, Bank of Hawaii Building, 134 West Soledad Avenue, P.O. Box BF, 96932-5027.
Telephone: 671-472-6813.
Fax: 671-477-4375.
Telex: 721-6445 CWCMI GM.
Saipan, Commonwealth of the Northern Mariana Islands Office: Carlsmith Building, Capitol Hill, P.O. Box 5241, 96950-5241.
Telephone: 670-322-3455.
Fax: 670-322-3368.
Los Angeles, California Office: 9th Floor, 444 South Flower Street, 90071-2901.
Telephone: 213-955-1200.
Fax: 213-623-0032.
Washington, D.C. Office: Suite 300, 1201 Pennsylvania Avenue, N.W., 20004-2401.
Telephone: 202-628-2228.
Fax: 202-628-2071.
Mexico City, Mexico Office: Carlsmith Ball, Sierra Nevada 119, Lomas de Chapultepec, 11000 Mexico, D.F.
Telephone: 52-5-520-8514, 52-5-520-8757.
Fax: 52-5-540-1545.
Mexico, D.F. Office of Carlsmith Ball, S.C. (Authorized to practice as foreign legal consultants in Mexico): Sierra Nevada 119, Lomas de Chapultepec, 11000 Mexico, D.F.
Telephone: 52-5-520-8514, 52-5-520-8757.
Fax: 52-5-540-1545.

MEMBERS OF FIRM

Joseph A. Ball (Resident at Los Angeles, California Office)
John F. Biehl (Resident at Saipan Office)
Edward E. Case
Albert H. Ebright (Resident at Los Angeles, California Office)
Steven M. Egesdal
Randall H. Endo (Resident at Maui, Hawaii Office)
Gary G. Grimmer
Philip D. Isaac (Resident at Hagatna, Guam Office)
David Patrick Ledger (Resident at Hagatna, Guam Office)
Katherine G. Leonard
Tom C. Leuteneker (Resident at Maui, Hawaii Office)
John P. Manaut
David S. Olson (Resident at Los Angeles, California Office)
John D. Osborn (Resident at Saipan Office)
James Polish (Resident at Los Angeles, California Office)
Marcia K. Schultz (Resident at Saipan Office)
Jonathan L. Smoller (Resident at Los Angeles, California Office)
Thomas R. Sylvester
Robert D. Triantos (Resident at Kailua-Kona, Hawaii Office)
Allen R. Wolff

ASSOCIATES

Bruce A. Bradley (Not admitted in HI; Resident at Hagatna, Guam Office)
Grace E. Jo (Resident, Los Angeles, California Office)
Brent K. Yamashita

For Complete List of Firm Personnel, See General Section

For full biographical listings, see the Martindale-Hubbell Law Directory

CHUN, KERR, DODD, BEAMAN & WONG (AV)

Suite 900, 745 Fort Street Mall, 96813
Telephone: 808-528-8200
Telecopier: 808-536-5869

(See Next Column)

CHUN, KERR, DODD, BEAMAN & WONG, *Honolulu—Continued*

MEMBERS OF FIRM

Edward Y. C. Chun
William H. Dodd
Andrew V. Beaman
Danton S. Wong
Leroy E. Colombe
Trudy Burns Stone

ASSOCIATES

Andrew R. Bunn
Trevor A. Brown
Tracy D. Tanaka
John S. Nitao

References: Bank of Hawaii; First Hawaiian Bank.

For full biographical listings, see the Martindale-Hubbell Law Directory

GOODSILL ANDERSON QUINN & STIFEL (AV)

Alii Place, Suite 1800, 1099 Alakea Street, P.O. Box 3196, 96801-3196
Telephone: 808-547-5600
FAX: 808-547-5880
Email: info@goodsill.com *URL:* http://www.goodsill.com

MEMBERS OF FIRM

Martin Anderson
David J. Dezzani
John R. Lacy
Thomas W. Williams, Jr.
William S. Miller
Jacqueline L. S. Earle
Gary M. Slovin
Lisa Woods Munger
Bruce L. Lamon
Mark B. Desmarais
Corlis J. Chang
Wayne H. Muraoka
Walter C. Davison
LindaLee K. Farm
Margaret Jenkins Leong
Carol Ann Eblen
Roy John Tjioe
A. Richard Philpott
Lennes N. Omuro
Derek R. Kobayashi

ASSOCIATES

Thomas L. Benedict
Edmund K. Saffery
Lisa A. Bail
Normand R. Lezy
Kathleen A. Kelly

Representative Clients: Bank of Hawaii; Chicago Title Ins. Co.; E. I. du Pont de Nemours & Company; Hawaiian Airlines, Inc.; Hawaiian Electric Industries, Inc.; Lorillard Tobacco Company; Shimizu Corporation.

For Complete List of Firm Personnel, See General Section

For full biographical listings, see the Martindale-Hubbell Law Directory

REINWALD, O'CONNOR & PLAYDON (AV)

(Formerly Anthony, Hoddick, Reinwald & O'Connor)
2400 Makai Tower, Grosvenor Center, P.O. Box 3199, 96801-3199
Telephone: 808-524-8350
Telecopier: 808-531-8628
Email: info@roplaw.com *URL:* http://www.roplaw.com

MEMBERS OF FIRM

Dennis E. W. O'Connor
George W. Playdon, Jr.
W. Thomas Fagan
Michael J. McGuigan

For full biographical listings, see the Martindale-Hubbell Law Directory

TAM, O'CONNOR, HENDERSON, TAIRA & YAMAUCHI ATTORNEYS AT LAW, A LAW CORPORATION (AV)

20th Floor, Central Pacific Plaza, 220 South King Street, 96813
Telephone: 808-545-3030
Fax: 808-523-8051
Fax: 808-537-6782
Email: lawyers@50thstatelaw.com

James K. Tam
Michael F. O'Connor
Harvey E. Henderson, Jr.
Lissa H. Andrews
Robert M. Yamauchi
Darryl M. Taira
Stuart M. Kodish

Wesley H. Ikeda
Russ S. Awakuni
Kevin W. Herring
Fred I. Waki

OF COUNSEL

Paul M. Dold

For full biographical listings, see the Martindale-Hubbell Law Directory

KAILUA, Honolulu Co.

WINER MEHEULA & DEVENS (AV)

970 North Kalaheo Avenue, Suite A-300, 96734
Telephone: 808-254-5855
Fax: 808-254-6872
Email: winer@pacificlaw.com *URL:* http://www.pacificlaw.com

MEMBERS OF FIRM

Andrew S. Winer
William K. Meheula
Vladimir Paul Devens

OF COUNSEL

David F. Fasi

ASSOCIATE

Blue H. Kaanehe

For full biographical listings, see the Martindale-Hubbell Law Directory

ILLINOIS

*BELLEVILLE,** St. Clair Co.

FREEARK, HARVEY, MENDILLO, DENNIS, WULLER & CAIN, P.C. (AV)

115 West Washington Street, P.O. Box 546, 62222
Telephone: 618-233-2686
Telecopier: 618-233-5677
Email: freeark@peaknet.net

Ray H. Freeark, Jr.
Ted R. Harvey, Jr.
James R. Mendillo
Ted W. Dennis
Ransom P. Wuller
Jeffery A. Cain

Michael P. Murphy
Denise Rusnack
W. Jeffrey Muskopf

Representative Clients: American Federation of Teachers, Local 434, Belleville, Illinois and 743, Granite City, Illinois.
Local Counsel for: Illinois State Medical Inter-Insurance Exchange, Chicago, Illinois; Sentry Insurance Co., Stevens Point, Wisconsin; General Casualty Cos., Springfield, Illinois and Sun Prairie, Wisconsin; Allstate Insurance Co., St. Louis, Missouri and Arlington Heights, Illinois; St. Paul Fire & Marine Insurance Co.; Travelers Insurance Co.; Northbrook Insurance Co., Arlington Heights, Illinois; Employers Insurance of Wausau, River Forest, Illinois and St. Louis, Missouri.

For full biographical listings, see the Martindale-Hubbell Law Directory

GAVIN LAW FIRM (AV)

NationsBank Building, 23 Public Square, Suite 415, 62220
Telephone: 618-236-0100
888-360-0100
Fax: 618-236-2684
Email: billg@gavinlaw.com *URL:* http://www.gavinlaw.com

William P. Gavin

For full biographical listings, see the Martindale-Hubbell Law Directory

NEVILLE, RICHARDS, DEFRANCO & WULLER (AV)

5 Park Place, 62226
Telephone: 618-277-0900
Facsimile: 618-277-0970
Email: nrdw@nrdw-law.com *URL:* http://www.nrdw-law.com

MEMBERS OF FIRM

James E. Neville
Timothy S. Richards
James E. DeFranco
Robert G. Wuller, Jr.

ASSOCIATES

Shari M. Brunton
Ellen M. Edmonds
Daniel L. Bradley
Matthew Charles Zittel

For full biographical listings, see the Martindale-Hubbell Law Directory

*BLOOMINGTON,** McLean Co.

DUNN, STANCZAK & WILLARD (AV)

1001 North Main Street, P.O. Box 3488, 61702-3488
Telephone: 309-828-6241
Fax: 309-828-8321
Email: Dunnlaw@aol.com

MEMBER OF FIRM

Mark T. Dunn

Representative Clients: Northeastern Illinois University; Governors State University; Western Illinois University; Chicago State University; First Federal Savings & Loan Association of Bloomington; Illinois Wesleyan University; Metropolitan Life Insurance Co., Agricultural Investments and Commercial Investments; Commerce Bank; Bluestem National Bank.

For Complete List of Firm Personnel, See General Section

For full biographical listings, see the Martindale-Hubbell Law Directory

CHAMPAIGN, Champaign Co.

MEYER, CAPEL, HIRSCHFELD, MUNCY, JAHN & ALDEEN, P.C. (AV)

306 West Church Street, P.O. Box 6750, 61826-6750
Telephone: 217-352-1800
Telecopier: 217-352-1083
Email: attorneys@meyercapel.com *URL:* http://www.meyercapel.com

James L. Capel, Jr. (1933-1991)
John C. Hirschfeld
Dennis K. Muncy
Francis J. Jahn
Donald R. Aldeen
John H. Elder
David B. Sholem
Mark D. Lipton

(See Next Column)

MEYER, CAPEL, HIRSCHFELD, MUNCY, JAHN & ALDEEN P.C.—*Continued*

Tracy J. Nugent
Richard T. West
Rusty W. Freeland
Lorna K. Geiler
Patrick T. Fitzgerald
Todd J. Black
Joseph D. Murphy
Neil R. Rafferty
James M. Mullady
William B. Moore
Evan D. Coobs
John J. Powers
Rochelle A. Funderburg

Matt C. Deering
Jeffrey M. Davis
Marjorie A. Harris
Gregory T. Mizen
Brian C. Lawlyes

OF COUNSEL

August C. Meyer, Jr.
Richard J. Winkel, Jr.
John H. McCord

Representative Clients: BankIllinois in Champaign; Bell Foods, Inc.; Christie Clinic; Illini Cablevision, Inc.; Kuck & Associates, Inc.; Midwest Television, Inc.; Parkland College.

For full biographical listings, see the Martindale-Hubbell Law Directory

*CHICAGO,** Cook Co.

ARONBERG GOLDGEHN DAVIS & GARMISA (AV)

Suite 3000 One IBM Plaza, 60611
Telephone: 312-828-9600
Telecopier: 312-828-9635
Email: agdglaw@aol.com
Schaumberg, Illinois Office: 1901 North Roselle Road, Suite 800, 60195.
Telephone: 847-985-4060.

MEMBERS OF FIRM

Christopher J. Bannon
Jay A. Frank
Mitchell S. Goldgehn
James J. Hickey
Nathan H. Lichtenstein
Marc W. O'Brien
Tami J. Reding-Brubaker
John M. Riccione
James A. Smith

ASSOCIATES

Lisa J. Brodsky
Howard J. Fishman
Paul A. Greenberg
William J. Serritella, Jr.

For Complete List of Firm Personnel, See General Section

For full biographical listings, see the Martindale-Hubbell Law Directory

BECKER & KAPLAN LLC (AV)

19 South La Salle Street Suite 1500, 60603
Telephone: 312-621-9500
Fax: 312-621-9011
Email: firm@beckerkaplan.com *URL:* http://www.beckerkaplan.com

Theodore M. Becker
Daniel S. Kaplan

Edward R. White
Michael J. Boxerman

For full biographical listings, see the Martindale-Hubbell Law Directory

CAHILL, CHRISTIAN & KUNKLE, LTD. (AV)

Santa Fe Building, 224 South Michigan Avenue, Suite 1300, 60604
Telephone: 312-341-1688
Fax: 312-341-1689
URL: http://www.cck.com

William J. Kunkle, Jr.
Roseann Oliver
William T. Cahill
John M. Christian
Lorna E. Propes
Scott B. Greene
Mary Kathryn Kelly
Suzanne M. Metzel
Matthew J. Gehringer
Steven E. Nieslawski
Michael K. Bartosz
Donald Lee Homyk

OF COUNSEL

Louis B. Garippo

Daniel J. Collins
Jeanne M. Cullen
Elizabeth A. Kaveny
Frederic T. Knape
David R. Nordwall
Elisha S. Rosenblum
Melisa G. Thompson

For full biographical listings, see the Martindale-Hubbell Law Directory

CLARK & DEGRAND (AV)

One South Wacker Drive, Suite 1495, 60606-4616
Telephone: 312-425-0500
Fax: 312-425-0501
Email: CandDeG@aol.com

MEMBERS OF FIRM

Donald C. Clark, Jr.
Luke DeGrand
Jennifer S. Holloway

(See Next Column)

ASSOCIATE

Tracey L. Wolfe

For full biographical listings, see the Martindale-Hubbell Law Directory

CLIFFORD LAW OFFICES, P.C. (AV)

120 North La Salle Street, 31st Floor, 60602
Telephone: 312-899-9090
1-800-899-0410
Fax: 312-251-1160
Email: RACA@CliffordLaw.com *URL:* http://www.cliffordlaw.com

Robert A. Clifford
Keith A. Hebeisen
Kevin P. Durkin
Thomas K. Prindable

Robert P. Walsh, Jr.
Susan A. Capra
Jeffrey J. Kroll
Richard F. Burke, Jr.
Matthew I. Baker
Timothy P. Rhatigan
Isobel S. Thomas
Michael S. Krzak
Timothy S. Tomasik
Brian Thomas Nash
Donald James Storino III
Sheri L. Tarr

OF COUNSEL

Robert P. Sheridan

For full biographical listings, see the Martindale-Hubbell Law Directory

ROBERT F. COLEMAN & ASSOCIATES (AV)

77 West Wacker Drive Suite 4800, 60601
Telephone: 312-444-1000
Telecopier: 312-444-1028
Email: rfca@sprynet.com

Kenneth P. Ross
Eugene J. Schiltz
Jerry S. Menge
Sean B. Crotty
Cassandra A. Crotty

For full biographical listings, see the Martindale-Hubbell Law Directory

CONNELLY & SCHROEDER (AV)

One North Franklin Street, Suite 1200, 60606-3421
Telephone: 312-251-9600
Fax: 312-251-9601
Geneva, Illinois Office: 1250 Executive Place, Suite 201.
Telephone: 630-232-6440.
FAX: 630-232-6450

MEMBERS OF FIRM

Michael P. Connelly
John L. Schroeder (Resident, Geneva Office)
Thomas F. Tobin
Raymond E. Stachnik
Daniel F. Konicek (Also at Geneva Office)
Eugene S. Kraus
Mary Lisa Kamins
Brandt R. Madsen
Robert J. Kartholl, Jr.

ASSOCIATES

Michelle L. Adams (Resident, Geneva Office)
Matthew Patrick Connelly
Thomas W. Dillon (Resident, Geneva Office)
John Michael Kelly
Colleen Konicek
Charina de los Reyes
Martha Swatek (Resident, Geneva Office)

For full biographical listings, see the Martindale-Hubbell Law Directory

CROWLEY BARRETT & KARABA, LTD. (AV)

Suite 2310 Two First National Plaza, 20 South Clark Street, 60603
Telephone: 312-726-2468
Fax: 312-726-2741

Patrick F. Crowley (1911-1974)
Frank A. Karaba (1921-1996)
Alan Rauh Orschel
Gregory M. White
Charles W. Siragusa
Thomas F. Karaba
Wade R. Joyner
Scott D.H. Redman

Jeffrey S. Burns
David C. Birks
Paul F. Markoff, IV

Reference: Harris Trust and Savings Bank.

For full biographical listings, see the Martindale-Hubbell Law Directory

EHRENBERG & FROST, P.C. (AV)

111 West Jackson Boulevard 15th Floor, 60604-3501
Telephone: 312-987-9766; 312-957-2022
Fax: 312-461-0338

Alan I. Ehrenberg
Scott C. Frost

For full biographical listings, see the Martindale-Hubbell Law Directory

FIELD & GOLAN (AV)

Three First National Plaza Suite 1500, 60602-4206
Telephone: 312-263-2300
Fax: 312-263-0939

(See Next Column)

FIELD & GOLAN, *Chicago—Continued*

MEMBERS OF FIRM

Robert E. Field
Stephen L. Golan
Margaret A. Christie
Donna F. Hartl

ASSOCIATES

Margaret A. Gisch
Matthew J. Cozzi
Anthony R. Taglia

OF COUNSEL

Leonard W. Golan
Stephen Edward Smith
Frank J. Dolan
John E. Vranicar

For full biographical listings, see the Martindale-Hubbell Law Directory

FIGLIULO & SILVERMAN, P.C. (AV)

10 South La Salle Street, Suite 3600, 60603
Telephone: 312-251-4600
Fax: 312-251-4610

James R. Figliulo
Peter A. Silverman
Carl A. Gigante
Brian P. Liston
Marc S. Porter
James H. Bowhay

James J. Sipchen, Jr.
Adam E. Bossov
Michael K. Desmond

For full biographical listings, see the Martindale-Hubbell Law Directory

FREEMAN, FREEMAN & SALZMAN, P.C. (AV)

401 North Michigan Avenue, Suite 3200, 60611-4207
Telephone: 312-222-5100
Facsimile: 312-822-0870

Lee A. Freeman (1909-1995)
Lee A. Freeman, Jr.
Jerrold E. Salzman
John F. Kinney
James T. Malysiak
Glynna W. Freeman
Phillip L. Stern
Chris C. Gair

Kevin P. Kappock
Jeffrey M. Osterkamp

For full biographical listings, see the Martindale-Hubbell Law Directory

GESSLER, HUGHES & SOCOL, LTD. (AV)

Three First National Plaza, Suite 2200, 60602
Telephone: 312-580-0100
Telecopy: 312-580-1994

Benjamin P. Beringer
Anjali Dayal
Mark S. Dym
George W. Gessler
John K. Hughes
Joshua Karsh
Peter M. Katsaros
Kimberley Marsh
Alex W. Miller
Terence J. Moran
Matthew J. Piers
Kalman D. Resnick
Frederick S. Rhine
Jonathan A. Rothstein
Michael P. Simkus
Donna Kaner Socol

Gary Chodorow
Ruth M. Dunning
S. Todd Neal
Mark A. Pellegrino
Steven C. Steinback
Dana H. Sukenik
J. Eric Vander Arend
Mark B. Weiner
Charles H. Wintersteen

OF COUNSEL

Darius S. Francescatti, M.D.
Susan R. Gzesh

For full biographical listings, see the Martindale-Hubbell Law Directory

MICHAEL T. HANNAFAN & ASSOCIATES, LTD. (AV)

One East Wacker Drive, Suite 2710, 60601
Telephone: 312-527-0055
Fax: 312-527-0220
Email: mthannafan@aol.com

Michael T. Hannafan

Cory A. Johnson

Reference: The Northern Trust Co.

For full biographical listings, see the Martindale-Hubbell Law Directory

HOLLIS AND JOHNSON (AV)

11 East Adams Street, Suite 501, 60603
Telephone: 312-427-0700
Fax: 312-427-8407
URL: http://www.digitalawyer.com/bankruptcy

Pamela S. Hollis
Donald E. Johnson

ASSOCIATE

Linda M. Kujaca

For full biographical listings, see the Martindale-Hubbell Law Directory

HOPKINS & SUTTER (AV)

A Partnership including Professional Corporations
Three First National Plaza, Suite 4100, 60602-4205
Telephone: 312-558-6600
Fax: 312-558-6538
Email: postmaster@hopsut.com *URL:* http://www.hopsut.com
Washington, D.C. Office: 888 Sixteenth Street, N.W.
Telephone: 202-835-8000.
Fax: 202-835-8136.
Troy, Michigan Office: 2800 Livernois, Suite 220.
Telephone: 248-740-6600.
Fax: 248-740-6613.

MEMBERS OF FIRM

Bryan S. Anderson
John T. Brooks
Antony S. Burt
Michael M. Conway
Mark Crane (P.C.)
Bruce W. Doughty
Bennett L. Epstein
Jay Erens
Robert C. Feldmeier
Michael A. Ficaro
Stephen E. Garcia
Diane Gianos
David B. Goroff
Paul F. Hanzlik
F. Thomas Hecht
Wm. Carlisle Herbert
Glen H. Kanwit
Dennis G. LaGory
Jeremiah Marsh (P.C.)
Mary Kay McCalla Martire
John W. McCaffrey
William J. McKenna, Jr.
Claudette P. Miller
Joel L. Miller
Marie C. Oldham
James D. Ossyra
Kathleen R. Pasulka-Brown
Robert W. Patterson (P.C.)
John P. Ratnaswamy
William E. Rattner
E. Glenn Rippie
John L. Rogers, III
Samuel K. Skinner
Michael B. Solow
David M. Spector
John F. Zabriskie
Christopher W. Zibart

For Complete List of Firm Personnel, See General Section

For full biographical listings, see the Martindale-Hubbell Law Directory

KAPLAN, BEGY & VON OHLEN (AV)

One First National Plaza 51st Floor, 60603
Telephone: 312-345-3000
Fax: 312-345-3119
URL: http://www.kbvlaw.com

MEMBERS OF FIRM

Fred C. Begy, III
Larry S. Kaplan
James D. Solon
Robert C. von Ohlen, Jr.
Joseph A. Bosco
Richard A. Walker
Mitchell J. Kanaan
Patrick J. Keating

ASSOCIATES

Keith S. Yamaguchi
Thomas C. Sokol
Robert K. Villa
Nicole Halpern Murphy
Telly Andrews
Tamara S. Dykstra

For full biographical listings, see the Martindale-Hubbell Law Directory

KUBASIAK, CREMIEUX, FYLSTRA, REIZEN & ROTUNNO, PROFESSIONAL CORPORATION (AV)

Two First National Plaza, 20 South Clark Street, Suite 2900, 60603
Telephone: 312-630-9600
Fax: 312-630-7939

Gerald E. Kubasiak
Richard J. Cremieux
Raymond A. Fylstra
Daniel J. Kubasiak
Richard S. Reizen
Steven J. Rotunno
Gregory A. Thorpe
Ellen Chapelle

Noël P. Goudreau
Scott A. Browdy
Jonathan S. Drage

OF COUNSEL

John A. Dienner, III

For full biographical listings, see the Martindale-Hubbell Law Directory

NORMAN J. LERUM (AV)

Suite 2100, 100 West Monroe Street, 60603
Telephone: 312-782-1087
Facsimile: 312-332-6020
Email: lerum@martindalemail.com *URL:* http://www.lawyers.com/lerumlaw

For full biographical listings, see the Martindale-Hubbell Law Directory

Chicago—Continued

McBride Baker & Coles (AV)

500 West Madison Street 40th Floor, 60661-2511
Telephone: 312-715-5700
Cable Address: "Chilaw"
Telex: 270258
Telecopier: 312-993-9350
Email: lastname@mbc.com *URL:* http://www.mbc.com
Oakbrook Terrace, Illinois Office: Suite 1000, One Mid America Plaza, 60181-4710.
Telephone: 630-954-2100.
Telecopier: 630-954-2112.

MEMBERS OF FIRM

Henry S. Allen, Jr.
Thomas P. Arden
Malcolm H. Brooks
John J. Cresto
Paul D. Frenz
Kenneth A. Jenero
Francis L. Keldermans
Clifton A. Lake
Richard S. Lauter
Donald G. Mulack
Robert W. Queeney
Richard A. Redmond
Mark A. Spognardi
William M. Stevens
Steven B. Varick
Michael L. Weissman
Richard R. Winter

OF COUNSEL

William J. Cooney
N. A. Jim Giambalvo
Geoffrey G. Gilbert
G. Gale Roberson, Jr.
Thomas P. Ward

ASSOCIATES

Naomi R. Angel
Marc L. Fogelberg
Steffanie N. Garrett
Rachel N. Lokken
Micah E. Marcus
Sarah E. Pace
Charles L. Philbrick
George M. Sanders
Phillip Michael Schreiber
Michele E. Sibley
Paul R. Simons
Peter J. Strand
Jonathan E. Strouse
Jeffrey M. Teske

For Complete List of Firm Personnel, See General Section

For full biographical listings, see the Martindale-Hubbell Law Directory

McFadden & Dillon, A Professional Corporation (AV)

135 South La Salle Street, Suite 2110, 60603-4402
Telephone: 312-201-8300
Facsimile: 312-201-0535
Email: mcfaddendillonlaw@ameritech.net

Roger J. McFadden
Thomas J. Dillon

Tyrrel J. Penn

For full biographical listings, see the Martindale-Hubbell Law Directory

Nisen & Elliott (AV)

200 West Adams Street, Suite 2500, 60606
Telephone: 312-346-7800
Telecopier: 312-346-9316

MEMBERS OF FIRM

Paul F. Gerbosi
Edward B. Mueller
Anthony Packard
Mark F. Zaenger
Michael J. Daley
John Foster Lesch
John K. Kneafsey
Michael H. Moirano
Robert O. Middleton
William G. Daluga, Jr.
Kenneth J. Rojc
Thomas V. McCauley
Helen M. Jensen
William A. Walker
Daniel P. Dawson
Michael J. Pavlicek

Robert Christie
Donald F. Froehlke
Thomas K. Juffernbruch
Brendan J. Kelly
Brian C. Kelly
Mary Rose C. Manczak
Bradley S. McCann
Brian D. Proctor

OF COUNSEL

Charles M. Nisen
Donald C. Shine

For full biographical listings, see the Martindale-Hubbell Law Directory

Oppenheimer Wolff & Donnelly (Illinois) (AV)

Two Prudential Plaza, 45th Floor, 180 North Stetson Avenue, 60601
Telephone: 312-616-1800
FAX: 312-616-5800
Email: webmaster@owdlaw.com *URL:* http://www.owdlaw.com
Oppenheimer Wolff & Donnelly LLP
Minneapolis, Minnesota Office: 3400 Plaza VII, 45 South Seventh Street. 55402.
Telephone: 612-607-7000.
FAX: 612-607-7100.
Amsterdam, The Netherlands Office: Keizergracht 241.
Telephone: 31-20-423-4555.
FAX: 31-20-423-4545.

(See Next Column)

Brussels, Belgium Office: Avenue Louise 240, Box 5, 1050.
Telephone: 32-2-626-0500.
FAX: 32-2-626-0510.
Geneva, Switzerland Office: Rue Gabriel Eynard, 6, 1205.
Telephone: (41/22) 311-7410.
FAX: (41/22) 311-7407.
New York, N.Y. Office: Citicorp Center, 153 East 53rd Street, 10022.
Telephone: 212-826-5000.
FAX: 212-486-0708.
Newport Beach, California Office: 500 Newport Center Drive, Suite 700, 92260.
Telephone: 949-719-6000.
FAX: 949-719-6020.
Paris, France Office: 53 Avenue Montaigne, 75008.
Telephone: (33/1) 44 95 03 50.
FAX: (33/1) 44 95 03 40.
St. Paul, Minnesota Office: 1700 First National Bank Building, 55101.
Telephone: 651-605-2000.
FAX: 651-605-2100.
Washington, D.C. Office: Oppenheimer Wolff Donnelly & Bayh LLP, 1350 Eye Street, N.W., Suite 200, 20005.
Telephone: 202-312-8000.
FAX: 202-312-8100.
Los Angeles, California Office: 2029 Century Park East, 38th Floor, 90067.
Telephone: 310-788-5000.
FAX: 310-277-1297.
San Jose, California Office: 101 Park Center Plaza, Suite 300, 95113.
Telephone: 408-795-3000.
FAX: 408-795-3100.

RESIDENT PARTNERS

Russell M. Pelton
Barry S. Maram
James A. Fletcher
Winston I. Lowe (Not admitted in IL)
William C. Sippel
David C. Bohrer
John Y. E. Lee
Martin K. LaPointe
Gregory S. Norrod
Rebecca R. Haller
Michael A. Chabraja
Kathryn C. Thomas

RESIDENT ASSOCIATES

Jeffrey A. Siderius
Thomas J. Litwiler
Lisa C. Breen
Vineet Gosain
Christopher E.V. Quinn
James D. Helenhouse
Lynn M. Geerdes
Michael G. Ryan
Colleen Young Kraus

RESIDENT OF COUNSEL

Robert H. Wheeler

For full biographical listings, see the Martindale-Hubbell Law Directory

Pavalon, Gifford, Laatsch & Marino (AV)

Two North La Salle Street, Suite 1600, 60602
Telephone: 312-419-7400
Fax: 312-419-7408
Email: pavgif@aol.com
Rockford, Illinois Office: 501 Seventh Street, Suite 501, 61104.
Telephone: 815-968-5100.

MEMBERS OF FIRM

Eugene I. Pavalon
Geoffrey L. Gifford
Gary K. Laatsch
Frank C. Marino
Henry Phillip Gruss

Christine Walsh Donnelly

For full biographical listings, see the Martindale-Hubbell Law Directory

Richard J. Prendergast, Ltd. (AV)

111 West Washington-Suite 1100, 60602-2768
Telephone: 312-641-0881
Fax: 312-641-3562
Email: rprendergastltd@msn.com *URL:* http://www.lawyers.com/prendergast

Richard J. Prendergast
James Prendergast

Ellen M. Murphy
Michael T. Layden
Deirdre Ann Close

For full biographical listings, see the Martindale-Hubbell Law Directory

Quinlan & Crisham, Ltd. (AV)

30 North La Salle Street, Suite 2900, 60602
Telephone: 312-263-0900
Telecopier: 312-263-5013

William R. Quinlan
Thomas M. Crisham
Thomas C. Hynes
Gino L. DiVito
Mary Patricia Benz
Michael C. Bruck
James R. Carroll
Thomas C. Hofbauer
John F. Kennedy
Jeffrey T. Kubes
Eugene E. Murphy, Jr.
Michael I Rothstein
Caesar A. Tabet
Cheryl I. Niro

(See Next Column)

QUINLAN & CRISHAM LTD., *Chicago—Continued*

Frank M. Adams, Jr.
Brian J. Alesia
Michael T. Beirne
Catherine J. Casey
Jasmine De La Torre
Karina H. DeHayes
Edward Fitzsimmons Dunne
Lisa M. Hegedus
Erin Bolan Hines
John N. Hourihane, Jr.
David M. Jenkins
J. Christopher Madden
Michelle A. Michalik
James A. Niewiara
Martin J. O'Hara
John P. O'Malley
J. Jeffrey Patton
Jean M. Prendergast
Melissa M. Riahei
John H. Scheid
Daniel L. Stanner
Michael A. Steigmann

For full biographical listings, see the Martindale-Hubbell Law Directory

PETER R. SONDERBY, P.C. (AV)

135 South La Salle Street Suite 1424, 60603
Telephone: 312-201-0999
Fax: 312-201-0749; 201-4559
Email: Psond@starnetinc.com

Peter R. Sonderby

For full biographical listings, see the Martindale-Hubbell Law Directory

STONE & MOORE, CHARTERED (AV)

30 North La Salle Street, Suite 4300, 60602
Telephone: 312-332-5656
Fax: 312-332-5858
URL: http://www.stonemoore.com
Merrillville, Indiana Office: 500 E. 86th Avenue, 46410.
Telephone: 219-736-5959.
Fax: 219-736-5858.
Wheaton, Illinois Office: 600 W. Roosevelt Road, Suite 1A, 60187.
Telephone: 630-221-9292.
Fax: 630-221-9393.

William G. Stone
Robert Charles Moore (Also at Wheaton, Illinois Office)
Raymond R. Pesavento
Rosario Cibella
Richard M. Johnson, Jr.
J. Murray Pinkston, III
Julie Osswald Hooven

Christian D. Ambler
Jeffrey W. Henning
Erica Lewis Battaglia
Kevin Kemp Lyons
Kristin E. Rooney
Daniel S. Schulz
Matthew B. Stephens
A. Christine Svenson
Douglas W. Walker

For full biographical listings, see the Martindale-Hubbell Law Directory

SUGAR, FRIEDBERG & FELSENTHAL (AV)

30 North La Salle Street, Suite 2600, 60602
Telephone: 312-704-9400
Telecopier: 312-372-7951
Cable: "SUGARFREE"

MEMBERS OF FIRM

Richard A. Sugar
Michael R. Friedberg
Steven A. Felsenthal
Andrew B. David
Leslie J. Weiss
Ira S. Neiman
Jonathan L. Mills
Etahn M. Cohen
Howard M. Helsinger
Robert F. Simon
Martin M. Weinstein
Charles H. Braun
Kathryn A. Erickson

ASSOCIATES

Aron L. Bornstein
Annette L. Brands
Kathryn T. Cha
Norman J. Ginsparg
William F. McGuinn
Suzanne J. Massel
Deanne Elizabeth Clarke

For full biographical listings, see the Martindale-Hubbell Law Directory

TORSHEN, SPREYER, GARMISA & SLOBIG, LTD. (AV)

105 West Adams Street, Suite 3200, 60603
Telephone: 312-372-9282
Fax: 312-372-7914
Email: torshen@ais.net

Jerome H. Torshen
Abigail Kay Spreyer
James K. Genden
Zoran Dragutinovich
Steven P. Garmisa
Robert J. Slobig
Thomas J. Ramsdell
Michael P. Bregenzer

Marlaine J. McVisk

For full biographical listings, see the Martindale-Hubbell Law Directory

WILLIAM S. WIGODA, LTD. (AV)

19 South LaSalle Street, Suite 1500, 60603-1401
Telephone: 312-214-4200
Fax: 312-332-4629
Email: wwigoda@aol.com

William S. Wigoda

OF COUNSEL

Linda Jakubs
Paul Goodman
Lori S. Loeb

For full biographical listings, see the Martindale-Hubbell Law Directory

WILDMAN, HARROLD, ALLEN & DIXON (AV)

225 West Wacker Drive, 30th Floor, 60606-1229
Telephone: 312-201-2000
Fax: 312-201-2555
Email: hennessy@whad.com *URL:* http://www.whad.com
Aurora, Illinois Office: 1961 W. Downer Place.
Telephone: 630-892-7021.
Fax: 630-892-7158.
Waukegan, Illinois Office: 404 West Water, P. O. Box 890.
Telephone: 847-625-5550.
Fax: 847-625-5555.
Lisle, Illinois Office: 4300 Commerce Court, Suite 320.
Telephone: 630-955-0555.
Fax: 630-955-0662
Toronto, Ontario correspondent Office: Keel Cottrelle. 36 Toronto Street, Suite 920.
Telephone: 416-367-2900.
Telefax: 416-367-2791.
Telex: 062-18660.

MEMBERS OF FIRM

John J. Arado
Brent R. Austin
Richard C. Bartelt
Fredrick H. Bates
Douglas R. Carlson
Leland H. Chait
Paul S. Chervin (Waukegan Office)
James A. Christman
Steven E. Danekas
Michael Dockterman
James P. Dorr
Jerald P. Esrick
Ira C. Feldman
James D. Fiffer
Donald Flayton
Kathy Pinkstaff Fox
John E. Frey
Robert E. Haley
H. Roderic Heard
Helaine Wachs Heydemann
Richard M. Hoffman
Anthony G. Hopp
Elizabeth Keiley
Anne Giddings Kimball
John S. Letchinger
Brian W. Lewis
Thomas M. Lynch
Joseph F. Madonia
Thomas I. Matyas
Michael L. McCluggage
Mark J. McCombs
Donald R. McGarrah
Mark P. Miller
James R. Morrin
Richard D. Murphy Jr.
Timothy G. Nickels
Douglas L. Prochnow
Fred E. Schulz
Donald J. Simantz (Resident, Aurora Office)
Lisa S. Simmons
David M. Simon
R. John Street
Robert A. Strelecky (Lisle Office)
Peter A. Tomaras
Louis P. Vitullo
David L. Weinstein
Craig M. White
Jonathan W. Young

OF COUNSEL

Thomas D. Allen
Diane G. Elder
Peter H. Fritts
Bernard Harrold

Karena J. Bierman
Brian W. Bilcer
Erin L. Bishop
Kristin M. Buchholz
Michael J. Castellino
David J. Chroust (Lisle Office)
Samuel S. Cohen
Kathie M. Contois
Helen A. Contos (Lisle Office)
Paul D. Cranley
Anne-Marie Dega
Vilia M. Drazdys
Mark L. Durbin
Lawrence W. Falbe
David S. Goles (Waukegan Office)
Kenneth M. Gorenberg
Douglas W. Hyman
James C. James, III (Aurora Office)
Michael A. Kaeding
Susan M. Kayser
Dara J. Keidan
Michone J. Kuhlman (Waukegan Office)
Jeffrey A. McIntyre
Ian J. McPheron
W. Scott Nehs
Martha D. Owens
Barbara M. Prohaska (Lisle Office)
Kevin B. Reid
Jennifer K. Walter
Susan M. Weis
Anita C. Wilson

For full biographical listings, see the Martindale-Hubbell Law Directory

*DECATUR,** Macon Co.

ERICKSON, DAVIS, MURPHY, JOHNSON, GRIFFITH & WALSH, LTD. (AV)

225 South Main Street, P.O. Box 25138, 62525-5138
Telephone: 217-428-0948
Fax: 217-428-0996
Email: lawyer@law225.com

(See Next Column)

Erickson, Davis, Murphy, Johnson, Griffith & Walsh Ltd.—*Continued*

Wayne E. Armstrong (1916-1977)
Frederick P. Erickson
Garry E. Davis
W. Scott Murphy
Evan H. Johnson
Thomas E. Griffith
Michael A. Walsh

Robert C. Bollinger
David T. Tanner

Representative Clients: A.E. Staley Manufacturing Company; Archer Daniels Midland Company; Cincinnati Insurance Company; Country Mutual Insurance Company; General Casualty Insurance Companies; Illinois Power Company; Millikin University; Reliance Insurance Company; St. Paul Insurance Co.; State Farm Insurance Co.; Western States Insurance Company.

For full biographical listings, see the Martindale-Hubbell Law Directory

GRANITE CITY, Madison Co.

Lueders, Robertson & Konzen (AV)

1939 Delmar Avenue, 62040
Telephone: 618-876-8500
Telecopier: 618-876-4534
Email: lrk.il@worldnet.att.net
Danville, Illinois Office: 809 1/2 North Gilbert, 61832.
Telephone: 217-443-0304.
Fax: 217-443-0375.

MEMBERS OF FIRM

Wesley Lueders (1896-1957)
Randall Robertson
Leo H. Konzen
R. Eric Robertson
Edward C. Fitzhenry, Jr.
Brian E. Konzen
Paul G. Foran

ASSOCIATE

Anthony R. Garavalia

Representative Clients: Ameritech; Mercantile Bank (Trust Division); Granite City Steel Division of National Steel Corporation; Allied Waste Industries, Inc.; Illinois Industrial Energy Consumers (IIEC) including Olin Corporation; Archers-Daniels-Midland Company; General Motors Corporation.

For full biographical listings, see the Martindale-Hubbell Law Directory

*KANKAKEE,** Kankakee Co.

Barmann, Kramer & Bohlen, P.C. (AV)

Suite 502, 200 East Court Street, P.O. Box 1787, 60901
Telephone: 815-939-1133
Fax: 815-939-0994

Glen R. Barmann
Christopher W. Bohlen
Michael D. Kramer

For Complete List of Firm Personnel, See General Section

For full biographical listings, see the Martindale-Hubbell Law Directory

LIBERTYVILLE, Lake Co.

James J. DeSanto A Professional Corporation (AV)

339 North Milwaukee Avenue, 60048
Telephone: 847-816-8100
Facsimile: 847-816-8126
Email: desanto@1connect.net

James J. DeSanto

For full biographical listings, see the Martindale-Hubbell Law Directory

*MARION,** Williamson Co.

Mitchell, Mitchell & Bradley (AV)

404 North Monroe, P.O. Box 488, 62959-2328
Telephone: 618-993-2134
Telecopier: 618-993-8702
Email: mmb@midwest.net *URL:* http://www.lawyers.com/mmb

J. C. Mitchell
Bruce W. Mitchell
John E. Bradley

OF COUNSEL

James E. Hopkins

Representative Clients: St. Paul Fire & Casualty Insurance Company; Liberty Mutual Insurance Company; Shelter Insurance Company; Atlantic Mutual Insurance Company; Farmer's Insurance Exchange; United States Fidelity and Guarantee Company; Horace Mann Insurance.

For full biographical listings, see the Martindale-Hubbell Law Directory

OAKBROOK TERRACE, DuPage Co.

McBride Baker & Coles (AV)

Suite 1000, One Mid America Plaza, 60181-4710
Telephone: 630-954-2100
Telecopier: 630-954-2112
URL: http://www.mbc.com
Chicago, Illinois Office: 500 West Madison Street, 40th Floor, 60661-2511.
Telephone: 312-715-5700.
Telecopier: 312-993-9350.

MEMBERS OF FIRM

Steven B. Bashaw
Eric L. Singer
Douglas C. Tibble
Jacqueline W. Vlaming
David E. Zajicek

ASSOCIATE

Eric D. Filkin

For Complete List of Firm Personnel, See General Section

For full biographical listings, see the Martindale-Hubbell Law Directory

*PEORIA,** Peoria Co.

Howard & Howard Attorneys, P.C. (AV)

The Creve Coeur Building, Suite 200, 321 Liberty Street, 61602-1403
Telephone: 309-672-1483
Telecopier: 309-672-1568
Kalamazoo, Michigan Office: The Michigan Building, Suite 200, 100 Portage Street.
Telephone: 616-382-1483.
Telecopier: 616-382-1568.
Bloomfield Hills, Michigan Office: The Pinehurst Office Center, Suite 101, 1400 North Woodward Avenue.
Telephone: 248-645-1483.
Telecopier: 248-645-1568.
Lansing, Michigan Office: Suite 500, The Phoenix Building, 222 Washington Square, North.
Telephone: 517-485-1483.
Telecopier: 517-485-1568.

Frederick G. Hoffman
Timothy J. Howard
Michael R. Lied
Scott R. Paulsen
Leonard W. Sachs
Jeffrey G. Sorenson

Representative Clients: For Representative Client list, see General Practice, Peoria, IL.

For Complete List of Firm Personnel, See General Section

For full biographical listings, see the Martindale-Hubbell Law Directory

VERNON HILLS, Lake Co.

Richards, Ralph & Schwab, Chartered (AV)

One Hawthorn Place, 175 East Hawthorn Parkway, Suite 345, 60061
Telephone: 847-367-9699
Fax: 847-367-9621
Email: dschwab@rr&s-chtd.com *URL:* http://www.lawyers.com/richardandschwab

Michael L. Ralph
Alan E. Richards
David J. Schwab

For full biographical listings, see the Martindale-Hubbell Law Directory

*WAUKEGAN,** Lake Co.

Salvi & Schostok, P.C. (AV)

Established 1982 as Law Offices of Patrick A. Salvi, P.C.
218 North Utica Street, 60085
Telephone: 847-249-1227
Telefax: 847-249-0138
Email: salvilaw.com *URL:* http://www.salvilaw.com
Chicago, Illinois Office: 181 West Madison, Suite 3525, 60602.
Telephone: 312-372-1227.
Telefax: 312-372-3720.

Patrick A. Salvi
Michael P. Schostok
David J. Pritchard (Resident, Chicago Office)

John Andrew Kornak
J. Matthew Dudley
Peter M. Trobe
Ellen C. Smith
Scott E. Preusen

OF COUNSEL

Bernard E. Grysen

References: First Midwest Bank, Waukegan, Illinois; Northern Trust Bank, Lake Forest, Illinois; Commercial Litigation Clients; Anderson Consulting, LLP.; Baxter Healthcare; Brunswick Corporation, Lake Forest, Illinois.

For full biographical listings, see the Martindale-Hubbell Law Directory

*WHEATON,** DuPage Co.

DONOVAN AND ROBERTS, P.C. (AV)

104 East Roosevelt Road, Suite 202, 60187
Telephone: 630-668-4211
Fax: 630-668-2076

Keith E. Roberts, Sr. | Keith E. (Chuck) Roberts, Jr.
Henry B. Vess, III

Marie F. Leach | Eric A. Burgeson
Robert S. Marcott | Kevin H. Saville

For full biographical listings, see the Martindale-Hubbell Law Directory

O'REILLY LAW OFFICES (AV)

1776 South Naperville Road, Suite 206-A, 60187
Telephone: 630-665-4444
Telecopier: 630-665-4442

Roger Kevin O'Reilly

Molly M. O'Reilly | John F. O'Reilly

For full biographical listings, see the Martindale-Hubbell Law Directory

ROLEWICK & GUTZKE, P.C. (AV)

Danada West Professional Center, 1776 South Naperville Road, Suite 104A, 60187-8133
Telephone: 630-653-1577
Fax: 630-653-1579
Email: rgpclaw@aol.com *URL:* http://www.lawyers.com/rolewickandgutzke

David F. Rolewick | Karen Johnson Guilde
John D. Gutzke | Christopher L. Cook

For full biographical listings, see the Martindale-Hubbell Law Directory

INDIANA

*CROWN POINT,** Lake Co.

EDWARD P. GRIMMER (AV)

603 N. Main Street, 46307-3233
Telephone: 219-662-1661
Fax: 219-663-4151
Email: Grimmerlaw@msn.com

Representative Clients: Furnished Upon Request.

For full biographical listings, see the Martindale-Hubbell Law Directory

*FORT WAYNE,** Allen Co.

ROTHBERG & LOGAN (AV)

(Formerly, Rothberg, Gallmeyer, Fruechtenicht & Logan)
2100 National City Center, 110 West Berry Street, P.O. Box 11647, 46859-1647
Telephone: 219-422-9454
Telefax: 219-422-1622

MEMBERS OF FIRM

Martin T. Fletcher, Sr. | Brian L. Nehrig
Gregory Martin Cole | Daniel G. McNamara

ASSOCIATE

Christine M. Stach

Counsel for: Parkview Hospital; Cameron Memorial Community Hospital; Norwest Bank Indiana, N.A.; Parkview Health System; Azar's, Incorporated; Fort Wayne-Allen County Airport Authority; Fort Wayne Public Transportation Corporation; Avis Industrial Corp.; Farm Credit Services of Mid-America, ASA; Slater Fort Wayne Federal Credit Union.

For Complete List of Firm Personnel, See General Section

For full biographical listings, see the Martindale-Hubbell Law Directory

SHIPLEY & ASSOCIATES (AV)

230 West Main Street, Suite 100, 46802-1612
Telephone: 219-422-2700
Fax: 219-424-2960
Email: shipley@iquest.net

Grant F. Shipley

ASSOCIATE

Deborah Wiers Vincent

Representative Clients: NBD Bank, N.A.; Fleet Capital Corp.

For full biographical listings, see the Martindale-Hubbell Law Directory

HAMMOND, Lake Co.

ABRAHAMSON, REED & ADLEY (AV)

200 Russell Street, 46320
Telephone: 219-937-1500
Fax: 219-937-3174

MEMBERS OF FIRM

Harold Abrahamson | Kenneth D. Reed
Michael C. Adley

ASSOCIATES

Scott R. Bilse | John P. Reed

References: Calumet National Bank, Hammond; Mercantile National Bank, Hammond.

For full biographical listings, see the Martindale-Hubbell Law Directory

*INDIANAPOLIS,** Marion Co.

CLARK, QUINN, MOSES & CLARK (AV)

One Indiana Square, Suite 2200, 46204-2011
Telephone: 317-637-1321
Fax: 317-687-2344
Email: lawyers@cqmc-law.com

MEMBERS OF FIRM

Alex M. Clark (1916-1991) | John M. Moses
James C. Clark | J. Murray Clark
Thomas Michael Quinn | Matthew R. Clark

ASSOCIATES

Michael D. Keele | Cameron F. Clark
Brigid O'Brien Shepherd

Representative Clients: Justus Companies; Davis Homes; Meijer Realty, Inc.; Lowe's; Marsh; MI Shottenstein; Indianapolis Colts; Fort Harrison Reuse Authority; Indianapolis Water Company; Kroger.

For full biographical listings, see the Martindale-Hubbell Law Directory

HOFFMAN DREWRY HANCOCK & SIMMONS (AV)

9100 Keystone Crossing, Suite 350, 46240
Telephone: 317-580-4848
Telecopier: 317-580-4855

Robert J. Hoffman | Richard S. Pitts
Michael F. Drewry | David B. Vornehm
William J. Hancock | Joseph M. Leone
David L. Simmons | Richard W. McMinn

OF COUNSEL

S. Douglas Trolson

For full biographical listings, see the Martindale-Hubbell Law Directory

HOPPER, GALLIHER & TUCKER, P.C. (AV)

Bank One Center/Circle, 111 Monument Circle, Suite 452, 46204-5170
Telephone: 317-635-5005
Facsimile: 317-634-2501

George W. Hopper | William J. Tucker
Mark R. Galliher | Ronald W. Buchmeier
Jeffrey E. Ramsey

Representative Clients: Banc One Corporation; National City Bank; Mutual Guaranty Corporation; I.T.T. Financial Services, Commercial Division; ABC Supply Co., Inc.; Sholodge, Inc.; Simon Debartolo Group, L.P.; IWC Resources Corp.; KRB Music Cos., Inc.; Whitewater Broadcasting Corp.

For full biographical listings, see the Martindale-Hubbell Law Directory

MCTURNAN & TURNER (AV)

2400 Market Tower, 10 West Market Street, 46204
Telephone: 317-464-8181
Telecopier: 317-464-8131

Lee B. McTurnan | Jacqueline Bowman Ponder
Wayne C. Turner | Steven M. Badger
Jackie M. Bennett, Jr. | John F. McCauley

For full biographical listings, see the Martindale-Hubbell Law Directory

ROCAP, WITCHGER & THRELKELD (AV)

One Indiana Square, Suite 2300, 46204
Telephone: 317-639-6281
FAX: 317-637-9056
Email: rocap@iquest.net

James E. Rocap, Sr. (1881-1969) | John T. Rocap (1909-1980)
Keith C. Reese (1920-1993)

MEMBERS OF FIRM

James D. Witchger | Richard A. Rocap
W. Brent Threlkeld | Thomas Todd Reynolds

(See Next Column)

ROCAP, WITCHGER & THRELKELD—*Continued*

ASSOCIATES

Robert A. Durham
Kandi K. Hidde
Robert F. Ahlgrim, Jr.
Kelley Bertoux Creveling
Tracy A. Arney
Edward A.B. Castaldo
Mark S. Maxwell

OF COUNSEL

James E. Rocap, Jr.
Joseph F. Quill
William C. Moore

Counsel for: Phillips Petroleum Co.; State Farm Mutual Auto Insurance Co.; Cessna Finance Corp.; American Family Insurance Group; The Travelers Insurance Co.

For full biographical listings, see the Martindale-Hubbell Law Directory

TABBERT HAHN EARNEST & WEDDLE (AV)

Suite 2100, One Indiana Square, 46204-2101
Telephone: 317-639-5444
Fax: 317-639-5232
Email: jtyrrell@tabberthahn.com *URL:* http://www.tabberthahn.com

Don A. Tabbert
Gregory F. Hahn
Lante K. Earnest
Robert G. Weddle
Mark K. Sullivan
Judy M. Tyrrell
Lara D. Engelking
Matthew W. Conner
William W. Mathews
Heather L. Fesko
Charles R. Whybrew

OF COUNSEL

James J. Nocon
William D. Lalley
Joseph W. Hammes
Dale E. Sporleder

For full biographical listings, see the Martindale-Hubbell Law Directory

IOWA

*DAVENPORT,** Scott Co.

GOSMA & GALLAGHER, P.L.C. (AV)

Quad City Bank Building, 4500 North Brady Street, Suite 200, 52806
Telephone: 319-388-8417
Fax: 319-388-9240
Email: lawfirm@gosma-gallagher.com
Bettendorf Office: 1989 Spruce Hills Drive.
Telephone: 319-355-5304.
Fax: 319-359-7711.

MEMBERS OF FIRM

Robert D. Wells (1904-1990)
Robert H. Gallagher
John S. Gosma
James G. Noth
Marie R. Rolling-Tarbox
David A. Millage
Robert S. Gallagher
Jane E. Zimmer

OF COUNSEL

Clay LeGrand
Nicholas W. LeGrand (Not admitted in IA)

References: American Bank and Trust Company, Rock Island; Great River Bank and Trust, Princeton.

For full biographical listings, see the Martindale-Hubbell Law Directory

WEST DES MOINES, Polk Co.

LAMARCA & LANDRY, P.C. (AV)

1300 50th Street, 50266
Telephone: 515-225-2600
Fax: 515-225-8581
Islamorada, Florida Office: 202 Biscayne Boulevard, 33036.
Telephone: 305-664-8527.

George A. LaMarca
Gregory W. Landry

Gary G. Mattson
Justin E. LaVan

OF COUNSEL

Martin R. Anderson
Samuel S. Duffey

For full biographical listings, see the Martindale-Hubbell Law Directory

KANSAS

*HUTCHINSON,** Reno Co.

GILLILAND & HAYES, P.A. A PROFESSIONAL ASSOCIATION (AV)

20 West 2nd Avenue, 2nd Floor, P.O. Box 2977, 67504-2977
Telephone: 316-662-0537
Facsimile: 316-669-9426
URL: http://www.gillilandhayes.com
Wichita, Kansas Office: The Orpheum Centre, Suite 300, 200 North Broadway, P.O. Box 49406.
Telephone: 316-262-2266.
Facsimile: 316-263-2202.
Kansas City, Missouri Office: 12th Floor, 3100 Broadway.
Telephone: 816-753-3100.
Facsimile: 816-753-2271.

Robert J. Gilliland
John F. Hayes
James R. Gilliland
John S. Schmidt
Bruce B. Waugh (Not admitted in KS; Resident, Kansas City, Missouri Office)
Michael R. O'Neal
Bradley D. Dillon
Gerald L. Green
David N. Zimmerman (Not admitted in KS; Resident, Kansas City, Missouri Office)
Scott J. Mann
Carol Z. Smith (Resident, Kansas City, Missouri Office)
Kathleen A. Hardee (Resident, Kansas City, Missouri Office)
Kendall R. Cunningham (Resident, Wichita Office)
Mark R. Maloney (Resident, Wichita Office)

Thomas A. Dower
Tracy Applegate Cole
Laura A. Hederstedt
Terri Roberts Munsell (Resident, Kansas City, Missouri Office)
Lisa M. Ward
Kimberly Breda Bushek (Resident, Kansas City, Missouri Office)
E. Thomas Pyle, III
Tara L. Bragg

OF COUNSEL

Robert P. Reams (Not admitted in KS; Resident, Kansas City, Missouri Office)

Representative Clients: Allied Group; Dillon Companies; Fidelity Deposit Co. of Maryland; Central Bank & Trust; CNA Insurance; Farm Bureau Mutual Insurance Co.; St. Paul Fire and Marine Insurance Co.; State Farm Insurance Co.; U.S. Fidelity Corp.

For full biographical listings, see the Martindale-Hubbell Law Directory

*KANSAS CITY,** Wyandotte Co.

WONER, GLENN, REEDER & GIRARD, P.A.

(See Topeka)

*LAWRENCE,** Douglas Co.

WONER, GLENN, REEDER & GIRARD, P.A.

(See Topeka)

OVERLAND PARK, Johnson Co.

WONER, GLENN, REEDER & GIRARD, P.A.

(See Topeka)

*TOPEKA,** Shawnee Co.

WONER, GLENN, REEDER & GIRARD, P.A. (AV)

A Partnership of Professional Corporations
534 South Kansas Avenue Suite 330, 66603-3424
Telephone: 785-235-5330
Fax: 785-235-1615
URL: http://www.lawyers.com/wgr&glaw
Email: bwoner@wonerglenn.com *URL:* http://www.wonerglenn.com
Wichita, Kansas Office: 155 N. Market, Suite 708.
Telephone: 316-264-8220.
Fax: 316-264-3012.

David S. Fricke
Timothy H. Girard
Grant M. Glenn
Leon B. Graves
Patricia A. Reeder
R. Patrick Riordan
Bruce J. Woner

For full biographical listings, see the Martindale-Hubbell Law Directory

*WICHITA,** Sedgwick Co.

GRACE, UNRUH & PRATT, L.C. (AV)

Suite 501, 155 North Market Street, 67202-1816
Telephone: 316-269-2006
FAX: 316-269-0437
Email: litigation@fn.net

(See Next Column)

GRACE, UNRUH & PRATT L.C., *Wichita—Continued*

Brian G. Grace
Terry L. Unruh
Corlin J. Pratt
Gilbert L. Guthrie
Sharon A. Werner
Kevin A. Grace

For full biographical listings, see the Martindale-Hubbell Law Directory

KAHRS, NELSON, FANNING, HITE & KELLOGG L.L.P. (AV)

200 W. Douglas, Suite 600, 67202
Telephone: 316-265-7761
Telecopier: 316-267-7803
URL: http://www.kahrsnelson.com

MEMBERS OF FIRM

William A. Kahrs (1904-1989)
Robert H. Nelson (1904-1977)
Darrell D. Kellogg (1931-1992)
Richard C. Hite
Richard L. Honeyman
Larry A. Withers
Gary A. Winfrey
Clark R. Nelson
Steven D. Gough
Scott J. Gunderson
Randy Troutt
Arthur S. Chalmers
Kim R. Martens
Linda S. Parks
Forrest James Robinson, Jr.
Don D. Gribble, II
John G. Pike
Alan R. Pfaff
Dennis V. Lacey
Donald N. Peterson, II
Lisa Adrian McPherson

ASSOCIATES

Jerry D. Hawkins
Jon E. Newman
Scott R. Schillings
Richard D. Crowder

OF COUNSEL

H. W. Fanning
Vince P. Wheeler

Representative Clients: Advance Chemical Dist., Inc.; Learjet Corp.; Hahner, Foreman & Harness, Contractors; New York Life Insurance Co.; General Motors Corp.; St. Paul Insurance Cos.

For full biographical listings, see the Martindale-Hubbell Law Directory

TRIPLETT, WOOLF & GARRETSON, LLC (AV)

2959 North Rock Road, Suite 300, 67226
Telephone: 316-630-8100
Fax: 316-630-8101
Email: twg@twgfirm.com

MEMBERS OF FIRM

John P. Woolf
James A. Walker
Timothy E. McKee
Eric B. Metz
Lee Thompson
Eric S. Strickler
Bradley A. Stout
Rachael K. Pirner
Jeffrey D. Leonard

ASSOCIATES

Jeffrey E. Goering
Jerald W. Rogers

Representative Clients: Anheuser-Busch Companies, Inc.; Brite Voice Systems, Inc.; Coleman Company, Inc.; Dow Chemical Co.; Friends University; KPMG Peat Marwick; National Plastics Color, Inc.; Total Petroleum, Inc.; Travelers Insurance Co.; Willis Corroon of Kansas, Inc.

For Complete List of Firm Personnel, See General Section

For full biographical listings, see the Martindale-Hubbell Law Directory

KENTUCKY

*BOWLING GREEN,** Warren Co.

BRODERICK & THORNTON (AV)

921 College Street, Phoenix Place, P.O. Box 3100, 42102-3100
Telephone: 270-782-6700
Facsimile: 270-782-3110

David F. Broderick
Steven O. Thornton

ASSOCIATES

Kenneth P. O'Brien
Andrew A. Stanford

Representative Clients: Allstate Insurance Co.; National City Bank, Kentucky; American States Insurance Co.; Capital Enterprise Insurance; Fireman's Fund Insurance Co.; Imperial Casualty & Indemnity; Indiana Lumbermen's Mutual Insurance; Kentucky Medical Insurance Co.; Scotty's Contracting & Stone, Inc.; St. Paul Insurance Co.

For full biographical listings, see the Martindale-Hubbell Law Directory

*LONDON,** Laurel Co.

TOOMS & HOUSE (AV)

310 West Fifth Street, P.O. Box 520, 40743-0520
Telephone: 606-864-4145
FAX: 606-864-4279

(See Next Column)

MEMBERS OF FIRM

Murray L. Brown (1894-1980)
Roy E. Tooms (1917-1986)
R. William Tooms
Brian C. House

ASSOCIATE

Roy G. Collins

Representative Clients: State Auto Mutual Insurance Co.; Grange Mutual Casualty Co.; Kentucky Farm Bureau Mutual Insurance Co.

For full biographical listings, see the Martindale-Hubbell Law Directory

*LOUISVILLE,** Jefferson Co.

MORGAN & POTTINGER, P.S.C. (AV)

601 West Main Street, 40202
Telephone: 502-589-2780
Telecopier: 502-585-3498
URL: http://www.morganandpottinger.com
Lexington, Kentucky Office: 133 West Short Street.
Telephone: 606-253-1900.
Telecopier: 606-255-2038.
New Albany, Indiana Office: 120 East Market Street.
Telephone: 812-948-0008.
Telecopier: 812-944-6215.

John T. McGarvey
James I. Murray
(Resident, Lexington Office)
Douglas Gene Sharp
John A. Majors
Scott T. Rickman
(Resident, Lexington Office)
Hal D. Friedman

COUNSEL

J. Jeffrey Cooke

For Complete List of Firm Personnel, See General Section

For full biographical listings, see the Martindale-Hubbell Law Directory

TILFORD, DOBBINS, ALEXANDER, BUCKAWAY & BLACK (AV)

Suite 1400, One Riverfront Plaza, 40202
Telephone: 502-584-6137
Fax: 502-584-2318

MEMBERS OF FIRM

Charles W. Dobbins (1916-1992)
Henry J. Tilford (1880-1968)
George S. Wetherby (1905-1954)
Lawrence W. Wetherby
(1908-1994)
John T. Metcalf (1890-1974)
Stuart E. Alexander
William A. Buckaway, Jr.
Charles W. Dobbins, Jr.
Terrell L. Black
Mark Wesley Dobbins
Stuart E. Alexander, III
John M. Nader

ASSOCIATES

John A. Wilmes
Sandra F. Keene
Patrick T. Schmidt
Thomas J.B. Hurst
H. Kevin Eddins
William J. Walsh, IV
Dana M. Taylor

OF COUNSEL

Randolph Noe
Carolyn K. Balleisen
Michael G. Karem

For full biographical listings, see the Martindale-Hubbell Law Directory

*PADUCAH,** McCracken Co.

DENTON & KEULER (AV)

Paducah Bank & Trust Company Building, 555 Jefferson Street, P.O. Box 929, 42001
Telephone: 502-443-8253
Fax: 502-442-6000
Email: dk@dklaw.com *URL:* http://www.dklaw.com

MEMBERS OF FIRM

David L. Kelly
Theodore S. Hutchins

ASSOCIATES

Glenn D. Denton
Stacey Ann Blankenship

Reference: The Paducah Bank & Trust Co.

For Complete List of Firm Personnel, See General Section

For full biographical listings, see the Martindale-Hubbell Law Directory

LOUISIANA

*BATON ROUGE,** East Baton Rouge Parish

KLEINPETER & KLEINPETER (AV)

1680 South Lobdell Avenue, Suite E, P.O. Box 66443, 70896
Telephone: 225-926-5093
Telecopier: 225-926-5318

(See Next Column)

KLEINPETER & KLEINPETER—*Continued*

MEMBERS OF FIRM

Robert L. Kleinpeter
R. Loren Kleinpeter

Representative Clients: Argonaut Insurance Co.; American Indemnity Co.; Allstate Insurance Co.; Consolidated American Inc. Co.; South Carolina Insurance Co.; TransAmerica Insurance Group; St. Paul Fire & Marine Insurance Co.; Scottsdale Insurance Co.; Fireman's Fund Insurance Co.; Western Heritage Insurance Co.

For full biographical listings, see the Martindale-Hubbell Law Directory

LONG LAW FIRM, L.L.P. (AV)

Suite 800 Two United Plaza, 8550 United Plaza Boulevard, 70809-7013
Telephone: 225-922-5110
Fax: 225-922-5105
Email: longlaw.com
Washington, D.C. Office: Market Square, Suite 750, 801 Pennsylvania Avenue, N.W., 20004-2167.
Telephone: 202-737-9212.
FAX: 202-624-0659.

MEMBERS OF FIRM

Russell B. Long
C. Kris Kirkpatrick
Michael A. Patterson
Joseph E. Juban
Albert Dale Clary
David L. Guerry
C. Stokes McConnell, Jr.

ASSOCIATES

Daniel D. Holliday, III
Jennifer J. Vosburg
Tracy Averett Morganti

OF COUNSEL

Melanie Peirron Patrick

For full biographical listings, see the Martindale-Hubbell Law Directory

POWERS & WILLARD, L.L.P. (AV)

7967 Office Park Boulevard, P.O. Box 15948, 70895
Telephone: 225-928-1951
Fax: 225-929-9834

MEMBERS OF FIRM

John Dale Powers
William E. Willard

ASSOCIATES

Neil H. Mixon
Lindsey J. Leavoy
Edwin L. Hightower
Andrew P. Sellers, Jr.
Suzanne K. Sasser
Kyle C. Marionneaux

General Counsel for: Audubon Insurance Co.
Louisiana Counsel for: Hancock Bank & Trust Co.; Hertz Corp.; Ciba-Geigy Corp.; Utica Mutual Insurance Co.

For full biographical listings, see the Martindale-Hubbell Law Directory

PREIS, BERGERON & ATCHISON (AV)

450 Laurel Street, Suite 1000, P.O. Box 2786, 70821-2786
Telephone: 225-387-0707
Facsimile: 225-344-0510
Email: preisber@aol.com

Phillip W. Preis
Kirk A. Bergeron
Ashley C. Atchison
Charles M. Gordon, Jr.

For full biographical listings, see the Martindale-Hubbell Law Directory

SEALE, SMITH, ZUBER & BARNETTE (AV)

Two United Plaza, Suite 200, 8550 United Plaza Boulevard, 70809
Telephone: 225-924-1600
Telecopier: 225-924-6100
Email: SSZB@WORLDNET.ATT.NET

Armbrust Gordon Seale (1913-1989)
Robert W. Smith (1922-1989)
Donald S. Zuber
Kenneth E. Barnette
William C. Kaufman III
John W. L. Swanner
James H. Morgan III
Ronald A. Seale
Charles K. Watts
Brent E. Kinchen
Myron A. Walker, Jr.
Daniel A. Reed
Lawrence R. Anderson, Jr.
Catherine S. Nobile
Anthony J. Russo, Jr.
Richard T. Reed

ASSOCIATE

Michael P. Bienvenu

OF COUNSEL

William H. Brown

Representative Clients: Farmers Insurance Group; St. Paul Fire and Marine Insurance Company; General Motors Acceptance Corporation; Bank One, Louisiana, N.A.
Reference: Bank One, Louisiana, N.A., Baton Rouge, Louisiana.

For full biographical listings, see the Martindale-Hubbell Law Directory

WATSON, BLANCHE, WILSON & POSNER (AV)

Registered Limited Liability Partnership
505 North Boulevard, P.O. Drawer 2995, 70821-2995
Telephone: 225-387-5511
Fax: 225-387-5972

Warren O. Watson (1893-1973)
Fred A. Blanche (1898-1977)
Charles W. Wilson (1910-1981)
Harvey H. Posner
Robert L. Roland
Alton J. Reine, Jr.
Peter T. Dazzio
Felix R. Weill
Richard S. Dunn
William E. Scott, III
Michael M. Remson
P. Chauvin Wilkinson, Jr.
Randall L. Champagne
René J. Pfefferle
P. Scott Jolly

ASSOCIATES

David G. Koch
Chris J. LeBlanc
Robert W. Robison, Jr.
Michael P. Wilson

Representative Clients: Citizens Savings Associations, F.A.; Community Coffee Company, Inc.; Louisiana Hospital Association; General Health System and affiliates.

For full biographical listings, see the Martindale-Hubbell Law Directory

*COVINGTON,** St. Tammany Parish

LAW OFFICES OF WILLIAM J. DUTEL (AV)

325 North New Hampshire Street, 70433
Telephone: 504-892-6474
Fax: 504-892-7307
Email: bdutel@fastband.com
New Orleans, Louisiana Office: 2960 Energy Centre, 1100 Poydras Street.
Telephone: 504-582-2429.

William J. Dutel

OF COUNSEL

Kimberly Kammler Dutel

For full biographical listings, see the Martindale-Hubbell Law Directory

*GRETNA,** Jefferson Parish

WINDHORST, GAUDRY, RANSON, HIGGINS & GREMILLION, L.L.C. (AV)

Oakwood Corporate Center, 401 Whitney Avenue Suite 500, P.O. Box 1910, 70056
Telephone: 504-362-2466; 367-9247
Telcopier: 504-362-5938
Email: wgrhg@gs.verio.net

Thomas L. Gaudry, Jr.
Daniel A. Ranson
Daryl A. Higgins
Gregory G. Gremillion
Wade A. Langlois, III
Michael D. Peytavin

OF COUNSEL

Fritz H. Windhorst (Retired)

Steven Dow Oliver
Thomas W. Darling
David J. Dowell, Jr.
John A Leslie
Walter Patrick Maestri
B. Wesley Pitts

Reference: Hibernia National Bank.

For full biographical listings, see the Martindale-Hubbell Law Directory

KENNER, Jefferson Parish

DEMARTINI, D'AQUILA & VOLK, A PROFESSIONAL LAW CORPORATION (AV)

3329 Florida Avenue, 70065
Telephone: 504-469-6699
Fax: 504-467-1866

Roy M. D'Aquila
Jerome M. Volk, Jr.
Jeffrey A. Jones
Ellen Mullins
Robert A. Contreras

Ronald J. Vega
Paul Wegmann

OF COUNSEL

Edward J. DeMartini
Aaron F. Broussard

Representative Clients: Jefferson Guaranty Bank; Hibernia National Bank; Regions Bank; Bay Savings Bank, F.S.B.; First American Bank and Trust; Federal Deposit Insurance Corp.; Citicorp Mortgage Inc.; Litton Loan Servicing, Inc.; Eustis Mortgage Corp.

For full biographical listings, see the Martindale-Hubbell Law Directory

*LAFAYETTE,** Lafayette Parish

DAVIDSON, MEAUX, SONNIER, MCELLIGOTT & SWIFT (AV)

810 South Buchanan Street, P.O. Drawer 2908, 70502
Telephone: 318-237-1660
Fax: 318-237-3676

(See Next Column)

DAVIDSON, MEAUX, SONNIER, MCELLIGOTT & SWIFT, *Lafayette—Continued*

MEMBERS OF FIRM

James J. Davidson, Jr. (1904-1990)	John G. Swift
V. Farley Sonnier (1942-1988)	Jeffrey A. Rhoades
Richard C. Meaux, Sr.	Philip A. Fontenot
James J. Davidson, III	Kyle L. Gideon
John E. McElligott, Jr.	Theodore G. Edwards, IV
	Mark C. Andrus

ASSOCIATES

John T. Andrishok	Christopher J. Piasecki

Nicholas J. Zeringue

OF COUNSEL

Jan Whitehead Swift

General Counsel: Southwest Louisiana Electric Membership Corp., Inc.; Macro Oil Co., Inc.; Dwight W. Andrus Insurance Agency; Lafayette Airport Commission.
Local Counsel: Southern Pacific Transportation Co.
Representative Clients: Highlands Insurance Co.; Wal-Mart Stores, Inc.; USAA.

For full biographical listings, see the Martindale-Hubbell Law Directory

WAYNE A. SHULLAW (AV)

600 Jefferson Street, Fifth Floor, Suite 502, P.O. Box 4815, 70502
Telephone: 318-266-2310
Fax: 318-266-2311

For full biographical listings, see the Martindale-Hubbell Law Directory

*LAKE CHARLES,** Calcasieu Parish

THE GRAY LAW FIRM A PROFESSIONAL LAW CORPORATION (AV)

Hibernia Tower, One Lakeshore Drive, Suite 900, P.O. Box 1467, 70602-1467
Telephone: 318-494-0694
Facsimile: 318-494-0697
Email: graylaw@graylawfirm.com

Andrew J. Gray, III	Anna R. Gray
David L. Sigler	Leslie Qvale Knox

Wade Thomas Visconte

For full biographical listings, see the Martindale-Hubbell Law Directory

METAIRIE, Jefferson Parish

THE DERBES LAW FIRM, L.L.C. (AV)

3027 Ridgelake Drive, 70002
Telephone: 504-837-1230
Fax: 504-837-2214
URL: http://www.DerbesLaw.com

Albert J. Derbes, III	Albert J. Derbes, IV

Eric J. Derbes

Julia C. Spear

For full biographical listings, see the Martindale-Hubbell Law Directory

NEWMAN, MATHIS, BRADY, WAKEFIELD & SPEDALE, A PROFESSIONAL LAW CORPORATION (AV)

212 Veterans Boulevard, 70005
Telephone: 504-837-9040
Telecopier: 504-834-6452
Email: newmanmath@aol.com *URL:* http://www.nmlaw.com
Baton Rouge, Louisiana Office: 3301 North Boulevard.
Telephone: 225-343-3456.
Telecopier: 225-336-9249.
New Orleans, Louisiana Office: 3723 Canal Street.
Telephone: 504-581-2552.

Ronald H. Newman (1937-1979)	Richard L. Crawford (Resident, Baton Rouge Office)
Robert A. Mathis	Joseph E. Fick, Jr. (Resident, New Orleans Office)
John D. Brady (Resident, Baton Rouge Office)	Mark C. Landry
Robert T. Wakefield	Clay J. LeGros
Charles E. Spedale (Resident, Baton Rouge Office)	Stephen J. Broussard

Gerard O. Salassi, IV

Keith M. Frey

For full biographical listings, see the Martindale-Hubbell Law Directory

*NEW ORLEANS,** Orleans Parish

BARTON, RICHARDSON, CANSECO & WHITNEY, L.L.P. (AV)

Southern Marine & Aviation Building, 610 Poydras Street, Suite 500, 70130
Telephone: 504-528-3635
Fax: 504-525-7208
Email: scivol@aol.com

James A. Barton, III	Jose S. Canseco
David R. Richardson	John F. Whitney

OF COUNSEL

Arden J. Lea	Raymond G. Hoffman, Jr.

For full biographical listings, see the Martindale-Hubbell Law Directory

CHAFFE, MCCALL, PHILLIPS, TOLER & SARPY, L.L.P. (AV)

A Partnership including a Professional Law Corporation
2300 Energy Centre, 1100 Poydras Street, 70163-2300
Telephone: 504-585-7000
Telecopier: 504-585-7075
Cable Address: "Denegre"
Telex: (AT&T) 460122 CMPTS
Email: cmptsno%chaffe@mcimail.com *URL:* http://www.chaffe.com
Baton Rouge, Louisiana Office: 202 Two United Plaza, 8550 United Plaza Boulevard.
Telephone: 504-922-4300.
Fax: 504-922-4304.
Caracas, Venezuela Office: Edificio Exa, Piso 10, Oficina PH-10, Avenida Venezuela entre Calles EL Retiro y Alameda, El Rosal.
Telephone: 011-582-953-4136.
Fax: 011-582-953-6518.

MEMBERS OF FIRM

Corinne Ann Morrison	Charles P. Blanchard
Robert S. Rooth	Merle F. Shoughrue
Keith Eric Gisleson	James C. Young
W. Anthony Toups, III	Scott C. Barney

ASSOCIATE

Earl F. Sundmaker, III

Representative Clients: Cendant Corp.; DePuy Orthopaedics, Inc.; Federal Deposit Insurance Corp.; Federal National Mortgage Assn.; Grinnell Corp.; Lafarge Corp.; Sears, Roebuck and Co.; The Rouse Co.; U.S. Sprint Corp.; USX Corporation.

For Complete List of Firm Personnel, See General Section

For full biographical listings, see the Martindale-Hubbell Law Directory

CORRERO FISHMAN HAYGOOD PHELPS WALMSLEY & CASTEIX, L.L.P. (AV)

Bank One Center, 46th Floor, 201 St. Charles Avenue, 70170-4600
Telephone: 504-586-5252
Fax: 504-586-5250

Esmond Phelps II	James R. Swanson

Loretta G. Mince

For full biographical listings, see the Martindale-Hubbell Law Directory

LUGENBUHL, BURKE, WHEATON, PECK, RANKIN & HUBBARD, A LAW CORPORATION (AV)

27th Floor, Pan-American Life Center, 601 Poydras Street, 70130-6017
Telephone: 504-568-1990
Telefax: 504-529-7418
URL: http://www.lawla.com
Gulfport, Mississippi Office: The Markham Building, 2301 14th Street, Suite 705.
Telephone: 228-865-1490.
Fax: 228-822-2170.

Charles E. Lugenbuhl	Nathan P. Horner, Jr.
Scott R. Wheaton, Jr.	Kristopher M. Redmann
Stewart F. Peck	James B. Persons (Resident, Gulfport, Mississippi Office)
S. Frazer Rankin	Claude F. Bosworth
Ralph S. Hubbard III	Gordon P. Wilson
Stanley J. Cohn	

J. Clayton Davie, Jr.

Loree Peacock Leboeuf	Simeon Bernard Reimonenq, Jr.
David B. Sharpe	Celeste Darmstadter Elliott
Mary Sprague Langston	Kristopher T. Wilson

Representative Clients: Baker Hughes, Inc.; Bank of Louisiana; E.N. Bisso & Son, Inc.; Brown & Root U.S.A., Inc.; Budget Rent A Car Corp.; Budget Rent A Car Systems, Inc.; The Center Marine Managers, Inc.; Central Gulf Towing Co., Inc.; Chrysler Capital Corp.; Citrus Lands of Louisiana, Inc.

For full biographical listings, see the Martindale-Hubbell Law Directory

New Orleans—Continued

MARTZELL & BICKFORD (AV)

A Partnership including a Professional Corporation
338 Lafayette Street, 70130-3244
Telephone: 504-581-9065
Fax: 504-581-7635
Email: mailbox@martzellbickford.com *URL:* http://www.martzellbickford.com

John R. Martzell (P.C.)
Scott R. Bickford

Regina O. Matthews
M. Suzanne Montero
Duggan F. Ellis
Richard A. Filce
Ray L. Rhymes

LEGAL SUPPORT PERSONNEL

LITIGATION ADMINISTRATOR

Christopher H. Sherwood

PARALEGALS

Jane B. Daigle
Connie L. Cosse
Mary Wiggenhorn

FIRM ADMINISTRATOR

Stephen C. Wolf (Certified Public Accountant)

For full biographical listings, see the Martindale-Hubbell Law Directory

MCGLINCHEY STAFFORD (AV)

A Professional Limited Liability Company
643 Magazine Street, 70130-3477
Telephone: 504-586-1200
Fax: 504-596-2800
TDD: (504) 596-2728
Telex: 584327
Cable Address: "MACSTAC"
Mailing Address: P.O. Box 60643, New Orleans, Louisiana, 70160-0643
Email: @mcglinchey.com *URL:* http://www.mcglinchey.com
Dallas, Texas Office: 2777 Stemmons Freeway, Suite 925, 75207-2401.
Telephone: 214-860-9700.
Fax: 214-860-9750.
Houston, Texas Office: 2727 Allen Parkway, Suite 1900, 77019.
Telephone: 713-520-1900.
Fax: 713-520-1025.
Baton Rouge, Louisiana Office: Ninth Floor, One American Place, 70825-0001.
Telephone: 504-383-9000.
Fax: 504-343-3076.
Jackson, Mississippi Office: Suite 1200, SkyTel Centre, 200 South Lamar Street, 39201.
Telephone: 601-960-8400.
Fax: 601-960-8406.
Lake Providence, Louisiana Office: 405 Morgan Street, 71254-2691.
Telephone: 318-559-1200.
Fax: 318-559-0609.
Monroe, Louisiana Office: Dean ONB Tower, 130 Desiard Street, Suite 807, 71201.
Telephone: 318-651-0807.
Fax: 318-651-0809.

MEMBERS OF FIRM

B. Franklin Martin, III, (P.C.)
Charles R. Penot, Jr.
Constance Charles Willems
Thomas A. Roberts
Rudy J. Cerone
Stephen P. Beiser
Anthony Rollo
Kevin L. O'Dea
Craig Lewis Caesar
Richard A. Aguilar
Stephen W. Rider
R. Keith Colvin

ASSOCIATES

Lauren L. Zimmermann
Edward L. Fenasci
David Ball
David S. Landry
Stephanie M. Sisson

MEMBERS OF FIRM

Michael David Ferachi (Resident, Baton Rouge Office)
Richard A. Curry (Resident, Baton Rouge Office)
Michael H. Rubin (Resident, Baton Rouge Office)
Jennifer Lynn Davis (Resident, Houston Office)
William H. Leech, Sr. (Resident, Jackson Office)
Mark D. Herbert (Resident, Jackson Office)
J. Scott Sheehan (Resident, Houston Office)
Joel W. Mohrman (Resident, Houston Office)
Rodolfo J. Aguilar, Jr. (Resident, Baton Rouge Office)
Paul S. West (Resident, Baton Rouge Office)

(See Next Column)

ASSOCIATES

Derrick B. Carson (Resident, Houston Office)
Donald Ray Cravins, Jr (Resident, Baton Rouge Office)
Jean-Paul Perrault (Resident, Baton Rouge Office)
David E. Harrell, Jr. (Resident, Houston Office)
Claude B. Anello (Resident, Houston Office)
Danice L. McKeehan (Resident, Dallas Office)
Vincent J. Bodin (Resident, Houston Office)

For full biographical listings, see the Martindale-Hubbell Law Directory

MILLING BENSON WOODWARD L.L.P. (AV)

A Partnership including Professional Law Corporations
Suite Twenty-Three Hundred, 909 Poydras Street, 70112-1017
Telephone: 504-569-7000
Telecopier: 504-569-7001
ABA net: 15656
MCI Mail: "Milling"
Email: milling@millinglaw.com
Lafayette, Louisiana Office: 101 La Rue France, Suite 200.
Telephone: 318-232-3929.
Telecopier: 318-233-4957.
Mandeville (North Shore), Louisiana Office: 2140 8th Street.
Telephone: 504-867-9622.
Telecopier: 504-867-8364.

MEMBERS OF FIRM

Neal D. Hobson (P.C.)
Peter M. Meisner (P.C.)
F. Frank Fontenot (P.C.)
Timothy T. Roniger (P.C.)
William C. Gambel (P.C.)
Michael M. Duran (P.C.)
James K. Irvin (P.C.)
Jay Corenswet (P.C.)
Jean M. Sweeney (P.C.)
Benjamin O. Schupp (P.C.)
J. Timothy Betbeze (P.C.)

SPECIAL COUNSEL

Roger C. Linde

ASSOCIATES

Sherry L. Tew
Murphy S. Christina
Sergio J. Alarcon
Rodrick E. Anderson
Stacie M. Hollis

See General Section for list of Representative Clients.

For Complete List of Firm Personnel, See General Section

For full biographical listings, see the Martindale-Hubbell Law Directory

MOULEDOUX, BLAND, LEGRAND & BRACKETT, LLC (AV)

Poydras Center, 650 Poydras Street, Suite 2150, 70130
Telephone: 504-595-3000
Fax: 504-522-2121
Email: admin@mblb.com *URL:* http://www.mblb.com

André J. Mouledoux
Alan Guy Brackett
Georges M. Legrand
David M. Flotte

For full biographical listings, see the Martindale-Hubbell Law Directory

ODOM & DES ROCHES, LLP (AV)

A Partnership including Professional Corporations
35th Floor, Bank One Center, 201 Saint Charles Avenue, 70170-3500
Telephone: 504-522-0077
Fax: 504-522-0078
Hahira, Georgia Office: 217 West Main Street, P.O. Box 523, 31632.
Telephone: 912-794-3412.
Fax: 912-794-3544.

John Gregory Odom, PLC
Stuart E. Des Roches

OF COUNSEL

Randall S. Acree (Resident, Hahira, Georgia Office)

For full biographical listings, see the Martindale-Hubbell Law Directory

SLATER LAW FIRM, A PROFESSIONAL CORPORATION (AV)

650 Poydras Street Suite 2600, 70130-6101
Telephone: 504-523-7333
Fax: 504-528-1080
URL: http://www.slaterlawfirm.com

Benjamin R. Slater, Jr.
Kevin M. Wheeler
Benjamin R. Slater, III
Anne Elise Brown
Mark E. Van Horn
Donald J. Miester, Jr.

Michael O. Waguespack
Sarah Ney
Cory Rabin Cahn
S. Joseph Welborn

SPECIAL COUNSEL

W. Malcolm Stevenson

Representative Clients: Norfolk Southern Corporation; New Orleans Steamship Association; The Quaker Oats Company; Anheuser-Busch, Incorporated; Patterson Pump Company; Diversified Foods and Seasonings, Inc.

For full biographical listings, see the Martindale-Hubbell Law Directory

New Orleans—Continued

WAGNER & BAGOT (AV)

Suite 2660, Poydras Center, 650 Poydras Street, 70130-6105
Telephone: 504-525-2141
Telecopier: 504-523-1587
TWX: 5106017673
ELN: 62928850
"INCISIVE"

Thomas P. Henican
Dana A. Henderson

For full biographical listings, see the Martindale-Hubbell Law Directory

WARD NELSON, LLC (AV)

1539 Jackson Avenue, 6th Floor, 70130
Telephone: 504-561-5000
Fax: 504-588-1334

MEMBERS OF FIRM

Joseph R. Ward, Jr.
Craig R. Nelson
Lisa A. Condrey

ASSOCIATES

Lynn H. Frank
James Everet Brouillette

OF COUNSEL

Christina Papastavros Fay

Representative Clients: Associated Aviation Underwriters; Associated International Underwriters; Colonial Penn Insurance; Fidelity & Casualty of New York; Gulf Insurance Co.; Prudential Property and Casualty Insurance Co.; RLI Insurance Group; State Farm Fire & Casualty Co.; State Farms Mutual Automobile Insurance Co.; The Weitz Company.

For full biographical listings, see the Martindale-Hubbell Law Directory

WILSON & BOWLING (AV)

A Partnership including Professional Law Corporations
Suite 2411, Bank One Center, 201 St. Charles Avenue, 70170
Telephone: 504-586-5200
Facsimile: 504-586-5201
Email: wilsbowl@gs.net
Gulfport, Mississippi Office: 715 Markham Building, 2301 14th Street, 39501.
Telephone: 228-575-6202.
Fax: 228-864-6227.

Gordon F. Wilson, Jr., (P.L.C.)
David A. Bowling (P.L.C.)

Jeanne B. Roques
Susannah Ross Cooley
John D. Acomb

For full biographical listings, see the Martindale-Hubbell Law Directory

*SHREVEPORT,** Caddo Parish

BLANCHARD, WALKER, O'QUIN & ROBERTS, A PROFESSIONAL LAW CORPORATION (AV)

Fourteenth Floor, Premier Bank Tower, 400 Texas Street, P.O. Drawer 1126, 71101
Telephone: 318-221-6858
Fax: 318-227-2967
Email: BWOR@BWOR.com
Bossier City, Louisiana Office: 2285 Benton Road, Suite B-201.
Telephone: 318-742-9255.
Fax: 318-742-9210.

John T. Cox, Jr.
W. Michael Adams
Robert W. Johnson
Edward Keith Carter
Paul M. Adkins
A. M. Stroud, III
Pamela G. Nathan

For Complete List of Firm Personnel, See General Section

For full biographical listings, see the Martindale-Hubbell Law Directory

SLIDELL, St. Tammany Parish

PATRICK J. BERRIGAN (P.L.C.) (AV)

770 Gause Boulevard, Suite B, P.O. Box 220, 70459
Telephone: 504-641-1070
Fax: 504-641-1073
Email: pjbplc@comm.net

Patrick J. Berrigan

Jenifer B. Besh
Judith Otero
Rodney J. Lacoste, Jr.
John W. Lindner, II

OF COUNSEL

Stephen A. Duczer

For full biographical listings, see the Martindale-Hubbell Law Directory

MAINE

*AUGUSTA,** Kennebec Co.

LIPMAN & KATZ, P.A. (AV)

227 Water Street, P.O. Box 1051, 04332-1051
Telephone: 207-622-3711
Telecopier: 207-622-7415
Email: lipmankatz@ibm.net

Sumner H. Lipman
David M. Lipman
Roger J. Katz
Robert J. Stolt
Keith R. Varner
Ronald E. Colby, III
Walter F. McKee

Karen E. Lipman
Tracie L. Adamson
Gregg D. Bernstein

OF COUNSEL

Joseph B. Campbell

For full biographical listings, see the Martindale-Hubbell Law Directory

*PORTLAND,** Cumberland Co.

BURNS RAY & DELANO, PROFESSIONAL ASSOCIATION (AV)

193 Middle Street, 04101-4062
Telephone: 207-775-3581
Facsimile: 207-775-3814
Email: mailcenter@brdlaw.com

George F. Burns
David P. Ray
Arnold C. Macdonald
Mary DeLano
Elizabeth A. Burns
Carrie A. Green

OF COUNSEL

Joanne F. Cole

Representative Clients: Maine Yankee Atomic Power Company; Tractebel Power, Inc.; Hancock Lumber Co., Inc.; Jackson Laboratory; Hague International (engineering); Aetna Life & Casualty Co.; The Hartford; Great American Insurance Co.; Wausau Insurance Co.

For full biographical listings, see the Martindale-Hubbell Law Directory

MARCUS, GRYGIEL & CLEGG, P.A. (AV)

100 Middle Street, East Tower, 04101-4102
Telephone: 207-828-8000
Fax: 207-773-3210
Email: firm@mgc-law.com

George J. Marcus
Jennie L. Clegg
Marilyn E. Mistretta
Lee H. Bals

Sean P. Joyce
Barbara G. Shaw
Michael J. Gartland
Regan M. Hornney

OF COUNSEL

Stephen G. Grygiel
Andrew Jeffrey Zulieve

For full biographical listings, see the Martindale-Hubbell Law Directory

PERKINS, OLSON & PRATT, P.A. (AV)

30 Milk Street, 04112
Telephone: 207-871-7159
Fax: 207-871-0521
Email: perkinspa@aol.com *URL:* http://www.lawyers.com/perkins&perkins

Donald W. Perkins
David J. Perkins
Richard P. Olson
Neal F. Pratt

For full biographical listings, see the Martindale-Hubbell Law Directory

PETRUCCELLI & MARTIN, LLP (AV)

50 Monument Square, P.O. Box 9733, 04104-5033
Telephone: 207-775-0200
Telecopier: 207-775-2360
Email: info@petruccellimartin.com *URL:* http://www.petruccellimartin.com

MEMBERS OF FIRM

Gerald F. Petruccelli
Joel C. Martin
Michael K. Martin
James B. Haddow
Linda C. Russell

Thomas C. Bradley
Bruce A. McGlauflin

Representative Clients: Bangor Hydro-Electric Co.; Chubb Insurance Co.; Coopers & Lybrand; Cumberland Farms; General Electric Capital Corp.; Maine Medical Center; Pine Tree Telephone & Telegraph Co.; KPMG Peat Marwick; Union Mutual Fire Insurance Co.; Vermont Mutual Insurance Co.

(See Next Column)

PETRUCCELLI & MARTIN LLP—*Continued*

For full biographical listings, see the Martindale-Hubbell Law Directory

VERRILL & DANA, LLP (AV)

One Portland Square, P.O. Box 586, 04112-0586
Telephone: 207-774-4000
Fax: 207-774-7499
Email: advice@verdan.com *URL:* http://www.verdan.com
Augusta, Maine Office: 45 Memorial Circle, P.O. Box 957.
Telephone: 207-623-3889.
Fax: 207-622-3117.
Kennebunk, Maine Office: 403-404 Lafayette Center, P.O. Box 147.
Telephone: 207-985-7193.
Fax: 207-985-3957.
Washington, D.C. Office: 400 North Capitol Street, Suite 585.
Telephone: 202-624-9733.
Fax: 202-393-5218.

OF COUNSEL

Roger A. Putnam

MEMBERS OF FIRM

Michael T. Healy
Andrew M. Horton
James G. Goggin
William C. Knowles
Gene R. Libby (Resident Partner, Kennebunk Office)
Michael J. Donlan (Resident Partner, Kennebunk Office)
Seth W. Brewster

ASSOCIATES

Hope K. Creal
Janet P. Judge
Jacqueline W. Rider

Counsel for: ASCAP; Bowdoin College; Fleet Bank; Hannaford Bros. Co.; Maine Blue Cross and Blue Shield; Maine Public Service Co.; Peoples Heritage Bank; Portland Water District.

For Complete List of Firm Personnel, See General Section

For full biographical listings, see the Martindale-Hubbell Law Directory

MARYLAND

*BALTIMORE,** (Independent City)

FREISHTAT & SANDLER (AV)

Suite 1500, One Calvert Plaza, 201 E. Baltimore Street, 21202
Telephone: 410-727-7740
FAX: 410-727-7356

MEMBERS OF FIRM

David Freishtat
Paul Mark Sandler
Raymond F. Altman
Raymond Daniel Burke
William Michael Mullen
Lloyd J. Snow
Stacie F. Dubnow

Roderick R. Barnes
Jeffrey S. Rosenfeld
Thomas K. Harris

OF COUNSEL

Lynn Weinberg

For full biographical listings, see the Martindale-Hubbell Law Directory

GALLAGHER, EVELIUS & JONES, LLP (AV)

Park Charles Suite 400, 218 North Charles Street, 21201
Telephone: 410-727-7702
Facsimile: 410-468-2786
URL: http://www.gejlaw.com

MEMBERS OF FIRM

Francis X. Gallagher (1928-1972)
C. Edward Jones (1908-1999)
John C. Evelius (Retired)
Richard O. Berndt
Thomas N. Biddison, Jr.
Robert R. Kern, Jr.
Saul E. Gilstein
Thomas B. Lewis
Bonnie Abrams Travieso
Stephen A. Goldberg
Linda H. Jones
Jack C. Tranter
Leslie B. Speed
Christopher J. Fritz
David E. Raderman
Peter E. Keith
Nita L. Schultz
Michael W. Skojec
Kathryn Kelley Hoskins
Mark P. Keener
Kevin J. Davidson
Eileen M. Lunga
Lori A. Nicolle
Kenneth S. Gross
Thomas C. Dame

ASSOCIATES

Valarie K. Oulds
Margaret Stevens Jacks
Matthew W. Oakey
Rebecca A. Weaver
Michael J. Henigan
David W. Kinkopf
Paul S. Caiola
Jason W. Gaarder
M. Kirsten Andrews

(See Next Column)

LEGAL ASSISTANTS

Patricia C. Quayle
Iris T. H. Heath
Connie L. Ennis
Margaret Graff
Margo Gibson Hughes
Jonathan T. Gillis
Brenda J. Heacock
Dwayne L. Rodeheaver

Representative Clients: Roman Catholic Archdiocese of Baltimore; The Shelter Group; Mercantile-Safe Deposit and Trust Co.; Mercy Medical Center, Inc.; Caronia Corporation.

For full biographical listings, see the Martindale-Hubbell Law Directory

MCDANIEL & MARSH (AV)

118 West Mulberry Street, 21201-3606
Telephone: 410-685-3810
Telecopier: 410-685-0203

William Alden McDaniel, Jr.
Jo Bennett Marsh

For full biographical listings, see the Martindale-Hubbell Law Directory

SCANLAN, ROSEN & SHAR, LLC (AV)

26 South Street, 21202-3399
Telephone: 410-244-1155
Fax: 410-244-1157
Email: lawyers@triallaw.com *URL:* http://www.triallaw.com

Alfred L. Scanlan, Jr.
Marc Seldin Rosen
Marcus Z. Shar
Michael Stuart Warshaw

Timothy Cronin Lynch
Neil E Duke
Kristofer P. Cubello

OF COUNSEL

Colleen A. Cavanaugh
Lee H. Caplan
J. Michael McWilliams

For full biographical listings, see the Martindale-Hubbell Law Directory

WRIGHT, CONSTABLE & SKEEN, LLP (AV)

One Charles Center, 16th Floor, 100 N. Charles Street, 21201
Telephone: 410-659-1300
Telex: 710 234-2383 CALDAS
Fax: 410-659-1350

MEMBERS OF FIRM

Wm. Pepper Constable (1882-1976)
John D. Wright (1903-1976)
George W. Constable (Retired)
Read A. McCaffrey (1913-1995)
William A. Skeen (Retired)
John Brentnall Powell, Jr.
Michael J. Abromaitis
Monte Fried
James W. Constable
David W. Skeen
James D. Skeen
Douglas G. Worrall
Kenneth F. Davies
Stephen F. White
Brian S. Goodman
Frederick L. Kobb
Paul F. Evelius
Lois A. Fenner McBride
Charles J. Morton, Jr.

ASSOCIATES

Mary Alice Smolarek
Catherine H. Bellinger
Carol J. Glover
Tracey D. King
David J. Shuster
Howard S. Stevens

COUNSEL

Francis N. Iglehart, Jr.
P. McEvoy Cromwell
C. Gordon Haines

Representative Clients: Conowingo Power Co.; Weyerhaeuser Co.; Commercial Credit Corp.; Noxell Corp.; Consolidated Rail Corp.; Murray Corp.; Atlantic Mutual Insurance Co.; Sea Containers, Ltd.; Great Atlantic & Pacific Tea Co.; Tyson Foods, Inc.

For full biographical listings, see the Martindale-Hubbell Law Directory

BETHESDA, Montgomery Co.

KARP, FROSH, LAPIDUS, WIGODSKY & NORWIND, P.A. (AV)

7475 Wisconsin Avenue, Suite 800, 20814
Telephone: 301-656-2111
Fax: 301-654-7748
Email: jackgold@erols.com
Washington, D.C. Office: 1150 Connecticut Avenue, N.W., Suite 900. 20036.
Telephone: 202-822-3777.
Fax: 202-828-4130.

Ronald A. Karp
Brian E. Frosh
Lawrence S. Lapidus
Jeffrey A. Wigodsky
Edward L. Norwind
J. Philip Kessel

Jack A. Gold
Donald C. Weinberg

OF COUNSEL

Douglas R. Smith
Stanley A. First (Not admitted in MD)
Roy I. Niedermayer
Maurice I. Burstein

For full biographical listings, see the Martindale-Hubbell Law Directory

Bethesda—Continued

RIDBERG, PRESS & SHERBILL (AV)

Three Bethesda Metro Center, Suite 650, 20814
Telephone: 301-913-5770
FAX: 301-913-5769

MEMBERS OF FIRM

Michael D. Ridberg
Fredric A. Press
Raymond J. Sherbill
Norman L. Eule

ASSOCIATES

Stuart A. Schwager
Paul D. Smolinsky

For full biographical listings, see the Martindale-Hubbell Law Directory

*EASTON,** Talbot Co.

EWING, DIETZ, TURNER & KEHOE, PROFESSIONAL ASSOCIATION (AV)

16 South Washington Street, P.O. Box 1146, 21601
Telephone: 410-822-1988
Fax: 410-820-5053
URL: http://www.edtklaw.com

L. Clark Ewing (1919-1998)
Philip E. L. Dietz, Jr.
Christopher B. Kehoe
John F. Hall
Karen M. Kaludis
Stephen H. Kehoe

Sharon M. Shilling

OF COUNSEL

Henry P. Turner

References: The Talbot Bank of Easton, Maryland; St. Michaels Bank.

For full biographical listings, see the Martindale-Hubbell Law Directory

GREENBELT, Prince Georges Co.

JOSEPH, GREENWALD AND LAAKE, P.A. (AV)

Capital Office Park, 6404 Ivy Lane, Suite 400, 20770
Telephone: 301-220-2200
Telecopier: 301-220-1214

Fred R. Joseph (1943-1997)
Andrew E. Greenwald
Walter E. Laake, Jr.
Stephen A. Friedman
Burt M. Kahn
Michael D. Jackley
Steven M. Pavsner
John Shay Parker
Barbara J. Gorinson
Timothy P. O'Brien
Jay P. Holland
David L. Bulitt
Timothy F. Maloney

Jerry D Miller
David Samuel Coaxum
Timothy S. Mitchell
Marc Eric Pasekoff
Dominique S. Johnson

For full biographical listings, see the Martindale-Hubbell Law Directory

RIVERDALE, Prince Georges Co.

MEYERS, BILLINGSLEY, RODBELL & ROSENBAUM, P.A. (AV)

Suite 400 Berkshire Building, 6801 Kenilworth Avenue, 20737-1385
Telephone: 301-699-5800
Fax: 301-779-5746
Email: mbrrlaw@martindalemail.com
Annapolis, Maryland Office: 95 Cathedral Street, Suite 100, 21401.
Telephone: 410-267-6670.
Fax: 410-267-8222.

William V. Meyers
Lance W. Billingsley
Paul B. Rodbell
Robert H. Rosenbaum
Russell E. Warfel
Linda C. Carter
Joseph B. Chazen
Michele LaRocca
Paul A. Turkheimer
David A. Carter

Frederick Stichnoth
Bud Stephen Tayman
M. Andree Green
Gina Marie Smith
Mindy Sue Kursban
M. Evan Meyers
Douglas C. Meister
David J. Martin

Reference: First National Bank of Maryland.

For full biographical listings, see the Martindale-Hubbell Law Directory

*ROCKVILLE,** Montgomery Co.

ANDERSON & QUINN (AV)

The Adams Law Center, 25 Wood Lane, 20850
Telephone: 301-762-3303
Fax: 301-762-3776
Email: rscanlon@andersonquinn.com

(See Next Column)

MEMBERS OF FIRM

Charles C. Collins (1900-1973)
Robert E. Anderson (Retired)
Francis X. Quinn
Donald P. Maiberger
Robert P. Scanlon
John A. Rego
Alice Kelley Scanlon

ASSOCIATES

Kerry S. McGeever
Timothy J. Mulreany
Todd P. Maiberger
Jennifer D. Burke
Marc N. Steren

Representative Clients: C & P Telephone; Allstate Insurance Co.; State Farm Mutual Automobile Insurance Co.; Liberty Mutual Insurance Co.; American International Adjustment Co.; Marriott Corp.

For full biographical listings, see the Martindale-Hubbell Law Directory

BARKLEY & KENNEDY, CHARTERED (AV)

Suite 1407, 51 Monroe Street, 20850
Telephone: 301-251-6600
FAX: 301-762-2606
Email: barkenlaw@erols.com *URL:* http://www.lawyers.com/barkenlaw

Brian E. Barkley
Daniel M. Kennedy, III

For full biographical listings, see the Martindale-Hubbell Law Directory

GARZA, REGAN & ROSENBLATT, P.C. (AV)

Eighteenth Floor One Metro Square 51 Monroe Street, 20850
Telephone: 301-340-8200
Fax: 301-294-6159
URL: http://www.garzanet.com
Greenbelt, Maryland Office: 6411 Ivy Lane, Suite 116.

Lawrence F. Regan, Jr.
Richard B. Rosenblatt

Linda M. Dorney

Representative Clients: Capital Bank; F & M Bank Allegiance; Mego Mortgage; Nova Mortgage.

For full biographical listings, see the Martindale-Hubbell Law Directory

HOFFMAN & LYONS, P.C. (AV)

Jackson Place, 966 Hungerford Drive, Suite 22, 20850-1714
Telephone: 301-838-9100
Telecopier: 301-838-9112
URL: http://www.lawyers.com/hoffmanlyonslaw

Joel I. Hoffman
Ronald E. Lyons

For full biographical listings, see the Martindale-Hubbell Law Directory

KING & ATTRIDGE (AV)

39 West Montgomery Avenue, 20850-4210
Telephone: 301-279-0780
Facsimile: 301-279-2988
URL: http://www.lawyers.com/king&attridgelaw

MEMBERS OF FIRM

John A. King
Patrick James Attridge

ASSOCIATES

Deirdre R. Horton
Kenneth D. Smith

For full biographical listings, see the Martindale-Hubbell Law Directory

STEIN, SPERLING, BENNETT, DE JONG, DRISCOLL, GREENFEIG & METRO, P.C. (AV)

25 West Middle Lane, 20850-2204
Telephone: 301-340-2020; 800-435-5230
Telecopier: 301-340-8217
Email: lawfirm@steinsperling.com
Falls Church, Virginia Office: 6245 Leesburg Pike, Suite 140, 22044.
Telephone: 703-237-0500.
Telecopier: 703-534-2899.

Millard S. Bennett
David C. Driscoll, Jr.
Jeffrey M. Schwaber

Jeffrey D. Goldstein
David W. Lease
Marc J. Smith
Debra Sue Grimes

For Complete List of Firm Personnel, See General Section

For full biographical listings, see the Martindale-Hubbell Law Directory

SILVER SPRING, Montgomery Co.

COGGINS, HARMAN & HEWITT (AV)

A Partnership of Professional Corporations
8905 Fairview Road, Suite 600, 20910
Telephone: 301-587-2880
Facsimile: 301-495-4990
Email: CHHlaw587@aol.com
Washington, D.C. Office: Suite 330, G Street Lobby, 655 15th Street, N.W.
Falls Church, Virginia Office: 254 North Washington Street.

William N. Coggins
John H. Harman
William E. Hewitt
John F. Davis

OF COUNSEL

Dale E. Duncan (Not admitted in MD)

For full biographical listings, see the Martindale-Hubbell Law Directory

LINOWES AND BLOCHER LLP (AV)

Suite 1000, 1010 Wayne Avenue, 20910-5600
Telephone: 301-588-8580
Telecopier: 301-495-9044
TTY/TDD: 301-588-3380
Email: inbox@linowes-law.com *URL:* http://www.linowes-law.com
Washington, D.C. Office: Suite 302, 1150 17th Street, N.W.
Telephone: 202-293-8510.
Telecopier: 202-293-8513.
Greenbelt, Maryland Office: Suite 202, 6411 Ivy Lane.
Telephone: 301-982-3382.
Telecopier: 301-982-0595.
Annapolis, Maryland Office: 145 Main Street.
Telephone: 410-268-0881.
Telecopier: 301-261-2603.
Frederick, Maryland Office: 228 West Patrick Street.
Telephone: 301-695-0244.
Telecopier: 301-663-6656.
Columbia, Maryland Office: Suite B215, 10015 Old Columbia Road.
Telephone: 410-312-5457.
Fax: 410-290-5285.

MEMBERS OF FIRM

Walter S. B. Childs (Resident Partner, Annapolis, Maryland office)
Gerald W. Heller
Robert C. Park, Jr.

ASSOCIATES

Jessica N. Drexler
James E. Gilbert

For Complete List of Firm Personnel, See General Section

For full biographical listings, see the Martindale-Hubbell Law Directory

MASSACHUSETTS

ACTON, Middlesex Co.

WILSON & ORCUTT, P.C. (AV)

201 Great Road, 01720
Telephone: 978-264-4770
Telecopier: 978-263-7142
Email: wilcutt@wilsonorcutt.com *URL:* http://www.wilsonorcutt.com

MEMBER OF FIRM

Daniel B. Greenberg

ASSOCIATE

Mark Burrell

For full biographical listings, see the Martindale-Hubbell Law Directory

*BOSTON,** Suffolk Co.

ADKINS & KELSTON, P.C. (AV)

90 Canal Street, 02114
Telephone: 617-367-1040
Fax: 617-742-8280
Email: a&k@sswg.com

David L. Kelston
Jason B. Adkins

Noah R. Rosmarin
Paula Isola

For full biographical listings, see the Martindale-Hubbell Law Directory

CRAIG AND MACAULEY, PROFESSIONAL CORPORATION (AV)

Federal Reserve Plaza, 600 Atlantic Avenue, 02210-2211
Telephone: 617-367-9500
Telecopier: 617-742-1788; 617-248-0886
URL: http://prospex.com/craig-macauley/

(See Next Column)

William F. Macauley
A. Van C. Lanckton
Richard E. Quinby
Stephen Wald
William R. Moorman, Jr.
Martin P. Desmery
Christopher J. Panos

For Complete List of Firm Personnel, See General Section

For full biographical listings, see the Martindale-Hubbell Law Directory

DANIELS LAW OFFICES, P.C. (AV)

One Center Plaza, 02108-1801
Telephone: 617-227-7300
Facsimile: 617-227-9643
Email: dlopc.com *URL:* http://www.dlopc.com

Richard S. Daniels, Jr.

Peter Dauksewicz
Karen J. Wisniowski
Kenneth W. Luke
Lynn M. Flury

For full biographical listings, see the Martindale-Hubbell Law Directory

HINCKLEY, ALLEN & SNYDER LLP (AV)

28 State Street, 30th Floor, 02109-1775
Telephone: 617-345-9000
Email: firm@haslaw.com *URL:* http://www.haslaw.com
Providence, Rhode Island Office: 1500 Fleet Center.
Telephone: 401-274-2000.
Fax: 401-277-9600. URL: http://www.hawlaw.com.

MEMBERS OF FIRM

David D. Barricelli (Not admitted in MA)
E. Jerome Batty (Not admitted in MA)
Jonathan Bell
Leon C. Boghossian III
Paul Bork
Stephen J. Carlotti (Not admitted in MA)
David Barry Connolly
Michael J. Connolly
Robert Corrente
Michael P. DeFanti
Eric F. Eisenberg
Malcolm Farmer, III
Margaret D. Farrell (Not admitted in MA)
Hugh J. Gorman, III
Gerard R. Goulet
William R. Grimm
Paul A. Hedstrom
Richard L. E. Jocelyn (Not admitted in MA)
Joel Lewin
Sandra Matrone Mack (Not admitted in MA)
Matthew T. Marcello, III (Not admitted in MA)
Frederick P. McClure
Paul F. O'Donnell, III
H. Peter Olsen (Not admitted in MA)
Julianne Palumbo
John J. Pendergast, III (Not admitted in MA)
Gerald J. Petros
Jeremy Ritzenberg
Charles E. Schaub, Jr.
Douglas F. Seaver
Herman Snyder
David R. Sullivan
Robert F. Sylvia
Howard E. Walker (Not admitted in MA)
Richard D. Wayne
John R. Allen (Retired)
Richard W. Billings (Retired)
Thomas J. Hogan (Retired)
Jacques V. Hopkins (Retired)
James A. Jackson (Retired)
James E. Keeley (Retired)
Robert F. Pickard (Retired)
Robert W. Shadd (Retired)
Richard F. Staples (Retired)
Edwin G. Torrance (Retired)

ASSOCIATES

Jessica M. Bettencourt (Not admitted in MA)
Mark Bianchi
Charles D. Blackman
Alexandra K. Callam
Brent R. Canning (Not admitted in MA)
Jane E. Cohen
Andrew D. Cummings
June E. Daniel (Not admitted in MA)
Kim Herman Goslant
Gloria Maria Gutierrez
Kelley Jordan-Price
Catherine S. Kim
Christopher W. Morog
Elena B. Olson
Timothy J. Perry
Michael J. Pisaturo
Leah A. Rochwarg
Lawrence W. Vernaglia
Joseph D. Whelan (Not admitted in MA)

OF COUNSEL

Willard R. Pope
Bentley Tobin
Joachim A. Weissfeld (Not admitted in MA)

For Complete List of Firm Personnel, See General Section

For full biographical listings, see the Martindale-Hubbell Law Directory

MENARD, MURPHY & WALSH LLP (AV)

One Financial Center, 02111
Telephone: 617-832-2500
Telecopier: 617-832-2550
Email: mmw@mmwlaw.com
Washington, D.C. Office: Farragut Park, 910 17th Street, NW, Suite 800, 20006.
Telephone: 202-293-3500.
Telecopier: 202-293-3596.

(See Next Column)

MENARD, MURPHY & WALSH LLP, *Boston—Continued*

Arthur P. Menard
Paul J. Murphy
Joseph H. Walsh
John E. Coyne
John S. Leonard

COUNSEL

Theodore E. Daiber

ASSOCIATES

Kevin G. Mahoney
Kevin P. Sweeney
Robert S. Steinberg

For full biographical listings, see the Martindale-Hubbell Law Directory

ROACH & CARPENTER, P.C. (AV)

24 School Street, 02108-5513
Telephone: 617-720-1800
Telefax: 617-720-0720
Email: lawyer@rc-law.com

Christine M. Roach
M. Ellen Carpenter
Alison L. Berman
Eric A. Howard

OF COUNSEL

Scott P. Lopez

For full biographical listings, see the Martindale-Hubbell Law Directory

SMITH & DUGGAN LLP (AV)

Two Center Plaza, 02108-1906
Telephone: 617-248-1900
Fax: 617-248-9320

MEMBERS OF FIRM

Scott A. Smith
Christopher A. Duggan
Garrick F. Cole
Thomas G. Cooper
H. Reed Witherby
Mark B. Rees

OF COUNSEL

John B. Savoca
Walter M. Foster
Paul W. Johnson
Thomas D. Herman

ASSOCIATES

Matthew J. Walko
Barbara E. Schultz
John J. Barrett, III
Kristen M. DeAngelo
Judith E. Michelman

For full biographical listings, see the Martindale-Hubbell Law Directory

SWARTZ & SWARTZ (AV)

10 Marshall Street, 02108
Telephone: 617-742-1900
Fax: 617-367-7193
Email: Attorney@Swartzlaw.com *URL:* http://www.Swartzlaw.com

Edward M. Swartz
Alan L. Cantor
Joseph A. Swartz
Victor A. Denaro
Joan E. Swartz
James A. Swartz
David P. Angueira
Jason Mark
Lisa V. Kaprielian

OF COUNSEL

Fredric A. Swartz

For full biographical listings, see the Martindale-Hubbell Law Directory

FRAMINGHAM, Middlesex Co.

DOMESTICO & BARRY (AV)

The Meadows, 161 Worcester Road, 01701
Telephone: 508-626-9000
Fax: 508-626-9001
Email: DandBLaw@aol.com

MEMBERS OF FIRM

Charles J. Domestico
Susan Moran-Barry
James A. Kobe

For full biographical listings, see the Martindale-Hubbell Law Directory

*SPRINGFIELD,** Hampden Co.

GOLD & VANARIA, P.C. (AV)

BankBoston Building, 1350 Main Street, Suite 1400, 01103-1627
Telephone: 413-747-7700
Fax: 413-747-9650
Email: govancoll@aol.com

Jerome S. Gold
Alan J. Vanaria

David A. Lavenburg
Kevin M. Brown

References: Norwest Bank Iowa, N.A. Card Services Division; Baystate Medical Center; Springfield Institution for Savings.

For full biographical listings, see the Martindale-Hubbell Law Directory

KAMBERG, BERMAN, P.C. (AV)

One Financial Plaza, 1350 Main Street, 01103-1628
Telephone: 413-781-1300
Facsimile: 413-732-0860
ABA/net: KAMBERGB
Email: kamberg@kamberg.com *URL:* http://www.kamberg.com

Abraham Kamberg (1895-1981)
Eugene B. Berman
Kerry David Strayer

References: Fleet Bank of Massachusetts, N.A.; Bank Boston/Springfield.

For full biographical listings, see the Martindale-Hubbell Law Directory

ROBINSON DONOVAN MADDEN & BARRY, P.C. (AV)

Suite 1600, Tower Square, 1500 Main Street, 01115-5609
Telephone: 413-732-2301
Fax: 413-785-4658
Email: service@robinson-donovan.com *URL:* http://www.robinson-donovan.com

Homans Robinson (1894-1973)
Lawrence M. Sinclair (1942-1986)
Milton J. Donovan (1906-1995)

RETIRED

John H. Madden, Jr.
Edward J. Barry
Richard S. Milstein

OF COUNSEL

Victor Rosenberg

SENIOR COUNSEL

Jonathan P. Rice

Gordon H. Wentworth
James H. Tourtelotte
Ronald C. Kidd
Jeffrey W. Roberts
Jeffrey L. McCormick
James F. Martin
Robert P. Cunningham
John C. Sikorski
Nancy Frankel Pelletier
Paul S. Weinberg
Frederica H. McCarthy
Matthew J. King
Neva Kaufman Rohan
Douglas F. Boyd
James K. Bodurtha
Keith A. Minoff
Patricia M. Rapinchuk
Kimberly Davis Crear

E. Paul Amata
Lisa A. Bongiovi (Not admitted in MA)
Edward J. Carroll, III
James D. Chadwell
John E. Garber
Patrick J. Markey
Carla W. Newton
Betsy Macmillan Stevens

Representative Clients: BankBoston, N.A.; United Cooperative Bank; Fleet National Bank; CNA; Commercial Union Insurance Co.; Hanover Insurance Group.

For full biographical listings, see the Martindale-Hubbell Law Directory

*WORCESTER,** Worcester Co.

MOUNTAIN, DEARBORN & WHITING LLP (AV)

370 Main Street, 01608
Telephone: 508-756-2423
Fax: 508-755-6640

MEMBERS OF FIRM

Alfred N. Whiting (1920-1989)
Thomas R. Mountain
Richard W. Dearborn
Samuel R. DeSimone
Henry W. Beth
Stuart A. Hammer
Francis J. Russell
Dale R. Harger
Mark W. Bloom
Donald J. O'Neil
Lawrence S. Delaney
Ann K. Molloy
Lisa D. Tingue

For full biographical listings, see the Martindale-Hubbell Law Directory

MICHIGAN

*ANN ARBOR,** Washtenaw Co.

BUTZEL LONG, A PROFESSIONAL CORPORATION (AV)

Suite 300, 350 South Main Street, 48104-2131
Telephone: 313-995-3110
Telecopier: 313-995-1777
Email: melnick@butzel.com *URL:* http://www.butzel.com
Detroit, Michigan Office: Suite 900, 150 West Jefferson.
Telephone: 313-225-7000.
Telecopier: 313-225-7080.
Birmingham, Michigan Office: Suite 200, 32270 Telegraph Road.
Telephone: 810-258-1616.
Telecopier: 810-258-1439.
Okemos, Michigan Office: Suite 300, 2127 University Park Drive.
Telephone: 517-372-6622.
Telecopier: 372-6672.

(See Next Column)

Bloomfield Hills—Continued

BEIER HOWLETT, PROFESSIONAL CORPORATION (AV)

200 East Long Lake Road, Suite 110, 48304-2361
Telephone: 248-645-9400
Fax: 248-645-9344
URL: http://www.beierhowlett.com

James L. Howlett
Daniel C. Devine
Lawrence R. Ternan
Stephen W. Jones
Frank S. Galgan
Kenneth J. Sorensen
Thomas J. Trenta
Mark W. Hafeli
Timothy J. Currier
Mary T. Schmitt Smith
Joseph F. Yamin
John D. Staran
Phyllis Aiuto Zimmerman
P. Daniel Christ
Lauren M. Underwood

Elizabeth A. Barrett Bonner
Mary M. Kucharek
Richard A. Joslin, Jr.
Michael C. Gibbons
Jon M. Midtgard
Paul L. Nystrom
Genevieve Dwaihy Hopkins
Jeffrey S. Kragt

OF COUNSEL

Dean G. Beier
Robert G. Waddell
Catherine J. Hulbert
Thomas V. Trainer

Representative Clients: BayCast, Inc.; C.J.Edwards Co., Inc; Magline Inc.; Industrial Experimental & Manufacturing Co., Inc.; A.M.Castle, Inc.; Flagstar Bank; Havenwyck Hospital; Magline, Inc.; MAC Valves, Inc.; Dimensional Control System, Inc.

For full biographical listings, see the Martindale-Hubbell Law Directory

COLOMBO AND COLOMBO, P.C. (AV)

1701 N. Woodward Avenue Suite 50, P.O. Box 2028, 48303-2028
Telephone: 248-645-9300
Facsimile: 248-645-5418
Email: C&C@Colombopc.com

Louis J. Colombo
Louis J. Colombo, Jr. (1911-1979)
Frederick Colombo
Charles A. LeFevre
John P. Hartwig
Lawrence F. Raniszeski
Robert Y. Weller, II
Michael J. O'Shaughnessy

Patrick J. Ennis
Michael J. Weikert

OF COUNSEL

Russell E. Knister
David J. Wellman
James H. Hudnut
Peter Leto (P.C.)

For full biographical listings, see the Martindale-Hubbell Law Directory

DAWDA, MANN, MULCAHY & SADLER, P.L.C. (AV)

1533 North Woodward Avenue Suite 200, 48304-2815
Telephone: 248-642-3700
Fax: 248-642-7791
Email: EMail@DMMS.Com

Suanne Tiberio Trimmer
Susan J. Sadler
Tyler D. Tennent
Sherwin E. Zamler
John Mucha, III
Keith James

Maureen B. Connaughton
John Gerald Gleeson, Jr.

Representative Clients: AEGON USA Realty Advisors, Inc.; AMB Property, LP; Cargill, Inc.; CB Commercial Real Estate; City Management; Ford Motor Company; Home Depot U.S.A., Inc.; Ladbroke Racing Corp.; Pep Boys; Wal-Mart Stores, Inc.

For full biographical listings, see the Martindale-Hubbell Law Directory

FEDERLEIN & KERANEN, P.C. (AV)

6895 Telegraph Road, 48301
Telephone: 248-647-9653
Fax: 248-647-9683
Email: firm@fk-law.com *URL:* http://www.fk-law.com
Detroit, Michigan Office: 407 East Fort, Suite 350.
Telephone: 313-965-6090.
Marquette, Michigan Office: 122 West Spring Street.
Telephone: 906-225-1770.
Fax: 906-225-1764.
Sault Ste. Marie, Michigan Office: 204 East Spruce Street.
Telephone: 906-635-6286.
Fax: 906-635-5390.

Walter J. Federlein
Thomas M. Keranen

Frederick F. Butters
Maria J. Bernard (Resident, Detroit Office)
Peter J. Cavanaugh
J. Christian Hauser (Resident, Detroit Office)
Gary Quesada
Jeffrey Michael Gallant

For full biographical listings, see the Martindale-Hubbell Law Directory

ROBERT HARRISON & ASSOCIATES (AV)

Bloomfield Office Pavilion, 2550 Telegraph Road, Suite 275, 48302
Telephone: 248-253-1800
Fax: 248-253-9446
URL: http://www.lawyers.com/harrison&associates

Robert S. Harrison

ASSOCIATES

Michael J. Rex
Michael James Harrison
Rachel M. Margules

References: Comerica Bank, Southfield; Huntington Banks of Michigan, W. Bloomfield.

For full biographical listings, see the Martindale-Hubbell Law Directory

HERTZ, SCHRAM & SARETSKY, P.C. (AV)

1760 South Telegraph Road, Suite 300, 48302
Telephone: 248-335-5000
Fax: 248-335-3346
Email: lawhss@aol.com *URL:* http://www.legalleaders.com

Bradley J. Schram
Howard Hertz
Gary M. Saretsky
Robert S. Hertzberg
Victor M. Norris
Steve J. Weiss
Robert Paul Geller
Walter J. Piszczatowski
Jeffrey A. Robbins
Mark L. Kowalsky

Dana A. Donohue
Miles D. Hart
Karen A. Gould
Paul K. Villarruel
Bradford T. Yaker
Michael F. Jacobson
Michael I. Zousmer
Brian Witus
Eva T. Cantarella
Eric Andrew Michaels

COUNSEL

Richard P. Zipser
Lisa M. Kavalhuna (Not admitted in MI)
James W. Burdick

OF COUNSEL

David L. Steinberg
Albert L. Holtz
Elmer L. Roller
Robert A. Canner
Harvey D. Geller (1928-1989)

For full biographical listings, see the Martindale-Hubbell Law Directory

HOWARD & HOWARD ATTORNEYS, P.C. (AV)

The Pinehurst Office Center, Suite 101, 1400 North Woodward Avenue, 48304-2855
Telephone: 248-645-1483
Telecopier: 248-645-1568
Kalamazoo, Michigan Office: The Michigan Building, Suite 200, 100 Portage Street.
Telephone: 616-382-1483.
Telecopier: 616-382-1568.
Lansing, Michigan Office: The Phoenix Building, Suite 500, 222 Washington Square, North.
Telephone: 517-485-1483.
Telecopier: 517-485-1568.
Peoria, Illinois Office: One Technology Plaza, Suite 600, 211 Fulton Street.
Telephone: 309-672-1483.
Telecopier: 309-672-1568.

Philip T. Carter
Carlene A. Caudill
Anthony P. Cho
Ronald R. Cook
Gregory L. Epstein
Kirkland W. Garey
Melanye K. Johnson
Douglas R. Kelly
Jon H. Kingsepp
Steven C. Kohl
David B. Lipski
Patrick M. McCarthy
Rhonda L. McCoy-Pfau
C. Douglas Moran
Bruce N. Moss
Mahesh K. Nayak
Brad A. Rayle
Jon Robert Steiger
Donald F. Tucker
Thomas H. Walters
James C. Wickens
Marla Gottlieb Zwas

Representative Clients: For Representative Client list, see General Practice, Bloomfield Hills, MI.

For Complete List of Firm Personnel, See General Section

For full biographical listings, see the Martindale-Hubbell Law Directory

PROVIZER & PHILLIPS, P.C. (AV)

6785 Telegraph Road, Suite 400, 48301
Telephone: 248-642-0444
Facsimile: 248-642-6661
Toll Free: 1-800-288-9080
URL: http://www.lawyers.com/provizer&phillips

Harold M. Provizer
Randall E. Phillips
Marilyn A. Madorsky
Noel F. Beck
Mark S. Baumkel

(See Next Column)

BUTZEL LONG A PROFESSIONAL CORPORATION—*Continued*

Grosse Pointe Farms, Michigan Office: Suite 260, 21 Kercheval.
Telephone: 313-886-5446.
Telecopier: 313-886-2114.
Boca Raton, Florida Office: Suite 411, 1200 North Federal Highway.
Telephone: 561-368-2151.
Telecopier: 561-368-4668.
Palm Beach Gardens, Florida Office: Suite 227, 11382 Prosperity Farms Road.
Telephone: 561-625-4442.
Telecopier: 561-625-6901.
Naples, Florida Office: Suite 705, 801 Laurel Oak Drive.
Telephone: 941-597-4500.
Telecopier: 941-597-5623.

John Henry Dudley, Jr.
Abba I. Friedman (Resident)
James E. Stewart (Resident)
Marissa W. Pollick (Resident)
Leonard M. Niehoff (Resident)
J. Michael Huget (Resident)

John C. Blattner (Resident)
Pamela M. Zauel

For full biographical listings, see the Martindale-Hubbell Law Directory

HOOPER, HATHAWAY, PRICE, BEUCHE & WALLACE (AV)

126 South Main Street, 48104
Telephone: 313-662-4426
Fax: 313-662-9559
Email: hhpbw@voyager.net

James R. Beuche
Bruce T. Wallace
Charles W. Borgsdorf
Anthony P. Patti
Angela L. Jackson
Kurtis R. Dumaw

Representative Clients: Avfuel Corporation; Bank of Ann Arbor; Castrol North America; Chem-Trend Incorporated; Ervin Industries, Inc.; First Martin Corporation; Glacier Hills, Inc.; Prestolite Electric, Inc.; Southern States Cooperative; E.B. Eddy Forest Products, Ltd.

For Complete List of Firm Personnel, See General Section

For full biographical listings, see the Martindale-Hubbell Law Directory

MILLER, CANFIELD, PADDOCK AND STONE, P.L.C. (AV)

A Professional Limited Liability Company
Founded in 1852 by Sidney Davy Miller
101 North Main Street, Seventh Floor, 48104-1400
Telephone: 734-663-2445
Fax: 734-747-7147
URL: http://www.millercanfield.com
Detroit, Michigan Office: 150 West Jefferson, Suite 2500, 48226-4415.
Telephone: 313-963-6420.
Fax: 313-496-7500.
Cable Address: "Stem Detroit."
Troy, Michigan Office: 840 West Long Lake Road, Suite 200, 48098.
Telephone: 248-879-2000.
Fax: 248-879-2001.
Grand Rapids, Michigan Office: 99 Monroe, N.W., Suite 1200, 49503-2639.
Telephone: 616-454-8656.
Fax: 616-776-6322.
Howell, Michigan Office: 121 South Barnard Street, Suite 4, 48843-2305.
Telephone: 517-546-7600.
Telecopier: 517-546-6974.
Kalamazoo, Michigan Office: 444 West Michigan Avenue, 49007-3752.
Telephone: 616-381-7030.
Fax: 616-382-0244.
Lansing, Michigan Office: One Michigan Avenue, Suite 900, 48933-1609.
Telephone: 517-487-2070.
Fax: 517-374-6304.
Monroe, Michigan Office: 214 East Elm Avenue, Suite 100, 48162-2682.
Telephone: 734-243-2000.
Fax: 734-243-0901.
Washington, D.C. Office: 1900 K Street, N.W., Suite 1150. 20006.
Telephone: 202-429-5575; 785-0600.
Fax: 202-331-1118; 785-1234.
Pensacola, Florida Office: 25 West Cedar, 32501.
Telephone: 850-469-1088.
Fax: 850-432-0677.
New York, New York Office: 1450 Broadway, 41st Floor, 10018.
Telephone: 212-704-4400.
Fax: 212-704-4410.
Gdynia, Poland Office: UL. Slaska 21, 81-319.
Telephone: 011-485-831-2808.
Fax: 011-48-58-628 6411.
Warsaw, Poland Office: UL. Nowogrodzkall, 5th Floor, 00-513.
Telephone: 011-4822 529 0200.
Fax: 011-4822 529 0201.
Katowice, Poland Office: UL. Francuska 35/37, 40-027.
Telephone: 011 (48-32) 757-2414.
Fax: 011 (48-32) 757-2483.

(See Next Column)

PRINCIPALS OF FIRM

Robert E. Gilbert
Gregory L. Curtner
Marta A. Manildi

Representative Firm Clients: Chrysler Corporation; Comerica, Incorporated; City of Detroit, Michigan; Detroit Tigers, Inc.; First of Michigan; Ford Motor Company; Ford Motor Credit Company; Great Lakes Bancorp; Henry Ford Hospital; INVETECH Company.

For Complete List of Firm Personnel, See General Section

For full biographical listings, see the Martindale-Hubbell Law Directory

BIRMINGHAM, Oakland Co.

BUTZEL LONG, A PROFESSIONAL CORPORATION (AV)

Suite 200, 32270 Telegraph Road, 48025
Telephone: 810-258-1616
Telecopier: 810-258-1439
Email: melnick@butzel.com *URL:* http://www.butzel.com
Detroit, Michigan Office: Suite 900, 150 West Jefferson.
Telephone: 313-225-7000.
Telecopier: 313-225-7080.
Okemos, Michigan Office: Suite 300, 2127 University Park Drive.
Telephone: 517-372-6622.
Telecopier: 517-372-6672.
Ann Arbor, Michigan Office: Suite 300, 350 South Main Street.
Telephone: 313-995-3110.
Telecopier: 313-995-1777.
Grosse Pointe Farms, Michigan Office: Suite 260, 21 Kercheval.
Telephone: 313-886-5446.
Telecopier: 313-886-2114.
Boca Raton, Florida Office: Suite 411, 1200 North Federal Highway.
Telephone: 561-368-2151.
Telecopier: 561-368-4668.
Palm Beach Gardens, Florida Office: Suite 227, 11382 Prosperity Farms Road.
Telephone: 561-625-4442.
Telecopier: 561-625-6901.
Naples, Florida Office: Suite 705, 801 Laurel Oak Drive.
Telephone: 941-597-4500.
Telecopier: 941-597-5623.

T. Gordon Scupholm II (Resident)
Thomas B. Radom (Resident)
Edward M. Kalinka (Resident)
Gordon J. Walker (Resident)
Alan S. Levine (Resident)
Eric J. Flessland (Resident)
Patrick A. Karbowski (Resident)
Ronald E. Reynolds (Resident)
Susan Klein Friedlaender (Resident)

Todd M. Fink (Resident)
Norman A. Yatooma (Resident)

For full biographical listings, see the Martindale-Hubbell Law Directory

HYMAN LIPPITT, P.C. (AV)

185 Oakland Avenue, Suite 300, 48009
Telephone: 248-646-8292
Facsimile: 248-646-8375
Email: hymalipp@tir.com

J. Leonard Hyman
Norman L. Lippitt
Douglas A. Hyman
Brian D. O'Keefe
H. Joel Newman
Nazli G. Sater
Kenneth F. Neuman
Terry S. Givens
Paul J. Fischer
John A. Sellers
Robert H. Lippitt
Roger L. Myers
Sally A. Rutledge
Joseph Pia
John P. Gonway
Leif K. Anderson
Jennifer S. Gold
Julie Lyons Kosovec
Dawn S. Spratley
Michael T. Price

For full biographical listings, see the Martindale-Hubbell Law Directory

BLOOMFIELD HILLS, Oakland Co.

ADKISON, NEED, GREEN & ALLEN (AV)

1533 North Woodward Avenue, Suite 210, 48304
Telephone: 248-540-7400
Fax: 248-540-7401
URL: http://www.adkisonneed.com

MEMBERS OF FIRM

Phillip G. Adkison
Gregory K. Need
Kelly A. Allen

ASSOCIATES

Miriam Blanks-Smart
Kevin M. Chudler

For Complete List of Firm Personnel, See General Section

For full biographical listings, see the Martindale-Hubbell Law Directory

PROVIZER & PHILLIPS P.C.—*Continued*

Constance S. Hall | Donald J. Parthum, Jr.

For full biographical listings, see the Martindale-Hubbell Law Directory

*DETROIT,** Wayne Co.

BUTZEL LONG, A PROFESSIONAL CORPORATION (AV)

Suite 900, 150 West Jefferson, 48226
Telephone: 313-225-7000
Telecopier: 313-225-7080
Email: melnick@butzel.com *URL:* http://www.butzel.com
Birmingham, Michigan Office: Suite 200, 32270 Telegraph Road.
Telephone: 810-258-1616.
Telecopier: 810-258-1439.
Okemos, Michigan Office: Suite 300, 2127 University Park Drive.
Telephone: 517-372-6622.
Telecopier: 517-372-6672.
Ann Arbor, Michigan Office: Suite 300, 350 South Main Street.
Telephone: 313-995-3110.
Telecopier: 313-995-1777.
Grosse Pointe Farms, Michigan Office: Suite 260, 21 Kercheval.
Telephone: 313-886-5446.
Telecopier: 313-886-2114.
Boca Raton, Florida Office: Suite 411, 1200 North Federal Highway.
Telephone: 561-368-2151.
Telecopier: 561-368-4668.
Palm Beach Gardens, Florida Office: Suite 227, 11382 Prosperity Farms Road.
Telephone: 561-625-4442.
Telecopier: 561-625-6901.
Naples, Florida Office: Suite 705, 801 Laurel Oak Drive.
Telephone: 941-597-4500.
Telecopier: 941-597-5623.

John Henry Dudley, Jr.
Richard E. Rassel
Abba I. Friedman (Ann Arbor)
Edward M. Kronk
Philip J. Kessler
Donald B. Miller
Dennis B. Schultz
Daniel P. Malone
Keefe A. Brooks
James E. Wynne
Michael J. Lavoie
Edward M. Kalinka (Birmingham)
Bruce L. Sendek
Marissa W. Pollick (Ann Arbor)
Leonard M. Niehoff (Ann Arbor)
David H. Oermann (Birmingham)
Eric J. Flessland (Birmingham)
Lynn Abraham Sheehy
Robert A. Boonin
J. Michael Huget (Ann Arbor)
Patrick A. Karbowski (Birmingham)
Ronald E. Reynolds (Birmingham)
Kenneth H. Adamczyk
Phillip C. Korovesis
James J. Urban (Okemos)
Susan Klein Friedlaender (Birmingham)

Representative Clients: Bridgestone/Firestone, Inc.; Detroit Diesel Corp.; The Detroit News, Inc.; Kelly Services; Merrill Lynch & Co., Inc.; Stroh Companies; Takata Corp.; TRW Automotive; The University of Michigan.

For full biographical listings, see the Martindale-Hubbell Law Directory

JAFFE, RAITT, HEUER & WEISS, PROFESSIONAL CORPORATION (AV)

One Woodward Avenue, Suite 2400, 48226
Telephone: 313-961-8380
Telecopier: 313-961-8358
Cable Address: "Jafsni"
Southfield,Michigan Office: Travelers Tower, Suite 1520.
Telephone: 313-961-8380.

Christopher A. Andreoff
R. Christopher Cataldo
Wallace H. Glendening
Larry K. Griffis
Jeffrey G. Heuer
Sharon J. LaDuke
Melanie LaFave
Susan S. Lichterman
Eric A. Linden
Brian G. Shannon
Joseph J. Shannon
Lawrence R. Shoffner
Arthur H. Siegal
George A. Sumnik
Jeffrey D. Weisserman
Thomas H. Williams

Lise Anne Barrera | Liam E. Hart

OF COUNSEL

David Griem | Carolyn Slasinski-Griem

Representative Clients: Michigan State Hospital Finance Auth.; The Stroh Brewery Co.; Unisys Corp.; Weiss Construction Co.

For Complete List of Firm Personnel, See General Section

For full biographical listings, see the Martindale-Hubbell Law Directory

MILLER, CANFIELD, PADDOCK AND STONE, P.L.C. (AV)

A Professional Limited Liability Company
Founded in 1852 by Sidney Davy Miller
150 West Jefferson, Suite 2500, 48226-4415
Telephone: 313-963-6420
Fax: 313-496-7500
Cable Address: "Stem Detroit"
URL: http://www.millercanfield.com
Ann Arbor, Michigan Office: 101 North Main Street, 7th Floor, 48104-1400.
Telephone: 734-663-2445.
Fax: 734-747-7147.
Troy, Michigan Office: 840 West Long Lake Road, Suite 200, 48098.
Telephone: 248-879-2000.
Fax: 248-879-2001.
Grand Rapids, Michigan Office: 99 Monroe, N.W., Suite 1200, 49503-2639.
Telephone: 616-454-8656.
Fax: 616-776-6322.
Howell, Michigan Office: 121 South Barnard Street, Suite 4, 48843-2305.
Telephone: 517-546-7600.
Telecopier: 517-546-6974.
Kalamazoo, Michigan Office: 444 West Michigan Avenue, 49007-3752.
Telephone: 616-381-7030.
Fax: 616-382-0244.
Lansing, Michigan Office: One Michigan Avenue, Suite 900, 48933-1609.
Telephone: 517-487-2070.
Fax: 517-374-6304.
Monroe, Michigan Office: 214 East Elm Avenue, Suite 100, 48162-2682.
Telephone: 734-243-2000.
Fax: 734-243-0901.
Washington, D.C. Office: 1900 K Street, N.W., Suite 1150. 20006.
Telephone: 202-429-5575; 785-0600.
Fax: 202-331-1118; 785-1234.
Pensacola, Florida Office: 25 West Cedar, 32501.
Telephone: 850-469-1088.
Fax: 850-432-0677.
New York, New York Office: 1450 Broadway, 41st Floor, 10018.
Telephone: 212-704-4400.
Fax: 212-704-4410.
Gdynia, Poland Office: UL. Slaska 21, 81-319.
Telephone: 011-485-831-2808.
Fax: 011-48-58-628 6411.
Warsaw, Poland Office: UL. Nowogrodzkall, 5th Floor, 00-513.
Telephone: 011-4822 529 0200.
Fax: 011-4822 529 0201.
Katowice, Poland Office: UL. Francuska 35/37, 40-027.
Telephone: 011 (48-32) 757-2414.
Fax: 011 (48-32) 757-2483.

PRINCIPALS OF FIRM

Carl H. von Ende
Gregory L. Curtner (Ann Arbor and New York, N.Y. Offices)
Joseph F. Galvin
Clarence L. Pozza, Jr.
Michael W. Hartmann
Peter W. Waldmeir
Michael P. Coakley
Le Roy L. Asher, Jr.
Steven A. Roach
Lawrence M. Dudek
Marta A. Manildi (Ann Arbor Office)
Kathryn L. Ossian
Frederick A. Acomb

OF COUNSEL/SENIOR COUNSEL

Gilbert E. Gove

ASSOCIATES

A. Michael Palizzi
Michael C. Fayz
Terence A. Thomas
Kimberly A. Paulson
Valarie Tatem Bomar
James M. Pelland

Representative Firm Clients: Chrysler Corporation; Comerica, Incorporated; City of Detroit, Michigan; Detroit Tigers, Inc.; First of Michigan; Ford Motor Company; Ford Motor Credit Company; Great Lakes Bancorp; Henry Ford Hospital; INVETECH Company.

For Complete List of Firm Personnel, See General Section

For full biographical listings, see the Martindale-Hubbell Law Directory

PYTELL & VARCHETTI, P.C. (AV)

18580 Mack Avenue, 48236
Telephone: 313-343-9200; 1-888-292-4LAW
Fax: 313-343-0207
Email: PROBATE@compuserve.com *URL:* http://www.MIprobate.com

Robert H. Pytell | Henry C. Pytell (1903-1988)
Paul E. Varchetti

For full biographical listings, see the Martindale-Hubbell Law Directory

TIMMIS & INMAN L.L.P. (AV)

300 Talon Centre, 48207
Telephone: 313-396-4200
Facsimile: 313-396-4228
Email: info@timmis-inman.com *URL:* http://www.timmis-inman.com

(See Next Column)

TIMMIS & INMAN L.L.P., *Detroit—Continued*

Michael T. Timmis
Robert E. Graziani
George A. Peck
Henry J. Brennan, III
Mark W. Peyser
Bradley J. Knickerbocker
George M. Malis

Michael F. Wais
Anthony J. Long
Michael J. Sheehan
John E.F. Gerlach

OF COUNSEL

William B. Fitzgerald

Representative Clients: Detroit Mortgage & Realty; DMR Fiancial Services, Inc.; J. Levin Sons Co.; Green Tree Financial Servicing Corp.; Hematology-Oncology Associates East, PC; Lakeshore Ear, Nose & Throat Center, PC; Micromanagement Systems, Inc.; Phoenix Crystal Corp.; Talon Surfaces LLC; Talon Automated Equipment Company.

For Complete List of Firm Personnel, See General Section

For full biographical listings, see the Martindale-Hubbell Law Directory

VANDEVEER GARZIA, PROFESSIONAL CORPORATION (AV)

Suite 1600, 333 West Fort Street, 48226
Telephone: 313-961-4880
Fax: 313-961-3822
Email: vg@voyager.net
Oakland County Office: 220 Park Street, Suite 300, Birmingham, Michigan.
Telephone: 810-645-0100.
Fax: 810-645-2430.

Fred L. Vandeveer (1879-1972)
James E. Haggerty, Sr. (1900-1966)
Leroy G. Vandeveer (1902-1981)
Buelle A. Doelle (1902-1985)
James E. Plastow, Jr.
Michael M. Hathaway
John J. Lynch, III (Resident, Oakland County Office)
Thomas M. Peters
James K. Thome
Gary Alan Miller
William L. Kiriazis
Daniel P. Steele
Shelley K. Miller (Resident, Oakland County Office)
Terrance P. Lynch
Dennis B. Cotter
Bruce E. Pearce
Hal O. Carroll
David B. Timmis (Resident, Oakland County Office)

Nancy A. Hensley
Dawn M. Twydell
Christian E. Hildebrandt (Resident, Oakland County Office)
Donald C. Brownell

Representative Clients: Bic Corp.; CNA Insurance Group; Travelers Insurance Co.; United States Aviation Underwriters; Goodyear Tire & Rubber Co.

For full biographical listings, see the Martindale-Hubbell Law Directory

WILLMARTH, TANOURY, RAMAR, CORBET, GARVES & SHAW (AV)

535 Griswold, Suite 1730, 48226-3602
Telephone: 313-964-6300
Fax: 313-964-6310
Email: mdwillth@home.net

MEMBERS OF FIRM

Daniel R. Corbet
Brian R. Garves
David R. Nauts
Anthony J. Paradiso
John M. Perrin
John J. Ramar
Bruce R. Shaw
William A. Tanoury
Mark D. Willmarth

ASSOCIATES

Marie C. Kennedy
Wayne Walker
Elizabeth L. Sokol
Robert S. Silverman
Carmine G. Paterra
Joseph J. Ceglarek, II
Derek Steven Wilczynski
Frank Hamidi
Kristen E. Skaff
Steven J. Bonasso
Colleen P. O'Connor
Lara R. Stutz
Eric G. Tucciarone
Michael P. Robach

For full biographical listings, see the Martindale-Hubbell Law Directory

FARMINGTON HILLS, Oakland Co.

BIRNKRANT & BIRNKRANT, P.C. (AV)

Hunters Square Office Building, 31555 West Fourteen Mile Road, Suite 201, 48334
Telephone: 248-932-7500
Facsimile: 248-932-5720

Jon J. Birnkrant
Sherwin M. Birnkrant

Dana Loewenstein

Representative Clients: Insurance Company of North America; CIGNA; City of Pontiac; ESIS; RHK Technology, Inc.; The Maccabees.

(See Next Column)

For full biographical listings, see the Martindale-Hubbell Law Directory

HALIW SICILIANO AND MYCHALOWYCH (AV)

37000 Grand River, Suite 350, 48335
Telephone: 248-442-0510
Fax: 248-442-0518
Email: hsmfirm@aol.com

MEMBERS OF FIRM

Andrew J. Haliw III
Joseph A. Siciliano
Andrew W. Mychalowych
Nanette Lynn Korpi
Raymond L. Feul
John N. Kaspers
David A. Monroe
Scott A. Decius
Katherine A. Jarred
Mark Gerard Chiesa

OF COUNSEL

Frank C. Kerr
Alphonse Tabaka
David Loeffler
William W. Decker, Jr.

For full biographical listings, see the Martindale-Hubbell Law Directory

*GRAND RAPIDS,** Kent Co.

BORRE, PETERSON, FOWLER & REENS, P.C. (AV)

300 Ottawa N.W., Suite 500, P.O. Box 1767, 49501-1767
Telephone: 616-459-1971
Fax: 616-459-2393
Email: 105162.1531@compuserve.com

William C. Reens
Frank H. Johnson
Harold E. Nelson

References: Old Kent Bank; NBD Bank/First Chicago Bank; The Huntington Bank.

For Complete List of Firm Personnel, See General Section

For full biographical listings, see the Martindale-Hubbell Law Directory

BUCHANAN, SILVER & BECKERING, P.L.C. (AV)

300 Ottawa N.W., Suite 800, 49503
Telephone: 616-458-2464
Fax: 616-458-0608
URL: http://www.bsblaw.com
Email: rbuchanan@bsblaw.com *URL:* http://www.lawyers.com/bsblaw

MEMBERS OF FIRM

John C. Buchanan
Lee T. Silver
Robert J. Buchanan
Jane M. Beckering

LEGAL SUPPORT PERSONNEL

Raymond E. Beckering, Jr., M.D. (Medical Consultant)

For full biographical listings, see the Martindale-Hubbell Law Directory

DE GROOT, KELLER, VINCENT & ALMASSIAN, P.L.C. (AV)

300 Trust Building, 40 Pearl Street, N.W., 49503
Telephone: 616-459-6251
Fax: 616-459-6352
Email: dkvkeller@aol.com

MEMBER OF FIRM

Brian D. Vincent

OF COUNSEL

Murray B. De Groot

For full biographical listings, see the Martindale-Hubbell Law Directory

GRUEL, MILLS, NIMS AND PYLMAN (AV)

50 Monroe Place, Suite 700 West, 49503
Telephone: 616-235-5500
Fax: 616-235-5550

MEMBERS OF FIRM

Grant J. Gruel
William F. Mills
J. Clarke Nims
Norman H. Pylman, II
Scott R. Melton
Brion J. Brooks
Thomas R. Behm
J. Paul Janes

Representative Clients: Aquinas College; Bell Helmet Co.; Blodgett Memorial Medical Center; Chem Central, Inc.; Cook Pump Co.; Grove, Inc.; NBDC; Heim Corp.

For full biographical listings, see the Martindale-Hubbell Law Directory

MCSHANE & BOWIE, P.L.C. (AV)

1100 Campau Square Plaza, 99 Monroe Avenue, N.W., P.O. Box 360, 49501-0360
Telephone: 616-732-5000
Fax: 616-732-5099

(See Next Column)

McShane & Bowie P.L.C.—*Continued*

MEMBERS OF FIRM

Terry J. Mroz
Steven E. Bratschie
Judy L. Walton

Representative Clients: Old Kent Bank; Amway Hotel Corp.; Randers Engineering, Inc.; BETA Design Group, Inc.; Wolverine Gas & Oil Co., Inc.; M. W. VanderVeen Co.

For Complete List of Firm Personnel, See General Section

For full biographical listings, see the Martindale-Hubbell Law Directory

Nelson and Kreuger, Professional Corporation (AV)

1010 McKay Tower, 146 Monroe Center, N.W., 49503
Telephone: 616-459-2112
Fax: 616-459-0657
URL: http://www.lawyers.com/nelsonkreuger

James R. Nelson
Steven L. Kreuger
Jon J. Schrotenboer

Representative Clients: Admiral Insurance Co.; Farm Bureau Insurance Group; Fireman's Fund Insurance Co.; Frankenmuth Mutual Insurance Co.; Great American Insurance Cos.; Hastings Mutual Insurance Co.; Michigan Educational Employees Insurance Co.; United States Fidelity & Guaranty; MLBA Limited Liability Pool.
Reference: Old Kent Bank.

For full biographical listings, see the Martindale-Hubbell Law Directory

Roberts, Betz & Bloss, P.C. (AV)

5005 Cascade Road SE, 49546-3724
Telephone: 616-285-8899
Telecopier: 616-285-0045

Connie R. Thacker

For full biographical listings, see the Martindale-Hubbell Law Directory

Schenk, Boncher and Prasher, P.C. (AV)

601 Three Mile Road NW, 49544-1601
Telephone: 616-647-8277
Fax: 616-647-0958
Email: sbp@voyager.net

Gary P. Schenk
Gregory G. Prasher
Frederick J. Boncher
Catherine M. Sullivan
Curtis D. Rypma

Daniel L. Burns

Reference: Huntington Bank.

For full biographical listings, see the Martindale-Hubbell Law Directory

HARBOR SPRINGS, Emmet Co.

Ramer, Moore & Glass (AV)

First Community Bank Building, One Hundred Spring Street Post Office Box 5, 49740
Telephone: 616-526-6214
Fax: 616-526-9343
http: //www.ramerandmoore.com
Email: jramer@ramerandmoore.com *URL:* http://www.lawyers.com/ramerandmoore

MEMBERS OF FIRM

James T. Ramer
Joel B. Moore
Charles F. Glass

Representative Clients: City of Harbor Springs; Roaring Brook Assn.; Forest Beach Assn.; Birchwood Farms Property Owners Assn.; Pride Hunters & Jumpers, Inc.; Black Forest Farm.

For full biographical listings, see the Martindale-Hubbell Law Directory

*HILLSDALE,** Hillsdale Co.

Parker, Hayes & Lovinger, P.C. (AV)

14-16 South Howell Street, P.O. Box 358, 49242
Telephone: 517-437-7210
Fax: 517-437-0260

James B. Parker
Lawrence L. Hayes, Jr.
John P. Lovinger

Representative Clients: Hillsdale County National Bank; Villages of Jonesville and Camden; Hillsdale County (Labor Counsel); Hillsdale College; Powell Petroleum Co.; Foulke Construction Co.; Somerset Township; Hillsdale Tool & Mfg. Co.

For full biographical listings, see the Martindale-Hubbell Law Directory

*KALAMAZOO,** Kalamazoo Co.

Paul F. Davidoff A Professional Corporation (AV)

405 West Michigan Avenue, Suite 130, P.O. Box 51066, 49005
Telephone: 616-388-2100
Fax: 616-388-5454
Email: pdavidoff@ameritech.net *URL:* http://www.lawyers.com/paulfdavidoff

Paul F. Davidoff

Reference: Old Kent Bank of Kalamazoo.

For full biographical listings, see the Martindale-Hubbell Law Directory

Howard & Howard Attorneys, P.C. (AV)

The Michigan Building, Suite 200, 100 Portage Street, 49007-4802
Telephone: 616-382-1483
Telecopier: 616-382-1568
Bloomfield Hills, Michigan Office: The Pinehurst Office Center, Suite 101, 1400 North Woodward Avenue.
Telephone: 248-645-1483.
Telecopier: 248-645-1568.
Lansing, Michigan Office: The Phoenix Building, Suite 500, 222 Washington Square North.
Telephone: 517-485-1483.
Telecopier: 517-485-1568.
Peoria, Illinois Office: One Technology Plaza, Suite 600, 211 Fulton Street.
Telephone: 309-672-1483.
Telecopier: 309-672-1568.

James H. Geary

Representative Clients: For Representative Client list, see General Practice, Kalamazoo, MI.

For Complete List of Firm Personnel, See General Section

For full biographical listings, see the Martindale-Hubbell Law Directory

Lewis & Allen, P.C. (AV)

Old Kent Bank Building, Suite 800, 136 East Michigan Avenue, 49007-3946
Telephone: 616-388-7600
Fax: 616-349-3831

Dean S. Lewis
W. Fred Allen, Jr.
Barry R. Smith
William A. Redmond
Stephen M. Denenfeld
Anne McGregor Fries
Gregory G. St. Arnauld
James M. Marquardt
Christopher T. Haenicke
Winfield J. Hollander (1906-1996)

LEGAL SUPPORT PERSONNEL

Dorothy B. Kelly

For full biographical listings, see the Martindale-Hubbell Law Directory

LANSING, Ingham Co.

Howard & Howard Attorneys, P.C. (AV)

The Phoenix Building, Suite 500, 222 Washington Square, North, 48933-1817
Telephone: 517-485-1483
Telecopier: 517-485-1568
Kalamazoo, Michigan Office: The Michigan Building, Suite 200, 100 Portage Street.
Telephone: 616-382-1483.
Telecopier: 616-382-1568.
Bloomfield Hills, Michigan Office: The Pinehurst Office Center, Suite 101, 1400 North Woodward Avenue.
Telephone: 248-645-1483.
Telecopier: 248-645-1568.
Peoria, Illinois Office: One Technology Plaza, Suite 600, 211 Fulton Street.
Telephone: 309-672-1483.
Telecopier: 309-672-1568.

Michael J. Brown
Ellen M. House-Harvath
Shannon A. Hunt
Robert D. Mollhagen
C. Douglas Moran

Representative Clients: For Representative Client list, see General Practice, Lansing, MI.

For Complete List of Firm Personnel, See General Section

For full biographical listings, see the Martindale-Hubbell Law Directory

Loomis, Ewert, Parsley, Davis & Gotting, P.C. (AV)

232 South Capitol Avenue, Suite 1000, 48933
Telephone: 517-482-2400
Facsimile: 517-482-0070

(See Next Column)

LOOMIS, EWERT, PARSLEY, DAVIS & GOTTING P.C., *Lansing—Continued*

Plummer Snyder (1900-1974)
Jack C. Davis (P.C.)
Karl L. Gotting (P.C.)
David M. Lick
Harvey J. Messing
James R. Neal
Kenneth W. Beall
Michael G. Oliva
Jeffrey W. Bracken
Catherine A. Jacobs
Ronald W. Bloomberg
Michael H. Rhodes
Howard J. Soifer
Jeffrey L. Green
Gary L. Field
James A. Ault
Sherri A. Wellman

Kelly K. Reed
Jeffrey S. Theuer
Daniel L. Pulter
Eldonna M. Ruddock
Kevin J. Roragen

OF COUNSEL

George W. Loomis
Quentin A. Ewert
William D. Parsley

Representative Clients: Altman Development Co.; Century Telephone Enterprises; Columbian Distribution, Inc.; Comerica Bank; Consumers Energy Co.; Southeastern Michigan Gas Enterprises, Inc.; Wal-Mart Stores, Inc.; Wisconsin Electric Power Co.

For full biographical listings, see the Martindale-Hubbell Law Directory

MCCLELLAND & ANDERSON, L.L.P. (AV)

1305 South Washington, 48933
Telephone: 517-482-4890
Fax: 517-482-4875
URL: http://www.mcclelland-anderson.com

Gregory L. McClelland
Melissa A. Hagen
Kelly A. Myers

Marc D. Matlock

For full biographical listings, see the Martindale-Hubbell Law Directory

*MUSKEGON,** Muskegon Co.

CULVER, SHERIDAN, KNOWLTON, EVEN & FRANKS, P.C. (AV)

250 Terrace Plaza, P.O. Box 629, 49443
Telephone: 231-724-4320
Telecopier: 231-724-4330
Email: cskef@novagate.com

Fred C. Culver, Jr.
James M. Sheridan
Michael M. Knowlton
Kevin B. Even
Eugene A. Franks

David E. Waterstradt
Foster D. Potter
Douglas Poland
Scott Knowlton
Joseph S. Bush

Representative Clients: SPX Corp.; National City Bank of Michigan/Illinois; Old Kent Bank of Grand Haven; Comerica Bank; NBD Bank; East Shore Chemical Company; Muskegon County Association of Realtors; Midland Groceries.

For full biographical listings, see the Martindale-Hubbell Law Directory

NOVI, Oakland Co.

LAW OFFICES OF SULLIVAN & LEAVITT, P.C. (AV)

22375 Haggerty Road, 48375
Telephone: 248-349-3980
Fax: 248-349-2810
Mailing Address: P.O. Box 5490, Northville, MI, 48167
Email: mjl@sullivanleavitt.com

Robert A. Sullivan (1917-1979)
Martin J. Leavitt

Paul E. Robinson
Michael J. Leavitt
Curtis R. Willner
Joseph Richard Mariniello, Jr.

OF COUNSEL

David Loeffler

Representative Clients: Aggregate Carriers of Michigan, Inc.; D & H Mack Kenworth Sales & Service, Inc.; Gordon F. Laramie Crane Co.; Premiere Video, Inc.; Palmer Moving & Storage, Inc.; Menlo Tool; Storage and Transport; Automated Benefit Services, Inc.; U.S. Health and Life Insurance Co.

For full biographical listings, see the Martindale-Hubbell Law Directory

ROCHESTER HILLS, Oakland Co.

SHERMETA, CHIMKO & KILPATRICK, P.C. (AV)

445 South Livernois, Suite 333, 48307
Telephone: 248-652-8200
Fax: 248-652-1292
Mailing Address: P.O. Box 5016, Rochester, Michigan, 48308
Detroit, Michigan Office: 211 West Fort Street, Suite 704, 48226.
Telephone: 313-961-4848.
Fax: 313-961-4365.
Grand Rapids, Michigan Office: 169 Louis Campau Prom., Suite 2B, 49503.
Telephone: 616-774-9258.
Fax: 616-774-9411.

Douglass H. Shermeta
Darryl J. Chimko
Richardo I. Kilpatrick
Barbara L. Adams
Henry J. Mittelstaedt III
Kelly L. Scola
Christopher E. McNeely

Robert L. Dzialo
Sheryl S. Zamplas
Lisa E. Gocha
Kevin C. Calhoun
Kristin J. Ermshler
James E. Hess
Kyle J. VonAllmen
Elizabeth M. Abood
Jessica Brown Allmand
Dina L. Centifanti
Tania A. Hricik DeVries
Sharon Denise Koerber
Heather L. Miserlian
Gregory J. Roth
Larysa Sawertailo
Tyra T. Brown
Brent M. Lamkin
Charles Milne
Paul J. Smigielski

For full biographical listings, see the Martindale-Hubbell Law Directory

SOUTHFIELD, Oakland Co.

YOUNG & ASSOCIATES, P.C. (AV)

Suite 305, Westview Office Center, 26200 American Drive, 48034
Telephone: 248-353-8620
Telecopier: 248-353-6559
Email: youngpc@aol.com

Rodger D. Young

Michael J. Fergestrom
Steven Susser
Jeffrey M. Macy
Terry Wuester Milne

For full biographical listings, see the Martindale-Hubbell Law Directory

*TRAVERSE CITY,** Grand Traverse Co.

DINGEMAN, DANCER & CHRISTOPHERSON, P.L.C. (AV)

100 Park Street, 49684
Telephone: 231-929-0500
Fax: 231-929-0504
Email: dingeman@dingemandancer.com *URL:* http://www.Dingemandancer.com

Mark R. Dancer
James A. Christopherson

Representative Clients: Texas Instruments, Inc.; Georgia-Pacific Corporation; Martin Marietta Magesia Specialities, Inc.; Elf Atochem North America, Inc.; Busch Oil Company; Lachine Oil Company; Charmilles Technologoes Corporation; Glawe Corporations; Stomberg Carlson Products, Inc.; L'DaRu Lakeside Resort.

For full biographical listings, see the Martindale-Hubbell Law Directory

SMITH & JOHNSON, ATTORNEYS, P.C. (AV)

603 Bay Street, P.O. Box 705, 49685
Telephone: 231-946-0700
Fax: 231-946-1735
Email: sjlaw@smith-johnson.com *URL:* http://www.smith-johnson.com
Lansing, Michigan Office: Suite 402, 116 West Ottawa Street.
Telephone: 517-482-5142.

Louis A. Smith
H. Wendell Johnson
Allen G. Anderson

Thomas A. Pezzetti
Timothy Paul Smith
Matthew D. Vermetten
Gary Allen Gardner

OF COUNSEL

Barbara Ann Assendelft

Representative Clients: Empire National Bank of Traverse City; Grand Traverse Mall Limited Partnership; Green Tree Acceptance, Inc.; Lansing Automakers' Federal Credit Union; Michigan Automobile Dealers Association; Cherry Capital Oldsmobile Cadillac L.L.C.; Bill Marsh Motors, Inc.; Northern Star Broadcasting, L.L.C.; Munson Healthcare; Republic Bank.

For full biographical listings, see the Martindale-Hubbell Law Directory

Traverse City—Continued

SULLIVAN & CROWLEY, P.C. (AV)

735 South Garfield, Suite 202, 49686
Telephone: 616-922-1888
Fax: 616-922-2221
Email: sullcro@GTII.com *URL:*
http://www.lawyers.com/sullivancrowleylaw

James I. Sullivan | Philip J. Crowley
Jeffrey J. Noorman

For full biographical listings, see the Martindale-Hubbell Law Directory

WALTON, SMITH, PHILLIPS & DIXON, P.C. (AV)

216 Cass Street, P.O. Box 549, 49685
Telephone: 616-947-7410
Fax: 616-947-5112

Geoff G. Smith | L. Kent Walton
Thomas L. Phillips

Representative Clients: The Travelers Insurance Cos.; Farm Bureau Insurance Group; TIG Insurance.
Reference: Huntington National Bank.

For full biographical listings, see the Martindale-Hubbell Law Directory

TROY, Oakland Co.

EGAN & MAZZARA, PLLC (AV)

Suite 621, 2301 West Big Beaver Road, 48084-3329
Telephone: 248-458-3000
Fax: 248-458-3005
URL: http://www.lawyers.com/egan&mazzara

Dennis K. Egan | Jack J. Mazzara

Sarah T. Chisholm

For full biographical listings, see the Martindale-Hubbell Law Directory

RANDALL J. GILLARY, P.C. (AV)

Suite 1020 Columbia Center, 201 W. Big Beaver, 48084
Telephone: 248-528-0440
Fax: 248-528-3412

Randall J. Gillary

Kevin P. Albus

For full biographical listings, see the Martindale-Hubbell Law Directory

HACKETT & MAXWELL, P.C. (AV)

City Center Building, Suite 1470, 888 West Big Beaver Road, 48084
Telephone: 810-362-2600
Fax: 810-362-3610
Email: hackmax@voyager.net

Patrick E. Hackett | Phillip B. Maxwell

Dennis W. Krakow | Mireille Leruth Phillips

For full biographical listings, see the Martindale-Hubbell Law Directory

JACOB & WEINGARTEN (AV)

2301 West Big Beaver Road, Suite 777, 48084-3300
Telephone: 248-649-1900
Facsimile: 248-649-2920
Email: law@jacobweingarten.com
North Palm Beach, Florida Office: P.O. Box 14037, 33408.
Telephone: 561-640-5600.

Howard S. Sher
Stephen M. Landau
Robert K. Siegel
Brian D. Figot
William L. Fischel
William R. Cohen

For full biographical listings, see the Martindale-Hubbell Law Directory

POLING, MCGAW & POLING, P.C. (AV)

Suite 275, 5435 Corporate Drive, 48098
Telephone: 248-641-0500
Telecopier: 248-641-0506
URL: http://www.lawyers.com/polingmcgaw&poling

Benson T. Buck (1926-1989)
Richard B. Poling
D. Douglas McGaw
Richard B. Poling, Jr.
Gregory C. Hamilton
Veronica B. O'Hara
James R. Parker
Shannon M. Acton

OF COUNSEL

Ralph S. Moore

Representative Clients: City of Troy; United States Fidelity & Guaranty Co.; Sentry Insurance Co.; Admiral Insurance; DeMaria Construction Co.; Leo Corporation; Aetna Casualty and Surety Co.; Concord Design; Pneumo-Abex.

For full biographical listings, see the Martindale-Hubbell Law Directory

SCHIER, DENEWETH & PARFITT, P.C. (AV)

888 West Big Beaver Road, Suite 610, 48084-4737
Telephone: 248-362-5600
Telecopier: 248-362-0073
Email: SDPlaw@aol.com *URL:* http://www.lawyers.com/schierlaw

Carl F. Schier
Ronald A. Deneweth
Chris Parfitt
Timothy P. Dugan
Janette E. Frank
Mark D. Sassak

OF COUNSEL

Edward A. Ryder | John J. Mallon

For full biographical listings, see the Martindale-Hubbell Law Directory

WESTLAND, Wayne Co.

ASKER, CHAPP & CLOS, P.C. (AV)

35551 Ford Road, Suite 100, 48185
Telephone: 734-326-2101
Fax: 734-595-9771
URL: http://www.lawyers.com/michigan
Torrance, California Office: 615 Hawaii Avenue, 90503.
Telephone: 310-320-5766.

Paul P. Asker
Sandra J. Chapp
Charles E. Clos
Gary E. Perlmuter
Brian J. Considine
J. Matthew Catchick, Jr.

For full biographical listings, see the Martindale-Hubbell Law Directory

COMMUNICATIONS LAW

ALABAMA

*BIRMINGHAM,** Jefferson Co.

BRADLEY ARANT ROSE & WHITE LLP (AV)

2001 Park Place, Suite 1400, P.O. Box 830709, 35283-0709
Telephone: 205-521-8000
Facsimile: 205-521-8800
Facsimile (SouthTrust Tower Office): 205-521-8500
URL: http://www.barw.com
Huntsville, Alabama Office: 200 Clinton Avenue West, Suite 900, 35801.
Telephone: 205-517-5100.
Facsimile: 205-533-5069.
Washington, D.C. Office: 801 Pennsylvania Avenue, NW, Suite 230, 20004.
Telephone: 202-347-8893.
Facsimile: 202-347-1684.

MEMBERS OF FIRM

Gary C. Huckaby (Resident, Huntsville Office)
E. Cutter Hughes Jr. (Resident, Huntsville Office)

Counsel for: SouthTrust Bank of Alabama, National Association; Energen, Corporation (formerly Alagasco, Inc.); Blount, Inc.; Torchmark Corp.; Russell Corp.; Coca-Cola Bottling Company United, Inc.; Ford Motor Co.; Walter Industries, Inc.; The Birmingham Post Co. (Post-Herald); The New York Times Co.

For Complete List of Firm Personnel, See General Section

For full biographical listings, see the Martindale-Hubbell Law Directory

BURR & FORMAN LLP (AV)

3100 SouthTrust Tower, 420 North 20th Street, P.O. Box 830719, 35283-0719
Telephone: 205-251-3000
Facsimile: 205-458-5100
URL: http://www.burr.com
Huntsville, Alabama Office: Suite 204, Regency Center, 400 Meridian Street.
Telephone: 205-551-0010.
Facsimile: 205-551-0043.
Atlanta, Georgia Office: Suite 1200, One Georgia Center, 600 West Peachtree Street, 30308.
Telephone: 404-815-3000.
Facsimile: 404-817-3244.

MEMBERS OF FIRM

John D. Clements
John F. DeBuys, Jr.

For Complete List of Firm Personnel, See General Section

For full biographical listings, see the Martindale-Hubbell Law Directory

JOHNSTON BARTON PROCTOR & POWELL LLP (AV)

2900 AmSouth/Harbert Plaza, 1901 Sixth Avenue North, 35203-2618
Telephone: 205-458-9400
Telecopier: 205-458-9500
Email: Law@JBPP.com

MEMBERS OF FIRM

Gilbert E. Johnston, Jr.
Hollinger F. Barnard
Robert S. Vance, Jr.

COUNSEL

Paul E. Toppins

OF COUNSEL

James C. Barton

ASSOCIATE

Anna R. Minor

Counsel for: Birmingham Broadcasting (WVTM-TV), Inc. (NBC-owned affiliate); The Birmingham News Co.; Consolidated Publishing Co. (publisher of the Anniston Star); Dick Broadcasting Co., Inc., of Alabama; Employers Reinsurance Company; Fox Group companies; MG Broadcasting of Birmingham (CBS affiliate); Media/Professional Insurance Agency, Inc.; Tennessee Valley Printing Co., Inc. (publisher of the Decatur Daily); The Tuscaloosa News (division of the New York Times Company).

For full biographical listings, see the Martindale-Hubbell Law Directory

*HUNTSVILLE,** Madison Co.

BRADLEY ARANT ROSE & WHITE LLP (AV)

200 Clinton Avenue West, Suite 900, 35801
Telephone: 205-517-5100
Facsimile: 205-517-5200
URL: http://www.barw.com
Birmingham, Alabama Office: 2001 Park Place, Suite 1400, P.O. Box 830709.
Telephone: 205-521-8000.
Facsimile: 205-521-8800. Facsimile (SouthTrust Tower Office): 205-521-8500.
Washington, D.C. Office: 801 Pennsylvania Avenue, NW, Suite 230, 20004.
Telephone: 202-347-8893.
Facsimile: 202-347-1684.

RESIDENT PARTNERS

Gary C. Huckaby
E. Cutter Hughes Jr.

For Complete List of Firm Personnel, See General Section

For full biographical listings, see the Martindale-Hubbell Law Directory

*MONTGOMERY,** Montgomery Co.

BRANTLEY & WILKERSON, P.C. (AV)

405 South Hull Street, P.O. Box 830, 36101-0830
Telephone: 334-265-1500
Fax: 334-265-0319
Email: ashley@brantleywilkerson.com *URL:* http://www.brantleywilkerson.com

Paul A. Brantley
Mark D. Wilkerson

Leah Snell Stephens

Representative Clients: ALLTEL; TDS; Digiph PCS, Inc.; KnoLogy; Technologies Management, Inc.

For full biographical listings, see the Martindale-Hubbell Law Directory

ARIZONA

*PHOENIX,** Maricopa Co.

FENNEMORE CRAIG, A PROFESSIONAL CORPORATION (AV)

3003 North Central Avenue, Suite 2600, 85012-2913
Telephone: 602-916-5000
Fax: 602-916-5999
Tucson, Arizona Office: One South Church Avenue, Suite 1000, 85701-1620.
Telephone: 520-879-6800.
Fax: 520-879-6899.

C. Webb Crockett
Timothy Berg

Theresa Dwyer

For Complete List of Firm Personnel, See General Section

For full biographical listings, see the Martindale-Hubbell Law Directory

ROSHKA HEYMAN & DEWULF, PLC (AV)

Two Arizona Center, 400 North 5th Street, Suite 1000, 85004
Telephone: 602-256-6100
Facsimile: 602-256-6800
Email: rheyman@rhd-law.com

Paul J. Roshka, Jr.
John E. DeWulf
Raymond S. Heyman
Darlene M. Wauro

Alan S. Baskin
Randall H. Warner
Linda D. Skon

For full biographical listings, see the Martindale-Hubbell Law Directory

ARKANSAS

*LITTLE ROCK,** Pulaski Co.

ROSE LAW FIRM, A PROFESSIONAL ASSOCIATION (AV)

120 East Fourth Street, 72201
Telephone: 501-375-9131
Telecopy: 501-375-1309

(See Next Column)

ROSE LAW FIRM A PROFESSIONAL ASSOCIATION, *Little Rock—Continued*

W. Wilson Jones
David L. Williams
Stephen N. Joiner
Michael N. Shannon

COUNSEL

Phillip Carroll

Counsel for: ALLTEL Corporation; Aluminum Company of America; Donrey Media Group Inc.; The Equitable Life Assurance Society of The United States; Bridgestone/Firestone Inc.; General Motors Corp.; The Prudential Insurance Company of America; Stephens Group, Inc.; Tyson Foods, Inc.

For Complete List of Firm Personnel, See General Section

For full biographical listings, see the Martindale-Hubbell Law Directory

CALIFORNIA

COSTA MESA, Orange Co.

RUTAN & TUCKER, LLP (AV)

A Partnership including Professional Corporations
611 Anton Boulevard, Fourteenth Floor, P.O. Box 1950, 92626-1998
Telephone: 714-641-5100; 213-625-7586
Telecopier: 714-546-9035
Email: rutan&tucker@rutan.com *URL:* http://www.rutan.com

MEMBER OF FIRM

William M. Marticorena

For Complete List of Firm Personnel, See General Section

For full biographical listings, see the Martindale-Hubbell Law Directory

FOLSOM, Sacramento Co.

THE BLEIER LAW FIRM (AV)

110 Blue Ravine Road, Suite 201, 95630
Telephone: 916-454-2100
Fax: 916-454-2121
Email: tblf@bleier.com *URL:* http://www.bleier.com

Brenton A. Bleier

ASSOCIATE

Bradford A. Bleier

For full biographical listings, see the Martindale-Hubbell Law Directory

*LOS ANGELES,** Los Angeles Co.

O'MELVENY & MYERS LLP (AV)

400 South Hope Street, 90071-2899
Telephone: 213-430-6000
Facsimile: 213-430-6407
Cable: MOMS
Telex: 674122
Email: omminfo@omm.com *URL:* http://www.omm.com
Century City, CA Office: 1999 Avenue of the Stars, Los Angeles, 90067-6035.
Telex: 674097. Tel: 310-553-6700.
Fax: 310-246-6779.
Newport Beach, CA Office: 610 Newport Center Drive, 92660-6429.
Telex: 4722088. Tel: 949-760-9600.
Fax: 949-823-6994.
San Francisco, CA Office: Embarcadero Center West, 275 Battery Street, 94111-3305. Tel: 415-984-8700.
Fax: 415-984-8701.
New York, NY Office: Citicorp Center, 153 East 53rd Street, 10022-4611.
Telex: 129165. Tel: 212-326-2000.
Fax: 212-326-2061.
Washington, DC Office: 555 13th Street, N.W., 20004-1109.
Cable: MOMSWSH.
Telex: 89622. Tel: 202-383-5300.
Fax: 202-383-5414.
London Office: O'Melveny & Myers, 3 Finsbury Square, London, EC2A 1LA, England. Tel: 44-171-256-8451. Fax 44-171-638-8205.
Tokyo Office: Akasaka Twin Tower, East 14F, 2-17-23, Akasaka, Minato-ku, Tokyo 107-0052, Japan. Tel: 03-5562-2800.
Fax: 03-5575-3840.
Hong Kong Office: O'Melveny & Myers, Suite 1905, Tower Two, Lippo Centre, 89 Queensway, Central, Hong Kong. Tel: 852-2523-8266.
Fax: 852-2522-1760.
Shanghai Office: Kerry Centre, 20F, 1515 Nanjing Road West, Shanghai, 200040 People's Republic of China. Tel: 86-21-5298-5600.
Fax: 86-21-5298-5500.

PARTNER

John H. Beisner (Washington, DC Office)

For Complete List of Firm Personnel, See General Section

For full biographical listings, see the Martindale-Hubbell Law Directory

*SAN DIEGO,** San Diego Co.

FERRIS & BRITTON, A PROFESSIONAL CORPORATION (AV)

1600 First National Bank Center, 401 West A Street, 92101
Telephone: 619-233-3131
Fax: 619-232-9316
Email: manager@ferrisbritton.com *URL:* http://www.ferrisbritton.com

Alfred G. Ferris
Christopher Q. Britton
Michael R. Weinstein

Representative Clients: California Cable Television Assoc.; Cox Communications, Inc.; Media One; Pacific Communications; Teleport Communications Group.

For Complete List of Firm Personnel, See General Section

For full biographical listings, see the Martindale-Hubbell Law Directory

COLORADO

*DENVER,** Denver Co.

GORSUCH KIRGIS LLP (AV)

Tower 1, Suite 1000, 1515 Arapahoe Street, 80202
Telephone: 303-376-5000
Fax: 303-376-5001

PARTNERS

Dudley P. Spiller
Peter R. Nadel

ASSOCIATES

Heather Anne Hawker
Julie Leamon Rosen

For full biographical listings, see the Martindale-Hubbell Law Directory

DISTRICT OF COLUMBIA

WASHINGTON, D.C. Co.

BAKER & HOSTETLER LLP (AV)

Washington Square, Suite 1100, 1050 Connecticut Avenue, N.W., 20036-5304
Telephone: 202-861-1500
Fax: 202-861-1783
To contact an attorney on the Internet use first initial and surname followed by @baker-hostetler.com
URL: http://www.bakerlaw.com
In Cleveland, Ohio: 3200 National City Center, 1900 East Ninth Street.
Telephone: 216-621-0200.
In Cincinnati, Ohio: 312 Walnut Street, Suite 2650.
Telephone: 513-929-3400.
In Columbus, Ohio: Capitol Square, Suite 2100, 65 East State Street.
Telephone: 614-228-1541.
In Denver, Colorado: 303 East 17th Avenue, Suite 1100.
Telephone: 303-861-0600.
In Houston, Texas: 1000 Louisiana, Suite 2000.
Telephone: 713-751-1600.
In Beverly Hills, California: 9150 Wilshire Boulevard, Suite 205.
Telephone: 310-385-7500.
In Long Beach, California: 300 Oceangate, Suite 620.
Telephone: 562-432-2827.
In Los Angeles, California: 600 Wilshire Boulevard.
Telephone: 213-624-2400.
In Orlando, Florida: SunBank Center, Suite 2300, 200 South Orange Avenue.
Telephone: 407-649-4000.

PARTNER

Kenneth C. Howard, Jr.

For Complete List of Firm Personnel, See General Section

For full biographical listings, see the Martindale-Hubbell Law Directory

BLOOSTON, MORDKOFSKY, JACKSON & DICKENS (AV)

2120 L Street, N.W., Suite 300, 20037
Telephone: 202-659-0830
Fax: 202-828-5568
Email: BMJD@CLARK.NET

MEMBERS OF FIRM

Harold Mordkofsky
Robert M. Jackson
Benjamin H. Dickens, Jr.
John A. Prendergast
Gerard J. Duffy
Andrew Brown

LEGISLATIVE CONSULTANT

Perry W. Woofter (Not admitted in DC)

(See Next Column)

BLOOSTON, MORDKOFSKY, JACKSON & DICKENS—*Continued*

ASSOCIATES

Richard D. Rubino
David Cary Mitchell
Michael B. Adams, Jr.
Laura A. Grasso (Not admitted in DC)

For full biographical listings, see the Martindale-Hubbell Law Directory

BLUMENFELD & COHEN (AV)

1625 Massachusetts Avenue, N.W., Suite 300, 20036
Telephone: 202-955-6300
Facsimile: 202-955-6460
Email: info@technologylaw.com *URL:* http://www.technologylaw.com
San Francisco, California Office: 4 Embarcadero Center, Suite 1170, 94111.
Telephone: 415-394-7500.
Facsimile: 415-394-7505.

MEMBERS OF FIRM

Jeffrey Blumenfeld
Gary M. Cohen
Glenn B. Manishin
Stephen P. Bowen (Not admitted in DC; Resident, San Francisco Office)
David M. Naseman (Not admitted in DC)
Christy C. Kunin
Elise P.W. Kiely

OF COUNSEL

Rand McQuinn

ASSOCIATES

Stephanie A. Joyce (Not admitted in DC)
Colin M. Alberts
Anita C. Taff-Rice (Not admitted in DC; Resident, San Francisco, California Office)
Aimee M. Cook (Resident, San Francisco, California Office)
Jeremy D. Marcus (Not admitted in DC)
Richard Bonkosky (Not admitted in DC; Resident, San Francisco, California Office)
Kristin L. Smith
James R. J. Scheltema (Not admitted in DC)

For full biographical listings, see the Martindale-Hubbell Law Directory

COHN AND MARKS (AV)

1920 N Street, N.W., Suite 300, 20036-1622
Telephone: 202-293-3860
Fax: 202-293-4827
URL: http://www.cohnmarks.com

MEMBERS OF FIRM

Joel H. Levy
Robert B. Jacobi
Roy R. Russo
Ronald A. Siegel
Lawrence N. Cohn
Richard A. Helmick
Wayne Coy, Jr.
J. Brian De Boice
Jerold L. Jacobs

ASSOCIATES

Susan Valerie Sachs
Kevin M. Goldberg
Joseph M. Di Scipio

OF COUNSEL

Marcus Cohn
Leonard H. Marks
Stanley S. Neustadt
Richard M. Schmidt, Jr.

For full biographical listings, see the Martindale-Hubbell Law Directory

COLE, RAYWID & BRAVERMAN, L.L.P. (AV)

1919 Pennsylvania Avenue, N.W., 20006
Telephone: 202-659-9750
Cable Address: "Crab"
Telecopier: 202-452-0067
URL: http://www.crblaw.com

John P. Cole, Jr.
Alan Raywid (1930-1991)
Burt A. Braverman
Robert L. James
John D. Seiver
Wesley R. Heppler
Paul Glist
David M. Silverman
James F. Ireland, III
Maurita K. Coley
Steven Jay Horvitz
Christopher W. Savage
Ann E. Flowers
Robert G. Scott, Jr.
Susan Whelan Westfall
Theresa A. Zeterberg
Karlyn D. Stanley
John Davidson Thomas
John Dodge

Frederick W. Giroux
Geoffrey C. Cook
Maria T. Browne
Donna Carrie Rattley
T. Scott Thompson
Adam S. Caldwell
Sandra G. Gibbs
Mark S. Kristiansen
Christin S. McMeley (Not admitted in DC)
Sara J. Kiernan (Not admitted in DC)
Heather M. Wilson
David N. Tobenkin

OF COUNSEL

Frances J. Chetwynd
Ellen S. Deutsch

For full biographical listings, see the Martindale-Hubbell Law Directory

DOW, LOHNES & ALBERTSON, PLLC (AV)

1200 New Hampshire Avenue, N.W. Suite 800, 20036-6802
Telephone: 202-776-2000
Facsimile: 202-776-2222
Email: info@dlalaw.com *URL:* http://www.dlalaw.com
Atlanta, Georgia Office: One Ravinia Drive, Suite 1600.
Telephone: 770-901-8800.
Telecopier: 770-901-8874.

MEMBERS OF THE FIRM

Michael D. Basile
Leonard J. Baxt (Chairman, Board of Directors)
Raymond G. Bender, Jr.
Barbara S. Esbin
Peter H. Feinberg
John R. Feore, Jr.
Ralph W. Hardy, Jr.
J.G. Harrington
Werner K. Hartenberger
Leonard Jervey Kennedy (Not admitted in DC)
John S. Logan
B. Dwight Perry (Managing Director)
Laura Hathaway Phillips
J. Christopher Redding
Kevin F. Reed
M. Anne Swanson

Christina Hosp Burrow
Kimberly L. Cook
Loretta J. Garcia
George L. Hanbury III
Kevin P. Latek
Gary S. Lutzker
Elizabeth Anne McGeary
Erik A. Moses
Carlos M. Nalda
Cecile Neuvens (Not admitted in DC)
Scott S. Patrick
Laura S. Roecklein
Nina Shafran

For Complete List of Firm Personnel, See General Section

For full biographical listings, see the Martindale-Hubbell Law Directory

FISHER WAYLAND COOPER LEADER & ZARAGOZA L.L.P. (AV)

A Registered Limited Liability Partnership
Suite 400, 2001 Pennsylvania Avenue, N.W., 20006-1851
Telephone: 202-659-3494
Facsimile: 202-296-6518
Email: fwclz@fwclz.com *URL:* http://www.fwclz.com

Ben S. Fisher (1890-1954)
Charles V. Wayland (1910-1980)
Martin R. Leader
Richard R. Zaragoza
Clifford M. Harrington
Kathryn R. Schmeltzer
Douglas Woloshin
David D. Oxenford
Barry H. Gottfried
Bruce D. Jacobs
Carroll John Yung
Glenn S. Richards
Robert C. Fisher
Scott R. Flick
Lauren Lynch Flick
Miles S. Mason

OF COUNSEL

Ben C. Fisher
Grover C. Cooper

ASSOCIATES

Dawn M. Sciarrino
Colette M. Capretz
Stephen J. Berman
Veronica D. McLaughlin
Stephanie Blessey Lilley
Jaqualin Friend Peterson
Cynthia D. Greer
Lara Strayer Meisner
David S. Konczal
Susan M. Hafeli
Tina R. Reynolds
Brendan Holland
Katherine Tong-Shin Suh
Max D. Gale (Not admitted in DC)
Joan E. Masters (Not admitted in DC)
Indra Sehdev Chalk (Not admitted in DC)

For full biographical listings, see the Martindale-Hubbell Law Directory

FLETCHER, HEALD & HILDRETH, P.L.C. (AV)

2000 L Street, NW, Suite 200, 20036
Telephone: 202-828-5700
Email: office@fhh-telcomlaw.com *URL:* http://www.fhh-telcomlaw.com
Arlington, Virginia Office: 1300 North 17th Street, 11th Floor.
Telephone: 703-812-0400.
Fax: 703-812-0486.

Paul D. P. Spearman (1936-1962)
Frank Roberson (1936-1961)
Russell Rowell (1948-1977)
Robert L. Heald (1956-1983)
Frank U. Fletcher (1939-1985)
Edward F. Kenehan (1960-1978)

MEMBERS OF FIRM

Richard Hildreth
James P. Riley
Leonard R. Raish
Vincent J. Curtis, Jr.
George Petrutsas
Frank R. Jazzo
Howard M. Weiss
Harry C. Martin
Paul J. Feldman
Kathleen Victory

SPECIAL COUNSEL

Susan A. Marshall

SENIOR ASSOCIATES

Ann Bavender
Anne Goodwin Crump
Andrew S. Kersting

ASSOCIATES

Alison J. Shapiro (Not admitted in DC)
Raymond J. Quianzon (Not admitted in DC)
Jennifer Dine Wagner

(See Next Column)

FLETCHER, HEALD & HILDRETH P.L.C., *Washington—Continued*

OF COUNSEL

Edward A. Caine
Eugene M. Lawson, Jr.
Mitchell Lazarus
Edward S. O'Neill
John Joseph Smith

For full biographical listings, see the Martindale-Hubbell Law Directory

GREGORY H. GUILLOT CHARTERED (AV)

International Square, 1825 I Street, N.W., Suite 400, 20006
Telephone: 202-955-1100
Facsimile: 202-955-1101
Email: ggmark@radix.net *URL:* http://www.ggmark.com

Gregory H. Guillot

Representative Clients: OASIS Corporation; OASIS, Ireland; Riverdance-The Show; Priority E.M.S., Inc.; The Publicate Corporation; Tropical Isle, Inc.; Dynamic Systems Development Method, Ltd.; TeddysoftBV (The Netherlands); AKP Services, Inc. d/b/a REPOSEARCH.

For full biographical listings, see the Martindale-Hubbell Law Directory

LEVINE, BLASZAK, BLOCK & BOOTHBY, LLP (AV)

2001 L Street, N.W., Suite 900, 20036
Telephone: 202-857-2550
Fax: 202-223-0833
URL: http://www.LB3Law.com

MEMBERS OF FIRM

Henry D. Levine
James S. Blaszak
Ellen G. Block
Colleen L. Boothby
Kevin S. DiLallo
Laura F. H. McDonald
David N. Baumann
D.E. Boehling

ASSOCIATES

Janine F. Goodman
Mark G. Johnston (Not admitted in DC)
Justin G. Castillo (Not admitted in DC)
Marc A. Lindsey (Not admitted in DC)
Andrew M. Brown
Bonnie R. Gerhardt

For full biographical listings, see the Martindale-Hubbell Law Directory

LEVINE SULLIVAN & KOCH, L.L.P. (AV)

1050 Seventeenth Street, N.W. Suite 800, 20036
Telephone: 202-508-1100
Facsimile: 202-861-9888
Email: info@lsklaw.com

MEMBERS OF FIRM

Lee Levine
Michael D. Sullivan
Elizabeth C. Koch
James E. Grossberg
Celeste Phillips (Not admitted in DC)
Seth D. Berlin

OF COUNSEL

Cameron A. Stracher

ASSOCIATES

Jay Ward Brown
Jacquelyn J. Orr (Not admitted in DC)
Ashley I. Kissinger

For full biographical listings, see the Martindale-Hubbell Law Directory

MIDLEN LAW CENTER (AV)

3238 Prospect Street, N.W., 20007-3214
Telephone: 202-333-1500
Facsimile: 202-333-6852
Email: john@midlen.com *URL:* http://www.midlen.com

John H. Midlen, Jr.

For full biographical listings, see the Martindale-Hubbell Law Directory

MILLER, CANFIELD, PADDOCK AND STONE, P.L.C. (AV)

A Professional Limited Liability Company
Founded in 1852 by Sidney Davy Miller
1900 K Street, N.W., Suite 1150, 20006
Telephone: 202-429-5575; 785-0600
Fax: 202-331-1118; 785-1234
URL: http://www.millercanfield.com
Detroit, Michigan Office: 150 West Jefferson, Suite 2500, 48226-4415.
Telephone: 313-963-6420.
Fax: 313-496-7500.
Cable Address: "Stem Detroit."
Ann Arbor, Michigan Office: 101 North Main Street, 7th Floor, 48104-1400.
Telephone: 734-663-2445.
Fax: 734-747-7147.
Troy, Michigan Office: 840 West Long Lake Road, Suite 200, 48098.
Telephone: 248-879-2000.
Fax: 248-879-2001.

(See Next Column)

Grand Rapids, Michigan Office: 99 Monroe, N.W., Suite 1200, 49503-2639.
Telephone: 616-454-8656.
Fax: 616-776-6322.
Howell, Michigan Office: 121 South Barnard Street, Suite 4, 48843-2305.
Telephone: 517-546-7600.
Telecopier: 517-546-6974.
Kalamazoo, Michigan Office: 444 West Michigan Avenue, 49007-3752.
Telephone: 616-381-7030.
Fax: 616-382-0244.
Lansing, Michigan Office: One Michigan Avenue, Suite 900, 48933-1609.
Telephone: 517-487-2070.
Fax: 517-374-6304.
Monroe, Michigan Office: 214 East Elm Avenue, Suite 100, 48162-2682.
Telephone: 734-243-2000.
Fax: 734-243-0901.
Pensacola, Florida Office: 25 West Cedar, 32501.
Telephone: 850-469-1088.
Fax: 850-432-0677.
New York, New York Office: 1450 Broadway, 41st Floor, 10018.
Telephone: 212-704-4400.
Fax: 212-704-4410.
Gdynia, Poland Office: UL. Slaska 21, 81-319.
Telephone: 011-485-831-2808.
Fax: 011-48-58-628 6411.
Warsaw, Poland Office: UL. Nowogrodzkall, 5th Floor, 00-513.
Telephone: 011-4822 529 0200.
Fax: 011-4822 529 0201.
Katowice, Poland Office: UL. Francuska 35/37, 40-027.
Telephone: 011 (48-32) 757-2414.
Fax: 011 (48-32) 757-2483.

OF COUNSEL/SENIOR COUNSEL

Tillman L. Lay

For full biographical listings, see the Martindale-Hubbell Law Directory

MILLER & VAN EATON, P.L.L.C. (AV)

1155 Connecticut Avenue, N.W., Suite 1000, 20036-4306
Telephone: 202-785-0600
Fax: 202-785-1234
Email: info2@millervaneaton.com *URL:* http://www.millervaneaton.com
San Francisco, California Office: 155 Montgomery Street, Suite 1410.
Telephone: 415-772-8127.
Fax: 415-434-2852.

Nicholas P. Miller
Joseph Van Eaton
William R. Malone
Frederick E. Ellrod III
Matthew C. Ames
William L. Lowery (Resident, San Francisco, California Office)
Frederick E. Dooley, Jr.
Marci Lynn Frischkorn (Not admitted in DC)

For full biographical listings, see the Martindale-Hubbell Law Directory

MINTZ, LEVIN, COHN, FERRIS, GLOVSKY AND POPEO, P.C. (AV)

701 Pennsylvania Avenue, N.W., 20004-2608
Telephone: 202-434-7300
Fax: 202-434-7400
Internet: Each Attorney's Internet Address takes the following form: first inital, last name @mintz.com (e.g., rmintz@mintz.com)
URL: http://www.mintz.com
Boston, Massachusetts Office: One Financial Center.
Telephone: 617-542-6000.
Fax: 617-542-2241.
Reston, Virginia Office: 12021 Sunset Hills Road, Suite 310.
Telephone: 703-464-4800.
Fax: 703-464-4895.

Charles D. Ferris
Frank W. Lloyd
Bruce D. Sokler
Howard J. Symons
Cameron F. Kerry (Resident, Boston, Mass. Office)

For Complete List of Firm Personnel, See General Section

For full biographical listings, see the Martindale-Hubbell Law Directory

MOIR & HARDMAN (AV)

1828 L. Street N.W., Suite 901, 20036-5104
Telephone: 202-872-8680
Fax: 202-872-8698

Brian R. Moir
Kenneth E. Hardman

For full biographical listings, see the Martindale-Hubbell Law Directory

PEPPER & CORAZZINI, L.L.P. (AV)

1776 K Street, N.W., 20006
Telephone: 202-296-0600
Telecopier: 202-296-5572
Email: pepcor@commlaw.com *URL:* http://www.commlaw.com

(See Next Column)

PEPPER & CORAZZINI L.L.P.—*Continued*

MEMBERS OF FIRM

Vincent A. Pepper
Robert F. Corazzini
Peter Gutmann
John F. Garziglia
Gregg P. Skall
Howard J. Barr

ASSOCIATES

Ellen Mandell Edmundson
Suzanne Spink Goodwyn (Not admitted in DC)
Michael H. Shacter
Patricia M. Chuh
Kristopher E. Twomey (Not admitted in DC)

For full biographical listings, see the Martindale-Hubbell Law Directory

PIERSON & BURNETT, L.L.P. (AV)

1667 K Street, N.W., Suite 801, 20006
Telephone: 202-466-3044
Fax: 202-466-3055
URL: http://www.comspacelaw.com

W. Theodore Pierson, Jr.
Dennis J. Burnett

David L. Lihani

For full biographical listings, see the Martindale-Hubbell Law Directory

VENABLE ATTORNEYS AT LAW VENABLE, BAETJER, HOWARD & CIVILETTI, LLP (AV)

A Partnership including Professional Corporations
Suite 1000, 1201 New York Avenue, N.W., 20005
Telephone: 202-962-4800
Fax: 202-962-8300
URL: http://www.venable.com
Baltimore, Maryland Office: Venable, Baetjer and Howard LLP, 1800 Mercantile Bank & Trust Building, 2 Hopkins Plaza.
Telephone: 410-244-7400.
Fax: 410-244-7742.
McLean, Virginia Office: Venable, Baetjer and Howard LLP, Suite 400, 2010 Corporate Ridge.
Telephone: 703-760-1600.
Fax: 703-821-8949.
Rockville, Maryland Office: Venable, Baetjer and Howard LLP, Suite 500, One Church Street, P. O. Box 1906.
Telephone: 301-217-5600.
Fax: 301-217-5617.
Towson, Maryland Office: Venable, Baetjer and Howard LLP, 210 Allegheny Avenue, P. O. Box 5517.
Telephone: 410-494-6200.
Fax: 410-821-0147.

MEMBERS OF FIRM

Edward F. Glynn, Jr.
Jeffrey D. Knowles
Ian D. Volner

OF COUNSEL

Frank Horton
Barbara L. Waite

For Complete List of Firm Personnel, See General Section

For full biographical listings, see the Martindale-Hubbell Law Directory

VERNER, LIIPFERT, BERNHARD, MCPHERSON AND HAND, CHARTERED (AV)

901 15th Street, N.W., 20005-2301
Telephone: 202-371-6000
Cable Address: "Verlip"
Fax: 202-371-6279
Email: verner.com *URL:* http://www.verner.com
Houston, Texas Office: 1111 Bagby, Suite 4700, 77002.
Telephone: 713-225-7200.
Fax: 713-752-2199.
Honolulu, Hawaii Office: 745 Fort Street, Suite 600, 96813.
Telephone: 808-566-0999.
Fax: 808-566-0995.
Austin, Texas Office: Suite 1440 San Jacinto Center, 98 San Jacinto Boulevard, 78701.
Telephone: 512-703-6000.
Fax: 512-703-6003.
Las Vegas, Nevada Affiliate Office: Gary C. Moss, Hughes Center, 3960 Howard Hughes Parkway, Suite 400, 89109.
Telephone: 702-737-3433.
Fax: 702-737-1612.
Miami, Florida Office: 3100 First Union Financial Center, 200 South Biscayne Boulevard, 33131.
Telephone: 305-371-8801.
Fax: 305-371-6545.

Thomas J. Keller
Erwin G. Krasnow
Lawrence E. Levinson (Not admitted in DC)
Lawrence R. Sidman

(See Next Column)

OF COUNSEL

Michael D. Berg
Philip R. Hochberg
Julian L. Shepard
David R. Siddall

For Complete List of Firm Personnel, See General Section

For full biographical listings, see the Martindale-Hubbell Law Directory

WILMER, CUTLER & PICKERING (AV)

2445 M Street, N.W., 20037-1420
Telephone: 202-663-6000
Fax: 202-663-6363
Email: Law@Wilmer.Com *URL:* http://www.wilmer.com
Baltimore, Maryland Office: 100 Light Street, 21202.
Telephone: 410-986-2800.
Fax: 410-986-2828.
New York, New York Office: 520 Madison Avenue, 10022.
Telephone: 212-230-8800.
Fax: 212-230-8888.
European Offices:
4 Carlton Gardens, London, SW1Y 5AA, England. Telephone: +44 (20) 7 872 1000.
Fax: +44 (20) 7 839 3537.
Rue de la Loi 15# Wetstraat, B-1040 Brussels, Belgium. Telephone: +32 (2) 285 49 00.
Fax: +32 (2) 285 49 49.
Friedrichstrasse 95, D-10117 Berlin, Germany. Telephone: +49 (30) 20 22 64 00.
Fax: +49 (30) 20 22 65 00.

MEMBERS OF FIRM

William T. Lake
David R. Johnson
John H. Harwood II
William R. Richardson, Jr.
W. Scott Blackmer
Thomas P. Olson
Patrick J. Carome
Lynn R. Charytan

SENIOR COUNSEL

J. Roger Wollenberg

COUNSEL

Joel Rosenbloom
Daniel B. Phythyon

For Complete List of Firm Personnel, See General Section

For full biographical listings, see the Martindale-Hubbell Law Directory

FLORIDA

*MIAMI,** Dade Co.

JOSEPH Z. FLEMING, P.A.

(See Ford & Harrison LLP, Miami, Florida)

GEORGIA

*ATLANTA,** Fulton Co.

CHOREY, TAYLOR & FEIL, A PROFESSIONAL CORPORATION (AV)

Suite 1700, The Lenox Building, 3399 Peachtree Road, N.E., 30326
Telephone: 404-841-3200
Facsimile: 404-841-3221
Email: ctf@ctflegal.com

Thomas V. Chorey, Jr.
John L. Taylor, Jr.
Matthew L. Hess

For Complete List of Firm Personnel, See General Section

For full biographical listings, see the Martindale-Hubbell Law Directory

HOLT NEY ZATCOFF & WASSERMAN, LLP (AV)

A Partnership including Professional Corporations
100 Galleria Parkway, Suite 600, 30339
Telephone: 770-956-9600
Facsimile: 770-956-1490
Email: mthomas@hnzw.com

MEMBERS OF FIRM

James M. Ney (P.C.)
J. Scott Jacobson
Stephen C. Greenberg
Brian P. Cain

ASSOCIATES

Thomas K. Anderson
Scott E. Morris

Representative Clients: Tower Com Development, Limited Partnership.

For Complete List of Firm Personnel, See General Section

For full biographical listings, see the Martindale-Hubbell Law Directory

Atlanta—Continued

LONG ALDRIDGE & NORMAN LLP (AV)

A Limited Liability Partnership including Professional Corporations
Suite 5300, 303 Peachtree Street, 30308
Telephone: 404-527-4000
Telecopier: 404-527-4198
Email: atlanta@lanlaw.com *URL:* http://www.lanlaw.com
Washington, D.C. Office: Suite 600, 701 Pennsylvania Avenue, N.W., 20004.
Telephone: 202-624-1200.
FAX: 202-624-1298.

MEMBERS OF FIRM

Wayne N. Bradley
Bruce P. Brown
L. Craig Dowdy
Jeffrey K. Haidet
H. Franklin Layson
Clay C. Long
Albert G. Norman, Jr.

SENIOR COUNSEL

F. T. Davis, Jr., (P.C.)

For Complete List of Firm Personnel, See General Section

For full biographical listings, see the Martindale-Hubbell Law Directory

HAWAII

*HONOLULU,** Honolulu Co.

GOODSILL ANDERSON QUINN & STIFEL (AV)

Alii Place, Suite 1800, 1099 Alakea Street, P.O. Box 3196, 96801-3196
Telephone: 808-547-5600
FAX: 808-547-5880
Email: info@goodsill.com *URL:* http://www.goodsill.com

MEMBERS OF FIRM

Thomas W. Williams, Jr.
Russell S. Kato
Audrey E. J. Ng
Kellie M. N. Sekiya

Representative Clients: PrimeCo Personal Communications, L.P.

For Complete List of Firm Personnel, See General Section

For full biographical listings, see the Martindale-Hubbell Law Directory

ILLINOIS

*CHICAGO,** Cook Co.

SAUNDERS & MONROE (AV)

1600 NBC Tower, 455 North Cityfront Plaza Drive, 60611
Telephone: 312-645-6000
Fax: 312-645-9848

MEMBERS OF FIRM

George L. Saunders, Jr.
Lee A. Monroe
Thomas F. Bush, Jr.
Matthew E. Van Tine
Thomas A. Doyle

OF COUNSEL

Victoria S. Kaplan

For full biographical listings, see the Martindale-Hubbell Law Directory

*PEORIA,** Peoria Co.

HOWARD & HOWARD ATTORNEYS, P.C. (AV)

The Creve Coeur Building, Suite 200, 321 Liberty Street, 61602-1403
Telephone: 309-672-1483
Telecopier: 309-672-1568
Kalamazoo, Michigan Office: The Michigan Building, Suite 200, 100 Portage Street.
Telephone: 616-382-1483.
Telecopier: 616-382-1568.
Bloomfield Hills, Michigan Office: The Pinehurst Office Center, Suite 101, 1400 North Woodward Avenue.
Telephone: 248-645-1483.
Telecopier: 248-645-1568.
Lansing, Michigan Office: Suite 500, The Phoenix Building, 222 Washington Square, North.
Telephone: 517-485-1483.
Telecopier: 517-485-1568.

Frederick G. Hoffman

Representative Clients: For Representative Client list, see General Practice, Peoria, IL.

(See Next Column)

For Complete List of Firm Personnel, See General Section

For full biographical listings, see the Martindale-Hubbell Law Directory

INDIANA

*INDIANAPOLIS,** Marion Co.

BOSE MCKINNEY & EVANS LLP (AV)

2700 First Indiana Plaza, 135 North Pennsylvania Street, 46204
Telephone: 317-684-5000
Facsimile: 317-684-5173
URL: http://www.boselaw.com
Indianapolis North Office: Suite 1500, 8888 Keystone Crossing, 46240.
Telephone: 317-574-3700.
Facsimile: 317-574-3716.

MEMBERS OF FIRM

Alan W. Becker
Kendall C. Crook
Ronald E. Elberger
David L. Wills

Representative Clients: David Letterman Companies; Columbia Management, Inc.; Emmis Communications Corp.; Apollo Communications Corporation; Hebdo Mag International; Atlanta Magazine; Nuvo News-Weekly; Indianapolis Monthly; Valcom, Inc.

For Complete List of Firm Personnel, See General Section

For full biographical listings, see the Martindale-Hubbell Law Directory

ICE MILLER DONADIO & RYAN (AV)

One American Square Box 82001, 46282-0002
Telephone: 317-236-2100
Fax: 317-236-2219
Email: info@imdr.com *URL:* http://www.imdr.com
South Bend, Indiana Office: 211 West Washington Street, Suite 2420.
Telephone: 219-234-7933.
Fax: 219-234-7965. Internet E-mail: info@imdr.com. Web Site Address: http://www.imdr.com.
Chicago, Illinois Office: 135 South LaSalle Street, Suite 4100.
Telephone: 312-726-1567.
Fax: 312-641-6263. Internet E-mail: info@imdr.com. Web Site Address: http://www.imdr.com.

MEMBERS OF FIRM

Jack R. Snyder
Thomas H. Ristine
Richard J. Thrapp
Michael A. Wilkins

OF COUNSEL

James B. Burroughs

ASSOCIATE

Paul H. Sinclair

Representative Clients: Indiana Broadcasters Assn.; Fairbanks Communications, Inc.; VideoIndiana, Inc.; Michiana Telecasting Corp.; National Broadcasting Co.; Sinclair Telecable, Inc.; Butler University; Taylor University; Great American Television & Radio Co.

For Complete List of Firm Personnel, See General Section

For full biographical listings, see the Martindale-Hubbell Law Directory

KANSAS

*TOPEKA,** Shawnee Co.

GOODELL, STRATTON, EDMONDS & PALMER, L.L.P. (AV)

515 South Kansas Avenue, 66603-3999
Telephone: 785-233-0593
Fax: 785-233-8870
Email: GSEP@CJNETWORKS.COM *URL:* http://www.cjnetworks.com/~gsep
Kansas City, Missouri Office: 10401 Holmes Road, Suite 280.
Telephone: 816-943-8577.

MEMBERS OF FIRM

Gerald L. Goodell
Arthur E. Palmer
John H. Stauffer, Jr.

SPECIAL COUNSEL

Curtis J. Waugh

Counsel for: Media Professional Insurance; Ogden Publications, Inc.; Mozark Publishing Company; Associated Press; Kansas Association of Broadcasters; Kansas Press Association; Reporters Committee for Freedom of the Press.

For Complete List of Firm Personnel, See General Section

For full biographical listings, see the Martindale-Hubbell Law Directory

KENTUCKY

*LEXINGTON,** Fayette Co.

STOLL, KEENON & PARK, LLP (AV)

201 E. Main Street, Suite 1000, 40507-1380
Telephone: 606-231-3000
Telecopier: 606-253-1093; 606-253-1027
URL: http://www.skp.com
Frankfort, Kentucky Office: 307 Washington Street, 40601.
Telephone: 502-875-6220.
Telecopier: 502-875-6235.
Henderson, Kentucky Office: 201 C North Main Street, 42420-3103.
Telephone: 270-831-1900.
Telecopier: 270-827-4060.
Louisville, Kentucky Office: 400 West Market Street, Suite 2650, 40202-3377.
Telephone: 502-568-9100.
Telecopier: 502-568-5700.

MEMBERS OF FIRM

Robert F. Houlihan, Jr. Dan M. Rose

Representative Clients: Lexington Herald Leader Co.; Knight-Ridder; GTE Of The South, GTE Products Corp.; BellSouth Mobility; Kentucky Press Assn.; Thompson Newspapers Inc.; Thoroughbred Racing Communications, Inc.; The Jockey Club.

For Complete List of Firm Personnel, See General Section

For full biographical listings, see the Martindale-Hubbell Law Directory

*LOUISVILLE,** Jefferson Co.

WYATT, TARRANT & COMBS (AV)

Citizens Plaza, 40202-2898
Telephone: 502-589-5235
Telecopier: 502-589-0309
URL: http://www.wyattfirm.com
Lexington, Kentucky Office: 1700 Lexington Financial Center.
Telephone: 606-233-2012.
Telecopier: 606-259-0649.
Frankfort, Kentucky Office: The Taylor-Scott Building, 311 West Main Street.
Telephone: 502-223-2104.
Telecopier: 502-227-7681.
New Albany, Indiana Office: The Elsby Building, 117 East Spring Street,
Telephone: 812-945-3561.
Telecopier: 812-949-2524.
Memphis, Tennessee Office: Crescent Center, Suite 650, 6075 Poplar Avenue.
Telephone: 901-537-1000.
Telecopier: 901-537-1010.
Nashville, Tennessee Office: 1500 Nashville City Center, 511 Union Street.
Telephone: 615-244-0020.
Telecopier: 615-256-1726.
Music Row, Nashville Office: 29 Music Square East.
Telephone: 615-255-6161.
Telecopier: 615-254-4490.
Hendersonville, Tennessee Office: 313 E. Main Street, Suite 1.
Telephone: 615-822-8822.
Telecopier: 615-824-4684.
Tri-Cities, Tennessee Office: Northeast Tennessee Business Park, 10368 Wallace Alley Street, Suite 6, Kingsport.
Telephone: 423-279-1825.
Telecopier: 423-279-9357.

MEMBERS OF FIRM

Edgar A. Zingman William H. Hollander

Representative Clients: Alpha Cellular Telephone Co.; BellSouth Telecommunications, Inc./South Central Bell; Clear Channel Radio, Inc.; Data Courier, Inc.; Kentucky Cable Television Assn.; McCann-Erickson of Louisville, Inc.; Shop at Home, Inc.; Telecable of Lexington; Thomas Nelson Publishers, Inc.; Trinity Broadcasting; WAVE-TV.

For Complete List of Firm Personnel, See General Section

For full biographical listings, see the Martindale-Hubbell Law Directory

LOUISIANA

*SHREVEPORT,** Caddo Parish

BARLOW AND HARDTNER L.C. (AV)

Tenth Floor, Louisiana Tower, 401 Edwards Street, 71101-3289
Telephone: 318-227-1131
Telecopier: 318-227-1141
Mailing Address: P.O. Box 8, Shreveport, Louisiana, 71161-0008

Joseph L. Shea, Jr. Jay A. Greenleaf

(See Next Column)

OF COUNSEL

Paula Hazelrig Hickman

Representative Clients: NorAm Energy Corp. (formerly Arkla, Inc.); Panhandle Eastern Corp.; Pennzoil Producing Co.; Ashland Oil, Inc.

For Complete List of Firm Personnel, See General Section

For full biographical listings, see the Martindale-Hubbell Law Directory

MAINE

*PORTLAND,** Cumberland Co.

PRETI, FLAHERTY, BELIVEAU, PACHIOS & HALEY, LLC (AV)

One City Center, P.O. Box 9546, 04112-9546
Telephone: 207-791-3000
Telecopier: 207-791-3111
Email: admin@preti.com *URL:* http://www.preti.com
Augusta, Maine Office: 45 Memorial Circle, P.O. Box 1058, 04332-1058.
Telephone: 207-623-5300.
Telefax: 207-623-2914.
Bath, Maine Office: Thirty Front Street, P.O. Box 665, 04530-0665.
Telephone: 207-443-5576.
Telefax: 207-443-6665.

MEMBERS OF FIRM

Severin M. Beliveau (Augusta Office)
Eric P. Stauffer
Jonathan S. Piper
Joseph G. Donahue (Augusta Office)
Ann R. Robinson (Augusta Office)
Mark B. LeDuc (Augusta Office)

ASSOCIATE

Kevin J. Beal

Representative Clients: Blethen-Maine Newspapers, Inc.; Maine Association of Broadcasters; Brunswick Publishing Co.; The Maine Times; State Cable; Public Cable Co.; Community Service Telephone Co.; Unitel, Inc.; Telephone Association of Maine.

For Complete List of Firm Personnel, See General Section

For full biographical listings, see the Martindale-Hubbell Law Directory

MARYLAND

*BALTIMORE,** (Independent City)

THOMAS & LIBOWITZ, P.A. (AV)

100 Light Street, Suite 1100, 21202-1053
Telephone: 410-752-2468
Fax: 410-752-2046; 752-2049; 752-0979
Email: thomasandlibowitz.com *URL:* http://www.thomasandlibowitz.com

Steven Anargyros Thomas
Michael S. Libowitz
Clinton R. Black, IV
C. Wayne Davis
Peter W. Taliaferro
Michael J. Collins

OF COUNSEL

Basil A. Thomas Susan M. Rittenhouse

LEGAL SUPPORT PERSONNEL

PARALEGALS

Melissa A. Johnson
Kelley Atkins
Kimberly Beard
Donna Janney

Representative Clients: Sinclair Broadcast Group, Inc. (Television and Radio stations); Roy Kirby & Sons, Inc. (Contractor); First Mariner Bank; Scandia Manufacturing Co. Inc. (Defense Contractor); Atlantic Automotive Corp. t/a Heritgage Automotive Group; Candy Express Franchising, Inc.; Wire Spectrum Services (Contractors-Transmission Tower Sites); Acrodyne Communications, Inc.; Alexis Logic Corporation (Software Developers); Selnic Corporation (Electronis Distributors); Liberty Mutual Insurance Company.

For full biographical listings, see the Martindale-Hubbell Law Directory

VENABLE ATTORNEYS AT LAW VENABLE, BAETJER AND HOWARD, LLP (AV)

A Partnership including Professional Corporations
1800 Mercantile Bank & Trust Building, 2 Hopkins Plaza, 21201
Telephone: 410-244-7400
Fax: 410-244-7742
URL: http://www.venable.com
Washington, D.C. Office: Venable, Baetjer, Howard & Civiletti LLP, Suite 1000, 1201 New York Avenue, N.W.
Telephone: 202-962-4800.
Fax: 202-962-8300.

(See Next Column)

VENABLE ATTORNEYS AT LAW VENABLE, BAETJER AND HOWARD, LLP, *Baltimore—Continued*

McLean, Virginia Office: Suite 400, 2010 Corporate Ridge.
Telephone: 703-760-1600.
Fax: 703-821-8949.
Rockville, Maryland Office: Suite 500, One Church Street, P. O. Box 1906.
Telephone: 301-217-5600.
Fax: 301-217-5617.
Towson, Maryland Office: 210 Allegheny Avenue, P. O. Box 5517.
Telephone: 410-494-6200.
Fax: 410-821-0147.

MEMBERS OF FIRM

Thomas P. Perkins, III (P.C.)
James A. Cole
Ian D. Volner (Not admitted in MD; Resident, Washington, D.C. Office)
Edward F. Glynn, Jr. (Resident, Washington, D.C. Office)
Jeffrey D. Knowles (Not admitted in MD; Resident, Washington, D.C. Office)

OF COUNSEL

Frank Horton (Not admitted in MD; Resident, Washington, D.C. Office)
Barbara L. Waite (Resident, Washington, D.C. Office)

For Complete List of Firm Personnel, See General Section

For full biographical listings, see the Martindale-Hubbell Law Directory

MASSACHUSETTS

*BOSTON,** Suffolk Co.

MINTZ, LEVIN, COHN, FERRIS, GLOVSKY AND POPEO, P.C. (AV)

One Financial Center, 02111
Telephone: 617-542-6000
FAX: 617-542-2241
Internet: Each Attorney's Internet Address takes the following form: first initial last name @mintz.com (e.g., rmintz@mintz.com)
URL: http://www.mintz.com
Washington, D.C. Office: 701 Pennsylvania Avenue, N.W. Suite 900.
Telephone: 202-434-7300.
Fax: 202-434-7400.
Reston, Virginia Office: 12021 Sunset Hills Road, Suite 310.
Telephone: 703-464-4800.
Fax: 703-464-4895.

Cameron F. Kerry
Charles D. Ferris (Resident, Washington, D.C. Office)
Frank W. Lloyd (Resident, Washington, D.C. Office)
Bruce D. Sokler (Resident, Washington, D.C. Office)
Howard J. Symons (Resident, Washington, D.C. Office)

For Complete List of Firm Personnel, See General Section

For full biographical listings, see the Martindale-Hubbell Law Directory

PALMER & DODGE LLP (AV)

One Beacon Street, 02108
Telephone: 617-573-0100
Facsimile: 617-227-4420
URL: http://www.palmerdodge.com

MEMBERS OF FIRM

James T. Barrett
Nathaniel S. Gardiner
Laurie S. Gill
Jeffrey F. Jones
Stanley Keller
David R. Pokross, Jr.
Kenneth W. Salinger
Thomas M. Spera
George Ticknor

SENIOR COUNSEL

Jay E. Gruber

For Complete List of Firm Personnel, See General Section

For full biographical listings, see the Martindale-Hubbell Law Directory

HINGHAM, Plymouth Co.

MALLOY & SULLIVAN LAWYERS PROFESSIONAL CORPORATION (AV)

59 Water Street, 02043
Telephone: 781-749-4141
Fax: 781-749-4109
Email: g.sullivan@worldnet.att.net
Email: mslpc@aol.com
Manchester, New Hampshire Office: 78 West Merrimack Street.
Telephone: 603-668-3737.
Fax: 603-668-5232.

(See Next Column)

Ralph Warren Sullivan (1921-1989)
Gregory V. Sullivan

OF COUNSEL

Richard A. Sullivan

For full biographical listings, see the Martindale-Hubbell Law Directory

MICHIGAN

BLOOMFIELD HILLS, Oakland Co.

ADKISON, NEED, GREEN & ALLEN (AV)

1533 North Woodward Avenue, Suite 210, 48304
Telephone: 248-540-7400
Fax: 248-540-7401
URL: http://www.adkisonneed.com

MEMBERS OF FIRM

Phillip G. Adkison
Gregory K. Need
Paul Green

ASSOCIATE

Richard D. Kuhn, Jr.

For Complete List of Firm Personnel, See General Section

For full biographical listings, see the Martindale-Hubbell Law Directory

*DETROIT,** Wayne Co.

BODMAN, LONGLEY & DAHLING LLP (AV)

34th Floor 100 Renaissance Center, 48243
Telephone: 313-259-7777
Fax: 313-393-7579
Email: info@bodmanlongley.com *URL:* http://www.bodmanlongley.com
Troy, Michigan Office: Suite 2020, 755 West Big Beaver Road.
Telephone: 248-362-2110.
Fax: 248-244-0780.
Ann Arbor, Michigan Office: 110 Miller, Suite 300.
Telephone: 734-761-3780.
Fax: 734-930-2494.
Northern Michigan Office: 229 Court Street, P.O. Box 405, Cheboygan.
Telephone: 231-627-4351.
Fax: 231-627-2802.

MEMBERS OF FIRM

Carson C. Grunewald
Kenneth R. Lango (Troy Office)
James A. Smith
James J. Walsh
Thomas J. Tallerico

For Representative Client List, See General Section

For Complete List of Firm Personnel, See General Section

For full biographical listings, see the Martindale-Hubbell Law Directory

HONIGMAN MILLER SCHWARTZ AND COHN (AV)

2290 First National Building, 660 Woodward Avenue, 48226
Telephone: 313-465-7000
Telecopier: 313-465-8000
Telex: 235705
Email: mvg@honigman.com *URL:* http://law.honigman.com
Lansing, Michigan Office: Phoenix Building, 222 North Washington Square, Suite 400, 48933-1800.
Telephone: 517-484-8282.

MEMBERS OF FIRM

Cameron J. Evans
Herschel P. Fink
Cynthia G. Thomas

ASSOCIATE

Andrew S. Doctoroff

Representative Clients: The Detroit Free Press; Knight-Ridder Inc.; ABC, Inc.; Crain Communications; Heritage Media Corp. (Mellus Newspapers, Dearborn Press and Guide, and News Herald Newspapers); Fox, Inc. (WJBK-TV) Channel 2; Paramount Stations Group (WKBD-TV) Channel 50, (WTVS-TV) Channel 56; American Society of Composers, Authors and Publishers (ASCAP).

For Complete List of Firm Personnel, See General Section

For full biographical listings, see the Martindale-Hubbell Law Directory

Detroit—Continued

MILLER, CANFIELD, PADDOCK AND STONE, P.L.C. (AV)

A Professional Limited Liability Company
Founded in 1852 by Sidney Davy Miller
150 West Jefferson, Suite 2500, 48226-4415
Telephone: 313-963-6420
Fax: 313-496-7500
Cable Address: "Stem Detroit"
URL: http://www.millercanfield.com
Ann Arbor, Michigan Office: 101 North Main Street, 7th Floor, 48104-1400.
Telephone: 734-663-2445.
Fax: 734-747-7147.
Troy, Michigan Office: 840 West Long Lake Road, Suite 200, 48098.
Telephone: 248-879-2000.
Fax: 248-879-2001.
Grand Rapids, Michigan Office: 99 Monroe, N.W., Suite 1200, 49503-2639.
Telephone: 616-454-8656.
Fax: 616-776-6322.
Howell, Michigan Office: 121 South Barnard Street, Suite 4, 48843-2305.
Telephone: 517-546-7600.
Telecopier: 517-546-6974.
Kalamazoo, Michigan Office: 444 West Michigan Avenue, 49007-3752.
Telephone: 616-381-7030.
Fax: 616-382-0244.
Lansing, Michigan Office: One Michigan Avenue, Suite 900, 48933-1609.
Telephone: 517-487-2070.
Fax: 517-374-6304.
Monroe, Michigan Office: 214 East Elm Avenue, Suite 100, 48162-2682.
Telephone: 734-243-2000.
Fax: 734-243-0901.
Washington, D.C. Office: 1900 K Street, N.W., Suite 1150. 20006.
Telephone: 202-429-5575; 785-0600.
Fax: 202-331-1118; 785-1234.
Pensacola, Florida Office: 25 West Cedar, 32501.
Telephone: 850-469-1088.
Fax: 850-432-0677.
New York, New York Office: 1450 Broadway, 41st Floor, 10018.
Telephone: 212-704-4400.
Fax: 212-704-4410.
Gdynia, Poland Office: UL. Slaska 21, 81-319.
Telephone: 011-485-831-2808.
Fax: 011-48-58-628 6411.
Warsaw, Poland Office: UL. Nowogrodzkall, 5th Floor, 00-513.
Telephone: 011-4822 529 0200.
Fax: 011-4822 529 0201.
Katowice, Poland Office: UL. Francuska 35/37, 40-027.
Telephone: 011 (48-32) 757-2414.
Fax: 011 (48-32) 757-2483.

PRINCIPALS OF FIRM

Carl H. von Ende
Richard T. Urbis

OF COUNSEL/SENIOR COUNSEL

Tillman L. Lay (Washington, D.C. Office)

ASSOCIATE

Michael C. Fayz

Representative Firm Clients: Chrysler Corporation; Comerica, Incorporated; City of Detroit, Michigan; Detroit Tigers, Inc.; First of Michigan; Ford Motor Company; Ford Motor Credit Company; Great Lakes Bancorp; Henry Ford Hospital; INVETECH Company.

For Complete List of Firm Personnel, See General Section

For full biographical listings, see the Martindale-Hubbell Law Directory

SOUTHFIELD, Oakland Co.

COLLINS, EINHORN, FARRELL & ULANOFF, A PROFESSIONAL CORPORATION (AV)

4000 Town Center, Suite 909, 48075-1473
Telephone: 248-355-4141
Facsimile: 248-355-2277

Morton H. Collins
Brian D. Einhorn
Clayton F. Farrell
Stuart A. Ulanoff
Dale J. McLellan
Kenneth C. Merritt
Noreen L. Slank
Michael J. Sullivan
Janice G. Hildenbrand
Neil W. MacCallum

Theresa M. Asoklis
Karen C. Liddle
Deborah A. Lujan
Shannon M. Kos
Kevin P. Moloughney
Susan P. Saltzman
Daniel E. Collins
J. Mark Cooney
David C. Anderson

For full biographical listings, see the Martindale-Hubbell Law Directory

COMPUTER LAW

ALABAMA

*BIRMINGHAM,** Jefferson Co.

BRADLEY ARANT ROSE & WHITE LLP (AV)

2001 Park Place, Suite 1400, P.O. Box 830709, 35283-0709
Telephone: 205-521-8000
Facsimile: 205-521-8800
Facsimile (SouthTrust Tower Office): 205-521-8500
URL: http://www.barw.com
Huntsville, Alabama Office: 200 Clinton Avenue West, Suite 900, 35801.
Telephone: 205-517-5100.
Facsimile: 205-533-5069.
Washington, D.C. Office: 801 Pennsylvania Avenue, NW, Suite 230, 20004.
Telephone: 202-347-8893.
Facsimile: 202-347-1684.

MEMBER OF FIRM

David Glenn Hymer

For Complete List of Firm Personnel, See General Section

For full biographical listings, see the Martindale-Hubbell Law Directory

ARIZONA

*PHOENIX,** Maricopa Co.

FENNEMORE CRAIG, A PROFESSIONAL CORPORATION (AV)

3003 North Central Avenue, Suite 2600, 85012-2913
Telephone: 602-916-5000
Fax: 602-916-5999
Tucson, Arizona Office: One South Church Avenue, Suite 1000, 85701-1620.
Telephone: 520-879-6800.
Fax: 520-879-6899.

C. Owen Paepke
Ray K. Harris

Paul F. Wille (Not admitted in AZ)
Stacie K. Smith
Sandra L. Etherton

For Complete List of Firm Personnel, See General Section

For full biographical listings, see the Martindale-Hubbell Law Directory

CALIFORNIA

COSTA MESA, Orange Co.

RUTAN & TUCKER, LLP (AV)

A Partnership including Professional Corporations
611 Anton Boulevard, Fourteenth Floor, P.O. Box 1950, 92626-1998
Telephone: 714-641-5100; 213-625-7586
Telecopier: 714-546-9035
Email: rutan&tucker@rutan.com *URL:* http://www.rutan.com

MEMBERS OF FIRM

Gilbert N. Kruger
Michael T. Hornak
Thomas J. Crane
Mark B. Frazier

ASSOCIATES

Kent M. Clayton
Treg A. Julander
B. Lynn Loschin

OF COUNSEL

Edward D. Sybesma, Jr. (P.C.)

For Complete List of Firm Personnel, See General Section

For full biographical listings, see the Martindale-Hubbell Law Directory

IRVINE, Orange Co.

THE ENTERPRISE COUNSEL GROUP (AV)

5 Park Plaza, 92614
Telephone: 949-553-2404
Fax: 949-553-2434
URL: http://www.enterprisecounsel.com

(See Next Column)

David A. Robinson
Corey E. Taylor
Susan M. Masson
Jeffrey Lewis

For full biographical listings, see the Martindale-Hubbell Law Directory

LAGUNA HILLS, Orange Co.

STETINA BRUNDA GARRED & BRUCKER, A PROFESSIONAL CORPORATION (AV)

24221 Calle De La Louisa, 4th Floor, 92653-3642
Telephone: 949-855-1246
Facsimile: 949-855-6371; 949-855-8986
Email: stetinabrundagarred&brucker@stetinalaw.com

Kit M. Stetina (Mr.)
Bruce B. Brunda
Mark B. Garred
William J. Brucker

Matthew A. Newboles
Thomas C. Naber (Not admitted in CA)
Darren S. Rimer
Eric L. Tanezaki
Eric K. Proul

LEGAL SUPPORT PERSONNEL

Kristy Kay Moore

For full biographical listings, see the Martindale-Hubbell Law Directory

*LOS ANGELES,** Los Angeles Co.

BLANC WILLIAMS JOHNSTON & KRONSTADT, LLP (AV)

A Partnership including Professional Corporations
Suite 1700, 1900 Avenue of the Stars, 90067
Telephone: 310-552-2500
Telecopier: 310-552-1191
Email: bwjk@bwjk.com

MEMBERS OF FIRM

Ronald L. Blanc (P.C.)
Harley J. Williams (P.C.)
Ronald L. Johnston (P.C.)
John A. Kronstadt
James R. Farrand
Richard T. McCoy III
Regina A. Stagg
John C. Rawls III
Daniel M. Grigsby
Suzanne V. Wilson
Dawn Weekes Glenn

James S. Blackburn
Vivian W. Yang
Allison Binder
Jennifer M. Lloyd
Mark S. Dancsecs

OF COUNSEL

Sol Rosenthal

Reference: Santa Monica Bank (Beverly Hills Office).

For full biographical listings, see the Martindale-Hubbell Law Directory

*SAN FRANCISCO,** San Francisco Co.

HAIGHT, BROWN & BONESTEEL, L.L.P. (AV)

A Partnership including Professional Corporations
100 Bush Street, 27th Floor, 94104-3902
Telephone: 415-986-7700
Telecopier: 415-986-6945
URL: http://www.hbblaw.com
Santa Monica, California Office: 1620 26th Street, Suite 4000 North, P.O. Box 680.
Telephone: 310-449-6000.
Telecopier: 310-829-5117.
Telex: 705837.
Santa Ana, California Office: Suite 900, 5 Hutton Centre Drive.
Telephone: 714-754-1100.
Telecopier: 714-754-0826.
Riverside, California Office: California Tower, 3737 Main Street, Suite 800.
Telephone: 909-341-8300.
Fax: 909-341-8309.
San Diego, California Office: 101 West Broadway, Suite 1000.
Telephone: 619-595-5583.
Fax: 619-595-7873.

RESIDENT MEMBER

David W. Evans

ASSOCIATE

Russell J. Smith

For full biographical listings, see the Martindale-Hubbell Law Directory

COLORADO

*DENVER,** Denver Co.

GORSUCH KIRGIS LLP (AV)

Tower 1, Suite 1000, 1515 Arapahoe Street, 80202
Telephone: 303-376-5000
Fax: 303-376-5001

PARTNERS

S. Lee Terry, Jr.
Cynthia Smith Cain

ASSOCIATE

Pantea M. Garroussi

LEGAL SUPPORT PERSONNEL

Lansing Wallace
Veronica Ehrenzeller

For full biographical listings, see the Martindale-Hubbell Law Directory

DISTRICT OF COLUMBIA

WASHINGTON, D.C. Co.

BARKATS & ASSOCIATES, CHARTERED, ATTORNEYS AND COUNSELORS AT LAW (AV)

1250 Eye Street, N.W., 20005
Telephone: 202-682-1396
Telecopier: 202-789-0895
URL: http://www.lawyers.com/barkatslaw
Paris, France Office: 24, Rue de Prony, 75017 Paris, France.
Telephone: 01 44 29 32 32.
Telecopier: 44 29 31 00.
Affiliated Law Firm: Robert J. Shutak, 1424 Fourth Street, Santa Monica, California 90401.
Telephone: 310-458-3343.
Telecopier: 301-451-0043.

MEMBER OF THE FIRM IN WASHINGTON, D.C.

Pierre-Philippe Barkats

ASSOCIATES

Robert Clifton Burns
Jeffrey Thomas Gutierrez (Not admitted in DC)
Pat James Kalellis (Not admitted in DC)

OF COUNSEL

Jerome K. Tankel
Jacques R. Beghain (Not admitted in the United States)

For full biographical listings, see the Martindale-Hubbell Law Directory

BLUMENFELD & COHEN (AV)

1625 Massachusetts Avenue, N.W., Suite 300, 20036
Telephone: 202-955-6300
Facsimile: 202-955-6460
Email: info@technologylaw.com *URL:* http://www.technologylaw.com
San Francisco, California Office: 4 Embarcadero Center, Suite 1170, 94111.
Telephone: 415-394-7500.
Facsimile: 415-394-7505.

MEMBERS OF FIRM

Jeffrey Blumenfeld
Gary M. Cohen
Glenn B. Manishin
Stephen P. Bowen (Not admitted in DC; Resident, San Francisco Office)
David M. Naseman (Not admitted in DC)
Elise P.W. Kiely

OF COUNSEL

Rand McQuinn

ASSOCIATES

Stephanie A. Joyce (Not admitted in DC)
Colin M. Alberts

For full biographical listings, see the Martindale-Hubbell Law Directory

FLORIDA

*MIAMI,** Dade Co.

MARTENS DUNAJ MARLOWE DAVIS & MARLOWE (AV)

Miami Center, Suite 880, 201 South Biscayne Boulevard, 33131
Telephone: 305-373-9977
Fax: 305-373-8877
Email: postmaster@miamilaw.net *URL:* http://www.miamilaw.net
New Port Richey, Florida Office: 8726 Old County Road 54, Suite E.
Telephone: 727-376-9599.
Fax: 727-376-3146. Email: postmaster@miamilaw.net. URL: http://www.miamilaw.net.

Sherryll Martens Dunaj
Ronald J. Marlowe
Gary L. Davis
Russell G. Marlowe
Linda G. McLoughlin
John L. Urban

For full biographical listings, see the Martindale-Hubbell Law Directory

*SARASOTA,** Sarasota Co.

WILSON, JOHNSON & JAFFER, P.A. (AV)

27 South Orange Avenue, 34236-5822
Telephone: 941-955-5800
Fax: 941-955-7353
Email: wilson@lawsites.com *URL:* http://www.lawsites.com

Clyde H. Wilson (1908-1994)
Robert M. Johnson
Clyde H. Wilson, Jr.
John S. Jaffer

For full biographical listings, see the Martindale-Hubbell Law Directory

*TALLAHASSEE,** Leon Co.

POLSTON, DEAN & HEALY, P.A. (AV)

Suite 900, Highpoint Center, 106 East College Avenue (32301), P.O. Box 1836, 32302-1836
Telephone: 850-513-0404
Fax: 850-681-0506
Email: polston@polstonlaw.com *URL:* http://www.lawyers.com/polstonlaw

Ricky L. Polston
James J. Dean
David P. Healy

For full biographical listings, see the Martindale-Hubbell Law Directory

*TAMPA,** Hillsborough Co.

BURTON & MURPHY (AV)

101 East Kennedy Boulevard Suite 1165, 33602
Telephone: 813-226-8500
Fax: 813-226-4266
Mailing Address: P.O. Box 172069, Tampa, Florida, 33672
Email: Attorneys@BurtonMurphy.com *URL:* http://www.BurtonMurphy.com

Steven G. Burton
Jeffrey D. Murphy
Charles G. Geitner

Beatriz M. Carta Wagman

For full biographical listings, see the Martindale-Hubbell Law Directory

GEORGIA

*ATLANTA,** Fulton Co.

LONG ALDRIDGE & NORMAN LLP (AV)

A Limited Liability Partnership including Professional Corporations
Suite 5300, 303 Peachtree Street, 30308
Telephone: 404-527-4000
Telecopier: 404-527-4198
Email: atlanta@lanlaw.com *URL:* http://www.lanlaw.com
Washington, D.C. Office: Suite 600, 701 Pennsylvania Avenue, N.W., 20004.
Telephone: 202-624-1200.
FAX: 202-624-1298.

MEMBERS OF FIRM

Maurice Ted Maloof
Ian K. Portnoy (Resident, Washington, D.C. Office)
Lisa W. Wannamaker
Charles E. Wilson, III

ASSOCIATES

Adam G. Mersereau
Julie Sonenshine Porter

(See Next Column)

LONG ALDRIDGE & NORMAN LLP—*Continued*

OF COUNSEL

Emily Gail Gunnells

For Complete List of Firm Personnel, See General Section

For full biographical listings, see the Martindale-Hubbell Law Directory

ILLINOIS

*CHICAGO,** Cook Co.

ARTHUR FAKES P.C.

(See Lombard)

HAMMAN & BENN (AV)

Suite 3300, 10 South La Salle Street, 60603-1002
Telephone: 312-372-2920
Facsimile: 312-372-7762

George W. Hamman
Marvin N. Benn
Dawn M. Cassie
Richard J. Superfine
Stephen J. Cassin
Jeanne M. Hoffmann
Jack Shore

OF COUNSEL

Jeffrey M. Carey
Ronald Olbrysh
Mitchell H. Saranow

For full biographical listings, see the Martindale-Hubbell Law Directory

MCBRIDE BAKER & COLES (AV)

500 West Madison Street 40th Floor, 60661-2511
Telephone: 312-715-5700
Cable Address: "Chilaw"
Telex: 270258
Telecopier: 312-993-9350
Email: lastname@mbc.com *URL:* http://www.mbc.com
Oakbrook Terrace, Illinois Office: Suite 1000, One Mid America Plaza, 60181-4710.
Telephone: 630-954-2100.
Telecopier: 630-954-2112.

MEMBERS OF FIRM

Thomas P. Arden
Andrew R. Basile
Malcolm H. Brooks
Donald G. Mulack
Elizabeth S. Perdue
Robert I. Schwimmer
Alan S. Wernick
Richard R. Winter
Larry M. Zanger

OF COUNSEL

Geoffrey G. Gilbert

ASSOCIATES

Marc L. Fogelberg
André C. Frieden
Sarah E. Pace
Peter J. Strand

For Complete List of Firm Personnel, See General Section

For full biographical listings, see the Martindale-Hubbell Law Directory

LOMBARD, DuPage Co.

ARTHUR FAKES P.C. (AV)

929 South Main Street, Suite 109, 60148
Telephone: 630-268-0600
Telecopier: 630-268-0642
Email: ARTFAKES@AOL.COM *URL:* http://www.lawyers.com/fakeslaw

Arthur Fakes

For full biographical listings, see the Martindale-Hubbell Law Directory

INDIANA

*INDIANAPOLIS,** Marion Co.

SOMMER & BARNARD, ATTORNEYS AT LAW, PC (AV)

4000 Bank One Tower, 111 Monument Circle, 46204
Telephone: 317-630-4000
FAX: 317-236-9802
Email: sandb@sommerbarnard.com
North Office: 8900 Keystone Crossing, Suite 1150, Indianapolis, Indiana, 46240-2134.
Telephone: 317-630-4000.
FAX: 317-844-4780.

(See Next Column)

William C. Barnard
Edward W. Harris, III
Gordon L. Pittenger

Representative Clients: Comerica Bank; Federal Express; Kimball International; Monsanto; TRW, Inc.

For Complete List of Firm Personnel, See General Section

For full biographical listings, see the Martindale-Hubbell Law Directory

MASSACHUSETTS

*BOSTON,** Suffolk Co.

HINCKLEY, ALLEN & SNYDER LLP (AV)

28 State Street, 30th Floor, 02109-1775
Telephone: 617-345-9000
Email: firm@haslaw.com *URL:* http://www.haslaw.com
Providence, Rhode Island Office: 1500 Fleet Center.
Telephone: 401-274-2000.
Fax: 401-277-9600. URL: http://www.hawlaw.com.

MEMBERS OF FIRM

Paula K. Andrews
David D. Barricelli (Not admitted in MA)
Jonathan Bell
Paul Bork
Stephen J. Carlotti (Not admitted in MA)
Joseph P. Curran (Not admitted in MA)
Michael P. DeFanti
Eric F. Eisenberg
Margaret D. Farrell (Not admitted in MA)
Pasco Gasbarro Jr.
Hugh J. Gorman, III
William R. Grimm
Richard L. E. Jocelyn (Not admitted in MA)
Elizabeth Murdock Myers
Paul F. O'Donnell, III
H. Peter Olsen (Not admitted in MA)
John J. Pendergast, III (Not admitted in MA)
Gerald J. Petros
Herman Snyder
David R. Sullivan
Robert F. Sylvia
Howard E. Walker (Not admitted in MA)
Richard D. Wayne

ASSOCIATES

Mark Bianchi
Andrew D. Cummings
June E. Daniel (Not admitted in MA)
Kelley Jordan-Price
Catherine S. Kim
Christopher W. Morog
Elena B. Olson
Joseph D. Whelan (Not admitted in MA)

For Complete List of Firm Personnel, See General Section

For full biographical listings, see the Martindale-Hubbell Law Directory

PALMER & DODGE LLP (AV)

One Beacon Street, 02108
Telephone: 617-573-0100
Facsimile: 617-227-4420
URL: http://www.palmerdodge.com

MEMBERS OF FIRM

F. Andrew Anderson
James T. Barrett
Matthew C. Dallett
Lynnette C. Fallon
Steven N. Farber
Mark A. Fischer
Nathaniel S. Gardiner
Stanley Keller
Michael J. Lacek
Francis C. Lynch
Michael Lytton
Maureen P. Manning
David R. Pokross, Jr.
John A. Rissman (Not admitted in MA)
Marc A. Rubenstein
Thomas M. Spera
Craig E. Stewart
John Taylor Williams

For Complete List of Firm Personnel, See General Section

For full biographical listings, see the Martindale-Hubbell Law Directory

MICHIGAN

BLOOMFIELD HILLS, Oakland Co.

ADKISON, NEED, GREEN & ALLEN (AV)

1533 North Woodward Avenue, Suite 210, 48304
Telephone: 248-540-7400
Fax: 248-540-7401
URL: http://www.adkisonneed.com

MEMBERS OF FIRM

Phillip G. Adkison
Gregory K. Need
Paul Green
Kelly A. Allen

(See Next Column)

ADKISON, NEED, GREEN & ALLEN, *Bloomfield Hills—Continued*

ASSOCIATES

Annette J. Benson
Kevin M. Chudler
Miriam Blanks-Smart
Richard D. Kuhn, Jr.
Nicki L. Weisberger

OF COUNSEL

John M. Fuleras
Thomas R. Curran, Jr.

For full biographical listings, see the Martindale-Hubbell Law Directory

PROVIZER & PHILLIPS, P.C. (AV)

6785 Telegraph Road, Suite 400, 48301
Telephone: 248-642-0444
Facsimile: 248-642-6661
Toll Free: 1-800-288-9080
URL: http://www.lawyers.com/provizer&phillips

Harold M. Provizer
Evan A. Zagoria
Randall E. Phillips
Noel F. Beck
Marilyn A. Madorsky
Mark S. Baumkel

Constance S. Hall
Donald J. Parthum, Jr.
Ellen C. Busch
Keith A. Castora
Gregory A. Nave

For full biographical listings, see the Martindale-Hubbell Law Directory

*DETROIT,** Wayne Co.

MILLER, CANFIELD, PADDOCK AND STONE, P.L.C. (AV)

A Professional Limited Liability Company
Founded in 1852 by Sidney Davy Miller
150 West Jefferson, Suite 2500, 48226-4415
Telephone: 313-963-6420
Fax: 313-496-7500
Cable Address: "Stem Detroit"
URL: http://www.millercanfield.com
Ann Arbor, Michigan Office: 101 North Main Street, 7th Floor, 48104-1400.
Telephone: 734-663-2445.
Fax: 734-747-7147.
Troy, Michigan Office: 840 West Long Lake Road, Suite 200, 48098.
Telephone: 248-879-2000.
Fax: 248-879-2001.
Grand Rapids, Michigan Office: 99 Monroe, N.W., Suite 1200, 49503-2639.
Telephone: 616-454-8656.
Fax: 616-776-6322.
Howell, Michigan Office: 121 South Barnard Street, Suite 4, 48843-2305.
Telephone: 517-546-7600.
Telecopier: 517-546-6974.
Kalamazoo, Michigan Office: 444 West Michigan Avenue, 49007-3752.
Telephone: 616-381-7030.
Fax: 616-382-0244.
Lansing, Michigan Office: One Michigan Avenue, Suite 900, 48933-1609.
Telephone: 517-487-2070.
Fax: 517-374-6304.
Monroe, Michigan Office: 214 East Elm Avenue, Suite 100, 48162-2682.
Telephone: 734-243-2000.
Fax: 734-243-0901.
Washington, D.C. Office: 1900 K Street, N.W., Suite 1150. 20006.
Telephone: 202-429-5575; 785-0600.
Fax: 202-331-1118; 785-1234.
Pensacola, Florida Office: 25 West Cedar, 32501.
Telephone: 850-469-1088.
Fax: 850-432-0677.
New York, New York Office: 1450 Broadway, 41st Floor, 10018.
Telephone: 212-704-4400.
Fax: 212-704-4410.
Gdynia, Poland Office: UL. Slaska 21, 81-319.
Telephone: 011-485-831-2808.
Fax: 011-48-58-628 6411.
Warsaw, Poland Office: UL. Nowogrodzkall, 5th Floor, 00-513.
Telephone: 011-4822 529 0200.
Fax: 011-4822 529 0201.
Katowice, Poland Office: UL. Francuska 35/37, 40-027.
Telephone: 011 (48-32) 757-2414.
Fax: 011 (48-32) 757-2483.

PRINCIPALS OF FIRM

Marjory G. Basile

Representative Firm Clients: Chrysler Corporation; Comerica, Incorporated; City of Detroit, Michigan; Detroit Tigers, Inc.; First of Michigan; Ford Motor Company; Ford Motor Credit Company; Great Lakes Bancorp; Henry Ford Hospital; INVETECH Company.

For Complete List of Firm Personnel, See General Section

For full biographical listings, see the Martindale-Hubbell Law Directory

*GRAND RAPIDS,** Kent Co.

MILLER, CANFIELD, PADDOCK AND STONE, P.L.C. (AV)

A Professional Limited Liability Company
Founded in 1852 by Sidney Davy Miller
99 Monroe, N.W. Suite 1200, 49503-2639
Telephone: 616-454-8656
Fax: 616-776-6322
URL: http://www.millercanfield.com
Detroit, Michigan Office: 150 West Jefferson, Suite 2500, 48226-4415.
Telephone: 313-963-6420.
Fax: 313-496-7500.
Cable Address: "Stem Detroit."
Ann Arbor, Michigan Office: 101 North Main Street, 7th Floor, 48104-1400.
Telephone: 734-663-2445.
Fax: 734-747-7147.
Troy, Michigan Office: 840 West Long Lake Road, Suite 200, 48098.
Telephone: 248-879-2000.
Fax: 248-879-2001.
Howell, Michigan Office: 121 South Barnard Street, Suite 4, 48843-2305.
Telephone: 517-546-7600.
Telecopier: 517-546-6974.
Kalamazoo, Michigan Office: 444 West Michigan Avenue, 49007-3752.
Telephone: 616-381-7030.
Fax: 616-382-0244.
Lansing, Michigan Office: One Michigan Avenue, Suite 900, 48933-1609.
Telephone: 517-487-2070.
Fax: 517-374-6304.
Monroe, Michigan Office: 214 East Elm Avenue, Suite 100, 48162-2682.
Telephone: 734-243-2000.
Fax: 734-243-0901.
Washington, D.C. Office: 1900 K Street, N.W., Suite 1150. 20006.
Telephone: 202-429-5575; 785-0600.
Fax: 202-331-1118; 785-1234.
Pensacola, Florida Office: 25 West Cedar, 32501.
Telephone: 850-469-1088.
Fax: 850-432-0677.
New York, New York Office: 1450 Broadway, 41st Floor, 10018.
Telephone: 212-704-4400.
Fax: 212-704-4410.
Gdynia, Poland Office: UL. Slaska 21, 81-319.
Telephone: 011-485-831-2808.
Fax: 011-48-58-628 6411.
Warsaw, Poland Office: UL. Nowogrodzkall, 5th Floor, 00-513.
Telephone: 011-4822 529 0200.
Fax: 011-4822 529 0201.
Katowice, Poland Office: UL. Francuska 35/37, 40-027.
Telephone: 011 (48-32) 757-2414.
Fax: 011 (48-32) 757-2483.

PRINCIPALS

Mark E. Putney

Representative Firm Clients: Chrysler Corporation; Comerica, Incorporated; City of Detroit, Michigan; Detroit Tigers, Inc.; First of Michigan; Ford Motor Company; Ford Motor Credit Company; Great Lakes Bancorp; Henry Ford Hospital; INVETECH Company.

For Complete List of Firm Personnel, See General Section

For full biographical listings, see the Martindale-Hubbell Law Directory

WARNER NORCROSS & JUDD LLP (AV)

900 Old Kent Building, 111 Lyon Street, N.W., 49503-2489
Telephone: 616-752-2000
Fax: 616-752-2500
URL: http://www.wnj.com
Muskegon, Michigan Office: 400 Terrace Plaza, P.O. Box 900.
Telephone: 231-727-2600.
Fax: 231-727-2699.
Holland, Michigan Office: Curtis Center, Suite 300, 170 College Avenue.
Telephone: 616-396-9800.
Fax: 616-396-3656.
Southfield, Michigan Office: 1000 Town Center, Suite 650.
Telephone: 248-223-5000.
Fax: 248-223-5005.

MEMBERS OF FIRM

Stephen C. Waterbury
Charles E. Burpee
Janet Percy Knaus

ASSOCIATES

Norbert F. Kugele
Michael P. Lunt
William P. Dani
Daniel K. DeWitt
James L. Scott II

For full biographical listings, see the Martindale-Hubbell Law Directory

*KALAMAZOO,** Kalamazoo Co.

Miller, Canfield, Paddock and Stone, P.L.C. (AV)

A Professional Limited Liability Company
Founded in 1852 by Sidney Davy Miller
444 West Michigan Avenue, 49007-3752
Telephone: 616-381-7030
Fax: 616-382-0244
URL: http://www.millercanfield.com
Detroit, Michigan Office: 150 West Jefferson, Suite 2500, 48226-4415.
Telephone: 313-963-6420.
Fax: 313-496-7500.
Cable Address: "Stem Detroit."
Ann Arbor, Michigan Office: 101 North Main Street, 7th Floor, 48104-1400.
Telephone: 734-663-2445.
Fax: 734-747-7147.
Troy, Michigan Office: 840 West Long Lake Road, Suite 200, 48098.
Telephone: 248-879-2000.
Fax: 248-879-2001.
Grand Rapids, Michigan Office: 99 Monroe, N.W., Suite 1200, 49503-2639.
Telephone: 616-454-8656.
Fax: 616-776-6322.
Howell, Michigan Office: 121 South Barnard Street, Suite 4, 48843-2305.
Telephone: 517-546-7600.
Telecopier: 517-546-6974.
Lansing, Michigan Office: One Michigan Avenue, Suite 900, 48933-1609.
Telephone: 517-487-2070.
Fax: 517-374-6304.
Monroe, Michigan Office: 214 East Elm Avenue, Suite 100, 48162-2682.
Telephone: 734-243-2000.
Fax: 734-243-0901.
Washington, D.C. Office: 1900 K Street, N.W., Suite 1150. 20006.
Telephone: 202-429-5575; 785-0600.
Fax: 202-331-1118; 785-1234.
Pensacola, Florida Office: 25 West Cedar, 32501.
Telephone: 850-469-1088.
Fax: 850-432-0677.
New York, New York Office: 1450 Broadway, 41st Floor, 10018.
Telephone: 212-704-4400.
Fax: 212-704-4410.
Gdynia, Poland Office: UL. Slaska 21, 81-319.
Telephone: 011-485-831-2808.
Fax: 011-48-58-628 6411.
Warsaw, Poland Office: UL. Nowogrodzkall, 5th Floor, 00-513.
Telephone: 011-4822 529 0200.
Fax: 011-4822 529 0201.
Katowice, Poland Office: UL. Francuska 35/37, 40-027.
Telephone: 011 (48-32) 757-2414.
Fax: 011 (48-32) 757-2483.

PRINCIPALS

Eric V. Brown, Jr.
Charles E. Ritter
John A. Campbell
Thomas P. Hustoles
John R. Cook
James G. Vantine, Jr.
Kevin M. McCarthy
Ronald E. Baylor
Thomas H. Van Dis
James E. Spurr
Steven M. Stankewicz
Vernon Bennett III
Pamela Chapman Enslen
Don M. Schmidt
Kurt N. Sherwood
Ballard Jay Yelton, III
John G. VanSlambrouck
Lori L. Purkey

OF COUNSEL/SENIOR COUNSEL

Eric V. Brown, Sr.
Gerard Thomas

RESIDENT SENIOR ATTORNEY

Leo P. Goddeyne

RESIDENT ASSOCIATES

Loyal A. Eldridge III
Kurt P. McCamman
Scott R. Sikkenga
James B. Thelen
Michael V. Camarota
Sarah S. Swallow
Oren R. Griffin
Stuart M. Heath

Representative Firm Clients: Chrysler Corporation; Comerica, Incorporated; City of Detroit, Michigan; Detroit Tigers, Inc.; First of Michigan; Ford Motor Company; Ford Motor Credit Company; Great Lakes Bancorp; Henry Ford Hospital; INVETECH Company.

For full biographical listings, see the Martindale-Hubbell Law Directory

TROY, Oakland Co.

Harness, Dickey & Pierce, P.L.C. (AV)

5445 Corporate Drive, Suite 400, 48098
Telephone: 248-641-1600
Cable Address: "PATENTS TROYMICHIGAN"
Telex: 287637 HARNES UR
Telefacsimile (All Groups): 248-641-0270
Email: info@hdp.com *URL:* http://www.hdp.com
Ann Arbor, Michigan Office: 301 East Liberty Street, Suite 555.
Telephone: 734-662-8000.
Telefacsimile: 734-662-7813.
Washington, D.C. Office: 888 Sixteenth Street, N.W.
Telephone: 202-835-7480.

MEMBERS OF FIRM

J. King Harness (1897-1977)
Arthur W. Dickey (1897-1964)
Hodgson S. Pierce (1896-1947)
Charles H. Blair
Joseph R. Papp
H. Keith Miller
James E. Stephenson (Resident at Ann Arbor Office)
Bernard J. Cantor
Christopher M. Brock
Richard L. Carlson
Ronald L. Hofer
Paul A. Keller
G. Gregory Schivley
Ronald W. Wangerow
Gregory A. Stobbs
Steven L. Oberholtzer (Resident at Ann Arbor Office)
Michael P. Brennan
Gordon K. Harris, Jr.
Stephen J. Foss
Gary L. Newtson
W. R. Duke Taylor (Also at Washington, D.C. Office)
Richard P. Vitek
Robert S. Nolan
Philip R. Warn
Philip E. Rettig
Mark D. Elchuk
Michael J. Schmidt
Lisabeth H. Coakley
Eric J. Sosenko (Resident at Ann Arbor Office)
Robert M. Siminski
Stephen T. Olson
Stanley M. Erjavac
Robert J. Lenihan, II
Douglas P. LaLone
David P. Utykanski
Thomas Traian Moga
Monte Lee Falcoff

ASSOCIATES

Michael R. Bascobert
John V. Biernacki
Anna M. Budde
Scott M. Confer (Resident at Ann Arbor Office)
Jeffrey M. Cox (Resident at Ann Arbor Office)
Christopher DeVries (Resident at Ann Arbor, Michigan Office)
Garrett C. Donley
Christopher A. Eusebi
Joseph M. Lafata
Timothy D. MacIntyre
Ryan W. Massey
David A. McClaughry
John A. Miller
George D. Moustakas
Douglas A. Mullen
George T. Schooff
Preston H. Smirman
Jeffrey L. Snyder
Joseph L. Stevenson
Bryant E. Wade
Donald G. Walker
Gregory A. Walters
Richard W. Warner
Michael D. Zalobsky

COUNSEL

Robert J. Wallace, Sr.
Charles R. Kiczek
Donald F. Scherer

Representative Clients: The Black and Decker Manufacturing Co.; Daimler-Chrysler Corp.; Emerson Electric Co.; General Motors Corp.; Kmart Corp.; La-Z-Boy Incorporated; Matsushita Electric; Seiko Epson Co.; Standard Products Co.; Sun Microsystems Laboratories Inc.

For full biographical listings, see the Martindale-Hubbell Law Directory

CONSTITUTIONAL LAW

ALABAMA

*BIRMINGHAM,** Jefferson Co.

THOMAS, MEANS, GILLIS, DEVLIN, ROBINSON & SEAY, P.C. (AV)

1035 Financial Center, 505 20th Street North, 35203-2605
Telephone: 205-328-7915
Fax: 205-214-6160
Mailing Address: P.O. Box 370497, Birmingham, AL, 35237-0447
Email: tmgpc.lawfirm@tmgpc.com *URL:* http://www.tmgpc.com
Montgomery, Alabama Office: 3121 Zelda Court, P.O. Drawer 5058, 36103-5058.
Telephone: 334-270-1033.
Fax: 334-260-9396. E-mail: tmgpc.lawfirm@tmgpc.com. URL: http://www.tmgpc.com
Atlanta, Georgia Office: The Chandler Building, Suite 300, 127 Peachtree Street N.E., 30303.
Telephone: 404-222-8400.
Fax: 404-222-0080. E-Mail: tmgpc.lawfir@tmgpc.com. URL: http://www.tmgpc.com

Kenneth L. Thomas (Resident)

James L. Richey (Resident)
Wendell J. Chambliss (Resident)
Lisa F. Brown (Resident)
Valerie L. Acoff (Resident)
Edward J. Berry (Resident)

For full biographical listings, see the Martindale-Hubbell Law Directory

*MOBILE,** Mobile Co.

SINTZ, CAMPBELL, DUKE & TAYLOR (AV)

3763 Professional Parkway, 36609
Telephone: 334-344-7241
Fax: 334-344-7400

MEMBERS OF FIRM

Peter V. Sintz (1940-1997)
Robert C. Campbell, III
Frank G. Taylor
Steven L. Terry

ASSOCIATES

Wm. Kyle Morris
Kathryn W. Petersen
Barry C. Prine

OF COUNSEL

Leon G. Duke

LEGAL SUPPORT PERSONEL

James A. Koblas

Representative Clients: Aetna C & S Insurance Co.; Mobile County School Board; Auto-Owners Insurance Co.; Argonaut Insurance Co.; Mostellar Medical Clinic; Scottsdale Insurance Co.; American International Group; Alabama School of Math and Science; Mobile County Sheriff's Office.

For full biographical listings, see the Martindale-Hubbell Law Directory

*MONTGOMERY,** Montgomery Co.

THOMAS, MEANS, GILLIS, DEVLIN, ROBINSON & SEAY, P.C. (AV)

3121 Zelda Court, P.O. Drawer 5058, 36103-5058
Telephone: 334-270-1033
Fax: 334-260-9396
Email: tmgpc.lawfirm@tmgpc.com *URL:* http://www.tmgpc.com
Birmingham, Alabama Office: 1035 Financial Center, 505 20th Street North, 35203. Mailing Address: P.O. Box 370447, Birmingham, AL., 35237-0447.
Telephone: 205-328-7915.
Fax: 205-214-6160. E-mail: tmgpc.lawfirm@tmgpc.com. URL: http://www.tmgpc.com
Atlanta, Georgia Office: The Chandler Building, Suite 300, 127 Peachtree Street, N.E., 30303.
Telephone: 404-222-8400.
Fax: 404-222-0080. E-Mail: tmgpc.lawfirm@tmgpc.com. URL: http://www.tmgpc.com

Kenneth L. Thomas (Resident, Birmingham, Alabama Office)
Tyrone C. Means
H. Lewis Gillis
Marvin A. Devlin (Resident, Atlanta, Georgia Office)
Mark E. Robinson (Resident, Atlanta, Georgia Office)
Quinton S. Seay (Resident, Atlanta, Georgia Office)

James L. Richey (Resident, Birmingham, Alabama Office)
Wendell J. Chambliss (Resident, Birmingham Office)
Lisa F. Brown (Resident, Birmingham, Alabama Office)
Valerie L. Acoff (Resident, Birmingham, Alabama Office)

(See Next Column)

John W. Adams, Jr.
Paul C. Williams
Jennifer D. Odom (Resident, Atlanta, Georgia Office)
Darnell D. Coley
Edward J. Berry (Resident, Birmingham, Alabama Office)
Thaddeus L. Hamilton (Resident, Birmingham, Alabama Office)

LEGAL SUPPORT PERSONNEL

Joyce L. Lehmann
Tonya White
Bryan Palmer
Felicia Kolley
John Baker (Office Administrator)
Cathy Allen
Lakesha Baker
Larry Holmes
Linda Steele
Mary Duncan
Pamela Watkins
Paula Mosely
Rodney Barganier
Tamara Venice
Linda Stoudemier

For full biographical listings, see the Martindale-Hubbell Law Directory

VOLZ, PRESTWOOD & HANAN, P.C. (AV)

350 Adams Avenue, P.O. Box 1910, 36102-1910
Telephone: 334-264-6401
Fax: 334-834-4954

Charles H. Volz, Jr.
Alvin T. Prestwood
Charles H. Volz, III
Ellis D. Hanan
Richard D. Lively
Judy H. Barganier

For full biographical listings, see the Martindale-Hubbell Law Directory

ARIZONA

*PHOENIX,** Maricopa Co.

FENNEMORE CRAIG, A PROFESSIONAL CORPORATION (AV)

3003 North Central Avenue, Suite 2600, 85012-2913
Telephone: 602-916-5000
Fax: 602-916-5999
Tucson, Arizona Office: One South Church Avenue, Suite 1000, 85701-1620.
Telephone: 520-879-6800.
Fax: 520-879-6899.

Timothy Berg

For Complete List of Firm Personnel, See General Section

For full biographical listings, see the Martindale-Hubbell Law Directory

ARKANSAS

*LITTLE ROCK,** Pulaski Co.

JOHN WESLEY HALL, JR. A PROFESSIONAL CORPORATION (AV)

523 West Third Street, 72201
Telephone: 501-371-9131
FAX: 501-378-0888
Email: jwh@johnwesley.com

John Wesley Hall, Jr.

For full biographical listings, see the Martindale-Hubbell Law Directory

CALIFORNIA

*BAKERSFIELD,** Kern Co.

BORTON, PETRINI & CONRON, LLP (AV)

The Borton, Petrini & Conron Building, 1600 Truxtun Avenue, 93301
Telephone: 661-322-3051
Voice Mail: 661-395-6700
Fax: 661-322-4628
Mailing Address: P.O. Box 2026, Bakersfield, California, 93303
Email: bpcbak@bpclaw.com *URL:* http://www.bpclaw.com
Other City Locations: Fresno, Los Angeles, Modesto, Redding, Sacramento, San Bernardino, San Diego, San Francisco, San Jose, San Luis Obispo, Santa Ana and Ventura.

MEMBER OF FIRM

George F. Martin

ASSOCIATES

Brian Jensen Stowell
Raymond G. Robinson
Dee H. Stasnopolis
Michael J. Stump

For Complete List of Firm Personnel, See General Section

For full biographical listings, see the Martindale-Hubbell Law Directory

*LOS ANGELES,** Los Angeles Co.

ROSSBACHER & ASSOCIATES (AV)

444 South Flower Street, Suite 2100, 90071-2922
Telephone: 213-895-6500
Fax: 213-895-6161
Email: rossbach@soca.com *URL:* http://www.rossbacher.com

MEMBER OF FIRM

Henry H. Rossbacher

ASSOCIATES

James S. Cahill — Clara I. Duran Reed
Nanci E. Nishimura — My T. Huynh

LEGAL SUPPORT PERSONNEL

Linda Connell (Legal Administrator) — Martha E. Guilmette (Paralegal)

For full biographical listings, see the Martindale-Hubbell Law Directory

*RIVERSIDE,** Riverside Co.

HAIGHT, BROWN & BONESTEEL, L.L.P. (AV)

A Partnership including Professional Corporations
California Tower, 3737 Main Street, Suite 800, 92501
Telephone: 909-341-8300
FAX: 909-341-8309
URL: http://www.hbblaw.com
Santa Monica, California Office: 1620 26th Street, Suite 4000 North, P.O. Box 680.
Telephone: 310-449-6000.
Telecopier: 310-829-5117.
Telex: 705837.
Santa Ana, California Office: Suite 900, 5 Hutton Centre Drive.
Telephone: 714-754-1100.
Telecopier: 714-754-0826.
San Francisco, California Office: 100 Bush Street, 27th Floor.
Telephone: 415-986-7700.
Fax: 415-986-6945.
San Diego, California Office: 101 West Broadway, Suite 1000.
Telephone: 619-595-5583.
Fax: 619-595-7873.

ASSOCIATE

Bonnie B. Bailey-Jones

For full biographical listings, see the Martindale-Hubbell Law Directory

*SAN FRANCISCO,** San Francisco Co.

REMCHO, JOHANSEN AND PURCELL (AV)

Suite 800, 220 Montgomery Street, 94104
Telephone: 415-398-6230
Fax: 415-398-7256
Email: Info@RJP.Com *URL:* http://www.rjp.com
Sacramento, California Office: U.S. Bank Plaza. Suite 2140, 980 Ninth Street, 95814.
Telephone: 916-264-1818.
Fax: 916-264-1824.

MEMBERS OF FIRM

Joseph Remcho — Robin B. Johansen
Kathleen J. Purcell

James C. Harrison — Thomas A. Willis

LEGAL SUPPORT PERSONNEL

Douglas Denton (Paralegal) — Ruth Fridhandler (Legal Administrator)

For full biographical listings, see the Martindale-Hubbell Law Directory

COLORADO

*DENVER,** Denver Co.

LAW OFFICES OF JOHN W. MCKENDREE (AV)

Creswell Mansion, 1244 Grant Street, 80203
Telephone: 303-861-8906
Fax: 303-861-7773
Email: Johnwmckendree@msn.com

ASSOCIATE

Elizabeth G. McKendree

Reference: Colorado National Bank.

For full biographical listings, see the Martindale-Hubbell Law Directory

CONNECTICUT

WESTPORT, Fairfield Co.

ANDREW B. BOWMAN (AV)

1804 Post Road East, 06880
Telephone: 203-259-0599
Fax: 203-255-2570
Email: andrew.bowman@snet.net

Reference: Peoples Bank.

For full biographical listings, see the Martindale-Hubbell Law Directory

DISTRICT OF COLUMBIA

WASHINGTON, D.C. Co.

COOPER CARVIN & ROSENTHAL, PLLC (AV)

Suite 200, 1500 K Street, N.W., 20005
Telephone: 202-220-9600
Fax: 202-220-9601
URL: http://www.coopercarvin.com

PARTNERS

Charles J. Cooper — Robert J. Cynkar
Michael A. Carvin — Michael W. Kirk
Steven S. Rosenthal — Alan K. Palmer
Vincent J. Colatriano — Jeffery A. Tomasevich

ASSOCIATES

R. Ted Cruz — Craig S. Lerner
Noel John Francisco (Not admitted in DC) — David H. Thompson
Hamish P.M. Hume — Douglas A. Tucker (Not admitted in DC)

OF COUNSEL

Kenneth L. Marcus — Andrew G. McBride

For full biographical listings, see the Martindale-Hubbell Law Directory

FLORIDA

*MIAMI,** Dade Co.

ROBBINS, TUNKEY, ROSS, AMSEL, RABEN & WAXMAN, P.A. (AV)

2250 Southwest Third Avenue, Fourth Floor, 33129
Telephone: Dade County 305-858-9550; Broward County 954-522-6244 (All Telephones Open 24 Hours); 1-800-226-9550
Fax: 305-858-7491
Email: RTR2250@AOL.COM *URL:* http://www.crimlawfirm.com

Frederick S. Robbins — Robert G. Amsel
William R. Tunkey — David Raben
Alan S. Ross — Benjamin S. Waxman

Mark R. Eiglarsh — Marco A. Vazquez (1968-1995)

Reference: Mellon United National Bank, Miami, Florida.

For full biographical listings, see the Martindale-Hubbell Law Directory

*TALLAHASSEE,** Leon Co.

POLSTON, DEAN & HEALY, P.A. (AV)

Suite 900, Highpoint Center, 106 East College Avenue (32301), P.O. Box 1836, 32302-1836
Telephone: 850-513-0404
Fax: 850-681-0506
Email: polston@polstonlaw.com *URL:* http://www.lawyers.com/polstonlaw

Ricky L. Polston — James J. Dean
David P. Healy

For full biographical listings, see the Martindale-Hubbell Law Directory

GEORGIA

*ATLANTA,** Fulton Co.

BONDURANT, MIXSON & ELMORE, LLP (AV)

1201 W. Peachtree Street Suite 3900, 30309
Telephone: 404-881-4100
Fax: 404-881-4111
URL: http://www.bondurant-mixson.com

MEMBERS OF FIRM

Emmet J. Bondurant II
H. Lamar Mixson
M. Jerome Elmore
Edward B. Krugman
Jeffrey O. Bramlett
John E. Floyd
Michael B. Terry
P. Richard Game
Jill A. Pryor
J. Scott McClain

Representative Clients: American Dairy Queen Corp.; Avon Products, Inc.; Bottlers of Coca-Cola, U.S.A.; Blue Circle of America; Delta Air Lines, Inc.; Fina Oil and Chemical Company; Four M Corporation; Penske Motorsports; Queen Carpets, Inc.; Ticketmaster Southeast.

For full biographical listings, see the Martindale-Hubbell Law Directory

MARYLAND

BETHESDA, Montgomery Co.

GARY HOWARD SIMPSON (AV)

9505 Kingsley Avenue, 20814
Telephone: 301-493-0345
Fax: 301-493-0347
Email: ghslaw@erols.com *URL:* http://www.lawyers.com/garyhsimpson

Alane Tempchin

OF COUNSEL

Krauthamer & Stahl, Chartered, Chevy Chase, Maryland

LEGAL SUPPORT PERSONNEL

Michelle Ratcliffe (Paralegal)
Joy Simpson (Paralegal)

For full biographical listings, see the Martindale-Hubbell Law Directory

MICHIGAN

*ANN ARBOR,** Washtenaw Co.

BUTZEL LONG, A PROFESSIONAL CORPORATION (AV)

Suite 300, 350 South Main Street, 48104-2131
Telephone: 313-995-3110
Telecopier: 313-995-1777
Email: melnick@butzel.com *URL:* http://www.butzel.com
Detroit, Michigan Office: Suite 900, 150 West Jefferson.
Telephone: 313-225-7000.
Telecopier: 313-225-7080.
Birmingham, Michigan Office: Suite 200, 32270 Telegraph Road.
Telephone: 810-258-1616.
Telecopier: 810-258-1439.
Okemos, Michigan Office: Suite 300, 2127 University Park Drive.
Telephone: 517-372-6622.
Telecopier: 372-6672.
Grosse Pointe Farms, Michigan Office: Suite 260, 21 Kercheval.
Telephone: 313-886-5446.
Telecopier: 313-886-2114.
Boca Raton, Florida Office: Suite 411, 1200 North Federal Highway.
Telephone: 561-368-2151.
Telecopier: 561-368-4668.
Palm Beach Gardens, Florida Office: Suite 227, 11382 Prosperity Farms Road.
Telephone: 561-625-4442.
Telecopier: 561-625-6901.
Naples, Florida Office: Suite 705, 801 Laurel Oak Drive.
Telephone: 941-597-4500.
Telecopier: 941-597-5623.

John Henry Dudley, Jr.
James E. Stewart (Resident)
Leonard M. Niehoff (Resident)
J. Michael Huget (Resident)

John C. Blattner (Resident)
Pamela M. Zauel

For full biographical listings, see the Martindale-Hubbell Law Directory

*DETROIT,** Wayne Co.

BUTZEL LONG, A PROFESSIONAL CORPORATION (AV)

Suite 900, 150 West Jefferson, 48226
Telephone: 313-225-7000
Telecopier: 313-225-7080
Email: melnick@butzel.com *URL:* http://www.butzel.com
Birmingham, Michigan Office: Suite 200, 32270 Telegraph Road.
Telephone: 810-258-1616.
Telecopier: 810-258-1439.
Okemos, Michigan Office: Suite 300, 2127 University Park Drive.
Telephone: 517-372-6622.
Telecopier: 517-372-6672.
Ann Arbor, Michigan Office: Suite 300, 350 South Main Street.
Telephone: 313-995-3110.
Telecopier: 313-995-1777.
Grosse Pointe Farms, Michigan Office: Suite 260, 21 Kercheval.
Telephone: 313-886-5446.
Telecopier: 313-886-2114.
Boca Raton, Florida Office: Suite 411, 1200 North Federal Highway.
Telephone: 561-368-2151.
Telecopier: 561-368-4668.
Palm Beach Gardens, Florida Office: Suite 227, 11382 Prosperity Farms Road.
Telephone: 561-625-4442.
Telecopier: 561-625-6901.
Naples, Florida Office: Suite 705, 801 Laurel Oak Drive.
Telephone: 941-597-4500.
Telecopier: 941-597-5623.

William M. Saxton
John Henry Dudley, Jr.
Richard E. Rassel
Philip J. Kessler
Donald B. Miller
Mark T. Nelson
Keefe A. Brooks
Leonard M. Niehoff (Ann Arbor)
Robert A. Boonin

Representative Clients: Detroit Newspapers; Bridgestone/Firestone; Complete Business Solutions, Inc.; Dayton Walther Corp.; General Dynamics; General Electric; Mobil Oil; Stroh Companies; TRW Automotive.

For full biographical listings, see the Martindale-Hubbell Law Directory

CONSTRUCTION LAW

ALABAMA

*BIRMINGHAM,** Jefferson Co.

BRADLEY ARANT ROSE & WHITE LLP (AV)

2001 Park Place, Suite 1400, P.O. Box 830709, 35283-0709
Telephone: 205-521-8000
Facsimile: 205-521-8800
Facsimile (SouthTrust Tower Office): 205-521-8500
URL: http://www.barw.com
Huntsville, Alabama Office: 200 Clinton Avenue West, Suite 900, 35801.
Telephone: 205-517-5100.
Facsimile: 205-533-5069.
Washington, D.C. Office: 801 Pennsylvania Avenue, NW, Suite 230, 20004.
Telephone: 202-347-8893.
Facsimile: 202-347-1684.

MEMBERS OF FIRM

Axel Bolvig III
G. Edward Cassady III
A. H. Gaede Jr.
David Glenn Hymer
Andrew J. Noble III
J. David Pugh
E. Mabry Rogers
Walter J. Sears III
H. Harold Stephens (Resident, Huntsville Office)

OF COUNSEL

Stanley D. Bynum

ASSOCIATES

James F. Archibald III
Joel E. Brown
Donna M. Crowe
Douglas E. Eckert
Fred M. Haston III
Arlan D. Lewis
Jeffrey P. Lisenby
Rodney L. Moss
Mary Carol White

For Complete List of Firm Personnel, See General Section

For full biographical listings, see the Martindale-Hubbell Law Directory

JOHNSTON BARTON PROCTOR & POWELL LLP (AV)

2900 AmSouth/Harbert Plaza, 1901 Sixth Avenue North, 35203-2618
Telephone: 205-458-9400
Telecopier: 205-458-9500
Email: Law@JBPP.com

MEMBERS OF FIRM

Charles L. Robinson
James C. Barton, Jr.
Thomas E. Walker
Oscar M. Price III
Anthony A. Joseph
James P. Pewitt
Lee M. Pope
Haskins W. Jones

OF COUNSEL

James C. Barton

ASSOCIATE

Keith Adrian Brown

General Counsel for: All-South Subcontractors, Inc.; Baptist Health System, Inc.; The Birmingham News Co..
Counsel for: Birmingham Broadcasting (WVTM TV), Inc. (NBC-Owned Affiliate); Jemison Investment Co.; Mid-South Steel, Inc.; Nimrod Long & Associates; Process Equipment Co.; Schreiber Corp., Inc.; Sirco Systems, Inc.

For full biographical listings, see the Martindale-Hubbell Law Directory

LIGHTFOOT, FRANKLIN & WHITE, L.L.C. (AV)

The Clark Building, 400 20th Street North, 35203
Telephone: 205-581-0700
Facsimile: 205-581-0799
Email: LFWlaw@LFWlaw.com *URL:* http://www.lfwlaw.com

M. Christian King
E. Glenn Waldrop, Jr.

For full biographical listings, see the Martindale-Hubbell Law Directory

SCHOEL, OGLE, LILES AND UPSHAW, LLP (AV)

600 Financial Center, 505 North 20th Street, P.O. Box 1865, 35201-1865
Telephone: 205-521-7000
Telecopier: 205-521-7007
Mailing Address: Drawer 1865, Birmingham, Alabama, 35201-1865

Jerry W. Schoel
Richard F. Ogle
Paul A. Liles
David O. Upshaw
Jann J. Rice

Reference: First Alabama Bank.

For full biographical listings, see the Martindale-Hubbell Law Directory

STARNES & ATCHISON LLP (AV)

100 Brookwood Place, 35209
Telephone: 205-868-6000
Telecopier: 205-868-6099
Mailing Address: P.O. Box 598512, 35259-8512
Email: information@starneslaw.com
Mobile, Alabama Office: Riverview Plaza, Suite 1106, 63 South Royal Street, 36602.
Telephone: 334-433-6049.

MEMBERS OF FIRM

W. Stancil Starnes
W. Michael Atchison
William Anthony Davis, III
L. Graves Stiff, III
Thomas Lawson Selden

ASSOCIATES

Sharon A. Woodard
Elise Beth May

Representative Clients: Harbert International; Brice Building Co., Inc.; Ellard Cont. Co., Inc.; Hallmark Builders, Inc.; Brasfield & Gorrie General Contractor, Inc.; Rives Construction Co.; Morris Shea Bridge Co.; Cowin & Company, Inc.; Daniel International.

For full biographical listings, see the Martindale-Hubbell Law Directory

*MOBILE,** Mobile Co.

ATCHISON, CROSBY, SAAD & BEEBE, P.C. (AV)

3030 Knollwood Drive, 36693
Telephone: 334-665-7200
Fax: 334-665-7250
URL: http://www.acsblaw.com

James E. Atchison
James H. Crosby
Elias J. Saad
Donald G. Beebe

Mona Ann Vivar
Jacqueline M. McConaha
Daryl A. Atchison

Representative Clients: City of Mobile; Alabama State Docks; Mobile Area Water and Sewer Board; Owens Corning, Inc.; Pilot Catastrophe Services, Inc.; Shell Oil Co.; Premdor,Inc.; Melvin Pierce Paint Co.; Commonwealth National Bank; Fiberglass Canada,Inc.

For full biographical listings, see the Martindale-Hubbell Law Directory

JOHNSTONE, ADAMS, BAILEY, GORDON AND HARRIS, L.L.C. (AV)

Royal St. Francis Building, 104 St. Francis Street, 8th Floor, P.O. Box 1988, 36633
Telephone: 334-432-7682
Facsimile: 334-432-0712 or 334-432-2800
Email: attorneys@JohnstoneAdams.com *URL:* http://www.JohnstoneAdams.com
Bay Minette, Alabama Office: Dahlberg Building, 107 Hand Avenue, P.O. Box 729, 36507.
Telephone: 334-937-9473.
Facsimile: 334-937-9475.

MEMBERS OF FIRM

I. David Cherniak
William Alexander Gray, Jr.
Lawrence J. Seiter

For Complete List of Firm Personnel, See General Section

For full biographical listings, see the Martindale-Hubbell Law Directory

*MONTGOMERY,** Montgomery Co.

PARNELL & CRUM, P.A. (AV)

641 South Lawrence Street, P.O. Box 2189, 36102
Telephone: 334-832-4202
Telecopier: 334-832-4703
Fax: 334-293-3550
Email: cnparnell@aol.com

Charles N. Parnell, III
G. Barton Crum

Robert J. Russell, Jr.
James McCauley Smith
Britt Batson Griggs
Angie Hubbard Ingram

Reference: Colonial Bank of Montgomery.

For full biographical listings, see the Martindale-Hubbell Law Directory

ARIZONA

*FLAGSTAFF,** Coconino Co.

MANGUM, WALL, STOOPS & WARDEN, P.L.L.C. (AV)

100 North Elden, P.O. Box 10, 86002
Telephone: 520-779-6951
Fax: 520-773-1312

(See Next Column)

MANGUM, WALL, STOOPS & WARDEN P.L.L.C., *Flagstaff—Continued*

H. Karl Mangum (1908-1993)

OF COUNSEL

Douglas J. Wall
Robert W. Warden
Daniel J. Stoops

MEMBERS OF FIRM

A. Dean Pickett
Melinda L. Garrahan
Stephen K. Smith
Michael H. Hinson

ASSOCIATES

Annette Star Lustgarten
R. Scott Currey
Rebecca Smith Currey
Melinda K. Jacquez
Franklin Hoover

Representative Clients: Northern Arizona University; Flagstaff Unified School District; Museum of Northern Arizona; Arizona School Board Association.
Local Counsel for: Bank of America-Arizona; Arizona Public Service; U.S-.A.A.; State Farm Fire & Casualty Insurance Co.; Property Development Co.

For Complete List of Firm Personnel, See General Section

For full biographical listings, see the Martindale-Hubbell Law Directory

MESA, Maricopa Co.

JACKSON WHITE GARDNER WEECH & WALKER, P.C. (AV)

40 North Center Street, Suite 200, 85201
Telephone: 480-464-1111
Fax: 480-464-5692
Statewide: 800-243-1160
Email: firm@azmesalaw.com *URL:* http://www.azmesalaw.com
Payson, Arizona Office: 708 East Highway 260, Suite C1-E.
Telephone: 520-472-8878.

Wayne L. Gardner
Bradley D. Weech
Eric M. Jackson
Richard A. White
Michael R. Pruitt
David L. Weed
J. Grant Walker
Roger R. Foote
Otto S. Shill, III

Eric K. Macdonald
Patricia A. Mancabelli
Kelly G. Black
Bobbie J. Rasmusson
Melody K. Seal
Maureen P. Kane
James L. Tanner

For full biographical listings, see the Martindale-Hubbell Law Directory

*PHOENIX,** Maricopa Co.

CARMICHAEL & POWELL, PROFESSIONAL CORPORATION (AV)

7301 North 16th Street, Suite 103, 85020-5224
Telephone: 602-861-0777
Facsimile: 602-870-0296

Ronald W. Carmichael
Sid A. Horwitz
Richard C. Gramlich

Stephen Manes

Representative Clients: Kawasaki Motors Corp., U.S.A.; Home Builders Association of Central Arizona; Firstar Metropolitan Bank & Trust; Wendy's International, Inc.; Innsuites International; Arizona Society of Architects; Diamond Key Homes, Inc.; Progressive Roofing; Boyer Electric.

For full biographical listings, see the Martindale-Hubbell Law Directory

DOYLE & WINTHROP, P.C. (AV)

2800 North Central Avenue Suite 1550, P.O. Box 10417, 85004
Telephone: 602-240-6711
Fax: 602-240-6951
Mailing Address: P.O. Box 10417, Phoenix, Arizona, 85064-0417
Las Vegas, Nevada Office: Edward D. Boyack, Esq., 2626 S. Rainbow Blvd., Suite 101, 89146.
Telephone: 702-873-1622.
Fax: 702-873-2280.

William H. Doyle
Angila L. Gallenstein

For full biographical listings, see the Martindale-Hubbell Law Directory

FENNEMORE CRAIG, A PROFESSIONAL CORPORATION (AV)

3003 North Central Avenue, Suite 2600, 85012-2913
Telephone: 602-916-5000
Fax: 602-916-5999
Tucson, Arizona Office: One South Church Avenue, Suite 1000, 85701-1620.
Telephone: 520-879-6800.
Fax: 520-879-6899.

Calvin H. Udall
John Randall Jefferies
Christopher L. Callahan
Keith L. Hendricks

(See Next Column)

LEGAL SUPPORT PERSONNEL

LEGAL ASSISTANTS

Julie Hodges

For Complete List of Firm Personnel, See General Section

For full biographical listings, see the Martindale-Hubbell Law Directory

GAONA MOORE, P.C. (AV)

National Bank Plaza, 3101 North Central Avenue, Suite 720, 85012
Telephone: 602-230-2636
Facsimile: 602-230-1377

David F. Gaona
Janice H. Moore

Tracey N. Fernandes

For full biographical listings, see the Martindale-Hubbell Law Directory

HORNE, BISTROW & DULBERG, P.C. (AV)

Renaissance Two, 40 North Central, Suite 2800, 85004
Telephone: 602-253-9700
Fax: 602-258-4805
Email: kcorson@azlitigation.com *URL:* http://www.azlitigation.com

Thomas C. Horne
Eric J. Bistrow
Michael S. Dulberg

Joel E. Sannes

For full biographical listings, see the Martindale-Hubbell Law Directory

JENNINGS, HAUG & CUNNINGHAM, L.L.P. (AV)

2800 North Central Avenue Suite Eighteen Hundred, 85004-1049
Telephone: 602-234-7800
Fax: 602-277-5595
Email: main@jhc-law.com

MEMBERS OF FIRM

Curtis A. Jennings
James L. Csontos
William F. Haug
Larry J. Crown
Jack R. Cunningham
Jeff R. Wilhelm
Dean Kim Lough
Edward Rubacha
Chad L. Schexnayder
Laurence R. Sharlot
Mark E. Barker
Dean M. Dinner
John G. Sinodis
Jorge Franco, Jr.

ASSOCIATES

K. Alan Holcomb
Lisa A. Shannon
Stephen J. Anthony

OF COUNSEL

James W. Washington (Not admitted in AZ)

For full biographical listings, see the Martindale-Hubbell Law Directory

RHEES, HOPKINS & KREAMER (AV)

100 West Clarendon Suite 700, 85013
Telephone: 602-263-6010
Fax: 602-263-6016
Email: rhk@primenet.com

MEMBERS OF FIRM

Michael L. Rhees
Joseph C. Kreamer
Stephen M. Hopkins
Kelly Brown

For full biographical listings, see the Martindale-Hubbell Law Directory

SHIMMEL, HILL, BISHOP & GRUENDER, P.C. (AV)

3700 North 24th Street, 85016
Telephone: 602-224-9500
Telecopier: 602-955-6176
URL: http://www.shimmelhill.com

Daniel F. Gruender
Margaret L. Steiner
Keith F. Overholt
Susan M. Swick
Scott J. Richardson
S. Gregory Jones
Joseph Wm. Kruchek
Glenn B. Hotchkiss
John W. Moody

OF COUNSEL

Charles A. Finch

Representative Clients: The Ashton Cos.; Associated General Contractors; Bashas' Stores; Black Mesa Pipeline Co.; CC Shops dba Cost Cutters Hairsetters; Christiania Bank; Citizen Auto Stage Line; Connecticut General Life Insurance Co.; Delta Airlines; Dunn Del Re Steel, Inc.

For full biographical listings, see the Martindale-Hubbell Law Directory

Phoenix—Continued

SNELL & WILMER L.L.P. (AV)

One Arizona Center, 85004-2202
Telephone: 602-382-6000
Fax: 602-382-6070
Email: postmaster@snellwilmer.com *URL:* http://www.swlaw.com
Tucson, Arizona Office: One South Church Avenue, Suite 1500, 85701-1612.
Telephone: 520-882-1200.
Fax: 520-884-1294.
Orange County Office: 1920 Main Street, Suite 1200, Irvine, California 92614-7230.
Telephone: 949-253-2700.
Fax: 949-955-2507.
Salt Lake City, Utah Office: 111 East Broadway, Suite 900, 84111-1004.
Telephone: 801-237-1900.
Fax: 801-237-1950.

MEMBERS OF FIRM

Richard K. Mallery
Gerard Morales
E. Jeffrey Walsh
Jay D. Wiley
James R. Condo
James J. Sienicki
Bob J. McCullough

Representative Clients: For list of Representative Clients, see end of biographical listings in the Martindale-Hubbell Law Directory.

For Complete List of Firm Personnel, See General Section

For full biographical listings, see the Martindale-Hubbell Law Directory

WARNER ANGLE ROPER & HALLAM PLC (AV)

3550 North Central Avenue, Suite 1500, 85012
Telephone: 602-264-7101
Fax: 602-234-0419

Edward (Ted) L. Roper
Stephen E. Jackson
Clark W. Watkin, Jr.
Dean J. Formanek
Kathryn Graham
John A. Buric
Jack D. Klausner

Chris R. Baniszewski
J. Brent Welker

Representative Clients: D.L. Withers Construction, Inc.; Martin K. Eby Construction Co., Inc.; Coreslab Structures; T.P. Acoustics; Pete King Construction; Butte Construction Co.; Nace Custom Homes; Fred Combs Construction; Centennial Homes; Douglas Allred Company.

For full biographical listings, see the Martindale-Hubbell Law Directory

WARNICKE & LITTLER, P.L.C. (AV)

2020 North Central Avenue, Fifth Floor, 85004-4506
Telephone: 602-256-0400
Fax: 602-256-0345
Email: wlittler@aol.com

Ronald E. Warnicke
Thomas E. Littler
Mark J. Giunta
Blake D. Gunn

For full biographical listings, see the Martindale-Hubbell Law Directory

SCOTTSDALE, Maricopa Co.

PESKIND HYMSON & GOLDSTEIN, P.C. (AV)

14595 North Scottsdale Road, Suite 14, 85254
Telephone: 602-991-9077
Fax: 602-443-8854
URL: http://www.legalcounselors.com

E. J. Peskind
David B. Goldstein

For full biographical listings, see the Martindale-Hubbell Law Directory

CALIFORNIA

ALAMO, Contra Costa Co.

LAW OFFICES OF DAVID M. BIRKA-WHITE (AV)

3240 Stone Valley Road West, Suite 102, 94507
Telephone: 925-838-2090
Facsimile: 925-362-9911
Email: d.birka-white@bending-weil.com *URL:* http://www.lawyers.com/birka-white

For full biographical listings, see the Martindale-Hubbell Law Directory

*BAKERSFIELD,** Kern Co.

BORTON, PETRINI & CONRON, LLP (AV)

The Borton, Petrini & Conron Building, 1600 Truxtun Avenue, 93301
Telephone: 661-322-3051
Voice Mail: 661-395-6700
Fax: 661-322-4628
Mailing Address: P.O. Box 2026, Bakersfield, California, 93303
Email: bpcbak@bpclaw.com *URL:* http://www.bpclaw.com
Other City Locations: Fresno, Los Angeles, Modesto, Redding, Sacramento, San Bernardino, San Diego, San Francisco, San Jose, San Luis Obispo, Santa Ana and Ventura.

MEMBERS OF FIRM

Stephen M. Dake
Richard E. Morton

ASSOCIATES

Stephen M. Crane
Raymond G. Robinson

For Complete List of Firm Personnel, See General Section

For full biographical listings, see the Martindale-Hubbell Law Directory

KLEIN, DENATALE, GOLDNER, COOPER, ROSENLIEB & KIMBALL, LLP (AV)

(Formerly Di Giorgio, Davis, Klein, Wegis, Duggan & Friedman)
ARCO Tower, 4550 California Avenue, Second Floor, 93309
Telephone: 661-395-1000
Telecopier: 661-326-0418
Mailing Address: P.O. Box 11172, Bakersfield, California, 93389-1172
Email: kleinlaw@kleinlaw.com

Anthony J. Klein (Inc.)
Barry L. Goldner

Representative Clients: Findley Construction; Kern High School District; Renfro-Russell & Associates, Inc.

For Complete List of Firm Personnel, See General Section

For full biographical listings, see the Martindale-Hubbell Law Directory

COSTA MESA, Orange Co.

RUTAN & TUCKER, LLP (AV)

A Partnership including Professional Corporations
611 Anton Boulevard, Fourteenth Floor, P.O. Box 1950, 92626-1998
Telephone: 714-641-5100; 213-625-7586
Telecopier: 714-546-9035
Email: rutan&tucker@rutan.com *URL:* http://www.rutan.com

MEMBERS OF FIRM

John B. Hurlbut, Jr.
Robert C. Braun
Thomas S. Salinger (P.C.)
David C. Larsen (P.C.)
Clifford E. Frieden
Michael D. Rubin
David J. Aleshire
Marcia A. Forsyth
William J. Caplan
Philip D. Kohn
Steven A. Nichols
Jayne Taylor Kacer
Stephen A. Ellis
Robert O. Owen
Adam N. Volkert
F. Kevin Brazil
Patrick D. McCalla
David H. Hochner

ASSOCIATES

Steven John Goon
Sean P. Farrell
Philip J. Blanchard
Charles A. Davenport, III

For Complete List of Firm Personnel, See General Section

For full biographical listings, see the Martindale-Hubbell Law Directory

EMERYVILLE, Alameda Co.

BISHOP, BARRY, HOWE, HANEY & RYDER, A PROFESSIONAL CORPORATION (AV)

Watergate Tower III, 2000 Powell Street, Suite 1425, 94608
Telephone: 510-596-0888
Fax: 510-596-0899
Email: FirmGeneral@BBHHR.com
San Francisco Office: 44 Montgomery Street, Suite 1300, 94104.
Telephone: 415-421-8550.

Nelson C. Barry
Drayton F. Howe, Jr.
Jeffrey N. Haney
Thomas O. Haran
Rebecca B. Aherne
Michael W. Bolechowski
Mark C. Raskoff
Patricia S. Lakner
Gregory R. de la Peña

J. Scott Wood
Mitchell J. Alward
Marco R. Sumarriva
Jane E. Carey
Mary Margaret Ryan
Thomas Edward Foran
John F. Cooke
Jean H. Hurricane
Daniel M. O'Connell
Lisa S. Wiggins
Edward M. Lai

(See Next Column)

BISHOP, BARRY, HOWE, HANEY & RYDER A PROFESSIONAL CORPORATION, *Emeryville—Continued*

OF COUNSEL

Lawrence S. Molton
David P. Osako

Representative Clients: Dome Construction Corp.; Gerling American; Masma Construction, Inc.; Prime Vest, Inc.; Risk Enterprises Management; TIG of Michigan; Westworth Development.

For full biographical listings, see the Martindale-Hubbell Law Directory

*FRESNO,** Fresno Co.

LANG, RICHERT & PATCH, A PROFESSIONAL CORPORATION (AV)

Fig Garden Financial Center, 5200 North Palm Avenue, 4th Floor, P.O. Box 40012, 93755
Telephone: 559-228-6700
Fax: 559-228-6727

William T. Richert (1937-1993)
Robert L. Patch, II
Val W. Saldaña
Douglas E. Noll
Michael T. Hertz
Victoria J. Salisch
Rene Lastreto, II
Charles Trudrung Taylor
Mark L. Creede
Peter N. Zeitler
Laurie L. Quigley
Tamara L. Equals
Douglas E. Griffin
Nabil E. Zumout

Christopher B. Dorian
Matthew W. Quall
Tracy E. Sagle
Julie K. Hill
Michelle Oleksa

OF COUNSEL

Frank H. Lang

References: Wells Fargo Bank (Fresno Main Office).

For full biographical listings, see the Martindale-Hubbell Law Directory

GLENDALE, Los Angeles Co.

GILL AND BALDWIN (AV)

130 North Brand Boulevard Fourth Floor, 91203
Telephone: 818-500-7755; 323-245-3131
Fax: 818-242-4305
URL: http://www.lawyers.com/g&blaw
Email: gillandbal@aol.com *URL:* http://www.gillandbaldwin.com

MEMBERS OF FIRM

John M. Carmack
Kirk S. MacDonald

Representative Clients: Morrison-Knudsen Corp.; Bireley Foundation.
Reference: Bank of Los Angeles.

For full biographical listings, see the Martindale-Hubbell Law Directory

O'ROURKE, ALLAN & FONG, LLP (AV)

100 West Broadway, Suite 1250, P.O. Box 10220, 91210
Telephone: 818-247-4303
Fax: 818-247-1451
Email: OAFLAW@aol.com

MEMBERS OF FIRM

Denis M. O'Rourke
Joan H. Allan
Roderick D. Fong

ASSOCIATES

Denise Michelle O'Rourke
Marina Manoukian
Toshiko Kobayashi

References: Verdugo Banking Co. (Glendale, California); Community Bank (Glendale, California).

For full biographical listings, see the Martindale-Hubbell Law Directory

IRVINE, Orange Co.

ANDRADE & ASSOCIATES (AV)

First Security Bank Building, 18401 Von Karman, Suite 350, 92612
Telephone: 949-553-1951
Telecopier: 949-553-0655
Email: andrade@andradelaw.com
San Diego, California Office: Tokia Bank Building, 3111 Camino Del Rio North, Suite 1100.
Telephone: 619-291-2481.
Las Vegas, Nevada Office: 3753 Howard Hughes Parkway, Suite 200.
Telephone: 888-553-1951.

MEMBER OF FIRM

Richard B. Andrade

ASSOCIATES

Frank A. Satalino
Lori A. McClaskey
Eric Rans
Deborah J. Taddeucci

Representative Clients: Advanco Constructor's, Inc.; American Insurance Company of North America; Fireman's Fund Insurance Co.; CIGNA Insurance Co.; Gentosi Builders, Inc.; Griffith Co.; Penhall Rentals; Steve Bubalo

(See Next Column)

Construction Co.; Sukut Construction, Inc.; United Rentals, Inc.; Veco International, Inc.

For full biographical listings, see the Martindale-Hubbell Law Directory

EISENBERG & FINK LLP (AV)

100 Pacifica, Suite 200, 92618
Telephone: 949-753-1500
Fax: 949-753-1516
Email: ef@ef-law.com *URL:* http://www.lawyers.com/ef-law

Lawrence S. Eisenberg
Steven A. Fink

Michael G. Mattern
Judith F. Zuckert

For full biographical listings, see the Martindale-Hubbell Law Directory

KASDAN, SIMONDS, MCINTYRE, EPSTEIN & MARTIN (AV)

2600 Michelson Drive, Tenth Floor, 92612-6510
Telephone: 949-851-9000
Fax: 949-833-9455
Email: info@ksmem.com *URL:* http://www.ksmem.com
San Jose, California Office: 111 West Saint John, Suite 850,
Telephone: 408-292-9220.
Fax: 408-292-9172. E Mail: INFO@KSMEM.com

MEMBERS OF FIRM

Kenneth S. Kasdan
Vance C. Simonds, Jr.
R. Donald McIntyre
David G. Epstein
Ronald B. Martin
Michael D. Turner

ASSOCIATES

Steven S. Hanagami
Randi Ellen Pinckes
Richard P. Riley
Wayne W. (Bill) Suojanen
Cathleen L. Mulligan
Heather A. Dozier
Melissa A. Pasek
James W. Markwith
Wendy Reed
Christopher J. Whelton
Daniel Peinado

Reference: Eldorado Bank.

For full biographical listings, see the Martindale-Hubbell Law Directory

LAGUNA BEACH, Orange Co.

NOKES, DAVIS & QUINN, A PROFESSIONAL CORPORATION (AV)

450 Ocean Avenue, 92651
Telephone: 949-376-3055
FAX: 949-376-3070
Email: ndqlaw@gte.net

Laurence P. Nokes
Thomas P. Davis
Thomas P. Quinn, Jr.

OF COUNSEL

Paul W. Davis

For full biographical listings, see the Martindale-Hubbell Law Directory

LONG BEACH, Los Angeles Co.

FORD, WALKER, HAGGERTY & BEHAR, PROFESSIONAL LAW CORPORATION (AV)

One World Trade Center, Twenty Seventh Floor, 90831
Telephone: 562-983-2500
Telecopier: 562-983-2555
Email: FWHB@FWHB.COM

G. Richard Ford
Timothy L. Walker
William C. Haggerty
Jeffrey S. Behar
Mark Steven Hennings
Donna Rogers Kirby
Tina Ivankovic Mangarpan
Joseph A. Heath
Robert J. Chavez
James D. Savage
Patrick J. Gibbs
Robert Reisinger

Arthur W. Schultz
Jon T. Moseley
Maxine J. Lebowitz
Timothy P. McDonald
K. Michele Williams
Stephen Ward Moore
James O. Miller
Stanley L. Scarlett
Scott A. Ritsema
Colleen A. Deziel
Thomas L. Gourdé
Patrick J. Stark
Shayne L. Wulterin
Charles J. Schmitt
John A. Haughton
Kristen C. Vine
Joel E. D. Odou
Christopher L. Mass
Robert Montes, Jr.
Alison S. Mathews
Tatia M. Tokunaga
Mark F. Wendorff
Anneke Joan Stewart
Pamela J. Paluga

OF COUNSEL

Theodore P. Shield, P.L.C.

For full biographical listings, see the Martindale-Hubbell Law Directory

COLLINS, COLLINS, MUIR & TRAVER LLP, *Pasadena—Continued*

ASSOCIATES

Robert H. Stellwagen, Jr.
Tomas A. Guterres
Christine E. Drage
Stephen W. Olson
Peter L. Stacy
Kien C. Tiet
Martha L. Cazeneuve
Howard Franco, Jr.
Jeffrey M. Hall
Michael M. Bergfeld
Jennifer M. Gregg

For full biographical listings, see the Martindale-Hubbell Law Directory

*SACRAMENTO,** Sacramento Co.

CAULFIELD, DAVIES & DONAHUE (AV)

3500 American River Drive, Suite 100, 95864
Telephone: 916-487-7700
Fax: 916-487-7091
Fairfield, California Office: Fairfield West Plaza, 1455 Oliver Road, Suite 130.
Telephone: 707-426-0223.

MEMBERS OF FIRM

Richard Hyland Caulfield
Robert E. Davies
James R. Donahue
Bruce E. Leonard
Matthew Paul Donahue
Brian C. Haydon

ASSOCIATES

Chance L. Trimm
Shawn C. Moore
Catherine A.J. Woodbridge

For full biographical listings, see the Martindale-Hubbell Law Directory

DAUER & THOMPSON (AV)

3455 American River Drive, Suite C, 95864
Telephone: 916-974-3400
Facsimile: 916-974-3405
Email: d&t@concourse.net

MEMBERS OF FIRM

Paul F. Dauer
James E. Thompson

Jennifer L. Dauer
Alan R. Barnes

For full biographical listings, see the Martindale-Hubbell Law Directory

HARDY ERICH BROWN & WILSON, A PROFESSIONAL CORPORATION (AV)

1000 G Street, 95814
Telephone: 916-449-3800
Fax: 916-449-3888
Mailing Address: P.O. Box 13530, Sacramento, California, 95853-4530
Email: hebw@hebw.com *URL:* http://www.hebw.com

Anthony D. Osmundson
Thomas C. Richards
David S. Worthington
L. Kent Wyatt
Brian H. Charter
Whitney A. Davis
John C. Miller, Jr.

Kristine E. Balogh
Lisa L. Palombo

Representative Clients: Champion Industries; The Chubb Insurance Company; Redman Industries; Reliant Building Materials; Risk Administration & ManagementCompany; Royal Insurance Company; Western Homes Corporation.

For full biographical listings, see the Martindale-Hubbell Law Directory

HARMATA LAW OFFICES (AV)

2201 Q Street, 95816
Telephone: 916-442-2842
Fax: 916-442-2015
Email: harmatalaw@aol.com *URL:* http://www.lawyers.com/harmatalaw

Donald D. Harmata

LEGAL SUPPORT PERSONNEL
PARALEGAL

Debra D. Morrow

Representative Clients: Control Data Corp.; Deloitte & Touche; General Electric Co.; Myers Electric, Inc.; Syblon-Reid Co.; Systemhouse Inc.; TRW, Inc.

For full biographical listings, see the Martindale-Hubbell Law Directory

HUNTER RICHEY DI BENEDETTO & BREWER, LLP (AV)

A Limited Liability Partnership
Renaissance Tower, 801 K Street, 23rd Floor, 95814-3525
Telephone: 916-491-3000
Facsimile: 916-491-3080
Email: hrdb@hrdb.com *URL:* http://www.hrdb.com

(See Next Column)

MEMBERS OF FIRM

William S. Hunter
Win R. Richey
Florence L. Di Benedetto
Roy E. Brewer
Anne E. Ferguson
James F. Geary
Janet C. Eisenbeis
Stephen C. Ruehmann
Sharon K. Sandeen
Jack V. Lovell
Patricia J. Hartman

OF COUNSEL

Laurie E. Davis

LEGAL SUPPORT PERSONNEL

Lori J. Moody (Paralegal)
Deborah M. Johnson (Paralegal)
Linda Jane Hall (Executive Assistant)
Jennifer E. Mueller (Legal Assistant)
Michele L. Nickell (Legal Assistant)
Lynetta G. Goodwin

For full biographical listings, see the Martindale-Hubbell Law Directory

LIVINGSTON & MATTESICH, LAW CORPORATION (AV)

1201 K Street, Suite 1100, 95814
Telephone: 916-442-1111
Fax: 916-448-1709
Email: l&m@lmlaw.net *URL:* http://www.lmlaw.net

Gene Livingston
James M. Mattesich
Carol Livingston
Rebecca M. Ceniceros
Emilio E. Varanini, III
Kenneth M. Malovos
Kathleen E. Finnerty
Joanna R. Mendoza

Steven P. Belzer
Jeffrey Leacox
Randy Pollack
Alice H. Choi
Stephen Craig Hunter
Matthew J. Goldman
Joel C. Baiocchi
Baldassaro (Bill) Di Capo
John McKinsey
Timothy E. Naccarato
Craig N. Lundgren
Mary Farrell Taylor
Brian Crone
Gay L. Carroll
Steven G. Churchwell

Representative Clients: Agra Foundations, Inc.; California Department of Corrections; California Department of Water Resources; Carter Pierce Mechanical; Combs Construction; H.J. Heinz Company; Hi-Voltage Wire Works, Inc.; Pisor Fence Company; Power Providers; Stonesfair Financial Corporation.

For full biographical listings, see the Martindale-Hubbell Law Directory

NAGELEY, MEREDITH & MILLER, INC. (AV)

8001 Folsom Boulevard, Suite 100, 95826
Telephone: 916-386-8282
Fax: 916-386-8952
Email: mail@mnlawfirm.com

Sam R. Nageley
Gregory A. Meredith
Andrea M. Miller
Lawrence N. Hensley
Craig S. MacGlashan
Janet M. Meredith
Carole Hansen Sharples
L. Alan Warwick
Drew M. Johnson
James C. Keowen
Duane S. Oliveira

For full biographical listings, see the Martindale-Hubbell Law Directory

PORTER, SCOTT, WEIBERG & DELEHANT, A PROFESSIONAL CORPORATION (AV)

350 University Avenue, Suite 200, 95825
Telephone: 916-929-1481
Fax: 916-927-3706
Email: pswdlaw@aol.com

Russell G. Porter
A. Irving Scott, Jr.
Edwin T. Weiberg
John W. Delehant
Anthony S. Warburg
Ned P. Telford
James K. Mirabell
Craig A. Caldwell
Terence J. Cassidy
Tom H. Bailey
Carl J. Calnero
Russ J. Wunderli
Nancy J. Sheehan
Norman V. Prior
Timothy M. Blaine
Stephen E. Horan
Carl L. Fessenden

Elisa Ungerman
Michael J. Baytosh
David A. Melton
Jennifer E. Duggan
Vanessa W. Whang
Dennis C. Huie
Michael W. Pott
Kellianne Akbar
Daniel M. Steinberg
Jack Woodside
Jonathan A. Corr
Kristina M. Hall
Alden J. Parker
Avery E. Dority
Robin Weideman
Denise A. Carnaroli
Lara S. Hilley
Sean Allen
Ralph R. Nevis
Darrin M. Menezes
Shane Singh

For full biographical listings, see the Martindale-Hubbell Law Directory

SELMAN • BREITMAN—*Continued*

Michelle E. Davis
Josh I. Keane
Michael Robert Hoffman
Natalie A. Barbanell
Kirk J. Retz
Paul A. Herp (Resident, San Francisco Office)
Greg M. Whaling (Resident, San Francisco Office)

Reference: City National Bank (Beverly Hills Branch).

For full biographical listings, see the Martindale-Hubbell Law Directory

GERALD T. YOSHIDA (AV)

12400 Wilshire Boulevard, Suite 400, 90025-1023
Telephone: 310-571-2756
Fax: 310-207-0954

Representative Clients: Vido Artukovich & Sons Construction; McKean Construction; Spiess Construction; Gierlich-Mitchell, Inc.; Hill Crane Service, Inc.; ACI General Engineering Contractors; A.A. Portanova & Sons, Inc.; Rough Terrain, Inc.; Altfillisch Construction; Ameron.

For full biographical listings, see the Martindale-Hubbell Law Directory

NEWPORT BEACH, Orange Co.

CAPRETZ & ASSOCIATES (AV)

5000 Birch Street, West Tower Suite 2500, 92660-2139
Telephone: 949-724-3000
Fax: 949-757-2635
URL: http://www.lawyers.com/capretzradcliffe
Email: crlawl@ix.netcom.com *URL:* http://www.CAPRETZ.com

MEMBER OF FIRM

James T. Capretz

OF COUNSEL

William B. Lawless (Not admitted in CA)

LEGAL SUPPORT PERSONNEL

Sandra L. Koop (Law Clerk)

For full biographical listings, see the Martindale-Hubbell Law Directory

MARK C. HARGAN (AV)

610 Newport Center Drive, Suite 700, 92660
Telephone: 949-851-1229
Fax: 949-851-5014
Email: mchargan@earthlink.net *URL:* http://www.lawyers.com/markchargan

For full biographical listings, see the Martindale-Hubbell Law Directory

MYERS & FLEMING, LLP (AV)

20301 Acacia Street, Suite 150, 92660
Telephone: 949-752-2001
Facsimile: 949-553-1413
Email: myersfleming@ocba.net *URL:* http://www.lawyers.com/myersfleming

Frank B. Myers
Dawn D. Fleming

For full biographical listings, see the Martindale-Hubbell Law Directory

*OAKLAND,** Alameda Co.

HAIMS, MACGOWAN, VALENTINO & PEEBLES, L.L.P. (AV)

490 Grand Avenue, 94610
Telephone: 510-835-0500
Facsimile: 510-835-2833

MEMBERS OF FIRM

Arnold B. Haims
Clyde L. MacGowan
Caroline N. Valentino
Dianne D. Peebles

For full biographical listings, see the Martindale-Hubbell Law Directory

PLAGEMAN, LUND & MILLER LLP (AV)

1999 Harrison, Suite 2700, 94612
Telephone: 510-273-8553
Fax: 510-273-8559

William H. Plageman, Jr.
Richard W. Lund
Debra J. Miller

ASSOCIATES

Timothy A. DeWitt
Maureen A. Kelly
Aneke M. Plimier
Susanne Meyer Brown
Paula J. Galleano

For full biographical listings, see the Martindale-Hubbell Law Directory

WULFSBERG REESE & SYKES, PROFESSIONAL CORPORATION (AV)

(Formerly Lempres & Wulfsberg, Professional Corporation)
Kaiser Center, 24th Floor, 300 Lakeside Drive, 94612
Telephone: 510-835-9100
Telecopier: 510-451-2170
San Francisco, California Office: 1 Maritime Plaza, Suite 1600, 94111.

Daniel N. Lempres (May 31, 1931 - March 19, 1987)
H. James Wulfsberg
Charles W. Reese, Jr.
Jeffrey A. Sykes
Timothy A. Colvig
Eric J. Firstman
Gregory R. Aker
Matthew D. Lempres
Mark A. Stump
David A. Rosenthal
Terri Ann Kim
Stephen L. Cali
William L. Darby

Charles A. Cobb
Paulette G. Andrews
J. Kevin Moore
Gillian Small, G.M.
Edward M. Callaghan
Donald S. Simon
David J. Hyndman

OF COUNSEL

Robert L. Hughes
Dianne K. Barry (Resident, San Francisco Office)

For full biographical listings, see the Martindale-Hubbell Law Directory

OXNARD, Ventura Co.

ENGLAND, WHITFIELD, SCHRÖEDER & TREDWAY, L.L.P. (AV)

300 Esplanade Drive, 6th Floor, 93030
Telephone: 805-485-9627
Ventura: 647-8237
Southern California Toll Free: 800-255-3485
Fax: 805-983-0297
URL: http://www.tsurf.com/ewst/

Theodore J. England
Anson M. Whitfield
Robert W. Schröeder
David W. Tredway
Robert A. McSorley
Stuart A. Comis
Mitchel B. Kahn
Mark A. Nelson
Eric J. Kananen
Mary E. Schröeder
Oscar C. Gonzalez
Madison M. Christian
Kurt Edward Kananen

Melissa E. Cohen
Linda Kathryn Ash
Mark T. Barney
Kevin L. Dorhout
Anthony M. Ramos
Gregory J. Ramirez

Representative Clients: Dah Chong Hong (automobile dealerships); Steve thomas BMW; Vreeland Cadillac, Inc.; Willamette Industries; The Port of Hueneme; Viola, Inc. (General Contracting); Santa Clara Chemical Co.; Nakamura Berry Growers; John Taft Electric Co.; Rodgers Mortgage Co.

For full biographical listings, see the Martindale-Hubbell Law Directory

PALO ALTO, Santa Clara Co.

GRIFFITHS & CASTLE, INC. (AV)

1755 Embarcadero Road Suite 150, 94303-0907
Telephone: 650-858-2300
Fax: 650-855-9386
Pleasant Hill, California Office: 3478 Buskirk, Suite 220. Zip: 94523-4346.
Telephone: 925-942-2710.
Fax: 925-942-2712.

John R. Griffiths
Thomas F. Castle
Jack A. Schwartzman
Anne M. Lawlor Goyette

For full biographical listings, see the Martindale-Hubbell Law Directory

PASADENA, Los Angeles Co.

COLLINS, COLLINS, MUIR & TRAVER LLP (AV)

Successor to Collins & Collins
Suite 300, 265 North Euclid, 91101
Telephone: 626-793-1163
FAX: 626-793-5982
Newport Beach, California Office: 333 Bayside Drive, 92660.
Telephone: 949-723-7700.
Fax: 949-723-7701.
Affiliated Offices: Drage, Olson & Tiet, LLP, 810 S. Casino Center Boulevard, Las Vegas, Nevada, 89101.
Telephone: 702-384-1600.
Fax: 702-384-1664.

MEMBERS OF FIRM

James E. Collins (1910-1987)
Robert J. Traver (Retired)
Paul L. Rupard (Retired)
John J. Collins
Samuel J. Muir
Frank J. D'Oro
Brian K. Stewart

(See Next Column)

*SAN DIEGO,** San Diego Co.

Barker Thomas & Walters, A Professional Law Corporation (AV)

1455 Frazee Road, Suite 800, 92108
Telephone: 619-682-4040
Facsimile: 619-220-7056
Email: info@btwlaw.com *URL:* http://www.btwlaw.com

Elizabeth A. Walters

Marsha E. Waldau
David J. Barnier
Robert G. Bernstein

For full biographical listings, see the Martindale-Hubbell Law Directory

Duke Gerstel Shearer, LLP (AV)

A Registered Limited Liability Partnership
Sixth Floor, 101 West Broadway, P.O. Box 85470, 92186-5470
Telephone: 619-232-0816
800-405-0816
Fax: 619-232-4661
Email: lawyers@dgsllp.com *URL:* http://www.dgsllp.com
Costa Mesa, California Office: 3200 Park Center Drive, Suite 1000, 92626.
Telephone: 949-551-8664, 800-405-0816.
Los Angeles, California Office: 10866 Wilshire Boulevard, Suite 1400, 90024.
Telephone: 310-475-7118, 800-405-0816.
San Francisco, California Office: 744 Montgomery Street, Fifth Floor, 94111.
Telephone: 415-773-0101.
Palm Springs, California Office: 1111 East Tahquitz Canyon Way, Suite 110, 92262.
Telephone: 760-322-7846.
Phoenix, Arizona Office: One Columbus Plaza, 3636 North Central Avenue, Suite 1200, 85012.
Telephone: 602-650-2060.
Fax: 602-650-2089.
Tucson, Arizona Office: 6969 East Sunrise Drive, Suite 102, 85750.
Telephone: 520-615-8858.
Fax: 520-615-1069.
Affiliate Las Vegas, Nevada Office: Parsons & Pursiano, LLP, City Center West, Suite 108, 7201 W. Lake Mead Boulevard, 89128.
Telephone: 702-384-9900.
Facsimile: 702-384-5900.

MEMBERS OF FIRM

Bryan R. Gerstel (A Professional Corporation)
William K. Shearer (A Professional Corporation)
Stephen V. Rupp (A Professional Corporation)
Andrew F. Lloyd (A Professional Corporation)
David T. Pursiano (A Professional Corporation)
Alan R. Johnston (A Professional Corporation)
Bryan R. Snyder (A Professional Corporation)
Robert D. Shoecraft
Dawn R. Brennan
Carolyn J. Kaye
Ronald M. Green
Eric W. Sachrison

ASSOCIATES

William E. Mayer
Michelle LeRoux Burton
Susan K. Stewart

Reference: Bank of Commerce.

For full biographical listings, see the Martindale-Hubbell Law Directory

Hovey & Kirby, A Professional Corporation (AV)

402 West Broadway, Suite 1500, 92101
Telephone: 619-685-4000
Fax: 619-685-4004
Email: administrator@hoveylaw.com

Gregg B. Hovey
M. Leslie Hovey

For full biographical listings, see the Martindale-Hubbell Law Directory

Kennerson Schwartz Semerdjian & Haile LLP (AV)

A Limited Liability Partnership
101 West Broadway, Suite 810, 92101
Telephone: 619-236-8821
Facsimile: 619-236-8827
URL: http://www.lawyers.com/ksshlaw

OF COUNSEL

Paul R. Kennerson

MEMBERS OF FIRM

Ross J. Schwartz
Dick A. Semerdjian
Jeffrey A. Haile

James R. Ballard
John K. Grant

For full biographical listings, see the Martindale-Hubbell Law Directory

Klinedinst, Fliehman & McKillop, A Professional Corporation (AV)

The Koll Center, 501 West Broadway, Suite 600, 92101-3584
Telephone: 619-239-8131
Fax: 619-238-8707
URL: http://www.kfmlaw.com
Orange County Office: Civic Center Law Building, 611 Civic Center Drive, Suite 250, Santa Ana, California, 92701.
Telephone: 714-542-1800.
Los Angeles, California Office: Wells Fargo Center, 333 South Grand Avenue, 33rd Floor, 90071.
Telephone: 213-625-8100.

SHAREHOLDERS

John D. Klinedinst
Donald R. McKillop, Sr.
G. William (Bill) Van De Weghe, Jr.
Thomas S. Ingrassia
Douglas A. Pettit
Gregory A. Garbacz
Arthur S. Moreau, III

Kendra J. Hall
Andrew N. Kohn
M. Shawn Payment
Kurt U. Campbell
G. Dale Britton
Susan S. Kohn
Heather L. Rosing
Debora A. Cappucci
Dayna Lyn Chmelka
Jennifer N. Lehman
Dennis C. Crovella
Carey L. Cooper
Kevin J. Gramling

PARALEGALS

Mary Ann Murphy-Brown
Cam B. Picano

Reference: Bank of America.

For full biographical listings, see the Martindale-Hubbell Law Directory

Maxie Rheinheimer Stephens & Vrevich, LLP (AV)

600 West Broadway, Suite 900, 92101
Telephone: 619-515-1155
Fax: 619-515-1159
Los Angeles, California Office: 555 South Flower Street, Suite 4640.
Telephone: 213-236-9878.
Fax: 213-489-7559.
Newport Beach, California Office: 110 Newport Center Drive, Suite 200.
Telephone: 714-644-8136.
Fax: 714-644-7526.
Sacramento, California Office: 400 Capital Mall, Suite 235.
Telephone: 916-444-5566.
Fax: 916-444-5494.
Las Vegas, Nevada Office: Law Office of Gary P. Sinkeldam, 4270 South Decatur Blvd., Suite B6-106.
Telephone: 702-968-8037.
Fax: 702-968-8069.

Robert C. Maxie
Jane A. Rheinheimer
Sean D. Stephens
Barry M. Vrevich

Christine L. Cornick
Suzanne Lovelace Smigliani
Ann Marie Thompson
Darin L. Wessel
Theodore Dikmen
Alison J. Barry
Marie K. Peluso
Jason R. Bogni

OF COUNSEL

Gary P. Sinkeldam
Cheryl D. Davidson

For full biographical listings, see the Martindale-Hubbell Law Directory

McCormick & Mitchell, A Professional Corporation (AV)

625 Broadway, Suite 1400, 92101
Telephone: 619-235-8444
Fax: 619-235-9432
Email: mccormickandmitchell@worldnet.att.net *URL:* http://www.lawyers.com/mccormicklaw

Glenn M. Mitchell (1938-1992)
John P. McCormick
Richard N. Appleton

Konrad M. Rasmussen
Deborah K. Garvin
Geoffrey E. Bishop

Reference: San Diego Trust & Savings.

For full biographical listings, see the Martindale-Hubbell Law Directory

Pope & Berger (AV)

550 West "C" Street, Seventeenth Floor, 92101
Telephone: 619-234-1222
Facsimile: 619-236-9677
Email: pope@pope-berger.com *URL:* http://www.pope-berger.com/

A. Mark Pope
Harvey C. Berger

ASSOCIATE

Timothy G. Williams

For full biographical listings, see the Martindale-Hubbell Law Directory

San Diego—Continued

SELDEN LAW FIRM (AV)

1230 Columbia Street, Suite 1060, 92101
Telephone: 619-515-1111
Facsimile: 619-515-1114
Email: lseldenii@aol.com
Las Vegas, Nevada Office: Selden, Lynch & Hopper, 501 South Rancho Drive, Suite C-12, 89106.
Telephone: 702-315-1115.
Facsimile: 702-315-1114.

Lynde Selden, II

For full biographical listings, see the Martindale-Hubbell Law Directory

THORSNES, BARTOLOTTA, MCGUIRE & PADILLA (AV)

A Partnership including Professional Corporations
Fifth Avenue Financial Center, 11th Floor, 2550 Fifth Avenue, 92103
Telephone: 619-236-9363
Fax: 619-236-9653
Email: TBMPmail@TBMP.com *URL:* http://www.tbmp.com

Michael T. Thorsnes (A.P.C., P.C.)
Vincent J. Bartolotta, Jr., (P.C.)
John F. McGuire (P.C.)
Kevin F. Quinn (P.C.)
C. Brant Noziska (P.C.)
Mitchell S. Golub (P.C.)
Palma Cesar Hooper (P.C.)
Neal H. Rockwood (P.C.)
Daral B. Mazzarella (P.C.)
R. Christian Hulburt (P.C.)

ASSOCIATES

Catherine A. Richardson
Jodi L. Hautaluoma
Douglas J. Billings
Scott A. Kennedy
Dori K. Rybacki
James T. Atkins
Leo Bartolotta
Jill E. Cleary
James B. Drimmer
Timothy J. Tatro

OF COUNSEL

Robert S. Kennedy

For full biographical listings, see the Martindale-Hubbell Law Directory

WINGERT GREBING BRUBAKER & RYAN LLP (AV)

A Limited Liability Partnership including Professional Corporations
One America Plaza, Seventh Floor, 600 West Broadway, 92101
Telephone: 619-232-8151
Facsimile: 619-232-4665
URL: http://www.wgbrlaw.com
Las Vegas, Nevada Office: Ryan Marks Johnson & Todd, 1120 Town Center Drive, Suite 200, 89144.
Telephone: 702-341-7870.
Fax: 702-341-8049.

MEMBERS OF FIRM

Charles R. Grebing (A Professional Corporation)
Alan K. Brubaker (A Professional Corporation)
Norman A. Ryan
James Goodwin
Shawn D. Morris
Robert M. Juskie
Dan H. Deuprey
Robert M. Caietti
Eileen Mulligan Marks
Christopher W. Todd
Robert L. Johnson
John S. Addams
Michael Sullivan
James J. Brown, Jr.
Terie M. Theis
Craig Gross

ASSOCIATES

Stephen C. Grebing
Brian P. Worthington
Marco B. Mercaldo
Solveig Store Deuprey
Kimberly Diane Howatt
Jay A. Kenyon
T. Steven Gregor
Jana M. Beck
Brad Lovelace

OF COUNSEL

William L. Todd, Jr.
John R. Wingert (A Professional Corporation)

LEGAL SUPPORT PERSONNEL

Carol C. Berry

representative Clients: Angelic Entertainment; Becton Dickinson; Brookfield Homes Pacific Inc.; California Casualty; Columbia/HCI; Cooper. of Amer. Physicians; Concan Davidson Homes; Discover R. Insurance; Farmers Insurance; Guaranty National.

For full biographical listings, see the Martindale-Hubbell Law Directory

*SAN FRANCISCO,** San Francisco Co.

STANLEY J. BELL A PROFESSIONAL CORPORATION (AV)

18th Floor, 505 Sansome Street, 94111
Telephone: 415-391-3700; San Jose: 408-295-1678
Fax: 415-391-3712
San Diego
San Diego, California Office: Suite 1200, 401 West A Street.
Telephone: 619-696-9445.

Stanley J. Bell

(See Next Column)

Samuel Boyd McCullagh
Sally G. Bergman
Steven J. Bell
J. Kevin Morrison
Craig William Morrison
Robert M. Dang
Frank C. Liuzzi
Hugh A. Donohoe

For full biographical listings, see the Martindale-Hubbell Law Directory

ERNEST BROWN & COMPANY A PROFESSIONAL CORPORATION (AV)

414 Jackson Street, Suite 401, 94111
Telephone: 415-249-0134
Fax: 415-249-0138
URL: http://www.ernestbrown.com
Email: starchris@aol.com *URL:* http://www.lawyers.com/ebrownlaw
San Diego, California Office: 4370 La Jolla Village Drive, Suite 400.
Telephone: 619-546-4368.
Fax: 619-546-9227.
Sacramento, California Office: 980 Ninth Street, 16th Floor.
Telephone: 916-449-9541.
Fax: 916-446-7104.

Ernest C. Brown

Robert C. Schneider (Resident, Phoenix, Arizona Office)
Clement K. Wong

Representative Clients: Ameron Chicago Bridge & Iron; Cleveland Marble; County of Orange; County Merced; City of Anaheim; Fluor Daniel; City of Fremont.

For full biographical listings, see the Martindale-Hubbell Law Directory

ROBERT D. CARROW (AV)

One Embarcadero Center, Suite 880, 94111
Telephone: 415-981-1691
Telecopier: 415-492-8419
Telex: 470562 LAW UI
Cable Address: "JURIS"
Email: robert@carrow.com *URL:* http://www.carrow.com/
London, England Chambers: 33 Bedford Row, WC1.
Telephone: +0171 242-6476.
Telecopier: +0171 831-6065.
San Rafael, California Office: 7 Mount Lassen Drive, Suite C134. 94903.
Telephone: 415-492-1225.
Telecopier: 415-492-8419.
(Also of Counsel to Goldstein & Musto, A Professional Corporation)

For full biographical listings, see the Martindale-Hubbell Law Directory

LEACH, MCGREEVY & BAUTISTA, LLP (AV)

2833 Laguna Street, 94123
Telephone: 415-775-4455
Telefax: 415-775-7435
Email: LMLawSF@aol,com
Southern California Office: 24752 Via San Fernando, Mission Viejo, CA 92692.
Telephone: 949-859-7464.

Theodore Tamba (1900-1973)
John T. Harmon (1928-1993)
David G. Leach
Richard E. McGreevy
A. Marquez Bautista
Robert W. Shinnick
Philip T. Kilduff
Peter C. Labrador

ASSOCIATES

John C. Connolly
Larry B. Carr
Annadel A. Almendras
David Emerson Beeby

OF COUNSEL

Lloyd F. Postel

For full biographical listings, see the Martindale-Hubbell Law Directory

MORGENSTEIN & JUBELIRER, LLP (AV)

One Market, Spear Street Tower, 32nd Floor, 94105
Telephone: 415-896-0666
Fax: 415-896-5592
Email: m&j@mj-sflaw.com

Marvin D. Morgenstein (Retired)
Eliot S. Jubelirer
Lee Ann Huntington
Jean L. Bertrand
Jeffrey R. Williams
James R. Balich
Rocky N. Unruh
James L. McGinnis
Charles W. LaGrave
William J. Carroll
John S. Worden
Wendi J. Berkowitz
Stephen M. Hankins
Bruce A. Wagman

(See Next Column)

MORGENSTEIN & JUBELIRER LLP—*Continued*

Lewis D. Barr
David H. Bromfield
Alexander P. Catalona
Michael "Cael" S. Davis
Roberta Nicol Dempster
Laura E. Gasser
Jill L. Gillen
Natasha L. Golding
Judith A. Holiber
Shawn D. Parrish
John J. Petry

For full biographical listings, see the Martindale-Hubbell Law Directory

MURPHY, PEARSON, BRADLEY & FEENEY, A PROFESSIONAL CORPORATION (AV)

88 Kearny Street, 10th Floor, 94108
Telephone: 415-788-1900
Telecopier: 415-393-8087
Email: IndividualsFirstInitialAndLastName@mpbf.com *URL:* http://www.mpbf.com
Sacramento, California Office: 701 University Avenue, Suite 150.
Telephone: 916-565-0300.
Fax: 916-565-1636.
San Jose, California Office: 80 South Market Street, 3rd Floor.
Telephone: 408-279-5792.
Facsimile: 408-279-5785.
Los Angeles, California Office: 11400 West Olympic Boulevard, Suite 249.
Telephone: 310-312-9565.
Fax: 310-312-9566.

Michael P. Bradley
Gregory A. Bastian (Resident, Sacramento Office)
Karen M. Goodman (Resident, Sacramento Office)
Gregg A. Thornton
Jane L. O'Hara Gamp

For Complete List of Firm Personnel, See General Section

For full biographical listings, see the Martindale-Hubbell Law Directory

SELTZER LAW GROUP (AV)

Suite 1300, Steuart Street Tower, One Market Plaza, 94105-1402
Telephone: 415-281-2154
Fax: 415-281-2194
Email: maseltzer@msn.com

Margaret A. Seltzer

For full biographical listings, see the Martindale-Hubbell Law Directory

STIMMEL, STIMMEL & SMITH, A PROFESSIONAL CORPORATION (AV)

100 Bush Street, Suite 850, 94104
Telephone: 415-392-2018
Fax: 415-391-2124
Email: stimmelpc@stimmel-law.com *URL:* http://www.stimmel-law.com

Norman S. Stimmel (1914-1991)
Lee D. Stimmel
Andrine K. Smith

OF COUNSEL

Jeffrey S. Rosen
Joanne M. Reming
Susan B. Jordan
Darrick T. Chase

For full biographical listings, see the Martindale-Hubbell Law Directory

WUERFEL & CHOLAKIAN, A PROFESSIONAL CORPORATION (AV)

555 Montgomery Street, Ninth Floor, 94111
Telephone: 415-398-1551; 800-992-5990
FAX: 415-398-3301
Email: sos@sflaw.net *URL:* http://www.sflaw.net
Santa Rosa, California Office: 131-A Stony Circle, Suite 515, 95401.
Telephones: 415-398-1551; 800-992-5990.
FAX: 415-398-1551.
Costa Mesa, California Office: Avenue of the Arts.
Telephone: 714-825-3590; 800-992-5990.

Mark D. Wuerfel
Kevin K. Cholakian
Julian J. Pardini
Nan R. Hooven
Sherri K. McElroy

SPECIAL COUNSEL

Dean C. Burnick
Charlene P. Rosack
Jonathan Gross
Michael A. Topp

Aaron D. Bigby
D. Clark Burton
Anthony J. Calero
Elizabeth A. Doyle
Linda L. Duiven
Jay E. Framson
Stephen D. Geist
Andrew A. Goode
David J. Heilman
Timothy S. Kirk
Stephen J. Liberatore
Anne Marie Master
Thomas A. Moore
Julianne Pinter

LEGAL SUPPORT PERSONNEL

Marla J. Kuresa (Legal Administrator)

For full biographical listings, see the Martindale-Hubbell Law Directory

*SAN JOSE,** Santa Clara Co.

LAW OFFICES OF THOMAS R. HOGAN (AV)

10 Almaden Boulevard, Suite 535, 95113-2258
Telephone: 408-292-7600
Facsimile: 408-292-7611
URL: http://www.lawyers.com/thomasrhogan
Email: trh@hoganlaw.com *URL:* http://www.hoganlaw.com

ASSOCIATE

Leslie Holmes

For full biographical listings, see the Martindale-Hubbell Law Directory

MAHL REHON WALWORTH & ROBERTS, A PROFESSIONAL CORPORATION (AV)

Ten Almaden Boulevard, Suite 550, 95113
Telephone: 408-494-0900
Fax: 408-494-0909
URL: http://www.mahlrehon.com

Susan J. Mahl
Peter M. Rehon
Janet R. Walworth
Lisa C. Roberts
Rogelio M. Ruíz

Phillip E. Maroc
Chris S. Friedrich
Francis X. Ferrer

For full biographical listings, see the Martindale-Hubbell Law Directory

MCMANIS, FAULKNER & MORGAN (AV)

160 West Santa Clara Street, 10th Floor, 95113
Telephone: 408-279-8700
Fax: 408-279-3244; 408-279-0494
Email: mfm@mfmlaw.com *URL:* http://www.mfmlaw.com

James McManis
William Faulkner
Donelle Morgan
Lisa Herrick
Michael Reedy
Erica Yew

Michelle Tidalgo
Colleen Duffy Smith
Lillian Wolf
Rebecca Hughes
Kalpana Vrudhula
Ray M. Baluyot
Catherine Bechtel
Arron Nesbitt

OF COUNSEL

Mary Arand

For full biographical listings, see the Martindale-Hubbell Law Directory

MILLER, MORTON, CAILLAT & NEVIS (AV)

50 West San Fernando Street, Suite 1300, 95113-2413
Telephone: 408-292-1765
Telecopier: 408-292-4484
URL: http://www.mmcn-law.com

Richard W. Morton (1916-1975)
Charles V. Caillat (1920-1990)
Harvey C. Miller (1906-1993)

MEMBERS OF FIRM

David L. Nevis
Francis J. Hughes
Peter A. Kline
Stevan C. Adelman
Joseph A. Scanlan, Jr.
Carolyn Tobiason Stuart
William K. Hurley
Peter V. Dessau

OF COUNSEL

Nancy F. Symons

ASSOCIATES

Kathryn E. Barrett
Katherine S. Pak
David I. Kornbluh
Christopher J. Hersey
Julie Neale Meyer

Representative Clients: Trammell Crow Residential; Yamaoka Builders, Inc.; B. T. Mancini Co., Inc.; Lennox International, Inc.; Greenbriar Homes Company; Hathaway-Dinwiddie Group; Hensel Phelps Construction Co.; Ray Helwig Plumbing & Heating Co.; Builders Exchange; Avalon Bay Communities.

For full biographical listings, see the Martindale-Hubbell Law Directory

REED, ELLIOTT, CREECH & ROTH (AV)

99 Almaden Boulevard, Eighth Floor, 95113
Telephone: 408-993-9911
Fax: 408-993-1335
URL: http://www.sjlegal.com

MEMBERS OF FIRM

John W. Elliott
Randall C. Creech
Thomas A. Elliott
Jeffrey S. Lawson
Peter A. Liebow
Raymond A. Brinson

ASSOCIATES

Lauren Berger
Nancy L. Mathis
Edward A. Kraus
Betty Chen
Bonnie L. Portis

(See Next Column)

REED, ELLIOTT, CREECH & ROTH, *San Jose—Continued*

OF COUNSEL

Steven J. Roth
Charles R. Reed
Thomas G. Perkins

Reference: Union Bank of California.

For full biographical listings, see the Martindale-Hubbell Law Directory

LAW OFFICES LESTER G. SACHS (AV)

1905 The Alameda, 95126-1428
Telephone: 408-296-1988

ASSOCIATE

James M. Ingram

For full biographical listings, see the Martindale-Hubbell Law Directory

SIMONCINI & ASSOCIATES (AV)

1694 The Alameda, 95126
Telephone: 408-280-7711
Facsimile: 408-280-1330
Email: kds@simoncini-law.com *URL:* http://www.simoncini-law.com

Kenneth D. Simoncini
Melanie D. Roberts
Marilynn J. Winters
Kerri A. Ridley

LEGAL SUPPORT PERSONNEL

Pamela A. Bauer (Paralegal - Case Manager)

For full biographical listings, see the Martindale-Hubbell Law Directory

TERRA LAW LLP (AV)

60 South Market Street, Suite 200, 95113
Telephone: 408-288-7325
Fax: 408-998-4895
Burlingame, California Office: 1350 Old Bayshore Highway, Suite 760, 94010.
Telephone: 650-685-7325.
Fax: 650-685-4895.

George H. Cole, Jr.
D. D. Hughmanick
R. Prescott Jaunich
Richard O. McDonald
Breck E. Milde
William L. Myers
Jane P. Relyea
Jason R. Biggs
Joan Paul
Ronald I. Rainey

Katharine L. Hardt-Mason
Thomas E. Rossmeissl

For full biographical listings, see the Martindale-Hubbell Law Directory

*SANTA ANA,** Orange Co.

CALLAHAN & BLAINE, A PROFESSIONAL LAW CORPORATION (AV)

3 Hutton Centre Drive, Suite 900, 92707
Telephone: 714-241-4444
Fax: 714-241-4445
Email: info@callahan-law.com *URL:* http://www.callahan-law.com

Daniel J. Callahan
Stephen E. Blaine

Jim P. Mahacek
Michael J. Sachs
Edward Susolik
Kathleen L. Dunham
Robyn Dimino
Reed N. Archambault
Nicki N. Eke
David Kam Ng
Douglas W. Schroeder

OF COUNSEL

Shelley M. Liberto
Walt D. Mahaffa

For full biographical listings, see the Martindale-Hubbell Law Directory

SANTA MONICA, Los Angeles Co.

BAKER, KEENER & NAHRA, LLP (AV)

2850 Ocean Park Boulevard, Suite 300, 90405-2936
Telephone: 310-399-0900
Fax: 310-399-1644
Email: general@bknlawyers.com *URL:* http://www.bknlawyers.com

MEMBERS OF FIRM

Robert C. Baker
Karl A. Keener
John P. Nahra
Michael H. Bailey
Steven T. Adams
Melissa S. Fink
Jeffrey P. Nolan
Constance A. Endelicato

Brenda K. Benson
Mitchell F. Mulbarger
James D. Hepworth
Phillip A. Baker
George P. Hawley
Thomas M. Mills
R. Jeffrey Neer
Wendy Wen Yun Chang

(See Next Column)

OF COUNSEL

Daniel P. Leonard

Reference: Wells Fargo Bank (Los Angeles Head Office).

For full biographical listings, see the Martindale-Hubbell Law Directory

WATERS, McCLUSKEY & BOEHLE (AV)

3250 Ocean Park Boulevard, Suite 300, 90405-3220
Telephone: 310-396-3411
Facsimile: 310-450-0925
Email: wmb@wmboehle.com
Santa Ana, California Office: Suite 1000, 200 West Santa Ana Boulevard.
Telephone: 714-953-4407.
Facsimile: 714-953-2118.

MEMBERS OF FIRM

William W. Waters (1898-1979)
Laurence R. Corcoran (1927-1987)
Fritz B. Hax
Wayne J. Boehle
Richard A. Wall (Resident, Santa Ana Office)
Timothy R. Lee
Gregg W. Brugger
Kevin G. McCluskey
Stacey B. Spurlock (Resident, Santa Ana Office)
Michael T. Montgomery

ASSOCIATES

Quyen H. Khuong (Resident, Santa Ana)
Christine Y. Chien (Resident, Santa Ana Office)
Portasha R. Moore
Julie C. Chang-Lee (Resident, Santa Ana Office)
Joseph C. Graven
Kirk Michael Olson (Resident, Santa Ana Office)
Brett C. Drouet

References: Bank of America; Santa Monica Business Park, Santa Monica; California National Bank, Los Angeles; First Republic, Los Angeles.

For full biographical listings, see the Martindale-Hubbell Law Directory

*SANTA ROSA,** Sonoma Co.

ABBEY, WEITZENBERG, HOFFMAN & EMERY, A PROFESSIONAL CORPORATION (AV)

1105 North Dutton Avenue, P.O. Box 1566, 95402
Telephone: 707-542-5050
Telecopier: 707-542-2589
Email: info@abbeylaw.com

W. Barton Weitzenberg

Representative Clients: Exchange Bank of Santa Rosa; Westamerica Bank; Northwestern Title Security Co.; Geyser Peak Winery; Santa Rosa City School District; Sonoma National Bank; Arrowood Vineyards & Winery; Friedman Bros. Hardware, Inc.; Bank of Lake County; Lasercraft, Inc.

For full biographical listings, see the Martindale-Hubbell Law Directory

WALNUT CREEK, Contra Costa Co.

FIELD, RICHARDSON & WILHELMY (AV)

Peri Executive Centre, 2033 North Main Street, Suite 900, 94596-3729
Telephone: 925-934-7700
Telecopier: 925-934-6090
Email: frwlaw@flash.net *URL:* http://www.frwlaw.com

MEMBERS

Robert C. Field
Robert W. Richardson
Alan J. Wilhelmy

OF COUNSEL

Donald L. Edgar

Reference: Civic Bank of Commerce (Walnut Creek Regional Office).

For full biographical listings, see the Martindale-Hubbell Law Directory

COLORADO

*COLORADO SPRINGS,** El Paso Co.

BELTZ, EDWARDS & SABO, L.L.P. (AV)

128 South Tejon, Suite 310, 80903
Telephone: 719-634-6620
Fax: 719-634-3142
Email: BES_LLP@aol.com *URL:* http://www.lawyers.com/beslaw
Other Colorado Springs, Colorado Office: 729 South Cascade, 80903.
Telephone: 719-473-4444.
Fax: 719-444-0186.

Daniel P. Edwards
W. Thomas Beltz
John W. Sabo, III

(See Next Column)

BELTZ, EDWARDS & SABO L.L.P.—*Continued*

ASSOCIATE

Daniel A. West

Representative Clients: Dows Investments, Inc.; Douglas Veltri Contracting; HBS, Inc.; Holmes Plumbing & Heating, Inc.; Jones Plumbing & Heating, LLC; Midway Development Company; Moldrite Products, Inc.; Newport Company; Nighthawk Industries, Inc.; RMG Engineers.

For full biographical listings, see the Martindale-Hubbell Law Directory

*DENVER,** Denver Co.

BRENMAN BROMBERG & TENENBAUM, P.C. (AV)

Mellon Financial Center Suite 1001, 1775 Sherman Street, 80203
Telephone: 303-894-0234
Fax: 303-839-1633
Email: bbt@bbtlaw.net

Albert Brenman
Thomas R. Bromberg
A. Thomas Tenenbaum
Steven W. McDonald

Sheryl A. Johnson
Judy A. Gooch

OF COUNSEL

Duane Woodard

For full biographical listings, see the Martindale-Hubbell Law Directory

GORSUCH KIRGIS LLP (AV)

Tower 1, Suite 1000, 1515 Arapahoe Street, 80202
Telephone: 303-376-5000
Fax: 303-376-5001

PARTNER

Philip E. Riedesel

LEGAL SUPPORT PERSONNEL

Lori Kully

For full biographical listings, see the Martindale-Hubbell Law Directory

THE MELLON LAW FIRM (AV)

2255 East Eighteenth Avenue Smith Mansion - Carriage House, 80206
Telephone: 303-320-5800
Facsimilie: 303-399-8038

MEMBERS OF FIRM

Joseph J. Mellon
Mary F. Mellon

For full biographical listings, see the Martindale-Hubbell Law Directory

MONTGOMERY LITTLE & MCGREW, P.C. (AV)

The Quadrant, 5445 DTC Parkway, Suite 800 (Englewood), 80111
Telephone: 303-773-8100
Telecopier: 303-220-0412
URL: http://www.mlmpc.com

David C. Little
William H. Knapp
Daniel P. Murphy
Timothy M. Schulte

LEGAL SUPPORT PERSONNEL

Carmen L. Antonio (Legal Assistant)

Representative Clients: BP Amoco; Bristol-Myers Squibb; Cyprus Minerals; Dillon Cos., Inc., d/b/a King Soopers; The St. Paul Insurance Cos.; University of Colorado Health Sciences Center; HealthOne; Design Professional Insurance Co.; Regency Realty Corp.; CNA.

For Complete List of Firm Personnel, See General Section

For full biographical listings, see the Martindale-Hubbell Law Directory

OTTEN, JOHNSON, ROBINSON, NEFF & RAGONETTI, P.C. (AV)

950 Seventeenth Street, 16th Floor, 80202
Telephone: 303-825-8400
Telecopier: 303-825-6525
URL: http://www.ojrnr.com

Thomas J. Ragonetti
Darrell G. Waas
Terence M. Ridley
Brad W. Schacht
R. Michael Shomo
David P. Hutchinson

Representative Clients: C.W. Fentress J.H. Bradburn & Associates, P.C.; Homart Development Co.; Leprino Foods Co.; Murata Outland Associates; TrizecHahn Centers, Inc.; Urban Design Group, Inc.; The Venture West Group.

For Complete List of Firm Personnel, See General Section

For full biographical listings, see the Martindale-Hubbell Law Directory

PREEO, SILVERMAN & GREEN, P.C. (AV)

1401 17th Street, Suite 800, 80202
Telephone: 303-296-4440
Fax: 303-296-3330

(See Next Column)

Robert L. Preeo
Eldon E. Silverman
Jersey M. Green
Martin J. Green
Gilbert R. Egle
Marilyn W. McWilliams
Timothy Kyle Jordan
Brandon S Culter

For full biographical listings, see the Martindale-Hubbell Law Directory

REIMAN & BAYAZ, P.C. (AV)

1600 Broadway, Suite 1340, 80202
Telephone: 303-860-1500
Fax: 303-839-4380
Email: rblaw@earthlink.net

Jeff Reiman
Marcie K. Bayaz

Debra D. Asimus

For full biographical listings, see the Martindale-Hubbell Law Directory

*GOLDEN,** Jefferson Co.

HOLLEY, ALBERTSON & POLK, P.C. (AV)

Suite 100, 1667 Cole Boulevard, 80401-3295
Telephone: 303-233-7838
Fax: 303-233-2860

George Alan Holley
Scott D. Albertson
Dennis B. Polk
Eric E. Torgersen
Howard R. Stone

Heather M. Davis

Reference: First Bank of Wheat Ridge.

For full biographical listings, see the Martindale-Hubbell Law Directory

CONNECTICUT

GLASTONBURY, Hartford Co.

TROWBRIDGE & BASINE, P.C. (AV)

45 Glastonbury Boulevard, 06033
Telephone: 860-633-3995
FAX: 860-633-3449

Robert L. Trowbridge
Robert B. Basine

For full biographical listings, see the Martindale-Hubbell Law Directory

GREENWICH, Fairfield Co.

ALBERT, WARD & JOHNSON, P.C. (AV)

125 Mason Street, P.O. Box 1668, 06836
Telephone: 203-661-8600
Telecopier: 203-661-8051

Tom S. Ward, Jr.
Scott R. Johnson
Jane D. Hogeman
Howard R. Wolfe
Christopher A. Kristoff
Vicki K. Comberiati

OF COUNSEL

David Albert
C. Robton Perelli-Minetti

For full biographical listings, see the Martindale-Hubbell Law Directory

*HARTFORD,** Hartford Co.

GORDON, MUIR AND FOLEY, LLP (AV)

Hartford Square North, Ten Columbus Boulevard, 06106-5123
Telephone: 860-525-5361
Telecopier: 860-525-4849
Email: admin@gmflaw.com *URL:* http://www.gmflaw.com

MEMBERS OF FIRM

William S. Gordon, Jr. (1946-1956)
George Muir (1939-1976)
Edward J. Foley (1955-1983)
Peter C. Schwartz
John J. Reid
John H. Goodrich, Jr.
R. Bradley Wolfe
Jon Stephen Berk
William J. Gallitto
Gerald R. Swirsky
Robert J. O'Brien
Philip J. O'Connor
Kenneth G. Williams
Mary Ann Santacroce
Mary Anne Alicia Charron
Andrew J. Hern
Reneé W. Dwyer
Patty G. Swan

ASSOCIATES

Doreen West Amata
Howard A. Steinman
Erik E. Roberts
Christopher J. Casciani

Reference: People's Bank.

For full biographical listings, see the Martindale-Hubbell Law Directory

Hartford—Continued

SOROKIN, GROSS & HYDE, P.C. (AV)

One Corporate Center, 06103
Telephone: 860-525-6645
Fax: 860-522-1781
Email: sorokin@sorokinlaw.com
Simsbury, Connecticut Office: 720 Hopmeadow Street.
Telephone: 860-651-9348.
Rocky Hill, Connecticut Office: 2360 Main Street.
Telephone: 860-563-9305.
Fax: 860-529-6931.

John J. Kindl
Richard C. Robinson

Gwen P. Weisberg

For Complete List of Firm Personnel, See General Section

For full biographical listings, see the Martindale-Hubbell Law Directory

DISTRICT OF COLUMBIA

WASHINGTON, D.C. Co.

BRAUDE & MARGULIES, P.C. (AV)

The Brawner Building, 888 Seventeenth Street, N.W., Suite 500, 20006
Telephone: 202-293-2993
Fax: 202-331-7916
Email: Braudemarg@aol.com

Herman M. Braude
Samuel M. Morrison, Jr.
Gerson B. Kramer

Stuart H. Sakwa
Stacie J. Broadwater

OF COUNSEL

J. Richard Margulies

For full biographical listings, see the Martindale-Hubbell Law Directory

THE FEINBERG GROUP, LLP (AV)

1120 20th Street, N.W. Suite 740 South, 20036-3437
Telephone: 202-371-1110
Fax: 202-962-9290
Email: kfeinberg@thefeinberggroup.com *URL:* http://www.krfassociates.com
New York, N.Y. Office: 780 3rd Avenue, Suite 2202.
Telephone: 212-527-9600.
Fax: 212-527-9611. Email: kfeinberg@thefeinberggroup.com.

PARTNERS

Kenneth R. Feinberg
Deborah E. Greenspan
Michael K. Rozen (Resident, New York Office)
Peter H. Woodin (Resident, New York Office)

ASSOCIATE

Fredric M. Brooks (Not admitted in DC)

SENIOR COUNSEL

Jacqueline E. Zins

For full biographical listings, see the Martindale-Hubbell Law Directory

KILCULLEN, WILSON AND KILCULLEN, CHARTERED (AV)

Suite 300, 1800 K Street, N.W., 20006
Telephone: 202-296-5700
Telecopier: 202-296-5706
Email: kwk@attny.com *URL:* http://www.attny.com

John L. Kilcullen (1916-1994)

MEMBERS

William H. Butterfield
Ronald E. Gilbertson
Christopher M. Johnson
Peter M. Kilcullen
Cyrus E. Phillips, IV
Walter A. I. Wilson

OF COUNSEL

Robert J. Gomez
Douglas K. Olson

For full biographical listings, see the Martindale-Hubbell Law Directory

SHAPIRO, LIFSCHITZ AND SCHRAM, P.C. (AV)

The Evening Star Building, 1101 Pennsylvania Avenue N.W. Suite 1050, 20004
Telephone: 202-347-4111
Facsimile: 202-347-8341
URL: http://www.slslaw.com
Greenbelt, Maryland Office: 6411 Ivy Lane, Suite 116, 20770.
Telephone: 202-347-4111.
Facsimile: 202-347-8341.

(See Next Column)

Ronald S. Shapiro
Judah Lifschitz
Steven H. Schram

Michael P. Van Voorhis
Robert A. Foster
Randal W. Wax
James D. McMichael
Thomas R. Bartman
Michelle Goldstein
Daniel Lasar

For full biographical listings, see the Martindale-Hubbell Law Directory

VENABLE ATTORNEYS AT LAW VENABLE, BAETJER, HOWARD & CIVILETTI, LLP (AV)

A Partnership including Professional Corporations
Suite 1000, 1201 New York Avenue, N.W., 20005
Telephone: 202-962-4800
Fax: 202-962-8300
URL: http://www.venable.com
Baltimore, Maryland Office: Venable, Baetjer and Howard LLP, 1800 Mercantile Bank & Trust Building, 2 Hopkins Plaza.
Telephone: 410-244-7400.
Fax: 410-244-7742.
McLean, Virginia Office: Venable, Baetjer and Howard LLP, Suite 400, 2010 Corporate Ridge.
Telephone: 703-760-1600.
Fax: 703-821-8949.
Rockville, Maryland Office: Venable, Baetjer and Howard LLP, Suite 500, One Church Street, P. O. Box 1906.
Telephone: 301-217-5600.
Fax: 301-217-5617.
Towson, Maryland Office: Venable, Baetjer and Howard LLP, 210 Allegheny Avenue, P. O. Box 5517.
Telephone: 410-494-6200.
Fax: 410-821-0147.

MEMBERS OF FIRM

James K. Archibald (Also at Baltimore, Maryland Office)
Maurice Baskin
Benjamin R. Civiletti (P.C.) (Also at Baltimore and Towson, Maryland Offices)
Jeffrey A. Dunn (Also at Baltimore, Maryland Office)
George F. Pappas (Also at Baltimore, Maryland Office)
James L. Shea (also at Baltimore, Maryland Office)

For Complete List of Firm Personnel, See General Section

For full biographical listings, see the Martindale-Hubbell Law Directory

WATT, TIEDER, HOFFAR & FITZGERALD, L.L.P. (AV)

601 Pennsylvania Avenue, N.W., Suite 900, 20004
Telephone: 703-749-1000
Telecopier: 703-893-8029
Email: contactus@wthf.com *URL:* http://www.wthf.com
McLean Virginia Office: 7929 Westpark Drive, Suite 400,
Telephone: 703-749-1000.
Telecopier: 703-893-8029.
Irvine California Office: 3 Park Plaza, Suite 1500.
Telephone: 949-852-6700.

MEMBERS OF FIRM

John B. Tieder, Jr.
Robert K. Cox

For full biographical listings, see the Martindale-Hubbell Law Directory

FLORIDA

BOCA RATON, Palm Beach Co.

LAW OFFICES OF ARTHUR C. KOSKI, P.A. (AV)

568 Yamato Road, 33431
Telephone: 561-989-8800
Facsimile: 561-989-3775
Email: akoski@worldnet.att.net

Arthur C. Koski
Frank J. Badach

Thomas A. Stewart

For full biographical listings, see the Martindale-Hubbell Law Directory

MICHAUD, BUSCHMANN, FOX, FERRARA & MITTELMARK, P.A. (AV)

33 Southeast 8th Street, 33432
Telephone: 561-392-0540
Fax: 561-392-0582
Email: Bocalaw@MBFFM.com *URL:* http://www.MBFFM.com

Scott H. Michaud
Paul Buschmann
Brian S. Fox
James T. Ferrara
Michael K. Mittelmark
Marc T. Millian

(See Next Column)

MICHAUD, BUSCHMANN, FOX, FERRARA & MITTELMARK P.A.—*Continued*

Marcy G. Blitz
Linda A. McCullough
Kimberly M. Hall

For full biographical listings, see the Martindale-Hubbell Law Directory

CORAL SPRINGS, Broward Co.

PERSHES & SCHWARTZ, P.A. (AV)

Suite 205, 2801 University Drive, 33065
Telephone: 954-341-2801
Fax: 954-341-9801
Email: pershlaw@gate.net *URL:* http://www.lawyers.com/p&slaw

Robert E. Pershes
Jay A. Schwartz

For full biographical listings, see the Martindale-Hubbell Law Directory

DAYTONA BEACH, Volusia Co.

KINSEY VINCENT PYLE, P.A. (AV)

150 South Palmetto Avenue, Box A, P.O. Box 1268, 32115-1268
Telephone: 904-252-1561
Telecopier: 904-254-8157

Roy E. Kinsey (1917-1984)
C. Aubrey Vincent, Jr. (1919-1977)
Frank L. Pyle (1919-1988)
S. LaRue Williams
J. Doyle Tumbleson
MaryEllen G. Koberg

Richard A. Burt

Representative Clients: Barnett Bank; The Chubb Corporation; Bellemead Development Corp.; American Development Corp.; Bellemead Realty, Inc.; The Oceans Condominiums; Daytona Beach Civil Service Board; Hudson International Consultants and Engineers; Foley and Associates Construction Co. Inc.; Commonwealth Land Title Insurance Co.

For full biographical listings, see the Martindale-Hubbell Law Directory

*FORT LAUDERDALE,** Broward Co.

CUMMINGS & SNYDER, P.A. (AV)

1600 Southeast 17th Street Causeway, P.O. Box 460327, 33346-1116
Telephone: 954-761-8700
Telecopier: 954-524-6927
Email: administrator@cummingslaw.com *URL:* http://www.cummingslaw.com
Tallahassee, Florida Office: 1004 DeSoto Park Drive, P.O. Box 589, 32302-0589.
Telephone: 850-878-3700.
Telecopier: 850-656-0329.

F. Alan Cummings

Bradley S. Copenhaver
Alejandro Espino

OF COUNSEL

James E. Glass

Representative Clients: American Bridge Company; American International Group; Dillingham Construction Holdings, Inc.; Hubbard Construction Company; Odebrecht Construction, Inc.; Reliance Surety Company; Traylor Bros., Inc.; Condotte America, Inc.; Seaboard Surety Company; Alabama Department of Transportation.

For full biographical listings, see the Martindale-Hubbell Law Directory

FERENCIK, LIBANOFF, BRANDT & BUSTAMANTE, P.A. (AV)

150 South Pine Island Road, Suite 400, 33324
Telephone: Dade County: 305-949-8003
Broward County: 954-474-8080
Fax: 954-474-7343
Email: RFerenci@Counsel.com *URL:* http://www.flbb@mindspring.com

Robert E. Ferencik, Jr.
Ira Libanoff
Alan C. (Peter) Brandt, Jr.
Nestor Bustamante III
Alexander J. Williams, Jr.

Jordana Lee Goldstein
Sandra Denise Kennedy
Gavin D. Caddy

OF COUNSEL

Carla Reece Gettlemen

For full biographical listings, see the Martindale-Hubbell Law Directory

LEIBY CONSTRUCTION LAW FIRM, PROFESSIONAL ASSOCIATION (AV)

Pine Island Commons, 8551 West Sunrise Boulevard, Suite 304, 33322
Telephone: 954-382-9199
Fax: 954-382-9063
URL: http://www.lawyers.com/leibylaw
Email: info@leibylaw.com *URL:* http://www.leibylaw.com

Larry R. Leiby
Salvatore H. Fasulo
Richard Eric Guttentag
Adam C. Linkhorst
Douglas J. Roberts
Michael E. Stearns
Kevin J. Taylor

For full biographical listings, see the Martindale-Hubbell Law Directory

*FORT MYERS,** Lee Co.

GOLDSTEIN, BUCKLEY, CECHMAN, RICE & PURTZ, P.A. (AV)

1515 Broadway, P.O. Box 2366, 33902-2366
Telephone: 941-334-1146
Fax: 941-334-3039
Email: info@gbclaw.com *URL:* http://www.GBClaw.com
Port Charlotte, Florida Office: Emerald Square, Suite 1, 2852 Tamiami Trail, 33952.
Telephone: 941-624-2393.
Fax: 941-624-2155.
Cape Coral, Florida Office: 1603 Hancock Bridge Parkway, 33990.
Telephone: 941-574-5575.
Fax: 941-574-9213.
Lehigh Acres, Florida Office: 1458 Lee Boulevard, Lee Boulevard Shopping Center, 33936.
Telephone: 941-368-6101.
Fax: 941-368-2461.
Naples, Florida Office: 4947 North Tamiami Trail, Suite 101, 34103.
Telephone: 941-262-4888.
Fax: 941-262-8716.

Stephen W. Buckley
J. Jeffrey Rice

Approved Attorneys for: Attorneys' Title Insurance Fund.

For Complete List of Firm Personnel, See General Section

For full biographical listings, see the Martindale-Hubbell Law Directory

*JACKSONVILLE,** Duval Co.

ALLEN, BRINTON, SIMMONS & MCCARTHY, P.A. (AV)

One Independent Drive, Suite 3200, 32202
Telephone: 904-353-8800
Fax: 904-353-8770

A. Graham Allen
William D. Brinton
Sidney S. Simmons, II
Edward McCarthy, III

Joelle Jackson Dillard

Representative Clients: Anheuser-Busch Companies, Inc.; Avis Rent A Car System, Inc.; Wood-Hopkins Contracting Co.; Petticoat Contracting; Great Lakes Dredge & Doch Co.; Hal Jones Contractor, Inc.; The Haskell Co.; Johnson & Johnson; Masthaed Industries, Inc.

For full biographical listings, see the Martindale-Hubbell Law Directory

HEDRICK, DEWBERRY & REGAN, P.A. (AV)

50 North Laura Street, Suite 2225, 32202
Telephone: 904-356-1300
Fax: 904-356-8050

Michael J. Dewberry
Alexandra Krueger Hedrick
Jeffrey C. Regan

Clinton Allen Wright III

For full biographical listings, see the Martindale-Hubbell Law Directory

LOBRANO & KINCAID, P.L. (AV)

Suite 1650 Independent Life Building, 1 Independent Drive, 32202
Telephone: 904-359-2100
Facsimile: 904-353-1332

Stephen D. Lobrano
Wade McK. Hampton

OF COUNSEL

W. Douglas Smith (Not admitted in FL)

For full biographical listings, see the Martindale-Hubbell Law Directory

*MIAMI,** Dade Co.

DANIELS, KASHTAN & FORNARIS, P.A. (AV)

241 Sevilla Avenue, Penthouse 2, 33134
Telephone: 305-448-7988
Telecopier: 305-448-7978
URL: http://www.dkflaw.com

(See Next Column)

DANIELS, KASHTAN & FORNARIS P.A., *Miami—Continued*

Richard G. Daniels | John E. Oramas
Michael F. Kashtan | Ana Latour Grande
Martha D. Fornaris | Albert Blair

Elizabeth M. Touma | Chad J. Schatzle
Tracey A. Wright | Joseph W. Carey
Mercy Blasa Piña | Christopher G. Berga
John M. Haney | Liane T. Alvarez
Omar Perez, Jr. | Ricardo Morales-Gomez

OF COUNSEL

Joseph W. Downs, III

Reference: Barnett Bank.

For full biographical listings, see the Martindale-Hubbell Law Directory

ELDER, KURZMAN & VACCARELLA, P.A. (AV)

Courvoisier Centre II, Suite 401 601 Brickell Key Drive, 33131
Telephone: 305-373-6065
Broward: 954-763-5304
Fax: 305-373-6066

David R. Elder | Michael J. Kurzman
Vincent F. Vaccarella

Kerry A. Hughes | Maury Lorne Udell

OF COUNSEL

Fredrica B. Elder

For full biographical listings, see the Martindale-Hubbell Law Directory

ROSENBERG, REISMAN & STEIN, LLP (AV)

One Southeast Third Avenue Suite 3050, 33131
Telephone: 305-358-2600
Telefax: 305-375-0328
URL: http://www.rrslaw.com

MEMBERS OF FIRM

Donald S. Rosenberg | Stephen H. Reisman
Joseph B. Reisman | Gary M. Stein
Richard E. Deutch, Jr.

Representative Clients: Turner Construction Co.; The Skylake State Bank.
Approved Attorneys for: Attorneys Title Insurance Fund; Lawyers Title Insurance Corp.
Reference: The Skylake State Bank.

For full biographical listings, see the Martindale-Hubbell Law Directory

SIEGFRIED, RIVERA, LERNER, DE LA TORRE & SOBEL, P.A. (AV)

Suite 1102, 201 Alhambra Circle (Coral Gables), 33134
Telephone: 305-442-3334
Fax: 305-443-3292
URL: http://www.siegfriedlaw.com

Steven M. Siegfried | Peter H. Edwards
Oscar R. Rivera | Stuart H. Sobel
Lisa A. Lerner | Maria Victoria Arias
Helio De La Torre | James F. Harrington
Elisabeth D. Kozlow

Gary Louis Brown | Fern F. Musselwhite
David B. Israel | Grissel C. Picot
Laura Michelle Manning | Marc C. Pugliese

OF COUNSEL

H. Hugh Mc Connell

For full biographical listings, see the Martindale-Hubbell Law Directory

WELBAUM, GUERNSEY, HINGSTON, GREENLEAF & GREGORY, L.L.P. (AV)

Penthouse Suite, 901 Ponce de Leon Boulevard (Coral Gables), 33134-3009
Telephone: 305-441-8900
Fax: 305-441-2255
Email: wghgglaw@bellsouth.net

MEMBERS OF FIRM

R. Earl Welbaum | Robert A. Hingston
Dan B. Guernsey | W. Frank Greenleaf
John H. Gregory

ASSOCIATES

Michael Yates | Michael Jay Rune, II

OF COUNSEL

René Sacasas

For full biographical listings, see the Martindale-Hubbell Law Directory

MOUNT DORA, Lake Co.

RICHARD S. BERGHOLTZ, P.A. (AV)

411 North Donnelly Street, Suite 207, P.O. Box 1789, 32756-1789
Telephone: 352-735-6938
Fax: 352-735-9283
Email: rsbpalaw@aol.com

Richard S. Bergholtz | Anne L. Bingler

Representative Clients: All-Interior Supply, Inc.; American Bronze Foundry; General Utilities Corporation; Henns Construction; Insurance General Contractors; MWM South, Inc.; Pleasants Hardware Company; Samafil Roofing and Waterproofing, Inc.; Siemens Cerberus Pyrotronics; Solmax Geosynthetics, Inc.

For full biographical listings, see the Martindale-Hubbell Law Directory

*NAPLES,** Collier Co.

QUARLES & BRADY LLP (AV)

Barnett Center, 4501 Tamiami Trail North Suite 300, 34103-3060
Telephone: 941-262-5959
Fax: 941-434-4999
URL: http://www.quarles.com
Milwaukee, Wisconsin Office: 411 East Wisconsin Avenue, 53202-4497.
Telephone: 414-277-5000.
Fax: 414-271-3552.
Madison, Wisconsin Office: Firstar Plaza, One South Pinckney Street, P.O. Box 2113, 53701-2113.
Telephone: 608-251-5000.
Fax: 608-251-9166.
West Palm Beach, Florida Office: 222 Lakeview Avenue, 4th Floor, 33401.
Telephone: 561-653-5000.
Fax: 561-653-5333.
Phoenix, Arizona Office: One Camelback Building, One East Camelback Road, Suite 400, 85012-1649.
Telephone: 602-230-5500.
Fax: 602-230-5598.
Chicago, Illinois Office: Quarles & Brady LLC, Citicorp Center, 500 West Madison Street, Suite 3700.
Telephone: 312-715-5000.
Fax: 312-715-5155.

PARTNERS

David L. Petersen | Robert E. Doyle, Jr.
F. Joseph McMackin, III | John D. Humphreville

ASSOCIATES

Mark Hubert Muller | James T. Demarest

For Complete List of Firm Personnel, See General Section

For full biographical listings, see the Martindale-Hubbell Law Directory

*ORLANDO,** Orange Co.

BAKER & HOSTETLER LLP (AV)

SunBank Center, Suite 2300, 200 South Orange Avenue, 32802-3432
Telephone: 407-649-4000
Fax: 407-841-0168
To contact an attorney on the Internet use first initial and surname followed by @baker-hostetler.com
URL: http://www.bakerlaw.com
In Cleveland, Ohio: 3200 National City Center, 1900 East Ninth Street.
Telephone: 216-621-0200.
In Cincinnati, Ohio: 312 Walnut Street, Suite 2650.
Telephone: 513-929-3400.
In Columbus, Ohio: Capitol Square, Suite 2100, 65 East State Street.
Telephone: 614-228-1541.
In Denver, Colorado: 303 East 17th Avenue, Suite 1100.
Telephone: 303-861-0600.
In Houston, Texas: 1000 Louisiana, Suite 2000.
Telephone: 713-751-1600.
In Long Beach, California: 300 Oceangate, Suite 620.
Telephone: 362-432-2827.
In Los Angeles, California: 600 Wilshire Boulevard.
Telephone: 213-624-2400.
In Washington, D. C.: Washington Square, Suite 1100, 1050 Connecticut Avenue, N.W.
Telephone: 202-861-1500.

PARTNER

John W. Foster, Sr.

For Complete List of Firm Personnel, See General Section

For full biographical listings, see the Martindale-Hubbell Law Directory

DEMPSEY & SASSO (AV)

Nations Bank Building, 390 North Orange Avenue, Suite 2700, P.O. Box 1980, 32802
Telephone: 407-422-5166
Telecopier: 407-422-8556
Email: demp-sas@magicnet.net

(See Next Column)

DEMPSEY & SASSO—*Continued*

Bernard H. Dempsey, Jr. | Michael C. Sasso

Brian D. Solomon | Jeffrey K. Grant
Barbara B. Smithers | Angelia J. Sheridan

For full biographical listings, see the Martindale-Hubbell Law Directory

NORMAN LINDER HULL, P.A. (AV)

537 North Magnolia Avenue, P.O. Box 2751, 32802
Telephone: 407-422-1235
Fax: 407-423-2842
Email: nlhull@ix.netcom.com *URL:* http://www.lawyers.com/hulllaw

Norman L. Hull

For full biographical listings, see the Martindale-Hubbell Law Directory

POHL & SHORT, P.A.

(See Winter Park)

RUSSELL LAW OFFICES, P.A. (AV)

537 North Magnolia Avenue, P.O. Box 886, 32802
Telephone: 407-422-1234
Telecopier: 407-423-2842
Email: RussLaw@compuserve.com *URL:* http://www.lawyers.com/russlaw

Rodney Laird Russell

Representative Clients: Cocoa Masonry, Inc.; Crane & Equipment Consulting, Inc.; Gaco Western, Inc.; Graybar Electric Co.; Grunau Company, Inc.; Haley Construction, Inc.; Steadman Steel Fabricators, Inc.; Turner Construction Co.; Uniroof Corp.; Vistana Resort Development, Inc.

For full biographical listings, see the Martindale-Hubbell Law Directory

*PENSACOLA,** Escambia Co.

YOUNG & ASSOCIATES, ATTORNEYS AT LAW, P.A. (AV)

Seville Tower, Seventh Floor, 226 South Palafox Place, 32501
Telephone: 850-432-2222
Fax: 850-432-1444
Tampa, Florida Office: 1517 Seventh Avenue, Suite C, 33605.
Telephone: 813-242-6262.
Fax: 813-342-6363.

B. Richard Young

Michael T. Bill | B. B. Boles, III
David A. Fugett | Ricardo J. Diaz
Peter S. Roumbos | James R. Barnes

For full biographical listings, see the Martindale-Hubbell Law Directory

*SARASOTA,** Sarasota Co.

BROWN CLARK, A PROFESSIONAL ASSOCIATION (AV)

Suite 500, Sarasota City Center, 1819 Main Street, 34236
Telephone: 941-957-3800
Telefax: 941-957-3888
Email: brownclark@mindspring.com *URL:* http://www.brownclark.com

Daryl J. Brown | Jennifer G. Maglio
William G. Christopher | Michael L. Morgan
Donald D. Clark | Robin S. Trupp

For full biographical listings, see the Martindale-Hubbell Law Directory

*STUART,** Martin Co.

MCCARTHY, SUMMERS, BOBKO, MCKEY, WOOD & SAWYER, P.A. (AV)

2081 East Ocean Boulevard, Second Floor, 34996
Telephone: 561-286-1700
Fax: 561-283-1803
URL: http://www.mcsumm.com

Terence P. McCarthy | Steven J. Wood
Robert P. Summers | Thomas R. Sawyer
Noel A. Bobko | Nicola J. Boone
John D. McKey, Jr. | Steven L. Perry

Kathryn C. Bass | Robert N. Maitland, II

Representative Clients: First National Bank and Trust Company of the Treasure Coast; Hydratech Utilities; Lost Lake at Hobe Sound; Gary Player Design Group; YMCA of Martin County; Shadow Lakes Groves, Inc.; Merrill Lynch Trust Co., (Florida); Wilmington Trust, FSB; The Huntington National Bank, N.A.; WSTU-Radio, WTCN-TV.

For full biographical listings, see the Martindale-Hubbell Law Directory

*TALLAHASSEE,** Leon Co.

CUMMINGS & SNYDER, P.A. (AV)

1004 DeSoto Park Drive, P.O. Box 589, 32302-0589
Telephone: 850-878-3700
Telecopier: 850-656-0329
Email: administrator@cummingslaw.com *URL:* http://www.cummingslaw.com
Fort Lauderdale, Florida Office: 1600 Southeast 17th Street Causeway, P.O. Box 460327, 33346-1116.
Telephone: 954-761-8700.
Telecopier: 954-524-6927.

F. Alan Cummings | Patricia Anne Hamilton Snyder

W. Guy McKenzie, Jr. | Daniel Te Young

Representative Clients: American Bridge Company; American International Group; Dillingham Construction Holdings, Inc.; Hubbard Construction Company; Odebrecht Construction, Inc.; Reliance Surety Company; Traylor Bros., Inc.; Condotte America, Inc.; Seaboard Surety Company; Alabama Department of Transportation.

For full biographical listings, see the Martindale-Hubbell Law Directory

*TAMPA,** Hillsborough Co.

MICHAEL C. ADDISON (AV)

Suite 1130, 220 East Madison Street, 33602
Telephone: 813-223-2000
Facsimile: 813-228-6000
Mailing Address: P.O. Box 2175, Tampa, Florida, 33601-2175
Email: michaeladdison@compuserve.com *URL:* http://www.lawyers.com/michaeladdison-law

For full biographical listings, see the Martindale-Hubbell Law Directory

JOHN W. BAKAS, JR. (AV)

201 East Kennedy Boulevard, Suite 400, 33602-5823
Telephone: 813-228-8015
Fax: 813-228-8208
Email: jbakas@aol.com *URL:* http://www.bakas.com

For full biographical listings, see the Martindale-Hubbell Law Directory

CAREY, O'MALLEY, WHITAKER & MANSON, P.A. (AV)

712 South Oregon Avenue, 33606
Telephone: 813-250-0577
Telecopier: 813-250-9898
Email: cowmpa@aol.com

Michael R. Carey | Daniel D. Whitaker
Andrew M. O'Malley | Douglas P. Manson
Randall P. Mueller

For full biographical listings, see the Martindale-Hubbell Law Directory

MEIROSE & FRISCIA, P.A. (AV)

500 North Westshore Boulevard, Suite 635, 33609
Telephone: 813-289-8800
Fax: 813-281-2005
Email: mftampa@worldnet.att.net

Leo H. Meirose, Jr. | Francis E. Friscia

Gregory Scott R. Haney

For full biographical listings, see the Martindale-Hubbell Law Directory

*VERO BEACH,** Indian River Co.

MOSS, HENDERSON, BLANTON & LANIER, P.A. (AV)

817 Beachland Boulevard, P.O. Box 3406, 32964-3406
Telephone: 561-231-1900
Fax: 561-231-4387

Steve L. Henderson | Fred L. Kretschmer, Jr.

Representative Clients: Aetna Life & Casualty; Alcoa Florida, Inc.; Florida Power & Light Co.; Insurance Company of North America; Liberty Mutual Insurance Co.; Sears, Roebuck & Co.; Sugar Cane Growers Cooperative of Florida; Norfolk Southern Corporation/North American Van Lines, Inc.

For Complete List of Firm Personnel, See General Section

For full biographical listings, see the Martindale-Hubbell Law Directory

*WEST PALM BEACH,** Palm Beach Co.

QUARLES & BRADY LLP (AV)

222 Lakeview Avenue, 4th Floor, 33401
Telephone: 561-653-5000
Fax: 561-653-5333
URL: http://www.quarles.com
Milwaukee, Wisconsin Office: 411 East Wisconsin Avenue, 53202-4497.
Telephone: 414-277-5000.
Fax: 414-271-3552.
Madison, Wisconsin Office: Firstar Plaza, One South Pinckney Street, P.O. Box 2113, 53701-2113.
Telephone: 608-251-5000.
Fax: 608-251-9166.
Naples, Florida Office: Barnett Center, 4501 Tamiami Trail North, Suite 300, 34103-3060.
Telephone: 941-262-5959.
Fax: 941-434-4999.
Phoenix, Arizona Office: One Camelback Building, One East Camelback Road, Suite 400, 85012-1649.
Telephone: 602-230-5500.
Fax: 602-230-5598.
Chicago, Illinois Office: Quarles & Brady LLC, Citicorp Center, 500 West Madison Street, Suite 3700.
Telephone: 312-715-5000.
Fax: 312-715-5155.

PARTNERS

J. Rodman Steele, Jr.
Ned R. Nashban
Gregory A. Nelson
Nancy Berz Colman
Joseph W. Bain
Robert J. Sacco

OF COUNSEL

John S. Sammond

ASSOCIATES

Mark D. Passler
Stanley A. Kim
Scott D. Paul
Steven M. Greenberg

BUSINESS MANAGEMENT SUPPORT PERSONNEL

OFFICE MANAGER

Nadean R. Stone

LEGAL ASSISTANTS

Jacquelyn Brookings
Carol Cavallerano
Linda C. Clemons
Leneah R. Davis
Susan Hess
Janet E. Townsend

For full biographical listings, see the Martindale-Hubbell Law Directory

WINTER PARK, Orange Co.

LYON KIRWIN, P.A. (AV®)

338 Morse Boulevard, Suite 150, 32789
Telephone: 407-740-6600
Facsimile: 407-740-6363

V. Frederic Lyon
Brian P. Kirwin
Bruce Alan Norris
Brian W. Bennett

James C. Washburn
Michelle B. Kane
Michael D. Chiumento, III

Representative Clients: American Express; Centex-Rooney; City of St. Petersburg; Clancy & Theys Construction Co.; Duke Engineering & Services; Florida Power Corp.; Sea World of Florida; Seminole County, Florida; Seminole County Public Schools; South Florida Water Management District; U.S. Steel.

For full biographical listings, see the Martindale-Hubbell Law Directory

POHL & SHORT, P.A. (AV)

280 West Canton Avenue, Suite 410, P.O. Box 3208, 32790
Telephone: 407-647-7645; 407-647-POHL
Telefax: 407-647-2314
Email: ps@pohlshort.com

Dwight I. Cool
Alexander S. Douglas II
Gary A. Forster
E. Givens Goodspeed
Mark A. Grimes
Robert S. Hoofman
Roger A. Kelly
Adam O. Kirwan
David J. Kohs
Frank L. Pohl
James Everett Shepherd V
Houston E. Short
John R. Simpson, Jr.

Representative Clients: American Generator Co.; Copelco Capital, Inc.; Denim U.S.A., Inc.; Ford Motor Credit Co.; Lodestar Technology, Inc.; Lutheran Brotherhood; SunTrust, N.A.; Trax, Inc.

For full biographical listings, see the Martindale-Hubbell Law Directory

VOSE, BLAU & HAYES (AV)

2705 West Fairbanks Avenue, 32789
Telephone: 407-645-3735
Fax: 407-628-5670
Email: bvose@vbh-law.com *URL:* http://www.vbh-law.com

(See Next Column)

Gretchen R. H. Vose
Leslie A. Blau
Rosemary H. Hayes

ASSOCIATES

Carolyn S. Crichton
Christina M. Page
Peter J. Meadows
Aubrey Harry Ducker, Jr.

For full biographical listings, see the Martindale-Hubbell Law Directory

GEORGIA

*ATLANTA,** Fulton Co.

BOVIS, KYLE & BURCH, LLC (AV)

A Limited Liability Corporation including Professional Corporations
Third Floor, 53 Perimeter Center East, 30346
Telephone: 770-391-9100
Telecopier: 770-668-0878
Email: bkb@boviskyle.com *URL:* http://www.boviskyle.com

John V. Burch (P.C.)
Gregory R. Veal
Timothy J. Burson

Christina A. Craddock

For Complete List of Firm Personnel, See General Section

For full biographical listings, see the Martindale-Hubbell Law Directory

MICHAEL L. CHAPMAN (AV)

Two Midtown Plaza, Suite 1100, 1349 West Peachtree Street, N.E., 30309
Telephone: 404-685-9600
FAX: 404-875-0666
URL: http://www.chapmanfirm.com

For full biographical listings, see the Martindale-Hubbell Law Directory

FREEMAN MATHIS & GARY, LLP (AV)

100 Galleria Parkway, 16th Floor, 30339-5959
Telephone: 770-818-0000
Fax: 770-937-9960
URL: http://www.fmglaw.com

MEMBER

T. Bart Gary

ASSOCIATE

Jefferson M. Allen

Representative Clients: AGCO Corporation; Abrams Construction Co.; C.W. Matthews Contracting Co.; Couch Construction, Inc.; Knight-Davidson Cos.; Rosser International; Superfos Construction (U.S.), Inc.; Security Capital Atlantic; The St. Paul Companies; Tensar Corp.

For full biographical listings, see the Martindale-Hubbell Law Directory

GRIFFIN COCHRANE & MARSHALL, A PROFESSIONAL CORPORATION (AV)

127 Peachtree Street, N.E. 14th Floor, 30303
Telephone: 404-523-2000
Fax: 404-523-9655

Harry L. Griffin, Jr.
Curtis W. Martin
Lee C. Davis
Jennifer Wheatley Fletcher
W. Henry Parkman
John Dean Marshall, Jr.
Michael C. Castellon
Craig Alan Courville
Melissa S. Dillon
F. Barry McCabe
Wm. Garth Snider

OF COUNSEL

Robert D. Marshall
John F. Elger

For full biographical listings, see the Martindale-Hubbell Law Directory

HENDRICK, PHILLIPS, SCHEMM & SALZMAN, A PROFESSIONAL CORPORATION (AV)

1800 Peachtree Center Tower, 230 Peachtree Street, N.W., 30303
Telephone: 404-522-1410
Fax: 404-522-9545

David R. Hendrick
Stephen M. Phillips
Neil C. Schemm
Martin R. Salzman
Victoria H. Tobin
William D. Flatt

James E. Rambeau, Jr.
Stephanie M. Warshal
Timothy A. Vanderver, III

Reference: First Union National Bank.

For full biographical listings, see the Martindale-Hubbell Law Directory

Atlanta—Continued

SMITH, CURRIE & HANCOCK LLP (AV)

2600 Harris Tower-Peachtree Center, 233 Peachtree Street, N.E., 30303-1530
Telephone: 404-521-3800
Telecopier: 404-688-0671
Email: smith-currie-hancock@worldnet.att.net *URL:* http://www.smithcurrie.com

MEMBERS OF FIRM

Overton A. Currie (Retired)
Luther P. House, Jr. (Retired)
Glower W. Jones (Retired)
Robert B. Ansley, Jr. (Retired)
Bert R. Oastler (Retired)
Aubrey L. Coleman, Jr.
Thomas E. Abernathy, IV
Philip L. Fortune
Thomas J. Kelleher, Jr.
Frank E. Riggs, Jr.
Ronald G. Robey
John T. Flynn
James F. Butler, III
Joseph C. Staak
Hubert J. Bell, Jr.
Philip E. Beck
James K. Bidgood, Jr.
S. Gregory Joy
Robert C. Chambers
Karl Dix, Jr.
John E. Menechino, Jr.
William L. Baggett, Jr.

ASSOCIATES

Mark V. Hanrahan
Eugene J. Heady
David A. Roberts
Deborah R. Murphey
Stacey L. Robinson
Eric L. Nelson
Anthony D. Lehman
Edward J. McNaughton

Construction Clients: Jacobs Engineering; Caddell Construction Co., Inc.; Turner Construction Co.; Martin K. Eby Construction Co., Inc.; Danis Industries Corp.; Georgia Chapter of Associated General Contractors; Georgia Highway Contractors Association; Massachusetts Water Resources Authority; City of Amarillo; S. P. McCarl's & Co.

For full biographical listings, see the Martindale-Hubbell Law Directory

SMITH, HOWARD & AJAX, LLP (AV)

300 Atlanta Financial Center South, 3333 Peachtree Road, N.E., 30326
Telephone: 404-239-1900
Fax: 404-239-1930

ASSOCIATE

Mark D. Gropp

OF COUNSEL

Larry S. McReynolds

Representative Clients: Construction Suppliers Association; Georgia Utility Contractors Association, Inc.; Concrete Products Association, Inc.; National Electrical Contractors Association; Conditioned Air Association of Georgia, Inc.; Masonry Contractors Association; Reynolds, Inc.; Doyle Dickerson Co.; United Electric Co.; D&N Electric Co.

For full biographical listings, see the Martindale-Hubbell Law Directory

WEINBERG, WHEELER, HUDGINS, GUNN & DIAL, LLC (AV)

999 Peachtree Street, N.E. Suite 2700, 30309
Telephone: 404-876-2700
Facsimile: 404-875-9433
Email: firm@wwhgd.com

MEMBERS OF FIRM

J. Kenneth Moorman
Robert G. Tanner
Patrick A. Thompson
David A. Dial
D. Lee Roberts, Jr.
Frederick N. Sager, Jr.

ASSOCIATES

Anandhi S. Rajan
Alan M. Maxwell
Beth E. Weitzman
Patrick Moore
Chloe E. Dallaire
Anna C. Palazzolo

Representative Clients: Alcatel Contracting (NA), Inc.; American International Group; Golder Associate, Inc.; Holder Corporation; MFS Network Technologies, Inc.; Travelers Property Casualty; H.B. Zachery Company.

For Complete List of Firm Personnel, See General Section

For full biographical listings, see the Martindale-Hubbell Law Directory

WEISZ & ASSOCIATES (AV)

Suite 900 Live Oak Center, 3475 Lenox Road, N.E., 30326-1232
Telephone: 404-233-7888
Facsimile: 404-261-1925
Email: prw1@bellsouth.net

Peter R. Weisz

ASSOCIATE

Cathy R. Nash

Representative Clients: L.M. Scofield Co.; S. Champion Constr. Co.; Deerfield Construction Co.; Cee Klein Accessories, LTD.
Reference: First Union National Bank.

For full biographical listings, see the Martindale-Hubbell Law Directory

MICHAEL WELCH (AV)

900 Circle 75 Parkway, Suite 1330, 30339
Telephone: 770-850-1900
Fax: 770-850-1967

For full biographical listings, see the Martindale-Hubbell Law Directory

*AUGUSTA,** Richmond Co.

HULL, TOWILL, NORMAN, BARRETT & SALLEY, A PROFESSIONAL CORPORATION (AV)

801 Broad Street, Suite 700, 30901
Telephone: 706-722-4481
Fax: 706-722-9779
Email: hullfirm@groupz.net *URL:* http://www.groupz.net/~advocate
Aiken, South Carolina Office: 111 Park Avenue, 29801.
Telephone: 803-648-4213.
Fax: 803-648-2601.

James M. Hull (1885-1975)
George B. Barrett (1894-1942)
Julian J. Willingham (1887-1963)
John Bell Towill (1907-1991)
Robert C. Norman (Retired, 1991)
W. Hale Barrett
Lawton Jordan, Jr.
Patrick J. Rice
Douglas D. Batchelor, Jr.
David E. Hudson
William H. Tucker (Not admitted in GA)
William F. Hammond
Mark S. Burgreen
George R. Hall
James B. Ellington
F. Michael Taylor
William J. Keogh, III
Edward J. Tarver
J. Noel Schweers, III
Susan D. Barrett
Ralph Emerson Hanna, III

James M. Holly (Not admitted in GA)
Timothy E. Moses
N. Shannon Gentry Lanier
Tara R. Simkins
Charles H. Weigle
Natalie A. Dopson
David C. Smith

OF COUNSEL

Julian B. Salley, Jr. (Not admitted in GA)

Counsel for: Morris Communications Corporation; Merry Land & Investment Company, Inc.; Castleberry/Snow's Brands, Inc.; Sun Trust Bank Augusta, N.A.; Georgia Power Co.; St. Joseph Hospital, Augusta, Georgia, Inc.; Norfolk Southern Corp.; Housing Authority of the City of Augusta; Georgia Press Association; Columbia County, Georgia.

For full biographical listings, see the Martindale-Hubbell Law Directory

*NEWNAN,** Coweta Co.

GLOVER & DAVIS, P.A. (AV)

10 Brown Street, P.O. Box 1038, 30264
Telephone: 770-683-6000
Fax: 770-683-6010
Peachtree City, Georgia Office: Suite 130, 200 Westpark Drive.
Telephone: 770-487-5834.
Fax: 770-487-3492.

J. Littleton Glover, Jr.
Alan W. Jackson

Peter A. Durham

Representative Clients: Batson-Cook Company and Construction Subsidiaries; Headley Construction Corporation; Stewart & Associates Construction, Inc.; Pyramid Masonry, Inc.; First Citizens Corporation and Banking Subsidiaries; Putnam-Greene Financial Corporation and Banking Subsidiaries; Peachtree National Bank.
Local Counsel for: West Georgia Farm Credit, ACA.

For Complete List of Firm Personnel, See General Section

For full biographical listings, see the Martindale-Hubbell Law Directory

HAWAII

*HONOLULU,** Honolulu Co.

AYABE, CHONG, NISHIMOTO, SIA & NAKAMURA (AV)

A Partnership including a Professional Corporation
Pauahi Tower, Suite 2500, 1001 Bishop Street, 96813
Telephone: 808-537-6119
Telecopier: 808-526-3491
Email: ACNSN@pixi.com

MEMBERS OF FIRM

Sidney K. Ayabe (P.C.)
Richard F. Nakamura
Jeffrey H. K. Sia
Kenneth T. Goya
Ann H. Aratani
Steven L. Goto

Representative Clients: Travelers Insurance Co.; St. Paul Fire and Marine Insurance Co.; The Employers Group of Insurance Companies; TIG Insurance Co.; Pacific Insurance Co.; Hartford Accident and Indemnity Co.; Continental Casualty Co.; CNA Insurance Co.; DTRIC.

(See Next Column)

AYABE, CHONG, NISHIMOTO, SIA & NAKAMURA, *Honolulu—Continued*

For full biographical listings, see the Martindale-Hubbell Law Directory

BAYS, DEAVER, HIATT, LUNG & ROSE (AV)

A Partnership including Professional Corporations
16th Floor, Alii Place, 1099 Alakea Street, P.O. Box 1760, 96806
Telephone: 808-523-9000
Telecopier: 808-533-4184
Telex: RCA 7238976
Email: bdhlr@aloha.net *URL:* http://www.bdhlr.com
Kamuela, Hawaii Office: Suite 204 Parker Square, 65-1279 Kawaihae Road.
Telephone: 808-885-3400.
Telecopier: 808-885-6765.

MEMBERS OF FIRM

A. Bernard Bays (A Law Corporation)
Phillip L. Deaver (A Law Corporation)
Jerry Michael Hiatt (A Law Corporation)
Harvey J. Lung (A Law Corporation)
Crystal K. Rose (A Law Corporation)
Jason N. Baba (A Law Corporation)
Michael W. Thomas
Karin L. Holma

ASSOCIATES

Mahilani E.K. Hiatt
Wendy J. Utsumi
Bruce Voss
Edward J. Corwin
Craig P. Wagnild
Rafael G. del Castillo
Kim A. Tomey
Liane L. Brown
Elizabeth A.C. Thompson

For full biographical listings, see the Martindale-Hubbell Law Directory

CARLSMITH BALL (AV)

A Partnership including Law Corporations
Suite 2200, Pacific Tower, 1001 Bishop Street, P.O. Box 656, 96809-3402
Telephone: 808-523-2500
Fax: 808-523-0842
Email: execdirector@carlsmith.com *URL:* http://www.carlsmith.com
Kapolei, Hawaii Office: Suite 318, Kapolei Building, 1001 Kamokila Boulevard, 96707.
Telephone: 808-523-2500.
Fax: 808-674-0850.
Wailuku, Maui Hawaii Office: Suite 400, One Main Plaza, 2200 Main Street, P.O. Box 1086, 96793-1086.
Telephone: 808-242-4535.
Fax: 808-244-4974.
Kailua-Kona, Hawaii Office: Suite 209, 75-1000 Henry Street, 96740.
Telephone: 808-329-6464.
Fax: 808-329-9450.
Hilo, Hawaii Office: 121 Waianuenue Avenue, P.O. Box 686, 96721-0686.
Telephone: 808-935-6644.
Fax: 808-935-7975.
Hagatna, Guam Office: Suite 401, Bank of Hawaii Building, 134 West Soledad Avenue, P.O. Box BF, 96932-5027.
Telephone: 671-472-6813.
Fax: 671-477-4375.
Telex: 721-6445 CWCMI GM.
Saipan, Commonwealth of the Northern Mariana Islands Office: Carlsmith Building, Capitol Hill, P.O. Box 5241, 96950-5241.
Telephone: 670-322-3455.
Fax: 670-322-3368.
Los Angeles, California Office: 9th Floor, 444 South Flower Street, 90071-2901.
Telephone: 213-955-1200.
Fax: 213-623-0032.
Washington, D.C. Office: Suite 300, 1201 Pennsylvania Avenue, N.W., 20004-2401.
Telephone: 202-628-2228.
Fax: 202-628-2071.
Mexico City, Mexico Office: Carlsmith Ball, Sierra Nevada 119, Lomas de Chapultepec, 11000 Mexico, D.F.
Telephone: 52-5-520-8514, 52-5-520-8757.
Fax: 52-5-540-1545.
Mexico, D.F. Office of Carlsmith Ball, S.C. (Authorized to practice as foreign legal consultants in Mexico): Sierra Nevada 119, Lomas de Chapultepec, 11000 Mexico, D.F.
Telephone: 52-5-520-8514, 52-5-520-8757.
Fax: 52-5-540-1545.

MEMBERS OF FIRM

Edward E. Case
John P. Manaut
Matthew M. Matsunaga
Thomas R. Sylvester
Allen R. Wolff

For Complete List of Firm Personnel, See General Section

For full biographical listings, see the Martindale-Hubbell Law Directory

GOODSILL ANDERSON QUINN & STIFEL (AV)

Alii Place, Suite 1800, 1099 Alakea Street, P.O. Box 3196, 96801-3196
Telephone: 808-547-5600
FAX: 808-547-5880
Email: info@goodsill.com *URL:* http://www.goodsill.com

MEMBERS OF FIRM

David J. Dezzani
Ronald H. W. Lum
John R. Lacy
Raymond S. Iwamoto
William S. Miller
Jacqueline L. S. Earle
Randall K. Steverson
Vincent A. Piekarski
Mark B. Desmarais
Corlis J. Chang
Mark F. Ito
Wayne H. Muraoka
Audrey E. J. Ng
Gail Otsuka Ayabe
Dale Edward F.T. Zane
LindaLee K. Farm
Carol Ann Eblen
Roy John Tjioe
Kellie M. N. Sekiya
Lennes N. Omuro

ASSOCIATES

Thomas L. Benedict
Edmund K. Saffery
Normand R. Lezy
Adrienne Y. Shimonishi

Representative Clients: Alaka'i Mechanical Corporation; Allied Construction; Castle & Cooke, Inc.; Dillingham Construction Pacific; Gentry Homes; Graham Murata Russell; Industrial Welding, Inc.; Shimizu Corporation; Takenaka (U.S.A.) Corporation.

For Complete List of Firm Personnel, See General Section

For full biographical listings, see the Martindale-Hubbell Law Directory

MIYAGI, NOHR & MYHRE (AV)

1001 Bishop Street, Suite 1200, 96813
Telephone: 808-524-2466
Fax: 808-524-2556

Melvyn M. Miyagi
Katharine M. Nohr
James V. Myhre
Michael H. Tsuchida
John E. Drotz

OF COUNSEL

Carleton B. Reid

Representative Clients: American International Group; State Farm Insurance; TIG Insurance; Crum & Forster; ITT Specialty Risk Services; Marriott International; The Hartford; USAA; Budget Rent A Car; Crawford & Company.

For full biographical listings, see the Martindale-Hubbell Law Directory

TOM & PETRUS (AV)

212 Merchant Street Suite 200, 96813
Telephone: 808-522-0800
Fax: 808-522-0809

MEMBERS OF FIRM

Michael D. Tom
Brad S. Petrus
Richard B. Miller

ASSOCIATES

Leslie H. Kondo
Stephen M. Teves
David R. Harada-Stone
Lauren K. Rauschenburg

COUNSEL

Lyle Minoru Ishida

Representative Clients: Dillingham Construction Pacific, Ltd.; JDH Construction Ltd.; Scottsdale Insurance Company; Dames & Moore; Delta Construction Corporation; Kapi'olani Health (Medical Center for Women and Children and Kapi'olani Medical Center at Pali Momi); St. Francis Health System (St. Francis Medical Center and St. Francis Medical Center West); Applied Technology Corporation; Nordic/PCL (HawaiiConvention Center); Morrison Knudsen Corp.

For full biographical listings, see the Martindale-Hubbell Law Directory

IDAHO

*BOISE,** Ada Co.

MEULEMAN & MILLER, L.L.P. (AV)

960 Broadway Avenue, Suite 400, P.O. Box 955, 83701
Telephone: 208-342-6066
Fax: 208-336-9712
Email: firm@lawidaho.com *URL:* http://www.lawidaho.com

MEMBERS OF FIRM

Wayne V. Meuleman
Robert L. Miller
Geoffrey J. McConnell

Representative Clients: Albertson's, Inc.; Associated General Contractors-Idaho Branch; C.M. Company, Inc.; Contractors Bonding & Insurance Co.; H-K Contractors, Inc.; Idaho Power Co.; Idaho State Building Authority; McAlvain Construction, Inc.; Wright Brothers; YMC Mechanical Contractors.

For full biographical listings, see the Martindale-Hubbell Law Directory

ILLINOIS

*CHICAGO,** Cook Co.

BECKER & KAPLAN LLC (AV)

19 South La Salle Street Suite 1500, 60603
Telephone: 312-621-9500
Fax: 312-621-9011
Email: firm@beckerkaplan.com *URL:* http://www.beckerkaplan.com

Theodore M. Becker
Daniel S. Kaplan

Edward R. White
Michael J. Boxerman

For full biographical listings, see the Martindale-Hubbell Law Directory

BLATT, HAMMESFAHR & EATON (AV)

333 W. Wacker Drive, Suite 1900, 60606
Telephone: 312-849-8000
FAX: 312-357-0198
Email: BHE@BHELAW.COM *URL:* HTTP://WWW.BHELAW.COM
New York, New York Office: 45 Broadway, 12th Floor.
Telephone: 212-363-1900.
Fax: 212-363-2600. Email: bhe@bhelaw.com.

MEMBERS OF FIRM

Hugo Chaviano
Larry R. Eaton

ASSOCIATES

Mary I. Babbo
Bruce M. Lichtcsien
Joseph G. Lyons

For full biographical listings, see the Martindale-Hubbell Law Directory

CAHILL, CHRISTIAN & KUNKLE, LTD. (AV)

Santa Fe Building, 224 South Michigan Avenue, Suite 1300, 60604
Telephone: 312-341-1688
Fax: 312-341-1689
URL: http://www.cck.com

William J. Kunkle, Jr.
Roseann Oliver
William T. Cahill
John M. Christian
Lorna E. Propes
Scott B. Greene
Mary Kathryn Kelly
Suzanne M. Metzel
Matthew J. Gehringer
Steven E. Nieslawski
Michael K. Bartosz
Donald Lee Homyk

OF COUNSEL

Louis B. Garippo

Daniel J. Collins
Jeanne M. Cullen
Elizabeth A. Kaveny
Frederic T. Knape
David R. Nordwall
Elisha S. Rosenblum
Melisa G. Thompson

For full biographical listings, see the Martindale-Hubbell Law Directory

FORAN & SCHULTZ (AV)

Suite 3000, 30 North La Salle Street, 60602
Telephone: 312-368-8330
Fax: 312-580-2600
Email: law@foran.com *URL:* http://www.Foran.com

MEMBERS OF FIRM

Richard G. Schultz
Stephen A. Gorman
Jeff D. Harris
Steven H. Gistenson

For full biographical listings, see the Martindale-Hubbell Law Directory

KAPLAN, BEGY & VON OHLEN (AV)

One First National Plaza 51st Floor, 60603
Telephone: 312-345-3000
Fax: 312-345-3119
URL: http://www.kbvlaw.com

MEMBERS OF FIRM

Fred C. Begy, III
Larry S. Kaplan
Robert C. von Ohlen, Jr.
Joseph A. Bosco
Richard A. Walker
Mitchell J. Kanaan
Patrick J. Keating

ASSOCIATES

Keith S. Yamaguchi
Thomas C. Sokol
Robert K. Villa
Nicole Halpern Murphy
Telly Andrews
Tamara S. Dykstra

For full biographical listings, see the Martindale-Hubbell Law Directory

LAWRENCE, KAMIN, SAUNDERS & UHLENHOP (AV)

208 South La Salle Street, Suite 1750, 60604-1188
Telephone: 312-372-1947
Telecopier: 312-372-2389
Email: LKSU@LKSU.com

MEMBERS OF FIRM

Kent Lawrence
David E. Muschler
Lawrence A. Rosen

ASSOCIATES

John S. Monical
Paul M. Weltlich

Representative Clients: Pepper Construction Co.; Landquist & Son, Inc.; O'-Neil Construction Co.; United States Fidelity and Guaranty; Lyons Electric Co.; Steiner Electric Company; St. Paul Financial Marine Insurance Co.; Seaboard Surety Co; Mellon Stuart Co.

For full biographical listings, see the Martindale-Hubbell Law Directory

SCHWARTZBERG, BARNETT & COHEN (AV)

55 West Monroe Street, 2400 Xerox Centre, 60603-5040
Telephone: 312-726-3555
Fax: 312-726-6299
Cable Address: "Justice"
Email: sb&c@twty.chi.il.us

MEMBERS OF FIRM

Ralph M. Schwartzberg (1939-1975)
Mark T. Barnett (1939-1970)
Hugh J. Schwartzberg
Benjamin H. Cohen

For full biographical listings, see the Martindale-Hubbell Law Directory

STONE & MOORE, CHARTERED (AV)

30 North La Salle Street, Suite 4300, 60602
Telephone: 312-332-5656
Fax: 312-332-5858
URL: http://www.stonemoore.com
Merrillville, Indiana Office: 500 E. 86th Avenue, 46410.
Telephone: 219-736-5959.
Fax: 219-736-5858.
Wheaton, Illinois Office: 600 W. Roosevelt Road, Suite 1A, 60187.
Telephone: 630-221-9292.
Fax: 630-221-9393.

William G. Stone
Robert Charles Moore (Also at Wheaton, Illinois Office)
Raymond R. Pesavento
Rosario Cibella
Richard M. Johnson, Jr.
J. Murray Pinkston, III
Julie Osswald Hooven

Christian D. Ambler
Jeffrey W. Henning
Erica Lewis Battaglia
Kevin Kemp Lyons
Kristin E. Rooney
Daniel S. Schulz
Matthew B. Stephens
A. Christine Svenson
Douglas W. Walker

For full biographical listings, see the Martindale-Hubbell Law Directory

INDIANA

*EVANSVILLE,** Vanderburgh Co.

ZIEMER, STAYMAN, WEITZEL & SHOULDERS, LLP (AV)

(Formerly Early, Arnold & Ziemer)
One Riverfront Place, 20 N.W. First Street 9th Floor, P.O. Box 916, 47706-0916
Telephone: 812-424-7575
Telecopier: 812-421-5089

MEMBERS OF FIRM

Robert F. Stayman
Mary Lee Schiff
David A. Guerrettaz

Reference: Old National Bank in Evansville.

For full biographical listings, see the Martindale-Hubbell Law Directory

*INDIANAPOLIS,** Marion Co.

BACKER & BACKER, A PROFESSIONAL CORPORATION (AV)

8710 North Meridian Street, 46260
Telephone: 317-571-0500
Telecopier: 317-571-0700
Email: sabacker@ameritech.net

Herbert J. Backer (1914-1995)
Stephen A. Backer

Reference: Bank One, Indianapolis.

For full biographical listings, see the Martindale-Hubbell Law Directory

Indianapolis—Continued

HOFFMAN DREWRY HANCOCK & SIMMONS (AV)

9100 Keystone Crossing, Suite 350, 46240
Telephone: 317-580-4848
Telecopier: 317-580-4855

Robert J. Hoffman
Michael F. Drewry
William J. Hancock
David L. Simmons
Richard S. Pitts
David B. Vornehm
Joseph M. Leone
Richard W. McMinn

OF COUNSEL

S. Douglas Trolson

For full biographical listings, see the Martindale-Hubbell Law Directory

HOVDE LAW FIRM (AV)

10585 North Meridian Street, Suite 345, P.O. Box 40849, 46240-0849
Telephone: 317-818-3100
Fax: 317-818-3111
Email: hovde@indy.net

F. Boyd Hovde
Frederick R. Hovde
Regina M. Poore
Robert T. Dassow

For full biographical listings, see the Martindale-Hubbell Law Directory

ICE MILLER DONADIO & RYAN (AV)

One American Square Box 82001, 46282-0002
Telephone: 317-236-2100
Fax: 317-236-2219
Email: info@imdr.com *URL:* http://www.imdr.com
South Bend, Indiana Office: 211 West Washington Street, Suite 2420.
Telephone: 219-234-7933.
Fax: 219-234-7965. Internet E-mail: info@imdr.com. Web Site Address: http://www.imdr.com.
Chicago, Illinois Office: 135 South LaSalle Street, Suite 4100.
Telephone: 312-726-1567.
Fax: 312-641-6263. Internet E-mail: info@imdr.com. Web Site Address: http://www.imdr.com.

MEMBERS OF FIRM

Arthur P. Kalleres
Michael H. Boldt
Gary J. Dankert
Phillip L. Bayt
Zeff A. Weiss
Alan H. Goldstein
Curtis W. McCauley

SENIOR COUNSEL

Mark D. Grant

OF COUNSEL

Susan Rogers Brooke
Stephanie Alden Smithey

Representative Clients: Huber, Hunt & Nichols; Howard Needles Tammen & Bergendoff; Geupel DeMars, Inc.; F.A. Wilhelm Construction Company, Inc.; CSO Architects, Inc.; Ratio Architects, Inc.; Shiel-Sexton Co., Inc.

For Complete List of Firm Personnel, See General Section

For full biographical listings, see the Martindale-Hubbell Law Directory

LOCKE REYNOLDS LLP (AV)

1000 Capital Center South, 201 North Illinois Street, 46204-4210
Telephone: 317-237-3800
Telecopier: 317-237-3900
Email: attys@locke.com *URL:* http://www.locke.com

Hugh E. Reynolds, Jr.
Steven J. Strawbridge
Julia Blackwell Gelinas
Terrence L. Brookie
James Dimos
John K. McDavid

Thomas F. Bedsole
Dean R. Brackenridge

Representative Clients: Cinergy/PSI Energy; CNA Surety Companies; F.A. Wilhelm Construction Co., Inc.; Fidelity & Deposit Co. of Maryland; Freitag-Weinhardt, Inc.; Great American Insurance Company; Hagerman Construction Corp.; J.S. Sweet Co. Inc.; Miller Pipeline Corporation.

For Complete List of Firm Personnel, See General Section

For full biographical listings, see the Martindale-Hubbell Law Directory

IOWA

*DES MOINES,** Polk Co.

FINLEY, ALT, SMITH, SCHARNBERG, CRAIG, HILMES & GAFFNEY, P.C. (AV)

604 Locust Street, Fourth Floor Equitable Building, 50309
Telephone: 515-288-0145
Telecopier: 515-288-2724

(See Next Column)

Jerry P. Alt

Representative Clients: ALAS; American Society of Composers, Authors and Publishers; Equitable Life Assurance Society of the U.S.; Federated Insurance Co.; Meredith Corp.
Iowa Attorneys for: Midwest Medical Insurance Co.
District Attorneys for: Norfolk & Southern Railroad; Soo Line Railroad Company.

For Complete List of Firm Personnel, See General Section

For full biographical listings, see the Martindale-Hubbell Law Directory

PINGEL & TEMPLER, P.C. (AV)

Suite 437 3737 Woodland Avenue (West Des Moines), P.O. Box 1991, 50309
Telephone: 515-225-3737
Fax: 515-225-9510

Jeffrey L. Goodman
John R. Perkins
Jeffrey D. Stone
John A. Templer, Jr.

For Complete List of Firm Personnel, See General Section

For full biographical listings, see the Martindale-Hubbell Law Directory

KANSAS

*HUTCHINSON,** Reno Co.

GILLILAND & HAYES, P.A. A PROFESSIONAL ASSOCIATION (AV)

20 West 2nd Avenue, 2nd Floor, P.O. Box 2977, 67504-2977
Telephone: 316-662-0537
Facsimile: 316-669-9426
URL: http://www.gillilandhayes.com
Wichita, Kansas Office: The Orpheum Centre, Suite 300, 200 North Broadway, P.O. Box 49406.
Telephone: 316-262-2266.
Facsimile: 316-263-2202.
Kansas City, Missouri Office: 12th Floor, 3100 Broadway.
Telephone: 816-753-3100.
Facsimile: 816-753-2271.

Robert J. Gilliland
John F. Hayes
James R. Gilliland
John S. Schmidt
Bruce B. Waugh (Not admitted in KS; Resident, Kansas City, Missouri Office)
Michael R. O'Neal
Bradley D. Dillon
Gerald L. Green
David N. Zimmerman (Not admitted in KS; Resident, Kansas City, Missouri Office)
Scott J. Mann
Carol Z. Smith (Resident, Kansas City, Missouri Office)
Kathleen A. Hardee (Resident, Kansas City, Missouri Office)
Kendall R. Cunningham (Resident, Wichita Office)
Mark R. Maloney (Resident, Wichita Office)

Thomas A. Dower
Tracy Applegate Cole
Laura A. Hederstedt
Terri Roberts Munsell (Resident, Kansas City, Missouri Office)
Lisa M. Ward
Kimberly Breda Bushek (Resident, Kansas City, Missouri Office)
E. Thomas Pyle, III
Tara L. Bragg

OF COUNSEL

Robert P. Reams (Not admitted in KS; Resident, Kansas City, Missouri Office)

Representative Clients: Allied Group; CNA Insurance; Dillon Companies; Fidelity Deposit Co. of Maryland; Central Bank & Trust; Leisure Hotel Corp.; Pine Development Company; St. Paul/USF&G; U.S. Fidelity Corp.

For full biographical listings, see the Martindale-Hubbell Law Directory

*WICHITA,** Sedgwick Co.

FOULSTON & SIEFKIN L.L.P. (AV)

700 NationsBank Financial Center, 67202
Telephone: 316-267-6371
Facsimile: 316-267-6345
URL: http://www.foulston.com
Topeka, Kansas Office: 1515 NationsBank Tower, 534 Kansas Avenue, 66603.
Telephone: 785-233-3600.
Fax: 785-233-1610.
Dodge City, Kansas Office: 810 Frontview, P.O. Box 1147, 67801.
Telephone: 316-227-8126.
Fax: 316-227-8451.
Member: Lex Mundi, The World's Leading Association of Independent Law Firms.

(See Next Column)

FOULSTON & SIEFKIN L.L.P.—*Continued*

MEMBERS OF FIRM

Robert L. Howard — Charles P. Efflandt
Mikel L. Stout — Wyatt A. Hoch

For Complete List of Firm Personnel, See General Section

For full biographical listings, see the Martindale-Hubbell Law Directory

TRIPLETT, WOOLF & GARRETSON, LLC (AV)

2959 North Rock Road, Suite 300, 67226
Telephone: 316-630-8100
Fax: 316-630-8101
Email: twg@twgfirm.com

MEMBERS OF FIRM

John P. Woolf — Jeffrey D. Leonard

Representative Clients: Anheuser-Busch Companies, Inc.; Brite Voice Systems, Inc.; Coleman Company, Inc.; Dow Chemical Co.; Friends University; KPMG Peat Marwick; National Plastics Color, Inc.; Total Petroleum, Inc.; Travelers Insurance Co.; Willis Corroon of Kansas, Inc.

For Complete List of Firm Personnel, See General Section

For full biographical listings, see the Martindale-Hubbell Law Directory

KENTUCKY

*LEXINGTON,** Fayette Co.

VIMONT & WILLS PLLC (AV)

Suite 300, 155 East Main Street, 40507-1317
Telephone: 606-252-2202
Telecopier: 606-259-2927
Email: vimont@lex.infi.net

Richard E. Vimont — Bernard F. Lovely, Jr.

J. Thomas Rawlings

For full biographical listings, see the Martindale-Hubbell Law Directory

*LOUISVILLE,** Jefferson Co.

HALL, RENDER, KILLIAN, HEATH & LYMAN PROFESSIONAL SERVICES CORPORATION (AV)

AEGON Center, Suite 1530, 400 West Market Street, 40202
Telephone: 502-568-1890
Fax: 502-568-4878
Email: hrkhl@hrkhl.com
Indianapolis, Indiana Office: Suite 2000, One American Square, Box 82064, 46282.
Telephone: 317-633-4884.
Fax: 317-633-4878.
Indianapolis North Office: Suite 820, 8402 Harcourt Road, 46260.
Telephone: 317-871-6222.
Fax: 317-338-3946.

Gerald L. Stovall — Samuel H. DeShazer

A. Courtney Guild, Jr. — Matthew W. Forsythe

For full biographical listings, see the Martindale-Hubbell Law Directory

LOUISIANA

*BATON ROUGE,** East Baton Rouge Parish

LAW OFFICES OF BERT K. ROBINSON (AV)

Suite F, 10481 Old Hammond Highway, 70816-8261
Telephone: 225-924-0296
Fax: 225-924-5288
Email: bkr@sdrlawfirm.com *URL:* http://www.constructionlaw.com

ASSOCIATE

Johanna R. Landreneau

Representative Clients: Metric Conductors, Inc.; Ferro Corporation; Merrick Construction Company, Inc.; Tri-State Road Boring, Inc.; V.A. Jones Construction Co.; Davis Construction Co.; Triple L Construction Co.; Louisiana Department of Transportation and Development; Traylor Bros. Construction; Louisiana House of Representatives.

For full biographical listings, see the Martindale-Hubbell Law Directory

*NEW ORLEANS,** Orleans Parish

LEAKE, ANDERSSON & MANN, L.L.P. (AV)

1700 Energy Centre, 1100 Poydras Street, 70163-1701
Telephone: 504-585-7500
Facsimile: 504-585-7775

W. Paul Andersson — Donald E. McKay, Jr.
Stanton E. Shuler, Jr.

OF COUNSEL

Robert E. Leake, Jr.

Representative Clients: Montgomery KONE Inc.; Solvation Services, Inc.; Professional Construction Services, Inc.

For Complete List of Firm Personnel, See General Section

For full biographical listings, see the Martindale-Hubbell Law Directory

MCGLINCHEY STAFFORD (AV)

A Professional Limited Liability Company
643 Magazine Street, 70130-3477
Telephone: 504-586-1200
Fax: 504-596-2800
TDD: (504) 596-2728
Telex: 584327
Cable Address: "MACSTAC"
Mailing Address: P.O. Box 60643, New Orleans, Louisiana, 70160-0643
Email: @mcglinchey.com *URL:* http://www.mcglinchey.com
Dallas, Texas Office: 2777 Stemmons Freeway, Suite 925, 75207-2401.
Telephone: 214-860-9700.
Fax: 214-860-9750.
Houston, Texas Office: 2727 Allen Parkway, Suite 1900, 77019.
Telephone: 713-520-1900.
Fax: 713-520-1025.
Baton Rouge, Louisiana Office: Ninth Floor, One American Place, 70825-0001.
Telephone: 504-383-9000.
Fax: 504-343-3076.
Jackson, Mississippi Office: Suite 1200, SkyTel Centre, 200 South Lamar Street, 39201.
Telephone: 601-960-8400.
Fax: 601-960-8406.
Lake Providence, Louisiana Office: 405 Morgan Street, 71254-2691.
Telephone: 318-559-1200.
Fax: 318-559-0609.
Monroe, Louisiana Office: Dean ONB Tower, 130 Desiard Street, Suite 807, 71201.
Telephone: 318-651-0807.
Fax: 318-651-0809.

MEMBERS OF FIRM

Henri Wolbrette, III, (P.C.) — Arthur H. Leith

MEMBERS OF FIRM

Mark D. Herbert (Resident, Jackson Office) — Samuel A. Bacot (Resident, Baton Rouge Office)

ASSOCIATES

Pamela L. Hancock (Resident, Jackson Office) — Vincent J. Bodin (Resident, Houston Office)

For full biographical listings, see the Martindale-Hubbell Law Directory

*SHREVEPORT,** Caddo Parish

BARLOW AND HARDTNER L.C. (AV)

Tenth Floor, Louisiana Tower, 401 Edwards Street, 71101-3289
Telephone: 318-227-1131
Telecopier: 318-227-1141
Mailing Address: P.O. Box 8, Shreveport, Louisiana, 71161-0008

Malcolm S. Murchison — David R. Taggart
Joseph L. Shea, Jr. — Michael B. Donald
Jay A. Greenleaf

Representative Clients: The Brinkman Corporation; T.L. James & Company, Inc.; NorAm Energy Corp. (formerly Arkla, Inc.); Central and South West Corporation; Panhandle Eastern Corp.; Pennzoil Producing Co.; Ashland Oil, Inc.; The Centex Construction Group; Southwestern Electric Power Company.

For Complete List of Firm Personnel, See General Section

For full biographical listings, see the Martindale-Hubbell Law Directory

WEEMS, SCHIMPF, HAYTER, GILSOUL & CARMOUCHE, (APLC) (AV)

912 Kings Highway, 71104
Telephone: 318-222-2100
Facsimile: 318-226-5100
URL: http://www.weems-law.com

(See Next Column)

Weems, Schimpf, Hayter, Gilsoul & Carmouche (APLC), *Shreveport—Continued*

John O. Hayter, III
Brian D. Landry

Representative Clients: Hand Construction Co., Inc.; Max Foote Construction Co., Inc.; La Quinta Inns, Inc.; Don M. Barron Contractor, Inc.; Northwest Louisiana Construction, Inc.; Jabar, Inc.; Con-Fab Welding, Inc.; Air-Ref, Inc.; Melvin Butler, Inc.; MONCLA Construction Co., Inc.; Reynolds Industrial Coatings, Inc.

For full biographical listings, see the Martindale-Hubbell Law Directory

MAINE

*PORTLAND,** Cumberland Co.

Burns Ray & DeLano, Professional Association (AV)

193 Middle Street, 04101-4062
Telephone: 207-775-3581
Facsimile: 207-775-3814
Email: mailcenter@brdlaw.com

George F. Burns
David P. Ray
Arnold C. Macdonald
Mary DeLano
Elizabeth A. Burns
Carrie A. Green

OF COUNSEL

Joanne F. Cole

Representative Clients: Tractebel Power, Inc.; Cianbro Corporation; Maine Yankee Atomic Power Company; Maine Drilling & Blasting, Inc.; Jackson Laboratory; Pinebrook Corporation; Sheridan Corp.; Hague International (engineering); Aetna Life & Casualty Co.; ITT Hartford.

For full biographical listings, see the Martindale-Hubbell Law Directory

Petruccelli & Martin, LLP (AV)

50 Monument Square, P.O. Box 9733, 04104-5033
Telephone: 207-775-0200
Telecopier: 207-775-2360
Email: info@petruccellimartin.com *URL:* http://www.petruccellimartin.com

MEMBERS OF FIRM

Gerald F. Petruccelli
Michael K. Martin

Representative Clients: Granger Northern Construction Co.; Seppala & Aho Construction Co.

For full biographical listings, see the Martindale-Hubbell Law Directory

Pierce Atwood (AV)

One Monument Square, 04101
Telephone: 207-791-1100
Fax: 207-791-1350
Email: info@PierceAtwood.com *URL:* http://www.pierceatwood.com
Augusta, Maine Office: 77 Winthrop Street.
Telephone: 207-622-6311.
Fax: 207-623-9367.
Newburyport, Massachusetts Office: 6 Harris Street.
Telephone: 978-465-9599.
Fax: 978-465-9945.

MEMBERS OF FIRM

Jotham D. Pierce, Jr.
John J. Aromando

ASSOCIATE

Debra L. Brown

For Complete List of Firm Personnel, See General Section

For full biographical listings, see the Martindale-Hubbell Law Directory

Thompson & Bowie (AV)

Three Canal Plaza, P.O. Box 4630, 04112
Telephone: 207-774-2500
Telecopier: 207-774-3591
Email: law@thompsonbowie.com

MEMBERS OF FIRM

Roy E. Thompson, Jr.
James M. Bowie
Daniel R. Mawhinney
Rebecca H. Farnum
Glenn H. Robinson
Frank W. DeLong, III
Michael E. Saucier
Mark V. Franco
Edward R. Benjamin, Jr.
Cathy S. Roberts
Paul C. Catsos

ASSOCIATES

Elizabeth Knox Peck
Thomas G. Diebold
Michael R. Bosse
Lisa M. Fitzgibbon

For full biographical listings, see the Martindale-Hubbell Law Directory

Verrill & Dana, LLP (AV)

One Portland Square, P.O. Box 586, 04112-0586
Telephone: 207-774-4000
Fax: 207-774-7499
Email: advice@verdan.com *URL:* http://www.verdan.com
Augusta, Maine Office: 45 Memorial Circle, P.O. Box 957.
Telephone: 207-623-3889.
Fax: 207-622-3117.
Kennebunk, Maine Office: 403-404 Lafayette Center, P.O. Box 147.
Telephone: 207-985-7193.
Fax: 207-985-3957.
Washington, D.C. Office: 400 North Capitol Street, Suite 585.
Telephone: 202-624-9733.
Fax: 202-393-5218.

OF COUNSEL

W. John Amerling
A. Robert Ruesch

Counsel for: ASCAP; Bowdoin College; Fleet Bank; Hannaford Bros. Co.; Maine Blue Cross and Blue Shield; Maine Public Service Co.; Peoples Heritage Bank; Portland Water District.

For Complete List of Firm Personnel, See General Section

For full biographical listings, see the Martindale-Hubbell Law Directory

MARYLAND

*BALTIMORE,** (Independent City)

Ferguson, Schetelich & Heffernan, P.A. (AV)

1401 NationsBank Center, 100 South Charles Street, 21201-2725
Telephone: 410-837-2200
Fax: 410-837-1188
URL: http://www.FSHLaw.com

Robert L. Ferguson, Jr.
Thomas J. Schetelich
Christopher J. Heffernan
Craig F. Ballew
Michael N. Russo, Jr.

Peter J. Basile
Ann D. Ware
Tracey J. McLauchlin
Michele P. Zahner
Michael K. Hourigan

For full biographical listings, see the Martindale-Hubbell Law Directory

Freishtat & Sandler (AV)

Suite 1500, One Calvert Plaza, 201 E. Baltimore Street, 21202
Telephone: 410-727-7740
FAX: 410-727-7356

MEMBERS OF FIRM

David Freishtat
Paul Mark Sandler
Raymond F. Altman
Raymond Daniel Burke
William Michael Mullen
Lloyd J. Snow
Stacie F. Dubnow

Roderick R. Barnes
Jeffrey S. Rosenfeld
Thomas K. Harris

OF COUNSEL

Lynn Weinberg

For full biographical listings, see the Martindale-Hubbell Law Directory

Kollman & Sheehan, P.A. (AV)

Sun Life Building, 20 South Charles Street, 21201-3225
Telephone: 410-727-4300
Telecopier: 410-727-4391
URL: http://www.kollman-sheehan.com

Frank L. Kollman
David M. Sheehan
Peter S. Saucier
Francis R. Laws
Darrell R. VanDeusen
Clifford B. Geiger

Bruce M. Luchansky
Richard P. Rieman, Jr.
Randi Klein Hyatt
Desmond Terrell McIlwain
Joseph R. Salko
Tracy L. Knight
Jeffrey A. Trueman

For full biographical listings, see the Martindale-Hubbell Law Directory

Baltimore—Continued

VENABLE ATTORNEYS AT LAW VENABLE, BAETJER AND HOWARD, LLP (AV)

A Partnership including Professional Corporations
1800 Mercantile Bank & Trust Building, 2 Hopkins Plaza, 21201
Telephone: 410-244-7400
Fax: 410-244-7742
URL: http://www.venable.com
Washington, D.C. Office: Venable, Baetjer, Howard & Civiletti LLP, Suite 1000, 1201 New York Avenue, N.W.
Telephone: 202-962-4800.
Fax: 202-962-8300.
McLean, Virginia Office: Suite 400, 2010 Corporate Ridge.
Telephone: 703-760-1600.
Fax: 703-821-8949.
Rockville, Maryland Office: Suite 500, One Church Street, P. O. Box 1906.
Telephone: 301-217-5600.
Fax: 301-217-5617.
Towson, Maryland Office: 210 Allegheny Avenue, P. O. Box 5517.
Telephone: 410-494-6200.
Fax: 410-821-0147.

MEMBERS OF FIRM

James A. Cole
Benjamin R. Civiletti (P.C.) (Also at Washington, D.C. and Towson, Maryland Offices)
John Henry Lewin, Jr. (P.C.)
Thomas J. Kenney, Jr. (P.C.)
Roger W. Titus (Resident, Rockville, Maryland Office)
John H. Zink, III (Resident, Towson, Maryland Office)
Paul T. Glasgow (Resident, Rockville, Maryland Office)
Joseph C. Wich, Jr. (Resident, Towson, Maryland Office)
Craig E. Smith
David G. Lane (Resident, McLean, Virginia Office)
A. Wayne Lalle, Jr. (Not admitted in MD; Resident, McLean, Virginia Office)
G. Stewart Webb, Jr.
James K. Archibald (Also at Washington, D.C. Office)
Jeffrey A. Dunn (Also at Washington, D.C. Office)
George F. Pappas (Also at Washington, D.C. Office)
Peter P. Parvis
James L. Shea (Also at Washington, D.C. Office)
Maurice Baskin (Resident, Washington, D.C. Office)
C. Carey Deeley, Jr. (Also at Towson, Maryland Office)
Christopher R. Mellott
M. King Hill, III (Resident, Towson, Maryland Office)
J. Michael Brennan (Resident, Towson, Maryland Office)
Herbert G. Smith, II (Not admitted in MD; Resident, Washington, D.C. Office)
David C. Mancini (Resident, McLean, Virginia Office)
Michael W. Robinson (Resident, McLean, Virginia Office)
Todd J. Horn
Christine M. McAnney (Not admitted in MD; Resident, McLean, Virginia Office)

ASSOCIATES

Paul D. Barker, Jr.
Daniel William China (Resident, Towson, Maryland Office)
Charles W. Durant (Not admitted in MD; Resident, McLean, Virginia Office)
Patricia A. Malone (Resident, Towson, Maryland Office)

For Complete List of Firm Personnel, See General Section

For full biographical listings, see the Martindale-Hubbell Law Directory

YOUNG & VALKENET, L.L.C. (AV)

Suite 707 The Susquehanna Building, 29 West Susquehanna Avenue, 21204
Telephone: 410-583-2414
Telefax: 410-583-2418

Thomas G. Young, III
Thomas C. Valkenet

For full biographical listings, see the Martindale-Hubbell Law Directory

*ROCKVILLE,** Montgomery Co.

KING & ATTRIDGE (AV)

39 West Montgomery Avenue, 20850-4210
Telephone: 301-279-0780
Facsimile: 301-279-2988
URL: http://www.lawyers.com/king&attridgelaw

MEMBERS OF FIRM

John A. King
Patrick James Attridge

ASSOCIATES

Deirdre R. Horton
Kenneth D. Smith

For full biographical listings, see the Martindale-Hubbell Law Directory

SILVER SPRING, Montgomery Co.

SAUNDERS & SCHMIELER (AV)

8737 Colesville Road, Suite L-200, 20910-3921
Telephone: 301-588-7717
Facsimile: 301-588-5073
Email: admin@sslawfirm.com *URL:* http://www.sslawfirm.com
Washington, D.C. Office: 1050 17th Street, N.W., #600
Telephone: 202-833-2999.
Baltimore, Maryland Office: Suite 2700, 111 South Calvert Street.
Telephone: 410-235-7558.
Arlington, Virginia Office: 2111 Wilson Boulevard, Suite 700.
Telephone: 703-243-1100.
Richmond, Virginia Office: 4900 Cutshaw Avenue.
Telephone: 804-353-9800.

MEMBER OF FIRM

Jeffrey R. Schmieler

ASSOCIATES

Nicole E. Ames
A. Benjamin Horton
Lucas F. Webster

For Complete List of Firm Personnel, See General Section

For full biographical listings, see the Martindale-Hubbell Law Directory

*TOWSON,** Baltimore Co.

MUDD, HARRISON & BURCH (AV)

105 West Chesapeake Avenue, 300 Jefferson Building, 21204
Telephone: 410-828-1335
FAX: 410-828-1042
Email: mhb@mhblaw.com

MEMBERS OF FIRM

John E. Mudd
T. Rogers Harrison (1949-1995)
Richard C. Burch
Douglas W. Biser
H. Patrick Stringer, Jr.
Andrew Janquitto

James R. Andersen
Matthew Paul Lalumia
Nancy C. Hopkins

OF COUNSEL

Wm. T. Russell, Jr.

For full biographical listings, see the Martindale-Hubbell Law Directory

VENABLE ATTORNEYS AT LAW VENABLE, BAETJER AND HOWARD, LLP (AV)

A Partnership including Professional Corporations
210 Allegheny Avenue, P.O. Box 5517, 21204
Telephone: 410-494-6200
Fax: 410-821-0147
URL: http://www.venable.com
Baltimore, Maryland Office: 1800 Mercantile Bank & Trust Building, 2 Hopkins Plaza.
Telephone: 410-244-7400.
Fax: 410-244-7742.
Washington, D.C. Office: Venable, Baetjer, Howard & Civiletti LLP, Suite 1000, 1201 New York Avenue, N.W.
Telephone: 202-962-4800.
Fax: 202-962-8300.
McLean, Virginia Office: Suite 400, 2010 Corporate Ridge.
Telephone: 703-760-1600.
Fax: 703-821-8949.
Rockville, Maryland Office: Suite 500, One Church Street, P. O. Box 1906.
Telephone: 301-217-5600.
Fax: 301-217-5617.

PARTNERS

Benjamin R. Civiletti (P.C.) (Also at Washington, D.C. and Baltimore, Maryland Offices)
John H. Zink, III
Joseph C. Wich, Jr.
C. Carey Deeley, Jr. (Also at Baltimore, Maryland Office)
M. King Hill, III
J. Michael Brennan

For Complete List of Firm Personnel, See General Section

For full biographical listings, see the Martindale-Hubbell Law Directory

MASSACHUSETTS

*BOSTON,** Suffolk Co.

CITY, HAYES, MEAGHER & DISSETTE, P.C. (AV)

50 Congress Street, 02109
Telephone: 617-523-3050
Telecopier: 617-523-5612

(See Next Column)

CITY, HAYES, MEAGHER & DISSETTE P.C., *Boston—Continued*

Robert D. City
James P. Hayes
Kieran B. Meagher
Michael J. Dissette

Martin R. Fisch
Philip B. Evans
Lewis R. Lear
Michael N. O'Connell, Jr.

For full biographical listings, see the Martindale-Hubbell Law Directory

HINCKLEY, ALLEN & SNYDER LLP (AV)

28 State Street, 30th Floor, 02109-1775
Telephone: 617-345-9000
Email: firm@haslaw.com *URL:* http://www.haslaw.com
Providence, Rhode Island Office: 1500 Fleet Center.
Telephone: 401-274-2000.
Fax: 401-277-9600. URL: http://www.hawlaw.com.

MEMBERS OF FIRM

David D. Barricelli (Not admitted in MA)
E. Jerome Batty (Not admitted in MA)
Paul Bork
Stephen J. Carlotti (Not admitted in MA)
David Barry Connolly
Michael P. DeFanti
Eric F. Eisenberg
Hugh J. Gorman, III
Alan P. Gottlieb
William R. Grimm
Paul A. Hedstrom
Richard L. E. Jocelyn (Not admitted in MA)
Joel Lewin
Matthew T. Marcello, III (Not admitted in MA)
Frederick P. McClure
Paul F. O'Donnell, III
H. Peter Olsen (Not admitted in MA)
John J. Pendergast, III (Not admitted in MA)
Gerald J. Petros
Jeremy Ritzenberg
David J. Rubin
Charles E. Schaub, Jr.
Douglas F. Seaver
Herman Snyder
David R. Sullivan
Robert F. Sylvia
Howard E. Walker (Not admitted in MA)
Richard D. Wayne

ASSOCIATES

Mark Bianchi
Alexandra K. Callam
Jane E. Cohen
Andrew D. Cummings
June E. Daniel (Not admitted in MA)
Kim Herman Goslant
Gloria Maria Gutierrez
Christopher P. Hamilton
Kelley Jordan-Price
Catherine S. Kim
Christopher W. Morog
Elena B. Olson
Michael T. Renaud
Joseph D. Whelan (Not admitted in MA)

OF COUNSEL

Willard Krasnow
Willard R. Pope

For Complete List of Firm Personnel, See General Section

For full biographical listings, see the Martindale-Hubbell Law Directory

LANGAN, DEMPSEY AND BRODIGAN (AV)

40 Broad Street Suite 220, 02109
Telephone: 617-542-1871
Telecopier: 617-482-1871

James M. Langan (1907-1998)
Daniel J. Dempsey (1945-1970)
Joseph J. Brodigan
James M. Langan, Jr.

William D. Gardiner
Joseph J. Brodigan, Jr.
Michael Brodigan

For full biographical listings, see the Martindale-Hubbell Law Directory

NATHANSON & GOLDBERG, A PROFESSIONAL CORPORATION (AV)

Two Oliver Street, 8th Floor, 02109-4901
Telephone: 617-210-4800
Fax: 617-210-4824
Email: natgolaw@earthlink.net *URL:* http://www.natgolaw.com

Alvin S. Nathanson
Arthur Goldberg
Shannon M. Fitzpatrick
José Centeio
Stuart J. Frank

For full biographical listings, see the Martindale-Hubbell Law Directory

PALMER & DODGE LLP (AV)

One Beacon Street, 02108
Telephone: 617-573-0100
Facsimile: 617-227-4420
URL: http://www.palmerdodge.com

MEMBERS OF FIRM

Michael J. Lacek
David R. Rodgers
Craig E. Stewart
Peter S. Terris
James M. Whalen

(See Next Column)

For Complete List of Firm Personnel, See General Section

For full biographical listings, see the Martindale-Hubbell Law Directory

ROCHE, CARENS & DEGIACOMO, P.C. (AV)

99 High Street, 02110
Telephone: 617-457-4000
Facsimile: 617-482-3868
Email: firm@rcdpc.com *URL:* http://www.rcdpc.com
Woburn, Massachusetts Office: 600 Unicorn Park Drive.
Telephone: 781-933-5505.

Richard J. Saletta
Loring A. Cook, III

For Complete List of Firm Personnel, See General Section

For full biographical listings, see the Martindale-Hubbell Law Directory

BROCKTON, Plymouth Co.

VINCENT P. CAHALANE, P.C. (AV)

478 Torrey Street, Suite 12, 02301-4696
Telephone: 508-588-1222
Fax: 508-584-4748
URL: http://www.lawyers.com/cahalanelaw

Vincent P. Cahalane
Robert J. Zullas
Julie A. Cahalane Cahill
Andrew H. P. Norton
Kristopher S. Stefani

For full biographical listings, see the Martindale-Hubbell Law Directory

*SPRINGFIELD,** Hampden Co.

ANNINO, DRAPER & MOORE, P.C. (AV)

1500 Main Street, Suite 1818, P.O. Box 15428, 01115
Telephone: 413-732-6400
Fax: 413-732-3339
Email: admatlaw@aol.com
Westfield, Massachusetts Office: 52 Court Street.
Telephone: 413-562-9829.

Calvin W. Annino, Jr.
Mark E. Draper
Louis S. Moore
Michael R. Siddall

For full biographical listings, see the Martindale-Hubbell Law Directory

ROBINSON DONOVAN MADDEN & BARRY, P.C. (AV)

Suite 1600, Tower Square, 1500 Main Street, 01115-5609
Telephone: 413-732-2301
Fax: 413-785-4658
Email: service@robinson-donovan.com *URL:* http://www.robinson-donovan.com

Homans Robinson (1894-1973)
Lawrence M. Sinclair (1942-1986)
Milton J. Donovan (1906-1995)

RETIRED

John H. Madden, Jr.
Edward J. Barry
Richard S. Milstein

OF COUNSEL

Victor Rosenberg

SENIOR COUNSEL

Jonathan P. Rice

Gordon H. Wentworth
James H. Tourtelotte
Ronald C. Kidd
Jeffrey W. Roberts
Jeffrey L. McCormick
James F. Martin
Robert P. Cunningham
John C. Sikorski
Nancy Frankel Pelletier
Paul S. Weinberg
Frederica H. McCarthy
Matthew J. King
Neva Kaufman Rohan
Douglas F. Boyd
James K. Bodurtha
Keith A. Minoff
Patricia M. Rapinchuk
Kimberly Davis Crear

E. Paul Amata
Lisa A. Bongiovi (Not admitted in MA)
Edward J. Carroll, III
James D. Chadwell
John E. Garber
Patrick J. Markey
Carla W. Newton
Betsy Macmillan Stevens

Representative Clients: BankBoston, N.A.; United Cooperative Bank; Fleet National Bank; CNA; Commercial Union Insurance Co.; Hanover Insurance Group.

For full biographical listings, see the Martindale-Hubbell Law Directory

MICHIGAN

BATTLE CREEK, Calhoun Co.

KREIS, ENDERLE, CALLANDER & HUDGINS, A PROFESSIONAL CORPORATION (AV)

One West Michigan Avenue, 49017
Telephone: 616-966-3000
Facsimile: 616-966-3022
Email: kech@kech.com *URL:* http://www.kech.com
Kalamazoo, Michigan Office: One Moorsbridge, P.O. Box 4010, 49003-4010.
Telephone: 616-324-3000.
Fax: 616-324-3010.

Alan G. Enderle (Resident, Kalamazoo Office)
Stephen J. Hessen (Resident, Kalamazoo Office)
Jeffrey D. Swenarton (Resident, Kalamazoo Office)

For Complete List of Firm Personnel, See General Section

For full biographical listings, see the Martindale-Hubbell Law Directory

BINGHAM FARMS, Oakland Co.

SMALL, TOTH, BALDRIDGE & VAN BELKUM, P.C. (AV)

30100 Telegraph Road Suite 250, 48025-4516
Telephone: 248-647-9595
Facsimile: 248-647-9599

Richard L. Small
John M. Toth
David M. Baldridge
Thomas G. Van Belkum
Keith P. Felty

Stephanie A. Griz-Kochkodan
Kristin Allen

Representative Clients: The Medical Protective Co.; Michigan Physicians Mutual Liability Insurance Co.; Physicians Insurance Company of Michigan; Shelby Insurance Group; Kemper Insurance Group; Michigan Society of Oral and Maxillofacial Surgeons; Michigan Association of Orthodontists; Michigan Association of Endodontists; AAMOS National; Mt Vernon Insurance Company.

For full biographical listings, see the Martindale-Hubbell Law Directory

BLOOMFIELD HILLS, Oakland Co.

DROLET, FREEMAN, COTTON & NORRIS, P.C. (AV)

33 Bloomfield Hills Parkway, Suite 100, 48304
Telephone: 248-642-2255
Fax: 248-642-6460
Email: droletfreeman@voyager.net

David G. Barnett (1915-1989)
H. William Freeman
J. Kingsley Cotton, III
Matthew C. Norris

Brian P. Henry
Suzanne S. Reynolds
Lauren D. Honet
David M. Blau

Representative Clients: Angelo Iafrate Construction Co.; ASC, Incorporated; Cadillac Asphalt Paving Co.; Carroll Packaging, Inc.; Choice Hotels International; Clawson Concrete Co.; Commerica Bank; Corrosion Control Engineering; Emcor; Farmington Public Schools.

For full biographical listings, see the Martindale-Hubbell Law Directory

FEDERLEIN & KERANEN, P.C. (AV)

6895 Telegraph Road, 48301
Telephone: 248-647-9653
Fax: 248-647-9683
Email: firm@fk-law.com *URL:* http://www.fk-law.com
Detroit, Michigan Office: 407 East Fort, Suite 350.
Telephone: 313-965-6090.
Marquette, Michigan Office: 122 West Spring Street.
Telephone: 906-225-1770.
Fax: 906-225-1764.
Sault Ste. Marie, Michigan Office: 204 East Spruce Street.
Telephone: 906-635-6286.
Fax: 906-635-5390.

Walter J. Federlein
Thomas M. Keranen

Frederick F. Butters
Maria J. Bernard (Resident, Detroit Office)
Peter J. Cavanaugh
J. Christian Hauser (Resident, Detroit Office)
Gary Quesada
Jeffrey Michael Gallant

For full biographical listings, see the Martindale-Hubbell Law Directory

PROVIZER & PHILLIPS, P.C. (AV)

6785 Telegraph Road, Suite 400, 48301
Telephone: 248-642-0444
Facsimile: 248-642-6661
Toll Free: 1-800-288-9080
URL: http://www.lawyers.com/provizer&phillips

Harold M. Provizer
Randall E. Phillips
Marilyn A. Madorsky
Noel F. Beck
Mark S. Baumkel

Constance S. Hall
Donald J. Parthum, Jr.

Representative Clients: Royal Ins. Group; Thomas Howell Group; Jefferson Ins. Co.

For full biographical listings, see the Martindale-Hubbell Law Directory

*DETROIT,** Wayne Co.

BODMAN, LONGLEY & DAHLING LLP (AV)

34th Floor 100 Renaissance Center, 48243
Telephone: 313-259-7777
Fax: 313-393-7579
Email: info@bodmanlongley.com *URL:* http://www.bodmanlongley.com
Troy, Michigan Office: Suite 2020, 755 West Big Beaver Road.
Telephone: 248-362-2110.
Fax: 248-244-0780.
Ann Arbor, Michigan Office: 110 Miller, Suite 300.
Telephone: 734-761-3780.
Fax: 734-930-2494.
Northern Michigan Office: 229 Court Street, P.O. Box 405, Cheboygan.
Telephone: 231-627-4351.
Fax: 231-627-2802.

MEMBERS OF FIRM

Walter O. Koch (Troy Office)
Michael B. Lewiston
Thomas A. Roach (Ann Arbor Office)
George G. Kemsley
David G. Chardavoyne
Thomas Van Dusen (Troy Office)
Robert J. Diehl, Jr.
F. Thomas Lewand
Michael A. Stack (Cheboygan Office)
Harvey W. Berman (Ann Arbor Office)
Jerold Lax (Ann Arbor Office)
Gary D. Reeves (Troy Office)
Sandra L. Sorini (Ann Arbor Office)

For Representative Client List, See General Section

For Complete List of Firm Personnel, See General Section

For full biographical listings, see the Martindale-Hubbell Law Directory

BUTZEL LONG, A PROFESSIONAL CORPORATION (AV)

Suite 900, 150 West Jefferson, 48226
Telephone: 313-225-7000
Telecopier: 313-225-7080
Email: melnick@butzel.com *URL:* http://www.butzel.com
Birmingham, Michigan Office: Suite 200, 32270 Telegraph Road.
Telephone: 810-258-1616.
Telecopier: 810-258-1439.
Okemos, Michigan Office: Suite 300, 2127 University Park Drive.
Telephone: 517-372-6622.
Telecopier: 517-372-6672.
Ann Arbor, Michigan Office: Suite 300, 350 South Main Street.
Telephone: 313-995-3110.
Telecopier: 313-995-1777.
Grosse Pointe Farms, Michigan Office: Suite 260, 21 Kercheval.
Telephone: 313-886-5446.
Telecopier: 313-886-2114.
Boca Raton, Florida Office: Suite 411, 1200 North Federal Highway.
Telephone: 561-368-2151.
Telecopier: 561-368-4668.
Palm Beach Gardens, Florida Office: Suite 227, 11382 Prosperity Farms Road.
Telephone: 561-625-4442.
Telecopier: 561-625-6901.
Naples, Florida Office: Suite 705, 801 Laurel Oak Drive.
Telephone: 941-597-4500.
Telecopier: 941-597-5623.

Robert J. Battista
Abba I. Friedman (Ann Arbor)
Dennis B. Schultz
Michael J. Lavoie
Marissa W. Pollick (Ann Arbor)
Eric J. Flessland (Birmingham)
Ronald E. Reynolds (Birmingham)
Kenneth H. Adamczyk
Richard T. Hewlett
James J. Urban (Okemos)
Eugene H. Boyle, Jr.

James J. Giszczak
Steven M. Ribiat
Michael F. Matheson (Okemos)

Representative Clients: Albert Kahn Associates, Inc.; Associated General Contractors; Associated Underground Contractors; Barton Malow Co.; Kajima International, Inc.; Michigan Road Builders Assn.; Perini Building Co.; Stroh Companies; The University of Michigan; William Beaumont Hospital.

(See Next Column)

BUTZEL LONG A PROFESSIONAL CORPORATION, *Detroit—Continued*

For full biographical listings, see the Martindale-Hubbell Law Directory

MILLER, CANFIELD, PADDOCK AND STONE, P.L.C. (AV)

A Professional Limited Liability Company
Founded in 1852 by Sidney Davy Miller
150 West Jefferson, Suite 2500, 48226-4415
Telephone: 313-963-6420
Fax: 313-496-7500
Cable Address: "Stem Detroit"
URL: http://www.millercanfield.com
Ann Arbor, Michigan Office: 101 North Main Street, 7th Floor, 48104-1400.
Telephone: 734-663-2445.
Fax: 734-747-7147.
Troy, Michigan Office: 840 West Long Lake Road, Suite 200, 48098.
Telephone: 248-879-2000.
Fax: 248-879-2001.
Grand Rapids, Michigan Office: 99 Monroe, N.W., Suite 1200, 49503-2639.
Telephone: 616-454-8656.
Fax: 616-776-6322.
Howell, Michigan Office: 121 South Barnard Street, Suite 4, 48843-2305.
Telephone: 517-546-7600.
Telecopier: 517-546-6974.
Kalamazoo, Michigan Office: 444 West Michigan Avenue, 49007-3752.
Telephone: 616-381-7030.
Fax: 616-382-0244.
Lansing, Michigan Office: One Michigan Avenue, Suite 900, 48933-1609.
Telephone: 517-487-2070.
Fax: 517-374-6304.
Monroe, Michigan Office: 214 East Elm Avenue, Suite 100, 48162-2682.
Telephone: 734-243-2000.
Fax: 734-243-0901.
Washington, D.C. Office: 1900 K Street, N.W., Suite 1150. 20006.
Telephone: 202-429-5575; 785-0600.
Fax: 202-331-1118; 785-1234.
Pensacola, Florida Office: 25 West Cedar, 32501.
Telephone: 850-469-1088.
Fax: 850-432-0677.
New York, New York Office: 1450 Broadway, 41st Floor, 10018.
Telephone: 212-704-4400.
Fax: 212-704-4410.
Gdynia, Poland Office: UL. Slaska 21, 81-319.
Telephone: 011-485-831-2808.
Fax: 011-48-58-628 6411.
Warsaw, Poland Office: UL. Nowogrodzkall, 5th Floor, 00-513.
Telephone: 011-4822 529 0200.
Fax: 011-4822 529 0201.
Katowice, Poland Office: UL. Francuska 35/37, 40-027.
Telephone: 011 (48-32) 757-2414.
Fax: 011 (48-32) 757-2483.

PRINCIPALS OF FIRM

Michael W. Hartmann
Richard A. Gaffin (Grand Rapids Office)
James E. Spurr (Kalamazoo Office)
Lawrence M. Dudek
Ronald E. Hodess (Troy Office)
Don M. Schmidt (Kalamazoo Office)
James R. Lancaster, Jr. (Lansing Office)

ASSOCIATES

Kurt P. McCamman (Kalamazoo Office)
Scott R. Sikkenga (Kalamazoo Office)

Representative Firm Clients: Chrysler Corporation; Comerica, Incorporated; City of Detroit, Michigan; Detroit Tigers, Inc.; First of Michigan; Ford Motor Company; Ford Motor Credit Company; Great Lakes Bancorp; Henry Ford Hospital; INVETECH Company.

For Complete List of Firm Personnel, See General Section

For full biographical listings, see the Martindale-Hubbell Law Directory

VANDEVEER GARZIA, PROFESSIONAL CORPORATION (AV)

Suite 1600, 333 West Fort Street, 48226
Telephone: 313-961-4880
Fax: 313-961-3822
Email: vg@voyager.net
Oakland County Office: 220 Park Street, Suite 300, Birmingham, Michigan.
Telephone: 810-645-0100.
Fax: 810-645-2430.

Fred L. Vandeveer (1879-1972)
James E. Haggerty, Sr. (1900-1966)
Leroy G. Vandeveer (1902-1981)
Buelle A. Doelle (1902-1985)
James E. Plastow, Jr.
Michael M. Hathaway
John J. Lynch, III (Resident, Oakland County Office)
Thomas M. Peters
James K. Thome
Gary Alan Miller
William L. Kiriazis
Daniel P. Steele

(See Next Column)

Shelley K. Miller (Resident, Oakland County Office)
Terrance P. Lynch
Dennis B. Cotter
Bruce E. Pearce
Hal O. Carroll
David B. Timmis (Resident, Oakland County Office)

Nancy A. Hensley
Dawn M. Twydell
Christian E. Hildebrandt (Resident, Oakland County Office)
Donald C. Brownell

Representative Clients: CNA Insurance Group; Travelers Insurance Co.

For full biographical listings, see the Martindale-Hubbell Law Directory

*GRAND RAPIDS,** Kent Co.

ROBERTS, BETZ & BLOSS, P.C. (AV)

5005 Cascade Road SE, 49546-3724
Telephone: 616-285-8899
Telecopier: 616-285-0045

Michael J. Roberts
Michael W. Betz
David J. Bloss
Gregory A. Block
Michael T. Small
Ralph M. Reisinger
Henry S. Emrich

Connie R. Thacker

For full biographical listings, see the Martindale-Hubbell Law Directory

TOLLEY, VANDENBOSCH, WALTON, KOROLEWICZ & BRENGLE, P.C. (AV)

1700 East Beltline, N.E., Suite 200, 49525-4512
Telephone: 616-447-1800
Fax: 616-447-1881

Peter R. Tolley
Michael C. Walton

For full biographical listings, see the Martindale-Hubbell Law Directory

*KALAMAZOO,** Kalamazoo Co.

KREIS, ENDERLE, CALLANDER & HUDGINS, A PROFESSIONAL CORPORATION (AV)

One Moorsbridge, P.O. Box 4010, 49003-4010
Telephone: 616-324-3000
Facsimile: 616-324-3010
Email: kech@kech.com *URL:* http://www.kech.com
Battle Creek, Michigan Office: One West Michigan Avenue, 49017.
Telephone: 616-966-3000.
Fax: 616-966-3022.

Alan G. Enderle
Stephen J. Hessen
Jeffrey D. Swenarton

For Complete List of Firm Personnel, See General Section

For full biographical listings, see the Martindale-Hubbell Law Directory

MILLER, CANFIELD, PADDOCK AND STONE, P.L.C. (AV)

A Professional Limited Liability Company
Founded in 1852 by Sidney Davy Miller
444 West Michigan Avenue, 49007-3752
Telephone: 616-381-7030
Fax: 616-382-0244
URL: http://www.millercanfield.com
Detroit, Michigan Office: 150 West Jefferson, Suite 2500, 48226-4415.
Telephone: 313-963-6420.
Fax: 313-496-7500.
Cable Address: "Stem Detroit."
Ann Arbor, Michigan Office: 101 North Main Street, 7th Floor, 48104-1400.
Telephone: 734-663-2445.
Fax: 734-747-7147.
Troy, Michigan Office: 840 West Long Lake Road, Suite 200, 48098.
Telephone: 248-879-2000.
Fax: 248-879-2001.
Grand Rapids, Michigan Office: 99 Monroe, N.W., Suite 1200, 49503-2639.
Telephone: 616-454-8656.
Fax: 616-776-6322.
Howell, Michigan Office: 121 South Barnard Street, Suite 4, 48843-2305.
Telephone: 517-546-7600.
Telecopier: 517-546-6974.
Lansing, Michigan Office: One Michigan Avenue, Suite 900, 48933-1609.
Telephone: 517-487-2070.
Fax: 517-374-6304.
Monroe, Michigan Office: 214 East Elm Avenue, Suite 100, 48162-2682.
Telephone: 734-243-2000.
Fax: 734-243-0901.
Washington, D.C. Office: 1900 K Street, N.W., Suite 1150. 20006.
Telephone: 202-429-5575; 785-0600.
Fax: 202-331-1118; 785-1234.

(See Next Column)

MILLER, CANFIELD, PADDOCK AND STONE P.L.C.—*Continued*

Pensacola, Florida Office: 25 West Cedar, 32501.
Telephone: 850-469-1088.
Fax: 850-432-0677.
New York, New York Office: 1450 Broadway, 41st Floor, 10018.
Telephone: 212-704-4400.
Fax: 212-704-4410.
Gdynia, Poland Office: UL. Slaska 21, 81-319.
Telephone: 011-485-831-2808.
Fax: 011-48-58-628 6411.
Warsaw, Poland Office: UL. Nowogrodzkall, 5th Floor, 00-513.
Telephone: 011-4822 529 0200.
Fax: 011-4822 529 0201.
Katowice, Poland Office: UL. Francuska 35/37, 40-027.
Telephone: 011 (48-32) 757-2414.
Fax: 011 (48-32) 757-2483.

PRINCIPALS

James E. Spurr
Don M. Schmidt

RESIDENT ASSOCIATES

Kurt P. McCamman
Scott R. Sikkenga

Representative Firm Clients: Chrysler Corporation; Comerica, Incorporated; City of Detroit, Michigan; Detroit Tigers, Inc.; First of Michigan; Ford Motor Company; Ford Motor Credit Company; Great Lakes Bancorp; Henry Ford Hospital; INVETECH Company.

For Complete List of Firm Personnel, See General Section

For full biographical listings, see the Martindale-Hubbell Law Directory

LANSING, Ingham Co.

MCCLELLAND & ANDERSON, L.L.P. (AV)

1305 South Washington, 48933
Telephone: 517-482-4890
Fax: 517-482-4875
URL: http://www.mcclelland-anderson.com

Gregory L. McClelland
Gail A. Anderson
David E. Pierson
Melissa A. Hagen
Kelly A. Myers

Marc D. Matlock
Jason W. Johnson

For full biographical listings, see the Martindale-Hubbell Law Directory

*MONROE,** Monroe Co.

BRAUNLICH, RUSSOW & BRAUNLICH, A PROFESSIONAL CORPORATION (AV)

111 South Macomb Street, 48161
Telephone: 734-241-8300
Fax: 734-241-7715

William J. Braunlich, Jr. (1924-1992)
Thomas P. Russow
William H. Braunlich

Philip A. Costello
Ann L. Nickel
Jeffrey A. Dulany, P.C.

LEGAL SUPPORT PERSONNEL

Ruth G. Flint

Representative Clients: State Farm Mutual Insurance Co.; Auto Club Insurance Assn.; Board of Road Commissioners, Monroe County; Port of Monroe; Monroe County Community College; City of Luna Pier; City of Petersburg; Auto-Owners Insurance Co.; Fremont Mutual Insurance Co.; Citizens Insurance Co. of America.

For full biographical listings, see the Martindale-Hubbell Law Directory

OKEMOS, Ingham Co.

BUTZEL LONG, A PROFESSIONAL CORPORATION (AV)

Suite 300, 2127 University Park Drive, 48864-5928
Telephone: 517-372-6622
Telecopier: 517-372-6672
Email: melnick@butzel.com *URL:* http://www.butzel.com
Detroit, Michigan Office: Suite 900, 150 West Jefferson.
Telephone: 313-225-7000.
Telecopier: 313-225-7080.
Birmingham, Michigan Office: Suite 200, 32270 Telegraph Road.
Telephone: 810-258-1616.
Telecopier: 810-258-1439.
Ann Arbor, Michigan Office: Suite 300, 350 South Main Street.
Telephone: 313-995-3110.
Telecopier: 313-995-1777.
Grosse Pointe Farms, Michigan Office: Suite 260, 21 Kercheval.
Telephone: 313-886-5446.
Telecopier: 313-886-2114.
Boca Raton, Florida Office: Suite 411, 1200 North Federal Highway.
Telephone: 561-368-2151.
Telecopier: 561-368-4668.

(See Next Column)

Palm Beach Gardens, Florida Office: Suite 227, 11382 Prosperity Farms Road.
Telephone: 561-625-4442.
Telecopier: 561-625-6901.
Naples, Florida Office: Suite 705, 801 Laurel Oak Drive.
Telephone: 941-597-4500.
Telecopier: 941-597-5623.

SENIOR ATTORNEYS

Max R. Hoffman, Jr.
Thomas L. Sparks

Michael F. Matheson

For full biographical listings, see the Martindale-Hubbell Law Directory

SOUTHFIELD, Oakland Co.

COLLINS, EINHORN, FARRELL & ULANOFF, A PROFESSIONAL CORPORATION (AV)

4000 Town Center, Suite 909, 48075-1473
Telephone: 248-355-4141
Facsimile: 248-355-2277

Dale J. McLellan
Kenneth C. Merritt

Kevin P. Moloughney

For full biographical listings, see the Martindale-Hubbell Law Directory

DE VINE & KOHN, PLLC (AV)

29800 Telegraph Road, 48034
Telephone: 248-353-6500
Fax: 248-353-2514

Clifford J. De Vine
Sheldon B. Kohn

For full biographical listings, see the Martindale-Hubbell Law Directory

ROSEN & LOVELL, P.C. (AV)

25505 West Twelve Mile Road Suite 1000, 48034-1811
Telephone: 248-213-2910
Fax: 248-948-6677

Paul A. Rosen

Alex J. Remick

For full biographical listings, see the Martindale-Hubbell Law Directory

TROY, Oakland Co.

POLING, MCGAW & POLING, P.C. (AV)

Suite 275, 5435 Corporate Drive, 48098
Telephone: 248-641-0500
Telecopier: 248-641-0506
URL: http://www.lawyers.com/polingmcgaw&poling

Benson T. Buck (1926-1989)
Richard B. Poling
D. Douglas McGaw
Richard B. Poling, Jr.
Gregory C. Hamilton
Veronica B. O'Hara
James R. Parker
Shannon M. Acton

OF COUNSEL

Ralph S. Moore

Representative Clients: City of Troy; United States Fidelity & Guaranty Co.; Sentry Insurance Co.; Admiral Insurance; DeMaria Construction Co.; Leo Corporation; Aetna Casualty and Surety Co.; Concord Design; Pneumo-Abex.

For full biographical listings, see the Martindale-Hubbell Law Directory

SCHIER, DENEWETH & PARFITT, P.C. (AV)

888 West Big Beaver Road, Suite 610, 48084-4737
Telephone: 248-362-5600
Telecopier: 248-362-0073
Email: SDPlaw@aol.com *URL:* http://www.lawyers.com/schierlaw

Carl F. Schier
Ronald A. Deneweth
Chris Parfitt
Timothy P. Dugan
Janette E. Frank
Mark D. Sassak

OF COUNSEL

Edward A. Ryder
John J. Mallon

References: Armond Cassil Company; Capital Contracting Co.; John Carlo, Inc.; Long Mechanical; Nagle Paving Company; P.K. Contracting, Inc.; R.W. Mead Company; Rainbow Construction Co. Inc.; Sunset Excavating; Centex Rodgers Construction Co.; Colasanti Corp.

For full biographical listings, see the Martindale-Hubbell Law Directory

Troy—Continued

STARK, REAGAN & FINNERTY, P.C. (AV)

Suite 202, 1111 West Long Lake Road, P.O. Box 7037, 48007-7037
Telephone: 248-641-9955
Facsimile: 248-641-9921
Email: @SRFPC.COM
Boca Raton, Florida Office: Suite 307B, 4800 North Federal Highway.
Telephone: 561-994-2266.
Traverse City, Michigan Office: 475 Eastwood Shores.
Telephone: 231-943-8230.
Facsimile: 231-943-8711.

Michael H. Whiting	Christopher E. LeVasseur
Kenneth M. Boyer	Daniel E. Chapman
Thomas H. Finnerty	William D. Girardot
R. Keith Stark	James R. Waldvogel
Joseph C. Bird	Jeffrey J. Fleury
Joseph A. Ahern	Michael D. FitzPatrick

OF COUNSEL

Harry S. Stark (Resident Of Counsel, Traverse City Office)	Willard M. Reagan
	James E. Beall

For full biographical listings, see the Martindale-Hubbell Law Directory

CORPORATE LAW

ALABAMA

*DECATUR,** Morgan Co.

HARRIS, CADDELL & SHANKS, P.C. (AV)

214 Johnston Street, S.E., P.O. Box 2688, 35602-2688
Telephone: 256-340-8000
Telecopier: 256-340-8040
Email: hcs@ala-net.com

Julian Harris (1904-1994)
Norman W. Harris (1907-1998)
Philip T. Shanks (Retired)
Charles L. Murphree (Retired)
John A. Caddell
Robert H. Harris
Jon H. Moores
Thomas A. Caddell
William E. Shinn, Jr.
Gary A. Phillips
Dow M. Perry, Jr.
Barnes F. Lovelace, Jr.
Jeffrey S. Brown
David W. Langston
Huel Harris

Attorneys for: First American Bank, Decatur, Alabama; SouthTrust Bank of Alabama (Morgan County); Morgan County Commission; The Industrial Development Board of the City of Decatur, Alabama; The Boeing Company; Amoco Chemical Co.; BellSouth Inc.; Auto-Owners Insurance Co.; ALFA Insurance Cos.; U.S.F. & G. Co.

For full biographical listings, see the Martindale-Hubbell Law Directory

*FORT PAYNE,** De Kalb Co.

SCRUGGS, JORDAN, DODD & DODD (AV)

207 Alabama Avenue, South, P.O. Box 681109, 35967
Telephone: 256-845-5932
Fax: 256-845-4325
Email: scruggs@peop.tdsnet.com *URL:* http://www.lawyers.com/scruggsjordandodd&dodd

William D. Scruggs, Jr.
Robert K. Jordan
J. David Dodd
E. Allen Dodd, Jr.
Holly Hendrickson

Representative Clients: State Farm Insurance Company; Allstate Insurance Co., Inc.; USF&G Insurance Co.; Nucor, Inc.; Ladd Engineering, Inc.; AL-ABAMA Band; First Federal Bank; Fritz Structural Steel, Inc.; Williamson Oil Co., Inc.

For full biographical listings, see the Martindale-Hubbell Law Directory

*GADSDEN,** Etowah Co.

INZER, HANEY, JOHNSON & MCWHORTER, P.A. (AV)

(Inzer, Suttle, Swann & Stivender)
Second Floor, Compass Bank Building, 601 Broad Street, P.O. Drawer 287, 35902-0287
Telephone: 256-546-1656
Telecopier: 256-546-1093
Email: inzerlaw@cybrtyme.com

James C. Inzer (1887-1967)
John A. Lusk, Jr. (1891-1970)
Hubert Burns (1915-1975)
Julius S. Swann, Sr. (1907-1989)
Frank J. Martin (1905-1992)
Roger C. Suttle (1910-1996)
James C. Inzer, Jr. (Of Counsel)
James C. Stivender (Of Counsel)
W. Roscoe Johnson, III
James C. Inzer, III
F. Michael Haney
Robert D. McWhorter, Jr.
James W. McGlaughn
Elizabeth Golson McGlaughn

Assistant Division Counsel for: Southern Railway System.
Attorneys for: General Motors Corp.; Gulf States Steel; Goodyear Tire and Rubber Co.; Alabama Power Co.; Southern Natural Gas Co.; Allstate Insurance Co.; Travelers Insurance Co.; Compass Bank; Cincinnati Insurance Co.

For full biographical listings, see the Martindale-Hubbell Law Directory

*HUNTSVILLE,** Madison Co.

STEPHENS, MILLIRONS, HARRISON & GAMMONS, P.C. (AV)

333 Franklin Street, P.O. Box 307, 35801
Telephone: 256-533-7711
Telecopier: 256-536-9388

Arthur M. Stephens
Paul L. Millirons
James G. Harrison
Robert C. Gammons

Douglas A. Baymiller
Steven J. Shaw

Representative Clients: SouthTrust Bank, N.A.,; Regions Mortgage, Inc.; Chase Manhattan Mortgage Corp.; Amiras, Inc. (d/b/a/ Buy-Wise Drugs); Huntsville Ford Tractor; Brookhill Management Group.

For full biographical listings, see the Martindale-Hubbell Law Directory

*MOBILE,** Mobile Co.

ATCHISON, CROSBY, SAAD & BEEBE, P.C. (AV)

3030 Knollwood Drive, 36693
Telephone: 334-665-7200
Fax: 334-665-7250
URL: http://www.acsblaw.com

James E. Atchison
James H. Crosby
Elias J. Saad
Donald G. Beebe

Mona Ann Vivar
Jacqueline M. McConaha
Daryl A. Atchison

Representative Clients: City of Mobile; Alabama State Docks; Mobile Area Water and Sewer Board; Owens Corning, Inc.; Pilot Catastrophe Services, Inc.; Shell Oil Co.; Premdor,Inc.; Melvin Pierce Paint Co.; Commonwealth National Bank; Fiberglass Canada,Inc.

For full biographical listings, see the Martindale-Hubbell Law Directory

SINTZ, CAMPBELL, DUKE & TAYLOR (AV)

3763 Professional Parkway, 36609
Telephone: 334-344-7241
Fax: 334-344-7400

MEMBERS OF FIRM

Peter V. Sintz (1940-1997)
Robert C. Campbell, III
Frank G. Taylor
Steven L. Terry

ASSOCIATES

Wm. Kyle Morris
Kathryn W. Petersen
Barry C. Prine

OF COUNSEL

Leon G. Duke

LEGAL SUPPORT PERSONEL

James A. Koblas

Representative Clients: Aetna C & S Insurance Co.; Mobile County School Board; Auto-Owners Insurance Co.; Argonaut Insurance Co.; Mostellar Medical Clinic; Scottsdale Insurance Co.; American International Group; Alabama School of Math and Science; Mobile County Sheriff's Office.

For full biographical listings, see the Martindale-Hubbell Law Directory

*MONTGOMERY,** Montgomery Co.

BALL, BALL, MATTHEWS & NOVAK, P.A. (AV)

2000 Interstate Park Drive, Suite 204, 36109
Telephone: 334-387-7680
Fax: 334-387-3222
Email: Firm@Ball-Ball.com

Fred S. Ball (1866-1942)
Charles A. Ball (1904-1969)
Fred S. Ball, Jr. (1896-1974)
Richard A. Ball (1906-1983)
John R. Matthews, Jr.
Richard A. Ball, Jr.
Tabor R. Novak, Jr.
Clyde C. Owen, Jr.
C. Winston Sheehan, Jr.
William H. Brittain II
E. Hamilton Wilson, Jr.
Richard E. Broughton
T. Cowin Knowles
Gerald C. Swann, Jr.
Mark T. Davis
James A. Rives

Fred B. Matthews
Allison L. Alford
Michael L. White
Emily C. Marks
Brandy A. Adkins
George R. Parker

LEGAL SUPPORT PERSONNEL

Lon Worley (Office Manager)

Counsel for: Beech Aircraft Corporation; Bell Helicopter Co.; John Deere Co.; Government Employees Insurance Co.; Chubb & Son; Cigna Co.; Chrysler Corp.; Associated Aviation Underwriters.

For full biographical listings, see the Martindale-Hubbell Law Directory

BRANTLEY & WILKERSON, P.C. (AV)

405 South Hull Street, P.O. Box 830, 36101-0830
Telephone: 334-265-1500
Fax: 334-265-0319
Email: ashley@brantleywilkerson.com *URL:* http://www.brantleywilkerson.com

Paul A. Brantley
Mark D. Wilkerson

Leah Snell Stephens

Representative Clients: MidCoast, Inc.; ALLTEL; Southeastern Cellular; TDS.
Reference: SouthTrust Bank, N.A.

For full biographical listings, see the Martindale-Hubbell Law Directory

*RUSSELLVILLE,** Franklin Co.

McDowell & Beason (AV)

(Formerly McDowell, Beason & Pilati)
507 North Jackson, P.O. Box 818, 35653
Telephone: 256-332-1660
Fax: 256-332-0318
Email: Legal@Getaway.Com

Daniel G. McDowell
Eddie Beason

OF COUNSEL

Joe Fine

Representative Clients: Citizens Bank & Savings Co. of Russellville; City of Phil Campbell; Russellville City Board of Education; Franklin County Board of Education; Mutual Savings Life Insurance Co.; State Farm Fire & Casualty Co.; State Farm Mutual Automobile Ins. Co.; Marshall Durbin Co.

For full biographical listings, see the Martindale-Hubbell Law Directory

ARIZONA

*FLAGSTAFF,** Coconino Co.

Mangum, Wall, Stoops & Warden, P.L.L.C. (AV)

100 North Elden, P.O. Box 10, 86002
Telephone: 520-779-6951
Fax: 520-773-1312

H. Karl Mangum (1908-1993)

OF COUNSEL

Douglas J. Wall
Robert W. Warden
Daniel J. Stoops

MEMBERS OF FIRM

A. Dean Pickett
Melinda L. Garrahan
Stephen K. Smith
Michael H. Hinson

ASSOCIATES

Annette Star Lustgarten
Melinda K. Jacquez
Rebecca Smith Currey
Franklin Hoover
R. Scott Currey
Brandon J. Kavanagh

LEGAL SUPPORT PERSONNEL

J.J. Feeney (Librarian/Research Analyst)
Diane M. Sulzer
Cathryn S. Rugg
Sheri A. Biro (Paralegal)
Dena L. Knoll (Paralegal)

Representative Clients: Northern Arizona University; Flagstaff Unified School District; Museum of Northern Arizona; Arizona School Board Association.
Local Counsel for: Bank of America-Arizona; Arizona Public Service; U.S-.A.A.; State Farm Fire & Casualty Insurance Co.; Property Development Co.

For full biographical listings, see the Martindale-Hubbell Law Directory

MESA, Maricopa Co.

Roberts & Rowley, Ltd. (AV)

63 East Main Street, Suite 501, 85201-7423
Telephone: 480-833-1113
Fax: 480-833-1114
URL: http://www.azlegal.com

Richard Roberts
Paul S. Rowley

Brian D. Strong
Jessica Carpenter
Kevin J. Chapman
Sean M. Sabo

For full biographical listings, see the Martindale-Hubbell Law Directory

*TUCSON,** Pima Co.

Daniel H. O'Connell, P.C. (AV)

3573 East Sunrise Drive, Suite 120, 85718-3206
Telephone: 520-615-9802
Telefax: 520-615-9789
Email: ben@dhopc.psemail.com *URL:* http://www.lawyers.com/danieloconnell-law

Daniel H. O'Connell

Benjamin J. Burnside

OF COUNSEL

Rosanne F. Lapan

Representative Clients: Empire West Cos.; Thermal Engineering, Inc.; Alban Medical Associates; Industrial Motor & Control, Inc.; Allergy Asthma Associates, P.C.
Reference: Bank of America.

For full biographical listings, see the Martindale-Hubbell Law Directory

ARKANSAS

*FORT SMITH,** Sebastian Co.

Gean, Gean & Gean (AV)

511 Garrison Avenue, 72901
Telephone: 501-783-1124
Fax: 501-783-2440

Roy Gean, Sr. (1894-1969)
Paul B. Gean
Roy R. Gean, Jr.
Roy R. Gean, III

ASSOCIATES

David C. Gean
Ellen Gean Pierce

Representative Clients: Federal Savings Bank of Rogers, Arkansas; First City Finance Corp.; First National Bank, Oklahoma; Commercial Credit Plan, Inc.; Associates, Financial Services Company of Oklahoma, Inc.; K & C Properties Real Estate Developers; Cyanede Plastics.

For full biographical listings, see the Martindale-Hubbell Law Directory

Warner, Smith & Harris, PLC (AV)

214 North Sixth Street, P.O. Box 1626, 72901
Telephone: 501-782-6041
Fax: 501-782-0841

Harry Preston Warner (1885-1969)
Cecil Randolph Warner (1890-1955)
Thomas G. Graves (1939-1971)
Douglas O. Smith, Jr.
C. Wayne Harris
Gerald L. DeLung
Patrick Neill Moore
Lillard Cody Hayes
G. Alan Wooten
James Melvin Dunn
John Alan Lewis
Joel D. Johnson
J. Randall McGinnis
Kathryn Stocks Campbell
R. Gregory Aclin

Jason Trevor Browning
Matthew C. Carter

OF COUNSEL

C. R. Warner, Jr.

Local Counsel for: Gerber Products Co.; Rheem Mfg. Co.; Planters Division, Nabisco Brands, Inc.; Owens Corning, Fiberglass, Inc.; General Motors Corp.; General Motors Acceptance Corp.; Hiram Walker & Sons, Inc.; Donrey Media Group; Fort Smith Public Housing Authority; Halcyon Communications.

For full biographical listings, see the Martindale-Hubbell Law Directory

*LITTLE ROCK,** Pulaski Co.

Chisenhall, Nestrud & Julian, P.A. (AV)

400 West Capitol, Suite 2840, 72201
Telephone: 501-372-5800
Telecopier: 501-372-4941
Email: cnjlaw@cnjlaw.com

Lawrence E. Chisenhall, Jr.
Jim L. Julian
Charles R. Nestrud
Ann P. Faitz
Michael T. Jackson

For full biographical listings, see the Martindale-Hubbell Law Directory

Rose Law Firm, A Professional Association (AV)

120 East Fourth Street, 72201
Telephone: 501-375-9131
Telecopy: 501-375-1309

George E. Campbell
William H. Kennedy, III
W. Wilson Jones
Ronald M. Clark
C. Brantly Buck
Kevin R. Burns

Counsel for: ALLTEL Corporation; Aluminum Company of America; Bridgestone/Firestone, Inc.; The Equitable Life Assurance Society of The United States; General Motors Corp.; The Prudential Insurance Company of America; Stephens Group Inc.; Tyson Foods, Inc.

For Complete List of Firm Personnel, See General Section

For full biographical listings, see the Martindale-Hubbell Law Directory

CALIFORNIA

*BAKERSFIELD,** Kern Co.

KLEIN, DENATALE, GOLDNER, COOPER, ROSENLIEB & KIMBALL, LLP (AV)

(Formerly Di Giorgio, Davis, Klein, Wegis, Duggan & Friedman)
ARCO Tower, 4550 California Avenue, Second Floor, 93309
Telephone: 661-395-1000
Telecopier: 661-326-0418
Mailing Address: P.O. Box 11172, Bakersfield, California, 93389-1172
Email: kleinlaw@kleinlaw.com

Thomas R. Davis (1920-1990)
Anthony J. Klein (Inc.)
Thomas V. DeNatale, Jr.
Barry L. Goldner
Jay L. Rosenlieb
David J. Cooper
Claude P. Kimball
William A. Bruce
Leonard K. Welsh
Christopher P. Burger
Ned E. Dunphy
Melvin L. Ehrlich
Kevin C. Findley
Krystyna L. Jamieson

T. Scott Belden
Catherine E. Bennett
David D. Blaine
Nicole M. Misner
Timothy G. Scanlon

OF COUNSEL

Bruce F. Bunker
Thomas C. Fallgatter
Craig D. Braun

Representative Clients: Bank of America; Great Western Bank; Mojave Pipeline Co.; Transamerican Title Insurance Co.; Dean Whittier Reynolds, Inc.; California Republic Bank; San Joaquin Bank; Nahama & Weagant Energy Co.; Freymiller Trucking, Inc.; Westinghouse Electric Co.

For full biographical listings, see the Martindale-Hubbell Law Directory

LAW OFFICES OF YOUNG WOOLDRIDGE (AV)

1800 30th Street, Fourth Floor, 93301
Telephone: 661-327-9661
Facsimile: 661-327-1087
Email: youngwooldridge@lightspeed.net *URL:* http://www.young.wooldridge.com

MEMBERS OF FIRM

Joseph Wooldridge (1913-1996)
A. Cameron Paulden (1927-1984)
Robert J. Self
G. Neil Farr
Michael R. Young
Ernest A. Conant
Steve W. Nichols
Larry R. Cox
Scott K. Kuney
Michael A. Kaia
Steven M. Torigiani
Scott D. Howry

ASSOCIATES

David F. Leon
Todd A. Gall
Mark H. Atkins
Christopher Finberg

OF COUNSEL

Edward M. Carpenter
John B. Young (Retired)

Representative Clients: Arvin-Edison Water Storage District; Motor City Truck Sales and Service.
References: Wells Fargo Bank; First Interstate Bank; California Republic Bank.

For full biographical listings, see the Martindale-Hubbell Law Directory

BEVERLY HILLS, Los Angeles Co.

HOCHMAN, SALKIN, RETTIG, TOSCHER & PEREZ, A PROFESSIONAL CORPORATION (AV)

9150 Wilshire Boulevard Suite 300, 90212-3414
Telephone: 310-281-3200; 273-1181
Fax: 310-859-1430
URL: http://www.taxlitigator.com

Bruce I. Hochman
Avram Salkin
Charles P. Rettig
Dennis Perez
Steven R. Toscher

OF COUNSEL

George DeRoy
Nathan Joseph Hochman

Stuart A. Simon
Steven D. Blanc
Michel R. Stein

Reference: Union Bank of California.

For full biographical listings, see the Martindale-Hubbell Law Directory

BREA, Orange Co.

BACON & MILLS, LLP (AV)

Three Pointe Drive, Suite 308, 92827
Telephone: 714-257-2100
Fax: 714-257-2101
Email: baconmills@earthlink.net *URL:* http://www.baconmills.com
Los Angeles, California Office: 800 Wilshire Boulevard, Suite 950.
Telephone: 213-486-6500.
Fax: 213-486-6552.

Robert L. Bacon
Theodore E. Bacon
John F. Norris

Representative Clients: Lucas Varity, PLC; Lucas Industries, Inc.; Columbia Showcase & Cabinet Co.; Cannon Fabrication, Inc.; Singer, Lewak, Greenbaum and Goldstein, LLP; Optical Components, Inc.; Femino Foundation; Coleman Foundation; Laguna Clay Co.

For full biographical listings, see the Martindale-Hubbell Law Directory

*FRESNO,** Fresno Co.

DIETRICH, GLASRUD, MALLEK & AUNE (AV)

An Association of Attorneys including Law Corporations
5250 North Palm Avenue, Suite 402, 93704
Telephone: 559-435-5250
Facsimile: 559-435-8776
Email: info@dgmalaw.com

Richard W. Dietrich (Inc.) (1930-1999)
Donald H. Glasrud (Inc.)
Robert A. Mallek Jr. (Inc.)
Richard E. Aune (Inc.)
Bruce A. Owdom
Thomas W. Isaac

Douglas D. Schorling
Leslie G. Miessner
Daniel J. Tekunoff

OF COUNSEL

Timothy J. Buchanan

Representative Clients: Fresno Surgery and Recovery Care Center; Helm Fertilizer, Inc.; Gragnani Farms; Wathen-Castanos, Inc.; Chicago Title Company; ABC, Inc.; The McClatchy Company; Monsanto Company; Armstrong World Industries, Inc.; Stewart Title Guaranty Company.

For full biographical listings, see the Martindale-Hubbell Law Directory

IRVINE, Orange Co.

SNELL & WILMER L.L.P. (AV)

1920 Main Street, Suite 1200, 92614-7230
Telephone: 949-253-2700
FAX: 949-955-2507
URL: http://www.swlaw.com
Phoenix, Arizona Office: One Arizona Center, 85004-2202.
Telephone: 602-382-6000.
Fax: 602-382-6070.
Tucson, Arizona Office: One South Church Avenue, Suite 1500, 85701-1630.
Telephone: 520-882-1200.
Fax: 520-884-1294.
Salt Lake City, Utah Office: 111 East Broadway, Suite 900, 84111-1004.
Telephone: 801-237-1900.
Fax: 801-237-1950.

MEMBERS OF FIRM

William S. O'Hare, Jr.
Nanette D. Sanders
William T. Gay
Roger A. Grad

ASSOCIATES

David S. Beard
Julie A. Douveas (Not admitted in CA)

Representative Clients: For list of Representative Clients, see end of biographical listings in the Martindale-Hubbell Law Directory.

For Complete List of Firm Personnel, See General Section

For full biographical listings, see the Martindale-Hubbell Law Directory

LONG BEACH, Los Angeles Co.

D. MICHAEL TRAINOTTI A PROFESSIONAL LAW CORPORATION (AV)

Suite 410, 200 Oceangate, 90802
Telephone: 562-590-8621
Fax: 562-590-8181
Email: mike@trainotti.com *URL:* http://www.trainotti.com

D. Michael Trainotti

Reference: Farmers & Merchants Bank; Harbor Bank.

For full biographical listings, see the Martindale-Hubbell Law Directory

*LOS ANGELES,** Los Angeles Co.

ALVARADO, SMITH & SANCHEZ, A PROFESSIONAL CORPORATION (AV)

611 West Sixth Street, Suite 2650, 90017
Telephone: 213-229-2400
Facsimile: 213-229-2499
URL: http://www.alvarado-smith.com
Irvine, California Office: 4 Park Plaza, Suite 1200, 92614.
Telephone: 949-955-6800.
Fax: 949-955-6899.

Raymond G. Alvarado
Ruben A. Smith
Maurice Sanchez
John M. Sorich
Raúl F. Salinas
Frances Q. Jett
Theresa Eileen Antonucci
Diane C. Barrio
Rosario M. Tobias

OF COUNSEL

Martin N. Burton

For full biographical listings, see the Martindale-Hubbell Law Directory

BRAND FARRAR & BUXBAUM LLP (AV)

515 South Flower Street, Suite 3500, 90071-2201
Telephone: 213-228-0288
Fax: 213-426-6222
Email: bfb-la@brandfarrar.com
Beijing (Peking), China Office: Suite 2518, China World Trade Centre, 1 Jian Guo Men Wai Avenue, Beijing, China.
Telephone: 86-10-6505-2288 Ext. 2523/2518.
Fax: 86-10-6505-2638. Email: bjbfbbj@public3.bta.net.cn
Chengdu, Sichuan, China Office: Suite 11A, Sichuan International Mansion, No. 1 Zhong Xi Shun Cheng Street, Chengdu, China.
Telephone: 86-28-652-1316.
Fax: 86-28-652-0547. Email: cdbfbcd@mail.sc.cninfo.net.
Chongqing, China Office: Suite 1510, Metropolitan Tower, 68 Zourong Lu, Chongqing, China.
Telephone: 86-23-6382-8381.
Fax: 86-23-6382-8373. Email: cqbfbcq@public.cta.cq.cn.
Guangzhou (Canton), China Office: Suite 1305, Main Tower, GITIC Plaza Hotel, 339 Huanshi Dong Road, Guangzhou, China.
Telephone: 86-20-8331-1888, Ext. 71305.
Fax: 86-20-8331-2671. Email: gzbfbgz@public.guangzhou.gd.cn.
Hong Kong, China Office: Brand Farrar Buxbaum LLP, 5/F., Landmark East, 12 Ice House Street, Central, Hong Kong, China.
Telephone: 852-2523-7001.
Fax: 852-2845-0947. Email: hkbfbhk@hk.super.net.
Los Angeles, California Office: Brand Farrar & Buxbaum LLP, Suite 3500, 515 South Flower Street, Los Angeles, California, 90071-2201.
Telephone: 213-228-0288.
Fax: 213-426-6222. Email: bfb-la@brandfarrar.com.
New York, New York Office: 275 Madison Avenue, 37th Floor, New York, New York, 10097.
Telephone: 212-286-0038.
Fax: 212-573-9077. Email: martineh@aol.com
Shanghai, China Office: Brand Farrar Buxbaum LLP, Suites 2611-12, Central Plaza, 227 Huangpi Bei Lu, Shanghai, China.
Telephone: 86-21-6375-8918.
Fax: 86-21-6375-8922. Email: shbfbsh@public2.sta.net.cn
Shenzhen, China Office: Suite 2103A, Shenzhen Development Center, Renmin Nan Lu, Shenzhen, China.
Telephone: 86-755-229-8009.
Fax: 86-755-229-8011. Email: szbfbsz@public.szptt.net.cn.
Ulaanbaatar, Mongolia Office: Brand Farrar Buxbaum LLP, 4/F., Time Center, No. 50 Baga Toiruu, Ulaanbaatar, Mongolia.
Telephone: 976-1-31-0711.
Fax: 976-1-32-5102. Email: mgbfbmg@magicnet.mn.
Xiamen, China Office: Suite 1182 Jian Ye Building, 28 Hubin North Road, Xiamen, China.
Telephone: 86-592-506-3059.
Fax: 86-592-511-1044. Email: xmbfbxm@public.xm.fj.cn.
Associated Office, Mumbai, Bombay, India: Shah & Sanghavi, Advocates, Solicitors & Notary, 114-A Mittal Court, Nariman Point, Mumbai 400 021 India.
Telephone: 91-22-285-5755/56 or 91-22-285-3592/93.
Fax: 91-22-284-5040.

PRINCIPALS

Michael A. Brand
David C. Buxbaum (China Offices)
Kenneth Y. Choy (Hong Kong Office)
Robert W. Dziubla
David W. Farrar
Amy E. Freilich
Margaret G. Graf
John Masao Iino
Charles K. Kolstad
Edward H. Martin (New York Office)
Gregory D. Trimarche
Li Zhuogen (China Offices)

OTHER ATTORNEYS RESIDENT IN LOS ANGELES OFFICE

Sherry L. Geyer
Joan M. Marquardt
James H. Service
Jeffrey S. Allen
Julia Sylva
Brian J. Kim
Lisa Teng

(See Next Column)

OTHER ATTORNEYS RESIDENT IN BEIJING OFFICE

Hao Xiaodong
Bin Zhao
Luo Rongping
Zhang Chunbo

OTHER ATTORNEYS RESIDENT IN CHENGDU, SICHUAN OFFICE

Zeng Xiangyu
Wu Wen

OTHER ATTORNEY RESIDENT IN CHONGQING OFFICE

Du Fei

OTHER ATTORNEYS RESIDENT IN GUANGZHOU OFFICE

Zou Wenyan (Not admitted in United States)
Feng Ruiding
Jia Guangxi

OTHER ATTORNEYS RESIDENT IN HONG KONG OFFICE

Shane F. Weir
Cheonghar Wong
N.T.S. Kularatne
Simon Woo
David William Gunson
Arthur Burton Crook
Simon K.C. Lee
Cheng Yuen Yi
Lo Wing Cheong
Nicholas C. McGrenra
Eva Y.N. Kwok

OTHER ATTORNEYS RESIDENT IN NEW YORK OFFICE

Vincent I. S. Hsieh (Of Counsel)
Jeffrey Schall
Jonathan Chun Wang

OTHER ATTORNEYS RESIDENT IN SHANGHAI OFFICE

Lin Yong
Wu Hong Liang
Tang Ying
Zhang Guoyao
Qi Zhenwen

OTHER ATTORNEYS RESIDENT IN SHENZHEN OFFICE

Zhong Wenya
Zhang He

OTHER ATTORNEYS RESIDENT IN ULAANBAATAR OFFICE

Byambaa Bayarmaa
Ajiv Enhktuya

OTHER ATTORNEY RESIDENT IN XIAMEN OFFICE

Deng Sheng

For full biographical listings, see the Martindale-Hubbell Law Directory

DARLING, HALL & RAE, LLP (AV)

520 South Grand Avenue, 7th Floor, 90071
Telephone: 213-627-8104
Fax: 213-627-7795
Email: darlinghallrae@compuserve.com

MEMBERS OF FIRM

Hugh W. Darling (1901-1986)
Edward S. Shattuck (1901-1965)
George Gaylord Gute (1922-1981)
Donald Keith Hall (1918-1984)
Matthew S. Rae, Jr.
Richard L. Stack
Edwin Freston

OF COUNSEL

Edward F. Pearson

Reference: City National Bank (Pershing Square Office, Los Angeles, California).

For full biographical listings, see the Martindale-Hubbell Law Directory

DONAHUE MESEREAU & LEIDS L.L.P. (AV)

A Limited Liability Partnership including Professional Corporations
1900 Avenue of the Stars Suite 2700, 90067
Telephone: 310-277-1441
Facsimile: 310-277-2888

Michael D. Donahue (A Professional Corporation)
Asher M. Leids
Dave Lenny
Kirsten L. Anderson
Jacqueline L. Shulman
Amy S. Novicoff (Not admitted in CA)
Julia A. Longjohn

OF COUNSEL

Thomas A. Mesereau, Jr. (A Professional Corporation)

For full biographical listings, see the Martindale-Hubbell Law Directory

EASTON & SCHIFF (AV)

A Partnership of Professional Corporations
1901 Avenue of the Stars Suite 1100, 90067
Telephone: 310-557-2436
FAX: 310-557-2432

MEMBERS OF FIRM

Harold Easton (P.C.)
Michael J. Schiff (P.C.)

References: Bank of America National Trust & Savings Assn. (Los Angeles Main Office); First Charter Bank (Beverly Hills).

For full biographical listings, see the Martindale-Hubbell Law Directory

INGLIS, LEDBETTER & GOWER (AV)

500 South Grand Avenue, 18th Floor, 90071-2612
Telephone: 213-627-6800
Facsimile: 213-622-2857

(See Next Column)

INGLIS, LEDBETTER & GOWER—*Continued*

MEMBERS OF FIRM

Michael K. Inglis
Steven K. Ledbetter
Richard S. Gower
Richard G. Ritchie
Gregory H. Gocke
John E. Hope

ASSOCIATE

Gregory J. Bramlage

LEGAL SUPPORT PERSONNEL

Suzanne Beyers (Paralegal)

Representative Clients: Barnes-Dyer Marketing, Inc.; Brehm Communications, Inc.; Eddings Brothers, Inc.; Global Manufacturers Corp.; Inter-Insurance Exchange of the Automobile Club of Southern California; Cecil Saydah Company; 6W Farms, Inc.; Prudential Property and Casualty Insurance Co.; SafariLand Ltd., Inc.; Thermal Equipment Corporation.

For full biographical listings, see the Martindale-Hubbell Law Directory

KESSLER & KESSLER, A LAW CORPORATION (AV)

2029 Century Park East, Suite 1520, 90067
Telephone: 310-552-9800
Fax: 310-552-0442
Email: kkalawcorp@aol.com

Warren J. Kessler
Joan B. Kessler
Lisa C. Alexander
Lisa K. Skaist

For full biographical listings, see the Martindale-Hubbell Law Directory

KNOPFLER & ROBERTSON, LLP (AV)

Suite 500, 21650 Oxnard Street (Woodland Hills), 91367
Telephone: 818-227-0770; 213-624-1111
Telefax: 818-227-0777
Irvine, California Office: 19800 MacArthur Boulevard, Suite 270, 92612.
Telephone: 714-261-6191.
Pleasanton, California Office: 400 Main Street, Suite 204, 94566.
Telephone: 510-425-7250.
Las Vegas, Nevada Office: Knopfler & Robertson in Association with Broom & Vaisbort, LLP, 3753 Howard Hughes Parkway, Suite 200, 89109.
Telephone: 702-792-2413.
Camarillo, California Office: 1200 Paseo, Suite 170, 93010.
Telephone: 805-482-1903; 800-CONDOLAW.
Fax: 805-484-5917.

George Knopfler
Alexander Robertson, IV
Deborah Broom
Richard A. Capella
Jonathan S. Vick
Edward D. Vaisbort
William G. Kelsberg

OF COUNSEL

Scott C. Haith
James P. Lingl (Resident, Camarillo Office)
Christina S. Robertson

Janice M. Michaels
James M. Pazos
Mark Rohrer
Craig Smith
Robert Nation
William S. Dunlevy (Resident, Camarillo Office)
Scott A. Hunter

For full biographical listings, see the Martindale-Hubbell Law Directory

KONOWIECKI & RANK LLP (AV)

A Partnership including a Professional Corporation
Library Tower, 633 West 5th Street, Suite 3500, 90071-2007
Telephone: 213-229-0990
Telefax: 213-229-0992

Peter C. Rank
Joseph S. Konowiecki
Michael C. Foster
Jon N. Manzanares
Kevin B. Kroeker
Peter Roan
Peter R. Mason
Denise E. Hanna
Edna M. Chism
Scott J. Moore
Robert C. Hayden
Gail D. Schubert

ASSOCIATES

Cynthia J. Billey
Michael J. Blake
Ana Castillo
Ronan Cohen
Richard A. Cross
Rosa Kwon Easton
I-Fan C. Go
Melinda A. Hess
Sandra Lee Hitt
Lynn E. Iba
Robert M. Kessler
Harry H.W. Kim
Thomas C. Knego
Stephen J. Krause
Phillip R. Maltin
John A. Mueller
Jeffrey D. Olster
Leslie Overfelt
Gary S. Pancer
Tallien Perry
Payman Pezhman
Harold C. Pope
Robin M. Prendergast
Ira L. Robinson
Michael B. Spencer
India S. Thompson
Keith A. Weaver
John A. Zrnich

(See Next Column)

Representative Clients: PacifiCare Health Systems, Inc.; Henry Mayo Newhall Memorial Hospital; Santa Clarita Health Care Assoc.; College Health Enterprises; Granada Hills Community Hospital; Redlands Community Hospital; Health Care Partners.
Reference: Bank of America.

For full biographical listings, see the Martindale-Hubbell Law Directory

RODI, POLLOCK, PETTKER, GALBRAITH & CAHILL, A LAW CORPORATION (AV)

444 South Flower Street, Suite 1700, 90071-2901
Telephone: 213-895-4900
Telecopiers: 213-895-4921; 895-4922; 895-4750
URL: http://www.rodipollock.com

Karl B. Rodi (1908-1982)
John D. Cahill
John D. Pettker
Daniel C. Bond (1942-1977)
William R. Christian
Henry P. Pramov, Jr.
John F. Cermak, Jr.
Allan E. Ceran
Elizabeth B. Blakely
Robert C. Norton
Tim G. Ceperley
Coralie Kupfer
Cris K. O'Neall
Scott E. Adamson
Margaret Rosenthal

Sonja A. Inglin
Michael A. Abraham
Kenneth A. Franklin
Richard Nessary
Donna Yamini
Wade E. Norwood
Deepak Nanda
David J. Elbaz

OF COUNSEL

John P. Pollock
James M. Galbraith

For full biographical listings, see the Martindale-Hubbell Law Directory

NEWPORT BEACH, Orange Co.

KRISTIN M. CANO (AV)

One Corporate Plaza, Suite 110, 92660
Telephone: 949-759-1505
FAX: 949-640-9535
URL: http://www.lawyers.com/kcano
Email: KristinCanoLawOffice@internetMCI.com *URL:* http://www.securities-law.com

For full biographical listings, see the Martindale-Hubbell Law Directory

MOZINGO & PRICE, LLP (AV)

One Newport Place, 1301 Dove Street, Suite 900, 92660
Telephone: 949-752-2255
Facsimile: 949-752-6636
Sacramento, California Office: US Bank Plaza, 980 Ninth Street, Suite 2120, 95814.
Telephone: 916-492-0525.
Facsimile: 916-492-0635.

MEMBERS OF FIRM

Glen R. Mozingo
Don G. Price
Jeffrey W. Fohrman

Representative Clients: Salomon Smith Barney-Charles Schwab; Keller, Collins, Hakopian & Leisure (Investment Advisors); American River Fire District; Merchants National Bank; Good & Roberts Construction, Inc.; Essex Insurance Co.; Integrated Environmental, Inc.; International Gateway Insurance Brokers; Coastal Pacific Funding Corp.

STEPP & BEAUCHAMP LLP (AV)

A Limited Liability Partnership of Professional Corporations
1301 Dove Street, Suite 460, 92660-2422
Telephone: 949-660-9700
Fax: 949-660-9010
Email: ndh@stepp-beauchamp.com *URL:* http://www.lawyers.com/stepp&beauchampllp

Thomas E. Stepp, Jr.
Mynette D. Beauchamp
Robert B. Beauchamp
Deron Matthew Colby
Michael J. Muellerleile

For full biographical listings, see the Martindale-Hubbell Law Directory

OXNARD, Ventura Co.

LOWTHORP, RICHARDS, MCMILLAN, MILLER, CONWAY & TEMPLEMAN, A PROFESSIONAL CORPORATION (AV)

300 Esplanade Drive, Suite 850, P.O. Box 5167, 93031
Telephone: 805-981-8555
Fax: 805-983-1967

Carl F. Lowthorp, Jr. (1933-1992)
Richard A. Richards
Robert C. McMillan
Paul A. Miller
Charles J. Conway, Jr.
Alan R. Templeman
Patrick T. Loughman
Glenn J. Campbell
John Q. Masteller

(See Next Column)

LOWTHORP, RICHARDS, MCMILLAN, MILLER, CONWAY & TEMPLEMAN A PROFESSIONAL CORPORATION, *Oxnard—Continued*

LEGAL SUPPORT PERSONNEL

Elizabeth T. Ladiana, CLA

Representative Clients: Pleasant Valley Mutual Water Co.; Friedrich Ranches, Inc.; Deardorff Jackson Co.; Pacific Coast Plastering; AGRX, Inc.; Terry Farms; Hurst Concrete Products; Chase Bros. Dairy; Dullam Nursery.
Reference: City National Bank.

For full biographical listings, see the Martindale-Hubbell Law Directory

PLEASANTON, Alameda Co.

JG, P.C. BUSINESS & CORPORATE LAW (AV)

5000 Hopyard Road, Suite 400, 94588
Telephone: 925-463-9600
Facsimile: 925-463-9644
Email: jgulseth@jgpc.com *URL:* http://www.jgpc.com

James H. Gulseth
Robert L. Taylor

LEGAL SUPPORT PERSONNEL

Jennifer Gray (Paralegal)

For full biographical listings, see the Martindale-Hubbell Law Directory

*REDWOOD CITY,** San Mateo Co.

HANNIG LAW FIRM LLP (AV)

2991 El Camino Real, Suite 100, 94061
Telephone: 650-482-3040
Facsimile: 650-482-2820
Email: tjh@hanniglaw.com *URL:* http://www.hanniglaw.com

Ted J. Hannig
H. Ann Liroff
David M. Rose

OF COUNSEL

John Antonakos
Michael D. Barry

For full biographical listings, see the Martindale-Hubbell Law Directory

*SAN DIEGO,** San Diego Co.

HAIGHT, BROWN & BONESTEEL, L.L.P. (AV)

A Partnership including Professional Corporations
101 West Broadway, Suite 1000, 92101-3544
Telephone: 619-595-5583
Telecopier: 619-595-7873
URL: http://www.hbblaw.com
Santa Monica, California Office: 1620 26th Street, Suite 4000 North, P.O. Box 680.
Telephone: 310-449-6000.
Telecopier: 310-829-5117.
Telex: 705837.
Santa Ana, California Office: Suite 900, 5 Hutton Centre Drive.
Telephone: 714-754-1100.
Telecopier: 714-754-0826.
Riverside, California Office: California Tower, 3737 Main Street, Suite 800.
Telephone: 909-341-8300.
Fax: 909-341-8309.
San Francisco, California Office: 101 Bush Street, 27th Floor.
Telephone: 415-986-7700.
Fax: 415-986-6945.

RESIDENT MEMBER

George R. Gonzalez

For full biographical listings, see the Martindale-Hubbell Law Directory

KENNERSON SCHWARTZ SEMERDJIAN & HAILE LLP (AV)

A Limited Liability Partnership
101 West Broadway, Suite 810, 92101
Telephone: 619-236-8821
Facsimile: 619-236-8827
URL: http://www.lawyers.com/ksshlaw

OF COUNSEL

Paul R. Kennerson

MEMBERS OF FIRM

Ross J. Schwartz
Dick A. Semerdjian
Jeffrey A. Haile

James R. Ballard
John K. Grant

For full biographical listings, see the Martindale-Hubbell Law Directory

*SAN FRANCISCO,** San Francisco Co.

STIMMEL, STIMMEL & SMITH, A PROFESSIONAL CORPORATION (AV)

100 Bush Street, Suite 850, 94104
Telephone: 415-392-2018
Fax: 415-391-2124
Email: stimmelpc@stimmel-law.com *URL:* http://www.stimmel-law.com

Norman S. Stimmel (1914-1991)
Lee D. Stimmel
Andrine K. Smith

OF COUNSEL

Jeffrey S. Rosen
Susan B. Jordan
Joanne M. Reming
Darrick T. Chase

For full biographical listings, see the Martindale-Hubbell Law Directory

*SAN JOSE,** Santa Clara Co.

HOPKINS & CARLEY, A LAW CORPORATION (AV)

Sixth Floor, 2 West Santa Clara Street, 95113-1824
Telephone: 408-286-9800
Facsimile: 408-998-4790
Mailing Address: P.O. Box 1469, San Jose, CA, 95109-1469
URL: http://www.hopkinscarley.com

Robert V. Hawn
Brian C. Finerty
Sharon L. Wong

OF COUNSEL

Clarence A. Kellogg Jr.
Lloyd Alvin Schmidt

Craig Lee Henderson
Andrew L. Romberger

For Complete List of Firm Personnel, See General Section

For full biographical listings, see the Martindale-Hubbell Law Directory

*SAN LUIS OBISPO,** San Luis Obispo Co.

ANDRE, MORRIS & BUTTERY, A PROFESSIONAL LAW CORPORATION (AV)

1102 Laurel Lane, P.O. Box 730, 93406-0730
Telephone: 805-543-4171
Fax: 805-543-0752
Email: amb@amblaw.com *URL:* http://www.amblaw.com

Michael J. Morris
J. Todd Mirolla
Scott W. Wall

William V. Douglass
Timothy L. Hodge

References: Bank of America National Trust and Savings Assn. (San Luis Obispo Main Branch); Mid-State Bank (San Luis Obispo).

For full biographical listings, see the Martindale-Hubbell Law Directory

*SANTA ROSA,** Sonoma Co.

ANDERSON, ZEIGLER, DISHAROON, GALLAGHER & GRAY, PROFESSIONAL CORPORATION (AV)

50 Old Courthouse Square, 5th Floor, P.O. Box 1498, 95404
Telephone: 707-545-4910
Fax: 707-544-0260
Other Santa Rosa, California Office: 6641 Oakmont Drive, 95409.
Telephone: 707-539-3880.
Petaluma, California Office: 17 Keller Street, 94952.
Telephone: 707-763-0937.

Edwin C. Anderson, Jr.
Kirt F. Zeigler
Robert Disharoon
Barbara Detrich Gallagher
Margaret M. Elliott
David G. Bjornstrom
Robert S. Rutherfurd
Christopher M. Mazzia
Tricia A. Shindledecker
Jeremy L. Olsan

Wendy D. Whitson
Daniel E. Post
Mary Catherine Doherty
Lisa Yoshida
Matthew E. Hannum

OF COUNSEL

John J. King, Jr.

LEGAL SUPPORT PERSONNEL

Edward J. Gibson
Daniel B. Flock (Director of Information)

For full biographical listings, see the Martindale-Hubbell Law Directory

COLORADO

*DENVER,** Denver Co.

BERLINER ZISSER WALTER & GALLEGOS, A PROFESSIONAL CORPORATION (AV)

One Norwest Center, 1700 Lincoln Street, Suite 4700, 80203-4547
Telephone: 303-830-1700
Facsimile: 303-830-1705
Email: bzwg@bzwg.com

Martin M. Berliner
David A. Zisser
Robert W. Walter
Larry D. Gallegos

Stacey L. Bowers

OF COUNSEL

Phillip C. Gans

For full biographical listings, see the Martindale-Hubbell Law Directory

BRENMAN BROMBERG & TENENBAUM, P.C. (AV)

Mellon Financial Center Suite 1001, 1775 Sherman Street, 80203
Telephone: 303-894-0234
Fax: 303-839-1633
Email: bbt@bbtlaw.net

Albert Brenman
Thomas R. Bromberg
A. Thomas Tenenbaum
Steven W. McDonald

Sheryl A. Johnson
Judy A. Gooch

OF COUNSEL

Duane Woodard

For full biographical listings, see the Martindale-Hubbell Law Directory

BROWNSTEIN HYATT & FARBER, P.C. (AV)

Twenty-Second Floor, 410 Seventeenth Street, 80202-4437
Telephone: 303-223-1100
Telecopier: 303-223-1111
Washington, D.C. Office: 1615 L Street, N.W., Suite 450, 20036.
Telephone: 202-296-7353.
Telecopier: 202-296-7009.
Glenwood Springs, Colorado Office: Box 357, 81602.
Telephone: 970-945-5302.
Telecopier: 970-945-4921.

Norman Brownstein
Steven W. Farber
Gary M. Reiff
Cole Finegan
Jeffrey M. Knetsch
Steven S. Siegel
John L. Ruppert
Steven C. Demby
Brent T. Slosky

SENIOR COUNSEL

John R. Garrett

OF COUNSEL

Jacquelyn Kilmer

Joshua J. Widoff
Robert M. Fogler
Ted J. Trimpa
Christopher D. Reiss
Mark J. Maichel
Tad S. Rogers
Jeffrey J. Schroeder

Representative Clients: Apollo Real Estate Advisors, L.P.; Atlantic Gulf Communities Corporation; Club Sports International; Color Spot Nurseries; Gart Sports Company; Kohlberg & Co.; Prometheus Partners, L.P.; Samsonite Corporation; U S WEST, Inc.; Vail Associates, Inc.

For Complete List of Firm Personnel, See General Section

For full biographical listings, see the Martindale-Hubbell Law Directory

FRIEDLOB SANDERSON RASKIN PAULSON & TOURTILLOTT, LLC (AV)

1400 Glenarm Place, 80202-5099
Telephone: 303-571-1400
Fax: 303-595-3159; 303-595-3970; 303-615-5472
Englewood, Colorado Office: 8400 East Prentice Avenue, 80111-2918.
Telephone: 303-571-1400.
Santa Cruz, California Office: 519 Seabright Avenue, Suite 208, 95062-3482.
Telephone: 813-460-3966.
Fax: 813-460-3968.

Raymond L. Friedlob
Gerald Raskin
John W. Kellogg

(See Next Column)

OF COUNSEL

Jack D. Feuer
Cameron A. Weist (Not admitted in CO; Resident Santa Cruz, California Office)

For full biographical listings, see the Martindale-Hubbell Law Directory

GORSUCH KIRGIS LLP (AV)

Tower 1, Suite 1000, 1515 Arapahoe Street, 80202
Telephone: 303-376-5000
Fax: 303-376-5001

PARTNERS

S. Lee Terry, Jr.
Cynthia Smith Cain

ASSOCIATES

Pantea M. Garroussi
Anastasia G. Khokhryakova

LEGAL SUPPORT PERSONNEL

Lansing Wallace
Veronica Ehrenzeller

For full biographical listings, see the Martindale-Hubbell Law Directory

HAMILTON AND FAATZ, A PROFESSIONAL CORPORATION (AV)

Suite 500 Colorado State Bank Building, 1600 Broadway, 80202-4905
Telephone: 303-830-0500
Facsimile: 303-860-7855
Email: HandF@HandF.com

Pierpont Fuller (1906-1983)
John M. Evans (1911-1984)
Dwight Alan Hamilton
Clyde A. Faatz, Jr.
John T. Willson
Michael E. Gurley
James H. Marlow
Jan E. Montgomery
Gregory W. Smith

Christopher J.W. Forrest
Cynthia Treadwell-Miller
Tal Diamant

OF COUNSEL

Kenneth W. Caughey

Representative Clients: Arapahoe County Public Airport Authority; Colorado Baptist General Convention; First Industrial Realty Trust; Masonic Temple Association of Denver; Meridian Investment Management Corp.; Public Employees' Retirement Association of Colorado; Randall and Blake, Inc.; Rocky Mountain Clothing Co.; South Denver Cardiology Associates, P.C.; Unisource Worldwide, Inc.

For full biographical listings, see the Martindale-Hubbell Law Directory

OTTEN, JOHNSON, ROBINSON, NEFF & RAGONETTI, P.C. (AV)

950 Seventeenth Street, 16th Floor, 80202
Telephone: 303-825-8400
Telecopier: 303-825-6525
URL: http://www.ojrnr.com

Arthur E. Otten, Jr.
A. Bruce Campbell
William R. Neff
Neil M. Goff
Blair L. Lockwood
Douglas R. Wright
Karen L. Barsch
John R. Marcil
Michael C. Villano
James D. Leonard
Paul D. Zier
Michael C. Matheson
C. Ander Smith
Jeffrey A. Sherman

Representative Clients: Amstar Group, Ltd.; The Broe Companies, Inc.; Coram Healthcare Corp.; Eagle Gaming, L.P.; Frontier Airlines; GeriMed of America, Inc.; Koala Corp.; Public Employees' Retirement Association of Colorado; StarTek, Inc.; TIC Holdings, Inc.; United General Financial Services, Inc.

For Complete List of Firm Personnel, See General Section

For full biographical listings, see the Martindale-Hubbell Law Directory

PREEO, SILVERMAN & GREEN, P.C. (AV)

1401 17th Street, Suite 800, 80202
Telephone: 303-296-4440
Fax: 303-296-3330

Robert L. Preeo
Eldon E. Silverman
Jersey M. Green
Martin J. Green
Gilbert R. Egle
Marilyn W. McWilliams
Timothy Kyle Jordan
Brandon S Culter

For full biographical listings, see the Martindale-Hubbell Law Directory

SENN LEWIS & VISCIANO, P.C. (AV)

1801 California Street, Suite 4300, 80202
Telephone: 303-298-1122
Facsimile: 303-296-9101

Mark A. Senn
Fredric J. Lewis
Frank W. Visciano
Stephen W. Arent
Ellen Kirschenbaum

(See Next Column)

SENN LEWIS & VISCIANO P.C., *Denver—Continued*

Rosemarie E. Delmonte
Mark A. Redmiles
Luis A. Toro
Margie J. Titus

OF COUNSEL

Lawrence A. Atler
Brenda Jansen

For Complete List of Firm Personnel, See General Section

For full biographical listings, see the Martindale-Hubbell Law Directory

ENGLEWOOD, Arapahoe Co.

NORTON • LIDSTONE, LLC (AV)

The Quadrant, 5445 DTC Parkway, Suite 850, 80111
Telephone: 303-221-5552
Fax: 303-221-5553
URL: http://www.lawyers.com/norton_lidstone_law

Michael J. Norton
Herrick K. Lidstone, Jr.

For full biographical listings, see the Martindale-Hubbell Law Directory

CONNECTICUT

DANBURY, Fairfield Co.

DRISCOLL, TALARICO, FRIZZELL, OLIVO & DRISCOLL (AV)

142 Deer Hill Avenue, 06810-7727
Telephone: 203-792-8333
Facsimile: 203-778-9570
Email: driscoll@javanet.com
Bethel, Connecticut Office: 235 Greenwood Avenue, 06801-2186.
Telephone: 203-744-5000; 743-5556.
Facsimile: 203-798-7790.
Southbury, Connecticut Office: Three Pomperaug Office Park, Suite 203, P.O. Box 252, 06488-0252.
Telephone: 203-264-9650.
Facsimile: 203-798-2175.

Julius J. Bielizna (1914-1988)
Kenneth H. Murray (1905-1984)
Herbert B. Wanderer (1902-1979)
James C. Driscoll, Jr. (Resident, Southbury Office)
Robert N. Talarico
Thomas A. Frizzell
Steven M. Olivo
James C. Driscoll, III (Resident, Bethel Office)
Jerome A. Mayer
Richard W. Hanna
D. Joseph Lane, Jr.
George S. Papazoglou

For full biographical listings, see the Martindale-Hubbell Law Directory

GREENWICH, Fairfield Co.

ALBERT, WARD & JOHNSON, P.C. (AV)

125 Mason Street, P.O. Box 1668, 06836
Telephone: 203-661-8600
Telecopier: 203-661-8051

Tom S. Ward, Jr.
Scott R. Johnson
Jane D. Hogeman
Howard R. Wolfe
Christopher A. Kristoff
Vicki K. Comberiati

OF COUNSEL

David Albert
C. Robton Perelli-Minetti

For full biographical listings, see the Martindale-Hubbell Law Directory

FOGARTY COHEN SELBY & NEMIROFF LLC (AV)

88 Field Point Road, P.O. Box 2508, 06836-2508
Telephone: 203-661-1000
Telefax: 203-629-7300

MEMBERS OF FIRM

James R. Fogarty
Bruce F. Cohen
Leland C. Selby
Andrew P. Nemiroff
Steven W. Russo

COUNSEL

Robert A. Epstein
Everett Fisher
Jennifer N. Boyd

ASSOCIATES

William Bradford Smith, Jr.
Carolyn Alexander Collins
Lawrence F. Reilly
Anne M. Piedade
Eric R. Posmantier

For full biographical listings, see the Martindale-Hubbell Law Directory

NEW LONDON, New London Co.

WALLER, SMITH & PALMER, P.C. (AV)

52 Eugene O'Neill Drive, P.O. Box 88, 06320
Telephone: 860-442-0367
Telecopier: 860-447-9915
Email: wspmain@snet.net *URL:* http://www.snetyp.com/wallersmithpalmer
Old Lyme Office: 103 Halls Road.
Telephone: 860-434-8063.
Telecopier: 860-434-9452. Email: wspol@snet.net

Tracy Waller (1862-1947)
J. Rodney Smith (1906-1979)
Birdsey G. Palmer (Retired)
William W. Miner
Robert P. Anderson, Jr.
Robert W. Marrion
Hughes Griffis
Edward B. O'Connell
Frederick B. Gahagan
Tracy M. Collins
Philip M. Johnstone
David P. Condon
Valerie Ann Votto
Charles C. Anderson

James F. Spallone

General Counsel For: Town of East Lyme.
Counsel For: Citizens Bank of Connecticut; Soneco/Northeastern, Inc.; The Nature Conservancy; Fleet Bank.
Local Counsel For: McCue Mortgage Co.; Citicorp Mortgage; U.S. Department of Housing and Urban Development.

For full biographical listings, see the Martindale-Hubbell Law Directory

STAMFORD, Fairfield Co.

CACACE, TUSCH & SANTAGATA (AV)

777 Summer Street, P.O. Box 15859, 06901-0859
Telephone: 203-327-2000
Telecopier: 203-353-3392
Email: lawcts@aol.com

MEMBERS OF FIRM

Michael J. Cacace
Mark P. Santagata
Paul T. Tusch
Richard S. Fisher

OF COUNSEL

Kenneth A. DellaRocco
Eric D. Grayson

ASSOCIATES

Edward F. Nemchek
Alice Ann Fitzpatrick
Ronald E. Kowalski II
Aamina Ahmad
Demaris Page Hetrick
Patrick L. Poeschl

LEGAL SUPPORT PERSONNEL

Eva L. Chan
Cynthia L. Mammone

For full biographical listings, see the Martindale-Hubbell Law Directory

CURTIS, BRINCKERHOFF & BARRETT, P.C. (AV)

666 Summer Street, 06901-1416
Telephone: 203-324-6777
Telecopier: 203-324-9621
Email: info@curtisbb.com

T. Ward Cleary (1916-1988)
Frederick M. Tobin
John Wayne Fox
Ward Frank Cleary
James D'Alton Murphy
Randolph T. Lovallo

OF COUNSEL

John D. Hertz
Jane F. Donovan
Richard L. Brinckerhoff
Patricia M. Gaug

Susan L. Stratton
Derek Gilman
Michael P. Murray
John J. Louizos

Counsel for: The F. A. Bartlett Tree Expert Co.; Town of Darien; Miller Automobile Corp.; Bolliger, Inc.; Titan Sports; People's Bank, Bridgeport; Fleet Bank; Federal Deposit Insurance Co.; William Pitt Foundation; Wood Logan Associates.

For full biographical listings, see the Martindale-Hubbell Law Directory

LAW OFFICES OF DONALD A. HERNER (AV)

One Landmark Square, 4th Floor, 06901
Telephone: 203-351-1020
Fax: 203-351-1029
Email: herner@erols.com *URL:* http://www.lawyers.com/donaldaherner

OF COUNSEL

Barbara J. Beghin (Not admitted in CT)

For full biographical listings, see the Martindale-Hubbell Law Directory

PHELAN & MITRI (AV)

One Atlantic Street, 06901
Telephone: 203-967-4140
Fax: 203-325-3056
Email: pmchart@pmchart.com *URL:* http://www.pmchart.com

(See Next Column)

PHELAN & MITRI—*Continued*

MEMBERS OF FIRM

William J. Phelan
Michael F. Mitri

ASSOCIATE

Edmund J. Cienava

For full biographical listings, see the Martindale-Hubbell Law Directory

WOFSEY, ROSEN, KWESKIN & KURIANSKY, LLP (AV)

600 Summer Street, 06901
Telephone: 203-327-2300
Fax: 203-967-9273

MEMBERS OF FIRM

Abraham Wofsey (1915-1944)
Michael Wofsey (1927-1951)
David M. Rosen (1926-1967)
Julius B. Kuriansky (1952-1992)
Sydney C. Kweskin (1946-1998)
Monroe Silverman
Howard C. Kaplan
Edward M. Kweskin
David M. Cohen
Marshall Goldberg
Stephen A. Finn
Judith Rosenberg
Mark H. Henderson
Steven D. Grushkin
Matthew J. Forstadt
Steven M. Frederick

OF COUNSEL

Saul Kwartin
Emanuel Margolis
Anthony R. Lorenzo

SPECIAL COUNSEL

Day R. Shields

ASSOCIATES

Joseph Brachfeld
Eric M. Higgins
William A. Harrison
Daniel M. Young
Angelo A. Ziotas

Representative Clients: Banque Paribas; Benenson Realty; Cellular Information Systems, Inc.; The Chase Manhattan Bank; First County Bank; Hartford Provision Co.; Louis Dreyfus Corp.; Norwalk Federation of Teachers; People's Bank; Ridgeway Shopping Center.

For full biographical listings, see the Martindale-Hubbell Law Directory

WESTPORT, Fairfield Co.

BERKOWITZ, TRAGER & TRAGER, LLC (AV)

253 Post Road West, P.O. Box 808, 06881
Telephone: 203-226-1001
Fax: 203-226-3801
Email: btt@bertralaw.com

Richard Berkowitz
Paul M. Berg
Samuel Febbraio, Jr.
Jay L. Goldstein
David A. Greenberg
Howard D. Komisar
Richard J. Preminger
Robert H. Rubin
Doris B. Shiller

OF COUNSEL

Philip Trager
Arthur E. Balbirer

For full biographical listings, see the Martindale-Hubbell Law Directory

DISTRICT OF COLUMBIA

WASHINGTON, D.C. Co.

CHARAPP, DEESE & WEISS, LLP (AV)

1901 Pennsylvania Avenue, N.W., Suite 1001, 20006
Telephone: 202-463-9100
Fax: 202-463-2091
Vienna, Virginia Office: 8300 Boone Boulevard, Suite 500, 22182.
Telephone 703-714-9576.
Bethesda, Maryland Office: 3 Bethesda Metro Center, Suite 700, 20814.
Telephone: 301-657-6258.
Richmond, Virginia Office: 2201 West Broad Street, Suite 201, 23220.
Telephone: 804-358-8680.
Fax: 804-358-3889.

Michael G. Charapp
C. Michael Deese
Brad D. Weiss

Sarah Daly Jackowski

OF COUNSEL

Edward H. Kim

For full biographical listings, see the Martindale-Hubbell Law Directory

THE CUNEO LAW GROUP, P.C. (AV)

317 Massachusetts Avenue, N.E. Suite 300, 20002
Telephone: 202-789-3960
Fax: 202-789-1813
Email: contact@cuneolaw.com *URL:* http://www.cuneolaw.com

(See Next Column)

Jonathan W. Cuneo
James J. Schweitzer
David W. Stanley
Michael G. Lenett

Arthur K. Park (Not admitted in DC)
Daniel Cohen (Not admitted in DC)

COUNSEL

Charles Tiefer

For full biographical listings, see the Martindale-Hubbell Law Directory

FLORIDA

*FORT LAUDERDALE,** Broward Co.

BRINKLEY, MCNERNEY, MORGAN, SOLOMON & TATUM, LLP (AV)

Suite 1800, New River Center, 200 East Las Olas Boulevard, P.O. Box 522, 33301-2209
Telephone: 954-522-2200
Facsimile: 954-522-9123
Email: lawfirm@brinkleymcnerney.com *URL:* http://www.brinkleymcnerney.com

W. Michael Brinkley
Michael J. McNerney
Philip J. Morgan
Harris K. Solomon
Thomas R. Tatum
Kenneth E. Keechl
Stephen L. Ziegler
Donald J. Lunny, Jr.
Roberta G. Stanley
Christopher M. Trapani
Kevin P. Crosby

Kenneth J. Joyce
Thomas J. Ansbro
David F. Hanley
Sean L. Wilson
Jonathan M. Streisfeld
W. Michael Brinkley, Jr.
Lindsey A. Payne
Marc K. Swickle
Kenneth A. Gordon
Juliette E. Lippman
Dawn M. Heisey
Veronica Vilarchao

OF COUNSEL

Amy R. Reeck

Approved Attorneys for: Attorneys' Title Insurance Fund; Chicago Title Insurance Co.; First American Title Insurance Co.

For full biographical listings, see the Martindale-Hubbell Law Directory

CURRAN & CURRAN (AV)

2400 East Commercial Boulevard, Suite 208, 33308
Telephone: 954-938-9922
Fax: 954-938-9923
Email: curran@compuserve.com

MEMBERS OF FIRM

Marshall G. Curran, Jr.
M. Glenn Curran, III

For full biographical listings, see the Martindale-Hubbell Law Directory

*FORT MYERS,** Lee Co.

HENDERSON, FRANKLIN, STARNES & HOLT, PROFESSIONAL ASSOCIATION (AV)

1715 Monroe Street, P.O. Box 280, 33902-0280
Telephone: 941-334-4121
Telecopier: 941-332-4494

Albert M. Frierson
Ernest H. Hatch, Jr.
Stephen L. Helgemo
Ronald W. Smalley
John A. Noland
William N. Horowitz
Gerald W. Pierce
J. Terrence Porter
Michael J. Corso
Vicki L. Sproat
Denis H. Noah
John W. Lewis
Craig Ferrante
James L. Nulman
Harold N. Hume, Jr.
Bruce M. Stanley Sr.
Daniel W. Sheppard
Russell P. Schropp
Chad J. Motes
Guy E. Whitesman
Steven G. Koeppel
Douglas B. Szabo
Charles J. Basinait
Randal H. Thomas
Robert C. Shearman
Andrew L. Ringers, Jr.
John F. Potanovic, Jr.
Thomas H. Gunderson
David K. Fowler
Paula F. Kelley
Jeffrey D. Kottkamp
J. Eric Stiffler
Thomas P. Clark
Theresa M. Kolish
Tricia A. Spivey
Cora Cisneros Molloy
Keith R. Kyle
Joseph M. Madden, Jr.
Danni Lynn Germano
Carlos A. Kelly
Elizabeth Wolt
Alane C. Laboda
Grace Gutierrez
Laurie Hannan-Anton
Neil R. Jetter

(See Next Column)

HENDERSON, FRANKLIN, STARNES & HOLT PROFESSIONAL ASSOCIATION, *Fort Myers—Continued*

Representative Clients: CIGNA Group; CSX Transportation, Inc.; Fireman's Fund Insurance Cos.; The Hartford Insurance Group; Huntington National Bank, N.A.; NationsBank, N.A.; Travelers/Aetna Insurance Group; Sprint-Florida, Inc.

For full biographical listings, see the Martindale-Hubbell Law Directory

*MIAMI,** Dade Co.

CAMNER, LIPSITZ AND POLLER, PROFESSIONAL ASSOCIATION (AV)

550 Biltmore Way, Suite 700 (Coral Gables), 33134
Telephone: 305-442-4994
Fax: 305-442-2389
URL: http://www.camner-lipsitz-poller.com

Alfred R. Camner
Marc Lipsitz
Neale J. Poller
Marsha D. Bilzin

Roger A. Preziosi
Adam Mitchell Neijna
Bridget Wong
David A. Messinger
Wendy Hill El Diery

OF COUNSEL

Anne Shari Camner
Thomas R. Blake

For full biographical listings, see the Martindale-Hubbell Law Directory

HAYDEN AND MILLIKEN, P.A. (AV)

Suite 63, 5915 Ponce de Leon Boulevard, 33146-2477
Telephone: 305-662-1523
Fax: 305-663-1358
Tampa, Florida Office: 615 De Leon Street 33606-2719.
Telephone: 813-251-1770.
Fax: 813-254-5436.
Cape Canaveral, Florida Office: 101 George King Boulevard, Suite 5, 32920,
Telephone: 407-868-0022.
Fax: 407-868-5060.

Reginald M. Hayden, Jr.
William Barry Milliken
William R. Boeringer
Timothy P. Shusta (Resident, Tampa, Florida Office)

Patrick M. Talbot

Representative Clients: Seaboard Marine, Ltd.; Tropical Shipping and Construction Co., Ltd.; Great American Insurance Co.; Marine Office of America Corp.; St. Paul Fire and Marine Insurance Co.; Britannia P & I; Newcastle P & I; Steamship Mutual; The Swedish Club.

For full biographical listings, see the Martindale-Hubbell Law Directory

HOLTZMAN, KRINZMAN, EQUELS & FURIA (AV)

2601 South Bayshore Drive, Suite 600, 33133
Telephone: 305-859-7700
Fax: 305-859-9996
Email: hkef@hkef.com *URL:* http://www.hkef.com
Orlando, Florida Office: 16 West Pine Street, 32801.
Telephone: 407-839-0095.
Fax: 407-839-2050.
Tallahassee, Florida Office: 542 East Park Avenue, 32301.
Telephone: 850-222-2900.
Fax: 850-222-2933.

Arthur J. Furia

Robert Quan Lee

For full biographical listings, see the Martindale-Hubbell Law Directory

SIEGFRIED, RIVERA, LERNER, DE LA TORRE & SOBEL, P.A. (AV)

Suite 1102, 201 Alhambra Circle (Coral Gables), 33134
Telephone: 305-442-3334
Fax: 305-443-3292
URL: http://www.siegfriedlaw.com

Steven M. Siegfried
Oscar R. Rivera
Lisa A. Lerner
Helio De La Torre
Peter H. Edwards
Stuart H. Sobel
Maria Victoria Arias
James F. Harrington
Elisabeth D. Kozlow

Gary Louis Brown
David B. Israel
Laura Michelle Manning
Fern F. Musselwhite
Grissel C. Picot
Marc C. Pugliese

OF COUNSEL

H. Hugh Mc Connell

For full biographical listings, see the Martindale-Hubbell Law Directory

PALM BEACH, Palm Beach Co.

AVIS & AVIS, P.A. (AV)

125 Worth Avenue, Suite 221, 33480
Telephone: 561-659-0200
Fax: 561-659-0942
Email: info@avislaw.com *URL:* http://www.avislaw.com

Warren E. Avis, Jr.
Deborah K. Avis

OF COUNSEL

Jill E. Kaufman
Richard D. Grow

Representative Clients: Florida Apple, Inc.; K-Rain Manufacturing Corp.; Sentry Paint Technology, Inc.; Palm Beach Precision Molding Co.; Arena Brands, Inc.; Wellington Industries, Inc.; Enterprise National Bank; Avis Enterprises; PAR Microsystems; Den-mat Corp.

For full biographical listings, see the Martindale-Hubbell Law Directory

*STUART,** Martin Co.

McCARTHY, SUMMERS, BOBKO, McKEY, WOOD & SAWYER, P.A. (AV)

2081 East Ocean Boulevard, Second Floor, 34996
Telephone: 561-286-1700
Fax: 561-283-1803
URL: http://www.mcsumm.com

Terence P. McCarthy
Robert P. Summers
Noel A. Bobko
John D. McKey, Jr.
Steven J. Wood
Thomas R. Sawyer
Nicola J. Boone
Steven L. Perry

Kathryn C. Bass
Robert N. Maitland, II

Representative Clients: First National Bank and Trust Company of the Treasure Coast; Hydratech Utilities; Lost Lake at Hobe Sound; Gary Player Design Group; YMCA of Martin County; Shadow Lakes Groves, Inc.; Merrill Lynch Trust Co., (Florida); Wilmington Trust, FSB; The Huntington National Bank, N.A.; WSTU-Radio, WTCN-TV.

For full biographical listings, see the Martindale-Hubbell Law Directory

*TALLAHASSEE,** Leon Co.

ROBERT S. HIGHTOWER (AV)

241 East Virginia Street, P.O. Box 4165, 32315-4165
Telephone: 850-222-3363
Telecopier: 850-222-0992
Email: rsh@hightowerlaw.com

Representative Clients: Apalachee Center for Human Services, Inc.; Clemons, Rutherford & Associates, Inc.; Medical Center Pharmacy, Inc. of Quincy; Prescott Supply Company, Inc.; Southern Medical Group, P.A.; Tallahassee Mack Sales, Inc.; Tallahassee Plastic Surgery Clinic; GTO, Inc.

For full biographical listings, see the Martindale-Hubbell Law Directory

*TAMPA,** Hillsborough Co.

HAYDEN AND MILLIKEN, P.A. (AV)

615 de Leon Street, 33606-2719
Telephone: 813-251-1770
Fax: 813-254-5436
Miami, Florida Office: Suite 63, 5915 Ponce de Leon Boulevard.
Telephone: 305-662-1523.
Fax: 305-663-1358.
Cape Canaveral, Florida Office: 101 George King Boulevard, Suite 5, 32920.
Telephone: 407-868-0022.
Fax: 407-868-5060.

Reginald M. Hayden, Jr.
William Barry Milliken
Timothy P. Shusta (Resident)

Matthew J. Valcourt

Representative Clients: Seaboard Marine, Ltd.; Tropical Shipping and Construction Co., Ltd.; Great American Insurance Co.; Marine Office of America Corp.; St. Paul Fire and Marine Insurance Co.; Britannia P & I; Newcastle P & I; Steamship Mutual.
Reference: Dadeland Bank.

For full biographical listings, see the Martindale-Hubbell Law Directory

KETCHEY HORAN, P.A. (AV)

100 North Tampa Street, Suite 1900, P.O. Box 500, 33601-0500
Telephone: 813-223-9395
Fax: 813-221-1348
Email: Stephanie@KetcheyHoran.com
Sun City Center, Florida Office: 1647 Sun City Center Plaza, Suite 200.
Telephone: 813-633-1200.

SHAREHOLDERS

John B. Neukamm

(See Next Column)

KETCHEY HORAN P.A.—*Continued*

ASSOCIATES

Alfred A. Colby
Christopher Charles Nash

For full biographical listings, see the Martindale-Hubbell Law Directory

VENICE, Sarasota Co.

MICHAEL D. HORLICK, P.A. (AV)

1314 E. Venice Avenue - Suite D, 34292
Telephone: 941-484-5656
Fax: 941-484-1650
Email: mhorlick@mdhpa.com *URL:* http://www.mdhpa.com

Michael D. Horlick

For full biographical listings, see the Martindale-Hubbell Law Directory

GEORGIA

*ATLANTA,** Fulton Co.

KREVOLIN & HORST, LLC (AV)

Suite 2150, 100 Colony Square, 1175 Peachtree Street, N.E., 30361
Telephone: 404-888-9700
Fax: 404-888-9577

Douglas P. Krevolin
Jeffrey D. Horst

Michael G. Regas II
Michael D. Flint

For full biographical listings, see the Martindale-Hubbell Law Directory

THOMAS E. MATTIMOE LLC (AV)

Suite 3700 • Promenade II, 1230 Peachtree Street, NE, 30309
Telephone: 404-870-9797
Fax: 404-870-9787
Email: tom@mattimoe.com

Thomas E. Mattimoe

For full biographical listings, see the Martindale-Hubbell Law Directory

*AUGUSTA,** Richmond Co.

FLETCHER, HARLEY & FLETCHER (AV)

429 Walker Street, P.O. Box 2084, 30903-2084
Telephone: 706-724-0558
Fax: 706-724-4730
URL: http://www.lawyers.com/fletcherharley&fletcher

MEMBERS OF FIRM

Leonard O. Fletcher, Jr.
C. Thompson Harley
W. Lawrence Fletcher

For full biographical listings, see the Martindale-Hubbell Law Directory

HULL, TOWILL, NORMAN, BARRETT & SALLEY, A PROFESSIONAL CORPORATION (AV)

801 Broad Street, Suite 700, 30901
Telephone: 706-722-4481
Fax: 706-722-9779
Email: hullfirm@groupz.net *URL:* http://www.groupz.net/~advocate
Aiken, South Carolina Office: 111 Park Avenue, 29801.
Telephone: 803-648-4213.
Fax: 803-648-2601.

James M. Hull (1885-1975)
George B. Barrett (1894-1942)
Julian J. Willingham (1887-1963)
John Bell Towill (1907-1991)
Robert C. Norman (Retired, 1991)
W. Hale Barrett
Lawton Jordan, Jr.
Patrick J. Rice
Douglas D. Batchelor, Jr.
David E. Hudson
William H. Tucker (Not admitted in GA)
William F. Hammond
Mark S. Burgreen
George R. Hall
James B. Ellington
F. Michael Taylor
William J. Keogh, III
Edward J. Tarver
J. Noel Schweers, III
Susan D. Barrett
Ralph Emerson Hanna, III

James M. Holly (Not admitted in GA)
Timothy E. Moses
N. Shannon Gentry Lanier
Tara R. Simkins
Charles H. Weigle
Natalie A. Dopson
David C. Smith

OF COUNSEL

Julian B. Salley, Jr. (Not admitted in GA)

Counsel for: Morris Communications Corporation; Merry Land & Investment Company, Inc.; Castleberry/Snow's Brands, Inc.; Sun Trust Bank Augusta, N.A.; Georgia Power Co.; St. Joseph Hospital, Augusta, Georgia, Inc.; Norfolk Southern Corp.; Housing Authority of the City of Augusta; Georgia Press Association; Columbia County, Georgia.

For full biographical listings, see the Martindale-Hubbell Law Directory

J. BENJAMIN KAY, III (AV)

808 First Union Bank Building, 30901
Telephone: 706-722-2008

Approved Attorney for: Lawyers Title Insurance Corp.
Reference: First Union National Bank of Georgia.
Representative Clients: American National Bank & Trust Company; Biotech Park, Inc.; Caterpillar Financial Services, Inc.; Davis-McGraw, Inc.; Ford Leasing Development Company; Ford Motor Credit Company; Gary Concrete Products, Inc.; Globe Life Insurance Company.

For full biographical listings, see the Martindale-Hubbell Law Directory

*GAINESVILLE,** Hall Co.

SMITH, GILLIAM AND WILLIAMS (AV)

200 Old Coca-Cola Building, 301 Green Street, N.W., P.O. Box 1098, 30503
Telephone: 770-536-3381
Fax: 770-531-1481
Email: SGWFirm@Applied.net

MEMBERS OF FIRM

R. Wilson Smith, Jr. (1906-1983)
John H. Smith
Steven P. Gilliam
Jerry A. Williams
Kelly Anne Miles
Bradley J. Patten
M. Tyler Smith

ASSOCIATE

Robert A. Weber, Jr.

General Counsel for: Gainesville Industrial Electric Co.; Georgia Mutual Insurance, a Stock Company; L & R Farms; H. Wilson Manufacturing Co.; Goforth Electrical Supply; North Georgia Petroleum Co.; Gibbs Management Group, Inc.

For full biographical listings, see the Martindale-Hubbell Law Directory

*JONESBORO,** Clayton Co.

GLAZE & GLAZE, P.C. (AV)

120 North McDonough Street, 30236
Telephone: 770-478-5555
Fax: 770-478-4555
Email: glaze@mindspring.com
Stockbridge, Georgia, 205A Corporate Center Drive, 30281. Telephone: 770-474-3347.

George E. Glaze
Kirby A. Glaze

Joe M. Harris, Jr.

For full biographical listings, see the Martindale-Hubbell Law Directory

NORCROSS, Gwinnett Co.

DEMING, PARKER, HOFFMAN, GREEN & CAMPBELL, P.C. (AV)

4851 Jimmy Carter Boulevard, 30093
Telephone: 770-564-2600
Fax: 770-564-2267
Covington, Georgia Office: Suite 11, 3236 Highway 278.
Telephone: 770-787-2600.
Fax: 770-564-2267.
Cumming, Georgia Office: 425 Tribble Gap Road, Suite 398, 30130.
Telephone: 770-889-2600.
Fax: 770-564-2267.

Michael D. Deming
Franklin E. Parker
Paul M. Hoffman
Jim R. Green, Jr.
Richard A. Campbell
Stephen R. Williams

OF COUNSEL

Robert E. Born
Richard K. Valldejuli, Jr.
Robert M.N. Shaker

Mark L. Wells
Christopher W. T. Daly
E. Nicole Harrison
Suzanne M. Boykin
Jeffrey C. Renz
David Black
Robert A. Leonard
Joan S. Pepe
Nadiyah Muhammad

For full biographical listings, see the Martindale-Hubbell Law Directory

WARNER ROBINS, Houston Co.

ROY N. COWART, P.C. (AV)

233 N. Houston Road Houston Mall Suite 114, P.O. Box 818, 31093
Telephone: 912-922-8515
Fax: 912-922-3184
Email: cowartpc@aol.com

(See Next Column)

ROY N. COWART, P.C., *Warner Robins—Continued*

Roy N. Cowart

Representative Clients: Shaheen Office Supply, Inc.; Maria H. Bartlett, M.D.; Surgical Associates, P.C.; Golden Key Realty, Inc.; Houston County Associates for Exceptional Children.

For full biographical listings, see the Martindale-Hubbell Law Directory

HAWAII

HONOLULU,* Honolulu Co.

CARLSMITH BALL (AV)

A Partnership including Law Corporations
Suite 2200, Pacific Tower, 1001 Bishop Street, P.O. Box 656, 96809-3402
Telephone: 808-523-2500
Fax: 808-523-0842
Email: execdirector@carlsmith.com *URL:* http://www.carlsmith.com
Kapolei, Hawaii Office: Suite 318, Kapolei Building, 1001 Kamokila Boulevard, 96707.
Telephone: 808-523-2500.
Fax: 808-674-0850.
Wailuku, Maui Hawaii Office: Suite 400, One Main Plaza, 2200 Main Street, P.O. Box 1086, 96793-1086.
Telephone: 808-242-4535.
Fax: 808-244-4974.
Kailua-Kona, Hawaii Office: Suite 209, 75-1000 Henry Street, 96740.
Telephone: 808-329-6464.
Fax: 808-329-9450.
Hilo, Hawaii Office: 121 Waianuenue Avenue, P.O. Box 686, 96721-0686.
Telephone: 808-935-6644.
Fax: 808-935-7975.
Hagatna, Guam Office: Suite 401, Bank of Hawaii Building, 134 West Soledad Avenue, P.O. Box BF, 96932-5027.
Telephone: 671-472-6813.
Fax: 671-477-4375.
Telex: 721-6445 CWCMI GM.
Saipan, Commonwealth of the Northern Mariana Islands Office: Carlsmith Building, Capitol Hill, P.O. Box 5241, 96950-5241.
Telephone: 670-322-3455.
Fax: 670-322-3368.
Los Angeles, California Office: 9th Floor, 444 South Flower Street, 90071-2901.
Telephone: 213-955-1200.
Fax: 213-623-0032.
Washington, D.C. Office: Suite 300, 1201 Pennsylvania Avenue, N.W., 20004-2401.
Telephone: 202-628-2228.
Fax: 202-628-2071.
Mexico City, Mexico Office: Carlsmith Ball, Sierra Nevada 119, Lomas de Chapultepec, 11000 Mexico, D.F.
Telephone: 52-5-520-8514, 52-5-520-8757.
Fax: 52-5-540-1545.
Mexico, D.F. Office of Carlsmith Ball, S.C. (Authorized to practice as foreign legal consultants in Mexico): Sierra Nevada 119, Lomas de Chapultepec, 11000 Mexico, D.F.
Telephone: 52-5-520-8514, 52-5-520-8757.
Fax: 52-5-540-1545.

MEMBERS OF FIRM

James H. Case (A Law Corporation)
Steven M. Egesdal
Paul Mullin Ganley (A Law Corporation)
Karl K. Kobayashi
Tim Lui-Kwan
Dean H. Robb
Lance F. Taniguchi

ASSOCIATE

Brent K. Yamashita

For Complete List of Firm Personnel, See General Section

For full biographical listings, see the Martindale-Hubbell Law Directory

TAM, O'CONNOR, HENDERSON, TAIRA & YAMAUCHI ATTORNEYS AT LAW, A LAW CORPORATION (AV)

20th Floor, Central Pacific Plaza, 220 South King Street, 96813
Telephone: 808-545-3030
Fax: 808-523-8051
Fax: 808-537-6782
Email: lawyers@50thstatelaw.com

James K. Tam
Michael F. O'Connor
Harvey E. Henderson, Jr.
Lissa H. Andrews
Robert M. Yamauchi
Darryl M. Taira
Stuart M. Kodish

Wesley H. Ikeda
Russ S. Awakuni
Kevin W. Herring
Fred I. Waki

(See Next Column)

OF COUNSEL

Paul M. Dold

For full biographical listings, see the Martindale-Hubbell Law Directory

ILLINOIS

CHICAGO,* Cook Co.

ARONBERG GOLDGEHN DAVIS & GARMISA (AV)

Suite 3000 One IBM Plaza, 60611
Telephone: 312-828-9600
Telecopier: 312-828-9635
Email: agdglaw@aol.com
Schaumberg, Illinois Office: 1901 North Roselle Road, Suite 800, 60195.
Telephone: 847-985-4060.

MEMBERS OF FIRM

William J. Garmisa
James S. Jarvis
Mitchell J. Melamed
Marc W. O'Brien
Ned S. Robertson
David H. Sachs
Robert N. Sodikoff
Andrew S. Williams

OF COUNSEL

Ronald J. Aronberg
Melvin A. Blum
Steven P. Davis
Steven H. Nemerovski
Charles E. Zeitlin

ASSOCIATES

Lisa J. Brodsky
Eric M. Brown
Mary Vidal Hays

For Complete List of Firm Personnel, See General Section

For full biographical listings, see the Martindale-Hubbell Law Directory

BLATT, HAMMESFAHR & EATON (AV)

333 W. Wacker Drive, Suite 1900, 60606
Telephone: 312-849-8000
FAX: 312-357-0198
Email: BHE@BHELAW.COM *URL:* HTTP://WWW.BHELAW.COM
New York, New York Office: 45 Broadway, 12th Floor.
Telephone: 212-363-1900.
Fax: 212-363-2600. Email: bhe@bhelaw.com.

MEMBERS OF FIRM

Richard L. Blatt
Larry R. Eaton

For full biographical listings, see the Martindale-Hubbell Law Directory

LAWRENCE, KAMIN, SAUNDERS & UHLENHOP (AV)

208 South La Salle Street, Suite 1750, 60604-1188
Telephone: 312-372-1947
Telecopier: 312-372-2389
Email: LKSU@LKSU.com

MEMBERS OF FIRM

Raymond E. Saunders
Paul B. Uhlenhop
Kent Lawrence
Kenneth S. Perlman
David E. Muschler
Charles J. Risch
Lawrence A. Rosen
Michael Wise
David L. Reich

ASSOCIATES

Peter E. Cooper
John S. Monical
Paul M. Weltlich

For full biographical listings, see the Martindale-Hubbell Law Directory

NISEN & ELLIOTT (AV)

200 West Adams Street, Suite 2500, 60606
Telephone: 312-346-7800
Telecopier: 312-346-9316

MEMBERS OF FIRM

Paul F. Gerbosi
Edward B. Mueller
Anthony Packard
Mark F. Zaenger
Michael J. Daley
John Foster Lesch
John K. Kneafsey
Michael H. Moirano
Robert O. Middleton
William G. Daluga, Jr.
Kenneth J. Rojc
Thomas V. McCauley
Helen M. Jensen
William A. Walker
Daniel P. Dawson
Michael J. Pavlicek

Robert Christie
Donald F. Froehlke
Thomas K. Juffernbruch
Brendan J. Kelly
Brian C. Kelly
Mary Rose C. Manczak
Bradley S. McCann
Brian D. Proctor

OF COUNSEL

Charles M. Nisen
Donald C. Shine

For full biographical listings, see the Martindale-Hubbell Law Directory

New Orleans—Continued

TARCZA & GELDERMAN, L.L.C. (AV)

Thirteen Ten Whitney Building, Two Twenty Eight St. Charles Avenue, 70130
Telephone: 504-525-6696
Fax: 504-525-6701

Robert E. Tarcza
G. Anthony Gelderman, III

ASSOCIATE

Juliet Puissegur Bland

For full biographical listings, see the Martindale-Hubbell Law Directory

TERRIBERRY, CARROLL & YANCEY, L.L.P. (AV)

3100 Energy Centre, 1100 Poydras Street, 70163-3100
Telephone: 504-523-6451
Cable Address: "Terrib"
Telex: 6821224 (WUI)
Fax: 504-524-3257
Email: info@terriberry.com

Benjamin W. Yancey (1906-1991)
Walter Carroll, Jr. (Retired)

MEMBERS OF FIRM

G. Edward Merritt
John A. Bolles
Charles F. Lozes
Robert J. Barbier
Hugh Ramsay Straub
David B. Lawton
Janet Wessler Marshall
D. Kirk Boswell
Gary A. Hemphill
Laurence R. De Buys, IV
Kevin J. LaVie
Stephen E. Mattesky
Gerald M. Baca
Michael M. Butterworth
John A. Scialdone

COUNSEL

Andrew T. Martinez
Cynthia Anne Wegmann

ASSOCIATES

Evans Martin Mcleod
Kenneth J. Gelpi, Jr.

OF COUNSEL

James L. Schupp, Jr.

Representative Clients: Assuranceforeningen Gard; Assuranceforeningen Skuld; The Britannia Club; Certain Underwriters at Lloyd's; The London Steam-Ship Owners' Mutual Insurance Assn. Ltd.; New Orleans Steamship Assn.; Nordisk Skibsrederforening (Northern Shipowners Defence Club); Scandinavian Marine Claims Office, Inc.; Steamship Mutual Underwriting Assn. Ltd.; United Kingdom Mutual Steam Ship Assurance Assn. Ltd.

For full biographical listings, see the Martindale-Hubbell Law Directory

MAINE

*BANGOR,** Penobscot Co.

GROSS, MINSKY, MOGUL & SINGAL, P.A. (AV)

Key Plaza, 23 Water Street, P.O. Box 917, 04402-0917
Telephone: 207-942-4644; 800-274-7124
Telecopier: 207-942-3699
Email: law@gmms.com

Edward I. Gross (1912-1999)
Jules L. Mogul (1930-1994)
George Z. Singal
Louis H. Kornreich
George C. Schelling
Edward W. Gould
Steven J. Mogul
James R. Wholly
Daniel A. Pileggi
Philip K. Clarke

Wayne P. Libhart (Retired)
Sandra L. Rothera
James S. Nixon

OF COUNSEL

Norman Minsky

Representative Client: Dahl Chase Pathology Associates.
Local Counsel for: The St. Paul Insurance Cos.; Aetna Life & Casualty Co.; Imperial Casualty & Indemnity Co.

For full biographical listings, see the Martindale-Hubbell Law Directory

BAR HARBOR, Hancock Co.

FENTON, CHAPMAN, FENTON, SMITH & KANE, P.A. (AV)

109 Main Street, P.O. Box B, 04609
Telephone: 207-288-3331
Fax: 207-288-9326
Email: fentonlawfirm@acadia.net *URL:* http://www.lawyers.com/fcfs&klaw

William Fenton
Douglas B. Chapman
Nathaniel R. Fenton
Chadbourn H. Smith
Daniel H. Kane (1940-1995)
Hancock Griffin, Jr. (1912-1980)

(See Next Column)

Margaret T. Jeffery

Reference: Bar Harbor Banking and Trust Co.

For full biographical listings, see the Martindale-Hubbell Law Directory

MARYLAND

*BALTIMORE,** (Independent City)

LAW OFFICE OF EDWARD L. BLANTON, JR., P.A. (AV)

404 Allegheny Avenue, 21204
Telephone: 410-296-8160
Fax: 410-821-8113

Peter T. McDowell

Representative Clients: Mortage Credit Reports, Inc.; G&L Drywall Inc.; Eco-Science Professionals, Inc.; National Campers & Hikers, Inc.; Paragon Management Systems, Inc.; Har-Tech Corp.
Reference: Mercantile-Safr Deposit & Trust Co.

For full biographical listings, see the Martindale-Hubbell Law Directory

GALLAGHER, EVELIUS & JONES, LLP (AV)

Park Charles Suite 400, 218 North Charles Street, 21201
Telephone: 410-727-7702
Facsimile: 410-468-2786
URL: http://www.gejlaw.com

MEMBERS OF FIRM

Francis X. Gallagher (1928-1972)
C. Edward Jones (1908-1999)
John C. Evelius (Retired)
Richard O. Berndt
Thomas N. Biddison, Jr.
Robert R. Kern, Jr.
Saul E. Gilstein
Thomas B. Lewis
Bonnie Abrams Travieso
Stephen A. Goldberg
Linda H. Jones
Jack C. Tranter
Leslie B. Speed
Christopher J. Fritz
David E. Raderman
Peter E. Keith
Nita L. Schultz
Michael W. Skojec
Kathryn Kelley Hoskins
Mark P. Keener
Kevin J. Davidson
Eileen M. Lunga
Lori A. Nicolle
Kenneth S. Gross
Thomas C. Dame

ASSOCIATES

Valarie K. Oulds
Margaret Stevens Jacks
Matthew W. Oakey
Rebecca A. Weaver
Michael J. Henigan
David W. Kinkopf
Paul S. Caiola
Jason W. Gaarder
M. Kirsten Andrews

LEGAL ASSISTANTS

Patricia C. Quayle
Iris T. H. Heath
Connie L. Ennis
Margaret Graff
Margo Gibson Hughes
Jonathan T. Gillis
Brenda J. Heacock
Dwayne L. Rodeheaver

Representative Clients: Roman Catholic Archdiocese of Baltimore; The Shelter Group; Mercy Medical Center, Inc.; Alban Tractor Company.

For full biographical listings, see the Martindale-Hubbell Law Directory

THOMAS & LIBOWITZ, P.A. (AV)

100 Light Street, Suite 1100, 21202-1053
Telephone: 410-752-2468
Fax: 410-752-2046; 752-2049; 752-0979
Email: thomasandlibowitz.com *URL:* http://www.thomasandlibowitz.com

Steven Anargyros Thomas
Clinton R. Black, IV
C. Wayne Davis
Peter W. Taliaferro
James E. Myers
Charles B. Jones

OF COUNSEL

Basil A. Thomas
Susan M. Rittenhouse

LEGAL SUPPORT PERSONNEL

PARALEGALS

Melissa A. Johnson
Kelley Atkins
Kimberly Beard
Donna Janney

Representative Clients: Sinclair Broadcast Group, Inc. (Television and Radio stations); Roy Kirby & Sons, Inc. (Contractor); First Mariner Bank; Scandia Manufacturing Co. Inc. (Defense Contractor); Atlantic Automotive Corp. t/a Heritgage Automotive Group; Candy Express Franchising, Inc.; Wire Spectrum Services (Contractors-Transmission Tower Sites); Acrodyne Communications, Inc.; Alexis Logic Corporation (Software Developers); Selnic Corporation (Electronis Distributors); Liberty Mutual Insurance Company.

For full biographical listings, see the Martindale-Hubbell Law Directory

Louisville—Continued

Pedley Zielke Gordinier Olt & Pence, PLLC (AV)

1150 Starks Building, 455 South Fourth Avenue, 40202
Telephone: 502-589-4600
Fax: 502-584-0422
Email: pzgop@undial.com

MEMBERS OF FIRM

Lawrence L. Pedley
Laurence J. Zielke
John K. Gordinier
Joseph M. Whittle
William W. Stodghill
Stephen B. Pence
Ronald L. Gaffney
John H. Dwyer, Jr.
Ilam E. Smith

OF COUNSEL

Schuyler J. Olt
Linda Shearer Speed

Caroline George Meena
Randal K. Perkins
Michael D. Ekman
Benjamin S. Schecter
Robert Bruce Bonar
Janice M. Theriot

For full biographical listings, see the Martindale-Hubbell Law Directory

LOUISIANA

*BATON ROUGE,** East Baton Rouge Parish

Powers & Willard, L.L.P. (AV)

7967 Office Park Boulevard, P.O. Box 15948, 70895
Telephone: 225-928-1951
Fax: 225-929-9834

MEMBERS OF FIRM

John Dale Powers
William E. Willard

ASSOCIATES

Neil H. Mixon
Lindsey J. Leavoy
Edwin L. Hightower
Andrew P. Sellers, Jr.
Suzanne K. Sasser
Kyle C. Marionneaux

General Counsel for: Audubon Insurance Co.
Louisiana Counsel for: Hancock Bank & Trust Co.; Hertz Corp.; Ciba-Geigy Corp.; Utica Mutual Insurance Co.

For full biographical listings, see the Martindale-Hubbell Law Directory

*COVINGTON,** St. Tammany Parish

Law Offices of William J. Dutel (AV)

325 North New Hampshire Street, 70433
Telephone: 504-892-6474
Fax: 504-892-7307
Email: bdutel@fastband.com
New Orleans, Louisiana Office: 2960 Energy Centre, 1100 Poydras Street.
Telephone: 504-582-2429.

William J. Dutel

OF COUNSEL

Kimberly Kammler Dutel

For full biographical listings, see the Martindale-Hubbell Law Directory

METAIRIE, Jefferson Parish

Henican, James & Cleveland (AV)

Suite 1200 Heritage Plaza, 111 Veterans Memorial Boulevard, 70005
Telephone: 504-837-8080
Facsimile: 504-833-0863
Mailing Address: P.O. Box 19300, New Orleans, Louisiana, 70179

MEMBERS OF FIRM

C. Ellis Henican (1905-1997)
Murray F. Cleveland (1913-1971)
Philip E. James, Jr.
Marshall G. Weaver
Edward N. George, III
Shawn M. Bridgewater

ASSOCIATES

Keith M. Benit
Jacob S. Capraro
David M. Packard

OF COUNSEL

Philip E. James
Louis V. Rand, II

Representative Clients: Better Business Bureau of New Orleans, Inc.; St. Paul Fire and Marine Insurance Co.; Stewart Enterprises, Inc.
Reference: Hibernia National Bank, New Orleans.

For full biographical listings, see the Martindale-Hubbell Law Directory

*NEW ORLEANS,** Orleans Parish

Correro Fishman Haygood Phelps Walmsley & Casteix, L.L.P. (AV)

Bank One Center, 46th Floor, 201 St. Charles Avenue, 70170-4600
Telephone: 504-586-5252
Fax: 504-586-5250

Anthony J. Correro, III
Louis Y. Fishman
Paul M. Haygood
Robert M. Walmsley, Jr.

Caroline B. Blitzer
Lloyd L. Drury, III

For full biographical listings, see the Martindale-Hubbell Law Directory

Lowe, Stein, Hoffman, Allweiss & Hauver, L.L.P. (AV)

One Shell Square, 701 Poydras Street Suite 3600, 70139-7735
Telephone: 504-581-2450
Telecopier: 504-581-2461

MEMBER OF FIRM

Mark S. Stein

Charlton D. Hunley
Barbara H. Weiss

For Complete List of Firm Personnel, See General Section

For full biographical listings, see the Martindale-Hubbell Law Directory

McGlinchey Stafford (AV)

A Professional Limited Liability Company
643 Magazine Street, 70130-3477
Telephone: 504-586-1200
Fax: 504-596-2800
TDD: (504) 596-2728
Telex: 584327
Cable Address: "MACSTAC"
Mailing Address: P.O. Box 60643, New Orleans, Louisiana, 70160-0643
Email: @mcglinchey.com *URL:* http://www.mcglinchey.com
Dallas, Texas Office: 2777 Stemmons Freeway, Suite 925, 75207-2401.
Telephone: 214-860-9700.
Fax: 214-860-9750.
Houston, Texas Office: 2727 Allen Parkway, Suite 1900, 77019.
Telephone: 713-520-1900.
Fax: 713-520-1025.
Baton Rouge, Louisiana Office: Ninth Floor, One American Place, 70825-0001.
Telephone: 504-383-9000.
Fax: 504-343-3076.
Jackson, Mississippi Office: Suite 1200, SkyTel Centre, 200 South Lamar Street, 39201.
Telephone: 601-960-8400.
Fax: 601-960-8406.
Lake Providence, Louisiana Office: 405 Morgan Street, 71254-2691.
Telephone: 318-559-1200.
Fax: 318-559-0609.
Monroe, Louisiana Office: Dean ONB Tower, 130 Desiard Street, Suite 807, 71201.
Telephone: 318-651-0807.
Fax: 318-651-0809.

MEMBERS OF FIRM

James M. Fantaci
Craig Lewis Caesar

ASSOCIATE

Jaye Andras Caffrey

MEMBERS OF FIRM

William S. Mendenhall (Resident, Jackson Office)
Stephen C. Edds (Resident, Jackson Office)
Richard A. Fogel (Resident, Dallas Office)

ASSOCIATES

Amy Kebert Elder (Resident, Jackson Office)
Claude B. Anello (Resident, Houston Office)
D. Jeffrey Wagner

For full biographical listings, see the Martindale-Hubbell Law Directory

Mouledoux, Bland, Legrand & Brackett, LLC (AV)

Poydras Center, 650 Poydras Street, Suite 2150, 70130
Telephone: 504-595-3000
Fax: 504-522-2121
Email: admin@mblb.com *URL:* http://www.mblb.com

André J. Mouledoux
Georges M. Legrand
Alan Guy Brackett
David M. Flotte

For full biographical listings, see the Martindale-Hubbell Law Directory

*ROCKVILLE,** Montgomery Co.

STEIN, SPERLING, BENNETT, DE JONG, DRISCOLL, GREENFEIG & METRO, P.C. (AV)

25 West Middle Lane, 20850-2204
Telephone: 301-340-2020; 800-435-5230
Telecopier: 301-340-8217
Email: lawfirm@steinsperling.com
Falls Church, Virginia Office: 6245 Leesburg Pike, Suite 140, 22044.
Telephone: 703-237-0500.
Telecopier: 703-534-2899.

Fred A. Balkin
Millard S. Bennett
David S. De Jong
David C. Driscoll, Jr.
Stuart S. Greenfeig
Ann G. Jakabcin
A. Howard Metro
Jeffrey M. Schwaber
Donald N. Sperling
Paul T. Stein

Jeffrey D. Goldstein
Jolie S. Deutschman
Karen Plave Goldstein
David W. Lease
Edward D. McGuire, Jr.
William J. Scott
Darcy A. Shoop
Marc J. Smith
Joseph D. Grandinetti, Jr. (Not admitted in MD)
Debra Sue Grimes

OF COUNSEL

Alan S. Kerxton

For full biographical listings, see the Martindale-Hubbell Law Directory

SILVER SPRING, Montgomery Co.

JONATHAN M. GENN (AV)

11900 Tech Road, 20904-1910
Telephone: 301-622-0100
Fax: 301-622-3507

For full biographical listings, see the Martindale-Hubbell Law Directory

MASSACHUSETTS

*BOSTON,** Suffolk Co.

BURNS & LEVINSON LLP (AV)

125 Summer Street, 02110-1624
Telephone: 617-345-3000
Telecopier: 617-345-3299
URL: http://www.burnslevinson.com
Hingham, Massachusetts Office: 175 Derby Street.
Telephone: 781-749-3810.
Telecopier: 781-749-3980.
Wellesley, Massachusetts Office: 60 Walnut Street.
Telephone: 781-235-1034.
Telecopier: 781-235-5975.

Raymond E. Baxter
Michael H. Goshko
Evelyn A. Haralampu
Mark J. Levinson
Steven J. Marullo
Howard D. Medwed
Robert C. Rives, Jr.
Frank A. Segall
Norman C. Spector
George N. Tobia, Jr.
Josef B. Volman

ASSOCIATES

Joseph Alexander, Jr.
Ann Connell Fox

For Complete List of Firm Personnel, See General Section

For full biographical listings, see the Martindale-Hubbell Law Directory

HINGHAM, Plymouth Co.

GILLIS & ANGLEY (AV)

Suite 227, 160 Old Derby Street, 02043
Telephone: 781-749-2432
Telecopier: 781-740-0768
Email: galaw@ici.net

MEMBERS OF FIRM

Ralph J. Gillis
Edward T. Angley

ASSOCIATE

Philip H. Barthel

For full biographical listings, see the Martindale-Hubbell Law Directory

HOLYOKE, Hampden Co.

LYON, FERRITER & FITZPATRICK, LLP (AV)

Whitney Place, 14 Bobala Road, 01040
Telephone: 413-536-4000
Fax: 413-536-3773
Email: lyonferr@aol.com

MEMBERS OF FIRM

Maurice J. Ferriter
Clarke S. Lyon
William D. Fitzpatrick
James F. Donnelly
Peter C. Connor
John J. Ferriter
Priscilla Fifield Chesky
Robert C. Sacco

ASSOCIATE

Robyn Andrea Porter

OF COUNSEL

William E. Begley

Representative Clients: Mount Holyoke College; Newspapers of New England, Inc.; Loomis House Retirement Community; Atlas Copco Compressors Inc.; Hazen Paper Company.

For full biographical listings, see the Martindale-Hubbell Law Directory

WELLESLEY, Norfolk Co.

WHITE & MCDERMOTT, P.C. (AV)

65 William Street, 02481
Telephone: 781-431-1700
Fax: 781-237-8120
Email: mail@WhiteMcD.com

David A. White
Scott F. McDermott
Sharon Goddard White
John L. Koenig

John J. McCarthy, Jr.
Kathleen Gregg
Sarah C. Wickham

For full biographical listings, see the Martindale-Hubbell Law Directory

MICHIGAN

*ANN ARBOR,** Washtenaw Co.

HOOPER, HATHAWAY, PRICE, BEUCHE & WALLACE (AV)

126 South Main Street, 48104
Telephone: 313-662-4426
Fax: 313-662-9559
Email: hhpbw@voyager.net

Charles W. Borgsdorf
Kurtis R. Dumaw

Representative Clients: Avfuel Corporation; Bank of Ann Arbor; Castrol North America; Chem-Trend Incorporated; Ervin Industries, Inc.; First Martin Corporation; Glacier Hills, Inc.; Prestolite Electric, Inc.; Southern States Cooperative; E.B. Eddy Forest Products, Ltd.

For Complete List of Firm Personnel, See General Section

For full biographical listings, see the Martindale-Hubbell Law Directory

PEAR SPERLING EGGAN & MUSKOVITZ, P.C. (AV)

Domino's Farms, 24 Frank Lloyd Wright Drive, 48105
Telephone: 734-665-4441
Fax: 734-665-8788
Email: peare@dominos.com
Ypsilanti, Michigan Offices: 5 South Washington Street.
Telephone: 734-483-3626 and 2164 Bellevue at Washtenaw.
Telephone: 734-483-7177.

Edwin L. Pear
Lawrence W. Sperling
Andrew M. Eggan
Melvin J. Muskovitz
Thomas E. Daniels
Joel F. Graziani
Paul R. Fransway
Francyne Stacey
Karl V. Fink
Scott H. Mandel
David E. Kempner
Jeffrey P. Thennisch

Counsel for: Domino's Pizza, Inc.; Townsend and Bottum, Inc.; Cleary College; Victory Lane Quick Oil Change Inc.; Citizens Banking Corp.; Washtenaw News Co., Inc.; Ann Arbor Transportation Authority; Meadowbrook Insurance Group; Michigan Municipal Liability & Property Pool.
Approved Attorneys for: Lawyers Title Insurance Corp.

For full biographical listings, see the Martindale-Hubbell Law Directory

BATTLE CREEK, Calhoun Co.

KREIS, ENDERLE, CALLANDER & HUDGINS, A PROFESSIONAL CORPORATION (AV)

One West Michigan Avenue, 49017
Telephone: 616-966-3000
Facsimile: 616-966-3022
Email: kech@kech.com *URL:* http://www.kech.com
Kalamazoo, Michigan Office: One Moorsbridge, P.O. Box 4010, 49003-4010.
Telephone: 616-324-3000.
Fax: 616-324-3010.

Russell A. Kreis (Resident, Kalamazoo Office)
Douglas L. Callander (Resident, Kalamazoo Office)
C. Reid Hudgins III (Resident, Kalamazoo Office)
Robert B. Borsos (Resident, Kalamazoo Office)
Jeffrey C. O'Brien (Resident, Kalamazoo Office)
Stephen J. Hessen (Resident, Kalamazoo Office)
Jeffery S. Rubel (Resident, Kalamazoo Office)
Thomas G. King (Resident, Kalamazoo Office)
Daniel P. McGlinn (Resident, Kalamazoo Office)
Raymond C. Schultz (Resident, Kalamazoo Office)
Jeffrey D. Swenarton (Resident, Kalamazoo Office)
James C. Boerigter (Resident, Kalamazoo Office)
John F. Koryto (Resident, Kalamazoo Office)
Janice Roark Peters (Resident, Kalamazoo Office)
Matthew S. DePerno (Resident, Kalamazoo Office)
Annette D. Nickel (Resident, Kalamazoo Office)
Peter F. Davis (Resident, Kalamazoo Office)
Manuel R. Rupe (Resident, Kalamazoo Office)

For Complete List of Firm Personnel, See General Section

For full biographical listings, see the Martindale-Hubbell Law Directory

BIRMINGHAM, Oakland Co.

HYMAN LIPPITT, P.C. (AV)

185 Oakland Avenue, Suite 300, 48009
Telephone: 248-646-8292
Facsimile: 248-646-8375
Email: hymalipp@tir.com

J. Leonard Hyman
Norman L. Lippitt
Douglas A. Hyman
Brian D. O'Keefe
H. Joel Newman
Nazli G. Sater
Kenneth F. Neuman
Terry S. Givens
Paul J. Fischer
John A. Sellers
Robert H. Lippitt
Roger L. Myers
Sally A. Rutledge
Joseph Pia
John P. Gonway
Leif K. Anderson
Jennifer S. Gold
Julie Lyons Kosovec
Dawn S. Spratley
Michael T. Price

For full biographical listings, see the Martindale-Hubbell Law Directory

BLOOMFIELD HILLS, Oakland Co.

ADKISON, NEED, GREEN & ALLEN (AV)

1533 North Woodward Avenue, Suite 210, 48304
Telephone: 248-540-7400
Fax: 248-540-7401
URL: http://www.adkisonneed.com

MEMBERS OF FIRM

Phillip G. Adkison
Gregory K. Need
Paul Green
Kelly A. Allen

ASSOCIATES

Annette J. Benson
Kevin M. Chudler
Richard D. Kuhn, Jr.

OF COUNSEL

John M. Fuleras
Thomas R. Curran, Jr.

For Complete List of Firm Personnel, See General Section

For full biographical listings, see the Martindale-Hubbell Law Directory

BEIER HOWLETT, PROFESSIONAL CORPORATION (AV)

200 East Long Lake Road, Suite 110, 48304-2361
Telephone: 248-645-9400
Fax: 248-645-9344
URL: http://www.beierhowlett.com

James L. Howlett
Daniel C. Devine
Lawrence R. Ternan
Stephen W. Jones
Frank S. Galgan
Kenneth J. Sorensen
Thomas J. Trenta
Mark W. Hafeli
Timothy J. Currier
Mary T. Schmitt Smith
Joseph F. Yamin
John D. Staran
Phyllis Aiuto Zimmerman
P. Daniel Christ
Lauren M. Underwood

(See Next Column)

Elizabeth A. Barrett Bonner
Mary M. Kucharek
Richard A. Joslin, Jr.
Michael C. Gibbons
Jon M. Midtgard
Paul L. Nystrom
Genevieve Dwaihy Hopkins
Jeffrey S. Kragt

OF COUNSEL

Dean G. Beier
Robert G. Waddell
Catherine J. Hulbert
Thomas V. Trainer

Representative Clients: Met Path of Michigan; American International Airways, Inc.; Caratron Industries, Inc.; Capricorn Capitol Group, Inc.; U.S. Farathane Corporation; Continental Wood Preservers; Four Star Transporatation, Inc.; Maxitrol Company; Interlink Computer Science, Inc.; The Oakland Press.

For full biographical listings, see the Martindale-Hubbell Law Directory

DAWDA, MANN, MULCAHY & SADLER, P.L.C. (AV)

1533 North Woodward Avenue Suite 200, 48304-2815
Telephone: 248-642-3700
Fax: 248-642-7791
Email: EMail@DMMS.Com

Michael D. Mulcahy
Edward C. Dawda
Curtis J. Mann
Paul A. Bringer
Glenn G. Ross
William L. Rosin
Todd A. Schafer

Daniel M. Halprin
Paul C. Apap
Daniel M. Israel
Wayne S. Segal
Nicole S. Leveque
Vincent J. Wilk
Richard S. Bailey

OF COUNSEL

Sidney W. Smith, Jr.

Representative Clients: AEGON USA Realty Advisors, Inc.; BASF Corp.; Cardell Corp.; DSP Technology, Inc.; Ford Motor Company; Home Depot U.S.A., Inc.; Ladbroke Racing Corp.; The Sherwin-Williams Company; Trammell Crow Company; Wal-Mart Stores, Inc.

For full biographical listings, see the Martindale-Hubbell Law Directory

HARDIG PARSONS PEDERSEN & STOUT, PLLC (AV)

74 West Long Lake Road, Suite 203, 48304
Telephone: 248-642-3500
Facsimile: 248-645-1128
URL: http://www.hpplaw.com
Charlevoix, Michigan Office: 212 Bridge Street. 49720.
Telephone: 616-547-1200.
Pawleys Island, South Caroline Office: 216 Highway 17. P.O. Box 1607. 29585.
Telephone: 803-237-9121.
West Palm Beach, Florida Office: 1450 North Bridge Tower. 515 North Flagler. 33401.
Telephone: 561-833-1622.

MEMBERS OF FIRM

Joseph L. Hardig, Jr.
Donald H. Parsons (Resident, Charlevoix Office)
Joseph L. Hardig, III
Edward C. Pedersen
Bradley S. Stout
John C. Benso (Not admitted in MI; Resident, Pawleys Island, South Carolina Office)

OF COUNSEL

John W. Henke
Patrick T. Barone
Gordon A. Snavely
Robert J. Cucco
Edward K. Pedersen, Jr.

For full biographical listings, see the Martindale-Hubbell Law Directory

*DETROIT,** Wayne Co.

BOOTHMAN, HEBERT & ELLER, P.C. (AV)

Marquette Building, 243 West Congress, Suite 950, 48226
Telephone: 313-964-0150
Fax: 313-964-2226
Email: boothman@mail.mich.com

Dale L. Hebert
Richard C. Boothman
Gary S. Eller

Edward C. Reynolds, Jr.
Marta J. Hoffman

Representative Clients: University of Michigan; Mutual Insurance Corporation of America; Emergency Physicians Medical Group; Pronational; HCR Manor Care, Inc.
Reference: Comerica Bank-Detroit.

For full biographical listings, see the Martindale-Hubbell Law Directory

TIMMIS & INMAN L.L.P. (AV)

300 Talon Centre, 48207
Telephone: 313-396-4200
Facsimile: 313-396-4228
Email: info@timmis-inman.com *URL:* http://www.timmis-inman.com

(See Next Column)

TIMMIS & INMAN L.L.P.—*Continued*

Michael T. Timmis
Robert E. Graziani
George A. Peck
Henry J. Brennan, III
Mark W. Peyser
Richard M. Miettinen
Bradley J. Knickerbocker
George M. Malis

Michael F. Wais
Erich J. D'Andrea
Shannon M. Nichols
Anthony J. Long
Alex N. Saleh
Michael J. Sheehan
Andrew D. Kehagiaras
John E.F. Gerlach
Jennifer A. Bourgoin

Representative Clients: Detroit Mortgage & Realty; DMR Fiancial Services, Inc.; J. Levin Sons Co.; Green Tree Financial Servicing Corp.; Hematology-Oncology Associates East, PC; Lakeshore Ear, Nose & Throat Center, PC; Micromanagement Systems, Inc.; Phoenix Crystal Corp.; Talon Surfaces LLC; Talon Automated Equipment Company.

For Complete List of Firm Personnel, See General Section

For full biographical listings, see the Martindale-Hubbell Law Directory

TROWBRIDGE LAW FIRM, P.C. (AV)

The Charles C. Trowbridge House, 1380 East Jefferson Avenue, 48207
Telephone: 313-259-6900
Fax: 313-259-3474

Stanley B. Dickson, Jr.
Stephen N. Leuchtman
Sarah W. Colegrove
Gary D. Dodds

OF COUNSEL
Robert M. Malecek

For full biographical listings, see the Martindale-Hubbell Law Directory

FARMINGTON HILLS, Oakland Co.

COUZENS, LANSKY, FEALK, ELLIS, ROEDER & LAZAR, P.C. (AV)

39395 West 12 Mile Road, Suite 200, 48331-2913
Telephone: 248-489-8600
Facsimile: 248-489-4156
Email: info@couzens.com *URL:* http://www.couzens.com

Sheldon A. Fealk
Jack S. Couzens, II
Jerry M. Ellis
Donald M. Lansky
Bruce J. Lazar
Alan C. Roeder
Renard J. Kolasa
Kathryn Gilson Sussman
Jeffrey A. Levine
Phillip L. Sternberg
Marc L. Prey
Lisa J. Walters
Stephen Scapelliti
Donald A. Wagner
Michael P. Witzke
Cyrus Raamin Kashef
Gregg A. Nathanson
David B. Deutsch
Mark S. Frankel

Roger E. Winkelman
Alisa A. Kwang
Turkia Awada Mullin
Raoul K. Maitra

Representative Clients: Provided upon request.
Reference: Michigan National Bank.

For full biographical listings, see the Martindale-Hubbell Law Directory

*FLINT,** Genesee Co.

GAULT DAVISON A PROFESSIONAL SERVICE CORPORATION (AV)

Tenth Floor, Northbank Center, 432 North Saginaw Street, 48502-2032
Telephone: 810-234-3633
Fax: 810-233-3387
Email: gltdav@tir.com *URL:* http://www.gaultdavison.com

Russell E. Bowers
Bernard L. McAra

Christine A. Waun

For full biographical listings, see the Martindale-Hubbell Law Directory

*GRAND RAPIDS,** Kent Co.

BORRE, PETERSON, FOWLER & REENS, P.C. (AV)

300 Ottawa N.W., Suite 500, P.O. Box 1767, 49501-1767
Telephone: 616-459-1971
Fax: 616-459-2393
Email: 105162.1531@compuserve.com

Glen V. Borre
James B. Peterson
Ben A. Fowler
William C. Reens
Frank H. Johnson
Mark D. Sevald
Harold E. Nelson
William R. Vander Sluis
William G. Krupar
John C. Arndts

Michelle H. Anthes

References: Old Kent Bank; NBD Bank/First Chicago Bank; The Huntington Bank.

(See Next Column)

For full biographical listings, see the Martindale-Hubbell Law Directory

DAY & SAWDEY, A PROFESSIONAL CORPORATION (AV)

200 Monroe Avenue, Suite 500, 49503-2217
Telephone: 616-774-8121
Telefax: 616-774-0168

George B. Kingston (1889-1965)
John R. Porter (1915-1975)
Charles E. Day, Jr.
C. Mark Stoppels
James B. Frakie
Larry A. Ver Merris
John Boyko, Jr.
Jonathan F. Thoits
Thomas J. Panik

Jeffrey A. VanMeter
Mary Rachel Pigorsh

OF COUNSEL
Robert W. Sawdey

For full biographical listings, see the Martindale-Hubbell Law Directory

MCSHANE & BOWIE, P.L.C. (AV)

1100 Campau Square Plaza, 99 Monroe Avenue, N.W., P.O. Box 360, 49501-0360
Telephone: 616-732-5000
Fax: 616-732-5099

MEMBERS OF FIRM

John F. Shape
Wayne P. Bryan
Richard A. Durell
Steven E. Bratschie

Representative Clients: Old Kent Bank; Amway Hotel Corp.; Randers Engineering, Inc.; Wolverine Gas & Oil Co., Inc.; M. W. VanderVeen Co.; Betten Imports, Inc.; Adac Plastics, Inc.; Toefco Engineering, Inc.; Mountain Ridge Development Corp.

For Complete List of Firm Personnel, See General Section

For full biographical listings, see the Martindale-Hubbell Law Directory

WARNER NORCROSS & JUDD LLP (AV)

900 Old Kent Building, 111 Lyon Street, N.W., 49503-2489
Telephone: 616-752-2000
Fax: 616-752-2500
URL: http://www.wnj.com
Muskegon, Michigan Office: 400 Terrace Plaza, P.O. Box 900.
Telephone: 231-727-2600.
Fax: 231-727-2699.
Holland, Michigan Office: Curtis Center, Suite 300, 170 College Avenue.
Telephone: 616-396-9800.
Fax: 616-396-3656.
Southfield, Michigan Office: 1000 Town Center, Suite 650.
Telephone: 248-223-5000.
Fax: 248-223-5005.

MEMBERS OF FIRM

George L. Whitfield
Charles E. McCallum
Jerome M. Smith
William K. Holmes
I. John Snider, II (Resident Member, Muskegon Office)
John R. Marquis (Resident Member, Holland Office)
James H. Breay
Robert H. Skilton, III (Resident Member, Southfield Office)
Ernest M. Sharpe
Vernon P. Saper
Hugh H. Makens
Gordon R. Lewis
Robert J. Chovanec
J. A. Cragwall, Jr.
Stephen R. Kretschman
W. Michael Van Haren
Michael L. Robinson
Eugene E. Smary
Thomas H. Thornhill (Resident Member, Muskegon Office)
Timothy Hillegonds
John G. Cameron, Jr.
John H. McKendry, Jr. (Resident Member, Muskegon Office)
Carl W. Dufendach
Stephen C. Waterbury
Rodney D. Martin
Richard E. Cassard
Alex J. DeYonker
John D. Dunn
William W. Hall
Bruce C. Young
Shane B. Hansen
Paul R. Jackson (Resident Member, Muskegon Office)
Janet Percy Knaus
Kathleen M. Hanenburg
Tracy T. Larsen
Sue O. Conway
Cameron S. DeLong
Jeffrey B. Power
Richard L. Bouma
Robert J. Jonker
Devin S. Schindler
Michael H. Schubert (Resident Member, Muskegon Office)
James Moskal
Mark K. Harder (Resident Member, Holland Office)
Jeffrey S. Battershall
Jeffrey A. Ott
Judith Lowitz Adler (Resident Member, Southfield Office)
Melvin G. Moseley, Jr.
Timothy L. Horner
R. Paul Guerre
Loren M. Andrulis
Susan Gell Meyers
Gordon J. Toering

(See Next Column)

WARNER NORCROSS & JUDD LLP, *Grand Rapids—Continued*

ASSOCIATES

Mark J. Wassink
Andrew D. Hakken
Michael P. Lunt
Michael K. Molitor
Melissa Nestico Collar
Tashia L. Rivard
John E. Kessler (Resident, Holland Office)
Steven D. Johnson (Resident, Muskegon Office)
Jonathan J. Siebers
Gregory E. Schmidt
Jaron J. Nyhof (Resident, Holland Office)

OF COUNSEL

Conrad A. Bradshaw
R. Malcolm Cumming
Roger H. Oetting

COUNSEL

Jerry D. Hanscum (Resident Member, Southfield Office)
Joseph M. Sweeney

For full biographical listings, see the Martindale-Hubbell Law Directory

GROSSE POINTE FARMS, Wayne Co.

ALLAN NEEF (AV)

18580 Mack Avenue, 48236
Telephone: 313-343-9200
Fax: 313-343-0207

For full biographical listings, see the Martindale-Hubbell Law Directory

*JACKSON,** Jackson Co.

MARCOUX, ALLEN, ABBOTT, SCHOMER & BOWER, P.C. (AV)

145 South Jackson Street, P.O. Box 787, 49204-0787
Telephone: 517-787-4100
Fax: 517-787-9455
Email: marcoux@jacksonmi.com

William J. Marcoux (Retired)
William O. Allen
William M. Abbott
John H. Schomer
Diane Y. Bower
William B. Nichols, Jr.
Robert T. Kendall, III
Timothy R. Allen
Richard C. Lindsey, Jr.

OF COUNSEL

Walter R. Boris
Lawrence L. Bullen
Philip M. Moilanen
Terry J. Klaasen
T. Harrison Stanton

For full biographical listings, see the Martindale-Hubbell Law Directory

*KALAMAZOO,** Kalamazoo Co.

EARLY, LENNON, PETERS & CROCKER, P.C. (AV)

900 Comerica Building, 49007-4752
Telephone: 616-381-8844
Fax: 616-349-8525
Email: elpc@michbar.org

George H. Lennon, III
John T. Peters, Jr.
David G. Crocker
Harold E. Fischer, Jr.
Lawrence M. Brenton
Gordon C. Miller
Blake D. Crocker
Robert M. Taylor
Patrick D. Crocker
Andrew J. Vorbrich
Nicolette G. Hahn
Robert G Lennon

OF COUNSEL

Vincent T. Early
C. H. Mullen
Thompson Bennett

Attorneys for: Aetna Insurance; Kemper Group; Medical Protective Co.; Zurich Insurance; Liberty Mutual; Home Insurance.

For full biographical listings, see the Martindale-Hubbell Law Directory

GEMRICH, MOSER, BOWSER, MURPHY & GRAHAM, LLP (AV)

222 South Westnedge Avenue, 49007
Telephone: 616-382-1030
Facsimile: 616-382-0703
Email: gmbl@net-link.net *URL:* http://www.lawyers.com/gmblaw

MEMBERS OF FIRM

William E. Bowser
Alfred J. Gemrich
Robert J. Moser
William K. Murphy
Scott Graham
David A. Lewis

References: Michigan National Bank; Leco Corp.; Checker Motors Corp.; Humphrey Products Co.; Kalamazoo College; Miller Davis Co.; RX Optical; Carl Walker Engineers, Inc.; SPX Corporation.

For full biographical listings, see the Martindale-Hubbell Law Directory

KREIS, ENDERLE, CALLANDER & HUDGINS, A PROFESSIONAL CORPORATION (AV)

One Moorsbridge, P.O. Box 4010, 49003-4010
Telephone: 616-324-3000
Facsimile: 616-324-3010
Email: kech@kech.com *URL:* http://www.kech.com
Battle Creek, Michigan Office: One West Michigan Avenue, 49017.
Telephone: 616-966-3000.
Fax: 616-966-3022.

Russell A. Kreis
Douglas L. Callander
C. Reid Hudgins III
Robert B. Borsos
Jeffrey C. O'Brien
Stephen J. Hessen
Jeffery S. Rubel
Thomas G. King
Daniel P. McGlinn
Raymond C. Schultz
Jeffrey D. Swenarton
James C. Boerigter
John F. Koryto
Janice Roark Peters
Matthew S. DePerno
Annette D. Nickel
Peter F. Davis
Manuel R. Rupe

For Complete List of Firm Personnel, See General Section

For full biographical listings, see the Martindale-Hubbell Law Directory

LEWIS & ALLEN, P.C. (AV)

Old Kent Bank Building, Suite 800, 136 East Michigan Avenue, 49007-3946
Telephone: 616-388-7600
Fax: 616-349-3831

Dean S. Lewis
W. Fred Allen, Jr.
Barry R. Smith
William A. Redmond
Stephen M. Denenfeld
Anne McGregor Fries
Gregory G. St. Arnauld
James M. Marquardt
Christopher T. Haenicke
Winfield J. Hollander (1906-1996)

LEGAL SUPPORT PERSONNEL

Dorothy B. Kelly

For full biographical listings, see the Martindale-Hubbell Law Directory

LANSING, Ingham Co.

LOOMIS, EWERT, PARSLEY, DAVIS & GOTTING, P.C. (AV)

232 South Capitol Avenue, Suite 1000, 48933
Telephone: 517-482-2400
Facsimile: 517-482-0070

Plummer Snyder (1900-1974)
Jack C. Davis (P.C.)
Karl L. Gotting (P.C.)
David M. Lick
Harvey J. Messing
James R. Neal
Kenneth W. Beall
Michael G. Oliva
Jeffrey W. Bracken
Catherine A. Jacobs
Ronald W. Bloomberg
Michael H. Rhodes
Howard J. Soifer
Jeffrey L. Green
Gary L. Field
James A. Ault
Sherri A. Wellman

Kelly K. Reed
Jeffrey S. Theuer
Daniel L. Pulter
Eldonna M. Ruddock
Kevin J. Roragen

OF COUNSEL

George W. Loomis
Quentin A. Ewert
William D. Parsley

Representative Clients: Altman Development Co.; Century Telephone Enterprises; Columbian Distribution, Inc.; Comerica Bank; Consumers Energy Co.; Southeastern Michigan Gas Enterprises, Inc.; Wal-Mart Stores, Inc.; Wisconsin Electric Power Co.

For full biographical listings, see the Martindale-Hubbell Law Directory

*MUSKEGON,** Muskegon Co.

LAGUE, NEWMAN & IRISH, A PROFESSIONAL CORPORATION (AV)

600 Terrace Plaza, P.O. Box 389, 49443
Telephone: 231-725-8148
Telecopier: 231-726-3404
Email: firm@lnilaw.com

Todd L. Helle
Richard C. Lague
J. Scott Timmer

LEGAL SUPPORT PERSONNEL

Rebecca A. McCroskey

General Counsel: Hackley Hospital & Medical Center; Kaydon Corp.; Cole's Quality Foods; Kurdziel Industries.
Local Counsel: SPX Corp.; Booth Newspapers Inc.; National City Bank; Neway Anchorlok International.

For Complete List of Firm Personnel, See General Section

For full biographical listings, see the Martindale-Hubbell Law Directory

NOVI, Oakland Co.

LAW OFFICES OF SULLIVAN & LEAVITT, P.C. (AV)

22375 Haggerty Road, 48375
Telephone: 248-349-3980
Fax: 248-349-2810
Mailing Address: P.O. Box 5490, Northville, MI, 48167
Email: mjl@sullivanleavitt.com

Robert A. Sullivan (1917-1979) Martin J. Leavitt

Paul E. Robinson
Michael J. Leavitt
Curtis R. Willner
Joseph Richard Mariniello, Jr.

OF COUNSEL

David Loeffler

Representative Clients: Aggregate Carriers of Michigan, Inc.; D & H Mack Kenworth Sales & Service, Inc.; Gordon F. Laramie Crane Co.; Premiere Video, Inc.; Palmer Moving & Storage, Inc.; Menlo Tool; Storage and Transport; Automated Benefit Services, Inc.; U.S. Health and Life Insurance Co.

For full biographical listings, see the Martindale-Hubbell Law Directory

SOUTHFIELD, Oakland Co.

MASON STEINHARDT JACOBS PERLMAN & PESICK, PROFESSIONAL CORPORATION (AV)

Suite 1500, 4000 Town Center, 48075-1415
Telephone: 248-358-2090
Fax: 248-358-3599
Email: admin@msjp.com *URL:* http://www.msjp.com

Gordon I. Ginsberg
Irving I. Boigon
Jack Schon
Frederick D. Steinhardt
John E. Jacobs
Michael B. Perlman
Jerome P. Pesick
Richard A. Polk
Neil S. Silver
L. Jeffrey Zauberman
Howard A. Lax
H. Adam Cohen
Diane Flagg Goldstein

Jeffrey B. Linden
David E. Nykanen
Jacquelyn L. Lane

OF COUNSEL

Walter B. Mason, Jr.
Erwin B. Ellmann
Walter J. Goldsmith
Randolph J. Friedman
Marvin C. Daitch

Representative Clients: Citibank, N.A.; City of Dearborn; DeMattia Development Co.; Forest City Enterprises; Michigan Wholesale Drug Assn.; Mortgage Bankers Association of Michigan; Nationwide Insurance Co.; City of Taylor; Union Labor Life Insurance Co.; Yellow Freight Systems, Inc.

For full biographical listings, see the Martindale-Hubbell Law Directory

SIEGEL, GREENFIELD, HAYES & GROSS, P.L.C. (AV)

2000 Town Center, Suite 2700, 48075-1318
Telephone: 248-386-5900
Facsimile: 248-354-3106
URL: http://www.lawyers.com/sghandglawfirm

MEMBERS OF FIRM

Robert W. Siegel
Norman E. Greenfield
Kelly M. Hayes
Robert A. Gross

OF COUNSEL

Steven H. Schwartz

For full biographical listings, see the Martindale-Hubbell Law Directory

*TRAVERSE CITY,** Grand Traverse Co.

BISHOP & HEINTZ, P.C. (AV)

440 W. Front at Oak Street, P.O. Box 707, 49685
Telephone: 616-946-4100
Fax: 616-946-8543
Email: info@bishop-heintztc.com *URL:* http://www.lawyers.com/bishopheintzlaw

Douglas S. Bishop
Patrick E. Heintz
David A. Cvengros
Steven R. Fox

OF COUNSEL

Arthur R. Curtis

Representative Clients: Old Kent Bank-Grand Traverse; Old Kent Bank & Trust Co.; NBD Bank, N.A.; Ball Aircraft, Inc.; Power Play International Inc.; National Cherry Festival; PDM Industries, Inc.; Bolthouse Machine Corp.; Corrections Management, Inc.; Buck Wilder, Inc.

For full biographical listings, see the Martindale-Hubbell Law Directory

CALCUTT CUNNINGHAM DAVISON ROGERS BOYNTON & PETTERSON, P.L.L.C. (AV)

109 East Front Street, Suite 300, 49684
Telephone: 616-947-4000
Fax: 616-947-4341
Email: cclawfirm@cclawfirm.com *URL:* http://www.cclawfirm.com

Robert B. Murchie (1894-1975)
Harry Calcutt (1918-1996)
William J. Cunningham (1942-1997)
William B. Calcutt
William M. Davison
Terry C. Rogers
Jack E. Boynton
Kenneth M. Petterson

ASSOCIATE

Adam M. Lett

General Counsel for: The Empire National Bank of Traverse City.
Local Counsel for: Union Oil Co.
Reference: The Empire National Bank of Traverse City.

For full biographical listings, see the Martindale-Hubbell Law Directory

DINGEMAN, DANCER & CHRISTOPHERSON, P.L.C. (AV)

100 Park Street, 49684
Telephone: 231-929-0500
Fax: 231-929-0504
Email: dingeman@dingemandancer.com *URL:* http://www.Dingemandancer.com

Daniel J. Dingeman
Mark R. Dancer
James A. Christopherson

ASSOCIATES

Brian L. Johnson
Michael J. Daray

Representative Clients: Old Kent Bank-Grand Traverse; Tuffy Mufflers of Traverse City, Ltd.; Venture Properties, Inc.; Hagerty Vintage Watercraft & Motor Vehicle Insurance; Heritage Broadcasting Group, Inc.

For full biographical listings, see the Martindale-Hubbell Law Directory

OLSON, NOONAN & BZDOK, P.C. (AV)

420 East Front Street, P.O. Box 2358, 49685-2358
Telephone: 616-946-0044
Fax: 616-946-4807

James M. Olson
John D. Noonan
Christopher M. Bzdok
Karen L. Ferguson
Scott W. Howard

For full biographical listings, see the Martindale-Hubbell Law Directory

RUNNING, WISE, FORD AND PHILLIPS, P.L.C. (AV)

326 State Street, P.O. Box 686, 49684
Telephone: 616-946-2700
Tele-Fax: 616-946-0857
Email: RWWFP@rwwfp.com

Harry T. Running (Deceased) William L. Wise (Retired)

MEMBERS OF FIRM

Richard W. Ford
Thomas J. Phillips
Sandra P. Howard
Kent E. Gerberding
Michael I. Conlon

ASSOCIATE

Bradley L. Putney

OF COUNSEL

Douglas J. Donaldson Miles C. Gerberding

For full biographical listings, see the Martindale-Hubbell Law Directory

SMITH & JOHNSON, ATTORNEYS, P.C. (AV)

603 Bay Street, P.O. Box 705, 49685
Telephone: 231-946-0700
Fax: 231-946-1735
Email: sjlaw@smith-johnson.com *URL:* http://www.smith-johnson.com
Lansing, Michigan Office: Suite 402, 116 West Ottawa Street.
Telephone: 517-482-5142.

Louis A. Smith
H. Wendell Johnson
Allen G. Anderson

Thomas A. Pezzetti
Timothy Paul Smith
Matthew D. Vermetten
Gary Allen Gardner

OF COUNSEL

Barbara Ann Assendelft

Representative Clients: Empire National Bank of Traverse City; Grand Traverse Mall Limited Partnership; Green Tree Acceptance, Inc.; Lansing Automakers' Federal Credit Union; Michigan Automobile Dealers Association; Cherry Capital Oldsmobile Cadillac L.L.C.; Bill Marsh Motors, Inc.; Northern Star Broadcasting, L.L.C.; Munson Healthcare; Republic Bank.

For full biographical listings, see the Martindale-Hubbell Law Directory

TROY, Oakland Co.

BOWEN, RADABAUGH, MILTON & BROWN, P.C. (AV)

4967 Crooks Road, Suite 150, 48098
Telephone: 248-641-8000
Fax: 248-641-8219
Email: brmb@brmb.com *URL:* http://www.brmb.com

Thomas R. Bowen
James M. Radabaugh
Lisa T. Milton
Susan Leigh Brown

Geoffrey D. Marshall
Mark P. Dunn

OF COUNSEL

Meri Craver Borin

For full biographical listings, see the Martindale-Hubbell Law Directory

HACKETT & MAXWELL, P.C. (AV)

City Center Building, Suite 1470, 888 West Big Beaver Road, 48084
Telephone: 810-362-2600
Fax: 810-362-3610
Email: hackmax@voyager.net

Patrick E. Hackett
Phillip B. Maxwell

Dennis W. Krakow
Mireille Leruth Phillips

For full biographical listings, see the Martindale-Hubbell Law Directory

POLING, McGAW & POLING, P.C. (AV)

Suite 275, 5435 Corporate Drive, 48098
Telephone: 248-641-0500
Telecopier: 248-641-0506
URL: http://www.lawyers.com/polingmcgaw&poling

Benson T. Buck (1926-1989)
Richard B. Poling
D. Douglas McGaw
Richard B. Poling, Jr.
Gregory C. Hamilton
Veronica B. O'Hara
James R. Parker
Shannon M. Acton

OF COUNSEL

Ralph S. Moore

Representative Clients: City of Troy; United States Fidelity & Guaranty Co.; Sentry Insurance Co.; Admiral Insurance; DeMaria Construction Co.; Leo Corporation; Aetna Casualty and Surety Co.; Concord Design; Pneumo-Abex.

For full biographical listings, see the Martindale-Hubbell Law Directory

YPSILANTI, Washtenaw Co.

PEAR SPERLING EGGAN & MUSKOVITZ, P.C. (AV)

5 South Washington Street, 48197
Telephone: 734-483-3626
Fax: 734-483-1107
Email: ameggan@ameritech.net
Ann Arbor, Michigan Office: Domino's Farms, 24 Frank Lloyd Wright Drive.
Telephone: 734-665-4441
Other Ypsilanti, Michigan Office: 2164 Bellevue at Washtenaw.
Telephone: 734-483-7177.

Lawrence W. Sperling
Andrew M. Eggan
Thomas E. Daniels

Counsel for: Domino's Pizza, Inc.; Citizens Banking Corp.; Townsend and Bottum, Inc.; The Credit Bureau of Ypsilanti; City of Ypsilanti (Labor Counsel); Michigan Municipal Worker's Compensation; Self-Insurance Fund.
Approved Attorneys for: Lawyers Title Insurance Corp.

For full biographical listings, see the Martindale-Hubbell Law Directory

CREDITORS RIGHTS

ALABAMA

*MOBILE,** Mobile Co.

Barry A. Friedman & Associates (AV)

257 St. Anthony Street, P.O. Box 2394, 36652-2394
Telephone: 334-439-7400
Fax: 334-432-2665
Email: baf75@aol.com

For full biographical listings, see the Martindale-Hubbell Law Directory

*MONTGOMERY,** Montgomery Co.

Parnell & Crum, P.A. (AV)

641 South Lawrence Street, P.O. Box 2189, 36102
Telephone: 334-832-4202
Telecopier: 334-832-4703
Fax: 334-293-3550
Email: cnparnell@aol.com

Charles N. Parnell, III
G. Barton Crum

Robert J. Russell, Jr.
Britt Batson Griggs
James McCauley Smith
Angie Hubbard Ingram

Reference: Colonial Bank of Montgomery.

For full biographical listings, see the Martindale-Hubbell Law Directory

ARIZONA

*PHOENIX,** Maricopa Co.

Davis & Lowe, P.C. (AV)

Suite 722, Security Building, 234 North Central Avenue, 85004
Telephone: 602-253-2882
Fax: 602-253-3088
Email: davislowe@prodigy.net

Edward E. Davis
Charles W. Lowe
Ilene J. Lashinsky

Representative Clients: Citgo Petroleum Corporation; Republic Companies; Tilden Financial Corp.; Douglas Allred Company; Fresh Quest Produce, Inc.
Reference: Firstar Metropolitan Bank.

For full biographical listings, see the Martindale-Hubbell Law Directory

Murphy & Posner, L.L.P. (AV)

3200 East Camelback Road, Suite 300, 85018
Telephone: 602-224-5900
Telecopier: 602-224-5754
Email: lawfirm@murphy-posner.com *URL:* http://www.murphy-posner.com

Terry L. Rakow
K. Bellamy Brown
Don A. Davis
Earl E. Berg

ASSOCIATES

Don C. Fletcher
Brooke U. Walker

Representative Clients: The Westcor Cos.; Westcor Partners; Prime Retail Group; Chase Manhattan Bank; Irwin Mortgage Corporation; Liberty Savings Bank; Capstead, Inc.; Kansas City Life Insurance Company.

For full biographical listings, see the Martindale-Hubbell Law Directory

Shannon & Fleming, P.C. (AV)

1649 East Bethany Home Road, 85016
Telephone: 602-277-6627
Fax: 602-277-6427

Mathew E. Shannon
Lawrence J. Fleming
L. Timothy Fleming

OF COUNSEL

Thomas W. McLellan

Representative Clients: Bank One Arizona, N.A.; West Publishing Co.; Fidelity & Deposit Company of Maryland; Associates Commercial Corporation; Walsh Brothers; Phoenix Newspapers, Inc.; American Credit Indemnity Co.; Syncor International Corporation; Banc One Financial Services; Bank One N.A., Arizona.

For full biographical listings, see the Martindale-Hubbell Law Directory

Shimmel, Hill, Bishop & Gruender, P.C. (AV)

3700 North 24th Street, 85016
Telephone: 602-224-9500
Telecopier: 602-955-6176
URL: http://www.shimmelhill.com

Joseph Wm. Kruchek
Margaret L. Steiner

Representative Clients: The Ashton Cos.; Associated General Contractors; Bashas' Stores; Black Mesa Pipeline Co.; CC Shops dba Cost Cutters Hairsetters; Christiania Bank; Citizen Auto Stage Line; Connecticut General Life Insurance Co.; Delta Airlines; Dunn Del Re Steel, Inc.

For full biographical listings, see the Martindale-Hubbell Law Directory

Skarecky & Holder, A Professional Association (AV)

Suite 300, 3130 North Third Avenue, 85013
Telephone: 602-248-0393
Fax: 602-266-4991

Dennis J. Skarecky
William W. Holder

Reference: Pacific Century Bank.

For full biographical listings, see the Martindale-Hubbell Law Directory

ARKANSAS

*LITTLE ROCK,** Pulaski Co.

Rose Law Firm, A Professional Association (AV)

120 East Fourth Street, 72201
Telephone: 501-375-9131
Telecopy: 501-375-1309

George E. Campbell
Charles W. Baker
Herbert C. Rule, III
John T. Hardin
Allen W. Bird, II
Stephen N. Joiner
Garland J. Garrett
Brian Rosenthal

Counsel for: ALLTEL Corporation; Aluminum Company of America; Bridgestone/Firestone, Inc.; The Equitable Life Assurance Society of The United States; General Motors Corp.; Mercantile Bank of Arkansas, N.A.; Bank of America, N.A.; The Prudential Insurance Company of America; Stephens Group Inc.; Tyson Foods, Inc.

For Complete List of Firm Personnel, See General Section

For full biographical listings, see the Martindale-Hubbell Law Directory

CALIFORNIA

COSTA MESA, Orange Co.

Albert, Weiland & Golden (AV)

Center Tower, 650 Town Center Drive, Suite 1350, 92626
Telephone: 714-966-1000
FAX: 714-966-1002
Email: awglawyers@aol.com

Theodor C. Albert
Michael J. Weiland
Jeffrey I. Golden

ASSOCIATES

Evan D. Smiley
Philip E. Strok
Lei Lei Wang Ekvall
Darlynn Campbell Morgan

OF COUNSEL

Marcus M. Kaufman
Jennifer Ann Golison
Steven J. Katzman

LEGAL SUPPORT PERSONNEL

PARALEGALS

Fran L. Russell
Patricia K. Nelson
Cynthia B. Meeker
Janet Hogan
Kim Sigismondo

For full biographical listings, see the Martindale-Hubbell Law Directory

*LOS ANGELES,** Los Angeles Co.

Ronald P. Slates, P.C. (AV)

548 South Spring Street, Suite 1012, 90013-2309
Telephone: 213-624-1515; 213-654-1461
Fax: 213-624-7536; 213-654-1463
Email: rslateslaw@aol.com *URL:* http://www.lawyers.com/slateslaw

Ronald P. Slates

Donald R. Ramenian

For full biographical listings, see the Martindale-Hubbell Law Directory

*SAN DIEGO,** San Diego Co.

LINDLEY, SCALES & CORBETT, A PROFESSIONAL CORPORATION (AV)

550 West C Street, Suite 1800, 92101
Telephone: 619-234-9181
Fax: 619-234-8475
Email: lsc@adnc.com

Luke R. Corbett

Representative Clients: Palomar Savings & Loan Assn.; McGraw-Hill Broadcasting Co.; Chicago Title Insurance Co.; San Diego Hospital Assn.; Bank United.

For full biographical listings, see the Martindale-Hubbell Law Directory

MIKKI ROSEMARY SULLIVAN (AV)

2139 First Avenue, 92101
Telephone: 619-233-0597
Fax: 619-557-9425
(Also Of Counsel to Miles D. Grant, A.P.C.)

For full biographical listings, see the Martindale-Hubbell Law Directory

*SAN FRANCISCO,** San Francisco Co.

HAIGHT, BROWN & BONESTEEL, L.L.P. (AV)

A Partnership including Professional Corporations
100 Bush Street, 27th Floor, 94104-3902
Telephone: 415-986-7700
Telecopier: 415-986-6945
URL: http://www.hbblaw.com
Santa Monica, California Office: 1620 26th Street, Suite 4000 North, P.O. Box 680.
Telephone: 310-449-6000.
Telecopier: 310-829-5117.
Telex: 705837.
Santa Ana, California Office: Suite 900, 5 Hutton Centre Drive.
Telephone: 714-754-1100.
Telecopier: 714-754-0826.
Riverside, California Office: California Tower, 3737 Main Street, Suite 800.
Telephone: 909-341-8300.
Fax: 909-341-8309.
San Diego, California Office: 101 West Broadway, Suite 1000.
Telephone: 619-595-5583.
Fax: 619-595-7873.

RESIDENT MEMBER

Daniel J. Kelly

For full biographical listings, see the Martindale-Hubbell Law Directory

*SAN JOSE,** Santa Clara Co.

TERRA LAW LLP (AV)

60 South Market Street, Suite 200, 95113
Telephone: 408-288-7325
Fax: 408-998-4895
Burlingame, California Office: 1350 Old Bayshore Highway, Suite 760, 94010.
Telephone: 650-685-7325.
Fax: 650-685-4895.

George H. Cole, Jr.
D. D. Hughmanick
R. Prescott Jaunich
Richard O. McDonald
Breck E. Milde
William L. Myers
Jane P. Relyea
Jason R. Biggs
Joan Paul
Ronald I. Rainey

Katharine L. Hardt-Mason
Thomas E. Rossmeissl

For full biographical listings, see the Martindale-Hubbell Law Directory

SANTA MONICA, Los Angeles Co.

GILCHRIST & RUTTER, PROFESSIONAL CORPORATION (AV)

Wilshire Palisades Building, 1299 Ocean Avenue, Suite 900, 90401
Telephone: 310-393-4000
Facsimile: 310-394-4700
Email: POSTMASTER@GRLAWYERS.COM *URL:* http://www.grlawyers.com
Los Angeles, California Office: 355 South Grand Avenue, Suite 4100.
Telephone: 213-617-8000.
Facsimile: 213-534-8001.

MEMBERS OF THE FIRM

Ellen K. Wolf
Michael S. Abrams

For full biographical listings, see the Martindale-Hubbell Law Directory

PARIS AND PARIS, LLP (AV)

Paris Law Building, 424 Pico Boulevard, 90405-1197
Telephone: 310-392-8722
Telecopier: 310-392-1768
Email: PandP424@aol.com *URL:* http://www.ParisandParis.com
San Rafael, California Office: PMB D, 4286 Redwood Highway, 94903.

Jeffrey A. Paris
Karen M. Paris
Murray A. Zeffren

OF COUNSEL

Reynold F. Paris
Bette S. Paris
Richard E. Paris

For full biographical listings, see the Martindale-Hubbell Law Directory

COLORADO

*DENVER,** Denver Co.

ARTHUR AND PERLMUTTER (AV)

2121 South Oneida Street, Suite 330, 80224
Telephone: 303-691-0205
FAX: 303-691-0227

MEMBER OF FIRM

Donald S. Perlmutter

OF COUNSEL

L. James Arthur

Representative Clients: Viking Freight Systems, Inc.; Conslidated Freightways; N.Y. State Higher Educ. Services; Utility Research and Management Co.; Farmers Insurance Group; Commercial Credit Corporation; Morgan Buildings & Spas; National Association of Credit Management, Rocky Mountain Affiliate.

For full biographical listings, see the Martindale-Hubbell Law Directory

LONGMONT, Boulder Co.

MILLER & COHEN, P.C. (AV)

344 Main Street, P.O. Box 1259, 80502-1259
Telephone: 303-772-0165
Nationally: 800-606-0165
Fax: 303-772-6450
Email: info@creditorsrights.com *URL:* http://www.creditorsrights.com

John Wayne Miller

Representative Clients: Bonded Collection Services of Longmont, Inc.; FirstBank of Longmont; First National Bank of Longmont.

For full biographical listings, see the Martindale-Hubbell Law Directory

CONNECTICUT

*BRIDGEPORT,** Fairfield Co.

ZEISLER & ZEISLER, P.C. (AV)

558 Clinton Avenue, P.O. Box 3186, 06605-0186
Telephone: 203-368-4234
Fax: 203-367-9678
Email: info@zeislaw.com *URL:* http://www.zeislaw.com
Westport Office: 25 Ford Road, Suite 2.
Telephone: 203-221-8066.
Fax: 203-222-4833.

Richard D. Zeisler
James G. Verrillo
James Berman
Craig I. Lifland
Jed Horwitt
Matthew K. Beatman
Dennis P. Anderson
Mark J. Rosen
Jeffrey Hellman

Lawrence S. Grossman
Stephen M. Kindseth
Johnpatrick O'Brien
Coleen Hurlie-Dunn
Gregory B. Schiller

OF COUNSEL

Robert M. Zeisler
Paul J. Pacifico

For full biographical listings, see the Martindale-Hubbell Law Directory

SHELTON, Fairfield Co.

GLENN M. REISMAN (AV)

Two Corporate Drive, Suite 650, P.O. Box 861, 06484-0861
Telephone: 203-944-3040
Fax: 203-944-3044
URL: http://www.ReismanLaw.com
Email: Glenn.Reisman@corporate.ge.com *URL:* http://www.CreditCollectionLaw.com

J. Michelle Reisman (Not admitted in CT)

For full biographical listings, see the Martindale-Hubbell Law Directory

FLORIDA

BOCA RATON, Palm Beach Co.

FURR AND COHEN, P.A. (AV)

Suite 412, 1499 W. Palmetto Park Road, 33486
Telephone: 561-395-0500
Broward: 954-421-0300
Fax: 561-338-7532
Email: thefirm@furrandcohenpa.com *URL:* http://www.furrandcohenpa.com

Robert C. Furr
Charles I. Cohen

Alvin S. Goldstein
Leslie Scott Osborne
Lisa J. Chaiklin Aflalo
Bradley Scott Shraiberg

OF COUNSEL

C. William Berger

For full biographical listings, see the Martindale-Hubbell Law Directory

*FORT LAUDERDALE,** Broward Co.

BERGER DAVIS & SINGERMAN (AV)

350 East Las Olas Boulevard, Suite 1000, 33301
Telephone: 954-525-9900
Fax: 954-523-2872
Email: jberger@bdslaw.com *URL:* http://www.bdslaw.com
Miami, Florida Office: 200 South Biscayne Boulevard, Suite 2950.
Telephone: 305-755-9500.
Fax: 305-714-4340.
Tallahassee, Florida Office: 215 South Monroe Street, Suite 705, 32301.
Telephone: 850-561-3010.
Fax: 850-561-3013.

James L. Berger
Mitchell W. Berger
Franklin H. Caplan (Resident, Miami Office)
James B. Davis
Henry H. (Bucky) Fox
Van P. Geeker (Resident, Tallahassee Office)
Jordi Guso (Resident, Miami Office)
Nick Jovanovich
Robert B. Judd
Manuel Kushner
Daniel Lampert
Dawn M. Meyers
John D. C. Newton, II (Resident, Tallahassee Office)
Samuel E. Poole III
Leonard K. Samuels
Laz L. Schneider
Paul Steven Singerman (Resident, Miami Office)
Daniel H. Thompson (Resident, Tallahassee Office)

Robert W. Barron
Maria St. John Daugherty
James Harris Fierberg (Resident, Miami Office)
Ilyse Wrubel Homer (Resident, Miami Office)
Sherry A. Lambson
Lisa D. MacClugage
Brian G. Rich (Resident, Miami Office)
Holiday Hunt Russell
Jonathan C. Vair (Resident, Miami Office)
Jeffrey Scott Wertman

OF COUNSEL

James C. Cunningham, Jr.
Fred Goldberg

For full biographical listings, see the Martindale-Hubbell Law Directory

KIPNIS TESCHER LIPPMAN & VALINSKY (AV)

100 Northeast Third Avenue, Suite 610, 33301
Telephone: 954-467-1964
Fax: 954-467-2264

MEMBERS OF FIRM

Alan G. Kipnis
Howard A. Tescher
Steven N. Lippman
Jay L. Valinsky

ASSOCIATES

Richard B. Storfer
Patricia Fox-Butler
Michelle L. LaRue

For full biographical listings, see the Martindale-Hubbell Law Directory

*MIAMI,** Dade Co.

MARKOWITZ, DAVIS, RINGEL & TRUSTY, P.A. (AV)

Two Datran Center, Suite 1225, 9130 South Dadeland Boulevard, 33156-7849
Telephone: 305-670-5000
Telecopier: 305-670-5011

Jerry M. Markowitz
Joseph I. Davis, Jr.
Candis Trusty
Thomas M. Messana

Ilan Markus

For full biographical listings, see the Martindale-Hubbell Law Directory

MISHAN, SLOTO, GREENBERG, HELLINGER & UDOLF, P.A. (AV)

Suite 2350, First Union Financial Center, 200 South Biscayne Boulevard, 33131
Telephone: 305-379-1792
Facsimile: 305-379-2328
Email: MishanSloto@COMPUSERVE.COM

Steven Mishan
James R. Sloto
Barry N. Greenberg
Andrew B. Hellinger
Bruce L. Udolf
Carol L. Cox
Alan M. Burger

Ana Cela Harris
Dara J. Collins
Steven J. Solomon
Coralee G. Penebad

For full biographical listings, see the Martindale-Hubbell Law Directory

WILLIAM L. RICHEY, P.A. (AV)

One Biscayne Tower, 2 South Biscayne Boulevard, Suite 3400, 33131-1897
Telephone: 305-372-8808
Fax: 305-372-3669
Email: wlr@richeylaw.com *URL:* http://www.lawyers.com/richeylaw
Palm City, Florida Office: 5501 S.W. Sunshine Farms Way, 34990-5696.
Telephone: 561-220-0558.
Fax: 305-372-3669.

William L. Richey (Also Of Counsel to Gunster, Yoakley, Valdes-Fauli & Stewart, P.A., Miami, Florida and Stuart, Florida)

For full biographical listings, see the Martindale-Hubbell Law Directory

SPRECHMAN & ASSOCIATES, P.A. (AV)

Nationsbank Building, 18305 Biscayne Boulevard, Suite 213, 33160-2172
Telephone: 305-931-0100
Facsimile: 305-936-0200
Email: sprechman@aol.com *URL:* http://www.sprechmanlaw.com

Steven B. Sprechman

Stacey S. Fisher
Scott E. Modlin
George J. Batarseh

For full biographical listings, see the Martindale-Hubbell Law Directory

*PENSACOLA,** Escambia Co.

PHILIP A. BATES (AV)

25 West Cedar Street, Suite 304, 32501
Telephone: 850-470-0091
Fax: 850-470-0441

For full biographical listings, see the Martindale-Hubbell Law Directory

*TAMPA,** Hillsborough Co.

KETCHEY HORAN, P.A. (AV)

100 North Tampa Street, Suite 1900, P.O. Box 500, 33601-0500
Telephone: 813-223-9395
Fax: 813-221-1348
Email: Stephanie@KetcheyHoran.com
Sun City Center, Florida Office: 1647 Sun City Center Plaza, Suite 200.
Telephone: 813-633-1200.

SHAREHOLDERS

Michael P. Horan
Charles F. Ketchey, Jr.
John B. Neukamm

ASSOCIATE

Alfred A. Colby

For full biographical listings, see the Martindale-Hubbell Law Directory

GEORGIA

*ATLANTA,** Fulton Co.

DAVID G. CROCKETT, P.C. (AV)

1950 Equitable Building, 100 Peachtree Street, N.W., 30303
Telephone: 404-522-4280
Telecopier: 404-589-9891
Email: CROCKLAW@BELLSOUTH.NET

David G. Crockett

Douglas L. Brooks

LEGAL SUPPORT PERSONNEL

Loraine B. Harps (Paralegal)

Approved Attorney for: Chicago Title Insurance Co.
Reference: NationsBank, N.A.

For full biographical listings, see the Martindale-Hubbell Law Directory

LAMBERTH, BONAPFEL, CIFELLI & STOKES, P.A. (AV)

Atlanta Financial Center, 3343 Peachtree Road, N.E. East Tower, Suite 550, 30326
Telephone: 404-262-7373
Fax: 404-262-9911

J. Michael Lamberth
James Craig Cifelli
Paul W. Bonapfel
Carter L. Stout
G. Frank Nason, IV
Gregory D. Ellis

Stuart F. Clayton, Jr.
A. Alexander Teel
Laura E. Woodson
Susan H. Seabury

OF COUNSEL

William H. Willson, Jr.

Reference: The Riverside Bank.

For full biographical listings, see the Martindale-Hubbell Law Directory

LONG ALDRIDGE & NORMAN LLP (AV)

A Limited Liability Partnership including Professional Corporations
Suite 5300, 303 Peachtree Street, 30308
Telephone: 404-527-4000
Telecopier: 404-527-4198
Email: atlanta@lanlaw.com *URL:* http://www.lanlaw.com
Washington, D.C. Office: Suite 600, 701 Pennsylvania Avenue, N.W., 20004.
Telephone: 202-624-1200.
FAX: 202-624-1298.

MEMBERS OF FIRM

John G. Aldridge
Deborah S. Ebel
Thomas D. Hall
Patrick M. McGeehan
Charles D. Weiss

OF COUNSEL

James W. Culbreth

For Complete List of Firm Personnel, See General Section

For full biographical listings, see the Martindale-Hubbell Law Directory

MACEY, WILENSKY, COHEN, WITTNER & KESSLER, LLP (AV)

285 Peachtree Center Avenue, Suite 600, 30303-1229
Telephone: 404-584-1200
Telecopier: 404-681-4355
Email: Lawyers@MaceyWilensky.com

MEMBERS OF FIRM

Morris W. Macey
Frank B. Wilensky
Neil C. Gordon
James R. Sacca
David B. Kurzweil

ASSOCIATES

Todd E. Hennings
Kristine M. Shryock
Louis G. McBryan

For Complete List of Firm Personnel, See General Section

For full biographical listings, see the Martindale-Hubbell Law Directory

LAW OFFICES OF PAMELA L. TREMAYNE (AV)

730 The Hurt Building, 50 Hurt Plaza, 30303
Telephone: 404-523-2800
Fax: 404-523-2806
URL: http://www.lawyers.com/tremayne

ASSOCIATE

Joseph B. Heimovics

Representative Clients: Fidelity National Bank, Commercial Credit; Peoples Financial Corp.; Probe Software Sciences, Ltd.; Probe U.S.A. Inc.

(See Next Column)

Approved Attorney for: Lawyers Title Insurance Corp.; Chicago Title Insurance.
Reference: Fidelity National Bank.

For full biographical listings, see the Martindale-Hubbell Law Directory

*AUGUSTA,** Richmond Co.

J. BENJAMIN KAY, III (AV)

808 First Union Bank Building, 30901
Telephone: 706-722-2008
Approved Attorney for: Lawyers Title Insurance Corp.
Reference: First Union National Bank of Georgia.
Representative Clients: American National Bank & Trust Company; Biotech Park, Inc.; Caterpillar Financial Services, Inc.; Davis-McGraw, Inc.; Ford Leasing Development Company; Ford Motor Credit Company; Gary Concrete Products, Inc.; Globe Life Insurance Company.

For full biographical listings, see the Martindale-Hubbell Law Directory

NORCROSS, Gwinnett Co.

THOMPSON, O'BRIEN, KEMP & NASUTI, P.C. (AV)

4845 Jimmy Carter Boulevard, 30093-3641
Telephone: 770-925-0111
Fax: 770-925-8597
Email: tokn@tokn.com

R. Michael Thompson
J. Patrick O'Brien
Donna N. Kemp
Albert F. Nasuti
Paul J. Morochnik

Paul B. Frickey
Bret T. Thrasher
Brian L. Hansen
Ronald F. Negin

OF COUNSEL

Betty H. Morris
Scott L. Dix

For full biographical listings, see the Martindale-Hubbell Law Directory

WALLACE & DE MAYO, P.C. (AV)

6356 Corley Road, 30071-1704
Telephone: 770-446-9996
Fax: 770-368-8331

Richard T. De Mayo
Douglas W. Wallace

SENIOR COUNSEL

Raymond N. Friedlander (Not admitted in GA)

Paul J. Gallo
Andrew J. Baird
Kristian Knochel

For full biographical listings, see the Martindale-Hubbell Law Directory

HAWAII

*HONOLULU,** Honolulu Co.

CARLSMITH BALL (AV)

A Partnership including Law Corporations
Suite 2200, Pacific Tower, 1001 Bishop Street, P.O. Box 656, 96809-3402
Telephone: 808-523-2500
Fax: 808-523-0842
Email: execdirector@carlsmith.com *URL:* http://www.carlsmith.com
Kapolei, Hawaii Office: Suite 318, Kapolei Building, 1001 Kamokila Boulevard, 96707.
Telephone: 808-523-2500.
Fax: 808-674-0850.
Wailuku, Maui Hawaii Office: Suite 400, One Main Plaza, 2200 Main Street, P.O. Box 1086, 96793-1086.
Telephone: 808-242-4535.
Fax: 808-244-4974.
Kailua-Kona, Hawaii Office: Suite 209, 75-1000 Henry Street, 96740.
Telephone: 808-329-6464.
Fax: 808-329-9450.
Hilo, Hawaii Office: 121 Waianuenue Avenue, P.O. Box 686, 96721-0686.
Telephone: 808-935-6644.
Fax: 808-935-7975.
Hagatna, Guam Office: Suite 401, Bank of Hawaii Building, 134 West Soledad Avenue, P.O. Box BF, 96932-5027.
Telephone: 671-472-6813.
Fax: 671-477-4375.
Telex: 721-6445 CWCMI GM.
Saipan, Commonwealth of the Northern Mariana Islands Office: Carlsmith Building, Capitol Hill, P.O. Box 5241, 96950-5241.
Telephone: 670-322-3455.
Fax: 670-322-3368.

(See Next Column)

CARLSMITH BALL—*Continued*

Los Angeles, California Office: 9th Floor, 444 South Flower Street, 90071-2901.
Telephone: 213-955-1200.
Fax: 213-623-0032.
Washington, D.C. Office: Suite 300, 1201 Pennsylvania Avenue, N.W., 20004-2401.
Telephone: 202-628-2228.
Fax: 202-628-2071.
Mexico City, Mexico Office: Carlsmith Ball, Sierra Nevada 119, Lomas de Chapultepec, 11000 Mexico, D.F.
Telephone: 52-5-520-8514, 52-5-520-8757.
Fax: 52-5-540-1545.
Mexico, D.F. Office of Carlsmith Ball, S.C. (Authorized to practice as foreign legal consultants in Mexico): Sierra Nevada 119, Lomas de Chapultepec, 11000 Mexico, D.F.
Telephone: 52-5-520-8514, 52-5-520-8757.
Fax: 52-5-540-1545.

MEMBERS OF FIRM

Michelle C. Imata
Matthew M. Matsunaga
Lawrence S. Okinaga (A Law Corporation)
Tom E. Roesser
J. Thomas Van Winkle (A Law Corporation)

For Complete List of Firm Personnel, See General Section

For full biographical listings, see the Martindale-Hubbell Law Directory

TAKUSHI, FUNAKI, WONG & STONE ATTORNEYS AT LAW, A LAW CORPORATION (AV)

Suite 1400 Grosvenor Center, 733 Bishop Street, 96813
Telephone: 808-543-9800
Fax: 808-543-9869
Email: tfwf@pixi.com

Roy E. Takushi
James T. Funaki
Alfred M. K. Wong
Robert M. Ehrhorn, Jr.
Dickson C. H. Lee
Peter T. Stone
James N. H. Yee
Ann L. Kurihara
Jacqueline Kong
Elizabeth A. Kane

For full biographical listings, see the Martindale-Hubbell Law Directory

ILLINOIS

*CHICAGO,** Cook Co.

BARNES & THORNBURG (AV)

2600 Chase Plaza, 10 South La Salle Street, 60603
Telephone: 312-357-1313
FAX: 312-759-5646
URL: http://www.btlaw.com
Indianapolis, Indiana Office: 11 South Meridian Street, 46204.
Telephone: 317-236-1313.
FAX: 317-231-7433.
Fort Wayne, Indiana Office: Suite 600, One Summit Square, 46802.
Telephone: 219-423-9440.
FAX: 219-424-8316.
South Bend, Indiana Office: 600 1st Source Bank Center, 100 North Michigan, 46601-1632.
Telephone: 219-233-1171.
FAX: 219-237-1125.
Elkhart, Indiana Office: 121 West Franklin Street, Suite 200, 46516.
Telephone: 219-293-0681.
FAX: 219-296-2535.
Washington, D.C. Office: 1401 Eye Street, N.W., Suite 500, 20005.
Telephone: 202-289-1313.
FAX: 202-289-1330.

MEMBER OF FIRM

William I. Kohn

ASSOCIATE

Kristan Quinn Laden

Representative Clients: AMPRO, Inc.; Chicago Football, LLC; Citizens Commercial Leasing Corporation; Commonwealth Edison Company; Harley-Davidson Motor Company; International Facilities Group, LLC; Marchesan Implementos E. Maquinas Agricoles Tatu SA; Ron Weber & Associates of Illinois, Inc.; Transtech Products Corporation; Whirlpool Corporation.

For Complete List of Firm Personnel, See General Section

For full biographical listings, see the Martindale-Hubbell Law Directory

WILDMAN, HARROLD, ALLEN & DIXON (AV)

225 West Wacker Drive, 30th Floor, 60606-1229
Telephone: 312-201-2000
Fax: 312-201-2555
Email: hennessy@whad.com *URL:* http://www.whad.com
Aurora, Illinois Office: 1961 W. Downer Place.
Telephone: 630-892-7021.
Fax: 630-892-7158.
Waukegan, Illinois Office: 404 West Water, P. O. Box 890.
Telephone: 847-625-5550.
Fax: 847-625-5555.
Lisle, Illinois Office: 4300 Commerce Court, Suite 320.
Telephone: 630-955-0555.
Fax: 630-955-0662
Toronto, Ontario correspondent Office: Keel Cottrelle. 36 Toronto Street, Suite 920.
Telephone: 416-367-2900.
Telefax: 416-367-2791.
Telex: 062-18660.

MEMBERS OF FIRM

John W. Costello
David J. Fischer
Alan B. Roth

For full biographical listings, see the Martindale-Hubbell Law Directory

INDIANA

ELKHART, Elkhart Co.

BARNES & THORNBURG (AV)

121 West Franklin Street, Suite 200, 46516
Telephone: 219-293-0681
FAX: 219-296-2535
URL: http://www.btlaw.com
Indianapolis, Indiana Office: 11 South Meridian Street, 46204.
Telephone: 317-236-1313.
FAX: 317-231-7433.
Fort Wayne, Indiana Office: Suite 600, One Summit Square, 46802.
Telephone: 219-423-9440.
FAX: 219-424-8316.
South Bend, Indiana Office: 600 1st Source Bank Center, 100 North Michigan, 46601-1632.
Telephone: 219-233-1171.
FAX: 219-237-1125.
Chicago, Illinois Office: 2600 Chase Plaza, 10 South La Salle Street, 60603.
Telephone: 312-357-1313.
FAX: 312-759-5646.
Washington, D.C. Office: 1401 Eye Street, N.W., Suite 500, 20005.
Telephone: 202-289-1313.
FAX: 202-289-1330.

MEMBER OF FIRM

Geoffrey K. Church

ASSOCIATE

Jennifer A. Bickley

Representative Clients: Bank One; Elkhart Community Schools; Elkhart General Hospital; Heywood Williams Group PLC; KeyBank National Association; Partners National Health Plans of Indiana, Inc.; Rieth-Riley Construction Co., Inc.; Skyline Corporation; Whirlpool Corporation.

For Complete List of Firm Personnel, See General Section

For full biographical listings, see the Martindale-Hubbell Law Directory

THORNE, GRODNIK, RANSEL, DUNCAN, BYRON, HOSTETLER & TRIPPEL, LLP (AV)

228 West High Street, 46516-3176
Telephone: 219-294-7473
FAX: 219-294-5390
Mishawaka, Indiana Office: 420 Lincoln Way West, P.O. Box 1210, 46544.
Telephone: 219-256-5660.
FAX: 219-674-6835.

MEMBERS OF FIRM

Charles H. Grodnik
J. Richard Ransel
Glenn L. Duncan
James R. Byron
Steven L. Hostetler
Michael A. Trippel

ASSOCIATES

W. Douglas Thorne
Gregg A. Hixenbaugh

OF COUNSEL

F. Richard Kramer
Joseph C. Zakas
William A. Thorne

Counsel for: Valley American Bank and Trust Co., Mishawaka, Indiana; NBD Bank.

For full biographical listings, see the Martindale-Hubbell Law Directory

*FORT WAYNE,** Allen Co.

BARNES & THORNBURG (AV)

Suite 600, One Summit Square, 46802
Telephone: 219-423-9440
FAX: 219-424-8316
URL: http://www.btlaw.com
Indianapolis, Indiana Office: 11 South Meridian Street, 46204.
Telephone: 317-236-1313.
FAX: 317-231-7433.
South Bend, Indiana Office: 600 1st Source Bank Center, 100 North Michigan, 46601-1632.
Telephone: 219-233-1171.
FAX: 219-237-1125.
Elkhart, Indiana Office: 121 West Franklin Street, Suite 200, 46516.
Telephone: 219-293-0681.
FAX: 219-296-2535.
Chicago, Illinois Office: 2600 Chase Plaza, 10 South La Salle Street, 60603.
Telephone: 312-357-1313.
FAX: 312-759-5646.
Washington, D.C. Office: 1401 Eye Street, N.W., Suite 500, 20005.
Telephone: 202-289-1313.
FAX: 202-289-1330.

MEMBER OF FIRM

Stephen L. Fink

ASSOCIATE

Matthew M. Hohman

Representative Clients: Demeter; Do it Best Corp.; EP Graphics, Inc.; Frick Services, Inc.; General Motors Corporation; Group Dekko International; Liberty Homes, Inc.; Lincoln National Corporation; Norwest Bank Indiana, N.A.; Zollner Pistons, L.L.C.

For Complete List of Firm Personnel, See General Section

For full biographical listings, see the Martindale-Hubbell Law Directory

HELMKE, BEAMS, BOYER & WAGNER (AV)

300 Metro Building, Berry & Harrison Streets, 46802-2242
Telephone: 219-422-7422
Telecopier: 219-422-6764
Email: hbbwdjb@aol.com
Email: rdboyer1@fortwayne.infi.net

MEMBERS OF FIRM

Walter E. Helmke (1901-1976)
Walter P. Helmke
R. David Boyer
Robert A. Wagner
J. Timothy McCaulay
Daniel J. Borgmann
Trina Glusenkamp Gould

ASSOCIATES

Payne D. Brown
R. David Boyer, II

OF COUNSEL

Glen J. Beams
William A. Berning

Representative Clients: Aalco Distributing Co., Inc.; Brotherhood Mutual Insurance Co.; Fremont Community Schools; Air-O-Mat, Inc.; Leo Distributors, Inc.; The City of Fort Wayne, Indiana; Foellinger Foundation, Inc.

For full biographical listings, see the Martindale-Hubbell Law Directory

*INDIANAPOLIS,** Marion Co.

BARNES & THORNBURG (AV)

11 South Meridian Street, 46204
Telephone: 317-236-1313
FAX: 317-231-7433; 317-231-7452
URL: http://www.btlaw.com
Fort Wayne, Indiana Office: Suite 600, One Summit Square, 46802.
Telephone: 219-423-9440.
FAX: 219-424-8316.
South Bend, Indiana Office: 600 1st Source Bank Center, 100 North Michigan, 46601-1632.
Telephone: 219-233-1171.
FAX: 219-237-1125.
Elkhart, Indiana Office: 121 West Franklin Street, Suite 200, 46516.
Telephone: 219-293-0681.
FAX: 219-296-2535.
Chicago, Illinois Office: 2600 Chase Plaza, 10 South La Salle Street, 60603.
Telephone: 312-357-1313.
FAX: 312-759-5646.
Washington, D.C. Office: 1401 Eye Street, N.W., Suite 500, 20005.
Telephone: 202-289-1313.
FAX: 202-289-1330.

MEMBERS OF FIRM

David M. Powlen
Michael K. McCrory
Alan K. Mills

OF COUNSEL

Edward A. Keirn

(See Next Column)

ASSOCIATES

Karen L. Kovalsky
Christine K. Jacobson
LaChelle D. Stepp

Representative Clients: Ameritech; DePuy Orthopaedics, Inc.; Dow AgroSciences; Eli Lilly and Company; Hillenbrand Industries; The Lincoln National Life Insurance Company; Purdue Research Foundation; Roche Diagnostics Corporation; Toyota Motor Corporation; Whirlpool Corporation.

For Complete List of Firm Personnel, See General Section

For full biographical listings, see the Martindale-Hubbell Law Directory

BUSCHMANN, CARR & SHANKS, PROFESSIONAL CORPORATION (AV)

1020 Market Tower, 10 West Market Street, 46204-2963
Telephone: 317-636-5511
Fax: 317-636-3661
Email: bcs@indy.net *URL:* http://www.buschmanncarr.com

C. Severin Buschmann (1896-1980)
John R. Carr, Jr.
John R. Carr, III
Bret S. Clement
Stephen R. Buschmann
Charles N. Doberneck
Gary L. Dilk
John N. Shanks II

Theresa A. Glass-Moody

OF COUNSEL

A. David Meyer

Representative Clients: Archer-Daniels Midland Co.; Ball Corp.; Industrial Valley Title Insurance; Creative Risk Management, Inc.; Deflecto Corporation; Glenfed Mortgage Corp.; Gates McDonald; Merchants National Bank & Trust Company of Muncie; Monumental Life Insurance Co.; National Council on Compensation Insurance.

For full biographical listings, see the Martindale-Hubbell Law Directory

HOPPER, GALLIHER & TUCKER, P.C. (AV)

Bank One Center/Circle, 111 Monument Circle, Suite 452, 46204-5170
Telephone: 317-635-5005
Facsimile: 317-634-2501

George W. Hopper
Mark R. Galliher
William J. Tucker
Ronald W. Buchmeier
Jeffrey E. Ramsey

Representative Clients: Banc One Corporation; National City Bank; Mutual Guaranty Corporation; I.T.T. Financial Services, Commercial Division; ABC Supply Co., Inc.; Sholodge, Inc.; Simon Debartolo Group, L.P.; IWC Resources Corp.; KRB Music Cos., Inc.; Whitewater Broadcasting Corp.

For full biographical listings, see the Martindale-Hubbell Law Directory

HOSTETLER & KOWALIK, P.C. (AV)

101 West Ohio Street Suite 2100, 46204
Telephone: 317-262-1001
Fax: 317-262-1010
Email: hoskow@indy.net *URL:* http://www.lawyers.com/hostetler&kowalik

Gary Lynn Hostetler
James S. Kowalik
David R. Krebs
J. Bradley Schooley
Timothy L. Black

For full biographical listings, see the Martindale-Hubbell Law Directory

ICE MILLER DONADIO & RYAN (AV)

One American Square Box 82001, 46282-0002
Telephone: 317-236-2100
Fax: 317-236-2219
Email: info@imdr.com *URL:* http://www.imdr.com
South Bend, Indiana Office: 211 West Washington Street, Suite 2420.
Telephone: 219-234-7933.
Fax: 219-234-7965. Internet E-mail: info@imdr.com. Web Site Address: http://www.imdr.com.
Chicago, Illinois Office: 135 South LaSalle Street, Suite 4100.
Telephone: 312-726-1567.
Fax: 312-641-6263. Internet E-mail: info@imdr.com. Web Site Address: http://www.imdr.com.

MEMBERS OF FIRM

Henry A. Efroymson
Dominic F. Polizzotto

OF COUNSEL

Peggy J. Naile
Susan Rogers Brooke

ASSOCIATES

John M. Hakes
Dennis H. Long

Representative Clients: National City Bank (Trust); Bank One, Indianapolis (Trust); Union County National Bank; Eastman Kodak Co.; Hewlett Packard Corp.; Phoenix Home Life Insurance; The National Bank of Indianapolis; Huntington National Bank; Transamerica Insurance Finance Corp.; Franchise Finance Corporations of America.

(See Next Column)

ICE MILLER DONADIO & RYAN—*Continued*

For Complete List of Firm Personnel, See General Section

For full biographical listings, see the Martindale-Hubbell Law Directory

*SOUTH BEND,** St. Joseph Co.

BARNES & THORNBURG (AV)

600 1st Source Bank Center, 100 North Michigan, 46601-1632
Telephone: 219-233-1171
FAX: 219-237-1125
URL: http://www.btlaw.com
Indianapolis, Indiana Office: 11 South Meridian Street, 46204.
Telephone: 317-236-1313.
FAX: 317-231-7433.
Fort Wayne, Indiana Office: Suite 600, One Summit Square, 46802.
Telephone: 219-423-9440.
FAX: 219-424-8316.
Elkhart, Indiana Office: 121 West Franklin Street, Suite 200, 46516.
Telephone: 219-293-0681.
FAX: 219-296-2535.
Chicago, Illinois Office: 2600 Chase Plaza, 10 South La Salle Street, 60603.
Telephone: 312-357-1313.
FAX: 312-759-5646.
Washington, D.C. Office: 1401 Eye Street, N.W., Suite 500, 20005.
Telephone: 202-289-1313.
FAX: 202-289-1330.

MEMBERS OF FIRM

Michael B. Watkins
Scott M. Keller
Michael D. Hardy

ASSOCIATES

Mark J. Adey
Adrianne L. Hoehner

Representative Clients: 1st Source Bank; AM General Corp.; Cadence Environmental Energy; Crowe, Chizek and Company L.L.P.; Gast Manufacturing Corporation; Memorial Hospital of South Bend; National Steel Corporation; University of Notre Dame; Whirlpool Corporation; Whiteford, Inc.

For Complete List of Firm Personnel, See General Section

For full biographical listings, see the Martindale-Hubbell Law Directory

IOWA

*CEDAR RAPIDS,** Linn Co.

MOYER & BERGMAN, P.L.C. (AV)

2720 First Avenue, N.E., 52406-1943
Telephone: 319-366-7331
Telecopier: 319-366-3668
Mailing Address: P.O. Box 1943,
Email: M&B@moyerbergman.com

MEMBER OF FIRM

Eric W. Lam

Representative Clients: National Oats Co., a division of Curtice-Burns, Inc.; CRST, Inc.; SSangyong (U.S.A.), Inc.; Maquoketa State Bank; Postville State Bank; Ag Services of America, Inc.; American Family Insurance Group.

For full biographical listings, see the Martindale-Hubbell Law Directory

*DES MOINES,** Polk Co.

HUBER, BOOK, CORTESE, HAPPE & BROWN, P.L.C. (AV)

317 Sixth Avenue, Suite 200, 50309-4127
Telephone: 515-243-4148
Fax: 515-243-5481
Email: huber@desmoineslaw.com

MEMBERS OF FIRM

James C. Huber
Richard G. Book
Joseph S. Cortese II
Joseph A. Happe
Terrence D. Brown
Patrick D. Smith

ASSOCIATES

Deborah M. Stein
William H. Grell
Jeffrey W. Lanz
R. Saffin Parrish

Representative Clients: Atlantic Mutual Cos.; CNA Insurance Cos.; Fireman's Fund American Insurance Companies; Great West Casualty Co.; Liberty Mutual Insurance Co.; Maryland Insurance Group; Prudential Property and Casualty Insurance Co.; USF&G Company.
Reference: Bank of America.

For full biographical listings, see the Martindale-Hubbell Law Directory

KENTUCKY

*LOUISVILLE,** Jefferson Co.

MAPOTHER & MAPOTHER (AV)

801 West Jefferson Street, 40202
Telephone: 502-587-5400
Fax: 502-587-5444
Email: mapother@mapother-atty.com *URL:* http://www.mapother-atty.com
Lexington, Kentucky Office: 100 East Vine Street, Suite 810.
Telephone: 606-253-0003.
Fax: 606-255-3961.
Jeffersonville, Indiana Office: 505 East Seventh Street.
Telephone: 812-288-5059.
Fax: 502-587-5444.
Cincinnati, Ohio Office: Kroger Building, Suite 2220, 1014 Vine Street.
Telephone: 513-381-4888.
Fax: 513-381-3117.
Huntington, West Virginia Office: Morris Building, Suite 701, 845 Fourth Avenue.
Telephone: 304-525-1185.
Fax: 304-529-3764.
Evansville, Indiana Office: 329 Main Street, Suite 602.
Telephone: 812-421-9108.
Fax: 812-421-9109.

MEMBERS OF FIRM

William R. Mapother
Thomas L. Canary, Jr.
Hollis L. Searcy
Charles M. Friedman

Roberta S. Dunlap (Resident, Evansville, Indiana Office)
Dean A. Langdon (Resident, Lexington, Kentucky Office)
Lee W. Grace
Brian E. Chapman (Resident, Cincinnati, Ohio Office)
T. Lawson McSwain, II
John D. Meyers (Resident, Lexington, Kentucky Office)
Lisa A. Herndon
Ronda C. Gunter (Resident, Huntington, West Virginia Office)
Steven B. Mulrooney
Dennis M. Ostrowski
Gerald O. Henderson, Jr. (Resident, Huntington, West Virginia Office)
Miles S. Apple
Joy B. Gilliam (Resident, Lexington, Kentucky Office)
Vincent A. Dimasi (Not admitted in KY; Resident, Cincinnati, Ohio Office)
Charlie W. Gordon

Representative Clients: Ford Motor Credit Co.; General Electric Capital Corp.; General Motors Acceptance Corp.; Nissan Motor Acceptance Corp.; Cuna Mutual Insurance Society; Kentucky Credit Union League; PNC Bank; Associates Financial Services Co.; Household Finance Corp.; Chrysler Financial Corp.

For full biographical listings, see the Martindale-Hubbell Law Directory

MORGAN & POTTINGER, P.S.C. (AV)

601 West Main Street, 40202
Telephone: 502-589-2780
Telecopier: 502-585-3498
URL: http://www.morganandpottinger.com
Lexington, Kentucky Office: 133 West Short Street.
Telephone: 606-253-1900.
Telecopier: 606-255-2038.
New Albany, Indiana Office: 120 East Market Street.
Telephone: 812-948-0008.
Telecopier: 812-944-6215.

Patrick E. Morgan
John T. McGarvey
C. Edward Hastie (Resident, Lexington Office)
M. Deane Stewart
James I. Murray (Resident, Lexington Office)
Douglas Gene Sharp
John A. Majors
Mark J. Sandlin
Scott T. Rickman (Resident, Lexington Office)
M. Thurman Senn
Hal D. Friedman

Thomas C. Fenton
Ruthanne Q. Whitt
Garret B. Hannegan (Resident, New Albany, Indiana Office)
Diane E. Bluhm (Not admitted in KY)
Laura Kincheloe (Resident, Lexington Office)
Drayer L. Bott
John Allan Combs (Resident, Lexington Office)
Jean T. Harrod

SENIOR COUNSEL

David C. Pottinger

COUNSEL

Elmer E. Morgan
J. Jeffrey Cooke

For full biographical listings, see the Martindale-Hubbell Law Directory

Louisville—Continued

ROTH FOLEY BRYANT & COOPER, PLLC (AV)

First Trust Centre, Suite 300S, 200 South Fifth Street, 40202-3236
Telephone: 502-569-7550
Fax: 502-540-0123
Email: RFBC.com

Irvin D. Foley
David M. Roth
David H. Cooper
Lisa Koch Bryant
K. Gail Russell
Christian L. Juckett

OF COUNSEL

James E. Fahey
David W. Gray

Representative Clients: Bank One, Kentucky, NA; Commonwealth Bank & Trust Co.; Farm Credit Services of Mid-America; First Citizens Bank of Hardin Co.; Great Financial Bank; Huntington National Bank; Huntington Acceptance Co.; People's State Bank.

For full biographical listings, see the Martindale-Hubbell Law Directory

MARYLAND

*ROCKVILLE,** Montgomery Co.

BARKLEY & KENNEDY, CHARTERED (AV)

Suite 1407, 51 Monroe Street, 20850
Telephone: 301-251-6600
FAX: 301-762-2606
Email: barkenlaw@erols.com *URL:* http://www.lawyers.com/barkenlaw

Brian E. Barkley
Daniel M. Kennedy, III

For full biographical listings, see the Martindale-Hubbell Law Directory

SILVER SPRING, Montgomery Co.

COGGINS, HARMAN & HEWITT (AV)

A Partnership of Professional Corporations
8905 Fairview Road, Suite 600, 20910
Telephone: 301-587-2880
Facsimile: 301-495-4990
Email: CHHlaw587@aol.com
Washington, D.C. Office: Suite 330, G Street Lobby, 655 15th Street, N.W.
Falls Church, Virginia Office: 254 North Washington Street.

William N. Coggins
John H. Harman
William E. Hewitt
John F. Davis

OF COUNSEL

Dale E. Duncan (Not admitted in MD)

For full biographical listings, see the Martindale-Hubbell Law Directory

*TOWSON,** Baltimore Co.

COHN, GOLDBERG & DEUTSCH, LLC (AV)

600 Baltimore Avenue, Suite 208, 21204-4084
Telephone: 410-296-2550
Fax: 410-296-2558
Email: RDeutsch@Cohn-Goldberg-Deutsch.com
Silver Spring, Maryland Office: 8630 Fenton Street, Suite 320, 20910.
Telephone: 301-585-9555.
Fax: 301-585-6292.

Edward S. Cohn
Stephen N. Goldberg
Ronald S. Deutsch

For full biographical listings, see the Martindale-Hubbell Law Directory

MASSACHUSETTS

*BOSTON,** Suffolk Co.

BURNS & LEVINSON LLP (AV)

125 Summer Street, 02110-1624
Telephone: 617-345-3000
Telecopier: 617-345-3299
URL: http://www.burnslevinson.com
Hingham, Massachusetts Office: 175 Derby Street.
Telephone: 781-749-3810.
Telecopier: 781-749-3980.
Wellesley, Massachusetts Office: 60 Walnut Street.
Telephone: 781-235-1034.
Telecopier: 781-235-5975.

(See Next Column)

Victor Bass
Raymond E. Baxter
Michael H. Goshko
Frederick S. Paulsen
Frank A. Segall
Norman C. Spector
Richard J. Tetrault
Stuart M. Van Tine
(Resident, Hingham Office)
Josef B. Volman
Robert W. Weinstein

ASSOCIATES

Christopher D. Guerin
Leslie B. Muldowney
Christina M. Murray

For Complete List of Firm Personnel, See General Section

For full biographical listings, see the Martindale-Hubbell Law Directory

DANIELS LAW OFFICES, P.C. (AV)

One Center Plaza, 02108-1801
Telephone: 617-227-7300
Facsimile: 617-227-9643
Email: dlopc.com *URL:* http://www.dlopc.com

Richard S. Daniels, Jr.

Peter Dauksewicz
Karen J. Wisniowski
Kenneth W. Luke
Lynn M. Flury

For full biographical listings, see the Martindale-Hubbell Law Directory

HINCKLEY, ALLEN & SNYDER LLP (AV)

28 State Street, 30th Floor, 02109-1775
Telephone: 617-345-9000
Email: firm@haslaw.com *URL:* http://www.haslaw.com
Providence, Rhode Island Office: 1500 Fleet Center.
Telephone: 401-274-2000.
Fax: 401-277-9600. URL: http://www.hawlaw.com.

MEMBERS OF FIRM

Paula K. Andrews
David D. Barricelli
(Not admitted in MA)
E. Jerome Batty
(Not admitted in MA)
Jonathan Bell
Paul Bork
Stephen J. Carlotti
(Not admitted in MA)
David Barry Connolly
Joseph P. Curran
(Not admitted in MA)
Michael P. DeFanti
Eric F. Eisenberg
Malcolm Farmer, III
Margaret D. Farrell
(Not admitted in MA)
Pasco Gasbarro Jr.
Hugh J. Gorman, III
Alan P. Gottlieb
William R. Grimm
Paul A. Hedstrom
Joel Lewin
Matthew T. Marcello, III
(Not admitted in MA)
Frederick P. McClure
Elizabeth Murdock Myers
Paul F. O'Donnell, III
H. Peter Olsen
(Not admitted in MA)
Gerald J. Petros
James O. Reavis
Jeremy Ritzenberg
Ralph J. Rivkind
David J. Rubin
Douglas F. Seaver
Scott E. Sheridan
Herman Snyder
David R. Sullivan
Robert F. Sylvia
Howard E. Walker
(Not admitted in MA)

ASSOCIATES

Mark Bianchi
Andrew D. Cummings
June E. Daniel
(Not admitted in MA)
Kim Herman Goslant
Gloria Maria Gutierrez
Kelley Jordan-Price
Catherine S. Kim
Christopher W. Morog
Joseph D. Whelan
(Not admitted in MA)

OF COUNSEL

Bentley Tobin

For Complete List of Firm Personnel, See General Section

For full biographical listings, see the Martindale-Hubbell Law Directory

*SPRINGFIELD,** Hampden Co.

GOLD & VANARIA, P.C. (AV)

BankBoston Building, 1350 Main Street, Suite 1400, 01103-1627
Telephone: 413-747-7700
Fax: 413-747-9650
Email: govancoll@aol.com

Jerome S. Gold
Alan J. Vanaria

David A. Lavenburg
Kevin M. Brown

References: Norwest Bank Iowa, N.A. Card Services Division; Baystate Medical Center; Springfield Institution for Savings.

For full biographical listings, see the Martindale-Hubbell Law Directory

MICHIGAN

*DETROIT,** Wayne Co.

BODMAN, LONGLEY & DAHLING LLP (AV)

34th Floor 100 Renaissance Center, 48243
Telephone: 313-259-7777
Fax: 313-393-7579
Email: info@bodmanlongley.com *URL:* http://www.bodmanlongley.com
Troy, Michigan Office: Suite 2020, 755 West Big Beaver Road.
Telephone: 248-362-2110.
Fax: 248-244-0780.
Ann Arbor, Michigan Office: 110 Miller, Suite 300.
Telephone: 734-761-3780.
Fax: 734-930-2494.
Northern Michigan Office: 229 Court Street, P.O. Box 405, Cheboygan.
Telephone: 231-627-4351.
Fax: 231-627-2802.

MEMBERS OF FIRM

Robert J. Diehl, Jr.
Lawrence P. Hanson (Cheboygan Office)
Ralph E. McDowell
Marc M. Bakst

ASSOCIATE

Brian R. Trumbauer

For Representataive Client list, See General Section

For Complete List of Firm Personnel, See General Section

For full biographical listings, see the Martindale-Hubbell Law Directory

MILLER, CANFIELD, PADDOCK AND STONE, P.L.C. (AV)

A Professional Limited Liability Company
Founded in 1852 by Sidney Davy Miller
150 West Jefferson, Suite 2500, 48226-4415
Telephone: 313-963-6420
Fax: 313-496-7500
Cable Address: "Stem Detroit"
URL: http://www.millercanfield.com
Ann Arbor, Michigan Office: 101 North Main Street, 7th Floor, 48104-1400.
Telephone: 734-663-2445.
Fax: 734-747-7147.
Troy, Michigan Office: 840 West Long Lake Road, Suite 200, 48098.
Telephone: 248-879-2000.
Fax: 248-879-2001.
Grand Rapids, Michigan Office: 99 Monroe, N.W., Suite 1200, 49503-2639.
Telephone: 616-454-8656.
Fax: 616-776-6322.
Howell, Michigan Office: 121 South Barnard Street, Suite 4, 48843-2305.
Telephone: 517-546-7600.
Telecopier: 517-546-6974.
Kalamazoo, Michigan Office: 444 West Michigan Avenue, 49007-3752.
Telephone: 616-381-7030.
Fax: 616-382-0244.
Lansing, Michigan Office: One Michigan Avenue, Suite 900, 48933-1609.
Telephone: 517-487-2070.
Fax: 517-374-6304.
Monroe, Michigan Office: 214 East Elm Avenue, Suite 100, 48162-2682.
Telephone: 734-243-2000.
Fax: 734-243-0901.
Washington, D.C. Office: 1900 K Street, N.W., Suite 1150. 20006.
Telephone: 202-429-5575; 785-0600.
Fax: 202-331-1118; 785-1234.
Pensacola, Florida Office: 25 West Cedar, 32501.
Telephone: 850-469-1088.
Fax: 850-432-0677.
New York, New York Office: 1450 Broadway, 41st Floor, 10018.
Telephone: 212-704-4400.
Fax: 212-704-4410.
Gdynia, Poland Office: UL. Slaska 21, 81-319.
Telephone: 011-485-831-2808.
Fax: 011-48-58-628 6411.
Warsaw, Poland Office: UL. Nowogrodzkall, 5th Floor, 00-513.
Telephone: 011-4822 529 0200.
Fax: 011-4822 529 0201.
Katowice, Poland Office: UL. Francuska 35/37, 40-027.
Telephone: 011 (48-32) 757-2414.
Fax: 011 (48-32) 757-2483.

PRINCIPALS OF FIRM

Terrence M. Crawford
Robert E. Lee Wright (Grand Rapids Offices)
Michael H. Traison
Jonathan S. Green
Donald J. Hutchinson
Lori L. Purkey (Kalamazoo Office)

(See Next Column)

ASSOCIATE

Stuart M. Heath (Kalamazoo Office)

Representative Firm Clients: Chrysler Corporation; Comerica, Incorporated; City of Detroit, Michigan; Detroit Tigers, Inc.; First of Michigan; Ford Motor Company; Ford Motor Credit Company; Great Lakes Bancorp; Henry Ford Hospital; INVETECH Company.

For Complete List of Firm Personnel, See General Section

For full biographical listings, see the Martindale-Hubbell Law Directory

PYTELL & VARCHETTI, P.C. (AV)

18580 Mack Avenue, 48236
Telephone: 313-343-9200; 1-888-292-4LAW
Fax: 313-343-0207
Email: PROBATE@compuserve.com *URL:* http://www.MIprobate.com

Robert H. Pytell
Henry C. Pytell (1903-1988)
Paul E. Varchetti

For full biographical listings, see the Martindale-Hubbell Law Directory

*GRAND RAPIDS,** Kent Co.

MILLER, CANFIELD, PADDOCK AND STONE, P.L.C. (AV)

A Professional Limited Liability Company
Founded in 1852 by Sidney Davy Miller
99 Monroe, N.W. Suite 1200, 49503-2639
Telephone: 616-454-8656
Fax: 616-776-6322
URL: http://www.millercanfield.com
Detroit, Michigan Office: 150 West Jefferson, Suite 2500, 48226-4415.
Telephone: 313-963-6420.
Fax: 313-496-7500.
Cable Address: "Stem Detroit."
Ann Arbor, Michigan Office: 101 North Main Street, 7th Floor, 48104-1400.
Telephone: 734-663-2445.
Fax: 734-747-7147.
Troy, Michigan Office: 840 West Long Lake Road, Suite 200, 48098.
Telephone: 248-879-2000.
Fax: 248-879-2001.
Howell, Michigan Office: 121 South Barnard Street, Suite 4, 48843-2305.
Telephone: 517-546-7600.
Telecopier: 517-546-6974.
Kalamazoo, Michigan Office: 444 West Michigan Avenue, 49007-3752.
Telephone: 616-381-7030.
Fax: 616-382-0244.
Lansing, Michigan Office: One Michigan Avenue, Suite 900, 48933-1609.
Telephone: 517-487-2070.
Fax: 517-374-6304.
Monroe, Michigan Office: 214 East Elm Avenue, Suite 100, 48162-2682.
Telephone: 734-243-2000.
Fax: 734-243-0901.
Washington, D.C. Office: 1900 K Street, N.W., Suite 1150. 20006.
Telephone: 202-429-5575; 785-0600.
Fax: 202-331-1118; 785-1234.
Pensacola, Florida Office: 25 West Cedar, 32501.
Telephone: 850-469-1088.
Fax: 850-432-0677.
New York, New York Office: 1450 Broadway, 41st Floor, 10018.
Telephone: 212-704-4400.
Fax: 212-704-4410.
Gdynia, Poland Office: UL. Slaska 21, 81-319.
Telephone: 011-485-831-2808.
Fax: 011-48-58-628 6411.
Warsaw, Poland Office: UL. Nowogrodzkall, 5th Floor, 00-513.
Telephone: 011-4822 529 0200.
Fax: 011-4822 529 0201.
Katowice, Poland Office: UL. Francuska 35/37, 40-027.
Telephone: 011 (48-32) 757-2414.
Fax: 011 (48-32) 757-2483.

PRINCIPALS

Robert E. Lee Wright

Representative Firm Clients: Chrysler Corporation; Comerica, Incorporated; City of Detroit, Michigan; Detroit Tigers, Inc.; First of Michigan; Ford Motor Company; Ford Motor Credit Company; Great Lakes Bancorp; Henry Ford Hospital; INVETECH Company.

For Complete List of Firm Personnel, See General Section

For full biographical listings, see the Martindale-Hubbell Law Directory

*KALAMAZOO,** Kalamazoo Co.

MILLER, CANFIELD, PADDOCK AND STONE, P.L.C. (AV)

A Professional Limited Liability Company
Founded in 1852 by Sidney Davy Miller
444 West Michigan Avenue, 49007-3752
Telephone: 616-381-7030
Fax: 616-382-0244
URL: http://www.millercanfield.com
Detroit, Michigan Office: 150 West Jefferson, Suite 2500, 48226-4415.
Telephone: 313-963-6420.
Fax: 313-496-7500.
Cable Address: "Stem Detroit."
Ann Arbor, Michigan Office: 101 North Main Street, 7th Floor, 48104-1400.
Telephone: 734-663-2445.
Fax: 734-747-7147.
Troy, Michigan Office: 840 West Long Lake Road, Suite 200, 48098.
Telephone: 248-879-2000.
Fax: 248-879-2001.
Grand Rapids, Michigan Office: 99 Monroe, N.W., Suite 1200, 49503-2639.
Telephone: 616-454-8656.
Fax: 616-776-6322.
Howell, Michigan Office: 121 South Barnard Street, Suite 4, 48843-2305.
Telephone: 517-546-7600.
Telecopier: 517-546-6974.
Lansing, Michigan Office: One Michigan Avenue, Suite 900, 48933-1609.
Telephone: 517-487-2070.
Fax: 517-374-6304.
Monroe, Michigan Office: 214 East Elm Avenue, Suite 100, 48162-2682.
Telephone: 734-243-2000.
Fax: 734-243-0901.
Washington, D.C. Office: 1900 K Street, N.W., Suite 1150. 20006.
Telephone: 202-429-5575; 785-0600.
Fax: 202-331-1118; 785-1234.
Pensacola, Florida Office: 25 West Cedar, 32501.
Telephone: 850-469-1088.
Fax: 850-432-0677.
New York, New York Office: 1450 Broadway, 41st Floor, 10018.
Telephone: 212-704-4400.
Fax: 212-704-4410.
Gdynia, Poland Office: UL. Slaska 21, 81-319.
Telephone: 011-485-831-2808.
Fax: 011-48-58-628 6411.
Warsaw, Poland Office: UL. Nowogrodzkall, 5th Floor, 00-513.
Telephone: 011-4822 529 0200.
Fax: 011-4822 529 0201.
Katowice, Poland Office: UL. Francuska 35/37, 40-027.
Telephone: 011 (48-32) 757-2414.
Fax: 011 (48-32) 757-2483.

PRINCIPALS

Lori L. Purkey

RESIDENT ASSOCIATE

Stuart M. Heath

Representative Firm Clients: Chrysler Corporation; Comerica, Incorporated; City of Detroit, Michigan; Detroit Tigers, Inc.; First of Michigan; Ford Motor Company; Ford Motor Credit Company; Great Lakes Bancorp; Henry Ford Hospital; INVETECH Company.

For Complete List of Firm Personnel, See General Section

For full biographical listings, see the Martindale-Hubbell Law Directory

SOUTHFIELD, Oakland Co.

GOLD LANGE & MAJOROS, P.C. (AV)

24901 Northwestern Highway, Suite 444, 48075
Telephone: 248-350-8220
Fax: 248-350-0519
Email: goldbricks@aol.com *URL:* http://www.lawyers.com/glm

Stuart A. Gold
John C. Lange
Elias Themistocles Majoros

Marilyn R. Somers
Ronna Stevens Gold
Deborah S. Rubin
Scott A. Gies

For full biographical listings, see the Martindale-Hubbell Law Directory

TROY, Oakland Co.

JACOB & WEINGARTEN (AV)

2301 West Big Beaver Road, Suite 777, 48084-3300
Telephone: 248-649-1900
Facsimile: 248-649-2920
Email: law@jacobweingarten.com
North Palm Beach, Florida Office: P.O. Box 14037, 33408.
Telephone: 561-640-5600.

Steven P. Schubiner
Howard S. Sher
Peter A. Nathan (Resident, North Palm Beach, Florida Office)
Robert K. Siegel
Scott Randall Schubiner

Representative Clients: Afco Credit Corporation; Archon Group, L.P.; IBM Credit Corp.; First Federal of Michigan; Zahn Associates, Inc.

For full biographical listings, see the Martindale-Hubbell Law Directory

CRIMINAL TRIAL PRACTICE

ALABAMA

*BAY MINETTE,** Baldwin Co.

BALL & KOONS (AV)

324 Courthouse Square, P.O. Drawer #1609, 36507
Telephone: 334-937-2303
Fax: 334-937-1243
URL: http://www.lawyers.com/ball&koons

E. E. Ball
Harold A. Koons, III

Reference: Regions Bank of Bay Minette.

For full biographical listings, see the Martindale-Hubbell Law Directory

*BIRMINGHAM,** Jefferson Co.

BAXLEY, DILLARD, DAUPHIN & MCKNIGHT (AV)

2008 3rd Avenue South, 35233
Telephone: 205-939-0995; 205-271-1100
Telecopier: 205-271-1108

MEMBERS OF FIRM

William J. Baxley
Joel E. Dillard
Charles A. Dauphin
Stewart D. McKnight, III
William C. Barclift
Betsy Palmer Collins
Donald R. James, Jr

ASSOCIATE

Elizabeth Louise Wood

For full biographical listings, see the Martindale-Hubbell Law Directory

GORHAM & WALDREP, P.C. (AV)

2101 6th Avenue North, Suite 700, 35203
Telephone: 205-254-3216; 251-9166
Telecopier: 205-324-3802
Email: info@gorham-waldrep.com *URL:* http://www.gorham-waldrep.com
Montgomery, Alabama Office: 250 Commerce Street, P.O. Box 4837, 36103-4837.
Telephone: 334-262-0777.
Telecopier: 334-262-0742.

Victor Kelley

Representative Clients: Jefferson County Personnel Board; Birmingham-Jefferson Civic Center Authority; The Water Works and Sewer Board of the City of Birmingham; City of Homewood; American Federation of Government Employees Local #1945; City of Pelham; Town of Kimberly; Alabama Tire Dealers Assn.; Southern States Body Shop Assn.

For Complete List of Firm Personnel, See General Section

For full biographical listings, see the Martindale-Hubbell Law Directory

REDDEN, MILLS & CLARK (AV)

940 Regions Bank Building, 417 North 20th Street, 35203
Telephone: 205-322-0457
Fax: 205-322-8481
URL: http://www.rmc-law.com

MEMBERS OF FIRM

L. Drew Redden
William H. Mills
William N. Clark
Gerald L. Miller
Stephen W. Shaw
Maxwell H. Pulliam, Jr.
Ronald J. Gault

References: SouthTrust Bank; Regions Bank.

For full biographical listings, see the Martindale-Hubbell Law Directory

*CHATOM,** Washington Co.

TURNER, ONDERDONK, KIMBROUGH & HOWELL, P.A. (AV)

1021 Central Avenue, P.O. Drawer 1389, 36518
Telephone: 334-847-2237
Fax: 334-847-3115
Email: firm@tokh.com *URL:* http://www.tokh.com
Mobile, Alabama Office: 1359 Dauphin Street.
Telephone: 334-432-2855.
Fax: 334-432-2863.

Edward P. Turner, Jr.
A. Michael Onderdonk
William A. Kimbrough, Jr. (Resident, Mobile Office)
Gordon K. Howell
Marc E. Bradley (Resident, Mobile Office)
Halron W. Turner
Frank Woodson (Resident, Mobile Office)
David M. Huggins (Resident, Mobile Office)
E. Tatum Turner

(See Next Column)

LEGAL SUPPORT PERSONNEL

Thomas E. Fuller

For full biographical listings, see the Martindale-Hubbell Law Directory

*HUNTSVILLE,** Madison Co.

MORRIS, CLOUD AND CONCHIN, P.C. (AV)

521 Madison Street, P.O. Box 248, 35804
Telephone: 256-534-0065
Fax: 256-539-0741

Harvey B. Morris (P.C.)
Joseph M. Cloud
Gary V. Conchin

Maureen "Mike" K. Cooper
Daniel B. Banks, Jr.

For full biographical listings, see the Martindale-Hubbell Law Directory

*MOBILE,** Mobile Co.

BRISKMAN & BINION, P.C. (AV)

205 Church Street, P.O. Box 43, 36601
Telephone: 334-433-7600
Fax: 334-433-4485
Email: briskman@zebra.net

Donald M. Briskman
Christ N. Coumanis
Kimberly C. Hodgson

A List of Representative Clients will be furnished upon request.
References: Regions Bank; AmSouth Bank, N.A.; Southtrust Bank of Mobile.

For Complete List of Firm Personnel, See General Section

For full biographical listings, see the Martindale-Hubbell Law Directory

CLARK, DEEN & COPELAND, P.C. (AV)

207 Church Street, P.O. Box 2705, 36652
Telephone: 334-433-5860
Telecopier: 334-433-0703
Email: Clark003@aol.com

Robert F. Clark
T. Jefferson Deen, III
W. Lloyd Copeland

Edward C. Blount, Jr.

For full biographical listings, see the Martindale-Hubbell Law Directory

HELMSING, SIMS & LEACH, P.C. (AV)

The Laclede Building, 150 Government Street, Suite 2000, P.O. Box 2767, 36652
Telephone: 334-432-5521
Telecopy: 334-432-0633

Larry U. Sims
Frederick G. Helmsing
John N. Leach, Jr.
Warren C. Herlong, Jr.
James B. Newman
Robert H. Rouse
Charles H. Dodson, Jr.
Joseph P. H. Babington
R. Alan Alexander
John J. Crowley, Jr.
Joseph D. Steadman
Todd S. Strohmeyer

William R. Lancaster
Robin Kilpatrick Fincher
John Townsend Dukes
John Casey Pipes
James Bradford Pittman, Jr.

For full biographical listings, see the Martindale-Hubbell Law Directory

*MONTGOMERY,** Montgomery Co.

ROBISON & BELSER, P.A. (AV)

200 Coosa Street, 36104
Telephone: 334-834-7000
Telecopier: 334-834-7011
Mailing Address: Drawer 1470, Montgomery, AL, 36102
Email: tsides@mont.mindspring.com

David B. Byrne, Jr.
John M. Bolton, III

General Counsel for: Montgomery County Board of Education.
Representative Clients: Union Bank & Trust Co.; Liberty National Life Insurance Co.; State Farm Mutual Fire & Casualty Co.

For full biographical listings, see the Martindale-Hubbell Law Directory

ALASKA

*ANCHORAGE,** Third Judicial District

Feldman & Orlansky (AV)

Suite 400, 500 L Street, 99501
Telephone: 907-272-3538
Telecopier: 907-274-0819
URL: http://www.frozenlaw.com

Jeffrey M. Feldman
Susan C. Orlansky

ASSOCIATE

James E. Fosler

LEGAL SUPPORT PERSONNEL

Wendy Bursiel Weber (Legal Assistant)

Reference: Key Bank of Alaska.

For full biographical listings, see the Martindale-Hubbell Law Directory

ARIZONA

*FLAGSTAFF,** Coconino Co.

Aspey, Watkins & Diesel, P.L.L.C. (AV)

123 North San Francisco, 3rd Floor, 86001
Telephone: 520-774-1478
Facsimile: 520-774-8404
Email: info@AWDLAW.com
Sedona, Arizona Office: 120 Soldier Pass Road.
Telephone: 520-282-5955.
Facsimile: 520-282-5962.
Cottonwood, Arizona Office: 2400 E. Highway 89A, Suite C.
Telephone: 520-639-1881.
Facsimile: 520-639-0272.

MEMBERS OF FIRM

Frederick M. Fritz Aspey
Harold L. Watkins
Louis M. Diesel
Bruce S. Griffen
Donald H. Bayles, Jr.
Kaign N. Christy
John J. Dempsey
Zachary J. Markham
James E. Ledbetter

Whitney Cunningham
Pernell Whynn McGuire
Stephen A. Thompson
Justin G. Vaughn
Janet Altschuler
Brett M. Hager
Mary E. Widdowson

Representative Clients: Farmer's Insurance Company of Arizona; Pepsi-Cola Bottling Company of Northern Arizona; Bill Luke's Chrysler-Plymouth, Inc.; First American Title Insurance Company; Transnation Title Insurance Co.; Page Electric Utility; Comprehensive Access Health Plan, Inc.; Northern Arizona Healthcare Corporation.
Reference: First Interstate Bank-Arizona, N.A., Flagstaff, Arizona.

For full biographical listings, see the Martindale-Hubbell Law Directory

MESA, Maricopa Co.

Law Offices of David Michael Cantor, P.C. (AV)

1839 South Alma School Road, Suite 250, 85210
Telephone: 602-831-5858; 888-822-6867
Fax: 602-831-5806
URL: http://www.dmcantor.com

David Michael Cantor

Robert P. Jarvis
Simone Anne Atkinson
Barry James Handler
Ron Ozer
Kristen Mckenzie Curry
John R. Gaertner, Jr.

COUNSEL

Alex B. Vakula

For full biographical listings, see the Martindale-Hubbell Law Directory

*PHOENIX,** Maricopa Co.

Michael V. Black (AV)

3550 North Central Avenue, Suite 1010, 85012
Telephone: 602-265-7200
Fax: 602-265-2431
URL: http://www.lawyers.com/michaelvblack

For full biographical listings, see the Martindale-Hubbell Law Directory

Burch & Cracchiolo, P.A. (AV)

702 East Osborn Road, Suite 200, 85014
Telephone: 602-274-7611
Fax: 602-234-0341
Mailing Address: P.O. Box 16882, Phoenix, AZ, 85011
Email: library@bcattorneys.com

Stephen E. Silver

Martha C. Patrick

For Complete List of Firm Personnel, See General Section

For full biographical listings, see the Martindale-Hubbell Law Directory

O. Joseph Chornenky, P.C. (AV)

Suite A209, 301 East Bethany Home Road, 85012
Telephone: 602-264-3289
Fax: 602-264-3779
Email: ojcpc@aol.com

O. Joseph Chornenky

For full biographical listings, see the Martindale-Hubbell Law Directory

Crowe & Scott, P.A. (AV)

1100 East Washington Suite 200, 85034-1090
Telephone: 602-252-2570
Fax: 602-252-1939
URL: http://www.lawyers.com/crowe&scott

Tom Crowe
Michael B. Scott (1945-1997)

Ginette M. Chinichian

For full biographical listings, see the Martindale-Hubbell Law Directory

Debus Kazan & Westerhausen, Ltd. (AV)

335 East Palm Lane, 85004
Telephone: 602-257-8900
Fax: 602-257-0723
Email: debusandkazan@uswest.com

Larry L. Debus
Lawrence Ian Kazan
Tracey Westerhausen

References: Firstar Metropolitan Bank; Citibank, Arizona.

For full biographical listings, see the Martindale-Hubbell Law Directory

David G. Derickson, P.C. (AV)

3636 North Central, Suite 1050, 85012
Telephone: 602-277-6072
Fax: 602-277-6078
Email: david.derickson@azbar.org

David G. Derickson

For full biographical listings, see the Martindale-Hubbell Law Directory

Feder Law Office, P.A. (AV)

Biltmore Pavilion, Suite 140, 2525 E. Arizona Biltmore Circle, 85016
Telephone: 602-257-0135
Fax: 602-954-8737
Mailing Address: P.O. Box 44560, Phoenix, Arizona, 85064-4560

Bruce Feder

For full biographical listings, see the Martindale-Hubbell Law Directory

Fennemore Craig, A Professional Corporation (AV)

3003 North Central Avenue, Suite 2600, 85012-2913
Telephone: 602-916-5000
Fax: 602-916-5999
Tucson, Arizona Office: One South Church Avenue, Suite 1000, 85701-1620.
Telephone: 520-879-6800.
Fax: 520-879-6899.

Jordan Green
Scott M. Finical
Christopher L. Callahan

James D. Burgess

LEGAL SUPPORT PERSONNEL

LEGAL ASSISTANTS

Ann V. Kooi

For Complete List of Firm Personnel, See General Section

For full biographical listings, see the Martindale-Hubbell Law Directory

Phoenix—Continued

RICHARD J. HERTZBERG (AV)

16 Luhrs Arcade 11 West Jefferson, 85003
Telephone: 602-253-1781
Fax: 602-253-0928

For full biographical listings, see the Martindale-Hubbell Law Directory

HOIDAL & HANNAH, P.L.C. (AV)

111 W. Monroe Street, Suite 1212, 85003-1732
Telephone: 602-254-0202
Fax: 602-258-9179

Thomas M. Hoidal — John R. Hannah

For full biographical listings, see the Martindale-Hubbell Law Directory

JOE KEILP, P.C. (AV)

1440 East Washington Street, Suite 100, 85034
Telephone: 602-252-0100
Fax: 602-252-0199
Email: joe@jktrial.com *URL:* http://www.jktrial.com

Joe Keilp

For full biographical listings, see the Martindale-Hubbell Law Directory

KIMERER & LAVELLE, P.L.C. (AV)

100 W. Clarendon Suite 2100, 85013
Telephone: 602-279-5900; 800-220-6817
Fax: 602-264-5566
Email: KimLav.com

Michael D. Kimerer — Clark L. Derrick
Lori L. Voepel

For full biographical listings, see the Martindale-Hubbell Law Directory

LEWIS AND ROCA, LLP (AV)

A Limited Liability Partnership including a Professional Corporation
40 North Central Avenue, 85004-4429
Telephone: 602-262-5311
Fax: 602-262-5747
Email: clientservice@lrlaw.com *URL:* http://www.lrlaw.com
Tucson, Arizona Office: One South Church Avenue, Suite 700, 86701-1620.
Telephone: 520-622-2090.
Fax: 520-622-3088. E-Mail: clientservice@lrlaw.com.
Las Vegas, Nevada Affiliated Office: Ashcraft and Heinz LLP, 3960 Howard Hughes Parkway, 89109.
Telephone: 702-990-3570.
Fax: 702-990-3571.

MEMBER OF FIRM
Dale A. Danneman
ASSOCIATE
Douglas J. McDonald

For Complete List of Firm Personnel, See General Section

For full biographical listings, see the Martindale-Hubbell Law Directory

MARTIN LIEBERMAN, P.C. (AV)

111 West Monroe, Suite 1650, 85003
Telephone: 602-254-5544
Fax: 602-254-9263
URL: http://www.lawyers.com/martin_lieberman

Martin Lieberman

For full biographical listings, see the Martindale-Hubbell Law Directory

MATHEW & MATHEW, P.C. (AV)

2525 East Camelback Road, Suite 750, 85016
Telephone: 602-381-8556
Facsimile: 602-381-8534
Email: Ivan.Mathew@AZBAR.Org
Email: Susan.Mathew@AZBAR.Org

Ivan K. Mathew — Susan T. Mathew

Reference: National Bank of Arizona; Johnson Bank, Arizona. .

For full biographical listings, see the Martindale-Hubbell Law Directory

MEHRENS AND WILEMON, P.A. (AV)

1005 North Second Street, 85004
Telephone: 602-258-5151
Fax: 602-257-8316
Email: craigm@goodnet.com

Craig Mehrens — Amy Wilemon

Reference: Firstar Metropolitan Bank & Trust.

For full biographical listings, see the Martindale-Hubbell Law Directory

THOMAS A. THINNES, P.A. (AV)

1005 North Second Street, 85004
Telephone: 602-257-8408
Fax: 602-257-8135

Thomas A. Thinnes

Reference: Firstar Metropolitan Bank & Trust.

For full biographical listings, see the Martindale-Hubbell Law Directory

TUCKER STROHM MILLER & TUCKER, P.C. (AV)

1136 East Campbell, 85014
Telephone: 602-279-3660
Fax: 602-279-2162
Email: rlslaw@worldnet.att.net

Richard L. Strohm

Nedra J. Bates

For full biographical listings, see the Martindale-Hubbell Law Directory

TUCSON, * Pima Co.

DONAU & BOLT (AV)

Suite 501, 3505 North Campbell Avenue, 85719-2033
Telephone: 520-795-8710
Fax: 520-795-0308

MEMBER OF FIRM
Alfred S. Donau III
ASSOCIATE
Keith A. Singer

For full biographical listings, see the Martindale-Hubbell Law Directory

HIRSH, BJORGAARD & ROGERS, P.L.C. (AV)

177 North Church Avenue, Suite 700, 85701-1119
Telephone: 520-624-4700
Fax: 520-624-4796

Robert J. Hirsh — David L. Bjorgaard
Jeffrey J. Rogers

For full biographical listings, see the Martindale-Hubbell Law Directory

HOOKER & RODRIGUEZ (AV)

2830 North Swan Road, Suite 120, 85712-1220
Telephone: 520-881-2333
800-280-2333
Telecopier: 520-325-0150
Email: rhooker@theriver.com

MEMBERS OF FIRM
Robert Hooker — Myrna Rodriguez

For full biographical listings, see the Martindale-Hubbell Law Directory

EDWARD HARRIS LABER, LTD. (AV)

33 North Tucson Boulevard, 85716
Telephone: 520-624-3000
Fax: 520-624-3332
Email: laber@azstarnet.com

Edward Harris Laber

For full biographical listings, see the Martindale-Hubbell Law Directory

WALTER B. NASH III, P.C. (AV)

Suite 4297, Guadalajara Building, La Placita, 110 South Church Avenue, P.O. Box 2310, 85702-2310
Telephone: 520-792-1613
Fax: 520-628-1079

Walter B. Nash III

William J. Kirchner

LEGAL SUPPORT PERSONNEL
Vicki L. Covey (Legal Assistant)

Reference: Bank One.

For full biographical listings, see the Martindale-Hubbell Law Directory

PICCARRETA & DAVIS, P.C. (AV)

145 South Sixth Avenue, 85701-2007
Telephone: 520-622-6900
Fax: 520-622-0521

(See Next Column)

PICCARRETA & DAVIS P.C., *Tucson—Continued*

Barry M. Davis
Carl A. Piccarreta
Michael L. Piccarreta
JoJene E. Mills
Jefferson Keenan

For full biographical listings, see the Martindale-Hubbell Law Directory

WILLIAM G. WALKER, P.C. (AV)

145 South Sixth Avenue, 85701
Telephone: 520-622-3330
Fax: 520-882-6833

William G. Walker

For full biographical listings, see the Martindale-Hubbell Law Directory

ARKANSAS

*LITTLE ROCK,** Pulaski Co.

JOHN WESLEY HALL, JR. A PROFESSIONAL CORPORATION (AV)

523 West Third Street, 72201
Telephone: 501-371-9131
FAX: 501-378-0888
Email: jwh@johnwesley.com

John Wesley Hall, Jr.

For full biographical listings, see the Martindale-Hubbell Law Directory

PERRONI AND JAMES (AV)

Stewart Building, 801 West Third Street, 72201
Telephone: 501-372-6555
Fax: 501-372-6333
Email: sperroni@aol.com *URL:* http://www.lawyers.com/perronianjames

Samuel A. Perroni
Patrick R. James (P.A.)
JaNan Arnold Davis (P.A.)
Susan L. Keller (P.A.)

LEGAL SUPPORT PERSONNEL

Sherry Joyce, CLA

References: Regions Bank, Little Rock, Ark.; Bank of Little Rock, Ark.

For full biographical listings, see the Martindale-Hubbell Law Directory

JEFF ROSENZWEIG (AV)

300 Spring Building, Suite 310, Third and Spring Streets, 72201
Telephone: 501-372-5247
FAX: 501-375-0067
Email: jrosenzweig@worldnet.att.com *URL:* http://www.lawyers.com/rosenzweiglaw

For full biographical listings, see the Martindale-Hubbell Law Directory

WILSON, ENGSTROM, CORUM & COULTER (AV)

809 West Third Street, P.O. Box 71, 72203
Telephone: 501-375-6453
FAX: 501-375-5914

MEMBERS OF FIRM

Roxanne Wilson (1947-1992)
Gary D. Corum
Stephen Engstrom
Nate Coulter

For full biographical listings, see the Martindale-Hubbell Law Directory

CALIFORNIA

*AUBURN,** Placer Co.

LEUPP, WACHOB & WOODALL (AV)

149 Court Street, 95603
Telephone: 530-888-1100
Fax: 530-888-1821
URL: http://www.lawyers.com/lwwlaw

MEMBERS OF FIRM

Thomas A. Leupp
Charles D. Wachob
Timothy S. Woodall

For full biographical listings, see the Martindale-Hubbell Law Directory

BEVERLY HILLS, Los Angeles Co.

HOCHMAN, SALKIN, RETTIG, TOSCHER & PEREZ, A PROFESSIONAL CORPORATION (AV)

9150 Wilshire Boulevard Suite 300, 90212-3414
Telephone: 310-281-3200; 273-1181
Fax: 310-859-1430
URL: http://www.taxlitigator.com

Bruce I. Hochman
Charles P. Rettig
Avram Salkin
Dennis Perez
Steven R. Toscher

OF COUNSEL

George DeRoy
Nathan Joseph Hochman
Stuart A. Simon
Steven D. Blanc
Michel R. Stein

Reference: Union Bank of California.

For full biographical listings, see the Martindale-Hubbell Law Directory

THE LAW OFFICES OF LAWRENCE TAYLOR (AV)

433 N. Camden Drive, Suite 600, 90210
Telephone: 310-860-9515
Email: taylor@law.net *URL:* http://www.duicenter.com
Carlsbad, California Office: 2131 Palomar Airport Road, Suite 300, 92009.
Telephone: 760-757-5579.
Irvine, California Office: 18101 Von Karman Avenue, Suite 350, 92612.
Telephone: 714-776-1566; 949-752-1550.
Long Beach, California Office: 3780 Kilroy Airport Way, Suite 310, 90806.
Telephone: 562-989-4774.
Fax: 562-989-0555.

Lawrence Taylor

For full biographical listings, see the Martindale-Hubbell Law Directory

BISHOP, Inyo Co.

DOUGLAS BUCHANAN (AV)

363 Academy Avenue, 93514
Telephone: 760-873-4211
Fax: 760-873-4007
Email: dbuchanan@QNET.com

OF COUNSEL

Ronald F. Sample
Susan A. Yeck

References: Dean Witter Reynolds, Bishop; Union Bank, Bishop.

For full biographical listings, see the Martindale-Hubbell Law Directory

CHULA VISTA, San Diego Co.

RAYMOND GEORGE ARAGON (AV)

P.O. Box 5342, 91912
Telephone: 619-338-4700
Fax: 619-267-4743

COSTA MESA, Orange Co.

THE LAW OFFICE OF JACK M. EARLEY (AV)

Imperial Bank Building, 695 Town Center Drive, Suite #1450, 92626-1924
Telephone: 714-241-9700
Facsimile: 714-979-9047

For full biographical listings, see the Martindale-Hubbell Law Directory

SCHULMAN & MCMILLAN, INCORPORATED (AV)

3200 Park Center Drive, Suite 600, 92626-7148
Telephone: 714-434-9596
Telecopier: 714-434-1823

Marshall M. Schulman

For full biographical listings, see the Martindale-Hubbell Law Directory

EMERYVILLE, Alameda Co.

JAMES JAY SELTZER (AV)

Watergate Towers, Tenth Floor, 2200 Powell Street, Suite 1035, 94608
Telephone: 510-596-2500
Telecopier: 510-596-2519
URL: http://www.secureadvise.com
Email: lawoffices@jjseltzer.com *URL:* http://www.lawyers.com/jamesjayseltzer

For full biographical listings, see the Martindale-Hubbell Law Directory

*FAIRFIELD,** Solano Co.

HONEYCHURCH AND FINKAS (AV)

Suite C, 823 Jefferson Street, 94533
Telephone: 707-429-3111
Fax: 707-429-4302
Email: honfinkas@aol.com

MEMBERS OF FIRM

Denis A. Honeychurch R. Anthony Finkas

For full biographical listings, see the Martindale-Hubbell Law Directory

*FRESNO,** Fresno Co.

NUTTALL BERMAN ATTORNEYS (AV)

A Partnership including a Professional Corporation
2333 Merced Street, 93721
Telephone: 559-233-2333
Fax: 559-233-6947
Email: nba@dfndr.com *URL:* http://www.dfndr.com

MEMBERS OF FIRM

Roger T. Nuttall (Inc.) Richard P. Berman

ASSOCIATE

Mark W. Coleman

For full biographical listings, see the Martindale-Hubbell Law Directory

FULLERTON, Orange Co.

CURRAN AND WATSON (AV)

Suite 290, 1235 North Harbor Boulevard, 92832
Telephone: 714-871-1138
Facsimile: 714-871-5620

MEMBERS OF FIRM

Richard J. Curran William G. Watson

For full biographical listings, see the Martindale-Hubbell Law Directory

GLENDALE, Los Angeles Co.

FLANAGAN, BOOTH, UNGER & MOSES (AV)

1156 North Brand Boulevard, 91202-2582
Telephone: 818-244-8694
Fax: 818-244-1852
Santa Ana, California Office: 1851 East First Street, Suite 805, 92705.
Telephone: 714-835-2607.
Fax: 714-835-4825.

MEMBERS OF FIRM

J. Michael Flanagan Charles J. Unger

ASSOCIATES

Michael T. Danis James A. Grover

For full biographical listings, see the Martindale-Hubbell Law Directory

IRVINE, Orange Co.

THE LAW OFFICES OF LAWRENCE TAYLOR (AV)

18101 Von Karman Avenue, Suite 350, 92612
Telephone: 714-776-1566; 949-752-1550
Fax: 562-989-0555
Email: taylor@law.net *URL:* http://www.duicenter.com
Beverly Hills, California Office: 433 N. Camden Drive, Suite 600, 90210.
Telephone: 310-860-9515.
Carlsbad, California Office: 2131 Palomar Airport Road, Suite 300, 92009.
Telephone: 760-757-5579.
Long Beach, California Office: 3780 Kilroy Airport Way, Suite 310.
Telephone: 562-989-4774.
Fax: 562-989-0555.

ASSOCIATES

Jeff Gold William L. Nelson, III
Nigel R. Witham

For full biographical listings, see the Martindale-Hubbell Law Directory

LONG BEACH, Los Angeles Co.

EDWARD P. GEORGE, JR., INC. A PROFESSIONAL CORPORATION (AV)

Suite 430, 5000 East Spring Street, 90815-1275
Telephone: 562-497-2900
Facsimile: 562-497-2904

Edward P. George, Jr. Timothy L. O'Reilly

OF COUNSEL

Albert C. S. Ramsey

Reference: City National Bank, Long Beach.

For full biographical listings, see the Martindale-Hubbell Law Directory

MOORE, RUTTER & EVANS (AV)

A Partnership including a Professional Corporation
555 East Ocean Boulevard, Suite 500, 90802-5090
Telephone: 562-435-4499
Facsimile: 562-495-4299
Email: mrelaw@gte.net *URL:* http://www.lawyers.com/moorerutter&evans
Huntington Beach, California Office: 2120 Main Street, Suite 250, 92648.
Telephone: 714-374-3333.
Fax: 714-374-9395

RESIDENT PARTNERS

Neal Moore Mark D. Rutter
William D. Evans (P.C.)

OF COUNSEL

Michael J. Emling

For full biographical listings, see the Martindale-Hubbell Law Directory

*LOS ANGELES,** Los Angeles Co.

BECK, DE CORSO, DALY, BARRERA & KREINDLER, A PROFESSIONAL LAW CORPORATION (AV)

601 West Fifth Street, 12th Floor, 90071-2025
Telephone: 213-688-1198
Fax: 213-489-7532
Email: beckdecorso@earthlink.net *URL:* http://www.beckdecorso.com

Mark E. Beck Teresa R. Barrera
Anthony A. De Corso Charles L. Kreindler
Bryan D. Daly Suzanne E. Tracy

Peter J. Diedrich Barbara E. Taylor
Stephen P. Jones

OF COUNSEL

Godfrey Isaac

For full biographical listings, see the Martindale-Hubbell Law Directory

HARLAND W. BRAUN PROFESSIONAL CORPORATION (AV)

Suite 1100, 2049 Century Park East, 90067
Telephone: 310-277-4777
Fax: 310-277-4045
http: //www.braunlaw.com
Email: HWBraunEsq@aol.com *URL:* http://www.lawyers.com/hwbrown

Harland W. Braun

Reference: Bank of America (Century City Office).

For full biographical listings, see the Martindale-Hubbell Law Directory

GERAGOS & GERAGOS (AV)

350 South Grand Avenue 39th Floor, 90071
Telephone: 213-625-3900
Fax: 213-625-1600

Paul J. Geragos Matthew J. Geragos
Mark J. Geragos Susan P. Strick
Shepard S. Kopp

OF COUNSEL

Mark M. Hathaway

For full biographical listings, see the Martindale-Hubbell Law Directory

KIRKLAND & ELLIS (AV)

A Partnership including Professional Corporations
777 South Figueroa Street, 90017
Telephone: 213-680-8400
Facsimile: 213-680-8500
URL: http://www.kirkland.com
Chicago, Illinois Office: 200 East Randolph Drive.
Telephone: 312-861-2000.
Telex: 25-4361.
Washington, D.C. Office: 655 Fifteenth Street, N.W.
Telephone: 202-879-5000.
Facsimile: (202)-879-5200.
New York, New York Office: Citicorp Center, 153 East 53rd Street.
Telephone: 212-446-4800.
Facsimile: (212)-446-4900.
London, England Office: International Financial Centre, Old Broad Street.
Telephone: 171-816-8700; New Telephone Effective April 1, 2000: 207-816-8700.
Facsimile: 171-816-8800.

MEMBER OF FIRM

Jan Lawrence Handzlik

For Complete List of Firm Personnel, See General Section

For full biographical listings, see the Martindale-Hubbell Law Directory

Los Angeles—Continued

JOSÉ Y. LAUCHENGCO, JR. (AV)

3545 Wilshire Boulevard, Suite 247, 90010
Telephone: 213-380-9897

For full biographical listings, see the Martindale-Hubbell Law Directory

O'MELVENY & MYERS LLP (AV)

400 South Hope Street, 90071-2899
Telephone: 213-430-6000
Facsimile: 213-430-6407
Cable: MOMS
Telex: 674122
Email: omminfo@omm.com *URL:* http://www.omm.com
Century City, CA Office: 1999 Avenue of the Stars, Los Angeles, 90067-6035.
Telex: 674097. Tel: 310-553-6700.
Fax: 310-246-6779.
Newport Beach, CA Office: 610 Newport Center Drive, 92660-6429.
Telex: 4722088. Tel: 949-760-9600.
Fax: 949-823-6994.
San Francisco, CA Office: Embarcadero Center West, 275 Battery Street, 94111-3305. Tel: 415-984-8700.
Fax: 415-984-8701.
New York, NY Office: Citicorp Center, 153 East 53rd Street, 10022-4611.
Telex: 129165. Tel: 212-326-2000.
Fax: 212-326-2061.
Washington, DC Office: 555 13th Street, N.W., 20004-1109.
Cable: MOMSWSH.
Telex: 89622. Tel: 202-383-5300.
Fax: 202-383-5414.
London Office: O'Melveny & Myers, 3 Finsbury Square, London, EC2A 1LA, England. Tel: 44-171-256-8451. Fax 44-171-638-8205.
Tokyo Office: Akasaka Twin Tower, East 14F, 2-17-23, Akasaka, Minato-ku, Tokyo 107-0052, Japan. Tel: 03-5562-2800.
Fax: 03-5575-3840.
Hong Kong Office: O'Melveny & Myers, Suite 1905, Tower Two, Lippo Centre, 89 Queensway, Central, Hong Kong. Tel: 852-2523-8266.
Fax: 852-2522-1760.
Shanghai Office: Kerry Centre, 20F, 1515 Nanjing Road West, Shanghai, 200040 People's Republic of China. Tel: 86-21-5298-5600.
Fax: 86-21-5298-5500.

PARTNER

James R. Asperger

For Complete List of Firm Personnel, See General Section

For full biographical listings, see the Martindale-Hubbell Law Directory

SIDLEY & BELL LLP (AV)

2940 Westwood Boulevard, Second Floor, 90064
Telephone: 310-229-8940
Fax: 310- 474-2541
Email: westlalaw@aol.com

Michael I. Sidley
Anthony E. Bell

For full biographical listings, see the Martindale-Hubbell Law Directory

ERROL H. STAMBLER (AV)

10880 Wilshire Boulevard, Suite 1050, 90024
Telephone: 310-473-4525
Fax: 310-470-3968
Email: estambler@aol.com *URL:* http://www.lawyers.com/errolstambler

For full biographical listings, see the Martindale-Hubbell Law Directory

TALCOTT, LIGHTFOOT, VANDEVELDE SADOWSKY, MEDVENE & LEVINE (AV)

Thirteenth Floor 655 South Hope Street, 90017
Telephone: 213-622-4750
Fax: 213-622-2690
Email: law@talcottlightfoot.com *URL:* http://www.talcottlightfoot.com

John S. Crouchley
Janet I. Levine
Michael J. Lightfoot
James H. Locklin
John P. Martin
Edward M. Medvene
Stephen B. Sadowsky
Robert M. Talcott
John D. Vandevelde
Melissa N. Widdifield
David K. Willingham

Reference: Sterling Bank, Los Angeles, California.

For full biographical listings, see the Martindale-Hubbell Law Directory

LAW OFFICES OF BARRY TARLOW A PROFESSIONAL CORPORATION (AV)

9119 Sunset Boulevard, 90069
Telephone: 310-278-2111
Cable Address: "Habeas"
Fax: 310-550-7055
Email: lobt@earthlink.net

(See Next Column)

Barry Tarlow

Mark O. Heaney
Blair Berk
Shereen J. Charlick

For full biographical listings, see the Martindale-Hubbell Law Directory

THE LAW OFFICES OF LAWRENCE TAYLOR

(See Long Beach)

NEWPORT BEACH, Orange Co.

LAW OFFICES OF JENNIFER L. KELLER (AV)

5160 Campus Drive, 92660-2101
Telephone: 949-476-8700
Fax: 949-476-0900
Email: jkeller@prodigy.net

For full biographical listings, see the Martindale-Hubbell Law Directory

*OAKLAND,** Alameda Co.

ROBERT J. BELES (AV)

#1 Kaiser Plaza, Suite 1750, 94612
Telephone: 510-836-0100
FAX: 510-832-3690
URL: http://www.lawyers.com/beleslaw

For full biographical listings, see the Martindale-Hubbell Law Directory

ORANGE, Orange Co.

ROBERT D. CHATTERTON (AV)

1400 Bank of America Tower, One City Boulevard West, 92668
Telephone: 714-547-8484
Facsimile: 714-634-2153

For full biographical listings, see the Martindale-Hubbell Law Directory

PALO ALTO, Santa Clara Co.

NOLAN, ARMSTRONG & BARTON, LLP (AV)

600 University Avenue, 94301
Telephone: 650-326-2980
Fax: 650-326-9704
Email: office@paloaltocrimlaw.com *URL:* http://www.paloaltocrimlaw.com

MEMBERS OF FIRM

Thomas J. Nolan
Michael W. Armstrong
Daniel L. Barton

ASSOCIATES

K. Kleigh Hathaway
Mara K. Goldman

LEGAL SUPPORT PERSONNEL

LEGAL ASSISTANTS

Marcia Hall
Dawn Phillips

For full biographical listings, see the Martindale-Hubbell Law Directory

PASADENA, Los Angeles Co.

W. MICHAEL MAYOCK (AV)

The Braley Building, Fourth Floor, 35 South Raymond Avenue, 91105
Telephone: 626-405-1465; 626-405-0158
FAX: 626-405-0158
Email: mlmayock@earthlink.net *URL:* http://www.lawyers.com/mayocklaw

Reference: Union Bank.

For full biographical listings, see the Martindale-Hubbell Law Directory

RICKARD SANTWIER (AV)

35 South Raymond Avenue Suite 301, 91105
Telephone: 626-449-6504; 323-681-4425
FAX: 323-681-4436
Email: santwier@pacbell.net

For full biographical listings, see the Martindale-Hubbell Law Directory

*RIVERSIDE,** Riverside Co.

STEVEN L. HARMON (AV)

The Loring Building, 3685 Main Street, Suite 250, 92501
Telephone: 909-787-6800
Fax: 909-787-6700

For full biographical listings, see the Martindale-Hubbell Law Directory

*SACRAMENTO,** Sacramento Co.

BLACKMON & SNELLINGS, LLP (AV)

U.S. Bank Plaza, 980 9th Street, Suite 2250, 95814
Telephone: 916-441-0824
Fax: 916-441-0970

MEMBERS OF FIRM

Clyde M. Blackmon — Hill C. Snellings

ASSOCIATES

Karen L. Hamilton — M. Allen Hopper

For full biographical listings, see the Martindale-Hubbell Law Directory

ROTHSCHILD, WISHEK & SANDS (AV)

901 "F" Street, Suite 200, 95814
Telephone: 916-444-9845
URL: http://www.lawyers.com/glsattylaw

MEMBERS OF FIRM

Michael Rothschild — M. Bradley Wishek

ASSOCIATES

Stacy Boulware Eurie — Jonathan C. Turner

OF COUNSEL

Michael S. Sands

For full biographical listings, see the Martindale-Hubbell Law Directory

STEVENS & O'CONNELL LLP (AV)

400 Capitol Mall, Suite 1400, 95814-4412
Telephone: 916-329-9111
Facsimile: 916-329-9110

Charles J. Stevens
George L. O'Connell
Richard Pachter
David A. Cheit
Craig C. Allison
Bradley A. Benbrook
Todd M. Noonan
Timothy P. Grieve

For full biographical listings, see the Martindale-Hubbell Law Directory

*SAN DIEGO,** San Diego Co.

DOUGLAS C. BROWN (AV)

Home Savings Tower, 225 Broadway, Suite 1210, 92101-5009
Telephone: 619-231-6158
Fax: 619-338-8375
Email: dcbrow@pacbell.net

For full biographical listings, see the Martindale-Hubbell Law Directory

JOHN G. COTSIRILOS (AV)

2442 Fourth Avenue, 92101
Telephone: 619-232-6022
Fax: 619-232-6052

For full biographical listings, see the Martindale-Hubbell Law Directory

JOHN A. CRAWFORD, JR. (AV)

1010 Second Avenue, Suite 2000, 92101
Telephone: 619-233-7012
Fax: 619-233-3172
URL: http://www.lawyers.com/johnacrawfordjrlaw

For full biographical listings, see the Martindale-Hubbell Law Directory

GRIMES & WARWICK (AV)

An Association of Sole Proprietorships
2664 Fourth Avenue, 92103-6515
Telephone: 619-232-9700
Fax: 619-232-8857

MEMBERS OF FIRM

Robert L. Grimes — Thomas J. Warwick, Jr.

ASSOCIATES

Gerard Jeffrey Wasson — Stephen T. Crandall

For full biographical listings, see the Martindale-Hubbell Law Directory

MICHAEL D. MCGLINN (AV)

5030 Camino de la Siesta, Suite 340, 92108
Telephone: 619-291-5115
Fax: 619-291-5999
Email: mmcglinn@simplyweb.net *URL:* http://www.lawyers.com/michaeldmcglinn

For full biographical listings, see the Martindale-Hubbell Law Directory

SELTZER CAPLAN MCMAHON & VITEK, A PROFESSIONAL CORPORATION (AV)

2100 Symphony Towers, 750 B Street, 92101
Telephone: 619-685-3003
Fax: 619-685-3100
URL: http://www.scwm.com

Charles L. Goldberg — Patrick Q. Hall

Representative Clients: Chicago Title; The Goodyear Tire & Rubber Co.; W.R. Grace & Co.—Conn.; McDonnell-Douglas Corp.; McMillin Communities; Western Financial Savings Bank.

For Complete List of Firm Personnel, See General Section

For full biographical listings, see the Martindale-Hubbell Law Directory

*SAN FRANCISCO,** San Francisco Co.

ROBERT D. CARROW (AV)

One Embarcadero Center, Suite 880, 94111
Telephone: 415-981-1691
Telecopier: 415-492-8419
Telex: 470562 LAW UI
Cable Address: "JURIS"
Email: robert@carrow.com *URL:* http://www.carrow.com/
London, England Chambers: 33 Bedford Row, WC1.
Telephone: +0171 242-6476.
Telecopier: +0171 831-6065.
San Rafael, California Office: 7 Mount Lassen Drive, Suite C134. 94903.
Telephone: 415-492-1225.
Telecopier: 415-492-8419.
(Also of Counsel to Goldstein & Musto, A Professional Corporation)

For full biographical listings, see the Martindale-Hubbell Law Directory

LADAR & LADAR (AV)

Suite 310, 507 Polk Street, 94102
Telephone: 415-928-2333
Fax: 415-928-4499

Jerrold M. Ladar — Joyce B. Ladar

ASSOCIATE

Erik Rapoport

For full biographical listings, see the Martindale-Hubbell Law Directory

HARRIET ROSS (AV)

One Sansome Street, Suite 2000, 94104
Telephone: 415-956-7655
Fax: 415-775-7491

For full biographical listings, see the Martindale-Hubbell Law Directory

JOHN M. RUNFOLA (AV)

465 California Street, Suite 400, 94101-1812
Telephone: 415-391-4243
Fax: 415-391-5161
Email: jrunfola@creative.net

Reference: Wells Fargo Bank.

For full biographical listings, see the Martindale-Hubbell Law Directory

GEORGE G. WALKER, INC. (AV)

Suite 635, 633 Battery Street, 94111
Telephone: 415-421-6911
Fax: 415-788-6787
Email: ggwalker@best.com *URL:* http://www.ggwalker.com

George G. Walker

For full biographical listings, see the Martindale-Hubbell Law Directory

*SAN JOSE,** Santa Clara Co.

GUYTON N. JINKERSON (AV)

50 West San Fernando Street Suite 400, 95113
Telephone: 408-297-8555
Fax: 408-494-9260
Email: gnj_law@email.msn.com *URL:* http://www.lawyers.com/jinkerson

For full biographical listings, see the Martindale-Hubbell Law Directory

MANCHESTER & WILLIAMS (AV)

An Association of Attorneys including Professional Corporations
100 Park Center Plaza, Suite 525, 95113
Telephone: 408-287-6193
Fax: 408-287-1554
Email: mwslaw@ix.netcom.com

(See Next Column)

MANCHESTER & WILLIAMS, *San Jose—Continued*

Steven R. Manchester (Inc.) John L. Williams (Inc.)
Kurt J. Seibert

LEGAL SUPPORT PERSONNEL

Elaine Evans (Legal/Administrative Assistant)

For full biographical listings, see the Martindale-Hubbell Law Directory

MCMANIS, FAULKNER & MORGAN (AV)

160 West Santa Clara Street, 10th Floor, 95113
Telephone: 408-279-8700
Fax: 408-279-3244; 408-279-0494
Email: mfm@mfmlaw.com *URL:* http://www.mfmlaw.com

James McManis
William Faulkner
Donelle Morgan
Lisa Herrick
Michael Reedy
Erica Yew

Michelle Tidalgo
Colleen Duffy Smith
Lillian Wolf
Rebecca Hughes
Kalpana Vrudhula
Ray M. Baluyot
Catherine Bechtel
Arron Nesbitt

OF COUNSEL

Mary Arand

For full biographical listings, see the Martindale-Hubbell Law Directory

THOMAS F. MUELLER A PROFESSIONAL CORPORATION (AV)

255 North Market Street, Suite 190, 95110
Telephone: 408-292-2434
Fax: 408-292-1264
Email: MuellerLaw@aol.com *URL:* http://www.members.aol.com/MuellerLaw/tfm1.html

Thomas F. Mueller

For full biographical listings, see the Martindale-Hubbell Law Directory

*SANTA BARBARA,** Santa Barbara Co.

SANGER & SWYSEN (AV)

233 East Carrillo Street, Suite C, 93101
Telephone: 805-962-4887
Fax: 805-963-7311
Email: rmsanger@gte.net *URL:* http://www.sangerswysen.com

Robert M. Sanger Catherine J. Swysen

ASSOCIATE

Barbara A. Carroll

For full biographical listings, see the Martindale-Hubbell Law Directory

SANTA MONICA, Los Angeles Co.

LAW OFFICES OF ROBERT BERKE (AV)

1717 Fourth Street, Third Floor, 90401
Telephone: 310-917-5599
Fax: 310-395-3884; 310-393-0405
Email: lawservices@earthlink.net *URL:* http://www.lorb.com

ASSOCIATE

Joseph A. Pertel

Representative Clients: L.A. County Bar Association Lawyer Referral Service; Santa Monica Bar Association Lawyer Referral Service.

For full biographical listings, see the Martindale-Hubbell Law Directory

NASATIR, HIRSCH & PODBERESKY (AV)

2115 Main Street, 90405
Telephone: 310-399-3259
Fax: 310-392-9029

MEMBERS OF FIRM

Michael D. Nasatir Richard G. Hirsch
Vicki I. Podberesky

ASSOCIATE

Tariq A. Khero

For full biographical listings, see the Martindale-Hubbell Law Directory

O'NEILL, LYSAGHT & SUN LLP (AV)

100 Wilshire Boulevard, Suite 700, 90401
Telephone: 310-451-5700
Telecopier: 310-399-7201

(See Next Column)

Brian O'Neill
Brian C. Lysaght
Frederick D. Friedman
Brian A. Sun
Yolanda Orozco
John M. Moscarino
Harriet Beegun Leva
Edward A. Klein
Robert L. Meylan
David E. Rosen
Paul D. Murphy

Ellyn S. Garofalo
Brian D. Hershman
Katharine A. Kates
Luan K. Phan
Kyle Y. Hoshide
Hersh Heather Elizabeth
Catherine D. Whiting

OF COUNSEL

J. Joseph Connolly

Reference: Wells Fargo Bank, Santa Monica.

For full biographical listings, see the Martindale-Hubbell Law Directory

TORRANCE, Los Angeles Co.

BIRD & BIRD, A LAW CORPORATION (AV)

3555 Torrance Boulevard, Suite 200, 90503-4816
Telephone: 310-316-2285
Fax: 310-316-7930
URL: http://www.lawyers.com/b&b_law

George Francis Bird, Jr. Karen Hunter Bird

Kimberly Gay Anderson

For full biographical listings, see the Martindale-Hubbell Law Directory

TUSTIN, Orange Co.

STAPLETON & STAPLETON, A PROFESSIONAL ASSOCIATION (AV)

Irvine Plaza Building, Suite 114, 17621 Irvine Boulevard, 92780
Telephone: 714-832-8003
Fax: 714-832-2007

Marlin G. Stapleton Marlin G. Stapleton, Jr.

For full biographical listings, see the Martindale-Hubbell Law Directory

*VENTURA,** Ventura Co.

JAY M. JOHNSON (AV)

770 County Square Drive, Suite 104, 93003
Telephone: 805-654-0400
Fax: 805-654-0326
Email: jaylaw@inreach.com

For full biographical listings, see the Martindale-Hubbell Law Directory

WHIPPLE AND VIELE, A PROFESSIONAL LAW CORPORATION (AV)

60 South California Street, 93001
Telephone: 805-643-8658; 643-8422
Fax: 805-653-6079

Edward A. Whipple

References: Wells Fargo Bank; American Commercial Bank.

For full biographical listings, see the Martindale-Hubbell Law Directory

COLORADO

*BOULDER,** Boulder Co.

HOWARD BITTMAN (AV)

1406 Pearl Street, Suite 200, 80302
Telephone: 303-443-2281
Fax: 303-443-2862
Email: bittmanh@aol.com *URL:* http://www.lawyers.com/howardbittman

For full biographical listings, see the Martindale-Hubbell Law Directory

ENWALL & GRANT, L.L.C. (AV)

720 Pearl Street, 80302
Telephone: 303-449-3891
Fax: 303-449-3992
Email: enwall@nilenet.com

Michael R. Enwall Barbara K. Grant

For full biographical listings, see the Martindale-Hubbell Law Directory

Boulder—Continued

LEONARD I. FRIELING, P.C. (AV)

1942 Broadway, Suite 314, 80302-5233
Telephone: 303-449-0092
Fax: 303-666-0956
Email: frieling@nilenet.com *URL:* http://www.LFrieling.com

Leonard I. Frieling

For full biographical listings, see the Martindale-Hubbell Law Directory

MCCORMICK AND CHRISTOPH, P.C. (AV)

1406 Pearl Street, Suite 200, 80302-5307
Telephone: 303-443-2281
Fax: 303-443-2862

G. Paul McCormick
James R. Christoph

For full biographical listings, see the Martindale-Hubbell Law Directory

MILLER AND HARRISON, LLC (AV)

2305 Broadway, 80304-4106
Telephone: 303-449-2830
Fax: 303-449-2198

MEMBERS OF FIRM

Robert Bruce Miller
David B. Harrison

ASSOCIATE

Joan Clifford

Reference: Norwest Bank.

For full biographical listings, see the Martindale-Hubbell Law Directory

PETER SCHILD (AV)

255 Canyon Boulevard, Suite 100, 80302
Telephone: 303-444-8720
Fax: 303-444-8720
Email: pschild@aol.com

For full biographical listings, see the Martindale-Hubbell Law Directory

*COLORADO SPRINGS,** El Paso Co.

GENTRY & HASKINS LLP (AV)

102 N. Cascade, Suite 220, 80903
Telephone: 719-635-1800
Telecopier: 719-635-1708
Email: haslaw@ibm.net *URL:* http://www.haslaw@ibm.ney

Elvin L. Gentry
Thomas M. Haskins, III

John L. Cyboron

Representative Clients: Western National Bank; The Citadel Bank; Lawyers Title InsuranceCorporation; High Valley Group; USF&G Insurance; K&R Products; Concept Restaurants; Intermountain Mortgage Corporation; Southwes Holdings Ltd.; Bennett Ravings/D.E. Frey Investments.

For full biographical listings, see the Martindale-Hubbell Law Directory

DENNIS W. HARTLEY, P.C. PROFESSIONAL CORPORATION (AV)

1749 S. 8th Street, Suite 5, 80906-1968
Telephone: 719-635-5521
FAX: 719-635-5760
Email: dennis@dennishartley.com

Dennis W. Hartley

Reference: First American Bank.

For full biographical listings, see the Martindale-Hubbell Law Directory

TEGTMEIER LAW FIRM, P.C. (AV)

518 North Nevada, Suite 200, 80903
Telephone: 719-473-5757
Telefax: 719-473-6767
Email: richard@worldclasslaw.com

Richard L. Tegtmeier

OF COUNSEL

Stephen A. Brunette

For full biographical listings, see the Martindale-Hubbell Law Directory

*DENVER,** Denver Co.

BIRGE & MAYERS, P.C. (AV)

1700 Broadway, Suite 1501, 80290
Telephone: 303-860-7100
Facsimile: 303-860-7338
URL: http://www.lawyers.com/birgemayerslaw
St. Louis, Missouri Office: 8000 Maryland Avenue, #250, 63105.
Telephone: 314-236-2203.
Telecopy: 314-236-2401.

(See Next Column)

Thomas D. Birge

Carla B. Minckley

SPECIAL COUNSEL

Terry L. Lister

For full biographical listings, see the Martindale-Hubbell Law Directory

BREGA & WINTERS P.C. (AV)

One Norwest Center, 1700 Lincoln Street, Suite 2222, 80203
Telephone: 303-866-9400
Fax: 303-861-9109
Greeley, Colorado Office: 1100 Tenth Street, Suite 402, 80631.
Telephone: 303-352-4805.
Fax: 303-352-6547.

James W. Bain
Stuart N. Bennett
Charles F. Brega
Robert R. Dormer
Wesley B. Howard, Jr.
William W. Hughes (Resident, Greeley Office)
Robert C. Kaufman
Ronald S. Loser
Brian A. Magoon
Loren L. Mall
Glenn W. Merrick
Pamela A. Shaddock (Resident, Greeley Office)
Jay John Schnell
Jerry D. Winters (Resident, Greeley Office)

Jennifer S. Fox
Julie Scroggins Frantz (Resident, Greeley Office)
Brent W. Houston
S. Scott Lasher
Bradley D. Laue (Resident, Greeley Office)
Eric B. Liebman
Kevin C. Massaro
Scott T. Rodgers

For full biographical listings, see the Martindale-Hubbell Law Directory

CANGES, IWASHKO & BETHKE, A PROFESSIONAL CORPORATION (AV)

303 East 17th Avenue Suite 400, 80203-1257
Telephone: 303-860-1900
Fax: 303-860-1665
URL: http://www.lawyers.com/ciblaw

E. Michael Canges
Nina A. Iwashko
Erich L. Bethke
James S. Bailey

Michelle L. Lukowicz

Reference: Norwest Bank Denver.

For full biographical listings, see the Martindale-Hubbell Law Directory

LAW OFFICES OF JOHN W. MCKENDREE (AV)

Creswell Mansion, 1244 Grant Street, 80203
Telephone: 303-861-8906
Fax: 303-861-7773
Email: Johnwmckendree@msn.com

ASSOCIATE

Elizabeth G. McKendree

Reference: Colorado National Bank.

For full biographical listings, see the Martindale-Hubbell Law Directory

NEWELL & MARTENS (AV)

A Partnership including a Professional Corporation
226 West Twelfth Avenue, 80204-3625
Telephone: 303-573-5253
FAX: 303-573-5257
Email: newellandmartens@mindspring.com *URL:* http://www.lawyers.com/newell&martenslaw

Steven R. Newell (P.C.)
Steven P. Martens

ASSOCIATE

Dane Torbenson

Reference: Vectra Bank.

For full biographical listings, see the Martindale-Hubbell Law Directory

DAVID A. OGILVIE, P.C. (AV)

Suite 3901, One Norwest Center, 1700 Lincoln Street, 80203
Telephone: 303-837-9991
Fax: 303-832-5010
Email: DAO9991@aol.com *URL:* http://www.lawyers.com/ogilvie

David A. Ogilvie

LEGAL SUPPORT PERSONNEL

Linda M. Nickolai (Legal Assistant)

Representative Clients: Dwight Deere Carter Trust; Sean Deere Carter Trust; Charles W. Swanson Trust.

(See Next Column)

DAVID A. OGILVIE, P.C., *Denver—Continued*

Reference: Norwest Bank Denver, N.A.

For full biographical listings, see the Martindale-Hubbell Law Directory

LARRY POZNER, P.C. (AV)

1890 Gaylord Street, 80206-1211
Telephone: 303-333-1890
Fax: 303-333-1041
Email: LPozner@aol.com

Larry S. Pozner

Reference: Guaranty Bank.

For full biographical listings, see the Martindale-Hubbell Law Directory

RICHILANO & RIDLEY, P.C. (AV)

1800 15th Street, Suite 101, 80202-1185
Telephone: 303-893-8000
Telecopier: 303-893-8055
Email: patridley@aol.com
Email: richilano@lawyernet.com

John M. Richilano
Patrick L. Ridley

For full biographical listings, see the Martindale-Hubbell Law Directory

ARTHUR M. SCHWARTZ, P.C. (AV)

Suite 420 1630 Welton Street, 80202
Telephone: 303-893-2500
Fax: 303-893-3349
Email: amspc1@aol.com *URL:* http://www.lawyers.com/arthurschwartz

Arthur M. Schwartz

Michael W. Gross
Cindy D. Schwartz
Gary M. Kramer

Reference: Wells Fargo Bank of Denver.

For full biographical listings, see the Martindale-Hubbell Law Directory

DANIEL T. SMITH (AV)

1900 Grant Street Suite 580, 80203-4305
Telephone: 303-860-8100
Fax: 303-860-8018

For full biographical listings, see the Martindale-Hubbell Law Directory

SPRINGER & STEINBERG, A PROFESSIONAL CORPORATION (AV)

Suite 1950, 1600 Broadway, 80202
Telephone: 303-861-2800
Fax: 303-832-7116

Jeffrey A. Springer
Harvey A. Steinberg
William R. Kelso
Amy Mandel Springer
Patricia J. Donahue

Reference: Norwest Bank of Denver.

For full biographical listings, see the Martindale-Hubbell Law Directory

CRAIG L. TRUMAN, P.C. (AV)

Suite 205, 1444 Wazee Street, 80202
Telephone: 303-595-8008
Fax: 303-595-9505

Craig L. Truman

For full biographical listings, see the Martindale-Hubbell Law Directory

LAKEWOOD, Jefferson Co.

POLIDORI, GEROME, FRANKLIN AND JACOBSON, L.L.C. (AV)

Suite 300, 550 South Wadsworth Boulevard, 80226
Telephone: 303-936-3300
Fax: 303-936-0125

Dennis J. Jacobson

For full biographical listings, see the Martindale-Hubbell Law Directory

CONNECTICUT

*BRIDGEPORT,** Fairfield Co.

GERALD E. BODELL (AV)

177 State Street Suite 401, 06604
Telephone: 203-335-8955
Fax: 203-366-6812
New York, New York Office: 36 West 44th Street, Suite 303.
Telephone: 212- 398-3778.
Fax: 212-398-3779.

For full biographical listings, see the Martindale-Hubbell Law Directory

DANBURY, Fairfield Co.

PINNEY, PAYNE, VAN LENTEN, BURRELL, WOLFE & DILLMAN, P.C. (AV)

Lee Farm Corporate Park, 83 Wooster Heights, P.O. Box 3499, 06813-3499
Telephone: 203-743-2721
Fax: 203-792-4759
URL: http://www.ppvlaw.com

Thomas W. Van Lenten
Hugh A. Burrell
Robert J. Wolfe
John M. Dillman
Martin A. Rader, Jr.
William S. Steele, Jr.
Sheldon A. Rosenbaum
Jackie Chan
Richard D. Arconti
Ted D. Backer
Joseph Dimyan
Daniel E. Casagrande
Kim E. Nolan
Wendy A. Grispin

Robin Edwards Otto
John H. Van Lenten

OF COUNSEL

A. Searle Pinney
Bobby S. Payne

Representative Clients: Savings Bank of Danbury.

For full biographical listings, see the Martindale-Hubbell Law Directory

*HARTFORD,** Hartford Co.

F. TIMOTHY MCNAMARA, P.C. (AV)

102 Oak Street, 06106
Telephone: 860-249-8458
Fax: 860-249-8850
Email: timothymcnamara@email.msn.com

F. Timothy McNamara

For full biographical listings, see the Martindale-Hubbell Law Directory

*NEW HAVEN,** New Haven Co.

WILLIAMS, POLAN & PATTIS, LLC (AV)

51 Elm Street, 06510
Telephone: 203-562-9931
Fax: 203-776-9494
Email: jrw@johnrwilliams.com

John R. Williams
Diane Polan
Norman A. Pattis

Katrena Engstrom
William S. Palmieri
Angelica N. Papastavros
Rosemarie Paine

References: Webster Bank; Citizens Bank.

For full biographical listings, see the Martindale-Hubbell Law Directory

STAMFORD, Fairfield Co.

SILVER, GOLUB & TEITELL LLP (AV)

184 Atlantic Street, P.O. Box 389, 06904
Telephone: 203-325-4491
Fax: 203-325-3769
Email: silvergolubteitell.com *URL:* http://www.sgtlaw.com

MEMBERS OF FIRM

David S. Golub
Ernest F. Teitell
John D. Josel
Mario DiNatale

For Complete List of Firm Personnel, See General Section

For full biographical listings, see the Martindale-Hubbell Law Directory

*VERNON,** Tolland Co.

FLAHERTY, MEISLER & COURTNEY (AV)

30 Lafayette Square, Suite 116, 06066-4554
Telephone: 860-872-7200
Fax: 860-875-6594
Email: FMACATTY@aol.com

(See Next Column)

FLAHERTY, MEISLER & COURTNEY—*Continued*

MEMBERS OF FIRM

Leo B. Flaherty Jr. (1923-1998) Arthur P. Meisler
Joseph D. Courtney

ASSOCIATE

Elizabeth C. Foran

Reference: Savings Bank of Rockville.

For full biographical listings, see the Martindale-Hubbell Law Directory

WESTPORT, Fairfield Co.

ANDREW B. BOWMAN (AV)

1804 Post Road East, 06880
Telephone: 203-259-0599
Fax: 203-255-2570
Email: andrew.bowman@snet.net

Reference: Peoples Bank.

For full biographical listings, see the Martindale-Hubbell Law Directory

DELAWARE

*WILMINGTON,** New Castle Co.

BIGGS AND BATTAGLIA (AV)

1800 Mellon Bank Center, P.O. Box 1489, 19899-1489
Telephone: 302-655-9677
Email: B-B@DOL.NET

MEMBERS OF FIRM

Victor F. Battaglia
Robert D. Goldberg
Philip B. Bartoshesky
Victor F. Battaglia, Jr.

For Complete List of Firm Personnel, See General Section

For full biographical listings, see the Martindale-Hubbell Law Directory

JOSEPH A. HURLEY, P.A. (AV)

1215 King Street, 19801
Telephone: 302-658-8980
Fax: 302-658-8987

Joseph A. Hurley

For full biographical listings, see the Martindale-Hubbell Law Directory

THE LYONS LAW FIRM (AV)

1526 Gilpin Avenue, P.O. Box 579, 19806
Telephone: 302-777-5698
Fax: 302-777-5051
Email: elyons@lyonslaw.com

Edmund Daniel Lyons
David J. Lyons

For full biographical listings, see the Martindale-Hubbell Law Directory

EUGENE J. MAURER, JR., P.A. (AV)

1201-A King Street, 19801
Telephone: 302-652-7900
Fax: 302-652-2173

Eugene J. Maurer, Jr.

LEGAL SUPPORT PERSONNEL

Carol Rende (Paralegal)

For full biographical listings, see the Martindale-Hubbell Law Directory

DISTRICT OF COLUMBIA

WASHINGTON, D.C. Co.

ASBILL, JUNKIN & MOFFITT, CHTD. (AV)

1615 New Hampshire Avenue, N.W., Suite 200, 20009
Telephone: 202-234-9000
Facsimile: 202-332-6480
Email: ajmchtd@erols.com *URL:* http://www.lawyers.com/asbill

Henry W. Asbill
Timothy deForest Junkin
William B. Moffitt (Not admitted in DC)

OF COUNSEL

Oscar I. Dodek, Jr.
Matthew L. Myers
W. Louis Hennessy

For full biographical listings, see the Martindale-Hubbell Law Directory

LAW OFFICES OF PLATO CACHERIS (AV)

Suite 730, 1100 Connecticut Avenue, North West, 20036
Telephone: 202-775-8700
Fax: 202-775-8702; 202-775-8722
Email: cacheris@erols.com *URL:* http://www.cacheris.com
Alexandria, Virginia Office: 120 North Alfred Street.
Telephone: 703-549-8181.

Plato Cacheris
Preston Burton
John F. Hundley

OF COUNSEL

Sydney J. Hoffmann

For full biographical listings, see the Martindale-Hubbell Law Directory

CAPLIN & DRYSDALE, CHARTERED (AV)

One Thomas Circle, N.W., 20005
Telephone: 202-862-5000
Cable Address: "Capdale"
Telex: 904001 CAPL UR WSH
Fax: 202-429-3301
URL: http://www.caplindrysdale.com
New York, N.Y. Office: 399 Park Avenue, 36th Floor.
Telephone: 212-319-7125.
Fax: 212-644-6755.

Mortimer M. Caplin
Thomas A. Troyer
David N. Webster
H. David Rosenbloom
Peter Van N. Lockwood
Richard W. Skillman
Patricia G. Lewis
Bernard S. Bailor
Albert G. Lauber, Jr.
Julie W. Davis
Trevor W. Swett III
James E. Salles
Craig A. Sharon
Catherine E. Livingston
Seth M. Green
Douglas D. Drysdale
Ralph A. Muoio
Elihu Inselbuch (Resident, New York Office)
Cono R. Namorato
Daniel B. Rosenbaum
Richard E. Timbie
Stafford Smiley
Scott D. Michel
Kent A. Mason
Robert A. Boisture
Milton Cerny
Matthew W. Frank
Jessica L. Katz
Christopher S. Rizek

Nathan D. Finch
Douglas N. Varley
Neal M. Kochman
Jason K. Bortz (Not admitted in DC)
April J. Adams (Not admitted in DC)
Elizabeth M. Sellers
Lloyd H. Mayer
Rita C. Tobin (Resident, New York Office)
H. Carter Hood (Not admitted in DC)

OF COUNSEL

Robert H. Elliott, Jr.
Myron C. Baum
Ann C. McMillan

For full biographical listings, see the Martindale-Hubbell Law Directory

JONES, DAY, REAVIS & POGUE (AV)

51 Louisiana Avenue, N.W., 20001-2113
Telephone: 202-879-3939
Telecopier: 202-626-1700
Email: counsel@jonesday.com *URL:* http://www.jonesday.com
In Atlanta, Georgia: 3500 SunTrust Plaza, 303 Peachtree Street.
Telephone: 404-521-3939.
Telecopier: 404-581-8330.
In Brussels, Belgium: Avenue Louise 480, 7th Floor, B-1050 Brussels.
Telephone: 32-2-645-14-11.
Telecopier: 32-2-645-14-45.
In Chicago, Illinois: 77 West Wacker.
Telephone: 312-782-3939.
Telecopier: 312-782-8585.
In Cleveland, Ohio: North Point, 901 Lakeside Avenue.
Telephone: 216-586-3939.
Telecopier: 216-579-0212.
In Columbus, Ohio: 1900 Huntington Center.
Telephone: 614-469-3939.
Telecopier: 614-461-4198.
In Dallas, Texas: 2727 North Harwood Street.
Telephone: 214-220-3939.
Telecopier: 214-969-5100.
In Frankfurt, Germany: Hochhaus am Park, Grüneburgweg 102, 60323, Frankfurt am Main.
Telephone: 49-69-9726-3939.
Telecopier: 49-69-9726-3993.
In Geneva, Switzerland: 20, rue de Candolle.
Telephone: 41-22-320-2339.
Telecopier: 41-22-320-1232.
In Hong Kong: 29th Floor, Entertainment Building, 30 Queen's Road Central.
Telephone: 852-2526-6895.
Telecopier: 852-2868-5871.

(See Next Column)

JONES, DAY, REAVIS & POGUE, *Washington—Continued*

In Irvine, California: 5 Park Plaza, Suite 1100.
Telephone: 949-851-3939.
Telecopier: 949-553-7539.
In London, England: Bucklersbury House, 3 Queen Victoria Street.
Telephone: 44-171-236-3939.
Telecopier: 44-171-236-1113.
In Los Angeles, California: 555 West Fifth Street, Suite 4600.
Telephone: 213-489-3939.
Telecopier: 213-243-2539.
In New Delhi, India (Associate Office): Pathak & Associates (an associate firm of Jones, Day, Reavis & Pogue), 1st Floor, Dr. Gopal Das Bhaven, 28 Barakhamba Road.
Telephone: 91-11-373-8793.; 91-11-335-7345.
Telecopier: 91-11-335-3761.
In New York, New York: 599 Lexington Avenue.
Telephone: 212-326-3939.
Telecopier: 212-755-7306.
In Paris, France: 120, rue du Faubourg Saint-Honoré.
Telephone: 33-1-56-59-39-39.
Telecopier: 33-1-56-59-39-38
In Pittsburgh, Pennsylvania: 500 Grant Street, 31st Floor.
Telephone: 412-391-3939.
Telecopier: 412-394-7959.
In Riyadh, Saudi Arabia: The International Law Firm (In Association with Jones, Day, Reavis & Pogue), Sulaymaniyah, Prince Mishari IBN, Abdulaziz Street, P.O. Box 22166.
Telephone: (966-1) 462-8866.
Telecopier: (966-1) 462-9001.
In Shanghai, China: 2805 Kerry Centre, 1515 Nanjing Road West.
Telephone: 86-21-5298-6568.
Telecopier: 86-21-5298-6569.
In Sydney, Australia: Governor Phillip Tower, Level 38, 1 Farrer Place.
Telephone: 61-2-9210-6921.
Telecopier: 61-2-9210-6926.
In Taipei, Taiwan: 8th Floor, 2 Tun Hwa South Road, Section 2.
Telephone: (886-2) 2704-6808.
Telecopier: (886-2) 2704-6791.
In Tokyo, Japan: Toranomon MT Building, 4th Floor, 10-3, Toranomon 3-Chome, Minato-Ku, Tokyo 105, Japan.
Telephone: 81-3-3433-3939.
Telecopier: 81-3-5401-2725.

MEMBERS OF FIRM IN WASHINGTON, D.C.

Joseph S. Iannucci
Michael Bradfield
Timothy B. Dyk
James T. O'Hara
J. Lawrence Manning, Jr.
Jonathan C. Rose
Sigmund T. Weiner
Andrew M. Kramer
James A. Wilderotter
Robert F. McDermott, Jr.
Joe Sims
James J. Graham
Mark K. Sisitsky
Junius C. McElveen, Jr.
Paul S. Ryerson
Tom D. Smith
Joseph M. David, Jr.
Clark Evans Downs
Willis J. Goldsmith
Phillip A. Proger
Thomas F. Cullen, Jr.
Robert S. Waters
Richard D. Avil, Jr.
Donald B. Ayer
Lawrence L. Lamade
David C. Roseman
Lester W. Droller
Raymond J. Wiacek
Stephen J. Brogan
Timothy J. Finn
Gregory M. Luce
Toby G. Singer
Geoffrey S. Stewart
Teresa A. Brooks
Kathryn M. Fenton
Peter F. Garvin, III
Kevin D. McDonald
Joseph F. Winterscheid
Kenneth J. Ayres
Charles A. James
Robert H. Klonoff
Mary Ellen Powers
Steven A. Teitelbaum
Peter J. Biersteker
Carolyn Y. Thompson
Christopher F. Dugan
Alison B. Marshall
Glen D. Nager
Adrian Wager-Zito
William V. O'Reilly
James D. Wareham
Michael P. Gurdak
David E. Miller
Gregory M. Shumaker
Kevin J. McIntyre
Candace A. Ridgway
James E. Gauch
R. Todd Johnson
Gregory G. Katsas

OF COUNSEL

Herbert J. Hansell (Not admitted in DC)
William E. Swope
Peter E. Heyward
Kent L. Killelea
Elliot D. Eder

COUNSEL

David A. Copus
Robert C. Jones
Jerome J. Zaucha
Stephen J. Goodman
Charles V. Stewart

ASSOCIATES

Heidi Hughes Bumpers
Neil A. Dellar
Mary L. Hale
Julia M. Broas
Kathleen Marie McChesney
James E. Anklam
Anthony P. Lalla
Steven J. Mintz
Edward K.M. Bilich
Gregory A. Castanias
Denise A. Fee
Edwin L. Fountain
William H. Oldach III
Daniel H. Bromberg
Stephen J. Jorden
Robin L. Juni
Martin V. Kirkwood
Elizabeth A. McLaughlin

(See Next Column)

ASSOCIATES (Continued)

Jesse A. Witten
Geoffrey K. Beach
Thomas M. Beck
Joseph A. Goldman
Blaney Harper
Lawrence D. Rosenberg
Michael R. Shumaker
Peter J. Wang
Jonathan Berman
Mandy Jones
Marcia Y. Lucas
Sarah Dryden Mackey
Mary-Helen Perry
Paul R. Reichert
Lynn A. Airasian
Mona Lisa Flicker
Michael L. Kolis
Jason F. Leif
Peter J. Love
Kevin C. Maclay
Sarah B. McClure
Pamela Sak
Catherine M. Stavrakis
Richard L. Winston
Todd C. Amidon
Kenneth B. Driver
Suzanne M. FitzGerald
Jacqueline M. Holmes
Julia E. McEvoy
John B. Nalbandian
Bevin M.B. Newman
Heather M. O'Shea (Not admitted in DC)
Sheryl Klemme Christmas
Karen M. Espaldon
Colette M. Hanson
Lisa Malloy Nardini
Leslie Overton
Laura Tuell Parcher
James D. Phipps (Not admitted in DC)
Stephen M. Polozie
Shelby L. Provencher
David S. Rutkowski
Beth T. Sigall
Aaron L. Agenbroad
Adam Candeub
T. Jeffrey Fitzgerald
Brian K. Grube (Not admitted in DC)
John B. Kennedy
Marli J.P. Kerrigan
Walid A. Khuri
Kathleen M. Laubenstein (Not admitted in DC)
John C. Martin
Joseph J. Migas
John S. Nagy (Not admitted in DC)
Sean G. Saxon (Not admitted in DC)
Susan V. Watson
J. Carter Andersen
Jack W. Campbell IV
Mia F. Cohen
Laura Talley Geyer
Mark L. Glassman
Carey G.B. Kerney
Stacy Renée Linden (Not admitted in DC)
Christopher J. Lovrien (Not admitted in DC)
Jennifer J. Gerstner Prozinski
J. Andrew Read
Portia A. Robert
Melissa D. Stear (Not admitted in DC)
Karen E. Van Horn (Not admitted in DC)
Margaret A. Ward
Jennifer A. Hunkler (Not admitted in DC)
Tamara Hardney Kassabian
Stuart M. Kuntz
Justin J. Roberts
Sheila L. Shadmand (Not admitted in DC)
Janie C.I. Sheng (Not admitted in DC)
Katherine A. Walther (Not admitted in DC)

SENIOR STAFF ATTORNEYS

Kevin B. Byrd
John P. McGrane, Jr.
Patrick L. Hubbard

STAFF ATTORNEYS

Brian J. McManus
Kenneth C. Terrell
Jenni R. Wallace
Jennifer A. Hay
Dara A. Lutz
Susan Q. Haines
Alison Colwell Snow (Not admitted in DC)
David S. Turbiner
Michael C. Kentoff
Lee A. Friedman

For full biographical listings, see the Martindale-Hubbell Law Directory

KING, PAGANO & HARRISON (AV)

1730 Pennsylvania Avenue, N.W., 20006
Telephone: 202-371-6800
Fax: 202-371-6770
URL: http://www.kph.com
New York, New York Office: 425 Park Avenue, 10022.
Telephone: 212-223-4000.
FAX: 212-223-4134.

MEMBERS OF FIRM

Jeffrey W. King
Keith J. Harrison
Steven Schaars
Jeffrey L. Poston

ASSOCIATE

Cheryl A. Maier

For full biographical listings, see the Martindale-Hubbell Law Directory

JOHN A. MCCAHILL (AV)

2021 L Street, N.W., Suite 300, 20036
Telephone: 202-861-0070
Fax: 202-861-2939
Email: Artabane@cais.com *URL:* http://www.lawyers.com/mccahilllaw
(Also Of Counsel, Artabane & Belden, P.C.)

For full biographical listings, see the Martindale-Hubbell Law Directory

THE ROBINSON LAW FIRM (AV)

Market Square, 717 D Street, N.W., 4th Floor, 20004
Telephone: 202-347-6100
Fax: 202-347-0081
URL: http://www.lawyers.com/robinsonlaw

(See Next Column)

THE ROBINSON LAW FIRM—*Continued*

MEMBER OF FIRM

Kenneth Michael Robinson

ASSOCIATES

Cameron Robinson Kourtesis (Not admitted in DC)
Nikolaos Panagiotis Kourtesis (Not admitted in DC)

For full biographical listings, see the Martindale-Hubbell Law Directory

TROUT & RICHARDS, P.L.L.C. (AV)

1742 N Street, N.W., 4th Floor, 20036
Telephone: 202-463-1920
Fax: 202-463-1925
Email: trlaw@troutrichards.com *URL:* http://www.troutrichards.com
Alexandria, Virginia Office: 301 North Pitt Street, 22314.
Telephone: 703-519-8840.

Robert P. Trout
John Thorpe Richards, Jr.

For full biographical listings, see the Martindale-Hubbell Law Directory

VENABLE ATTORNEYS AT LAW VENABLE, BAETJER, HOWARD & CIVILETTI, LLP (AV)

A Partnership including Professional Corporations
Suite 1000, 1201 New York Avenue, N.W., 20005
Telephone: 202-962-4800
Fax: 202-962-8300
URL: http://www.venable.com
Baltimore, Maryland Office: Venable, Baetjer and Howard LLP, 1800 Mercantile Bank & Trust Building, 2 Hopkins Plaza.
Telephone: 410-244-7400.
Fax: 410-244-7742.
McLean, Virginia Office: Venable, Baetjer and Howard LLP, Suite 400, 2010 Corporate Ridge.
Telephone: 703-760-1600.
Fax: 703-821-8949.
Rockville, Maryland Office: Venable, Baetjer and Howard LLP, Suite 500, One Church Street, P. O. Box 1906.
Telephone: 301-217-5600.
Fax: 301-217-5617.
Towson, Maryland Office: Venable, Baetjer and Howard LLP, 210 Allegheny Avenue, P. O. Box 5517.
Telephone: 410-494-6200.
Fax: 410-821-0147.

MEMBERS OF FIRM

Joseph G. Block
Benjamin R. Civiletti (P.C.) (Also at Baltimore and Towson, Maryland Offices)
William D. Coston
David W. Goewey
Gary M. Hnath
Amy Berman Jackson
Thomas J. Kelly, Jr.
Michael Schatzow (Also at Baltimore, Maryland Office)
Judson W. Starr (Also at Baltimore and Towson, Maryland Offices)

For Complete List of Firm Personnel, See General Section

For full biographical listings, see the Martindale-Hubbell Law Directory

WEHNER & YORK (AV)

1029 Vermont Avenue, N.W. Suite 300, 20005
Telephone: 202-543-2700
Facsimile: 202-543-2023
Email: litigation@wehner-york-law.com *URL:* http://www.lawyers.com/w&ylaw
Bridgeport, West Virginia Office: Grande Meadows, Saltwell Road and Route 73, Suite 230.
Telephone: 304-592-3400. E-Mail: litigation@wehner-york-law.com.

MEMBERS OF FIRM

Stephen V. Wehner
Michael M. York

ASSOCIATES

Gregory M. Kline (Not admitted in DC)
Charles Hildebrandt (Not admitted in DC)
Damien V. Alexander

LEGAL SUPPORT PERSONNEL

Charleen Hamrick (Legal Assistant)

For full biographical listings, see the Martindale-Hubbell Law Directory

WILLIAMS & CONNOLLY (AV)

725 Twelfth Street, N.W., 20005-5901
Telephone: 202-434-5000
Fax: 202-434-5029

MEMBERS OF FIRM

Jeremiah C. Collins
David Povich
Steven M. Umin
John W. Vardaman
Paul Martin Wolff
J. Alan Galbraith
John G. Kester
William E. McDaniels
Brendan V. Sullivan, Jr.
Aubrey M. Daniel, III
Richard M. Cooper
Gerald A. Feffer
Robert P. Watkins
Jerry L. Shulman

(See Next Column)

MEMBERS OF FIRM (Continued)

Lawrence Lucchino
Lewis H. Ferguson, III
Robert B. Barnett
David E. Kendall
Gregory B. Craig
John J. Buckley, Jr.
Terrence O'Donnell
John K. Villa
Barry S. Simon
Kevin T. Baine
Stephen L. Urbanczyk
Philip J. Ward
James A. Bruton, III
Peter J. Kahn
Lon S. Babby
Michael S. Sundermeyer
James T. Fuller, III
David D. Aufhauser
Bruce R. Genderson
Carolyn H. Williams
Frank Lane Heard III
Steven R. Kuney
Gerson A. Zweifach
Paul Mogin
Howard W. Gutman
Nancy F. Lesser
Richard S. Hoffman
Steven A. Steinbach
Mark S. Levinstein
Mary Greer Clark
Victoria Radd Rollins
Daniel Franklin Katz
Nicole K. Seligman
Robert M. Krasne
Kathleen L. Beggs
William R. Murray, Jr.
Eva Petko Esber
Stephen D. Raber
David C. Kiernan
Lon E. Musslewhite
Robin E. Jacobsohn
Charles A. Sweet
Heidi K. Hubbard
Glenn J. Pfadenhauer
George A. Borden
Robert J. Shaughnessy
Jonathan P. Graham
Allen P. Waxman
David S. Blatt
Ari S. Zymelman
Joseph D. Piorkowski, Jr.
Regina G. Maloney
Dane H. Butswinkas
Laurie S. Fulton

OF COUNSEL

Vincent J. Fuller
Raymond W. Bergan
Lyman G. Friedman

COUNSEL

Eric M. Braun

For Complete List of Firm Personnel, See General Section

For full biographical listings, see the Martindale-Hubbell Law Directory

WILMER, CUTLER & PICKERING (AV)

2445 M Street, N.W., 20037-1420
Telephone: 202-663-6000
Fax: 202-663-6363
Email: Law@Wilmer.Com *URL:* http://www.wilmer.com
Baltimore, Maryland Office: 100 Light Street, 21202.
Telephone: 410-986-2800.
Fax: 410-986-2828.
New York, New York Office: 520 Madison Avenue, 10022.
Telephone: 212-230-8800.
Fax: 212-230-8888.
European Offices:
4 Carlton Gardens, London, SW1Y 5AA, England. Telephone: +44 (20) 7 872 1000.
Fax: +44 (20) 7 839 3537.
Rue de la Loi 15# Wetstraat, B-1040 Brussels, Belgium. Telephone: +32 (2) 285 49 00.
Fax: +32 (2) 285 49 49.
Friedrichstrasse 95, D-10117 Berlin, Germany. Telephone: +49 (30) 20 22 64 00.
Fax: +49 (30) 20 22 65 00.

MEMBERS OF FIRM

Stephen H. Sachs
Louis R. Cohen
Michael R. Klein
Paul J. Mode, Jr.
Stephen F. Black
Gary D. Wilson
Michael L. Burack
William J. Kolasky, Jr.
A. Stephen Hut, Jr.
John Rounsaville, Jr.
Roger M. Witten
Andrew B. Weissman
Lynn Bregman
William R. McLucas
Harry J. Weiss
Bruce E. Coolidge
Juanita A. Crowley
John Payton
Andrew N. Vollmer
Bruce M. Berman
Thomas F. Connell
Charles E. Davidow
Philip D. Anker
Joseph K. Brenner
Carol Clayton
Thomas P. Olson
Patrick J. Carome
Jane C. Sherburne
David P. Donovan
Howard M. Shapiro
Roger W. Yoerges
Lewis J. Liman (Not admitted in DC; Resident, New York, New York Office)
Steven M. Dunne

COUNSEL

Brent J. Gurney
Jeffrey E. McFadden

For Complete List of Firm Personnel, See General Section

For full biographical listings, see the Martindale-Hubbell Law Directory

Washington—Continued

ZUCKERMAN, SPAEDER, GOLDSTEIN, TAYLOR & KOLKER, L.L.P. (AV)

1201 Connecticut Avenue, N.W., Suite 1200, 20036-2638
Telephone: 202-778-1800
Fax: 202-822-8106
Email: counsel@zuckerman.com
Miami, Florida Office: Zuckerman, Spaeder, Taylor & Evans, L.L.P., 201 South Biscayne Boulevard, Suite 900.
Telephones: 305-358-5000; 305-579-0110; Broward County: 305-523-0277.
Fax: 305-579-9749.
Ft. Lauderdale, Florida Office: Zuckerman, Spaeder, Taylor & Evans, L.L.P., One East Broward Boulevard, Suite 700.
Telephone: 954-356-0463.
Fax: 954-356-0406.
Baltimore, Maryland Office: Zuckerman, Spaeder, Goldstein, Taylor & Better, L.L.P., Suite 2440, 100 East Pratt Street.
Telephone: 410-332-0444.
Fax: 410-659-0436.
Tampa, Florida Office: Zuckerman, Spaeder, Taylor & Evans, L.L.P., 401 East Jackson Street, Suite 2525.
Telephone: 813-221-1010.
Fax: 813-223-7961.
New York, N.Y. Office: Zuckerman, Spaeder, Goldstein, Taylor & Kolker, L.L.P., 1114 Avenue of the Americas, 27th Floor, Grace Building.
Telephone: 212-479-6500.
Fax: 212-479-6512.
Vienna, Virginia Office: 8230 Leesburg Pike, Suite 501, Tysons Corner.
Telephone: 703-821-5594.
Fax: 703-821-9410.

MEMBERS OF FIRM

Roger E. Zuckerman
Roger C. Spaeder
William W. Taylor, III
Herbert Better (Resident, Baltimore, Maryland Office)
Michael S. Pasano (Miami and Ft. Lauderdale, Florida Offices)
Steven M. Salky
Morris Weinberg, Jr. (Resident, Tampa, Florida Office)
Blair G. Brown
Martin S. Himeles, Jr. (Resident, Baltimore, Maryland Office)
Edward J. M. Little (Resident, New York, N.Y. Office)
Graeme W. Bush
Thomas B. Mason
Cyril V. Smith (Resident, Baltimore, Maryland Office)
Guy A. Rasco (Resident, Miami, Florida Office)
Stephen J. Bronis (Resident, Miami, Florida Office)

COUNSEL

Lee Fugate (Resident, Tampa, Florida Office)

ASSOCIATE

Norman L. Eisen

Reference: Sovran Bank/DC National.

For full biographical listings, see the Martindale-Hubbell Law Directory

FLORIDA

*BARTOW,** Polk Co.

RICHARD D. MARS, P.A. (AV)

343 West Davidson Street, Suite 103, P.O. Box 1276, 33830-3765
Telephone: 941-533-0855
Telecopier: 941-534-3500
Email: RDMBAR@AOL.COM

Richard D. Mars

For full biographical listings, see the Martindale-Hubbell Law Directory

*CLEARWATER,** Pinellas Co.

BAUER, CRIDER & PELLEGRINO (AV)

1550 South Highland Avenue, Suite C, 33756
Telephone: 727-446-4800
Fax: 727-447-1443
Email: info@bcpcriminallaw.com *URL:* http://www.bcpcriminallaw.com
Tampa, Florida Office: One Urban Centre, Suite 750, 4830 West Kennedy Boulevard, 33609.
Telephone: 813-286-4300. E-Mail: info@bcpcriminallaw.com.

MEMBERS OF FIRM

Robert O. Bauer, Jr.
Ronnie G. Crider
Victor J. Pellegrino (Resident, Tampa Office)

David R. Parry

LEGAL SUPPORT PERSONNEL

Stephanie Stangle
Cindy Beaudet

For full biographical listings, see the Martindale-Hubbell Law Directory

JOHN D. FERNANDEZ, P.A. (AV)

918 Drew Street, 33755
Telephone: 727-461-4441
Fax: 727-442-4423
Email: jfernand@gate.net

John D. Fernandez

For full biographical listings, see the Martindale-Hubbell Law Directory

KWALL, SHOWERS & COLEMAN, P.A. (AV)

133 North Fort Harrison Avenue, 33755
Telephone: 727-441-4947
Telecopier: 727-447-3158
Email: kwall@worldnet.att.net *URL:* http://www.usalaw.com/adminlaw/

Louis Kwall
Gregory K. Showers
Sherwood S. (Flip) Coleman

For Complete List of Firm Personnel, See General Section

For full biographical listings, see the Martindale-Hubbell Law Directory

GEORGE E. TRAGOS (AV)

600 Cleveland Street Suite 700, 33755
Telephone: 727-441-9030; Tampa: 813-223-6405
Fax: 727-441-9254
Email: greeklaw@gte.net *URL:* http://www.greeklaw.com

For full biographical listings, see the Martindale-Hubbell Law Directory

CORAL GABLES, Dade Co.

JOEL HIRSCHHORN, P.A. (AV)

Douglas Centre-Penthouse One, 2600 Douglas Road, 33134
Telephone: 305-445-5320
Telefax: 305-446-1766

Joel Hirschhorn

Brian H. Bieber

Representative Clients: Former President of GDC 1B Public; Former President of Centrust 13B Bank; Former President of American Saving & Loan 10B Bank; Playboy Enterprises, Inc.; City of Miami Beach; Avis Rent-a-Car System, Inc.; International Fast Foods Corp.

For full biographical listings, see the Martindale-Hubbell Law Directory

*DADE CITY,** Pasco Co.

GREENFELDER, MANDER, HANSON, MURPHY & DWYER (AV)

14217 Third Street, 33523
Telephone: 352-567-0411
Fax: 352-567-7758
Email: GMHMandD@aol.com

MEMBERS OF FIRM

Albert R. Mander, III
T. Philip Hanson, Jr.

For full biographical listings, see the Martindale-Hubbell Law Directory

DAYTONA BEACH, Volusia Co.

LANDIS, GRAHAM, FRENCH, HUSFELD, SHERMAN & FORD, P.A. (AV)

Formerly Hull, Landis, Graham & French
543 South Ridgewood Avenue, 32114
Telephone: 904-252-4717
Fax: 904-253-7352
Email: firm@landispa.com *URL:* http://www.landispa.com
De Land, Florida Office: 145 East Rich Avenue, P.O. Box 48.
Telephone: 904-734-3451.
Deltona, Florida Office: 204 Medical Arts Center, 1555 Saxon Boulevard.
Telephone: 407-574-1461.
Fax: 407-574-0242.

Erskine W. Landis (1900-1967)
John L. Graham (1905-1978)
Thorwald J. Husfeld (1926-1995)
Richard S. Graham
William E. Sherman
Sam N. Masters

Carol Lumb Allen (Resident)
Janet M. Strickland

OF COUNSEL

J. Compton French (Retired)

Counsel for: School Board of Volusia County; Walmart Stores, Inc.; Delco Oil, Inc.; West Volusia Hospital Authority; South Florida Natural Gas Co.; Florida Public Utilities Co.; Volusia County Industrial Development Authority; Florida United Methodist Children's Home: Volusia County Educational Facilities Authority.

For full biographical listings, see the Martindale-Hubbell Law Directory

*FORT LAUDERDALE,** Broward Co.

BLACKMORE & BLACKMORE (AV)

320 Southeast 10th Court, 33316
Telephone: 954-522-0418; 1-800-646-2786
Fax: 954-522-4974
Email: adelelaw@bellsouth.net *URL:* http://www.lawyers.com/blackmore

MEMBERS OF FIRM

Robert W. Blackmore — Adele M. Blackmore

For full biographical listings, see the Martindale-Hubbell Law Directory

BOGENSCHUTZ & DUTKO, P.A. (AV)

600 South Andrews Avenue, Suite 500, 33301
Telephone: 954-764-2500
Fax: 954-764-5040
URL: http://www.lawyers.com/bogenschutz&dutko

J. David Bogenschutz — Michael E. Dutko
Mary H. McCleary

For full biographical listings, see the Martindale-Hubbell Law Directory

LAW OFFICES OF BRAVERMAN AND ROSSI, P.A. (AV)

625 Northeast Third Avenue, 33304
Telephone: 954-524-0505
Telefax: 954-527-4805
Email: Braver1@aol.com *URL:* http://www.BravermanRossi.com

Alan Jay Braverman — Steve Rossi

Michael A. Hymowitz — Bennett Braverman

OF COUNSEL

Robert L. Bogen — Steven F. Squire

Reference: SunTrust.

For full biographical listings, see the Martindale-Hubbell Law Directory

JOHN R. HOWES A PROFESSIONAL ASSOCIATION (AV)

633 Southeast Third Avenue, Suite 4F, P.O. Box 697, 33302
Telephone: 954-763-6003; 305-945-2854 (Miami-Dade)
Fax: 954-462-2255
Email: buldophin@aol.com

John R. Howes

LEGAL SUPPORT PERSONNEL

Marcella Mirande-Ketcham

For full biographical listings, see the Martindale-Hubbell Law Directory

GARY KOLLIN, P.A. (AV)

8211 West Broward Boulevard, Suite 420, 33324
Telephone: 954-723-9999
Telefax: 954-475-2279
Email: Kollin@earthlink.net *URL:* http://www.lawyers.com/gary_kollin-attorney

Gary Kollin

For full biographical listings, see the Martindale-Hubbell Law Directory

HILLIARD E. MOLDOF, P.A. (AV)

1311 Southeast Second Avenue, 33316
Telephone: 954-462-1005
Facsimile: 954-463-9869
Email: crimlaw@gate.net

Hilliard E. Moldof

For full biographical listings, see the Martindale-Hubbell Law Directory

RICHARD L. ROSENBAUM (AV)

Suite 1500, One East Broward Boulevard, 33301
Telephone: 954-522-7000
Facsimile: 954-522-7003
Email: rlrappeal@aol.com *URL:* http://www.lawyers.com/richardlrosenbaum

ASSOCIATE

Denise A. Bregoff

For full biographical listings, see the Martindale-Hubbell Law Directory

H. DOHN WILLIAMS, JR., P.A. (AV)

721 N.E. 3rd Avenue, P.O. Box 1722, 33302
Telephone: 954-523-5432
Boca Raton: 561-367-7900
Fax: 954-527-5565
Email: hdohn@ibm.net

(See Next Column)

H. Dohn Williams, Jr.

For full biographical listings, see the Martindale-Hubbell Law Directory

*GAINESVILLE,** Alachua Co.

THOMAS W. KURRUS (AV)

Suite 11, 204 West University Avenue, P.O. Box 838, 32602
Telephone: 352-377-2332 or 1-800-781-2332
Fax: 352-375-6249
Email: tomkurrus@earthlink.net *URL:* http://www.lawyers.com/tomkurrus

For full biographical listings, see the Martindale-Hubbell Law Directory

*JACKSONVILLE,** Duval Co.

SUZANNE BASS (AV)

24 North Market Street, Suite 400, 32202
Telephone: 904-356-9740
Fax: 904-350-1910
Email: bass@jaxlawyer.com *URL:* http://www.jaxlawyer.com

For full biographical listings, see the Martindale-Hubbell Law Directory

M. ALAN CEBALLOS, P.A. (AV)

The Old Title & Trust Company Building, 200 East Forsyth Street, 32202
Telephone: 904-353-3000
Fax: 904-353-5801
URL: http://www.lawyers.com/ceballoslaw

M. Alan Ceballos

For full biographical listings, see the Martindale-Hubbell Law Directory

HUGH COTNEY, P.A. (AV)

905 Blackstone Building, 233 East Bay Street, 32202-3417
Telephone: 904-356-0162
FAX: 904-355-5170

Hugh Cotney

Representative Clients: First Insuramerica of Florida, Inc.; Deaf Services Center, Inc.

For full biographical listings, see the Martindale-Hubbell Law Directory

WILLIAM C. A. MOULDER, P.A. (AV)

One San Jose Place, Suite 20, 32257
Telephone: 904-262-7600
Fax: 904-262-7608
Email: wcamlaw@mindspring.com *URL:* http://www.lawyers.com/moulderlaw

William C. A. Moulder

LEGAL SUPPORT PERSONNEL

Eloise Mullen (Legal Assistant) — Jeanine D. Leone (Firm Administrator)
Rebecca Pringle (Legal Secretary)
John Robert Leone (C.P.A./Tax Consultant in areas of Dissolution of Marriage)

References: First Guaranty Bank & Trust Company of Jacksonville; First Union Bank of Jacksonville.

For full biographical listings, see the Martindale-Hubbell Law Directory

SHEPPARD, WHITE & THOMAS, P.A. (AV)

215 Washington Street, 32202
Telephone: 904-356-9661
Facsimile: 904-356-9667
Email: sheppardwhitethomas@worldnet.att.com

Wm. J. Sheppard — Elizabeth L. White
D. Gray Thomas

Adam Benjamin Allen — Leslie C. Scott

For full biographical listings, see the Martindale-Hubbell Law Directory

*MIAMI,** Dade Co.

WILLIAM AARON (AV)

Miami Center, Suite 880, 201 South Biscayne Boulevard, 33131
Telephone: 305-371-5800
Cable Address: "Worldlaw"
Fax: 305-373-8877
Email: aaron@miamilaw.net *URL:* http://www.lawyers.com/us-criminallaw

For full biographical listings, see the Martindale-Hubbell Law Directory

Miami—Continued

ARAGON, BURLINGTON, WEIL & CROCKETT, P.A. (AV)

Office in the Grove - Penthouse, 2699 South Bayshore Drive, 33133
Telephone: 305-858-2900
Telefax: 305-858-5261
Email: info@abwc.com

Rudolph F. Aragon
Robert K. Burlington
Jeffrey B. Crockett
Ronald P. Weil
Paul J. Schwiep
Kevin C. Kaplan
Daniel F. Blonsky
Ava Borrasso
Sean R. Santini

For full biographical listings, see the Martindale-Hubbell Law Directory

JOSEPH BEELER, P.A. (AV)

Suite 300, 3050 Biscayne Boulevard, 33137
Telephone: 305-576-3050
Facsimile: 305-576-8080
Email: jbeeler@counsel.com *URL:* http://www.lawyers.com/beelerlaw

Joseph Beeler

H. Eugene Lindsey, III

For full biographical listings, see the Martindale-Hubbell Law Directory

BIERMAN, SHOHAT, LOEWY & KLEIN, PROFESSIONAL ASSOCIATION (AV)

Penthouse Two, 800 Brickell Avenue, 33131-2944
Telephone: 305-358-7000
Facsimile: 305-358-4010

Donald I. Bierman
Edward R. Shohat
Ira N. Loewy
Theodore Klein

Michael A. Pizzi, Jr.

Reference: United National Bank of Miami.

For full biographical listings, see the Martindale-Hubbell Law Directory

BILL CLAY, II, P.A. (AV)

11440 North Kendall Drive Penthouse 400, 33176
Telephone: 305-595-0866
Fax: 305-595-9732
Email: BillClayPA@worldnet.att.net

William "Bill" Clay

For full biographical listings, see the Martindale-Hubbell Law Directory

ESSEN, ESSEN, SUSANECK, CANET & LIPSON, P.A. (AV)

20801 Biscayne Boulevard, Suite 402 (Aventura), 33180
Telephone: 305-935-6680
1-888-303-7736
Fax: 305-935-2314
Email: ressen@richardessen.com *URL:* http://www.RichardEssen.com
West Palm Beach, Florida Office: Commerce Centre, 324 Datura Street, Suite 145.
Telephone: 561-833-0626.
Fax: 561-833-0728.
Naples, Florida Office: 2500 Airport Road, Suite 306, 34112. .
Telephone: 888-303-7736.
Fax: 305-935-2314.

Ben Essen (Deceased)
Richard Essen
Fredrick R. Susaneck (Resident, West Palm Beach Office)
Carlos A. Canet
Alan T. Lipson
Jose L. Fernandez
Lloyd H. Goldburgh
Randy Goodis
Andrew Parks
Michael Braxton

For full biographical listings, see the Martindale-Hubbell Law Directory

FERRELL SCHULTZ CARTER & FERTEL, P.A. (AV)

201 South Biscayne Boulevard Miami Center, 34th Floor, 33131-4325
Telephone: 305-371-8585
Telecopier: 305-371-5732
Email: receptionist@ferrellscf.com *URL:* http://www.ferrellscf.com

Milton M. Ferrell, Jr.
Alan K. Fertel

Reference: City National Bank of Florida.

For full biographical listings, see the Martindale-Hubbell Law Directory

DAVID M. GARVIN, P.A. (AV)

1200 Brickell Avenue, Suite 1480, 33131
Telephone: 305-371-8101
Fax: 305-371-8848
Email: ontrial2@aol.com

(See Next Column)

David M. Garvin

For full biographical listings, see the Martindale-Hubbell Law Directory

ALBERT J. KRIEGER, P.A. (AV)

1899 South Bayshore Drive, 33133
Telephone: 305-854-0050
Fax: 305-285-1761
Email: ajkriegerlaw@ibm.net

Albert J. Krieger

OF COUNSEL

Susan W. Van Dusen
Scott A. Srebnick

For full biographical listings, see the Martindale-Hubbell Law Directory

PAUL D. LAZARUS (AV)

Penthouse Two, 800 Brickell Avenue, 33131
Telephone: 305-539-0606
Fax: 305-539-1100
Email: trier700@aol.com *URL:* http://www.lawyers.com/miamicriminallaw

For full biographical listings, see the Martindale-Hubbell Law Directory

THE LAW OFFICES OF RONALD S. LOWY (AV)

5615 Lagorce Drive Penthouse, 33140
Telephone: 305-673-5699
Telecopier: 305-865-1809
Email: rlowyesq@bellsouth.net

Representative Clients: Tate Enterprises; British Airways, PLC; Alleghany Mutual Co.; SunTrust of Miami; Crescent Heights Companies.

For full biographical listings, see the Martindale-Hubbell Law Directory

CLARK D. MERVIS (AV)

Grove Forest Plaza, Suite 202, 2937 Southwest 27th Avenue (Coconut Grove), 33133-3703
Telephone: 305-443-1600
Fax: 305-445-9666

For full biographical listings, see the Martindale-Hubbell Law Directory

MOSCOWITZ STARKMAN & MAGOLNICK (AV)

100 Southeast 2nd Street Suite 3700, 33131
Telephone: 305-379-8300
Facsimile: 305-379-4404
Email: law@msmmiami.com *URL:* http://www.lawyers.com/msm-law

MEMBERS OF FIRM

Joel S. Magolnick
Jane Wollner Moscowitz
Norman A. Moscowitz
Jay Starkman

ASSOCIATES

Jennifer B. Glinsky
Mitchell R. Katz
Farah J. Korn
Lizbeth M. Michel

OF COUNSEL

Bradley L. Mirkin

For full biographical listings, see the Martindale-Hubbell Law Directory

PODHURST, ORSECK, JOSEFSBERG, EATON, MEADOW, OLIN & PERWIN, P.A. (AV)

Suite 800 City National Bank Building, 25 West Flagler Street, 33130-1780
Telephone: 305-358-2800; Fort Lauderdale: 954-463-4346
Fax: 305-358-2382
Email: Info@podhurst.com *URL:* http://www.wwdir.com/podhurst.html

Robert C. Josefsberg

References: City National Bank of Miami; Mellon United National Bank of Miami.

For Complete List of Firm Personnel, See General Section

For full biographical listings, see the Martindale-Hubbell Law Directory

WILLIAM L. RICHEY, P.A. (AV)

One Biscayne Tower, 2 South Biscayne Boulevard, Suite 3400, 33131-1897
Telephone: 305-372-8808
Fax: 305-372-3669
Email: wlr@richeylaw.com *URL:* http://www.lawyers.com/richeylaw
Palm City, Florida Office: 5501 S.W. Sunshine Farms Way, 34990-5696.
Telephone: 561-220-0558.
Fax: 305-372-3669.

William L. Richey (Also Of Counsel to Gunster, Yoakley, Valdes-Fauli & Stewart, P.A., Miami, Florida and Stuart, Florida)

For full biographical listings, see the Martindale-Hubbell Law Directory

Miami—Continued

Robbins, Tunkey, Ross, Amsel, Raben & Waxman, P.A. (AV)

2250 Southwest Third Avenue, Fourth Floor, 33129
Telephone: Dade County 305-858-9550; Broward County 954-522-6244 (All Telephones Open 24 Hours); 1-800-226-9550
Fax: 305-858-7491
Email: RTR2250@AOL.COM *URL:* http://www.crimlawfirm.com

Frederick S. Robbins
William R. Tunkey
Alan S. Ross
Robert G. Amsel
David Raben
Benjamin S. Waxman

Mark R. Eiglarsh
Marco A. Vazquez (1968-1995)

Reference: Mellon United National Bank, Miami, Florida.

For full biographical listings, see the Martindale-Hubbell Law Directory

Michael J. Rosen, P.A. (AV)

2400 South Dixie Highway Suite 105, 33133-3141
Telephone: 305-858-9700
Fax: 305-858-7299
Email: MJRPALAW@aol.com *URL:* http://www.lawyers.com/mjrpalaw

Michael J. Rosen

For full biographical listings, see the Martindale-Hubbell Law Directory

Sands & Moskowitz, P.A. (AV)

300 Bayview Executive Plaza, 3225 Aviation Avenue (Coconut Grove), 33133
Telephone: 305-285-1500
Fax: 305-285-0699
URL: http://www.lawyers.com/sandsandmoskowitzpa

Leonard A. Sands
Jay R. Moskowitz

For full biographical listings, see the Martindale-Hubbell Law Directory

Thornton & Rothman, P.A. (AV)

200 South Biscayne Boulevard, Suite 3420 First Union Financial Center, 33131
Telephone: 305-358-9000
Fax: 305-374-5747
Email: rothman2@sprynet.com *URL:* http://www.lawyers.com/thornton&rothman

John W. Thornton, Jr.
David B. Rothman

For full biographical listings, see the Martindale-Hubbell Law Directory

Jeffrey S. Weiner, P.A. (AV)

Two Datran Center Nineteenth Floor, Suite 1910, 9130 South Dadeland Boulevard, 33156-7858
Telephone: 305 670-9939
Fax: 305 670-9299
Email: lawfirm@jeffweiner.com
Boca Raton, Florida Office: Mizner Park. 327 Plaza Real, Suite 215, 33432.

Jeffrey S. Weiner

Mycki L. Ratzan
Michael B. Cohen
Jason M. Wandner

LEGAL SUPPORT PERSONNEL

Duchess Weiner (Law Office Administrator)

For full biographical listings, see the Martindale-Hubbell Law Directory

*MONTICELLO,** Jefferson Co.

David W. Collins (AV)

310 North Jefferson Street, 32344
Telephone: 850-997-5100
Fax: 850-997-3542

For full biographical listings, see the Martindale-Hubbell Law Directory

*NAPLES,** Collier Co.

McDonnell Trial Lawyers (AV)

1165 Eighth Street South, 34102
Telephone: 941-434-7711; 1-800-873-8060
Fax: 941-434-5629
Email: attyfirstname@mcdonnelltriallawyers. com
URL: http://www.lawyers.com/mtl

Michael McDonnell

ASSOCIATE

Gary Layne Green

For full biographical listings, see the Martindale-Hubbell Law Directory

NORTH PALM BEACH, Palm Beach Co.

Craig R. Wilson, P.A. (AV)

Crystal Tree Office Centre, Suite 415, 1201 U.S. Highway 1, 33408
Telephone: 561-626-6300
Fax: 561-627-2288
URL: http://www.lawyers.com/craigrwilson

Craig R. Wilson

Reference: First Union Bank of Palm Beach County.

For full biographical listings, see the Martindale-Hubbell Law Directory

*OCALA,** Marion Co.

Charles R. Holloman, P.A. (AV)

1515 East Silver Springs Boulevard, Suite 120 East, 34470
Telephone: 352-867-0766
Fax: 352-351-9217
Email: maddogfirm@aol.com *URL:* http://www.maddogfirm.com

Charles R. Holloman, Jr.

For full biographical listings, see the Martindale-Hubbell Law Directory

*ORLANDO,** Orange Co.

Barnett, Barclay & Springmann, P.A. (AV)

501 Mariposa Street, P.O. Box 1667, 32802
Telephone: 407-425-4245
Telecopier: 407-423-4332
Email: barnettlaw@mpinet.net *URL:* http://www.lawyers.com/bbslaw

William B. Barnett
Henry B. Rothblatt (1916-1985)
Bert W. Barclay
Franz F. Springmann

For full biographical listings, see the Martindale-Hubbell Law Directory

Robert J. Buonauro, P.A. (AV)

390 North Orange Avenue, Suite 1630, 32801
Telephone: 407-841-1940
Fax: 407-649-1936
Email: Robert@Buonauro.com

Robert J. Buonauro

For full biographical listings, see the Martindale-Hubbell Law Directory

James M. Campbell (AV)

111 North Orange Avenue, Suite 700, 32801
Telephone: 407-841-9860
Fax: 407-843-3738
Email: JMC47@aol.com

ASSOCIATE

Elizabeth Renee Joy

Reference: Citrus Bank.

For full biographical listings, see the Martindale-Hubbell Law Directory

Russell E. Crawford (AV)

Nations Bank Center, 390 North Orange Avenue Suite 2100, 32801
Telephone: 407-425-8659

Reference: Nations Bank.

For full biographical listings, see the Martindale-Hubbell Law Directory

Dempsey & Sasso (AV)

Nations Bank Building, 390 North Orange Avenue, Suite 2700, P.O. Box 1980, 32802
Telephone: 407-422-5166
Telecopier: 407-422-8556
Email: demp-sas@magicnet.net

Bernard H. Dempsey, Jr.
Michael C. Sasso

Brian D. Solomon
Barbara B. Smithers
Jeffrey K. Grant
Angelia J. Sheridan

For full biographical listings, see the Martindale-Hubbell Law Directory

W. Ford Duane (AV)

37 North Orange Avenue Suite 300, 32801-2425
Telephone: 407-481-9449
Fax: 407-481-2199
Email: hvei@intellistar.net

For full biographical listings, see the Martindale-Hubbell Law Directory

Orlando—Continued

THOMAS F. EGAN, P.A. (AV)

204 Park Lake Street, 32803
Telephone: 407-849-1055
Fax: 407-849-1094
Email: eganatty@aol.com

Thomas F. Egan

For full biographical listings, see the Martindale-Hubbell Law Directory

LAW OFFICES OF HORWITZ & FUSSELL A PROFESSIONAL ASSOCIATION (AV)

17 East Pine Street, 32801
Telephone: 407-843-7733
Fax: 407-849-1321

Mark L. Horwitz — David Dean Fussell

Glen J. Ioffredo

For full biographical listings, see the Martindale-Hubbell Law Directory

STUART I. HYMAN, P.A. (AV)

1520 East Amelia Street, 32803-5490
Telephone: 407-896-0536
Fax: 407-896-0540

Stuart I. Hyman

For full biographical listings, see the Martindale-Hubbell Law Directory

LEVENTHAL & SLAUGHTER, P.A. (AV)

Suite 700, 111 North Orange Avenue, 32801
Telephone: 407-849-6161
Telecopier: 407-843-3738

Robert A. Leventhal — Harrison T. Slaughter, Jr.

For full biographical listings, see the Martindale-Hubbell Law Directory

DONALD A. LYKKEBAK (AV)

390 North Orange Avenue, Suite 2100, 32801
Telephone: 407-425-4044
Fax: 407-425-0007
Email: dalykkebak@aol.com *URL:* http://www.lawyers.com/lykkebak

For full biographical listings, see the Martindale-Hubbell Law Directory

J. CHENEY MASON, P.A. (AV)

Barnett Bank Center, 390 North Orange Avenue, Suite 2100, 32801
Telephone: 407-843-5785
Fax: 407-422-6858

J. Cheney Mason

For full biographical listings, see the Martindale-Hubbell Law Directory

LAW OFFICES OF MARK E. NEJAME, P.A. (AV)

1 South Orange Avenue Suite 304, 32801
Telephone: 407-245-1232
Fax: 407-245-2980
Email: nejamem@nejamelaw.com *URL:* http://nejamelaw.com

Mark Elias NeJame

Joe D. Harrington — Eric H. Barker

For full biographical listings, see the Martindale-Hubbell Law Directory

LAW OFFICE OF KENTON V. SANDS (AV)

250 North Orange Avenue, Suite 1700-Penthouse, 32801
Telephone: 407-423-3421
Fax: 407-423-4735
Email: ksands@bellsouth.net *URL:* http://www.lawyers.com/sandslaw

For full biographical listings, see the Martindale-Hubbell Law Directory

WILLIAM J. SHEAFFER, P.A. (AV)

609 East Central Boulevard, 32801
Telephone: 407-423-1066
Fax: 407-648-0683
Email: defenselaw@cwix.com *URL:* http://www.lawyers.com/orlandocriminallaw

William J. Sheaffer

For full biographical listings, see the Martindale-Hubbell Law Directory

JOHN L. WOODARD, III (AV)

The Taylor Building, 320 North Magnolia Avenue, Suite A-6, 32801
Telephone: 407-843-1889; 800-940-5708
Fax: 407-422-9068

For full biographical listings, see the Martindale-Hubbell Law Directory

*SARASOTA,** Sarasota Co.

JAMES R. DIRMANN, P.A. (AV)

2180 Main Street, Suite A, 34237
Telephone: 941-366-7997
FAX: 941-955-7797
Email: jdirm@aol.com *URL:* http://www.lawyers.com/jdirm

James R. Dirmann

Reference: First Union National Bank.

For full biographical listings, see the Martindale-Hubbell Law Directory

JOHN M. FITZGIBBONS (AV)

22 South Tuttle Avenue, Suite 4, 34237
Telephone: 941-953-5697
Tampa, Florida Office: 707 North Franklin Street, Suite 700.
Telephone: 813-221-8800.
Fax: 813-228-9813

Kay Neiss Klein

*STUART,** Martin Co.

FRIERSON & WATSON (AV)

A Partnership of Professional Associations
3601 S.E. Ocean Boulevard, Suite 4, 34996
Telephone: 561-288-1880
Fax: 561-288-1887
URL: http://www.lawyers.com/robertw,watsonlaw

Robert J. Watson (P.A.) — Robin Wesley Frierson (P.A.)

For full biographical listings, see the Martindale-Hubbell Law Directory

*TALLAHASSEE,** Leon Co.

BROOKS, LEBOEUF, BENNETT & FOSTER, P.A. (AV)

863 East Park Avenue, 32301
Telephone: 850-222-2000
Fax: 850-222-9757

Ronald W. Brooks — Rhonda S. Bennett
Dean R. LeBoeuf — Matthew K. Foster

For full biographical listings, see the Martindale-Hubbell Law Directory

KITCHEN, JUDKINS, SIMPSON & HIGH (AV)

1102 North Gadsden Street, 32303
Telephone: 850-222-6040
Telecopier: 850-561-1471

E. C. Deeno Kitchen — Larry D. Simpson
James P. Judkins — Robert King High, Jr.

ASSOCIATE

Paul M. Villeneuve — Thomas J. Schulte, Jr.

OF COUNSEL

John R. Overchuck

For full biographical listings, see the Martindale-Hubbell Law Directory

*TAMPA,** Hillsborough Co.

BAUER, CRIDER & PELLEGRINO (AV)

One Urban Centre, Suite 750, 4830 West Kennedy Boulevard, 33609
Telephone: 813-286-4300
Email: info@bcpcriminallaw.com
Email: Vpelle6544@aol.com *URL:* http://www.bcpcriminallaw.com
Clearwater, Florida Office: 1550 South Highland Avenue, Suite C. 33756.
Telephone: 727-446-4800.
Fax: 727-447-1443. E-mail: info@bcpcriminallaw.com.

Victor J. Pellegrino

LEGAL SUPPORT PERSONNEL

Liz Quirk — Teresa Carlevale

For full biographical listings, see the Martindale-Hubbell Law Directory

RONALD K. CACCIATORE, P.A. (AV)

100 North Tampa Street, Suite 2835, 33602
Telephone: 813-223-4831
Facsimile: 813-223-2737

(See Next Column)

RONALD K. CACCIATORE, P.A.—*Continued*

Ronald K. Cacciatore

Reference: The Bank of Tampa.

For full biographical listings, see the Martindale-Hubbell Law Directory

THE LAW FIRM OF COHEN, JAYSON & FOSTER, P.A. (AV)

First of America Plaza, Suite 1700, 201 East Kennedy Boulevard, P.O. Box 172538, 33672-0538
Telephone: 813-225-1655
Fax: 813-225-1921
URL: http://www.cjfslawfirm.com

Barry A. Cohen
Christopher P. Jayson
Todd Foster
Mark H. Wright

E. Patrick Buntz
Michael A. Gold

For full biographical listings, see the Martindale-Hubbell Law Directory

JOHN M. FITZGIBBONS (AV)

707 North Franklin Street, Suite 700, 33602-4441
Telephone: 813-221-8800
Fax: 813-228-9813
Sarasota, Florida Office: 22 South Tuttle Avenue, Suite 4, 34237.
Telephone: 941-953-5697.

Kay Neiss Klein

For full biographical listings, see the Martindale-Hubbell Law Directory

THOMAS F. GRANAHAN, P.A. (AV)

1906 North Tampa Street, 33602-2133
Telephone: 813-229-1084
Fax: 813-228-6820
Email: granahan@mindspring.com

Thomas F. Granahan

For full biographical listings, see the Martindale-Hubbell Law Directory

MARCELINO J. HUERTA, III, P.A. (AV)

501 East Kennedy Boulevard Suite 1220, 33602
Telephone: 813-229-7623
Telefax: 813-228-0903
URL: http://www.lawyers.com/huertalaw

Marcelino J. Huerta, III

For full biographical listings, see the Martindale-Hubbell Law Directory

KYNES, MARKMAN & FELMAN, P.A. (AV)

P.O. Box 3396, 33601
Telephone: 813-229-1118
Facsimile: 813-221-6750

James H. Kynes (1953-1993)
Stuart C. Markman
James E. Felman
Susan H. Freemon

For full biographical listings, see the Martindale-Hubbell Law Directory

ANTHONY J. LASPADA, P.A. (AV)

1802 North Morgan Street, 33602
Telephone: 813-223-6048
Pinellas Line: 813-894-1788
Fax: 813-228-9471

Anthony J. LaSpada

Joseph A. Eustace, Jr.

For full biographical listings, see the Martindale-Hubbell Law Directory

JOHN F. LAURO, P.A. (AV)

Barnett Plaza, 101 East Kennedy Boulevard, Suite 3950, 33602
Telephone: 813-222-8990
FAX: 813-222-8991

John F. Lauro

For full biographical listings, see the Martindale-Hubbell Law Directory

LEVINE, HIRSCH, SEGALL & BRENNAN, P.A. (AV)

First Union Center, 100 South Ashley Drive, Suite 1600, P.O. Box 3429, 33601-3429
Telephone: 813-229-6585
Telecopier: 813-229-7210
Email: lhsb@lhsblaw.com

(See Next Column)

Arnold D. Levine
Richard A. Hirsch
Stephen L. Segall
Edward M. Brennan

For full biographical listings, see the Martindale-Hubbell Law Directory

MANEY, DAMSKER & JONES, P.A. (AV)

606 Madison Street, P.O. Box 172009, 33672-0009
Telephone: 813-228-7371
Fax: 813-223-4846

David A. Maney

For full biographical listings, see the Martindale-Hubbell Law Directory

LAW OFFICES OF MERKLE & MAGRI, P.A. (AV)

5510 West LaSalle Street, 33607
Telephone: 813-281-9000; Clearwater, 727-441-2699
Fax: 813-281-2223

Robert W. Merkle
Joseph D. Magri
Ward A. Meythaler
David J. Plante
Gerard J. Roble

For full biographical listings, see the Martindale-Hubbell Law Directory

ROBERT P. POLLI, P.A. (AV)

Barnett Bank Plaza, 101 East Kennedy Boulevard, Suite 1265, 33602
Telephone: 813-222-8350
Fax: Available Upon Request

Robert P. Polli

For full biographical listings, see the Martindale-Hubbell Law Directory

SUAREZ & WARDELL, P.A. (AV)

400 North Tampa Street, Suite 2950, 33602
Telephone: 813-229-2224
Fax: 813-221-8013
Email: S-W-Law@ix.netcom.com *URL:* http://www.lawyers.com/swlaw

Eddie A. Suarez
James A. Wardell

Julia Best Chase

For full biographical listings, see the Martindale-Hubbell Law Directory

*WEST PALM BEACH,** Palm Beach Co.

RICHARD G. LUBIN, P.A. (AV)

Second Floor, Flagler Plaza, 1217 South Flagler Drive, 33401
Telephone: 561-655-2040
Fax: 561-655-2182
Email: LubinLaw@aol.com

Richard G. Lubin
Nancy H. Hamill (1938-1980)

John Olea
Kirk C. Volker

For full biographical listings, see the Martindale-Hubbell Law Directory

ROTH AND DUNCAN, P.A. (AV)

Northbridge Centre, Suite 325, 515 North Flagler Drive, 33401
Telephone: 561-655-5529
Telecopier: 561-655-7818
Mailing Address: P.O. Box 770, 33402

David Roth
Douglas Duncan

For full biographical listings, see the Martindale-Hubbell Law Directory

TIERNEY & HAUGHWOUT (AV)

324 Datura Street Commerce Center, Suite 250, 33401
Telephone: 561-655-7601
Fax: 561-655-7344

MEMBERS OF FIRM

John F. Tierney, III
Carey Haughwout

LEGAL SUPPORT PERSONNEL

Jana L. Gillette
Kelly M. Manning

For full biographical listings, see the Martindale-Hubbell Law Directory

WINTER PARK, Orange Co.

FREDERICK R. MANN, JR., P.A. (AV)

The Taylor Building, Suite A, 312 Park Avenue North, 32789
Telephone: 407-599-7200
Fax: 407-599-7221

Frederick R. Mann, Jr.

For full biographical listings, see the Martindale-Hubbell Law Directory

Winter Park—Continued

LAW OFFICES OF CHANDLER R. MULLER, P.A. (AV)

1150 Louisiana Avenue, Suite 2, P.O. Box 2128, 32789
Telephone: 407-647-8200
Fax: 407-645-3000
URL: http://www.lawyers.com/chanmuller

Chandler R. Muller

For full biographical listings, see the Martindale-Hubbell Law Directory

GEORGIA

*ALBANY,** Dougherty Co.

DONALDSON, BELL & PICKETT, P.C. (AV)

127 North Westover Boulevard, P.O. Box 1607, 31708-0639
Telephone: 912-439-8987
Facsimile: 912-439-0150
Email: DoBePi@worldnet.att.net

George P. Donaldson, III
R. Ripley Bell, Jr.
Mark L. Pickett

For full biographical listings, see the Martindale-Hubbell Law Directory

*ATHENS,** Clarke Co.

COOK, NOELL, TOLLEY, BATES & MICHAEL, LLP (AV)

304 East Washington Street, P.O. Box 1927, 30603
Telephone: 706-549-6111
Fax: 706-548-0956

MEMBERS OF FIRM

J. Vincent Cook
Edward D. Tolley
John S. Noell, Jr.
Robert B. Bates
M. Kim Michael

Ronald E. Houser

For full biographical listings, see the Martindale-Hubbell Law Directory

*ATLANTA,** Fulton Co.

C. MICHAEL ABBOTT, P.C. (AV)

The Grand, 75 Fourteenth Street, Suite 2500, 30309-3644
Telephone: 404-885-1994
Fax: 404-885-1677
Email: cmabbott@mindspring.com

Michael Abbott

For full biographical listings, see the Martindale-Hubbell Law Directory

JAKE ARBES (AV)

2300 Harris Tower, 233 Peachtree Street, N.E., 30303
Telephone: 404-522-1980
FAX: 404-588-0648
Email: arbesjak@avana.net

For full biographical listings, see the Martindale-Hubbell Law Directory

BRENDA JOY BERNSTEIN, P.C. (AV)

800 The Grant Building, 44 Broad Street N.W., 30303
Telephone: 404-522-1200
Fax: 404-577-3600
Email: bjbernstein@mindspring.com *URL:* http://www.lawyers.com/bjbernstein

Brenda Joy (B.J.) Bernstein

For full biographical listings, see the Martindale-Hubbell Law Directory

BONDURANT, MIXSON & ELMORE, LLP (AV)

1201 W. Peachtree Street Suite 3900, 30309
Telephone: 404-881-4100
Fax: 404-881-4111
URL: http://www.bondurant-mixson.com

MEMBERS OF FIRM

Emmet J. Bondurant II
John E. Floyd
H. Lamar Mixson
Michael B. Terry
M. Jerome Elmore
P. Richard Game
Edward B. Krugman
Jill A. Pryor
Jeffrey O. Bramlett
J. Scott McClain

Representative Clients: American Dairy Queen Corp.; Avon Products, Inc.; Bottlers of Coca-Cola, U.S.A.; Blue Circle of America; Delta Air Lines, Inc.; Fina Oil and Chemical Company; Four M Corporation; Penske Motorsports; Queen Carpets, Inc.; Ticketmaster Southeast.

For full biographical listings, see the Martindale-Hubbell Law Directory

R. DAVID BOTTS (AV)

152 Nassau Street, N.W., 30303
Telephone: 404-524-0606
FAX: 404-524-0607
Email: dbotts@bellsouth.net

For full biographical listings, see the Martindale-Hubbell Law Directory

FINESTONE & MORRIS (AV)

2500 Tower Place, Suite 2540, 3340 Peachtree Road, N.E., 30326
Telephone: 404-262-2500
Telecopier: 404-231-1930
Email: administrator@fmattorneys.com *URL:* http://www.lawyers.com/f&mlaw

MEMBER OF FIRM

Bruce H. Morris

Reference: NationsBank.

For full biographical listings, see the Martindale-Hubbell Law Directory

GARLAND, SAMUEL & LOEB, P.C. (AV)

3151 Maple Drive, N.E., 30305
Telephone: 404-262-2225
Fax: 404-365-5041
Email: triallaw@atlanta.com

Edward T. M. Garland
Donald F. Samuel

For full biographical listings, see the Martindale-Hubbell Law Directory

HEAD, THOMAS & WEBB, LLC (AV)

Building 12, Suite 100, 750 Hammond Drive, N.E., 30328-5532
Telephone: 404-250-1113
Fax: 404-250-1494
URL: http://www.lawyers.com/dui
Email: wchead@absolutely-not-guilty.com *URL:* http://www.drunkdrivingdefense.com

William C. Head
Thomas J. Thomas
J. Lee Webb

Gregory Allen Willis
Lawrence Abram Kohn

For full biographical listings, see the Martindale-Hubbell Law Directory

THOMAS E. MADDOX, JR., P.C. (AV)

3521 Habersham at Northlake (Tucker), 30084-4001
Telephone: 770-414-8055
Telecopier: 770-414-8755
Email: tommylaw@worldnet.att.net

Thomas E. Maddox, Jr.

LEGAL SUPPORT PERSONNEL

Matthew K. Johnson, Jr.

For full biographical listings, see the Martindale-Hubbell Law Directory

STEVEN H. SADOW, P.C. (AV)

800 Grant Building, 44 Broad Street, N.W., 30303
Telephone: 404-577-1400
Fax: 404-577-3600
Email: steve8300@mindspring.com

Steven H. Sadow

For full biographical listings, see the Martindale-Hubbell Law Directory

*AUGUSTA,** Richmond Co.

RICHARD E. ALLEN (AV)

440 Greene Street, 30901
Telephone: 706-724-4466
Fax: 706-722-1677
Email: RALLENLAW@AOL.COM

For full biographical listings, see the Martindale-Hubbell Law Directory

GARRETT & GILLIARD (AV)

SunTrust Bank Building, 801 Broad Street, Suite 1001, 30901
Telephone: 706-724-1896
Fax: 706-724-0047
Email: g+g313@GroupZ.net *URL:* http://www.lawyers.com/g&glaw

MEMBERS OF FIRM

Michael C. Garrett
Kirk Emerson Gilliard

LEGAL SUPPORT PERSONNEL

Becky Padgett (Paralegal)

For full biographical listings, see the Martindale-Hubbell Law Directory

BUFORD, Gwinnett Co.

CHANDLER & BRITT, LLC (AV)

A Firm of Professional Corporations
4350 South Lee Street, 30518
Telephone: 770-271-2991
Fax: 770-271-2986
Email: chandlerbrittllc@mindspring.com

MEMBERS OF FIRM

Richard B. Chandler, Jr. (P.C.)
Walt M. Britt (P.C.)
Gregory D. Jay (P.C.)
W. Wade Beavers (P.C.)
Luther H. Beck, Jr.

Deborah F. Weiss

For full biographical listings, see the Martindale-Hubbell Law Directory

*DOUGLASVILLE,** Douglas Co.

KENNETH W. KRONTZ, P.C. (AV)

8493 Campbellton Street, 30134
Telephone: 770-577-1500
Fax: 770-920-0059
Email: K1444@XXINET.COM

Kenneth W. Krontz

For full biographical listings, see the Martindale-Hubbell Law Directory

*GAINESVILLE,** Hall Co.

DAVID A. POWELL (AV)

604 Green Street, N.E., Suite 3, 30501
Telephone: 770-287-1300
Fax: 770-287-0033
Email: dapowell@earthlink.net

For full biographical listings, see the Martindale-Hubbell Law Directory

KINGSLAND, Camden Co.

JOHN J. OSSICK, JR., P.C. (AV)

P.O. Box 1087 230 South Lee Street, 31548
Telephone: 912-729-5864
Fax: 912-729-2230
Email: ossick@gate.net

John J. Ossick, Jr.

Representative Clients: City of Kingsland Downtown Development Authority; Cumberland Transport, Inc.; Southeastern Bank.

For full biographical listings, see the Martindale-Hubbell Law Directory

NORCROSS, Gwinnett Co.

DEMING, PARKER, HOFFMAN, GREEN & CAMPBELL, P.C. (AV)

4851 Jimmy Carter Boulevard, 30093
Telephone: 770-564-2600
Fax: 770-564-2267
Covington, Georgia Office: Suite 11, 3236 Highway 278.
Telephone: 770-787-2600.
Fax: 770-564-2267.
Cumming, Georgia Office: 425 Tribble Gap Road, Suite 398, 30130.
Telephone: 770-889-2600.
Fax: 770-564-2267.

Michael D. Deming
Franklin E. Parker
Paul M. Hoffman
Jim R. Green, Jr.
Richard A. Campbell
Stephen R. Williams

OF COUNSEL

Robert E. Born

Mark L. Wells
Christopher W. T. Daly
E. Nicole Harrison
Suzanne M. Boykin

For full biographical listings, see the Martindale-Hubbell Law Directory

*OCILLA,** Irwin Co.

WALTERS, DAVIS & PUJADAS, P.C. (AV)

South Cherry Street, P.O. Box 247, 31774
Telephone: 912-468-7472; 468-9433
Fax: 912-468-9022

W. Emory Walters
J. Harvey Davis
Thomas E. Pujadas
C. Vinson Walters, II

Attorneys for: Irwin County Board of Education; First State Bank of Ocilla; Irwin County; Wilcox County.
Local Counsel for: Georgia Farm Bureau Mutual Insurance Co.
Approved Attorneys for: Kaiser Aluminum & Chemical Sales, Inc.; Lawyers Title Insurance Corp.; Ticor Title Insurance Co.; Farmers Home Administration; Federal Land Bank of Columbia.

(See Next Column)

For Complete List of Firm Personnel, See General Section

For full biographical listings, see the Martindale-Hubbell Law Directory

*SUMMERVILLE,** Chattooga Co.

COOK & CONNELLY (AV)

128 South Commerce Street, P.O. Box 370, 30747
Telephone: 706-857-3421
Fax: 706-857-1520

MEMBERS OF FIRM

Bobby Lee Cook
A. Cecil Palmour (1913-1980)
Bobby Lee Cook, Jr. (1950-1995)
L. Branch S. Connelly

For full biographical listings, see the Martindale-Hubbell Law Directory

*VALDOSTA,** Lowndes Co.

DODD AND DENNIS, P.C. (AV)

613 N. Patterson Street, P.O. Box 1066, 31603-1066
Telephone: 912-242-4470
Telefax: 912-245-7731
URL: http://www.lawyers.com/dodd&dennis
Email: doddlaw@mail.datasys.net *URL:* http://www.doddlaw.com

Roger J. Dodd
Sam D. Dennis

References: First Union Bank; First State Bank and Trust Co.; Park Avenue Bank.

For full biographical listings, see the Martindale-Hubbell Law Directory

HAWAII

*HONOLULU,** Honolulu Co.

EDMUNDS MAKI VERGA & THORN (AV)

Suite 2104, Davies Pacific Center, 841 Bishop Street, 96813
Telephone: 808-524-2000
Telecopier: 808-528-3585

John S. Edmunds
Paul Maki
Ronald J. Verga
Elise Owens Thorn
Joy S. Omonaka
Wesley D. Shimazu

Reference: Bank of Hawaii.

For full biographical listings, see the Martindale-Hubbell Law Directory

DAVID W. HALL ATTORNEY AT LAW, A LAW CORPORATION (AV)

Dillingham Transportation Building, Suite 236, 735 Bishop Street, 96813
Telephone: 808-526-0402
Fax: 808-526-0404
URL: http://www.lawyers.com/hall_firm

David W. Hall

For full biographical listings, see the Martindale-Hubbell Law Directory

BROOK HART ATTORNEY AT LAW, A LAW CORPORATION (AV)

Suite 610 Melim Building, 333 Queen Street, 96813
Telephone: 808-526-0811
Fax: 808-531-2677
Email: hartlaw@hawaii.rr.com

Brook Hart

For full biographical listings, see the Martindale-Hubbell Law Directory

RENEE M. L. YUEN ATTORNEY AT LAW, A LAW CORPORATION (AV)

Haseko Center, 820 Mililani Street, Suite 702A, 96813-2937
Telephone: 808-523-0125
Facsimile: 808-523-0127
Email: yuenlaw@hawaii.rr.com

Renee M. L. Yuen

For full biographical listings, see the Martindale-Hubbell Law Directory

ILLINOIS

*CHICAGO,** Cook Co.

ALLAN A. ACKERMAN, P.C. (AV)

2000 North Clifton Avenue, 60614-4120
Telephone: 312-332-2891; 332-2863
Fax: 773-871-3304
Email: doctrips@aol.com

Allan A. Ackerman

For full biographical listings, see the Martindale-Hubbell Law Directory

ROBERT H. ARONSON (AV)

Suite 714, 100 West Monroe Street, 60603
Telephone: 312-372-7123
FAX: 312-372-1247

For full biographical listings, see the Martindale-Hubbell Law Directory

THOMAS ANTHONY DURKIN, P.C. (AV)

53 West Jackson Boulevard, Suite 615, 60604
Telephone: 312-922-8980
Fax: 312-922-2055

Thomas Anthony Durkin

For full biographical listings, see the Martindale-Hubbell Law Directory

FORAN & SCHULTZ (AV)

Suite 3000, 30 North La Salle Street, 60602
Telephone: 312-368-8330
Fax: 312-580-2600
Email: law@foran.com *URL:* http://www.Foran.com

MEMBERS OF FIRM

Thomas A. Foran
Jeff D. Harris
Richard G. Schultz
Jack J. Carriglio
Jeffrey C. Blumenthal

ASSOCIATE

Charles M. Baum

OF COUNSEL

Harry G. Comerford

For full biographical listings, see the Martindale-Hubbell Law Directory

JONES, DAY, REAVIS & POGUE (AV)

77 West Wacker, 60601-1692
Telephone: 312-782-3939
Telecopier: 312-782-8585
Email: counsel@jonesday.com *URL:* http://www.jonesday.com
In Atlanta, Georgia: 3500 SunTrust Plaza, 303 Peachtree Street.
Telephone: 404-521-3939.
Telecopier: 404-581-8330. 34000 Brussels, Belgium: Avenue Louise 480, 7th Floor, B-1050 Brussels.
Telephone: 32-2-645-14-11.
Telecopier: 32-2-645-14-45.
In Cleveland, Ohio: North Point, 901 Lakeside Avenue.
Telephone: 216-586-3939.
Telecopier: 216-579-0212.
In Columbus, Ohio: 1900 Huntington Center.
Telephone: 614-469-3939.
Telecopier: 614-461-4198.
In Dallas, Texas: 2727 North Harwood Street.
Telephone: 214-220-3939.
Telecopier: 214-969-5100.
In Frankfurt, Germany: Hochhaus am Park, Grüneburgweg 102, 60323 Frankfurt am Main.
Telephone: 49-69-9726-3939.
Telecopier: 49-69-9726-3993.
In Geneva, Switzerland: 20, rue de Candolle.
Telephone: 41-22-320-2339.
Telecopier: 41-22-320-1232.
In Hong Kong: 29th Floor, Entertainment Building, 30 Queen's Road Central.
Telephone: 852-2526-6895.
Telecopier: 852-2868-5871 or 852-2868-5699.
In Irvine, California: 5 Park Plaza, Suite 1100.
Telephone: 949-851-3939.
Telecopier: 949-553-7539.
In London, England: Bucklersbury House, 3 Queen Victoria Street.
Telephone: 44-171-236-3939.
Telecopier: 44-171-236-1113.
In Los Angeles, California: 555 West Fifth Street, Suite 4600.
Telephone: 213-489-3939.
Telecopier: 213-243-2539.

(See Next Column)

In New Delhi, India (Associate Office): Pathak & Associates (an associate firm of Jones, Day, Reavis & Pogue), 1st Floor, Dr. Gopal Das Bhaven, 28 Barakhamba Road.
Telephone: 91-11-373-8793; 91-11-335-7345.
Telecopier: 91-11-335-3761.
In New York, New York: 599 Lexington Avenue.
Telephone: 212-326-3939.
Telecopier: 212-755-7306.
In Paris, France: 120, rue du Faubourg Saint-Honoré.
Telephone: 33-1-56-59-39-39.
Telecopier: 33-1-56-59-39-38
In Pittsburgh, Pennsylvania: 500 Grant Street, 31st Floor.
Telephone: 412-391-3939.
Telecopier: 412-394-7959.
In Riyadh, Saudi Arabia: The International Law Firm (In Association with Jones, Day, Reavis & Pogue), Sulaymaniyah, Prince Mishari IBN, Abdulaziz Street, P.O. Box 22166.
Telephone: (966-1) 462-8866.
Telecopier: (966-1) 462-9001.
In Shanghai, China: 2805 Kerry Centre, 1515 Nanjing Road West.
Telephone: 86-21-5298-6568.
Telecopier: 86-21-5298-6569.
In Sydney, Australia: Governor Phillip Tower, Level 38, 1 Farrer Place.
Telephone: 61-2-9210-6921.
Telecopier: 61-2-9210-6926.
In Taipei, Taiwan: 8th Floor, 2 Tun Hwa South Road, Section 2.
Telephone: (886-2) 2704-6808.
Telecopier: (886-2) 2704-6791.
In Tokyo, Japan: Toranomon MT Building, 4th Floor, 10-3, Toranomon 3-Chome, 34200o-ku, Tokyo 105, Japan.
Telephone: 81-3-3433-3939.
Telecopier: 81-3-5401-2725.
In Washington, D.C.: 51 Louisiana Avenue, N.W.
Telephone: 202-879-3939.
Telecopier: 202-626-1700.

MEMBER OF FIRM IN CHICAGO

Daniel E. Reidy

For Complete List of Firm Personnel, See General Section

For full biographical listings, see the Martindale-Hubbell Law Directory

THE LAW OFFICES OF JED STONE, LTD. (AV)

434 West Ontario Street, Suite 400, 60610
Telephone: 312-943-7881
Fax: 312-943-7978
Email: jeds716442@aol.com

Jed Stone

John Curnyn

For full biographical listings, see the Martindale-Hubbell Law Directory

CRAIG D. TOBIN & ASSOCIATES (AV)

Three First National Plaza, Suite 535, 60602
Telephone: 312-641-1321
Fax: 312-641-5220
Email: ctobin@barristers.com

Craig D. Tobin

For full biographical listings, see the Martindale-Hubbell Law Directory

WILDMAN, HARROLD, ALLEN & DIXON (AV)

225 West Wacker Drive, 30th Floor, 60606-1229
Telephone: 312-201-2000
Fax: 312-201-2555
Email: hennessy@whad.com *URL:* http://www.whad.com
Aurora, Illinois Office: 1961 W. Downer Place.
Telephone: 630-892-7021.
Fax: 630-892-7158.
Waukegan, Illinois Office: 404 West Water, P. O. Box 890.
Telephone: 847-625-5550.
Fax: 847-625-5555.
Lisle, Illinois Office: 4300 Commerce Court, Suite 320.
Telephone: 630-955-0555.
Fax: 630-955-0662
Toronto, Ontario correspondent Office: Keel Cottrelle. 36 Toronto Street, Suite 920.
Telephone: 416-367-2900.
Telefax: 416-367-2791.
Telex: 062-18660.

MEMBERS OF FIRM

Michael Dockterman
Timothy G. Nickels
Lisa S. Simmons

OF COUNSEL

Bernard Harrold

W. Scott Nehs

For full biographical listings, see the Martindale-Hubbell Law Directory

COLLINSVILLE, Madison Co.

DUNHAM, BOMAN & LESKERA (AV)

300 West Clay Street, 62234
Telephone: 618-344-7734
Telecopier: 618-344-3853
Belleville Office: 208 N. High.
Telephone: 618-235-7222.
Telecopier: 618-236-2800; 618-236-1899.

John W. Leskera
William L. Berry
Eric C. Young
Robert D. Francis
John L. Bitzer

For full biographical listings, see the Martindale-Hubbell Law Directory

*EDWARDSVILLE,** Madison Co.

LUCCO BROWN & MUDGE (AV)

224 St. Louis Street, P.O. Box 539, 62025
Telephone: 618-656-2321
Fax: 618-656-2363
Email: lbm@plantnet.com

Dick H. Mudge, Jr. (1919-1978)
J. William Lucco
Joseph R. Brown, Jr.
William A. Mudge

ASSOCIATES

Michael Shaheen
Billie L. Johnson

Reference: Bank of Edwardsville, Edwardsville, Illinois.

For full biographical listings, see the Martindale-Hubbell Law Directory

*GENEVA,** Kane Co.

SCHAFFNER & VAN DER SNICK, P.C. (AV)

115 Campbell Street, P.O. Box 101, 60134-2733
Telephone: 630-232-8900
Fax: 630-232-8908

Harry Schaffner
J. Brick Van Der Snick

Christine V Carney
Brian E. Leach

For full biographical listings, see the Martindale-Hubbell Law Directory

*ROCK ISLAND,** Rock Island Co.

WINSTEIN, KAVENSKY & WALLACE (AV)

4th Floor, Rock Island Bank Building, 224 18th Street, P.O. Box 4298, 61201
Telephone: 309-794-1515; 800-747-1527
Fax: 309-794-9929

MEMBERS OF FIRM

Stewart R. Winstein
David L. Cunningham

Local Regional Counsel for: United Auto Workers.
Reference: First National Bank of Quad Cities.

For full biographical listings, see the Martindale-Hubbell Law Directory

*SPRINGFIELD,** Sangamon Co.

METNICK, CHERRY & FRAZIER (AV)

Second Floor, Myers Building, 1 West Old State Capitol Plaza, P.O. Box 12140, 62791
Telephone: 217-753-4242
Telefax: 217-753-4642
Email: SPRINGLAW@AOL.COM

MEMBERS OF FIRM

Michael B. Metnick
Richard D. Frazier

ASSOCIATE

Kathryn Saltmarsh

For full biographical listings, see the Martindale-Hubbell Law Directory

*WAUKEGAN,** Lake Co.

ROBERT P. WILL & ASSOCIATES (AV)

7 South County Street, 60085
Telephone: 847-336-4440

MEMBER OF FIRM

Robert P. Will, Jr.

For full biographical listings, see the Martindale-Hubbell Law Directory

INDIANA

CARMEL, Hamilton Co.

KNOWLES & ASSOCIATES, LLC (AV)

811 South Range Line Road, 46032
Telephone: 317-848-4360
Telecopier: 317-848-4363
Email: knowlesassociates@worldnet.att.net *URL:* http://www.lawyers.com/knowles

William W. Knowles

D. Brandon Johnston

For full biographical listings, see the Martindale-Hubbell Law Directory

*EVANSVILLE,** Vanderburgh Co.

GLENN A. GRAMPP (AV)

Suite 400, 111 S.E. 3rd Street, P.O. Box 3401, 47733
Telephone: 812-464-8800
Fax: 812-422-8832
Reference: Citizens National Bank.

For full biographical listings, see the Martindale-Hubbell Law Directory

*INDIANAPOLIS,** Marion Co.

TABBERT HAHN EARNEST & WEDDLE (AV)

Suite 2100, One Indiana Square, 46204-2101
Telephone: 317-639-5444
Fax: 317-639-5232
Email: jtyrrell@tabberthahn.com *URL:* http://www.tabberthahn.com

Don A. Tabbert
Gregory F. Hahn
Lante K. Earnest
Robert G. Weddle
Mark K. Sullivan
Judy M. Tyrrell
Lara D. Engelking
Matthew W. Conner
William W. Mathews
Heather L. Fesko
Charles R. Whybrew

OF COUNSEL

James J. Nocon
William D. Lalley
Joseph W. Hammes
Dale E. Sporleder

For full biographical listings, see the Martindale-Hubbell Law Directory

MERRILLVILLE, Lake Co.

MARCE GONZALEZ, JR. (AV)

Connecticut Center, 9120 Connecticut, Suite D, 46410
Telephone: 219-769-3030
FAX: 219-769-3031

For full biographical listings, see the Martindale-Hubbell Law Directory

IOWA

*DES MOINES,** Polk Co.

THE ROSENBERG LAW FIRM (AV)

1010 Insurance Exchange Building, 505 Fifth Avenue, 50309
Telephone: 515-243-7600
Email: bdr@worldnet.att.net

MEMBERS OF FIRM

Raymond Rosenberg
Dean A. Stowers
Brent D. Rosenberg

Reference: Firstar Bank, Des Moines, Iowa.

For full biographical listings, see the Martindale-Hubbell Law Directory

*IOWA CITY,** Johnson Co.

JOHNSTON, POTTERFIELD & NATHANSON, P.C. (AV)

1902 Broadway, P.O. Box 3400, 52244
Telephone: 319-354-1712
Fax: 319-354-7265
URL: http://www.lawyers.com/johnstonlaw
Cedar Rapids Office: 129 First Avenue, S.W., P.O. Box 74210.
Telephone: 319-366-1000.
Fax: 319-366-6973.
Waterloo Office: 1506 LaPorte Road, P.O. Box 2787.
Telephone: 319-235-3000.
Fax: 319-235-2108.

(See Next Column)

JOHNSTON, POTTERFIELD & NATHANSON P.C., *Iowa City—Continued*

Joseph C. Johnston
Henry E. Nathanson
Amanda Potterfield
Cathy L. Fitzmaurice
David Burbidge

OF COUNSEL

Carl J. Goetz, Jr.

For full biographical listings, see the Martindale-Hubbell Law Directory

KANSAS

*WICHITA,** Sedgwick Co.

YOUNG, BOGLE, McCAUSLAND, WELLS & BLANCHARD, P.A. (AV)

106 West Douglas, Suite 923, 67202
Telephone: 316-265-7841
Facsimile: 316-265-3956
Email: ybmwblaw@aol.com

Paul S. McCausland
Patrick C. Blanchard

Representative Client: CJA Panel, D.Kan.

For Complete List of Firm Personnel, See General Section

For full biographical listings, see the Martindale-Hubbell Law Directory

KENTUCKY

*BOWLING GREEN,** Warren Co.

MILLIKEN LAW FIRM (AV)

410 East Tenth Avenue, P.O. Box 1640, 42102-1640
Telephone: 502-843-0800
Fax: 502-842-1237

W. Currie Milliken
Wesley V. Milliken

Reference: Firstar Bank, Bowling Green, Kentucky; Citizens First, Bowling Green, Kentucky.

For full biographical listings, see the Martindale-Hubbell Law Directory

COVINGTON, Kenton Co.

ROBERT E. SANDERS AND ASSOCIATES, P.S.C. (AV)

The Charles H. Fisk House, 1017 Russell Street, 41011-3052
Telephone: 606-491-3000
Fax: 606-655-4642
Email: resanders@worldnet.att.net

Robert E. Sanders

Jeffrey M. Sanders
J. Pierre Tismo
Delana S. Pierce

LEGAL SUPPORT PERSONNEL

Shirley L. Sanders
Sandra A. Sturgeon
Sheila D. Rachal

For full biographical listings, see the Martindale-Hubbell Law Directory

TALIAFERRO, MEHLING, SHIROONI & CARRAN (AV)

1005 Madison Avenue, P.O. Box 468, 41012-0468
Telephone: 606-291-9900
Fax: 606-291-3014

MEMBERS OF FIRM

Philip Taliaferro, III
Lucinda C. Shirooni
Christopher J. Mehling
Robert W. Carran

ASSOCIATES

Howard L. Tankersley
Jerome N. Epping, Jr.
Alice G. Keys
Michelle Snodgrass-Deimling

OF COUNSEL

Norbert J. Bischoff
F. Edward Worland, Jr.

For full biographical listings, see the Martindale-Hubbell Law Directory

*LEXINGTON,** Fayette Co.

McCOY & WEST (AV)

309 North Broadway, 40507
Telephone: 606-254-6363
FAX: 606-233-4234

MEMBERS OF FIRM

R. Burl McCoy, Jr.
John Kevin West

(See Next Column)

Charles E. Beal, II
Tonya S. Conner

For full biographical listings, see the Martindale-Hubbell Law Directory

ROBERTS & SMITH (AV)

167 West Main Street Suite 200, 40507-1701
Telephone: 606-233-1104
Fax: 606-255-6438
Email: LRob70165@aol.com

MEMBERS OF FIRM

Larry S. Roberts
Kenneth W. Smith

For full biographical listings, see the Martindale-Hubbell Law Directory

*LOUISVILLE,** Jefferson Co.

JAY LAMBERT (AV)

8701 Black Cherry Court, 40202
Telephone: 502-583-2831
Fax: 502-583-3701
Email: jlambert@iglou.com *URL:* http://www.iglou.com/lambertandlambert

For full biographical listings, see the Martindale-Hubbell Law Directory

*MOUNT VERNON,** Rockcastle Co.

CLONTZ & COX (AV)

Courthouse, 115 Richmond, P.O. Box 1350, 40456
Telephone: 606-256-5111
Fax: 606-256-2036

MEMBERS OF FIRM

Carl R. Clontz
Jerry J. Cox
John E. Clontz

ASSOCIATE

Jerome S. Fish, II

Representative Clients: The Bank of Mt. Vernon; Citizens Bank, Brodhead, Kentucky; Kentucky Farm Bureau Mutual Insurance Co.; Louisville Title Division of Commonwealth Land Title Insurance Co.
Reference: The Bank of Mt. Vernon, Mt. Vernon, Kentucky.

For full biographical listings, see the Martindale-Hubbell Law Directory

*PADUCAH,** McCracken Co.

LEN W. OGDEN, JR. (AV)

The Sinnott House, 228 North 9th Street, 42001-1850
Telephone: 502-444-0232
Fax: 502-444-0239
Email: lenogden@apex.net

For full biographical listings, see the Martindale-Hubbell Law Directory

LOUISIANA

*BATON ROUGE,** East Baton Rouge Parish

JAMES E. BOREN (AV)

830 Main Street, 70802
Telephone: 225-387-5786
Fax: 225-336-4667
Email: JBOREN6000@AOL.COM

For full biographical listings, see the Martindale-Hubbell Law Directory

deGRAVELLES, PALMINTIER & HOLTHAUS (AV)

628 St. Louis Street, 70802-0628
Telephone: 225-344-3735
Fax: 225-336-1146

MEMBERS OF FIRM

John W. deGravelles
Michael C. Palmintier
Craig F. Holthaus

ASSOCIATE

Scott H. Frugé

OF COUNSEL

David W. Robinson

LEGAL SUPPORT PERSONNEL

Jimmie W. Murvin (Paralegal)

For full biographical listings, see the Martindale-Hubbell Law Directory

Baton Rouge—Continued

M. MICHELE FOURNET (AV)

715 St. Ferdinand, 70802
Telephone: 225-383-5107
Fax: 225-383-5131
Email: lawoffic@intersurf.com

For full biographical listings, see the Martindale-Hubbell Law Directory

UNGLESBY, KOCH & REYNOLDS (AV)

246 Napoleon Street, 70802
Telephone: 225-387-0120
Fax: 225-336-4355
Email: unglkoch@premier.net

Lewis O. Unglesby
Karl J. Koch
Aidan C. Reynolds

For full biographical listings, see the Martindale-Hubbell Law Directory

*MINDEN,** Webster Parish

JAMES M. JOHNSON (AV)

105 Pearl Street, P.O. Box 1015, 71058-1015
Telephone: 318-377-4978
Toll Free: 877-827-4294
Fax: 318-377-9026

For full biographical listings, see the Martindale-Hubbell Law Directory

*MONROE,** Ouachita Parish

DAVENPORT, FILES & KELLY, L.L.P. (AV)

1509 Lamy Lane, P.O. Box 4787, 71211-4787
Telephone: 318-387-6453
FAX: 318-323-6533
Email: dfk@dfklaw.com

Thos. W. Davenport (1909-1962)
Wm. G. Kelly, Jr.
Thomas W. Davenport, Jr.
Jack B. Files
Mike C. Sanders
Ramsey L. Ogg
Michael J. Fontenot
M. Shane Craighead

W. David Hammett
Carey B. Underwood

STAFF ATTORNEY
Stacy L. Guice

Representative Clients: American International Group (AIG); Burlington Motor Carriers; Chubb Group; Crum & Forster Group; Delta Airlines, Inc.; GAINSCO; GEICO; Highlands Ins. Co.; Trinity Universal Ins. Co.; Zurich-American Insurance Companies.

For full biographical listings, see the Martindale-Hubbell Law Directory

*NEW ORLEANS,** Orleans Parish

CAPITELLI & WICKER (AV)

2950 Energy Centre, 1100 Poydras Street, 70163-2950
Telephone: 504-582-2425
Fax: 504-582-2422
Email: cw4law@bellsouth.net

Ralph Capitelli
T. Carey Wicker, III
Paul Michael Elvir, Jr.

For full biographical listings, see the Martindale-Hubbell Law Directory

GAINSBURGH, BENJAMIN, DAVID, MEUNIER & WARSHAUER (AV)

2800 Energy Centre, 1100 Poydras, 70163-2800
Telephone: 504-522-2304
Telecopier: 504-528-9973
Email: DPHILLIPS@GAINSBEN.COM

MEMBERS OF FIRM
Irving J. Warshauer
Madeleine M. Landrieu

For Complete List of Firm Personnel, See General Section

For full biographical listings, see the Martindale-Hubbell Law Directory

MARTZELL & BICKFORD (AV)

A Partnership including a Professional Corporation
338 Lafayette Street, 70130-3244
Telephone: 504-581-9065
Fax: 504-581-7635
Email: mailbox@martzellbickford.com *URL:* http://www.martzellbickford.com

John R. Martzell (P.C.)
Scott R. Bickford

Regina O. Matthews
Duggan F. Ellis
M. Suzanne Montero
Richard A. Filce
Ray L. Rhymes

(See Next Column)

LEGAL SUPPORT PERSONNEL
LITIGATION ADMINISTRATOR
Christopher H. Sherwood
PARALEGALS
Jane B. Daigle
Connie L. Cosse
Mary Wiggenhorn
FIRM ADMINISTRATOR
Stephen C. Wolf (Certified Public Accountant)

For full biographical listings, see the Martindale-Hubbell Law Directory

LAW OFFICES OF RICHARD W. WESTLING, L.L.C. (AV)

Poydras Center, 650 Poydras Street, Suite 2135, 70130
Telephone: 504-525-0600
Facsimile: 504-525-0641
Email: westling@communique.net *URL:* http://www.lawyers.com/westling

Richard W. Westling

For full biographical listings, see the Martindale-Hubbell Law Directory

RALPH S. WHALEN, JR. (AV)

3170 Energy Centre, 1100 Poydras Street, 70163
Telephone: 504-582-2333
Fax: 504-582-2332
Covington, Louisiana Office: 325 North New Hampshire Street.
Telephone: 504-893-7506.

For full biographical listings, see the Martindale-Hubbell Law Directory

*SHREVEPORT,** Caddo Parish

BLANCHARD, WALKER, O'QUIN & ROBERTS, A PROFESSIONAL LAW CORPORATION (AV)

Fourteenth Floor, Premier Bank Tower, 400 Texas Street, P.O. Drawer 1126, 71101
Telephone: 318-221-6858
Fax: 318-227-2967
Email: BWOR@BWOR.com
Bossier City, Louisiana Office: 2285 Benton Road, Suite B-201.
Telephone: 318-742-9255.
Fax: 318-742-9210.

A. M. Stroud, III
Stacey D. Williams

For Complete List of Firm Personnel, See General Section

For full biographical listings, see the Martindale-Hubbell Law Directory

MAINE

*AUGUSTA,** Kennebec Co.

PIERCE ATWOOD (AV)

77 Winthrop Street, 04330
Telephone: 207-622-6311
Fax: 207-623-9367
Email: info@PierceAtwood.com *URL:* http://www.pierceatwood.com
Portland, Maine Office: One Monument Square.
Telephone: 207-791-1100.
Fax: 207-791-1350.
Newburyport, Massachusetts Office: 6 Harris Street.
Telephone: 978-465-9599.
Fax: 978-465-9945.

MEMBER OF FIRM
Malcolm L. Lyons

For Complete List of Firm Personnel, See General Section

For full biographical listings, see the Martindale-Hubbell Law Directory

*BANGOR,** Penobscot Co.

GROSS, MINSKY, MOGUL & SINGAL, P.A. (AV)

Key Plaza, 23 Water Street, P.O. Box 917, 04402-0917
Telephone: 207-942-4644; 800-274-7124
Telecopier: 207-942-3699
Email: law@gmms.com

Edward I. Gross (1912-1999)
Jules L. Mogul (1930-1994)
George Z. Singal
Louis H. Kornreich
George C. Schelling
Edward W. Gould
Steven J. Mogul
James R. Wholly
Daniel A. Pileggi
Philip K. Clarke

Wayne P. Libhart (Retired)
Sandra L. Rothera
James S. Nixon

(See Next Column)

GROSS, MINSKY, MOGUL & SINGAL P.A., *Bangor—Continued*

OF COUNSEL

Norman Minsky

Representative Client: Dahl Chase Pathology Associates.
Local Counsel for: The St. Paul Insurance Cos.; Aetna Life & Casualty Co.; Imperial Casualty & Indemnity Co.

For full biographical listings, see the Martindale-Hubbell Law Directory

*PORTLAND,** Cumberland Co.

PIERCE ATWOOD (AV)

One Monument Square, 04101
Telephone: 207-791-1100
Fax: 207-791-1350
Email: info@PierceAtwood.com *URL:* http://www.pierceatwood.com
Augusta, Maine Office: 77 Winthrop Street.
Telephone: 207-622-6311.
Fax: 207-623-9367.
Newburyport, Massachusetts Office: 6 Harris Street.
Telephone: 978-465-9599.
Fax: 978-465-9945.

MEMBERS OF FIRM

Ralph I. Lancaster, Jr.
Malcolm L. Lyons (Resident, Augusta Office)
Peter W. Culley
James R. Erwin
Kevin F. Gordon

For Complete List of Firm Personnel, See General Section

For full biographical listings, see the Martindale-Hubbell Law Directory

*SKOWHEGAN,** Somerset Co.

WRIGHT & MILLS, P.A. (AV)

218 Water Street, P.O. Box 9, 04976-0009
Telephone: 207-474-3324
Telefax: 207-474-3609
Email: millslaw@somtel.com

S. Peter Mills
Paul P. Sumberg
Janet T. Mills
Kenneth A. Lexier
Robert H. Conkling

Representative Clients: Design Professionals Insurance Co., New Jersey; Solon Manufacturing Co., Solon, Maine; Kleinschmidt Associates-Engineers, Pittsfield, Maine; Acheron Engineering, Newport, Maine; E.W. Littlefield-Contractors, Hartland, Maine; WBRC-Architects, Bangor, Maine; Town of Skowhegan; Town of Norridgewock.

For full biographical listings, see the Martindale-Hubbell Law Directory

MARYLAND

*ANNAPOLIS,** Anne Arundel Co.

DALNEKOFF & MASON, P.A. (AV)

Suite 301 West Court Building, 2448 Holly Avenue, 21401-3177
Telephone: 410-841-6500; 266-0544
D.C.: 301-261-8671
Fax: 410-224-4135
Email: info@dalnekoffmason.com *URL:* http://www.dalnekoffmason.com
Affiliated with: Morgan and Hendrick, 317 Whitehead Street, Key West, Florida.
Telephone: 305-296-5676.

Carol S. Craig
Barry J. Dalnekoff
Mark E. Mason
Royal G. Shannonhouse, III
Nelson R. Stewart
Thomas J. Voigt
Erin D. Gable

OF COUNSEL

Leonard E. Moodispaw
Matthew S. Evans, Jr.

Reference: NationsBank, Annapolis, Maryland.

For full biographical listings, see the Martindale-Hubbell Law Directory

*BALTIMORE,** (Independent City)

ALBRIGHT BROWN & GOERTEMILLER, LLC (AV)

120 East Baltimore Street, Suite 2150, 21202
Telephone: 410-244-0350
Facsimile: 410-244-0356
Elkton, Maryland Office: 205 East Main Street. 21921.
Telephone: 410-398-3850.
Fax: 410-398-0666.

(See Next Column)

David F. Albright
C. Thomas Brown
Benjamin R. Goertemiller

For full biographical listings, see the Martindale-Hubbell Law Directory

HAROLD I. GLASER (AV)

Suite 1717, 201 North Charles Street, 21201
Telephone: 410-244-8822
Fax: 410-625-1028
Email: HIGlaser@aol.com

MEMBER OF FIRM

Michael S. Glushakow

For full biographical listings, see the Martindale-Hubbell Law Directory

MARTIN, SNYDER & BERNSTEIN, P.A. (AV)

Redwood Tower, Suite 2000, 217 East Redwood Street, 21202
Telephone: 410-547-7163
Facsimile: 410-547-1605

Gerard P. Martin
David L. Snyder
Gregg L. Bernstein

Kimberly Dunn Spelman
Caroline DeLisle Ciraolo
Steven F. Wrobel
Denis J. Charlesworth

OF COUNSEL

Steven J. Sibel

LEGAL SUPPORT PERSONNEL

Joanna L. Trela (Administrator)
D'Ann Auty (Paralegal)

For full biographical listings, see the Martindale-Hubbell Law Directory

MCDANIEL & MARSH (AV)

118 West Mulberry Street, 21201-3606
Telephone: 410-685-3810
Telecopier: 410-685-0203

William Alden McDaniel, Jr.
Jo Bennett Marsh

For full biographical listings, see the Martindale-Hubbell Law Directory

MEHLMAN & GREENBLATT, LLC (AV)

1838 Greene Tree Road, Suite 360, 21208
Telephone: 410-486-4790
Fax: 410-486-4360
URL: http://www.lawyers.com/mehlman&greenblatt

Gerson B. Mehlman
Gary R. Greenblatt
Frederic C. Heyman
Francis X. Leary
Constance M. Hare

For full biographical listings, see the Martindale-Hubbell Law Directory

REDMOND, BURGIN & GUTIERREZ, P.A. (AV)

1301, The Fidelity Building, 210 North Charles Street, 21202
Telephone: 410-752-1555
Fax: 410-752-1064
URL: http://www.RBGLAW.com
Upper Marlboro, Maryland Office: 14746 Main Street.
Telephone: 301-952-1555.

Maria Cristina Gutierrez

Mark B. Martin
Joseph I. Tivvis, Jr.
Rita Pazniokas

For Complete List of Firm Personnel, See General Section

For full biographical listings, see the Martindale-Hubbell Law Directory

VENABLE ATTORNEYS AT LAW VENABLE, BAETJER AND HOWARD, LLP (AV)

A Partnership including Professional Corporations
1800 Mercantile Bank & Trust Building, 2 Hopkins Plaza, 21201
Telephone: 410-244-7400
Fax: 410-244-7742
URL: http://www.venable.com
Washington, D.C. Office: Venable, Baetjer, Howard & Civiletti LLP, Suite 1000, 1201 New York Avenue, N.W.
Telephone: 202-962-4800.
Fax: 202-962-8300.
McLean, Virginia Office: Suite 400, 2010 Corporate Ridge.
Telephone: 703-760-1600.
Fax: 703-821-8949.
Rockville, Maryland Office: Suite 500, One Church Street, P. O. Box 1906.
Telephone: 301-217-5600.
Fax: 301-217-5617.
Towson, Maryland Office: 210 Allegheny Avenue, P. O. Box 5517.
Telephone: 410-494-6200.
Fax: 410-821-0147.

(See Next Column)

VENABLE ATTORNEYS AT LAW VENABLE, BAETJER AND HOWARD, LLP—*Continued*

MEMBERS OF FIRM

Benjamin R. Civiletti (P.C.) (Also at Washington, D.C. and Towson, Maryland Offices)
John Henry Lewin, Jr. (P.C.)
Joseph G. Block (Not admitted in MD; Resident, Washington, D.C. Office)
Michael Schatzow (Also at Washington, D.C. Office)
Judson W. Starr (Not admitted in MD; Also at Washington, D.C. and Towson, Maryland Offices)
William D. Coston (Not admitted in MD; Resident, Washington, D.C. Office)
Amy Berman Jackson (Not admitted in MD; Resident, Washington, D.C. Office)
Thomas J. Kelly, Jr. (Not admitted in MD; Resident, Washington, D.C. Office)
Gary M. Hnath (Resident, Washington, D.C. Office)
Mitchell Y. Mirviss
Geoffrey R. Garinther (Also at Towson, Maryland Office)
Terri L. Turner
David W. Goewey (Not admitted in MD; Resident, Washington, D.C. Office)

ASSOCIATE

Paul D. Barker, Jr.

For Complete List of Firm Personnel, See General Section

For full biographical listings, see the Martindale-Hubbell Law Directory

*BEL AIR,** Harford Co.

BROWN, BROWN & BROWN, A PROFESSIONAL ASSOCIATION (AV)

200 South Main Street, 21014
Telephone: 410-838-5500
Baltimore: 410-879-2220
Fax: 410-893-0402

A. Freeborn Brown (1915-1998)
T. Carroll Brown
Augustus F. Brown
Albert J. A. Young

Harold Douglas Norton
Christopher R. vanRoden
David E. Carey

Attorneys for: Baltimore Gas & Electric Co.; Chesapeake & Potomac Telephone Co.; Aberdeen Proving Ground Federal Credit Union; First National Bank of Maryland; Bell Atlantic Mobile Systems; First Harbor Securities; Maryland Portable Concrete, Inc.
Approved Counsel for: The Chicago Title Insurance Co. of Maryland, Inc.

For full biographical listings, see the Martindale-Hubbell Law Directory

*ELLICOTT CITY,** Howard Co.

GERALD M. RICHMAN (AV)

Suite 204, 3454 Ellicott Center Drive, 21043-4128
Telephone: 410-465-6666
FAX: 410-465-8964
Email: GMRPALAW@AOL.COM *URL:* http://www.lawyers.com/gmrichmanlaw

For full biographical listings, see the Martindale-Hubbell Law Directory

GREENBELT, Prince Georges Co.

RICHARD P. ARNOLD (AV)

Greenway Professional Center East, Suite 314 7525 Greenway Center Drive, 20770
Telephone: 301-474-5550
Fax: 301-345-0975

For full biographical listings, see the Martindale-Hubbell Law Directory

STANLEY S. PICKETT (AV)

Suite 414 Capital Office Park, 6411 Ivy Lane, 20770
Telephone: 301-513-0613
Fax: 301-513-0618
Email: lossp@intr.net

Stanley Sinclair Pickett

ASSOCIATES

Gordon J. Brumback
Stacy S. Pickett Trimble

LEGAL SUPPORT PERSONNEL

Vivian A. Wolfe (Paralegal)

Representative Clients: B.F. Saul Co.; McDonald and Eudy Printers, Inc.; Condominium Management, Inc.; Long & Foster Realtors; Mitron Systems Corp.; Glenanden Housing Authority; Community Associations, Inc.; Hagmer Management, Inc.; Quantum Management, Inc.

For full biographical listings, see the Martindale-Hubbell Law Directory

*LA PLATA,** Charles Co.

MUDD, MUDD & FITZGERALD, P.A. (AV)

106 St. Mary's Avenue, P.O. Box 310, 20646
Telephone: 301-934-9541
FAX: 301-934-8178

John F. Mudd (1885-1950)
F. DeSales Mudd (1909-1972)
Thomas F. Mudd
John F. Mudd
Stephen P. Fitzgerald

John E. Ray

Local Counsel for: County First Bank (La Plata); Potomac Electric Power Co.; The Hartford Insurance Group; Maryland Bank & Trust Co.; Chicago Title Insurance Co.; Peninsula Title Insurance Co.; Colonial Farm Credit Agric. Credit Assn.
Counsel for: Interstate General Corporation; SMO, Inc.

For full biographical listings, see the Martindale-Hubbell Law Directory

OCEAN CITY, Worcester Co.

AYRES, JENKINS, GORDY & ALMAND, P.A. (AV)

5200-B Coastal Highway, 21842
Telephone: 410-723-1400
Fax: 410-723-1861
Email: ajga@beachin.net
Berlin, Maryland Office: 11047 Race Track Road (Ocean Pines).
Telephone: 410-641-5033.
Fax: 410-641-6926.

Guy R. Ayres, III
M. Dean Jenkins
Harold B. Gordy, Jr. (Resident, Berlin Office)
James W. Almand
William E. Esham, III
Mark Spencer Cropper

Paul Timmons Haskell

References: Calvin B. Taylor Banking Co.; Peninsula Bank.

For full biographical listings, see the Martindale-Hubbell Law Directory

COURTLAND K. TOWNSEND, JR. CHARTERED (AV)

The Executive Building, Suite 101, 7200 Coastal Highway, 21842
Telephone: 410-524-4300
FAX: 410-524-4953

Courtland K. Townsend, Jr.

For full biographical listings, see the Martindale-Hubbell Law Directory

OWINGS MILLS, Baltimore Co.

LEONARD H. SHAPIRO (AV)

The Owings Centre, 10220 South Dolfield Road Suite 203, 21117-3660
Telephone: 410-363-3311
Fax: 410-581-7020
Email: LHShapiro@aol.com

Marie Fischer Cooke

For full biographical listings, see the Martindale-Hubbell Law Directory

*ROCKVILLE,** Montgomery Co.

ARMSTRONG, DONOHUE, CEPPOS & VAUGHAN, CHARTERED (AV)

Suite 101, 204 Monroe Street, 20850
Telephone: 301-251-0440
Telecopier: 301-279-5929

Larry A. Ceppos
John C. Monahan
Benjamin S. Vaughan

For full biographical listings, see the Martindale-Hubbell Law Directory

CATTERTON, KEMP & GREENBERG, P.A. (AV)

Suite 215, 200 A Monroe Street, 20850
Telephone: 301-294-0460
FAX: 301-294-4568
Email: PFKemp@aol.com

Judith R. Catterton
Paul F. Kemp
Robert A. Greenberg

Linda M. Schaefer

OF COUNSEL

Jane Macht

For full biographical listings, see the Martindale-Hubbell Law Directory

Rockville—Continued

HEENEY, ARMSTRONG & HEENEY (AV)

Adams Law Center, 29 Wood Lane, 20850
Telephone: 301-762-8585
Fax: 301-309-1461

MEMBERS OF FIRM

Robert C. Heeney (1922-1981) Thomas L. Heeney
Philip H. Armstrong

ASSOCIATES

Matthew W. Black Jr. Jennifer B. Page

Reference: Crestar Bank, Rockville, Maryland.

For full biographical listings, see the Martindale-Hubbell Law Directory

STEIN, SPERLING, BENNETT, DE JONG, DRISCOLL, GREENFEIG & METRO, P.C. (AV)

25 West Middle Lane, 20850-2204
Telephone: 301-340-2020; 800-435-5230
Telecopier: 301-340-8217
Email: lawfirm@steinsperling.com
Falls Church, Virginia Office: 6245 Leesburg Pike, Suite 140, 22044.
Telephone: 703-237-0500.
Telecopier: 703-534-2899.

David C. Driscoll, Jr. Paul T. Stein

David W. Lease Debra Sue Grimes

For Complete List of Firm Personnel, See General Section

For full biographical listings, see the Martindale-Hubbell Law Directory

*SALISBURY,** Wicomico Co.

ANTHENELLI & OTWAY (AV)

108 The Plaza, P.O. Box 4096, 21801
Telephone: 410-749-3900
Fax: 410-749-8577

MEMBERS OF FIRM

James V. Anthenelli James L. Otway

ASSOCIATE

John K. Phoebus

For full biographical listings, see the Martindale-Hubbell Law Directory

DUVALL & DUVALL, L.L.P. (AV)

108 East Market Street, P.O. Box 4077, 21803-4077
Telephone: 410-548-1010
Fax: 410-548-1045
Email: billduva@shore.intercom.net

MEMBERS OF FIRM

William G. Duvall Richard M. Duvall

Reference: Nations Bank.

For full biographical listings, see the Martindale-Hubbell Law Directory

WEBB, BURNETT, JACKSON, CORNBROOKS, WILBER, VORHIS & DOUSE, LLP (AV)

115 Broad Street, P.O. Box 910, 21801
Telephone: 410-742-3176
Fax: 410-742-0438
Email: webnett@shore.intercom.net

MEMBERS OF FIRM

Frederick W. C. Webb (1889-1956)
John W. T. Webb (1918-1990)
K. King Burnett
W. Newton Jackson, 3rd
Ernest I. Cornbrooks, III
Paul D. Wilber
David A. Vorhis
David B. Douse

ASSOCIATE

Chris Schiller Mason

Counsel for: First National Bank of Maryland (Salisbury branch); K & L Microwave, Inc.; Peninsula General Hospital Medical Center.
Local Attorneys for: State Farm Insurance Cos.; Nationwide Insurance Cos.; Travelers Insurance Co.; United States Fidelity & Guaranty Co.; Aetna Casualty & Surety Co.; Insurance Company of North America.

For full biographical listings, see the Martindale-Hubbell Law Directory

*TOWSON,** Baltimore Co.

FREEMAN, WOLFE & GREENBAUM, P.A. (AV)

409 Washington Avenue Suite 300, 21204
Telephone: 410-321-8400
Fax: 410-321-8407
Email: Lawyers@fwglaw.com

(See Next Column)

Steven R. Freeman Thomas D. Wolfe
David A. Greenbaum

LEGAL SUPPORT PERSONNEL

Mary E. Stielper Joan M. Johnson (Office Administrator)

For full biographical listings, see the Martindale-Hubbell Law Directory

NOLAN, PLUMHOFF & WILLIAMS, CHARTERED (AV)

Suite 700, Nottingham Centre, 502 Washington Avenue, 21204-4528
Telephone: 410-823-7800
Fax: 410-296-2765
Email: npw@nolanplumhoff.com

Newton A. Williams

For Complete List of Firm Personnel, See General Section

For full biographical listings, see the Martindale-Hubbell Law Directory

*UPPER MARLBORO,** Prince Georges Co.

KNIGHT, MANZI, NUSSBAUM & LAPLACA, P.C. (AV)

14440 Old Mill Road, 20772
Telephone: 301-952-0100
Annapolis/Baltimore: 410-792-3786
Fax: 301-952-0221

William E. Knight
Robert A. Manzi
Ronald M. Miller
William C. Brennan, Jr.
Harry J. Trainor, Jr.
Andrew W. Nussbaum
Raymond G. LaPlaca
John F. Shay, Jr.
Sheldon L. Gnatt
Daniel A. LaPlaca
Gail Borjeson Viens
Roger C. Thomas
Monica M. Haley-Pierson
Daniel F. Lynch III
Norman D. Rivera

Robert L. Lombardo Brent M. Ahalt
Amy B. Glaser Terry L. Bell

For full biographical listings, see the Martindale-Hubbell Law Directory

MASSACHUSETTS

*BOSTON,** Suffolk Co.

ADKINS & KELSTON, P.C. (AV)

90 Canal Street, 02114
Telephone: 617-367-1040
Fax: 617-742-8280
Email: a&k@sswg.com

David L. Kelston Jason B. Adkins

Noah R. Rosmarin Paula Isola

For full biographical listings, see the Martindale-Hubbell Law Directory

HRONES AND GARRITY (AV)

Lewis Wharf, Bay 232, 02110-3927
Telephone: 617-227-4019
Fax: 617-227-3908
Email: Azhro@aol.com *URL:* http://www.lawyers.com/hrones
Londonderry, New Hampshire Office: 14 Londonderry Road.
Telephone: 603-434-4106.
Fax: 603-434-9356.
Concord, Massachusetts Office: 39 Winslow Street.
Telephone: 978-287-5634.

Stephen B. Hrones Paul J. Garrity

Aderonke O. Lipede

Reference: Shawmut Bank NA.

For full biographical listings, see the Martindale-Hubbell Law Directory

LAW OFFICE OF SCOTT P. LOPEZ (AV)

24 School Street, 8th Floor, 02108
Telephone: 617-742-5700
Fax: 617-742-5715
Email: lopez@lopezlaw.com *URL:* http://www.lopezlaw.com
(Also Of Counsel, Roach & Carpenter, P.C.)

For full biographical listings, see the Martindale-Hubbell Law Directory

Boston—Continued

Mintz, Levin, Cohn, Ferris, Glovsky and Popeo, P.C. (AV)

One Financial Center, 02111
Telephone: 617-542-6000
FAX: 617-542-2241
Internet: Each Attorney's Internet Address takes the following form: first initial last name @mintz.com (e.g., rmintz@mintz.com)
URL: http://www.mintz.com
Washington, D.C. Office: 701 Pennsylvania Avenue, N.W. Suite 900.
Telephone: 202-434-7300.
Fax: 202-434-7400.
Reston, Virginia Office: 12021 Sunset Hills Road, Suite 310.
Telephone: 703-464-4800.
Fax: 703-464-4895.

R. Robert Popeo | John K. Markey
Thomas R. Murtagh | Michael S. Gardener
Tracy A. Miner

For Complete List of Firm Personnel, See General Section

For full biographical listings, see the Martindale-Hubbell Law Directory

Oteri, Weinberg & Lawson, P.A. (AV)

The Statler Building, 20 Park Plaza, Suite 905, 02116
Telephone: 617-227-3700
Fax: 617-338-9538

Joseph S. Oteri | Martin G. Weinberg
James W. Lawson

Prince, Lobel & Tye LLP (AV)

585 Commercial Street, 02109-1024
Telephone: 617-367-2202
Fax: 617-523-0977

MEMBERS OF FIRM

Elliot D. Lobel, P.C. | Walter B. Prince

ASSOCIATE

Nancy A. Dolberg

For Complete List of Firm Personnel, See General Section

For full biographical listings, see the Martindale-Hubbell Law Directory

Rankin & Sultan (AV)

One Commercial Wharf North Second Floor, 02110
Telephone: 617-720-0011
Fax: 617-742-0701
Email: office@rankin-sultan.com

Charles W. Rankin | James L. Sultan

ASSOCIATE

Catherine J. Hinton

For full biographical listings, see the Martindale-Hubbell Law Directory

Martin R. Rosenthal (AV)

65A Atlantic Avenue, 02110
Telephone: 617-742-0606
Fax: 617-367-1407
Email: martyros@world.std.com

For full biographical listings, see the Martindale-Hubbell Law Directory

Sheketoff & Homan (AV)

One McKinley Square, Third Floor, 02109
Telephone: 617-367-3449
Fax: 617-723-1710
Email: sandh2@aol.com

MEMBERS OF FIRM

Robert L. Sheketoff | Kimberly Homan

For full biographical listings, see the Martindale-Hubbell Law Directory

Zalkind, Rodriguez, Lunt & Duncan (AV)

65A Atlantic Avenue, 02110
Telephone: 617-742-6020
Facsimile: 617-742-3269
Email: office@zrld.com

MEMBERS OF FIRM

Norman S. Zalkind | Elizabeth A. Lunt
David Duncan

ASSOCIATES

Inga S. Bernstein | William B. Van Lonkhuyzen

OF COUNSEL

Barbara Equen Rodriguez | John Ward

For full biographical listings, see the Martindale-Hubbell Law Directory

FITCHBURG, Worcester Co.

O'Connor and Ryan, P.C. (AV)

61 Academy Street, 01420
Telephone: 978-345-4166
Fax: 978-343-8416

John M. O'Connor | Edward P. Ryan, Jr.

Eugene P. O'Donnell, Jr.

For full biographical listings, see the Martindale-Hubbell Law Directory

FRANKLIN, Norfolk Co.

Cataldo Law Offices, LLP (AV)

55 West Central Street, P.O. Box 435, 02038
Telephone: 508-528-2400
Fax: 508-520-0699

Paul A. Cataldo | Joseph P. Cataldo

ASSOCIATE

Cheryl A. Tracy

References: The Benjamin Franklin Savings Bank.

For full biographical listings, see the Martindale-Hubbell Law Directory

SOMERSET, Bristol Co.

Sabra & Aspden, Professional Association (AV)

1026 County Street, 02726
Telephone: 508-674-0890
Fax: 508-679-5998
Email: sabra@efortress.com

Steven P. Sabra | Matthew Mark Aspden

For full biographical listings, see the Martindale-Hubbell Law Directory

*WORCESTER,** Worcester Co.

Glickman, Sugarman, Kneeland & Gribouski (AV)

11 Harvard Street, P.O. Box 2917, 01613
Telephone: 508-756-6206
Fax: 508-831-0443

MEMBERS OF FIRM

Melvyn Glickman | David J. Kneeland, Jr.
David W. Sugarman | James Gribouski

ASSOCIATES

Joe Boynton | Wayne M. LeBlanc
James F. Scola

Representative Clients: Country Bank for Savings; Clinton Savings Bank.
References: Country Bank for Savings.

For full biographical listings, see the Martindale-Hubbell Law Directory

MICHIGAN

*ANN ARBOR,** Washtenaw Co.

Ferris & Salter, P.C. (AV)

4158 Washtenaw Avenue, 48108
Telephone: 734-677-2020
Fax: 734-677-3277
Email: ferrissalt@aol.com *URL:* http://www.ferris-salter.com

Don Ferris

For full biographical listings, see the Martindale-Hubbell Law Directory

Hooper, Hathaway, Price, Beuche & Wallace (AV)

126 South Main Street, 48104
Telephone: 313-662-4426
Fax: 313-662-9559
Email: hhpbw@voyager.net

OF COUNSEL

James A. Evashevski

Representative Clients: Avfuel Corporation; Bank of Ann Arbor; Castrol North America; Chem-Trend Incorporated; Ervin Industries, Inc.; First Martin Corporation; Glacier Hills, Inc.; Prestolite Electric, Inc.; Southern States Cooperative; E.B. Eddy Forest Products, Ltd.

For Complete List of Firm Personnel, See General Section

For full biographical listings, see the Martindale-Hubbell Law Directory

BLOOMFIELD HILLS, Oakland Co.

BAUM & ASSOCIATES (AV)

200 East Long Lake Road Suite 180, 48304
Telephone: 248-647-6890
Fax: 248-647-4727
Email: baumlaw@worldnet.att.net *URL:* http://www.lawyers.com/baumlaw

Martin S. Baum

For full biographical listings, see the Martindale-Hubbell Law Directory

ROBERT HARRISON & ASSOCIATES (AV)

Bloomfield Office Pavilion, 2550 Telegraph Road, Suite 275, 48302
Telephone: 248-253-1800
Fax: 248-253-9446
URL: http://www.lawyers.com/harrison&associates

Robert S. Harrison

ASSOCIATES

Michael J. Rex
Michael James Harrison
Rachel M. Margules

References: Comerica Bank, Southfield; Huntington Banks of Michigan, W. Bloomfield.

For full biographical listings, see the Martindale-Hubbell Law Directory

*DETROIT,** Wayne Co.

DAVID F. DUMOUCHEL, P.C. (AV)

150 West Jefferson, Suite 900, 48226-4430
Telephone: 313-225-7004
Email: dumouchd@butzel.com

David F. DuMouchel

For full biographical listings, see the Martindale-Hubbell Law Directory

S. ALLEN EARLY & ASSOCIATES (AV)

163 Madison Avenue Suite 229, 48226
Telephone: 313-962-2320
Fax: 313-962-2341

S. Allen Early

Suzanna Kostovski

For full biographical listings, see the Martindale-Hubbell Law Directory

DAVID GRIEM (AV)

One Woodward Avenue, Suite 2400, 48226
Telephone: 313-961-8380
Email: dgriem@jafferaitt.com *URL:* http://www.jafferaitt.com
Mount Clemens, Michigan Office: 14 First Street, 48043.
Telephone: 313-465-4900.

For full biographical listings, see the Martindale-Hubbell Law Directory

HONIGMAN MILLER SCHWARTZ AND COHN (AV)

2290 First National Building, 660 Woodward Avenue, 48226
Telephone: 313-465-7000
Telecopier: 313-465-8000
Telex: 235705
Email: mvg@honigman.com *URL:* http://law.honigman.com
Lansing, Michigan Office: Phoenix Building, 222 North Washington Square, Suite 400, 48933-1800.
Telephone: 517-484-8282.

MEMBERS OF FIRM

Mark R. Werder
Richard E. Zuckerman

For Complete List of Firm Personnel, See General Section

For full biographical listings, see the Martindale-Hubbell Law Directory

MARK J. KRIGER (AV)

645 Griswold Street, Suite 1817, 48226
Telephone: 313-967-0100
Email: kriger@ix.netcom.com *URL:* http://www.lawyers.com/markkriger
Southfield, Michigan Office: 29800 Telegraph Road.
Telephone: 248-353-6500.

For full biographical listings, see the Martindale-Hubbell Law Directory

KENNETH M. MOGILL (AV)

One Kennedy Square Building, Suite 1930, 719 Griswold, 48226
Telephone: 313-962-7210
Fax: 313-961-7799
(Also Member Mogill, Posner & Cohen)

For full biographical listings, see the Martindale-Hubbell Law Directory

CAROLE M. STANYAR (AV)

Suite 1938, One Kennedy Square, 48226
Telephone: 313-963-7222
Fax: 313-963-6490

For full biographical listings, see the Martindale-Hubbell Law Directory

VANDER MALE, BELLAMY, GILCHRIST, VANDE VUSSE & CAFFERTY (AV)

333 West Fort, Suite 1100, 48226
Telephone: 313-964-3070
Fax: 313-628-4701
Email: HEALTHLAWYERS@wwnet.net

MEMBERS OF FIRM

Frederick B. Bellamy
Bruce A. Vande Vusse
Alan G. Gilchrist
Michael S. Cafferty
Keith J. Soltis

ASSOCIATES

Joseph E. Kozely, Jr.
Michael P. Risko
Lawrence David Rosenstock

For full biographical listings, see the Martindale-Hubbell Law Directory

*GRAND RAPIDS,** Kent Co.

DAVID A. DODGE, P.C. (AV)

200 North Division Avenue, 49503
Telephone: 616-459-3850
Fax: 616-459-4909

David A. Dodge

For full biographical listings, see the Martindale-Hubbell Law Directory

WILLEY & CHAMBERLAIN, L.L.P. (AV)

940 Trust Building, 40 Pearl Street, N.W., 49503
Telephone: 616-458-2212
Fax: 616-458-1158

Larry C. Willey
Charles E. Chamberlain, Jr.

ASSOCIATES

Raymond E. Beckering, III
Julie F. Thelen

For full biographical listings, see the Martindale-Hubbell Law Directory

*MOUNT CLEMENS,** Macomb Co.

DAVID GRIEM (AV)

14 First Street, 48043
Telephone: 810-465-4900
Email: dgriem@jafferaitt.com *URL:* http://www.jafferaitt.com
Detroit, Michigan Office: One Woodward Avenue, Suite 2400, 48226.
Telephone: 313-961-8380.

For full biographical listings, see the Martindale-Hubbell Law Directory

SOUTHFIELD, Oakland Co.

MORGANROTH & MORGANROTH (AV)

3000 Town Center, Suite 1500, 48075
Telephone: 248-355-3084
Fax: 248-355-3017
URL: http://www.lawyers.com/morganrothlawfirm
New York, N.Y. Office: 156 W. 56th Street, Suite 1101. 10019.
Telephone: 212-586-5905.
Fax: 212-586-7302.

MEMBERS OF FIRM

Mayer Morganroth
Cherie Morganroth
Jeffrey B. Morganroth
Jason Ross Hirsch

Representative Clients: APCOA,Inc.; ; Mayor Coleman Young (Detroit); John Z. DeLorean; Realtek Industries, Inc.; Dr. Jack Kevorkian; Carolyn Warmus; Edward J. Holland, Jr.; Lyndon LaRouche; Thomas Warmus; Walter Keating.

For full biographical listings, see the Martindale-Hubbell Law Directory

SOMMERS, SCHWARTZ, SILVER & SCHWARTZ, P.C. (AV)

2000 Town Center, Suite 900, 48075
Telephone: 248-355-0300
Telecopier: 248-746-4001
Plymouth, Michigan Office: 747 South Main Street.
Telephone: 313-455-4250.

Lawrence Warren
David M. Black
Justin C. Ravitz
Matthew G. Curtis

General Counsel for: City of Taylor; Township of Van Buren.
Representative Clients: Don Lee Distributors; Rite-Aid of Michigan.

For Complete List of Firm Personnel, See General Section

For full biographical listings, see the Martindale-Hubbell Law Directory

EDUCATION LAW

ALABAMA

*DOTHAN,** Houston Co.

HARDWICK, HAUSE & SEGREST (AV)

212 North Lena Street, P.O. Box 1469, 36302
Telephone: 334-794-4144
Fax: 334-671-9330
URL: http://www.lawyers.com/hhslawfirm

W. G. Hardwick (1910-1993) William G. Hause (Retired)

MEMBERS OF FIRM

Jere C. Segrest
Kevin Walding
Tina Whitehead Stamps

Counsel for: Dothan City Board of Education; American General Life & Accident Ins. Co.; General Motors Acceptance Corp.; Alabama Power Co.; Liberty National Life Ins. Co.; CBI-Equifax, Inc.; Houston County Board of Education; Cincinnati Insurance Companies.

For full biographical listings, see the Martindale-Hubbell Law Directory

*MOBILE,** Mobile Co.

SINTZ, CAMPBELL, DUKE & TAYLOR (AV)

3763 Professional Parkway, 36609
Telephone: 334-344-7241
Fax: 334-344-7400

MEMBERS OF FIRM

Peter V. Sintz (1940-1997)
Robert C. Campbell, III
Frank G. Taylor
Steven L. Terry

ASSOCIATES

Wm. Kyle Morris
Kathryn W. Petersen
Barry C. Prine

OF COUNSEL

Leon G. Duke

LEGAL SUPPORT PERSONEL

James A. Koblas

Representative Clients: Aetna C & S Insurance Co.; Mobile County School Board; Auto-Owners Insurance Co.; Argonaut Insurance Co.; Mostellar Medical Clinic; Scottsdale Insurance Co.; American International Group; Alabama School of Math and Science; Mobile County Sheriff's Office.

For full biographical listings, see the Martindale-Hubbell Law Directory

ARIZONA

MESA, Maricopa Co.

UDALL, SHUMWAY, BLACKHURST, ALLEN & LYONS, P.C. (AV)

30 West First Street, 85201-1446
Telephone: 480-461-5300
Facsimile: 480-461-5398
Email: usbalsea@vtc.net
Willcox, Arizona Office: 135 East Maley.
Telephone: 602-384-3389.
Fax: 602-384-2280.

David K. Udall
Dale R. Shumway
Dennis P. Blackhurst
John H. Lyons
Barry C. Dickerson
Steven H. Everts
Clark R. Richter
Roger C. Decker
Peter W. Taylor
Denise Lowell-Britt
Stephen L. West

David R. Schwartz
Robert M. Jarrett, Jr. (Resident, Willcox Office)
Brian T. Allen
Curtis M. Chipman
April A. Speelmon

Representative Clients: Mesa Public Schools; Ticor Title; University of Arizona; Wal-Mart Stores, Inc.; Church of Jesus Christ of Latter Day Saints.

For full biographical listings, see the Martindale-Hubbell Law Directory

ARKANSAS

*LITTLE ROCK,** Pulaski Co.

LASER, WILSON, BUFFORD & WATTS, P.A. (AV)

101 South Spring Street, Suite 300, 72201-2488
Telephone: 501-376-2981
Telecopier: 501-376-2417
Email: laser@laserlaw.com

Dan F. Bufford Alfred F. Angulo, Jr.

Brian A. Brown

Representative Clients: Allstate Insurance Co.; American International Insurance Group; Continental Insurance Cos.; Farm Bureau Insurance Cos. (Casualty & Fire); Farmers Insurance Group; GAB Business Services, Inc.; St. Paul Insurance Cos.; Scottsdale Insurance Co.; State Farm Auto (Fire) Insurance Cos.

For Complete List of Firm Personnel, See General Section

For full biographical listings, see the Martindale-Hubbell Law Directory

CALIFORNIA

*OAKLAND,** Alameda Co.

LOMBARDI, LOPER & CONANT, LLP (AV)

1999 Harrison Street, Suite 1950, 94612
Telephone: 510-433-2600
Fax: 510-433-2699

Ralph A. Lombardi
Bruce P. Loper
Matthew S. Conant
Chris P. Lavdiotis
Peter O. Glaessner
Timothy J. McCaffery
GayLynn Renee Kirn

Jeffrey D Hosking
Joseph Blaise Adams
Paul S. Lecky

OF COUNSEL

George S. Peyton, Jr.
Linda C. Roodhouse
Lori A. Sebransky

For full biographical listings, see the Martindale-Hubbell Law Directory

OXNARD, Ventura Co.

ENGLAND, WHITFIELD, SCHRÖEDER & TREDWAY, L.L.P. (AV)

300 Esplanade Drive, 6th Floor, 93030
Telephone: 805-485-9627
Ventura: 647-8237
Southern California Toll Free: 800-255-3485
Fax: 805-983-0297
URL: http://www.tsurf.com/ewst/

Theodore J. England
Anson M. Whitfield
Robert W. Schröeder
David W. Tredway
Robert A. McSorley
Stuart A. Comis
Mitchel B. Kahn
Mark A. Nelson
Eric J. Kananen
Mary E. Schröeder
Oscar C. Gonzalez
Madison M. Christian
Kurt Edward Kananen

Melissa E. Cohen
Linda Kathryn Ash
Mark T. Barney
Kevin L. Dorhout
Anthony M. Ramos
Gregory J. Ramirez

Representative Clients: Dah Chong Hong (automobile dealerships); Steve thomas BMW; Vreeland Cadillac, Inc.; Willamette Industries; The Port of Hueneme; Viola, Inc. (General Contracting); Santa Clara Chemical Co.; Nakamura Berry Growers; John Taft Electric Co.; Rodgers Mortgage Co.

For full biographical listings, see the Martindale-Hubbell Law Directory

COLORADO

*DENVER,** Denver Co.

SEMPLE, MILLER & MOONEY, P.C. (AV)

1120 Lincoln Street, Suite 1308, 80203
Telephone: 303-595-0941
Fax: 303-861-9608
Email: smdm@relay.hcp.net

(See Next Column)

SEMPLE, MILLER & MOONEY P.C., *Denver—Continued*

Martin Semple
Reese Miller
Patrick B. Mooney
Christopher E. Gdowski

Kathleen Marie Shannon
Frederick C. Kuhlwilm
Elizabeth J. Hyatt
Julie C. Tolleson

Representative Clients: Denver Public Schools; Adams County School District No. 50; Roaring Forks School District RE-1; Widefield Public Schools.

For full biographical listings, see the Martindale-Hubbell Law Directory

FLORIDA

WINTER PARK, Orange Co.

HADDOCK PROFESSIONAL ASSOCIATION (AV)

3260 University Boulevard, Suite 210, 32792
Telephone: 407-679-6171
Fax: 407-679-8810
Email: ehaddock@fullsail.com
Mailing Address: P.O. Box 5148, Winter Park, FL, 32793-5148
Email: edhaddock@aol.com

Edward E. Haddock, Jr.

Approved Attorneys For: American Pioneer Title Insurance Co.
Reference: Colonial Bank, Orlando, Florida.

For full biographical listings, see the Martindale-Hubbell Law Directory

ILLINOIS

*BLOOMINGTON,** McLean Co.

DUNN, STANCZAK & WILLARD (AV)

1001 North Main Street, P.O. Box 3488, 61702-3488
Telephone: 309-828-6241
Fax: 309-828-8321
Email: Dunnlaw@aol.com

MEMBERS OF FIRM

Richard F. Dunn (1888-1963)
Mark T. Dunn
David L. Stanczak
Donald A. Willard

ASSOCIATE

Thomas J. Arkell

OF COUNSEL

Louis F. Ulbrich
Richard T. Dunn

Representative Clients: Northeastern Illinois University; Governors State University; Western Illinois University; Chicago State University; First Federal Savings & Loan Association of Bloomington; Illinois Wesleyan University; Metropolitan Life Insurance Co., Agricultural Investments and Commercial Investments; Commerce Bank; Bluestem National Bank.

For full biographical listings, see the Martindale-Hubbell Law Directory

*CHICAGO,** Cook Co.

FRANCZEK SULLIVAN P.C. (AV)

Suite 3400, 300 South Wacker Drive, 60606-6785
Telephone: 312-986-0300
FAX: 312-986-9192
URL: http://www.nlfpc.com

Anthony J. Crement
J. Todd Faulkner
James C. Franczek, Jr.
Ronald J. Hein, Jr.
Lisa A. Lopatka
Bruce C. Mackey
Robert E. Mann
Paul A. Millichap
David P. Radelet
John A. Relias
Michael I. Richardson
Charles P. Rose
Sally J. Scott
William R. Sullivan, Jr.
Andrea R. Waintroob
Patricia J. Whitten
James J. Zuehl

Shelli L. Boyer
Sheila M. Conroy
Terrence T. Creamer
Erika Dillon
Edward N. Druck
Gregory D. Isbell
Thomas Koutsouvas
Darcy L. Kriha
Jeffrey M. Kropp
Jeremy C. Moritz
Alec Rubenstein
Leah D. Gidron
Jennifer L. Schilling
Michael A. Warner, Jr.
Anne Elizabeth Wilson

OF COUNSEL

Michael Z. Green
Wesley A. Wildman
John L. Wren

(See Next Column)

LEGAL SUPPORT PERSONNEL

Caty E. Kearney

For full biographical listings, see the Martindale-Hubbell Law Directory

INDIANA

ELKHART, Elkhart Co.

THORNE, GRODNIK, RANSEL, DUNCAN, BYRON, HOSTETLER & TRIPPEL, LLP (AV)

228 West High Street, 46516-3176
Telephone: 219-294-7473
FAX: 219-294-5390
Mishawaka, Indiana Office: 420 Lincoln Way West, P.O. Box 1210, 46544.
Telephone: 219-256-5660.
FAX: 219-674-6835.

MEMBERS OF FIRM

Charles H. Grodnik
J. Richard Ransel
Glenn L. Duncan
James R. Byron
Steven L. Hostetler
Michael A. Trippel

ASSOCIATES

W. Douglas Thorne
Gregg A. Hixenbaugh

OF COUNSEL

F. Richard Kramer
Joseph C. Zakas
William A. Thorne

Counsel for: Valley American Bank and Trust Co., Mishawaka, Indiana; NBD Bank.

For full biographical listings, see the Martindale-Hubbell Law Directory

MARYLAND

*BALTIMORE,** (Independent City)

GALLAGHER, EVELIUS & JONES, LLP (AV)

Park Charles Suite 400, 218 North Charles Street, 21201
Telephone: 410-727-7702
Facsimile: 410-468-2786
URL: http://www.gejlaw.com

MEMBERS OF FIRM

Francis X. Gallagher (1928-1972)
C. Edward Jones (1908-1999)
John C. Evelius (Retired)
Richard O. Berndt
Thomas N. Biddison, Jr.
Robert R. Kern, Jr.
Saul E. Gilstein
Thomas B. Lewis
Bonnie Abrams Travieso
Stephen A. Goldberg
Linda H. Jones
Jack C. Tranter
Leslie B. Speed
Christopher J. Fritz
David E. Raderman
Peter E. Keith
Nita L. Schultz
Michael W. Skojec
Kathryn Kelley Hoskins
Mark P. Keener
Kevin J. Davidson
Eileen M. Lunga
Lori A. Nicolle
Kenneth S. Gross
Thomas C. Dame

ASSOCIATES

Valarie K. Oulds
Margaret Stevens Jacks
Matthew W. Oakey
Rebecca A. Weaver
Michael J. Henigan
David W. Kinkopf
Paul S. Caiola
Jason W. Gaarder
M. Kirsten Andrews

LEGAL ASSISTANTS

Patricia C. Quayle
Iris T. H. Heath
Connie L. Ennis
Margaret Graff
Margo Gibson Hughes
Jonathan T. Gillis
Brenda J. Heacock
Dwayne L. Rodeheaver

Representative Clients: Roman Catholic Archdiocese of Baltimore; The Shelter Group; Mercantile-Safe Deposit and Trust Co.; The Enterprise Social Investment Corp.; Mercy Medical Center, Inc.

For full biographical listings, see the Martindale-Hubbell Law Directory

MASSACHUSETTS

*BOSTON,** Suffolk Co.

PALMER & DODGE LLP (AV)

One Beacon Street, 02108
Telephone: 617-573-0100
Facsimile: 617-227-4420
URL: http://www.palmerdodge.com

MEMBERS OF FIRM

F. Andrew Anderson
Neil P. Arkuss
Michael R. Brown
Jean M. DeLuca
Mark A. Fischer
Malcolm E. Hindin
Jeffrey F. Jones
Daryl J. Lapp
Scott P. Lewis
Judith A. Malone
Thomas W. Merrill
Arthur B. Page
David R. Rodgers
Elizabeth P. Seaman
Thomas M. Spera
Craig E. Stewart
Russell B. Swapp
Jeffrey Swope
James M. Whalen
Donald F. Winter
R. Robert Woodburn, Jr.

COUNSEL

Kathryn Cochrane Murphy
Marianna C. Pierce

ASSOCIATE

Jordana B. Glasgow

For Complete List of Firm Personnel, See General Section

For full biographical listings, see the Martindale-Hubbell Law Directory

STONEMAN, CHANDLER & MILLER LLP (AV)

99 High Street, 02110
Telephone: 617-542-6789
Telecopier: 617-556-8989

MEMBERS OF FIRM

Alan S. Miller
Robert Chandler
Carol Chandler
Kay H. Hodge
Robert G. Fraser
Macon P. Magee
Miriam K. Freedman
Rebecca Bryant

ASSOCIATES

Nancy Norfolk Nevils
Geoffrey R. Bok
Joan Lerner Stein
Karen Shaffer Levy
Sandra L. Moody
Ronald M. Jacobs
Andrew L. Rodman
John M. Simon
(Not admitted in MA)

For full biographical listings, see the Martindale-Hubbell Law Directory

ELDER LAW

ARIZONA

MESA, Maricopa Co.

Jackson White Gardner Weech & Walker, P.C. (AV)
40 North Center Street, Suite 200, 85201
Telephone: 480-464-1111
Fax: 480-464-5692
Statewide: 800-243-1160
Email: firm@azmesalaw.com *URL:* http://www.azmesalaw.com
Payson, Arizona Office: 708 East Highway 260, Suite C1-E.
Telephone: 520-472-8878.

Wayne L. Gardner
Eric M. Jackson
Michael R. Pruitt
J. Grant Walker
Bradley D. Weech
Richard A. White
David L. Weed
Roger R. Foote
Otto S. Shill, III

Eric K. Macdonald
Kelly G. Black
Melody K. Seal
Patricia A. Mancabelli
Bobbie J. Rasmusson
Maureen P. Kane
James L. Tanner

For full biographical listings, see the Martindale-Hubbell Law Directory

SCOTTSDALE, Maricopa Co.

Paul J. Buser (AV Ⓣ)
7633 East Acoma Drive, Suite 106, 85260-3486
Telephone: 480-951-1222
Fax: 480-951-2568
Email: pjbazlit@worldnet.att.net *URL:* http://www.lawyers.com/paulbusercactuslaw

For full biographical listings, see the Martindale-Hubbell Law Directory

CALIFORNIA

IRVINE, Orange Co.

Stevens & Kramer, A Professional Corporation (AV)
18022 Cowan, Suite 200D, 92614-6808
Telephone: 949-253-9553
Fax: 949-253-9643
Agoura Hills, California Office: 30401 W. Agoura Road, Suite 102.
Telephone: 818-879-1699.
Fax: 818-879-1673.

Carl R. Stevens

Lee E. Burrows
Javier H. Van Oordt

For full biographical listings, see the Martindale-Hubbell Law Directory

LAGUNA HILLS, Orange Co.

Stanton T. Mathews & Associates, A Law Corp. (AV)
24012 Calle de la Plata, Suite 320, 92653
Telephone: 949-586-2235
Email: Triallaw@flash.net
Email: stm@injurytriallaw.com *URL:* http://www.injurytriallaw.com

Stanton T. Mathews

Paul W. Ralph
Ronald B. Funk

LEGAL SUPPORT PERSONNEL
PARALEGAL/ADMINISTRATOR
Sharing Garrett-Anderson
LEGAL ASSISTANT
Cheri C. Wickam

For full biographical listings, see the Martindale-Hubbell Law Directory

*SAN DIEGO,** San Diego Co.

The Law Offices of Birger Greg Bacino, APC (AV)
3033 Fifth Avenue, Suite 301, 92103
Telephone: 800-801-4878
Fax: 619-299-0086
URL: http://www.bacinolaw.com
Washington, D.C. Office: 1201 Pennsylvania Avenue, Suite 300, 20004.
Telephone: 800-801-4878.

(See Next Column)

Houston, Texas Office: 510 Bering Street, Suite 300, 77057.
Telephone: 800-801-4878.

Birger Greg Bacino
Richard P. Verlasky
Philip Aman

OF COUNSEL

Patricia M. Sayre
Michael B. Sayre
Anthony J. DeLellis

For full biographical listings, see the Martindale-Hubbell Law Directory

Duke Gerstel Shearer, LLP (AV)
A Registered Limited Liability Partnership
Sixth Floor, 101 West Broadway, P.O. Box 85470, 92186-5470
Telephone: 619-232-0816
800-405-0816
Fax: 619-232-4661
Email: lawyers@dgsllp.com *URL:* http://www.dgsllp.com
Costa Mesa, California Office: 3200 Park Center Drive, Suite 1000, 92626.
Telephone: 949-551-8664, 800-405-0816.
Los Angeles, California Office: 10866 Wilshire Boulevard, Suite 1400, 90024.
Telephone: 310-475-7118, 800-405-0816.
San Francisco, California Office: 744 Montgomery Street, Fifth Floor, 94111.
Telephone: 415-773-0101.
Palm Springs, California Office: 1111 East Tahquitz Canyon Way, Suite 110, 92262.
Telephone: 760-322-7846.
Phoenix, Arizona Office: One Columbus Plaza, 3636 North Central Avenue, Suite 1200, 85012.
Telephone: 602-650-2060.
Fax: 602-650-2089.
Tucson, Arizona Office: 6969 East Sunrise Drive, Suite 102, 85750.
Telephone: 520-615-8858.
Fax: 520-615-1069.
Affiliate Las Vegas, Nevada Office: Parsons & Pursiano, LLP, City Center West, Suite 108, 7201 W. Lake Mead Boulevard, 89128.
Telephone: 702-384-9900.
Facsimile: 702-384-5900.

MEMBER OF FIRM
Ronald M. Green

Reference: Bank of Commerce.

For full biographical listings, see the Martindale-Hubbell Law Directory

COLORADO

*DENVER,** Denver Co.

Michael L. Gilbert (AV)
Suite 850, 50 South Steele Street, 80209-2809
Telephone: 303-320-4580
Fax: 303-320-0648
Email: mgilbert@csn.net

For full biographical listings, see the Martindale-Hubbell Law Directory

M. Kent Olsen (AV)
650 South Cherry Street, Suite 1250, 80246
Telephone: 303-329-4670
Facsimile: 303-329-4671

Representative Clients: Colorado Association of Homes & Services for the Aging; Allied Jewish Housing; Karis, Inc.; Colorado State Bank; Bank of Cherry Creek.

For full biographical listings, see the Martindale-Hubbell Law Directory

CONNECTICUT

STAMFORD, Fairfield Co.

Curtis, Brinckerhoff & Barrett, P.C. (AV)
666 Summer Street, 06901-1416
Telephone: 203-324-6777
Telecopier: 203-324-9621
Email: info@curtisbb.com

T. Ward Cleary (1916-1988)
Frederick M. Tobin
John Wayne Fox
Ward Frank Cleary
James D'Alton Murphy
Randolph T. Lovallo

OF COUNSEL

John D. Hertz
Jane F. Donovan
Richard L. Brinckerhoff
Patricia M. Gaug

(See Next Column)

CURTIS, BRINCKERHOFF & BARRETT P.C., *Stamford—Continued*

Susan L. Stratton
Derek Gilman
Michael P. Murray
John J. Louizos

Counsel for: The F. A. Bartlett Tree Expert Co.; Town of Darien; Miller Automobile Corp.; Bolliger, Inc.; Titan Sports; People's Bank, Bridgeport; Fleet Bank; Federal Deposit Insurance Co.; William Pitt Foundation; Wood Logan Associates.

For full biographical listings, see the Martindale-Hubbell Law Directory

FLORIDA

BOCA RATON, Palm Beach Co.

LAW OFFICES OF CARTER & THOMAS LLP (AV)

1200 North Federal Highway, Suite 312, 33432
Telephone: 561-368-9900
Broward 954-427-0933
Fax: 561-368-0293
Email: carterboca@aol.com

John E. Carter
Donald Joseph Thomas

Colleen M. Stiger

For full biographical listings, see the Martindale-Hubbell Law Directory

*FORT LAUDERDALE,** Broward Co.

KENNETH R. MIKOS, P.A. (AV)

2780 East Oakland Park Boulevard, 33306
Telephone: 954-566-7200
Facsimile: 954-566-1568

Kenneth R. Mikos

Douglas F. Hoffman

Special Counsel to: Fort Lauderdale Civil Service Board.

For full biographical listings, see the Martindale-Hubbell Law Directory

KANSAS

*TOPEKA,** Shawnee Co.

GOODELL, STRATTON, EDMONDS & PALMER, L.L.P. (AV)

515 South Kansas Avenue, 66603-3999
Telephone: 785-233-0593
Fax: 785-233-8870
Email: GSEP@CJNETWORKS.COM *URL:*
http://www.cjnetworks.com/~gsep
Kansas City, Missouri Office: 10401 Holmes Road, Suite 280.
Telephone: 816-943-8577.

SPECIAL COUNSEL

Marta Fisher Linenberger

Counsel for: Columbian National Title Insurance Co.; Central Regional Dental Testing Service, Inc.; Heartland Community Bankers Association; The Menninger Foundation; Topeka Chamber of Commerce; Washburn University of Topeka; Reser's Fine Foods; ConAgra; Monfort, Inc.

For Complete List of Firm Personnel, See General Section

For full biographical listings, see the Martindale-Hubbell Law Directory

MASSACHUSETTS

*SPRINGFIELD,** Hampden Co.

ANNINO, DRAPER & MOORE, P.C. (AV)

1500 Main Street, Suite 1818, P.O. Box 15428, 01115
Telephone: 413-732-6400
Fax: 413-732-3339
Email: admatlaw@aol.com
Westfield, Massachusetts Office: 52 Court Street.
Telephone: 413-562-9829.

Calvin W. Annino, Jr.
Mark E. Draper
Louis S. Moore
Michael R. Siddall

For full biographical listings, see the Martindale-Hubbell Law Directory

MICHIGAN

BLOOMFIELD HILLS, Oakland Co.

PROVIZER & PHILLIPS, P.C. (AV)

6785 Telegraph Road, Suite 400, 48301
Telephone: 248-642-0444
Facsimile: 248-642-6661
Toll Free: 1-800-288-9080
URL: http://www.lawyers.com/provizer&phillips

Harold M. Provizer
Randall E. Phillips
Marilyn A. Madorsky
Evan A. Zagoria
Noel F. Beck
Mark S. Baumkel

Constance S. Hall
Ellen C. Busch
Donald J. Parthum, Jr.
Keith A. Castora
Gregory A. Nave

For full biographical listings, see the Martindale-Hubbell Law Directory

EMINENT DOMAIN

ARIZONA

*PHOENIX,** Maricopa Co.

DUSHOFF & MCCALL, A PROFESSIONAL CORPORATION (AV)

Two Renaissance Square, Suite 1000, 40 North Central, 85004
Telephone: 602-254-3800
Fax: 602-258-2551
URL: http://www.dushoff@neta.com

Jay Dushoff
Jack E. McCall (1942-1995)
Michael Riikola
Leonard M. Bell

Patrick J. McGill
Robert H. Kreutzer

LEGAL SUPPORT PERSONNEL

Thomas M. Flynn

For full biographical listings, see the Martindale-Hubbell Law Directory

CALIFORNIA

COSTA MESA, Orange Co.

MCCORMICK, KIDMAN & BEHRENS, LLP (AV)

A Partnership of Professional Corporations
Imperial Bank Building, 695 Town Center Drive Suite 1400, 92626-7187
Telephone: 714-755-3100
Fax: 714-755-3110; 1-800-755-3125
Email: mkb1@ix.netcom.com
Sacramento, California Office: 980 Ninth Street. 16th Floor. 95814-2736.
Telephone: 916-449-9533.
Fax: 916-446-7104.
Effective April 1, 1999 the new address will be: Imperial Bank Building, 695 Town Center Drive, Suite 400.

MEMBERS OF FIRM

Homer L. (Mike) McCormick, Jr., (P.C.)
Arthur G. Kidman (P.C.)
Russell G. Behrens (P.C.)
Suzanne M. Tague (P.C.)
Janet R. Morningstar (P.C.)
Keith E. McCullough (P.C.)

ASSOCIATES

David D. Boyer
Paeter E. Garcia
Gary D. Grant
Edward L. Bertrand

For full biographical listings, see the Martindale-Hubbell Law Directory

FOLSOM, Sacramento Co.

THE BLEIER LAW FIRM (AV)

110 Blue Ravine Road, Suite 201, 95630
Telephone: 916-454-2100
Fax: 916-454-2121
Email: tblf@bleier.com *URL:* http://www.bleier.com

Brenton A. Bleier

ASSOCIATE

Bradford A. Bleier

For full biographical listings, see the Martindale-Hubbell Law Directory

*LOS ANGELES,** Los Angeles Co.

BARBOSA GARCIA LLP (AV)

A Partnership including a Professional Corporation
801 South Grand Avenue Suite 300, 90017-4621
Telephone: 213-612-0800
Fax: 213-612-8085

Henry S. Barbosa (P.C.)
Lorie A. Campos
Kenneth T. Fong
Bonifacio Bonny Garcia (P.C.)
Michael L. Kadish
John F. Lagle
Peter E. Langsfeld
Benjamin D. Nieberg
Gary W. Park
Roberta R. Sistos
Jonathan B. Stone
Rajeev M. Talwani
Sylvia J. Trujillo
Thuy-Whien Vuong
John G. Yslas

OF COUNSEL

Albert A. Erkel, Jr.

SPECIAL COUNSEL

Adrienne D. Konigar
Joyce E. Paul
Melvin D. Peters

(See Next Column)

LEGAL SUPPORT PERSONNEL

Victor M. Estrada (Paralegal)
Janice H. Minamoto (Paralegal)

For full biographical listings, see the Martindale-Hubbell Law Directory

DEMETRIOU, DEL GUERCIO, SPRINGER & MOYER, LLP (AV)

801 South Grand Avenue, 10th Floor, 90017
Telephone: 213-624-8407
Telecopy: 213-624-0174
Email: ddsm@juno.com

MEMBERS OF FIRM

Jeffrey Z. B. Springer
Jennifer T. Taggart
Bradley D. Pierce
Wendy M. Conole
Brian D. Langa
Silvia Saucedo

OF COUNSEL

Richard A. Del Guercio

Reference: Bank of America, L.A. Main Office, Los Angeles, Calif.

For full biographical listings, see the Martindale-Hubbell Law Directory

HILL, FARRER & BURRILL LLP (AV)

A Limited Liability Partnership including Professional Corporations
37th Floor, One California Plaza, 300 South Grand Avenue, 90071-3147
Telephone: 213-620-0460
Fax: 213-624-4840
URL: http://www.hfbllp.com

MEMBERS OF FIRM

William M. Bitting (P.C.)
Kevin H. Brogan (P.C.)
Benjamin B. Salvaty (P.C.)
Jennifer Cook Lewis
Jennifer L. Pancake
Byron T. Ball
Paul M. Porter

For Complete List of Firm Personnel, See General Section

For full biographical listings, see the Martindale-Hubbell Law Directory

OLIVER, VOSE, SANDIFER, MURPHY & LEE, A PROFESSIONAL CORPORATION (AV)

Figueroa Courtyard, Second Floor, 281 South Figueroa Street, 90012
Telephone: 213-621-2000
Telecopier: 213-621-2211

Charles S. Vose
Connie Cooke Sandifer
James Duff Murphy
Edward W. Lee
Roger W. Springer
Arthur J. Hazarabedian

Bradley E. Wohlenberg
Timothy J. Chung
Kristin L. Mendenhall

Representative Clients: Cities of Anaheim, Bell, Brea, Calabasas and Carson.
Agency Counsel Clients: Anaheim Housing Authority; Anaheim Redevelopment Agency; Brea Redevelopment Agency; Buena Park Redevelopment Authority; Compton Redevelopment Agency.

For full biographical listings, see the Martindale-Hubbell Law Directory

*SACRAMENTO,** Sacramento Co.

LIVINGSTON & MATTESICH, LAW CORPORATION (AV)

1201 K Street, Suite 1100, 95814
Telephone: 916-442-1111
Fax: 916-448-1709
Email: l&m@lmlaw.net *URL:* http://www.lmlaw.net

Gene Livingston
James M. Mattesich
Carol Livingston
Rebecca M. Ceniceros
Emilio E. Varanini, III
Kenneth M. Malovos
Kathleen E. Finnerty
Joanna R. Mendoza

Steven P. Belzer
Jeffrey Leacox
Randy Pollack
Alice H. Choi
Stephen Craig Hunter
Matthew J. Goldman
Joel C. Baiocchi
Baldassaro (Bill) Di Capo
John McKinsey
Timothy E. Naccarato
Craig N. Lundgren
Mary Farrell Taylor
Brian Crone
Gay L. Carroll
Steven G. Churchwell

Representative Clients: City of Redding; City of Rocklin; County of Del Norte; Tahoe Regional Planning Agency.

For full biographical listings, see the Martindale-Hubbell Law Directory

*SAN DIEGO,** San Diego Co.

THORSNES, BARTOLOTTA, MCGUIRE & PADILLA (AV)

A Partnership including Professional Corporations
Fifth Avenue Financial Center, 11th Floor, 2550 Fifth Avenue, 92103
Telephone: 619-236-9363
Fax: 619-236-9653
Email: TBMPmail@TBMP.com *URL:* http://www.tbmp.com

(See Next Column)

THORSNES, BARTOLOTTA, MCGUIRE & PADILLA, *San Diego—Continued*

Michael T. Thorsnes (A.P.C., P.C.)
Vincent J. Bartolotta, Jr., (P.C.)
John F. McGuire (P.C.)
Kevin F. Quinn (P.C.)
C. Brant Noziska (P.C.)
Mitchell S. Golub (P.C.)
Palma Cesar Hooper (P.C.)
Neal H. Rockwood (P.C.)
Daral B. Mazzarella (P.C.)
R. Christian Hulburt (P.C.)

ASSOCIATES

Catherine A. Richardson
Jodi L. Hautaluoma
Douglas J. Billings
Scott A. Kennedy
Dori K. Rybacki
James T. Atkins
Leo Bartolotta
Jill E. Cleary
James B. Drimmer
Timothy J. Tatro

OF COUNSEL

Robert S. Kennedy

For full biographical listings, see the Martindale-Hubbell Law Directory

SANTA MONICA, Los Angeles Co.

BERGER & NORTON, A LAW CORPORATION (AV)

1620 26th Street Suite 200 South, 90404
Telephone: 310-449-1000
Fax: 310-449-5000
URL: http://www.bergernorton.com

Michael M. Berger
Richard D. Norton
Ann E. Kelly
George M. Soneff
Edward G. Burg
Craig M. Collins
Pamela Schmidt

Kisu Shin
Sophie A. Castillo

OF COUNSEL

Gideon Kanner

For full biographical listings, see the Martindale-Hubbell Law Directory

WALNUT CREEK, Contra Costa Co.

LAW OFFICES OF THOMAS C. NAGLE A PROFESSIONAL CORPORATION (AV)

500 Ygnacio Valley Road Suite 325, 94596
Telephone: 925-938-2299
Fax: 925-933-3793
Email: tcnagle@ix.netcom.com

Thomas C. Nagle

Sharon M. Nagle

For full biographical listings, see the Martindale-Hubbell Law Directory

COLORADO

*DENVER,** Denver Co.

OTTEN, JOHNSON, ROBINSON, NEFF & RAGONETTI, P.C. (AV)

950 Seventeenth Street, 16th Floor, 80202
Telephone: 303-825-8400
Telecopier: 303-825-6525
URL: http://www.ojrnr.com

Kenneth K. Skogg
Karen L. Brody
Katherine L. Ruff

Representative Clients: Anschutz Family Trust; The Broe Cos.; Fuller & Company; Gun Club Farms, LLP; Kiewit Construction Group, Inc.; La-Farge Corp.; Nevin Gun Club, LLC; Trillium Corp; TrizecHahn Centers, Inc.; U S WEST, Inc.; Wells Fargo Bank; Western Mobile, Inc.

For Complete List of Firm Personnel, See General Section

For full biographical listings, see the Martindale-Hubbell Law Directory

CONNECTICUT

STAMFORD, Fairfield Co.

CURTIS, BRINCKERHOFF & BARRETT, P.C. (AV)

666 Summer Street, 06901-1416
Telephone: 203-324-6777
Telecopier: 203-324-9621
Email: info@curtisbb.com

(See Next Column)

T. Ward Cleary (1916-1988)
Frederick M. Tobin
John Wayne Fox
Ward Frank Cleary
James D'Alton Murphy
Randolph T. Lovallo

OF COUNSEL

John D. Hertz
Jane F. Donovan
Richard L. Brinckerhoff
Patricia M. Gaug

Susan L. Stratton
Derek Gilman
Michael P. Murray
John J. Louizos

Counsel for: The F. A. Bartlett Tree Expert Co.; Town of Darien; Miller Automobile Corp.; Bolliger, Inc.; Titan Sports; People's Bank, Bridgeport; Fleet Bank; Federal Deposit Insurance Co.; William Pitt Foundation; Wood Logan Associates.

For full biographical listings, see the Martindale-Hubbell Law Directory

FLORIDA

*BRADENTON,** Manatee Co.

GRIMES GOEBEL GRIMES HAWKINS & GLADFELTER, P.A. (AV)

The Professional Building, 1023 Manatee Avenue West, P.O. Box 1550, 34206
Telephone: 941-748-0151
Fax: 941-748-0158
Email: ggghg@gte.net
Tampa, Florida Office: Old Hyde Park Village, 1509 West Swann Avenue, Suite 275.
Telephone: 813-258-2557.
Fax: 813-258-2327.

William C. Grimes
Caleb J. Grimes
William S. Galvano

Counsel for: Schroeder Manatee Inc. (Agriculture and Land Development); Lombardo & Skipper & Foley, Inc. (Civil Engineers); CCI Environmental Services, Inc. (Environmental Consultants); Creekwood Investors, Ltd.; Old Hyde Park Village Center, Ltd.; First Federal Savings & Loan Association of Florida.
Approved Attorneys for: Lawyers Title Insurance Corp.; Chicago Title Insurance Co.; Attorneys Title Insurance Fund.

For full biographical listings, see the Martindale-Hubbell Law Directory

*CLEARWATER,** Pinellas Co.

GAINES & HELINGER (AV)

209 Turner Street, 33756
Telephone: 727-446-2889
Fax: 727-443-7794
Email: MWGainespa@aol.com

Michael W. Gaines
James A. Helinger, Jr.

For full biographical listings, see the Martindale-Hubbell Law Directory

*MIAMI,** Dade Co.

EARLE & PATCHEN, PROFESSIONAL ASSOCIATION (AV)

1000 Brickell Avenue Suite 1112, 33131
Telephone: 305-372-1112
Fax: 305-372-3691
Email: earlepatchen@lawyers.com

William George Earle
Brian P. Patchen

Reference: Mellon United National Bank.

For full biographical listings, see the Martindale-Hubbell Law Directory

*ORLANDO,** Orange Co.

FIXEL & MAGUIRE (AV)

2816 East Robinson Street, Suite 250, 32803
Telephone: 407-228-9522
Fax: 407-228-9665
URL: http://www.fla-eminentdomain.com
Tallahassee Office: 211 South Gadsden Street.
Telephone: 850-681-1800.
Fax: 850-681-9017.

Joe W. Fixel
Raymer F. Maguire, III

Craig B. Willis

Representative Clients: Condemnees: Allen Morris Co.; Franklin Carriage Gate Shopping Center, Ltd.; Miccosukee Village Shopping Center, Ltd.; Nick Nicholas Ford, Inc.; Weaver Oil Co.; United Fuel Corp.; Majik Market Convenience Stores. Condemnors: Collier County Board of County Commissioners; Hillsborough County Board of County Commissioners.

(See Next Column)

FIXEL & MAGUIRE—*Continued*

Reference: Barnett Bank.

For full biographical listings, see the Martindale-Hubbell Law Directory

WILSON, LEAVITT & SMALL, P.A. (AV)

437 North Magnolia Avenue, 32801-1524
Telephone: 407-843-4321
Fax: 407-423-1505
Email: wlspa@aol.com *URL:* http://www.lawyers.com/eminentdomain

J. Christy Wilson, III
Mark R. Leavitt
Jay W. Small
Kurt H. Garber

Representative Clients: Circle K; Cumberland Farms; Hardee's Food Systems; Mobil Oil; Public Storage; Southland Corp.; U.S.F.& G.; Oerther Foods; Seventh Day Adventists; McDonald's Corporation.

For full biographical listings, see the Martindale-Hubbell Law Directory

PALM BEACH, Palm Beach Co.

PAUL A. TURK, JR., P.A. (AV)

324 Royal Palm Way, Suite 303, 33480
Telephone: 561-655-5807
Fax: 561-655-3775

Paul A. Turk, Jr.

For full biographical listings, see the Martindale-Hubbell Law Directory

*TALLAHASSEE,** Leon Co.

FIXEL & MAGUIRE (AV)

211 South Gadsden Street, 32301
Telephone: 850-681-1800
Fax: 850-681-9017
Email: jfixel@fla-eminentdomain.com *URL:* http://www.fla-eminentdomain.com
Orlando Office: 2816 East Robinson Street, Suite 250, 32803.
Telephone: 407-228-9522.
Fax: 407-228-9665.

Joe W. Fixel
Raymer F. Maguire, III

Craig B. Willis

Representative Clients: Florida Mining and Materials, Inc.; Sun Trust Bank; State Farm Insurance; Allen Morris Co.; Nick Nicholas Ford; Burger King; Bill Salter Outdoor Advertising; Capital Agriculture Property Services, Inc.; Housing and Neighborhood Development of Central Florida; United Fuel Corp.

For full biographical listings, see the Martindale-Hubbell Law Directory

*TAMPA,** Hillsborough Co.

BRICKLEMYER SMOLKER & BOLVES, P.A. (AV)

500 East Kennedy Boulevard, Suite 200, 33602-4708
Telephone: 813-223-3888
Fax: 813-228-6422
Email: bsb@bsbpropertylaw.com *URL:* http://www.bsbpropertylaw.com

Keith W. Bricklemyer
David Smolker
Brian A. Bolves
Jay J. Bartlett
Douglas C. Roland
David M. Corry
Richard A. Schlosser
Gregory J. Orcutt

R. Michael Brooks
Deborah M. Schmitt

OF COUNSEL

J.A. Jurgens

For full biographical listings, see the Martindale-Hubbell Law Directory

SACHS & WERDINE, P.A. (AV)

601 Bayshore Boulevard, Suite 840, 33606
Telephone: 813-253-3755
Fax: 813-258-8299
Email: www.sachs-werdine@mindspring.com

Marc I. Sachs
Frederick S. Werdine

D. Tobyn DeYoung

For full biographical listings, see the Martindale-Hubbell Law Directory

ILLINOIS

*CHICAGO,** Cook Co.

FIGLIULO & SILVERMAN, P.C. (AV)

10 South La Salle Street, Suite 3600, 60603
Telephone: 312-251-4600
Fax: 312-251-4610

James R. Figliulo
Peter A. Silverman
Carl A. Gigante
Brian P. Liston
Marc S. Porter
James H. Bowhay

James J. Sipchen, Jr.
Adam E. Bossov
Michael K. Desmond

For full biographical listings, see the Martindale-Hubbell Law Directory

FORAN & SCHULTZ (AV)

Suite 3000, 30 North La Salle Street, 60602
Telephone: 312-368-8330
Fax: 312-580-2600
Email: law@foran.com *URL:* http://www.Foran.com

MEMBERS OF FIRM

Thomas A. Foran
Richard G. Schultz
Stephen A. Gorman
Jeff D. Harris
Jack J. Carriglio
Steven H. Gistenson
Brooke R. Whitted
Jeffrey C. Blumenthal
Teresa F. Frisbie

OF COUNSEL

Robert J. Weber

For full biographical listings, see the Martindale-Hubbell Law Directory

LOUISIANA

*LAKE CHARLES,** Calcasieu Parish

THE GRAY LAW FIRM A PROFESSIONAL LAW CORPORATION (AV)

Hibernia Tower, One Lakeshore Drive, Suite 900, P.O. Box 1467, 70602-1467
Telephone: 318-494-0694
Facsimile: 318-494-0697
Email: graylaw@graylawfirm.com

Andrew J. Gray, III
David L. Sigler
Anna R. Gray
Leslie Qvale Knox

Wade Thomas Visconte

For full biographical listings, see the Martindale-Hubbell Law Directory

MICHIGAN

TROY, Oakland Co.

ACKERMAN & ACKERMAN, P.C. (AV)

3001 West Big Beaver Road Suite 508, 48084-3102
Telephone: 248-643-9550
Toll Free: 1-800-284-1155
URL: http://www.ackerman-ackerman.com

Irving B. Ackerman (1910-1999)
Alan T. Ackerman
Stephon B. Bagne
Darius W. Dynkowski

For full biographical listings, see the Martindale-Hubbell Law Directory

EMPLOYMENT BENEFITS LAW

ALABAMA

*BIRMINGHAM,** Jefferson Co.

BRADLEY ARANT ROSE & WHITE LLP (AV)

2001 Park Place, Suite 1400, P.O. Box 830709, 35283-0709
Telephone: 205-521-8000
Facsimile: 205-521-8800
Facsimile (SouthTrust Tower Office): 205-521-8500
URL: http://www.barw.com
Huntsville, Alabama Office: 200 Clinton Avenue West, Suite 900, 35801.
Telephone: 205-517-5100.
Facsimile: 205-533-5069.
Washington, D.C. Office: 801 Pennsylvania Avenue, NW, Suite 230, 20004.
Telephone: 202-347-8893.
Facsimile: 202-347-1684.

MEMBERS OF FIRM

James S. Christie Jr.
John James Coleman Jr.
Kevin J. Henderson
Robert G. Johnson
James Walker May

ASSOCIATES

Kelly Hubbard Estes
Abdul K. Kallon
T. Matthew Miller

For Complete List of Firm Personnel, See General Section

For full biographical listings, see the Martindale-Hubbell Law Directory

GORDON, SILBERMAN, WIGGINS & CHILDS, P.C. (AV)

1400 SouthTrust Tower, 420 North 20th Street, 35203
Telephone: 205-328-0640
Facsimilie: 205-254-1500
Washington, D.C. Office: 1621 Connecticut Avenue, N.W., Suite 400.
Telephone: 202-238-0690.
Facsimilie: 202-238-0968.

RESIDENT SHAREHOLDERS

Wilbur G. Silberman
Bruce L. Gordon
Robert L. Wiggins, Jr.
Robert F. Childs, Jr.
Augustus J. Beck, Jr.
Harvey L. Wachsman
Ray D. Gibbons
C. Michael Quinn
Dennis George Pantazis
Terrill W. Sanders
James Mendelsohn
Richard J. Ebbinghouse
Ann K. Wiggins
Samuel Fisher
Ann C. Robertson
Mark P. Williams
Timothy D. Davis
Joseph H. Calvin, III
Linda J. Peacock
Deborah A. Mattison

RESIDENT ASSOCIATES

Byron R. Perkins
Jon C. Goldfarb
Gregory O. Wiggins
Lee Winston
Rocco Calamusa, Jr.

OF COUNSEL

Robert H. Loeb

For Complete List of Firm Personnel, See General Section

For full biographical listings, see the Martindale-Hubbell Law Directory

LUSK, FRALEY, MCALISTER & SIMMS, P.C. (AV)

Suite 1700 AmSouth/Harbert Plaza, 1901 Sixth Avenue North, 35203
Telephone: 205-323-7100
Fax: 205-323-7050
Email: Lusk-Fraley.com

Donald D. Lusk
John M. Fraley
David L. McAlister
Keri Donald Simms
Kenneth A. Dowdy
David Lawrence Dean
David Thurston White, III
Susan Gilman McAlister
Payton Caldwell Lusk
Leslie Ann Caldwell

For full biographical listings, see the Martindale-Hubbell Law Directory

*MOBILE,** Mobile Co.

ARMBRECHT, JACKSON, DEMOUY, CROWE, HOLMES & REEVES, L.L.C. (AV)

1300 Riverview Plaza, P.O. Box 290, 36601
Telephone: 334-405-1300
Facsimile: 334-432-6843; 433-3821
Email: adc@ajlaw.com

MEMBERS OF FIRM

William B. Harvey
Broox G. Holmes, Jr.

(See Next Column)

ASSOCIATE

Leah P. Ladd

Representative Clients: Cooper/T. Smith Stevedoring Co., Inc.; Loyal American Life Insurance Co.; Mobile Gas Service Corp.; Mobile Steamship Ass'n -- International Longshoremen's Pension, Welfare & Vacation Plans; Southern Pine Inspection Bureau; TACA Airlines, S.A.; United Bank; WKRG-TV-Channel 5.

For Complete List of Firm Personnel, See General Section

For full biographical listings, see the Martindale-Hubbell Law Directory

JOHNSTONE, ADAMS, BAILEY, GORDON AND HARRIS, L.L.C. (AV)

Royal St. Francis Building, 104 St. Francis Street, 8th Floor, P.O. Box 1988, 36633
Telephone: 334-432-7682
Facsimile: 334-432-0712 or 334-432-2800
Email: attorneys@JohnstoneAdams.com *URL:* http://www.JohnstoneAdams.com
Bay Minette, Alabama Office: Dahlberg Building, 107 Hand Avenue, P.O. Box 729, 36507.
Telephone: 334-937-9473.
Facsimile: 334-937-9475.

MEMBERS OF FIRM

Ben H. Harris, Jr.
E. Watson Smith
Joseph M. Allen, Jr.
Wade B. Perry, Jr.
Celia J. Collins
R. Gregory Watts
Tracy P. Turner

OF COUNSEL

Brock B. Gordon

For Complete List of Firm Personnel, See General Section

For full biographical listings, see the Martindale-Hubbell Law Directory

*MONTGOMERY,** Montgomery Co.

VOLZ, PRESTWOOD & HANAN, P.C. (AV)

350 Adams Avenue, P.O. Box 1910, 36102-1910
Telephone: 334-264-6401
Fax: 334-834-4954

Charles H. Volz, Jr.
Alvin T. Prestwood
Charles H. Volz, III
Ellis D. Hanan
Richard D. Lively
Judy H. Barganier

For full biographical listings, see the Martindale-Hubbell Law Directory

ARIZONA

*PHOENIX,** Maricopa Co.

BACON & DEAR, PLC (AV)

340 East Palm Lane, Suite 240, 85004
Telephone: 602-256-6700
Fax: 602-257-0600

MEMBERS

Roxana C. Bacon
Diane M. Dear

ASSOCIATES

Eric R. Bowman (Not admitted in AZ)
Danielle L. Ventura

For full biographical listings, see the Martindale-Hubbell Law Directory

EHMANN & HILLER, P.C. (AV)

2525 East Camelback Road, Suite 720, 85016
Telephone: 602-956-5050
Telecopier: 602-468-9775
Email: nhiller@home.com

Anthony V. Ehmann
Neil H. Hiller
John G. Pattullo
John F. Daniels, III

References: Harris Trust Bank of Arizona; Bank One, Arizona, N.A. (Trust Department); M&I Thunderbird Bank; Marshall & Ilsley Trust Company of Arizona; Wells Fargo Bank, N.A.; Colonial Trust Company; National Bank of Arizona.

For full biographical listings, see the Martindale-Hubbell Law Directory

FENNEMORE CRAIG, A PROFESSIONAL CORPORATION (AV)

3003 North Central Avenue, Suite 2600, 85012-2913
Telephone: 602-916-5000
Fax: 602-916-5999
Tucson, Arizona Office: One South Church Avenue, Suite 1000, 85701-1620.
Telephone: 520-879-6800.
Fax: 520-879-6899.

(See Next Column)

FENNEMORE CRAIG A PROFESSIONAL CORPORATION, *Phoenix—Continued*

Cynthia L. Shupe — Karen Ciupak McConnell
David N. Heap — J. Barry Shelley
James J. Trimble

Joel B. Shapiro

LEGAL SUPPORT PERSONNEL

LEGAL ASSISTANTS

Ann V. Kooi

For Complete List of Firm Personnel, See General Section

For full biographical listings, see the Martindale-Hubbell Law Directory

SHIMMEL, HILL, BISHOP & GRUENDER, P.C. (AV)

3700 North 24th Street, 85016
Telephone: 602-224-9500
Telecopier: 602-955-6176
URL: http://www.shimmelhill.com

Daniel F. Gruender — Keith F. Overholt

Representative Clients: Arizona Laborers', Teamsters' and Cement Masons, Local 395 Pension Annuity, Health and Welfare and Vacation Trust Funds; Arizona State Carpenters' Pension, Annuity, Health and Welfare and Vacation Trust Funds; The Ashton Cos.; Associated General Contractors; Bashas' Stores; Black Mesa Pipeline Co.; Citizen Auto Stage Line; Dunn Del Re Steel, Inc.; Operating Engineers' Local 428 Pension, Annuity and Health and Welfare and Vacation Trust Funds; Phoenix Area Pipe Trades Joint Apprenticeship Committee.

For full biographical listings, see the Martindale-Hubbell Law Directory

SNELL & WILMER L.L.P. (AV)

One Arizona Center, 85004-2202
Telephone: 602-382-6000
Fax: 602-382-6070
Email: postmaster@snellwilmer.com *URL:* http://www.swlaw.com
Tucson, Arizona Office: One South Church Avenue, Suite 1500, 85701-1612.
Telephone: 520-882-1200.
Fax: 520-884-1294.
Orange County Office: 1920 Main Street, Suite 1200, Irvine, California 92614-7230.
Telephone: 949-253-2700.
Fax: 949-955-2507.
Salt Lake City, Utah Office: 111 East Broadway, Suite 900, 84111-1004.
Telephone: 801-237-1900.
Fax: 801-237-1950.

MEMBERS OF FIRM

Thomas R. Hoecker — Marvin S. Swift, Jr.

ASSOCIATES

Nancy Kay Campbell — Nancy J. Caplette
Catherine Wehling

Representative Clients: For list of Representative Clients, see end of biographical listings in the Martindale-Hubbell Law Directory.

For Complete List of Firm Personnel, See General Section

For full biographical listings, see the Martindale-Hubbell Law Directory

ARKANSAS

*LITTLE ROCK,** Pulaski Co.

ROSE LAW FIRM, A PROFESSIONAL ASSOCIATION (AV)

120 East Fourth Street, 72201
Telephone: 501-375-9131
Telecopy: 501-375-1309

Tim Boe — David P. Martin
Kathryn Bennett Perkins

Counsel for: Aluminum Company of America; Bridgestone/Firestone, Inc.; The Equitable Life Assurance Society of The United States; General Motors Corp.; The Prudential Insurance Company of America; Stephens Group Inc.; TCBY Enterprises, Inc.; Tyson Foods, Inc.

For Complete List of Firm Personnel, See General Section

For full biographical listings, see the Martindale-Hubbell Law Directory

CALIFORNIA

COSTA MESA, Orange Co.

RUTAN & TUCKER, LLP (AV)

A Partnership including Professional Corporations
611 Anton Boulevard, Fourteenth Floor, P.O. Box 1950, 92626-1998
Telephone: 714-641-5100; 213-625-7586
Telecopier: 714-546-9035
Email: rutan&tucker@rutan.com *URL:* http://www.rutan.com

MEMBER OF FIRM

David C. Larsen (P.C.)

For Complete List of Firm Personnel, See General Section

For full biographical listings, see the Martindale-Hubbell Law Directory

*LOS ANGELES,** Los Angeles Co.

MICHAEL ANTIN A LAW CORPORATION (AV)

10880 Wilshire Boulevard Suite 1010, 90024
Telephone: 310-470-0049
Fax: 310-470-0322
Email: mantin@ix.netcom.com *URL:* http://www.lawyers.com/atlaw

Michael Antin

For full biographical listings, see the Martindale-Hubbell Law Directory

BRUCKER MORRA & HILTUNEN, A PROFESSIONAL CORPORATION (AV)

10880 Wilshire Boulevard, Suite 2210, 90024
Telephone: 310-475-7540
Fax: 310-470-4806
URL: http://www.lawyers.com/pensionlawyers
Email: abrucker@pensionlawyers.com *URL:* http://www.pensionlawyers.com

Alex M. Brucker — Scott E. Hiltunen
Linda Russano Morra — Michael L. Cotter
Robert Turkel

For full biographical listings, see the Martindale-Hubbell Law Directory

DECARLO, CONNOR & SELVO, A PROFESSIONAL CORPORATION (AV)

500 South Virgil Avenue, Fourth Floor, 90020-1430
Telephone: 213-738-7959
Fax: 213-738-1813
Email: dcs@deconsel.com
Washington, D.C. Office: 101 Constitution Avenue, N.W., Suite 322.
Telephone: 202-547-8300.
Fax: 202-547-9303.

John T. DeCarlo — Patrick T. Connor
Gerald V. Selvo

Daniel J. Hall — Daniel M. Shanley
Lee S. Feldman — Brian F. Quinn (Resident, Washington D.C., Office)
Margaret Rawls Gifford — Willow J. Prall (Resident, Washington, D.C. Office)
Desmond C. Lee
Enrique Guieb Gutierrez
Kathleen M. Jorgenson

Representative Clients: Carpenters Pension Trust for Southern California; Palm Springs Riviera Hotel & Resort; Office and Professional Employees International Union Pension Fund; United Brotherhood of Carpenters and Joiners of America; United Brotherhood of Carpenters Pension Fund.

For full biographical listings, see the Martindale-Hubbell Law Directory

O'MELVENY & MYERS LLP (AV)

400 South Hope Street, 90071-2899
Telephone: 213-430-6000
Facsimile: 213-430-6407
Cable: MOMS
Telex: 674122
Email: omminfo@omm.com *URL:* http://www.omm.com
Century City, CA Office: 1999 Avenue of the Stars, Los Angeles, 90067-6035.
Telex: 674097. Tel: 310-553-6700.
Fax: 310-246-6779.
Newport Beach, CA Office: 610 Newport Center Drive, 92660-6429.
Telex: 4722088. Tel: 949-760-9600.
Fax: 949-823-6994.
San Francisco, CA Office: Embarcadero Center West, 275 Battery Street, 94111-3305. Tel: 415-984-8700.
Fax: 415-984-8701.
New York, NY Office: Citicorp Center, 153 East 53rd Street, 10022-4611.
Telex: 129165. Tel: 212-326-2000.
Fax: 212-326-2061.

(See Next Column)

O'MELVENY & MYERS LLP—*Continued*

Washington, DC Office: 555 13th Street, N.W., 20004-1109.
Cable: MOMSWSH.
Telex: 89622. Tel: 202-383-5300.
Fax: 202-383-5414.
London Office: O'Melveny & Myers, 3 Finsbury Square, London, EC2A 1LA, England. Tel: 44-171-256-8451. Fax 44-171-638-8205.
Tokyo Office: Akasaka Twin Tower, East 14F, 2-17-23, Akasaka, Minato-ku, Tokyo 107-0052, Japan. Tel: 03-5562-2800.
Fax: 03-5575-3840.
Hong Kong Office: O'Melveny & Myers, Suite 1905, Tower Two, Lippo Centre, 89 Queensway, Central, Hong Kong. Tel: 852-2523-8266.
Fax: 852-2522-1760.
Shanghai Office: Kerry Centre, 20F, 1515 Nanjing Road West, Shanghai, 200040 People's Republic of China. Tel: 86-21-5298-5600.
Fax: 86-21-5298-5500.

PARTNER

David E. Gordon

For Complete List of Firm Personnel, See General Section

For full biographical listings, see the Martindale-Hubbell Law Directory

RODI, POLLOCK, PETTKER, GALBRAITH & CAHILL, A LAW CORPORATION (AV)

444 South Flower Street, Suite 1700, 90071-2901
Telephone: 213-895-4900
Telecopiers: 213-895-4921; 895-4922; 895-4750
URL: http://www.rodipollock.com

Karl B. Rodi (1908-1982)
John D. Cahill
John D. Pettker
Daniel C. Bond (1942-1977)
William R. Christian
Henry P. Pramov, Jr.
John F. Cermak, Jr.
Allan E. Ceran
Elizabeth B. Blakely
Robert C. Norton
Tim G. Ceperley
Coralie Kupfer
Cris K. O'Neall
Scott E. Adamson
Margaret Rosenthal

Sonja A. Inglin
Michael A. Abraham
Kenneth A. Franklin
Richard Nessary
Donna Yamini
Wade E. Norwood
Deepak Nanda
David J. Elbaz

OF COUNSEL

John P. Pollock
James M. Galbraith

For full biographical listings, see the Martindale-Hubbell Law Directory

SCHWARTZ, STEINSAPIR, DOHRMANN & SOMMERS, LLP (AV)

6300 Wilshire Boulevard, Suite 2000, 90048
Telephone: 323-655-4700
Fax: 323-655-4488
Pittsburgh, Pennsylvania Office: 1007 Mt. Royal Boulevard, 15223.
Telephone: 412-492-8797.
Fax: 412-492-8978.

MEMBERS OF FIRM

Laurence D. Steinsapir
Robert M. Dohrmann
Richard D. Sommers
Stuart Libicki
Michael R. Feinberg
Michael D. Four
Margo A. Feinberg
Henry M. Willis
D. William Heine, Jr.
Claude Cazzulino
Dolly M. Gee

ASSOCIATES

Erika A. Zucker
Janet L. Woods

For full biographical listings, see the Martindale-Hubbell Law Directory

ONTARIO, San Bernardino Co.

COVINGTON & CROWE LLP (AV)

1131 West Sixth Street, P.O. Box 1515, 91762
Telephone: 909-983-9393
Fax: 909-391-6762
URL: http://www.covcrowe.com

MEMBERS OF FIRM

Maurice G. Covington (1908-1997)
Harold A. Bailin (1930-1988)
Samuel P. Crowe
George W. Porter
Robert E. Dougherty
Donald G. Haslam
Robert F. Schauer
Jette R. Anderson
Audrey A. Perri
Tracy L. Tibbals
Melanie Fisch
R. Douglas Donesky
Tammy S. Jager
Katrina West

ASSOCIATES

J. Michael Kaler
Eric S. Vail
Khymberli S. Apaloo

OF COUNSEL

Edward A. Hopson

For full biographical listings, see the Martindale-Hubbell Law Directory

*SACRAMENTO,** Sacramento Co.

MATHENY SEARS LINKERT & LONG, LLP (AV)

3638 American River Drive, P.O. Box 13711, 95853-4711
Telephone: 916-978-3434
Fax: 916-978-3430
Email: info@msll.com *URL:* http://www.msll.com

MEMBERS OF FIRM

Henry G. Matheny (1933-1984)
Douglas A. Sears
Richard S. Linkert
Ernest A. Long
Joann Georgallis
Kent M. Luckey
Matthew C. Jaime
Michael A. Bishop
Robert B. Berrigan
Ronald E. Enabnit
Eric R. Wiesel

ASSOCIATES

Andrea Croak Christensen
Michael G. Jones
Eric M. Bonzell
Mary Elizabeth Wood
Paul Richard Baleria
James F. Curran
Andreas C. Rockas
Timothy P. Chang

OF COUNSEL

James C. Damir

LEGAL SUPPORT PERSONNEL

PARALEGALS

Frances Studer
Lynell Rae Steed
Jennifer Bachman

For full biographical listings, see the Martindale-Hubbell Law Directory

*SAN DIEGO,** San Diego Co.

MERRILL, SCHULTZ & WOLDS, LIMITED (AV)

First National Bank Building, Suite 2550, 401 West "A" Street, 92101
Telephone: 619-234-4525
Telecopier: 619-234-9740
Email: mswltd@mswltd.com

Stephen J. Schultz
David P. Wolds
Mark T. Bennett

John M. Julius, III
Laura B. Riesenberg

OF COUNSEL

Michael E. Merrill
William R. Kuntz, Jr.

Representative Clients: Associated General Contractors of America, San Diego Chapter, Inc.; Associated General Contractors Health and Welfare, Retirement, and Apprenticeship and Training Trust Funds; San Diego Opera Association; La Jolla Beach & Tennis Club; ABC Framers, Commercial and Residential Drywall Councils Health Insurance Trust Funds; Douglas E. Barnhart, Inc.; Blake Construction; United Way of San Diego County/-Health Way Trust Fund; San Diego Construction Councils; McCarthy Brothers Company.

For full biographical listings, see the Martindale-Hubbell Law Directory

STEPHENSON, WORLEY, GARRATT, SCHWARTZ, GARFIELD & PRAIRIE (AV)

A Limited Liability Partnership
401 "B" Street, Suite 2400, 92101-4200
Telephone: 619-696-3500
Fax: 619-696-3555
Email: SDLAW@swgsgp.com

MEMBERS OF FIRM

Gary J. Stephenson
Donald R. Worley
Gregory C. M. Garratt
William J. Schwartz, Jr.
Michael W. Prairie
Timothy K. Garfield
Laurel Lee Hyde

OF COUNSEL

Kent H. Foster
Elaine L. Chan
Ralph E. Hughes

Reference: Bank of Commerce.

For full biographical listings, see the Martindale-Hubbell Law Directory

*SAN FRANCISCO,** San Francisco Co.

LUDWIG GOLDBERG & KRENZEL, A PROFESSIONAL CORPORATION (AV)

36th Floor, 50 California Street, 94111
Telephone: 415-788-7200
Fax: 415-433-6496
URL: http://www.lgklaw.com

Laurence A. Goldberg
Jeffrey F. Krenzel
Karen D. Ng
Marcus Wilson

OF COUNSEL

Ronald L. Ludwig

For full biographical listings, see the Martindale-Hubbell Law Directory

San Francisco—Continued

MURPHY, PEARSON, BRADLEY & FEENEY, A PROFESSIONAL CORPORATION (AV)

88 Kearny Street, 10th Floor, 94108
Telephone: 415-788-1900
Telecopier: 415-393-8087
Email: IndividualsFirstInitialAndLastName@mpbf.com *URL:* http://www.mpbf.com
Sacramento, California Office: 701 University Avenue, Suite 150.
Telephone: 916-565-0300.
Fax: 916-565-1636.
San Jose, California Office: 80 South Market Street, 3rd Floor.
Telephone: 408-279-5792.
Facsimile: 408-279-5785.
Los Angeles, California Office: 11400 West Olympic Boulevard, Suite 249.
Telephone: 310-312-9565.
Fax: 310-312-9566.

Karen M. Goodman (Resident, Sacramento Office)
Mark S. Perelman
Gregg A. Thornton
Jane L. O'Hara Gamp

For Complete List of Firm Personnel, See General Section

For full biographical listings, see the Martindale-Hubbell Law Directory

PAHL & GOSSELIN, A PROFESSIONAL CORPORATION (AV)

601 Montgomery Street Suite 325, 94111
Telephone: 415-356-8300
Telecopier: 415-356-8319
San Jose, California Office: 160 West Santa Clara Street. Fourteenth Floor, 95113.
Telephone: 408-286-5100.
Telecopier: 408-286-5722. Email: mail@pahl-gosselin.com.

Thomas M. Gosselin
Michael J. Vartain
Stephen D. Pahl (Resident, San Jose Office)

Kenneth L. Kann
Susan S. Hahm Walker
Lisa E. Barnett

For full biographical listings, see the Martindale-Hubbell Law Directory

WALKUP, MELODIA, KELLY & ECHEVERRIA, A PROFESSIONAL CORPORATION (AV)

26th Floor, 650 California Street, 94108
Telephone: 415-981-7210
Fax: 415-391-6965

Paul V. Melodia
Ronald H. Wecht
Daniel J. Kelly
Michael A. Kelly
John Echeverria
Kevin L. Domecus
Richard H. Schoenberger

Cynthia F. Newton
Douglas S. Saeltzer
Michael J. Recupero
Khaldoun A. Baghdadi
Doris Cheng

OF COUNSEL

John D. Link
Wesley Sokolosky

Reference: Bank of California, San Francisco Main Office, 400 California Street, San Francisco, Calif. 94104.

For full biographical listings, see the Martindale-Hubbell Law Directory

*SANTA ANA,** Orange Co.

BEAM, BROBECK & WEST (AV)

600 West Santa Ana Boulevard, Suite 1000, 92701
Telephone: 714-558-3944
Fax: 714-568-0129

MEMBERS OF FIRM

Byron J. Beam
Kirk H. Nakamura
David J. Brobeck, Jr.
Daniel R. Sullivan
John E. West
Charles W. Matheis, Jr.

ASSOCIATES

Gregory L. Rippetoe
Kermit D. Marsh
Jennifer J. Miller
Kelly A. Fortin
Donald S. Zalewski
Barbara J. Salvini
David R. Rosenberg
Lil G. Delcampo
Louise M. Douville
Michael J. Peffer
L. Steven Hattendorf

Representative Clients: Aetna Insurance Co.; American General Life Insurance Co.; American Hospital Supply; Carl Warren & Co.; Casualty Insurance Co.; City of Anaheim; City of Fullerton; City of Newport Beach; Empire Insurance Cos.; Physicians Interindemnity.

For full biographical listings, see the Martindale-Hubbell Law Directory

CONNECTICUT

*HARTFORD,** Hartford Co.

SOROKIN, GROSS & HYDE, P.C. (AV)

One Corporate Center, 06103
Telephone: 860-525-6645
Fax: 860-522-1781
Email: sorokin@sorokinlaw.com
Simsbury, Connecticut Office: 720 Hopmeadow Street.
Telephone: 860-651-9348.
Rocky Hill, Connecticut Office: 2360 Main Street.
Telephone: 860-563-9305.
Fax: 860-529-6931.

Sharon Kowal Freilich
Barrie K. Wetstone

For Complete List of Firm Personnel, See General Section

For full biographical listings, see the Martindale-Hubbell Law Directory

SOUTHPORT, Fairfield Co.

BRODY, WILKINSON AND OBER, P.C. (AV)

2507 Post Road, 06490
Telephone: 203-319-7100
Fax: 203-254-1772

Seth O. L. Brody
Robert L. Teicher
Peter Wilkinson
Ronald B. Noren
Frank Fritz Ober
Peter T. Mott
S. Giles Payne
Thomas J. Walsh, Jr.
James E. Rice
Diane F. Martucci
William J. Britt
Seth L. Cooper
Barbara S. Miller
Douglas R. Brown
Charles S. Brody (1894-1976)

OF COUNSEL

Bruce E. Dillingham
Roy W. Moore, III

For full biographical listings, see the Martindale-Hubbell Law Directory

DELAWARE

*WILMINGTON,** New Castle Co.

POTTER ANDERSON & CORROON LLP (AV)

Hercules Plaza, 1313 N. Market Street, P.O. Box 951, 19899-0951
Telephone: 302-984-6000
Fax: 302-658-1192
URL: http://www.attys.pacdelaware.com

MEMBERS OF FIRM

Mary E. Copper
Kathleen Furey McDonough

ASSOCIATE

Wendy K. Voss

Representative Clients: KAO Corporation of America; The Andrew Jergens Company; Conectiv, Inc.; E.I. du Pont de Nemours & Co.; The Equitable Life Assurance Society of the United States; Winterthur Museum; Metropolitan Life Insurance Company.

For Complete List of Firm Personnel, See General Section

For full biographical listings, see the Martindale-Hubbell Law Directory

DISTRICT OF COLUMBIA

WASHINGTON, D.C. Co.

COHEN, MILSTEIN, HAUSFELD & TOLL, P.L.L.C. (AV)

West Tower, Suite 500, 1100 New York Avenue, N.W., 20005-3964
Telephone: 202-408-4600
Facsimile: 202-408-4699
Email: lawinfo@cmht.com *URL:* http://www.CMHT.com
Seattle, Washington Office: 999 Third Avenue, Suite 3600.
Telephone: 206-521-0080.
Facsimile: 206-521-0166.

MEMBERS OF FIRM

Jerry S. Cohen (1925-1995)
Lisa M. Mezzetti
Herbert E. Milstein
Andrew N. Friedman
Michael D. Hausfeld
Richard S. Lewis
Steven J. Toll (Resident, Seattle, Washington Office)
Daniel S. Sommers
Daniel A. Small
Ann C. Yahner
Gary E. Mason

(See Next Column)

COHEN, MILSTEIN, HAUSFELD & TOLL P.L.L.C.—*Continued*

MEMBERS OF FIRM (Continued)

Joseph M. Sellers
Sharon A. Snyder
Mark S. Willis (Not admitted in DC)

ASSOCIATES

Lori G. Feldman (Resident, Seattle, Washington Office)
Paul T. Gallagher
Christine E. Webber
Alexander E. Barnett
Matthew James Ide (Resident, Seattle, Washington Office)
Matthew F. Pawa
Suzette M. Malveaux
Mary N. Strimel
Kristopher A. Kinkade (Resident, Seattle, Washington Office)
Agnieszka M. Fryszman
Deborah J. Vagins
Ari Karen
Charles E. Tompkins
Tamara J. Driscoll (Resident, Seattle, Washington Office)
Elizabeth Haines Cronise
Donna Solen
Lesli C. Esposito (Not admitted in DC)

OF COUNSEL

Margaret G. Farrell

For full biographical listings, see the Martindale-Hubbell Law Directory

---

CONNER & WINTERS, A PROFESSIONAL CORPORATION (AV)

1050 Seventeenth Street, N.W., Suite 810, 20036-5503
Telephone: 202-783-5711
Facsimile: 202-783-5720
Email: postmaster@cwlaw.com
Tulsa, Oklahoma Office: 3700 First Place Tower, 15 East 5th Street, 74103-4344.
Telephone: 918-586-5711.
Facsimile: 918-586-8982.
Oklahoma City, Oklahoma Office: One Leadership Square, 211 North Robinson, Suite 1700, 73102-7101.
Telephone: 405-272-5711.
Facsimile: 405-232-2695.
Fayetteville, Arkansas Office: Conner & Winters, P.L.L.C., 100 West Center Street, Suite 200, 72701-6081.
Telephone: 501-582-5711.
Facsimile: 501-587-1426.

G. Daniel Miller (Not admitted in DC)
Carol V. Calhoun

Erica L. Summers

OF COUNSEL

Henry Rose

For full biographical listings, see the Martindale-Hubbell Law Directory

---

THE FEINBERG GROUP, LLP (AV)

1120 20th Street, N.W. Suite 740 South, 20036-3437
Telephone: 202-371-1110
Fax: 202-962-9290
Email: kfeinberg@thefeinberggroup.com *URL:* http://www.krfassociates.com
New York, N.Y. Office: 780 3rd Avenue, Suite 2202.
Telephone: 212-527-9600.
Fax: 212-527-9611. Email: kfeinberg@thefeinberggroup.com.

PARTNERS

Kenneth R. Feinberg
Deborah E. Greenspan
Michael K. Rozen (Resident, New York Office)
Peter H. Woodin (Resident, New York Office)

ASSOCIATE

Fredric M. Brooks (Not admitted in DC)

SENIOR COUNSEL

Jacqueline E. Zins

For full biographical listings, see the Martindale-Hubbell Law Directory

---

SCHMELTZER, APTAKER & SHEPARD, P.C. (AV)

The Watergate, Suite 1000, 2600 Virginia Avenue, N.W., 20037-1905
Telephone: 202-333-8800
Cable Address: "Ship"
Telex: 440517
Facsimile: 202-337-6065
Email: sas@saslaw.com *URL:* http://www.saspc.com
Los Angeles, California Office: 1999 Avenue of the Stars, Twenty-Seventh Floor, 90067-4095.
Telephone: 310-557-2966.
FAX: 310-286-6610.

Ira M. Shepard
Paul M. Heylman

For full biographical listings, see the Martindale-Hubbell Law Directory

---

SLEVIN & HART, P.C. (AV)

1625 Massachusetts Avenue, N.W., Suite 450, 20036
Telephone: 202-797-8700
FAX: 202-234-8231
Email: Slevin&Hart@compuserve.com

Barry S. Slevin
Thomas J. Hart
Fredrick M. Marx
Jeffrey S. Endick
Marc H. Rifkind
Sharon McNeilly Goodman
Allison A. Madan

Lynn A. Bowers
Elizabeth M. Dalzell
Jennifer C. Holmes
Sandra Mazliah
John M. McIntire
Colleen R. Robertson
Malcolm C. Slee (Not admitted in DC)
Laura Barton Stack

For full biographical listings, see the Martindale-Hubbell Law Directory

---

VENABLE ATTORNEYS AT LAW VENABLE, BAETJER, HOWARD & CIVILETTI, LLP (AV)

A Partnership including Professional Corporations
Suite 1000, 1201 New York Avenue, N.W., 20005
Telephone: 202-962-4800
Fax: 202-962-8300
URL: http://www.venable.com
Baltimore, Maryland Office: Venable, Baetjer and Howard LLP, 1800 Mercantile Bank & Trust Building, 2 Hopkins Plaza.
Telephone: 410-244-7400.
Fax: 410-244-7742.
McLean, Virginia Office: Venable, Baetjer and Howard LLP, Suite 400, 2010 Corporate Ridge.
Telephone: 703-760-1600.
Fax: 703-821-8949.
Rockville, Maryland Office: Venable, Baetjer and Howard LLP, Suite 500, One Church Street, P. O. Box 1906.
Telephone: 301-217-5600.
Fax: 301-217-5617.
Towson, Maryland Office: Venable, Baetjer and Howard LLP, 210 Allegheny Avenue, P. O. Box 5517.
Telephone: 410-494-6200.
Fax: 410-821-0147.

MEMBERS OF FIRM

Maurice Baskin
George F. Pappas (Also at Baltimore, Maryland Office)

For Complete List of Firm Personnel, See General Section

For full biographical listings, see the Martindale-Hubbell Law Directory

---

FLORIDA

*MIAMI,** Dade Co.

CLARKE SILVERGLATE WILLIAMS & MONTGOMERY (AV)

A Partnership of Professional Corporations
100 North Biscayne Boulevard Suite 2401, 33132
Telephone: 305-377-0700
Facsimile: 305-377-3001
Chicago, Illinois Office: Williams & Montgomery Ltd., 20 North Wacker Drive, Suite 2100.
Telephone: 312-443-3200.
Telex: 206598.
Facsimile: 312-443-1323.
Waukegan, Illinois Office: Williams & Montgomery Ltd., 20 S. Utica.
Telephone: 847-360-1220.
Wheaton, Illinois Office: Williams & Montgomery Ltd., 310 S. County Farm Road.
Telephone: 630-690-3200.
Joliet, Illinois Office: Williams & Montgomery Ltd., 81 North Chicago Avenue.
Telephone: 815-727-2653.

Mercer K. Clarke
Spencer H. Silverglate

OF COUNSEL

Henry H. Bolz, III

ASSOCIATES

Kelly Anne Luther
Richard R. Cochran
William J. Dimmig
Cynthia R. Bernard
Spencer T. Kuvin
Francisco Ramos, Jr.
Edward J. Pfister
John C. Schlesinger

For full biographical listings, see the Martindale-Hubbell Law Directory

GEORGIA

*ATLANTA,** Fulton Co.

Elarbee, Thompson & Trapnell, LLP (AV)

800 International Tower, 229 Peachtree Street, N.E., 30303
Telephone: 404-659-6700
Fax: 404-222-9718
Email: info@elarbeethompson.com *URL:* http://www.elarbeethompson.com

MEMBERS OF FIRM

Fred W. Elarbee, Jr. (1925-1986)
Robert L. Thompson
John R. Trapnell
David M. Vaughan
John Lewis Sapp
William M. Earnest
Walter O. Lambeth, Jr.
Joseph M. Freeman
Stanford G. Wilson
Brent L. Wilson
Victor A. Cavanaugh
Nancy F. Reynolds
Sharon Parker Morgan
Mark D. Halverson
R. Read Gignilliat
Douglas H. Duerr
Victor J. Maya
William Drummond Deveney
Kelly Michael Hundley

ASSOCIATES

Patrick L. Lail
Kenneth N. Winkler
Laura K. Johnson
G. Cornelius Nevitt
Scott E. Atwood
Alisa L. Pittman
Richard M. Escoffery
C. Shawn Jones
Jeffrey B. Kent
Lance P. McMillian
Annette A. Idalski
Nicole A. Richardson

Representative Clients: Cox Communications, Inc.; Dunlop Tire Corp.; National Service Industries; Atlanta Gas Light Co.; Brown & Williamson Tobacco Corp.; Engelhard Corp.; Louisiana-Pacific Corp.; MCI WorldCom; Florida Power and Light Co.; Southwire Co.

For full biographical listings, see the Martindale-Hubbell Law Directory

Fisher & Phillips LLP (AV)

A Limited Liability Partnership including Professional Corporations and Professional Associations
1500 Resurgens Plaza, 945 East Paces Ferry Road, N.E., 30326
Telephone: 404-231-1400
Telecopier: 404-240-4249
Email: fp@laborlawyers.com *URL:* http://www.laborlawyers.com
Fort Lauderdale, Florida Office: Suite 2300 NationsBank Tower, One Financial Plaza, 33394.
Telephone: 954-525-4800.
Telecopier: 954-525-8739.
Redwood City, California Office: Suite 345, Three Lagoon Drive, 94065.
Telephone: 650-592-6160.
Telecopier: 650-592-6385.
Newport Beach, California Office: 4675 MacArthur Court, Suite 550, 92660.
Telephone: 949-851-2424.
Telecopier: 949-851-0152.
New Orleans, Louisiana Office: 201 St. Charles Avenue, Suite 3710, 70170.
Telephone: 504-522-3303.
Telecopier: 504-529-3850.
Houston, Texas Office: 6850 Chase Tower, 600 Travis, 77002.
Telephone: 713-227-5410.
Telecopier: 713-236-6949.
Chicago, Illinois Office: 420 Marquette Building, 140 South Dearborn Street, 60603.
Telephone: 312-346-8061.
Telecopier: 312-346-3179.

MEMBERS OF FIRM

Robert C. Christenson
Sandra Mills Feingerts (Resident Partner, New Orleans, Louisiana Office)
Paul T. Ryan

OF COUNSEL

Susan Whittington Leidner (Resident, New Orleans, Louisiana Office)

ASSOCIATES

Carlton C. Pilger
Debbie A. Dickinson
Daniel G. Taylor
Sheldon J. Blumling

Representative Clients: Arvida/JMB Partners; Atlantic Gulf Communities Corp.; Eastern Asiatic Corp.; The Flagler System, Inc.; Hyatt Corp.; Johnstown America Corp.; Pneumo Abex Corp.

For full biographical listings, see the Martindale-Hubbell Law Directory

Long Aldridge & Norman LLP (AV)

A Limited Liability Partnership including Professional Corporations
Suite 5300, 303 Peachtree Street, 30308
Telephone: 404-527-4000
Telecopier: 404-527-4198
Email: atlanta@lanlaw.com *URL:* http://www.lanlaw.com
Washington, D.C. Office: Suite 600, 701 Pennsylvania Avenue, N.W., 20004.
Telephone: 202-624-1200.
FAX: 202-624-1298.

MEMBER OF FIRM

Patricia E. Tate

ASSOCIATE

Sheridan Bracken Johnson

For Complete List of Firm Personnel, See General Section

For full biographical listings, see the Martindale-Hubbell Law Directory

*COLUMBUS,** Muscogee Co.

Hatcher, Stubbs, Land, Hollis & Rothschild (AV)

A Limited Liability Partnership
Suite 500 The Corporate Center, 233 12th Street, P.O. Box 2707, 31902-2707
Telephone: 706-324-0201
Telecopier: 706-322-7747
Email: mailman@hatcherstubbs.com

MEMBERS OF FIRM

Morton A. Harris
Charles T. Staples
James E. Humes, II
Alan F. Rothschild, Jr.

ASSOCIATE

Bradley R. Coppedge

General Counsel for: SunTrust Bank, West Georgia, N.A.; TOM'S Foods Inc.; Muscogee County Board of Education; St. Francis Hospital, Inc.; Georgia Crown Distributing Co.

For Complete List of Firm Personnel, See General Section

For full biographical listings, see the Martindale-Hubbell Law Directory

HAWAII

*HONOLULU,** Honolulu Co.

Carlsmith Ball (AV)

A Partnership including Law Corporations
Suite 2200, Pacific Tower, 1001 Bishop Street, P.O. Box 656, 96809-3402
Telephone: 808-523-2500
Fax: 808-523-0842
Email: execdirector@carlsmith.com *URL:* http://www.carlsmith.com
Kapolei, Hawaii Office: Suite 318, Kapolei Building, 1001 Kamokila Boulevard, 96707.
Telephone: 808-523-2500.
Fax: 808-674-0850.
Wailuku, Maui Hawaii Office: Suite 400, One Main Plaza, 2200 Main Street, P.O. Box 1086, 96793-1086.
Telephone: 808-242-4535.
Fax: 808-244-4974.
Kailua-Kona, Hawaii Office: Suite 209, 75-1000 Henry Street, 96740.
Telephone: 808-329-6464.
Fax: 808-329-9450.
Hilo, Hawaii Office: 121 Waianuenue Avenue, P.O. Box 686, 96721-0686.
Telephone: 808-935-6644.
Fax: 808-935-7975.
Hagatna, Guam Office: Suite 401, Bank of Hawaii Building, 134 West Soledad Avenue, P.O. Box BF, 96932-5027.
Telephone: 671-472-6813.
Fax: 671-477-4375.
Telex: 721-6445 CWCMI GM.
Saipan, Commonwealth of the Northern Mariana Islands Office: Carlsmith Building, Capitol Hill, P.O. Box 5241, 96950-5241.
Telephone: 670-322-3455.
Fax: 670-322-3368.
Los Angeles, California Office: 9th Floor, 444 South Flower Street, 90071-2901.
Telephone: 213-955-1200.
Fax: 213-623-0032.
Washington, D.C. Office: Suite 300, 1201 Pennsylvania Avenue, N.W., 20004-2401.
Telephone: 202-628-2228.
Fax: 202-628-2071.
Mexico City, Mexico Office: Carlsmith Ball, Sierra Nevada 119, Lomas de Chapultepec, 11000 Mexico, D.F.
Telephone: 52-5-520-8514, 52-5-520-8757.
Fax: 52-5-540-1545.

(See Next Column)

CARLSMITH BALL—*Continued*

Mexico, D.F. Office of Carlsmith Ball, S.C. (Authorized to practice as foreign legal consultants in Mexico): Sierra Nevada 119, Lomas de Chapultepec, 11000 Mexico, D.F.
Telephone: 52-5-520-8514, 52-5-520-8757.
Fax: 52-5-540-1545.

MEMBERS OF FIRM

Anna M. Elento-Sneed
John C. Khil
Harry Y. Oda
James L. Starshak

ASSOCIATE

Joanne L. Grimes

OF COUNSEL

Lorraine S. Klevansky

For Complete List of Firm Personnel, See General Section

For full biographical listings, see the Martindale-Hubbell Law Directory

TAM, O'CONNOR, HENDERSON, TAIRA & YAMAUCHI ATTORNEYS AT LAW, A LAW CORPORATION (AV)

20th Floor, Central Pacific Plaza, 220 South King Street, 96813
Telephone: 808-545-3030
Fax: 808-523-8051
Fax: 808-537-6782
Email: lawyers@50thstatelaw.com

James K. Tam
Michael F. O'Connor
Harvey E. Henderson, Jr.
Lissa H. Andrews
Robert M. Yamauchi
Darryl M. Taira
Stuart M. Kodish

Wesley H. Ikeda
Russ S. Awakuni
Kevin W. Herring
Fred I. Waki

OF COUNSEL

Paul M. Dold

For full biographical listings, see the Martindale-Hubbell Law Directory

ILLINOIS

*CHICAGO,** Cook Co.

FRANCZEK SULLIVAN P.C. (AV)

Suite 3400, 300 South Wacker Drive, 60606-6785
Telephone: 312-986-0300
FAX: 312-986-9192
URL: http://www.nlfpc.com

Anthony J. Crement
J. Todd Faulkner
James C. Franczek, Jr.
Ronald J. Hein, Jr.
Lisa A. Lopatka
Bruce C. Mackey
Robert E. Mann
Paul A. Millichap
David P. Radelet
John A. Relias
Michael I. Richardson
Charles P. Rose
Sally J. Scott
William R. Sullivan, Jr.
Andrea R. Waintroob
Patricia J. Whitten
James J. Zuehl

Shelli L. Boyer
Sheila M. Conroy
Terrence T. Creamer
Erika Dillon
Edward N. Druck
Gregory D. Isbell
Thomas Koutsouvas
Darcy L. Kriha
Jeffrey M. Kropp
Jeremy C. Moritz
Alec Rubenstein
Leah D. Gidron
Jennifer L. Schilling
Michael A. Warner, Jr.
Anne Elizabeth Wilson

OF COUNSEL

Michael Z. Green
Wesley A. Wildman
John L. Wren

LEGAL SUPPORT PERSONNEL

Caty E. Kearney

For full biographical listings, see the Martindale-Hubbell Law Directory

HOWARD GORDON KAPLAN, LTD. (AV)

180 North La Salle Street, 28th Floor, 60601
Telephone: 312-641-2555
Facsimile No.: 312-641-6265
Email: howie641@aol.com

Howard Gordon Kaplan
Leonard J. Brenner
Rhonda D. Kaplan-Katz

For full biographical listings, see the Martindale-Hubbell Law Directory

LANER, MUCHIN, DOMBROW, BECKER, LEVIN AND TOMINBERG, LTD. (AV)

515 North State Street, Suite 2800, 60610
Telephone: 312-467-9800
Fax: 312-467-9479

Lawrence F. Doppelt (1935-1979)
Arthur B. Muchin
Anthony E. Dombrow
William L. Becker
Alan M. Levin
Carl S. Tominberg
Mark L. Juster
Gary Alan Wincek
Michael Klupchak
Joseph H. Yastrow
Joseph M. Gagliardo
Robert H. Brown
James J. Convery
Robert S. Letchinger
Violet M. Clark
James F. Vanek
Jeffrey P. Carren
Jane E. Shaffer
Jill P. O'Brien
Neil P. Stern
Thomas Vasiljevich
Thomas Bradley
Scott A. Gore
Jeffrey S. Fowler
Maureen A. Gorman
Clifford R. Perry, III

Mark W. Bennett
Robert T. Bernstein
Alejandro Caffarelli
Deborah Glaser Chagal
Robert S. Forman
Andrew S. Goldberg
Gregory R. James, Jr.
Jennifer A. Naber
Katherine O. Porter
Marc J. Siegel

OF COUNSEL

Isaiah S. Dorfman
Herman J. De Koven
Seymour Cohen
Richard W. Laner

References: NBD Bank Chicago; Illinois; La Salle National Bank & Trust Co.

For full biographical listings, see the Martindale-Hubbell Law Directory

MCBRIDE BAKER & COLES (AV)

500 West Madison Street 40th Floor, 60661-2511
Telephone: 312-715-5700
Cable Address: "Chilaw"
Telex: 270258
Telecopier: 312-993-9350
Email: lastname@mbc.com *URL:* http://www.mbc.com
Oakbrook Terrace, Illinois Office: Suite 1000, One Mid America Plaza, 60181-4710.
Telephone: 630-954-2100.
Telecopier: 630-954-2112.

MEMBERS OF FIRM

David Ackerman
Martin J. Campanella
Kenneth A. Jenero
Thomas J. Kinasz
Patrick W. Kocian
Steven R. Lifson
Anne Hamblin Schiave

OF COUNSEL

William J. Cooney

ASSOCIATES

Brian D. Hector
Jonathan E. Strouse

For Complete List of Firm Personnel, See General Section

For full biographical listings, see the Martindale-Hubbell Law Directory

NISEN & ELLIOTT (AV)

200 West Adams Street, Suite 2500, 60606
Telephone: 312-346-7800
Telecopier: 312-346-9316

MEMBERS OF FIRM

Paul F. Gerbosi
Edward B. Mueller
Anthony Packard
Mark F. Zaenger
Michael J. Daley
John Foster Lesch
John K. Kneafsey
Michael H. Moirano
Robert O. Middleton
William G. Daluga, Jr.
Kenneth J. Rojc
Thomas V. McCauley
Helen M. Jensen
William A. Walker
Daniel P. Dawson
Michael J. Pavlicek

Robert Christie
Donald F. Froehlke
Thomas K. Juffernbruch
Brendan J. Kelly
Brian C. Kelly
Mary Rose C. Manczak
Bradley S. McCann
Brian D. Proctor

OF COUNSEL

Charles M. Nisen
Donald C. Shine

For full biographical listings, see the Martindale-Hubbell Law Directory

Chicago—Continued

SCARIANO, ELLCH, HIMES, SRAGA AND PETRARCA, CHARTERED (AV)

Two Prudential Plaza 180 North Stetson Suite 3100, 60601-6224
Telephone: 312-565-3100
Facsimile: 312-565-0000
Chicago Heights, Illinois Office: 1450 Aberdeen, 60411.
Telephone: 708-755-1900.
Facsimile: 708-755-0000.

Anthony G. Scariano
Robert H. Ellch
A. Lynn Himes
Alan T. Sraga
Justino D. Petrarca
Lawrence Jay Weiner
John M. Izzo
Raymond A. Hauser
Kathleen Roche Hirsman
Daniel M. Boyle
Teri E. Engler
Rosanne Ciambrone

Kelly A. Hayden
Todd K. Hayden
Christopher L. Petrarca
Sarah E. Joyce
Joel R. DeTella
Susan H. Walter (Resident)
Brian J. Fahey
David A. Harley
Bradley C. Coleman
Christina Sepiol
Alan M. Mullins
John E. Fester
Michael Alan DeBartolo

OF COUNSEL

John Kralovec

For full biographical listings, see the Martindale-Hubbell Law Directory

INDIANA

*INDIANAPOLIS,** Marion Co.

ICE MILLER DONADIO & RYAN (AV)

One American Square Box 82001, 46282-0002
Telephone: 317-236-2100
Fax: 317-236-2219
Email: info@imdr.com *URL:* http://www.imdr.com
South Bend, Indiana Office: 211 West Washington Street, Suite 2420.
Telephone: 219-234-7933.
Fax: 219-234-7965. Internet E-mail: info@imdr.com. Web Site Address: http://www.imdr.com.
Chicago, Illinois Office: 135 South LaSalle Street, Suite 4100.
Telephone: 312-726-1567.
Fax: 312-641-6263. Internet E-mail: info@imdr.com. Web Site Address: http://www.imdr.com.

MEMBERS OF FIRM

James D. Kemper
Terry A. M. Mumford
Michael H. Boldt
Gary J. Dankert
E. Van Olson
Marc W. Sciscoe
Mary Beth Braitman
Melissa Proffitt Reese

OF COUNSEL

Catherine R. Reese
Stephanie Alden Smithey

ASSOCIATES

Craig C. Burke
Tara L. Schulstad
Yeiena Fertman
Michael Griffin
Kathleen Marie Sheil Scheidt

For Complete List of Firm Personnel, See General Section

For full biographical listings, see the Martindale-Hubbell Law Directory

*LAFAYETTE,** Tippecanoe Co.

STUART & BRANIGIN (AV)

The Life Building, 300 Main Street, Suite 800, P.O. Box 1010, 47902-1010
Telephone: 765-423-1561
Telecopier: 765-742-8175
Email: sb@stuartlaw.com *URL:* http://www.stuartlaw.com
Indianapolis, Indiana Office: Suite 1401, 8888 Keystone Crossing, 46240.
Telephone: 317-574-7245.
Fax: 317-574-7050.

MEMBERS OF FIRM

Allison Ellsworth Stuart (1886-1950)
Roger D. Branigin (1902-1975)
Roger D. Branigin, Jr.
Thomas L. Ryan
Thomas R. McCully
Larry R. Fisher
Nina B. Kirkpatrick
Mark Lillianfeld
Stephen R. Pennell
Anthony S. Benton
Erik D. Spykman
William E. Emerick
John C. Duffey
Bruce McSpadden
Mark E. DeYoung

(See Next Column)

Thomas B. Parent
Laura L. Bowker
Kevin D. Nicoson
Susan K. Roberts
John M. Stuckey
Deborah B. Trice
William P. Kealey
David A. Starkweather
Geoffrey L. Blazi

SENIOR COUNSEL

Russell H. Hart

COUNSEL

John F. Bodle
James V. McGlone

ASSOCIATES

Elizabeth B. Searle
Marianne Mitten Owen
David A. Locke
Karen Orr McClure
Ann Marie Waldron
Barry L. Loftus

General Counsel for: The Lafayette Life Insurance Co.; INB National Bank, N.W.; Lafayette Home Hospital, Inc.

State Counsel for: Norfolk & Western Railway Co.

Mr. Ryan is Counsel to: The Trustees of Purdue University.

Representative Clients: Aluminum Company of America; Liberty Mutual Insurance Group.

For full biographical listings, see the Martindale-Hubbell Law Directory

*VALPARAISO,** Porter Co.

HOEPPNER WAGNER & EVANS LLP (AV)

103 East Lincolnway, P.O. Box 2357, 46384-2357
Telephone: 219-464-4961; 800-879-2246 (IN, IL)
Fax: 219-465-0603
Email: hwe@hwelaw.com *URL:* http://www.hwelaw.com
Merrillville, Indiana Office: Twin Towers, Suite 606 South, 1000 East 80th Place, P.O. Box 10627, 46419-0627.
Telephone: 219-769-6552; 800-263-1466 (IN, IL).
Fax: 219-738-2349. Email: hwe@hwelaw.com

MEMBERS OF FIRM

John E. Hughes (Resident, Merrillville Office)
James L. Jorgensen
F. Joseph Jaskowiak (Resident, Merrillville Office)
Mark E. Schmidtke

ASSOCIATES

Lauren K. Kroeger
Tina M. Bengs

Representative Clients: American Family Insurance Group; Bank One; Bethlehem Steel Corp.; CNA Insurance Co.; National Steel Corp.; Okaya Electric America, Inc.; State Farm Insurance Cos.; Toys R Us Corp.; Valparaiso University; Whiteco Industries, Inc.

For Complete List of Firm Personnel, See General Section

For full biographical listings, see the Martindale-Hubbell Law Directory

IOWA

*DES MOINES,** Polk Co.

FINLEY, ALT, SMITH, SCHARNBERG, CRAIG, HILMES & GAFFNEY, P.C. (AV)

604 Locust Street, Fourth Floor Equitable Building, 50309
Telephone: 515-288-0145
Telecopier: 515-288-2724

David C. Craig

Representative Clients: ALAS; American Society of Composers, Authors and Publishers; Equitable Life Assurance Society of the U.S.; Federated Insurance Co.; Meredith Corp.
Iowa Attorneys for: Midwest Medical Insurance Co.
District Attorneys for: Norfolk & Southern Railroad; Soo Line Railroad Company.

For Complete List of Firm Personnel, See General Section

For full biographical listings, see the Martindale-Hubbell Law Directory

KANSAS

*HUTCHINSON,** Reno Co.

Gilliland & Hayes, P.A. A Professional Association (AV)

20 West 2nd Avenue, 2nd Floor, P.O. Box 2977, 67504-2977
Telephone: 316-662-0537
Facsimile: 316-669-9426
URL: http://www.gillilandhayes.com
Wichita, Kansas Office: The Orpheum Centre, Suite 300, 200 North Broadway, P.O. Box 49406.
Telephone: 316-262-2266.
Facsimile: 316-263-2202.
Kansas City, Missouri Office: 12th Floor, 3100 Broadway.
Telephone: 816-753-3100.
Facsimile: 816-753-2271.

Robert J. Gilliland
John F. Hayes
James R. Gilliland
John S. Schmidt
Bruce B. Waugh (Not admitted in KS; Resident, Kansas City, Missouri Office)
Michael R. O'Neal
Bradley D. Dillon
Gerald L. Green
David N. Zimmerman (Not admitted in KS; Resident, Kansas City, Missouri Office)
Scott J. Mann
Carol Z. Smith (Resident, Kansas City, Missouri Office)
Kathleen A. Hardee (Resident, Kansas City, Missouri Office)
Kendall R. Cunningham (Resident, Wichita Office)
Mark R. Maloney (Resident, Wichita Office)

Thomas A. Dower
Tracy Applegate Cole
Laura A. Hederstedt
Terri Roberts Munsell (Resident, Kansas City, Missouri Office)
Lisa M. Ward
Kimberly Breda Bushek (Resident, Kansas City, Missouri Office)
E. Thomas Pyle, III
Tara L. Bragg

OF COUNSEL

Robert P. Reams (Not admitted in KS; Resident, Kansas City, Missouri Office)

Representative Clients: CNA Insurance; Dillon Companies; Fidelity Deposit Co. of Maryland; Hutchinson Clinic; Hutchinson Hospital Corp.; Central Bank & Trust; Collins Industries; Kansas City Poster Display Company; Sirloin Stockade International; TSW Products.

For full biographical listings, see the Martindale-Hubbell Law Directory

*TOPEKA,** Shawnee Co.

Foulston & Siefkin L.L.P. (AV)

1515 NationsBank Tower, 534 Kansas Avenue, 66603
Telephone: 785-233-3600
Fax: 785-233-1610
URL: http://www.foulston.com
Wichita, Kansas Office: 100 North Broadway, 700 NationsBank Financial Center, 67202.
Telephone: 316-267-6371.
Fax: 316-267-6345.
Dodge City, Kansas Office: 810 Frontview, P.O. Box 1147, 67801.
Telephone: 316-227-8126.
Fax: 316-227-8451.
Member: Lex Mundi, The World's Leading Association of Independent Law Firms.

MEMBER OF FIRM

James P. Rankin

For full biographical listings, see the Martindale-Hubbell Law Directory

*WICHITA,** Sedgwick Co.

Foulston & Siefkin L.L.P. (AV)

700 NationsBank Financial Center, 67202
Telephone: 316-267-6371
Facsimile: 316-267-6345
URL: http://www.foulston.com
Topeka, Kansas Office: 1515 NationsBank Tower, 534 Kansas Avenue, 66603.
Telephone: 785-233-3600.
Fax: 785-233-1610.
Dodge City, Kansas Office: 810 Frontview, P.O. Box 1147, 67801.
Telephone: 316-227-8126.
Fax: 316-227-8451.
Member: Lex Mundi, The World's Leading Association of Independent Law Firms.

MEMBERS OF FIRM

James P. Rankin (Resident, Topeka Office)
Douglas L. Hanisch
Kevin J. Arnel
Jay M. Rector

(See Next Column)

For Complete List of Firm Personnel, See General Section

For full biographical listings, see the Martindale-Hubbell Law Directory

KENTUCKY

*LEXINGTON,** Fayette Co.

Stoll, Keenon & Park, LLP (AV)

201 E. Main Street, Suite 1000, 40507-1380
Telephone: 606-231-3000
Telecopier: 606-253-1093; 606-253-1027
URL: http://www.skp.com
Frankfort, Kentucky Office: 307 Washington Street, 40601.
Telephone: 502-875-6220.
Telecopier: 502-875-6235.
Henderson, Kentucky Office: 201 C North Main Street, 42420-3103.
Telephone: 270-831-1900.
Telecopier: 270-827-4060.
Louisville, Kentucky Office: 400 West Market Street, Suite 2650, 40202-3377.
Telephone: 502-568-9100.
Telecopier: 502-568-5700.

MEMBER OF FIRM

C. Joseph Beavin

ASSOCIATE

Lindsey W. Ingram, III

Representative Clients: Lexmark International, Inc.; Bank One, Lexington, NA; Farmers Capital Bank Corp.; International Business Machines Corp.; Keeneland Association; ATR Wire & Cable; Matsushita Home Appliance Corporation; Link-Belt Construction Equipment Co.; Whitaker Bank Corporation of Kentucky; VicWest Steel.

For Complete List of Firm Personnel, See General Section

For full biographical listings, see the Martindale-Hubbell Law Directory

LOUISIANA

*NEW ORLEANS,** Orleans Parish

McGlinchey Stafford (AV)

A Professional Limited Liability Company
643 Magazine Street, 70130-3477
Telephone: 504-586-1200
Fax: 504-596-2800
TDD: (504) 596-2728
Telex: 584327
Cable Address: "MACSTAC"
Mailing Address: P.O. Box 60643, New Orleans, Louisiana, 70160-0643
Email: @mcglinchey.com *URL:* http://www.mcglinchey.com
Dallas, Texas Office: 2777 Stemmons Freeway, Suite 925, 75207-2401.
Telephone: 214-860-9700.
Fax: 214-860-9750.
Houston, Texas Office: 2727 Allen Parkway, Suite 1900, 77019.
Telephone: 713-520-1900.
Fax: 713-520-1025.
Baton Rouge, Louisiana Office: Ninth Floor, One American Place, 70825-0001.
Telephone: 504-383-9000.
Fax: 504-343-3076.
Jackson, Mississippi Office: Suite 1200, SkyTel Centre, 200 South Lamar Street, 39201.
Telephone: 601-960-8400.
Fax: 601-960-8406.
Lake Providence, Louisiana Office: 405 Morgan Street, 71254-2691.
Telephone: 318-559-1200.
Fax: 318-559-0609.
Monroe, Louisiana Office: Dean ONB Tower, 130 Desiard Street, Suite 807, 71201.
Telephone: 318-651-0807.
Fax: 318-651-0809.

MEMBER OF FIRM

Katherine Conklin

MEMBER OF FIRM

Mark A. Sanders (Resident, Houston Office)

For full biographical listings, see the Martindale-Hubbell Law Directory

MAINE

*PORTLAND,** Cumberland Co.

BENNETT BENNETT AND TROIANO, P.A. (AV)

Suite 300, 121 Middle Street, P.O. Box 7799, 04112-7799
Telephone: 207-773-4775
Telecopier: 207-774-2366
Email: lawyers@bennettlegal.com *URL:* http://www.bennettlegal.com

Herbert H. Bennett (1928-1992)
Peter Bennett
Jeffrey Bennett
Joseph A. Troiano
Frederick B. Finberg

Julie A. Boesky

OF COUNSEL

Jonathan M. Dunitz

Counsel for: Associated Grocers of New England; General Star Indemnity Company; Coca Cola Bottling Company of Northern New England, Inc.; Northern Utilities/Bay State Gas; Pratt & Whitney (Division of United Technologies); Primerica Financial Services (Citigroup); Sprague Energy (C.H. Sprague & Son); Perrier Group of America, Inc.; Lepage Bakeries, Inc. (Country Kitchen); Texaco, Inc.

For full biographical listings, see the Martindale-Hubbell Law Directory

VERRILL & DANA, LLP (AV)

One Portland Square, P.O. Box 586, 04112-0586
Telephone: 207-774-4000
Fax: 207-774-7499
Email: advice@verdan.com *URL:* http://www.verdan.com
Augusta, Maine Office: 45 Memorial Circle, P.O. Box 957.
Telephone: 207-623-3889.
Fax: 207-622-3117.
Kennebunk, Maine Office: 403-404 Lafayette Center, P.O. Box 147.
Telephone: 207-985-7193.
Fax: 207-985-3957.
Washington, D.C. Office: 400 North Capitol Street, Suite 585.
Telephone: 202-624-9733.
Fax: 202-393-5218.

MEMBERS OF FIRM

Gregg H. Ginn
Kimberly S. Couch
Lisa S. Boehm
Suzanne E. Meeker
Eric D. Altholz

ASSOCIATES

Kevin G. Anderson
Kenneth F. Ginder

Counsel for: ASCAP; Bowdoin College; Fleet Bank; Hannaford Bros. Co.; Maine Blue Cross and Blue Shield; Maine Public Service Co.; Peoples Heritage Bank; Portland Water District.

For Complete List of Firm Personnel, See General Section

For full biographical listings, see the Martindale-Hubbell Law Directory

SOUTH PORTLAND, Cumberland Co.

VAN MEER & BELANGER, P.A. (AV)

25 Long Creek Drive, 04106
Telephone: 207-871-7500
Fax: 207-871-7505
Email: VBLAW@GWI.NET

Thomas J. Van Meer
Norman R. Belanger
D. Kelley Young
Richard N. Bryant

Betts J. Gorsky
Mary McQuillen

For full biographical listings, see the Martindale-Hubbell Law Directory

MARYLAND

*BALTIMORE,** (Independent City)

REDMOND, BURGIN & GUTIERREZ, P.A. (AV)

1301, The Fidelity Building, 210 North Charles Street, 21202
Telephone: 410-752-1555
Fax: 410-752-1064
URL: http://www.RBGLAW.com
Upper Marlboro, Maryland Office: 14746 Main Street.
Telephone: 301-952-1555.

Harold L. Burgin

(See Next Column)

Mark B. Martin

For Complete List of Firm Personnel, See General Section

For full biographical listings, see the Martindale-Hubbell Law Directory

VENABLE ATTORNEYS AT LAW VENABLE, BAETJER AND HOWARD, LLP (AV)

A Partnership including Professional Corporations
1800 Mercantile Bank & Trust Building, 2 Hopkins Plaza, 21201
Telephone: 410-244-7400
Fax: 410-244-7742
URL: http://www.venable.com
Washington, D.C. Office: Venable, Baetjer, Howard & Civiletti LLP, Suite 1000, 1201 New York Avenue, N.W.
Telephone: 202-962-4800.
Fax: 202-962-8300.
McLean, Virginia Office: Suite 400, 2010 Corporate Ridge.
Telephone: 703-760-1600.
Fax: 703-821-8949.
Rockville, Maryland Office: Suite 500, One Church Street, P. O. Box 1906.
Telephone: 301-217-5600.
Fax: 301-217-5617.
Towson, Maryland Office: 210 Allegheny Avenue, P. O. Box 5517.
Telephone: 410-494-6200.
Fax: 410-821-0147.

MEMBERS OF FIRM

Barbara E. Schlaff
G. Stewart Webb, Jr.
Jana Howard Carey (P.C.)
George F. Pappas (Also at Washington, D.C. Office)
Jeffrey P. Ayres (P.C.)
Kenneth R. Hoffman (Also at Washington, D.C. Office)
Maurice Baskin (Resident, Washington, D.C. Office)
James A. Dunbar (Resident, Towson, Maryland Office)
Robert L. Waldman
John A. Wilhelm (Not admitted in MD; Resident, McLean, Virginia Office)
Michael W. Robinson (Resident, McLean, Virginia Office)
Todd J. Horn
John A. McCauley

OF COUNSEL

A. Samuel Cook (P.C.) (Resident, Towson, Maryland Office)

ASSOCIATES

Louis B. Barr
Thora A. Johnson

For Complete List of Firm Personnel, See General Section

For full biographical listings, see the Martindale-Hubbell Law Directory

MASSACHUSETTS

*BOSTON,** Suffolk Co.

HINCKLEY, ALLEN & SNYDER LLP (AV)

28 State Street, 30th Floor, 02109-1775
Telephone: 617-345-9000
Email: firm@haslaw.com *URL:* http://www.haslaw.com
Providence, Rhode Island Office: 1500 Fleet Center.
Telephone: 401-274-2000.
Fax: 401-277-9600. URL: http://www.hawlaw.com.

MEMBERS OF FIRM

David D. Barricelli (Not admitted in MA)
Jonathan Bell
Paul Bork
Stephen J. Carlotti (Not admitted in MA)
Michael P. DeFanti
Eric F. Eisenberg
Malcolm Farmer, III
William R. Grimm
Richard L. E. Jocelyn (Not admitted in MA)
Michael J. Kelly
Frederick P. McClure
Elizabeth Murdock Myers
H. Peter Olsen (Not admitted in MA)
Julianne Palumbo
John J. Pendergast, III (Not admitted in MA)
Charles E. Schaub, Jr.
Douglas F. Seaver
David R. Sullivan
Robert F. Sylvia
Howard E. Walker (Not admitted in MA)
Richard D. Wayne

ASSOCIATES

Mark Bianchi
Kelley Jordan-Price
Catherine S. Kim
Christopher W. Morog
Elena B. Olson
Joseph D. Whelan (Not admitted in MA)

OF COUNSEL

Willard Krasnow

For Complete List of Firm Personnel, See General Section

For full biographical listings, see the Martindale-Hubbell Law Directory

Boston—Continued

PALMER & DODGE LLP (AV)

One Beacon Street, 02108
Telephone: 617-573-0100
Facsimile: 617-227-4420
URL: http://www.palmerdodge.com

MEMBER OF FIRM

Malcolm E. Hindin

For Complete List of Firm Personnel, See General Section

For full biographical listings, see the Martindale-Hubbell Law Directory

*SPRINGFIELD,** Hampden Co.

SKOLER, ABBOTT & PRESSER, P.C. (AV)

Suite 2000, One Monarch Place, 01144
Telephone: 413-737-4753
Fax: 413-787-1941
Email: SAP@skoler-abbott.com
Worcester, Massachusetts Office: 30 Park Avenue.
Telephone: 508-757-5335.

Martin E. Skoler (1932-1991)
Jay M. Presser
Ralph F. Abbott, Jr.
John H. Glenn
Rosemary J. Nevins

Richard U. Stubbs, Jr.
Marylou Fabbo
Jo-Ann W. Davis

OF COUNSEL

Martin Fleisher

Representative Clients: Baystate Medical Center; Kanzaki Specialty Papers; Smith & Wesson; Spalding, Division of Questor Corp.

For full biographical listings, see the Martindale-Hubbell Law Directory

*WORCESTER,** Worcester Co.

SKOLER, ABBOTT & PRESSER, P.C. (AV)

30 Park Avenue, 01605
Telephone: 508-757-5335
Email: SAP@skoler-abbott.com
Springfield, Massachusetts Office: Suite 2000, One Monarch Place.
Telephone: 413-737-4753.
Fax: 413-787-1941.

Martin E. Skoler (1932-1991)
Jay M. Presser
Ralph F. Abbott, Jr.
John H. Glenn
Rosemary J. Nevins

Richard U. Stubbs, Jr.
Marylou Fabbo
Jo-Ann W. Davis

OF COUNSEL

Martin Fleisher

Representative Clients: American Optical Co.; Erving Paper Mills; Baystate Medical Center; Smith & Wesson; Spalding, Sports Worldwide; Polar Beverages; Ree & Rolled Trread Co.

For full biographical listings, see the Martindale-Hubbell Law Directory

MICHIGAN

*ANN ARBOR,** Washtenaw Co.

HOOPER, HATHAWAY, PRICE, BEUCHE & WALLACE (AV)

126 South Main Street, 48104
Telephone: 313-662-4426
Fax: 313-662-9559
Email: hhpbw@voyager.net

Bruce T. Wallace
Charles W. Borgsdorf
Susan T. Cannell

Representative Clients: Avfuel Corporation; Bank of Ann Arbor; Castrol North America; Chem-Trend Incorporated; Ervin Industries, Inc.; First Martin Corporation; Glacier Hills, Inc.; Prestolite Electric, Inc.; Southern States Cooperative; E.B. Eddy Forest Products, Ltd.

For Complete List of Firm Personnel, See General Section

For full biographical listings, see the Martindale-Hubbell Law Directory

BATTLE CREEK, Calhoun Co.

KREIS, ENDERLE, CALLANDER & HUDGINS, A PROFESSIONAL CORPORATION (AV)

One West Michigan Avenue, 49017
Telephone: 616-966-3000
Facsimile: 616-966-3022
Email: kech@kech.com *URL:* http://www.kech.com
Kalamazoo, Michigan Office: One Moorsbridge, P.O. Box 4010, 49003-4010.
Telephone: 616-324-3000.
Fax: 616-324-3010.

C. Reid Hudgins III (Resident, Kalamazoo Office)
Matthew S. DePerno (Resident, Kalamazoo Office)
Janice Roark Peters (Resident, Kalamazoo Office)

For Complete List of Firm Personnel, See General Section

For full biographical listings, see the Martindale-Hubbell Law Directory

BLOOMFIELD HILLS, Oakland Co.

PROVIZER & PHILLIPS, P.C. (AV)

6785 Telegraph Road, Suite 400, 48301
Telephone: 248-642-0444
Facsimile: 248-642-6661
Toll Free: 1-800-288-9080
URL: http://www.lawyers.com/provizer&phillips

Harold M. Provizer
Randall E. Phillips
Marilyn A. Madorsky

Ellen C. Busch

For full biographical listings, see the Martindale-Hubbell Law Directory

*DETROIT,** Wayne Co.

ABBOTT, NICHOLSON, QUILTER, ESSHAKI & YOUNGBLOOD, P.C. (AV)

300 River Place, Suite 3000, 48207-4225
Telephone: 313-566-2500
Telecopier: 313-566-2502
Email: anqey@anqey.com *URL:* http://www.anqey.com

C. Richard Abbott
John R. Nicholson
Thomas R. Quilter III
Gene J. Esshaki
John F. Youngblood
James B. Perry
Carl F. Jarboe
Jay A. Kennedy
Timothy A. Stoepker
Timothy J. Kramer
Norbert T. Madison, Jr.
William D. Gilbride, Jr.
Mary P. Nelson
Michael R. Blum
Anne Warren Bagno
Thomas J. Giachino

Eric J. Girdler
Jill A. Bankey
Daniel G. Kielczewski
George P. Butler III
Christopher P. Baker
Faith M. Gaudaen
Susan T. Rapp
Sean A. Fraser
Christopher T. Koch
Scott C. Cadieux (Not admitted in MI)

OF COUNSEL

Thomas C. Shumaker
Lisa R. Gorman

For full biographical listings, see the Martindale-Hubbell Law Directory

BUTZEL LONG, A PROFESSIONAL CORPORATION (AV)

Suite 900, 150 West Jefferson, 48226
Telephone: 313-225-7000
Telecopier: 313-225-7080
Email: melnick@butzel.com *URL:* http://www.butzel.com
Birmingham, Michigan Office: Suite 200, 32270 Telegraph Road.
Telephone: 810-258-1616.
Telecopier: 810-258-1439.
Okemos, Michigan Office: Suite 300, 2127 University Park Drive.
Telephone: 517-372-6622.
Telecopier: 517-372-6672.
Ann Arbor, Michigan Office: Suite 300, 350 South Main Street.
Telephone: 313-995-3110.
Telecopier: 313-995-1777.
Grosse Pointe Farms, Michigan Office: Suite 260, 21 Kercheval.
Telephone: 313-886-5446.
Telecopier: 313-886-2114.
Boca Raton, Florida Office: Suite 411, 1200 North Federal Highway.
Telephone: 561-368-2151.
Telecopier: 561-368-4668.
Palm Beach Gardens, Florida Office: Suite 227, 11382 Prosperity Farms Road.
Telephone: 561-625-4442.
Telecopier: 561-625-6901.

(See Next Column)

BUTZEL LONG A PROFESSIONAL CORPORATION, *Detroit—Continued*

Naples, Florida Office: Suite 705, 801 Laurel Oak Drive.
Telephone: 941-597-4500.
Telecopier: 941-597-5623.

Paul L. Triemstra (Birmingham)
Alexander B. Bragdon
Mark T. Nelson
Michael D. Guzick (Birmingham)
Jordan S. Schreier (Ann Arbor)

Antoinette M. Pilzner

Representative Clients: Central Michigan University; Detroit Diesel Corp.; The Detroit News, Inc.; Kelly Services; Merrill Lynch & Co., Inc.; Mt. Clemens General Hospital; Stroh Companies; Takata Corp.; TRW Automotive; The University of Michigan.

For full biographical listings, see the Martindale-Hubbell Law Directory

CHARFOOS, REITER, PETERSON, HOLMQUIST & PILCHAK, P.C. (AV)

476 State of Michigan Plaza Building, 1200 Sixth Street, 48226
Telephone: 313-961-7011
Email: CRPHP@crphp.com
Farmington Hills, Michigan Office: 30500 Northwestern Highway, Suite 400.
Telephone: 248-626-7300.
Fax: 248-626-7305.

Myron B. Charfoos
James A. Reiter
Daniel Peterson
C. John Holmquist, Jr.
William E. Pilchak
Daniel G. Cohen

Kenneth E. Jones
Deborah S. Dorland
Danial J. Hébert
Robert C. Tice

Nedra D. Campbell

For full biographical listings, see the Martindale-Hubbell Law Directory

JAFFE, RAITT, HEUER & WEISS, PROFESSIONAL CORPORATION (AV)

One Woodward Avenue, Suite 2400, 48226
Telephone: 313-961-8380
Telecopier: 313-961-8358
Cable Address: "Jafsni"
Southfield,Michigan Office: Travelers Tower, Suite 1520.
Telephone: 313-961-8380.

Karen F. R. Grotberg (Not admitted in MI)
Michael A. Rajt
Joseph J. Shannon
Arthur A. Weiss
Thomas H. Williams

Thomas L. Shaevsky

Representative Clients: Masco Tech, Inc.; Sisters of Mercy - Province of Detroit; The Stroh Brewery Company; Unisys Corporation.

For Complete List of Firm Personnel, See General Section

For full biographical listings, see the Martindale-Hubbell Law Directory

KELLER, THOMA, SCHWARZE, SCHWARZE, DUBAY & KATZ, P.C. (AV)

440 East Congress, 5th Floor, 48226
Telephone: 313-965-7610
Fax: 313-965-4480
Bingham Farms, Michigan Office: 30150 Telegraph Road, Suite 444, 48025.
Telephone: 248-642-5218.

Anthony J. Heckemeyer

Counsel for: Livonia Public Schools; Ludington News Co., Inc.
Representative Clients: Borg-Warner Corp.; E & L Transport Co.; The Kroger Co.; Holnam, Inc.
Public Employer Clients: City of Farmington Hills; City of Flint; City of Grosse Pointe Woods; Saginaw Public Schools.

For Complete List of Firm Personnel, See General Section

For full biographical listings, see the Martindale-Hubbell Law Directory

MILLER, CANFIELD, PADDOCK AND STONE, P.L.C. (AV)

A Professional Limited Liability Company
Founded in 1852 by Sidney Davy Miller
150 West Jefferson, Suite 2500, 48226-4415
Telephone: 313-963-6420
Fax: 313-496-7500
Cable Address: "Stem Detroit"
URL: http://www.millercanfield.com
Ann Arbor, Michigan Office: 101 North Main Street, 7th Floor, 48104-1400.
Telephone: 734-663-2445.
Fax: 734-747-7147.

(See Next Column)

Troy, Michigan Office: 840 West Long Lake Road, Suite 200, 48098.
Telephone: 248-879-2000.
Fax: 248-879-2001.
Grand Rapids, Michigan Office: 99 Monroe, N.W., Suite 1200, 49503-2639.
Telephone: 616-454-8656.
Fax: 616-776-6322.
Howell, Michigan Office: 121 South Barnard Street, Suite 4, 48843-2305.
Telephone: 517-546-7600.
Telecopier: 517-546-6974.
Kalamazoo, Michigan Office: 444 West Michigan Avenue, 49007-3752.
Telephone: 616-381-7030.
Fax: 616-382-0244.
Lansing, Michigan Office: One Michigan Avenue, Suite 900, 48933-1609.
Telephone: 517-487-2070.
Fax: 517-374-6304.
Monroe, Michigan Office: 214 East Elm Avenue, Suite 100, 48162-2682.
Telephone: 734-243-2000.
Fax: 734-243-0901.
Washington, D.C. Office: 1900 K Street, N.W., Suite 1150. 20006.
Telephone: 202-429-5575; 785-0600.
Fax: 202-331-1118; 785-1234.
Pensacola, Florida Office: 25 West Cedar, 32501.
Telephone: 850-469-1088.
Fax: 850-432-0677.
New York, New York Office: 1450 Broadway, 41st Floor, 10018.
Telephone: 212-704-4400.
Fax: 212-704-4410.
Gdynia, Poland Office: UL. Slaska 21, 81-319.
Telephone: 011-485-831-2808.
Fax: 011-48-58-628 6411.
Warsaw, Poland Office: UL. Nowogrodzkall, 5th Floor, 00-513.
Telephone: 011-4822 529 0200.
Fax: 011-4822 529 0201.
Katowice, Poland Office: UL. Francuska 35/37, 40-027.
Telephone: 011 (48-32) 757-2414.
Fax: 011 (48-32) 757-2483.

PRINCIPALS OF FIRM

Robert S. Ketchum
Orin D. Brustad
John A. Campbell (Kalamazoo Office)
Deborah W. Thompson
Brant A. Freer
Richard I. Loebl

OF COUNSEL/SENIOR COUNSEL

Joseph F. Maycock, Jr.

Representative Firm Clients: Chrysler Corporation; Comerica, Incorporated; City of Detroit, Michigan; Detroit Tigers, Inc.; First of Michigan; Ford Motor Company; Ford Motor Credit Company; Great Lakes Bancorp; Henry Ford Hospital; INVETECH Company.

For Complete List of Firm Personnel, See General Section

For full biographical listings, see the Martindale-Hubbell Law Directory

TIMMIS & INMAN L.L.P. (AV)

300 Talon Centre, 48207
Telephone: 313-396-4200
Facsimile: 313-396-4228
Email: info@timmis-inman.com *URL:* http://www.timmis-inman.com

Michael T. Timmis
Robert E. Graziani
George A. Peck
Henry J. Brennan, III
Mark W. Peyser
Richard M. Miettinen
Bradley J. Knickerbocker
George M. Malis

Michael F. Wais
Erich J. D'Andrea
Shannon M. Nichols
Anthony J. Long

OF COUNSEL

William B. Fitzgerald

LEGAL SUPPORT PERSONNEL

PARALEGALS

Linda M. Bierl

Representative Clients: Detroit Mortgage & Realty; DMR Fiancial Services, Inc.; J. Levin Sons Co.; Green Tree Financial Servicing Corp.; Hematology-Oncology Associates East, PC; Lakeshore Ear, Nose & Throat Center, PC; Micromanagement Systems, Inc.; Phoenix Crystal Corp.; Talon Surfaces LLC; Talon Automated Equipment Company.

For Complete List of Firm Personnel, See General Section

For full biographical listings, see the Martindale-Hubbell Law Directory

FARMINGTON HILLS, Oakland Co.

CHARFOOS, REITER, PETERSON, HOLMQUIST & PILCHAK, P.C. (AV)

30500 Northwestern Highway, Suite 400, 48334-3179
Telephone: 248-626-7300
Facsimile: 248-626-7305
Email: CRPHP@crphp.com
Detroit, Michigan Office: 1200 Sixth Street.
Telephone: 313-961-7011.

(See Next Column)

CHARFOOS, REITER, PETERSON, HOLMQUIST & PILCHAK P.C.—*Continued*

Myron B. Charfoos
James A. Reiter
Daniel Peterson
C. John Holmquist, Jr.
William E. Pilchak
Daniel G. Cohen

Kenneth E. Jones
Deborah S. Dorland
Danial J. Hébert
Robert C. Tice
Nedra D. Campbell

For full biographical listings, see the Martindale-Hubbell Law Directory

---

COUZENS, LANSKY, FEALK, ELLIS, ROEDER & LAZAR, P.C. (AV)

39395 West 12 Mile Road, Suite 200, 48331-2913
Telephone: 248-489-8600
Facsimile: 248-489-4156
Email: info@couzens.com *URL:* http://www.couzens.com

Sheldon A. Fealk
Bruce J. Lazar
Jeffrey A. Levine
Phillip L. Sternberg
Marc L. Prey
Stephen Scapelliti
Cyrus Raamin Kashef

Representative Clients: Provided upon request.
Reference: Michigan National Bank.

For Complete List of Firm Personnel, See General Section

For full biographical listings, see the Martindale-Hubbell Law Directory

---

*GRAND RAPIDS,** Kent Co.

WARNER NORCROSS & JUDD LLP (AV)

900 Old Kent Building, 111 Lyon Street, N.W., 49503-2489
Telephone: 616-752-2000
Fax: 616-752-2500
URL: http://www.wnj.com
Muskegon, Michigan Office: 400 Terrace Plaza, P.O. Box 900.
Telephone: 231-727-2600.
Fax: 231-727-2699.
Holland, Michigan Office: Curtis Center, Suite 300, 170 College Avenue.
Telephone: 616-396-9800.
Fax: 616-396-3656.
Southfield, Michigan Office: 1000 Town Center, Suite 650.
Telephone: 248-223-5000.
Fax: 248-223-5005.

MEMBERS OF FIRM

George L. Whitfield
Vernon P. Saper
John H. McKendry, Jr. (Resident Member, Muskegon Office)
Sue O. Conway
Anthony J. Kolenic, Jr. (Resident Member, Muskegon Office)

ASSOCIATES

James L. Scott II
John E. Kessler (Resident, Holland Office)
Amy O'Meara Chambers

For full biographical listings, see the Martindale-Hubbell Law Directory

---

*KALAMAZOO,** Kalamazoo Co.

KREIS, ENDERLE, CALLANDER & HUDGINS, A PROFESSIONAL CORPORATION (AV)

One Moorsbridge, P.O. Box 4010, 49003-4010
Telephone: 616-324-3000
Facsimile: 616-324-3010
Email: kech@kech.com *URL:* http://www.kech.com
Battle Creek, Michigan Office: One West Michigan Avenue, 49017.
Telephone: 616-966-3000.
Fax: 616-966-3022.

C. Reid Hudgins III
Janice Roark Peters
Matthew S. DePerno

For Complete List of Firm Personnel, See General Section

For full biographical listings, see the Martindale-Hubbell Law Directory

---

MILLER, CANFIELD, PADDOCK AND STONE, P.L.C. (AV)

A Professional Limited Liability Company
Founded in 1852 by Sidney Davy Miller
444 West Michigan Avenue, 49007-3752
Telephone: 616-381-7030
Fax: 616-382-0244
URL: http://www.millercanfield.com
Detroit, Michigan Office: 150 West Jefferson, Suite 2500, 48226-4415.
Telephone: 313-963-6420.
Fax: 313-496-7500.
Cable Address: "Stem Detroit."

(See Next Column)

Ann Arbor, Michigan Office: 101 North Main Street, 7th Floor, 48104-1400.
Telephone: 734-663-2445.
Fax: 734-747-7147.
Troy, Michigan Office: 840 West Long Lake Road, Suite 200, 48098.
Telephone: 248-879-2000.
Fax: 248-879-2001.
Grand Rapids, Michigan Office: 99 Monroe, N.W., Suite 1200, 49503-2639.
Telephone: 616-454-8656.
Fax: 616-776-6322.
Howell, Michigan Office: 121 South Barnard Street, Suite 4, 48843-2305.
Telephone: 517-546-7600.
Telecopier: 517-546-6974.
Lansing, Michigan Office: One Michigan Avenue, Suite 900, 48933-1609.
Telephone: 517-487-2070.
Fax: 517-374-6304.
Monroe, Michigan Office: 214 East Elm Avenue, Suite 100, 48162-2682.
Telephone: 734-243-2000.
Fax: 734-243-0901.
Washington, D.C. Office: 1900 K Street, N.W., Suite 1150. 20006.
Telephone: 202-429-5575; 785-0600.
Fax: 202-331-1118; 785-1234.
Pensacola, Florida Office: 25 West Cedar, 32501.
Telephone: 850-469-1088.
Fax: 850-432-0677.
New York, New York Office: 1450 Broadway, 41st Floor, 10018.
Telephone: 212-704-4400.
Fax: 212-704-4410.
Gdynia, Poland Office: UL. Slaska 21, 81-319.
Telephone: 011-485-831-2808.
Fax: 011-48-58-628 6411.
Warsaw, Poland Office: UL. Nowogrodzkall, 5th Floor, 00-513.
Telephone: 011-4822 529 0200.
Fax: 011-4822 529 0201.
Katowice, Poland Office: UL. Francuska 35/37, 40-027.
Telephone: 011 (48-32) 757-2414.
Fax: 011 (48-32) 757-2483.

PRINCIPALS

John A. Campbell

Representative Firm Clients: Chrysler Corporation; Comerica, Incorporated; City of Detroit, Michigan; Detroit Tigers, Inc.; First of Michigan; Ford Motor Company; Ford Motor Credit Company; Great Lakes Bancorp; Henry Ford Hospital; INVETECH Company.

For Complete List of Firm Personnel, See General Section

For full biographical listings, see the Martindale-Hubbell Law Directory

---

LANSING, Ingham Co.

FOSTER, SWIFT, COLLINS & SMITH, P.C. (AV)

313 South Washington Square, 48933-2193
Telephone: 517-371-8100
Telecopier: 517-371-8200
URL: http://www.fosterswift.com
Farmington Hills, Michigan Office: 32300 Northwestern Highway, Suite 230.
Telephone: 248-539-9900.
Fax: 248-851-7504.

Stephen I. Jurmu
Sherry A. Stein
Stephen J. Lowney
Patricia A. Calore
Eric E. Doster
Matt G. Hrebec

LEGAL SUPPORT PERSONNEL

LEGAL ASSISTANTS

Jaxine L. Wintjen, CLA

For Complete List of Firm Personnel, See General Section

For full biographical listings, see the Martindale-Hubbell Law Directory

---

FRASER TREBILCOCK DAVIS & FOSTER, P.C. (AV)

1000 Michigan National Tower, 48933
Telephone: 517-482-5800
Fax: 517-482-0887
URL: http://WWW.FTDF.COM
Detroit, Michigan Office: One Woodward Avenue, Suite 1550.
Telephone: 313-237-7300.
Fax: 313-961-1651.

Darrell A. Lindman
David D. Waddell

Counsel for: Ingham Regional Medical Center; Michigan Catholic Conference; Michigan Farm Bureau; Weyco, Inc.

For full biographical listings, see the Martindale-Hubbell Law Directory

SOUTHFIELD, Oakland Co.

MADDIN, HAUSER, WARTELL, ROTH, HELLER & PESSES, P.C. (AV)

Third Floor Essex Centre, 28400 Northwestern Highway, P.O. Box 215, 48037
Telephone: 248-354-4030, 355-5200
Telefax: 248-354-1422

Milton M. Maddin (1902-1984)
Michael W. Maddin
Mark R. Hauser
C. Robert Wartell
Richard J. Maddin
Richard F. Roth
Harvey R. Heller
Ian D. Pesses
Michael S. Leib
Robert D. Kaplow
William E. Sigler
Stewart C. W. Weiner
Charles M. Lax
Stuart M. Bordman
Steven D. Sallen
Gregory J. Gamalski
Julie Chenot Mayer
Nathaniel H. Simpson
Ronald A. Sollish
Lowell D. Salesin

Mark H. Fink
Steven M. Wolock
Lori E. Talsky
Stephen E. Handelman
Ronald M. Stern
Martin Scott Frenkel
Gary M. Remer
Jennifer S. Sternberg
George V. Cassar, Jr.
Adam J. Goldstein

OF COUNSEL

Bruce N. Goldman

Reference: Comerica Bank.

For full biographical listings, see the Martindale-Hubbell Law Directory

SOMMERS, SCHWARTZ, SILVER & SCHWARTZ, P.C. (AV)

2000 Town Center, Suite 900, 48075
Telephone: 248-355-0300
Telecopier: 248-746-4001
Plymouth, Michigan Office: 747 South Main Street.
Telephone: 313-455-4250.

Steven J. Schwartz

Marcy B. Spitz
Ericka M. Jackson

General Counsel for: City of Taylor; Foodland Distributors; C.A. Muer Corporation; Vlasic & Company; Nederlander Corporation; Midwest Health Centers, P.C.
Representative Clients: Michigan National Bank; Universal Underwriters Insurance Co.; Rite-Aid of Michigan.

For Complete List of Firm Personnel, See General Section

For full biographical listings, see the Martindale-Hubbell Law Directory

TROY, Oakland Co.

POLING, MCGAW & POLING, P.C. (AV)

Suite 275, 5435 Corporate Drive, 48098
Telephone: 248-641-0500
Telecopier: 248-641-0506
URL: http://www.lawyers.com/polingmcgaw&poling

Benson T. Buck (1926-1989)
Richard B. Poling
D. Douglas McGaw
Richard B. Poling, Jr.
Gregory C. Hamilton
Veronica B. O'Hara
James R. Parker
Shannon M. Acton

OF COUNSEL

Ralph S. Moore

Representative Clients: City of Troy; United States Fidelity & Guaranty Co.; Sentry Insurance Co.; Admiral Insurance; DeMaria Construction Co.; Leo Corporation; Aetna Casualty and Surety Co.; Concord Design; Pneumo-Abex.

For full biographical listings, see the Martindale-Hubbell Law Directory

STARK, REAGAN & FINNERTY, P.C. (AV)

Suite 202, 1111 West Long Lake Road, P.O. Box 7037, 48007-7037
Telephone: 248-641-9955
Facsimile: 248-641-9921
Email: @SRFPC.COM
Boca Raton, Florida Office: Suite 307B, 4800 North Federal Highway.
Telephone: 561-994-2266.
Traverse City, Michigan Office: 475 Eastwood Shores.
Telephone: 231-943-8230.
Facsimile: 231-943-8711.

Michael H. Whiting
Kenneth M. Boyer
Thomas H. Finnerty
R. Keith Stark
Joseph C. Bird
Joseph A. Ahern
Christopher E. LeVasseur
Daniel E. Chapman
William D. Girardot
James R. Waldvogel
Jeffrey J. Fleury
Michael D. FitzPatrick

OF COUNSEL

Harry S. Stark (Resident Of Counsel, Traverse City Office)
Willard M. Reagan
James E. Beall

For full biographical listings, see the Martindale-Hubbell Law Directory

ENERGY LAW

CALIFORNIA

*BAKERSFIELD,** Kern Co.

Borton, Petrini & Conron, LLP (AV)

The Borton, Petrini & Conron Building, 1600 Truxtun Avenue, 93301
Telephone: 661-322-3051
Voice Mail: 661-395-6700
Fax: 661-322-4628
Mailing Address: P.O. Box 2026, Bakersfield, California, 93303
Email: bpcbak@bpclaw.com *URL:* http://www.bpclaw.com
Other City Locations: Fresno, Los Angeles, Modesto, Redding, Sacramento, San Bernardino, San Diego, San Francisco, San Jose, San Luis Obispo, Santa Ana and Ventura.

MEMBERS OF FIRM

John F. Petrini
Stephen M. Dake
Calvin R. Stead

ASSOCIATES

Brian Jensen Stowell
Timothy B. Liebaert
Valana K. Timroth
William R. Olson

For Complete List of Firm Personnel, See General Section

For full biographical listings, see the Martindale-Hubbell Law Directory

*SACRAMENTO,** Sacramento Co.

Grattan & Galati (AV)

Renaissance Tower, 801 K Street, Penthouse Suite, 95814
Telephone: 916-441-6575
Fax: 916-441-6553
Email: scarey@grattangalati.com *URL:* http://www.lawyers.com/grattan&galati

John P. Grattan, Jr.
Scott A. Galati

LEGAL SUPPORT PERSONNEL

Sandra A. Carey

For full biographical listings, see the Martindale-Hubbell Law Directory

Livingston & Mattesich, Law Corporation (AV)

1201 K Street, Suite 1100, 95814
Telephone: 916-442-1111
Fax: 916-448-1709
Email: l&m@lmlaw.net *URL:* http://www.lmlaw.net

Gene Livingston
James M. Mattesich
Carol Livingston
Rebecca M. Ceniceros
Emilio E. Varanini, III
Kenneth M. Malovos
Kathleen E. Finnerty
Joanna R. Mendoza

Steven P. Belzer
Jeffrey Leacox
Randy Pollack
Alice H. Choi
Stephen Craig Hunter
Matthew J. Goldman
Joel C. Baiocchi
Baldassaro (Bill) Di Capo
John McKinsey
Timothy E. Naccarato
Craig N. Lundgren
Mary Farrell Taylor
Brian Crone
Gay L. Carroll
Steven G. Churchwell

Representative Clients: NRG Energy, Inc.; Southern Energy, Inc.; Sunlaw Cogeneration Partners; Thermo Ecotek Corporation; Turlock Irrigation District.

For full biographical listings, see the Martindale-Hubbell Law Directory

*SAN JOSE,** Santa Clara Co.

Reed, Elliott, Creech & Roth (AV)

99 Almaden Boulevard, Eighth Floor, 95113
Telephone: 408-993-9911
Fax: 408-993-1335
URL: http://www.sjlegal.com

MEMBERS OF FIRM

John W. Elliott
Randall C. Creech
Thomas A. Elliott
Jeffrey S. Lawson
Peter A. Liebow
Raymond A. Brinson

ASSOCIATES

Lauren Berger
Nancy L. Mathis
Edward A. Kraus
Betty Chen
Bonnie L. Portis

(See Next Column)

OF COUNSEL

Steven J. Roth
Charles R. Reed
Thomas G. Perkins

Reference: Union Bank of California.

For full biographical listings, see the Martindale-Hubbell Law Directory

*SANTA BARBARA,** Santa Barbara Co.

Hollister & Brace, A Professional Corporation (AV)

1126 Santa Barbara Street, P.O. Box 630, 93101
Telephone: 805-963-6711
Fax: 805-965-0329
Email: hblaw@hbsb.com

William A. Brace (Retired)
J. James Hollister, III (Retired)
John S. Poucher
Richard C. Monk
George A. Rempe, III
Steven Evans Kirby
Bradford F. Ginder
John G. Busby
Susan H. McCollum
Robert L. Brace
Marcus Scott Bird
Charles W. Willey (P.C.)
Alexis W. Willey
Peter L. Candy

Attorneys For: Western States Petroleum Assoc.; California Independent Petroleum Assoc.; Venoco, Inc.; Torch Energy Advisors.

For full biographical listings, see the Martindale-Hubbell Law Directory

COLORADO

*DENVER,** Denver Co.

Dufford & Brown, P.C. (AV)

1700 Broadway, Suite 1700, 80290-1701
Telephone: 303-861-8013
Facsimile: 303-832-3804
Colorado Springs, Colorado Office: 101 N. Tejon, Suite 410.
Telephone: 719-471-0559.
Facsimile: 719-471-0583.
Affiliated Office: Solomon, Pearl, Blum & Quinn, L.L.P., New York, NY and Denver, Colorado.

Richard L. Fanyo

Representative Clients: Rocky Mountain Steel Mills; Cyprus Climax Molybdenum Co., Inc.

For Complete List of Firm Personnel, See General Section

For full biographical listings, see the Martindale-Hubbell Law Directory

CONNECTICUT

*HARTFORD,** Hartford Co.

Killian, Donohue & Shipman, LLC (AV)

363 Main Street, 06106-1885
Telephone: 860-560-1977
Telecopier: 860-249-6638
Email: lawyers@killiandonohueshipman.com
Simsbury, Connecticut Office: 141 West Street.
Telephone: 860-658-0436.
Telecopier: 860-249-6638.

Robert K. Killian, Jr.
Thomas J. Donohue, Jr.
Mark S. Shipman
Lawrence S. Shipman

For full biographical listings, see the Martindale-Hubbell Law Directory

DISTRICT OF COLUMBIA

WASHINGTON, D.C. Co.

Betts & Holt (AV)

815 Connecticut Avenue N.W., Suite 1201, 20006
Telephone: 202-530-3380
Fax: 202-530-3389

Kirk Howard Betts
James H. Holt
Jill M. Barker

For full biographical listings, see the Martindale-Hubbell Law Directory

Washington—Continued

BRUDER, GENTILE & MARCOUX, L.L.P. (AV)

1100 New York Avenue, N.W., Suite 510 East, 20005-3934
Telephone: 202-783-1350
Telecopiers: 202-737-9117; 347-2644
Email: bgmstaff@brugen.com *URL:* http://www.brugen.com

George F. Bruder (Retired)
Carmen L. Gentile
Albert R. Simonds, Jr. (Retired)
J. Michel Marcoux
David E. Goroff
Gary E. Guy
James H. McGrew
Thomas L. Blackburn

Antonia A. Frost
David Martin Connelly
Gary D. Levenson

OF COUNSEL

Peter K. Matt

For full biographical listings, see the Martindale-Hubbell Law Directory

BRUNENKANT & HASKELL, LLP (AV)

805 15th Street, N.W., Suite 1101, 20005
Telephone: 202-408-0700
Fax: 202-408-5959
Email: brunenkant@bh-law.com

Jon L. Brunenkant
Mark R. Haskell
James W. Moeller

ASSOCIATES

Cheryl J. Walker
Melissa L. Lauderdale
Christie L. Richart (Not admitted in DC)

For full biographical listings, see the Martindale-Hubbell Law Directory

CAMERON MCKENNA LLP (AV)

2175 K Street, N.W. Fifth Floor, 20036
Telephone: 202-466-0060
Fax: 202-466-0077
Email: info@cammckenna.com *URL:* http://www.cmck.com
Associated offices in: Almaty, Brussels, Budapest, Hong Kong, London, Aberdeen, Bristol, Moscow, Prague, Toronto, Tashkent, Warsaw, Utrecht, Copenhagen, Stuttgart, Stockholm, Amsterdam, Hilversum, Arnhem, Dusseldorf, Berlin, Leipzig, Frankfurt, Chemnitz.
(Please refer to London entry for more details).

PARTNERS

Joel F. Zipp
George H. Williams, Jr.
Reinier H. J. H. Lock
Amy S. Koch
Michael S. Hindus (Resident, San Francisco, California Office)
Andrzej M. Blach (Resident, Warsaw Office)

COUNSEL

Robert C. Platt

SENIOR ASSOCIATE

Bridget Shahan

ASSOCIATES

Gunnar Birgisson
Phi H.D. Nguyen (Not admitted in DC)
Matthew E. Ross

For full biographical listings, see the Martindale-Hubbell Law Directory

CUTLER & STANFIELD, L.L.P. (AV)

700 Fourteenth Street, N.W. 10th Floor, 20005-2014
Telephone: 202-624-8400
Fax: 202-624-8410
Denver, Colorado Office: 1675 Broadway, 80202.
Telephone: 303-825-7000.
FAX: 303-825-7005.

MEMBERS OF FIRM

Eliot R. Cutler
Jeffrey L. Stanfield
Sheila D. Jones
Perry M. Rosen
Peter J. Kirsch
Barry Conaty
Stephen H. Kaplan (Not admitted in DC)
Sarah M. Rockwell (Not admitted in DC)
Thomas D. Roth

OF COUNSEL

Byron Keith Huffman, Jr.

ASSOCIATES

Katherine Boonin Andrus
Joel D. Armstrong (Not admitted in DC)
Françoise M. Carrier
Polly B. Jessen (Not admitted in DC)
William G. Malley
Elizabeth A. Mitchell (Resident at Denver, Colorado Office)
Dana C. Nifosi
W. Eric Pilsk
Timothy A. Pohle
John E. Putnam
Daniel S. Reimer (Not admitted in DC)
Andrew T. Swers
Sara E. Wilensky

For full biographical listings, see the Martindale-Hubbell Law Directory

VERNER, LIIPFERT, BERNHARD, MCPHERSON AND HAND, CHARTERED (AV)

901 15th Street, N.W., 20005-2301
Telephone: 202-371-6000
Cable Address: "Verlip"
Fax: 202-371-6279
Email: verner.com *URL:* http://www.verner.com
Houston, Texas Office: 1111 Bagby, Suite 4700, 77002.
Telephone: 713-225-7200.
Fax: 713-752-2199.
Honolulu, Hawaii Office: 745 Fort Street, Suite 600, 96813.
Telephone: 808-566-0999.
Fax: 808-566-0995.
Austin, Texas Office: Suite 1440 San Jacinto Center, 98 San Jacinto Boulevard, 78701.
Telephone: 512-703-6000.
Fax: 512-703-6003.
Las Vegas, Nevada Affiliate Office: Gary C. Moss, Hughes Center, 3960 Howard Hughes Parkway, Suite 400, 89109.
Telephone: 702-737-3433.
Fax: 702-737-1612.
Miami, Florida Office: 3100 First Union Financial Center, 200 South Biscayne Boulevard, 33131.
Telephone: 305-371-8801.
Fax: 305-371-6545.

R. Stuart Broom (Not admitted in DC)
J. Cathy Fogel
Gary J. Klein
Paul E. Nordstrom
Glen L. Ortman
Sherry A. Quirk
Deborah A. Swanstrom
Clinton A. Vince
John H. Zentay

OF COUNSEL

Phillip A. Holder (Resident, Austin, Texas Office)
Regina Y. Speed-Bost (Not admitted in DC)

For Complete List of Firm Personnel, See General Section

For full biographical listings, see the Martindale-Hubbell Law Directory

FLORIDA

*TALLAHASSEE,** Leon Co.

LANDERS & PARSONS (AV)

310 West College Avenue, P.O. Box 271, 32302
Telephone: 850-681-0311
Telecopier: 850-224-5595

MEMBERS OF FIRM

Joseph W. Landers, Jr.
Philip S. Parsons
Fred A. McCormack
John T. LaVia, III
Robert Scheffel Wright
David S. Dee
Leslie J. Paugh

LEGAL SUPPORT PERSONNEL

Victoria J. Tschinkel

For full biographical listings, see the Martindale-Hubbell Law Directory

HAWAII

*HONOLULU,** Honolulu Co.

CARLSMITH BALL (AV)

A Partnership including Law Corporations
Suite 2200, Pacific Tower, 1001 Bishop Street, P.O. Box 656, 96809-3402
Telephone: 808-523-2500
Fax: 808-523-0842
Email: execdirector@carlsmith.com *URL:* http://www.carlsmith.com
Kapolei, Hawaii Office: Suite 318, Kapolei Building, 1001 Kamokila Boulevard, 96707.
Telephone: 808-523-2500.
Fax: 808-674-0850.
Wailuku, Maui Hawaii Office: Suite 400, One Main Plaza, 2200 Main Street, P.O. Box 1086, 96793-1086.
Telephone: 808-242-4535.
Fax: 808-244-4974.
Kailua-Kona, Hawaii Office: Suite 209, 75-1000 Henry Street, 96740.
Telephone: 808-329-6464.
Fax: 808-329-9450.
Hilo, Hawaii Office: 121 Waianuenue Avenue, P.O. Box 686, 96721-0686.
Telephone: 808-935-6644.
Fax: 808-935-7975.

(See Next Column)

CARLSMITH BALL—*Continued*

Hagatna, Guam Office: Suite 401, Bank of Hawaii Building, 134 West Soledad Avenue, P.O. Box BF, 96932-5027.
Telephone: 671-472-6813.
Fax: 671-477-4375.
Telex: 721-6445 CWCMI GM.
Saipan, Commonwealth of the Northern Mariana Islands Office: Carlsmith Building, Capitol Hill, P.O. Box 5241, 96950-5241.
Telephone: 670-322-3455.
Fax: 670-322-3368.
Los Angeles, California Office: 9th Floor, 444 South Flower Street, 90071-2901.
Telephone: 213-955-1200.
Fax: 213-623-0032.
Washington, D.C. Office: Suite 300, 1201 Pennsylvania Avenue, N.W., 20004-2401.
Telephone: 202-628-2228.
Fax: 202-628-2071.
Mexico City, Mexico Office: Carlsmith Ball, Sierra Nevada 119, Lomas de Chapultepec, 11000 Mexico, D.F.
Telephone: 52-5-520-8514, 52-5-520-8757.
Fax: 52-5-540-1545.
Mexico, D.F. Office of Carlsmith Ball, S.C. (Authorized to practice as foreign legal consultants in Mexico): Sierra Nevada 119, Lomas de Chapultepec, 11000 Mexico, D.F.
Telephone: 52-5-520-8514, 52-5-520-8757.
Fax: 52-5-540-1545.

MEMBERS OF FIRM

Ian L. Sandison
William C. Williams, Jr. (Not admitted in HI)

For Complete List of Firm Personnel, See General Section

For full biographical listings, see the Martindale-Hubbell Law Directory

ILLINOIS

GRANITE CITY, Madison Co.

LUEDERS, ROBERTSON & KONZEN (AV)

1939 Delmar Avenue, 62040
Telephone: 618-876-8500
Telecopier: 618-876-4534
Email: lrk.il@worldnet.att.net
Danville, Illinois Office: 809 1/2 North Gilbert, 61832.
Telephone: 217-443-0304.
Fax: 217-443-0375.

MEMBERS OF FIRM

Wesley Lueders (1896-1957)
Randall Robertson
Leo H. Konzen
R. Eric Robertson
Edward C. Fitzhenry, Jr.
Brian E. Konzen
Paul G. Foran

ASSOCIATE

Anthony R. Garavalia

Representative Clients: Ameritech; Mercantile Bank (Trust Division); Granite City Steel Division of National Steel Corporation; Allied Waste Industries, Inc.; Illinois Industrial Energy Consumers (IIEC) including Olin Corporation; Archers-Daniels-Midland Company; General Motors Corporation.

For full biographical listings, see the Martindale-Hubbell Law Directory

LOUISIANA

*LAFAYETTE,** Lafayette Parish

ONEBANE, BERNARD, TORIAN, DIAZ, McNAMARA & ABELL (AV)

Suite 600, Versailles Centre, 102 Versailles Boulevard, P.O. Box 3507, 70502
Telephone: 318-237-2660
Telecopier: 318-266-1232
Email: info@onebane.com
Monroe, Louisiana Office: 1900 N. 18th Street, Suite 420, P.O. Box 2255, 71207.
Telephone: 318-340-0220.
Fax: 318-340-0110.

Joseph Onebane (1917-1987)
John G. Torian, II (1936-1991)
James E. Diaz
Timothy J. McNamara
Edward C. Abell, Jr.
Lawrence L. Lewis, III
Robert M. Mahony
Daniel G. Fournerat
Douglas W. Truxillo
Randall C. Songy
Michael G. Durand
Greg Guidry
Joseph L. Lemoine, Jr.
Mark L. Riley

(See Next Column)

Graham N. Smith
Gordon T. Whitman
Gary P. Kraus
Richard J. Petre, Jr.
Charles J. Boudreaux, Jr.
James R. Shelton
Thomas G. Smart
Roger E. Ishee
Jennifer M. Kleinpeter
Steven C. Lanza
Joel P. Babineaux

Alison M. Brumley
Jesse D. Lambert
Brent G. Sonnier
Cary B. Bryson
Maria F. Manuel
Greg R. Mier
Jennifer L. Smith
Janice Church Reeves
Mark B. Oliver
Chanelle T. Delahoussaye
Aimee L. Williams
A.G. "Alec" Alexander, III
Terry J. Blanchard
William E. Bourgeois (Resident, Monroe, Louisiana Office)

OF COUNSEL

William E. Kellner

Representative Clients: American Explorer, Inc.; Chesapeake Operating, Inc.; Louisiana Independent Oil & Gas Assn.; Marathon Oil Co.; Mobil Exploration and Producing, U.S., Inc.; Ocean Energy, Inc.; Pennzoil; Phillips Petroleum Co..; Shell Offshore, Inc.; Spirt Energy 76.

For full biographical listings, see the Martindale-Hubbell Law Directory

*NEW ORLEANS,** Orleans Parish

LEE, FUTRELL & PERLES, L.L.P. (AV)

Suite 2409, 201 St. Charles Avenue, 70170-2409
Telephone: 504-569-1725
Fax: 504-569-1726
Email: mgr@leefutrell.com *URL:* http://www.lawyers.com/lf&plaw

Gary A. Lee
John Maurice Futrell
Richard M. Perles

Representative Clients: Certain Underwriters at Lloyd's, London; Institute of London Underwriters Companies.

For full biographical listings, see the Martindale-Hubbell Law Directory

MILLING BENSON WOODWARD L.L.P. (AV)

A Partnership including Professional Law Corporations
Suite Twenty-Three Hundred, 909 Poydras Street, 70112-1017
Telephone: 504-569-7000
Telecopier: 504-569-7001
ABA net: 15656
MCI Mail: "Milling"
Email: milling@millinglaw.com
Lafayette, Louisiana Office: 101 La Rue France, Suite 200.
Telephone: 318-232-3929.
Telecopier: 318-233-4957.
Mandeville (North Shore), Louisiana Office: 2140 8th Street.
Telephone: 504-867-9622.
Telecopier: 504-867-8364.

MEMBER OF FIRM

David Conroy (P.C.)

MANDEVILLE (NORTH SHORE) OFFICE
RESIDENT MEMBER OF FIRM

McChord Carrico (P.C.)

See General Section for list of Representative Clients.

For Complete List of Firm Personnel, See General Section

For full biographical listings, see the Martindale-Hubbell Law Directory

*SHREVEPORT,** Caddo Parish

BLANCHARD, WALKER, O'QUIN & ROBERTS, A PROFESSIONAL LAW CORPORATION (AV)

Fourteenth Floor, Premier Bank Tower, 400 Texas Street, P.O. Drawer 1126, 71101
Telephone: 318-221-6858
Fax: 318-227-2967
Email: BWOR@BWOR.com
Bossier City, Louisiana Office: 2285 Benton Road, Suite B-201.
Telephone: 318-742-9255.
Fax: 318-742-9210.

Gilbert L. Hetherwick
J. David Garrett
Cecil W. Talley
Michael E. Riddick
Leslie Idom Kalmbach

For Complete List of Firm Personnel, See General Section

For full biographical listings, see the Martindale-Hubbell Law Directory

MASSACHUSETTS

*BOSTON,** Suffolk Co.

HINCKLEY, ALLEN & SNYDER LLP (AV)

28 State Street, 30th Floor, 02109-1775
Telephone: 617-345-9000
Email: firm@haslaw.com *URL:* http://www.haslaw.com
Providence, Rhode Island Office: 1500 Fleet Center.
Telephone: 401-274-2000.
Fax: 401-277-9600. URL: http://www.hawlaw.com.

MEMBERS OF FIRM

David D. Barricelli (Not admitted in MA)
E. Jerome Batty (Not admitted in MA)
Jonathan Bell
Paul Bork
Stephen J. Carlotti (Not admitted in MA)
David Barry Connolly
Michael P. DeFanti
Eric F. Eisenberg
Malcolm Farmer, III
Pasco Gasbarro Jr.
William R. Grimm
Paul A. Hedstrom
Joel Lewin
Sandra Matrone Mack (Not admitted in MA)
H. Peter Olsen (Not admitted in MA)
John J. Pendergast, III (Not admitted in MA)
Gerald J. Petros
Charles E. Schaub, Jr.
Douglas F. Seaver
David R. Sullivan
Robert F. Sylvia
Howard E. Walker (Not admitted in MA)
Richard D. Wayne

ASSOCIATES

Alexandra K. Callam
Kelley Jordan-Price

OF COUNSEL

Willard R. Pope

For Complete List of Firm Personnel, See General Section

For full biographical listings, see the Martindale-Hubbell Law Directory

ENVIRONMENTAL LAW

ALABAMA

*BIRMINGHAM,** Jefferson Co.

BRADLEY ARANT ROSE & WHITE LLP (AV)

2001 Park Place, Suite 1400, P.O. Box 830709, 35283-0709
Telephone: 205-521-8000
Facsimile: 205-521-8800
Facsimile (SouthTrust Tower Office): 205-521-8500
URL: http://www.barw.com
Huntsville, Alabama Office: 200 Clinton Avenue West, Suite 900, 35801.
Telephone: 205-517-5100.
Facsimile: 205-533-5069.
Washington, D.C. Office: 801 Pennsylvania Avenue, NW, Suite 230, 20004.
Telephone: 202-347-8893.
Facsimile: 202-347-1684.

MEMBERS OF FIRM

Joseph S. Bird III
Axel Bolvig III
T. Michael Brown
G. Edward Cassady III
Michael S. Denniston
Denson Nauls Franklin III
John E. Goodman
M. Williams Goodwyn Jr.
Patrick H. Graves Jr. (Resident, Huntsville Office)
Andrew Robert Greene
John E. Hagefstration Jr.
John G. Harrell
George Bryan Harris
Gary C. Huckaby (Resident, Huntsville Office)
Norman Jetmundsen Jr.
Joseph B. Mays Jr.
John H. Morrow
E. Mabry Rogers
Sid J. Trant
Bobby C. Underwood
Meade Whitaker, Jr.

OF COUNSEL

Macbeth Wagnon Jr. (Retired)

ASSOCIATES

Matthew A. Aiken
Hugh Chester Boston III
Jeffrey P. Lisenby
David E. Roth
Anne Marie Seibel
Joseph E. Smith
Rusha C. Smith
Laura P. Washburn (Not admitted in AL)

For Complete List of Firm Personnel, See General Section

For full biographical listings, see the Martindale-Hubbell Law Directory

BURR & FORMAN LLP (AV)

3100 SouthTrust Tower, 420 North 20th Street, P.O. Box 830719, 35283-0719
Telephone: 205-251-3000
Facsimile: 205-458-5100
URL: http://www.burr.com
Huntsville, Alabama Office: Suite 204, Regency Center, 400 Meridian Street.
Telephone: 205-551-0010.
Facsimile: 205-551-0043.
Atlanta, Georgia Office: Suite 1200, One Georgia Center, 600 West Peachtree Street, 30308.
Telephone: 404-815-3000.
Facsimile: 404-817-3244.

MEMBERS OF FIRM

D. Frank Davis
John F. DeBuys, Jr.
James Ross Forman, III
Mark McCarroll Lawson

For Complete List of Firm Personnel, See General Section

For full biographical listings, see the Martindale-Hubbell Law Directory

HOGAN, SMITH & ALSPAUGH, P.C. (AV)

2323 Second Avenue, North, 35203
Telephone: 205-324-5635
Telecopier: 205-324-5637
Email: Chris@Hogan-Smith.com *URL:* http://www.hsa-pc.com

William W. Smith
M. Clay Alspaugh
R. Benjamin Hogan, III
Ronald R. Crook
Richard D. Stratton
Benjamin E. Baker, Jr.

Reference: Regions Bank.

For full biographical listings, see the Martindale-Hubbell Law Directory

LIGHTFOOT, FRANKLIN & WHITE, L.L.C. (AV)

The Clark Building, 400 20th Street North, 35203
Telephone: 205-581-0700
Facsimile: 205-581-0799
Email: LFWlaw@LFWlaw.com *URL:* http://www.lfwlaw.com

(See Next Column)

Warren B. Lightfoot
Jere F. White, Jr.
John M. Johnson
Adam K. Peck
Harlan I. Prater, IV
William S. Cox, III
Jackson R. Sharman, III

John Q. Somerville
Suzanne Alldredge
William Larkin Radney, IV

For full biographical listings, see the Martindale-Hubbell Law Directory

SPAIN & GILLON, L.L.C. (AV)

The Zinszer Building, 2117 2nd Avenue North, 35203
Telephone: 205-328-4100
Telecopier: 205-324-8866
Email: ddh@spain-gillon.com *URL:* http://lawlinks.com:80/atty/al/sggbn.html

MEMBERS OF FIRM

Eugene P. Stutts
Samuel H. Frazier
Alton B. Parker, Jr.
David S. Maxey

General Counsel for: Piggly Wiggly Alabama Distributing Co.; Alabama Insurance Guaranty Association; Alabama Life and Disability Insurance Guaranty Association; Koppers Industries; Jefferson County Board of Health.
Counsel for: Alabama Department of Environmental Management, Inc.; City of Birmingham; Jefferson County Health Department.

For Complete List of Firm Personnel, See General Section

For full biographical listings, see the Martindale-Hubbell Law Directory

STARNES & ATCHISON LLP (AV)

100 Brookwood Place, 35209
Telephone: 205-868-6000
Telecopier: 205-868-6099
Mailing Address: P.O. Box 598512, 35259-8512
Email: information@starneslaw.com
Mobile, Alabama Office: Riverview Plaza, Suite 1106, 63 South Royal Street, 36602.
Telephone: 334-433-6049.

MEMBERS OF FIRM

W. Stancil Starnes
W. Michael Atchison
William Anthony Davis, III
L. Graves Stiff, III
J. Bentley Owens, III
Robert P. Mackenzie, III
Thomas Lawson Selden

ASSOCIATES

Jeannie Bugg Walston
Rik S. Tozzi

Representative Clients: Ciba-Geigy Corp.; Wyerhaeuser, Inc.; Browning-Ferris Industries, Inc.; Nobel Insurance Co.; Drummond Co., Inc.; Mobile Infirmary Medical Center; Hoffman-La Roche, Inc.

For full biographical listings, see the Martindale-Hubbell Law Directory

*HUNTSVILLE,** Madison Co.

BRADLEY ARANT ROSE & WHITE LLP (AV)

200 Clinton Avenue West, Suite 900, 35801
Telephone: 205-517-5100
Facsimile: 205-517-5200
URL: http://www.barw.com
Birmingham, Alabama Office: 2001 Park Place, Suite 1400, P.O. Box 830709.
Telephone: 205-521-8000.
Facsimile: 205-521-8800. Facsimile (SouthTrust Tower Office): 205-521-8500.
Washington, D.C. Office: 801 Pennsylvania Avenue, NW, Suite 230, 20004.
Telephone: 202-347-8893.
Facsimile: 202-347-1684.

RESIDENT PARTNERS

Patrick H Graves Jr.
Gary C. Huckaby

For Complete List of Firm Personnel, See General Section

For full biographical listings, see the Martindale-Hubbell Law Directory

*MOBILE,** Mobile Co.

ATCHISON, CROSBY, SAAD & BEEBE, P.C. (AV)

3030 Knollwood Drive, 36693
Telephone: 334-665-7200
Fax: 334-665-7250
URL: http://www.acsblaw.com

James E. Atchison
James H. Crosby
Elias J. Saad
Donald G. Beebe

Mona Ann Vivar
Jacqueline M. McConaha
Daryl A. Atchison

Representative Clients: City of Mobile; Alabama State Docks; Mobile Area Water and Sewer Board; Owens Corning, Inc.; Pilot Catastrophe Services, Inc.; Shell Oil Co.; Premdor,Inc.; Melvin Pierce Paint Co.; Commonwealth National Bank; Fiberglass Canada,Inc.

(See Next Column)

ATCHISON, CROSBY, SAAD & BEEBE P.C., *Mobile—Continued*

For full biographical listings, see the Martindale-Hubbell Law Directory

JOHNSTONE, ADAMS, BAILEY, GORDON AND HARRIS, L.L.C. (AV)

Royal St. Francis Building, 104 St. Francis Street, 8th Floor, P.O. Box 1988, 36633
Telephone: 334-432-7682
Facsimile: 334-432-0712 or 334-432-2800
Email: attorneys@JohnstoneAdams.com *URL:* http://www.JohnstoneAdams.com
Bay Minette, Alabama Office: Dahlberg Building, 107 Hand Avenue, P.O. Box 729, 36507.
Telephone: 334-937-9473.
Facsimile: 334-937-9475.

MEMBERS OF FIRM

Ben H. Harris, Jr.
Alan C. Christian
Tracy P. Turner

OF COUNSEL

Brock B. Gordon

For Complete List of Firm Personnel, See General Section

For full biographical listings, see the Martindale-Hubbell Law Directory

LYONS, PIPES & COOK, P.C. (AV)

2 North Royal Street, P.O. Box 2727, 36652-2727
Telephone: 334-432-4481
Cable Address: "Lysea"
Telecopier: 334-433-1820
URL: http://www.LPCLaw.com

Wesley Pipes
Norton W. Brooker, Jr.
Cooper C. Thurber
Walter M. Cook, Jr.
W. David Johnson, Jr.
Caroline C. McCarthy

Representative Clients: Esenjay Petroleum Corporation; Shell Oil Company; Spectacor Management Group.

For Complete List of Firm Personnel, See General Section

For full biographical listings, see the Martindale-Hubbell Law Directory

VICKERS, RIIS, MURRAY AND CURRAN, L.L.C. (AV)

8th Floor, Regions Bank Building, 106 Saint Francis Street, P.O. Box 2568, 36652
Telephone: 334-432-9772
Fax: 334-432-9781
Email: vickersriis.com

MEMBERS OF FIRM

Edwin J. Curran, Jr.
Frank Grey Redditt, Jr.
Thomas E. Sharp, III
J. Marshall Gardner
L. Thomas Styron
C. Richard Wilkins

For Complete List of Firm Personnel, See General Section

For full biographical listings, see the Martindale-Hubbell Law Directory

*MONTGOMERY,** Montgomery Co.

KAUFMAN & ROTHFEDER, P.C. (AV)

2740 Zelda Road, Drawer 4540, 36103-4540
Telephone: 334-244-1111
Fax: 334-244-1969
Email: firm@krlegal.com *URL:* http://www.krlegal.com

Samuel Kaufman
Alan E. Rothfeder
Jo Karen Parr
Thomas R. DeBray
Robert E. L. Gilpin
George W. Thomas
Carla Cole Gilmore

Counsel for: Dale Medical Center; Evergreen Medical Center; Community Health Systems, Inc.; The Russell Hospital Corporation.

For full biographical listings, see the Martindale-Hubbell Law Directory

NIX, HOLTSFORD & VERCELLI, P.C. (AV)

300 A Water Street, Suite 300, P.O. Box 4128, 36103
Telephone: 334-262-2006
Fax: 334-834-3616
Email: NHV@JUNO.COM

H. E. Nix, Jr.
Alex L. Holtsford, Jr.
Charles E. Vercelli, Jr.
Floyd R. Gilliland, Jr.
T. Randall Lyons
Steven A. Higgins
Kenneth A. Hitson, Jr.

David P. Stevens
Todd E. Hughes
Rick A. Howard
Stacy Anne Linn
Jay S. Tuley

(See Next Column)

LEGAL SUPPORT PERSONNEL

Richard M. Seibert (Firm Manager)
Ashley Collins (Paralegal)
Monica E. Jayroe (Paralegal)
Suzanne H. Long (Legal Assistant)
Kelley S. Tracy (Paralegal)

Representative Clients: Alabama Chemical Association; Alabama League of Municipalities; Coastal Chemical Co.; Dupont Chemical Co.; Gay & Taylor; Tennessee Farmers Cooperative; Terra International; Ranger Insurance Co.; United States Fidelity & Guaranty Co.

For full biographical listings, see the Martindale-Hubbell Law Directory

ALASKA

*ANCHORAGE,** Third Judicial District

DELANEY, WILES, HAYES, GERETY, ELLIS & YOUNG, INC. (AV)

1007 West Third Avenue, Suite 400, 99501
Telephone: 907-279-3581
Fax: 907-277-1331
Email: dwhge@alaska.net

Stephen M. Ellis

Clyde E. Sniffen, Jr.

Representative Clients: Carr-Gottstein Foods Co.; Chevron Corporation; Arco Alaska Inc.; Alyeska Pipeline Service Co.; Phillips Petroleum Company; Matanuska Electric Association; Nana Regional Corporation; Bering Straits Native Corporation; Mobil Oil Company; Seibu, Inc.

For Complete List of Firm Personnel, See General Section

For full biographical listings, see the Martindole-Hubbell Law Directory

*JUNEAU,** First Judicial District

RUDDY, BRADLEY, KOLKHORST & REGES, A PROFESSIONAL CORPORATION (AV)

Jordan Creek Center, 8800 Glacier Highway, Suite 223, P.O. Box 34338, 99801
Telephone: 907-789-0047
Fax: 907-789-0783
Email: rbklaw@alaska.net *URL:* http://www.alaska.net/~rbklaw/

William G. Ruddy
Robert K. Reges, Jr.

Representative Clients: State of Alaska, Department of Environmental Conservation; BP Exploration (Alaska) Inc.; Goldbelt Inc.; Markel Essex Insurance Co.; Alaskans for Juneau.

For full biographical listings, see the Martindale-Hubbell Law Directory

ARIZONA

*PHOENIX,** Maricopa Co.

BURCH & CRACCHIOLO, P.A. (AV)

702 East Osborn Road, Suite 200, 85014
Telephone: 602-274-7611
Fax: 602-234-0341
Mailing Address: P.O. Box 16882, Phoenix, AZ, 85011
Email: library@bcattorneys.com

Daniel Cracchiolo
Daniel R. Malinski
Edwin D. Fleming
Ralph D. Harris

Representative Clients: Bashas' Inc.; Farmers Insurance Group; U-Haul International, Inc.

For Complete List of Firm Personnel, See General Section

For full biographical listings, see the Martindale-Hubbell Law Directory

FENNEMORE CRAIG, A PROFESSIONAL CORPORATION (AV)

3003 North Central Avenue, Suite 2600, 85012-2913
Telephone: 602-916-5000
Fax: 602-916-5999
Tucson, Arizona Office: One South Church Avenue, Suite 1000, 85701-1620.
Telephone: 520-879-6800.
Fax: 520-879-6899.

James W. Johnson
Phillip F. Fargotstein
Norman D. James
Christopher L. Callahan
Robert J. Kramer
John M. Pearce
Douglas C. Northup

(See Next Column)

FENNEMORE CRAIG A PROFESSIONAL CORPORATION—*Continued*

Scott H. Thomas
Jay L. Shapiro
Karen Errant
David M. Call
Lawrence E. Palles
(Not admitted in AZ)

LEGAL SUPPORT PERSONNEL

LEGAL ASSISTANTS

Beverly Cooper

For Complete List of Firm Personnel, See General Section

For full biographical listings, see the Martindale-Hubbell Law Directory

JENNINGS, STROUSS & SALMON, P.L.C. (AV)

A Professional Limited Liability Company
One Renaissance Square, Two North Central Avenue, 85004-2393
Telephone: 602-262-5911
Fax: 602-253-3255
Email: info@jsslaw.com *URL:* http://www.jsslaw.com
Arrowhead Office: 16150 North Arrowhead Fountains Center Drive, Suite 250, Peoria, Arizona.
Telephone: 623-878-2222.
Fax: 623-878-1333.

David J. Calverley
Richard N. Morrison
George Esahak-Gage
Shiela B. Schmidt

ASSOCIATES

Andrew B. Turk
C. David Martinez

For Complete List of Firm Personnel, See General Section

For full biographical listings, see the Martindale-Hubbell Law Directory

KIMERER & LAVELLE, P.L.C. (AV)

100 W. Clarendon Suite 2100, 85013
Telephone: 602-279-5900; 800-220-6817
Fax: 602-264-5566
Email: KimLav.com

Teri Dyan McCall

Representative Clients: The National Basketball Association; Aetna Insurance Co.; Kaibab Industries; Centric Jones Constructors; B & B Masonry; Western Block.

For full biographical listings, see the Martindale-Hubbell Law Directory

LEWIS AND ROCA, LLP (AV)

A Limited Liability Partnership including a Professional Corporation
40 North Central Avenue, 85004-4429
Telephone: 602-262-5311
Fax: 602-262-5747
Email: clientservice@lrlaw.com *URL:* http://www.lrlaw.com
Tucson, Arizona Office: One South Church Avenue, Suite 700, 86701-1620.
Telephone: 520-622-2090.
Fax: 520-622-3088. E-Mail: clientservice@lrlaw.com.
Las Vegas, Nevada Affiliated Office: Ashcraft and Heinz LLP, 3960 Howard Hughes Parkway, 89109.
Telephone: 702-990-3570.
Fax: 702-990-3571.

MEMBERS OF FIRM

Newman R. Porter
Robert F. Roos
Amy R. Porter
Steven J. Burr

ASSOCIATES

Michael L. Denby
Amy L. McAllister

Representative Clients: Arizona Hospital Assn.; ASARCO Inc.; Digital Equipment Corp.; Intel Corp.; Lockheed Aeromod Center, Inc.; Woodstuff Manufacturing.

For Complete List of Firm Personnel, See General Section

For full biographical listings, see the Martindale-Hubbell Law Directory

MUCHMORE & WALLWORK, A PROFESSIONAL CORPORATION (AV)

2700 North Central Avenue, Suite 1225, 85004-1165
Telephone: 602-240-6699
Data: 602-240-6698
Facsimile: 602-240-6697
Email: muchwork@mmww.com *URL:* http://www.mmww.com

Charles J. Muchmore
Nicholas J. Wallwork
Fredric D. Bellamy

SENIOR COUNSEL

Steve Owens

COUNSEL

Bridget S. Bade

(See Next Column)

Christopher D. Payne
Carolina L. Carver
Margaret Benny Hurst
Mindy K. Brinker

OF COUNSEL

Leslie Kyman Cooper
George H. King

LEGAL SUPPORT PERSONNEL

Gloria A. Torres (Administrator)
James R. Potts (Systems Administrator and Litigation Support Manager)
Gale James (Finance Manager)

Representative Clients: AgrEvo USA Company; BHP Copper, Inc.; Chevron U.S.A., Inc.; Cyprus Amax Minerals Company; Homes by Dave Brown, Inc.; National Indemnity Insurance Company; Standard Insurance Company; Washington Mills Electro Minerals Corporation; Cadbury Beverages, Inc.; Eisenberg Company.

For full biographical listings, see the Martindale-Hubbell Law Directory

QUARLES & BRADY LLP (AV)

One Camelback Building, One East Camelback Road, Suite 400, 85012-1649
Telephone: 602-230-5500
Fax: 602-230-5598
URL: http://www.quarles.com
Milwaukee, Wisconsin Office: 411 East Wisconsin Avenue.
Telephone: 414-277-5000.
Fax: 414-271-3552.
Madison, Wisconsin Office: First Wisconsin Plaza, One South Pinckney Street, P.O. Box 2113.
Telephone: 608-251-5000.
Fax: 608-251-9166.
West Palm Beach, Florida Office: 222 Lakeview Avenue, 4th Floor.
Telephone: 407-653-5000.
Fax: 407-653-5333.
Naples, Florida Office: Barnett Center, 4501 Tamiami Trail North, Suite 300.
Telephone: 813-262-5959.
Fax: 813-434-4999.
Chicago, Illinois Office: Quarles & Brady LLC, Citicorp Center, 500 West Madison Street, Suite 3700.
Telephone: 312-715-5000.
Fax: 312-715-5155.

MEMBERS OF THE FIRM

P. Robert Fannin
James D. Vieregg
David G. Beauchamp
Daniel L. Muchow

ASSOCIATE

Jeffrey A. Sandquist

For full biographical listings, see the Martindale-Hubbell Law Directory

SNELL & WILMER L.L.P. (AV)

One Arizona Center, 85004-2202
Telephone: 602-382-6000
Fax: 602-382-6070
Email: postmaster@snellwilmer.com *URL:* http://www.swlaw.com
Tucson, Arizona Office: One South Church Avenue, Suite 1500, 85701-1612.
Telephone: 520-882-1200.
Fax: 520-884-1294.
Orange County Office: 1920 Main Street, Suite 1200, Irvine, California 92614-7230.
Telephone: 949-253-2700.
Fax: 949-955-2507.
Salt Lake City, Utah Office: 111 East Broadway, Suite 900, 84111-1004.
Telephone: 801-237-1900.
Fax: 801-237-1950.

MEMBERS OF FIRM

Steven M. Wheeler
Richard W. Shapiro
Carlos D. Ronstadt
Robert B. Hoffman
G. Van Velsor Wolf, Jr.
Jeffrey Webb Crockett

SENIOR ATTORNEY

Thomas L. Mumaw

ASSOCIATES

Jeffrey Breck Guldner
Robert Henry
Patrick J. Paul

Representative Clients: For list of Representative Clients, see end of biographical listings in the Martindale-Hubbell Law Directory.

For Complete List of Firm Personnel, See General Section

For full biographical listings, see the Martindale-Hubbell Law Directory

SCOTTSDALE, Maricopa Co.

SPARKS, TEHAN & RYLEY, P.C. (AV)

7503 First Street, 85251-4573
Telephone: 480-949-1339
Fax: 480-949-7587

(See Next Column)

SPARKS, TEHAN & RYLEY P.C., *Scottsdale—Continued*

Joe P. Sparks | Kevin T. Tehan
John H. Ryley

LEGAL SUPPORT PERSONNEL

Pamela L. Sparks | Joshua Morgan Sparks
Catherine L. McComb

References: Bank One, Arizona, Trust Department; Northern Trust Bank of Arizona, N.A.; Wells Fargo Bank of Arizona.

For full biographical listings, see the Martindale-Hubbell Law Directory

*TUCSON,** Pima Co.

CHANDLER, TULLAR, UDALL & REDHAIR, L.L.P. (AV)

1700 Bank of America Plaza, 33 North Stone Avenue, 85701-1415
Telephone: 520-623-4353
Telefax: 520-792-3426

MEMBERS OF FIRM

Thomas Chandler
Steven Weatherspoon
Dwight M. Whitley, Jr.
John J. Brady

ASSOCIATE

Stephen L. Wetherell

Representative Clients: Arizona Electric Power Cooperative, Inc.; Atlantic Richfield Co.; CNA Insurance; Farmers Insurance Exchange; MICA; Chubb Insurance Group; State Farm Mutual Insurance Companies.
Reference: Arizona Bank.

For Complete List of Firm Personnel, See General Section

For full biographical listings, see the Martindale-Hubbell Law Directory

SNELL & WILMER L.L.P. (AV)

One South Church Avenue, Suite 1500, 85701-1612
Telephone: 520-882-1200
Fax: 520-884-1294
URL: http://www.swlaw.com
Phoenix, Arizona Office: One Arizona Center, 85004-2202.
Telephone: 602-382-6000.
Fax: 602-382-6070.
Orange County Office: 1920 Main Street, Suite 1200, Irvine, California 92614-7230.
Telephone: 949-253-2700.
Fax: 949-955-2507.
Salt Lake City, Utah Office: 111 East Broadway, Suite 900, 84111-1004.
Telephone: 801-237-1900.
Fax: 801-237-1950.

MEMBERS OF FIRM

Marjorie R. Perry | William N. Poorten, III

OF COUNSEL

Clague A. Van Slyke

Representative Clients: For list of Representative Clients, see end of biographical listings in the Martindale-Hubbell Law Directory.

For full biographical listings, see the Martindale-Hubbell Law Directory

STRICKLAND & STRICKLAND, P.C. (AV)

4400 E. Broadway, Suite 700, 85711-3517
Telephone: 520-795-8727
Fax: 520-795-5649

William E. Strickland | William E. Strickland, Jr.
Robert F. Palmquist

Representative Client: AkChin Indian Community.
Reference: Bank One (formerly Valley National Bank).

ARKANSAS

*LITTLE ROCK,** Pulaski Co.

CHISENHALL, NESTRUD & JULIAN, P.A. (AV)

400 West Capitol, Suite 2840, 72201
Telephone: 501-372-5800
Telecopier: 501-372-4941
Email: cnjlaw@cnjlaw.com

Lawrence E. Chisenhall, Jr.
Charles R. Nestrud
Jim L. Julian
Ann P. Faitz
Michael T. Jackson

For full biographical listings, see the Martindale-Hubbell Law Directory

ROSE LAW FIRM, A PROFESSIONAL ASSOCIATION (AV)

120 East Fourth Street, 72201
Telephone: 501-375-9131
Telecopy: 501-375-1309

(See Next Column)

Herbert C. Rule, III
Allen W. Bird, II
Garland J. Garrett
Stephen N. Joiner
Amy Lee Stewart
Brian Rosenthal
David P. Martin
Michael G. Smith
Kathryn Bennett Perkins
Michael N. Shannon

Counsel for: ALLTEL Corporation; Aluminum Company of America; Bridgestone/Firestone, Inc.; The Equitable Life Assurance Society of The United States; General Motors Corp.; The Prudential Insurance Company of America; Stephens Group Inc.; Tyson Foods, Inc.

For Complete List of Firm Personnel, See General Section

For full biographical listings, see the Martindale-Hubbell Law Directory

CALIFORNIA

APTOS, Santa Cruz Co.

DENNIS J. KEHOE A LAW CORPORATION (AV)

311 Bonita Drive, 95003
Telephone: 408-662-8444
Fax: 408-662-0227

Dennis J. Kehoe

For full biographical listings, see the Martindale-Hubbell Law Directory

*BAKERSFIELD,** Kern Co.

BORTON, PETRINI & CONRON, LLP (AV)

The Borton, Petrini & Conron Building, 1600 Truxtun Avenue, 93301
Telephone: 661-322-3051
Voice Mail: 661-395-6700
Fax: 661-322-4628
Mailing Address: P.O. Box 2026, Bakersfield, California, 93303
Email: bpcbak@bpclaw.com *URL:* http://www.bpclaw.com
Other City Locations: Fresno, Los Angeles, Modesto, Redding, Sacramento, San Bernardino, San Diego, San Francisco, San Jose, San Luis Obispo, Santa Ana and Ventura.

MEMBERS OF FIRM

George F. Martin | Richard E. Morton
Calvin R. Stead

ASSOCIATE

Timothy B. Liebaert

For Complete List of Firm Personnel, See General Section

For full biographical listings, see the Martindale-Hubbell Law Directory

KLEIN, DENATALE, GOLDNER, COOPER, ROSENLIEB & KIMBALL, LLP (AV)

(Formerly Di Giorgio, Davis, Klein, Wegis, Duggan & Friedman)
ARCO Tower, 4550 California Avenue, Second Floor, 93309
Telephone: 661-395-1000
Telecopier: 661-326-0418
Mailing Address: P.O. Box 11172, Bakersfield, California, 93389-1172
Email: kleinlaw@kleinlaw.com

Anthony J. Klein (Inc.)
David J. Cooper
Christopher P. Burger
Melvin L. Ehrlich

Representative Clients: JACO Oil Company; City of Visalia; City of Farmersville; Destec, Inc.; Sandyland Nursery; Boggiato Produce, Inc.; Occidental Oil & Gas; Chevron USA Production Company.

For Complete List of Firm Personnel, See General Section

For full biographical listings, see the Martindale-Hubbell Law Directory

CARLSBAD, San Diego Co.

GATZKE, DILLON & BALLANCE (AV)

A Partnership
Suite 200, 1921 Palomar Oaks Way, 92008
Telephone: 760-431-9501
Fax: 760-431-9512

MEMBERS OF FIRM

Michael Scott Gatzke | Mark J. Dillon
Lori D. Ballance

ASSOCIATES

Michael S. Haberkorn
Stephen F. Tee
Jill Dian Skinner
Tom Deak
Sophia R. Ray
Anne E. Bickel

For full biographical listings, see the Martindale-Hubbell Law Directory

COSTA MESA, Orange Co.

FELDHAKE, AUGUST & ROQUEMORE (AV)

Plaza Tower, Suite 1730, 600 Anton Boulevard, 92626-7124
Telephone: 714-438-3885
Fax: 714-438-3888
Email: farlaw@hqonline.com

Robert J. Feldhake
Kenneth S. August
Lisa A. Roquemore
Joshua M. Wolff

ASSOCIATES

Dimitri P. Gross
Supriya Kakkar
Katherine A. Slayton

OF COUNSEL

Arthur J. Swerdloff
Arthur M. Wilcox, Jr.

For full biographical listings, see the Martindale-Hubbell Law Directory

MCCORMICK, KIDMAN & BEHRENS, LLP (AV)

A Partnership of Professional Corporations
Imperial Bank Building, 695 Town Center Drive Suite 1400, 92626-7187
Telephone: 714-755-3100
Fax: 714-755-3110; 1-800-755-3125
Email: mkb1@ix.netcom.com
Sacramento, California Office: 980 Ninth Street. 16th Floor. 95814-2736.
Telephone: 916-449-9533.
Fax: 916-446-7104.
Effective April 1, 1999 the new address will be: Imperial Bank Building, 695 Town Center Drive, Suite 400.

MEMBERS OF FIRM

Homer L. (Mike) McCormick, Jr., (P.C.)
Arthur G. Kidman (P.C.)
Russell G. Behrens (P.C.)
Suzanne M. Tague (P.C.)
Janet R. Morningstar (P.C.)
Keith E. McCullough (P.C.)

ASSOCIATES

David D. Boyer
Paeter E. Garcia
Gary D. Grant
Edward L. Bertrand

For full biographical listings, see the Martindale-Hubbell Law Directory

RUTAN & TUCKER, LLP (AV)

A Partnership including Professional Corporations
611 Anton Boulevard, Fourteenth Floor, P.O. Box 1950, 92626-1998
Telephone: 714-641-5100; 213-625-7586
Telecopier: 714-546-9035
Email: rutan&tucker@rutan.com *URL:* http://www.rutan.com

MEMBERS OF FIRM

Leonard A. Hampel, Jr.
Michael D. Rubin
Robert S. Bower
David J. Aleshire
Philip D. Kohn
Joel D. Kuperberg
Mary M. Green
Mark B. Frazier
Richard Montevideo
Elizabeth L. Martyn
Kim D. Thompson
Hans Van Ligten
Adam N. Volkert
F. Kevin Brazil
Layne H. Melzer
Lien Ski Harrison
Patrick D. McCalla
S. Daniel Harbottle
Paul J. Sievers

For Complete List of Firm Personnel, See General Section

For full biographical listings, see the Martindale-Hubbell Law Directory

EMERYVILLE, Alameda Co.

BISHOP, BARRY, HOWE, HANEY & RYDER, A PROFESSIONAL CORPORATION (AV)

Watergate Tower III, 2000 Powell Street, Suite 1425, 94608
Telephone: 510-596-0888
Fax: 510-596-0899
Email: FirmGeneral@BBHHR.com
San Francisco Office: 44 Montgomery Street, Suite 1300, 94104.
Telephone: 415-421-8550.

Ross R. Ryder (1940-1989)
Nelson C. Barry
Drayton F. Howe, Jr.
Jeffrey N. Haney
Thomas O. Haran
Rebecca B. Aherne
Michael W. Bolechowski
Mark C. Raskoff
Patricia S. Lakner
Gregory R. de la Peña

J. Scott Wood
Mitchell J. Alward
Marco R. Sumarriva
Jane E. Carey
Carol L. Healey
Mary Margaret Ryan
Thomas Edward Foran
John F. Cooke
Jean H. Hurricane
Daniel M. O'Connell
Lisa S. Wiggins
Edward M. Lai

(See Next Column)

OF COUNSEL

Lawrence S. Molton
David P. Osako

Representative Clients: American Excess & Surplus Ins. Co. (AESIC); Argonaut Ins. Co.; CGU Insurance; Farmers Insurance; Firemans Fund Ins. Co.; General Reinsurance Co.; Gerling American Ins. Co.; Great American Ins. Company; Royal/SunAlliance; TIG.

For full biographical listings, see the Martindale-Hubbell Law Directory

FOLSOM, Sacramento Co.

THE BLEIER LAW FIRM (AV)

110 Blue Ravine Road, Suite 201, 95630
Telephone: 916-454-2100
Fax: 916-454-2121
Email: tblf@bleier.com *URL:* http://www.bleier.com

Brenton A. Bleier

ASSOCIATE

Bradford A. Bleier

For full biographical listings, see the Martindale-Hubbell Law Directory

*FRESNO,** Fresno Co.

DOWLING, AARON & KEELER, INCORPORATED (AV)

6051 North Fresno Street, Suite 200, 93710
Telephone: 559-432-4500
Fax: 559-432-4590
Email: dak@daklaw.com *URL:* http://www.daklaw.com
Bakersfield, California Office: 110 South Mt. Claire, Suite 203. 93309.
Telephone: 661-396-0451. Web Site: http://www.daklaw.com.

Philip David Kopp
Gary M. Fachin
Francine Marie Kanne
Christopher A. Brown
James C. Sherwood

Reference: Wells Fargo Bank (Main).

For Complete List of Firm Personnel, See General Section

For full biographical listings, see the Martindale-Hubbell Law Directory

LANG, RICHERT & PATCH, A PROFESSIONAL CORPORATION (AV)

Fig Garden Financial Center, 5200 North Palm Avenue, 4th Floor, P.O. Box 40012, 93755
Telephone: 559-228-6700
Fax: 559-228-6727

William T. Richert (1937-1993)
Robert L. Patch, II
Val W. Saldaña
Douglas E. Noll
Michael T. Hertz
Victoria J. Salisch
Rene Lastreto, II
Charles Trudrung Taylor
Mark L. Creede
Peter N. Zeitler
Laurie L. Quigley
Tamara L. Equals
Douglas E. Griffin
Nabil E. Zumout

Christopher B. Dorian
Matthew W. Quall
Tracy E. Sagle
Julie K. Hill
Michelle Oleksa

OF COUNSEL

Frank H. Lang

References: Wells Fargo Bank (Fresno Main Office).

For full biographical listings, see the Martindale-Hubbell Law Directory

SAGASER, FRANSON & JONES, A PROFESSIONAL CORPORATION (AV)

2445 Capitol Street, Second Floor, P.O. Box 1632, 93717-1632
Telephone: 559-233-4800
Fax: 559-233-9330

Howard A. Sagaser
Eric K. Hansen (1952-1996)
Donald R. Franson, Jr.
Timothy Jones
Kristi R. Culver Kapetan
Elise M. Shebelut Krause
Nancy A. Maler
W. Allen Bennett
Mark D. Kruthers
Michael S. Helsley
Jamie Katzman

For full biographical listings, see the Martindale-Hubbell Law Directory

GLENDALE, Los Angeles Co.

BRIGHT AND BROWN (AV)

550 North Brand Boulevard, Suite 2100, 91203
Telephone: 818-243-2121; 213-489-1414
Facsimile: 818-243-3225
Email: attorneys@brightandbrown.com

(See Next Column)

BRIGHT AND BROWN, *Glendale—Continued*

James S. Bright
Gregory C. Brown
Maureen J. Bright
John Quirk
Brian L. Becker

ASSOCIATES

PhillipaL. Altmann
Kristin L. Gamble

For full biographical listings, see the Martindale-Hubbell Law Directory

GOLD RIVER, Sacramento Co.

HACKARD, HOLT & HELLER (AV)

11335 Gold Express Drive, Suite 155, 95670
Telephone: 916-853-3000
Facsimile: 916-853-3010
Email: tholt@hackardlaw.com *URL:* http://www.hackardlaw.com

MEMBERS OF FIRM

Michael A. Hackard
Theodore J. Holt

OF COUNSEL

Steven M. Heller
Paige M. Hibbert

ASSOCIATES

David R. Zarka
Jenny M. Fickel
Eric L. Graves
Gregory W. Bayless

For full biographical listings, see the Martindale-Hubbell Law Directory

IRVINE, Orange Co.

MAHER & MAHER, LLP (AV)

18500 Von Karman Avenue, Suite 700, 92612
Telephone: 949-721-7555
Fax: 949-721-7444
Email: mmaher@maherlaw.com

Michael K. Maher
Cynthia R. Maher

For full biographical listings, see the Martindale-Hubbell Law Directory

LAW OFFICES OF SUSAN M. TRAGER A PROFESSIONAL CORPORATION (AV)

The Landmark Building, 2100 S. E. Main Street, Suite 104, 92614
Telephone: 949-752-8971
Telefax: 949-863-9804
Email: smt@tragerlaw.com

Susan M. Trager

OF COUNSEL

Eric S. Norby

Representative Client: San Luis Rey Municipal Water District.
Reference: Sanwa Bank California.

For full biographical listings, see the Martindale-Hubbell Law Directory

LONG BEACH, Los Angeles Co.

CAMERON, PEARLSON & GALE (AV)

One World Trade Center, Suite 1600, 90831-1600
Telephone: 562-436-3888
Telecopier: 562-437-1967
URL: http://www.cpglawyers.com
URL: http://www.lawyers.com/cmp&glaw

MEMBERS OF FIRM

Timothy C. Cameron
Charles M. Gale
Paul R. Pearlson

ASSOCIATES

Dana K. Anderson, Jr.
Susan R. Loh

For full biographical listings, see the Martindale-Hubbell Law Directory

TAUBMAN, SIMPSON, YOUNG & SULENTOR (AV)

249 East Ocean Boulevard, Suite 700, P.O. Box 22670, 90801-5670
Telephone: 562-436-9201
FAX: 562-590-9695
Email: thefirm@tsyslaw.com

E. C. Denio (1864-1952)
Geo. A. Hart (1881-1967)
Geo. P. Taubman, Jr. (1897-1970)
Matthew C. Simpson (1900-1988)
Roger W. Young
William J. Sulentor
Peter M. Williams
Maria M. Rohaidy
Stuart C. Talley

Attorneys for: Bixby Land Co.; Renick Cadillac, Inc.; Oil Operators Inc.
Local Counsel: Crown Cork & Seal Co., Inc.

For full biographical listings, see the Martindale-Hubbell Law Directory

WOOLLEY RUSSELL & JOHNSON (AV)

444 West Ocean Boulevard, Suite 1700, 90802
Telephone: 562-495-6000
Telecopier: 562-435-1359
Email: mail@transportlawyers.com *URL:* http://www.transportlawyers.com
Port Hueneme, California Office: 105 East Port Hueneme Road, 93041.
Telephone: 562-495-6000.
Fax: 562-435-1359.

MEMBERS OF FIRM

David E. R. Woolley
Thomas A. Russell
Philip L. Johnson

ASSOCIATE

Thomas G. Walsh

LEGAL SUPPORT PERSONNEL

PARALEGAL

Dawn C. Breaux

For full biographical listings, see the Martindale-Hubbell Law Directory

*LOS ANGELES,** Los Angeles Co.

ALVARADO, SMITH & SANCHEZ, A PROFESSIONAL CORPORATION (AV)

611 West Sixth Street, Suite 2650, 90017
Telephone: 213-229-2400
Facsimile: 213-229-2499
URL: http://www.alvarado-smith.com
Irvine, California Office: 4 Park Plaza, Suite 1200, 92614.
Telephone: 949-955-6800.
Fax: 949-955-6899.

Raymond G. Alvarado
Ruben A. Smith
Maurice Sanchez
John M. Sorich
Raúl F. Salinas
Frances Q. Jett
Theresa Eileen Antonucci
Diane C. Barrio
Rosario M. Tobias

OF COUNSEL

Martin N. Burton

For full biographical listings, see the Martindale-Hubbell Law Directory

BAKER & HOSTETLER LLP (AV)

600 Wilshire Boulevard, 90017-3212
Telephone: 213-624-2400
FAX: 213-975-1740
To contact an attorney on the Internet use first initial and surname followed by @baker-hostetler.com
URL: http://www.bakerlaw.com
In Cleveland, Ohio: 3200 National City Center, 1900 East Ninth Street.
Telephone: 216-621-0200.
In Cincinnati, Ohio: 312 Walnut Street, Suite 2650.
Telephone: 513-929-3400.
In Columbus, Ohio: Capitol Square, Suite 2100, 65 East State Street.
Telephone: 614-228-1541.
In Denver, Colorado: 303 East 17th Avenue, Suite 1100.
Telephone: 303-861-0600.
In Houston, Texas: 1000 Louisiana, Suite 2000.
Telephone: 713-751-1600.
In Long Beach, California: 300 Oceangate, Suite 620.
Telephone: 562-432-2827.
In Orlando, Florida: SunBank Center, Suite 2300, 200 South Orange Avenue.
Telephone: 407-649-4000.
In Washington, D. C.: Washington Square, Suite 1100, 1050 Connecticut Avenue, N.W.
Telephone: 202-861-1500.

Edward J. McCutchen (1857-1933)
Harold A. Black (1895-1970)
George Harnagel (1903-1962)
G. William Shea (1911-1986)

OFFICE MANAGING PARTNER

Peter W. James (Managing Partner, Los Angeles and Long Beach, California Offices)

PARTNERS

Angela C. Agrusa
Penny M. Costa
David A. Destino
Jonathan R. Hodes
Jack I. Samet
Bill E. Schroeder
Patrick J. Cain
Richard A. Deeb
Gary L. Gilbert
Thomas G. Roberts
David C. Sampson
Glen A. Smith
Teresa R. Tracy

ASSOCIATES

Kathleen E. Bailey
Nigel E. Jacques
Brian A. Ross
Marcos M. Tarango
Megan E. Gray
Andrew Lurie
Wendy E. Stanford
Kimberly R. Wells
Cranston J. Williams

(See Next Column)

BAKER & HOSTETLER LLP—*Continued*

OF COUNSEL

Lisa F. Hinchliffe

RETIRED PARTNERS

G. Richard Doty
Howard J. Privett

For full biographical listings, see the Martindale-Hubbell Law Directory

CLARK & TREVITHICK, A PROFESSIONAL CORPORATION (AV)

800 Wilshire Boulevard, 12th Floor, 90017
Telephone: 213-629-5700
Telecopier: 213-624-9441
Email: postmaster@clarktrev.com
San Francisco, California Office: 456 Montgomery Street, 20th Floor.
Telephone: 415-288-6520.
Fax: 415-398-2820.

Philip W. Bartenetti
Vincent Tricarico
Leonard Brazil
Arturo Santana Jr.

For Complete List of Firm Personnel, See General Section

For full biographical listings, see the Martindale-Hubbell Law Directory

DEMETRIOU, DEL GUERCIO, SPRINGER & MOYER, LLP (AV)

801 South Grand Avenue, 10th Floor, 90017
Telephone: 213-624-8407
Telecopy: 213-624-0174
Email: ddsm@juno.com

MEMBERS OF FIRM

Jeffrey Z. B. Springer
Craig A. Moyer
Stephen A. Del Guercio
Michael A. Francis
Regina Liudzius Cobb
Jennifer T. Taggart
Bradley D. Pierce
Wendy M. Conole
Brian D. Langa
Silvia Saucedo

OF COUNSEL

Ronald J. Del Guercio

Reference: Bank of America, L.A. Main Office, Los Angeles, Calif.

For full biographical listings, see the Martindale-Hubbell Law Directory

GORDON, EDELSTEIN, KREPACK, GRANT, FELTON & GOLDSTEIN (AV)

Suite 1800, 3580 Wilshire Boulevard, 90010
Telephone: 213-739-7000; 213-487-1520
Fax: 213-386-1671
Email: geklaw.com

Roger L. Gordon
Mark Edelstein
Howard D. Krepack
Sherry E. Grant
Richard I. Felton
Irwin L. Goldstein
Steven J. Kleifield
David A. Goldstein

OF COUNSEL

Joshua M. Merliss

ASSOCIATES

Eugenia L. Steele
Vincent F. Bennett
Adam D. Dombchik
Jennifer S. Weisman

For full biographical listings, see the Martindale-Hubbell Law Directory

IVERSON, YOAKUM, PAPIANO & HATCH (AV)

One Wilshire Building, 27th Floor 624 South Grand Avenue, 90017
Telephone: 213-624-7444
Telecopier: 213-629-4563

Paul E. Iverson (1907-1975)
Frank B. Yoakum, Jr. (1906-1991)

MEMBERS OF FIRM

Patrick M. Mc Adam
Arnold D. Larson
John M. Garrick

ASSOCIATES

Douglas C. Pease
Andrew K. Doty
Melissa A. Immel
Mary P. Lightfoot
Mark Pearson
Adam F. Burke
Scott A. Horton

OF COUNSEL

R. Noel Hatch

Representative Clients: Lockheed Corp.; International Paper; Bridgestone/-Firestone, Inc.
Reference: Bank of America (Los Angeles Head Office).

For Complete List of Firm Personnel, See General Section

For full biographical listings, see the Martindale-Hubbell Law Directory

KNOPFLER & ROBERTSON, LLP (AV)

Suite 500, 21650 Oxnard Street (Woodland Hills), 91367
Telephone: 818-227-0770; 213-624-1111
Telefax: 818-227-0777
Irvine, California Office: 19800 MacArthur Boulevard, Suite 270, 92612.
Telephone: 714-261-6191.
Pleasanton, California Office: 400 Main Street, Suite 204, 94566.
Telephone: 510-425-7250.
Las Vegas, Nevada Office: Knopfler & Robertson in Association with Broom & Vaisbort, LLP, 3753 Howard Hughes Parkway, Suite 200, 89109.
Telephone: 702-792-2413.
Camarillo, California Office: 1200 Paseo, Suite 170, 93010.
Telephone: 805-482-1903; 800-CONDOLAW.
Fax: 805-484-5917.

George Knopfler
Alexander Robertson, IV
Deborah Broom
Richard A. Capella
Jonathan S. Vick
Edward D. Vaisbort
William G. Kelsberg

OF COUNSEL

Scott C. Haith
James P. Lingl (Resident, Camarillo Office)
Christina S. Robertson

Janice M. Michaels
James M. Pazos
Mark Rohrer
Craig Smith
Robert Nation
William S. Dunlevy (Resident, Camarillo Office)
Scott A. Hunter

For full biographical listings, see the Martindale-Hubbell Law Directory

LOEB & LOEB LLP (AV)

A Limited Liability Partnership including Professional Corporations
Suite 1800, 1000 Wilshire Boulevard, 90017-2475
Telephone: 213-688-3400
Facsimile: 213-688-3460
Email: info@loeb.com *URL:* http://www.loeb.com
Century City, California Office: Suite 2200, 10100 Santa Monica Boulevard, Los Angeles, 90067-4164.
Telephone: 310-282-2000.
Facsimile: 310-282-2192.
New York, N.Y. Office: 345 Park Avenue, 10154-0037.
Telephone: 212-407-4000.
Facsimile: 212-407-4990.
Nashville, Tennessee Office: 45 Music Square West, 37203-3205.
Telephone: 615-749-8300;
Facsimile: 615-749-8308.
Rome, Italy Office: Piazza Digione 1, 00197.
Telephone: 011-3906-808-8456.
Facsimile: 011-3906-808-8288.

MEMBERS OF FIRM

Brant H. Dveirin
Malissa Hathaway McKeith

ASSOCIATES

Nina B. Luban (New York City Office)
Martha Siefert-Sharp

For Complete List of Firm Personnel, See General Section

For full biographical listings, see the Martindale-Hubbell Law Directory

MITCHELL, SILBERBERG & KNUPP LLP (AV)

A Partnership including Professional Corporations
11377 West Olympic Boulevard, 90064
Telephone: 310-312-2000
Fax: 310-312-3100
Email: info@msk.com *URL:* http://www.msk.com

MEMBERS OF FIRM

Arthur Fine (A Professional Corporation)
John E. Hatherley (A Professional Corporation)
Marvin Leon (A Professional Corporation)
Jean Pierre Nogues (A Professional Corporation)

OF COUNSEL

Douglas W. Bordewieck

References: Wells Fargo Bank, N.A.; Merrill, Lynch.

For Complete List of Firm Personnel, See General Section

For full biographical listings, see the Martindale-Hubbell Law Directory

OLIVER, VOSE, SANDIFER, MURPHY & LEE, A PROFESSIONAL CORPORATION (AV)

Figueroa Courtyard, Second Floor, 281 South Figueroa Street, 90012
Telephone: 213-621-2000
Telecopier: 213-621-2211

(See Next Column)

OLIVER, VOSE, SANDIFER, MURPHY & LEE A PROFESSIONAL CORPORATION, *Los Angeles—Continued*

Charles S. Vose
Connie Cooke Sandifer
James Duff Murphy
Edward W. Lee
Roger W. Springer
Arthur J. Hazarabedian

Bradley E. Wohlenberg
Timothy J. Chung
Kristin L. Mendenhall

Representative Clients: Cities of Anaheim, Bell, Brea, Calabasas and Carson. *Agency Counsel Clients:* Anaheim Housing Authority; Anaheim Redevelopment Agency; Brea Redevelopment Agency; Buena Park Redevelopment Authority; Compton Redevelopment Agency.

For full biographical listings, see the Martindale-Hubbell Law Directory

O'MELVENY & MYERS LLP (AV)

400 South Hope Street, 90071-2899
Telephone: 213-430-6000
Facsimile: 213-430-6407
Cable: MOMS
Telex: 674122
Email: omminfo@omm.com *URL:* http://www.omm.com
Century City, CA Office: 1999 Avenue of the Stars, Los Angeles, 90067-6035.
Telex: 674097. Tel: 310-553-6700.
Fax: 310-246-6779.
Newport Beach, CA Office: 610 Newport Center Drive, 92660-6429.
Telex: 4722088. Tel: 949-760-9600.
Fax: 949-823-6994.
San Francisco, CA Office: Embarcadero Center West, 275 Battery Street, 94111-3305. Tel: 415-984-8700.
Fax: 415-984-8701.
New York, NY Office: Citicorp Center, 153 East 53rd Street, 10022-4611.
Telex: 129165. Tel: 212-326-2000.
Fax: 212-326-2061.
Washington, DC Office: 555 13th Street, N.W., 20004-1109.
Cable: MOMSWSH.
Telex: 89622. Tel: 202-383-5300.
Fax: 202-383-5414.
London Office: O'Melveny & Myers, 3 Finsbury Square, London, EC2A 1LA, England. Tel: 44-171-256-8451. Fax 44-171-638-8205.
Tokyo Office: Akasaka Twin Tower, East 14F, 2-17-23, Akasaka, Minato-ku, Tokyo 107-0052, Japan. Tel: 03-5562-2800.
Fax: 03-5575-3840.
Hong Kong Office: O'Melveny & Myers, Suite 1905, Tower Two, Lippo Centre, 89 Queensway, Central, Hong Kong. Tel: 852-2523-8266.
Fax: 852-2522-1760.
Shanghai Office: Kerry Centre, 20F, 1515 Nanjing Road West, Shanghai, 200040 People's Republic of China. Tel: 86-21-5298-5600.
Fax: 86-21-5298-5500.

PARTNER

Mitchell B. Menzer

For Complete List of Firm Personnel, See General Section

For full biographical listings, see the Martindale-Hubbell Law Directory

OPPENHEIMER WOLFF & DONNELLY LLP (AV)

2029 Century Park East 38th Floor, 90067
Telephone: 310-788-5000
FAX: 310-277-1297
Email: oppenheimer.com
Minneapolis, Minnesota Office: 3300 Plaza VII, 45 South Seventh Street. 55402.
Telephone: 612-607-7000.
FAX: 612-607-7100.
Amsterdam, The Netherlands Office: Keizergracht 241.
Telephone: 31-20-423-4555.
FAX: 312-20-423-4545.
Brussels, Belgium Office: Avenue Louise 240, Box 5, 1050.
Telephone: 32-2-626-0500.
FAX: 32-2-626-0510.
Geneva, Switzerland Office: Rue Gabriel Eynard, 6, 1205.
Telephone: (41/22) 311-7410.
FAX: (41/22) 311-4707.
Newport Beach, California Office: 500 Newport Center Drive, Suite 700, 92660.
Telephone: 949-823-6000.
FAX: 949-823-6100.
New York, N.Y. Office: The Chrysler East Building, 19th Floor, 666 Third Avenue, 10017.
Telephone: 212-826-5000.
FAX: 212-486-0708.
Paris, France Office: 35 Boulevard des Capucines, 75002.
Telephone: (33/1) 53 45 40 00.
FAX: (33/1) 53 45 40 10.
St. Paul, Minnesota Office: 1700 First National Bank Building, 55101.
Telephone: 651-605-2000.
FAX: 651-605-2100.

(See Next Column)

Washington, D.C. Office: Oppenheimer Wolff Donnelly & Bayh LLP, 1350 Eye Street, N.W., Suite 200, 20005.
Telephone: 202-312-8000.
FAX: 202-312-8100.
Palo Alto, California Office: 3373 Hillview Avenue, Suite 200, 94304.
Telephone: 650-320-4000.
FAX: 650-320-4100.
Chicago, Illinois Office: Oppenheimer Wolff & Donnelly (Illinois), Two Prudential Plaza, 45th Floor, 180 North Stetson Avenue, 60601.
Telephone: 312-616-1800.
Fax: 312-616-5800.

RESIDENT PARTNERS

Alan C. Rose
William Poms
Guy Porter Smith
Charles Berman
Gary E. Lande
Louis J. Bovasso
Michael D. Harris
Mark P. Wine
Gregory B. Wood
Christopher Darrow
Jane Shay Wald
Douglas N. Larson
David J. Oldenkamp
Marc E. Brown
W. Mark Levinson
J. Patrick Weir
Charles Rosenberg
Michael B. Farber
Mark L. Jubelt
Alan P. Block
Scott R. Hansen

RESIDENT ASSOCIATES

Sandra M. Parker
Cynthia A. Lock
Joel D. Voelzke
Aimee Y. Wong
George L. Fountain
Barbara J. Quinn
Ronald S. Tamura
Joon M. Khang
Jake A. Taylor
Sung I. Oh

Reference: City National Bank (Century Plaza Office, Century City).

For full biographical listings, see the Martindale-Hubbell Law Directory

THE O'TOOLE LAW FIRM (AV)

601 South Figueroa Street, Suite 4100, 90017
Telephone: 213-630-4200
Facsimile: 213-683-1148
Email: otoolelaw@earthlink.net

Patricia M. O'Toole

For full biographical listings, see the Martindale-Hubbell Law Directory

RODI, POLLOCK, PETTKER, GALBRAITH & CAHILL, A LAW CORPORATION (AV)

444 South Flower Street, Suite 1700, 90071-2901
Telephone: 213-895-4900
Telecopiers: 213-895-4921; 895-4922; 895-4750
URL: http://www.rodipollock.com

Karl B. Rodi (1908-1982)
John D. Cahill
John D. Pettker
Daniel C. Bond (1942-1977)
William R. Christian
Henry P. Pramov, Jr.
John F. Cermak, Jr.
Allan E. Ceran
Elizabeth B. Blakely
Robert C. Norton
Tim G. Ceperley
Coralie Kupfer
Cris K. O'Neall
Scott E. Adamson
Margaret Rosenthal

Sonja A. Inglin
Michael A. Abraham
Kenneth A. Franklin
Richard Nessary
Donna Yamini
Wade E. Norwood
Deepak Nanda
David J. Elbaz

OF COUNSEL

John P. Pollock
James M. Galbraith

For full biographical listings, see the Martindale-Hubbell Law Directory

*OAKLAND,** Alameda Co.

FILICE, BROWN, EASSA & MCLEOD, LLP (AV)

1999 Harrison Street, 18th Floor, 94612
Telephone: 510-444-3131
Fax: 510-839-7940

Gennaro A. Filice III
Eugene Brown, Jr.
Robert D. Eassa
Bruce E. McLeod
Raymond J. Bergez
Nicholas D. Kayhan
John A. De Pasquale
Peter A. Strotz
Richard V. Normington III
Amee A. Mikacich
Stephen J. Valen

Jennifer Walker O'Sullivan
Jason J. Curliano
Kristin Ashurst Hughes
Lisa M. Brown
Jennifer K. Pearce
Constance J. McNeil
Michael H. Kim
Carla M. Nakata
Katrina C. Decker

(See Next Column)

FILICE, BROWN, EASSA & MCLEOD LLP—*Continued*

OF COUNSEL

Barrie Engel
Paul R. Johnson

Representative Clients: Astra Zeneca, Inc.; ChemCentral Corp.; Chevron Corp. Dow Chemical Co.; Ethyl Corporation; ICI Americas, Inc.; Rhodia, Inc.; Rhom & Haas Co.; Tosco Refining Co.; Unocal Corp.

For full biographical listings, see the Martindale-Hubbell Law Directory

HAIMS, MACGOWAN, VALENTINO & PEEBLES, L.L.P. (AV)

490 Grand Avenue, 94610
Telephone: 510-835-0500
Facsimile: 510-835-2833

MEMBERS OF FIRM

Arnold B. Haims
Clyde L. MacGowan
Caroline N. Valentino
Dianne D. Peebles

For full biographical listings, see the Martindale-Hubbell Law Directory

ORANGE, Orange Co.

WALSWORTH, FRANKLIN, BEVINS & MCCALL (AV)

1 City Boulevard West, Fifth Floor, 92868-3604
Telephone: 714-634-2522
LAW-FAX: 714-634-0686
Email: info@wfbm.com
San Francisco, California Office: 550 Montgomery Street, Eighth Floor, 94111-2534.
Telephone: 415-781-7072.
Fax: 415-391-6258.
Santa Barbara, California Office: 827 State Street, Suite 23, 93101.
Telephone: 805-957-0091
Fax: 805-962-7760.

Jeffrey P. Walsworth
Ferdie F. Franklin
Ronald H. Bevins, Jr.
Michael T. McCall
Noel Edlin (Resident, San Francisco Office)
Nicholas A. Cipiti
Lawrence E. Duffy, Jr.
Sandra G. Kennedy
Robert M. Channel (Resident, San Francisco Office)
Stephen M. Nichols
James A. Anton
Randall J. Lee (Resident, San Francisco Office)
John S. Murray
Cyrian B. Tabuena (Resident, San Francisco Office)
Cindy R. Hughes
Laurie E. Sherwood (Resident, San Francisco Office)
Allan W. Ruggles
Houston M. Watson, II
Mary A. Watson
Sharon L. Clisham (Resident, San Francisco Office)
Ingrid K. Campagne (Resident, San Francisco Office)
Deidre F. Cohen
Robyn Sherain Geary
Jennifer A. Cormier (Resident, San Francisco Office)
Karol H. Ingber
Peter D. Nitschke
Lisa M. Martin
Christi M. Gotvald (Resident, San Francisco Office)
Geoffrey S. Long (Resident, San Francisco Office)
Richard R. Ames (Resident, San Francisco Office)
Daniel C. Sigler
Kimberly A. Moses
Michelle M. Castro (Resident, San Francisco Office)
Ellen V. Lockridge (Resident, San Francisco Office)
Jeffrey E. Park
Eric S. McIntosh
Christian J. Ziegler
George M. Snyder
Colleen B. Dougherty
Stamos T. Akrivos (Resident, San Francisco Office)
Margaret Flynn Mahaffey (Resident, San Francisco Office)
Andrew A. Nelson (Resident, San Francisco Office)
Cynthia S. Sandoval (Resident, San Francisco Office)
Jennifer A. Niles (Resident, San Francisco Office)
Scott S. Shepardson
Lisa R. King
Allison L. Fischer
Karen M. Johnson

For full biographical listings, see the Martindale-Hubbell Law Directory

PALO ALTO, Santa Clara Co.

OPPENHEIMER WOLFF & DONNELLY LLP (AV)

3373 Hillview Avenue, Suite 200, 94304
Telephone: 650-320-4000
FAX: 650-320-4100
Email: oppenheimer.com
Minneapolis, Minnesota Office: 3300 Plaza VII, 45 South Seventh Street. 55402.
Telephone: 612-607-7000.
FAX: 612-607-7100.
Amsterdam, The Netherlands Office: Keizergracht 241.
Telephone: 31-20-423-4555.
FAX: 312-20-423-4545.
Brussels, Belgium Office: Avenue Louise 240, Box 5, 1050.
Telephone: 32-2-626-0500.
FAX: 32-2-626-0510.
Geneva, Switzerland Office: Rue Gabriel Eynard, 6, 1205.
Telephone: (41/22) 311-7410.
FAX: (41/22) 311-4707.

(See Next Column)

Newport Beach, California Office: 500 Newport Center Drive, Suite 700, 92660.
Telephone: 949-823-6000.
FAX: 949-823-6100.
New York, N.Y. Office: The Chrysler East Building, 19th Floor, 666 Third Avenue, 10017.
Telephone: 212-826-5000.
FAX: 212-486-0708.
Paris, France Office: 35 Boulevard des Capucines, 75002.
Telephone: (33/1) 53 45 40 00.
FAX: (33/1) 53 45 40 10.
St. Paul, Minnesota Office: 1700 First National Bank Building, 55101.
Telephone: 651-605-2000.
FAX: 651-605-2100.
Washington, D.C. Office: Oppenheimer Wolff Donnelly & Bayh LLP, 1350 Eye Street, N.W., Suite 200, 20005.
Telephone: 202-312-8000.
FAX: 202-312-8100.
Los Angeles, California Office: 2029 Century Park East, 38th Floor, 90067.
Telephone: 310-788-5000.
FAX: 310-277-1297.
Chicago, Illinois Office: Oppenheimer Wolff & Donnelly (Illinois), Two Prudential Plaza, 45th Floor, 180 North Stetson Avenue, 60601.
Telephone: 312-616-1800.
Fax: 312-616-5800.

RESIDENT PARTNER

E. Patrick Ellisen

Reference: City National Bank (Century Plaza Office, Century City).

For full biographical listings, see the Martindale-Hubbell Law Directory

PASADENA, Los Angeles Co.

FREEBURG, JUDY & NETTELS (AV)

600 South Lake Avenue, Suite 500, 91106
Telephone: 626-585-4150
Fax: 626-585-0718
Tustin, California Office: 440 West First Street, Suite 102, 92780-3047.
Telephone: 714-508-1800.
Facsimile: 714-508-1809.

Steven J. Freeburg
J. Lawrence Judy
Charles F. Nettels

ASSOCIATES

Ingall W. Bull, Jr.
Richard B. Castle
Cynthia B. Schaldenbrand (Resident, Tustin Office)
Holly A. McNulty
Karen S. Freeburg
Jennifer D. Helsel
Carla Lynn Crochet (Resident, Tustin Office)
Edward William Burns

For full biographical listings, see the Martindale-Hubbell Law Directory

LAGERLOF, SENECAL, BRADLEY, GOSNEY & KRUSE, LLP (AV)

301 North Lake Avenue, 10th Floor, 91101-4108
Telephone: 626-793-9400
FAX: 626-793-5900
Email: mail@lagerlof.com

MEMBERS OF FIRM

Joseph J. Burris (1913-1980)
Stanley C. Lagerlof (1915-1998)
H. Jess Senecal
Jack T. Swafford
John F. Bradley
Timothy J. Gosney
William F. Kruse
Thomas S. Bunn, III
Andrew D. Turner
Rebecca J. Thyne
James D. Ciampa

ASSOCIATE

Shaun O. Kwon

Representative Clients: Gallo Glass Company; Orthopaedic Hospital; North American Chemical Company; Palmdale Water District; Public Water Agencies Group; Ventura Port District; Walnut Valley Water District; Metric Construction Co., Inc.

For full biographical listings, see the Martindale-Hubbell Law Directory

*SACRAMENTO,** Sacramento Co.

DIEPENBROCK & COSTA (AV)

455 University Avenue, Suite 300, 95825
Telephone: 916-565-6222
Fax: 916-565-6220
Email: dpc@diepcos.com

MEMBERS OF FIRM

Anthony C. Diepenbrock
Daniel P. Costa

ASSOCIATES

John P. Cotter
Nora E. Dwyer
Evan D. Williams
Scott W. DePeel
Paul R. Cotter
Jean M. O'Sullivan

Representative Clients: American Nuclear Insurer; Caldwell International; Central States of Omaha; Century Surety Co.; CIGNA; Citation; Colonial Penn; Connecticut Speciality Insurance Co.; Federated Mutual; Fleming & Hall.

(See Next Column)

DIEPENBROCK & COSTA, *Sacramento—Continued*

For full biographical listings, see the Martindale-Hubbell Law Directory

DOWNEY, BRAND, SEYMOUR & ROHWER LLP (AV)

Suite 1050, 555 Capitol Mall, 95814
Telephone: 916-441-0131
FAX: 916-441-4021
Email: downey@dbsr.com *URL:* http://www.dbsr.com

MEMBERS OF FIRM

Stephen J. Meyer
Judy H. Hersher
Steven H. Goldberg
Katharine E. Wagner
Patrick G. Mitchell
David R.E. Aladjem
William H. Koch

COUNSEL

Taylor O. Miller

ASSOCIATES

Michael N. Mills
R. Bruce Steubing
Ann L. Trowbridge
Deborah A. Wordham

Counsel for: Roseburg Forest Products Co.; California Department of Conservation; Sunsweet Growers, Inc.; Libby Owens Ford; Evergreen Holdings, Inc.; F.D.I.C.; Procter & Gamble Co.; Raley's; Sacramento-Yolo Port District; The Hertz Corp.

For Complete List of Firm Personnel, See General Section

For full biographical listings, see the Martindale-Hubbell Law Directory

GRATTAN & GALATI (AV)

Renaissance Tower, 801 K Street, Penthouse Suite, 95814
Telephone: 916-441-6575
Fax: 916-441-6553
Email: scarey@grattangalati.com *URL:* http://www.lawyers.com/grattan&galati

John P. Grattan, Jr.
Scott A. Galati

LEGAL SUPPORT PERSONNEL

Sandra A. Carey

For full biographical listings, see the Martindale-Hubbell Law Directory

GREBEN & ASSOCIATES (AV)

Wells Fargo Center, 400 Capitol Mall, Suite 1100, 95814
Telephone: 916-558-6148
Fax: 916-447-2414
Email: jgreben@pacbell.net *URL:* http://www.lawyers.com/greben&associates

Jan Adam Greben

ASSOCIATE

Daniel Chester

For full biographical listings, see the Martindale-Hubbell Law Directory

HARDY ERICH BROWN & WILSON, A PROFESSIONAL CORPORATION (AV)

1000 G Street, 95814
Telephone: 916-449-3800
Fax: 916-449-3888
Mailing Address: P.O. Box 13530, Sacramento, California, 95853-4530
Email: hebw@hebw.com *URL:* http://www.hebw.com

Anthony D. Osmundson
Thomas C. Richards
John Quincy Brown, III
David S. Worthington
L. Kent Wyatt
Bruce E. Salenko
Brian H. Charter
Richard L. Alley
Whitney A. Davis
John C. Miller, Jr.
Michael J. Nelson

Kristine E. Balogh
Reginald A. Dunn

Representative Clients: Aircraft Services International Group; The Dexter Corporation; Fireman's Fund Insurance Company; Liberty Mutual Insurance Company; The Goodyear Tire & Rubber Company; Royal Insurance Company; Travelers Insurance Company; VIAD Corporation; Wausau Insurance Company; Zurich American Insurance Company.

For full biographical listings, see the Martindale-Hubbell Law Directory

HUNTER RICHEY DI BENEDETTO & BREWER, LLP (AV)

A Limited Liability Partnership
Renaissance Tower, 801 K Street, 23rd Floor, 95814-3525
Telephone: 916-491-3000
Facsimile: 916-491-3080
Email: hrdb@hrdb.com *URL:* http://www.hrdb.com

(See Next Column)

MEMBERS OF FIRM

William S. Hunter
Win R. Richey
Florence L. Di Benedetto
Roy E. Brewer
Anne E. Ferguson
James F. Geary
Janet C. Eisenbeis
Stephen C. Ruehmann
Sharon K. Sandeen
Jack V. Lovell
Patricia J. Hartman

OF COUNSEL

Laurie E. Davis

LEGAL SUPPORT PERSONNEL

Lori J. Moody (Paralegal)
Deborah M. Johnson (Paralegal)
Linda Jane Hall (Executive Assistant)
Jennifer E. Mueller (Legal Assistant)
Michele L. Nickell (Legal Assistant)
Lynetta G. Goodwin

For full biographical listings, see the Martindale-Hubbell Law Directory

LIVINGSTON & MATTESICH, LAW CORPORATION (AV)

1201 K Street, Suite 1100, 95814
Telephone: 916-442-1111
Fax: 916-448-1709
Email: l&m@lmlaw.net *URL:* http://www.lmlaw.net

Gene Livingston
James M. Mattesich
Carol Livingston
Rebecca M. Ceniceros
Emilio E. Varanini, III
Kenneth M. Malovos
Kathleen E. Finnerty
Joanna R. Mendoza

Steven P. Belzer
Jeffrey Leacox
Randy Pollack
Alice H. Choi
Stephen Craig Hunter
Matthew J. Goldman
Joel C. Baiocchi
Baldassaro (Bill) Di Capo
John McKinsey
Timothy E. Naccarato
Craig N. Lundgren
Mary Farrell Taylor
Brian Crone
Gay L. Carroll
Steven G. Churchwell

Representative Clients: 3M Comapny; Apollinaris & Schweppes, GMBH & Co.; Calvin Klein Cosmetics Company; Lyondell Chemical Company; Oxygenated Fuels Association; Styrene Information and Research Center; The Cosmetic, Toiletry and Fragrance Association; Vulcan Materials; Weider Nutrition Group.

For full biographical listings, see the Martindale-Hubbell Law Directory

REMY, THOMAS AND MOOSE, LLP (AV)

455 Capitol Mall, Suite 210, 95814
Telephone: 916-443-2745
Fax: 916-443-9017
Email: RANDT@CWO.COM *URL:* http://www.cwo.com/~randt/

MEMBERS OF FIRM

Michael Helge Remy
Tina A. Thomas
James G. Moose
Whitman F. Manley

ASSOCIATES

John H. Mattox
Andrea M. Klein
Sheryl Schaffner Freeman
Erik K. Spiess
Jennifer S. Holman
Marian A. King

OF COUNSEL

Brian J. Plant

Representative Clients: Metropolitan Water District; Euron Oil and Gas; County of Butte; City of San Rafael; AKT Developments.

For full biographical listings, see the Martindale-Hubbell Law Directory

RICHARD M. ROSS (AV)

400 Capitol Mall, Suite 900, 95814-4407
Telephone: 916-449-3908
Fax: 916-444-0270
Email: rross000@counsel.com

For full biographical listings, see the Martindale-Hubbell Law Directory

STEVENS & O'CONNELL LLP (AV)

400 Capitol Mall, Suite 1400, 95814-4412
Telephone: 916-329-9111
Facsimile: 916-329-9110

Charles J. Stevens
George L. O'Connell
Richard Pachter
David A. Cheit
Craig C. Allison
Bradley A. Benbrook
Todd M. Noonan
Timothy P. Grieve

For full biographical listings, see the Martindale-Hubbell Law Directory

*SAN DIEGO,** San Diego Co.

HAIGHT, BROWN & BONESTEEL, L.L.P. (AV)

A Partnership including Professional Corporations
101 West Broadway, Suite 1000, 92101-3544
Telephone: 619-595-5583
Telecopier: 619-595-7873
URL: http://www.hbblaw.com
Santa Monica, California Office: 1620 26th Street, Suite 4000 North, P.O. Box 680.
Telephone: 310-449-6000.
Telecopier: 310-829-5117.
Telex: 705837.
Santa Ana, California Office: Suite 900, 5 Hutton Centre Drive.
Telephone: 714-754-1100.
Telecopier: 714-754-0826.
Riverside, California Office: California Tower, 3737 Main Street, Suite 800.
Telephone: 909-341-8300.
Fax: 909-341-8309.
San Francisco, California Office: 101 Bush Street, 27th Floor.
Telephone: 415-986-7700.
Fax: 415-986-6945.

RESIDENT MEMBER
Terrell A. Quealy

For full biographical listings, see the Martindale-Hubbell Law Directory

HOVEY & KIRBY, A PROFESSIONAL CORPORATION (AV)

402 West Broadway, Suite 1500, 92101
Telephone: 619-685-4000
Fax: 619-685-4004
Email: administrator@hoveylaw.com

Gregg B. Hovey
Geraldine A. Valdez

For full biographical listings, see the Martindale-Hubbell Law Directory

LUCE, FORWARD, HAMILTON & SCRIPPS LLP (AV)

A Partnership including Professional Corporations
600 West Broadway, Suite 2600, 92101
Telephone: 619-236-1414
Fax: 619-232-8311
URL: http://www.luce.com
La Jolla, California Office: 4275 Executive Square, Suite 800, 92037.
Telephone: 858-455-6611.
Fax: 858-232-8311.
Los Angeles, California Office: 777 South Figueroa, Suite 3600, 90017.
Telephone: 213-892-4992.
Fax: 213-892-7731.
San Francisco, California Office: 121 Spear Street, Suite 200, 94105.
Telephone: 415-356-4600.
Fax: 415-356-4610.
New York, N.Y. Office: Citicorp Center, 153 East 53rd Street, 26th Floor, 10022.
Telephone: 212-754-1414.
Fax: 212-644-9727.
Chicago, Illinois Office: 180 North La Salle Street, Suite 3110, 60601.
Telephone: 312-641-0580.
Fax: 312-641-0380.

Christopher J. Healey
John W. Leslie
Stephen L. Marsh
Steven P. McDonald
Jon K. Wactor (Resident, San Francisco Office)

OF COUNSEL
Robert E. McGinnis

ASSOCIATES
Jonathan Schneeweiss
James G. Waian

For Complete List of Firm Personnel, See General Section

For full biographical listings, see the Martindale-Hubbell Law Directory

*SAN FRANCISCO,** San Francisco Co.

ALDEN ARONOVSKY & SAX LLP (AV)

235 Montgomery Street, 28th Floor, 94104-2902
Telephone: 415-732-5820
Facsimile: 415-732-5840
Email: law@aaslaw.com

MEMBERS OF FIRM
David W. Alden
Ronald G. Aronovsky
Brian M. Sax (1945-1997)

ASSOCIATES
Jeffrey S. Koppelmaa
Sherry A. Glassman

For full biographical listings, see the Martindale-Hubbell Law Directory

ALICE SUET YEE BARKLEY (AV)

30 Blackstone Court, 94123
Telephone: 415-775-0495
Facsimile: 415-775-6466

For full biographical listings, see the Martindale-Hubbell Law Directory

HAIGHT, BROWN & BONESTEEL, L.L.P. (AV)

A Partnership including Professional Corporations
100 Bush Street, 27th Floor, 94104-3902
Telephone: 415-986-7700
Telecopier: 415-986-6945
URL: http://www.hbblaw.com
Santa Monica, California Office: 1620 26th Street, Suite 4000 North, P.O. Box 680.
Telephone: 310-449-6000.
Telecopier: 310-829-5117.
Telex: 705837.
Santa Ana, California Office: Suite 900, 5 Hutton Centre Drive.
Telephone: 714-754-1100.
Telecopier: 714-754-0826.
Riverside, California Office: California Tower, 3737 Main Street, Suite 800.
Telephone: 909-341-8300.
Fax: 909-341-8309.
San Diego, California Office: 101 West Broadway, Suite 1000.
Telephone: 619-595-5583.
Fax: 619-595-7873.

RESIDENT MEMBER
Lisa L. Oberg

For full biographical listings, see the Martindale-Hubbell Law Directory

KAUFMAN & LOGAN LLP (AV)

111 Pine Street, Suite 1300, 94111
Telephone: 415-392-6677
Telecopier: 415-391-4639

MEMBERS OF FIRM
Jeffrey Kaufman
Peter J. Logan
Garrett L. Cecchini
W. Martin Tellegen
Richard A. Eggerth

ASSOCIATES
Nancy S. Coan
Sandra L. Cross
Gerald F. Ellersdorfer
Paul A. Peters
Paulette Donsavage
George D. Vanberg-Wolff

OF COUNSEL
Gerhard Stoll

LEGAL SUPPORT PERSONNEL
PARALEGALS
Karen L. Dunn, CLA
T. Patrick Bridenstine
Adrienne Levin
Paula R. Brawley

For full biographical listings, see the Martindale-Hubbell Law Directory

LEACH, MCGREEVY & BAUTISTA, LLP (AV)

2833 Laguna Street, 94123
Telephone: 415-775-4455
Telefax: 415-775-7435
Email: LMLawSF@aol,com
Southern California Office: 24752 Via San Fernando, Mission Viejo, CA 92692.
Telephone: 949-859-7464.

Theodore Tamba (1900-1973)
John T. Harmon (1928-1993)
David G. Leach
Richard E. McGreevy
A. Marquez Bautista
Robert W. Shinnick
Philip T. Kilduff
Peter C. Labrador

ASSOCIATES
John C. Connolly
Larry B. Carr
Annadel A. Almendras
David Emerson Beeby

OF COUNSEL
Lloyd F. Postel

For full biographical listings, see the Martindale-Hubbell Law Directory

LIEFF, CABRASER, HEIMANN & BERNSTEIN, LLP (AV)

Embarcadero Center West, 30th Floor, 275 Battery Street, 94111
Telephone: 415-956-1000
Telecopier: 415-956-1008
Email: mail@lchb.com *URL:* http://www.lchb.com
New York, N.Y. Office: 10 Rockefeller Plaza, 12th Floor, 10020-1903.
Telephone: 212-218-6600.
Fax: 212-218-6608.

Robert L. Lieff
Elizabeth J. Cabraser
Richard M. Heimann
William Bernstein
William B. Hirsch
James M. Finberg
Karen E. Karpen
Joseph R. Saveri
Donald C. Arbitblit

(See Next Column)

LIEFF, CABRASER, HEIMANN & BERNSTEIN LLP, *San Francisco—Continued*

Steven E. Fineman (Resident, New York, N.Y. Office)
Robert J. Nelson
Jacqueline E. Mottek
Morris A. Ratner
Melanie M. Piech
Kelly M. Dermody
Jonathan D. Selbin
Richard M. Franco
Barry R. Himmelstein
Joshua P. Davis
Michael W. Sobol
Robert G. Eisler (Resident, New York, N.Y. Office)

Jennie L. Anderson
Lori E. Andrus
Caryn Becker
Joan T. Brown (Not admitted in CA)
Stephen H. Cassidy
Paulina do Amaral
Eric B. Fastiff
Hector D. Geribon (Resident, New York, N.Y. Office)
Pierce Gore
Rebecca M. Katz (Resident, New York, N.Y. Office)
Lisa J. Leebove
Karen J. Mandel (Resident, New York, N.Y. Office)
Scott P. Nealey
Erik L. Shawn (Resident, New York, N.Y. Office)
David S. Stellings (Resident, New York, N.Y. Office)
Steven M. Tindall
Fabrice N. Vincent
Jonathan M. Watkins
Heather A. Woodard
Yu-Yee Wu

For full biographical listings, see the Martindale-Hubbell Law Directory

MORGENSTEIN & JUBELIRER, LLP (AV)

One Market, Spear Street Tower, 32nd Floor, 94105
Telephone: 415-896-0666
Fax: 415-896-5592
Email: m&j@mj-sflaw.com

Marvin D. Morgenstein (Retired)
Eliot S. Jubelirer
Lee Ann Huntington
Jean L. Bertrand
Jeffrey R. Williams
James R. Balich
Rocky N. Unruh
James L. McGinnis
Charles W. LaGrave
William J. Carroll
John S. Worden
Wendi J. Berkowitz
Stephen M. Hankins
Bruce A. Wagman

Lewis D. Barr
David H. Bromfield
Alexander P. Catalona
Michael "Cael" S. Davis
Roberta Nicol Dempster
Laura E. Gasser
Jill L. Gillen
Natasha L. Golding
Judith A. Holiber
Shawn D. Parrish
John J. Petry

For full biographical listings, see the Martindale-Hubbell Law Directory

SCADDEN, HAMILTON & RYAN (AV)

220 Montgomery Street, 13th Floor, 94104-3410
Telephone: 415-362-5116
Telecopier: 415-362-4214
URL: http://www.shrlaw.com

James G. Scadden
Robert P. Hamilton
Robert J. Ryan
James P. Cunningham

Charles O. Thompson
Eileen Santana Wright
Vincent C. Milani
Timothy K. Killelea

LEGAL SUPPORT PERSONNEL

Edwin L. Lilley
Dennis Prime
Mary Sue Schroeder

For full biographical listings, see the Martindale-Hubbell Law Directory

VOGL & MEREDITH (AV)

456 Montgomery Street, 20th Floor, 94104
Telephone: 415-398-0200
Facsimile: 415-398-2820

Samuel E. Meredith
David R. Vogl
John P. Walovich
Jean N. Yeh
Thomas S. Clifton

Nicole L. Meredith
Dennis Gildea
Michael S. Burke
Martin Ross Sances
Joshua A. Ridless
David G. Valdez

For full biographical listings, see the Martindale-Hubbell Law Directory

*SAN JOSE,** Santa Clara Co.

HOPKINS & CARLEY, A LAW CORPORATION (AV)

Sixth Floor, 2 West Santa Clara Street, 95113-1824
Telephone: 408-286-9800
Facsimile: 408-998-4790
Mailing Address: P.O. Box 1469, San Jose, CA, 95109-1469
URL: http://www.hopkinscarley.com

(See Next Column)

William S. Klein

For Complete List of Firm Personnel, See General Section

For full biographical listings, see the Martindale-Hubbell Law Directory

MCMANIS, FAULKNER & MORGAN (AV)

160 West Santa Clara Street, 10th Floor, 95113
Telephone: 408-279-8700
Fax: 408-279-3244; 408-279-0494
Email: mfm@mfmlaw.com *URL:* http://www.mfmlaw.com

James McManis
William Faulkner
Donelle Morgan
Lisa Herrick
Michael Reedy
Erica Yew

Michelle Tidalgo
Colleen Duffy Smith
Lillian Wolf
Rebecca Hughes
Kalpana Vrudhula
Ray M. Baluyot
Catherine Bechtel
Arron Nesbitt

OF COUNSEL

Mary Arand

For full biographical listings, see the Martindale-Hubbell Law Directory

REED, ELLIOTT, CREECH & ROTH (AV)

99 Almaden Boulevard, Eighth Floor, 95113
Telephone: 408-993-9911
Fax: 408-993-1335
URL: http://www.sjlegal.com

MEMBERS OF FIRM

John W. Elliott
Randall C. Creech
Thomas A. Elliott
Jeffrey S. Lawson
Peter A. Liebow
Raymond A. Brinson

ASSOCIATES

Lauren Berger
Nancy L. Mathis
Edward A. Kraus
Betty Chen
Bonnie L. Portis

OF COUNSEL

Steven J. Roth
Charles R. Reed
Thomas G. Perkins

Reference: Union Bank of California.

For full biographical listings, see the Martindale-Hubbell Law Directory

*SAN LUIS OBISPO,** San Luis Obispo Co.

ANDRE, MORRIS & BUTTERY, A PROFESSIONAL LAW CORPORATION (AV)

1102 Laurel Lane, P.O. Box 730, 93406-0730
Telephone: 805-543-4171
Fax: 805-543-0752
Email: amb@amblaw.com *URL:* http://www.amblaw.com

Michael J. Morris
James C. Buttery

Mary E. McAlister
Kevin D. Morris
William V. Douglass

References: Bank of America National Trust and Savings Assn. (San Luis Obispo Main Branch); Mid-State Bank (San Luis Obispo).

For full biographical listings, see the Martindale-Hubbell Law Directory

*SANTA ANA,** Orange Co.

CALLAHAN & BLAINE, A PROFESSIONAL LAW CORPORATION (AV)

3 Hutton Centre Drive, Suite 900, 92707
Telephone: 714-241-4444
Fax: 714-241-4445
Email: info@callahan-law.com *URL:* http://www.callahan-law.com

Daniel J. Callahan
Stephen E. Blaine

Jim P. Mahacek
Michael J. Sachs
Edward Susolik
Kathleen L. Dunham
Robyn Dimino
Reed N. Archambault
Nicki N. Eke
David Kam Ng
Douglas W. Schroeder

OF COUNSEL

Shelley M. Liberto
Walt D. Mahaffa

For full biographical listings, see the Martindale-Hubbell Law Directory

Santa Ana—Continued

CASSIDY, WARNER, LANE & WINSTEAD, A PROFESSIONAL CORPORATION (AV)

600 West Santa Ana Boulevard, Suite 700, 92701
Telephone: 714-835-9431
Fax: 714-835-5264
Email: cdaly@cassidywarner.com

B. Kent Warner
Timothy X. Lane
Bruce A. Winstead

David C. Olson
Glen A. Stebens

OF COUNSEL

Alvin M. Cassidy

For full biographical listings, see the Martindale-Hubbell Law Directory

*SANTA BARBARA,** Santa Barbara Co.

HOLLISTER & BRACE, A PROFESSIONAL CORPORATION (AV)

1126 Santa Barbara Street, P.O. Box 630, 93101
Telephone: 805-963-6711
Fax: 805-965-0329
Email: hblaw@hbsb.com

William A. Brace (Retired)
J. James Hollister, III (Retired)
John S. Poucher
Richard C. Monk
George A. Rempe, III
Steven Evans Kirby
Bradford F. Ginder
John G. Busby
Susan H. McCollum
Robert L. Brace
Marcus Scott Bird
Charles W. Willey (P.C.)
Alexis W. Willey
Peter L. Candy

Attorneys For: Environmental Research Foundation, Inc.; Buellflat Rock Co.; Celite Corp.

For full biographical listings, see the Martindale-Hubbell Law Directory

SANTA MONICA, Los Angeles Co.

HAIGHT, BROWN & BONESTEEL, L.L.P. (AV)

A Partnership including Professional Corporations
1620 26th Street, Suite 4000 North, P.O. Box 680, 90404
Telephone: 310-449-6000
Telecopier: 310-829-5117
Telex: 705837
URL: http://www.hbblaw.com
Santa Ana, California Office: Suite 900, 5 Hutton Centre Drive.
Telephone: 714-754-1100.
Telecopier: 714-754-0826.
Riverside, California Office: California Tower, 3737 Main Street, Suite 800.
Telephone: 909-341-8300.
Fax: 909-341-8309.
San Francisco, California Office: 101 Bush Street, 27th Floor.
Telephone: 415-986-7700.
Fax: 415-986-6945.
San Diego, California Office: 101 West Broadway, Suite 1000.
Telephone: 619-595-5583.
Fax: 619-595-7873.

MEMBERS OF FIRM

Steven L. Hoch (A Professional Corporation)
William J. Sayers
Jeffrey B. Margulies
Farah Sohaili Nicol

ASSOCIATES

Joanne Lembert Rosen
Karen B. Goldberg
Nana Nakano
Susan M. Weisenberg
Asmi A. Shah

For full biographical listings, see the Martindale-Hubbell Law Directory

TORRANCE, Los Angeles Co.

FINER, KIM & STEARNS (AV)

An Association of Professional Corporations
City National Bank Building, 3424 Carson Street, Suite 500, 90503
Telephone: 310-214-1477
Telecopier: 310-214-0764
Email: finerkimstearns@pobox.com *URL:* http://www.finerkimstearnslaw.com

W. A. Finer (A Professional Corporation)
Robert David Ciaccio
Robert B. Parsons

OF COUNSEL

Bennett A. Rheingold
Ryan E. Stearns

For Complete List of Firm Personnel, See General Section

For full biographical listings, see the Martindale-Hubbell Law Directory

*VENTURA,** Ventura Co.

STRAUSS • URITZ A PROFESSIONAL CORPORATION (AV)

290 Maple Court, Suite 200, 93003
Telephone: 805-644-7458
Fax: 805-644-4325
Email: mail@venturalaw.com *URL:* http://www.venturalaw.com

Curt W. Uritz

For full biographical listings, see the Martindale-Hubbell Law Directory

TAYLOR MCCORD, A LAW CORPORATION (AV)

721 East Main Street, P.O. Box 1477, 93002
Telephone: 805-648-4700
Email: vtafamlaw@aol.com

Richard L. Taylor
Robert L. McCord, Jr.
David L. Praver

Patrick Cherry
Susan D. Siple
Rebbecca F. Calderwood

LEGAL SUPPORT PERSONNEL

PARALEGALS

Stephanie Gibson
Adele Rubino (Certified Legal Assistant, California Advanced Specialist)
Diane Lovato

For full biographical listings, see the Martindale-Hubbell Law Directory

COLORADO

*ASPEN,** Pitkin Co.

PATRICK & STOWELL, P.C. (AV)

730 East Durant Street, Suite 200, 81611
Telephone: 970-920-1028
Fax: 970-925-6847
Email: info@waterlaw.com *URL:* http://www.waterlaw.com

Kevin L. Patrick
Brian L. Stowell

Scott Carpenter Miller
Kristin L. Howse
Ramsey L. Kropf

For full biographical listings, see the Martindale-Hubbell Law Directory

*BOULDER,** Boulder Co.

TRINE & METCALF, P.C. (AV)

1435 Arapahoe Avenue, 80302-6390
Telephone: 303-442-0173
Fax: 303-443-7677
Email: firm@trine-metcalf.com *URL:* http://www.trine-metcalf.com

William A. Trine
J. Conard Metcalf

T. Michael Kennedy

Reference: Norwest Bank of Boulder.

For full biographical listings, see the Martindale-Hubbell Law Directory

VRANESH AND RAISCH, L.L.P. (AV)

1720 14th Street, Suite 200, P.O. Box 871, 80306-0871
Telephone: 303-443-6151
Telecopier: 303-443-9586
Email: attorneys@vraneshraisch.com

MEMBERS OF FIRM

Jerry W. Raisch
John R. Henderson
Michael D. Shimmin
Eugene J. Riordan
Paul J. Zilis
George Vranesh (1926-1997)

Richard Woodruff Curran

OF COUNSEL

Asimakis (Maki) P. Iatridis

Representative Clients: Cyprus Climax Metals Co.; City of Fort Collins; Colorado Association of Commerce and Industry; County of Arapahoe; Eastman Kodak Company; Hendricks Mining Company; Independence Mining Co.; Metro Wastewater Reclamation District; Waste Management of North America.

For full biographical listings, see the Martindale-Hubbell Law Directory

*DENVER,** Denver Co.

BAKER & HOSTETLER LLP (AV)

303 East 17th Avenue, Suite 1100, 80203-1264
Telephone: 303-861-0600
FAX: 303-861-7805
To contact an attorney on the Internet use first initial and surname followed by @baker-hostetler.com
URL: http://www.bakerlaw.com
In Cleveland, Ohio: 3200 National City Center, 1900 East Ninth Street.
Telephone: 216-621-0200.
In Cincinnati, Ohio: 312 Walnut Street, Suite 2650.
Telephone: 513-929-3400.
In Columbus, Ohio: Capitol Square, Suite 2100, 65 East State Street.
Telephone: 614-228-1541.
In Houston, Texas: 1000 Louisiana, Suite 2000.
Telephone: 713-751-1600.
In Beverly Hills, California: 9150 Wilshire Boulevard, Suite 205.
Telephone: 310-385-7500.
In Long Beach, California: 300 Oceangate, Suite 620.
Telephone: 562-432-2827.
In Los Angeles, California: 600 Wilshire Boulevard.
Telephone: 213-624-2400.
In Orlando, Florida: SunBank Center, Suite 2300, 200 South Orange Avenue.
Telephone: 407-649-4000.
In Washington, D. C.: Washington Square, Suite 1100, 1050 Connecticut Avenue, N.W.
Telephone: 202-861-1500.

OFFICE MANAGING PARTNER

Raymond L. Sutton, Jr.

PARTNERS

Timothy R. Beyer
Mary Price Birk
Gregory S. Brown
Alfred C. Chidester
James A. Clark
Marc D. Flink
Gerald H. Hansen
James M. King
Peter J. Korneffel, Jr.
Phillip S. Lorenzo
Richard S. Mandelson
William R. Marsh
James R. Martin
Michael G. Martin
Thomas H. Maxfield
John B. Moorhead
Laurin D. Quiat
Stuart G. Rifkin
Michael J. Roche
Cassandra G. Sasso
David L. Starbuck
Douglas M. Tisdale
Victor L. Wallace, II

ASSOCIATES

Jeanne A. Carroll
Fay Chu Fong
Theresa J. Collier
L. Andrew Cooper
Paul S. Enockson
Ronald Lyle Hellbusch
Steven A. Klenda
Rebecca C. Lovell
Munir R. Meghjee
Demetri E. (Rico) Munn
Stephanie S. Padilla
David J. Ringelman
Thomas B. Romer
R. Scott Smith (Not admitted in CO)
Michelle M. St. Pierre
Jennifer N. Story

RETIRED PARTNERS

Keith Anderson
Fred M. Winner

For full biographical listings, see the Martindale-Hubbell Law Directory

BALLARD SPAHR ANDREWS & INGERSOLL, LLP (AV)

Seventeenth Street Plaza Building, Suite 2300, 1225 17th Street, 80202-5596
Telephone: 303-292-2400
Fax: 303-296-3956
URL: http://www.ballardspahr.com
Baltimore, Maryland Office: 300 East Lombard Street. 19th Floor.
Telephone: 410-528-5600.
Fax: 410-528-5650.
Camden, New Jersey Office: 800 Hudson Square, 5th Floor.
Telephone: 856-541-5577.
Fax: 856-541-8272.
Philadelphia, Pennsylvania Office: 1735 Market Street, 51st Floor.
Telephone: 215-665-8500.
Fax: 215-864-8999.
Salt Lake City, Utah Office: One Utah Center, Suite 1200, 201 South Main Street.
Telephone: 801-531-3000.
Fax: 801-531-3001.
Voorhees, New Jersey Office: Suite 100, 1101 Laurel Oak Drive.
Telephone: 856-627-8555.
Fax: 856-627-1153.
Washington, D.C. Office: Suite 1000 South, 601 13th Street, N.W.
Telephone: 202-661-2200.
Fax: 202-661-2299.

Elizabeth H. Temkin

OF COUNSEL

Denise S. Maes

(See Next Column)

Virginia Morton Creighton
Suzanna Kay Moran
Kristin M. Tita

For Complete List of Firm Personnel, See General Section

For full biographical listings, see the Martindale-Hubbell Law Directory

BERENBAUM, WEINSHIENK & EASON, P.C. (AV)

Suite 2600 Republic Plaza, 370 17th Street, 80202
Telephone: 303-825-0800
Facsimile: 303-629-7610
Email: berenbaum1@aol.com *URL:* http://www.BWELaw.com

James L. Kurtz-Phelan
Larry R. Martinez
Dean G. Panos

Representative Clients: Home Depot; Sprint Spectrum, L.P.; Town of Vail, Colorado; First Union Corporation; City of Englewood, Colorado; Oakwood Homes; Karman, Inc.; Wells Fargo Bank, N.A.; Berkshire Life Insurance Co.; Trinity Ventures.

For full biographical listings, see the Martindale-Hubbell Law Directory

BROWNSTEIN HYATT & FARBER, P.C. (AV)

Twenty-Second Floor, 410 Seventeenth Street, 80202-4437
Telephone: 303-223-1100
Telecopier: 303-223-1111
Washington, D.C. Office: 1615 L Street, N.W., Suite 450, 20036.
Telephone: 202-296-7353.
Telecopier: 202-296-7009.
Glenwood Springs, Colorado Office: Box 357, 81602.
Telephone: 970-945-5302.
Telecopier: 970-945-4921.

Andrew W. Loewi
Stanley L. Garnett
Wayne F. Forman
Hubert A. Farbes, Jr.
Mark J. Mathews

SENIOR COUNSEL

James S. Lochhead (Resident, Glenwood Springs, Colorado Office)
Gale A. Norton

SPECIAL COUNSEL

Richard P. Barkley

Beth Doherty Quinn
David S. Chipman
Ted J. Trimpa
Andrew L. Spielman
Chad G. Asarch

Representative Clients: Forest City Development; The Hertz Corporation; Kohlberg & Co.; New Century Energies, Inc.; The Prudential Insurance Company of America; Ravinia, LLC; Richmond Homes; SunAmerica, Inc.; Trammell Crow Company; Trillium Corporation.

For Complete List of Firm Personnel, See General Section

For full biographical listings, see the Martindale-Hubbell Law Directory

CARLSON, HAMMOND & PADDOCK, L.L.C. (AV)

1700 Lincoln Street, Suite 3900, 80203
Telephone: 303-861-9000
Telefax: 303-861-9026
Email: CHP@ECentral.com

MEMBERS OF FIRM

John Undem Carlson (1940-1992)
Mary Mead Hammond
William A. Paddock
Lee Heinrick Johnson
Peter C. Fleming

Elizabeth Pollock

Representative Clients: Arch Coal Co.; Board of Water Works of Pueblo Colorado; City of Colorado Springs; Colorado Water Resources & Power Development Authority; Forbes Inc.; Irrigationists' Association; OXY USA, Inc.; Rio Grande Water Users Assn.; San Luis Valley Water Conservancy District; City of Westminster.

For full biographical listings, see the Martindale-Hubbell Law Directory

DUFFORD & BROWN, P.C. (AV)

1700 Broadway, Suite 1700, 80290-1701
Telephone: 303-861-8013
Facsimile: 303-832-3804
Colorado Springs, Colorado Office: 101 N. Tejon, Suite 410.
Telephone: 719-471-0559.
Facsimile: 719-471-0583.
Affiliated Office: Solomon, Pearl, Blum & Quinn, L.L.P., New York, NY and Denver, Colorado.

William C. Robb
Richard L. Fanyo
Eugene F. Megyesy, Jr.
Craig B. Shaffer

(See Next Column)

DUFFORD & BROWN P.C.—*Continued*

Joanne Herlihy

Representative Clients: A. O. Smith Corp.; Asarco, Inc.; CF&I Steel, L.P.; Chemical Waste Management, Inc.; ChevronShale Oil Company; Coors Brewing Company; Echo Bay Mines, Ltd.-Sunnyside Gold Co.; Homestake Mining Company; Kerr Coal Company; Trapper Mining Inc.; WMX Technologies, Inc.

For Complete List of Firm Personnel, See General Section

For full biographical listings, see the Martindale-Hubbell Law Directory

FRIEDLOB SANDERSON RASKIN PAULSON & TOURTILLOTT, LLC (AV)

1400 Glenarm Place, 80202-5099
Telephone: 303-571-1400
Fax: 303-595-3159; 303-595-3970; 303-615-5472
Englewood, Colorado Office: 8400 East Prentice Avenue, 80111-2918.
Telephone: 303-571-1400.
Santa Cruz, California Office: 519 Seabright Avenue, Suite 208, 95062-3482.
Telephone: 813-460-3966.
Fax: 813-460-3968.

James W. Sanderson
Christopher R. Paulson
W. B. Tourtillott
Paul M. Seby
Brian M. Nazarenus

Carolyn Burr
Matthew G. Paulson

For full biographical listings, see the Martindale-Hubbell Law Directory

GORSUCH KIRGIS LLP (AV)

Tower 1, Suite 1000, 1515 Arapahoe Street, 80202
Telephone: 303-376-5000
Fax: 303-376-5001

PARTNER

Peter R. Nadel

For full biographical listings, see the Martindale-Hubbell Law Directory

HOLLY I. HOLDER, P.C. (AV)

518 Seventeenth Street Suite 1500, 80202
Telephone: 303-534-3636
Fax: 303-534-6905
Email: holderpc@aol.com

Holly I. Holder

Priscilla S. Fulmer
Carmen Sower Hall

LEGAL SUPPORT PERSONNEL

Gary J. Crosby (Paralegal)
Dean C. Stalnaker (Paralegal)

For full biographical listings, see the Martindale-Hubbell Law Directory

HOLME ROBERTS & OWEN LLP (AV)

Suite 4100, 1700 Lincoln, 80203
Telephone: 303-861-7000
Telecopier: 303-866-0200
Email: hro@hro.com *URL:* http://www.hro.com
Boulder, Colorado Office: Suite 400, 1401 Pearl Street.
Telephone: 303-444-5955.
Telecopier: 303-444-1063.
Colorado Springs, Colorado Office: Suite 1300, 90 South Cascade Avenue.
Telephone: 719-473-3800.
Telecopier: 719-633-1518.
Salt Lake City, Utah Office: Suite 1100, 111 East Broadway.
Telephone: 801-521-5800.
Telecopier: 801-521-9639.
London, England Office: Heathcoat House, 3rd Floor, 20 Savile Row.
Telephone: 011-44-171-494-5600.
Telecopier: 011-44-171-287-9344.

PARTNERS OF FIRM

Dennis L. Arfmann
Linnea Brown
Thomas F. Cope
Daniel J. Dunn
Colin G. Harris
Henry W. Ipsen
Kenneth W. Lund
John D. McCarthy
Charlotte Louise Neitzel
Robert Tuchman

SPECIAL COUNSEL

Richard A. Oertli

SENIOR COUNSEL

A. Edgar Benton
Edward E. Stevenson

ASSOCIATES

Kelly K. Calocci
Katheryn Jarvis Coggon
Matthew J. Lepore
E. Blaine Rawson (Salt Lake City Office)
Lisa A. Schuh
Brent A. Tracy

(See Next Column)

For Complete List of Firm Personnel, See General Section

For full biographical listings, see the Martindale-Hubbell Law Directory

LEVY & LAMBDIN, P.C. (AV)

Plaza Tower One, Suite 900, 6400 South Fiddlers Green Circle (Englewood), 80111
Telephone: 303-796-2900
Telecopier: 303-796-2081

Marc R. Levy
Suzanne J. Lambdin
Stuart D. Morse
Karen Hannah Wheeler

Martha C. Ferris
Gerald D. Pratt
Michael S. Power
Janet S. Bouffard
Stephanie Ann Montague
Brian J. Waters
Ivan A. Sarkissian
Lelia Kathleen Chaney
Jane E. Hershey

For full biographical listings, see the Martindale-Hubbell Law Directory

MARKUSSON, GREEN & JARVIS, P.C. (AV)

Suite 2300, 1050 Seventeenth Street, 80265
Telephone: 303-572-4200
Fax: 303-595-3780

James K. Green
H. Keith Jarvis
Dennis H. Markusson
Thomas E. Napp

Kirstin G. Lindberg
Jason L. Romero
William B. Stanton
William T. Webb
Ashley E. Moller

For full biographical listings, see the Martindale-Hubbell Law Directory

OTTEN, JOHNSON, ROBINSON, NEFF & RAGONETTI, P.C. (AV)

950 Seventeenth Street, 16th Floor, 80202
Telephone: 303-825-8400
Telecopier: 303-825-6525
URL: http://www.ojrnr.com

Hugh Q. Gottschalk
Nicole J. Hanak
Berkeley I. Vogelsang

OF COUNSEL

Barbara J. Green

For Complete List of Firm Personnel, See General Section

For full biographical listings, see the Martindale-Hubbell Law Directory

ROOT & SCHINDLER, P.C. (AV)

410 17th Street, Suite 460, 80202
Telephone: 303-572-1235
Fax: 303-572-1256
Email: rootschi@ix.netcom.com

Thomas E. Root
Ronald I. Schindler

For full biographical listings, see the Martindale-Hubbell Law Directory

TREECE, ALFREY, MUSAT & BOSWORTH, P.C. (AV)

999 18th Street, Suite 1600, 80202
Telephone: 303-292-2700
Facsimile: 303-295-0414
Email: tamb@tamblaw.com *URL:* http://www.tamblaw.com

Robert S. Treece
Thomas N. Alfrey
Arthur H. Bosworth, II

For full biographical listings, see the Martindale-Hubbell Law Directory

VRANESH AND RAISCH, L.L.P.

(See Boulder)

WELBORN SULLIVAN MECK & TOOLEY, P.C. (AV)

1775 Sherman Street, Suite 1800, 80203-4318
Telephone: 303-376-4490
Facsimile: 303-376-4495
Email: wsmt@aol.com

John F. Welborn
Scott L. Sells
Stephen A. Bain

Representative Clients: Colorado Oil & Gas Association; Evergreen Resources, Inc.; Vessels Oil & Gas Company; Western Mining Corporation (USA); WMC Exploration Inc.

For Complete List of Firm Personnel, See General Section

For full biographical listings, see the Martindale-Hubbell Law Directory

CONNECTICUT

GLASTONBURY, Hartford Co.

TROWBRIDGE & BASINE, P.C. (AV)

45 Glastonbury Boulevard, 06033
Telephone: 860-633-3995
FAX: 860-633-3449

Robert L. Trowbridge
Robert B. Basine

For full biographical listings, see the Martindale-Hubbell Law Directory

*HARTFORD,** Hartford Co.

AUSTIN CAREY, JR., P.C. (AV)

Gothic Park, Suite 200, 43 Woodland Street, 06105-2340
Telephone: 860-724-0012
Fax: 860-724-1211
Email: acarey@compuserve.com

Austin Carey, Jr.

For full biographical listings, see the Martindale-Hubbell Law Directory

SHIPMAN & GOODWIN LLP (AV)

One American Row, 06103-2819
Telephone: 860-251-5000
Telecopier: 860-251-5099
Email: www@goodwin.com *URL:* http://shipman-goodwin.com
Lakeville, Connecticut Office: 12 Porter Street.
Telephone: 203-435-2539.
Stamford, Connecticut Office: One Landmark Square.
Telephone: 203-324-8100.

MEMBERS OF FIRM

Coleman H. Casey
Charles L. Howard
Paul D. Sanson
John E. Wertam
Timothy S. Hollister

ASSOCIATES

Joseph P. Williams
Eric W. Alletzhauser

Representative Clients: Hartford Hospital; Lego Systems; Stanadyne, Inc.; Wheelabrator Environmental Systems; Cumberland Farms, Inc.; Waste Management, Inc.

For Complete List of Firm Personnel, See General Section

For full biographical listings, see the Martindale-Hubbell Law Directory

DELAWARE

*WILMINGTON,** New Castle Co.

POTTER ANDERSON & CORROON LLP (AV)

Hercules Plaza, 1313 N. Market Street, P.O. Box 951, 19899-0951
Telephone: 302-984-6000
Fax: 302-658-1192
URL: http://www.attys.pacdelaware.com

MEMBERS OF FIRM

W. Harding Drane, Jr.
Harold I. Salmons, III

Representative Clients: Conectiv, Inc.; U.S. Generating Co.; International Petroleum Corporation; KAO Infosystems Company; The Andrew Jergens Company; High Point Chemical Corporation; Rodel, Inc.; Hercules, Inc.; Conrail; Amtrak.

For Complete List of Firm Personnel, See General Section

For full biographical listings, see the Martindale-Hubbell Law Directory

DISTRICT OF COLUMBIA

WASHINGTON, D.C. Co.

BAISE, MILLER & FREER, P.C. (AV)

1020 19th Street NW, Suite 400, 20036
Telephone: 202-331-9100
Fax: 202-331-9060
Email: Baisemill@aol.com *URL:* http://www.dclaw.net
Charlottesville, Virginia Office: 100 Court Square Annex, Suite B, 22902.
Telephone: 804-970-7999.
Fax: 804-970-5046.

(See Next Column)

Gary H. Baise
Eric P. Bock (Not admitted in DC)
Anson M. Keller
Marshall Lee Miller
Mark L. Shaffer
Robert E. Freer, Jr.
Michael S. Levy
Paul Clinton Harris, Sr. (Resident, Charlottesville, Virginia Office)
Cyndra H. Van Clief (Resident, Charlottesville, Virginia Office)
Elva M. Holland (Not admitted in DC)

Charlotte E. Gillespie
Elizabeth S. Poliner
David G. Zanardi (Not admitted in DC)

OF COUNSEL

Guy Vander Jagt (Not admitted in DC)
Alexander McMillan Bullock

For full biographical listings, see the Martindale-Hubbell Law Directory

BAKER BOTTS L.L.P. (AV)

A Registered Limited Liability Partnership
The Warner, 1299 Pennsylvania Avenue, N.W., 20004-2400
Telephone: 202-639-7700
Fax: 202-639-7832
Email: postmaster@bakerbotts.com *URL:* http://www.bakerbotts.com
Houston, Texas Office: One Shell Plaza, 910 Louisiana.
Telephone: 713-229-1234.
Austin, Texas Office: 1600 San Jacinto Center, 98 San Jacinto Boulevard.
Telephone: 512-322-2500.
Dallas, Texas Office: 2001 Ross Avenue.
Telephone: 214-953-6500.
New York, New York Office: 599 Lexington Avenue.
Telephone: 212-705-5000.
Moscow, Russia Office: 10 ul. Bolshaya Dimitrovka (formerly Pushkinskaya), 103031.
Telephone: 7095/921-5300 (Local); 7501/929-7070 (International).
London, England Office: 45 Ludgate Hill.
Telephone: 0171-778-1400 (Local); 011-44-171-778-1400 (International).
Baku, Azerbaijan Office: 6-10 Vagif Mustafa-zadeh Street, Third Floor, Icheri Sheher, 370004.
Telephone: 994-12-97-63-88 (Local); 011-994-12-97-63-88 (International).

MEMBERS OF FIRM

J. Patrick Berry
William M. Bumpers
Thomas J. Eastment
Steven R. Hunsicker
Bruce F. Kiely
Mark K. Lewis
Randolph Quaile McManus

SPECIAL COUNSEL

Debra Raggio Bolton

ASSOCIATES

Joshua B. Frank
Debra J. Jezouit
Mary Ann Poirier

For Complete List of Firm Personnel, See General Section

For full biographical listings, see the Martindale-Hubbell Law Directory

BAKER & HOSTETLER LLP (AV)

Washington Square, Suite 1100, 1050 Connecticut Avenue, N.W., 20036-5304
Telephone: 202-861-1500
Fax: 202-861-1783
To contact an attorney on the Internet use first initial and surname followed by @baker-hostetler.com
URL: http://www.bakerlaw.com
In Cleveland, Ohio: 3200 National City Center, 1900 East Ninth Street.
Telephone: 216-621-0200.
In Cincinnati, Ohio: 312 Walnut Street, Suite 2650.
Telephone: 513-929-3400.
In Columbus, Ohio: Capitol Square, Suite 2100, 65 East State Street.
Telephone: 614-228-1541.
In Denver, Colorado: 303 East 17th Avenue, Suite 1100.
Telephone: 303-861-0600.
In Houston, Texas: 1000 Louisiana, Suite 2000.
Telephone: 713-751-1600.
In Beverly Hills, California: 9150 Wilshire Boulevard, Suite 205.
Telephone: 310-385-7500.
In Long Beach, California: 300 Oceangate, Suite 620.
Telephone: 562-432-2827.
In Los Angeles, California: 600 Wilshire Boulevard.
Telephone: 213-624-2400.
In Orlando, Florida: SunBank Center, Suite 2300, 200 South Orange Avenue.
Telephone: 407-649-4000.

PARTNER

Kenneth D. Woodrow

For Complete List of Firm Personnel, See General Section

For full biographical listings, see the Martindale-Hubbell Law Directory

Washington—Continued

CARR GOODSON WARNER, A PROFESSIONAL CORPORATION (AV)

1301 K Street, N.W., Suite 400, East Tower, 20005-3300
Telephone: 202-310-5500
Telecopier: 202-310-5555
Email: (attorney initials)@cgw-law.com *URL:* http://www.carrgoodsonwarner.com
Vienna, Virginia Office: Tycon Towers, 8000 Towers Crescent Drive, Suite 1350, 22182.
Telephone: 703-691-8818.
Baltimore, Maryland Office: 401 East Pratt Street, Suite 1622, The World Trade Center, 21202.
Telephone: 410-752-1570.
Rockville, Maryland Office: 31 Wood Lane, 20850.
Telephone: 301-424-7024.

Margaret H. Warner
M. Miller Baker
William J. Carter
Mark A. Collins
Gregory A. Krauss
James G. Rizzo

SENIOR COUNSEL

Peter K. Tompa

Edward M. Andries
Matthew J. Cuccias (Not admitted in DC)
Ngoc H. Lam (Not admitted in DC)
Brian M. Tauscher

For Complete List of Firm Personnel, See General Section

For full biographical listings, see the Martindale-Hubbell Law Directory

COHEN, MILSTEIN, HAUSFELD & TOLL, P.L.L.C. (AV)

West Tower, Suite 500, 1100 New York Avenue, N.W., 20005-3964
Telephone: 202-408-4600
Facsimile: 202-408-4699
Email: lawinfo@cmht.com *URL:* http://www.CMHT.com
Seattle, Washington Office: 999 Third Avenue, Suite 3600.
Telephone: 206-521-0080.
Facsimile: 206-521-0166.

MEMBERS OF FIRM

Jerry S. Cohen (1925-1995)
Herbert E. Milstein
Michael D. Hausfeld
Steven J. Toll (Resident, Seattle, Washington Office)
Ann C. Yahner
Lisa M. Mezzetti
Andrew N. Friedman
Richard S. Lewis
Daniel S. Sommers
Daniel A. Small
Gary E. Mason
Joseph M. Sellers
Sharon A. Snyder
Mark S. Willis (Not admitted in DC)

ASSOCIATES

Lori G. Feldman (Resident, Seattle, Washington Office)
Paul T. Gallagher
Christine E. Webber
Alexander E. Barnett
Matthew James Ide (Resident, Seattle, Washington Office)
Matthew F. Pawa
Suzette M. Malveaux
Mary N. Strimel
Kristopher A. Kinkade (Resident, Seattle, Washington Office)
Agnieszka M. Fryszman
Deborah J. Vagins
Ari Karen
Charles E. Tompkins
Tamara J. Driscoll (Resident, Seattle, Washington Office)
Elizabeth Haines Cronise
Donna Solen
Lesli C. Esposito (Not admitted in DC)

OF COUNSEL

Margaret G. Farrell

For full biographical listings, see the Martindale-Hubbell Law Directory

CUTLER & STANFIELD, L.L.P. (AV)

700 Fourteenth Street, N.W. 10th Floor, 20005-2014
Telephone: 202-624-8400
Fax: 202-624-8410
Denver, Colorado Office: 1675 Broadway, 80202.
Telephone: 303-825-7000.
FAX: 303-825-7005.

MEMBERS OF FIRM

Eliot R. Cutler
Jeffrey L. Stanfield
Sheila D. Jones
Perry M. Rosen
Peter J. Kirsch
Barry Conaty
Stephen H. Kaplan (Not admitted in DC)
Sarah M. Rockwell (Not admitted in DC)
Thomas D. Roth

OF COUNSEL

Byron Keith Huffman, Jr.

(See Next Column)

ASSOCIATES

Katherine Boonin Andrus
Joel D. Armstrong (Not admitted in DC)
Françoise M. Carrier
Polly B. Jessen (Not admitted in DC)
William G. Malley
Elizabeth A. Mitchell (Resident at Denver, Colorado Office)
Dana C. Nifosi
W. Eric Pilsk
Timothy A. Pohle
John E. Putnam
Daniel S. Reimer (Not admitted in DC)
Andrew T. Swers
Sara E. Wilensky

For full biographical listings, see the Martindale-Hubbell Law Directory

LEWIS & MUNDAY, A PROFESSIONAL CORPORATION (AV)

(Formerly Lewis, Clay & Munday, P.C.)
1120 Connecticut Avenue, Suite 280, 20036
Telephone: 202-835-0616
Fax: 202-833-3316
Email: karen.brown@lewis-pc.com *URL:* http://www.lewis-pc.com
Detroit, Michigan Office: 1300 First National Building, 660 Woodward Avenue. 48226-3531.
Telephone: 313-961-2550.
Fax: 313-961-1270.
Boston, Massachusetts Office: 101 Federal Street, Suite 1900. 02110.
Telephone: 617-478-0553.
Fax: 617-478-0543.

Karen Kendrick Brown (Resident)

For full biographical listings, see the Martindale-Hubbell Law Directory

OPPENHEIMER WOLFF DONNELLY & BAYH LLP (AV)

1350 Eye Street, N.W. Suite 200, 20005
Telephone: 202-312-8000
FAX: 202-312-8100
URL: http://www.owdlaw.com
Oppenheimer Wolff & Donnelly LLP
Minneapolis, Minnesota Office: 3300 Plaza VII, 45 South Seventh Street. 55402.
Telephone: 612-607-7000.
FAX: 612-607-7100.
Amsterdam, The Netherlands Office: Keizergracht 241.
Telephone: 31-20-423-4555.
FAX: 31-20-423-4545.
Brussels, Belgium Office: Avenue Louise 240, Box 5, 1050.
Telephone: 32-2-626-0500.
FAX: 32-2-626-0510.
Geneva, Switzerland Office: Rue Gabriel Eynard, 6, 1206.
Telephone: (41/22) 311-7410.
FAX: (41/22) 311-7407.
New York, N.Y. Office: Citicorp Center, 153 East 53rd Street, 10022.
Telephone: 212-826-5000.
FAX: 212-486-0708.
Newport Beach, California Office: 500 Newport Center Drive, Suite 700, 92660.
Telephone: 949-719-6000.
FAX: 949-719-6020.
Paris, France Office: 53 Avenue Montaigne, 75008.
Telephone: (33/1) 44 95 03 50.
FAX: (33/1) 44 95 03 40.
St. Paul, Minnesota Office: 1700 First National Bank Building, 55101.
Telephone: 651-605-2000.
FAX: 651-605-2100.
Los Angeles, California Office: 2029 Century Park East, 38th Floor, 90067.
Telephone: 310-788-5000.
FAX: 310-277-1297.
Palo Alto, California Office: 3373 Hillview Avenue, Suite 200, 94304.
Telephone: 650-320-4000.
FAX: 650-320-4100.
Chicago, Illinois Office: Oppenheimer Wolff & Donnelly (Illinois), Two Prudential Plaza, 45th Floor, 180 North Stetson Avenue, 60601.
Telephone: 312-616-1800.
Fax: 312-616-5800.

RESIDENT PARTNERS

Margaret N. Strand
Carole Stern
Karen M. Hansen (Not admitted in DC)

RESIDENT ASSOCIATE

Lynn A. Bulan

For full biographical listings, see the Martindale-Hubbell Law Directory

Washington—Continued

VENABLE ATTORNEYS AT LAW VENABLE, BAETJER, HOWARD & CIVILETTI, LLP (AV)

A Partnership including Professional Corporations
Suite 1000, 1201 New York Avenue, N.W., 20005
Telephone: 202-962-4800
Fax: 202-962-8300
URL: http://www.venable.com
Baltimore, Maryland Office: Venable, Baetjer and Howard LLP, 1800 Mercantile Bank & Trust Building, 2 Hopkins Plaza.
Telephone: 410-244-7400.
Fax: 410-244-7742.
McLean, Virginia Office: Venable, Baetjer and Howard LLP, Suite 400, 2010 Corporate Ridge.
Telephone: 703-760-1600.
Fax: 703-821-8949.
Rockville, Maryland Office: Venable, Baetjer and Howard LLP, Suite 500, One Church Street, P. O. Box 1906.
Telephone: 301-217-5600.
Fax: 301-217-5617.
Towson, Maryland Office: Venable, Baetjer and Howard LLP, 210 Allegheny Avenue, P. O. Box 5517.
Telephone: 410-494-6200.
Fax: 410-821-0147.

MEMBERS OF FIRM

James K. Archibald (Also at Baltimore, Maryland Office)
Joseph G. Block
Anthony M. Carey (Not admitted in DC; Also at Baltimore, Maryland Office)
Benjamin R. Civiletti (P.C.) (Also at Baltimore and Towson, Maryland Offices)
John F. Cooney
Jeffrey A. Dunn (Also at Baltimore, Maryland Office)
Thomas J. Kelly, Jr.
Brock R. Landry
John J. Pavlick, Jr.
Michael Schatzow (Also at Baltimore, Maryland Office)
James L. Shea (also at Baltimore, Maryland Office)
Judson W. Starr (Also at Baltimore and Towson, Maryland Offices)

ASSOCIATE

Gregory S. Braker

For Complete List of Firm Personnel, See General Section

For full biographical listings, see the Martindale-Hubbell Law Directory

VERNER, LIIPFERT, BERNHARD, MCPHERSON AND HAND, CHARTERED (AV)

901 15th Street, N.W., 20005-2301
Telephone: 202-371-6000
Cable Address: "Verlip"
Fax: 202-371-6279
Email: verner.com *URL:* http://www.verner.com
Houston, Texas Office: 1111 Bagby, Suite 4700, 77002.
Telephone: 713-225-7200.
Fax: 713-752-2199.
Honolulu, Hawaii Office: 745 Fort Street, Suite 600, 96813.
Telephone: 808-566-0999.
Fax: 808-566-0995.
Austin, Texas Office: Suite 1440 San Jacinto Center, 98 San Jacinto Boulevard, 78701.
Telephone: 512-703-6000.
Fax: 512-703-6003.
Las Vegas, Nevada Affiliate Office: Gary C. Moss, Hughes Center, 3960 Howard Hughes Parkway, Suite 400, 89109.
Telephone: 702-737-3433.
Fax: 702-737-1612.
Miami, Florida Office: 3100 First Union Financial Center, 200 South Biscayne Boulevard, 33131.
Telephone: 305-371-8801.
Fax: 305-371-6545.

R. Stuart Broom (Not admitted in DC)
Gary J. Klein
Edward J. McGrath
Paul E. Nordstrom
Neil T. Proto
Sherry A. Quirk
Clinton A. Vince

OF COUNSEL

James K. Jackson
Stanley W. Legro

For Complete List of Firm Personnel, See General Section

For full biographical listings, see the Martindale-Hubbell Law Directory

WATT, TIEDER, HOFFAR & FITZGERALD, L.L.P. (AV)

601 Pennsylvania Avenue, N.W., Suite 900, 20004
Telephone: 703-749-1000
Telecopier: 703-893-8029
Email: contactus@wthf.com *URL:* http://www.wthf.com
McLean Virginia Office: 7929 Westpark Drive, Suite 400,
Telephone: 703-749-1000.
Telecopier: 703-893-8029.
Irvine California Office: 3 Park Plaza, Suite 1500.
Telephone: 949-852-6700.

(See Next Column)

MEMBERS OF FIRM

John B. Tieder, Jr.
Robert K. Cox

For full biographical listings, see the Martindale-Hubbell Law Directory

WILMER, CUTLER & PICKERING (AV)

2445 M Street, N.W., 20037-1420
Telephone: 202-663-6000
Fax: 202-663-6363
Email: Law@Wilmer.Com *URL:* http://www.wilmer.com
Baltimore, Maryland Office: 100 Light Street, 21202.
Telephone: 410-986-2800.
Fax: 410-986-2828.
New York, New York Office: 520 Madison Avenue, 10022.
Telephone: 212-230-8800.
Fax: 212-230-8888.
European Offices:
4 Carlton Gardens, London, SW1Y 5AA, England. Telephone: +44 (20) 7 872 1000.
Fax: +44 (20) 7 839 3537.
Rue de la Loi 15# Wetstraat, B-1040 Brussels, Belgium. Telephone: +32 (2) 285 49 00.
Fax: +32 (2) 285 49 49.
Friedrichstrasse 95, D-10117 Berlin, Germany. Telephone: +49 (30) 20 22 64 00.
Fax: +49 (30) 20 22 65 00.

MEMBERS OF FIRM

C. Boyden Gray
Neil J. King
Daniel H. Squire
Carol Clayton
Laura B. Ahearn
James R. Wrathall

COUNSEL

William A. Butler
Glynn D. Key
Martin Seyfarth (Not admitted in DC; Resident, European Office, Berlin, Germany)

For Complete List of Firm Personnel, See General Section

For full biographical listings, see the Martindale-Hubbell Law Directory

ZEVNIK HORTON GUIBORD MCGOVERN PALMER & FOGNANI, L.L.P. (AV)

The Warner Building, 1299 Pennsylvania Avenue, N.W. Ninth Floor, 20004
Telephone: 202-824-0950
Facsimile: 202-824-0955
Email: law@dc.zhgm.com *URL:* http://www.zevnik.com
Boston, Massachusetts Office: One International Place, Fourteenth Floor.
Telephone: 617-790-2970.
Facsimile: 617-790-2910.
San Francisco, California Office: 225 Bush Street, Seventeenth Floor.
Telephone: 415-364-6300.
Facsimile: 415-364-6333.
Los Angeles, California Office: 333 South Grande Avenue, Twenty First Floor.
Telephone: 213-437-5200.
Facsimile: 213-437-5222.
New York, New York Office: 1330 Avenue of the Americas, Eleventh Floor.
Telephone: 212-407-0600.
Facsimile: 212-407-0606.
Chicago, Illinois Office: 77 West Wacker Drive, Thirty Third Floor.
Telephone: 312-977-2500.
Facsimile: 312-977-2560.
London, England Office: 4 Kings Bench Walk, Temple, London EC4Y 7DL.
Telephone: 171-822-8822.
Facsimile: 171-822-8844.
San Diego, California Office: 101 West Broadway, Seventeenth Floor.
Telephone: 619-515-9600.
Facsimile: 619-515-9628.
Denver, Colorado Office: 555 Seventeenth Street, Twenty Sixth Floor.
Telephone: 303-382-6200.
Facsimile: 303-382-6210.
Woodcliff Lake, New Jersey Office: 50 Tice Boulevard, First Floor.
Telephone: 201-476-9600.
Facsimile: 201-476-9666.
Philadelphia, Pennsylvania Office: 620 Chestnut Street, Tenth Floor.
Telephone: 215-440-8450.
Facsimile: 215-440-8459.

Paul Anton Zevnik
Michel Yves Horton (Resident, Los Angeles, California Office)
Barbara B. Guibord (Resident, Chicago, Illinois Office)
Patrick Michael McGovern (Resident, New York, New York Office)
David G. Palmer (Resident, Denver, Colorado Office)
John D. Fognani (Resident, Denver, Colorado Office)
Joseph G. Homsy (Resident, Chicago, Illinois Office)
John K. Crossman (Resident, New York, New York Office)
Jonathan L. Osborne
John W. Roberts (Resident, Chicago, Illinois Office)

(See Next Column)

ZEVNIK HORTON GUIBORD MCGOVERN PALMER & FOGNANI L.L.P.—*Continued*

Steven E. Knott (Resident, Los Angeles, California Office)
Kenneth D. Polin (Resident, San Diego, California Office)
Steven G. Rowles (Resident, San Diego, California Office)
Charles J. Malaret (Resident, Los Angeles, California Office)
Michael John Miguel (Resident, Boston, Massachusetts Office)
Lea Leadbeater (Not admitted in DC; Resident, Chicago, Illinois Office)

Michael J. Wilson
Gregory M. Cork (Not admitted in DC)
Yolanda C. Griffin
Dolores R. Lyons (Not admitted in DC)

For full biographical listings, see the Martindale-Hubbell Law Directory

FLORIDA

*FORT LAUDERDALE,** Broward Co.

KRUPNICK CAMPBELL MALONE ROSELLI BUSER SLAMA HANCOCK MCNELIS LIBERMAN & MCKEE, P.A. (AV)

700 Southeast 3rd Avenue, Suite 100, 33316-1186
Telephone: 954-763-8181; 877-763-8181 (Toll Free)
Fax: 954-763-8292
Email: information@krupnicklaw.com *URL:* http://www.krupnicklaw.com

Jon E. Krupnick
Walter G. Campbell, Jr.
Kevin A. Malone
Richard J. Roselli
Thomas E. Buser
Joseph J. Slama
Kelly D. Hancock
Lisa A. McNelis
Scott S. Liberman
Robert J. McKee

Carlos Acevedo (Not admitted in FL)
Louis R. Battista
Ivan F. Cabrera
Robert D. Erben
Kelley Badger Gelb
Sean J. Greene
Holly Debra Krulik
Michael J. Ryan

OF COUNSEL

Ben J. Weaver
Dianne Jay Weaver

Reference: Mellon United National Bank.

For full biographical listings, see the Martindale-Hubbell Law Directory

TRIPP SCOTT (AV)

110 S.E. 6th Street, P.O. Box 14245, 33301
Telephone: 954-525-7500
Telecopier: 954-761-8475
URL: http://www.trippscott.com

Norman D. Tripp
James A. Scott
Dennis Dustin Smith
Peter G. Herman
Garry W. Johnson
Kimberly A. Gilmour
Richard D. Heller
Gregory A. McLaughlin
Steven C. Elkin
Daniel E. Taylor
Matthew Zifrony
Edward J. Pozzuoli
William J. Gross

OF COUNSEL

Welcom H. Watson, Jr.

ASSOCIATES

Laura L. Hess
Scott J. Jordan
Tammy L. Knight
Paul Octavio Lopez
Milagros (Millie) G. Muñoz
Loren K. Newman
Richard J. Simeone
Heather S. Tripp
Jeffrey S. Wood
Christine T. Yates

Representative Clients: Alamo Rent A Car, Inc.; Atlas Waste Magic Recyclers, Inc.; AutoNation; Broward County; The Sports Authority, Inc.

For full biographical listings, see the Martindale-Hubbell Law Directory

*JACKSONVILLE,** Duval Co.

BROWN, TERRELL, HOGAN, ELLIS, MCCLAMMA & YEGELWEL, P.A. (AV)

Suite 804 Blackstone Building, 233 East Bay Street, 32202-3417
Telephone: 904-632-2424
Fax: 904-632-2027
Email: mail@bthemy-law.com *URL:* http://www.bthemy-law.com

Thomas R. Brown
James T. Terrell
Wayne Hogan
Timothy D. Ellis
T. Edward McClamma
Evan J. Yegelwel
Thomas E. Duffy, Jr.
Christopher G. Burns
Anita Pryor
Alan M. Pickert

Carroll Cayer
Michael S. Sharrit
Theodore Samuel Pina, Jr.
Mark E. Calvin
Leslie A. Goller
Patricia M. Dodson
Jennifer Kolinski Millis

Reference: NCNB.

For full biographical listings, see the Martindale-Hubbell Law Directory

PAPPAS METCALF JENKS MILLER & REINSCH, P.A. (AV)

200 West Forsyth Street, Suite 1400, 32202-4327
Telephone: 904-353-1980
Telecopier: 904-353-5217
Email: pmj@papmet.com

Thomas M. Jenks
Robert A. Leapley, Jr.
John G. Metcalf
Frank Estes Miller
M. Lynn Pappas
Mark A. Reinsch

Christina P. Gillam
Gary B. Davenport
G. Todd Cottrill
Thomas Ingram

LEGAL SUPPORT PERSONNEL

Mary Beth Wimmer
Glenna Thompson (Paralegal)
Donna F. Demetree (Paralegal)

For full biographical listings, see the Martindale-Hubbell Law Directory

SMITH HULSEY & BUSEY (AV)

1800 First Union National Bank Tower, 225 Water Street, P.O. Box 53315, 32201-3315
Telephone: 904-359-7700
Facsimile: 904-359-7708; 353-9908
Email: vsharp@smithhulsey.com

Lloyd Smith (1915-1987)

MEMBERS OF FIRM

Stephen D. Busey
Earl E. Googe, Jr.
Jeanne E. Helton
Cynthia C. Jackson
G. Preston Keyes
Richard E. Klein
William E. Kuntz
Lauren P. Langham
M. Richard Lewis, Jr.
John F. MacLennan
Raymond R. Magley
E. Owen McCuller, Jr.
James H. Post
Bryan L. Putnal
E. Lanny Russell
Joel Settembrini, Jr.
Tim E. Sleeth
John R. Smith, Jr.
Harry M. Wilson, III

Brandon L. Ayscue
Brannon B. Belcastro
James A. Bolling, Jr.
Charmaine T.M. Chiu
Ryan C. Curtis
Michael R. Freed
Reynold N. Hoover
Michael J. Ivan, Jr.
Tonya L. Janney
Charles H. Keller
Bradley R. Markey
R. Leanne McKnight
Bert J. Millis
Stephen D. Moore, Jr.
Jon L. Swergold

OF COUNSEL

Mark Hulsey
John E. Thrasher

Representative Clients: ATP Tour, Inc; Baptist/St. Vincent's Health System, Inc.; Browning-Ferris Industries, Inc.; First Union National Bank of Florida; Florida Rock Industries, Inc.; PGA Tour, Inc.; KPMG Peat Marwick; The Regency Group, Inc.; The Ritz-Carlton Hotel Co.; University of Florida.

For full biographical listings, see the Martindale-Hubbell Law Directory

LAKELAND, Polk Co.

PETERSON & MYERS, P.A. (AV)

100 East Main Street, P.O. Box 24628, 33802-4628
Telephone: 941-683-6511; 676-6934
Telecopier: 941-682-8031
Lake Wales, Florida Office: 130 East Central Avenue, P.O. Box 1079.
Telephones: 941-676-7611; 683-8942.
Winter Haven, Florida Office: Lake Region Plaza, 141 5th Street, N.W., P.O. Drawer 7608.
Telephone: 941-294-3360.

M. David Alexander, III
Philip O. Allen
Jack P. Brandon
Kristen Marie Buzzanca
Debra Leigh Cline
J. Davis Connor
Dennis G. Corrick
Roy A. Craig, Jr.
Clinton A. Curtis
Jacob C. Dykxhoorn
Joseph A. Geary
Maria "Mia" Gerber
Jonn D. Hoppe
Dennis P. Johnson
Kevin C. Knowlton
Douglas A. Lockwood, III
Corneal B. Myers
E. Blake Paul
Robert E. Puterbaugh
Thomas B. Putnam, Jr.
Deborah A. Ruster
Stephen R. Senn
Andrea Teves Smith
Keith H. Wadsworth
Kerry M. Wilson

General Counsel for: SunTrust Bank Mid-Florida, N.A.; Lakeland Regional Medical Center, Inc.; Housing Finance Authority of Polk County.

(See Next Column)

PETERSON & MYERS P.A., *Lakeland—Continued*

Representative Clients: NationsBank, N.A.; First Union National Bank; Mutual Wholesale Co.; Ben Hill Griffin, Inc.; E. R. Jahna Industries, Inc.
Approved Attorneys for: Attorneys' Title Insurance Fund; Equitable Life Assurance Society of the United States.

For full biographical listings, see the Martindale-Hubbell Law Directory

LAKE WALES, Polk Co.

PETERSON & MYERS, P.A. (AV)
130 East Central Avenue, P.O. Box 1079, 33853
Telephone: 941-676-7611; 683-8942
Telecopier: 941-676-0643
Lakeland, Florida Office: 100 East Main Street, P.O. Box 24628.
Telephones: 941-683-6511; 676-6934.
Winter Haven, Florida Office: Lake Region Plaza, 141 5th Street, N.W., P.O. Drawer 7608.
Telephone: 941-294-3360.

M. David Alexander, III
Philip O. Allen
Jack P. Brandon
Kristen Marie Buzzanca
Debra Leigh Cline
J. Davis Connor
Dennis G. Corrick
Roy A. Craig, Jr.
Clinton A. Curtis
Jacob C. Dykxhoorn
Joseph A. Geary
Maria "Mia" Gerber
Jonn D. Hoppe
Dennis P. Johnson
Kevin C. Knowlton
Douglas A. Lockwood, III
Corneal B. Myers
E. Blake Paul
Robert E. Puterbaugh
Thomas B. Putnam, Jr.
Deborah A. Ruster
Stephen R. Senn
Andrea Teves Smith
Keith H. Wadsworth
Kerry M. Wilson

General Counsel for: SunTrust Bank Mid-Florida, N.A.; Lakeland Regional Medical Center, Inc.; Housing Finance Authority of Polk County.
Representative Clients: NationsBank, N.A.; First Union National Bank; Mutual Wholesale Co.; Ben Hill Griffin, Inc.; E. R. Jahna Industries, Inc.
Approved Attorneys for: Attorneys' Title Insurance Fund; Equitable Life Assurance Society of the United States.

For full biographical listings, see the Martindale-Hubbell Law Directory

*MIAMI,** Dade Co.

EARL, BLANK, KAVANAUGH & STOTTS, PROFESSIONAL ASSOCIATION (AV)
Suite 3760, One Biscayne Tower, Two South Biscayne Boulevard, 33131
Telephone: 305-358-3000
FAX: 305-358-5079
Email: ebkslaw.com *URL:* http://www.ebkslaw.com

William L. Earl
Robert H. Blank
Judith Smith Kavanaugh
Dennis M. Stotts
Stephen R. Verbit

Reference: NationsBank, N.A.

For full biographical listings, see the Martindale-Hubbell Law Directory

JOSEPH Z. FLEMING, P.A.
(See Ford & Harrison LLP, Miami, Florida)

NAGIN GALLOP FIGUEREDO, P.A. (AV)
3225 Aviation Avenue - Third Floor, 33133-4741
Telephone: 305-854-5353
Facsimile: 305-854-5351

Stephen E. Nagin
Earl G. Gallop
Luis R. Figueredo
Scott L. Cagan
Eve A. Boutsis
Jeffrey B. Mallory

For full biographical listings, see the Martindale-Hubbell Law Directory

JEFFREY S. WEINER, P.A. (AV)
Two Datran Center Nineteenth Floor, Suite 1910, 9130 South Dadeland Boulevard, 33156-7858
Telephone: 305 670-9939
Fax: 305 670-9299
Email: lawfirm@jeffweiner.com
Boca Raton, Florida Office: Mizner Park. 327 Plaza Real, Suite 215, 33432.

Jeffrey S. Weiner

Mycki L. Ratzan
Michael B. Cohen
Jason M. Wandner

LEGAL SUPPORT PERSONNEL

Duchess Weiner (Law Office Administrator)

For full biographical listings, see the Martindale-Hubbell Law Directory

*ORLANDO,** Orange Co.

BEST & ANDERSON, P.A. (AV)
1201 East Robinson Street, 32801
Telephone: 407-425-2985
Email: cab@bestandanderson.com *URL:* http://www.bestandanderson.com
Crystal River, Florida Office: Executive Center Condos, 7655 West Gulf to Lake Highway, Suite 6, 34429.
Telephone: 352-795-1107.
Melbourne, Florida Office: Healthsouth Marina Towers, 709 South Harbor City Boulevard, Suite 270, 32901.
Telephone: 407-727-9923.

David R. Best
George H. "Dutch" Anderson, III

Angela O'Neil
James William Nuebel
Lora L. Wilson
Louis Allen DeFreitas, Jr.

For full biographical listings, see the Martindale-Hubbell Law Directory

PUGH AND VAN BUREN (AV)
218 Annie Street, 32806
Telephone: 407-843-5840
Email: igpugh@aol.com *URL:* http://www.lawyers.com/pvblaw

Irby G. Pugh
Tye W. Van Buren

For full biographical listings, see the Martindale-Hubbell Law Directory

WILSON, LEAVITT & SMALL, P.A. (AV)
437 North Magnolia Avenue, 32801-1524
Telephone: 407-843-4321
Fax: 407-423-1505
Email: wlspa@aol.com *URL:* http://www.lawyers.com/eminentdomain

J. Christy Wilson, III
Mark R. Leavitt
Jay W. Small
Kurt H. Garber

Representative Clients: Circle K; Cumberland Farms; Hardee's Food Systems; Mobil Oil; Public Storage; Southland Corp.; U.S.F.& G.; Oerther Foods; Seventh Day Adventists; McDonald's Corporation.

For full biographical listings, see the Martindale-Hubbell Law Directory

*ST. AUGUSTINE,** St. Johns Co.

DOBSON & BROWN, P.A. (AV)
66 Cuna Street, Suite A, 32084
Telephone: 904-824-9032
Fax: 904-824-9236
Email: dblaw@aug.com *URL:* http://www.lawdb.com

Geoffrey B. Dobson
Ronald W Brown

For full biographical listings, see the Martindale-Hubbell Law Directory

UPCHURCH, BAILEY & UPCHURCH, P.A. (AV)
780 North Ponce de Leon Boulevard, P.O. Drawer 3007, 32085-3007
Telephone: 904-829-9066
Facsimile: 904-825-4862
Email: info@ubulaw.com

John D. Bailey, Jr.
Frank D. Upchurch, III
Sidney F. Ansbacher
Stephen A. Faustini

Representative Clients: Flagler Hospital, Inc.; Marine Supply & Oil Co.; Hercules, Inc.; Florida Rock & Tank Lines, Inc.; Island Food Stores, Inc.; Envirotech Southeast, Inc.; McAllisar Towing & Transportation, Inc.; Mobro Marine, Inc.; Kimmins Recycling Corporation; Homosassa Special Water District.

For Complete List of Firm Personnel, See General Section

For full biographical listings, see the Martindale-Hubbell Law Directory

*SARASOTA,** Sarasota Co.

EARL, BLANK, KAVANAUGH & STOTTS, PROFESSIONAL ASSOCIATION

(See Miami)

*TALLAHASSEE,** Leon Co.

AMUNDSEN, MOORE & TORPY (AV)
502 East Park Avenue, P.O. Drawer 1759, 32302
Telephone: 850-425-2444
Facsimile: 850-425-2447
Email: ammolaw@nettally.com
Melbourne, Florida Office: Amundsen, Moore & Torpy, 202 North Harbor City Boulevard, Suite 300, 32935.
Telephone: 407-255-2332.
Facsimile: 407-253-2546.

(See Next Column)

AMUNDSEN, MOORE & TORPY—*Continued*

Paul H. Amundsen — Richard W. Moore

Rodolfo Nuñez — Julia E. Smith

OF COUNSEL

Byron B. Mathews, Jr.

For full biographical listings, see the Martindale-Hubbell Law Directory

LANDERS & PARSONS (AV)

310 West College Avenue, P.O. Box 271, 32302
Telephone: 850-681-0311
Telecopier: 850-224-5595

MEMBERS OF FIRM

Joseph W. Landers, Jr. — John T. LaVia, III
Philip S. Parsons — Robert Scheffel Wright
Fred A. McCormack — David S. Dee
Leslie J. Paugh

LEGAL SUPPORT PERSONNEL

Victoria J. Tschinkel

For full biographical listings, see the Martindale-Hubbell Law Directory

ROSE, SUNDSTROM & BENTLEY, LLP (AV)

2548 Blairstone Pines Drive, P.O. Box 1567, 32301-1567
Telephone: 850-877-6555
Telecopier: 850-656-4029
URL: http://www.rsbattorneys.com

MEMBERS OF FIRM

Chris H. Bentley (P.A.) — John R. Jenkins (P.A.)
Martin S. Friedman (P.A.) — William E. Sundstrom (P.A.)
Diane D. Tremor (P.A.)

Representative Clients: Aloha Utilities, Inc.; Autry Petroleum Co.; Bonita Springs Utility, Inc; City of Apalachicola; Destec Energy; East Central Florida Services, Inc.; Utility Board of Key West; Clay County Water and Sewer Authority; Liberty Waste, Inc.
Reference: Capital City Bank, Tallahassee.

For full biographical listings, see the Martindale-Hubbell Law Directory

*TAMPA,** Hillsborough Co.

CAREY, O'MALLEY, WHITAKER & MANSON, P.A. (AV)

712 South Oregon Avenue, 33606
Telephone: 813-250-0577
Telecopier: 813-250-9898
Email: cowmpa@aol.com

Michael R. Carey — Daniel D. Whitaker
Andrew M. O'Malley — Douglas P. Manson
Randall P. Mueller

For full biographical listings, see the Martindale-Hubbell Law Directory

DE LA PARTE, GILBERT & BALES, PROFESSIONAL ASSOCIATION (AV)

101 East Kennedy, Suite 3400, P.O. Box 2350, 33601-2350
Telephone: 813-229-2775
FAX: 813-229-2712

Louis A. de la Parte (Founder, Retired) — L. David de la Parte
Richard A. Gilbert — Patrick J. McNamara
Edward P. de la Parte, Jr. — Michael A. Skelton
John Calhoun Bales — David M. Caldevilla
David Dallas Dickey

Ronald Anthony Christaldi — Charles W. Crabtree, Jr
Charles Robert Fletcher — Michael S. Dorris

For full biographical listings, see the Martindale-Hubbell Law Directory

WINTER HAVEN, Polk Co.

PETERSON & MYERS, P.A. (AV)

Lake Region Plaza, 141 5th Street N.W., P.O. Drawer 7608, 33883-7608
Telephone: 941-294-3360
Lake Wales, Florida Office: 130 East Central Avenue, P.O. Box 1079.
Telephones: 941-676-7611; 683-8942.
Lakeland, Florida Office: 100 East Main Street, P.O. Box 24628.
Telephones: 941-683-6511; 676-6934.

M. David Alexander, III — Clinton A. Curtis
Philip O. Allen — Jacob C. Dykxhoorn
Jack P. Brandon — Joseph A. Geary
Kristen Marie Buzzanca — Maria "Mia" Gerber
Debra Leigh Cline — Jonn D. Hoppe
J. Davis Connor — Dennis P. Johnson
Dennis G. Corrick — Kevin C. Knowlton
Roy A. Craig, Jr. — Douglas A. Lockwood, III

(See Next Column)

Corneal B. Myers — Deborah A. Ruster
E. Blake Paul — Stephen R. Senn
Robert E. Puterbaugh — Andrea Teves Smith
Thomas B. Putnam, Jr. — Keith H. Wadsworth
Kerry M. Wilson

General Counsel for: SunTrust Bank Mid-Florida, N.A.; Lakeland Regional Medical Center, Inc.; Housing Finance Authority of Polk County.
Representative Clients: NationsBank, N.A.; First Union National Bank; Mutual Wholesale Co.; Ben Hill Griffin, Inc.; E. R. Jahna Industries, Inc.
Approved Attorneys for: Attorneys' Title Insurance Fund; Equitable Life Assurance Society of the United States.

For full biographical listings, see the Martindale-Hubbell Law Directory

WINTER PARK, Orange Co.

VOSE, BLAU & HAYES (AV)

2705 West Fairbanks Avenue, 32789
Telephone: 407-645-3735
Fax: 407-628-5670
Email: bvose@vbh-law.com *URL:* http://www.vbh-law.com

Gretchen R. H. Vose — Leslie A. Blau
Rosemary H. Hayes

ASSOCIATES

Carolyn S. Crichton — Peter J. Meadows
Christina M. Page — Aubrey Harry Ducker, Jr.

For full biographical listings, see the Martindale-Hubbell Law Directory

GEORGIA

*ATLANTA,** Fulton Co.

BONDURANT, MIXSON & ELMORE, LLP (AV)

1201 W. Peachtree Street Suite 3900, 30309
Telephone: 404-881-4100
Fax: 404-881-4111
URL: http://www.bondurant-mixson.com

MEMBERS OF FIRM

Emmet J. Bondurant II — John E. Floyd
H. Lamar Mixson — Michael B. Terry
M. Jerome Elmore — P. Richard Game
Edward B. Krugman — Jill A. Pryor
Jeffrey O. Bramlett — J. Scott McClain

Representative Clients: American Dairy Queen Corp.; Avon Products, Inc.; Bottlers of Coca-Cola, U.S.A.; Blue Circle of America; Delta Air Lines, Inc.; Fina Oil and Chemical Company; Four M Corporation; Penske Motorsports; Queen Carpets, Inc.; Ticketmaster Southeast.

For full biographical listings, see the Martindale-Hubbell Law Directory

BOVIS, KYLE & BURCH, LLC (AV)

A Limited Liability Corporation including Professional Corporations
Third Floor, 53 Perimeter Center East, 30346
Telephone: 770-391-9100
Telecopier: 770-668-0878
Email: bkb@boviskyle.com *URL:* http://www.boviskyle.com

John M. Bovis (P.C.) — Charles M. Medlin
James E. Singer — John H. Peavy Jr.

For Complete List of Firm Personnel, See General Section

For full biographical listings, see the Martindale-Hubbell Law Directory

FREEMAN, WRIGHT & HERMAN (AV)

3060 Peachtree Road, N.W. Suite 720, 30305-2240
Telephone: 404-262-2962
Fax: 404-237-1926
Email: bhi@bellsouth.net

MEMBERS OF FIRM

Joe C. Freeman, Jr. — Arnold Wright, Jr.
Robert L. Herman

For full biographical listings, see the Martindale-Hubbell Law Directory

HAWKINS & PARNELL, LLP (AV)

4000 SunTrust Plaza, 303 Peachtree Street, N.E., 30308-3243
Telephone: 404-614-7400
Fax: 404-614-7500
Email: relliott@hplegal.com *URL:* http://www.hawkinsparnell.com

(See Next Column)

HAWKINS & PARNELL LLP, *Atlanta—Continued*

MEMBERS OF FIRM

J. Bruce Welch
Albert H. Parnell
A. Timothy Jones
Alan F. Herman
H. Lane Young, II
Frank C. Bedinger, III
William H. Major, III
Jack N. Sibley
Warner S. Fox
Robert U. Wright
Michael E. Hutchins
Ollie M. Harton
Kevin J. Bahr
Roger M. Goode
Dennis J. Manganiello

ASSOCIATES

Allen L. Broughton
Stephen Michael Bowers
Michael J. Crist

Representative Clients: Ashland Oil, Inc.; Georgia-Pacific Corp.; Ericsson, Inc.; Monsanto Corporation; Commercial Union Insurance Co.; Terminix; Mobay Corp.; Apollo Industries; GAF Corporation; Celanese, Ltd.

For Complete List of Firm Personnel, See General Section

For full biographical listings, see the Martindale-Hubbell Law Directory

HOLT NEY ZATCOFF & WASSERMAN, LLP (AV)

A Partnership including Professional Corporations
100 Galleria Parkway, Suite 600, 30339
Telephone: 770-956-9600
Facsimile: 770-956-1490
Email: mthomas@hnzw.com

MEMBERS OF FIRM

J. Scott Jacobson
Richard P. Vornholt
Jay Frank Castle

Representative Clients: Safety-Kleen Corp.; Cummins South, Inc.; Gables Residential Trust; The University Financing Foundation, Inc.; Trammell Crow Residential; NationsBank N.A.

For Complete List of Firm Personnel, See General Section

For full biographical listings, see the Martindale-Hubbell Law Directory

LONG ALDRIDGE & NORMAN LLP (AV)

A Limited Liability Partnership including Professional Corporations
Suite 5300, 303 Peachtree Street, 30308
Telephone: 404-527-4000
Telecopier: 404-527-4198
Email: atlanta@lanlaw.com *URL:* http://www.lanlaw.com
Washington, D.C. Office: Suite 600, 701 Pennsylvania Avenue, N.W., 20004.
Telephone: 202-624-1200.
FAX: 202-624-1298.

MEMBERS OF FIRM

Phillip A. Bradley
Barbara H. Gallo
James D. Levine

ASSOCIATES

Daniel H. Sherman IV
Robert Todd Silliman

For Complete List of Firm Personnel, See General Section

For full biographical listings, see the Martindale-Hubbell Law Directory

SMITH, CURRIE & HANCOCK LLP (AV)

2600 Harris Tower-Peachtree Center, 233 Peachtree Street, N.E., 30303-1530
Telephone: 404-521-3800
Telecopier: 404-688-0671
Email: smith-currie-hancock@worldnet.att.net *URL:* http://www.smithcurrie.com

MEMBERS OF FIRM

Bert R. Oastler (Retired)
Frank E. Riggs, Jr.
James F. Butler, III
James K. Bidgood, Jr.
Robert C. Chambers

ASSOCIATES

Deborah R. Murphey
Stacey L. Robinson

Construction Clients: Jacobs Engineering; Williams Group; IT Corp.; Envirocon, Inc.; Asbestos Free,Inc.

For full biographical listings, see the Martindale-Hubbell Law Directory

*AUGUSTA,** Richmond Co.

HULL, TOWILL, NORMAN, BARRETT & SALLEY, A PROFESSIONAL CORPORATION (AV)

801 Broad Street, Suite 700, 30901
Telephone: 706-722-4481
Fax: 706-722-9779
Email: hullfirm@groupz.net *URL:* http://www.groupz.net/~advocate
Aiken, South Carolina Office: 111 Park Avenue, 29801.
Telephone: 803-648-4213.
Fax: 803-648-2601.

(See Next Column)

James M. Hull (1885-1975)
George B. Barrett (1894-1942)
Julian J. Willingham (1887-1963)
John Bell Towill (1907-1991)
Robert C. Norman (Retired, 1991)
W. Hale Barrett
Lawton Jordan, Jr.
Patrick J. Rice
Douglas D. Batchelor, Jr.
David E. Hudson
William H. Tucker (Not admitted in GA)
William F. Hammond
Mark S. Burgreen
George R. Hall
James B. Ellington
F. Michael Taylor
William J. Keogh, III
Edward J. Tarver
J. Noel Schweers, III
Susan D. Barrett
Ralph Emerson Hanna, III

James M. Holly (Not admitted in GA)
Timothy E. Moses
N. Shannon Gentry Lanier
Tara R. Simkins
Charles H. Weigle
Natalie A. Dopson
David C. Smith

OF COUNSEL

Julian B. Salley, Jr. (Not admitted in GA)

Counsel for: Morris Communications Corporation; Merry Land & Investment Company, Inc.; Castleberry/Snow's Brands, Inc.; Sun Trust Bank Augusta, N.A.; Georgia Power Co.; St. Joseph Hospital, Augusta, Georgia, Inc.; Norfolk Southern Corp.; Housing Authority of the City of Augusta; Georgia Press Association; Columbia County, Georgia.

For full biographical listings, see the Martindale-Hubbell Law Directory

*SAVANNAH,** Chatham Co.

BOUHAN, WILLIAMS & LEVY LLP (AV)

The Armstrong House, 447 Bull Street, P.O. Box 2139, 31402-2139
Telephone: 912-236-2491
Fax: 912-233-0811
Email: bouhan@bellsouth.net

MEMBER OF FIRM

Ann Marie Stack

General Counsel for: Savannah Electric and Power Co.; Wachovia Bank of Georgia, N.A.; Southeastern Maritime Co.; Solomons Co.; Fiduciary Services Corp.; Peeples Industry, Inc.; Board of Education of the City of Savannah and County of Chatham; The Branigar Organization, Inc.

For Complete List of Firm Personnel, See General Section

For full biographical listings, see the Martindale-Hubbell Law Directory

HUNTER, MACLEAN, EXLEY & DUNN, P.C. (AV)

200 East St. Julian Street, P.O. Box 9848, 31412
Telephone: 912-236-0261
Cable Address: "Ancan"
Telecopier: 912-236-4936
Telex: 54-6483
Email: hmed.com *URL:* http://www.bobbs@hmed.com
Atlanta, Georgia Office: The Peachtree, 1355 Peachtree Street, N.E., Suite 640.
Telephone: 404-876-3611.
Fax: 404-870-2025.

John M. Hewson, III
Andrew H. Ernst
Triece Gignilliat Ziblut

Representative Clients: Great Dane Trailers; Atlantic Wood Industries, Inc.; CSX, Inc.; Savannah Economic Developments Authority; TIC Southeast.

For Complete List of Firm Personnel, See General Section

For full biographical listings, see the Martindale-Hubbell Law Directory

HAWAII

*HONOLULU,** Honolulu Co.

CARLSMITH BALL (AV)

A Partnership including Law Corporations
Suite 2200, Pacific Tower, 1001 Bishop Street, P.O. Box 656, 96809-3402
Telephone: 808-523-2500
Fax: 808-523-0842
Email: execdirector@carlsmith.com *URL:* http://www.carlsmith.com
Kapolei, Hawaii Office: Suite 318, Kapolei Building, 1001 Kamokila Boulevard, 96707.
Telephone: 808-523-2500.
Fax: 808-674-0850.
Wailuku, Maui Hawaii Office: Suite 400, One Main Plaza, 2200 Main Street, P.O. Box 1086, 96793-1086.
Telephone: 808-242-4535.
Fax: 808-244-4974.
Kailua-Kona, Hawaii Office: Suite 209, 75-1000 Henry Street, 96740.
Telephone: 808-329-6464.
Fax: 808-329-9450.

(See Next Column)

CARLSMITH BALL—*Continued*

Hilo, Hawaii Office: 121 Waianuenue Avenue, P.O. Box 686, 96721-0686.
Telephone: 808-935-6644.
Fax: 808-935-7975.
Hagatna, Guam Office: Suite 401, Bank of Hawaii Building, 134 West Soledad Avenue, P.O. Box BF, 96932-5027.
Telephone: 671-472-6813.
Fax: 671-477-4375.
Telex: 721-6445 CWCMI GM.
Saipan, Commonwealth of the Northern Mariana Islands Office: Carlsmith Building, Capitol Hill, P.O. Box 5241, 96950-5241.
Telephone: 670-322-3455.
Fax: 670-322-3368.
Los Angeles, California Office: 9th Floor, 444 South Flower Street, 90071-2901.
Telephone: 213-955-1200.
Fax: 213-623-0032.
Washington, D.C. Office: Suite 300, 1201 Pennsylvania Avenue, N.W., 20004-2401.
Telephone: 202-628-2228.
Fax: 202-628-2071.
Mexico City, Mexico Office: Carlsmith Ball, Sierra Nevada 119, Lomas de Chapultepec, 11000 Mexico, D.F.
Telephone: 52-5-520-8514, 52-5-520-8757.
Fax: 52-5-540-1545.
Mexico, D.F. Office of Carlsmith Ball, S.C. (Authorized to practice as foreign legal consultants in Mexico): Sierra Nevada 119, Lomas de Chapultepec, 11000 Mexico, D.F.
Telephone: 52-5-520-8514, 52-5-520-8757.
Fax: 52-5-540-1545.

MEMBERS OF FIRM

Daniel A. Bent
Eric A. James
Katherine G. Leonard
Ian L. Sandison

OF COUNSEL

Tom K. Houston (Resident at Los Angeles, California Office)
Edward M. Ranger (Resident at Mexico Office)

For Complete List of Firm Personnel, See General Section

For full biographical listings, see the Martindale-Hubbell Law Directory

GOODSILL ANDERSON QUINN & STIFEL (AV)

Alii Place, Suite 1800, 1099 Alakea Street, P.O. Box 3196, 96801-3196
Telephone: 808-547-5600
FAX: 808-547-5880
Email: info@goodsill.com *URL:* http://www.goodsill.com

MEMBERS OF FIRM

Gary M. Slovin
Lisa Woods Munger

ASSOCIATE

Lisa A. Bail

Representative Clients: AMFAC/JMB Hawaii, Inc.; Chevron USA; Hawaiian Electric Industries, Inc.

For Complete List of Firm Personnel, See General Section

For full biographical listings, see the Martindale-Hubbell Law Directory

IDAHO

*BOISE,** Ada Co.

ELAM & BURKE, A PROFESSIONAL ASSOCIATION (AV)

Key Financial Center, 702 West Idaho Street, P.O. Box 1539, 83701
Telephone: 208-343-5454
Telecopier: 208-384-5844
Email: eblaw@elamburke.com

Carl P. Burke
John Magel
William G. Dryden
Scott L. Campbell

Angela D. Schaer

Representative Clients: Morrison-Knudsen, Inc.; Pechiney Corp.; Dow Corning Corporation; State Farm Insurance Cos.; Sinclair Oil Co. d/b/a/ Sun Valley Co.; Farmers Insurance Group; Thompson Creek Mining Co.

For Complete List of Firm Personnel, See General Section

For full biographical listings, see the Martindale-Hubbell Law Directory

KETCHUM, Blaine Co.

JAMES L. KENNEDY, JR. (AV)

340 Second Street East, P.O. Box 2165, 83340
Telephone: 208-726-8255
Fax: 208-726-4886

Reference: First Interstate Bank of Idaho, N.A. (Ketchum-Sun Valley Branch); First Security Bank of Idaho, N.A. (Ketchum Branch)

(See Next Column)

For full biographical listings, see the Martindale-Hubbell Law Directory

ILLINOIS

AURORA, Kane Co.

MURPHY, HUPP, FOOTE, MIELKE AND KINNALLY (AV)

North Island Center, P.O. Box 5030, 60507
Telephone: 630-844-0056
Fax: 630-844-1905
Email: mhfmk@insnet.com

MEMBERS OF FIRM

William C. Murphy
Robert B. Hupp
Robert M. Foote
Craig S. Mielke
Patrick M. Kinnally
Paul G. Krentz
Joseph C. Loran
Gerald K. Hodge

Timothy D. O'Neil
Matthew J. Herman

Representative Clients: American Telephone & Telegraph Co.; Fox Valley Park District; Lyon Metal Products; Kane County Forest Preserve District; Hollywood Casino; Employers Mutual Insurance Co.; Forty-Eight Insulations, Inc.; UNR Asbestos Disease Trust; Richards-Wilcox Co.; National Bank & Trust Company of Syracuse.

For full biographical listings, see the Martindale-Hubbell Law Directory

*BELLEVILLE,** St. Clair Co.

GAVIN LAW FIRM (AV)

NationsBank Building, 23 Public Square, Suite 415, 62220
Telephone: 618-236-0100
888-360-0100
Fax: 618-236-2684
Email: billg@gavinlaw.com *URL:* http://www.gavinlaw.com

William P. Gavin

For full biographical listings, see the Martindale-Hubbell Law Directory

*CHICAGO,** Cook Co.

ANSPACH & ASSOCIATES (AV)

111 West Washington Street, Suite 1435, 60602
Telephone: 312-407-7888
Facsimile: 312-407-7889
Email: KANSPACH@primenet.com

Kenneth G. Anspach

Representative Clients: A. H. Harris & Sons, Inc.; Cooper Tire & Rubber Company; Chase Products Co.; Deerfield Federal Savings; Graham Paint & Varnish Co., Inc.; Mid-City National Bank of Chicago; Monarch Tile, Inc.; W. R. Meadows, Inc.

For full biographical listings, see the Martindale-Hubbell Law Directory

BLATT, HAMMESFAHR & EATON (AV)

333 W. Wacker Drive, Suite 1900, 60606
Telephone: 312-849-8000
FAX: 312-357-0198
Email: BHE@BHELAW.COM *URL:* HTTP://WWW.BHELAW.COM
New York, New York Office: 45 Broadway, 12th Floor.
Telephone: 212-363-1900.
Fax: 212-363-2600. Email: bhe@bhelaw.com.

MEMBERS OF FIRM

Richard L. Blatt
Larry R. Eaton
Robert W. Hammesfahr
Gregory D. Hopp
Josh M. Kantrow
Kathleen A. McQueeny

ASSOCIATES

Frederic C. Goodwill, II
Ryan M. Henderson
Bruce M. Lichtcsien

For full biographical listings, see the Martindale-Hubbell Law Directory

THE BROWN ENVIRONMENTAL LAW GROUP, P.C. (AV)

35 East Wacker Drive Suite 1356, 60601
Telephone: 312-236-1450
Fax: 312-236-1451
Email: brownelg@frontiernet.net

Johnine J. Brown

Sheila H. Deely

Representative Clients: Avondale Federal Savings Bank; Berger Excavating Contractors, Inc.; Browning-Ferris Industries of Illinois, Inc.; Elmhurst-Chicago Stone Company; Hamilton Partners, Inc.; Hartz Construction Co.; Home Builders Association of Greater Chicago; United Homes of Illinois; Wiseman-Hughes Enterprises, Inc.

(See Next Column)

THE BROWN ENVIRONMENTAL LAW GROUP, P.C., *Chicago—Continued*

For full biographical listings, see the Martindale-Hubbell Law Directory

CAHILL, CHRISTIAN & KUNKLE, LTD. (AV)

Santa Fe Building, 224 South Michigan Avenue, Suite 1300, 60604
Telephone: 312-341-1688
Fax: 312-341-1689
URL: http://www.cck.com

William J. Kunkle, Jr.
Roseann Oliver
William T. Cahill
John M. Christian
Lorna E. Propes
Scott B. Greene
Mary Kathryn Kelly
Suzanne M. Metzel
Matthew J. Gehringer
Steven E. Nieslawski
Michael K. Bartosz
Donald Lee Homyk

OF COUNSEL

Louis B. Garippo

Daniel J. Collins
Jeanne M. Cullen
Elizabeth A. Kaveny
Frederic T. Knape
David R. Nordwall
Elisha S. Rosenblum
Melisa G. Thompson

For full biographical listings, see the Martindale-Hubbell Law Directory

JOHNSON & BELL, LTD. (AV)

Suite 2200, 222 North La Salle Street, 60601
Telephone: 312-372-0770
Facsimile: 312-372-9818
Waukegan, Illinois Office: Nine North County Street, Suite G-1, 60085.
Telephone: 847-662-7458.
Facsimile: 847-662-7366.
Highland, Indiana Office: 900 Indianapolis Boulevard, Suite A, 46322.
Telephone: 219-923-5250.
Facsimile: 219-923-6170.

John W. Bell
Frederick S. Mueller
Daniel C. Murray
William J. Anaya

References available upon request.

For full biographical listings, see the Martindale-Hubbell Law Directory

THE MARTIN LAW FIRM (AV)

111 West Washington Street, Suite 1815, 60602
Telephone: 312-236-2000
Fax: 312-236-2036
Email: mmartinlaw@aol.com

Maureen Martin

Representative Clients: Avondale Federal Savings Bank; Benjamin Moore & Co.; Browning-Ferris Industries of Illinois, Inc.; Chicago Trust Co.; Heidelberg Web Press, Inc.; Gallagher & Henry; Hartz Construction Co.; Metropolitan Water Reclamation District of Greater Chicago; Midas Realty Corp.; Sprague Farms.

For full biographical listings, see the Martindale-Hubbell Law Directory

MCBRIDE BAKER & COLES (AV)

500 West Madison Street 40th Floor, 60661-2511
Telephone: 312-715-5700
Cable Address: "Chilaw"
Telex: 270258
Telecopier: 312-993-9350
Email: lastname@mbc.com *URL:* http://www.mbc.com
Oakbrook Terrace, Illinois Office: Suite 1000, One Mid America Plaza, 60181-4710.
Telephone: 630-954-2100.
Telecopier: 630-954-2112.

MEMBERS OF FIRM

Malcolm H. Brooks
Clifton A. Lake
Richard A. Redmond
Mark J. Steger
William M. Stevens
Steven B. Varick

OF COUNSEL

Joseph S. Wright, Jr.

ASSOCIATE

Christopher J. Rosette

For Complete List of Firm Personnel, See General Section

For full biographical listings, see the Martindale-Hubbell Law Directory

WILDMAN, HARROLD, ALLEN & DIXON (AV)

225 West Wacker Drive, 30th Floor, 60606-1229
Telephone: 312-201-2000
Fax: 312-201-2555
Email: hennessy@whad.com *URL:* http://www.whad.com
Aurora, Illinois Office: 1961 W. Downer Place.
Telephone: 630-892-7021.
Fax: 630-892-7158.

(See Next Column)

Waukegan, Illinois Office: 404 West Water, P. O. Box 890.
Telephone: 847-625-5550.
Fax: 847-625-5555.
Lisle, Illinois Office: 4300 Commerce Court, Suite 320.
Telephone: 630-955-0555.
Fax: 630-955-0662
Toronto, Ontario correspondent Office: Keel Cottrelle. 36 Toronto Street, Suite 920.
Telephone: 416-367-2900.
Telefax: 416-367-2791.
Telex: 062-18660.

MEMBERS OF FIRM

Thomas W. Daggett
Steven E. Danekas
John E. Frey
H. Roderic Heard
Anthony G. Hopp
Brian W. Lewis
Joseph F. Madonia
James R. Morrin
Robert L. Shuftan
David M. Simon
Linda E. Spring (Waukegan Office)
Sanford M. Stein
James B. Vogts

OF COUNSEL

Bernard Harrold

Leo P. Dombrowski
Lawrence W. Falbe
Ian J. McPheron

For full biographical listings, see the Martindale-Hubbell Law Directory

MATTOON, Coles Co.

CRAIG & CRAIG (AV)

1807 Broadway, P.O. Box 689, 61938-0689
Telephone: 217-234-6481
Telecopier: 217-234-6486; 258-8292
Email: craiglaw@advant.com
Mount Vernon, Illinois Office: 115 North 7th Street.
Telephone: 618-244-7511.

MEMBERS OF FIRM

Craig Van Meter (1895-1981)
Fred H. Kelly (1894-1971)
Robert M. Werden (1908-1969)
George N. Gilkerson (1911-1985)
John P. Ewart
Richard F. Record, Jr.
Stephen L. Corn
Robert G. Grierson
Gregory C. Ray
Paul R. Lynch (Resident, Mount Vernon Office)
Kenneth F. Werts (Resident, Mount Vernon Office)
John L. Barger

ASSOCIATES

Kathleen M. Stockwell
Kristine M. Tuttle
Julie A. Webb (Resident, Mount Vernon Office)
John M. O'Driscoll
Duane A. Deters
Katy C. Fain (Resident, Mount Vernon Office)
Erin E. Wisner
John F. Watson

OF COUNSEL

Jack E. Horsley

Representative Clients: Freeman United Coal Mining Co.; Natural Gas Pipeline Company of America; Marathon Oil Company; Howell Paving, Inc.; Illinois Central R.R. Co.; Consolidated Communications Inc.; Lake Land College; Scattering Fork Drainage District of Douglas County, Illinois.

For full biographical listings, see the Martindale-Hubbell Law Directory

*PEORIA,** Peoria Co.

HOWARD & HOWARD ATTORNEYS, P.C. (AV)

The Creve Coeur Building, Suite 200, 321 Liberty Street, 61602-1403
Telephone: 309-672-1483
Telecopier: 309-672-1568
Kalamazoo, Michigan Office: The Michigan Building, Suite 200, 100 Portage Street.
Telephone: 616-382-1483.
Telecopier: 616-382-1568.
Bloomfield Hills, Michigan Office: The Pinehurst Office Center, Suite 101, 1400 North Woodward Avenue.
Telephone: 248-645-1483.
Telecopier: 248-645-1568.
Lansing, Michigan Office: Suite 500, The Phoenix Building, 222 Washington Square, North.
Telephone: 517-485-1483.
Telecopier: 517-485-1568.

Jon S. Faletto
Frederick G. Hoffman
Diana M. Jagiella

Representative Clients: For Representative Client list, see General Practice, Peoria, IL.

For Complete List of Firm Personnel, See General Section

For full biographical listings, see the Martindale-Hubbell Law Directory

INDIANA

*EVANSVILLE,** Vanderburgh Co.

FINE & HATFIELD, A PROFESSIONAL CORPORATION (AV)

520 N.W. Second Street, P.O. Box 779, 47705-0779
Telephone: 812-425-3592
Telecopier: 812-421-4269
Email: Fine@Fine-Hatfield.com *URL:* http://www.Fine-Hatfield.com

Thomas H. Bryan

A List of Representative Clients Furnished Upon Request.

For full biographical listings, see the Martindale-Hubbell Law Directory

KAHN, DEES, DONOVAN & KAHN, LLP (AV)

Fifth Main Financial Plaza, Suite 305, P.O. Box 3646, 47735-3646
Telephone: 812-423-3183
Fax: 812-423-3841
Email: evvlaw@k2d2.com

MEMBERS OF FIRM

Alan N. Shovers
Brian P. Williams
G. Michael Schopmeyer
Jeffrey K. Helfrich
Kent A. Brasseale II

ASSOCIATE

Allison K. Comstock

Representative Clients: Enviro Group, Inc.; D. Patrick, Inc.; Deaconess Hospital, Inc.; Geo. Koch Sons, Inc.; Red Spot Paint & Varnish Co., Inc.; Sterling Boiler & Mechanical, Inc.; Windsor Plastics, Inc.; Princeton Mining Company, Inc.; Locust Street Company, Inc.

For Complete List of Firm Personnel, See General Section

For full biographical listings, see the Martindale-Hubbell Law Directory

*INDIANAPOLIS,** Marion Co.

BOSE MCKINNEY & EVANS LLP (AV)

2700 First Indiana Plaza, 135 North Pennsylvania Street, 46204
Telephone: 317-684-5000
Facsimile: 317-684-5173
URL: http://www.boselaw.com
Indianapolis North Office: Suite 1500, 8888 Keystone Crossing, 46240.
Telephone: 317-574-3700.
Facsimile: 317-574-3716.

MEMBERS OF FIRM

James C. Carlino
Kathleen G. Lucas
Daniel P. McInerny
Theodore J. Nowacki
L. Parvin Price
C. Joseph Russell

ASSOCIATES

Lisa McKinney Goldner
Melinda R. Shapiro

Representative Clients: BP Amoco Corp.; Centre Properties; Duke Realty Limited Partnership; Eli Lilly & Co.; Estes Express Lines; First Indiana Bank; First Industrial Realty Trust, Inc.; Indiana Pork Producers Association; United States Steel Carnegie Pension Fund.

For Complete List of Firm Personnel, See General Section

For full biographical listings, see the Martindale-Hubbell Law Directory

ICE MILLER DONADIO & RYAN (AV)

One American Square Box 82001, 46282-0002
Telephone: 317-236-2100
Fax: 317-236-2219
Email: info@imdr.com *URL:* http://www.imdr.com
South Bend, Indiana Office: 211 West Washington Street, Suite 2420.
Telephone: 219-234-7933.
Fax: 219-234-7965. Internet E-mail: info@imdr.com. Web Site Address: http://www.imdr.com.
Chicago, Illinois Office: 135 South LaSalle Street, Suite 4100.
Telephone: 312-726-1567.
Fax: 312-641-6263. Internet E-mail: info@imdr.com. Web Site Address: http://www.imdr.com.

MEMBERS OF FIRM

Phillip R. Scaletta, III
Susan B. Tabler
Terri Ann Czajka

SENIOR COUNSEL

Bradley L. Williams

STAFF ATTORNEY

Dana G. Meier

ASSOCIATES

Brent W. Huber
Jennifer Weflen

Representative Clients: Amoco Oil Corp.; Avesta-Sheffield, Inc.; BAA, L.CC./Indianapolis Airport Authority; Exide Corp.; Reilly Industries, Inc.; United Dominion Industries; Ontario Corporation; Guide Corporation; Magnequench International; Delco Remy America.

(See Next Column)

For Complete List of Firm Personnel, See General Section

For full biographical listings, see the Martindale-Hubbell Law Directory

JOHNSON SMITH PENCE & HEATH LLP (AV)

One Indiana Square Suite 1800, 46204
Telephone: 317-634-9777
Telecopier: 317-636-9061
Email: firm@jsplaw.com *URL:* http://www.jsplaw.com
Washington, D.C. Office: 555 Twelfth Street, N.W., Suite 650.
Telephone: 202-737-5410.
Fax: 202-737-5411.

MEMBERS OF FIRM

Robert M. Baker III
Thomas A. Barnard
David R. Day
G. Ronald Heath
Linda L. Pence

ASSOCIATE

Melina Maniatis Kennedy

For Complete List of Firm Personnel, See General Section

For full biographical listings, see the Martindale-Hubbell Law Directory

PLEWS SHADLEY RACHER & BRAUN (AV)

1346 North Delaware Street, 46202-2415
Telephone: 317-637-0700
Telecopier: 317-637-0710
Email: psrb@psrb.com
Mishawaka, Indiana Office: 4440 Edison Lake Parkway, 46545.
Telephone: 219-273-1010.
Fax: 219-271-2050.

MEMBERS OF FIRM

George M. Plews
Sue A. Shadley
Peter M. Racher
Christopher J. Braun
Jeffrey D. Claflin
Frederick D. Emhardt
Leonardo D. Robinson
S. Curtis DeVoe
John B. Bridge
Stephen A. Studer (Resident, Mishawaka Office)

ASSOCIATES

Jeffrey A. Townsend
Jeffrey D. Featherstun
Donna C. Marron
Thomas A. John
Carol S. Comer
John D. Moriarty
Alexandra S. Lipps
Michael W. Skorupka

OF COUNSEL

Christine C. H. Plews
Mary Ann Fuchs Saggese
John H. Lloyd, IV (Resident, Mishawaka Office)

For full biographical listings, see the Martindale-Hubbell Law Directory

SOMMER & BARNARD, ATTORNEYS AT LAW, PC (AV)

4000 Bank One Tower, 111 Monument Circle, 46204
Telephone: 317-630-4000
FAX: 317-236-9802
Email: sandb@sommerbarnard.com
North Office: 8900 Keystone Crossing, Suite 1150, Indianapolis, Indiana, 46240-2134.
Telephone: 317-630-4000.
FAX: 317-844-4780.

Frank J. Deveau
Robert R. Clark
Lawrence A. Vanore
Donald C. Biggs

Representative Clients: Comerica Bank; Federal Express; Kimball International; Monsanto; TRW, Inc.

For Complete List of Firm Personnel, See General Section

For full biographical listings, see the Martindale-Hubbell Law Directory

STARK DONINGER & SMITH (AV)

Suite 700, 50 South Meridian Street, 46204
Telephone: 317-638-2400
Fax: 317-633-6618; 633-6619

MEMBERS OF FIRM

John C. Stark
Bruce E. Smith
John W. Van Buskirk
Richard W. Dyar
Patricia Seasor Bailey
Brian J. Tuohy
Mark A. Bailey
Lewis E. Willis, Jr.
Thomas A. Brodnik

ASSOCIATES

Richard B. Kaufman
Paul T. Belch
John J. Moore
Dennis R. Tyler

COUNSEL

Clarence H. Doninger
Gregory S. Fehribach
Robert D. Maas
William K. Byrum

Representative Clients: American Testing & Engineering Corp.; Speedco, Inc.; SJC, Inc.

For full biographical listings, see the Martindale-Hubbell Law Directory

Indianapolis—Continued

TABBERT HAHN EARNEST & WEDDLE (AV)

Suite 2100, One Indiana Square, 46204-2101
Telephone: 317-639-5444
Fax: 317-639-5232
Email: jtyrrell@tabberthahn.com *URL:* http://www.tabberthahn.com

Mark K. Sullivan William W. Mathews

For full biographical listings, see the Martindale-Hubbell Law Directory

*LAFAYETTE,** Tippecanoe Co.

STUART & BRANIGIN (AV)

The Life Building, 300 Main Street, Suite 800, P.O. Box 1010, 47902-1010
Telephone: 765-423-1561
Telecopier: 765-742-8175
Email: sb@stuartlaw.com *URL:* http://www.stuartlaw.com
Indianapolis, Indiana Office: Suite 1401, 8888 Keystone Crossing, 46240.
Telephone: 317-574-7245.
Fax: 317-574-7050.

MEMBERS OF FIRM

Allison Ellsworth Stuart (1886-1950)
Roger D. Branigin (1902-1975)
Roger D. Branigin, Jr.
Thomas L. Ryan
Thomas R. McCully
Larry R. Fisher
Nina B. Kirkpatrick
Mark Lillianfeld
Stephen R. Pennell
Anthony S. Benton
Erik D. Spykman
William E. Emerick
John C. Duffey
Bruce McSpadden
Mark E. DeYoung
Thomas B. Parent
Laura L. Bowker
Kevin D. Nicoson
Susan K. Roberts
John M. Stuckey
Deborah B. Trice
William P. Kealey
David A. Starkweather
Geoffrey L. Blazi

SENIOR COUNSEL

Russell H. Hart

COUNSEL

John F. Bodle James V. McGlone

ASSOCIATES

Elizabeth B. Searle
Marianne Mitten Owen
David A. Locke
Karen Orr McClure
Ann Marie Waldron
Barry L. Loftus

General Counsel for: The Lafayette Life Insurance Co.; INB National Bank, N.W.; Lafayette Home Hospital, Inc.
State Counsel for: Norfolk & Western Railway Co.
Mr. Ryan is Counsel to: The Trustees of Purdue University.
Representative Clients: Aluminum Company of America; Liberty Mutual Insurance Group.

For full biographical listings, see the Martindale-Hubbell Law Directory

*SOUTH BEND,** St. Joseph Co.

DORAN • BLACKMOND LLP (AV)

1700 Valley American Bank Building, 211 W. Washington Street, 46601
Telephone: 219-288-1800
Fax: 219-236-4265

MEMBERS OF FIRM

M. Edward Doran (1895-1982) John E. Doran
Don G. Blackmond

ASSOCIATES

Don Gregory Blackmond Peter J. Van Dyke
Lynn M. Butcher

OF COUNSEL

A. Howard Williams

For full biographical listings, see the Martindale-Hubbell Law Directory

KANSAS

OVERLAND PARK, Johnson Co.

SHAMBERG, JOHNSON & BERGMAN, CHARTERED (AV)

Suite 355, 4551 West 107th Street, 66207
Telephone: 913-642-0600
Fax: 913-642-9629
Email: mail@sjblaw.com *URL:* http://www.sjblaw.com
Kansas City, Kansas Office: Suite M-4, One Security Plaza.
Telephone: 913-281-1900.
Kansas City, Missouri Office: Suite 205, Scarritt Arcade Building, 819 Walnut.
Telephone: 816-556-9431.

(See Next Column)

Lynn R. Johnson Victor A. Bergman
John M. Parisi

Steven G. Brown Steve N. Six

OF COUNSEL

John E. Shamberg

For full biographical listings, see the Martindale-Hubbell Law Directory

*TOPEKA,** Shawnee Co.

GOODELL, STRATTON, EDMONDS & PALMER, L.L.P. (AV)

515 South Kansas Avenue, 66603-3999
Telephone: 785-233-0593
Fax: 785-233-8870
Email: GSEP@CJNETWORKS.COM *URL:* http://www.cjnetworks.com/~gsep
Kansas City, Missouri Office: 10401 Holmes Road, Suite 280.
Telephone: 816-943-8577.

MEMBERS OF FIRM

Gerald L. Goodell Wayne T. Stratton
N. Larry Bork

SPECIAL COUNSEL

Curtis J. Waugh

Local Counsel for: Farm Bureau Mutual Insurance Co.; St. Paul Fire & Marine Insurance Co.; Washburn University of Topeka; HydroFlex, Inc.; Bartlett & West Engineers.
General Counsel for: American Home Life Insurance Co.; Columbian National Title Insurance Co.; Kansas Medical Society; Kansas Hospital Association.

For Complete List of Firm Personnel, See General Section

For full biographical listings, see the Martindale-Hubbell Law Directory

*WICHITA,** Sedgwick Co.

DEPEW AND GILLEN, L.L.C. (AV)

151 North Main, Suite 800, 67202-1409
Telephone: 316-262-4000
Facsimile: 316-265-3819
Email: DG@DEPEWGILLEN.COM *URL:* HTTP://WWW.DEPEWGILLEN.COM

Randall K. Rathbun Charles C. Steincamp

For Complete List of Firm Personnel, See General Section

For full biographical listings, see the Martindale-Hubbell Law Directory

FOULSTON & SIEFKIN L.L.P. (AV)

700 NationsBank Financial Center, 67202
Telephone: 316-267-6371
Facsimile: 316-267-6345
URL: http://www.foulston.com
Topeka, Kansas Office: 1515 NationsBank Tower, 534 Kansas Avenue, 66603.
Telephone: 785-233-3600.
Fax: 785-233-1610.
Dodge City, Kansas Office: 810 Frontview, P.O. Box 1147, 67801.
Telephone: 316-227-8126.
Fax: 316-227-8451.
Member: Lex Mundi, The World's Leading Association of Independent Law Firms.

MEMBERS OF FIRM

Charles P. Efflandt Wyatt A. Hoch

SPECIAL COUNSEL

David M. Traster John C. Peck

For Complete List of Firm Personnel, See General Section

For full biographical listings, see the Martindale-Hubbell Law Directory

YOUNG, BOGLE, MCCAUSLAND, WELLS & BLANCHARD, P.A. (AV)

106 West Douglas, Suite 923, 67202
Telephone: 316-265-7841
Facsimile: 316-265-3956
Email: ybmwblaw@aol.com

Glenn D. Young, Jr. Paul S. McCausland
J. Michael Peters

Representative Clients: Bridgestone/Firestone Inc.; Deere & Co.; Citibank; Metropolitan Life Insurance Co.; Equitable Assurance Society of the United States; Geotechnical Services, Inc.; Greif Bros. Corp.; Geotechnical Services, Inc.

For Complete List of Firm Personnel, See General Section

For full biographical listings, see the Martindale-Hubbell Law Directory

KENTUCKY

COVINGTON, Kenton Co.

ROBERT E. SANDERS AND ASSOCIATES, P.S.C. (AV)

The Charles H. Fisk House, 1017 Russell Street, 41011-3052
Telephone: 606-491-3000
Fax: 606-655-4642
Email: resanders@worldnet.att.net

Robert E. Sanders

Jeffrey M. Sanders
J. Pierre Tismo
Delana S. Pierce

LEGAL SUPPORT PERSONNEL

Shirley L. Sanders
Sandra A. Sturgeon
Sheila D. Rachal

For full biographical listings, see the Martindale-Hubbell Law Directory

*LEXINGTON,** Fayette Co.

STOLL, KEENON & PARK, LLP (AV)

201 E. Main Street, Suite 1000, 40507-1380
Telephone: 606-231-3000
Telecopier: 606-253-1093; 606-253-1027
URL: http://www.skp.com
Frankfort, Kentucky Office: 307 Washington Street, 40601.
Telephone: 502-875-6220.
Telecopier: 502-875-6235.
Henderson, Kentucky Office: 201 C North Main Street, 42420-3103.
Telephone: 270-831-1900.
Telecopier: 270-827-4060.
Louisville, Kentucky Office: 400 West Market Street, Suite 2650, 40202-3377.
Telephone: 502-568-9100.
Telecopier: 502-568-5700.

MEMBERS OF FIRM

Samuel D. Hinkle IV
David E. Fleenor
Lea Pauley Goff
Culver V. Halliday
John Browning Park

Representative Clients: Bank One, Lexington, NA; C. Lee Cook; Cintech Industrial Coatings; Farmers Capital Bank Corp.; FOSROC; Link Belt Construction Equipment Co.; General Motors Corp.; International Business Machines Corp.; Rockwell International Corp.; Swifty Oil Co.

For Complete List of Firm Personnel, See General Section

For full biographical listings, see the Martindale-Hubbell Law Directory

*LOUISVILLE,** Jefferson Co.

MIDDLETON & REUTLINGER, P.S.C. (AV)

2500 Brown and Williamson Tower, 40202-3410
Telephone: 502-584-1135
Fax: 502-561-0442
URL: http://middreut.com
Jeffersonville, Indiana Office: 530 East Court Avenue, 47130.
Telephone: 812-282-1132.
Fax: 812-282-3188.

Charles G. Middleton, III
John W. Bilby
Kathiejane Oehler
James E. Milliman

Terri Elms Phelps

For Complete List of Firm Personnel, See General Section

For full biographical listings, see the Martindale-Hubbell Law Directory

WOODWARD, HOBSON & FULTON (AV)

2500 National City Tower, 101 South Fifth Street, 40202
Telephone: 502-581-8000
Fax: 502-581-8111
Email: WHF@IGLOU.COM
Lexington, Kentucky Office: PNC Bank Plaza, 200 West Vine Street, Suite 500.
Telephone: 606-244-7100.
Telecopier: 606-244-7111.

MEMBERS OF FIRM

Harry K. Herren
Thomas A. Hoy

ASSOCIATE

Christopher R. Fitzpatrick

Representative Clients: Custom Resins; Sun Refining and Marketing; Koppers Industries, Inc.; Concord Custom Cleaners; Hechingers; OPTA Food Ingredients; Owensboro Grain; Rumpke Waste Systems; United Waste.

(See Next Column)

For Complete List of Firm Personnel, See General Section

For full biographical listings, see the Martindale-Hubbell Law Directory

LOUISIANA

*BATON ROUGE,** East Baton Rouge Parish

ATKINSON, PERRY, ATKINSON & BALHOFF, L.L.C. (AV)

7520 Perkins Road, Suite 260, P.O. Box 83260, 70884-3260
Telephone: 504-767-7730
Fax: 504-767-7967
Email: apabllc@msn.com

Daniel R. Atkinson
John W. Perry, Jr.
Daniel R. Atkinson, Jr.
Daniel J. Balhoff
Joseph W. Mengis

ASSOCIATE

Barbara G. Baier

LEGAL SUPPORT PERSONNEL

Becky Bourgeois (Legal Secretary/Paralegal)
Renee Bordelon (Legal Secretary/Paralegal)
Sue Rivere (Legal Secretary)
Cindy Martrain (Paralegal)
Wendy Cotton (Legal Secretary)

For full biographical listings, see the Martindale-Hubbell Law Directory

KEAN, MILLER, HAWTHORNE, D'ARMOND, McCOWAN & JARMAN, L.L.P. (AV)

22nd Floor, One American Place, 70825
Telephone: 225-387-0999
Fax: 225-388-9133
Mailing Address: P.O. Box 3513, Baton Rouge, Louisiana, 70821
URL: http://WWW.KMLAW.COM
New Orleans, Louisiana Office: Energy Centre, Suite 1560, 1100 Poydras Street, 70163.
Telephone: 504-585-3050.
Fax: 504-585-3051.
Plaquemine, Louisiana Office: Suite 10, 23425 Railroad Avenue, 70764.
Telephone: 225-687-9845.
Fax: 225-382-3445.
Lake Charles, Louisiana Office: One Lakeshore Drive, Suite 1220, 70629.
Telephone: 318-430-0350.
Fax: 318-436-5566.
Covington, Louisiana Office: 503 North New Hampshire Street, P.O. Box 3096, 70433.
Telephone: 504-875-0400.
Fax: 504-875-0500.

MEMBERS OF FIRM

Charles S. McCowan, Jr.
G. William Jarman
Leonard L. Kilgore III
Maureen N. Harbourt
M. Dwayne Johnson
J. Carter Wilkinson
Sandra L. Edwards
James P. Doré
Katherine W. King
Charles S. McCowan III
Esteban Herrera, Jr.
J. Randy Young
Yul D. Lorio (Resident, Lake Charles Office)

Robert M. Hoyland
Julie Parelman Silbert (Resident, New Orleans Office)
Melissa M. Cresson
Amy deGeneres Berret
Kyle B. Beall
Jennifer G. Gary (Resident, Lake Charles Office)

Representative Clients: Amoco Production Company, Houston, TX; BASF Corporation, Parsippany, NJ; CONDEA Vista Company, Houston, TX; Exxon Company, U.S.A., Baton Rouge, LA; Georgia-Pacific Corporation, Atlanta, GA; Joslyn Manufacturing Corporation, Franklin Park, IL; Louisiana Chemical Association, Baton Rouge, LA; Lyondell Petrochemical Company/Lyondell Chemicals Worldwide, Inc., Houston, TX; PPG Industries, Inc., Pittsburgh, PA; Transcontinental Gas Pipe Line Company, Houston, TX.

For full biographical listings, see the Martindale-Hubbell Law Directory

SHOCKEY & ZIOBER, A PROFESSIONAL LAW CORPORATION (AV)

5551 Corporate Boulevard, Suite 3-A, P.O. Box 80286, 70898-0286
Telephone: 225-929-8929
Telecopier: 225-928-7694

John David Ziober

For full biographical listings, see the Martindale-Hubbell Law Directory

*LAFAYETTE,** Lafayette Parish

ONEBANE, BERNARD, TORIAN, DIAZ, MCNAMARA & ABELL (AV)

Suite 600, Versailles Centre, 102 Versailles Boulevard, P.O. Box 3507, 70502
Telephone: 318-237-2660
Telecopier: 318-266-1232
Email: info@onebane.com
Monroe, Louisiana Office: 1900 N. 18th Street, Suite 420, P.O. Box 2255, 71207.
Telephone: 318-340-0220.
Fax: 318-340-0110.

Joseph Onebane (1917-1987)
John G. Torian, II (1936-1991)
James E. Diaz
Timothy J. McNamara
Edward C. Abell, Jr.
Lawrence L. Lewis, III
Robert M. Mahony
Daniel G. Fournerat
Douglas W. Truxillo
Randall C. Songy
Michael G. Durand
Greg Guidry
Joseph L. Lemoine, Jr.
Mark L. Riley
Graham N. Smith
Gordon T. Whitman
Gary P. Kraus
Richard J. Petre, Jr.
Charles J. Boudreaux, Jr.
James R. Shelton
Thomas G. Smart
Roger E. Ishee
Jennifer M. Kleinpeter
Steven C. Lanza
Joel P. Babineaux

Alison M. Brumley
Jesse D. Lambert
Brent G. Sonnier
Cary B. Bryson
Maria F. Manuel
Greg R. Mier
Jennifer L. Smith
Janice Church Reeves
Mark B. Oliver
Chanelle T. Delahoussaye
Aimee L. Williams
A.G. "Alec" Alexander, III
Terry J. Blanchard
William E. Bourgeois (Resident, Monroe, Louisiana Office)

OF COUNSEL
William E. Kellner

Representative Clients: Allstate Insurance Co.; Coastal Chemical Co., Inc.; Coastal Fluids Technology; FMC Corp.; Highlands Insurance Co.; Interstate Insurance Group; Kraft Foods, Inc.; Louisiana Independent Oil & Gas Assn.; Royal-Globe Insurance Co.; Terra International, Inc.

For full biographical listings, see the Martindale-Hubbell Law Directory

*NEW ORLEANS,** Orleans Parish

BOGGS, LOEHN & RODRIGUE (AV)

A Partnership including Law Corporations
Suite 1850, Entergy Building, 639 Loyola Avenue, 70130-3597
Telephone: 504-523-7090
Fax: 504-581-6822
Email: BLAR@bellsouth.net

Charles A. Boggs (A Law Corporation)
Thomas E. Loehn (A Law Corporation)
Edward A. Rodrigue, Jr., (A Law Corporation)

Anne E. Medo
Matthew B. Moreland

Reference: First National Bank of Commerce, New Orleans, La.

For full biographical listings, see the Martindale-Hubbell Law Directory

BURKE & MAYER, A PROFESSIONAL LAW CORPORATION (AV)

Twentieth Floor, Energy Centre, 1100 Poydras Street, 70163-2000
Telephone: 504-569-2900
Telefacsimile: 504-569-2099
URL: http://www. Burke-Mayer.com

Gibbons Burke (1902-1989)
James G. Burke, Jr.
Charles B. Mayer
David L. Carrigee
William B. Schwartz
Daniel E. Knowles, III
Bernard H. Ticer
Andrew C. Wilson
Wm. Daniel Wellons
Robert D. Hoffman, Jr.
Donna M. Young
Brien J. Fricke
JeanPaul P. Overton

William B. Hidalgo
Jedd S. Malish
Cindy Galpin Martin

Representative Clients: All American Marine Slip/American Marine Insurance Group; American Bureau of Shipping; AON Companies; Bender Shipbuilding & Repair Co., Inc.; Blessey Marine Services, Inc.; British Companies and Lloyds Underwriters; Carnival Cruise Lines, Inc.; CARI Corp.; Chiquita Brands Intl.; Consolidated Grain & Barge Co.

For full biographical listings, see the Martindale-Hubbell Law Directory

FRILOT, PARTRIDGE, KOHNKE & CLEMENTS, L.C. (AV)

3600 Energy Centre, 1100 Poydras Street, 70163-3600
Telephone: 504-599-8000
Telecopier: 504-599-8100
Email: postmaster@fpkc.com *URL:* http://www.fpkc.com

Francis H. Brown, III
James H. Brown, Jr.
George E. Cain, Jr.
Michael T. Cali
Miles P. Clements
Andrew S. de Klerk
George A. Frilot, III (A Professional Law Corp.)
John J. Hainkel, III
Edward F. Kohnke, IV
Allen J. Krouse, III
J. Dwight LeBlanc, III
Douglas P. Matthews
Kenneth A. Mayeaux
Robert B. McNeal
Wayne K. McNeil
Patrick J. McShane
Joseph N. Mole
David A. Olson
Scott S. Partridge
Greg A. Pellegrini
Michael R. Phillips
James F. Shuey
James R. Silverstein
Peter E. Sperling
Patrick A. Talley (P.C.)
Patricia E. Weeks

Sidney A. Backstrom
Joel Edwin Cape (Not admitted in LA)
Nairda T. Lesa Colón
Bruce Arne Cranner
Frederick T. Greschner, Jr.
Brant David Imperatore
Stephanie Ann May
Michael B. North

For full biographical listings, see the Martindale-Hubbell Law Directory

GAINSBURGH, BENJAMIN, DAVID, MEUNIER & WARSHAUER (AV)

2800 Energy Centre, 1100 Poydras, 70163-2800
Telephone: 504-522-2304
Telecopier: 504-528-9973
Email: DPHILLIPS@GAINSBEN.COM

MEMBERS OF FIRM

Robert J. David
Gerald E. Meunier
Irving J. Warshauer
Stevan C. Dittman
Madeleine M. Landrieu
Darryl M. Phillips
Jeffrey A. Mitchell

ASSOCIATE
Gary B. Roth

For Complete List of Firm Personnel, See General Section

For full biographical listings, see the Martindale-Hubbell Law Directory

GORDON, ARATA, MCCOLLAM, DUPLANTIS & EAGAN, L.L.P. (AV)

A Registered Limited Liability Partnership including Professional Law Corporations
201 St. Charles Avenue, Suite 4000, 70170-4000
Telephone: 504-582-1111
Fax: 504-582-1121
Lafayette, Louisiana Office: 625 East Kaliste Saloom Road.
Telephone: 318-237-0132.
Fax: 318-237-3451.
Baton Rouge, Louisiana Office: 1400 One American Place.
Telephone: 225-381-9643.
Fax: 225-336-9763.

MEMBERS OF FIRM

John A. Gordon (A P.L.C.)
John M. McCollam (A P.L.C.)
Guy E. Wall
Cynthia A. Nicholson

ASSOCIATES

Martin P. Averill
Andrée M. Braud
Fernand L. Laudumiey, IV

LAFAYETTE OFFICE
RESIDENT MEMBER OF FIRM
William F. Bailey

RESIDENT ASSOCIATES

Denis C. Swords
Gregory G. Duplantis

Representative Clients: Apache Corp.; Bass Enterprises Production Co.; Burlington Resources Oil & Gas Co.; CNG Producing Co.; Duke Energy Corp.; Highlands Insurance Co.; Taylor Energy Co.; Torch Oil & Gas Co.; Union Pacific Resources Co.; XCL Ltd.

For Complete List of Firm Personnel, See General Section

For full biographical listings, see the Martindale-Hubbell Law Directory

New Orleans—Continued

LUGENBUHL, BURKE, WHEATON, PECK, RANKIN & HUBBARD, A LAW CORPORATION (AV)

27th Floor, Pan-American Life Center, 601 Poydras Street, 70130-6017
Telephone: 504-568-1990
Telefax: 504-529-7418
URL: http://www.lawla.com
Gulfport, Mississippi Office: The Markham Building, 2301 14th Street, Suite 705.
Telephone: 228-865-1490.
Fax: 228-822-2170.

Charles E. Lugenbuhl
Scott R. Wheaton, Jr.
Stewart F. Peck
S. Frazer Rankin
Ralph S. Hubbard III
Stanley J. Cohn
Nathan P. Horner, Jr.
Kristopher M. Redmann
James B. Persons (Resident, Gulfport, Mississippi Office)
Claude F. Bosworth
Gordon P. Wilson
J. Clayton Davie, Jr.

Loree Peacock Leboeuf
David B. Sharpe
Mary Sprague Langston
Simeon Bernard Reimonenq, Jr.
Celeste Darmstadter Elliott
Kristopher T. Wilson

Representative Clients: Baker Hughes, Inc.; Bank of Louisiana; E.N. Bisso & Son, Inc.; Brown & Root U.S.A., Inc.; Budget Rent A Car Corp.; Budget Rent A Car Systems, Inc.; The Center Marine Managers, Inc.; Central Gulf Towing Co., Inc.; Chrysler Capital Corp.; Citrus Lands of Louisiana, Inc.

For full biographical listings, see the Martindale-Hubbell Law Directory

---

MARTZELL & BICKFORD (AV)

A Partnership including a Professional Corporation
338 Lafayette Street, 70130-3244
Telephone: 504-581-9065
Fax: 504-581-7635
Email: mailbox@martzellbickford.com *URL:* http://www.martzellbickford.com

John R. Martzell (P.C.)
Scott R. Bickford

Regina O. Matthews
Duggan F. Ellis
M. Suzanne Montero
Richard A. Filce
Ray L. Rhymes

LEGAL SUPPORT PERSONNEL

LITIGATION ADMINISTRATOR

Christopher H. Sherwood

PARALEGALS

Jane B. Daigle
Connie L. Cosse
Mary Wiggenhorn

FIRM ADMINISTRATOR

Stephen C. Wolf (Certified Public Accountant)

For full biographical listings, see the Martindale-Hubbell Law Directory

---

McGLINCHEY STAFFORD (AV)

A Professional Limited Liability Company
643 Magazine Street, 70130-3477
Telephone: 504-586-1200
Fax: 504-596-2800
TDD: (504) 596-2728
Telex: 584327
Cable Address: "MACSTAC"
Mailing Address: P.O. Box 60643, New Orleans, Louisiana, 70160-0643
Email: @mcglinchey.com *URL:* http://www.mcglinchey.com
Dallas, Texas Office: 2777 Stemmons Freeway, Suite 925, 75207-2401.
Telephone: 214-860-9700.
Fax: 214-860-9750.
Houston, Texas Office: 2727 Allen Parkway, Suite 1900, 77019.
Telephone: 713-520-1900.
Fax: 713-520-1025.
Baton Rouge, Louisiana Office: Ninth Floor, One American Place, 70825-0001.
Telephone: 504-383-9000.
Fax: 504-343-3076.
Jackson, Mississippi Office: Suite 1200, SkyTel Centre, 200 South Lamar Street, 39201.
Telephone: 601-960-8400.
Fax: 601-960-8406.
Lake Providence, Louisiana Office: 405 Morgan Street, 71254-2691.
Telephone: 318-559-1200.
Fax: 318-559-0609.
Monroe, Louisiana Office: Dean ONB Tower, 130 Desiard Street, Suite 807, 71201.
Telephone: 318-651-0807.
Fax: 318-651-0809.

MEMBERS OF FIRM

Henri Wolbrette, III, (P.C.)
Eric A. Shuman

(See Next Column)

ASSOCIATES

Margaret Woolverton Triebes
Dwayne C. Jefferson

MEMBER OF FIRM

Richard A. Curry (Resident, Baton Rouge Office)

For full biographical listings, see the Martindale-Hubbell Law Directory

---

PHELPS DUNBAR, L.L.P. (AV)

Texaco Center, 400 Poydras Street, 70130-3245
Telephone: 504-566-1311
Telecopier: 504-568-9130, 504-568-9007
Cable Address: "Howspencer"
Telex: 584125 WU
Telex: 6821155 WUI
Email: info@phelps.com
Baton Rouge, Louisiana Office: Suite 701, 445 North Boulevard, P.O. Box 4412.
Telephone: 225-346-0285.
Telecopier: 225-381-9197.
Jackson, Mississippi Office: Suite 500, SkyTel Centre, 200 South Lamar Street, P.O. Box 23066.
Telephone: 601-352-2300.
Telecopier: 601-360-9777.
Tupelo, Mississippi Office: Seventh Floor, One Mississippi Plaza, P.O. Box 1220.
Telephone: 662-842-7907.
Telecopier: 662-842-3873.
Houston, Texas Office: Suite 900, 3040 Post Oak Boulevard.
Telephone: 713-626-1386.
Telecopier: 713-626-1388.
London, England Office: Suite 731, Level 7, Lloyd's, 1 Lime Street, London EC3M 7DQ England.
Telephone: 011-44-207-929-4765.
Telecopier: 011-44-207-929-0046.
Telex: 987321.

RESIDENT PARTNER

Steven J. Levine (Resident, Baton Rouge, Louisiana Office)

RESIDENT ASSOCIATES

Rebecca Bellows Crawford (Resident, Baton Rouge, Louisiana Office)
Eric T. Hamer (Not admitted in LA; Resident, Jackson, Mississippi Office)
Gwen P. Harmon (Resident, Baton Rouge Office)
Patrick O'Hara (Resident, Baton Rouge, Louisiana Office)
Sheila T. Walet

Representative Clients: CONDEA Vista Company; Energy Development Corp.; GATX Terminals Corp.; Rubicon Inc.; Underwriters at Lloyd's, London; Union Pacific Railroad Company; Union Tank Car Company, Inc.; Waste Management, Inc.

For Complete List of Firm Personnel, See General Section

For full biographical listings, see the Martindale-Hubbell Law Directory

---

PLAUCHÉ MASELLI LANDRY & PARKERSON L.L.P. (AV)

Bank One Center, Suite 4240, 201 St. Charles Avenue, 70170-4240
Telephone: 504-582-1142
Fax: 504-582-1172
URL: http://www.pmlpnola.com

MEMBERS OF FIRM

Andrew L. Plauché, Jr.
Joseph Maselli, Jr.
Arthur W. Landry
G. Bruce Parkerson
Robert E Caraway, III

ASSOCIATES

Mark E. Young
Thomas L. Hutchinson
Cherie T. Burlett
Kenan S. Rand, Jr.
Elizabeth Salzer Schell
J. Marie Rudd
Wendy K. Lappenga
Deborah F. Malveaux
Diane S. Mitnik
Lori P. Moser

Reference: Bank One of Louisiana.

For full biographical listings, see the Martindale-Hubbell Law Directory

---

PULASKI, GIEGER & LABORDE, L.L.C. (AV)

Suite 4800, One Shell Square, 701 Poydras Street, 70139
Telephone: 504-561-0400
Telecopier: 504-561-1011
Covington, Louisiana Office: 434 North Columbia Street, Suite 200, 70433.
Telephone: 504-561-0400.
Telecopier: 504-809-9677.

Marjorie Randall Brown

For full biographical listings, see the Martindale-Hubbell Law Directory

---

SLATER LAW FIRM, A PROFESSIONAL CORPORATION (AV)

650 Poydras Street Suite 2600, 70130-6101
Telephone: 504-523-7333
Fax: 504-528-1080
URL: http://www.slaterlawfirm.com

(See Next Column)

SLATER LAW FIRM A PROFESSIONAL CORPORATION, *New Orleans—Continued*

Benjamin R. Slater, Jr.
Benjamin R. Slater, III
Mark E. Van Horn
Kevin M. Wheeler
Anne Elise Brown
Donald J. Miester, Jr.

Michael O. Waguespack
Cory Rabin Cahn
Sarah Ney
S. Joseph Welborn

SPECIAL COUNSEL

W. Malcolm Stevenson

Representative Clients: Norfolk Southern Corporation.

For full biographical listings, see the Martindale-Hubbell Law Directory

WAGNER & BAGOT (AV)

Suite 2660, Poydras Center, 650 Poydras Street, 70130-6105
Telephone: 504-525-2141
Telecopier: 504-523-1587
TWX: 5106017673
ELN: 62928850
"INCISIVE"

Thomas J. Wagner
Michael H. Bagot, Jr.

Thomas A. Rayer, Jr.
Brian P. Brancato
Thomas P. Henican
Dana A. Henderson

For full biographical listings, see the Martindale-Hubbell Law Directory

WILSON & BOWLING (AV)

A Partnership including Professional Law Corporations
Suite 2411, Bank One Center, 201 St. Charles Avenue, 70170
Telephone: 504-586-5200
Facsimile: 504-586-5201
Email: wilsbowl@gs.net
Gulfport, Mississippi Office: 715 Markham Building, 2301 14th Street, 39501.
Telephone: 228-575-6202.
Fax: 228-864-6227.

Gordon F. Wilson, Jr., (P.L.C.)
David A. Bowling (P.L.C.)

Jeanne B. Roques
Susannah Ross Cooley
John D. Acomb

For full biographical listings, see the Martindale-Hubbell Law Directory

*SHREVEPORT,** Caddo Parish

BARLOW AND HARDTNER L.C. (AV)

Tenth Floor, Louisiana Tower, 401 Edwards Street, 71101-3289
Telephone: 318-227-1131
Telecopier: 318-227-1141
Mailing Address: P.O. Box 8, Shreveport, Louisiana, 71161-0008

Malcolm S. Murchison
Joseph L. Shea, Jr.
Michael B. Donald

Representative Clients: Ashland Oil, Inc.; The Brinkmann Corporation; Central Louisiana Electric Co., Inc.; NorAm Energy Corp. (formerly Arkla, Inc.); Central and South West Corporation; Panhandle Eastern Corp.; Texas Eastern Corp.; Pennzoil Producing Co.; Ashland Oil, Inc.; TE Products Pipeline Company.

For Complete List of Firm Personnel, See General Section

For full biographical listings, see the Martindale-Hubbell Law Directory

BLANCHARD, WALKER, O'QUIN & ROBERTS, A PROFESSIONAL LAW CORPORATION (AV)

Fourteenth Floor, Premier Bank Tower, 400 Texas Street, P.O. Drawer 1126, 71101
Telephone: 318-221-6858
Fax: 318-227-2967
Email: BWOR@BWOR.com
Bossier City, Louisiana Office: 2285 Benton Road, Suite B-201.
Telephone: 318-742-9255.
Fax: 318-742-9210.

W. Michael Adams
Michael E. Riddick

For Complete List of Firm Personnel, See General Section

For full biographical listings, see the Martindale-Hubbell Law Directory

WILKINSON, CARMODY & GILLIAM (AV)

1700 Beck Building, 400 Travis Street, P.O. Box 1707, 71166
Telephone: 318-221-4196
Telecopier: 318-221-3705
Email: wcg1895@aol.com

(See Next Column)

MEMBERS OF FIRM

John D. Wilkinson (1867-1929)
William Scott Wilkinson (1895-1985)
Arthur R. Carmody, Jr.
Bobby S. Gilliam
Mark E. Gilliam
William Allen Haynes

Representative Clients: Farmers Insurance Group; Home Federal Savings & Loan Association of Shreveport; The Kansas City Southern Railway Co.; KTAL-TV; Lincoln National Life Insurance Co.; Mobil Oil Co.; Schumpert Medical Center; Sears, Roebuck & Co.; Southern Pacific Transportation Co.; Southwestern Electric Power Co.

For full biographical listings, see the Martindale-Hubbell Law Directory

MAINE

*BANGOR,** Penobscot Co.

EATON, PEABODY, BRADFORD & VEAGUE, P.A. (AV)

Fleet Center-Exchange Street, P.O. Box 1210, 04402-1210
Telephone: 207-947-0111
Telecopier: 207-942-3040
Email: eaton@eatonpeabody.com *URL:* http://www.eatonpeabody.com
Augusta, Maine Office: 77 Sewall Street, Suite 3000.
Telephone: 207-622-3747.
Telecopier: 207-622-9732.
Blue Hill, Maine Office: One East Blue Hill Road.
Telephone: 207-374-2812.
Telecopier: 207-374-2548.
Brunswick, Maine Office: 167 Park Row.
Telephone: 207-729-1144.
Telecopier: 207-729-1140.
Dover-Foxcroft, Maine Office: 30 East Main Street.
Telephone: 207-564-8378.
Telecopier: 207-564-7059.

Edward D. Leonard, III
P. Andrew Hamilton
Dorisann B. W. Wagner (Resident, Augusta Office)
Roger L. Huber

OF COUNSEL

Martin L. Wilk (Resident, Brunswick Office)

William V. Ferdinand, Jr. (Resident, Augusta Office)

For Complete List of Firm Personnel, See General Section

For full biographical listings, see the Martindale-Hubbell Law Directory

BAR HARBOR, Hancock Co.

FENTON, CHAPMAN, FENTON, SMITH & KANE, P.A. (AV)

109 Main Street, P.O. Box B, 04609
Telephone: 207-288-3331
Fax: 207-288-9326
Email: fentonlawfirm@acadia.net *URL:* http://www.lawyers.com/fcfs&klaw

William Fenton
Douglas B. Chapman
Nathaniel R. Fenton
Chadbourn H. Smith

Margaret T. Jeffery

Reference: Bar Harbor Banking and Trust Co.

For Complete List of Firm Personnel, See General Section

For full biographical listings, see the Martindale-Hubbell Law Directory

*PORTLAND,** Cumberland Co.

FRIEDMAN BABCOCK & GAYTHWAITE (AV)

Suite 400, Six City Center, P.O. Box 4726, 04112-4726
Telephone: 207-761-0900
Telecopier: 207-761-0186
Email: info@fbg-law.com *URL:* http://www.fbg-law.com

MEMBERS OF FIRM

Harold J. Friedman
Ernest J. Babcock
Martha C. Gaythwaite
Karen Frink Wolf
Jennifer S. Riggle
Laurence H. Leavitt
Elizabeth A. Germani
Michelle Allott
Tracy D. Hill

ASSOCIATES

Susan J. Guerette
L. John Topchik
Sally A. Morris
Catherine C. Miller
Kieran N. Shields
Evan Smith

For full biographical listings, see the Martindale-Hubbell Law Directory

Portland—Continued

Jensen Baird Gardner & Henry (AV)

Ten Free Street, P.O. Box 4510, 04112-4510
Telephone: 207-775-7271
Telecopier: 207-775-7935
Email: info@jbgh.com *URL:* http://www.jbgh.com
York County Office: 11 Main Street, Suite 4, Kennebunk, Maine, 04043.
Telephone: 207-985-4676.
Telecopier: 207-985-4932.

MEMBERS OF FIRM

Walter E. Webber
Nicholas S. Nadzo
Leslie E. Lowry, III

ASSOCIATE

Natalie L. Burns

Representative Clients: Steego Auto Parts Co.; St. Lawrence & Atlantic Railroad; Regional Waste Systems; Mid-Maine Waste Action Corp.; Pratt & Whitney; Shaw's Supermarkets; Marine Atlantic; Town of Sanford; Yankee Ford.

For Complete List of Firm Personnel, See General Section

For full biographical listings, see the Martindale-Hubbell Law Directory

Petruccelli & Martin, LLP (AV)

50 Monument Square, P.O. Box 9733, 04104-5033
Telephone: 207-775-0200
Telecopier: 207-775-2360
Email: info@petruccellimartin.com *URL:* http://www.petruccellimartin.com

MEMBERS OF FIRM

Gerald F. Petruccelli
Linda C. Russell

Thomas C. Bradley

Representative Clients: Brunswick Associates Trust; Cumberland Farms; Town of Jay, Maine.

For full biographical listings, see the Martindale-Hubbell Law Directory

Pierce Atwood (AV)

One Monument Square, 04101
Telephone: 207-791-1100
Fax: 207-791-1350
Email: info@PierceAtwood.com *URL:* http://www.pierceatwood.com
Augusta, Maine Office: 77 Winthrop Street.
Telephone: 207-622-6311.
Fax: 207-623-9367.
Newburyport, Massachusetts Office: 6 Harris Street.
Telephone: 978-465-9599.
Fax: 978-465-9945.

MEMBERS OF FIRM

John D. Delahanty
Thomas R. Doyle
Philip F. W. Ahrens, III
Kenneth Fairbanks Gray
William E. Taylor
Dixon P. Pike
Matthew D. Manahan

ASSOCIATES

Kate L. Geoffroy
David P. Littell
Helen L. Edmonds (Resident, Augusta Office)
Ande A. Smith

For Complete List of Firm Personnel, See General Section

For full biographical listings, see the Martindale-Hubbell Law Directory

Preti, Flaherty, Beliveau, Pachios & Haley, LLC (AV)

One City Center, P.O. Box 9546, 04112-9546
Telephone: 207-791-3000
Telecopier: 207-791-3111
Email: admin@preti.com *URL:* http://www.preti.com
Augusta, Maine Office: 45 Memorial Circle, P.O. Box 1058, 04332-1058.
Telephone: 207-623-5300.
Telefax: 207-623-2914.
Bath, Maine Office: Thirty Front Street, P.O. Box 665, 04530-0665.
Telephone: 207-443-5576.
Telefax: 207-443-6665.

MEMBERS OF FIRM

Severin M. Beliveau (Augusta Office)
Harold C. Pachios
Michael J. Gentile (Augusta Office)
Virginia E. Davis (Augusta Office)
Michael Kaplan
David B. Van Slyke
Ann R. Robinson (Augusta Office)
John P. McVeigh
Jeanne T. Cohn-Connor
John S. Rudd

(See Next Column)

ASSOCIATES

Tracey G. Burton (Bath Office)
Sigmund D. Schutz
Sharon G. Newman (Not admitted in ME)

Representative Clients: Bangor Hydro-Electric Co.; Maine Turnpike Authority; Maine Oil Dealers Assn.; American Ash Recycling Corp.; HoltraChem Manufacturing Co.; Hyland Lumber; Blethen-Maine Newspapers, Inc.; Safety Kleen Corp.; National Semiconductor; Hannaford Brothers Co.

For Complete List of Firm Personnel, See General Section

For full biographical listings, see the Martindale-Hubbell Law Directory

Verrill & Dana, LLP (AV)

One Portland Square, P.O. Box 586, 04112-0586
Telephone: 207-774-4000
Fax: 207-774-7499
Email: advice@verdan.com *URL:* http://www.verdan.com
Augusta, Maine Office: 45 Memorial Circle, P.O. Box 957.
Telephone: 207-623-3889.
Fax: 207-622-3117.
Kennebunk, Maine Office: 403-404 Lafayette Center, P.O. Box 147.
Telephone: 207-985-7193.
Fax: 207-985-3957.
Washington, D.C. Office: 400 North Capitol Street, Suite 585.
Telephone: 202-624-9733.
Fax: 202-393-5218.

MEMBERS OF FIRM

James T. Kilbreth, III
Robert E. Cleaves, IV
Juliet T. Browne

ASSOCIATES

Hope K. Creal
Sean M. Mahoney
Jeffrey A. Meyers

Counsel for: ASCAP; Bowdoin College; Fleet Bank; Hannaford Bros. Co.; Maine Blue Cross and Blue Shield; Maine Public Service Co.; Peoples Heritage Bank; Portland Water District.

For Complete List of Firm Personnel, See General Section

For full biographical listings, see the Martindale-Hubbell Law Directory

Wright & Coon, P.A. (AV)

Four Canal Plaza, P.O. Box 7526, 04112
Telephone: 207-775-7722
Fax: 207-772-7045
Email: lexfori@lexfori.com

Steven F. Wright
John R. Coon
Brita J. Forssberg

For full biographical listings, see the Martindale-Hubbell Law Directory

MARYLAND

*ANNAPOLIS,** Anne Arundel Co.

Council, Baradel, Kosmerl & Nolan, P.A. (AV)

125 West Street, Fourth Floor, P.O. Box 2289, 21404-2289
Telephone: 410-268-6600
Baltimore: 410-269-6190
Washington, D.C.: 301-261-2247
FAX: 410-269-8409
Email: cbkn@cbknlaw.com

Ronald E. Council
Ronald A. Baradel
Wayne T. Kosmerl
James P. Nolan
William F. Flood, III
Kevin M. Schaeffer
Donna McCabe Schaeffer
Frederick C. Sussman

John Naumann Strange
Susan T. Ford
Edwin H. Staples, II
Susan Stobbart Shapiro

OF COUNSEL

George N. Manis
Nicholas Goldsborough

Representative Clients: Anne Arundel County; Annapolis Bank and Trust; Bank of Maryland; State Farm Mutual Automobile Insurance Co.; Annapolis Yacht Club; Annapolis Yacht Sales, Inc.

For full biographical listings, see the Martindale-Hubbell Law Directory

*BALTIMORE,** (Independent City)

Ferguson, Schetelich & Heffernan, P.A. (AV)

1401 NationsBank Center, 100 South Charles Street, 21201-2725
Telephone: 410-837-2200
Fax: 410-837-1188
URL: http://www.FSHLaw.com

(See Next Column)

FERGUSON, SCHETELICH & HEFFERNAN P.A., *Baltimore—Continued*

Robert L. Ferguson, Jr.
Thomas J. Schetelich
Christopher J. Heffernan
Craig F. Ballew
Michael N. Russo, Jr.

Peter J. Basile
Ann D. Ware
Tracey J. McLauchlin
Michele P. Zahner
Michael K. Hourigan

For full biographical listings, see the Martindale-Hubbell Law Directory

VENABLE ATTORNEYS AT LAW VENABLE, BAETJER AND HOWARD, LLP (AV)

A Partnership including Professional Corporations
1800 Mercantile Bank & Trust Building, 2 Hopkins Plaza, 21201
Telephone: 410-244-7400
Fax: 410-244-7742
URL: http://www.venable.com
Washington, D.C. Office: Venable, Baetjer, Howard & Civiletti LLP, Suite 1000, 1201 New York Avenue, N.W.
Telephone: 202-962-4800.
Fax: 202-962-8300.
McLean, Virginia Office: Suite 400, 2010 Corporate Ridge.
Telephone: 703-760-1600.
Fax: 703-821-8949.
Rockville, Maryland Office: Suite 500, One Church Street, P. O. Box 1906.
Telephone: 301-217-5600.
Fax: 301-217-5617.
Towson, Maryland Office: 210 Allegheny Avenue, P. O. Box 5517.
Telephone: 410-494-6200.
Fax: 410-821-0147.

MEMBERS OF FIRM

Benjamin R. Civiletti (P.C.) (Also at Washington, D.C. and Towson, Maryland Offices)
Anthony M. Carey (Also at Washington, D.C. Office)
John Henry Lewin, Jr. (P.C.)
Robert G. Smith (P.C.)
John G. Milliken (Not admitted in MD; Resident, McLean, Virginia Office)
Joseph C. Wich, Jr. (Resident, Towson, Maryland Office)
Joseph G. Block (Not admitted in MD; Resident, Washington, D.C. Office)
Michael Schatzow (Also at Washington, D.C. Office)
John F. Cooney (Not admitted in MD; Resident, Washington, D.C. Office)
Brock R. Landry (Not admitted in MD; Resident, Washington, D.C. Office)
James K. Archibald (Also at Washington, D.C. Office)
Judson W. Starr (Not admitted in MD; Also at Washington, D.C. and Towson, Maryland Offices)
Jeffrey A. Dunn (Also at Washington, D.C. Office)
James L. Shea (Also at Washington, D.C. Office)
Brigid E. Kenney
John J. Pavlick, Jr. (Not admitted in MD; Resident, Washington, D.C. Office)
Christopher R. Mellott
M. King Hill, III (Resident, Towson, Maryland Office)
James A. Dunbar (Resident, Towson, Maryland Office)
Ronald W. Taylor
Thomas J. Kelly, Jr. (Not admitted in MD; Resident, Washington, D.C. Office)
David C. Mancini (Resident, McLean, Virginia Office)
Kevin L. Shepherd
Mitchell Y. Mirviss
Thomas M. Lingan
Christine M. McAnney (Not admitted in MD; Resident, McLean, Virginia Office)

OF COUNSEL

Judith A. Armold (Also at Washington, D.C. Office)

ASSOCIATES

Gregory S. Braker (Resident, Washington, D.C. Office)
Thomas H. Strong

For Complete List of Firm Personnel, See General Section

For full biographical listings, see the Martindale-Hubbell Law Directory

*SALISBURY,** Wicomico Co.

ADKINS, POTTS & SMETHURST, L.L.P. (AV)

Suite 600, One Plaza East, P.O. Box 4247, 21803-4247
Telephone: 410-749-0161
Fax: 410-749-5021

MEMBER OF FIRM

Raymond Stevens Smethurst, Jr.

Representative Clients: Bell Atlantic NYNEX Mobile; Campbell Soup Company; Delmarva Power & Light Co.; Shopco Group; WBOC-TV.

For full biographical listings, see the Martindale-Hubbell Law Directory

SILVER SPRING, Montgomery Co.

LINOWES AND BLOCHER LLP (AV)

Suite 1000, 1010 Wayne Avenue, 20910-5600
Telephone: 301-588-8580
Telecopier: 301-495-9044
TTY/TDD: 301-588-3380
Email: inbox@linowes-law.com *URL:* http://www.linowes-law.com
Washington, D.C. Office: Suite 302, 1150 17th Street, N.W.
Telephone: 202-293-8510.
Telecopier: 202-293-8513.
Greenbelt, Maryland Office: Suite 202, 6411 Ivy Lane.
Telephone: 301-982-3382.
Telecopier: 301-982-0595.
Annapolis, Maryland Office: 145 Main Street.
Telephone: 410-268-0881.
Telecopier: 301-261-2603.
Frederick, Maryland Office: 228 West Patrick Street.
Telephone: 301-695-0244.
Telecopier: 301-663-6656.
Columbia, Maryland Office: Suite B215, 10015 Old Columbia Road.
Telephone: 410-312-5457.
Fax: 410-290-5285.

MEMBERS OF FIRM

Kathryn J. Dahl (Resident Partner, Annapolis, Maryland office)
John J. Delaney
Lawrence R. Liebesman
David M. Plott (Resident Partner, Annapolis, Maryland office)
James B. Witkin

ASSOCIATES

Rafe Petersen
Emily J. Vaias

For Complete List of Firm Personnel, See General Section

For full biographical listings, see the Martindale-Hubbell Law Directory

SAUNDERS & SCHMIELER (AV)

8737 Colesville Road, Suite L-200, 20910-3921
Telephone: 301-588-7717
Facsimile: 301-588-5073
Email: admin@sslawfirm.com *URL:* http://www.sslawfirm.com
Washington, D.C. Office: 1050 17th Street, N.W., #600
Telephone: 202-833-2999.
Baltimore, Maryland Office: Suite 2700, 111 South Calvert Street.
Telephone: 410-235-7558.
Arlington, Virginia Office: 2111 Wilson Boulevard, Suite 700.
Telephone: 703-243-1100.
Richmond, Virginia Office: 4900 Cutshaw Avenue.
Telephone: 804-353-9800.

MEMBER OF FIRM

Jeffrey R. Schmieler

ASSOCIATES

Nicole E. Ames
A. Benjamin Horton
Lucas F. Webster

For Complete List of Firm Personnel, See General Section

For full biographical listings, see the Martindale-Hubbell Law Directory

*TOWSON,** Baltimore Co.

WHITNEY & BOGRIS, LLP (AV)

401 Washington Avenue, Twelfth Floor, 21204
Telephone: 410-583-8000
Fax: 410-583-8031
Email: HGWC@worldnet.att.net

MEMBERS OF FIRM

Daniel W. Whitney
George D. Bogris

ASSOCIATES

Kathleen D. Leslie
Henry Russell
Sandra A. Tofte
Michael A. Giacomazza
Arlene L. Sew
Gerald S. Gaetano (Not admitted in MD)
Scott A. McCabe (Not admitted in MD)
Jeffrey C. Shipley

OF COUNSEL

Joseph E. Dever
David L. Feldstein
Ronald V. Miller, Jr.

For full biographical listings, see the Martindale-Hubbell Law Directory

MASSACHUSETTS

*BOSTON,** Suffolk Co.

BARRON & STADFELD, P.C. (AV)

50 Staniford Street, Suite 200, 02114
Telephone: 617-723-9800
Telecopier: 617-523-8359
Email: barron@barronstad.com *URL:* HTTP://WWW.BARRONSTAD.COM
Hyannis, Massachusetts Office: 258 Winter Street.
Telephone: 617-778-6622.

Bernard A. Dwork
David P. Dwork
Julie Taylor Moran

For Complete List of Firm Personnel, See General Section

For full biographical listings, see the Martindale-Hubbell Law Directory

KOPELMAN AND PAIGE, P.C. (AV)

Park Square Building, 31 St. James Avenue, 7th Floor, 02116
Telephone: 617-556-0007
Fax: 617-654-1735

Leonard Kopelman
Donald G. Paige
Elizabeth A. Lane
Joyce F. Frank
John W. Giorgio
Barbara J. Saint Andre
Joel B. Bard
Everett Joseph Marder
Patrick J. Costello
Anne-Marie M. Hyland
Deborah Eliason
Richard Bowen

William Hewig, III
Judith Chanoux Cutler
Brian W. Riley

For Complete List of Firm Personnel, See General Section

For full biographical listings, see the Martindale-Hubbell Law Directory

McGREGOR & ASSOCIATES, P.C. (AV)

60 Temple Place, 02111
Telephone: 617-338-6464
Fax: 617-338-0737
URL: http://www.mcgregorlaw.com

Gregor I. McGregor
Nathaniel Stevens
Michael J. O'Neill

LEGAL SUPPORT PERSONNEL

Ralph R. Willmer, A.I.C.P. (Environmental Planner)
Ezra H. Glenn

For full biographical listings, see the Martindale-Hubbell Law Directory

PALMER & DODGE LLP (AV)

One Beacon Street, 02108
Telephone: 617-573-0100
Facsimile: 617-227-4420
URL: http://www.palmerdodge.com

MEMBERS OF FIRM

Charles E. DeWitt, Jr.
William L. Lahey
Scott P. Lewis
Raymond M. Murphy
David R. Rodgers
Kenneth W. Salinger
James M. Whalen

For Complete List of Firm Personnel, See General Section

For full biographical listings, see the Martindale-Hubbell Law Directory

SWARTZ & SWARTZ (AV)

10 Marshall Street, 02108
Telephone: 617-742-1900
Fax: 617-367-7193
Email: Attorney@Swartzlaw.com *URL:* http://www.Swartzlaw.com

Edward M. Swartz
Alan L. Cantor
Joseph A. Swartz
Victor A. Denaro
Joan E. Swartz
James A. Swartz
David P. Angueira
Jason Mark
Lisa V. Kaprielian

OF COUNSEL

Fredric A. Swartz

For full biographical listings, see the Martindale-Hubbell Law Directory

*SPRINGFIELD,** Hampden Co.

ANNINO, DRAPER & MOORE, P.C. (AV)

1500 Main Street, Suite 1818, P.O. Box 15428, 01115
Telephone: 413-732-6400
Fax: 413-732-3339
Email: admatlaw@aol.com
Westfield, Massachusetts Office: 52 Court Street.
Telephone: 413-562-9829.

Calvin W. Annino, Jr.
Mark E. Draper
Louis S. Moore
Michael R. Siddall

For full biographical listings, see the Martindale-Hubbell Law Directory

MICHIGAN

*ANN ARBOR,** Washtenaw Co.

BRAUN KENDRICK FINKBEINER PLC (AV)

First National Building, 210 S. Main, Suite 700, 48104
Telephone: 313-995-4100
Telecopier: 313-995-4798
Email: ALBFIE@BKF-LAW.COM *URL:* http://www.bkf-law.com
Bay City, Michigan Office: 201 Phoenix Building, P.O. Box 2039.
Telephone: 517-895-8505.
Telecopier: 517-895-8437.
Saginaw, Michigan Office: 101 N. Washington, Suite 812.
Telephone: 517-753-3461.
Telecopier: 517-753-3951.
Saginaw Township, Michigan Office: 5800 Gratiot Road, Suite 107, P.O. Box 5169.
Telephone: 517-799-8692.
Fax: 517-799-4666.
Mt. Pleasant, Michigan Office: 805 North Brown.
Telephone: 517-775-7404.
Telecopier: 517-775-3764.

Barry M. Levine

Representative Clients: The Dow Chemical Co.; General Motors Corp.; Merrill, Lynch, Inc.; Saginaw General Hospital; Saginaw News; The Wickes Foundation.

For Complete List of Firm Personnel, See General Section

For full biographical listings, see the Martindale-Hubbell Law Directory

HOOPER, HATHAWAY, PRICE, BEUCHE & WALLACE (AV)

126 South Main Street, 48104
Telephone: 313-662-4426
Fax: 313-662-9559
Email: hhpbw@voyager.net

Bruce T. Wallace
William J. Stapleton

Representative Clients: Avfuel Corporation; Bank of Ann Arbor; Castrol North America; Chem-Trend Incorporated; Ervin Industries, Inc.; First Martin Corporation; Glacier Hills, Inc.; Prestolite Electric, Inc.; Southern States Cooperative; E.B. Eddy Forest Products, Ltd.

For Complete List of Firm Personnel, See General Section

For full biographical listings, see the Martindale-Hubbell Law Directory

BATTLE CREEK, Calhoun Co.

KREIS, ENDERLE, CALLANDER & HUDGINS, A PROFESSIONAL CORPORATION (AV)

One West Michigan Avenue, 49017
Telephone: 616-966-3000
Facsimile: 616-966-3022
Email: kech@kech.com *URL:* http://www.kech.com
Kalamazoo, Michigan Office: One Moorsbridge, P.O. Box 4010, 49003-4010.
Telephone: 616-324-3000.
Fax: 616-324-3010.

Alan G. Enderle (Resident, Kalamazoo Office)
Jeffrey D. Swenarton (Resident, Kalamazoo Office)
Peter F. Davis (Resident, Kalamazoo Office)

For Complete List of Firm Personnel, See General Section

For full biographical listings, see the Martindale-Hubbell Law Directory

*BAY CITY,** Bay Co.

BRAUN KENDRICK FINKBEINER PLC (AV)

201 Phoenix Building, P.O. Box 2039, 48708
Telephone: 517-895-8505
Telecopier: 517-895-8437
Email: ALBFIE@BKF-LAW.COM *URL:* http://www.bkf-law.com
Saginaw, Michigan Office: 101 N. Washington, Suite 812. 8th Floor Second National Bank Building.
Telephone: 517-753-3461.
Telecopier: 517-753-3951.
Saginaw Township, Michigan Office: 5800 Gratiot Road, Suite 107, P.O. Box 5169.
Telephone: 517-799-8692.
Fax: 517-799-4666.
Ann Arbor, Michigan Office: First National Building. 201 S. Main, Suite 700.
Telephone: 313-995-4100.
Telecopier: 313-995-4798.
Mt. Pleasant, Michigan Office: 805 North Brown.
Telephone: 517-775-7404.
Telecopier: 517-775-3764.

Ralph J. Isackson
Frank M. Quinn
Gregory E. Meter
Daniel S. Opperman
Gregory T. Demers
Jeffrey C. Wilson

Michael E. Wooley

Representative Clients: Bay Health Systems; Catholic Federal Credit Union; City of Saginaw; City of Vassar; City of Zilwaukee; Corporate Service; Cox Cable.

For full biographical listings, see the Martindale-Hubbell Law Directory

BLOOMFIELD HILLS, Oakland Co.

JON H. BERKEY, P.C. (AV)

1700 North Woodward Avenue, Suite 101, 48304-2249
Telephone: 248-593-6460
Fax: 248-593-6470
URL: http://www.lawyers.com/jonberkeylaw

Jon H. Berkey

Anthony A. Yezbick

OF COUNSEL

Kenneth J. Wrobel, Jr.

For full biographical listings, see the Martindale-Hubbell Law Directory

DAWDA, MANN, MULCAHY & SADLER, P.L.C. (AV)

1533 North Woodward Avenue Suite 200, 48304-2815
Telephone: 248-642-3700
Fax: 248-642-7791
Email: EMail@DMMS.Com

Susan J. Sadler
Tyler D. Tennent
Sherwin E. Zamler
John Mucha, III

Maureen B. Connaughton
John Gerald Gleeson, Jr.

Representative Clients: Allied Waste Industries, Inc.; BASF Corp.; Cardell Corp.; Cargill, Inc.; Home Depot U.S.A., Inc.; Ladbroke Racing Corp.; Lockheed Martin Corp.; The Sherwin-Williams Company; Trammell Crow Company; Wal-Mart Stores, Inc.

For full biographical listings, see the Martindale-Hubbell Law Directory

HOWARD & HOWARD ATTORNEYS, P.C. (AV)

The Pinehurst Office Center, Suite 101, 1400 North Woodward Avenue, 48304-2855
Telephone: 248-645-1483
Telecopier: 248-645-1568
Kalamazoo, Michigan Office: The Michigan Building, Suite 200, 100 Portage Street.
Telephone: 616-382-1483.
Telecopier: 616-382-1568.
Lansing, Michigan Office: The Phoenix Building, Suite 500, 222 Washington Square, North.
Telephone: 517-485-1483.
Telecopier: 517-485-1568.
Peoria, Illinois Office: One Technology Plaza, Suite 600, 211 Fulton Street.
Telephone: 309-672-1483.
Telecopier: 309-672-1568.

Chris T. Danikolas
Charles E. Dunn
Steven C. Kohl
Susan E. Padley
Gary A. Peters
Brian J. Renaud
Rhonda L. Ross

Representative Clients: For Representative Client list, see General Practice, Bloomfield Hills, MI.

(See Next Column)

For Complete List of Firm Personnel, See General Section

For full biographical listings, see the Martindale-Hubbell Law Directory

PROVIZER & PHILLIPS, P.C. (AV)

6785 Telegraph Road, Suite 400, 48301
Telephone: 248-642-0444
Facsimile: 248-642-6661
Toll Free: 1-800-288-9080
URL: http://www.lawyers.com/provizer&phillips

Harold M. Provizer
Randall E. Phillips
Marilyn A. Madorsky
Noel F. Beck

Constance S. Hall
Donald J. Parthum, Jr.
Gregory A. Nave

Representative Clients: Jefferson Ins. Co.; Reliance National Ins. Group; Ken Modell (Personal Representative); Mort Novak (Personal Representative of the Estate of Garavaglia).

For full biographical listings, see the Martindale-Hubbell Law Directory

*DETROIT,** Wayne Co.

BODMAN, LONGLEY & DAHLING LLP (AV)

34th Floor 100 Renaissance Center, 48243
Telephone: 313-259-7777
Fax: 313-393-7579
Email: info@bodmanlongley.com *URL:* http://www.bodmanlongley.com
Troy, Michigan Office: Suite 2020, 755 West Big Beaver Road.
Telephone: 248-362-2110.
Fax: 248-244-0780.
Ann Arbor, Michigan Office: 110 Miller, Suite 300.
Telephone: 734-761-3780.
Fax: 734-930-2494.
Northern Michigan Office: 229 Court Street, P.O. Box 405, Cheboygan.
Telephone: 231-627-4351.
Fax: 231-627-2802.

MEMBERS OF FIRM

James A. Smith
David G. Chardavoyne
Fredrick J. Dindoffer
Michael A. Stack (Cheboygan Office)
R. Craig Hupp

ASSOCIATES

Cortney E. Goldberg
Margaret M. Wood
Kurt M. Brauer

For Representative Client List, See General Section

For Complete List of Firm Personnel, See General Section

For full biographical listings, see the Martindale-Hubbell Law Directory

BUTZEL LONG, A PROFESSIONAL CORPORATION (AV)

Suite 900, 150 West Jefferson, 48226
Telephone: 313-225-7000
Telecopier: 313-225-7080
Email: melnick@butzel.com *URL:* http://www.butzel.com
Birmingham, Michigan Office: Suite 200, 32270 Telegraph Road.
Telephone: 810-258-1616.
Telecopier: 810-258-1439.
Okemos, Michigan Office: Suite 300, 2127 University Park Drive.
Telephone: 517-372-6622.
Telecopier: 517-372-6672.
Ann Arbor, Michigan Office: Suite 300, 350 South Main Street.
Telephone: 313-995-3110.
Telecopier: 313-995-1777.
Grosse Pointe Farms, Michigan Office: Suite 260, 21 Kercheval.
Telephone: 313-886-5446.
Telecopier: 313-886-2114.
Boca Raton, Florida Office: Suite 411, 1200 North Federal Highway.
Telephone: 561-368-2151.
Telecopier: 561-368-4668.
Palm Beach Gardens, Florida Office: Suite 227, 11382 Prosperity Farms Road.
Telephone: 561-625-4442.
Telecopier: 561-625-6901.
Naples, Florida Office: Suite 705, 801 Laurel Oak Drive.
Telephone: 941-597-4500.
Telecopier: 941-597-5623.

John Henry Dudley, Jr.
Jack D. Shumate (Birmingham)
Donald B. Miller
Leonard F. Charla
James E. Wynne
Michael J. Lavoie

SENIOR ATTORNEY

Saulius K. Mikalonis

Elizabeth A. DuMouchelle
James A. Gray, III

Representative Clients: Associated General Contractors; Complete Business Solutions, Inc.; General Dynamics Corp.; General Electric Co.; Indian Head Industries, Inc.; McKesson Corp.; McLouth Steel; TRW Automotive.

For full biographical listings, see the Martindale-Hubbell Law Directory

Detroit—Continued

DICKINSON WRIGHT PLLC (AV)

500 Woodward Avenue, Suite 4000, 48226-3425
Telephone: 313-223-3500
Facsimile: 313-223-3598
URL: http://www.dickinson-wright.com
Bloomfield Hills, Michigan Office: 525 North Woodward Avenue, Suite 2000.
Telephone: 248-433-7200.
Facsimile: 248-433-7274.
Grand Rapids, Michigan Office: 200 Ottawa Avenue, N.W., Suite 900.
Telephone: 616-458-1300.
Facsimile: 616-458-6753.
Lansing, Michigan Office: Suite 200, 215 South Washington Square.
Telephone: 517-371-1730.
Facsimile: 517-487-4700.
Washington, D.C. Office: Suite 800, 1901 L Street, N.W.
Telephone: 202-457-0160.
Facsimile: 202-659-1559.

MEMBERS OF FIRM

Margaret A. Coughlin
Keith J. Lerminiaux
Sharon R. Newlon
Claudia Rast
Herbert G. Sparrow, III

For Representative Client list, see General Section.

For Complete List of Firm Personnel, See General Section

For full biographical listings, see the Martindale-Hubbell Law Directory

DYKEMA GOSSETT PLLC (AV)

400 Renaissance Center, 48243-1668
Telephone: 313-568-6800
Fax: 313-568-6545
Email: mstarrs@dykema.com *URL:* http://www.dykema.com
Ann Arbor, Michigan Office: 315 East Eisenhower Parkway, Suite 100, 48108-3306.
Telephone: 734-214-7660.
Fax: 734-214-7696.
Bloomfield Hills, Michigan Office: 1577 North Woodward Avenue, Suite 300, 48304-2820.
Telephone: 248-203-0700.
Fax: 248-203-0763.
Chicago, Illinois Office: 55 East Monroe Street, Suite 3050, 60603-5709.
Telephone: 312-551-4900.
Fax: 312-551-4919.
Grand Rapids, Michigan Office: Suite 700, 300 Ottawa Avenue, N.W., 49503-2304.
Telephone: 616-776-7500.
Fax: 616-776-7573.
Lansing, Michigan Office: 800 Michigan National Tower, 48933-1707.
Telephone: 517-374-9100.
Fax: 517-374-9191.
Washington, D.C. Office: Franklin Square, Suite 300 West, 1300 I Street, N.W., 20005-3306.
Telephone: 202-522-8600.
Fax: 202-522-8669.
Affiliated Office: Via Matconi, 3, 40122 Bologna, Italy.
Telephone: 011-39-51-228222.
Fax: 011-39-51-6593580.

MEMBERS OF FIRM

Joseph C. Basta
James W. Collier
John A. Ferroli (Resident at Grand Rapids Office)
Grant P. Gilezan
Mark D. Jacobs
Jerome I. Maynard (Member in Charge of Chicago Office)
David L. Tripp

ASSOCIATES

Scott D. Broekstra (Resident at Grand Rapids Office)
Sharon A. Salinas (Not admitted in MI; Resident at Chicago Office)
William R. Schikora
Nicholas G. Zotos

For Complete List of Firm Personnel, See General Section

For full biographical listings, see the Martindale-Hubbell Law Directory

HAYDUK, ANDREWS & HYPNAR, P.C. (AV)

1700 Buhl Building, 535 Griswold, 48226
Telephone: 313-962-4500
Fax: 313-964-6577
Email: hahpc3@aol.com

Mark S. Hayduk
Robin K. Andrews
Mark A. Hypnar

Sean Angus McPhillips
Francis J. Lagrou

Representative Clients: Farmers Insurance Group; Admiral Insurance Co.; Heritage Ins. Alexis; Meijer, Inc.; Condon & Forsyth; Pinkerton's Inc.; Vik Brothers Ins.; Investors Ins. Group.

(See Next Column)

For full biographical listings, see the Martindale-Hubbell Law Directory

HONIGMAN MILLER SCHWARTZ AND COHN (AV)

2290 First National Building, 660 Woodward Avenue, 48226
Telephone: 313-465-7000
Telecopier: 313-465-8000
Telex: 235705
Email: mvg@honigman.com *URL:* http://law.honigman.com
Lansing, Michigan Office: Phoenix Building, 222 North Washington Square, Suite 400, 48933-1800.
Telephone: 517-484-8282.

MEMBERS OF FIRM

Christopher J. Dunsky
Kenneth C. Gold
S. Lee Johnson
Steven C. Nadeau
Brian J. Negele
John D. Pirich (Lansing, Michigan Office)
Joseph M. Polito
Grant R. Trigger
William A. Wichers II
Jeffrey L. Woolstrum
Ruth E. Zimmerman (Lansing, Michigan Office)

ASSOCIATE

Stuart J. Weiss

Representative Clients: Auto Alliance International Inc. (formerly Mazda Motor Manufacturing (USA) Corporation); Consumers Power Company; The Detroit Edison Company; Ford Motor Company; General Motors Corporation; Hughes Aircraft Company; Hughes Missile Systems Company; Edw. C. Levy Co.; Masco Corporation and its affiliates; Morton International, Inc.

For Complete List of Firm Personnel, See General Section

For full biographical listings, see the Martindale-Hubbell Law Directory

JAFFE, RAITT, HEUER & WEISS, PROFESSIONAL CORPORATION (AV)

One Woodward Avenue, Suite 2400, 48226
Telephone: 313-961-8380
Telecopier: 313-961-8358
Cable Address: "Jafsni"
Southfield, Michigan Office: Travelers Tower, Suite 1520.
Telephone: 313-961-8380.

Jeffrey G. Heuer
Eric A. Linden
Arthur H. Siegal

For Complete List of Firm Personnel, See General Section

For full biographical listings, see the Martindale-Hubbell Law Directory

KITCH DRUTCHAS WAGNER DENARDIS & VALITUTTI, A PROFESSIONAL CORPORATION (AV)

One Woodward, Tenth Floor, 48226-3499
Telephone: 313-965-7900
Fax: 313-965-7403
URL: http://www.kitch.com
Lansing, Michigan Office: 120 Washington Square, North, Suite 280, One Michigan Avenue, 48933-1609.
Telephone: 517-372-6430.
Fax: 517-372-0441.
Macomb County Office: Towne Square Development, 10 South Main Street, Suite 301, Mount Clemens, 48043-7903.
Telephone: 810-463-9770.
Fax: 810-463-8994.
Toledo, Ohio Office: 405 Madison Avenue, Suite 1500, 43604-1235.
Telephone: 419-243-4006.
Fax: 419-243-7333.
Marquette, Michigan Office: Old City Hall, 220 West Washington, Suite 500, 49855-4344.
Telephone: 906-228-0001.
Fax: 906-228-0003.
Ann Arbor, Michigan Office: 303 Detroit Street, Suite 400, P.O. Box 8610, 48107-8610.
Telephone: 734-994-7600.
Fax: 734-994-7626.
Grand Rapids, Michigan Office: 300 Ottawa, NW, Suite 210, 49503.
Telephone: 616-456-8384.
Fax: 616-456-8795.

FIRM PRINCIPALS

Ronald E. Wagner (Managing Principal)
Richard S. Baron

FIRM ASSOCIATE PRINCIPALS

Anthony J. Nellis

FIRM SENIOR ASSOCIATE

Jeffrey A. Magid

For Complete List of Firm Personnel, See General Section

For full biographical listings, see the Martindale-Hubbell Law Directory

Detroit—Continued

LEWIS & MUNDAY, A PROFESSIONAL CORPORATION (AV)

(Formerly Lewis, Clay & Munday, P.C.)
1300 First National Building, 660 Woodward Avenue, 48226-3531
Telephone: 313-961-2550
Fax: 313-961-1270
Email: camille.miller@lewis-pc.com *URL:* http://www.lewis-pc.com
Washington, D.C. Office: 1120 Connecticut Avenue, Suite 280. 20036.
Telephone: 202-835-0616.
Fax: 202-833-3316.
Boston, Massachusetts Office: 101 Federal Street, Suite 1900. 02110.
Telephone: 617-478-0553.
Fax: 617-478-0543.

David Baker Lewis
Reuben A. Munday
Camille Stearns Miller
Jacqueline H. Sellers
David N. Zacks
Thomas J. Guyer
Blair A. Person
Karen Kendrick Brown (Resident, Washington, D.C. Office)
Susan D. Hoffman
Hans J. Massaquoi, Jr.

Althea Lynn Simpson
Donica Thomas Varner
Kris W. Krueger
Cylenthia LaToye Miller
Joseph N. Ejbeh
Yolanda R. Bates
Caroletta L. Edgar-Sprinkle
Derek G. McBride
Ayanna Weber
Deborah Jean Williamson
Darice Elizabeth Weber
Krystal M. Gardner
Syeda Taqi

COUNSEL

G. Allen Bass (Resident, Boston, Massachusetts Office)
Leamon R. Sowell, Jr.
Gail Pabarue Bennett
Roger M. Groves
Carol H. Rodriguez
Linda M. Bruton
Brian J. Kott

OF COUNSEL

Otis M. Smith (1922-1994)
Herbert O. Reid, Sr. (1915-1991)

Representative Clients: Aetna Life & Casualty Co.; Chrysler Motors Corp.; Chrysler Financial Corp.; MCI Communications Corp.; City of Detroit; City of Detroit Building Authority; City of Detroit Downtown Development Authority; Consolidated Rail Corp. (Conrail); Equitable Life Assurance Society of the United States.

For full biographical listings, see the Martindale-Hubbell Law Directory

MILLER, CANFIELD, PADDOCK AND STONE, P.L.C. (AV)

A Professional Limited Liability Company
Founded in 1852 by Sidney Davy Miller
150 West Jefferson, Suite 2500, 48226-4415
Telephone: 313-963-6420
Fax: 313-496-7500
Cable Address: "Stem Detroit"
URL: http://www.millercanfield.com
Ann Arbor, Michigan Office: 101 North Main Street, 7th Floor, 48104-1400.
Telephone: 734-663-2445.
Fax: 734-747-7147.
Troy, Michigan Office: 840 West Long Lake Road, Suite 200, 48098.
Telephone: 248-879-2000.
Fax: 248-879-2001.
Grand Rapids, Michigan Office: 99 Monroe, N.W., Suite 1200, 49503-2639.
Telephone: 616-454-8656.
Fax: 616-776-6322.
Howell, Michigan Office: 121 South Barnard Street, Suite 4, 48843-2305.
Telephone: 517-546-7600.
Telecopier: 517-546-6974.
Kalamazoo, Michigan Office: 444 West Michigan Avenue, 49007-3752.
Telephone: 616-381-7030.
Fax: 616-382-0244.
Lansing, Michigan Office: One Michigan Avenue, Suite 900, 48933-1609.
Telephone: 517-487-2070.
Fax: 517-374-6304.
Monroe, Michigan Office: 214 East Elm Avenue, Suite 100, 48162-2682.
Telephone: 734-243-2000.
Fax: 734-243-0901.
Washington, D.C. Office: 1900 K Street, N.W., Suite 1150. 20006.
Telephone: 202-429-5575; 785-0600.
Fax: 202-331-1118; 785-1234.
Pensacola, Florida Office: 25 West Cedar, 32501.
Telephone: 850-469-1088.
Fax: 850-432-0677.
New York, New York Office: 1450 Broadway, 41st Floor, 10018.
Telephone: 212-704-4400.
Fax: 212-704-4410.
Gdynia, Poland Office: UL. Slaska 21, 81-319.
Telephone: 011-485-831-2808.
Fax: 011-48-58-628 6411.
Warsaw, Poland Office: UL. Nowogrodzkall, 5th Floor, 00-513.
Telephone: 011-4822 529 0200.
Fax: 011-4822 529 0201.

(See Next Column)

Katowice, Poland Office: UL. Francuska 35/37, 40-027.
Telephone: 011 (48-32) 757-2414.
Fax: 011 (48-32) 757-2483.

PRINCIPALS OF FIRM

Allyn D. Kantor (Ann Arbor Office)
Frank L. Andrews (Troy Office)
Thomas C. Phillips (Lansing Office)
Ronald E. Baylor (Kalamazoo Office)
Douglas W. Crim (Grand Rapids Office)
Ronald E. Hodess (Troy Office)
Steven E. Chester (Lansing Office)
James R. Lancaster, Jr. (Lansing Office)

ASSOCIATE

Anna M. Maiuri (Troy Office)

Representative Firm Clients: Chrysler Corporation; Comerica, Incorporated; City of Detroit, Michigan; Detroit Tigers, Inc.; First of Michigan; Ford Motor Company; Ford Motor Credit Company; Great Lakes Bancorp; Henry Ford Hospital; INVETECH Company.

For Complete List of Firm Personnel, See General Section

For full biographical listings, see the Martindale-Hubbell Law Directory

TIMMIS & INMAN L.L.P. (AV)

300 Talon Centre, 48207
Telephone: 313-396-4200
Facsimile: 313-396-4228
Email: info@timmis-inman.com *URL:* http://www.timmis-inman.com

Robert E. Graziani
Mark W. Peyser
Richard M. Miettinen
Bradley J. Knickerbocker

Representative Clients: CNA Insurance Companies; Continental Insurance; Transamerica Insurance; AIG Technical Services, Inc.; J. Levin Sons Co.

For Complete List of Firm Personnel, See General Section

For full biographical listings, see the Martindale-Hubbell Law Directory

*FLINT,** Genesee Co.

GAULT DAVISON A PROFESSIONAL SERVICE CORPORATION (AV)

Tenth Floor, Northbank Center, 432 North Saginaw Street, 48502-2032
Telephone: 810-234-3633
Fax: 810-233-3387
Email: gltdav@tir.com *URL:* http://www.gaultdavison.com

Frederick L. Schmoll, III

Kevin A. Lavalle
Christopher L. Toot

Representative Clients: Al Serra Automobile Cos.; Shoney's, Inc.; City of Flint; Vic Canever Chevrolet Co.; Oil Chem, Inc.; Richfield Iron Works, Inc.; Wakeland Oil Co.; Millburn Peat Co.

For full biographical listings, see the Martindale-Hubbell Law Directory

*GRAND RAPIDS,** Kent Co.

BORRE, PETERSON, FOWLER & REENS, P.C. (AV)

300 Ottawa N.W., Suite 500, P.O. Box 1767, 49501-1767
Telephone: 616-459-1971
Fax: 616-459-2393
Email: 105162.1531@compuserve.com

Mark D. Sevald

References: NBD Bank/First Chicago Bank; The Huntington Bank.

For Complete List of Firm Personnel, See General Section

For full biographical listings, see the Martindale-Hubbell Law Directory

BOS & GLAZIER, P.L.C. (AV)

300 Ottawa N.W., Suite 800, 49503
Telephone: 616-458-6814
Fax: 616-458-0608
Email: bglazier@bosglazier.com *URL:* http://www.bosglazier.com

Carole D. Bos
Bradley K. Glazier
Susan Wilson Keener

ASSOCIATES

Gwen E. Buday
Thomas S. Olsson

For full biographical listings, see the Martindale-Hubbell Law Directory

GRUEL, MILLS, NIMS AND PYLMAN (AV)

50 Monroe Place, Suite 700 West, 49503
Telephone: 616-235-5500
Fax: 616-235-5550

MEMBERS OF FIRM

Grant J. Gruel
William F. Mills
J. Clarke Nims
Norman H. Pylman, II
Scott R. Melton
Brion J. Brooks
Thomas R. Behm
J. Paul Janes

(See Next Column)

GRUEL, MILLS, NIMS AND PYLMAN—*Continued*

Representative Clients: Aquinas College; Bell Helmet Co.; Blodgett Memorial Medical Center; Chem Central, Inc.; Cook Pump Co.; Grove, Inc.; NBDC; Heim Corp.

For full biographical listings, see the Martindale-Hubbell Law Directory

MILLER, CANFIELD, PADDOCK AND STONE, P.L.C. (AV)

A Professional Limited Liability Company
Founded in 1852 by Sidney Davy Miller
99 Monroe, N.W. Suite 1200, 49503-2639
Telephone: 616-454-8656
Fax: 616-776-6322
URL: http://www.millercanfield.com
Detroit, Michigan Office: 150 West Jefferson, Suite 2500, 48226-4415.
Telephone: 313-963-6420.
Fax: 313-496-7500.
Cable Address: "Stem Detroit."
Ann Arbor, Michigan Office: 101 North Main Street, 7th Floor, 48104-1400.
Telephone: 734-663-2445.
Fax: 734-747-7147.
Troy, Michigan Office: 840 West Long Lake Road, Suite 200, 48098.
Telephone: 248-879-2000.
Fax: 248-879-2001.
Howell, Michigan Office: 121 South Barnard Street, Suite 4, 48843-2305.
Telephone: 517-546-7600.
Telecopier: 517-546-6974.
Kalamazoo, Michigan Office: 444 West Michigan Avenue, 49007-3752.
Telephone: 616-381-7030.
Fax: 616-382-0244.
Lansing, Michigan Office: One Michigan Avenue, Suite 900, 48933-1609.
Telephone: 517-487-2070.
Fax: 517-374-6304.
Monroe, Michigan Office: 214 East Elm Avenue, Suite 100, 48162-2682.
Telephone: 734-243-2000.
Fax: 734-243-0901.
Washington, D.C. Office: 1900 K Street, N.W., Suite 1150. 20006.
Telephone: 202-429-5575; 785-0600.
Fax: 202-331-1118; 785-1234.
Pensacola, Florida Office: 25 West Cedar, 32501.
Telephone: 850-469-1088.
Fax: 850-432-0677.
New York, New York Office: 1450 Broadway, 41st Floor, 10018.
Telephone: 212-704-4400.
Fax: 212-704-4410.
Gdynia, Poland Office: UL. Slaska 21, 81-319.
Telephone: 011-485-831-2808.
Fax: 011-48-58-628 6411.
Warsaw, Poland Office: UL. Nowogrodzkall, 5th Floor, 00-513.
Telephone: 011-4822 529 0200.
Fax: 011-4822 529 0201.
Katowice, Poland Office: UL. Francuska 35/37, 40-027.
Telephone: 011 (48-32) 757-2414.
Fax: 011 (48-32) 757-2483.

PRINCIPALS

Douglas W. Crim

Representative Firm Clients: Chrysler Corporation; Comerica, Incorporated; City of Detroit, Michigan; Detroit Tigers, Inc.; First of Michigan; Ford Motor Company; Ford Motor Credit Company; Great Lakes Bancorp; Henry Ford Hospital; INVETECH Company.

For Complete List of Firm Personnel, See General Section

For full biographical listings, see the Martindale-Hubbell Law Directory

ROBERTS, BETZ & BLOSS, P.C. (AV)

5005 Cascade Road SE, 49546-3724
Telephone: 616-285-8899
Telecopier: 616-285-0045

Michael W. Betz
David J. Bloss
Michael T. Small
Ralph M. Reisinger

Connie R. Thacker

For full biographical listings, see the Martindale-Hubbell Law Directory

SCHENK, BONCHER AND PRASHER, P.C. (AV)

601 Three Mile Road NW, 49544-1601
Telephone: 616-647-8277
Fax: 616-647-0958
Email: sbp@voyager.net

Gary P. Schenk
Frederick J. Boncher
Gregory G. Prasher
Catherine M. Sullivan
Curtis D. Rypma

(See Next Column)

Daniel L. Burns

Reference: Huntington Bank.

For full biographical listings, see the Martindale-Hubbell Law Directory

WARNER NORCROSS & JUDD LLP (AV)

900 Old Kent Building, 111 Lyon Street, N.W., 49503-2489
Telephone: 616-752-2000
Fax: 616-752-2500
URL: http://www.wnj.com
Muskegon, Michigan Office: 400 Terrace Plaza, P.O. Box 900.
Telephone: 231-727-2600.
Fax: 231-727-2699.
Holland, Michigan Office: Curtis Center, Suite 300, 170 College Avenue.
Telephone: 616-396-9800.
Fax: 616-396-3656.
Southfield, Michigan Office: 1000 Town Center, Suite 650.
Telephone: 248-223-5000.
Fax: 248-223-5005.

MEMBERS OF FIRM

John D. Tully
Michael L. Robinson
Eugene E. Smary
Paul T. Sorensen
John D. Dunn
John V. Byl
Scott D. Hubbard
Robert J. Jonker
Devin S. Schindler
Michael H. Schubert (Resident Member, Muskegon Office)
William C. Fulkerson
Melvin G. Moseley, Jr.

ASSOCIATES

Kenneth W. Vermeulen
Mark E. Brouwer
Dennis J. Donohue
Daniel K. DeWitt

For full biographical listings, see the Martindale-Hubbell Law Directory

HOLLAND, Ottawa Co.

CUNNINGHAM DALMAN, P.C. (AV)

321 Settlers Road, P.O. Box 1767, 49422-1767
Telephone: 616-392-1821
Fax: 616-392-4769
Email: cunndalm@crossover.net *URL:* http://www.holland-law.com

Gordon H. Cunningham
Ronald L. Dalman
Max R. Murphy
James A. Bidol
Andrew J. Mulder
Kenneth B. Breese
Jeffrey K. Helder
Ronald J. Vander Veen
David M. Zessin
Mark H. Zietlow
Randall S. Schipper
Susan E. Vroegop
Joel G. Bouwens

Gregory J. McCoy
Jason M. Milstone
Aaron Leal
Dawn J. Ward

Representative Clients: Waste Management of Michigan; Huntington National Bank; First of America Bank-Holland, N.A.; Ameribank; City of Holland; The Title Office; Donnelly Corp.

For full biographical listings, see the Martindale-Hubbell Law Directory

*KALAMAZOO,** Kalamazoo Co.

KREIS, ENDERLE, CALLANDER & HUDGINS, A PROFESSIONAL CORPORATION (AV)

One Moorsbridge, P.O. Box 4010, 49003-4010
Telephone: 616-324-3000
Facsimile: 616-324-3010
Email: kech@kech.com *URL:* http://www.kech.com
Battle Creek, Michigan Office: One West Michigan Avenue, 49017.
Telephone: 616-966-3000.
Fax: 616-966-3022.

Alan G. Enderle
Jeffrey D. Swenarton
Peter F. Davis

For Complete List of Firm Personnel, See General Section

For full biographical listings, see the Martindale-Hubbell Law Directory

MILLER, CANFIELD, PADDOCK AND STONE, P.L.C. (AV)

A Professional Limited Liability Company
Founded in 1852 by Sidney Davy Miller
444 West Michigan Avenue, 49007-3752
Telephone: 616-381-7030
Fax: 616-382-0244
URL: http://www.millercanfield.com
Detroit, Michigan Office: 150 West Jefferson, Suite 2500, 48226-4415.
Telephone: 313-963-6420.
Fax: 313-496-7500.
Cable Address: "Stem Detroit."
Ann Arbor, Michigan Office: 101 North Main Street, 7th Floor, 48104-1400.
Telephone: 734-663-2445.
Fax: 734-747-7147.

(See Next Column)

MILLER, CANFIELD, PADDOCK AND STONE P.L.C., *Kalamazoo—Continued*

Troy, Michigan Office: 840 West Long Lake Road, Suite 200, 48098.
Telephone: 248-879-2000.
Fax: 248-879-2001.
Grand Rapids, Michigan Office: 99 Monroe, N.W., Suite 1200, 49503-2639.
Telephone: 616-454-8656.
Fax: 616-776-6322.
Howell, Michigan Office: 121 South Barnard Street, Suite 4, 48843-2305.
Telephone: 517-546-7600.
Telecopier: 517-546-6974.
Lansing, Michigan Office: One Michigan Avenue, Suite 900, 48933-1609.
Telephone: 517-487-2070.
Fax: 517-374-6304.
Monroe, Michigan Office: 214 East Elm Avenue, Suite 100, 48162-2682.
Telephone: 734-243-2000.
Fax: 734-243-0901.
Washington, D.C. Office: 1900 K Street, N.W., Suite 1150. 20006.
Telephone: 202-429-5575; 785-0600.
Fax: 202-331-1118; 785-1234.
Pensacola, Florida Office: 25 West Cedar, 32501.
Telephone: 850-469-1088.
Fax: 850-432-0677.
New York, New York Office: 1450 Broadway, 41st Floor, 10018.
Telephone: 212-704-4400.
Fax: 212-704-4410.
Gdynia, Poland Office: UL. Slaska 21, 81-319.
Telephone: 011-485-831-2808.
Fax: 011-48-58-628 6411.
Warsaw, Poland Office: UL. Nowogrodzkall, 5th Floor, 00-513.
Telephone: 011-4822 529 0200.
Fax: 011-4822 529 0201.
Katowice, Poland Office: UL. Francuska 35/37, 40-027.
Telephone: 011 (48-32) 757-2414.
Fax: 011 (48-32) 757-2483.

PRINCIPALS

Eric V. Brown, Jr.
John R. Cook
Ronald E. Baylor

Representative Firm Clients: Chrysler Corporation; Comerica, Incorporated; City of Detroit, Michigan; Detroit Tigers, Inc.; First of Michigan; Ford Motor Company; Ford Motor Credit Company; Great Lakes Bancorp; Henry Ford Hospital; INVETECH Company.

For Complete List of Firm Personnel, See General Section

For full biographical listings, see the Martindale-Hubbell Law Directory

LANSING, Ingham Co.

FOSTER, SWIFT, COLLINS & SMITH, P.C. (AV)

313 South Washington Square, 48933-2193
Telephone: 517-371-8100
Telecopier: 517-371-8200
URL: http://www.fosterswift.com
Farmington Hills, Michigan Office: 32300 Northwestern Highway, Suite 230.
Telephone: 248-539-9900.
Fax: 248-851-7504.

Webb A. Smith
Stephen O. Schultz
Charles E. Barbieri
James B. Jensen, Jr.
James B. Croom
Brent A. Titus
Kenneth T. Brooks
Nancy L. Kahn
Michael R. Huber

For Complete List of Firm Personnel, See General Section

For full biographical listings, see the Martindale-Hubbell Law Directory

FRASER TREBILCOCK DAVIS & FOSTER, P.C. (AV)

1000 Michigan National Tower, 48933
Telephone: 517-482-5800
Fax: 517-482-0887
URL: http://WWW.FTDF.COM
Detroit, Michigan Office: One Woodward Avenue, Suite 1550.
Telephone: 313-237-7300.
Fax: 313-961-1651.

Douglas J. Austin
Stephen L. Burlingame
Michael H. Perry
Thomas J. Waters

OF COUNSEL

Donald A. Hines

Counsel for: Snell Environmental Group; Mason Family Enterprises; STRATA Environmental Services; RCO Engineering, Inc.; General Aviation; Eaton Technologies; Growth Environmental Services, Inc.; Growth Resources, Inc.

For full biographical listings, see the Martindale-Hubbell Law Directory

HONIGMAN MILLER SCHWARTZ AND COHN (AV)

A Partnership including Professional Corporations
222 North Washington Square, Suite 400, 48933-1800
Telephone: 517-484-8282
Telecopier: 517-484-8286
Email: mvg@honigman.com *URL:* http://law.honigman.com
Detroit, Michigan Office: 2290 First National Building, 660 Woodward Avenue, 48226.
Telephone: 313-465-7000.

MEMBERS

Frederick M. Baker, Jr.
John D. Pirich

General Counsel for: Dart Container Corp; Forbes-Cohen Properties (The Lansing Mall); Michigan Hospital Association.
Legal or Special Counsel for: Champion International; Greater Detroit Resource Recovery Authority.

For Complete List of Firm Personnel, See General Section

For full biographical listings, see the Martindale-Hubbell Law Directory

MILLER, CANFIELD, PADDOCK AND STONE, P.L.C. (AV)

A Professional Limited Liability Company
Founded in 1852 by Sidney Davy Miller
Suite 900, One Michigan Avenue, 48933-1609
Telephone: 517-487-2070
Fax: 517-374-6304
URL: http://www.millercanfield.com
Detroit, Michigan Office: 150 West Jefferson, Suite 2500, 48226-4415.
Telephone: 313-963-6420.
Fax: 313-496-7500.
Cable Address: "Stem Detroit."
Ann Arbor, Michigan Office: 101 North Main Street, 7th Floor, 48104-1400.
Telephone: 734-663-2445.
Fax: 734-747-7147.
Troy, Michigan Office: 840 West Long Lake Road, Suite 200, 48098.
Telephone: 248-879-2000.
Fax: 248-879-2001.
Grand Rapids, Michigan Office: 99 Monroe, N.W., Suite 1200, 49503-2639.
Telephone: 616-454-8656.
Fax: 616-776-6322.
Howell, Michigan Office: 121 South Barnard Street, Suite 4, 48843-2305.
Telephone: 517-546-7600.
Telecopier: 517-546-6974.
Kalamazoo, Michigan Office: 444 West Michigan Avenue, 49007-3752.
Telephone: 616-381-7030.
Fax: 616-382-0244.
Monroe, Michigan Office: 214 East Elm Avenue, Suite 100, 48162-2682.
Telephone: 734-243-2000.
Fax: 734-243-0901.
Washington, D.C. Office: 1900 K Street, N.W., Suite 1150. 20006.
Telephone: 202-429-5575; 785-0600.
Fax: 202-331-1118; 785-1234.
Pensacola, Florida Office: 25 West Cedar, 32501.
Telephone: 850-469-1088.
Fax: 850-432-0677.
New York, New York Office: 1450 Broadway, 41st Floor, 10018.
Telephone: 212-704-4400.
Fax: 212-704-4410.
Gdynia, Poland Office: UL. Slaska 21, 81-319.
Telephone: 011-485-831-2808.
Fax: 011-48-58-628 6411.
Warsaw, Poland Office: UL. Nowogrodzkall, 5th Floor, 00-513.
Telephone: 011-4822 529 0200.
Fax: 011-4822 529 0201.
Katowice, Poland Office: UL. Francuska 35/37, 40-027.
Telephone: 011 (48-32) 757-2414.
Fax: 011 (48-32) 757-2483.

RESIDENT PRINCIPALS

Thomas C. Phillips
Steven E. Chester
James R. Lancaster, Jr.

Representative Firm Clients: Chrysler Corporation; Comerica, Incorporated; City of Detroit, Michigan; Detroit Tigers, Inc.; First of Michigan; Ford Motor Company; Ford Motor Credit Company; Great Lakes Bancorp; Henry Ford Hospital; INVETECH Company.

For Complete List of Firm Personnel, See General Section

For full biographical listings, see the Martindale-Hubbell Law Directory

*MONROE,** Monroe Co.

BRAUNLICH, RUSSOW & BRAUNLICH, A PROFESSIONAL CORPORATION (AV)

111 South Macomb Street, 48161
Telephone: 734-241-8300
Fax: 734-241-7715

(See Next Column)

BRAUNLICH, RUSSOW & BRAUNLICH A PROFESSIONAL CORPORATION—*Continued*

William J. Braunlich, Jr. (1924-1992)
Thomas P. Russow
William H. Braunlich

Philip A. Costello
Ann L. Nickel
Jeffrey A. Dulany, P.C.

LEGAL SUPPORT PERSONNEL

Ruth G. Flint

Representative Clients: State Farm Mutual Insurance Co.; Auto Club Insurance Assn.; Board of Road Commissioners, Monroe County; Port of Monroe; Monroe County Community College; City of Luna Pier; City of Petersburg; Auto-Owners Insurance Co.; Fremont Mutual Insurance Co.; Citizens Insurance Co. of America.

For full biographical listings, see the Martindale-Hubbell Law Directory

*MOUNT PLEASANT,** Isabella Co.

LYNCH, GALLAGHER, LYNCH & MARTINEAU, P.L.L.C. (AV)

555 North Main Street, P.O. Box 446, 48858
Telephone: 517-773-9961
Fax: 517-773-2107
Email: lglm@power-net.net
Lansing, Michigan Office: 2400 Lake Lansing Road, Suite B.
Telephone: 517-485-0400.
Fax: 517-485-0402.

MEMBERS OF FIRM

Edward N. Lynch (1908-1984)
Byron P. Gallagher
John J. Lynch
Steven W. Martineau
Paula K. Manis (Resident at Lansing Office)
Michael J. Hackett
Richard J. Garcia
Nancy E. Gallagher
Jennifer M. Galloway

Representative Clients: Amoco Production, Co.; Liquid Transport, Inc.; Central Concrete Products; Central Michigan University; Northern Michigan Oil and Gas Corp.

For full biographical listings, see the Martindale-Hubbell Law Directory

*MUSKEGON,** Muskegon Co.

LAGUE, NEWMAN & IRISH, A PROFESSIONAL CORPORATION (AV)

600 Terrace Plaza, P.O. Box 389, 49443
Telephone: 231-725-8148
Telecopier: 231-726-3404
Email: firm@lnilaw.com

Eric R. Gielow
Alvin D. Treado

LEGAL SUPPORT PERSONNEL

Lynette E. Reichert

General Counsel: Brenner Oil Company; Cole's Quality Foods; G. Van Dyken Disposal; Great Lakes Aquarium & Research; Hackley Hospital & Medical Center; Kurdziel Industries; Ottawa Corp.; Quality Plating Co.; Resource Recovery Corporation; Seabrook Plastics.

For Complete List of Firm Personnel, See General Section

For full biographical listings, see the Martindale-Hubbell Law Directory

*SAGINAW,** Saginaw Co.

BRAUN KENDRICK FINKBEINER PLC (AV)

101 N. Washington Suite 812, 48607-1297
Telephone: 517-753-3461
Telecopier: 517-753-3951
Email: ALBFIE@BKF-LAW.COM *URL:* http://www.bkf-law.com
Saginaw Township Office, Michigan Office: 5800 Gratiot Road, Suite 107, P.O. Box 5169. Telephone 517-799-8692.
Fax: 517-799-4666.
Bay City, Michigan Office: 201 Phoenix Building, P.O. Box 2039.
Telephone: 517-895-8505.
Telecopier: 517-895-8437.
Ann Arbor, Michigan Office: First National Building. 201 S. Main, Suite 700.
Telephone: 313-995-4100.
Telecopier: 313-995-4798.
Mt. Pleasant, Michigan Office: 805 North Brown.
Telephone: 517-775-7404.
Telecopier: 517-775-3764.

Thomas R. Luplow
John A. Decker
Barry M. Levine
Glenn L. Fitkin
Brian S. Makaric

Representative Clients: The Dow Chemical Co.; General Motors Corp.; Merrill, Lynch, Inc.; Saginaw General Hospital; Saginaw News; The Wickes Foundation.

(See Next Column)

For Complete List of Firm Personnel, See General Section

For full biographical listings, see the Martindale-Hubbell Law Directory

SOUTHFIELD, Oakland Co.

COLLINS, EINHORN, FARRELL & ULANOFF, A PROFESSIONAL CORPORATION (AV)

4000 Town Center, Suite 909, 48075-1473
Telephone: 248-355-4141
Facsimile: 248-355-2277

Morton H. Collins
Brian D. Einhorn
Clayton F. Farrell
Stuart A. Ulanoff
Dale J. McLellan
Kenneth C. Merritt
Noreen L. Slank
Michael J. Sullivan
Janice G. Hildenbrand
Neil W. MacCallum

Theresa M. Asoklis
Karen C. Liddle
Deborah A. Lujan
Shannon M. Kos
Kevin P. Moloughney
Susan P. Saltzman
Daniel E. Collins
J. Mark Cooney
David C. Anderson

For full biographical listings, see the Martindale-Hubbell Law Directory

MASON STEINHARDT JACOBS PERLMAN & PESICK, PROFESSIONAL CORPORATION (AV)

Suite 1500, 4000 Town Center, 48075-1415
Telephone: 248-358-2090
Fax: 248-358-3599
Email: admin@msjp.com *URL:* http://www.msjp.com

John E. Jacobs
Michael B. Perlman
Neil S. Silver

Representative Clients: Citibank, N.A.; City of Dearborn; DeMattia Development Co.; Forest City Enterprises; Michigan Wholesale Drug Assn.; Mortgage Bankers Association of Michigan; Nationwide Insurance Co.; City of Taylor; Union Labor Life Insurance Co.; Yellow Freight Systems, Inc.

For Complete List of Firm Personnel, See General Section

For full biographical listings, see the Martindale-Hubbell Law Directory

SOMMERS, SCHWARTZ, SILVER & SCHWARTZ, P.C. (AV)

2000 Town Center, Suite 900, 48075
Telephone: 248-355-0300
Telecopier: 248-746-4001
Plymouth, Michigan Office: 747 South Main Street.
Telephone: 313-455-4250.

James J. Vlasic
David M. Black

General Counsel for: City of Taylor; Foodland Distributors; C.A. Muer Corporation; Vlasic & Company; Nederlander Corporation; Midwest Health Centers, P.C.
Representative Clients: Michigan National Bank; Universal Underwriters Insurance Co.

For Complete List of Firm Personnel, See General Section

For full biographical listings, see the Martindale-Hubbell Law Directory

*TRAVERSE CITY,** Grand Traverse Co.

DINGEMAN, DANCER & CHRISTOPHERSON, P.L.C. (AV)

100 Park Street, 49684
Telephone: 231-929-0500
Fax: 231-929-0504
Email: dingeman@dingemandancer.com *URL:* http://www.Dingemandancer.com

Mark R. Dancer

Representative Clients: Texas Instruments, Inc.; Georgia-Pacific Corporation; Martin Marietta Magesia Specialities, Inc.; Elf Atochem North America, Inc.; Busch Oil Company; Lachine Oil Company; Charmilles Technologoes Corporation; Glawe Corporations; Stomberg Carlson Products, Inc.; L'DaRu Lakeside Resort.

For full biographical listings, see the Martindale-Hubbell Law Directory

OLSON, NOONAN & BZDOK, P.C. (AV)

420 East Front Street, P.O. Box 2358, 49685-2358
Telephone: 616-946-0044
Fax: 616-946-4807

James M. Olson
John D. Noonan
Christopher M. Bzdok
Karen L. Ferguson
Scott W. Howard

For full biographical listings, see the Martindale-Hubbell Law Directory

Traverse City—Continued

Sullivan & Crowley, P.C. (AV)

735 South Garfield, Suite 202, 49686
Telephone: 616-922-1888
Fax: 616-922-2221
Email: sullcro@GTII.com *URL:* http://www.lawyers.com/sullivancrowleylaw

James I. Sullivan
Philip J. Crowley
Jeffrey J. Noorman

For full biographical listings, see the Martindale-Hubbell Law Directory

TROY, Oakland Co.

Hainer & Berman, P.C. (AV)

888 West Big Beaver, Suite 1400, 48084
Telephone: 248-244-8424
Fax: 248-244-8455

Michael J. Hainer
Leonard K. Berman
Kay E. Malaney

Drew S. Norton
Paul S. Miller

OF COUNSEL

Michael A. Kus
Robert F. Riley
Mark S. Demorest

Representative Clients: American Empire Surplus Lines Insurance Co.; Biomass Energy Systems, Inc.; Bridgestone/Firestone, Inc.; Central Distributors of Beer, Inc.; Champion Enterprises, Inc.; City Management Corp.; Clarklift of Detroit, Inc.; Federal Reserve Bank of Chicago; Hotel Investment Services, Inc.; M&O Marketing, Inc.

For full biographical listings, see the Martindale-Hubbell Law Directory

Holahan, Malloy, Maybaugh, Monnich & Delie (AV)

Suite 100, 2690 Crooks Road, 48084-4700
Telephone: 248-362-4747
Fax: 248-362-4779
East Tawas, Michigan Office: 910 East Bay Street.
Telephone: 517-362-4747.
Fax: 517-362-7331.

MEMBERS OF FIRM

J. Michael Malloy, III
James D. Maybaugh
John R. Monnich
David L. Delie, Jr.

OF COUNSEL

Thomas H. O'Connor
Maureen Holahan (Retired; Resident, East Tawas Office)

For full biographical listings, see the Martindale-Hubbell Law Directory

Poling, McGaw & Poling, P.C. (AV)

Suite 275, 5435 Corporate Drive, 48098
Telephone: 248-641-0500
Telecopier: 248-641-0506
URL: http://www.lawyers.com/polingmcgaw&poling

Benson T. Buck (1926-1989)
Richard B. Poling
D. Douglas McGaw
Richard B. Poling, Jr.
Gregory C. Hamilton
Veronica B. O'Hara
James R. Parker
Shannon M. Acton

OF COUNSEL

Ralph S. Moore

Representative Clients: City of Troy; United States Fidelity & Guaranty Co.; Sentry Insurance Co.; Admiral Insurance; DeMaria Construction Co.; Leo Corporation; Aetna Casualty and Surety Co.; Concord Design; Pneumo-Abex.

For full biographical listings, see the Martindale-Hubbell Law Directory

WEST BLOOMFIELD, Oakland Co.

Cheatham, Estes & Hollman, P.C. (AV)

5777 West Maple Road, Suite 130, P.O. Box 255002, 48325-5002
Telephone: 248-932-2000
Fax: 248-932-2008

Charles C. Cheatham
Lee Estes
Mary E. Hollman

Christopher P. Jelinek

COUNSEL

Lynn L. Lower

For full biographical listings, see the Martindale-Hubbell Law Directory

FAMILY LAW

ALABAMA

*BIRMINGHAM,** Jefferson Co.

BRADLEY ARANT ROSE & WHITE LLP (AV)
2001 Park Place, Suite 1400, P.O. Box 830709, 35283-0709
Telephone: 205-521-8000
Facsimile: 205-521-8800
Facsimile (SouthTrust Tower Office): 205-521-8500
URL: http://www.barw.com
Huntsville, Alabama Office: 200 Clinton Avenue West, Suite 900, 35801.
Telephone: 205-517-5100.
Facsimile: 205-533-5069.
Washington, D.C. Office: 801 Pennsylvania Avenue, NW, Suite 230, 20004.
Telephone: 202-347-8893.
Facsimile: 202-347-1684.

MEMBER OF FIRM

Patrick H. Graves Jr. (Resident, Huntsville Office)

For Complete List of Firm Personnel, See General Section

For full biographical listings, see the Martindale-Hubbell Law Directory

CRITTENDEN • MARTIN (AV)
Suite 1044, Park Place Tower, P.O. Box 11545, 35201
Telephone: 205-324-9494
Fax: 205-324-8086

MEMBERS OF FIRM

Judith S. Crittenden
Virginia Lanair Martin

Latresia Lewis Kinnell

For full biographical listings, see the Martindale-Hubbell Law Directory

GORHAM & WALDREP, P.C. (AV)
2101 6th Avenue North, Suite 700, 35203
Telephone: 205-254-3216; 251-9166
Telecopier: 205-324-3802
Email: info@gorham-waldrep.com *URL:* http://www.gorham-waldrep.com
Montgomery, Alabama Office: 250 Commerce Street, P.O. Box 4837, 36103-4837.
Telephone: 334-262-0777.
Telecopier: 334-262-0742.

Charles W. Gorham

Kim Davidson

Representative Clients: Jefferson County Personnel Board; Birmingham-Jefferson Civic Center Authority; The Water Works and Sewer Board of the City of Birmingham; City of Homewood; American Federation of Government Employees Local #1945; City of Pelham; Town of Kimberly; Alabama Tire Dealers Assn.; Southern States Body Shop Assn.

For Complete List of Firm Personnel, See General Section

For full biographical listings, see the Martindale-Hubbell Law Directory

REDDEN, MILLS & CLARK (AV)
940 Regions Bank Building, 417 North 20th Street, 35203
Telephone: 205-322-0457
Fax: 205-322-8481
URL: http://www.rmc-law.com

MEMBERS OF FIRM

L. Drew Redden
William H. Mills
William N. Clark
Gerald L. Miller
Stephen W. Shaw
Maxwell H. Pulliam, Jr.
Ronald J. Gault

References: SouthTrust Bank; Regions Bank.

For full biographical listings, see the Martindale-Hubbell Law Directory

*HUNTSVILLE,** Madison Co.

STEPHENS, MILLIRONS, HARRISON & GAMMONS, P.C. (AV)
333 Franklin Street, P.O. Box 307, 35801
Telephone: 256-533-7711
Telecopier: 256-536-9388

Arthur M. Stephens
Paul L. Millirons
James G. Harrison
Robert C. Gammons

Douglas A. Baymiller
Steven J. Shaw

For full biographical listings, see the Martindale-Hubbell Law Directory

*MOBILE,** Mobile Co.

BRISKMAN & BINION, P.C. (AV)
205 Church Street, P.O. Box 43, 36601
Telephone: 334-433-7600
Fax: 334-433-4485
Email: briskman@zebra.net

Donald M. Briskman
Christ N. Coumanis
Kimberly C. Hodgson

A List of Representative Clients will be furnished upon request.
References: Regions Bank; AmSouth Bank, N.A.; Southtrust Bank of Mobile.

For Complete List of Firm Personnel, See General Section

For full biographical listings, see the Martindale-Hubbell Law Directory

DAVID P. BROOME (AV)
AmSouth Bank Building, 107 St. Francis Street Suite 1408, 36633
Telephone: 334-432-9933
Fax: 334-432-9706
Mailing Address: P.O. Box 1944, Mobile, Alabama, 36633-1944
Email: broomelaw@aol.com

LEGAL SUPPORT PERSONNEL

Heidi Marie Fundinger

References: AmSouth Bank, NA; The Bank of Mobile.

For full biographical listings, see the Martindale-Hubbell Law Directory

*MONTGOMERY,** Montgomery Co.

PARNELL & CRUM, P.A. (AV)
641 South Lawrence Street, P.O. Box 2189, 36102
Telephone: 334-832-4202
Telecopier: 334-832-4703
Fax: 334-293-3550
Email: cnparnell@aol.com

Charles N. Parnell, III
G. Barton Crum

Robert J. Russell, Jr.
James McCauley Smith
Britt Batson Griggs
Angie Hubbard Ingram

Reference: Colonial Bank of Montgomery.

For full biographical listings, see the Martindale-Hubbell Law Directory

ROBISON & BELSER, P.A. (AV)
200 Coosa Street, 36104
Telephone: 334-834-7000
Telecopier: 334-834-7011
Mailing Address: Drawer 1470, Montgomery, AL, 36102
Email: tsides@mont.mindspring.com

David B. Byrne, Jr.

General Counsel for: Montgomery County Board of Education.
Representative Clients: Union Bank & Trust Co.; Liberty National Life Insurance Co.; State Farm Mutual Fire & Casualty Co.

For full biographical listings, see the Martindale-Hubbell Law Directory

TURNER, WILSON & SAWYER (AV)
428 South Lawrence Street, P.O. Box 98, 36104
Telephone: 334-262-2756
Fax: 334-262-2759
Email: turnerone@mindspring.com

MEMBERS OF FIRM

Wayne P. Turner
Terry P. Wilson
William P. Sawyer

LEGAL SUPPORT PERSONNEL

Dorothy Bennett (Paralegal)
Kelly Westbrook
Cara Morales (Paralegal)

For full biographical listings, see the Martindale-Hubbell Law Directory

ARIZONA

*FLAGSTAFF,** Coconino Co.

HUFFORD, HORSTMAN, MONGINI, PARNELL & MCCARTHY, P.C. (AV)
323 North Leroux Street, P.O. Box B, 86002-0808
Telephone: 520-774-1453
Fax: 520-779-3621

(See Next Column)

HUFFORD, HORSTMAN, MONGINI, PARNELL & MCCARTHY P.C., *Flagstaff—Continued*

C. Benson Hufford
Patrice M. Horstman
Michael E.J. Mongini
Eve A. Parnell
Philip (Jay) McCarthy, Jr.

E. Duane Weston

LEGAL SUPPORT PERSONNEL

R. Gehl Tucker (Legal Assistant)
Doris Utzinger (Legal Assistant)
Vickie Belman (Legal Assistant)
Jan Blackman (Paralegal)
Dawn L. Karsten (Paralegal)

Reference: Norwest Bank Arizona, N.A.

For full biographical listings, see the Martindale-Hubbell Law Directory

MANGUM, WALL, STOOPS & WARDEN, P.L.L.C. (AV)

100 North Elden, P.O. Box 10, 86002
Telephone: 520-779-6951
Fax: 520-773-1312

H. Karl Mangum (1908-1993)

OF COUNSEL

Douglas J. Wall
Robert W. Warden
Daniel J. Stoops

MEMBERS OF FIRM

A. Dean Pickett
Stephen K. Smith
Melinda L. Garrahan
Michael H. Hinson

ASSOCIATES

Annette Star Lustgarten
Rebecca Smith Currey
R. Scott Currey
Melinda K. Jacquez
Franklin Hoover

Representative Clients: Northern Arizona University; Flagstaff Unified School District; Museum of Northern Arizona; Arizona School Board Association.
Local Counsel for: Bank of America-Arizona; Arizona Public Service; U.S.A.A.; State Farm Fire & Casualty Insurance Co.; Property Development Co.

For Complete List of Firm Personnel, See General Section

For full biographical listings, see the Martindale-Hubbell Law Directory

LAKE HAVASU CITY, Mohave Co.

WACHTEL, BIEHN & MALM (AV)

2240 McCulloch Boulevard, 86403
Telephone: 520-855-5115
Fax: 520-855-5211
Email: wbm1@ctaz.com

FOUNDER

Wing Wachtel (1927-1997)

MEMBERS OF FIRM

Don Biehn
Denis R. Malm
James B. Wyss
Steven A. Biehn
Jill Wachtel Davis
Steven Eric Mundy

For full biographical listings, see the Martindale-Hubbell Law Directory

MESA, Maricopa Co.

UDALL, SHUMWAY, BLACKHURST, ALLEN & LYONS, P.C. (AV)

30 West First Street, 85201-1446
Telephone: 480-461-5300
Facsimile: 480-461-5398
Email: usbalsea@vtc.net
Willcox, Arizona Office: 135 East Maley.
Telephone: 602-384-3389.
Fax: 602-384-2280.

David K. Udall
Dale R. Shumway
Dennis P. Blackhurst
John H. Lyons
Barry C. Dickerson
Steven H. Everts
Clark R. Richter
Roger C. Decker
Peter W. Taylor
Denise Lowell-Britt
Stephen L. West

David R. Schwartz
Robert M. Jarrett, Jr. (Resident, Willcox Office)
Brian T. Allen
Curtis M. Chipman
April A. Speelmon

Representative Clients: Mesa Public Schools; Ticor Title; University of Arizona; Wal-Mart Stores, Inc.; Church of Jesus Christ of Latter Day Saints.

For full biographical listings, see the Martindale-Hubbell Law Directory

*PHOENIX,** Maricopa Co.

DAVID W. ADLER (AV)

4141 West Bethany Home Road, Suite 1, 85019
Telephone: 602-266-6010
Fax: 602-787-9897
Mailing Address: P.O. Box 22188, Phoenix, Arizona, 85028-2188

For full biographical listings, see the Martindale-Hubbell Law Directory

BURCH & CRACCHIOLO, P.A. (AV)

702 East Osborn Road, Suite 200, 85014
Telephone: 602-274-7611
Fax: 602-234-0341
Mailing Address: P.O. Box 16882, Phoenix, AZ, 85011
Email: library@bcattorneys.com

Donald W. Lindholm

Thomas A. Longfellow
Steven M. Serrano

Representative Clients: Bashas' Inc.; Farmers Insurance Group; U-Haul International, Inc.

For Complete List of Firm Personnel, See General Section

For full biographical listings, see the Martindale-Hubbell Law Directory

COHEN AND FROMM, P.C. (AV)

2198 East Camelback Road, Suite 365, 85016-4742
Telephone: 602-955-1515
Facsimile: 602-955-0509

Bruce R. Cohen
Sandra J. Fromm

Stephen R. Smith
Jennifer G. Gadow

LEGAL SUPPORT PERSONNEL

PARALEGALS

Karen L. Wilhelm
Kelly S. Gilliland

For full biographical listings, see the Martindale-Hubbell Law Directory

HIRSCH LAW OFFICE, P.C. (AV)

4614 East Shea Boulevard Suite D250, 85028
Telephone: 602-996-9544
Fax: 602-494-0815

Lawrence D. Hirsch
Iva S. Hirsch

For full biographical listings, see the Martindale-Hubbell Law Directory

JENSEN & KELLEY, P.A. (AV)

3101 North Central Avenue, Suite 820, 85012
Telephone: 602-230-1118
Fax: 602-230-9622
URL: http://www.azfamilylaw.com

Robert A. Jensen
Brian E. Kelley

Paul G. Schmidt
Therese R. McElwee

For full biographical listings, see the Martindale-Hubbell Law Directory

MACLEAN & JACQUES, LTD. (AV)

Suite 202, 40 East Virginia, 85004
Telephone: 602-263-5771
FAX: 602-279-5569

John H. MacLean (1932-1992)
Raoul T. Jacques

Cary T. Inabinet
Macre S. Inabinet

LEGAL SUPPORT PERSONNEL

Sharon Petterson

For full biographical listings, see the Martindale-Hubbell Law Directory

MARISCAL, WEEKS, MCINTYRE & FRIEDLANDER, P.A. (AV)

2901 North Central Avenue Suite 200, 85012-2705
Telephone: 602-285-5000
Fax: 602-285-5100

Leonce A. Richard
Robert L. Schwartz
Steven D. Wolfson
Dana M. Levy
Claudia D. Work

References: Northern Trust Bank of Arizona; National Bank of Arizona.

For Complete List of Firm Personnel, See General Section

For full biographical listings, see the Martindale-Hubbell Law Directory

Phoenix—Continued

Mark & Pearlstein, P.A. (AV)

Suite 150 The Brookstone, 2025 North Third Street, 85004
Telephone: 602-257-0200
Fax: 602-271-4711
Email: mplaw@primenet.com

Leonard J. Mark — Mr. Lynn M. Pearlstein

OF COUNSEL

Stephen G. Campbell

For full biographical listings, see the Martindale-Hubbell Law Directory

Sheldon Mitchell, Ltd. (AV)

The Brookstone, 340 E. Palm Lane Suite A-300, 85004-4531
Telephone: 602-712-1900
Fax: 602-712-9303

Sheldon Mitchell

Tammy Padgett

Reference: Norwest Bank.

For full biographical listings, see the Martindale-Hubbell Law Directory

Mueller & Gallios, P.C. (AV)

Country Club Manor, 1221 East Osborn Road, Suite 200, 85014
Telephone: 602-274-7272
Telecopier: 602-279-0863

James W. Mueller — Aris J. Gallios

Donna J. Hamilton

Reference: Bank of America, Arizona.

For full biographical listings, see the Martindale-Hubbell Law Directory

Shimmel, Hill, Bishop & Gruender, P.C. (AV)

3700 North 24th Street, 85016
Telephone: 602-224-9500
Telecopier: 602-955-6176
URL: http://www.shimmelhill.com

Margaret L. Steiner — Susan M. Swick

For full biographical listings, see the Martindale-Hubbell Law Directory

Judith M. Wolf, P.C. (AV)

The Esplanade, 2525 East Camelback Road, Suite 710, 85016
Telephone: 602-852-5566
Facsimile: 602-852-5560
Email: judith@arizonamediation.com *URL:* http://www.Arizonamediation.com

Judith M. Wolf

For full biographical listings, see the Martindale-Hubbell Law Directory

*PRESCOTT,** Yavapai Co.

Favour, Moore & Wilhelmsen, A Professional Association (AV)

1580 Plaza West Drive, P.O. Box 1391, 86302
Telephone: 520-445-2444
Fax: 520-771-0450
Email: fmw@primenet.com

John M. Favour — Mark M. Moore
David K. Wilhelmsen

Representative Client: Yavapai Title Co.
Reference: Bank of America.

For Complete List of Firm Personnel, See General Section

For full biographical listings, see the Martindale-Hubbell Law Directory

SCOTTSDALE, Maricopa Co.

Paul J. Buser (AV㉮)

7633 East Acoma Drive, Suite 106, 85260-3486
Telephone: 480-951-1222
Fax: 480-951-2568
Email: pjbazlit@worldnet.att.net *URL:* http://www.lawyers.com/paulbusercactuslaw

For full biographical listings, see the Martindale-Hubbell Law Directory

Campana, Vieh, Shore, Owens & Loeb (AV)

4422 North Civic Center Plaza, Suite 101, 85251
Telephone: 480-707-5000
Fax: 480-707-5005

(See Next Column)

Richard V. Campana — William F. Shore, III
James E. Vieh — Bernard C. Owens
Donald O. Loeb

LEGAL SUPPORT PERSONNEL

Lois V. Johnson (Legal Assistant)

For full biographical listings, see the Martindale-Hubbell Law Directory

Peskind Hymson & Goldstein, P.C. (AV)

14595 North Scottsdale Road, Suite 14, 85254
Telephone: 602-991-9077
Fax: 602-443-8854
URL: http://www.legalcounselors.com

Marilee Miller Clarke — Jeffrey A. Leyton

For full biographical listings, see the Martindale-Hubbell Law Directory

*TUCSON,** Pima Co.

Law Office of Margrit E. Cromwell (AV)

325 West Franklin, #111, 85701
Telephone: 520-624-8371
Fax: 520-792-9736

For full biographical listings, see the Martindale-Hubbell Law Directory

Donau & Bolt (AV)

Suite 501, 3505 North Campbell Avenue, 85719-2033
Telephone: 520-795-8710
Fax: 520-795-0308

MEMBER OF FIRM

John R. Bolt

ASSOCIATE

Keith A. Singer

For full biographical listings, see the Martindale-Hubbell Law Directory

David H. Lieberthal (AV)

Bank of America Building, 33 North Stone Avenue, Suite 2100, 85701
Telephone: 520-622-6793
Fax: 520-624-2816
Email: dhl@azstarnet.com

For full biographical listings, see the Martindale-Hubbell Law Directory

Joseph H. Riley, Jr. (AV)

Suite 401, Pioneer Plaza, 100 North Stone Avenue, P.O. Box 1642, 85702
Telephone: 520-622-6422
Fax: 520-622-0049

Reference: Arizona Bank.

For full biographical listings, see the Martindale-Hubbell Law Directory

Salese & McCarthy, P.C. (AV)

300 North Main Suite 203, 85701-8287
Telephone: 520-623-0341
Fax: 520-628-9495

Armand Salese — Kathleen Alistair McCarthy

For full biographical listings, see the Martindale-Hubbell Law Directory

Stompoly, Stroud, Glicksman & Erickson, P.C. (AV)

1820 Norwest Tower, One South Church Avenue, 85702
Telephone: 520-628-8300
Telefax: 520-628-9948
Mailing Address: P.O. Box 190, Tucson, AZ, 85702-0190

James L. Stroud

For Complete List of Firm Personnel, See General Section

For full biographical listings, see the Martindale-Hubbell Law Directory

CALIFORNIA

ARCADIA, Los Angeles Co.

Helms, Hanrahan & Myers (AV)

Suite 685 Towne Centre Building, 150 North Santa Anita Avenue, 91006
Telephone: 626-445-1177
Fax: 626-445-2085
Email: helmsj@aol.com *URL:* http://www.lawyers.com/hhmlaw

(See Next Column)

HELMS, HANRAHAN & MYERS, *Arcadia—Continued*

Sterling E. Myers

Reference: Bank of America National Trust & Savings Assn. (Arcadia Branch).

For Complete List of Firm Personnel, See General Section

For full biographical listings, see the Martindale-Hubbell Law Directory

BEVERLY HILLS, Los Angeles Co.

ROBERT A. ADELMAN A LAW CORPORATION (AV)

9454 Wilshire Boulevard Suite PH-29, 90212-2937
Telephone: 310-858-1201
Fax: 310-858-6558

Robert A. Adelman

Reference: City National Bank.

For full biographical listings, see the Martindale-Hubbell Law Directory

COLMAN-SCHWIMMER & WARREN, A PROFESSIONAL LAW CORPORATION (AV)

9595 Wilshire Boulevard, Suite 810, 90212
Telephone: 310-273-2818
Fax: 310-273-8549

Arlene Colman-Schwimmer
Edie Wittick Warren
Nancy Burt

For full biographical listings, see the Martindale-Hubbell Law Directory

LAW OFFICES OF NORMAN M. DOLIN (AV)

9100 Wilshire Boulevard, Suite 601 East Tower, 90212
Telephone: 310-247-4850
Fax: 310-247-4856

ASSOCIATES

Lynn Langley
Ani M. Garikian
Marilyn D. York

For full biographical listings, see the Martindale-Hubbell Law Directory

LAW OFFICES OF NEAL RAYMOND HERSH (AV)

9150 Wilshire Boulevard, Suite 209, 90212
Telephone: 310-786-1910
Fax: 310-786-1917
Email: hershlaw@pacbell.net *URL:* http://www.lawyers.com/nealhersh
(Also Of Counsel to Stephen R. Kahn)

ASSOCIATES

Lori M. Vogelsang
Carole H. Cohen
Allan S. Morton

OF COUNSEL

Raoul Lionel Felder (Not admitted in CA)
Simon Taub

For full biographical listings, see the Martindale-Hubbell Law Directory

JAFFE AND CLEMENS (AV)

A Partnership including Professional Corporations
Suite 1000, 433 North Camden Drive, 90210
Telephone: 310-550-7477
Telecopier: 310-271-8313

Daniel J. Jaffe (A Professional Corporation)
Bruce A. Clemens (A Professional Corporation)
William S. Ryden

ASSOCIATES

David M. Luboff
Mark L. Levinson
Richard Mackay
Cynthia S. Monaco (On Leave)
Linda R. Snyder
Steven M. Rubenstein

For full biographical listings, see the Martindale-Hubbell Law Directory

KAUFMAN & YOUNG, A PROFESSIONAL CORPORATION (AV)

121 South Beverly Drive, 90212-3002
Telephone: 310-275-5132
Los Angeles: 213-272-7807
Fax: 310-275-2919

Robert S. Kaufman
Kenneth M. Young
Marcy L. Kenerson
Scott K. Robinson

OF COUNSEL

Lance S. Spiegel

Reference: City National Bank (Beverly Hills Main Office Branch).

For full biographical listings, see the Martindale-Hubbell Law Directory

KOLODNY & ANTEAU (AV)

9100 Wilshire Boulevard 9th Floor, West Tower, 90212
Telephone: 310-271-5533
Fax: 310-271-3918

MEMBERS OF FIRM

Stephen A. Kolodny
Ronald W. Anteau
Harlee M. Gasmer

Peter T. Hermes
William J. Glucksman
Lauren S. Petkin
Nicole L. Currer

OF COUNSEL

Terry Levich Ross

For full biographical listings, see the Martindale-Hubbell Law Directory

CARLSBAD, San Diego Co.

DANIEL V. BURKE (AV)

Suite One, 2755 Jefferson Street, P.O. Box 1988, 92008
Telephone: 760-434-3330
Fax: 760-434-4958
Email: dburkeatty@aol.com *URL:* http://www.dburke.com

For full biographical listings, see the Martindale-Hubbell Law Directory

INDIAN WELLS, Riverside Co.

LAW OFFICES OF VIRGINIA S. CRISTE (AV)

45-200 Club Drive, Suite B, 92210
Telephone: 760-345-2200
Fax: 760-345-5516
Email: vcriste@aol.com

For full biographical listings, see the Martindale-Hubbell Law Directory

IRVINE, Orange Co.

RAY HENDRICKSON (AV)

University Tower, Suite 700, 4199 Campus Drive, 92612
Telephone: 949-833-0101; 854-8800
Fax: 949-854-4897
Email: RayEsqPhD@Prodigy.met *URL:* http://www.lawyers.com/hendrickson

References: Manufacturers Bank, Newport Beach, California.

For full biographical listings, see the Martindale-Hubbell Law Directory

LAW OFFICES OF GEORGE M. KORNIEVSKY A PROFESSIONAL CORPORATION (AV)

18881 Von Karman Avenue, Suite 1260, 92612
Telephone: 949-724-0888
Fax: 949-752-7035
Email: kornievsky@toughbutfair.com *URL:* http://www.toughbutfair.com

George M. Kornievsky

For full biographical listings, see the Martindale-Hubbell Law Directory

LAGUNA BEACH, Orange Co.

NOKES, DAVIS & QUINN, A PROFESSIONAL CORPORATION (AV)

450 Ocean Avenue, 92651
Telephone: 949-376-3055
FAX: 949-376-3070
Email: ndqlaw@gte.net

Laurence P. Nokes
Thomas P. Davis
Thomas P. Quinn, Jr.

OF COUNSEL

Paul W. Davis

For full biographical listings, see the Martindale-Hubbell Law Directory

LA HABRA, Orange Co.

C. LARRY FANCHER (AV)

440 East La Habra Boulevard, 90631
Telephone: 714-870-9972; 562-691-1300
Fax: 562-697-8477

For full biographical listings, see the Martindale-Hubbell Law Directory

LONG BEACH, Los Angeles Co.

BRANDON & YARC, LLP (AV)

Limited Liability Partnership
200 Oceangate, Suite 1500, 90802-4302
Telephone: 562-901-9800
Fax: 562-983-9383
Email: LEBBGY@aol.com

(See Next Column)

BRANDON & YARC LLP—*Continued*

Lisa E. Brandon | Mariellen Yarc

ASSOCIATE

Derek B. Vosskuhler

For full biographical listings, see the Martindale-Hubbell Law Directory

*LOS ANGELES,** Los Angeles Co.

DECAROLIS, SAENZ & TROPE, LLP (AV)

1801 Century Park East 26th Floor, 90067
Telephone: 310-552-2444
Facsimile: 310-552-0441
Email: pdecarolis@mindspring.com *URL:* http://www.lawyers.com/decarsape

Patrick DeCarolis, Jr. | Edgar A. Saenz
Michael L. Trope

For full biographical listings, see the Martindale-Hubbell Law Directory

LAW OFFICES OF ROBERT W. EISFELDER, P.C. (AV)

11755 Wilshire Boulevard, Suite 2150, 90025-1543
Telephone: 310-820-4500
Facsimile: 310-826-0683

Robert W. Eisfelder

John Thayer Clark

For full biographical listings, see the Martindale-Hubbell Law Directory

GOLDMAN & KAGON, LAW CORPORATION (AV)

1801 Century Park East, Suite 2222, 90067
Telephone: 310-552-1707
Telecopier: 310-552-7938
URL: http://www.goldmankagon.com

Terry Mc Niff | Jared Laskin

COUNSEL

A. David Kagon

For Complete List of Firm Personnel, See General Section

For full biographical listings, see the Martindale-Hubbell Law Directory

HARRIS • GINSBERG LLP (AV)

11755 Wilshire Boulevard, Suite 950, 90025
Telephone: 310-444-6333
Fax: 310-444-6330
lginsberg@harris-ginsberg.com
Email: sharris@harris-ginsberg.com

MEMBERS OF FIRM

Suzanne Harris | Larry A. Ginsberg

Andrea A. Fugate | Laurel Tuvim Amaya

OF COUNSEL

Pamela Somers

For full biographical listings, see the Martindale-Hubbell Law Directory

LAWRENCE E. LEONE (AV)

12100 Wilshire Boulevard, Suite 1500 Fifteenth Floor, 90025
Telephone: 310-450-2130
Fax: 310-450-2611
Email: lelcfls@aol.com

For full biographical listings, see the Martindale-Hubbell Law Directory

MOSTEN & TUFFIAS (AV)

11601 Wilshire Boulevard, Suite 1840, 90025-1754
Telephone: 310-473-7611
Facsimile: 310-473-7422
Email: mosten@mediate.com *URL:* http://www.mediate.com/mosten

MEMBERS OF FIRM

Forrest S. Mosten | Heidi S. Tuffias

For full biographical listings, see the Martindale-Hubbell Law Directory

F. PATRICIA MUDIE A PROFESSIONAL CORPORATION (AV)

12100 Wilshire Boulevard, Suite 1650, 90025-1506
Telephone: 310-820-5505
Fax: 310-207-1030
Email: fpmudie@earthlink.net

F. Patricia Mudie

For full biographical listings, see the Martindale-Hubbell Law Directory

NACHSHIN & WESTON, LLP (AV)

A Limited Liability Partnership including Professional Corporations
Suite 2240, 11755 Wilshire Boulevard, 90025
Telephone: 310-478-6868
Telefax: 310-473-8112
Email: info@nwdivorce.com *URL:* http://www.nwdivorce.com

Robert J. Nachshin (A Professional Corporation) | Scott N. Weston (A Professional Corporation)

ASSOCIATES

Stephanie I. Blum | Joseph A. Langlois

For full biographical listings, see the Martindale-Hubbell Law Directory

BEATRICE H. NEMLAHA, P.C. (AV)

11377 West Olympic Boulevard, 90064-1683
Telephone: 310-914-7911
Fax: 310-312-3787

Beatrice H. Nemlaha

For full biographical listings, see the Martindale-Hubbell Law Directory

LAW OFFICES OF MILES J. RUBIN (AV)

Second Floor, West Tower, 11377 West Olympic Boulevard, 90064-1683
Telephone: 310-312-3222
Fax: 310-312-3205
Email: milesjrubin@compuserve.com *URL:* http://www.lawyers.com/milesrubin

Lauri Kritt Martin

OF COUNSEL

Linda Cukier

For full biographical listings, see the Martindale-Hubbell Law Directory

TROPE AND TROPE (AV)

12121 Wilshire Boulevard, Suite 801, 90025
Telephone: 310-207-8228
Fax: 310-826-1122

MEMBERS OF FIRM

Sorrell Trope | Steven Knowles
Eugene L. Trope | Mark S. Patt
Maryanne La Guardia | Bruce E. Cooperman
Anne Campbell Kiley

ASSOCIATES

John A. Ellis | Patricia A. Johnson
Thomas Paine Dunlap | James A. Durant
Donna Beck Weaver | Fahi Takesh
Robert B. Clayton | Geniveve Joan Ruskus
Ann Dobbs | Daniel B. Rubanowitz
Susan E. Wiesner | Frederick D. Hale
Lisa R. Krieger | William R. Waldman
Susannah J. Braffman

For full biographical listings, see the Martindale-Hubbell Law Directory

WASSER, ROSENSON & CARTER (AV)

Suite 1200, One Century Plaza, 2029 Century Park East (Century City), 90067
Telephone: 310-277-7117
Fax: 310-553-1793
Email: wrclaw@wrclaw.com *URL:* http://www.wrclaw.com

MEMBERS OF FIRM

Dennis M. Wasser | S. David Rosenson
Susan K. Carter

ASSOCIATES

John A. Foley | Laura Allison Wasser
Laura Landesman | Melanie D. Mandles

For full biographical listings, see the Martindale-Hubbell Law Directory

ZOLLA AND MEYER (AV)

A Partnership including a Professional Corporation
Suite 1020, 2029 Century Park East, 90067
Telephone: 310-277-0725
Facsimile: 310-277-3784
Email: familylaw@zmlalaw.com *URL:* http://www.zmlalaw.com/familylaw

MEMBERS OF FIRM

Marshall S. Zolla (A P.C.) | Lisa Helfend Meyer

ASSOCIATES

Doreen Marie Olson | Cori Gayle Stockman
Dana Lowy | Alison J. Stein

Reference: City National Bank, Beverly Hills.

For full biographical listings, see the Martindale-Hubbell Law Directory

MOUNTAIN VIEW, Santa Clara Co.

J. NORMAN BAKER (AV)

San Antonio Center, 2570 El Camino Real West, Suite 504, 94040
Telephone: 650-941-0604
Fax: 650-941-0119

Reference: Bank of the West (Los Altos Branch).

For full biographical listings, see the Martindale-Hubbell Law Directory

*NAPA,** Napa Co.

GAW, VAN MALE, SMITH, MYERS & MIROGLIO, A PROFESSIONAL LAW CORPORATION (AV)

944 Main Street, 94559-3045
Telephone: 707-252-9000
Telecopier: 707-252-0792
URL: http://www.gvmsmm.com
Fairfield, California Office: Corporate Plaza. 1261 Travis Boulevard, Suite 350, 94533-4801.
Telephone: 707-425-1250.
Fax: 707-425-1255.
Redlands, California Office: 300 E. State Street, Suite 101, 92372-5200.
Telephone: 909-798-3190.
Fax: 909-798-3092.

Nicholas R. Van Male
Joyce L. Elliott
Joseph M. Scalise

Reference: The Vintage Bank.

For full biographical listings, see the Martindale-Hubbell Law Directory

NEWPORT BEACH, Orange Co.

THOMAS A. BERNAUER A PROFESSIONAL CORPORATION (AV)

500 Newport Center Drive, Suite 950, 92660
Telephone: 949-720-1313
Fax: 949-720-7457

Thomas A. Bernauer

LEGAL SUPPORT PERSONNEL

Michele Minick

For full biographical listings, see the Martindale-Hubbell Law Directory

*OAKLAND,** Alameda Co.

LAW OFFICES OF LORIN B. BLUM (AV)

1939 Harrison Street, Suite 618, 94612-3533
Telephone: 510-465-3927
Fax: 510-465-4222
Email: Lorin@Blumlaw.com
Walnut Creek, California Office: 1350 Carlback Avenue, Suite 335, 94596.
Telephone: 510-933-6125.

ASSOCIATES

Sharon M. Braz
Donna Tsifrin

LEGAL SUPPORT PERSONNEL

Sandra L. Kellum
Amy Drackert
Dolores Rutzen

For full biographical listings, see the Martindale-Hubbell Law Directory

GARRETT C. DAILEY (AV)

519 - 17th Street, 7th Floor, 94612
Telephone: 510-465-3920
Fax: 510-465-7348
Email: BriefCase@aol.com

Reference: Wells Fargo Bank (Oakland City Center Office).

For full biographical listings, see the Martindale-Hubbell Law Directory

ROBERT D. MCGUINESS (AV)

1939 Harrison Street, Suite 310, 94612
Telephone: 510-273-8870
Fax: 510-273-8830

For full biographical listings, see the Martindale-Hubbell Law Directory

ONTARIO, San Bernardino Co.

COVINGTON & CROWE LLP (AV)

1131 West Sixth Street, P.O. Box 1515, 91762
Telephone: 909-983-9393
Fax: 909-391-6762
URL: http://www.covcrowe.com

(See Next Column)

MEMBERS OF FIRM

Maurice G. Covington (1908-1997)
Harold A. Bailin (1930-1988)
Samuel P. Crowe
George W. Porter
Robert E. Dougherty
Donald G. Haslam
Robert F. Schauer
Jette R. Anderson
Audrey A. Perri
Tracy L. Tibbals
Melanie Fisch
R. Douglas Donesky
Tammy S. Jager
Katrina West

ASSOCIATES

J. Michael Kaler
Eric S. Vail
Khymberli S. Apaloo

OF COUNSEL

Edward A. Hopson

For full biographical listings, see the Martindale-Hubbell Law Directory

ORANGE, Orange Co.

MINYARD AND MORRIS, LLP (AV)

One City Boulevard West, 11th Floor, Suite 1100, 92868
Telephone: 714-937-1020
Facsimile: 714-978-6060

MEMBERS OF FIRM

Mark E. Minyard
Michael A. Morris

ASSOCIATES

Lonnie K. Seide
Kenneth T. Demmerle
James R. Parke
Robert McLaughlin
Steven G. Hittelman
Nancy E. McAllister
John S. Cowhig
Kevin G. Musulas

For full biographical listings, see the Martindale-Hubbell Law Directory

PALM SPRINGS, Riverside Co.

SCHLECHT, SHEVLIN & SHOENBERGER, A LAW CORPORATION (AV)

801 East Tahquitz Canyon Way, Suite 100, P.O. Box 2744, 92263-2744
Telephone: 760-320-7161
Facsimile: 760-323-1758
Email: ssslaw@gte.net *URL:* http://www.ssslaw.com

Jon A. Shoenberger

David Darrin

For Complete List of Firm Personnel, See General Section

For full biographical listings, see the Martindale-Hubbell Law Directory

PALO ALTO, Santa Clara Co.

FLICKER & KERIN (AV)

Suite 460, 285 Hamilton, P.O. Box 840, 94302
Telephone: 650-321-0947
Fax: 650-326-9722

MEMBERS OF FIRM

Michael R. Flicker
Anthony J. Kerin, III
Rhesa C. Rubin

ASSOCIATES

Cheri A. Bell
Eleni Adamis

For full biographical listings, see the Martindale-Hubbell Law Directory

JOHN E. MILLER (AV)

250 Cambridge Avenue, Suite 102, 94306-1504
Telephone: 650-321-8886
Fax: 650-321-8998

ASSOCIATE

Matthew P. Pachkowski

Reference: Bank of the West.

For full biographical listings, see the Martindale-Hubbell Law Directory

LINCOLN A. MITCHELL (AV)

Suite 300, 550 Hamilton Avenue, 94301
Telephone: 650-321-5003
Fax: 650-326-2404

For full biographical listings, see the Martindale-Hubbell Law Directory

PASADENA, Los Angeles Co.

GARY W. KEARNEY (AV)
Suite 410, 225 South Lake Avenue, 91101-3005
Telephone: 626-796-9621
Telecopier: 626-796-6839
Email: gary@kearney-law.com
URL: http://www.lawyers.com/kearney_familylaw
Email: info@kearney-law.com *URL:* http://www.kearney-law.com

ASSOCIATE
Ronald K. Ziff

For full biographical listings, see the Martindale-Hubbell Law Directory

*SACRAMENTO,** Sacramento Co.

BARTHOLOMEW, WASZNICKY & MOLINARO LLP (AV)
1006 Fourth Street, 8th Floor, 95814
Telephone: 916-443-2055
Fax: 916-443-8287
URL: http://www.divorcepage.com
Email: info@divorcepage.com *URL:* http://www.lawyers.com/divorcepage

MEMBERS OF FIRM
Hal D. Bartholomew
Diane Wasznicky
Mary C. Molinaro

ASSOCIATE
Noel C. Murray

For full biographical listings, see the Martindale-Hubbell Law Directory

JAMES M. MIZE (AV)
3620 American River Drive, Suite 250, 95864
Telephone: 916-485-2211
Fax: 916-485-1934
Email: mize@alum.calberkeley.org

For full biographical listings, see the Martindale-Hubbell Law Directory

JOHN W. MUNSILL (AV)
12150 Tributary Point Drive, Suite 110 (Gold River), 95670
Telephone: 916-985-5601
Fax: 916-985-5604
Email: munsilaw@sna.com

For full biographical listings, see the Martindale-Hubbell Law Directory

WOODRUFF, O'HAIR & POSNER, INC. A LAW CORPORATION (AV)
2251 Fair Oaks Boulevard, Suite 100, 95825
Telephone: 916-920-0211
Telecopier: 916-920-0241

D. Thomas Woodruff
Robert J. O'Hair
Jeffrey J. Posner

For full biographical listings, see the Martindale-Hubbell Law Directory

*SAN BERNARDINO,** San Bernardino Co.

STEVEN A. BECKER A PROFESSIONAL LAW CORPORATION (AV)
315 West Sixth Street, 92401
Telephone: 909-888-2211
Fax: 909-381-0586

Steven A. Becker
Patricia L. Huberty

For full biographical listings, see the Martindale-Hubbell Law Directory

*SAN DIEGO,** San Diego Co.

E. GREGORY ALFORD (AV)
1551 Fourth Avenue, Suite 301, 92101
Telephone: 619-232-4734
FAX: 619-239-3345
Email: alfordlaw@aol.com *URL:* http://www.galfordlaw.com

ASSOCIATE
Sandra L. Mayberry

For full biographical listings, see the Martindale-Hubbell Law Directory

LUCE, FORWARD, HAMILTON & SCRIPPS LLP (AV)
A Partnership including Professional Corporations
600 West Broadway, Suite 2600, 92101
Telephone: 619-236-1414
Fax: 619-232-8311
URL: http://www.luce.com
La Jolla, California Office: 4275 Executive Square, Suite 800, 92037.
Telephone: 858-455-6611.
Fax: 858-232-8311.
Los Angeles, California Office: 777 South Figueroa, Suite 3600, 90017.
Telephone: 213-892-4992.
Fax: 213-892-7731.
San Francisco, California Office: 121 Spear Street, Suite 200, 94105.
Telephone: 415-356-4600.
Fax: 415-356-4610.
New York, N.Y. Office: Citicorp Center, 153 East 53rd Street, 26th Floor, 10022.
Telephone: 212-754-1414.
Fax: 212-644-9727.
Chicago, Illinois Office: 180 North La Salle Street, Suite 3110, 60601.
Telephone: 312-641-0580.
Fax: 312-641-0380.

Susanne J. Stanford

ASSOCIATES
Frank J. Kros
Elizabeth R. Potter

For Complete List of Firm Personnel, See General Section

For full biographical listings, see the Martindale-Hubbell Law Directory

OLINS, FOERSTER & HAYES (AV)
A Legal Liability Partnership including A Professional Corporation
2214 Second Avenue, 92101
Telephone: 619-238-1601
Fax: 619-238-1613
URL: http://www.ofh.com
Santa Ana, California Office: 1314 West Fifth Street, Suite C, 92703.
Telephone: 714-836-9777.
Fax: 714-954-1156.

MEMBERS OF FIRM
Douglas F. Olins
Barrett J. Foerster (A P.C.)
Dennis J. Hayes

ASSOCIATES
Laura H. Miller
John C. Zucconi
Barbara J. Ginsberg (Resident, Santa Ana Office)

For full biographical listings, see the Martindale-Hubbell Law Directory

STOCKS AND FENTIN, LLP (AV)
600 "B" Street, Suite 2050, 92101
Telephone: 619-231-2025
Facsimile: 619-231-2024
Email: info@stocksfentin.com *URL:* http://www.lawyers.com/stocks&fentin

Janis K. Stocks
Hildy L. Fentin

ASSOCIATE
Kristine Pogalies

For full biographical listings, see the Martindale-Hubbell Law Directory

VELTMANN & LETO (AV)
1620 Fifth Avenue, Suite 700, 92101-2743
Telephone: 619-232-7384
Fax: 619-232-2236

MEMBERS OF FIRM
James S. Veltmann
Nicholas A. Leto, Jr.

ASSOCIATE
Lisa A. Flores

Reference: Bank of Southern California.

For full biographical listings, see the Martindale-Hubbell Law Directory

*SAN FRANCISCO,** San Francisco Co.

BLEY AND BLEY (AV)
555 Montgomery Street, Suite 605, 94111
Telephone: 415-982-7311
Fax: 415-982-7278

Bertrand A. Bley (1903-1992)
Stephen Bruce Bley
Casimir A. Wilson
Samantha Bley DeJean
Richard S. Weil

For full biographical listings, see the Martindale-Hubbell Law Directory

San Francisco—Continued

G. William Filley (AV)

5455 Anza Street, 94121
Telephone: 415-956-5912
Fax: 415-221-7965
Email: filleyatty@aol.com

For full biographical listings, see the Martindale-Hubbell Law Directory

Hersh FamilyLaw Practice, A Professional Corporation (AV)

One Maritime Plaza, Suite 1040, 94111
Telephone: 415-788-2200
Telecopier: 415-394-0222
Email: mail@hershfamlaw.com *URL:* http://www.lawyers.com/hersh

Jill Hersh

Jessica N. Metoyer
Wendy K. Reimer
Jenny Wald

For full biographical listings, see the Martindale-Hubbell Law Directory

MacInnis, Donner & Koplowitz (AV)

Suite 222, 465 California Street, 94104
Telephone: 415-434-2400
FAX: 415-433-1917

MEMBERS OF FIRM

James Martin MacInnis (1914-1979)
Conrad Donner
Edward A. Koplowitz

For full biographical listings, see the Martindale-Hubbell Law Directory

*SAN JOSE,** Santa Clara Co.

Dok, Levy & Perrin (AV)

An Association of Attorneys including a Professional Corporation
1550 The Alameda, Suite 300, 95126
Telephone: 408-287-7790
Fax: 408-280-5748
Email: lawfirm@ix.netcom.com *URL:* http://www.netcom.com/~lawfirm

William L. Dok (Inc.)
Michael R. Levy
Lawrence J. Perrin

For full biographical listings, see the Martindale-Hubbell Law Directory

Hammer & Jacobs (AV)

160 West Santa Clara Street, Suite 600, 95113-2227
Telephone: 408-297-8400
Fax: 408-297-8488

Philip L. Hammer
Paul E. Jacobs

ASSOCIATES

Sally Reed Meggs
David A. Gonzalez

For full biographical listings, see the Martindale-Hubbell Law Directory

McManis, Faulkner & Morgan (AV)

160 West Santa Clara Street, 10th Floor, 95113
Telephone: 408-279-8700
Fax: 408-279-3244; 408-279-0494
Email: mfm@mfmlaw.com *URL:* http://www.mfmlaw.com

James McManis
William Faulkner
Donelle Morgan
Lisa Herrick
Michael Reedy
Erica Yew

Michelle Tidalgo
Colleen Duffy Smith
Lillian Wolf
Rebecca Hughes
Kalpana Vrudhula
Ray M. Baluyot
Catherine Bechtel
Arron Nesbitt

OF COUNSEL

Mary Arand

For full biographical listings, see the Martindale-Hubbell Law Directory

SAN MATEO, San Mateo Co.

Norris & Rossi LLP (AV)

777 Mariners Island Boulevard, Suite 575, P.O. Box 5446, 94404-1588
Telephone: 650-571-0600
Fax: 650-571-0835

MEMBERS OF FIRM

Lana L. Norris
Anne Marie Rossi

ASSOCIATES

Ann Karole Nylander
Kathleen Robertson

(See Next Column)

LEGAL SUPPORT PERSONNEL

J. Bridget Peterson-Paquette

For full biographical listings, see the Martindale-Hubbell Law Directory

*SAN RAFAEL,** Marin Co.

Richard Barry and Sharon Mah (AV)

An Association - Not a Partnership
Courthouse Square, 1000 Fourth Street, Suite 650, P.O. Box 151257, 94915-1257
Telephone: 415-453-0360
Fax: 415-453-9193

Richard F. Barry
Sharon F. Mah

For full biographical listings, see the Martindale-Hubbell Law Directory

SAN RAMON, Contra Costa Co.

Weiler & Borst, LLP (AV)

Bishop Ranch Business Park, Two Annabel Lane, Suite 200, 94583
Telephone: 925-275-0855
Telecopier: 925-830-8787
Email: tgb@weilerlaw.com
Email: ldw@weilerlaw.com *URL:* http://www.weilerlaw.com

Leonard D. Weiler (PC)
Thomas G. Borst

For full biographical listings, see the Martindale-Hubbell Law Directory

*SANTA BARBARA,** Santa Barbara Co.

Angle, Carlson, Goldrick & Roberts (AV)

A Partnership including a Professional Corporation
200 East Carrillo Street, Suite 310, 93101
Telephone: 805-963-7400
Fax: 805-963-7610

Robert O. Angle
Arthur W. Carlson (A P.C.)
Miles T. Goldrick
Paul A. Roberts

For full biographical listings, see the Martindale-Hubbell Law Directory

SANTA MONICA, Los Angeles Co.

Kelly & Hammers, A Professional Corporation (AV)

501 Santa Monica Boulevard, Suite 701, P.O. Box 1490, 90406-1490
Telephone: 310-393-0236
Email: JMK@kellyhammers.com *URL:* http://www.kellyhammers.com

J. Michael Kelly
Barbara K. Hammers

William M. Strachan
Clarke Logan Young
Craig Nadai

For full biographical listings, see the Martindale-Hubbell Law Directory

THOUSAND OAKS, Ventura Co.

Cohen, Alexander & Clayton, A Professional Corporation (AV)

One Boardwalk, Suite 102, 91360-5799
Telephone: 805-497-0802
Fax: 805-373-6082
Email: lawcac@ix.netcom.com

Charles W. Cohen
Leonard Alexander
Raymond C. Clayton
Ruth D. Morrow
Marguerite A. Wilson

Thomas S. Cohen

Representative Clients: Comsat General Corp.; Conejo Valley Chamber of Commerce; South Coast Area Transit.

For full biographical listings, see the Martindale-Hubbell Law Directory

TORRANCE, Los Angeles Co.

McGaughey & Spirito (AV)

2377 Crenshaw Boulevard, Suite 310, 90501
Telephone: 310-787-8783
Fax: 310-787-9937

MEMBERS OF FIRM

Terence C. McGaughey
Joseph P. Spirito Jr.

ASSOCIATE

Steven Spitzer

Reference: Bay Cities National Bank.

For full biographical listings, see the Martindale-Hubbell Law Directory

Torrance—Continued

MOORE, BRYAN & SCHROFF, A LAW CORPORATION (AV)
Suite 490 California Bank & Trust Tower, 21515 Hawthorne Boulevard, 90503
Telephone: 310-540-8855
Fax: 310-316-1307
Email: mail@cmoorelaw.com

Christopher M. Moore
Sharon A. Bryan
Rebecca Lee Tomlinson Schroff

Kimberly K Davidson

For full biographical listings, see the Martindale-Hubbell Law Directory

TUSTIN, Orange Co.

STAPLETON & STAPLETON, A PROFESSIONAL ASSOCIATION (AV)
Irvine Plaza Building, Suite 114, 17621 Irvine Boulevard, 92780
Telephone: 714-832-8003
Fax: 714-832-2007

Marlin G. Stapleton
Marlin G. Stapleton, Jr.

For full biographical listings, see the Martindale-Hubbell Law Directory

*VENTURA,** Ventura Co.

JAY M. JOHNSON (AV)
770 County Square Drive, Suite 104, 93003
Telephone: 805-654-0400
Fax: 805-654-0326
Email: jaylaw@inreach.com

For full biographical listings, see the Martindale-Hubbell Law Directory

SMITH AND NOWLIN (AV)
950 County Square Drive, Suite 108, 93003
Telephone: 805-650-8188
FAX: 805-650-0741

Herbert D. Nowlin
OF COUNSEL
Leonard H. Smith

For full biographical listings, see the Martindale-Hubbell Law Directory

TAYLOR McCORD, A LAW CORPORATION (AV)
721 East Main Street, P.O. Box 1477, 93002
Telephone: 805-648-4700
Email: vtafamlaw@aol.com

Richard L. Taylor
Robert L. McCord, Jr.
David L. Praver

Patrick Cherry
Susan D. Siple
Rebbecca F. Calderwood

LEGAL SUPPORT PERSONNEL
PARALEGALS

Stephanie Gibson
Diane Lovato
Adele Rubino (Certified Legal Assistant, California Advanced Specialist)

For full biographical listings, see the Martindale-Hubbell Law Directory

WHIPPLE AND VIELE, A PROFESSIONAL LAW CORPORATION (AV)
60 South California Street, 93001
Telephone: 805-643-8658; 643-8422
Fax: 805-653-6079

Terry James Viele

References: Wells Fargo Bank; American Commercial Bank.

For full biographical listings, see the Martindale-Hubbell Law Directory

VISTA, San Diego Co.

JAMES A. HENNENHOEFER A PROFESSIONAL CORPORATION (AV)
316 South Melrose Drive, Suite 200, 92083-6618
Telephone: 760-941-2260
Facsimile: 760-945-1805
Email: jahesq@aol.com *URL:* http://www.lawyers.com/jhennen

James A. Hennenhoefer
Rolf G. Steeve, Jr.

LEGAL SUPPORT PERSONNEL

Claudia Vess
Liz Franciscus

For full biographical listings, see the Martindale-Hubbell Law Directory

WOODLAND HILLS, Los Angeles Co.

LEON F. BENNETT (AV)
6400 Canoga Avenue, Suite 354, 91367-2425
Telephone: 818-888-7731
Fax: 818-888-7674
URL: http://www.lawyers.com/leonfbennettlaw

ASSOCIATE
Debra J. Przelomiec

For full biographical listings, see the Martindale-Hubbell Law Directory

LAURENCE R. GOLDMAN (AV)
21700 Oxnard Street, Suite 1750, 91367
Telephone: 818-888-0299
Facsimile: 818-888-5602
URL: http://www.lawyers.com/laurencergoldman

For full biographical listings, see the Martindale-Hubbell Law Directory

COLORADO

*ASPEN,** Pitkin Co.

OATES, KNEZEVICH & GARDENSWARTZ, P.C. (AV)
Aspen Plaza Building, 3rd Floor, 533 East Hopkins Avenue, 81611
Telephone: 970-920-1700
Fax: 970-920-1121
Email: ohkg@rof.net

Leonard M. Oates
Ted D. Gardenswartz
Richard A. Knezevich
David B. Kelly

David B. Mueller

OF COUNSEL

John Thomas Kelly
Michael Feigenbaum

For full biographical listings, see the Martindale-Hubbell Law Directory

*BOULDER,** Boulder Co.

HOWARD BITTMAN (AV)
1406 Pearl Street, Suite 200, 80302
Telephone: 303-443-2281
Fax: 303-443-2862
Email: bittmanh@aol.com *URL:* http://www.lawyers.com/howardbittman

For full biographical listings, see the Martindale-Hubbell Law Directory

THORBURN, SAKOL & THRONE (AV)
A Partnership of Professional Corporations
255 Canyon Boulevard at Cloud Creek, Suite 100, 80302-4954
Telephone: 303-449-1873
Fax: 303-447-9840
Email: bsakol@prodigy.net

MEMBER OF FIRM
Barre M. Sakol (P.C.)

Reference: Bank One of Boulder.

For full biographical listings, see the Martindale-Hubbell Law Directory

*COLORADO SPRINGS,** El Paso Co.

BELTZ, EDWARDS & SABO, L.L.P. (AV)
128 South Tejon, Suite 310, 80903
Telephone: 719-634-6620
Fax: 719-634-3142
Email: BES_LLP@aol.com *URL:* http://www.lawyers.com/beslaw
Other Colorado Springs, Colorado Office: 729 South Cascade, 80903.
Telephone: 719-473-4444.
Fax: 719-444-0186.

Daniel P. Edwards
W. Thomas Beltz
John W. Sabo, III

ASSOCIATE
Daniel A. West

Representative Clients: A.M.I. Industries, Inc.; Analytical Surveys, Inc.; A.C. Israel Enterprises, Inc.; Boddington Lumber Co., Inc.; Cardiovascular Surgeons of Colorado Springs, P.C.; Colorado Springs Radiologists, P.C.; Digital, Inc.; Music Semi-Conductors, Inc.; Schlage Lock Co.; Texas Instruments.

For full biographical listings, see the Martindale-Hubbell Law Directory

Colorado Springs—Continued

KANE, DONLEY & JOHNSON, P.C. (AV)

90 South Cascade Avenue, Suite 830, 80903
Telephone: 719-471-1650
Fax: 719-471-1663
Mailing Address: P.O. Box 1119, Colorado Springs, CO, 80901
Email: kdandjpc@earthlink.net

Jerry A. Donley
Jack E. Donley
Mark H. Kane
David M. Johnson
Hayden W. Kane, II

William A. Palmer
Katherine L. Hays

OF COUNSEL

Hayden W. Kane

Representative Clients: American International Companies; Shelter Insurance Co.; Metropolitan Insurance Co.
Reference: State Bank & Trust and Bank One.

For full biographical listings, see the Martindale-Hubbell Law Directory

*DENVER,** Denver Co.

CANGES, IWASHKO & BETHKE, A PROFESSIONAL CORPORATION (AV)

303 East 17th Avenue Suite 400, 80203-1257
Telephone: 303-860-1900
Fax: 303-860-1665
URL: http://www.lawyers.com/ciblaw

E. Michael Canges
Erich L. Bethke
Nina A. Iwashko
James S. Bailey

Michelle L. Lukowicz

Reference: Norwest Bank Denver.

For full biographical listings, see the Martindale-Hubbell Law Directory

STEPHEN J. HARHAI (AV)

1928 East Eighteenth Avenue, 80206
Telephone: 303-329-8300
Fax: 303-329-8119

Jerald N. Marrs

For full biographical listings, see the Martindale-Hubbell Law Directory

STANLEY G. LIPKIN (AV)

1380 Lawrence Street, Suite 300, 80204
Telephone: 303-446-8300
FAX: 303-572-7804
Email: lipkinlaw@aol.com *URL:* http://www.lawyers.com/stanleylipkinlaw

ASSOCIATE

Rose Mary Zapor

For full biographical listings, see the Martindale-Hubbell Law Directory

LITVAK, LITVAK, MEHRTENS & EPSTEIN, PROFESSIONAL CORPORATION (AV)

1900 Grant Street, Suite 590, 80203-4305
Telephone: 303-837-0757
Fax: 303-839-9826
Email: FamilyAtty@aol.com *URL:* http://www.FamilyAtty.com

Lawrence Litvak
Timothy R. J. Mehrtens
Ronald D. Litvak
Steven B. Epstein
William Troy Romero

Christina Lynn Huiatt Patierno
Paula J. Smith
Janine C. Manchester

For full biographical listings, see the Martindale-Hubbell Law Directory

THOMAS P. MALONE & ASSOCIATES, P.C. (AV)

Suite 600, 950 South Cherry Street, 80246
Telephone: 303-757-8300
Fax: 303-757-8001
Email: ThomMalone@aol.com *URL:* http://www.lawyers.com/malonelaw

Thomas P. Malone

OF COUNSEL

Judith Beggs Pierson

For full biographical listings, see the Martindale-Hubbell Law Directory

MCGUANE AND HOGAN LLP (AV)

A Partnership including Professional Corporations
Suite 910-N, The Galleria, 720 South Colorado Boulevard, 80246
Telephone: 303-691-9600
Fax: 303-691-9900
Email: McGuane.Hogan@lawyernet.com *URL:* http://www.lawyers.com/mcguaneandhogan
Aspen, Colorado Office: Plaza 117, Suite 302, 117 Aspen Airport Business Center, 81611.
Telephone: 970-920-7645.
Fax: 970-920-7695.

Frank L. McGuane, Jr.
Kathleen A. Hogan

ASSOCIATE

Brenda L. Storey

For full biographical listings, see the Martindale-Hubbell Law Directory

LAW OFFICES OF JOHN W. MCKENDREE (AV)

Creswell Mansion, 1244 Grant Street, 80203
Telephone: 303-861-8906
Fax: 303-861-7773
Email: Johnwmckendree@msn.com

ASSOCIATE

Elizabeth G. McKendree

Reference: Colorado National Bank.

For full biographical listings, see the Martindale-Hubbell Law Directory

HOWARD B. ZUCKER (AV)

1660 Wynkoop, Suite 1100, 80202
Telephone: 303-758-6790
Fax: 303-534-0725
Email: howbull@aol.com
(Also Special Counsel to Gelt, Fleishman & Sterling)

For full biographical listings, see the Martindale-Hubbell Law Directory

GREENWOOD VILLAGE, Arapahoe Co.

ROBERT T. HINDS, JR. AND ASSOCIATES, P.C. (AV)

8490 East Crescent Parkway, Suite 395, 80111
Telephone: 303-224-9000
Fax: 303-224-9099
Email: rhinds@legalfile.com

Robert T. Hinds, Jr.

Lucy Hojo Denson
Robert T. Hinds, III
Angela R. Arkin

OF COUNSEL

Dr. Howard I. Rosenberg

For full biographical listings, see the Martindale-Hubbell Law Directory

LAKEWOOD, Jefferson Co.

POLIDORI, GEROME, FRANKLIN AND JACOBSON, L.L.C. (AV)

Suite 300, 550 South Wadsworth Boulevard, 80226
Telephone: 303-936-3300
Fax: 303-936-0125

Gary L. Polidori
Peter L. Franklin
Dennis J. Jacobson
Lesleigh Wiggs Monahan

Sandra Kreshek
Patricia M. Woods

For full biographical listings, see the Martindale-Hubbell Law Directory

*LITTLETON,** Arapahoe Co.

DOROTHY H. TOMASETTI (AV)

Suite 740 26 West Dry Creek Circle, 80465
Telephone: 303-730-8477
Fax: 303-798-4637
Email: DTOMASET@Legalfile.com

For full biographical listings, see the Martindale-Hubbell Law Directory

LONE TREE, Douglas Co.

GUTTERMAN, CARLTON & HECKENBACH, L.L.P. (AV)

8375 South Willow Street, Suite 300 (Park Meadows), 80124
Telephone: 303-858-8000
Fax: 303-858-8001

David W. Heckenbach
Diane Carlton
Sheila M. Gutterman

ASSOCIATES

Laura Lynne Ammarell
Denise A. Cook
Marie Avery Moses

(See Next Column)

GUTTERMAN, CARLTON & HECKENBACH L.L.P.—*Continued*

SPECIAL COUNSEL

Marc J. Kaplan Suzanne Griffiths

For full biographical listings, see the Martindale-Hubbell Law Directory

*MONTROSE,** Montrose Co.

EDWARD D. DURHAM (AV)

543 South Second Street, P.O. Box 1721, 81402
Telephone: 970-249-2274
Fax: 970-249-6482; 970-249-6592

Reference: Norwest Bank of Montrose.

For full biographical listings, see the Martindale-Hubbell Law Directory

WESTMINSTER, Adams Co.

CIANCIO & JONSEN, P.C. (AV)

12000 North Pecos Street Suite 200, 80234-2079
Telephone: 303-451-0300
Fax: 303-280-0614
Email: ciancio@csn.net
Email: jonsen@csn.net

Gene A. Ciancio Eric R. Jonsen

Cynthia M. Ciancio

For full biographical listings, see the Martindale-Hubbell Law Directory

CONNECTICUT

DARIEN, Fairfield Co.

MILLAR & AMBRETTE (AV)

23 Old King's Highway South, 06820-1267
Telephone: 203-655-7931
FAX: 203-656-2055

MEMBERS OF FIRM

Samuel D. B. Millar, Jr. L. Conrad Ambrette

OF COUNSEL

Peter M. Ryan

ASSOCIATE

Patricia Moreland Gross

For full biographical listings, see the Martindale-Hubbell Law Directory

GREENWICH, Fairfield Co.

GARY I. COHEN (AV)

781 North Street, 06831
Telephone: 203-622-8787
Facsimile: 203-622-8798
Email: GICLAW@AOL.COM

ASSOCIATE

Marci E. Finkelstein

For full biographical listings, see the Martindale-Hubbell Law Directory

WAYNE D. EFFRON, P.C. (AV)

165 West Putnam Avenue, P.O. Box 499, 06830
Telephone: 203-622-1160
Fax: 203-622-4004
Email: effronlaw@effronlaw.com

Wayne D. Effron
Brian M. Yard
Allen Gary Palmer
Kristen M. Smith

OF COUNSEL

Joel M. Kaye

For full biographical listings, see the Martindale-Hubbell Law Directory

HOLLAND KAUFMANN & BARTELS, LLC (AV)

289 Greenwich Avenue, 06830-6595
Telephone: 203-869-5600
Fax: 203-869-4648

Alexander J. Holland
Charles B. Kaufmann, III
Philip H. Bartels
Harold R. Burke
Jean Mills Aranha
Lori E. Romano
John C. Fusco

OF COUNSEL

Beth K. Hansson

For full biographical listings, see the Martindale-Hubbell Law Directory

SCHOONMAKER, GEORGE & COLIN, P.C. (AV)

5 Edgewood Avenue, P.O. Box 5059, 06831-5059
Telephone: 203-862-5000
Fax: 203-862-5099
URL: http://www.SandG.com

Samuel V. Schoonmaker, III
Cynthia Coulter George
Thomas D. Colin
Samuel V. Schoonmaker IV
Melissa J. Needle

For full biographical listings, see the Martindale-Hubbell Law Directory

THOMAS M. SHANLEY (AV)

140 Greenwich Avenue, 06830
Telephone: 203-622-9004
FAX: 203-622-3086
Email: tmshanley@snet.net

For full biographical listings, see the Martindale-Hubbell Law Directory

*HARTFORD,** Hartford Co.

JACKSON, O'KEEFE AND PHELAN (AV)

36 Russ Street, 06106-1571
Telephone: 860-278-4040
Fax: 860-527-2500
West Hartford, Connecticut Office: 62 LaSalle Road.
Telephone: 860-521-7500.
Fax: 860-561-5399.
Bethlehem, Connecticut Office: 423 Munger Lane. Telephone/
Fax: 203-266-5255.

MEMBERS OF FIRM

Jay W. Jackson
Andrew J. O'Keefe
Denise Martino Phelan
Matthew J. O'Keefe
Michael E. Riley
Peter K. O'Keefe
Philip R. Dunn, Jr.
Kathryn M. Cunningham
Joseph M. Busher, Jr.
Kristen E. Scholhamer

Representative Clients: Travelers Aetna Property Casualty Co.; ITT Hartford; Liberty Mutual Insurance Co.; Connecticut Medical Insurance Co.

For full biographical listings, see the Martindale-Hubbell Law Directory

SOROKIN, GROSS & HYDE, P.C. (AV)

One Corporate Center, 06103
Telephone: 860-525-6645
Fax: 860-522-1781
Email: sorokin@sorokinlaw.com
Simsbury, Connecticut Office: 720 Hopmeadow Street.
Telephone: 860-651-9348.
Rocky Hill, Connecticut Office: 2360 Main Street.
Telephone: 860-563-9305.
Fax: 860-529-6931.

Lisa A. Magliochetti
Lewis Rabinovitz
Richard D. Tulisano (Resident, Rocky Hill Office)

OF COUNSEL

Ethel Silver Sorokin

For Complete List of Firm Personnel, See General Section

For full biographical listings, see the Martindale-Hubbell Law Directory

*NEW HAVEN,** New Haven Co.

ROSEN & DOLAN, P.C. (AV)

400 Orange Street, 06511
Telephone: 203-787-3513
Fax: 203-789-1605
Email: davidrosen@snet.net
Email: sapincus@snet.net

Edward J. Dolan

Reference: Peoples Bank.

For Complete List of Firm Personnel, See General Section

For full biographical listings, see the Martindale-Hubbell Law Directory

SUSMAN, DUFFY & SEGALOFF, P.C. (AV)

55 Whitney Avenue, 06510-1300
Telephone: 203-624-9830
Fax: 203-562-8430
Mailing Address: P.O. Box 1684, New Haven, Connecticut, 06507-1684

Allen H. Duffy (1931-1986)
Michael Susman
James H. Segaloff
Joseph E. Faughnan
Susan W. Wolfson
Laura M. Sklaver
Andrew R. Lubin
James J. Perito
Matthew C. Susman
Thomas E. Katon

Jennifer L. Schancupp
Peter G. Kruzynski
Vincent J. Candelora
Karen Baldwin Kravetz

(See Next Column)

SUSMAN, DUFFY & SEGALOFF P.C., *New Haven—Continued*

OF COUNSEL

Diana C. Ballard
David P. Hambleton

For full biographical listings, see the Martindale-Hubbell Law Directory

JEAN L. WELTY (AV)

385 Orange Street, P.O. Box 1662, 06507
Telephone: 203-781-0877
Fax: 203-781-0899

Reference: People's Bank.

For full biographical listings, see the Martindale-Hubbell Law Directory

STAMFORD, Fairfield Co.

CURTIS, BRINCKERHOFF & BARRETT, P.C. (AV)

666 Summer Street, 06901-1416
Telephone: 203-324-6777
Telecopier: 203-324-9621
Email: info@curtisbb.com

T. Ward Cleary (1916-1988)
Frederick M. Tobin
John Wayne Fox
Ward Frank Cleary
James D'Alton Murphy
Randolph T. Lovallo

OF COUNSEL

John D. Hertz
Jane F. Donovan
Richard L. Brinckerhoff
Patricia M. Gaug

Susan L. Stratton
Derek Gilman
Michael P. Murray
John J. Louizos

Counsel for: The F. A. Bartlett Tree Expert Co.; Town of Darien; Miller Automobile Corp.; Bolliger, Inc.; Titan Sports; People's Bank, Bridgeport; Fleet Bank; Federal Deposit Insurance Co.; William Pitt Foundation; Wood Logan Associates.

For full biographical listings, see the Martindale-Hubbell Law Directory

PIAZZA & PICKEL (AV)

112 Prospect Street, P.O. Box 15390, 06901
Telephone: 203-348-2465
Fax: 203-964-9509
Email: aap@piazza-pickel.com *URL:* http://www.piazza-pickel.com

Anthony A. Piazza
Alan Scott Pickel

ASSOCIATES

Tara C.F. Ryan
Michelle M. Napoli

For full biographical listings, see the Martindale-Hubbell Law Directory

SILVER, GOLUB & TEITELL LLP (AV)

184 Atlantic Street, P.O. Box 389, 06904
Telephone: 203-325-4491
Fax: 203-325-3769
Email: silvergolubteitell.com *URL:* http://www.sgtlaw.com

MEMBERS OF FIRM

Richard A. Silver
Elaine T. Silver

For Complete List of Firm Personnel, See General Section

For full biographical listings, see the Martindale-Hubbell Law Directory

WOFSEY, ROSEN, KWESKIN & KURIANSKY, LLP (AV)

600 Summer Street, 06901
Telephone: 203-327-2300
Fax: 203-967-9273

MEMBERS OF FIRM

Abraham Wofsey (1915-1944)
Michael Wofsey (1927-1951)
David M. Rosen (1926-1967)
Julius B. Kuriansky (1952-1992)
Sydney C. Kweskin (1946-1998)
Monroe Silverman
Howard C. Kaplan
Edward M. Kweskin
David M. Cohen
Marshall Goldberg
Stephen A. Finn
Judith Rosenberg
Mark H. Henderson
Steven D. Grushkin
Matthew J. Forstadt
Steven M. Frederick

OF COUNSEL

Saul Kwartin
Emanuel Margolis
Anthony R. Lorenzo

SPECIAL COUNSEL

Day R. Shields

ASSOCIATES

Joseph Brachfeld
Eric M. Higgins
William A. Harrison
Daniel M. Young
Angelo A. Ziotas

Representative Clients: Banque Paribas; Benenson Realty; Cellular Information Systems, Inc.; The Chase Manhattan Bank; First County Bank; Hartford Provision Co.; Louis Dreyfus Corp.; Norwalk Federation of Teachers; People's Bank; Ridgeway Shopping Center.

(See Next Column)

For full biographical listings, see the Martindale-Hubbell Law Directory

WEST HARTFORD, Hartford Co.

BERMAN, BOURNS & CURRIE, LLC (AV)

970 Farmington Avenue, P.O. Box 271837, 06127-1837
Telephone: 860-232-4471
Fax: 860-523-4605

John A. Berman
Courtney B. Bourns

Mary Beth Anderson
Steven R. Dembo
Annemarie Burnham

OF COUNSEL

John K. Currie

For full biographical listings, see the Martindale-Hubbell Law Directory

WESTPORT, Fairfield Co.

NUSBAUM & PARRINO, P.C. (AV)

212 Post Road West, 06880
Telephone: 203-226-8181
Fax: 203-454-9937

Edward Nusbaum
Thomas P. Parrino

Harold W. Haldeman

OF COUNSEL

Susan A. Moch

For full biographical listings, see the Martindale-Hubbell Law Directory

RUTKIN AND OLDHAM, L.L.C (AV)

321 Riverside Avenue, P.O. Box 295, 06881
Telephone: 203-227-7301
Fax: 203-222-9295
Email: aradvocate@aol.com
Greenwich Office: 125 Mason Street, 06830.
Telephone: 203-869-7277.

Arnold H. Rutkin
Sarah S. Oldham

OF COUNSEL

Kathleen A. Hogan

For full biographical listings, see the Martindale-Hubbell Law Directory

DISTRICT OF COLUMBIA

WASHINGTON, D.C. Co.

DIANE M. BRENNEMAN (AV)

601 Pennsylvania Avenue, N.W., Ninth Floor, 20004
Telephone: 202-393-2121
Fax: 202-393-6911
Email: dbrenneman@mat.net *URL:* http://www.lawyers.com/dianembrennemanlaw
(Also Of Counsel, O'Reilly, Mark & Peelman, L.L.C.)

For full biographical listings, see the Martindale-Hubbell Law Directory

FELDESMAN, TUCKER, LEIFER, FIDELL & BANK LLP (AV)

2001 L Street, N.W., 2nd Floor, 20036
Telephone: 202-466-8960
Telefax: 202-293-8103
Rockville, Maryland Office: One Church Street, Suite 800.
Telephone: 301-279-6770.
Falls Church, Virginia Office: 5661 Columbia Pike, Suite 200.
Telephone: 703-671-5800.

Margaret H. Long (1940-1990)

MEMBERS OF FIRM

James L. Feldesman
Marna S. Tucker
Jacqueline C. Leifer
Eugene R. Fidell
Rita M. Bank
Pamela B. Forbes
Mary S. Pence
Jonathan M. Dana
Beth Goodman
Edward T. Waters
Roger A. Schwartz
Michael B. Glomb
Tanya A. Harvey
Richard C. Shadyac, Jr.
David P. Sheldon
Bruce F. Hoffmeister
M. Toni Waldman

(See Next Column)

FELDESMAN, TUCKER, LEIFER, FIDELL & BANK LLP—*Continued*

ASSOCIATES

Robin A. Clark
Jennifer P. Rosenberg
Garrett L. Lee
Marcie H. Zakheim
Kathy S. Ghiladi
Daniel L. Gray
Mary Price
Savalle C. Sims
Alice J. Gallin-Dwyer
Elizabeth A. Greczek
Jennifer L. Dziedzic
Alan J. Van Luven

For full biographical listings, see the Martindale-Hubbell Law Directory

LAW OFFICES OF GARFINKLE & ASSOCIATES (AV)

1150 Connecticut Avenue, N.W., Suite 505, 20036
Telephone: 202-457-0200
Facsimile: 202-857-0550
URL: http://www.lawyers.com/washingtonartlaw

Ann M. Garfinkle

ASSOCIATE

Laura A. Possessky

OF COUNSEL

Austin P. Frum (Retired)

For full biographical listings, see the Martindale-Hubbell Law Directory

THE LEWIS LAW FIRM A PROFESSIONAL CORPORATION (AV)

805 15th Street, N.W. Suite 200, 20005
Telephone: 202-408-0655
Fax: 202-408-9826
URL: http://www.lewislawfirm.com
Fairfax, Virginia Office: Suite 100, 10306 Eaton Place.
Telephone: 703-691-8686.
Rockville, Maryland Office: Suite 402, 11921 Rockville Pike, 20852.

Glenn C. Lewis

Wendy Helene Schwartz
Leslie Weber Hoffman (Resident, Fairfax, Virginia Office)
Daniel G. Dannenbaum
Keira Lynne Schwartz
Robin L. Robb
Gregory R. Nugent
Jeffrey Howard Skatoff
David B. Kauffman
David H. Spratt
Catherine M. Reese
Barbara E. Sosnick
Aresh Homayoun (Not admitted in DC)
Amy L. Svatek (Not admitted in DC)

LEGAL SUPPORT PERSONNEL

Kim Ella Clarkson (Paralegal Coordinator)
Jacqueline Robinson (Paralegal)
Sherrie L. White (Paralegal)

For full biographical listings, see the Martindale-Hubbell Law Directory

RAVDIN & WOFFORD, A PROFESSIONAL CORPORATION (AV)

1700 K Street, N.W., Suite 650, 20006
Telephone: 202-429-5551
Fax: 202-429-5553
URL: http://www.lawyers.com/ravdin&wofford

Linda J. Ravdin
Cindy Lynn Wofford

Kelly J. Capps
Lisa N. Seltzer (Not admitted in DC)

For full biographical listings, see the Martindale-Hubbell Law Directory

FLORIDA

BOCA RATON, Palm Beach Co.

JOEL H. FELDMAN, P.A. (AV)

Suite 207, Tower D, Sanctuary Centre, 4800 North Federal Highway, 33431
Telephone: 561-392-4400
Fax: 561-392-1521
Email: jhf@gate.net *URL:* http://www.joelhfeldman.com

Joel H. Feldman

Adam B. Sklar

For full biographical listings, see the Martindale-Hubbell Law Directory

FURR AND COHEN, P.A. (AV)

Suite 412, 1499 W. Palmetto Park Road, 33486
Telephone: 561-395-0500
Broward: 954-421-0300
Fax: 561-338-7532
Email: thefirm@furrandcohenpa.com *URL:* http://www.furrandcohenpa.com

Robert C. Furr
Charles I. Cohen

Alvin S. Goldstein
Leslie Scott Osborne
Lisa J. Chaiklin Aflalo
Bradley Scott Shraiberg

OF COUNSEL

C. William Berger

For full biographical listings, see the Martindale-Hubbell Law Directory

HUNT, COOK, RIGGS, MEHR & MILLER, P.A. (AV)

2200 Corporate Boulevard, N.W. Suite 401, 33431
Telephone: 561-997-9223
Telecopier: 561-997-6224
Email: admin@huntcook.com *URL:* http://www.huntcook.com

Robert J. Hunt
Joseph R. Cook
David A. Riggs
Ryna E. Mehr
Lawrence J. Miller
Andrew M. Gross
Susan E. Greenberg

David A. Greene
Sonja Trom Eayrs
Benjamin A. Jablow
Holly M. O'Neill

OF COUNSEL

Andrea G. Alpern

For full biographical listings, see the Martindale-Hubbell Law Directory

WEISS & HANDLER, P.A. (AV)

Suite 218A, One Boca Place, 2255 Glades Road, 33431-7313
Telephone: 561-997-9995
Broward: 954-421-5101
Palm Beach: 561-734-8008
Telecopier: 561-997-5280
Email: weisshand@aol.com
West Palm Beach, Florida Office: 505 South Flagler Drive, Suite 1331, 33401.
Telephone: 561-655-3433.
New York, NY Office: 45 Rockefeller Plaza, Suite 1501.
Telephone: 212-332-2900.

Howard I. Weiss
Henry B. Handler

Manuel R. Comras
Donald Feldman
William M. Franz
David K. Friedman
Carol A. Kartagener
Allison L. Kay
Bruce A. Harris
Howard M. Rudolph (Resident, West Palm Beach Office)
Stacy E. Welt

OF COUNSEL

Malcolm L. Stein (Not admitted in FL)
Harry Winderman

For full biographical listings, see the Martindale-Hubbell Law Directory

*BRADENTON,** Manatee Co.

LARRY K. COLEMAN (AV)

The Riverview Center, Suite 100, 1111 Third Avenue West, 34205
Telephone: 941-747-1234
Fax: 941-747-1236
Email: lcoleman@gte.net

LEGAL SUPPORT PERSONNEL

Nancy A. Martin (Certified Legal Assistant)

For full biographical listings, see the Martindale-Hubbell Law Directory

EDWARD B. SOBEL (AV)

Suite 206, 4900 Manatee Avenue, West, 34209
Telephone: 941-746-1203
Fax: 941-746-2094
URL: http://www.lawyers.com/edwardbsobel

For full biographical listings, see the Martindale-Hubbell Law Directory

*CLEARWATER,** Pinellas Co.

BOYER AND SCHILTZ, P.A. (AV)

P.O. Box 10655, 34617-8655
Telephone: 727-733-2154
Fax: 727-734-0333
Email: wboyerpa@aol.com

(See Next Column)

BOYER AND SCHILTZ P.A., *Clearwater—Continued*

Wayne J. Boyer
Scott E. Schiltz

LEGAL SUPPORT PERSONNEL

Linda D. Abbott (Certified Legal Assistant)
Patricia A. Miller (Certified Legal Assistant)

For full biographical listings, see the Martindale-Hubbell Law Directory

ANN LOUGHRIDGE KERR (AV)

425 South Garden Avenue, 33756
Telephone: 727-443-6787
Fax: 727-442-1251
URL: http://www.lawyers.com/kerrlaw
Tampa, Florida Office: 601 East Twiggs Street, Suite 200.
Telephone: 813-229-7251.
Fax: 727-442-1251.

For full biographical listings, see the Martindale-Hubbell Law Directory

KOCH & HARRINGTON, P.A. (AV)

200 North Garden Avenue, Suite "A", 33755
Telephone: 727-446-6248
Fax: 727-446-9113
Email: kochharr@gte.net

Ky M. Koch
Jennifer C. Harrington

Juliann Karenko

LEGAL SUPPORT PERSONNEL

Karen Wendt

For full biographical listings, see the Martindale-Hubbell Law Directory

CORAL GABLES, Dade Co.

MERLIN & HERTZ, P.A. (AV)

95 Merrick Way, Suite 420, 33134-5310
Telephone: 305-448-1555
Facsimile: 305-448-5337
Email: rmerlin@merlinlaw.com *URL:* http://www.lawyers.com/merlin&hertz

Robert J. Merlin
Christy L. Hertz

For full biographical listings, see the Martindale-Hubbell Law Directory

*FORT LAUDERDALE,** Broward Co.

AMLONG & AMLONG, P.A. (AV)

Second Floor, 500 Northeast Fourth Street, 33301-1154
Telephone: 954-462-1983
Fax: 954-523-3192

Karen Coolman Amlong
William R. Amlong

Judith M. Alexander
Randall Lane Bloom
Alain E. Boileau
Jennifer E. Daley

For full biographical listings, see the Martindale-Hubbell Law Directory

LAW OFFICES OF BRAVERMAN AND ROSSI, P.A. (AV)

625 Northeast Third Avenue, 33304
Telephone: 954-524-0505
Telefax: 954-527-4805
Email: Braver1@aol.com *URL:* http://www.BravermanRossi.com

Alan Jay Braverman
Steve Rossi

Michael A. Hymowitz
Bennett Braverman

OF COUNSEL

Robert L. Bogen
Steven F. Squire

Reference: SunTrust.

For full biographical listings, see the Martindale-Hubbell Law Directory

GORDON C. BRYDGER, P.A. (AV)

600 South Andrews Avenue, Suite 601, 33301-2802
Telephone: 954-527-2855
Fax: 954-527-4166
URL: http://www.lawyers.com/gordonbrydgerpa

Gordon C. Brydger

Carin Marie Porras

For full biographical listings, see the Martindale-Hubbell Law Directory

SHELLEY M. MITCHELL (AV)

Suite 103, 212 S.E. 8th Street, 33316
Telephone: 954-523-8311
Fax: 954-523-4707

For full biographical listings, see the Martindale-Hubbell Law Directory

RAAB & RAAB (AV)

621 South Federal Highway, Suite 2, 33301
Telephone: 954-523-7877
Fax: 954-523-9691
Email: raab-raab@juno.com *URL:* http://www.divorcesource.com/FL/DS/raab&raab.html

Howard Raab
Ariel Raab

For full biographical listings, see the Martindale-Hubbell Law Directory

*FORT MYERS,** Lee Co.

SHELDON E. FINMAN, P.A. (AV)

2215 First Street, P.O. Drawer 1380, 33902-1380
Telephone: 941-332-4543
Email: sfinman@ibm.net

Sheldon E. Finman

For full biographical listings, see the Martindale-Hubbell Law Directory

ROBERTS & ENGVALSON, P.A. (AV)

1920 Victoria Avenue, 33901
Telephone: 941-332-7273
Fax: 941-332-3320

Charles M. Roberts
Kinley I. Engvalson
Lori W. Clifford

LEGAL SUPPORT PERSONNEL

Carolyn Glover (Legal Assistant)

For full biographical listings, see the Martindale-Hubbell Law Directory

HOLLYWOOD, Broward Co.

STEVEN A. MASON, P.A. (AV)

3363 Sheridan Street, Suite 201, 33021
Telephone: 954-963-5900
Fax: 954-985-9811
Email: passat902@aol.com *URL:* http://www.lawyers.com/stevenmasonpa

Steven A. Mason

Representative Clients: T.S.I., Inc.; Southern Security Bank; Dental Centers of America.

For full biographical listings, see the Martindale-Hubbell Law Directory

*JACKSONVILLE,** Duval Co.

GLENN K. ALLEN A PROFESSIONAL ASSOCIATION (AV)

The Plaza Building, 353 East Forsyth Street, 32202-2822
Telephone: 904-355-7506
Facsimile: 904-353-8814
URL: http://www.glennallenpa.com
Email: GKA@glennallenpa.com *URL:* http://www.lawyers.com/glennallen

Glenn K. Allen

Jennifer Workinger Fites

For full biographical listings, see the Martindale-Hubbell Law Directory

COKER, MYERS, SCHICKEL, SORENSON, HIGGINBOTHAM & GREEN, P.A. (AV)

136 East Bay Street, P.O. Box 1860, 32201
Telephone: 904-356-6071
Fax: 904-353-2425

Howard C. Coker
M. Wayne Myers
John J. Schickel
Charles A. Sorenson
Wm. Earl Higginbotham
Samuel H. Lanier
J. Thomas McKeel
Mark M. Green
R. Daniel Noey
Ronald M. Owen
John Moffitt Howell
James H. Daniel
Richard R. Alexander

For full biographical listings, see the Martindale-Hubbell Law Directory

MAHON & FARLEY, P.A. (AV)

350 East Adams Street, 32202
Telephone: 904-354-4300
Fax: 904-354-4658

(See Next Column)

MAHON & FARLEY P.A.—*Continued*

Lacy Mahon (1891-1968) Harry B. Mahon
Joseph S. Farley, Jr.

References: First Guaranty Bank & Trust; Coastline Federal Credit Union.

For full biographical listings, see the Martindale-Hubbell Law Directory

WILLIAM C. A. MOULDER, P.A. (AV)

One San Jose Place, Suite 20, 32257
Telephone: 904-262-7600
Fax: 904-262-7608
Email: wcamlaw@mindspring.com *URL:* http://www.lawyers.com/moulderlaw

William C. A. Moulder

LEGAL SUPPORT PERSONNEL

Eloise Mullen (Legal Assistant) Jeanine D. Leone
Rebecca Pringle (Firm Administrator)
(Legal Secretary)
John Robert Leone (C.P.A./Tax Consultant in areas of Dissolution of Marriage)

References: First Guaranty Bank & Trust Company of Jacksonville; First Union Bank of Jacksonville.

For full biographical listings, see the Martindale-Hubbell Law Directory

RICHARD L. NICHOLS (AV)

3000 Hartley Road, Suite 5, 32257
Telephone: 904-886-7010
Fax: 904-886-7282

For full biographical listings, see the Martindale-Hubbell Law Directory

LAW OFFICE OF BARRY S. SINOFF, P.A. (AV)

6960 Bonneval Road, Suite 202, 32216-6076
Telephone: 904-296-2299
Telecopier: 904-296-8900
Email: bsinoff@bellsouth.net

Barry S. Sinoff

LEGAL SUPPORT PERSONNEL

Patricia J. Abraham (Paralegal)

For full biographical listings, see the Martindale-Hubbell Law Directory

LAKE ALFRED, Polk Co.

SMITH AND HAMM, P.A. (AV)

170 East Haines Boulevard, P.O. Box 1145, 33850
Telephone: 941-956-1119
Fax: 941-956-3905

Douglas H. Smith William C. Hamm, Jr.
Victor Smith

LAKE PARK, Palm Beach Co.

MARTIN L. HAINES, III CHARTERED (AV)

501 North Federal Highway, 33403
Telephone: 561-863-5400
Fax: 561-863-3420
Mailing Address: P.O. Box 14790, North Palm Beach, FL, 33408
Email: mlhaines@bellsouth.net

Martin L. Haines, III

Rosemarie W. Guerini Jeffrey S. D'Amore

Approved Attorney for: Lawyers Title Guaranty Fund.

For full biographical listings, see the Martindale-Hubbell Law Directory

LAKE WORTH, Palm Beach Co.

RENICK, SINGER AND KAMBER (AV)

1530 North Federal Highway, 33460
Telephone: 561-582-6644
Fax: 561-533-7975

Kenneth H. Renick Leonard I. Singer
Cathy L. Kamber

*MIAMI,** Dade Co.

LAW OFFICES OF ELIZABETH S. BAKER, P.A. (AV)

601 Brickell Key Drive, Suite 801, 33131-2649
Telephone: 305-373-7077
Facsimile: 305-373-7078
Email: bakeresq@bellsouth.net

(See Next Column)

Elizabeth S. Baker

For full biographical listings, see the Martindale-Hubbell Law Directory

CARUANA AND LORENZEN, P.A. (AV)

1000 Courthouse Tower, 44 West Flagler Street, 33130
Telephone: 305-371-7972
Fax: 305-358-6907

Albert G. Caruana Dirk Lorenzen
Melissa Jill Jacobs

For full biographical listings, see the Martindale-Hubbell Law Directory

MARILYN J. W. CESARANO, P.A. (AV)

Suite 550, 999 Ponce de Leon Boulevard (Coral Gables), 33134
Telephone: 305-446-2020
Facsimile: 305-442-4371

Marilyn J. W. Cesarano

For full biographical listings, see the Martindale-Hubbell Law Directory

CYNTHIA L. GREENE, P.A. (AV)

9150 S.W. 87th Avenue, Suite 200, 33176
Telephone: 305-274-3848
Fax: 305-274-7630
Email: clgpa@aol.com *URL:* http://www.lawyers.com/clgpa

Cynthia L. Greene

Laura Davis Smith

For full biographical listings, see the Martindale-Hubbell Law Directory

HALL, DAVID AND JOSEPH, P.A. (AV)

Penthouse 1428 Brickell Avenue, P.O. Box 019113, 33131-9113
Telephone: 305-374-5030
Fax: 305-374-5033

Andrew C. Hall Christopher M. David
Allan A. Joseph

Adam S. Hall Ilene Schnall
Michael L Cotzen Santiago A. Cueto
Kimberly S. Rogers

For full biographical listings, see the Martindale-Hubbell Law Directory

ANDREW M. LEINOFF & ASSOCIATES, P.A. (AV)

Suite 206, 1500 San Remo Avenue (Coral Gables), 33146
Telephone: 305-661-1556
Fax: 305-665-2555
Email: amlfamatt@aol.com

Andrew M. Leinoff

Natalie Scharf Lemos Seth E. Schneiderman

For full biographical listings, see the Martindale-Hubbell Law Directory

*ORLANDO,** Orange Co.

BARNETT, BARCLAY & SPRINGMANN, P.A. (AV)

501 Mariposa Street, P.O. Box 1667, 32802
Telephone: 407-425-4245
Telecopier: 407-423-4332
Email: barnettlaw@mpinet.net *URL:* http://www.lawyers.com/bbslaw

William B. Barnett Bert W. Barclay
Henry B. Rothblatt (1916-1985) Franz F. Springmann

For full biographical listings, see the Martindale-Hubbell Law Directory

JAMES M. CAMPBELL (AV)

111 North Orange Avenue, Suite 700, 32801
Telephone: 407-841-9860
Fax: 407-843-3738
Email: JMC47@aol.com

ASSOCIATE

Elizabeth Renee Joy

Reference: Citrus Bank.

For full biographical listings, see the Martindale-Hubbell Law Directory

JEFF B. CLARK, P.A. (AV)

Bank of Central Florida Building, 105 East Robinson Street, Suite 300, 32801
Telephone: 407-422-0516
Fax: 407-872-8683
Mailing Address: P.O. Box 1949, 32802-1949
Email: jbclark@gdi.net

(See Next Column)

JEFF B. CLARK, P.A., *Orlando—Continued*

Jeff B. Clark

Representative Clients: Regal Marine Industries, Inc.; Florida Citrus Sports Association, Inc.
Reference: Bank of Central Florida/Orlando.

For full biographical listings, see the Martindale-Hubbell Law Directory

LAW FIRM OF STANTON L. COBB, P.A. (AV)

3319 Maguire Boulevard, Suite 120, 32803
Telephone: 407-895-6966
Fax: 407-895-6955
Mailing Address: P.O. Box 149223, 32814-9223
Email: stancobb@flfamilylaw.com

Stanton L. Cobb

For full biographical listings, see the Martindale-Hubbell Law Directory

PETER CUSHING (AV)

801 North Magnolia Avenue, Suite 318, 32803
Telephone: 407-841-4543
Fax: 407-841-1135
Email: Cushing12@aol.com *URL:* http://members.aol.com/Cushing12/MilitaryDivorce

For full biographical listings, see the Martindale-Hubbell Law Directory

J. CHENEY MASON, P.A. (AV)

Barnett Bank Center, 390 North Orange Avenue, Suite 2100, 32801
Telephone: 407-843-5785
Fax: 407-422-6858

J. Cheney Mason

For full biographical listings, see the Martindale-Hubbell Law Directory

KENNETH D. MORSE A PROFESSIONAL ASSOCIATION (AV)

390 North Orange Avenue, Suite 2100, 32801
Telephone: 407-422-2411
Fax: 407-422-2451
URL: http://www.morselaw.com
URL: http://www.lawyers.com/morselaw

Kenneth D. Morse

For full biographical listings, see the Martindale-Hubbell Law Directory

MICHAEL R. WALSH (AV)

326 North Fern Creek Avenue, 32803
Telephone: 407-896-9431
Fax: 407-898-2724
URL: http://www.lawyers.com/walshlaw

For full biographical listings, see the Martindale-Hubbell Law Directory

POMPANO BEACH, Broward Co.

HARRY D. DENNIS, JR. (AV)

1401 East Atlantic Boulevard, 33060
Telephone: 954-946-0360
Fax: 954-946-9382
Email: HDDJan@worldnet.att.net

For full biographical listings, see the Martindale-Hubbell Law Directory

*ST. AUGUSTINE,** St. Johns Co.

MILLER, SHINE & BRYAN, P.A. (AV)

97 Orange Street, P.O. Box 3376, 32085-3376
Telephone: 904-824-0484
Email: msbpa@aol.com

Joe C. Miller, II
Judith G. Shine
Linda Logan Bryan

For full biographical listings, see the Martindale-Hubbell Law Directory

ST. PETERSBURG, Pinellas Co.

RALEIGH –LEE– GREENE III (AV)

401 Fourth Street North, 33701
Telephone: 727-821-2900
Fax: 727-822-7686

(See Next Column)

Raleigh "Lee" Greene III

*SANFORD,** Seminole Co.

HUTCHISON, MAMELE & COOVER, P.A. (AV)

Park-Fulton Building, 230 North Park Avenue, P.O. Box 1149, 32771
Telephone: 407-322-4051
Fax: 407-330-0966

William C. Hutchison, Jr. (1928-1991)
Richard L. Mamele
Stephen H. Coover

OF COUNSEL

Timothy R. Askew, Jr.

Representative Clients: Sun Trust; Seminole County Port Authority; Sanford Airport Authority.
Approved Attorneys for: Attorney's Title Insurance Fund, Inc.
Reference: Sun Trust, N.A.

For full biographical listings, see the Martindale-Hubbell Law Directory

STENSTROM, MCINTOSH, COLBERT, WHIGHAM & SIMMONS, P.A. (AV)

200 West First, Suite 22, P.O. Box 4848, 32772-4848
Telephone: 407-322-2171
Fax: 407-330-2379
Orlando/Winterpark Telephone: 407-834-5119
DeLand/DeBary Telephone: 407-668-1479
URL: http://www.stenstrom.com

Thomas E. Whigham (1952-1988)
Douglas Stenstrom (Retired)
William L. Colbert
Franklin C. Whigham
Clayton D. Simmons
Robert K. McIntosh
Donna L. Surratt-McIntosh
William E. Reischmann, Jr.

Catherine D. Reischmann
James J. Partlow
Dawn M. Harrison

OF COUNSEL

Kenneth W. McIntosh
S. Kirby Moncrief

Representative Clients: City of Sanford; City of Oviedo; City of Casselberry; Seminole Community College; City of Lake Mary; Sanford Housing Authority; City of DeBary; Seminole Soccer Club, Inc.; Tuskawilla Homeowners' Association; South Seminole-North Orange Wastewater Transmission Authority.

For full biographical listings, see the Martindale-Hubbell Law Directory

*SARASOTA,** Sarasota Co.

EDWARD B. SOBEL

(See Bradenton)

SHALIMAR, Okaloosa Co.

STEPHEN S. POCHE, P.A. (AV)

1270 North Eglin Parkway, Suite C-14, P.O. Box 130, 32579
Telephone: 850-651-4466
Fax: 850-651-3499
Email: ssp@emeraldcoast.com

Stephen S. Poche

Tonya C. Petermann

For full biographical listings, see the Martindale-Hubbell Law Directory

WEBSTER, BRANNON & BISORDI, P.A. (AV)

12 Old Ferry Road, P.O. Box 876, 32579
Telephone: 850-651-0354
Fax: 850-651-5958
Email: mtwlaw@cybertron.com *URL:* http://www.mtwlaw.com

Michael T. Webster
Curtis W. Brannon
Anthony C. Bisordi

LEGAL SUPPORT PERSONNEL

Pam Abney
Laura Cato (Legal Assistant)
Gay Parks (Legal Assistant)
Mayenda Gale (Legal Assistant)

For full biographical listings, see the Martindale-Hubbell Law Directory

*STUART,** Martin Co.

RUSSELL J. FERRARO, JR. AND ASSOCIATES, P.A. (AV)

3601 East Ocean Boulevard, Suite 201 (Sewall's Point), 34996-6737
Telephone: 561-221-0600
Fax: 561-220-0640
Email: rjfjrpa@bellsouth.net

Russell J. Ferraro, Jr.

(See Next Column)

RUSSELL J. FERRARO, JR. AND ASSOCIATES, P.A.—*Continued*

Jennifer C. Allen

LEGAL SUPPORT PERSONNEL

Dorthea M. Duncan (Certified Legal Assistant)

For full biographical listings, see the Martindale-Hubbell Law Directory

McCARTHY, SUMMERS, BOBKO, McKEY, WOOD & SAWYER, P.A. (AV)

2081 East Ocean Boulevard, Second Floor, 34996
Telephone: 561-286-1700
Fax: 561-283-1803
URL: http://www.mcsumm.com

Terence P. McCarthy
Robert P. Summers
Noel A. Bobko
John D. McKey, Jr.
Steven J. Wood
Thomas R. Sawyer
Nicola J. Boone
Steven L. Perry

Kathryn C. Bass
Robert N. Maitland, II

Representative Clients: First National Bank and Trust Company of the Treasure Coast; Hydratech Utilities; Lost Lake at Hobe Sound; Gary Player Design Group; YMCA of Martin County; Shadow Lakes Groves, Inc.; Merrill Lynch Trust Co., (Florida); Wilmington Trust, FSB; The Huntington National Bank, N.A.; WSTU-Radio, WTCN-TV.

For full biographical listings, see the Martindale-Hubbell Law Directory

*TALLAHASSEE,** Leon Co.

McFARLAIN, WILEY, CASSEDY & JONES, PROFESSIONAL ASSOCIATION (AV)

215 South Monroe Street, Suite 600, P.O. Box 2174, 32316-2174
Telephone: 850-222-2107
Telecopier: 850-222-8475
Email: firm@mcfarlain.com *URL:* http://www.mcfarlain.com

Richard C. McFarlain
William B. Wiley
Douglas P. Jones
Charles A. Stampelos
H. Darrell White, Jr.
Christopher Barkas
Harold R. Mardenborough, Jr.
Terrell C. Madigan

Robert A. McNeely
P. David Brannon

LEGAL SUPPORT PERSONNEL

Diane L. Doll (Office Manager)

For full biographical listings, see the Martindale-Hubbell Law Directory

*TAMPA,** Hillsborough Co.

ALLEN, DELL, FRANK & TRINKLE, P.A. (AV)

1240 Barnett Plaza, 101 East Kennedy Boulevard, P.O. Box 2111, 33601
Telephone: 813-223-5351
Telecopier: 813-229-6682

Stewart C. Eggert
Joseph G. Heyck, Jr.
Michael N. Brown
Marian P. McCulloch
Robert A. Mora
Benjamin G. Morris
A. Christopher Kasten, II
Richard A. Harrison
James S. Eggert
Donald W. Stanley, Jr.
John W. Wilcox
William L. Yanger
M. David Linton
Tabatha A. Liebert
J. Bert Grandoff

Tamlyn Sbar
Craig A. Jorgensen

OF COUNSEL

Ralph C. Dell

Representative Clients: Tampa International Airport; Bank of Tampa; Seminole Electric Cooperative Inc.; Tampa General Healthcare; Tampa Greyhound Track; Tampa Bay Water, A Regional Water Supply Authority.

For full biographical listings, see the Martindale-Hubbell Law Directory

RAYMOND A. ALLEY, JR., P.A. (AV)

805 West Azeele, 33606
Telephone: 813-251-8778
Fax: 813-254-3892
Email: ralleyjrpa@aol.com

Raymond A. Alley, Jr.
Donald L. Gilbert

LEGAL SUPPORT PERSONNEL

Cheryl A. Call

For full biographical listings, see the Martindale-Hubbell Law Directory

NANCY HUTCHESON HARRIS, P.A. (AV)

Barristers Building, 505 East Jackson Street, Suite 306, 33602
Telephone: 813-223-5421
Fax: 813-223-6127

Nancy Hutcheson Harris

For full biographical listings, see the Martindale-Hubbell Law Directory

ANN LOUGHRIDGE KERR (AV)

601 East Twiggs Street Suite 200, 33602
Telephone: 813-229-7251
Fax: 727-442-1251
URL: http://www.lawyers.com/kerrlaw
Clearwater, Florida Office: 425 South Garden Avenue.
Telephone: 727-443-6787.
Fax: 727-442-1251.

For full biographical listings, see the Martindale-Hubbell Law Directory

LEVINE, HIRSCH, SEGALL & BRENNAN, P.A. (AV)

First Union Center, 100 South Ashley Drive, Suite 1600, P.O. Box 3429, 33601-3429
Telephone: 813-229-6585
Telecopier: 813-229-7210
Email: lhsb@lhsblaw.com

Arnold D. Levine
Richard A. Hirsch
Stephen L. Segall
Edward M. Brennan

For full biographical listings, see the Martindale-Hubbell Law Directory

MANEY, DAMSKER & JONES, P.A. (AV)

606 Madison Street, P.O. Box 172009, 33672-0009
Telephone: 813-228-7371
Fax: 813-223-4846

David A. Maney

Lorena L. Kiely
Patricia F. Kuhlman

For full biographical listings, see the Martindale-Hubbell Law Directory

RICHARD G. PIPPINGER, P.A. (AV)

13907 North Dale Mabry Highway Suite 202, 33618
Telephone: 813-265-0301
Fax: 813-265-0831
Email: attyrgp@aol.com

Richard G. Pippinger

For full biographical listings, see the Martindale-Hubbell Law Directory

RONALD S. REED, P.A. (AV)

202 South Westland Avenue, 33606-1744
Telephone: 813-251-2162
Fax: 813-254-9046

Ronald S. Reed

For full biographical listings, see the Martindale-Hubbell Law Directory

SESSUMS, MASON & BLACK, P.A. (AV)

307 South Magnolia Avenue, 33606
Telephone: 813-251-9200
FAX: 813-254-6841

Stephen W. Sessums
Miriam E. Mason
Caroline Kapusta Black

Alexander Caballero

For full biographical listings, see the Martindale-Hubbell Law Directory

*VERO BEACH,** Indian River Co.

G. RUSSELL PETERSEN, P.A. (AV)

3339 Cardinal Drive, Suite 200, 32963
Telephone: 561-234-1501
Fax: 561-231-3923
Email: sunshine@gate.net

G. Russell Petersen

Representative Clients: General Motors Corp.; General Motors Acceptance Corp.; Royal Indemnity Co.; The St. Paul Seaboard Insurance Co.
Reference: Sun Bank of Indian River County; Southtrust Bank.

For full biographical listings, see the Martindale-Hubbell Law Directory

*WEST PALM BEACH,** Palm Beach Co.

FARISH, FARISH & ROMANI (AV)

316 Banyan Boulevard, P.O. Box 4118, 33402
Telephone: 561-659-3500
1-800-401-4LAW
Fax: 561-655-3158
Email: farish@bellsouth.net

MEMBERS OF FIRM

Joseph D. Farish (1892-1977) Joseph D. Farish, Jr.
Robert V. Romani

ASSOCIATES

S. Emory Rogers Peter M. Bassaline

LEGAL SUPPORT PERSONNEL

Ken P. Beelner

References: 1st Union Bank.

For full biographical listings, see the Martindale-Hubbell Law Directory

LEWIS KAPNER, P.A. (AV)

Suite 1402, One Clearlake Centre, 250 Australian Avenue South, P.O. Box 1428, 33402
Telephone: 561-655-3000
Delray/Ft. Lauderdale: 305-930-9191
Fax: 561-655-8899
Email: KAPNER1@aol.com
Boca Raton Office: 621 Northwest 53rd Street.
Telephone: 305-930-9191.

Lewis Kapner Victoria A. Calebrese
Michael C. Spain

For full biographical listings, see the Martindale-Hubbell Law Directory

KEITH H. PARK, P.A. (AV)

Suite 200, 2240 Palm Beach Lakes Boulevard, P.O. Box 3563, 33402
Telephone: 561-686-7711
Fax: 561-686-8021
Email: kparkpa@unidial.com

Keith H. Park

For full biographical listings, see the Martindale-Hubbell Law Directory

RONALD SALES, P.A. (AV)

1601 Forum Place Suite 906, 33401
Telephone: 561-688-6446
Fax: 561-697-1866

Ronald Sales

Reference: Palm Beach National Bank & Trust Co., Palm Beach, Florida.

For full biographical listings, see the Martindale-Hubbell Law Directory

SASSER, CESTERO & SASSER, P.A. (AV)

1800 Australian Avenue, South, Suite 203, P.O. Box 2907, 33402
Telephone: 561-689-4378
Fax: 561-689-4652
URL: http://www.sasserlaw.com

Donald J. Sasser Jorge M. Cestero

Reference: First Union National Bank of Florida.

For Complete List of Firm Personnel, See General Section

For full biographical listings, see the Martindale-Hubbell Law Directory

LAW OFFICES OF ROBERT M.W. SHALHOUB, P.A. (AV)

Suite 1107, One Clearlake Center, 250 Australian Avenue South, 33401
Telephone: 561-835-1102
FAX: 561-835-1777
Email: RMSHALHOUB@aol.com

Robert M. W. Shalhoub C. Debra Welch

For full biographical listings, see the Martindale-Hubbell Law Directory

MICHAEL P. WALSH, P.A. (AV)

501 South Flagler Drive, Suite 306, 33401-5911
Telephone: 561-659-3989
Fax: 561-659-3822
Email: MPWPA@aol.com *URL:* http://www.lawyers.com/michaelwalsh

Michael P. Walsh

For full biographical listings, see the Martindale-Hubbell Law Directory

JOEL M. WEISSMAN, P.A. (AV)

An Association of Professional Associations
515 North Flager Drive, Suite 1100, 33401
Telephone: 561-655-4655
Fax: 561-832-1421
Email: jmwlawyer@aol.com

Joel M. Weissman Doreen Yaffa

For full biographical listings, see the Martindale-Hubbell Law Directory

WINTER HAVEN, Polk Co.

PETERSON & MYERS, P.A. (AV)

Lake Region Plaza, 141 5th Street N.W., P.O. Drawer 7608, 33883-7608
Telephone: 941-294-3360
Lake Wales, Florida Office: 130 East Central Avenue, P.O. Box 1079.
Telephones: 941-676-7611; 683-8942.
Lakeland, Florida Office: 100 East Main Street, P.O. Box 24628.
Telephones: 941-683-6511; 676-6934.

M. David Alexander, III
Philip O. Allen
Jack P. Brandon
Kristen Marie Buzzanca
Debra Leigh Cline
J. Davis Connor
Dennis G. Corrick
Roy A. Craig, Jr.
Clinton A. Curtis
Jacob C. Dykxhoorn
Joseph A. Geary
Maria "Mia" Gerber
Jonn D. Hoppe
Dennis P. Johnson
Kevin C. Knowlton
Douglas A. Lockwood, III
Corneal B. Myers
E. Blake Paul
Robert E. Puterbaugh
Thomas B. Putnam, Jr.
Deborah A. Ruster
Stephen R. Senn
Andrea Teves Smith
Keith H. Wadsworth
Kerry M. Wilson

General Counsel for: SunTrust Bank Mid-Florida, N.A.; Lakeland Regional Medical Center, Inc.; Housing Finance Authority of Polk County.
Representative Clients: NationsBank, N.A.; First Union National Bank; Mutual Wholesale Co.; Ben Hill Griffin, Inc.; E. R. Jahna Industries, Inc.
Approved Attorneys for: Attorneys' Title Insurance Fund; Equitable Life Assurance Society of the United States.

For full biographical listings, see the Martindale-Hubbell Law Directory

WINTER PARK, Orange Co.

WENDY L. AIKIN, P.A. (AV)

288 Park Avenue North, 32789
Telephone: 407-644-4040
Fax: 407-644-4414
Email: aikinlaw@aol.com *URL:* http://www.lawyers.com/wendyaikin

Wendy L. Aikin

OF COUNSEL

Donald N. Crowell Brenda Lee London

For full biographical listings, see the Martindale-Hubbell Law Directory

GEORGIA

*ATLANTA,** Fulton Co.

LAWRENCE A. COOPER (AV)

Resurgens Plaza, Suite 1770 945 East Paces Ferry Road, 30326
Telephone: 404-814-0000
Fax: 404-816-8900
Email: lacooperaty@mindspring.com *URL:* http://www.lawyers.com/lacooperaty

For full biographical listings, see the Martindale-Hubbell Law Directory

DILLARD & GALLOWAY, LLC (AV)

1500 Monarch Plaza, 3414 Peachtree Road, NE, 30326
Telephone: 404-965-3680
Telecopier: 404-965-3670

MEMBERS OF FIRM

G. Douglas Dillard Andrea Cantrell Jones
William Woodson Galloway W. Trav Carter

For full biographical listings, see the Martindale-Hubbell Law Directory

GRAY & GILLILAND, P.C. (AV)

400 Perimeter Center Terrace, Suite 1050, 30346-1239
Telephone: 770-392-4800
Telecopy: 770-392-4808

John C. Gray
T. Cullen Gilliland
Charles A. Ratz
Melissa A. Garrett
T. Jeffery Lehman
Robert W. Browning

(See Next Column)

GRAY & GILLILAND P.C.—*Continued*

P. Steven Kratsch
OF COUNSEL
E. Reid Garrett
David S. Currie
Mark B. Bullman

For full biographical listings, see the Martindale-Hubbell Law Directory

HOFFMAN & FOWLER, LLP (AV)

A Partnership of Professional Corporations
5040 Roswell Road, N.E. Suite 250, 30342
Telephone: 404-256-6464
Fax: 404-256-1422

MEMBERS OF FIRM
Clifford G. Hoffman (P.C.)
Michael C. Fowler (P.C.)
LEGAL SUPPORT PERSONNEL
Penny J. Farr (Paralegal)

For full biographical listings, see the Martindale-Hubbell Law Directory

KESSLER & SCHWARZ, P.C. (AV)

Centennial Tower, Suite 3500, 101 Marietta Street, 30303
Telephone: 404-688-8810
Fax: 404-681-2205
Email: mail@kesslerschwarz.com *URL:* http://www.kesslerschwarz.com

Randall M. Kessler
Barry P. Schwarz

Monica Ann Toback
Marvin L. Solomiany
PARALEGALS
Nancy B. Miller
Mako Goss
Stacy Horton Smith

For full biographical listings, see the Martindale-Hubbell Law Directory

LONG ALDRIDGE & NORMAN LLP (AV)

A Limited Liability Partnership including Professional Corporations
Suite 5300, 303 Peachtree Street, 30308
Telephone: 404-527-4000
Telecopier: 404-527-4198
Email: atlanta@lanlaw.com *URL:* http://www.lanlaw.com
Washington, D.C. Office: Suite 600, 701 Pennsylvania Avenue, N.W., 20004.
Telephone: 202-624-1200.
FAX: 202-624-1298.

MEMBERS OF FIRM
Deborah S. Ebel
Steven J. Labovitz

For Complete List of Firm Personnel, See General Section

For full biographical listings, see the Martindale-Hubbell Law Directory

PIERCE & YOUNG (AV)

Building 1700, 2255 Cumberland Parkway Northwest, 30339-4575
Telephone: 770-435-0500
Telecopier: 770-435-0362

MEMBERS OF FIRM
J. Wayne Pierce
Richard M. Young
Christy A. Dunkelberger

For full biographical listings, see the Martindale-Hubbell Law Directory

STERN & EDLIN, P.C. (AV)

225 West Wieuca Road, N.E., 30342
Telephone: 404-256-0010
Fax: 404-851-9081
Email: stern-edlin.com

George S. Stern (Partner)
Janis Y. Dickman (Partner)
Shiel G. Edlin (Partner)
Carla F. Stern (Partner)

Heidi Geiger (Senior Associate)
William J. Piercy

Reference: NationsBank.

For full biographical listings, see the Martindale-Hubbell Law Directory

LAW OFFICES OF PAMELA L. TREMAYNE (AV)

730 The Hurt Building, 50 Hurt Plaza, 30303
Telephone: 404-523-2800
Fax: 404-523-2806
URL: http://www.lawyers.com/tremayne

ASSOCIATE
Joseph B. Heimovics

Representative Clients: Fidelity National Bank, Commercial Credit; Peoples Financial Corp.; Probe Software Sciences, Ltd.; Probe U.S.A. Inc.

(See Next Column)

Approved Attorney for: Lawyers Title Insurance Corp.; Chicago Title Insurance.
Reference: Fidelity National Bank.

For full biographical listings, see the Martindale-Hubbell Law Directory

TURNER, TURNER & TURNER PROFESSIONAL CORPORATION (AV)

500 Century Springs East, 6100 Lake Forrest Drive, 30328
Telephone: 404-250-0946
Fax: 404-250-1360

Russell G. Turner, Sr. (1896-1981)
Jack P. Turner
Nelson Goss Turner
Gregory R. Miller

Stuart S. Gordan

Representative Clients: NationsBank.

For full biographical listings, see the Martindale-Hubbell Law Directory

WARNER, MAYOUE & BATES, P.C. (AV)

Riverwood 100 Building, Suite 2300 3350 Riverwood Parkway, 30339
Telephone: 770-951-2700
Facsimile: 770-951-2200
URL: http://www.wmb-law.com

C. Wilbur Warner, Jr.
Robert D. Boyd
John C. Mayoue
John Lind Collar, Jr.
Edward E. Bates, Jr.
Richard M. Nolen
Alvah O. Smith
Margaret R. Martin
R. Scott Berryman

Andree D. Delgado
Hope Celeste Barbian Allen
Pamela Jean Gray
Paul J. Coburn

For full biographical listings, see the Martindale-Hubbell Law Directory

*AUGUSTA,** Richmond Co.

RICHARD E. ALLEN (AV)

440 Greene Street, 30901
Telephone: 706-724-4466
Fax: 706-722-1677
Email: RALLENLAW@AOL.COM

For full biographical listings, see the Martindale-Hubbell Law Directory

SURRETT & COLEMAN, P.A. (AV)

901 Suntrust Bank Building, P.O. Box 1497, 30903
Telephone: 706-722-3301
Telecopier: 706-722-3318
Email: ecoleman@groupz.net

Carl J. Surrett
Edward J. Coleman, III

Representative Clients: Sears, Roebuck & Co.; American Home Assurance Co.; Great Southwest Fire Insurance Co.; Duke Buick, Inc.; American Southern Insurance Co.; Scottsdale Insurance Co.; Providence Washington Insurance Co.; Nautilus Insurance Co.

For full biographical listings, see the Martindale-Hubbell Law Directory

*CARROLLTON,** Carroll Co.

HEAD, HEAD & HEAD (AV)

516 Newnan Street, P.O. Box 508, 30117
Telephone: 770-832-9697
Fax: 770-834-1800

MEMBERS OF FIRM
Henry C. Head
James B. Head
David C. Head

For full biographical listings, see the Martindale-Hubbell Law Directory

*DECATUR,** De Kalb Co.

SIMMONS, WARREN, SZCZECKO & MCFEE, PROFESSIONAL ASSOCIATION (AV)

315 West Ponce de Leon Avenue, Suite 850, 30030
Telephone: 404-378-1711
Fax: 404-377-6101

M. T. Simmons, Jr.
Joseph Szczecko

For full biographical listings, see the Martindale-Hubbell Law Directory

*DOUGLASVILLE,** Douglas Co.

KENNETH W. KRONTZ, P.C. (AV)

8493 Campbellton Street, 30134
Telephone: 770-577-1500
Fax: 770-920-0059
Email: K1444@XXINET.COM

(See Next Column)

KENNETH W. KRONTZ, P.C., *Douglasville—Continued*

Kenneth W. Krontz

For full biographical listings, see the Martindale-Hubbell Law Directory

*GAINESVILLE,** Hall Co.

DAVID A. POWELL (AV)

604 Green Street, N.E., Suite 3, 30501
Telephone: 770-287-1300
Fax: 770-287-0033
Email: dapowell@earthlink.net

For full biographical listings, see the Martindale-Hubbell Law Directory

*JONESBORO,** Clayton Co.

JAMES J. MACIE (AV)

2212 Emerald Drive, 30236
Telephone: 770-478-4155
Fax: 770-471-2053
Email: jjmacie@aol.com
Atlanta, Georgia Office: 400 Colony Square, Suite 1940, 1201 Peachtree Street.
Telephone: 770-478-4155.
Fax: 770-471-2053.

For full biographical listings, see the Martindale-Hubbell Law Directory

*LAWRENCEVILLE,** Gwinnett Co.

ANDERSEN, DAVIDSON & TATE, P.C. (AV)

1505 Lakes Parkway, Suite 100, P.O. Box 2000, 30043
Telephone: 770-822-0900
Telecopier: 770-822-9680
Email: a-dt@mindspring.com

Thomas J. Andersen
Gerald Davidson, Jr.
Thomas T. Tate
Jeffrey R. Mahaffey
William M. Ray, II
Kathleen B. Guy
R. Bradley Carr

Tracey D. Mason
Michael J. Hay
Stephen J. Tyde, Jr.

OF COUNSEL

Ethel D. Andersen
Tanya Andrews Eades

References: Sun Trust Bank; The Bank of Gwinnett County; Chicago Title Insurance Co.; Title Insurance Company of Minnesota.

For full biographical listings, see the Martindale-Hubbell Law Directory

MICHAEL C. MURPHY (AV)

390 West Crogan Street Suite 301, 30045
Telephone: 770-682-5952
Fax: 770-682-5113
Email: michaelcmurphy@worldnet.att.net

For full biographical listings, see the Martindale-Hubbell Law Directory

*MACON,** Bibb Co.

STONE, KAPLAN & CHAPMAN, P.C. (AV)

701 Nottingham Drive, P.O. Box 56701, 31208-6701
Telephone: 912-741-0060
FAX: 912-741-7971
Email: stonelaw@cyberhighway.net

Kice H. Stone, Jr.
Lise S. Kaplan
Claire C. Chapman

Suzanne Rohrbeck

LEGAL SUPPORT PERSONNEL

Karen B. Jones (Paralegal)

Reference: Wachovia.

For full biographical listings, see the Martindale-Hubbell Law Directory

*MARIETTA,** Cobb Co.

BROWNING & TANKSLEY, LLP (AV)

Suite 225, 166 Anderson Street, 30060
Telephone: 770-424-1500
Fax: 770-424-1740

MEMBER OF FIRM

Thomas J. Browning

OF COUNSEL

George T. Smith

For full biographical listings, see the Martindale-Hubbell Law Directory

CUSTER & HILL, P.C. (AV)

324 Cherokee Street, P.O. Box 1224, 30061
Telephone: 770-429-8300
Fax: 770-429-8338
Email: custerhill@mindspring.com

Lawrence B. Custer
Douglas A. Hill

Vic Brown Hill

Reference: Nations Bank.

For full biographical listings, see the Martindale-Hubbell Law Directory

LAW OFFICES OF DEBBIE CROSBY PELEROSE, P.C. (AV)

707 Whitlock Avenue Suite D-29, 30064
Telephone: 770-794-0204
Facsimile: 770 794-9895
Email: lawpelerosepc@mindspring.com *URL:* http://www.lawyers.com/peleroselaw

Debbie C. Pelerose

Jennifer E. Jacobson

For full biographical listings, see the Martindale-Hubbell Law Directory

*MCDONOUGH,** Henry Co.

SMITH, WELCH & BRITTAIN (AV)

200 The Commerce Building, 235 Keys Ferry Street, P.O. Box 31, 30253
Telephone: 770-957-3937
Fax: 770-957-9165
Stockbridge, Georgia Office: 1239 Eagle's Landing Parkway.
Telephone: 770-389-4864.
Fax: 770-389-5157.

MEMBERS OF FIRM

Ernest M. Smith (1911-1992)
A. J. Welch, Jr.
J. Mark Brittain (Resident, Stockbridge Office)
E. Gilmore Maxwell

ASSOCIATES

Thomas Bruce McFarland
John P. Webb (Resident, Stockbridge Office)
Katharyne Clark Johnson
Tricia B. Smith
Bruce R. Vail

Representative Clients: Atlanta Motor Speedway, Inc.; Bellamy-Strickland Chevrolet, Inc.; Columbia/HCA Healthcare Corp.; Ceramic and Metal Coatings Corp.; Cities of Hampton, Locust Grove and Stockbridge; Georgia Farm Bureau Mutual Insurance; Killearn Properties, Inc. of Georgia; RSKCO, Inc.

For full biographical listings, see the Martindale-Hubbell Law Directory

*NEWNAN,** Coweta Co.

ROSENZWEIG, JONES & MACNABB, P.C. (AV)

32 South Court Square, P.O. Box 220, 30264
Telephone: 770-253-3282
Fax: 770-251-7262

George C. Rosenzweig
Sidney Pope Jones, Jr.
Joseph P. MacNabb

Douglas L. Dreyer
Jonathan W. Hickman

Approved Attorneys for: Lawyers Title Insurance Corp.; Chicago Title Insurance Co.

For Complete List of Firm Personnel, See General Section

For full biographical listings, see the Martindale-Hubbell Law Directory

*TIFTON,** Tift Co.

THOMAS H. PITTMAN (AV)

211 North Park Avenue, 31794
Telephone: 912-388-1222
Fax: 912-388-9222
Email: THPlwyr@SurfSouth.Com *URL:* http://www.lawyers.com/thomaspittmanlaw

For full biographical listings, see the Martindale-Hubbell Law Directory

*VALDOSTA,** Lowndes Co.

DODD AND DENNIS, P.C. (AV)

613 N. Patterson Street, P.O. Box 1066, 31603-1066
Telephone: 912-242-4470
Telefax: 912-245-7731
URL: http://www.lawyers.com/dodd&dennis
Email: doddlaw@mail.datasys.net *URL:* http://www.doddlaw.com

Roger J. Dodd
Sam D. Dennis

References: First Union Bank; First State Bank and Trust Co.; Park Avenue Bank.

(See Next Column)

DODD AND DENNIS P.C.—*Continued*

For full biographical listings, see the Martindale-Hubbell Law Directory

HAWAII

*HONOLULU,** Honolulu Co.

STIRLING & KLEINTOP (AV)

20th Floor, 1100 Alakea Street, 96813
Telephone: 808-524-5183
FAX: 808-528-0261
Email: S&K@hifamlaw.com

MEMBERS OF FIRM

Thomas L. Stirling, Jr.
Charles T. Kleintop (Managing Partner)

Steven L. Hartley
Dyan M. Medeiros
Renee M. Yoshimura

LEGAL SUPPORT PERSONNEL

Danette L. Okino
Deborah W. Huebler
Amelia Y. Dolim
Melinda K. Enos
Adelle Takaoka

For full biographical listings, see the Martindale-Hubbell Law Directory

TAKUSHI, FUNAKI, WONG & STONE ATTORNEYS AT LAW, A LAW CORPORATION (AV)

Suite 1400 Grosvenor Center, 733 Bishop Street, 96813
Telephone: 808-543-9800
Fax: 808-543-9869
Email: tfwf@pixi.com

Roy E. Takushi
James T. Funaki
Alfred M. K. Wong
Robert M. Ehrhorn, Jr.
Dickson C. H. Lee
Peter T. Stone
James N. H. Yee
Ann L. Kurihara
Jacqueline Kong
Elizabeth A. Kane

For full biographical listings, see the Martindale-Hubbell Law Directory

MICHAEL J. Y. WONG (AV)

2222 Central Pacific Plaza, 220 South King Street, 96813
Telephone: 808-536-1855
Fax: 808-536-1857

For full biographical listings, see the Martindale-Hubbell Law Directory

IDAHO

KETCHUM, Blaine Co.

KNEELAND, KORB, COLLIER & LEGG (AV)

Kneeland Professional Building, 128 Saddle Road, Suite 103, P.O. Box 249, 83340
Telephone: 208-726-9311
Telecopier: 208-726-4515
Email: kneeland@micron.net

MEMBERS OF FIRM

Robert Korb, III
Bruce J. Collier
Ann Legg
Michael Dorazio

OF COUNSEL

G.R. Kneeland

Reference: First Security Bank of Idaho, N. A.

For full biographical listings, see the Martindale-Hubbell Law Directory

ILLINOIS

*CHICAGO,** Cook Co.

ARONBERG GOLDGEHN DAVIS & GARMISA (AV)

Suite 3000 One IBM Plaza, 60611
Telephone: 312-828-9600
Telecopier: 312-828-9635
Email: agdglaw@aol.com
Schaumberg, Illinois Office: 1901 North Roselle Road, Suite 800, 60195.
Telephone: 847-985-4060.

(See Next Column)

MEMBER OF FIRM

Jay A. Frank

OF COUNSEL

Melvin A. Blum

ASSOCIATE

Elizabeth Olen Lazzara

For Complete List of Firm Personnel, See General Section

For full biographical listings, see the Martindale-Hubbell Law Directory

MARSHALL J. AUERBACH & ASSOCIATES, LTD. (AV)

180 North La Salle Street, Suite 2307, 60601
Telephone: 312-853-3300
Fax: 312-853-1043

Marshall J. Auerbach

Pamela J. Kuzniar

For full biographical listings, see the Martindale-Hubbell Law Directory

FORREST S. BAYARD (AV)

150 North Wacker Drive, Suite 2570, 60606
Telephone: 312-236-3828
Fax: 312-704-6746
Email: fsblaw@aol.com *URL:* http://www.lawyers.com/forrestsbayard

For full biographical listings, see the Martindale-Hubbell Law Directory

SUSAN CHRISTINE HADDAD (AV)

Suite 3600, Three First National Plaza, 60602
Telephone: 312-236-2298
FAX: 312-236-0089

For full biographical listings, see the Martindale-Hubbell Law Directory

KALCHEIM, SCHATZ & BERGER (AV)

A Partnership including Professional Corporations
161 North Clark Street, 28th Floor, 60601
Telephone: 312-782-3456
FAX: 312-782-8463
Lake Forest, Lake County, Illinois Office: 920 South Waukegan Road.
Telephone: 847-295-0550.
Fax: 847-295-0560.

MEMBERS OF FIRM

Michael W. Kalcheim (P.C.)
Barry A. Schatz (P.C.)
Michael J. Berger (P.C.)
David H. Levy (P.C.)
Michael S. Cohen
Mary J. Clark (Resident Partner-in-Charge, Lake Forest Office)
Andrew D. Eichner
Leon I. Finkel

Jason G. Adess
Jacalyn Birnbaum
Jennifer Cantrell
Julia K. Carpenter (Resident, Lake Forest Office)
Jack Ehrlich
Rhonda L. Kerns
David S. Kerpel (Resident, Lake Forest)
Debbie K. Lerner (Not admitted in IL)
David M. Goldman
Nanette A. McCarthy
Michael S. Sabath

For full biographical listings, see the Martindale-Hubbell Law Directory

LAKE, TOBACK & YAVITZ (AV)

A Partnership including a Professional Corporation
Chicago Title Tower, Suite 2200, 161 North Clark Street, 60601
Telephone: 312-726-7111
Fax: 312-726-2385

MEMBERS OF FIRM

Steven R. Lake
Alan Jay Toback
David B. Yavitz, Ltd.
Ross S. Levey
Sharon M. Warning
Karen P. O'Neill

For full biographical listings, see the Martindale-Hubbell Law Directory

MANDEL, LIPTON AND STEVENSON LIMITED (AV)

Suite 2900, 120 North La Salle Street, 60602
Telephone: 312-236-7080
Facsimile: 312-236-0781

Alfred R. Lipton
Leonard M. Malkin
R. Peter Carey
Henry A. Waller
Kathleen Roseborough
Richard A. Lifshitz
Terry Yale Feiertag
Uve R. Jerzy
Carolyn E. Winter
Leo G. Aubel

Andrés J. Gallegos
Jennifer R. Shapiro
Joan Comiskey

(See Next Column)

MANDEL, LIPTON AND STEVENSON LIMITED, *Chicago—Continued*

OF COUNSEL

Richard L. Mandel
Nicholas Stevenson

LEGAL SUPPORT PERSONNEL

Jacqueline Steffens (Paralegal)

References: Northern Trust Co.; American National Bank of Chicago; La Salle Bank FSB.

For full biographical listings, see the Martindale-Hubbell Law Directory

THE MINTON FIRM (AV)

Suite 1950, 222 North La Salle Street, 60601
Telephone: 312-641-2500
Fax: 312-641-6688
Suburban Office: 1600 Golf Road, Suite 1200, Rolling Meadows, Illinois.
Telephone: 847-981-8070.
Fax: 847-981-5006.

MEMBERS OF FIRM

Michael Harry Minton
James P. Powers

ASSOCIATE

Ann Marie Ahern

For full biographical listings, see the Martindale-Hubbell Law Directory

NOTTAGE AND WARD (AV)

Ten North Dearborn Street, Penthouse, 60602
Telephone: 312-332-2915
Fax: 312-332-3075

MEMBERS OF FIRM

Rosaire M. Nottage
Eunice Ward

ASSOCIATES

Richard Allen Wilson
Meighan Templin
Jennifer Schick

For full biographical listings, see the Martindale-Hubbell Law Directory

DAVID P. PASULKA & ASSOCIATES, P.C. (AV)

Three First National Plaza, 70 West Madison Street, Suite 650, 60602
Telephone: 312-236-9150
Fax: 312-236-9157

David P. Pasulka

Sally Ann Martin

For full biographical listings, see the Martindale-Hubbell Law Directory

RINELLA AND RINELLA, LTD. (AV)

Suite 3400, One North La Salle Street, 60602
Telephone: 312-236-5454
Fax: 312-236-6975
URL: http://www.lawyers.com/rinellaandrinella

Samuel A. Rinella (1906-1982)
Kathryn B. Rinella (1906-1991)
Bernard B. Rinella
Joseph G. Phelps
Walter J. Monco
Steven D. Gerage

Maricarol Lacy

For full biographical listings, see the Martindale-Hubbell Law Directory

SCHILLER, DU CANTO AND FLECK (AV)

200 North La Salle Street, Suite 2700, 60601
Telephone: 312-641-5560
Fax: 312-641-6361
Lake Forest, Illinois Office: Suite 300, 207 East Westminster Avenue.
Telephone: 847-615-8300.
Fax: 847-615-8284.
Wheaton, Illinois Office: 300 South County Farm Road, Suite A.
Telephone: 630-665-5800.
Fax: 630-665-6082.

MEMBERS OF FIRM

Joseph N. Du Canto
Donald C. Schiller
Charles J. Fleck
David H. Hopkins
Benjamin S. Mackoff
Arnold B. Stein
James B. O'Brien
Burton S. Hochberg
Carlton R. Marcyan (Resident, Wheaton Office)
Sarane Crowther Siewerth
Michael J. Cummins
Timothy M. Daw (Resident, Wheaton Office)
Harold G. Field (Resident, Wheaton Office)
Anita Bolaños

(See Next Column)

ASSOCIATES

Andrea K. Muchin
David A. King (Resident, Wheaton Office)
Karen Pinkert-Lieb
Daniel R. Stefani
Celia G. Gamrath
Eric L. Schulman
Stuart A. Reid (Resident, Lake Forest Office)
Paul H. Chanan
Mario R. Ventrelli
Jacqueline J. Torshen
Jennifer L. Dillon

OF COUNSEL

Sidney S. Schiller

For full biographical listings, see the Martindale-Hubbell Law Directory

SCHWARTZBERG, BARNETT & COHEN (AV)

55 West Monroe Street, 2400 Xerox Centre, 60603-5040
Telephone: 312-726-3555
Fax: 312-726-6299
Cable Address: "Justice"
Email: sb&c@twty.chi.il.us

MEMBERS OF FIRM

Ralph M. Schwartzberg (1939-1975)
Mark T. Barnett (1939-1970)
Hugh J. Schwartzberg
Benjamin H. Cohen

For full biographical listings, see the Martindale-Hubbell Law Directory

LAW OFFICES OF LESLIE L. VEON (AV)

Ten South La Salle Street, Suite 3320, 60603-1002
Telephone: 312-578-1721
Facsimile: 312-578-1743

ASSOCIATE

Christina M. Dardick

For full biographical listings, see the Martindale-Hubbell Law Directory

WILLIAM S. WIGODA, LTD. (AV)

19 South LaSalle Street, Suite 1500, 60603-1401
Telephone: 312-214-4200
Fax: 312-332-4629
Email: wwigoda@aol.com

William S. Wigoda

OF COUNSEL

Linda Jakubs
Paul Goodman
Lori S. Loeb

For full biographical listings, see the Martindale-Hubbell Law Directory

CRYSTAL LAKE, McHenry Co.

ZUKOWSKI, ROGERS, FLOOD & MCARDLE (AV)

50 Virginia Street, 60014-4126
Telephone: 815-459-2050
Facsimile: 815-459-9057
Email: zrfm@stans.com *URL:* http://www.zrfmlaw.com
Chicago, Illinois Office: 100 South Wacker Drive, Suite 1502.
Telephone: 312-407-7700.
Facsimile: 312-332-1901.

PARTNERS

H. David Rogers
Richard G. Flood
David W. McArdle
Jeannine A. Thoms
Stuart D. Gordon
Kevin J. O'Brien
Michael J. Chmiel
Kathleen Field Orr

ASSOCIATES

Melissa J. Cooney
Kelly A. Cahill
Michael J. Smoron
E. Regan Daniels Shepley
Michael S. Drella
Timothy P. Dwyer
Paul A. Zukowski
Tracey Anne Wertman
Jenette M Schwemler

OF COUNSEL

Timothy J. Curran
Francis S. Lorenz

For full biographical listings, see the Martindale-Hubbell Law Directory

*GENEVA,** Kane Co.

SCHAFFNER & VAN DER SNICK, P.C. (AV)

115 Campbell Street, P.O. Box 101, 60134-2733
Telephone: 630-232-8900
Fax: 630-232-8908

Harry Schaffner
J. Brick Van Der Snick

Christine V Carney
Brian E. Leach

For full biographical listings, see the Martindale-Hubbell Law Directory

LAKE FOREST, Lake Co.

SCHILLER, DU CANTO AND FLECK (AV)

Suite 300, 207 East Westminster Avenue, 60045-1857
Telephone: 847-615-8300
Fax: 847-615-8284
Chicago, Illinois Office: 200 North La Salle Street, Suite 2700.
Telephone: 312-641-5560.
Fax: 312-641-6361.
Wheaton, Illinois Office: 300 South County Farm Road, Suite A.
Telephone: 630-665-5800.
Fax: 630-665-6082.

RESIDENT PARTNERS

Charles J. Fleck — Michael J. Cummins

RESIDENT ASSOCIATE

Stuart A. Reid

For full biographical listings, see the Martindale-Hubbell Law Directory

PALOS HEIGHTS, Cook Co.

JAMES ANTHONY PALMISANO, LTD. (AV)

7000 West 127th Street, 60463
Telephone: 708-923-1220
URL: http://www.lawyers.com/jamesanthonypalmisanoltd

James A. Palmisano

For full biographical listings, see the Martindale-Hubbell Law Directory

*PEORIA,** Peoria Co.

WINGET & KANE (AV)

Commerce Bank Building, 416 Main Street, Suite 807, 61602
Telephone: 309-674-2310
Fax: 309-674-9722

MEMBERS OF FIRM

Walter W. Winget — James F. Kane

ASSOCIATE

Nicole V. Nemec

Representative Client: Davison-Fulton Ltd.
References: Commerce Bank.

For full biographical listings, see the Martindale-Hubbell Law Directory

*SPRINGFIELD,** Sangamon Co.

METNICK, CHERRY & FRAZIER (AV)

Second Floor, Myers Building, 1 West Old State Capitol Plaza, P.O. Box 12140, 62791
Telephone: 217-753-4242
Telefax: 217-753-4642
Email: SPRINGLAW@AOL.COM

MEMBERS OF FIRM

Michael B. Metnick — Diana N. Cherry

For full biographical listings, see the Martindale-Hubbell Law Directory

*WAUKEGAN,** Lake Co.

DIVER, GRACH, QUADE & MASINI (AV)

Bank of Waukegan Building, 111 North County Street, 60085
Telephone: 847-662-8611
FAX: 847-662-2960

MEMBERS OF FIRM

Clarence W. Diver (1883-1962)
Thomas W. Diver
Brian S. Grach
David R. Quade
Robert J. Masini
Sarah P. Lessman
David L. Hazan

Heidi J. Aavang
Donna-Jo Rodden Vorderstrasse
Paula Vincich Randall

A list of Representative Clients will be furnished upon request.
Reference: First Midwest Bank of Waukegan.

For full biographical listings, see the Martindale-Hubbell Law Directory

INDIANA

*COLUMBUS,** Bartholomew Co.

SHARPNACK, BIGLEY, DAVID & RUMPLE (AV)

321 Washington Street, P.O. Box 310, 47202-0310
Telephone: 812-372-1553
Fax: 812-372-1567
Email: sbdr@hsonline.net

(See Next Column)

MEMBERS OF FIRM

John A. Stroh — Joan Tupin Crites

For Complete List of Firm Personnel, See General Section

For full biographical listings, see the Martindale-Hubbell Law Directory

*FORT WAYNE,** Allen Co.

ROTHBERG & LOGAN (AV)

(Formerly, Rothberg, Gallmeyer, Fruechtenicht & Logan)
2100 National City Center, 110 West Berry Street, P.O. Box 11647, 46859-1647
Telephone: 219-422-9454
Telefax: 219-422-1622

MEMBERS OF FIRM

Thomas D. Logan — Anne Carney

Counsel for: Parkview Hospital; Cameron Memorial Community Hospital; Norwest Bank Indiana, N.A.; Parkview Health System; Azar's, Incorporated; Fort Wayne-Allen County Airport Authority; Fort Wayne Public Transportation Corporation; Avis Industrial Corp.; Farm Credit Services of Mid-America, ASA; Slater Fort Wayne Federal Credit Union.

For Complete List of Firm Personnel, See General Section

For full biographical listings, see the Martindale-Hubbell Law Directory

*INDIANAPOLIS,** Marion Co.

COHEN, GARELICK & GLAZIER, A PROFESSIONAL CORPORATION (AV)

Suite 800, Keystone Crossing Plaza, 8888 Keystone Crossing Boulevard, 46240
Telephone: 317-573-8888
Telecopier: 317-574-3855
Email: chuckindy@aol.com *URL:* http://www.indianapolislawyers.com

Samuel J. Mantel (1893-1978)
Thomas D. Mantel (Retired)
Charles A. Cohen
Robert A. Garelick
Steven J. Glazier
Sandra Lazarus Rothbaum
Steven M. Crell
Bradley H. Cohen
Jill Elizabeth Goldenberg

Bryan S. Redding

OF COUNSEL

Joseph J. Reiswerg — Richard L. Darst

Reference: NBD Bank.

For full biographical listings, see the Martindale-Hubbell Law Directory

MIROFF, CROSS & KLINEMAN (AV)

An Association, Not a Partnership
Suite 1000, Two Market Square Center, 251 East Ohio Street, 46204-2133
Telephone: 317-264-1040
Telecopier: 317-264-1039

Franklin I. Miroff
Nancy L. Cross
Monty K. Woolsey
Penny Robinson

OF COUNSEL

James M. Klineman
Stephen J. Klineman
Audrey K. Grossman
Susanne B. Jones

For full biographical listings, see the Martindale-Hubbell Law Directory

PHELPS & FARA (AV)

Indiana Bar Center, 230 East Ohio, Sixth Floor, 46204-2149
Telephone: 317-637-7575
Facsimile: 317-685-1106
Email: pandf@phelpsandfana.com

MEMBERS OF FIRM

Gale M. Phelps — Thomas A. Fara (Retired)

ASSOCIATES

Michael Cheerva — Melissa J. Avery

For full biographical listings, see the Martindale-Hubbell Law Directory

*NOBLESVILLE,** Hamilton Co.

CHURCH, CHURCH, HITTLE & ANTRIM (AV)

938 Conner Street, P.O. Box 10, 46061-0010
Telephone: 317-773-2190
Telecopier: 317-773-5320
Email: cchadoug@msn.com

MEMBERS OF FIRM

Douglas D. Church
Jack G. Hittle
J. Michael Antrim
Martin E. Risacher
Bruce M. Bittner
Brian J. Zaiger
Leslie Craig Henderzahs
Jordan D. Church

(See Next Column)

CHURCH, CHURCH, HITTLE & ANTRIM, *Noblesville—Continued*

OF COUNSEL

Manson E. Church

Representative Clients: Noblesville Schools; Westfield-Washington Schools; Community Bank; Metrobank; Towns of Westfield, Fishers and Pendleton; Reynolds Farm Equipment Co.; Weihe Engineering; Historic Railroad Multijurisdictional Port Authority.

For full biographical listings, see the Martindale-Hubbell Law Directory

IOWA

*COUNCIL BLUFFS,** Pottawattamie Co.

SHELDON GALLNER, P.C. (AV)

300 West Broadway, Suite 145, P.O. Box 1588, 51503
Telephone: 712-323-0999
Fax: 712-323-0814
URL: http://www.lawyers.com/gallnerlaw

Sheldon M. Gallner — Laura Laubenthal Pattermann

Eric C. Hanson

For full biographical listings, see the Martindale-Hubbell Law Directory

*IOWA CITY,** Johnson Co.

JOHNSTON, POTTERFIELD & NATHANSON, P.C. (AV)

1902 Broadway, P.O. Box 3400, 52244
Telephone: 319-354-1712
Fax: 319-354-7265
URL: http://www.lawyers.com/johnstonlaw
Cedar Rapids Office: 129 First Avenue, S.W., P.O. Box 74210.
Telephone: 319-366-1000.
Fax: 319-366-6973.
Waterloo Office: 1506 LaPorte Road, P.O. Box 2787.
Telephone: 319-235-3000.
Fax: 319-235-2108.

Joseph C. Johnston — Henry E. Nathanson
Amanda Potterfield — Cathy L. Fitzmaurice
David Burbidge

OF COUNSEL

Carl J. Goetz, Jr.

For full biographical listings, see the Martindale-Hubbell Law Directory

KANSAS

PRAIRIE VILLAGE, Johnson Co.

DAVID P. WOODBURY (AV)

Executive Building, Suite 125, 4121 West 83rd Street, 66208-5317
Telephone: 913-642-1144
Fax: 913-642-1175
Email: jayhawk@abanet.org

For full biographical listings, see the Martindale-Hubbell Law Directory

*TOPEKA,** Shawnee Co.

WRIGHT, HENSON, SOMERS, SEBELIUS, CLARK & BAKER, LLP (AV)

Commerce Bank Building, 100 Southeast Ninth Street, 2nd Floor, P.O. Box 3555, 66601-3555
Telephone: 785-232-2200
FAX: 785-232-3344
Email: wrighthenson@wrighthenson.com *URL:* http://www.wrighthenson.com

MEMBERS OF FIRM

Dale L. Somers — Evelyn Zabel Wilson

ASSOCIATE

John H. Hutton

For Complete List of Firm Personnel, See General Section

For full biographical listings, see the Martindale-Hubbell Law Directory

*WICHITA,** Sedgwick Co.

LAMBDIN, JOHNSON, HERLOCKER, SODERBERG & LAMBDIN, CHARTERED (AV)

830 North Main, P.O. Box 797, 67201-0797
Telephone: 316-265-3285
Fax: 316-265-1303

Donald E. Lambdin — Ann Gottberg Soderberg
David N. Johnson — Lucy L. Herlocker
Lisa L. Lambdin

Reference: Intrust Bank, NA.

For full biographical listings, see the Martindale-Hubbell Law Directory

KENTUCKY

COVINGTON, Kenton Co.

TALIAFERRO, MEHLING, SHIROONI & CARRAN (AV)

1005 Madison Avenue, P.O. Box 468, 41012-0468
Telephone: 606-291-9900
Fax: 606-291-3014

MEMBERS OF FIRM

Philip Taliaferro, III — Lucinda C. Shirooni
Christopher J. Mehling — Robert W. Carran

ASSOCIATES

Howard L. Tankersley — Jerome N. Epping, Jr.
Alice G. Keys — Michelle Snodgrass-Deimling

OF COUNSEL

Norbert J. Bischoff — F. Edward Worland, Jr.

For full biographical listings, see the Martindale-Hubbell Law Directory

*GLASGOW,** Barren Co.

HERBERT & HERBERT (AV)

135 North Public Square, P.O. Box 1000, 42141
Telephone: 502-651-9000
Fax: 502-651-3317
Email: h&hlaw@glasgow-ky.com

MEMBERS OF FIRM

H. Jefferson Herbert, Jr. — Betty Reece Herbert

ASSOCIATES

Brian K. Pack — Wesley W. Stephens

For full biographical listings, see the Martindale-Hubbell Law Directory

*LEXINGTON,** Fayette Co.

STOLL, KEENON & PARK, LLP (AV)

201 E. Main Street, Suite 1000, 40507-1380
Telephone: 606-231-3000
Telecopier: 606-253-1093; 606-253-1027
URL: http://www.skp.com
Frankfort, Kentucky Office: 307 Washington Street, 40601.
Telephone: 502-875-6220.
Telecopier: 502-875-6235.
Henderson, Kentucky Office: 201 C North Main Street, 42420-3103.
Telephone: 270-831-1900.
Telecopier: 270-827-4060.
Louisville, Kentucky Office: 400 West Market Street, Suite 2650, 40202-3377.
Telephone: 502-568-9100.
Telecopier: 502-568-5700.

MEMBER OF FIRM

Anita M. Britton

ASSOCIATES

Susan Beverly Jones — Crystal Lynn Osborne

For Complete List of Firm Personnel, See General Section

For full biographical listings, see the Martindale-Hubbell Law Directory

VIMONT & WILLS PLLC (AV)

Suite 300, 155 East Main Street, 40507-1317
Telephone: 606-252-2202
Telecopier: 606-259-2927
Email: vimont@lex.infi.net

Richard E. Vimont — Fred E. Fugazzi, Jr.

Richard A. Whitaker

For full biographical listings, see the Martindale-Hubbell Law Directory

*LOUISVILLE,** Jefferson Co.

Roth Foley Bryant & Cooper, PLLC (AV)

First Trust Centre, Suite 300S, 200 South Fifth Street, 40202-3236
Telephone: 502-569-7550
Fax: 502-540-0123
Email: RFBC.com

Irvin D. Foley
David M. Roth
David H. Cooper
Lisa Koch Bryant
K. Gail Russell
Christian L. Juckett

OF COUNSEL

James E. Fahey
David W. Gray

Representative Clients: Bank One, Kentucky, N.A.; Huntington National Bank; Commonwealth Bank & Trust Co.; Farm Credit Services of Mid-America; Century Indemnity Co.; Travelers Casualty and Insurance Co.; Tumbleweed, LLC; John R. Gains Thoroughbreds, LLC; ARM Financial Group, Inc.; Osborn Enterprises.

For full biographical listings, see the Martindale-Hubbell Law Directory

LOUISIANA

*MINDEN,** Webster Parish

James M. Johnson (AV)

105 Pearl Street, P.O. Box 1015, 71058-1015
Telephone: 318-377-4978
Toll Free: 877-827-4294
Fax: 318-377-9026

For full biographical listings, see the Martindale-Hubbell Law Directory

*MONROE,** Ouachita Parish

McLeod Verlander (AV)

A Partnership including Professional Law Corporations
1900 North 18th Street, Suite 610, P.O. Box 2270, 71207-2270
Telephone: 318-325-7000
Telecopier: 318-324-0580
Email: mv@mv-law.com *URL:* http://www.lawyers.com/mvlaw

MEMBERS OF FIRM

Robert P. McLeod (P.L.C.)
David E. Verlander, III (P.L.C.)

Rick W. Duplissey
Donald C. Douglas, Jr.
Laurie J. Burkett

For full biographical listings, see the Martindale-Hubbell Law Directory

*NEW ORLEANS,** Orleans Parish

Lowe, Stein, Hoffman, Allweiss & Hauver, L.L.P. (AV)

One Shell Square, 701 Poydras Street Suite 3600, 70139-7735
Telephone: 504-581-2450
Telecopier: 504-581-2461

MEMBERS OF FIRM

Robert C. Lowe
Mitchell J. Hoffman
Terence L. Hauver
Ellen Widen Kessler
Suzette Marie Smith
David M. Prados

Kermit L. Roux, III
Paula H. Lee
Stanley Dale Broome

For Complete List of Firm Personnel, See General Section

For full biographical listings, see the Martindale-Hubbell Law Directory

Edith H. Morris (AV)

1515 Poydras Street, Suite 1870, 70112
Telephone: 504-524-3781
Facsimile: 504-561-0228

Bernadette Rocco Lee
Suzanne Ecuyer Bayle

For full biographical listings, see the Martindale-Hubbell Law Directory

Moseley & Associates, A Professional Law Corporation (AV)

866 Camp Street, 70130
Telephone: 504-523-5220
Fax: 504-523-5225
Email: rockslaw@aol.com

(See Next Column)

Rockne L. Moseley
Janet M. Ahern

For full biographical listings, see the Martindale-Hubbell Law Directory

*SHREVEPORT,** Caddo Parish

Sockrider, Bolin, Anglin & Batte, A Professional Law Corporation (AV)

327 Crockett Street, 71101
Telephone: 318-221-5503
Fax: 318-221-3849

John R. Pleasant (1905-1983)
H. F. Sockrider, Jr.
James E. Bolin, Jr.
D. Rex Anglin
Gregory H. Batte

For full biographical listings, see the Martindale-Hubbell Law Directory

SLIDELL, St. Tammany Parish

Oster & Wegener, A P.L.C. (AV)

(Formerly Gauche, Wegener & Oster)
1344 Gause Boulevard West, P.O. Box 5747, 70469-5747
Telephone: 504-639-9000
Fax: 504-639-9096
Email: WEG10@communique.net

Edmund T. Wegener (1910-1982)
Raymond Gauche (1888-1983)
Robert J. Oster (1919-1995)
Edmund T. Wegener, Jr.

OF COUNSEL

Steven D. Peterson

LEGAL SUPPORT PERSONNEL

Darlene Eiermann Wegener (Paralegal)

Reference: Whitney National Bank of New Orleans.

For full biographical listings, see the Martindale-Hubbell Law Directory

MARYLAND

*ANNAPOLIS,** Anne Arundel Co.

Brassel & Baldwin, P.A. (AV)

112 West Street, 21401
Telephone: 410-216-7900
DC Metro: 301-261-2199
Fax: 410-974-6019
URL: http://www.brasselbaldwin.com
Baltimore, Maryland Office: The B & O Building, Suite 920. 2 North Charles Street, 21201-3754.
Telephone: 410-974-6000.
Fax: 410-385-2939.

Rignal W. Baldwin, Jr.
Jon W. Brassel

Jonathan P. Kagan
Mary Coale Baldwin
Alexander John May

OF COUNSEL

Richard T. Stansbury (Resident, Baltimore, Maryland Office)

For full biographical listings, see the Martindale-Hubbell Law Directory

Council, Baradel, Kosmerl & Nolan, P.A. (AV)

125 West Street, Fourth Floor, P.O. Box 2289, 21404-2289
Telephone: 410-268-6600
Baltimore: 410-269-6190
Washington, D.C.: 301-261-2247
FAX: 410-269-8409
Email: cbkn@cbknlaw.com

Ronald E. Council
Ronald A. Baradel
Wayne T. Kosmerl
James P. Nolan
William F. Flood, III
Kevin M. Schaeffer
Donna McCabe Schaeffer
Frederick C. Sussman

John Naumann Strange
Susan T. Ford
Edwin H. Staples, II
Susan Stobbart Shapiro

OF COUNSEL

George N. Manis
Nicholas Goldsborough

Representative Clients: Anne Arundel County; Annapolis Bank and Trust; Bank of Maryland; State Farm Mutual Automobile Insurance Co.; Annapolis Yacht Club; Annapolis Yacht Sales, Inc.

For full biographical listings, see the Martindale-Hubbell Law Directory

Annapolis—Continued

DALNEKOFF & MASON, P.A. (AV)

Suite 301 West Court Building, 2448 Holly Avenue, 21401-3177
Telephone: 410-841-6500; 266-0544
D.C.: 301-261-8671
Fax: 410-224-4135
Email: info@dalnekoffmason.com *URL:* http://www.dalnekoffmason.com
Affiliated with: Morgan and Hendrick, 317 Whitehead Street, Key West, Florida.
Telephone: 305-296-5676.

Carol S. Craig
Barry J. Dalnekoff
Mark E. Mason
Royal G. Shannonhouse, III
Nelson R. Stewart
Thomas J. Voigt

Erin D. Gable

OF COUNSEL

Leonard E. Moodispaw
Matthew S. Evans, Jr.

Reference: NationsBank, Annapolis, Maryland.

For full biographical listings, see the Martindale-Hubbell Law Directory

HYATT, PETERS & WEBER (AV)

1919 West Street, P.O. Box 6635, 21401
Telephone: 410-266-0626
Fax: 410-841-5065
Email: info@hyatt.hpwsb.com *URL:* http://www.hpwlaw.com

Alan J. Hyatt
Paula J. Peters
Paul J. Weber

ASSOCIATES

Sara H. Arthur
Sharon M. Grosfeld
Gregg M. Weinberg
Jonathan A. Hodgson
John L. Hill
Arlette K. Bright
Bruce F. Bright (Not admitted in MD)

OF COUNSEL

Steven G. Tyler

For full biographical listings, see the Martindale-Hubbell Law Directory

ROGER A. PERKINS (AV)

Suite 202, The Courtyards, 133 Defense Highway, 21401
Telephone: 410-266-3558
Baltimore: 410-841-6368
FAX: 410-841-6466
Email: roger@perkinslaw.com *URL:* http://www.lawyers.com/perkinslaw

For full biographical listings, see the Martindale-Hubbell Law Directory

*BALTIMORE,** (Independent City)

LAW OFFICES OF SALLY B. GOLD (AV)

Fidelity Building, 210 North Charles Street, Suite 1025, 21201
Telephone: 410-962-8343
Fax: 410-962-8319
Email: sgold@min.net

LEGAL SUPPORT PERSONNEL

Erin Devaney (Paralegal)
Tracey Jones (Paralegal)
Charmaine Sheeler (Paralegal)

For full biographical listings, see the Martindale-Hubbell Law Directory

LAW OFFICE OF JULIE ELLEN LANDAU (AV)

201 North Charles Street, 19th Floor, 21201
Telephone: 410-625-1100
Fax: 410-625-2174
Email: JLandau@Landaulaw.com

For full biographical listings, see the Martindale-Hubbell Law Directory

REDMOND, BURGIN & GUTIERREZ, P.A. (AV)

1301, The Fidelity Building, 210 North Charles Street, 21202
Telephone: 410-752-1555
Fax: 410-752-1064
URL: http://www.RBGLAW.com
Upper Marlboro, Maryland Office: 14746 Main Street.
Telephone: 301-952-1555.

Leonard C. Redmond, III
Harold L. Burgin

Bambi Glenn

For Complete List of Firm Personnel, See General Section

For full biographical listings, see the Martindale-Hubbell Law Directory

THOMAS & LIBOWITZ, P.A. (AV)

100 Light Street, Suite 1100, 21202-1053
Telephone: 410-752-2468
Fax: 410-752-2046; 752-2049; 752-0979
Email: thomasandlibowitz.com *URL:* http://www.thomasandlibowitz.com

Michael S. Libowitz
David P. Chaisson

Representative Clients: Sinclair Broadcast Group, Inc. (Television and Radio stations); Roy Kirby & Sons, Inc. (Contractor); First Mariner Bank; Scandia Manufacturing Co. Inc. (Defense Contractor); Atlantic Automotive Corp. t/a Heritgage Automotive Group; Candy Express Franchising, Inc.; Wire Spectrum Services (Contractors-Transmission Tower Sites); Acrodyne Communications, Inc.; Alexis Logic Corporation (Software Developers); Selnic Corporation (Electronis Distributors); Liberty Mutual Insurance Company.

For full biographical listings, see the Martindale-Hubbell Law Directory

VENABLE ATTORNEYS AT LAW VENABLE, BAETJER AND HOWARD, LLP (AV)

A Partnership including Professional Corporations
1800 Mercantile Bank & Trust Building, 2 Hopkins Plaza, 21201
Telephone: 410-244-7400
Fax: 410-244-7742
URL: http://www.venable.com
Washington, D.C. Office: Venable, Baetjer, Howard & Civiletti LLP, Suite 1000, 1201 New York Avenue, N.W.
Telephone: 202-962-4800.
Fax: 202-962-8300.
McLean, Virginia Office: Suite 400, 2010 Corporate Ridge.
Telephone: 703-760-1600.
Fax: 703-821-8949.
Rockville, Maryland Office: Suite 500, One Church Street, P. O. Box 1906.
Telephone: 301-217-5600.
Fax: 301-217-5617.
Towson, Maryland Office: 210 Allegheny Avenue, P. O. Box 5517.
Telephone: 410-494-6200.
Fax: 410-821-0147.

MEMBERS OF FIRM

John H. Zink, III (Resident, Towson, Maryland Office)
Paul T. Glasgow (Resident, Rockville, Maryland Office)
Craig E. Smith
Michael Schatzow (Also at Washington, D.C. Office)
Christopher R. Mellott
Mitchell Y. Mirviss
Michael W. Robinson (Resident, McLean, Virginia Office)
John A. McCauley
Vicki Margolis (Also at Washington, D.C. Office)

ASSOCIATES

Carla Draluck Craft (Resident, Washington, D.C. Office)
Patricia A. Malone (Resident, Towson, Maryland Office)

For Complete List of Firm Personnel, See General Section

For full biographical listings, see the Martindale-Hubbell Law Directory

*BEL AIR,** Harford Co.

BROWN, BROWN & BROWN, A PROFESSIONAL ASSOCIATION (AV)

200 South Main Street, 21014
Telephone: 410-838-5500
Baltimore: 410-879-2220
Fax: 410-893-0402

A. Freeborn Brown (1915-1998)
T. Carroll Brown
Augustus F. Brown
Albert J. A. Young

Harold Douglas Norton
Christopher R. vanRoden
David E. Carey

Attorneys for: Baltimore Gas & Electric Co.; Chesapeake & Potomac Telephone Co.; Aberdeen Proving Ground Federal Credit Union; First National Bank of Maryland; Bell Atlantic Mobile Systems; First Harbor Securities; Maryland Portable Concrete, Inc.
Approved Counsel for: The Chicago Title Insurance Co. of Maryland, Inc.

For full biographical listings, see the Martindale-Hubbell Law Directory

BETHESDA, Montgomery Co.

MOSS, STRICKLER & SACHITANO, P.A. (AV)

Suite 700 N, 4550 Montgomery Avenue, 20814
Telephone: 301-657-8805
Facsimile: 301-657-8815
Email: mss@mss-law.com

Stephen E. Moss
Scott Michael Strickler
Nancy A. Sachitano

Hadrian N. Hatfield
Jonathan J. Biedron
Aubrey L. Moss

(See Next Column)

MOSS, STRICKLER & SACHITANO P.A.—*Continued*

LEGAL ASSISTANTS

Tri Bostelman
Beverly Feldman
Marcie Laderman

For full biographical listings, see the Martindale-Hubbell Law Directory

PARADISO, DACK, TAUB & OLER, P.C. (AV)

3 Bethesda Metro Center Suite 645, 20814
Telephone: 301-986-7900
Fax: 301-986-4001
Vienna, Virginia Office: Suite 750, 8045 Leesburg Pike.
Telephone: 703-917-9030.
Fax: 703-917-9060.
Washington, D.C. Office: Sixth Floor, 1201 Connecticut Avenue, N.W.

Joseph C. Paradiso
Robin B. Taub
Leonard J. Dack
Carren S. Oler
Steven J. Gaba

For full biographical listings, see the Martindale-Hubbell Law Directory

*EASTON,** Talbot Co.

EWING, DIETZ, TURNER & KEHOE, PROFESSIONAL ASSOCIATION (AV)

16 South Washington Street, P.O. Box 1146, 21601
Telephone: 410-822-1988
Fax: 410-820-5053
URL: http://www.edtklaw.com

L. Clark Ewing (1919-1998)
John F. Hall
Philip E. L. Dietz, Jr.
Karen M. Kaludis
Christopher B. Kehoe
Stephen H. Kehoe

Sharon M. Shilling

OF COUNSEL

Henry P. Turner

References: The Talbot Bank of Easton, Maryland; St. Michaels Bank.

For full biographical listings, see the Martindale-Hubbell Law Directory

GAITHERSBURG, Montgomery Co.

BRODSKY, GREENBLATT & RENEHAN, CHARTERED (AV)

16061 Comprint Circle, 20877-1321
Telephone: 301-869-1700
Fax: 301-926-7844

Jackson Brodsky (Retired)
Jeffrey N. Greenblatt
Bryan Renehan

Brian K. Pearlstein
Ellen L. Lee

OF COUNSEL

John S. Weaver

LEGAL SUPPORT PERSONNEL

Nancy Devers (Paralegal)

Reference: First Union Bank.

For full biographical listings, see the Martindale-Hubbell Law Directory

GREENBELT, Prince Georges Co.

STANLEY S. PICKETT (AV)

Suite 414 Capital Office Park, 6411 Ivy Lane, 20770
Telephone: 301-513-0613
Fax: 301-513-0618
Email: lossp@intr.net

Stanley Sinclair Pickett

ASSOCIATES

Gordon J. Brumback
Stacy S. Pickett Trimble

LEGAL SUPPORT PERSONNEL

Vivian A. Wolfe (Paralegal)

Representative Clients: B.F. Saul Co.; McDonald and Eudy Printers, Inc.; Condominium Management, Inc.; Long & Foster Realtors; Mitron Systems Corp.; Glenanden Housing Authority; Community Associations, Inc.; Hagmer Management, Inc.; Quantum Management, Inc.

For full biographical listings, see the Martindale-Hubbell Law Directory

*LA PLATA,** Charles Co.

MUDD, MUDD & FITZGERALD, P.A. (AV)

106 St. Mary's Avenue, P.O. Box 310, 20646
Telephone: 301-934-9541
FAX: 301-934-8178

(See Next Column)

John F. Mudd (1885-1950)
Thomas F. Mudd
F. DeSales Mudd (1909-1972)
John F. Mudd
Stephen P. Fitzgerald

John E. Ray

Local Counsel for: County First Bank (La Plata); Potomac Electric Power Co.; The Hartford Insurance Group; Maryland Bank & Trust Co.; Chicago Title Insurance Co.; Peninsula Title Insurance Co.; Colonial Farm Credit Agric. Credit Assn.
Counsel for: Interstate General Corporation; SMO, Inc.

For full biographical listings, see the Martindale-Hubbell Law Directory

LAUREL, Prince Georges Co.

ALLEN J. KRUGER, P.A. (AV)

8381 Cherry Lane, 20707
Telephone: 301-953-7440
Fax: 301-953-7444

Allen J. Kruger

Elizabeth A. Proctor

For full biographical listings, see the Martindale-Hubbell Law Directory

*ROCKVILLE,** Montgomery Co.

JO BENSON FOGEL, P.A. (AV)

Georgetowne Park, 5900 Hubbard Drive, 20852
Telephone: 301-468-2288
FAX: 301-881-9074
Email: jfogelpa@aol.com *URL:* http://www.lawyers.com/jobensonfogellaw

Jo Benson Fogel

For full biographical listings, see the Martindale-Hubbell Law Directory

HASPEL & MEISELMAN, CHARTERED (AV)

77 South Washington Street Suite 200, 20850
Telephone: 301-424-8840
Fax: 301-424-0569
Email: lhaspel@aol.com *URL:* http://www.lawyers.com/mydivorce

Linda Haspel
Neal J. Meiselman
Gwendolen C. Lesh McLeod

Melissa Suzanne Polito
Diana Magazine Schobel

For full biographical listings, see the Martindale-Hubbell Law Directory

CHERYL LYNN HEPFER (AV)

220 North Adams Street, 20850
Telephone: 301-762-5500
Fax: 301-294-2270
Email: law@hepfer.com *URL:* http://www.lawyers.com/hepferlaw
Upper Marlboro, Maryland Office: 14346 Old Marlboro Pike.
Telephone: 301-627-7900.
Fax: 301-627-7905.

Geraldine Welikson Hess
Sharri B. Freedman

For full biographical listings, see the Martindale-Hubbell Law Directory

STEIN, SPERLING, BENNETT, DE JONG, DRISCOLL, GREENFEIG & METRO, P.C. (AV)

25 West Middle Lane, 20850-2204
Telephone: 301-340-2020; 800-435-5230
Telecopier: 301-340-8217
Email: lawfirm@steinsperling.com
Falls Church, Virginia Office: 6245 Leesburg Pike, Suite 140, 22044.
Telephone: 703-237-0500.
Telecopier: 703-534-2899.

David C. Driscoll, Jr.
Stuart S. Greenfeig
Paul T. Stein

Darcy A. Shoop

For Complete List of Firm Personnel, See General Section
For full biographical listings, see the Martindale-Hubbell Law Directory

*TOWSON,** Baltimore Co.

MUDD, HARRISON & BURCH (AV)

105 West Chesapeake Avenue, 300 Jefferson Building, 21204
Telephone: 410-828-1335
FAX: 410-828-1042
Email: mhb@mhblaw.com

(See Next Column)

MUDD, HARRISON & BURCH, *Towson—Continued*

MEMBERS OF FIRM

John E. Mudd
T. Rogers Harrison (1949-1995)
Richard C. Burch
Douglas W. Biser
H. Patrick Stringer, Jr.
Andrew Janquitto

James R. Andersen
Matthew Paul Lalumia
Nancy C. Hopkins

OF COUNSEL

Wm. T. Russell, Jr.

For full biographical listings, see the Martindale-Hubbell Law Directory

*UPPER MARLBORO,** Prince Georges Co.

KNIGHT, MANZI, NUSSBAUM & LAPLACA, P.C. (AV)

14440 Old Mill Road, 20772
Telephone: 301-952-0100
Annapolis/Baltimore: 410-792-3786
Fax: 301-952-0221

William E. Knight
Robert A. Manzi
Ronald M. Miller
William C. Brennan, Jr.
Harry J. Trainor, Jr.
Andrew W. Nussbaum
Raymond G. LaPlaca
John F. Shay, Jr.
Sheldon L. Gnatt
Daniel A. LaPlaca
Gail Borjeson Viens
Roger C. Thomas
Monica M. Haley-Pierson
Daniel F. Lynch III
Norman D. Rivera

Robert L. Lombardo
Amy B. Glaser
Brent M. Ahalt
Terry L. Bell

For full biographical listings, see the Martindale-Hubbell Law Directory

MASSACHUSETTS

*BOSTON,** Suffolk Co.

ATWOOD & CHERNY (AV)

Dexter House, 393 Commonwealth Avenue, 02115-1802
Telephone: 617-262-6400
Telecopier: 617-421-9482

Jacob M. Atwood
David E. Cherny

OF COUNSEL

Margaret F. McGovern

For full biographical listings, see the Martindale-Hubbell Law Directory

FRIEDMAN & ATHERTON (AV)

(Formerly Friedman, Atherton, King & Turner)
(Formerly Friedman, Atherton, Sisson & Kozol)
Exchange Place, 53 State Street, 02109-2803
Telephone: 617-227-5540
Telecopier: 617-523-1559

Lee M. Friedman (1897-1957)
Percy A. Atherton (1903-1940)
Frank L. Kozol (1927-1993)
Robert D. Kozol (1938-1999)

OF COUNSEL

Frank H. Shapiro

MEMBERS OF FIRM

Joel A. Kozol
Lee H. Kozol
William I. Cowin
Richard M. Zinner
Matthew S. Kozol
David M. Kozol

ASSOCIATES

Christine P. Deshler
Angela M. Kalivas
Janet Kenton-Walker
Olive E. Larson
David A. Rich
Meredith Anne Rosenthal
Herbert Weinberg

COUNSEL

Paul S. Alpert
Thomas C. Bailey
Michael P. Morizio

For full biographical listings, see the Martindale-Hubbell Law Directory

GELB & GELB LLP (AV)

20 Custom House Street, 02110
Telephone: 617-345-0010
Facsimile: 617-345-0009
Email: g&g@gelbgelb.com *URL:* http://www.gelbgelb.com

MEMBERS OF FIRM

Richard M. Gelb
Gail Kleven Gelb

(See Next Column)

Aaron J. Bullwinkel
Brian G. Cafferty

For full biographical listings, see the Martindale-Hubbell Law Directory

MENARD, MURPHY & WALSH LLP (AV)

One Financial Center, 02111
Telephone: 617-832-2500
Telecopier: 617-832-2550
Email: mmw@mmwlaw.com
Washington, D.C. Office: Farragut Park, 910 17th Street, NW, Suite 800, 20006.
Telephone: 202-293-3500.
Telecopier: 202-293-3596.

Arthur P. Menard
Paul J. Murphy
Joseph H. Walsh
John E. Coyne
John S. Leonard

COUNSEL

Theodore E. Daiber

ASSOCIATES

Kevin G. Mahoney
Kevin P. Sweeney
Robert S. Steinberg

For full biographical listings, see the Martindale-Hubbell Law Directory

PACKENHAM, SCHMIDT & FEDERICO, P.C. (AV)

Four Longfellow Place, 35th Floor, 02114-2832
Telephone: 617-742-6565
Fax: 617-742-0292

Richard D. Packenham
Mary H. Schmidt
Phyllis E. Federico

Jennifer Rivera-Ulwick
Nicole R. Manny

OF COUNSEL

W. Sanford Durland III

For full biographical listings, see the Martindale-Hubbell Law Directory

PRINCE, LOBEL & TYE LLP (AV)

585 Commercial Street, 02109-1024
Telephone: 617-367-2202
Fax: 617-523-0977

MEMBERS OF FIRM

Donald G. Tye
Nancy A. Freed

ASSOCIATES

Linda M. Medonis
Pasquale DeSantis
Kathryn Dowling Silveria

OF COUNSEL

Lenore Zug Lobel

For Complete List of Firm Personnel, See General Section

For full biographical listings, see the Martindale-Hubbell Law Directory

ROCHE, CARENS & DEGIACOMO, P.C. (AV)

99 High Street, 02110
Telephone: 617-457-4000
Facsimile: 617-482-3868
Email: firm@rcdpc.com *URL:* http://www.rcdpc.com
Woburn, Massachusetts Office: 600 Unicorn Park Drive.
Telephone: 781-933-5505.

James R. DeGiacomo
Joan P. Armstrong

Beth L. Powers

For Complete List of Firm Personnel, See General Section

For full biographical listings, see the Martindale-Hubbell Law Directory

TRAVERS & GARGAS, P.C. (AV)

75 Federal Street, 02110
Telephone: 617-423-3000
Facsimile: 617-423-5880
Email: travers@socialaw.com

Margaret S. Travers
Melanie J. Gargas

For full biographical listings, see the Martindale-Hubbell Law Directory

WITMER, KARP, WARNER & THUOTTE LLP (AV)

28 State Street, 02109
Telephone: 617-248-0550
Telefax: 617-248-0607
Email: wkwt@28state.com

(See Next Column)

WITMER, KARP, WARNER & THUOTTE LLP—*Continued*

Ronald A. Witmer
Eric H. Karp
Mark J. Warner
Robert W. Thuotte

ASSOCIATES

Elisabeth A. Pelletier
Daniel J. Dwyer
Melanie B. Jacobs
Laura W. Gal

For full biographical listings, see the Martindale-Hubbell Law Directory

*CAMBRIDGE,** Middlesex Co.

BENJAMIN & BENSON (AV)

Bulfinch Square, 43 Thorndike Street, 02141
Telephone: 617-577-1515
Fax: 617-577-0595
Email: rfbjb@aol.com

Roberta F. Benjamin
Jon Benson

ASSOCIATE

Phyllis K. Kolman

For full biographical listings, see the Martindale-Hubbell Law Directory

FITCHBURG, Worcester Co.

O'CONNOR AND RYAN, P.C. (AV)

61 Academy Street, 01420
Telephone: 978-345-4166
Fax: 978-343-8416

John M. O'Connor
Edward P. Ryan, Jr.

Eugene P. O'Donnell, Jr.

For full biographical listings, see the Martindale-Hubbell Law Directory

FRAMINGHAM, Middlesex Co.

HARGRAVES, KARB, WILCOX & GALVANI, LLP (AV)

The Corporate Center, 550 Cochituate Road, P.O. Box 966, 01701
Telephone: 508-620-0140
Fax: 508-875-7728
Email: Hargrave@ultranet.com *URL:* http://www.ultranet.com/~Hargrave

MEMBERS OF FIRM

Paul V. Galvani
William H. Mayer
William M. Pezzoni
Mark R. Haranas
Robert P. Jachowicz
Evans J. Carter

Charlene Denise Oliveira Cabral

OF COUNSEL

Victor H. Galvani
Brenda S. Steinberg

Counsel for: Framingham Cooperative Bank; Framingham Housing Authority; Wayland Housing Authority.
Local Counsel for: General Motors Corp. (Westwood, Mass.); Bose Corp.; Consolidated Rail Corp.; Kens Foods, Inc.; Framingham Ford.

For full biographical listings, see the Martindale-Hubbell Law Directory

FRANKLIN, Norfolk Co.

CATALDO LAW OFFICES, LLP (AV)

55 West Central Street, P.O. Box 435, 02038
Telephone: 508-528-2400
Fax: 508-520-0699

Paul A. Cataldo
Joseph P. Cataldo

ASSOCIATE

Cheryl A. Tracy

References: The Benjamin Franklin Savings Bank.

For full biographical listings, see the Martindale-Hubbell Law Directory

*PLYMOUTH,** Plymouth Co.

MILES AND MILES, A PROFESSIONAL ASSOCIATION (AV)

159 Samoset Street, 02360-4815
Telephone: 508-746-2660
Fax: 508-746-3838
Duxbury, Massachusetts Office: 907 Tremont Street, P.O. Box 1686, 02331-1686.
Telephone: 781-934-5474

Frankland W. L. Miles (1897-1974)
Frankland W. L. Miles, Jr.
John Grother Miles

For full biographical listings, see the Martindale-Hubbell Law Directory

MICHIGAN

*ANN ARBOR,** Washtenaw Co.

HOOPER, HATHAWAY, PRICE, BEUCHE & WALLACE (AV)

126 South Main Street, 48104
Telephone: 313-662-4426
Fax: 313-662-9559
Email: hhpbw@voyager.net

OF COUNSEL

James A. Evashevski

Representative Clients: Avfuel Corporation; Bank of Ann Arbor; Castrol North America; Chem-Trend Incorporated; Ervin Industries, Inc.; First Martin Corporation; Glacier Hills, Inc.; Prestolite Electric, Inc.; Southern States Cooperative; E.B. Eddy Forest Products, Ltd.

For Complete List of Firm Personnel, See General Section

For full biographical listings, see the Martindale-Hubbell Law Directory

JEAN LEDWITH KING (AV)

Suite 289, 255 East Liberty Street, 48104-2120
Telephone: 734-662-1334
Fax: 734-332-1042
Email: jking@ic.net

Reference: Comerica Bank.

For full biographical listings, see the Martindale-Hubbell Law Directory

NICHOLS, SACKS, SLANK & SWEET, A PROFESSIONAL CORPORATION (AV)

121 W. Washington Street, Suite 300, 48104
Telephone: 734-994-3000
Fax: 734-994-1557
Email: info@nsss.com *URL:* http://www.nsss.com

Margaret J. Nichols
Monika Holzer Sacks (Ms.)
Eileen J. Slank
Rebecca G. Sweet
Karen S. Sendelbach

References: Society Bank-Ann Arbor; Comerica Bank-Ann Arbor.

For full biographical listings, see the Martindale-Hubbell Law Directory

PEAR SPERLING EGGAN & MUSKOVITZ, P.C. (AV)

Domino's Farms, 24 Frank Lloyd Wright Drive, 48105
Telephone: 734-665-4441
Fax: 734-665-8788
Email: peare@dominos.com
Ypsilanti, Michigan Offices: 5 South Washington Street.
Telephone: 734-483-3626 and 2164 Bellevue at Washtenaw.
Telephone: 734-483-7177.

Edwin L. Pear
Andrew M. Eggan
Thomas E. Daniels
Paul R. Fransway
Francyne Stacey

Counsel For: Domino's Pizza, Inc.; Townsend and Bottum, Inc.; The Credit Bureau of Ypsilanti; Margolis Nursery, Inc.; Wiards Orchards.

For Complete List of Firm Personnel, See General Section

For full biographical listings, see the Martindale-Hubbell Law Directory

BATTLE CREEK, Calhoun Co.

KREIS, ENDERLE, CALLANDER & HUDGINS, A PROFESSIONAL CORPORATION (AV)

One West Michigan Avenue, 49017
Telephone: 616-966-3000
Facsimile: 616-966-3022
Email: kech@kech.com *URL:* http://www.kech.com
Kalamazoo, Michigan Office: One Moorsbridge, P.O. Box 4010, 49003-4010.
Telephone: 616-324-3000.
Fax: 616-324-3010.

Russell A. Kreis (Resident, Kalamazoo Office)
Jeffery S. Rubel (Resident, Kalamazoo Office)
James C. Boerigter (Resident, Kalamazoo Office)
Annette D. Nickel (Resident, Kalamazoo Office)

For Complete List of Firm Personnel, See General Section

For full biographical listings, see the Martindale-Hubbell Law Directory

BINGHAM FARMS, Oakland Co.

HARVEY I. HAUER, P.C. (AV)

30100 Telegraph Road, Suite 221, 48025
Telephone: 248-258-0800
Facsimile: 248-258-2750
URL: http://www.lawyers.com/harveyhauer

(See Next Column)

HARVEY I. HAUER, P.C., *Bingham Farms—Continued*

Harvey I. Hauer

Nicole J. Hauer

For full biographical listings, see the Martindale-Hubbell Law Directory

SHELDON G. LARKY (AV)

Suite 3350, 30600 Telegraph Road, 48025-4533
Telephone: 248-642-4660

For full biographical listings, see the Martindale-Hubbell Law Directory

BIRMINGHAM, Oakland Co.

BUTZEL LONG, A PROFESSIONAL CORPORATION (AV)

Suite 200, 32270 Telegraph Road, 48025
Telephone: 810-258-1616
Telecopier: 810-258-1439
Email: melnick@butzel.com *URL:* http://www.butzel.com
Detroit, Michigan Office: Suite 900, 150 West Jefferson.
Telephone: 313-225-7000.
Telecopier: 313-225-7080.
Okemos, Michigan Office: Suite 300, 2127 University Park Drive.
Telephone: 517-372-6622.
Telecopier: 517-372-6672.
Ann Arbor, Michigan Office: Suite 300, 350 South Main Street.
Telephone: 313-995-3110.
Telecopier: 313-995-1777.
Grosse Pointe Farms, Michigan Office: Suite 260, 21 Kercheval.
Telephone: 313-886-5446.
Telecopier: 313-886-2114.
Boca Raton, Florida Office: Suite 411, 1200 North Federal Highway.
Telephone: 561-368-2151.
Telecopier: 561-368-4668.
Palm Beach Gardens, Florida Office: Suite 227, 11382 Prosperity Farms Road.
Telephone: 561-625-4442.
Telecopier: 561-625-6901.
Naples, Florida Office: Suite 705, 801 Laurel Oak Drive.
Telephone: 941-597-4500.
Telecopier: 941-597-5623.

Edward D. Gold (Resident)
Frederick G. Buesser, III (Resident)
T. Gordon Scupholm II (Resident)

OF COUNSEL

David William Potts (Resident)

Patricia E. Nessel (Resident)
Estelle Lopez Kwartowitz (Resident)

For full biographical listings, see the Martindale-Hubbell Law Directory

HYMAN LIPPITT, P.C. (AV)

185 Oakland Avenue, Suite 300, 48009
Telephone: 248-646-8292
Facsimile: 248-646-8375
Email: hymalipp@tir.com

J. Leonard Hyman
Norman L. Lippitt
Douglas A. Hyman
Brian D. O'Keefe
H. Joel Newman
Nazli G. Sater
Kenneth F. Neuman
Terry S. Givens
Paul J. Fischer
John A. Sellers
Robert H. Lippitt
Roger L. Myers
Sally A. Rutledge
Joseph Pia
John P. Gonway
Leif K. Anderson
Jennifer S. Gold
Julie Lyons Kosovec
Dawn S. Spratley
Michael T. Price

For full biographical listings, see the Martindale-Hubbell Law Directory

MORGANROTH, MORGANROTH, JACKMAN & NYE, P.C. (AV)

Suite 410, 300 Park Street, 48009
Telephone: 248-594-4200
Telecopier: 248-594-4204
Email: fmmman1@aol.com *URL:* http://www.lawyers.com/morganrothlawfirm

Fred Morganroth
Janice Morganroth
Wade P. Jackman
Leslie M. Nye
Patricia A. Kasody-Coyle

For full biographical listings, see the Martindale-Hubbell Law Directory

BLOOMFIELD HILLS, Oakland Co.

ADKISON, NEED, GREEN & ALLEN (AV)

1533 North Woodward Avenue, Suite 210, 48304
Telephone: 248-540-7400
Fax: 248-540-7401
URL: http://www.adkisonneed.com

MEMBER OF FIRM

Kelly A. Allen

ASSOCIATE

Annette J. Benson

For Complete List of Firm Personnel, See General Section

For full biographical listings, see the Martindale-Hubbell Law Directory

BEIER HOWLETT, PROFESSIONAL CORPORATION (AV)

200 East Long Lake Road, Suite 110, 48304-2361
Telephone: 248-645-9400
Fax: 248-645-9344
URL: http://www.beierhowlett.com

James L. Howlett
Daniel C. Devine
Lawrence R. Ternan
Stephen W. Jones
Frank S. Galgan
Kenneth J. Sorensen
Thomas J. Trenta
Mark W. Hafeli
Timothy J. Currier
Mary T. Schmitt Smith
Joseph F. Yamin
John D. Staran
Phyllis Aiuto Zimmerman
P. Daniel Christ
Lauren M. Underwood

Elizabeth A. Barrett Bonner
Mary M. Kucharek
Richard A. Joslin, Jr.
Michael C. Gibbons
Jon M. Midtgard
Paul L. Nystrom
Genevieve Dwaihy Hopkins
Jeffrey S. Kragt

OF COUNSEL

Dean G. Beier
Robert G. Waddell
Catherine J. Hulbert
Thomas V. Trainer

For full biographical listings, see the Martindale-Hubbell Law Directory

BUESSER, BUESSER, BLACK, LYNCH, FRYHOFF & GRAHAM, P.C. (AV)

505 North Woodward Avenue, Suite 1000, 48304
Telephone: 248-642-7880
Telecopier: 248-642-9319
Email: jimw@buesserlaw.com *URL:* http://www.buesserlaw.com

Frederick G. Buesser, Jr. (1916-1993)
William R. Buesser
Michael J. Black
William O. Lynch
Timothy T. Fryhoff
Ronald F. Graham
L. James Wilson

Neil K. Disney
Ronald C. Paul
Diane M. Buettner

OF COUNSEL

Charles E. Blank
Susan E. Cohen

Representative Clients: Wayne County Medical Society; Frances P. Rhoades Memorial Foundation; Detroit Country Day School; Air-Way Manufacturing Co.; American States University Co.; Holiday Inns, Inc.; The Promus Companies Incorporated; Premo Pharmaceutical Co.; Citizens Insurance Co. of America; Michigan River Corp.

For full biographical listings, see the Martindale-Hubbell Law Directory

HENRY S. GORNBEIN (AV)

4190 Telegraph Road, Suite 3000, 48302
Telephone: 248-594-3444
Fax: 248-594-3222
URL: http://www.lawyers.com/henrygornbein
Email: henry@divorce-online.com *URL:* http://www.divorce-online.com
Reference: Comerica Bank, Farmington Hills, Michigan.

For full biographical listings, see the Martindale-Hubbell Law Directory

HARDIG PARSONS PEDERSEN & STOUT, PLLC (AV)

74 West Long Lake Road, Suite 203, 48304
Telephone: 248-642-3500
Facsimile: 248-645-1128
URL: http://www.hpplaw.com
Charlevoix, Michigan Office: 212 Bridge Street. 49720.
Telephone: 616-547-1200.
Pawleys Island, South Caroline Office: 216 Highway 17. P.O. Box 1607. 29585.
Telephone: 803-237-9121.
West Palm Beach, Florida Office: 1450 North Bridge Tower. 515 North Flagler. 33401.
Telephone: 561-833-1622.

(See Next Column)

HARDIG PARSONS PEDERSEN & STOUT PLLC—*Continued*

MEMBERS OF FIRM

Joseph L. Hardig, Jr.
Donald H. Parsons (Resident, Charlevoix Office)
Joseph L. Hardig, III
Edward C. Pedersen
Bradley S. Stout
John C. Benso (Not admitted in MI; Resident, Pawleys Island, South Carolina Office)

OF COUNSEL

John W. Henke
Patrick T. Barone
Gordon A. Snavely
Robert J. Cucco
Edward K. Pedersen, Jr.

For full biographical listings, see the Martindale-Hubbell Law Directory

HERTZ, SCHRAM & SARETSKY, P.C. (AV)

1760 South Telegraph Road, Suite 300, 48302
Telephone: 248-335-5000
Fax: 248-335-3346
Email: lawhss@aol.com *URL:* http://www.legalleaders.com

Bradley J. Schram
Howard Hertz
Gary M. Saretsky
Robert S. Hertzberg
Victor M. Norris
Steve J. Weiss
Robert Paul Geller
Walter J. Piszczatowski
Jeffrey A. Robbins
Mark L. Kowalsky

Dana A. Donohue
Miles D. Hart
Karen A. Gould
Paul K. Villarruel
Bradford T. Yaker
Michael F. Jacobson
Michael I. Zousmer
Brian Witus
Eva T. Cantarella
Eric Andrew Michaels

COUNSEL

Richard P. Zipser
Lisa M. Kavalhuna (Not admitted in MI)
James W. Burdick

OF COUNSEL

David L. Steinberg
Albert L. Holtz
Elmer L. Roller
Robert A. Canner
Harvey D. Geller (1928-1989)

For full biographical listings, see the Martindale-Hubbell Law Directory

MEYER, KIRK, SNYDER & SAFFORD, PLLC (AV)

Suite 100, 100 West Long Lake Road, 48304
Telephone: 248-647-5111
Telecopier: 248-647-6079
Email: mkss@michbar.org
Detroit, Michigan Office: 1400 Ford Building, 615 Griswold, 48226.
Telephone: 313-961-1261.

George E. Snyder
Boyd C. Farnam

Representative Clients: Available Upon Request.

For full biographical listings, see the Martindale-Hubbell Law Directory

*DETROIT,** Wayne Co.

ABBOTT, NICHOLSON, QUILTER, ESSHAKI & YOUNGBLOOD, P.C. (AV)

300 River Place, Suite 3000, 48207-4225
Telephone: 313-566-2500
Telecopier: 313-566-2502
Email: anqey@anqey.com *URL:* http://www.anqey.com

C. Richard Abbott
John R. Nicholson
Thomas R. Quilter III
Gene J. Esshaki
John F. Youngblood
James B. Perry
Carl F. Jarboe
Jay A. Kennedy
Timothy A. Stoepker
Timothy J. Kramer
Norbert T. Madison, Jr.
William D. Gilbride, Jr.
Mary P. Nelson
Michael R. Blum
Anne Warren Bagno
Thomas J. Giachino

Eric J. Girdler
Jill A. Bankey
Daniel G. Kielczewski
George P. Butler III
Christopher P. Baker

OF COUNSEL

Thomas C. Shumaker
Lisa R. Gorman

For full biographical listings, see the Martindale-Hubbell Law Directory

BEVERLY CLARK, P.C. (AV)

440 East Congress, Suite 4R, 48226-2917
Telephone: 313-961-4440
Fax: 313-961-5830
URL: http://www.lawyers.com/beverlyclark

Beverly Clark

For full biographical listings, see the Martindale-Hubbell Law Directory

JAFFE, RAITT, HEUER & WEISS, PROFESSIONAL CORPORATION (AV)

One Woodward Avenue, Suite 2400, 48226
Telephone: 313-961-8380
Telecopier: 313-961-8358
Cable Address: "Jafsni"
Southfield, Michigan Office: Travelers Tower, Suite 1520.
Telephone: 313-961-8380.

Joel S. Golden
Sharon J. LaDuke
Susan S. Lichterman

For Complete List of Firm Personnel, See General Section

For full biographical listings, see the Martindale-Hubbell Law Directory

MEYER, KIRK, SNYDER & SAFFORD, PLLC (AV)

1400 Ford Building, 615 Griswold, 48226
Telephone: 313-961-1261
Fax: 248-647-6079
Bloomfield Hills, Michigan Office: Suite 100, 100 West Long Lake Road.
Telephone: 248-647-5111.
Telecopier: 248-647-6079.

George H. Meyer
George E. Snyder
Boyd C. Farnam

Representative Clients: Available Upon Request.

For full biographical listings, see the Martindale-Hubbell Law Directory

PRATHER & ASSOCIATES, P.C. (AV)

3800 Penobscot Building, 48226-4220
Telephone: 313-962-7722
Facsimile: 313-962-2653

Kenneth E. Prather

For full biographical listings, see the Martindale-Hubbell Law Directory

WULFMEIER & OTTENWESS, PLC (AV)

The Buhl Building, 535 Griswold Suite 850, 48226
Telephone: 313-965-2121
Facsimile: 313-965-7680
Email: law@wulf-ott.com *URL:* http://www.wulf-ott.com
Ann Arbor Office: 320 N. Main Street, Suite 102, 48104.
Telephone: 734-761-1900.
Facsimile: 734-769-0433.

LeRoy H. Wulfmeier, III
David M. Ottenwess
Cheryl L. Chandler
Daniel J. Dulworth
John J. Moran
Stephanie L. Pappas

For full biographical listings, see the Martindale-Hubbell Law Directory

FARMINGTON HILLS, Oakland Co.

MICHAEL H. GOLOB (AV)

30300 Northwestern Highway, Suite 300, 48334
Telephone: 248-855-2626
Fax: 248-932-4009

For full biographical listings, see the Martindale-Hubbell Law Directory

FLAT ROCK, Wayne Co.

TUCHOW & TRAHEY (AV)

26316 Telegraph Road, 48134
Telephone: 734-782-2900
Fax: 734-782-2123
Bloomfield Hills, Michigan Office: Americenter of Bloomfield Hills, Seven West Square Lake Road.
Telephone: 313-963-7633.
Fax: 313-782-2123.

MEMBERS OF FIRM

Gerald Tuchow
Stephen J. Trahey

Reference: Old Kent Bank.

For full biographical listings, see the Martindale-Hubbell Law Directory

*GRAND RAPIDS,** Kent Co.

ROBERT B. RELPH (AV)

1303 McKay Tower, 49503
Telephone: 616-235-1300
Fax: 616-235-0113

For full biographical listings, see the Martindale-Hubbell Law Directory

ZERRENNER & ROANE (AV)

Grand Plaza Place, Suite 450, 220 Lyon Square, N.W., 49503
Telephone: 616-774-4414
Fax: 616-774-8203

(See Next Column)

ZERRENNER & ROANE, *Grand Rapids—Continued*

James W. Zerrenner | Richard A. Roane

For full biographical listings, see the Martindale-Hubbell Law Directory

GROSSE POINTE, Wayne Co.

JAMES ALLE (AV)

16824 Kercheval Place, Suite 201, 48230
Telephone: 313-882-0200
Facsimile: 313-882-6231

ASSOCIATE

Lynn M. Capp

For full biographical listings, see the Martindale-Hubbell Law Directory

HOLLAND, Ottawa Co.

CUNNINGHAM DALMAN, P.C. (AV)

321 Settlers Road, P.O. Box 1767, 49422-1767
Telephone: 616-392-1821
Fax: 616-392-4769
Email: cunndalm@crossover.net *URL:* http://www.holland-law.com

Gordon H. Cunningham
Ronald L. Dalman
Max R. Murphy
James A. Bidol
Andrew J. Mulder
Kenneth B. Breese
Jeffrey K. Helder
Ronald J. Vander Veen
David M. Zessin
Mark H. Zietlow
Randall S. Schipper
Susan E. Vroegop
Joel G. Bouwens

Gregory J. McCoy
Jason M. Milstone
Aaron Leal
Dawn J. Ward

Representative Clients: Huntington National Bank; First of America Bank-Holland, N.A.; Ameribank; City of Holland; Auto Club Insurance Assn. (AAA); American States Insurance Co.; Holland Economic Development Corp.; Hope College; Western Theological Seminary.
Reference: Huntington National Bank.

For full biographical listings, see the Martindale-Hubbell Law Directory

*KALAMAZOO,** Kalamazoo Co.

KREIS, ENDERLE, CALLANDER & HUDGINS, A PROFESSIONAL CORPORATION (AV)

One Moorsbridge, P.O. Box 4010, 49003-4010
Telephone: 616-324-3000
Facsimile: 616-324-3010
Email: kech@kech.com *URL:* http://www.kech.com
Battle Creek, Michigan Office: One West Michigan Avenue, 49017.
Telephone: 616-966-3000.
Fax: 616-966-3022.

Russell A. Kreis
Jeffery S. Rubel
James C. Boerigter
Annette D. Nickel

For Complete List of Firm Personnel, See General Section

For full biographical listings, see the Martindale-Hubbell Law Directory

LEWIS & ALLEN, P.C. (AV)

Old Kent Bank Building, Suite 800, 136 East Michigan Avenue, 49007-3946
Telephone: 616-388-7600
Fax: 616-349-3831

Dean S. Lewis
W. Fred Allen, Jr.
Barry R. Smith
William A. Redmond
Stephen M. Denenfeld
Anne McGregor Fries
Gregory G. St. Arnauld
James M. Marquardt
Christopher T. Haenicke
Winfield J. Hollander (1906-1996)

LEGAL SUPPORT PERSONNEL

Dorothy B. Kelly

For full biographical listings, see the Martindale-Hubbell Law Directory

*MIDLAND,** Midland Co.

CURRIE KENDALL POLASKY MEISEL, PLC (AV)

6024 Eastman Avenue, P.O. Box 2765, 48641-2765
Telephone: 517-839-0300
Fax: 517-832-0077
Saginaw, Michigan Office: 4800 Fashion Square Boulevard, Suite 100, 48603.
Telephone: 517-792-9300; 517-792-1111.
Fax: 517-792-7000; 517-793-6597.

(See Next Column)

Gilbert A. Currie (1882-1960)
Gilbert A. Currie (1923-1998)
Peter J. Kendall (1961-1999)
William C. Collins
Ramon F. Rolf, Jr.
Daniel J. Cline
Peter A. Poznak
Julia A. Close
Jeffrey N. Dyer
Jonathan E. Lauderbach
Amy E. Wilson
Cheryl L. Whitman
Todd M. Gambrell
Frank M. Polasky (Resident, Saginaw Office)
Robert H. Meisel (Resident, Saginaw Office)
Michael H. Allen (Resident, Saginaw Office)
Larry L. Preston (Resident, Saginaw Office)
David J. Kolat (Resident, Saginaw Office)
M. Randall Jurrens (Resident, Saginaw Office)
John E. Gannon (Resident, Saginaw Office)
Carolyn Pollock Cary (Resident, Saginaw Office)
John D. Jolley (Resident, Saginaw Office)
W. Jay Brown (Resident, Saginaw Office)

OF COUNSEL

James A. Kendall

Counsel for: Chemical Financial Corp.; Chemical Bank & Trust Co.; Saginaw Valley State University; Northwood University; The Midland Foundation; Elsa U. Pardee Foundation; Rollin M. Gerstacker Foundation; Charles J. Strosacker Foundation.

For full biographical listings, see the Martindale-Hubbell Law Directory

*SAGINAW,** Saginaw Co.

CURRIE KENDALL POLASKY MEISEL, PLC (AV)

4800 Fashion Square Boulevard, Suite 100, 48603
Telephone: 517-792-1111; 517-792-9300
Fax: 517-793-6597; 517-792-7000
Midland, Michigan Office: 6024 Eastman Avenue, P.O. Box, 2765.
Telephone: 517-839-0300.
Fax: 517-832-0077.

Frank M. Polasky
Robert H. Meisel
Michael H. Allen
Larry L. Preston
David J. Kolat
M. Randall Jurrens
John E. Gannon
Carolyn Pollock Cary
John D. Jolley
W. Jay Brown
William C. Collins (Resident, Midland Office)
Ramon F. Rolf, Jr. (Resident, Midland Office)
Daniel J. Cline (Resident, Midland Office)
Peter A. Poznak (Resident, Midland Office)
Julia A. Close (Resident, Midland Office)
Jeffrey N. Dyer (Resident, Midland Office)
Jonathan E. Lauderbach (Resident, Midland Office)
Amy E. Wilson (Resident, Midland Office)
Cheryl L. Whitman (Resident, Midland Office)
Todd M. Gambrell (Resident, Midland Office)

OF COUNSEL

James A. Kendall (Resident, Midland Office)

Counsel for: Chemical Financial Corp.; Chemical Bank & Trust Co.; Saginaw Valley State University; Northwood University; The Midland Foundation; Elsa U. Pardee Foundation; Rollin M. Gerstacker Foundation; Charles J. Strosacker Foundation.

For full biographical listings, see the Martindale-Hubbell Law Directory

SOUTHFIELD, Oakland Co.

SCHWARTZ & JALKANEN, P.C. (AV)

24400 Northwestern Highway, Suite 200, 48075-6821
Telephone: 248-352-2555
Facsimile: 248-352-5963

Melvin R. Schwartz
Arthur W. Jalkanen
Karl Eric Hannum

Gregory A. Light
David C. Dixon

For full biographical listings, see the Martindale-Hubbell Law Directory

SOMMERS, SCHWARTZ, SILVER & SCHWARTZ, P.C. (AV)

2000 Town Center, Suite 900, 48075
Telephone: 248-355-0300
Telecopier: 248-746-4001
Plymouth, Michigan Office: 747 South Main Street.
Telephone: 313-455-4250.

Lawrence Warren
William M. Brukoff

General Counsel for: City of Taylor; Foodland Distributors; C.A. Muer Corporation; Vlasic & Company; Nederlander Corporation; Midwest Health Centers, P.C.
Representative Clients: Michigan National Bank; Universal Underwriters Insurance Co.; Don Lee Distributors; Rite-Aid of Michigan.

For Complete List of Firm Personnel, See General Section

For full biographical listings, see the Martindale-Hubbell Law Directory

SYLVAN LAKE, Oakland Co.

Betty L. Lowenthal (AV)

2055 Orchard Lake Road, 48320
Telephone: 248-334-9938
Fax: 248-858-8508
Email: lowenthalb@aol.com *URL:* http://www.lawyers.com/lowenthalb

For full biographical listings, see the Martindale-Hubbell Law Directory

*TRAVERSE CITY,** Grand Traverse Co.

Smith & Johnson, Attorneys, P.C. (AV)

603 Bay Street, P.O. Box 705, 49685
Telephone: 231-946-0700
Fax: 231-946-1735
Email: sjlaw@smith-johnson.com *URL:* http://www.smith-johnson.com
Lansing, Michigan Office: Suite 402, 116 West Ottawa Street.
Telephone: 517-482-5142.

Louis A. Smith
H. Wendell Johnson
Allen G. Anderson

Thomas A. Pezzetti
Timothy Paul Smith
Matthew D. Vermetten
Gary Allen Gardner

OF COUNSEL

Barbara Ann Assendelft

Representative Clients: Empire National Bank of Traverse City; Grand Traverse Mall Limited Partnership; Green Tree Acceptance, Inc.; Lansing Automakers' Federal Credit Union; Michigan Automobile Dealers Association; Cherry Capital Oldsmobile Cadillac L.L.C.; Bill Marsh Motors, Inc.; Northern Star Broadcasting, L.L.C.; Munson Healthcare; Republic Bank.

For full biographical listings, see the Martindale-Hubbell Law Directory

TROY, Oakland Co.

Bookholder & Bassett, P.C. (AV)

Long Lake Crossings, 1301 West Long Lake Road, Suite 355, 48098-6349
Telephone: 248-641-0100
Fax: 248-641-0109
Email: info@bookholderbassett.com *URL:* http://www.lawyers.com/bookholder&bassett

Ronald M. Bookholder
Scott Bassett

Patricia S. Leary

For full biographical listings, see the Martindale-Hubbell Law Directory

Poling, McGaw & Poling, P.C. (AV)

Suite 275, 5435 Corporate Drive, 48098
Telephone: 248-641-0500
Telecopier: 248-641-0506
URL: http://www.lawyers.com/polingmcgaw&poling

Benson T. Buck (1926-1989)
Richard B. Poling
D. Douglas McGaw
Richard B. Poling, Jr.
Gregory C. Hamilton
Veronica B. O'Hara
James R. Parker
Shannon M. Acton

OF COUNSEL

Ralph S. Moore

Representative Clients: City of Troy; United States Fidelity & Guaranty Co.; Sentry Insurance Co.; Admiral Insurance; DeMaria Construction Co.; Leo Corporation; Aetna Casualty and Surety Co.; Concord Design; Pneumo-Abex.

For full biographical listings, see the Martindale-Hubbell Law Directory

YPSILANTI, Washtenaw Co.

Pear Sperling Eggan & Muskovitz, P.C. (AV)

5 South Washington Street, 48197
Telephone: 734-483-3626
Fax: 734-483-1107
Email: ameggan@ameritech.net
Ann Arbor, Michigan Office: Domino's Farms, 24 Frank Lloyd Wright Drive.
Telephone: 734-665-4441
Other Ypsilanti, Michigan Office: 2164 Bellevue at Washtenaw.
Telephone: 734-483-7177.

Lawrence W. Sperling
Andrew M. Eggan
Thomas E. Daniels

Counsel for: Domino's Pizza, Inc.; Citizens Banking Corp.; Townsend and Bottum, Inc.; The Credit Bureau of Ypsilanti; City of Ypsilanti (Labor Counsel); Michigan Municipal Worker's Compensation; Self-Insurance Fund.
Approved Attorneys for: Lawyers Title Insurance Corp.

For full biographical listings, see the Martindale-Hubbell Law Directory

FRANCHISE LAW

CALIFORNIA

RANCHO SANTA MARGARITA, Orange Co.

FRANCHISE LAW TEAM (AV)

30021 Tomas, Suite 260, 92688
Telephone: 949-459-7474
Toll Free Number: 888-276-2976
Fax: 949-459-7772
Email: franmail@franchiselawteam.com *URL:* http://www.franchiselawteam.com

Robin Day Glenn

Reference: Bank of America, Rancho Santa Margarita Branch.

For full biographical listings, see the Martindale-Hubbell Law Directory

COLORADO

*DENVER,** Denver Co.

SMITH McCULLOUGH, P.C. (AV)

Suite 900, 4643 South Ulster Street, 80237
Telephone: 303-221-6000
Fax: 303-221-6001
Email: info@smithmc.com *URL:* http://www.smithmc.com

Thomas S. Smith
Kim I. McCullough
Douglas R. Ferguson
Jeffrey J. Cowman
Harold R. Bruno, III
Steven M. Feder
Theresa M. Mehringer

Lynne M. Hanson
Garrett M. Tuttle
Mark A. Meyer
Kevin J. Kanouff
Gennaro M. DeSantis

For full biographical listings, see the Martindale-Hubbell Law Directory

WHEELER TRIGG & KENNEDY, P.C. (AV)

Suite 3600, 1801 California Street, 80202
Telephone: 303-292-2525
Telecopier: 303-294-1879
Email: info@wtklaw.com *URL:* http://www.wtklaw.com
Roslyn, New York Office: 1800 Northern Boulevard, Suite 208, 11576.
Telephone: 516-484-9701.
Fax: 516-484-6362.

Mark F. Kennedy
Gwen J. Young
Christopher J. Meyer

Sean D. Baker
Bryan D. Cross

For full biographical listings, see the Martindale-Hubbell Law Directory

ILLINOIS

*CHICAGO,** Cook Co.

BECKER & KAPLAN LLC (AV)

19 South La Salle Street Suite 1500, 60603
Telephone: 312-621-9500
Fax: 312-621-9011
Email: firm@beckerkaplan.com *URL:* http://www.beckerkaplan.com

Theodore M. Becker
Daniel S. Kaplan

Edward R. White
Michael J. Boxerman

For full biographical listings, see the Martindale-Hubbell Law Directory

MARYLAND

*BALTIMORE,** (Independent City)

THOMAS & LIBOWITZ, P.A. (AV)

100 Light Street, Suite 1100, 21202-1053
Telephone: 410-752-2468
Fax: 410-752-2046; 752-2049; 752-0979
Email: thomasandlibowitz.com *URL:* http://www.thomasandlibowitz.com

Clinton R. Black, IV
James E. Myers

Representative Clients: Sinclair Broadcast Group, Inc. (Television and Radio stations); Roy Kirby & Sons, Inc. (Contractor); First Mariner Bank; Scandia Manufacturing Co. Inc. (Defense Contractor); Atlantic Automotive Corp. t/a Heritgage Automotive Group; Candy Express Franchising, Inc.; Wire Spectrum Services (Contractors-Transmission Tower Sites); Acrodyne Communications, Inc.; Alexis Logic Corporation (Software Developers); Selnic Corporation (Electronis Distributors); Liberty Mutual Insurance Company.

For full biographical listings, see the Martindale-Hubbell Law Directory

*TOWSON,** Baltimore Co.

ELLYN L. BROWN CHARTERED (AV)

600 Washington Avenue, Suite 100, 21204
Telephone: 410-823-4200
Fax: 410-823-4201
Email: ellynbrown@worldnet.att.net

Ellyn L. Brown

For full biographical listings, see the Martindale-Hubbell Law Directory

MASSACHUSETTS

*BOSTON,** Suffolk Co.

LAW OFFICES OF HAROLD BROWN & ASSOCIATES (AV)

66 Long Wharf, 02110
Telephone: 617-720-4200
Fax: 617-720-0240
Email: brownlaw@world.std.com *URL:* http://www.franchise-counsel.com

L. Michael Hankes
Linda J. Keogh
Andrea B Aptowitz
Rory A. Valas

For full biographical listings, see the Martindale-Hubbell Law Directory

MICHIGAN

*ANN ARBOR,** Washtenaw Co.

PEAR SPERLING EGGAN & MUSKOVITZ, P.C. (AV)

Domino's Farms, 24 Frank Lloyd Wright Drive, 48105
Telephone: 734-665-4441
Fax: 734-665-8788
Email: peare@dominos.com
Ypsilanti, Michigan Offices: 5 South Washington Street.
Telephone: 734-483-3626 and 2164 Bellevue at Washtenaw.
Telephone: 734-483-7177.

Edwin L. Pear
Lawrence W. Sperling
Andrew M. Eggan
Melvin J. Muskovitz
Thomas E. Daniels
Joel F. Graziani
Paul R. Fransway
Francyne Stacey
Karl V. Fink
Scott H. Mandel
David E. Kempner
Jeffrey P. Thennisch

Counsel for: Domino's Pizza, Inc.; Townsend and Bottum, Inc.; Cleary College; Victory Lane Quick Oil Change Inc.; Citizens Banking Corp.; Washtenaw News Co., Inc.; Ann Arbor Transportation Authority; Meadowbrook Insurance Group; Michigan Municipal Liability & Property Pool.
Approved Attorneys for: Lawyers Title Insurance Corp.

For full biographical listings, see the Martindale-Hubbell Law Directory

YPSILANTI, Washtenaw Co.

PEAR SPERLING EGGAN & MUSKOVITZ, P.C. (AV)

5 South Washington Street, 48197
Telephone: 734-483-3626
Fax: 734-483-1107
Email: ameggan@ameritech.net
Ann Arbor, Michigan Office: Domino's Farms, 24 Frank Lloyd Wright Drive.
Telephone: 734-665-4441

(See Next Column)

PEAR SPERLING EGGAN & MUSKOVITZ P.C., *Ypsilanti—Continued*

Other Ypsilanti, Michigan Office: 2164 Bellevue at Washtenaw. *Telephone:* 734-483-7177.

Lawrence W. Sperling — Andrew M. Eggan — Thomas E. Daniels

Counsel for: Domino's Pizza, Inc.; Citizens Banking Corp.; Townsend and Bottum, Inc.; The Credit Bureau of Ypsilanti; City of Ypsilanti (Labor Counsel); Michigan Municipal Worker's Compensation; Self-Insurance Fund. *Approved Attorneys for:* Lawyers Title Insurance Corp.

For full biographical listings, see the Martindale-Hubbell Law Directory

GENERAL PRACTICE

ALABAMA

ALBERTVILLE, Marshall Co.

GULLAHORN & HARE, P.C. (AV)

310 West Main Street, P.O. Box 1669, 35950
Telephone: 256-878-1891
Fax: 256-878-1965
Email: g-hpc@cybertyme.com

Charles R. Hare, Jr. | John C. Gullahorn

Representative Clients: First Bank of Boaz; The Home Bank; Peoples Independent Bank of Boaz; AmSouth Bank; Compass Bank; Albertville Industrial Development Board; Boaz Industrial Development Board; Marshall-Dekalb Electric Cooperative; Olympia Construction, Inc.

For full biographical listings, see the Martindale-Hubbell Law Directory

*ANDALUSIA,** Covington Co.

ALBRITTONS, CLIFTON, ALVERSON & MOODY, P.C. (AV)

(Powell, Albritton & Albritton)
(Albrittons & Rankin)
(Albrittons, Givhan, Clifton & Alverson)
(Albrittons & Givhan)
109 Opp Avenue, P.O. Box 880, 36420
Telephone: 334-222-3177
Telecopier: 334-222-2696

Ed. T. Albritton (1857-1925)
Wm. Harold Albritton, Sr. (1881-1929)
Dempsey M. Powell (1863-1949)
Albert L. Rankin (1909-1970)
Robert Bynum Albritton (1905-1983)
William H. Albritton, Jr. (1907-1983)
James Marvin Albritton (1915-1987)
James R. Clifton
William Harold Albritton, IV
William B. Alverson, Jr.
Thomas B. Albritton
Julie S. Moody

Benjamin M. Bowden

General Counsel for: Coca-Cola Bottling Co. of Andalusia; Opp-Micolas Cotton Mills.
Attorneys for: First Alabama Bank; Alabama Power Co.; The Travelers; Liberty Mutual Ins. Co; Kemper Insurance; Crum & Forster Insurance Cos; CSX Transporation.

For full biographical listings, see the Martindale-Hubbell Law Directory

POWELL, PEEK & WEAVER (AV)

201 East Troy Street, Drawer 969, 36420
Telephone: 334-222-4103
Facsimile: 334-222-4105
Email: ppw@alaweb.com

MEMBERS OF FIRM

Abner R. Powell (1875-1940)
Abner R. Powell, Jr. (1916-1987)
Abner R. Powell, III
John M. Peek
Gary L. Weaver
Abner Riley Powell, IV

Representative Clients: State Farm Insurance Group; ALFA Insurance Companies; U.S.F.& G. Co.; CNA Insurance; Auto Owners Insurance Co.; Southern Guaranty Co.; Covington County Bank; Colonial Bank of Opp, Alabama.

For full biographical listings, see the Martindale-Hubbell Law Directory

*ATHENS,** Limestone Co.

PATTON, LATHAM, LEGGE & COLE (AV)

Professional Building, 315 West Market Street, P.O. Box 470, 35612
Telephone: 256-232-2010
Fax: 256-230-0610
Email: pllclaw@hiwaay.net

MEMBERS OF FIRM

Roy B. Patton (1885-1954)
David U. Patton (Retired)
Byrd R. Latham
Winston V. Legge, Jr.
P. Michael Cole
Claire Jones Tinney

Local Counsel for: Alabama Gas Corp.; Alabama Power Co.; Avis; Bell South Telecommunications; Blue Cross and Blue Shield of Alabama; State Farm Life Insurance Co.; State Farm Mutual Automobile Insurance Co.; Travelers Insurance Co.; United States Fidelity and Guaranty Co.; Wausau Insurance Company.

For full biographical listings, see the Martindale-Hubbell Law Directory

*BAY MINETTE,** Baldwin Co.

CHASON & CHASON, P.C. (AV)

300 D'Olive Street, P.O. Box 100, 36507
Telephone: 334-937-2191
Fax: 334-937-2101

John Chason (1904-1992)
John Earle Chason
Allan R. Chason

Jessica M. McDill

Representative Clients: International Paper Co.; CSX Transportation, Inc.; Baldwin County Electric Membership Corp.; State Farm Mutual Insurance Co.; Peoples Fertilizer Co.; Kimberly-Clark Tissue Company; Uniroyal Chemical Company, Inc.; John Hancock Mutual Life Insurance Co.; Chubb Group of Insurance Cos.; Champion International Corporation.

For full biographical listings, see the Martindale-Hubbell Law Directory

JOHNSTONE, ADAMS, BAILEY, GORDON AND HARRIS, L.L.C. (AV)

Dahlberg Building, 104 Hand Avenue, P.O. Box 729, 36507
Telephone: 334-937-9473
Facsimile: 334-937-9475
Email: attorneys@JohnstoneAdams.com *URL:* http://www.JohnstoneAdams.com
Mobile, Alabama Office: Royal St. Francis Building, 104 St. Francis Street, P.O. Box 1988, 36633.
Telephone: 334-432-7682.
Facsimile: 334-432-2800; 432-0712.

MEMBER OF FIRM

Charles C. Simpson, III (Resident)

For full biographical listings, see the Martindale-Hubbell Law Directory

*BIRMINGHAM,** Jefferson Co.

BALCH & BINGHAM LLP (AV)

1710 Sixth Avenue North, P.O. Box 306, 35201-0306
Telephone: 205-251-8100
Facsimile: 205-226-8798
URL: http://www.balch.com
Other Birmingham, Alabama Office: 1901 Sixth Avenue North, 35203.
Telephone: 205-251-8100.
Facsimile: 205-226-8799.
Montgomery, Alabama Office: The Winter Building, 2 Dexter Avenue, 36104.
Telephone: 334-834-6500.
Facsimile: 334-269-3115.
Huntsville, Alabama Office: 655 Gallatin Street, 35801.
Telephone: 205-551-0171.
Facsimile: 205-512-0119.
Washington, D.C. Office: 1275 Pennsylvania Avenue, N.W., 10th Floor, 20004.
Telephone: 202-347-6000.
Facsimile: 202-347-6001.

William Logan Martin (1883-1959)
Schuyler A. Baker (1915-1990)

COUNSEL

S. Eason Balch
John Bingham
Harold A. Bowron, Jr.
Frederick R. Eames (Resident, Washington, D.C. Office)
Joseph M. Farley
B. Judson Hennington, III
Robert L. Loftin, III
M. Roland Nachman, Jr. (Resident, Montgomery Office)
Barbara K. Olson (Resident, Washington, D.C. Office)
Maury D. Smith (Resident, Montgomery Office)
William J. Ward

MEMBERS OF FIRM

John S. Bowman (Resident, Montgomery Office)
Charles M. Crook (Resident, Montgomery Office)
Sterling G. Culpepper, Jr. (Resident, Montgomery Office)
Edward S. Allen
Warren H. Goodwyn (Resident, Montgomery Office)
H. Hampton Boles
Michael L. Edwards
Marshall Timberlake
Walter M. Beale, Jr.
James F. Hughey, Jr.
S. Eason Balch, Jr.
S. Allen Baker, Jr.
J. Foster Clark
Randolph H. Lanier
David R. Boyd (Resident, Montgomery Office)
John Richard Carrigan
Lee H. Zell
William E. Shanks, Jr.
T. Dwight Sloan
William H. Satterfield
Steven G. McKinney
Steven F. Casey
Malcolm N. Carmichael (Resident, Montgomery Office)
Richard L. Pearson
James A. Bradford
Dan H. McCrary
William P. Cobb, II (Resident, Montgomery Office)
Alan T. Rogers
James A. Byram, Jr. (Resident, Montgomery Office)
William S. Wright
Susan Bevill Livingston
John J. Coleman, III
John F. Mandt

(See Next Column)

BALCH & BINGHAM LLP, *Birmingham—Continued*

MEMBERS OF FIRM (Continued)

Michael D. Waters (Resident, Montgomery Office)
M. Stanford Blanton
T. Kurt Miller
J. Thomas Francis, Jr.
Timothy J. Tracy
Clark R. Hammond
W. Joseph McCorkle, Jr. (Resident, Montgomery Office)
Patrick J. McCormick, III (Resident, Washington, D.C. Office)
Will Hill Tankersley, Jr.
Suzanne Ashe
Mark A. Crosswhite
Leonard Charles Tillman
Dorman Walker (Resident, Montgomery Office)
Alex B. Leath, III
Cavender Crosby Kimble
Daniel M. Wilson (Resident, Huntsville Office)
Michael D. Freeman
James H. Hancock, Jr.
Robin G. Laurie (Resident, Montgomery Office)
Jesse Stringer Vogtle, Jr.
Donald R. Jones, Jr. (Resident, Montgomery Office)
Charles B. Paterson (Resident, Montgomery Office)
Felton W. Smith
Lois Smith Woodward
Leslie M. Allen (Resident, Montgomery Office)
Gregory Carl Cook
Lyle David Larson
Phillip Anthony Nichols
John Russell Campbell
Marcel L. Debruge
R. Bruce Barze, Jr.
David B. Block (Resident, Huntsville Office)
Matthew W. Bowden
Leigh Anne Hodge
C. Grady Moore, III
Lisa Johnson Sharp

ASSOCIATES

William D. Lineberry
Teresa G. Minor
N. DeWayne Pope
John W. McCullough
Douglas B. Kauffman
Josephine Rose Wright
Craig A. Parker
Timothy John Segers
Andrew W. Tunnell
Cynthia G. Burnside
John D. Pickering
Tom S. Roper
Charles A. Burkhart
Robert P. Fowler
Robert M. D. Mercer (Not admitted in AL)
Spencer M. Taylor
Angela F. Thornhill
Yvonne Norris Beshany
Carl Lenford Evans, Jr. (Resident, Montgomery Office)
Jenelle D. Evans
James L. Noles, Jr.
Kimberly Katherine Till
Mark E. Tindal
Monica L. Warmbrod
William S. Blair
Gregory P. Butrus
Sean B. Cunningham (Resident, Washington, D.C. Office)
Bingham D. Edwards, Jr.
Theresa R. Jenkins (Resident, Montgomery Office)
Eric B. Langley
J. Thomas Longino, IV
Jennifer R. McCain
J. Beth Moscarelli (Resident, Montgomery Office)
Leslie Caren Paulus (Resident, Huntsville Office)
M. Ann Skipper
Wendy Ann Zarzaur

OF COUNSEL

Edward M. Rogers, Jr. (Resident, Washington, D.C. Office)
Harold Williams

Counsel for: Alabama Power Co.; Blue Cross and Blue Shield of Alabama; The Boeing Company; Brasfield & Gorrie, Inc.; Compass Bancshares, Inc.; Harbert Corp.; Kimberly-Clark Corp.; Southern Company Services, Inc.; Southern Research Institute; Vesta Insurance Group, Inc.

For full biographical listings, see the Martindale-Hubbell Law Directory

BERKOWITZ, LEFKOVITS, ISOM & KUSHNER, A PROFESSIONAL CORPORATION (AV)

SouthTrust Tower, 420 North Twentieth Street, Suite 1600, 35203-5202
Telephone: 205-328-0480
Telecopier: 205-322-8007
URL: http://www.blik.com

A. Berkowitz (1907-1985)
Arnold K. Lefkovits
Chervis Isom
Harold B. Kushner
B. G. Minisman, Jr.
Henry I Frohsin
Edward P. Meyerson
David A. Larsen
Barry S. Marks
J. Forrest Hinton
Anne W. Mitchell
Susan S. Wagner
Frank S. James III
D. J. Simonetti
Patricia Clotfelter
Steven B. Corenblum
Wesley C. Redmond
Denise W. Killebrew
Andrew J. Potts
Thomas J. Mahoney, Jr.
Thomas O. Kolb
Lana K. Hawkins (Not admitted in AL)
Michael R. Silberman
Richard A. Pizitz, Jr.
Walton E. Williams III
Nancy C. Hughes

OF COUNSEL

Linda S. Lehe

(See Next Column)

N. Andrew Rotenstreich
Ellen Elizabeth Henderson
Hewes T. Hull
Matthew W. Barnes
Stanley W. Logan
Lee T. Clanton
Alane A. Phillips
Andrew R. Chambless
Kirsten Hunt Kowalski
Robert Buchanan Phillips, II
Adam Joshua Sigman

For full biographical listings, see the Martindale-Hubbell Law Directory

BISHOP, COLVIN, JOHNSON & KENT (AV)

317-20th Street, North, P.O. Box 370404, 35237
Telephone: 205-251-2881
Fax: 205-254-3987
Email: BCJK@BELLSOUTH.NET

MEMBERS OF FIRM

Maurice F. Bishop (1913-1982)
Gerald D. Colvin, Jr.
Carl E. Johnson, Jr.
Burgin H. Kent
Gerald DeWitt (Whit) Colvin, III

Representative Clients: Miller Transporters, Inc.; United Van Lines, Inc.; Western Steel, Inc.; Alabama Building Products, Inc.; The City of Trussville, Alabama; Utilities Board of the City of Trussville, Alabama; Jefferson County Board of Education; University of Montevallo; Milan Express, Inc.
Reference: AmSouth Bank, N.A.

For full biographical listings, see the Martindale-Hubbell Law Directory

BRADLEY ARANT ROSE & WHITE LLP (AV)

2001 Park Place, Suite 1400, P.O. Box 830709, 35283-0709
Telephone: 205-521-8000
Facsimile: 205-521-8800
Facsimile (SouthTrust Tower Office): 205-521-8500
URL: http://www.barw.com
Huntsville, Alabama Office: 200 Clinton Avenue West, Suite 900, 35801.
Telephone: 205-517-5100.
Facsimile: 205-533-5069.
Washington, D.C. Office: 801 Pennsylvania Avenue, NW, Suite 230, 20004.
Telephone: 202-347-8893.
Facsimile: 202-347-1684.

MEMBERS OF FIRM

John P. Adams
Mary Louise Ahearn (1934-1985)
James Patrick Alexander
Douglas Arant (1897-1987)
Charles A. J. Beavers Jr.
Joseph S. Bird III
Axel Bolvig III
Lee C. Bradley Jr. (1897-1999)
T. Michael Brown
Hall B. Bryant III (Resident, Huntsville Office)
Philip J. Carroll III
Thomas Neely Carruthers Jr.
G. Edward Cassady III
James S. Christie Jr.
Kenneth B. Cole, Jr. (Resident, Huntsville Office)
Brittin Turner Coleman
John James Coleman Jr.
J. Paul Compton Jr.
Deane K. Corliss
Forrest K. Covington
Stewart M. Cox
J. Patrick Darby
Paige Maddox Davis
Michael S. Denniston
L. Susan Doss
J. David Dresher
Denson Nauls Franklin III
Sherri Tucker Freeman
Stuart Joseph Frentz
Linda A. Friedman
A. H. Gaede Jr.
James W. Gewin
John E. Goodman
M. Williams Goodwyn Jr.
Patrick H. Graves Jr. (Resident, Huntsville Office)
Andrew Robert Greene
Stephen K. Greene
P. Nicholas Greenwood
John B. Grenier (Resident, Huntsville Office)
John E. Hagefstration Jr.
John William Hargrove
John G. Harrell
George Bryan Harris
Carleta Roberts Hawley
Warne S. Heath (Resident, Huntsville Office)
Kevin J. Henderson
William L. Hinds Jr.
Gary C. Huckaby (Resident, Huntsville Office)
E. Cutter Hughes Jr. (Resident, Huntsville Office)
James Donald Hughes
David Glenn Hymer
Norman Jetmundsen Jr.
Robert G. Johnson
William W. Johnson Jr. (1943-1984)
Matthew H. Lembke
T. Barr Linton (Not admitted in AL)
Thad Gladden Long
Scott E. Ludwig (Resident, Huntsville Office)
James Walker May
Joseph B. Mays Jr.
Michael D. McKibben
Hobart A. McWhorter Jr.
John K. Molen
Bernard A. Monaghan (1916-1987)
Richard H. Monk III
Stephen R. Monk
John H. Morrow
Andrew J. Noble III
Virginia Calvert Patterson
Michael R. Pennington
J. David Pugh
E. Mabry Rogers
Wm. Alfred Rose (1900-1981)
James E. Rotch
Walter J. Sears III
Charles R. Smith Jr. (Resident, Huntsville Office)
Wm. Allen Smyly (1954-1993)
Robert K. Spotswood
Jay D. St. Clair
H. Harold Stephens (Resident, Huntsville Office)
Luther J. Strange, III
Sid J. Trant
Bobby C. Underwood
Laurence Duncan Vinson Jr.
Robert C. Walthall
Paul S. Ware
John D. Watson III
Meade Whitaker, Jr.

(See Next Column)

BRADLEY ARANT ROSE & WHITE LLP—*Continued*

MEMBERS OF FIRM (Continued)

John P. Whittington
Ellene Winn (1911-1986)
Kenneth T. Wyatt
Ralph Howard Yeilding
Anne R. Yuengert
Alan K. Zeigler

OF COUNSEL

Stanley D. Bynum
Lant B. Davis
J. Robert Fleenor
S. Revelle Gwyn (Resident, Huntsville Office)
J. Reese Murray
Scott M. Phelps
Romaine S. Scott Jr.
Edward M. Selfe
Macbeth Wagnon Jr. (Retired)
C. Larimore Whitaker
Wm. Bew White Jr. (Retired)
John N. Wrinkle

COUNSEL

Amy K. Myers
Jack W. Selden

ASSOCIATES

Matthew A. Aiken
F. Wendall Allen
Julia Spazzarini Aquila (Resident, Huntsville Office)
James F. Archibald III
Helena F. Barkworth
Jay R. Bender
Dylan C. Black
Jolee Hancock Bollinger
Hugh Chester Boston III
Joel E. Brown
James W. Childs, Jr.
Lynne R. Connery
Matthew W. Cooper
Donna M. Crowe
Rebecca G. DePalma
Lesley S. DeRamus
Denise Avery Dodson
Douglas E. Eckert
Julie S. Elmer
Kelly Hubbard Estes
Thomas M. Goodrich
Alan R. Hanson
Fred M. Haston III
K. Wood Herren
Erika Jenke-Huber (Resident, Huntsville Office)
Nathan W. Johnson
Abdul K. Kallon
Ronald H. Kent Jr.
George P. Kobler (Resident, Huntsville Office)
Margaret Smith Kubiszyn
David M. Lawson
Arlan D. Lewis
Jeffrey P. Lisenby
Kimberly B. Martin (Resident, Huntsville Office)
Justin T. McDonald
Angus N. McFadden
Jennifer Byers McLeod (Resident, Huntsville Office)
T. Matthew Miller
Rodney L. Moss
Dorothy D. Pak
Kenneth M. Perry
Caroline Lewis Powell
David E. Roth
June K. Rowell
Anne Marie Seibel
Richard L. Sharff Jr.
Delores J. Simmons
Frederic L. Smith, Jr.
Joseph E. Smith
Rusha C. Smith
Scott B. Smith
John W. Smith T
Paul Sykes
Rebecca Thai (Resident, Huntsville Office)
Tracy M. Thompson
Arnold W. Umbach III
Laura P. Washburn (Not admitted in AL)
James H. White
Mary Carol White
J. Keith Windle

Counsel for: SouthTrust Bank of Alabama, National Association; Energen Corporation; Blount, Inc.; Torchmark Corp.; Russell Corp.; Coca-Cola Bottling Company United, Inc.; Ford Motor Co.; Walter Industries, Inc.; The Birmingham Post Co. (Post-Herald); The New York Times Co.

For full biographical listings, see the Martindale-Hubbell Law Directory

BURR & FORMAN LLP (AV)

3100 SouthTrust Tower, 420 North 20th Street, P.O. Box 830719, 35283-0719
Telephone: 205-251-3000
Facsimile: 205-458-5100
URL: http://www.burr.com
Huntsville, Alabama Office: Suite 204, Regency Center, 400 Meridian Street.
Telephone: 205-551-0010.
Facsimile: 205-551-0043.
Atlanta, Georgia Office: Suite 1200, One Georgia Center, 600 West Peachtree Street, 30308.
Telephone: 404-815-3000.
Facsimile: 404-817-3244.

Borden H. Burr (1876-1952)
James R. Forman (1880-1942)
Mark L. Taliaferro (1906-1981)
Andrew J. Thomas (1897-1984)

MEMBERS OF FIRM

Louis H. Anders, Jr.
Jeffrey T. Baker
Henry Graham Beene
Paul P. Bolus
Patricia Powell Burke
"Ginger" M. Busby
Eric L. Carlton
John D. Clements
D. Frank Davis
John F. DeBuys, Jr.
David D. Dowd, III
Robert Hunt Dunlap, Jr. (Resident, Atlanta, Georgia Office)
David A. Elliott
John W. Evans (Resident, Huntsville, Alabama Office)
Ronald W. Farley
Gary W. Farris (Resident, Atlanta, Georgia Office)
Deborah P. Fisher
Richard A. Fishman (Resident, Atlanta, Georgia Office)
F. A. Flowers, III
James Ross Forman, III
Gerald P. Gillespy
Robert S. W. Given
Peter A. Grammas
Michael L. Hall

(See Next Column)

MEMBERS OF FIRM (Continued)

Gregory F. Harley (Resident, Atlanta, Georgia Office)
Victor L. Hayslip
David Tully Hazell (Resident, Atlanta, Georgia Office)
William S. Hereford
J. Fredric Ingram
W. Benjamin Johnson
William C. Knight, Jr.
Mark McCarroll Lawson
L. Tennent Lee, III (Resident, Huntsville, Alabama Office)
Joseph W. Letzer
J. Patrick Logan
Gary M. London
E. Clayton Lowe, Jr.
Michael L. Lucas
Timothy M. Lupinacci
Warren C. Matthews
George F. Maynard (Resident, Atlanta, Georgia Office)
William T. McKenzie (Resident, Atlanta, Georgia Office)
Gail Livingston Mills
Dwight L. Mixson, Jr.
John T. Mooresmith
John C. Morrow
C. Read Morton, Jr. (Resident, Atlanta, Georgia Office)
Dent M. Morton
William F. Murray, Jr.
Samuel W. Oliver, Jr.
Marvin Glenn Perry, Jr.
J. Hunter Phillips, III
J. Fred Powell
Gene T. Price
Bruce A. Rawls
James B. Rhoads (Resident, Atlanta, Georgia Office)
James J. Robinson
S. Dagnal Rowe (Resident, Huntsville, Alabama Office)
Robert B. Rubin
Robert H. Rutherford, Jr.
James Dean Spratt, Jr. (Resident, Atlanta, Georgia Office)
Jack P. Stephenson, Jr.
Carol H. Stewart
Joseph G. Stewart
Mark Taliaferro, Jr.
George M. Taylor, III
W. Lee Thuston
A. Brand Walton
Paul O. Woodall
R. Michael Yarbro

OF COUNSEL

Samuel H. Burr
James R. Forman, Jr.
William K. Murray
A. Jackson Noble, Jr.
C. V. Stelzenmuller
Robert G. Tate

ASSOCIATES

Robert Eugene Battle
Rebecca W. Block
Howard E. Bogard
Luanne M. Bonnie (Resident, Atlanta, Georgia Office)
Stephen J. Bumgarner
S. Mark Burr (Resident, Atlanta, Georgia Office)
William C. Byrd, II
D. Christopher Carson
Edward R. Christian
William C. Collins, Jr. (Resident, Atlanta, Georgia Office)
Clark A. Cooper
Allen D. Cope
Wendy Cornett
Damon P. Denney
Walter A. Dodgen (Resident, Huntsville, Alabama Office)
Erich N. Durlacher (Resident, Atlanta, Georgia Office)
Cameron Turner Earnhardt
James Earnest Fleenor, Jr.
Eric Franz
Ashley H. Hattaway
Brent D. Hitson
Gary Lane Howard
Lori L. Howland
Alycia K. Jastrebski
Richard C. Keller
Reid Stephens Manley
Ricky J. McKinney
Patrick G. Nelson (Resident, Huntsville, Alabama Office)
John E. Norris
David B. O'Dell
Allan G. Overton (Resident, Atlanta, Georgia Office)
Jerry F. Perkins, Jr
Joel (Jay) A. Price, Jr.
James Charles Stanley II
Cynthia F. Stephenson
Cary Tynes Wahlheim
J. Andrew Watson, III (Resident, Huntsville, Alabama Office)
Harlan F. Winn, III

LEGAL SUPPORT PERSONNEL

J. Michael Tarpley (Director of Administration)

For full biographical listings, see the Martindale-Hubbell Law Directory

CABANISS, JOHNSTON, GARDNER, DUMAS & O'NEAL (AV)

Park Place Tower, 2001 Park Place North, Suite 700, P.O. Box 830612, 35283-0612
Telephone: 205-716-5200
Fax: 205-716-5389
Email: bgm@cabaniss.com *URL:* http://www.cabaniss.com
Mobile, Alabama Office: 700 Riverview Plaza, P.O. Box 2906.
Telephone: 334-433-6961.
Fax: 334-415-7350.

Edward H. Cabaniss (1857-1936)
Forney Johnston (1879-1965)
Lucien D. Gardner, Jr. (1903-1988)
M. Camper O'Neal (1907-1989)

MEMBERS OF FIRM

William F. Gardner
Crawford S. McGivaren, Jr.
Sydney F. Frazier, Jr.
Benjamen T. Rowe (Resident, Mobile Office)
William A. Robinson (Resident, Mobile Office)
Patrick H. Sims (Resident, Mobile Office)
Donald J. Stewart (Resident, Mobile Office)
Roy J. Crawford
William K. Thomas
F. Gerald Burnett
David S. Dunkle
C. Fred Daniels
David L. Kane (Resident, Mobile Office)
R. Boyd Miller (Resident, Mobile Office)
R. Carlton Smyly
Steve A. Tucker
Sandy G. Robinson (Resident, Mobile Office)

(See Next Column)

CABANISS, JOHNSTON, GARDNER, DUMAS & O'NEAL, *Birmingham—Continued*

MEMBERS OF FIRM (Continued)

R. Taylor Abbot, Jr.
Herbert H. West, Jr.
Richard Eldon Davis
Melanie Merkle Bass
John M. Graham

COUNSEL

L. Murray Alley

OF COUNSEL

Joseph F. Johnston
E. T. Brown, Jr.

ASSOCIATES

Diane H. Crawley
Joseph V. Musso
Rebecca D. Parks (Resident, Mobile Office)
Ian D. Rosenthal (Resident, Mobile Office)
Annette Lanning Kinderman
Michael E. Turner
Jarrod J. White (Resident, Mobile Office)
Stephen Andrew Walsh
Mark E. House

Counsel for: Schuler Industries, Inc.; Carraway Methodist Health Systems; Doster Construction Co., Inc.; Liberty Mutual Insurance Co.; MacMillan Bloedel Packaging, Inc.; Norfolk Southern Corp.; O'Neal Steel, Inc.

For full biographical listings, see the Martindale-Hubbell Law Directory

CORLEY, MONCUS & WARD, P.C. (AV)

400 Shades Creek Parkway, Suite 100, P.O. Box 59807, 35259
Telephone: 205-879-5959
Telecopier: 205-871-4411

Claude McCain Moncus
James S. Ward
Ezra B. Perry, Jr.
F. Lane Finch, Jr.

Carla C. Ray

For full biographical listings, see the Martindale-Hubbell Law Directory

DOMINICK, FLETCHER, YEILDING, WOOD & LLOYD, P.A. (AV)

2121 Highland Avenue, 35209
Telephone: 205-939-0033
URL: http://members.aol.com/dfywandl/lawyer.htm

Frank Dominick
Walter Fletcher
Manly Yeilding
J. Fred Wood, Jr.
Susan Dominick Doughton
J. Terrell McElheny
Sammye Oden Kok
Brian T. Williams
C. Clark Collier
Mary P. Thornton
Judy Bateman Shepura
Steven C. Pearson

Christopher A. Bottcher
Lisa Hudson Dorough

OF COUNSEL

Lee B. Lloyd

Counsel for: Amerex Corp.; Citizens Federal Savings Bank; St. Vincent's Hospital; Birmingham-Southern College; Castle Mortgage Corporation; Kappler Safety Group; Integrated Health Services, Inc.; Thornton Construction Company, Inc.

For full biographical listings, see the Martindale-Hubbell Law Directory

GORDON, SILBERMAN, WIGGINS & CHILDS, P.C. (AV)

1400 SouthTrust Tower, 420 North 20th Street, 35203
Telephone: 205-328-0640
Facsimilie: 205-254-1500
Washington, D.C. Office: 1621 Connecticut Avenue, N.W., Suite 400.
Telephone: 202-238-0690.
Facsimile: 202-238-0968.

Louis Silberman (1889-1976)
Robert S. Gordon (1914-1983)

RESIDENT SHAREHOLDERS

Wilbur G. Silberman
Bruce L. Gordon
Robert L. Wiggins, Jr.
Robert F. Childs, Jr.
Augustus J. Beck, Jr.
Harvey L. Wachsman
Ray D. Gibbons
C. Michael Quinn
Dennis George Pantazis
Terrill W. Sanders
James Mendelsohn
Richard J. Ebbinghouse
Ann K. Wiggins
Samuel Fisher
Ann C. Robertson
Mark P. Williams
Timothy D. Davis
Joseph H. Calvin, III
Linda J. Peacock
Deborah A. Mattison

RESIDENT ASSOCIATES

Paul H. Webb
Timothy C. Gann
Byron R. Perkins
Jon C. Goldfarb
Gregory O. Wiggins
Lee Winston
Rocco Calamusa, Jr.
Brian M. Clark
Joel S. Isenberg
Craig L. Lowell
Sandra B. Reiss
Laura M. Hitt
Kyle T. Smith
Maury S. Weiner
Robbie Steele Martin
Abigail P. van Alstyne
Rand A. Linton
Jill O. Radwin
Kell A. Simon
Nicole L. Gordon
Russell W. Adams
Kimberly C. Page

(See Next Column)

RESIDENT ASSOCIATES (Continued)

Scott A. Gilliland
Eden Brown Gaines
Karen Gurley Kolaczek
Edward McFarland Johnson

OF COUNSEL

Robert H. Loeb

For full biographical listings, see the Martindale-Hubbell Law Directory

GORHAM & WALDREP, P.C. (AV)

2101 6th Avenue North, Suite 700, 35203
Telephone: 205-254-3216; 251-9166
Telecopier: 205-324-3802
Email: info@gorham-waldrep.com *URL:* http://www.gorham-waldrep.com
Montgomery, Alabama Office: 250 Commerce Street, P.O. Box 4837, 36103-4837.
Telephone: 334-262-0777.
Telecopier: 334-262-0742.

Charles W. Gorham
Charlie D. Waldrep
Thomas L. Stewart
Michael G. Kendrick
LaVeeda Morgan Battle
John T. Natter
Frank G. Alfano
Kay L. McNabb Cason
Victor Kelley
K. Mark Parnell

Tamara Harris Johnson
John A. Lentine
Victoria Franklin-Sisson
Mary H. Thompson
Leslie Miller Klasing
Timothy M. Fulmer
Kenneth A. Hairston
Phillip Eugene Kinney
Donna Eich Brooks
Kim Davidson
Myron Cordell Penn

OF COUNSEL

Giles Gilpin Perkins

Representative Clients: Jefferson County Personnel Board; Birmingham-Jefferson Civic Center Authority; The Water Works and Sewer Board of the City of Birmingham; City of Homewood; American Federation of Government Employees Local #1945; City of Pelham; Town of Kimberly; Alabama Tire Dealers Assn.; Southern States Body Shop Assn.

For full biographical listings, see the Martindale-Hubbell Law Directory

HALL, CONERLY, MUDD & BOLVIG, P.C. (AV)

1400 Financial Center, 505 North 20th Street, 35203-2626
Telephone: 205-251-8143

Jack J. Hall
Edward O. Conerly
William A. Mudd
C. Peter Bolvig
Jack J. Hall, Jr.

Christy Lynn Campbell Osborne
Paul C. Garrison
Kerry Phillip Luke
Sia Marie Kantargis
Linda Hinson Ambrose
P. Ted Colquett
Jerry D. Redmond, Jr.
David R. Wells

Counsel for: ALFA Insurance Cos.; Allstate Insurance Co.; Insurance Company of North America; Crum & Forster Insurance Co.; Canal Insurance Co.; Argonaut Insurance Co.; Chubb Pacific Indemnity Group; Commercial Union Cos.; General Accident Group.

For full biographical listings, see the Martindale-Hubbell Law Directory

HASKELL SLAUGHTER & YOUNG, L.L.C. (AV)

1200 AmSouth/Harbert Plaza, 1901 Sixth Avenue North, 35203
Telephone: 205-251-1000
Facsimile: 205-324-1133
Email: hsy@hsy.com
Montgomery, Alabama Office: 305 South Lawrence Street, P.O. Box 4660. 36103-4660.
Telephone: 334-265-8573.
Facsimile: 334-264-7945.

Wyatt Rushton Haskell
William M. Slaughter
Frank M. Young, III
Robert E. Lee Garner
Benjamin B. Spratling III
Thomas T. Gallion, III (Resident, Montgomery Office)
Robert D. Shattuck, Jr.
E. Alston Ray
James C. Huckaby, Jr.
Mark Edward Ezell
Stephen L. Poer
Thomas E. Reynolds
Beverly P. Baker
Ross N. Cohen
Constance C. Walker (Resident, Montgomery Office)
Richard H. Walston
Gwen L. Windle
Michael K. K. Choy
Carter H. Dukes
Frank Hampton McFadden, Jr.
John W. Scott
R. Scott Williams

OF COUNSEL

Donald T. Locke (Not admitted in AL)

Georgia Sullivan Roberson
James A. Patton, Jr.
Lynn Reynolds
Joseph N. Harden
Kimberly L. Hager
Matthew T. Franklin
S. Jason Nabors

(See Next Column)

HASKELL SLAUGHTER & YOUNG L.L.C.—*Continued*

Representative Clients: The Banc Corporation; The Bank; City of Birmingham; The Equitable Life Assurance Society of the United States; Federal Deposit Insurance Corporation; HEALTHSOUTH Corporation/HEALTHSOUTH Medical Centers; Montgomery County, Alabama; USX Corporation.

For full biographical listings, see the Martindale-Hubbell Law Directory

PARSONS, LEE & JULIANO, P.C. (AV)

2200 AmSouth/Harbert Plaza, 1901 Sixth Avenue, North, P.O. Box 371088, 35237-1088
Telephone: 205-326-6600
Fax: 205-324-7097

Robert E. Parsons
Jasper P. Juliano
Marcus W. Lee
Marda W. Sydnor
David A. Lee
John M. Bergquist
Paul J. DeMarco
Deborah Ann Payne
Dorothy A. Powell
David Samuel Snoddy

For full biographical listings, see the Martindale-Hubbell Law Directory

SCHOEL, OGLE, LILES AND UPSHAW, LLP (AV)

600 Financial Center, 505 North 20th Street, P.O. Box 1865, 35201-1865
Telephone: 205-521-7000
Telecopier: 205-521-7007
Mailing Address: Drawer 1865, Birmingham, Alabama, 35201-1865

Jerry W. Schoel
Richard F. Ogle
Paul A. Liles
David O. Upshaw
Jann J. Rice

Reference: First Alabama Bank.

For full biographical listings, see the Martindale-Hubbell Law Directory

SPAIN & GILLON, L.L.C. (AV)

The Zinszer Building, 2117 2nd Avenue North, 35203
Telephone: 205-328-4100
Telecopier: 205-324-8866
Email: ddh@spain-gillon.com *URL:* http://lawlinks.com:80/atty/al/sggbn.html

MEMBERS OF FIRM

H. Hobart Grooms, Jr.
Ollie L. Blan, Jr.
John P. McKleroy, Jr.
Eugene P. Stutts
Samuel H. Frazier
Alton B. Parker, Jr.
Charles D. Stewart
Elizabeth Ann McMahan
Glenn E. Estess, Jr.
J. Sanford Mullins, III
Harold H. Goings
Paul S. Leonard
Paul L. Sotherland
Robert L. Williams
Gary A. Parker
David S. Maxey
W. Gregory Smith
Steve R. Burford
Earl H. Lawson, Jr.
Howard K. Glick
James P. Rea

OF COUNSEL

Richard S. Riley
Ralph B. Tate
Ira L. Burleson
J. W. Gillon (1900-1992)
John P. Ansley (1914-1998).

ASSOCIATES

Karen B. Johns
Mark W. Macoy
Peter McKeever Wright
Kerry Ann Lahey
Carrie P. Walthall
Anthony C. Portera
David P. Donahue
Myla Calhoun Choy

General Counsel for: Piggly Wiggly Alabama Distributing Co.; Alabama Insurance Guaranty Association; Alabama Life and Disability Insurance Guaranty Association; Alabama Insurance Underwriters Association; Auburn University Foundation.
Counsel for: The Minnesota Life Insurance Co.; Government Employees Insurance Co.; Massachusetts Mutual Life Insurance Co.

For full biographical listings, see the Martindale-Hubbell Law Directory

WALSTON, WELLS, ANDERSON & BAINS, LLP (AV)

Suite 500 Financial Center, 505 20th Street North, 35203
Telephone: 205-251-9600
Telecopier: 205-251-0700
Mailing Address: P.O. Box 830642, Birmingham, AL, 35283-0642

Robert H. Walston (Retired)
Frank C. Galloway, Jr.
Lawrence Dumas, III
C. Henry Marston
Vernon L. Wells, II
James L. Birchall
Michael C. Quillen
David B. Anderson
Larry B. Childs
William R. Sylvester
Kay K. Bains
Heyward C. Hosch III
Ronald A. Levitt
Elizabeth Champlin Bishop
C. Ellis Brazeal, III
David B. Walston
Anne Stone Sumblin
Emily Sides Bonds
Julia Boaz Cooper

OF COUNSEL

Edward J. Ashton
Jerry Dean Hillman

(See Next Column)

ASSOCIATES

Randall D. Quarles
N. Christian Glenos
Barry A. Brock
Dawn Helms Sharff
Elizabeth M. Davis
David B. Ringelstein, II
J. David Moore
Erin O. Brooks
Alan Michael Warfield
Benjamin Earl Waller
Tracy H. Beauchamp

For full biographical listings, see the Martindale-Hubbell Law Directory

*BREWTON,** Escambia Co.

OTTS, MOORE & JORDAN (AV)

401 Evergreen Avenue, P.O. Box 467, 36427
Telephone: 334-867-7724
Fax: 334-867-2624

MEMBERS OF FIRM

John Thaddeus Moore
J. David Jordan

OF COUNSEL

Lee M. Otts

ASSOCIATE

James Eric Coale

Representative Clients: Container Corporation of America; First National Bank, Brewton; Southern Pine Electric Cooperative; Exxon Corp.; Mobil-GC Corp.; Pennzoil Exploration & Production Co.; T.R. Miller Mill Co., Inc.; Texaco, Inc.
Approved Attorneys for: Mississippi Valley Title Insurance Co.; Auto Owners Insurance Co.

For full biographical listings, see the Martindale-Hubbell Law Directory

THOMPSON, GARRETT & HINES (AV)

218 Belleville Avenue, P.O. Box 387, 36427-0387
Telephone: 334-867-6063
Fax: 334-867-6067
Atmore, Alabama Office: 101 3rd Avenue, P.O. Box 737.
Telephone: 205-368-4999.

MEMBERS OF FIRM

Joe B. Thompson, Jr.
Broox G. Garrett, Jr.
Edward T. Hines

Counsel for: First National Bank, Brewton, Alabama; Alabama Power Co.; State Farm Insurance Co.; Southern Guaranty Insurance Cos.; First National Bank of Atmore; Cities of Atmore, Brewton; Escambia County Board of Education; Brewton City Board of Education; T.R. Miller Mill, Co.; Knud Nielsen Company, Inc.

For full biographical listings, see the Martindale-Hubbell Law Directory

*CENTRE,** Cherokee Co.

KEENER & KEENER (AV)

150 East Main Street, P.O. Box 604, 35960
Telephone: 256-927-5518

Irby A. Keener (1900-1965)
Irby A. Keener, Jr.

*CHATOM,** Washington Co.

TURNER, ONDERDONK, KIMBROUGH & HOWELL, P.A. (AV)

1021 Central Avenue, P.O. Drawer 1389, 36518
Telephone: 334-847-2237
Fax: 334-847-3115
Email: firm@tokh.com *URL:* http://www.tokh.com
Mobile, Alabama Office: 1359 Dauphin Street.
Telephone: 334-432-2855.
Fax: 334-432-2863.

Edward P. Turner, Jr.
A. Michael Onderdonk
William A. Kimbrough, Jr. (Resident, Mobile Office)
Gordon K. Howell
Marc E. Bradley (Resident, Mobile Office)
Halron W. Turner
Frank Woodson (Resident, Mobile Office)
David M. Huggins (Resident, Mobile Office)
E. Tatum Turner

LEGAL SUPPORT PERSONNEL

Thomas E. Fuller

For full biographical listings, see the Martindale-Hubbell Law Directory

*CULLMAN,** Cullman Co.

JOHN DAVID KNIGHT (AV)

114 Downtown Plaza, 35055
Telephone: 256-739-4347
Fax: 256-739-4348
Email: pattyk@hiwaay.net

For full biographical listings, see the Martindale-Hubbell Law Directory

*DECATUR,** Morgan Co.

EYSTER, KEY, TUBB, WEAVER & ROTH (AV)

Eyster Building, 402 East Moulton Street, S.E., P.O. Box 1607, 35602
Telephone: 256-353-6761
Fax: 256-353-6767

John C. Eyster (1863-1926)
Charles H. Eyster, Sr. (1888-1964)
Wm. B. Eyster (1921-1995)

MEMBERS OF FIRM

John S. Key
J. Glynn Tubb
Lawrence C. Weaver
Nicholas B. Roth
J. Witty Allen
William L. Middleton, III
James G. Adams, Jr.
John R. Baggette, Jr.
Jenny L. Mcleroy

General Counsel for: Alabama Farmers Cooperative.
Regional Counsel for: AmSouth Bank.
Local Counsel for: Allstate Insurance Co.; Champion International Corp; Goodyear; Liberty Mutual Insurance Co.; Saginaw Steering Gear Division, General Motors Corp.; State Farm Mutual Automobile Insurance Co.; 3M; The Travelers.

For full biographical listings, see the Martindale-Hubbell Law Directory

HARRIS, CADDELL & SHANKS, P.C. (AV)

214 Johnston Street, S.E., P.O. Box 2688, 35602-2688
Telephone: 256-340-8000
Telecopier: 256-340-8040
Email: hcs@ala-net.com

Julian Harris (1904-1994)
Norman W. Harris (1907-1998)
Philip T. Shanks (Retired)
Charles L. Murphree (Retired)
John A. Caddell
Robert H. Harris
Jon H. Moores
Thomas A. Caddell
William E. Shinn, Jr.
Gary A. Phillips
Dow M. Perry, Jr.
Barnes F. Lovelace, Jr.
Jeffrey S. Brown
David W. Langston
Huel Harris

Attorneys for: First American Bank, Decatur, Alabama; SouthTrust Bank of Alabama (Morgan County); Morgan County Commission; The Industrial Development Board of the City of Decatur, Alabama; The Boeing Company; Amoco Chemical Co.; BellSouth Inc.; Auto-Owners Insurance Co.; ALFA Insurance Cos.; U.S.F. & G. Co.

For full biographical listings, see the Martindale-Hubbell Law Directory

DEMOPOLIS, Marengo Co.

LLOYD, DINNING, BOGGS & DINNING (AV)

Lloyd & Dinning Building, 501 North Walnut Avenue, P.O. Drawer 740, 36732
Telephone: 334-289-0556
Telefax: 334-289-5506
Linden, Alabama Office: 201 E. Coats Avenue, P.O. Box 545.
Telephone: 205-295-8782.

MEMBERS OF FIRM

Hugh A. Lloyd
Woodford W. Dinning (1915-1998)
Thomas H. Boggs, Jr.
Woodford W. Dinning, Jr.

ASSOCIATE

Gregory S. Griggers

Attorneys for: Robertson Banking Co.; Board of Education, City of Demopolis; Black Warrior Electric Membership Corp.; Bryan W. Whitfield Memorial Hospital; Citadel Cement Corp.; City of Linden; Marengo County Commission.

For full biographical listings, see the Martindale-Hubbell Law Directory

MANLEY, TRAEGER, PERRY & STAPP (AV)

111 South Walnut Avenue, 36732-0590
Telephone: 334-289-1384
Fax: 334-289-5384
Mailing Address: P.O. Box 590, Demopolis, Alabama, 36732-0590

Richard S. Manley
William H. Traeger, III
Taylor T. Perry, Jr.
K. Scott Stapp

For full biographical listings, see the Martindale-Hubbell Law Directory

*DOTHAN,** Houston Co.

COBB & SHEALY, P.A. (AV)

206 North Lena Street, P.O. Box 6346, 36302
Telephone: 334-794-8526
Fax: 334-677-0030
URL: http://www.cobb-shealy.com

(See Next Column)

Herman W. Cobb
Steadman S. Shealy, Jr.
Raymond Todd Derrick
Richard Elder Crum
James H. Pike
Joseph A. Morris
Brian T. Mosholder
Joseph D. Talmadge, Jr.

Representative Clients: Travelers Insurance; Nationwide Insurance; Auto-Owners Insurance; Employers Casualty of Texas; Safeco Insurance; Federated Insurance; Universal Underwriters; National Security Insurance; Great Central Insurance.
Approved Title Attorneys for: Mississippi Valley Title Ins. Co.

For full biographical listings, see the Martindale-Hubbell Law Directory

HARDWICK, HAUSE & SEGREST (AV)

212 North Lena Street, P.O. Box 1469, 36302
Telephone: 334-794-4144
Fax: 334-671-9330
URL: http://www.lawyers.com/hhslawfirm

W. G. Hardwick (1910-1993)
William G. Hause (Retired)

MEMBERS OF FIRM

Jere C. Segrest
Kevin Walding
Tina Whitehead Stamps

Counsel for: Dothan City Board of Education; American General Life & Accident Ins. Co.; General Motors Acceptance Corp.; Alabama Power Co.; Liberty National Life Ins. Co.; CBI-Equifax, Inc.; Houston County Board of Education; Cincinnati Insurance Companies.

For full biographical listings, see the Martindale-Hubbell Law Directory

LEE & MCINISH (AV)

238 West Main Street, P.O. Box 1665, 36302
Telephone: 334-792-4156
Facsimile: 334-794-8342
Email: leemc@graceba.net

MEMBERS OF FIRM

W. L. Lee (1873-1944)
Alto V. Lee, III (1915-1987)
William L. Lee, III
Alan C. Livingston
William C. Carn, III
Peter A. McInish
Jerry M. White

ASSOCIATES

William L. Lee, IV
William W. Nichols
William C. White, II

OF COUNSEL

H. Dwight McInish

Counsel for: Seaboard Coast Line Railroad Co.; Atlanta & St. Andrews Bay Railroad Co.; ALFA; U. S. F. & G. Co.; Maryland Casualty Co.; Continental Insurance Cos.; Royal-Globe Group; Slocomb National Bank; GTE South.

For full biographical listings, see the Martindale-Hubbell Law Directory

ENTERPRISE, Coffee Co.

CASSADY, FULLER & MARSH, LLP (AV)

203 East Lee Avenue, P.O. Box 310910, 36331
Telephone: 334-347-2626
Telecopier: 334-393-1396

MEMBERS OF FIRM

Joe C. Cassady
Kenneth T. Fuller
M. Dale Marsh
Joe C. Cassady, Jr.
R. Rainer Cotter, III

Representative Clients: RegionsBank; Enterprise Health Care Authority; Sessions Co., Inc.; Allstate; State Farm Mutual Insurance Co.; Community Bank & Trust Co.; Conagra, Inc.
Approved Attorneys for: First American Title Insurance Co.

For full biographical listings, see the Martindale-Hubbell Law Directory

J. E. SAWYER, JR. (AV)

203 South Edwards Street, 36330
Telephone: 334-347-6447
Fax: 334-347-8217
Email: sawyer@entercomp.com

ASSOCIATE

Stanley P. Walker

For full biographical listings, see the Martindale-Hubbell Law Directory

EUFAULA, Barbour Co.

WILLIAM V. NEVILLE, JR. (AV)

302 East Broad Street, P.O. Box 337, 36072-0337
Telephone: 334-687-5183
Fax: 334-687-6602
Email: anna@neville.com *URL:* http://www.lawyers.com/williamvneville

For full biographical listings, see the Martindale-Hubbell Law Directory

*FORT PAYNE,** De Kalb Co.

SCRUGGS, JORDAN, DODD & DODD (AV)

207 Alabama Avenue, South, P.O. Box 681109, 35967
Telephone: 256-845-5932
Fax: 256-845-4325
Email: scruggs@peop.tdsnet.com *URL:* http://www.lawyers.com/scruggsjordandodd&dodd

William D. Scruggs, Jr.
Robert K. Jordan
J. David Dodd
E. Allen Dodd, Jr.
Holly Hendrickson

Representative Clients: State Farm Insurance Company; Allstate Insurance Co., Inc.; USF&G Insurance Co.; Nucor, Inc.; Ladd Engineering, Inc.; ALABAMA Band; First Federal Bank; Fritz Structural Steel, Inc.; Williamson Oil Co., Inc.

For full biographical listings, see the Martindale-Hubbell Law Directory

*GADSDEN,** Etowah Co.

FORD AND HOWARD, P.C. (AV)

(Formerly Ford & Associates)
The Lancaster Building, 645 Walnut Street, Suite 5, P.O. Box 388, 35902
Telephone: 256-546-5432
Fax: 256-546-5435
Email: fordfirm@aol.com

George P. Ford
H. Edgar Howard

Bradley Williams Cornett
Vann Allan Spray

OF COUNSEL

Elizabeth R. Howard

Reference: AmSouth Bank, N.A.

For full biographical listings, see the Martindale-Hubbell Law Directory

INZER, HANEY, JOHNSON & MCWHORTER, P.A. (AV)

(Inzer, Suttle, Swann & Stivender)
Second Floor, Compass Bank Building, 601 Broad Street, P.O. Drawer 287, 35902-0287
Telephone: 256-546-1656
Telecopier: 256-546-1093
Email: inzerlaw@cybrtyme.com

James C. Inzer (1887-1967)
John A. Lusk, Jr. (1891-1970)
Hubert Burns (1915-1975)
Julius S. Swann, Sr. (1907-1989)
Frank J. Martin (1905-1992)
Roger C. Suttle (1910-1996)
James C. Inzer, Jr. (Of Counsel)
James C. Stivender (Of Counsel)
W. Roscoe Johnson, III
James C. Inzer, III
F. Michael Haney
Robert D. McWhorter, Jr.
James W. McGlaughn
Elizabeth Golson McGlaughn

Assistant Division Counsel for: Southern Railway System.
Attorneys for: General Motors Corp.; Gulf States Steel; Goodyear Tire and Rubber Co.; Alabama Power Co.; Southern Natural Gas Co.; Allstate Insurance Co.; Travelers Insurance Co.; Compass Bank; Cincinnati Insurance Co.

For full biographical listings, see the Martindale-Hubbell Law Directory

*GENEVA,** Geneva Co.

JOHN L. KNOWLES (AV)

202 North Glenn Street, P.O. Box 850, 36340-0850
Telephone: 334-684-9606
Telecopier: 334-684-6369

For full biographical listings, see the Martindale-Hubbell Law Directory

*GUNTERSVILLE,** Marshall Co.

LUSK & LUSK (AV)

452 Gunter Avenue, P.O. Box 609, 35976
Telephone: 256-582-3248
Fax: 256-582-3215

MEMBERS OF FIRM

Marion F. Lusk (1896-1986)
Louis B. Lusk

Representative Clients: AmSouth Bank of Alabama, Guntersville; United States Fidelity & Guaranty Co.; The Travelers Insurance Co.; St. Paul Cos.; ALFA Mutual Insurance Cos.; Hartford Group; Liberty Mutual Insurance Co.; Allstate Insurance Co.; Home of New York Group.

For full biographical listings, see the Martindale-Hubbell Law Directory

*HUNTSVILLE,** Madison Co.

BRADLEY ARANT ROSE & WHITE LLP (AV)

200 Clinton Avenue West, Suite 900, 35801
Telephone: 205-517-5100
Facsimile: 205-517-5200
URL: http://www.barw.com
Birmingham, Alabama Office: 2001 Park Place, Suite 1400, P.O. Box 830709.
Telephone: 205-521-8000.
Facsimile: 205-521-8800. Facsimile (SouthTrust Tower Office): 205-521-8500.
Washington, D.C. Office: 801 Pennsylvania Avenue, NW, Suite 230, 20004.
Telephone: 202-347-8893.
Facsimile: 202-347-1684.

RESIDENT PARTNERS

Hall B. Bryant III
Kenneth B. Cole, Jr. (Not admitted in AL)
Patrick H Graves Jr.
Warne S. Heath
Gary C. Huckaby
E. Cutter Hughes Jr.
Scott E. Ludwig
Charles R. Smith Jr.
H. Harold Stephens
Luther J. Strange, III

OF COUNSEL

S. Revelle Gwyn

RESIDENT ASSOCIATES

Julia Spazzarini Aquila
Erika Jenke-Huber
George P. Kobler
Kimberly B. Martin
Jennifer Byers McLeod
Rebecca Thai

Counsel for: SouthTrust Bank of Alabama, National Association; Energen Corporation; Blount, Inc.; Torchmark Corp.; Russell Corp.; Coca-Cola Bottling Company United, Inc.; Ford Motor Co.; Walter Industries, Inc.; The Birmingham Post Co. (Post-Herald); The New York Times Co.

For full biographical listings, see the Martindale-Hubbell Law Directory

STEPHENS, MILLIRONS, HARRISON & GAMMONS, P.C. (AV)

333 Franklin Street, P.O. Box 307, 35801
Telephone: 256-533-7711
Telecopier: 256-536-9388

Arthur M. Stephens
Paul L. Millirons
James G. Harrison
Robert C. Gammons

Douglas A. Baymiller
Steven J. Shaw

Representative Clients: SouthTrust Bank, N.A.,; Regions Mortgage, Inc.; Chase Manhattan Mortgage Corp.; Amiras, Inc. (d/b/a/ Buy-Wise Drugs); Huntsville Ford Tractor; Brookhill Management Group.

For full biographical listings, see the Martindale-Hubbell Law Directory

*MOBILE,** Mobile Co.

ARMBRECHT, JACKSON, DEMOUY, CROWE, HOLMES & REEVES, L.L.C. (AV)

1300 Riverview Plaza, P.O. Box 290, 36601
Telephone: 334-405-1300
Facsimile: 334-432-6843; 433-3821
Email: adc@ajlaw.com

MEMBERS OF FIRM

Rae M. Crowe
Broox G. Holmes
W. Boyd Reeves
E. B. Peebles III
William B. Harvey
Kirk C. Shaw
Norman E. Waldrop, Jr.
Conrad P. Armbrecht
Grover E. Asmus II
David A. Bagwell
Douglas L. Brown
Donald C. Radcliff
Christopher I. Gruenewald
M. Kathleen Miller
Edward A. Dean
David E. Hudgens
James Dale Smith
Duane A. Graham
Wm. Steele Holman II
Broox G. Holmes, Jr.
James E. Robertson, Jr.
Scott G. Brown
Clifford C. Brady
Richard W. Franklin
Thomas P. Oldweiler
Rodney R. Cate
James F. Watkins

OF COUNSEL

Marshall J. DeMouy

ASSOCIATES

P. Vincent Gaddy
Timothy D. Ryan
Leah P. Ladd
Tamela E. Esham
A. Edwin Stuardi, III
J. Walton Jackson
Sam David Knight
Christopher B. Estes

Representative Clients: American Security Insurance Co. (Regional Counsel); American Security Group (Regional Counsel); AmSouth Bank (Regional Counsel); Burlington Northern Railroad Co. (District Counsel); International Paper Co.; Kimberly-Clark Corp.; Loyal American Life Insurance Co.; Mutual Assurance, Inc.; Travelers Insurance Co.

For full biographical listings, see the Martindale-Hubbell Law Directory

Mobile—Continued

BRISKMAN & BINION, P.C. (AV)

205 Church Street, P.O. Box 43, 36601
Telephone: 334-433-7600
Fax: 334-433-4485
Email: briskman@zebra.net

Donald M. Briskman
Mack B. Binion
Christ N. Coumanis
Kimberly C. Hodgson

A List of Representative Clients will be furnished upon request.
References: Regions Bank; AmSouth Bank, N.A.; Southtrust Bank of Mobile.

For full biographical listings, see the Martindale-Hubbell Law Directory

CABANISS, JOHNSTON, GARDNER, DUMAS & O'NEAL (AV)

700 Riverview Plaza, P.O. Box 2906, 36652
Telephone: 334-433-6961
Fax: 334-415-7350
Email: bgm@cabaniss.com *URL:* http://www.cabaniss.com
Birmingham, Alabama Office: Park Place Tower. 2001 Park Place North, Suite 700. P.O. Box 830612.
Telephone: 205-716-5200.
Fax: 205-716-5389.

MEMBERS OF FIRM

Benjamen T. Rowe (Resident)
William A. Robinson (Resident)
Patrick H. Sims (Resident)
Donald J. Stewart (Resident)
William K. Thomas
David L. Kane (Resident)
R. Boyd Miller (Resident)
Sandy G. Robinson (Resident)

ASSOCIATES

Rebecca D. Parks (Resident)
Ian D. Rosenthal (Resident)
Jarrod J. White (Resident)

Representative Clients: Liberty Mutual Insurance Co.; Liberty National Life Insurance Co.; Rohr Aeroservices; International Paper Company; Boise Cascade Corporation; Employers Reinsurance Co.; Montgomery Kone, Inc.; UOP; Vanity Fair Intimates, Inc.

For full biographical listings, see the Martindale-Hubbell Law Directory

CUNNINGHAM, BOUNDS, YANCE, CROWDER & BROWN, L.L.C. (AV)

1601 Dauphin Street, P.O. Box 66705, 36660
Telephone: 334-471-6191
Fax: 334-479-1031
Email: adm@cbycb.com

James A. Yance
John T. Crowder, Jr.
Robert T. Cunningham, Jr.
Joseph M. Brown, Jr.
Gregory B. Breedlove
Michael A. Worel
David G. Wirtes, Jr.
Toby D. Brown
Reggie Copeland, Jr.
Richard T. Dorman

J. Stephen Legg
George M. Dent, III

OF COUNSEL

Richard Bounds
Robert T. Cunningham
J. Kenyon Rainer, Sr., M.D., J.D.

References: Regions Bank; AmSouth Bank, N.A.

For full biographical listings, see the Martindale-Hubbell Law Directory

FINKBOHNER AND LAWLER, L.L.C. (AV)

169 Dauphin Street Suite 300, P.O. Box 3085, 36652
Telephone: 334-438-5871
Fax: 334-432-8052
Email: finkbohnerlawlerllc@zebra.net

MEMBERS OF FIRM

George W. Finkbohner, Jr.
John L. Lawler
George W. Finkbohner, III
Royce A. Ray, III

For full biographical listings, see the Martindale-Hubbell Law Directory

HELMSING, SIMS & LEACH, P.C. (AV)

The Laclede Building, 150 Government Street, Suite 2000, P.O. Box 2767, 36652
Telephone: 334-432-5521
Telecopy: 334-432-0633

Larry U. Sims
Frederick G. Helmsing
John N. Leach, Jr.
Warren C. Herlong, Jr.
James B. Newman
Robert H. Rouse
Charles H. Dodson, Jr.
Joseph P. H. Babington
R. Alan Alexander
John J. Crowley, Jr.
Joseph D. Steadman
Todd S. Strohmeyer

(See Next Column)

William R. Lancaster
Robin Kilpatrick Fincher
John Townsend Dukes
John Casey Pipes
James Bradford Pittman, Jr.

For full biographical listings, see the Martindale-Hubbell Law Directory

INGE, TWITTY & DUFFY (AV)

1410 Regions Bank Building, 56 St. Joseph Street, P.O. Box 1109, 36633
Telephone: 334-433-3200
Facsimile: 334-433-3444

MEMBERS OF FIRM

James J. Duffy, Jr.
James J. Duffy, III

Francis H. Inge (1902-1959)
Thos. E. Twitty (1901-1975)
Richard H. Inge (1912-1980)

For full biographical listings, see the Martindale-Hubbell Law Directory

JOHNSTONE, ADAMS, BAILEY, GORDON AND HARRIS, L.L.C. (AV)

Royal St. Francis Building, 104 St. Francis Street, 8th Floor, P.O. Box 1988, 36633
Telephone: 334-432-7682
Facsimile: 334-432-0712 or 334-432-2800
Email: attorneys@JohnstoneAdams.com *URL:* http://www.JohnstoneAdams.com
Bay Minette, Alabama Office: Dahlberg Building, 107 Hand Avenue, P.O. Box 729, 36507.
Telephone: 334-937-9473.
Facsimile: 334-937-9475.

MEMBERS OF FIRM

Charles B. Bailey, Jr.
Ben H. Harris, Jr.
William H. Hardie, Jr.
E. Watson Smith
Joseph M. Allen, Jr.
I. David Cherniak
David C. Hannan
Wade B. Perry, Jr.
Thomas S. Rue
Alan C. Christian
Celia J. Collins
R. Gregory Watts
Charles C. Simpson, III
William Alexander Gray, Jr.
Robert S. Frost
Tracy P. Turner
Lawrence J. Seiter
E. Erich Bergdolt

ASSOCIATES

E. Russell March, III
Scott Alton Browning
Craig Bryant Morris
John Robert Parker
Katherine Parks Nelson
F. Inge Johnstone

OF COUNSEL

Robert F. Adams
Brock B. Gordon

For full biographical listings, see the Martindale-Hubbell Law Directory

LYONS, PIPES & COOK, P.C. (AV)

2 North Royal Street, P.O. Box 2727, 36652-2727
Telephone: 334-432-4481
Cable Address: "Lysea"
Telecopier: 334-433-1820
URL: http://www.LPCLaw.com

Joseph H. Lyons (1874-1957)
Sam W. Pipes, III (1916-1982)
Walter M. Cook (1915-1988)
Wesley Pipes
Norton W. Brooker, Jr.
Cooper C. Thurber
Marion A. Quina, Jr.
Thomas F. Garth
Walter M. Cook, Jr.
W. David Johnson, Jr.
Joseph J. Minus, Jr.
Caroline C. McCarthy
William E. Shreve, Jr.
Kenneth A. Nixon
Daniel S. Cushing
Allen E. Graham
Michael C. Niemeyer
M. Warren Butler
S. Wesley Pipes, V
James D. Jeffries, Jr.
Roger E. Cole
S. Andrew Scharfenberg, Jr
Ginger L. Pierce
Philip A. Stroud

Ryan T. Northrup

General Counsel: Inchcape Shipping Services.
Counsel: The Hertz Corp.; McKenzie Tank Lines, Inc.; SCNO Barge Lines, Inc.; Scott Paper Co.; Shell Oil Corp.
Trial Counsel: Aetna Life & Casualty Co.; Chubb Group of Insurance Companies.

For full biographical listings, see the Martindale-Hubbell Law Directory

AUGUSTINE MEAHER, III, P.C. (AV)

107 St. Francis Street, Suite 2118, 36602-3321
Telephone: 334-432-9971
Fax: 334-432-9978

Augustine Meaher, III

References: Bank of Mobile, Mobile, Alabama; AmSouth Bank, Mobile, Alabama.

For full biographical listings, see the Martindale-Hubbell Law Directory

Mobile—Continued

TURNER, ONDERDONK, KIMBROUGH & HOWELL, P.A. (AV)

1359 Dauphin Street, 36604
Telephone: 334-432-2855
FAX: 334-432-2863
URL: http://www.tokhmobile.com
Chatom, Alabama Office: 1021 Central Avenue, P.O. Drawer 1389.
Telephone: 334-847-2237.
Fax: 334-847-3115.

Edward P. Turner, Jr.
A. Michael Onderdonk
William A. Kimbrough, Jr. (Resident)
Gordon K. Howell
Marc E. Bradley
Halron W. Turner
Frank Woodson (Resident)
David M. Huggins (Resident)
E. Tatum Turner

LEGAL SUPPORT PERSONNEL

Thomas E. Fuller

For full biographical listings, see the Martindale-Hubbell Law Directory

VICKERS, RIIS, MURRAY AND CURRAN, L.L.C. (AV)

8th Floor, Regions Bank Building, 106 Saint Francis Street, P.O. Box 2568, 36652
Telephone: 334-432-9772
Fax: 334-432-9781
Email: vickersriis.com

MEMBERS OF FIRM

Marion R. Vickers (1901-1995)
Marion R. Vickers, Jr. (1935-1989)
Erling Riis, Jr.
J. Manson Murray
Edwin J. Curran, Jr.
J. W. Goodloe, Jr.
E. L. McCafferty, III
Zebulon M. P. Inge, Jr.
Frank Grey Redditt, Jr.
Thomas E. Sharp, III
Ronald P. Davis
J. Marshall Gardner
M. Kathryn Knight
L. Thomas Styron
C. Richard Wilkins
Terry A. Moore

Timothy A. Clarke
Evan Austill, Jr.

Representative Clients: Mobile Forest Products, Inc.; Azalea Aviation, Inc.; Midstream Fuel Services; McPhillips Manufacturing Co., Inc.; Spring Hill College; Steiner Shipyard, Inc.; Marine Office of America Corp.; Cummins Alabama, Inc.; Ben M. Radcliff Contractor, Inc.

For full biographical listings, see the Martindale-Hubbell Law Directory

*MONTGOMERY,** Montgomery Co.

AZAR & AZAR, L.L.C. (AV)

260 Washington Avenue, P.O. Box 2028, 36197
Telephone: 334-265-8551
Fax: 334-264-9453

MEMBERS OF FIRM

Edward J. Azar
George B. Azar

ASSOCIATES

Robert D. Reynolds
Charles W. Edmondson
Zack M. Azar
William D. Azar

OF COUNSEL

Elizabeth C. Wible

General Counsel For: Resurrection Catholic Missions of the South, Inc.; City of St. Jude, Inc.; Jerry Kyser Builder, Inc.; Buffalo's American Grille; Nathan Watson Builder, Inc.; H & B Construction Co., Inc.; AAA Mini-Storage Warehouses; Medical Clinic Board of the City of Montgomery - Montco Center; Credit Union Attorneys Legal Directory; Accounts Receivable Management.

For full biographical listings, see the Martindale-Hubbell Law Directory

BALL, BALL, MATTHEWS & NOVAK, P.A. (AV)

2000 Interstate Park Drive, Suite 204, 36109
Telephone: 334-387-7680
Fax: 334-387-3222
Email: Firm@Ball-Ball.com

Fred S. Ball (1866-1942)
Charles A. Ball (1904-1969)
Fred S. Ball, Jr. (1896-1974)
Richard A. Ball (1906-1983)
John R. Matthews, Jr.
Richard A. Ball, Jr.
Tabor R. Novak, Jr.
Clyde C. Owen, Jr.
C. Winston Sheehan, Jr.
William H. Brittain II
E. Hamilton Wilson, Jr.
Richard E. Broughton
T. Cowin Knowles
Gerald C. Swann, Jr.
Mark T. Davis
James A. Rives

Fred B. Matthews
Allison L. Alford
Michael L. White
Emily C. Marks
Brandy A. Adkins
George R. Parker

(See Next Column)

LEGAL SUPPORT PERSONNEL

Lon Worley (Office Manager)

Counsel for: Beech Aircraft Corporation; Bell Helicopter Co.; John Deere Co.; Government Employees Insurance Co.; Chubb & Son; Cigna Co.; Chrysler Corp.; Associated Aviation Underwriters.

For full biographical listings, see the Martindale-Hubbell Law Directory

HASKELL SLAUGHTER YOUNG & GALLION, L.L.C. (AV)

305 South Lawrence Street, P.O. Box 4660, 36103-4660
Telephone: 334-265-8573
Facsimile: 334-264-7945
Email: hsymont@actworld.net
Birmingham, Alabama Office: 1200 AmSouth/Harbert Plaza, 1901 Sixth Avenue North. 35203
Telephone: 205-251-1000.
Facsimile: 205-324-1133.

Thomas T. Gallion, III
Constance C. Walker

Representative Clients: City of Birmingham; The Equitable Life Assurance Society of the United States; Federal Deposit Insurance Corporation; HEALTHSOUTH Corporation/HEALTHSOUTH Medical Centers; Montgomery County, Alabama; USX Corporation.

For full biographical listings, see the Martindale-Hubbell Law Directory

HILL, HILL, CARTER, FRANCO, COLE & BLACK, P.C. (AV)

425 South Perry Street, P.O. Box 116, 36101-0116
Telephone: 334-834-7600
Fax: 334-263-5969

Thomas B. Hill, Jr. (1903-1984)
Wm. Inge Hill (1911-1995)
James T. Stovall (1905-1972)
James J. Carter (1913-1985)
William A. Oldacre (1932-1973)
Ralph A. Franco
T. Bowen Hill, III
Harry Cole
Robert C. Black, Sr.
William I. Hill, II
John M. Milling, Jr.
William Inge Hill, Jr.
Gerald W. Hartley
Randall Morgan
Robert W. Bradford, Jr.
David E. Allred
Laura L. Crum
Mark A. Franco
Joana S. Ellis
John R. Bradwell
William C. McGowin
Robert C. Black, Jr.
Thomas C. Tankersley

Pamela Pelekis Swan
Elizabeth Brannen Carter
Doy Leale McCall, III
Erika Perrone Tatum

Representative Clients: The Aetna Group; The State Farm Group; ALFA; General Electric Co.; General Motors Corp; Blue Cross and Blue Shield of Alabama; Allstate Insurance Co.; Winn-Dixie Stores, Inc.; Scottsdale Insurance Co.; National Casualty Co.

For full biographical listings, see the Martindale-Hubbell Law Directory

VOLZ, PRESTWOOD & HANAN, P.C. (AV)

350 Adams Avenue, P.O. Box 1910, 36102-1910
Telephone: 334-264-6401
Fax: 334-834-4954

Charles H. Volz, Jr.
Alvin T. Prestwood
Charles H. Volz, III
Ellis D. Hanan
Richard D. Lively
Judy H. Barganier

For full biographical listings, see the Martindale-Hubbell Law Directory

PELL CITY, St. Clair Co.

BLAIR AND PARSONS (AV)

St. Clair Land Title Building, 1711 Cogswell Avenue, 35125
Telephone: 205-884-3440
Fax: 205-884-3442

MEMBERS OF FIRM

A. Dwight Blair
Elizabeth S. Parsons

Representative Clients: Colonial Bank; Metro Bank; Am South Bank; State Farm Mutual Insurance Cos; ALFA Mutual Insurance Co.; Allstate Insurance Co.; St. Paul Insurance Cos.; Auto Owners Insurance Co.; Reliance Insurance Cos.; National Bank of Commerce.

For full biographical listings, see the Martindale-Hubbell Law Directory

*RUSSELLVILLE,** Franklin Co.

MCDOWELL & BEASON (AV)

(Formerly McDowell, Beason & Pilati)
507 North Jackson, P.O. Box 818, 35653
Telephone: 256-332-1660
Fax: 256-332-0318
Email: Legal@Getaway.Com

Daniel G. McDowell
Eddie Beason

(See Next Column)

McDowell & Beason, *Russellville—Continued*

OF COUNSEL

Joe Fine

Representative Clients: Citizens Bank & Savings Co. of Russellville; City of Phil Campbell; Russellville City Board of Education; Franklin County Board of Education; Mutual Savings Life Insurance Co.; State Farm Fire & Casualty Co.; State Farm Mutual Automobile Ins. Co.; Marshall Durbin Co.

For full biographical listings, see the Martindale-Hubbell Law Directory

*SELMA,** Dallas Co.

Hobbs & Hain, P.C. (AV)

707 Selma Avenue, P.O. Box 1190, 36701
Telephone: 334-874-6683
Facsimile: 334-872-8435
Email: hobbsandhain@zebra.net

Samuel Earle Hobbs (1917-1994)
Ralph N. Hobbs
Bruce V. Hain (1915-1995)
Barry R. Bennett
James B. McNeill, Jr.

Counsel for: Industrial Development Board of the City of Selma; Roy S. Jones Realty Co., Inc.; Jones Oil Co., Inc.

For full biographical listings, see the Martindale-Hubbell Law Directory

Pitts, Pitts & Thompson (AV)

Suite 201 AmSouth Bank Building, Drawer 537, 36702-0537
Telephone: 334-875-7213
Fax: 334-874-8218

MEMBERS OF FIRM

Arthur M. Pitts (1880-1955)
Philip Henry Pitts
W. McLean Pitts (1911-1982)
J. Garrison Thompson

ASSOCIATE

Rickman E. Williams, III

LEGAL SUPPORT PERSONNEL

Ruby Jo Caver (Paralegal)

Local Attorneys for: U. S. F. & G. Co.; St. Paul Mercury Insurance Cos.; Maryland Casualty Co.; Traveler's Insurance Co.; CSX Transportation; City of Selma.
Approved Attorneys for: Lawyers Title Insurance Corp.; Farm Credit Bank of Texas.

For full biographical listings, see the Martindale-Hubbell Law Directory

Reeves & Stewart, P.C. (AV)

Regions Bank Building, 101 Church Street, P.O. Box 457, 36702-0457
Telephone: 334-875-7236
Fax: 334-875-7625

Archie T. Reeves, Jr.
Robert E. Armstrong, III
B. Kincey Green, Jr.
Allen S. Reeves

Local Attorneys for: State Farm Mutual Automobile Insurance Cos.; St. Paul Insurance Cos.; International Paper Co.; Regions Bank; Alabama Power Co.; South Central Bell Telephone; Alabama Gas Corp.; Columbia-HCA, Inc.; CSX Transportation.
Assistant Division Counsel for: Norfolk Southern Corp.

For full biographical listings, see the Martindale-Hubbell Law Directory

*TROY,** Pike Co.

Calhoun, Faulk, Watkins & Faircloth, L.L.C. (AV)

78 South Court Square, P.O. Box 489, 36081
Telephone: 334-566-7200
Fax: 334-566-7584

Richard F. Calhoun
William Keith Watkins
Joseph E. Faulk
Robert Curry Faircloth
James G. Clower (Retired)

General Counsel for: City of Troy; City of Brundidge; Regions Bank, Troy; First National Bank of Brundidge; Troy City Board of Education; Pike County Board of Education; South Alabama Electric Cooperative, Inc.; Airtek Engineering, Inc.

For full biographical listings, see the Martindale-Hubbell Law Directory

*TUSCALOOSA,** Tuscaloosa Co.

Davidson, Wiggins, Jones & Coleman, P.C. (AV)

2625 Eighth Street, P.O. Box 1939, 35403
Telephone: 205-759-5771
Fax: 205-752-8259
Email: wiggins@dbtech.net
Email: tj@dbtech.net

G. Stephen Wiggins
Thomas R. Jones, Jr.
Charles M. Coleman

(See Next Column)

Randal Kevin Davis
J. Paul Zimmerman
Roman Ashley Shaul

OF COUNSEL

M. McCoy Davidson

Representative Clients: Peco Foods, Inc.; St. Paul Companies, Inc.; Illinois-Central Railroad Co.; The Travelers Group; Mutual Assurance, Inc.; Cigna Insurance Companies; Zenith Insurance Company; Industrial Development Board of the City of Tuscaloosa, Alabama; Nationwide Insurance Company; Blue Cross and Blue Shield of Alabama.

For full biographical listings, see the Martindale-Hubbell Law Directory

Donald, Randall, Donald & Tipton (AV)

Ninth Floor, AmSouth Building, 2330 University Boulevard, P.O. Box 2155, 35403
Telephone: 205-758-2585
Fax: 205-758-2593
Email: drdtlaw@bellsouth.net

MEMBERS OF FIRM

William J. Donald
William J. Donald, III
B. Wayne Randall
Ritchie L. Tipton

ASSOCIATES

Laurie K. Pratt
Elizabeth Utsey Sadler
John R. Franks, Jr.

References: AmSouth Bank; The Bank of Vernon.

For full biographical listings, see the Martindale-Hubbell Law Directory

Hubbard, Smith, McIlwain, Brakefield & Browder, P.C. (AV)

808 Lurleen Wallace Boulevard, North, P.O. Box 2427, 35403
Telephone: 205-345-6789
Telecopier: 205-759-1195

Perry Hubbard (1921-1991)
W. Marcus Brakefield
Michael D. Smith
Herbert E. "Chip" Browder
Christopher L. McIlwain
Justice D. Smyth, III

Elizabeth Faxon Colwick
Gary E. Sullivan

Counsel for: Randall Publishing Co.; United States Fidelity & Guaranty Co.; Chubb Group of Insurance Cos.; West Alabama Health Services; City of Eutaw; Kimberly-Clark Corp.; Regions Bank; City of Tuscaloosa; West Alabama Bank & Trust; Tuscaloosa County Industrial Development Authority.

For full biographical listings, see the Martindale-Hubbell Law Directory

Owens & Almond, LLP (AV)

2606 8th Street, P.O. Box 2487, 35403-2487
Telephone: 205-750-0750
Facsimile: 205-750-0355
Email: owensalm@dbtech.net

John A. Owens
M. Bradley Almond
Apsilah Owens Millsaps

Anna Northington Hutcheson

For full biographical listings, see the Martindale-Hubbell Law Directory

Rosen, Cook, Sledge, Davis, Cade & Shattuck, P.A. (AV)

2117 Jack Warner Parkway, P.O. Box 2727, 35403-2727
Telephone: 205-344-5000
Fax: 205-758-8358

Gordon Rosen
Ronald L. Davis
J. Sydney Cook, III
Joseph W. Cade
James J. Sledge
R. Cooper Shattuck

Paige M. Carpenter
Leon Y. Sadler, IV
Joseph K. Beach
William Bradford Roane, Jr.
Jeffrey Carl Smith
Jerry C. Oldshue, Jr.
John T. Fisher, Jr.

Counsel for: Hunt Refining Company; National Bank of the South; Security Federal Bank; City of Northport; City of Brookwood.
Local Counsel for: AmSouth Bank; United States Fidelity & Guaranty Co.; Kemper Insurance Group; State Farm Insurance Companies; Commercial Union Insurance Cos.

For full biographical listings, see the Martindale-Hubbell Law Directory

Turner & Turner, P.C. (AV)

1426 22nd Avenue, P.O. Drawer 2688, 35403
Telephone: 205-752-1502
Fax: 205-345-7229
Email: JTurner003@aol.com

(See Next Column)

TURNER & TURNER P.C.—*Continued*

James A. Turner
Louise I. Turner
James D. Turner

Thomas D. Bobitt, II
Brian D. Turner

Representative Clients: B.F. Goodrich Alabama Employees Federal Credit Union; Friday Lumber Company, Inc.; W.G. Sullivan Lumber Company, Inc.; Barkley Pontiac Cadillac-GMC Trucks; Landmark Oldsmobile; Haverty's Credit Service; Weyerhauser Credit Union; Warrior Tractor and Equipment Company.

For full biographical listings, see the Martindale-Hubbell Law Directory

ZEANAH, HUST, SUMMERFORD, DAVIS, JONES & WILLIAMSON, L.L.C. (AV)

Seventh Floor, AmSouth Bank Building, P.O. Box 1310, 35403
Telephone: 205-349-1383
Fax: 205-391-1319
Email: ZHSDJ@mail.dbtech.net

MEMBERS OF FIRM

Olin W. Zeanah (1922-1987)
Wilbor J. Hust, Jr.
E. Clark Summerford
Kenneth D. Davis
Christopher H. Jones
Beverly Smith Williamson

OF COUNSEL

Marvin T. Ormond

Representative Clients: Alfa Insurance Cos.; Hartford Insurance Group; Home Insurance Co.; Nationwide Insurance Co.; Alabama Power Co.; Liberty Mutual Insurance Co.; The Uniroyal Goodrich Tire Co.

For full biographical listings, see the Martindale-Hubbell Law Directory

ALASKA

*ANCHORAGE,** Third Judicial District

DELANEY, WILES, HAYES, GERETY, ELLIS & YOUNG, INC. (AV)

1007 West Third Avenue, Suite 400, 99501
Telephone: 907-279-3581
Fax: 907-277-1331
Email: dwhge@alaska.net

Daniel A. Gerety
Stephen M. Ellis
Clay A. Young
William E. Moseley
James B. Friderici
Andrew Guidi
Howard A. Lazar
Donald C. Thomas
Timothy J. Lamb
Cynthia L. Ducey
Donna M. Meyers
Jeffrey P. Stark

Clyde E. Sniffen, Jr.
Amy E. Headrick

OF COUNSEL

James J. Delaney
George N. Hayes
Stanley H. Reitman
J. D. Cellars

Representative Clients: Carr-Gottstein Foods Co.; Chevron Corporation; Arco Alaska Inc.; Alyeska Pipeline Service Co.; Phillips Petroleum Company; Matanuska Electric Association; Nana Regional Corporation; Bering Straits Native Corporation; Mobil Oil Company; Seibu, Inc.

For full biographical listings, see the Martindale-Hubbell Law Directory

HOLMES WEDDLE & BARCOTT, A PROFESSIONAL CORPORATION (AV)

701 West Eighth Avenue, Suite 700, 99501-3408
Telephone: 907-274-0666
Telecopier: 907-277-4657
Email: INFO@ANC.HWB-LAW.COM
Seattle, Washington Office: 999 Third Avenue, Suite 2600.
Telephone: 206-292-8008.
Telecopier: 206-340-0289.

Michael M. Holmes (Resident at the Seattle, Washington Office)
Randall J. Weddle
Michael A. Barcott (Resident at the Seattle, Washington Office)
Timothy A. McKeever
Constance E. Livsey
Theresa Hennemann
Elizabeth D. Goudreau
Matthew D. Regan

OF COUNSEL

Richard B. Brown

Suzanne K. Ishii-Regan
William W. Whitaker
Robert Jospeh Bredesen
Jon Goltz

For full biographical listings, see the Martindale-Hubbell Law Directory

ROBERTSON, MONAGLE & EASTAUGH, A PROFESSIONAL CORPORATION (AV)

1400 West Benson Boulevard Suite 315, 99503
Telephone: 907-277-6693
Telecopy: 907-279-1959
Juneau, Alaska Office: Goldbelt Place Office Building, 801 West 10th Street, Suite 300.
Telephone: 907-586-3340.
Telecopy: 907-586-6818.
Arlington, Virginia Office: Arlington Courthouse Plaza II, 2300 Clarendon Boulevard, Suite 1010.
Telephone: 703-527-4414.
Telecopy: 703-527-0421.

Royal Arch Gunnison (1873-1918)
R. E. Robertson (1885-1961)
M. E. Monagle (1902-1985)
Frederick O. Eastaugh (1913-1992)
Leroy J. Barker
L. G. Berry
Harold E. Snow, Jr.
Julia Barrows Bockmon
Stacy K. Steinberg
Wayne G. Dawson
Brad D. De Noble

LEGAL SUPPORT PERSONNEL

LEGAL ASSISTANTS

Chloe Clark-Berry
Deborah Sims

Representative Clients: Alaska Pulp Corp.; Associated Aviation Underwriters; Brunswick Corp.; Fireman's Fund Insurance Group; U.S. Aviation Insurance Group; U.S. Borax Chemical Corp.

For full biographical listings, see the Martindale-Hubbell Law Directory

*JUNEAU,** First Judicial District

ROBERTSON, MONAGLE & EASTAUGH, A PROFESSIONAL CORPORATION (AV)

Goldbelt Place Office Building, 801 West 10th Street, Suite 300, 99801
Telephone: 907-586-3340
Telecopy: 907-586-6818
Anchorage, Alaska Office: 1400 West Benson Boulevard, Suite 315.
Telephone: 907-277-6693.
Telecopy: 907-279-1959.
Arlington, Virginia Office: Arlington Courthouse Plaza II, 2300 Clarendon Boulevard, Suite 1010.
Telephone: 703-527-4414.
Telecopy: 703-527-0421.

RESIDENT PERSONNEL

James F. Clark
Paul M. Hoffman
Robert Blasco
Terry L. Thurbon
Daniel J. Boone
Ruth R. Hamilton
Amy S. Gurton

For full biographical listings, see the Martindale-Hubbell Law Directory

KODIAK, Third Judicial District

JAMIN, EBELL, SCHMITT & MASON, A PROFESSIONAL CORPORATION (AV)

323 Carolyn Street, 99615
Telephone: 907-486-6024
Telecopier: 907-486-6112
Seattle, Washington Office: 605 1st Avenue, Suite 300.
Telephone: 206-622-7634.
Telecopier: 206-623-7521.

Matthew D. Jamin
C. Walter Ebell (Resident, Seattle, Washington Office)
Alan L. Schmitt
Walter W. Mason (Resident, Seattle, Washington Office)

Karen E. Bendler (Resident, Seattle, Washington Office)
Stephen B. Wallace

For full biographical listings, see the Martindale-Hubbell Law Directory

ARIZONA

*FLAGSTAFF,** Coconino Co.

MANGUM, WALL, STOOPS & WARDEN, P.L.L.C. (AV)

100 North Elden, P.O. Box 10, 86002
Telephone: 520-779-6951
Fax: 520-773-1312

H. Karl Mangum (1908-1993)

OF COUNSEL

Douglas J. Wall
Robert W. Warden
Daniel J. Stoops

(See Next Column)

MANGUM, WALL, STOOPS & WARDEN P.L.L.C., *Flagstaff—Continued*

MEMBERS OF FIRM

A. Dean Pickett
Stephen K. Smith
Melinda L. Garrahan
Michael H. Hinson

ASSOCIATES

Annette Star Lustgarten
Rebecca Smith Currey
R. Scott Currey
Melinda K. Jacquez
Franklin Hoover
Brandon J. Kavanagh

LEGAL SUPPORT PERSONNEL

J.J. Feeney (Librarian/Research Analyst)
Sheri A. Biro (Paralegal)
Diane M. Sulzer
Cathryn S. Rugg
Dena L. Knoll (Paralegal)

Representative Clients: Northern Arizona University; Flagstaff Unified School District; Museum of Northern Arizona; Arizona School Board Association.
Local Counsel for: Bank of America-Arizona; Arizona Public Service; U.S-.A.A.; State Farm Fire & Casualty Insurance Co.; Property Development Co.

For full biographical listings, see the Martindale-Hubbell Law Directory

GLENDALE, Maricopa Co.

MEAD & ASSOCIATES (AV)

6670 West Cactus Road, Suite A-105, 85304-1656
Telephone: 623-412-2508
Fax: 623-878-9153
After Hours: 602-547-0908

Terrance C. Mead

ASSOCIATES

Judith E. Abramsohn
Danielle H. Riordan
Martin A. Bihn
Kenn Martin Hanson

Representative Clients: American Medical Security, Inc.; Arizona Department of Public Safety Local Retirement Board.

For full biographical listings, see the Martindale-Hubbell Law Directory

*PHOENIX,** Maricopa Co.

ANDERSON, BRODY, LEVINSON, WEISER & HORWITZ, P.A. (AV)

1112 West Camelback Road, 85013
Telephone: 602-234-0563
Fax: 602-234-2952
Email: pmw@andersonbrody.com *URL:* http://www.andersonbrody.com

Donald E. Anderson
Jeffrey H. Levinson
Paul M. Weiser
Jamie A. Brody
Ronald M. Horwitz
Bradley D. Gardner
Alan M. Levinsky
Janessa E. Shtabsky
Jan Grossman
David L. O'Daniel
Steven M. Fox
Gail I. Schwartzbard

For full biographical listings, see the Martindale-Hubbell Law Directory

JAMES T. BIALAC (AV)

Suite 8 Luhrs Arcade, 11 West Jefferson Street, 85003
Telephone: 602-258-8441
Fax: 602-258-8443
Mailing Address: P.O. Box 4095, 85030

BURCH & CRACCHIOLO, P.A. (AV)

702 East Osborn Road, Suite 200, 85014
Telephone: 602-274-7611
Fax: 602-234-0341
Mailing Address: P.O. Box 16882, Phoenix, AZ, 85011
Email: library@bcattorneys.com

Daniel Cracchiolo
Stephen E. Silver
Brian Kaven
Guadalupe Iniguez
Brad S. Ostroff
Daryl Manhart
Ian Neale
Edwin C. Bull
Bryan F. Murphy
Linda A. Finnegan
Andrew Abraham
Clare H. Abel
Donald W. Lindholm
F. Michael Carroll
Daniel R. Malinski
Edwin D. Fleming
Ralph D. Harris
David M. Villadolid
Marvin Davis

Amy DeLaplace Howland
Susanne E. Ingold
Theodore (Todd) Julian
Steven J. Lippman
Thomas A. Longfellow
Martha C. Patrick
Mitchell J. Resnick
Jordan J. Rich
Steven M. Serrano
James M. Stipe

OF COUNSEL

Frank Haze Burch
Donna Platt Boros
Howard C. Meyers

Representative Clients: Bashas' Inc.; Farmers Insurance Group; U-Haul International, Inc.

(See Next Column)

For full biographical listings, see the Martindale-Hubbell Law Directory

FENNEMORE CRAIG, A PROFESSIONAL CORPORATION (AV)

3003 North Central Avenue, Suite 2600, 85012-2913
Telephone: 602-916-5000
Fax: 602-916-5999
Tucson, Arizona Office: One South Church Avenue, Suite 1000, 85701-1620.
Telephone: 520-879-6800.
Fax: 520-879-6899.

Calvin H. Udall
James Powers
James M. Bush
Arthur D. Ehrenreich
C. Webb Crockett
Kenneth J. Sherk
Neal Kurn
Robert P. Robinson
Michael Preston Green
John D. Everroad
James W. Johnson
Robert J. Hackett
Jay S. Ruffner
Jordan Green
Louis F. Comus, Jr.
Donald R. Gilbert
Ronald L. Ballard
Timothy J. Burke
Ronald J. Stolkin
Stephen M. Savage
Roger T. Hargrove
William L. Kurtz
Mark A. Nesvig
David T. Maddox
George T. Cole
Lauren J. Caster
Timothy Berg
C. Owen Paepke
William L. Thorpe
Charles M. King
David T. Cox
Cynthia L. Shupe
Michael V. Mulchay
Phillip F. Fargotstein
Paul J. Mooney
Cathy L. Reece
David A. Weatherwax
Graeme Hancock
Rita A. Eisenfeld
David N. Heap
Don J. Miner
Norman D. James
Ray K. Harris
Margaret R. Gallogly
Scott M. Finical
Andrew M. Federhar
Gregg Hanks
Karen Ciupak McConnell
Jay S. Kramer
Christopher L. Callahan
Jim L. Wright
Bryan A. Albue
David E. Vieweg
J. Barry Shelley
Christopher P. Staring
Janet W. Lord
John Randall Jefferies
John J. Balitis, Jr.
James J. Trimble
Janice Procter-Murphy
Robert J. Kramer
John M. Pearce
Jean Marie Sullivan
Keith L. Hendricks
W. T. Eggleston, Jr.
M. Virginia Perry
Douglas C. Northup
Marc H. Lamber
Kendis K. Muscheid
Stephen A. Good

SENIOR COUNSEL

Stanley S. Weithorn (Not admitted in AZ)

John E. Kofron
Paul E. Wolf
Theresa Dwyer
Mark H. Brain
Scott H. Thomas
Elizabeth M. Behnke
Paul F. Wille (Not admitted in AZ)
Susan Marie Ciupak
Jeffrey S. Pitcher
Stacie K. Smith
Dewain D. Fox
Jeffrey S. Silvyn
Amy Abdo Anderson
Jay L. Shapiro
James D. Burgess
Scott L. Altes
Mary Beth Phillips
Sandra L. Etherton
Erin E. Flaharty
Thomas F. O'Malley, III
Karen Errant
Janna B. Day
Susan M. Wissink
David M. Call
Vera E. Munoz
Sal J. Rivera
Joel B. Shapiro
Theodore D. Setzer
Paul A. Krulisky
Barney M. Holtzman
Audrey V. Dorch (Not admitted in AZ)
Stacey A. Kelly
Michelle G. Marshall
Joseph Sciarrotta, Jr.
Scott W. Hyder
William S. Gates
John D. Bethea
Lori A. Higuera
Rosa Mroz
Tracey Ann Ager
Jane Proctor
Kenneth J. Lee
Kim S. Alvarado
Lawrence E. Palles (Not admitted in AZ)
Thomas D. Ulreich
Michele L. Tyler
Kenneth W. Miller
Drew C. Flowers
Charles D. Mitchell, Jr.

LEGAL SUPPORT PERSONNEL

LEGAL ASSISTANTS

Claudia E. Anderson
Beverly Cooper
Vicki Montei
Nancy E. Esser
Jane Friedman
Joyce Herron
Julie Hodges
Donna M. Horwitz
Ann V. Kooi
Margaret Larson
Carol Levine
Margaret Moore
Marie Morrell
Claudia L. Parks
Charlene Sarich
Amy Thompson
Karen Tomb
Alison Vander Ark

For full biographical listings, see the Martindale-Hubbell Law Directory

Phoenix—Continued

GOODSON, MANLEY & DURFEE, P.L.C. (AV)

The Brookstone Building, 2025 North 3rd Street, Suite 200, 85004-1471
Telephone: 602-252-5110
Fax: 602-257-1883
URL: http://www.gmdlaw.com
Email: gmdlaw@primenet.com *URL:*
http://www.lawyers.com/goodson__manley__durfee

John F. Goodson
Colleen C. Manley
Richard E. Durfee, Jr.
Benjamin D. Benedict

A list of Representative Clients will be furnished upon request.
Reference: Pacific Century Bank.

For full biographical listings, see the Martindale-Hubbell Law Directory

JENNINGS, STROUSS & SALMON, P.L.C. (AV)

A Professional Limited Liability Company
One Renaissance Square, Two North Central Avenue, 85004-2393
Telephone: 602-262-5911
Fax: 602-253-3255
Email: info@jsslaw.com *URL:* http://www.jsslaw.com
Arrowhead Office: 16150 North Arrowhead Fountains Center Drive, Suite 250, Peoria, Arizona.
Telephone: 623-878-2222.
Fax: 623-878-1333.

John R. Christian
Gary G. Keltner
Lee E. Esch
Richard L. Lassen
T. Patrick Flood
W. Michael Flood
I. Douglas Dunipace
Douglas G. Zimmerman
Gerald W. Alston
Michael G. Helms
Robert J. Novak
George C. Spilsbury
John G. Sestak, Jr.
Philip J. MacDonnell
David J. Calverley
Kenneth C. Sundlof, Jr.
Douglas F. Behm
Rita A. Meiser
Joseph W. Mott
Leland M. Jones
Gerrit M. Steenblik
Gary L. Lassen
Richard N. Morrison
Anne L. Kleindienst
David Brnilovich
John C. West
Joen M. Schaefer
Jay A. Fradkin
Michael R. Palumbo
David W. Kash
Glenn J. Carter
H. Christian Bode
James M. Ackerman
George Esahak-Gage
Robert J. Werner
Ernest Calderón
Wendy D. Woodrow
Michael V. Perry
Dean C. Robertson
Brian N. Spector
Michael J. O'Connor
Scott K. Oberg
John J. Egbert
Michael J. Farrell
Shiela B. Schmidt
Robert D. Haws
Jennifer M. Bligh
Kim D. Steinmetz
Cody M. Hall
David B. Earl
Lydia A. Jones
Richard K. Delo
R. Quinn De Angelis, Jr.

OF COUNSEL

Gary L. Stuart
Ann M. Dumenil

ASSOCIATES

Herbert T. Swafford
Cynthia A. Coates
Gordon Lewis
Stephanie A. McRae
Andrew B. Turk
Scott M. Berg
Bryan S. VanMeveren
Stacey A. Dowdell
Scott Rhodes
John P. Robertson, II
Johnny J. Sorenson
Jeffrey C. Whitley
C. David Martinez
Kimberly J. Cilke
Carolyn D. Craft
Anoma T. Nolan
Kevin R. Robling

Representative Clients: Bank One Arizona, NA; Best Western International, Inc.; CNA Insurance Co.; Karsten Manufacturing; Mutual Insurance Company of Arizona; Salt River Project; Shamrock Foods Co.; Southwest Gas Corp.; Sun Health Corporation; Western Agricultural Insurance Group.

For full biographical listings, see the Martindale-Hubbell Law Directory

LEWIS AND ROCA, LLP (AV)

A Limited Liability Partnership including a Professional Corporation
40 North Central Avenue, 85004-4429
Telephone: 602-262-5311
Fax: 602-262-5747
Email: clientservice@lrlaw.com *URL:* http://www.lrlaw.com
Tucson, Arizona Office: One South Church Avenue, Suite 700, 86701-1620.
Telephone: 520-622-2090.
Fax: 520-622-3088. E-Mail: clientservice@lrlaw.com.
Las Vegas, Nevada Affiliated Office: Ashcraft and Heinz LLP, 3960 Howard Hughes Parkway, 89109.
Telephone: 702-990-3570.
Fax: 702-990-3571.

(See Next Column)

MEMBERS OF FIRM

Orme Lewis (1903-1990)
Edwin Beauchamp (1916-1964)
Joseph E. McGarry
Peter D. Baird
Merton E. Marks (P.C.)
Richard N. Goldsmith
Richard S. Cohen
David E. Manch
Patricia K. Norris
Patrick Derdenger
Foster Robberson
Michael J. Holden
Amy R. Porter
George L. Paul
Thomas G. Ryan
Jesse B. Simpson
James K. Kloss
Brent C. Gardner
Cathy M. Holt
Steven J. Hulsman
Carl F. Mariano
Christopher J. Brelje
Kenneth Van Winkle, Jr.
Steven J. Burr
L. Keith Beauchamp
Hope Leibsohn
Douglas L. Christian
Richard A. Halloran
Geoffrey H. Walker
Thel W. Casper
Paul M. Roca (1911-1979)
John P. Frank
Gerald K. Smith
Douglas L. Irish
Douglas R. Chandler
R. Kent Klein
Susan M. Freeman
Randolph J. Haines
José A. Cárdenas
Dale A. Danneman
Thomas H. Campbell
Newman R. Porter
Sheila Carmody
D. Randall Stokes
Stephen M. Bressler
Scott DeWald
Robert F. Roos
Mary Ellen Simonson
James T. Acuff, Jr.
Rosemarie Christofolo
Bryant D. Barber
Bret A. Maidman
Robert H. McKirgan
Pamela B. Petersen
Jane E. Reddin
Craig W. Phillips
Greg S. Como
Kevin G. Hunter
Janell M. Adams
Glenn D. Forcucci
Anderson L. Carper

ASSOCIATES

Ann-Martha Andrews
Randy Papetti
Todd E. Hale
J. Henk Taylor
Michael L. Denby
Kent J. Hammond
Douglas J. McDonald
Stephanie M. Cerasano
Leanne Dodds-Eastman
Gena LoPresto Sluga
Daniel A. Goldfried
Amy L. McAllister
Robert G. Fisher
Lawrence E. Thompson
Mark Egan
Michael Hallam
Debra A. Gordon
John R. Rapasky
Jennifer A. Van Kirk
(Not admitted in AZ)
Dawn M. Bergin
David B. Gass
Bruce E. Samuels
Barry A. Willits
Tracy M. Durchslag
Robert K. Lewis
Stephen W. Tully
W. Todd Coleman
Maria E. Morales
Michael Christian
Eric G. Maxfield
Lynn M. Allen
Jon Weiss
Mark Wenker
Warren M. Denetsosie
Katherine Philippakis
Kevin C. Nicholas
Amy E. Altshuler
Stephen E. Silverman
Donald J. Baier

OF COUNSEL

Lyman A. Manser
James L. Hohnbaum
Julie M. Arvo MacKenzie
Dona A. Nutini
Cindy A. Beard
(Not admitted in AZ)
Jeremy E. Butler
Barbara Anstey Hoerner
David A. Kelly
Joseph A. Mislove
Gregory Y. Harris
Frances J. Haynes
Thomas J. Morgan

Representative Clients: Arizona Public Service; Blood Systems, Inc.; CIT Corp.; City of Phoenix; The Dial Corp; E.I. du Pont de Nemours and Co.; MCI Communications, Corp.; The Prudential Insurance Company of America; Samaritan Health System; Smith Barney Shearson, Inc.

For full biographical listings, see the Martindale-Hubbell Law Directory

MARISCAL, WEEKS, MCINTYRE & FRIEDLANDER, P.A. (AV)

2901 North Central Avenue Suite 200, 85012-2705
Telephone: 602-285-5000
Fax: 602-285-5100

Phillip Weeks (1936-1999)
Donald N. McIntyre
(1932-1999)
Richard A. Friedlander
Gerald Gaffaney
William Novotny
Michael S. Rubin
Gary L. Birnbaum
Robert A. Shull
Peter A. Winkler
Michael R. Scheurich
Fred C. Fathe
Les Raatz
Andrew L. Pringle
Brian M. Mueller
Anne L. Tiffen
P. Bruce Converse
Terry L. Tedesco
James T. Braselton
Leonce A. Richard
Scott A. Holcomb
David J. Ouimette
D. Samuel Coffman
Kenneth A. Hodson
Michael D. Hool
Robert L. Schwartz
David I. Thompson
Steven D. Wolfson
Scot L. Claus
David D. Rodgers
Dana M. Levy
Claudia D. Work
Cathy L. Knapp
Valerie Costa-Sheedy
Allison R. Shiff
Cassandra M. Wambaugh

(See Next Column)

MARISCAL, WEEKS, MCINTYRE & FRIEDLANDER P.A., *Phoenix—Continued*

References: Northern Trust Bank of Arizona; National Bank of Arizona.

For full biographical listings, see the Martindale-Hubbell Law Directory

MOHR, HACKETT, PEDERSON, BLAKLEY & RANDOLPH, P.C. (AV)

2800 North Central Avenue, Suite 1100, 85004-1043
Telephone: 602-240-3000
Fax: 602-240-6600
Email: Info@mhplaw.com

William C. Blakley (1946-1987)
Robert C. Hackett
Gordon A. Mohr
Arthur W. Pederson
John M. Randolph
Thomas K. Chenal
Peter N. Spiller
David W. Dow
M. Maureen Anders
Gregory W. Falls
Azim Q. Hameed
Thomas C. Axelsen
John J. Nicgorski
Thomas M. Quigley
Michael W. Wright
Daniel P. Beeks
Carolyn Ratti Matthews
Nathaniel B. Rose
Karen L. Karr
Joseph R. Meaney
Daniel J. Kiley
Kathryn E. Maxwell

For full biographical listings, see the Martindale-Hubbell Law Directory

SNELL & WILMER L.L.P. (AV)

One Arizona Center, 85004-2202
Telephone: 602-382-6000
Fax: 602-382-6070
Email: postmaster@snellwilmer.com *URL:* http://www.swlaw.com
Tucson, Arizona Office: One South Church Avenue, Suite 1500, 85701-1612.
Telephone: 520-882-1200.
Fax: 520-884-1294.
Orange County Office: 1920 Main Street, Suite 1200, Irvine, California 92614-7230.
Telephone: 949-253-2700.
Fax: 949-955-2507.
Salt Lake City, Utah Office: 111 East Broadway, Suite 900, 84111-1004.
Telephone: 801-237-1900.
Fax: 801-237-1950.

MEMBERS OF FIRM

John J. Bouma
Robert C. Bates
Warren E. Platt
William A. Hicks, III
Peter J. Rathwell
Steven M. Wheeler
Joseph T. Melczer, III
Gerard Morales
Barry D. Halpern
James R. Condo
Richard W. Sheffield
Arthur P. Greenfield
Thomas R. Hoecker
Charles A. Pulaski, Jr.
Matthew P. Feeney
Arthur T. Anderson
Quinn Williams
Richard W. Shapiro
Jody Kathleen Pokorski
Heidi McNeil Staudenmaier
Alex B. Marconi
E. Jeffrey Walsh
Michael K. Kelly
Katherine M. Harmeyer
George J. Coleman, III
Kevin J. Parker
Charles E. James, Jr.
Christopher H. Bayley
Robert R. Kinas
Richard D. Blau
Patrick X. Fowler
Brian J. Foster
Patrick G. Byrne
Marvin S. Swift, Jr.
Patricia Lee Refo
GinaMarie Rossano
John C. Vryhof
Jeffrey Webb Crockett
Daniel J. Noblitt
Lisa M. Coulter
Richard B. Stagg
Shaukat A. Karjeker
Richard K. Mallery
Jon S. Cohen
Jay D. Wiley
George H. Lyons
Daniel J. McAuliffe
Douglas W. Seitz
William R. Hayden
Robert B. Hoffman
Joel P. Hoxie
Lonnie J. Williams, Jr.
Vaughn A. Crawford
David A. Sprentall
Suzanne McCann
Terry Morris Roman
Donald L. Gaffney
Joyce Kline Wright
Rebecca A. Winterscheidt
Craig K. Williams
Timothy G. O'Neill
G. Van Velsor Wolf, Jr.
David E. Weiss, Jr.
Steven D. Pidgeon
Martha E. Gibbs
James J. Sienicki
Janet E. Barton
Donald H. Smith
Steven S. Guy
Nicholas J. Wood
Samuel C. Cowley
Charles P. Keller
Barbara J. Dawson
Bob J. McCullough
Prithviraj S. Sivananthan
Charles F. Hauff, Jr.
Carlos D. Ronstadt
Timothy J. Casey
Paul J. Giancola
Maria Nutile
L. Frederick Williams, Jr.
Michael M. Donahey
Gerard E. Wimberly, Jr.
Sid Leach (Not admitted in AZ)

OF COUNSEL

Edward Jacobson

SENIOR ATTORNEYS

Cheryl A. Ikegami
Thomas L. Mumaw

(See Next Column)

ASSOCIATES

Jennifer Abracht-Smith
Andrew S. Ashworth
Roberta E. Berger
Michael Byorick (Not admitted in AZ)
Nancy Kay Campbell
Nancy J. Caplette
David J. Carroll
J. Michael Christopher
Stephanie R. Derby
Sharon L. Fabian
Brigitte Finley
Dora Fitzpatrick
Robert Lee Fraley
Brad A. Gazaway
Dan W. Goldfine
Elizabeth A. Guth
Andrew Foster Halaby
Robert Henry
Steven D. Jerome
Robert M. Kort
Monica A. Limón-Wynn
Kristin Major
Craig A. Marquiz
Brian C. Miller
James B. Morse (Not admitted in AZ)
Daren W. Perkins
Daniel R. Pote
DeShon Pullen
Michael S. Rafford
Michelle L. Ray
Brian Roberts
Kenneth G. Royer
Barbara Ryan
Shahpar Shahpar
Leslie A. Smith
Mark M. Takahashi
Stephanie Vithoulkas
Todd J. Weiss
Donald Zavala
Joseph G. Adams
Denise L. Atwood
Damon L. Boyd
M. Lawrence Brown
Terri N.A. Buccino
David Caplan
Brett A. Carlson
Deborah M. Chess
Anthony Joseph Coury
Kelly Druten
Todd Feltus
John A. Fisher
Elizabeth A. Fox
Stacy Gabriel
Elicia D. Giroux
Jeffrey Breck Guldner
Jennifer L. Hadley
Robert M. Hayward
Karen Lynn Hunnicutt
Brad L. Kerby
Amy L. Leinen
Todd Cannon Lockwood
Michael B. Maledon
L. Drew Metcalf
Kevin T. Miller
Mark D. Ohre
Patrick J. Paul
Cynthia Pillote
Howard J. Powers, II
Stephanie Quincy
David E. Rauch
Heidi J. Richter
Rosario A. Rodriguez
Philip Randolph Rudd
Lori A. Schmig
Gretchen N. Smith
Howard Sobelman
Barry C. Toone
Catherine Wehling
Jay Douglas Wiley, II
Laura J. Zeman

Representative Clients: For list of Representative Clients, see end of biographical listings in the Martindale-Hubbell Law Directory.

For full biographical listings, see the Martindale-Hubbell Law Directory

SQUIRE, SANDERS & DEMPSEY L.L.P. (AV)

Two Renaissance Square, 40 North Central Avenue, Suite 2700, 85004-4498
Telephone: 602-528-4000
Fax: 602-253-8129
URL: http://www.ssd.com
Cleveland, Ohio Office: 4900 Key Tower, 127 Public Square, Cleveland, Ohio 44114-1304.
Telephone: 216-479-8500.
Fax: 216-479-8780.
Columbus, Ohio Office: 1300 Huntington Center, 41 South High Street, Columbus, Ohio 43215-6150.
Telephone: 614-365-2700.
Fax: 614-365-2499.
Houston, Texas Office: 6250 Chase Tower, 600 Travis Street, Houston, Texas 77002-3007.
Telephone: 713-546-5850.
Fax: 713-546-5830.
Jacksonville, Florida Office: One Enterprise Center, Suite 2100, 225 Water Street, Jacksonville, Florida 32202-4424.
Telephone: 904-366-2420.
Fax: 904-356-2986.
Miami, Florida Office: 201 South Biscayne Boulevard, 2900 Miami Center, Miami, Florida 33131-4330.
Telephone: 305-577-8700.
Fax: 305-358-1425.
New York, New York Office: 350 Park Avenue, New York, New York 10022-6002.
Telephone: 212-872-9800.
Fax: 212-872-9815.
Washington, D.C. Office: 1201 Pennsylvania Avenue, N.W., Suite 500, Washington, D.C. 20004-2491.
Telephone: 202-626-6600.
Fax: 202-626-6780.
Bratislava, Slovak Republic Office: Zochova 5, 811 03 Bratislava, Slovak Republic.
Telephone: 421-7-5441-7611.
Fax: 42-1-7-6280-2212.
Brussels, Belgium Office: Avenue Louise, 165-Box 15, 1050 Brussels, Belgium.
Telephone: 32-2-627-1111.
Fax: 32-2-627-1100.

(See Next Column)

SQUIRE, SANDERS & DEMPSEY L.L.P.—*Continued*

Budapest, Hungary Office: H-1062 Budapest, Andrassy ut. 64, Budapest, Hungary.
Telephone: 36-1-428-7111.
Fax: 36-1-428-7100.
Kyiv, Ukraine Office: 14A Yaroslaviv Val, Kyiv 252034, Ukraine.
Telephone: 38-044-228-8687.
Fax: 38-044-228-4938.
London, England Office: Royex House, Aldermanbury Square, London EC2V 7HR.
Telephone: 44-171-776-5200.
Fax: 44-171-776-5233.
Madrid, Spain Office: Calle Velazquez 108-110, 28006 Madrid, Spain.
Telephone: 34-91-590-2420.
Fax: 34-91-590-2421.
Moscow, Russian Federation Office: 13 Khokhlovskiy Lane, Moscow 109028, Russian Federation.
Telephone: 7-503-956-3750.
Fax: 7-503-956-3635.
Prague, Czech Republic Office: Václavské náměst 1 57/813, 110 00 Praha 1, Czech Republic.
Telephone: 420-2-2166-2111.
Fax: 420-2-2166-2222.
Hong Kong Office: Rooms 1101-2 St. George's Building, 2 Ice House Street, Central, Hong Kong.
Telephone: 852-2509-9732.
Fax: 852-2509-9772.
Taipei, Taiwan Office: 14F, 116 Nanking East Road, Sec. 2, Taipei, Taiwan, Republic of China.
Telephone: 886-2-2531-2888.
Fax: 886-2-2571-6199.

PARTNERS

James L. Adler, Jr.
Mitchel B. Axler (Not admitted in AZ)
Carl M. Bennett
Cary B. Edgar
Craig D. Hansen
Christopher D. Johnson
David W. Kreutzberg
Michael A. Lechter
K. David Lindner
Robert L. Matia
Timothy W. Moser
Mark A. Nadeau
William L. Nelson
Robert H. Olson
Karen L. Peters
Cynthia A. Ricketts
Richard F. Ross
Thomas J. Salerno
Norman C. Storey
Christopher D. Thomas
Donald A. Wall

OF COUNSEL

Hugh A. Madden
Bruce E. Martin (Not admitted in AZ)

ASSOCIATES

Joel J. Agena
Benjamin D. Aguilera
Ann-Marie Anderson
Rawle Andrews, Jr. (Not admitted in AZ)
Scott T. Ashby
William R. Bachand (Not admitted in AZ)
Kevin J. Bonner
Joseph M. Crabb
Cynthia Crockett
Karl S. Dahlquist
Mark W. Daliere
Brian P. Dolasinski
Dane K. Fernandes (Not admitted in AZ)
Gregory R. Hall
Jonathan E. Hess
Christopher E. Kevane
Sandra J. Kimm
David M. Klein
Jordan A. Kroop
Hugh H. Marthinsen
André H. Merrett (Not admitted in AZ)
Timothy C. Nash (Not admitted in AZ)
Natasha M. Price
David E. Rogers (Not admitted in AZ)
Claudia T. Salomon
Mark A. Schmidt
Renée E.Sandler Shamblin
James D. Smith
Renée E. Tetreault
Sara A. Thacker

For full biographical listings, see the Martindale-Hubbell Law Directory

---

STEPTOE & JOHNSON LLP (AV)

Two Renaissance Square, 40 N. Central, 24th Floor, 85004
Telephone: 602-257-5200
Fax: 602-257-5299
Email: wrehm@steptoe.com *URL:* http://www.steptoe.com
Washington, D.C. Office: 1330 Connecticut Avenue, N.W. 20036.
Telephone: 202-429-3000.
Fax: 202-429-9204.
Cable Address: "Stepjohn".
Los Angeles, California Office: 633 West Fifth Street, Suite 700, 90071.
Telephone: 213-439-9400.
Fax: 213-439-9599.
Moscow, Russia Office: Steptoe & Johnson International. 25 Tsvetnoy Boulevard, Building 3, Moscow, Russia.
Telephone: 011-7-501-258-5250.
Fax: 011-7-501-258-5251.
Almaty, Kazakhstan Office: Steptoe & Johnson Company (Almaty), 4 Republic Square, Rooms 501-508, 480065.
Telephone: 011-7-(3272)-50-1125.
Fax: 011-7(3272)-581-650.

(See Next Column)

PARTNERS

Lawrence A. Katz
James G. Derouin
Bruce E. Meyerson
Francis J. Burke, Jr.
David J. Bodney
Floyd P. Bienstock
George Ian Brandon
Kevin L. Olson
Monica L. Goebel

OF COUNSEL

Barbara R. Goldberg
Bennett Evan Cooper
Scot C. Stirling

SPECIAL COUNSEL

Kevin M. Judiscak

ASSOCIATES

Lisa Morganstern Bickel
Anthony J. Blackwell
Brian A. Cabianca
Elizabeth A. Schallop Call
Rebecca Kozloff Collins
Alan R. Davis
Catharine D. Ellingsen
Michael B. Gerdes
Stacey F. Gottlieb
Sara M. Hankins
Mark G. Kisicki
Christopher A. LaVoy
David R. Nelson
Jon T. Neumann
John B Nickerson
Sandra K. Sanders
Peter B. Swann
Andrew J. Sweet
James M. Torre
Kathryn E. Underwood
Mari I. Valenzuela
Steven D. Wheeless

For full biographical listings, see the Martindale-Hubbell Law Directory

---

*PRESCOTT,** Yavapai Co.

FAVOUR, MOORE & WILHELMSEN, A PROFESSIONAL ASSOCIATION (AV)

1580 Plaza West Drive, P.O. Box 1391, 86302
Telephone: 520-445-2444
Fax: 520-771-0450
Email: fmw@primenet.com

John M. Favour
Mark M. Moore
David K. Wilhelmsen

Lollie A. Roberts (Not admitted in AZ)
Robert A. Miller

Representative Client: Yavapai Title Co.
Reference: Bank of America.

For full biographical listings, see the Martindale-Hubbell Law Directory

---

MURPHY, LUTEY, SCHMITT & BECK, P.L.L.C. (AV)

Elks Building, 117 East Gurley Street, 86301
Telephone: 520-445-6860
Fax: 520-445-6488
Email: MLSB@GOODNET.COM
Yuma, Arizona Office: Valley Professional Plaza, 1763 West Twenty-Fourth Street, Suite 200.
Telephone: 520-726-0314.
Fax: 520-341-1079.
Kingman, Arizona Office: 2601 Stockton Hill Road, Suite H8.
Telephone: 520-718-0888; 1-800-281-0822.

MEMBERS OF FIRM

Thelton D. Beck
Michael R. Murphy
Selmer D. Lutey
Robert E. Schmitt
Dan A. Wilson
Alex B. Vakula

Scott K. Risley

Counsel for: State Farm Mutual Automobile Insurance Co.; Allstate Insurance Co.; Farmers Insurance; Western Agricultural Insurance Co.;
Local Counsel for: Bank One Arizona, NA; The Stockmen's Bank.
Representative Clients: Prescott College; Galpin Ford, Inc.; Sedona-Oak Creek Airport Authority; Yavapai County Fair Association (Prescott Downs).

For full biographical listings, see the Martindale-Hubbell Law Directory

---

SCOTTSDALE, Maricopa Co.

SACKS TIERNEY P.A. (AV)

4250 North Civic Center Boulevard, 85251
Telephone: 480-425-2600
Facsimile: 480-970-4610
Email: ST@sackstierney.com
Phoenix, Arizona Office: Two North Central Avenue, Suite 1960. 85004.
Telephone: 480-435-2600.
Fax: 480-970-4610.

Seymour Sacks
Marvin S. Cohen
David C. Tierney
Stephen Aron Benson
Michael R. Rooney
Robert G. Kimball
Stephen P. Linzer
Marcia J. Busching
Randall S. Yavitz
Sharon Brook Shively
James W. Armstrong
Steven M. Goldstein
Judith M. Dworkin
Robert J. Lord

(See Next Column)

SACKS TIERNEY P.A., *Scottsdale—Continued*

Sharon S. Moyer
Candess J. Hunter
Lori R. Miller
Brian E. Ditsch

Sharyl Poulson Speaker
Steven W. Bienstock
Andrew Lane de Mars
Scott B. Cohen
Mark D. Dillon
John L. Habib
W. Kevin Bell
Isabel M. Humphrey
Julie A. Inderlied
Laura G. Meyer
Stephen A. Wolf

Reference: M&I Thunderbird Bank.

For full biographical listings, see the Martindale-Hubbell Law Directory

*TUCSON,** Pima Co.

CHANDLER, TULLAR, UDALL & REDHAIR, L.L.P. (AV)

1700 Bank of America Plaza, 33 North Stone Avenue, 85701-1415
Telephone: 520-623-4353
Telefax: 520-792-3426

MEMBERS OF FIRM

Thomas Chandler
D. B. Udall
Jack Redhair
Steven Weatherspoon
Edwin M. Gaines, Jr.
Dwight M. Whitley, Jr.
E. Hardy Smith
John J. Brady
Charles V. Harrington
Kurt Kroese

ASSOCIATES

Lori A. Petersen
Elizabeth D. Bushell
Christopher R. Pennison
Charles Alexander Davis
Michael Scott Redhair
Sue Ann Welch
Stephen L. Wetherell
Edward Moomjian, II

Representative Clients: Arizona Electric Power Cooperative, Inc.; Atlantic Richfield Co.; CNA Insurance; Farmers Insurance Exchange; MICA; Chubb Insurance Group; State Farm Mutual Insurance Companies.
Reference: Arizona Bank.

For full biographical listings, see the Martindale-Hubbell Law Directory

FENNEMORE CRAIG, A PROFESSIONAL CORPORATION (AV)

Suite 1000, One South Church Avenue, 85701-1620
Telephone: 520-879-6800
Fax: 520-879-6899
Phoenix, Arizona Office: 3003 North Central Avenue, Suite 2600, 85012-2913.
Telephone: 602-916-5000.
Fax: 602-916-5999.

Ronald J. Stolkin
Andrew M. Federhar
Christopher P. Staring

John E. Kofron
Paul E. Wolf
Jeffrey S. Silvyn
Amy Abdo Anderson
Barney M. Holtzman

LEGAL SUPPORT PERSONNEL

LEGAL ASSISTANTS

Jane Friedman
Susan Chesser

For full biographical listings, see the Martindale-Hubbell Law Directory

GABROY, ROLLMAN & BOSSÉ, P.C. (AV)

3507 North Campbell Avenue, Suite 111, 85719
Telephone: 520-320-1300
Telefax: 520-320-0717
Email: admin@gabroylaw.com

Steven L. Bossé
Richard M. Rollman
John Gabroy
Ronald M. Lehman
Fred A. Farsjo
Lyle D. Aldridge
Ronna L. Fickbohm

Richard A. Brown
Nicole Gabroy-Ayaz

For full biographical listings, see the Martindale-Hubbell Law Directory

GOERING, ROBERTS, BERKMAN, RUBIN & BROGNA, P.C. (AV)

Suite 302, 1840 East River Road, 85718
Telephone: 520-577-9300
Fax: 520-577-0848
Email: grbrb@aol.com

Scott Goering
Howard T. Roberts, Jr.
David L. Berkman
William L. Rubin
Carmine A. Brogna
Christopher L. Enos

Representative Clients: Fireman's Fund Insurance; Safeco Insurance; Royal Insurance; Sentry Insurance; American International Group; Farmers Insurance; USAA; Country Companies; Cigna.
Reference: Bank One.

For full biographical listings, see the Martindale-Hubbell Law Directory

HARALSON, MILLER, PITT & MCANALLY, P.L.C. (AV)

One South Church Avenue Suite 900, 85701
Telephone: 520-792-3836
Telecopier: 520-624-5080
Email: mpmpc@azstarnet.com

Barry N. Akin (1939-1988)
Dale Haralson, P.C.
G. Eugene Isaak
Gerald Maltz
Janice A. Wezelman
T. Patrick Griffin
Philip J. Hall
Grace McIlvain
Thomas G. Cotter
Lindsay E. Brew
Armando Rivera
Gus Aragón, Jr.
Carole A. Summers
Bradley P. Miller

OF COUNSEL

Richard L. McAnally

RETIRED

Robert F. Miller
Donald Pitt

Representative Clients: Bell Atlantic Metro Mobile; Farmers Investment Co.; Forest City Enterprises; Vince Granatelli Racing; KVOA Channel 4 TV; Newmont Mining Corp.; S.L. Industries, Inc.; Tucson Unified School District; University of Arizona Foundation.

For full biographical listings, see the Martindale-Hubbell Law Directory

HAZLETT & WILKES (AV)

310 South Williams Boulevard, Suite 305, 85711
Telephone: 520-790-9663
Fax: 520-790-9616
Email: hazlettwilkes@juno.com

MEMBERS OF FIRM

Carl E. Hazlett
James M. Wilkes

ASSOCIATE

Thomas M. Bayham

For full biographical listings, see the Martindale-Hubbell Law Directory

STOMPOLY, STROUD, GLICKSMAN & ERICKSON, P.C. (AV)

1820 Norwest Tower, One South Church Avenue, 85702
Telephone: 520-628-8300
Telefax: 520-628-9948
Mailing Address: P.O. Box 190, Tucson, AZ, 85702-0190

John G. Stompoly
James L. Stroud
Elliot A. Glicksman
George Erickson

For full biographical listings, see the Martindale-Hubbell Law Directory

ARKANSAS

*ARKADELPHIA,** Clark Co.

WRIGHT, CHANEY, BERRY, DANIEL, SLAUGHTER & HUGHES, P.A. (AV)

303 Professional Park Drive, P.O. Drawer 947, 71923
Telephone: 501-246-6796
Telefax: 501-246-2178
Email: dchaney@arklaw.com *URL:* http://www.arklaw.com

William G. Wright
Donald P. Chaney, Jr.
Travis R. Berry
LeAnne Daniel
Eric G. Hughes
Edward M. Slaughter
Rodney Moore

Counsel for: Elk Horn Bank and Trust Co.; Farm Bureau Mutual Insurance Company of Arkansas, Inc.; Southern Farm Bureau Casualty Insurance Co.; Underwriters Adjustment Co.; Nationwide Insurance Co.; Central Production Credit Assn.; Shelter Insurance Co.; Colonial Insurance Co.
Approved Attorneys for: Farmers Home Administration; American Title Insurance Co.

For full biographical listings, see the Martindale-Hubbell Law Directory

*ASHDOWN,** Little River Co.

BISHOP & BISHOP (AV)

171 West Main Street, P.O. Box 609, 71822
Telephone: 870-898-5058
Fax: 870-898-8110

MEMBERS OF FIRM

Eric W. Bishop
Eric T. Bishop

Representative Clients: The First National Bank, Ashdown; First National Bank of De Queen; Citizens National Bank of Nashville; Little River County Rural Development Authority; E-Z Mart Stores, Inc.; Little River Memorial Hospital; Bank of Waldron; First National Bank of Howard County; First Guaranty Ins. Co.

(See Next Column)

BISHOP & BISHOP—*Continued*

Agents for: Lawyers Title Insurance Corp.

For full biographical listings, see the Martindale-Hubbell Law Directory

*BATESVILLE,** Independence Co.

BLAIR, STROUD & DAVIDSON (AV)

Suite 201, 500 East Main, P.O. Box 2135, 72503-2135
Telephone: 870-793-8350
Fax: 870-793-3989
Email: blast@cei.net

MEMBERS OF FIRM

H. David Blair
Robert D. Stroud
J. Scott Davidson

For full biographical listings, see the Martindale-Hubbell Law Directory

*BLYTHEVILLE,** Mississippi Co.

OSCAR FENDLER (AV)

104 North Sixth Street, P.O. Box 548, 72316-0548
Telephone: 870-763-6891
Facsimile: 870-763-6892

Representative Clients: Farmers Bank & Trust Co., Blytheville; Drainage District No. 16, Miss. Co., Ark.; Lee Wilson & Co.; S.J. Cohen Co.; Ashmore Bros. & Brown; Skyline Steel Corp.; Arkansas Steel Processing, Inc.; Merchants & Planters Bank, Manila; Manila Depot Committee, Inc.

*CAMDEN,** Ouachita Co.

HARRELL & LINDSEY, P.A. (AV)

201 Jackson Street, S.W., P.O. Box K, 71711
Telephone: 870-836-7725
Fax: 870-836-4643
URL: http://www.lawyers.com/harrelllaw

Searcy W. Harrell, Jr.
Paul E. Lindsey

Christina S. Carr

For full biographical listings, see the Martindale-Hubbell Law Directory

ALLEN P. ROBERTS, P.A. (AV)

325 Jefferson Street, S.W., P.O. Box 280, 71711-0280
Telephone: 870-836-5310
FAX: 870-836-9662
Email: aroberts@cei.net

Allen P. Roberts

Representative Clients: International Paper Co.; Camden Fairview School District; The City of Camden; Byars Oil Co.; American Fuel Cell & Coated Fabrics Co.; Star City School District; Highland Resources, Inc.; Circle B Logging Co.; First National Bank, Magnolia, Arkansas.

For full biographical listings, see the Martindale-Hubbell Law Directory

*EL DORADO,** Union Co.

COMPTON, PREWETT, THOMAS & HICKEY, P.A. (AV)

423 North Washington Avenue, P.O. Box 1917, 71731-1917
Telephone: 870-862-3478
Fax: 870-862-7228

Walter L. Brown (1893-1972)
Robert C. Compton
William I. Prewett
Floyd M. Thomas, Jr.
Joseph Hickey
Roger W. Landes
Robin J. Carroll

Ted Botner

LEGAL SUPPORT PERSONNEL

Jerri L. Agerton (Paralegal)

General Counsel for: National Bank of Commerce of El Dorado; Cross Oil Refining & Marketing, Inc.
Local Counsel for: Figgie International, Inc.; Farmers Insurance Group; Employers Mutual Companies.
Representative Clients: Murphy Oil Corp.; El Dorado Chemical Co.; El Dorado Industrial Development Corp.

For full biographical listings, see the Martindale-Hubbell Law Directory

CRUMPLER O'CONNOR & WYNNE (AV)

1501 West Block Street, 71730-5300
Telephone: 870-863-8118
FAX: 870-863-8110
Email: WJWGSW@aol.com

(See Next Column)

Claude B. Crumpler (1890-1978)
John A. O'Connor, Jr. (1913-1988)
William J. Wynne

A list of Representative Clients will be furnished upon request.

SHACKLEFORD, PHILLIPS, WINELAND & RATCLIFF, P.A. (AV)

100 East Church Street, P.O. Box 1718, 71731-1718
Telephone: 870-862-5523
FAX: 870-862-9443
Email: SPWR@IPA.NET

John M. Shackleford (1896-1968)
Dennis L. Shackleford
Norwood Phillips
Teresa Wineland
Brian H. Ratcliff
Michelle H. Cauley

OF COUNSEL

John M. Shackleford, Jr.

Representative Insurance Clients: American Interstate Insurance Co.; CIGNA Cos.; CNA Insurance Co.; Commercial Union Insurance Co.; Fireman's Fund Insurance Co.; General Accident Insurance Co.; Liberty Mutual Insurance Co.; Medical Protective Insurance Co.; The St. Paul Cos.; Zurich Insurance Co.

For full biographical listings, see the Martindale-Hubbell Law Directory

*FAYETTEVILLE,** Washington Co.

BALL & MOURTON, LTD., PLLC (AV)

A Professional Limited Liability Company
Suite 700, E.J. Ball Plaza, P.O. Box 1948, 72702
Telephone: 501-442-6213
Fax: 501-442-6233
Email: contact@ballandmourton.com *URL:* http://www.BallandMourton.com
Siloam Springs, Arkansas Office: 106 South Broadway. P.O. Box 1348, 72761.
Telephone: 501-524-2337.
Fax: 501-524-3693.

E. J. Ball
Kenneth R. Mourton
John T. Lee
Rayburn W. Green

David G. Bercaw
J. Michael Threet
Joseph D. Reece
Shannon L. Poore

OF COUNSEL

Neal R. Pendergraft

Representative Clients: Arkansas Western Gas Co.; Coors of Western Arkansas, Inc.; Rebel Enterprises, Inc.; Southwestern Energy Co.; Stephens Production Co.; Ohlendorf Investment Co.; Central Health Corporation; McIlroy Bank & Trust.

For full biographical listings, see the Martindale-Hubbell Law Directory

BASSETT LAW FIRM (AV)

221 North College Avenue, P.O. Box 3618, 72702-3618
Telephone: 501-521-9996
Fax: 501-521-9600
Email: places212@aol.com

MEMBERS OF FIRM

Woodson W. Bassett, Jr.
Woodson W. Bassett, III
Tod C. Bassett
Wm. Robert Still, Jr.
Walker Dale Garrett
Curtis L. Nebben
Earl Buddy Chadick, Jr.
Angela M. Doss
Gary V. Weeks
J. David Wall
Vincent O. Chadick
James M. Graves
Scott Edward Wray
Shannon L. Fant

Representative Clients: Hartford Insurance Group; Tyson Foods, Inc.; Scottsdale Insurance Co.; St. Paul Fire and Marine Insurance Co.; AIG Aviation Ins. Co.; WAUSAU; USAA; Baldor Corp.; Wal-Mart Stores, Inc.

For full biographical listings, see the Martindale-Hubbell Law Directory

CONNER & WINTERS, P.L.L.C. (AV)

100 West Center Street, Suite 200, 72701-6081
Telephone: 501-582-5711
Facsimile: 501-587-1426
Email: postmaster@cwlaw.com
Tulsa, Oklahoma Office: Conner & Winters, A Professional Corporation, 3700 First Place Tower, 15 East 5th Street, 74103-4344.
Telephone: 918-586-5711.
Facsimile: 918-586-8982.
Oklahoma City, Oklahoma Office: Conner & Winters, A Professional Corporation, One Leadership Square, 211 North Robinson, Suite 1700, 73102-7101.
Telephone: 405-272-5711.
Facsimile: 405-232-2695.

(See Next Column)

CONNER & WINTERS P.L.L.C., *Fayetteville—Continued*

Washington, D.C. Office: Conner & Winters, A Professional Corporation, 1101 Seventeenth Street, N.W., Suite 606, 20036-4704.
Telephone: 202-783-5711.
Facsimile: 202-783-5720.

John R. Elrod
Greg S. Scharlau
Ruth Ann Wisener

Burton E. Stacy, Jr.
Terri Dill Chadick
Vicki S. Bronson

OF COUNSEL

D. Randy Laney

OFFICE PERSONNEL
TULSA, OKLAHOMA

John E. Barry
Henry G. Will
Joseph J. McCain, Jr.
Lynnwood R. Moore, Jr.
Robert A. Curry
Steven W. McGrath
John T. Schmidt
D. Richard Funk
Randolph L. Jones, Jr.
P. David Newsome, Jr.
J. Ronald Petrikin
Larry B. Lipe
James E. Green, Jr.
Martin R. Wing
John W. Ingraham
Andrew R. Turner
Douglas M. Rather
Gentra Abbey Sorem
R. Kevin Redwine
Deirdre O'Neil E. Dexter
Tony W. Haynie
Bruce W. Freeman
David R. Cordell
Paul E. Braden
Robert J. Melgaard
R. Mark Solano
C. Raymond Patton, Jr.
P. Scott Hathaway
John A. Bugg
Lawrence A. Hall
Timothy T. Trump
Mark E. Dreyer
Nancy E. Vaughn
Gregory D. Renberg
John M. Matheson

Katherine Gallagher Coyle
Anne B. Sublett
Rebecca Sellers Woodward
Beverly K. Smith
Melodie Freeman-Burney
Jacalyn W. Peter
M. Sean Radcliffe
Robert D. James
David H. Herrold
Fern Holland
Elizabeth K. Giddens
Jonathan M. Cinocca

OF COUNSEL

Charles C. Killin
James R. Ryan
Russell H. Harbaugh, Jr.
Debbie L. Blackwell
David O. Cordell

RETIRED SHAREHOLDERS

Robert L. McGowen
John S. Athens

OFFICE PERSONNEL
OKLAHOMA CITY, OKLAHOMA

Peter B. Bradford
Raymond E. Tompkins
Irwin H. Steinhorn
John W. Funk
Kiran A. Phansalkar
Timothy J. Bomhoff
Mitchell D. Blackburn
P. Blake Allen
Mark H. Bennett

L. Don Smitherman
Laura L. McCasland
Cecily H. Murray

OF COUNSEL

S. Paul Hammons

OFFICE PERSONNEL
WASHINGTON, D.C.

G. Daniel Miller
Carol V. Calhoun

Erica L. Summers

OF COUNSEL

Henry Rose

For full biographical listings, see the Martindale-Hubbell Law Directory

DAVIS, COX & WRIGHT, PLC (AV)

19 East Mountain Street, P.O. Drawer 1688, 72702-1688
Telephone: 501-521-7600
Fax: 501-521-7661
Email: daviscoxwright@dcw-plc.com *URL:* http://www.dcw-plc.com

Sidney P. Davis, Jr.
Walter B. Cox
Tilden P. Wright, III
Constance G. Clark
William Jackson Butt, II
Kelly P. Carithers
Don A. Taylor
Paul H. Taylor
John G. Trice
Laura J. Andress

Mark W. Dossett
S. Lance Cox
Robin Miller

Representative Clients: Arkansas Farm Bureau Insurance Cos.; Fireman's Fund Insurance Group; St. Paul Insurance Cos; Chrysler Motors Corp.; Kemper Insurance Group; Kawasaki Motors Corp.; CIGNA; CNA Insurance Companies.

For full biographical listings, see the Martindale-Hubbell Law Directory

*FORREST CITY,** St. Francis Co.

BUTLER, HICKY & LONG (AV)

A Partnership of Professional Corporations
2216 North Washington Street, P.O. Box 989, 72335
Telephone: 870-633-4611
FAX: 870-633-6848
Email: bhlfirm@IPA.NET

MEMBERS OF FIRM

Philip Hicky (Ltd.)
Fletcher Long, Jr. (P.A.)

ASSOCIATE

Rita Reed Harris

Representative Clients: First National Bank of Eastern Arkansas; Southern Farm Bureau Insurance Cos.; United States Aviation Underwriters Group; National Aviation Underwriters; Hartford Accident and Indemnity Co.; Peoples Implement Co.; Virginia Insurance Reciprocal.

For full biographical listings, see the Martindale-Hubbell Law Directory

W. FRANK MORLEDGE, P.A. (AV)

205 North Washington, P.O. Box 912, 72335
Telephone: 870-633-9531
Fax: 870-633-2219

W. Frank Morledge

Representative Clients: Union Planters National Bank; Hughes Grain Corp.; Don Edmondson Foods, Inc.; Forrest City Ready Mix Concrete Co.; Thomas International; Japan Forest Industries; Wynne Progress Publishing, Inc.; East Arkansas Community College.

For full biographical listings, see the Martindale-Hubbell Law Directory

*FORT SMITH,** Sebastian Co.

DAILY & WOODS, P.L.L.C. (AV)

Stephens Office Building, 623 Garrison Avenue, P.O. Box 1446, 72902
Telephone: 501-782-0361
Fax: 501-782-6160
Email: DailyWoods@aol.com

MEMBERS OF FIRM

Ben Core
Jerry L. Canfield
Thomas A. Daily
Wyman R. Wade, Jr.
Stanley A. Leasure
Douglas M. Carson

ASSOCIATES

Todd Patrick Lewis
Barry D. Neal
Leigh M. Chiles

OF COUNSEL

James E. West

Counsel for: Claims Management, Inc. (Wal-Mart); Arkla, Inc.; City of Fort Smith; Commercial Union Insurance Cos.; Pennzoil Exploration and Production Co.; Silvey Cos., Inc.; Metropolitan Life Insurance Co.; Chevron U.S.A., Inc.

For full biographical listings, see the Martindale-Hubbell Law Directory

LEDBETTER, COGBILL, ARNOLD & HARRISON, LLP (AV)

622 Parker Avenue, P.O. Box 185, 72902-0185
Telephone: 501-782-7294
Fax: 501-782-1493

MEMBERS OF FIRM

Charles R. Ledbetter
J. Michael Cogbill
James A. Arnold, II
Ronald D. Harrison
E. Diane Graham
R. Ray Fulmer, II

ASSOCIATES

Rebecca D. Hattabaugh
Virginia C. Trammell
Daniel A. Stewart

Representative Clients: General: First National Bank of Fort Smith; Bank of Mansfield; Commercial Bank at Alma.
Local Attorneys for: Liberty Mutual Insurance Co.; St Paul Insurance Cos.

For full biographical listings, see the Martindale-Hubbell Law Directory

ROBERTSON, BEASLEY, COWAN & KETCHAM, PLLC (AV)

615 North B Street, P.O. Box 23, 72902
Telephone: 501-782-7911
Fax: 501-782-7964
Email: RBCK@CEI.NET
Waldron, Arkansas Office: 205 South Main Street, 72958.
Telephone: 501-637-1197.
Fax: 501-782-7964.

MEMBERS OF FIRM

Donald P. Callaway (1935-1984)
Thomas E. Robertson, Jr.
John R. Beasley
Kenneth W. Cowan
Matthew J. Ketcham

(See Next Column)

ROBERTSON, BEASLEY, COWAN & KETCHAM PLLC—*Continued*

Representative Clients: The Aetna Casualty & Surety Co.; James River - Dixie Cup; Arkansas-Oklahoma Gas Corp.; Beverage Products Corp. (Pepsi-Cola); The Prudential Insurance Company of America; Sentry - Dairyland Insurance Co; General Tire and Rubber; Quanex Corp.; The Fort Smith Municipal Airport Commission; Southern Steel & Wire Co.

For full biographical listings, see the Martindale-Hubbell Law Directory

SHAW LAW FIRM (AV)

4615 Free Ferry Road, P.O. Box 2767, 72913-2767
Telephone: 501-484-8229
Fax: 501-484-5792
Email: lawbank@aol.com

Bruce H. Shaw (1904-1990) Richard B. Shaw (1927-1988)

MEMBER OF FIRM

J. Michael Shaw

Representative Clients: Bank of Mansfield; Mid-South Dredging Company; Jeffrey Sand Company; Hickory Springs Manufacturing Co.; Morrison-Quirk Grain Company; General Electric; Trane; CAC Inc.; Baldor Electric Company; Southern Marine Construction Inc.

For full biographical listings, see the Martindale-Hubbell Law Directory

*HOT SPRINGS NATIONAL PARK,** Garland Co.

RICHARD H. WOOTTON, P.A. (AV)

Rix Professional Center, 1401 Malvern, Suite 180, 71901
Telephone: 501-623-2593
Fax: 501-623-1485

Richard H. Wootton

Attorney for: American Surety Co.; Jefferson Standard Life Insurance Co.; Zurich American Insurance Co.; Western Surety Co; National Life & Accident Co.
Approved Attorneys for: Lawyers Title Insurance Corp.; Chicago Title Insurance Co.; Chubb Insurance Co.

For full biographical listings, see the Martindale-Hubbell Law Directory

*JONESBORO,** Craighead Co.

BARRETT & DEACON, A PROFESSIONAL ASSOCIATION (AV)

Union Planters Bank Building, 300 South Church Street, P.O. Box 1700, 72403
Telephone: 870-931-1700
Fax: 870-931-1800

Joe C. Barrett (1897-1980)
John C. Deacon
J. Barry Deacon
Ralph W. Waddell
Paul D. Waddell
D. Price Marshall, Jr.
James D. Bradbury

Kevin W. Cole
Robert S. Jones
Jennifer S. Cameron
James F. Gramling, Jr

For full biographical listings, see the Martindale-Hubbell Law Directory

MOONEY LAW FIRM (AV)

401 South Main Street, P.O. Box 1423, 72403-1423
Telephone: 870-935-5847
Fax: 870-935-4438
Email: mlf@insolwwb.net

MEMBERS OF FIRM

Charles M. Mooney
Charles M (Skip) Mooney, Jr.
Christopher R. Thyer
H. Clarke Mixon, III

Representative Clients: Simmons First Bank of Jonesboro; The Bert Cruse Agency, Inc.; Prudential Insurance Company of America.
Approved Attorneys for: Chicago Title Co.; Chelsea Title & Guaranty Co.; Commerce Title Guaranty Co.; Lawyers Title Insurance Corp.
References: Simmons First Bank of Jonesboro; First Bank of Arkansas; Union Planters Bank of Jonesboro.

For full biographical listings, see the Martindale-Hubbell Law Directory

SNELLGROVE, LANGLEY, LOVETT & CULPEPPER (AV)

Second Floor, 111 East Huntington, P.O. Box 1346, 72403-1346
Telephone: 870-932-8357
Fax: 870-932-5488

MEMBERS OF FIRM

G. D. Walker (1910-1989)
Frank Snellgrove, Jr.
Stanley R. Langley
Glenn Lovett, Jr.
Malcolm Culpepper
D. Todd Williams
Michael E. Mullally

(See Next Column)

ASSOCIATE

Anita Perkins Leonard

Representative Clients: Union Planters Bank, N.A. (formerly Mercantile Bank); Regions Bank; Travelers Insurance Co.; Aetna Insurance Co.; ITT Hartford Insurance Co.; Commercial Union Insurance Co.; CNA Insurance Group; State Farm Insurance Cos.; Columbia Mutual Insurance Co.; Bituminous Insurance Co.

For full biographical listings, see the Martindale-Hubbell Law Directory

WOMACK, LANDIS, PHELPS, MCNEILL & MCDANIEL, A PROFESSIONAL ASSOCIATION (AV)

Century Center, 301 West Washington, P.O. Box 3077, 72403
Telephone: 870-932-0900
Fax: 870-932-2553
URL: http//www.wlpmm-firm.com

Tom D. Womack
Carl David Landis
John V. Phelps
Paul D. McNeill
Lucinda McDaniel
Richard A. Lusby
Jeffrey W. Puryear

Mark Alan Mayfield
David Christopher Gardner
Dan Clark Young
Jeffrey L. Singleton

Representative Clients: Arkansas State University; Bank of Trumann; E.C. Barton & Co.; E. Ritter & Co.; Kraft General Foods Corp.; Northeast Arkansas Clinic; St. Paul Insurance Cos.; Shelter Insurance Co.; United States Fidelity & Guaranty Co.

For full biographical listings, see the Martindale-Hubbell Law Directory

*LITTLE ROCK,** Pulaski Co.

BARBER, MCCASKILL, JONES & HALE, P.A. (AV)

2700 Regions Center, 400 West Capitol Avenue, 72201-3414
Telephone: 501-372-6175
Telecopier: 501-375-2802

Azro L. Barber (1885-1979)
Elbert A. Henry (1889-1966)
John B. Thurman (1912-1971)
Austin McCaskill, Sr.
Glenn W. Jones
Michael E. Hale
John S. Cherry, Jr.
Robert L. Henry, III
Micheal L. Alexander
William H. Edwards, Jr.
G. Spence Fricke
Gail Ponder Gaines
Michael J. Emerson
R. Kenny McCulloch
Tim A. Cheatham
Joseph F. Kolb
Scott Michael Strauss
Baucum Fulk
D. Keith Fortner
Wendy Scholtens Wood
Morris L. Williams, III
Michelle Bass Miller

Attorneys for: AFCO Steel; AFCO Metals, Inc.; Associated Aviation Underwriters; CNA Insurance Companies; Fireman's Fund Insurance Co.; General Motors Corp.; Gennett Co., Inc.; General Motors Acceptance Corp.; Hanover Insurance Co.; Royal Insurance.

For full biographical listings, see the Martindale-Hubbell Law Directory

CEARLEY LAW FIRM, P.A. (AV)

Centre Place, Second Floor, 212 Center Street, 72201
Telephone: 501-372-5600
Fax: 501-374-3463
Email: bcearley@CearleyLawFirm.com *URL:* http://www.CearleyLawFirm.com

Robert M. Cearley, Jr.

Counsel for: Arkansas Bankers Association; Greyhound Lines, Inc.; Arkansas State Medical Board.

For full biographical listings, see the Martindale-Hubbell Law Directory

DOVER & DIXON, P.A. (AV)

425 West Capitol, Suite 3700, 72201
Telephone: 501-375-9151
Telecopier: 501-375-6484
URL: http://www.doverdixon.com

Darrell D. Dover
Philip E. Dixon
Thomas S. Stone
Steve L. Riggs
Joseph H. Purvis
Charles W. Reynolds
John B. Peace
Wm. Dean Overstreet
Gary B. Rogers
Michael R. Johns
W. Michael Reif
Patrick E. Hollingsworth
David A. Couch
M. Darren O'Quinn
Monte D. Estes
Jennifer M. Browne

Representative Clients: Wood Manufacturing Company, Inc. (Ranger Boats); J.B. Hunt; Transport Services, Inc.; Affiliated Foods; Southwest, Inc.; St. Vincent Infirmary; First Commercial Bank; Arkansas Teacher Retirement System; Assurance Alliance, Inc.; Connecticut Mutual Life Insurance; Old Republic National Title Insurance Company.

For full biographical listings, see the Martindale-Hubbell Law Directory

Little Rock—Continued

FRIDAY, ELDREDGE & CLARK (AV)

A Limited Liability Partnership of Individuals and Professional Associations
Formerly, Smith, Williams, Friday, Eldredge & Clark
2000 Regions Center, 400 West Capitol Avenue, 72201-3493
Telephone: 501-376-2011
Telecopier: 501-376-2147
Email: fecmh@fec.net

MEMBERS OF FIRM

William H. Sutton (P.A.)
James W. Moore
Byron M. Eiseman, Jr. (P.A.)
Joe D. Bell (P.A.)
James A. Buttry (P.A.)
Frederick S. Ursery (P.A.)
Oscar E. Davis, Jr. (P.A.)
James C. Clark, Jr. (P.A.)
Thomas P. Leggett (P.A.)
John Dewey Watson (P.A.)
Paul B. Benham, III (P.A.)
Larry W. Burks (P.A.)
A. Wyckliff Nisbet, Jr. (P.A.)
James E. Harris (P.A.)
J. Phillip Malcom (P.A.)
James M. Simpson, Jr. (P.A.)
James M. Saxton (P.A.)
J. Shepherd Russell, III (P.A.)
Donald H. Bacon (P.A.)
W. Thomas Baxter (P.A.)
Barry E. Coplin (P.A.)
Richard D. Taylor (P.A.)
Joseph B. Hurst, Jr. (P.A.)
Elizabeth Robben Murray (P.A.)
Christopher J. Heller (P.A.)
Laura Hensley Smith (P.A.)
Robert S. Shafer (P.A.)
William Mell Griffin III (P.A.)
Michael Scott Moore (P.A.)
Diane S. Mackey (P.A.)
Walter M. Ebel, III (P.A.)
Kevin A. Crass (P.A.)
William A. Waddell, Jr. (P.A.)
Scott J. Lancaster (P.A.)
M. Gayle Corley (P.A.)
Robert B. Beach, Jr. (P.A.)
J. Lee Brown (P.A.)
James C. Baker (P.A.)
Harry A. Light (P.A.)
Scott H. Tucker (P.A.)
Guy Alton Wade (P.A.)
Price C. Gardner (P.A.)
Tonia P. Jones (P.A.)
David D. Wilson (P.A.)
Jeffrey H. Moore (P.A.)
David M. Graf (P.A.)
Carla G. Spainhour (P.A.)
John C. Fendley, Jr. (P.A.)
Jonann E. Coniglio (P.A.)
R. Christopher Lawson (P.A.)
Gregory D. Taylor (P.A.)
Tony L. Wilcox (P.A.)
Fran C. Hickman (P.A.)
Betty J. Demory (P.A.)

ASSOCIATES

Lynda M. Johnson
James W. Smith
Clifford W. Plunkett
Daniel Lee Herrington
K. Coleman Westbrook, Jr.
Allison Cornwell
Ellen M. Owens
Helene Norcross Rayder
Jason B. Hendren
Susan N. Childers
Bruce B. Tidwell
Christopher A. Averitt
Kelly Murphy McQueen
Joseph P. McKay

COUNSEL

William J. Smith
John T. Williams (1909-1988)
Herschel H. Friday (1922-1994)
William A. Eldredge, Jr. (1925-1996)
Robert V. Light (1930-1996)
B. S. Clark
William L. Terry
William L. Patton, Jr.
H. T. Larzelere, Jr. (P.A.)
John C. Echols (P.A.)

Counsel for: Union Pacific System; St. Paul Insurance Co.; Liberty Mutual Insurance Co.; Cigna Property & Casualty Co.; Entergy Arkansas, Inc.; Dillard's, Inc.; Browning Arms Co.; Aetna Casualty & Surety Co.; ALLTEL Corp.; Acxiom Corp.

For full biographical listings, see the Martindale-Hubbell Law Directory

HILBURN, CALHOON, HARPER, PRUNISKI & CALHOUN, LTD. (AV)

P.O. Box 1256, 72203-1256
Telephone: 501-372-0110
Fax: 501-372-2029
Email: hilburn@aristotle.net
North Little Rock, Arkansas Office: Eighth Floor, Mercantile Bank Building, One Riverfront Place, P.O. Box 5551, 72119.
Telephone: 501-372-0110.
Fax: 501-372-2029.

Sam Hilburn
Ken F. Calhoon
Ernest H. Harper, Jr.
John E. Pruniski, III
John C. Calhoun, Jr.
David M. Fuqua
James M. McHaney, Jr.
Phil Campbell
J. Maurice Rogers
Paula Jamell Storeygard
Carrold E. Ray
Scott Thomas Vaughn
Susan Gordon Gunter
James D. Lawson
Mark K. Halter
Michael E. Hartje, Jr.

Pamela Moseley Roberts
Randy L. Grice
Traci Harris LaCerra

Representative Clients: Mercantile Bank of Arkansas, N.A.; Merrill Lynch Pierce Fenner & Smith, Inc.; Allstate Insurance Company.

For full biographical listings, see the Martindale-Hubbell Law Directory

HORNE, HOLLINGSWORTH & PARKER, A PROFESSIONAL ASSOCIATION (AV)

401 West Capitol, Suite 501, P.O. Box 3363, 72203
Telephone: 501-376-4731
Fax: 501-372-7142

Walter W. Davidson (1936-1999)
Allan W. Horne
Cyril Hollingsworth
Michael O. Parker
James P. Beachboard
Mark H. Allison
Joyce Bradley Babin
Laura G. Wiltshire
Bradley Sean Chafin
M. Joshua Leicht

OF COUNSEL

Garland W. Binns, Jr.

Representative Clients: Associated Industries of Arkansas, Inc.; Arkansas Blue Cross and Blue Shield; J.B. Hunt Transport, Inc.; American Insurance Association; Arkansas Kraft Corp. Div., Green Bay Packaging, Inc.; Gaylord Container Corp.; Southern Pioneer Life Insurance Co.; Robinette-Burnett Construction Co.; Fleming Companies, Inc.

For full biographical listings, see the Martindale-Hubbell Law Directory

KEMP, DUCKETT, SPRADLEY, CURRY & ARNOLD (AV)

A Partnership including Professional Associations
Suite 1300, 111 Center Street, 72201
Telephone: 501-372-7243
Fax: 501-372-5553

Hal Joseph Kemp (P.A.)
James M. Duckett
J. Mark Spradley
Stephen L. Curry
Benjamin F. Arnold
James E. Smith, Jr.

Representative Clients: Ticor Title Insurance Co.; Chicago Title Insurance Co.; Beach Enterprises, Inc.; Commercial Union Insurance.

For full biographical listings, see the Martindale-Hubbell Law Directory

LASER, WILSON, BUFFORD & WATTS, P.A. (AV)

101 South Spring Street, Suite 300, 72201-2488
Telephone: 501-376-2981
Telecopier: 501-376-2417
Email: laser@laserlaw.com

Sam Laser
Dan F. Bufford
Richard N. Watts
Frank B. Newell
J. Kendal "Ken" Cook
Alfred F. Angulo, Jr.
David M. Donovan
Kevin J. Staten

Brian A. Brown
Karen J. Hughes
Thomas J. Diaz
Keith Martin McPherson
Deborah S. Denton
Andy L. Turner
Donna L. Gay
Sara A. Farris

OF COUNSEL

Ralph R. Wilson

Representative Clients: Allstate Insurance Co.; American International Insurance Group; Continental Insurance Cos.; Farm Bureau Insurance Cos. (Casualty & Fire); Farmers Insurance Group; GAB Business Services, Inc.; St. Paul Insurance Cos.; Scottsdale Insurance Co.; State Farm Auto (Fire) Insurance Cos.

For full biographical listings, see the Martindale-Hubbell Law Directory

ROSE LAW FIRM, A PROFESSIONAL ASSOCIATION (AV)

120 East Fourth Street, 72201
Telephone: 501-375-9131
Telecopy: 501-375-1309

George E. Campbell
Herbert C. Rule, III
W. Wilson Jones
Allen W. Bird, II
C. Brantly Buck
Tim Boe
M. Jane Dickey
William H. Kennedy, III
Ronald M. Clark
Garland J. Garrett
Charles W. Baker
David L. Williams
Kevin R. Burns
Richard T. Donovan
John T. Hardin
Stephen N. Joiner
Amy Lee Stewart
Brian Rosenthal
Bryant K. Cranford
David P. Martin
Michael G. Smith
Kathryn Bennett Perkins
Michael N. Shannon

COUNSEL

J. Gaston Williamson
Phillip Carroll
W. Dane Clay

Craig S. Lair
Jennifer B. Hendren
Mark Davis
Kevin Keech
John D. Coulter

Counsel for: ALLTEL Corporation; Aluminum Company of America; Bridgestone/Firestone, Inc.; The Equitable Life Assurance Society of The United States; General Motors Corp.; The Prudential Insurance Company of America; Stephens Group Inc.; Tyson Foods, Inc.

For full biographical listings, see the Martindale-Hubbell Law Directory

Little Rock—Continued

WILLIAM F. SHERMAN (AV)

Suite 504, Pyramid Place, 221 West Second Street, 72201
Telephone: 501-372-3148
FAX: 501-372-2630

For full biographical listings, see the Martindale-Hubbell Law Directory

WILLIAMS & ANDERSON (AV)

Registered Limited Liability Partnership
Twenty-Second Floor, 111 Center Street, 72201
Telephone: 501-372-0800
Fax: 501-372-6453
Email: info@williamsanderson.com *URL:* http://www.williamsanderson.com

MEMBERS OF FIRM

W. Jackson Williams
Philip S. Anderson
Peter G. Kumpe
David F. Menz
Steven W. Quattlebaum
John E. Tull, III
Timothy W. Grooms
J. Leon Holmes
James E. Hathaway III
Thomas G. Williams
Patrick A. Burrow

Edie R. Ervin
Stephen B. Niswanger
T. David Gillespie
Kristine Gerhard Baker
Robert F. Thompson III
Charles S. Harmon

Representative Clients: Arkansas Democrat-Gazette, Inc.; Arkansas Development Finance Authority; Camden News Publishing Company; Coca-Cola Enterprises, Inc.; Entergy Corporation; Metrocentre Improvement District No. 1 of the City of Little Rock; Potlatch Corporation; Texaco Inc.; Roman Catholic Diocese of Little Rock; Wal-Mart Stores, Inc.

For full biographical listings, see the Martindale-Hubbell Law Directory

*MONTICELLO,** Drew Co.

BALL, BARTON & HOFFMAN, A PROFESSIONAL ASSOCIATION (AV)

North Main at Oakland, 71655
Telephone: 870-367-6288
Fax: 870-367-7851
Mailing Address: P.O. Box 507, Monticello, Arkansas, 71657

Lamar Williamson (1887-1974)
Adrian Williamson (1892-1982)
Walter W. Barton
David D. Hoffman

OF COUNSEL

William K. Ball

Representative Clients: Crossett Division of Georgia-Pacific Corp.; Union Bank & Trust Co.; Sea Ark Marine, Inc.; Monticello School District; Southern Farm Bureau Casualty Insurance Co.; R. A. Pickens & Son; Arkansas Land & Cattle Co.; State Auto Insurance; U.S.A.A.

JAMES A. ROSS, JR. LAW OFFICE (AV)

(Formerly Ross & Ross)
115 East Shelton Avenue, P.O. Box 209, 71655
Telephone: 870-367-5351
Fax: 870-367-2221
Email: jrosslaw@seark.net

James A. Ross (1911-1983)
James A. Ross, Jr.

ASSOCIATE

LeAnne P. Burch

For full biographical listings, see the Martindale-Hubbell Law Directory

*NEWPORT,** Jackson Co.

BOYCE & BOYCE, A PROFESSIONAL ASSOCIATION (AV)

515 Second Street, 72112
Telephone: 870-523-5242
Fax: 870-523-5196

Wayne Boyce
Edward W. Boyce, III

For full biographical listings, see the Martindale-Hubbell Law Directory

*PARAGOULD,** Greene Co.

BRANCH, THOMPSON, PHILHOURS & WARMATH, A PROFESSIONAL ASSOCIATION (AV)

414 West Court Street, 72450-4293
Telephone: 870-239-9581
Fax: 870-239-4859
Email: btpw@paragouldlawyer.com

Robert F. Thompson
Randy F. Philhours
Jeffrey T. Branch
Allen L. Warmath

(See Next Column)

Curtis Wayne Hitt

Representative Clients: Tenneco, Inc.; Piggott Community Hospital; City of Paragould; Northeast Arkansas Employment & Training Services.
Approved Attorneys for: American Title Insurance Co.

For full biographical listings, see the Martindale-Hubbell Law Directory

*PINE BLUFF,** Jefferson Co.

BRIDGES, YOUNG, MATTHEWS & DRAKE PLC (AV)

315 East Eighth Avenue, P.O. Box 7808, 71611
Telephone: 870-534-5532
Fax: 870-534-5582
Email: bridges@arkansas.net

Stephen A. Matthews
Ted N. Drake
Joseph A. Strode
Jack A. McNulty
Terry F. Wynne
James L. (Lee) Moore, III
Michael J. Dennis
David L. Sims
R. Scott Morgan
Jeffrey H. Dixon
Carrington E. (Cary) Young
James C. Moser, Jr.

John P. (Jack) Talbot

OF COUNSEL

Paul B. Young

Representative Clients: Central Moloney, Inc.; International Paper Co.; Pine Bluff National Bank; Hartford Insurance Group; CNA Insurance Companies; Jefferson Regional Medical Center; Florida Drum Co., Inc.; Southern Bag Corp.; Terra International, Inc.

For full biographical listings, see the Martindale-Hubbell Law Directory

RAMSAY, BRIDGFORTH, HARRELSON & STARLING (AV)

11th Floor, Simmons First National Building, P.O. Drawer 8509, 71611
Telephone: 870-535-9000
Fax: 870-535-8544

MEMBERS OF FIRM

William Franklin Coleman (1870-1956)
Nicholas J. Gantt, Jr. (1879-1975)
Marion J. Starling, Jr. (1941-1990)
William C. Bridgforth
F. Daniel Harrelson
Spencer F. Robinson
Phillip A. Raley
Rosalind M. Mouser
William M. Bridgforth
David R. Bridgforth
Christopher C. May
Anthony A. Hilliard

OF COUNSEL

Louis L. Ramsay, Jr.

Representative Clients: Simmons First National Bank; Pine Bluff Sand & Gravel Co.; Stant, Inc.; McGeorge Contracting Co., Inc.; Television Station KATV.

For full biographical listings, see the Martindale-Hubbell Law Directory

*PRESCOTT,** Nevada Co.

MCKENZIE, MCRAE, VASSER & BARBER, PLLC (AV)

A Professional Limited Liability Company
McKenzie Building, 122 East Second South, P.O. Box 599, 71857-0599
Telephone: 870-887-2601
FAX: 870-887-5504
Email: mckenzie@occ.com

William V. Tompkins (1861-1953)
Charles H. Tompkins (1889-1975)
Horace H. McKenzie (1905-1996)

OF COUNSEL

Duncan L. McRae

MEMBERS OF FIRM

James H. McKenzie
Albert Glenn Vasser
Barry D. Barber
Joseph P. Graham

Attorneys for: The Bank of Prescott; Bank of Delight; Citizens National Bank, Hope; Farm Credit Services of Southwest, Arkansas; Arkla, Inc.; United States Fidelity & Guaranty Co.; Hudson Foods, Inc.; Potlatch Corporation; The Firestone Tire & Rubber Co.; Logan Grocer Co.

For full biographical listings, see the Martindale-Hubbell Law Directory

*RUSSELLVILLE,** Pope Co.

LAWS & MURDOCH, P.A. (AV)

200 South Arkansas, P.O. Box 3000, 72801
Telephone: 501-968-1168
Fax: 501-968-5590
Email: alaws@cei.net

(See Next Column)

LAWS & MURDOCH P.A., *Russellville—Continued*

Ike Allen Laws, Jr. | Ike Allen Laws, III
Timothy W. Murdoch | Hugh R. Laws

Representative Clients: Koch Oklahoma Midstream Services Co.; NationsBank of Russellville; Bibler Bros, Inc.; Pope County Levee District; Sonat Exploration Co.; Tri County Regional Water Distribution District; Robinson, Inc.; Sundiro-Impuls America, Inc.
Approved Attorneys for: Old Republic Title Co.
Reference: Simmons First Bank of Russellville.

For full biographical listings, see the Martindale-Hubbell Law Directory

SPRINGDALE, Washington Co.

CYPERT, CROUCH, CLARK & HARWELL (AV)

111 Holcomb Street, P.O. Box 1400, 72765-4496
Telephone: 501-751-5222
Fax: 501-751-5777
Email: nwark.com

Courtney C. Crouch (1912-1975) | William M. Clark, Jr.
James E. Crouch | Charles L. Harwell

ASSOCIATES

R. Jeffrey Reynerson | Marcus W. Van Pelt

SENIOR COUNSEL

James D. Cypert

OF COUNSEL

Stanley W. Ludwig

General Counsel for: First National Bank of Springdale; Northwest Health Systems; Springdale School District.
Representative Clients: Purina Mills, Inc.; Swift-Eckrich, Inc.; Arkansas and Missouri RRCO.
Insurance Clients: American National Property and Casualty Co.; Liberty Mutual; Fireman's Fund; Chicago Title.

For full biographical listings, see the Martindale-Hubbell Law Directory

*TEXARKANA,** Miller Co.

DUNN, NUTTER, MORGAN & SHAW (AV)

State Line Plaza, 6th Floor, P.O. Box 8030, 71854-5945
Telephone: 870-773-5651
Texas Telephone: 903-793-5651
Telecopier: 870-772-2037
Email: lawfirm@dnms.com *URL:* http://www.dnms.com

MEMBERS OF FIRM

Willis B. Smith (1926-1980) | R. Gary Nutter
Charles M. Conway (1925-1976) | Charles A. Morgan
James N. Nutt (1949-1983) | Nelson V. Shaw
Alex G. Sanderson (1912-1996) | R. David Freeze
Winford L. Dunn, Jr. | W. David Carter

ASSOCIATES

Jeff M. Addison | Adam O. Fellows
Tina R. Green | Samuel Scott Karr

OF COUNSEL

Hayes C. McClerkin

LEGAL SUPPORT PERSONNEL

LEGAL ASSISTANTS

Myra Conaway Wells | Sonja L. Oliver

Representative Clients: Reliant Energy, Incorporated; Regions Bank; Prudential Insurance Company of America; CNA Insurance Cos.; Cigna Insurance Cos.; First Federal Savings & Loan Assn.; St. Michael Health Care Center; Southwest Arkansas Water District; Mobil Oil Co.; Southwest Arkansas Electric Cooperative Corp.

For full biographical listings, see the Martindale-Hubbell Law Directory

WEST MEMPHIS, Crittenden Co.

RIEVES & MAYTON (AV)

304 East Broadway, P.O. Box 1359, 72303
Telephone: 870-735-3420
Telecopier: 870-735-4678
Email: rieves.mayton@worldnet.att.net
Little Rock, Arkansas Office: Suite 1719, First Commercial Building, 400 West Capitol.
Telephone: 501-376-0504.
Telecopier: 501-372-3482.

MEMBERS OF FIRM

Elton A. Rieves, Jr. (1909-1984) | Michael R. Mayton
Elton A. Rieves, III | Elton A. Rieves, IV

ASSOCIATES

David S. Wilson, III | Eric Newkirk

For full biographical listings, see the Martindale-Hubbell Law Directory

SLOAN, RUBENS & PEEPLES (AV)

An Association of Lawyers
600 North Missouri Street, P.O. Box 768, 72303
Telephone: 870-735-5500
Telecopy: 870-735-2624

Edward J. Rubens (1913-1977) | Kent J. Rubens
Ralph W. Sloan (1915-1996) | David C. Peeples
J. Michael Stephenson

OF COUNSEL

Edward B. Johnson (Not admitted in AR)

General Counsel for: Bank of West Memphis; Crittenden Publishing Co., Inc.; West Memphis School District; Razorback Concrete Company; Flash Market, Inc.
Representative Clients: Arkansas School Boards Association-Risk Management Association; Vanliner Insurance; Builder's Transport, Inc.; Citizens Bank Marion; Marion School District.

For full biographical listings, see the Martindale-Hubbell Law Directory

CALIFORNIA

ARCADIA, Los Angeles Co.

HELMS, HANRAHAN & MYERS (AV)

Suite 685 Towne Centre Building, 150 North Santa Anita Avenue, 91006
Telephone: 626-445-1177
Fax: 626-445-2085
Email: helmsj@aol.com *URL:* http://www.lawyers.com/hhmlaw

James R. Helms, Jr. | James J. Hanrahan
Sterling E. Myers

LEGAL SUPPORT PERSONNEL

PARALEGAL

Michelle L. Upp

Reference: Bank of America National Trust & Savings Assn. (Arcadia Branch).

For full biographical listings, see the Martindale-Hubbell Law Directory

*BAKERSFIELD,** Kern Co.

BORTON, PETRINI & CONRON, LLP (AV)

The Borton, Petrini & Conron Building, 1600 Truxtun Avenue, 93301
Telephone: 661-322-3051
Voice Mail: 661-395-6700
Fax: 661-322-4628
Mailing Address: P.O. Box 2026, Bakersfield, California, 93303
Email: bpcbak@bpclaw.com *URL:* http://www.bpclaw.com
Other City Locations: Fresno, Los Angeles, Modesto, Redding, Sacramento, San Bernardino, San Diego, San Francisco, San Jose, San Luis Obispo, Santa Ana and Ventura.

MEMBERS OF FIRM

Fred E. Borton (1877-1948) | John F. Petrini
James Petrini (1897-1978) | Stephen M. Dake
Harry M. Conron (1907-1971) | Paul Lafranchise
Kenneth D. Pinsent (1953-1984) | Richard E. Morton
George F. Martin | Calvin R. Stead
Richard E. Hitchcock | Steve Karcher
Victoria R. Allard-Bernhardt

ASSOCIATES

William G. Welzenbach | John W. Fox
Stephen M. Crane | Timothy B. Liebaert
Brian Jensen Stowell | Valana K. Timroth
Richard D. Brown | Clayton A. Mack
Raymond G. Robinson | Michael J. Stump
Dee H. Stasnopolis | William R. Olson
Lori M. Cullman | Jonathan L. Shugart
Michael S. Abril | Rebecca T. Ishaq
Randall Steven Joyce | Susan D. (Johnson) Salvucci

OF COUNSEL

Roy J. Gargano | Jere N. Sullivan, Sr.

For full biographical listings, see the Martindale-Hubbell Law Directory

KLEIN, DENATALE, GOLDNER, COOPER, ROSENLIEB & KIMBALL, LLP (AV)

(Formerly Di Giorgio, Davis, Klein, Wegis, Duggan & Friedman)
ARCO Tower, 4550 California Avenue, Second Floor, 93309
Telephone: 661-395-1000
Telecopier: 661-326-0418
Mailing Address: P.O. Box 11172, Bakersfield, California, 93389-1172
Email: kleinlaw@kleinlaw.com

(See Next Column)

KLEIN, DENATALE, GOLDNER, COOPER, ROSENLIEB & KIMBALL LLP—*Continued*

Thomas R. Davis (1920-1990)
Anthony J. Klein (Inc.)
Thomas V. DeNatale, Jr.
Barry L. Goldner
Jay L. Rosenlieb
David J. Cooper
Claude P. Kimball
William A. Bruce
Leonard K. Welsh
Christopher P. Burger
Ned E. Dunphy
Melvin L. Ehrlich
Kevin C. Findley
Krystyna L. Jamieson

T. Scott Belden
Catherine E. Bennett
David D. Blaine
Nicole M. Misner
Timothy G. Scanlon

OF COUNSEL

Bruce F. Bunker
Thomas C. Fallgatter
Craig D. Braun

Representative Clients: Bank of America; Great Western Bank; Mojave Pipeline Co.; Transamerican Title Insurance Co.; Dean Whittier Reynolds, Inc.; California Republic Bank; San Joaquin Bank; Nahama & Weagant Energy Co.; Freymiller Trucking, Inc.; Westinghouse Electric Co.

For full biographical listings, see the Martindale-Hubbell Law Directory

ROBINSON, PALMER & LOGAN (AV)

Suite 150, 3434 Truxtun Avenue, 93301
Telephone: 805-323-8277
Fax: 805-323-4205
Email: RPLLAW@AOL.COM

MEMBERS OF FIRM

Oliver U. Robinson
William D. Palmer
Gary L. Logan

ASSOCIATES

Marshall S. Fontes
David T. Ungar

For full biographical listings, see the Martindale-Hubbell Law Directory

LAW OFFICES OF YOUNG WOOLDRIDGE (AV)

1800 30th Street, Fourth Floor, 93301
Telephone: 661-327-9661
Facsimile: 661-327-1087
Email: youngwooldridge@lightspeed.net *URL:* http://www.young.wooldridge.com

MEMBERS OF FIRM

Joseph Wooldridge (1913-1996)
A. Cameron Paulden (1927-1984)
Robert J. Self
G. Neil Farr
Michael R. Young
Ernest A. Conant
Steve W. Nichols
Larry R. Cox
Scott K. Kuney
Michael A. Kaia
Steven M. Torigiani
Scott D. Howry

ASSOCIATES

David F. Leon
Todd A. Gall
Mark H. Atkins
Christopher Finberg

OF COUNSEL

Edward M. Carpenter
John B. Young (Retired)

Representative Clients: Arvin-Edison Water Storage District; Motor City Truck Sales and Service.
References: Wells Fargo Bank; First Interstate Bank; California Republic Bank.

For full biographical listings, see the Martindale-Hubbell Law Directory

BEVERLY HILLS, Los Angeles Co.

TURNER, AUBERT & FRIEDMAN, LLP (AV)

Formerly Turner, Gerstenfeld, Wilk & Tigerman
Suite 510, 8383 Wilshire Boulevard, 90211
Telephone: 323-653-3900
Facsimile: 323-653-3021

MEMBERS OF FIRM

Rubin M. Turner
Ronald D. Aubert
Edward Friedman
Michael J. Hanna

ASSOCIATES

Dortha Larene Pyles
Steven A. Morris
Diane H. Pappas

OF COUNSEL

Yelena Yeruhim

For full biographical listings, see the Martindale-Hubbell Law Directory

BISHOP, Inyo Co.

DOUGLAS BUCHANAN (AV)

363 Academy Avenue, 93514
Telephone: 760-873-4211
Fax: 760-873-4007
Email: dbuchanan@QNET.com

OF COUNSEL

Ronald F. Sample
Susan A. Yeck

References: Dean Witter Reynolds, Bishop; Union Bank, Bishop.

For full biographical listings, see the Martindale-Hubbell Law Directory

BURLINGAME, San Mateo Co.

CARR, MCCLELLAN, INGERSOLL, THOMPSON & HORN, PROFESSIONAL CORPORATION (AV)

216 Park Road, P.O. Box 513, 94011-0513
Telephone: 650-342-9600
Telecopier: 650-342-7685
Email: cmith@cmithlaw.com
San Francisco, California Office: Suite 1120, Four Embarcadero Center.
Telephone: 415-362-1400.
Telecopier: 415-362-5149.

E. H. Cosgriff (1880-1947)
J. Ed McClellan (1895-1985)
Robert R. Thompson (1921-1995)
Norman I. Book, Jr.
Marion L. Brown
L. Michael Telleen
Lage E. Andersen
Keith P. Bartel
Mark A. Cassanego
Laurence M. May
Michael J. McQuaid
Penelope Creasey Greenberg
James R. Cody
Edward J. Willig, III
W. George Wailes
Carol B. Schwartz
Lori A. Lutzker
Jeremy W. Katz
Lisa Hayhurst Stalteri
Steven D. Anderson

SPECIAL COUNSEL

Elise Clowes
Daniel R. Morris

CHAIRMAN EMERITUS

Albert J. Horn

John M. Andersen
Gitanjali Mohindra
Terese M. Raddie
Don W. Robinson
Quynh T. Tran
Michelle Leu Zaccone

OF COUNSEL

Luther M. Carr (Retired)
Frank B. Ingersoll, Jr. (Retired)
Cyrus J. McMillan (Retired)
David C. Carr (Retired)
Robert A. Nebrig (Retired)

For full biographical listings, see the Martindale-Hubbell Law Directory

CHULA VISTA, San Diego Co.

ATHERTON & ALLEN (AV)

210 Towne Centre Professional Building, 345 "F" Street, 91910
Telephone: 619-420-6869
Email: daveallen@estplanlaw.com

MEMBERS OF FIRM

Harvey H. Atherton (1881-1972)
Keith Atherton (1912-1998)
David R. Allen

For full biographical listings, see the Martindale-Hubbell Law Directory

CORONA, Riverside Co.

CLAYSON, MANN, YAEGER & HANSEN, A PROFESSIONAL LAW CORPORATION (AV)

Clayson Law Building, 601 South Main Street, P.O. Box 1447, 92878-1447
Telephone: 909-737-1910
Riverside: 909-689-7241
Fax: 909-737-4384

Walter S. Clayson (1887-1972)
E. Spurgeon Rothrock (1918-1979)
Roy H. Mann
Derrill E. Yaeger
Gary K. Rosenzweig
Kent A. Hansen
Roland C. Bainer
David R. Saunders
Sallie Barnett
Barry M. Walker

Counsel for: Lee Lake Municipal Water District; Palo Verde Irrigation District; Loma Linda University.
Local Counsel: Minnesota Mining & Manufacturing Co.; U.S.A. Waste.

For full biographical listings, see the Martindale-Hubbell Law Directory

COSTA MESA, Orange Co.

FELDHAKE, AUGUST & ROQUEMORE (AV)

Plaza Tower, Suite 1730, 600 Anton Boulevard, 92626-7124
Telephone: 714-438-3885
Fax: 714-438-3888
Email: farlaw@hqonline.com

Robert J. Feldhake
Lisa A. Roquemore
Kenneth S. August
Joshua M. Wolff

ASSOCIATES

Dimitri P. Gross
Supriya Kakkar
Katherine A. Slayton

OF COUNSEL

Arthur J. Swerdloff
Arthur M. Wilcox, Jr.

For full biographical listings, see the Martindale-Hubbell Law Directory

McCORMICK, KIDMAN & BEHRENS, LLP (AV)

A Partnership of Professional Corporations
Imperial Bank Building, 695 Town Center Drive Suite 1400, 92626-7187
Telephone: 714-755-3100
Fax: 714-755-3110; 1-800-755-3125
Email: mkb1@ix.netcom.com
Sacramento, California Office: 980 Ninth Street. 16th Floor. 95814-2736.
Telephone: 916-449-9533.
Fax: 916-446-7104.
Effective April 1, 1999 the new address will be: Imperial Bank Building, 695 Town Center Drive, Suite 400.

MEMBERS OF FIRM

Homer L. (Mike) McCormick, Jr., (P.C.)
Russell G. Behrens (P.C.)
Suzanne M. Tague (P.C.)
Arthur G. Kidman (P.C.)
Janet R. Morningstar (P.C.)
Keith E. McCullough (P.C.)

ASSOCIATES

David D. Boyer
Gary D. Grant
Paeter E. Garcia
Edward L. Bertrand

For full biographical listings, see the Martindale-Hubbell Law Directory

PAUL, HASTINGS, JANOFSKY & WALKER LLP (AV)

A Limited Liability Partnership including Professional Corporations
Firm Established in 1951; Office in 1974
695 Town Center Drive, 92626-1924
Telephone: 714-668-6200
Fax: 714-979-1921
URL: http://www.phjw.com
Atlanta, Georgia Office: 24th Floor, 600 Peachtree Street, N.E.
Telephone: 404-815-2400.
Los Angeles, California Office: 555 South Flower Street.
Telephone: 213-683-6000.
New York, New York Office: 399 Park Avenue.
Telephone: 212-318-6000.
San Francisco, California Office: 345 California Street.
Telephone: 415-835-1600.
Stamford, Connecticut Office: 1055 Washington Boulevard.
Telephone: 203-961-7400.
Washington, D.C. Office: 1299 Pennsylvania Avenue, N.W.
Telephone: 202-508-9500.
Tokyo, Japan Office: Ark Mori Building, 12-32 Akasaka, P.O. Box 577, 1-Chome, Minato-Ku.
Telephone: (03) 3586-4711.
London, England Office: The International Financial Centre, 25 Old Broad Street.
Telephone: (011) 44-171-562-4000.
ATTORNEY E-MAIL ADDRESSES: first initial middle initial last name @phjw.com (e.g. rmasbill@phjw.com)

COUNSEL

Oliver F. Green
Lee G. Paul

MEMBERS OF FIRM

Stephen D. Cooke
Matthew A. Hodel
Glenn D. Dassoff
Michael A. Hood
Janet Toll Davidson
Donald L. Morrow
John F. Della Grotta
David S. Phelps
John S. Gibson
Douglas A. Schaaf
Howard C. Hay
William J. Simpson
Peter J. Tennyson

SENIOR COUNSEL

Robert R. Burge
James W. Hamilton
John E. Trinnaman

OF COUNSEL

Jessica S. Dorman-Davis
John F. Simonis
Sean A. O'Brien
Darla L. Yancey

(See Next Column)

ASSOCIATES

Terry Jon Allen
Monica L. Martelli
Andrea D. Bishop
Scott R. Miller
Glenn L. Briggs
Veronica Louise Nitschke
Robert P. Bryant
Catherine Patiño Patton
Shelly J. Darby
Mark Zdzislaw Prochowski (Not admitted in CA)
Colleen T. Dorney
Jay C. Gandhi
Daniel A. Sonenshine
Daniel M. Glassman
Peter M. Stone
Deirdre M. Kelly
Daniel J. Tangeman
Lisa M. LaFourcade
Michael W. Traynham
Neil D. Lansing
Joanna Joyce Weiss
Jeffrey Scott Marks
Ralph H. Winter

For full biographical listings, see the Martindale-Hubbell Law Directory

RUTAN & TUCKER, LLP (AV)

A Partnership including Professional Corporations
611 Anton Boulevard, Fourteenth Floor, P.O. Box 1950, 92626-1998
Telephone: 714-641-5100; 213-625-7586
Telecopier: 714-546-9035
Email: rutan&tucker@rutan.com *URL:* http://www.rutan.com

MEMBERS OF FIRM

James R. Moore (P.C.)
Michael F. Sitzer
Paul Frederic Marx
Thomas J. Crane
Richard A. Curnutt
Mark B. Frazier
Leonard A. Hampel, Jr.
Penelope Parmes
John B. Hurlbut, Jr.
M. Katherine Jenson
Michael W. Immell
Duke Wahlquist
Milford W. Dahl, Jr.
Richard Montevideo
Theodore I. Wallace, Jr. (P.C.)
Lori Sarner Smith
Gilbert N. Kruger
Ernest W. Klatte III
Joseph D. Carruth
Elizabeth L. Martyn
Richard P. Sims
Kim D. Thompson
James B. O'Neal
Jayne Taylor Kacer
Robert C. Braun
David B. Cosgrove
Thomas S. Salinger (P.C.)
Hans Van Ligten
David C. Larsen (P.C.)
Stephen A. Ellis
Clifford E. Frieden
Matthew K. Ross
Michael D. Rubin
Jeffrey Wertheimer
Ira G. Rivin (P.C.)
Robert O. Owen
Jeffrey M. Oderman (P.C.)
Adam N. Volkert
Stan Wolcott (P.C.)
Jeffrey A. Goldfarb
Robert S. Bower
F. Kevin Brazil
David J. Aleshire
Layne H. Melzer
Marcia A. Forsyth
Lien Ski Harrison
William M. Marticorena
Elise K. Traynum
James L. Morris
Larry A. Cerutti
William J. Caplan
Carol D. Carty
Michael T. Hornak
Patrick D. McCalla
Philip D. Kohn
Richard K. Howell
Joel D. Kuperberg
James S. Weisz (P.C.)
Steven A. Nichols
David H. Hochner
Thomas G. Brockington
A. Patrick Muñoz
William W. Wynder
S. Daniel Harbottle
Evridiki (Vicki) Dallas
Paul J. Sievers
Randall M. Babbush
Joseph Louis Maga III
Mary M. Green
Kraig C. Kilger

SPECIAL COUNSEL

Debra Dunn Steel
Michael K. Slattery
Dan Slater

ASSOCIATES

Kent M. Clayton
Deja Marie Hemingway
Mark D. Budensiek
Julie K. Whang
Steven John Goon
Denise L. Mester
Douglas J. Dennington
W. Andrew Moore
Treg A. Julander
Alison Tsao
Todd O. Litfin
Charles A. Davenport, III
Kara S. Carlson
Daniel L. Gebert
Eric L. Dunn
Julie L. Drew
Fred Galante
Natasha L. Pavia
Cristy Lomenzo Parker
Richard D. Arko
Jeffrey T. Melching
Mark M. Malovos
Sean P. Farrell
Nikki Nguyen
Marlene Pose Jurgensen
Matthew L. Nelson
April L. Walter
Jeff C. Risher
Karen E. Walter
Jennifer S. Anderson
Natalie Sibbald Dundas
John T. Bradley
Alison M. Barbarosh
Alison L. Rossman
John W. Hamilton, Jr.
Allison Lemoine-Bui
John A. Ramirez
William Heath Ihrke
B. Lynn Loschin
Karen Lynn Martinez
Philip J. Blanchard
Chyi G. Chen
Terence J. Gallagher
T. Lan Nguyen
Robert E. King
Lisa V. Nicholas
George A. Gallegos

OF COUNSEL

Edward D. Sybesma, Jr. (P.C.)
David J. Garibaldi III

For full biographical listings, see the Martindale-Hubbell Law Directory

*EL CENTRO,** Imperial Co.

EWING, JOHNSON, GRAVES & DRISKILL, PROFESSIONAL LAW CORPORATION (AV)

636 State Street, 92243
Telephone: 760-352-6371
Telecopier: 760-353-5355
Email: info@ejgd.com
Palm Springs, California Office: 1111 East Tahquitz Canyon Way, Suite 110.
San Diego, California Office: 401 'B'Street, Suite 2100.

William J. Ewing
Charles G. Johnson
James K. Graves
Mitchell A. Driskill

Vance Bryan McAlister

Representative Clients: Bonanza Farms, Inc.; Kandal Insurance Agency; Imperial Printers; Robert Hawk Farming; Foss Accountancy Corp.; T. C. Worthy Cash & Carry, Inc.; Val Rock, Inc.; Southland Geotechnical; I.V. Radiology Group; Phillips Cattle Co.

For full biographical listings, see the Martindale-Hubbell Law Directory

GRAY CARY WARE & FREIDENRICH LLP (AV)

Gray Cary Established in 1927
Ware & Freidenrich Established in 1969
1224 State Street, P.O. Box 2890, 92244
Telephone: 760-353-6140
Telecopier: 760-353-6228
Email: info@graycary.com *URL:* http://www.graycary.com
San Diego, California Office: 401 B Street, Suite 1700, 92101-4297. 619-699-2700.
Telecopier: 619-236-1048.
San Diego/Golden Triangle, California Office: 4365 Executive Drive, Suite 1600, 92121.
Telephone: 858-677-1400.
Telecopier: 858-677-1477.
Palo Alto, California Office: 400 Hamilton Avenue, 94301-1825.
Telephone: 650-833-2000.
Telecopier: 650-327-3699.
La Jolla, California Office: 1200 Prospect Street, Suite 575, 92037.
Telephone: 858-456-3000.
Telecopier: 858-456-3075.
San Francisco, California Office: 139 Townsend Street, Suite 400, 94107-1922.
Telephone: 415-836-2500.
Telecopier: 415-836-9220.
Austin, Texas Office: 100 Congress Avenue, Suite 1440, 78701-4042.
Telephone: 512-457-7000.
Telecopier: 512-457-7070.
Sacramento, California Office: 400 Capitol Mall, Suite 2100, 95814.
Telephone: 916-930-3200.
Fax: 916-930-3201.

Jay W. Jeffcoat
Merrill F. Storms, Jr.

Representative Clients: American Bankers Life; Asgrow Seed; Boise Cascade; California State Automobile Assn.; Helena Chemical Co.; Hospital Council of San Diego and Imperial Counties; Imperial Valley Press/Brawley News; Unocal; Valley Independent Bank.

For full biographical listings, see the Martindale-Hubbell Law Directory

HORTON, KNOX, CARTER & FOOTE (AV)

Law Building, 895 Broadway, 92243
Telephone: 760-352-2821
Telefax: 760-352-8540
Email: hkcf@earthlink.net
Brawley Office: 195 South Second Street.
Telephone: 760-344-2360.
Fax: 760-344-9778.

MEMBERS OF FIRM

Harry W. Horton (1892-1966)
James H. Carter (1918-1978)
Reginald L. Knox, Jr. (1916-1996)
Orlando B. Foote, III
John Penn Carter, III
Frank A. Oswalt, III
Dennis H. Morita
Philip J. Krum, Jr.
Mercedes Z. Wheeler (Resident, Brawley Office)

ASSOCIATES

Patrick M. Pace (Resident, Brawley Office)
Ruth Bermudez Montenegro
Jeffrey M. Garber
Steve Escalera
Mark V. Santa-Romana

OF COUNSEL

Paul D. Engstrand

Representative Clients: Automobile Club of Southern Calif.; Imperial Irrigation District; Union Pacific Co.; Reliance Insurance Cos.; Pioneer Memorial Hospital District; City of Imperial; San Diego Gas & Electric Co.; Chevron U.S.A.; Bixby Land Co.

For full biographical listings, see the Martindale-Hubbell Law Directory

EMERYVILLE, Alameda Co.

LEGAL STRATEGIES GROUP (AV)

5905 Christie Avenue, 94608
Telephone: 510-450-9600
Fax: 510-450-9601
URL: http://www.lsglaw.com

SHAREHOLDERS

Ralph C. Alldredge
Timothy R. Cahn
Joshua R. Floum
Karen S. Frank
Gregory S. Gilchrist
Peter H. Goldsmith
Vincent L. Johnson
Leigh A. Kirmssé
Louise E. Ma
Maureen A. Sheehy
Heather A. Young

OF COUNSEL

Robert J. Vizas

ASSOCIATE

Jeffrey N. Hyman

AFFILIATE COUNSEL

Christine A. Amatruda
Gia L. Cincone
R. Dennis Claessens (Not admitted in CA)
Gregory P. Farnham
Ariela Freed
Jennifer Connors Hayes
Daniel J. Kroll
Jonathan P. Marvin
Paul J. Neibergs
Margaret R. O'Donnell
William Michael Quinn, Jr.
Nancy Lee Tang

For full biographical listings, see the Martindale-Hubbell Law Directory

*EUREKA,** Humboldt Co.

MITCHELL, BRISSO, DELANEY & VRIEZE (AV)

814 Seventh Street, P.O. Drawer 1008, 95502
Telephone: 707-443-5643
Fax: 707-444-9586
Email: mitchlaw@humboldt1.com

MEMBERS OF FIRM

Clifford B. Mitchell
Nancy K. Delaney
Paul A. Brisso
John M. Vrieze
William F. Mitchell

ASSOCIATES

Russell Scott Gans
Nicholas R. Kloeppel

RETIRED PARTNER

Robert C. Dedekam

Representative Clients: Louisiana-Pacific Corp.; City of Eureka; Housing Authority; St. Joseph Health Systems; California Automobile Assn.; K Mart; Hertz Corp.; Walmart; StairMaster Sports/Medical Products, Inc.; Montgomery Ward.

For full biographical listings, see the Martindale-Hubbell Law Directory

*FRESNO,** Fresno Co.

BAKER, MANOCK & JENSEN, A PROFESSIONAL CORPORATION (AV)

5260 North Palm, Suite 421, 93704
Telephone: 209-432-5400
Fax: 209-432-5620
Email: bmj@bmj-law.com *URL:* http://www.bmj-law.com

John H. Baker
Kendall L. Manock
Douglas B. Jensen
Donald R. Fischbach
Robert G. Fishman
Howard M. Zidenberg
John L. B. Smith
George L. Strasser
Joseph M. Marchini
Craig A. Houghton
Andrew R. Weiss
Mark W. Snauffer
James E. Shekoyan
Carl R. Refuerzo
John G. Michael
Christopher L. Campbell
Robert D. Wilkinson
Jeffrey A. Jaech
Lisa M. Martin
Gayle D. Hearst
Glenn J. Holder
Mark B. Canepa
Douglas M. Larsen
Michael W. Goldring
William M. White
Kathleen A. Meehan
Richard S. Salinas
Peter G. Bertling

David E. Holland
Charles K. Manock
Matthew E. Hoffman
James M. Cipolla
Kristine R. Cerro
Jeffrey R. Ahronian
Keith M. White
Michelle E. Guardado
Stephanie L. Hamilton
Linda Berg Othman
Scott G. Cross
Pa Lai Lee

OF COUNSEL

Leonard I. Meyers
James E. Ganulin
Otto E. Berg

Representative Clients: Bank of America NT&SA; Challenge Dairy Products, Inc.; Fresno Metropolitan Flood Control District; Metropolitan Life Insurance Co.; Norcal Mutual Insurance Co.; Wells Fargo Bank, N.A.; Sun-Maid Growers of California.

(See Next Column)

BAKER, MANOCK & JENSEN A PROFESSIONAL CORPORATION, *Fresno—Continued*

For full biographical listings, see the Martindale-Hubbell Law Directory

DOWLING, AARON & KEELER, INCORPORATED (AV)

6051 North Fresno Street, Suite 200, 93710
Telephone: 559-432-4500
Fax: 559-432-4590
Email: dak@daklaw.com *URL:* http://www.daklaw.com
Bakersfield, California Office: 110 South Mt. Claire, Suite 203. 93309.
Telephone: 661-396-0451. Web Site: http://www.daklaw.com.

Michael D. Dowling
Richard M. Aaron
William J. Keeler, Jr.
Stephen M. Blumberg
William T. McLaughlin, II
Bruce S. Fraser
Philip David Kopp
John C. Ganahl
Dale Ikeda
Adolfo M. Corona
Gary M. Fachin
Francine Marie Kanne
Christopher A. Brown
James C. Sherwood
David J. Weiland

Larry B. Lindenau
Kenton J. Klassen
Timothy R. Sullivan
Michael P. Dowling
Leigh W. Burnside
Justin D. Harris
Catherine Anne Amador

OF COUNSEL

Daniel K. Whitehurst
Morris M. Sherr
Blaine Pettitt

Reference: Wells Fargo Bank (Main).

For full biographical listings, see the Martindale-Hubbell Law Directory

LANG, RICHERT & PATCH, A PROFESSIONAL CORPORATION (AV)

Fig Garden Financial Center, 5200 North Palm Avenue, 4th Floor, P.O. Box 40012, 93755
Telephone: 559-228-6700
Fax: 559-228-6727

William T. Richert (1937-1993)
Robert L. Patch, II
Val W. Saldaña
Douglas E. Noll
Michael T. Hertz
Victoria J. Salisch
Rene Lastreto, II
Charles Trudrung Taylor
Mark L. Creede
Peter N. Zeitler
Laurie L. Quigley
Tamara L. Equals
Douglas E. Griffin
Nabil E. Zumout

Christopher B. Dorian
Matthew W. Quall
Tracy E. Sagle
Julie K. Hill
Michelle Oleksa

OF COUNSEL

Frank H. Lang

References: Wells Fargo Bank (Fresno Main Office).

For full biographical listings, see the Martindale-Hubbell Law Directory

*HANFORD,** Kings Co.

GRISWOLD, LASALLE, COBB, DOWD & GIN, L.L.P. (AV)

311 North Douty Street, 93230
Telephone: 209-584-6656
Facsimile: 209-582-3106
Email: glcdgllp@lightspeed.net

Lyman D. Griswold (Retired)
Steven W. Cobb (1947-1993)

MEMBERS OF FIRM

Michael E. LaSalle
Robert M. Dowd
Robert W. Gin
Randy L. Edwards

ASSOCIATES

Jim D. Lee
Jeffrey L. Levinson
Raymond L. Carlson
Ty Naoto Mizote
Scott M. Marconda
Jennifer Farrington
Matthew S. Kish
Gregory E. Bullard

Representative Clients: Badasci Land Leveling, Inc.; David A. Bush, Inc.; Calcot, Ltd.; Kings County Housing Authority; Kings County Water District; Hanford Mall; Silvas Oil Co.; Stone Land Co.; World Wide Sires; Toyota Motor Co.

For full biographical listings, see the Martindale-Hubbell Law Directory

HAYWARD, Alameda Co.

HALEY, PURCHIO, SAKAI & SMITH (AV)

P.O. Box 450, 22320 Foothill Boulevard, Suite 620, 94543
Telephone: 510-538-6400

MEMBERS OF FIRM

John K. Smith
Robert Sakai
Cynthia K. Birmingham

(See Next Column)

OF COUNSEL

John J. Purchio (1915-1997)
Donald A. Pearce (1898-1982)
Marlin W. Haley (1910-1993)

Representative Clients: City Center Commercial (Shopping Center); Oak Hills, Walnut Hills, Creekwood (Apartment Complexes); R. Zaballos & Sons (General Contractors); Hospital Associates; Wolf Investment Co.; Mission Valley Rock Co. (quarry); Sunol Golf & Recreation Co. (golf course).

For full biographical listings, see the Martindale-Hubbell Law Directory

INDIO, Riverside Co.

THOMAS T. ANDERSON, P.C. (AV)

45-926 Oasis Street, 92201
Telephone: 760-347-3364
Fax: 760-347-5572
Email: ttapc@aol.com *URL:* http://www.anderson-law-firm.com

Thomas T. Anderson

David M. Chapman
Samuel F. Trussell

Reference: City National Bank.

For full biographical listings, see the Martindale-Hubbell Law Directory

IRVINE, Orange Co.

ALLEN, MATKINS, LECK, GAMBLE & MALLORY LLP (AV)

A Limited Liability Partnership including Professional Corporations
Fourth Floor, 18400 Von Karman, 92612
Telephone: 949-553-1313
Telecopier: 949-553-8354
Los Angeles, California Office: Seventh Floor, 515 South Figueroa Street, 90071.
Telephone: 213-622-5555.
Telecopier: 213-620-8816.
San Diego, California Office: 501 West Broadway, Ninth Floor, 92101.
Telephone: 619-233-1155.
Facsimile: 619-233-1158.
West Los Angeles, California Office: 1999 Avenue of the Stars, 90067.
Telephone: 310-788-2400.
Fax: 310-788-2410.
San Francisco, California Office: 333 Bush Street, Seventeenth Floor, 94104-2806.
Telephone: 415-837-1515.
Fax: 415-837-1516.

PARTNERS

John C. Gamble
Thomas C. Foster (Resident)
R. Michael Joyce (Resident)
Lawrence D. Lewis (P.C.) (Resident)
Monica E. Olson (Resident)
Thomas E. Gibbs (Resident)
Dwight L. Armstrong (Resident)
Paul D. O'Connor (Resident)
Richard E. Stinehart (Resident)
Stephen R. Thames (Resident)
Anne E. Klokow (Resident)
David W. Wensley (Resident)
Gary S. McKitterick (Resident)
Patrick J. Grady (Resident)
Robert M. Hamilton (Resident)
Vincent M. Coscino (Resident)
Bradley N. Schweitzer (Resident)
Pamela L. Andes (Resident)
Michael S. Greger (Resident)
Stephen J. Kepler (Resident)

RESIDENT ASSOCIATES

Catherine M. Page
Leslie Tucker Fischer
A. Kristine Floyd
Michael A. Alvarado
Mary Kay Ruck
Susan E. Graham
Drew M. Emmel
Cynthia B. Paulsen
John W. Kittleson
Sandra A. Jacobson
Scott D. Howie
Daniel R. Foster
Laura B. Finkelstein
Bruce W. Hepler
A. Kenneth Hennesay, Jr.
Anne Marie LaPlace
Jeanne M. Jorgensen
Louis T. Antosh, Jr.
Christa Stern Eilers
Steven E. Creamer
Joseph S. Stuart
Timothy J. Hoban
William R. Ahern, III
Christine Kormanik
Mark Edward Foster
Elizabeth A. Markey
Brad H. Nielsen

OF COUNSEL

S. Lee Hancock

For full biographical listings, see the Martindale-Hubbell Law Directory

BORCHARD & WILLOUGHBY, A PROFESSIONAL CORPORATION (AV)

18881 Von Karman Avenue, Suite 1400, 92612
Telephone: 949-263-0424
Fax: 949-263-1913

Michael D. Borchard
Michael L. Willoughby
Mark A. Rodriguez

Stephanie A. Pittaluga

For full biographical listings, see the Martindale-Hubbell Law Directory

Irvine—Continued

BROBECK, PHLEGER & HARRISON LLP (AV)

A Partnership including a Professional Corporation
38 Technology Drive, 92618
Telephone: 949-790-6300
Facsimile: 949-790-6301
Email: info@brobeck.com *URL:* http://www.brobeck.com/
San Francisco, California Office: Spear Street Tower, One Market.
Telephone: 415-442-0900.
Facsimile: 415-442-1010.
Palo Alto, California Office: Two Embarcadero Place, 2200 Geng Road.
Telephone: 650-424-0160.
Facsimile: 650-496-2885.
Los Angeles, California Office: 550 South Hope Street.
Telephone: 213-489-4060.
Facsimile: 213-745-3345.
San Diego, California Office: 550 West C Street, Suite 1300.
Telephone: 619-234-1966.
Facsimile: 619-236-1403.
Austin, Texas Office: 301 Congress Avenue, Suite 1200.
Telephone: 512-477-5495.
Facsimile: 512-477-5813.
Denver, Colorado Office: 370 Interlocken Boulevard, Suite 500.
Telephone:
Telephone: 303-410-2000.
Facsimile: 303-410-2199.
New York, N.Y. Office: 1633 Broadway, 47th Floor.
Telephone: 212-581-1600.
Facsimile: 212-586-7878.
Washington, D.C. Office: 701 Pennsylvania Avenue, NW, Suite 220.
Telephone: 202-220-6000.
Facsimile: 202-824-0949.
London, England Office: Brobeck Hale and Dorr International, Hasilwood House, 60 Bishopsgate, London EC2N 4AJ.
Telephone: 011 44 171 638 6688.
Facsimile: 011 44 171 638 5888.

OFFICE LEADER

Bruce R. Hallett

PARTNERS

Patrick Arrington
Ellen S. Bancroft
Roger M. Cohen
Kevin D. DeBré
Richard A. Fink
Laura B. Hunter
Drew Jones
Kathlene W. Lowe
Greg T. Williams
Gabrielle M. Wirth

SENIOR COUNSEL

Caleb J. (Jeff) Brinton, IV

OF COUNSEL

Keven F. Baxter
Jeffrey S. Rovner

ASSOCIATES

John S. Baker
Joseph H. Chi
Sue L. Collins
Colleen Erin Curtin
Ethan D. Feffer
R. Scott Feldmann
Craig S. Gunther
Elizabeth T. Hall
Amy J. Hansen
Beverly A. Johnson
Joo R. Kang
Christine P. Le
(Not admitted in CA)
Patty H. Le
Barbara J. Miller
Bryan L. Ngo
Matthew W. Paskerian
Kathleen M. Ratz Graham
Scott R. Santagata
Mark D. Servino
Marrie K. Stone
Kourosh Vossoughi
Kandy L. Williams
Michael E. Zahm, Jr.

For full biographical listings, see the Martindale-Hubbell Law Directory

CROWELL & MORING LLP (AV)

2010 Main Street, Suite 1200, 92614-7217
Telephone: 949-263-8400
Fax: 949-263-8414
URL: http://www.crowellmoring.com
Washington, D.C. Office: 1001 Pennsylvania Avenue, N.W.
Telephone: 202-624-2500.
Fax: 202-628-5116.
London, England Office: Crowell & Moring, 180 Fleet Street, EC4A 2HG.
Telephone: 44-207-413-0011.
Fax: 44-207-413-0333.

MEMBERS OF FIRM

Donald E. Sovie
Randall L. Erickson
Jean-Pierre Swennen
(Not admitted in CA)
Michael D. Newman
Donald E. Bradley

OF COUNSEL

Steven P. Rice
Peter B. Ackerman

(See Next Column)

ASSOCIATES

Diane Smith Daruty
Wendy G. Macy
Deborah E. Colaner
Glenn A. Rowley
Rosemary K. Robinson
Bronwyn Whittaker Petersen
Brian Russ
(Not admitted in CA)

For full biographical listings, see the Martindale-Hubbell Law Directory

JONES, DAY, REAVIS & POGUE (AV)

5 Park Plaza, Suite 1100, 92614
Telephone: 949-851-3939
Telecopier: 949-553-7539
Email: counsel@jonesday.com *URL:* http://www.jonesday.com
In Los Angeles, California: 555 West Fifth Street, Suite 4600.
Telephone: 213-489-3939.
Telecopier: 213-243-2539.
In Atlanta, Georgia: 3500 SunTrust Plaza, 303 Peachtree Street.
Telephone: 404-521-3939.
Telecopier: 404-581-8330.
In Brussels, Belgium: Avenue Louise 480, 7th Floor, B-1050 Brussels.
Telephone: 32-2-645-14-11.
Telecopier: 32-2-645-14-45.
In Chicago, Illinois: 77 West Wacker.
Telephone: 312-782-3939.
Telecopier: 312-782-8585.
In Cleveland, Ohio: North Point, 901 Lakeside Avenue.
Telephone: 216-586-3939.
Telecopier: 216-579-0212.
In Columbus, Ohio: 1900 Huntington Center.
Telephone: 614-469-3939.
Telecopier: 614-461-4198.
In Dallas, Texas: 2727 North Harwood Street.
Telephone: 214-220-3939.
Telecopier: 214-969-5100.
In Frankfurt, Germany: Hochhaus am Park, Grüneburgweg 102, 60323 Frankfurt am Main.
Telephone: 49-69-9726-3939.
Telecopier: 49-69-9726-3993.
In Geneva, Switzerland: 20, rue de Candolle.
Telephone: 41-22-320-2339.
Telecopier: 41-22-320-1232.
In Hong Kong: 29th Floor, Entertainment Building, 30 Queen's Road Central.
Telephone: 852-2526-6895.
Telecopier: 852-2868-5871.
In London, England: Bucklersbury House, 3 Queen Victoria Street.
Telephone: 44-20-7236-3939.
Telecopier: 44-20-7236-1113.
In New York, New York: 599 Lexington Avenue.
Telephone: 212-326-3939.
Telecopier: 212-755-7306.
In Paris, France: 120, rue du Faubourg Saint-Honoré.
Telephone: 33-1-56-59-3939.
Telecopier: 33-1-56-59-3938
In Pittsburgh, Pennsylvania: 500 Grant Street, 31st Floor.
Telephone: 412-391-3939.
Telecopier: 412-394-7959.
In Riyadh, Saudi Arabia: The International Law Firm (In Association with Jones, Day, Reavis & Pogue), Sulaymaniyah, Prince Mishari IBN, Abdulaziz Street, P.O. Box 22166.
Telephone: (966-1) 462-8866.
Telecopier: (966-1) 462-9001.
In Shanghai, China: 2805 Kerry Centre, 1515 Nanjing Road West.
Telephone: 86-21-5298-6568.
Telecopier: 86-21-5298-6569.
In Sydney, Australia: Governor Phillip Tower, Level 38, 1 Farrer Place.
Telephone: 61-2-9210-6921.
Telecopier: 61-2-9210-6926.
In Taipei, Taiwan: 8th Floor, 2 Tun Hwa South Road, Section 2.
Telephone: (886-2) 2704-6808.
Telecopier: (886-2) 2704-6791.
In Tokyo, Japan: Toranomon 45 Mori Building, 3th Floor, 1-5, Toranomon 5-Chome, Minato-ku, Tokyo 105, Japan.
Telephone: 81-3-3433-3939.
Telecopier: 81-3-5401-2725.
In Washington, D.C.: 51 Louisiana Avenue, N.W.
Telephone: 202-879-3939.
Telecopier: 202-626-1700.

MEMBERS OF FIRM IN IRVINE

Thomas R. Malcolm
Richard J. Grabowski

ASSOCIATES

Mark D. Kemple
Marc K. Callahan
Jeffrey B. Kirzner
Michelle M. Blum
Randy G. Gerchick
James L. Poth
Darryl E. Towell
Scott D. Kirkner
Edward M. Hall

For full biographical listings, see the Martindale-Hubbell Law Directory

Irvine—Continued

MAHER & MAHER, LLP (AV)

18500 Von Karman Avenue, Suite 700, 92612
Telephone: 949-721-7555
Fax: 949-721-7444
Email: mmaher@maherlaw.com

Michael K. Maher
Cynthia R. Maher

For full biographical listings, see the Martindale-Hubbell Law Directory

PALMIERI, TYLER, WIENER, WILHELM & WALDRON, LLP (AV)

A Limited Liability Partnership including Professional Corporations
East Tower - Suite 1300, 2603 Main Street, P.O. Box 19712, 92614-6228
Telephone: 949-851-9400
Telecopier: 949-851-1554; 851-3844; 757-1225
Email: general@ptwww.com

MEMBERS OF FIRM

Angelo J. Palmieri (1926-1996)
Robert F. Waldron (1927-1998)
Alan H. Wiener (A Professional Corporation)
Robert C. Ihrke (A Professional Corporation)
James E. Wilhelm (A Professional Corporation)
Dennis G. Tyler (A Professional Corporation)
Michael J. Greene (A Professional Corporation)
Frank C. Rothrock (A Professional Corporation)
Dennis W. Ghan (A Professional Corporation)
David D. Parr (A Professional Corporation)
Charles H. Kanter (A Professional Corporation)
George J. Wall
L. Richard Rawls
Patrick A. Hennessey
Don Fisher
Gregory N. Weiler
Warren A. Williams
John R. Lister
Bruce W. Dannemeyer
Cynthia M. Wolcott
Joel P. Kew
Michelle M. Fujimoto
Gary C. Weisberg
Michael H. Leifer
Scott R. Carpenter
Richard A. Salus

ASSOCIATES

Norman J. Rodich
D. Susan Wiens
Ronald M. Cole
Lucee S. Kirka
Lori K. Davies
Paul B. La Scala
Michael L. D'Angelo
Charles S. Krolikowski
Michael J. Sarrao
Troy Thomas
James R. McCoy, Jr.
Elizabeth Davis Terry
Darolyn Y. Hamada
Raymond W. Sakai
Stephen A. Scheck
Andrew H. Fesler
Elise L. Enomoto
Chadwick L. Mills

For full biographical listings, see the Martindale-Hubbell Law Directory

SNELL & WILMER L.L.P. (AV)

1920 Main Street, Suite 1200, 92614-7230
Telephone: 949-253-2700
FAX: 949-955-2507
URL: http://www.swlaw.com
Phoenix, Arizona Office: One Arizona Center, 85004-2202.
Telephone: 602-382-6000.
Fax: 602-382-6070.
Tucson, Arizona Office: One South Church Avenue, Suite 1500, 85701-1630.
Telephone: 520-882-1200.
Fax: 520-884-1294.
Salt Lake City, Utah Office: 111 East Broadway, Suite 900, 84111-1004.
Telephone: 801-237-1900.
Fax: 801-237-1950.

MEMBERS OF FIRM

Robert J. Gibson
Arthur P. Greenfield
Creighton D. Mills
Steven T. Graham
William S. O'Hare, Jr.
Gary A. Wolensky
Charles W. Hurst
David W. Evans
Richard A. Derevan
Randolph T. Moore
Nanette D. Sanders
Luke A. Torres
Frank Cronin
Christy D. Joseph
Ellen L. Darling
Martin W. Taylor
Julianne Sartain
William T. Gay
Roger A. Grad
Alexander L. Conti

SENIOR ATTORNEY

Gerda M. Roy

ASSOCIATES

Lori Arvanitidis
David S. Beard
Zachary L. Berman
Tiffanny Brosnan
John A. Chatowski
Julie A. Douveas (Not admitted in CA)
Janet Lynn Hurdle
Marlene Klein
Henry G. Kohlmann
Deborah Mallgrave
Maxy Rush Otuteye
Sarah Petty
Michael B. Reynolds
Daniel S. Rodman
C. Athena Roussos
Sean Michael Sherlock
Yvonne A. Yung

Representative Clients: For list of Representative Clients, see end of biographical listings in the Martindale-Hubbell Law Directory.

(See Next Column)

For full biographical listings, see the Martindale-Hubbell Law Directory

LAGUNA BEACH, Orange Co.

WARREN FINLEY (AV)

564 Vista Lane, 92651
Telephone: 949-494-8960
Facsimile: 949-497-8477
Email: WFinley@SurEmail.com *URL:* http://www.SurEmail.com/finley

For full biographical listings, see the Martindale-Hubbell Law Directory

LA JOLLA, San Diego Co.

GRAY CARY WARE & FREIDENRICH LLP (AV)

1200 Prospect Street, Suite 575, 92037-3610
Telephone: 858-456-3000
Telecopier: 858-456-3075
Email: info@graycary.com *URL:* http://www.graycary.com
San Diego, California Office: 401 B Street, Suite 1700, 92101-4297. 619-699-2700.
Telecopier: 619-236-1048.
San Diego/Golden Triangle, California Office: 4365 Executive Drive, Suite 1600, 92121.
Telephone: 858-677-1400.
Telecopier: 858-677-1477.
Palo Alto, California Office: 400 Hamilton Avenue, 94301-1825.
Telephone: 650-833-2000.
Telecopier: 650-327-3699.
El Centro, California Office: 1224 State Street, P.O. Box 2890, 92244.
Telephone: 760-353-6140.
Telecopier: 760-353-6228.
San Francisco, California Office: 139 Townsend Street, Suite 400, 94107-1922.
Telephone: 415-836-2500.
Telecopier: 415-836-9220.
Austin, Texas Office: 100 Congress Avenue, Suite 1440, 78701-4042.
Telephone: 512-457-7000.
Telecopier: 512-457-7070.
Sacramento, California Office: 400 Capitol Mall, Suite 2100, 95814.
Telephone: 916-930-3200.
Fax: 916-930-3201.

Theodore J. Cranston (Resident, San Diego/Golden Triangle Office)
Melitta Fleck (Resident, San Diego/Golden Triangle Office)
Karl Zobell (Resident)

Representative Clients: The Copley Press, Inc.; Home Capital Corp.; Dr. Seuss Foundation; Ernest W. Hahn, Inc.; Imperial Corporation of America; La Jolla Bank & Trust Co.; La Jolla Real Estate Brokers Association; Merrill, Lynch, Pierce, Fenner & Smith; Scripps Clinic and Research Foundation; Timkin-Sturgis Foundation.

For full biographical listings, see the Martindale-Hubbell Law Directory

MULVANEY, KAHAN & BARRY, A PROFESSIONAL CORPORATION (AV)

Suite 315, 875 Prospect Street, P.O. Box 1168, 92038-1168
Telephone: 619-454-1780
Fax: 619-454-1792
San Diego, California Office: Seventeenth Floor, First National Bank Center, 401 West "A" Street.
Telephone: 619-238-1010.
Fax: 619-238-1981.
Los Angeles, California Office: Union Bank Plaza, 445 South Figueroa Street, Suite 2600.
Telephone: 213-612-7765.
Orange, California Office: The Koll Center, 500 North State College Boulevard, Suite 440.
Telephone: 714-634-7069.
Fax: 714-939-8000.

Thomas A. Henry, Jr.

For full biographical listings, see the Martindale-Hubbell Law Directory

LONG BEACH, Los Angeles Co.

LAW OFFICES OF JAMES H. ACKERMAN (AV)

Suite 1440, One World Trade Center, 90831-1440
Telephone: 562-436-9911
Cable Address: "Jimack"
Telecopier: 562-436-1897

References: Farmers and Merchants Bank (Long Beach Main Office); California Bank and Trust (Long Beach Main Office).

For full biographical listings, see the Martindale-Hubbell Law Directory

Long Beach—Continued

BAKER & HOSTETLER LLP (AV)

300 Oceangate, Suite 620, 90802-6807
Telephone: 562-432-2827
FAX: 562-432-6698
To contact an attorney on the Internet use first initial and surname followed by @baker-hostetler.com
URL: http://www.bakerlaw.com
In Cleveland, Ohio: 3200 National City Center, 1900 East Ninth Street.
Telephone: 216-621-0200.
In Cincinnati, Ohio: 312 Walnut Street, Suite 2650.
Telephone: 513-929-3400.
In Columbus, Ohio: Capitol Square, Suite 2100, 65 East State Street.
Telephone: 614-228-1541.
In Denver, Colorado: 303 East 17th Avenue, Suite 1100.
Telephone: 303-861-0600.
In Houston, Texas: 1000 Louisiana, Suite 2000.
Telephone: 713-751-1600.
In Los Angeles, California: 600 Wilshire Boulevard.
Telephone: 213-624-2400.
In Orlando, Florida: SunBank Center, Suite 2300, 200 South Orange Avenue.
Telephone: 407-649-4000.
In Washington, D. C.: Washington Square, Suite 1100, 1050 Connecticut Avenue, N.W.
Telephone: 202-861-1500.

OFFICE MANAGING PARTNER

Peter W. James (Managing Partner, Los Angeles and Long Beach, California Offices)
Sheldon A. Gebb (Managing Partner, Long Beach, California Office)

PARTNER IN CHARGE

Robert E. Coppola (Partner in Charge)

PARTNERS

David A. Kettel
George T. Mooradian
Christina L. Owen

ASSOCIATES

Theodore H. Adkinson
Cynthia F. Catalino
Leah E. Delancey
George M. Jones

OF COUNSEL

Herbert W. Kalmbach

For full biographical listings, see the Martindale-Hubbell Law Directory

---

CAYER, KILSTOFTE & CRATON, A PROFESSIONAL LAW CORPORATION (AV)

Suite 700, 444 West Ocean Boulevard, 90802
Telephone: 562-435-6008
Fax: 562-435-3704
Email: CKCCRC@AOL.COM

John J. Cayer
Stephen R. Kilstofte
Curt R. Craton

Cortlen R. Hauge

For full biographical listings, see the Martindale-Hubbell Law Directory

---

FORD, WALKER, HAGGERTY & BEHAR, PROFESSIONAL LAW CORPORATION (AV)

One World Trade Center, Twenty Seventh Floor, 90831
Telephone: 562-983-2500
Telecopier: 562-983-2555
Email: FWHB@FWHB.COM

G. Richard Ford
Timothy L. Walker
William C. Haggerty
Jeffrey S. Behar
Mark Steven Hennings
Donna Rogers Kirby
Tina Ivankovic Mangarpan
Joseph A. Heath
Robert J. Chavez
James D. Savage
Patrick J. Gibbs
Robert Reisinger

Arthur W. Schultz
Jon T. Moseley
Maxine J. Lebowitz
Timothy P. McDonald
K. Michele Williams
Stephen Ward Moore
James O. Miller
Stanley L. Scarlett
Scott A. Ritsema
Colleen A. Deziel
Thomas L. Gourdé
Patrick J. Stark
Shayne L. Wulterin
Charles J. Schmitt
John A. Haughton
Kristen C. Vine
Joel E. D. Odou
Christopher L. Mass
Robert Montes, Jr.
Alison S. Mathews
Tatia M. Tokunaga
Mark F. Wendorff
Anneke Joan Stewart
Pamela J. Paluga

OF COUNSEL

Theodore P. Shield, P.L.C.

For full biographical listings, see the Martindale-Hubbell Law Directory

WOOLLEY RUSSELL & JOHNSON (AV)

444 West Ocean Boulevard, Suite 1700, 90802
Telephone: 562-495-6000
Telecopier: 562-435-1359
Email: mail@transportlawyers.com *URL:* http://www.transportlawyers.com
Port Hueneme, California Office: 105 East Port Hueneme Road, 93041.
Telephone: 562-495-6000.
Fax: 562-435-1359.

MEMBERS OF FIRM

David E. R. Woolley
Thomas A. Russell
Philip L. Johnson

ASSOCIATE

Thomas G. Walsh

LEGAL SUPPORT PERSONNEL

PARALEGAL

Dawn C. Breaux

For full biographical listings, see the Martindale-Hubbell Law Directory

---

*LOS ANGELES,** Los Angeles Co.

ALLEN, MATKINS, LECK, GAMBLE & MALLORY LLP (AV)

A Limited Liability Partnership including Professional Corporations
Seventh Floor, 515 South Figueroa Street, 90071
Telephone: 213-622-5555
Telecopier: 213-620-8816
Irvine, California Office: Fourth Floor, 18400 Von Karman, 92612.
Telephone: 949-553-1313.
Telecopier: 949-553-8354.
San Diego, California Office: 501 West Broadway, Ninth Floor, 92101.
Telephone: 619-233-1155.
Facsimile: 619-233-1158.
West Los Angeles, California Office: 1999 Avenue of the Stars, Suite 1800, 90067.
Telephone: 310-788-2400.
Fax: 310-788-2410.
San Francisco, California Office: 333 Bush Street, Seventeenth Floor, 94104-2806.
Telephone: 415-837-1515.
Fax: 415-837-1516.

PARTNERS

Frederick L. Allen
John C. Gamble (Resident, Orange County and San Francisco Offices)
Brian C. Leck
Richard C. Mallory (Resident, San Francisco Office)
Michael L. Matkins
Marvin E. Garrett
Thomas C. Foster (Resident, Irvine Office)
Robert J. Cathcart
R. Michael Joyce (Resident, Irvine Office)
Gerben Hoeksma
Thomas W. Henning
Patrick E. Breen
Lawrence D. Lewis (P.C.) (Resident, Irvine Office)
George T. McDonnell
Michael F. Sfregola
Guy Rounsaville, Jr. (Resident, San Francisco Office)
David A. B. Burton (P.C.)
Monica E. Olson (Resident, Irvine Office)
Thomas E. Gibbs (Resident, Irvine Office)
Vernon C. Gauntt (Resident, San Diego Office)
Dwight L. Armstrong (Resident, Irvine Office)
Paul D. O'Connor (Resident, Irvine Office)
David L. Osias (San Diego and Los Angeles Offices)
William R. Harmsen
Debra Dison Hall
Anton N. Natsis (Resident, West Los Angeles Office)
George J. Berger (Resident, San Diego Office)
Michael C. Pruter (Resident, San Diego Office)
Michael H. Cerrina
Richard E. Stinehart (Resident, Irvine Office)
Stephen R. Thames (Resident, Irvine Office)
Dana I. Schiffman (Resident, San Diego Office)
Anne E. Klokow (Resident, Irvine Office)
Neil N. Gluck
David W. Wensley (Resident, Irvine Office)
Gary S. McKitterick (Resident, Irvine Office)
Patrick J. Grady (Resident, Irvine Office)
Thomas J. Masenga
Ray B. Gliner (Resident, San Diego Office)
Charles N. Kenworthy (Resident, West Los Angeles Office)
Anthony J. Oliva
Mark J. Grushkin
Michael P. Durkee (Resident, San Francisco Office)
Lindbergh Porter, Jr. (Resident, San Francisco Office)
Michael D. Ryan
Edwin W. Green
Ronald K. Clausen (Resident, San Francisco Office)
Ellen B. Spellman
Robert M. Hamilton (Resident, Irvine Office)
David R. Zaro
Janet A. Winnick
H. Christian L'Orange (Resident, San Francisco Office)
Robert R. Barnes (Resident, San Diego Office)
Vincent M. Coscino (Resident, Irvine Office)
Jeffrey R. Patterson (Resident, San Diego Office)
Jerold B. Neuman (P.C.)
Mark R. Hartney
John M. Tipton (Resident, West Los Angeles Office)
Nancy Lundeen (Resident, San Francisco Office)
Joe M. Davidson (Resident, San Diego Office)

(See Next Column)

ALLEN, MATKINS, LECK, GAMBLE & MALLORY LLP, *Los Angeles—Continued*

PARTNERS (Continued)

Craig D. Swanson (Resident, San Diego Office)
Gregory G. Gorman
George W. Kuney (Resident, San Diego Office)
Michael J. Kiely
Cheryl S. Prell
Bradley N. Schweitzer (Resident, Irvine Office)
Pamela L. Andes (Resident, Irvine Office)
Samuel H. Stein
Michael S. Greger (Resident, Irvine Office)
Robert A. Lurie (Resident, West Los Angeles Office)
Stephen J. Kepler (Resident, Irvine Office)
Mark J. Kelson (Resident, West Los Angeles Office)

ASSOCIATES

Henry Einar Fink
Rebecca L. Gundzik
Adela Carrasco
Catherine M. Page (Resident, Irvine Office)
Leslie Tucker Fischer (Resident, Irvine Office)
A. Kristine Floyd (Resident, Irvine Office)
Jennifer M. Casey
Cynthia Eder Bouza
Claudia Stone (Resident, West Los Angeles Office)
Michael A. Alvarado (Resident, Irvine Office)
Mary Kay Ruck (Resident, Irvine Office)
Eric J. Shelby (Resident, West Los Angeles Office)
Susan E. Graham (Resident, Irvine Office)
Martin L. Togni (Resident, San Diego Office)
Robert D. Jaffe
Stephen P. Lieske (Resident, San Francisco Office)
Loraine L. Pedowitz (Resident, San Diego Office)
Karen L. Lawlor
Drew M. Emmel (Resident, Irvine Office)
Dana R. Stone (Resident, San Francisco Office)
David H. Blackwell (Resident, San Francisco Office)
Cynthia B. Paulsen (Resident, Irvine Office)
Peter J. Roth
Thomas B. Crosbie (Resident, San Diego Office)
Rebecca Ann Thompson
Sandra J. Young (Resident, San Diego Office)
Christie M. Musser (Resident, San Francisco Office)
Bradley P. Kaplan (Resident, San Francisco Office)
Mark J. Hattam (Resident, San Diego Office)
Michael R. Farrell
Steven E. Creamer (Resident, Irvine Office)
David Y. Otsuka (Resident, San Francisco Office)
Steve Wellington (Resident, San Diego Office)
Ann Marie Maas (Resident, San Diego Office)
Todd E. Whitman
Allison L. Malin (Resident, West Los Angeles Office)
Kari Mason Desgalier (Resident, San Diego Office)
Kelly J. Brinkman (Resident, San Diego Office)
Lee A. Edlund (Resident, San Francisco Office)
John W. Kittleson (Resident, Irvine Office)
Sonia J. Ransom
Hazel Marlee Brandt (Resident, San Francisco Office)
Kimberly A. Donlon
Jeffrey N. Strug
Allen B. Walburn (Resident, San Diego Office)
Sandra A. Jacobson (Resident, Irvine Office)
Sharon Saslow (Resident, San Diego Office)
Deborah L. Babb (Resident, San Francisco Office)
Scott D. Howie (Resident, Irvine Office)
Scott Wilson Hatter
Charles D. Jarrell
Daniel R. Foster (Resident, Irvine Office)
Kathryn D. Horning (Resident, San Diego Office)
Francis N. Scollan
Darren A. Manibog
Laura B. Finkelstein (Resident, Irvine Office)
Bruce W. Hepler (Resident, Irvine Office)
A. Kenneth Hennesay, Jr. (Resident, Irvine Office)
Anne Marie LaPlace (Resident, Irvine Office)
Theodore M. Gizewski (Resident, San Francisco Office)
Jeanne M. Jorgensen (Resident, Irvine Office)
Lisa N. Machii
Kevin M. Ehrhart
Heidi K. Eick
Carrie H. Crockett (Resident, San Francisco Office)
Todd Chapman (Resident, San Francisco Office)
Gregg S. Pasternack (Resident, West Los Angeles Office)
Louis T. Antosh, Jr. (Resident, Irvine Office)
Angie Y. Yoon
Christa Stern Eilers (Resident, Irvine Office)
Hillary J. Post
Joseph S. Stuart (Resident, Irvine Office)
Timothy J. Hoban (Resident, Irvine Office)
William R. Ahern, III (Resident, Irvine Office)
Kushal S. Bhakta
Lisa R. Kamrath
Christine Kormanik (Resident, Irvine Office)
Patrick Austin Perry
Jennie Lau (Resident, San Francisco Office)
Cynthia Hinshaw Wertz (Resident, San Francisco Office)
Dawnmarie I. Saunders (Resident, San Diego Office)
Michael J. Holmes (Resident, San Diego Office)
Mark Edward Foster (Resident, Irvine Office)
Matthew J. Mahan
Natasha Lynn Hyman
Jennifer Erin Bromiley
Elizabeth A. Markey (Resident, Irvine Office)
Matthew J. Ertman (Resident, Irvine Office)
Brad H. Nielsen (Resident, Irvine Office)

(See Next Column)

ASSOCIATES (Continued)

Michael J. Betz (Resident, San Francisco Office)
Christopher B. Hansmeyer (Resident, San Diego Office)
Vanessa Alvarez (Resident, San Francisco Office)

OF COUNSEL

John G. Davies (Resident, San Diego Office)
Michael J. Murphy
S. Lee Hancock (At Irvine and San Diego Offices)
Henry Lerner (Resident, San Francisco Office)
James M. Tervo (Resident, San Francisco Office)
Madeleine E. Sloane (Resident, San Francisco Office)
Roberta V. Romberg (Resident, San Francisco Office)

Reference: Wells Fargo Bank (Los Angeles Main Office).

For full biographical listings, see the Martindale-Hubbell Law Directory

---

ALSCHULER GROSSMAN STEIN & KAHAN LLP (AV)

2049 Century Park East, Thirty-Ninth Floor, 90067-3213
Telephone: 310-277-1226
Fax: 310-552-6077
Email: info@agsk.com *URL:* http://www.agsk.com

MEMBERS OF FIRM

Daniel Alberstone
Bruce D. Andelson
Marilyn Barrett
Bennett A. Bigman
Jeffrey C. Briggs
Michael L. Cypers
Rebecca Edelson
Bruce A. Friedman (P.C.)
Patricia Gandras-Alperin
Marshall B. Grossman (P.C.)
Susan Grueneberg
Marcia J. Harris
Johnnie A. James
Robert L. Kahan
Frank Kaplan (P.C.)
Lance Jon Kimmel
Dana N. Levitt (P.C.)
Ann Loeb
Kenneth S. Meyers
Steven E. Peden
Samuel R. Pryor
Gwyn Quillen
John A. Schwimmer
Michael A. Sherman
William S. Small (P.C.)
Stanton L. Stein
Bruce Warner (P.C.)
Mary Lee Wegner

ASSOCIATES

Jesse J. Contreras
David B. Dreyfus
Matthew C. Elstein
Joseph T. Gauthier
Michael R. Heimbold
Adrienne D. Herman
Grant E. Kinsel
Kathleen H. Langan
Sally S. Liu
Jonathan A. Loeb
Kevin B. Martin
Grant P. Michaelson
A. Ron Milkes
Melissa Miller
Dana Milmeister
Philip H. R. Nevinny
Jeremy E. Pendrey

OF COUNSEL

David G. Baram
Karen Kaplowitz (P.C.)

LEGAL SUPPORT PERSONNEL

John J. Moohr (Executive Director)
Denise J. Grigst (Library Director)

For full biographical listings, see the Martindale-Hubbell Law Directory

---

ANDREWS & KURTH L.L.P. (AV)

Suite 4200, 601 S. Figueroa Street, 90017
Telephone: 213-896-3100
Telecopier: 213-896-3137
Email: webmaster@andrews-kurth.com *URL:* http://www.andrews-kurth.com
Houston, Texas Office: Suite 4200, 600 Travis, 77002.
Telephone: 713-220-4200.
Telecopier: 713-220-4285. E-Mail: webmaster@andrews-kurth.com.
Washington, D.C. Office: Suite 300, 1701 Pennsylvania Avenue, N.W.
Telephone: 202-662-2700.
Telecopier: 202-662-2739.
Dallas, Texas Office: 1717 Main Street, Suite 3700.
Telephone: 214-659-4400.
Telecopier: 214-659-4401.
The Woodlands, Texas Office: Suite 150, 2170 Buckthorne Place, 77380.
Telephone: 713-220-4801.
Telecopier: 713-220-4815.
New York, N.Y. Office: 805 Third Avenue.
Telephone: 212-850-2800.
Telecopier: 212-850-2929.
London, England Office: 2 Creed Court, 5-11 Ludgate Hill, EC4M 7AA.
Telephone: 0171-236-3456.
Telecopier: 0171-236-4276.

MEMBERS OF FIRM

Jon L. R. Dalberg
Gregg J. Loubier
Ralph W. Tarr

OF COUNSEL

Diane C. Weil

ASSOCIATES

Trudi J. Lesser
C. John M. Melissinos
Carolyn Y. Morgan
Pamela M. Roberson

For full biographical listings, see the Martindale-Hubbell Law Directory

Los Angeles—Continued

ARTER & HADDEN LLP (AV)

725 South Figueroa Street, Suite 3400, 90017-5418
Telephone: 213-430-3000
Cable Address: "Oslaw"
Facsimile: 213-617-9255
URL: http://www.arterhadden.com
In Cleveland, Ohio: 1100 Huntington Building, 925 Euclid Avenue.
Telephone: 216-696-1100.
Fax: 216-696-2645.
In Columbus, Ohio: Suite 1200, One Columbus, 10 West Broad Street.
Fax: 614-221-0479.
Telephone: 614-221-3155.
In Dayton, Ohio: Kettering Tower, Suite 2310, 40 North Main Street.
Telephone: 937-223-4701.
Fax: 937-223-0170.
In Washington, D.C.: 1801 K Street, N.W., Suite 400K.
Telephone: 202-775-7100.
Fax: 202-857-0172.
In Dallas, Texas: 1717 Main Street, Suite 4100.
Telephone: 214-761-2100.
Fax: 214-741-7139.
In Irvine, California: Five Park Plaza, Suite 1000, Jamboree Center, 92714.
Telephone: 949-252-7500.
Fax: 949-833-9604.
In Austin, Texas: 100 Congress Avenue, Suite 1800.
Telephone: 512-479-6403.
Fax: 512-469-5505.
In San Antonio, Texas: One Riverwalk Place, 700 North Saint Mary's Street, Suite 800, 78205.
Telephone: 210-805-8497.
Fax: 210-805-8519.
In San Francisco, California: Two Embarcadero Center, 5th Floor, 94111.
Telephone: 415-617-2100.
Fax: 415-912-3636.
In Sacramento, California: Wells Fargo Center, 400 Capitol Mall, Suite 900, 95814.
Telephone: 916-449-3917.
Fax: 916-449-8249.
In San Diego, California: 402 West Broadway, Sixth Floor, 92101.
Telephone: 619-238-0001.
Fax: 619-238-8333.
In Woodland Hills, California: 5959 Topanga Canyon Boulevard, Suite 244, 91367.
Telephone: 818-712-0036.
Fax: 818-346-6502.

MEMBERS OF FIRM

Viviana Amzel (Not admitted in CA)
Robert P. Andreani
Victor M. Bartholetti
Breton A. Bocchieri
James S. Bryan
Steven J. Coté
Leslie E. Criswell
Jay M. Davis
William S. Davis
David R. Decker
Daniel W. Douglass
Edwin W. Duncan
Gerald M. Fisher
Jack Goldman
Wayne S. Grajewski
Paul D. Hesse
David M. Hershorin
John L. Hosack
Curtiss L. Isler
John E. James
Bart L. Kessel
Craig G. Kline
Michael S. Kogan
Julie Dean Larsen
Roger Erik Marken
Bruce H. Newman
Maura B. O'Connor
Kay Rustand
Andrea Y. Slade
Neil M. Sunkin
John R. Tate
Frederick J. Ufkes
Ronald Warner
Harriet M. Welch
Kim W. West
Roxanne M. Wilson
Joseph S. Wu
Michael C. Zellers
Tod I. Zuckerman

RETIRED PARTNERS

James E. Durbin
Robert Henigson
Reed A. Stout

OF COUNSEL

William A. Boeck
Eric D. Dean
Richard D. De Luce
Charles R. Diaz
Robert L. Dickson
Victoria Ying Jin
Daniel A. Lev
Edwin K. Marzec
Kenneth J. Murphy
Aaron M. Peck
Urban J. Schreiner
Juliana Stamato
Norma J. Williams

ASSOCIATES

Paul F. Arentz
Lisa A. Atty
Mark Aveis
Julian Bach
Russell T. Bates
Mollie F. Benedict
Susan C. Bergemann
Brett Michael Broderick
Freya L. Christian (Not admitted in CA)
Robert A. Cocchia
Albert F. Davis
Katessa Charles Davis
Michael Drury
Wendy C. Freedman
David M. Gillen
Margaret A. Glynn
Mark E. Gustafson
Jean A. Hobart
Jill M. Holt
Janice Rourke Hugener
Erik L. Jackson

(See Next Column)

ASSOCIATES (Continued)

Richard A. Janisch
Yale K. Kim
Michelle McAloon
Danielle E. Miller
Christina O. Nyhan
Denise Kabakow Rasmussen
David C. Read
Maria Ronchetto
Anne K. Samuelson
Evan Scheffel
Sandra M. Schwarzmann
Reem J. Shamieh
Melissa K. Stack
Ronald M. Stone
Alex Tarkian
Stephanie C. Tydlaska
Jürgen K. Vollrath
Nicole E. Waters
Matthew L. Wein
Eric R. Wilson

Representative Clients: Chevron Corp.; American International Group; ADT, Inc.; PacTel Properties; The Bank of California, N.A.; Brunswick Corp.; Reliance Steel & Aluminum Co.; Scope Industries; National Railroad Passenger Car; Boral Industries, Inc.

For full biographical listings, see the Martindale-Hubbell Law Directory

---

BAKER & HOSTETLER LLP (AV)

600 Wilshire Boulevard, 90017-3212
Telephone: 213-624-2400
FAX: 213-975-1740
To contact an attorney on the Internet use first initial and surname followed by @baker-hostetler.com
URL: http://www.bakerlaw.com
In Cleveland, Ohio: 3200 National City Center, 1900 East Ninth Street.
Telephone: 216-621-0200.
In Cincinnati, Ohio: 312 Walnut Street, Suite 2650.
Telephone: 513-929-3400.
In Columbus, Ohio: Capitol Square, Suite 2100, 65 East State Street.
Telephone: 614-228-1541.
In Denver, Colorado: 303 East 17th Avenue, Suite 1100.
Telephone: 303-861-0600.
In Houston, Texas: 1000 Louisiana, Suite 2000.
Telephone: 713-751-1600.
In Long Beach, California: 300 Oceangate, Suite 620.
Telephone: 562-432-2827.
In Orlando, Florida: SunBank Center, Suite 2300, 200 South Orange Avenue.
Telephone: 407-649-4000.
In Washington, D. C.: Washington Square, Suite 1100, 1050 Connecticut Avenue, N.W.
Telephone: 202-861-1500.

Edward J. McCutchen (1857-1933)
Harold A. Black (1895-1970)
George Harnagel (1903-1962)
G. William Shea (1911-1986)

OFFICE MANAGING PARTNER

Peter W. James (Managing Partner, Los Angeles and Long Beach, California Offices)

PARTNERS

Angela C. Agrusa
Penny M. Costa
David A. Destino
Jonathan R. Hodes
Jack I. Samet
Bill E. Schroeder
Patrick J. Cain
Richard A. Deeb
Gary L. Gilbert
Thomas G. Roberts
David C. Sampson
Glen A. Smith
Teresa R. Tracy

ASSOCIATES

Kathleen E. Bailey
Nigel E. Jacques
Brian A. Ross
Marcos M. Tarango
Megan E. Gray
Andrew Lurie
Wendy E. Stanford
Kimberly R. Wells
Cranston J. Williams

OF COUNSEL

Lisa F. Hinchliffe

RETIRED PARTNERS

G. Richard Doty
Howard J. Privett

For full biographical listings, see the Martindale-Hubbell Law Directory

---

BELCHER, HENZIE & BIEGENZAHN, A PROFESSIONAL CORPORATION (AV)

333 South Hope Street, Suite 3650, 90071-1479
Telephone: 213-624-8293
Telecopier: 213-576-9964

Frank B. Belcher (1891-1979)
Leo J. Biegenzahn (1926-1996)
David Bernard (1931-1978)
John S. Curtis
E. Lee Horton
William T. DelHagen
Julia Azrael
Jeffrey L. Horwith
Raymond E. Hane, III

Georgette Renata Herget
John Erin McOsker
Paul R. Flaherty
Ian C. Fusselman
Jeffrey D. Wolf
Debby Lynne Zajac

(See Next Column)

BELCHER, HENZIE & BIEGENZAHN A PROFESSIONAL CORPORATION, *Los Angeles—Continued*

OF COUNSEL

George M. Henzie

Reference: Bank of America (Los Angeles Main Office).

For full biographical listings, see the Martindale-Hubbell Law Directory

LAW OFFICES OF DAVID B. BLOOM A PROFESSIONAL CORPORATION (AV)

3325 Wilshire Boulevard, Ninth Floor, 90010
Telephone: 323-938-5248; 384-4088
Telecopier: 213-385-2009

David B. Bloom

Stephen S. Monroe (A Professional Corporation)	Susan Carole Jay
Raphael A. Rosemblat	Edward Idell
James E. Adler	Sandra Kamenir
Roy A. Levun	Steven Wayne Lazarus
Jonathan Udell	Andrew Edward Briseno
	Shelley M. Gould

Ted L. Travis

For full biographical listings, see the Martindale-Hubbell Law Directory

BROBECK, PHLEGER & HARRISON LLP (AV)

A Partnership including a Professional Corporation
550 South Hope Street, 90071-2604
Telephone: 213-489-4060
Facsimile: 213-745-3345
Email: info@brobeck.com *URL:* http://www.brobeck.com/
San Francisco, California Office: Spear Street Tower, One Market.
Telephone: 415-442-0900.
Facsimile: 415-442-1010.
Palo Alto, California Office: Two Embarcadero Place, 2200 Geng Road.
Telephone: 650-424-0160.
Facsimile: 650-496-2885.
San Diego, California Office: 550 West C Street, Suite 1300.
Telephone: 619-234-1966.
Facsimile: 619-236-1403.
Irvine, California Office: 38 Technology Drive.
Telephone: 949-790-6300.
Facsimile: 949-790-6301.
Austin, Texas Office: 301 Congress Avenue, Suite 1200.
Telephone: 512-477-5495.
Facsimile: 512-477-5813.
Denver, Colorado Office: 370 Interlocken Boulevard, Suite 500.
Telephone: 303-410-2000.
Facsimile: 303-420-2199.
New York, N.Y. Office: 1633 Broadway, 47th Floor.
Telephone: 212-581-1600.
Facsimile: 212-586-7878.
Washington, D.C. Office: 701 Pennsylvania Avenue, NW, Suite 220.
Telephone: 202-220-6000.
Facsimile: 202-824-0949.
London, England Office: Brobeck Hale and Dorr International, Hasilwood House, 60 Bishopsgate, London EC2N 4AJ.
Telephone: 011 44 171 638 6688.
Facsimile: 011 44 171 638 5888.

OFFICE LEADER

Thomas P. Burke

PARTNERS

Kenneth R. Bender	Richard S. Odom
Linda J. Bozung	Debra E. Pole
Gregg A. Farley	Howard M. Privette
William B. Fitzgerald	David L. Schrader
David M. Halbreich	William K. Swank
Susan B. Hall	Jeffrey S. Turner
Jeffery D. Hermann	Daniel J. Tyukody, Jr.
John Francis Hilson	Kenneth L. Waggoner
Jamie L. Johnson	Gerard J. Walsh
George H. Link	John J. Wasilczyk

Michael T. Zarro

SENIOR COUNSEL

Marcia Z. Gordon	Thomas H. Petrides

Raymond T. Sung

OF COUNSEL

William K. Dial	James D. Prendergast
Joan M. Goddard	Lynn A. Robertson
Earle D. Miller	Allen Z. Sussman

Perrie M. Weiner

ASSOCIATES

Michael L. Armstrong	Robert C. Bigler
A. Rick Atwood, Jr.	Michael W. Chou
Raymond P. Barkes	Richard L. Daniels
Sarah J. Barney	Torey J. Favarote

(See Next Column)

ASSOCIATES (Continued)

Rita M. Herscovici	Douglas C. Rawles
Ryan S. Hong	Lorelei D. Ritchie (Not admitted in CA)
Bruce M. Jacobs	Konrad F. Schreier, III
Bryan P. Jacobsen	Allison N. Shue
Wayne E. Johnson	Joel D. Siegel
Kevin M. Kemper	Aaron Sonnhalter
Lilly Kim	Edward D. Totino
Scott W. Langley	Michael C. Tu
Howard L. Magee	Kathleen MacFarlane Waters
Richard T. Marquez	Robert D. Weber
Adam H. Mindle	Pamela J. Yates
Cromwell R. Montgomery	Gregg Zucker
Lauren M. Raskin	

For full biographical listings, see the Martindale-Hubbell Law Directory

CARLSMITH BALL (AV)

A Partnership including Law Corporations
9th Floor, 444 South Flower Street, 90071-2901
Telephone: 213-955-1200
Fax: 213-623-0032
Email: execdirector@carlsmith.com *URL:* http://www.carlsmith.com
Honolulu, Hawaii Office: Suite 2200, Pacific Tower, 1001 Bishop Street. P.O. Box 656, 96809-3402.
Telephone: 808-523-2500.
Fax: 808-523-0842.
Kapolei, Hawaii Office: Suite 318, Kapolei Building, 1001 Kamokila Boulevard, 96707.
Telephone: 808-523-2500.
Fax: 808-674-0850.
Wailuku, Maui Hawaii Office: Suite 400, One Main Plaza, 2200 Main Street, P.O. Box 1086, 96793-1086.
Telephone: 808-242-4535.
Fax: 808-244-4974.
Kailua-Kona, Hawaii Office: Suite 209, 75-1000 Henry Street, 96740.
Telephone: 808-329-6464.
Fax: 808-329-9450.
Hilo, Hawaii Office: 121 Waianuenue Avenue, P.O. Box 686, 96721-0686.
Telephone: 808-935-6644.
Fax: 808-935-7975.
Hagatna, Guam Office: Suite 401, Bank of Hawaii Building, 134 West Soledad Avenue, P.O. Box BF, 96932-5027.
Telephone: 671-472-6813.
Fax: 671-477-4375.
Telex: 721-6445 CWCMI GM.
Saipan, Commonwealth of the Northern Mariana Islands Office: Carlsmith Building, Capitol Hill, P.O. Box 5241, 96950-5241.
Telephone: 670-322-3455.
Fax: 670-322-3368.
Washington, D.C. Office: 1201 Pennsylvania Avenue, N.W., Suite 300, 20004-2401.
Telephone: 202-628-2228.
Fax: 202-628-2071.
Mexico City, Mexico Office: Sierra Nevada 119, Lomas de Chapultepec, 11000 Mexico, D.F.
Telephone: 52-5-520-8514, 52-5-520-8757.
Fax: 52-5-540-1545.
Mexico, D.F. Office of Carlsmith Ball, S.C. (Authorized to practice as foreign legal consultants in Mexico): Sierra Nevada 119, Lomas de Chapultepec, 11000 Mexico, D.F.
Telephone: 52-5-520-8514, 52-5-520-8757.
Fax: 52-5-540-1545.

RESIDENT PARTNERS

Annie Kun Baker	Terrence A. Everett
Joseph A. Ball	Robert F. Kull
Roger B. Baymiller	Randolph G. Muhlestein
Michael I. Blaylock	James Polish
Stephen L. Bradford	Jonathan L. Smoller
Albert H. Ebright	Donald C. Williams

RESIDENT ASSOCIATES

Deborah Elise Barack (Not admitted in CA)	Patricia Cymerman
	Grace E. Jo

RESIDENT OF COUNSEL

Herbert G. Baerwitz	John R. McDonough
Tom K. Houston	Ole R. Sandberg

Robert R. Thornton

For full biographical listings, see the Martindale-Hubbell Law Directory

CHADBOURNE & PARKE LLP (AV)

601 South Figueroa Street, 90017
Telephone: 213-892-1000; 800-892-2043
Facsimile: 213-622-9865
New York, N.Y. Office: 30 Rockefeller Plaza, 10112.
Telephone: 212-408-5100.
Facsimile: 212-541-5369.
Washington, D.C. Office: 1200 New Hampshire Avenue, N.W., Suite 300, 20036.
Telephone: 202-974-5600.
Facsimile: 202-974-5602.

(See Next Column)

CHADBOURNE & PARKE LLP—*Continued*

London, England Affiliate Office: Chadbourne & Parke, a multinational partnership of Registered Foreign Lawyers and Solicitors, Regis House, 45 King William Street, London, EC4R 9AN.
Telephone: 44-171-337-8000.
Facsimile: 44-171-337-8001.
Moscow, Russia Office: 52/5 Kosmodamianskaya Nab., 113054.
Telephone: 7095-974-2424.
Facsimile: 7095-974-2425. International satellite lines via U.S.:
Telephone: 212-408-1190.
Facsimile: 212-408-1199.
Hong Kong, China Office: 1701A The Hong Kong Club Building, 3A Chater Road, Central, Hong Kong.
Telephone: 852-2842-5400.
Facsimile: 852-2521-7527.

PARTNERS

Peter R. Chaffetz
Jay R. Henneberry
Kenneth J. Langan
Richard J. Ney

RESIDENT COUNSEL

William J. Kelley, III
Carl Thomas

RESIDENT ASSOCIATES

Robin D. Ball
Nadine S. Koobatian
Kenneth J. Lorge
Marvin D. Mohn
James F.B. Sawyer
Herbert S. Smith
Susan M. St. Denis

For full biographical listings, see the Martindale-Hubbell Law Directory

CLARK & TREVITHICK, A PROFESSIONAL CORPORATION (AV)

800 Wilshire Boulevard, 12th Floor, 90017
Telephone: 213-629-5700
Telecopier: 213-624-9441
Email: postmaster@clarktrev.com
San Francisco, California Office: 456 Montgomery Street, 20th Floor.
Telephone: 415-288-6520.
Fax: 415-398-2820.

Donald P. Clark
Alexander C. McGilvray, Jr.
Philip W. Bartenetti
Kevin P. Fiore
Vincent Tricarico
John A. Lapinski
Leonard Brazil
Dean I. Friedman
Robert F. DeMeter
Michael K. Wofford
Leslie R. Horowitz
Brent A. Reinke
Arturo Santana Jr.
James S. Arico
Robert W. Renken

OF COUNSEL

Dolores Cordell
Judith Ilene Bloom
John A. Tucker, Jr.
Raimund Freihube

For full biographical listings, see the Martindale-Hubbell Law Directory

COTKIN, COLLINS & GINSBURG, A PROFESSIONAL CORPORATION (AV)

555 South Flower Street, 18th Floor, 90071-2319
Telephone: 213-688-9350
FAX: 213-688-9351
URL: http://www.cotkincollinsginsburg.com
Santa Ana, California Office: 200 West Santa Ana Boulevard, Suite 800.
Telephone: 714-835-2330.
FAX: 714-835-2209.

Raphael Cotkin
James P. Collins, Jr. (Resident, Santa Ana Office)
William H. Ginsburg
Steven L. Paine
William D. Naeve (Resident, Santa Ana Office)
Terry C. Leuin
Roger W. Simpson
Joan M. Dolinsky
Robert G. Wilson
David A. Winkle (Resident, Santa Ana Office)
Karen C. Freitas
Brian R. Hill (Resident, Santa Ana Office)
Douglas A. Greer
Myrna L. D'Incognito
Kenneth S. Kleeger

Gregory A. Sargenti (Resident, Santa Ana Office)
Terry L. Kesinger (Resident, Santa Ana Office)
Ellen M. Tipping (Resident, Santa Ana Office)
Cooper W. Collins (Resident, Santa Ana Office)
Shannon L. Fernandez
David P. Nemecek, Jr

References: Mellon 1st Business Bank, Los Angeles; Bank of America.

For full biographical listings, see the Martindale-Hubbell Law Directory

DAAR & NEWMAN, PROFESSIONAL CORPORATION (AV)

Suite 2500, 865 South Figueroa Street, 90017-2567
Telephone: 213-892-0999
FAX: 213-892-1066
Email: lawyers@daarnewman.com *URL:* http://www.daarnewman.com

(See Next Column)

David Daar
Michael R. Newman
Jeffery J. Daar
Marsha McLean-Utley
Michael J. White

OF COUNSEL

Rodney W. Loeb
William F. White, Jr.
Samuel T. Rees
Leo S. Rich

LEGAL SUPPORT PERSONNEL

Joe A. Morton
Frank E. Raab

Representative Clients: Allianz Insurance Co.; American Income Life Insurance Co.; American Life and Casualty Insurance Co.; Balboa Insurance Co.; California Casualty Insurance Co.; National Benefit Life Insurance Co.; Capital Life Insurance Co.; Charter National Life; Columbian Mutual Life; Connecticut Mutual Life Insurance Co.

For full biographical listings, see the Martindale-Hubbell Law Directory

DAVIS & FOX (AV)

1901 Avenue of the Stars, Suite 400, 90067
Telephone: 310-286-2915
Fax: 310-286-2916

Calvin E. Davis
Steven A. Fox
Elizabeth A. Kooyman
John J. Stumreiter
Amy L. Freisleben
Barbara Kekich
Gregory M. Sinderbrand

For full biographical listings, see the Martindale-Hubbell Law Directory

GIBSON, DUNN & CRUTCHER LLP (AV)

333 South Grand Avenue, 90071-3197
Telephone: 213-229-7000
Telecopier: 213-229-7520; 213-229-7268
Century City, Los Angeles, California Office: 2029 Century Park East.
Telephone: 310-552-8500.
Telecopier: 310-551-8741.
Irvine, California Office: 4 Park Plaza.
Telephone: 949-451-3800.
Telecopier: 949-451-4220.
San Diego, California Office: 401 West A Street, Suite 1900.
Telephone: 619-544-8000.
Telecopier: 619-544-8190.
San Francisco, California Office: One Montgomery Street, Telesis Tower, 26th Floor and 31st Floor.
Telephone: 415-393-8200.
Telecopier: 415-986-5309.
Palo Alto, California Office: 1530 Page Mill Road.
Telephone: 650-849-5300.
Telecopier: 650-849-5333.
Denver, Colorado Office: 1801 California Street, Suite 4200.
Telephone: 303-298-5700.
Telecopier: 303-296-5310.
Washington, D.C. Office: 1050 Connecticut Avenue, N.W.
Telephone: 202-955-8500.
Telecopier: 202-467-0539.
New York, New York Office: 200 Park Avenue.
Telephone: 212-351-4000.
Telecopier: 212-351-4035; 212-351-4018.
Cable Address: GIBTRASK NEWYORK.
Dallas, Texas Office: 1717 Main Street, Suite 5400.
Telephone: 214-698-3100.
Telecopier: 214-698-3400.
Paris, France Office: 166, ru du Faubourg Saint Honoré.
Telephone: 011-33-01-56-43-13-00.
Telecopier: 011-33-01-56-43-13-33.
London, England Office: 30/35 Pall Mall, SW1Y 5LP.
Telephone: 011-44-171-925-0440.
Telecopier: 011-44-171-925-2465.

Jas. A. Gibson (1852-1922)
W. E. Dunn (1861-1925)
Albert Crutcher (1860-1931)

PARTNERS

Robert S. Warren
Ronald E. Gother
Robert E. Cooper
Ronald S. Beard (Irvine and Los Angeles Offices)
John H. Sharer
Wesley G. Howell, Jr. (New York City and Los Angeles, California Offices)
John F. Olson (Washington, D.C. Office)
Andrew E. Bogen
Robert K. Montgomery (Century City and Los Angeles Offices)
Theodore B. Olson (Los Angeles and Washington, D.C. Offices)
John J. Swenson
John T. Behrendt (New York City Office)
William J. Kilberg (Washington, D.C. Office)
Bruce D. Meyer
Peter L. Baumbusch (Washington, D.C. Office)
Christopher H. Buckley, Jr. (Washington, D.C. Office)
William Stinehart, Jr. (Century City Office)
Kenneth E. Ristau, Jr. (Irvine Office)
Dean Stern
Jack H. Halgren
Roy J. Schmidt, Jr.
John A. Ruskey
Fred F. Gregory
Kenneth W. Anderson
Stephen M. Blitz (Denver, Colorado Office)
James G. Phillipp

(See Next Column)

GIBSON, DUNN & CRUTCHER LLP, *Los Angeles—Continued*

PARTNERS (Continued)

Blake T. Franklin (New York City Office)
David A. Cathcart
Robert C. Bonner (Washington, D.C. and Los Angeles, California Offices)
Steven Alan Meiers
Arthur L. Sherwood
Richard A. Strong
Richard D. Hall
R. Randall Huff
Lawrence Calof (Palo Alto Office)
John Edd Stepp, Jr. (Century City Office)
Charles C. Ivie
Meldon E. Levine (Century City and Washington, D.C. Offices)
J. Anthony Sinclitico, III (San Diego Office)
Joseph H. Price (Washington, D.C. Office)
James C. Opel
Martin Carl Washton
Cantwell Faulkner Muckenfuss III (Washington, D.C. Office)
Scott August Kruse
Wayne W. Smith (Los Angeles and Irvine Offices)
Richard Paul Levy
Dennis A. Gladwell (Irvine Office)
S. David Blinn (Los Angeles and Irvine Offices)
Irwin F. Sentilles, III (Dallas, Texas Office)
Aulana L. Peters (Los Angeles and Washington, D.C. Offices)
Gerard J. Kenny (Irvine Office)
James P. Clark (Century City Office)
John A. Herfort (New York City Office)
Lawrence J. Hohlt (New York City Office)
Jerry J. Strochlic (New York City Office)
Bennett L. Silverman
Kirk A. Patrick
Thomas E. Holliday
Peter F. Ziegler
Stephen C. Johnson (Dallas, Texas Office)
Gordon A. Schaller (Irvine Office)
David R. Johnson (Washington, D.C. Office)
Donald Harrison (Washington, D.C. Office)
Richard Michael Russo (Denver, Colorado Office)
Phillip L. Bosl
Wayne A. Schrader (Washington, D.C. Office)
Robert W. Loewen (Irvine Office)
Anthony Bonanno (London, England Office)
Peter H. Turza (Washington, D.C. Office)
Charles F. Feldman (New York City Office)
Conor D. Reilly (New York City Office)
Dennis B. Arnold
Steven R. Finley (New York City Office)
Andrew H. Levy (New York City Office)
Martin B. McNamara (Dallas, Texas Office)
Michael L. Denger (Washington, D.C. Office)
F. Joseph Warin (Washington, D.C. Office)
Charles M. Schwartz (Dallas, Texas Office)
Lawrence J. Ulman
Daniel J. Plaine (Washington, D.C. Office)
Robert Everett Dean (Irvine Office)
Thomas D. Magill (Irvine Office)
George B. Curtis (Denver, Colorado Office)
William D. Claster (Irvine Office)
Joseph P. Busch III (Irvine Office)
Pamela Lynn Hemminger
Daniel Q. Callister (Washington, D.C. Office)
Fred L. Pillon (San Francisco Office)
Denis R. Salmon (Palo Alto Office)
Larry C. Boyd (Irvine Office)
E. Michael Greaney (Irvine, California and New York, N.Y. Offices)
Nancy P. McClelland
Howard B. Adler (Washington, D.C. Office)
Karen H. Clark (Irvine Office)
Dhiya El-Saden
D. Jansing Baker (New York City Office)
Robert S. Metzger
Jack M. Weiss (New York City Office)
Gilbert D. Porter (New York City Office)
William L. Hudson (San Francisco Office)
Dean J. Kitchens
Jeffrey Reid Hudson
Charles A. Larson (Century City Office)
Mark W. Shurtleff (Irvine Office)
Christopher J. Martin (Palo Alto Office)
Peter Sullivan
Shari Leinwand (Century City Office)
Gary L. Justice
Jonathan K. Layne
Scott A. Fink (San Francisco Office)
Gail Ellen Lees
Marjorie Ehrich Lewis
David West
Russell C. Hansen (Century City Office)
William Edward Wegner
Meryl L. Young (San Diego Office)
Larry L. Simms (Washington, D.C. Office)
John H. Sturc (Washington, D.C. Office)
Jonathan C. Dickey (Palo Alto Office)
Joseph Kattan (Washington, D.C. Office)
Scott R. Hoyt (Dallas, Texas Office)
Mitchell A. Karlan (New York City Office)
Thomas C. McGraw (Dallas, Texas Office)
Hatef Behnia
Joel A. Feuer
Kenneth M. Doran (Los Angeles and Century City Offices)
J. Nicholson Thomas
Karen E. Bertero
Robert C. Eager (Washington, D.C. Office)
Robert L. Weigel (New York City Office)
Mark E. Weber
Todd H. Baker (San Francisco Office)
Douglas D. Smith (San Francisco Office)
Stephan H. Haimo (New York City Office)
William A. Gray (New York City Office)

PARTNERS (Continued)

(See Next Column)

David J. Grais (New York City Office)
Harlan P. Cohen (Dallas, Texas Office)
Glenn K. Beaton (Denver, Colorado Office)
John M. Vaught (Denver, Colorado Office)
Stephen L. Tolles
Cheryl D. Justice
Jeffrey T. Thomas (Irvine Office)
Steven Eugene Sletten
Baruch A. Fellner (Washington, D.C. Office)
Craig H. Millet (Irvine Office)
Patrick W. Dennis
Michael A. Rosenthal (Dallas, Texas Office)
Jennifer Bellah-Maguire
Joel S. Sanders (San Francisco Office)
Rory Michael Hernandez
Arthur David Pasternak (Washington, D.C. Office)
Paul R. Harter (London, England Office)
Terence P. Ross (Washington, D.C. Office)
Kathryn Anne Coleman (San Francisco Office)
John C. Millian (Washington, D.C. Office)
Brian D. Kilb
Wayne M. Barsky (Century City Office)
Robert B. Krakow (Dallas, Texas Office)
M. Byron Wilder (Dallas, Texas Office)
Robert E. Palmer (Irvine Office)
Steven P. Buffone (New York City Office)
Mark S. Pécheck
Daniel G. Swanson
Gregory J. Kerwin (Denver, Colorado Office)
Scott A. Edelman (Los Angeles and Century City Offices)
David B. Pendarvis (San Diego Office)
David B. Rosenauer (New York City Office)
Randy Michael Mastro (New York City Office)
Raymond B. Ludwiszewski (Washington, D.C. Office)
Larry V. Smith (Dallas, Texas Office)
Amy R. Forbes
David I. Schiller (Dallas, Texas Office)
John R. Crews (Dallas, Texas Office)
Kenneth R. Lamb (San Francisco Office)
Joerg H. Esdorn (New York City Office)
Daniel S. Floyd
Robert Francis Serio (New York City Office)
David L. Herbert (Dallas, Texas Office)
Amy G. Rudnick (Washington, D.C. Office)
Steven A. Ruben
Paul S. Issler
Kay Ellen Kochenderfer
Richard J. Doren
Jesse Sharf
Sean P. Griffiths (New York City Office)
Julia A. Dahlberg (Washington, D.C. Office)
Patricia S. Radez (San Francisco Office)
Timothy J. Hatch
Bradford P. Weirick
James P. Ricciardi (New York City Office)
David Alan Battaglia
Theodore J. Boutrous, Jr. (Los Angeles, California and Washington, D.C. Offices)
Kevin S. Rosen
Janet Vance (New York City Office)
Judith A. Lee (Washington, D.C. Office)
David H. Kennedy (Palo Alto Office)
A. James Isbester (San Francisco Office)
Bernard Grinspan (Paris, France Office)
Jeffrey M. Trinklein (Dallas, Texas Office)
Ronald O. Mueller (Washington, D.C. Office)
Timothy J. Kay (Irvine Office)
Douglas R. Cox (Washington, D.C. Office)
Geniene B. Stillwell (Irvine Office)
Chad S. Hummel
Steven R. Shoemate (New York City Office)
Gregory Toll Davidson (Palo Alto Office)
Kimberly S. McGovern (San Francisco Office)
Susan M. Marcella
Thomas G. Hungar (Washington, D.C. Office)
D. Eric Remensperger
Jeffrey D. Dintzer
Gregory J. Conklin (San Francisco Office)
Deborah J. Clarke
Adam H. Offenhartz (New York City Office)
Rodney J. Stone
David W. Mayo (New York City Office)
Thomas J.P. McHenry
Teresa Joanning Farrell (Irvine Office)
Gregory L. Surman
Gareth T. Evans
Janet M. Weiss (New York City Office)
Linda L. Curtis
Oscar Garza (Irvine Office)
Alan N. Bick (Irvine Office)
Michael F. Flanagan (Washington, D.C. Office)
Andrea E. Neuman (Irvine Office)
Eugene Scalia (Washington, D.C. Office)
M. Sean Royall (Washington, D.C. Office)
Peter J. Beshar (New York City Office)
Wendy M. Singer (London, England and Paris, France Offices) (European Partner)
Christopher J. Bellini (Washington, D.C. and Riyadh, Saudi Arabia Offices)
Stephanie R. Bess (London, England Office) (European Partner)
Stephanie Tsacoumis (Washington, D.C. Office)
David J. Furman (New York City Office)
Miguel A. Estrada (Washington, D.C. Office)
Alan V. Samson (London, England Office)
Scott M. Knutson (Irvine Office)
Karl G. Nelson (Dallas, Texas Office)
William A. MacArthur
Kristine R. Robertson
John M. Williams, III (Irvine Office)
Steven K. Talley (Denver, Colorado Office)
Ignacio M. Foncillas (New York City Office)
Mark A. Perry (Washington, D.C. Office)
Frédérique Sauvage (Paris, France Office)

(See Next Column)

GIBSON, DUNN & CRUTCHER LLP—*Continued*

ADVISORY COUNSELS

Sherman Seymour Welpton, Jr.
Julian O. von Kalinowski
F. Daniel Frost
Sharp Whitmore (San Diego Office)
Francis M. Wheat
Arthur W. Schmutz
Norman B. Barker
James R. Hutter
Robert D. Burch (Century City Office)
John L. Endicott
John J. Hanson
Jerome C. Byrne
George W. Bermant (Denver, Colorado Office)
Willard Z. Carr, Jr.
G. Edward Fitzgerald
Stephen E. Tallent (Washington, D.C. Office)
Russell L. Johnson
Thomas B. Pitcher (Irvine Office)
Charles K. Marquis (New York City Office)
George H. Whitney
Frank L. Mallory (Irvine Office)
John T. Pigott (Century City Office)
Raymond L. Curran
Dean C. Dunlavey
Roy D. Miller
Herbert Kraus
Irwin F. Woodland
James M. Murphy
Charles S. Battles, Jr.
Robert T. Gelber
Paul G. Bower
Charles R. Collins (San Francisco Office)
Bruce L. Gitelson (Palo Alto Office)
Leo G. Ziffren (Century City Office)
Bruce A. Toor
Ralph C. Wintrode (Irvine Office)
Dwight L. Nye (Dallas, Texas Office)
John C. Wells (Irvine Office)
James R. Martin
Lester Ziffren (Century City Office)
Michael E. Alpert (San Diego Office)
Robert Forgnone
C. Ransom Samuelson II
Peter J. Wallison (Washington, D.C. Office)
J. Michael Brennan (Irvine Office)
Jonathan M. Landers (San Francisco Office)
John J.A. Hossenlopp (New York City Office)
Jane Lindsey Wingfield

OF COUNSELS

John A. Arguelles (Irvine Office)
Kevin W. Barrett (New York City Office)
Gracia M. Berg (Washington, D.C. Office)
Kimberly L. Bick (Irvine Office)
Paul Blankenstein (Washington, D.C. Office)
Susan B. Burr (Palo Alto Office)
Bernard W. Crotty
Andrea F. Dynes (Washington, D.C. Office)
Jonathan B. Eddison (Irvine Office)
Stanton P. Eigenbrodt (Dallas, Texas Office)
Deborah S. Feinerman (Century City Office)
Daniel J. Fetterman (New York City Office)
Joanne Franzel (New York City Office)
Amy L. Goodman (Washington, D.C. Office)
Alan J. Gordee (Irvine Office)
Nicola T. Hanna (San Diego Office)
Mark B. Holton (New York City Office)
William H. Horton, Jr. (New York City Office)
Steven B. Jackman (New York City Office)
Michael J. Keliher (Dallas, Texas Office)
Jong Han Kim (Irvine Office)
Andrew A. Lance (New York City Office)
Michelle Alison Lewis (Washington, D.C. Office)
Richard G. Lyon (Dallas, Texas Office)
Clifton J. McFarland
Leonard J. McGill (Irvine Office)
Marcellus Antonio McRae
John O'Halloran (Century City Office)
Gonzalo Pardo de Zela (New York City Office)
Malcolm R. Pfunder (Washington, D.C. Office)
Diana Gale Richard (Washington, D.C. Office)
Victoria P. Rostow (Washington, D.C. Office)
Cynthia L. Salmen
Marianne Shipp (Irvine Office)
John E. Stoner (Irvine Office)

TECHNOLOGY COUNSEL

Adam S. Bendell
Daryl T. Teshima

SENIOR TRADE COUNSEL

Gregory S. Menegaz (Washington, D.C. Office)

SPECIAL COUNSELS

Deborah E. Miller (New York City Office)
Derry Dean Sparlin Jr. (Washington, D.C. Office)
April McGandy Evans
Thomas D. Boyle (Dallas, Texas Office)
Steven James Johnson (Palo Alto Office)
Kevin R. Nowicki (San Diego Office)

ASSOCIATES

Peter C. D'Apice (Dallas, Texas Office)
Walter J. Scott, Jr. (Dallas, Texas Office)
Jeffrey T. Gilleran (Washington, D.C. Office)
Joan M. Steinmann (Century City and Los Angeles Offices)
J. Fred Neuman (Irvine Office)
Jeffrey B. Conner (Not admitted in CA)
Jeffrey H. Reeves (Irvine Office)
Marshall R. King (New York City Office)
Scott J. Calfas
Audrey S. Trundle (New York City Office)
Antoinette D. Paglia
Mark J. Payne (Irvine Office)
Tanya S. McVeigh (San Francisco Office)
Kathrin E. Sears (Palo Alto Office)

(See Next Column)

ASSOCIATES (Continued)

James C. Dougherty (Washington, D.C. Office)
Leeanna Izuel
Noël C. Lohr
Merritt R. Blakeslee (Washington, D.C. Office)
Steven S. Kimball (San Francisco Office)
James P. Fogelman
Timothy L. Alger
Michael P. De Simone (New York City Office)
Leslie Ellen Moore (New York City Office)
Patricia E. Foley (Denver, Colorado Office)
Sharyl P. Bilas (Irvine Office)
Michael A. Levy (San Francisco Office)
Chris D. Biondi (New York City Office)
Elise D. Charbonnet (Washington, D.C. Office)
Lawrence J. La Sala (New York City Office)
David A. Segal (Irvine Office)
Peter P. Murphy (Washington, D.C. Office)
H. Mark Lyon (Palo Alto Office)
Paul J. Collins (Palo Alto Office)
Bryan B. Arnold
Yvonne M. Dutton (San Diego Office)
Alan R. Struble (Dallas, Texas Office)
Daniel W. Nelson (Washington, D.C. Office)
Leslie Y. Kim
Debra Alligood White (Washington, D.C. Office)
Jeffrey A. Fiarman (Washington, D.C. Office)
Monique Michal Drake (Denver, Colorado Office)
T. Michael Crimmins (Denver, Colorado Office)
Timothy J. Hart
Peter E. Seley (Washington, D.C. Office)
Lindsey F. Buss (Washington, D.C. Office)
D. Jarrett Arp (Washington, D.C. Office)
Kathleen M. Vanderziel
Jon G. Shepherd (Dallas, Texas Office)
Jason C. Murray (Los Angeles and Century City Offices)
Jonathan K. Tycko (Washington, D.C. Office)
Kimberly Ann Udovic
Thomas S. Jones (Irvine Office)
O. Rey Rodriguez (Dallas, Texas Office)
Jessica Lee (Denver, Colorado Office)
Deborah A. Cussen (Washington, D.C. Office)
Georgiana G. Rodiger
Pamela B. Stein (Dallas, Texas Office)
Peter T. Heilmann (San Francisco Office)
Richard T. Joffe (New York City Office)
Michael A. Sitzman (San Francisco Office)
Anthony C. Providenti (New York City Office)
Felix Sotomayor (New York City Office)
Shanda K. Beach (Irvine Office)
Eugene Y. Ferrer (New York City Office)
Gary T. Chow (Irvine Office)
Charles R. Bogle (New York City Office)
Thomas G. Mackey
Frederick A. Walters (New York City Office)
Rebecca Sanhueza (San Francisco Office)
Shelley R. Meacham
William M. Rustum (New York City Office)
Mary Sikra Thomas
Laura C. Roche (San Francisco Office)
Hilary Joy Hatch
Michael L. Reed (San Francisco Office)
Christopher D. Dusseault
Jeffrey E. Oraker (Denver, Colorado Office)
Simone Procas (New York City Office)
Christina Rooke Jones (San Francisco Office)
Adam E. Muchnick (Irvine Office)
Sue J. Nam (New York City Office)
C. Glen Morris (Dallas, Texas Office)
Hillary S. Zilz (New York City Office)
Brette S. Simon
Bradley J. Muro (New York City Office)
James A. Deets (Dallas, Texas Office)
Wendy A. Learmont Hallgren (Irvine Office)
Mary A. Donovan (Irvine Office)
David J. Fraser (Irvine Office)
G. Leland Dutcher, Jr. (Century City Office)
Lisa A. Fontenot (San Francisco Office)
Stanley Sze (Palo Alto Office)
David A. Zonana (Palo Alto Office)
Alice W. Detwiler (Washington, D.C. Office)
David W.T. Daniels (Washington, D.C. Office)
Andrew D. Rotstein (New York City Office)
John J. Fetters (Not admitted in CA)
Deborah J. Verdile (New York City Office)
Seth A. Miller (Century City Office)
J. Andrew Ward (New York City Office)
Robert M. Zimmerman (New York City Office)
Andrew E. Burrows (Palo Alto Office)
David P. Simonds (New York City Office)
Thomas D. Bunton (San Diego Office)
Michael J. Hartley
Heather A. Spriggs (Irvine Office)
Diana L. Preston (Washington, D.C. Office)
Louis R. Dienes (New York City Office)
Stephen R. Smerek (Not admitted in CA)
Helen M. Corcoran (New York City Office)
Robert R. Stark, Jr. (Denver, Colorado Office)
John C. Conway
James P. Maniscalco
Todd D. Kantorczyk (Washington, D.C. Office)
Connie J. Rand (San Diego Office)
Lisa A. Alfaro (New York City Office)
Jeff Augustini (Irvine Office)
Wendy A. Lutzker
Todd S. Cohen (New York City Office)
Michele J. Herschkowitz (New York City Office)

(See Next Column)

GIBSON, DUNN & CRUTCHER LLP, *Los Angeles—Continued*

ASSOCIATES (Continued)

Laurie McLaughlin (New York City Office)
Samuel G. Liversidge
Timothy S. Lykowski
Stewart L. McDowell (San Francisco Office)
Thomas C. Sheehan (New York City Office)
Hassan A. Zavareei (Washington, D.C. Office)
Michael Pierovich (Palo Alto Office)
Kevin F. Mabrey
Robert H. Pritchard, Jr. (New York City Office)
Karin L. Wolff (New York City Office)
Gavin A. Beske (Washington, D.C. Office)
S. Elizabeth Foster (New York City Office)
Jesse S. Finlayson (Irvine Office)
Colleen McMillin McCall (Dallas, Texas Office)
Aron Friedman (Washington, D.C. Office)
Seth M.M. Stodder (Washington, D.C. Office)
Jean D. Billyou (Irvine Office)
Abril Bedarf Turner (Irvine Office)
Roger P. Capriotti
Larry M. Furst (Century City Office)
Susanne M. MacIntosh
N. Kenneth Burraston (San Francisco Office)
William B. Holloway, Jr. (Dallas, Texas Office)
Steven R. Mitchell (Dallas, Texas Office)
Sonya L. Karpowich (Irvine Office)
Clay R. Stevens (Irvine Office)
Elizabeth S. Bluestein
John P. Newell
Thomas J. Fitzpatrick, Jr. (Irvine Office)
Dianna M. Nixon (New York City Office)
Ronit E. Attlesey (Irvine Office)
Jennifer P. Ashley (Irvine Office)
Samuel A. Mills (Dallas, Texas Office)
Peter F. Weinberg (Denver, Colorado Office)
Antoinette DeCamp
Amy L. Neuhardt (New York City Office)
Hill B. Wellford, III (Washington, D.C. Office)
Victoria C. Shapiro (Century City Office)
Paul DeCamp
Crystal E. Wright
John J. Hopkins (Dallas, Texas Office)
Robert S. Case (Dallas, Texas Office)
Robert G. Haiman (Dallas, Texas Office)
Roger W. Bivans (Dallas, Texas Office)
M. Natasha Labovitz (New York City Office)
Christopher S. Dallas (Irvine Office)
John C. Troutman (Irvine Office)
Joshua F. Cender (New York City Office)
Elizabeth A. Warke (Irvine Office)
Deborah J. Katz (Washington, D.C. Office)
James R. Ponichtera (New York City Office)
Theresa M. Melson
Michelle H. Tremain

Jeffrey D. Firestone (Washington, D.C. Office)
Amanda L. Riley (San Francisco Office)
Beau Claire Stacom
George C. Tung (Irvine Office)
James P. Ursomarso (Washington, D.C. Office)
Susan K. Zamzow (New York City Office)
Michelle Hodges (Irvine Office)
Gavin E. Hill (Dallas, Texas Office)
Jacqueline E. Coleman (Washington, D.C. Office)
William E. Thomson
Juan Manuel Trujillo (New York City Office)
Dora Arash
James P. Arguelles (San Diego Office)
Wesley L. Hsu (Century City Office)
Benjamin C. Burkhart (London, England Office)
Michael P. Lambert
Marni J. Roder (New York City Office)
Judith A. Smith (Denver, Colorado Office)
Andrea Sloan Pink (Irvine Office)
Monica J. Burick (Irvine Office)
Elisabeth C. Watson
James M. Schober (Dallas, Texas Office)
Suzy C. Kaster (San Francisco Office)
Michael R. Williams (Irvine Office)
Kevin C. Shea (New York City Office)
Marshall S. Sprung
Frances K. Greenleaf
Margaret L. Fitzpatrick (San Francisco Office)
David B. Salmons (Washington, D.C. Office)
Brian C. Goebel
Ariane M. Horn (New York City Office)
Nicole B. Hancock
Joseph D. Matal (Washington, D.C. Office)
William A. Wargo
Mark S. Lahive
Linn A. Brady (New York City Office)
Guy P. Glazier
Amy E. Davis (New York City Office)
Andrew S. Tulumello (Washington, D.C. Office)
Joshua A. Kreinberg
Nhan T. Vu (Irvine Office)
Jonathan M. Eisenberg (San Francisco Office)
Jonathan C. Mosher (Irvine Office)
Henry A. Lanman (New York City Office)
Scott M. Davies (Denver, Colorado Office)
Charles H. Haake (Irvine Office)
Kwame J. Granderson
Stephen C. McKenna (Denver, Colorado Office)
Glenn E. Schoenfeld (New York City Office)
Pamela H. Black
Robert R. Chai-Onn
J. Owen Borum (Denver, Colorado Office)
Paul D. Weckerly (Irvine Office)
Brett H. Oberst
Jeff J. Jeon
Richard Ting
John P. Babel (Irvine Office)
Anna U. Nguyen

ASSOCIATES (Continued)

(See Next Column)

Aleem Raja (San Francisco Office)
Brad W. Cleveringa
Rachel E. Courtney (San Francisco Office)
Karen R. Gulkin (New York City Office)
Oksana M. Komarnyckyj (Irvine Office)
Brian Tran
Harvey Jang
Anton W. Leung
Gregory L. Doll (Century City Office)
Jodee M. Flint (Washington, D.C. Office)
Daniel S. Kim (Not admitted in CA)
Brian R. Gin (Palo Alto Office)
Ralph P. Brescia (Century City Office)
Jonathan D. Twombly (New York City Office)
Michele L. Maryott (Irvine Office)
Montgomery N. Kosma (Washington, D.C. Office)
Amanda Dalton Bourne
Ross E. Davies (Washington, D.C. Office)
Lisa A. Murray (Washington, D.C. Office)
Brendan P. Ryan (New York City Office)
Kristina M. Woodworth
Denis A. Curran (Palo Alto Office)
Casey M. Nault (Century City Office)
Peter W. Wardle
Thomas H. Dupree, Jr. (Washington, D.C. Office)
Cindy A. Purifoy
Cheryl M. Stanton (Washington, D.C. Office)
Amanda R. Wheeland (Irvine Office)
John Christopher Wood (Washington, D.C. Office)
Megan A. Barnett (Washington, D.C. Office)
Shannon C. Saalfield (Dallas, Texas Office)
Michael G. Honeymar, Jr. (New York City Office)
Jennifer W. Chaloemtiarana (San Francisco Office)
Rachel L. Sagan (Irvine Office)
Kenneth B. Stratton (Palo Alto Office)
Kristopher E. Moldovan (Dallas, Texas Office)
Sarah A. Donch (Dallas, Texas Office)
Peter A. Christou (San Francisco Office)
Michael J. Scanlon (Washington, D.C. Office)
Karen M. Howard
Jennifer A. Turnock
Christopher H. Norton
Christopher R. LaQuay

Bryn A. Sappington (Dallas, Texas Office)
Richard T. Archibald (Dallas, Texas Office)
Michael S. Brophy (Century City Office)
Aaron G. York (Dallas, Texas Office)
Charles H. Jeanfreau (New York City Office)
Peter D. Sunukjian (Irvine Office)
Mara V.J. Senn (Washington, D.C. Office)
Stephanie A. Bailiff (Irvine Office)
Cecilia V. Estolano
Janet E. Moser (San Diego Office)
Jennifer K. Schreck (Denver, Colorado Office)
Robert L. Bruce (Irvine Office)
Richard J. Brown (New York City Office)
Shashi K. Hanuman
Peter E. Masaitis
John B. Stone (San Francisco Office)
Lucille S. Leonard (Denver, Colorado Office)
Clinton P. Johnston (New York City Office)
Janelle S. Padilla (Dallas, Texas Office)
J. Warren Rissier
Craig A. Bruens (New York City Office)
Leslie M. Kelly (Denver, Colorado Office)
Denise McGinn (New York City Office)
Apik Minassian
Melinda A. Tisch (San Francisco Office)
Michele D. Carter
Deborah L. Shirley
Daniel E. Giddings
Aric H. Wu (New York City Office)
Christopher Bosland (Washington, D.C. Office)
Tilda L. Cho
John Z. Chen
Jeffrey A. Le Sage
Juliet M. Hanna (Denver, Colorado Office)
Ryan A. Murr (Irvine Office)
Joel D. Scott (Century City Office)
Jason C. Schwartz (Washington, D.C. Office)
Samantha D. Hardy (San Diego Office)
Ethan D. Dettmer (San Francisco Office)
Albert Y. Kim (Washington, D.C. Office)
Steven D. Buchholz (Palo Alto Office)
Kathryn E. Nealon (New York City Office)
Mark E. Papadopoulos (Washington, D.C. Office)

STAFF ATTORNEYS

Katherine A. Bacal (San Diego Office)
David Brier (New York City Office)
Tammy J. Evans
Carlos A. Garcia (Washington, D.C. Office)
Eric F. Hinton (Washington, D.C. Office)
Brian R. Kirchoff (Irvine Office)
Sharon W. Koplan (Dallas, Texas Office)

Jeanne M. Lempert (San Francisco Office)
Linda Noonan (Washington, D.C. Office)
Roberto Redondo (New York City Office)
Martha L. Sjogreen (New York City Office)
Melinda D. Waterman (Irvine Office)

For full biographical listings, see the Martindale-Hubbell Law Directory

Los Angeles—Continued

GOLDMAN & KAGON, LAW CORPORATION (AV)

1801 Century Park East, Suite 2222, 90067
Telephone: 310-552-1707
Telecopier: 310-552-7938
URL: http://www.goldmankagon.com

Mark A. Goldman
Barry Felsen
Charles D. Meyer
Christopher B. Fagan
Terry Mc Niff
Jared Laskin
Edmund S. Schaffer

COUNSEL

A. David Kagon

For full biographical listings, see the Martindale-Hubbell Law Directory

GRAHAM & JAMES LLP (AV)

14th Floor, 801 South Figueroa Street, 90017
Telephone: 213-624-2500
Telecopier: 213-623-4581
Email: dtakeuchi@gj.com *URL:* http://www.gj.com
Other offices located in: San Francisco, Orange County, Palo Alto and Sacramento, California; Seattle, Washington; Washington, D.C.; New York, New York; Milan, Italy; Beijing, China; Tokyo, Japan; London, England.
Associated Offices: Deacons Graham & James, Hong Kong, Sydney, Melbourne, Brisbane, Perth and Canberra, Australia.
Affiliated Offices: Deacons Graham & James, Hanoi and Ho Chi Minh City, Vietnam; Taipei, Taiwan and Bangkok, Thailand; In association with Dewi Soeharto & Rekan, Jakarta, Indonesia; Graham & James in affiliation with Taylor Joynson Garrett, London, England, Bucharest, Romania and Brussels, Belgium; Kau, Dusseldorf, Germany; Mishare M. Al-Ghazali & Partners, Safat, Kuwait; Law Firm of Salah Al-Hejailan, Jeddah and Riyadh, Saudi Arabia; Yeo Wee Kiong & Partners, Singapore.

David B. Abel
Jorge Arciniega
Hidetoshi Asakura
Vincent J. Belusko
James H. Broderick, Jr.
Jeffrey A. Chester
Hillel T. Cohn
Henry S. David
David L. Fehrman
Rodney A. Fujii
Benjamin E. Goldman
Randolph H. Gustafson
Yasuhiro Hagihara (Not admitted in CA)
David L. Henty
John C. Holberton
William J. James
Cheryl Lee Johnson
Allen Choo Kim
Joon Yong Kim
Ken Kurosu
Thomas T. Liu
Stuart L. Merkadeau
David T. Miyamoto
John T. Nagai
Stephen T. Owens
Denis H. Oyakawa
Don A. Proudfoot, Jr.
Minda R. Schechter
Brian E. Schield
Allan A. Shenoi
Eric Shih
Wayne M. Smith
Derrick K. Takeuchi
Martin J. Trupiano
Les J. Weinstein
Barry Leigh Weissman

SENIOR COUNSEL

Patrick J. Fields

OF COUNSEL

Richard P. Manson
William W. Wells

ASSOCIATES

Nancy Battelstein
Paul S. Berra
Alexandra A. Bodnar
Eric Cha
Terrence D. Garnett
Joseph R. Keating (Not admitted in CA)
Stefan J. Kirchanski
Anthony J. Luna
Sandra K. Lau
Robert McArthur
Rie Miyake
Hisako Muramatsu
Martin M. Noonen
David J. Roberts
Bobby J. Ryu
Erika L. Schreiber
Paul D. Swanson
Andy Hiroshi Takatsuka
Andrew H. Thorson
Todd W. Wight
Rami S. Yanni
Jennifer S. Yount

For full biographical listings, see the Martindale-Hubbell Law Directory

GREENBERG GLUSKER FIELDS CLAMAN & MACHTINGER LLP (AV)

21st Floor, 1900 Avenue of the Stars (Century City), 90067
Telephone: 310-553-3610
Fax: 310-553-0687
URL: http://www.ggfcm.com

MEMBERS OF FIRM

Arthur N. Greenberg
Sidney J. Machtinger
Stephen Claman
Bertram Fields
Harvey R. Friedman
Bernard Shearer
Jon J. Gallo
Paula J. Peters
Michael K. Collins
John L. Child
C. Bruce Levine
Michael A. Greene
Garrett L. Hanken
Norman H. Levine
William A. Halama
James E. Hornstein
Robert S. Chapman
Robert F. Marshall

(See Next Column)

MEMBERS OF FIRM (Continued)

Robert E. Bennett, Jr.
Marc S. Cohen
Charles N. Shephard
Dennis B. Ellman
Gary L. Kaplan
Lawrence Y. Iser
Martin H. Webster
Michael V. Bales
Henry D. Finkelstein
Elizabeth Watson
Jill A. Cossman
Roger L. Funk
Richard A. Kale
Arnold D. Kahn
Nancy A. Bertrando
Bonnie E. Eskenazi
Glenn A. Dryfoos
Richard E. Posell
Jeffrey Spitz
Steven J. Lurie
Lee A. Dresie
Marc M. Stern
David E. Cranston
Patricia A. Millett
Jeffrey A. Krieger
Edward N. Sabin
Paul A. Blechner
Dale J. Goldsmith
Karl E. Block
Ann Kane Smith
Jonathan B. Sokol

OF COUNSEL

Jean Morris

RETIRED

Philip Glusker

ASSOCIATES

Nancy C. Hsieh
Darryl W. Cluster
Carla M. Roberts
Sheri E. Porath
Stephanie H. Gold
Stephen S. Smith
Karen E. Pointer
Kristen L. Spanier
Barry D. Kellman
Mona S. Amer
Stephen B. Espinoza
Laura A. Zwicker
Hillary S. Bibicoff
Michelle Marie Lynn
Alison F. Clarke
Heidi M. Binford
Audrey J. Henninger
Matthew N. Falley
Aaron J Moss
JoAn H. Cho
Bob Baradaran
Jessica D. Lazarus
Michael D. McLachlan
Anna Y. Joo
Sarah K. Aubrey
Julia R. Haye
Thomas D. Martin
Michael G. Morgan
Robert S. Tippett
Jeffrey A. Backhus
Lorraine B. Echavarria
Veena D. Persaud
Andrew T. Kugler
David K. Eldan
Daniel P. Hoffer
Kurt Zimmerman
Ricardo P. Cestero
Matt Galsor

Reference: Wells Fargo Bank, 1801 Ave. of the Stars, Los Angeles, CA 90067.

For full biographical listings, see the Martindale-Hubbell Law Directory

HILL, FARRER & BURRILL LLP (AV)

A Limited Liability Partnership including Professional Corporations
37th Floor, One California Plaza, 300 South Grand Avenue, 90071-3147
Telephone: 213-620-0460
Fax: 213-624-4840
URL: http://www.hfbllp.com

William M. Farrer (1894-1971)
Alfred J. Hill (1881-1953)
Stanley S. Burrill (1902-1957)

MEMBERS OF FIRM

Kyle D. Brown (P.C.)
William M. Bitting (P.C.)
Stuart H. Young, Jr., (P.C.)
Steven W. Bacon (P.C.)
Wm. Harold Borthwick (P.C.)
Arthur B. Cook, II, (P.C.)
George Koide (P.C.)
Jonathan M. Brandler (P.C.)
Scott L. Gilmore (P.C.)
Kevin H. Brogan (P.C.)
James A. Bowles (P.C.)
Neil D. Martin (P.C.)
Michael J. DiBiase (P.C.)
Alfred M. Clark, III, (P.C.)
Daniel J. McCarthy (P.C.)
Ronald W. Novotny (P.C.)
Benjamin B. Salvaty (P.C.)
Dean E. Dennis (P.C.)
Thomas F. Reed
Suzanne J. Holland (P.C.)
William A. White (P.C.)
James R. Evans, Jr., (P.C.)
G. Cresswell Templeton III, (P.C.)
Michael S. Turner (P.C.)
Michelle A. Meghrouni (P.C.)
Ian M. Green (P.C.)
R. Curtis Ballantyne
Jennifer Cook Lewis
Jennifer L. Pancake
Byron T. Ball
Paul M. Porter

OF COUNSEL

Leon S. Angvire (P.C.)
Stanley E. Tobin (P.C.)
Jack R. White (P.C.)
James G. Johnson (P.C.)

RETIRED

Carl M. Gould
Vincent C. Page
William C. Farrer (P.C.)
Edwin H. Franzen (P.C.)
Darlene Fischer Phillips (P.C.)

ASSOCIATES

Dean A. Reeves
Arnold D. Woo
Karen S. Seigel
Laurie W. Wilson-Espinosa
Warren J. Higgins
Stacey A. Sullivan
John M. Byrne
Robert P. Silverstein

For full biographical listings, see the Martindale-Hubbell Law Directory

Los Angeles—Continued

IRELL & MANELLA LLP (AV)

A Law Partnership including Professional Corporations
Suite 900, 1800 Avenue of the Stars (Century City), 90067-4276
Telephone: 310-277-1010
Telecopier: 310-203-7199
URL: http://www.irell.com
Downtown Los Angeles Office: Suite 3300, 333 South Hope Street, 90071-3042.
Telephone: 213-620-1555.
Telecopier: 213-229-0515.
Newport Beach, California Office: Suite 400, 840 Newport Center Drive, 92660-6324.
Telephone: 949-760-0991.
Telecopier: 949-760-5200.

MEMBERS OF FIRM

Eugene M. Berger (1892-1944)
Arthur Manella (1917-1997)
Allan J. Abshez
James N. Adler (P.C.)
Scott D. Baskin (P.C.) (Resident at Newport Beach)
Richard L. Bernacchi (P.C.)
Richard M. Birnholz
Keith P. Bishop (Resident at Newport Beach)
Sheri A. Bluebond (Downtown Los Angeles Office)
Richard H. Borow (P.C.)
Elliot N. Brown
Norman E. Brunell
Christine W. S. Byrd
Frank A. Caput (Resident at Newport Beach)
Louis M. Castruccio (P.C.)
Morgan Chu
Richard de Bodo
James F. Elliott
Scott M. Epstein
Michael G. Ermer (Resident at Newport Beach)
Dorette S. Feit
Kevin L. Finch
John C. Fossum (P.C.) (Resident at Newport Beach)
Elliot G. Freier
Paul N. Frimmer (P.C.)
Gary N. Frischling
Roy S. Geiger (Downtown Los Angeles Office)
Martin N. Gelfand
David I. Gindler
Andra Barmash Greene (Resident at Newport Beach)
Peter J. Gregora
Andrew W. Gross
Kenneth R. Heitz
Catherine H. Helm
Brian J. Hennigan (Downtown Los Angeles Office)
Louis A. Huskins (P.C.)
Milton B. Hyman (P.C.)
Edebeatu C. Ibekwe
Ken Ikari (Downtown Los Angeles Office)
Anthony T. Iler (Downtown Los Angeles Office)
Meredith S. Jackson
Thomas W. Johnson, Jr. (Resident at Newport Beach)
Sandra Gerson Kanengiser
Edmund M. Kaufman (P.C.) (Downtown Los Angeles Office)
Kyle S. Kawakami (Resident at Newport Beach)
Richard B. Kendall
J. Christopher Kennedy (Downtown Los Angeles Office)
Thomas A. Kirschbaum
Bruce D. Kuyper
Daniel P. Lefler
Joan L. Lesser (P.C.)
Joseph M. Lipner
Marc S. Maister (Resident at Newport Beach)
Steven A. Marenberg
C. Kevin McGeehan
Richard J. McNeil (Resident at Newport Beach)
Ashok W. Mukhey
Layn R. Phillips (Resident at Newport Beach)
Anthony W. Pierotti (Resident at Newport Beach)
S. Thomas Pollack
Joel Rabinovitz (P.C.)
Lois J. Scali
David A. Schwarz
Alvin G. Segel
Marvin S. Shapiro (P.C.)
Richard M. Sherman, Jr.,(P.C.) (Resident at Newport Beach)
Henry Shields, Jr., (P.C.)
Clark B. Siegel
David Siegel
Steven L. Sloca
Gregory R. Smith
Howard J. Steinberg (Downtown Los Angeles Office)
Jonathan H. Steinberg
Steven E. Thomas
Ronald B. Tischler (P.C.)
Eric A. Webber (Downtown Los Angeles Office)
Bruce A. Wessel
Ian C. Wiener
Alexander F. Wiles
Richard C. Wirthlin (Downtown Los Angeles Office)
Werner F. Wolfen (P.C.) (Retired)
Juliette Youngblood
Rob C. Zeitinger
Edward Zeldow

OF COUNSEL

Jeffrey L. Arrington
Thomas H. Bienert Jr. (Resident at Newport Beach)
Charles A. Collier, Jr.
John J. Cost (P.C.) (Downtown Los Angeles Office)
Wendy G. Glenn
Lawrence E. Irell
John M. Nakashima (Resident at Newport Beach)
David Nimmer
Alvaro Pascotto
Steven H. Shiffrin
Leslie A. Sowle (Not admitted in CA)
Robert W. Stedman (P.C.) (Resident at Newport Beach)
Lawrence M. Stone (P.C.)
Michael H. Strub, Jr.
John Leo Wagner (Resident at Newport Beach)
Ted S. Ward
William D. Warren (Not admitted in CA)
Wendy A. Wolf

(See Next Column)

ASSOCIATES

Matthew S. Alexander
Alvin M. Ashley (Resident at Newport Beach)
Paul J. Backofen
Giselle M. Barth
Spencer E. Bendell (Downtown Los Angeles Office)
James P. Berklas Jr. (Downtown Los Angeles Office)
Nicola J. Bird
Marc Blau
Jody M. Borrelli
Laura W. Brill
David C. Brown (Downtown Los Angeles Office)
Stacie L. Butts (Resident at Newport Beach)
Elizabeth A. Camacho
Eric B. Carlson
Douglas H. Carsten
Charles C. Cavanagh
Albert B. Choi (Downtown Los Angeles Office)
Peter T. Christensen (Resident at Newport Beach)
David C. Codell
Mary MacIsaac Coleman
Leigh Taylor Combs (Resident at Newport Beach)
Graham L. W. Day
Christine D'Angelo
Charles E. Elder
Marc A. Fenster
Theodore H. Frank
Joseph M. Freeman
Perry M. Goldberg
Craig A. Grossman
Jeremy D. Halpern (Downtown Los Angeles Office)
Benjamin Hattenbach
Jason P. Hendler
Stephanie Kaufman Hernand
Victor W. Hwang
Andrei Iancu
Anton D. Jensen (Resident at Newport Beach)
Carrie E. Johnson
Jonathan S. Kagan
Richard D. Kim
R. Carter Kirkwood
Gregory B. Klein
Jennifer M. Kowal
Fernanda Lai
Soyeon (Karen) Pak Laub (Resident at Newport Beach)
Brian D. Ledahl
Richard Ung-Jin Lee (Downtown Los Angeles Office)
Tami K. Lefko
Lee M. Liedecke
Michael M. Lowe (Downtown Los Angeles Office)
Samuel Kai Lu
Benjamin R. Martin
Damian Martinez
Melissa R. McCormick (Resident at Newport Beach)
Roman Melnik
Abraham C. Meltzer
Philip H. Miller
Harry A. Mittleman
Arthur J. Ochoa
Ben D. Orlanski (Downtown Los Angeles Office)
Lisa N. Partain
Elizabeth K. Penfil (Resident at Newport Beach)
Seth E. Pierce
Stevie Pyon (Downtown Los Angeles Office)
Flavio Rose
David J. Rosmann
Noah B. Salamon (Resident at Newport Beach)
Matthew Sant (Resident at Newport Beach)
Karin Schwindt
Laura A. Seigle
Jeffrey N. Shapiro
Cheryl M. Sheinkopf
Nicholas R. Simmons
Geoffrey Trachtenberg (Resident at Newport Beach)
Lore A. Unt
Craig Varnen
Bradley W. Voss
Ryan Z. Walker
Peter J. Wied
Michael R. Williams (Resident at Newport Beach)
Sharon Wong
Richard Zelichov

For full biographical listings, see the Martindale-Hubbell Law Directory

IVERSON, YOAKUM, PAPIANO & HATCH (AV)

One Wilshire Building, 27th Floor 624 South Grand Avenue, 90017
Telephone: 213-624-7444
Telecopier: 213-629-4563

Paul E. Iverson (1907-1975)
Frank B. Yoakum, Jr. (1906-1991)

MEMBERS OF FIRM

Neil Papiano
Dennis A. Page
Patrick M. Mc Adam
Arnold D. Larson
John M. Garrick

ASSOCIATES

Douglas C. Pease
Andrew K. Doty
Melissa A. Immel
Mary P. Lightfoot
Mark Pearson
Gioia M. Fasi
Adam F. Burke
Scott A. Horton

OF COUNSEL

R. Noel Hatch

Representative Clients: Lockheed Corp.; International Paper; Bridgestone/-Firestone, Inc.
Reference: Bank of America (Los Angeles Head Office).

For full biographical listings, see the Martindale-Hubbell Law Directory

JONES, DAY, REAVIS & POGUE (AV)

555 West Fifth Street Suite 4600, 90013-1025
Telephone: 213-489-3939
Telecopier: 213-243-2539
Email: counsel@jonesday.com *URL:* http://www.jonesday.com
In Irvine, California: 5 Park Plaza, Suite 1100.
Telephone: 949-851-3939.
Telecopier: 949-553-7539.
In Atlanta, Georgia: 3500 SunTrust Plaza, 303 Peachtree Street.
Telephone: 404-521-3939.
Telecopier: 404-581-8330.

(See Next Column)

JONES, DAY, REAVIS & POGUE—*Continued*

In Brussels, Belgium: Avenue Louise 480, 7th Floor, B-1050 Brussels.
Telephone: 32-2-645-14-11.
Telecopier: 32-2-645-14-45.
In Chicago, Illinois: 77 West Wacker.
Telephone: 312-782-3939.
Telecopier: 312-782-8585.
In Cleveland, Ohio: North Point, 901 Lakeside Avenue.
Telephone: 216-586-3939.
Telecopier: 216-579-0212.
In Columbus, Ohio: 1900 Huntington Center.
Telephone: 614-469-3939.
Telecopier: 614-461-4198.
In Dallas, Texas: 2727 North Harwood Street.
Telephone: 214-220-3939.
Telecopier: 214-969-5100.
In Frankfurt, Germany: Hochhaus am Park, Grüneburgweg 102, 60323 Frankfurt am Main.
Telephone: 49-69-9726-3939.
Telecopier: 49-69-9726-3993.
In Geneva, Switzerland: 20, rue de Candolle.
Telephone: 41-22-320-2339.
Telecopier: 41-22-320-1232.
In Hong Kong: 29th Floor, Entertainment Building, 30 Queen's Road Central.
Telephone: 852-2526-6895.
Telecopier: 852-2868-5871.
In London England: Bucklersbury House, 3 Queen Victoria Street.
Telephone: 44-20-7236-3939.
Telecopier: 44-20-7236-1113.
In New York, New York: 599 Lexington Avenue.
Telephone: 212-326-3939.
Telecopier: 212-755-7306.
In Paris, France: 120, rue du Faubourg Saint-Honoré.
Telephone: 33-1-56-59-3939.
Telecopier: 33-1-56-59-3938
In Pittsburgh, Pennsylvania: 500 Grant Street, 31st Floor.
Telephone: 412-391-3939.
Telecopier: 412-394-7959.
In Riyadh, Saudi Arabia: The International Law Firm (In Association with Jones, Day, Reavis & Pogue), Sulaymaniyah, Prince Mishari IBN, Abdulaziz Street, P.O. Box 22166.
Telephone: (966-1) 462-8866.
Telecopier: (966-1) 462-9001.
In Shanghai, China: 2805 Kerry Centre, 1515 Nanjing Road West.
Telephone: 86-21-5298-6568.
Telecopier: 86-21-5298-6569.
In Sydney, Australia: Governor Phillip Tower, Level 38, 1 Farrer Place.
Telephone: 61-2-9210-6921.
Telecopier: 61-2-9210-6926.
In Taipei, Taiwan: 8th Floor, 2 Tun Hwa South Road, Section 2.
Telephone: (886-2) 2704-6808.
Telecopier: (886-2) 2704-6791.
In Tokyo, Japan: Toranomon 45 Mori Building, 3th Floor, 1-5, Toranomon 5-Chome, Minato-ku, Tokyo 105, Japan.
Telephone: 81-3-3433-3939.
Telecopier: 81-3-5401-2725.
In Washington, D.C.: 51 Louisiana Avenue, N.W.
Telephone: 202-879-3939.
Telecopier: 202-626-1700.

MEMBERS OF FIRM IN LOS ANGELES

Bertram R. Zweig
William J. Emanuel
James F. Childs, Jr.
William G. Wilson
Ross E. Stromberg
Gerald W. Palmer
Victor G. Savikas
Elwood Lui
Frederick L. McKnight
Dean B. Allison
Norman A. Pedersen
David S. Boyce
Andrew J. Demetriou
Thomas R. Mueller
Dulcie D. Brand
Peter G. McAllen
Thomas M. McMahon
Eric V. Rowen
Daniel J. McLoon
Patricia A. Van Dyke
Scott D. Bertzyk
Sarah Heck Griffin
Jeffrey A. LeVee
Lester O. Brown
Kevin G. McBride
David J. DiMeglio
Kevin A. Dorse
Catherine A. Ehrgott
Daniel D. McMillan

OF COUNSEL

Richard H. Koppes
David C. Zucker
Marsha E. Durko

ASSOCIATES

Jane L. Henning
Erich R. Luschei
Mary J. Garnett
Robert M. Gilchrest
Jeffrey A. Miller
Kenneth A. Remson
Philip E. Cook
Ricky L. Shackelford
Valerie A. Brown
Mary K. Hartigan
Suzanne Cate Jones
Mark M. Kassabian
Maria K. Nelson
Gary W. Nugent
Wendy L. Thomas
Lynne E. Mallya
Susanne L. Meline
Amy A. Stathos
Harry I. Johnson III
Erin E. Nolan

(See Next Column)

ASSOCIATES (Continued)

Kirstin D. Poirier-Whitley
Marc T. Rasich
John S. Sasaki
Karen R. Thorland
Kathryn E. LaQuay
Susanne E. Stamey
Erin L. Burke
Eugenia L. Castruccio
Vince L. Farhat
Gregory S.G. Klatt
Allan Z. Litovsky
Ann-Marie Niccolai
Holger C. Besch
David R. Brightman
William J. Brown, Jr.
Jacqueline A. Bruce-Chinery
Susan A. Clark
Stephanie A. Collins
Julie S. Gabler
Emma Killick
John J. Murphy
Jeremy J. Osher
Elizabeth Rees
Courtney M. Schaberg
Barbara Velasco
Michelle C. Brathwaite
Francesca D. Harewood
Haeji Hong
Lee T. Kuo
H. Jacob Lager
Pauline Massih
Monica M. Randazzo
Sarah A. Silbert
Chelsea A. Sneed
John A. Vogt
Joan Wasylenki
Gregory J. Mann
Alexandra Shin

For full biographical listings, see the Martindale-Hubbell Law Directory

KAYE, SCHOLER, FIERMAN, HAYS & HANDLER, LLP (AV)

A New York Limited Liability Partnership
1999 Avenue of the Stars, Suite 1600, 90067-6048
Telephone: 310-788-1000
Facsimile: 310-788-1200
URL: http://www.kayescholer.com
New York, N.Y.: 425 Park Avenue, 10022-3598.
Telephone: 212-836-8000.
Telex: 234860 KAY UR.
Facsimile: 212-836-8689.
Washington, D.C.: McPherson Building, 901 Fifteenth Street, N.W., Suite 1100, 20005-2327.
Telephone: 202-682-3500.
Facsimile: 202-682-3580.
West Palm Beach, Florida: Phillips Point, West Tower 1002, 777 South Flagler Drive, 33401.
Telephone: 561-802-3230.
Facsimile: 561-802-3217.
Hong Kong: No. 1 Harbor View Street, Central.
Telephone: 852-28458989.
Facsimile: 852-28452389.
Shanghai, China: Suite 405 Shanghai Centre, 1376 Nanjing Xi Lu, 200040.
Telephone: 86-21-62797356.
Facsimile: 86-21-62797351.

MEMBERS OF FIRM

Aton Arbisser
Robert Barnes
Russ Alan Cashdan
T. Brent Costello
Barry L. Dastin
Michael D. Fernhoff
Jeffrey S. Gordon
Peter L. Haviland
Sheri Jeffrey
Barry H. Lawrence
Ronald L. Leibow
Joseph M. Malinowski
Michael A. Santoro
Regina T. Shanney-Saborsky

SPECIAL COUNSEL

Cruz Reynoso

COUNSEL

Michael J. Eliasberg
Carole E. Handler
Ronald E. Levinson
B.J. Yankowitz

ASSOCIATES

Andrew W. Ash
Lawrence B. Behrendt
Gordon M. Bobb (Not admitted in CA)
Reid Hunter Breitman
Julian Brew
Ashleigh A. Danker
Jon E. Gelb
Stephanie Granato
Gina Guerra
James R. Hoskinson, Jr.
Asher Isaacs
Jason E. Miller (Not admitted in CA)
Quimby Pierce
Alison Genevieve Regan
Sergey Trakhtenberg
Rhonda Renee Trotter
Jeremy M. Weitz

For full biographical listings, see the Martindale-Hubbell Law Directory

KIRKLAND & ELLIS (AV)

A Partnership including Professional Corporations
777 South Figueroa Street, 90017
Telephone: 213-680-8400
Facsimile: 213-680-8500
URL: http://www.kirkland.com
Chicago, Illinois Office: 200 East Randolph Drive.
Telephone: 312-861-2000.
Telex: 25-4361.
Washington, D.C. Office: 655 Fifteenth Street, N.W.
Telephone: 202-879-5000.
Facsimile: (202)-879-5200.
New York, New York Office: Citicorp Center, 153 East 53rd Street.
Telephone: 212-446-4800.
Facsimile: (212)-446-4900.

(See Next Column)

KIRKLAND & ELLIS, *Los Angeles—Continued*

London, England Office: International Financial Centre, Old Broad Street.
Telephone: 171-816-8700; New Telephone Effective April 1, 2000: 207-816-8700.
Facsimile: 171-816-8800.

MEMBERS OF FIRM

April L. Ammeter
Michael E. Baumann
Steven E. Bledsoe
Mary Blodgett
Martin R. Boles
Boaz M. Brickman
Jeffrey S. Davidson
Eva Herbst Davis
Joseph M. Graham Jr.
Jan Lawrence Handzlik
Catherine C. Hwang
Robert G. Krupka (P.C.)
Eric C. Liebeler
Alexander F. MacKinnon
Christopher Rebel J. Pace
Andrew E. Paris
Tony L. Richardson
Rick Richmond
David S. Shukan
John A. Zackrison

ASSOCIATES

JoLee M. Adamich
C. Robert Boldt
Damian D. Capozzola
Brent L. Caslin
Bindu Chandrabose
Adam J. Chester
Marc H. Cohen
Sarretta C. Coomes
Mark T. Cramer
Dean M. Fink (Not admitted in CA)
Marcie L. Gardner
Patrik M. Griego
Eric W. Hagen
Shannon M. Hansen
Viddell L. Heard Jr.
Christopher J. Heck
Melissa D. Ingalls
Michelle M. Inouye
Eric R. Lamison
Michael S. McCauley
Stephen H. McClain
Brian McKeever
Sydne Squire Michel
James A. Nicholas
G. Charles Nierlich
Xanath Owens
Charles C. Pak
R. Alexander Pilmer
Tracy B. Rane
James B. Ransom
Heiko Kai Schultz
Marc L. Turman

For full biographical listings, see the Martindale-Hubbell Law Directory

KNAPP, MARSH, JONES & DORAN, L.L.P. (AV)

Suite 1400, Manulife Plaza, 515 South Figueroa Street, 90071-3329
Telephone: 213-627-8471
Telecopier: 213-627-7897

MEMBERS OF FIRM

B. Richard Marsh
Thomas A. Doran
James G. Jones
Daniel V. Hyde
Gary H. Giesler
Wesley G. Beverlin
Patricia M. Schnegg
Janette Sarmiento Knowlton

ASSOCIATES

Paul J. Beck
Alexander Shipman
Scott M. Olken
Brian D. Peters
Stephanie A. Jones
Edward D. Castro

For full biographical listings, see the Martindale-Hubbell Law Directory

LAGERLOF, SENECAL, BRADLEY, GOSNEY & KRUSE, LLP

(See Pasadena)

LATHAM & WATKINS (AV)

633 West Fifth Street, Suite 4000, 90071
Telephone: 213-485-1234
Telecopier: 213-891-8763
TWX: 910-321-3733
Cable Address: "Lathwat"
URL: http://www.lw.com
Costa Mesa, California Office: 650 Town Center Drive, Suite 2000.
Telephone: 714-540-1235.
Menlo Park, California Office: 135 Commonwealth Drive.
Telephone: 650-328-4600.
San Diego, California Office: 701 B Street, Suite 2100.
Telephone: 619-236-1234.
San Francisco, California Office: 505 Montgomery Street, Suite 1990.
Telephone: 415-391-0600.
Washington, D.C. Office: 1001 Pennsylvania Avenue, N.W., Suite 1300.
Telephone: 202-637-2200.
Chicago, Illinois Office: Sears Tower, Suite 5800.
Telephone: 312-876-7700.
Newark, New Jersey Office: One Newark Center.
Telephone: 201-639-1234.
Fax: 201-639-7298.
New York, N.Y. Office: 885 Third Avenue, Suite 1000.
Telephone: 212-906-1200.
London, England Office: 99 Bishopsgate, Eleventh Floor, EC2M 3XF.
Telephone: +-44-207-710-1000.
Telecopier: +-44-171-374 4460.
Moscow, Russia Office: Ducat II, Ulitsa Gasheka 7, Suite 900, 125047.
Telephone: +7-(095) 785-1234.
Fax: +7-(095) 785-1235.
Hong Kong Office: No. 9 Queen's Road Central, 22nd Floor, Suite 2205A.
Telephone: 011-852-2522-7886.
Fax: 011-852-2522-7006.

(See Next Column)

Tokyo, Japan Office: Infini Akasaka, 8-7-15 Akasaka, Minato-Ku, Tokyo 107, Japan.
Telephone: 011 81 3 3423-3970.
Fax: 011 81 3 3423-3971.
Singapore Office: 80 Raffles Place, #14-20, UOB Plaza 2, Singapore, 048624.
Telephone: (65) 536-1161.
Fax: (65) 536-1171.

Paul R. Watkins (1899-1973)
Dana Latham (1898-1974)
Ira M. Price, II (1919-1968)

MEMBERS OF FIRM

Michael Bruce Abelson
Mary Rose Alexander (Chicago, Illinois Office)
Nicholas W. Allard (Washington, D.C. Office)
Jon D. Anderson (Costa Mesa Office)
A. Victor Antola
James L. Arnone
Steven Atlee
Susan S. Azad
J. Douglas Bacon (Chicago, Illinois Office)
Teresa D. Baer (Washington, D.C. Office)
Donald P. Baker
David W. Barby (Costa Mesa Office)
James H. Barker, III (Washington, D.C. Office)
James D. C. Barrall
David Judson Barrett (New York City Office)
James R. Barrett (Washington, D.C. Office)
Randall C. Bassett
Marc D. Bassewitz (Chicago, Illinois Office)
Steven M. Bauer (San Francisco Office)
James P. Beaubien
Mark D. Beckett (New York City Office)
Joseph I. Bentley (Costa Mesa Office)
Peter H. Benzian (San Diego Office)
Eric L. Bernthal (Washington, D.C. Office)
Joseph A. Bevash (Hong Kong and Singapore Offices)
Dorn G. Bishop (San Diego Office)
Kevin C. Blauch (New York City Office)
Elizabeth A. Blendell
Kenneth E. Blohm (San Francisco Office)
Dena L. Bloom
Joseph Blum (London, England Office)
Ian B. Blumenstein (New York City Office)
David C. Boatwright (San Diego Office)
Thomas G. Bost
Sharon Y. Bowen (New York City Office)
Stephen S. Bowen (Chicago, Illinois Office)
Scott O. Bowie (New York City Office)
Kevin Charles Boyle (Washington, D.C. Office)
James E. Brandt (New York City Office)
Robert K. Break (Costa Mesa Office)
Jed W. Brickner (New York City Office)
Michael J. Brody
Gay L. Bronson (London, England Office)
Karen Smith Bryan
Michael J. Carroll (Costa Mesa Office)
Brian G. Cartwright
E. William Cattan, Jr. (Singapore Office)
William J. Cernius (Costa Mesa Office)
Richard L. Chadakoff (New York City Office)
James A. Cherney (Chicago, Illinois Office)
Michael Chertoff (Newark, New Jersey, New York City and Washington, D.C. Offices)
John J. Clair, Jr.
Alan B. Clark
Barry M. Clarkson (San Diego Office)
Glen B. Collyer
Kenneth Conboy (New York City Office)
Richard A. Conn, Jr. (Washington, D.C. Office)
Terrence J. Connolly (New York City Office)
Philip E. Coviello (New York City Office)
Robert D. Crockett
Charles S. Crompton, III (Menlo Park Office)
Timothy P. Crudo (San Francisco Office)
David G. Crumbaugh (Chicago Office)
Robert E. Currie (Costa Mesa Office)
Cynthia H. Cwik-Martin (San Diego Office)
Robert P. Dahlquist (San Diego Office)
Robin D. Dal Soglio
James W. Daniels (Costa Mesa Office)
Kirk A. Davenport (New York City Office)
Paul H. Dawes (Menlo Park Office)
Francis K. Decker, Jr. (New York City Office)
Robert M. Dell (San Francisco Office)
Steven Della Rocca (New York City Office)
Jon D. Demorest (San Diego Office)
Paul R. DeMuro (Also at San Francisco Office)
Peter W. Devereaux
Gary L. Dickson
Thomas W. Dobson
James W. Doran (Chicago Office)
Dean G. Dunlavey (Costa Mesa Office)
Tracy K. Edmonson (San Francisco Office)
Bryant B. Edwards
Thomas A. Edwards (San Diego Office)
Gary M. Epstein (Washington, D.C. Office)
Gregory A. Ezring (New York City Office)
Joseph B. Farrell (Costa Mesa Office)
Michael Scott Feeley
Anthony I. Fenwick (Menlo Park Office)
Ora T. Fisher (Menlo Park Office)
Samuel A. Fishman (New York City Office)
Kenneth M. Fitzgerald (San Diego Office)
Mark A. Flagel
David C. Flattum (Costa Mesa Office)
Wayne S. Flick

(See Next Column)

LATHAM & WATKINS—*Continued*

MEMBERS OF FIRM (Continued)

Martin N. Flics (New York City Office)
David S. Foster (Chicago, Illinois Office)
Douglas A. Freedman (Chicago Office)
Kelley Michael Gale (San Diego Office)
Thomas G. Gallatin, Jr. (New York City Office)
Paul A. Galleberg
Christopher W. Garrett (San Diego Office)
Mark D. Gerstein (Chicago Office)
Ernest J. Getto
William J. Gibbons (Chicago, Illinois Office)
Peter M. Gilhuly
Anya Goldin (Moscow, Russia Office)
Robert G. Goldman (Chicago, Illinois Office)
Roger S. Goldman (Washington, D.C. Office)
David A. Gordon (New York City Office)
Robert A. Greenspon (New York City Office)
McGee Grigsby (Washington, D.C. Office)
Virginia Sollenberger Grogan (Costa Mesa Office)
Robert J. Gunther, Jr. (New York City Office)
Scott R. Haber (San Francisco Office)
David A. Hahn (San Diego Office)
Ronald W. Hanson (Chicago, Illinois Office)
Timothy B. Hardwicke (Chicago, Illinois Office)
Mark A. Harris (Chicago, Illinois Office)
Christopher Harrison (London, England Office)
Marian A. Harvey
Julia A. Hatcher (Washington, D.C. Office)
Carolyne R. Hathaway (Washington, D.C. Office)
Russell Hayman
Allen D. Haynie (San Diego Office)
David R. Hazelton (Washington, D.C. Office)
David S. Heller (Chicago, Illinois Office)
Scott C. Herlihy (Washington, D.C. Office)
Michael K. Hertz (New York City Office)
James I. Hisiger (New York City Office)
Jeffrey R. Holmstead (Washington, D.C. Office)
R. Ronald Hopkinson (New York City Office)
Bruce P. Howard
Robert M. Howard (San Diego Office)
Maria Pilar Hoye
John J. Huber (Washington, D.C. Office)
Robin M. Hulshizer (Chicago Office)
Paul J. Hunt (Washington, D.C. Office)
James G. Hunter, Jr. (Chicago, Illinois Office)
Nancy Scheurwater Hunter (Chicago, Illinois Office)
Geoffrey K. Hurley (New York City Office)
Peter Huston (San Francisco Office)
Cary K. Hyden (Costa Mesa Office)
Ursula H. Hyman
Michael S. Immordino (London, England Office)
Linda M. Inscoe (San Francisco Office)
John M. Jameson
Dean T. Janis (San Diego Office)
John P. Janka (Washington, D.C. Office)
Everett C. Johnson, Jr. (Washington, D.C. Office)
Martha Barnhart Jordan
Mary Ellen Kanoff
Christopher L. Kaufman (Menlo Park Office)
James V. Kearney (New York City Office)
Pamela Brown Kelly
William C. Kelly, Jr. (Washington, D.C. Office)
John H. Kenney (San Francisco Office)
Peter F. Kerman (Menlo Park Office)
Roger H. Kimmel (New York City Office)
John J. Kirby, Jr. (New York City Office)
Betty-Jane Kirwan
Scott P. Klein
Sosi Biricik Klijian (San Diego Office)
Robert A. Klyman
Robert A. Koenig
Brian C. Krisberg (New York City Office)
Joel E. Krischer
Joseph M. Kronsnoble (Chicago, Illinois Office)
Stuart S. Kurlander (Washington, D.C. Office)
Katherine A. Lauer (San Diego Office)
Bruce R. Lederman
David V. Lee
Daniel T. Lennon (Washington, D.C. Office)
Laurence H. Levine (Chicago, Illinois Office)
Richard A. Levy (Chicago, Illinois Office)
Jiyeon Lee Lim (New York City Office)
Raymond Yung Lin (New York City Office)
Gregory P. Lindstrom (San Francisco Office)
Robert A. Long
Walter P. Loughlin (New York City Office)
Curtis P. Lu (Washington, D.C. Office)
Gene A. Lucero
Christopher D. Lueking (Chicago, Illinois Office)
G. Andrew Lundberg
Michael S. Lurey
John P. Lynch (Chicago, Illinois Office)
John J. Lyons
Karl S. Lytz (San Francisco Office)
Joel H. Mack (San Diego Office)
Maureen E. Mahoney (Washington, D.C. Office)
Ellen L. Marks (Chicago, Illinois Office)
Victoria E. Marmorstein
Juli Wilson Marshall (Chicago, Illinois Office)
Takashi Matsumoto (Tokyo, Japan Office)
Marcus A. McDaniel
David J. McLean
David C. Meckler (Costa Mesa Office)
William J. Meeske
Mark S. Mester (Chicago, Illinois Office)
Paul I. Meyer (San Diego Office)
George J. Mihlsten

MEMBERS OF FIRM (Continued)

(See Next Column)

David Miles (London, England Office)
Milton A. Miller
Jeffrey G. Moran (Chicago, Illinois Office)
David L. Mulliken (San Diego Office)
Bennett J. Murphy
Kevin M. Murphy (Chicago, Illinois Office)
Dale K. Neal
Bernard E. Nelson (London, England Office)
David A. Nelson (Chicago, Illinois Office)
Donald P. Newell (San Diego Office)
John M. Newell
Mark E. Newell (Washington, D.C. Office)
Dennis B. Nordstrom (London, England Office)
Gary Olson
J. Drew Page (San Diego Office)
Catherine E. Palmer (New York City Office)
Pamela S. Palmer
Thomas L. Patten (Washington, D.C. Office)
Edith R. Perez
Cary R. Perlman (Chicago, Illinois Office)
Jeffrey T. Pero (San Francisco Office)
Philip J. Perzek (Chicago, Illinois Office)
Jerry R. Peters (San Francisco Office)
Alan W. Pettis (Costa Mesa Office)
Thomas L. Pfister
Gregory N. Pimstone
Christopher R. Plaut (New York City Office)
Bruce J. Prager (New York City Office)
Michael A. Pucker (Chicago, Illinois Office)
Mark S. Pulliam (San Diego Office)
David S. Raab (New York City Office)
Marc W. Rappel
David K. Rathgeber (Chicago, Illinois Office)
Richard W. Raushenbush (San Francisco Office)
William K. Rawson (Washington, D.C. Office)
George A. Rice (Chicago, Illinois Office)
Anthony J. Richmond (Menlo Park Office)
Maureen A. Riley (New York City Office)
James F. Ritter (Washington, D.C. Office)
David Booth Rogers
James F. Rogers (Washington, D.C. Office)
Robert M. Romano (New York City Office)
Michael G. Romey
J. Thomas Rosch (San Francisco Office)
Robert J. Rosenberg (New York City Office)
Bruce E. Rosenblum (Washington, D.C. Office)
Cynthia A. Rotell
Alan I. Rothenberg
Charles K. Ruck (Costa Mesa Office)
Mary B. Ruhl
Kevin A. Russell (Chicago, Illinois Office)
Miles N. Ruthberg
John L. Sachs (Washington, D.C. Office)
Thomas C. Sadler
Irving Salem (New York City Office)
Barry A. Sanders
Glenda Sanders (Costa Mesa Office)
Russell F. Sauer, Jr.
Linda Schilling (Costa Mesa Office)
Nancy L. Schimmel (Chicago, Illinois Office)
Linda S. Schurman (Chicago, Illinois Office)
David L. Schwartz (Washington, D.C. Office)
Donald L. Schwartz (Chicago Office)
Patrick T. Seaver (Costa Mesa Office)
Selvyn Seidel (New York City Office)
Daniel K. Settelmayer
David L. Shapiro (Chicago, Illinois Office)
Edward J. Shapiro (Washington, D.C. Office)
Bruce P. Shepherd (San Diego Office)
John B. Sherrell
Michael J. Shockro
Barry J. Shotts (San Diego Office)
John D. Shyer (New York City Office)
Patricia Timko Sinclair
Paul N. Singarella (Costa Mesa Office)
Andrew D. Singer (San Diego Office)
Edward Sonnenschein, Jr.
Lucinda Starrett
Mark A. Stegemoeller (London, England Office)
Joshua Stein (New York City Office)
Laurence J. Stein
Erica H. Steinberger (New York City Office)
Eric A. Stern (Washington, D.C. Office)
Michael W. Sturrock (Singapore, Office)
Joseph D. Sullivan (Washington, D.C. Office)
Robert M. Sussman (Washington, D.C. Office)
Pheng Theng Tan (Washington, D.C. Office)
Job Taylor, III (New York City Office)
Bruce A. Tester (Costa Mesa Office)
Reba W. Thomas
Morris A. Thurston (Costa Mesa Office)
R. Brian Timmons (Costa Mesa Office)
Paul D. Tosetti
Charles Stephen Treat (San Francisco Office)
Richard M. Trobman (New York City Office)
A. Brent Truitt (New York City Office)
James E. Tyrrell, Jr. (Newark, New Jersey Office)
Richard B. Ulmer Jr. (San Francisco Office)
Michael P. Vandenbergh (Washington, D.C. Office)
David H. Vena
Perry J. Viscounty (Costa Mesa Office)
William H. Voge (New York City Office)
Lisa A. Von Eschen
Peter A. Wald (San Francisco Office)
John F. Walker, Jr.
John D. Watson, Jr. (Washington, D.C. Office)
Michael J. Weaver (San Diego Office)
Samuel R. Weiner
Susan Paulsrud Welch
W. Harrison Wellford (Washington, D.C. Office)

MEMBERS OF FIRM (Continued)

(See Next Column)

LATHAM & WATKINS, *Los Angeles—Continued*

Mary K. Westbrook
(Costa Mesa Office)
Joseph J. Wheeler
(San Diego Office)
Kristine L. Wilkes
(San Diego Office)
Beth A. Wilkinson
(Washington, D.C. Office)
Kimberly L. Wilkinson
(San Francisco Office)
Kirk A. Wilkinson
Hugh Steven Wilson
Peter J. Wilson
(Costa Mesa Office)
Peter L. Winik
(Washington, D.C. Office)
Vernon M. Winters
(Menlo Park Office)
Richard L. Wirthlin
Carl E. Witschy
(Chicago, Illinois Office)
Scott N. Wolfe
(San Diego Office)
Kenneth A. Wolfson
(Costa Mesa Office)
Robert A. Wyman, Jr.
David A. York
(Menlo Park Office)
Roger M. Zaitzeff
(New York City Office)
Leonard A. Zax
(Washington, D.C. Office)
Richard S. Zbur
Fredric J. Zepp
(San Francisco Office)
Robert A. Zuccaro
(New York City Office)

OF COUNSEL

Carlos Alvarez
(New York City Office)
Jennifer C. Archie
(Washington, D.C. Office)
Philip F. Belleville
Elissa Ganbarg Benudis
(New York City Office)
Kim Natalie Alicia Boras
William C. Bottger, Jr.
Richard P. Bress
(Washington, D.C. Office)
Karen Brinkmann
(Washington, D.C. Office)
Stephen M. Burgin
Bernard C. Byrnes
(New York City Office)
Nigel Campion-Smith
(London, England Office)
Adele K. Cardoza
(Costa Mesa Office)
Richard Carver
James O. Copley
(Newark, New Jersey Office)
William F. Delvac
Jean M. Donnelly
(Costa Mesa Office)
Marla Becker Dunn
(New York City Office)
David W. Fleming
Mark S. Fowler
(Washington, D.C. Office)
Irwin Goldbloom
(Washington, D.C. Office)
Jeffrey S. Haber
Alan N. Halkett
Scott P. Jacobs
Donna Jones (San Diego Office)
Desiree Icaza Kellogg
(San Diego Office)
Beth R. Klein
(New York City Office)
Kathleen J. Kravitz
David S. Langer
(New York Office)
David M. Leive
(Washington, D.C. Office)
Steven J. Levine
(San Diego Office)
Karen R. Leviton
John R. Light
Kimberly M. McCormick
(San Diego Office)
L. Susan McGinnis
John P. McLoughlin
Kenneth L. McWilliams
(Washington, D.C. Office)
Mark I. Michigan
(New York City Office)
Gregory K. Miller
(San Francisco Office)
William R. Nicholas
Andrew Marc Paley
Austin H. Peck, Jr.
Gregory M. Pettigrew
Philip L. Reynolds (Retired)
Judith B. M. Romaine
(New York Office)
Esther R. Scherb
(Washington, D.C. Office)
Regina M. Schlatter
(Costa Mesa Office)
Bruce John Shih
Lev S. Simkin
(Moscow, Russia Office)
J. Wesley Skow
(San Francisco Office)
Maureen Smith
(New York City Office)
Scott R. Smith
(New York City Office)
John R. Stahr
(Costa Mesa Office)
Clinton R. Stevenson
John C. Stiska
(San Diego Office)
H. Randall Stoke
John S. Welch
Robert B. Wessling
Kenneth R. Whiting, Jr.
(San Francisco Office)
E. Marcellus Williamson
(Washington, D.C. Office)
Yanlei Wu
(Washington, D.C. Office)
Louise Zeitzew

ASSOCIATES

Tracy Abels
Tanya Nadra Marie Acker
Alan S. Adler
David B. Allen
(Costa Mesa Office)
Louis G. Alonso
(San Diego Office)
Melissa S. Alwang
(New York Office)
Anna B. Amarandos
(Costa Mesa Office)
Eric T. Andrews
(Washington, D.C. Office)
Susan Leckrone Anhalt
Meghan L. Archdeacon
(Washington, D.C. Office)
Howard L. Armstrong
(San Diego Office)
Kimberly Arouh
(San Diego Office)
John B. Ashley
(New York City Office)
Josef S. Athanas
(Chicago, Illinois Office)
David Franklin Azad
(Washington, D.C. Office)
Linda A. Bagley
(Menlo Park Office)
Patricia L. Ball
(New York City Office)
Lee Ann Bambach
(Washington, D.C. Office)
Rita Fournier Barnett
(Costa Mesa Office)
Michele D. Barney
David A. Barrett
(Washington, D.C. Office)
Holly M. Bauer
(San Francisco Office)

(See Next Column)

ASSOCIATES (Continued)

Vicky L. Beasley
(Washington, D.C. Office)
Adel F. Bebawy
David A. Becker
(Washington, D.C. Office)
Marisa J. Beeney
(New York City Office)
Jonn R. Beeson
(Costa Mesa Office)
Michael A. Bell
(Washington, D.C. Office)
Denise R. Ben-Attar
(New York City Office)
Sony Ben-Moshe
(San Diego Office)
Kelly J. Bendell
Michelle Duncan Bergman
(New York City Office)
Meredith A. Berlin
(Chicago Office)
Lisa Binder
Justin C. Bird
(San Diego Office)
Robert J. Blair
(San Diego Office)
James S. Blank
(New York City Office)
Stephen D. Blevit
Erik S. Bliss (San Diego Office)
David J. Blue (New York Office)
Michael A. Bond
(London, England Office)
Patricia L. Bonheyo
(San Francisco Office)
Jeryl A. Bowers
(Not admitted in CA)
Cheryl Vigder Brause
(New York City Office)
Catherine S. Bridge
Mary E. Britton
(Washington, D.C. Office)
Elizabeth Coppage Brown
Mark E. Brubaker
Sara R. Bucholtz
(New York City Office)
Jennifer Buczek
(New York Office)
Bradley A. Bugdanowitz
(San Francisco Office)
Malgorzata Bula-Duane
(Tokyo Office)
Hugh L. Burns
(New York City Office)
Chris Burt
Robert E. Burwell
(San Diego Office)
Laura I. Bushnell
(Menlo Park Office)
Orla Butler
(London, England Office)
Alejandro E. Camacho
Richard R. Cameron
(Washington, D.C. Office)
Barbara L. Cammarata
(San Diego Office)
William S. Carnell
(Washington, D.C. Office)
Ramona R. Carroll
(Washington, D.C. Office)
Margret M. Caruso
(New York City Office)
Stephen F. Case
(San Diego Office)
Jan Alex Castro
(Moscow, Russia Office)
Meera Joshi Cattafesta
(New York Office)
Lorraine Charlton
(London, England Office)
Connie C. Chen
Rowland I. Cheng
(Singapore Office)
Sue J. Choi
(Washington, D.C. Office)
David E. Christensen
(San Diego Office)
Julianne L. Chun
Elizabeth L. Churchwell
(Chicago Office)
Ann Claassen
(Washington, D.C. Office)
Cheryl Miller Coe
(Washington, D.C. Office)
Adam B. Cohen
(New York City Office)
Miriam T. Cole
(Chicago, Illinois Office)
Lisa Plunkett Conlon
(Chicago, Illinois Office)
Blair G. Connelly
(New York City Office)
Charles W. Cox, II
Kenneth D. Crews
(Chicago, Illinois Office)
Neil Cummings
Eric L. Czech
(New York City Office)
William D'Angelo, III
(Costa Mesa Office)
Jason D'Elia (San Diego Office)
David S. Dantzic
(Washington, D.C. Office)
Roman E. Darmer, II
(Costa Mesa Office)
Ben Davies
(London, England Office)
Geoffrey Davies (London Office)
William C. Davisson, III
(Menlo Park Office)
Estela de Llanos
Harold R. DeGraff
(Menlo Park Office)
Elspeth K. Deily
(San Francisco Office)
Scott J. Depta
(San Diego Office)
Rene M. Devlin (Chicago Office)
Deborah E. Dezelan
(Chicago Office)
Simon J. Dickens
(London, England Office)
Christopher M. DiMuro
(Newark, New Jersey Office)
Ona Alston Dosunmu
(Washington, D.C. Office)
Diana Slyfield Doyle
(Chicago Office)
Jon S. Drumwright
(Chicago Office)
Daniel S. Duane
(Tokyo, Japan Office)
Alexandra F. Dufresne
(Chicago, Office)
Thomas E. Duley
(Menlo Park Office)
Derek D. Dundas
(Costa Mesa Office)
James R. Dutro
(San Francisco Office)
Lisa K. Eastwood
(New York City Office)
Karen E. Eberle (Menlo Park, California Office)
Linda Harrison Edwards
Sarah M. Ekdahl
(Chicago, Illinois Office)
Christopher L. Elwell
Blair A. England
(New York Office)
Bart Scott Epstein
(Washington, D.C. Office)
Kevin B. Espinola
(Costa Mesa Office)
Michael R. Etzioni
Vernita Fairley
(San Francisco Office)
Peter J. Falconer
(Chicago Office)
Rachelle Fan
(New York City Office)
Sabrina Y. T. Fang
(Hong Kong Office)
James J. Farrell
Michael R. Fassler
(San Francisco Office)
Amber R. FauntLeRoy
Andrew A. Faye
(London, England Office)
Tamar Feder
(Not admitted in CA)
Mark Feldman
(New York City Office)
Martin T. Felli
(New York City Office)
Edward M. Fentin

(See Next Column)

LATHAM & WATKINS—*Continued*

ASSOCIATES (Continued)

Rachael Fink
(New York City Office)
Mark A. Finkelstein
(Costa Mesa Office)
Alice S. Fisher
(Washington, D.C. Office)
Will B. Fitton
(San Francisco Office)
Susan P. Flattum
Jared G. Flinn
(San Diego Office)
Patricia I. Folan-Gump
(San Francisco Office)
David N. Fong
(Not admitted in CA)
Angelee Fox
Tad J. Freese
(San Francisco Office)
Joshua R. Frieman
Laura Gabriel
(San Francisco Office)
Zhun Julie Gao
Craig M. Garner
(San Diego Office)
Ana R. Genender
Amy R. George
(New York City Office)
Patrick Gibbs
(Chicago, Illinois Office)
Scott H. Gingold
(Chicago Office)
John Giouroukakis
(New York City Office)
Carrie Girgenti
(New York Office)
Holly Gladstone
(New York Office)
Brian L. Glassberg
(Washington, D.C. Office)
Michael Joseph Golden
(Washington, D.C. Office)
Alanna J. Goldman
Lisa P. Gomez
(San Diego Office)
Lyudmila Gorbatova
(Moscow, Russian Office)
Jeevan Gore (Costa Mesa Office)
Evan Gourvitz
(San Francisco Office)
Jonathan Green
(London, England Office)
Jeffrey B. Greenberg
(New York Office)
Tisha M. Greene
Dru Greenhalgh
(San Diego Office)
Gabriel G. Gregg
Christine M. Gregorski
(San Diego Office)
Jane Greyf (New York Office)
Douglas A. Griffin
(New York City Office)
Regina L. Griffin
(New York City Office)
Belinda B. Grondin
(New York City Office)
Patricia Guerrero
(San Francisco Office)
Jennifer E. Gully
Kathleen Raven Gurrola
(Chicago Office)
Laura W. Guthrie
(San Francisco Office)
Michael J. Gyr
(Washington, D.C. Office)
M. Christopher Hall
(New York City Office)
Karen R. Han
(New York Office)
Amos E. Hartston
Sarah A. Hefty (Chicago Office)
Leigh A. Hellner-Cord
(New York City Office)
Melinda P. Heppberger
(San Francisco Office)
David M. Hernand
Vincent H. Herron
Donna Herzing
(San Francisco Office)
Jeannette M. Hill-Yonis

Jens H. Hillen
(Menlo Park Office)
Perry J. Hindin
(Washington, D.C. Office)
J. Scott Hodgkins
Alexander D. Hoehn-Saric
(New York Office)
Lynne S. Hoffenberg
(Washington, D.C. Office)
Julie K. Hoffman
(Washington, D.C. Office)
Kyle W. Hoffman
(San Diego Office)
Blythe A. Holden
John G. Holland
(Washington, D.C. Office)
Joseph E. Hopkins
(Newark, New Jersey Office)
Darrin A. Hostetler
(San Diego Office)
Jill M. Houlahan
(San Diego Office)
Peggy Huang
(Menlo Park Office)
Andrew D. Irwin
(Washington, D.C. Office)
Eva Izsak-Niimura
(New York City Office)
Keith Jackson
Nicole E. Jaeger
(San Francisco Office)
Marc D. Jaffe
(New York City Office)
Collie F. James, IV
(Costa Mesa Office)
Eric H. Jaso
(Newark, New Jersey Office)
Jonathan M. Jenkins
C. Chad Johnson
(New York City Office)
Jared W. Johnson
(Washington, D.C. Office)
Jennifer L. Johnson
(New York City Office)
Michele Johnson
(Costa Mesa Office)
Nandan M. Joshi
(Washington, D.C. Office)
David O. Kahn
Jeeun P. Kahng
(Not admitted in CA)
Michael Kalachman
(Chicago, Illinois Office)
Gary A. Kashar
Reyaz A. Kassamali
(New York Office)
Jeffrey L. Kateman
Dean M. Kato
Thomas E. Keim, Jr.
(Chicago, Illinois Office)
Robert F. Kennedy
(New York City Office)
Shayne Kennedy
(Costa Mesa Office)
Katherine Allen Kessler
(New York Office)
Daniel Byong Kim
(Not admitted in CA)
Monica Yung-Min Kim
(Menlo Park Office)
Julie V. King
(Costa Mesa Office)
Jena Kirsch (San Diego Office)
Satoko Kishi
(San Francisco Office)
Mark Klaassen
(Washington, D.C. Office)
Heidi E. Klein
(San Francisco Office)
Stephan E. Klein
(San Francisco Office)
Julian Thomas Kleindorfer
(Chicago, Illinois Office)
Trena Lee Klohe
(Washington, D.C. Office)
Stephanie H. Knutson
(Costa Mesa Office)
William Paul Koenig
(Chicago, Illinois Office)

ASSOCIATES (Continued)

(See Next Column)

Bradley E. Kotler
(Chicago, Illinois Office)
Dmitri A. Kounitsa
(Moscow, Russian Office)
Lisa M. Koven
Lindsey C. Kozberg
Elizabeth Opper Kraemer
(Chicago Office)
Marlen Kruzhkov
(New York Office)
David L. Kuiper
(Costa Mesa Office)
John M. Kuriyama
Julie Y. Kwok
Peter M. Labonski
(New York City Office)
Christina Y. Lai
(Menlo Park Office)
Catherine Lamb
(San Francisco Office)
Deborah C. Lambe
G. Steven Lambert
Dennis D. Lamont
(New York City Office)
Arthur S. Landerholm
(Washington, D.C. Office)
Cheston J. Larson
(San Diego Office)
Lino J. Lauro
Michael J. Lawrence
Timothy C. Layton
(Washington, D.C. Office)
Robert S. Leach
Audrey Lee
Belinda S. Lee
Deborah T. Lee
Jeffrey K. Lee
(Washington, D.C. Office)
Namee Lee
Sangyeup Lee
(New York City Office)
David A. Levitt
(San Francisco Office)
Matthew R. Lewis
(Washington, D.C. Office)
Jennifer T. Li (New York Office)
Anna C. Lincoln
(Washington, D.C. Office)
Dana N. Linker
(San Francisco Office)
Nancy Carr Lippa
(New York Office)
Keven K. Lippert
(San Diego Office)
Joshua E. Little
(San Diego Office)
Jennifer C. Loach
(New York Office)
Angelo Lombardo
Sarah S. Londergan
(Chicago, Illinois Office)
David L. London
(Washington, D.C. Office)
Gregory O. Lunt
Carl A. Lux
James K. Lynch
(San Francisco Office)
Robert A. Magnanini
(Newark, New Jersey Office)
Damon P. Mamalakis
Jennifer L. Mandigo
(Washington, D.C. Office)
Brian A. Manson
John C. Marchese
(Chicago, Illinois Office)
Kathleen M. Marcus
(Costa Mesa Office)
Daniel L. Martens
Matthew T. Martens
(Newark, New Jersey Office)
David H. Martin
Kevin C. May (Chicago Office)
Martha Ann Mazzone
(Washington, D.C. Office)
Daniel G. McBride
(San Francisco Office)
Joseph G. McCarthy
(Costa Mesa Office)
Douglas F. McCormick
(Costa Mesa Office)
Erica McFarquhar
(Washington, D.C. Office)

Christian B. McGrath
(Chicago, Illinois Office)
Stephen P. McGrath
(Menlo Park Office)
Susan E. McNeil
(Washington, D.C. Office)
Mary McShane
(New York Office)
Nicholas G. Mehler
(New York Office)
Clifford Mentrup
(Chicago, Illinois Office)
Philip M. Midgen
Jason T. Miller
Jeffrey L. Miller
Peter J. Millones, Jr.
(New York City Office)
Michael Mills
Scott K. Milsten
(San Francisco Office)
Michael G. Mishik
Loren M. Montgomery
Richard J. Mooney
(San Francisco Office)
Patricia A. Moran
(New York City Office)
David T. Morris
(San Francisco Office)
Kenneth R. Morris
(San Francisco Office)
Rafael F. Muilenburg
(San Diego Office)
Amy G. Nefouse
(San Diego Office)
Laura H. Neuwirth
(Washington, D.C. Office)
Stephen J. Newman
Wayne G. Nitti
Elena C. Norman
(New York Office)
Steven J. Novatney
(Chicago Office)
Ann K. O'Brien
Claudia M. O'Brien
(Washington, D.C. Office)
Alice O'Connor
(London, England Office)
Lynley A. Ogilvie
(Washington, D.C. Office)
Michael G. Oleinik
Steven J. Olson
Omer Oztan
(New York City Office)
Francis Y. Park
Jacklyn J. Park
Julia E. Parry (San Diego Office)
Darryl A. Parson
(New York City Office)
David B. Pearson
(Washington, D.C. Office)
Wendy Imatani Peloso
(Costa Mesa Office)
Michèle O. Penzer
(New York City Office)
Leslie A. Pereira
Robert W. Perrin
Christopher J. Peters
(Chicago, Illinois Office)
Corinne M. Plummer
(Washington, D.C Office)
Amy Sapper Poling
(San Diego Office)
Elizabeth Enayati Powers
(Menlo Park Office)
Jon L. Praed
(Washington, D.C. Office)
Michele M. Pyle
(New York City Office)
Scott R. Raber
(San Francisco Office)
Shireen Bitha Rahnema
Francisco J. Ramirez
(New York Office)
Paula Wilson Render
(Chicago Office)
Ann Marie Richardson
(New York City Office)
Annette C. Rivera-Zayas
(Chicago Office)
Jennifer Root (San Diego Office)
Reuben Rosen
(San Diego Office)

ASSOCIATES (Continued)

(See Next Column)

LATHAM & WATKINS, *Los Angeles—Continued*

Sarah K. Rosen
(San Diego Office)
Brett Rosenblatt
Allison C. Rosenstock
(San Diego Office)
Lisa Ann T. Ruggiero
(Newark, New Jersey Office)
Andrea L. Russi
Brian L. Saliman
(Washington, D.C. Office)
Lucantonio N. Salvi
(London, England Office)
Stephen J. Salvucci
(Costa Mesa Office)
Sharadchandra A. Samy
(New York City Office)
Nehal Sanghavi
(New York Office)
Taitt Sato (San Francisco Office)
Jennifer Upham Saunders
Gregory M. Saylin
(Costa Mesa Office)
Jennifer L. Scafe
(San Francisco Office)
Daniel Scott Schecter
Dawn D. Schiller
(Chicago, Illinois Office)
Alexandra W. Schlesinger
(New York City Office)
Deidre L. Schneider
(San Diego Office)
Kenneth A. Schuhmacher
(London, England Office)
Kenneth G. Schuler
(Chicago, Illinois Office)
Steven H. Schulman
(Washington, D.C. Office)
Robert J. Schulze
Jocelyn M. Seitzman
(London, England Office)
Nadia A. Shabaik
Patrick H. Shannon
(Washington, D.C. Office)
Erin S. Shaw (Chicago Office)
R. Scott Shean
(Costa Mesa Office)
Kashif Z. Sheikh
(New York City Office)
Jennifer Silber
(Washington, D.C. Office)
Jessica I. Silberman
Joseph A. Simei
(Washington, D.C. Office)
Adam K. Simpson
(San Diego Office)
Phillip B. Slater
(London, England Office)
Juliette Smith
(New York City Office)
Lenora Smith
(Chicago, Illinois Office)
Michael D. Smith
(Chicago, Illinois Office)
Theodore K. Smith
(Washington, D.C. Office)
A. Bridget Sorenson
Amy F. Sorenson
(San Francisco Office)
Kelly J. Sosnow
Shane M. Spradlin
(Washington, D.C. Office)
Allon Stabinsky
(Menlo Park, Office)
John C. Steele
Sylvia A. Stein
(Chicago, Illinois Office)
Michael A. Steinig
(Washington, D.C. Office)
Shanda M. Stephenson
(Costa Mesa Office)
Jeffrey Ross Stern
(New York City Office)
Stacey Sternberg
David M. Stewart
(New York City Office)
Mitchell D. Stocks
(Hong Kong Office)
Craig A. Stoehr
(New York City Office)
Laurie M. Stone

Vivian Clara Strache
(Washington, D.C. Office)
Diana L. Strauss
(San Diego Office)
Gavin Stuttard
(Costa Mesa Office)
Joseph A. Sullivan
(Chicago, Illinois Office)
Hyen-ae Jane Sung
(San Francisco Office)
Neal C. Svalstad
Stephen A. Swedlow
(Chicago Office)
Hoyt Y. Sze
(San Francisco Office)
Kristina Garcia Szurkus
(San Diego Office)
Niveen Tadros
John C. Tang (New York Office)
Bruce D. Taterka
(Newark, New Jersey Office)
David M. Taub
William C. Tayler
(San Diego Office)
Amy R. Teresso
(Costa Mesa, Office)
Stephen R. Tetro, II
(Chicago, Illinois Office)
Rachel W. Thorn
(New York City Office)
Monica K. Thurmond
(New York City Office)
Gwyn Goodson Timms
(San Diego Office)
John R. Tinkham
(Chicago, Illinois Office)
Jeffrey A. Tochner
(New York City Office)
Kathleen M. O'Prey Truman
John B. Turner
(Not admitted in CA)
Monique Valbuena
(Washington, D.C. Office)
Jan-Marc van der Schee
(Menlo Park Office)
Julie Vaughan
(London, England Office)
Ryan J. Victor
William A. Voxman
Minh N. Vu
(Washington, D.C. Office)
Ayesha K. Waheed
(London, England Office)
Matthew W. Walch
(Chicago, Illinois Office)
Scott L. Weber
(Newark, New Jersey Office)
Eric Whitaker
(San Francisco Office)
Gialisa Whitchurch
(Costa Mesa Office)
Kelly P. Whiting
C. Blake T. Williams
Andrew S. Williamson
(San Francisco Office)
Bradd L. Williamson
(New York City Office)
Jill N. Willis (San Diego Office)
Michael S. Winderman
(New York City Office)
Jamie L. Wine
Paul M. Winters
(Washington, D.C. Office)
Teri L. Witteman
K. Matthew Wong
(New York City Office)
Carolyn R. Worsley
(New York City Office)
Michael S. Wroblewski
(Washington, D.C. Office)
Jenny Chin Wu
(Washington, D.C. Office)
Jeffrey W. Wutzke
(San Francisco Office)
Joseph M. Yaffe
(Costa Mesa Office)
Loan Chu Yip
(New York City Office)
Mary J. Yoo
Dominic K.L. Yoong

ASSOCIATES (Continued)

(See Next Column)

Daiske Yoshida
(New York Office)
Roland S. Young
(New York City Office)
Kelly Yuan (New York Office)
Stephanie R. Ziesel
(San Francisco Office)

For full biographical listings, see the Martindale-Hubbell Law Directory

LEWIS, D'AMATO, BRISBOIS & BISGAARD LLP (AV)

A Limited Liability Partnership including Professional Corporations
Suite 1200, 221 North Figueroa Street, 90012
Telephone: 213-250-1800
Telex: 194508
Fax: 213-250-7900
Email: firmwide@ldbb.com *URL:* http://www.ldbb.com
San Diego, California Office: 550 West C Street, Suite 800, 92101.
Telephone: 619-233-1006.
Fax: 619-233-8627.
San Francisco, California Office: One Sansome Street, 14th Floor, 94104.
Telephone: 415-362-2580.
Fax: 415-434-0882.
Costa Mesa, California Office: 650 Town Center Drive, Suite 1400, 92626.
Telephone: 714-545-9200.
Fax: 714-850-1030.
Sacramento, California Office: 2500 Venture Oaks Way, 95833.
Telephone: 916-564-5400.
Fax: 916-564-5444.
San Bernardino, California Office: 650 East Hospitality Lane, Suite 600, 92408.
Telephone: 909-387-1130.
Fax: 909-387-1138.
Affiliated Offices:
Beltran, Leal & Medina, 221 North Figueroa Street, Los Angeles, California, 90012. Telephone: 213-580-7900.
Fax: 213-580-0055.
Lee & Hong, 221 North Figueroa Street, Los Angeles, California 90012.
Telephone: 213-250-7780.
Fax: 213-250-8150.

MEMBERS OF FIRM

Robert F. Lewis (P.C.)
Roy M. Brisbois (P.C.)
Christopher P. Bisgaard (P.C.)
David E. Reynolds (P.C.)
Mary G. Whitaker (P.C.)
David N. Makous
Barry G. Kaiman (P.C.)
Scott Lichtig
Steven R. Lewis
Timothy R. Graves
James D. Fraser
Raul L. Martinez (P.C.)
Dennis R. Kasper
Steven Mark Levy
Bartley L. Becker
Eric C. Castro
Lawrence N. Halperin
Thomas Rittenburg
Lance A. Selfridge
John H. Shimada
Gary L. Effron
Joseph K. Hegedus
Judith A. Zipkin
Gordon J. Calhoun
Richard B. Wolf
Paul Y. Lee
David E. Long
Cathey A. Stricker
Elise D. Klein
Joseph C. Owens
William John Rea, Jr.
Jana I. Lubert
Judith M. Tishkoff
Howard G. Rath, Jr.
Mercedes Cruz
Leon M. Cooper
Laura E. Inlow
Douglas R. Irvine
Timothy J. Watson
Gregory P. Martin
L. Robert De Stefano
Peter F. Harris
Brad Krasnoff
Penny Paxton
Howard A. Slavin
Joseph C. Campo
Edward F. Morrison, Jr.
Cary L. Wood
Patrick R. Broadway
Raimo H. Kaasik
Jonathon Kaplan
Steven E. Meyer
Christina M. Slatton
John L. Barber
David Isenberg
Thomas S. Kiddé
Larry W. Mitchell
Gary S. Rattet
Amy L. Goldman
Alan R. Zuckerman
Kenneth D. Watnick
Gregory G. Lynch
Blenda Eyvazzadeh
Donald G. Forgey
Christopher C. Love
Manuel Saldaña

OF COUNSEL

Sheldon H. Sloan

ASSOCIATES

Julie M. Azevedo
Leo A. Bautista
Stephen N. Besser
Larry J. Brock
Keri Lynn Bush
John S. Christopher
Christopher E. Deal
Daniel C. DeCarlo
Julie M. DeRose
Bridget A. Esquibias
Lawrence A. Eugenio
Christopher R. Green
Christopher J. Greenleaf
Meriam E. Hamilton
Jerry C. J. Huang
Karen E. Vaughey Marble
Christopher McGrath
Pilar Morin
Matthew S. Pascale
Surekha A. Pessis
Francis Ryu
Michael D. Schwarzmann
Robert L. Slaughter III
Ryan C. Squire
Larry A. Schwartz
Antoinette R. Tutt

(See Next Column)

LEWIS, D'AMATO, BRISBOIS & BISGAARD LLP—*Continued*

ASSOCIATES (Continued)

Glen S. Umeda
Julie A. Veltkamp
Raquel Vidal
Helen Ting-Shan Wang
Timothy R. Windham

For full biographical listings, see the Martindale-Hubbell Law Directory

LOEB & LOEB LLP (AV)

A Limited Liability Partnership including Professional Corporations
Suite 1800, 1000 Wilshire Boulevard, 90017-2475
Telephone: 213-688-3400
Facsimile: 213-688-3460
Email: info@loeb.com *URL:* http://www.loeb.com
Century City, California Office: Suite 2200, 10100 Santa Monica Boulevard, Los Angeles, 90067-4164.
Telephone: 310-282-2000.
Facsimile: 310-282-2192.
New York, N.Y. Office: 345 Park Avenue, 10154-0037.
Telephone: 212-407-4000.
Facsimile: 212-407-4990.
Nashville, Tennessee Office: 45 Music Square West, 37203-3205.
Telephone: 615-749-8300;
Facsimile: 615-749-8308.
Rome, Italy Office: Piazza Digione 1, 00197.
Telephone: 011-3906-808-8456.
Facsimile: 011-3906-808-8288.

MEMBERS OF FIRM

Joseph P. Loeb (1883-1974)
Edwin J. Loeb (1886-1970)
Mortimer H. Hess (1889-1968)
Phillip E. Adler (A P.C.)
Christopher K. Aidun (New York City Office)
Harriet B. Alexson
Kenneth B. Anderson (New York City Office)
John Arao
Roger M. Arar (New York City Office)
Curtis W. Bajak
Donald L. B. Baraf (New York City Office)
Robert S. Barry, Jr.
Michael D. Beck (A P.C.) (New York City Office)
Kenneth R. Benbassat
Michele E. Beuerlein
Marguerite L. Bui
David H. Carlin (New York City Office)
Marc Chamlin (New York City Office)
Andrew S. Clare (A P.C.)
Kevin E. Coventon
Terence F. Cuff
John J. Dellaverson (A P.C.) (Century City Office)
Lorenzo De Sanctis (Rome, Italy Office)
Brant H. Dveirin
Linda F. Edell (Nashville, Tennessee Office)
David B. Eizenman (New York City Office)
Craig A. Emanuel (Century City Office)
Carla J. Feldman
Jay Fenster (New York City Office)
David L. Ficksman
David C. Fischer (New York City Office)
Keith G. Fleer (Century City Office)
John T. Frankenheimer (A P.C.) (Century City Office)
Kenneth D. Freeman (New York City Office)
Andrew S. Garb (A P.C.)
Helen Gavaris (New York City Office)
Seth D. Gelblum (New York City Office)
James P. Goodkind (Century City Office)
David W. Grace (Century City Office)
Fred B. Griffin
Lawrence B. Gutcho
Joseph P. Heffernan (A P.C.)
Karen Nielsen Higgins
Stanley M. Johnson (New York City Office)
Lance N. Jurich
Michael Bryce Kinney (New York City Office)
John F. Lang (New York City Office)
Jerome L. Levine (New York City Office)
Andrew E. Lippmann (New York City Office)
Jeffrey M. Loeb
Stuart Lubitz (Century City Office)
William J. Marlow (New York City Office)
Michael A. Mayerson (Century City Office)
Malissa Hathaway McKeith
Sharon S. Mequet
Robert A. Meyer
Stephen R. Mick (Century City Office)
Charles H. Miller (New York City Office)
Malcolm L. Mimms, Jr., (A P.C.) (Nashville, Tennessee Office)
Douglas E. Mirell
Daniel G. Murphy
Anthony Murray (A P.C.)
David C. Nelson
Susan V. Noonoo
Diane B. Paul
Nigel G. Pearson (Century City Office)
Robert L. Pelz (New York City Office)
Steven J. Peña (Century City Office)
Martin R. Pollner (New York City Office)
Guendalina Ponti (Rome, Italy Office)
Robert S. Reich (New York City Office)
Jai H. Rho (Century City Office)
Victor A. Rodgers
Thomas E. Rohlf (A P.C.)
Andrew M. Ross (New York City Office)
Stanford K. Rubin (A P.C.) (Century City Office)
Stephen L. Saltzman (Century City Office)
David M. Satnick (New York City Office)
David S. Schaefer (New York City Office)
P. Gregory Schwed (New York City Office)
Scott I. Schneider (New York City Office)
Paul A. Sczudlo

(See Next Column)

MEMBERS OF FIRM (Continued)

Terri J. Seligman (New York City Office)
Peter S. Selvin
Brian R. Socolow (New York City Office)
Lee N. Steiner (New York City Office)
Rebel R. Steiner, Jr. (Century City Office)
Bruce M. Stiglitz (A P.C.)
Richard P. Streicher (New York City Office)
Adam F. Streisand
Alan J. Tarr (New York City Office)
James D. Taylor (New York City Office)
Irwin J. Tenenbaum (Century City Office)
Robert N. Treiman
Ronald Weinstein
Bruce J. Wexler (New York City Office)
Alan W. Wilken
Susan Williams (Century City Office)
William H. Wright (Century City Office)
Michael P. Zweig (New York City Office)

OF COUNSEL

Harold D. Berkowitz (A P.C.) (Century City Office)
James R. Birnberg
Frank E. Feder (A P.C.) (Century City and New York Offices)
Howard I. Friedman (A P.C.)
Marvin Greene (A P.C.)
Robert A. Holtzman
Harold I. Kahen (New York City Office)
Alden G. Pearce (A P.C.)
Alfred I. Rothman
Bernard M. Silbert (Century City Office)
Harvey L. Silbert (Century City Office)
Myron L. Slobodien (Century City Office)
John S. Warren

SENIOR COUNSEL

Dorie G. Choderker (Century City Office)
Richard Garmise (New York City Office)
Miriam J. Golbert (Century City Office)
Louis A. Mok (Century City Office)
Harry S. Prawer (New York City Office)
Michael J. Ram (Century City Office)
Laurie S. Ruckel (New York City Office)
John P. Scherlacher (Century City Office)

ASSOCIATES

Leah Antonio-Ketcham (Century City Office)
Paula G. Atkinson
Lisa M. Burkdall
David A. Byrnes (Century City Office)
Christian D. Carbone (New York City Office)
Ying Chen (Century City Office)
Paula K. Colbath (New York City Office)
Shanda W. Connolly
Craig B. Cooper
Yasir Elbiali
F. Jason Far-hadian (Century City Office)
Amedeo F. Ferraro
Kenneth R. Florin (New York City Office)
Ana Maria Z. Fredgren
Daniel J. Friedman
Kevin Friedmann
Irving S. Gomez
Philip J. Graves
Barbara D. Griff (New York City Office)
James R. Guerette (New York City Office)
Patrick P. Gunn
Victoria K. Harvey
Molly S. Heger
Lisa L. Horlick
Ronald L. Israel (New York City Office)
Roni A. Jacobson (New York City Office)
Jennifer Jewett (Not admitted in CA)
Robert B. Lachenauer (New York City Office)
Michael J. Linowes (New York City Office)
Lynda C. Loigman (New York Office)
Nina B. Luban (New York City Office)
David L. Lubitz (Century City Office)
Sonya Makunga
Vivek K. Malhotra
Todd M. Malynn
Denise McIntosh-Stevens (Nashville, Tennessee Office)
Randolf S. Mendelsohn (Century City Office)
Samuel Mark Mizrahi (New York City Office)
Miles V. Mogulescu (Century City Office)
Thu Minh Nguyen
August W. Pelton
Michelle Oyler Saifer (Century City Office)
Deborah L. Saltzman (New York City Office)
Jay D. Sanders
Gregory R. Schenz (Century City Office)
Gail E. Sharps (New York City Office)
Edward F. Shermn Jr. (Century City Office)
Riccardo Siciliani (Rome, Italy Office)
Martha Siefert-Sharp
Karen L. Silverman
Philippa J. Smith (New York City Office)
Jill H. Talley
Don Thornburgh
James Urbanic
Corinna M. Wong
Jonathan M. Wight
Gavin M. Wise (Not admitted in the United States) (Century City Office)
Wein-ing Yang (Century City Office)
Maria L. Zanfini (New York City Office)
Robin Zeidel (New York City Office)

For full biographical listings, see the Martindale-Hubbell Law Directory

Los Angeles—Continued

LORD, BISSELL & BROOK (AV)

300 South Grand Avenue, 90071-3200
Telephone: 213-485-1500
Telecopy: 213-485-1200
Telex: 18-1135
Email: info@lordbissell.com *URL:* http://www.lordbissell.com
Chicago, Illinois Office: Suites 2600-3600 Harris Bank Building, 115 South LaSalle Street, 60603.
Telephone: 312-443-0700.
Telecopy: 312-443-0336.
Cable Address: "Lowirco".
Telex: 25-0336.
Atlanta, Georgia Office: One Atlantic Center, 1201 West Peachtree Street, N.W., Suite 3700, 30309.
Telephone: 404-870-4600.
Telecopy: 404-872-5547.
Rockford, Illinois Office: 120 West State Street, Suite 200, 61101.
Telephone: 815-963-8050.
New York, N.Y. Office: One Penn Plaza, Suite 3935, 10119.
Telephone: 212-947-4700.
Facsimile: 212-947-1202.

RESIDENT PARTNERS

Charles A. Adamek
Gail M. Baev
Kirk A. Borchardt
C. Guerry Collins
Cynthia M. Frey
David F. Hauge
Jacqueline Redin Klein
Jeffrey S. Kravitz
LouCinda Laughlin
Mitchell J. Popham
Keith G. Wileman

OF COUNSEL

Brenda Adams Bissett

RESIDENT ASSOCIATES

Michael S. Blanton
Christopher M. Brainard
Stephen L. Cope
Robert S. Crowder
Charissa Dorian
Franklin T. Dunn
Mark S. Fall
James B. Green
(Not admitted in CA)
John M. Hochhausler
Elizabeth Klippi
Jeri Rouse Looney
George D. Lozano
Lisa A. Navarro
Karen N. Pavia
Karen A. Soomekh
James H. Wynn

For full biographical listings, see the Martindale-Hubbell Law Directory

MANATT, PHELPS & PHILLIPS, LLP (AV)

A Limited Liability Partnership including Professional Corporations
Trident Center, East Tower, 11355 West Olympic Boulevard, 90064
Telephone: 310-312-4000
Fax: 310-312-4224
Telex: 21-5653
Email: mpp@manatt.com
Washington, D.C. Office: 1500 M Street, N.W., Suite 700.
Telephone: 202-463-4300.
Fax: 202-463-4394.
Nashville, Tennessee Office: 1233 17th Avenue South.
Telephone: 615-327-2600.
Fax: 615-327-2044.
Palo Alto, California Office: 3030 Hansen Way.
Telephone: 650-812-1300.
Fax: 650-213-0260.
Sacramento, California Office: 1215 K Street, Suite 1900.
Telephone: 916-552-2300.
Fax: 916-552-2323.

MEMBERS OF FIRM

Charles T. Manatt (P.C.)
Thomas D. Phelps (P.C.)
L. Lee Phillips (P.C.)
Gordon M. Bava (P.C.)
Wilsie H. Adams, Jr. (Resident, Washington, D.C. Office)
Irwin P. Altschuler (Resident, Washington, D.C. Office)
David R. Amerine (Resident, Washington, D.C. Office)
Robert B. Anderson (Resident, Palo Alto Office)
Lisa Barton-Olt (Resident, Palo Alto Office)
Ronald S. Barak
Thomas L. Barton (Resident, Palo Alto Office)
Ellen Berkowitz
Barrie D. Berman (Resident, Washington, D.C. Office)
Donna R. Black
Robert A. Blair (P.C.) (Resident, Washington, D.C. Office)
Lawrence J. Blake
T. Hale Boggs (P.C.) (Resident, Palo Alto Office)
David T. Bradford (Resident, Nashville, Tennessee Office)
Donald R. Brown
William S. Brunsten (P.C.)
Alan M. Brunswick
Jack W. Buechner (Resident, Washington, D.C. Office)
Chris A. Carlson
Catherine A. Conway
William P. Cook (Resident, Washington, D.C. Office)
Jay L. Cooper
Jerry W. Cox (Resident, Washington, D.C. Office)
June Langston (Walton) DeHart (Resident, Washington, D.C. Office)
Craig J. de Recat
Robert N. Duran
Gene R. Elerding
Robert M. Eller
David Elson
Andrew Erskine (P.C.)

(See Next Column)

MEMBERS OF FIRM (Continued)

Diane L. Faber
Angelo C. Falcone
Donald J. Fitzgerald
David R. Foley (Resident, Palo Alto Office)
Dan Forman
Peter R. Gilbert (Resident, Washington, D.C. Office)
Mary Ann Gilleece (Resident, Washington, D.C. Office)
Amy L. Gilson (Resident, Palo Alto Office)
Geoffrey P. Gitner (Resident, Washington, D.C. Office)
Seth Gold
Donna Fields Goldstein
Marc P. Goodman
T.J. (Mick) Grasmick
Andrea Jane Grefe
Carl Grumer
Scott D. Harrington
Daniel B. Hayes
David W. Herbst (Resident, Palo Alto Office)
Robert E. Hinerfeld
Maria D. Hummer (P.C.)
Paul H. Irving
James R. Jones (Resident, Washington, D.C. Office)
Robert J. Kabel (Resident, Washington, D.C. Office)
Ivan L. Kallick
Andrew M. Katzenstein
Joseph F. Kelly (Resident, Washington, D.C. Office)
Terri Donna Keville
George David Kieffer
Sandra R. King
David M. Klaus (Resident, Washington, D.C. Office)
Kenneth L. Kraus (Resident, Nashville, Tennessee Office)
Barry S. Landsberg
John I. Lazar
Mark S. Lee
Tin Kin Lee
Monte M. Lemann II
Lizbeth R. Levinson (Resident, Washington, D.C. Office)
Margaret Levy
Stanley W. Levy
John F. Libby
Abbe David Lowell (Resident, Washington, D.C. Office)
Edward L. Lublin (Resident, Washington, D.C. Office)
Eileen Lyon
Barry E. Mallen
Gerald A. Margolis
Laurence M. Marks
William R. Martin (Resident, Washington, D.C. Office)
Thomas J. McDermott Jr.
Thomas R. McMorrow (Resident, Sacramento Office)
Sherwin L. Memel (P.C.)
Alan E. Morelli
James P. Mulkeen
Jeffrey S. Neeley (Resident, Washington, D.C. Office)
Kevin O'Connell
Thomas P. Ondeck (Resident, Washington, D.C. Office)
Jerrold F. Petruzzelli (Resident, Palo Alto Office)
Jill M. Pietrini
Robert H. Platt
Steven J. Plinio
William T. Quicksilver (P.C.)
B. Michael Rauh (Resident, Washington, D.C. Office)
John L. Ray (Resident, Washington, D.C. Office)
Harold P. Reichwald
James H. Roberts III (Resident, Washington, D.C. Office)
Harvey Rochman
Christopher L. Rudd
Stephen M. Ryan (Resident, Washington, D.C. Office)
John Sarafopoulos
Alan U. Schwartz
James Richard Schwartz
Brad William Seiling
Lawrence S. Sher (Resident, Washington, D.C. Office)
Martin Shulman (Resident, Washington, D.C. Office)
Tina M. Singh (Resident, Palo Alto Office)
James M. Smith (Resident, Palo Alto Office)
Laurie L. Soriano
Lisa Specht
Donald S. Stein (Resident, Washington, D.C. Office)
Robert L. Sullivan (Resident, Nashville, Tennessee Office)
Ronald B. Turovsky
Leonard D. Venger
Vincent M. Waldman
Charles E. Washburn Jr.
Jessica A. Wasserman (Resident, Washington, D.C. Office)
Priscilla Wheeler (Resident, Palo Alto Office)
Nancy H. Wojtas
Alan T. Yoshitake
Thomas A. Zaccaro

OF COUNSEL

Katrina L. Breuner
Roger L. Ellison
Dennis B. Franks
Joseph Horacek III, (P.C.)
Mark D. Johnson
Arnold D. Kassoy
Alan R. Polsky
Martin E. Steere
Barbara Timmer (Resident, Washington, D.C. Office)
Geoffrey T. Tong
Martha A. Warriner
Abby B. Wayne
Melissa Weeks Weaver
Gail Anderson Windisch (Firm General Counsel)
Ronald M. Wisla (Resident, Washington, D.C. Office)
Shari Mulrooney Wollman
Angela Wong

COUNSEL

Neal M. Williams (Resident, Palo Alto Office)

ASSOCIATES

David Ammons
Roger Armstrong
Sharon B. Bauman
Elizabeth H. Bellamy
Susan A. Beveridge
Staci Blevins
Alexander H. Bromley
Kenneth L. Burry
Eric J. Custer
J. Andrew Douglas
Peter R. Duchesneau
Scott E. Gluck
Hal D. Goldflam
Mark E. Goldman
Kim Green
Tanya C. Greig
Maureen M. Home
Susan C. V. Jones
Noah E. Jussim
Matthew P. Kanny
Randall W. Keen
Jeffrey A. Kohn
Jeffrey A. Mannisto
Jonathan A. Meretsky
Craig D. Miller
Tara N. Morris
Brenda B. Nelson
Matthew X. Oster
Albert Y. Park
Raúl Pérez

(See Next Column)

MANATT, PHELPS & PHILLIPS LLP—*Continued*

ASSOCIATES (Continued)

Adam Pines	Kristi M. Springer
Cameron A. Port	S. Daniel Stein
Sam Puathasnanon	Barry L. Tobias
Pegheen Rhyne	Kathrin A. Wanner
Kenneth D. Rozell	Norman Y. Wong
Andrew L. Satenberg	Jack S. Yeh
Marlene R. Schwartz	Miwon Yi
Eric Sherman	Candace Anne Younger

For full biographical listings, see the Martindale-Hubbell Law Directory

MAYER, BROWN & PLATT (AV)

350 South Grand Avenue, 25th Floor, 90071-1503
Telephone: 213-229-9500
Facsimile: 213-625-0248
Telex: 188089
Cable: LEMAYLA
URL: http://www.mayerbrown.com
Chicago, Illinois Office: 190 South LaSalle Street, 60603-3441.
Telephone: (312) 782-0600.
Facsimile: (312) 701-7711.
Telex: 190404.
Cable: LEMAY.
Berlin, Germany Office: Breite Strasse 29, Muehlendamm, 10178.
Telephone: 011-49-30-2060-7710.
Facsimile: 011-49-30-2060-7744.
Charlotte, North Carolina Office: 100 North Tryon Street, Suite 2400.
Telephone: (704) 444-3500.
Fax: (704) 377-2033.
Cologne, Germany Office: Kaiser-Wilhelm-Ring 27-29, 50672.
Telephone: 011-49-221-5771-100.
Facsimile: 011-49-221-5771-199.
Houston, Texas Office: 700 Louisiana Street, Suite 3600, 77002-2730.
Telephone: (713) 221-1651.
Facsimile: (713) 224-6410.
Telex: 775809.
Cable: LEMAYHOU.
London, England Office: Bucklersbury House, 3 Queen Victoria Street, London, EC4N 8EL, England.
Telephone: 011-44-171-246-6200.
Facsimile: 011-44-171-329-4465.
Telex: 8811095.
Cable: LEMAYLDN.
Los Angeles, California Office: 350 South Grand Avenue, 25th Floor, 90071-1503.
Telephone: (213) 229-9500.
Facsimile: (213) 625-0248.
Telex: 188089.
Cable: LEMAYLA.
New York, New York Office: 1675 Broadway, 10019-5820.
Telephone: (212) 506-2500.
Facsimile: (212) 262-1910.
Telex: 701842.
Cable: LEMAYEN.
Washington, D.C. Office: 1909 K Street, N.W., 20006-1101.
Telephone: (202) 263-3000.
Facsimile: (202) 263-3300.
Telex: 892603.
Cable: LEMAYDC.
Representative Offices:
Ashgabat, Turkmenistan: 28 Gogol Street, 744000.
Telephone: 011-99-312-355247.
Facsimile: 011-99-312-510074.
Bishkek, Kyrgyz Republic: 66 Kalyka Akieva Str. 720010.
Telephone: 011-996-312-65-02-56.
Facsimile: 011-996-312-65-09-80.
Tashkent, Republic of Uzbekistan: 3rd Floor, 1 Turab Tula Street, 700003.
Telephone: 011-998-71-1206-627.
Facsimile: 011-998-71-1206-329.
Mexico City, Mexico, D.F., Independent Mexico Correspondent: Jáuregui, Navarrete, Nader y Rojas, S.C., Torre Arcos, Paseo de los Tamarindos No. 400-B. Col. Bosques de las Lomas, 05120.
Telephone: 011-525-267-45-00.
Facsimile: 011-525-267-45-99.
Paris, France, Independent Paris Correspondent: Lambert & Lee, 13 Avenue Hoche, 75008.
Telephone: 011-33-1-53-53-43-43.
Facsimile: 011-33-1-53-96-03-83.

PARTNERS

Teresa A. Beaudet	Brian E. Newhouse
Louis P. Eatman	Philip R. Recht
L. Bruce Fischer	William J. Robinson
Douglas B. Frank	Peter K. Rosen
Lorie Soares Griffen	Kevin L. Shaw
Michael F. Kerr	Neil M. Soltman
Kenneth E. Kohler	Todd Evan Stark
Fredrick S. Levin	Pierre Vogelenzang
Gregory R. McClintock	James R. Walther
Alec G. Nedelman	Don L. Weaver

(See Next Column)

COUNSEL

Michael C. Kelcy	Andrew J. Starrels
Christopher P. Murphy	Kimberly S. Winick

ASSOCIATES

Brian Aronson	Jerome M.F. Jauffret
David C. Bolstad	Maureen G. Johnson
Susan J. Booth	Jenny Ae-Ru Ko
Jennifer L. Brockett	Bruce H. Levine
Beth Y. Brotz	Raffi K. Mansourian
Boise A. Ding	Mark A. Mears
Margaret S. Giles	John Nadolenco
Anthony G. Graham	Maria M. Rabassa
Richard Greta	Drasan R. Scranton
Miriam B. Jaffe	Matthew P. Seeberger

For full biographical listings, see the Martindale-Hubbell Law Directory

MCCUTCHEN, DOYLE, BROWN & ENERSEN, LLP (AV)

355 South Grand Avenue Suite 4400, 90071-1560
Telephone: 213-680-6400
Facsimile: 213-680-6499
Email: postmaster@mdbe.com *URL:* http://www.mccutchen.com
San Francisco, California Office: Three Embarcadero Center, 94111-4067.
Telephone: 415-393-2000.
Facsimile: 415-393-2286 (G I, II, III).
Walnut Creek, California Office: 1331 North California Boulevard, Post Office Box V, 94596-4502.
Telephone: 510-937-8000.
Facsimile: 510-975-5390.
Palo Alto, California Office: 3150 Porter Drive, 94304.
Telephone: 650-849-4400.
Fax: 650-849-4800.
Taipei, Taiwan Republic of China Office: International Trade Building, Tenth Floor, 333 Keelung Road, Section 1, 110.
Telephone: 886-2-723-5000.
Facsimile: 886-2-757-6070.

MEMBERS OF FIRM

Jill F. Cooper	Susan L. Hoffman
Colleen P. Doyle	Michael B. Lubic
James J. Dragna	John C. Morrissey
Richard C. Field	Rick R. Rothman
Debra L. Fischer	Patricia L. Shanks
William H. Freedman	William E. Thomson, Jr.

COUNSEL

Heather C. Beatty	John D. Schlotterbeck
Karen A. Caffee	Clayton J. Vreeland
George B. Newhouse, Jr.	Sandra Hughes Waddell
Nancy Mayfield Saunders	Pamela F. Worth

ASSOCIATES

Mary Moss Appleton	Heather Hoecherl
Barbra Barnett	Matthew A. Lesnick
David K. Bowles (Not admitted in CA)	Diana Martin
	Michael S. McDonough
Bryan K. Brown	Deborah A. Nolan
P. Scott Burton	Cory O'Donnell
Edwin A. Carlson	M. Abigail Page
Stephen P. Charbonnet	Christopher E. Prince
Greg A. Christianson	Allyson W. Sonenshine
Mary J. Decker	Catherine M. Stites
Byron P. Gee	Shiraz D. Tangri (Not admitted in CA)
Douglas A. Gravelle	
Kristi Lynn Gudoski	Maj-Le R. Tate
Tiffany R. Hedgpeth	Regina R. Wong

Vincent K. Yip

For full biographical listings, see the Martindale-Hubbell Law Directory

MILBANK, TWEED, HADLEY & MCCLOY LLP (AV)

601 South Figueroa Street, 90017
Telephone: 213-892-4000
Fax: 213-629-5063
Email: postmaster@milbank.com *URL:* http://www.milbank.com
New York, New York Office: 1 Chase Manhattan Plaza, 10005-1413.
Telephone: 212-530-5000.
Fax: 212- 530-5219.
Midtown Office: 375 Park Avenue, Suite 3601, 10152.
Telephone: 212-530-5800.
Fax: 212-530-0158.
Washington, D.C. Office: International Square Building, Suite 1100, 1825 Eye Street, N.W., 20006.
Telephone: 202-835-7500.
Fax: 202-835-7586.
Tokyo, Japan Office: Fukoku Seimei Building, 2-2, Uchisaiwai-cho 2-Chome, Chiyoda-ku, Tokyo 100-0011, Japan.
Telephone: 011-81-3-3504-1050.
Fax: 011-81-3-3595-2790, 011-81-3-3595-2840.
London, England Office: Dashwood House, 69 Old Broad Street, London, EC2M 1QS.
Telephone: 011-44-207-448-3000.
Fax: 011-44-207-448-3029.

(See Next Column)

MILBANK, TWEED, HADLEY & McCLOY LLP, *Los Angeles—Continued*

Hong Kong Office: 3007 Alexandra House, 16 Charter Road.
Telephone: 011-852-2571-4888.
Fax: 011-852-2840-0792, 011-8522-845-9046.
Singapore Office: 14-00 Caltex House, 30 Raffles Place, 048622.
Telephone: 011-65-428-2400.
Fax: 011-65-428-2500.
Moscow, Russia Office: 24/27 Sadovaya-Samotyochnya, Moscow, 103051.
Telephone: 011-7-501-258-5015.
Fax: 011-7-501-258-5014.

PARTNERS

Paul S. Aronzon
Kenneth J. Baronsky
Deborah Baumgart
Devan D. Beck
Linda Dakin-Grimm
Edwin F. Feo
Simon Friedman
C. Stephen Howard
David A. Lamb
Robert Jay Moore
Ted Obrzut
Eric H. Schunk
Neil J Wertlieb
Karen B. Wong

OF COUNSEL

Alan M. Fenning
John A. Funk (Not admitted in CA)

ASSOCIATES

Sally Agel
Taline A. Aharonian
John C. Ashby
Dino Barajas
Sabina Bhalla
Gabriel Kristopher Coy
Jeanette B. Cruz
Michael Dayen
Uttam Dhillon
R. Lee Garner III
Brett D. Goldblatt
Chandra L. Gooding
John Joseph Griggs
Elliot D. Hinds
David J. Impastato
Sharon E. Jackson
Edward V. Kayukov
Edward K. Kim
Nicholas L. Kondoleon
Thomas R. Kreller
Tobin D. Lippert
Melainie K. Mansfield
Allan T. Marks
Bredt D. Martin
Richard A. Mathurin
Matthew E. McDonald
Kevin R. McSpadden
Fred Neufeld
Michael C. Newman
Steven C. Papkin (Not admitted in CA)
William J. Peters
Steven A. Rivers
Kendrick F. Royer
Anat Sideman (Not admitted in CA)
Wayne Song
Juliet L. Stone
Tiziana Sucharitkul
Roland K. Tellis
Nancy Toross
M. Benjamin Valerio
Scott Vick
Anne C. Winston
Eugena Yasnogorodsky
David B. Zolkin

For full biographical listings, see the Martindale-Hubbell Law Directory

MITCHELL, SILBERBERG & KNUPP LLP (AV)

A Partnership including Professional Corporations
11377 West Olympic Boulevard, 90064
Telephone: 310-312-2000
Fax: 310-312-3100
Email: info@msk.com *URL:* http://www.msk.com

Shepard Mitchell (1908-1979)
M. B. Silberberg (1908-1965)
Guy Knupp (1907-1970)

MEMBERS OF FIRM

Anthony A. Adler (A Professional Corporation)
Miriam Claire Beezy (A Professional Corporation)
Patricia H. Benson (A Professional Corporation)
Allan E. Biblin (A Professional Corporation)
George M. Borkowski (A Professional Corporation)
Tracy L. Thornburg Cahill (A Professional Corporation)
William L. Cole (A Professional Corporation)
Danna L. Cook (A Professional Corporation)
Lucia E. Coyoca (A Professional Corporation)
Allan B. Cutrow (A Professional Corporation)
Philip Davis (A Professional Corporation)
Ronald A. DiNicola (A Professional Corporation)
Larry C. Drapkin (A Professional Corporation)
Jeffrey K. Eisen (A Professional Corporation)
Arthur Fine (A Professional Corporation)
Russell J. Frackman (A Professional Corporation)
Harold Friedman (A Professional Corporation)
Kevin Gaut (A Professional Corporation)
Peter B. Gelblum (A Professional Corporation)
Lawrence A. Ginsberg (A Professional Corporation)
Frida Popik Glucoft (A Professional Corporation)
Lessing E. Gold (A Professional Corporation)
Ron R. Goldie (A Professional Corporation)
Jeffrey D. Goldman (A Professional Corporation)
Allen J. Gross (A Professional Corporation)
John E. Hatherley (A Professional Corporation)
Yakub Hazzard (A Professional Corporation)
Richard S. Hessenius (A Professional Corporation)
Hayward J. Kaiser (A Professional Corporation)
Andrew E. Katz (A Professional Corporation)
David J. Katz (A Professional Corporation)
Deborah P. Koeffler (A Professional Corporation)

(See Next Column)

MEMBERS OF FIRM (Continued)

John M. Kuechle (A Professional Corporation)
Thomas P. Lambert (A Professional Corporation)
Chester I. Lappen (A Professional Corporation)
Marvin Leon (A Professional Corporation)
Christopher B. Leonard (A Professional Corporation)
Adam Levin (A Professional Corporation)
Lawrence A. Michaels (A Professional Corporation)
Yvette Molinaro (A Professional Corporation)
Mark R. Moskowitz (A Professional Corporation)
David Wheeler Newman (A Professional Corporation)
Jean Pierre Nogues (A Professional Corporation)
Alan L. Pepper (A Professional Corporation)
Daniel M. Petrocelli (A Professional Corporation)
J. Eugene Salomon, Jr. (A Professional Corporation)
David P. Schack (A Professional Corporation)
Steven M. Schneider (A Professional Corporation)
John L. Segal (A Professional Corporation)
Thomas P. Seltz (A Professional Corporation)
Steven E. Shapiro (A Professional Corporation)
Richard B. Sheldon, Jr. (A Professional Corporation)
Roger Sherman (A Professional Corporation)
Roy L. Shults (A Professional Corporation)
David A. Steinberg (A Professional Corporation)
Eugene H. Veenhuis (A Professional Corporation)
Mark A. Wasserman (A Professional Corporation)
Elia Weinbach (A Professional Corporation)
Robert C. Welsh (A Professional Corporation)

OF COUNSEL

Richard E. Ackerknecht
Douglas W. Bordewieck
Marvin A. Demoff (A Professional Corporation)
Bernard Donnenfeld
Daniel M. Freedman
William M. Kaplan (A Professional Corporation)
Stephen D. Marks (A Professional Corporation)
A. Catherine Norian
Jan Powers (A Professional Corporation)
Douglas R. Ring (A Professional Corporation)
Kim H. Swartz
H. Wayne Taylor

ASSOCIATES

Lisa M. Baker
Brenda S. Barton
Drew E. Breuder
Dana Anderson Childers
Daniel J. Cooper
Jeffrey D. Davine
Karl de Costa
Peter M. DelVecchio
Allison L. Demoff
Angelike I. Dexter
Jason H. Farber
Celine M. Guillou
Jocelyn M. Gutiérrez
Jeannette Hahm
Alec Harrell
Carolyn Hoff
Craig E. Holden
Carolyn S. Javier
Sara A. Kapp
Jason Krischer
Marc E. Mayer
Haven G. Morgan-Hubbard
Gamze Onur
Karin Pagnanelli
Brent Rabowsky
Matt J. Railo
Jeffrey L. Richardson
Kim Y. Richardson
David Scott Rugendorf
Alison A. Sanders
Jenny Schneider
Howard D. Shapiro
Jill H. Silfen
Lee Anne Steinberg
Eric M. Steinert
Suzanne M. Steinke
Joseph G. Swan
Wayne R. Terry
Michael J. Zerman

References: Wells Fargo Bank, N.A.; Merrill, Lynch.

For full biographical listings, see the Martindale-Hubbell Law Directory

MONTELEONE & McCRORY, LLP (AV)

A Limited Liability Partnership including Professional Corporations
725 South Figueroa Street Suite 3750, 90017-5402
Telephone: 213-612-9900
FAX: 213-612-9930
Email: montmcc@pacbell.net
Santa Ana, California Office: Suite 750, 1551 North Tustin Avenue, 92705.
Telephone: 714-565-3170.
Fax: 714-565-3184.

Stephen Monteleone (1886-1962)
Darrell P. McCrory (Retired)
G. Robert Hale (P.C.)
Patrick J. Duffy, III (P.C.)
Michael F. Minchella (P.C.)
Thomas P. McGuire (P.C.)
Philip C. Putnam (P.C.)
Joseph A. Miller (P.C.)
Donald J. Shields
David C. Romyn

Andrew W. Hawthorne
Jeffrey S. Hurst
William R. Baerg
Steven B. Copeland
Dennis C. Tulsiak
Scott R. Lane
Matthew S. Rork
Keith E. Davis
Sandra S. Fujiyama
Nilay A. Shah
Cha-Hee Nagashima Lee
William J. Ingalsbe (P.C.) (Resident, Santa Ana Office)
Diana M. Dron (Resident, Santa Ana Office)
Barry J. Jensen (Resident, Santa Ana Office)
Gerald W. Mouzis (Resident, Santa Ana Office)

(See Next Column)

MONTELEONE & MCCRORY LLP—*Continued*

OF COUNSEL

Joseph C. Malpasuto

For full biographical listings, see the Martindale-Hubbell Law Directory

MUNGER, TOLLES & OLSON LLP (AV)

A Law Partnership including Professional Corporations
355 South Grand Avenue 35th Floor, 90071
Telephone: 213-683-9100
Cable Address: "Muntoll"
Telex: 677574
Telecopier: 213-687-3702
URL: http://www.mto.com
San Francisco, California Office: 33 New Montgomery Street, Suite 1900.
Telephone: 415-512-4000.
FAX: 415-512-4077.

MEMBERS OF FIRM

Frederick B. Warder, Jr. (1932-1972)
Peter R. Taft (A Professional Corporation)
Robert K. Johnson (A Professional Corporation)
Alan V. Friedman (A Professional Corporation)
Ronald L. Olson (A Professional Corporation)
Dennis E. Kinnaird (A Professional Corporation)
Richard S. Volpert
Simon M. Lorne
Dennis C. Brown (A Professional Corporation)
Robert E. Denham
Jeffrey I. Weinberger
Melvyn H. Wald (1947-1992)
Robert L. Adler
Cary B. Lerman
Charles D. Siegal
Ronald K. Meyer
Gregory P. Stone
Vilma S. Martinez
Brad D. Brian
Bradley S. Phillips
George M. Garvey
Rita J. Miller
William D. Temko
Steven L. Guise (A Professional Corporation)
Robert B. Knauss
R. Gregory Morgan
Stephen M. Kristovich
John W. Spiegel
Terry E. Sanchez
Steven M. Perry
Ruth E. Fisher
Mark B. Helm
Joseph D. Lee
Michael R. Doyen
Michael E. Soloff
Gregory D. Phillips
John B. Frank
Lawrence C. Barth
Kathleen M. McDowell
Glenn D. Pomerantz
Thomas B. Walper
Ronald C. Hausmann (Resident, San Francisco Office)
Patrick J. Cafferty, Jr. (Resident, San Francisco Office)
Jay Masa Fujitani
O'Malley M. Miller
Sandra A. Seville-Jones
Mark H. Epstein
Henry Weissmann
Kevin S. Allred
Marc A. Becker
Cynthia L. Burch
Bart H. Williams
Jeffrey A. Heintz
Judith T. Kitano
Kristin Linsley Myles (Resident, San Francisco Office)
Marc T. G. Dworsky
Jerome C. Roth (Resident, San Francisco Office)
Stephen D. Rose
Jeffrey L. Bleich (Resident, San Francisco Office)
Garth T. Vincent
Ted G. Dane
Mark Shinderman
Stuart N. Senator
Martin D. Bern (Resident, San Francisco Office)
Daniel P. Collins
Steven B. Weisburd
Edward C. Hagerott, Jr.
Richard E. Drooyan
Robert L. DellAngelo
Bruce A. Abbott
Jonathan E. Altman
Mary Ann Lyman
Michael J. O'Sullivan
Kelly M. Klaus (Resident, San Francisco Office)
David B. Goldman

OF COUNSEL

Richard D. Esbenshade (A Professional Corporation)

ASSOCIATES

Marsha Hymanson
Monica Wahl Shaffer
Susan R. Szabo
Bernardo Silva
Kristin Sherratt Escalante
Gregg W. Kettles
Ilana B. Rubenstein
John C. Ulin
Burton A. Gross (Resident, San Francisco Office)
Steven W. Hawkins
David M. Rosenzweig
David C. Dinielli
Kevin S. Masuda
Andrea J. Weiss
Peter A. Detre (Resident, San Francisco Office)
Steven H. Usdan
Devon A. Gold
Jose F. Sanchez
Michael E. Greaney
Hojoon Hwang (Resident, San Francisco Office)
Douglas A. Axel
Rachel M. Capoccia
Bruce Hamilton Searby
Jonathan R. Levey
Melinda J. Demsky (Resident, San Francisco Office)
David H. Fry (Resident, San Francisco Office)
Stephen E. Morrissey
Janice M. Kroll
Tamerlin J. Godley
Pamela Barnes
Gail M.L. Mosse (Resident, San Francisco Office)
Linda S. Goldman
Douglas M. Fuchs
Dana S. Treister
Todd E. Molz
Linda M. Burrow
Lisa J. Demsky
Andrew Corydon Finch
Malcolm A. Heinicke (Resident, San Francisco Office)
Donovan Cocas
Stephen Sorensen
Mark Woolway
Lisa Wiens-Sinko

(See Next Column)

ASSOCIATES (Continued)

Tung Yin
Michael R. Barsa
James C. Rutten
Sean P. Gates
Mark J. Johnston
J. Martin Willhite
Natalie Pages Stone
Paul A. Davis
Richard C. St. John
Hamilton Chan, Jr.
Brett J. Rodda
Aaron Harrison
Avital T. Zer-Ilan (Resident, San Francisco Office)

Reference: City National Bank.

For full biographical listings, see the Martindale-Hubbell Law Directory

O'MELVENY & MYERS LLP (AV)

400 South Hope Street, 90071-2899
Telephone: 213-430-6000
Facsimile: 213-430-6407
Cable: MOMS
Telex: 674122
Email: omminfo@omm.com *URL:* http://www.omm.com
Century City, CA Office: 1999 Avenue of the Stars, Los Angeles, 90067-6035.
Telex: 674097. Tel: 310-553-6700.
Fax: 310-246-6779.
Newport Beach, CA Office: 610 Newport Center Drive, 92660-6429.
Telex: 4722088. Tel: 949-760-9600.
Fax: 949-823-6994.
San Francisco, CA Office: Embarcadero Center West, 275 Battery Street, 94111-3305. Tel: 415-984-8700.
Fax: 415-984-8701.
New York, NY Office: Citicorp Center, 153 East 53rd Street, 10022-4611.
Telex: 129165. Tel: 212-326-2000.
Fax: 212-326-2061.
Washington, DC Office: 555 13th Street, N.W., 20004-1109.
Cable: MOMSWSH.
Telex: 89622. Tel: 202-383-5300.
Fax: 202-383-5414.
London Office: O'Melveny & Myers, 3 Finsbury Square, London, EC2A 1LA, England. Tel: 44-171-256-8451. Fax 44-171-638-8205.
Tokyo Office: Akasaka Twin Tower, East 14F, 2-17-23, Akasaka, Minato-ku, Tokyo 107-0052, Japan. Tel: 03-5562-2800.
Fax: 03-5575-3840.
Hong Kong Office: O'Melveny & Myers, Suite 1905, Tower Two, Lippo Centre, 89 Queensway, Central, Hong Kong. Tel: 852-2523-8266.
Fax: 852-2522-1760.
Shanghai Office: Kerry Centre, 20F, 1515 Nanjing Road West, Shanghai, 200040 People's Republic of China. Tel: 86-21-5298-5600.
Fax: 86-21-5298-5500.

SENIOR PARTNER

Warren Christopher (Century City and Los Angeles, CA Offices)

PARTNERS

Douglas W. Abendroth (Newport Beach, CA Office)
Wallace M. Allan
Russell G. Allen (Newport Beach, CA Office)
Kermit W. Almstedt (Washington, DC Office)
John L. Altieri, Jr. (New York, NY Office)
Brian C. Anderson (Washington, DC Office)
D. Stephen Antion (Century City, CA Office)
Dale M. Araki (Tokyo, Japan Office; may also be contacted through the Los Angeles, CA Office)
Seth Aronson
James R. Asperger
Thomas W. Baxter
David T. Beddow (Washington, DC Office)
John H. Beisner (Washington, DC Office)
Debra S. Belaga (San Francisco, CA Office)
Charles W. Bender
Brian M. Berliner
Kendall R. Bishop (Century City and Los Angeles, CA Offices)
Leah Margaret Bishop (Century City, CA Office)
Robert D. Blashek, III (Century City, CA Office)
Donald T. Bliss, Jr. (Washington, DC Office)
Stan Blumenfeld
Richard A. Boehmer
Daniel H. Bookin (San Francisco, CA Office)
Jennifer L. Borow (Century City, CA Office)
Rigdon H. Boykin (New York, NY Office)
Brian D. Boyle (Washington, DC Office)
Avery R. Brown
Greyson Lee Bryan
Joseph A. Calabrese (Century City, CA Office)
Donald G. Carden (New York, NY Office)
Jerry W. Carlton (Newport Beach, CA Office)
Cormac J. Carney (Newport Beach, CA Office)
David W. Cartwright (Century City, CA Office)
Dale M. Cendali (New York, NY Office)
Howard Chao (Hong Kong, China and Shanghai, China Offices; may also be contacted through the Los Angeles, CA Office)
Martin S. Checov (San Francisco, CA Office)
Denise M. Clolery (New York, NY and Century City, CA Offices)
Alan M. Cohen (New York, NY Office)
James W. Colbert, III
William N. Cooney
Stephen A. Cowan (San Francisco, CA Office)
Arthur B. Culvahouse, Jr. (Washington, DC Office)
Michael A. Curley (New York, NY Office)
Brian S. Currey

(See Next Column)

O'MELVENY & MYERS LLP, *Los Angeles—Continued*

PARTNERS (Continued)

Howard F. Daniels
John F. Daum
Walter E. Dellinger (Washington, DC Office)
James H. De Meules
George C. Demos (Los Angeles and Newport Beach, CA Offices)
Daniel A. Deshon, IV (Hong Kong, China Office)
Douglas E. Dexter (San Francisco, CA Office)
Charles P. Diamond (Century City and Los Angeles, CA Offices)
Roderick G. Dorman
Robert S. Draper
Karen Dreyfus (Newport Beach, CA Office)
Scott H. Dunham
Robert N. Eccles (Washington, DC Office)
Steven L. Edwards (Newport Beach, CA Office)
David P. Enzminger
David G. Estes (San Francisco, CA Office)
Michael J. Fairclough
Marc F. Feinstein
Robert E. Ferdon (New York, NY Office)
Jose W. Fernandez (New York, NY Office)
Richard N. Fisher
Cliff H. Fonstein (Washington, DC and New York, NY Offices)
Charles W. Fournier (New York, NY Office)
Andrew J. Frackman (New York, NY Office)
Kenneth J. Friedman (New York, NY Office)
Patricia Frobes (Newport Beach and Los Angeles, CA Offices)
David R. Garcia (Century City, CA Office)
Travis C. Gibbs
Martin Glenn (New York, NY Office)
Richard B. Goetz
Gregory W. Goff
David E. Gordon
Kent V. Graham (Century City, CA Office)
Pamela C. Gray (Newport Beach and Los Angeles, CA Offices)
Linda Boyd Griffey
Steven L. Grossman (Century City, CA Office)
Catherine Burcham Hagen (Newport Beach and Los Angeles, CA Offices)
Christopher D. Hall (London, England and New York, NY Offices)
Stephen J. Harburg (Washington, DC Office)
John D. Hardy, Jr.
Adam C. Harris (New York, NY Office)
Adrian Michael Harris (London, England Office)
David L. Hayes (Newport Beach, CA Office)
Robert D. Haymer (Century City, CA Office)
Peter T. Healy (San Francisco, CA Office)
Howard M. Heitner
David Lynn Herron
J. Jay Herron (Newport Beach, CA Office)
Jack B. Hicks III
B. Boyd Hight
Bruce A. Hiler (Washington, DC Office)
Michael S. Hobel (Century City, CA Office)
Chris A. Hollinger
Mark C. Holscher
Gary N. Horlick (Washington, DC Office)
Sandra Segal Ikuta (Los Angeles and San Francisco, CA Offices)
Yongjin Im (New York, NY Office)
Wayne Jacobsen (Newport Beach, CA Office)
Tom A. Jerman (Washington, DC Office)
David J. Johnson, Jr.
Evan M. Jones
Richard M. Jones
Jeffrey M. Judd (San Francisco, CA Office)
Christopher N. Kandel (London, England Office)
Phillip R. Kaplan (Newport Beach, CA Office)
Allison M. Keller (Century City, CA Office)
Peter C. Kelley (Century City, CA Office)
Holly E. Kendig
Jeffrey W. Kilduff (Washington, DC Office)
David E. Killough (San Francisco and Los Angeles, CA Offices)
Joseph K. Kim
Louis B. Kimmelman (New York, NY Office)
Matthew T. Kirby (Los Angeles, CA and New York, NY Offices)
F. Curt Kirschner, Jr. (San Francisco, CA Office)
Ronald Klain (Washington, DC Office)
Paul R. Koepff (New York, NY Offices)
Jeffrey I. Kohn (New York, NY Office)
C. Douglas Kranwinkle (New York, NY and Los Angeles, CA Offices)
Malcolm M. Kratzer (New York, NY Office)
David A. Krinsky (Newport Beach, CA Office)
Gordon E. Krischer
Stanford G. Ladner (New York, NY Office)
Thomas J. Leary (Newport Beach, CA Office)
Elizabeth A. Leckie (New York, NY Office)
C. James Levin
Charles C. Lifland
David G. Litt (Washington, DC Office)
Ben H. Logan, III
Warren R. Loui (Los Angeles and Century City, CA Offices)
Patrick Lynch
Joseph M. Malkin (San Francisco, CA Offices)
James P. Marlin (New York, NY Office)
Cheryl White Mason (San Francisco and Los Angeles, CA Offices)
Jill H. Matichak (San Francisco and Los Angeles, CA Offices)
Michael G. McGuinness
Frederick B. McLane
Paul G. McNamara
Mitchell B. Menzer
Scott A. Meyerhoff (Newport Beach, CA Office)
Paul E. Mosley (Newport Beach, CA Office)
F. Thomas Muller, Jr.
Christopher C. Murray (Century City, CA Office)
Michael Newman

PARTNERS (Continued)

(*See Next Column*)

Charles F. Niemeth (New York, NY and Century City, CA Offices)
Jeffery L. Norton (New York, NY Office)
William J. O'Brien
James Odell (New York, NY Office)
Christine M. Olsen
M. Randall Oppenheimer (Century City, CA Office)
Kenneth R. O'Rourke
Peter V. Pantaleo (New York, NY Office)
Dean Pappas (Century City, CA Office)
Stephen P. Pepe (Newport Beach and Los Angeles, CA Offices)
David G. Pommerening (Washington, DC Office)
Laurence G. Preble (Los Angeles, CA and New York, NY Offices)
Bruce E. Prigoff (San Francisco, CA Office)
Alan Rader (Century City and Los Angeles, CA Offices)
Ira H. Raphaelson (Washington, DC Office)
David J. Reis (San Francisco, CA Office)
Eric A.S. Richards
Frederick A. Richman (Century City, CA Office)
George A. Riley (San Francisco, CA Office)
Robert A. Rizzi (Washington, DC Office)
John A. Rogovin (Washington, DC Office)
Jeffrey J. Rosen (New York, NY and Washington, DC Offices)
Richard R. Ross (Century City, CA Office)
Frank L. Rugani (Newport Beach, CA Office)
Mark A. Samuels
Kathryn A. Sanders
William H. Satchell (Washington, DC and New York, NY Offices)
Stephen Scharf (Century City, CA Office)
Carl R. Schenker, Jr. (Washington, DC Office)
Patricia A. Schmiege (San Francisco, CA Office)
Robert M. Schwartz (Century City, CA Office)
Ralph J. Shapira
Peter O. Shinevar (New York, NY Office)
Robert A. Siegel
Gary J. Singer (Newport Beach, CA Office)
Gary Mitchel Smith (New York, NY Office)
Linda Jane Smith (Century City and Los Angeles, CA Offices)
Steven L. Smith (San Francisco, CA Office)
Darin W. Snyder (San Francisco, CA Office)
Masood Sohaili
Stephanie I. Splane (San Francisco, CA Office)
John W. Stamper
Mark R. Steinberg
Stephen J. Stern
Gregory B. Thorpe
Henry C. Thumann
Stuart P. Tobisman (Century City and Los Angeles, CA Offices)
Todd R. Triller (New York, NY Office)
Lawrence P. Tu (Hong Kong, China Office)
Michael F. Tubach (San Francisco, CA Office)
Ko-Yung Tung (New York, NY Office)
Kenneth J. Turnbull (New York, NY Office)
Suzzanne Uhland (Newport Beach and Los Angeles, CA Offices)
James R. Ukropina
Robert C. Vanderet
Framroze M. Virjee
Ulrich Wagner (New York, NY Office)
Diana L. Walker
Larry A. Walraven (Newport Beach, CA Office)
Richard C. Warmer (San Francisco, CA Office)
Stephen H. Warren
David D. Watts
David I. Weil (Century City, CA Office)
Dean M. Weiner
Jacqueline A. Weiss (New York, NY Office)
John E. Welch (Washington, DC Office)
Pamela Lynne Westhoff
Robert J. White
Robert E. Willett
Brett J. Williamson (Newport Beach, CA Office)
Michael A. Wisnev
Charles C. Wolf
W. Mark Wood
Alfred M. Wurglitz (Washington, DC Office)
Michael G. Yoder (Newport Beach, CA Office)
Joel B. Zweibel (New York, NY Office)

INTERNATIONAL PARTNER

Simon Walker (Hong Kong, China Office)

SENIOR COUNSELLOR

William T. Coleman, Jr. (Washington, DC Office)

SENIOR COUNSEL

Francis J. Burgweger, Jr. (New York, NY Office)

OF COUNSEL

William G. Adams (Newport Beach, CA Office)
Barton Beek (Newport Beach, CA Office)
Joel S. Burton (Washington, DC Office)
R. Bradbury Clark
Bertrand M. Cooper
Samuel Estreicher (New York, NY Office)
Christine C. Ewell
Philip D. Irwin
Lowell C. Martindale, Jr. (Newport Beach and San Francisco, CA Offices)
Edward J. McAniff (Los Angeles and San Francisco, CA Offices)
John G. Niles
Owen Olpin
Gilbert T. Ray
Susan S. Richardson (Washington, DC Office)
John H. Roney
Lawrence J. Sheehan (Century City, CA Office)
William W. Vaughn

(*See Next Column*)

O'MELVENY & MYERS LLP—*Continued*

SPECIAL COUNSEL

Paul M. Alfieri
(New York, NY Office)
Iman J. Anabtawi
(Century City, CA Office)
Bernard C. Barmann, Jr.
Rosemary B. Boller
(New York, NY Office)
Laura C. Bremer
(San Francisco, CA Office)
Richard W. Buckner
Nadia St. George Burgard
(Washington, DC Office)
Thomas G. Carruthers
(New York, NY Office)
Apalla U. Chopra
Carla J. Christofferson
(Century City, CA Office)
Peggy Ann Clarke
(Washington, DC Office)
Steven M. Cooper
Regina Covitt
(Century City, CA Office)
Scott J. Daruty
(Newport Beach, CA Office)
Ralph P. DeSanto
(New York, NY Office)
Thomas J. Di Resta
(New York, NY Office)
Mary P. Donlevy
(Newport Beach, CA Office)
Kate W. Duchene
Daniel M. Dunn
(New York, NY Office)
David R. Eberhart
(San Francisco, CA Office)
Debbie J. Gezon
(Not admitted in CA)
Joseph G. Giannola
(New York, NY Office)
Robert A. Grauman
(New York, NY Office)
Allan I. Grossman
Karen R. Growdon
Lawrence M. Hadley
Kevin M. Harr
Pamela Harris
(Washington, DC Office)
Michael Hawkins
(Newport Beach, CA Office)
Harold Henderson
(Washington, DC Office)
Lawrence J. Hilton
(Newport Beach, CA Office)
David A. Hollander
David I. Hurwitz
Neil Scot Jahss
Teresa L. Johnson
(San Francisco, CA Office)
Carol A. Johnston
(Century City, CA Office)
David S. Kitchen
John A. Laco
Frances Elizabeth Lossing
Robert J. Lowe
(Century City, CA Office)
Michael M. Maddigan
Ann Catherine Menard
Crystal Nix
(Washington, DC Office)
Patrick M. Norton
(Shanghai, China Office)
Jane Nowotny
Peter Obstler
(San Francisco, CA Office)
Gregory R. Oxford
Lynn E. Parseghian
(Washington, DC Office)
Daniel F. Passage
Gregory P. Patti, Jr.
(New York, NY Office)
Achilles M. Perry
(New York, NY Office)
Stuart S. Poloner
(New York, NY Office)
Claudia E. Ray
(New York, NY Office)
Lori E. Romley
(San Francisco, CA Office)
Tancred V. Schiavoni, III
(New York, NY Office)
Scott Schrader
(New York, NY Office)
Ayaz R. Shaikh
(New York, NY Office)
Ian Simmons
(Washington, DC Office)
Craig W. Smith
Valerie A. Smith
Mark E. Thierfelder
(New York, NY Office)
Diana M. Torres
Karen Mary Wahle
(Washington, DC Office)
Marc Philip Wane
Michael A. Williamson
David A. Wimmer
Masami Yamamoto

ASSOCIATES

Hirobumi Abe
(Tokyo, Japan Office)
Peter R. Afrasiabi
(Newport Beach, CA Office)
Zeeshan Ahmedani
(New York, NY Office)
Christiana M. Ajalat
(Newport Beach, CA Office)
Susan C. Alker
Terrence R. Allen
(Newport Beach, CA Office)
Dipanwita Deb Amar
(San Francisco, CA Office)
Kavita Amar
Paula E. Ambrosini
Andrew C. Ambruoso
(New York, NY Office)
Eric J. Amdursky
(San Francisco, CA Office)
Jeremy T. Amen
(Century City, CA Office)
Catherine M. Ames
(New York, NY Office)
David J. Anderson
(Washington, DC Office)
Floy E. Andrews
Hazim H. Ansari
(Newport Beach, CA Office)
Tina F. Antonakakis
(New York, NY Office)
Christopher W. Arledge
(Newport Beach, CA Office)
Samir B. Armaly
H. Tomás Arostegui
(Century City, CA Office)
Felipe J. Arroyo
Jennifer J. Austin
(Century City, CA Office)
Jeffrey A. Barker
(Century City, CA Office)
Brian D. Beck
Evelyn Becker
(Washington, DC Office)
Astrid C. Becker-Celik
(San Francisco, CA Office)
Angela M. Bellanca
(Century City, CA Office)
Richard D. Beller
Robert E. Benfield
(Century City, CA Office)
Mark Binger
(Newport Beach, CA Office)
William F. Birchfield III
(San Francisco, CA Office)
Alexis D. Bircoll
(Century City, CA Office)
Michael D. Birnbaum
(New York, NY Office)
Jay Blaivas
(New York, NY Office)
Jonathan L. Blinderman
Martin Bogue
(New York, NY Office)
Debra L. Boyd
Benjamin G. Bradshaw
(Washington, DC Office)

(See Next Column)

ASSOCIATES (Continued)

Christopher D. Brearton
(Century City, CA Office)
Donald Breese
Eric Breitman
(New York, NY Office)
Michele Brinker
(Newport Beach, CA Office)
Carmine J. Broccole
(New York, NY Office)
Brian P. Brooks
(Washington, DC Office)
Leila R. Brown
Michael P. Brown
(San Francisco, CA Office)
J. Taylor Browning
Emily Brubaker
Glenn R. Butterton
(Washington, DC Office)
Kenneth R. Button
Tasneem Campwala
(Century City, CA Office)
Michael C. Camuñez
Kristen V. Campana
(New York, NY Office)
John J. Cardenas
Jeffrey J. Carlisle
(Washington, DC Office)
Diane P. Carman
(New York, NY Office)
Kevin B. Carter
Priscila E. Castillo
Rodrigo A. Castro-Silva
(Century City, CA Office)
Yar R. Chaikovsky
Ann C. Chan
Nick Chatterton
(London, England Office)
Kristina Cheh
Stephen Chen
Dennis Hohn Cho
C. Brophy Christensen, Jr.
(San Francisco, CA Office)
John Christianakis
(London, England Office)
Sang-Ah Deborah Chun
Henry H. Chung
(New York, NY Office)
Paul Cirino
(New York, NY Office)
Gregory Clark
(Newport Beach, CA Office)
Melissa Clemens
(Not admitted in CA)
Matthew W. Close
Shane K. Cobb
(London, England Office)
Andréa D. Cohen
Jason F. Cohen
(New York, NY Office)
Sheri E. Cohen
Derrick Coleman
Charles F. Connolly
(Washington, DC Office)
Jacqueline E. Cowden
(Newport Beach, CA Office)
Frank M. Crance
(Newport Beach, CA Office)
Raphael Dang-Quang Cung
Joanne M. Darkey
(New York, NY Office)
Scott K. Davidson
(Newport Beach, CA Office)
Robert L. Davis
(Newport Beach, CA Office)
Teresa E. Dawson
(Washington, DC Office)
Edward A. Deibert
(San Francisco, CA Office)
Antonio A. Del Pino
(New York, NY Office)
Emily A. Dephoure
(Not admitted in CA)
Kendra M. Deter
(Newport Beach, CA Office)
Michael Devins
(New York, NY Office)
Rafael Diaz-Granados
(New York, NY Office)
Marisa Di Meglio
(New York, NY Office)
Andrew Dolak
(Newport Beach, CA Office)
Stephen Dorrough
(Shanghai, China Office)
Patrick N. Downes
Bradford David Duea
(Century City, CA Office)
Martha Dye
(Washington, DC Office)
Mark C. Easton
Randall W. Edwards
(San Francisco, CA Office)
Jeffrey S. Eisenberg
Steven G. Eisner
Matthew Erramouspe
(Century City, CA Office)
Timothy Brian Evans
(Not admitted in CA)
Daniel E. Farrington
(Washington, DC Office)
John M. Fedorko
(New York, NY Office)
Jeffrey A. Fehervari
(Washington, DC Office)
Danielle F. Fern
Olivia D. A. Fields
Robert F. Fisher
Matthew Fojut
Suzanne Rich Folsom
(Washington, DC Office)
Charlotte E. Forssander
(New York, NY Office)
Lesley G. Freeman
(Century City, CA Office)
Aleks S. Frimershtein
Richard M. Froehlich
(New York, NY Office)
Jess B. Frost
Karen Fujii
(New York, NY Office)
Shervin I. Gabayan
(Century City, CA Office)
Dennis R. Gallagher
Anne Elizabeth Garrett
Scott A. Gartner
(Century City, CA Office)
Weni C. Gieseking
Neil K. Gilman
(Washington, DC Office)
Mitchell A. Gluck
(New York, NY Office)
Jeffrey D. Goldberg
Victoria A. Graff
Nancy E. Grauman
Todd A. Green
(Newport Beach, CA Office)
Adam M. Greenfield
(New York, NY Office)
Jennifer G. Grenert
(New York, NY Office)
Jonathan L. Griffith
(Washington, DC Office)
Alyssa A. Grikscheit
(New York, NY Office)
Nicolas Groffman
(Shanghai, China Office)
Julia A. Guizan
(Newport Beach, CA Office)
Seth Gustafson
(San Francisco, CA Office)
Carrielyn D. Guymon
(Washington, DC Office)
Jonathan Hacker
(Washington, DC Office)
Afshin Hakim
Esther Han
(Washington, DC Office)
Jason Harman
(New York, NY Office)
Deborah Hauser
(San Francisco, CA Office)
Katharine B. Hazlett
(Washington, DC Office)
Jeff S. Hegedus
(Century City, CA Office)
Wendy Heller
(Century City, CA Office)
Rebecca B. Hilberman
(Washington, DC Office)
Bradford R. Hise
(San Francisco, CA Office)
Chadwick A. Ho
(Century City, CA Office)

(See Next Column)

O'MELVENY & MYERS LLP, *Los Angeles—Continued*

ASSOCIATES (Continued)

Mark Ho (Shanghai and Hong Kong, China Offices)
Bonnie L. Hobbs (Not admitted in CA)
Eric J. Hoffman (Newport Beach, CA Office)
Michael J. Holden (New York, NY Office)
Kristin Holland (New York, NY Office)
Rebekah Holman
Paul Horwitz (Washington, DC Office)
Jennifer Howard (New York, NY Office)
Lane Huang (Shanghai, China Office)
Diana J. Hunt
Brian Hutchings (New York, NY Office)
Jacquelyn Inserra (New York, NY Office)
Jill Irvin (New York, NY Office)
Benjamin R. Jacewicz (Washington, DC Office)
Kimberly A. Jackson (Washington, DC Office)
Eric D. Jacobs (New York, NY Office)
Kevin D. Jaffe (New York, NY Office)
James Paul Jenal
Victor Jih (Century City, CA Office)
Thomas P. Jirgil (Century City, CA Office)
Melissa Joe (Newport Beach, CA Office)
Eric S. Johnson (New York, NY Office)
James L. Johnston (New York, NY Office)
Cameron Johnstone (Washington, DC Office)
Mizuho Kameoka (New York, NY Office)
Mitchell A. Kamin (Not admitted in CA)
Hyun S. Kim (New York, NY Office)
Ammu R. Kirtane (San Francisco, CA Office)
Jenny G. Ko (San Francisco, CA Office)
Selene S. Ko (Washington, DC Office)
Hayley J. Kondon
Michael Kopp (San Francisco, CA Office)
Sarah M. Kopp (Washington, DC Office)
Joshua D. Kussman (San Francisco, CA Office)
Teresa Kwong (Washington, DC Office)
Christopher M. Lal (Newport Beach, CA Office)
Catherine Lamb (London, England Office)
Veronique Lanthier (Washington, DC Office)
Jennifer E. Laser (Century City, CA Office)
Jose A. Lau Dan (New York, NY Office)
Amy J. Laurendeau (Newport Beach, CA Office)
Elisabeth Layton (Washington, DC Office)
Samuel M. Leaf (New York, NY Office)
David E. Lederman
Anna Lee (New York, NY Office)
Deanna Lee (Century City, CA Office)
Euffi D. Lee (Century City, CA Office)
James C. Lee
Sonia Y. Lee
Alan Lefkowitz (Washington, DC Office)
Robert J. Lemons (New York, NY Office)
Khai LeQuang (Newport Beach, CA Office)
Stella S. Leung (Hong Kong, China Office)
Adam G. Levine
Lance I. Levine (New York, NY Office)
Barry P. Levinson (New York, NY Office)
Alfred P. Levitt (New York, NY Office)
Erich F. Lichtblau (San Francisco, CA Office)
Richard J. Lind (Washington, DC Office)
Katherine Lipel
Francine J. Lipman (Newport Beach, CA Office)
Robert G. Loewy (Newport Beach, CA Office)
Amy J. Longo (Newport Beach, CA Office)
Eva M. Luchini (Century City, CA Office)
Christopher Lui
John J. Lulejian
Kerry A. Lyon
Dana C. MacGrath (New York, NY Office)
Suann C. MacIsaac (Not admitted in CA)
Lauren Mahler (New York, NY Office)
Jeremy Maltby (New York, NY Office)
Prētha Mani
Andrew S. Mansfield (Century City, CA Office)
Stefanie I. Markman (Century City, CA Office)
James V. Martin (Washington, DC Office)
Rebecca Martin (New York, NY Office)
Christine E. Martin-Nicholson (London, England Office)
Cynthia Martinez
Shannon M. Mason (Century City, CA Office)
Christopher J. Matarese (Newport Beach, CA Office)
Keri N. Matthews (New York, NY Office)
Brian T. May
Timothy B. McCaffrey, Jr.
Jordan McCollum
Deborah N. McFarland (New York, NY Office)
Delenia H. McIver
Joseph R. McKechnie, Jr. (New York, NY Office)
Dana McMahon (New York, NY Office)
Peter J. McPartlin (Century City, CA Office)
Heather E. McPhail
Caroline K. Menes (New York, NY Office)
Michael A. Meyer (Washington, DC Office)
Marissa B. Molé (New York, NY Office)
Michael T. Moon
Luc Moritz
Stan A. Mortensen (Newport Beach, CA Office)
Kristin H. Mowry (Washington, DC Office)
Jean Murphy
Felicia H. Murray (New York, NY Office)
Allison Rose Musante
Richard E. Myers II
Darren K. Nakano (Century City, CA Office)

ASSOCIATES (Continued)

(*See Next Column*)

Vicki A. Nash (Newport Beach, CA Office)
Michael J. Neary
Carlos Needham (Not admitted in CA)
Kathleen A. Nelson (Century City, CA Office)
David B. Newdorf (San Francisco, CA Office)
John F. Niblock (Washington, DC Office)
Jason A. Nicoll (New York, NY Office)
Brent J. North (Newport Beach, CA Office)
Colleen Ann O'Neil (New York, NY Office)
Shinyung Oh (San Francisco, CA Office)
Yasuko Okamoto (New York, NY Office)
Kevin Oliver
Matthew L. Olmsted (Washington, DC Office)
David L. Orlic
Scott S. Packman (Century City, CA Office)
Kathleen M. Pakenham (New York, NY Office)
Vivek V. Pande
Jeehye Park (New York, NY Office)
Paul Park (San Francisco, CA Office)
Un Kyung Park (San Francisco, CA Office)
Kenneth G. Parker (Newport Beach, CA Office)
Austen L. Parrish
James Pearl (Century City, CA Office)
J. Weston Peterson (New York, NY Office)
Michael Pettingill (San Francisco, CA Office)
Jonathan L. Pettit
Steven Lee Pickering (San Francisco, CA Office)
David Pierce (Newport Beach, CA Office)
Stuart C. Plunkett (San Francisco, CA Office)
Annette L. Poblete (New York, NY Office)
Gregory Y. Porter (Washington, DC Office)
Laura C. Prager (New York, NY Office)
Sandeep Qusba (New York, NY Office)
Vikram Raghavan (New York, NY Office)
Najma Q. Rana (New York, NY Office)
Lauren G. Rasmus (New York, NY Office)
A. Yasmine Rassam (New York, NY Office)
Ossie Ravid (Century City, CA Office)
Lawrence H. Reif (New York, NY Office)
Maria J. Reilly (New York, NY Office)
Laurel A. Remington
Andrea Joseph Restivo (Newport Beach, CA Office)
Ray J. Reyes (Not admitted in CA)
Karen Rhodes
Christopher Rider (New York, NY Office)
Laura B. Riley
Kelly Riordan (Washington, DC Office)
Thomas M. Riordan
Patrick R. Rizzi (Washington, DC Office)
Mark W. Robertson
Gregory Robins
Scharn Robinson (Washington, DC Office)
Donald H. Rolfe
Paul A. Rose (Century City, CA Office)
Todd D. Rosenberg (Washington, DC Office)
Alexander Rosenstein (New York, NY Office)
Michael T. Rosenthal (Not admitted in CA)
Patrick Ross
Erin Cooper Rotgin (Washington, DC Office)
Christine M. Roth (Washington, DC Office)
Valerie Granfield Roush (Washington, DC Office)
Benjamin Rozwood
Shannon Rust (Newport Beach, CA Office)
Katharine Sabich-Robison
Deborah J. Saltzman
Paul Salvaty
William T. Salzmann
Mark Saulino (New York, NY Office)
Mark C. Scarsi
Diana Scherer (Newport Beach, CA Office)
Martin L. Schmelkin (New York, NY Office)
Matthew Schneider (New York, NY Office)
Daniel A. Schulze (San Francisco, CA Office)
Peter J. Shakow
Stephen C. Shannon (Washington, DC Office)
Rachel Shapiro (Washington, DC Office)
Sam S. Shaulson (New York, NY Office)
Megan L. Sheetz (New York, NY Office)
Ting-Ting Shi (New York, NY Office)
Jimmy M. Shin
Katherine Sieck (Newport Beach, CA Office)
James P. Sileneck (New York, NY Office)
Ashley S. H. Sim
Luann L. Simmons (San Francisco, CA Office)
Hunter Simon (Century City, CA Office)
Nancy M. Solomon
Whitty Somvichian (San Francisco, CA Office)
Steven E. Soule
Geoffrey J. Spolyar
W. Douglas Sprague (San Francisco, CA Office)
Srikanth Srinivasan (Washington, DC Office)
Stamatios Stamoulis (New York, NY Office)
Brandi R. Steege (Newport Beach, CA Office)
Erika Aronson Stern (New York, NY Office)
Robert Stern (New York, NY Office)
Summer Stevens
Karen L. Stevenson (Century City, CA Office)
William J. Stuckwisch (Washington, DC Office)
Christine H. Suh
Adam J. Sullins (Century City, CA Office)
Dean E. Sussman
Robert M. Swerdlow
Christine Tam
Thomas J. Tarala (London, England Office)
Gary S. Tell (Washington, DC Office)
Andor D. Terner (Newport Beach, CA Office)
Mark Christopher Teuton (Newport Beach, CA Office)
Judy W. Tieh (New York, NY Office)
Sharon L. Tomkins

ASSOCIATES (Continued)

(*See Next Column*)

O'MELVENY & MYERS LLP—*Continued*

Rik Toulon
(Century City, CA Office)
Glenn A. Trager
Andrew J. Trask
(Washington, DC Office)
Hannibal Travis
(San Francisco, CA Office)
Ashok K. Tripathi
David V. Trulio
Jarlon Tsang
Darren S. Tucker
(Washington, DC Office)
Ronald J. Turiello, Jr.
(New York, NY Office)
Mark T. Uyeda
Andrew J. Varner
(Washington, DC Office)
Hernan D. Vera
Joseph Viola
(New York, NY Office)
Scott M. Voelz (Los Angeles and Century City, CA Offices)
Dani L. Vogt
(Century City, CA Office)
Michelle Curtis Vonderhaar
(London, England Office)
Robert Wachter
(San Francisco, CA Office)
Matthias H. Wagener
Jeffrey W. Walbridge
(Newport Beach, CA Office)
Walker J. Wallace
(Shanghai, China Office)
Abbey Walsh
(New York, NY Office)
Stephanie M. Walter
(San Francisco, CA Office)
Nan Wang
(Hong Kong, China Office)
Eric L. Webb
(Newport Beach, CA Office)
Loren J. Weber
(Newport Beach, CA Office)
Nicole Weber
(New York, NY Office)
Carolyn Wessling
Jonathan D. West
(Century City, CA Office)
Heather G. White
Molly M. White
Christopher A. Whytock
(Newport Beach, CA Office)
Martine Apollon Wicks
(New York, NY Office)
Marc S. Williams
Elisabeth A. Wing
(Not admitted in CA)
Robert Winter
(Washington, DC Office)
Allen C. P. Wong
(Hong Kong, China Office)
Andrew Wong
(Newport Beach, CA Office)
Jeffrey A. Wortman
Daniel Wu
Lin Xia (New York, NY Office)
Ryan K. Yagura
Kevin Yamaga-Karns (Tokyo, Japan and Los Angeles, CA Offices)
Craig Yamakawa
(Tokyo, Japan Office)
Troy M. Yoshino
(San Francisco, CA Office)
Spencer H.C. Yu
Eric Zabinski
(Century City, CA Office)
Lydia R. Zaidman
(New York, NY Office)
Yi Zhang
(Hong Kong, China Office)

For full biographical listings, see the Martindale-Hubbell Law Directory

PAUL, HASTINGS, JANOFSKY & WALKER LLP (AV)

A Limited Liability Partnership including Professional Corporations
555 South Flower Street, 90071-2371
Telephone: 213-683-6000
Fax: 213-627-0705
URL: http://www.phjw.com
Atlanta, Georgia Office: 24th Floor, 600 Peachtree Street, N.E.
Telephone: 404-815-2400.
New York, New York Office: 399 Park Avenue.
Telephone: 212-318-6000.
Orange County, California Office: 695 Town Center Drive, Costa Mesa.
Telephone: 714-668-6200.
San Francisco, California Office: 345 California Street.
Telephone: 415-835-1600.
Stamford, Connecticut Office: 1055 Washington Boulevard.
Telephone: 203-961-7400.
Washington, D.C. Office: 1299 Pennsylvania Avenue, N.W.
Telephone: 202-508-9500.
Tokyo, Japan Office: Ark Mori Building, 12-32 Akasaka, P.O. Box 577, 1-Chome, Minato-Ku.
Telephone: (03) 3586-4711.
London, England Office: The International Financial Centre, 25 Old Broad Street.
Telephone: (011) 44-171-562-4000.
ATTORNEY E-MAIL ADDRESSES: first initial middle initial last name @phjw.com (e.g. rmasbill@phjw.com)

Robert Pusey Hastings (1910-1996)

COUNSEL

Leonard S. Janofsky
Charles M. Walker

MEMBERS OF FIRM

George W. Abele
Nancy L. Abell
Carl T. Anderson
Toshiyuki Arai
Mark W. Atkinson
Alan J. Barton
Stephen L. Berry
Woodson Toliver Besson (P.C.)
Thomas P. Brennan (P.C.)
John H. Brinsley
Jamie Broder
Siobhan McBreen Burke
Robert E. Carlson
Roxanne E. Christ
Eve Mary Coddon
Donald A. Daucher
Barbra L. Davis
Robert M. Dudnik
Linda M. Edwards
Philip N. Feder
Hydee R. Feldstein
Norman A. Futami
David L. Gersh
Michael Glazer
Paul Grossman
Melinda L. Hayes
Nancy L. Iredale (P.C.)
Eric H. Joss
Nancy N. Kennerly-Miller
Rick S. Kirkbride
J. Al Latham, Jr.
Michael K. Lindsey

(See Next Column)

MEMBERS OF FIRM (Continued)

Ethan Lipsig
M. Guy Maisnik
Robert A. Miller, Jr.
Greg M. Nitzkowski
Belinda K. Orem
Ronald M. Oster (P.C.)
Michael L. Owen
James Franklin Owens
John E. Porter
Patrick A. Ramsey
Robert S. Span
Alan K. Steinbrecher
George E. Stephens, Jr.
Kaoruhiko Suzuki
Geoffrey L. Thomas (P.C.)
William Stewart Waldo
Robert F. Walker
David M. Walsh
Alan Wade Weakland
Thomas S. Wisialowski
Kenneth J. Yood
James A. Zapp

SENIOR COUNSEL

Robert A. DeWitt (P.C.)
Dennis H. Vaughn

OF COUNSEL

Patricia M. Berry
Julian B. Decyk
Jan Elizabeth Eakins
Steven A. Fein
Michele A. Freedenthal
Anna M. Graves
Matthew I. Lamishaw
Martin C. Mead
Lisa A. Popovich
James A. Rice
Anthony J. Rossi
Christine A. Scheuneman
Beverly A. Tiffany
Katherine A. Traxler
Jeffrey G. Varga
William P. Wade
Michael S. Woodward
Clarisse W. J. Young

ASSOCIATES

Leslie L. Abbott
Kelly J. Aran
Courtney D. Armstrong
Elena R. Baca
Jennifer Stivers Baldocchi
Michele L. Barber
Sasha Edward Barbour
Margaret Frick Bertisch
Alison R. Blum
David A. Blumenfeld
Martin A. Boskovich
Steven S. Choi
Chad C. Conwell
Jami I. Copeland
William A. Crowfoot
S. Mark Denham
Melissa R. DeVita
Carolyn M. Domen-Broshears
Dennis S. Ellis
Steven W. Farnsworth
Margo E. Freedman
Andrew R. Gilmour
Allison B. Gruettner
Joshua G. Hamilton
Joy M. Harris
(Not admitted in CA)
Stephen H. Harris
Andrew W. Heger
Laura E. Henry
Stacy M. Hopkins
Dawn E. Horrocks
Peter M. Huie
Robert M. Keane, Jr.
Tara K. Kelly
Lisa L. Kim
Judith M. Kline
Cheryl L. Kopitzke
Lisa E. Krakow
Daniel J. Krasner
Douglas E. Lahammer
John K. Lee
Richard Y. Lee
Kevin K. Leung
Michelle L. Lieteau
(Not admitted in CA)
Robert L. Madok
Kelly Martin
Kathleen L. McAchran
Christina L. McEnerney
Kristen L. McMichael
Amy R. Melner
Cara D. Miller
J. Clark Miller
Henry J. Moravec III
C. Miguel Moreno
Glori J. Norwitt
John C. Oakes
Jessica Pae
Parag Patel
Bradley S. Pauley
Rajnish Puri
Josh S. Ridout
David M. Ritchie
Carl W. Robertson, Jr.
David A. Rosenblum
(Not admitted in CA)
Derek V. Roth
Alfred Sanchez, Jr.
Kelley L. Sbarbaro
Craig S. Seligman
Glenna Shen
Jacob M. Simon
Derek E. Smith
Stephen P. Sonnenberg
David A. Sudeck
Sana Swe
Todd D. Thibodo
Michael L. Turrill
Deborah S. Weiser
Carlos W. Williams
Christopher A. Wilson
Heather Morgan Wood
Julie Arias Young
Caroline Zuk
Arthur L. Zwickel

For full biographical listings, see the Martindale-Hubbell Law Directory

PILLSBURY MADISON & SUTRO LLP (AV)

Citicorp Plaza, 725 South Figueroa Street, Suite 1200, 90017-5443
Telephone: 213-488-7100
Fax: 213-629-1033
Email: pillsburylaw.com *URL:* http://pillsburylaw.com
Costa Mesa, California Office: 650 Town Center Drive, 7th Floor, 92626.
Telephone: 714-436-6800.
Fax: 714-436-2800.
Silicon Valley Office: 2550 Hanover Street, Palo Alto, 94034.
Telephone: 650-233-4500.
Fax: 650-233-4545.
Sacramento, California Office: 400 Capitol Mall, Suite 1700, 95814.
Telephone: 916-329-4700.
Fax: 916-441-3583.
San Diego, California Office: 101 West Broadway, Suite 1800, 92101.
Telephone: 619-234-5000.
Fax: 619-236-1995.
San Francisco, California Office: 50 Fremont Street, 94105.
Telephone: 415-983-1000.
Fax: 415-983-1200.

(See Next Column)

PILLSBURY MADISON & SUTRO LLP, *Los Angeles—Continued*

Washington, D.C. Office: 1100 New York Avenue, N.W., Ninth Floor, 20005.
Telephone: 202-861-3000.
Fax: 202-822-0944.
Vienna, Virginia Office: 8330 Boone Boulevard, Suite 400, 22182.
Telephone: 703-744-7600.
Fax: 703-744-7605.
New York, New York Office: 375 Park Avenue, Suite 3108, 10152.
Telephone: 212-826-1060.
Fax: 212-826-9255. One Liberty Plaza, 165 Broadway, 51st Floor.
Telephone: 212-374-1890.
Fax: 212-374-1852.
Tokyo, Japan Office: Pillsbury Madison & Sutro, Gaikokuho Jimu Bengoshi Jimusho, 5th Floor, Samon Eleven Building, 3-1, Samon-cho, Shinjuku-ku, Tokyo 160 Japan.
Telephone: 800-729-9830; 011-813-3354-3531.
Fax: 011-813-3354-3534.

MEMBERS OF FIRM

Dimitrios P. Biller
Anthon S. Cannon, Jr.
Kenneth R. Chiate
Anthony R. Delling
Jerone J. English
Michael J. Finnegan
Kent B. Goss
Amy D. Hogue
Sidney K. Kanazawa
Christopher J. McNevin
Catherine D. Meyer
Margaret L. Milam
Robert L. Morrison
Dana P. Newman
Charles E. Patterson
James M. Rishwain, Jr.
Matthew R. Rogers
Robert V. Slattery Jr.
William E. Stoner
Reed S. Waddell
William S. Waller
Roger R. Wise
Lawrence D. Bradley, Jr.
Jan H. Cate
Barbara L. Croutch
John J. Duffy
Evan Finkel
William B. Freeman
David L. Hayutin
Yuji Iwanaga
Jennie L. La Prade
Donald W. Meaders
Michael E. Meyer
Nancy G. Morrison
J. Richard Morrissey
Jackie K. Park
Edward A. Perron
Patrick G. Rogan
Kenneth N. Russak
Sheryl E. Stein
Marshall M. Taylor
Robert L. Wallan
John W. Whitaker
Gordon K. Wright
Richard H. Zaitlen

OF COUNSEL

Susan G. Fillichio
Deborah S. Thoren-Peden

SENIOR COUNSEL

Ian R. Barrett
Stewart S. Harrison
Steven W. Smyrski

ASSOCIATES

Bruce A. Baldwin
Gregory L. Brett
Carolyn C. Burger
Eric S. Chen
Jason N. Chung
Leanna B. Einbinder
Jason R. Erb
Jason David Finkle
Joel B. German
Joshua A. Gratch
Yvonne Lu Groen
Julie Huang
Kelly A. Kightlinger
G. Allen McNamee, III
Jiji Park
David S. Rauch
Laura Eames Sax
Samantha D. Slotkin
Kalman Steinberg
Marcus G. Whittle
J. Douglas Bishop
Kimberly L. Buffington
Christopher J. Chaudoir
Jennifer K. Chun
Sybille Dreuth
Sheri F. Eisner
Michael J. Erlinger
Aaron E. Friedland
Valerie M. Goo
Blaine I. Green
Sabina A. Helton
Rebecca Nell Kaufman
Christopher S. Lipp
Paul G. Nagy
Christopher H. Patay
H. Marc Rupp
Vivian S. Shin
Anthony J. Stanley
Bernard R. Ussery
Richard Kon Yoon

For full biographical listings, see the Martindale-Hubbell Law Directory

PROSKAUER ROSE LLP (AV)

2049 Century Park East, Suite 3200, 90067-3206
Telephone: 310-557-2900
FAX: 310-557-2193
URL: http://www.proskauer.com
New York, New York Office: 1585 Broadway.
Telephone: 212-969-3000.
Fax: 212-969-2900.
Washington, D.C. Office: 1233 Twentieth Street, N.W., Suite 800.
Telephone: 202-416-6800.
Fax: 202-416-6899.
Boca Raton, Florida Office: One Boca Place, Suite 340 West, 2255 Glades Road.
Telephone: 561-241-7400.
Fax: 561-241-7145.
Newark, New Jersey Office: One Newark Center.
Telephone: 973-274-3200.
Fax: 973-274-3299.

(See Next Column)

Paris, France Office: Proskauer Rose, 68, rue du Faubourg Saint-Honoré.
Telephone: +33-1-53-05-60-00.
Fax: +33-1-53-05-60-05.

MEMBERS OF FIRM

Howard D. Behar
Harold M. Brody
Scott P. Cooper
Thomas W. Dollinger
Mitchell M. Gaswirth
Bernard D. Gold
Barry C. Groveman
Paul D. Rubenstein
David R. Scheidemantle
Marvin Sears
Arthur F. Silbergeld
Lois D. Thompson
Scott J. Witlin
Martin S. Zohn

RESIDENT ASSOCIATES

Aaron P. Allan
William M. Brockschmidt
Jennifer M. Crome
Steven J. Elkins
Tanya L. Forsheit
Christopher E. Harding
Jeff Garcia Hilger
Gloria C. Jan
Gregory J. Patterson
Michael A. Ramos
Mark R. Rehe
Mary H. Rose
Deborah J. Sager
Stephanie T. Sasaki
Scott Silver
Tracy L. Turner
Donald S. Urrabazo
Rachelle S. Visconte
James M. Wakefield
Carolyn R. Young

For full biographical listings, see the Martindale-Hubbell Law Directory

ROPERS, MAJESKI, KOHN & BENTLEY, A PROFESSIONAL CORPORATION (AV)

515 South Flower Street, Suite 2100, 90071
Telephone: 213-312-2000
Fax: 213-312-2001
URL: http://www.ropers.com
Redwood City, California Office: 1001 Marshall Street.
Telephone: 650-364-8200.
Fax: 650-367-0997.
San Jose, California Office: 80 North 1st Street.
Telephone: 408-287-6262.
Fax: 408-297-6819.
San Francisco, California Office: 333 Market Street, Suite 3150.
Telephone: 415-543-4800.
Fax: 415-274-6301.
New York, New York Office: 1 World Trade Center, 85th Floor.
Telephone: 212-432-4300.
Fax: 212-432-4303.

Stephen J. Erigero
Frank T. Sabaitis (Resident)
Marta B. Arriandiaga
Allan E. Anderson (Resident)
Jeffrey S. Pollak

Michael W. Parks
Ernest E. Price
Andrew D. Castricone
Bradley P. Boyer
Robin L. Jacobs
Gerald B. Malanga
Queena C. Ho
Kristine M. Paden
Samuel J. Woo
Sabrina Kong
John C. Lee
Louis R. Chao
Kim Karelis
Brett M. Middleton
Jeffrey S. Bolender
Maureen C. O'Hara
Todd M. Thacker
Timothy L. Skelton
Chad A. Harris

For full biographical listings, see the Martindale-Hubbell Law Directory

SHEPPARD, MULLIN, RICHTER & HAMPTON LLP (AV)

A Limited Liability Partnership including Professional Corporations
Forty-Eighth Floor, 333 South Hope Street, 90071-1448
Telephone: 213-620-1780
Telecopier: 213-620-1398
Email: info@smrh.com *URL:* http://www.smrh.com
Orange County, California Office: 650 Town Center Drive, 4th Floor, Costa Mesa.
Telephone. 714-513-5100.
Telecopier: 714-513-5130. Home Page Address: http://www.smrh.com.
San Francisco, California Office: Seventeenth Floor, Four Embarcadero Center.
Telephone: 415-434-9100.
Telecopier: 415-434-3947. Home Page Address: http://www.smrh.com.
San Diego, California Office: Nineteenth Floor, 501 West Broadway.
Telephone: 619-338-6500.
Telecopier: 619-234-3815. Home Page Address: http://www.smrh.com.

COUNSEL

Gordon F. Hampton (1912-1996)
J. Stanley Mullin (Retired)
George R. Richter, Jr. (Retired)
James C. Sheppard (1898-1964)
Matthew K. Fong
Gerald N. Gordon
David A. Maddux *
Myrl R. Scott *
Frank Simpson, III (1926-1993)

PARTNERS

Michael H. Ahrens (San Francisco Office)
Philip F. Atkins-Pattenson (San Francisco Office)
Charles F. Barker
Robert S. Beall (Orange County Office)
John D. Berchild, Jr.
John R. Bonn (Los Angeles and San Diego Offices)

(See Next Column)

SHEPPARD, MULLIN, RICHTER & HAMPTON LLP—*Continued*

PARTNERS (Continued)

David M. Bosko (Orange County Office)
Arthur Wm. Brown, Jr.
Thomas M. Brown
James R. Brueggemann
Richard W. Brunette, Jr.
James M. Burgess
Anthony R. Callobre
Steven W. Cardoza (Orange County Office)
Justine Mary Casey (Orange County Office)
Michael J. Changaris (San Diego Office)
David B. Chidlaw (San Diego Office)
Dennis Childs (San Diego Office)
Gary A. Clark
John D. Collins * (San Diego Office)
Thomas A. Counts (San Francisco Office)
Joseph F. Coyne, Jr.
André J. Cronthall
Jonathan C. Curtis
Phillip A. Davis
Dean A. Demetre (Orange County Office)
Polly Dennis Towill
Domenic C. Drago (San Diego Office)
Juliette M. Ebert (San Francisco Office)
Frank Falzetta
Merrill R. Francis *
Geraldine A. Freeman (San Francisco Office)
Richard M. Freeman * (San Diego Office)
Marsha D. Galinsky
Robert S. Gerber (San Diego Office)
John J. Giovannone (Orange County Office)
Randolph B. Godshall (Orange County Office)
Joseph G. Gorman, Jr. *
Andrew J. Guilford (Orange County Office)
Guy N. Halgren (San Diego Office)
Gary L. Halling (San Francisco Office)
Harold E. Hamersmith
Douglas R. Hart
Suzanne J. Heeg
Kelly L. Hensley
Don T. Hibner, Jr.
James Blythe Hodge * (San Francisco Office)
John D. Hussey *
Frank William Iaffaldano
Tracey A. Kennedy
Richard L. Kintz (San Diego Office)
Robert L. Layton
Brent R. Liljestrom (Orange County Office)
James A. Lonergan
Gregory A. Long *
Richard L. Lotts *
Charles H. MacNab, Jr. (San Francisco Office)
David M. Madway (San Francisco Office)
Philip A. Magen (San Diego Office)
Paul S. Malingagio
William T. Manierre (San Francisco Office)
Alan H. Martin (Orange County Office)
Candace L. Matson
David J. McCarty
Charles E. McCormick
Ryan D. McCortney (Orange County Office)
M. Elizabeth McDaniel (San Francisco Office)
Otis McGee, Jr. (San Francisco Office)
James F. McShane
Peter M. Menard
James J. Mittermiller (San Diego Office)
Michael R. Moore (San Diego Office)
A. John Murphy, Jr. (San Francisco Office)
Christopher B. Neils (San Diego Office)
Mark L. Nelson
Thomas D. Nevins (San Francisco Office)
Jon W. Newby
Steven C. Nock (Orange County Office)
Wesley L Nutten, III * (1929-1993)
Kathyleen A. O'Brien
Joel R. Ohlgren
Mark T. Okuma
Prentice L. O'Leary *
Stephen J. O'Neil
T. William Opdyke
Tyler M. Paetkau (San Francisco Office)
John R. Pennington
Joseph E. Petrillo (San Francisco Office)
Robert H. Philibosian
Terrence V. Ponsford (San Francisco Office)
Fred R. Puglisi
Paul F. Rafferty (Orange County Office)
Kent R. Raygor
Nancy Baldwin Reimann
Paul M. Reitler *
James M. René
Mark Riera
Scott F. Roybal
Jack H. Rubens
John F. Runkel, Jr. (San Francisco Office)
Theodore A. Russell (San Francisco Office)
D. Ronald Ryland (San Francisco Office)
Robert G. Sbardellati (San Diego Office)
William M. Scott IV
Pierce T. Selwood *
Michelle Sherman
Randal B. Short (San Francisco Office)
Richard J. Simmons
John R. Simon * (Orange County Office)
James J. Slaby, Jr.
Mark K. Slater (San Francisco Office)
Dianne Baquet Smith
Martin J. Smith
Mark A. Spitzer
Richard L. Stone
Joan H. Story (San Francisco Office)
R. Marshall Tanner (Orange County Office)
Finley L. Taylor * (Orange County Office)
Laura S. Taylor (San Diego Office)
Timothy B. Taylor (San Diego Office)
Robert A. Thompson (San Francisco Office)
Amy L. Tranckino (San Diego Office)
David C. Ulich
Robert J. Uram (San Francisco Office)
Carlton A. Varner *
Edward D. Vogel (San Diego Office)
Kirk Wallace
William V. Whelan (San Diego Office)

PARTNERS (Continued)

(See Next Column)

Loretta A. Wider (San Francisco Office)
Robert E. Williams
Roy G. Wuchitech
William R. Wyatt (San Francisco Office)
John A. Yacovelle (San Diego Office)

SPECIAL COUNSEL

Fredric I. Albert (Orange County Office)
Kenneth J. Carl
Douglas J. Farmer (San Francisco Office)
Frederick V. Geisler
Rebecca V. Hlebasko (San Francisco Office)
Joseph B. Hudson, Jr.
Kristen A. Jensen (San Francisco Office)
Helen J. Lauderdale
Scott J. Lochner
Ethna M. S. Piazza (San Diego Office)
Maria C. Pracher (San Francisco Office)
Michael J. St. Denis
John H. Sears (San Francisco Office)

SENIOR ATTORNEYS

Donna R. Andrews (San Francisco Office)
Nancy Brandel
Mary K. Hedley (San Francisco Office)
Donna L. Hueckel
Harold S. Marenus
David John Richardson
Ellen R.Z. Rosen
Lisa H. Rosenlund (San Francisco Office)
Steven A. Ross
Betty J. Santohigashi (San Diego Office)
Steven L. Satz (Orange County Office)
Sheldon M. Siegel (San Francisco Office)
Barry Sullivan

OF COUNSEL

Thomas R. Sheppard *
Stephen C. Taylor *

ASSOCIATES

Cindy Thomas Archer (Orange County Office)
John O. Beanum
Jeffrey N. Boozell
Amy R. Brownstein
Scott A. Brutocao
Oral Caglar
Dana R. Cherney (San Diego Office)
Randall J. Clement (Orange County Office)
Gretchen W. Corbell
Sarah D. Keller Cox
Brian M. Daucher (Orange County Office)
Lisa N. Davis
Hooman Dayani
Wendi J. Delmendo (San Francisco Office)
K. Kristine Dunn
Julie A. Dunne (San Diego Office)
Robert A. Endries
Timothy Lee Epp
Matthew J. Erwin (Orange County Office)
Victor H. Fann
Kate R. Fitz (San Francisco Office)
Richard M. Foehr (San Francisco Office)
Grant P. Fondo (San Francisco Office)
Linda D. Fox (San Diego Office)
Christine Y. Friedman (San Diego Office)
John E. Friedrichs
Christopher L. Frost
Jason R. Gasper
Travis M. Gemoets
Gregory B. Genske (San Francisco Office)
Greg L. Gerardi (San Diego Office)
John F. Golembesky (San Diego Office)
Mary E. Gram
Mark S. Greenstone
John A. Griecci
Derek R. Havel
Judy Hawthorne-Waters (San Francisco Office)
Jeanine L. Hayes
Jonathan P. Hersey (San Francisco Office)
Karen L. Imbernino (Orange County Office)
Chris E. Jaenike (San Francisco Office)
Kenneth E. James (San Diego Office)
Stacey E. James (San Diego Office)
Scott B. Joachim (San Diego Office)
Amy L. Johnson
Frank J. Johnson, Jr. (San Diego Office)
Bryan A. Kabahar
Jim R. Karpiak (San Francisco Office)
Jeffrey A. Kaye
Andrea Kelly-Smethurst (San Francisco Office)
Marie B. Kenny (San Diego Office)
Diane P. Kong (San Francisco Office)
Peter A. Krause
Greg S. Labate (Orange County Office)
Matthew L. Levy
Ted C. Lindquist, III (San Francisco Office)
Kristin N. Locke
Melissa P. Lopez
Michael L. Ludwig
Mary E. Lynch (Orange County Office)
Aaron J. Malo (Orange County Office)
Joseph P. Martinez II (San Francisco Office)
Susan S. Matsui (Orange County Office)
Kevin K. McAleenan
Gavin T. McCraley
Amy S. McDowell
Daniel B. Mestaz
Justine Meyers (San Francisco Office)
Jacqueline R. Mijuskovic (San Francisco Office)
Justine Witt Milani (San Francisco Office)
Rachelle Miles (Orange County Office)
Steven L. Miller
Kristine L. Mostofizadeh (San Francisco Office)
Elena Muravina
Keith A. Newburry
Katharine D. Newman
Carmela Dunn Nicholas (San Diego Office)
Sean P. O'Connor (Orange County Office)
Isabelle L. Ord (Orange County Office)
Richard H. Otera
David J. Paik
Daniel W. Park

(See Next Column)

SHEPPARD, MULLIN, RICHTER & HAMPTON LLP, *Los Angeles—Continued*

ASSOCIATES (Continued)

A. Dale Parker
Jeffrey J. Parker
Berj K. Parseghian
John D. Pernick
(San Francisco Office)
Linda Pino
(San Francisco Office)
Kellilyn W. Porter
Tyson H. Powell
(San Francisco Office)
Jeffrey K. Rehfeld
(San Francisco Office)
Patrick G. C. Rezzo
(San Diego Office)
Renée Louise Robin
(San Francisco Office)
Amelia D. Sanchez
(San Diego Office)
Stacy Gamble Shaw
Bernard C. Shek
(San Francisco Office)
Robert M. Shore
Kimberly C. Simonds
(San Francisco Office)
Beth S. Sonnenklar
Martha H. Sottosanti
(San Diego Office)
Thomas N. Stephens
(Orange County Office)
Michael D. Stewart
(Orange County Office)
Robert T. Sturgeon
Ronald J. Thommarson
(Orange County Office)
Michael J. Thompson
Keith R. Thorell
Lei K. Udell (San Diego Office)
David A. Urban
Ketan S. Vakil
Carlo Van den Bosch
Sascha von Mende
Mark D. Watkins
(Orange County Office)
Richard P. Wickline
Tara L. Wilcox
(San Diego Office)
Steven H. Winick
(San Francisco Office)
Tawnya R. Wojciechowski
(Orange County Office)
R. Anthony Young

*Professional Corporation

For full biographical listings, see the Martindale-Hubbell Law Directory

SONNENSCHEIN NATH & ROSENTHAL (AV)

601 South Figueroa Street, Suite 1500, 90017
Telephone: 213-623-9300
Telecopier: 213-623-9924
URL: http://www.sonnenschein.com
Chicago, Illinois Office: Suite 8000 Sears Tower, 233 South Wacker Drive.
Telephone: 312-876-8000.
Cable Address: "Sonberk".
Telex: 25-3526.
Facsimile: 312-876-7934.
New York, N.Y. Office: 1221 Avenue of the Americas, 24th Floor.
Telephone: 212-768-6700.
Facsimile: 212-391-1247.
Washington, D.C. Office: 1301 K Street, N.W., Suite 600 East Tower.
Telephone: 202-408-6400.
Fax: 202-408-6399.
San Francisco, California Office: 685 Market Street, 6th Floor.
Telephone: 415-882-5000.
Facsimile: 415-543-5472.
St. Louis, Missouri Office: One Metropolitan Square, Suite 3000.
Telephone: 314-241-1800.
Facsimile: 314-259-5959.
Kansas City, Missouri Office: Suite 1100, 4520 Main Street, 64111.
Telephone: 816-932-4400.
Facsimile: 816-531-7545.
London, England Office: Sonnenscheins, Royex House, Aldermanbury Square, EC2V 7HR.
Telephone: 0207-600-2222.
Facsimile: 0207-600-2221.

John J. Allen
Percy Anderson
James E. Barnett
Michael J. Bayard
Charles R. Campbell, Jr.
Anthony Capobianco
Dennis S. Diaz
Martin J. Foley
Matthew C. Fragner
Brent Matthew Giddens
Robert D. Girard
Peter J. Gurfein
Mark T. Hansen
Scott L. Jones
Kevin P. Kamraczewski
Ronald D. Kent
Neal R. Marder
Lee T. Paterson
Laura R. Petroff
Pamela K. Prickett
Edwin B. Reeser, III
Michael W. Ring
Robert L. Schuchard
Robert F. Scoular
J. A. Shafran
David L. Volk
Susan M. Walker
Henry S. Zangwill

OF COUNSEL

Karen L. Bizzini
Bryan C. Jackson
Grace E. Mueller

ASSOCIATES

David S. Alverson
Judith M. Beall
Kerry E. Branch
Jeffry Butler
Weston A. Edwards
Michael S. Gould
Charles W. Hokanson
Stephanie K. Joiner
Laurie K. Jones
Matthew I. Kaplan
Jessie A. Kohler
John R. Miller
Evan R. Moses
James R. Moss, Jr.
Terrence R. Pace
Henry S. Robles
Frank Saidara
Steven R. Smith

(See Next Column)

ASSOCIATES (Continued)

T. Mark Smith
Amanda C. Sommerfeld
Daniela P. Stoutenburg
John E. Walker
Laura Ann Wytsma

For full biographical listings, see the Martindale-Hubbell Law Directory

STEPTOE & JOHNSON LLP (AV)

633 West Fifth Street, Suite 700, 90071
Telephone: 213-439-9400
Fax: 213-439-9599
Email: wrehm@steptoe.com *URL:* http://www.steptoe.com
Washington, D.C. Office: 1330 Connecticut Avenue, N.W. 20036.
Telephone: 202-429-3000.
Fax: 202-429-3902.
Cable Address: "Stepjohn".
Phoenix, Arizona Office: Two Renaissance Square, 40 N. Central Avenue, 24th Floor, 85004.
Telephone: 602-257-5200.
Fax: 602-257-5299.

MEMBERS

Laurence F. Janssen
Theodore E. Rhodes
Charles C. Read
Lawrence P. Riff
Steven J. Barber
Kevin C. Mayer

OF COUNSEL

Edward G. Gregory
Kathryn R. Janssen
Ruth D. Kahn
Lloyd C. Loomis

ASSOCIATES

Daniel R. Blakey
W. Chelsea Chen
Sheri T. Cheung
Carol A. Juhas
Troy A. Paredes
Larry R. Schmadeka
Jay E. Smith
Cynthia T. Soldwedel

For full biographical listings, see the Martindale-Hubbell Law Directory

STROOCK & STROOCK & LAVAN LLP (AV)

2029 Century Park East, Suite 1800, 90067-3086
Telephone: 310-556-5800
Telecopier: 310-556-5959
Cable Address: "Plastroock, L.A."
Telex: Plastroock LSA 677190 (Domestic and International)
Email: infola@stroock.com *URL:* http://www.stroock.com
New York, N.Y. Office: 180 Maiden Lane, New York, NY, 10038-4982.
Telephone: 212-806-5400.
Telecopiers: 212-806-6006; 212-806-5919; 212-806-6086; 212-425-9509; 212-806-6176. Email: info@stroock.com
New York Conference Center: 767 Third Avenue, New York, N.Y., 10017-2023.
Telephones: 212-806-5767; 5768; 5769; 5770.
Telecopier: 212-421-6234. Email: info@stroock.com
Boston, Massachusetts Office: 100 Federal Street, Boston, MA., 02110-1813.
Telephone: 617-482-6800.
Fax: 617-330-5111. Email: infoboston@stroock.com
Miami, Florida Office: First Union Financial Center, 200 South Biscayne Boulevard, Suite 3300, Miami, FL., 33131-2385.
Telephone: 305-358-9900.
Telecopier: 305-789-9302. Email: infomiami@stroock.com
Washington, D.C. Office: 1150 Seventeenth Street, N.W., Suite 600, Washington, D.C., 20036-4652.
Telephone: 202-452-9250.
Telecopier: 202-293-2293. Email: infodc@stroock.com

RESIDENT PARTNERS

Gregory A. Bray
Richard S. Forman
Barry B. Langberg
Schuyler M. Moore
Michael F. Perlis
Glenn D. Smith
Julia B. Strickland
Chauncey M. Swalwell

OF COUNSEL

Gerald J. Mehlman
Robert M. Shafton
Michael M. Umansky

SPECIAL COUNSEL

Deborah Drooz
D. Wayne Jeffries
Alan Z. Yudkowsky

RETIRED PARTNER

Merrill E. Jenkins

Judith L. Anderson
Wrenn E. Chais
Mary C. Costa
Stephanie E. Deaner
James W. Denison
Karen R. Dinino
John L. Filippone
Jennifer L. Gentin
Mark D. Grossman
Adam L. Gubner
Jody M. Heitner
(Not admitted in CA)
Gary S. Hiller
Richard R. Johnson
Stuart Johnson
JiAe Kim
Susan D. Koot
Pamela L. Kunath
Mitchell J. Langberg
Mary D. Manesis

(See Next Column)

STROOCK & STROOCK & LAVAN LLP—*Continued*

Heather A. McConnell
David W. Moon
Andrew W. Moritz
Randy J. Myricks
Michael J. Niborski
Scott M. Pearson
Daniel A. Rozansky
Lisa M. Simonetti
Carol M.L. Smithson
James J. Thompson
Matthew C. Thompson
Robyn B. Tuerk
Mark A. Vega

For full biographical listings, see the Martindale-Hubbell Law Directory

SULLIVAN & CROMWELL (AV)

1888 Century Park East, 90067-1725
Telephone: 310-712-6600
Telecopier: 310-712-8800
URL: http://www.sullcrom.com
New York City Office: 125 Broad Street, 10004-2498.
Telephone: 212-558-4000.
Telex: 62694.
Telecopier: 212-558-3588 or 212-514-5706.
Washington, D.C. Office: 1701 Pennsylvania Avenue, N.W., 20006-5805.
Telephone: 202-956-7500.
Telecopier: 202-293-6330.
Paris Office: 8, Place Vendôme, 75001 Paris, France.
Telephone: (011)(331) 44 50 60 00.
Telex: 240654.
Telecopier: (011)(331) 44 50 60 60 or (011)(331) 42 60 56 36.
London Office: St. Olave's House, 9a Ironmonger Lane, London EC2V 8EY, England.
Telephone: (011)(44207) 710 6500.
Telecopier: (011)(44207) 710 6565.
Melbourne Office: 101 Collins Street, Melbourne, Victoria 3000, Australia.
Telephone: (011)(613) 9635-1500.
Telecopier: (011)(613) 9654-2422.
Tokyo Office: Sullivan & Cromwell, Gaikokuho Jimu Bengoshi Jimusho, Akai Law Offices (Registered Associated Offices), Otemachi First Square East Tower 16F, 5-1, Otemachi 1-chome, Chiyoda-ku, Tokyo 100-0004, Japan.
Telephone: (011)(813) 3213-6140.
Telecopier: (011)(813) 3213-6470 or (011)(813) 3213-6477.
Hong Kong Office: 28th Floor, Nine Queen's Road, Central, Hong Kong.
Telephone: (011)(852) 2826-8688.
Telecopier: (011)(852) 2522-2280.
Frankfurt Office: Neue Mainzer Strasse 52, 60311 Frankfurt, Germany.
Telephone: (011)(4969) 7191 26-0.
Telecopier: (011)(4969) 7191 26-10.
Beijing Office: The Beijing Representative Office of Sullivan & Cromwell, Suite 501, China World Trade Center, No. 1 Jianguo Menwai Avenue, Beijing 100004, P.R.C.
Telephone: (011)(86) 10 6505 6120.
Telecopier: (011)(86) 10 6505 6136.

PARTNERS IN LOS ANGELES

Stanley F. Farrar
Frank H. Golay, Jr.
Robert A. Sacks
Alison S. Ressler
Michael H. Steinberg
John L. Savva
Steven B. Stokdyk

OF COUNSEL IN LOS ANGELES

Charles F. Rechlin

ASSOCIATES IN LOS ANGELES

Patrick S. Brown
Brendan P. Cullen
Kristen J. Dayley
Ondraus Jenkins
Albert Yun-Quan Liu
James R. Oehler
Jennifer H. Painter
David A. Rivera
Daniel E. Sobelsohn
Rosslyn Coldwell Stevens
Steven W. Thomas
James J. Vieceli III
Sheri M. Watts

For full biographical listings, see the Martindale-Hubbell Law Directory

THELEN REID & PRIEST LLP (AV)

34th Floor, 333 South Grand Avenue, 90071
Telephone: 213-621-9800
Fax: 213-623-4742
URL: http://www.thelenreid.com
San Francisco, California Office: 101 Second Street, Suite 1800.
Telephone: 415-371-1200.
Fax: 415-371-1211.
San Jose, California Office: 17th Floor, 333 West San Carlos Street.
Telephone: 408-292-5800.
Fax: 408-287-8040.
New York, New York Office: 40 West 57th Street.
Telephone: 212-603-2000.
Fax: 212-603-2001.
Washington, D.C. Office: Market Square, 701 Pennsylvania Avenue, N.W.
Telephone: 202-508-4000.
Fax: 202-508-4321.

(See Next Column)

David L. Bacon
Charles S. Birenbaum
Robert G. Campbell
John B. Clark
Curtis A. Cole
W. Glenn Cornell
Mark S. Geraghty
Joseph E. Herman
Thomas E. Hill
Linda S. Husar
Remy Kessler
Michael R. Lindsay
Valarie H. Macht
James J. Moak
Walter K. Oetzell
Timothy L. Pierce
Cheryl L. Schreck
John L. Viola
Lonnie E. Woolverton (P.C.)

OF COUNSEL

James Acret
William F. Holbrook
David E. Novitski

SPECIAL COUNSEL

Peggy A. Gerber
Jeffrey S. Sinek

ASSOCIATES

Richard E. Bromley
Mark D. Campbell
Raymond M. Collins
Nicole M. Duckett
Kathryn P. Fletcher
Gary H. Green II
Gayle I. Jenkins
Darci M. Jump
Cheryl H. Karz
Rebecca Yuan Lawlor
Mimi M. Lee
Sharon A. Ligorsky
Brooks P. Marshall
Hardy Ray Murphy
Charles E. Rampenthal

Representative Clients: The Bechtel Group of Companies; Hydril Co.; Industrial Indemnity Co.; Kaiser Aluminum & Chemical Corp.

For full biographical listings, see the Martindale-Hubbell Law Directory

TUTTLE & TAYLOR, A LAW CORPORATION (AV)

355 South Grand Avenue Fortieth Floor, 90071-3102
Telephone: 213-683-0600
Facsimile: 213-683-0225
Email: info@ttlaw.com *URL:* http://www.tuttletaylor.com
Washington, D.C. Office: Tuttle, Taylor & Heron, 1025 Thomas Jefferson Street, N.W. 20007-5201.
Telephone: 202-342-1300.
Facsimile: 202-342-5880.

Edward W. Tuttle (1877-1960)
Edward E. Tuttle (1907-1996)
Robert G. Taylor
Merlin W. Call
Frank C. Christl
Patrick L. Shreve
C. David Anderson
Richard S. Berger
Alan E. Friedman
Timi Anyon Hallem
Charles L. Woltmann
Marjorie S. Steinberg
Douglas W. Beck
John Arthur Moe, II
Mark A. Borenstein
Nancy E. Howard
Marc L. Brown
Michael H. Bierman
Louis E. Kempinsky
Gregory D. Schetina
Diann H. Kim
Marla J. Aspinwall
Robin D. Wiener
Laura J. Carroll
Edward A. Mendoza
Jeffrey D. Wexler
Julio A. Thompson
John R. Dent
Marnie S. Carlin
Kate Schneider Gold
Dahni K. Tsuboi

Sam S. Oh
Michelle M. Carroll
Kathryn E. Olson
Thomas I. Dupuis
Shannon Sullivan Martinez
Steven M. Rogers
Jeffrey S. Karr
Julie M. Ruhlin
Kristen E. Green
Kelley B. Poleynard
Linda K. Thomas
Katherine Perkins Ross
Priya Sridharan
Diana Echeveste
R. Stephen Roehler

OF COUNSEL

Julian B. Heron, Jr. (Resident, Washington, D.C. Office)
Phillip L. Fraas (Resident, Washington, D.C. Office)
Pamela G. Bothwell

Reference: Union Bank, 455 South Figueroa Street, Main Office (Los Angeles, California).

For full biographical listings, see the Martindale-Hubbell Law Directory

MANHATTAN BEACH, Los Angeles Co.

STEINBERG BARNESS FOSTER & FOLEY LLP (AV)

1334 Park View Avenue, Suite 100, 90266
Telephone: 310-546-8160
Telecopier: 310-546-8189
Email: sbgf@ix.netcom.com

MEMBERS OF FIRM

Alex Steinberg
Daniel I. Barness
Douglas B. Foster
Shannon M. Foley

ASSOCIATES

William R. (Randy) Kirkpatrick
Jeff M. Lee
Kimberly Ann White

(See Next Column)

STEINBERG BARNESS FOSTER & FOLEY LLP, *Manhattan Beach—Continued*

OF COUNSEL

Jordan G. Barness
Ronald D. Hariri (Not admitted in CA)

References: California United Bank; Wells Fargo Bank; Citizens Commerical Trust & Savings Bank; Bank of America.

For full biographical listings, see the Martindale-Hubbell Law Directory

*MARTINEZ,** Contra Costa Co.

BERNARD F. CUMMINS (AV)

917 Las Juntas Street, P.O. Box 351, 94553
Telephone: 925-228-3001
Fax: 925-228-6825

For full biographical listings, see the Martindale-Hubbell Law Directory

MENLO PARK, San Mateo Co.

COOLEY GODWARD LLP (AV)

3000 Sand Hill Road, Building 3, Suite 230, 94025-7116
Telephone: 650-843-5000
Fax: 650-854-2691
Email: webmaster@cooley.com *URL:* http://www.cooley.com
Palo Alto, California Office: Five Palo Alto Square, 3000 El Camino Real.
Telephone: 650-843-5000.
Fax: 650-857-0663.
San Francisco, California Office: 20th Floor, One Maritime Plaza.
Telephone: 415-693-2000.
Fax: 415-951-3699.
San Diego, California Office: 4365 Executive Drive, Suite 1100.
Telephone: 619-550-6000.
Fax: 619-453-3555.
Boulder, Colorado Office: 2595 Canyon Boulevard, Suite 250.
Telephone: 303-546-4000.
Fax: 303-546-4099.
Denver, Colorado Office: One Tabor Center, 1200 17th Street, Suite 2100.
Telephone: 303-606-4800.
Fax: 303-606-4899.
Kirkland, Washington Office: 5200 Carillon Point.
Telephone: 425-893-7700.
Fax: 425-893-7777.
Reston, Virginia Office: 2002 Edmund Halley Drive, Suite 300.
Telephone: 703-262-8000.
Fax: 703-262-8100.

PARTNERS

John A. Dado
Craig E. Dauchy
Mark P. Tanoury

ASSOCIATES

Stephanie A. Anagnostou
Nicole C. Deiger
Catherine A. Dring
James F. Fulton, Jr.
John Geschke
Ryan E. Naftulin
Vincent P. Pangrazio
Stephanie Parr
Elaine H. Tseng (Not admitted in CA)
Craig R. Venable

LEGAL SUPPORT PERSONNEL

SPECIALISTS

Bobbi Milliken

For full biographical listings, see the Martindale-Hubbell Law Directory

JORGENSON, SIEGEL, MCCLURE & FLEGEL, LLP (AV)

Suite 210, 1100 Alma Street, 94025-3392
Telephone: 415-324-9300
Fax: 415-324-0227
URL: http://www.jsmf.com

MEMBERS OF FIRM

John D. Jorgenson
Marvin S. Siegel
William L. McClure
John L. Flegel
Margaret A. Sloan

ASSOCIATES

Dan K. Siegel
Jennifer H. Friedman
Mindie S. Romanowsky

OF COUNSEL

Helene L. Leichter

Counsel for: City of Menlo Park.
References: Mid-Peninsula Bank (Palo Alto).

For full biographical listings, see the Martindale-Hubbell Law Directory

*MERCED,** Merced Co.

ALLEN, POLGAR, PROIETTI & FAGALDE (AV)

1640 "N" Street, Suite 200, P.O. Box 2184, 95344
Telephone: 209-723-4372
Fax: 209-723-7397
URL: http://www.mercedlaw.com
Mariposa, California Office: 5079 Highway 140. P.O. Box 1907.
Telephone: 209-966-3007.
Fax: 209-742-6353.

MEMBERS OF FIRM

Terry L. Allen
Gary B. Polgar
Donald J. Proietti
Michael A. Fagalde
Jeffrey S. Kaufman
F. Dana Walton (Resident, Mariposa Office)
Brian L. McCabe
Paul C. Lo
Susan L. Albertoni
Karen R. Spinardi

LEGAL SUPPORT PERSONNEL

Timothy J. Kolb (Paralegal)
Conrad J. Kranz (Paralegal)
Bethanne Dowlan (Paralegal)
Karen E. Kaufman (Paralegal)

For full biographical listings, see the Martindale-Hubbell Law Directory

MISSION VIEJO, Orange Co.

THE BUCKLEY FIRM, P.C. (AV)

Suite 200, 26522 La Alameda, 92691
Telephone: 949-348-8300
Facsimile: 949-348-8310
Email: TBF__law@ix.netcom.com
Email: TBFlaw@ix.netcom.com *URL:* http://www.buckleyfirm.com

Lawrence J. Buckley
John W. Klein
Paula Scotland
John R. Beisner

OF COUNSEL

Timothy D. Carlyle
Jonathan C. Cavett
Sam M. Muriella
Edgar C. Smith, III

Reference: Union Bank of California

For full biographical listings, see the Martindale-Hubbell Law Directory

*MODESTO,** Stanislaus Co.

CRABTREE, SCHMIDT, ZEFF, JACOBS & FARRAR (AV)

1100 14th Street, Second Floor, Suite E, P.O. Box 3307, 95353
Telephone: 209-522-5231
Fax: 209-526-0632

MEMBERS OF FIRM

Robert W. Crabtree
Walter J. Schmidt
Thomas D. Zeff
Nan Cohan Jacobs
E. Daniel Farrar

ASSOCIATE

Bonnie J. Anderson

Counsel for: Great American Insurance Co.; United Pacific/Reliance Insurance Co.; Hahn Property Management Corp.; Kemper Insurance Co.; State Farm Fire & Casualty; National Can Co.; Central Valley Production Credit Assn.; WestAmerica Bank.

For full biographical listings, see the Martindale-Hubbell Law Directory

DAMRELL, NELSON, SCHRIMP, PALLIOS & LADINE, A PROFESSIONAL CORPORATION (AV)

1601 I Street, Fifth Floor, 95354
Telephone: 209-526-3500
Fax: 209-526-3534
Email: general@dnspl.com
Oakdale, California Office: 703 West "F" Street, P.O. Drawer C.
Telephone: 209-848-3500.
Fax: 209-848-3400.

Frank C. Damrell (1898-1988)
Duane L. Nelson
Roger M. Schrimp
Steven G. Pallios
Wray F. Ladine
Matthew O. Pacher
Fred A. Silva

James F. Lewis
Michelle Burke McKenzie
Clinton P. Walker
Shana A. Bagley
Amy Elliott Neumann
Stephen V. Imburg
Curtis M. Fiorini
Gerry Preciado
Lisa W. Chao
Khanh T. Tran

Representative Clients: American Honda Motor Co., Inc.; Bronco Wine Co.; E. & J. Gallo Winery; Gallo Glass Co.; Norfolk Southern Corp.; Pep Boys of California, Inc.; W. R. Grace & Co.; United Rentals, Inc.; Tenet Healthcare Corporation.

For full biographical listings, see the Martindale-Hubbell Law Directory

MORRO BAY, San Luis Obispo Co.

OGLE, MERZON & KIRSCHNER (AV)

A Partnership including a Professional Corporation
770 Morro Bay Boulevard, P.O. Box 720, 93443-0720
Telephone: 805-772-7353
Fax: 805-772-7713
San Luis Obispo, California Office: P.O. Box 1855, 93406.
Telephone: 805-543-0295.

Charles E. Ogle (A Professional Corporation)
James B. Merzon
Charles G. Kirschner
Charles Patrick Ogle

For full biographical listings, see the Martindale-Hubbell Law Directory

NEWPORT BEACH, Orange Co.

CAPRETZ & ASSOCIATES (AV)

5000 Birch Street, West Tower Suite 2500, 92660-2139
Telephone: 949-724-3000
Fax: 949-757-2635
URL: http://www.lawyers.com/capretzradcliffe
Email: crlawl@ix.netcom.com *URL:* http://www.CAPRETZ.com

MEMBERS OF FIRM

James T. Capretz

OF COUNSEL

William B. Lawless (Not admitted in CA)

LEGAL SUPPORT PERSONNEL

Sandra L. Koop (Law Clerk)

For full biographical listings, see the Martindale-Hubbell Law Directory

STRADLING YOCCA CARLSON & RAUTH, A PROFESSIONAL CORPORATION (AV)

660 Newport Center Drive, Suite 1600, 92660-6441
Telephone: 949-725-4000
Facsimile: 949-725-4100
Mailing Address: P.O. Box 7680, 92658-7680
Email: info@sycr.com *URL:* http://www.sycr.com
San Francisco, California Office: 44 Montgomery Street, Suite 2950, 94104-4803.
Telephone: 415-283-2240.
Facsimile: 415-283-2255.

Fritz R. Stradling
Nick E. Yocca
C. Craig Carlson
William R. Rauth III
K. C. Schaaf
Richard C. Goodman
John J. Murphy
Thomas P. Clark, Jr.
Ben A. Frydman
David R. McEwen
Paul L. Gale
Rudolph C. Shepard
Robert J. Kane
Bruce C. Stuart
E. Kurt Yeager
Robert J. Whalen
Robert E. Rich
Randall J. Sherman
Bruce Feuchter
Mark J. Huebsch
David G. Casnocha (Resident, San Francisco Office)
Karen A. Ellis
Bruce D. May
Donald J. Hamman
John J. Swigart, Jr.
Celeste Stahl Brady
Douglas S. Brown
Julie McCoy Akins
Lawrence B. Cohn
Stephen T. Freeman
Carol L. Lew
Michael E. Flynn
Julie M. Porter
Gary A. Pemberton
Denise Harbaugh Hering
Jon E. Goetz
Russell A. Miller (Resident, San Francisco Office)
J. Michael Vaughn
John F. Cannon
Douglas J. Evertz
Sean Tierney (Resident, San Francisco Office)
Richard T. Needham
James Robert Roth (Resident, San Francisco Office)
Shivbir S. Grewal

Michael A. Zablocki
Neila R. Bernstein
Nicholas J. Yocca
Cheryl A. Dow
Robert Craig Wallace
Mark L. Skaist
Jeffrey B. Coyne
David E. Lafitte
Andrea Levitan Reeves
Steven M. Hanle
Holly A. Ellis
Christopher D. Ivey
Lee Kolodny
David E. Outwater
Numan J. Siddiqi
Marc G. Alcser
Brent N. Triff
Michele McCormick Troyan
Gary J. Vyneman
Thomas N. Williams
Allison Fong Greenberg
Peter D. Taylor
Christine A. Miller
Sandra A. Galle
Daniel P. Murphy
M. Candice Bryner
Michael D. Cobb
Melanie McCall Houk
Geoffrey M. Moore
Steven R. Pacelli
John R. Williams
Theodore J. Cody
Brian J. Maas
Sandra A. Milligan
Jason H. Anderson
John C. Kang
LeeAnn B. Napolitana (Resident, San Francisco Office)
Allison E. Burns
Daniel Conway Flynn
Brian Forbath

(See Next Column)

Timothy F. O'Brien, Jr.
Timothy N. Stickler
Gayle Davis
Jennifer A. Trusso
Kinnari P. Shah (Resident, San Francisco Office)
Jeffrey F. Allen (Not admitted in CA)
Thong (Tom) D. Le
Lara A. Saunders
Kathryn A. Deutsch (Not admitted in CA)
Edward S. Kim

OF COUNSEL

John E. Breckenridge
Rena C. Stone
Robert J. Matthews
Michael K. Maher
Cynthia R. Maher

For full biographical listings, see the Martindale-Hubbell Law Directory

*OAKLAND,** Alameda Co.

BURNHAM & BROWN, A PROFESSIONAL CORPORATION (AV)

1901 Harrison Street, 11th Floor, P.O. Box 119, 94604
Telephone: 510-444-6800
Fax: 510-835-6666

Arthur Jay Moore, Jr. (1918-1984)
Clark J. Burnham
Gregory D. Brown
Robert J. Lyman
Eric R. Haas
Scott C. Finch
Steven M. Marden
Monica Dell'Osso
Susan Feldsted Halman
Gary R. Selvin
James L. Wraith
Richard J. Finn
John J. Verber
Cathy L. Arias
Thomas M. Downey
Paul D. Caleo
David H. Waters
David S. Webster
Bradley M. Zamczyk

SPECIAL COUNSEL

Mark A. Koop

Daniel B. Alweiss
Heather D. Bihr
James F. Blake
Kimberly Ann Blake
Kurt R. Bockes
Robert M. Bodzin
Caryn Bortnick
Lisa M. Cappelluti
Jeanine K. Clasen
Keri L. Faseler
Pamela Fastiff Ellman
Susan E. Firtch
Jeffrey Stephen Gillespie
Alison F. Greene
James F. Hodgkins
John K. Kirby
Joanna MacQueen
Gregory H. McCormick
John P. McGill
Paola C. McNamara
Molly J. Mrowka
Ulla M. Pajala
Dean Pollack
Walter C. Rundin, III
Jennifer J. Sarkozy
Beverly J. Smith
Darrell T. Thompson
Sarah Valentine

Representative Clients: The Travelers Insurance Co.; U.S. Fidelity & Guaranty Co.; Home Insurance Co.; County of Alameda; City of Livermore; Shell Oil Co.

For full biographical listings, see the Martindale-Hubbell Law Directory

FILICE, BROWN, EASSA & MCLEOD, LLP (AV)

1999 Harrison Street, 18th Floor, 94612
Telephone: 510-444-3131
Fax: 510-839-7940

Gennaro A. Filice III
Eugene Brown, Jr.
Robert D. Eassa
Bruce E. McLeod
Raymond J. Bergez
Nicholas D. Kayhan
John A. De Pasquale
Peter A. Strotz
Richard V. Normington III
Amee A. Mikacich
Stephen J. Valen

Jennifer Walker O'Sullivan
Jason J. Curliano
Kristin Ashurst Hughes
Lisa M. Brown
Jennifer K. Pearce
Constance J. McNeil
Michael H. Kim
Carla M. Nakata
Katrina C. Decker

OF COUNSEL

Barrie Engel
Paul R. Johnson

Representative Clients: AstraZeneca, Inc.; Chevron Corp.; Dow Chemical Co.; Fort Motor Co.; ICI Americas, Inc.; Long's Drug Stores California; PPG Industries, Inc.; Rhodia, Inc.; Tosco Refining Co.; Unocal Corp.

For full biographical listings, see the Martindale-Hubbell Law Directory

FITZGERALD, ABBOTT & BEARDSLEY LLP (AV)

A Partnership including Professional Corporations
1221 Broadway, 21st Floor, P.O. Box 12867, 94602-2867
Telephone: 510-451-3300
Telecopy: 510-451-1527
Email: inbox@fablaw.com *URL:* http://www.fablaw.com

(See Next Column)

FITZGERALD, ABBOTT & BEARDSLEY LLP, *Oakland—Continued*

MEMBERS OF FIRM

Robert M. Fitzgerald (1858-1934)
Carl H. Abbott (1867-1933)
Charles A. Beardsley (1882-1963)
James C. Soper (Inc.)
Philip M. Jelley (Inc.)
Gerald C. Smith
Lawrence R. Shepp
Richard T. White
Michael P. Walsh
J. Brittain Habegger
Virginia Palmer
Timothy H. Smallsreed
Barry H. Epstein
Stephen M. Judson
Stephen M. Williams
Kristin A. Pace
Michael M.K. Sebree
Sarah E. Robertson

ASSOCIATES

Philip E. Drysdale
Jay M. Goldman
Paul Stanton Kibel
Michael S. Ward
Fatima Brunson Evans
Dena R. Graff

Attorneys for: Peterson Tractor Co.; Sunset View Cemetery Assn.; Bigge Crane & Rigging Corp.; Gillig Corp.
Local Counsel for: Exxon Corp.

For full biographical listings, see the Martindale-Hubbell Law Directory

HAIMS, MACGOWAN, VALENTINO & PEEBLES, L.L.P. (AV)

490 Grand Avenue, 94610
Telephone: 510-835-0500
Facsimile: 510-835-2833

MEMBERS OF FIRM

Arnold B. Haims
Clyde L. MacGowan
Caroline N. Valentino
Dianne D. Peebles

For full biographical listings, see the Martindale-Hubbell Law Directory

ONTARIO, San Bernardino Co.

COVINGTON & CROWE LLP (AV)

1131 West Sixth Street, P.O. Box 1515, 91762
Telephone: 909-983-9393
Fax: 909-391-6762
URL: http://www.covcrowe.com

MEMBERS OF FIRM

Maurice G. Covington (1908-1997)
Harold A. Bailin (1930-1988)
Samuel P. Crowe
George W. Porter
Robert E. Dougherty
Donald G. Haslam
Robert F. Schauer
Jette R. Anderson
Audrey A. Perri
Tracy L. Tibbals
Melanie Fisch
R. Douglas Donesky
Tammy S. Jager
Katrina West

ASSOCIATES

J. Michael Kaler
Eric S. Vail
Khymberli S. Apaloo

OF COUNSEL

Edward A. Hopson

For full biographical listings, see the Martindale-Hubbell Law Directory

OXNARD, Ventura Co.

ENGLAND & COHEN, LLP (AV)

300 Esplanade Drive Financial Plaza Tower, Suite 380, 93030
Telephone: 805-983-8181; California Toll Free: 800-675-6166
Fax: 805-983-8813

MEMBERS OF FIRM

Robert B. England
Randall A. Cohen

For full biographical listings, see the Martindale-Hubbell Law Directory

NORDMAN, CORMANY, HAIR & COMPTON (AV)

1000 Town Center Drive, Sixth Floor, P.O. Box 9100, 93031-9100
Telephone: 805-485-1000
Telecopier: 805-988-8387; 988-8397
Email: atty@nchc.com *URL:* http://www.nchc.com

Ben E. Nordman, Founder (1913-1985)

MEMBERS OF FIRM

William H. Hair
Robert L. Compton
Marc L. Charney
Ronald H. Gill
Larry L. Hines
Kenneth M. High, Jr.
Michael C. O'Brien
Laura K. McAvoy
Randall H. George
Janet Anne Reese
Paul W. Kurzeka
Anthony H. Trembley
Jonathan Fraser Light
William E. Winfield
Gerald M. Etchingham
Christopher K. Kitasaki
Scott B. Samsky
Guy C. Parvex, Jr.
John A. Slezak
Susan M. Seemiller
Glenn J. Dickinson
Nancy Miller

OF COUNSEL

Ralph L. Cormany
Louis A. Cappadona

(See Next Column)

ASSOCIATES

Terry Anne Buchanan
Lorraine H. Clark
Ilene Friend Mickens
Dien Le
Ellen Marie Bass

Representative Clients: Berry Petroleum Co.; BRE Properties, Inc.; Kmart Corp.; Saticoy Lemon Assn.; The Procter & Gamble Paper Products Co.; The Prudential Insurance Company of America; Saticoy Sanitary District; Ojai Valley Sanitary District; Carpinteria Sanitary District; Bell Canyon Community Services District.

For full biographical listings, see the Martindale-Hubbell Law Directory

PALM SPRINGS, Riverside Co.

SCHLECHT, SHEVLIN & SHOENBERGER, A LAW CORPORATION (AV)

801 East Tahquitz Canyon Way, Suite 100, P.O. Box 2744, 92263-2744
Telephone: 760-320-7161
Facsimile: 760-323-1758
Email: ssslaw@gte.net *URL:* http://www.ssslaw.com

James M. Schlecht
John C. Shevlin
Jon A. Shoenberger
Daniel T. Johnson

David Darrin

Representative Clients: Outdoor Resorts of America; The Escrow Connection; Palm Hills Land Corp.; Shadowrock; Palm Springs Marquis.

For full biographical listings, see the Martindale-Hubbell Law Directory

PALO ALTO, Santa Clara Co.

BAKER & MCKENZIE (AV)

660 Hansen Way, P.O. Box 60309, 94304
Telephone: (650) 856-2400
Intn'l. Dialing: (1-650) 856-2400
Facsimile: (1-650) 856-9299
URL: http://www.bakerinfo.com
Associated Offices of Baker & McKenzie in: Almaty, Amsterdam, Bahrain, Baku, Bangkok, Barcelona, Beijing, Berlin, Bogotá, Brasília, Brussels, Budapest, Buenos Aires, Cairo, Caracas, Chicago, Dallas, Düsseldorf, Frankfurt, Geneva, Hanoi, Ho Chi Minh City, Hong Kong, Houston, Hsinchu, Juárez, Kiev, London, Madrid, Manila, Melbourne, México City, Miami, Milan, Monterrey, Moscow, München, New York, Paris, Prague, Rio de Janeiro, Riyadh, Rome, St. Petersburg, San Diego, San Francisco, Santiago, São Paulo, Singapore, Stockholm, Sydney, Taipei, Tijuana, Tokyo, Toronto, Valencia, Warsaw, Washington, D.C. and Zürich.
Correspondent Law Firm: Hadiputranto, Hadinoto & Partners, Jakarta.

MEMBERS OF FIRM

Cole R. Capener
Robin A. Chesler
Maurice S. Emmer
Tod L. Gamlen
Cynthia L. Jackson
John C. Klotsche (Not admitted in CA)
Antoinette F. Konski
Michael J. Madda
Susan H. Nycum
John M. Peterson, Jr.
J. Pat Powers
André M. Saltoun
Gary D. Sprague

NATIONAL PARTNERS

Jon M. Appleton
Michael Bumbaca

OF COUNSEL

Mary E. Wynne

ASSOCIATES

Eric H. Anderson
Aimee E. Arost
Andrew P. Crousore (Not admitted in CA)
Susan F. Eandi
Scott H. Frewing
Andrew J. Gottlieb
Rachel Hersey
Stewart R. Lipeles
Louise C. Ober
Taylor S. Reid
Joanne L. Siu
Nicholas L. Spyros, Jr.
Michelle J. Wachs

For full biographical listings, see the Martindale-Hubbell Law Directory

BROBECK, PHLEGER & HARRISON LLP (AV)

A Partnership including a Professional Corporation
Two Embarcadero Place, 2200 Geng Road, 94303
Telephone: 650-424-0160
Facsimile: 650-496-2885
Email: info@brobeck.com *URL:* http://www.brobeck.com/
San Francisco, California Office: Spear Street Tower, One Market.
Telephone: 415-442-0900.
Facsimile: 415-442-0900.
Los Angeles, California Office: 550 South Hope Street.
Telephone: 213-489-4060.
Facsimile: 213-745-3345.
San Diego, California Office: 550 West C Street, Suite 1300.
Telephone: 619-234-1966.
Facsimile: 619-236-1403.
Irvine, California Office: 38 Technology Drive.
Telephone: 949-790-6300.
Facsimile: 949-790-6301.

(See Next Column)

BROBECK, PHLEGER & HARRISON LLP—*Continued*

Austin, Texas Office: 301 Congress Avenue, Suite 1200.
Telephone: 512-477-5495.
Facsimile: 512-477-5813.
Denver, Colorado Office: 370 Interlocken Boulevard, Suite 500.
Telephone: 303-410-2000.
Facsimile: 303-410-2199.
New York, N.Y. Office: 1633 Broadway, 47th Floor.
Telephone: 212-581-1600.
Facsimile: 212-586-7878.
Washington, D.C. Office: 701 Pennsylvania Avenue, NW, Suite 220.
Telephone: 202-220-6000.
Facsimile: 202-824-0949.
London, England Office: Brobeck Hale and Dorr International, Hasilwood House, 60 Bishopsgate, London EC2N 4AJ.
Telephone: 011 44 171 638 6688.
Facsimile: 011 44 171 638 5888.

OFFICE LEADER

Therese A. Mrozek

PARTNERS

William C. Anderson
Mark H. Boxer
Armando Castro
Patricia G. Copeland
Timothy R. Curry
S. James DiBernardo
J. Stephan Dolezalek
James J. Elacqua
Noemi C. Espinosa
David M. Furbush
Daniel R. Hansen
Rod J. Howard
Meredith Nelson Landy
Warren T. Lazarow
Curtis L. Mo (Not admitted in CA)
Luther Kent Orton
Michael A. Plumleigh
Zaitun Poonja
Karen Y. Spencer

SENIOR COUNSEL

Thomas H. Carlson
Karen H. Peteros

OF COUNSEL

Stephen M. Kociol
Melinda Collins Riechert
Gary Shapiro
Julie A. Vehrenkamp

ASSOCIATES

Craig Y. Allison
Paul J. André
Jonathan D. Baker
Robert J. Blanch, Jr.
Peter S. Buckland
William Wei-Li Chuang
Richard J. Colosimo (Not admitted in CA)
Brian E. Covotta
Heather M. Cox
Michael C. Doran
Michelle Falkoff
David Allen Foster
Carol R. Freeman
Colby R. Gartin
Hanna Casper George
Henock F. Gessesse
Nicholas S. Gikkas
Jonathan Gilliland
Scot A. Griffin
Christina Tavella Hall
Daniel R. Harris
Kimberley Erin Henningsen
Pamela B. Hiatt
Sheryl L. Howell
Andrew R. Hull
Gregory C. Jackson
Lee David Jackson (Not admitted in CA)
Brian L. Johnsrud
Rahul Kapoor (Not admitted in CA)
Michael B. King
Lisa Kobialka
Robert Kramer (Not admitted in CA)
Richard C. Leska
J. Omar Mahmud
David A. Makarechian (Not admitted in CA)
Krista J. Martinelli
Gregory W. Mathis
Richard B. Meamber (Not admitted in CA)
John S. Mills (Not admitted in CA)
David G. Odrich
Peter D. Rosenthal
Anna Ruiz Rothbart
Valerie L. Russell
Jeannine Y. Sano
Vahe H. Sarrafian
Valerie Schulthies
Hooman Shahlavi
Jonathan P. Shanberge (Not admitted in CA)
Jonathan G. Shapiro
Paul L. Sieben
Mary Ann Stretch
Andrew N. Thomases
Alan K. Tse
Allyson M. Willoughby
Janet Lee Wilson
Joseph K. Wyatt
Elizabeth A. R. Yee

For full biographical listings, see the Martindale-Hubbell Law Directory

COOLEY GODWARD LLP (AV)

Five Palo Alto Square, 3000 El Camino Real, 94306-2155
Telephone: 650-843-5000
Fax: 650-857-0663
Email: webmaster@cooley.com *URL:* http://www.cooley.com
San Francisco, California Office: 20th Floor, One Maritime Plaza.
Telephone: 415-693-2000.
Fax: 415-951-3699.
San Diego, California Office: 4365 Executive Drive, Suite 1100.
Telephone: 619-550-6000.
Fax: 619-453-3555.
Menlo Park, California Office: 3000 Sand Hill Road, Building 3, Suite 230.
Telephone: 650-843-5000.
Fax: 650-854-2691.
Boulder, Colorado Office: 2595 Canyon Boulevard, Suite 250.
Telephone: 303-546-4000.
Fax: 303-546-4099.

(See Next Column)

Denver, Colorado Office: One Tabor Center, 1200 17th Street, Suite 2100.
Telephone: 303-606-4800.
Fax: 303-606-4899.
Kirkland, Washington Office: 5200 Carillon Point.
Telephone: 425-893-7700.
Fax: 425-893-7777.
Reston, Virginia Office: 2002 Edmund Halley Drive, Suite 300.
Telephone: 703-262-8000.
Fax: 703-262-8100.

PARTNERS

Frederick D. Baron
Brandon D. Baum
Lois K. Benes
Robert J. Benson
Lee F. Benton
Robert J. Brigham
Richard E. Climan
Janet L. Cullum
Julia Loewy Davidson
Scott D. Devereaux
John Charles Dwyer
Stephen W. Fackler
Keith A. Flaum
William S. Freeman
Michelle Greer Galloway
Matthew B. Hemington
Willis E. Higgins
Suzanne Sawochka Hooper
Ronald L. Jacobson
Eric C. Jensen
Robert L. Jones
Barclay J. Kamb
James C. Kitch
Anthony R. Klein
Barbara A. Kosacz
Martin L. Lagod
Tharan Gregory Lanier
Andrei M. Manoliu
Deborah A. Marshall
Pamela J. Martinson
Alan C. Mendelson
Timothy J. Moore
Stephen C. Neal
Craig P. Opperman
Timothy G. Patterson
Anne Harris Peck
Mark B. Pitchford
Patrick A. Pohlen
Jeffrey G. Randall
Julie M. Robinson
Diane Wilkins Savage
Nicholas J. Spaeth (Not admitted in CA)
Michael Stern
Gregory C. Tenhoff
William S. Veatch
Brett D. White
Toni Pryor Wise
Darryl M. Woo
Christopher O. B. Wright

SPECIAL COUNSEL

Frederick J. Dorey
Shelley Precivale Eberle
Richard M. Goldman
James R. Jones
Peter R. Leal
Tom M. Moran
Gary H. Ritchey
Deidre Lynn Sparks
Gretchen R. Stroud
Andrea H. Vachss
Marianne T. Wolf

OF COUNSEL

Glenn J. Borromeo
Brian C. Cunningham
John W. Girvin, Jr.
Richard L. Neeley

ASSOCIATES

Matthias Alder
Kathleen N. Allen
Gregg H. Alton
Brian J. Ankenbrandt
Sean K. Arend
Nina M. Ashton
Laura A. Berezin
Luke J. Bergstrom (Not admitted in CA)
Susan D. Berney-Key
Ray Bilbeaux
Todd S. Bontemps
Gianna M. Bosko
J. Derek Boswell
Wendy Brenner
John P Brockland (Not admitted in CA)
Deborah L. Budach
James T. Bushnell
Linda A. F. Callison
Andrea R. Cohen
Vincent Colianni
Erika C. Collins
Carolyn L. Craig
L. Michelle Cutrer
P. Francois de Villiers
Jennifer Fonner DiNucci
Jason Doren
Brian Draves
David T. Emerson
Thomas L. Ewing
Stuart A. Fagin
Lisa A. Feldman
Molly Brown Forstall
Edward A. Frueh
Eric Goldman
Lynne M. Golochnik
Kevin D. Gonzalez (Not admitted in CA)
Alan K. Grebene
Tanya Greene (Not admitted in CA)
Nina Grover
Judith A. Hasko
Evelyn G. Heilbrunn
Anne M. Hilbert
Gordon K. Ho
Colin D. Horst
Peter Hsieh
Paul D. Huie
Rujiporn Tita Kanthatham (Not admitted in CA)
Larissa A.J. Kehoe
Edward B. Kile
Rachel E. Kosmal
Stephanie N. Kroon
David J. Lawson (Not admitted in CA)
David N. Lawson
Janet Lee
Wendy L. Lee (Not admitted in CA)
David E. Lillevand
Marcella Lillis
Margaret C. Livnah
Annie O. Loo
Deborah J. Ludewig
Hilary Luros
Thomas L. MacMitchell
Lisa A. Mammel
John D. Marple
John T. McKenna
Faina Medzonsky
Jason A. Mendelson
Susan L. Meyer
Jana R. Miller
Michael D. Morehead
Michele E. Moreland
Todd C. Murtha
Tahir J. Naim
Glenn Gerard Nash
Jeremy D. Nelson
Max P. Ochoa
James Oh
William R. Pierznik
Lori Ellis Ploeger (Not admitted in CA)
Patrick C. Pope
William F. Porter
Marya A. Postner
Mary E. Powell

(See Next Column)

COOLEY GODWARD LLP, *Palo Alto—Continued*

ASSOCIATES (Continued)

Paul T. Quinlan (Not admitted in CA)
Rakesh Ramde
Eric M. Reifschneider
Ricardo Rodriguez
Mark V. Roeder
Sarah Greden Rogers
Stephen N. Rosenfield
Gregory Alan Rutchik
Gurjeev K. Sachdeva
Cheryl L. Sakowski
Robert M. Saman
Alexis Schatten
Charles A. Schwab
Luma Serrano
Joanne Marshall Shea
Matthew W. Sonsini
Debbi R. Stern
Christopher J. Sundermeier
Paul H. Sunshine
Jonathan H. Takei
Marilyn N. Taketa
Barbara E. Tanzillo
Theresa V. Tao
Andrew C. Temkin
Timothy S. Teter
Anthony J. Tilghman III
Vicki Ting
Todd Torr
Joi C. True
Tomas C. Tovar
Jennifer A. Ulveling
David M. Urso
Julia Vax
Erin M. Verneris
Marjorie C. Wagman
Kathryn A. Walker
Michael L. Weiner
Clay C. Wheeler
Donna M. Whooley
Julie D. Wicklund (Not admitted in United States)
John F. Wicks
David L. Wilke
Stuart K. Wilks
Lara A. Williams
Jennifer L. Wong
Alison Wright
Ya-Ting Yang
Robyn Zorea

PATENT AGENTS

Alexandra J. Baran
James A. Bradburne
Karen E. Flick
Michelle S. Rhyu

LEGAL SUPPORT PERSONNEL

SPECIALISTS

Shellie Anderson
Steven Dean
Jane R. Johnstone
Linda M. Rigas

SENIOR PARALEGALS

Mary E. Ahern
Laura A. Carey
Maryan C. Carroll
Susan E. Gonzalez
Juel D. Gudaitis
Dina K. Kanaya
Janet L. LaPointe
Sally B. Lavecchia
Richard M. Renfree
Eric J. Steiner
Kristine S. Tamashiro
Gary A. Thunell
Valerie Vorres
Diane Wallis

For full biographical listings, see the Martindale-Hubbell Law Directory

GRAHAM & JAMES LLP (AV)

600 Hansen Way, 94304
Telephone: 650-856-6500
Telecopier: 650-856-3619
Email: thuber@gj.com *URL:* http://www.gj.com
Other offices located in: San Francisco, Los Angeles, Orange County and Sacramento, California; Seattle, Washington; Washington, D.C.; New York, New York; Milan, Italy; Beijing, China; Tokyo, Japan; London, England.
Associated Offices: Deacons Graham & James, Hong Kong, Sydney, Melbourne, Brisbane, Perth and Canberra, Australia.
Affiliated Offices: Deacons Graham & James, Hanoi and Ho Chi Minh City, Vietnam; Taipei, Taiwan and Bangkok, Thailand; In association with Dewi Soeharto & Rekan, Jakarta, Indonesia; Graham & James in affiliation with Taylor Joynson Garrett, London, England, Bucharest, Romania and Brussels, Belgium; Kau, Dusseldorf, Germany; Mishare M. Al-Ghazali & Partners, Safat, Kuwait; Law Firm of Salah Al-Hejailan, Jeddah and Riyadh, Saudi Arabia; Yeo Wee Kiong & Partners, Singapore.

MEMBERS OF FIRM

Donald R. Davis
David S. Elkins
Ronald S. Lemieux
Robert E. Patterson
Thomas R. Radcliffe

COUNSEL

Michael E. Sobel

RESIDENT ASSOCIATES

Nicole Kamian Bilbeaux
Cecelia A. Gassner
Brien B. Kirk
Bruce W. Phillips
Bruce J. Rome
Benjamin M. Rubin
Marc A. Sockol

For full biographical listings, see the Martindale-Hubbell Law Directory

GRAY CARY WARE & FREIDENRICH LLP (AV)

Gray Cary Established in 1927
Ware & Freidenrich Established in 1969
400 Hamilton Avenue, 94301-1825
Telephone: 650-833-2000
Telex: 348-372
Telecopier: 650-327-3699
Email: info@graycary.com *URL:* http://www.graycary.com
San Diego, California Office: 401 B Street, Suite 1700, 92101-4297
619-699-2700.
Telecopier: 619-236-1048.

(See Next Column)

San Diego/Golden Triangle, California Office: 4365 Executive Drive, Suite 1600, 92121.
Telephone: 858-677-1400.
Telecopier: 858-677-1477.
La Jolla, California Office: 1200 Prospect Street, Suite 575, 92037-3610.
Telephone: 858-456-3000.
Telecopier: 858-456-3075.
El Centro, California Office: 1224 State Street, P.O. Box 2890, 92244.
Telephone: 760-353-6140.
Telecopier: 760-353-6228.
San Francisco, California Office: 139 Townsend Street, Suite 400, 94107-1922.
Telephone: 415-836-2500.
Telecopier: 415-836-9220.
Austin, Texas Office: 100 Congress Avenue, Suite 1440, 78701-4042.
Telephone: 512-457-7000.
Telecopier: 512-457-7070.
Sacramento, California Office: 400 Capitol Mall, Suite 2100, 95814.
Telephone: 916-930-3200.
Fax: 916-930-3201.

James E. Anderson
Paul A. Blumenstein
Hope A. Case
Lawrence A. Cogan
Steven G. Cohen
David Colker
Edward P. Davis, Jr.
David Henry Dolkas
Maureen S. Dorney
Russell S. Elmer
Ian N. Feinberg
Mark Fowler
Diane Holt Frankle
Thomas M. French
Thomas W. Furlong
Gregory M. Gallo
Penny Howe Gallo
Françoise Gilbert
Hugh Goodwin, Jr.
David F. Gross
John B. Hale
Linda M. Hayes
William H. Hoffman
David Alan Hubb
Jeffrey R. Ii
Margaret H. Kavalaris
James M. Koshland
Jeffrey J. Lederman
Patrick J. McGaraghan
Marvin Meisel
Martin H. Myers
Nels Raymond Nelsen
David J. Plewa
James Pooley
Mark F. Radcliffe
Arthur C. Rinsky
Bradley J. Rock
Robert T. Russell
Bruce E. Schaeffer
John W. Schlicher
Daniel K. Seubert
John R. Shuman, Jr.
Wayne P. Sobon
Joe C. Sorenson
Jay M. Spitzen
Lillian G. Stenfeldt
Dennis C. Sullivan
R. Allyn Taylor
Craig M. Tighe
Jeffrey A. Trant
Andrew Paul Valentine
Richard I. Yankwich
Barry N. Young
Andrew D. Zeif (Not admitted in CA)

Whitney Pollack Ames
Jeffrey D. Aronson
Julie M. Bardacke
Kathleen Salas Bass
Edward H. Batts
Carole H. Bellis
Marcy Berkman
David S. Bloch
Jeffrey Burke
Susan E. Bunnell
Stephen O. Carlson
Kathleen Cattani
James M. Chadwick
Pinaki Chakravorty
Lee Cheng
William W. Choe
David Chow
Daniel R. Cook
Dan W. Cooperider
Jenelle C. L. Cox
Andrea J. Cummings
Pamela R. Davis
W. Russell Davis
M. Elizabeth Day
Brian V. Donnelly
John M. Fogg
Virginia Hewitt Fogg
William J. Frimel
Lynn E. Fullerton
Heather L. Gaede
Bradley J. Gersich
William G. Goldman
Benjamin G. Griebe
Amanda Groves
Mary M. Hamaker
Julie Fabian Haniger
Michelle R. Harbottle
Maureen C. Harrison
H. Katerina Hertzog
Broady R. Hodder (Not admitted in CA)
Matthew E. Horsley
Julie L. Hsu
Victoria N. Kaempf
Kris M. Kamali
Chirag V. Karia
Adam C. Kates
Esther S. Kim
Lawrence C. King
Allison P. Koehler
Paul K. Lauher
Victoria W-Y Lee
Kim Levy
Bill Littlewood
Timothy W. Lohse
Craig Malina
Christine McCarthy
S. Tye Menser
Sean E. Morley
Michael P. Mount
Marilyn M. Munoz
Elizabeth M. O'Callahan
L. Scott Oliver
Narendra B. Patel
Virginia Pearcy
Marvin G. Peña
Jon C. Perry
Wendy M. Pizarro
Haleh Rahjoo
Sally J. Rau
Magan Ray
Susan D. Resley
David B. Rockower
Joshua E. rosenfeld
Michael G. Schwartz
Eliane R. Setton
Shaban Shakoori
Jacqueline R. Sparks
Jill Andrews Sprague (Not admitted in CA)
Michael C. Standlee
David R. Stevens
Kimberly N. Van Voorhis
Zoila E. Villacorta
Derek J. Westberg
Jason A. Whong

(See Next Column)

GRAY CARY WARE & FREIDENRICH LLP—*Continued*

Megan Rae Whyman
Kristi A. Wilkens
(Not admitted in CA)
Aileen G. Wu
Heather Yohn

RETIRED PARTNERS

John Freidenrich
Leonard Ware

OF COUNSEL

Peter M. Astiz
Audrey Barris
Joan S. Kato
Nicole Lance

Representative Clients: Automobile Club of South California; Bank of America; Brooktree Corp.; C. A. Parr (Agencies), Ltd.; IMED; Pacific Bell; McMillin Development Co.; Scripps Clinic and Research Found.; SeaWorld, Inc.; Underwriters at Lloyds.

For full biographical listings, see the Martindale-Hubbell Law Directory

---

WILSON SONSINI GOODRICH & ROSATI, PROFESSIONAL CORPORATION (AV)

650 Page Mill Road, 94304-1050
Telephone: 650-493-9300
Telex: 345500 wilson pla
Fax: 650-493-6811
Email: wsgr@wsgr.com *URL:* http://www.wsgr.com
Kirkland, Washington Office: 5300 Carillon Point, 98033.
Telephone: 425-576-5800.
Fax: 425-576-5899.
Austin, Texas Office: 8911 Capitol of Texas Highway North, Suite 3350, 78759.
Telephone: 512-338-5400.
Fax: 512-338-5499.

Aaron J. Alter
Fred W. Alvarez
Aileen L. Arrieta
Alan K. Austin
Jonathan Axelrad
Michael Barclay
Suzanne Y. Bell
David J. Berger
Steven V. Bernard
Kurt J. Berney
Steven L. Berson
Mark A. Bertelsen
Jerome F. Birn, Jr.
Kathleen Borrero Bloch
Jeffrey M. Bloom
Steven E. Bochner
Mark E. Bonham
Donald E. Bradley
Harry B. Bremond
Andrew P. Bridges
Robert D. Brownell
Steve L. Camahort
Trevor J. Chaplick
Peter P. Chen
Douglas J. Clark
Robert Claassen
Bruce A. Cohen
Kenneth A. Clark
Douglas H. Collom
Charles T. C. Compton
Susan A. Creighton
Leo P. Cunningham
Michael J. Danaher
Paul Davis
Selim B. Day
Thomas C. DeFilipps
James A. DiBoise
Michael S. Dorf
Francis W. Dubreuil
Keith E. Eggleton
Nevan C. Elam
Vera M. Elson
Brian C. Erb
Boris Feldman
Robert P. Feldman
Chris F. Fennell
Mark D. Flanagan
Elizabeth R. Flint
Herbert P. Fockler
John A. Fore
Roger Edward George
Selwyn B. Goldberg
Sarah Ann Good
John B. Goodrich
Marc E. Gottschalk
Irwin R. Gross
Dana Haviland
Andrew J. Hirsch
David M. Hoffmeister
Ivan H. Humphreys
Gail Clayton Husick
Robert B. Jack
Neil A. Jeffries
Terry T. Johnson
Michael J. Kennedy
David A. Killam
Catherine S. Kirkman
Thomas Christopher Klein
Jared L. Kopel
Martin W. Korman
Peter LaBoskey
Michael A. Ladra
David L. Larson
Robert P. Latta
Douglas M. Laurice
Nina Locker
Jose F. Macias
Page Mailliard
Katharine A. Martin
Henry P. Massey, Jr.
J. Casey McGlynn
Bruce M. McNamara
Christopher D. Mitchell
Daniel R. Mitz
Michael J. Murphy
Bradford C. O'Brien
Judith Mayer O'Brien
Michael Occhiolini
Michael J. O'Donnell
Michael Okada
James C. Otteson
Donna M. Petkanics
David Priebe
Gary L. Reback
Mark L. Reinstra
Susan Pasquinelli Reinstra
Paul H. Roeder
John V. Roos
Ulrico S. Rosales
Mario M. Rosati
Michele E. Rose
Ronald M. Roth
Alisande M. Rozynko
Ignacio E. Salceda
Robert D. Sanchez
Jeffrey D. Saper
Elizabeth M. Saunders
Steven M. Schatz
Arthur F. Schneiderman
Michael L. Schultz
Timothy T. Scott
David J. Segre
Stephanie Sharron
John T. Sheridan
Ron E. Shulman
Kenneth M. Siegel
Laurie B. Smilan
Larry W. Sonsini
Timothy J. Sparks
Roger D. Stern

(See Next Column)

David S. Steuer
Blair W. Stewart, Jr.
Rodney G. Strickland, Jr.
J. Robert Suffoletta, Jr.
Debra S. Summers
Barry E. Taylor
Bruce G. Vanyo
Issac J. Vaughn
Ann Yvonne Walker
David J. Weitz
Kenneth B. Wilson
Lloyd Winawer
Neil Jay Wolff
Eric W. Wright
Howard S. Zeprun

COUNSEL

Stephen P. Berke
Christian L. Castle
Gerald G. Chacon, Jr.
Douglas Keith Krohn
Mark Parnes
Richard L. Picheny
Joanne R. Scully

SPECIAL COUNSEL

Megan J. Carroll
Janice Leyrer Fall
Cheryl Weisbard Foung
Monica Mucchetti
Jon O. Nygaard
Ian J. Stock
Kimberly Paul Zapata

David Abraham
Theodore Allegaert
Jason R. Altieri
Linda Graham Alvarez
(Not admitted in CA)
Paul D. Anawalt
Bryan C. Anderson
Richard S. Arnold, Jr.
Robert C. Atherton III
Richard S. Au
(Not admitted in CA)
Jon Christopher Avina
Carl A. Baier
Steven S. Baik
Colleen Bal
Thomas I. Barnett
Ralph J. Barry
Shantanu Basu
Mark B. Baudler
Mark D. Beariault
(Not admitted in CA)
Julie Ann Bell
Steven J. Benerofe
Braden L. Berg
Peter H. Bergman
Allison L. Berry
Whit Bissell
Jill K. Bjorkholm
Jonathan M. Block
Elizabeth A. Blomberg
Lauren I. Boro
Jason D. Borrevik
Susan Bower
David R. Bowman
Jill Hubbard Bowman
Kelly R. Boyd
David R. Boyko
Michelle N. Branch
Jason M. Brady
Jason David Brandwene
Mark D. Brazeal
Cynthia T. Bright
Judith E. Brown
Thomas G. Brown
John J. Bruckner
Noah A. Brumfield
David Richard Burtt
Deanna M. Butler
Jennifer L. Cahill
Mary Cabanski-Evers
Gidon M. Caine
Mark J. Casper
Michael D. Celio
C. Paul Chalmers
Jonathan G. Chance
(Not admitted in CA)
Carmen I-Hua Chang
Deborah M. Chang
Michael D. Charney
Pablo L. Chavez
Oliver K. Chee
Priya Sara Cherian
Hanley Chew
Taylor B. Chi
Gregory Chin
Roger J. Chin
Gina M. Christopher
Benjamin L. Chun
Tobias D. Chun
(Not admitted in CA)
Patrick S. Chung
Ariana M. Chung-Han
Stefan V. Clulow
Wendy Theophilos Coleman
Anton Theodore Commissaris
Krystilyn Corbett
Angela Corsilles
(Not admitted in CA)
Barbara B. Courtney
David B. Crawford
James C. Creigh
Norman R. Cruz
Linda M. Cuny
Robert E. Curry, III
Joseph F. Daniels
Lisa A. Davis
Robert E. Dawson
(Not admitted in CA)
Robert G. Day
David Dayan
(Not admitted in CA)
Michael A. De Angelis
Kenneth J. Deleon
David Thomas Della Rocca
(Not admitted in CA)
Robert S. Devens, Jr.
Sanjiv S. Dhawan
Dale A.J. Dietrich (Not admitted in the United States)
Kristin A. Dillehay
Bret M. DiMarco
Adam R. Dolinko
Michael H. Domesick
(Not admitted in CA)
Thomas M. Dono, Jr.
(Not admitted in CA)
Darin H. Donovan
Tracy Donsky
Thomas D. Drescher
(Not admitted in CA)
Tamara Duncan
Cynthia A. Dy
Margo M. Eakin
Joseph M. Eandi
Kent Wycliffe Easter
Dale M. Edmondson
Sara L. Eisner
(Not admitted in CA)
Michael S. Ellis
U. P. Peter Eng
Peri B. Erlanger
Wade Estey
Gail Etzion
Jeannie Y. Evans
Geoffrey M. Ezgar
Stacy Amity Feld
Bradley L. Finkelstein
Eric J. Finseth
Mark E. Fleisher
Diane Jean Fong
Regina M.C. Fong
(Not admitted in CA)
Kimberley A. Fonner
Brenda R. Frank
Joseph Douglas Fuqua, Jr.
David Y. Gan
Gary M. Gansle
Alice C. Garber
Kristin A. Garcia
Robert R. Ghoorah
Patricia L. Gibbon
Stephen E. Gillette
Josh Goldfoot
Laura R. Grant

(See Next Column)

WILSON SONSINI GOODRICH & ROSATI PROFESSIONAL CORPORATION, *Palo Alto—Continued*

Jason L. Gray
Lisa C. Green
Cynthia M. Greene
(Not admitted in CA)
Michelle D. Gregory
Richard L. Gregory, Jr.
Steven D. Guggenheim
(Not admitted in CA)
Ava M. Hahn
Judy G. Hamel
Ramsey Hanna
Jay D. Hansen
Sara Duval Harrington
Paul W. Hartzel
(Not admitted in CA)
Nicole M. Healy
Peter S. Heinecke
Jeffrey J. Hessekiel
Elizabeth C. Hewitt
Anne S. High
Lawrence S. Hing
Betty Ho
Melissa V. Hollatz
Ted S. Hollifield
Mark Hooshmand
Brandon G. Howald
David A. Hsu
(Not admitted in CA)
Kathleen D. Huryn
Robert T. Ishii
(Not admitted in CA)
Anna Itoi
Barbara A. Izzo
Micah R. Jacobs
David P. Jedrzejek
Karen Jennings
James F. Jensen
Carolynn W. Jones
Antone F. Johnson
Jeffrey David Jonker
Raju S. Judge
Kevin A. Kakareka
(Not admitted in CA)
Kevin E. Keller
Christine Kendrick
Adit M. Khorana
Anthony T. Kikuta
Annah S. Kim
Jeanie Kim
Stephen E. Kim
Bryan King
David Alan King
(Not admitted in CA)
David R. King
Rick Kline
Sandra P. Knox
Andrea D. Kohn
(Not admitted in CA)
Alexander E. Kolar
Robert F. Kornegay, Jr.
Donna L. Kotake
David H. Kramer
Susan P. Krause
GermainD. Labat, III
Mark Labaton
Tracy Tosh Lane
Craig N. Lang
David L. Lansky
Thomas G. LaWer
Elizabeth D. Lear
Edward T. Lee
In Lee (Not admitted in CA)
Andrew Leibnitz
Michael B. Levin
Justin D. Levinson
Jonathan Levy
Jeffrey Lin
Nathan E. Linn
(Not admitted in CA)
Teri A. Little
John K. Liu
Steven Liu
Carl Loeffler
Laurie-Ann Mei Inn Look
Thomas J. Lorr
Rachel S. Lovejoy
(Not admitted in CA)
Ilan Lovinsky
(Not admitted in CA)
Michael D. Lowenstein

Glenn J. Luinenburg
Angenette M. Lynch
Junling Ma
(Not admitted in CA)
Melissa M. Maccarone
Matthew MacKenzie
Zurvan Mahamedi
Laura A. Malinasky
John Mao
Jerry Marcus
Stacy B. Margolies
(Not admitted in CA)
Jill D. Marsal
Eileen Marshall
Armen S. Martin
Thomas J. Martin
Nancy D. Martindale
Debera L. Massahos
Brian McDaniel
Lisa G. McFall
Kirk McInnis
Ruth Ann McNees
Heather Meeker
Shailesh Mehra
Margaret T. Miles
J. Gregg Miller, Jr.
Torrey J. Miller
Rebecca A. Mitchells
Adriene Mixon
John R. Moore
Kelly Ames Morehead
Su-Jim Lee Moreland
Thomas D. Morell
Susan Cleary Morse
Caine T. Moss
Kenneth W. Muller
Maurine M. Murtagh
Eveline Mutsaers
Akihito Nakamachi
Usha Narayanan
Todd A. Nelson
Steve S. Nikkhou
John C. Nishi
Jill L. Nissen
Craig D. Norris
Burke F. Norton
Paul Velasco Obico
David P. O'Brien
William M. O'Callaghan
Jennifer A. Ochs
Paul A. Okada
Erik Oliver
Karla K. Padilla
Michael J. Panepucci
Touraj Parang
Anil Patel
Joseph Aaron Pierce
Alexander D. Phillips
Michael D. Pogue
Dorrian Porter
Russell A. Powell
(Not admitted in CA)
Charles J. Prober
Vincent J. Presti, III
(Not admitted in CA)
Thomas E. Pyke
Sheldon J. Quan
Helen Emma Quinn
Anjani Ragade
Anand Rao
Jaideep P. Reddy
(Not admitted in CA)
Matthew R. Reed
Amy E. Rees
Maura Rees
Audrey S. Garfield Reich
Julia Reigel
Rosemary G. Reilly
Christine L. Richardson
Kent R. Richardson
Michael J. Richter
(Not admitted in CA)
William L. Richter
(Not admitted in CA)
Erik F. Riegler
Sharon Levine Ring
Terence J. Roberts
Stephen D. Robinson
Stephen Dane Rockwell
RoseAnn Marie Rotandaro

(See Next Column)

Randall D. Roth
(Not admitted in CA)
Stephanie L. Ruby
Michael S. Russell
Adam G. Safwat
John Y. Sasaki
David J. Saul
Thomas I. Savage
Richard J. Schachtili
Gali Schaham
Caitlin Schmid
Kari C. Schoening
Otto R. Scholtz
(Not admitted in CA)
Julia Schwartzman
Jennifer Sarah Seibly
Ariana N. Seldman
Bahram Seyedin-Noor
Shahram Seyedin-Noor
David M. Serepca
Mary E. Shannon
Behrooz Shariati
Shari A. Shepard
(Not admitted in CA)
John P. Shinn
Paul B. Shinn
James P.A. Shulman
Richard Jay Silverstein
Clay B. Simpson
John L. Slafsky
Yaphet L. Smith
Ellen H. Solomon
Seungtaik Song
Susan L. Stapleton
Felix S. Sterling
John P. Stigi III
(Not admitted in CA)
Jinntung Su
Betsey Sue
Linda Ya-Ning Sung
Yoichiro Taku
Marc P. Taxay
(Not admitted in CA)

Robert S. Tesler
(Not admitted in CA)
Carol A. Timm
Ephrat Toshav
Marina C. Tsatalis
Daniel W. Turbow
Diane E. Turriff
John D. van Loben Sels
(Not admitted in CA)
Alicia J. Vasquez
Edward F. Vermeer
John D. Villarreal
M. Linda Waissar
(Not admitted in CA)
David C. Wang
Stephen Warhola
Martin J. Waters III
(Not admitted in CA)
Gregory Lewis Watts
Virginia W. Wei
Michael D. Weisberg
Seth R. Weissman
Stephen M. Welles
(Not admitted in CA)
David West
Robert F. Westover
Howard Wettan
James T. Whaley
Michelle L. Whipkey
Shannon D. Whisenant
Seth W. Wiener
Don S. Williams
George A. Willman
Catherine H. Winterburn
Lisa J. Wirnowski
John L. Wollman
Christine Wong
Richard L. Woodworth
Timothy R. Yee
Jenny C. Yeh
(Not admitted in CA)
James C. Yoon
Daniel K. Yuen

Lior Zorea

For full biographical listings, see the Martindale-Hubbell Law Directory

*REDDING,** Shasta Co.

CARR, KENNEDY, PETERSON & FROST, A LAW CORPORATION (AV)

420 Redcliff Drive, P.O. Box 492396, 96049
Telephone: 530-222-2100
Fax: 530-222-0504
Email: info@ckpf.com

Francis Carr (1875-1944)
Lawrence J. Kennedy, Sr. (1883-1975)
Laurence J. Kennedy, Jr. (1918-1986)
Laurence W. Carr (1912-1991)
R. Russ Peterson

Daniel S. Frost
Robert M. Harding
Evan L. Delgado
Stephen H. Baker
Michael P. Ashby
Randall C. Nelson
Robert A. West

Representative Clients: Catholic Health Care West; Chicago Title Insurance Co.; CH2M Hill California, Inc.; Design Professional Insurance Co.; Fruit Growers Supply Co.; Louisiana-Pacific Corp.; PacifiCorp; Rayonier, Inc.; Roseburg Lumber Co.; Stewart Title Insurance Co.

For full biographical listings, see the Martindale-Hubbell Law Directory

REDLANDS, San Bernardino Co.

DILL & SHOWLER (AV)

411 Brookside Avenue, 92373
Telephone: 909-793-2377
Fax: 909-798-6557

MEMBERS OF FIRM

Fred H. Dill
Scott Showler

Representative Clients: Homestead Supplies, Inc.; Riverside County Lumber Co.; Lois Lauer Realty, Inc.; Kivett-Teeters Coldwell Banker; Green Valley Escrow; Redlands Centennial Bank.

For full biographical listings, see the Martindale-Hubbell Law Directory

*REDWOOD CITY,** San Mateo Co.

ROPERS, MAJESKI, KOHN & BENTLEY, A PROFESSIONAL CORPORATION (AV)

1001 Marshall Street, 94063
Telephone: 650-364-8200
Fax: 650-367-0997
URL: http://www.ropers.com
San Jose, California Office: 80 North 1st Street.
Telephone: 408-287-6262.
Fax: 408-297-6819.
San Francisco, California Office: 333 Market Street, Suite 3150.
Telephone: 415-543-4800.
Fax: 415-274-6301.
Los Angeles, California Office: 515 South Flower Street, Suite 2100.
Telephone: 213-312-2000.
Fax: 213-312-2001.
New York, New York Office: 1 World Trade Center, 85th Floor.
Telephone: 212-432-4300.
Fax: 212-432-4303.

Harold Ropers (1905-1966)
John M. Rubens (1936-1993)
Eugene J. Majeski
John M. Bentley
Michael J. Brady
Frank J. Pagliaro, Jr.
John S. Simonson
Daniel E. Alberti
Mark G. Bonino
Richard K. Wilson
Stephen M. Hayes
Katherine S. Clark
Lawrence M. Guslani
David J. Miclean
Pamela E. Cogan
Colin R. Campbell
Brad W. Blocker
Marc D. Rosati
Thomas H. Clarke, Jr.
Robert P. Andris, II
Todd A. Roberts
David M. McLaughlin
Robert G. Ittig
Francois G. Laugier
Susan H. Handelman
Kevin G. McCurdy
Stephen P. Ellingson
Chi-Hung A. Chan
John A. Rowland
Jeffrey W. Allen (Resident)
Paul D. Herbert (Resident)
Raymond A. Greene III
Dean A. Pappas (Resident)
Richard M. Williams (Resident)

OF COUNSEL

Ron W. Fields
Walter C. Kohn
James H. McKibben

Linda J. Dvorak
Peter C. Suhr
Laura L. Reidenbach
Brian R. Davis
Kimberly A. Donovan
Robert P. Soran
Ida Samawi Skikos
Terry Anastassiou
Timothy K. Branson
Eva Yablonsky
Whitney E. Davisson
Cynthia G. Lawrence
Bruce Hunter Hinze (Resident)
Matthew A. Bisbee
Mary P. McCurdy
Mark E. Inbody
Karen Lynn Prodromo (Not admitted in CA)
Kathryn L. Courtney
Brian Richard Blackman
Lucy Fong Wang

For full biographical listings, see the Martindale-Hubbell Law Directory

*SACRAMENTO,** Sacramento Co.

DOWNEY, BRAND, SEYMOUR & ROHWER LLP (AV)

Suite 1050, 555 Capitol Mall, 95814
Telephone: 916-441-0131
FAX: 916-441-4021
Email: downey@dbsr.com *URL:* http://www.dbsr.com

MEMBERS OF FIRM

Stephen W. Downey (1926-1959)
Clyde H. Brand (1926-1964)
Harry B. Seymour (1926-1977)
John F. Downey (1930-1991)
Otto Rohwer (1931—)
James A. Willett
D. Steven Blake
James M. Day, Jr.
Thomas N. Cooper
Stephen J. Meyer
Daniel James McVeigh
Fred A. Dawkins
Roberta L. Franklin
James L. Deeringer
Kevin M. O'Brien
R. Dale Ginter
David E. Lindgren
Dan L. Carroll
Stephen G. Stwora-Hail
Judy H. Hersher
Steven P. Saxton
James M. Nelson
Julie A. Carter
Steven H. Goldberg
Julia L. Jenness
Jeffrey M. Koewler
Mary J. Martinelli
Katharine E. Wagner
William R. Warne
Patrick G. Mitchell
Arthur G. Woodward
David R.E. Aladjem
Sean B. Murphy
Silvio Reggiardo, III
Daniel J. Coyle
Joseph G. De Angelis
Heather B. Lee
William H. Koch
Rhonda Canby
Michael O. Gualco
Jane E. Luckhardt

COUNSEL

Barbara L. Berg
Taylor O. Miller
Bruce Dravis

(See Next Column)

OF COUNSEL

George Basye
Philip A. Stohr
John J. Hamlyn, Jr.

ASSOCIATES

Bernhard D. Baltaxe
Matthew C. Bradford
Michael L.F. Buck
Jacqueline U. Dosick
David R. Feniger
Jeffrey S. Galvin
Tory E. Griffin
Jennifer Harder
Thomas A. Henry
Tracy K. Hunckler
Robert M. McCormick
Scott D. McElhern
Michael N. Mills
Mike Mireles
Mary-Beth Moylan
John O'Malley
Karin S. Phalen
Jason E. Rios
Lisa L. Ruth
Scott L. Shapiro
Helen Singmaster-Hernández
R. Bruce Steubing
Robert G. Strauch
Richard K. Sueyoshi
Marshall W. Taylor
Robert J. Taylor, Jr.
Michael J. Thomas
Ann L. Trowbridge
Gwyn-Mohr Tully
Maria E. Valdez
Debbie J. Vorous
Deborah A. Wordham

Representative Clients: Hertz Corp.; Raley's and Bel Air Supermarkets; Sacramento Municipal Utility District; Steelcase, Inc.

For full biographical listings, see the Martindale-Hubbell Law Directory

FRIEDMAN, COLLARD, CUTTER & PANNETON, PROFESSIONAL CORPORATION (AV)

7750 College Town Drive, Suite 300, 95826
Telephone: 916-381-9011
Telecopier: 916-381-7048

Morton L. Friedman
William H. Collard
C. Brooks Cutter
John Panneton
Eric J. Ratinoff
Ron Winters

For full biographical listings, see the Martindale-Hubbell Law Directory

HARMATA LAW OFFICES (AV)

2201 Q Street, 95816
Telephone: 916-442-2842
Fax: 916-442-2015
Email: harmatalaw@aol.com *URL:* http://www.lawyers.com/harmatalaw

Donald D. Harmata

LEGAL SUPPORT PERSONNEL
PARALEGAL

Debra D. Morrow

Representative Clients: Control Data Corp.; Deloitte & Touche; General Electric Co.; Myers Electric, Inc.; Syblon-Reid Co.; Systemhouse Inc.; TRW, Inc.

For full biographical listings, see the Martindale-Hubbell Law Directory

LIVINGSTON & MATTESICH, LAW CORPORATION (AV)

1201 K Street, Suite 1100, 95814
Telephone: 916-442-1111
Fax: 916-448-1709
Email: l&m@lmlaw.net *URL:* http://www.lmlaw.net

Gene Livingston
James M. Mattesich
Carol Livingston
Rebecca M. Ceniceros
Emilio E. Varanini, III
Kenneth M. Malovos
Kathleen E. Finnerty
Joanna R. Mendoza

Steven P. Belzer
Jeffrey Leacox
Randy Pollack
Alice H. Choi
Stephen Craig Hunter
Matthew J. Goldman
Joel C. Baiocchi
Baldassaro (Bill) Di Capo
John McKinsey
Timothy E. Naccarato
Craig N. Lundgren
Mary Farrell Taylor
Brian Crone
Gay L. Carroll
Steven G. Churchwell

Representative Clients: H&R Block Tax Services, Inc.; California Grocers Association; Childrens World Learning Center; P.G. Design Electronics, Inc.; Aetna Leasing Co.; Payless Cashways, Inc.; Town & Country Lutheran Church and School.

For full biographical listings, see the Martindale-Hubbell Law Directory

McDONOUGH, HOLLAND & ALLEN, A PROFESSIONAL CORPORATION (AV)

9th Floor, 555 Capitol Mall, 95814
Telephone: 916-444-3900
Fax: 916-444-8334
URL: http://www.mhalaw.com
Yuba City, California Office: 422 Century Park Drive, Suite A, P.O. Box 776.
Telephone: 530-674-9761.
Fax: 530-671-0990.

(See Next Column)

McDonough, Holland & Allen A Professional Corporation, *Sacramento—Continued*

Oakland, California Office: 1999 Harrison Street, Suite 1300.
Telephone: 510-273-8780.
Fax: 510-839-9104.

Martin McDonough (1915-1987)
Alfred E. Holland (Retired)
Bruce F. Allen (Retired)
Joseph E. Coomes, Jr.
David J. Spottiswood
Richard W. Nichols
Donald C. Poole
Richard W. Osen
Richard E. Brandt
G. Richard Brown
David W. Post
Susan K. Edling
David F. Beatty
Michael T. Fogarty
Natalie E. West (Resident, Oakland Office)
Ann H. O'Connell
Robert W. O'Connor
Jeffry R. Jones
T. Brent Hawkins
James M. Ruddick (Resident, Yuba City Office)
Dawn H. Cole
Sharon Day Roseme
Susan L. Schoenig
James L. Leet
Mark A. Wasser
Virginia A. Cahill
Harriet A. Steiner
William A. Lichtig
Edward J. Quinn, Jr.
Mark Gorton
Robert R. Rubin
Morgan T. Jones, III
Patricia D. Elliott
William C. Hilson, Jr.
Iris P. Yang
Cathy Deubel Salenko
Craig Labadie (Resident, Oakland Office)
Jack D. Brown (Resident, Yuba City Office)
Thomas L. Hill (Resident, Yuba City Office)
Nancy P. Lee
Mary E. Olden
Edward J. Wright, Jr.
Michelle Marchetta Kenyon (Resident, Oakland Office)
Michele M. Clark
Stephen L. Goff
Michael K. Iwahiro
Glenn W. Peterson
David L. Krotine
Timothy P. Hayes (Resident, Yuba City Office)
Todd M. Bailey
Marcia L. Augsburger
Nancy T. Templeton
David E. Macchiavelli
Kent William Silvester
Daniel V. Martinez (Resident, Yuba City Office)
Steven A. Lamon
Jan Patrick Sherry
Paul C. Anderson (Resident, Oakland Office)
L. Stuart List

Jeremy S. Millstone
Torene L.M. Schwab
Julie Raney
Stacey N. Sheston
André K. Campbell
Tyson M. Shower
Christopher Hart Doyle
Eric N. Robinson
Seth Merewitz
James Clarke
Laura J. Fowler
Thomas F. Morrison
Rocco R. Paternoster

OF COUNSEL

V. Barlow Goff
Ann Taylor Schwing
Zachary M. Smith
Clement J. Dougherty, Jr.
Marci R. Coglianese
Linda R. Beck (Resident, Oakland Office)
Richard G. Rypinski (Resident, Oakland Office)
John R. Briggs

Representative Clients: Sutter Health and Affiliated Entities; California Public Employees Retirement System; Robert C. Powell Properties; A. Teichert & Son, Inc.; Las Vegas, Nevada Redevelopment Agency; NEC Electronics; The Money Store;Weyerhaeuser Venture Co.; City of Davis.

For full biographical listings, see the Martindale-Hubbell Law Directory

*SALINAS,** Monterey Co.

Noland, Hamerly, Etienne & Hoss, A Professional Corporation (AV)

333 Salinas Street, P.O. Box 2510, 93902-2510
Telephone: 831-424-1414; 831-372-7525
Fax: 831-424-1975
Monterey, California Office: 660 Camino Aguajito Road, Third Floor.
Telephone: 831-647-3080.
Fax: 831-647-3083.
King City, California Office: 104 South Vanderhurst, Suite D, 93930.
Telephone: 831-386-1080.
Fax: 831-386-1083.

Harry L. Noland (1904-1991)
Paul M. Hamerly
Myron E. Etienne, Jr.
James D. Schwefel, Jr.
Stephen W. Pearson
Lloyd W. Lowrey, Jr.
Anne K. Secker
Paula Robinson
Werner D. ("Randy") Meyenberg, III
Michael P. Masuda
Christine P. Gianascol
Lisa Nakata
Laura A. Davis
Dale E. Grindrod
John E. Kesecker

OF COUNSEL

Martin J. May
Jerome F. Politzer, Jr.
Blanca E. Zarazua
Peter T. Hoss

Representative Clients: Quail Lodge, Inc.; J. M. Smucker Company; McCormick & Co.; Tanimura & Antle; Fresh Express; Mann Packing Co.; First National Bank of Central California; Household International; Robert Talbott, Inc.; El Aguila Food Products, Inc.

For full biographical listings, see the Martindale-Hubbell Law Directory

*SAN BERNARDINO,** San Bernardino Co.

Wilson, Borror, Dunn & Davis, LLP (AV)

Suite 307, The Bank of California Building, 255 North D Street, 92401
Telephone: 909-884-8855
Fax: 909-884-5161

MEMBERS OF FIRM

Fred A. Wilson (1886-1973)
Wm. H. Wilson (1915-1981)
James R. Dunn
Thomas M. Davis
Sarah L. Overton

ASSOCIATES

S. Mark Strain
C. Victor Wear

OF COUNSEL

Caywood J. Borror

Representative Clients: Travelers Insurance Co.; Rockwell International; Westinghouse Air Brake Co.; Goodyear Tire and Rubber Co.; Home Insurance Co.; Cities of: Redlands, Chino, Colton, San Bernardino, Upland, Yucapia and Corona; Lloyd's of London; Universal Health Services, Inc.-;Lawyer's Mutual Insurance; Unified School Districts of Rialto and Fontana.

For full biographical listings, see the Martindale-Hubbell Law Directory

*SAN DIEGO,** San Diego Co.

Allen, Matkins, Leck, Gamble & Mallory LLP (AV)

A Limited Liability Partnership including Professional Corporations
501 West Broadway, Ninth Floor, 92101
Telephone: 619-233-1155
Facsimile: 619-233-1158
Los Angeles, California Office: Seventh Floor, 515 South Figueroa Street, 90071.
Telephone: 213-622-5555.
Telecopier: 213-620-8816.
Irvine, California Office: Fourth Floor, 18400 Von Karman, 92612.
Telephone: 949-553-1313.
Telecopier: 949-553-8354.
West Los Angeles, California Office: 1999 Avenue of the Stars, 90067.
Telephone: 310-788-2400.
Fax: 310-788-2410.
San Francisco, California Office: 333 Bush Street, Seventeenth Floor, 94104-2806.
Telephone: 412-837-1515.
Fax: 415-837-1516.

PARTNERS

Vernon C. Gauntt (Resident)
David L. Osias
George J. Berger (Resident)
Michael C. Pruter (Resident)
Dana I. Schiffman (Resident)
Ray B. Gliner (Resident)
Ellen B. Spellman
Robert R. Barnes (Resident)
Jeffrey R. Patterson (Resident)
Joe M. Davidson (Resident)
Craig D. Swanson (Resident)
George W. Kuney (Resident)

ASSOCIATES

Martin L. Togni (Resident)
Loraine L. Pedowitz (Resident)
Thomas B. Crosbie (Resident)
Sandra J. Young (Resident)
Mark J. Hattam (Resident)
Steve Wellington (Resident)
Ann Marie Maas (Resident)
Kari Mason Desgalier (Resident)
Kelly J. Brinkman (Resident)
Allen B. Walburn (Resident)
Sharon Saslow (Resident)
Kathryn D. Horning (Resident)
Dawnmarie I. Saunders (Resident)
Michael J. Holmes (Resident)

OF COUNSEL

John G. Davies (Resident)
S. Lee Hancock

Reference: Wells Fargo Bank (Los Angeles Main Office).

For full biographical listings, see the Martindale-Hubbell Law Directory

Bacalski, Byrne & Koska (AV)

A Partnership including a Professional Corporation
24th Floor, Emerald Plaza 402 West Broadway, 92101
Telephone: 619-239-4340
Fax: 619-239-0116
Email: lawbbk@lawbbk.com

A. Daniel Bacalski Jr. (A Professional Corporation)
Margaret M. Byrne
William K. Koska
Richard R. Roy
David P. Ramirez
Andrew J. Marton
Susie J. Kater

Kerry F. Kawamura
Christopher John Workman
David B. Monks
Matthew J. Evans
Wendy L. Tucker
Christopher S. Trunzo
Stephen M. Lerner

Representative Clients: Ohio Casualty Insurance Co.; American Insurance Group.
Reference: San Diego National Bank.

For full biographical listings, see the Martindale-Hubbell Law Directory

San Diego—Continued

BAKER & MCKENZIE (AV)

101 West Broadway, Twelfth Floor, 92101
Telephone: (619) 236-1441; (800) 786-1022
Intl. Dialing: (1-619) 236-1441
Facsimile: (1-619) 236-0429
URL: http://www.bakerinfo.com
Associated Offices of Baker & McKenzie in: Almaty, Amsterdam, Bahrain, Baku, Bangkok, Barcelona, Beijing, Berlin, Bogotá, Brasília, Brussels, Budapest, Buenos Aires, Cairo, Caracas, Chicago, Dallas, Düsseldorf, Frankfurt, Geneva, Hanoi, Ho Chi Minh City, Hong Kong, Houston, Hsinchu, Juárez, Kiev, London, Madrid, Manila, Melbourne, México City, Miami, Milan, Monterrey, Moscow, Münich, New York, Palo Alto, Paris, Prague, Rio de Janeiro, Riyadh, Rome, St. Petersburg, San Francisco, Santiago, São Paulo, Singapore, Stockholm, Sydney, Taipei, Tijuana, Tokyo, Toronto, Valencia, Warsaw, Washington, D.C. and Zürich.
Correspondent Law Firm: Hadiputranto, Hadinoto & Partners, Jakarta.

MEMBERS OF FIRM

Charles H. Dick, Jr.
David C. Doyle
Thomas W. Ferrell
John J. Hentrich
Clark H. Libenson
Ali M. M. Mojdehi
Pamela J. Naughton
Abby B. Silverman

NATIONAL PARTNERS

Mitchell P. Brook
Craig I. Celniker (Not admitted in CA)
Ernest Cordero, Jr.
Carlos D. Heredia
Michael P. McCloskey
Maria E. Nuñez
Claire Wright

OF COUNSEL

Edward T. Butler

ASSOCIATES

Alison Priske Adema
Christopher M. Alexander
James P. Armstrong
Steven E. Comer
Shannon M. Dailey
Brett D. Ekins
Charles S. Evendorff
Cynthia A. Freeland
Koji F. Fukumura
Kenji L. Funahashi
Christina E. Giorgio (Not admitted in CA)
Michelle B. Graham
Robert M. Harkins, Jr.
Helen S. Irza
Peter W. Ito
Richard C. Kim
Cory J. King
William J. Kolegraff
Moses Mares
Michael A. Roybal (Not admitted in CA)
Susan I. Santana
Renee S. Schor
Joseph W. Secondine, Jr.
Andrew B. Serwin
Michael J. Shea
Michael W. Vella
Nellwyn W. Voorhies
George C. Yu
Juan E. Zúñiga

For full biographical listings, see the Martindale-Hubbell Law Directory

BROBECK, PHLEGER & HARRISON LLP (AV)

A Partnership including a Professional Corporation
550 West C Street Suite 1300, 92101
Telephone: 619-234-1966
Facsimile: 619-236-1403 (13th Floor); 619-234-3848 (12th Floor)
Email: info@brobeck.com *URL:* http://www.brobeck.com/
San Francisco, California Office: Spear Street Tower, One Market.
Telephone: 415-442-0900.
Facsimile: 415-442-0900.
Palo Alto, California Office: Two Embarcadero Place, 2200 Geng Road.
Telephone: 650-424-0160.
Facsimile: 650-496-2885.
Los Angeles, California Office: 550 South Hope Street.
Telephone: 213-489-4060.
Facsimile: 213-745-3345.
Irvine, California Office: 38 Technology Drive.
Telephone: 949-790-6300.
Facsimile: 949-790-6301.
Austin, Texas Office: 301 Congress Avenue, Suite 1200.
Telephone: 512-477-5495.
Facsimile: 512-477-5813.
Denver, Colorado Office: 370 Interlocken Boulevard, Suite 500.
Telephone: 303-410-2000.
Facsimile: 303-410-2199.
New York, N.Y. Office: 1633 Broadway, 47th Floor.
Telephone: 212-581-1600.
Facsimile: 212-586-7878.
Washington, D.C. Office: 701 Pennsylvania Avenue, NW, Suite 220.
Telephone: 202-220-6000.
Facsimile: 202-824-0949.
London, England Office: Brobeck Hale and Dorr International, Hasilwood House, 60 Bishopsgate, London EC2N 4AJ.
Telephone: 011 44 171 638 6688.
Facsimile: 011 44 171 638 5888.

OFFICE LEADER

Faye H. Russell

(See Next Column)

PARTNERS

Craig S. Andrews
Theodore W. Graham
Jennifer A. Kearns
Daniel G. Lamb, Jr.
Christopher H. McGrath
Martin Clark Nichols
Richard L. Parker
Maria K. Pum
William F. Sullivan
Hayden J. Trubitt
Mary L. Walker

SENIOR COUNSEL

Jeffrey Garfinkle

ASSOCIATES

Jonathan D. Andrews
Edith A. Bauer
William S. Biel
Ross L. Burningham
Kristen E. Caverly
Robert H. Cutler (Not admitted in CA)
Tracey Lynn Kovall De Lange
Carey J. Fox (Not admitted in CA)
Thomas E. Hornish
Craig E. Hunsaker
Jason B. Isaacs
Michael S. Kagnoff
Alan S. Kholos
Lance S. Kurata
Michelle A. Lara
Brian D. Martin
Colleen Elizabeth O'Leary
Sean T. Prosser
Kandace W. Richardson
Eddie Rodriguez
Scott G. Sand
Jason Schauer
Sherry E. Schnell
Maria Sendra
Kirt W. Shuldberg
Joel S. Smith
Hamilton Southworth III
Kimberly S. Steckling
Matthew B. Swartz
Jeffrey C. Thacker
Michael S. Umansky
Kathleen M. Walker (Not admitted in CA)

For full biographical listings, see the Martindale-Hubbell Law Directory

COOLEY GODWARD LLP (AV)

4365 Executive Drive, Suite 1100, 92121-2128
Telephone: 619-550-6000
Fax: 619-453-3555
Email: webmaster@cooley.com *URL:* http://www.cooley.com
Palo Alto, California Office: Five Palo Alto Square, 300 El Camino Real.
Telephone: 650-843-5000.
Fax: 650-857-0663.
San Francisco, California Office: 20th Floor, One Maritime Plaza.
Telephone: 415-693-2000.
Fax: 415-951-3699.
Menlo Park, California Office: 3000 Sand Hill Road, Building 3, Suite 230.
Telephone: 650-843-5000.
Fax: 650-854-2691.
Boulder, Colorado Office: 2595 Canyon Boulevard, Suite 250.
Telephone: 303-546-4000.
Fax: 303-546-4099.
Denver, Colorado Office: One Tabor Center, 1200 17th Street, Suite 2100.
Telephone: 303-606-4800.
Fax: 303-606-4899.
Kirkland, Washington Office: 5200 Carillon Point.
Telephone: 425-893-7700.
Fax: 425-893-7777.
Reston, Virginia Office: 2002 Edmund Halley Drive, Suite 300.
Telephone: 703-262-8000.
Fax: 703-262-8100.

PARTNERS

Barbara L. Borden
Lance W. Bridges
Susan P. Bushor
Lynda Kay Chandler
Thomas A. Coll
M. Wainwright Fishburn, Jr.
Jeremy D. Glaser
William E. Grauer
J. Christopher Jaczko
Eric J. Loumeau
Frederick T. Muto
D. Bradley Peck
Michael G. Rhodes
Anthony M. Stiegler
Stephen P. Swinton

SPECIAL COUNSEL

Kevin James Zimmer
Ron S. Zollman

ASSOCIATES

Jane K. Adams
Carrie Battilega
David B. Berger
Blake T. Bilstad
Lauren D. Boyd
Dennis Calderon
Ethan Christensen
Randall Lee Clark
Scott R. Cutler
Micha "Mitch" Danzig
Nancy E. Denyes
Anne-Marie Dinius
Michelle C. Doolin
James V. Fazio, III
Amy S. Hellenkamp
Christopher J. Kearns
Adam Lenain
Patrick M. Maloney
Micaela H. Martín
Larry W. Nishnick
Seth A. Rafkin
Elizabeth E. Reed
Carl R. Sanchez
Philip C. Tencer
Lina Pitesa Waage
Kent M. Walker
Steven M. Weiss
Denise L. Woolard

LEGAL SUPPORT PERSONNEL

SENIOR PARALEGALS

Deborah R. Cravets
Cynthia Deatrick
Sharon K. Ritchie

(See Next Column)

COOLEY GODWARD LLP, *San Diego—Continued*

SPECIALISTS

Denise L. Stark | Stephen M. Valois

For full biographical listings, see the Martindale-Hubbell Law Directory

DETISCH & CHRISTENSEN (AV)

444 West C Street, Suite 200, 92101
Telephone: 619-236-9343
Fax: 619-236-8307
Email: dclaw@adnc.com

MEMBERS OF FIRM

Charles B. Christensen | Donald W. Detisch

ASSOCIATES

Sean D. Schwerdtfeger | Carl E. Sizemore
John Frederick Smith

OF COUNSEL

Harold O. Valderhaug

For full biographical listings, see the Martindale-Hubbell Law Directory

FERRIS & BRITTON, A PROFESSIONAL CORPORATION (AV)

1600 First National Bank Center, 401 West A Street, 92101
Telephone: 619-233-3131
Fax: 619-232-9316
Email: manager@ferrisbritton.com *URL:* http://www.ferrisbritton.com

Alfred G. Ferris
Christopher Q. Britton
Steven J. Pynes
Tamara K. Fogg
Michael R. Weinstein
Gary T. Moyer
Richard S. Bayer
Margaret Prodanov

Eric M. Volkert

OF COUNSEL

James J. Granby

Representative Clients: Cox Communications, Inc.; Datel, Inc.; Exxon; Frontier Analytics, Inc.; Media One, Inc.; Peninsula Bank; Structural Bioinformatics, Inc.; Teleport Communications Group; Southwest Airlines.

For full biographical listings, see the Martindale-Hubbell Law Directory

FOLEY & LARDNER (AV)

402 West Broadway, 23rd Floor, 92101-3542
Telephone: 619-234-6655
Facsimile: 619-234-3510
Email: foleylardner@worldnet.att.net *URL:* http://www.foleylardner.com
Los Angeles, California Office: 2029 Century Park East, 35th Floor.
Telephone: 310-277-2223.
Fax: 310-557-8475.
Sacramento, California Office: 300 Capitol Mall, Suite 1125.
Telephone: 916-443-8005.
Fax: 916-443-2240.
San Francisco, California Office: One Maritime Plaza, Sixth Floor.
Telephone: 415-434-4484.
Fax: 415-434-4507.
Denver, Colorado Office: 1999 Broadway, Suite 2560.
Telephone: 303-297-0260.
Fax: 303-297-0266.
Washington, D.C. Office: Washington Harbour, Suite 500, 3000 K Street, N.W.
Telephone: 202-672-5300.
Telex: 904136 (Foley Lard Wash).
Facsimile: 202-672-5399.
Jacksonville, Florida Office: The Greenleaf Building, 200 Laura Street. P.O. Box 240.
Telephone: 904-359-2000.
Facsimile: 904-359-8700.
Orlando, Florida Office: Suite 1800, 111 North Orange Avenue, P.O. Box 2193.
Telephone: 407-423-7656.
Facsimile: 407-648-1743.
Tallahassee, Florida Office: 300 East Park Avenue, P.O. Box 1454.
Telephone: 850-222-6100.
Facsimile: 850-561-6475.
Tampa, Florida Offices: Suite 2700, One Hundred N. Tampa Street, P.O. Box 3391.
Telephones: 813-229-2300; Pinellas County: 813-442-3296.
Facsimile: 813-221-4210.
West Palm Beach, Florida Office: Suite 200, Phillips Point East Tower, 777 South Flagler Drive.
Telephone: 561-655-5050.
Facsimile: 561-655-6925.
Chicago, Illinois Office: Suite 3300, One IBM Plaza, 330 N. Wabash Avenue.
Telephone: 312-755-1900.
Facsimile: 312-755-1925.

(See Next Column)

Annapolis, Maryland Office: Suite 102, 175 Admiral Cochrane Drive.
Telephone: 410-266-8077.
Telex: 899149 (Oldtownpat).
Facsimile: 410-266-8664.
Madison, Wisconsin Office: Verex Plaza, 150 East Gilman Street, P.O. Box 1497.
Telephone: 608-257-5035.
Facsimile: 608-258-4258.
Milwaukee, Wisconsin Office: Firstar Center, 777 East Wisconsin Avenue.
Telephone: 414-271-2400.
Telex: 26-819 (Foley Lard Mil).
Facsimile: 414-297-4900.
Brussels, Belgium Office: Avenue Louise, 283.
Telephone: 32-2-646-2777.
Facsimile: 32-2-646-7574.

PARTNERS

Laurie A. Axford
Edsell M. Eady, Jr.
Robert E. Goldstein
Samuel F. Hoffman
Carol Isackson
Larry L. Marshall
Michael G. McCarty
Gregory V. Moser
George L. Root, Jr.
R. Michael Scarano, Jr.

OF COUNSEL

Mary K. Norvell

SPECIAL COUNSEL

Joseph M. Lesko | Stacy L. Taylor

ASSOCIATES

Julie C. Ashby
Margaret M. Duncan
Lynn R. Goodfellow
Darrell L. Pugh
Diane M. Racicot
Steven J. Simerlein
Susanne C. Washington
Barry S. Wilson

For full biographical listings, see the Martindale-Hubbell Law Directory

GRAY CARY WARE & FREIDENRICH LLP (AV)

Gray Cary Established in 1927
Ware & Freidenrich Established in 1969
401 "B" Street, Suite 1700, 92101-4297
Telephone: 619-699-2700
Telecopier: 619-236-1048
Email: info@graycary.com *URL:* http://www.graycary.com
San Diego/Golden Triangle, California Office: 4365 Executive Drive, Suite 1600, 92121.
Telephone: 858-677-1400.
Telecopier: 858-677-1477.
Palo Alto, California Office: 400 Hamilton Avenue, 94301-1825.
Telephone: 650-833-2000.
Telecopier: 650-327-3699.
La Jolla, California Office: 1200 Prospect Street, Suite 575, 92037-3610.
Telephone: 858-456-3000.
Telecopier: 858-456-3075.
El Centro, California Office: 1224 State Street, P.O. Box 2890, 92244.
Telephone: 760-353-6140.
Telecopier: 760-353-6228.
San Francisco, California Office: 139 Townsend Street, Suite 400, 94107-1922.
Telephone: 415-836-2500.
Telecopier: 415-836-9220.
Austin, Texas Office: 100 Congress Avenue, Suite 1440, 78701-4042.
Telephone: 512-457-7000.
Telecopier: 512-457-7070.
Sacramento, California Office: 400 Capitol Mall, Suite 2100, 95814.
Telephone: 916-930-3200.
Fax: 916-930-3201.

Maria R. Acker
John Allcock
Brian L. Behmer
Robert W. Bell, Jr.
Cathy A. Bencivengo
J. Rod Betts
Charles E. Black
William S. Boggs
Ann K. Bradley
Robert W. Brownlie
John Howard Clowes (Resident, San Francisco Office)
Guylyn R. Cummins
Jeffry A. Davis
Charles L. Deem
Joseph A. Delaney
Nancy O. Dix
L. B. Chip Edleson
Janis S. Fagan
Brian L. Forbes
Brian A. Foster
Mark H. Hamer
James T. Hannink
Jay D. Hanson
James W. Huston
Jay W. Jeffcoat
Kathryn E. Karcher
Margaret H. Kavalaris (Resident, Palo Alto Office)
Randall Evan Kay
Robert C. Longstreth
Richard F. Luther
Diane L. Mack
Guillermo Marrero
William McCurine, Jr.
Terrance A. Meador
Lisa C. Merrill
Marcelle E. Mihaila
David E. Monahan
Tracy L. Nation
J. Terence O'Malley
Barbara Jean Orr
Alexander H. Rogers
Terry D. Ross
Don G. Rushing
Jeffrey M. Shohet (Resident, San Diego/Golden Triangle Office)
Merrill F. Storms, Jr.
Lawrence I. Tannenbaum
Michael S. Tracy
David E. Watson
Shirli Fabbri Weiss

(See Next Column)

GRAY CARY WARE & FREIDENRICH LLP—*Continued*

Amy T. Wintersheimer
Mark C. Zebrowski
Karen M. ZoBell
Karl Zobell
(Resident, La Jolla Office)

Heather M. Ace
Marianne F. Adriatico
Marta B. Almli
Timothy Blackford
Erin Bosman
Stewart M. Brown
John P. Cleary
Curtis Cotton
Sean C. Cunningham
Sanjeev Date
Travis L. Dodd
Erin Downey
Emily Durkee
Timothy N. Ellis
John E. Fitzsimmons
Charles D. Gavrilovich
Ronit Gechter
John E. Giust
Andrew M. Greene
December Greene
John M. Guaragna
Licia Heffernan
Robert Hicks
Duane S. Horning
Charles E. Houston, Jr.
Christina Hwang
Nancy Kawano (Resident, San Diego/Golden Triangle Office)
Kenneth A. Kecskes
Mary A. Lehman
Karla A. Lyon
Gerald Maliszewski
Emily Maxwell
David McClure
Richard T. Mulloy
Danielle S. Murray
Michelle E. Nepomuceno
John J. Oskorep
Daniel T. Pascucci
Joann F. Peters
Lisa Pondrom
Paul A. Reynolds
James M. Sarnecky
Mary B. Scott
Randy Socol
Sharon B. Spivak
Nancy L. Stagg
Eric D. Swenson
Tali Tuchin
Geneva Wasserman
Christopher M. Young
Troy Zander

CONSULTING PARTNERS

Robert Ames
Richard Alexander Burt
Frederick P. Crowell
(Consulting Partner)
R. Reaves Elledge, Jr.
Sterling Hutcheson

OF COUNSEL

H. Cushman Dow
William N. Kammer
Browning E. Marean, III
Don L. Nay
Ralph M. Pray, III
James K. Smith
Kristin J. Westphal

GOLDEN TRIANGLE OFFICE

Robert W. Ayling
Neil P. Balmert
Mildred Basden
T. Knox Bell
Theodore J. Cranston
Elisabeth Eisner
Melitta Fleck
David B. Geerdes
Lisa A. Haile
Matt A. Kirmayer
Paul E. Kreutz
Cameron Jay Rains
Douglas J. Rein
Stephen E. Reiter
Rebecca K. Schmitt
Richard B. Thorp
(Not admitted in CA)
Ellen H. Whelan

Jeffrey T. Baglio
Christopher P. Bifone
Michael J. Brown
James E. Cartoni
Laura Giese
Joseph T. Holland
Richard J. Imbra
Paul B. Johnson
Sheila R. Kirschenbaum
June M. Learn
Mark T. Lee
Mark C. Lehberg
Marty B. Lorenzo
Laura D. Ravine
Theodore D. Rolf
Adam P. Schwenker
Gennady Shnaider
Christopher M. Smith
Scott M. Stanton
Ramsey R. Stewart
Anne H. West

OF COUNSEL

Jill F. Kalliomaa

Representative Clients: Automobile Club of South California; Bank of America; Brooktree Corp.; Pacific Bell; McMillin Development Co.

For full biographical listings, see the Martindale-Hubbell Law Directory

HIGGS, FLETCHER & MACK LLP (AV)

2000 First National Bank Building, 401 West "A" Street, Suite 2600, 92101
Telephone: 619-236-1551
Telecopier: 619-696-1410
Email: info@higgslaw.com

MEMBERS OF FIRM

Henry Pitts Mack (1909-1974)
DeWitt A. Higgs (1907-1994)
Joe N. Turner
Craig D. Higgs
J. Tim Konold
Harry L. Carter
Franklin T. Lloyd
Michael F. Boyle
John Morris
Kurt L. Kicklighter
John L. Morrell
David R. Clark
M. Cory Brown
Patricia P. Hollenbeck
James M. Peterson
Charles V. Berwanger
Susan Moriarty Hack
Bernard L. Kleinke
Martin A. Eliopulos
Peter S. Doody
Michael Langs
Mark K. Stender
Daniel C. Herbert
Phillip C. Samouris

(See Next Column)

MEMBERS OF FIRM (Continued)

Anna Frustaglio-Roppo
William M. Low
Richard D. Barton
Steven J. Cologne
Gregory W. Pollack
James J. Reynolds
Susan E. Basinger
Marianne Barth
William A. Miller
Richard J. Elliott

OF COUNSEL

Ferdinand T. Fletcher
Margaret Anne Payne
John W. Netterblad

SPECIAL COUNSEL

James E. Fox
S. Wayne Rosenbaum
Thomas E. Sharkey
James E. Chodzko

ASSOCIATES

Liong Lie Gan Penfield
Michael T. Quinn
Lauri Croce Streeter
Alexis Sean Gutierrez
Mary R. Robberson
Heidi Maley
R. Michael Jones
Jon R. Williams
Julia C. Nelson
Robert N. Hocker
Catherine Morrison
Arthur A. Wellman, Jr.
Douglas W. Lytle
Melinda J. Mahony
Thomas J. Tobin
Loren G. Freestone
Margaret E. Mangin

For full biographical listings, see the Martindale-Hubbell Law Directory

KING & BALLOW (AV)

2700 Symphony Towers, 750 B Street, 92101
Telephone: 619-236-9401
Fax: 619-236-9437
URL: http://www.king-ballow.com
Nashville, Tennessee Office: Union Street Plaza, 315 Union Street, Suite 1100. 37201.
Telephone: 615-259-3456.
Fax: 615-254-7907.

MEMBERS OF FIRM

Frank S. King, Jr.
(Not admitted in CA)
Robert L. Ballow
(Not admitted in CA)
Richard C. Lowe
(Not admitted in CA)
R. Eddie Wayland
(Not admitted in CA)
Paul H. Duvall (Resident)
Douglas R. Pierce
(Not admitted in CA)
Mark E. Hunt
(Not admitted in CA)
Lynn Siegel (Resident)

ASSOCIATES

James P. Thompson
(Not admitted in CA)
D'Lesli M. Davis
(Not admitted in CA)
Andrew S. Naylor
(Not admitted in CA)
Denise A. Nash (Resident)
Martina M. Stolar (Resident)

Representative Clients: City of Corodado and La Mesa, California; Ingram Micro, Inc., Santa Ana, California; Sullivan Graphics, Inc., Brentwood, Tennessee; Union-Tribune Publishing Co., San Diego, California; Herco Technology, Speedy Circuits, Huntington Beach, California; KCAL-TV, Los Angeles, California; Los Angeles Newspaper Group, Los Angeles, CA.

For full biographical listings, see the Martindale-Hubbell Law Directory

LUCE, FORWARD, HAMILTON & SCRIPPS LLP (AV)

A Partnership including Professional Corporations
600 West Broadway, Suite 2600, 92101
Telephone: 619-236-1414
Fax: 619-232-8311
URL: http://www.luce.com
La Jolla, California Office: 4275 Executive Square, Suite 800, 92037.
Telephone: 858-455-6611.
Fax: 858-232-8311.
Los Angeles, California Office: 777 South Figueroa, Suite 3600, 90017.
Telephone: 213-892-4992.
Fax: 213-892-7731.
San Francisco, California Office: 121 Spear Street, Suite 200, 94105.
Telephone: 415-356-4600.
Fax: 415-356-4610.
New York, N.Y. Office: Citicorp Center, 153 East 53rd Street, 26th Floor, 10022.
Telephone: 212-754-1414.
Fax: 212-644-9727.
Chicago, Illinois Office: 180 North La Salle Street, Suite 3110, 60601.
Telephone: 312-641-0580.
Fax: 312-641-0380.

MEMBERS OF FIRM

Edgar A. Luce (1881-1958)
F. Tudor Scripps, Jr.
(1908-1963)
Charles H. Forward (1886-1981)
Thomas M. Hamilton (Retired)

G. Edward Arledge
Christopher K. Barnette
Craig K. Beam
Robert J. Bell
Kathryn A. Bernert
Terrence L. Bingman
Charles A. Bird
Mikel R. Bistrow
Callie A. Bjurstrom
John W. Brooks
Craig R. Brown (Resident, New York, N.Y. Office)

(See Next Column)

LUCE, FORWARD, HAMILTON & SCRIPPS LLP, *San Diego—Continued*

(Continued)

Robert D. Buell (Managing Partner)
Marjorie J. Burchett
Kevin A. Cahill
Christopher Celentino
Jack G. Charney
Jeffrey A. Chine
Huhnsik Chung (Resident, New York, N.Y. Office)
Sean L. Collin
Robert G. Copeland
Robin D. Craig-Olson (Resident, San Francisco Office)
R. Randal Crispen
Cathy L. Croshaw (Resident, San Francisco Office)
Charles A. Danaher
Dennis J. Doucette
Robert J. Durham, Jr.
William T. Earley
Marc J. Feldman
Martin D. Fern (Resident, Los Angeles Office)
Jeffrey L. Fillerup (Resident, San Francisco Office)
James E. Fitzgerald (Resident, Los Angeles Office)
Mary F. Gillick
Nancy J. Gleason (Resident, Chicago, Illinois Office)
Roger C. Haerr
Mark Hagarty
Peter K. Hahn
Mark W. Hansen
Christopher J. Healey
Rex Heeseman (Resident, Los Angeles Office)
Charles L. Hellerich
James B. Hicks (Resident, Los Angeles Office)
Valentine S. Hoy, VIII
David M. Hymer
Phillip L. Jelsma
Michael L. Jensen
Kathy A. Jorrie (Resident, Los Angeles Office)
Peter H. Klee
Lawrence J. Kouns
Kimball Ann Lane (Resident, New York, N.Y. Office)
Mitchell L. Lathrop (Resident, New York, N.Y. Office)
John W. Leslie
Robert A. Levy
Allan E. Low (Resident, San Francisco Office)
Margaret M. Mann
Mark L. Mann
Stephen L. Marsh
Thomas A. May
Steven P. McDonald
John B. McNeece III
Cary W. Miller
Thomas M. Murray
Timothy R. Pestotnik
John L. Riedl
Daniel N. Riesenberg
Robert H. Roe
Ronald W. Rouse
Mary L. Russell
Craig A. Schloss
Theodore R. Scott
Nancy T. Scull
Scott W. Sonne
Otto E. Sorensen
Richard R. Spirra
Susanne J. Stanford
Robert G. Steiner
Darryl Steinhause
Edward Patrick "Pat" Swan, Jr.
Stephen T. Toohill
Frederick R. Vandeveer
Jon K. Wactor (Resident, San Francisco Office)
Pamela Wagner
Steven S. Wall
Kathy P. Waring
Andrew J. Waxler (Resident, Los Angeles Office)
William J. A. Weir (Resident, San Francisco Office)
Robert L. Young

OF COUNSEL

Michael T. Andrew
Stephen R. Brown
Gerald S. Davee
Robert E. McGinnis
Thomas R. Newman (Resident, New York, N.Y. Office)
Gregory D. Roper
William A. Yale

SPECIAL COUNSEL

Roger D. Brown
Gretchen S. Carner (Resident, Los Angeles Office)
Karla R. Kelly
Philip J. McGuire (Resident, Chicago, Illinois Office)

ASSOCIATES

Laura S. Adams
Melissa M. Allenby
Nathan S. Arrington
Jennifer R. Barragan (Resident, San Francisco Office)
Nancy L. Beattie
Richard J. Bergstrom
Lynn Borkenhagen
Dustin P. Branch
Michael L. Branch
John T. Brooks
Thomas A. Butler
Guillermo Cabrera
Valerie R. Cardenas
Kathryn M. S. Catherwood
Cathie A. Childs
David M. Clark
John P. Cooley
Holly Traube Cordova
Gus Cruger
Cindy Dobler Davis
Steven J. Davis
Patricia Dee-Bilka (Resident, New York, N.Y. Office)
Kelly Capen Douglas
John D. Edson
Christopher H. Findley
Brian C. Fish
Aurelia E. Flores
Jana Ford-Harder
Michael G. Fraunces
Seth M. Friedman
Ronald D. Getchey
Russell A. Gold
James A. Goniea (Resident, San Francisco Office)
Angela J. Hansen
Paula L. Harrington
Maria C. Heredia
Lynne D. Kaelin
Carol K. Kao
Jason L. Kent
Stephanie E. Kish
David R. Krause-Leemon (Resident, Los Angeles Office)
Frank J. Kros
Jeanne M. Malitz
Erin E. Martens (Resident, Los Angeles Office)
Heather L. McCloskey (Resident, Los Angeles Office)
Christine M. Megna (Resident, New York, N.Y. Office)
Erit S. Meitlis (Resident, New York, N.Y. Office)
Bridget Klein Moorhead
Lisa Pach (Resident, Chicago, Illinois Office)
Tami Johnson Penner
William G. Peterson
Michelle M. Porter
Elizabeth R. Potter
Carrie G. Pratt (Resident, San Francisco Office)

(See Next Column)

ASSOCIATES (Continued)

Lucinda Y. Quan
Michael G. Ramsey
William R. Reiter II
Jonathan Schneeweiss
Stephanie K. Shingleton (Not admitted in CA)
Edward H. Sikorski (Not admitted in CA)
Lourdes M. Slater (Resident, New York, N.Y. Office)
David J. Smith
Marjorie A. Stender
Philip J. Sullivan
Mia D. Thompson (Resident, Los Angeles Office)
Tisha P. Underwood
John D. Vaughn
Julie A. Vogelzang
James G. Waian
Sonia S. Waisman
Blaze D. Waleski (Resident, New York, N.Y. Office)
Mina S. Yang

For full biographical listings, see the Martindale-Hubbell Law Directory

MULVANEY, KAHAN & BARRY, A PROFESSIONAL CORPORATION (AV)

Seventeenth Floor, First National Bank Center, 401 West "A" Street, 92101-7994
Telephone: 619-238-1010
Fax: 619-238-1981
Email: mkb@mkblaw.com
Los Angeles, California Office: Union Bank Plaza, 445 South Figueroa Street, Suite 2600.
Telephone: 213-612-7765.
La Jolla, California Office: Suite 315, 875 Prospect Street, P.O. Box 1168.
Telephone: 619-454-1780.
Fax: 619-454-1792.
Orange, California Office: The Koll Center, 500 North State College Boulevard, Suite 440.
Telephone: 714-634-7069.
Fax: 714-939-8000.

James F. Mulvaney
Lawrence Kahan
Everett G. Barry, Jr.
Robert A. Linn
Paula Rotenberg
Melissa A. Blackburn
Mark R. Raftery
John A. Mayers
Robin L. Cahill
Kristin L. Yokomoto
Darren John Devlin

OF COUNSEL

Rex B. Beatty
Derrick W. Samuelson (Not admitted in CA)

Representative Clients: Air Products & Chemicals, Inc.; Aoki Construction (CA) Co., Ltd.; AT&T Capital Corp.; BellSouth Communications Systems, Inc.; ITT Corp.; NationsBank; Phoenix Home Life Mutual Insurance Co.; Textron Financial Corporation; Union Bank; Wells Fargo Bank.

For full biographical listings, see the Martindale-Hubbell Law Directory

THE PAGE FIRM, A P.C. (AV)

401 B Street, Suite 2100, 92101-4244
Telephone: 619-231-1822
Fax: 619-231-1877
URL: http://www.lawyers.com/pagefirm

Richard W. Page

For full biographical listings, see the Martindale-Hubbell Law Directory

PILLSBURY MADISON & SUTRO LLP (AV)

101 West Broadway, Suite 1800, 92101-8219
Telephone: 619-234-5000
FAX: 619-236-1995
Email: pillsburylaw.com *URL:* http://pillsburylaw.com
Costa Mesa, California Office: 650 Town Center Drive, 7th Floor, 92626.
Telephone: 714-436-6800.
Fax: 714-436-2800.
Los Angeles, California Office: Citicorp Plaza, 725 South Figueroa, Suite 1200, 90017.
Telephone: 213-488-7100.
Fax: 213-629-1033.
New York, New York Office: 375 Park Avenue, Suite 3108, 10152.
Telephone: 212-826-1060.
Fax: 212-826-9255.
Silicon Valley Office: 2550 Hanover Street, Palo Alto, 94034.
Telephone: 650-233-4500.
Fax: 650-233-4545.
Sacramento, California Office: 400 Capitol Mall, Suite 1700, 95814.
Telephone: 916-329-4700.
Fax: 916-441-3583.
San Francisco, California Office: 50 Fremont Street, 94105.
Telephone: 415-983-1000.
Fax: 415-983-1200.
Washington, D.C. Office: 1100 New York Avenue, N.W., Ninth Floor, 20005.
Telephone: 202-861-3000.
Fax: 202-822-0944.
Vienna, Virginia Office: 8330 Boone Boulevard, Suite 400, 22182.
Telephone: 703-744-7600.
Fax: 703-744-7605.

(See Next Column)

PILLSBURY MADISON & SUTRO LLP—*Continued*

Tokyo, Japan Office: Pillsbury Madison & Sutro, Gaikokuho Jimu Bengoshi Jimusho, 5th Floor, Samon Eleven Building, 3-1, Samon-cho, Shinjuku-ku, Tokyo 160 Japan.
Telephone: 800-729-9830; 011-813-3354-3531.
Fax: 011-813-3354-3534.

MEMBERS OF FIRM

John M. Dunn
K. Micheal Garrett
P. Garth Gartrell
T. Michael Hird
Sue J. Hodges
George S. Howard, Jr.
Anita M. Kirkpatrick
Eric A. Kremer
Daniel C. Minteer
Patrick C. Shea
David R. Snyder
Douglas R. Tribble
Mark R. Wicker
Angela M. Yates
Eric C. Young

OF COUNSEL

John E. Burke
Matthew S. Walker

SENIOR COUNSEL

Christopher B. Latham
David M. Logan
Kimberly A. Mc Donnell
Warren H. Nelson, Jr.
Richard M. Segal
Jan H. Webster

ASSOCIATES

Christine K. Besnard
Wayne B. Brown
Martha L. Carpenter
Robert J. Driscoll
Jena Kirsch Joyce
Laura K. Licht
Kathryn L. Partrick
Thomas A. Rector
Jon P. Rodrigue
Elizabeth A. Ryner
Michelle L. Wilson

For full biographical listings, see the Martindale-Hubbell Law Directory

SELTZER CAPLAN MCMAHON & VITEK, A PROFESSIONAL CORPORATION (AV)

2100 Symphony Towers, 750 B Street, 92101
Telephone: 619-685-3003
Fax: 619-685-3100
URL: http://www.scwm.com

Floyd Wilkins, Jr. (Retired)
Norman T. Seltzer
Robert Caplan
Gerald L. McMahon
Reginald A. Vitek
Stephen D. Royer
David J. Dorne
James R. Dawe
Brian T. Seltzer
Elizabeth A. Smith
Julie P. Dubick
Joyce A. McCoy
Dennis J. Wickham
John H. Alspaugh
James P. Delphey
Craig E. Courter
Elinor T. Merideth
Michael G. Nardi
Thomas F. Steinke
Neal P. Panish
Sean T. Hargaden
Vera P. Pardee
Michael R. Seyle
David S. Minton
Adrienne Jeffrey
David J. Zubkoff
John D. Hershberger
Charles L. Goldberg
Patrick Q. Hall
Gregory E. Flynn
Michael A. Leone
Daniel A. Andrist
J. Scott Scheper

Elisa A. Brandes
Kelly Rae Waggonner
Lee E. Hejmanowski
Christine M. Dabrowski
Christopher J. Weaver
Laura H. Roppe
Genevieve Chesnut
Scott W. Sigman
Mary Christine Tennison
Andrew D. Brooks
Steven K. Jonker
Paul R. Datnow
Daniel E. Eaton
Jennifer L. Hardy
Marnie S. Skeen
Romy A. Selati
David M. Greeley
Troy A. Kingshaven
Charles B. Witham
William K. Browning
Jennifer N. Long
Jason J. Belice

STAFF ATTORNEY

John M. Toscano (Not admitted in CA)

OF COUNSEL

Julie Genthner Lopez
Patricia Garcia
Kathleen Furness
Victor A. Vilaplana

Representative Clients: Chicago Title; The Goodyear Tire & Rubber Co.; W.R. Grace & Co.—Conn.; McDonnell-Douglas Corp.; McMillin Communities; Western Financial Savings Bank.

For full biographical listings, see the Martindale-Hubbell Law Directory

SPARBER, FERGUSON, PONDER & RYAN, A PROFESSIONAL LAW CORPORATION (AV)

Imperial Bank Building, 701 "B" Street, Tenth Floor, 92101-8103
Telephone: 619-239-3600
Facsimile: 619-239-5601

Richard E. Sparber
James P. Ferguson
John E. Ponder
Greg J. Ryan
Richard J. Annen
Daniel F. Morrin
Gary B. Rudolph

(See Next Column)

Todd R. Gabriel
Carol R. McGinnis
William P. Fennell
Jack Anderson
Gregory L. Lusitana
Jill D. Perry
Melvin E. Morris
Peter A. Zamoyski
Yosina M. Lissebeck

OF COUNSEL

Michael D. Nagle

LEGAL SUPPORT PERSONNEL

LEGAL ADMINISTRATOR

Beverly K. Driscoll

For full biographical listings, see the Martindale-Hubbell Law Directory

*SAN FRANCISCO,** San Francisco Co.

ALLEN, MATKINS, LECK, GAMBLE & MALLORY LLP (AV)

A Limited Liability Partnership including Professional Corporations
333 Bush Street, Seventeenth Floor, 94104-2806
Telephone: 415-837-1515
Fax: 415-837-1516
Los Angeles, California Office: Seventh Floor, 515 South Figueroa Street. 90071.
Telephone: 213-622-5555.
Telecopier: 213-620-8816.
Irvine, California Office: Fourth Floor, 18400 Von Karman, 92612.
Telephone: 949-553-1313.
Telecopier: 949-553-8354.
San Diego, California Office: 501 West Broadway, Ninth Floor, 92101.
Telephone: 619-233-1155.
Facsimile: 619-233-1158.
West Los Angeles, California Office: 1999 Avenue of the Stars, Suite 1800, 90067.
Telephone: 310-788-2400.
Fax: 310-788-2410.

PARTNERS

Richard C. Mallory (Resident)
John C. Gamble
Guy Rounsaville, Jr. (Resident)
Michael P. Durkee (Resident)
H. Christian L'Orange (Resident)
Ronald K. Clausen (Resident)
Lindbergh Porter, Jr. (Resident)
Nancy Lundeen (Resident)

ASSOCIATES

Stephen P. Lieske (Resident)
Dana R. Stone (Resident)
David H. Blackwell (Resident)
Christie M. Musser (Resident)
Bradley P. Kaplan (Resident)
Hazel Marlee Brandt (Resident)
Lee A. Edlund (Resident)
Deborah L. Babb (Resident)
David Y. Otsuka (Resident)
Theodore M. Gizewski (Resident)
Carrie H. Crockett (Resident)
Todd Chapman (Resident)
Cynthia Hinshaw Wertz (Resident)
Jennie Lau (Resident)
Michael J. Betz (Resident)

OF COUNSEL

Henry Lerner
James M. Tervo
Madeleine E. Sloane
Roberta V. Romberg (Resident)

For full biographical listings, see the Martindale-Hubbell Law Directory

BAKER & MCKENZIE (AV)

Two Embarcadero Center 24th Floor, 94111-3909
Telephone: (415) 576-3000
Intl. Dialing: (1-415) 576-3000
Facsimiles: (1-415) 576-3099; 576-3098
URL: http://www.bakerinfo.com
Associated Offices of Baker & McKenzie in: Almaty, Amsterdam, Bahrain, Baku, Bangkok, Barcelona, Beijing, Berlin, Bogotá, Brasília, Brussels, Budapest, Buenos Aires, Cairo, Caracas, Chicago, Dallas, Düsseldorf, Frankfurt, Geneva, Hanoi, Ho Chi Minh City, Hong Kong, Houston, Hsinchu, Juárez, Kiev, London, Madrid, Manila, Melbourne, México City, Miami, Milan, Monterrey, Moscow, Münich, New York, Palo Alto, Paris, Prague, Rio de Janeiro, Riyadh, Rome, St. Petersburg, San Diego, Santiago, São Paulo, Singapore, Stockholm, Sydney, Taipei, Tijuana, Tokyo, Toronto, Valencia, Warsaw, Washington, D.C. and Zürich.
Correspondent Law Firm: Hadiputranto, Hadinoto & Partners, Jakarta.

MEMBERS OF FIRM

Michael E. Arruda
Deborah A. Bailey-Wells
Russell Baker (1901-1979)
Frank S. Bayley
Edward D. Burmeister
Klaus H. Burmeister
Judy V. Davidoff
Peter J. Engstr[illegible]
Howard F. Fine
Virginia L. Gibson
Bruce H. Jackson
George H. Kalikman
Jonathan S. Kitchen
John F. McKenzie
Timothy A. Tosta
Kent F. Wisner

NATIONAL PARTNERS

Bartley B. Baer
Peter R. Denwood
Tyrrell M. Prosser

(See Next Column)

BAKER & MCKENZIE, *San Francisco—Continued*

OF COUNSEL

David G. Ellsworth
J. Michael Goulding
Bill O. Hing
Dennis Keeley
Bonnie K. Levitt
C. Matthew Schulz
Kerry Shapiro
Richard P. Walker

ASSOCIATES

Edward S. Atkinson, Jr.
Suzanne Awad
Majda Barazzutti
Daniel J. Barry
Allison S.Y. Chang (Not admitted in CA)
Timothy D. Cremin
Lothar Determann (Not admitted in United States)
Edward Young Chul Dhong
Valerie Diamond
Jon F. Doyle (Not admitted in CA)
Maureen M. Duffy
Eric L. Dupré
Aaron X. Fellmeth
Sean M. Fischer
Christopher van Gundy
Dina Hamdy
Mae Y. Ho
Mark J. Jarrett
Peter Y. Malyshev
Robert G. Marshall II
Lance C. Martin
Kerry E. Medd (Not admitted in United States)
Charles V. Moseley
Margreet G. Nijhof
Lynda M. Ruiz
Irina A. Shestakova (Not admitted in CA)
Joyce Y. Smith
Elena V. Speed
Craig P. Tanner
Beneba J. Thomas
Yen B. Trac
Robert A. Trodella
A. Alyce Werdel
Sharon P. Yau

For full biographical listings, see the Martindale-Hubbell Law Directory

---

BEVERIDGE & DIAMOND LLP (AV)

One Sansome Street, Suite 3400, 94104-4438
Telephone: 415-397-0100
Telecopier: 415-397-4238
URL: http://www.beveridgediamond.com
Sacramento, California Office: Suite 1860, 400 Capitol Mall, 95814-4407.
Telephone: 916-553-4533.
Telecopier: 916-553-4539.
Washington, D.C. Office: Beveridge & Diamond, P.C. 1350 I Street, N.W., Suite 700, 20005-3311.
Telephone: 202-789-6000.
Telecopier: 202-789-6190.
New York, N.Y. Office: Beveridge & Diamond, P.C. 15th Floor, 477 Madison Avenue, 10022-5802.
Telephone: 212-702-5400.
Telecopier: 212-702-5450.
Saddle Brook, New Jersey Office: Beveridge & Diamond, Park 80 West, Plaza II Suite 200, 07663-5836.
Telephone: 201-585-8162.
Telecopier: 201-368-1944.
Baltimore, Maryland Office: Beveridge & Diamond, P.C., Suite 2210, 201 North Charles Street, 21201-4150.
Telephone: 410-230-3850.
Telecopier: 410-230-3868.

Lawrence S. Bazel
James T. Burroughs
David D. Cooke
Robert P. Doty
Jennifer L. Hernandez
James L. Meeder
Daniel J. O'Hanlon
Robert D. Wyatt

OF COUNSEL

Laurence G. Chaset
Marc J. Ebbin

SENIOR ATTORNEY

Eileen M. Nottoli

Laura S. Bernard
Stuart I. Block
Alexander G. Crockett
Diane Korbel
John L. Kortum
Elizabeth A. Lake
Janet C. Loduca
Karen Lynn Peterson
Tamsen Plume
Katherine B. Reilly
Gregory A. Ritter
Christine Wade Griffith
Zachary R. Walton

For full biographical listings, see the Martindale-Hubbell Law Directory

---

BROBECK, PHLEGER & HARRISON LLP (AV)

A Partnership including a Professional Corporation
Spear Street Tower, One Market, 94105
Telephone: 415-442-0900
Facsimile: 415-442-1010
Email: info@brobeck.com *URL:* http://www.brobeck.com
Los Angeles, California Office: 550 South Hope Street.
Telephone: 213-489-4060.
Facsimile: 213-745-3345.
Palo Alto, California Office: Two Embarcadero Place, 2200 Geng Road.
Telephone: 650-424-0160.
Facsimile: 650-496-2885.
San Diego, California Office: 550 West C Street, Suite 1300.
Telephone: 619-234-1966.
Facsimile: 619-236-1403 (13th Floor); 619-234-3848 (12th Floor).

(See Next Column)

Irvine, California Office: 38 Technology Drive.
Telephone: 949-790-6300.
Facsimile: 949-790-6301.
Austin, Texas Office: 301 Congress Avenue, Suite 1200.
Telephone: 512-477-5495.
Facsimile: 512-477-5813.
Denver, Colorado Office: 370 Interlocken Boulevard, Suite 500.
Telephone: 303-410-2000.
Facsimile: 303-410-2199.
New York, N.Y. Office: 1633 Broadway, 47th Floor.
Telephone: 212-581-1600.
Facsimile: 212-586-7878.
Washington, D.C. Office: 701 Pennsylvania Avenue, NW, Suite 220.
Telephone: 202-220-6000.
Facsimile: 202-824-0949.
London, England Office: Brobeck Hale and Dorr International, Hasilwood House, 60 Bishopsgate, London EC2N 4AJ.
Telephone: 011 44 171 638 6688.
Facsimile: 011 44 171 638 5888.

CHAIRMAN

Tower C. Snow, Jr.

MANAGING PARTNER

James E. Burns, Jr.

PARTNERS

Rochelle D. Alpert
James P. Baker
Grady M. Bolding
Donald J. Bouey
Sara B. Brody
David J. Brown
Donald W. Brown
Rollin B. Chippey, II
Roy E. Crawford, III
George A. Cumming, Jr.
Susan R. Diamond
Brendan G. Dolan
Rebecca D. Eisen
G. Larry Engel
Gary S. Fergus
Vincent P. Finigan, Jr.
Stephen R. Finn
Kevin B. Fisher
Tom M. Freeman
Anthony O. Garvin
Nora L. Gibson
A. Bruce Gilmore
Lawrence J. Gornick
Franklin Brockway Gowdy
Michael B. Green
Max Gutierrez, Jr.
Mortimer H. Hartwell
George A. Hisert
Frederick D. Holden, Jr.
Barry W. Homer
William R. Irwin
Karen Johnson-McKewan
Jeffrey S. Kingston
Molly Moriarty Lane
John W. Larson
F. Daniel Leventhal
William A. Levin
Robert C. Livsey
Mark E. McKeen
Roderick A. McLeod
Timothy A. Meltzer
James L. Miller
Michael E. Molland
Ronald B. Moskovitz
Kevin P. Muck
John D. Muller
Carla B. Oakley
James N. Penrod
Thomas M. Peterson
Barbara Pletcher
Michael F. Potter
James H. Quirk
Laura J. Remington
Diane S. Rice
Robert A. Rich
Kent M. Roger
J. Michael Shepherd
Joseph K. Siino
Stephen M. Snyder
W. Scott Thomas
Michael D. Torpey
William E. Trautman
George D. Tuttle
Douglas G. Van Gessel
Robert P. Varian
L. Christopher Vejnoska
Nicholas B. Waranoff
Cecily A. Waterman
David E. Weiss
Kelly C. Wooster
Ronald S. Wynn
Douglas M. Young

SENIOR COUNSEL

Stephen M. Knaster
Jayne Loughry
Eileen M. Malley
Tracy Thompson

OF COUNSEL

Keven F. Baxter
William S. Boyd
Barbara A. Clark
Peter C. Coleman (Not admitted in CA)
Marilyn Fisher
Ivan M. Gold
William L. Harvey
Otto C. Holz
Eliza M. Rodrigues
Susan P. Vomund

ASSOCIATES

Michael D. Adams
Ronit Michelle Alcheck
Kathryn J. Allen
Paul A. Andronico
Ted F. Angus, Jr.
V. Elise Bigelow
Margo N. Bradish
Janet Brody
John A. Burke
Shelby L. Carter
Moira L. Dawson
Laura Miller de Petra
David F. Dedyo
Sahil W. Desai
Matthew R. Drake
Lindsay C. Freeman
Erin E. Giacoppo
Tanya Herrera
Angela Christine Hilt
Edith M. Hofmeister
Howard Holderness III
Stephanie A. Hopkins
William W. Huckins
Catherine A. Jackson
Linda R. Jones
Jeffrey A. Kaiser
Roberto J. Kampfner
Scott D. Karchmer
Deborah L. Kartiganer
Steven S. Kaufhold
Elizabeth M. Khachigian
John C. Kirke
Edward A. Kleinhaus
James N. Kramer
Savita N. Krishna
Bernice Lynn Lake

(See Next Column)

BROBECK, PHLEGER & HARRISON LLP—*Continued*

ASSOCIATES (Continued)

Jeanine Marie Larrea
David C. Lee
Elisa S. Lee
Kahala Lee
James A. Lico
Gregory L. Lippetz
Renée T. Machi
Kenneth A. MacKay
Jori K. Mandelman
Mary Beth Mayo
Nikki S. McKennedy
Eric Meckley
Peter P. Meringolo
Lauren M. Michals
Martha Oberle O'Malley
Tavan L. R. Pechet (Not admitted in CA)
Michael J. Penner
Peter M. Phleger
Jennifer Smith Ray
Randall A. Richmond
Elizabeth L. Riles
Maura Roe
Shelli Rosenfeld
Jeffrey A. Rossman
Tracey S. Ryniec
Brett Schuman
Kristen L. Schutjer (Not admitted in CA)
Patrick J. Shea (Not admitted in CA)
Erika B. Smith
Stacey E. Stillman
Kathryn M. Taylor
Isabel Traugott
Gregory W. Tschider III (Not admitted in CA)
Julie Unmacht
Dorothy Vinski
RobURT J. Waldow
Shelley E. Wharton
Sarah C. Wilson
Thomas R. Wilson
David J. Wood

For full biographical listings, see the Martindale-Hubbell Law Directory

COOLEY GODWARD LLP (AV)

20th Floor, One Maritime Plaza, 94111-3580
Telephone: 415-693-2000
Fax: 415-951-3699
Email: webmaster@cooley.com *URL:* http://www.cooley.com
Palo Alto, California Office: Five Palo Alto Square, 3000 El Camino Real.
Telephone: 650-843-5000.
Fax: 650-857-0663.
San Diego, California Office: 4365 Executive Drive, Suite 1100.
Telephone: 619-550-6000.
Fax: 619-453-3555.
Menlo Park, California Office: 3000 Sand Hill Road, Building 3, Suite 230.
Telephone: 650-843-5000.
Fax: 650-854-2691.
Boulder, Colorado Office: 2595 Canyon Boulevard, Suite 250.
Telephone: 303-546-4000.
Fax: 303-546-4099.
Denver, Colorado Office: One Tabor Center, 1200 17th Street, Suite 2100.
Telephone: 303-606-4800.
Fax: 303-606-4899.
Kirkland, Washington Office: 5200 Carillon Point.
Telephone: 425-893-7700.
Fax: 425-893-7777.
Reston, Virginia Office: 2002 Edmund Halley Drive, Suite 300.
Telephone: 703-262-8000.
Fax: 703-262-8100.

PARTNERS

Augustus Castro (1911-1995)
Edwin E. Huddleson, Jr. (1914-1995)
Arthur E. Cooley (1882-1972)
Louis V. Crowley (1887-1971)
H. Rowan Gaither, Jr. (1909-1961)
Thomas A. H. Hartwell (1927-1990)
Andrew Kopperud (1924-1973)
Kenneth J. Adelson
Gordon C. Atkinson
Andrew R. Basile, Jr. (Not admitted in CA)
John L. Cardoza
Peter H. Carson
Jamie E. Chung
Paul Churchill
John W. Crittenden
James Donato
Robert L. Eisenbach, III
Kimberly D. Fanning
Daniel W. Frank
Richard H. Frank
Steven L. Friedlander
William G. Gaede, III
James C. Gaither
Kenneth L. Guernsey
J. Michael Kelly
Karen J. Kubin
Paul J. Laveroni
Samuel M. Livermore
Ann M. Mooney
Webb B. Morrow, III
Lance Director Nagel
Susan Cooper Philpot
Anna B. Pope
Thomas Z. Reicher
Paul A. Renne
Benjamin K. Riley
Yvonne Gonzalez Rogers
Joseph P. Russoniello
Martin S. Schenker
Joseph A. Scherer
Anita F. Stork
Myron G. Sugarman
Michael J. Sullivan
Michael Traynor
Christopher A. Westover
Jeffrey S. Zimman

OF COUNSEL

Anthony C. Gilbert
William W. Godward
Bradford Jeffries
Paul M. Little
Erving Sodos
Frank D. Tatum, Jr.

SPECIAL COUNSEL

Barry A. Graynor
Cydney S. Posner
Sandra B. Price
Randi Silverman

(See Next Column)

ASSOCIATES

Robert Ajemian
Dina E. Alexander
Jodie M. Bourdet
Matthew D. Brown
Tracie L. Brown
Michelle Brownlee
Thea M. Chester
Randall K. H. Ching
Julie Conner
Mara Eleina Conway (Not admitted in CA)
Christina G. Cordoza
Juan Cornejo
Bradley C. Crawford
Steve Daetz
Karen Siobhan Daly
Carrie Anderson Daniel
Shashikala Deb
Kirk Dizon
Virginia C. Edwards
Jennifer Shiu-Li Fan (Not admitted in CA)
Stephen M. Fronk
Juli A. Gammon
Nate A. Garhart
David E. Garrett
Susan P. Gibbs
Rachel Nico Halpren
Steven R. Harmon
Michael W. Hauptman
Tamara Hinds
Monica K. Hoppe
Kathleen A. Howard
Craig D. Jacoby
Isobel Ann Jones
Edward A. Kleinhans
Sarah L. Kowalski
Hans Lapping
J. David Larsen
Rochelle S. Levy
Felice P. Liang
Jeffrey T. Lindgren
Michael D. Lisi
Timothy J. Lucey
Cecilia Meei-Wenn Mao
Kathleen T. McCarthy
Heather McCormick
Malu S. Mercado
Tsan Merritt-Poree
Maricel Mojares-Moore (Not admitted in CA)
Alison J. Morbey
Jennifer J. Nam
J. Timothy Nardell
Eugene M. Pak
David Joseph Paul
Kristin Pedersen
Alan C. Perkins (Not admitted in CA)
Kathleen G. Philips
Ann E. Polus
Laura M. Randall
Miles Roeder (Not admitted in CA)
Susan L. Ruebush
Erin Sawyer
Charles M. Schaible
Myles B. Silton
Esme C. Smith
Karyn R. Smith
Lea Anne Storum
Alan Tafapolsky
Angelique Tremble
Eric S. Vanderpool
A. James Vazquez-Azpiri
Stacie A. Wallace
Kathryn M. Wheble
Elizabeth A. Willes
Peter M. O. Wong
Timothy S. G. Young

LEGAL SUPPORT PERSONNEL

SPECIALISTS

Mariana M. Brothers
Tomoko T. Flynn
Joni Gok
Phyllis A. O'Dea

SENIOR PARALEGALS

Michelle Barroca
Ron A. Metzger
C. Kim Miller
Diana G. Moore
Joyce E. Stackpole

For full biographical listings, see the Martindale-Hubbell Law Directory

DUANE, MORRIS & HECKSCHER LLP (AV)

100 Spear Street, 94105
Telephone: 415-371-2200
Fax: 415-371-2201
URL: http://www.duanemorris.com
Philadelphia, Pennsylvania Office: Suite 4200, One Liberty Place.
Telephone: 215-979-1000.
Fax: 215-979-1020.
New York, New York Office: 380 Lexington Avenue.
Telephone: 212-692-1000.
Fax: 212-692-1020.
Chicago, Illinois Office: 227 West Monroe Street, Suite 3400.
Telephone: 312-499-6700.
Fax: 312-499-6701.
Washington, D.C. Office: 1667 K Street, N.W., Suite 700.
Telephone: 202-776-7800.
Fax: 202-776-7801.
Boston, Massachusetts Office: One International Place, 14th Floor.
Telephone: 617-598-3100.
Fax: 617-598-3101.
Miami, Florida Office: 200 South Biscayne Boulevard, Suite 3410.
Telephone: 305-571-5550.
Fax: 302-571-5560.
Wilmington, Delaware Office: 1201 Market Street, Suite 1500.
Telephone: 302-571-5550.
Fax: 302-571-5560.
Harrisburg, Pennsylvania Office: 305 North Front Street, 5th Floor, P.O. Box 1003.
Telephone: 717-237-5500.
Fax: 717-232-4015.
Wayne, Pennsylvania Office: 735 Chesterbrook Boulevard, Suite 300.
Telephone: 610-647-3555.
Fax: 610-640-2619.
Cherry Hill, New Jersey Office: 51 Haddonfield Road, Suite 340.
Telephone: 856-488-7300.
Fax: 856-488-7021.
Newark, New Jersey Office: One Riverfront Plaza.
Telephone: 973-424-2000.
Fax: 973-424-2001.

(See Next Column)

DUANE, MORRIS & HECKSCHER LLP, *San Francisco—Continued*

Palm Beach, Florida Office: 249 Royal Palm Way, Suite 403.
Telephone: 561-366-5400.
Fax: 561-366-5401.
Allentown, Pennsylvania Office: 968 Postal Road, Suite 200, P.O. Box 90400.
Telephone: 610-266-3650.
Fax: 610-266-3651.
Houston, Texas Office: One Greenway Plaza, Suite 500.
Telephone: 713-552-9900.
Fax: 713-552-0109.
Dover, Delaware Office: 314 S. State Street.
Telephone: 302-736-0156.
Fax: 302-736-0336.
Bangor, Maine Office: 15 Columbia Street, 4th Floor.
Telephone: 207-990-4800.
Fax: 207-990-4804.
Princeton, New Jersey Office: Princeton Forrestal Village, 116 Village Boulevard, Suite 200.
Telephone: 609-734-4323.
Fax: 609-734-4387.

RESIDENT PARTNERS

Thomas M. Berliner (Partner-in-Charge, San Francisco, California Office)
Joseph M. Burton
M. Elizabeth Graham
George D. Niespolo
Mark P. Rapazzini

ASSOCIATES

Lina M. Brenner
Thomas F. Chan
Colin L. Pearce

For full biographical listings, see the Martindale-Hubbell Law Directory

FOLEY & LARDNER (AV)

One Maritime Plaza, 6th Floor, 94111-3404
Telephone: 415-434-4484
Facsimile: 415-434-4507
Email: foleylardner@worldnet.att.net *URL:* http://www.foleylardner.com
Los Angeles, California Office: 2029 Century Park East, 35th Floor.
Telephone: 310-277-2223.
Fax: 310-557-8475.
Sacramento, California Office: 300 Capitol Mall, Suite 1125.
Telephone: 916-443-8005.
Fax: 916-443-2240.
San Diego, California Office: 402 West Broadway, 23rd Floor.
Telephone: 619-234-6655.
Fax: 619-234-3510.
Denver, Colorado Office: 1999 Broadway, Suite 2560.
Telephone: 303-297-0260.
Fax: 303-297-0266.
Washington, D.C. Office: Washington Harbour, Suite 500, 3000 K Street, N.W.
Telephone: 202-672-5300.
Telex: 904136 (Foley Lard Wash).
Facsimile: 202-672-5399.
Jacksonville, Florida Office: The Greenleaf Building, 200 Laura Street. P.O. Box 240.
Telephone: 904-359-2000.
Facsimile: 904-359-8700.
Orlando, Florida Office: Suite 1800, 111 North Orange Avenue, P.O. Box 2193.
Telephone: 407-423-7656.
Facsimile: 407-648-1743.
Tallahassee, Florida Office: 300 East Park Avenue, P.O. Box 1454.
Telephone: 850-222-6100.
Facsimile: 850-561-6475.
Tampa, Florida Offices: Suite 2700, One Hundred N. Tampa Street, P.O. Box 3391.
Telephones: 813-229-2300; Pinellas County: 813-442-3296.
Facsimile: 813-221-4210.
West Palm Beach, Florida Office: Suite 200, Phillips Point East Tower, 777 South Flagler Drive.
Telephone: 561-655-5050.
Facsimile: 561-655-6925.
Chicago, Illinois Office: Suite 3300, One IBM Plaza, 330 N. Wabash Avenue.
Telephone: 312-755-1900.
Facsimile: 312-755-1925.
Annapolis, Maryland Office: Suite 102, 175 Admiral Cochrane Drive.
Telephone: 410-266-8077.
Telex: 899149 (Oldtownpat).
Facsimile: 410-266-8664.
Madison, Wisconsin Office: Verex Plaza, 150 East Gilman Street, P.O. Box 1497.
Telephone: 608-257-5035.
Facsimile: 608-258-4258.
Milwaukee, Wisconsin Office: Firstar Center, 777 East Wisconsin Avenue.
Telephone: 414-271-2400.
Telex: 26-819 (Foley Lard Mil).
Facsimile: 414-297-4900.
Brussels, Belgium Office: Avenue Louise, 283.
Telephone: 32-2-646-2777.
Facsimile: 32-2-646-7574.

(See Next Column)

PARTNERS

William B. Alberti
Laurence R. Arnold
Thomas F. Carlucci
Thomas L. Driscoll
Edsell M. Eady, Jr.
Carl H. Hitchner
Jonathan M. Lindeke
Gregory W. McClune
Shirley J. Paine
Stephen W. Parrish
Ingeborg E. Penner
Mark E. Reagan
Mark T. Schieble
Dorothy J. Stephens
Paul A. Stewart
Judith A. Waltz

SPECIAL COUNSEL

Kenneth L. Burgess (Not admitted in CA)
Cathleen Desjardins
Lawrence C. Jensen

ASSOCIATES

Sam N. Dawood
John H. Douglas
Mark A. Johnson
Jennifer G. Krengel
Paula C. Ohliger
Anna Rienhardt
Alice J. Um (Not admitted in CA)
Danny W. Wan

For full biographical listings, see the Martindale-Hubbell Law Directory

FOLGER LEVIN & KAHN LLP (AV)

Embarcadero Center West, 275 Battery Street, 23rd Floor, 94111
Telephone: 415-986-2800
Fax: 415-986-2827
URL: http://www.flk.com
Los Angeles, California Office: 28th Floor, 1900 Avenue of the Stars.
Telephone: 310-556-3700.
FAX: 310-556-3770.

MEMBERS OF FIRM

John P. Levin
Peter M. Folger
Michael A. Kahn
William A. Norris (Resident in Los Angeles Office)
Donald E. Kelley, Jr.
Thomas P. Laffey (Resident in Los Angeles Office)
Scott W. Bowen (Resident in Los Angeles Office)
Samuel R. Miller
Mary C. Castle
Richard Keenan
Roger B. Mead
Douglas W. Sullivan
Teressa K. Lippert
Margaret R. Dollbaum
James Goldberg
Lisa McCabe van Krieken
Gregory D. Call
Janice B. Lawrence
Susan W. Ansberry
Thomas F. Koegel
Katharine Livingston
Adam Sachs
Wesley D. Hurst (Resident in Los Angeles Office)
J. Daniel Sharp
Margaret E. Murray
Christopher B. Conner

ASSOCIATES

Deborah W. Pulido
Carol Kerr (Resident in Los Angeles Office)
M. Kay Martin
Julie M. Kennedy
Roland Valayre
Dominique R. Shelton (Resident in Los Angeles Office)
Kevin D. Caton
Kenneth R. Hillier
Theresa I. McFarland
Michael F. Kelleher
Raquel L. Wilkening
Jiyun Cameron Lee
Theresa A. Nagle
Karen Jensen Petrulakis
Beatrice B. Nguyen
Ernst A. Halperin
Jessica M. Karner
Nancy E. Yaffe (Resident in Los Angeles Office)
Lynne S. Bourgault
Stuart J. Mackey
Kristina K. Chamorro
Mary Anne Weiss
Denelle M. Dixon-Thayer
Jennifer A. Salzman (Resident in Los Angeles Office)
Kereth Frankel Klein
Jennifer Lurie
Janine L. Scancarelli
Timothy Sullivan
Tania L. Davis
Jane J. Felton (Resident in Los Angeles Office)
Julie L. Fieber
Andrew J. Davis

For full biographical listings, see the Martindale-Hubbell Law Directory

GRAHAM & JAMES LLP (AV)

One Maritime Plaza, Suite 300, 94111
Telephone: 415-954-0200
Telecopier: 415-391-2493
Email: twoofter@gj.com *URL:* http://www.gj.com
Other offices located in: Los Angeles, Orange County, Palo Alto and Sacramento California; Seattle, Washington; Washington, D.C.; New York, New York; Milan, Italy; Beijing, China; Tokyo, Japan; London, England.
Associated Offices: Deacons Graham & James, Hong Kong, Sydney, Melbourne, Brisbane, Perth and Canberra, Australia.
Affiliated Offices: Deacons Graham & James, Hanoi and Ho Chi Minh City, Vietnam; Taipei, Taiwan and Bangkok, Thailand; In association with Dewi Soeharto & Rekan, Jakarta, Indonesia; Graham & James in affiliation with Taylor Joynson Garrett, London, England, Bucharest, Romania and Brussels, Belgium; Kau, Dusseldorf, Germany; Mishare M. Al-Ghazali & Partners, Safat, Kuwait; Law Firm of Salah Al-Hejailan, Jeddah and Riyadh, Saudi Arabia; Yeo Wee Kiong & Partners, Singapore.

(See Next Column)

GRAHAM & JAMES LLP—*Continued*

Maureen Bennett	Caroline H. Mead
Mitsuru Claire Chino	Michael R. Moyle
Mark C. Dosker	David M. Niebauer
Diane L. Gibson	Rodney R. Patula
David C. Kenny	Noriyuki Shimoda
Nathan Lane III	Nicholas Unkovic
Michael D. Levin	Thomas H. Woofter
David M. Lofholm	Philip R. Zender

OF COUNSEL

Alexander D. Calhoun

ASSOCIATES

P. Craig Cardon	Caren Jenkins
Priscilla J. Cortez	Remsen M. Kinne, IV
Melissa E. Davidson	Richard MacBride
Matthew Dickstein (Not admitted in CA)	Joseph Meckes
	Catharina Yoosun Min
Quoc-Huy D. Do	Ayako Onoda
Darryl E. Hendrix	Lisa Palter
Achim W. Hoelzle	Serafina Sands

Constance J. Yu

For full biographical listings, see the Martindale-Hubbell Law Directory

GRAY CARY WARE & FREIDENRICH LLP (AV)

Gray Cary Established in 1927
Ware & Freidenrich Established in 1969
139 Townsend Street, Suite 400, 94107-1922
Telephone: 415-836-2500
Telecopier: 415-836-9220
Email: info@graycary.com *URL:* http://www.graycary.com
San Diego, California Office: 401 B Street, Suite 1700, 92101-4297. 619-699-2700.
Telecopier: 619-736-1048.
San Diego/Golden Triangle, California Office: 4365 Executive Drive, Suite 1600, 92121.
Telephone: 858-677-1400.
Telecopier: 858-677-1477.
Palo Alto, California Office: 400 Hamilton Avenue, 94301-1825.
Telephone: 650-833-2000.
Telecopier: 650-327-3699.
La Jolla, California Office: 1200 Prospect Street, Suite 575, 92037-3610.
Telephone: 858-456-3000.
Telecopier: 858-456-3075.
El Centro, California Office: 1224 State Street, P.O. Box 2890, 92244.
Telephone: 760-353-6140.
Telecopier: 760-353-6228.
Austin, Texas Office: 100 Congress Avenue, Suite 1440, 78701.
Telephone: 512-457-7000.
Telecopier: 512-457-7070.
Sacramento, California Office: 400 Capitol Mall, Suite 2100, 95814.
Telephone: 916-930-3200.
Fax: 916-930-3201.

John Allcock (Resident, San Diego Office)	David E. Monahan (Resident, San Diego Office)
John A. Anzur	J. Martin Robertson
William S. Boggs (Resident, San Diego Office)	Dianne B. Salesin
	Stacy Snowman
John Howard Clowes	Karen K. Williams
Margaret H. Kavalaris (Resident, Palo Alto Office)	

Nicole D. Alston	Joanna Edelstein
James M. Brennan	Michael B. Gebhardt
Pamela B. Burke	Brooke S. Geffs
Trevor A. Cox	Andrew M. Jacobson
Kellian Hall Dowd (Not admitted in CA)	Margaret M. Powers
	Jinah K. Yun (Not admitted in CA)

Representative Clients: Automobile Club of South California; Bank of America; Brooktree Corp.; C. A. Parr (Agencies), Ltd.; IMED; Pacific Bell; McMillin Development Co.; Scripps Clinic and Research Found.; SeaWorld, Inc.; Underwriters at Lloyds.

For full biographical listings, see the Martindale-Hubbell Law Directory

HANCOCK ROTHERT & BUNSHOFT LLP (AV)

2nd Floor, Four Embarcadero Center, 94111-4168
Telephone: 415-981-5550
Telecopy: 415-955-2599
URL: http://www.hrblaw.com
Los Angeles, California Office: 17th Floor, 515 South Figueroa Street, 90071-3334.
Telephone: 213-623-7777.
Telecopy: 213-623-5405.
Tahoe City, California Office: Lighthouse Center, 850 North Lake Boulevard, Suite 15, P.O. Box 7199, 96145-7199.
Telephone: 530-583-7767.
Telecopy: 530-581-3215.

(See Next Column)

London Office: Forum House, 35 Great St. Helens, 4th Floor, London EC3A 6HH, England.
Telephone: 071-220-7567.
Telecopy: 071-220-7609.

SAN FRANCISCO BASED MEMBERS OF FIRM

Barry L. Bunshoft	Brian A. Kelly
James P. Barber	Dominica Cortum Anderson
Paul D. Nelson	Paul J. Killion
Richard L. Seabolt	Eric J. Sinrod
Philip R. Matthews	Michael A. Gevertz
Ray L. Wong	Peter J. Whalen
Robert C. Hendrickson	L. Savannah Lichtman
Paul S. Rosenlund	W. Andrew Miller
Nancy B. Ranney	Colleen A. Cassidy
Andrew K. Gordon	Reginald D. Davis
Ronald E. Ruma	Heidi Honora Frenzel
Michael L. Donovan	Lorraine P. Ocheltree
William J. Baron	Joan N. D'Ambrosio
William J. Casey	Maximilian H. Stern

OF COUNSEL

George L. Waddell

SENIOR COUNSEL

Mary Cavins Anderson

ASSOCIATES

Kenneth D. Ayers	Maribel D. Osborne
Eileen M. Hansen	Robert M. Fineman
Suzanne Ryder Fogarty	Elizabeth C. Gaither
John R. Garnett	James P. Koelzer
John L. Slebir	Kate Cutler
David A. Gabianelli	Ann Marie Heimberger
Kevin M. Haithcox	Jeffrey W. Reyna
Merton A. Howard	Eva C. Russell
Beth Pennington	Eleanor M. Roman
Monica M. Slakey	Julie A. Marquis
Charles E. Webb	Scott M. Bloom
Stephen H. Sutro	Tung-On Kong
Craig W. Wallace	Barak D. Jolish
Joleen C. Lenihan	James Birkelund
Edward J. Tafe	Dina D. Nobles
Dina E. Micheletti	Robert D. Goodson

For full biographical listings, see the Martindale-Hubbell Law Directory

HANSON, BRIDGETT, MARCUS, VLAHOS & RUDY, LLP (AV)

23rd Floor, 333 Market Street, 94105
Telephone: 415-777-3200
Facsimile: 415-541-9366
Email: hanson@hansonbridgett.com *URL:* http://www.hansonbridgett.com
Marin County, California Office: 80 East Sir Francis Drake Boulevard, Larkspur, California, 94939.
Telephone: 415-925-8400.
Fax: 415-925-8409.

MEMBERS OF FIRM

Raymond L. Hanson (1912-1996)	Allan D. Jergesen
	Kim T. Schoknecht
Gerald D. Marcus	Bonnie Kathleen Gibson
John J. Vlahos	Howard W. Ashcraft, Jr.
Sidney Rudy	Joel S. Goldman
William J. Bush	Rory J. Campbell
Ronald C. Peterson	Jacquelyn J. Garman
Richard N. Rapoport	David W. Baer
David J. Miller	Madeline Chun
Laurence W. Kessenick	Linda E. Klamm
Ray E. McDevitt	Peter Dmytryk
Douglas H. Barton	Susan G. O'Neill
Jerrold C. Schaefer	Patrick M. Glenn
James D. Holden	W. Daniel Clinton
Paul A. Gordon	David C. Longinotti
Michael A. Duncheon	Pamela S. Kaufmann
William D. Taylor	Diane Marie O'Malley
Fred B. Weil	Jeffrey M. Chu
Craig J. Cannizzo	Michael N. Conneran
Steven V. Schnier	Jonathan S. Storper
Theodore A. Hellman	Andrew G. Giacomini
Kevin M. O'Donnell	James A. Napoli
Stephen L. Taber	Constance M. Hiatt
Joan L. Cassman	Patrick T. Miyaki
Stephen B. Peck	Richard J. Stratton

Lawrence M. Cirelli

ASSOCIATES

Lisa M. Pooley	Gilson S. Riecken
Michael B. McNaughton	Terry A. Rogan
Sandra L. Rappaport	Jennifer G. Hagedorn
Lisa K. Puntillo	Amy J. Wright
Bettina E. Moore	Garner K. Weng
Eric V. Tao	Sonya C. Hong
Allison M. Woodall	Hussein M. Saffouri
Glenda M. Zarbock	Christopher G. Monahan
Leah S. Goldberg	Kurt A. Franklin
Walter R. Schneider	S. Anne Johnson

(See Next Column)

HANSON, BRIDGETT, MARCUS, VLAHOS & RUDY LLP, *San Francisco—Continued*

ASSOCIATES (Continued)

Keren D. Gilbert
Carrie J. Grove
Rudolph Reyes
Gordon D. McAuley
David S. Gehrig
Cynthia L. Laberge
Teresa Viskovich Pahl
Therese M. Leone
Thomas E. McGrath
Alexa A. Sullivan

OF COUNSEL

Arthur T. Bridgett (Retired)
Daniel W. Baker
Robert E. Simms
John W. Broad
Sarah D. Mott
Gary T. Giacomini
William A. Hickey

Representative Clients: Blue Cross and Blue Shield Assn.; Blue Diamond Growers; California Association of Homes for the Aging; CH2M Hill; City of Millbrae; Golden Gate Bridge; Levi Strauss & Co.; PG&E Energy Systems; The Fairmont Hotel; University of California; Wells Fargo Bank, N.A.

For full biographical listings, see the Martindale-Hubbell Law Directory

HOLLAND & KNIGHT LLP (AV)

44 Montgomery Street, Suite 4050, 94104
Telephone: 415-743-6900
Fax: 415-743-6910
Email: hklaw.com *URL:* http://www.hklaw.com
Atlanta, Georgia Office: 1201 West Peachtree Street, N.E., Suite 2000.
Telephone: 404-817-8500.
Fax: 404-881-0470.
Boston, Massachusetts Office: One Beacon Street.
Telephone: 617-523-2700.
Fax: 617-523-6850.
Bradenton, Florida Office: 1001 3rd Avenue West, Suite 600.
Telephone: 941-748-7076.
Fax: 941-747-9774.
Falls Church, Virginia Office: 3110 Fairview Park Drive, Suite 900.
Telephone: 703-645-8600.
Fax: 703-645-8610.
Fort Lauderdale, Florida Office: One East Broward Boulevard, Suite 1300.
Telephone: 954-525-1000.
Fax: 954-463-2030.
Jacksonville, Florida Office: 50 North Laura Street, Suite 3900.
Telephone: 904-353-2000.
Fax: 904-358-1872.
Lakeland, Florida Office: 92 Lake Wire Drive.
Telephone: 941-682-1161.
Fax: 941-688-1186.
Melbourne, Florida Office: 1499 South Harbor City Boulevard, Suite 201.
Telephone: 407-951-1776.
Fax: 407-951-1849.
Miami, Florida Office: 701 Brickell Avenue, Suite 3000.
Telephone: 305-374-8500.
Fax: 305-789-7799.
New York, New York Office: 195 Broadway, 24th Floor
Telephone: 212-513-3200.
Fax: 212-385-9010.
Orlando, Florida Office: 200 South Orange Avenue, Suite 2600.
Telephone: 407-425-8500.
Fax: 407-244-5288.
Providence, Rhode Island Office: 50 Exchange Terrace, Suite 300, Union Station Plaza.
Telephone: 401-751-8500.
Fax: 401-553-6850.
St. Petersburg, Florida Office: 200 Central Avenue, Suite 1600.
Telephone: 727-896-7171.
Fax: 727-822-8048.
Tallahassee, Florida Office: 315 South Calhoun Street, Suite 600.
Telephone: 850-224-7000.
Fax: 850-224-8832.
Tampa, Florida Office: 400 North Ashley Drive, Suite 2300.
Telephone: 813-227-8500.
Fax: 813-229-0134.
Washington, D.C. Office: 2100 Pennsylvania Avenue, N.W., Suite 400.
Telephone: 202-955-3000.
Fax: 202-955-5564.
West Palm Beach, Florida Office: 625 North Flagler Drive, Suite 700.
Telephone: 561-833-2000.
Fax: 561-650-8399.
Mexico City, Mexico Office: HOLLAND & KNIGHT-GALLÁSTEGUI Y LOZANO, S.C. (Joint Venture Office) Avenida Paseo de los Tamarindos No. 400, Torre "B" - 2° Piso, Col. Bosques d las Lomas, C.P. 05120 Mexico, D.F.
Telephone: 011-525-261-1866.
Fax: 011-525-261-1867.
Tel Aviv, Israel Office: Holland & Knight LTD, 23 Derech Petach-Tikva, 18th Floor.
Telephone: +011-972-3-566-7666.
Fax: +011-972-3-566-7667.
Buenos Aires, Argentina Office: San Martin 323--Piso 18, 1004.
Telephone: +54-11 4324-7600.
Fax: +54-11 4324-7601.

SAN FRANCISCO MEMBERS AND ASSOCIATES

Lynn K. Cadwalader
Charles L. Coleman, III
William B. Piels
Constance M. Ridder
Audrey L. Sung
Matthew P. Vafidis
Vernon C. Watters
Thomas A. Zimmer

Donna L. Langley
Naomi Meyers
Mark L. Venardi

SENIOR COUNSEL

Alexis S. M. Chiu

For full biographical listings, see the Martindale-Hubbell Law Directory

LANDELS RIPLEY & DIAMOND, LLP (AV)

Hills Plaza, 350 The Embarcadero, 94105
Telephone: 415-512-8700
Fax: 415-512-8750
URL: http://www.landels.com

MEMBERS OF FIRM

Edward D. Landels (1899-1991)
Earl M. Ripley (Retired)
Philip E. Diamond (Retired)
John H. Bickel (Retired).
Sanford Svetcov
Robert J. Breakstone
James A. Bruen
Yaroslav Sochynsky
John F. Barg
Stewart H. Foreman
Jon Enscoe
Stephen C. Lewis
Bruce W. Laidlaw
Margaret Hart Edwards
Theodore A. Griffinger, Jr.
Richard C. Coffin
Kathleen M. Meagher
Paul P. Spaulding, III
Deborah J. Schmall
Stafford Matthews
Thomas D. Trapp
Deborah K. Miller
Paul Zieff
R. Christopher Locke
Scott D. Rogers
Michael H. Zischke
Jonathan A. Funk
Brian S. Haughton
Matthew J. Geyer
Gregory L. Germain
Beth S. Jordan
Robert L. Hines
Deborah K. Tellier
Jonathan Polland
R. Morgan Gilhuly
John D. Fiero
Jennifer G. Redmond
Richard S. Winer
Peter S. Modlin
Neil L. Shapiro
David P. Lanferman
Carolyn A. Lown
Deborah M. Castles
Stephen C. Ryan
Phillip D. Sasso
Michelle D. Kahn
Suheil J. Totah
Peter A. Mastromonaco
Steven R. Charno
Brian E. Nussbaum
Jeffrey S. Sloan

SPECIAL COUNSEL

Barbara Cohen Stikker
Anne R. Knowles

ASSOCIATES

Geoffrey H. Yost
Michelle J. Hirth
James H. Colopy
Jason S. Cohen
Jan E. Ellard
JoAnna L. Brooks
Kevin M. Corbett
Carrie Suzanne Knopf
Michelle Howard
Matthew J. Schenck
Michael C. Li
Juliette L. Hirt
Sarah A. Longstreth
Gary Van Housen
Janine Keck Massey
Scott M. Sellwood
Alex G. Hanafi
Scott C. Smith
Jennifer Kathleen Randlett
Laura L. Buchanan

Representative Clients: Bank of America; California Mortgage Bankers Association; Catellus Development Corp.; General Electric Co.; Metropolitan Life Insurance Co.; Occidental Petroleum Corp.; Union Oil Co.; WMX Technologies, Inc.; Levi Strauss & Co.; Pacific Gas & Electric Co.; California Federal Bank; Waste Management of North America, Inc.

For full biographical listings, see the Martindale-Hubbell Law Directory

LELAND, PARACHINI, STEINBERG, MATZGER & MELNICK, L.L.P. (AV)

27th Floor, 333 Market Street, 94105
Telephone: 415-957-1800
FAX: 415-974-1520
Email: postmaster@lpslaw.com *URL:* http://www.lpslaw.com
Los Angeles, California Office: 500 South Grand Avenue, Suite 1100.
Telephone: 213-623-7505;
Fax: 213-623-7595

Herbert A. Leland (1907-1984)

PARTNERS

James M. Allen
Christopher J. Donnelly
Harvey L. Gould
Craig A. Kepler
Nina P. Kwan
Steven B. Mains
Paul J. Matzger
David H. Melnick
Donald G. Parachini
Merrill E. Steinberg
Neil E. Taxy
Kenneth R. Wachtel
Peter K. Wolff, Jr.

ASSOCIATES

Molly F. Jacobson
Amy N. Paul
Lissa L. Rapoport
Michael L. Violanti

(See Next Column)

LELAND, PARACHINI, STEINBERG, MATZGER & MELNICK L.L.P.—*Continued*

SENIOR COUNSEL

David J. Block
Karen Valentia Clopton
Carroll J. Collins III
Martha L. Daetwyler
Edward Vail Pollack (A Professional Corporation)
Gayle Nin Rosenkrantz
Leland R. Selna, Jr.
Stephan R. Silen
Lynn R. Yamashita

For full biographical listings, see the Martindale-Hubbell Law Directory

LITTLER MENDELSON, A PROFESSIONAL CORPORATION (AV)

650 California Street, 20th Floor, 94108-2693
Telephone: 415-433-1940
Facsimile: 415-399-8490
URL: http://www.littler.com
Offices located in: Phoenix, Arizona, California -- Bakersfield, Fresno, Los Angeles, Oakland, Palm Desert, Sacramento, San Diego, San Jose, Santa Maria, Santa Rosa, Stockton and Walnut Creek; Denver, Colorado; Washington, D.C.; Atlanta, Georgia; Chicago, Illinois; Baltimore, Maryland; Minneapolis, Minnesota; Reno and Las Vegas, Nevada (a partnership with Hicks & Walt); Morristown, New Jersey; New York, New York; Dallas and Houston, Texas; and Seattle and Yakima, Washington

Arthur Mendelson (Retired)
Wesley J. Fastiff
George J. Tichy, II
Wendy L. Tice-Wallner
Joseph A. Schwachter
Robert M. Lieber
Jordan L. Bloom
Garry G. Mathiason
Alan S. Levins
Randolph C. Roeder
William F. Terheyden
Nancy L. Ober
John M. Skonberg
Robert G. Hulteng
Robert Kelton Carrol
R. Brian Dixon
David S. Durham
Paula Champagne
Richard N. Hill
Michele J. Silak
Patricia A. Shepherd
Jeffrey M. Tanenbaum
Jennifer J. Walt
Scott D. Rechtschaffen
Nancy E. Pritikin
Stephen C. Tedesco
Philip L. Ross
David F. Byrnes
Ronald J. Holland II
Carolyn Sue Petrouski
Daniel A. Croley
Robert Leinwand
John C. Fish, Jr.
Marjorie S. Fochtman
Karen E. Ford
Eric A. Grover

G. J. Stillson MacDonnell
Lou Ann Bassan
Rod M. Fliegel
Arthur M. Eidelhoch
Ann M. Wicks
Robert T. Landau
Salimé Samii
Michael Hoffman
Tram-Anh T. Frank
David S. Warner
Michael Mankes
Kristin E. Hutchins
Karen A. Sundermier
Susan A.P. Woodhouse
Elizabeth Toole
Bethany M. Kaye
Michelle R. Barrett
Alma S. Beck
Amy M. Krause
Barbara M. Russell
Valarie L. Sharpe
Anthony J. Sperber
Richard Spitalnik
C. Robert Sturm
Natalie A. Pierce
Stacey A. Zartler
Tracy L. Parola
Ronald A. Peters
Dionysia Johnson-Massie (Not admitted in CA)
Blake W. Martell
L. Julius M. Turman (Not admitted in CA)

For full biographical listings, see the Martindale-Hubbell Law Directory

LONG & LEVIT LLP (AV)

A Limited Liability Partnership
101 California Street, Suite 2300, 94111
Telephone: 415-397-2222
Telex: 340924 HOME OFC SFO-LONG & LEVIT
Facsimile: 415-397-6392
URL: http://www.longlevit.com
Los Angeles, California Office: 601 S. Figueroa, 37th Floor.
Telephone: 213-356-5900.
Facsimile: 213-613-0664.

PARTNERS

Percy V. Long (1870-1953)
Bert W. Levit (1903-1980)
John B. Hook
Howard M. Garfield
Joseph P. McMonigle
Marsha Lee Morrow
Edward F. Donohue, III
Robert C. Chiles
Gerald Gamliel Weisbach
J. Michael Higginbotham
Steven Sharafian
Jeanette Traverso
Richard James Sciaroni
Jennifer Wong Suzuki
Kathleen M. Ewins
Peter L. Isola
Karen L. Uno

(See Next Column)

RESIDENT ASSOCIATES

David A. Astengo
Jennifer A. Becker
John P. Bevan
Corey Shapiro Cherkas
Allison Lane Cooper
Bruce N. Furukawa
Jason A. Geller
Stefan S. Lawrence
Douglas J. Melton
Laurence Scott Near
John H. Quinn
Jennifer Stewart
Clark T. Thiel
Seth E. Watkins
Judith Ann Whitehouse

SPECIAL COUNSEL

Merle J. Panick
Peter B. Molgaard

For full biographical listings, see the Martindale-Hubbell Law Directory

McCUTCHEN, DOYLE, BROWN & ENERSEN, LLP (AV)

Three Embarcadero Center, 94111-4067
Telephone: 415-393-2000
Facsimile: 415-393-2286 (G I, II, III)
Email: postmaster@mdbe.com *URL:* http://www.mccutchen.com
Los Angeles, California Office: 355 South Grand Avenue, Suite 4400, 90071-1560.
Telephone: 213-680-6400.
Facsimile: 213-680-6499.
Walnut Creek, California Office: 1331 North California Boulevard, 94596-4502.
Telephone: 510-937-8000.
Facsimile: 510-975-5390.
Palo Alto, California Office: 3150 Porter Drive, 94304.
Telephone: 650-849-4400.
Fax: 650-849-4800.
Taipei, Taiwan Republic of China Office: International Trade Building, Tenth Floor, 333 Keelung Road, Section 1, 110.
Telephone: 886-2-723-5000.
Facsimile: 886-2-757-6070.

MEMBERS OF FIRM

David M. Balabanian
Dale E. Barnes, Jr.
William Bates, III
Michael I. Begert
Christopher P. Berka (Resident, Palo Alto Office)
Gregory L. Bowling
Susan S. Briggs
Robert Minge Brown (1911-1994)
Ross E. Campbell (Resident, Palo Alto Office)
Byde W. Clawson (Resident, Palo Alto Office)
Jill F. Cooper (Resident, Los Angeles Office)
Robert E. Cox (San Francisco and Palo Alto Offices)
Charles William Craycroft (Resident, Palo Alto Office)
Nora C. Cregan
Daniel J. Curtin, Jr. (Resident, Walnut Creek Office)
Bartley C. Deamer (San Francisco and Palo Alto Offices)
Anne M. Deibert
Carol K. Dillon (Resident, Palo Alto Office)
Colleen P. Doyle (Managing Partner, Los Angeles Office)
James J. Dragna (Resident, Los Angeles Office)
Robert L. Ebe
Roger D. Ehlers
Henry D. Evans, Jr.
Richard C. Field (Resident, Los Angeles Office)
Debra L. Fischer (Resident, Los Angeles Office)
James C. Fowler
John W. Fowler (Resident, Palo Alto Office)
William H. Freedman (Resident, Los Angeles Office)
Angel A. Garganta
Warren E. George
Barry P. Goode
Michael L. Greene (Resident, Walnut Creek Office)
David M. Heilbron
Stephen D. Hibbard
Frank M. Hinman
Christopher B. Hockett
Susan L. Hoffman (Resident, Los Angeles Office)
Terry J. Houlihan
Holly A. House
Geoffrey M. Howard
James L. Hunt
Mary T. Huser (Resident, Palo Alto Office)
Karen E. Silverman Johnson
Dawn L. Judd (Resident, Palo Alto Office)
Alan B. Kalin (Resident, Palo Alto Office)
Karen L. Kennard
James P. Kleinberg (Resident, Palo Alto Office)
Stephen L. Kostka (Resident, Walnut Creek Office)
Leslie G. Landau
James Boyd Lewis
Robert A. Lewis
Michael J. Loeb (San Francisco and Palo Alto Offices)
Jane Elizabeth Lovell
John B. Lowry
Michael B. Lubic (Resident, Los Angeles Office)
Raymond Charles Marshall
Edward J. McCutchen (1857-1933)
Beth A. McGowen (Resident, Palo Alto Office)
Edward S. Merrill (San Francisco and Palo Alto Offices)
Robert E. Merritt (Resident, Walnut Creek Office)
Randy E. Michelson
Robert A. Mills
Gary H. Moore (San Francisco and Palo Alto Offices)
John C. Morrissey (Resident, Los Angeles Office)
David E. Moser
Karen J. Nardi
Trenton H. Norris
Lior O. Nuchi (Resident, Palo Alto Office)
Lynn H. Pasahow
Sara Louise Peterson
Alfred C. Pfeiffer, Jr.
Donn P. Pickett
Michael J. Plishner
Thomas G. Reddy
John R. Reese
Geoffrey L. Robinson (Resident, Walnut Creek Office)
James M. Rockett
Rick R. Rothman (Resident, Los Angeles Office)

(See Next Column)

McCutchen, Doyle, Brown & Enersen LLP, *San Francisco—Continued*

MEMBERS OF FIRM (Continued)

Jonathan H. Sakol
James Severson
Patricia L. Shanks
Charlene Sachi Shimada
Robert E. Sims
Sanford M. Skaggs (Resident and Managing Partner, Walnut Creek Office)
Edward L. Strohbehn, Jr.
Cecily T. Talbert
William E. Thomson, Jr. (Resident, Los Angeles Office)
Daniel M. Wall
Harlan Wendell (Resident, Palo Alto Office)
Thomas B. Worth

Stephen A. Zovickian

COUNSEL

Brent M. Abel (Retired Partner)
Marilee J. Allan
Eric J. Baysinger (Resident, Palo Alto Office)
Heather C. Beatty (Resident, Los Angeles Office)
Joshua A. Bloom
Neil Boorstyn
Robert A. Brundage
Karen A. Caffee (Resident, Los Angeles Office)
Joan C. Y. Chen (Resident, Taipei, Taiwan Office)
David D. Chow (Resident, Taipei, Taiwan Office)
Henry A. Cirillo
Marie A. Cooper (Resident, Walnut Creek Office)
Claire T. Cormier (Resident, Palo Alto Office)
Morris M. Doyle (1909-1998)
Sally A. Drach
Burnham Enersen
Jacqueline C. Fu (Resident, Taipei Office)
Eli W. Gould (Resident, Palo Alto Office)
Grant Guerra (Resident, Walnut Creek Office)
Emily M. Haliday (Resident, Palo Alto Office)
John N. Hauser
Alan S. Hodes (Resident, Palo Alto Office)
Susan K. Hoerger (Resident, Palo Alto Office)
Owen Jameson
Julie A. Jones (Resident, Walnut Creek Office)
Mark O. Kasanin
Frank B. Kennamer
Jack G. Knebel
Christine L. Kopitzke
Stephanie Simonds Lamarre
Kathleen A. McDonald (Resident, Walnut Creek Office)
George B. Newhouse, Jr. (Resident, Los Angeles Office)
Barry R. Ogilby
Venrice R. Palmer
Norman B. Richards
Nancy Mayfield Saunders (Resident, Los Angeles Office)
John D. Schlotterbeck (Resident, Los Angeles Office)
Barbara J. Schussman (Resident, Walnut Creek Office)
M. Johanna Sherlin (Resident, Walnut Creek Office)
Carissa M. Smith (Resident, Palo Alto Office)
Nina K. Srejovic
Keith D. Ungles
Clayton J. Vreeland (Resident, Los Angeles Office)
Sandra Hughes Waddell (Resident, Los Angeles Office)
Mary Catherine Wirth
Pamela F. Worth (Resident, Palo Alto Office)

ASSOCIATES

Richard H. Acker
Monty Agarwal
Dorothy I. Anderson (Resident, Walnut Creek Office)
Mary Moss Appleton (Resident, Los Angeles Office)
Rebecca M. Archer
Peter B. Axelrod
Asha Lata Badrinath
Christine Banks
Philip Barilovits (Resident, Palo Alto Office)
Barbra Barnett (Resident, Los Angeles Office)
Ann Marie Bender
Jeffrey A. Benz (Resident, Walnut Creek Office)
Itzel D. Berrio
Margaret Bielak
David K. Bowles (Resident, Los Angeles Office)
Sheryl Brooks (Resident, Los Angeles Office)
Bryan K. Brown (Resident, Los Angeles Office)
P. Scott Burton (Resident, Los Angeles Office)
Ladd Cahoon
John W. Calkins
Edwin A. Carlson (Resident, Los Angeles Office)
Amy Chang (Resident, Palo Alto Office)
Anne Chapman
Stephen P. Charbonnet (Resident, Los Angeles Office)
Jesus Chavez (Resident, Los Angeles Office)
Winnie L. Chern (Resident, Taipei, Taiwan Office)
David P. Chiappetta
Abby Cogswell
Jason M. Cohen
Greg A. Christianson (Resident, Los Angeles Office)
Saideh Dadras (Resident, Palo Alto Office)
Anthony E. Davis
Mary J. Decker (Resident, Los Angeles Office)
Mark K. de Langis
Andrea P. Deshazo
William F. Dietrich
Darren Donnelly (Resident, Palo Alto Office)
Kevin M. Epstein
Salah Esmaili
David Fallek
Anthony T. Falzone
Philip Ferrari
Lonnie Finkel
Maxwell Fox (Resident, Los Angeles Office)
Joy Fuyuno
Lisa Beth Goldberg
Douglas A. Gravelle (Resident, Los Angeles Office)
Matthew S. Gray
Kristi Lynn Gudoski (Resident, Los Angeles Office)
Simona S. Gurevich
J. David Hadden (Resident, Palo Alto Office)
Rita A. Hao
Kara Hatfield (Resident, Palo Alto Office)
James Hawley (Resident, Palo Alto Office)
Peter S. Hayes (Resident, Walnut Creek Office)

(See Next Column)

ASSOCIATES (Continued)

Tiffany R. Hedgpeth (Resident, Los Angeles Office)
Thomas Hixson
John Hoar
Linda Hoda (Resident, Palo Alto Office)
Heather Hoecherl
Alex C. Hung (Resident, Taipei, Taiwan Office)
Margaret Chu Ikeya (Resident, Palo Alto Office)
Jennifer James (Resident, Palo Alto Office)
Jennifer L. Jonak
Paige K. Kaplan
Maha Khalaf (Resident, Palo Alto Office)
Thomas F. Kennedy
Erica L. Kuerbis (Resident, Palo Alto Office)
Joyce Kuo
Hartley M. Kuhn
Thomas Eilif Kuhnle (Resident, Palo Alto Office)
Mark L. Lasser
Matthew A. Lesnick
Zahavah Levine
Claire T. Lin (Resident, Taipei, Taiwan Office)
John L. Lin (Resident, Palo Alto Office)
Aimee D. Long
David Maher (Resident, Palo Alto Office)
Diana Martin (Resident, Los Angeles Office)
Debera Masahos (Resident, Palo Alto Office)
Ronald M. Mastroianni
Devan McCarty (Resident, Palo Alto Office)
Michael S. McDonough (Resident, Los Angeles Office)
Michael McFadden (Resident, Walnut Creek Office)
Daniel D. Meyers (Resident, Palo Alto Office)
Gilman T. Miller (Not admitted in CA)
Weston C. Miller (Resident, Palo Alto Office)
Michael G. Nichols
Deborah A. Nolan (Resident, Los Angeles Office)
Cory O'Donnell
M. Abigail Page (Resident, Los Angeles Office)
Gina Pavlovic (Resident, Palo Alto Office)
Eric F. Pierson
Sean Platt (Resident, Palo Alto Office)
Christopher E. Prince (Resident, Los Angeles Office)
Michael T. Pyle (Resident, Palo Alto Office)
Orit Regwan (Resident, Los Angeles Office)
Kalyani Robbins
Kim L. Robinson
Neal A. Rubin (Resident, Palo Alto Office)
Viveka Ågren Rydell
Jacob J. Schatz
Rita P. Schmidt (Resident, Palo Alto Office)
Caitlin A. Schneider
Natasha Sen
Karen Shaw (Resident, Palo Alto Office)
Michael J. Shuster
Sindy Jill Siegel
R. James Slaughter
James Grant Snell (Resident, Palo Alto Office)
Allyson W. Sonenshine
Carter M. Stewart
Keslie Stewart
Catherine M. Stites (Resident, Los Angeles Office)
Sara Takasugi (Resident, Los Angeles Office)
Shiraz D. Tangri (Resident, Los Angeles Office)
Maj-Le R. Tate (Resident, Los Angeles Office)
Jason Taylor (Resident, Palo Alto Office)
Han N. Tran
Lindsey A. Urbina
Brett R. Waxdeck
Lisa D. Weil (Resident, Walnut Creek Office)
Colin West
Katharine L. West (Resident, Palo Alto Office)
Nadia Wetzler
Jamie Weyand
Christina M. Wheeler
Regina R. Wong (Resident, Los Angeles Office)
Rajiv Yadav (Resident, Los Angeles Office)
Vincent K. Yip (Resident, Los Angeles Office)
Jason A. Yurasek
David J. Zack
Shawn Jennifer Zovod (Resident, Walnut Creek Office)
Laura J. Zuckerman

For full biographical listings, see the Martindale-Hubbell Law Directory

---

Morgenstein & Jubelirer, LLP (AV)

One Market, Spear Street Tower, 32nd Floor, 94105
Telephone: 415-896-0666
Fax: 415-896-5592
Email: m&j@mj-sflaw.com

Marvin D. Morgenstein (Retired)
Eliot S. Jubelirer
Lee Ann Huntington
Jean L. Bertrand
Jeffrey R. Williams
James R. Balich
Rocky N. Unruh
James L. McGinnis
Charles W. LaGrave
William J. Carroll
John S. Worden
Wendi J. Berkowitz
Stephen M. Hankins

Bruce A. Wagman

Lewis D. Barr
David H. Bromfield
Alexander P. Catalona
Michael "Cael" S. Davis
Roberta Nicol Dempster
Laura E. Gasser
Jill L. Gillen
Natasha L. Golding
Judith A. Holiber
Shawn D. Parrish

John J. Petry

For full biographical listings, see the Martindale-Hubbell Law Directory

San Francisco—Continued

MORRISON & FOERSTER LLP (AV)

425 Market Street, 94105-2482
Telephone: 415-268-7000
Facsimile: 415-268-7522
URL: http://www.mofo.com
Other offices located in: Los Angeles, New York, Washington, D.C., Buenos Aires, London, Brussels, Beijing, Hong Kong, Singapore, Tokyo, Irvine, San Diego, Sacramento, Palo Alto, Walnut Creek, and Denver.

MEMBERS OF FIRM

Michael J. Agoglia
Peter Aitelli
Elizabeth P. Allor
Carl E. Anduri, Jr.
David E. Baudler
David B. Bayless
James P. Bennett
Roland E. Brandel
James J. Brosnahan
John W. Campbell, III
Annette P. Carnegie
Cedric C. Chao
Vincent J. Chiarello
Michèle B. Corash
Gregory P. Dresser
Stephen C. Durant
Gordon P. Erspamer (San Francisco and Walnut Creek Offices)
Jordan Eth
Craig B. Etlin
Robert L. Falk
Jill Feldman
Stephen L. Feldman
Kathleen V. Fisher
Paul Flum
Paul T. Friedman
Terri A. Garland
James J. Garrett (San Francisco and Walnut Creek Offices)
David A. Gold (San Francisco and Walnut Creek Offices)
Melvin R. Goldman
Arturo J. Gonzalez
Zane O. Gresham (San Francisco and Buenos Aires Offices)
Gavin B. Grover
Laurie S. Hane
Peter W. Hanschen
Nancy L. Hayes
Douglas L. Hendricks
Charles F. Hoyng
Michael A. Jacobs
Peter B. Kanter
Grant L. Kim
Richard S. Kinyon
Thomas F. Kostic
Matthew I. Kreeger
Rachel Krevans
Ray Larroca
Adam A. Lewis
Jack W. Londen
Bruce Alan Mann
James F. McCabe
Patrick R. McCabe
Harold J. McElhinny
Marla J. Miller
Charles J. Moll III
Andrew E. Monach
Portia R. Moore
Preston Moore
R. Clark Morrison (San Francisco, Walnut Creek and Sacramento Offices)
Michael G. O'Bryan
Stuart J. Offer
Mitchell J. Olejko
Wesley E. Overson, Jr.
Angela L. Padilla
Peter J. Pfister
Michael S. Powlen
Penelope Athene Preovolos
Darryl P. Rains
Pamela J. Reed (San Francisco and Walnut Creek Offices)
M. Ellen Robb
Robert A. Saltzberg
Barry S. Sandals
Lori A. Schechter
James M. Schurz
William I. Schwartz
Carl J. (Kim) Seneker II
Linda E. Shostak
Amy L. Silverstein
Thomas H. Steele
Anders E. Stenstedt
Tamu K. Sudduth
Jennifer Lee Taylor
James M. Tobin
Robert S. Townsend
Keith C. Wetmore

SENIOR OF COUNSEL

John P. Austin
Paul E. Homrighausen
James E. Merritt
James C. Paras
Robert D. Raven
Marshall L. Small

OF COUNSEL

Lloyd W. Aubry, Jr.
Erwin J. Basinski
James E. Boddy, Jr.
Ruth N. Borenstein
Ellen Borgersen
Douglas B. Evans
Stephen P. Freccero
Lynn M. Garney
Paul Goldstein
Lawrence R. Katzin
Sylvie K. Kern
Patricia S. Mar
Ross D. Meador
Diane E. Pritchard
David G. Robertson
April Hopkins Rox
Richard G. Stephenson
Arne D. Wagner
Mary E. Wand
Lulu Yen

ASSOCIATES

Edwin P. Antolin
Dana S. Baker
Brooks M. Beard
Julia Belian (Not admitted in CA)
Lawrence B. Berroya
James L. S. Bouldin
Stephen R. Brady
Kenneth W. Brakebill
Elizabeth A. Brown
Kelly M. Brown
Carolyn Beasley Burton
Daphne E. Butler
Brian F. Chase
Maria Chedid
Karl H. Christiansen
Thomas Chuang
Frederick S. Chung
Jason A. Crotty
Matthew S. Crowley
Deborah A. Davis
Kenneth A. Davis (Not admitted in CA)
Ilene Diamond
Jonathan S. Dickstein
L. Kathleen Durousseau
Kimberly A. Eckhart
Landon R. Edmond
Jill D. Fairbrother
Daniel F. Feldman
Dorothy L. Fernandez
Mary A. Ferrer
William M. Fleishhacker
Ronald P. Flynn
David Goldenberg
Brian W. Hayle (Not admitted in CA)
Zachariah A. Higgins

(See Next Column)

ASSOCIATES (Continued)

Elena Kondos Hillman
Douglas G. Hodder (Not admitted in CA)
John Hou
Lynn M. Humphreys
Paul E. Jahn
Bruce Elwood Johnson
Ararat Kapouytian
Ruth Ann Keene
John A. Kelley
Charles Kim
Christina V. Kirk-Kazhe
James H. Laws (Not admitted in CA)
Nancy M. Lisewski
Jaclyn Liu
Erinn M. Lopez
Susan H. MacCormac
Joy S. MacIntyre
Vlasta Maric
David J. Martz
Jennifer E. Matz
Veronica K. McGregor
James R. McGuire
Jill Neiman
Christine S. Neuhoff
Thomas P. O'Toole
John A. Pacheco
Stephen E. Paffrath
E. John Park
Pamela Pasti
Christopher A. Patz
Lois K. Perrin
Brian N. Poll
Emmalena K. Quesada
Johanna W. Roberts
Peter E. Romo III
P. Rupert Russell
Yolanda M. Sanders
Lisa Scheff
Tessa J. Schwartz
Katherine Shlaudeman
Martha P. Siegel
Walter M. Stella
Mae Tai
Kristin Taylor
Olive Lee Thaler
Michelle D. Traylor
Thomas L. Treffert
Alison Tucher
Pamela Ty
Xavier C. Vasquez
Valerie A. Villanueva
Richard L. Villasenor
Stephan C. Wagner
Kristian E. Wiggert
Russell J. Wood (Not admitted in CA)
Margaret L. Wu
David H. Youssefi (Not admitted in CA)

LEGAL SUPPORT PERSONNEL

LEGAL ANALYSTS

Eric R. Roberts (Senior Litigation Analyst)
Stephen R. Sara (Director, Tax Analysis)
Reagan S. Wade
Gary S. Yellin

ENVIRONMENTAL ANALYSTS

Lynne F. Anderson
Brooke C.F. Ashworth (Environmental Analyst)
Susan Prentice Linden
Robert J. Reinhard

PATENT AGENTS

Mark R. Carter
Franklin Y. Han

For full biographical listings, see the Martindale-Hubbell Law Directory

---

MURPHY, PEARSON, BRADLEY & FEENEY, A PROFESSIONAL CORPORATION (AV)

88 Kearny Street, 10th Floor, 94108
Telephone: 415-788-1900
Telecopier: 415-393-8087
Email: IndividualsFirstInitialAndLastName@mpbf.com *URL:* http://www.mpbf.com
Sacramento, California Office: 701 University Avenue, Suite 150.
Telephone: 916-565-0300.
Fax: 916-565-1636.
San Jose, California Office: 80 South Market Street, 3rd Floor.
Telephone: 408-279-5792.
Facsimile: 408-279-5785.
Los Angeles, California Office: 11400 West Olympic Boulevard, Suite 249.
Telephone: 310-312-9565.
Fax: 310-312-9566.

James A. Murphy
Arthur V. Pearson
Michael P. Bradley
John H. Feeney
Gregory A. Bastian (Resident, Sacramento Office)
Timothy J. Halloran
Karen M. Goodman (Resident, Sacramento Office)
Mark S. Perelman
Mark Ellis (Resident, Sacramento Office)
William S. Kronenberg
Gregg A. Thornton
Jane L. O'Hara Gamp
Alexander J. Berline
Margaret M. Schneck (Resident, San Jose Office)

Michele Z. Allen (Resident, San Jose Office)
Thomas N. Bell (Resident, Sacramento Office)
Alec Hunter Boyd
Shoshana Y. Chazan
Dennis W. Chiu (Resident, San Jose Office)
June D. Coleman (Resident, Sacramento Office)
Barbara A. Cotter
Peggy S. Doyle
Jan L. Gardiner (Resident, Sacramento Office)
John P. Girarde
Michael D. Haupt
Christian P. Hurley (Resident, Sacramento Office)
Anna Kapetanakos
Theresa M. La Voie (Resident, Sacramento Office)
Peter J. Linn
Joan E. Low
Anne F. Marchant
Aaron Karl McClellan
Bernard M. McGuire
Quinn Adele Moody
Van Thuc Nguyen (Resident, Sacramento Office)
Jessica B. Rudin

(See Next Column)

MURPHY, PEARSON, BRADLEY & FEENEY A PROFESSIONAL CORPORATION, *San Francisco—Continued*

John A. Safyurtlu
Kelli L. Taylor
(Resident, Sacramento Office)
Sylvia Wahba
Richard Sung Wang
Harlan B. Watkins

For full biographical listings, see the Martindale-Hubbell Law Directory

ORRICK, HERRINGTON & SUTCLIFFE LLP (AV)

Old Federal Reserve Bank Building, 400 Sansome Street, 94111
Telephone: 415-392-1122
Telecopier: 415-773-5759
URL: http://www.orrick.com
Los Angeles, California Office: 777 South Figueroa Street.
Telephone: 213-629-2020.
Telecopier: 213-612-2499.
New York, New York Office: 666 Fifth Avenue.
Telephone: 212-506-5000.
Telecopier: 212-506-5151.
Sacramento, California Office: 400 Capitol Mall.
Telephone: 916-447-9200.
Telecopier: 916-329-4900.
Singapore Office: 10 Collyer Quay, #23-08 Ocean Building, Singapore.
Telephone: 011-65-538-6116.
Telecopier: 011-65-538-0606.
Washington, D.C. Office: Washington Harbour, 3050 K Street, N.W.
Telephone: 202-339-8400.
Telecopier: 202-339-8500.
Menlo Park, California Office: 1020 Marsh Road.
Telephone: 650-614-7400.
Telecopier: 650-614-7401.
Tokyo, Japan Office: 11th Floor, Main Tower, Akasaka Twin Towers, 17-22 Akasaka 2-Chome.
Telephone: 011-81-3-3224-2900.
Telecopier: 011-81-3-3224-2901.
London, England Office: 1 Threadneedle Street.
Telephone: 011-44-171-638-1584.
Telecopier: 011-44-171-628-0078.
Seattle, Washington Office: 999 Third Avenue, Suite 3800.
Telephone: 206-224-5690.
Fax: 206-224-6207.

SAN FRANCISCO, CALIFORNIA
MEMBERS OF FIRM

William F. Alderman
David T. Alexander
Denise Alter
Ralph H. Baxter, Jr.
Elaine R. Bayus
Daniel R. Bedford
William D. Berry
Paul C. Borden
Steven A. Brick
Fred A. Brown
Charles C. Cardall
Barbara Caulfield
Mark J. Coleman
Thomas Y. Coleman
Mary A. Collins
Dean E. Criddle
Roger L. Davis
Stanley J. Dirks
Raymond G. Ellis
Robert P. Feyer
Grant Finlayson
Carlo S. Fowler
Richard A. Gilbert
Robert J. Gloistein
Richard Grey
Richard D. Harroch
John M. Hartenstein
Gary A. Herrmann
Richard I. Hiscocks
Leslie P. Jay
Lawrence T. Kane
Mary Ellen Kazimer
Thomas P. Klein
John H. Knox
Mark R. Levie
Michael H. Liever
Peter Lillevand
Gary Louie
Steven C. Malvey
Dora Mao
Jesse W. Markham
Thomas C. Mitchell
William G. Murray
Noel W. Nellis
Jonathan M. Ocker
Tracy Preston
M. J. Pritchett
Greg R. Riddle
Marie B. Riehle
William L. Riley
Paul J. Sax
John F. Seegal
Gary R. Siniscalco
Richard V. Smith
Stephen A. Spitz
Alan Talkington
Ralph C. Walker
Jeffrey S. White
Kenneth G. Whyburn
Jeffrey D. Wohl
George G. Wolf
Cameron W. Wolfe, Jr.
George A. Yuhas

OF COUNSEL

Michael A. Beckius
Martha Everett
Maria Gray
Teri Jackson
Bruce S. Klafter
William J. Kramer
Philip C. Morgan
Catherine K. O'Connell
Peter E. Root
Douglas C. Sands
Samuel A. Sperry
James V. Telfer
John Van Cott
(Not admitted in CA)
Adrienne D. Weil
Neal L. Wolf

ASSOCIATES

Branda N. Andrade
John M. Beer
Pamela H. Bennett
Gregory D. Bibbes
Rebecca Bond
Bruce J. Bozzo
Thomas R. Brida
Jeffrey R. Brown
Bradley Bruner
Jessica L. Cahen
G. Blake Campbell
David Castillo
Laurie Chambers

(See Next Column)

ASSOCIATES (Continued)

Aileen T. Chang
(Not admitted in CA)
Nancy M. Clock
Brett E. Cooper
Oswald B. Cousins
Mark Davis
Ana Marie del Rio
Adriana Duffy
Peter Duong
Christine Fitzpatrick
Michael T. Frank
Kathy Woeber Gardner
Bruce J. Grant
Adam J. Gutride
Brian A. Hahn
Nancy Harris
David M. Hasen
Susan M. Heaney
Dolph M. Hellman
Mats Hellsten
Lynne T. Hirata
Jill V. Jackson
John H. Kanberg
Heidi Keefe
Jennifer J. Kordestani
Barbara Lange
Lisa G. Lawson
Kathleen A. Leak
Nicole S. Lipman
Douglas D. Mandell
Ellen McDonald
Shannon M. McGriff-Smith
Cynthia L. Mire
(Not admitted in CA)
Todd Mitchell
Genevieve M. Moore
Chad O'Neal Muilenberg
Tamara E. Nam
Miranda Nye
Myra J. Pasek
Scott Pasternack
Kimberly Peterson
Scott M. Porter
Richard Rahm
David C. Ritchey
Kenneth D. Roux
Paul Rubin
Seth Safier
Gregory C. Schick
Lisa M. Schull
Jacob Schwarz
David A. Sobul
Margaret U. Song
Rita E. Tautkus
Troy Thompson
Aaron C. Timm
Howard Ullman
(Not admitted in CA)
Daniel Yost

LONDON, ENGLAND
MEMBERS OF FIRM

Ian Johnson
Martin Stewart-Smith
Michael Voldstad
Paul Weiffenbach

LOS ANGELES, CALIFORNIA
RESIDENT PARTNERS

Alan G. Benjamin
J. Keith Biancamano
William W. Bothwell
Lori A. Bowman
William B. Campbell
Eugene Carron
Gerald L. Chaleff
Blase P. Dillingham
Earl A. Glick
Todd E. Gordinier
Greg Harrington
W. Douglas Kari
Peter V. Leparulo
Michael A. McAndrews
Richard C. Mendelson
Mary H. Neale
Gary D. Samson
Larry D. Sobel
Payne L. Templeton
Paul A. Webber
Bradley S. White

MENLO PARK, CALIFORNIA
MEMBERS OF FIRM

William L. Anthony
W. Reece Bader
Peter Cohn
Robert E. Freitas
G. Hopkins Guy, III
Lynne C. Hermle
Geoffrey P. Leonard
Sean A. Lincoln
Terrence P. McMahon
Christopher R. Ottenweller
Gary E. Weiss
Eric L. Wesenberg

NEW YORK, NEW YORK
MEMBERS OF FIRM

Paul Abramson
Peter A. Bicks
Charles W. Bradley
Bradford S. Breen
Peter Bucci
Charles N. Burger
Colman J. Burke
Fred C. Byers, Jr.
James J. Capra, Jr.
Michael B. Carlinsky
Richard Chirls
J. Peter Coll, Jr.
Jeffrey A. Conciatori
Robert A. Cote
Katharine I. Crost
Duncan Darrow
Michael Delikat
Edward M. DeSear
Joseph Evall
Rubi Finkelstein
Robert A. Fippinger
Lawrence B. Fisher
Stephen G. Foresta
Charles W. Gerdts, III
Howard M. Goldwasser
Lawrence B. Goodwin
F. Susan Gottlieb
Arnold Gulkowitz
Eileen B. Heitzler
Robert M. Isackson
David R. Jewell
William L. Kandel
Mitchell S. Kaplan
John J. Keohane
Alan M. Knoll
Peter J. Korda
Martin H. Levenglick
Herbert J. Levine
Carl F. Lyon, Jr.
John A. MacKerron
Richard W. Mark
Daniel Mathews
Lorraine S. McGowen
Michael R. Meyers
Robert B. Michel
Sam Scott Miller
Christopher J. Moore
Barbara Moses
P. Quinn Moss
David Nirenberg
Joshua E. Raff
Clayton Reynolds
Jill L. Rosenberg
Ira G. Rosenstein
Al B. Sawyers
Stephen K. Sawyier
William C. Seligman
Albert Simons, III
Louis H. Singer
James L. Stengel
Corey A. Tessler
Daniel J. Thomasch
Diana Weiss
Neil T. Wolk

(See Next Column)

ORRICK, HERRINGTON & SUTCLIFFE LLP—*Continued*

SACRAMENTO, CALIFORNIA
MEMBERS OF FIRM

Norman C. Hile
Perry E. Israel
Cynthia J. Larsen
Marc A. Levinson
Timothy J. Long
Iain Mickle
John R. Myers
Cynthia L. Remmers
Thomas J. Welsh

SINGAPORE
MEMBERS OF FIRM

Kenneth S. Aboud
William R. Campbell
Bruce R. Schulberg

TOKYO
MEMBERS OF FIRM

R. Michael Bacon
Christopher Lewis
Dennis P. Martin

WASHINGTON, D.C.
MEMBERS OF FIRM

Cameron L. Cowan
Margaret A. de Lisser
Felicia B. Graham
David S. Katz
Keith W. Kriebel
Douglas L. Madsen
Edwin G. Oswald

For full biographical listings, see the Martindale-Hubbell Law Directory

PAUL, HASTINGS, JANOFSKY & WALKER LLP (AV)

A Limited Liability Partnership including Professional Corporations
Firm Established in 1951; Office in 1997
345 California Street, 94104-2635
Telephone: 415-835-1600
Fax: 415-835-2700
URL: http://www.phjw.com
Atlanta, Georgia Office: 24th Floor, 600 Peachtree Street, N.E.
Telephone: 404-815-2400.
Costa Mesa, California Office: 695 Town Center Drive.
Telephone: 714-668-6200.
Los Angeles, California Office: 555 South Flower Street.
Telephone: 213-683-6000.
New York, New York Office: 399 Park Avenue.
Telephone: 212-318-6000.
Stamford, Connecticut Office: 1055 Washington Boulevard.
Telephone: 203-961-7400.
Washington, D.C. Office: 1299 Pennsylvania Avenue, N.W.
Telephone: 202-508-9500.
Tokyo, Japan Office: Ark Mori Building, 12-32 Akasaka, P.O. Box 577, 1-Chome, Minato-Ku.
Telephone: (03) 3586-4711.
London, England Office: The International Financial Centre, 25 Old Broad Street.
Telephone: (011) 44-171-562-4000.
ATTORNEY E-MAIL ADDRESSES: first initial middle initial last name @phjw.com (e.g. rmasbill@phjw.com)

MEMBERS OF FIRM

Julie Allecta
Paul W. Cane, Jr.
Grace A. Carter
Sandra A. Golze
David A. Hearth
Daniel B. Higgins
Ned N. Isokawa
Rosemary Mahar Kirbach
Mitchell E. Nichter
John A. Reding
Charles V. Thornton
Peter H. Weiner
Gayl A. Westendorf
M. Kirby C. Wilcox

OF COUNSEL

Barry N. Endick
Bruce W. Hyman
Paul A. Reiner
William W. Schofield, Jr.

ASSOCIATES

Noelle L. Aaron
Kelly Quigley Applegate
Julie E. Blank
Christine E. Cahill (Not admitted in CA)
William S. Choy
Andrea L. Clay
M. Elizabeth Deane
Darek A. DeFreece
Stephanie A. Doria
Shannon S. Fallick
Maria Graesser
E. Jeffrey Grube
Gary S. Hand (Not admitted in CA)
Gordon E. Hart
Christina G. Hong
Todd A. Huge
Katherine C. Huibonhoa (Not admitted in CA)
John F. Hyland
Ken Kimura (Not admitted in CA)
Kelvin K. Leung
Star Lightner
Peter C. Meier
Thao H. Ngo
John P. Phillips
Peter S. Rukin
Laurie A. Sanders
Glenn C. Shrader
Keith M. Sutton
Raymond J. Tittmann
Louisa G. Weix
Hilton S. Williams
Junie Yoon (Not admitted in CA)
Philip B. Young (Not admitted in CA)
Anne F. Zinkin

For full biographical listings, see the Martindale-Hubbell Law Directory

PILLSBURY MADISON & SUTRO LLP (AV)

50 Fremont Street, 94105
Telephone: 415-983-1000
FAX: 415-983-1200
Email: pillsburylaw.com *URL:* http://pillsburylaw.com
Costa Mesa, California Office: 650 Town Center Drive, 7th Floor, 92626.
Telephone: 714-436-6800.
Fax: 714-436-2800.
Los Angeles, California Office: Citicorp Plaza, 725 South Figueroa Street, Suite 1200, 90017.
Telephone: 213-488-7100.
Fax: 213-629-1033.
Silicon Valley Office: 2550 Hanover Street, Palo Alto, 94034.
Telephone: 650-233-4500.
Fax: 650-233-4545.
New York, New York Office: 375 Park Avenue, Suite 3108, 10152.
Telephone: 212-826-1060.
Fax: 212-826-9255.
Sacramento, California Office: 400 Capitol Mall, Suite 1700, 95814.
Telephone: 916-329-4700.
Fax: 916-441-3583.
San Diego, California Office: 101 West Broadway, Suite 1800, 92101.
Telephone: 619-234-5000.
Fax: 619-236-1995.
Washington, D.C. Office: 1100 New York Avenue, N.W., Ninth Floor, 20005.
Telephone: 202-861-3000.
Fax: 202-822-0944.
Vienna, Virginia Office: 8330 Boone Boulevard, Suite 400, 22182.
Telephone: 703-744-7600.
Fax: 703-744-7605.
Tokyo, Japan Office: Pillsbury Madison & Sutro, Gaikokuho Jimu Bengoshi Jimusho, 5th Floor, Samon Eleven Building, 3-1, Samon-cho, Shinjuku-ku, Tokyo 160 Japan.
Telephone: 800-729-9830; 011-813-3354-3531.
Fax: 011-813-3354-3534.

MEMBERS OF FIRM

Christopher R. Ball
Michael R. Barr
W. Patrick Bengtsson
Mark A. Beskind
William E. Bonano
Ronald E. Bornstein
Gary E. Botto
Timothy P. Burns
Brian C. Burr
Christopher L. Byers
Terrence A. Callan
Nathaniel M. Cartmell III
James P. Clough
Robert W. Cosby
Mary B. Cranston
Karen A. Dempsey
Julie A. Divola
Richard M. Eigner
Bruce A. Ericson
David R. Farabee
William O. Fisher
Sarah G. Flanagan
Kevin M. Fong
William Gaus
Robert B. Gex IV
Deene Goodlaw
John M. Grenfell
Paul R. Griffin
George P. Haley
Michael J. Halloran
Laura E. Hannusch
John T. Hansen
Shawn E. Hanson
Henry A. Hernandez
Robert C. Herr
William J. Hoehler
Lawrence L. Hoenig
David E. Hopmann
Timothy R. Jacobs
Robert A. James
Jonathan D. Joseph
Terry M. Kee
Alson R. Kemp, Jr.
Richard L. Kirkpatrick
David L. Klott
David R. Lamarre
Thomas V. Loran III
Frederick K. Lowell
Courtney M. Lynch
Richard Maggio
Patrick C. Marshall
Stephen J. Martin
Bruce W. McDiarmid
William C. Miller
Frederick D. Minnes
M. David Minnick
Robert A. Mittelstaedt
Ruth Modisette
Margaret McCandless Niver
Richard W. Odgers
Rodney R. Peck
Alfred L. Pepin, Jr.
Robert C. Phelps
Roxane A. Polidora
Marcia L. Pope
Jay E. Powell
Edward L. Quevedo
Toni Rembe
Margaret N. Rosegay
Jeffrey S. Ross
Jerry W. Ross
D. Stanley Rowland
Steven L. Saxe
James M. Seff
Elisa W. Smith
Glenn Q. Snyder
Sharon M. Solomon
Thomas E. Sparks, Jr.
Robert J. Spjut
Michael J. Steel
Reginald D. Steer
Craig E. Stewart
Stephen Stublarec
Robert E. Sullivan
Chinin Tana
Patrick S. Thompson
James O'M. Tingle
Ronald E. Van Buskirk
Jeffrey M. Vesely
Gregg F. Vignos
Philip S. Warden
Paula M. Weber
Robert M. Westberg
Blair W. White
Carole V. White
Mark N. White
Linda C. Williams
Andrea A. Wirum
Stanton D. Wong
Patricia A. Young

OF COUNSEL

James M. Canty
Maureen E. Corcoran
Cameo F. Jones
Richard E. Nielsen
Karren M. Shorofsky

(See Next Column)

PILLSBURY MADISON & SUTRO LLP, *San Francisco—Continued*

SENIOR COUNSEL

Gregor Baer
Thomas G. Blomberg, Jr.
Gregory P. Broome
Michael J. Kass
Patrick W. Lawler
Andrew D. Mastin
Caroline N. Mitchell
Victoria R. Nuetzel
Richard P. Rados
Eduardo G. Roy
Cydney A. Tune
Kim S. Zeldin

ASSOCIATES

Michael D. Alper
Brett H. Bailey
Natalie A. Beccia
Tula Bogdanos
Brent W. Brougher
Norman F. Carlin
Lisa F. Cetlin
Daniel Cullum
J. Daniel Davis
Patrick J. Devine
John M. Dick
Matthew D. Disco
Thi Bao Do
Robert J. Edwards
Margaret N. Fitzgerald
Emily E. Flynn
Ellyn Freed
William P. Fuller
Tanuja V. Garde (Not admitted in CA)
Laura C. Gustafson
Rebecca M. Hale
Judith A. Hall
Alice K. Hayashi
James L. Heideman
William A. Hines
Joseph K. Hollinger
S. Christian (Christy) Holman
Justin D. Hovey
Karen E. Jaenike
Amy L. Kerxton
David M. Koeninger
Andrew Lanphere
Lindy M. Lilien
Claudia J. Lowder
Alexandre B. Makler (Not admitted in CA)
Anita D. Mayo
Mark R. Mengelberg
Theresa G. Moran
Daniel B. Myers
Felton T. Newell, Jr.
Henry S. Noyes
Caroline E. Papas
Philip J. Pogledich
Dean M. Poulakidas
Edward E. Powell, Jr.
Paula Quintiliani
Christine S. Ring
Katherine Salo Ritchey
Catherine A. Roundy (Not admitted in CA)
Suzanne R. Scheiner
Margaret S. Schroeder
Christine M. Shen
Linda P. Shih
Morgan R. Smock
Naomi L. Snyder
Amy E. Spence
Savitha Sridharan
Andrea P. Sumits
Wendy S. Tien (Not admitted in CA)
Matthew P. Vandall
Jason M. Venner
Laura E. Watts
Mark D. Weideman
Amy Weitzenberg
Brian M. Wong
Monique L. Wright
Karen M. Yan
Michael T. Yu

For full biographical listings, see the Martindale-Hubbell Law Directory

---

ROPERS, MAJESKI, KOHN & BENTLEY, A PROFESSIONAL CORPORATION (AV)

333 Market Street, Suite 3150, 94105
Telephone: 415-543-4800
Fax: 415-274-6301
URL: http://www.ropers.com
Redwood City, California Office: 1001 Marshall Street.
Telephone: 650-364-8200.
Fax: 650-367-0997.
San Jose, California Office: 80 North 1st Street.
Telephone: 408-287-6262.
Fax: 408-297-6819.
Los Angeles, California Office: 515 South Flower Street, Suite 2100.
Telephone: 213-312-2000.
Fax: 213-312-2001.
New York, New York Office: 1 World Trade Center, 85th Floor.
Telephone: 212-432-4300.
Fax: 212-432-4303.

John A. Koeppel (Resident)
James A. Lassart (Resident)
Stacey L. Pratt (Resident)
Lawrence O. Monin
Adrian G. Driscoll (Resident)
George G. Weickhardt

Mary Ellen Gambino
Joseph P. Breen
Larry A. Reback
Monica G. Farrell
Pamela J. Zanger

OF COUNSEL

Andre V. Tolpegin

For full biographical listings, see the Martindale-Hubbell Law Directory

---

SEDGWICK, DETERT, MORAN & ARNOLD (AV)

A Partnership including Professional Corporations
16th Floor, One Embarcadero Center, 94111-3628
Telephone: 415-781-7900
Fax: 415-781-2635
URL: http://www.sdma.com
Los Angeles, California Office: 801 South Figueroa Street, 18th Floor.
Telephone: 213-426-6900.
Fax: 213-426-6921.

(See Next Column)

New York, New York Office: 125 Broad Street, 39th Floor.
Telephone: 212-422-0202.
Fax: 212-422-0925.
Telex:
Irvine, California Office: 3 Park Plaza, 17th Floor.
Telephone: 949-852-8200.
Fax: 949-852-8282.
Chicago, Illinois Office: The Rookery Building, Seventh Floor, 209 South La Salle Street.
Telephone: 312-641-9050.
Fax: 312-641-9530.
London, England Office: Candlewick House, 120 Cannon Street, EC4N 6LR.
Telephone: +44 020-7929-1829.
Fax: +44 020-7929-1808.
Telex: 927037.
Zurich, Switzerland Office: Spluegenstrasse 3, CH-8002.
Telephone: 0411-201-1730.
Fax: 0411-201-4404.

MEMBERS OF FIRM

P. Beach Kuhl *
Kevin J. Dunne *
Stephen W. Jones *
Gregory C. Read *
David E. Bordon *
W. Bruce Wold *
Cynthia H. Plevin *
Lane J. Ashley
Warren J. Krauss
Paul B. Lahaderne
Berridge R. Marsh
Michael B. McGeehon
Nicholas W. Heldt
Michael F. Healy
Rebecca A. Hull
Steven D. Roland
Steven D. Wasserman
Scott D. Mroz
David De Busschere
Paul J. Riehle
Stuart W. Miller
Kathleen D. Patterson
Frederick D. Baker
Martin J. O'Leary
Eugene V. Elsbree III
Christopher A. Nedeau
Alan H. Packer
Stephanie A. Sheridan
Steven P. Burke
James S. Brown
Earl L. Hagström
Micki S. Singer
Julia A. Molander
James P. Diwik
Charles T. Sheldon
Elizabeth A. Collier
Wayne A. Wolff

OF COUNSEL

William C. Judge *
Roger W. Sleight *

SPECIAL COUNSEL

Randall G. Block
Kathryn H. Edwards
Gary C. Sheppard

ASSOCIATES

Marie J. Giardina
Michael C. Scanlon, Jr.
Shelley L. Brittman
Constance A. Leahy
Alicia J. Donahue
Katharine Demgen
Kirk Christopher Jenkins
Melinda Knupp-Walker
Holly A. Harris
Stephen A. Schram
Denise Trani-Morris
James Yuanxin Li
Diane D. Papan
Janet M. Alexander
Shannon Ball Jones
Sarah E. Lucas
Noreen E. McDermott
Gayle L. Gough
Teresa McLoughlin Rice
David E. Faliszek
Mark J. Hancock
Thomas F. Kopshever
William J. Lutz (Not admitted in CA)
Jonathan T. Rodriguez
Elizabeth Yelland Lara
Eric W. Schnurpfeil
Peter J. Messrobian
Bryan W. Vereschagin
Carol J. Stair
Paul W. Windust
Elizabeth C. Branham
Michael L. Fox
Linh N. Ha
Elizabeth M. Dillon (Not admitted in CA)
Diane T. Gorczyca
William C. Rogers, Jr.
Margaret Krinsky Schultz
Stephanie Barclay
Matthew G. Dudley
Robert E. Tonn
Marc Brainich
Stella Fey Epling
Matthew A. Fischer
Ian W. Freeman
Matthew C. Lovell
Rebecca M. Biernat
James P. Donahue
Richard Payne
David A. Schnider
Alexander H. Tynberg
Sharon R. Terris

*A Professional Corporation

For full biographical listings, see the Martindale-Hubbell Law Directory

---

SHARTSIS, FRIESE & GINSBURG LLP (AV)

One Maritime Plaza, Eighteenth Floor, 94111
Telephone: 415-421-6500
FAX: 415-421-2922
URL: www.sfglaw.com

Robert Charles Friese
Arthur J. Shartsis
Mary Jo Shartsis
Robert D. Evans
Douglas L. Hammer
Ronald Hayes Malone
Joel Zeldin
John P. Broadhurst
David H. Kremer
Charles R. Rice
Anthony B. Leuin
Douglas Mo
Robert E. Schaberg
Tracy L. Salisbury
Jeffrey A. O'Connell
Carolyn R. Klasco

(See Next Column)

SHARTSIS, FRIESE & GINSBURG LLP—*Continued*

Eric M. Sippel
Jonathan M. Kennedy
Adam Elsesser
Steven O. Gasser
Barbara W. Staman
Zesara C. Chan
Geoffrey W. Haynes
Christopher J. Rupright
Carolyn S. Reiser
Robert Charles Ward

Carl D. Ciochon
James P. Martin
Jahan P. Raissi
Frank A. Cialone
John F. Milani
Christina M. O'Brien
Joan C. Tao
Neil J. Koren
Jonathan Streifer
Katherine F. Jen
Alissa A. McQuitty
Adrian J. Sawyer
Colleen Elizabeth Butler

SENIOR COUNSEL

Alan J. Robin

OF COUNSEL

Monique Alonso
Maryanne Minalga
Winnifred C. Ward
Joan L. Grant
Ellyn Roberts
Mary Kay Kennedy

For full biographical listings, see the Martindale-Hubbell Law Directory

SHEARMAN & STERLING (AV)

555 California Street, 94104-1522
Telephone: (415) 616-1100
Fax: (415) 616-1199
URL: http://www.shearman.com
New York, N.Y. Office: 599 Lexington Avenue, New York, New York, 10022-6069.
Telephone: (212) 848-4000.
Telex: 667290 Num Lau.
Fax: (212) 848-7179.
Abu Dhabi, United Arab Emirates Office: Butti Al Otaiba Building, 13th Floor, Suite 1302, Sheikh Khalifa Street, P.O. Box 2948.
Telephone: (971-2) 6274477.
Fax: (971-2) 6268933.
Beijing, People's Republic of China Office: Suite #2205, Capital Mansion, No. 6, Xin Yuan Nan Road. Chao Yang District, Beijing, 100004.
Telephone: (86-10) 6465-2299.
Fax: (86-10) 6465-4578.
Düsseldorf, Federal Republic of Germany Office: Couvenstrasse 8 40211 Düsseldorf.
Telephone: (49 211) 178 88-0.
Fax: (49 211) 178 88-88.
Frankfurt, Federal Republic of Germany Office: Trianon Building, Mainzer Landstrasse 16, 60325 Frankfurt am Main.
Telephone: (49-69) 9711-1000.
Fax: (49-69) 9711-1100.
Hong Kong Office: Standard Chartered Bank Building, 4 Des Voeux Road, Central.
Telephone: (852) 2978-8000.
Fax: (852) 2978-8099.
London, England Office: Broadgate West, 9 Appold Street, London EC2A 2AP.
Telephone: (44-020) 7655-5000.
Fax: (44-020) 7655-5500.
Menlo Park, California Office: 1550 El Camino Real, 94025-4100.
Telephone: (650) 330-2200.
Fax: (650) 330-2299.
Paris, France Office: 114, avenue des Champs-Elysées, 75008.
Telephone: (33-1) 53-89-7000.
Fax: (33-1) 53-89-7070.
Singapore Office: 6 Battery Road #25-03 Singapore 049909.
Telephone: (65) 230-3800.
Fax: (65) 230-3899.
Tokyo, Japan Office: Fukoku Seimei Building, 5th Fl. 2-2-2, Uchisaiwaicho, Chiyoda-ku, Tokyo 100-0011, Japan.
Telephone: (81 3) 5251-1601.
Fax: (81 3) 5251-1602.
Toronto, Ontario, Canada Office: Commerce Court West, Suite 4405, P.O. Box 247, M5L 1E8.
Telephone: (416) 360-8484.
Fax: (416) 360-2958.
Washington, D.C. Office: 801 Pennsylvania Avenue, N.W., 20004-2604.
Telephone: (202) 508-8000.
Fax: (202) 508-8100.

RESIDENT PARTNERS

William H. Hinman (Managing Partner, San Francisco and Menlo Park)
Laurence E. Crouch
Christopher D. Dillon
Jeffrey S. Facter
Kevin P. Kennedy
Dean S. Krystowski
Susan S. Muck
Steven E. Sherman
Alan F. Denenberg

OF COUNSEL

Steven M. Herman (Not admitted in CA)

For full biographical listings, see the Martindale-Hubbell Law Directory

SKJERVEN, MORRILL, MACPHERSON, FRANKLIN & FRIEL LLP (AV)

Suite 800, 601 California Street, 94108
Telephone: 415-986-8383
Telecopier: 415-982-7372
Newport Beach, California Office; Suite 330, 610 Newport Center Drive.
Telephone: 949-718-6780.
Telecopier: 949-718-6799.
San Jose, California Office: Suite 700, 25 Metro Drive.
Telephone: 408-453-9200.
Telecopier: 408-453-7979.
Austin, Texas Office: Suite 300 West, 9600 Great Hills Trail.
Telephone: 512-794-3600.
Telecopier: 512-794-3601.

MEMBERS OF FIRM

Edward V. Anderson (Also at San Jose Office)
Justin T. Beck (Resident, San Jose Office)
David G. Farrington (Resident, San Jose Office)
Thomas J. Friel, Jr. (Also at San Jose Office)
Vernon H. Granneman (Resident, San Jose Office)
Beth L. Hamilton (Resident, San Jose Office)
David W. Heid (Resident, San Jose Office)
Alexandra J. Horne (Resident, San Jose Office)
Russell L. Johnson (Resident, San Jose Office)
Peter H. Kang (Resident, San Jose Office)
Norman R. Klivans, Jr. (Resident, San Jose Office)
Edward C. Kwok (Resident, San Jose Office)
Steven M. Levitan (Resident, San Jose Office)
Alan H. MacPherson (Resident, San Jose and Newport Beach Offices)
David T. Millers (Resident, San Jose Office)
Robert B. Morrill (Also at San Jose Office)
Thomas P. O'Donnell (Resident, San Jose Office)
Brian D. Ogonowsky (Resident, San Jose Office)
James E. Parsons (Resident, San Jose Office)
Matthew T. Powers (Resident, San Jose Office)
Randolf J. Rice (Resident, San Jose Office)
David E. Steuber (Resident, San Jose Office)
Georgia K. Van Zanten (Resident, San Jose Office)

Reference: Bank of America.

For full biographical listings, see the Martindale-Hubbell Law Directory

SONNENSCHEIN NATH & ROSENTHAL (AV)

6th Floor, 685 Market Street, 94105
Telephone: 415-882-5000
Telecopier: 415-543-5472
URL: http://www.sonnenschein.com
Chicago, Illinois Office: Suite 8000 Sears Tower, 233 South Wacker Drive.
Telephone: 312-876-8000.
Cable Address: "Sonberk".
Telex: 25-3526.
Facsimile: 312-876-7934.
New York, N.Y. Office: 1221 Avenue of the Americas, 24th Floor.
Telephone: 212-768-6700.
Facsimile: 212-391-1247.
Washington, D.C. Office: 1301 K Street, N.W., Suite 600, East Tower.
Telephone: 202-408-6400.
Facsimile: 202-408-6399.
Los Angeles, California Office: Suite 1500, 601 South Figueroa Street.
Telephone: 213-623-9300.
Facsimile: 213-623-9924.
St. Louis, Missouri Office: One Metropolitan Square, Suite 3000.
Telephone: 314-241-1800.
Facsimile: 314-259-5959.
Kansas City, Missouri Office: Suite 1100, 4520 Main Street, 64111.
Telephone: 816-932-4400.
Facsimile: 816-531-7545.
London, England Office: Sonnenscheins, Royex House, Aldermanbury Square, EC2V 7HR.
Telephone: 0207-600-2222.
Facsimile: 0207-600-2221.

RESIDENT PARTNERS

Gayle M. Athanacio
Michael A. Barnes
Robin M. Edwards
Steven H. Frankel
Paul E. B. Glad
Gary A. Hernandez
Oliver L. Holmes
Curtis E. A. Karnow
Mark J. Linderman
Matthew F. Lintner
Sandra R. McCandless
Cynthia L. Mellema
Philip A. O'Connell, Jr.
Ivor E. Samson
Arnold P. Schuster
Peter A. Smalbach
Charles Spiegel
John Leland Williams
Nicholas C. Yost

OF COUNSEL

Jon K. Adams
Mary Kay Lacey
Kara S. Navarro

(See Next Column)

SONNENSCHEIN NATH & ROSENTHAL, *San Francisco—Continued*

RESIDENT ASSOCIATES

Terence M. Abad
Cheryl Dyer Berg
Susan E. Bloch
Brook Bernard Bond
Alice L. Busching
Donald M. Carley
C. N. Coby Cohen
Theodore Correl
Terri Marie Esparza
Bryce P. Goeking
Daniel R. Guggenheim
Thomas M. Hanson
Sonia Renee Martin
Sean McEneaney
Jennifer A. Moore (Not admitted in CA)
Maria J. Morga
Erin O'Neal Muilenburg
Emily S. Nozick
Demian L. Pay
Elena Ro
Diane Sovereign
Gillian W. Thackray
Letitia Rei Todd
Elizabeth A. Tosaris
Kelly B. Valen
Kevin Vilke
Paula M. Yost
Virginia K. Young

For full biographical listings, see the Martindale-Hubbell Law Directory

STEEFEL, LEVITT & WEISS, A PROFESSIONAL CORPORATION (AV)

30th Floor, One Embarcadero Center, 94111
Telephone: 415-788-0900
Fax: 415-788-2019
Email: slw@steefel.com
Stamford, Connecticut Office: Six Landmark Square, Fourth Floor, 06901-2792.
Telephone: 203-359-5605.
Fax: 203-359-5805.

Edward R. Steefel
Alvin T. Levitt
Lenard G. Weiss
Harvey S. Schochet
Michael J. Lawson
Christine A. Murphy
Janet C. Norris
Marvin B. Pearlstein
Harvey L. Leiderman
Michael D. Early
Clayton B. Gantz
Craig P. Wood
Barry W. Lee
Jordan P. Rose
James F. Eastman
Stephen S. Mayne
Daryl S. Landy
Sheldon H. Wolfe
Jill S. Dodd
Richard J. Tannenbaum (Resident, Stamford, Connecticut Office)
Mark Fogelman
Andrew A. Bassak
Lisa M. Carvalho
Anthony J. Justman
Elizabeth A. Erskine
Peter N. Larson

Cesar A. Alvarado
Saralyn M.C. Ang
Linda M. Balok
Raymond A. Chenault
Adria I. Cheng
Miles Cooley
Joseph E. Floren
Karen Frasier-Kolligs
Jennifer Billiet George
James M. Grady
Ted W. Harrison (Not admitted in CA)
E. Venessa Henlon
Andrea Hackett Henningsen
Ashley Ilangwa
Scott B. Johnson
James D. Lee
Angela Y. Liang
Vladislav V. Luskin
Robert B. Mison
Dena L. Narbaitz
Jeff C. Nguyen
Laudan S. Raissi
Kevin D. Reese
Jonathan M. Reymann
Gary D. Rothstein
Jacqueline H. Sung
Paul L. Svitenko
Jojiro Takano

OF COUNSEL

Gary J. Shapiro
Leonard R. Stein
Raymond F. Triana

LEGAL SUPPORT PERSONNEL

Esther Thal (General Manager)

For full biographical listings, see the Martindale-Hubbell Law Directory

THELEN REID & PRIEST LLP (AV)

101 Second Street, Suite 1800, 94111-3995
Telephone: 415-371-1200
Fax: 415-371-1211
URL: http://www.thelenreid.com
Los Angeles, California Office: 34th Floor, 333 South Grand Avenue.
Telephone: 213-621-9800.
Fax: 213-623-4742.
San Jose, California Office: 17th Floor, 333 West San Carlos Street.
Telephone: 408-292-5800.
Fax: 408-287-8040.
New York, New York Office: 40 West 57th Street.
Telephone: 212-603-2000.
Fax: 212-603-2001.
Washington, D.C. Office: Market Square, 701 Pennsylvania Avenue, N.W.
Telephone: 202-508-4000.
Fax: 202-508-4321.

(See Next Column)

MEMBERS OF FIRM

Max Thelen (1880-1972)
Paul S. Marrin (1894-1980)
Gordon Johnson (1905-1985)
A. Barlow Ferguson (1918-1992)
R. Tyler Andersen
Jon T. Anderson
George T. Argyris
Anthony J. Barron
Karl D. Belgum
Paul W. Berning
David V. Biesemeyer
Charles S. Birenbaum
Robert M. Blum
James R. Bridges
Walter F. Brown, Jr.
David Buoncristiani
Wynne S. Carvill
John B. Clark
James C. Collins
Helen Leah Conroy
Nicole A. Dillingham
Robert A. Dolinko
Gregg N. Dulik
Gary L. Fontana
John R. Foote
David S. Foster
Stephen J. Fowler
Jarrett L. Fugh
Adam F. Gambel
Richard N. Gary (Chairman)
Thomas B. Glascock
Bonnie A. Glatzer
Christine Haas
Michael C. Hallerud
James P. Hargarten
Ted W. Harris
John R. Heisse II
James T. Hendrick
Michelle L. Johnson
Kent Jonas
Jennifer Kuenster
Richard A. Lapping
Thomas W. Lathram
Kent W. Lindsay
Kit Choy Loke
Ronald F. Lopez
Daven G. Lowhurst
Karen L. Mathes
Rauer L. Meyer
R. David Mishel
John M. Mooney
Dean A. Morehous, Jr.
Nancy L. Murray
Fredric C. Nelson
Bradford A. Nilsson
Kevin O'Brien
Stephen V. O'Neal
Philip W. Peters
Philip R. Placier
Robert B. Pringle
John W. Ralls
James A. Riddle
Donald D. Roberts
Hilary N. Rowen
Kerry E. Shea
Leslie E. Sherman
Daniel R. Sovocool
Robert B. Thum
Robert A. Weikert
Mark P. Weitzel
James R. Willcox

OF COUNSEL

Steven L. Hock (Managing Partner)
Gregory R. Shaughnessy

SAN FRANCISCO SPECIAL COUNSEL

Carolyn Collins
Allison A. Davis
Dana W. Fox
David L. Suddendorf

SAN FRANCISCO ASSOCIATES

Shiela T. Addiego
Adam R. Alper
Christopher D. Baker
Joshua Baker
Jeffrey S. Bosley
Deborah J. Broyles
Sheri A. Byrne
Kelly Lynn Canady
Paul A. Carlson
Ava H. Chan
Louis J. Cisz, III
Melissa Newel Conour
James M. Conway
John C. Corcoran
Carissa Carol Wong Coze
Elizabeth C. Crandall
David F. Crutcher
Fernando L. Delmendo
Charles M. Dyke
Anthony B. Fong
Mary A. Francis
Scott L. Gardner
Stephen T. Grimsrud
Gustavo Grunbaum
Scott E. Hennigh
Karen A. Henry
Constance E. Johnson
Jordan C. Kahn
Alexander Klibaner
Arthur T. Kolios (Not admitted in CA)
Paul V. Lankford
David M. Laser
Andrew Lloyd
Julia L. Maibach
Thomas J. McHugh
Thomas M. McInerney
Kathryn E. McQueen
Michael P. Mihalek
Monika Birgit Gruter Morhenn
Javad Mostofizadeh
James J. Ostertag
Ellen M. Papadakis
Ross M. Petty
Kimberly M. Phillips (Not admitted in CA)
Marion I. Quesenbery
Roberta R. Rendahl
Alexandra Ross
Bradford S. Simon
Carol A. Sobczak
Robert Spagat
Becky L. Troutman (Not admitted in CA)
Tanya K. Tudor
Stacey L. West
Julia Whitelaw
Marlene J. Williams
Kristina K. Woolbright
Hong-Sze A. Yu

Representative Clients: The Bechtel Group of Companies; Hydril Company; Industrial Indemnity Company; Kaiser Aluminum & Chemical Corporation.

For full biographical listings, see the Martindale-Hubbell Law Directory

---

*SAN JOSE,** Santa Clara Co.

LAW OFFICES OF THOMAS R. HOGAN (AV)

10 Almaden Boulevard, Suite 535, 95113-2258
Telephone: 408-292-7600
Facsimile: 408-292-7611
URL: http://www.lawyers.com/thomasrhogan
Email: trh@hoganlaw.com *URL:* http://www.hoganlaw.com

(See Next Column)

LAW OFFICES OF THOMAS R. HOGAN—*Continued*

ASSOCIATE

Leslie Holmes

For full biographical listings, see the Martindale-Hubbell Law Directory

HOPKINS & CARLEY, A LAW CORPORATION (AV)

Sixth Floor, 2 West Santa Clara Street, 95113-1824
Telephone: 408-286-9800
Facsimile: 408-998-4790
Mailing Address: P.O. Box 1469, San Jose, CA, 95109-1469
URL: http://www.hopkinscarley.com

John F. Hopkins
Robert D. Wenzel
Garth E. Pickett
Dunham B. Sherer
Arthur V. Plank
Stephen J. Kottmeier
Anthony J. McCarthy
Jon Michaelson
James M. Hager
Charles H. Packer
Ross G. Adler
Robert V. Hawn
Jeffrey E. Essner
William S. Klein
Robert O. Whyte
Brian C. Finerty
Jay M. Ross
Linda Larson Usoz
Sharon L. Wong
J. Randall Toch

OF COUNSEL

Clarence A. Kellogg Jr.
Theodore J. Biagini
Donald J. Pagel
Lloyd Alvin Schmidt
Gail M. Hashimoto

Jennifer M. Cunneen
John W. Easterbrook
Mark R. Figueiredo
Perry S. Goldman
Craig Lee Henderson
G. Trent Morrow
Tamara B. Pow
Christine Baddell Redfield
Andrew L. Romberger
Eleanor C. Schuermann
Jamie R. Shelden
Philippe A. Toudic
Phillip K. Wang
Denise Y. Yamamoto

For full biographical listings, see the Martindale-Hubbell Law Directory

MILLER, MORTON, CAILLAT & NEVIS (AV)

50 West San Fernando Street, Suite 1300, 95113-2413
Telephone: 408-292-1765
Telecopier: 408-292-4484
URL: http://www.mmcn-law.com

Richard W. Morton (1916-1975)
Charles V. Caillat (1920-1990)
Harvey C. Miller (1906-1993)

MEMBERS OF FIRM

David L. Nevis
Francis J. Hughes
Peter A. Kline
Stevan C. Adelman
Joseph A. Scanlan, Jr.
Carolyn Tobiason Stuart
William K. Hurley
Peter V. Dessau

OF COUNSEL

Nancy F. Symons

ASSOCIATES

Kathryn E. Barrett
Katherine S. Pak
David I. Kornbluh
Christopher J. Hersey
Julie Neale Meyer

Representative Clients: Trammell Crow Residential; Joe Kerley Lincoln Mercury Co.; Milligan News Co.; Joseph George Distributors; Santa Clara Dental Society; Avalon Bay Communities; Bershire Life Insurance Co; Hathaway-Dinwiddie Group; South Bay Circuits; John Alden Life Insurance Co.

For full biographical listings, see the Martindale-Hubbell Law Directory

ROPERS, MAJESKI, KOHN & BENTLEY, A PROFESSIONAL CORPORATION (AV)

80 North 1st Street, 95113
Telephone: 408-287-6262
Fax: 408-297-6819
URL: http://www.ropers.com
Redwood City, California Office: 1001 Marshall Street.
Telephone: 650-364-8200.
Fax: 650-367-0997.
San Francisco, California Office: 333 Market Street, Suite 3150.
Telephone: 415-274-6301.
Fax: 415-512-1574.
Los Angeles, California Office: 515 South Flower Street, Suite 2100,
Telephone: 213-312-2000.
Fax: 213-312-2001.
New York, New York Office: 1 World Trade Center, 85th Floor.
Telephone: 212-432-4300.
Fax: 212-432-4303.

(See Next Column)

Robert S. Luft (Resident)
Dennis J. Ward (Resident)
Michael J. Ioannou (Resident)
Stephan A. Barber (Resident)
Kevin P. Cody (Resident)
George E. Clause (Resident)
Curtis R. Tingley (Resident)
James C. Hyde
David B. Draper
Michael Ropers (Resident)
Stephen A. Scott

Daniel R. Kirwan (Resident)
J. Mark Thacker (Resident)
Douglas W. Dal Cielo
Anne S. Hilleary
Lita Monique Verrier
Bruce Piontkowski
Jonathan M. Schwartz
Nicole E. Rossi
Gregory D. Lopez
Mia P. Mosher
Richard Carter Mosher
Sean R. O'Halloran

For full biographical listings, see the Martindale-Hubbell Law Directory

SKJERVEN, MORRILL, MACPHERSON, FRANKLIN & FRIEL LLP (AV)

Suite 700, 25 Metro Drive, 95110
Telephone: 408-453-9200
Telecopier: 408-453-7979
Newport Beach, California Office: Suite 330, 610 Newport Center Drive.
Telephone: 949-718-6780.
Telecopier: 949-718-6799.
San Francisco, California Office: Suite 800, 601 California Street.
Telephone: 415-986-8383.
Telecopier: 415-982-7372.
Austin, Texas Office: Suite 300 West, 9600 Great Hills Trail.
Telephone: 512-794-3600.
Telecopier: 512-794-3601.

MEMBERS OF FIRM

Michael P. Adams (Resident, Austin, Texas Office)
Bryan K. Anderson
Edward V. Anderson
Justin T. Beck
Kent B. Chambers (Resident, Austin, Texas Office)
David G. Farrington
Thomas J. Friel, Jr.
Vernon H. Granneman
Beth L. Hamilton
David W. Heid
Alexandra J. Horne
Russell L. Johnson
Philip L. Judson (Resident, Austin, Texas Office)
Peter H. Kang
Norman R. Klivans, Jr.
Ken J. Koestner (Resident, Newport Beach, California Office)
Edward C. Kwok
Steven M. Levitan
Alan H. MacPherson
David T. Millers
Robert B. Morrill
Thomas P. O'Donnell
Brian D. Ogonowsky
James E. Parsons
Matthew T. Powers
Randolf J. Rice
David E. Steuber
Omkarmurthy K. Suryadevara
Stephen A. Terrile (Resident, Austin, Texas Office)
Georgia K. Van Zanten
Philip W. Woo

ASSOCIATES

Christopher B. Allenby
Patrick D. Benedicto
Rory G. Bens
Matthew J. Brigham
Craig J. Bristol
J. Melissa Brown
Richard F. Cauley
Carmen C. Cook
Bas de Blank
Mayankkumar M. Dixit (Not admitted in CA)
Teague I. Donahey
Gary J. Edwards
Scott D. Goss
Michael J. Halbert
Suzanne A. Heinrich
Elizabeth A. Hemphill
Judith S.H. Hom
David C. Hsia
Cameron K. Kerrigan (Not admitted in CA)
Kenneth S. Korea
Jennifer M. Lantz
Rachel V. Leiterman
Paul E. Lewkowicz
Steven F. Lincoln
John A. Livingstone
Fabio E. Marino
Hugh H. Matsubayashi
Brian E. Mitchell
John A. Morely
Richard J. Nelson
Victoria L. Nicholson
Paul J. Niewiadomski
Ivonne Prieto
L. Scott Primak
Judith A. Recchio
Barmak S. Sani
Kristin A. Snyder
Suzanne C. Sordello
Maria S. Spustek
Daniel P. Stewart (Not admitted in CA)
Clark S. Stone
Dianne L. Sweeney
Ardeshir Tabibi

OF COUNSEL

Frank S. Hiscox
Michael Shenker
John T. Winburn (Not admitted in CA)
George Wolken, Jr. (Not admitted in CA)

TECHNICAL COUNSEL

Ronald J. Meetin

Reference: Bank of America.

For full biographical listings, see the Martindale-Hubbell Law Directory

San Jose—Continued

THELEN REID & PRIEST LLP (AV)

17th Floor, 333 West San Carlos Street, 95110-2701
Telephone: 408-292-5800
Fax: 408-287-8040
URL: http://www.thelenreid.com
San Francisco, California Office: 101 Second Street, Suite 1800.
Telephone: 415-371-1200.
Fax: 415-371-1211.
Los Angeles, California Office: 34th Floor, 333 South Grand Avenue.
Telephone: 213-621-9800.
Fax: 213-623-4742.
New York, New York Office: 40 West 57th Street.
Telephone: 212-603-2000.
Fax: 212-603-2001.
Washington, D.C. Office: Market Square, 701 Pennsylvania Avenue, N.W.
Telephone: 202-508-4000.
Fax: 202-508-4321.

RESIDENT PARTNERS

Paul A. Bruno
Robert E. Camors, Jr.
Jay L. Margulies
Kenneth L. Nissly
Gregory Paul O'Hara
Susan G. van Keulen

RESIDENT ASSOCIATES

Lisa A. Carmody
W. Samuel Niece
Susan Roeder
Karen G. Semke
Jeffrey M. Ratinoff

Representative Clients: The Bechtel Group of Companies; Hydril Co.; Industrial Indemnity Co.; Kaiser Aluminum & Chemical Corp.

For full biographical listings, see the Martindale-Hubbell Law Directory

*SAN LUIS OBISPO,** San Luis Obispo Co.

SINSHEIMER, SCHIEBELHUT & BAGGETT, A PROFESSIONAL CORPORATION (AV)

1010 Peach Street, P.O. Box 31, 93406
Telephone: 805-541-2800
Fax: 805-541-2802
Email: info@ssblaw.com
Paso Robles, California Office: 1200 Vine Street.
Telephone: 805-238-2300.
Fax: 805-238-2322.

Warren A. Sinsheimer, III
Robert K. Schiebelhut
K. Robin Baggett
Martin J. Tangeman
Thomas M. Duggan
Martin P. Moroski (Resident Paso Robles Office)
David A. Juhnke
Steven J. Adamski
Thomas D. Green
M. Suzanne Fryer
Thomas J. Madden, III (Resident, Paso Robles Office)
Steven M. Chanley

Maria Hutkin
Linda Somers Smith
John E.D. Nicholson

Reference: Wells Fargo Bank, N.A.

For full biographical listings, see the Martindale-Hubbell Law Directory

*SANTA ANA,** Orange Co.

BEAM, BROBECK & WEST (AV)

600 West Santa Ana Boulevard, Suite 1000, 92701
Telephone: 714-558-3944
Fax: 714-568-0129

MEMBERS OF FIRM

Byron J. Beam
David J. Brobeck, Jr.
John E. West
Kirk H. Nakamura
Daniel R. Sullivan
Charles W. Matheis, Jr.

ASSOCIATES

Gregory L. Rippetoe
Jennifer J. Miller
Donald S. Zalewski
David R. Rosenberg
Louise M. Douville
Kermit D. Marsh
Kelly A. Fortin
Barbara J. Salvini
Lil G. Delcampo
Michael J. Peffer
L. Steven Hattendorf

Representative Clients: Aetna Insurance Co.; American General Life Insurance Co.; American Hospital Supply; Carl Warren & Co.; Casualty Insurance Co.; City of Anaheim; City of Fullerton; City of Newport Beach; Empire Insurance Cos.; Physicians Interindemnity.

For full biographical listings, see the Martindale-Hubbell Law Directory

CALLAHAN & BLAINE, A PROFESSIONAL LAW CORPORATION (AV)

3 Hutton Centre Drive, Suite 900, 92707
Telephone: 714-241-4444
Fax: 714-241-4445
Email: info@callahan-law.com *URL:* http://www.callahan-law.com

(See Next Column)

Daniel J. Callahan
Stephen E. Blaine

Jim P. Mahacek
Michael J. Sachs
Edward Susolik
Kathleen L. Dunham
Robyn Dimino
Reed N. Archambault
Nicki N. Eke
David Kam Ng
Douglas W. Schroeder

OF COUNSEL

Shelley M. Liberto
Walt D. Mahaffa

For full biographical listings, see the Martindale-Hubbell Law Directory

COTKIN, COLLINS & GINSBURG, A PROFESSIONAL CORPORATION (AV)

200 West Santa Ana Boulevard, Suite 800, 92701
Telephone: 714-835-2330
FAX: 714-835-2209
URL: http://www.cotkincollinsginsburg.com
Los Angeles, California Office: 555 South Flower Street, 18th Floor.
Telephone: 213-688-9350.
FAX: 213-688-9351.

Raphael Cotkin (Resident, Los Angeles Office)
James P. Collins, Jr.
William H. Ginsburg (Resident, Los Angeles Office)
Steven L. Paine (Resident, Los Angeles Office)
William D. Naeve
Terry C. Leuin (Resident, Los Angeles Office)
Roger W. Simpson (Resident, Los Angeles Office)
Joan M. Dolinsky (Resident, Los Angeles Office)
Robert G. Wilson (Resident, Los Angeles Office)
David A. Winkle
Karen C. Freitas (Resident, Los Angeles Office)
Brian R. Hill
Douglas A. Greer (Resident, Los Angeles Office)
Myrna L. D'Incognito (Resident, Los Angeles Office)
Kenneth S. Kleeger (Resident, Los Angeles Office)

Gregory A. Sargenti
Terry L. Kesinger
Ellen M. Tipping
Cooper W. Collins
Shannon L. Fernandez (Resident, Los Angeles Office)
David P. Nemecek, Jr (Resident, Los Angeles Office)

References: Mellon 1st Business Bank, Los Angeles; Bank of America.

For full biographical listings, see the Martindale-Hubbell Law Directory

*SANTA BARBARA,** Santa Barbara Co.

ALLEN AND KIMBELL, LLP (AV)

317 East Carrillo Street, 93101
Telephone: 805-963-8611
Fax: 805-962-1940
URL: http://www.AKLaw.net

MEMBERS OF FIRM

W. Joe Bush
Charles D. Kimbell
Paul A. Graziano
Steven K. McGuire
John H. Parke

ASSOCIATES

Jennifer J. Tice
David H. Barton
Christine Ray

OF COUNSEL

George H. Allen

Reference: Santa Barbara Bank.

For full biographical listings, see the Martindale-Hubbell Law Directory

*SANTA CRUZ,** Santa Cruz Co.

BOSSO, WILLIAMS, SACHS, BOOK, ATACK & GALLAGHER, A PROFESSIONAL CORPORATION (AV)

133 Mission Street, Suite 280, P.O. Box 1822, 95061
Telephone: 831-426-8484
Fax: 831-423-2839
Email: admin@sclawfirm.com

Robert E. Bosso
Lloyd R. Williams
Philip M. Sachs
Charlene B. Atack
John M. Gallagher

Catherine A. Rodoni
Pascha R. Moller Stevens

LEGAL SUPPORT PERSONNEL

Virginia Calhoun

Representative Clients: Santa Cruz Seaside Co.; World Savings & Loan; Coast Dairies & Land Co.; Sunset Farms, Inc.; Valley Packing Service, Inc.; Soquel Creek Water District.
References: Coast Commercial Bank (Santa Cruz); Pacific Western Bank.

For full biographical listings, see the Martindale-Hubbell Law Directory

SANTA MARIA, Santa Barbara Co.

TWITCHELL AND RICE (AV)

215 North Lincoln Street, P.O. Box 520, 93456-0520
Telephone: 805-925-2611
Telecopier: 805-925-1635
Email: trlaw@best1.net

MEMBERS OF FIRM

T. A. Twitchell (1902-1955)
William C. Rice (1924-1960)
Maurice F. Twitchell
Burton J. Twitchell
W. Kenneth Rice

Vincent T. Martinez

A list of Representative Clients and References will be furnished upon request.

For full biographical listings, see the Martindale-Hubbell Law Directory

*SANTA ROSA,** Sonoma Co.

ANDERSON, ZEIGLER, DISHAROON, GALLAGHER & GRAY, PROFESSIONAL CORPORATION (AV)

50 Old Courthouse Square, 5th Floor, P.O. Box 1498, 95404
Telephone: 707-545-4910
Fax: 707-544-0260
Other Santa Rosa, California Office: 6641 Oakmont Drive, 95409.
Telephone: 707-539-3880.
Petaluma, California Office: 17 Keller Street, 94952.
Telephone: 707-763-0937.

Edwin C. Anderson, Jr.
Kirt F. Zeigler
Robert Disharoon
Barbara Detrich Gallagher
Margaret M. Elliott
David G. Bjornstrom
Robert S. Rutherfurd
Christopher M. Mazzia
Tricia A. Shindledecker
Jeremy L. Olsan

Wendy D. Whitson
Daniel E. Post
Mary Catherine Doherty
Lisa Yoshida
Matthew E. Hannum

OF COUNSEL

John J. King, Jr.

LEGAL SUPPORT PERSONNEL

Edward J. Gibson
Daniel B. Flock (Director of Information)

For full biographical listings, see the Martindale-Hubbell Law Directory

O'BRIEN WATTERS & DAVIS, LLP (AV)

Suite 200, 3510 Unocal Place, 95402-3759
Telephone: 707-545-7010
Telecopier: 707-544-2861
Email: info@obrienlaw.com

John R. O'Brien
Michael G. Watters
Daniel E. Davis
Robert A. Pratt

Deborah G. Corlett
Alan M. Steinberg
James A. Coleman

OF COUNSEL

Toni L. Griffin

Representative Clients: Honda of Santa Rosa; Manly Olds-GMC; Ronald Fream Design Group (golfplan), Ltd; Santa Rosa Medical Park; Sonoma County Wineries Association; Parker Plastics, Inc.; Shamrock Materials, Inc.; Sonoma County Community Foundation; Mesa/Boogie Ltd.; Everett Graphics, Inc.
Reference: National Bank of the Redwoods.

For full biographical listings, see the Martindale-Hubbell Law Directory

*STOCKTON,** San Joaquin Co.

BRAY, GEIGER, RUDQUIST & NUSS (AV)

400 Bank of Stockton Building, 311 East Main Street, 95202-2904
Telephone: 209-948-0434
Fax: 209-948-9451
Email: bgrn@inreach.com *URL:* http://www.stocktonet.com/bgrn

MEMBERS OF FIRM

Dennis Donald Geiger
John B. Rudquist
James T. C. Nuss
Alan R. Coon
Anthony S. Guerriero
Steven P. Emrick
Laureen J. Keen
Peter A. Viri

OF COUNSEL

Mark S. Bray (1928-1999)

Representative Clients: Bank of Stockton; Guaranty Federal Bank, F.S.B.; Imperial Holly Corp.; Georgia-Pacific Corp.; South San Joaquin Irrigation District; Stockton Newspapers Inc.; University of the Pacific.

For full biographical listings, see the Martindale-Hubbell Law Directory

KROLOFF, BELCHER, SMART, PERRY & CHRISTOPHERSON (AV)

7540 Shoreline Drive, P.O. Box 692050, 95269-2050
Telephone: 209-478-2000
Fax: 209-478-0354

FOUNDING PARTNERS

Yale S. Kroloff (1907-1987)
Richard Belcher (1913-1997)

MEMBERS OF FIRM

Claude H. Smart, Jr.
Thomas O. Perry
Gary Christopherson
J. Douglas Van Sant
Orlie L. Curtis
Christopher H. Engh
Elizabeth Humphreys
Velma K. Lim
Robert J. Harrington
Kim A. Smith
Kathleen M. Abdallah
Ron A. Northup

OF COUNSEL

Robert B. Sternfels

ASSOCIATES

Clarence Chan
G. Rich Gillespie
Allison D. Cherry

Counsel for: Bank of America; Lend Lease Agri-Business, Inc.; Foster Farms; The Grupe Company; Tudor Construction; Cottage Bakery, Inc.
Representative Clients: Amador County; Catholic Healthcare West; Crestwood Hospitals, Inc.; Dameron Hospital; Lodi Metal Tech, Inc.; Truck Insurance Exchange.

For full biographical listings, see the Martindale-Hubbell Law Directory

NEUMILLER & BEARDSLEE, A PROFESSIONAL CORPORATION (AV)

5th Floor, Waterfront Office Towers II, P.O. Box 20, 95201-3020
Telephone: 209-948-8200
Fax: 209-948-4910
Email: is@neumiller.com *URL:* http://www.neumiller.com

Charles L. Neumiller (1873-1933)
George A. Ditz (1889-1971)
Irving L. Neumiller (1899-1970)
Robert L. Beardslee (1905-1999)
Thomas J. Shephard, Sr.
Duncan R. McPherson
Rudy V. Bilawski
Robert C. Morrison
James R. Dyke
John W. Stovall
Paul N. Balestracci
Daniel J. Schroeder
Clifford W. Stevens
Daniel S. Truax

OF COUNSEL

Christopher A. Greene
K. Robert Foster

Gregory T. Meath
Eric J. Nims
Christine Leigh Kroger
Rod A. Attebery
Anita C. Demps
Anthony L. Vignolo
Saroya J. Leonardini

Representative Clients: Roman Catholic Bishop of Stockton; Equitable Insurance Co.; The Grupe Cos.; St. Joseph's Regional Health System & Medical Center; Teichert Aggregate; Trimark Communities.

For full biographical listings, see the Martindale-Hubbell Law Directory

STEINHEIMER, RIGGIO, HAYDEL & MORDAUNT, A PROFESSIONAL LAW CORPORATION (AV)

400 East Main Street, Suite 600, 95290-0600
Telephone: 209-464-8732
Fax: 209-464-9165
Sonora, California Office: 38 North Washington Street, Suite A.
Telephone: 209-532-1424.
Fax: 209-532-4233.
Affiliated Office: Law Offices of M. Max Steinheimer, 301 Flint Street, Reno, Nevada 89505-3295.
Telephone: 702-322-2240.

M. Max Steinheimer
Donald M. Riggio
Douglas A. Haydel
Michael R. Mordaunt
Peter J. Kelly
Mark F. Ornellas
William D. Johnson
Kate Powell Segerstrom (Resident, Sonora Office)
Kevin M. Seibert
Elizabeth R. Bogart
Frank R. Perrott

Corinne K. Reynolds
Neal C. Lutterman
Daniel C. Cederborg
Rachelle C. Sanchez
Robert T. Waters
Nicole E. Bader
Amy Plomteaux
James Mark Mylles

Counsel for: Pacific Gas and Electric Co.; Kleinfelder Inc.; Turlock Irrigation District.
Insurance Clients: Allied Insurance Group; Design Professional Insurance Co.; The Doctors Co.; Kemper Insurance Co.; Norcal Mutual Insurance Co.; The Travelers.

For full biographical listings, see the Martindale-Hubbell Law Directory

THOUSAND OAKS, Ventura Co.

COHEN, ALEXANDER & CLAYTON, A PROFESSIONAL CORPORATION (AV)

One Boardwalk, Suite 102, 91360-5799
Telephone: 805-497-0802
Fax: 805-373-6082
Email: lawcac@ix.netcom.com

Charles W. Cohen
Raymond C. Clayton
Leonard Alexander
Ruth D. Morrow
Marguerite A. Wilson

Thomas S. Cohen

Representative Clients: Comsat General Corp.; Conejo Valley Chamber of Commerce; South Coast Area Transit.

For full biographical listings, see the Martindale-Hubbell Law Directory

TORRANCE, Los Angeles Co.

FINER, KIM & STEARNS (AV)

An Association of Professional Corporations
City National Bank Building, 3424 Carson Street, Suite 500, 90503
Telephone: 310-214-1477
Telecopier: 310-214-0764
Email: finerkimstearns@pobox.com *URL:* http://www.finerkimstearnslaw.com

Harry J. Kim (A Professional Corporation)
Robert David Ciaccio
W. A. Finer (A Professional Corporation)
Robert B. Parsons

OF COUNSEL

Bennett A. Rheingold
Ryan E. Stearns

LEGAL SUPPORT PERSONNEL

Marcia E. Talbert
Daphne Fenwick

For full biographical listings, see the Martindale-Hubbell Law Directory

UPLAND, San Bernardino Co.

ALTHOUSE & McDONOUGH (AV)

Second Floor, Metro Commerce Bank Building, 188 North Euclid Avenue, P.O. Box 698, 91785
Telephone: 909-985-9828
Telecopier: 909-985-3282
Email: AltandMcD@aol.com *URL:* http://www.Alt-McD.com

Charles S. Althouse
James E. Bamber (1947-1989)
Elizabeth A. McDonough

References: Metro Commerce Bank, Upland, California; Upland Bank, Upland, California.

For full biographical listings, see the Martindale-Hubbell Law Directory

VALLEJO, Solano Co.

DUNN, ROGASKI, PREOVOLOS & WEBER (AV)

241 Georgia Street, P.O. Box 1072, 94590
Telephone: 707-553-1555
Fax: 707-553-9043

MEMBERS OF FIRM

Robert C. Dunn
Michael J. Preovolos
Chester A. Rogaski, Jr.
Howard R. Weber

ASSOCIATES

Jill Noonan
Jon A.C. Vonder Haar
Jeffrey S. Olds
Leeanne Y. Patterson

Representative Clients: Norcal Mutual Insurance Co.; Nationwide Insurance Co.; Medical Insurance Exchange of California; California Insurance Guarantee Assn.; Scottsdale Insurance Co.; CAP/MPT; Kaiser Foundation Hospitals.
Reference: Bank of America, NT & SA.

For full biographical listings, see the Martindale-Hubbell Law Directory

*VENTURA,** Ventura Co.

NORMAN, DOWLER, SAWYER, ISRAEL, WALKER & BARTON (AV)

A Limited Liability Partnership
840 County Square Drive, 93003
Telephone: 805-654-0911
Fax: 805-654-1902

Richard M. Norman
Michael M. Israel
Peter C. Dowler
Michael G. Walker
Robert M. Sawyer
Loye M. Barton

(See Next Column)

ASSOCIATES

Eugenia M. Bernacchi
Thomas J. Hutchinson
Scott M. Norman

OF COUNSEL

James D. Loebl

For full biographical listings, see the Martindale-Hubbell Law Directory

WALNUT CREEK, Contra Costa Co.

McCUTCHEN, DOYLE, BROWN & ENERSEN, LLP (AV)

1331 North California Boulevard, P.O. Box Post Office Box V, 94596-4502
Telephone: 510-937-8000
Facsimile: 510-975-5390
Email: postmaster@mdbe.com *URL:* http://www.mccutchen.com
San Francisco, California Office: Three Embarcadero Center, 94111-4067.
Telephone: 415-393-2000.
Facsimile: 415-393-2286 (G I, II, III).
Los Angeles, California Office: 355 South Grand Avenue, Suite 4400, 90071-1560.
Telephone: 213-680-6400.
Facsimile: 213-680-6499.
Palo Alto, California Office: 3150 Porter Drive, 94304.
Telephone: 650-849-4400.
Fax: 650-849-4800.
Taipei, Taiwan Republic of China Office: International Trade Building, Tenth Floor, 333 Keelung Road, Section 1, 110.
Telephone: 886-2-723-5000.
Facsimile: 886-2-757-6070.

MEMBERS OF FIRM

Daniel J. Curtin, Jr.
Robert E. Merritt
Michael L. Greene
Geoffrey L. Robinson
Stephen L. Kostka
Sanford M. Skaggs (Managing Partner, Walnut Creek Office)

COUNSEL

Marie A. Cooper
Kathleen A. McDonald
Grant Guerra
Barbara J. Schussman
Julie A. Jones
M. Johanna Sherlin

ASSOCIATES

Dorothy I. Anderson
Peter S. Hayes
Jeffrey A. Benz
Lisa D. Weil
Shawn Jennifer Zovod

For full biographical listings, see the Martindale-Hubbell Law Directory

WATSONVILLE, Santa Cruz Co.

GRUNSKY, EBEY, FARRAR & HOWELL, A PROFESSIONAL CORPORATION (AV)

240 Westgate Drive, 95076
Telephone: 831-722-2444
Fax: 831-722-6153
Email: gefh@grunskylaw.com
Monterey, California Office: 5 Harris Court, Building N, Suite 3, 93940.
Telephone: 831-645-7900.
Fax: 831-646-8484.

Donald L. Grunsky (Retired)
Alan J. Smith
Frederick H. Ebey
Robert E. Wall, III
James S. Farrar
Mark E. Myers (Resident, Monterey Office)
Dennis P. Howell (Resident, Monterey Office)
David S. Spini
Thomas N. Griffin
Kathleen Ann Franke

Leslie J. Karst
Katherine R. Hotchkiss
Elaine Richelieu
Gavin E. Kogan
Michael Tunink
Dorothy E. Lank

Local Counsel for: Dominican Santa Cruz Hospital; Regents of U.C.; California-State Automobile Assn.; State Farm Insurance Cos.; Granite Construction Co.; Berman Enterprises; Watsonville Community Hospital; California Strawberry Commission; Monterey Bay Banking Corp.; City of Watsonville; Safeway, Inc.

For full biographical listings, see the Martindale-Hubbell Law Directory

WHITTIER, Los Angeles Co.

THOMSON & NELSON, A PROFESSIONAL LAW CORPORATION (AV)

15111 East Whittier Boulevard, Suite 400, 90603-2189
Telephone: 562-945-3536
714-680-0674
Telecopier: 562-693-2866
URL: http://www.lawyers.com/tnlaw

Alexander D. Thomson
John G. Nelson

Representative Clients: Blue Hills Nursery; Great Western Hotels Corp.; ICBO Evaluation Service, Inc.; International Conference of Building Officials; Shima Pearl, Inc.; Sunset Tropicals, Inc.; Trico Trading Co.

(See Next Column)

THOMSON & NELSON A PROFESSIONAL LAW CORPORATION—*Continued*

For full biographical listings, see the Martindale-Hubbell Law Directory

COLORADO

*ASPEN,** Pitkin Co.

AUSTIN, PEIRCE & SMITH, P.C. (AV)

Suite 205, 600 East Hopkins Avenue, 81611
Telephone: 970-925-2600
FAX: 970-925-4720
Email: aps_aspen@aol.com

Ronald D. Austin — Frederick F. Peirce
Thomas Fenton Smith

John M. Lassalette

Counsel for: Chase Manhattan of Colorado, Inc.; Clark's Market; Coates, Reid & Waldron Property Management, Inc.; Crystal Palace Corp.; Snowmass Shopping Center; Coldwell Banker The Aspen Brokers, Ltd.; William Poss & Assoc., Architects; Snowmass Village Resort Association; Aspen/-Pitkin County Housing Authority.

For full biographical listings, see the Martindale-Hubbell Law Directory

J. NICHOLAS MCGRATH, P.C. (AV)

Suite 203, 600 East Hopkins Avenue, 81611
Telephone: 970-925-2612
Telecopier: 970-925-4402
Email: jnm@jnmpc.com *URL:* http://www.jnmpc.com

J. Nicholas McGrath

Representative Clients: Alpine Surveys, Inc.; Aspen Alps Condominium Assn.; Aspen Center for Physics; Gant Condominium Assn.; Old Hundred Condominum Assn; North of Nell Condominum Assn.

For full biographical listings, see the Martindale-Hubbell Law Directory

OATES, KNEZEVICH & GARDENSWARTZ, P.C. (AV)

Aspen Plaza Building, 3rd Floor, 533 East Hopkins Avenue, 81611
Telephone: 970-920-1700
Fax: 970-920-1121
Email: ohkg@rof.net

Leonard M. Oates — Ted D. Gardenswartz
Richard A. Knezevich — David B. Kelly

David B. Mueller

OF COUNSEL

John Thomas Kelly — Michael Feigenbaum

For full biographical listings, see the Martindale-Hubbell Law Directory

*BOULDER,** Boulder Co.

COOLEY GODWARD LLP (AV)

2595 Canyon Boulevard, Suite 250, 80302-6737
Telephone: 303-546-4000
Fax: 303-546-4099
Email: webmaster@cooley.com *URL:* http://www.cooley.com
San Francisco, California Office: 20th Floor, One Maritime Plaza.
Telephone: 415-693-2000.
Fax: 415-951-3699.
Palo Alto, California Office: Five Palo Alto Square, 3000 El Camino Real.
Telephone: 650-843-5000.
Fax: 650-857-0663.
Menlo Park, California Office: 3000 Sand Hill Road, Building 3 Suite 230.
Telephone: 650-843-5000.
Fax: 650-854-2691.
San Diego, California Office: 4365 Executive Drive, Suite 1100.
Telephone: 619-550-6000.
Fax: 619-453-3555.
Denver, Colorado Office: One Tabor Center, 1200 17th Street, Suite 2100.
Telephone: 303-606-4800.
Fax: 303-606-4899.
Kirkland, Washington Office: 5200 Carillon Point.
Telephone: 425-893-7700.
Fax: 425-893-7777.
Reston, Virginia Office: 2002 Edmund Halley Drive, Suite 300.
Telephone: 703-262-8000.
Fax: 703-620-5380.

PARTNERS

James H. Carroll — James C. T. Linfield
William J. Leone — James E. Nesland
Michael L. Platt

(See Next Column)

ASSOCIATES

Aaron S. Brodsky — Kenlyn J. Kolleen (Not admitted in CO)
Andrew D. Dickinson — Sean May
Lisa S. Dumaw — Laura Majerfeld Medina
Steven Dupont — Rex R. O'Neal
Brent D. Fassett — Melissa K. Richards
Craig C. Garby — Richard P. Salgado
Peter A. Gergely — Mark Seneker
Bernard L. Hatcher — Wendy W. Tuey
Marc L. Jacuzzi

LEGAL SUPPORT PERSONNEL

SPECIALISTS

Katherine E. Duplay — Robin K. Lee

For full biographical listings, see the Martindale-Hubbell Law Directory

HOLME ROBERTS & OWEN LLP (AV)

Suite 400, 1401 Pearl Street, 80302
Telephone: 303-444-5955
Telecopier: 303-444-1063
Email: hro@hro.com *URL:* http://www.hro.com
Denver, Colorado Office: Suite 4100, 1700 Lincoln.
Telephone: 303-861-7000.
Telecopier: 303-866-0200.
Colorado Springs, Colorado Office: Suite 1300, 90 South Cascade Avenue.
Telephone: 719-473-3800.
Telecopier: 719-633-1518.
Salt Lake City, Utah Office: Suite 1100, 111 East Broadway.
Telephone: 801-521-5800.
Telecopier: 801-521-9639.
London, England Office: Heathcoat House, 3rd Floor, 20 Savile Row.
Telephone: 011-44-171-494-5600.
Telecopier: 011-44-171-287-9344.

PARTNERS OF FIRM

Kent A. Fischmann — Jill K. Rood
Christopher J. Kulish — John B. Wood

OF COUNSEL

Kay M. Small

ASSOCIATE

Vikki Lynn Wulf

For full biographical listings, see the Martindale-Hubbell Law Directory

*CASTLE ROCK,** Douglas Co.

FOLKESTAD & FAZEKAS, P.C. (AV)

316 Wilcox Street, 80104-2495
Telephone: 303-688-3045
FAX: 303-688-3189
Email: Firm@Folkestad-Fazekas.com

James B. Folkestad — Ernest F. Fazekas, II

Aaron W. Barrick — Marc C. Patoile
James M. Hunsaker

Representative Clients: Jackson Creek Ranch, LLC; Ashcroft Homes of Denver LLC.
References: First National Bank of Castle Rock; Castle Rock Bank.

For full biographical listings, see the Martindale-Hubbell Law Directory

*COLORADO SPRINGS,** El Paso Co.

BELTZ, EDWARDS & SABO, L.L.P. (AV)

128 South Tejon, Suite 310, 80903
Telephone: 719-634-6620
Fax: 719-634-3142
Email: BES_LLP@aol.com *URL:* http://www.lawyers.com/beslaw
Other Colorado Springs, Colorado Office: 729 South Cascade, 80903.
Telephone: 719-473-4444.
Fax: 719-444-0186.

Daniel P. Edwards — W. Thomas Beltz
John W. Sabo, III

ASSOCIATE

Daniel A. West

Representative Clients: A.M.I. Industries, Inc.; Analytical Surveys, Inc.; A.C. Israel Enterprises, Inc.; Boddington Lumber Co., Inc.; Cardiovascular Surgeons of Colorado Springs, P.C.; Colorado Springs Radiologists, P.C.; Digital, Inc.; Music Semi-Conductors, Inc.; Schlage Lock Co.; Texas Instruments.

For full biographical listings, see the Martindale-Hubbell Law Directory

Colorado Springs—Continued

HALL & EVANS, L.L.C. (AV)

Suite 600, 102 South Tejon Street, 80903-2264
Telephone: 719-578-5600
Fax: 719-635-7458
Email: hallevans@hallevans.com *URL:* http://www.hallevans.com
Denver, Colorado Office: Suite 1700, 1200 Seventeenth Street, 80202.
Telephone: 303-628-3300.
Fax: 303-628-3368.
Washington, D.C. Office: Suite 610, 1341 G. Street, N.W., 20005.
Telephone: 202-638-4633.
Fax: 202-408-5146.

COLORADO SPRINGS RESIDENT ATTORNEYS

MEMBERS

S. Kent Karber | Michael L. Luchetta

ASSOCIATES

Troy R. Olsen | Daniel L. Rosenberg

Representative Clients: American Insurance Association; Chrysler Corporation; Continental Airlines, Inc.; Jacor Broadcasting Corporation of Colorado, Inc.; Monfort, Inc.; National Railroad Passenger Corporation (AMTRAK); Northern Telecom Inc. (NORTEL); Safeco Insurance Company of America.

For full biographical listings, see the Martindale-Hubbell Law Directory

HOGAN & HARTSON L.L.P. (AV)

Two North Cascade Avenue, Suite 1300, 80903
Telephone: 719-448-5900
Fax: 719-448-5922
Washington, D.C. Office: Columbia Square, 555 13th Street, N.W.
Telephone: 206-637-5600.
Telex: 89-2757.
Cable Address: "Hogander Washington".
Fax: 202-637-5910.
Brussels, Belgium Office: Avenue des Arts 41, 1040.
Telephone: (32.2) 505.09.11.
Fax: (32.2) 505.09.96.
Budapest, Hungary (Affiliated Office): Nagy & Pintér, Hogan & Hartson Law Office, Bank Center, Granite Tower, 9th Floor, Budapest V., Szabadsag ter 7, 1944 Hungary.
Telephone: (36-1) 302-9050.
Fax: (36-1) 302-9060.
London, England Office: 21 Garlick Hill, EC4V 2AU.
Telephone: (44 171) 815 1200.
Fax: (44 171) 329 0299.
Moscow, Russia Office: 33/2 Usacheva Street, Building 3, 119048.
Telephone: (7095) 245-5190. Intl.
Telephone: (7501) 907-0451.
Fax: (7095) 245-5192. Int'l
Fax: (7501) 907-0462.
Paris, France (Affiliated Office): Cariddi, Mee, Rué, Avocats Associés à la Cour de Paris, 12, rue de la Paix, 75002.
Telephone: (33-1) 42.61.57.71.
Fax: (33-1) 42.61.79.21.
Prague, Czech Republic (Affiliated Office): Hogan & Hartson, Advokátní Kanceláře, Trziste 13, 118 00.
Telephone: (420-2) 2211-7111.
Fax: (420-2) 2421-5105.
Warsaw, Poland Office: Hogan & Hartson Sp.zo.o, Atrium Tower, Al. Jana Pawla II 25, 00-854.
Telephone: (48-22) 653-4200.
Fax: (48-22) 653-4250.
Baltimore, Maryland Office: 111 South Calvert Street.
Telephone. 410-659-2700.
Fax: 410-539-6981.
Rockville, Maryland Office: 600 Jefferson Plaza, Suite 203.
Telephone: 301-315-2206.
Fax: 301-315-9046.
Broomfield, Colorado Office: 370 Interlocken Boulevard, Fourth Floor.
Telephone: 303-474-1960.
Fax: 303-474-1961.
Denver, Colorado Office: One Tabor Center, Suite 1500, 1200 Seventeenth Street.
Telephone: 303-899-7300.
Fax: 303-899-7333.
Los Angeles, California Office: Biltmore Tower, 500 S. Grand Avenue, Suite 1900.
Telephone: 213-337-6700.
Fax: 213-337-6701.
Newport Beach, California Office: 4675 MacArthur Court, Suite 670.
Telephone: 949-250-4550.
Fax: 949-833-0976.
McLean, Virginia Office: 8300 Greensboro Drive.
Telephone: 703-610-6100.
Fax: 703-610-6200.
New York, New York Office: 885 Third Avenue, 26th Floor.
Telephone: 212-409-9800.
Fax: 212-409-9801.

(See Next Column)

PARTNERS

John W. Cook (Resident) | Donis G. Walker (Also at Denver, Colorado Office)
William J. Kubida

COUNSEL

Jeffrey S. George

ASSOCIATES

Amy S. Koretz | Virginia Starr Morgan

For full biographical listings, see the Martindale-Hubbell Law Directory

HOLME ROBERTS & OWEN LLP (AV)

Suite 1300, 90 South Cascade Avenue, 80903
Telephone: 719-473-3800
Telecopier: 719-633-1518
Email: hro@hro.com *URL:* http://www.hro.com
Denver, Colorado Office: Suite 4100, 1700 Lincoln.
Telephone: 303-861-7000.
Telecopier: 303-866-0200.
Boulder, Colorado Office: Suite 400, 1401 Pearl Street.
Telephone: 303-444-5955.
Telecopier: 303-444-1063.
Salt Lake City, Utah Office: Suite 1100, 111 East Broadway.
Telephone: 801-521-5800.
Telecopier: 801-521-9639.
London, England Office: Heathcoat House 3rd Floor, 20 Savile Row.
Telephone: 011-44-171-494-5600.
Telecopier: 011-44-171-287-9344.

PARTNERS OF FIRM

Susan E. Duffey Campbell | Brent E. Rychener
Steve L. Gaines | Steven B. Smith
David W. Isbell | John R. Wylie
Richard L. Nagl | Richard R. Young (Managing Partner)

SENIOR COUNSEL

Sharon A. Thomas

ASSOCIATES

Ashley Warren Jordaan | Tammy H. Kraemer
Hendrik F. Jordaan | Stuart J. Lark
Brent P. Karasiuk | Tonya Feit Lark
Deborah S. Menkins

For full biographical listings, see the Martindale-Hubbell Law Directory

KANE, DONLEY & JOHNSON, P.C. (AV)

90 South Cascade Avenue, Suite 830, 80903
Telephone: 719-471-1650
Fax: 719-471-1663
Mailing Address: P.O. Box 1119, Colorado Springs, CO, 80901
Email: kdandjpc@earthlink.net

Jerry A. Donley | Jack E. Donley
Mark H. Kane | David M. Johnson
Hayden W. Kane, II

William A. Palmer | Katherine L. Hays

OF COUNSEL

Hayden W. Kane

Representative Clients: American International Companies; Shelter Insurance Co.; Metropolitan Insurance Co.
Reference: State Bank & Trust and Bank One.

For full biographical listings, see the Martindale-Hubbell Law Directory

MULLIKEN, GLEASON, WEINER & WHITNEY, P.C. (AV)

Alamo Corporate Center, 102 South Tejon, Suite 700, 80903
Telephone: 719-635-8750
Telecopier: 719-635-8706

Steven K. Mulliken | Murray I. Weiner
Edward A. Gleason | Christopher D. Whitney

Mary Kominek Linden | Gregory M. O'Boyle
Carla L. Baker

OF COUNSEL

Janet K. Williams

For full biographical listings, see the Martindale-Hubbell Law Directory

RETHERFORD, MULLEN, JOHNSON & BRUCE, L.L.C. (AV)

415 South Sahwatch, P.O. Box 1580, 80901
Telephone: 719-475-2014
Toll Free: 1-800-281-2014
Fax: 719-630-1267
Email: info@rmjblaw.com

(See Next Column)

RETHERFORD, MULLEN, JOHNSON & BRUCE L.L.C.—*Continued*

MEMBERS OF FIRM

Jerry A. Retherford
J. Stephen Mullen
Anthony A. Johnson
Neil C. Bruce
Patrick R. Salt
Lori M. Moore

ASSOCIATES

Timothy E. Reilly
Debra P. DeRee

OF COUNSEL

Marilyn Brock Doig
Patricia L. Peterson

Reference: Norwest Banks; Colorado Springs Memorial Hospital.

For full biographical listings, see the Martindale-Hubbell Law Directory

SHERMAN & HOWARD L.L.C. (AV)

Attorneys and Counselors at Law
Suite 1500, 90 South Cascade Avenue, 80903
Telephone: 719-475-2440
Telecopier: 719-635-4576
Denver, Colorado Office: 633 17th Street, Suite 3000, 80202.
Telephone: 303-297-2900.
Las Vegas, Nevada Office: Swendseid & Stern, a member in Sherman & Howard L.L.C., 317 Sixth Street, 89101.
Telephone: 702-387-6073
Reno, Nevada Office: Swendseid & Stern, a member in Sherman & Howard L.L.C., 50 West Liberty Street, Suite 660, 89501.
Telephone: 702-323-1980.

Ben S. Wendelken (1899-1991)
William A. Baker (1913-1991)
Raymond M. Deeny
Durward E. Timmons, Jr.
N. Dawn Webber
Glenn H. Schlabs
Bruce A. Kolbezen
Milton L. "Skip" Smith, III

COUNSEL

William L. Sasz

Howard M. Diamond
Brenda K. (Buege) Heinicke
Edward J. Butler
Patrick R. Scully

Representative Clients: El Pomar Foundation Co.; Ampex, Inc.; Broadmoor Hotel, Inc.; Signal Processing Technologies, Inc.; The Gazette.
References: Colorado National Bank-Exchange; First National Bank, Colorado Springs; United Bank of Colorado Springs.

For full biographical listings, see the Martindale-Hubbell Law Directory

*DENVER,** Denver Co.

BAILEY & PETERSON, P.C. (AV)

Lincoln Center, 1660 Lincoln Street, Suite 3175, 80264-3101
Telephone: 303-837-1660
Facsimile: 303-837-0097
Email: bailey@b-p-law.com *URL:* http://www.aescon.com/b-p-law
Vail, Colorado Office: Weststar Bank Building, 108 South Frontage Road West, Suite 204, 81657.
Telephone: 970-476-0092.
Facsimile: 970-476-0099.
Edwards, Colorado Office: P.O. Box 449, 429 Edwards Access Road, Suite 203, 81632.
Telephone: 970-926-9255.
Facsimile: 970-926-9298.

James S. Bailey, Jr. (Resident)
Jay K. Peterson (Resident, Vail Office)

Randall M. Livingston (Resident)
Neil L. Arney
Cynthia J. Jones

OF COUNSEL

Lawrence A. Eskwith (Resident, Edwards Office)

For full biographical listings, see the Martindale-Hubbell Law Directory

BAKER & HOSTETLER LLP (AV)

303 East 17th Avenue, Suite 1100, 80203-1264
Telephone: 303-861-0600
FAX: 303-861-7805
To contact an attorney on the Internet use first initial and surname followed by @baker-hostetler.com
URL: http://www.bakerlaw.com
In Cleveland, Ohio: 3200 National City Center, 1900 East Ninth Street.
Telephone: 216-621-0200.
In Cincinnati, Ohio: 312 Walnut Street, Suite 2650.
Telephone: 513-929-3400.
In Columbus, Ohio: Capitol Square, Suite 2100, 65 East State Street.
Telephone: 614-228-1541.
In Houston, Texas: 1000 Louisiana, Suite 2000.
Telephone: 713-751-1600.
In Beverly Hills, California: 9150 Wilshire Boulevard, Suite 205.
Telephone: 310-385-7500.
In Long Beach, California: 300 Oceangate, Suite 620.
Telephone: 562-432-2827.

(See Next Column)

In Los Angeles, California: 600 Wilshire Boulevard.
Telephone: 213-624-2400.
In Orlando, Florida: SunBank Center, Suite 2300, 200 South Orange Avenue.
Telephone: 407-649-4000.
In Washington, D. C.: Washington Square, Suite 1100, 1050 Connecticut Avenue, N.W.
Telephone: 202-861-1500.

OFFICE MANAGING PARTNER

Raymond L. Sutton, Jr.

PARTNERS

Timothy R. Beyer
Mary Price Birk
Gregory S. Brown
Alfred C. Chidester
James A. Clark
Marc D. Flink
Gerald H. Hansen
James M. King
Peter J. Korneffel, Jr.
Phillip S. Lorenzo
Richard S. Mandelson
William R. Marsh
James R. Martin
Michael G. Martin
Thomas H. Maxfield
John B. Moorhead
Laurin D. Quiat
Stuart G. Rifkin
Michael J. Roche
Cassandra G. Sasso
David L. Starbuck
Douglas M. Tisdale
Victor L. Wallace, II

ASSOCIATES

Jeanne A. Carroll
Fay Chu Fong
Theresa J. Collier
L. Andrew Cooper
Paul S. Enockson
Ronald Lyle Hellbusch
Steven A. Klenda
Rebecca C. Lovell
Munir R. Meghjee
Demetri E. (Rico) Munn
Stephanie S. Padilla
David J. Ringelman
Thomas B. Romer
R. Scott Smith (Not admitted in CO)
Michelle M. St. Pierre
Jennifer N. Story

RETIRED PARTNERS

Keith Anderson
Fred M. Winner

For full biographical listings, see the Martindale-Hubbell Law Directory

BALLARD SPAHR ANDREWS & INGERSOLL, LLP (AV)

Seventeenth Street Plaza Building, Suite 2300, 1225 17th Street, 80202-5596
Telephone: 303-292-2400
Fax: 303-296-3956
URL: http://www.ballardspahr.com
Baltimore, Maryland Office: 300 East Lombard Street. 19th Floor.
Telephone: 410-528-5600.
Fax: 410-528-5650.
Camden, New Jersey Office: 800 Hudson Square, 5th Floor.
Telephone: 856-541-5577.
Fax: 856-541-8272.
Philadelphia, Pennsylvania Office: 1735 Market Street, 51st Floor.
Telephone: 215-665-8500.
Fax: 215-864-8999.
Salt Lake City, Utah Office: One Utah Center, Suite 1200, 201 South Main Street.
Telephone: 801-531-3000.
Fax: 801-531-3001.
Voorhees, New Jersey Office: Suite 100, 1101 Laurel Oak Drive.
Telephone: 856-627-8555.
Fax: 856-627-1153.
Washington, D.C. Office: Suite 1000 South, 601 13th Street, N.W.
Telephone: 202-661-2200.
Fax: 202-661-2299.

Roger C. Cohen
Roger V. Davidson
Thomas H. Duncan
Leslie A. Eaton
Loring E. Harkness III
Michael E. Lindsay
Beverly J. Quail
Kevin Michael Shea
Jeffrey L. Smith
Elizabeth H. Temkin
Roger P. Thomasch

SPECIAL COUNSEL

Frank A. Brame, III

OF COUNSEL

Jon Bernhardt
W. Michael Clowdus
Jeffrey R. Davine
Rebecca Wilcox Dow
Denise S. Maes
Peggy E. Montaño
Terrance A. Noyes
Andrew L. Pidcock
Sarah P. Tasker

Andrew J. Creighton
Virginia Morton Creighton
John S. Gaensbauer
Matthew J. Hogan
Wade A. Houser
Kaye A. Jacuzzi
Richard C. Jennings
Dwight R. Landes
Suzanna Kay Moran
Christopher W. Payne
Laura B. Redstone
Cindy L. Robinson
William T. Slamkowski
Kristin M. Tita
Stephanie Michelle Woods

For full biographical listings, see the Martindale-Hubbell Law Directory

Denver—Continued

BREGA & WINTERS P.C. (AV)

One Norwest Center, 1700 Lincoln Street, Suite 2222, 80203
Telephone: 303-866-9400
Fax: 303-861-9109
Greeley, Colorado Office: 1100 Tenth Street, Suite 402, 80631.
Telephone: 303-352-4805.
Fax: 303-352-6547.

James W. Bain
Stuart N. Bennett
Charles F. Brega
Robert R. Dormer
Wesley B. Howard, Jr.
William W. Hughes (Resident, Greeley Office)
Robert C. Kaufman
Ronald S. Loser
Brian A. Magoon
Loren L. Mall
Glenn W. Merrick
Pamela A. Shaddock (Resident, Greeley Office)
Jay John Schnell
Jerry D. Winters (Resident, Greeley Office)

Jennifer S. Fox
Julie Scroggins Frantz (Resident, Greeley Office)
Brent W. Houston
S. Scott Lasher
Bradley D. Laue (Resident, Greeley Office)
Eric B. Liebman
Kevin C. Massaro
Scott T. Rodgers

For full biographical listings, see the Martindale-Hubbell Law Directory

BROWNSTEIN HYATT & FARBER, P.C. (AV)

Twenty-Second Floor, 410 Seventeenth Street, 80202-4437
Telephone: 303-223-1100
Telecopier: 303-223-1111
Washington, D.C. Office: 1615 L Street, N.W., Suite 450, 20036.
Telephone: 202-296-7353.
Telecopier: 202-296-7009.
Glenwood Springs, Colorado Office: Box 357, 81602.
Telephone: 970-945-5302.
Telecopier: 970-945-4921.

Norman Brownstein
Steven W. Farber
Mark F. Leonard
Edward N. Barad
John R. Call
Steven M. Sommers
Ronald B. Merrill
Lynda A. McNeive
Laura Jean Christman
Andrew W. Loewi
Wayne H. Hykan
Stanley L. Garnett
Michael J. Sternick
Gary M. Reiff
Michael R. McGinnis
Lisa Hogan
Wayne F. Forman
Bruce A. James
Thomas J. Mancuso
Cole Finegan
Jeffrey M. Knetsch
Hubert A. Farbes, Jr.
Terence C. Gill
Steven S. Siegel
John L. Ruppert
Gregory W. Berger
Robert Kaufmann
Steven C. Demby
William T. Brack (Resident, Washington, D.C. Office)
Brent T. Slosky
Jay F. Kamlet
Ana Lazo Tenzer
Mark J. Mathews

SENIOR COUNSEL

John R. Garrett
James S. Lochhead (Resident, Glenwood Springs, Colorado Office)
Thomas H. Hudson (Resident, Washington, D.C. Office)
Gale A. Norton

OF COUNSEL

Jack N. Hyatt
Ann B. Riley
Jacquelyn Kilmer
Lawrence Bass

SPECIAL COUNSEL

Lynne M. Hufnagel
Mark T. Shipley
Richard P. Barkley
David E. Tenzer
Robert P. Coyne

Howard J. Pollack
Ellen O. Kauffmann
Joshua J. Widoff
Beth Doherty Quinn
Kent C. Veio
Lea Ann T. Groesser
David S. Chipman
Joseph F. Capello
Robert M. Fogler
Ted J. Trimpa
Jeanine M. Anderson
Christopher D. Reiss
Mark J. Maichel
Tad S. Rogers
Gregory A. Vallin
Christina G. Grasso
James D. Sloan
Andrew L. Spielman
Patricia L. Gruber
A.W. Victoria Jacobs
Suzanne R. Kalutkiewicz
Travis A. Willock
Chad G. Asarch
Michael H. Harper
David L. Bernhardt (Resident, Washington, D.C. Office)
J. David Hershberger
Adam J. Agron
Jennifer C. Robinson
Meghan W. Martinez
Kurt B. Colburn
Richard A. Hardaway
Alisa B. Burns
Jeffrey J. Schroeder
Brett M. Perry

Representative Clients: Columbia/HCA Healthcare Corp.; Global Crossing; The Hertz Corporation; KeyBank; SunAmerica Inc.; Trammell Crow Company; United Air Lines, Inc.; U.S. Home Corporation; U S WEST, Inc.; Vail Associates, Inc.

(See Next Column)

For full biographical listings, see the Martindale-Hubbell Law Directory

COOLEY GODWARD LLP (AV)

One Tabor Center, 1200 17th Street, Suite 2100, 80202-5835
Telephone: 303-606-4800
Fax: 303-606-4899
Email: webmaster@cooley.com *URL:* http://www.cooley.com
San Francisco, California Office: 20th Floor, One Maritime Plaza.
Telephone: 415-693-2000.
Fax: 415-951-3699.
Palo Alto, California Office: Five Palo Alto Square, 3000 El Camino Real.
Telephone: 650-843-5000.
Fax: 650-857-0663.
Menlo Park, California Office: 3000 Sand Hill Road, Building 3 Suite 230.
Telephone: 650-843-5000.
Fax: 650-854-2691.
Boulder, Colorado Office: 2595 Canyon Boulevard, Suite 250.
Telephone: 303-546-4000.
Fax: 303-546-4099.
San Diego, California Office: 4365 Executive Drive, Suite 1100.
Telephone: 619-550-6000.
Fax: 619-453-3555.
Kirkland, Washington Office: 5200 Carillon Point.
Telephone: 425-893-7700.
Fax: 425-893-7777.
Reston, Virginia Office: 2002 Edmund Hadley Drive, Suite 300.
Telephone: 703-262-8000.
Fax: 703-620-5380.

PARTNERS

James H. Carroll
William J. Leone
James C. T. Linfield
James E. Nesland
Michael L. Platt

ASSOCIATES

Aaron S. Brodsky
Andrew D. Dickinson
Lisa S. Dumaw
Steven Dupont
Brent D. Fassett
Craig C. Garby
Peter A. Gergely
Bernard L. Hatcher
Marc L. Jacuzzi
Kenlyn J. Kolleen (Not admitted in CO)
Sean May
Laura Majerfeld Medina
Rex R. O'Neal
Melissa K. Richards
Richard P. Salgado
Mark Seneker
Wendy W. Tuey

LEGAL SUPPORT PERSONNEL

SPECIALISTS

Katherine E. Duplay
Robin K. Lee

For full biographical listings, see the Martindale-Hubbell Law Directory

DAVIS, GRAHAM & STUBBS LLP (AV)

A Limited Liability Partnership
Suite 4700, 370 Seventeenth Street, P.O. Box 185, 80201-0185
Telephone: 303-892-9400
Fax: (303) 893-1379
Cable Address: "Davgram, Denver"
Telex: 413726 DGS DVR UD
Email: dgs@dgslaw.com
Boulder, Colorado Office: Suite 200, 4410 Arapahoe Avenue, Viewpoint on the Parkway.
Telephone: 303-544-5900.
Fax: 303-544-5997

PARTNERS

Wanda J. Abel
Thomas C. Bell
William A. Bianco
Mark D. Bingham
Charles D. Bybee
Charles L. Casteel
James E. Culhane
Brian T. Dolan
William J. Duffy
John A. Francis
Roger L. Freeman
Daniel E. Friesen
Michael J. Gallagher
Laura B. Gill
David R. Hammond
Dale R. Harris
Paul Hilton
Richard P. Holme
Marcia Chadwick Holt
Randall E. Hubbard
John R. Jacus
Carole K. Jeffery
Thomas P. Johnson
Charles L. Kaiser
Martin J. Katz
Glen E. Keller, Jr.
Robert W. Lawrence
Ronald R. Levine, II
Alan M. Loeb
Andrew M. Low
Paula J. Martin
Judith M. Matlock
John L. McCabe
John G. McGrath
Thomas B. McNamara
Joseph P. McMahon, Jr.
Gale T. Miller
Zach C. Miller
Sara Kraeski (Resident, Boulder Office)
Laura J. Nagle
Laurence E. Nemirow
Michael M. Page
Neil Peck
Kurt M. Petersen
Patricia Peterson
Jeffrey R. Pilkington
Christopher L. Richardson (Resident, Boulder Office)
Janet A. Savage
John M. Roche
Anthony J. Shaheen
Sheldon H. Smith
Jacqueline L. Studer (Resident, Boulder Office)
Randall Weeks
Lester R. Woodward
Gail L. Wurtzler

(See Next Column)

DAVIS, GRAHAM & STUBBS LLP—*Continued*

OF COUNSEL

Richard Marden Davis (1912-1987)
Donald S. Graham
Donald S. Stubbs (1908-1996)
Deborah J. Friedman
Janet N. Harris
Robert H. Harry
Donald W. Hoagland
George M. Hopfenbeck, Jr.
Clyde O. Martz
Barbara J. Mueller
Jennings J. Newcom (Not admitted in CO)
Quigg Newton, Jr.
Thomas S. Nichols
Donald J. O'Connor
Celia F. Rankin (Not admitted in CO; Resident, Boulder Office)
Robert S. Rich
John M. Sayre
Pamela S. Sbar
Ted R. Sikora, II
Jean Justyn Sirkin
James D. Voorhees

ASSOCIATES

Robert P. Attai
Joel Benson
Jonathan D. Bergman
Jeffrey R. Brandel (Not admitted in CO)
Charles A. Breer
William H. Brierly
Lon A. Burke
Alison C. Conover (Not admitted in CO)
Kristin W. Dale
Claire E. Douthit
Susan J. Geer
Catherine A. Hance
Christopher Kamper
Kenzo Kawanabe
Kristen Kirmer
Cynthia R. Kok
Christine Kessler Lamb
Daniel P. Meehan
Dean C. Miller
Jeannine L. Miller (Not admitted in CO)
Patricia M. Mitchell
Melissa A. Mograss (Not admitted in CO; Resident, Boulder Office)
Brett C. Painter
Jeffrey M. Quick (Resident, Boulder Office)
Geoffrey H. Simon
Shana M. Solomon
David J. Willbrand (Resident, Boulder Office)
Michael Nikolaos Stefanoudakis

For full biographical listings, see the Martindale-Hubbell Law Directory

HERBERT A. DELAP & ASSOCIATES, P.C. (AV)

1776 Lincoln Street, Suite 1300, 80203-1030
Telephone: 303-837-8521
Fax: 303-830-2832

Herbert A. Delap

For full biographical listings, see the Martindale-Hubbell Law Directory

DUFFORD & BROWN, P.C. (AV)

1700 Broadway, Suite 1700, 80290-1701
Telephone: 303-861-8013
Facsimile: 303-832-3804
Colorado Springs, Colorado Office: 101 N. Tejon, Suite 410.
Telephone: 719-471-0559.
Facsimile: 719-471-0583.
Affiliated Office: Solomon, Pearl, Blum & Quinn, L.L.P., New York, NY and Denver, Colorado.

Philip G. Dufford
Thomas G. Brown
Dale Tooley (1933-1985)
David W. Furgason
William C. Robb
Richard L. Fanyo
Jack F. Ross
Eugene F. Megyesy, Jr.
Randall J. Feuerstein
S. Kirk Ingebretsen
Peggy J. Anderson
Craig B. Shaffer
Scott J. Mikulecky
Lawrence D. Stone
Thomas E. J. Hazard

Terry Jo Epstein
Joanne Herlihy
Lisa Ann Lee
Michael Roch
Nili Abrahamsson
Jodie L. Behrmann

OF COUNSEL

Morris B. Hecox, Jr.
Claude M. Maer, Jr.
Scott Swenson

Representative Clients: CF&I Steel L.P.; The Colorado and Wyoming Railway Co.; Echo Bay Mines, Ltd.-Sunnyside Gold Co.; Hall and Hall Mortgage Corp.; Hewlett-Packard Co.; Coors Brewing Company; Starbucks Coffee Co.; Stewart & Stevenson Services, Inc.; CF&I Steel L.P.

For full biographical listings, see the Martindale-Hubbell Law Directory

FAEGRE & BENSON LLP (AV)

2500 Republic Plaza, 370 Seventeenth Street, 80202-4004
Telephone: 303-592-9000
Facsimile: 303-820-0600
Email: postmaster@faegre.com *URL:* http://www.faegre.com
Minneapolis, Minnesota: 2200 Norwest Center, 90 South Seventh Street, 55402-3901.
Telephone: 612-336-3000.
Facsimile: 612-336-3026.
Des Moines, Iowa: 400 Capital Square, 400 Locust Street, 50309-2335.
Telephone: 515-248-9000.
Facsimile: 515-248-9010.

(See Next Column)

London, England: Faegre Benson Hobson Audley, 7 Pilgrim Street, EC4V 6DR.
Telephone: 0171-450-4510.
Facsimile: 0171-450-4544.
Frankfurt, Germany: Wiesenau 1, 60323 Frankfurt am Main.
Telephone: 011-49-69-971-227-0.
Facsimile: 011-49-69-971-227-70.

RESIDENT MEMBERS

John D. Shively
Bruce W. Sattler
Dirk W. De Roos
William J. Campbell
Thomas B. Kelley
Michael S. McCarthy
Michael J. Cook
Gerald A. Niederman
James R. Spaanstra
Leslie A. Fields
Catherine A. Lemon
Elizabeth A. MacDonald
Russell O. Stewart
Linda L. Rockwood
Diane B. Davies
Charlotte Wiessner
J. William Callison
Natalie Hanlon-Leh
Michael J. Pankow
Jeanne M. Coleman

OF COUNSEL

Frederic K. Conover, II

SPECIAL COUNSEL

Charles D. Calvin
J. David Arkell
Richard F. Busch II
Jo Frances Walsh
Gail D. Zirkelbach (Not admitted in CO)
Julie L. Bernard

STAFF ATTORNEY

Jeffrey H. Desautels

Joseph M. Montano (Retired)

RESIDENT ASSOCIATES

Adrienne O'Connell McNamara
Jack R. Sperber
Colin C. Deihl
Ann C. McCullough
Laury E. Bowman
Bret R. Gunnell
Steven D. Zansberg
Benjamin M. Chin
K. Megan Doberneck
Carol A. Deck
Janet L. McDaniel
Luis M. Agosto
Jennifer Bradfield
Christopher P. Beall
Jessica F. Toll
Catherine A. Traugott
Kristi B. Tyler
Peggy Pei-Ru Chiu

For full biographical listings, see the Martindale-Hubbell Law Directory

FOLEY & LARDNER (AV Ⓣ)

1999 Broadway, Suite 2560, 80202
Telephone: 303-297-0260
Fax: 303-297-0266
Email: foleylardner@worldnet.att.net *URL:* http://www.foleylardner.com
Los Angeles, California Office: 2029 Century Park East, 35th Floor.
Telephone: 310-277-2223.
Fax: 310-557-8475.
Sacramento, California Office: 300 Capitol Mall, Suite 1125.
Telephone: 916-443-8005.
Fax: 916-443-2240.
San Diego, California Office: 402 West Broadway, 23rd Floor.
Telephone: 619-234-6655.
Fax: 619-234-3510.
San Francisco, California Office: One Maritime Plaza, Sixth Floor.
Telephone: 415-434-4484.
Fax: 415-434-4507.
Washington, D.C. Office: Washington Harbour, Suite 500, 3000 K Street, N.W.
Telephone: 202-672-5300.
Telex: 904136 (Foley Lard Wash).
Facsimile: 202-672-5399.
Jacksonville, Florida Office: The Greenleaf Building, 200 Laura Street. P.O. Box 240.
Telephone: 904-359-2000.
Facsimile: 904-359-8700.
Orlando, Florida Office: Suite 1800, 111 North Orange Avenue, P.O. Box 2193.
Telephone: 407-423-7656.
Facsimile: 407-648-1743.
Tallahassee, Florida Office: 300 East Park Avenue, P.O. Box 1454.
Telephone: 850-222-6100.
Facsimile: 850-561-6475.
Tampa, Florida Offices: Suite 2700, One Hundred N. Tampa Street, P.O. Box 3391.
Telephones: 813-229-2300; Pinellas County: 813-442-3296.
Facsimile: 813-221-4210.
West Palm Beach, Florida Office: Suite 200, Phillips Point East Tower, 777 South Flagler Drive.
Telephone: 561-655-5050.
Facsimile: 561-655-6925.
Chicago, Illinois Office: Suite 3300, One IBM Plaza, 330 N. Wabash Avenue.
Telephone: 312-755-1900.
Facsimile: 312-755-1925.
Annapolis, Maryland Office: Suite 102, 175 Admiral Cochrane Drive.
Telephone: 410-266-8077.
Telex: 899149 (Oldtownpat).
Facsimile: 410-266-8664.

(See Next Column)

FOLEY & LARDNER, *Denver—Continued*

Madison, Wisconsin Office: Verex Plaza, 150 East Gilman Street, P.O. Box 1497.
Telephone: 608-257-5035.
Facsimile: 608-258-4258.
Milwaukee, Wisconsin Office: Firstar Center, 777 East Wisconsin Avenue.
Telephone: 414-271-2400.
Telex: 26-819 (Foley Lard Mil).
Facsimile: 414-297-4900.
Brussels, Belgium Office: Avenue Louise, 283.
Telephone: 32-2-646-2777.
Facsimile: 32-2-646-7574.

Jeffrey N. Costakos (Not admitted in CO)
Richard W. Johns
Robyn A. Meinhardt

RESIDENT ASSOCIATE

M. Jennifer Harwell (Not admitted in CO)

For full biographical listings, see the Martindale-Hubbell Law Directory

HALABY CROSS & SCHLUTER (AV)

Suite 1400, 1873 South Bellaire Street, 80222
Telephone: 303-691-5300
Fax: 303-691-5307

Theodore S. Halaby
Jonathan A. Cross
Leslie L. Schluter

ASSOCIATES

Andrew J. Carafelli
E. James Wilder, IV
Matthew A. Samuelson
Sue Ann Haskell
Marc C. Diamant

For full biographical listings, see the Martindale-Hubbell Law Directory

HALL & EVANS, L.L.C. (AV)

Suite 1700, 1200 Seventeenth Street, 80202
Telephone: 303-628-3300
Fax: 303-628-3368
Email: hallevans@hallevans.com *URL:* http://www.hallevans.com
Colorado Springs, Colorado Office: Suite 600, 102 South Tejon Street, 80903-2664.
Telephone: 719-578-5600.
Fax: 719-635-7458.
Washington, D.C. Office: Suite 610, 1341 G. Street, N.W., 20005.
Telephone: 202-638-4633.
Fax: 202-408-5146.

MEMBERS

Ronald V. Yegge (1905-1970)
Don R. Evans (1925-1976)
Richard D. Hall (1916-1997)
Eugene O. Daniels
Edward H. Widmann
Richard A. Hanneman
David R. Brougham
Samuel David Cheris
Peter F. Jones
Bruce A. Menk
Jeffery B. Stalder
James W. Britt
Eugene R. Commander
Daniel R. Satriana, Jr.
Kevin E. O'Brien
C. Willing Browne
Chris A. Mattison
Robert M. Ferm
Alan Epstein
Paul R. Franke, III
Charles Greenhouse
John E. Bolmer, II
Kenneth H. Lyman
Clinton P. Swift
Joyce H. Nakamura
Thomas R. Dolven
Robert J. McCormick
Matthew Y. Biscan
Thomas J. Lyons
Patricia Jean Clisham
David N. Schachter
F. Gregory McKenna

OF COUNSEL

Brooke Wunnicke

SPECIAL COUNSEL

H. F. Riebesell, Jr.
Malcolm S. Mead
Vincent A. Zarlengo
Robert J. Vincze
Thomas M. List
David F. Murray
Jeffrey Bartholomew
Thomas L. Beam
Walter J. Downing
Fredrick T. Martinez
Josh A. Marks

ASSOCIATES

Edward J. Adkins
W. Alexa Chiang
Beth A. Dickhaus (Not admitted in CO)
William H. Eikenberry
Steven M. Gutierrez
Bradley Joseph Haight (Not admitted in CO)
Joyce L. Jenkins
George Koons, III
Melanie B. Lewis
C. Chandler Lippitt
Marianne E. Pierce
Deborah Ann Purcell
Matthew Damon Ramirez
Andrew D. Ringel
John Gregory Scott
Richard S. Shea
Tatiana Taylor
Hugo Teufel, III
Jesús M. Vázquez, Jr.
Lynne A. Weitzel

Representative Clients: American Insurance Association; Chrysler Corporation; Continental Airlines, Inc.; Jacor Braodcasting Corporation of Colorado, Inc.; Monfort, Inc.; National Railroad Passenger Corporation (AMTRAK); Northern Telecom Inc. (NORTEL); Safeco Insurance Company of America.

(See Next Column)

For full biographical listings, see the Martindale-Hubbell Law Directory

HAMILTON AND FAATZ, A PROFESSIONAL CORPORATION (AV)

Suite 500 Colorado State Bank Building, 1600 Broadway, 80202-4905
Telephone: 303-830-0500
Facsimile: 303-860-7855
Email: HandF@HandF.com

Pierpont Fuller (1906-1983)
John M. Evans (1911-1984)
Dwight Alan Hamilton
Clyde A. Faatz, Jr.
John T. Willson
Michael E. Gurley
James H. Marlow
Jan E. Montgomery
Gregory W. Smith

Christopher J.W. Forrest
Cynthia Treadwell-Miller
Tal Diamant

OF COUNSEL

Kenneth W. Caughey

Representative Clients: Arapahoe County Public Airport Authority; Colorado Baptist General Convention; First Industrial Realty Trust; Masonic Temple Association of Denver; Meridian Investment Management Corp.; Public Employees' Retirement Association of Colorado; Randall and Blake, Inc.; Rocky Mountain Clothing Co.; South Denver Cardiology Associates, P.C.; Unisource Worldwide, Inc.

For full biographical listings, see the Martindale-Hubbell Law Directory

HOGAN & HARTSON L.L.P. (AV)

One Tabor Center Suite 1500, 1200 Seventeenth Street, 80202
Telephone: 303-899-7300
Fax: 303-899-7333
Washington, D.C. Office: Columbia Square, 555 13th Street, N.W.
Telephone: 206-637-5600.
Telex: 89-2757.
Cable Address: "Hogander Washington".
Fax: 202-637-5910.
Brussels, Belgium Office: Avenue des Arts 41, 1040.
Telephone: (32.2) 505.09.11.
Fax: (32.2) 505.09.96.
Budapest, Hungary (Affiliated Office): Nagy & Pintér, Hogan & Hartson Law Office, Bank Center, Granite Tower, 9th Floor, Budapest V., Szabadsag ter 7, 1944 Hungary.
Telephone: (36-1) 302-9050.
Fax: (36-1) 302-9060.
London, England Office: 21 Garlick Hill, EC4V 2AU.
Telephone: (44 171) 815 1200.
Fax: (44 171) 329 0299.
Moscow, Russia Office: 33/2 Usacheva Street, Building 3, 119048.
Telephone: (7095) 245-5190. Int'l
Telephone: (7501) 907-0451.
Fax: (7095) 245-5192. Int'l
Fax: (7501) 907-0462.
Paris, France (Affiliated Office): Cariddi, Mee, Rué, Avocats Associés à la Cour de Paris, 12, rue de la Paix, 75002.
Telephone: (33-1) 42.61.57.71.
Fax: (33-1) 42.61.79.21.
Prague, Czech Republic (Affiliated Office): Hogan & Hartson, Advokátní Kanceláře, Trziste 13, 118 00.
Telephone: (420-2) 2211-7111.
Fax: (420-2) 2421-5105.
Warsaw, Poland Office: Hogan & Hartson Sp.zo.o, Atrium Tower, Al. Jana Pawla II 25, 00-854.
Telephone: (48-22) 653-4200.
Fax: (48-22) 653-4250.
Baltimore, Maryland Office: 111 South Calvert Street.
Telephone: 410-659-2700.
Fax: 410-539-6981.
Rockville, Maryland Office: 600 Jefferson Plaza, Suite 203.
Telephone: 301-315-2206.
Fax: 301-315-9046.
Broomfield, Colorado Office: 370 Interlocken Boulevard, Fourth Floor.
Telephone: 303-474-1960.
Fax: 303-474-1961.
Colorado Springs, Colorado Office: Two North Cascade Avenue, Suite 1300.
Telephone: 719-448-5900.
Fax: 719-448-5922.
Los Angeles, California Office: Biltmore Tower, 500 S. Grand Avenue, Suite 1900.
Telephone: 213-337-6700.
Fax: 213-337-6701.
Newport Beach, California Office: 4675 MacArthur Court, Suite 670.
Telephone: 949-250-4550.
Fax: 949-833-0976.
McLean, Virginia Office: 8300 Greensboro Drive.
Telephone: 703-610-6100.
Fax: 703-610-6200.
New York, New York Office: 885 Third Avenue, 26th Floor.
Telephone: 212-409-9800.
Fax: 212-409-9801.

(See Next Column)

HOGAN & HARTSON L.L.P.—*Continued*

PARTNERS

Edwin P. Aro
Helen Clark Atkeson
Kathryn Webb Bradley
Carol W. Burton
Michael L. Cheroutes (Also at Washington, D.C. and Warsaw, Poland Offices)
Nancy Andreas Clodfelter
Ty Cobb (Not admitted in CO; Also at Washington, D.C. Office)
Steven A. Cohen
Kevin D. Evans
John P. Fitzgerald (Also at Washington, D.C. Office)
Sean R. Gallagher
John M. Gardner
Whitney A. Holmes
Douglas A. Pluss
Scott H. Reisch
David J. Scott
Niki Frangos Tuttle
Craig A. Umbaugh
Donis G. Walker (Also at Colorado Springs, Colorado Office)

OF COUNSEL

H. Thomas Coghill
David E. Skaggs (Also at Washington, D.C. Office)
Jac K. Sperling

ASSOCIATES

Kelly R. Berg
Suzanne M. Bonnet
Kimberly A. Casey
Lisa Reckler Cohn
Sarah L. Kinnick
David L. London
Christopher A. Marks
Theodore D. Matula
Charles T. Mitchell
Kate Turshen Schroepfer
Jussi P. Snellman
Phyllis V. Wan
Peter H. Walsh
Paul E. Washington
Robert E. Witwer

For full biographical listings, see the Martindale-Hubbell Law Directory

HOLLAND & HART LLP (AV)

Suite 3200, 555 Seventeenth Street, P.O. Box 8749, 80201
Telephone: 303-295-8000
Telecopier: 303-295-8261
Email: info@hollandhart.com *URL:* http://www.hollandhart.com
Regional Offices:
Denver Tech Center, Greenwood Village, Colorado
Aspen, Colorado
Boulder, Colorado
Colorado Springs, Colorado
Boise, Idaho
Billings, Montana
Salt Lake City, Utah
Cheyenne, Wyoming, Holland & Hart, A Partnership including Professional Corporations
Jackson, Wyoming, Holland & Hart, A Partnership including Professional Corporations

MEMBERS OF FIRM

Josiah G. Holland (1900-1975)
Stephen H. Hart (1908-1993)
Harry L. Hobson (Retired)
Gordon G. Greiner
William E. Murane
H. Gregory Austin
John S. Castellano
Dennis M. Jackson
Robert E. Benson
Stephen H. Foster (Not admitted in CO)
Richard M. Koon
Robert T. Connery
Michael D. Martin
Jack L. Smith
Jesse B. Heath, Jr.
Mark R. Levy
Wiley E. Mayne, Jr.
Gregory A. Eurich
Ronald M. Martin
Ronald A. Lehmann
Gregory Russell Piché
John Arthur Ramsey
Jane Michaels
James E. Hartley
Peter C. Houtsma
Betty Carter Arkell
Paul D. Phillips
John M. Husband
Daniel R. Frost
Joseph W. Halpern
John F. Shepherd
Davis O. O'Connor
Jeffrey T. Johnson
Mark D. Safty
Kevin S. Crandell
Jeanine Feriancek
Elizabeth A. Sharrer
Mary Ellen Scanlan
Scott S. Barker
Anne J. Castle
John C. Tredennick, Jr.
Maureen Reidy Witt
Elizabeth Ann Phelan
Jack M. Englert, Jr.
A. Bruce Jones
John R. Maxfield
Holly Stein Sollod
Geraldine A. Brimmer
Sandra R. Goldman
Marcy G. Glenn
Michael S. Beaver
Denise W. Kennedy
Steven C. Choquette
Scott Havlick
David E. Crandall
Debra S. Fagan
Karen Sweeney
Risa L. Wolf-Smith
J. Kevin Bridston
Judith A. (Jude) Biggs
Craig E. Stewart
David D. Powell, Jr.
Steven W. Black
Patricia Dean
Brian M. Mumaugh
Heidi S. Glance
Shari R. Baker
Stephen Masciocchi
Jane Oglesby Francis

(See Next Column)

OF COUNSEL

John L. J. Hart (1904-1986)
David Butler
Susani N.H. Dixon
Lynn Bolinske Dolven
Kevin W. Johnson (Not admitted in CO)
Robert R. Keatinge
William C. McClearn
Thomas R. O'Donnell
Christopher L. Thorne
Stephen P. Villano
Lawrence E. Volmert

SPECIAL COUNSEL

Douglas L. Abbott
James J. Gonzales
Jane Lowell Montgomery

ASSOCIATES

Jennifer VanDerbur Atler
Megan Connor Bertron
Virginia L. Briggs
Elizabeth Carney
Cynthia Ullem Christy
Lynn A. Cleveland
Catherine C. Crane
Elizabeth Loring Crane
Lori A. Dixon
Mark D. Ebel
Stephanie B. Edinger
Nicole A. Elias
Maria Teresa (Terry) Fox
Traci R. Garner (Not admitted in CO)
Martin W. Gitlin
Daniel J. Glivar
Jimmy Goh
Christina Groll
Charles P. Henderson
Eric L. Hilty
Arthur A. Hundhausen
Laura S. Hundley
Lee Frederick Johnston
Brian Kinnear
William L. Lawrence
Jude Normand Leblanc
Teresa D. Locke
Veronica J. May
Billi R. McCullough
Lee R. Osman
Lawrence L. Ostema
James A. Pinto
Kami A. Pomerantz
M. Scott Regan
Lusanna J. Ro
Alan D. Schuchman
Tiffany West Smink
Nancy Trethewey
Ido Tuchman
Monique A. Tuttle
Valerie W. Tyler

LEGAL SUPPORT PERSONNEL

Minou Bohlin
Karen Ohnemus Lisko

ASPEN, COLORADO ATTORNEYS

Arthur C. Daily
Arthur B. Ferguson, Jr.
Ginger E. Margolin
Harry Shulman
Thomas J. Todd

BOULDER, COLORADO ATTORNEYS

Judith A. (Jude) Biggs
Robert G. Crouch
Donald A. Degnan
Timothy P. Getzoff
Earl C. Hancock
Scott Havlick
Laura S. Hundley
Camron R. Kuelthau
Stuart T. Langley
Robert W. Planchard
Timothy M. Rastello
Francis A. Sirr

COLORADO SPRINGS, COLORADO ATTORNEYS

William K. Brown (Resident)
Edward H. Flitton (Resident)
Robert Hamilton Kelly (Resident)
Ronald A. Lehmann
Ronald M. Martin
Wendy J. Pifher
David Scott Prince
Elaine Holland Turner
Carey L. Wall

DENVER TECH CENTER, GREENWOOD VILLAGE, COLORADO ATTORNEYS

Michael S. Beaver
Perry L. Glantz
C. William Groscup
Karol L. Kahalley
William W. Maywhort
Todd W. Miller
Robert Alan Poe
Robert M. Pomeroy, Jr.
John Arthur Ramsey
Paul J. Schlauch
Jeffrey Robert Thomas
Christopher H. Toll
Maureen Reidy Witt
Rachel A. Yates

BOISE, IDAHO RESIDENT ATTORNEYS

Steven B. Andersen
Walter H. Bithell
Steven C. Bowman
Amanda K. Brailsford
Shelly H. Cozakos
Jeffrey T. Drake
Robert A. Faucher
Murray D. Feldman
Kurt D. Holzer
Linda B. Jones
J. Frederick Mack
Ted C. Murdock
William G. Myers III
Douglas R. Nash
Andrea P. Patterson
Larry E. Prince
B. Newal Squyres
Bradley J. Wiskirchen

BILLINGS, MONTANA ATTORNEYS

Jeanne Matthews Bender
David R. Chisholm
Stephen H. Foster
Kyle A. Gray
Charles E. Hansberry
Robert A. Lorenz
Paul D. Miller
W. Scott Mitchell
Elizabeth A. Nedrow
Donald W. Quander

SALT LAKE CITY UTAH RESIDENT ATTORNEYS

Barbara Bagnasacco
James L. Barnett
Ashby D. Boyle, II
Susie Inskeep Hindley
H. Matthew Horlacher
Brent E. Johnson
Bruce N. Lemons
Patrick McBride
David R. Rudd
Norman M. White
Scott F. Young

(See Next Column)

HOLLAND & HART LLP, *Denver—Continued*

CHEYENNE, WYOMING ATTORNEYS

James R. Belcher (P.C.)
Teresa Burkett Buffington
Bradley T. Cave (P.C.)
William R. Dabney
Patrick R. Day (P.C.)
David G. Ditto
Edward W. Harris
Melissa Larkin Hughes
Jack D. Palma, II (P.C.)
Thomas L. Sansonetti (P.C.)
Richard Schneebeck (P.C.)
Donald I. Schultz (P.C.)
Lawrence J. Wolfe (P.C.)

JACKSON, WYOMING ATTORNEYS

Michael J. Brennan
Stephen R. Duerr
Paula Fleck
John L. Gallinger (P.C.)
Marilyn S. Kite (P.C.)
Joe M. Teig (P.C.)

For full biographical listings, see the Martindale-Hubbell Law Directory

HOLME ROBERTS & OWEN LLP (AV)

Suite 4100, 1700 Lincoln, 80203
Telephone: 303-861-7000
Telecopier: 303-866-0200
Email: hro@hro.com *URL:* http://www.hro.com
Boulder, Colorado Office: Suite 400, 1401 Pearl Street.
Telephone: 303-444-5955.
Telecopier: 303-444-1063.
Colorado Springs, Colorado Office: Suite 1300, 90 South Cascade Avenue.
Telephone: 719-473-3800.
Telecopier: 719-633-1518.
Salt Lake City, Utah Office: Suite 1100, 111 East Broadway.
Telephone: 801-521-5800.
Telecopier: 801-521-9639.
London, England Office: Heathcoat House, 3rd Floor, 20 Savile Row.
Telephone: 011-44-171-494-5600.
Telecopier: 011-44-171-287-9344.

PARTNERS OF FIRM

Dennis L. Arfmann
Daron J. Arnold
John P. Babb
Robert H. Bach
Donald K. Bain
Duncan E. Barber
Diane S. Barrett
Blaine J. Benard (Salt Lake City Office)
Bruce F. Black
Boyd N. Boland
Ross E. Breyfogle
Elizabeth E. Brown
Linnea Brown
Charles B. Bruce, Jr.
Mark K. Buchi (Salt Lake City Office)
James D. Butler
James E. Bye
Susan E. Duffey Campbell (Colorado Springs Office)
Phillip R. Clark
G. Kevin Conwick
Thomas F. Cope
James F. Cress
Carolyn E. Daniels
Spencer T. Denison
Judson W. Detrick
Daniel J. Dunn
Elizabeth T. Dunning (Salt Lake City Office)
Adam R. Eaton
Frank Erisman
Kent A. Fischmann (Boulder Office)
Richard L. Gabriel
Steve L. Gaines (Colorado Springs Office)
Nancy J. Gegenheimer
Mary L. Groves
George M. Haley, III (Salt Lake City Office)
Colin G. Harris
Lynn Parker Hendrix
Paul D. Holleman
Robert A. Holmes
Donald J. Hopkins
Mark M. Hrenya
William S. Huff
Henry W. Ipsen
David W. Isbell (Colorado Springs Office)
Garth B. Jensen
Eric E. Johnson
Bruce R. Kohler (Resident Managing Partner, London, England Office)
Sherri Heckel Kuhlmann
Christopher J. Kulish (Boulder Office)
Lawrence L. Levin
Bruce L. Likoff
Martin D. Litt
David H. Little (Salt Lake City Office)
Kenneth W. Lund
Daniel C. Lynch
McKay Marsden (Managing Partner, Salt Lake City Office)
Thomas R. Marsh
Manuel L. Martinez
George G. Matava
John D. McCarthy
John V. McDermott
David T. Mitzner
Joseph W. Morrisey, Jr.
Richard L. Nagl (Colorado Springs Office)
Charlotte Louise Neitzel
Nick Nimmo
K. Preston Oade, Jr.
Susan L. (Jones) Oakes
Renée W. O'Rourke
Katherine Jean Peck
John R. Posthumus
Charles A. Ramunno
Steven B. Richardson
Thomas A. Richardson
Judith L. Roberts
Martha Traudt Collins Rolle (London, England Office)
Jill K. Rood (Boulder Office)
Brent E. Rychener (Colorado Springs Office)
W. Dean Salter
Greggory J. Savage (Salt Lake City Office)
Steven B. Smith (Colorado Springs Office)
David S. Steefel
Jan N. Steiert
Robert L. Stolebarger (Salt Lake City Office)
Mary Hurley Stuart
Paul G. Thompson (London, England Office)
Gary R. Thorup (Salt Lake City Office)
Paul V. Timmins
Patricia C. Tisdale
Robert Tuchman
Stephanie M. Tuthill
John A. Warnick (Not admitted in CO)
John R. Webb
Robert J. Welter

(See Next Column)

PARTNERS OF FIRM (Continued)

Francis R. Wheeler
David B. Wilson
Richard G. Wohlgenant
John B. Wood (Boulder Office)
John R. Wylie (Colorado Springs Office)
Richard R. Young (Managing Partner, Colorado Springs Office)

OF COUNSEL

Harold S. Bloomenthal
Karen Campbell Jenson (Salt Lake City Office)
Frank E. Moss (Salt Lake City Office)
Richard L. Schrepferman
Kay M. Small (Boulder Office)
Ted P. Stockmar

SPECIAL COUNSEL

Charles E. Berry
Carolyn Cox (Salt Lake City Office)
Rita I. Ehrman
James L. Johnson
Karen Schauble Leaffer
Richard A. Oertli
Linda K. Wackwitz
Norman H. Wright

SENIOR COUNSEL

A. Edgar Benton
Steven E. Christoffersen
Louise Betcher Staab
Edward E. Stevenson
Sharon A. Thomas (Colorado Springs Office)
Lawrence M. Zavadil

ASSOCIATES

Mark A. Adams
Lisa McGee Allen (London, England Office)
Merry H. Balson
Robert Boyd Berube
Troy R. Braegger
Kelly K. Calocci
Brian A. Carpenter
Pattie S. Christensen (Salt Lake City Office)
Katheryn Jarvis Coggon
Kelly M. Condon
Jennifer A. D'Alessandro
Nancy L. Dempsey
Jeffrey A. Divney
Denise Pino Erwin
Matthew N. Evans (Salt Lake City Office)
Elizabeth K. Flaagan
Thomas A. Geraghty, Jr.
Sherry A. Gonzales
Elizabeth A. González
Stanley J. Gradisar
Peter O. Hansen
Michael J. Hofmann
William C. Holland
Kenneth J. Johnson
Ashley Warren Jordaan (Colorado Springs Office)
Hendrik F. Jordaan (Colorado Springs Office)
Brent P. Karasiuk (Colorado Springs Office)
Donald I. J. Kelso
Tammy H. Kraemer (Colorado Springs Office)
Ann E. Lane
Stuart J. Lark (Colorado Springs Office)
Tonya Feit Lark (Colorado Springs Office)
Matthew J. Lepore
M. Mashenka Lundberg
Matt A. Mayer
Deborah S. Menkins (Colorado Springs Office)
Joli A. Messer-Liebrock
Jennifer Nelson (Salt Lake City Office)
Roxane J. Perruso
J. Daniel Phelan
E. Blaine Rawson (Salt Lake City Office)
Thad W. Renaud
Richard F. Rodriguez
Jill W. Rose-Tappert
Michelle M. Rose-Hughes
Tara M. Schiller (London, England Office)
Lisa A. Schuh
Annette M. Schüller (London, England Office)
Alec C. Sherod (Not admitted in CO)
Kevin Joseph Simon (Salt Lake City Office)
William A. Skewes, II
John M. Stafford
Lori S. Stefanoudakis
Brent A. Tracy
Paul M. Wilson (Salt Lake City Office)
Maria V. Woods
Vikki Lynn Wulf (Boulder Office)
Thomas E. Yearout
Steven P. Young (Salt Lake City Office)
Philip C. Zimmerman

LEGAL SUPPORT PERSONNEL

Mark E. Estes (Director of Library Services)
Cynthia J. Hyman (Legal Recruiting Administrator)

For full biographical listings, see the Martindale-Hubbell Law Directory

KUTAK ROCK (AV)

Suite 2900, 717 Seventeenth Street, 80202-3329
Telephone: 303-297-2400
Fax: 303-292-7799
URL: http://www.kutakrock.com
Atlanta, Georgia Office: Suite 2100, 225 Peachtree Street, NE, 30303-1731.
Telephone: 404-222-4600.
Facsimile: 404-222-4654.
Kansas City, Missouri Office: One Main Plaza, Suite 810, 4435 Main Street, 64111-7727.
Telephone: 816-960-0090.
Telefax: 816-960-0041.
Little Rock, Arkansas Office: Suite 1100, 425 West Capitol Avenue, 72201-3409.
Telephone: 501-975-3000.
Facsimile: 501-975-3001.
New York, New York Office: 650 Fifth Avenue, 10019-6108.
Telephone: 212-713-6480.
Facsimile: 212-713-6481.

(See Next Column)

KUTAK ROCK—*Continued*

Oklahoma City, Oklahoma Office: Suite 475, 6305 Waterford Boulevard, 73118-1116.
Telephone: 405-848-2475.
Facsimile: 405-842-5748.
Omaha, Nebraska Office: The Omaha Building, 1650 Farnam Street, 68102-2186.
Telephone: 402-346-6000.
Facsimile: 402-346-1148.
Phoenix, Arizona Office: 16th Floor, 3300 North Central Avenue, 85012-2516.
Telephone: 602-285-1700.
Facsimile: 602-285-1868.
Pittsburgh, Pennsylvania Office: 1214 Frick Building, 437 Grant Street, 15219-6002.
Telephone: 412-261-6720.
Facsimile: 412-261-6717.
Washington, D.C. Office: Suite 1000, 1101 Connecticut Avenue, NW, 20036-4374.
Telephone: 202-828-2400.
Facsimile: 202-828-2488.
Newport Beach, California Office: Suite 450, 620 Newport Center Drive, 92660-8019.
Telephone: 949-718-6700.
Facsimile: 949-718-6708.

MEMBERS OF FIRM

James D. Arundel	David A. Caprera
Paul E. Belitz	M. Lou Raders
Robert D. Irvin	Scott H. Beck
Michael K. Reppe	Sam S. Balisy (Not admitted in CO)
Larry L. Carlile	Cindy S. Birley
John H. Bernstein	William C. Gorham
Michael R. Johnson	Thomas M. Peltz
Robert J. Ahrenholz	Diana C. Fields
Thane R. Hodson	Saranne K Maxwell
Peter D. Willis	Peggy Ann Richter
Robert C. Roth, Jr.	Richard L. Buddin
Michael T. Lambert	Anne M. Gish
Frederic H. Marienthal III	Dominic A. Lloyd
Peter E. Robinson	

John P. Jones

OF COUNSEL

Lydia A. Mangan	Tana K. Simard
Gerard V. Reardon	Paula J. McCann (Not admitted in CO)
Mark L. Sabey	J. Gregory Whitehair
Melvin B. Sabey	

Donald R. Stover

ASSOCIATES

Craig N. Johnson	Trenton H. Johnson
Matthew J. Rita	Michael G. Thomas
Kathryn K. Heet	Margaret M. Groscup
Amy E. Campbell (Not admitted in CO)	Amy A. Sumner
Jennifer K. Barrett	Michael J. Zieg
Bryce H. Beecher (Not admitted in CO)	Thomas C. Weihe
	Joshua M. Kerstein
	Anita Luck (Not admitted in CO)

For full biographical listings, see the Martindale-Hubbell Law Directory

LONG & JAUDON, P.C. (AV)

The Bailey Mansion, 1600 Ogden Street, 80218-1414
Telephone: 303-832-1122
FAX: 303-832-1348

Lawrence A. Long (1908-1992)	Michael T. McConnell
Joseph C. Jaudon, Jr.	Stephen P. Hopkins
David B. Higgins	Michael T. DePinto (1956-1995)
James A. Dierker	Alan D. Avery
Frederick W. Long	Cecelia A. Fleischner
Gary B. Blum	Walter N. Houghtaling

Christine Anne Craigmile

Sheri Hood Roswell	Michael Rosenberg
David H. Yun	David M. McLain
James Michael Miletich	Jennifer J. Gifford
Traci L. Van Pelt	Susan A. Jones
Thomas J. Kresl	(Not admitted in CO)

Christopher D. Yvars

OF COUNSEL

Linda L. Siderius

Representative Clients: Keystone Resorts, Inc.; King Soopers, Inc. (Dillon Companies, Inc.); St. Joseph Hospital; Watersaver; Travelers Property Casualty Company; The Doctors Co.; Home Insurance Co.; Baxter Healthcare; CNA.

For full biographical listings, see the Martindale-Hubbell Law Directory

MONTGOMERY LITTLE & MCGREW, P.C. (AV)

The Quadrant, 5445 DTC Parkway, Suite 800 (Englewood), 80111
Telephone: 303-773-8100
Telecopier: 303-220-0412
URL: http://www.mlmpc.com

Roy E. Montgomery (1907-1986)	Daniel P. Murphy
Robert R. Montgomery	Michael H. Smith
David C. Little	Rebecca B. Givens
Dan McGrew	Robert N. Spencer
James J. Soran, III	John R. Riley
Richard L. Murray, Jr.	Christopher B. Little
Kevin J. Kuhn	Karen B. Best
Robert J. Beattie	Timothy M. Schulte
William H. Knapp	Carole Salamaha
Debra Piazza	Joel A. Mayo
	Patrick T. O'Rourke

Julie J. Collett

OF COUNSEL

J. Bayard Young	Thomas C. Deline

David M. Treadwell

LEGAL SUPPORT PERSONNEL

Rodney R. Germeroth (Director of Administration)	Tammy L. Jackson (Legal Assistant)
Mary Kay Ackley (Legal Assistant)	Debbie L. Kirke (Legal Assistant)
Julie M. Alvarez (Legal Assistant)	Kelly W. Roberge (Legal Assistant)
Carmen L. Antonio (Legal Assistant)	Monica L. Sharp (Legal Assistant)
Margaret M. Green (Legal Assistant)	

Representative Clients: BP Amoco; Bristol-Myers Squibb; Colorado Medical Society; Cyprus Minerals; Dillon Cos., Inc., d/b/a King Soopers; The St. Paul Insurance Cos.; University of Colorado Health Sciences Center; HealthOne; Westport Insurance Group; COPIC.

For full biographical listings, see the Martindale-Hubbell Law Directory

MYER, SWANSON, ADAMS & WOLF, P.C. (AV)

The Colorado State Bank Building, 1600 Broadway, Suite 1480, 80202-4915
Telephone: 303-866-9800
Facsimile: 303-866-9818

Fred E. Neef (1910-1986)	Allan B. Adams
Rendle Myer (1929-1999)	Thomas J. Wolf

John M. Anderson	Karen S. Proc

OF COUNSEL

Robert Swanson

Representative Clients: The Oppenheimer Funds; Panorama Series Fund; The Centennial Trusts; Mile High Chapter of American Red Cross; Master Lease; Heartland Management Co.; Kan-Build of Colorado, Inc.
Reference: The Colorado State Bank and Trust of Denver.

For full biographical listings, see the Martindale-Hubbell Law Directory

OTTEN, JOHNSON, ROBINSON, NEFF & RAGONETTI, P.C. (AV)

950 Seventeenth Street, 16th Floor, 80202
Telephone: 303-825-8400
Telecopier: 303-825-6525
URL: http://www.ojrnr.com

Arthur E. Otten, Jr.	Karen L. Barsch
William F. Schoeberlein	Brad W. Schacht
Frank L. Robinson	R. Michael Shomo
Bruce B. Johnson	David P. Hutchinson
A. Bruce Campbell	John R. Marcil
William R. Neff	Michael C. Villano
Thomas J. Ragonetti	Todd A. Fredrickson
David W. Stark	Mark F. Copertino
Lawrence W. Marquess	James D. Leonard
Darrell G. Waas	Darin Mackender
Robert C. Fisher, Jr.	Victoria L. Hellmer
Neil M. Goff	Patricia C. Campbell
Blair L. Lockwood	Christopher T. Toll
Douglas R. Wright	J. Bart Johnson
Hugh Q. Gottschalk	Karen L. Brody
J. Thomas Macdonald	James C. Ellenberger
John D. Sternberg	Patricia A. Thatcher
Michael Westover	Heidi G. Duston
Randall G. Alt	Nancy L. Lipson
Daniel M. Minzer	Munsey L. Ayers, Jr.
Kevin A. Gliwa	Paul D. Zier
P. Kathleen Lower	Michael C. Matheson
David T. Brennan	C. Ander Smith
Kathleen M. Bottagaro	Jeffrey A. Sherman
Terence M. Ridley	Nicole J. Hanak
Kenneth K. Skogg	Carolyn J. Fairless

(See Next Column)

OTTEN, JOHNSON, ROBINSON, NEFF & RAGONETTI P.C., *Denver—Continued*

Cheryl A. Malcolm
Katherine L. Ruff
Lenn A. Moldenhauer
Brian P. Jumps
Berkeley I. Vogelsang

OF COUNSEL

Barbara J. Kelley
Barbara J. Green

Representative Clients: Aetna Life Insurance Co.; The Broe Companies; Conoco Inc.; Coram Healthcare Corp.; Eagle Gaming, L.P.; Frontier Airlines; GeriMed of America, Inc.; KN Energy, Inc.; Public Employees' Retirement Association of Colorado; StarTek, Inc.; TrizecHahn Centers, Inc.; U.S. Bank National Association; U S WEST Financial Services, Inc.

For full biographical listings, see the Martindale-Hubbell Law Directory

PENDLETON, FRIEDBERG, WILSON & HENNESSEY, P.C. (AV)

Seventeenth & Grant Building, Suite 1000, 303 East 17th Avenue, 80203
Telephone: 303-839-1204
Telecopier: 303-831-0786

Brian Pendleton
Alan C. Friedberg
Robert F. Wilson
Richard F. Hennessey
F. Stephen Collins
Michael E. Romero
Susan M. Hargleroad
Joel W. Cantrick
Nancy R. Crow
William S. Martin
Stephen J. Ismert

Noriko K. Nakamura
John Christopher Haas
Timothy M. Kratz
Kathryn A. Wingard
John E. Horneck

SPECIAL COUNSEL

Paul G. Bursiek
Jeffrey R. Fiske

Reference: Norwest Bank of Denver.

For full biographical listings, see the Martindale-Hubbell Law Directory

SENN LEWIS & VISCIANO, P.C. (AV)

1801 California Street, Suite 4300, 80202
Telephone: 303-298-1122
Facsimile: 303-296-9101

Mark A. Senn
Fredric J. Lewis
Frank W. Visciano
Stephen W. Arent
Ellen Kirschenbaum

Martha J. Bohling
Rosemarie E. Delmonte
Mark A. Redmiles
Rufus C. "Butch" Taylor, Jr.
David C. Camp
Luis A. Toro
Margie J. Titus
Hazel I. Lee
Vivian Lee Perla
Joel S. Rosenstein

OF COUNSEL

Lawrence A. Atler
Brenda Jansen
Lynn S. Jordan

For full biographical listings, see the Martindale-Hubbell Law Directory

SHERMAN & HOWARD L.L.C. (AV)

Attorneys and Counselors at Law
633 Seventeenth Street, Suite 3000, 80202
Telephone: 303-297-2900
Telecopier: 303-298-0940
Colorado Springs, Colorado Office: Suite 1500, 90 South Cascade Avenue, 80903.
Telephone: 719-475-2440.
Las Vegas, Nevada Office: Swendseid & Stern, a member in Sherman & Howard L.L.C., 317 Sixth Street, 89101.
Telephone: 702-387-6073.
Reno, Nevada Office: Swendseid & Stern, a member in Sherman & Howard L.L.C., 50 West Liberty Street, Suite 660, 89501.
Telephone: 702-323-1980.

James H. Pershing (1863-1948)
Robert Graham Bosworth (1888-1954)
Lewis A. Dick (1889-1954)
Fritz A. Nagel (1891-1978)
Clyde C. Dawson (1905-1979)
Samuel S. Sherman, Jr. (1909-1988)
Winston S. Howard (Retired)
James L. Cunningham
Douglas M. Cain
Duane F. Wurzer
E. Lee Dale
Christopher Lane
Kurt A. Kaufmann
R. Michael Sanchez
Andrew L. Blair, Jr.
Howard B. Gelt
Charles W. Newcom
Mark L. Fulford
James F. Wood
Robert P. Mitchell
Kenneth B. Siegel
David Thomas III
Cynthia C. Benson
Joseph J. Bronesky
John O. Swendseid (Las Vegas and Reno, Nevada Offices)
Robert L. Brown
Dee P. Wisor
Arlene S. Bobrow
Raymond M. Deeny (Colorado Springs Office)
W.V. Bernie Siebert
Stanley M. Raine
Theodore A. Olsen

(See Next Column)

Paul Curtis Daw
Ronald M. Eddy
Durward E. Timmons, Jr. (Colorado Springs Office)
Rebecca Anderson Fischer
Steven D. Miller
Peggy Berning Knight
B. Scott Pullara
Jennifer Stern (Las Vegas and Reno, Nevada Offices)
Richard N. Baer
Leanne B. DeVos
Joanne F. Norris
Leslie A. Nichols
Stefan D. Stein
Amy L. Hirter
Lawrence W. Treece
Calvin T. Hanson
N. Dawn Webber (Colorado Springs Office)
Glenn H. Schlabs (Colorado Springs Office)
Karen L. Chapman
Robert Mintz
Diana M. Wendel
Hugh J. McClearn
William T. Diss
Edmond F. Noel, Jr.
Richard K. Parks
Cynthia P. Delaney
Bruce A. Kolbezen (Colorado Springs Office)
Robert A. Hykan
Blake T. Jordan
Carol V. Berger
James P. Lane
Kathleen A. Odle
Doran L. Matzke
Andrew W. Volin
Michael Dubetz, Jr.
Milton L. "Skip" Smith, III (Colorado Springs Office)
John W. Mill
Deborah Land Buckley
Kendra S. Follett (Las Vegas and Reno, Nevada Offices)
Paul J. McCue
Kimberley H. Tyson

COUNSEL

John W. Low
Garth C. Grissom
Michael D. Groshek
James E. Hautzinger
Gary L. Greer
Paul E. Roberts
Barbara Weil Gall
Joan Blaik
James R. McMaster
Stephanie J. Griffin
William L. Sasz (Colorado Springs Office)
Bridget K. Sullivan

Carol Hildebrand
Christopher R. Mosley
Joseph M. Dencker
Jeffrey S. Lyons
Peter A. Cal
Gregory J. Ramos
Peter J. Whitmore
Heather Fox Vickles
Emily F. Keimig
Jennifer M. Mardosz
Cherry J. Hearn
Howard M. Diamond
Kurt L. Gottschall
Ted C. Tow, III
Bryan D. Biesterfeld
William A. Wright
Brenda K. (Buege) Heinicke (Colorado Springs Office)
Edward J. Butler (Colorado Springs Office)
Ronald M. Pierce
Wendy G. Ramsey
Noel M. Franklin
Elizabeth S. McKelvey
Allison H. Lee
Cynthia M. Stovall
Michael P. Gleason
Patrick R. Scully (Colorado Springs Office)
Vicki L. Bussard
Kirsten B. Stewart (Not admitted in CO)
Dawn A. Leporati
Stina A. Bonkoski
Scott W. Shaver
Dallas Lain
Gregory T. Densen
Rachel P. Dauer
Michael A. Hammell
Carrie Lamitie
Michael A. Bushell
Lauren A. McLaughlin
Brian David Zall

Representative Clients: BACE Industries, LLC; Flatiron Structures Co. LLC; Hanifen, Imhoff Inc.; Hathaway Corp.; J.D. Edwards & Co.; Newmont Gold Company; Public Employees' Retirement Assn.; Tele-Communications, Inc.; United Artists Theatre Circuit, Inc.; U.S. West Communications, Inc.

For full biographical listings, see the Martindale-Hubbell Law Directory

WALDBAUM, CORN, KOFF AND BERGER, P.C. (AV)

303 East Seventeenth Avenue, Suite 940, 80203-1262
Telephone: 303-861-1166
Telecopier: 303-861-0601

Leonard N. Waldbaum
Douglas B. Koff
Robert O. Corn
Michael H. Berger
Scot M. Peterson
Eben P. Clark

Representative Clients: Bestop, Inc.; CIMA Energy Corporation; Contact Lens Association of Ophthalmologists, Inc. (CLAO); Hayashida Farms, Inc.; J.A. Balistreri Farms, Inc.; OraLabs, Inc.; Premier Enterprises, Inc.; Raintree Homes, Inc.; The Staubach Co.; Western Optical, Inc.

For full biographical listings, see the Martindale-Hubbell Law Directory

WALTERS & JOYCE, P.C. (AV)

2015 York Street, 80205
Telephone: 303-322-1404
FAX: 303-377-5668

William E. Walters, III
Craig D. Joyce

Anne Baudino Holton

OF COUNSEL

Julia T. Waggener

Reference: Norwest Bank of Buckingham Square; Mountain States Bank.

For full biographical listings, see the Martindale-Hubbell Law Directory

Denver—Continued

WELBORN SULLIVAN MECK & TOOLEY, P.C. (AV)

1775 Sherman Street, Suite 1800, 80203-4318
Telephone: 303-376-4490
Facsimile: 303-376-4495
Email: wsmt@aol.com

John F. Welborn
Stephen J. Sullivan
John F. Meck
Keith D. Tooley
Kendor P. Jones
Brian S. Tooley
Scott L. Sells
Mary V. Laitos
Molly Sommerville
Thomas C. McKee
William R. Rapson
Stephen A. Bain
Amy E. Mang
Danielle V. Smith

OF COUNSEL

Robert F. Welborn

SPECIAL COUNSEL

Jan G. Laitos
Norman S. Early, Jr.

Representative Clients: The Joslin Dry Goods Company; K.P. Kauffman Company; McNeel International; Mercantile Stores, Inc.; Palace Construction Company; Pitney Bowes, Inc.; Union Pacific Resources Company; Western Mining Corporation (USA); WMC Exploration Inc.

For full biographical listings, see the Martindale-Hubbell Law Directory

*DURANGO,** La Plata Co.

FRANK J. ANESI (AV)

Suite 220, 835 East Second Avenue, P.O. Box 2185, 81302
Telephone: 970-247-9246
Fax: 970-259-2793
Email: fjanesi@frontier.net

References: First National Bank of Durango; Burns Bank, Durango.

For full biographical listings, see the Martindale-Hubbell Law Directory

MAYNES, BRADFORD, SHIPPS & SHEFTEL LLP (AV)

West Building, Suite 123, 835 East Second Avenue, P.O. Box 2717, 81302
Telephone: 970-247-1755
Fax: 970-247-8827
Email: mbss@frontier.net *URL:* http://www.mbssllp.com

MEMBERS OF FIRM

Frank E. (Sam) Maynes
Byron V. Bradford (1907-1985)
Thomas H. Shipps
Janice C. Sheftel
Sam W. Maynes
Patricia A. Hall
John Barlow Spear
Geoffrey M. Craig

Counsel for: Southwestern Water Conservation District; San Miguel and La Plata Water Conservancy Districts; La Plata Electric Association, Inc. (REA); Southern Ute Indian Tribe; South Durango Water District; Dolores Water Conservancy District; Animas-La Plata Water Conservancy District; State Farm Insurance.

For full biographical listings, see the Martindale-Hubbell Law Directory

ENGLEWOOD, Arapahoe Co.

BANTA, HOYT, EVERALL & FARRINGTON, L.L.C. (AV)

Suite 240E, 5690 DTC Boulevard, 80111-3232
Telephone: 303-220-8000
Fax: 303-220-0153

Richard J. Banta
Stephen G. Everall
Darryl L. Farrington

OF COUNSEL

R. Val Hoyt

Representative Clients: Cherry Creek School District No. 5; Colorado School District Self Insurance Pool; Copper Mountain Consolidated Metropolitan District; Kiewit Western Co.; Littleton Public Schools; National Union Fire Insurance Co. (local); South Arapahoe Santation District.

For full biographical listings, see the Martindale-Hubbell Law Directory

*FORT COLLINS,** Larimer Co.

ALLEN, VAHRENWALD & JOHNSON, LLC (AV)

Eleventh Floor, Key Bank Building, 125 South Howes, P.O. Box 608, 80522
Telephone: 970-482-5058
Fax: 970-482-5175
Email: arvlaw@concentric.net

MEMBERS OF FIRM

William H. Allen (1917-1990)
Jack D. Vahrenwald
Donald E. Johnson, Jr.
J. Brian McMahill
Russell B. Sanford
Allan S. Massey

ASSOCIATE

Mason C. Mitchell

Representative Clients: Everitt Enterprises, Inc. (Real Estate Development); LaPorte Water and Sanitation District; Foothills Fashion Mall (Shopping Center); Community First National Bank, Fort Collins.

(See Next Column)

References: First National Bank of Fort Collins, N.A.; Community First National Bank, Fort Collins.

For full biographical listings, see the Martindale-Hubbell Law Directory

DWYER, HUDDLESON & RAY, P.C. (AV)

Tenth Floor, First Tower, 215 West Oak Street Drawer J, 80522
Telephone: 970-482-1056
Facsimile: 970-482-3840
Email: info@dhr-law.com *URL:* http://www.dhr-law.com

David E. Dwyer
Charles R. Huddleson
Steven B. Ray
James E. Ringenberg
Stephen J. Jouard
Joel M. Funk
Megan Hayes
Kent E. Sutherland

General Counsel for: First National Bank; Columbine Health Systems, Inc.; Steele's Market, Inc.; Orthopaedic Center of the Rockies.
Counsel for: Hewlett-Packard Co.; Leggett & Platt Inc.; Platte River Power Authority; Woodward Governor Co.; Stelbar Oil Corp.; Advanced Energy Industries Co., Inc.

For full biographical listings, see the Martindale-Hubbell Law Directory

FISCHER, BROWN & GUNN, P.C. (AV)

8th Floor, First Tower, 215 West Oak Street, P.O. Box Q, 80521
Telephone: 970-407-9000
Facsimile: 970-407-1055
Email: fbg@frii.com

Ward H. Fischer (1929-1996)
William H. Brown
William C. Gunn
William R. Fischer
Margaret A. Brown
Margaret A. Althoff

Daniel K. Brown

General Counsel for: First National Bank; The Water Supply and Storage Co.; Cache La Poudre Water Users Assn.
Counsel for: Eastman Kodak Co.; The City of Northglenn; The City of Littleton; The City of Brighton.

For full biographical listings, see the Martindale-Hubbell Law Directory

MARCH & LILEY, P.C. (AV)

110 East Oak Street, Suite 200, 80524
Telephone: 970-482-4322
Fax: 970-482-5719
Email: marchlaw@verinet.com *URL:* http://www.lawyers.com/march&lileylaw

Arthur E. March (1909-1981)
Arthur E. March, Jr.
Lucia A. Liley
J. Brad March

Edward M. Yosses

Local Counsel for: The Genesee Co.; U.S. Homes Corp.; McDonalds Corp.
General Counsel for: Schrader Oil Co.; Bartran & Co.; Sitzman-Mitchell & Co.; Giuliano & Father Construction, Inc.; Fort Collins Downtown Development Authority; Town of Wellington; Town of Timnath.

For full biographical listings, see the Martindale-Hubbell Law Directory

*GLENWOOD SPRINGS,** Garfield Co.

BALCOMB & GREEN, P.C. (AV)

818 Colorado Avenue, P.O. Drawer 790, 81602
Telephone: 970-945-6546, 945-2371
Fax: 970-945-8902

John A. Thulson
Edward Mulhall, Jr.
Scott M. Balcomb
Lawrence R. Green
Timothy A. Thulson
Lori J.M. Satterfield
Edward Bryan Olszewski

David Sandoval
Dendy M. Heisel
Christopher L. Coyle
Jefferson J. Cheney

OF COUNSEL

Kenneth Balcomb

General Counsel for: Ski Sunlight, Inc.
Local Counsel for: Farm Credit Services.

For full biographical listings, see the Martindale-Hubbell Law Directory

*GOLDEN,** Jefferson Co.

BUSCH PROFESSIONAL CORPORATION (AV)

1767-A Denver West Boulevard, Suite 39, 80401
Telephone: 303-215-0050
Fax: 303-742-2396

Robert G. Busch

(See Next Column)

BUSCH PROFESSIONAL CORPORATION, *Golden—Continued*

Robert G. Busch

For full biographical listings, see the Martindale-Hubbell Law Directory

FLEMING, PATTRIDGE & RUNNERSTROM, P.C. (AV)

1200 Arapahoe Street, 80401-1198
Telephone: 303-279-2563
Fax: 303-279-2677

Robert G. Fleming (Retired)
Frederick J. Pattridge (Retired)
Lars R. Runnerstrom

Michelle A. Dobbins
Marilana S. "Marnie" Walsh

Counsel for: Metrolist, Inc.; Ardourel Construction Co.; The Foss Co.; Meyer Home Center, Inc.; Mesa Meadows Land Co.

For full biographical listings, see the Martindale-Hubbell Law Directory

*GRAND JUNCTION,** Mesa Co.

HOSKIN, FARINA, ALDRICH & KAMPF, PROFESSIONAL CORPORATION (AV)

Bank of Colorado Building, 200 Grand Avenue, Suite 400, P.O. Box 40, 81502
Telephone: 970-242-4903
FAX: 970-241-3760

Gregory K. Hoskin
Terrance L. Farina
Frederick G. Aldrich
Gregg K. Kampf
Curtis G. Taylor
David M. Scanga
David A. Younger
Michael J. Russell
John T. Howe
Matthew G. Weber

John Siddeek
Gregory L. Ryan
Loretta (Laurie) A. Cahill

Attorneys for: Great American First Savings Bank, FSB; Central Bank of Grand Junction; Grand Valley National Bank; City Market, Inc.; Rangely School District RE-4; Rocky Mountain Health Maintenance Organization; Unocal Corp.; Equitable Life Assurance Society; Grand Valley Rural Power Lines, Inc.; Pepsi-Cola Bottling Group.

For full biographical listings, see the Martindale-Hubbell Law Directory

*GREELEY,** Weld Co.

WITWER, OLDENBURG, BARRY & BEDINGFIELD, LLP (AV)

Suite 760, 822 7th Street, 80631
Telephone: 970-352-3161
Facsimile: 970-352-3165

MEMBERS OF FIRM

Stow L. Witwer, Jr.
R. Sam Oldenburg
John J. Barry
Jeffrey T. Bedingfield
Jacqueline Johnson
Charles A. Karowsky (Retired)

Patrick M. Groom
Timothy V. Clancy

Representative Clients: Bank One-Greely; Greeley School District; Aims Junior College; John Hancock Mutual Life Insurance Co.; Phelps-Tointon, Inc.

For full biographical listings, see the Martindale-Hubbell Law Directory

*LAMAR,** Prowers Co.

SHINN, STEERMAN & SHINN (AV)

200 West Elm Street, P.O. Box 390, 81052
Telephone: 719-336-4313
Fax: 719-336-4315
URL: http://www.lawyers.com/shinnsteerman&shinn

MEMBERS OF FIRM

Carl M. Shinn
Wendy S. Shinn
Donald L. Steerman

Counsel for: Amity Canal; District 67 Ditch Assn.; County of Cheyenne, Colorado; County of Kiowa, Colorado; Ragsdale Farms, Inc.; Scherler Farms; Hatcher Farms, Inc.; Buffalo Canal Co.; Four States Feedyard, Inc.; Ordway Feedyard Limited, Ltd.

For full biographical listings, see the Martindale-Hubbell Law Directory

LONGMONT, Boulder Co.

GRANT & GRANT, LLP (AV)

436 Coffman Street, Suite 200, 80502-0908
Telephone: 303-776-3100
Facsimile: 303-774-2349
Email: law@grant-grant.com

Wallace H. Grant
Cameron A. Grant

(See Next Column)

ASSOCIATES

Edward R. Gorab

OF COUNSEL

William J. McCarren

LEGAL SUPPORT PERSONNEL

Khileen B. Flynn (Paralegal)
Tom R. Kiteley (Estate & Financial Planning Consultant)

For full biographical listings, see the Martindale-Hubbell Law Directory

LOVELAND, Larimer Co.

HAMMOND AND CLARK (AV)

Suite 418 Bank One Building, 200 East 7th Street, 80537
Telephone: 970-667-1023
Fax: 970-669-9380
Email: LAHLawyer@aol.com

MEMBERS OF FIRM

Lynn A. Hammond
Roger E. Clark
Jon-Mark C. Patterson

Representative Clients: Hewlett-Packard Co.; City of Loveland (Water Matters); Ward Construction Company; Loveland Ready-Mix, Inc.; Action, Inc.; Lundeen Sculptures, Ltd.; Ostermiller Studios.
Reference: Bank One, Colorado; Home State Bank; First National Bank.

For full biographical listings, see the Martindale-Hubbell Law Directory

*MONTROSE,** Montrose Co.

EDWARD D. DURHAM (AV)

543 South Second Street, P.O. Box 1721, 81402
Telephone: 970-249-2274
Fax: 970-249-6482; 970-249-6592

Reference: Norwest Bank of Montrose.

For full biographical listings, see the Martindale-Hubbell Law Directory

SOUTH FORK, Rio Grande Co.

GORDON H. ROWE, JR. (AV)

0020 West Lodge Drive, P.O. Box 1273, 81154
Telephone: 719-873-1740
Fax: 719-873-1742
Albuquerque, New Mexico Office: Rowe & Rowe, A Professional Corporation, 1200 Pennsylvania N.E., Suite 2B, 87110.
Telephone: 505-232-2800.
Fax: 505-268-7027.

OF COUNSEL

Gordon H. Rowe, III

ASSOCIATE

Charles C. Powers

Representative Clients: Tri-Me Potato Co.; Lariat Irrigation Co.; Rio Grande & San Luis Irrigation Co.; Rio Grande & Piedra Ditch Co.; Emerald Ranch.
Counsel for: Bank of Monte Vista.
Approved Attorney for: Attorneys Title Guaranty Fund, Inc.
Reference: Bank of Monte Vista.

For full biographical listings, see the Martindale-Hubbell Law Directory

VAIL, Eagle Co.

DUNN, ABPLANALP & MAURIELLO, P.C. (AV)

Suite 300 Weststar Bank Building, 108 South Frontage Road West, 81657-5087
Telephone: 970-476-0300
Telecopier: 970-476-4765
Email: vaillaw@vail.net *URL:* http://www.lawyers.com/vaillaw

John W. Dunn
Arthur A. Abplanalp, Jr.
Diane Herman Mauriello
Carrie A. Hendon

OF COUNSEL

Jerry W. Hannah

LEGAL SUPPORT PERSONNEL

Karen M. Dunn (Paralegal)

For full biographical listings, see the Martindale-Hubbell Law Directory

OTTO, PORTERFIELD & POST, LLC (AV)

51 Eagle Road, P.O. Box 3149, 81658-3149
Telephone: 970-949-5380
Fax: 970-845-9135
Email: wbrucep@vail.net

Frederick S. Otto
Wendell B. Porterfield, Jr.
William J. Post

(See Next Column)

OTTO, PORTERFIELD & POST LLC—*Continued*

Ann E. Hutchison

References: 1st Bank of Vail; WestStar Bank.

For full biographical listings, see the Martindale-Hubbell Law Directory

CONNECTICUT

*BRIDGEPORT,** Fairfield Co.

COHEN AND WOLF, P.C. (AV)

1115 Broad Street, 06604
Telephone: 203-368-0211
Facsimile: 203-576-8504
Danbury, Connecticut Office: 158 Deer Hill Avenue.
Telephone: 203-792-2771.
Facsimile: 203-791-8149.
Stamford, Connecticut Office: 112 Prospect Street.
Telephone: 203-964-9907.
Facsimile: 203-576-8504.
Westport, Connecticut Office: 190 Main Street.
Telephone: 203-222-1034.
Facsimile: 203-227-1373.

Herbert L. Cohen (1905-1983)
Austin K. Wolf
Richard L. Albrecht
Jonathan S. Bowman
Irving J. Kern
Martin J. Albert
Stewart I. Edelstein
Neil R. Marcus (Resident at Danbury Office)
David L. Grogins (Resident at Danbury Office)
Greta E. Solomon
Robin A. Kahn (Resident at Danbury Office)
Richard G. Kent
Richard Slavin
Daniel S. Nagel
Richard J. Di Marco
David B. Zabel
Mark A. Kirsch
David M. Levine
Joseph G. Walsh (Resident at Danbury Office)
David A. Ball
Jocelyn B. Hurwitz
Stuart M. Katz
Monte E. Frank (Resident at Danbury Office)
Patricia C. Sullivan
Vincent M. Marino

SPECIAL COUNSEL

G. Kenneth Bernhard

OF COUNSEL

Martin F. Wolf
Robert J. Ashkins
Stuart A. Epstein
Jack E. McGregor

LEGAL SUPPORT PERSONNEL

Sherry E. Sopin

For full biographical listings, see the Martindale-Hubbell Law Directory

GOLDSTEIN AND PECK, P.C. (AV)

1087 Broad Street, P.O. Box 1538, 06601
Telephone: 203-334-9421
Telefax: 203-334-6949
Westport, Connecticut Office: 190 Main Street, P.O. Box 5031.
Telephone: 203-226-7488.
Telefax: 203-334-6949.

David Goldstein (1898-1992)
William J. Kupinse, Jr.
Walter A. Flynn, Jr.
Eugene E. Cederbaum
John G. Dzurik
Dennis M. Laccavole
Kathleen H. Allsup
Robert L. Cavanaugh, Jr.
Jo-Ann R. Sensale

OF COUNSEL

Peter B. O'Connell

Representative Clients: Bee Publishing Co., Inc.; The Chase Manhattan Bank; Great American Insurance Companies; Physicians Health Services, Inc.; Town of Westport; Greenwich Board of Education; Newtown Savings Bank; People's Bank.

For full biographical listings, see the Martindale-Hubbell Law Directory

WILLIAMS, COONEY & SHEEHY (AV)

One Lafayette Circle, 06604
Telephone: 203-331-0888
Telecopier: 203-331-0896
Email: wilcooshee@aol.com

MEMBERS OF FIRM

Ronald D. Williams
Robert J. Cooney
Edward Maum Sheehy
Dion W. Moore
Ronald D. Williams, Jr.
Francis A. Smith, Jr. (1951-1989)

(See Next Column)

Suzannah Kim Nigro
Michael Richard Brandt

Representative Clients: Connecticut Medical Insurance Co.; Zimmer Manufacturing Co.; Textron-Lycoming; The Stop & Shop Companies, Inc.; Fleet Bank; Podiatry Insurance Company of America; Town of Easton, Conn.

For full biographical listings, see the Martindale-Hubbell Law Directory

ZELDES, NEEDLE & COOPER, A PROFESSIONAL CORPORATION (AV)

1000 Lafayette Boulevard, P.O. Box 1740, 06601-1740
Telephone: 203-333-9441
Telecopiers: 203-333-1489; 579-2933
Email: znclaw.com

Jacob D. Zeldes
Charles M. Needle
Robert S. Cooper
Alfred J. Jennings, Jr.
Stuart Bear
Frank J. Silvestri, Jr.
Robert A. Harris
Gregory J. Cava
David P. Atkins
Maximino Medina, Jr.
Jonathan B. Orleans
Shelley R. Sadin
Edward R. Scofield
David P. Friedman
Leslie Paier Aceto
Ann M. VanDeventer

Patrick J. Fitzgerald
Martin L. McCann
S. Dave Vatti
Douglas J. Varga
Marcy Tench Stovall
Marie A. Casper
Sarah W. Poston
Anthony R. Minchella
Kevin C. Kelly
Robert A. Pacelli, Jr.
Robert M. Frost, Jr.

OF COUNSEL

John R. Bryk
Sheryl J. Rosander

Representative Clients: Jeneric/Pentron, Inc.; Pace Motor Lines, Inc.; C.W. Pond Contractors, Inc.; Rudel Machinery Co. Inc.; U.S. Surgical Corp.

For full biographical listings, see the Martindale-Hubbell Law Directory

DANIELSON, Windham Co.

JACKSON HARRIS BURLINGAME & HUBERT, LLC (AV)

245 Main Street, 06239
Telephone: 860-774-9627
Fax: 860-774-5784

MEMBERS OF FIRM

George H. Jackson, III
John K. Harris, Jr.
Stephen J. Burlingame
David M. Hubert

Representative Client: New London Trust, F.S.B.

For full biographical listings, see the Martindale-Hubbell Law Directory

DARIEN, Fairfield Co.

MILLAR & AMBRETTE (AV)

23 Old King's Highway South, 06820-1267
Telephone: 203-655-7931
FAX: 203-656-2055

MEMBERS OF FIRM

Samuel D. B. Millar, Jr.
L. Conrad Ambrette

OF COUNSEL

Peter M. Ryan

ASSOCIATE

Patricia Moreland Gross

For full biographical listings, see the Martindale-Hubbell Law Directory

GREENWICH, Fairfield Co.

ALBERT, WARD & JOHNSON, P.C. (AV)

125 Mason Street, P.O. Box 1668, 06836
Telephone: 203-661-8600
Telecopier: 203-661-8051

Tom S. Ward, Jr.
Scott R. Johnson
Jane D. Hogeman
Howard R. Wolfe
Christopher A. Kristoff
Vicki K. Comberiati

OF COUNSEL

David Albert
C. Robton Perelli-Minetti

For full biographical listings, see the Martindale-Hubbell Law Directory

FOGARTY COHEN SELBY & NEMIROFF LLC (AV)

88 Field Point Road, P.O. Box 2508, 06836-2508
Telephone: 203-661-1000
Telefax: 203-629-7300

MEMBERS OF FIRM

James R. Fogarty
Bruce F. Cohen
Leland C. Selby
Andrew P. Nemiroff
Steven W. Russo

(See Next Column)

FOGARTY COHEN SELBY & NEMIROFF LLC, *Greenwich—Continued*

COUNSEL

Robert A. Epstein
Everett Fisher
Jennifer N. Boyd

ASSOCIATES

William Bradford Smith, Jr.
Lawrence F. Reilly
Carolyn Alexander Collins
Anne M. Piedade
Eric R. Posmantier

For full biographical listings, see the Martindale-Hubbell Law Directory

HOLLAND KAUFMANN & BARTELS, LLC (AV)

289 Greenwich Avenue, 06830-6595
Telephone: 203-869-5600
Fax: 203-869-4648

Alexander J. Holland
Harold R. Burke
Charles B. Kaufmann, III
Jean Mills Aranha
Philip H. Bartels
Lori E. Romano
John C. Fusco

OF COUNSEL

Beth K. Hansson

For full biographical listings, see the Martindale-Hubbell Law Directory

IVEY, BARNUM & O'MARA, LLC (AV)

170 Mason Street, P.O. Box 1689, 06830
Telephone: 203-661-6000
Telecopier: 203-661-9462
Email: general@ibolaw.com *URL:* http://www.ibolaw.com

MEMBERS OF FIRM

Michael J. Allen
Donat C. Marchand
Robert C. Barnum, Jr.
Miles F. McDonald, Jr.
Edward D. Cosden, Jr.
Edwin J. O'Mara, Jr.
Wilmot L. Harris, Jr.
Jennifer D. Port
William I. Haslun II
Karla Pankratz Ray
Juerg A. Heim
Remy A. Rodas
Michael J. Jones
Gregory A. Saum
Edward T. Krumeich, Jr.
Lorraine Slavin
Steven B. Steinmetz

ASSOCIATES

Raymond G. Baghdady
Jennifer B. Kallenbach
John E. Chaffee
Deborah A. Kelly
Scott P. DeMartino
Melissa Townsend Klauberg
Stephan B. Grozinger
Cynthia L. Singer

OF COUNSEL

James W. Cuminale
Deirdre A Martini
Philip R. McKnight

For full biographical listings, see the Martindale-Hubbell Law Directory

WHITMAN BREED ABBOTT & MORGAN LLP (AV)

100 Field Point Road, 06830
Telephone: 203-869-3800
Telecopier: 203-869-1951
URL: http://www.wbam.com
New York, N.Y. Office: 200 Park Avenue.
Telephone: 212-351-3000.
Los Angeles, California Office: 633 West Fifth Street.
Telephone: 213-896-2400.
Newark, New Jersey Office: One Gateway Center.
Telephone: 973-621-2230.
Palm Beach, Florida Office: 220 Sunrise Avenue.
Telephone: 407-832-5458.
London, England Office: 11 Waterloo Place.
Telephone: 71-839-3226.
Telex: 917881.
Tokyo, Japan Office: Suite 450, New Otemachi Building, 2-2-1 Otemachi, Chiyoda-Ku, Tokyo 100.
Telephone: 81-3-3242-1289.
Beirut, Lebanon Office: Tyan & Associes, 22, La Sagesse Street-Rmeil, Lebanon.
Telephone: (961) (1) 56 16 73; (961) (1) 56 16 74.
Fax: (961) (1) 56 14 35.

PARTNERS

Charles E. Coates, III
Robert C. O'Brien
James A. Fulton
Harry E. Peden, Jr.
Thomas F. Hartch
Harry E. Peden, III
Richard F. Lawler
Charles W. Pieterse
Anthony M. Macleod
James C. Riley
Richard E. Mancuso
David P. Tuttle
Kevin A. Walsh

COUNSEL

Michael B. Weir (Not admitted in CT)

RETIRED PARTNER

Jacob R. Lynch

(See Next Column)

ASSOCIATES

Ann Dudley Belknap
Eric T. Kaplan
Margaret E. Conboy
Henry K. Snyder
Margaret Ann Triolo

For full biographical listings, see the Martindale-Hubbell Law Directory

*HARTFORD,** Hartford Co.

BINGHAM DANA LLP (AV)

100 Pearl Street, 06103
Telephone: 860-244-3770
Telefax: 860-527-5188
Email: info@bingham.com *URL:* http://www.bingham.com
Boston, Massachusetts Office: 150 Federal Street.
Telephone: 617-951-8000.
Telecopy: 617-951-8736.
London, England Office: 39 Victoria Street, SWIH 0EE.
Telephone: 011-44-71-799-2646.
Telecopy: 011-44-71-799-2654.
Washington, D.C. Office: 1200 19th Street, N.W., Suite 400.
Telephone: 202-778-6150.
Telecopy: 202-778-6155.
Los Angeles, California Office: The Wells Fargo Center, 333 South Grand Avenue, Suite 1570.
Telephone: 213-687-2700.
Fax: 213-617-9109.
New York, New York Office: 399 Park Avenue.
Telephone: 212-318-7700.
Fax: 212-752-5378.

PARTNERS

Jonathan B. Alter
Eric W. Johnson
Frank A. Appicelli
William E. Kelly
G. Eric Brunstad, Jr.
Ben M. Krowicki
David M. Cain
George A. McKeon (Of Counsel)
Richard F. Casher
John B. D'Agostino
Peter M. Nolin
Timothy B. DeSieno
Gregory W. Nye
Robert M. Dombroff
Thomas F. O'Connor
Chester L. Fisher III
Mark Oland
Douglas E. Fiske
Thomas J. O'Shea
Evan D. Flaschen
Daniel I. Papermaster
Deborah Samuels Freeman
Michael J. Reilly
F. Mark Fucci
James Scott Rollins
Richard A. Gitlin
Stuart D. Rosen
James Greenfield
James G. Scantling
Gary S. Hammersmith
Ronald J. Silverman
Edwin Gordon Hebb, Jr.
Bruce C. Silvers
Harold S. Horwich
R. Jeffrey Smith
Jeffrey L. Williams

RESIDENT OF COUNSEL

Robert M. Borden
John D. Inwood
Scott A. Falk
Peter H. Levine
Judith H. Friedman
James P. Maher
Ann M. Siczewicz

RESIDENT ASSOCIATES

Jacqueline Smith Anderson
Christine C. Peaslee
Nicole J. Anker
Andrew H. Pinkowski
Deborah M. Bibbins
Nora E. Pistey (Not admitted in CT)
Patti Lynn Boss
Kevin P. Braun
Denise R. Polivy
John M. Casanova (Not admitted in CT)
Patricia Ann Shackelford
David Silber
Raymond A. Colla, Jr.
Vi R. Smalley
William H. Erickson
Anthony J. Smits
Anna M. Gustafson
Patrick J. Trostle
William J. Lehman
Michael P. Ungaro
Timothy P. Lynch
Oscar Urizar
Theodore C. Morris
Steven S. Wheeler
Michael B. Nadolski
Jeffrey B. Zeman

For full biographical listings, see the Martindale-Hubbell Law Directory

DAY, BERRY & HOWARD LLP (AV)

CityPlace I, 06103-3499
Telephone: 860-275-0100
Telecopier: 860-275-0343
Email: postmaster@dbh.com *URL:* http://www.dbh.com
Greenwich, Connecticut Office: One East Putnam Avenue.
Telephone: 203-862-7800.
Stamford, Connecticut Office: One Canterbury Green.
Telephone: 203-977-7300.
Telecopier: 203-977-7301.
Boston, Massachusetts Office: 260 Franklin Street.
Telephone: 617-345-4600.
Telecopier: 617-345-4745.

(See Next Column)

DAY, BERRY & HOWARD LLP—*Continued*

MEMBERS OF FIRM IN HARTFORD

Edward M. Day (1872-1947)
Joseph Francis Berry (1880-1953)
Lawrence Augustus Howard (1881-1960)
J. Danford Anthony, Jr.
Paul N. Belval
Robert A. Brooks
Harold C. Buckingham, Jr.
Dean M. Cordiano
William H. Cuddy
Rodney J. Dillman
David T. Doot
Glenn W. Dowd
David J. Elliott
Michael W. Elsass
Steven M. Fast
Diane M. Fitzgerald
Daniel L. FitzMaurice
Charles W. Fortune
Gerald Garfield
Steven M. Greenspan
Thomas J. Groark, Jr.
Jeffrey G. Grody
Michael F. Halloran
J. Roger Hanlon
Mitchell R. Harris
Richard D. Harris
Thomas F. Harrison
Tricia A. Haught
Paula Lacey Herman
Robert P. Knickerbocker, Jr.
Myles J. Laffey
Charles H. Lenore
Timothy R. Lyman
Richard C. MacKenzie
Frank J. Marco
Daniel S. Matos
Ernest J. Mattei
Paul F. McAlenney
Ann G. Monaghan
Joseph A. Moniz
Francis H. Morrison III
John B. Nolan
Richard M. Reynolds
James H. Rotondo
Edmund M. See
James Sicilian
Robert G. Siegel
Felix J. Springer
James J. Tancredi
Allan B. Taylor
Robert M. Taylor III
Lyn Gammill Walker
Philip S. Walker
Richard J. Wasserman
Thomas R. Wildman
Paul D. Williams
Martin Wolman
Albert Zakarian

ASSOCIATES OF FIRM IN HARTFORD

Elizabeth A. Alquist
Esther R. Aronson
Sarah C. Baskin
Gary M. Becker
Matthew J. Becker
Jan I. Berlage
Judith A. Blank
Christopher J. Boccaccio
John E. Bonini
Mario R. Borelli
Michael A. Bucci
James W. Caley
Sam S.F. Caligiuri
James J. Carroll
Peter Chadwick
Victoria Woodin Chavey
Kristin G. Cianflone
Robert W. Clark
Florence K. S. Davis
B. Dane Dudley
David A. Fitzgerald
Tracy A. Gaudet
Patrick M. Gerity
Michelle D. Gouin
Tara J. Hart-Nova
Kevin B. Hawkins
Honor S. Heath
Eric R. Jones
Peter R. Knight
Paul A. Lagasse
Jennifer K. Lawson
Jonathan M. Lewis
Robert J. Lewton
Ronald E. Lyles
Carolyn B. Martino
Kelly G. Miley
Raymond F. Miller
Jessica Joan Mitchell
Kathleen Dondero Monnes
Priya S. Morganstern
Nancy Kase O'Brasky
Robert J. O'Hara
Rebecca Matthews Parent
Robert L. Rispoli
Deborah S. Russo
Daniel A. Schwartz
Namita Tripathi Shah
Kathleen A. Shea
Michael P. Shea
Robin L. Smith
Steven Steinmetz
Eric L. Sussman
Andrew R. Wallace
Lane T. Watson
Philip S. Wellman
Shawn T. Wooden

OF COUNSEL

C. Duane Blinn
George H. Cain
John C. Glezen
Raymond B. Green
James R. McIntosh
A. Peter Quinn, Jr. (Not admitted in CT)

COUNSEL

Rosemary G. Ayers
Douglas W. Gillette
Joseph L. Hammer
Edward F. Krzanowski
Stephen B. Middlebrook
Scott P. Myers
Ernest C. Mysogland
Kevin J. O'Connor

RESIDENT PARTNERS IN BOSTON OFFICE

David B. Broughel
Lewis A. Burleigh
Daniel J. Carragher
Jeffrey A. Clopeck
Nancy M. Cullen
George L. Cushing
Charles Donelan
Bruce D. Hickey
William A. Hunter
James A. McGraw
J. Charles Mokriski
Francis H. Morrison III
Ross A. Pascal
William Shields
H. Lawrence Tafe III
Kenneth E. Werner
Cynthia J. Williams

PARTNERS IN STAMFORD OFFICE

Jerome Berkman
Martin L. Budd
Michael P. Byrne
Patricia A. Carpenter
Michael G. Considine
Ronald Osburn Dederick
Thomas D. Goldberg
F. Lee Griffith III
Gregory A. Hayes
Robert J. Miller
Kenneth W. Ritt
Sabino Rodriguez III
Daniel L. Schwartz
Felix J. Springer

(See Next Column)

PARTNERS IN STAMFORD OFFICE (Continued)

James F. Stapleton
David A. Swerdloff
Stanley A. Twardy, Jr.
Amy K. Wilfert

PARTNERS IN GREENWICH OFFICE

Ronald Osburn Dederick
Gregory A. Hayes
Robert J. Miller
Amy K. Wilfert

RESIDENT COUNSEL IN BOSTON OFFICE

Stephen G. Howard
Frank A. Libby, Jr.
Richard S. Novak
Eric K. Runge

OF COUNSEL IN STAMFORD OFFICE

Emil H. Frankel

RESIDENT COUNSEL IN STAMFORD OFFICE

Andrew P. Gaillard
James O'Connor
Paulette Wunsch

RESIDENT ASSOCIATES IN BOSTON OFFICE

Scott C. Altonian
John G. Balboni
Bonnie J. Crowley
Tricia F. Deraska
Andrea Falcione
Jonathan I. Handler
Louise A. Handler
Rahul A. Kalke
John P. McLafferty
Kathleen S. Moore
Mary Theresa Moran
Jason W. Morgan
Faith B. Nirenstein
John J. Phillips
Kenneth C. Pickering
Anton Richard Reinert
Kent D.B. Sinclair
Maura D. Sullivan
Craig J. Tiedemann

ASSOCIATES IN STAMFORD OFFICE

R. Scott Beach
Tricia S. Begg
William L. Brewer
Viktoria K. Cech-Vinhais
Richard P. Colbert
M. Kate Curran
Richard D. Edwards
Sarah Moore Fass
Kenneth W. Gage
Lorey Rives Leddy
Natasha M. Lipcan
Catherine Dugan O'Connor
Thomas J. O'Neill
Jennifer L. Slager
Ann Lisa Spletzer
Fritz Strohmeyer
Elena Tourchinskaya
Jonathan B. Tropp
Theodore J. Whitehead

ASSOCIATE IN GREENWICH OFFICE

Viktoria K. Cech-Vinhais

For full biographical listings, see the Martindale-Hubbell Law Directory

GORDON, MUIR AND FOLEY, LLP (AV)

Hartford Square North, Ten Columbus Boulevard, 06106-5123
Telephone: 860-525-5361
Telecopier: 860-525-4849
Email: admin@gmflaw.com *URL:* http://www.gmflaw.com

MEMBERS OF FIRM

William S. Gordon, Jr. (1946-1956)
George Muir (1939-1976)
Edward J. Foley (1955-1983)
Peter C. Schwartz
John J. Reid
John H. Goodrich, Jr.
R. Bradley Wolfe
Jon Stephen Berk
William J. Gallitto
Gerald R. Swirsky
Robert J. O'Brien
Philip J. O'Connor
Kenneth G. Williams
Mary Ann Santacroce
Mary Anne Alicia Charron
Andrew J. Hern
Reneé W. Dwyer
Patty G. Swan

ASSOCIATES

Doreen West Amata
Howard A. Steinman
Erik E. Roberts
Christopher J. Casciani

Reference: People's Bank.

For full biographical listings, see the Martindale-Hubbell Law Directory

GOULD, KILLIAN & WYNNE (AV)

280 Trumbull Street, 25th Floor, 06103-3595
Telephone: 860-278-1270
Telecopier: 860-244-9290

MEMBERS OF FIRM

Samuel Gould (1905-1994)
Robert K. Killian
Francis J. Wynne
Martin A. Gould
Mark W. Baronas
William F. Healey
Nancy E. Gould
Robert O. Wynne

For full biographical listings, see the Martindale-Hubbell Law Directory

HALLORAN & SAGE LLP (AV)

One Goodwin Square, 225 Asylum Street, 06103
Telephone: 860-522-6103
Fax: 860-548-0006
URL: http://www.halloran-sage.com
Middletown, Connecticut Office: 300 Plaza Middlesex, 06457.
Telephone: 860-346-8641.
Fax: 860-344-1641.
Westport, Connecticut Office: 315 Post Road West, 06880-4739.
Telephone: 203-227-2855.
Fax: 203-227-6992.

(See Next Column)

HALLORAN & SAGE LLP, *Hartford—Continued*

MEMBERS OF FIRM

Joseph G. Lynch
Joseph T. Sweeney
George Royster
Arthur P. McGowan, Jr.
John W. Lemega
Robert C. Engstrom
Vincent M. Marino (Middletown Office)
Richard C. Tynan
William P. Borchert
Thomas J. Hagarty, Jr.
Paul V. Knopf
Brian J. Donnell
James J. Szerejko
William J. McGrath, Jr.
Dennis C. Cavanaugh
Christopher J. Lynch
Paul D. Meade
Joseph G. Fortner, Jr.
Stephen P. Fogerty (Westport Office)
Peter G. Boucher
Jean M. D'Aquila
Steven H. Malitz
John B. Farley
Mark R. Cramer
David B. Losee
Harris B. Appelman
Mark T. Altermatt
Henry M. Beck, Jr.
Susan O'Donnell
Bruce H. Raymond
Kevin M. Roche
David G. Hill
Daniel P. Scapellati
James M. Sconzo
Robert B. Cox
Thomas P. O'Dea, Jr. (Westport Office)

COUNSEL

Irwin D. Mittelman (Middletown Office)
Dan E. LaBelle (Westport Office)
Duncan J. Forsyth
Lisa M. Kowtko (Westport Office)
Ann M. Catino

ASSOCIATES

Donna-Maria Lonergan
Robert M. Barrack
Richard P. Roberts
Gregory R. Faulkner
John S. Rosania
Lynda A. Barry
John W. Dietz (Westport Office)
Brian P. Leaming
Michael S. Taylor
Mark T. Livesay
Thomas P. Lambert (Westport Office)
Robert A. Rhodes (Westport Office)
James V. Somers
James A. Alissi
Laura A. Zaino
John B. Kennelly
Melinda M. Decker
Jodie R. Small
Reed A. Slatas
Janice D. Lai
James M. Celentano
Kathleen A. St. Onge
Melissa S. Rotenberg
John J. Robinson
Martin A. Onorato
David R. Levesque
Mony B. P. Yin
Brett M. Szczesny (Westport Office)
Wendi L. Boyden
Alan P. Curto
Mark Sheehan
Kevin J. Greene
Michelle J. Bond
Brian C. Clifford
Kevin E. Majewski
Daryl C. Capuano

For full biographical listings, see the Martindale-Hubbell Law Directory

HOWD & LUDORF (AV)

65 Wethersfield Avenue, 06114
Telephone: 860-249-1361
Fax: 860-522-9549
Email: handl@ix.netcom.com

MEMBERS OF FIRM

John R. Lilliendahl, III
John J. Bogdanski
Philip T. Newbury, Jr.
Thomas R. Gerarde
Mark J. Claflin
Christopher M. Vossler
William F. Corrigan
David S. Monastersky
Michael J. Rose
Michael T. McCormack
Colette S. Griffin
Elizabeth Fitzsimmons Mucci
Elissa A. Flanagan
Melinda P. Frechette
Keith E. Marquis
Paul Erickson
Daniel C. DeMerchant

RETIRED

Edward S. Ludorf

Representative Clients: CIGNA; Reliance; Daimler Chrysler; Toyota; Harsco; Ladder Management; Baxter International; Black & Decker; Texaco; Windsor Insurance Co.

For full biographical listings, see the Martindale-Hubbell Law Directory

JACKSON, O'KEEFE AND PHELAN (AV)

36 Russ Street, 06106-1571
Telephone: 860-278-4040
Fax: 860-527-2500
West Hartford, Connecticut Office: 62 LaSalle Road.
Telephone: 860-521-7500.
Fax: 860-561-5399.
Bethlehem, Connecticut Office: 423 Munger Lane. Telephone/
Fax: 203-266-5255.

MEMBERS OF FIRM

Jay W. Jackson
Andrew J. O'Keefe
Denise Martino Phelan
Matthew J. O'Keefe
Michael E. Riley
Peter K. O'Keefe
Philip R. Dunn, Jr.
Kathryn M. Cunningham
Joseph M. Busher, Jr.
Kristen E. Scholhamer

(See Next Column)

Representative Clients: Travelers Aetna Property Casualty Co.; ITT Hartford; Liberty Mutual Insurance Co.; Connecticut Medical Insurance Co.

For full biographical listings, see the Martindale-Hubbell Law Directory

KENNY, BRIMMER, MELLEY & MAHONEY (AV)

5 Grand Street, 06106
Telephone: 860-527-4226
FAX: 860-527-0214

Joseph P. Kenny (1920-1993)

MEMBERS OF FIRM

William J. Melley, III
Richard C. Mahoney
Anita M. Varunes
Dennis F. McCarthy

ASSOCIATES

Shannon K. McCarthy
Flora Pizzoferrato

OF COUNSEL

Leslie R. Brimmer

Representative Clients: Allstate Insurance Co.; Peerless Insurance Co.; Berkshire Mutual Fire Insurance Co.; Dorchester Mutual Fire Insurance Co.; Abington Mutual Fire Insurance Co.

For full biographical listings, see the Martindale-Hubbell Law Directory

REID AND RIEGE, P.C. (AV)

One State Street, 06103
Telephone: 860-278-1150
FAX: 860-240-1002
West Hartford, Connecticut Office: 65 LaSalle Road.
Telephone: 860-232-6565.
FAX: 860-232-6066.
Lakeville, Connecticut Office: 322 Main Street.
Telephone: 860-435-9894.
FAX: 860-240-1002.
Woodbury, Connecticut Office: 47 Sherman Hill Road.
Telephone: 203-267-6680.
FAX: 860-240-1002.

Robert C. McNally
James C. Ervin, Jr.
Andrew J. Howat
Travers T. Auburn
Maurice T. FitzMaurice
Bruce M. Lutsk
Maynard R. Miller, Jr.
Michael L. Coyle
Suzanne S. Bocchini
John J. Jacobson
John E. D'Amico
Lawrence H. Lissitzyn
Frederick J. Mullen, Jr.
Edmund A. Mikolowsky
Robert U. Sattin
John M. Horak
Edward F. Spinella
Craig L. Sylvester
Robert M. Mulé
Eileen M. Marks
Earl F. McMahon
Christopher J. Sowden
Jon P. Newton
Mark X. Ryan
John D. Newman
Joseph K. Fortier
Thomas M. Armstrong
Eric A. Henzy
Alan Birmingham
John V. Galiette
Dominic Fulco, III

Karen L. Brand
Robert C. Reichert
Douglas K. Knight
Theodore A. Donahue, Jr.
Michael T. Wade
Jennifer Ventres Filler
James B. Schomburg
Kevin M. Tighe
Louis J. Donofrio
Ames B. Shea
Haripriya M. Hannan

OF COUNSEL

Raymond J. Payne
Clifford S. Burdge, Jr.

For full biographical listings, see the Martindale-Hubbell Law Directory

ROGIN, NASSAU, CAPLAN, LASSMAN & HIRTLE, LLC (AV)

CityPlace I, 22nd Floor, 185 Asylum Street, 06103-3460
Telephone: 860-278-7480
Fax: 860-278-2179

MEMBERS OF FIRM

Robert L. Hirtle
Steven D. Bartelstone
David M. Call
Paul B. Zolan
David J. Heinlein
Lewis K. Wise
Joan G. Engel
Thomas M. Divine
Mark A. Rosenblum
Barry S. Feigenbaum
Donald G. Gaudreau
Peter S. Sorokin
Iris June Brown
Benjamin Engel
Lawrence G. Rosenthal

ASSOCIATES

Clara A. Porcello
Mark J. Lassman
Brendan T. Flynn
Elizabeth R. Houde
Jonathan M. Starble
Monique R. Polidoro
Lisa M. Anderson

OF COUNSEL

Jerome E. Caplan
Edwin A. Lassman

(See Next Column)

ROGIN, NASSAU, CAPLAN, LASSMAN & HIRTLE LLC—*Continued*

RETIRED

Edward S. Rogin (Retired)
Louis E. Nassau (Retired)

For full biographical listings, see the Martindale-Hubbell Law Directory

SHIPMAN & GOODWIN LLP (AV)

One American Row, 06103-2819
Telephone: 860-251-5000
Telecopier: 860-251-5099
Email: www@goodwin.com *URL:* http://shipman-goodwin.com
Lakeville, Connecticut Office: 12 Porter Street.
Telephone: 203-435-2539.
Stamford, Connecticut Office: One Landmark Square.
Telephone: 203-324-8100.

MEMBERS OF FIRM

Paul W. Orth
Robert J. Cathcart
Francis M. Dooley (Lakeville Office)
Theodore M. Space
Stuyvesant K. Bearns (Lakeville Office)
Alex Lloyd
Daniel P. Brown, Jr.
James T. Betts
Brian Clemow
Ira H. Goldman
Scott L. Murphy
Coleman H. Casey
Brenda A. Eckert
John E. Kreitler
Peter W. Benner
Thomas B. Mooney
Thomas F. Tresselt
John T. Harris
Robert L. Wyld
Charles L. Howard
John H. Lawrence, Jr.
James W. Bergenn
Paul D. Sanson
Saranne P. Murray
Alan E. Lieberman
William G. Rock
Donna L. Brooks
Linda L. Yoder
John E. Wertam
Richard I. Cohen
Timothy S. Hollister
Joan W. Feldman
Richard A. Mills, Jr.
Deborah Smith Frisone
Mark K. Ostrowski
Paul R. Pescatello
Stephen K. Gellman
Thomas P. Flynn
Louis B. Schatz
Leslie L. Davenport
Patrick J. McHale
Glenn M. Cunningham
Burton Kainen
Gary S. Starr
Diana Garfield
Susan M. Wright
Miguel A. Escalera, Jr.
Janet S. Stulting
Howard L. Pierce
Bruce A. Chudwick
Katherine J. Lambert
Allan P. Weeks
Christine L. Chinni
Susan C. Freedman
Kimberly A. Mango
Julie A. Manning

COUNSEL

Mary Jo Blain Andrews
Vaughan Finn
Arnold K. Shimelman
Marcus D. Wilkinson
Gerald P. Stergio

ASSOCIATES

Sheila A. Huddleston
Maria A. Gulluni
Natalie W. Welsh
Joseph P. Williams
Stephanie M. Gitlin
Joseph W. McQuade
Anne H. Littlefield
Henry J. Zaccardi
Jennifer Brown Mailly
Ross H. Garber
Kathleen M. LaManna
Barbara N. Weady
Jennifer Bullock Majewski
David M. Jones
Jennifer L. Veshia
Anne E. K. Dacey
Patrick Fahey
Susan G. Fentin
Eric W. Alletzhauser
Martha Watts Prestley
Thomas K. Jones
Sheldon D. Myers
Jennifer L. Dixon
James W. Shaughnessy
Jason M. Price
Maureen J. Anderson
Donald R. Ballman
Lisa L. Banatoski
Jeffrey W. Hussey
Amy R. Kirschbaum
Brian W. Kniesly
Robert C. Scott
Lisa Denise Gladke
Craig S. Meuser
Maura B. Murphy Osborne
Morgan P. Rueckert
Nathaniel Selleck
Bryon W. Harmon

OF COUNSEL

Warren S. Randall
Charles B. Milliken
Robert L. Rosensweig
George C. Jepsen (Stamford Office)

Representative Clients: Aetna Casualty & Surety Co.; Agri-Mark, Inc.; Anthem Blue Cross & Blue Shield of Connecticut.; City of Hartford; The Dexter Corp.; Bank of Boston Connecticut; Hartford Hospital; Stanadyne, Inc.; United Technologies Corp.; Yankee Energy System, Inc.

For full biographical listings, see the Martindale-Hubbell Law Directory

SOROKIN, GROSS & HYDE, P.C. (AV)

One Corporate Center, 06103
Telephone: 860-525-6645
Fax: 860-522-1781
Email: sorokin@sorokinlaw.com
Simsbury, Connecticut Office: 720 Hopmeadow Street.
Telephone: 860-651-9348.
Rocky Hill, Connecticut Office: 2360 Main Street.
Telephone: 860-563-9305.
Fax: 860-529-6931.

(See Next Column)

Jeffery P. Apuzzo
Morris W. Banks
James G. Dowling, Jr.
Sharon Kowal Freilich
Andrew C. Glassman
Barry D. Greene
Joshua A. Hawks-Ladds
John J. Kindl
Lisa A. Magliochetti
Jeffrey R. Martin
Alan S. Parker
Lewis Rabinovitz
Keith D. Robbins
Richard C. Robinson
Bruce H. Stanger
Richard D. Tulisano (Resident, Rocky Hill Office)
Barrie K. Wetstone

Rod W. Farrell
Margaret M. Murphy
Jeffrey R. Neidle
Gwen P. Weisberg

OF COUNSEL

Joseph D. Hurwitz
Charles R. Moore, Jr.
Paula G. Pressman
Ethel Silver Sorokin

For full biographical listings, see the Martindale-Hubbell Law Directory

TYLER COOPER & ALCORN, LLP (AV)

CityPlace, 06103-3488
Telephone: 860-725-6200
Telecopier: 860-278-3802
URL: http://www.tylercooper.com
New Haven, Connecticut Office: 205 Church Street.
Telephone: 203-784-8200.
Telecopier: 203-789-2133.
Stamford, Connecticut Office: One Landmark Square.
Telephone: 203-348-5555.
Telecopier: 203-348-3875.
Greenwich, Connecticut Office: 675 Steamboat Road.
Telephone: 203-869-2000.
Telecopier: 203-869-2001.
Madison, Connecticut Office: 23 Woodland Road.
Telephone: 203-318-3600.
Telecopier: 203-218-3609.

MEMBERS OF FIRM

Ralph Gregory Elliot
Lewis Segal
William H. Champlin III
Robert J. Metzler II
William W. Bouton III
Thomas C. Clark
Mark V. Connolly
William S. Fish, Jr.
Kevin McCann
David J. Wiese
Fillis W. Stober
Thomas S. Marrion
Kevin G. Ferrigno
William F. Cummings
Glory Martyn Lena

OF COUNSEL

William S. Rogers
Roger E. Koontz

COUNSEL

Kurt W. Johnson

RESIDENT ASSOCIATES

Barry M. Winnick
David Lammey
Christopher Markham Haddad
Carol L. Loomis
Elizabeth M. Smith

Representative Clients: Purolator Courier Corp.; American Society of Composers, Authors and Publishers (ASCAP); The Hartford Courant Co.; Sears, Roebuck & Co.; Shearson Lehman Brothers; Prudential Securities Inc.; Aetna Life and Casualty Co.; The Travelers Companies.

For full biographical listings, see the Martindale-Hubbell Law Directory

WIGGIN & DANA (AV)

One CityPlace, 06103-3402
Telephone: 860-297-3700
Fax: 860-525-9380
URL: http://www.wiggin.com
New Haven, Connecticut Office: One Century Tower.
Telephone: 203-498-4400.
Telefax: 203-782-2889.
Stamford, Connecticut Office: Three Stamford Plaza, 301 Tresser Boulevard.
Telephone: 203-363-7600.
Telefax: 203-363-7676.

MEMBERS OF FIRM

Peter J. Lefeber
Valerie A. Seiling (Resident)
Patrick J. Monahan, II (Resident)
Robert M. Langer (Resident)
Maureen Weaver (Resident)
Stephen B. Harris (Resident)

RESIDENT COUNSEL

Sharyn B. Zuch
Marcia Kenny Keegan

RESIDENT ASSOCIATES

Catherine P. Baatz
Lori R. Clark
Michelle Wilcox DeBarge
Daniel J. Klau
Nicholas J. Maglio
Karen E. Overchuk
Lisa J. Reimer
Peter M. Wendzel

For full biographical listings, see the Martindale-Hubbell Law Directory

LAKEVILLE, Litchfield Co.

SHIPMAN & GOODWIN LLP (AV)

12 Porter Street, 06039
Telephone: 860-435-2539
Telecopier: 860-435-0011
Email: www@goodwin.com *URL:* http://shipman-goodwin.com
Hartford, Connecticut Office: One American Row.
Telephone: 203-251-5000.
Stamford, Connecticut Office: One Landmark Square.
Telephone: 203-324-8100.

MEMBERS

Francis M. Dooley
Stuyvesant K. Bearns

Representative Clients: American Title Insurance Co.; Berkshire Construction Co.; Colonial Bank and Trust Co., Sharon; Lakeville Journal, Inc.; Lawyers Title Insurance Co.; Salisbury Bank & Trust Co., Lakeville, Conn.

For full biographical listings, see the Martindale-Hubbell Law Directory

*LITCHFIELD,** Litchfield Co.

CRAMER & ANDERSON LLP (AV)

46 West Street, P.O. Box 278, 06759-0278
Telephone: 860-567-8718
Telecopier: 860-567-4531
Email: cramerlaw@snet.net
Danbury, Connecticut Office: 68 North Street.
Telephone: 203-790-7747.
Kent, Connecticut Office: Kent Green, P.O. Box 333.
Telephone: 860-927-3568.
New Milford, Connecticut Office: 51 Main Street.
Telephone: 860-355-2631.
Washington Depot, Connecticut Office: 2 Green Hill Road, P.O. Box 321.
Telephone: 860-868-0527.

MEMBERS OF FIRM

David Cramer (1902-1981)
Clayton L. Blick
Perley H. Grimes, Jr.
Robert L. Fisher, Jr.
William C. Franklin
Barry S. Moller
Maurice A. Goldstein (Resident, New Milford Office)
Grant J. Nelson (Resident, Kent Office)
Reginald William H. Fairbairn (Resident, Washington Depot Office)
Randall J. Breeckner (Resident, New Milford Office)
Arthur C. Weinshank (Resident, New Milford Office)
David P. Burke (Resident, Danbury Office)
Joseph A. Saffi (Resident, Danbury Office)
D. Randall DiBella (Resident, New Milford Office)
Mitchell J. Melnick (Resident, New Milford Office)
John D. Tower (Resident, New Milford Office)

ASSOCIATES

James D. Hirschfield
Denise M. Cloutier
Lisa L. Buzaid (Resident, New Milford Office)
Barbara W. Reynolds (Resident, New Milford Office)

OF COUNSEL

Robert M. FitzGerald
Stephen N. Hume (Resident, New Milford Office)
Henry B. Anderson (Resident, New Milford Office)
Paul B. Altermatt (Resident, New Milford Office)

Counsel for: Town of Cornwall; First National Bank of Litchfield; Marriott Corp.; Neeltran, Inc.; New Milford Hospital, Inc.; NMBT (formerly known as The New Milford Bank & Trust); Canterbury School; New Milford Savings Bank; South Kent School; Marvelwood School.

For full biographical listings, see the Martindale-Hubbell Law Directory

*MIDDLETOWN,** Middlesex Co.

HALLORAN & SAGE LLP (AV)

300 Plaza Middlesex, 06457
Telephone: 860-346-8641
Fax: 860-344-1641
Hartford, Connecticut Office: One Goodwin Square, 225 Asylum Street, 06103.
Telephone: 860-522-6103.
Fax: 860-548-0006.
Westport, Connecticut Office: 315 Post Road West, 06880-4739.
Telephone: 203-227-2855.
Fax: 203-227-6992.

RESIDENT PARTNER

Vincent M. Marino

(See Next Column)

COUNSEL

Irwin D. Mittelman

MILFORD, New Haven Co.

BERCHEM, MOSES & DEVLIN, A PROFESSIONAL CORPORATION (AV)

75 Broad Street, 06460-3363
Telephone: 203-783-1200
Facsimile: 203-878-2235; 203-877-8422
URL: http://www.bmd-law.com

Robert L. Berchem
Marsha Belman Moses
Michael P. Devlin
Stephen W. Studer
Richard J. Buturla
Floyd J. Dugas
Kenneth R. Plumb
Lawrence B. Pellegrino

Brian A. Lema
Warren L. Holcomb
Michelle C. Laubin
Jonathan David Berchem
Dean R. Singewald

For full biographical listings, see the Martindale-Hubbell Law Directory

HARLOW, ADAMS & FRIEDMAN, P.C. (AV)

300 Bic Drive, 06460-3508
Telephone: 203-878-0661
Fax: 203-878-9568
Email: attorney@quidproquo.com

William D. Harlow (1921-1988)
George W. Adams, III
Dana Eric Friedman
Theodore H. Shumaker
Stephen P. Wright
Michael P. A. Williams
Eric R. Gaynor
Joseph A. Kubic
James M. Nugent
James R. Winkel

For full biographical listings, see the Martindale-Hubbell Law Directory

NEW BRITAIN, Hartford Co.

JANUSZEWSKI, MCQUILLAN AND DENIGRIS (AV)

165 West Main Street, P.O. Box 150, 06050-0150
Telephone: 860-225-7667
Fax: 860-826-1814
Email: JMDNBCT@WORLDNET.ATT.NET

MEMBERS OF FIRM

Paul J. McQuillan
Nicholas E. DeNigris
John C. Matulis, Jr.
Steven D. Anderson
Martin McQuillan

OF COUNSEL

Edward Januszewski (Retired)

Representative Clients: The Peoples Savings Bank of New Britain, Inc.; Tilcon, Inc.; Acmat, Inc.

For full biographical listings, see the Martindale-Hubbell Law Directory

*NEW HAVEN,** New Haven Co.

CARMODY & TORRANCE LLP (AV)

195 Church Street, P.O. Box 1950, 06509-1950
Telephone: 203-777-5501
Facsimile: 203-784-3199
Waterbury, Connecticut Office: 50 Leavenworth Street. P.O. Box 1110, 06721-1110.
Telephone: 203-573-1200.
Facsimile: 203-575-2600.
Southbury, Connecticut Office: 900 Main Street South. P.O. Box 410, 06488-0410.
Telephone: 203-264-7882.
Facsimile: 203-264-7847.

MEMBERS OF FIRM

Anthony M. Fitzgerald
Charles F. Corcoran, III
Thomas R. Candrick, Jr.
Susan Seidler Chambers
Ann Harris Rubin
Thomas J. Sansone
Ann Hedges Zucker
Christopher Rooney
Steven G. Mednick

ASSOCIATES

Heena Kapadia
Howard K. Levine
David J. Vegliante
Joshua L. Milrad
Naomi B. Graubard
Amy B. Levy (Resident)

Representative Clients: Algonquin Gas Transmission Co.; Bank of Boston, N.A.; Bell Atlantic Mobile; Anthem Blue Cross & Blue Shield of Connecticut, Inc.; MacDermid, Inc.; Northeast Utilities; Timex Corp.; Waterbury Hospital.
Trial Counsel for: Aetna Life and Casualty; St. Paul Fire & Marine Insurance.

For full biographical listings, see the Martindale-Hubbell Law Directory

New Haven—Continued

William H. Clendenen, Jr. A Professional Corporation (AV)

400 Orange Street, P.O. Box 301, 06502-0301
Telephone: 203-787-1183
Fax: 203-787-2847

William H. Clendenen, Jr.

James E. Clifford
Nancy L. Walker
Thomas C. Pellegrino

For full biographical listings, see the Martindale-Hubbell Law Directory

Gallagher & Calistro (AV)

1377 Boulevard, P.O. Box 1925, 06509
Telephone: 203-624-4165
Fax: 203-865-5598

William F. Gallagher
Roger B. Calistro
Cynthia C. Bott
Barbara L. Cox
Kurt D. Koehler
Thomas J. Airone

For full biographical listings, see the Martindale-Hubbell Law Directory

Jacobs, Grudberg, Belt & Dow, P.C. (AV)

350 Orange Street, P.O. Box 606, 06503
Telephone: 203-772-3100
Fax: 203-772-1691
Email: jacobslaw@jacobslaw.com *URL:* http://www.jacobslaw.com

Israel J. Jacobs (1918-1963)
Howard A. Jacobs
Ira B. Grudberg
David L. Belt
William F. Dow, III
Jonathan Katz
Susan H. Bartholomew
Charles B. Price, Jr.
William M. Bloss
Shirley V. Hoogstra
David T. Grudberg
David A. Leff

Steven J. DeFrank
Alinor C. Sterling
Phillip A. Escoriaza
Marybeth C. Gauthier
Bernard C. Christianson

For full biographical listings, see the Martindale-Hubbell Law Directory

Rosen & Dolan, P.C. (AV)

400 Orange Street, 06511
Telephone: 203-787-3513
Fax: 203-789-1605
Email: davidrosen@snet.net
Email: sapincus@snet.net

David N. Rosen
Edward J. Dolan

Stephen M. Pincus

Reference: Peoples Bank.

For full biographical listings, see the Martindale-Hubbell Law Directory

Tyler Cooper & Alcorn, LLP (AV)

205 Church Street, P.O. Box 1936, 06509-1910
Telephone: 203-784-8200
Telecopier: 203-789-2133
URL: http://www.tylercooper.com
Hartford, Connecticut Office: CityPlace.
Telephone: 860-725-6200.
Telecopier: 860-278-3802.
Stamford, Connecticut Office: One Landmark Square.
Telephone: 203-348-5555.
Telecopier: 203-348-3875.
Greenwich, Connecticut Office: 675 Steamboat Road.
Telephone: 203-869-2000.
Telecopier: 203-869-2001.
Madison, Connecticut Office: 23 Woodland Road.
Telephone: 203-318-3600.
Telecopier: 203-318-3609.

MEMBERS OF FIRM

Ralph Gregory Elliot (Resident at Hartford Office)
Michael J. Dorney
Bruce Lewellyn
Joseph C. Lee (Managing Partner of the Firm)
Lewis Segal (Resident at Hartford Office)
Irving S. Schloss
Jon T. Hirschoff
William H. Champlin III (Resident at Hartford Office)
Timothy W. Bingham
David W. Schneider
Robert W. Allen
Richard W. Bowerman
George E. O'Brien, Jr.
Robert J. Metzler II (Resident at Hartford Office)
Ronald J. Cohen
Margaret P. Mason
William W. Bouton III (Resident at Hartford Office)
Thomas C. Clark (Resident at Hartford Office)
Mark V. Connolly (Resident at Hartford Office)

(See Next Column)

MEMBERS OF FIRM (Continued)

William S. Fish, Jr. (Resident at Hartford Office)
Kevin McCann (Resident at Hartford Office)
David J. Wiese (Resident at Hartford Office)
Emmett E. Brown III (Resident at Stamford Office)
Ben A. Solnit
Jacqueline DeAndrus Bucar
Fillis W. Stober (Resident at Hartford Office)
Thomas S. Marrion (Resident at Hartford Office)
Christopher P. McCormack
Christopher L. Ulrich (Resident at Stamford Office)
Kevin G. Ferrigno (Resident at Hartford Office)
Lori B. Alexander
Greg R. Barringer
William F. Cummings (Resident at Hartford Office)
Patricia E. Reilly
Noble F. Allen
Glory Martyn Lena (Resident at Hartford Office)

OF COUNSEL

Richard G. Bell
Milton P. DeVane
James R. Greenfield
William R. Murphy
William S. Rogers (Resident at Hartford Office)
Roger E. Koontz (Resident at Hartford Office)

SENIOR COUNSEL

Henry W. Pascarella (Resident at Greenwich Office)

COUNSEL

Nan Budde Chequer (Resident at Stamford Office)
Kurt W. Johnson (Resident at Hartford Office)
Kathleen A. Maher

ASSOCIATES

Charles R. Andres
Shawn L. O'Sullivan
Barry M. Winnick (Resident at Hartford Office)
Robert B. Flynn
Renee M. Reed
Niclas A. Ferland
Antonio Ponvert III
Timothy P. Pothin
Lisa N. Davis
James R. Bryne
S. Peter Sachner
Eleanor Stuart DeVane
Robert C. Hinton
Michael C. D'Agostino
Paul E. Monaghan, Jr.
Paul L. Bader
Christopher Markham Haddad (Resident at Hartford Office)
Timothy P. Jensen
David Lammey (Resident at Hartford Office)
Angela Shenk
Carol L. Loomis (Resident at Hartford Office)
Cassandra S. Pascarella
Elizabeth M. Smith (Resident at Hartford Office)

Counsel for: Echlin, Inc.; Hospital of St. Raphael; The Stanley Works; The Southern Connecticut Gas Co.; Southern New England Telephone Co.; Science Park Development Corp.; Connecticut American Water Co.; General Electric Co.

For full biographical listings, see the Martindale-Hubbell Law Directory

Wiggin & Dana (AV)

One Century Tower, 06508-1832
Telephone: 203-498-4400
Telefax: 203-782-2889
URL: http://www.wiggin.com
Hartford, Connecticut Office: One CityPlace.
Telephone: 203-297-3700.
Fax: 203-525-9380.
Stamford, Connecticut Office: Three Stamford Plaza, 301 Tresser Boulevard.
Telephone: 203-363-7600.
Telefax: 203-363-7676.

MEMBERS OF FIRM

Frederick H. Wiggin (1882-1963)
J. Dwight Dana (1889-1951)
John Q. Tilson
John W. Barnett
William C. Baskin, Jr.
Robert F. Cavanagh
Charles C. Kingsley
William J. Doyle
David P. Faulkner
Noel E. Hanf
Shaun S. Sullivan
Jeremy G. Zimmermann
J. Michael Eisner
Norman Fineberg
William H. Prout, Jr.
Linda L. Randell
D. Terence Jones
Mark R. Kravitz
Melinda A. Agsten
Edward Wood Dunham
Norman J. Fleming
Peter J. Lefeber
John G. Zandy
Sherry L. Dominick
Alan G. Schwartz
Valerie A. Seiling (Resident, Hartford Office)
Bennett J. Bernblum
Susan J. Bryson
William G. Millman, Jr.
Jeanette Carpenter Schreiber
Patrick J. Monahan, II (Resident, Hartford Office)
Peter H. Gruen
Mary R. Norris
Maureen Weaver (Resident, Hartford Office)
Robert M. Langer (Resident, Hartford Office)
James F. Farrington, Jr. (Resident, Stamford Office)
Karen L. Clute
John F. Conway
Leonard Leader (Resident, Stamford Office)
Jeffrey R. Babbin
Ian E. Bjorkman
Dale L. Carlson
William A. Simons (Not admitted in CT)
David B. Fein (Resident, Stamford Office)
William A. Perrone (Resident, Stamford Office)
Merton G. Gollaher
Stephen B. Harris (Resident, Hartford Office)
Phyllis M. Pari
Gregory S. Rosenblatt
Francis J. Duffin

(See Next Column)

WIGGIN & DANA, *New Haven—Continued*

MEMBERS OF FIRM (Continued)

Kevin M. Kennedy
Michael Grundei (Resident, Stamford Office)
Patricia Kavee Melick (Not admitted in CT; Resident, Stamford Office)
Mark S. Flynn (Resident, Stamford Office)
William J. Speranza (Resident, Stamford Office)
Amy Ghory Winnick

SENIOR COUNSEL

William E. Craig
S. Robert Jelley
Robert M. McAnerney (Resident, Stamford Office)
Charles N. Schenck, III

COUNSEL

Penny Quinn Seaman
Sharyn B. Zuch (Not admitted in CT; Resident, Hartford Office)
Marcia Kenny Keegan (Resident, Hartford Office)

OF COUNSEL

Martin H. Dodd

ASSOCIATES

William John Albinger
Jeffrey Russell Ambroziak
Ann K. Anderson
Bethany L. Appleby
Rachel B. Arnedt
Catherine P. Baatz (Resident, Hartford Office)
Tina Clark Beamon
Patricia R. Beauregard
Eileen Reynolds Becker
Penelope I. Bellamy
Louis A. Bevilacqua (Resident, Stamford Office)
James H. Bicks (Not admitted in CT; Resident, Stamford Office)
Carolyn C. Brady
Isabel E. Chenoweth
Lori R. Clark (Resident, Hartford Office)
Patrick J. Corcoran
James O. Craven
Kevin Paul Dean
Michelle Wilcox DeBarge (Resident, Hartford Office)
Timothy A. Diemand
Tanya J. Dobash (Resident, Stamford Office)
Patty A. Fairweather
Todd E. Garabedian (Not admitted in CT)
Jessie A. Gilbert (Resident, Stamford Office)
David C. Grigsby
Jonathan W. Haray
Nancy Guller Hayt
Mark W. Heaphy
Lisa Page Heslin
Nicole M. Hoffmeister (Resident, Stamford Office)
Paul G. Holland, Jr. (Resident, Stamford Office)
John C. Huggins
Stuart C. Johnson
Charles J. Keegan (Not admitted in CT)
Edward M. Kennedy, Jr.
Daniel J. Klau (Resident, Hartford Office)
Sigrid E. Kun
Tracey M. Lane
Monica C. Lewis
Kenneth W. Lord (Not admitted in CT; Resident, Stamford Office)
Richard H. Lugli
Nicholas J. Maglio (Resident, Hartford Office)
Bruce L. McDermott
Benedicta McGrath (Resident, Stamford Office)
Steven D. Meyers
Christine Owens Morgan
Richard F. Nace, Jr.
Stewart E. Newman
David J. O'Callaghan
Karen E. Overchuk (Resident, Hartford Office)
W. Glen Pierson
Lisa J. Reimer (Resident, Hartford Office)
Meredith Gordon Remigino
George H. Richards II
Joan Allen Rowe
Steven F. Rowell
Alisa T. Rulnick
Jennifer B. Rubin (Resident, Stamford Office)
Joseph A. SanFilippo (Not admitted in CT)
William B. Slate (Not admitted in CT)
Joseph R. Tristine
Suzanne E. Wachsstock (Resident, Stamford Office)
Peter M. Wendzel (Resident, Hartford Office)

For full biographical listings, see the Martindale-Hubbell Law Directory

NEW LONDON, New London Co.

WALLER, SMITH & PALMER, P.C. (AV)

52 Eugene O'Neill Drive, P.O. Box 88, 06320
Telephone: 860-442-0367
Telecopier: 860-447-9915
Email: wspmain@snet.net *URL:* http://www.snetyp.com/wallersmithpalmer
Old Lyme Office: 103 Halls Road.
Telephone: 860-434-8063.
Telecopier: 860-434-9452. Email: wspol@snet.net

Tracy Waller (1862-1947)
J. Rodney Smith (1906-1979)
Birdsey G. Palmer (Retired)
William W. Miner
Robert P. Anderson, Jr.
Robert W. Marrion
Hughes Griffis
Edward B. O'Connell
Frederick B. Gahagan
Tracy M. Collins
Philip M. Johnstone
David P. Condon
Valerie Ann Votto
Charles C. Anderson

James F. Spallone

General Counsel For: Town of East Lyme.
Counsel For: Citizens Bank of Connecticut; Soneco/Northeastern, Inc.; The Nature Conservancy; Fleet Bank.

(See Next Column)

Local Counsel For: McCue Mortgage Co.; Citicorp Mortgage; U.S. Department of Housing and Urban Development.

For full biographical listings, see the Martindale-Hubbell Law Directory

NORWALK, Fairfield Co.

TIERNEY, ZULLO, FLAHERTY & MURPHY, P.C. (AV)

134 East Avenue, P.O. Box 2028-Belden Station, 06852
Telephone: 203-853-7000
Fax: 203-838-4829

Thomas Tierney
Frank N. Zullo
Thomas A. Flaherty
Frank W. Murphy
Reuben S. Midler
Gary Lorusso
Andrew F. Kordas
Barbara Coughlan
Elizabeth A.B. Suchy
Creighton M. English

OF COUNSEL

Thomas A. Keating, Jr.
Vincent Gallogly

References: First Union Bank of Connecticut; Fleet Bank.

For full biographical listings, see the Martindale-Hubbell Law Directory

OLD LYME, New London Co.

WALLER, SMITH & PALMER, P.C. (AV)

103 Halls Road, 06371
Telephone: 860-434-8063
Telecopier: 860-434-9452
Email: wspol@snet.net *URL:* http://www.snetyp.com/wallersmithpalmer
New London Office: 52 Eugene O'Neill Drive.
Telephone: 860-442-0367.
Telecopier: 860-447-9915. Email: wspmain@snet.net

Robert W. Marrion
Frederick B. Gahagan
Valerie Ann Votto

For full biographical listings, see the Martindale-Hubbell Law Directory

SOUTHBURY, New Haven Co.

SECOR, CASSIDY & MCPARTLAND, P.C. (AV)

Successors to Bronson, Lewis, Upson & Secor; Lewis, Hart, Upson & Secor; Upson, Secor, Greene & Cassidy and Upson, Secor, Cassidy & McPartland, P.C.
900 Main Street South, 06488
Telephone: 203-264-8223
Fax: 203-264-6730
Email: scm@ctlawyers.com *URL:* http://www.ctlawyers.com
Waterbury, Connecticut Office: 41 Church Street, P.O. Box 2818.
Telephone: 203-757-9261.
Fax: 203-756-5762.

James R. Healey (Resident)

James J. Flaherty, Jr.

Attorneys for: The Mattatuck Museum; American Republican, Inc.; Hubbard-Hall, Inc.; The Siemon Co.; Engineered Sinterings and Plastics, Inc.; Boutin Industries; County Line Buick-Nissan, Inc.

For full biographical listings, see the Martindale-Hubbell Law Directory

STAMFORD, Fairfield Co.

CURTIS, BRINCKERHOFF & BARRETT, P.C. (AV)

666 Summer Street, 06901-1416
Telephone: 203-324-6777
Telecopier: 203-324-9621
Email: info@curtisbb.com

T. Ward Cleary (1916-1988)
Frederick M. Tobin
John Wayne Fox
Ward Frank Cleary
James D'Alton Murphy
Randolph T. Lovallo

OF COUNSEL

John D. Hertz
Jane F. Donovan
Richard L. Brinckerhoff
Patricia M. Gaug

Susan L. Stratton
Derek Gilman
Michael P. Murray
John J. Louizos

Counsel for: The F. A. Bartlett Tree Expert Co.; Town of Darien; Miller Automobile Corp.; Bolliger, Inc.; Titan Sports; People's Bank, Bridgeport; Fleet Bank; Federal Deposit Insurance Co.; William Pitt Foundation; Wood Logan Associates.

For full biographical listings, see the Martindale-Hubbell Law Directory

Stamford—Continued

DAY, BERRY & HOWARD LLP (AV)

One Canterbury Green, 06901
Telephone: 203-977-7300
Telecopier: 203-977-7301
Email: postmaster@dbh.com *URL:* http://www.dbh.com
Greenwich, Connecticut Office: One East Putnam Avenue.
Telephone: 203-862-7800.
Hartford, Connecticut Office: CityPlace I.
Telephone: 860-275-0100.
Telecopier: 860-275-0343.
Boston, Massachusetts Office: 260 Franklin Street.
Telephone: 617-345-4600.
Telecopier: 617-439-4453.

MEMBERS OF FIRM IN STAMFORD

Jerome Berkman
Martin L. Budd
Michael P. Byrne
Patricia A. Carpenter
Michael G. Considine
Ronald Osburn Dederick
Thomas D. Goldberg
F. Lee Griffith III
Gregory A. Hayes
Robert J. Miller
Kenneth W. Ritt
Sabino Rodriguez III
Daniel L. Schwartz
Felix J. Springer
James F. Stapleton
David A. Swerdloff
Stanley A. Twardy, Jr.
Amy K. Wilfert

ASSOCIATES OF FIRM IN STAMFORD

R. Scott Beach
Tricia S. Begg
William L. Brewer
Viktoria K. Cech-Vinhais
Richard P. Colbert
M. Kate Curran
Richard D. Edwards
Sarah Moore Fass
Kenneth W. Gage
Lorey Rives Leddy
(Not admitted in CT)
Natasha M. Lipcan
Catherine Dugan O'Connor
Thomas J. O'Neill
Jennifer L. Slager
(Not admitted in CT)
Ann Lisa Spletzer
Fritz Strohmeyer
Elena Tourchinskaya
Jonathan B. Tropp
Theodore J. Whitehead

OF COUNSEL IN STAMFORD

Emil H. Frankel

COUNSEL IN STAMFORD

Andrew P. Gaillard
James O'Connor
Paulette Wunsch
(Not admitted in CT)

For full biographical listings, see the Martindale-Hubbell Law Directory

HEALY & BAILLIE, LLP (AV Ⓣ)

Stamford Harbor Park, 333 Ludlow Street, 06902-6987
Telephone: 203-961-7250
Telecopier: 203-357-7909
Email: reception@healy.com *URL:* http://www.healy.com
New York, N.Y. Office: 29 Broadway, 10006-3293.
Telephone: 212-943-3980.
Telecopier: 212-425-0131. Email: reception@healy.com.
Hong Kong Office: Healy & Baillie, Suite 1303, Dina House, Ruttonjee Centre, 11 Duddell Street, Central.
Telephone: 852-2537-8628.
Telecopier: 852-2521-9072. Email: gryu@healy.com.hk.

RESIDENT PARTNER

John W. Wall

For full biographical listings, see the Martindale-Hubbell Law Directory

NEVILLE SHAVER HUBBARD & McLEAN (AV Ⓣ)

Three Landmark Square, 06901
Telephone: 203-363-5300
Telecopier: 203-363-5323
Email: firm@nevillaw.com
New York, N.Y. Office: 444 Madison Avenue, 25th Floor.
Telephone: 212-989-5300;
Telecopier: 212-989-5323.

Richard M. Neville
(Not admitted in CT)
Alan H. McLean
D. Seeley Hubbard

Alan M. Shaver
John P. Maloney
(Not admitted in CT)
Roger J. Pearson

For full biographical listings, see the Martindale-Hubbell Law Directory

PAUL, HASTINGS, JANOFSKY & WALKER LLP (AV)

A Limited Liability Partnership including Professional Corporations
1055 Washington Boulevard, 06901-2217
Telephone: 203-961-7400
Fax: 203-359-3031
URL: http://www.phjw.com
Atlanta, Georgia Office: 24th Floor, 600 Peachtree Street, N.E.
Telephone: 404-815-2400.
Los Angeles, California Office: 555 South Flower Street.
Telephone: 213-683-6000.

(See Next Column)

New York, New York Office: 399 Park Avenue.
Telephone: 212-318-6000.
Orange County, California Office: 695 Town Center Drive, Costa Mesa.
Telephone: 714-668-6200.
San Francisco, California Office: 345 California Street.
Telephone: 415-835-1600.
Washington, D.C. Office: 1299 Pennsylvania Avenue, N.W.
Telephone: 202-508-9500.
Tokyo, Japan Office: Ark Mori Building, 12-32 Akasaka, P.O. Box 577, 1-Chome, Minato-Ku.
Telephone: (03) 3556-4711.
London, England Office: The International Financial Centre, 25 Old Broad Street.
Telephone: (011) 44-171-562-4000.
ATTORNEY E-MAIL ADDRESSES: first initial middle initial last name @phjw.com (e.g. rmasbill@phjw.com)

MEMBERS OF FIRM

Jonathan Birenbaum
Douglas C. Conroy
Christopher H. Craig
Mary C. Dollarhide
Esteban A. Ferrer, III
Kurt W. Hansson
John D. Hawkins, Jr.
Mario J. Ippolito
Charles T. Lee
John S. McGeeney
David E. Rabin
Patrick W. Shea
David E. Snediker
Carla R. Walworth

SENIOR COUNSEL

Christopher A. Barreca

OF COUNSEL

Karen Y. Bitar
Elizabeth Adolff Brower
Harold N. Eddy, Jr.
John W. Hamlin
Andrew S. Holmes
Robert A. Horowitz
Leslie A. Plaskon

ASSOCIATES

Matthew S. Antonetti
James R. Bliss
Jennifer A. Magyar Bologna
Eric R. Bootsma
Adam S. Bozek
Shannon T. Browne
(Not admitted in CT)
David G. Call
Michelle J. Cohn
Louis K. Fisher
Richard B. Furey
(Not admitted in CT)
Joshua D. Goodman
Sarah E. Graves
Joseph A. Guay
(Not admitted in CT)
T. Anthony Howell
(Not admitted in CT)
Claudia N. Humphrey
(Not admitted in CT)
Gregory F. Lang
Eric T. Levine
Paul C. Marazita
Diane L. Matt
Karen E. McArthur
Philip J. Paseltiner
Suzanne Marie Pepe-Robbins
Bonnie Pierson-Murphy
Allison Beth Rosenberg
Peter M. Schultz
(Not admitted in CT)
Yolanda Y. Seals
Evan S. Seideman
Brit K. Seifert
H. William Smith III
Toby S. Soli
John P. Staikos
Neil B. Stekloff
Holly M. Strutt

For full biographical listings, see the Martindale-Hubbell Law Directory

ROSENBLUM & FILAN, L.L.C. (AV Ⓣ)

One Landmark Square, 06901
Telephone: 203-358-9200
Fax: 203-358-0687
Email: counsel@rosenblumfilan.com *URL:* http://www.rosenblumfilan.com
White Plains, New York Office: 50 Main Street.
Telephone: 914-686-6100.
Fax: 914-686-6140.
New York, New York Office: 400 Madison Avenue.
Telephone: 212-888-8001.
Fax: 212-888-3331.

MEMBERS OF FIRM

Patrick J. Filan
James B. Rosenblum
Alan S. Rubenstein
Samuel Tannenbaum
James S. Newfield

James F. Biondo
James A. Mahar

OF COUNSEL

Theodore J. Greene

For full biographical listings, see the Martindale-Hubbell Law Directory

RYAN, RYAN, JOHNSON & DELUCA, LLP (AV)

80 Fourth Street, P.O. Box 3057, 06905
Telephone: 203-357-9200
FAX: 203-357-7915
Email: ryanlaw@rrjmd.com
New York, New York Office: Park Avenue Atrium, 237 Park Avenue.
Telephone: 212-551-1430.

(See Next Column)

RYAN, RYAN, JOHNSON & DELUCA LLP, *Stamford—Continued*

MEMBERS OF FIRM

Daniel E. Ryan, Jr.
Daniel E. Ryan, III
W. Patrick Ryan
Michael T. Ryan
J. Paul Johnson
Kevin M. Tepas
Charles A. Deluca
Robert C.E. Laney
John F. Leydon, Jr.

OF COUNSEL

Charles M. McCaghey

ASSOCIATES

Beverly J. Hunt
Robert O. Hickey
Darren P. Renner
Danielle DiBerardini-Albrecht
Catherine S. Nietzel
Joseph N. DeFilippo
Janine M. Kelly
Jennifer R. Mazzella
Robert R. Statchen
Brock T. Dubin

For full biographical listings, see the Martindale-Hubbell Law Directory

SHIPMAN & GOODWIN LLP (AV)

One Landmark Square, 06901
Telephone: 203-324-8100
Telecopier: 203-324-8199
Email: www@goodwin.com *URL:* http://shipman-goodwin.com
Hartford, Connecticut Office: One American Row.
Telephone: 203-251-5000.
Lakeville, Connecticut Office: 12 Porter Street.
Telephone: 203-435-2539.

PARTNERS

Michael L. Widland
Steven M. Gold
Barry C. Hawkins
Donald R. Gustafson
Lewis G. Schwartz
Robin G. Frederick
Frederick S. Gold
Robert M. Wonneberger

COUNSEL

Michael J. Palmieri

OF COUNSEL

George C. Jepsen

ASSOCIATES

Jennifer A. Hauhuth
Cathy L. Bromberg (Not admitted in CT)
Shari M. Goodstein
Raymond M. Bernstein
Bart F. Peters
Suzanne Lee Cartledge
Timothy D. DiResta
Aline B. Goldbach
R. Michael Meo, Jr.

For full biographical listings, see the Martindale-Hubbell Law Directory

SILVER, GOLUB & TEITELL LLP (AV)

184 Atlantic Street, P.O. Box 389, 06904
Telephone: 203-325-4491
Fax: 203-325-3769
Email: silvergolubteitell.com *URL:* http://www.sgtlaw.com

MEMBERS OF FIRM

Richard A. Silver
Elaine T. Silver
David S. Golub
John D. Josel
Ernest F. Teitell
Mario DiNatale
Patricia M. Haugh (1942-1988)
Jonathan M. Levine

Marilyn J. Ramos
Kathleen L. Brandt
Richard H. Greenwood
Paul A. Slager (Not admitted in CT)
Mary G. Curry
Brad C. Gustafson

For full biographical listings, see the Martindale-Hubbell Law Directory

TYLER COOPER & ALCORN, LLP (AV)

One Landmark Square, 06901-2501
Telephone: 203-348-5555
Telecopier: 203-348-3875
URL: http://www.tylercooper.com
Hartford, Connecticut Office: CityPlace.
Telephone: 860-725-6200.
Telecopier: 860-278-3802.
New Haven, Connecticut Office: 205 Church Street.
Telephone: 203-784-8200.
Telecopier: 203-789-2133.
Greenwich, Connecticut Office: 675 Steamboat Road.
Telephone: 203-869-2000.
Telecopier: 203-869-2001.
Madison, Connecticut Office: 23 Woodland Road.
Telephone: 203-318-3600.
Telecopier: 203-318-3609.

MEMBERS OF FIRM

Emmett E. Brown III (Resident)
Christopher L. Ulrich (Resident)

COUNSEL

Nan Budde Chequer (Resident)

For full biographical listings, see the Martindale-Hubbell Law Directory

WIGGIN & DANA (AV)

Three Stamford Plaza, 301 Tresser Boulevard, 06901-3234
Telephone: 203-363-7600
Telefax: 203-363-7676
URL: http://www.wiggin.com
New Haven, Connecticut Office: One Century Tower.
Telephone: 203-498-4400.
Telefax: 203-782-2889.
Hartford, Connecticut Office: One CityPlace.
Telephone: 203-297-3700.
FAX: 203-525-9380.

MEMBERS OF FIRM

James F. Farrington, Jr. (Resident)
Michael Grundei (Resident)
Leonard Leader (Resident)
Patricia Kavee Melick (Not admitted in CT; Resident)
David B. Fein (Resident)
Mark S. Flynn (Resident)
William A. Perrone (Resident)
William J. Speranza (Resident)

RESIDENT SENIOR COUNSEL

Robert M. McAnerney (Resident)

ASSOCIATES

Louis A. Bevilacqua (Resident)
Paul G. Holland, Jr. (Resident)
James H. Bicks (Not admitted in CT; Resident)
Kenneth W. Lord (Not admitted in CT; Resident)
Tanya J. Dobash (Not admitted in CT)
Benedicta McGrath (Resident)
Jessie A. Gilbert (Resident)
Jennifer B. Rubin (Resident)
Nicole M. Hoffmeister (Resident)
Suzanne E. Wachsstock (Resident)

For full biographical listings, see the Martindale-Hubbell Law Directory

WINTHROP, STIMSON, PUTNAM & ROBERTS (AV)

Financial Centre, 695 East Main Street, P.O. Box 6760, 06904-6760
Telephone: 203-348-2300
Telefax: 203-965-8226
URL: http://www.winstim.com
New York, N.Y. Office: One Battery Park Plaza, 10004.
Telephone: 212-858-1000.
Fax: 212-858-1500.
Washington, D.C. Office: 1133 Connecticut Avenue, N.W., 20036.
Telephone: 202-775-9800.
Fax: 202-833-8491.
Palm Beach, Florida Office: 125 Worth Avenue, 33480.
Telephone: 561-655-7297.
Fax: 561-833-6726.
London, England Office: 2 Throgmorton Avenue, London, EC2N 2DL, England.
Telephone: O11-44171-628-4931.
Fax: 011-44171-638-0443.
Tokyo, Japan Office: 608 Atagoyama Bengoshi Building 6-7, Atago 1-chome, Minato-ku, Tokyo 105 Japan.
Telephone: 011-813-3437-9740.
Fax: 011-813-3437-9261.
Hong Kong, China Office: 2505 Asia Pacific Finance Tower, Citibank Plaza, 3 Garden Road, Central.
Telephone: 011-852-2530-3400.
Fax: 011-852-2530-3355.
Singapore Office: 6 Battery Road #38-01/B, Singapore 049909.
Telephone: 65-227-4700.
Fax: 65-227-4711.

MEMBERS OF FIRM

Thomas F. Clauss, Jr.
Kent S. Nevins
Frode Jensen, III
Robert J. Rawn
G. William Sisley

COUNSEL

Arthur W. Hooper, Jr.

ASSOCIATES

George P. Barbaresi (Not admitted in CT)
David Singer (Not admitted in CT)
Kristin Chach
Cozata Solloway
Stephen J. Curley
William L. Sturman, Jr.
Seth L. Kaplan
Vicki E. Volper
Kelly J. McClure
Karin Weiner
Lori Iannotti Zyskowski

For full biographical listings, see the Martindale-Hubbell Law Directory

WOFSEY, ROSEN, KWESKIN & KURIANSKY, LLP (AV)

600 Summer Street, 06901
Telephone: 203-327-2300
Fax: 203-967-9273

MEMBERS OF FIRM

Abraham Wofsey (1915-1944)
Howard C. Kaplan
Michael Wofsey (1927-1951)
Edward M. Kweskin
David M. Rosen (1926-1967)
David M. Cohen
Julius B. Kuriansky (1952-1992)
Marshall Goldberg
Sydney C. Kweskin (1946-1998)
Stephen A. Finn
Monroe Silverman
Judith Rosenberg

(See Next Column)

WOFSEY, ROSEN, KWESKIN & KURIANSKY LLP—*Continued*

MEMBERS OF FIRM (Continued)

Mark H. Henderson
Steven D. Grushkin
Matthew J. Forstadt
Steven M. Frederick

OF COUNSEL

Saul Kwartin
Emanuel Margolis
Anthony R. Lorenzo

SPECIAL COUNSEL

Day R. Shields

ASSOCIATES

Joseph Brachfeld
Eric M. Higgins
William A. Harrison
Daniel M. Young
Angelo A. Ziotas

Representative Clients: Banque Paribas; Benenson Realty; Cellular Information Systems, Inc.; The Chase Manhattan Bank; First County Bank; Hartford Provision Co.; Louis Dreyfus Corp.; Norwalk Federation of Teachers; People's Bank; Ridgeway Shopping Center.

For full biographical listings, see the Martindale-Hubbell Law Directory

*VERNON,** Tolland Co.

FLAHERTY, MEISLER & COURTNEY (AV)

30 Lafayette Square, Suite 116, 06066-4554
Telephone: 860-872-7200
Fax: 860-875-6594
Email: FMACATTY@aol.com

MEMBERS OF FIRM

Leo B. Flaherty Jr. (1923-1998)
Arthur P. Meisler
Joseph D. Courtney

ASSOCIATE

Elizabeth C. Foran

Reference: Savings Bank of Rockville.

For full biographical listings, see the Martindale-Hubbell Law Directory

WATERBURY, New Haven Co.

CARMODY & TORRANCE LLP (AV)

50 Leavenworth Street, P.O. Box 1110, 06721-1110
Telephone: 203-573-1200
Facsimile: 203-575-2600
New Haven, Connecticut Office: 195 Church Street, P.O. Box 1950, 06509-1950.
Telephone: 203-777-5501.
Facsimile: 203-784-3199.
Southbury, Connecticut Office: 900 Main Street South. P.O. Box 410, 06488-0410.
Telephone: 203-264-7882.
Facsimile: 203-264-7847.

MEMBERS OF FIRM

Timothy R. Carmody
Joseph F. Budny
Anthony M. Fitzgerald (Resident, New Haven Office)
Norman K. Jellinghaus
Kenneth J. Pocius
Burton Z. Alter
Charles F. Corcoran, III (Resident, New Haven Office)
James K. Robertson, Jr.
Thomas R. Candrick, Jr. (Resident, New Haven Office)
Trudie Ross Hamilton
Augustus R. Southworth III
David L. Sfara
John D. Yarbrough, Jr.
Maureen Danehy Cox
Mark J. Malaspina
Susan Seidler Chambers (Resident, New Haven Office)
D. Charles Stohler
Ann Harris Rubin (Resident, New Haven Office)
Marianne Barbino Dubuque
Thomas J. Sansone (Resident, New Haven Office)
Joseph A. Wellington
Joseph L. Kinsella
Ann Hedges Zucker (Resident, New Haven Office)
Kathleen Lenehan Nastri
Christopher Rooney (Resident, New Haven Office)
Joseph E. Dornfried
M. Anne Peters
Michael J. Reardon
Steven G. Mednick (Resident, New Haven Office)
Brian T. Henebry
Paul S. Tagatac
Arthur G. Schaier (Not admitted in CT)

OF COUNSEL

G. Bradford Palmer
Walter F. Torrance, Jr.
Thomas L. Brayton
Lisa E. Wnuck (Resident, Southbury Office)
Deborah Whitlock Madden

COUNSEL

Brian L. Smith

ASSOCIATES

Rona C. Lynch
Joseph J. Packtor
Giovanna Tiberii Weller
Heena Kapadia (Resident, New Haven Office)
Christine I. Andrew
Howard K. Levine (Resident, New Haven Office)
David J. Vegliante (Resident, New Haven Office)
John R. Horvack, Jr.
Kristin Connors
Jennifer E. Sills
Richard L. Street
Beth Bryan Critton
George Monteiro Moreira

(See Next Column)

ASSOCIATES (Continued)

Mariella LaRosa
William M. O'Donnell, III
Leslie Gold McPadden
Joshua L. Milrad (Resident, New Haven Office)
Naomi B. Graubard (Resident, New Haven Office)
Domenico Zaino, Jr.
Michael K. Kinney
Sandra K. Davis
Michael L. Ferguson
Matthew R. Peterson
Susan LoFaso Henebry
Amy B. Levy (Resident, New Haven Office)

Representative Clients: Algonquin Gas Transmission Co.; Bank of Boston, N.A.; Bell Atlantic Mobile; Anthem Blue Cross & Blue Shield of Connecticut, Inc.; MacDermid, Inc.; Northeast Utilities; Timex Corp.; Waterbury Hospital.
Trial Counsel for: Aetna Life and Casualty; St. Paul Fire & Marine Insurance.

For full biographical listings, see the Martindale-Hubbell Law Directory

GAGER & PETERSON, LLP (AV)

One Exchange Place, P.O. Box 2480, 06722-2480
Telephone: 203-597-5100
Telecopier: 203-757-7888
Bethel, Connecticut Office: 2 Stony Hill Road.
Telephone: 203-207-5400.
Telecopier: 203-207-5407.
Litchfield, Connecticut Office: 49 Commons Drive, P.O. Box 1544.
Telephone: 860-567-0828.
Telecopier: 860-567-5844.
Sharon, Connecticut Office: 25 West Main Street, P.O. Box 158.
Telephone: 860-364-5531.
Telecopier: 860-364-5805.
Southbury, Connecticut Office: 325 Main Street South.
Telephone: 203-262-6600.
Telecopier: 203-262-6780.

SECOR, CASSIDY & MCPARTLAND, P.C. (AV)

Successors to Bronson, Lewis, Upson & Secor; Lewis, Hart, Upson & Secor; Upson, Secor, Greene & Cassidy and Upson, Secor, Cassidy & McPartland, P.C.
41 Church Street, P.O. Box 2818, 06723-2818
Telephone: 203-757-9261
Fax: 203-756-5762
Email: scm@ctlawyers.com *URL:* http://www.ctlawyers.com
Southbury, Connecticut Office: 900 Main Street South.
Telephone: 203-264-8223.
Fax: 203-264-6730.

Nath'l R. Bronson (1860-1949)
Lawrence L. Lewis (1881-1965)
Charles E. Hart (1884-1972)
J. Warren Upson (1903-1992)
John H. Cassidy, Jr.
Donald McPartland
W. Fielding Secor
James R. Healey (Resident, Southbury Office)
Gail E. McTaggart
Thomas G. Parisot
Elizabeth A. Bozzuto
Patrick W. Finn
David J. Bozzuto

Donald C. McPartland
James J. Flaherty, Jr.

COUNSEL

William J. Secor, Jr.
Milton A. Seymour

Attorneys for: The Mattatuck Museum; American Republican, Inc.; Hubbard-Hall, Inc.; The Siemon Co.; Engineered Sinterings and Plastics, Inc.; Boutin Industries; County Line Buick-Nissan, Inc.

For full biographical listings, see the Martindale-Hubbell Law Directory

TINLEY, NASTRI, RENEHAN & DOST, LLP (AV)

60 North Main Street, 2nd Floor, 06702
Telephone: 203-596-9030
Fax: 203-596-9036
URL: http://www.tnrdlaw.com

Jeffrey J. Tinley
Robert Nastri, Jr.
Richard P. Renehan
Mark W. Dost

ASSOCIATES

Marilyn N. Toland
Stephen E. Pliakas
Lisa J. Marotta

Representative Clients: Gar-San Corp.; General Electric Capital Commercial Automotive Finance, Inc.; Mobil Oil Corp.; Teikyo Post University; The May Department Stores Company; Watertown Construction Company, Inc.

For full biographical listings, see the Martindale-Hubbell Law Directory

WEST HARTFORD, Hartford Co.

BERMAN, BOURNS & CURRIE, LLC (AV)

970 Farmington Avenue, P.O. Box 271837, 06127-1837
Telephone: 860-232-4471
Fax: 860-523-4605

John A. Berman
Courtney B. Bourns

(See Next Column)

BERMAN, BOURNS & CURRIE LLC, *West Hartford—Continued*

Mary Beth Anderson
Steven R. Dembo
Annemarie Burnham

OF COUNSEL

John K. Currie

For full biographical listings, see the Martindale-Hubbell Law Directory

JOHN C. PETERS, P.C. (AV)

61 South Main Street, Suite 204, P.O. Box 270047, 06127-0047
Telephone: 860-313-0255
Direct Dial: 860-983-0540
Facsimile: 860-313-0257
Email: Pete31@aol.com

John C. Peters

For full biographical listings, see the Martindale-Hubbell Law Directory

WESTPORT, Fairfield Co.

BLAZZARD, GRODD & HASENAUER, P.C. (AV)

943 Post Road East, P.O. Box 5108, 06881
Telephone: 203-226-7866
Telecopier: 203-454-4855
Lauderdale-By-the-Sea Office: Suite 207, W. Tradewinds Avenue, 33308.
Telephone: 954-771-6667.
Facsimile: 954-771-7689. E-Mail: BGHFL@AOL.COM

Norse N. Blazzard
Leslie E. Grodd
Judith A. Hasenauer
William E. Hasenauer
Raymond A. O'Hara, III
Lynn Korman Stone

Peter L. Cejas (Not admitted in CT)

For full biographical listings, see the Martindale-Hubbell Law Directory

GOLDSTEIN AND PECK, P.C. (AV)

190 Main Street, P.O. Box 5031, 06881
Telephone: 203-226-7488
Telefax: 203-334-6949
Bridgeport, Connecticut Office: 1087 Broad Street, P.O. Box 1538.
Telephone: 203-334-9421.
Telefax: 203-334-6949.

David Goldstein (1898-1992)
William J. Kupinse, Jr.
Walter A. Flynn, Jr.
Eugene E. Cederbaum
John G. Dzurik
Dennis M. Laccavole
Kathleen H. Allsup
Robert L. Cavanaugh, Jr.
Jo-Ann R. Sensale

OF COUNSEL

Peter B. O'Connell

Representative Clients: Bee Publishing Co., Inc.; The Chase Manhattan Bank; Great American Insurance Companies; Physicians Health Services, Inc.; Town of Westport; Greenwich Board of Education; Newtown Savings Bank; People's Bank.

For full biographical listings, see the Martindale-Hubbell Law Directory

LEVETT ROCKWOOD P.C. (AV)

33 Riverside Avenue, P.O. Box 5116, 06881
Telephone: 203-222-0885
Telecopier: 203-226-8025

Suzanne B. Albani
Robert O. Barberi
Edward B. Chansky
Madeleine F. Grossman
Dorit Schutzengel Heimer
Cheryl L. Johnson
Marc J. Kurzman
David R. Levett
Judy A. Rabkin
Sharon M. Schweitzer
Steven M. Siegelaub
Peter H. Struzzi
Barbara A. Young

OF COUNSEL

William O. Rockwood, Jr.

Debra R. Cardinali
Stephen M. Cowherd
Christopher M. Graham
Robin K. Higgins
Douglas R. Sansted
Rodger F. Smith, Jr.
Patricia D. Weitzman

Representative Clients: Cannondale Corp.; Caradon, Inc.; DataViz, Inc.; Dooney & Bourke, Inc.; GAF Corporation; Heyman Properties; Hospital of Saint Raphael; Marketing Corporation of America; Olin Corporation; St. Vincent's Medical Center.

For full biographical listings, see the Martindale-Hubbell Law Directory

TIROLA & HERRING (AV)

1221 Post Road East, P.O. Box 631, 06881
Telephone: 203-226-8926
Fax: 203-226-9500
Email: TirolaLaw@aol.com
New York, New York Office: Suite 4E, 10 Sheridan Square, 10014.

MEMBERS OF FIRM

Vincent S. Tirola
Charles Fredericks, Jr.
Elizabeth C. Seeley
Buddy O. H. Herring

Dan Shaban
Susannah Jacobson
Thomas C. Cusa

OF COUNSEL

C. Michael Carter
Alan D. Lieberson

Reference: The Westport Bank and Trust Co.

For full biographical listings, see the Martindale-Hubbell Law Directory

DELAWARE

*DOVER,** Kent Co.

MORRIS, JAMES, HITCHENS & WILLIAMS, LLP (AV)

Suite 202, 32 West Loockerman Street, 19904-7356
Telephone: 302-678-8815
Telecopier: 302-678-9063
URL: http://www.morrisjames.com
Wilmington, Delaware Office: 222 Delaware Avenue. P.O. Box 2306, 19899-2306.
Telephone: 302-888-6800.
Telecopier: 302-571-1750.
Newark, Delaware Office: 22 Polly Drummond Hill Road, 19711-5703.
Telephone: 302-368-4200.
Fax: 302-368-6259.

RESIDENT PARTNER

Glenn E. Hitchens

RESIDENT ASSOCIATE

Mary L. Sutherland

For full biographical listings, see the Martindale-Hubbell Law Directory

PRICKETT, JONES & ELLIOTT, P.A. (AV)

11 North State Street, 19901
Telephone: 302-674-3841
Telecopier: 302-674-5864
Email: attorneys@prickett.com *URL:* http://www.prickett.com
Wilmington, Delaware Office: 1310 King Street.
Telephone: 302-888-6500.
Kennett Square, Pennsylvania Office: 217 West State Street.
Telephone: 610-444-1573.

RESIDENT MEMBERS

Wayne N. Elliott
Gary F. Traynor
John W. Paradee

RESIDENT ASSOCIATES

Rebecca Batson Kidner
William G. Bush, IV

For full biographical listings, see the Martindale-Hubbell Law Directory

SCHMITTINGER & RODRIGUEZ, PROFESSIONAL ASSOCIATION (AV)

414 South State Street, 19901
Telephone: 302-674-0140
FAX: 302-674-1830
Email: attorneys@schmittrod.com
Wilmington, Delaware Office: 1300 North Market Street, Suite 205.
Telephone: 302-652-3676.
Fax: 302-652-8788.
Rehoboth Beach, Delaware Office: 4602 Highway One.
Telephone: 302-227-1400.
Fax: 302-645-1843.
Odessa, Delaware Office: Odessa Professional Park, P.O. Box 626.
Telephone: 302-378-1697.
Fax: 302-378-1659.

Harold Schmittinger
Nicholas H. Rodriguez
Paul H. Boswell
John J. Schmittinger
Bruce C. Ennis
Douglas B. Catts
William D. Fletcher, Jr.
William A. Denman
Catherine T. Hickey
William W. Pepper Sr.
Craig T. Eliassen
Crystal L. Carey
Scott E. Chambers
Mardi F. Pyott
David A. Boswell (Resident, Rehoboth Beach, Delaware Office)
Noel E. Primos
Walt F. Schmittinger

(See Next Column)

SCHMITTINGER & RODRIGUEZ PROFESSIONAL ASSOCIATION—*Continued*

Jeffrey J Clark
Kathy S. Gravell (Resident, Odessa, Delaware Office)
R. Scott Kappes (Resident, Wilmington, Delaware Office)
Beth Buzzell Miller

Representative Clients: Chesapeake Utilities Corp.; City of Dover.

For full biographical listings, see the Martindale-Hubbell Law Directory

*GEORGETOWN,** Sussex Co.

WILSON, HALBROOK & BAYARD, PROFESSIONAL ASSOCIATION (AV)

107 West Market Street, P.O. Box 690, 19947
Telephone: 302-856-0015
Telecopier: 302-856-7116

Houston Wilson (1910-1980)
Eugene H. Bayard
Clayton E. Bunting
Dennis L. Schrader
Robert G. Gibbs
Eric C. Howard
Mark D. Olson
Vivian Medinilla Longo

RETIRED

Robert L. Halbrook

Representative Clients: Delaware National Bank; Townsend's Inc.; Allen Family Foods, Inc.; Burris Foods, Inc.; J.G. Townsend, Jr. & Co.; Sussex County; Nanticoke Homes, Inc.; First State Packaging, Inc.
Approved Attorneys for: Ticor Title Insurance Co.; First American Title Insurance Co.
References: Delaware National Bank; Wilmington Trust Co.

For full biographical listings, see the Martindale-Hubbell Law Directory

YOUNG CONAWAY STARGATT & TAYLOR, LLP (AV)

110 West Pine Street, 19947
Telephone: 302-856-3571
Telecopy: 302-856-9338
Email: ycst@ycst.com
Wilmington, Delaware Office: 11th Floor, Rodney Square North, P.O. Box 391.
Telephone: 302-571-6600.
Telecopy: 302-571-1253.

MEMBERS OF FIRM

H. James Conaway, Jr. (1922-1990)
Craig A. Karsnitz (Resident)

ASSOCIATE

E. Scott Bradley

For full biographical listings, see the Martindale-Hubbell Law Directory

NEWARK, New Castle Co.

MORRIS, JAMES, HITCHENS & WILLIAMS, LLP (AV)

22 Polly Drummond Hill Road, 19711-5703
Telephone: 302-368-4200
Telecopier: 302-368-6259
URL: http://www.morrisjames.com
Wilmington, Delaware Office: 222 Delaware Avenue, P.O. Box 2306, 19899-2306.
Telephone: 302-888-6800.
Telecopier: 302-571-1750.
Dover, Delaware Office: Suite 202, 32 West Loockerman Street, 19904-7356.
Telephone: 302-678-8815.
Telecopier: 302-678-9063.

RESIDENT ATTORNEYS

Kevin G. Healy
Francis J. Jones, Jr.

For full biographical listings, see the Martindale-Hubbell Law Directory

*WILMINGTON,** New Castle Co.

ASHBY & GEDDES (AV)

One Rodney Square, P.O. Box 1150, 19899
Telephone: 302-654-1888
Fax: 302-654-2067

MEMBERS OF FIRM

Lawrence C. Ashby
James McC. Geddes
Stephen E. Jenkins
Randall E. Robbins
Steven J. Balick
Regina A. Iorii
William P. Bowden
Richard D. Heins
Philip Trainer, Jr.

ASSOCIATES

Amy Arnott Quinlan
Steven T. Margolin
Christopher S. Sontchi
Richard I.G. Jones, Jr.
Aaron A. Garber (Not admitted in DE)

For full biographical listings, see the Martindale-Hubbell Law Directory

BIGGS AND BATTAGLIA (AV)

1800 Mellon Bank Center, P.O. Box 1489, 19899-1489
Telephone: 302-655-9677
Email: B-B@DOL.NET

MEMBERS OF FIRM

Victor F. Battaglia
Robert D. Goldberg
Robert K. Beste, Jr.
Philip B. Bartoshesky
Victor F. Battaglia, Jr.
Linda F. Shopland
Nancy E. Whinnery

OF COUNSEL

John Biggs, III
Gerard P. Kavanaugh, Sr.
S. Bernard Ableman

For full biographical listings, see the Martindale-Hubbell Law Directory

CONNOLLY BOVE LODGE & HUTZ LLP (AV)

1220 Market Street, P.O. Box 2207, 19899-2207
Telephone: 302-658-9141
Telecopier: 302-658-5614
Email: cblhlaw@cblhlaw.com *URL:* http://www.cblhlaw.com

Arthur G. Connolly (Retired)
James M. Mulligan, Jr.
Arthur G. Connolly, Jr.
Rudolf E. Hutz
Harold Pezzner
Richard M. Beck (Not admitted in DE)
Paul E. Crawford
Stanley C. Macel, III
Thomas M. Meshbesher
Henry E. Gallagher, Jr.
George Pazuniak
N. Richard Powers
Richard David Levin
John A. Clark, III
Jeffrey B. Bove
James J. Woods, Jr.
Collins J. Seitz, Jr.
Edward F. Eaton
Charles J. Durante
Patricia Smink Rogowski
Mary W. Bourke
Robert G. McMorrow, Jr. (Not admitted in DE)
R. Eric Hutz
Arthur G. Connolly, III
William E. McShane (Not admitted in DE)
James D. Heisman
Jeffrey C. Wisler
John D. Fairchild (Not admitted in DE)
William E. Lambert (Not admitted in DE)
M. Edward Danberg
Ashley I. Pezzner
Anne Love Barnett
Matthew F. Boyer
Gerard M. O'Rourke
Francis DiGiovanni
Karen C. Bifferato
Samuel D. Brickley II
Thomas A. Stevens
Oleh V. Bilynsky
Allan Neal Kutzenco (Not admitted in DE)
Frank Z. Yang (Not admitted in DE)
James M. Olsen
Eric J. Evain

For full biographical listings, see the Martindale-Hubbell Law Directory

DUANE, MORRIS & HECKSCHER LLP (AV)

1201 Market Street, 19801
Telephone: 302-571-5550
Fax: 302-571-5560
URL: http://www.duanemorris.com
Philadelphia, Pennsylvania Office: Suite 4200, One Liberty Place.
Telephone: 215-979-1000.
Fax: 215-979-1020.
New York, New York Office: 380 Lexington Avenue.
Telephone: 212-692-1000.
Fax: 212-692-1020.
Chicago, Illinois Office: 227 West Monroe Street, Suite 3400.
Telephone: 312-499-6700.
Fax: 312-499-6701.
Washington, D.C. Office: 1667 K Street, N.W., Suite 700.
Telephone: 202-776-7800.
Fax: 202-776-7801.
San Francisco, California Office: 100 Spear Street.
Telephone: 415-371-2200.
Fax: 415-371-2201.
Boston, Massachusetts Office: One International Place, 14th Floor.
Telephone: 617-598-3100.
Fax: 617-598-3101.
Miami, Florida Office: 200 South Biscayne Boulevard, Suite 3140.
Telephone: 305-960-2200.
Fax: 305-960-2201.
Harrisburg, Pennsylvania Office: 305 North Front Street, 5th Floor, P.O. Box 1003.
Telephone: 717-237-5500.
Fax: 717-232-4015
Wayne, Pennsylvania Office: 735 Chesterbrook Boulevard, Suite 300.
Telephone: 610-647-3555.
Fax: 610-640-2619.
Cherry Hill, New Jersey Office: 51 Haddonfield Road, Suite 340.
Telephone: 856-488-7300.
Fax: 856-488-7021.
Newark, New Jersey Office: One Riverfront Plaza.
Telephone: 973-424-2000.
Fax: 973-424-2001.
Palm Beach, Florida Office: 249 Royal Palm Way, Suite 403.
Telephone: 561-366-5400.
Fax: 561-366-5401.

(See Next Column)

DUANE, MORRIS & HECKSCHER LLP, *Wilmington—Continued*

Allentown, Pennsylvania Office: 968 Postal Road, Suite 200, P.O. Box 90400.
Telephone: 610-266-3650.
Fax: 610-266-3651.
Houston, Texas Office: One Greenway Plaza, Suite 500.
Telephone: 713-552-9900.
Fax: 713-552-0109.
Dover, Delaware Office: 314 S. State Street.
Telephone: 302-736-0156.
Fax: 302-736-0336.

RESIDENT PARTNERS

Teresa K. D. Currier
Richard A. Forsten
John F. Grossbauer
Daniel F. Lindley
William E. Manning
Bonnie L. Metz
Thomas P. Preston
Judith Nichols Renzulli
David S. Swayze (Partner-in-Charge, Wilmington)
J. Richard Tucker (Not admitted in DE)

RESIDENT ASSOCIATES

A. Kimberly Brosseit (Not admitted in DE)
Mary F. Caloway
Richard S. Cobb
Frances Gauthier
John G. Harris (Not admitted in DE)
Adam G. Landis
Daniel B. Rath
Christine P. Schiltz
Michael W. Teichman
Jan A. T. Van Amerongen, Jr.

For full biographical listings, see the Martindale-Hubbell Law Directory

McCARTER & ENGLISH, LLP (AV)

Mellon Bank Center, 919 Market Street, 19899
Telephone: 302-654-8010
Telecopier: 302-654-0795
URL: http://www.mccarter.com
Newark, New Jersey Office: Four Gateway Center, 100 Mulberry Street. P.O. Box 652.
Telephone: 973-622-4444.
Telecopier: 973-624-7070.
Cherry Hill, New Jersey Office: 1820 Chapel Avenue West, Suite 380.
Telephone: 609-662-8444.
Telecopier: 609-662-6203.
New York, New York Office: Suite 2247, One World Trade Center.
Telephone: 212-466-9018.
Telecopier: 212-432-6568.
Boca Raton, Florida Office: 2255 Glades Road, Suite 319-A.
Telephone: 561-994-6262.
Telecopier: 561-241-0798.
Philadelphia, Pennsylvania Office: One Commerce Square, 2005 Market Street, Suite 3600.
Telephone: 215-557-7700.
Telecopier: 215-557-6544.

RESIDENT PARTNERS

Robert B. Anderson
Paul A. Bradley

SPECIAL COUNSEL

W. Wade W. Scott

ASSOCIATE

Elizabeth A. Saurman

For full biographical listings, see the Martindale-Hubbell Law Directory

MORRIS, JAMES, HITCHENS & WILLIAMS, LLP (AV)

222 Delaware Avenue, P.O. Box 2306, 19899-2306
Telephone: 302-888-6800
Telecopier: 302-571-1750
URL: http://www.morrisjames.com
Dover, Delaware Office: Suite 202, 32 West Loockerman Street, 19904-7356.
Telephone: 302-678-8815.
Telecopier: 302-678-9063.
Newark, Delaware Office: 22 Polly Drummond Hill Road, 19711-5703.
Telephone: 302-368-4200.
Fax: 302-368-6259.

MEMBERS OF FIRM

Henry N. Herndon, Jr.
George C. Hering, III
Grover C. Brown
William R. Hitchens, Jr.
Richard P. Beck
Glenn E. Hitchens (Resident at Dover)
Edward M. McNally
Norris P. Wright
James W. Semple
David H. Williams
P. Clarkson Collins, Jr.
Richard Galperin
Steven R. Director
Richard D. Kirk
Lewis H. Lazarus
Michael M. Ledyard
Francis J. Jones, Jr. (Resident, Newark, Delaware Office)
Daniel P. McCollom
Barbara MacDonald
Robert L. Symonds, Jr.
Stephen M. Miller
John D. Demmy
Mary M. Culley
Joseph R. Slights, III
Sherry C. McReynolds
Neal C. Belgam
Laura Sunstein Murphy

(See Next Column)

MEMBERS OF FIRM (Continued)

Kevin G. Healy (Resident, Newark, Delaware Office)
Nicholas J. Caggiano, Jr.
Michael J. Maimone
Lewis C. Ledyard, III
Joseph C. Schoell

ASSOCIATES

Gretchen Ann Bender
Norman M. Powell
Eileen K. Andersen
Gretchen S. Knight
Ellen Marie Cooper
John T. Meli, Jr.
Matthew J. O'Toole
Francis J. Schanne
Michael A. Weidinger
Mary L. Sutherland (Resident at Dover)
Stephanie M. Tarabicos
Nancy W. Law
Roger D. Anderson
James E. Drnec
Ricardo Palacio

For full biographical listings, see the Martindale-Hubbell Law Directory

MORRIS, NICHOLS, ARSHT & TUNNELL (AV)

1201 North Market Street, P.O. Box 1347, 19899-1347
Telephone: 302-658-9200
Telecopier: 302-658-3989
URL: http://www.mnat.com

MEMBERS OF FIRM

Richard L. Sutton
Johannes R. Krahmer
O. Francis Biondi
Lewis S. Black, Jr.
Paul Welsh
William O. LaMotte, III
Douglas E. Whitney
William H. Sudell, Jr.
Martin P. Tully
Thomas R. Hunt, Jr.
A. Gilchrist Sparks, III
Richard D. Allen
David Ley Hamilton
John F. Johnston
Walter C. Tuthill
Donald F. Parsons, Jr.
Jack B. Blumenfeld
Donald Nelson Isken
Donald E. Reid
Denison H. Hatch, Jr.
Thomas C. Grimm
Kenneth J. Nachbar
Andrew M. Johnston
Mary B. Graham
Michael Houghton
Matthew B. Lehr
Thomas R. Pulsifer
Jon E. Abramczyk
Alan J. Stone
Louis G. Hering
Frederick H. Alexander
R. Judson Scaggs, Jr.
William M. Lafferty
Karen Jacobs Louden
Donna L. Culver
Julia Heaney
Jonathan I. Lessner
Robert J. Dehney
Colm F. Connolly

ASSOCIATES

Rachel A. Dwares
Jeffrey R. Wolters
Maryellen Noreika
David J. Teklits
S. Mark Hurd
Rodger D. Smith
Lisa K. W. Crossland
Eric D. Schwartz
Lucinda C. Cucuzzella
Mona A. Lee
Stanford L. Stevenson, III
J. Andrew Huffman
Derek C. Abbott
Jessica Zeldin
Bradley James Enna
David A. Harris
Elizabeth A. Brown
Patricia A. O'Neill
Gregory W. Werkheiser
Wendy L. Walter
Christopher F. Carlton
Stephanie L. Nagel
Joelle E. Polesky
Richard W. Ellis
Francis X. Gorman
John D. Pirnot
Megan E. Ward

COUNSEL

Andrew B. Kirkpatrick, Jr.
David A. Drexler
Walter L. Pepperman, II

DECEASED PARTNERS

Hugh M. Morris (1878-1966)
Alexander L. Nichols (1906-1985)
James M. Tunnell, Jr. (1910-1986)
S. Samuel Arsht (1910-1999)

Representative Clients: AstraZeneca Inc.; The Chase Manhattan Bank (USA); The Coca-Cola Company; Data General Corporation; Ford Motor Company; J.P. Morgan & Co. Incorporated; McDonald's Corporation; Merck & Co., Inc.; Texaco Inc.; U S West, Inc.

For full biographical listings, see the Martindale-Hubbell Law Directory

PEPPER HAMILTON LLP (AV)

1201 Market Street, Suite 1600, P.O. Box 1709, 19899-1709
Telephone: 302-777-6500
Telecopy: 302-656-8865
Email: phinfo@pepperlaw.com *URL:* http://www.pepperlaw.com
Philadelphia, Pennsylvania Office: 3000 Two Logan Square, Eighteenth and Arch Streets, 19103-2799.
Telephone: 215-981-4000.
Fax: 215-981-4750.
Washington, D.C. Office: Hamilton Square, 600 Fourteenth Street, N.W. 20005-2004.
Telephone: 202-220-1200.
Fax: 202-220-1665.
Detroit, Michigan Office: 100 Renaissance Center, 36th Floor, 48243-1157.
Telephone: 313-259-7110.
Fax: 313-259-7926.

(See Next Column)

PEPPER HAMILTON LLP—*Continued*

New York, New York Office: 750 Lexington Avenue, Suite 600, 10022-1200.
Telephone: 212-813-9668.
Fax: 212-813-9802.
Pittsburgh, Pennsylvania Office: 500 Grant Street, 50th Floor, 15219-2502.
Telephone: 412-454-5000.
Fax: 412-281-0717.
Harrisburg, Pennsylvania Office: 200 One Keystone Plaza, North Front and Market Streets, P.O. Box 1181, 17108-1181.
Telephone: 717-255-1155.
Fax: 717-238-0575.
Berwyn, Pennsylvania Office: 1235 Westlakes Drive, Suite 400, 19312-2401.
Telephone: 610-640-7800.
Fax: 610-640-7835.
Cherry Hill, New Jersey Office: LibertyView Building, Suite 420, 457 Haddonfield Road, 08002-2220.
Telephone: 856-910-7200.
Fax: 856-665-7743.

PARTNERS

Richard P. Eckman	M. Duncan Grant
David M. Fournier	Christopher J. Lamb
David B. Stratton	

ASSOCIATES

Deneen L. Donnley-Evans	Sean P. McDevitt
Tara L. Lattomus	Barbara E. McDonald
Monica Leigh Loftin	Benjamin Strauss
Andrea Beth Unterberger	

For full biographical listings, see the Martindale-Hubbell Law Directory

POTTER ANDERSON & CORROON LLP (AV)

Hercules Plaza, 1313 N. Market Street, P.O. Box 951, 19899-0951
Telephone: 302-984-6000
Fax: 302-658-1192
URL: http://www.attys.pacdelaware.com

MEMBERS OF FIRM

Charles S. Crompton, Jr.	Mary E. Copper
Robert K. Payson	W. Laird Stabler, III
Leonard S. Togman	Richard L. Horwitz
Richard E. Poole	Michael B. Tumas
Michael D. Goldman	Kathleen Furey McDonough
James F. Burnett	Laurie Selber Silverstein
Daniel F. Wolcott, Jr.	Peter J. Walsh, Jr.
Charles S. McDowell	Stephen C. Norman
David B. Brown	Arthur L. Dent
Somers S. Price, Jr.	Harold I. Salmons, III
Donald J. Wolfe, Jr.	William R. Denny
Gregory A. Inskip	Philip A. Rovner
David J. Baldwin	Jennifer Gimler Brady
John E. James	Scott E. Waxman
W. Harding Drane, Jr.	Joanne Ceballos
Mark A. Morton	

COUNSEL

Robert P. Barnett	Michael B. Keehan
W. Laird Stabler, Jr.	

OF COUNSEL

John P. Sinclair	Hugh Corroon
Blaine T. Phillips	Joseph H. Geoghegan
Richard L. McMahon	

SENIOR ATTORNEY

Frederick H. Altergott

ASSOCIATES

Wendy K. Voss	John A. Ciccarone
Kevin R. Shannon	Gregory M. Johnson
Todd L. Goodman	Alisha K. Hiner
Michael A. Pittenger	(Not admitted in DE)
Matthew E. Fischer	John J. Quinn, III
William A. Hazeltine	Michael A. Steinberg
Eileen M. Filliben	(Not admitted in DE)
Emilie R. Ninan	Alissa Balotti Anderson
Gregory J. Feulner	William J. Dorgan
(Not admitted in DE)	Peter R. Macleod
Deborah A. Cuoco	Brian C. Ralston
Andrew T. O'Neill	Elihu E. Allinson, III

Counsel for: ConRail; Conectiv, Inc.; Hercules Inc.; Corporation Trust Co.; General Motors Corp.; Chrysler Corp.; Citicorp.; Mazda Motor of America, Inc.; E.I. duPont de Nemours & Company, Inc.

For full biographical listings, see the Martindale-Hubbell Law Directory

PRICKETT, JONES & ELLIOTT, P.A. (AV)

1310 King Street, P.O. Box 1328, 19899-1328
Telephone: 302-888-6500
Telecopier: 302-658-8111; 658-7257
Email: attorneys@prickett.com *URL:* http://www.prickett.com
Dover, Delaware Office: 11 North State Street.
Telephone: 302-674-3841.

(See Next Column)

Kennett Square, Pennsylvania Office: 217 West State Street.
Telephone: 610-444-1573.

OF COUNSEL

William Prickett	Paul M. Lukoff
William S. Prickett (1862-1926)	Elizabeth M. McGeever
William Prickett (1894-1964)	William J. Martin, III
Richard I. G. Jones	Joseph Grey
Wayne N. Elliott	Gary F. Traynor
Mason E. Turner, Jr.	(Resident at Dover Office)
James L. Holzman	John W. Paradee
John H. Small	(Resident at Dover Office)
Michael Hanrahan	Ronald A. Brown, Jr.
David E. Brand	Bruce E. Jameson
Wayne J. Carey	Thomas A. Mullen
F. Peter Conaty, Jr.	

Rebecca Batson Kidner	William G. Bush, IV
(Resident at Dover Office)	(Resident at Dover Office)
Barbara Snapp Danberg	Elizabeth A. Wilburn
William H. Lunger	Sheldon K. Rennie
Paul A. Fioravanti, Jr.	

Representative Clients: Computer Associates International; Connectiv Power Delivery (Delmarva Power & Light); PHICO Insurance Company.

For full biographical listings, see the Martindale-Hubbell Law Directory

RICHARDS, LAYTON & FINGER, P.A. (AV)

One Rodney Square, P.O. Box 551, 19899
Telephone: 302-658-6541
Telecopier: 302-658-6548

Richard J. Abrams	Gregory P. Williams
Charles F. Richards, Jr.	Paul M. Altman
Thomas P. Sweeney	Gregory V. Varallo
Pierre S. du Pont	Mark J. Gentile
Robert H. Richards, III	Robert J. Krapf
R. Franklin Balotti	Kevin G. Abrams
Martin I. Lubaroff	Eric A. Mazie
Richard G. Elliott, Jr.	Robert W. Whetzel
Wendell Fenton	W. Donald Sparks, II
Allen M. Terrell, Jr.	C. Stephen Bigler
Daniel M. Kristol	Charles Malcolm Cochran, IV
Glenn C. Kenton	Anne C. Foster
Richard G. Bacon	Cynthia Deans Kaiser
Stephen E. Herrmann	Daniel A. Dreisbach
Julian H. Baumann, Jr.	James G. Leyden, Jr.
Daniel L. Klein	Frederick L. Cottrell, III
Donald A. Bussard	Bernard J. Kelley
William J. Wade	Robert J. Stearn, Jr.
Thomas L. Ambro	William A. Yemc
Jesse A. Finkelstein	Mark D. Collins
Samuel A. Nolen	Lisa A. Schmidt
Thomas A. Beck	Doneene Keemer Damon
John A. Parkins, Jr.	William J. Haubert

Michael D. Allen	Tracy L. McGloin
Jennifer C. Bebko	Dawn A. Miello
Thad J. Bracegirdle	Jocelyn D. Margolin
David S. Conway	John S. Mills
Catherine G. Dearlove	Jeffrey L. Moyer
Daniel J. DeFranceschi	Daniel J. Munley
Raymond J. DiCamillo	Dennis W. O'Neill
John T. Dorsey	(Not admitted in DE)
Richard J. Facciolo	Mark V. Purpura
(Not admitted in DE)	Srinivas M. Raju
Eric N. Feldman	Leanne J. Reese
Brigitte V. Fresco	Michael K. Reilly
Dominick T. Gattuso	Deirdre M. Richards
Melanie L. George	(Not admitted in DE)
Christine M. Gorgone	Christopher D. Romaine
Megan Semple Greenberg	Janine M. Salomone
Paul N. Heath	Eric A. Schwartzman
Kelly A. Herring	Jeremy R. Schwer
Tara J. Hoffner	Chad M. Shandler
Geoffrey S. Kercsmar	Russell C. Silberglied
John H. Knight	Deborah E. Spivack
(Not admitted in DE)	Michael R. Stein
Thomas H. Kovach	(Not admitted in DE)
(Not admitted in DE)	Melissa K. Stubenberg
Peter B. Ladig	(Not admitted in DE)
Gregory W. Ladner	James Tobia
J. Travis Laster	Helen L. Winslow

For full biographical listings, see the Martindale-Hubbell Law Directory

SMITH, KATZENSTEIN & FURLOW LLP (AV)

The Corporate Plaza, 800 Delaware Avenue, P.O. Box 410, 19899
Telephone: 302-652-8400
Fax: 302-652-8405
Email: info@skfdelaware.com *URL:* http://www.SKFDelaware.com

(See Next Column)

SMITH, KATZENSTEIN & FURLOW LLP, *Wilmington—Continued*

MEMBERS OF FIRM

Craig B. Smith
Robert J. Katzenstein
David A. Jenkins
Laurence V. Cronin
Brett D. Fallon
Charles E. Butler

Michele C. Gott
Kathleen M. Miller

OF COUNSEL

Clark W. Furlow
Anne E. Bookout

For full biographical listings, see the Martindale-Hubbell Law Directory

YOUNG CONAWAY STARGATT & TAYLOR, LLP (AV)

Eleventh Floor, Rodney Square North, P.O. Box 391, 19899-0391
Telephone: 302-571-6600
Telecopy: 302-571-1253
Email: ycst@ycst.com *URL:* http://www.ycst.com
Georgetown, Delaware Office: 110 West Pine Street.
Telephone: 302-856-3571.
Telecopy: 302-856-9338.

MEMBERS OF FIRM

H. Albert Young (1904-1982)
H. James Conaway, Jr. (1922-1990)
Bruce M. Stargatt
Stuart B. Young
Ben T. Castle
Sheldon A. Weinstein
Sheldon N. Sandler
Richard A. Levine
Richard A. Zappa
Frederick William Iobst
David C. McBride
Richard H. Morse
Joseph M. Nicholson
John Vincent Alexander
Barry M. Willoughby
Josy W. Ingersoll
Anthony G. Flynn
Jerome K. Grossman
Eugene A. DiPrinzio
James L. Patton, Jr.
Robert L. Thomas
William D. Johnston
Timothy J. Snyder
Laura Davis Jones
Bruce L. Silverstein
William W. Bowser
Larry J. Tarabicos
Richard A. DiLiberto, Jr.
Melanie K. Sharp
Cassandra Faline Kaminski
Richard J. A. Popper
Jan R. Jurden
Teresa A. Cheek
Sasson David Peress
Neilli Mullen Walsh
Janet Z. Charlton
Robert S. Brady
Joel A. Waite
James P. Hughes, Jr.
Brent C. Shaffer

OF COUNSEL

William F. Taylor
Edward B. Maxwell, 2nd

ASSOCIATES

M. Blake Cleary
Richard H. Cross, Jr.
Matthew P. Denn
Richard A. Estacio (Not admitted in DE)
Drewry N. Fennell
Danielle B. Gibbs
Lisa B. Goodman
Craig D. Grear
Edwin J. Harron
Scott A. Holt
Timothy Jay Houseal
Edward J. Kosmowski (Not admitted in DE)
Martin S. Lessner
Maureen D. Luke
Pauline K. Morgan
Michael R. Nestor
Nicole M. Orfanello
John J. Paschetto
Stephen Rahaim
Brendan Linehan Shannon
John W. Shaw
Leon L. Vinokur
Natalie S. Wolf
Christian Douglas Wright
Matthew G. Zaleski, III

GEORGETOWN, DELAWARE OFFICE

RESIDENT PARTNERS

Craig A. Karsnitz

ASSOCIATE

E. Scott Bradley

For full biographical listings, see the Martindale-Hubbell Law Directory

DISTRICT OF COLUMBIA

WASHINGTON, D.C. Co.

AKIN, GUMP, STRAUSS, HAUER & FELD, L.L.P. (AV)

A Registered Limited Liability Partnership including Professional Corporations
1333 New Hampshire Avenue, N.W., Suite 400, 20036
Telephone: 202-887-4000
Fax: 202-887-4288
URL: http://www.akingump.com
Dallas, Texas Office: 1700 Pacific Avenue, Suite 4100.
Telephone: 214-969-2800.
FAX: 214-969-4343.
Austin, Texas Office: Frost Bank Plaza, 816 Congress Avenue, Suite 1900.
Telephone: 512-499-6200.
Fax: 512-499-6290.

(See Next Column)

San Antonio, Texas Office: 300 Convent Street, Suite 1500.
Telephone: 210-281-7000.
Houston, Texas Office: 1900 Pennzoil Place-South Tower, 711 Louisiana Street.
Telephone: 713-220-5800.
New York, New York Office: 590 Madison Avenue.
Telephone: 212-872-1000.
Fax: 212-872-1002.
Philadelphia, Pennsylvania Office: One Commerce Square, 2005 Market Street, Suite 2200.
Telephone: 215-965-1200.
Fax: 215-965-1210.
Brussels, Belgium Office: Akin, Gump, Strauss, Hauer & Feld, 65 Avenue Louise, P.B. #7, 1050.
Telephone: (+32 2) 535-29-11.
Moscow, Russia Office: Ducat Place II, 7 Gasheka Street, Moscow 123056.
Telephone: 011/7-095-974-2411.
Fax: 011/7-095-974-2412.
Los Angeles, California Office: 2029 Century Park East, Suite 2600.
Telephone: 310-229-1000.
Fax: 310-229-1001.
London, England Office: Akin, Gump, Strauss, Hauer & Feld, One Angel Court.
Telephone: 011/44-171-726-9600.
Fax: 011/44-171-726-9610.

MEMBERS OF FIRM

Donald C. Alexander
Edward John Allera
Richard N Appel
Victoria A. Baylin (Not admitted in DC)
Andrew G. Berg
William A. Bianco
Janet C. Boyd
Linda S. Broyhill
David P. Callet (P.C.)
J. David Carlin
Patricia A. Casey
Joel M. Cohn (P.C.)
Warren E. Connelly
Colleen M. Coyle
Tom W. Davidson
Smith W. Davis (P.C.)
Sylvia A. de Leon
Frank J. Donatelli
David A. Donohoe (P.C.)
Marilyn L. Doria
John M. Dowd
David H. Eisenstat
Joseph P. Esposito (P.C.)
Cheryl Adams Falvey
James S. Friedlander
David Geanacopoulos
Richard M. Gittleman
Lawrence J. Goffney, Jr. (Not admitted in DC)
Avrum M. Goldberg
Larry S. Gondelman
Spencer S. Griffith
Paul E. Gutermann
Scott M. Heimberg
Frank H. Henneburg
Paul B. Hewitt
Laurence J. Hoffman
William G. Hundley
Howard B. Jacobson
Joel Jankowsky (P.C.)
Owen M. Johnson, Jr., (P.C.)
Ronald M. Johnson
Vernon E. Jordan, Jr.
Daniel Joseph
Donald Michael Kaye
Sukhan Kim
Merrill L. Kramer (P.C.)
James C. Langdon, Jr.
Malcolm Lassman (P.C.)
Vladimir Lechtman
Roy P. Lessy, Jr.
Lawrence D. Levien (P.C.)
Donald R. Livingston
Jorge Lopez, Jr.
Terence J. Lynam
Mark J. MacDougall
Kathryn D. MacKinnon
Michael J. Madigan (P.C.)
Michael S. Mandel
Michael S. Marcus (P.C.)
R. Bruce McLean
Thomas P. McLish
Luis R. Mejia
Bruce S. Mendelsohn
Michael J. Mueller
Daniel L. Nash
Robin M. Nuschler
David B. Palmer
Russell W. Parks, Jr.
Duane H. Pellervo
Anthony T. Pierce
Robert G. Pinco
Donald R. Pongrace
Michael Quigley
Dennis M. Race
Franz R. Rassman
Steven R. Ross
Jerry E. Rothrock
Edward L. Rubinoff (P.C.)
George R. Salem (P.C.)
Robert Salcido
Stanley J. Samorajczyk (P.C.)
Randall L. Sarosdy
Sanford M. Saunders, Jr.
C. Stevens Seale (Not admitted in DC)
Donald E. Segal
Earl L. Segal
Jeffrey K. Sherwood
Barney J. Skladany, Jr.
Valerie A. Slater
Roxane N. Sokolove
Jonathan S. Spaeth
Daniel L. Spiegel
C. Fairley Spillman
Robert S. Strauss
Larry E. Tanenbaum
L. Kay Tatum
Henry A. Terhune
W. Randolph Teslik (P.C.)
Leslie M. Turner
Charles L. Warren
S. Bruce Wilson
Richard L. Wyatt, Jr. (P.C.)
Clifford J. Zatz
Jay D. Zeiler

ASSOCIATES

Stephanie M. Agli
Carrie Hill Allen
William F. Allen
Paige S. Anderson
Richard W. Black (Not admitted in DC)
Karen L. Bland
Sanjoy K. Bose
Victoria L. Botvin
Robert T. Bradford
Dean S. Brockbank
Katherine D. Brodie
David A. Catania
Risa B. Cherry
Timothy J. Choppin
Joel A. Christie
Patrick J. Christmas, II
Michael L. Converse
Erin Dozier (Not admitted in DC)
Dmitri I. Dubograev
Christopher P. Edelson
Robin A. Fastenau
Michael Ferrans

(See Next Column)

AKIN, GUMP, STRAUSS, HAUER & FELD L.L.P.—*Continued*

ASSOCIATES (Continued)

Catherine J. Finnegan
Laura E. FitzRandolph
Mary Ellen Fleck
Thomas R. Freeman
Heather French
(Not admitted in DC)
Karen M. Ginsberg
Brian S. Gleicher
Karen E. Goldmeier
Alison Leigh Gray
Michele S. Greif
Todd H. Halpern
(Not admitted in DC)
Jonathan H. Hambrick
Michael Hamra
Anne T. Hickey
Beth L. Hirschfelder
M. Leah Hudson
(Not admitted in DC)
Michael J. Huppe
Elizabeth A. Hyman
Sylvia F. James
Charles W. Johnson, IV
Mary L. Johnson
Steven G. Johnston
Janine L. Jones
Daniel H. Jorjani
Jonathan R. Joyce
(Not admitted in DC)
Kenneth P. Kaplan
Jeffrey M. King
Jo-Ellyn Sakowitz Klein
Robert H. Kluge, III
(Not admitted in DC)
Jonathan M. Krell
(Not admitted in DC)
Kevin M. Lally
(Not admitted in DC)
Paul J. Larsen
(Not admitted in DC)
Phillip R. Marchesiello
Elizabeth A. Matthews
Thomas J. McCarthy
(Not admitted in DC)
Mikaela A. McDermott
(Not admitted in DC)
Daniel F. McInnis
Tracy B. McKibben
Scott D. McKinney
Sydney H. Mintzer
Jill D. Morganbesser
Richard J. Mrizek
(Not admitted in DC)
James J. Murphy
Cristina G. Niccolini
(Not admitted in DC)
David J. Ohrenstein
Beth J. Olson
Ardra M. O'Neal
(Not admitted in DC)
Amy E. Overton
Mona Papillon
(Not admitted in DC)
Chan Park
(Not admitted in DC)
J. David Park
Evangeline C. Paschal
Laurent C. Pavageau
Elizabeth C. Peterson
Daniel E. Pollner
David H. Quigley
John M. Rafferty
Aaron J. Reed
John M. Remy
Mark E. Ricardo
(Not admitted in DC)
Thais L. Richardson
Bruce G. Rosen
Matthew A. Rossi
Reed L. Russell
(Not admitted in DC)
George N. Sapio
Jennifer McKeone Saunders
Scott E. Seewald
Kristine L. Sendek
Rajat R. Shah
W. Dixon Shay, III
Djaouida Siaci
(Not admitted in DC)
Dana E. Singiser
(Not admitted in DC)
Richard H. Sinkfield, III
James O. Smith
David G. Socie
Kimberly M. Stallings
Catherine McCallie Stavlas
Todd M. Stenerson
Theodore M. Sullivan
(Not admitted in DC)
Anthony W. Swisher
Esther G. Tamburo
Jason E. Tankel
(Not admitted in DC)
Joshua C. Toll
Thomas B. Trimble
James R. Tucker, Jr.
(Not admitted in DC)
Andrea T. Vavonese
Jedd B. Vertman
Lisa A. Weinman
(Not admitted in DC)
Robin Mahler Weisman
Zachary N. Wittenberg
(Not admitted in DC)
Stacey L. Wruble
Elizabeth R. Yang

COUNSEL

Sam J. Alberts
Stephen J. Claeys
Maryellen Connor
Sean G. D'Arcy
Shari L. Fleishman
Vicki Scheer Foster
Stefan A. Hagerup
Gary A. Heimberg
John R. Jacob
Kathleen A. Kenealy
Robert G. Lian, Jr.
Carl L. Liederman
Alan S. Macdonald
Michele Harrington Murphy
J. Steven Patterson
Wynn H. Segall
Elizabeth Wells Skaggs
Mark D. Taylor

SENIOR COUNSEL

Kenneth D. Alderfer
Paul A. Belvin
Richard P. Bonsignore
Alex Chartove
Marlene M. Colucci
Larisa E. Dobriansky
William J. Farah
Edwin P. Geils
Lars-Erik A. Hjelm
Susan Heck Lent
Patrick F. J. Macrory
Paul E. Mirengoff
Kenneth E. Natale
James C. Osborne, Jr.
William E. Potts, Jr.
Stark Ritchie
James P. Scanlan
Scott A. Spear
(Not admitted in DC)
Dawn E. Starr
Steven A. Weiler
Samuel Wolff
Mark M. Yacura

For full biographical listings, see the Martindale-Hubbell Law Directory

ALLEN, JOHNSON, ALEXANDER & KARP, P.A. (AV)

1707 L Street, N.W., Suite 1050, 20036
Telephone: 202-828-4141
Fax: 202-429-8798
Email: ajakdc@aol.com
Baltimore, Maryland Office: Suite 1540, 100 East Pratt Street.
Telephone: 410-727-5000.

D'Ana E. Johnson
George B. Breen

Representative Clients: Scottsdale Insurance Co.; Nautilus Insurance Co.; Jefferson Insurance Co.; Liberty Mutual Insurance Co.; Avis Rent-A-Car; Otis Elevator Co.; Montgomery Elevator Co.; Admiral Insurance Co.; Local Government Insurance Trust; Penn National Insurance Co.

For full biographical listings, see the Martindale-Hubbell Law Directory

ANDERSON KILL & OLICK, L.L.P. (AV)

2000 Pennsylvania Avenue, N.W. Suite 7500, 20006
Telephone: 202-728-3100
Fax: 202-728-3199
Email: akodc@andersonkill.com *URL:* http://www.andersonkill.com
New York, N.Y. Office: Anderson Kill & Olick, P.C., 1251 Avenue of the Americas.
Telephone: 212-278-1000.
Fax: 212-278-1733
Philadelphia, Pennsylvania Office: Anderson Kill & Olick, P.C., 1600 Market Street.
Telephone: 215-568-4202.
Fax: 215-568-4573.
Newark, New Jersey Office: Anderson Kill & Olick, P.C. One Gateway Center, Suite 901.
Telephone: 973-642-5858.
Fax: 973-621-6361.
Chicago, Illinois Office: Anderson Kill & Olick, 227 West Monroe Street, Mezzanine Level.
Telephone: 312-857-2500.
Fax: 312-857-0122.

Paula M. Bresnan Gibson
(Not admitted in DC)
Steven J. Dolmanish
(Not admitted in DC)
Michele A. Gallagher
Lorelie S. Masters
Rhonda D. Orin
Lia B. Royle
(Not admitted in DC)
Koorosh Talieh

For full biographical listings, see the Martindale-Hubbell Law Directory

ANDREWS & KURTH L.L.P. (AV)

A Registered Limited Liability Partnership
Suite 300, 1701 Pennsylvania Avenue, N.W., 20006
Telephone: 202-662-2700
Telecopier: 202-662-2739
Email: webmaster@andrews-kurth.com *URL:* http://www.andrews-kurth.com
Houston, Texas Office: Suite 4200, 600 Travis, 77002.
Telephone: 713-220-4200.
Telecopier: 713-220-4285. E-Mail: webmaster@andrews-kurth.com.
Dallas, Texas Office: 1717 Main Street, Suite 3700.
Telephone: 214-659-4400.
Telecopier: 214-659-4401.
The Woodlands, Texas Office: Suite 150, 2170 Buckthorne Place, 77380.
Telephone: 713-220-4801.
Telecopier: 713-220-4815.
Los Angeles, California Office: Suite 4200, 601 South Figueroa Street.
Telephone: 213-896-3100.
Telecopier: 213-896-3137.
New York, N.Y. Office: 805 Third Avenue, 10022.
Telephone: 212-850-2800.
Telecopier: 212-850-2929.
London, England Office: 2 Creed Court, 5-11 Ludgate Hill, EC4M 7AA.
Telephone: 0171-236-3456.
Telecopier: 0171-236-4276.

MEMBERS OF FIRM

James A. Blalock III
Michael J. Fremuth
Catherine S. Gallagher
Richard C. Green
Anthony J. Ivancovich
Judy A. Johnson
Thomas R. Kline
Jay G. Martin
Kenneth M. Minesinger
(Not admitted in DC)
Shemin V. Proctor
Mark F. Sundback
Bruce A. Templeton
Kenneth L. Wiseman

OF COUNSEL

Hu A. Benton
Dorothea W. Dickerman
Douglas V. Rigler
Thomas E. Starnes
Craig B. Young

ASSOCIATES

Charles M. Crout
(Not admitted in DC)
Kristina Ann Mack
(Not admitted in DC)
Julie Nolan Papa
(Not admitted in DC)
Scott A. Richie
Kevin D. Ryan
(Not admitted in DC)
David S. Shaffer
Sylvia L. Sironi
(Not admitted in DC)

(See Next Column)

ANDREWS & KURTH L.L.P., *Washington—Continued*

ASSOCIATES (Continued)

Peter J. Thompson
Richard F. Trimber (Not admitted in DC)
Gabriel B. Valle (Not admitted in DC)

SENIOR ATTORNEY

Johanna S. Coulter (Not admitted in DC)

For full biographical listings, see the Martindale-Hubbell Law Directory

ARNOLD & PORTER (AV)

Thurman Arnold Building, 555 Twelfth Street, N.W., 20004-1202
Telephone: 202-942-5000
Cable Address: "Arfopo"
Telecopy: 202-942-5999
URL: http://www.arnoldporter.com
Los Angeles, California Office: 44th Floor, 777 South Figueroa Street, 90017-2513.
Telephone: 213-243-4000.
Telecopy: 213-243-4199.
Denver, Colorado Office: 1700 Lincoln Street, 80203-4540.
Telephone: 303-863-1000.
Telecopy: 303-832-0428.
New York, New York Office: 399 Park Avenue, 10022-4690.
Telephone: 212-715-1000.
Telecopy: 212-715-1399.
The United Kingdom Office: Tower 42, 25 Old Broad Street, London, England, EC2N 1HQ.
Telephone: 011-44-0171-786-6100.
FAX: 011-44-0171-786-6299.

WASHINGTON, D.C. OFFICE

MEMBERS OF FIRM

Bruce A. Adams
Richard M. Alexander
David B. Apatoff
Geoffrey F. Aronow
Richard E. Baltz
Leonard H. Becker
Donald O. Beers
Kathleen A. Behan
Alexander E. Bennett
Paul S. Berger
David B. Bergman
Michael L. Bernstein
Blake A. Biles
Edward E. Bintz
Peter K. Bleakley
Brooksley Born
Jeffrey A. Burt
Michael Caglioti
Susan Booth Cassidy
Howard Neil Cayne
Bruce M. Chadwick
Jerome I. Chapman
Martha L. Cochran
Robert B. Conley
William Edro Cook, Jr.
James L. Cooper
George E. Covucci
Patricia Ann Dean
Eli Whitney Debevoise, II
Jacqueline R. Denning
Norman Diamond
Steven S. Diamond
A. Patrick Doyle
David S. Eggert
Steven R. Englund
Richard S. Ewing
Deborah L. Feinstein
Roger P. Fendrich
Richard M. Firestone
James F. Fitzpatrick
Samuel A. Flax
Sonia (Turcotte) Fois
Theodore D. Frank
David F. Freeman, Jr.
Milton V. Freeman
Melvin C. Garbow
Murray R. Garnick
Robert A. Garrett
David P. Gersch
Neil M. Goodman
Michael D. Goodwin
Patrick J. Grant
Julius M. Greisman
Peter T. Grossi, Jr.
Drew A. Harker
Cathy Hoffman
Philip W. Horton
Roberta Lazarus Horton
Joseph G. Howe, III
Richard L. Hubbard
Gary E. Humes
Darryl W. Jackson
Richard A. Johnson
Robert J. Jones
James P. Joseph
Kenneth I. Juster
Steven Kaplan
Andrew T. Karron
Hadrian R. Katz
David R. Kentoff
Werner Kronstein
M. Sean Laane
Stuart J. Land
J. Stephen Lawrence, Jr.
Kenneth A. Letzler
Arthur N. Levine
Daniel Martin Lewis
Jack L. Lipson
Robert S. Litt
Steven P. Lockman
Richard M. Lucas
Dennis G. Lyons
Helene B. Madonick
Robert E. Mannion
Jonathan S. Martel
Mark R. Merley
Michael B. Mierzewski
Thomas H. Milch
Bruce L. Montgomery
Susan T. Morita
S. Lee Narrow
Irvin B. Nathan
Anne J. O'Brien
Charles D. Ossola
Robert B. Ott
Andrew Pace
L. Stevenson Parker
Jennifer S. Perkins
Stephanie M. Phillipps
Stephen W. Porter
Jack Quinn
Claire E. Reade
Steven G. Reade
Thomas W. Richardson
Walter J. Rockler
William D. Rogers
Richard L. Rosen
Robert D. Rosenbaum
Stanford G. Ross
Eric A. Rubel
Michael J. Rufkahr
Stephen M. Sacks
James J. Sandman
Ronald A. Schechter
K. Peter Schmidt
Lawrence A. Schneider
Scott B. Schreiber
Matthew J. Seiden
Michael T. Shor
Norman M. Sinel

(See Next Column)

WASHINGTON, D.C. OFFICE

MEMBERS OF FIRM (Continued)

Jeffrey H. Smith
Michael N. Sohn
Michael S. Solender
Lester Sotsky
Mary Gabrielle Sprague
Mark H. Stumpf
Bryan J. Tomasek
Asim Varma
G. Duane Vieth
William W. Vodra
Douglas L. Wald
Daniel Waldman
Robert N. Weiner
Joseph D. West
Leslie Wharton
Robert H. Winter
Jay Kelly Wright
Thurman Arnold (1891-1969)
Paul A. Porter (1904-1975)
William L. McGovern (1913-1977)
B. Howell Hill (1922-1977)
James R. McAlee (1931-1985)
David H. Lloyd (1938-1988)
James A. Dobkin (1968-1999)
Mason C. Brown (1945-1994)
Thomas J. McGrew (1942-1995)
Nancy K. Mintz (1942-1996)
Charles H. Cochran (1946-1997)
Vivian Lee Hobbs (1954-1997)
Carolyn E. Agger (1909-1997)
Elizabeth Weightman (1962-1998)

OF COUNSEL

J. Bradway Butler
Karen L. Casser
Timothy R. Dewitt
Michael A. Lee
Thomas E. Silfen
Melvin Spaeth
James T. Walsh

SPECIAL COUNSEL

Waltraut Susanne Addy
Theodore S. Boone
Mary E. Cassidy
Peter J. Cinquegrani
March Coleman
Marcia Ann Cranberg
Lawrence E. Culleen
Beth S. DeSimone
Michael R. Geske
Howard L. Hyde
Jean E. Kalicki
David E. Korn
Joan G. Ochs
Nancy L. Perkins
Randal M. Shaheen
Peter B. Szegedy-Maszak
Sharon L. Taylor

ASSOCIATES

Eric L. Alexander
Richard G. Alexander
Bruce H. Andrews
Michael C. Augustini
Layli Miller Bashir
Richard B. Benenson
Judith Bernstein-Gaeta
Laura Respess Biddle
L. Elizabeth Bowles
Heather Cameron
Daniel A. Cantor
Arturo Caraballo
William J. Carmody
William P. Cejudo
Scott A. Chambers
Lisa ReVeal Chavarria
Perry S. Clegg
Linda B. Coe
Sharon Beth Cohn
Roger P. Colinvaux
Pelayo Coll
Jeffrey J. Connaughton
Robert S. Conway
Robert M. Cooper
D. Michael Cormaney
Kathleen M. Courtis
Katherine Culliton
Michael D. Daneker
David G. Dargatis
William S. Dean
Mark E. DeWitt
Ranjit S. Dhindsa
Jamellah L. Ellis
Christina Maria Erickson
Paul Scott Feira
Justine Anne Fitzgerald
Holly R. Fogler
John A. Freedman
Paul D. Freshour
Paul Alexander Friedman
Matthew L. Gannon
Matthew W. Garber
Jeffrey D. Gerrish
Jonathan Gleklen
Gary R. Greenstein
Kristen L. Gustafson
Jeffrey L. Handwerker
Myles R. Hansen
Catherine A. Hazlitt
Scott D. Helsel
Susan E. Hendrickson
Courtney E. Ingraffia
Stephen E. Jones
Michael A. Johnson
Sarah Elizabeth Kahn
Beth R. Kallet
Simon Kann
Roy A. Katriel
Matthew D. Keiser
Timothy J. Kelly
Thomas L. Klein
Helene T. Krasnoff
Barry Kreiswirth
Carol Williams Lally
Bertrand R. Lanciault III
Gordon Lederman
Mitchell D. Lee
Wendy J. Levenson
Joel Garner Levi
Gregory H. Levine
Jeffrey A. Liesemer
Franklin R. Liss
Nicolas T. Maduros
Christopher D. Man
Robert E. Mascola
John C. Massaro
Duane J. Mauney
Rosemary Maxwell
Robert A. McCarter III
Amy L. McGinnis
Laura K. McNally
Mark A. Merva
Kendall Millard
Randall K. Miller
Mark J. Montano
Wilson D. Mudge
Stevenson O. Munro
Leslie A. Nickel
David M. Orta
Amanda J. Paracuellos
Daniel S. Pariser
Douglas S. Pelley
Amy K. Phillips
Annalisa Pizzarello
Ian Plant
Kenneth L. Pollack
Stacy J. Pollock
Nicholas Porritt
Thorn L. Pozen
Elissa J. Preheim
Lisa A. Price
Michael D. Raibman
Prakash Rajamani
Amy E. Ralph
David A Rhodes
Jeff Richman
Amy B. Rifkind
James M. Rosenthal
Julie B. Rottenberg
Anika K. Sanders
Peter J. Schildkraut
Kenneth L. Schwartz

(See Next Column)

ARNOLD & PORTER—*Continued*

ASSOCIATES (Continued)

P. Moni SenGupta
Jule L. Sigall
Edward H. Sisson
Darren C. Skinner
Carey W. Smith
James E. Smith
Julie K. Stapel
Tim Stelzig
Ellen Hochstedler Steury
Jonathan R. Streeter
Steve C. Suk
Eric Suter
Thomas D. Sydnor, II
Flora Szilagyi
Joy Taylor
Cathlene A. Tharp
Kevin T. Traskos
Anne McBride Walker
Amy E. Weissman
Erica Y. Williams
Christopher Winters
Amy J. Yanoff
Michael D. Yeh
Cynthia Finn Yuffee
Elliott Zenick
Walter F. Zenner

For full biographical listings, see the Martindale-Hubbell Law Directory

ARTER & HADDEN LLP (AV)

1801 K Street, N.W., Suite 400K, 20006
Telephone: 202-775-7100
Facsimile: 202-857-0172
URL: http://www.arterhadden.com
In Cleveland, Ohio: 1100 Huntington Building, 925 Euclid Avenue, 44115-1475.
Telephone: 216-696-1100.
Fax: 216-696-2645.
In Columbus, Ohio: Suite 1200, One Columbus, 10 West Broad Street, 43215-3422.
Telephone: 614-221-3155.
Fax: 614-221-0479.
In Dallas, Texas: 1717 Main Street, Suite 4100, 75201-4605.
Telephone: 214-761-2100.
Fax: 214-741-7139.
In Dayton, Ohio: Suite 2310, 40 North Main Street, 45423.
Telephone: 973-223-4701.
Fax: 937-223-0170.
In Los Angeles, California: 725 South Figueroa Street, Suite 3400, 90017.
Telephone: 213-430-3000.
Fax: 212-617-9255.
In Irvine, California: Five Park Plaza, Suite 1000, Jamboree Center, 92714.
Telephone: 949-252-7500.
Fax: 949-833-9604.
In Austin, Texas: 100 Congress Avenue, Suite 1800, 78701.
Telephone: 512-479-6403.
Fax: 512-469-3552.
In San Antonio, Texas: One Riverwalk Place, 700 North Saint Mary's Street, Suite 900, 78205.
Telephone: 210-805-8497.
Fax: 210-805-8519.
In San Francisco, California: Two Embarcadero Center, 5th Floor, 94111.
Telephone: 415-617-2100.
Fax: 415-912-3636.
In Sacramento, California: Wells Fargo Center, 400 Capitol Center Mall, Suite 900, 95814.
Telephone: 916-449-3917.
Fax: 916-449-8249.
In San Diego, California: 402 West Broadway, Sixth Floor, 92101.
Telephone: 619-238-0001.
Fax: 619-238-8333.
In Woodland Hills, California: 5959 Topanga Canyon Boulevard, Suite 244, 91367.
Telephone: 818-712-0036.
Fax: 818-346-6502.

MEMBERS OF FIRM

Charles K. Arter (1875-1957)
Peter L. Canzano
William K. Dabaghi
Richard A. Dean
Lawrence R. Freedman
Paul H. Friedman
Roger P. Furey
Joseph V. Gatti
William L. Gehrig
Lawrence H. Gesner
Michael R. Goodstein
Philip M. Horowitz
James Grier Hoyt
Paula A. Jameson
W. James Jonas, III
William K. Keane
John A. Hadden (1886-1979)
Laura Metcoff Klaus
Howard M. Liberman
Thomas G. Loeffler
John D. Maddox
David L. Miller
Jerry A. Moore III
Michael P. Murphy
Michael J. Pollack
Jerold I. Schneider
David J. Shaffer
Thomas K. Slattery
Francis R. Snodgrass
Mark E. Solomons
Evelyn M. Suarez
James U. Troup
Allan J. Weiner

OF COUNSEL

Myles J. Ambrose
Franklin Blackstone, III
Carla Calobrisi
Madeliene H. Dobbins
(Not admitted in DC)
Karen Rapaport Esser
Jerome A. Hochberg
Robert H. Jackson
Jodi Mintzer Krame
Patricia Adams McQuillen
Thomas H. Odom
Lawrence M. Sung
Robert J. Ungar
Mark Van Bergh

(See Next Column)

ASSOCIATES

Marc R. Baluda
Corina R. Caplan
Richard L. Davis
Sylvia D. Davis
Oonagh L. Deasy
(Not admitted in DC)
Gregory S. Feder
Elizabeth A. Hammond
Joanna S. Han
(Not admitted in DC)
Rachelle A. Kagan
Robert Richard Kaplan, Jr.
(Not admitted in DC)
Caroline A. Leonard
Jonathan W. Lipshie
James H. Lister
Matthew J. Murcko
Rebecca A. Naser
W. William Prochot
Peter J. Riebling
Brian D. Robinson
Ronald A. Schmidt
(Not admitted in DC)
Naomi S. Travers
Amy Wilmot
Alexandra Zelikson

Reference: The Century Bank, Washington, D.C.

For full biographical listings, see the Martindale-Hubbell Law Directory

BAKER BOTTS L.L.P. (AV)

A Registered Limited Liability Partnership
The Warner, 1299 Pennsylvania Avenue, N.W., 20004-2400
Telephone: 202-639-7700
Fax: 202-639-7832
Email: postmaster@bakerbotts.com *URL:* http://www.bakerbotts.com
Houston, Texas Office: One Shell Plaza, 910 Louisiana.
Telephone: 713-229-1234.
Austin, Texas Office: 1600 San Jacinto Center, 98 San Jacinto Boulevard.
Telephone: 512-322-2500.
Dallas, Texas Office: 2001 Ross Avenue.
Telephone: 214-953-6500.
New York, New York Office: 599 Lexington Avenue.
Telephone: 212-705-5000.
Moscow, Russia Office: 10 ul. Bolshaya Dimitrovka (formerly Pushkinskaya), 103031.
Telephone: 7095/921-5300 (Local); 7501/929-7070 (International).
London, England Office: 45 Ludgate Hill.
Telephone: 0171-778-1400 (Local); 011-44-171-778-1400 (International).
Baku, Azerbaijan Office: 6-10 Vagif Mustafa-zadeh Street, Third Floor, Icheri Sheher, 370004.
Telephone: 994-12-97-63-88 (Local); 011-994-12-97-63-88 (International).

MEMBERS OF FIRM

James A. Baker IV
James Addison Baker, III
(Not admitted in DC)
J. Patrick Berry
William M. Bumpers
O. Donaldson Chapoton
Kevin B. Dent
Diana L. Dietrich
James R. Doty
Thomas J. Eastment
Leslie Anne Freiman
Steven R. Hunsicker
Bruce F. Kiely
William D. Kramer
Steven L. Leifer
Mark K. Lewis
Martin T. Lutz
Randolph Quaile McManus
Harold D. Murry, Jr.
Scott F. Partridge
Nancy M. Persechino
B. Donovan Picard
David N. Powers
James Remenick
Daniel J. Riley
Mary C. Spearing
(Not admitted in DC)
Jeffrey A. Stonerock
David A. Super
Rodger L. Tate
Kirk K. Van Tine

SPECIAL COUNSEL

James B. Arpin
Debra Raggio Bolton
Robert J. Bohme
(Not admitted in DC)
Jay M. Cantor
Robert L. Troike

ASSOCIATES

Steven A. Alerding
Jessie Marie Brooks
Floyd B. Chapman
Dylan Cors
Wendy L. Cox
Michael P. Coyle
Kelly Riley Donovan
Courtney Eden
(Not admitted in DC)
Jacqueline H. Fine
Joshua B. Frank
Michael A. Gold
Gregory J. Golden
Peter K. Grose
Renu K. Gupta
(Not admitted in DC)
Lois McKenna Henry
Debra J. Jezouit
Jon B. Jordan
Jane Boland Keough
Robert A. King
(Not admitted in DC)
Meredith M. Lackey
(Not admitted in DC)
Paul T. Luther
William F. Nixon
Nikesh R. Patel
Clara M. Poffenberger
Mary Ann Poirier
Laurence H. Posorske
Martin Schaefermeier
Lynn M. Schug
(Not admitted in DC)
James F. H. Scott
(Not admitted in DC)
Andrew Skale
(Not admitted in DC)
Tamar C. Stanley
Clifford E. Stevens, Jr.
(Not admitted in DC)
O. Kevin Vincent
Wendy Barrett Warren
Jennifer J. Yi
Susan Aldrich Zoch

For full biographical listings, see the Martindale-Hubbell Law Directory

Washington—Continued

BAKER & DANIELS (AV)

805 15th Street, Suite 700, 20005
Telephone: 202-312-7440
Fax: 202-312-7441
URL: http://www.bakerdaniels.com
Indianapolis, Indiana Office: 300 North Meridian Street, 46204.
Telephone: 317-237-0300.
Fort Wayne, Indiana Office: 111 East Wayne Street, Suite 800, 46802.
Telephone: 219-424-8000.
South Bend, Indiana Office: First Bank Building, 205 West Jefferson Boulevard, 46601.
Telephone: 219-234-4149.
Elkhart, Indiana Office: 301 B South Main Street, Suite 307, 46516.
Telephone: 219-296-6000.
Qingdao, China Office: Room C, 13th Floor, Qingdao Beer Building, May 4th Square, 35 Donghai Road, 266071.
Telephone: +011-86-532-575-1051.
Fax: +011-86-532-575-1055.

MEMBERS OF FIRM

Anne Slaughter Andrew (Not admitted in DC)
Frank S. Swain (Resident)
Mark W. Weller (Not admitted in DC; Resident)

For full biographical listings, see the Martindale-Hubbell Law Directory

BAKER & HOSTETLER LLP (AV)

Washington Square, Suite 1100, 1050 Connecticut Avenue, N.W., 20036-5304
Telephone: 202-861-1500
Fax: 202-861-1783
To contact an attorney on the Internet use first initial and surname followed by @baker-hostetler.com
URL: http://www.bakerlaw.com
In Cleveland, Ohio: 3200 National City Center, 1900 East Ninth Street.
Telephone: 216-621-0200.
In Cincinnati, Ohio: 312 Walnut Street, Suite 2650.
Telephone: 513-929-3400.
In Columbus, Ohio: Capitol Square, Suite 2100, 65 East State Street.
Telephone: 614-228-1541.
In Denver, Colorado: 303 East 17th Avenue, Suite 1100.
Telephone: 303-861-0600.
In Houston, Texas: 1000 Louisiana, Suite 2000.
Telephone: 713-751-1600.
In Beverly Hills, California: 9150 Wilshire Boulevard, Suite 205.
Telephone: 310-385-7500.
In Long Beach, California: 300 Oceangate, Suite 620.
Telephone: 562-432-2827.
In Los Angeles, California: 600 Wilshire Boulevard.
Telephone: 213-624-2400.
In Orlando, Florida: SunBank Center, Suite 2300, 200 South Orange Avenue.
Telephone: 407-649-4000.

OFFICE MANAGING PARTNER

William H. Schweitzer (Managing Partner, Washington, D.C. Office)

PARTNERS

Edward Jay Beckwith
Ralph G. Blasey, III
Bruce J. Casino
Frederick W. Chockley, III
Gerald A. Connell
William F. Conroy
William J. Conti
Barry J. Cutler
Mark A. Cymrot
Matthew J. Dolan
Lee T. Ellis, Jr.
David J. Fischer
Ann K. Ford
Kelly Matthews Gerber
Frederick H. Graefe
David Alistair Grant
Leonard C. Greenebaum
Brian S. Harvey
Richard A. Hauser
Kenneth C. Howard, Jr.
Robert D. Lystad
David L. Marshall
Mario V. Mirabelli
Shelby F. Mitchell
Thomas R. Mounteer
Betty Southard Murphy
Roger A. Pies
Bruce W. Sanford
Belinda Jayne Scrimenti
Louis R. Sernoff
Lee H. Simowitz
Mark H. Tidman
Alan S. Ward
Kenneth D. Woodrow
Joanne W. Young (Resident)
Henry G. Zapruder

ASSOCIATES

Alissa J. Altongy
Marc A. Antonetti
Mark I. Bailen
Johnine P. Barnes-Pannell (Not admitted in DC)
Jennifer L. Blum
Bruce D. Brown
David S. Chung (Not admitted in DC)
Jennifer B Dine (Not admitted in DC)
Andrew J. Durkovic (Not admitted in DC)
Ana V. Farach
Judith A. Farrand
David Morgan Giles
Anne E. Hawkes (Not admitted in DC)
Samuel L. Hendrix
Meghan E. Muldoon (Not admitted in DC)
Brice D. Prince
Laurel E. Queeno
Suvarna Umakant Rajguru (Not admitted in DC)
Lisa K. Rushton

(See Next Column)

ASSOCIATES (Continued)

Elizabeth A Scully (Not admitted in DC)
Christopher T. Stephen (Not admitted in DC)
David S. Wachen
Ronald F. Wick

OF COUNSEL

E. Mark Braden
Jenifer M. Brown
Luis A. Galliani (Not admitted in United States)
Peder A. Garske
David M. Kirstein
Julia A. Oas
Madeleine B. Schaller
Guy Vander Jagt

RETIRED PARTNERS

Samuel K. Abrams
Webb C. Hayes, III
Richard H. Jones
Sargent Karch
Harlan Pomeroy

For full biographical listings, see the Martindale-Hubbell Law Directory

BAKER & MCKENZIE (AV)

815 Connecticut Avenue, N.W., 20006-4078
Telephone: (202) 452-7000
Intn'l. Dialing: (1-202) 452-7000
Facsimiles: (1-202) 452-7074, 452-7073, 452-7072
Email: washington.info@bakernet.com *URL:* http://www.bakerinfo.com
Associated Offices of Baker & McKenzie in: Almaty, Amsterdam, Bahrain, Baku, Bangkok, Barcelona, Beijing, Berlin, Bogotá, Brasília, Brussels, Budapest, Buenos Aires, Cairo, Caracas, Chicago, Dallas, Düsseldorf, Frankfurt, Geneva, Hanoi, Ho Chi Minh City, Hong Kong, Houston, Hsinchu, Juárez, Kiev, London, Madrid, Manila, Melbourne, México City, Miami, Milan, Monterrey, Moscow, Münich, New York, Palo Alto, Paris, Prague, Rio de Janeiro, Riyadh, Rome, St. Petersburg, San Diego, San Francisco, Santiago, São Paulo, Singapore, Stockholm, Sydney, Taipei, Tijuana, Tokyo, Toronto, Valencia, Warsaw and Zürich.
Correspondent Law Firm: Hadiputranto, Hadinoto & Partners, Jakarta.

MEMBERS OF FIRM

Mary C. Bennett
David A. Clanton
Nicholas F. Coward
W. Warren Crowdus, III (Not admitted in DC)
Edward E. Dyson
Thomas J. Egan, Jr.
Teresa A. Gleason
Daniel L. Goelzer
Jonathan W. Gottlieb
Dennis I. Meyer
Kevin M. O'Brien
Marc R. Paul
B. Thomas Peele III
C. David Swenson
Leonard B. Terr
Eugene Theroux
A. Duane Webber
Michael J. Zimmer

NATIONAL PARTNERS

John Francis Fitzpatrick (Not admitted in DC)
David J. Laing
Rachael E. Schwartz
Richard L. Slowinski
Lynda S. Zengerle

OF COUNSEL

Howard Adler, Jr.
Susan G. Braden
John W. Polk
John R. Reilly

RESIDENT ASSOCIATES

Margaret R. Blake
Gregory W. Bowman (Not admitted in DC)
Phoebe W. Brown (Not admitted in DC)
Brian F. Burke
Shaleim M. Carmichael
John A. Cohen
David S. Cole
R. Campbell Connell
Samir S. Desai
Harry A. Franks, Jr.
Dirk Gifford (Not admitted in DC)
Barry S. Goldsmith
Anne H. Harrison
Kenneth R. Hayduk
Janet K. Kim
Scott A. Knott (Not admitted in DC)
Jeffery P. Maydew (Not admitted in DC)
Jean A. Milner (Not admitted in DC)
Michael E. Murphy (Not admitted in DC)
Richard A. Scully
Michelle R. Wildstein (Not admitted in DC)

For full biographical listings, see the Martindale-Hubbell Law Directory

BALLARD SPAHR ANDREWS & INGERSOLL, LLP (AV)

Suite 1000 South, 601 13th Street, N.W., 20005-3807
Telephone: 202-661-2200
Fax: 202-661-2299
URL: http://www.ballardspahr.com
Baltimore, Maryland Office: 300 East Lombard Street, 19th Floor.
Telephone: 410-528-5600.
Fax: 410-528-5650.
Camden, New Jersey Office: 800 Hudson Square, 5th Floor.
Telephone: 856-541-5577.
Fax: 856-541-8772.
Denver, Colorado Office: Seventeenth Street Plaza Building, Suite 2300, 1225 17th Street.
Telephone: 303-292-2400.
Fax: 303-296-3956.
Philadelphia, Pennsylvania Office: 1735 Market Street, 51st Floor.
Telephone: 215-665-8500.
Fax: 215-834-8999.

(See Next Column)

BALLARD SPAHR ANDREWS & INGERSOLL LLP—*Continued*

Salt Lake City, Utah Office: 201 South Main Street, Suite 1200.
Telephone: 801-531-3000.
Fax: 801-531-3001.
Voorhees, New Jersey Office: Suite 100, 1101 Laurel Oak Drive.
Telephone: 856-627-8555.
Fax: 856-627-1153.

Nancy V. Alquist (Not admitted in DC)
Frederic L. Ballard, Jr.
Paul K. Casey
Joseph A. Fanone
Mary Jo George (Not admitted in DC)
Charles S. Henck
Justin P. Klein
F. Joseph Nealon
Linda B. Schakel
Howard H. Shafferman
Allan R. Winn
Kelly Mitchell Wrenn

OF COUNSEL

Katherine L. Bishop (Not admitted in DC)
Thomas R. Burns
James P. Cooke
J. Joseph Cullen (Not admitted in DC)
B. Cheryl Terio (Not admitted in DC)

Langhorne Ambrose (Not admitted in DC)
Jari Carlton Cannon (Not admitted in DC)
Eileen M. Greenbaum
Kirsten E. Keating
Marina Kravets (Not admitted in DC)
Kenneth J. Labach
Jeffrey W. Larroca
Ronald Andrew Lien (Not admitted in DC)
Paul J. Miller (Not admitted in DC)
Constantinos G. Panagopoulos
Ann Marie H. Peters
Vicky Tsilas
Kurt E. Van Engen (Not admitted in DC)
John A. Washington, Jr.

For full biographical listings, see the Martindale-Hubbell Law Directory

---

BARNES & THORNBURG (AV)

1401 Eye Street, N.W., Suite 500, 20005
Telephone: 202-289-1313
FAX: 202-289-1330
URL: http://www.btlaw.com
Indianapolis, Indiana Office: 11 South Meridian Street, 46204.
Telephone: 317-236-1313.
FAX: 317-231-7433.
Fort Wayne, Indiana Office: Suite 600, One Summit Square, 46802.
Telephone: 219-423-9440.
FAX: 219-424-8316.
South Bend, Indiana Office: 600 1st Source Bank Center, 100 North Michigan, 46601-1632.
Telephone: 219-233-1171.
FAX: 219-237-1125.
Elkhart, Indiana Office: 121 West Franklin Street, Suite 200, 46516.
Telephone: 219-293-0681.
FAX: 219-296-2535.
Chicago, Illinois Office: 2600 Chase Plaza, 10 South La Salle Street, 60603.
Telephone: 312-357-1313.
FAX: 312-759-5646.

PARTNERS

Randolph J. Stayin
Perry Palan
Richard H. Streeter
Mark J. Andrews
Paul K. Brooks
Joseph D. Lewis

OF COUNSEL

Mark M. Newman
Paul E. Fahrenkopf (Not admitted in DC)

Representative Intellectual Property Clients: CNF Transportation, Inc.; Food Processing Machinery and Supplies Association; G.S. Roofing Products Company, Inc.; Laidlaw Transportation, Inc.; National Candle Association; National Older Worker Career Center; Pittston Company; Society of Travel Agents in Government; Water and Wastewater Equipment Manufacturers Association; Wheat Gluten Industry Council.

For full biographical listings, see the Martindale-Hubbell Law Directory

---

BEVERIDGE & DIAMOND, P.C. (AV)

1350 I Street, N.W., Suite 700, 20005-3311
Telephone: 202-789-6000
Telecopier: 202-789-6190
URL: http://www.beveridgediamond.com
New York, N.Y. Office: 15th Floor, 477 Madison Avenue, 10022-5802.
Telephone: 212-702-5400.
Telecopier: 212-702-5450.
San Francisco, California Office: Beveridge & Diamond LLP, Suite 3400, One Sansome Street, 94104-4438.
Telephone: 415-397-0100.
Telecopier: 415-397-4238.
Sacramento, California Office: Beveridge & Diamond LLP, Suite 1860, 400 Capitol Mall, 95814-4407.
Telephone: 916-553-4533.
Telecopier: 916-553-4539.
Saddle Brook, New Jersey Office: Beveridge & Diamond, Park 80 West, Plaza II Suite 200, 07663-5836.

(See Next Column)

Baltimore, Maryland Office: Suite 2210, 201 North Charles Street, 21201-4150.
Telephone: 410-230-3850.
Telecopier: 410-230-3868.

Karl S. Bourdeau
Robert Brager (Also at Baltimore, MD Office)
Dean H. Cannon
Richard S. Davis
Henry L. Diamond
David M. Friedland
Aaron H. Goldberg
John S. Guttmann, Jr. (Also at New York, NY Office)
Paul E. Hagen
John N. Hanson
Harold Himmelman
Steven M. Jawetz
David S. Krakoff
Cynthia Ann Lewis
Christopher W. Mahoney
Brenda Mallory
Donald J. Patterson, Jr.
Christopher F. Regan
Thomas Richichi
Harold L. Segall
James B. Slaughter
Gary J. Smith
Kathryn E. Szmuszkovicz
Mark A. Turco (Also at Baltimore, MD Office)
Fred R. Wagner
Benjamin F. Wilson
Nancy N. Young

OF COUNSEL

Gus Bauman
Albert J. Beveridge, III
Jonathan Z. Cannon
David A. McKay

SENIOR ATTORNEY

Terry F. Quill

Stephen M. Arner
Kathryn Yessian Aspegren
Brian L. Doster
Jason A. Dunn (Not admitted in DC)
Richard J. Ferris, Jr.
Tammie M. Gregg (Not admitted in DC)
Leah A. Gregor
Matthew C. Holloran
Susan D. Loyd (Not admitted in DC)
Robert J. Phocas
Christina Guerola Sarchio
Justin A. Savage (Not admitted in DC)
Caroline Tipton
John B. Weiner
David M. Williamson

For full biographical listings, see the Martindale-Hubbell Law Directory

---

BINGHAM DANA LLP (AV)

1120 20th Street, N.W., 20036
Telephone: 202-778-6150
Telecopy: 202-778-6155
Email: info@bingham.com *URL:* http://www.bingham.com
Boston, Massachusetts Office: 150 Federal Street.
Telephone: 617-951-8000.
Telecopy: 617-951-8736.
Hartford, Connecticut Office: One State Street.
Telephone: 860-240-2700.
Fax: 860-240-2800.
Los Angeles, California Office: The Wells Fargo Center, 333 South Grand Avenue, Suite 1570.
Telephone: 213-687-2700.
Fax: 213-617-9109.
New York, New York Office: 399 Park Avenue.
Telephone: 212-318-7700.
Fax: 212-752-5378.
London, England Office: 39 Victoria Street, SWIH 0EE.
Telephone: 011-44-71-799-2646.
Telecopy: 011-44-71-799-2654.
Singapore Office: Level 15 Prudential Tower, 30 Cecil Street, 049712.
Telephone: 011.65.232.2768.
Fax: 011.65.232.2888.

RESIDENT PARTNERS

Roger D. Feldman
Yoshihide Ito (Not admitted in DC)
Paul J. Lambert
Edward R. Leahy
Barry P. Rosenthal
Peter D. Schellie
Roger L. Selfe
Neal E. Sullivan
Erica H. Weiss

OF COUNSEL

Bonnie S. Temple
Joseph P. Pelican

RESIDENT ASSOCIATES

Matthew R. Bowsher (Not admitted in DC)
Margaret Kadel Eck
Gerard P. Finn
Jennifer L. Hilliard (Not admitted in DC)
Kara Ann Parmelee (Not admitted in DC)
J. Michael Pickett

For full biographical listings, see the Martindale-Hubbell Law Directory

Washington—Continued

BROWN & WOOD LLP (AV)

1666 K Street, N.W., Suite 700, 20006-1208
Telephone: 202-533-1300
Telecopier: 202-533-1399
URL: http://www.brownwoodlaw.com
Los Angeles, California Office: 10877 Wilshire Boulevard, 90024.
Telephone: 310-443-0200.
New York, New York Office: One World Trade Center, 10048-0557.
Telephone: 212-839-5300.
San Francisco, California Office: 555 California Street, 94104-1715.
Telephone: 415-772-1200.
London, England Office: Brown & Wood, Princes Court, 7 Princes Street, EC2R 8AQ.
Telephone: 011-44-171-778-1800.
Hong Kong Office: Brown & Wood, Bank of China Tower, 1 Garden Road, Central.
Telephone: 011-852-2509-7888.
Beijing, China Office: 3527, China World Tower, China World Trade Center 1, Jian Guo Men Wai Avenue.
Telephone: 011-8610-6505-5359; 011-8610-6505-1807.

RESIDENT PARTNERS

John Arnholz
Jay Gordon Cohen
(Not admitted in DC)
Edward E. Gainor
Frank R. Goldstein
Robert M. Huber
John K. Hughes
David R. Kuney
Thomas J. Lyden
(Not admitted in DC)
Jaemin Park
(Not admitted in DC)
R. Nicholas Singh
H. John Steele
William E. Sudow

COUNSEL

Joseph V. Jest
Timothy Sadler

RESIDENT ASSOCIATES

Stacy R. Dees
Barbara Jean Endres
Matthew J. Fitzgerald
Kimberly W. Gordon
(Not admitted in DC)
Robert J. Gross
(Not admitted in DC)
Nick A. Henderson
Jeffrey R. Johnson
Phillip John Kardis
Darius R. Kingsley
Jennifer W. Lewis
Stephen H. McElhennon
(Not admitted in DC)
Byung Joon Min
Peter C. Morreale
Hanna Tedla Teshome
Craig Harrison Weise
James Z. Zhang

For full biographical listings, see the Martindale-Hubbell Law Directory

CAHILL GORDON & REINDEL (AV)

A Partnership including a Professional Corporation
1990 K Street, N.W., 20006-1103
Telephone: 202-862-8900
Facsimile: 202-862-8958
New York, N.Y. Office: 80 Pine Street.
Telephone: 212-701-3000.
European Office: 19 rue François 1er, 75008, Paris, France.
Telephone: 33.1-47.20.10.50.

RESIDENT PARTNER

Donald J. Mulvihill

COUNSEL

Corydon B. Dunham

RESIDENT ASSOCIATES

Barbara O. Brincefield
Stephen A. Myrow
Jonathan Sherman
(Not admitted in DC)
Kathy Silberthau Strom
Sanjay Wadhwa
(Not admitted in DC)

For full biographical listings, see the Martindale-Hubbell Law Directory

CARLSMITH BALL (AV)

A Partnership including Law Corporations
1201 Pennsylvania Avenue, N.W., Suite 300, 20004-2401
Telephone: 202-628-2228
Fax: 202-628-2071
Email: execdirector@carlsmith.com *URL:* http://www.carlsmith.com
Honolulu, Hawaii Office: Suite 2200, Pacific Tower, 1001 Bishop Street. P.O. Box 656, 96809-3402.
Telephone: 808-523-2500.
Fax: 808-523-0842.
Kapolei, Hawaii Office: Suite 318, Kapolei Building, 1001 Kamokila Boulevard, 96707.
Telephone: 808-523-2500.
Fax: 808-674-0850.
Wailuku, Maui Hawaii Office: Suite 400, One Main Plaza, 2200 Main Street, P.O. Box 1086, 96793-1086.
Telephone: 808-242-4535.
Fax: 808-244-4974.
Kailua-Kona, Hawaii Office: Suite 209, 75-1000 Henry Street, 96740.
Telephone: 808-329-6464.
Fax: 808-329-9450.

(See Next Column)

Hilo, Hawaii Office: 121 Waianuenue Avenue, P.O. Box 686, 96721-0686.
Telephone: 808-935-6644.
Fax: 808-935-7975.
Hagatna, Guam Office: Suite 401, Bank of Hawaii Building, 134 West Soledad Avenue, P.O. Box BF, 96932-5027.
Telephone: 671-472-6813.
Fax: 671-477-4375.
Telex: 721-6445 CWCMI GM.
Saipan, Commonwealth of the Northern Mariana Islands Office: Carlsmith Building, Capitol Hill, P.O. Box 5241, 96950-5241.
Telephone: 670-322-3455.
Fax: 670-322-3368.
Los Angeles, California Office: 9th Floor, 444 South Flower Street, 90071-2901.
Telephone: 213-955-1200.
Fax: 213-623-0032.
Mexico City, Mexico Office: Carlsmith Ball, Sierra Nevada 119, Lomas de Chapultepec, 11000 Mexico, D.F.
Telephone: 52-5-520-8514, 52-5-520-8757.
Fax: 52-5-540-1545.
Mexico, D.F. Office of Carlsmith Ball, S.C. (Authorized to practice as foreign legal consultants in Mexico): Sierra Nevada 119, Lomas de Chapultepec, 11000 Mexico, D.F.
Telephone: 52-5-520-8514, 52-5-520-8757.
Fax: 52-5-540-1545.

RESIDENT PARTNER

Nancy M. Beckner

For full biographical listings, see the Martindale-Hubbell Law Directory

CARR GOODSON WARNER, A PROFESSIONAL CORPORATION (AV)

1301 K Street, N.W., Suite 400, East Tower, 20005-3300
Telephone: 202-310-5500
Telecopier: 202-310-5555
Email: (attorney initials)@cgw-law.com *URL:* http://www.carrgoodsonwarner.com
Vienna, Virginia Office: Tycon Towers, 8000 Towers Crescent Drive, Suite 1350, 22182.
Telephone: 703-691-8818.
Baltimore, Maryland Office: 401 East Pratt Street, Suite 1622, The World Trade Center, 21202.
Telephone: 410-752-1570.
Rockville, Maryland Office: 31 Wood Lane, 20850.
Telephone: 301-424-7024.

Lawrence E. Carr, Jr.
Robert W. Goodson
Margaret H. Warner
M. Miller Baker
William J. Carter
Mark A. Collins
Catherine A. Hanrahan
David H. Jacobs
(Not admitted in DC)
Gregory A. Krauss
Robert E. Madden
Paul J. Maloney
Thomas L. McCally
Kevin M. Murphy
James G. Rizzo
Jan E. Simonsen

SENIOR COUNSEL

Peter K. Tompa

OF COUNSEL

Edward J. Krill

Juan M. Anderson
(Not admitted in DC)
Edward M. Andries
Kimberley S. Baxter
(Not admitted in DC)
Janette M. Blee
(Not admitted in DC)
Laura K. Biederman
(Not admitted in DC)
Matthew J. Cuccias
(Not admitted in DC)
Maureen A. Delaney
David J. Finucane
Pamela S. Fox
Shadonna E. Hale
Ngoc H. Lam
(Not admitted in DC)
Robert L. Magielnicki, Jr.
(Not admitted in DC)
Tina M. Maiolo
Dennis J. Quinn
Lori A.F. Ridgeway
Richard B. Rogers
Angela W. Russell
James P. Steele
Spencer K. Stephens
Ki Jun Sung
Brian M. Tauscher
Alan D. Titus
Manuel S. Varela
Timothy J. Wolf
Gloria A. Worch

For full biographical listings, see the Martindale-Hubbell Law Directory

CHADBOURNE & PARKE LLP (AV)

1200 New Hampshire Avenue, N.W., 20036
Telephone: 202-974-5600
Facsimile: 202-974-5602
New York, N.Y. Office: 30 Rockefeller Plaza, 10112.
Telephone: 212-408-5100.
Facsimile: 212-541-5369.
Los Angeles, California Office: 601 South Figueroa Street, 90017.
Telephone: 213-892-1000.
Facsimile: 213-622-9865.

(See Next Column)

CHADBOURNE & PARKE LLP—*Continued*

London, England Affiliate Office: Chadbourne & Parke, a multinational partnership of Registered Foreign Lawyers and Solicitors, Regis House, 45 King William Street, London EC4R 9AN.
Telephone: 44-171-337-8000.
Facsimile: 44-171-337-8001.
Moscow, Russia Office: 52/5 Kosmodamianskaya, 113054.
Telephone: 7095-974-2424.
Facsimile: 7095-974-2425. International satellite via US:
Telephone: 212-408-1190.
Facsimile: 212-408-1199.
Hong Kong, China Office: 1701 The Hong Kong Club Building, 3A Chater Road, Central, Hong Kong.
Telephone: 852-2842-5400.
Facsimile: 852-2521-7527.

PARTNERS

William S. D'Amico
Peter F. Fitzgerald
Andrew A. Giaccia
Cornelius J. Golden, Jr.
Kenneth W. Hansen (Not admitted in DC)
Tracey W. Laws
Keith Martin
John B. O'Sullivan
William K. Perry
David M. Raim
David K. Schumacher
Robert F. Shapiro
Ellen H. Woodbury (Not admitted in DC)

RESIDENT COUNSEL

Noam Ayali (Not admitted in DC)
Lynn N. Hargis
Susan C. Maxson
Don J. Mros

RESIDENT OF COUNSEL

Edmund E. Harvey

RESIDENT ASSOCIATES

Todd E. Alexander (Not admitted in DC)
Bonnie K. Arthur
Meaghan McGrath Beaumont
Roy S. Belden
Rohit Chaudhry (Not admitted in DC)
Carey G. Child
Lisa C. Dorr
Philip J. Goodman
Thomas G. Hohenthaner
Heléna M. Klumpp
Samuel R. Kwon (Not admitted in DC)
Joy L. Langford
Ellen M. MacDonald
Kristin L. Meikle
James W. Scarrow
William H. Schmidt, Jr.
John R. R. Tormey
Luis F. Torres
Mary Patricia Zeglin
Laura Cohen Zimmitti

STAFF ATTORNEY

Kathryn L. Cervon
Samantha Thayer (Not admitted in DC)

For full biographical listings, see the Martindale-Hubbell Law Directory

CLEARY, GOTTLIEB, STEEN & HAMILTON (AV)

2000 Pennsylvania Avenue, N.W. Suite 9000, 20006-1801
Telephone: 202-974-1500
Facsimile: 202-974-1999
New York, New York Office: One Liberty Plaza, New York, N.Y. 10006.
Telephone: 212-225-2000.
Paris, France Office: 41, Avenue de Friedland, 75008 Paris, France.
Telephone: 33-1-40-74-68-00.
Brussels, Belgium Office: Rue de la Loi 23, 1040 Brussels, Belgium.
Telephone: 32-2-287-2000.
London, England Office: City Place House, 55 Basinghall Street, London EC2V 5EH England.
Telephone: 44-71-614-2200.
Hong Kong Office: 39th Floor, Bank of China Tower, One Garden Road, Hong Kong.
Telephone: 852-2521-4122.
Tokyo, Japan Office: Cleary, Gottlieb, Steen & Hamilton Gaikokuho Jimu Bengoshi Jimusho, 20th Floor, Shin Kasumigaseki Building, 3-2, Kasumigaseki 3-Chome, Chiyoda-Ku, Tokyo 100-0013, Japan.
Telephone: 81-3-3595-3911.
Frankfurt, Germany Office: Main Tower, Neve Mainzer Strasse 52, 60311 Frankfurt am Main, Germany.
Telephone: 49-69-971-03-0.
Rome, Italy Office: Piazza de Spagna 15, 00187 Rome, Italy.
Telephone: 39-06-69-52-22-1.

COUNSEL

Robert C. Barnard
Fred D. Turnage
Douglas E. Kliever
Daniel B. Silver

WASHINGTON, D.C. PARTNERS

Donald L. Morgan
J. Eugene Marans
Kenneth L. Bachman, Jr.
Charles F. Lettow
Richard deC. Hinds
Sara D. Schotland
John S. Magney
Mark Leddy
John C. Murphy, Jr.
George S. Cary
Janet L. Weller
Mitchell S. Dupler
Linda J. Soldo
Giovanni P. Prezioso
John T. Byam
Matthew D. Slater
Steven N. Robinson
Michael R. Lazerwitz
David I. Gelfand
Ricardo A. Anzaldúa-Montoya

(See Next Column)

SPECIAL COUNSEL

W. Richard Bidstrup
Scott N. Benedict
Linda S. Matlack
Kevin A. Griffin

ASSOCIATES

Robin M. Bergen
Barbara W. Bernstein
Brent E. Binge (Not admitted in DC)
Marcilynn A. Burke
Derek M. Bush
Brian Byrne
Kimble C. Cannon
Natalie G. Coburn
Robert W. Cook
L. Burton Davis
Onnig H. Dombalagian
John L. Farry
James Filippatos (Not admitted in DC)
William S. Fultz (Not admitted in DC)
Erik F. Gerding
Scott R. Goodwin
Kristofer W. Hess
Richard B. Holbrook, Jr.
Steven J. Kaiser
Elizabeth L. Katkin
Karen A. Kerr
Elke M. Krauland (Not admitted in DC)
James D. Livingstone (Not admitted in DC)
Michael A. Mazzuchi
Joyce E. McCarty
Dipali B. Mehta (Not admitted in DC)
Paolo Morante
Mark W. Nelson
Andrew K. Niebler (Not admitted in DC)
Eruch P. Nowrojee
Henry Kwasi Prempeh
Mitchell L. Rabinowitz
Emily Ryo (Not admitted in DC)
David S. Snyder
Michael L. Travers
Timothy A. Vogel
Michael W. Waldron
Robert K. Williams

For full biographical listings, see the Martindale-Hubbell Law Directory

CLIFFORD CHANCE ROGERS & WELLS LLP (AV)

607 Fourteenth Street, N.W., 20005-2018
Telephone: 202-434-0700
Facsimile: 202-434-0800
URL: http://www.cliffordchance.com
Amsterdam, The Netherlands Office: Apollolaan 171, 1077 AS Amsterdam, P.O. Box 7301, 1007 JH.
Telephone: +31 20 5777111.
Fax: +31 20 5777222.
Bangkok, Thailand Office: Sindhorn Building Tower 3, 21st Floor, 130-132 Wireless Road, Pathumwan, 10330.
Telephone: +66 2 263 2250.
Fax: +66 2 263 2240.
Barcelona, Spain Office: Pau Claris 102, 08009.
Telephone: +34 93 344 2200.
Fax: +34 93 344 2222.
Brussels, Belgium Office: Avenue Louise 65, Box 2, 1050.
Telephone: +32 2 533 59 11.
Fax: +32 2 533 59 59.
Budapest, Hungary Office: Madách Trade Center, Madách Imre Út 14, 1075.
Telephone: +36 1 268 1600.
Fax: +36 1 268 1610.
Dubai, United Arab Emirates Office: 18th Floor, Dubai World Trade Centre, P.O. Box 9380.
Telephone: +971 4 3314333.
Fax: +971 4 3313990/314565.
Düsseldorf, Germany Office: Viktoriaplatz 2, 40477.
Telephone: +49 211 862 11 0.
Fax: +49 211 862 11 555.
Frankfurt am Main, Germany Office: Oberlindau 54-56, D-60323.
Telephone: +49 69 971 55 0.
Fax: +49 69 971 55 555.
Hanoi, Vietnam Office: International Centre, Unit 02, Second Floor, 17 Ngo Quyen Street.
Telephone: +84 4 8241520.
Fax: +84 4 8241560.
Ho Chi Minh City, Vietnam Office: 172C Nguyen Dinh Chieu Street, District 3.
Telephone: +4 8 8226406.
Fax: +84 8 8226410.
Hong Kong Office: 30th Floor, Jardine House, One Connaught Place.
Telephone: +852 2810 0229.
Fax: +852 2810 4708/4858/4743.
London, England Office: 200 Aldersgate Street, EC1A 4JJ.
Telephone: +44 (0)207 600 1000.
Fax: +44 (0)207 600 5555.
Madrid, Spain Office: Paseo de la Castellana 110, 28046.
Telephone: +34 91 590 75 00.
Fax: +34 91 590 75 75.
Milan, Italy Associated Office: Grimaldi e Clifford Chance, Via Clerici 7, 20121.
Telephone: +39 02 806 341.
Fax: +39 02 806 34200.
Moscow, Russia Office: Ul. Sadovaya-Samotechnaya 24/27, Second Floor, 103051.
Telephone: +7 501 258 50 50.
Fax: +7 501 258 50 51.
New York, New York Office: 200 Park Avenue, 10166-0153.
Telephone: 212-878-8000.
Facsimile: 212-878-8375. Email: email@cliffordchance.com.
Telex: 234493 RKWUR.

(See Next Column)

CLIFFORD CHANCE ROGERS & WELLS LLP, *Washington—Continued*

Padua, Italy Associated Office: Grimaldi e Clifford Chance, Via Felice Cavallotti 4, 35124.
Telephone: +39 049 8042511.
Fax: +39 049 8805900.
Paris, France Office: 112 avenue Kléber, BP 163 Trocadéro, 75770 Paris Cedex 16.
Telephone: +33 1 44 05 52 52.
Fax: +33 1 44 05 52 00.
Prague, Czech Republic Office: Charles Bridge Centre, Krizovnické nám. 2, 110 00 Prague 1.
Telephone: +420 2 2409 7410.
Fax: +420 2 2409 7411.
Rome, Italy Associated Office: Grimaldi e Clifford Chance, Via Mercadante, 32, 00 198.
Telephone: +39 06 844 651.
Fax: +39 06 844 65200.
São Paulo, Brazil Office: Rua Helena, 260, 6th Floor, São Paulo -SP, 04552-050.
Telephone: +55 11 3049 3188.
Fax: +55 11 3049 3198.
Shanghai, People's Republic of China Office: Suite 730, Shanghai Centre, 1376 Nanjing Xi Lu, 200040.
Telephone: +86 21 6279 8461.
Fax: +86 21 6279 8462.
Singapore Office: 16 Collyer Quay #10-00, Hitachi Tower, 049318.
Telephone: +65 5351855.
Fax: +65 5356855.
Tokyo, Japan Office: 6th Floor, South Hill Nagatacho Building, 11-30 Nagatacho 1-chome, Chiyoda-ku, 100.
Telephone: +81 3 3581 4311.
Fax: +81 3 3593 0651.
Warsaw, Poland Office: Norway House, ul. Lwowska 19, 00-660.
Telephone: +48 22 627 11 77.
Fax: +48 22 627 14 66.

SENIOR PARTNER

William P. Rogers

PARTNERS

Kevin J. Arquit
Jeremy A. Connick (Not admitted in United States)
Anthony F. Essaye
David J. Evans
Kenneth A. Gallo
Ira D. Hammerman
Sara P. Hanks
John Paul Ketels
Steven A. Newborn
Michael A. O'Shea
Anthony J. Renzi, Jr.
David A. Schulz (Not admitted in DC)
Rodney N.T. Short (Not admitted in United States)
William Silverman
Joseph J. Simons
Ryan Trainer
Dale C. Turza

COUNSEL

Leiv H. Blad, Jr.
David D. DiBari
James C. Egan, Jr.
Douglas J. Heffner
Jon Randall Roellke
Carrie A. Simon
John M. Sipple, Jr.
Laura A. Wilkinson

CONSULTANTS

Jon McCormick
Virginia L. Snider

ASSOCIATES

Michael R. Albrecht
Matthew D. Adler
Carrie M. Anderson
Tracy E. Ballard
Amy E. Beargie
Lacy D. Berrington
James J. Black
Sean E. Callahan
Bret A. Campbell
Marianne T. Caulfield
Kathleen Chouai (Not admitted in DC)
Frank C. Cimino, Jr.
Charles M. Cole
Patricia C. Crowley
Julia Symon de Kluiver
Kelly Keimig Elsea (Not admitted in DC)
Richard P. Ferrin
Paul R. Frontczak
Steven F. Gatti
Laurence B. Giraud (Not admitted in DC)
Michael J. King
George D. Kleinfeld
Thomas C. Koonce
Lisa C. Barton Kranz (Not admitted in DC)
Denise Landers (Not admitted in DC)
Joanne C. Lewers
Jeffery C. Lowe
Catherine Marsh (Not admitted in United States)
Prakash H. Mehta
Katherine Wells Meighan
Ashley Anne Meise
Jennifer J. Mink
Scott B. Murray
Brian K. O'Bleness
Mark S. Pesso
Timothy P. Peterson (Not admitted in DC)
Carlos E. Provencio
Matthew J. Reilly (Not admitted in DC)
Charles J. Rinaldi
Christopher D. Roberti
Nicholas M. Roegner (Not admitted in DC)
John E. Scribner
Robyn Shields
Lisa D. Tymann
Lee K. Van Voorhis
Nicholas C. Wong (Not admitted in United States)
Therese Marie Woods
Glen M. Zwicker

For full biographical listings, see the Martindale-Hubbell Law Directory

COVINGTON & BURLING (AV)

1201 Pennsylvania Avenue, N.W., P.O. Box 7566, 20044-7566
Telephone: 202-662-6000
Fax: 202-662-6291
Email: postmaster@cov.com *URL:* http://www.cov.com
San Francisco, California Office: 601 California Street, Suite 1900, 94108.
Telephone: 415-591-6000.
New York, N.Y. Office: 1330 Avenue of the Americas, 10019.
Telephone: 212-841-1000.
Telecopier: 212-841-1010.
London, England Office: Leconfield House, Curzon Street, W1Y 8A5.
Telephone: 011-44-71-495-5655.
Fax: 011-44-71-495-3101.
Brussels, Belgium Office: 44 Avenue des Arts (Bte. 8), 1040.
Telephone: 011-32-2-549-5230.
Fax: 011-32-2-502-1598.

PARTNERS

Dana T. Ackerly II
Harvey M. Applebaum
James R. Atwood
Bruce A. Baird
Patricia A. Barald
Thomas O. Barnett
Michael St. Patrick Baxter
Bruce C. Bennett (Resident, New York, N.Y. Office)
Paul J. Berman
Jonathan D. Blake
Doris Blazek-White
Peter W. L. Bogaert (Resident, Brussels, Belgium Office)
Eric C. Bosset
Richard A. Brady
Lanny A. Breuer
Edward C. Britton
Caroline M. Brown
David N. Brown
E. Edward Bruce
John G. Buchanan, III
Charles E. Buffon
Bobby R. Burchfield
Russell H. Carpenter, Jr.
Warren G. Caywood, Jr. (Resident, New York, N.Y. Office)
Leonard Chazen (Resident, New York, N.Y. Office)
George M. Chester, Jr.
Brice M. Clagett
William R. Collins (Resident, New York, N.Y. Office)
Richard D. Copaken
Carolyn F. Corwin
Evan R. Cox (Resident, San Francisco, California Office)
Fiona Crawley (Resident, London, England Office)
Michael E. Cutler
Roderick Allen DeArment
John B. Denniston
Allen N. Dixon (Resident, London, England Office)
Mitchell F. Dolin
John C. Dugan
Herbert Dym
Clausen Ely, Jr.
Anna Engh
Nicholas W. Fels
Matthew E. Fishbein (Resident, New York, N.Y. Office)
Ellen J. Flannery
Andrew H. Friedman
Robert J. Gage
Marialuisa S. Gallozzi
Oscar M. Garibaldi
Theodore L. Garrett
Deborah A. Garza
Corinne A. Goldstein
Linda C. Goldstein (Resident, New York, N.Y. Office)
Saul B. Goodman
John P. Gourary (Resident, New York, N.Y. Office)
William F. Greaney
Joanne B. Grossman
Eugene D. Gulland
David W. Haller (Resident, New York, N.Y. Office)
Newman T. Halvorson, Jr.
Robert P. Haney, Jr. (Resident, New York, N.Y. Office)
David L. Harfst (Resident, Brussels, Belgium Office)
J. Michael Hemmer
Anthony Herman
Timothy C. Hester
David H. Hickman
Harry G. Hives (Resident, New York, N.Y. Office)
Michael B. Hopkins (Resident, New York, N.Y. Office)
Michael S. Horne
Jasper A. Howard
Philip K. Howard (Resident, New York, N.Y. Office)
John A. Hurvitz
Peter Barton Hutt
Jeffrey G. Huvelle
Stephen A. Infante (Resident, New York, N.Y. Office)
William D. Iverson
O. Thomas Johnson, Jr.
Elizabeth T. Kessenides (Resident, New York, N.Y. Office)
Mark F. Kightlinger (Resident, Brussels, Belgium Office)
Richard F. Kingham (Resident, London, England Office)
Bruce N. Kuhlik
Eugene I. Lambert
D. Michael Lefever
Bingham B. Leverich
Jack P. Levin (Resident, New York, N.Y. Office)
Gregg H. Levy
Michael R. Levy
Charles E. Lister (Resident, London, England Office)
S. William Livingston, Jr.
J. Jay Lobell (Resident, New York, N.Y. Office)
Robert A. Long, Jr.
Mark H. Lynch
Daniel M. Mandil (Resident, New York, N.Y. Office)
Aaron R. Marcu (Resident, New York, N.Y. Office)
David Lawrence Meyer
Charles A. Miller
Allan B. Moore (Resident, London, England Office)
Amy N. Moore
Peter J. Nickles
William M. Paul
Ronald A. Pearlman
C. William Phillips (Resident, New York, N.Y. Office)
Mark E. Plotkin
Hilary Prescott (Resident, London, England Office)
David H. Remes
Arvid E. Roach II
Neil K. Roman
Steven J. Rosenbaum
Charles F.C. Ruff
Charles F. (Rick) Rule
John Peter Rupp
Robert N. Sayler
Richard C. Shea
Laurence A. Silverman (Resident, New York, N.Y. Office)
Andrew W. Singer
Christopher N. Sipes
William P. Skinner
Jay T. Smith
John Thomas Smith, II

(See Next Column)

COVINGTON & BURLING—*Continued*

PARTNERS (Continued)

Scott F. Smith (Resident, New York, N.Y. Office)
James C. Snipes (Resident, San Francisco, California Office)
Rebecca Snow
Stuart C. Stock
Philipp U. Tamussino (Resident, Brussels, Belgium Office)
Carolyn E. Taylor (Resident, New York, N.Y. Office)
Keith A. Teel
Phyllis D. Thompson
Lee J. Tiedrich
Henriette A. Tielemans (Not admitted in United States) (Resident, Brussels, Belgium Office)
Allan J. Topol
Peter D. Trooboff
Seth A. Tucker
Kelly Vance (Resident, New York, N.Y. Office)
John Vanderstar
John M. Vine
Ralph C. Voltmer, Jr.
Theodore Voorhees, Jr.
Gerard J. Waldron
J. D. Weinberg (Resident, New York, N.Y. Office)
Harris Weinstein
Mark A. Weiss
Stephen A. Weiswasser
Albert L. Wells (Resident, New York, N.Y. Office)
Reeves C. Westbrook
Wesley S. Williams, Jr.
Thomas S. Williamson, Jr.
Bruce Sandess Wilson
Kurt A. Wimmer
Sonya D. Winner (Resident, San Francisco, California Office)

SENIOR COUNSEL

Edwin S. Cohen
John L. Ellicott
Daniel M. Gribbon
David B. Isbell
James C. McKay
Alfred H. Moses
Roberts B. Owen
John H. Schafer
Stanley L. Temko
J. Randolph Wilson
Edwin M. Zimmerman

OF COUNSEL

Patrick S. Davies
Julie M. Edmond
Herbert Estreicher
Kathleen T. Gallagher-Duff
James A. Goold
David R. Grace
R. Laird Hart
W. Andrew Jack
Eric G. Lasker
Brian E. Lebowitz
Benedict M. Lenhart
Richard A. Merrill
Alan A. Pemberton
Douglas E. Phillips
Elliott Schulder
Laurie C. Self
Robert Edward Shaw
Robert B. Stevens (Resident, London, England Office)
Sarah E. Taylor
Edward S. West

SPECIAL COUNSEL

David W. Addis
Dennis B. Auerbach
Susan L. Burke
Stephen Calkins
Michael J. Cicero
Scott David Feldstein
William H. Fitz
Thomas W. Krause
Michael Gary Michaelson
James S. Portnoy
Karen K. Schwartz
Joyce Payne Yette

ASSOCIATES

Charles S. Abell
Karen A. Ballotta
Bryan Beier
Thomas W. Beimers (Not admitted in DC)
Michael R. Bergmann
Molly E. Bishop (Not admitted in DC)
P. Robert Broeren, Jr.
Jennifer A. Burt
Charles J. Butler (Not admitted in DC)
Kurt G. Calia
Susanne Carnell
Michael A. Carrier
Michael K. Catoe
George F. Cicotte (Not admitted in DC)
Kipp A. Coddington
Tracey H. Cohen
Angela M. Cooper
Thomas L. Cubbage III
Catherine Janine Dargan
Michael S. Dawson
John T. Delacourt
Andrea L. Dennis
Edward H. Dixon
Kathleen J. Donnelly
Ronald G. Dove
Kenneth J. Drexler
Phillip E. Dube (Not admitted in DC)
Richard Dulik
Erin M. Egan
Kimberly K. Egan
Christine E. Enemark
Alessio D. Evangelista
Michael J. Fanelli
Lisa M. Farabee
Peter L. Flanagan
Lawrence Stewart Fox
Michael J. Francese
Coleen Friel (Not admitted in DC)
Evelyn J. Furse
Laura B. Gasho
Adam W. Goldberg
Ellen P. Goodman
Sara L. Gottovi
Eric D. Greenberg
Gideon Y. Grunfeld
Miriam J. Guggenheim
Suneeta Hazra
Andrew J. Heimert
Michael X. Imbroscio
H. Stuart Irvin, Jr.
Robin Jacobson
Rana Jazayerli
Jennifer Anne Johnson
Russell P. Kanjorski
Faith D. Kasparian (Not admitted in DC)
Georgia Kazakis
Robert K. Kelner (Not admitted in DC)
Ann-Kelley Kemper
Patrick S. Kim
Erika King
Coleen Klasmeier
Rukesh Korde (Not admitted in DC)
Karen Kramer (Not admitted in DC)
Christine L. Kurek
Joan L. Kutcher
Krista Labelle
Michael Scott Labson
Monique J. La Fleur

(See Next Column)

ASSOCIATES (Continued)

Marie A. Lavalleye
Melissa Lawrence
Linda L. LeCraw
Emily Leonard
M. Elizabeth Leverage
Amy L. Levine
Jason A. Levine
Andrew D. Levy
Catherine E. Long
Adriana S. Luedke
John F. C. Luedke
Cara Maggioni
Gerard N. Magliocca
Stanford Kenneth McCoy
William Carroll Muffett (Not admitted in DC)
Ralph M. Muoio (Not admitted in DC)
David G. Nason
Robert S. Newman
Kevin C. Newsom
Keith A. Noreika
Adam E. Pachter
Chong S. Park
Elizabeth Pearsall (Not admitted in DC)
Jean M. Perron
Eric Phillips
Anthony R. Picarello, Jr.
Jennifer Plitsch (Not admitted in DC)
Mark E. Porada
Diana L. Puknys
Edward Holden Rippey
Michael L. Rosenthal
Philip J. Rosenthal
Kristina Rosette
Simone Ross
Salvatore G. Rotella, Jr.
James P. A. Ryan
Anthony Saldana
John Scheib
A. Christopher Sega
Kevin Shortill
Alexei M. Silverman
Bruce P. Smith
Richard W. Smith (Not admitted in DC)
Elizabeth A. Snodgrass
Jeremy D. Spector
Lisa J. Stevenson
Chad Y. Tang
Jonathan Taub
Peter Z. Teluk
Henry P. Ting
P. Andrew Torrez (Not admitted in DC)
Kimberly Vasconi
Anthony J. Vlatas
William C. Waller
Grail Peyton Walsh
Edward J. Walters
George L. Washington, Jr.
Andrew Watson
Glen D. Weinstein
Alane C. Weixel
Grady Lee White
Jeffrey L. White
Robert Wick
Jarrett Williams
Mary Newcomer Williams
Michele J. Woods
Anthony S. Yoo
Peter Zern

For full biographical listings, see the Martindale-Hubbell Law Directory

CROWELL & MORING LLP (AV)

1001 Pennsylvania Avenue, N.W., 20004-2595
Telephone: 202-624-2500
Fax: 202-628-5116
URL: http://www.crowellmoring.com
Irvine, California Office: 2010 Main Street, Suite 1200.
Telephone: 949-263-8400.
Fax: 949-263-8414.
London, England Office: Crowell & Moring, 180 Fleet Street, EC4A 2HG.
Telephone: 44-207-413-0011.
Fax: 44-207-413-0333.

MEMBERS OF FIRM

Frederick Moring
Brian C. Elmer
Patrick W. Lee
W. Stanfield Johnson
Peter B. Work
Victor E. Schwartz
Ridgway M. Hall, Jr.
Harold J. Heltzer
Richard L. Beizer
Donald L. Flexner
R. Bruce Keiner, Jr.
Steven P. Quarles
Jeffrey H. Howard
Thomas P. Humphrey
Michael M. Levy
John A. Macleod
Kent R. Morrison
Barry E. Cohen
Marc F. Efron
Joseph M. Oliver, Jr.
Timothy M. Biddle
Herbert J. Martin
Richard McMillan, Jr.
Dana C. Contratto
George D. Ruttinger
Richard E. Schwartz
Howard M. Weinman
Karen Hastie Williams
Terry L. Albertson
Nancy S. Bryson
James P. Denvir, III
JoAnn E. Macbeth
Peter J. Romatowski
Wm. Randolph Smith
Fred S. Souk
John I. Stewart, Jr.
Frederick W. Claybrook, Jr.
Robert T. Ebert
Thomas P. Gies
Andrew H. Marks
William P. O'Neill
James J. Regan
Jennifer N. Waters
Rosemary M. Collyer
Kenneth M. Bruntel
Robert C. Davis, Jr.
Warren J. DeVecchio
Clifford B. Hendler
Thomas C. Means
John T. Scott, III
Shauna E. Alonge
Clifton S. Elgarten
Laurel Pyke Malson
Stuart H. Newberger
David B. Siegel
Robert M. Halperin
Raymond F. Monroe
Robert L. Willmore
Alan W.H. Gourley
Mark D. Plevin
David Z. Bodenheimer
R. Timothy McCrum
M. Lisanne Crowley
Kent A. Gardiner
Mark E. Baker
Ellen Moran Dwyer
Lawrence J. Gotts
Luther Zeigler
Paul William Kalish
J. Michael Klise
William D. Wallace
Michael D. Bednarek
Scott L. Winkelman
Charles C. Hwang
Steven C. Schnitzer
Kathryn Dean Kirmayer
Jeane A. Thomas
Alexandre de Gramont
Kris David Meade

(See Next Column)

CROWELL & MORING LLP, *Washington—Continued*

SENIOR COUNSEL

Eldon H. Crowell
Roger N. Boyd
L. Graeme Bell, III

OF COUNSEL

Richard J. Bednar
Edward M. Green
Robert P. Charrow
Michael J. Cooper (Not admitted in DC)
Lloyd M. Weinerman
Linda S. Bruggeman
Lorraine Berman Halloway
Bonnie A. Sullivan
Anne M. ("Nancy") Wheeler
Daryl A. Lander
Kathryn A. Underhill
Edward M. Barberic
Elizabeth M. Roesel
William L. Anderson
Edward Jackson
Amy J. Mauser
David M. Schnorrenberg
Aslan Baghdadi
Mark A. Behrens
Glenn D. Grant
Kathleen E. Karelis
Jonathan Hale Pittman

PUBLIC SERVICE COUNSEL

Susan M. Hoffman

Thomas R. Lundquist (Special Counsel)

ASSOCIATES

Richard J. Mannix
Bazil Facchina
Janine L. Gregory
Linn Kaiser Redway
Laurel A. Bedig
Steven P. Taub
John E. McCarthy, Jr.
Stephanie B. N. Renzi
Terence F. Flynn
Christine C. D'Alessandro
Ariel R. David
Mark R. Koehn
Christopher McGuire
Ellen B. Steen
Matthew S. R. Bewig
Stephen M. Byers
Lisa Taeko Greenlees
Jerome A. Murphy
Peter W. Paulsen
Tracy A. Roman
Carolyn P. Carmody
Monica G. Parham
Karen A. Rosenthal
Christine Elizabeth Stroh
Andrew W. Bagley
Jacqueline E. Davis
Christopher E. Kaczmarek
Leah Lorber
Jeffrey A. Spector
Joseph W. C. Warren
Christopher H. Wood
Paul Alp
Tara Weinstock Blanchard
John I. Blanck, Jr.
Reed Michael Brodsky
Scott E. Gant
James Anthony Garcia
Rodrigo "Diego" Garcia, Jr.
Michael S. Lee
Andy Liu
Bennett J. Matelson
Barry M. Parsons
Dawn Millman Popp
Michele T. St. Mary
Felicia Goldberg Schweitzer
Cheryl A. Solomon
Thomas Newton Bolling
Sarah H. Garb
Jeffrey E. Greene
Kimberly K. Hartwell
David C. Isaacson
Michone T. Johnson (Not admitted in DC)
Kenneth F. Rossman IV
Simeon M. Schopf
Sarah J. Zimmerman
Beverly L. Blank
Emma K. Burton
Benjamin T. Butler
Bridget E. Calhoun (Not admitted in DC)
Poh C. Chua
Derek Dickinson
Deborah W. Feinstein
Michael Richard Finley
Daniel R. Forman (Not admitted in DC)
Edward B. Glennon
Michael G. Grable
Christopher J. Huber
Leavy Mathews III
Daniel A. Sasse (Not admitted in DC)
Sarah L. Seager
Jennifer Brooke Tomchin
Dylana Leigh Blum (Not admitted in DC)
Michele M. Burris
Tejpal Singh Chawla
Miguel H. Del Toro
Kesha Danyeil Evans (Not admitted in DC)
Adam C. Gajadharsingh
Jennifer G. Glass
David L. Haga
Marcos E. Hasbun
Sarah C. Lindsey
Alan W. Lowrey
Joseph P. Mastrosimone
Lisa A. Meengs
Kirsten L. Nathanson
Aryeh S. Portnoy
Susan M. Roach (Not admitted in DC)
Fabio Roman Silva (Not admitted in DC)
Paul A. Walker (Not admitted in DC)

For full biographical listings, see the Martindale-Hubbell Law Directory

---

CURTIS, MALLET-PREVOST, COLT & MOSLE LLP (AV)

Suite 1205L, 1801 K Street, N.W., 20006
Telephone: 202-452-7373
Telecopier: 202-452-7333
Email: info@cm-p.com *URL:* http://www.cm-p.com
New York, N.Y. Office: 101 Park Avenue.
Telephone: 212-696-6000.
Telecopier: 212-697-1559.
Newark, New Jersey Office: One Gateway Center, Suite 403.
Telephone: 973-622-0605.
Telecopier: 973-622-5646.
Houston, Texas Office: 2 Houston, Center, 909 Fannin Street, Suite 3725.
Telephone: 713-759-9555.
Telecopier: 713-759-0712.
Stamford, Connecticut Office: One Canterbury Green.
Telephone: 203-359-6200.
Telecopier: 203-328-2617.

(See Next Column)

Mexico City, D.F., Mexico Office: Curtis, Mallet-Prevost, Colt & Mosle, Ruben Dario 281, Piso 9, Col. Bosque de Chapultepec, 11580 Mexico, D.F.
Telephone: 525-282-0444.
Telecopier: 525-282-0637.
Paris, France Office: 15 rue d'Astorg, 75008.
Telephone: 42-66-39-10.
Telecopier: 42-66-39-62 .
London, England Office: Two Throgmorton Avenue, EC2N 2DL.
Telephone: 0207-638-7957.
Telecopier: 0207-638-5512.
Frankfurt am Main 1, Germany Office: Staufenstrasse 42.
Telephone: 69-971-4420.
Telecopier: 69-17 33 99.
Muscat, Sultanate of Oman Office: P.O. Box 200, Jewel Beach-134.
Telephone: 968-607-725.
Telecopier: 968-607-724.
Milan, Italy Office: Curtis, Mallet-Prevost, Colt & Mosle, Piazzale Principessa Clotilde 8, 20121.
Telephone: (39) 02-2900-2932.
Telecopier: (39) 02-657-5969.

RESIDENT PARTNERS

Preston Brown
Samuel Rosenthal
Jeffrey I. Zuckerman

For full biographical listings, see the Martindale-Hubbell Law Directory

---

DAVIS POLK & WARDWELL (AV)

1300 I Street, N.W., 20005
Telephone: 202-962-7000
Fax: 202-962-7111
URL: http://www.dpw.com
New York, N.Y. Office: 450 Lexington Avenue, 10017.
Telephone: 212-450-4000.
Fax: 212-450-4800.
Menlo Park, California Office: 1600 El Camino Real, Menlo Park, California, 94025.
Telephone: 650-752-2000.
Fax: 650-752-2195.
Paris, France Office: 15, avenue Matignon, 75008 Paris, France.
Telephone: 33-01-56-59-36-00.
Fax: 33-01-56-59-36-90.
London, England Office: 99 Gresham Street, London, EC2V 7NG, England.
Telephone: 44-171-418-1300.
Fax: 44-171-418-1400.
Tokyo, Japan Office: Akasaka Twin Tower East, 11th Floor, 17-22, Akasaka 2-Chome, Minato-ku, Tokyo 107-0052, Japan.
Telephone: 81-3-5561-4421. Fax (main): 81-3-5561-4425.
Frankfurt, Germany Office: MesseTurm, 60308 Frankfurt am Main, Germany.
Telephone: 49-69-97-57-03-0.
Fax: 49-69-74-77-44.
Hong Kong, China Office: The Hong Kong Club Building, 3A Chater Road, Hong Kong.
Telephone: 852-2533-3300.
Fax: 852-2533-3388.

MEMBERS OF FIRM

Stephen H. Case
Scott W. Muller
Jordan Luke
Dana L. Trier

RESIDENT COUNSEL

Margaret M. Ayres
Theodore A. Doremus, Jr.
Robert W. Weaver

For full biographical listings, see the Martindale-Hubbell Law Directory

---

DEBEVOISE & PLIMPTON (AV)

555 13th Street N.W., 20004
Telephone: 202-383-8000
Telecopier: 202-383-8118
New York, N.Y. Office: 875 Third Avenue, 10022.
Telephone: 212-909-6000.
Telex: (Domestic) 148377 DEBSTEVE NYK.
Telecopier: (212) 909-6836.
Paris, France Office: 21 Avenue George V 75008.
Telephone: (33-1) 40 73 12 12.
Telecopier: (33-1) 47 20 50 82.
Telex: 648141F DPPAR.
London, England Office: Old Broad Street, EC2N 1HQ.
Telephone: (44-71) 786-9000.
Telex: 884569 DPLON G.
Telecopier: (44-71) 588-4180.
Hong Kong Office: 13/F Entertainment Building, 30 Queen's Road Central.
Telephone: 852-2160-9800.
Fax: 852-2810-9828.
Moscow, Russia Representative Office: Debevoise & Plimpton, LLC, Bolshoi Palashevsky Pereulok 13/2, 4th Floor, 103104.
Telephone: 7 (095 or 503) 956-3858.
Fax: 7 (095 or 503) 956-3868.

(See Next Column)

DEBEVOISE & PLIMPTON—*Continued*

MEMBERS OF FIRM

Judah Best
Ralph C. Ferrara
Loren Kieve
Marcia L. MacHarg
Jeffrey P. Cunard
Colby A. Smith
(Not admitted in DC)

COUNSEL

Ann M. Ashton
Paul C. Palmer
Phillip D. Parker
Herbert C. Thomas

RETIRED PARTNER

Robert J. Geniesse

ASSOCIATES

Scott N. Auby
Barton B. Clark
Gregg S. Farano
Sean K. Hornbeck
Elizabeth N. Kaplan
Philip S. Khinda
Lothar A. Kneifel
Paul F. Sheridan, Jr.
Jonathan R. Tuttle

For full biographical listings, see the Martindale-Hubbell Law Directory

DECHERT PRICE & RHOADS (AV)

1775 Eye Street, N.W., 20006
Telephone: 202-261-3300
Telefax: 202-261-3333
URL: http://www.dechert.com
Philadelphia, Pennsylvania: 4000 Bell Atlantic Tower, 1717 Arch Street, 19103-2793.
Telephone: 215-994-4000.
New York, New York: 30 Rockefeller Plaza, 10112.
Telephone: 212-698-3500.
Harrisburg, Pennsylvania: Thirty North Third Street, 17101-1603.
Telephone: 717-237-2000.
Princeton, New Jersey: Princeton Pike Corporate Center, P.O. Box 5218, 08543-5218.
Telephone: 609-620-3200.
Boston, Massachusetts: Ten Post Office Square South, 12th Floor, 02109-4603.
Telephone: 617-728-7100.
Hartford, Connecticut: 90 State House Square, 06103-3702.
Telephone: 860-524-3999.
London, England: 2 Serjeants' Inn, EC4Y 1LT.
Telephone: (0171) 583-5353. (Also see Titmuss Sainer Dechert).
Brussels, Belgium: 65 Avenue Louise, 1050.
Telephone: (02) 535-5411.
Paris, France: 55, avenue Kléber, 76116.
Telephone: 33-(0) 1-53 65 05 00.

RESIDENT PARTNERS

Joseph J. Aronica
James E. Ballowe, Jr.
Sander M. Bieber
Catherine Botticelli
Frank J. Eisenhart
Ruth S. Epstein
David J. Harris
Robert W. Helm
Jane A. Kanter
Bettina M. Lawton
I. Lewis Libby
Allan S. Mostoff
Jack W. Murphy
Jeffrey S. Puretz
Theodore Sonde
Wallace L. Timmeny
Donald Zarin

OF COUNSEL

Arthur W. Leibold Jr.

RESIDENT COUNSEL

Susan C. Ervin
Carmen Guzman Lowrey
(Not admitted in DC)
Mary S. Head
Ralph Oman

RESIDENT ASSOCIATES

Olivia P. Adler
Karen L. Anderberg
Vincent J. Badolato
Janet A. Broeckel
(Not admitted in DC)
Dilia M. Caballero
Ethan D. Corey
Douglas P. Dick
Mary Teresa Anastasia Doud
(Not admitted in DC)
Jennifer A. Epstein
(Not admitted in DC)
Jennifer L. Kim
Dennis J. Lawson
Randy G. Legg
John H. Lively
Michael J. McDonough
(Not admitted in DC)
Laura A. Novack
(Not admitted in DC)
Keith T. Robinson
Meha Shah
Janene M. Smith
Patrick W.D. Turley
Michael A. Valerio
David A. Vaughan
Neal J. Wilson
Scott Michael Zoltowski

For full biographical listings, see the Martindale-Hubbell Law Directory

DEWEY BALLANTINE LLP (AV)

1775 Pennsylvania Avenue, N.W., 20006-4605
Telephone: 202-862-1000; Telecopier: 202-862-1093
Cable Address: "Dewbalaw"
N.Y., N.Y., L.A., Calif., Budapest, Hungary, Prague, Czech Republic & Warsaw, Poland
URL: http://www.deweyballantine.com
Other offices: New York, New York; Los Angeles, California; London, England; Hong Kong; Budapest, Hungary; Prague, Czech Republic; and Warsaw, Poland.

RESIDENT PARTNERS

J. Bradford Anwyll
Donna M. Attanasio
James F. Bowe, Jr.
Joseph K. Dowley
Zori G. Ferkin
Thomas R. Howell
Gerald A. Kafka
Andrew W. Kentz
Felix B. Laughlin
Myles V. Lynk
W. Clark McFadden II
Earle H. O'Donnell
Joseph M. Pari
John A. Ragosta
Howard J. Rosenstock
John J. Salmon
Michael H. Stein
Martha J. Talley
Robert H.C. Wilkerson
Alan Wm. Wolff

COUNSEL

Harry Lewis Clark
Anna-Liza B. Harris

OF COUNSEL

Julia Dryden English
Laurel W. Glassman
Scotta E. McFarland
(Not admitted in DC)
Keith M. Schwartz
Bradford L. Ward

For full biographical listings, see the Martindale-Hubbell Law Directory

DICKINSON WRIGHT PLLC (AV)

Suite 800, 1901 L Street, N.W., 20036-3506
Telephone: 202-457-0160
Facsimile: 202-659-1559
URL: http://www.dickinson-wright.com
Detroit, Michigan Office: 500 Woodward Avenue, Suite 4000.
Telephone: 313-223-3500.
Facsimile: 313-223-3598.
Bloomfield Hills, Michigan Office: 525 North Woodward Avenue, Suite 2000.
Telephone: 248-433-7200.
Facsimile: 248-433-7274.
Grand Rapids, Michigan Office: 200 Ottawa Avenue, N.W., Suite 900.
Telephone: 616-458-1300.
Facsimile: 616-458-6753.
Lansing, Michigan Office: Suite 200, 215 South Washington Square.
Telephone: 517-371-1730.
Facsimile: 517-487-4700.

RESIDENT MEMBERS

Marc A. Bergsman
Conrad J. Clark
William E. Elwood
David R. Haarz
Samuel D. Littlepage
Jeffrey M. Petrash

RESIDENT OF COUNSEL

Christopher W. Brody
Laurinda L. Hicks
Lucien N. Nedzi
J. John Shimazaki

For full biographical listings, see the Martindale-Hubbell Law Directory

DICKSTEIN SHAPIRO MORIN & OSHINSKY LLP (AV)

2101 L Street, N.W., 20037-1526
Telephone: 202-785-9700
Fax: 202-887-0689
URL: http://www.dsmo.com
New York, New York Office: 1177 Avenue of the Americas, 41st Floor, 10036-2714.
Telephone: 212-835-1400.
Fax: 212-997-9880.
Correspondent Office, St. Petersburg, Russia: Russian-American Law Firm, Lermontovsky Prospect 7/12, 190008. Local
Telephone: 114-5660. International
Telephone: 850-1430.

MEMBERS OF FIRM

Kenneth L. Adams
John Agar
Lee A. Alexander
Angelo V. Arcadipane
George T. Boggs
James W. Brady, Jr.
Paul Bennett Bran
Karen L. Bush
Henry C. Cashen II
Leslie R. Cohen
Robin L. Cohen (Resident, New York, N.Y. Office)
Richard J. Conway
Thomas J. D'Amico
Ida Wurczinger Draim
Stephen A. Dvorkin (Resident, New York, N.Y. Office)
Larry F. Eisenstat
David L. Elkind
Emanuel Faust, Jr.
Margaret Feinstein
Howard N. Feldman
Barry J. Fleishman
Lawrence D. Garr
Scott D. Gilbert
Allan B. Goldstein
G. Michael Green
Donald A. Gregory
Jon David Grossman
Robert J. Higgins
Gary M. Hoffman
R. Bruce Holcomb
J. Andrew Jackson
Howard S. Jatlow

(See Next Column)

DICKSTEIN SHAPIRO MORIN & OSHINSKY LLP, *Washington—Continued*

MEMBERS OF FIRM (Continued)

Jeffrey M. Johnson
Peter Hafner Jost
Peter J. Kadzik
Leslie A. Kaplan
George Kaufmann (1931-1990)
Leon B. Kellner
Deborah P. Kelly
James D. Kelly
David B. Killalea
William D. Kingery, Jr.
Joel B. Kleinman
Joseph E. Kolick, Jr.
Mark H. Kolman
John T. Kotelly
Albert H. Kramer
Rachel S. Kronowitz
Arthur J. Lafave III
Neil Lefkowitz
Richard J. Leveridge
Barry Wm. Levine
Daniel M. Litt
Frederick M. Lowther
Patrick Winston Lynch
Kenneth M. Lyons
Matthew G. Maloney
Elaine Metlin
Andrew P. Miller
G. Joseph Minetti (1907-1993)
M. J. Mintz
Ira R. Mitzner
Peter W. Morgan
Kenneth R. Morrow
David M. Nadler
Michael E. Nannes
Bernard Nash
Bette M. Orr
Jerold Oshinsky
Mark A. Packman
Lewis J. Paper
David Patton Parker
Corrine Propas Parver
Woody N. Peterson
George R. Pitts
Ira H. Polon
Charles M. Pratt (Resident, New York, N.Y. Office)
Adam Proujansky
Frank C. Razzano
Gabrielle S. Roth
Charles W. Saber
Murray D. Sacks
Francis J. Sailer
Howard Schiffman
Richard Schramm (1941-1991)
Elizabeth A. Sherwin (Resident, New York, N.Y. Office)
Richard D. Shore
Justin D. Simon
Kenneth M. Simon
James vanR. Springer
Paul R. Taskier
Edward Tessler (Resident, New York, N.Y. Office)
Mark J. Thronson
Beth L. Webb
Stephan G. Weil
Kent T. Withycombe
Rebecca Wright
L. Andrew Zausner

SENIOR COUNSEL

Sidney Dickstein
Seymour Glanzer
Sallie H. Helm
Charles H. Morin
David I. Shapiro
Joseph D. Tydings

OF COUNSEL

Robert F. Aldrich
Laura Hamilton Calaluca
Michael Carowitz
Michael D. Cox
George E. Johnson
Robert Mangas (Not admitted in DC)
Harold K. McCombs, Jr.
Amy Marmer Nice
Stanford E. Parris
Mark L. Perlis
Steven John Roman
Walter J. Walvick

COUNSEL

Geoffrey Bestor
Linda J. Chase
Joan M. Darby
Michael J. DeCarlo
Michael R. Engleman (Not admitted in DC)
Joel A. Fischman
Katherine J. Henry
Allan C. Hubbard
Mark Kotlarsky
Isaac Lyumkis
Bryan T. McGinnis
Edward G. Modell
Charlotte Rothenberg Rosen

PRINCIPAL

Douglas N. Jacobson (Not admitted in DC)

ASSOCIATES

Kelli A. Andrews
Therman A. Baker, Jr.
Ruxandra Barbulescu (Not admitted in DC)
Anthony E. Bell
Robyn R. Bender (Not admitted in DC)
Eric A. Bensky
Matthew Steven Bergman
Amy L. Bogart (Not admitted in DC)
Donald L. Bowman (Not admitted in DC)
Julie A. Campbell (Not admitted in DC)
John M. Catalano (Not admitted in DC)
Daniel T. Chaudoin
Jonathan M. Cohen
Jeremy A. Cubert
Estelina L. Dallett
Merle Miller DeLancey, Jr.
Jeffery B. Denning
Jennifer M. Eck
Charles Ernest Edgar, IV
Carmela N. Edmunds
David L. Engelhardt
April N. Everette
Jacob S. Farber
Sabrina A. Farrar (Not admitted in DC)
Laura Beth Feigin
Elizabeth H. Feinberg (Not admitted in DC)
Ted J. Feldman
Janet C. Fisher
Laurence E. Fisher
Robert Friedman (Resident, New York, N.Y. Office)
John R. Fuisz
Valerie M. Furman
Keisha A. Gary
Lloyd A. Gelwan (Resident, New York, N.Y. Office)
Michael I. Gilman
Jonathan C. Gold
Jonathan M. Goodman (Resident, New York, N.Y. Office)
Scott D. Greenspan
Kevin M. Haley
Teresa L. Harvey
Elizabeth B. Haywood
Maria Colsey Heard
Jennifer Tara Geter Holubar
Lina Horchani (Not admitted in DC)
Samuel L. Jefferson, Jr.

(See Next Column)

ASSOCIATES (Continued)

Michael S. Kimberling (Not admitted in DC)
Donna Burdyck King
Paul W. Kisslinger (Not admitted in DC)
Jorge Kotelanski
Stefan M. Krantz
Brian A. Lemm
Selena J. Linde
Paul R. Lucey
Marilyn T. Lynch (Not admitted in DC)
Shelly M. Lynn (Not admitted in DC)
Carla M. Marcolin
James Robertson Martin
Andrew J. McFarland (Not admitted in DC)
Tara L. Mehrbach
Patrick S. Menasco
Charles L. Miller, Jr.
Frances J. Miller
Lisa M. R. Miller
Gianni Minutoli
David J. Mlodinoff (Resident, New York, N.Y. Office)
Robert James Moss
Nicole K Mueller
Michelle T. Nash
Guy S. Neal
Bridget O'Connor
Jonathan C. Odell
Ann Odelson (Resident, New York, N.Y. Office)
Benjamin R. Ogletree (Not admitted in DC)
Edwin Oh (Not admitted in DC)
Eric Oliver
Richard P. Perrin
Robert W. Pommer, III
R. Edward Poole
William E. Powell III
Benjamin R. Preston (Not admitted in DC)
Paul L. Ratcliffe (Not admitted in DC)
Tina M. Reynolds
Jeffrey Rhodes
Esteban Antonio Rockett (Not admitted in DC)
Michael J. Rustum
Joseph J. Samarias
Gretchen Schott
Edward E. Sharkey (Not admitted in DC)
Michael T. Sharkey
Nicole Cober Shumate
Kristi Singleton (Not admitted in DC)
Michelle D. Smith
Divonne Smoyer
Patricia M. Steele
Mark Edward Strickland (Not admitted in DC)
Paul C. Sullivan
Laura J. V. Szabo
Salvatore P. Tamburo (Not admitted in DC)
Kate Tapley
Jodi Trulove
Adam Vann (Not admitted in DC)
Laura A. Vikander
Janet Baker Walker (Not admitted in DC)
Jason D. Wallach
Steven M. Weinstein
Bradley D. Wine
James M. Wines
Adam S. Ziffer (Resident, New York, N.Y. Office)
Jean E. Zimmerman (Resident, New York, N.Y. Office)

For full biographical listings, see the Martindale-Hubbell Law Directory

DOW, LOHNES & ALBERTSON, PLLC (AV)

1200 New Hampshire Avenue, N.W. Suite 800, 20036-6802
Telephone: 202-776-2000
Facsimile: 202-776-2222
Email: info@dlalaw.com *URL:* http://www.dlalaw.com
Atlanta, Georgia Office: One Ravinia Drive, Suite 1600.
Telephone: 770-901-8800.
Telecopier: 770-901-8874.

MEMBERS OF THE FIRM

Corinne M. Antley
Michael D. Basile
Leonard J. Baxt (Chairman, Board of Directors)
Raymond G. Bender, Jr.
Richard L. Braunstein
Lisa C. Bureau
James M. Burger
Blain B. Butner
John T. Byrnes, Jr.
Peter C. Canfield (Resident, Atlanta, Georgia Office)
James A. Demetry (Resident, Atlanta, Georgia Office)
William S. Dudzinsky Jr.
Barbara S. Esbin
Peter H. Feinberg
John R. Feore, Jr.
Patricia A. Francis
Linda A. Fritts
Michael B. Goldstein
Todd D. Gray
Joyce Trimble Gwadz
Ralph W. Hardy, Jr.
J.G. Harrington
Jonathan D. Hart
Werner K. Hartenberger
Michael D. Hays
Michael A. Hepburn
David A. Hildebrandt
Jonathan B. Hill
J. Michael Hines
R. Dale Hughes (Resident, Atlanta, Georgia Office)
John C. Jost
Timothy J. Kelley
Leonard Jervey Kennedy (Not admitted in DC)
Michael Kovaka
Paul R. Lang
John S. Logan
Bernard J. Long, Jr.
Stephanie M. Loughlin
Judith A. Mather
Richard P. McHugh
John W. McNamara (Resident, Atlanta, Georgia Office)
Margaret L. Miller
David E. Mills
Edward J. O'Connell
Timothy J. O'Rourke
B. Dwight Perry (Managing Director)
Thomas J. Peters IV (Resident, Atlanta, Georgia Office)
Laura Hathaway Phillips
John H. Pomeroy
Mary K. Qualiana
J. Christopher Redding
Kevin F. Reed
Curtis A. Ritter
Kenneth D. Salomon
Stuart A. Sheldon
Sean R. Smith (Resident, Atlanta, Georgia Office)
Mitchell H. Stabbe
M. Anne Swanson
James A. Treanor, III
John D. Ward
Leslie H. Wiesenfelder
David Daniel Wild
Richard A. Wilhelm (Resident, Atlanta, Georgia Office)
David J. Wittenstein

(See Next Column)

DOW, LOHNES & ALBERTSON PLLC—*Continued*

Adisa P. Bakari
Steven E. Blumenthal (Resident, Atlanta, Georgia Office)
Kevin P. Brandon
Christina Hosp Burrow
Laurent M. Campo (Not admitted in DC)
Peter C. Cassat
Thomas M. Clyde (Resident, Atlanta, Georgia Office)
Jill C. Coan (Resident, Atlanta, Georgia Office)
Peter D. Coffman (Resident, Atlanta, Georgia Office)
Kimberly L. Cook
Cynthia L. Counts (Resident, Atlanta, Georgia Office)
Scott D. Dailard
W. Bruce Delmonico (Resident, Atlanta, Georgia Office)
Richard S. Denning (Resident, Atlanta, Georgia Office)
Whiting G. Dimock (Not admitted in DC)
Loretta J. Garcia
Jeffrey J. Gee
Aaron A. Ghais
Jonathon C. Glass
Lars Golumbic (Not admitted in DC)
George L. Hanbury III
Laura S. Harper
John E. Hinding
Joseph R. House
Lawrence T. Humphrey (Resident, Atlanta, Georgia Office)
Bradley R. Jacobsen (Not admitted in DC)
Jeffrey A. Jaeckel
Aaron Kanter (Not admitted in DC)
Anna Hong Kim (Not admitted in DC)
Kevin J. Kuzas
Kevin P. Latek
Jacqueline C. Lee
Rebecca A. Littleton (Resident, Atlanta, Georgia Office)
Tracy Anderson Locklin (Not admitted in DC)
Stephen E. Lopez
Gary S. Lutzker
Brian T. Mangino
David L. Martin (Not admitted in DC)
Sherry Booth Mastrostefano
Elizabeth Anne McGeary
J. Kevin Mills
Erik A. Moses
Carlos M. Nalda
Cecile Neuvens (Not admitted in DC)
Christine J. Newcomb
Scott S. Patrick
Karen A. Post
Leslie S. Price (Resident, Atlanta, Georgia Office)
Heather A. Purcell
Brooks C. Rathet (Resident, Atlanta, Georgia Office)
Elizabeth M. Roberts
Laura S. Roecklein
Prabha Raja Rollins
Elisa P. Rosen
Andrew B. Rosenstein
Barry Rothberg (Not admitted in DC)
Michael D. Rothberg
James R. Saxenian
Carolyn Schafer
Nina Shafran
Randall R. Smith (Resident, Atlanta, Georgia Office)
Linda J. Tarlow
Kathleen M. Tomcho (Resident, Atlanta, Georgia Office)
Thomas D. Twedt
Suzanne M. Underwald
Steven E. Wagner (Not admitted in DC)
Jay P. Walters
E. Adam Webb (Resident, Atlanta, Georgia Office)
Beth D. Wilkinson (Resident, Atlanta, Georgia Office)
Jill M. Wood (Resident, Atlanta, Georgia Office)
Allison S. Yamamoto

SENIOR COUNSEL

Daniel W. Toohey
Christina S. Wadyka

OF COUNSEL

Fayette B. Dow (1881-1962)
Gaylen D. Kemp (Resident, Atlanta, Georgia Office)
Horace L. Lohnes (1897-1954)
Fred W. Albertson
Thomas J. Schoenbaum (Resident, Atlanta, Georgia Office)

CONSULTANT

James Sears Bryant

For full biographical listings, see the Martindale-Hubbell Law Directory

DRINKER BIDDLE & REATH LLP (AV)

A Pennsylvania Limited Liability Partnership
1500 K Street, N.W., Suite 1100, 20005-1208
Telephone: 202-842-8800
Fax: 202-842-8465.
Cable Address: "Debemac"
URL: http://www.dbr.com
Philadelphia, Pennsylvania Office: Philadelphia National Bank Building, 1345 Chestnut Street.
Telephone: 215-988-2700.
Telefax: 215-988-2757.
Florham Park, New Jersey Office: Drinker Biddle & Shanley LLp, 500 Campus Drive,
Telephone: 973-360-1100.
Fax: 973-285-1625.
Princeton, New Jersey Office: Suite 300, 105 College Road East.
Telephone: 609-716-6500.
Telefax: 609-799-7000.
Berwyn, Pennsylvania Office: Suite 300, 1000 Westlakes Drive.
Telephone: 610-993-2200.
Telefax: 610-993-8585.
New York, New York Office: 89th Floor, One World Trade Center.
Telephone: 212-321-1812.
Telecopier: 1-212-466-0569.

(See Next Column)

RESIDENT PARTNERS

Joe D. Edge
Michael L. Gassmann
John C. Hockenbury
Alan J. Joaquin
Joseph F. Johnston, Jr.
Richard A. Levan
Douglas M. Mangel
Joaquin A. Marquez
Philip J. Mause
Michael J. McManus
James A. Meyers
M. Howard Morse
Mark L. Pelesh
John W. Pettit
Michael J. Remington
Richard M. Singer
Robert A. Skitol

OF COUNSEL

John P. Bankson, Jr.
Robert N. Cook
Kenneth E. Ryan

RESIDENT ASSOCIATES

Steven M. Chernoff (Not admitted in DC)
Brian A. Coleman
Mark F. Dever
Amy E. Carroll
Dina M. Gold
Timothy R. Hughes (Not admitted in DC)
Jeffrey J. Lopez
Elizabeth A. Marshall
Janet R. McFadden
Tina M. Pidgeon
John R. Przypyszny

LEGAL SUPPORT PERSONNEL
SPECIALIST (NON-LAWYER)

Sharon H. Bob (Higher Education Specialist on Policy and Regulation)

For full biographical listings, see the Martindale-Hubbell Law Directory

DUANE, MORRIS & HECKSCHER LLP (AV)

1667 K Street, N.W., Suite 700, 20006-1608
Telephone: 202-776-7800
Fax: 202-776-7801
URL: http://www.duanemorris.com
Philadelphia, Pennsylvania Office: Suite 4200, One Liberty Place.
Telephone: 215-979-1000.
Fax: 215-979-1020.
New York, New York Office: 380 Lexington Avenue.
Telephone: 212-692-1000.
Fax: 212-692-1020.
Chicago, Illinois Office: 227 West Monroe Street, Suite 3400.
Telephone: 312-499-6700.
Fax: 312-499-6701.
San Francisco, California Office: 100 Spear Street.
Telephone: 415-371-2200.
Fax: 415-371-2201.
Boston, Massachusetts Office: One International Place, 14th Floor.
Telephone: 617-598-3100.
Fax: 617-598-3101.
Miami, Florida Office: 200 South Biscayne Boulevard, Suite 3410.
Telephone: 305-960-2200.
Fax: 305-960-2201.
Wilmington, Delaware Office: 1201 Market Street, Suite 1500.
Telephone: 302-571-5550.
Fax: 302-571-5560.
Harrisburg, Pennsylvania Office: 305 North Front Street, 5th Floor, P.O. Box 1003.
Telephone: 717-237-5500.
Fax: 717-232-4015.
Wayne, Pennsylvania Office: 735 Chesterbrook Boulevard, Suite 300.
Telephone: 610-647-3555.
Fax: 610-640-2619.
Cherry Hill, New Jersey Office: 51 Haddonfield Road, Suite 340.
Telephone: 856-488-7300.
Fax: 856-488-7021.
Newark, New Jersey Office: One Riverfront Plaza.
Telephone: 973-424-2000.
Fax: 973-424-2001.
Palm Beach, Florida Office: 249 Royal Palm Way, Suite 403.
Telephone: 561-366-5400.
Fax: 561-366-5401.
Allentown, Pennsylvania Office: 968 Postal Road, Suite 200, P.O. Box 90400.
Telephone: 610-266-3650.
Fax: 610-266-3651.
Houston, Texas Office: One Greenway Plaza, Suite 500.
Telephone: 713-552-9900.
Fax: 713-552-0109.
Dover, Delaware Office: 314 S. State Street.
Telephone: 302-736-0156.
Fax: 302-736-0336.
Bangor, Maine Office: 15 Columbia Street, 4th Floor.
Telephone: 207-990-4800.
Fax: 207-990-4804.
Princeton, New Jersey Office: Princeton Forrestal Village, 116 Village Boulevard, Suite 200.
Telephone: 609-734-4323.
Fax: 609-734-4387.

(See Next Column)

DUANE, MORRIS & HECKSCHER LLP, *Washington—Continued*

PARTNERS

Brian D. Alprin
Jeffrey P. Bloom
Shirley A. Coffield
Christopher L. Crosswhite
Keith H. Ellis
John W. Griffin
Sheila Slocum Hollis (Partner-in-Charge, Washington, D.C.)
Mark L. Itzkoff
Brad C. Johnson
Laurence S. Lese
Andrew E. Mishkin
Mark F. Pretzat
David H. Robbins
Denyse Sabagh
Stephen L. Teichler

ASSOCIATE

Mary Ann Ralls

SPECIAL COUNSEL

Catherine Carl Wakelyn

For full biographical listings, see the Martindale-Hubbell Law Directory

DYKEMA GOSSETT PLLC (AV)

Franklin Square, Suite 300 West, 1300 I Street, N.W., 20005-3306
Telephone: 202-522-8600
Fax: 202-522-8669
Email: mstarrs@dykema.com *URL:* http://www.dykema.com
Ann Arbor, Michigan Office: 315 East Eisenhower Parkway, Suite 100, 48108-3306.
Telephone: 734-214-7660.
Fax: 734-214-7696.
Bloomfield Hills, Michigan Office: 1577 North Woodward Avenue, Suite 300, 48304-2820.
Telephone: 248-203-0700.
Fax: 248-203-0763.
Chicago, Illinois Office: 55 East Monroe Street, Suite 3050, 60603-5709.
Telephone: 312-551-4900.
Fax: 312-551-4919.
Detroit, Michigan Office: 400 Renaissance Center, 48243-1668.
Telephone: 313-568-6800.
Fax: 313-568-6545.
Grand Rapids, Michigan Office: Suite 700, 300 Ottawa Avenue, N.W., 49503-2304.
Telephone: 616-776-7500.
Fax: 616-776-7573.
Lansing, Michigan Office: 800 Michigan National Tower, 48933-1707.
Telephone: 517-374-9100.
Fax: 517-374-9191.
Affiliated Office: Via Matconi, 3, 40122 Bologna, Italy.
Telephone: 011-39-51-228222.
Fax: 011-39-51-6593580.

RESIDENT MEMBERS

Charles R. Bernardini (Not admitted in DC)
William H. Carroll
Steven A. Diaz
Edward A. Groobert
D. Biard MacGuineas
Howard E. O'Leary, Jr.
Fred L. Woodworth (Member in Charge)
Stephen H. Zimmerman (Not admitted in DC)

OF COUNSEL

Hilary Stephen Cairnie

RESIDENT ASSOCIATES

Judy Parker Jenkins

For full biographical listings, see the Martindale-Hubbell Law Directory

ECKERT SEAMANS CHERIN & MELLOTT, LLC (AV)

Suite 700, 1250 24th Street, N.W., 20037
Telephone: 202-659-6600
Facsimile: 202-659-6699
Email: escm.d.c.@escm.com *URL:* http://www.escm.com
Pittsburgh, Pennsylvania Office: 44th Floor, 600 Grant Street.
Telephone: 412-566-6000.
Facsimile: 412-566-6099.
Harrisburg, Pennsylvania Office: 213 Market Street, Eighth Floor.
Telephone: 717-237-6000.
Facsimile: 717-237-6019.
Philadelphia, Pennsylvania Office: 1515 Market Street, Ninth Floor.
Telephone: 215-851-8400.
Facsimile: 215-851-8383.
Boston, Massachusetts Office: One International Place, 18th Floor.
Telephone: 617-342-6800.
Facsimile: 617-342-6899.
Fort Lauderdale, Florida Office: Las Olas Centre, Suite 800, 450 East Las Olas Boulevard.
Telephone: 954-523-0400.
Facsimile: 954-523-7002.
Haddonfield, New Jersey Office: 36 Tanner Street, Second Floor.
Telephone: 609-427-6240.
Facsimile: 609-427-0611.

(See Next Column)

MEMBERS OF FIRM

Anthony A. Anderson
Keith L. Baker
C. Jonathan Benner
Edward J. Gill, Jr.
Edward R. Noonan
Jane Sutter Starke
George J. Wallace
Michael A. Wiegard
G. Kent Woodman

SPECIAL COUNSEL

Sean T. Connaughton
R. Lawrence Coughlin
Leonard L. Fleisig

RESIDENT ASSOCIATES

Anita C. Canovas (Not admitted in DC)
Timi E. Nickerson
Jeffrey E. Weinstein

For full biographical listings, see the Martindale-Hubbell Law Directory

THE FEINBERG GROUP, LLP (AV)

1120 20th Street, N.W. Suite 740 South, 20036-3437
Telephone: 202-371-1110
Fax: 202-962-9290
Email: kfeinberg@thefeinberggroup.com *URL:* http://www.krfassociates.com
New York, N.Y. Office: 780 3rd Avenue, Suite 2202.
Telephone: 212-527-9600.
Fax: 212-527-9611. Email: kfeinberg@thefeinberggroup.com.

PARTNERS

Kenneth R. Feinberg
Deborah E. Greenspan
Michael K. Rozen (Resident, New York Office)
Peter H. Woodin (Resident, New York Office)

ASSOCIATE

Fredric M. Brooks (Not admitted in DC)

SENIOR COUNSEL

Jacqueline E. Zins

For full biographical listings, see the Martindale-Hubbell Law Directory

FISHER WAYLAND COOPER LEADER & ZARAGOZA L.L.P. (AV)

A Registered Limited Liability Partnership
Suite 400, 2001 Pennsylvania Avenue, N.W., 20006-1851
Telephone: 202-659-3494
Facsimile: 202-296-6518
Email: fwclz@fwclz.com *URL:* http://www.fwclz.com

Ben S. Fisher (1890-1954)
Charles V. Wayland (1910-1980)
Martin R. Leader
Richard R. Zaragoza
Clifford M. Harrington
Kathryn R. Schmeltzer
Douglas Woloshin
David D. Oxenford
Barry H. Gottfried
Bruce D. Jacobs
Carroll John Yung
Glenn S. Richards
Robert C. Fisher
Scott R. Flick
Lauren Lynch Flick
Miles S. Mason

OF COUNSEL

Ben C. Fisher
Grover C. Cooper

ASSOCIATES

Dawn M. Sciarrino
Colette M. Capretz
Stephen J. Berman
Veronica D. McLaughlin
Stephanie Blessey Lilley
Jaqualin Friend Peterson
Cynthia D. Greer
Lara Strayer Meisner
David S. Konczal
Susan M. Hafeli
Tina R. Reynolds
Brendan Holland
Katherine Tong-Shin Suh
Max D. Gale (Not admitted in DC)
Joan E. Masters (Not admitted in DC)
Indra Sehdev Chalk (Not admitted in DC)

For full biographical listings, see the Martindale-Hubbell Law Directory

FOLEY, HOAG & ELIOT LLP (AV)

1747 Pennsylvania Avenue, N.W., 20006
Telephone: 202-223-1200
Telecopier: 202-785-6687
URL: http://www.fhe.com
Boston, Massachusetts Office: One Post Office Square.
Telephone: 617-832-1000.
Telecopier: 617-832-7000.

MEMBERS OF FIRM

John L. Burke, Jr.
James T. Montgomery, Jr.
Paul S. Reichler

COUNSEL

Janis H. Brennan
Stephanie Cutler
Marie Beatrice Grause
Traci Duvall Humes
Alima Joned

ASSOCIATES

Melissa E. Crow
Daniel M. Malabonga
Danell Palladine Dean

For full biographical listings, see the Martindale-Hubbell Law Directory

Washington—Continued

FOLEY & LARDNER (AV)

Washington Harbour, Suite 500, 3000 K Street, N.W., 20007-5109
Telephone: 202-672-5300
Facsimile: 202-672-5399
Telex: 904136 (FoleyLard Wash)
Email: foleylardner@worldnet.att.net *URL:* http://www.foleylardner.com
Los Angeles, California Office: 2029 Century Park East, 35th Floor.
Telephone: 310-277-2223.
Fax: 310-557-8475.
Sacramento, California Office: 300 Capitol Mall, Suite 1125.
Telephone: 916-443-8005.
Fax: 916-443-2240.
San Diego, California Office: 402 West Broadway, 23rd Floor.
Telephone: 619-234-6655.
Fax: 619-234-3510.
San Francisco, California Office: One Maritime Plaza, Sixth Floor.
Telephone: 415-434-4484.
Fax: 415-434-4507.
Denver, Colorado Office: 1999 Broadway, Suite 2560.
Telephone: 303-297-0260.
Fax: 303-297-0266.
Jacksonville, Florida Office: The Greenleaf Building, 200 Laura Street. P.O. Box 240.
Telephone: 904-359-2000.
Facsimile: 904-359-8700.
Orlando, Florida Office: Suite 1800, 111 North Orange Avenue, P.O. Box 2193.
Telephone: 407-423-7656.
Facsimile: 407-648-1743.
Tallahassee, Florida Office: 300 East Park Avenue, P.O. Box 1454.
Telephone: 850-222-6100.
Facsimile: 850-561-6475.
Tampa, Florida Offices: Suite 2700, One Hundred N. Tampa Street, P.O. Box 3391.
Telephones: 813-229-2300; Pinellas County: 813-442-3296.
Facsimile: 813-221-4210.
West Palm Beach, Florida Office: Suite 200, Phillips Point East Tower, 777 South Flagler Drive.
Telephone: 561-655-5050.
Facsimile: 561-655-6925.
Chicago, Illinois Office: Suite 3300, One IBM Plaza, 330 N. Wabash Avenue.
Telephone: 312-755-1900.
Facsimile: 312-755-1925.
Annapolis, Maryland Office: Suite 102, 175 Admiral Cochrane Drive.
Telephone: 410-266-8077.
Telex: 899149 (Oldtownpat).
Facsimile: 410-266-8664.
Madison, Wisconsin Office: Verex Plaza, 150 East Gilman Street, P.O. Box 1497.
Telephone: 608-257-5035.
Facsimile: 608-258-4258.
Milwaukee, Wisconsin Office: Firstar Center, 777 East Wisconsin Avenue.
Telephone: 414-271-2400.
Telex: 26-819 (Foley Lard Mil).
Facsimile: 414-297-4900.
Brussels, Belgium Office: Avenue Louise, 283.
Telephone: 32-2-646-2777.
Facsimile: 32-2-646-7574.

PARTNERS

Stephen A. Bent
James N. Bierman
David A. Blumenthal
Robert A. Burka
Alan I. Cantor
Steven B. Chameides
Paul E. Cooney
William T. Ellis
John J. Feldhaus (Not admitted in DC)
Howard W. Fogt, Jr.
Patricia D. Granados
John P. Isacson, Jr.
Mary Cynthia Atchley Jester
Michael D. Kaminski
Kenneth E. Krosin
Jack L. Lahr
Glenn Law
Melinda F. Levitt
Richard Linn
Peter C. Linzmeyer
Peter G. Mack
Lisa S. Mankofsky
Brian J. McNamara
Sybil Meloy
Paul R. Monsees
Richard C. Peet
George E. Quillin (Not admitted in DC)
David A. Sacks
Colin G. Sandercock
Jacqueline Marie Saue
Bernhard D. Saxe
Charles F. Schill
Richard L. Schwaab
Arthur Schwartz
Larry L. Shatzer II
Jay N. Varon
J. Mark Waxman (Not admitted in DC; Resident also at Los Angeles, California Office)
Harold C. Wegner
Martin J. Weinstein
Kenneth B. Winer
Samuel J. Winer
Yoichiro Yamaguchi (Not admitted in DC)
Jeff Zimmerman
Gary M. Zinkgraf

RETIRED PARTNERS

Edwin Jason Dryer
Donald D. Jeffery

OF COUNSEL

Barbara Ann McDowell (Not admitted in DC)

(See Next Column)

SPECIAL COUNSEL

Theodore H. Bornstein
Jayme A. Huleatt
Susan Ann Richards
James A. Sprowl

RESIDENT ASSOCIATES

Pavan Kumar Agarwal
Phillip John Articola
George C. Beck
George C. Best (Not admitted in DC)
Paul M. Booth
Todd J. Burns
Beth A. Burrous
Robert W. Busby Jr.
Aaron C. Chatterjee
Matthew R. Cohen
Ronald Coslick
Simon E. Dance
Brian J. Dorini
Joseph D. Edmondson, Jr.
Lloyd N. Fantroy
Rebecca R. Fry
Allison C. George
Stacy L. Holmes
Bryan B. House (Not admitted in DC)
Ronald J. Kamis
Jennifer Kane (Not admitted in DC)
Mary Michelle Kile
Lyle Kimms
Ivonne Mena King
Susan M. C. Kovarovics
Johnny A. Kumar
Kening Li (Not admitted in DC)
Thomas W. Mac Allister (Not admitted in DC)
Stephen B. Maebius
Jeffrey G. Micklos (Not admitted in DC)
Marvin A. Motsenbocker
Nalini K. Pande
Andrew E. Rawlins
Norman J. Rich (Not admitted in DC)
Thomas M. Rizzo
Gary S. Rovner
Alan D. Rutenberg
Michele M. Schafer
Ankur D. Shah
James M. Silbermann
Samuel B. Sterrett, Jr.
C. Anthony Trambley

For full biographical listings, see the Martindale-Hubbell Law Directory

FREEDMAN, LEVY, KROLL & SIMONDS (AV)

Suite 825, 1050 Connecticut Avenue, N.W., 20036-5366
Telephone: 202-457-5100
Cable Address: "Attorneys"
Telecopier: 202-457-5151
Email: flks@flks.com *URL:* http://www.flks.com

MEMBERS OF FIRM

Walter Freedman
Peter E. Panarites
Gary O. Cohen
Jay W. Freedman
Arthur H. Bill
Thomas C. Lauerman
Richard G. Stoll
Marc B. Dorfman
John H. Chettle
Lawrence G. McBride
Emil Hirsch
Thomas L. James
David P. Novello
Richard T. Choi
Bruce A. Rosenblum

OF COUNSEL

Arnold Levy
Milton P. Kroll
Jerome H. Simonds

SPECIAL COUNSEL

Norman C. Bensley (Not admitted in DC)
Gregor B. McCurdy
Leo F. Orenstein

ASSOCIATES

Patrick J. Kearney
David Seth Sanders
Marvin C. Lunde, III (Not admitted in DC)

For full biographical listings, see the Martindale-Hubbell Law Directory

FRIED, FRANK, HARRIS, SHRIVER & JACOBSON (AV)

A Partnership including Professional Corporations
Suite 800, 1001 Pennsylvania Avenue, N.W., 20004-2505
Telephone: 202-639-7000
Telecopy: 202-639-7008
Email: info@ffhsj.com
New York, New York Office: One New York Plaza.
Telephone: 212-859-8000.
Cable Address: "Steric New York." W.U. Intl.
Telex: 662119. W.U. Domestic: 128173.
Telecopier: 212-859-4000 (Dex 6200).
Los Angeles, California Office: 350 South Grand Avenue, 32nd Floor.
Telephone: 213-473-2000.
London, England Office: 4 Chiswell Street, London EC1Y 4UP.
Telephone: 011-44-171-972-9600.
Fax: 011-44-171-972-9602.
Other London, England Office: International Securities Unit, 21 Wilson Street, London EC2M 2TX.
Telephone: 011-44-171-825-3093.
Paris, France Office: 7, Rue Royale, 75008.
Telephone: (011 331) 40-17-04-04.
Fax: (011 331) 40-17-08-30.

WASHINGTON, D.C. PARTNERS

David L. Ansell
David E. Birenbaum
John T. Boese
John W. Chierichella
Peter V. Z. Cobb (Not admitted in DC)
Paul H. Falon
Stephen I. Glover
Jack B. Gordon
Karl A. Groskaufmanis
David B. Hardison
Dixie Lynn Johnson
Gregory P. Joseph (Not admitted in DC)
Robert E. Juceam (Not admitted in DC)

(See Next Column)

FRIED, FRANK, HARRIS, SHRIVER & JACOBSON, *Washington—Continued*

WASHINGTON, D.C. PARTNERS (Continued)

Alan S. Kaden
Jay R. Kraemer
Robert H. Ledig
Daniel E. Loeb
James J. McCullough
Deneen J. Melander
Matt T. Morley
Harvey L. Pitt
Elliot E. Polebaum
Richard A. Sauber
James H. Schropp
Richard A. Steinwurtzel
William H. Taft, IV
Vasiliki B. Tsaganos
Andrew P. Varney
Michael L. Waldman
Thomas P. Vartanian

OF COUNSEL

Milton Eisenberg (P.C.)
Joel R. Feidelman (P.C.)
Martin D. Ginsburg (P.C.)
Max M. Kampelman
Marcus A. Rowden
Sargent Shriver
Daniel M. Singer
Louis D. Victorino

SPECIAL COUNSEL

Douglas W. Baruch
Mark J. Dorsey
Michele E. Foster
Douglas E. Perry

ASSOCIATES

Jonathan S. Aronie
Alisa Babitz
James P. Baetzhold
Lawrence R. Bard
Stephen R. Bauer
Tommy P. Beaudreau (Not admitted in DC)
Beth Hilliard Colleye
Yolanda Marie Demianczuk (Not admitted in DC)
Arlene R. Dick
Urvi M. Doshi (Not admitted in DC)
Scott M. Faga (Not admitted in DC)
Mark J. Fajfar
Dawn E. Faris
Robin B. First
Brandon M. Fitzgerald
Lisa A. Fuller
Janet G. Gamer
Thomas M. Glassic
Gejaa Temesgien Gobena (Not admitted in DC)
Michelle Berk Gold
K. Susan Grafton
Karen T. Grisez
Brian Scott Higgins (Not admitted in DC)
Consuelo J. Hitchcock
Lanae Holbrook
J. Todd Hutchins
Jonathan M. Jacobs
Shelby L. Katz
James S. Kennell
Charles W. Lockyer, Jr.
JoEllen Lotvedt Legg
Jay D. Majors
Julia A. McDonough
R. Patrick Murphy
Tanya Y. Murphy (Not admitted in DC)
Elton F. Norman
Paul H. Pashkoff
Stacy L. Paxson
Anne B. Perry
Catherine Evans Pollack
Renuka E. Rao (Not admitted in DC)
Steven E. Rindner
Michael J. Rivera
Christopher M. Salter
Benjamin Salzillo
Peter H. Schwartz
Jonathan P. Scott
Andrew Dieter Skowronek (Not admitted in DC)
Thomas Peter Smith, Jr. (Not admitted in DC)
Timothy W. Staley
Sharan Kaur Suri (Not admitted in DC)
Larisa Avner Trainor
Nina Y. Wang
Robert C. Westerfeldt
Edward B. Whittemore
Kathryn Keating Winters
David B. Wiseman

For full biographical listings, see the Martindale-Hubbell Law Directory

GRAHAM & JAMES LLP (AV)

Suite 700, 2000 M Street, N.W., 20036
Telephone: 202-463-0800
Telecopier: 202-463-0823
Email: rbank@gj.com *URL:* http://www.gj.com
Other offices located in: San Francisco, Los Angeles, Orange County, Palo Alto and Sacramento, California; Seattle, Washington; New York, New York; Milan, Italy; Beijing, China; Tokyo, Japan; London, England.
Associated Offices: Deacons Graham & James, Hong Kong, Sydney, Melbourne, Brisbane, Perth and Canberra, Australia.
Affiliated Offices: Deacons Graham & James, Hanoi and Ho Chi Minh City, Vietnam; Taipei, Taiwan and Bangkok, Thailand; In association with Dewi Soeharto & Rekan, Jakarta, Indonesia; Graham & James in affiliation with Taylor Joynson Garrett, London, England, Bucharest, Romania and Brussels, Belgium; Kau, Dusseldorf, Germany; Mishare M. Al-Ghazali & Partners, Safat, Kuwait; Law Firm of Salah Al-Hejailan, Jeddah and Riyadh, Saudi Arabia; Yeo Wee Kiong & Partners, Singapore.

OF COUNSEL

Richard K. Bank (Resident)

MEMBERS OF FIRM

Lawrence D. Blume (Resident, New York, N.Y. Office)
Grace Parke Fremlin (Resident, New York, N.Y. Office)
Brian S. Goldstein (Resident, New York, N.Y. Office)
Yasuhiro Hagihara (Resident, Los Angeles, California Office)
Irwin M. Rosenthal (Resident, New York, N.Y. Office)
Les J. Weinstein (Resident, Los Angeles, California Office)
Steven S. Weiser (Resident, New York, N.Y. Office)
Barry Leigh Weissman (Resident, Los Angeles, California Office)

SPECIAL COUNSEL

Phillip Ashman (Resident, Orange County, California Office)

(See Next Column)

ASSOCIATES

Mark S. Burton (Resident, San Francisco, California Office)
John P. Lasala (Resident, New York, N.Y. Office)
Eugene Serban (Resident, New York, N.Y. Office)

For full biographical listings, see the Martindale-Hubbell Law Directory

HALE AND DORR LLP (AV)

A Partnership including Professional Corporations
1455 Pennsylvania Avenue, N.W., 20004
Telephone: 202-942-8400
Cable Address: "Hafis Wsh"
Telecopier: 202-942-8484
URL: http://www.haledorr.com
Boston, Massachusetts Office: 60 State Street.
Telephone: 617-526-6000.
Cable Address: "Hafis."
Telex: 94-0472.
Telecopier: Domestic 617-526-5000; 617-742-9108.

MEMBERS OF FIRM

John C. Christie, Jr. (Resident)
James L. Quarles III (Resident)
Mark A. Heller (Resident)
Allen H. Fox (Resident)
Jay P. Urwitz (Resident)
Paul G. Wallach (Resident)
Michael D. Esch (Resident)
Steven S. Snider (Resident)
David Sylvester (Resident)
Jeffrey J. Davidson (Resident)
Gilbert B. Kaplan (Resident)
Kenneth H. Slade
William G. McElwain (Resident)
William F. Leahy (Resident)
Brent B. Siler (Resident)
Kenneth R. Meade (Resident)
Henry N. Wixon (Resident)
Paul V. Rogers (Not admitted in DC; Resident)
Louise Nicholson Howe (Resident)
Kathleen M. Weinstein (Resident)
David A. Wilson (Resident)
Scott M. Alter (Resident)
Sean P. Sherman (Resident)
Wendy E. Anderson (Resident)
Barry J. Hurewitz
Jane A. Kalinski
Melisa Moonan
James G. Votaw

COUNSEL

Miriam R. Gamson
Paul W. Jameson (Resident)
Cris R. Revaz
William F. Winslow

RESIDENT ASSOCIATES

Eric S. Andreas (Not admitted in DC)
Alexander D. Baldwin
Michael S. Buckner (Not admitted in DC)
Kerry Burke (Not admitted in DC)
Jeffrey C. Dorsey (Not admitted in DC)
James M. Dowd (Not admitted in DC)
Charles V. Ghoorah
Edward D. Grieff
Michael Q. Hyde
Karin J. Kysilka (Not admitted in DC)
Karen Lowy Tinsky (Not admitted in DC)
Daniel D. McCawley (Not admitted in DC)
Carol McGee
Stephanie Philbin
Natalie L. Reed (Not admitted in DC)
Kerry Pyle Rubin (Not admitted in DC)
Andrew P. Schoeffler (Not admitted in DC)
David A. Suski (Not admitted in DC)

Hy David Rubenstein

For full biographical listings, see the Martindale-Hubbell Law Directory

HOGAN & HARTSON L.L.P. (AV)

Columbia Square, 555 13th Street, N.W., 20004-1109
Telephone: 202-637-5600
Telex: 89-2757
Cable Address: "Hogander Washington"
Fax: 202-637-5910
URL: http://www.hhlaw.com
Brussels, Belgium Office: Avenue des Arts 41, 1040.
Telephone: (32.2) 505.09.11.
Fax: (32.2) 505.09.96.
Budapest, Hungary (Affiliated Office): Nagy & Pintér, Hogan & Hartson Law Office, Bank Center, Granite Tower, 9th Floor, Budapest V., Szabadsag ter 7, 1944 Hungary.
Telephone: (36-1) 302-9050.
Fax: (36-1) 302-9060.
London, England Office: One Angel Court, EC2R 7HJ.
Telephone: +(44) 207-367-0200.
Fax: +(44) 207-367-0220.
Moscow, Russia Office: 33/2 Usacheva Street, Building 3, 119048.
Telephone: (7095) 245-5190. Int'l
Telephone: (7501) 907-0451.
Fax: (7095) 245-5192. Int'l
Fax: (7501) 907-0462.
Paris, France (Affiliated Office): Cariddi, Mee, Rué, Avocats Associés à la Cour de Paris, 12, rue de la Paix, 75002.
Telephone: (33-1) 42.61.57.71.
Fax: (33-1) 42.61.79.21.

(See Next Column)

HOGAN & HARTSON L.L.P.—*Continued*

Prague, Czech Republic (Affiliated Office): Hogan & Hartson, Advokátnií Kanceláře, v.o.s., Trziste 13, 118 00.
Telephone: (420-2) 2211-7111.
Fax: (420-2) 2421-5105.
Warsaw, Poland Office: Hogan & Hartson Sp.zo.o, Atrium Tower, Al. Jana Pawla II 25, 00-854.
Telephone: (48-22) 653-4200.
Fax: (48-22) 653-4250.
Baltimore, Maryland Office: 111 South Calvert Street.
Telephone: 410-659-2700.
Fax: 410-539-6981.
Rockville, Maryland Office: 600 Jefferson Plaza, Suite 203.
Telephone: 301-315-2206.
Fax: 301-315-9046.
Boulder, Colorado Office: 1800 Broadway, Suite 200.
Telephone: 720-406-5300.
Fax: 720-406-5301.
Colorado Springs, Colorado Office: Two North Cascade Avenue, Suite 1300.
Telephone: 719-448-5900.
Fax: 719-448-5922.
Denver, Colorado Office: One Tabor Center, Suite 1500, 1200 Seventeenth Street.
Telephone: 303-899-7300.
Fax: 303-899-7333.
Los Angeles, California Office: Biltmore Tower, 500 S. Grand Avenue, Suite 1900.
Telephone: 213-337-6700.
Fax: 213-337-6701.
Newport Beach, California Office: 4675 MacArthur Court, Suite 670.
Telephone: 949-250-4550.
Fax: 949-833-0976.
McLean, Virginia Office: 8300 Greensboro Drive.
Telephone: 703-610-6100.
Fax: 703-610-6200.
New York, New York Office: 885 Third Avenue, 26th Floor.
Telephone: 212-409-9800.
Fax: 212-409-9801.

MEMBERS OF FIRM

Frank J. Hogan (1877-1944)
Nelson T. Hartson (1887-1976)
Jonathan L. Abram
Gil A. Abramson (Resident, Baltimore, Maryland Office)
Donna Lady Alpi
Patricia Riley Ambrose
Jeanne S. Archibald
Edwin P. Aro (Resident, Denver, Colorado Office)
Robert L. Asher (Resident, London, England Office)
Deborah Taylor Ashford
Helen Clark Atkeson (Resident, Denver, Colorado Office)
Steven E. Ballew
James T. Banks
Michael D. Barnes
George P. Barsness
Raymond J. Batla, Jr. (Also at London, England and Budapest, Hungary Offices)
George Beall (Resident, Baltimore, Maryland Office)
Richard K.A. Becker (Resident, McLean, Virginia Office)
Joseph C. Bell (Also at Warsaw, Poland Office)
Barbara Bennett
A. Lee Bentley, III
Weatherly Lowe Bentley
Lee E. Berner (Resident, McLean, Virginia Office)
Lisa Bonanno
David W. Bonser
John W. Borkowski (Also practicing individually in New Orleans, Louisiana)
Donna A. Boswell
William J. Bowman
Marc H. Bozeman (Resident, Los Angeles, California Office)
William A. Bradford, Jr.
Kathryn Webb Bradley (Resident, Denver, Colorado Office)
Robert P. Brady
Patricia A. Brannan
Rebecca B. Bronson (Resident, Moscow, Russia Office)
Stanley J. Brown (Rockville, Maryland and McLean, Virginia Offices)
Thomas N. Bulleit, Jr.
David W. Burgett
Carol W. Burton (Resident, Denver, Colorado Office)
Raymond S. Calamaro
Alan F. Cariddi (Resident, Paris, France)
George U. Carneal
Robert B. Cave
Michael L. Cheroutes (Not admitted in DC; Also at Denver, Colorado and Warsaw, Poland Offices)
Alphonso A. Christian, II
Claudette M. Christian
Nancy Andreas Clodfelter (Resident, Denver, Colorado Office)
Ty Cobb (Also at Denver, Colorado Office)
Steven A. Cohen (Resident, Denver, Colorado Office)
Vincent H. Cohen
Michael D. Colglazier (Resident, Baltimore, Maryland Office)
Joseph G. Connolly, Jr.
Jonathan A. Constine
John W. Cook (Resident, Colorado Springs, Colorado Office)
Robert L. Corn-Revere
Michele C. Coyle (Resident, Los Angeles, California Office)
Colin W. Craik (Prague, Czech Republic and London, England Offices)
Dean W. Crowell
Charles B. Curtis
Daniel M. Davidson
Edward S. Desmarais, Jr.
Sara-Ann Determan
John F. Dienelt
Edward C. Dolan
Agnes Pek Dover
Edward C. Duckers
Robert B. Duncan (Also at McLean, Virginia Office)
Isabel P. Dunst
Alan L. Dye
Bijan-Emmanuel Eghbal (Resident, Paris France Office)
Claud v. S. Eley (Resident, Brussels, Belgium Office)

(See Next Column)

MEMBERS OF FIRM (Continued)

E. Tazewell Ellett
Kevin D. Evans (Resident, Denver, Colorado Office)
Frank J. Fahrenkopf, Jr.
Michele C. Farquhar
Prentiss E. Feagles
Douglas A. Fellman
John P. Fitzgerald (Also at Denver, Colorado Office)
Howard I. Flack
William P. Flanagan
Jonathan S. Franklin
Amy Bowerman Freed (Resident, Baltimore, Maryland Office)
Sean R. Gallagher (Resident, Denver, Colorado Office)
Aleksander Galos (Resident, Warsaw, Poland Office)
John M. Gardner (Resident, Denver, Colorado Office)
James A. Gede, Jr. (Resident, Baltimore, Maryland Office)
James R. Ghiselli (Resident, Boulder, Colorado Office)
Gerald E. Gilbert (Resident, McLean, Virginia Office)
Bruce W. Gilchrist
Gardner F. Gillespie
C. Michael Gilliland
J. Warren Gorrell, Jr. (Also at New York, N.Y. Office)
Kevin G. Gralley (Resident, Baltimore, Maryland Office)
Darrel J. Grinstead
Christopher J. Hagan
Martin J. Hahn
Benton R. Hammond
Karen M. Hardwick
Anthony S. Harrington
Joseph M. Hassett
Catriona Hatton (Resident, Brussels, Belgium Office)
Melinda Reid Hatton
Kenneth J. Hautman (Resident, McLean, Virginia Office)
Elizabeth Blossom Heffernan
David J. Hensler
Patrick F. Hofer
Steven P. Hollman
Whitney A. Holmes (Resident, Denver, Colorado Office)
Howard M. Holstein
Janet Pitterle Holt
Craig A. Hoover
Richard T. Horan, Jr. (Resident, McLean, Virginia Office)
James A. Hourihan
William Mike House
Eve N. Howard
Stephen J. Immelt (Resident, Baltimore, Maryland Office)
Maciej Jamka (Resident, Warsaw, Poland Office)
Harry T. Jones, Jr.
Jonathan S. Kahan
Robert H. Kapp
Steven M. Kaufman
John C. Keeney, Jr.
J. Clinton Kelly (Resident, Baltimore, Maryland Office)
Nevin J. Kelly
J. Hovey Kemp
Robert J. Kenney, Jr.
Michael L. Kidney
David A. Kikel
Andrew J. Kilcarr
Carol Weld King
David P. King (Resident, Baltimore, Maryland Office)
Duncan S. Klinedinst (Resident, McLean, Virginia Office)
Diane A. Koonjy
Edward L. Korwek
William J. Kubida (Resident, Colorado Springs, Colorado Office)
Gary Jay Kushner
Kevin J. Lanigan
Mark J. Larson
Philip C. Larson
C. Stephen Lawrence (Resident, Newport Beach, California Office)
Stephan E. Lawton
Thomas B. Leary
Dirk Leermakers (Resident, Brussels, Belgium Office)
Robert F. Leibenluft
Lewis E. Leibowitz
David G. Leitch
Scott R. Lilienthal
John R. Lilyestrom
Kevin J. Lipson
Timothy A. Lloyd
Laura E. Loeb
Walter G. Lohr, Jr. (Resident, Baltimore, Maryland Office)
Ellen R. Lokker
Milan Lovíšek (Resident, Prague, Czech Republic Office)
Jeffrey Alan Lowe
Daniel H. Maccoby (Resident, London, England Office)
David B. H. Martin, Jr.
Thene M. Martin (Resident, Baltimore, Maryland Office)
Warren H. Maruyama
Mary Anne Mason
John P. Mathis
George W. Mayo, Jr.
Mark E. Mazo
Mark S. McConnell
Janet L. McDavid
Thomas L. McGovern III
James G. McMillan
Bruce C. Mee (Resident, Paris, France)
George H. Mernick, III
Martin Michaelson
Kathleen M. Miko
Evan Miller
George W. Miller
H. Todd Miller
Randy E. Miller
Barbara F. Mishkin
Austin S. Mittler
William L. Monts, III
Jean S. Moore
Dennis K. Moyer (Resident, McLean, Virginia Office)
Steven A. Museles
Kornelia Nagy-Koppany (Not admitted in United States)
William L. Neff
Karol Lyn Newman
William D. Nussbaum
Gerald E. Oberst, Jr. (Resident, Brussels, Belgium Office)
Maureen O'Bryon
Bob Glen Odle
Linda L. Oliver
Nancy Doerr O'Neil (Not admitted in DC; Also at Baltimore, Maryland Office)
Christopher D. Ozeroff (Resident, Boulder, Colorado Office)
Christine M. Pallares (Resident, New York, N.Y. Office)
Bruce E. Parmley
Richard J. Parrino (Resident, McLean, Virginia Office)
Bert R. Peña
Robert B. Pender, Jr.
Patrick K. Perrin (Resident, Boulder, Colorado Office)
M. Elizabeth Peters
Douglas A. Pluss (Resident, Denver, Colorado Office)
Daniel B. Poneman
Lisa Lee Poole
Philip D. Porter (Resident, McLean, Virginia Office)
John M. Potter (Resident, Los Angeles, California Office)
E. Barrett Prettyman, Jr.
Michael A. Proett (Resident, London, England Office)
Gerard J. Prud'homme
Patrick M. Raher

(See Next Column)

HOGAN & HARTSON L.L.P., *Washington—Continued*

MEMBERS OF FIRM (Continued)

Scott H. Reisch (Resident, Denver, Colorado Office)
Terri Steinhaus Reiskin
Thomas E. Repke (Resident, Baltimore, Maryland Office)
Marissa G. Repp
William S. Reyner, Jr.
Leslie S. Ritts
John G. Roberts, Jr.
William R. Roberts (Managing Partner, Boulder, Colorado Office)
Steven A. Robins (Rockville, Maryland and McLean, Virginia Offices)
Richard S. Rodin
Paul G. Rogers
Peter A. Rohrbach
Peter J. Romeo
James J. Rosenhauer
Mace J. Rosenstein
Steven J. Routh
Fabrice Rué (Resident, Paris, France)
James P. Ruggeri
Richard T. Saas
David J. Saylor
Todd D. Schafer (Resident, Moscow, Russia Office)
William C. Schmidt
Jeffrey G. Schneider (Resident, New York, N.Y. Office)
David J. Scott (Resident, Denver, Colorado Office)
James E. Showen
Howard S. Silver
Michael J. Silver (Resident, Baltimore, Maryland Office)
Richard S. Silverman
Paul C. Skelly
Edward C. Sledge (Resident, Baltimore, Maryland Office)
Maree F. Sneed
Allen R. Snyder
Clyde H. Sorrell, Jr.
Lorraine Sostowski
Peter S. Spivack
Timothy Charles Stanceu
John S. Stanton
Krzysztof Stefanowicz (Resident, Warsaw, Poland Office)
Stuart G. Stein
Steven B. Steinborn
Clifford D. Stromberg
Rose Ann C. Sullivan (Resident, Colorado Springs, Colorado Office)
Jan Tanzer (Resident, Prague, Czech Republic Office)
Peter W. Tredick
Helen R. Trilling
Andrew J. Trubin (Resident, New York, N.Y. Office)
Albert W. Turnbull
Niki Frangos Tuttle (Resident, Denver, Colorado Office)
Ralph S. Tyler (Resident, Baltimore, Maryland Office)
Craig H. Ulman
Craig A. Umbaugh (Resident, Denver, Colorado Office)
Christine A. Varney
Ann Morgan Vickery
Eric Von Salzen
Robert J. Waldman
Donis G. Walker (Denver and Colorado Springs, Colorado Offices)
Richard L.A. Weiner (Resident, Brussels, Belgium Office)
T. Clark Weymouth
Douglas P. Wheeler
Zdzislaw W. Wieckowski (Resident, Warsaw, Poland Office)
Michael Cunningham Williams
Edward C. Wilson, Jr.
Ronald J. Wiltsie, II
Joel S. Winnik
Pamela G. Winthrop
Erik B. Wulff
Michael K. Wyatt
Emily M. Yinger (Resident, McLean, Virginia Office)
Joseph H. Young (Resident, Baltimore, Maryland Office)

COUNSEL

Audrey J. Anderson
Merry C. Anderson
Margaret A. Athay
Dale E. Bonner (Resident, Los Angeles, California Office)
Pavel Bradac (Resident, Prague, Czech Republic Office)
Donald C. Brown Jr.
Lance D. Bultena
Maryanne Courtney
Jeffrey S. George (Resident, Colorado Springs, Colorado Office)
Jacquelyn E. Grillon
Michele Sasse Harrington (Resident, McLean, Virginia Office)
Karis A. Hastings
Lynn G. Kamarck
Mark A. Kass
Joseph G. Krauss
Gerald J. S. Laporte
Ildiko Laszlo (Resident, Budapest, Hungary Office)
Timothy J. Lockhart (Resident, McLean, Virginia Office)
Helen P. McClure
Jeffrey W. Munk
Helen A. Nastasia (Resident, McLean, Virginia Office)
Aurel Pinter (Resident, Budapest, Hungary Office)
Sharis Arnold Pozen
Robert N. Rabecs
Margaret E. Roggensack
Robert C. Satrom (Resident, Moscow, Russia Office)
Ellen Siegler
David L. Sieradzki
Robert L. Spencer
Stephen G. Vaskov

INTERNATIONAL COUNSEL

Christine Bougis (Resident, Paris, France Office)
Vuong Van Bac (Resident, Paris, France Office)
Paul W. Virtue (Not admitted in DC)

OF COUNSEL

John P. Arness
Iwo Byczewski (Resident, Warsaw, Poland Office)
H. Thomas Coghill (Resident, Denver, Colorado Office)
Marvin J. Diamond
Robert J. Elliott
Robert M. Jeffers
Bogudar Kordasiewicz (Resident, Warsaw, Poland Office)
Dennis J. Lehr
Lee Loevinger
Sherwin J. Markman
Seymour S. Mintz
John J. Ross
David E. Skaggs (Not admitted in DC; Also at Denver, Colorado Office)
Jerome N. Sonosky
Jac K. Sperling (Resident, Denver, Colorado Office)
Bruce S. Wolff
Clayton K. Yeutter

(See Next Column)

RESIDENT ASSOCIATES

Roger P. Alford
Nalini P. Anand
Ana Cristina Arumi
Rose Marie L. Audette
Daniel D. Barnhizer
Suzanne A. Barr
H. Christopher Bartolomucci
John B. Beckman (Not admitted in DC)
Jonathan Bender
Leslie Anne Benton
Peter R. Bisio
Robert M. Blue
Pamela Morris Blumenthal
Jennifer A. Bonanno
Joseph M. Boyle
Ronald P. Brower
Catherine T. Brown
René E. Browne
Andrea M. Bruce
Brooke Bumpers
Paul A. Burkett
Mary Ellen Callahan
Bruce D. Campbell Jr.
Christopher P. Cardaci
Irene Florence Chang
James C. Chen
Carol B. Chesley (Not admitted in DC)
Brian S. Chilton
Jessica C. Clark
Kaija M. Clark (Not admitted in DC)
Karen Renfree Clark
Laurie A. Clarke
Tracy-Elizabeth Clay
Jacqueline P. Cleary
Susan M. Cook
Andrea T. Cummings (Not admitted in DC)
Alice T. Valder Curran
William J. Curtin, III
David F. Cutter
Scott M. Deutchman
M. Colette Devine
Kristen A. Donoghue
Yaron Dori
Alexander E. Dreier
Daniel F. Duchovny
William L. Elder
Jonathan Engler
Jody M. Foster
Anthony J. Franze
Jodi K. Fredrickson (Not admitted in DC)
Deborah Schwager Froling
Jennifer Bush Furey
Andrea Gacki
Lily M. Garcia
Gregory G. Garre
John F. Gaul
Joseph E. Gilligan
Victoria W. Girard
Stephanie J. Gold
F. Joseph Gormley (Not admitted in DC)
Justine Young Gottshall
William D. Gould
Andrea F. Grable (Not admitted in DC)
Catherine R. Guttman-McCabe
Christopher R. Hall (Not admitted in DC)
Lisa A. Harig
Lorane F. Hebert (Not admitted in DC)
E. Desmond Hogan
Janice Marchiafava Hogan
Stephen P. Holman
Kevin Huffman (Not admitted in DC)
James A. Hutchinson
Jamila E. Jefferson
Sten A. Jensen
Deen Kaplan
R. Daniel Keating (Not admitted in DC)
Valerie E. Keller
Christopher L. Killion
Alethia N. King (Not admitted in DC)
Douglas A. Klein
Michele A. Kulerman
Jennifer J. Kulynych (Not admitted in DC)
S. Gregg Kunzi
Stephen Kuperberg (Not admitted in DC)
Stuart M. Langbein
Helene C. Lasker
Mitchell J. Lazris
Allison B. Leader
Coates Lear (Not admitted in DC)
Mark D. Learn
F. William LeBeau
Adam K. Levin
Craig A. Lewis
Ronald G. London
Harriette H. Lopp (Not admitted in DC)
Paul D. Manca
Timothy C. Maples (Not admitted in DC)
Lynda K. Marshall
Michael F. Mason (Not admitted in DC)
Brian E. Mazurek
Susan Rotatori McAuliffe
John E. McCarrick
Scott D. McClure
Tovan McDaniel
John J. McDonald
Scott A. McIntosh
Cynthia M. McKnight
Margaret E.K. Middleton
Kathy Marlo Miljanic
Jeremy B. Miller
R. Latane Montague, IV (Not admitted in DC)
Thomas C. Morey
Steven F. Morris
Christopher K. Murphy
Joseph M. Murphy
Jeffrey C. Nelson
J. Patrick Nevins
Molly Sullivan Newberry
David Newmann
Timothy D. Palmer
Alexia Pappas
Jeffrey D. Pariser
Alexander J. Park
Mark Paulding
Melissa Jones Pelczynski
Scott D. Peterman
Kathryn A. Peterson (Not admitted in DC)
Kathleen R. Philpott
G. Laurence Plaisted
Stephen F. Propst
Jennifer A. Purvis
Omyra M. Ramsingh
Siobhan C. Rausch (Not admitted in DC)
Michael J. Reedich (Not admitted in DC)
Jonathan T. Rees
Victor L. Reid
James S. Rixse
Margaret Rhinelander Rizzi
Beth L. Roberts
Corey W. Roush (Not admitted in DC)
Melissa L. Roy
Amit Saluja (Not admitted in DC)
Sherri A. Braden Sampson
Atul Saran (Not admitted in DC)
Christopher A. Schindler
Julie Mathews Schuetze
Matthew L. Schwartz
Kelleen McGinnis Scott
Catherine S. Seery
W. Ming Shao
Jeffrey K. Shapiro
Charles E. Sieving (Not admitted in DC)
Scott G. Silverstein
David W. Small
Elizabeth D. Smith
Gina M. Spade
Kimberly J. Stahlman
Deborah Kim Staudinger
Jolanta Sterbenz
Lowell R. Stern

(See Next Column)

HOGAN & HARTSON L.L.P.—*Continued*

RESIDENT ASSOCIATES (Continued)

Catherine E. Stetson
Joy E. Sturm
Cynthia G. Swann
Ellen F. Swennes
Marta I. Tanenhaus
Farinaz S. Tehrani
Kyra A. Todd
Patrick D. Traylor
James K. Trefil
Shawna R. Tunnell
Joseph Turitz
Robert Tyler
(Not admitted in DC)
Katharine T. Vestal
David M. Viscovich
Kevin L. Vold
Nicholas A. Widnell
Gordon C. Wilson
David A. Winter
Stephen J. Zempolich
Allison K. Zidlicky
Kimberly D. Ziropoulos

For full biographical listings, see the Martindale-Hubbell Law Directory

HOLLAND & KNIGHT LLP (AV)

2100 Pennsylvania Avenue, N.W., Suite 400, 20037
Telephone: 202-955-3000
Fax: 202-955-5564
URL: http://www.hklaw.com
Atlanta, Georgia Office: 1201 West Peachtree Street, N.E., Suite 2000.
Telephone: 404-817-8500.
Fax: 404-881-0470.
Boston, Massachusetts Office: One Beacon Street.
Telephone: 617-523-2700.
Fax: 617-523-6850.
Falls Church, Virginia Office: 3110 Fairview Park Drive, Suite 900.
Telephone: 703-645-8600.
Fax: 703-645-8610.
Fort Lauderdale, Florida Office: One East Broward Boulevard, Suite 1300.
Telephone: 954-525-1000.
Fax: 954-463-2030.
Jacksonville, Florida Office: 50 North Laura Street, Suite 3900.
Telephone: 904-353-2000.
Fax: 904-358-1872.
Lakeland, Florida Office: 92 Lake Wire Drive.
Telephone: 941-682-1161.
Fax: 941-688-1186.
Melbourne, Florida Office: 1499 South Harbor City Boulevard, Suite 201.
Telephone: 407-951-1776.
Fax: 407-951-1849.
Miami, Florida Office: 701 Brickell Avenue, Suite 3000.
Telephone: 305-374-8500.
Fax: 305-789-7799.
New York, New York Office: 195 Broadway, 24th Floor.
Telephone: 212-513-3200.
Fax: 212-385-9010.
Orlando, Florida Office: 200 South Orange Avenue, Suite 2600.
Telephone: 407-425-8500.
Fax: 407-244-5288.
San Francisco, California Office: 44 Montgomery Street, Suite 4050.
Telephone: 415-743-6900.
Fax: 415-743-6910.
St. Petersburg, Florida Office: 200 Central Avenue, Suite 1600.
Telephone: 813-896-7171.
Fax: 813-822-8048.
Tallahassee, Florida Office: 315 South Calhoun Street, Suite 600.
Telephone: 850-224-7000.
Fax: 850-224-8832.
Tampa, Florida Office: 400 North Ashley Drive, Suite 2300.
Telephone: 813-227-8500.
Fax: 813-229-0134.
West Palm Beach, Florida Office: 625 North Flagler Drive, Suite 700.
Telephone: 561-833-2000.
Fax: 561-650-8399.
Providence, Rhode Island Office: 50 Exchange Terrace, Suite 300, Union Station Plaza.
Telephone: 401-751-8500.
Fax: 401-553-6850.
Mexico City, Mexico Office: HOLLAND & KNIGHT-GALLÁSTEGUI Y LOZANO, S.C. (Joint Venture Office) Avenida Paseo de los Tamarindos No. 400, Torre "B" - 2° Piso, Col. Bosques d las Lomas, C.P. 05120 Mexico, D.F.
Telephone: 011-525-261-1866.
Fax: 011-525-261-1867.
Tel Aviv, Israel Office: 23 Derech Petach-Tikva, 18th Floor.
Telephone: +011 972 (3) 566-7666.
Fax: +011 972 (3) 566-7667.
Buenos Aires, Argentina Office: San Martin 323--Piso 18, 1004.
Telephone: +54-11-4324-7600.
Fax: +54-11 4324-7601.

WASHINGTON, D.C. MEMBERS AND ASSOCIATES

Michael E. Anderson
Brant Baber
Markham Ball
Timothy J. Bloomfield
Stephen A. Bogorad
David W. Briggs
Henry J. Brothers II
John A. Buchman
Harold R. Bucholtz
Melinda Burrows
Tanja H. Castro
J. Michael Cavanaugh
Robert M. Chasnow
Louise B. Cobbs
Mark D. Colley
George A. Dalley
G. Richard Dunnells
Richard O. Duvall

(See Next Column)

WASHINGTON, D.C. MEMBERS AND ASSOCIATES (Continued)

Stuart S. Dye
Amy L. Edwards
Eric Fishman
Richard M. Gold
Steven D. Gordon
T. Wayne Gray
Christopher B. Hanback
Robin Belton Hayes
Dennis M. Horn
Edward W. Hummers, Jr.
Thomas J. Hutton
Martin J. Jaron, Jr.
Susan E. Juroe
David S. Kahn
Richard E. Lear
Patricia Y. Lee
Jerry Levine
George T. Magee
Peter T. Meszoly
David P. Metzger
Nelson F. Migdal
William J. Mutryn
Christopher A. Myers
La Fonte Nesbitt
Stephen D. Niles
Ronald A. Oleynik
Timothy P. O'Shea
(Not admitted in DC)
Eugene M. Propper
Stephen J. Powell
Robert L. Rhodes, Jr.
Marvin Rosenberg
Michael J. Ruane
Alban Salaman
Janis B. Schiff
Christopher "Kip" Schwartz
Stephen Brett Shapiro
Gerald E. Sikorski
Richard P. Sills
Theodore S. Silva, Jr.
David C. Silver
Judy G. Sinkin
Andrew W. Stephenson
Scott Andrew Sterling
Jeffrey B. Stern
Janet R. Studley
Charles Welch Tiedemann
David A. Vaughan
Alan P. Vollmann
Susan Lee Voss
Frederick P. Waite
Mel S. Weinberger
Stephen J. Weiss
Lawrence J. Wolk

SENIOR COUNSEL

Joel D. Bonfiglio
Dennis L. Bryant
Sharon K. Freiman
Alvin J. Geske
Keith D. Lind
Jim J. Marquez
Donald H. Meiers
Frank K. Peterson
Sung Park Reynolds
Roderic L. Woodson

John M. Burkman
Christopher L. Camarra
(Not admitted in DC)
Keith Clausen
Amy Decker Cook
Kara L. Daniels
(Not admitted in DC)
Jonathan M. Epstein
Philip Tucker Evans
Jonathan A. Greenberg
Margaret A. Hackbarth
Michelle D. Hertz
Craig A. Holman
Eric B. Holmberg
John G. Kelly
(Not admitted in DC)
Eileen C. Lee
Thomas D. Leland
Christopher G. Margand
Selwa Masri
(Not admitted in DC)
David M. Matuszewski
Leslie S. McAdoo-Brobson
David A. O'Connor
Bryan R. Phillips
(Not admitted in DC)
Scott M. Pritchett
Thomas F. Railsback
J. Steven Rich
Leo G. Rydzewski
Samuel J. Salario, Jr.
Curtis L. Sano
(Not admitted in DC)
Tara A. Scanlon
Kristen E. Schmeelcke
Prasad Sharma
Randall W. Sifers
Theodore Washington Small, Jr.
Bernard L. Smith
Jennifer M. Smith
C. Dennis Southard IV
Leslie S. Spitalney
Kimberly Young

OF COUNSEL

Stuart Marshall Bloch
Philip N. Hogen
(Not admitted in DC)
William B. Ingersoll
Richard S. Weinstein
(Not admitted in DC)
Robert T. Wray

For full biographical listings, see the Martindale-Hubbell Law Directory

HOPKINS & SUTTER (AV)

A Partnership including Professional Corporations
888 Sixteenth Street, N.W., 20006
Telephone: 202-835-8000
Fax: 202-835-8136
Email: postmaster@hopsut.com *URL:* http://www.hopsut.com
Chicago, Illinois Office: Three First National Plaza.
Telephone: 312-558-6600.
Telex: 206231.
Fax: 312-558-6538.
Troy, Michigan Office: 2800 Livernois, Suite 220.
Telephone: 248-740-6600.
Fax: 248-740-6613.

PARTNERS

Jonathan P. Biller
(Not admitted in DC)
John G. DeGooyer
Thomas R. Devine
Murray Drabkin
Mary Gayle Holden
(Not admitted in DC)
Donald M. Itzkoff
Steven C. Lambert
Jerris Leonard
Francis O. McDermott
Philip A. Nacke
Gordon O. Pehrson, Jr.
David T. Ralston, Jr.
Jamie Palter Rennert
Richard F. Riley, Jr.
Perry D. Robinson

(See Next Column)

HOPKINS & SUTTER, *Washington—Continued*

PARTNERS (Continued)

Samuel K. Skinner (Not admitted in DC)
Charles A. Spitulnik
Daniel F. Stenger
Charles Michael Tobin
Robert P. vom Eigen

SENIOR COUNSEL

K. Martin Worthy

OF COUNSEL

Donald G. Brotzman
Henry Roemer McPhee

COUNSEL

Basil Cole (Not admitted in DC)
Edward A. McCabe

ASSOCIATES

Rachel Danish Campbell
Bobby L. Dexter
Karen M. Grane
Walter C. Hazlitt, Jr.
Jeffrey S. Newman (Not admitted in DC)
Robert K. Temple (Not admitted in DC)
Roderick B. Williams

For full biographical listings, see the Martindale-Hubbell Law Directory

HOWREY & SIMON (AV)

1299 Pennsylvania Avenue, N.W., 20004-2402
Telephone: 202-783-0800
Fax: 202-383-6610
URL: http://www.howrey.com
Los Angeles, California Office: Suite 1400, 550 South Hope Street, 90071-2604.
Telephone: 213-892-1800.
Fax: 213-892-2300.
Menlo Park, California Office: 301 Ravenswood Avenue, 94025.
Telephone: 650-463-8100.
Fax: 650-463-8400.

COUNSEL

Terrence C. Sheehy
William Simon
David C. Murchison
Harold F. Baker

MEMBERS OF FIRM

Robert G. Abrams
Stephen Angle
Scott Arnold
Jeffrey I. Auerbach
Richard E. Ayres
Gregory L. Baker
Michael J. Bell
Darren B. Bernhard
John Bodner, Jr.
Ray S. Bolze
Timothy E. Boyle
John DeQ. Briggs, III
Robert J. Brookhiser, Jr.
Kenneth W. Brothers
John F. Bruce
Robert M. Bruskin
Patricia G. Butler
John G. Calender
Allen Cannon III
Matthew J. Clark
Richard B. Clifford, Jr.
Michael Paul Austern Cohen
Richard T. Colman
Gregory J. Commins, Jr.
Chris Comuntzis
Michael G. Cowie
Basil C. Culyba
Martin F. Cunniff
Lee P. Curtis
James F. Davis
Mindy G. Davis
David C. Eddy
W. Neil Eggleston
Jeffrey N. Eisenstein (Not admitted in DC)
Charles J. (Tim) Engel, III
Scott E. Flick
Joel M. Freed
John G. Froemming
Jerrold J. Ganzfried
Thomas E. Gilbertsen
Cecilia H. Gonzalez
Charles E. Graf
Jonathan G. Graves
Allen B. Green
Robert L. Green, Jr.
Alan M. Grimaldi
Edward Han
Stuart H. Harris
Philip H. Hecht
John E. Heintz
Edward P. Henneberry
Roxann E. Henry
Thomas N. Heyer
Robert H. Huey
Michael J. Hurley
Thomas A. Isaacson
Marcia Press Kaplan
Richard H. Kjeldgaard
Roger A. Klein
James G. Kress
Lisa I. Latorre
Joseph P. Lavelle
Ezra C. Levine
Mark I. Levy
Karen Louise Manos
Elizabeth B. McCallum
Rosemary H. McEnery
Katherine D. McManus
Joseph A. Micallef
Helen Katherine Michael
Richard D. Milone, Jr.
Peter E. Moll
Harriet Mountcastle-Walsh
P. Todd Mullins
Reed W. Neuman
John W. Nields, Jr.
Rodney J. Nydam
William R. O'Brien
Christopher N. Olsen
James W. Olson
Joseph A. Ostoyich
John C. Peirce
Eberhard W. Pfaller, Jr.
Keith E. Pugh, Jr.
Bert C. Reiser
Richard A. Ripley
Howard T. Rosenblatt
John J. Rosenthal
Robert F. Ruyak
Lisa J. Saks
Ralph J. Savarese
Mark C. Schechter
Marc G. Schildkraut
Edward B. Schwartz
Frederick F. Shaheen
Anthony W. Shaw
Harvey G. Sherzer
Laura S. Shores
Robert H. Shulman
Michael J. Songer
Gary Thompson
Brian D. Wallach
William L. Webber
Mark D. Wegener
David B. Weinberg
William K. West, Jr.
A. Duncan Whitaker

(See Next Column)

MEMBERS OF FIRM (Continued)

Stephen R. Whitt (Not admitted in DC)
Marguerite Smith Willis
Alan M. Wiseman
Carmine R. Zarlenga
Margaret M. Zwisler

OF COUNSEL

Kerry L. Adams
Nancy L. Boughton (Not admitted in DC)
Jan Christensen
Robert C. Fallon
Gregory F. Intoccia
William E. Marames
Andrea G. Reister
Kent R. Stevens (Not admitted in DC)
Linda L. Walsh

SPECIAL COUNSEL

Juliana M. Cofrancesco
Gilbert S. Keteltas
Jeffrey M. Lenser

ASSOCIATES

Brent H. Allen (Not admitted in DC)
Michele Arington
Timothy K. Armstrong
William D. Belanger
Alexander B. Berger
Michael A. Berta
Erik Bertin
Bradford E. Biegon
Diane E. Bieri
Kimberly M. Bonner
LaShanda D. Branch
Julie K. Brof
David Penn Burns
Celine T. Callahan
George D. Cannon, Jr.
Daniel S. Carlineo
Deborah Ann Carpentier
Cono A. Carrano
Elizabeth J. Chandler
Donald J. Carney (Not admitted in DC)
Jillian E. Charles
Hollis T. Chen
Michael N. Clark (Not admitted in DC)
Kelly A. Clement
June E. Cohan
Joseph V. Colaianni, Jr.
Kathryn R. Colburn
Brian H. Corcoran
Robert H. Cox
Nathan K. Cummings
Sarah E. Davis
Lara A. Degenhart
Kenneth W. Donnelly
Stephen G. Dormer (Not admitted in DC)
Donna Drake (Not admitted in DC)
Thomas M. Dunham
Teresa E. Dykes (Not admitted in DC)
Dawn A. Ellison (Not admitted in DC)
Maria Farinella
Patrick D. Farrington
Edward L. Ferguson, Jr.
Thomas C. Fiala
Alan M. Fisch
Meryl S. Fishman
Amy R. Fitzpatrick
Colin Foley (Not admitted in DC)
James J. Fournier
Therese K. Francese
Michael R. Gartman
Robert A. Geckle, Jr.
Julie B. Greenisen
Jacqueline I. Grise
Alexander J. Hadjis
Danielle D. Hallcom (Not admitted in DC)
Kenneth N. Hickox, Jr.
Steven F. Hill
Jason Foster Hoffman (Not admitted in DC)
Brian A. Howie
Robert P. Jacobs
Michelle E. Jones
Pamela S. Kane
Ellen R. Kennedy (Not admitted in DC)
Cecil E. Key
Melissa B. Kimmel
David J. Kulik
Andrew Lazerow (Not admitted in DC)
Charles A. Loughlin
Margaret D. Macdonald
Keith R. Marino
David R. Marsh
Linda A. Mayer (Not admitted in DC)
James A. Maysonett (Not admitted in DC)
Eric J. McCarthy
Jennifer K. McDannell
Lawrence McDonough
Christopher W. Meyer
Polly A. Myers
Victor J. Miller
Matthew J. Moore
David M. Morris
Paul E. Murray
Mitchel Neurock (Not admitted in DC)
Nancy A. Noonan
Danielle R. Oddo (Not admitted in DC)
Bradley J. Olson
Douglas S. Onley
Timothy D. Osterhaus (Not admitted in DC)
Hae-Chan Park (Not admitted in DC)
Geoffrey C. Pemble
Jason Penfield (Not admitted in DC)
Michael A. Rahman
Jeanne-Marie S. Raymond
Karen M. Robinson (Not admitted in DC)
Robert D. Rowe
Kristen S. Scammon
Bradley J. Schlozman (Not admitted in DC)
Michael J. Schofield
Jason D. Smith
Tracy A. Heinzman Smith
John F. Stanton
Rachel Lisa Strong
Terry L. Sullivan
Todd M. Tidgewell (Not admitted in DC)
Peter L. Tracey (Not admitted in DC)
Margaret Vierbuchen
Mary F. Walters
Evan Jeffrey Werbel
Matthew S. Wild
Karen B. Williams
Matthew M. Wolf
Robert Jones Worrall
Elaine T. L. Wu
W. Hartmann Young
John H. Zacharia

For full biographical listings, see the Martindale-Hubbell Law Directory

Washington—Continued

JACKSON & CAMPBELL, P.C. (AV)

One Lafayette Centre, 300 South Tower, 1120-20th Street, N.W., 20036
Telephone: 202-457-1600
Telecopier: 202-457-1678
Email: JCLAWFIRM@AOL.COM
Rockville, Maryland Office: Suite 225, 200 A Monroe Street.
Telephone: 301-340-0450.
Baltimore, Maryland Office: 111 S. Calvert Street, Suite 2700.
Telephone: 410-385-5343.
Vienna, Virginia Office: 8300 Boone Boulevard, Suite 500.
Telephone: 703-522-1330.

Peter F. Axelrad
James E. Brammer
John J. Brennan, III
Richard W. Bryan
Arthur D. Burger
James E. Cervenak
Douglas W. Charnas
Robert Clayton Cooper
David H. Cox
Timothy R. Dingilian
Benjamin W. Dulany
Arthur C. Elgin, Jr.
Patricia D. Gurne
Vernon W. Johnson, III
Robert N. Kelly
Richard S. Kuhl
Peter Lipresti
Warren C. Lutz
John J. Matteo
Scott Alton Mills
Nicholas S. McConnell
John J. McDermott
Madonna A. McGwin
M. Elizabeth Medaglia
James R. Michal
Philip L. O'Neill
Tonia Jones Powell
Mary Lynn Reed
Robert E. Rider, Jr.
James P. Schaller
Alan R. Swendiman
Donald L. Uttrich
Xiaohua Zhao
(Not admitted in DC)

OF COUNSEL

Michael Paige

Raymond P. Ausrotas
Hollis B. Brewer III
Janet A. Brown
Kristan M. Cassidy
Kenneth C. Crickman
Elisa A. Eisenberg
Edward J. Estrada
Mark A. Goodin
Thomas F. Gristina
Tiffany A. Hosey
John P. Malloy
(Not admitted in DC)
Jennifer E. Mandell
Erin N. McGonagle
John C. Muccifori
(Not admitted in DC)
Susan Phillips
Ann Marie Terzaken
Bruce K. Trauben
Liliana E. Ward

For full biographical listings, see the Martindale-Hubbell Law Directory

JACKSON & KELLY (AV)

2401 Pennsylvania Avenue, N.W., Suite 400, 20037
Telephone: 202-973-0200
Fax: 202-973-0232
Email: info@jacksonkelly.com *URL:* http://www.jacksonkelly.com
Charleston, West Virginia Office: 1600 Laidley Tower, P.O. Box 553.
Telephone: 304-340-1000.
Fax: 304-340-1130.
Martinsburg, West Virginia Office: 300 Foxcroft Avenue, P.O. Box 1068.
Telephone: 304-263-8800.
Fax: 304-263-7110.
Morgantown, West Virginia Office: 6000 Hampton Center, P.O. Box 619.
Telephone: 304-599-3000.
Fax: 304-285-2040.
New Martinsville, West Virginia Office: 256 Russell Avenue, P.O. Box 68.
Telephone: 304-455-1751.
Fax: 304-455-6314.
Parkersburg, West Virginia Office: 412 Market Street, Suite 202, P.O. Box 1144.
Telephone: 304-424-3490.
Fax: 304-424-3499.
Fairmont, West Virginia Office: 1000 Technology Drive, Suite 1310.
Telephone: 304-368-2000.
Fax: 304-368-2020.
Lexington, Kentucky Office: 175 East Main Street, Suite 500, P.O. Box 2150.
Telephone: 606-255-9500.
Fax: 606-281-6478.
Denver, Colorado Office: Suite 2710, 1660 Lincoln Street.
Telephone: 303-390-0003.
Fax: 303-390-0040.
Wheeling, West Virginia Office: 1144 Market Street.
Telephone: 304-233-4000.
Fax: 304-233-4077.

MEMBERS OF FIRM

Thad S. Huffman
(Administrative Manager)
G. Lindsay Simmons
John K. McDonald

OF COUNSEL

Louis J. Ferrara (Not admitted in DC)

For full biographical listings, see the Martindale-Hubbell Law Directory

JONES, DAY, REAVIS & POGUE (AV)

51 Louisiana Avenue, N.W., 20001-2113
Telephone: 202-879-3939
Telecopier: 202-626-1700
Email: counsel@jonesday.com *URL:* http://www.jonesday.com
In Atlanta, Georgia: 3500 SunTrust Plaza, 303 Peachtree Street.
Telephone: 404-521-3939.
Telecopier: 404-581-8330.
In Brussels, Belgium: Avenue Louise 480, 7th Floor, B-1050 Brussels.
Telephone: 32-2-645-14-11.
Telecopier: 32-2-645-14-45.
In Chicago, Illinois: 77 West Wacker.
Telephone: 312-782-3939.
Telecopier: 312-782-8585.
In Cleveland, Ohio: North Point, 901 Lakeside Avenue.
Telephone: 216-586-3939.
Telecopier: 216-579-0212.
In Columbus, Ohio: 1900 Huntington Center.
Telephone: 614-469-3939.
Telecopier: 614-461-4198.
In Dallas, Texas: 2727 North Harwood Street.
Telephone: 214-220-3939.
Telecopier: 214-969-5100.
In Frankfurt, Germany: Hochhaus am Park, Grüneburgweg 102, 60323, Frankfurt am Main.
Telephone: 49-69-9726-3939.
Telecopier: 49-69-9726-3993.
In Geneva, Switzerland: 20, rue de Candolle.
Telephone: 41-22-320-2339.
Telecopier: 41-22-320-1232.
In Hong Kong: 29th Floor, Entertainment Building, 30 Queen's Road Central.
Telephone: 852-2526-6895.
Telecopier: 852-2868-5871.
In Irvine, California: 5 Park Plaza, Suite 1100.
Telephone: 949-851-3939.
Telecopier: 949-553-7539.
In London, England: Bucklersbury House, 3 Queen Victoria Street.
Telephone: 44-171-236-3939.
Telecopier: 44-171-236-1113.
In Los Angeles, California: 555 West Fifth Street, Suite 4600.
Telephone: 213-489-3939.
Telecopier: 213-243-2539.
In New Delhi, India (Associate Office): Pathak & Associates (an associate firm of Jones, Day, Reavis & Pogue), 1st Floor, Dr. Gopal Das Bhaven, 28 Barakhamba Road.
Telephone: 91-11-373-8793.; 91-11-335-7345.
Telecopier: 91-11-335-3761.
In New York, New York: 599 Lexington Avenue.
Telephone: 212-326-3939.
Telecopier: 212-755-7306.
In Paris, France: 120, rue du Faubourg Saint-Honoré.
Telephone: 33-1-56-59-39-39.
Telecopier: 33-1-56-59-39-38
In Pittsburgh, Pennsylvania: 500 Grant Street, 31st Floor.
Telephone: 412-391-3939.
Telecopier: 412-394-7959.
In Riyadh, Saudi Arabia: The International Law Firm (In Association with Jones, Day, Reavis & Pogue), Sulaymaniyah, Prince Mishari IBN, Abdulaziz Street, P.O. Box 22166.
Telephone: (966-1) 462-8866.
Telecopier: (966-1) 462-9001.
In Shanghai, China: 2805 Kerry Centre, 1515 Nanjing Road West.
Telephone: 86-21-5298-6568.
Telecopier: 86-21-5298-6569.
In Sydney, Australia: Governor Phillip Tower, Level 38, 1 Farrer Place.
Telephone: 61-2-9210-6921.
Telecopier: 61-2-9210-6926.
In Taipei, Taiwan: 8th Floor, 2 Tun Hwa South Road, Section 2.
Telephone: (886-2) 2704-6808.
Telecopier: (886-2) 2704-6791.
In Tokyo, Japan: Toranomon MT Building, 4th Floor, 10-3, Toranomon 3-Chome, Minato-Ku, Tokyo 105, Japan.
Telephone: 81-3-3433-3939.
Telecopier: 81-3-5401-2725.

MEMBERS OF FIRM IN WASHINGTON, D.C.

Joseph S. Iannucci
Michael Bradfield
Timothy B. Dyk
James T. O'Hara
J. Lawrence Manning, Jr.
Jonathan C. Rose
Sigmund T. Weiner
Andrew M. Kramer
James A. Wilderotter
Robert F. McDermott, Jr.
Joe Sims
James J. Graham
Mark K. Sisitsky
Junius C. McElveen, Jr.
Paul S. Ryerson
Tom D. Smith
Joseph M. David, Jr.
Clark Evans Downs
Willis J. Goldsmith
Phillip A. Proger
Thomas F. Cullen, Jr.
Robert S. Waters
Richard D. Avil, Jr.
Donald B. Ayer
Lawrence L. Lamade
David C. Roseman
Lester W. Droller
Raymond J. Wiacek
Stephen J. Brogan
Timothy J. Finn
Gregory M. Luce
Toby G. Singer
Geoffrey S. Stewart
Teresa A. Brooks

(See Next Column)

JONES, DAY, REAVIS & POGUE, *Washington—Continued*

MEMBERS OF FIRM IN WASHINGTON, D.C. (Continued)

Kathryn M. Fenton
Peter F. Garvin, III
Kevin D. McDonald
Joseph F. Winterscheid
Kenneth J. Ayres
Charles A. James
Robert H. Klonoff
Mary Ellen Powers
Steven A. Teitelbaum
Peter J. Biersteker
Carolyn Y. Thompson
Christopher F. Dugan
Alison B. Marshall
Glen D. Nager
Adrian Wager-Zito
William V. O'Reilly
James D. Wareham
Michael P. Gurdak
David E. Miller
Gregory M. Shumaker
Kevin J. McIntyre
Candace A. Ridgway
James E. Gauch
R. Todd Johnson
Gregory G. Katsas

OF COUNSEL

Herbert J. Hansell (Not admitted in DC)
William E. Swope
Peter E. Heyward
Kent L. Killelea
Elliot D. Eder

COUNSEL

David A. Copus
Robert C. Jones
Jerome J. Zaucha
Stephen J. Goodman
Charles V. Stewart

ASSOCIATES

Heidi Hughes Bumpers
Neil A. Dellar
Mary L. Hale
Julia M. Broas
Kathleen Marie McChesney
James E. Anklam
Anthony P. Lalla
Steven J. Mintz
Edward K.M. Bilich
Gregory A. Castanias
Denise A. Fee
Edwin L. Fountain
William H. Oldach III
Daniel H. Bromberg
Stephen J. Jorden
Robin L. Juni
Martin V. Kirkwood
Elizabeth A. McLaughlin
Jesse A. Witten
Geoffrey K. Beach
Thomas M. Beck
Joseph A. Goldman
Blaney Harper
Lawrence D. Rosenberg
Michael R. Shumaker
Peter J. Wang
Jonathan Berman
Mandy Jones
Marcia Y. Lucas
Sarah Dryden Mackey
Mary-Helen Perry
Paul R. Reichert
Lynn A. Airasian
Mona Lisa Flicker
Michael L. Kolis
Jason F. Leif
Peter J. Love
Kevin C. Maclay
Sarah B. McClure
Pamela Sak
Catherine M. Stavrakis
Richard L. Winston
Todd C. Amidon
Kenneth B. Driver
Suzanne M. FitzGerald
Jacqueline M. Holmes
Julia E. McEvoy
John B. Nalbandian
Bevin M.B. Newman
Heather M. O'Shea (Not admitted in DC)
Sheryl Klemme Christmas
Karen M. Espaldon
Colette M. Hanson
Lisa Malloy Nardini
Leslie Overton
Laura Tuell Parcher
James D. Phipps (Not admitted in DC)
Stephen M. Polozie
Shelby L. Provencher
David S. Rutkowski
Beth T. Sigall
Aaron L. Agenbroad
Adam Candeub
T. Jeffrey Fitzgerald
Brian K. Grube (Not admitted in DC)
John B. Kennedy
Marli J.P. Kerrigan
Walid A. Khuri
Kathleen M. Laubenstein (Not admitted in DC)
John C. Martin
Joseph J. Migas
John S. Nagy (Not admitted in DC)
Sean G. Saxon (Not admitted in DC)
Susan V. Watson
J. Carter Andersen
Jack W. Campbell IV
Mia F. Cohen
Laura Talley Geyer
Mark L. Glassman
Carey G.B. Kerney
Stacy Renée Linden (Not admitted in DC)
Christopher J. Lovrien (Not admitted in DC)
Jennifer J. Gerstner Prozinski
J. Andrew Read
Portia A. Robert
Melissa D. Stear (Not admitted in DC)
Karen E. Van Horn (Not admitted in DC)
Margaret A. Ward
Jennifer A. Hunkler (Not admitted in DC)
Tamara Hardney Kassabian
Stuart M. Kuntz
Justin J. Roberts
Sheila L. Shadmand (Not admitted in DC)
Janie C.I. Sheng (Not admitted in DC)
Katherine A. Walther (Not admitted in DC)

SENIOR STAFF ATTORNEYS

Kevin B. Byrd
John P. McGrane, Jr.
Patrick L. Hubbard

STAFF ATTORNEYS

Brian J. McManus
Kenneth C. Terrell
Jenni R. Wallace
Jennifer A. Hay
Dara A. Lutz
Susan Q. Haines
Alison Colwell Snow (Not admitted in DC)
David S. Turbiner
Michael C. Kentoff
Lee A. Friedman

For full biographical listings, see the Martindale-Hubbell Law Directory

KAYE, SCHOLER, FIERMAN, HAYS & HANDLER, LLP (AV)

A New York Limited Liability Partnership
McPherson Building, 901 Fifteenth Street, N.W., Suite 1100, 20005-2327
Telephone: 202-682-3500
Facsimile: 202-682-3580
URL: http://WWW.kayescholer.com
New York, N.Y.: 425 Park Avenue, 10022-3598.
Telephone: 212-836-8000.
Telex: 234860 KAY UR.
Facsimile: 212-836-8689.
Los Angeles, California: 1999 Avenue of the Stars, Suite 1600, 90067-6048.
Telephone: 310-788-1000.
Facsimile: 310-788-1200.
West Palm Beach, Florida Office: Phillips Point, West Tower 1002, 777 South Flagler Drive, 33401.
Telephone: 561-802-3230.
Facsimile: 561-802-3217.
Hong Kong: No. 1 Harbor View Street, Central.
Telephone: 852-28458989.
Facsimile: 852-28452389.
Shanghai, China: Suite 405 Shanghai Centre, 1376 Nanjing Xi Lu, 200040.
Telephone: 86-21-62797356.
Facsimile: 86-21-62797351.

RESIDENT PARTNERS

Sylvia M. Becker
David O. Bickart
Donald B. Cameron, Jr.
G. Christopher Griner
Ronald K. Henry
Michael P. House
Julie C. Mendoza
Kerry Alan Scanlon
Jason L. Shrinsky
Randall L. Speck

SPECIAL COUNSEL

William S. Eberle (P.A.) (Not admitted in DC)
Steven L. Schwarcz (Not admitted in DC)

COUNSEL

Christopher R. Brewster
Bruce Alan Eisen
Farhad Jalinous
Raymond Paretzky
R. Will Planert
John P. Rynkiewicz (Not admitted in DC)
John W. Schryber
James M. Weitzman

RESIDENT ASSOCIATES

Todd B. Elmer (Not admitted in DC)
Dean C. Garfield
Craig Guthery (Not admitted in DC)
John R. Miles
Brady W. Mills
Allan Gary Moskowitz
Randi S. Turner
Deborah L. Wengel

For full biographical listings, see the Martindale-Hubbell Law Directory

KIRKLAND & ELLIS (AV)

A Partnership including Professional Corporations
655 Fifteenth Street, N.W., Suite 1200, 20005
Telephone: 202-879-5000
Telex: 89-2320
Facsimile: 202-879-5200
URL: http://www.kirkland.com
Chicago, Illinois Office: 200 East Randolph Drive.
Telephone: 312-861-2000.
Telex: 25-4361.
Los Angeles, California Office: 777 South Figueroa Street.
Telephone: 213-680-8400.
Facsimile: 213-680-8500.
New York, New York Office: Citicorp Center, 153 East 53rd Street.
Telephone: 212-446-4800.
Facsimile: (212)-446-4900.
London, England Office: International Financial Centre, Old Broad Street.
Telephone: 171-816-8700; New Telephone Effective April 1, 2000: 207-816-8700.
Facsimile: 171-816-8800.

MEMBERS OF FIRM

Jay I. Alexander
Eugene F. Assaf
Daniel F. Attridge
James F. Basile
Kenneth N. Bass
Steven Gill Bradbury
Paul F. Brinkman
Kathleen A. Buck
Karen McCartan DeSantis
Maureen A. Donley-Hoopes
Edward C. Donovan
Stuart A. C. Drake
James Worth Draughn, Jr.
Michael T. Edsall
Jack M. Feder
Robert R. Gasaway
James P. Gillespie
Mark E. Grummer
Barbara Mack Harding
Timothy S. Hardy
Mitchell F. Hertz
John S. Irving, Jr.
Michael D. Jones
Brett M. Kavanaugh
Stephen D. Knight
Mark L. Kovner
Brian R. Land
Christopher Landau
Jay P. Lefkowitz
Walter H. Lohmann, Jr.
Jeffrey A. Manley
Dawn Danzeisen Marchant
Gerald F. Masoudi
John Gibson Mullan
Susan M. O'Sullivan
Richard L. Perkal
Patrick F. Philbin
Bruce H. Rabinovitz
Jeffrey A. Rosen
Robert S. Ryland
Tefft W. Smith
Kenneth W. Starr

(See Next Column)

KIRKLAND & ELLIS—*Continued*

MEMBERS OF FIRM (Continued)

Robert Timothy Stephenson
Jennifer L. Stevens
Laurence A. Urgenson
Karen Natalie Walker
Edward W. Warren (P.C.)
Kenneth G. Weigel
Steven M. Wellner
L. Mark Wine (P.C.)
Thomas D. Yannucci
Mark D. Young

OF COUNSEL

Terrance L. Bessey
Janet A. Forest
James S. Hostetler
David G. Norrell
Constance O'Keefe
Frederick M. Rowe
James D. Senger

ASSOCIATES

Pamela Aronson
Laura R. Bach
Reatha A. Baker
Michael S. Becker
Jason Beckerman
Brant W. Bishop
Paul J. Bohr (Not admitted in DC)
Jennifer R. Brosnahan
Zhonette Brown
L. Rachel Buckner
Thomas A. Clare
Jeffrey B. Clark
Andrew B. Clubok
Elizabeth Lee Deeley (Not admitted in DC)
Daniel T. Donovan
Charles E. Duross
Kenneth J. Dyer
Joseph A. Eisert
Susan Kathleen Fitch
David B. Florenzo
Laura Fraedrich
John P. Frantz
Jeffrey Friedenberg (Not admitted in DC)
Jennifer G. Gardner
Amy Marie Harvey
Eric Hecker (Not admitted in DC)
Leigh A. Hyer
Geoffrey S. Irwin (Not admitted in DC)
Traci L. Jones (Not admitted in DC)
Daryl Joseffer
Kelion N. Kasler (Not admitted in DC)
Colin R. Kass
Andrew B. Kay
Antony B. Klapper
Anthony W. Lacosta (Not admitted in DC)
David L. Lambert
Sean Byrne Litton (Not admitted in DC)
Gregg F. LoCascio
Kevin M. Loftus
Robert G. Marks
Mark E. McKane
Granta Y. Nakayama
Michelle T. Palmer
Ashley Charles Parrish (Not admitted in DC)
Cathleen P. Peterson
Craig S. Primis
David Pruitt (Not admitted in DC)
Lewis T. Putman, Jr.
Richard A. Rice, Jr.
Christina M. Sarris
David P. Steinberger (Not admitted in DC)
Martha Phillips Stuart
David P. Swenson
Theodore W. Ullyot
James E. Williams
John F. Wood

For full biographical listings, see the Martindale-Hubbell Law Directory

KUTAK ROCK (AV)

Suite 1000, 1101 Connecticut Avenue, N.W., 20036-4374
Telephone: 202-828-2400
Fax: 202-828-2488
URL: http://www.kutakrock.com
Atlanta, Georgia Office: Suite 2100, 225 Peachtree Street, NE, 30303-1731.
Telephone: 404-222-4600.
Facsimile: 404-222-4654.
Denver, Colorado Office: Suite 2900, 717 Seventeenth Street, 80202-3329.
Telephone: 303-297-2400.
Facsimile: 303-292-7799.
Kansas City, Missouri Office: One Main Plaza, Suite 810, 4435 Main Street, 64111-7727.
Telephone: 816-960-0090.
Telefax: 816-960-0041.
Little Rock, Arkansas Office: Suite 1100, 425 West Capitol Avenue, 72201-3409.
Telephone: 501-975-3000.
Facsimile: 501-975-3001.
New York, New York Office: 650 Fifth Avenue, 10019-6108.
Telephone: 212-713-6480.
Facsimile: 212-713-6481.
Oklahoma City, Oklahoma Office: Suite 475, 6305 Waterford Boulevard, 73118-1116.
Telephone: 405-848-2475.
Facsimile: 405-842-5748.
Omaha, Nebraska Office: The Omaha Building, 1650 Farnam Street, 68102-2186.
Telephone: 402-346-6000.
Facsimile: 402-346-1148.
Phoenix, Arizona Office: 16th Floor, 3300 North Central Avenue, 85012-2516.
Telephone: 602-285-1700.
Facsimile: 602-285-1868.
Pittsburgh, Pennsylvania Office: 1214 Frick Building, 437 Grant Street, 15219-6002.
Telephone: 412-261-6720.
Facsimile: 412-261-6717.

(See Next Column)

Newport Beach, California Office: Suite 450, 620 Newport Center Drive, 92660-8019.
Telephone: 949-718-6700.
Facsimile: 949-718-6708.

MEMBERS OF FIRM

W. Kimball Griffith
Joseph A. Ingrisano
Mitchell J. Bragin
Robert L. Magielnicki
George R. Schlossberg
Matthew G. Ash
Daniel J. Goldberg
Edward B. Crosland, Jr.
Barry P. Steinberg
Margo BeVier Stern
Alan D. Strasser
Jeffrey S. Jacobovitz
Gilbert W. Boyce
Paul D. Borja (Not admitted in DC)
Alicia A. Terry
Daniel H. Burd
Jeffrey S. Ballard

OF COUNSEL

Joseph Mark Poerio (Not admitted in DC)

ASSOCIATES

Adam Augustine Carter
Seth David Kirshenberg
Eric R. Keller
Philip J. Berkowitz
Holly H. Sadeghian
Jeffrey W. Epstein
Rhonda D. Bond-Collins
Michael G. Rafferty
Tiffani K. Whittaker

For full biographical listings, see the Martindale-Hubbell Law Directory

LEFTWICH & DOUGLAS, P.L.L.C. (AV)

Suite 600, 1401 New York Avenue, N.W., 20005
Telephone: 202-434-9100
Facsimile: 202-783-3420
URL: http://www.lawyers.com/leftwich&douglaslaw

Frederick A. Douglas
Nicholas S. Penn
Natalie O. Ludaway

Curtis A. Boykin
Thomas D. Bridenbaugh
Nicole C. Mason (Not admitted in DC)
David B. Mintz
Nat N. Polito
Rebecca Lynn Taylor
Darryl A. Toler

OF COUNSEL

Leonard A. Sacks

For full biographical listings, see the Martindale-Hubbell Law Directory

MAYER, BROWN & PLATT (AV)

1909 K Street, N.W., 20006-1101
Telephone: (202) 263-3000
Facsimile: (202) 263-3300
Telex: 892603
Cable: LE MAYDC
URL: http://www.mayerbrown.com
Chicago, Illinois Office: 190 South LaSalle Street, 60603-3441.
Telephone: (312) 782-0600.
Facsimile: (312) 701-7711.
Telex: 190404.
Cable: LEMAY.
Berlin, Germany Office: Breite Strasse 29, Muehlendamm, 10178.
Telephone: 011-49-30-2060-7710.
Facsimile: 011-49-30-2060-7744.
Charlotte, North Carolina Office: 100 North Tryon Street, Suite 2400.
Telephone: (704) 444-3500.
Fax: (704) 377-2033.
Cologne, Germany Office: Kaiser-Wilhelm-Ring 27-29, 50672.
Telephone: 011-49-221-5771-100.
Facsimile: 011-49-221-5771-199.
Houston, Texas Office: 700 Louisiana Street, Suite 3600, 77002-2730.
Telephone: (713) 221-1651.
Facsimile: (713) 224-6410.
Telex: 775809.
Cable: LEMAYHOU.
London, England Office: Bucklersbury House, 3 Queen Victoria Street, London, EC4N 8EL, England.
Telephone: 011-44-171-246-6200.
Facsimile: 011-44-171-329-4465.
Telex: 8811095.
Cable: LEMAYLDN.
Los Angeles, California Office: 350 South Grand Avenue, 25th Floor, 90071-1503.
Telephone: (213) 229-9500.
Facsimile: (213) 625-0248.
Telex: 188089.
Cable: LEMAYLA.
New York, New York Office: 1675 Broadway, 10019-5820.
Telephone: (212) 506-2500.
Facsimile: (212) 262-1910.
Telex: 701842.
Cable: LEMAYEN.
Representative Offices:
Ashgabat, Turkmenistan: 28 Gogol Street, 744000.
Telephone: 011-99-312-355247.
Facsimile: 011-99-312-510074.

(See Next Column)

MAYER, BROWN & PLATT, *Washington—Continued*

Bishkek, Kyrgyz Republic: 66 Kalyka Akieva Str. 720001.
Telephone: 011-996-312-65-02-56.
Facsimile: 011-996-312-65-09-80.
Tashkent, Republic of Uzbekistan: 3rd Floor, 1 Turab Tula Street, 700003.
Telephones: 011-998-71-1206-627.
Facsimile: 011-998-71-1206-329.
Mexico City, Mexico, D.F., Independent Mexico Correspondent: Jáuregui, Navarrete, Nader y Rojas, S.C., Torre Arcos, Paseo de los Tamarindos No. 400-B. Col. Bosques de las Lomas, 05120.
Telephone: 011-525-267-45-00.
Facsimile: 011-525-267-45-98.
Paris, France, Independent Paris Correspondent: Lambert & Lee, 13 Avenue Hoche, 75008.
Telephone: 011-33-1-53-53-43-43.
Facsimile: 011-33-1-53-96-03-83.

PARTNERS

Diane E. Ambler
Robert E. Bloch
David I. Bloom
Kim Marie Kozaczek Boylan
C. Cabell Chinnis, Jr.
Robert P. Davis
Kerry Lynn Edwards
Roy T. Englert, Jr.
Donald M. Falk
Richard J. Favretto
Andrew L. Frey
Marc Gary
Kenneth S. Geller
Mark H. Gitenstein
Werner J. Hein
Charles M. Horn
Robert M. Jenkins, III
Erika Z. Jones
Michael Kantor
Timothy E. Keehan
Simeon M. Kriesberg
Kathryn A. Kusske
Philip Allen Lacovara
Daniel A. Masur
Jerry L. Oppenheimer
Gary A. Orseck
Carolyn P. Osolinik
Stuart P. Pergament
Scott P. Perlman
Mitchell D. Raup
Lawrence S. Robbins
Mark W. Ryan
John P. Schmitz
Brian W. Smith
Adrian L. Steel, Jr.
John J. Sullivan
Robert H. Swart
Evan M. Tager
Charles S. Triplett
Alan E. Untereiner
Keith J. Willner

SENIOR COUNSEL

David B. Finnegan

SPECIAL COUNSEL

David Hyman
Charles Rothfeld

COUNSEL

Carol J. Bilzi
Thomas B. Burnside (Not admitted in DC)
Kathy Kresch Ingber
Andrew J. Morris
Howard A. Parelskin

ASSOCIATES

Michael J. Alter
Marc S. Berger (Not admitted in DC)
Robert L. Bronston (Not admitted in DC)
Jay S. Brown
Kelley E. Campbell (Not admitted in DC)
Craig W. Canetti
Peter C. Choharis
Elizabeth A. Clark (Not admitted in DC)
Thomas B. Colby (Not admitted in DC)
Julian P. Gehman
Craig Isenberg (Not admitted in DC)
John W. Jarrell, Jr.
Laura H. Jones
Kimberly B. Kiefer
Michael E. Lackey, Jr.
Brian Kenneth Lee
Edward S. Lee
Lisa L. Levine
Susan J. Luken
Emily W. Mao
Jennifer C. Maloney
Rita W. Morales
Scott A. Morehouse
Wendy L. Morris
Miriam R. Nemetz
Andrew A. Nicely
Michael G. Palek (Not admitted in DC)
Ronald D. Parisotto
Eileen Penner
C. Dirk Peterson
Jeffrey A. Rackow
Lee H. Rubin
Timothy R. Ryan (Not admitted in DC)
Adam C. Sloane
Kristin Hart Smith
Lily Fu Swenson
Sharon Swingle
Jeffrey P. Taft (Not admitted in DC)
Jodi L. Valeri
Arthur C. Walker, Jr.
Gary A. Winters
Joseph E. Yesutis

For full biographical listings, see the Martindale-Hubbell Law Directory

MCGUIRE, WOODS, BATTLE & BOOTHE LLP (AV)

Washington Square, 1050 Connecticut Avenue, N.W., Suite 1200, 20036-5317
Telephone: 202-857-1700
Fax: 202-857-1737
Email: info@mwbb.com *URL:* http://www.mwbb.com
Atlanta, Georgia Office: 285 Peachtree Center Avenue, N.E., Suite 2200, Marquis Tower Two, 30303-1234.
Telephone: 404-443-5500.
Fax: 404-443-5599.
Baltimore, Maryland Office: 7 Saint Paul Street, Suite 1000, 21202-1671.
Telephone: 410-659-4400.
Fax: 410-659-4599.

(See Next Column)

Charlotte, North Carolina Offices: 3700 Bank of America Plaza, 101 South Tryon Street, 28280.
Telephone: 704-373-8999.
Fax: 704-373-8980 and Bank of America Corporate Center, Suite 2900, 100 North Tryon Street, 28202.
Telephone: 704-373-8999.
Fax: 704-373-8935.
Charlottesville, Virginia Office: Court Square Building, 310 Fourth Street, N.E., Suite 300, P.O. Box 1288, 22902-1288.
Telephone: 804-977-2500.
Fax: 804-980-2222.
Chicago, Illinois Office: R.R. Donnelly Building, 77 West Wacker Drive, Suite 4500, 60601-1635.
Telephone: 312-849-3699.
Fax: 312-849-3690.
Jacksonville, Florida Office: 50 North Laura Street, 32202-3635.
Telephone: 904-798-3200.
Fax: 904-798-3207.
McLean, (Tysons Corner) Virginia Office: 1750 Tysons Boulevard, Suite 1800, 22102-3892.
Telephone: 703-712-5000.
Fax: 703-712-5050.
Norfolk, Virginia Office: World Trade Center, 101 West Main Street, Suite 9000, 23510-1655.
Telephone: 757-640-3700.
Fax: 757-640-3701.
Richmond, Virginia Office: One James Center, 901 East Cary Street, 23219-4030.
Telephone: 804-775-1000.
Fax: 804-775-1061.
Almaty, Republic of Kazakhstan Office: Park Palace, 41 Kazibek Bi Street, 2nd Floor, 480100.
Telephone: 7-3272-608-300.
Fax: 7-3272-608-305.
Brussels, Belgium Office: 250 Avenue Louise, Bte. 64, 1050.
Telephone: 32-2-629-42-11.
Fax: 32-2-629-42-22.
Moscow, Russia Office: Paveltskaya Square, 1 Valovaya Street, 7th Floor, 13054.
Telephone: 7-502-937-0774.
Fax: 7-502-937-0776.

MEMBERS OF FIRM

Robert J. Bittman (Not admitted in DC)
James D. Bridgeman
Michael W. Clancy
James M. Costan
William E. Donnelly
Steven D. Kittrell
David J. Levenson
Thomas J. McGonigle
David H. Pankey
Larry D. Sharp
George J. Terwilliger III
Sharon K. Tucker (Not admitted in DC)

RETIRED PARTNER

Clifford R. Oviatt Jr.

ASSOCIATES

Joel M. Baranowski
Neal J. Cabral
Bradley J. Daves
George W. Erikson Jr. (Not admitted in DC)
Jewell Lim Esposito
Laurie A. Hartman
Robert P. Howard, Jr.
Laura McNeill Hutcheson
Leyla Gainievna Kalniazova
Stephen A. Katsurinis
David W. Kiefer (Not admitted in DC)
Karen Lloyd
Ian C. Lofwall (Not admitted in DC)
Saima Makhdoom (Not admitted in DC)
William G. Miller
Lawrence P. Sandor
Kurt T. Slawson
Virginia Leggett Stevenson

For full biographical listings, see the Martindale-Hubbell Law Directory

MILBANK, TWEED, HADLEY & MCCLOY LLP (AV)

International Square Building, Suite 1100, 1825 Eye Street, N.W., 20006
Telephone: 202-835-7500
Fax: 202-835-7586
Email: postmaster@milbank.com *URL:* http://www.milbank.com
New York, New York Offices: 1 Chase Manhattan Plaza, 10005-1413.
Telephone: 212-530-5000.
Fax: 212-530-5219. ABA/net: MilbankNY.
Midtown Office: 375 Park Avenue, Suite 3601, 10152.
Los Angeles, California Office: 601 South Figueroa Street, 90017.
Telephone: 213-892-4000.
Fax: 213-629-5063.
Tokyo, Japan Office: Fukoku Seimei Building, 2-2, Uchisaiwai-cho 2-Chome, Chiyoda-ku, Tokyo 100-0011, Japan.
Telephone: 011-81-3-3504-1050.
Telephone: 011-81-3-3504-1050.
Fax: 011-81-3-3595-2790, 011-81-3-3595-2840.
London, England Office: Dashwood House, 69 Old Broad Street, London, EC2M 1QS.
Telephone: 44-207-448-3000.
Fax: 44-207-448-3029.
Hong Kong: 3007 Alexandra House, 16 Chater Road.
Telephone: 852-2971-4888.
Fax: 852-2840-0792, 852-2854-9046.

(See Next Column)

MILBANK, TWEED, HADLEY & McCLOY LLP—*Continued*

Singapore Office: 14-00 Caltex House, 30 Raffles Place, 048622.
Telephone: 65-428-2400.
Fax: 65-428-2500.
Moscow, Russia Office: 24/27 Sadovaya-Samotyochnya, Moscow, 103051.
Telephone: 7-501-258-5015.
Fax: 7-501-258-5014.

PARTNERS

Glenn S. Gerstell
Mark A. Kantor
Robert F. Lawrence
John E. Shockey
Richard C. Tufaro
William H. Webster

RETIRED PARTNER

Elliot L. Richardson

OF COUNSEL

Fred W. Reinke

ASSOCIATES

Peter M. Anderson
Katherine Aydin
Michael C. Bisignano
David S. Cohen
Nicholas DeCarlo
Hillary S. DeNigro
Seth D. Garland
Kathryn E. Hoff-Patrinos
Julie M. Jacobs
Michael H. Jacobs
Hilary R. Kao
Dean A. Manson
William Jackson Matney, Jr.
Barbara J. Melby (Not admitted in DC)
Dara A. Panahy (Not admitted in DC)
Felice Roggen
Franceska O. Schroeder
Walter L. Stone
Carla J. Urquhart
Andrew R. Walker
A. Joseph Warburton (Not admitted in DC)
Elizabeth A. Zelinka

For full biographical listings, see the Martindale-Hubbell Law Directory

MINTZ, LEVIN, COHN, FERRIS, GLOVSKY AND POPEO, P.C. (AV)

701 Pennsylvania Avenue, N.W., 20004-2608
Telephone: 202-434-7300
Fax: 202-434-7400
Internet: Each Attorney's Internet Address takes the following form: first inital, last name @mintz.com (e.g., rmintz@mintz.com)
URL: http://www.mintz.com
Boston, Massachusetts Office: One Financial Center.
Telephone: 617-542-6000.
Fax: 617-542-2241.
Reston, Virginia Office: 12021 Sunset Hills Road, Suite 310.
Telephone: 703-464-4800.
Fax: 703-464-4895.

Francis X. Meaney
Charles D. Ferris
William C. Brashares
Frank W. Lloyd
Raymond D. Cotton
Hope S. Foster
Jerome Gotkin (Resident, Boston, Massachusetts Office)
R. Robert Popeo (Resident, Boston, Massachusetts Office)
Thomas M. Antone, IV
Bruce D. Sokler
Alvin J. Lorman
Benjamin J. Griffin
Peter M. Kazon
Charles Alan Samuels
Howard J. Symons
Cameron F. Kerry (Resident, Boston, Mass. Office)
Bradley L. Kelly
David R. Ford
Richard M. Graf
James A. Kirkland
Christopher J. Harvie
Cherie R. Kiser
Sara F. Seidman
William A. Davis
James L. Casserly

OF COUNSEL

Michael Faber
Michael H. Pryor

A. Sheba Chacko
Lisa Marie Sylvia
Deena Godshall Roth
Laura J. Oberbroeckling
Gil M. Strobel
Stephen F. Thurber
James J. Valentino
Tara M. Corvo
David M. Janas
Peter M. Bloom
Eric S. Tower
Aliza A. Danoff
Fernando R. Laguarda
Michelle Marie Mundt
Britton N. Murray (Not admitted in DC)
Uzoma C. Onyeije
Casey Anderson (Not admitted in DC)
Douglas W. Macdonald (Not admitted in DC)
David T. Shapiro (Not admitted in DC)
Bryan T. Bookhard
Amy L. Bushyeager
Valerie E. Hurt
Colin Thomas Roskey (Not admitted in DC)

For full biographical listings, see the Martindale-Hubbell Law Directory

O'CONNOR & HANNAN, L.L.P. (AV)

Suite 500, 1666 K Street, N.W., 20006
Telephone: 202-887-1400
Telecopy: 202-466-2198
Vienna, Virginia Office: 8300 Boone Boulevard, Suite 554.
Telephone: 703-714-6670.
Fax: 703-848-4586.

(See Next Column)

Madrid, Spain Office: La Rinconada, 6, 3°.
Telephone: +34-1-575-0944; +34-1-357-2251.
Fax: +34-1-577-0759.

MEMBERS OF FIRM

Patrick J. O'Connor
Joe A. Walters
Thomas H. Quinn
David R. Melincoff
Patrick E. O'Donnell
F. Gordon Lee
George J. Mannina, Jr.
Robert M. Adler
Timothy W. Jenkins
Stephen N. Shulman
James W. Symington
Larry Pressler
J. Craig Potter
Christina W. Fleps
Gary C. Adler
John M. Himmelberg
John S. Jagiela (Not admitted in DC)
Michael P. Carvalho
Roy C. Coffee III (Not admitted in DC)

NON-ATTORNEY MEMBER

Thomas J. Corcoran

Craig A. Koenigs
Frederick T. Dombo III

OF COUNSEL

David L. Hill
Albert P. Lindemann, Jr.
Charles R. McCarthy, Jr.
William W. Nickerson
Thomas Henry Quinn, Jr.
Audrey P. Rasmussen
Thomas J. Schneider
Moshe Schuldinger

For full biographical listings, see the Martindale-Hubbell Law Directory

PATTON BOGGS LLP (AV)

2550 M Street, N.W., 20037-1350
Telephone: 202-457-6000
Telecopier: 202-457-6315
Email: info@pattonboggs.com *URL:* http://www.pattonboggs.com
Anchorage, Alaska Office: Suite 504, 1031 W. Fourth Avenue, 99501.
Telephone: 907-277-4900.
Facsimile: 907-277-4117.
Dallas, Texas Office: 2001 Ross Avenue, Suite 3000, 75201.
Telephone: 214-758-1500.
Facsimile: 214-758-1550.
Denver, Colorado Office: Suite 1900, 1660 Lincoln Street, 80264.
Telephone: 303-830-1776.
Facsimile: 303-894-9239.
Seattle, Washington Office: Suite 1400, 1000 Second Avenue, 98104.
Telephone: 206-382-0200.
Facsimile: 206-382-0363.

MEMBERS OF FIRM

James R. Patton, Jr.
George Blow (Retired)
Joseph L. Brand
Thomas Hale Boggs, Jr.
Timothy J. May
Elliot H. Cole
J. Gordon Arbuckle
David C. Todd
Richard Alan Earle
Robert H. Koehler
David B. Robinson
John H. Vogel
Allan Abbot Tuttle
John L. Oberdorfer
Timothy A. Vanderver, Jr.
Middleton A. Martin
Garret G. Rasmussen
James B. Christian, Jr.
David E. Dunn, III
Ronald S. Liebman
J. Kirk Wade
Stuart M. Pape
Steven M. Schneebaum
Cliff Massa III
Shaoul Aslan
Donald V. Moorehead
Frank R. Samolis
Don A. Allen
George M. Borababy
Jeffrey T. Smith
Katharine R. Boyce
George J. Schutzer
Scott N. Stone
John F. Jonas
Kenneth J. Gumbiner (Not admitted in DC)
Duane Alan Siler
Russell V. Randle
Jean Veeder MacHarg
Dean M. Dilley
John C. Martin
Deborah M. Lodge
Mitchell R. Berger
Donald H. Pearlman
Daniel H. Margolis
Jeffrey L. Turner
Charles E. Talisman
W. Caffey Norman III
Paul A. J. Wilson
Mary Elizabeth Bosco
Read Kemp McCaffrey
Ross E. Eichberg
Geoffrey G. Davis
Charles H. Camp
James R. Stuart, III
Martha M. Kendrick
Kenneth A. Grigg, Jr.
Michael A. Curto
James A. Reeder
Philip S. Kaplan
Daniel E. Waltz
Herbert W. Hecht, II
Timothy B. Mills
Benjamin L. Ginsberg
Henry Chajet
Mark N. Savit
Robert S. Brams
David J. Farber
Daniel A. Kracov
Benjamin G. Chew
Robert C. Jones
Richard M. Stolbach
Paul C. Besozzi
Stephen Diaz Gavin
J. Jeffrey Craven
Joseph E. Schmitz
Penelope S. Farthing
James A. Hughes, Jr.
Robert K. Taylor
Edward J. Newberry
Michael J. Schaengold
John J. Deschauer, Jr.
Parker E. Brugge
Elliott P. Laws
Michelle D. Bernard
Michael J. Nardotti, Jr.
Benjamin O. Tayloe, Jr.
Michael N. Druckman
G. Kendrick Macdowell
Darryl D. Nirenberg
Mary M. Sjoquist
Joseph G. Passaic, Jr.

(See Next Column)

PATTON BOGGS LLP, *Washington—Continued*

MEMBERS OF FIRM (Continued)

Timothy A. Chorba
Florence Weatherly Prioleau
Lanny J. Davis
Jonathan R. Yarowsky
Joseph V. Colaianni
Nancy A. Murray
Michael T. Platt
James N. Schwarz
George P. Levendis
Douglas B. Mishkin
Stephen J. Kott (Not admitted in DC)
William E. Slade
Eric A. Kuwana
Peter D. Robertson

ASSOCIATES

Denise A. Vanison
Jamal Laurence El-Hindi
Laura C. Tayloe
Elizabeth E. Ring
Aubrey A. Rothrock, III
Christy Gherlein Slade
Edward S. Wisneski (Not admitted in DC)
Jeanne M. Liedtka
Thomas C. Downs
Donald F. McGahn, II
Michael T. Wood
Jeffrey L. Ross
David A. Colodny
Philip A. Bangert
Jennifer A. Wiegleb (Not admitted in DC)
Adele L. Abrams
Norah Virginia Dabney
Janet Fitzpatrick
Douglas C. Proxmire
Susan B. Bastress
Harold H. Kim
Jon Paul Morris
Stephen H. Sherman
Lisa Lynne Hawkins
Elizabeth Baltzan
Elizabeth C. Vella
Jennifer Bastian Schettewi
Rodney A. Grandon
Susan Mathiascheck
Robert A. Hager
Willa B. Perlmutter
F. Cooper Ward
Sean Patrick Clancy
Carl F. Lettow
Andrew M. Rosenberg (Not admitted in DC)
Staci D. Coleman
Amy C. Davine
Jonathan D. Robbins
Stephen S. (Todd) Anderson, Jr. (Not admitted in DC)
Jennifer J. Spokes
Geoffrey W. Ryan
John Spitaleri Shaw
Michael T. Palmer
David A. Bocian (Not admitted in DC)
Philip G. Feigen
Michele J. Bianco
Lloyd H. Spencer, III (Not admitted in DC)
Marcus E. Rosenlehner (Not Admitted in the United States) (Foreign Associate)
Paul D. Rubin
Bing Xu (Not admitted in DC)
Laurence E. Stein (Not admitted in DC)
Elizabeth W. Ho
Carol L. Hoshall
Jay L. Eizenstat (Not admitted in DC)
Matthew Reece (Not admitted in DC)
Andrew M. Friedman
Amy B. Chasanov (Not admitted in DC)
Lisa A. Hunt (Not admitted in DC)
Lisa A. Lavelle
Alyssa T. Senzel
Robert K. Tompkins
Jennifer A. Goldstein
Michael Bloomquist (Not admitted in DC)
Andrew Zimmitti (Not admitted in DC)
Thomas O'Donoghue (Not admitted in DC)
William McGinley (Not admitted in DC)
Christopher Hellmich (Not admitted in DC)
Karen L. Marangi (Not admitted in DC)
David M. Tafuri
Jonathan C. Pavony
Crystal Gothard (Not admitted in DC)
J. Yost Conner, Jr. (Not admitted in DC)
Vincente L. Martinez (Not admitted in DC)
Gal N. Kaufman
T. Michael Guiffre (Not admitted in DC)
Matthew D. Cutts (Not admitted in DC)
Daniel R. Volkmuth (Not admitted in DC)
Michael E. Klein (Not admitted in DC)
Lisa M. Dwyer (Not admitted in DC)
Mary A. Montebello (Not admitted in DC)
R. Brian Hendrix (Not admitted in DC)
Shannon W. Conway (Not admitted in DC)
Grace D. O'Malley (Not admitted in DC)
Daniel Valente
Robyn M. Underwood (Not admitted in DC)

OF COUNSEL

Peter O. Evenson (Not admitted in DC)
John C. Camp
William C. Foster
Gregory H. Laughlin (Not admitted in DC)
Thomas P. O'Donnell
Anne M. Miano
Graham G. Wisner
Brian C. Lopina
Francis X. Gindhart
Lansing B. Lee, III
Gregory S. Walden
Clayton Lee Hough
Daniel R. Addison
Thomas L. Siebert
Marie L. Miller

PUBLIC SERVICE COUNSEL

Melanie K. Gerber

LEGAL SUPPORT PERSONNEL

TRANSPORTATION POLICY CONSULTANT

Carolina L. Mederos

CHIEF ECONOMIC CONSULTANT

David G. Raboy

ECONOMICS CONSULTANT

Teri L. Simpson

(See Next Column)

LEGISLATIVE AFFAIRS SPECIALIST

John F. Kelly, Jr.

SENIOR HEALTH POLICY ADVISOR

JoAnn V. Willis

PUBLIC POLICY SPECIALISTS

Michael A. Brown
Elena M. Giberga (Legislative Affairs Specialist)
Michael J. Hettinger

For full biographical listings, see the Martindale-Hubbell Law Directory

PAUL, HASTINGS, JANOFSKY & WALKER LLP (AV)

A Limited Liability Partnership including Professional Corporations
1299 Pennsylvania Avenue, N.W., 20004-2400
Telephone: 202-508-9500
Fax: 202-508-9700
Atlanta, Georgia Office: 24th Floor, 600 Peachtree Street, N.E.
Telephone: 404-815-2400.
Los Angeles, California Office: 555 South Flower Street.
Telephone: 213-683-6000.
New York, New York Office: 399 Park Avenue.
Telephone: 212-318-6000.
Orange County, California Office: 695 Town Center Drive, Costa Mesa.
Telephone: 714-668-6200.
San Francisco, California Office: 345 California Street.
Telephone: 415-835-1600.
Stamford, Connecticut Office: 1055 Washington Boulevard.
Telephone: 203-961-7400.
Tokyo, Japan Office: Ark Mori Building, 12-32 Akasaka, P.O. Box 577, 1-Chome, Minato-Ku.
Telephone: (03) 3586-4711.
London, England Office: The International Financial Centre, 25 Old Broad Street.
Telephone: (011) 44-171-562-4000.
ATTORNEY E-MAIL ADDRESSES: first initial middle initial last name @phjw.com (e.g. rmasbill@phjw.com)

MEMBERS OF FIRM

E. Lawrence Barcella, Jr.
Barbara Berish Brown
R. Bruce Dickson
E. Donald Elliott
Ralph B. Everett
Zachary D. Fasman
Scott M. Flicker
John J. Gallagher
Jon A. Geier
John Griffith Johnson, Jr.
G. Hamilton Loeb
Carl W. Northrop
Charles A. Patrizia
William Thomas Reeder, Jr.
Bruce D. Ryan
William A. Schmidt
Kenneth M. Willner

SENIOR COUNSEL

Judith Richards Hope
Paul L. Perito

OF COUNSEL

Kirby D. Behre
Claudia Treadwell Callaway
Edwin I. Colodny
William D. DeGrandis
Wendell M. Faria
George R. A. Jones
Michael J. Metzger
Neal D. Mollen
Robert S. Plotkin
Robert E. Pokusa
Margaret H. Spurlin
Erin M. Sweeney
Gregory R. Watchman
Gerald H. Yamada

ASSOCIATES

Steven D. Allison (Not admitted in DC)
Quisaira Y. Almanzar
A. Eduardo Balarezo
Daniel R. Ball
Eric Berger
Gina M. Boscarino
David D. Burns
Kathrine L. Calderazzi
Michelle Weisberg Cohen
Christopher A. Cole
Dianne C. Coombs
Christine M. Crowe
Behnam Dayanim
Keith R. Fentonmiller
Elizabeth M. Georges
Intra L. Germanis
Claudia Hinsch (Not admitted in DC)
Jennifer L. Hong
Karen R. Hunter
A. Jeff Ifrah
Carol A. Kelley
P. Susan Lively
Chester A. McPherson
W. Glenn Merten (Not admitted in DC)
Ellen C. Rice
Seth C. Silber
Jocelyn M. Sturdivant
Jenny C. Wu
Kimberly M. Zywicki

For full biographical listings, see the Martindale-Hubbell Law Directory

PAUL, WEISS, RIFKIND, WHARTON & GARRISON (AV)

1615 L Street, NW Suite 1300, 20036-5694
Telephone: 202-223-7300
TDD 202-223-7490
Facsimile: 202-223-7420
New York, N.Y. Office: 1285 Avenue of the Americas, 10019-6064.
Telephones: 212-373-3000, TDD 212-373-2000.
Facsimile: 212-757-3990.
Paris, France Office: 62, rue du Faubourg Saint-Honoré, 75008.
Telephone: (33-1) 53.43.14.14.
Facsimile: (33-1) 53.43.00.23.

(See Next Column)

PAUL, WEISS, RIFKIND, WHARTON & GARRISON—*Continued*

Tokyo, Japan Office: Fukoku Seimei Building, 2-2 Uchisaiwaicho 2-chome, Chiyoda-ku, Tokyo 100-0011, Japan.
Telephone: (81-3) 3597-8101.
Facsimile: (81-3)3597-8120.
Beijing, China Office: 2918 China World Tower II, No.1 Jianguomenwai Dajie, 100004.
Telephone: (86-10) 6505-6822.
Facsimile: (86-10) 6505-6830.
Hong Kong, China Office: 12th Floor, Hong Kong Club Building, 3A Chater Road, Central Hong Kong.
Telephone: (011-852) 2536-9933.
Facsimile: 011 (852) 2536-9622.

RESIDENT PARTNERS

Terence J. Fortune
Robert E. Montgomery, Jr.
Robert P. Parker
Warren B. Rudman
Dale M. Sarro
Phillip L. Spector
Stuart G. Steingold

COUNSEL

Richard S. Elliott
Soon-Yub Samuel Kwon
Jeffrey H. Olson
Laura B. Sherman

RESIDENT ASSOCIATES

Swati Agrawal
Patrick S. Campbell
Matthew Chavez
Diane C. Gaylor
Gaela K. Gehring-Flores (Not admitted in DC)
Carl W. Hampe
Erik C. Luchs
Aseel M. Rabie
David J. Weiler
Matthew H. Wheelock (Not admitted in DC)

For full biographical listings, see the Martindale-Hubbell Law Directory

PEPPER HAMILTON LLP (AV)

Hamilton Square, 600 Fourteenth Street, N.W., 20005-2004
Telephone: 202-220-1200
Telecopy: 202-220-1665
Email: phinfo@pepperlaw.com *URL:* http://www.pepperlaw.com
Philadelphia, Pennsylvania Office: 3000 Two Logan Square, Eighteenth and Arch Streets, 19103-2799.
Telephone: 215-981-4000.
Fax: 215-981-4750.
Detroit, Michigan Office: 100 Renaissance Center, 36th Floor, 48243-1157.
Telephone: 313-259-7110.
Fax: 313-259-7926.
New York, New York Office: 750 Lexington Avenue, Suite 600, 10022-1200.
Telephone: 212-813-9668.
Fax: 212-813-9802.
Wilmington, Delaware Office: 1201 Market Street, Suite 1600, P.O. Box 1709, 19899-1709.
Telephone: 302-777-6500.
Fax: 302-656-8865.
Pittsburgh, Pennsylvania Office: 500 Grant Street, 50th Floor, 15219-2502.
Telephone: 412-454-5000.
Fax: 412-281-0717.
Harrisburg, Pennsylvania Office: 200 One Keystone Plaza, North Front and Market Streets, P.O. Box 1181, 17108-1181.
Telephone: 717-255-1155.
Fax: 717-238-0575.
Berwyn, Pennsylvania Office: 1235 Westlakes Drive, Suite 400, 19312-2401.
Telephone: 610-640-7800.
Fax: 610-640-7835.
Cherry Hill, New Jersey Office: LibertyView Building, Suite 420, 457 Haddonfield Road, 08002-2220.
Telephone: 856-910-7200.
Fax: 856-665-7743.

PARTNERS

George A. Lehner (Chair, Washington Office Management Committee)
John J. Burke
Irah H. Donner
K. Stewart Evans, Jr.
Elliot J. Feldman
Donald H. Green
John B. Huffaker
Marc D. Machlin
Edward A. McCullough
Cynthia A. Metzler
John Will Ongman
Daniel I. Prywes
Frank M. Rapoport
Sheldon L. Schreiberg
Michael B. Staebler (Not admitted in DC)
Stephen M. Truitt
Gilberto M. Villacorta
William J. Walsh
John H. Weber
David A. Wormser

OF COUNSEL

John F. DePodesta (Not admitted in DC)
Mark L. Hogge
Robert B. Joselow
William S. Ramsey (Not admitted in DC)
Martin D. Teckler
Donna Lee Yesner

(See Next Column)

ASSOCIATES

Charles H. Carpenter
Patrick C. Chi (Not admitted in DC)
Gregory C. Dorris
Scott E. Fireison
Gianna M. Julian-Arnold (Not admitted in DC)
Benjamin M. Kahrl (Not admitted in DC)
Suresh Koshy
O'Kelly E. McWilliams, III
Corinne M. Pouliquen
Elizabeth D. Rodriguez
Elizabeth M. Stanley
Christine C. Waldmann
Christine Quickenden Washington (Not admitted in DC)
David M. Young

For full biographical listings, see the Martindale-Hubbell Law Directory

PERKINS COIE LLP (AV)

607 Fourteenth Street, N.W., 20005
Telephone: 202-628-6600
Facsimile: 202-434-1690
Email: perkins@perkinscoie.com *URL:* http://www.perkinscoie.com
Seattle, Washington: 1201 Third Avenue, Suite 4800, 98101-3099.
Telephone: 206-583-8888.
Facsimile: 206-583-8500.
Anchorage, Alaska: 1029 West Third Avenue, Suite 300, 99501-1970.
Telephone: 907-279-8561.
Facsimile: 907-276-3108.
Santa Monica, California: 1620 26th Street, Suite 600 South, 90404.
Telephone: 310-788-9900.
Facsimile: 310-788-3399.
Menlo Park, California: 135 Commonwealth Drive, Suite 250, 94025-1105.
Telephone: 650-752-6000.
Facsimile: 650-752-6050.
San Francisco, California: 180 Townsend Street, 94107-1909.
Telephone: 415-781-3200.
Facsimile: 415-781-2525.
Denver, Colorado: World Trade Center, 1675 Broadway, Suite 2800, 80202-0462.
Telephone: 303-571-6100.
Facsimile: 303-571-6111.
Boise, Idaho: 714 West State Street, Suite 110, 83702.
Telephone: 208-343-3434.
Facsimile: 208-343-3232.
Olympia, Washington: 1110 Capitol Way South, Suite 405, 98501-2251.
Telephone: 360-956-3300.
Facsimile: 360-956-1208.
Portland, Oregon: 1211 Southwest Fifth Avenue, Suite 1500, 97204-3715.
Telephone: 503-727-2000.
Facsimile: 503-727-2222.
Bellevue, Washington: Suite 1800, One Bellevue Center, 411 - 108th Avenue N.E., 98004-5584.
Telephone: 425-453-6980.
Facsimile: 425-453-7350.
Spokane, Washington: North 221 Wall Street, Suite 600, 99201-0826.
Telephone: 509-624-2212.
Facsimile: 509-458-3399.
Taipei, Taiwan, R.O.C.: 8/F, Cathay United Bank Tower, 85 Jen Ai Rd., Section 4.
Telephone: 886-2-2778-1177.
Facsimile: 886-2-2777-9898.
Hong Kong: 17/F, Standard Charter Bank Building, 4 Des Voeux Road Central.
Telephone: 852-2878-1177.
Facsimile: 852-2524-9988.
Canada: Strategic Alliance with Russell & Dumoulin, 1700-1075 West Georgia Street, Vancouver, B.C. V6E 3G2.
Telephone: 604-631-3131.

PARTNERS

Robert F. Bauer
Donald C. Baur
Judith L. Corley
John M. Devaney
Donald J. Friedman
Mary Rose Hughes
Kerry B. Long
Guy R. Martin
Barry J. Reingold
Yoshihiro Saito
Kara M. Sacilotto
Benjamin S. Sharp
Thomas V. Vakerics
John M. Vassiliades
Martin P. Willard
Jeffrey A. Wool (Not admitted in DC)

OF COUNSEL

Thomas L. Adams, Jr.
Wilford H. "Buzz" Fawcett
Irving Gastfreund (Also at Santa Monica, California Office)
Cassandra F. Lentchner (Not admitted in DC)
B. Holly Schadler
Helen P. Starr
Ellen L. Weintraub
Lis Wiehl (Not admitted in DC; Also at Seattle, Washington Office)

RESIDENT ASSOCIATES

Andrea Anderson
Kelly A. Cameron
Alyssa Chumnanvech
Cynthia H. Clark
Marc E. Elias
Andrew E. Falk
Stephanie A. Handwerger
Marc D. Latman
Adam L. Schless
Brian G. Svoboda
Mark T. Wasden
Sloane Anders Wildman

For full biographical listings, see the Martindale-Hubbell Law Directory

Washington—Continued

PILLSBURY MADISON & SUTRO LLP (AV)

1100 New York Avenue, N.W., Ninth Floor, 20005-3918
Telephone: 202-861-3000
Fax: 202-822-0944
Email: pillsburylaw.com *URL:* http://pillsburylaw.com
Costa Mesa, California Office: 650 Town Center Drive, 7th Floor, 92626.
Telephone: 714-436-6800.
Fax: 714-436-2800.
Los Angeles, California Office: Citicorp Plaza, 725 South Figueroa, Suite 1200, 90017.
Telephone: 213-488-7100.
Fax: 213-629-1033.
New York, New York Office: 375 Park Avenue, Suite 3108, 10152.
Telephone: 212-826-1060.
Fax: 212-826-9255.
Silicon Valley Office: 2550 Hanover Street, Palo Alto, 94034.
Telephone: 650-233-4500.
Fax: 650-233-4545.
Sacramento, California Office: 400 Capitol Mall, Suite 1700, 95814.
Telephone: 916-329-4700.
Fax: 916-441-3583.
San Diego, California Office: 101 West Broadway, Suite 1800, 92101.
Telephone: 619-234-5000.
Fax: 619-236-1995.
San Francisco, California Office: 50 Fremont Street, 94105.
Telephone: 415-983-1000.
Fax: 415-983-1200.
Vienna, Virginia Office: 8330 Boone Boulevard, Suite 400, 22182.
Telephone: 703-744-7600.
Fax: 703-744-7605.
Tokyo, Japan Office: Pillsbury Madison & Sutro, Gaikokuho Jimu Bengoshi Jimusho, 5th Floor, Samon Eleven Building, 3-1, Samon-cho, Shinjuku-ku, Tokyo 160 Japan.
Telephone: 800-729-9830; 011-813-3354-3531.
Fax: 011-813-3354-3534.

MEMBERS OF FIRM

Jack S. Barufka
Donald J. Bird
Susan Tucker Brown
Terry Calvani (Not admitted in DC)
Kendrew H. Colton
Michael A. Conley (Not admitted in DC)
Michael R. Dzwonczyk
Lynn E. Eccleston
G. Paul Edgell
Jay M. Finkelstein
Stephen C. Glazier
Barry P. Golob
Peter W. Gowdey
Robert A. Gutkin (Not admitted in DC)
Adam R. Hess
Kevin E. Joyce
Timothy J. Klima
G. Lloyd Knight, Jr.
Paul N. Kokulis
Dale S. Lazar
Raymond F. Lippitt
Carl G. Love
Paul F. McQuade
Ruth N. Morduch
Mark G. Paulson (Not admitted in DC)
Glenn J. Perry
W. Jeffrey Schmidt
George M. Sirilla
Raymond L. Sweigart
Paul E. White, Jr.
Arthur Wineburg

OF COUNSEL

Robert J. Walters

SENIOR COUNSEL

Theresa Fenelon Falk

ASSOCIATES

William P. Atkins
Gregory P. Brummett (Not admitted in DC)
Samuel P. Burkholder (Not admitted in DC)
Janine A. Carlan (Not admitted in DC)
Cecil S. Chung
Bryan Patrick Collins (Not admitted in DC)
Henry J. Daley (Not admitted in DC)
Lisa Ann Dunner
Barbara M. Flaherty
Paul G. Griffin (Not admitted in DC)
Kerry Hartman (Not admitted in DC)
Ann S. Hobbs
Richard C. Irving (Not admitted in DC)
Thomas A. Isaacson (Not admitted in DC)
Jeffrey David Karceski
Paul W. Kruse
David W. Long (Not admitted in DC)
Raymond Y. Mah (Not admitted in DC)
Anthony L. Miele (Not admitted in DC)
Heather Morin (Not admitted in DC)
Christopher P. Murphy
Dongkwan James Pak (Not admitted in DC)
Paul L. Sharer
Brian Siritzky (Not admitted in DC)
David S. Taylor
Perry E. Van Over
Richard Wydeven
Patricia R. Zeigler

For full biographical listings, see the Martindale-Hubbell Law Directory

PIPER MARBURY RUDNICK & WOLFE LLP (AV)

1200 Nineteenth Street, N.W., 20036-2430
Telephone: 202-861-3900
FAX: 202-223-2085
Email: lawfirm@piperrudnick.com *URL:* http://www.piperrudnick.com
Other Washington, D.C. Office: 1201 New York Avenue, N.W., Penthouse, 20005-3919.
Telephone: 202-712-7200.
Telecopier: 202-712-7222.
Chicago, Illinois Office: Piper Marbury Rudnick & Wolfe, 203 North La Salle Street, Suite 1800, 60601-1293.
Telephone: 312-368-4000.
Telecopier: 312-236-7516.
Telex: 754347.
Tampa, Florida Office: 101 East Kennedy Boulevard, Suite 2001, 33602-5133.
Telephone: 813-229-2111.
Telecopier: 813-229-1447.
Baltimore, Maryland Office: 36 South Charles Street, 21201-3018.
Telephone: 410-539-2530.
FAX: 410-539-0489.
Dallas, Texas Office: 1717 Main Street, Suite 4600, 75201-2605.
Telephone: 214-743-4500.
New York, N.Y. Office: 1251 Avenue of the Americas, 10020-1104.
Telephone: 212-835-6000.
FAX: 212-835-6001.
Philadelphia, Pennsylvania Office: 3400 Two Logan Square, 18th & Arch Streets, 19103-2762.
Telephone: 215-656-3300.
FAX: 215-656-3301.
Easton, Maryland Office: 117 Bay Street, 21601-2703.
Telephone: 410-820-4460.
FAX: 410-820-4463.
Princeton, New Jersey Office: 116 Village Boulevard, Suite 200, Princeton Forrestal Village, 08540.
Telephone: 609-951-2252.
FAX: 609-951-2216.
Reston, Virginia Office: 1850 Centennial Park Drive, Suite 610, Commerce Executive Park III, 20191.
Telephone: 703-391-7100.
Fax: 703-309-5299.

MEMBERS OF FIRM

David H. Bamberger
William D. Blakely
Gary P. Blitz
Benjamin S. Boyd
Michael F. Brockmeyer (Not admitted in DC)
Daniel J. Carrigan
David Clarke, Jr.
Philip L. Cohan
John E. Corette, III
David B. Dempsey
Jay Gary Finkelstein
David J. Fisher (Not admitted in DC; Also at Baltimore, MD and New York, N.Y. Offices)
Mary E. Gately
Leonard L. Gordon
Douglas H. Green
Thomas L. Hanley
Larry D. Harris
Adam S. Hoffinger
E. Leslie Hoffman III (Not admitted in DC)
Deborah E. Jennings
Lawrence M. Katz (Not admitted in DC)
Jill K. Kerxton
Sheldon Krantz
Jeffrey F. Liss
Steven J. Mandell
Edwin M. Martin, Jr.
Deborah R. Meshulam
J. Brian Molloy
Cynthia J. Morris
Mark Muedeking
Kevin P. Mullen
Robert B. Murphy
Stephen R. Mysliwiec
Lewis A. Noonberg
Stephen L. Owen
Ronald L. Plesser
Alan C. Porter
James P. Rathvon
Richard P. Rector
Anthony H. Rickert
Theodore D. Segal
Earl J. Silbert
Gregory A. Smith
Stanley R. Soya
Nancy A. Spangler (Also at Reston, Virginia Office)
Kenneth G. Starling
Ernest M. Stern (Resident)
Mark J. Tauber
Carl L. Vacketta
Richard J. Vacura
Charles B. Wayne
Sandra Jarva Weiss
William R. Weissman
John T. Westermeier, Jr.
Thomas C. Wheeler
Anthony L. Young

OF COUNSEL

Lucinda J. Bach
Emilio W. Cividanes
Cary M. Feldman
E. Ashton Johnston
Randall B. Lowe
Stuart Mendelsohn
Cynthia K. Nicholson
Richard J. Oparil

PARTNER EMERITUS

Toni K. Allen
Nathan B. Feinstein

RESIDENT ASSOCIATES

Carolyn M. Bamberger
J. Darrel Barros (Not admitted in DC)
Alisa M. Bergman (Not admitted in DC)
Timothy P. Branigan
R. Timothy Bryan (Not admitted in DC)
Mark Wayne Carmean (Not admitted in DC)
Kris O. Carter
Sulee J. Clay (Not admitted in DC)
William J. Crowley (Not admitted in DC)
Elizabeth R. Dewey
Chandra Emery
Erik M. Feig (Not admitted in DC)

(See Next Column)

PIPER MARBURY RUDNICK & WOLFE LLP—*Continued*

RESIDENT ASSOCIATES (Continued)

Ada Fernandez (Not admitted in DC)
Lisa Wong Fitch (Not admitted in DC; Also at Baltimore, Maryland)
Steven E. Friedman
Heather E. Gange
Monica Derbes Gibson (Not admitted in DC)
Lorrie A. Giventer
Scott N. Godes (Not admitted in DC)
Keara M. Gordon (Not admitted in DC)
Steven J. Groseclose
Carol Guy-Jackson
James J. Halpert (Resident)
David P. Handler (Not admitted in DC)
Daniel M. Horrigan
Janice W. Housey
Tami J. Howie (Not admitted in DC)
Charles M. Inokon (Not admitted in DC)
Paul W. Jamieson
Brian R. Kennedy
Sean J. Klein (Not admitted in DC)
William Michael Klimon (Not admitted in DC)
Michael G. Langan
Amy Susan Leavens
Tashir J. Lee
Alan R. Lewine (Not admitted in DC)
Bradley K. McConnell (Not admitted in DC)
Robert L. McKay, Jr.
J. Todd Metcalf (Not admitted in DC)
Sara Z. Moghadam (Not admitted in DC)
John L. Moore, Jr.
Eric S. Namrow (Not admitted in DC)
Anant S. Narayanan (Not admitted in DC)
Michael T. Novak (Not admitted in DC)
Sharon S. Y. Park
Christian E. Plaza (Also in Baltimore, MD Office)
Susan H. Pope (Not admitted in DC)
Andrew M. Price
Adam D. Resnick
William F. Reynolds, Jr.
Susan B. Ross (Not admitted in DC)
Robert A. Salerno
Edward S. Scheideman (Not admitted in DC)
Mark I. Schwartz
Anoop G. Shroff
Amy L. Schaner Stanley (Not admitted in DC)
Sheila Stark
James Michael Sullivan
Holly Emrick Svetz
Jane Kwok Ping Tam
Marisa C. Terrenzi
Marianne Mancino Thiede
William F. Tilghman (Not admitted in DC)
Eric S. Wechselblatt (Not admitted in DC)
Janice L. Weiner (Not admitted in DC)
Geoffrey T. Willard (Not admitted in DC)
Alec Zacaroli (Not admitted in DC)

NEW YORK AVENUE OFFICE

MEMBERS OF FIRM

Perry C. Ausbrook
Jay A. Epstien
Steven K. Fedder
Steven B. Feirman
Thomas Galli
Barry M. Heller
Deborah J. Israel
Jeffrey R. Keitelman
Mark A. Kirsch
Frederick L. Klein
H. Bret Lowell
Howard R. Majev
Caroline E. Petro
Lee J. Plave
John M. Tifford
Philip F. Zeidman

ASSOCIATES

Regina B. Amolsch
David L. Cahn
Brian M. Colson
James A. Crolle III
Mary Jane DeWeese
John J. Dwyer
E. O'Brien Kelley (Not admitted in DC)
Frank A. Marino
John D. Muir, Jr.
Reed P. Sexter
William Arthur Smith, II (Not admitted in DC)
Tracy L. Steele
Gerald C. Wells

OF COUNSEL

Robert M. Hall
Petrina M. Markowitz
Timothy Edward Trinka (Not admitted in DC)

For full biographical listings, see the Martindale-Hubbell Law Directory

PORTER WRIGHT MORRIS & ARTHUR LLP (AV)

1667 K Street, N.W., Suite 1100, 20006-1605
Telephone: 202-778-3000; (800-456-7962)
Fax: 202-778-3063
Email: dca@porterwright.com *URL:* http://www.porterwright.com
Columbus, Ohio Office: 41 South High Street, 43215-6194.
Telephones: 614-227-2000; (800-533-2794).
Fax: 614-227-2100. Internet: cmh@porterwright.com.
Dayton, Ohio Office: One Dayton Centre, One South Main Street, Suite 1600, 45402-2028.
Telephones: 937-449-6810; (800-533-4434).
Fax: 937-449-6820. Internet: day@porterwright. com.
Cincinnati, Ohio Office: 250 E. Fifth Street, Suite 2200, 45202-4199.
Telephones: 513-381-4700; (800-582-5813).
Fax: 513-421-0991. Internet: cvg@porterwright.com.
Cleveland, Ohio Office: 925 Euclid Avenue, Suite 1700, 44115-1483.
Telephones: 216-443-9000; (800-824-1980).
Fax: 216-443-9011. Internet: cle@porterwright.com.
Naples, Florida Office: 5801 Pelican Bay Boulevard, Suite 300, 34108-2709.
Telephones: 941-593-2900; (800-876-7962).
Fax: 941-593-2990. Internet: apf@porterwright.com.

(See Next Column)

MEMBERS OF FIRM

David L. Douglass
Alison MacDonald Duncan
E. Jay Finkel
Leslie Alan Glick
Thomas O. Gorman
Judd L. Kessler
Mark L. Lezell
William P. McGrath, Jr.
James E. Pohlman (Not admitted in DC)
W. Scott Simmer
Mitchell A. Stearn

RESIDENT ASSOCIATES

Alfred Campos (Not admitted in DC)
Terra E. Castaldi (Not admitted in DC)
Kristie G. Haynes
John E. Hedstrom
Claire C. Robinson May
Aisha Q. Murray
Thomas J. Poulin (Not admitted in DC)
Robert T. Rhoad
Virginia E. Richards
Heather J. Stewart
Josephine J. Tao
Renata S. Vasconcellos (Not admitted in DC)

RESIDENT OF COUNSEL

Bart S. Fisher
James R. Hagerty
Theresa W. Hajost
Alan C. Nessman
Patrice M. Pitts
James C. Stearns

For full biographical listings, see the Martindale-Hubbell Law Directory

POWELL, GOLDSTEIN, FRAZER & MURPHY LLP (AV)

6th Floor, 1001 Pennsylvania Avenue, N.W., 20004
Telephone: 202-347-0066
Fax: 202-624-7222
URL: http://www.pgfm.com
Atlanta, Georgia Office: Sixteenth Floor, 191 Peachtree Street, N.E., 30303.
Telephone: 404-572-6600.
Telecopier: 404-572-6999.

RESIDENT MEMBERS

Elliott B. Adler
J. Gail Bancroft
Richard M. Belanger
Joseph M. Berl
Jerome A. Breed
Ralph J. Caccia
Kelly Cameron
Anne B. Camper
Michael H. Chanin
William C. Crenshaw
Michael P. Daniels
Butler C. Derrick, Jr.
William Gerald Driggers
Keith A. Dunsmore (Not admitted in DC)
Neil R. Ellis
Michael E. Fine
Lawrence R. Fullerton
Larry S. Gage
Ronald S. Gart
Elizabeth Cole Hafner
David C. Hammond
Harry Huge
Brett G. Kappel
John J. Knapp
Jeffrey P. Kushan (Not admitted in DC)
Simon Lazarus, III
Niall P. Meagher
N. David Palmeter
Alan K. Parver
Daniel M. Price
Charles H. Roistacher
Allen S. Rugg
Michael I. Sanders
Peter W. Segal
W. Bruce Shirk
Andrew W. Shoyer
Andrew J. Strenio, Jr.
Peter O. Suchman
Susan J. Thomas
Robert Torresen, Jr.
Mark Traphagen
Colin W. Uckert
William H.E. von Oehsen
Lawrence R. Walders
Wayne M. Zell

OF COUNSEL

Jessica C. Abrahams
Andrew I. Gavil
David Ginsburg
G. Lee Skillington

COUNSEL

Susan A. Cobb
Charlotte Collins (Not admitted in DC)
Barbara D.A. Eyman
Robert N. Falk
Michael J. Grace
Leonard J. Henzke, Jr.
Brenda A. Jacobs

RESIDENT ASSOCIATES

John E. Bagwell, III
Andre Barlow (Not admitted in DC)
Camille Bennett (Not admitted in DC)
Marinn F. Carlson (Not admitted in DC)
G. A. "Jay" Chadwick, IV
Robert G. Coberly
Daniel C. Cornette (Not admitted in DC)
Lisa Ann Crosby
Maria T. DiGivlian (Not admitted in DC)
Valerie J. Eastwood (Not admitted in DC)
Lorenzo F. Exposito
Gayle Forst
Leigh A. Fraiser
Todd J. Friedbacher
Robert L. Galbreath
Diane Greenlee
Robin Heimann-McGhee
Alexander Koff
Sheryl Krongold
Edward W. Lam (Not admitted in DC)
Anne M. Lewis
Mary Baroody Lowe
Charles A. Luband (Not admitted in DC)
Susan M. Mathews
Richard A. Medway
James E. Mendenhall
Amy H. Nemko
William Compton Poling, Jr (Not admitted in DC)
David C. Quam
Aileen M. Reilly
J. Christopher Rodgers (Not admitted in DC)
Donna Marie Rodney (Not admitted in DC)
Cindy K. Share (Not admitted in DC)
Stephen R. Smith

(See Next Column)

POWELL, GOLDSTEIN, FRAZER & MURPHY LLP, *Washington—Continued*

RESIDENT ASSOCIATES (Continued)

Steven K. Stranne
Adam W. Walsh
(Not admitted in DC)
Leslie S. Yang
(Not admitted in DC)

FOREIGN COUNSEL

Stanimir A. Alexandrov

For full biographical listings, see the Martindale-Hubbell Law Directory

PROSKAUER ROSE LLP (AV)

1233 Twentieth Street, N.W. Suite 800, 20036-2396
Telephone: 202-416-6800
FAX: 202-416-6899
URL: http://www.proskauer.com
New York, New York Office: 1585 Broadway.
Telephone: 212-969-3000.
Fax: 212-969-2900.
Los Angeles, California Office: 2049 Century Park East, Suite 3200.
Telephone: 310-557-2900.
Fax: 310-557-2193.
Boca Raton, Florida Office: One Boca Place, Suite 340 West, 2255 Glades Road.
Telephone: 407-241-7400.
Fax: 561-241-7145.
Newark, New Jersey Office: One Newark Center.
Telephone: 973-274-3200.
Fax: 973-274-3299.
Paris, France Office: Proskauer Rose, 68, rue du Faubourg Saint-Honoré.
Telephone: +33-1-53-05-60-00.
Fax: +33-1-53-05-60-05.

MEMBERS OF FIRM

Jon A. Baumgarten
Mark J. Biros
Joseph E. Casson
Warren L. Dennis
Malcolm J. Harkins, III
Richard H. Rowe
Christopher Wolf

WASHINGTON, D.C.
SENIOR COUNSEL

Thomas H. Brock
Alec W. Farr
James P. Holloway
Lionel E. Pashkoff
Stephen D. Solomon

WASHINGTON, D.C. ASSOCIATES

Mary Ellen Allen
Margaret J. Babb
Christine D. Bachman
Anita M. Bahauddin
(Not admitted in DC)
Susan Brinkerhoff
(Not admitted in DC)
William R. Cowden
Timothy E. Delahunt
(Not admitted in DC)
Brian Elsbernd
Amybeth Garcia-Bokor
Michael C. Hochman
Brian E. Kamoie
(Not admitted in DC)
Julia McMillen
(Not admitted in DC)
Richard E. Ramsay
Cheralyn E. Schessler
Pamela B. Small
Megan H. Tinker
(Not admitted in DC)
Susan A. Turner

For full biographical listings, see the Martindale-Hubbell Law Directory

LAW OFFICES OF LEWIS A. RIVLIN, P.C. (AV)

7th Floor, 1146 19th Street, N.W., 20036
Telephone: 240-401-4959
Fax: 202-496-1647
Affiliated Office: Dr. Carlos Alfredo Lopez Guevara, Lopez, Lopez y Asociados, Suite 12-B, Piso 12, Banco Aliado Tower, Calle Ricardo Arias, Panama, Republica de Panama.
Telephone: 507-263-7670.
Telefax: 507-264-5052.
Affiliated Office: Takeshi Maruyama, Tokyo, Japan.
Telephone: 813-3 541-4781.
Telefax: 813-5 41-3005.

Lewis A. Rivlin

For full biographical listings, see the Martindale-Hubbell Law Directory

ROPES & GRAY (AV)

One Franklin Square, 1301 K Street, NW, Suite 800 East, 20005-3333
Telephone: 202-626-3900
Telecopy: 202-626-3961
Email: postmaster@ropesgray.com *URL:* http://www.ropesgray.com
Boston, Massachusetts Office: One International Place.
Telephone: 617-951-7000.
Fax: 617-951-7050.
Providence, Rhode Island Office: 30 Kennedy Plaza.
Telephone: 401-455-4400.
Fax: 401-455-4401.

(See Next Column)

RESIDENT MEMBERS

Michael Nussbaum
Robert H. Morse
Thomas M. Susman
Russell A. Gaudreau, Jr.
Martin E. Lybecker
Samuel J. Buffone
Colburn T. Cherney
J. Daniel Berry
Mark A. Greenwood
David O. Stewart
Alan G. Priest
Peter M. Brody
Thomas B. Smith

RESIDENT ASSOCIATES

Dina L. Michels
Mary C. Hennessey
J. Steven Baughman
Alyssa Albertelli
Jennifer D. McNasby
Moira T. Roberts
Colleen H. McDuffie
David J. Baum
Catherine Carroll
(Not admitted in DC)
Marc L. Kesselman
Kelly B. Kramer
Todd M. Richman
Jodi R. Goldstein
(Not admitted in DC)

For full biographical listings, see the Martindale-Hubbell Law Directory

SCHIFF HARDIN & WAITE (AV)

A Partnership including Professional Corporations
Founded 1864
1101 Connecticut Avenue, N.W., 20036
Telephone: 202-778-6400
Facsimile: 202-778-6460
URL: http://www.schiffhardin.com
Chicago, Illinois Office: 6600 Sears Tower, 60606.
Telephone: 312-258-5500.
Facsimile: 312-258-5600.
TWX: 910-221-2463.
Merrillville, Indiana Office: 8585 Broadway, Suite 842, 46410.
Telephone: 219-738-3820.
Facsimile: 219-738-3826.
Dublin, Ireland Office: 34 Fitzwilliam Square.
Telephone: +353-1-662-8080.
Facsimile: +353-1-661-1053.

RESIDENT PARTNERS

Edward J. Finn
Barbara K. Heffernan
Andrew M. Klein
Gearold L. Knowles
Howard L. Kramer
André E. Owens

SPECIAL PARTNER

Drexel D. Journey

RESIDENT OF COUNSEL

John W. Glendening, Jr.
Edwin S. Rockefeller
John S. Schmid

COUNSEL

M. Thompson Rattray

RESIDENT ASSOCIATE

Debra Ann Palmer

For full biographical listings, see the Martindale-Hubbell Law Directory

SEWARD & KISSEL LLP (AV)

(Smith & Martin 1890)
1200 G Street, N.W. Suite 350, 20005
Telephone: 202-737-8833
Cable Address: "Sewkis New York"
Telex: 23-9046; 62-0982
Facsimile: 202-737-5184
New York, New York Office: One Battery Park Plaza.
Telephone: 212-574-1200.
Facsimile: 212-480-8421.

RESIDENT PARTNERS

Anthony C. J. Nuland
Paul T. Clark
D. Edwin Schmelzer

RESIDENT COUNSEL

Kathleen K. Clarke
Kevin M. Broadwater

RESIDENT ASSOCIATE

Frederick H. Sherley (Not admitted in DC)

For full biographical listings, see the Martindale-Hubbell Law Directory

SHEARMAN & STERLING (AV)

801 Pennsylvania Avenue, N.W., 9th Floor, 20004-2604
Telephone: (202) 508-8000
Fax: (202) 508-8100
URL: http://www.shearman.com
New York, N.Y. Office: 599 Lexington Avenue, New York, New York, 1002-6069.
Telephone: (212) 848-4000.
Telex: 667290. Num Lau.
Fax: (212) 848-7179.
Abu Dhabi, United Arab Emirates Office: Butti Al Otaiba Building, 13th Floor, Suite 1302, Sheikh Khalifa Street, P.O. Box 2948.
Telephone: (971-2) 274477.
Fax: (971-2) 268933.

(See Next Column)

SHEARMAN & STERLING—*Continued*

Beijing, People's Republic of China Office: Suite #2205, Capital Mansion, No. 6, Xin Yuan Nan Road. Chao Yang District, Beijing, 100004.
Telephone: (86-10) 6465-2299.
Fax: (86-10) 6465-4578.
Düsseldorf, Federal Republic of Germany Office: Couvenstrasse 8 40211 Düsseldorf.
Telephone: (49 211) 178 88-0.
Fax: (49 211) 178 88-88.
Frankfurt, Federal Republic of Germany Office: Mainzer Landstrasse 16, 60325 Frankfurt am Main.
Telephone: (49-69) 9711-1000.
Fax: (49-69) 9711-1100.
Hong Kong Office: Standard Chartered Bank Building, 4 Des Voeux Road, Central.
Telephone: (852) 2978-8000.
Fax: (852) 2978-8099.
London, England Office: 199 Bishopsgate, London EC2M 3TY.
Telephone: (44-171) 920-9000.
Fax: (44-171) 920-9020.
Menlo Park, California Office: 1550 El Camino Real, 94025-4100.
Telephone: (650) 330-2200.
Fax: (650) 330-2299.
Paris, France Office: 114, avenue des Champs-Elysées, 75008.
Telephone: (33-1) 53-89-7000.
Fax: (33-1) 53-89-7070.
San Francisco, California Office: 555 California Street, 94104-1522.
Telephone: (415) 616-1100.
Fax: (415) 616-1199.
Singapore Office: 6 Battery Road, #25-03. Singapore, 049909. Telephone (65) 230-3800.
Fax: (65) 230-3899.
Tokyo, Japan Office: Fukoku Seimei Building, 5th Fl. 2-2-2, Uchisaiwaicho, Chiyoda-ku, Tokyo 100-0011. Japan.
Telephone: (81 3) 5251-1601.
Fax: (81 3) 5251-1602.
Toronto, Ontario, Canada Office: Commerce Court West, Suite 4405, P.O. Box 247, M5L 1E8.
Telephone: (416) 360-8484.
Fax: (416) 360-2958.

RESIDENT PARTNERS

Thomas S. Martin (Managing Partner)
Barry P. Barbash
Robert A. Bergquist
Jonathan L. Greenblatt
Alfred C. Groff
Stephen James Marzen
Linda C. Quinn
Robert A. Rudnick
Frank R. Strong
Steven C. Sunshine
Thomas B. Wilner
Jeffrey M. Winton

OF COUNSEL

Edward Bransilver

COUNSEL

Wendy E. Ackerman
Abigail Arms
Karen Hess McMillan
James F. Warren

For full biographical listings, see the Martindale-Hubbell Law Directory

SIDLEY & AUSTIN (AV)

A Partnership including Professional Corporations
1722 Eye Street, N.W., 20006
Telephone: 202-736-8000
Telecopier: 202-736-8711
Email: info@sidley.com *URL:* http://www.sidley.com/
Chicago, Illinois Office: 48th Floor, Bank One Plaza, 10 South Dearborn Street, 60603.
Telephone: 312-853-7000.
Telecopier: 312-853-7036.
Dallas, Texas Office: 717 North Harwood, Suite 3400, 75201.
Telephone: 214-981-3300.
Telecopier: 214-981-3400.
London, England Office: 1 Threadneedle Street, EC2R 8AW.
Telephone: 011-44-171-360-3600.
Telecopier: 011-44-171-626-7937.
Los Angeles, California Office: 555 West Fifth Street, 40th Floor, 90013-1010.
Telephone: 213-896-6000.
Telecopier: 213-896-6600.
New York, New York Office: 875 Third Avenue, 10022.
Telephone: 212-906-2000.
Telecopier: 212-906-2021.
Singapore Office: 6 Battery Road, #38-01A, Singapore 049909.
Telephone: 011-65-230-3900.
Facsimile: 011-65-230-3939.
Tokyo, Japan Office: Taisho Seimei Hibiya Building, 7th Floor, 9-1, Yurakucho, 1-Chome, Chiyoda-Ku, 100.
Telephone: 011-81-3-3218-5900.
Facsimile: 011-891-3-3218-5922.
Shanghai, China Office: Room F2-G, 19/F Jiushi, Renaissance Mansion, 918 Middle Huai Hai Road, Shanghai 200020.
Telephone: 86.21.6415.6269.
Fax: 86.21.6415.6270.

(See Next Column)

Hong Kong Office: Two Exchange Square, Suite 3403-5, Central Hong Kong.
Telephone: 852.2901.3800.
Fax: 852.2901.3850.

PARTNERS

I. Scott Bass
Christopher L. Bell
James F. Bendernagel, Jr.
Bradford A. Berenson
Jeffrey S. Berlin
Frederic G. Berner, Jr.
Richard D. Bernstein
Raymond A. Bonner
Samuel B. Boxerman
David T. Buente, Jr.
C. John Buresh
Ann E. Bushmiller
Robert J. Conlan, Jr.
James L. Connaughton
Jacqueline Gerson Cooper
Thomas G. Echikson
William S. Eckland
Krista L. Edwards
Eugene R. Elrod
Ronald S. Flagg
Alan C. Geolot
Jeffrey T. Green
Thomas C. Green
Joseph R. Guerra
Samuel I. Gutter
Mark E. Haddad
Kevin Hawley
Stephen S. Hill
Mark D. Hopson
James Alan Huizinga
Terence M. Hynes
George W. Jones, Jr.
Paul E. Kalb
Peter D. Keisler
David L. Lawson
David M. Levy
David J. Lewis
Angus Macbeth
Lorrie M. Marcil
David Michael Miles
Lawrence A. Miller
G. Paul Moates
Michael A. Nemeroff
G. Philip Nowak
Francis J. O'Toole
Carter G. Phillips
Karen A. Popp
Joseph C. Port, Jr.
Vincent F. Prada
Alan Charles Raul
P. David Richardson, II
Melvin Rishe
Constance A. Sadler
Gene C. Schaerr
Mark D. Schneider
Virginia A. Seitz
Langley R. Shook
Joel Singer
Howard J. Stanislawski
Julia E. Sullivan
David Teitelbaum
Kathryn B. Thomson
Joseph B. Tompkins, Jr.
Thomas P. Van Wazer
R. Clark Wadlow
Michael D. Warden
Marc D. Wassermann
R. Merinda Wilson
Elroy H. Wolff
Thomas H. Yancey

COUNSEL

Myles E. Flint (Not admitted in DC)
Richard L. Larach
Stephen B. Lyons
Mark E. Martin
Gary P. Quigley
Donald H. Smith
John F. Wester
Richard E. Young

ASSOCIATES

Anil K. Abraham
Clinton F. Beckner
Scott M. Bohannon
Luisa Caro
Margaret S. Demers
John Fee
Joel D. Feinberg
Marisa A. Gomez
Griffith L. Green
Karin L. Green (Not admitted in DC)
Christina J. Grigorian
Mark P. Guerrera
Achiezer Guggenheim (Not admitted in DC)
Alan Gura
Dima S. Hakura
Paul A. Hemmersbaugh
Michael J. Hunseder
Kurt H. Jacobs
Jennifer L. Janss (Not admitted in DC)
Brian C. Kalt (Not admitted in DC)
Rudolph M. Kammerer (Not admitted in DC)
Lawrence D. Kaplan
Stephen B. Kinnaird
Kristin G. Koehler (Not admitted in DC)
Colleen M. Lauerman (Not admitted in DC)
Greer O. Lautrup
Trey N. Mayfield
Nuala McConnell
Edward R. McNicholas
Daniel Meron
Joseph S. Miller (Not admitted in DC)
Juan P. Morillo (Not admitted in DC)
Robert C. Nissen
Christine Liverzani Prame
Mary C. Ragsdale
Nathan C. Sheers
Michael C. Sloan
Stephen F. Smith (Not admitted in DC)
James A. Tartal (Not admitted in DC)
Frank R. Volpe
Claudia A. Von-Pervieux
Heather M. Walloch (Not admitted in DC)
Carl D. Wasserman
Michael F. Wasserman
Andrew E. Weis (Not admitted in DC)
James P. Young
Paul J. Zidlicky

For full biographical listings, see the Martindale-Hubbell Law Directory

SONNENSCHEIN NATH & ROSENTHAL (AV)

1301 K Street, N.W. Suite 600 East Tower, 20005
Telephone: 202-408-6400
Fax: 202-408-6399
URL: http://www.sonnenschein.com
Chicago, Illinois Office: Suite 8000 Sears Tower, 233 South Wacker Drive.
Telephone: 312-876-8000.
Cable Address: "Sonberk".
Telex: 25-3526.
Facsimile: 312-876-7934.

(See Next Column)

SONNENSCHEIN NATH & ROSENTHAL, *Washington—Continued*

New York, N.Y. Office: 1221 Avenue of the Americas, 24th Floor.
Telephone: 212-768-6700.
Facsimile: 212-391-1247.
San Francisco, California Office: 685 Market Street, 6th Floor.
Telephone: 415-882-5000.
Facsimile: 415-543-5472.
Los Angeles, California Office: 601 South Figueroa Street, Suite 1500.
Telephone: 213-623-9300.
Facsimile: 213-623-9924.
St. Louis, Missouri Office: One Metropolitan Square, Suite 3000.
Telephone: 314-241-1800.
Facsimile: 314-259-5959.
Kansas City, Missouri Office: Suite 1100, 4520 Main Street, 64111.
Telephone: 816-932-4400.
Facsimile: 816-531-7545.
London, England Office: Sonnenscheins, Royex House, Aldermanbury Square, EC2V 7HR.
Telephone: 0207-600-2222.
Facsimile: 0207-600-2221.

RESIDENT PARTNERS

Amy L. Bess	Roger W. Patrick
Todd R. Eskelsen	Kenneth J. Pfaehler
Elizabeth A. Ferrell	Caryl A. Potter, III
Lisa J. Gilden	Douglas E. Rosenthal
John S. Hahn	Kirk R. Ruthenberg
Joseph P. Hornyak	Michael A. Schlanger
Stuart E. Hunt	Albert W. Shay
Fred L. Levy	Jeffrey L. Snyder
Lawrence Z. Lorber	Ronald E. Stauffer
Michael R. Maryn	Jerome P. Weiss (Deceased, 1934-1996)

OF COUNSEL

Donald P. Arnavas	Frances J. Henderson

L. John Osborn

RESIDENT ASSOCIATES

Daniel D. Barnowski	Allyson B. Handler
Imanta M. Bergmanis	Keith J. Hwang
Anne M. Bertsch (Not admitted in DC)	Leslie E. Klein (Not admitted in DC)
John J. Calkins	Raymond Victor Lee
Lynn A. Clements	William F. Lee (Not admitted in DC)
William E. Copley, III (Not admitted in DC)	Marci Rose Levine
Hilary Duke (Not admitted in DC)	Lisa A. MacVittie
	Stephanie L. Marn
Catherine B. Gardner	Drew W. Marrocco
John T. Gilbertson (Not admitted in DC)	Julie Anna Potts
	Alexander H. Schaefer (Not admitted in DC)
Wendy B. Goodman (Not admitted in DC)	David J. Tess

For full biographical listings, see the Martindale-Hubbell Law Directory

---

SQUIRE, SANDERS & DEMPSEY L.L.P. (AV)

1201 Pennsylvania Avenue, N.W., Suite 500, 20004-2491
Telephone: 202-626-6600
Fax: 202-626-6780
URL: http://www.ssd.com
Cleveland, Ohio Office: 4900 Key Tower, 127 Public Square, Cleveland, Ohio 44114-1304.
Telephone: 216-479-8500.
Fax: 216-479-8780.
Columbus, Ohio Office: 1300 Huntington Center, 41 South High Street, Columbus, Ohio 43215-6150.
Telephone: 614-365-2700.
Fax: 614-365-2499.
Houston, Texas Office: 6250 Chase Tower, 600 Travis Street, Houston, Texas 77002-3007.
Telephone: 713-546-5850.
Fax: 713-546-5830.
Jacksonville, Florida Office: One Enterprise Center, Suite 2100, 225 Water Street, Jacksonville, Florida 32202-4424.
Telephone: 904-366-2420.
Fax: 904-356-2986.
Miami, Florida Office: 201 South Biscayne Boulevard, 2900 Miami Center, Miami, Florida 33131-4330.
Telephone: 305-577-8700.
Fax: 305-358-1425.
New York, New York Office: 350 Park Avenue, New York, New York 10022-6002.
Telephone: 212-872-9800.
Fax: 212-872-9815.
Phoenix, Arizona Office: Two Renaissance Square, 40 North Central Avenue, Suite 2700, Phoenix, Arizona 85004-4498.
Telephone: 602-528-4000.
Fax: 602-253-8129.
Bratislava, Slovak Republic Office: Zochova 5, 811 03 Bratislava, Slovak Republic.
Telephone: 421-7-5441-7611.
Fax: 42-1-7-6280-2212.

(See Next Column)

Brussels, Belgium Office: Avenue Louise, 165-Box 15, 1050 Brussels, Belgium.
Telephone: 32-2-627-1111.
Fax: 32-2-627-1100.
Budapest, Hungary Office: H-1062 Budapest, Andrassy ut. 64, Budapest, Hungary.
Telephone: 36-1-428-7111.
Fax: 36-1-428-7100.
Kyiv, Ukraine Office: 14A Yaroslaviv Val, Kyiv 252034, Ukraine.
Telephone: 38-044-228-8687.
Fax: 38-044-228-4938.
London, England Office: Royex House, Aldermanbury Square, London EC2V 7HR.
Telephone: 44-171-776-5200.
Fax: 44-171-776-5233.
Madrid, Spain Office: Calle Velazquez 108-110, 28006 Madrid, Spain.
Telephone: 34-91-590-2420.
Fax: 34-91-590-2421.
Moscow, Russian Federation Office: 13 Khokhlovskiy Lane, Moscow 109028, Russian Federation.
Telephone: 7-503-956-3750.
Fax: 7-503-956-3635.
Prague, Czech Republic Office: Václavské náměst 1 57/813, 110 00 Praha 1, Czech Republic.
Telephone: 420-2-2166-2111.
Fax: 420-2-2166-2222.
Hong Kong Office: Rooms 1101-2 St. George's Building, 2 Ice House Street, Central, Hong Kong.
Telephone: 852-2509-9732.
Fax: 852-2509-9772.
Taipei, Taiwan Office: 14F, 116 Nanking East Road, Sec. 2, Taipei, Taiwan, Republic of China.
Telephone: 886-2-2531-2888.
Fax: 886-2-2571-6199.

PARTNERS

John H. C. Barron Jr.	Glenn W. Letham
Roland J. Behm	Herbert E. Marks
Timothy W. Bergin	William A. Mogel
Sam Black	James P. Murphy
Alan L. Briggs	Jonathan Jacob Nadler
Donald T. Bucklin	David A. Nall
James V. Dick	Paul A. O'Hop, Jr.
Charles F. Donley II	Robert D. Papkin
Arnold Fieldman	Douglas L. Povich
Edward A. Geltman	Barry A. Pupkin
Coralyn Goode	Edward W. Sauer
John C. Henry, Jr.	Marshall Sanford Sinick
John A. Howell	Channing D. Strother, Jr.
Robert B. Kelly	Ritchie T. Thomas
Scott T. Kragie	Nancy A. White
Henry W. Lavine	Robert I. White

Glenn M. Young

COUNSEL

Thomas J. Quigley (Retired)

OF COUNSEL

Susan Bierman	Edward J. Hawkins
Ann R. Brashear	Francis S. Rath
Elizabeth Glass Geltman	David Schmeltzer
Mark E. Greenwold	Judith Jurin Semo

ASSOCIATES

Benigno E. Bartolome, Jr. (Not admitted in DC)	Brian J. McHugh
	Alvaro J. Mestre
Heather M. Boals	Bruce A. Olcott
Amy L. Brown	William O'Neill (Not admitted in DC)
John A. Burlingame	
William M. Carter, Jr. (Not admitted in DC)	Mark D. Poindexter
	Kelly Anne Quinn
Andrew W. Cohen	Matthew McLean Rabin (Not admitted in DC)
Keith E. Dobbins	
Heidi Duncan (Not admitted in DC)	C. Russell Shearer (Not admitted in DC)
Christopher Howe Gordon (Not admitted in DC)	Thomas E. Skilton
	Robert E. Stup, Jr.
Lisa Goekjian Henneberry	James P. Wehner
Kevin S. Levey	Richard J. Wickham, Jr. (Not admitted in DC)
Ruth Ann Lowery	

For full biographical listings, see the Martindale-Hubbell Law Directory

---

STEPTOE & JOHNSON LLP (AV)

1330 Connecticut Avenue, N.W., 20036
Telephone: 202-429-3000
Fax: 202-429-3902
Cable Address: "Stepjohn"
Email: wrehm@steptoe.com *URL:* http://www.steptoe.com
Phoenix, Arizona Office: Two Renaissance Square, 40 N. Central Avenue, 24th Floor, 85004.
Telephone: 602-257-5200.
Fax: 602-257-5299.
Los Angeles, California Office: 633 West Fifth Street, Suite 700, 90071.
Telephone: 213-439-9400.
Fax: 213-439-9599.

(See Next Column)

STEPTOE & JOHNSON LLP—*Continued*

MEMBERS

Calvin H. Cobb, Jr.
Monroe Leigh
Richard P. Taylor
John E. Nolan
Robert D. Wallick
James P. Holden
Betty Jo Christian
Robert E. Jordan III
Matthew J. Zinn
Richard H. Weise
P. Robert Fannin (Resident, Phoenix, Arizona Office)
Robert E. McLaughlin
James T. Halverson
Martin D. Schneiderman
Richard O. Cunningham
David L. Roll
Richard H. Porter
Sheldon E. Hochberg
Lawrence A. Katz (Resident, Phoenix, Arizona Office)
Laurence F. Janssen (Resident, Los Angeles, California Office)
Kenneth I. Jonson
Theodore E. Rhodes (Resident, Los Angeles, California Office)
J. A. Bouknight, Jr.
James G. Derouin (Resident, Phoenix, Arizona Office)
Ronald S. Cooper
Terence P. Quinn
Roger E. Warin
John R. Labovitz
F. Michael Kail
Mark J. Silverman
William Karas
John T. Collins
Steven H. Brose
Robert W. Fleishman
Howard H. Stahl
W. George Grandison
Arthur L. Bailey
Bruce E. Meyerson (Resident, Phoenix, Arizona Office)
Herbert C. Shelley
Edmund W. Burke
Morgan D. Hodgson
Douglas G. Green
Frederick S. Frei
Ellen d'Alelio
Mark F. Horning
Christopher T. Lutz
Samuel T. Perkins
James B. Vasile
Ellen M. McNamara
Paul J. Ondrasik, Jr.
Thomas C. Collier, Jr.
Reid H. Weingarten
Charles C. Read
Stewart A. Baker
Charles G. Cole
Susan H. Serling
Francis J. Burke, Jr. (Resident, Phoenix, Arizona Office)
Joel D. Kaufman
Filiberto Agusti
Thomas P. Barletta
Timothy M. Walsh
Peter L. Wellington
Olin L. Wethington
Daryl A. (Sandy) Chamblee
Anthony C. Epstein
Stephen A. Fennell
Seth Goldberg
Samuel M. Sipe, Jr.
Maureen O'Keefe Ward
Gary A. Morgans
J. William Koegel, Jr.
Anne E. Moran
Steven Reed
Daniel C. Sauls
David J. Bodney (Resident, Phoenix, Arizona Office)
David B. Raskin
Blake D. Rubin
Melanie F. Nussdorf
Philip L. Malet
Antonia B. Ianniello
Edward J. Krauland
J. Walker Johnson
Erik L. Kitchen
Floyd P. Bienstock (Resident, Phoenix, Arizona Office)
Gary J. Rinkerman
Stephen L. Sulzer
George Ian Brandon (Resident, Phoenix, Arizona Office)
Kevin L. Olson (Resident, Phoenix, Arizona Office)
Mark P. Fitzsimmons
Scott H. Katzman
Steven J. Ross
Jane I. Ryan
Lawrence P. Riff (Resident, Los Angeles, California Office)
Carol A. Rhees
Jerald S. Howe Jr.
Virginia L. White-Mahaffey
David H. Coburn
Anthony J. LaRocca
Alfred M. Mamlet
Steven K. Davidson
Harry Lee
Mark A. Moran
Thomas M. Barba
William T. Hassler
Linda S. Stein
Cynthia L. Quarterman
Gregory M. Giammittorio
Richard L. Roberts
Mark J. Hulkower
Monica L. Goebel (Resident, Phoenix, Arizona Office)
Pantelis Michalopoulos
Steven J. Barber (Resident, Los Angeles, California Office)
Stuart T. F. Huang
M. Jean Schlesinger
Edward R. Mackiewicz
James B. Moorhead
Steven B. Teplinsky
Peter Lichtenbaum
Wendy Gerlach Briggs (Resident, Phoenix, Arizona Office)
Caroline Gaudet (Not admitted in DC)
Kevin C. Mayer (Resident, Los Angeles, California Office)
Matthew D. Lerner
Eric C. Emerson

OF COUNSEL

Cecil J. Olmstead
Richard Diamond
Kenneth D. Ludwig
Richard A. Whiting
Stanley Smilack
William K. Condrell
Sara Beth Watson
Carol A. Mitchell
Scott A. Harman
Joseph E. Stubbs
Edward J. Twomey
Errol R. Patterson
Ellen Kohn
John J. Duffy
James M. Talens
Edward G. Gregory (Resident, Los Angeles, California Office)
Kathryn R. Janssen (Resident, Los Angeles, California Office)
Ruth D. Kahn (Resident, Los Angeles, California Office)
Mary Woodson (Molly) Poag
Sara E. Hauptfuehrer
Barbara R. Goldberg (Resident, Phoenix, Arizona Office)
Savery M. Gradoville
Carolyn Doozan Clayton
Bennett Evan Cooper (Resident, Phoenix, Arizona Office)
Sidney P. Levinson
Leonard S. Kolsky (Not admitted in DC)
Alice Alexandra Kipel

(See Next Column)

OF COUNSEL (Continued)

Lloyd C. Loomis (Resident, Los Angeles, California Office)
Thomas J. Trendl
Scot C. Stirling (Resident, Phoenix, Arizona Office)
John L. Jacobus
Jennifer L. Key
Mark G. Kisicki (Resident, Phoenix, Arizona Office)
Kenneth J. Sheehan

SPECIAL COUNSEL

John Flyger
Marcia R. Mitnick
Kevin M. Judiscak (Resident, Phoenix, Arizona Office)
Sharon Hyman Schick
Marlene L. Stein

ASSOCIATES

Benjamin R. Achenbach, Jr.
Sonia Baldia (Not admitted in United States)
Bruce J. Barnard
Jean Male Baxley
Deon Woods Bell
Matias Bendersky (Not admitted in the United States)
Bruce C. Bishop
Melineh B. Blackwell
Peter D. Blumberg
Gordon M. Clay
Carlynne S. Cockrum
Shannen W. Coffin
Thomas M. Contois
L. Benjamin Ederington
Mark C. Elmer
Andrea C. Evans
Kenneth P. Ewing
Omer C. Eyal (Not admitted in DC)
Wm. Fletcher Fairey
James S. Felt
Jonathan I. Forrest
Sherry I. Gilman
Catherine M. Giovannoni
Rebecca A. Goldman
Carol R. Gosain
Kathleen M. Graber
Cheryl L. Grant
Susan Harthill
Brian M. Heberlig
Leslie R. Hoffman
Amy L. Howe
Paul R. Hurst
Julie M. Jackson
Leo J. Jennings
Barbara K. Kagan
B. Kelly Kiser
Galina V. Kolomietz (Not admitted in DC)
Lindsey B. Lang
Anja Lehmann
Brian J. Leske
Margaret A. Lin (Not admitted in DC)
Mark A. Machi
Andrea R. Macintosh
Shannon P. MacMichael
Lark T. Mallory
Catherine Jurgensmeyer Martin
Gregory S. McCue
Tekedra V. McGee
Mary T. Mitchell (Not admitted in DC)
Viet H. Ngo
John F. O'Connor, Jr
Patrick O'Donnell
Raymond E. Patricco
Marc A. Paul
Libretta A. Porta
Gwendolyn Prothro
L. Matthew Quigley
T. Robert Rehm, Jr.
James A. "Del" Renigar
Mary J. Reyburn
Carrie Aleen Rhoads
Rhonda M. Rivens
Julia Court Ryan
Colleen Sechrest
Eric G. Serron
Maury D. Shenk
Andrew J. Sloniewsky
Matthew L. Stennes (Not admitted in DC)
Catherine A. Szilagyi (Not admitted in DC)
David N. Tanenbaum
Cynthia L. Taub
Stephanie A. Taylor
Brian J. Telpner
Shaun Leland Terrill (Not admitted in DC)
David G. Tewksbury (Not admitted in DC)
Richard R. Verma
Michael J. Vernick
Julie A.S. Vinyard
Andrew J. Weinstein
Elaine Weiss (Not admitted in DC)
Ripple L. Weistling (Not admitted in DC)
Greg R. Yates (Not admitted in DC)
Matthew Yeo
Lisa M. Zarlenga
Tracy Zorpette

For full biographical listings, see the Martindale-Hubbell Law Directory

STEWART AND STEWART (AV)

Suite 200, 2100 M Street, N.W., 20037-1207
Telephone: 202-785-4185
Telecopier: 202-466-1286; 466-1287; 466-1288
Email: general@stewartlaw.com
Moscow, Russia Office: Leninskiy Prospect, Dom 42, Corpus 1, Suite 1562, Moscow 117119.
Telephone: 011-7-95-938-7775.
Fax: 011-7-95-938-7648. Email: stewart@pol.ru
Charleroi, Belgium Office: Boulevard Dewandre 13, B6000 Charleroi.
Telephone: 011-32-7-132-5131.
Fax: 011-32-7-132-3526. Email: spinoitwese@compuserve.com

Eugene L. Stewart, Founder (1920-1998)

MEMBERS OF FIRM

Terence P. Stewart
James R. Cannon, Jr.
Wesley K. Caine
William A. Fennell
Geert De Prest
Alan M. Dunn

ASSOCIATES

David S. Johanson
Dennis R. Nuxoll
Marta Maria Prado (Not admitted in DC)

(See Next Column)

STEWART AND STEWART, *Washington—Continued*

OF COUNSEL

Bernard Spinoit (Not admitted in the United States)
Lane Steven Hurewitz
Patrick John McDonough (Not admitted in DC)
Amy S. Dwyer
Eric P. Salonen
James R. Holbein (Not admitted in DC)

For full biographical listings, see the Martindale-Hubbell Law Directory

STROOCK & STROOCK & LAVAN LLP (AV)

1150 Seventeenth Street, N.W. Suite 600, 20036-4652
Telephone: 202-452-9250
Telecopier: 202-293-2293
Email: infodc@stroock.com *URL:* http://www.strock.com
New York, N.Y. Office: 180 Maiden Lane, New York, NY, 10038.
Telephone: 212-806-5400.
Telecopiers: 212-806-6006; 212-806-5919; 212-806-6086; 212-425-9509; 212-806-6176. Email: info@stroock.com
New York Conference Center: 767 Third Avenue, New York, N.Y., 10017-2023.
Telephones: 212-806-5767; 5768; 5769; 5770.
Telecopier: 212-421-6234. Email: info@stroock.com
Boston, Massachusetts Office: 100 Federal Street, Boston, Massachusetts 02110-1813.
Telephone: 617-482-6800.
Fax: 617-330-5111. Email: infoboston@stroock.com
Budapest, Hungary Office: East-West Business Center, Rákóczi út 1-3, H-1088 Budapest, Hungary.
Telephone: 011-36-1-266-9520; 011-36-1-266-7770.
Telecopier: 011-36-1-266-9279. Email: stroock@stroock.hu
Los Angeles, California Office: 2029 Century Park East, Suite 1800, Los Angeles, Ca., 90067-3086.
Telephone: 310-556-5800.
Telecopier: 310-556-5959. Email: infola@stroock.com
Miami, Florida Office: First Union Financial Center, 200 South Biscayne Boulevard, Suite 3300, Miami, Fl., 33131-2385.
Telephone: 305-358-9900.
Telecopier: 305-789-9302. Email: infomiami@stroock.com

RESIDENT PARTNER

Richard K. Eaton

RETIRED PARTNER

Walter Pozen

For full biographical listings, see the Martindale-Hubbell Law Directory

SULLIVAN & CROMWELL (AV)

1701 Pennsylvania Avenue, N.W., 20006-5805
Telephone: 202-956-7500
Telecopier: 202-293-6330
URL: http://www.sullcrom.com
New York City Office: 125 Broad Street, 10004-2498.
Telephone: 212-558-4000.
Telex: 62694.
Telecopier: 212-558-3588 or 212-514-5706.
Los Angeles, California Office: 1888 Century Park East, 90067-1725.
Telephone: 310-712-6600.
Telecopier: 310-712-8800.
Paris Office: 8, Place Vendôme, 75001 Paris, France.
Telephone: (011)(331) 44 50 60 00.
Telex: 240654.
Telecopier: (011)(331) 44 50 60 60 or (011)(331) 42 60 56 36.
London Office: St. Olave's House, 9a Ironmonger Lane, London EC2V 8EY, England.
Telephone: (011)(44207) 710 6500.
Telecopier: (011)(44207) 710 6565.
Melbourne Office: 101 Collins Street, Melbourne, Victoria 3000, Australia.
Telephone: (011)(613) 9635-1500.
Telecopier: (011)(613) 9654-2422.
Tokyo Office: Sullivan & Cromwell, Gaikokuho Jimu Bengoshi Jimusho, Akai Law Offices (Registered Associated Offices), Otemachi First Square East Tower 16F, 5-1, Otemachi 1-chome, Chiyoda-ku, Tokyo 100-0004, Japan.
Telephone: (011)(813) 3213-6140.
Telecopier: (011)(813) 3213-6470 or (011)(813) 3213-6477.
Hong Kong Office: 28th Floor, Nine Queen's Road, Central, Hong Kong.
Telephone: (011)(852) 2826-8688.
Telecopier: (011)(852) 2522-2280.
Frankfurt Office: Neue Mainzer Strasse 52, 60322 Frankfurt, Germany.
Telephone: (011)(4969) 7191 26-0.
Telecopier: (011)(4969) 7191 26-10.
Beijing Office: The Beijing Representative Office of Sullivan & Cromwell, Suite 501, China World Trade Center, No. 1 Jianguo Menwai Avenue, Beijing 100004, P.R.C.
Telephone: (011)(86) 10 6505 6120.
Telecopier: (011)(86) 10 6505 6136.

PARTNERS IN WASHINGTON, D.C.

Edwin D. Williamson
H. Rodgin Cohen (Not admitted in DC)
Robert H. Craft, Jr.
Margaret K. Pfeiffer
Daryl A. Libow
Dennis C. Sullivan

(See Next Column)

OF COUNSEL IN WASHINGTON, D.C.

Janet Thiele Geldzahler
Douglas Mark McCall

SPECIAL COUNSEL IN WASHINGTON, D.C.

William J. Brown
Thomas R. Leuba
Paul J. McElroy

ASSOCIATES IN WASHINGTON, D.C.

Adel B. Al-Ali (Not admitted in United States)
Toryah S. Cameron (Not admitted in DC)
Anna Maria Kuzmik
Lee Ann Anderson McCall
Charles C. Moore (Not admitted in DC)
Chidi J. Ogene (Not admitted in DC)
Kathryn E. Rorer
Samantha Evans Ross
Timothy E. Sheil
Michael K. Sopchick
Joy Marzilli Willing (Not admitted in DC)
Andrew W. Winden (Not admitted in DC)
Christopher M. Zochowski

For full biographical listings, see the Martindale-Hubbell Law Directory

THELEN REID & PRIEST LLP (AV)

Market Square, 701 Pennsylvania Avenue, N.W., 20004-2608
Telephone: 202-508-4000
Facsimile: 202-508-4321
URL: http://www.thelenreid.com
San Francisco, California Office: Two Embarcadero Center.
Telephone: 415-392-6320.
Fax: 415-421-1068.
Los Angeles, California Office: 34th Floor, 333 South Grand Avenue.
Telephone: 213-621-9800.
Fax: 213-623-4742.
San Jose, California Office: 17th Floor, 333 West San Carlos Street.
Telephone: 408-292-5800.
Fax: 408-287-8040.
New York, New York Office: 40 West 57th Street.
Telephone: 212-603-2000.
Fax: 212-603-2001.

Howard A. Cooper
Benjamin I. Delancy (Not admitted in DC)
Deborah A. DeMasi
Mark Fox Evens
Lee M. Goodwin
Robert T. Hall, III
Steven S. Honigman
Nathaniel A. Humphries
David E. Jacobson
William A. Kirk, Jr.
Richard J. Leidl
Phillip G. Lookadoo
Allen S. Melser
Stephan M. Minikes
James K. Mitchell
Gregory G. Pavin (Not admitted in DC)
Mark J. Riedy
John R. Schaefgen, Jr.
Kenneth B. Weiner

OF COUNSEL

Raymond F. Dacek
Andrew F. MacDonald
Edward L. Pittman
Richard Y. Roberts

RESIDENT ASSOCIATES

Nancy J. Eskenazi
Raymond C. Glenny
Jose Joaquin Ledesma (Not admitted in DC)
Ambari Prakash (Not admitted in DC)
Martha Groves Pugh
Linda J. Shapiro
Luis Oscar Souffront
Mary Margaret Utterback

SPECIALISTS AND ADVISORS

Amy E. Angelier (Legislative Representative)
Barry I. Berkoff
Nancy K. West

For full biographical listings, see the Martindale-Hubbell Law Directory

THOMPSON COBURN LLP (AV)

Suite 900, 700-14th Street, N.W., 20005-2010
Telephone: 202-508-1000
Telecopier: 202-508-1010
Email: info@thompsoncoburn.com *URL:* http://www.thompsoncoburn.com
St. Louis, Missouri Office: One Mercantile Center.
Telephone: 314-552-6000.
Telecopier: 314-552-7000.
Belleville, Illinois Office: 525 West Main Street.
Telephone: 618-277-4700.
Telecopier: 618-236-3434.
Billings, Montana Office: Norwest Center, 175 North 27th Street, Suite 903, 59101.
Telephone: 406-896-4100.
Fax: 406-896-4199.

MEMBERS OF FIRM

Milton D. Andrews
John V. Austin
Murray J. Belman
Bonnie S. Blair
Warren L. Dean, Jr.
Michael A. Greenspan
Andrew A. Jaxa-Debicki (Not admitted in DC)
Marjorie F. Krumholz
Barbara B. Powell
Edward J. Sheppard, IV
Patricia N. Snyder
Gerald D. Stoltz
Marcela B. Stras
David R. Straus

(See Next Column)

THOMPSON COBURN LLP—*Continued*

ASSOCIATES

Mercia Elayne Arnold (Not admitted in DC)
Eileen P. Brown
Jacqueline T. Colclough
Judith "Jan" Elston
Matthew H. Kaiser (Not admitted in DC)
Heather Leigh Miller
David M. Schwartz

Representative Clients: American Municipal Power-Ohio, Inc.; Appleton Papers, Inc.; Cold Finished Steel Bar Institute; Comerica, Inc.; GATX Capital Corporation; Riso, Inc.; Shell Bermuda (Overseas) Limited; Summit Bancorp; Tata Consultancy Services; Venepal, S.A.C.A.; World Bank.

For full biographical listings, see the Martindale-Hubbell Law Directory

TUTTLE, TAYLOR & HERON (AV)

1025 Thomas Jefferson Street, N.W., 20007-5201
Telephone: 202-342-1300
Facsimile: 202-342-5880
Email: ttandh@erols.com
Los Angeles, California Office: Tuttle & Taylor, A Law Corporation, 355 South Grand Avenue, 40th Floor, 90071-3102.
Telephone: 213-683-0600.
Facsimile: 213-683-0225.

OF COUNSEL

Julian B. Heron, Jr.
Phillip L. Fraas

For full biographical listings, see the Martindale-Hubbell Law Directory

VENABLE ATTORNEYS AT LAW VENABLE, BAETJER, HOWARD & CIVILETTI, LLP (AV)

A Partnership including Professional Corporations
Suite 1000, 1201 New York Avenue, N.W., 20005
Telephone: 202-962-4800
Fax: 202-962-8300
URL: http://www.venable.com
Baltimore, Maryland Office: Venable, Baetjer and Howard LLP, 1800 Mercantile Bank & Trust Building, 2 Hopkins Plaza.
Telephone: 410-244-7400.
Fax: 410-244-7742.
McLean, Virginia Office: Venable, Baetjer and Howard LLP, Suite 400, 2010 Corporate Ridge.
Telephone: 703-760-1600.
Fax: 703-821-8949.
Rockville, Maryland Office: Venable, Baetjer and Howard LLP, Suite 500, One Church Street, P. O. Box 1906.
Telephone: 301-217-5600.
Fax: 301-217-5617.
Towson, Maryland Office: Venable, Baetjer and Howard LLP, 210 Allegheny Avenue, P. O. Box 5517.
Telephone: 410-494-6200.
Fax: 410-821-0147.

MEMBERS OF FIRM

David G. Adams
Robert G. Ames (Also at Baltimore, Maryland Office)
Alan S. Anderson
James K. Archibald (Also at Baltimore, Maryland Office)
Maurice Baskin
Kenneth C. Bass, III (Also at McLean, Virginia Office)
John B. Beaty
Lawrence B. Bernard
Connie N. Bertram
Joseph G. Block
Robert J. Bolger, Jr. (Also at Baltimore, Maryland Office)
Neal D. Borden (Not admitted in DC; Also at Baltimore, Maryland Office)
James R. Burdett
Anthony M. Carey (Not admitted in DC; Also at Baltimore, Maryland Office)
Wallace E. Christner (Also at Baltimore, Maryland Office)
Arthur E. Cirulnick
Benjamin R. Civiletti (P.C.) (Also at Baltimore and Towson, Maryland Offices)
Roger A. Colaizzi
Bryson L. Cook (P.C.) (Not admitted in DC; Also at Baltimore, Maryland Office)
John F. Cooney
William D. Coston
Jeffrey A. Dunn (Also at Baltimore, Maryland Office)
Craig A. Emden
Anita J. Finkelstein
Michael R. Flyer
Andrew Fois
Robert J. Frank
Stuart M. Ginsberg
Ronald R. Glancz
Edward F. Glynn, Jr.
David W. Goewey
Michael A. Gollin
Robert Gene Gottlieb
Jan K. Guben (Not admitted in DC; Also at Baltimore, Maryland Office)
John S. Harper
Mark B. Harrison
Gregory B. Hauptman
Gary M. Hnath
Kenneth R. Hoffman (Also at Baltimore, Maryland Office)
Kenneth G. Hurwitz (Also at Baltimore, Maryland Office)
Amy Berman Jackson
Paul T. Kaplun
Lawrence A. Katz
Joshua J. Kaufman
Gabor J. Kelemen (Not admitted in DC)
Thomas J. Kelly, Jr.
Robert Kinberg
Jeffrey D. Knowles
Norman N. Kunitz
Brock R. Landry
Fernand A. Lavallee
Stephen E. Leach
Geoffrey M. Levitt
Thomas J. Madden
David M. Malone
Mary Ann Mancini

(See Next Column)

MEMBERS OF FIRM (Continued)

Vicki Margolis (Also at Baltimore, Maryland Office)
Charles R. "Rod" Marvin, Jr.
Lindsay Beardsworth Meyer
Daniel L. Morgan
Andrea I. O'Brien
Jerry R. O'Conor
George F. Pappas (Also at Baltimore, Maryland Office)
Thomas L. Patterson
John J. Pavlick, Jr.
Julie A. Petruzzelli
Todd H. Reuben
Tamara Schiebel Rickman
Mary Jane Saunders
Michael Schatzow (Also at Baltimore, Maryland Office)
Michael A. Schlesinger
John W. Schneller
Marina V. Schneller
James E. Scott (Not admitted in DC)
David E. Sellinger
James L. Shea (also at Baltimore, Maryland Office)
Joe A. Shull
Kenneth S. Slaughter
Herbert G. Smith, II
George H. Spencer
Judson W. Starr (Also at Baltimore and Towson, Maryland Offices)
Patrick J. Stewart (Also at Baltimore, Maryland Office)
Wayne G. Travell
Gerard Treanor
Stefan F. Tucker
Ian D. Volner
Ashley J. Wells
Judith L. Wheat
N. Frank Wiggins
Allen Wood

OF COUNSEL

Susan G. Blumenthal
Thomas J. Cooper
David G. Dickman
Susan T. Edlavitch
Gary D. Hailey
Frank Horton
Rebecca E. Pearson (Not admitted in DC)
Robert G. Rathbun (Not admitted in DC)
Janet F. Satterthwaite
Gary L. Shaffer (Not admitted in DC)
Jeffrey S. Tenenbaum
Ariel Vannier (Also at Baltimore, Maryland Office)
Barbara L. Waite

ASSOCIATES

A. Hope Adams
Theodore W. Atkinson
Marcia A. Auberger
Purvi Badiani (Not admitted in DC)
Jennifer N. Baraban (Not admitted in DC)
Nathan A. Beaver
Gregory S. Braker
Patricia Russell Brown
Fei-Fei Chao
Pier-Alysia M. Coyne (Not admitted in DC)
Carla Draluck Craft
Donald P. Creston
Kimberly A. Crowder
Peter J. Curtin (Also at Baltimore, Maryland Office)
James Nicholas Czaban
Rosemary E. Dailey
Paul A. Debolt
Kathleen S. Dolan (Not admitted in DC)
Maureen E. Donahue
Patricia A. Exposito
Catherine A. Ferguson
Andrew S. Gold (Not admitted in DC)
Rebecca L. Goldsmith (Not admitted in DC)
Kenyatta S. Green (Not admitted in DC)
Matthew B. Greiner
Keith G. Haddaway
John C. Hardwick, Jr.
Andrew M. Herzig
Linda A. Hildreth
David W. Hotes (Not admitted in DC)
Jeremy K. Huffman
Davida H. Isaacs
Jane J. Johansen (Not admitted in DC)
Matthew F. Kadish
Jordan Lee Klingsberg
Mary Ann Knoeckel
Melissa E. Lamb (Not admitted in DC)
Michael P. Leary (Not admitted in DC)
Jeanny K. Lee
Erik J. Lichter (Not admitted in DC)
Karen E. Mason (Not admitted in DC)
Heather L. McDowell
Jeannette C. Meacham (Not admitted in DC)
Emily A. Miller
John P. Moy (Not admitted in DC)
Thomas V. Mulrine
Rebecca Nassab
Chellis E. Neal
William T. Nesbitt (Not admitted in DC)
Jeanne Louise Newlon
Monica Charisse Parchment
Jill I. Prater
Andrew Douglas Price
Johana A. Reed
Martin L. Saad
Michael A. Sartori
Joshua N. Schopf (Not admitted in DC)
Sara T. Schumacher (Not admitted in DC)
Jagpreet Singh
Christine M. Sorge
Melissa Landau Steinman
Dale C. Van Demark (Not admitted in DC)
Catherine M. Voorhees
Gregory L. Waddoups (Not admitted in DC)
Robin Waugh-Farretta (Not admitted in DC)
Rita L. Wecker
Eric J. Weierstall (Not admitted in DC)
Samantha M. Williams
Kristin K. Woody
Damon W. D. Wright
George Abe Zachariah
John M. Zaremba
Scott A. Zebrak

For full biographical listings, see the Martindale-Hubbell Law Directory

Washington—Continued

VERNER, LIIPFERT, BERNHARD, MCPHERSON AND HAND, CHARTERED (AV)

901 15th Street, N.W., 20005-2301
Telephone: 202-371-6000
Cable Address: "Verlip"
Fax: 202-371-6279
Email: verner.com *URL:* http://www.verner.com
Houston, Texas Office: 1111 Bagby, Suite 4700, 77002.
Telephone: 713-225-7200.
Fax: 713-752-2199.
Honolulu, Hawaii Office: 745 Fort Street, Suite 600, 96813.
Telephone: 808-566-0999.
Fax: 808-566-0995.
Austin, Texas Office: Suite 1440 San Jacinto Center, 98 San Jacinto Boulevard, 78701.
Telephone: 512-703-6000.
Fax: 512-703-6003.
Las Vegas, Nevada Affiliate Office: Gary C. Moss, Hughes Center, 3960 Howard Hughes Parkway, Suite 400, 89109.
Telephone: 702-737-3433.
Fax: 702-737-1612.
Miami, Florida Office: 3100 First Union Financial Center, 200 South Biscayne Boulevard, 33131.
Telephone: 305-371-8801.
Fax: 305-371-6545.

Lloyd M. Bentsen (Resident, Houston, Texas Office)
Berl Bernhard
Graham Kerin Blair (Resident, Houston, Texas Office)
James J. Blanchard (Not admitted in DC)
R. Stuart Broom (Not admitted in DC)
Steven A. Buxbaum (Resident, Houston, Texas Office)
Brendan D. Cook (Resident, Houston, Texas Office)
Hopewell H. Darneille, III
Andrew D. Eskin
William C. Evans
J. Cathy Fogel
Harold I. Freilich
Andrea Jill Grant
Douglas W. Hall
Lloyd N. Hand
James F. Hibey
Jane Hickie (Not admitted in DC)
Patrick L. Hughes (Resident, Houston, Texas Office)
Thomas M. Ingoldsby
Dwight E. Jefferson (Resident, Houston, Texas Office)
Kenric D. Kattner (Resident, Houston, Texas Office)
Thomas J. Keller
Gary J. Klein
Erwin G. Krasnow
Kyung S. Lee (Resident, Houston, Texas Office)
Lawrence E. Levinson (Not admitted in DC)
Don Charles Lewis
Harriet Lipkin
Jorge Luis Lopez (Resident, Miami, Florida Office)
Joseph L. Manson, III
Edward J. McGrath
Harry McPherson
John P. Melko (Resident, Houston, Texas Office)
Martin Mendelsohn
John A. Merrigan
Brian A. Mizoguchi
Gary C. Moss (Resident, Las Vegas, Nevada Office)
Ronald B. Natalie
Paul E. Nordstrom
Glen L. Ortman
Peter S. Pantaleo
Lenard M. Parkins (Resident, Houston, Texas Office)
Russell E. Pommer
Neil T. Proto
Sherry A. Quirk
Michael J. Roberts
Ignacio E. Sanchez (Resident, Miami, Florida Office)
John C. Shawde (Resident, Miami, Florida Office)
William R. Sherman
Lawrence R. Sidman
Keith D. Spickelmier (Resident, Houston, Texas Office)
Cynthia M. Surrisi (Resident, Honolulu, Hawaii Office)
Deborah A. Swanstrom
Michael D. Sydow (Resident, Houston, Texas Office)
Susan O'Hearn Temkin
James M. Verner (Emeritus)
Clinton A. Vince
John D. Waihee, III (Resident, Honolulu, Hawaii Office)
Eric T. Werner
Robert T. Wright, Jr. (Resident, Miami, Florida Office)
William A. Zeitler
John H. Zentay

SPECIAL COUNSEL

Daniel R. Coats (Not admitted in DC)
Robert J. Dole (Not admitted in DC)
George J. Mitchell

SENIOR COUNSEL

Wayne S. Bishop
Alvaro Cifuentes de Castro

SENIOR ADVISOR

Ann W. Richards (Resident, Austin, Texas Office)

OF COUNSEL

Gregg S. Avitabile
Howell E. Begle, Jr.
Michael D. Berg
David A. Brakebill (Resident, Houston, Texas Office)
Leonard Garment
Philip R. Hochberg
John R. Hohlt (Resident, Houston, Texas Office)
Phillip A. Holder (Resident, Austin, Texas Office)
James K. Jackson
David B. Jacobsohn
J. Robert Kirk
Ronald J. Kormanik (Resident, Houston, Texas Office)
Stanley W. Legro
Frederick J. McConville
Brenda G. Meister (Not admitted in DC)
John R. Mietus, Jr.
Trey A. Monsour (Resident, Houston, Texas Office)

(See Next Column)

OF COUNSEL (Continued)

John R. Myrdal (Resident, Honolulu, Hawaii Office)
Mikol S. B. Neilson
Renton L. K. Nip (Resident, Honolulu, Hawaii Office)
Nell Payne
Steven R. Phillips
Richard H. Saltsman
Gene Schleppenbach
Julian L. Shepard
David R. Siddall
Regina Y. Speed-Bost (Not admitted in DC)
Lauraine D. Sullivan (Not admitted in DC)
Michael A. Taylor
Celeste M. Wasielewski

SENIOR ATTORNEYS

Paula W. Chong (Resident, Honolulu, Hawaii Office)
Sherry Lane Deaver (Resident, Houston, Texas Office)
Lori A. Hood (Resident, Houston, Texas Office)
JoAnn Lippman (Resident, Houston, Texas Office)

Pablo Acosta (Resident, Miami, Florida Office)
Kimberly C. Ayers
Hever M. Bascon, Jr. (Not admitted in DC)
Matthew C. Bernstein
Jamie E. Brown
Adrienne E. Clair
Michael J. Condron
Julia J. Decker (Resident, Houston, Texas Office)
Patricia A. Deem
Andrea R. Dillman (Resident, Houston, Texas Office)
Kellie A. Donnelly
Lawrence Duncan, III
Paul F. Donsbach (Resident, Honolulu, Hawaii Office)
Rick A. Eckerson (Resident, Houston, Texas Office)
David A. Fitzgerald
Henry Flores (Resident, Houston, Texas Office)
Lisa M. Fowlkes
Bradley O. Haque
Mary L. Harrell (Resident, Houston, Texas Office)
Noelle Montano Hawley
Alan N. Hernandez
Karl V. Hopkins (Resident, Houston, Texas Office)
Thomas A. Howley (Resident, Houston, Texas Office)
Lisa K. Hsiao
Juan Carlos Iturregui
Steven R. Johnson
John M. R. Kneuer (Not admitted in DC)
Maxim B. Litvak (Resident, Houston, Texas Office)
Jenifer J. Martin
Karen Turner McWilliams
William H. Minor
Sharon L. Nelson (Resident, Law Vegas, Nevada Office)
James A. Pickup (Not admitted in DC)
Michael M. Pratt
Robin E. Remis Shichman
Timothy M. Rutten (Not admitted in DC)
Layn M. Saint-Louis
Susannah Wellford Shakow
Karen M. Stengel
John H. Sterne, Jr. (Not admitted in DC)
Coke Morgan Stewart
Gopal Swaminathan
Jennifer H. Tribulski (Not admitted in DC)
Orlando E. Vidal
Jessica A. Wallace
Linda M. Weinberg
Linda J. Willard
Theresa Youngblood
Michael A. Yuffee
Andre J. Zamorano (Resident, Miami, Florida Office)
Marnie Weller Zebrak (Not admitted in DC)

LEGAL SUPPORT PERSONNEL

Suzanne D. Cartwright (Director of Urban Development)
Denis J. Dwyer (Director of Legislative and Federal Affairs)
Rosemary B. Freeman (Director of Public Affairs)
Marla Grossman (Director of Federal Affairs)
Vicki Hart (Director of Legislative and Federal Affairs)
Maria Fabiana Jorge (Director, Latin American Affairs)
Cristina Krasow (Legislative Consultant)
Sara W. Morris (Telecommunications Consultant)
Janice R. Moskowitz (Transactions Specialist)
Nancy A. Sheliga (Legislative Consultant)
David A. Weiss (Director of Trade Policy)

For full biographical listings, see the Martindale-Hubbell Law Directory

---

VINSON & ELKINS L.L.P. (AV)

A Registered Limited Liability Partnership
The Willard Office Building, 1455 Pennsylvania Avenue, N.W., 20004-1008
Telephone: 202-639-6500
Fax: 202-639-6604
URL: http://www.velaw.com
Austin, Texas Office: One American Center Suite 2700, 600 Congress Avenue, Austin, Texas, 78701-3200.
Telephone: 512-495-8400.
Fax: 512-495-8612.
Beijing, China Office: 20/F, Beijing Silver Tower, No. 2, Dong San Huan Bei Lu, Chaoyang District, 100027.
Telephone: +86-10-6410-6300.
Fax: +86-10-6410-6360.
Dallas, Texas Office: 3700 Trammell Crow Center, 2001 Ross Avenue, Dallas, Texas, 75201-2975.
Telephone: 214-220-7700.
Fax: 214-220-7716.
Houston, Texas Office: 2300 First City Tower, 1001 Fannin, Houston, Texas, 77002-6760.
Telephone: 713-758-2222.
Fax: 713-758-2346.

(See Next Column)

VINSON & ELKINS L.L.P.—*Continued*

London, England Office: Regis House, 8th Floor, 45 King William Street, London, EC4R 9AN, England.
Telephone: (44-171) 618-6000.
Fax: (44-171) 618-6001.
Moscow, Russia Office: 16 Ulitsa Spiridonovka, Second Floor, 103001 Moscow, Russia.
Telephone: (7-095) 956-1995. Local
Fax: (7-095) 956-1996. U.S. Satellite
Fax: (212) 803-0142.
New York, N.Y. Office: 1325 Avenue of the Americas, 17th Floor, New York, N.Y., 10019.
Telephone: 917-206-8000.
Fax: 917-206-8100.
Singapore Office: 6 Battery Road, #39-01, Singapore, 049909.
Telephone: (65) 536-8300.
Fax: (65) 536-8311. Avenue, N.W., Washington, D.C., 20004-1008.

RESIDENT PARTNERS

Michael A. Andrews (Not admitted in DC)
David T. Andril
Alden L. Atkins
Dennis M. Barry
C. Michael Buxton
John E. Chapoton
Michael R. Charness
David B. Cohen
Ky P. Ewing, Jr.
Kevin A. Gaynor
Michael J. Henke
George C. Hopkins
Neil W. Imus
David R. Johnson
Theodore W. Kassinger
Gary M. Kotara
Cathy A. Lewis
Kathleen C. Little
Richard D. Marks
Robert A. Mazer
Elizabeth Anne Moler
Larry A. Oday
Mark R. Spivak
John D. Taurman
Charles D. Tetrault
Michael D. Thomson
Mark H. Tuohey, III
Christine L. Vaughn
Adam Wenner
Anita Rutkowski Wilson
Paul L. Yde

RESIDENT OF COUNSEL

Becky M. Bruner
Christopher P. B. Erckert (Not admitted in DC)
Tegan M. Flynn
Mark S. Laufman
William E. Lawler, III
Albert D. Shuldiner
Gregory C. Staple
Samuel B. Sterrett

RESIDENT ASSOCIATES

Virginia Navarrete Brooks
Christopher K. Carr
Vanessa Y. Chandler (Not admitted in DC)
Christopher M. Dawe (Not admitted in DC)
John S. Decker
Debra J. Duncan
Benjamin Erulkar
James R. Farnsworth
John M. Faust
Judith M. Feldt (Not admitted in DC)
Robert S. Field (Not admitted in DC)
Joseph E. Hunsader (Not admitted in DC)
Mark Reid Klupt
Douglas J. Lanzo
Greta L.H. Lichtenbaum
Benjamin S. Lippard (Not admitted in DC)
Bruce C. McCulloch (Not admitted in DC)
Leah E. Medway
Timothy M. Murphy
Philip A. Nickles
Daniel A. Petalas (Not admitted in DC)
Laura Brodbeck Phillips (Not admitted in DC)
R. Edward Price
Cary D. Pugh
Suzanne D. Reifman
Judith M. Rosenberg
Robert J. Rothwell (Not admitted in DC)
Michael A. Sanzo
Jerome A. Swindell
Megan H. Troy (Not admitted in DC)

For full biographical listings, see the Martindale-Hubbell Law Directory

VORYS, SATER, SEYMOUR AND PEASE LLP (AV)

11th Floor, 1828 L Street, N.W., 20036-5104
Telephone: 202-467-8800
Telex: 440693
Telecopier: 202-467-8900
URL: http://www.vssp.com
Columbus, Ohio Office: 52 East Gay Street, P.O. Box 1008, 43216-1008.
Telephone: 614-464-6400.
Telex: 241348.
Telecopier: 614-464-6350.
Cleveland, Ohio Office: 2100 One Cleveland Center, 1375 East Ninth Street, 44114-1724.
Telephone: 216-479-6100.
Telecopier: 216-479-6060.
Cincinnati, Ohio Office: Suite 2100, 221 East Fourth Street, P.O. Box 0236, 45201-0236.
Telephone: 513-723-4000.
Telecopier: 513-723-4056.
Alexandria, Virginia Office: 277 South Washington Street, Suite 310, 22314.
Telephone: 703-549-4282.
Facsimile: 703-549-4492.

Joseph D. Lonardo

(See Next Column)

James K. Alford
Cory M. Amron
Steven R. Becker
Thomas R. Boland
Pamela A. Bresnahan
Stephen H. Brown (Not admitted in DC)
Jean-Marc Brun
James M. Burns
Laura Westfall Casey (Not admitted in DC)
D. Richard Froelke
Warren W. Glick
Richard J. Leon
Robert E. Levine
Thomas B. Magee
Peter A. Martin
Nihar R. Mohanty
Mark J. Palchick
Michael Sean Purcell
Mitchell W. Shapiro
Nelson H. Shapiro
Ronald E. Shapiro
George W. Swenson, Jr.
Randal C. Teague
Barry D. Umansky
John W. Wilmer, Jr.

For full biographical listings, see the Martindale-Hubbell Law Directory

WHITE & CASE (AV)

Limited Liability Partnership
601 Thirteenth Street, NW, Suite 600 South, 20005-3807
Telephone: 202-626-3600
Facsimile: 202-639-9355
URL: http://www.whitecase.com
Los Angeles, California:
Telephone: 213-620-7700.
Facsimile: 213-687-0758; 213-452-2330; 213-452-2331.
Palo Alto, California:
Telephone: 650-213-0300.
Facsimile: 650-213-8158.
San Francisco, California:
Telephone: 415-544-1100.
Facsimile: 415-544-0202.
Miami, Florida:
Telephone: 305-371-2700.
Facsimile: 305-358-5744; 305-358-5766.
New York, New York:
Telephone: 212-819-8200.
Facsimile: 212-354-8113.
Bratislava, Slovak Republic:
Telephone: (421-7) 5441-5100.
Facsimile: (421-7) 5441-6100.
Brussels, Belgium:
Telephone: (32-2) 219-16-20.
Facsimile: (32-2) 219-16-26.
Budapest, Hungary: Réczicza Law Firm White & Case LLP.
Telephone: (36-1) 488-5200.
Facsimile: (36-1) 488-5299.
Frankfurt, Germany:
Telephone: (49-69) 713-77-(0).
Facsimile: (49-69) 713-77-100.
Helsinki, Finland: Asianajotoimisto White & Case Oy.
Telephone: (358-9) 228-641.
Facsimile: (358-9) 228-64228.
Istanbul, Turkey:
Telephone: (90-212) 275-75-33.
Facsimile: (90-212) 275-75-43.
London, England:
Telephone: (44-20) 7600-7300.
Facsimile: (44-20) 7600-7030.
Moscow, Russia:
Telephone: (7-095) 787-3000.
Facsimile: (7-095) 787-3001.
Paris, France:
Telephone: (33-1) 55-04-15-15.
Facsimile: (33-1) 55-04-15-16.
Prague, Czech Republic:
Telephone: (420-2) 2481-1796.
Facsimile: (420-2) 2481-0252.
Stockholm, Sweden: White & Case Advokat AB.
Telephone: (46-8) 506-323-00.
Facsimile: (46-8) 611-21-22.
Warsaw, Poland: White & Case (Poland) Sp. z o.o.
Telephone: (48-22) 625-33-33; (48-22) 622-67-67; (43-89) 12-19-06.
Facsimile: (48-22) 628-22-28.
Johannesburg, Republic of South Africa:
Telephone: 27 (11) 884-7689.
Facsimile: 27 (11) 884-7229.
Almaty, Kazakhstan:
Telephone: (7-3272) 50-74-91.
Facsimile: (7-3272) 50-74-93.
Ankara, Turkey:
Telephone: (90-312) 442-5680.
Facsimile: (90-312) 442-5691/4.
Bangkok, Thailand: White & Case (Thailand) Limited.
Telephone: (662) 656-1721 to 32.
Facsimile: (662) 656-1733/34.
Bombay/Mumbai, India: Liaison Office, (91-22) 282-6300/01/02/03.
Facsimile: (91-22) 282-6305.
Hanoi, Vietnam:
Telephone: (84-4) 934-5355.
Facsimile: (84-4) 934-5356.

(See Next Column)

WHITE & CASE, *Washington—Continued*

Ho Chi Minh City, Vietnam:
Telephone: (84-8) 821-0888.
Facsimile: (84-8) 823-6902.
Hong Kong:
Telephone: (852) 2822-8700.
Facsimile: (852) 2845-9070.
Singapore, Republic of Singapore:
Telephone: (65) 225-6000.
Facsimile: (65) 225-6009.
Tokyo, Japan: White & Case Kandabashi Law Offices.
Telephone: (81-3) 3259-0200.
Facsimile: (81-3) 3259-0150.
Jeddah, Saudi Arabia: Law Office of Hassan Mahassni,
Telephone: (966-2) 665-4353.
Facsimile: (966-2) 669-2996.
Riyadh, Saudi Arabia: Law Office of Hassan Mahassni,
Telephone: (966-1) 464-4006.
Facsimile: (966-1) 465-1348.
Mexico City, Mexico: White & Case, S.C.
Telephone: (52) 5-540-9600.
Facsimile: (52) 5-540-9699.
São Paulo, SP, Brazil:
Telephone: (55-11) 5505-0170.
Facsimile: (55-11) 5505-0174.
Bombay/Mumbai, India: Associated Law Firm; India Law Services (ILS).
Telephones: (91-22) 284-1995; (91-22) 284-1847.
Facsimile: (91-22) 285-0824.
New Delhi, India: Associated Law Firm; India Law Services (ILS).
Telephone: (91-11) 697-1602/3/4.
Facsimile: (91-11) 698-8860.

PARTNERS

Charles N. Brower
Linda E. Carlisle
William J. Clinton
Christopher F. Corr
Christopher M. Curran
Bruce N. Davis
Victor J. DeSantis
J. Mark Gidley
David P. Houlihan
David W. Hunt
Carolyn B. Lamm
Carmen D. Legato
William P. McClure
J. Roger Mentz
Edward R. Neaher, Jr.
Robert D. Paul
Gregory J. Spak
Walter J. Spak

COUNSEL

Ellen M. Jakovic
Anne D. Smith

ASSOCIATES

Jocelyn A. Aqua
Christina C. Benson
Vincent Bowen
Patrick J. Browne, Jr.
Richard J. Burke
Carolyn Campbell
Peter J. Carney
Daniel S. Chen (Not admitted in DC)
Elizabeth L. Cheney (Not admitted in DC)
Gustav Chiarello (Not admitted in DC)
Kevin C. Clayton
Jaime M. Crowe
Jennifer M. Curley (Not admitted in DC)
Stephane P. Des Lauriers (Not admitted in DC)
Denise L. Diaz
David L. Elmont (Not admitted in DC)
Nicole Erb (Not admitted in DC)
Lynn H. Fabrizio (Not admitted in DC)
Rumei Clarice Furman (Not admitted in DC)
Robert G. Gosselink
Gregg A. Hand
Eckhard R. Hellbeck (Not admitted in DC)
Douglas M. Jasinski
Richard G. King
Geoffrey B. Lanning (Not admitted in DC)
Judd Lawler
Bleu Kuwanyantiwa Lawless (Not admitted in DC)
Adams C. Lee
Micah A. Levy (Not admitted in DC)
John W. Owczarski
Frank Panopoulos
George L. Paul
Stephen R. Payne (Not admitted in DC)
Mark A. Shalaby
Abby Cohen Smutny
Eric P. Spooner
Lee A. Steven (Not admitted in DC)
Peter P. Thieman
Mara E. R. Topping (Not admitted in DC)
Osamu Umejima
Lyle B. Vander Schaaf
Francis A. Vasquez, Jr.
Margaret G. Wachenfeld (Not admitted in DC)
Kristin D. Wells (Not admitted in DC)
Laura M. Wilson
J. Christian Word
Kristina Zissis

For full biographical listings, see the Martindale-Hubbell Law Directory

WHITEFORD, TAYLOR & PRESTON L.L.P. (AV)

1025 Connecticut Avenue, N.W., 20036-5405
Telephone: 202-659-6800
Fax: 202-331-0573
Email: wt&pllp@wtplaw.com *URL:* http://www.wtplaw.com
Baltimore, Maryland Office: 7 Saint Paul Street.
Telephone: 410-347-8700.
Fax: 410-752-7092.
Towson, Maryland Office: 210 West Pennsylvania Avenue.
Telephone: 410-832-2000.
Fax: 410-832-2015.

(See Next Column)

Columbia, Maryland Office: 10440 Little Patuxent Parkway.
Telephone: 410-884-0700.
Fax: 410-884-0719.
Alexandria, Virginia Office: 1317 King Street.
Telephone: 703-836-5742.
Fax: 703-836-0265.

PARTNERS

Glenn R. Bonard
Joseph D. Douglass
John J. Hathway
Kenneth J. Ingram
Arthur P. Rogers
Andrew J. Terrell

OF COUNSEL

Edward S. Cogen
Lee A. Satterfield
C. William Tayler

RESIDENT ASSOCIATES

Karen A. Doner
Jane Saindon Dudley (Not admitted in DC)
Julianne Erin Dymowski
Mary Kaitlin McSally
Diane Preston Moore
Valerie L. Tetro (Not admitted in DC)

For full biographical listings, see the Martindale-Hubbell Law Directory

WILEY, REIN & FIELDING (AV)

1776 K Street, N.W., 20006-2304
Telephone: 202-719-7000
Facsimile: 202-719-7207
URL: http://www.wrf.com

MEMBERS OF FIRM

Richard E. Wiley
Bert W. Rein
Fred F. Fielding
Thomas W. Brunner
James H. Wallace, Jr.
Charles Owen Verrill, Jr.
Rand L. Allen
Andrew S. Krulwich
R. Michael Senkowski
Lawrence W. Secrest, III
Richard J. Bodorff
Laura A. Foggan
Jeffrey S. Linder
Walter J. Andrews
Jan Witold Baran
William A. Roberts, III
Thomas W. Queen
John B. Wyss
Richard L. McConnell
Bruce L. McDonald
Clifford M. Sloan
Peter J. Klarfeld
Matthew S. Simchak
Carl R. Ramey
Philip J. Davis
Stuart F. Carwile
James R. W. Bayes
Robert J. Butler
Nathaniel F. Emmons
Bruce G. Joseph
Thomas W. Kirby
Robert L. Pettit
Jim Slattery
Daniel E. Troy
Keith S. Watson
Arthur I. Cantor
Robert A. Smith
Samuel D. Walker
Dag Wilkinson
Peter D. Ross
Peter D. Shields
Paul E. Misener
J. Timothy Hobbs
William B. Baker
Alan H. Price
Gregory J. Vogt
Edwin O. Bailey
David E. Hilliard
Trevor Potter
Hugh Latimer
John B. Reynolds, III
Thomas B. Griffith
Daniel J. Standish
James T. Bruce, III
John A. Hodges
Katherine M. Harris
Jerry V. Haines
John L. Bartlett
Richard C. Lowery
James C. Rubinger
Donna Coleman Gregg
Susan D. Sawtelle
Marilyn E. Kerst
John E. Barry
Lon A. Berk
Paul F. Khoury
Carol A. Laham
Eileen P. Bradner
Kirk J. Nahra
Michael L. Sturm
Frank Winston, Jr.
Russell D. Duncan
Dominic T. Bodensteiner
David R. Hill
John R. Shane
Nancy J. Victory
Eric W. DeSilva
Wayne D. Johnsen
Dale E. Hausman
Todd M. Stansbury
Barbara Van Gelder
Alex M. Azar II
Gregory L. Masters
David W. Koch
Bruce A. McDonald
Rosemary C. Harold
Karen A. Kincaid
Gregory Lyons
William A. McGrath

OF COUNSEL

Howard H. Bell (Not admitted in DC)
Robert E. Boone, Jr.
Tyrone Brown
Christine E. Connelly
Kurt E. DeSoto
Elizabeth Ann Eastwood
Carl R. Frank
Stephen D. Halliday
Phillip H. Harrington
Mary Jo Manning
Peter D. O'Connell
Marnie K. Sarver

ASSOCIATES

Karyn K. Ablin
Thomas W. Antonucci
Mary E. Borja
Timothy C. Brightbill
Dorann Bunkin
John M. Burgett
Jennifer Chung (Not admitted in DC)
C. Russell Clause
Kara Lee Copley
Jason P. Cronic
Catherine M. Crutcher
Anatolio B. Cruz III
Scott D. Delacourt
Marjorie J. Dickman
Alicia M. Dixon

(See Next Column)

WILEY, REIN & FIELDING—*Continued*

ASSOCIATES (Continued)

John W. Dunfee
Brook A. Edinger
Marisa Gallehr Faunce
Jodi L. Feldman
David O. Ferry
Meredith Fuchs
Thomas S. Garrett
Elizabeth E. Goldin
Edward J. Grass
Christopher Guttman-McCabe
N. Christopher Hardee
Martha E. Heller
Tanja E. Hens
Anne E. Hoge
Timothy Holbrook
John B. Hoover
David A. Huberman
Paul E. Janaskie
Leslie Johnson-Pujo
Kirk L. Jowers
Kenneth D. Katkin
Christopher Kelly
Kathleen A. Kirby
E. Joseph Knoll, III
Anil Koshy (Not admitted in DC)
Diane L. Krawczun
Kenneth J. Krisko
Keith Kuder
T. Eric Lai
Eric W. Leonard
William Lieth
Hope W.D. Linzer
Andrew K. Long
Eric J. Mahr
Kevin J. Maynard
Scott M. McCaleb
Amyli A. McDaniel
Nicole M. McGinnis (Not admitted in DC)
Jennifer B. Miller (Not admitted in DC)
Brian Nuterangelo
John F. Papandrea
Leslie A. Platt
Paula Lynn Primost
Howard M. Radzely
Benjamin B. Reed
Kristina Reynolds (Not admitted in DC)
Christopher L. Robbins
Oren Rosenthal
Michael A. Rotker
Jennifer A. Shah
Daniel J. Shonkwiler
Daniel A. Silien
David B. Silverman (Not admitted in DC)
Timothy J. Simeone
Daniel J. Smith
Rachel E. Smith
Craig A. Sperling
Sandra Tvarian Stevens
Nicole Telecki
Alysa Beth Wakin (Not admitted in DC)
Jennifer D. Wheatley
John C. Yang
Suzanne Yelen

For full biographical listings, see the Martindale-Hubbell Law Directory

WILKES, ARTIS, HEDRICK & LANE, CHARTERED (AV)

Suite 3000, 1666 K Street, N.W., 20006-2897
Telephone: 202-457-7800
URL: http://www.wilkesartis.com
Annapolis, Maryland Office: Suite 400, 47 State Circle.
Telephone: 410-263-7800.
Bethesda, Maryland Office: Suite 800, 3 Bethesda Metro Center.
Telephone: 301-654-7800.
Greenbelt, Maryland Office: Suite 500, 6305 Ivy Lane.
Telephone: 301-345-7700.
Fairfax, Virginia Office: Suite 600, 11320 Random Hills Road.
Telephone: 703-385-8000.
Waldorf, Maryland Office: Suite 101, 1 Post Office Road.
Telephone: 301-638-7500; 301-843-7610 (Metro).

James C. Wilkes (1899-1968)
James E. Artis (1907-1978)
David M. Bond
Stephen J. Braun (Resident, Waldorf, Maryland Office)
Charles A. Camalier, III
Ilene Baxt Campbell (Resident, Fairfax, Virginia Office)
Jerald S. Cohn
Christopher H. Collins
James P. Downey (Resident, Fairfax, Virginia Office)
Timothy Dugan (Resident, Bethesda, Maryland)
Maureen Ellen Dwyer
John T. Epting
Jonathan L. Farmer
Nancy G. Fax (Resident, Bethesda, Maryland Office)
Phil T. Feola
Stanley J. Fineman
David A. Fuss
Norman M. Glasgow
Norman M. Glasgow, Jr.
Larry A. Gordon (Resident, Bethesda, Maryland Office)
Robert L. Gorham
Robert M. Gurss
Patricia Ann Harris (Resident, Bethesda, Maryland Office)
Robert R. Harris (Resident, Bethesda, Maryland Office)
Allen Jones, Jr.
Eric S. Kassoff (Resident, Bethesda, Maryland Office)
Samuel P. Kastner
Paul J. Kiernan
Jonathan I. Kipnis (Resident, Greenbelt, Maryland Office)
William Kominers (Resident, Bethesda, Maryland Office)
John D. Lane
Lawrence G. Lerman (Resident, Bethesda, Maryland Office)
Kenneth A. Max (Resident, Bethesda, Maryland Office)
Thomas G. McGarry
Gerard P. Panaro
Allison Carney Prince
John E. Prominski, Jr.
Whayne S. Quin
Jonathan P. Rak (Resident, Fairfax, Virginia Office)
Mark S. Randall
Richard K. Reed (Resident, Greenbelt Maryland Office)
John H. Rust, Jr. (Resident, Fairfax, Virginia Office)
David H. Saffern
Kenneth L. Samuelson
Frank W. Stearns (Resident at Fairfax, Virginia Office)
Dana Brewington Stebbins
Stuart A. Turow
Lois J. Vermillion
Lorraine J. Webb (Resident, Waldorf, Maryland Office)
Joseph B. Whitebread, Jr.
David L. Winstead
Ramsey L. Woodworth

(See Next Column)

Matthew G. Ahrens (Resident, Fairfax, Virginia Office)
Antonio M. Barros, Jr.
Ronald A. Brown (Resident, Waldorf, Maryland Office)
Lisa L. Jackson (Resident, Greenbelt, Maryland Office)
Kathleen A. Marthaler (Resident, Bethesda, Maryland Office)
Marc E. Miller
Mark F. Rogers (Resident, Bethesda, Maryland Office)
Brian P. Rohde (Resident, Greenbelt, Maryland Office)
Karin M. Ryan
Sarah E. Shaw
Stacy Plotkin Silber (Resident, Greenbelt, Maryland Office)
Martin P. Sullivan
Paul A Tummonds, Jr

For full biographical listings, see the Martindale-Hubbell Law Directory

WILLIAMS & CONNOLLY (AV)

725 Twelfth Street, N.W., 20005-5901
Telephone: 202-434-5000
Fax: 202-434-5029

MEMBERS OF FIRM

Edward Bennett Williams (1920-1988)
Paul R. Connolly (1922-1978)
Jeremiah C. Collins
David Povich
Steven M. Umin
John W. Vardaman
Paul Martin Wolff
J. Alan Galbraith
John G. Kester
William E. McDaniels
Brendan V. Sullivan, Jr.
Aubrey M. Daniel, III
Richard M. Cooper
Gerald A. Feffer
Robert P. Watkins
Jerry L. Shulman
Lawrence Lucchino
Lewis H. Ferguson, III
Robert B. Barnett
David E. Kendall
Gregory B. Craig
John J. Buckley, Jr.
Terrence O'Donnell
John K. Villa
Barry S. Simon
Kevin T. Baine
Stephen L. Urbanczyk
Philip J. Ward
James A. Bruton, III
Peter J. Kahn
Lon S. Babby
Michael S. Sundermeyer
James T. Fuller, III
David D. Aufhauser
Bruce R. Genderson
Carolyn H. Williams
Frank Lane Heard III
Steven R. Kuney
Gerson A. Zweifach
Paul Mogin
Howard W. Gutman
Nancy F. Lesser
Richard S. Hoffman
Steven A. Steinbach
Mark S. Levinstein
Mary Greer Clark
Victoria Radd Rollins
Daniel Franklin Katz
Nicole K. Seligman
Robert M. Krasne
Kathleen L. Beggs
William R. Murray, Jr.
Eva Petko Esber
Stephen D. Raber
David C. Kiernan
Lon E. Musslewhite
Robin E. Jacobsohn
Charles A. Sweet
Heidi K. Hubbard
Glenn J. Pfadenhauer
George A. Borden
Robert J. Shaughnessy
Jonathan P. Graham
Allen P. Waxman
David S. Blatt
Ari S. Zymelman
Joseph D. Piorkowski, Jr.
Regina G. Maloney
Dane H. Butswinkas
Laurie S. Fulton
Dennis M. Black
Philip A. Sechler
Lynda Schuler
Charles D. Niemeier
Paul K. Dueffert
R. Hackney Wiegmann
Jacqueline E. Maitland Davies
Robert M. Cary
Kevin M. Hodges

Eric A. Kuhl
Paul A. Murphy
David M. Zinn
Joseph G. Petrosinelli
Steven M. Farina
Sharon L. Davis
Kevin M. Downey
Paul B. Gaffney
Thomas G. Hentoff
Julie L. Ferguson Queen
Emmet T. Flood
Robert A. Van Kirk
Marcie R. Ziegler
Kenneth C. Smurzynski
John E. Schmidtlein
Jonathan Banks
Mark A. Smith
Michael K. Ross
Matthew J. Herrington
Suzanne H. Woods
Craig D. Singer
Julie C. Hilden
James L. Tanner, Jr.
Kathleen H. Quimby
Sherry A. Ingram
J. Andrew Keyes
Nicole Chapin Duke
Julia B. Shelton
Gilbert O. Greenman
Maurita Elaine Horn
Enu A. Mainigi
Michael L. Wang
Michael F. O'Connor
Oliver Garcia
Paul T. Hourihan
Paul C. Rauser
William J. Bachman
Stacey M. Bosshardt
Margaret A. Keeley
Ann H. Rakestraw
Elizabeth A. Davidson
Helen I. Dooley
John C. Shipley, Jr.
Jeffrey S. Bucholtz
Kristin E. Adler
William D. Langford, Jr.
Theodore W. Ruger
Charles C. Moore
James Gibson
Mary-Rose Papandrea
Malachi B. Jones, Jr.
Edward J. Bennett
Kathleen M. Ryan
Mara Walker Murphy
Scott E. Williams
Tobin J. Romero
Beth A. Levene
Kathleen L. Jennings
Kirsten M. Schimpff
Eric R. Delinsky
Kathleen M. Grillo
Stephanie Wank Kofman

(See Next Column)

WILLIAMS & CONNOLLY, *Washington—Continued*

Glen Donath
Lisa M. Duggan
Thomas G. Ward
Elizabeth Lin
Alicia L. Marti
Megan E. Rupp
Melissa A. Weiland
Bethany E. Matz
Bonnie H. Dunninger
Charles T. Kimmett, Jr.
Adam L. Perlman
Michael J. Leotta
Russell D. Covey
Andrew W. Rudge
Deneen C. Howell
Matthew S. Amatruda (Not admitted in DC)
Jason M. Levien (Not admitted in DC)
David H. Angeli
David C. Rieveschl
Laura P. Stout
Diana R. Hartstein (Not admitted in DC)
Stephen A. Beck (Not admitted in DC)
Mary Beth Long (Not admitted in DC)
John E. Joiner (Not admitted in DC)
Michael P. Matthews
Luba Shur

OF COUNSEL

Vincent J. Fuller
Raymond W. Bergan
Lyman G. Friedman

COUNSEL

Jane E. Genster
Kumiki Gibson
Eric M. Braun

For full biographical listings, see the Martindale-Hubbell Law Directory

WILLKIE FARR & GALLAGHER (AV)

Three Lafayette Centre, 1155 21st Street, N.W., 20036-3384
Telephone: 202-328-8000
Fax: 202-887-8979
New York, N.Y. Office: The Equitable Center, 787 Seventh Avenue, 10019-6099.
Telephone: 212-728-8000.
Fax: 212-728-8111.
Paris, France Office: 21-23 rue de la Ville l'Evêque, 75008.
Telephone: 011-33-1-53-43-45-00.
Fax: 011-33-1-40-06-96-06.
London, England Office: 35 Wilson Street, EC2M 2SJ.
Telephone: 011-44-171-696-9060.
Fax: 011-44-171-417-9191.

RESIDENT MEMBERS

William H. Barringer
Stephen R. Bell
Sue D. Blumenfeld
Kevin B. Clark
John P. Dean
Christopher A. Dunn
James P. Durling
Michael H. Hammer
David P. Murray
Steven M. Oster
Kenneth J. Pierce
Philip L. Verveer
Theodore C. Whitehouse

RESIDENT COUNSEL

Brian Conboy
Noel Hemmendinger
Russell L. Smith

RESIDENT ASSOCIATES

F. Alexander Amrein
Jay T. Angelo
James M. Assey, Jr.
Miriam A. Bishop
Randy Branitsky
Francis M. Buono
A. Renée Callahan
Lucy G. Carlson
Lisa K. Coleman
Carolyn W. Conkling
Gregory K. Conway
Joseph G. Davis
David M. Don
Jennifer A. Donaldson
Julia K. Eppard (Not admitted in DC)
Jonathan A. Friedman (Not admitted in DC)
D. Gunnar Halley
Michael G. Jones
Thomas Jones
Bonni Fine Kaufman
Sophie J. Keefer
Angie W. Kronenberg
Robert L. LaFrankie
Jennifer L. Desmond McCarthy
John i McGrew
Kevin M. Miller (Not admitted in DC)
Matthew R. Nicely
George O. Nwanze
Christian E. O'Connell (Not admitted in DC)
Daniel L. Porter
Gabriel R. Sanz-Rexach
Conrad J. Smucker
Scott E. Stewart
Christopher S. Stokes
Pamela S. Strauss
Lise K. Strom
Raymond F. Sullivan, Jr.
Andrew E. Thomas
Sean M. Thornton
Nicos L. Tsilas
Karl von Schriltz (Not admitted in DC)
Richard F. Waddington (Not admitted in DC)
David M. Waters
Jacqueline A. Weisman
Teresa S. Werner (Not admitted in DC)
Lois G. Wye

For full biographical listings, see the Martindale-Hubbell Law Directory

WILMER, CUTLER & PICKERING (AV)

2445 M Street, N.W., 20037-1420
Telephone: 202-663-6000
Fax: 202-663-6363
Email: Law@Wilmer.Com *URL:* http://www.wilmer.com
Baltimore, Maryland Office: 100 Light Street, 21202.
Telephone: 410-986-2800.
Fax: 410-986-2828.
New York, New York Office: 520 Madison Avenue, 10022.
Telephone: 212-230-8800.
Fax: 212-230-8888.
European Offices:
4 Carlton Gardens, London, SW1Y 5AA, England. Telephone: +44 (20) 7 872 1000.
Fax: +44 (20) 7 839 3537.
Rue de la Loi 15# Wetstraat, B-1040 Brussels, Belgium. Telephone: +32 (2) 285 49 00.
Fax: +32 (2) 285 49 49.
Friedrichstrasse 95, D-10117 Berlin, Germany. Telephone: +49 (30) 20 22 64 00.
Fax: +49 (30) 20 22 65 00.

Richard H. Wilmer (1892-1976)

MEMBERS OF FIRM

Daniel K. Mayers
Stephen H. Sachs
James S. Campbell
Dennis M. Flannery
Louis R. Cohen
Michael R. Klein
F. David Lake, Jr.
Jeffrey M. Lang
Paul J. Mode, Jr.
Stephen F. Black
C. Boyden Gray
Ronald J. Greene
Gary D. Wilson
C. Loring Jetton, Jr.
William T. Lake
Michael L. Burack
Michael S. Helfer
Neil J. King
Dieter G. F. Lange (Not admitted in DC; Resident, European Office, London, England)
Charles S. Levy
Robert B. McCaw
Richard W. Cass
Kenneth W. Gideon
William J. Kolasky, Jr.
A. Stephen Hut, Jr.
David R. Johnson
Mark Pollak (Not admitted in DC; Resident, Baltimore, Maryland Office)
John Rounsaville, Jr.
Roger M. Witten
Robert C. Cassidy, Jr.
John D. Greenwald (Not admitted in DC)
John H. Harwood II
Roberto Dañino
Mary Carolyn Cox
Christopher R. Lipsett
William J. Perlstein
Marianne K. Smythe
Andrew B. Weissman
Lynn Bregman
William R. McLucas
Stephen P. Doyle
William R. Richardson, Jr.
George P. Stamas
Harry J. Weiss
Brandon Becker
Russell J. Bruemmer
Bruce E. Coolidge
Juanita A. Crowley
Robert M. Kimmitt
Paul Mitchard (Not admitted in DC; Resident, European Office, London, England)
John Payton
William J. Wilkins
Andrew N. Vollmer
Thomas W. White
Jeffrey N. Shane
Matthias Wissmann (Not admitted in DC; Resident, European Office, Berlin, Germany)
Bruce M. Berman
Thomas F. Connell
Charles E. Davidow
Terrill A. Hyde
Duane D. Morse
James S. Venit (Not admitted in DC; Resident, European Office, Brussels, Belgium)
Dr. Andreas Weitbrecht (Not admitted in DC; Resident, European Offices, Berlin, Germany and Brussels, Belgium)
John H. Ratliff (Not admitted in DC; Resident, European Office, Brussels, Belgium)
Robert B. Bell
Daniel H. Squire
W. Scott Blackmer
Gary B. Born (European Offices, London, England and Berlin, Germany)
John B. Watkins V
Philip D. Anker
Joseph K. Brenner
Matthew A. Chambers
Carol Clayton
Meredith B. Cross
Thomas P. Olson
Patrick J. Carome
Jane C. Sherburne
Sheila C. Cheston
David P. Donovan
Paul A. von Hehn (Not admitted in DC; Resident, European Office, Brussels, Belgium)
Marc C. Hansen (Not admitted in DC; Resident, European Office, Brussels, Belgium)
Andrew K. Parnell (Not admitted in DC; Resident, European Office, London, England)
Howard M. Shapiro
Roger W. Yoerges
Laura B. Ahearn
Mark D. Cahn
Eric R. Markus
Jeremy N. Rubenstein
Jorge E. Alers
Mark A. Dewire
Paul S. Dwyer Jr.
Eric J. Mogilnicki
Robert B. Stack
Lewis J. Liman (Not admitted in DC; Resident, New York, New York Office)
R. Scott Kilgore
Thomas E.D. Millspaugh (Not admitted in DC; Resident, Baltimore, Maryland Office)
James R. Wrathall
Yoon-Young Lee
Gail C. Bernstein
Steven F. Cherry
Susan P. Crawford
Robert F. Hoyt
Dr. Natalie Lübben (Not admitted in DC; Resident, European Office, Berlin, Germany)
Lynn R. Charytan

(See Next Column)

WILMER, CUTLER & PICKERING—*Continued*

MEMBERS OF FIRM (Continued)

Steven M. Dunne
Michael R. Holter (Not admitted in DC; Resident, European Office, London, England)
Thomas Mueller (Resident, European Office, Brussels, Belgium)
Christian L. Duvernoy (Resident, European Office, Brussels, Belgium)
James W. Lowe
Ali M. Stoeppelwerth
Denise Esposito
Erik H. Corwin
Gregorio B. Cater
Soo J. Yim
Timothy E. Stumpff
James E. Anderson
Dr. Roland Steinmeyer (Not admitted in DC; Resident, European Office, Berlin, Germany)

SENIOR COUNSEL

Lloyd N. Cutler
John H. Pickering
J. Roger Wollenberg

COUNSEL

Lester Nurick
Max O. Truitt, Jr.
Joel Rosenbloom
William A. Butler
Leonard M. Shambon
Patricia A. Sherman
William J. Flanagan
John J. Kallaugher (Not admitted in DC; European Offices, London, England and Brussels, Belgium)
Marcia A. Wiss
Carol H. Fishman
Joseph E. Killory, Jr.
Christopher J. Herrling
Roger J. Patterson
Daniel B. Phythyon
Joanne F. Catanese (Not admitted in DC; Resident, Baltimore, Maryland Office)
Robert G. Bagnall
Brent J. Gurney
Nancy L. Manzer
Glynn D. Key
Leon B. Greenfield
Ronald I. Meltzer
Jeffrey E. McFadden
Brian J. Menkes
Martin Seyfarth (Not admitted in DC; Resident, European Office, Berlin, Germany)

OF COUNSEL

Andrea Ann Timko

ASSOCIATES

William F. Adkinson, Jr.
David J. Aveni (Not admitted in DC)
Jeffrey D. Ayer
Carol J. Banta
George A. Baptista
Andreas Bardong (Not admitted in DC; Resident, European Office, Brussels, Belgium)
Brigida Benitez
David C. Berry (Not admitted in DC)
Karan Bhatia
Francesca Elisabeth Bignami
Laura Blood
Matthew A. Brill
Clifton L. Brinson (Not admitted in DC)
Christopher T. Bruneau
Kevin M. Carroll
Marticha L. Cary
David J. Charles
Steve Charnovitz (Not admitted in DC)
Melanie D. Coates
Karen L. Cohen
Nicholas P. Coleman
J. Barclay Collins, III
Bryan Corbett (Not admitted in DC)
Amber L. Cottle
Jean-Michel Coumes (Not admitted in DC; Resident, European Office, Brussels, Belgium)
Lowry A. Crook (Not admitted in DC)
Christopher R.L. Davies (Not admitted in DC)
Jonathan G. Davis
Stuart F. Delery
Dr. Britta Delmas (Not admitted in DC; Resident, European Office, Berlin, Germany Office)
Andrea De Matteis (Resident, European Office, Brussels, Belgium)
Flavia Distefano (Not admitted in DC; Resident, European Office, Brussels, Belgium)
Colleen Doherty-Minicozzi
Jennifer M. Drogula
Paul R. Eckert
Van W. Ellis
Sara E. Emley
Lara A. Englund
Gail Susan Ennis (Not admitted in DC; Resident, Baltimore, Maryland Office)
Stephanie C. Evans
Gregory J. Ewald
Laura E. Fein
Luis A. Feldstein-Soto
Lydia Alix Fillingham
Steven P. Finizio
David Flickinger
Jonathan J. Frankel
Nancy E. Furman
Daniel M. Gallagher, Jr. (Not admitted in DC)
Eric S. Galler
Katherine H. Gibson
Allison Clara Goodman Gold
Craig Goldblatt
Michael E. Gordon
Lynsey N. Graham (Not admitted in DC)
Tarnisha A. Graves
David Gray
Maura E. Griffin
Jennifer Grishkin
Franca E. Harris (Resident, New York, New York Office)
Wilhelm M.A. Hartung (Not admitted in DC; Resident, European Office, Berlin, Germany)
Andrew M. Herman
Laura A. Heymann
Eric J. Hougen
Matthew Huggins
Jeffrey S. Hydrick
Samir Jain
Manijeh Nan Kargahi (Not admitted in DC)
Rachael D. Kent
Ruth E. Kent
Jason J. Kilborn
Satish M. Kini
Sara Needleman Kline
Gregory Scott Knell (Not admitted in DC)

(See Next Column)

ASSOCIATES (Continued)

Mary E. Kostel (Not admitted in DC)
David M. Kreeger (Not admitted in DC)
Amy T. Kreiger
Hite Colby Lane (Not admitted in DC)
Robert H. Lantz
Michael Leffel (Not admitted in DC)
Andrew J. Lorentz
David A. Luigs
Cherie L. Macauley
Susan A. MacIntyre (Not admitted in DC)
Jeanine L. Magurshak (Not admitted in DC)
Denise Manning-Cabrol
Jonathan M. Mastrangelo
John Maull
Deirdre A. McDonnell (Not admitted in DC)
Michael A. McKenzie
Francisco Medina
Justin Menezes (Not admitted in DC; Resident, European Office, Brussels, Belgium)
Carol Messito (Not admitted in DC)
Juan A. Millán
Karen M. Mincavage (Not admitted in DC)
Margaret C. Minifie
David S. Molot (Not admitted in DC)
Sophie Moonen (Not admitted in DC; Resident, European Office, Brussels, Belgium)
Peter J. Mucchetti (Not admitted in DC)
John C. Nagel
Kimberly D. Ockene (Not admitted in DC)
James Francis O'Reilly (Not admitted in DC)
Jonathan E. Paikin (Not admitted in DC)
IJay Palansky
Kimberly Parker
Gordon Pearson
Hester Maria Peirce
Ann R. Perry
Christian C.D. Petersen
Ursula Bass (Not admitted in DC)
Colin Benjamin Picker
Harold E. Pizzetta, III (Not admitted in DC)
Michael Plotnick
Jean Paul M. Poitras (Not admitted in DC; Resident, European Office, Brussels, Belgium)
Jay V. Prabhu
Matthew P. Previn (Resident, New York, New York Office)
Joseph R. Profaizer (Not admitted in DC; Resident, European Office, London, England)
Augusto Repetto (Not admitted in DC)
Janet Durholz Ridge
Christine Sarudy Roberts
Lyle Roberts (Not admitted in DC)
Erika L. Robinson
Tonya Robinson (Not admitted in DC)
Alex E. Rogers
Steven Rosen (Not admitted in DC)
Jeffrey A. Roth
David M. Rubenstein
Nader Hossain Salehi
M. Kathryn Schafer (Not admitted in DC)
Alec Scheiner
Reinhard Schu (Not admitted in DC; Resident, European Office, London, England)
Dr. Thorsten Seidel (Not admitted in DC; Resident, European Office, Berlin, Germany)
Thomas E. Sharp (Not admitted in DC)
Mark S. Shelton
Christopher P. Simkins (Not admitted in DC)
Erika K. Singer
David M. Sohn
Laurie Michelle Stegman
Natacha D. Steimer (Not admitted in DC)
Beth A. Stekler
Sabrina Tardy (Not admitted in DC)
Daniel L. Torbenson (Not admitted in DC)
John A. Trenor
Julie A. Veach
Sven B. Völcker (Not admitted in DC; Resident, European Office, Brussels, Belgium)
Esmée Gräfin Von Der Groeben (Not admitted in DC; Resident, European Office, Berlin, Germany)
Jutta von Falkenhausen (Not admitted in DC; Resident, European Office, Berlin, Germany)
Joshua D. Weinberg (Not admitted in DC)
Stephen A. Weisbrod
William E. White (Not admitted in DC)
Todd E. Wiench (Not admitted in DC)
Deborah M. Wiggin
Manley Williams
David M. Wohlstadter
Jolie F. Zimmerman (Not admitted in DC)
Todd Zubler

For full biographical listings, see the Martindale-Hubbell Law Directory

WINSTON & STRAWN (AV)

1400 L Street, N.W., 20005-3502
Telephone: 202-371-5700
Telex: 440574 INTLAW UI
Telecopier: 202-371-5950
Email: postmaster@winston.com *URL:* http://www.winston.com
Chicago, Illinois Office: 35 West Wacker Drive, 60601.
Telephone: 315-558-5600.
Cable Address: "Winston Chicago."
Facsimile: 312-558-5700.
New York, N.Y. Office: 200 Park Avenue, 10166-4193.
Telephone: 212-294-6700.
Telecopier: 212-294-4700.
Cable Address: "Coledeitz, NYK."
Telex: (RCA) 232459.
Los Angeles, California Office: 444 South Flower, 10th Floor, 90071-2911.
Telephone: 213-615-1700.
Geneva, Switzerland Office: 43 Rue du Rhone, 1204.
Telephone: (4122) 7810506.
Fax: (4122) 7810361.

(See Next Column)

WINSTON & STRAWN, *Washington—Continued*

Paris, France Office: 21 Avenue Victor Hugo. 75116.
Telephone: 331-5364- 8282.
Fax: 331-5364-8220.

MEMBERS OF FIRM

J. Michael McGarry, III (Resident)
Nicholas S. Reynolds (Resident)
Dean L. Overman (Resident)
Donald K. Dankner (Resident)
William J. Madden, Jr. (Resident)
John P. Proctor (Resident)
Edward F. Gerwin, Jr. (Resident)
John R. Keys, Jr. (Resident)
Leonard W. Belter (Resident)
Richard C. Browne (Resident)
Thomas M. Buchanan (Resident)
Peter N. Hiebert (Resident)
Eric L. Hirschhorn (Resident)
Frederick J. Killion (Resident)
John C. Kirtland (Resident)
Michael R. Lemov (Resident)
Malcolm H. Philips, Jr. (Resident)
Robert M. Rader (Resident)
Mark J. Wetterhahn (Resident)
John E. Williams (Resident)
David A. Repka (Resident)
Margaret A. Hill (Resident)
John A. Waits, II (Resident)
James H. Burnley IV (Resident)
Beryl F. Anthony, Jr. (Not admitted in DC; Resident)
Norman R. Vander Clute (Resident)
Benjamin P. Fishburne, III (Resident)
Barry J. Hart (Resident)
Charles L. Kinney (Resident)
James R. Curtiss (Resident)
Sheldon L. Trubatch (Resident)
Robert A. Mangrum (Resident)
William G. Miossi
James T. Pitts (Resident)
John Albert Whittaker, IV (Resident)
Timothy M. Broas (Resident)
Gordon Alan Coffee (Resident)
Richard A. Hibey (Resident)
Christopher C. McIsaac (Resident)
Eric W. Bloom (Resident)
Michael L. Sibarium (Resident)
Thomas L. Mills (Resident)
Constantine G. Papavizas (Resident)
Jeffrey G. Berman (Resident)
Edmund D. Cooke, Jr. (Resident)
Peter M. Kirby (Resident)
John Fehrenbach (Resident)
William N. Hall (Resident)
William A. Anderson, II (Resident)
Patrick L. Schmidt (Resident)
Guy A. Morley (Resident)
Joan B. Tucker Fife (Resident)
Michael I. Raschid (Resident)
Kathryn M. Sutton (Resident)
Carol A. Joffe (Resident)
Charles B. Molster, III (Resident)
Eric J. Marcotte
Donn C. Meindertsma (Resident)
Thomas C. Poindexter (Resident)
Vincent D. Salvatore, Jr. (Resident)
Deborah Gage Haude (Not admitted in DC)
Daniel G. Grove (Resident)
Robert Linn Draper (Resident)
Mary E. Wall (Resident)
David C. Romm (Resident)
Garry R. Boehlert (Not admitted in DC; Resident)
James E. Sharp (Resident)

OF COUNSEL

Robert M. Bor
Carl J. Peckinpaugh
John L. Napier
David W. Raymond
Joseph B. Knotts, Jr. (Resident)
Lawrence I. Kiern (Resident)

SENIOR ATTORNEYS

Anne W. Cottingham
William A. Horin
Chuncheng Lian

ASSOCIATES

John R. Ates
Michael K. Atkinson
Faton A. Bacaj
Lori A. Bean
Robert A. Berger
Dennis W. Bishop (Not admitted in DC)
H. Allen Black III (Not admitted in DC)
M. Carter DeLorme (Not admitted in DC)
Jeanne M. Dennis
Elizabeth J. Dillon (Not admitted in DC)
Michael Thomas Dyson
Paul S. Ebert
F. Stanley Echols
Gerald P. Farano
Donald P. Ferraro
Adam S. Feuerstein
Carey William Fleming (Not admitted in DC)
Rodolphe O. Gelly (Not admitted in DC)
Eric P. Gotting (Not admitted in DC)
Douglas N. Greenburg
Karen L. Grubber
John F. Guyot
Cynthia L. Hansen (Not admitted in DC)
Sunshine Hernandez (Not admitted in DC)
Robert A. Kaplan (Not admitted in DC)
Charles B. Klein
Andreas H. Leskovsek
Jay L. Levine
Melissa B. Levine (Not admitted in DC)
Jeffrey W. Mayes
Donald W. McLaughlin, Jr.
Marc Zaki Michael (Not admitted in DC)
Angela M. Moore (Not admitted in DC)
Francisco J. Pavia
Sandra L. Pearlman
Crane M. Pomerantz (Not admitted in DC)
Garth D. Richmond (Not admitted in DC)
Douglas J. Rosinski (Not admitted in DC)
Jared Richard Silverman (Not admitted in DC)
Gregory K. Smith (Not admitted in DC)
William B. Fenning Steinman
Thomas M. Stimson (Not admitted in DC)
Frank J. Supik
Raymond B. Wuslich

(See Next Column)

STAFF ATTORNEYS

Pamela A. Rons
Susan S. Yim

For full biographical listings, see the Martindale-Hubbell Law Directory

WINTHROP, STIMSON, PUTNAM & ROBERTS (AV)

1133 Connecticut Avenue, N.W., 20036
Telephone: 202-775-9800
Fax: 202-833-8491
URL: http://www.winstim.com
New York, N.Y. Office: One Battery Park Plaza, 10004.
Telephone: 212-858-1000.
Fax: 212-858-1500.
Stamford, Connecticut Office: Financial Centre, 695 East Main Street, P.O. Box 6760, 06904-6760.
Telephone: 203-348-2300.
Fax: 203-965-8226.
Palm Beach, Florida Office: 125 Worth Avenue, 33480.
Telephone: 561-655-7297.
Fax: 561-833-6726.
London, England Office: 54 Lombard Street, London EC3V 9DH, England.
Telephone: 011 0171 648 9200.
Fax: 011 0171 283 1656.
Tokyo, Japan Office: 608 Atagoyama Bengoshi Building 6-7, Atago 1-chome, Minato-ku, Tokyo 105 Japan.
Telephone: 011-813-3437-9740.
Fax: 011-813-3437-9261.
Hong Kong, China Office: 2505 Asia Pacific Finance Tower, Citibank Plaza, 3 Garden Road, Central.
Telephone: 011-852-2530-3400.
Fax: 011-852-2530-3355.
Singapore Office: 6 Battery Road #38-01/B, Singapore 049909.
Telephone: 65-227-4700.
Fax: 65-227-4711.

RESIDENT PARTNERS

Isaac D. Benkin
Donald A. Carr
John E. Gillick
Gerald D. Morgan, Jr.
Kenneth P. Quinn (Not admitted in DC)
Mary Ann Walker
Christopher R. Wall

COUNSEL

Roy G. Bowman
Marvin T. Griff
Aileen Meyer
C. Christopher Parlin
Peter S. Watson (Not admitted in DC)

RESIDENT ASSOCIATES

David S. Christy, Jr.
Thomas M. deButts
William H. Espinosa
James L. Gallagher
Asaf Hahami (Not admitted in DC)
Kelly Hewitt
Maren D. Lee
Michael J. Levitin
Neil L. Levy
Joshua I. Romanow
Paul W. Terry
William L. Thomas

For full biographical listings, see the Martindale-Hubbell Law Directory

FLORIDA

*BARTOW,** Polk Co.

FROST & SAUNDERS, P.A. (AV)

395 South Central Avenue, P.O. Box 2188, 33830
Telephone: 941-533-0314; 800-533-0967
Telecopier: 941-533-8985
Email: jfrost1985@aol.com

John W. Frost, II
Thomas C. Saunders
Richard E. "Rick" Dantzler
John Marc Tamayo
Mark A. Sessums
Robert J. Aranda
Peter W. Van den Boom
Nicholas D. Zorn, Jr.

Reference: Community National Bank, Bartow.

For full biographical listings, see the Martindale-Hubbell Law Directory

BOCA RATON, Palm Beach Co.

BROAD AND CASSEL (AV)

A Partnership including Professional Associations
Corporate Centre at Boca Raton, Suite 300, 7777 Glades Road, 33434
Telephone: 561-483-7000
Telecopier: 561-483-7321
URL: http://www.broadandcassel.com
Fort Lauderdale, Florida Office: Suite 1130, Broward Financial Centre, 500 E. Broward Boulevard, 33394.
Telephone: 954-764-7060.
Miami, Florida Office: Miami Center, 201 South Biscayne Boulevard, Suite 3000, 33131.
Telephone: 305-373-9400.

(See Next Column)

BROAD AND CASSEL—*Continued*

Orlando, Florida Office: 390 N. Orange Avenue, Suite 1100, 32801.
Telephone: 407-839-4200.
Tallahassee, Florida Office: 215 South Monroe Street, Suite 400, 32302.
Telephone: 850-681-6810.
Tampa, Florida Office: 100 North Tampa, Suite 3500, 33602.
Telephone: 813-225-3020.
West Palm Beach, Florida Office: The Reflections Office Centre, 400 Australian Avenue, South, Fifth Floor, 33401.
Telephone: 561-832-3300.

PARTNERS

Jeffrey A. Deutch (P.A.)
Richard B. MacFarland (P.A.)
Arvin J. Jaffe (P.A.)
James J. Wheeler (P.A.)
Kenneth Edelman (P.A.)
Jodi B. Laurence (P.A.)
David J. Powers (P.A.)

ASSOCIATES

Theodore Eliot Deutch
Marcy H. Kammerman
Carl S. Rosen
Michael Doar
Zelica Quigley
Lee Ann Tranford

OF COUNSEL

Michael D. Karsch

For full biographical listings, see the Martindale-Hubbell Law Directory

HUNT, COOK, RIGGS, MEHR & MILLER, P.A. (AV)

2200 Corporate Boulevard, N.W. Suite 401, 33431
Telephone: 561-997-9223
Telecopier: 561-997-6224
Email: admin@huntcook.com *URL:* http://www.huntcook.com

Robert J. Hunt
Joseph R. Cook
David A. Riggs
Ryna E. Mehr
Lawrence J. Miller
Andrew M. Gross
Susan E. Greenberg

David A. Greene
Sonja Trom Eayrs
Benjamin A. Jablow
Holly M. O'Neill

OF COUNSEL

Andrea G. Alpern

For full biographical listings, see the Martindale-Hubbell Law Directory

PROSKAUER ROSE LLP (AV)

One Boca Place, Suite 340 West, 2255 Glades Road, 33431-7360
Telephone: 561-241-7400 Toll Free: 800-432-7746
FAX: 561-241-7145
N.Y., N.Y., Wash., D.C., L.A. & San Fran., Calif., Paris, Fra. & Newark, N.J.
URL: http://www.proskauer.com
New York, New York Office: 1585 Broadway.
Telephone: 212-969-3000.
Fax: 212-969-2900.
Washington, D.C. Office: 1233 Twentieth Street, N.W., Suite 800.
Telephone: 202-416-6800.
Fax: 202-416-6899.
Los Angeles, California Office: 2049 Century Park East, Suite 3200.
Telephone: 310-557-2900.
Fax: 310-557-2193.
Newark, New Jersey Office: One Newark Center.
Telephone: 973-274-3200.
Fax: 973-274-3299.
Paris, France Office: Proskauer Rose, 68, rue du Faubourg Saint-Honoré.
Telephone: +33-1-53-05-60-00.
Fax: +33-1-53-05-60-05.

MEMBERS OF FIRM

Jay S. Blumenkopf
Howard K. Coates, Jr.
Joseph Erdman
Albert W. Gortz
Allan H. Weitzman
Christopher C. Wheeler

SENIOR COUNSEL

Kristina B. Pett
George A. Pincus
Donald E. Thompson, II
Matthew H. Triggs

ASSOCIATES

Mary F. April
Gayle Coleman
Jonathan M. Fordin
John M. Fox-Snider
Joshua B. Frank
Wendy L. Furman
David J. George
Marcy Hahn-Saperstein
Walter J. Harvey
Robert Jacobowitz
Jeannine Cline Jacobson
Stuart T. Kapp
George D. Karibjanian
Andrew D. Levy
Daniel L. Leyton
Michael S. Metta
Julie M. Mihelich
Mara Lerner Robbins
Justin Michael Senior
Susan H. Stern
Michael R. Tricarico

For full biographical listings, see the Martindale-Hubbell Law Directory

*BROOKSVILLE,** Hernando Co.

MCGEE & MASON, P.A. (AV)

101 South Main Street, P.O. Box 1900, 34605-1900
Telephone: 352-796-0795
Facsimile: 352-796-0235
Email: jmmason@innet.com
Spring Hill, Florida, Office: 4074 Commercial Way (U.S. 19), 34606-2397.
Telephone: 352-686-1028.

Joseph M. Mason, Jr.
Richard E. McGee, Sr.

Counsel For: SunTrust Bank, Nature Coast; City of Weeki Wachee, Florida; W.W. Hospitality Company, L.L.C.; Weeki Wachee Springs, L.L.C.; Coastal Engineering Associates, Inc.; Coastal Architects, Inc.; Hernando County Mining Association, Inc.; Cliff's Septic Service, Inc.; Dobson Construction, Inc.; Cal Wilson Tractor Service, Inc.
Local Counsel For: Walgreen Co.; Albertson's Inc.; Developers Diversified, Inc.; Richland Properties, Inc.; Trammell Crow Co.; Batson-Cook, Inc.; The Deeb Companies; Horne Properties, Inc.; The Regency Organization; Jireh, Inc.

For full biographical listings, see the Martindale-Hubbell Law Directory

*CLEARWATER,** Pinellas Co.

JOHNSON, BLAKELY, POPE, BOKOR, RUPPEL & BURNS, P.A. (AV)

911 Chestnut Street, P.O. Box 1368, 33756
Telephone: 727-461-1818
Telecopier: 727-441-8617
Tampa, Florida Office: 100 N. Tampa Street, Suite 1800, P.O. Box 1100.
Telephone: 813-225-2500.
Telecopier: 813-223-7118.
Naples, Florida Office: 975 Sixth Avenue South.
Telephone: 941-435-0035.
Telecopier: 941-435-9992.

E. D. Armstrong III
John T. Blakely
Bruce H. Bokor
Guy M. Burns
Michael T. Cronin
Elizabeth J. Daniels
Marion Hale
Scott C. Ilgenfritz
Frank R. Jakes
Timothy A. Johnson, Jr.
Roger A. Larson
John R. Lawson, Jr.
Michael G. Little
Michael C. Markham
F. Wallace Pope, Jr.
Dennis G. Ruppel
Charles A. Samarkos
John Schaefer
Philip M. Shasteen
Joan M. Vecchioli
Julius J. Zschau

Sharon E. Krick
Stephanie T. Marquardt
Amber F. Williams
Peter A. Rivellini
Robert V. Potter, Jr.
Steven H. Weinberger

For full biographical listings, see the Martindale-Hubbell Law Directory

KWALL, SHOWERS & COLEMAN, P.A. (AV)

133 North Fort Harrison Avenue, 33755
Telephone: 727-441-4947
Telecopier: 727-447-3158
Email: kwall@worldnet.att.net *URL:* http://www.usalaw.com/adminlaw/

Louis Kwall
Gregory K. Showers
Sherwood S. (Flip) Coleman
Elizabeth M. Gannon

For full biographical listings, see the Martindale-Hubbell Law Directory

DAYTONA BEACH, Volusia Co.

LANDIS, GRAHAM, FRENCH, HUSFELD, SHERMAN & FORD, P.A. (AV)

Formerly Hull, Landis, Graham & French
543 South Ridgewood Avenue, 32114
Telephone: 904-252-4717
Fax: 904-253-7352
Email: firm@landispa.com *URL:* http://www.landispa.com
De Land, Florida Office: 145 East Rich Avenue, P.O. Box 48.
Telephone: 904-734-3451.
Deltona, Florida Office: 204 Medical Arts Center, 1555 Saxon Boulevard.
Telephone: 407-574-1461.
Fax: 407-574-0242.

Erskine W. Landis (1900-1967)
John L. Graham (1905-1978)
Thorwald J. Husfeld (1926-1995)
Richard S. Graham
William E. Sherman
Sam N. Masters

Carol Lumb Allen (Resident)
Janet M. Strickland

OF COUNSEL

J. Compton French (Retired)

Counsel for: School Board of Volusia County; Walmart Stores, Inc.; Delco Oil, Inc.; West Volusia Hospital Authority; South Florida Natural Gas Co.; Florida Public Utilities Co.; Volusia County Industrial Development Au-

(See Next Column)

LANDIS, GRAHAM, FRENCH, HUSFELD, SHERMAN & FORD P.A., *Daytona Beach—Continued*

thority; Florida United Methodist Children's Home: Volusia County Educational Facilities Authority.

For full biographical listings, see the Martindale-Hubbell Law Directory

DEERFIELD BEACH, Broward Co.

PATTERSON & HARMON, P.A. (AV)

665 S.E. 10th Street, 33441
Telephone: 954-421-7700
Fax: 954-421-7956
Email: gpbh@mindspring.com

George A. Patterson — Blake M. Harmon

Representative Clients: Butler Properties, Ltd.; Powerline Development, Inc.; Rivertown Apartments, Inc.; Rivertown Manor Condominium Association; Reliance Enterprises; Ransco Development, Inc.
Approved Attorneys for: Attorneys' Title Insurance Fund; Chicago Title Insurance Co.
Reference: First Union National Bank of Florida.

For full biographical listings, see the Martindale-Hubbell Law Directory

*DELAND,** Volusia Co.

LANDIS, GRAHAM, FRENCH, HUSFELD, SHERMAN & FORD, P.A. (AV)

Formerly Hull, Landis, Graham & French
145 East Rich Avenue, P.O. Box 48, 32721-0048
Telephone: 904-734-3451
Fax: 904-736-1350
Email: firm@landispa.com *URL:* http://www.landispa.com
Daytona Beach, Florida Office: 543 South Ridgewood Avenue, 32114.
Telephone: 904-252-4717.
Fax: 904-258-7352.
Deltona, Florida Office: 204 Medical Arts Center, 1555 Saxon Boulevard.
Telephone: 407-574-1461.
Fax: 407-574-0242.

Erskine W. Landis (1900-1967)
John L. Graham (1905-1978)
Thorwald J. Husfeld (1926-1995)
William E. Sherman
Richard S. Graham (Daytona Beach Office)
William A. Ottinger (Deltona Office)
Joe G. Dykes, Jr.
Frank A. Ford, Jr.
Sam N. Masters (Daytona Beach Office)

Edwin Channing Coolidge, Jr.
Carol Lumb Allen (Resident, Daytona Beach Office)
Janet M. Strickland
Steven N. Gosney

OF COUNSEL

Frank A. Ford, Sr.
J. Compton French (Daytona Beach Office; Retired)

Counsel for: School Board of Volusia County; Walmart Stores, Inc.; Delco Oil, Inc.; West Volusia Hospital Authority; South Florida Natural Gas Co.; Florida Public Utilities Co.; Volusia County Industrial Development Authority; Florida United Methodist Children's Home; Volusia County Educational Facilities Authority.

For full biographical listings, see the Martindale-Hubbell Law Directory

DELRAY BEACH, Palm Beach Co.

SIMON & SCHMIDT (AV)

100 N.E. Fifth Avenue, P.O. Box 2020, 33447
Telephone: 561-278-2601
Fax: 561-265-0286

MEMBERS OF FIRM

Ernest G. Simon — David W. Schmidt

Reference: Sun Trust Bank South Florida.

For full biographical listings, see the Martindale-Hubbell Law Directory

DELTONA, Volusia Co.

LANDIS, GRAHAM, FRENCH, HUSFELD, SHERMAN & FORD, P.A. (AV)

204 Medical Arts Center, 1555 Saxon Boulevard, 32725
Telephone: 407-574-1461
Fax: 407-574-0242
Email: firm@landispa.com *URL:* http://www.landispa.com
Daytona Beach, Florida Office: 543 South Ridgewood Avenue, 32114.
Telephone: 904-252-4717.
Fax: 904-253-7352.
De Land, Florida Office: 145 East Rich Avenue, P.O. Box 48.
Telephone: 904-734-3451.

(See Next Column)

William A. Ottinger

Counsel for: School Board of Volusia County; Walmart Stores, Inc.; Delco Oil, Inc.; West Volusia Hospital Authority; South Florida Natural Gas Co.; Florida Public Utilities Co.; Volusia County Industrial Development Authority; Florida United Methodist Children's Home; Volusia County Educational Facilities Authority.

For full biographical listings, see the Martindale-Hubbell Law Directory

*FORT LAUDERDALE,** Broward Co.

BROAD AND CASSEL (AV)

A Partnership including Professional Associations
Suite 1130, Broward Financial Centre, 500 E. Broward Boulevard, 33394
Telephone: 954-764-7060
Telecopier: 954-761-8135
URL: http://www.broadandcassel.com
Boca Raton, Florida Office: Corporate Centre at Boca Raton, Suite 300, 7777 Glades Road, 33434.
Telephone: 561-483-7000.
Miami, Florida Office: Miami Center, 201 South Biscayne Boulevard, Suite 3000, 33131.
Telephone: 305-373-9400.
Orlando, Florida Office: 390 N. Orange Avenue, Suite 1100, 32801.
Telephone: 407-839-4200.
Tallahassee, Florida Office: 215 South Monroe Street, Suite 400, 32302.
Telephone: 850-681-6810.
Tampa, Florida Office: 100 North Tampa, Suite 3500, 33602.
Telephone: 813-225-3020.
West Palm Beach, Florida Office: The Reflections Office Centre, 400 Australian Avenue, South, Fifth Floor, 33401.
Telephone: 561-832-3300.

RESIDENT PARTNERS

Martin R. Press (P.A.)
William C. Phillippi (P.A.)
Gabriel L. Imperato (P.A.)
Andrew Cotzin (P.A.)
Anne Novick Branan (P.A.)

RESIDENT ASSOCIATES

Bernard M. Cassidy
Michael Manthei
Steve L. Waserstein
Steven J. Silverman
Lester J. Perling
Maria C. Montenegro
Lu-ann Mancini Dominguez
Craig Hamilton Smith
Amy C. Grable

OF COUNSEL

Jeanne K. Damirgian

For full biographical listings, see the Martindale-Hubbell Law Directory

CONRAD & SCHERER (AV)

A Partnership of Professional Associations
Eighth Floor, 633 South Federal Highway, P.O. Box 14723, 33302
Telephone: 954-462-5500
Facsimile: 954-463-9244
Miami, Florida Office: 44 West Flagler Street, Suite 402, 33130.
Telephone: 305-856-9920.
Facsimile: 305-374-4408.

MEMBERS OF FIRM

William R. Scherer, Jr., (P.A.)
Gary S. Genovese (P.A.)
William V. Carcioppolo (P.A.)
Linda Rae Spaulding (P.A.)
Reid A. Cocalis (P.A.)
Willie Earl Hall (P.A.)
Ronald A. FitzGerald
James F. Carroll
Paul R. Larkin, Jr.
Dominic L. Brandy

OF COUNSEL

Rex Conrad

ASSOCIATES

Albert L. Frevola, Jr.
William R. Scherer, III
Vanessa A. Reynolds
Douglas Todd Marx
Janine Renee Kalagher
James A. Epstein
Angel Petti
Nicholas William Romanello
Shari L. McCartney
Catherine M. Rodriguez
Wendy A. Delvecchio

Local Counsel for: American Home Assurance Group; Caterpillar Tractor Co.; Division of Risk Management, State of Florida; Florida East Coast Railway; Fort Motor Co.; Liberty Mutual Insurance Co.; Ryder Truck Lines; Unigard Insurance Group.
Approved Attorneys for: Attorneys' Title Insurance Fund.
Reference: Barnett Bank of Fort Lauderdale.

For full biographical listings, see the Martindale-Hubbell Law Directory

ESLER & LINDIE, P.A. (AV)

Suite 300 The Advocate Building, 315 S.E. Seventh Street, 33301
Telephone: 954-764-5400
FAX: 954-764-5408
Email: eslerandlindie@martindalemail.com *URL:* http://www.lawyers.com/esler&lindie

(See Next Column)

ESLER & LINDIE P.A.—*Continued*

Gary A. Esler	Beth G. Lindie

Representative Clients: The Chubb Group of Insurance Cos.; Fireman's Fund Insurance Co.; State of Florida-Department of Risk Management; Marriott Corp.; Mobile America Insurance Group, Inc.; Ohio Casualty Insurance Co.
Reference: Capital Bank.

For full biographical listings, see the Martindale-Hubbell Law Directory

HEINRICH GORDON HARGROVE WEIHE & JAMES, P.A. (AV)

500 East Broward Boulevard, Suite 1000, 33394-3092
Telephone: 954-527-2800
Facsimile: 954-524-9481
Email: talexander@heinrichgordon.com *URL:* http://www.heinrichgordon.com
Orlando, Florida Office: 201 South Orange Avenue, Suite 1015.
Telephone: 407-317-9117.
Facsimile: 407-317-9114.

Elicia D. Blackwell	Eric L. Lundt
Mark R. Boyd	Scott A. Markowitz
Todd E. Brant	Moises Melendez
William Kent Brown	Jeffrey A. O'Keefe
Bruce A. Chaimowitz	Steven H. Osber
Thomas A. Dye	Hans Ottinot
Richard G. Gordon	Cristina M. Pierson
Thomas A. Groendyke	Valerie Shea
John R. Hargrove	Gilbert E. Theissen
Eugene L. Heinrich	Kenneth W. Waterway
Richard P. Hermann, II	Bruce A. Weihe
Gordon James, III	Clifford A. Wolff

OF COUNSEL

Hugh L. Carey (Not admitted in FL)

For full biographical listings, see the Martindale-Hubbell Law Directory

HOLLAND & KNIGHT LLP (AV)

One East Broward Boulevard, Suite 1300, 33301-4811
Telephone: 954-525-1000
Fax: 954-463-2030
Mailing Address: P.O. Box 14070, 33302-4070,
Email: hklaw.com *URL:* http://www.hklaw.com
Atlanta, Georgia Office: 1201 West Peachtree Street, N.E., Suite 2000.
Telephone: 404-817-8500.
Fax: 404-881-0470.
Boston, Massachusetts Office: One Beacon Street.
Telephone: 617-523-2700.
Fax: 617-523-6850.
Bradenton, Florida Office: 1001 3rd Avenue West, Suite 600.
Telephone: 941-748-7076.
Fax: 941-747-9774.
Falls Church, Virginia Office: 3110 Fairview Park Drive, Suite 900.
Telephone: 703-645-8600.
Fax: 703-645-8610.
Jacksonville, Florida Office: 50 North Laura Street, Suite 3900.
Telephone: 904-353-2000.
Fax: 904-358-1872.
Lakeland, Florida Office: 92 Lake Wire Drive.
Telephone: 941-682-1161.
Fax: 941-688-1186.
Melbourne, Florida Office: 1499 South Harbor City Boulevard, Suite 201.
Telephone: 407-951-1776.
Fax: 407-951-1849.
Miami, Florida Office: 701 Brickell Avenue, Suite 3000.
Telephone: 305-374-8500.
Fax: 305-789-7799.
New York, New York Office: 195 Broadway, 24th Floor.
Telephone: 212-513-3200.
Fax: 212-385-9010.
Orlando, Florida Office: 200 South Orange Avenue, Suite 2600.
Telephone: 407-425-8500.
Fax: 407-244-5288.
Providence, Rhode Island Office: 50 Exchange Terrace, Suite 300, Union Station Plaza.
Telephone: 401-751-8500.
Fax: 401-553-6850.
San Francisco, California Office: 44 Montgomery Street, Suite 4050.
Telephone: 415-743-6900.
Fax: 415-743-6910.
St. Petersburg, Florida Office: 200 Central Avenue Suite 1600.
Telephone: 727-896-7171.
Fax: 727-822-8048.
Tallahassee, Florida Office: 315 South Calhoun Street, Suite 600.
Telephone: 850-224-7000.
Fax: 850-224-8832.
Tampa, Florida Office: 400 North Ashley Drive, Suite 2300.
Telephone: 813-227-8500.
Fax: 813-229-0134.
Washington, D.C. Office: 2100 Pennsylvania Avenue, N.W., Suite 400.
Telephone: 2002-955-3000.
Fax: 202-955-5564.

(See Next Column)

West Palm Beach, Florida Office: 625 North Flagler Drive, Suite 700.
Telephone: 561-833-2000.
Fax: 561-650-8399.
Mexico City, Mexico Office: HOLLAND & KNIGHT-GALLÁSTEGUI Y LOZANO, S.C. (Joint Venture Office) Avenida Paseo de los Tamarindos No. 400, Torre "B" - 2° Piso, Col. Bosques d las Lomas, C.P. 05120 Mexico, D.F.
Telephone: 011-525-261-1866.
Fax: 011-525-261-1867.
Tel Aviv, Israel Office: Holland & Knight LTD, 23 Derech Petach-Tikva, 18th Floor.
Telephone: +011-972-3-566-7666.
Fax: +011-972-3-566-7667.
Buenos Aires, Argentina Office: San Martin 323--Piso 18, 1004.
Telephone: +54-11-4324-7600.
Fax: +54-11 4324-7601.

FORT LAUDERDALE MEMBERS AND ASSOCIATES

Constance R. Barnhart	Marie Lefere
Michael J. Carbo	Timothy C. Leixner
Curtis R. Cowan	Thomas Holland Loffredo
Susan F. Delegal	Jonathan S. Marcus
Irwin J. Fayne	Stephen B. Moss
Robert E. Ferris, Jr.	Robbin Newman
Lawrence H. Goldberg	James M. Norman
Paul S. Gravenhorst	William B. Sherman
Joel K. Gustafson	Donald S. Showalter
Lori R. Hartglass	Martin J. Shuham
Richard C. Hutchison	Steven Sonberg
Thomas L. Kautz	Jay A. Taplin
Heather C. Keith	Roma W. Theus, II
Gerald L. Knight	Douglas A. Walker
Judith Epstein Kreitzer	Philip E. Ward

Paul Young

SENIOR COUNSEL

Suzanne W. Schwartz	Alexander F. Vitale

Brett D. Carroll	Brett D. Marley
Daniel C. Crilly	Nicholas G. Milano
Michelle M. DeRosa	Paul H. Minoff
Eric K. Gabrielle	Patricia Nance
Deborah Packer Goodall	Denise D. Riley
Adam J. Hodkin	Heather S. Rogers
Brian K. Hole	D. Ronald Surbey
Janna Peters Lhota	Arnold M. Zipper

For full biographical listings, see the Martindale-Hubbell Law Directory

KRUPNICK CAMPBELL MALONE ROSELLI BUSER SLAMA HANCOCK MCNELIS LIBERMAN & MCKEE, P.A. (AV)

700 Southeast 3rd Avenue, Suite 100, 33316-1186
Telephone: 954-763-8181; 877-763-8181 (Toll Free)
Fax: 954-763-8292
Email: information@krupnicklaw.com *URL:* http://www.krupnicklaw.com

Jon E. Krupnick	Joseph J. Slama
Walter G. Campbell, Jr.	Kelly D. Hancock
Kevin A. Malone	Lisa A. McNelis
Richard J. Roselli	Scott S. Liberman
Thomas E. Buser	Robert J. McKee

Carlos Acevedo (Not admitted in FL)	Robert D. Erben
	Kelley Badger Gelb
Louis R. Battista	Sean J. Greene
Ivan F. Cabrera	Holly Debra Krulik

Michael J. Ryan

OF COUNSEL

Ben J. Weaver	Dianne Jay Weaver

Reference: Mellon United National Bank.

For full biographical listings, see the Martindale-Hubbell Law Directory

PETERS ROBERTSON DEMAHY PARSONS MOWERS PASSARO & DRAKE P.A. (AV)

506 S.E. 8th Street, 33316
Telephone: 954-761-8999
Fax: 954-761-8990
Miami, Florida Office: Suite 600, Ingraham Building, 25 Southeast 2nd Avenue.
Telephone: 305-374-3103.
Fax: 305-377-9805.
Fort Myers, Florida Office: Key West Professional Centre, 1342 Colonial Boulevard, Suite 45.
Telephone: 941-936-1129.
Fax: 941-936-4036.
West Palm Beach, Florida Office: Galleria International Building, 301 Clematis Street, Suite 3000.
Telephone: 407-832-9698.
Fax: 407-832-8355.

Geralyn M. Passaro (Resident)

(See Next Column)

PETERS ROBERTSON DEMAHY PARSONS MOWERS PASSARO & DRAKE P.A., *Fort Lauderdale—Continued*

Scott J. Brook (Resident)
Michael A. Bryant (Resident)
Kimberly M. Valashinas (Resident)

Representative Clients: Auto-Owners Insurance Co.; Dade County School Board; Employers Reinsurance Group; Gallagher Bassett Insurance Service; Maryland Casualty Co.

For full biographical listings, see the Martindale-Hubbell Law Directory

RUDEN, MCCLOSKY, SMITH, SCHUSTER & RUSSELL, P.A. (AV)

200 East Broward Boulevard, P.O. Box 1900, 33302
Telephone: 954-764-6660
Telecopier: 954-764-4996
Email: info@ruden.com *URL:* http://www.ruden.com
Miami, Florida Office: Suite 1900, 701 Brickell Avenue.
Telephone: 305-789-2700.
Tallahassee, Florida Office: Suite 815, 215 South Monroe Street.
Telephone: 904-681-9027.
Naples, Florida Office: 5150 N. Tamiami Trail, Suite 602.
Telephone: 941-659-1100.
Sarasota, Florida Office: Suite 600, 1549 Ringling Boulevard.
Telephone: 941-365-0140.
St. Petersburg, Florida Office: Suite 1700, 150 Second Avenue North, P.O. Box 14034.
Telephone: 727-895-1971.
Tampa, Florida Office: 401 East Jackson Street, 27th Floor.
Telephone: 813-221-8027.
West Palm Beach, Florida Office: Suite 800, 222 Lakeview Avenue.
Telephone: 561-838-4500.

Simon Ruden (1915-1967)
Jeffrey A. Baskies
David K. Blattner
Thomas R. Bolf
Robert C. Brighton, Jr. (Not admitted in FL)
Michele Kane Cummings
Joseph T. Ducanis Jr.
John L. Farquhar
Scott J. Fuerst
Denise J. Ganz
Diane J. Geller
Melinda S. Gentile
W. Wyndham Geyer, Jr.
Bruce D. Goorland
Mark F. Grant
Bryan S. Greenberg
Thomas O. Katz
Beth-Ann Ellenberg Krimsky
Michael H. Krul
Barry A. Mandelkorn
Scott H. Margol
Donald C. McClosky
Brian S. McHugh
Dennis D. Mele
Robert H. Miltenberger, II
Susan Patrey Motley
Marc S. Nurik
Kevin J. O'Grady
John H. Pelzer
Maria L. Periharos Spiliopoulos
Terrence Russell
Carl Schuster
John L. Shiekman
Peter D. Slavis
Glenn N. Smith
Barry E. Somerstein
Mark K. Somerstein
Edwin J. Stacker
Glen A. Stankee
Elliot M. Stern

Sharon Attas
Brooke Davis Austin
Steven Robert Braten
Jerry Peter Brodsky
Dale Alan Bruschi
Genevre Ferrero
Daniella Friedman
John R. Keller
Richard E. Landman
Robert B. Lochrie, III
James A. Lovegren
Scott H Marder
Olivia S. Matuszak
Deborah M. McTigue
Bonnie L. Miskel
Jacqueline F. Monte
John P. Moore, Jr.
Kristie J. Myers
Matthew S. Nelles
Paul B. Ranis
Richard K. Resch
Jennifer J. Robinson
Stephen M. Rubin
Amy J. Salsburg
Brian Jay Samuels
Lillian A. Ser
Todd I. Stone
Heidi Howard Tandy
Stephanie J. Toothaker
Douglas S. Wilens
Andrew D. Zaron

OF COUNSEL

Bruno L. Di Giulian
Samuel S. Fields
Sherman A. Katz
Mark S. Schecter

SPECIAL COUNSEL

Mortyn K. Zietz (Not admitted in FL)

For full biographical listings, see the Martindale-Hubbell Law Directory

WALTON LANTAFF SCHROEDER & CARSON (AV)

A Partnership including Professional Associations
Blackstone Building, Third Floor, 707 Southeast Third Avenue, 33302
Telephone: 954-463-8456
Telecopier: 954-763-6294
Email: dtharp@waltonlantaff.com *URL:* http://www.waltonlantaff.com
Miami, Florida Office: 9350 Financial Centre, 9350 South Dixie Highway.
Telephone: 305-379-6411 and 305-671-1300.
Telecopier: 305-670-7065.

(See Next Column)

West Palm Beach, Florida Office: United National Bank Tower, Suite 800, 1645 Palm Beach Lakes Boulevard.
Telephone: 561-689-6700.
Telecopier: 561-689-2647.

RESIDENT PARTNERS

Jonathan J. Davis
Beth J. Leahy
Richard G. Rosenblum
Deborah Poore Knight
Warren Brown

RESIDENT ASSOCIATES

Danilo J. Iglesias
Edward M. Harvey, Jr.

For full biographical listings, see the Martindale-Hubbell Law Directory

*FORT MYERS,** Lee Co.

GOLDSTEIN, BUCKLEY, CECHMAN, RICE & PURTZ, P.A. (AV)

1515 Broadway, P.O. Box 2366, 33902-2366
Telephone: 941-334-1146
Fax: 941-334-3039
Email: info@gbclaw.com *URL:* http://www.GBClaw.com
Port Charlotte, Florida Office: Emerald Square, Suite 1, 2852 Tamiami Trail, 33952.
Telephone: 941-624-2393.
Fax: 941-624-2155.
Cape Coral, Florida Office: 1603 Hancock Bridge Parkway, 33990.
Telephone: 941-574-5575.
Fax: 941-574-9213.
Lehigh Acres, Florida Office: 1458 Lee Boulevard, Lee Boulevard Shopping Center, 33936.
Telephone: 941-368-6101.
Fax: 941-368-2461.
Naples, Florida Office: 4947 North Tamiami Trail, Suite 101, 34103.
Telephone: 941-262-4888.
Fax: 941-262-8716.

Ray Goldstein
Stephen W. Buckley
John B. Cechman
J. Jeffrey Rice
Richard Lee Purtz
George J. Mitar
Raymond L. Racila
Luis E. Insignares
Scot D. Goldberg
Jerome A. Sico
Michael M. Noone
David M. Goldberg

Approved Attorneys for: Attorneys' Title Insurance Fund.

For full biographical listings, see the Martindale-Hubbell Law Directory

HENDERSON, FRANKLIN, STARNES & HOLT, PROFESSIONAL ASSOCIATION (AV)

1715 Monroe Street, P.O. Box 280, 33902-0280
Telephone: 941-334-4121
Telecopier: 941-332-4494

Albert M. Frierson
Ernest H. Hatch, Jr.
Stephen L. Helgemo
Ronald W. Smalley
John A. Noland
William N. Horowitz
Gerald W. Pierce
J. Terrence Porter
Michael J. Corso
Vicki L. Sproat
Denis H. Noah
John W. Lewis
Craig Ferrante
James L. Nulman
Harold N. Hume, Jr.
Bruce M. Stanley Sr.
Daniel W. Sheppard
Russell P. Schropp
Chad J. Motes
Guy E. Whitesman
Steven G. Koeppel
Douglas B. Szabo
Charles J. Basinait
Randal H. Thomas
Robert C. Shearman
Andrew L. Ringers, Jr.
John F. Potanovic, Jr.
Thomas H. Gunderson
David K. Fowler
Paula F. Kelley
Jeffrey D. Kottkamp
J. Eric Stiffler
Thomas P. Clark
Theresa M. Kolish
Tricia A. Spivey
Cora Cisneros Molloy
Keith R. Kyle
Joseph M. Madden, Jr.
Danni Lynn Germano
Carlos A. Kelly
Elizabeth Wolt
Alane C. Laboda
Grace Gutierrez
Laurie Hannan-Anton
Neil R. Jetter

Representative Clients: CIGNA Group; CSX Transportation, Inc.; Fireman's Fund Insurance Cos.; The Hartford Insurance Group; Huntington National Bank, N.A.; NationsBank, N.A.; Travelers/Aetna Insurance Group; Sprint-Florida, Inc.

For full biographical listings, see the Martindale-Hubbell Law Directory

PETERS ROBERTSON DEMAHY PARSONS MOWERS PASSARO & DRAKE P.A. (AV)

Key West Professional Centre, 1342 Colonial Boulevard, Suite 45, 33907
Telephone: 941-936-1129
Fax: 941-936-4036
Miami, Florida Office: Suite 600, Ingraham Building, 25 Southeast 2nd Avenue.
Telephone: 305-374-3103.
Fax: 305-377-9805.

(See Next Column)

PETERS ROBERTSON DEMAHY PARSONS MOWERS PASSARO & DRAKE P.A.—*Continued*

Fort Lauderdale, Florida Office: 506 South East B Street.
Telephone: 954-761-8999.
Fax: 954-761-8990.
West Palm Beach, Florida Office: Galleria International Building, 301 Clematis Street, Suite 3000.
Telephone: 407-832-9698.
Fax: 407-832-8355.

Steven B. Sundook (Resident)

Representative Clients: Auto-Owners Insurance Co.; Dade County School Board; Employers Reinsurance Group; Gallagher Bassett Insurance Service; Maryland Casualty Co.

For full biographical listings, see the Martindale-Hubbell Law Directory

*FORT PIERCE,** St. Lucie Co.

BRENNAN, HAYSKAR, JEFFERSON, WALKER & SCHWERER, PROFESSIONAL ASSOCIATION (AV)

515-519 South Indian River Drive, P.O. Box 3779, 34948-3779
Telephone: 561-461-2310
Fax: 561-468-6580

John T. Brennan
Thad H. Carlton (1906-1965)
Stephen G. Hayskar
Bradford L. Jefferson
Robert V. Schwerer
James T. Walker

Garrison M. Dundas
Steven R. McCain

Representative Clients: Allstate Insurance Co.; Auto Owners Insurance Co.; Canal Insurance Co.; City of Fort Pierce; City of Stuart; First Union National Bank; First National Bank & Trust Co. of the Treasure Coast; Florida Farm Bureau Insurance Group; Kemper Insurance Group.

For full biographical listings, see the Martindale-Hubbell Law Directory

FORT WALTON BEACH, Okaloosa Co.

SMITH, GRIMSLEY, BAUMAN, PINKERTON, PETERMANN & WELLS (AV)

A Partnership of Professional Associations
25 Walter Martin Avenue, P.O. Box 2379, 32549
Telephone: 904-243-8194
Telecopier: 904-664-5728

MEMBERS OF FIRM

Walter J. Smith (P.A.)
James W. Grimsley (P.A.)
Steven B. Bauman (P.A.)
Drew S. Pinkerton (P.A.)
Richard P. Petermann (P.A.)
Kelvin Clyde Wells (P.A.)

Representative Clients: First City Bank of Fort Walton; Regions Bank; First Alabama Bank; Vanguard Bank; AmSouth Bank; Ready Bank of Ft. Walton; Eglin BMW-Mazda; Preston Hood Chevrolet; Noland Co.; Abbott Realty Services.

For full biographical listings, see the Martindale-Hubbell Law Directory

HOLLYWOOD, Broward Co.

MILLER, SCHWARTZ AND MILLER, P.A. (AV)

2535 Hollywood Boulevard, 33020
Telephone: Hollywood: 954-924-0300
Miami: 625-3630
Telefax: 954-961-2124
Mailing Address: P.O. Box 7259, Hollywood, Florida, 33081-1259

Joseph L. Schwartz
James Fox Miller
A. Matthew Miller
Robert M. Schwartz
Charles Fox Miller

Approved Attorneys for: Attorneys' Title Insurance Fund.
Reference: First Union National Bank of Florida, Hollywood, Florida.

For full biographical listings, see the Martindale-Hubbell Law Directory

*JACKSONVILLE,** Duval Co.

FOLEY & LARDNER (AV)

The Greenleaf Building, 200 Laura Street, P.O. Box 240, 32201-0240
Telephone: 904-359-2000
Facsimile: 904-359-8700
Email: foleylardner@worldnet.att.net *URL:* http://www.foleylardner.com
Los Angeles, California Office: 2029 Century Park East, 35th Floor.
Telephone: 310-277-2223.
Fax: 310-557-8475.
Sacramento, California Office: 300 Capitol Mall, Suite 1125.
Telephone: 916-443-8005.
Fax: 916-443-2240.
San Diego, California Office: 402 West Broadway, 23rd Floor.
Telephone: 619-234-6655.
Fax: 619-234-3510.

(See Next Column)

San Francisco, California Office: One Maritime Plaza, Sixth Floor.
Telephone: 415-434-4484.
Fax: 415-434-4507.
Denver, Colorado Office: 1999 Broadway, Suite 2560.
Telephone: 303-297-0260.
Fax: 303-297-0266.
Washington, D.C. Office: Washington Harbour, Suite 500, 3000 K Street, N.W.
Telephone: 202-672-5300.
Telex: 904136 (Foley Lard Wash).
Facsimile: 202-672-5399.
Orlando, Florida Office: Suite 1800, 111 North Orange Avenue, P.O. Box 2193.
Telephone: 407-423-7656.
Facsimile: 407-648-1743.
Tallahassee, Florida Office: 300 East Park Avenue, P.O. Box 1454.
Telephone: 850-222-6100.
Facsimile: 850-561-6475.
Tampa, Florida Offices: Suite 2700, One Hundred N. Tampa Street, P.O. Box 3391.
Telephones: 813-229-2300; Pinellas County: 813-442-3296.
Facsimile: 813-221-4210.
West Palm Beach, Florida Office: Suite 200, Phillips Point East Tower, 777 South Flagler Drive.
Telephone: 561-655-5050.
Facsimile: 561-655-6925.
Chicago, Illinois Office: Suite 3300, One IBM Plaza, 330 N. Wabash Avenue.
Telephone: 312-755-1900.
Facsimile: 312-755-1925.
Annapolis, Maryland Office: Suite 102, 175 Admiral Cochrane Drive.
Telephone: 410-266-8077.
Telex: 899149 (Oldtownpat).
Facsimile: 410-266-8664.
Madison, Wisconsin Office: Verex Plaza, 150 East Gilman Street, P.O. Box 1497.
Telephone: 608-257-5035.
Facsimile: 608-258-4258.
Milwaukee, Wisconsin Office: Firstar Center, 777 East Wisconsin Avenue.
Telephone: 414-271-2400.
Telex: 26-819 (Foley Lard Mil).
Facsimile: 414-297-4900.
Brussels, Belgium Office: Avenue Louise, 283.
Telephone: 32-2-646-2777.
Facsimile: 32-2-646-7574.

PARTNERS

Robert S. Bernstein
Tracy S. Carlin
John W. Caven, Jr.
Allan P. Clark
Charles E. Commander, III
David C. Cook
Gardner F. Davis
Guy O. Farmer II
Charles V. Hedrick
Chanley T. Howell
Kevin E. Hyde
Bradley R. Johnson
Linda Yayoi Kelso
William D. King
Kevin P. Leasure
Chauncey W. Lever, Jr.
Emerson M. Lotzia
Jean M. Mangu
E. Robert Meek
Sybil Meloy
Luther F. Sadler, Jr.
John T. Sefton
Robert H. Sturgess
John A. Tucker
John M. Welch, Jr.
Steven A. Werber

OF COUNSEL

Paul C. Vance

RETIRED PARTNER

Thomas B. Slade, III

RESIDENT ASSOCIATES

Charles B. Bennett
Matthew G. Breuer
Jenny L. Cisne
John P. Cole
Julia Brooke Davis
Latasha Garrison
Miriam Krestul Greenhut
Melissa O. Hanson
Matthew Stuart McAfee
Jeffrey M. McFarland
John S. Mills
Lora Tarle Monahan
Christina E. Parrish
James Wesley Poppell
James B. Porter
Scott D. Richburg
Juliana Rowland
Dabney D. Ware
Karen F. Webb

For full biographical listings, see the Martindale-Hubbell Law Directory

HOLLAND & KNIGHT LLP (AV)

50 North Laura Street, Suite 3900, 32202
Telephone: 904-353-2000
Fax: 904-358-1872
Mailing Address: P.O. Box 52687, 32201
Email: hklaw.com *URL:* http://www.hklaw.com
Atlanta, Georgia Office: 1201 West Peachtree Street, N.E., Suite 2000.
Telephone: 404-817-8500.
Fax: 404-881-0470.
Boston, Massachusetts Office: One Beacon Street.
Telephone: 617-523-2700.
Fax: 617-523-6850.
Bradenton, Florida Office: 1001 3rd Avenue West, Suite 600.
Telephone: 941-748-7076.
Fax: 941-747-9774.

(See Next Column)

HOLLAND & KNIGHT LLP, *Jacksonville—Continued*

Falls Church, Virginia Office: 3110 Fairview Park Drive, Suite 900.
Telephone: 703-645-8600.
Fax: 703-645-8610.
Fort Lauderdale, Florida Office: One East Broward Boulevard, Suite 1300.
Telephone: 954-525-1000.
Fax: 954-463-2030.
Lakeland, Florida Office: 92 Lake Wire Drive.
Telephone: 941-682-1161.
Fax: 941-688-1186.
Melbourne, Florida Office: 1499 South Harbor City Boulevard, Suite 201.
Telephone: 407-951-1776.
Fax: 407-951-1849.
Miami, Florida Office: 701 Brickell Avenue, Suite 3000.
Telephone: 305-374-8500.
Fax: 305-789-7799.
New York, New York Office: 195 Broadway, 24th Floor.
Telephone: 212-513-3200.
Fax: 212-385-9010.
Orlando, Florida Office: 200 South Orange Avenue, Suite 2600.
Telephone: 407-425-8500.
Fax: 407-244-5288.
Providence, Rhode Island Office: 50 Exchange Terrace, Suite 300, Union Station Plaza. Telephone-401-751-8500.
Fax: 401-553-6850.
San Francisco, California Office: 44 Montgomery Street, Suite 4050.
Telephone: 415-743-6900.
Fax: 415-743-6910.
St. Petersburg, Florida Office: 200 Central Avenue, Suite 1600.
Telephone: 727-896-7171.
Fax: 727-822-8048.
Tallahassee, Florida Office: 315 South Calhoun Street, Suite 600.
Telephone: 850-224-7000.
Fax: 850-224-8832.
Tampa, Florida Office: 400 North Ashley Drive, Suite 2300.
Telephone: 813-227-8500.
Fax: 813-229-0134.
Washington, D.C. Office: 2100 Pennsylvania Avenue, N.W., Suite 400.
Telephone: 202-955-3000.
Fax: 202-955-5564.
West Palm Beach Office: 625 North Flagler Drive, Suite 700.
Telephone: 561-833-2000.
Fax: 561-650-8399.
Mexico City, Mexico Office: HOLLAND & KNIGHT-GALLÁSTEGUI Y LOZANO, S.C. (Joint Venture Office) Avenida Paseo de los Tamarindos No. 400, Torre "B" - 2° Piso, Col. Bosques d las Lomas, C.P. 05120 Mexico, D.F.
Telephone: 011-525-261-1866.
Fax: 011-525-261-1867.
Tel Aviv, Israel Office: Holland & Knight LTD, 23 Derech Petach-Tikva, 18th Floor.
Telephone: +011-972-3-566-7666.
Fax: +011-972-3-566-7667.
Buenos Aires, Argentina Office: San Martin 323--Piso 18, 1004. Telephone +54-11-4324-7600.
Fax: +54-11 4324-7601.

JACKSONVILLE MEMBERS AND ASSOCIATES

Mark G. Alexander
Barry C. Averitt
Robert J. Beckham
L. Kinder Cannon, III
Matthew P. Coglianese
Timothy J. Conner
Robert M. Dees
Raymond Ehrlich
Robert R. Feagin, III
Babette L. Fletcher
Charlene Francis
Fred D. Franklin, Jr.
George D. Gabel, Jr.
John F. Germany, Jr.
T. Malcolm Graham
Christopher J. Greene
Lawrence J. Hamilton II
Suzanne Meyer Judas
Linda Connor Kane
Michael F. Killea
Adam J. Kohl
Sharon Strayer Learch
Frederick J. Lotterhos, III
James L. Main
Scott D. Makar
John M. McNatt, Jr.
John J. Mikals
Drew W. Prusiecki
Chad S. Roberts
George E. Schulz, Jr.
Leonard A. Selber
M. Kami Smith
Michael G. Tanner
Donald W. Wallis
Alan M. Weiss

Crystal J. Adkins
Thomas E. Bishop
Michael L. Buckner
Christopher G. Commander
R. Raye Curry
Tammy D. Dawson
Margaret Widman Dees
Wyman R. Duggan
Craig D. Feiser
Peter P. Hargitai
E. Clayton Harland, II
Reese J. Henderson, Jr.
Nancy Hogshead
Todd C. Johnson
James R. McCain, Jr.
Charles S. McCall
Carol Mirando
Judy C. Ossi
Frederick D. Page
Patricia R. Sher
Adrian G. Soud
Catherine J. Tackett
Melissa S. Turra
Alan S. Wachs
Gregory Williamson
Christina Yeager

(See Next Column)

OF COUNSEL

J. Shepard Bryan, Jr.
Thomas M. Fiorentino
Philip Selber

For full biographical listings, see the Martindale-Hubbell Law Directory

---

MARKS GRAY (AV)

Suite 800, 1200 Riverplace Boulevard, 32207
Telephone: 904-398-0900
Telecopier: 904-399-8440
Mailing Address: P.O. Box 447, 32201
Email: mginfo@marksgray.com

Richard P. Marks (1876-1942)
Francis Michael Holt (1884-1946)
James A. Yates (1885-1960)
Sam R. Marks (1885-1973)
Harry T. Gray (1890-1975)
Francis P. Conroy (1912-1991)
Delbridge L. Gibbs (1917-1992)
James C. Rinaman, Jr.
H. Franklin Perritt, Jr.
Victor M. Halbach, Jr.
Gerald W. Weedon
Nicholas V. Pulignano, Jr.
William M. Corley
Jeptha F. Barbour
Susan Smith Erdelyi
Robert E. Broach
Alan K. Ragan
Stephen B. Gallagher
L. Johnson Sarber, III

Daniel A. Nicholas
Daniel K. Bean
Katherine D. Vince
Sonya Harrell Hoener
Allison Hunnicutt Hauser
Edward L. Birk

OF COUNSEL

Linda Cobb Ingham

Representative Clients: American International Group; American President Lines, Ltd.; Amerisure Insurance Group; Anesthesiologists' Professional Assurance Trust; Associated Aviation Underwriters; Baxter Healthcare Corp.; Merrill Lynch Pierce, Fenner & Smith, Inc.; Nations Bank; Scottsdale Insurance Company.
Of Counsel to: Cone, Yong, Stewart & Houston, P.A., Jacksonville, FL.

For full biographical listings, see the Martindale-Hubbell Law Directory

---

MARTIN, ADE, BIRCHFIELD & MICKLER, P.A. (AV)

One Independent Drive Suite 3000, Post Office Box 59, 32201
Telephone: 904-354-2050
Fax: 904-354-5842

James L. Ade
Lynda R. Aycock
W. O. Birchfield
Timothy A. Burleigh
Charles L. Cranford
Stephen H. Durant
T. William Glocker
Stephen D. Halker
Sharon Roberts Henderson
Barbara Christie Johnston
Ralph H. Martin
Robert O. Mickler
John D. Milton, Jr.
Daniel B. Nunn, Jr.
Scott G. Schildberg
Michael D. Whalen
Gary Wilkinson

Jason E. Campbell
Michael E. Goodbread, Jr.
James A. Nolan

Representative Clients: Deerwood/Gate Lands; General Waterworks Corp.; Wilma South Corp.; First Union National Bank of Florida; Mac Papers, Inc.; Tree of Life, Inc.; United Water Florida, Inc.

For full biographical listings, see the Martindale-Hubbell Law Directory

---

McGUIRE, WOODS, BATTLE & BOOTHE LLP (AV)

50 North Laura Street Suite 3300, 32202-3635
Telephone: 904-798-3200
Fax: 904-798-3207
Email: info@mwbb.com *URL:* http://www.mwbb.com
Atlanta, Georgia Office: 285 Peachtree Center Avenue, N.E., Suite 2200, Marquis Tower Two, 30303-1234.
Telephone: 404-443-5500.
Fax: 404-443-5599.
Baltimore, Maryland Office: 7 Saint Paul Street, Suite 1000, 21202-1671.
Telephone: 410-659-4400.
Fax: 410-659-4599.
Charlotte, North Carolina Offices: 3700 Bank of America Plaza, 101 South Tryon Street, 28280.
Telephone: 704-373-8999.
Fax: 704-373-8999 and Bank of America Corporate Center, Suite 2900, 100 North Tryon Street, 28202.
Telephone: 704-373-8999.
Fax: 704-373-8935.
Charlottesville, Virginia Office: Court Square Building, 310 Fourth Street, N.E., Suite 300, P.O. Box 1288, 22902-1288.
Telephone: 804-977-2500.
Fax: 804-980-2222.
Chicago, Illinois Office: 77 West Wacker Drive, Suite 4500, 60601-1635.
Telephone: 312-849-3699.
Fax: 312-849-3690.
McLean, (Tysons Corner) Virginia Office: 1750 Tysons Boulevard, Suite 1800, 22102-3892.
Telephone: 703-712-5000.
Fax: 703-712-5050.

(See Next Column)

McGuire, Woods, Battle & Boothe LLP—*Continued*

New York, New York Office: 9 West 57th Street, Suite 1620, 10019.
Telephone: 212-319-1572.
Fax: 212-319-5466.
Norfolk, Virginia Office: World Trade Center, 101 West Main Street, Suite 9000, 23510-1655.
Telephone: 757-640-3700.
Fax: 757-640-3701.
Richmond, Virginia Office: One James Center, 901 East Cary Street, 23219-4030.
Telephone: 804-775-1000.
Fax: 804-775-1061.
Washington, D.C. Office: Washington Square, 1050 Connecticut Avenue, N.W., Suite 1200, 20036-5317.
Telephone: 202-857-1700.
Fax: 202-857-1737.
Almaty, Republic of Kazakhstan Office: Park Palace, 41 Kazibek Bi Street, 2nd Floor, 480100.
Telephone: 7-3272-608-300.
Fax: 7-3272-608-305.
Brussels, Belgium Office: 250 Avenue Louise, Boite 64, 1050.
Telephone: 32-2-629-42-11.
Fax: 32-2-629-42-22.
Moscow, Russia Office: Paveletskaya Square, 1 Valovaya Street, 7th Floor, 13054.
Telephone: 7-502-937-0774.
Fax: 7-502-937-0776.

MEMBERS OF FIRM

Donald D. Anderson
James I. Vance Berry, Jr.
Scott S. Cairns
Karen M. Chastain
Marshall M. Criser
Michael F. Dawes
William W. Deem
David K. Etheridge
Nathan D. Goldman
Kenneth M. Keefe, Jr.
Richard N. Margulies
Christine Rieger Milton
Ann Roberts Purdue
C. Daniel Rice
Halcyon E. Skinner
Gresham R. Stoneburner
J. Cameron Story, III
David M. Wells

OF COUNSEL

William H. Adams III

ASSOCIATES

Patricia D. Barksdale
R. Eric Bilik
Thomas R. Brice
Michael R. Cavendish
W. Curtis Caywood IV (Not admitted in FL)
Mark C. Dearing
Steven B. Greenhut
Gwen Hutcheson Griggs
Marcia Morales Howard
Allison Warren Keller
Frank A. Lonegro
Ann M. Meadows
Erin O. O'Brien
James L. Purcell, Jr.
Devin J. Reed
Stacy Lynn Watson
Edward M. Whelan (Not admitted in FL)
Jeffrey S. York

For full biographical listings, see the Martindale-Hubbell Law Directory

Moseley, Warren, Prichard & Parrish, P.A. (AV)

501 West Bay Street, 32202
Telephone: 904-356-1306
Telecopier: 904-354-0194
Cable Address: "Ragland"
Email: firm@mwpplaw.com

Reuben Ragland (1882-1954)
Louis Kurz (1891-1965)
E. Dale Joyner (1943-1993)
James F. Moseley
Robert E. Warren
Joseph W. Prichard, Jr.
Robert B. Parrish
Andrew J. Knight II
Richard K. Jones
James F. Moseley, Jr.
Phillip A. Buhler

Stanley M. Weston
Kimberly Held Israel
Tracy A. Chesser
Michael A. Garfield
Eric Lee Hearn
Samuel Allen Maroon

OF COUNSEL

James E. Williams
Neil C. Taylor

Counsel for: CSX Transportation; Britannia Steam Ship Insurance Assn., Ltd.; The West of England Protection & Indemnity Assn. (Luxembourg); Crowley American Transport Services, Inc.; United Kingdom Mutual Steamship Assurance Assn., Ltd. (Bermuda); The London Steam-Ship Owners' Mutual Insurance Assn., Ltd.

For full biographical listings, see the Martindale-Hubbell Law Directory

Pappas Metcalf Jenks Miller & Reinsch, P.A. (AV)

200 West Forsyth Street, Suite 1400, 32202-4327
Telephone: 904-353-1980
Telecopier: 904-353-5217
Email: pmj@papmet.com

Thomas M. Jenks
Robert A. Leapley, Jr.
John G. Metcalf
Frank Estes Miller
M. Lynn Pappas
Mark A. Reinsch

(See Next Column)

Christina P. Gillam
Gary B. Davenport
G. Todd Cottrill
Thomas Ingram

LEGAL SUPPORT PERSONNEL

Mary Beth Wimmer
Glenna Thompson (Paralegal)
Donna F. Demetree (Paralegal)

For full biographical listings, see the Martindale-Hubbell Law Directory

Squire, Sanders & Dempsey L.L.P. (AV)

One Enterprise Center Suite 2100, 225 Water Street, 32202-4424
Telephone: 904-366-2420
Fax: 904-356-2986
URL: http://www.ssd.com
Cincinnati, Ohio Office: PNC Center, 201 East Fifth Street, Suite 1700, Cincinnati, Ohio 45202.
Telephone: 513-361-1200.
Fax: 513-361-1201.
Cleveland, Ohio Office: 4900 Key Tower, 127 Public Square, Cleveland, Ohio 44114-1304.
Telephone: 216-479-8500.
Fax: 216-479-8780.
Columbus, Ohio Office: 1300 Huntington Center, 41 South High Street, Columbus, Ohio 43215-6150.
Telephone: 614-365-2700.
Fax: 614-365-2499.
Houston, Texas Office: 6250 Chase Tower, 600 Travis Street, Houston, Texas 77002-3007.
Telephone: 713-546-5850.
Fax: 713-546-5830.
Miami, Florida Office: 201 South Biscayne Boulevard, 2900 Miami Center, Miami, Florida 33131-4330.
Telephone: 305-577-8700.
Fax: 305-358-1425.
New York, New York Office: 350 Park Avenue, New York, New York 10022-6002.
Telephone: 212-872-9800.
Fax: 212-872-9815.
Phoenix, Arizona Office: Two Renaissance Square, 40 North Central Avenue, Suite 2700, Phoenix, Arizona 85004-4498.
Telephone: 602-528-4000.
Fax: 602-253-8129.
Washington, D.C. Office: 1201 Pennsylvania Avenue, N.W., Suite 500, Washington, D.C. 20004-2491.
Telephone: 202-626-6600.
Fax: 202-626-6780.
Almaty, Kazakhstan Office: 141 Ablay Khan Avenue, Second Floor, Almaty, Kazakhstan 480091.
Telephone: +73-27-50-11-25.
Fax: +73-27-50-11-25.
Bratislava, Slovak Republic Office: Zochova 5, 811 03 Bratislava, Slov k Republic.
Telephone: 421-7-5441-7611.
Fax: 42-1-7-6280-2212.
Brussels, Belgium Office: Avenue Louise, 165-Box 15, 1050 Brussels, Belgium.
Telephone: 32-2-627-1111.
Fax: 32-2-627-1100.
Budapest, Hungary Office: H-1062 Budapest, Andrassy ut. 64, Budapest, Hungary.
Telephone: 36-1-428-7111.
Fax: 36-1-428-7100.
Kyiv, Ukraine Office: 14A Yaroslaviv Val, Kyiv 252034, Ukraine.
Telephone: 38-044-228-8687.
Fax: 38-044-228-4938.
London, England Office: Royex House, Aldermanbury Square, London EC2V 7HR.
Telephone: 44-171-776-5200.
Fax: 44-171-776-5233.
Madrid, Spain Office: Calle Velazquez 108-110, 28006 Madrid, Spain.
Telephone: 34-91-590-2420.
Fax: 34-91-590-2421.
Moscow, Russian Federation Office: Paveletskaya Square II, 1 Valovaya Street, 5th Floor, Moscow 113054, Russian Federation.
Telephone: 7-503-956-3750.
Fax: 7-503-956-3635.
Prague, Czech Republic Office: Václavské náměst 1 57/813, 110 00 Praha 1, Czech Republic.
Telephone: 420-2-2166-2111.
Fax: 420-2-2166-2222.
Hong Kong Office: Rooms 1101-2 St. George's Building, 2 Ice House Street, Central, Hong Kong.
Telephone: 852-2509-9732.
Fax: 852-2509-9772.
Taipei, Taiwan Office: 14F, 116 Nanking East Road, Sec. 2, Taipei, Taiwan, Republic of China.
Telephone: 886-2-2531-2888.
Fax: 886-2-2571-6199.

PARTNER

Robert O. Freeman

(See Next Column)

SQUIRE, SANDERS & DEMPSEY L.L.P., *Jacksonville—Continued*

OF COUNSEL

Alexandra M. MacLennan

For full biographical listings, see the Martindale-Hubbell Law Directory

KEY BISCAYNE, Dade Co.

ROBERTS & SALAZAR, L.L.P. (AV)

The Professionals' Building of Key Biscayne, 50 West Mashta Drive, 33149
Telephone: 305-361-1383
Fax: 305-361-0385

Norman T. Roberts
Lisette Pie Salazar

OF COUNSEL

Marc A. Kuperman

Reference: SunTrust Bank Miami, N.A. (Key Biscayne Branch).

For full biographical listings, see the Martindale-Hubbell Law Directory

*LAKE CITY,** Columbia Co.

BRANNON, BROWN, HALEY, ROBINSON & BULLOCK, P.A. (AV)

10 North Columbia Street, P.O. Box 1029, 32056
Telephone: 904-752-3213
Fax: 904-755-4524

W. Brantley Brannon (1907-1985)
Clarence E. Brown (1911-1997)
William J. Haley
Thomas W. Brown
Bruce W. Robinson
Stephen C. Bullock
David M. Robertson
J. Rhett Bullard

Counsel for: Timco; Florida Farm Bureau Insurance Co.; Florida Power & Light Co.; Maryland Casualty Co.; Suwannee River Water Management District.

For full biographical listings, see the Martindale-Hubbell Law Directory

DARBY, PEELE, BOWDOIN, PAYNE & KENNON (AV)

A Partnership including Professional Associations
327 North Hernando Street, P.O. Drawer 1707, 32056
Telephone: 904-752-4120
Fax: 904-755-4569

Herbert F. Darby (P.A.)
S. Austin Peele (P.A.)
W. Roderick Bowdoin (P.A.)
M. Blair Payne
Thomas J. Kennon, III

Representative Clients: City of Jasper; City of Lake City; First Federal Savings Bank of Florida; General Motors Acceptance Corp.; NationsBank N.A. (South); Town of White Springs; Rayonier, Inc.

For full biographical listings, see the Martindale-Hubbell Law Directory

LAKELAND, Polk Co.

HAHN, MCCLURG, WATSON, GRIFFITH & BUSH, P.A. (AV)

101 South Florida Avenue, 33801-4619
Telephone: 941-688-7747
Telecopier: 941-683-4582
Mailing Address: P.O. Box 38, 33802-0038
Email: lawfirm@hahnmcclurg.com *URL:* http://www.hmwgb@gte.net

James P. Hahn
E.V. McClurg
Stephen C. Watson
John R. Griffith
Philip H. Bush
James M. Craig, II

General Counsel: Huntington National Bank, Lakeland, Florida; Florida-First Bank, Lakeland, Florida; Publix Super Markets, Inc.
Approved Attorneys For: Attorneys' Title Insurance Fund; American Title Insurance Co.; Title & Trust Company of Florida; Federal Land Bank of Columbia, Columbia, S.C.
Reference: Huntington National Bank, Lakeland, Florida.

For full biographical listings, see the Martindale-Hubbell Law Directory

HARRIS, MIDYETTE & DARBY, P.A. (AV)

2012 South Florida Avenue, P.O. Box 2451, 33806-2451
Telephone: 941-683-7567
FAX: 941-688-8099

Christy F. Harris (Mr.)
William M. Midyette, III
Ben H. Darby, Jr.

Diane E. Hill
Lisa S. Dobson

Approved Attorneys for: Attorneys' Title Insurance Fund.
References: NationsBank, Lakeland, Florida; Watkins Motor Lines, Inc.; Tampa Armature Works, Inc.; Carter, Belcourt & Atkinson, C.P.A.'s; International Speedway Corporation.

For full biographical listings, see the Martindale-Hubbell Law Directory

HOLLAND & KNIGHT LLP (AV)

92 Lake Wire Drive, 33815
Telephone: 941-682-1161
Fax: 941-688-1186
Mailing Address: P.O. Box 32092, 33802
Email: hklaw.com *URL:* http://www.hklaw.com
Atlanta, Georgia Office: 1201 West Peachtree Street, N.E., Suite 2000.
Telephone: 404-817-8500.
Fax: 404-881-0470.
Boston, Massachusetts Office: One Beacon Street.
Telephone: 617-523-2700.
Fax: 617-523-6850.
Bradenton, Florida Office: 1001 3rd Avenue West, Suite 600.
Telephone: 941-748-7076.
Fax: 941-747-9774.
Falls Church, Virginia Office: 3110 Fairview Park Drive, Suite 900.
Telephone: 703-645-8600.
Fax: 703-645-8610.
Fort Lauderdale, Florida Office: One East Broward Boulevard, Suite 1300.
Telephone: 954-525-1000.
Fax: 954-463-2030.
Jacksonville, Florida Office: 50 North Laura Street, Suite 3900.
Telephone: 904-353-2000.
Fax: 904-358-1872.
Melbourne, Florida Office: 1499 South Harbor City Boulevard, Suite 201.
Telephone: 407-951-1776.
Fax: 407-951-1849.
Miami, Florida Office: 701 Brickell Avenue, Suite 3000.
Telephone: 305-374-8500.
Fax: 305-787-7799.
New York, New York Office: 195 Broadway, 24th Floor.
Telephone: 212-513-3200.
Fax: 212-385-9010.
Orlando, Florida Office: 200 South Orange Avenue, Suite 2600.
Telephone: 407-425-8500.
Fax: 407-244-5288.
Providence, Rhode Island Office: 50 Exchange Terrace, Suite 300, Union Station Plaza.
Telephone: 401-751-8500.
Fax: 401-553-6850.
San Francisco, California Office: 44 Montgomery Street, Suite 4050.
Telephone: 415-743-6900.
Fax: 415-743-6910.
St. Petersburg, Florida Office: 200 Central Avenue, Suite 1600.
Telephone: 727-896-7171.
Fax: 727-822-8048.
Tallahassee, Florida Office: 315 South Calhoun Street, Suite 600.
Telephone: 850-224-7000.
Fax: 850-224-8832.
Tampa, Florida Office: 400 North Ashley Drive, Suite 2300.
Telephone: 813-227-8500.
Fax: 813-229-0134.
Washington, D.C. Office: 2100 Pennsylvania Avenue, N.W., Suite 400.
Telephone: 202-955-3000.
Fax: 202-955-5564.
West Palm Beach, Florida Office: 625 North Flagler Drive, Suite 700.
Telephone: 561-833-2000.
Fax: 561-650-8399.
Mexico City, Mexico Office: HOLLAND & KNIGHT-GALLÁSTEGUI Y LOZANO, S.C. (Joint Venture Office) Avenida Paseo de los Tamarindos No. 400, Torre "B" - 2° Piso, Col. Bosques d las Lomas, C.P. 05120 Mexico, D.F.
Telephone: 011-525-261-1866.
Fax: 011-525-261-1867.
Tel Aviv, Israel Office: Holland & Knight LTD, 23 Derech Petach-Tikva, 18th Floor.
Telephone: +011-972-3-566-7666.
Fax: +011-972-3-566-7667.
Buenos Aires, Argentina Office: San Martin 323--Piso 18, 1004.
Telephone: +54-11 4324-7600. +54-11 4324-7601.

LAKELAND MEMBERS AND ASSOCIATES

Randall C. Clement
William S. Dufoe
William O. E. Henry
D. Burke Kibler, III
Henry M. Kittleson
Edward F. Koren
C. Parkhill Mays, Jr.
Henry M. Morgan, Jr.
Robert P. Murray
Harry M. Sawyer, Jr.
Richard B. Stephens, Jr.
Richard L. Stockton
Edward W. Vogel, III

Barbara Willman Davis
Walter E. Engle, III
A. Brent Geohagan
Sandra Graham Sheets

For full biographical listings, see the Martindale-Hubbell Law Directory

LANE, TROHN, BERTRAND & VREELAND, P.A. (AV)

One Lake Morton Drive, P.O. Box 3, 33802-0003
Telephone: 941-284-2200
Telecopier: 941-688-0310
URL: http://www.lanetrohn.com

(See Next Column)

LANE, TROHN, BERTRAND & VREELAND P.A.—*Continued*

A. H. Lane (Retired)
Robert L. Trohn
Robert J. Bertrand
John K. Vreeland
Christopher M. Fear
Gary S. Rabin
Robert M. Brush
Kingswood Sprott, Jr.
Hank B. Campbell
Patrick J. Murphy
Mitchell D. Franks
Janet M. Stuart
Robert G. Stokes
Mark N. Miller
Jonathan B. Trohn
T. W. Weeks, III
Neil A. Roddenbery

Stephen B. French
Jack P. James, III
E. Alexander Pujol
David D. Hallock, Jr.
Louise Wilkinson Spivey
Mark G. Capron
Connie C. Durrence

Counsel for: Ewell Industries, Inc.
Local Counsel for: Auto Owners Insurance Co.; Liberty Mutual Insurance Co.; St. Paul Fire & Marine Insurance Cos.; State Farm Insurance Cos.
Approved Attorneys for: Attorneys' Title Insurance Fund.

For full biographical listings, see the Martindale-Hubbell Law Directory

MARTIN & MARTIN, P.A. (AV)
200 Lake Morton Drive, 33801
Telephone: 941-688-7611
Telefax: 941-688-7329
Email: mdmartin@gate.net *URL:* http://www.martinpa.com

E. Snow Martin
E. Snow Martin, Jr.
Michael D. Martin

For full biographical listings, see the Martindale-Hubbell Law Directory

PETERSON & MYERS, P.A. (AV)
100 East Main Street, P.O. Box 24628, 33802-4628
Telephone: 941-683-6511; 676-6934
Telecopier: 941-682-8031
Lake Wales, Florida Office: 130 East Central Avenue, P.O. Box 1079.
Telephones: 941-676-7611; 683-8942.
Winter Haven, Florida Office: Lake Region Plaza, 141 5th Street, N.W., P.O. Drawer 7608.
Telephone: 941-294-3360.

M. David Alexander, III
Philip O. Allen
Jack P. Brandon
Kristen Marie Buzzanca
Debra Leigh Cline
J. Davis Connor
Dennis G. Corrick
Roy A. Craig, Jr.
Clinton A. Curtis
Jacob C. Dykxhoorn
Joseph A. Geary
Maria "Mia" Gerber
Jonn D. Hoppe
Dennis P. Johnson
Kevin C. Knowlton
Douglas A. Lockwood, III
Corneal B. Myers
E. Blake Paul
Robert E. Puterbaugh
Thomas B. Putnam, Jr.
Deborah A. Ruster
Stephen R. Senn
Andrea Teves Smith
Keith H. Wadsworth
Kerry M. Wilson

General Counsel for: SunTrust Bank Mid-Florida, N.A.; Lakeland Regional Medical Center, Inc.; Housing Finance Authority of Polk County.
Representative Clients: NationsBank, N.A.; First Union National Bank; Mutual Wholesale Co.; Ben Hill Griffin, Inc.; E. R. Jahna Industries, Inc.
Approved Attorneys for: Attorneys' Title Insurance Fund; Equitable Life Assurance Society of the United States.

For full biographical listings, see the Martindale-Hubbell Law Directory

LAKE PLACID, Highlands Co.

SWAINE, HARRIS, SHEEHAN & McCLURE, P.A. (AV)
212 Interlake Boulevard, P.O. Box 548, 33852
Telephone: 941-465-2811
Fax: 941-465-6999
Email: lplaw@ct.net *URL:* http://www.lawyers.com/shsmlaw
Sebring, Florida Office: 425 South Commerce Avenue.
Telephone: 813-385-1549.
Fax: 813-471-0008. E-Mail: shsmlaw@ct.net.

J. Michael Swaine
Bert J. Harris, III
John K. McClure
J. Timothy Sheehan

Kimberly L. Sapp

Representative Clients: Barnett Bank of Highlands County; Lykes Bros., Inc; City of Sebring; City of Lake Placid; Lakeshore Mall.
Approved Attorneys for: Attorneys' Title Insurance Corp.

For full biographical listings, see the Martindale-Hubbell Law Directory

LAKE WALES, Polk Co.

PETERSON & MYERS, P.A. (AV)
130 East Central Avenue, P.O. Box 1079, 33853
Telephone: 941-676-7611; 683-8942
Telecopier: 941-676-0643
Lakeland, Florida Office: 100 East Main Street, P.O. Box 24628.
Telephones: 941-683-6511; 676-6934.
Winter Haven, Florida Office: Lake Region Plaza, 141 5th Street, N.W., P.O. Drawer 7608.
Telephone: 941-294-3360.

M. David Alexander, III
Philip O. Allen
Jack P. Brandon
Kristen Marie Buzzanca
Debra Leigh Cline
J. Davis Connor
Dennis G. Corrick
Roy A. Craig, Jr.
Clinton A. Curtis
Jacob C. Dykxhoorn
Joseph A. Geary
Maria "Mia" Gerber
Jonn D. Hoppe
Dennis P. Johnson
Kevin C. Knowlton
Douglas A. Lockwood, III
Corneal B. Myers
E. Blake Paul
Robert E. Puterbaugh
Thomas B. Putnam, Jr.
Deborah A. Ruster
Stephen R. Senn
Andrea Teves Smith
Keith H. Wadsworth
Kerry M. Wilson

General Counsel for: SunTrust Bank Mid-Florida, N.A.; Lakeland Regional Medical Center, Inc.; Housing Finance Authority of Polk County.
Representative Clients: NationsBank, N.A.; First Union National Bank; Mutual Wholesale Co.; Ben Hill Griffin, Inc.; E. R. Jahna Industries, Inc.
Approved Attorneys for: Attorneys' Title Insurance Fund; Equitable Life Assurance Society of the United States.

For full biographical listings, see the Martindale-Hubbell Law Directory

LEESBURG, Lake Co.

AUSTIN & PEPPERMAN (AV)
Suite C, 1321 Citizens Boulevard, P.O. Drawer 490200, 34749-0200
Telephone: 352-728-1020
Fax: 352-728-0595
URL: http://www.aust-pep.com

Robert E. Austin, Jr.
Carla R. Pepperman

ASSOCIATES

Reda J. Stewart
Bradford D. Fisher

Representative Clients: Allstate Insurance Co.; American Excess Insurance Co.; American Re-Insurance Co.; Florida Rock Industries, Inc.; Goodyear Tire & Rubber Co.; Great American Insurance Co.

For full biographical listings, see the Martindale-Hubbell Law Directory

MELBOURNE, Brevard Co.

HOLLAND & KNIGHT LLP (AV)
1499 South Harbor City Boulevard Suite 201, 32901
Telephone: 407-951-1776
Fax: 407-951-1849
Mailing Address: P.O. Box 1288, 33601-1288
Email: hklaw.com *URL:* http://www.hklaw.com
Atlanta, Georgia Office: 1201 West Peachtree Street, N.E., Suite 2000.
Telephone: 404-817-8500.
Fax: 404-881-0470.
Boston, Massachusetts Office: One Beacon Street.
Telephone: 617-523-2700.
Fax: 617-523-6850.
Bradenton, Florida Office: 1001 3rd Avenue West, Suite 600.
Telephone: 941-748-7076.
Fax: 941-747-9774.
Falls Church, Virginia Office: 3110 Fairview Park Drive, Suite 900.
Telephone: 703-645-8600.
Fax: 703-645-8610.
Fort Lauderdale, Florida Office: One East Broward Boulevard, Suite 1300.
Telephone: 954-525-1000.
Fax: 954-463-2030.
Jacksonville, Florida Office: 50 North Laura Street, Suite 3900.
Telephone: 904-353-2000.
Fax: 904-358-1872.
Lakeland, Florida Office: 92 Lake Wire Drive.
Telephone: 941-682-1161.
Fax: 941-688-1186.
Miami, Florida Office: 701 Brickell Avenue, Suite 3000.
Telephone: 305-374-8500.
Fax: 305-789-7799.
New York, New York Office: 195 Broadway, 24th Floor.
Telephone: 212-513-3200.
Fax: 212-385-9010.
Orlando, Florida Office: 200 South Orange Avenue, Suite 2600.
Telephone: 407-425-8500.
Fax: 407-244-5288.

(See Next Column)

HOLLAND & KNIGHT LLP, *Melbourne—Continued*

Providence, Rhode Island Office: 50 Exchange Terrace, Suite 300, Union Station Plaza.
Telephone: 401-751-8500.
Fax: 401-553-6850.
San Francisco, California Office: 44 Montgomery Street, Suite 4050.
Telephone: 415-743-6900.
Fax: 415-743-6910.
St. Petersburg, Florida Office: 200 Central Avenue, Suite 1600.
Telephone: 727-896-7171.
Fax: 727-822-8048.
Tallahassee, Florida Office: 315 South Calhoun Street, Suite 600.
Telephone: 850-224-7000.
Fax: 850-224-8832.
Tampa, Florida Office: 400 North Ashley Drive, Suite 2300.
Telephone: 813-227-8500.
Fax: 813-229-0134.
Washington, D.C. Office: 2100 Pennsylvania Avenue, N.W., Suite 400.
Telephone: 202-955-3000.
Fax: 202-955-5564.
West Palm Beach, Florida Office: 625 North Flagler Drive, Suite 700.
Telephone: 561-833-2000.
Fax: 561-650-8399.
Mexico City, Mexico Office: HOLLAND & KNIGHT-GALLÁSTEGUI Y LOZANO, S.C. (Joint Venture Office) Avenida Paseo de los Tamarindos No. 400, Torre "B" - 2° Piso, Col. Bosques d las Lomas, C.P. 05120 Mexico, D.F.
Telephone: 011-525-261-1866.
Fax: 011-525-261-1867.
Tel Aviv, Israel Office: Holland & Knight LTD, 23 Derech Petach-Tikva, 18th Floor.
Telephone: +011-972-3-566-7666.
Fax: +011-972-3-566-7667.
Buenos Aires, Argentina Office: San Martin 323--Piso 18, 1004.
Telephone: +54-11 4324-7600.
Fax: +54-11 4324-7601. 34000

MELBOURNE MEMBERS AND ASSOCIATES

Andrew S. Hament — Hubert C. Normile, Jr.
Patrick F. Healy — William C. Potter
Clifton A. McClelland, Jr. — Erik P. Shuman

SENIOR COUNSEL

Mark D. Shuman

ASSOCIATES

Joseph G. Colombo — Robert J. Crohan, Jr.
Timothy M. Williams

For full biographical listings, see the Martindale-Hubbell Law Directory

NANCE, CACCIATORE AND HAMILTON (AV)

525 North Harbor City Boulevard, 32935
Telephone: 321-254-8416
Fax: 321-259-8243
Email: nancacc@iu.net

MEMBERS OF FIRM

James H. Nance — Charles G. Barger, Jr.
S. Sammy Cacciatore — James N. Nance
John N. Hamilton — Sammy M. Cacciatore

Reference: The Bank.

For full biographical listings, see the Martindale-Hubbell Law Directory

*MIAMI,** Dade Co.

ADAMS & ADAMS (AV)

5th Floor, Concord Building, 66 West Flagler Street, 33130
Telephone: 305-371-3333
Broward: 954-728-8770
Telecopier: 305-372-3987

Richard B. Adams (1926-1983) — Richard B. Adams, Jr.
R. Wade Adams

ASSOCIATES

Andrew D. Stone — Peter G. Walsh

LEGAL SUPPORT PERSONNEL

Sonia Torres

For full biographical listings, see the Martindale-Hubbell Law Directory

ANGONES, HUNTER, McCLURE, LYNCH & WILLIAMS, P.A. (AV)

Ninth Floor-Concord Building, 66 West Flagler Street, 33130-1805
Telephone: 305-371-5000
Fort Lauderdale: 954-728-9112
Fax: 305-371-3948
Fort Lauderdale, Florida Office: Suite 203N Justice Building, 524 South Andrews Avenue.
Telephone: 954-779-3456.
Fax: 954-832-0037.

(See Next Column)

Frank R. Angones — Christopher J. Lynch
Steven Kent Hunter — Stewart D. Williams
John McClure — B. Scott Hunter
Leopoldo Garcia, Jr.

Thomas W. Paradise (Resident, Fort Lauderdale Office) — Carlton A. Bober (Resident, Fort Lauderdale Office)
Donna Joy Hunter — Surama Suarez
Lourdes Alfonsin Ruiz — Juan Lucas Alvarez
Kara D. Phinney — Cheri R. Lazar
C. David Durkee — Christopher L. McClure

Insurance Clients: Allstate Insurance Co.; Prudential Property & Casualty Insurance Co.; Travelers Insurance Co.; Rollins Hudig Hall Healthcare Risk, Inc.

For full biographical listings, see the Martindale-Hubbell Law Directory

BAKER & McKENZIE (AV)

1200 Brickell Avenue 19th Floor, 33131
Telephone: (305) 789-8900
Intn'l. Dialing: (1-305) 789-8900
Facsimile: (1-305) 789-8953
URL: http://www.bakerinfo.com
Associated Offices of Baker & McKenzie in: Almaty, Amsterdam, Bahrain, Baku, Bangkok, Barcelona, Beijing, Berlin, Bogotá, Brasília, Brussels, Budapest, Buenos Aires, Cairo, Caracas, Chicago, Dallas, Düsseldorf, Frankfurt, Geneva, Hanoi, Ho Chi Minh City, Hong Kong, Houston, Hsinchu, Juárez, Kiev, London, Madrid, Manila, Melbourne, México City, Milan, Monterrey, Moscow, Münich, New York, Palo Alto, Paris, Prague, Rio de Janeiro, Riyadh, Rome, St. Petersburg, San Diego, San Francisco, Santiago, São Paulo, Singapore, Stockholm, Sydney, Taipei, Tijuana, Tokyo, Toronto, Valencia, Warsaw, Washington, D.C. and Zürich.
Correspondent Law Firm: Hadiputranto, Hadinoto & Partners, Jakarta.

MEMBERS OF FIRM

Donald J. Hayden — Andrew Hulsh
Robert F. Hudson, Jr. — Noel H. Nation
Eugene A. Rostov

NATIONAL PARTNERS

James H. Barrett — R. Allen Naudé
Charles Lea Hume — Anthony J. O'Donnell, Jr.
Keith Wasserstrom

ASSOCIATES

Jeffrey F. D. Bogert — Anna A. Krimshtein
Lorne S. Cantor — Jonas C. Packer
J. Mario Fontes, Jr. — Rahul P. Ranadive
Jordan Matthew Keusch — Ozzie A. Schindler
Laura K. Wendell

For full biographical listings, see the Martindale-Hubbell Law Directory

BIERMAN, SHOHAT, LOEWY & KLEIN, PROFESSIONAL ASSOCIATION (AV)

Penthouse Two, 800 Brickell Avenue, 33131-2944
Telephone: 305-358-7000
Facsimile: 305-358-4010

Donald I. Bierman — Ira N. Loewy
Edward R. Shohat — Theodore Klein

Michael A. Pizzi, Jr.

Reference: United National Bank of Miami.

For full biographical listings, see the Martindale-Hubbell Law Directory

BILZIN SUMBERG DUNN PRICE & AXELROD LLP (AV)

A Partnership of Professional Associations
First Union Financial Center, 200 South Biscayne Boulevard Suite 2500, 33131
Telephone: 305-374-7580
Telecopier: 305-374-7593
Email: info@bilzin.com

MEMBERS OF FIRM

Brian L. Bilzin (P.A.) — Alan J. Kazan (P.A.)
John C. Sumberg (P.A.) — Audrey Alterman Ellis (P.A.)
Richard Dunn (P.A.) — Marjie C. Nealon (P.A.)
Stanley B. Price (P.A.) — David W. Trench (P.A.)
Alan D. Axelrod (P.A.) — Mitchell E. Widom (P.A.)
Alvin D. Lodish (P.A.) — Albert E. Dotson, Jr. (P.A.)
Eileen Ball Mehta (P.A.) — Jacob J. Givner (P.A.)
Richard M. Goldstein (P.A.) — Howard E. Nelson (P.A.)
Carter N. McDowell (P.A.) — Steven D. Lear (P.A.)
Martin A. Schwartz (P.A.) — Lester L. Goldstein (P.A.)
James W. Shindell (P.A.)

COUNSEL

Richard D. Mondre (P.A.) — Arnold A. Brown
Marc J. Stone (P.A.) — Marc J. Sternbaum

(See Next Column)

Bilzin Sumberg Dunn Price & Axelrod LLP—*Continued*

ASSOCIATES

Brian Scott Adler
Suzanne M. Amaducci
Christopher D. Brown
Sherril M. Colombo
Allyn S. Danzeisen
J. Ronald Denman
Paul J. Durham
Daron S. Fitch
A. Vicky Leiva Garcia-Toledo
Nancy B. Glimcher
Raquel M. Gonzalez
Frank Guerra, Jr.
David R. Hazouri
Scott D. Kravetz
John M. Kuhn
Michael W. Larkin
Adam D. Lustig
Deborah R. Mayo
Lissette Benitez Ortiz
Jerry B. Proctor
Charles H. Ratner
Christopher Hahn Saia
Eric Saida
William A. Salgado
Teresa J. Urda
Lynn S. Waterman

For full biographical listings, see the Martindale-Hubbell Law Directory

Broad and Cassel (AV)

A Partnership including Professional Associations
Miami Center, 201 South Biscayne Boulevard, Suite 3000, 33131
Telephone: 305-373-9400
Telecopier: 305-373-9443
URL: http://www.broadandcassel.com
Boca Raton, Florida Office: Corporate Centre at Boca Raton, Suite 300, 7777 Glades Road, 33434.
Telephone: 561-483-7000.
Fort Lauderdale, Florida Office: Suite 1130, Broward Financial Centre, 500 E. Broward Boulevard, 33394.
Telephone: 954-764-7060.
Orlando, Florida Office: 390 N. Orange Avenue, Suite 1100, 32801.
Telephone: 407-839-4200.
Tallahassee, Florida Office: 215 South Monroe Street, Suite 400, 32302.
Telephone: 850-681-6810.
Tampa, Florida Office: 100 North Tampa, Suite 3500, 33602.
Telephone: 813-225-3020.
West Palm Beach, Florida Office: The Reflections Office Center, 400 Australian Avenue, South, Fifth Floor, 33401.
Telephone: 561-832-3300.

MEMBERS OF FIRM

Murray D. Shear (P.A.)
Mike Segal (P.A.) (Managing Partner)
Michael A. Dribin (P.A.)
Alan S. Lederman (P.A.)
Jose I. Rojas (P.A.)
Nina S. Gordon (P.A.)
A. Jeffry Robinson (P.A.)
Dale S. Bergman (P.A.)
Dawn Lankford Bowling (P.A.)
Kathleen L. Deutsch (P.A.)
Michael Paul Bennett (P.A.)
Thomas J. Palmieri (P.A.)
Gary Edward Lehman (P.A.)
Gary M. Carman
Ronald A. Shapo (P.A.)
David A. Freedman (P.A.)
Leonard H. Bloom (P.A.)
Joanne B. Erde (P.A.)

ASSOCIATES

Tamara Carmichael
Rose M. Parish-Ramón
Frank H. Henry
Neil F. McGuinness
Rodger L. Hochman
Joseph I. Emas
Jana Marie Yaw
Lee-Anne Perkins
Martin Pico
Alberto I. de Cardenas
Robin E. Carney
Melissa S. Channing
Miriam A. Alfonso
Joshua B. Weingard
Marcus Bodet

OF COUNSEL

Shepard Broad
Alvin Cassel
Norman Broad

Counsel for: Bank of Central Florida.
Local Counsel for: Barnett Banks, Inc.; Republic National Bank.

For full biographical listings, see the Martindale-Hubbell Law Directory

Camner, Lipsitz and Poller, Professional Association (AV)

550 Biltmore Way, Suite 700 (Coral Gables), 33134
Telephone: 305-442-4994
Fax: 305-442-2389
URL: http://www.camner-lipsitz-poller.com

Alfred R. Camner
Marc Lipsitz
Neale J. Poller
Marsha D. Bilzin

Roger A. Preziosi
Adam Mitchell Neijna
Bridget Wong
David A. Messinger
Wendy Hill El Diery

OF COUNSEL

Anne Shari Camner
Thomas R. Blake

For full biographical listings, see the Martindale-Hubbell Law Directory

Carlton, Fields, Ward, Emmanuel, Smith & Cutler, P.A. (AV)

4000 International Place, 100 S.E. Second Street, P.O. Box 019101, 33131-9101
Telephone: 305-530-0050
Fax: 305-530-0055
URL: http://www.carltonfields.com
Orlando, Florida Office: Citrus Center, 255 South Orange Avenue, Suite 1600, 32801-3488, P.O. Box 1171, 32802-1171.
Telephone: 407-849-0300.
Pensacola, Florida Office: Harbourview Building, 25 West Cedar Street, 4th Floor, 32501-5974, P.O. Box 12426, 32582-2426.
Telephone: 850-434-0142.
St. Petersburg, Florida Office: One Progress Plaza, 200 Central Avenue, Suite 2300, 33701-4352, P.O. Box 2861, 33731-2861.
Telephone: 727-821-7000.
Tallahassee, Florida Office: 215 South Monroe Street, Suite 500, 32301-1866, P.O Drawer 1900, 32302-0190.
Telephone: 850-224-1585.
Tampa, Florida Office: One Harbour Place, 777 South Harbour Island Boulevard, 33602-5799, P.O. Box 3239, 33601-3239.
Telephone: 813-223-7000.
West Palm Beach, Florida Office: Esperanté, 222 Lakeview Avenue, Suite 1400, 33401-6149, P.O. Box 150, 33402-0150.
Telephone: 561-659-7070.

Gregory M. Cesarano
Douglas J. Chumbley
Ignacio G. del Valle
John D. Golden
Bruce Charles King
Jose A. Loredo
Wendy Frank Lumish
Raquel M. Matas
Jason M. Murray
Paul L. Nettleton
Edith G. Osman
Gary M. Pappas
Benjamine Reid
Paul T. Reid
Emmet J. Schwartzman
Lea Ann Souza-Rasile
Jay A. Steinman
Patricia Halvorson Thompson

OF COUNSEL

Nancy Hagan Henry

Jeffrey A. Cohen
Corey Collins
Neil A. Covone
Jorge I.G. Del Valle
Amy E. Furness
Robert W. Hudson
John Fitzgerald Kennedy
Maria Charles McGuinness
Ana M. Morales
Janeen L. Rivers
K. Renee Schimkat (Not admitted in FL)
Alicia E. Shick
Karen M. Stanford
William H. Strop
Daniel R. Vega
Carlos A. Zumpano

For full biographical listings, see the Martindale-Hubbell Law Directory

Colson, Hicks, Eidson, Colson, Matthews, Martinez & Mendoza (AV)

Floor 47 First Union Financial Center, 200 South Biscayne Boulevard, 33131-2351
Telephone: 305-373-5400
Fax: 305-374-4796
URL: http://www.colson.com/

MEMBERS OF FIRM

William M. Hicks (1928-1996)
Bill Colson
Mike Eidson
Dean C. Colson
Joseph M. Matthews
Roberto Martinez
Enid Duany Mendoza
Julie Braman Kane
Robert H. Fernandez
Joseph J. Kalbac, Jr.
Daniel Uhlfelder

Reference: Northern Trust Bank of Florida.

For full biographical listings, see the Martindale-Hubbell Law Directory

Duane, Morris & Heckscher LLP (AV)

200 South Biscayne Boulevard, Suite 3410, 33131
Telephone: 305-960-2200
Fax: 305-960-2201
URL: http://www.duanemorris.com
Philadelphia, Pennsylvania Office: Suite 4200, One Liberty Place.
Telephone: 215-979-1000.
Fax: 215-979-1020.
New York, New York Office: 380 Lexington Avenue.
Telephone: 212-692-1000.
Fax: 212-692-1020.
Chicago, Illinois Office: 227 West Monroe Street, Suite 3400.
Telephone: 312-499-6700.
Fax: 312-499-6701.
Washington, D.C. Office: 1667 K Street, N.W., Suite 700.
Telephone: 202-776-7800.
Fax: 202-776-7801.
San Francisco, California Office: 100 Spear Street.
Telephone: 415-371-2200.
Fax: 415-371-2201.
Boston, Massachusetts Office: One International Place, 14th Floor.
Telephone: 617-598-3100.
Fax: 617-598-3101.

(See Next Column)

DUANE, MORRIS & HECKSCHER LLP, *Miami—Continued*

Wilmington, Delaware Office: 1201 Market Street, Suite 1500.
Telephone: 302-571-5550.
Fax: 302-571-5560.
Harrisburg, Pennsylvania Office: 305 North Front Street, 5th Floor, P.O. Box 1003.
Telephone: 717-237-5500.
Fax: 717-232-4015.
Wayne, Pennsylvania Office: 735 Chesterbrook Boulevard, Suite 300.
Telephone: 610-647-3555.
Fax: 610-640-2619.
Cherry Hill, New Jersey Office: 51 Haddonfield Road, Suite 340.
Telephone: 856-488-7300.
Fax: 856-488-7021.
Newark, New Jersey Office: One Riverfront Plaza.
Telephone: 973-424-2000.
Fax: 973-424-2001.
Palm Beach, Florida Office: 249 Royal Palm Way, Suite 403.
Telephone: 561-366-5400.
Fax: 561-366-5401.
Allentown, Pennsylvania Office: 968 Postal Road, Suite 200, P.O. Box 90400.
Telephone: 610-266-3650.
Fax: 610-266-3651.
Houston, Texas Office: One Greenway Plaza, Suite 500.
Telephone: 713-552-9900.
Fax: 713-552-0109.
Dover, Delaware Office: 314 S. State Street.
Telephone: 302-736-0156.
Fax: 302-736-0336.
Bangor, Maine Office: 15 Columbia Street, 4th Floor.
Telephone: 207-990-4800.
Fax: 207-990-4804.
Princeton, New Jersey Office: Princeton Forrestal Village, 116 Village Boulevard, Suite 200.
Telephone: 609-734-4323.
Fax: 609-734-4387.

RESIDENT PARTNERS

Harvey W. Gurland, Jr.
James E. McDonald
William R. Nuernberg
Charles C. Papy, III (Partner-in-Charge, Miami, Florida Office)
Walter J. Stanton III

RESIDENT ASSOCIATES

Jeffrey R. Margolis
Lynne H. Nowell
Lida Rodriguez-Taseff

SPECIAL COUNSEL

Joan A. Keston

For full biographical listings, see the Martindale-Hubbell Law Directory

HARDY, BISSETT & TEICHNER, P.A. (AV)

501 Northeast First Avenue, 33132
Telephone: 305-358-6200
Broward: 954-462-6377
Fax: 305-577-8230

G. Jack Hardy
G. William Bissett
Lee Philip Teichner

Lyle E. Shapiro

Representative Clients: International Paper Co.; Bridgestone/Firestone, Inc.; American International Underwriters; American International Group, Inc.; Crown Equipment Corp.; The Budd Company; Loewen Group International, Inc.; St. Paul Insurance Company; Titan International, Inc.; Sunstate Manufactured Homes of Georgia, Inc. d/b/a Peach State Homes, Inc.

For full biographical listings, see the Martindale-Hubbell Law Directory

HICKS & ANDERSON, P.A. (AV)

Suite 2402 New World Tower, 100 North Biscayne Boulevard, 33132
Telephone: 305-374-8171
Fax: 305-372-8038

Mark Hicks
Ralph O. Anderson
Jean Kneale

Gary A. Magnarini
Cindy L. Ebenfeld
Dinah S. Stein
David J. Maher
Rick A. Piccolo
Lisa Rodriguez
Kelly Gibson

OF COUNSEL

James E. Tribble
Roger L. Blackburn

For full biographical listings, see the Martindale-Hubbell Law Directory

HOLLAND & KNIGHT LLP (AV)

701 Brickell Avenue, Suite 3000, 33131
Telephone: 305-374-8500
Fax: 305-789-7799
Mailing Address: P.O. Box 015441, 33101
Email: hklaw.com *URL:* http://www.hklaw.com
Atlanta, Georgia Office: 1201 West Peachtree Street, N.E., Suite 2000.
Telephone: 404-817-8500.
Fax: 404-881-0470.
Boston, Massachusetts Office: One Beacon Street.
Telephone: 617-523-2700.
Fax: 617-523-6850.
Bradenton, Florida Office: 1001 3rd Avenue West, Suite 600.
Telephone: 941-748-7076.
Fax: 941-747-9774.
Falls Church, Virginia Office: 3110 Fairview Park Drive, Suite 900.
Telephone: 703-645-8600.
Fax: 703-645-8610.
Fort Lauderdale, Florida Office: One East Broward Boulevard, Suite 1300.
Telephone: 954-525-1000.
Fax: 954-463-2030.
Jacksonville, Florida Office: 50 North Laura Street, Suite 3900.
Telephone: 904-353-2000.
Fax: 904-358-1872.
Lakeland, Florida Office: 92 Lake Wire Drive.
Telephone: 941-682-1161.
Fax: 941-688-1186.
Melbourne, Florida Office: 1499 South Harbor City Boulevard, Suite 201.
Telephone: 407-951-1776.
Fax: 407-951-1849.
New York, New York Office: 195 Broadway, 24th Floor.
Telephone: 212-513-3200.
Fax: 212-385-9010.
Orlando, Florida Office: 200 South Orange Avenue, Suite 2600.
Telephone: 407-425-8500.
Fax: 407-244-5288.
Providence, Rhode Island Office: 50 Exchange Terrace, Suite 300, Union Station Plaza.
Telephone: 401-751-8500.
Fax: 401-553-6850.
San Francisco, California Office: 44 Montgomery Street, Suite 4050.
Telephone: 415-743-6900.
Fax: 415-743-6910.
St. Petersburg, Florida Office: 200 Central Avenue, Suite 1600.
Telephone: 727-896-7171.
Fax: 727-822-8048.
Tallahassee, Florida Office: 315 South Calhoun Street, Suite 600.
Telephone: 850-224-7000.
Fax: 850-224-8832.
Tampa, Florida Office: 400 North Ashley Drive, Suite 2300.
Telephone: 813-227-8500.
Fax: 813-229-0134.
Washington, D.C. Office: 2100 Pennsylvania Avenue, N.W., Suite 400.
Telephone: 202-955-3000.
Fax: 202-955-5564.
West Palm Beach, Florida Office: 625 North Flagler Drive, Suite 700.
Telephone: 561-833-2000.
Fax: 561-650-8399.
Mexico City, Mexico Office: HOLLAND & KNIGHT-GALLÁSTEGUI Y LOZANO, S.C. (Joint Venture Office) Avenida Paseo de los Tamarindos No. 400, Torre "B" - 2° Piso, Col. Bosques de las Lomas, C.P. 05120 Mexico, D.F.
Telephone: 011-525-261-1866.
Fax: 011-525-261-1867.
Tel Aviv, Israel Office: Holland & Knight LTD, 23 Derech Petach-Tikva, 18th Floor.
Telephone: +011-972-3-566-7666.
Fax: +011-972-3-566-7667.
Buenos Aires, Argentina Office: San Martin 323--Piso 18, 1004.
Telephone: +54-11 4324-7600.
Fax: +54-11 4324-7601. 34200

MIAMI MEMBERS AND ASSOCIATES

Ronald Albert Jr.
Susan H. Aprill
Mark I. Aronson
Alcides I. Ávila
Gregory A. Baldwin
Margarita Barreto
Robert G. Beatty
Christopher Noel Bellows
Rachel Blechman
William R. Bloom
Sanford L. Bohrer
John Campbell
Mirta (Mikki) Canton
Kelly-Ann Gibbs Cartwright
Jose A. Casal
Matthew P. Coglianese
Bruce Jay Colan
J. Thomas Cookson
Luis A. Cordero
J. Raul Cosio
Douglas F. Darbut
R. Thomas Farrar
Martin Fine
Robert J. Friedman
Teresita Garcia
Daniel Gelber
James S. Groh
Steven H. Hagen
John F. Halula
William F. Hamilton
Eugenio Hernandez
Jorge L. Hernandez-Toraño
Linda Collins Hertz
Stuart K. Hoffman
Lucinda A. Hofmann
John M. Hogan
Marilyn J. Holifield
Bernard Jacobson
Adolfo E. Jimenez
Judith M. Korchin
Lee F. Lasris
Barbara Ehrich Locke

(See Next Column)

HOLLAND & KNIGHT LLP—*Continued*

MIAMI MEMBERS AND ASSOCIATES (Continued)

Amelia Rea Maguire
George Mencio, Jr.
Michael T. Moore
Tracy Nichols
Daniel S. Pearson
James M. Porter
Peter Prieto
Craig V. Rasile
Wilfredo A. Rodriguez
José E. Sirvén
Chesterfield Smith
Lenore C. Smith
Robert H. Smith
Steven Sonberg
Bruce Stone
Laurie A. Thompson
Lynn C. Washington
Andrew H. Weinstein
James D. Wing

Jeffrey Bast
Rodney H. Bell
Juan D. Bendeck
Christopher W. Boyett
Louise McAlpin Brais
Dana L. Choi
Jose E. Cil
Diamela del Castillo
Norma De Miguel
Josias N. Dewey
Frances Gail Faigenblat
Emilio Fernandez
Dalia Merced· s Garcia
Marco Ferri
Alex M. Gonzalez
Sylvia B. Gonzalez
Belinda Ann Hatzenbuhler
Patricia M. Hernandez
Olga L. Kazakevitch
Kenneth D. Kossow
Robert J. Kuntz, Jr.
Tiffani G. Lee
Robert K. Levenson
Daniel O. Mena
Judith M. Mercier
Sheri E. Nott
Ilene Linda Pabian
Leon N. Patricios
Jorge E. Reynardus
Vivian Rodriguez Riveiro
Ambarina A. Rodriguez
Erika R. Royal
Vanessa P. Sciarra
Paul K. Silverberg
Darcy Lynn Van Kirk
George A. Villasana
Hava B. Villaverde
Lori K. Weems
Dwayne E. Williams

OF COUNSEL

George D. Perlman
Roderick N. Petrey

For full biographical listings, see the Martindale-Hubbell Law Directory

KENNY NACHWALTER SEYMOUR ARNOLD CRITCHLOW & SPECTOR, PROFESSIONAL ASSOCIATION (AV)

1100 Miami Center, 201 South Biscayne Boulevard, 33131-4327
Telephone: 305-373-1000
Facsimile: 305-372-1861
Email: admin@knsacs.com
Rogersville, Tennessee Office: 107 East Main Street, Suite 301.
Telephone: 423-272-5300.
Facsimile: 423-272-4961.

James J. Kenny
Michael Nachwalter
Thomas H. Seymour
Richard Alan Arnold
Richard H. Critchlow
Brian F. Spector
Kevin J. Murray
William J. Blechman
Harry R. Schafer
Deborah Sampieri Corbishley
David H. Lichter
Scott E. Perwin
Jeffrey T. Foreman
Pamela I. Perry
Lauren C. Ravkind
Katherine Clark Silverglate
Amanda M. McGovern
Paul C. Huck, Jr.
Robert D.W. Landon, III
Maria J. Beguiristain

Representative Clients: Albertson's, Inc.; American Bankers Insurance Group; Cartier, Inc.; Ethan Allen, Inc.; Federated Department Stores, Inc.; The Florida Bar; GTE Directories Corp.; Siemens Credit Corp.; GTE Florida; Columbia HCA.

For full biographical listings, see the Martindale-Hubbell Law Directory

KUTNER, RUBINOFF, BUSH & LERNER (AV)

501 N.E. 1st Avenue, P.O. Box 9700, 33101
Telephone: 305-358-6200; Broward: 954-462-6377
Fax: 305-577-8230
Email: Kutner@KRBL.com

MEMBERS OF FIRM

Arno Kutner
Edward G. Rubinoff
Kenneth J. Bush
Susan Scrivani Lerner

ASSOCIATE

Andrew M. Moss

For full biographical listings, see the Martindale-Hubbell Law Directory

LEESFIELD, LEIGHTON, RUBIO & MAHFOOD, P.A. (AV)

2350 South Dixie Highway, 33133
Telephone: 305-854-4900; 800-836-6400 (toll free)
Fax: 305-854-8266
Email: LEESFIELD@AOL.COM *URL:* http://www.LLRM.com
Key West, Florida Office: 615 1/2 Whitehead Street.
Telephone: 305-296-1342.
Fax: 305-294-1793.

Ira H. Leesfield
John Elliott Leighton
Maria L. Rubio
George G. Mahfood

(See Next Column)

Robert B. Boyers
Patricia M. Kennedy (P.A.)

For full biographical listings, see the Martindale-Hubbell Law Directory

LEVINE & PARTNERS, P.A. (AV)

1110 Brickell Avenue, 7th Floor, 33131
Telephone: Dade: 305-372-1350
Telefax: 305-372-1352
URL: http://www.levinelawfirm.com

I. Stanley Levine
Robert J. Levine
Suzan Jon Jacobs
Alan W. Levine
Allan S. Reiss
Judith L. Gelber

For full biographical listings, see the Martindale-Hubbell Law Directory

LAW OFFICE OF WILLIAM P. MCCAUGHAN (AV)

Suite 2803 World Trade Center, 80 S.W. Eighth Street, 33130
Telephone: 305-577-0058
Fax: 305-372-0526
Email: WPMLAW@BellSouth.net

For full biographical listings, see the Martindale-Hubbell Law Directory

MURAI, WALD, BIONDO & MORENO, P.A. (AV)

9th Floor Ingraham Building, 25 Southeast 2nd Avenue, 33131
Telephone: 305-358-5900
Fax: 305-358-9490
Email: mwbm@gate.net

Rene V. Murai
Gerald B. Wald
Gerald J. Biondo
M. Cristina Moreno
Cristina Echarte Brochin

Antonio Arzola
Maria Victoria Currais
Lynette Ebeoglu McGuinness

Reference: Union Planters Bank.

For full biographical listings, see the Martindale-Hubbell Law Directory

PERTNOY, SOLOWSKY, ALLEN & HABER, P.A. (AV)

Museum Tower, Suite 2000, 150 West Flagler Street, 33130
Telephone: 305-371-2223
Fax: 305-373-2073
URL: http://www.psahlaw.com

Sidney M. Pertnoy
Jay Solowsky
Richard Lewis Allen
David B. Haber

Alfred I. Hopkins
Leah Lariviere
Montgomery Blair Sibley

For full biographical listings, see the Martindale-Hubbell Law Directory

PETERS ROBERTSON DEMAHY PARSONS MOWERS PASSARO & DRAKE P.A. (AV)

Suite 600, Ingraham Building, 25 Southeast 2nd Avenue, 33131-1691
Telephone: 305-374-3103
Fax: 305-377-9805
Email: pmckay@peterson.com
Fort Lauderdale, Florida Office: 506 S.E. 8th Street.
Telephone: 954-761-8999.
Fax: 954-761-8990.
Fort Myers, Florida Office: Key West Professional Centre, 1342 Colonial Boulevard, Suite 45.
Telephone: 941-936-1129.
Fax: 941-936-4036.
West Palm Beach, Florida Office: Galleria International Building, 301 Clematis Street, Suite 3000.
Telephone: 407-832-9698.
Fax: 407-832-8355.

John R. W. Parsons
Neil P. Robertson
Jeffrey A. Mowers
Geralyn M. Passaro (Resident, Fort Lauderdale Office)
Pete L. DeMahy
Kenneth R. Drake

OF COUNSEL

Roger G. Welcher
Jackson L. Peters
Kenneth J. Smith

Steven B. Sundook (Resident, Fort Myers Office)
Scott J. Brook (Resident, Fort Lauderdale Office)
Z. Suzanne Arbide
Michael T. Flury
David Abramovici
Kimberly M. Valashinas (Resident, Fort Lauderdale Office)
Michael A. Bryant (Resident, Fort Lauderdale Office)

Representative Clients: Auto-Owners Insurance Co.; Dade County School Board; Employers Reinsurance Group; Gallagher Bassett Insurance Service; Maryland Casualty Co.

(See Next Column)

PETERS ROBERTSON DEMAHY PARSONS MOWERS PASSARO & DRAKE P.A., *Miami—Continued*

For full biographical listings, see the Martindale-Hubbell Law Directory

PODHURST, ORSECK, JOSEFSBERG, EATON, MEADOW, OLIN & PERWIN, P.A. (AV)

Suite 800 City National Bank Building, 25 West Flagler Street, 33130-1780
Telephone: 305-358-2800; Fort Lauderdale: 954-463-4346
Fax: 305-358-2382
Email: Info@podhurst.com *URL:* http://www.wwdir.com/podhurst.html

Aaron Podhurst
Robert Orseck (1934-1978)
Robert C. Josefsberg
Joel D. Eaton
Barry L. Meadow
Michael S. Olin
Joel S. Perwin
Steven C. Marks
Victor M. Diaz, Jr.
Katherine W. Ezell

Xavier Martínez

OF COUNSEL

Walter H. Beckham, Jr.
Karen Podhurst Dern

References: City National Bank of Miami; Mellon United National Bank of Miami.

For full biographical listings, see the Martindale-Hubbell Law Directory

SAMS & LISTER, P.A. (AV)

73255 West 63 Avenue, Suite 201, 33143
Telephone: 305-740-5401
Fax: 305-740-5425

Murray Sams, Jr.
David P. Lister

Arthur B. Stark

For full biographical listings, see the Martindale-Hubbell Law Directory

SHUTTS & BOWEN LLP (AV)

A Partnership including Professional Associations
1500 Miami Center, 201 South Biscayne Boulevard, 33131
Telephone: 305-358-6300
Telefax: 305-381-9982
Email: MCONNORS@SHUTTS-LAW.COM *URL:* HTTP://WWW.SHUTTS-LAW.COM
Orlando, Florida Office: 20 North Orange Avenue, Suite 1000.
Telephone: 407-423-3200.
Fax: 407-425-8316.
West Palm Beach, Florida Office: One Clearlake Centre, 250 Australian Avenue, Suite 500.
Telephone: 561-835-8500.
Fax: 561-650-8530.
Tallahassee, Florida Office: 215 South Monroe Street, Suite 804.
Telephone: 850-521-0600.
Fax: 850-521-0604.
Fort Lauderdale, Florida Office: First Union Center, Suite 2000, 200 East Broward Boulevard.
Telephone: 954-524-5505.
Fax: 954-524-5506.
Amsterdam, The Netherlands Office: Shutts & Bowen, B.V., Europa Boulevard 59, 1083 AD, Amsterdam.
Telephone: (31 20) 661-0969.
Fax: (31 20) 642-1475.
London, England Office: 43 Grosvenor Street, London W1X 9PG.
Telephone: 441-71-493-4840.
Telefax: 441-71-493-4299.

MEMBERS OF FIRM

Frank B. Shutts (1870-1947)
Crate D. Bowen (1871-1959)
Gary M. Bagliebter
Kimberly Lynn Barbar (Resident at Fort Lauderdale Office)
Brian L. Belt
Arnold L. Berman (Resident at West Palm Beach Office)
Joseph D. Bolton
Bowman Brown (P.A.)
Andrew M. Brumby (Resident at Orlando Office)
Judith A. Burke
Sidney C. Calloway (Resident to Fort Lauderdale Office)
Sheila M. Cesarano
Gary J. Cohen
Jonathan Cohen
John J. Copelan, Jr. (Resident at Fort Lauderdale Office)
Kevin D. Cowan
Luis A. de Armas
Jean-Charles Dibbs
James F. Durham, II
James A. Farrell (Also Resident at West Palm Beach Office)
Charles Robinson Fawsett (P.A.)
Terry B. Fein
Robert G. Fracasso, Jr.
Robert A. Freyer (Resident at Orlando Office)
Roger Friedbauer
David A. Gart (Resident at West Palm Beach Office)
Scott A. Glass (Resident at Orlando Office)
Michael L. Gore (Resident at Orlando Office)
Michael J. Grindstaff (P.A.) (Resident at Orlando Office)
Robert E. Gunn (P.A.) (Resident at West Palm Beach Office)
Edmund T. Henry, III

(See Next Column)

MEMBERS OF FIRM (Continued)

Mary Ruth Houston (Resident at Orlando Office)
J. Gregory Humphries (Resident at Orlando Office)
William N. Jacobs
Brian M. Jones (Resident at Orlando Office)
Rod Jones (Resident at Orlando Office)
Roger S. Kobert
John Thomas Kolinski
Jeffrey M. Landau
Richard M. Leslie (P.A.)
Stephen N. Lipton (Resident at Fort Lauderdale Office)
Maxine Master Long
Don A. Lynn (P.A.)
Lee D. Mackson
Antonio Martinez, Jr., (P.A.)
David B. McCrea (P.A.)
William G. McCullough
Joseph F. McSorley (Resident at West Palm Beach Office)
John E. Meagher
Arthur J. Menor (Resident at West Palm Beach Office)
C. Richard Morgan
Patrick M. Muldowney (Resident at Orlando Office)
Timothy J. Murphy
Phillip G. Newcomm (P.A.)
Louis Nostro
I. Ed Pantaleon (Resident at Orlando Office)
Harold E. Patricoff Jr.
George I. Platt, III (Resident Manager at Fort Lauderdale Office)
Geoffrey Randall
Margaret A. Rolando
Stephen L. Roof
Allan M. Rubin (Resident at Fort Lauderdale Office)
Raul J. Salas
Robert A. Savill (Resident at Orlando Office)
Alfred G. Smith, II
William F. Smith
Robert C. Sommerville (P.A.) (Resident; West Palm Beach Office)
Mark D. Thomson (Resident at Orlando Office)
Robert A. Wainger
Joseph Donald Wasil
Arnold M. Weiner
John B. White (P.A.)
James G. Willard (Resident at Orlando Office)
Scott G. Williams (Resident at West Palm Beach Office)
Kenneth W. Wright (Resident at Orlando Office)

ASSOCIATES

Jeannette E. Albo
Michael R. Ansay (Resident at West Palm Beach Office)
Jennifer J. Ator
Elizabeth R. Blandon
Leann M. Brezinsky (Resident at Orlando Office)
John E. Calles
Suzanne M. Driscoll (Resident at Fort Lauderdale Office)
Philip M. Feanny (Resident at Fort Lauderdale Office)
Jonathan D. Gerber (Resident at West Palm Beach Office)
Stacey L. Goldberg
Robert B. Goldman (Resident at West Palm Beach Office)
Joseph M. Goldstein (Resident at Fort Lauderdale Office)
Florentino L. Gonzalez
René J. González-Llorens
Bradley S. Gould (Resident at Fort Lauderdale Office)
Meredith A. Harper (Resident at Orlando Office)
Michael V. Herskowitz
Mark D. Hobson
Michael H. Hoffman
Jonathan Z. Kurry
David P. Lederman
Daniel T. O'Keefe (Resident, Orlando Office)
Edward J. O'Sheehan (Resident at Fort Lauderdale Office)
Mark L. Pateman (Resident at West Palm Beach Office)
Dario A. Perez
Jennifer L. Perry (Resident at Orlando Office)
Susan J. Pontigas
Vanessa L. Prieto (Resident at Fort Lauderdale Office)
Michael J. Rosenbaum
Joey Schlosberg
Derek A. Schwartz
Angela D. Shaw (Resident at Orlando Office)
Neil B. Shoter (Resident, West Palm Beach Office)
Miguel A. Silva
Scott K. Spivack (Resident at Orland Office)
David Tetrick, Jr. (Resident at Orlando Office)
Eric J. Thorn (Resident, Tallahassee Office)
Stephen K. Tilbrook (Resident, Fort Lauderdale Office)
Geoffrey L. Travis
Robert W. Vale
Bryan Wells
Wanda B. Whigham

OF COUNSEL

George J. Brusky (Not admitted in FL)
John S. Chowning (P.A.)
John R. Day (P.A.)
Andrew L. Gordon
Stephen J. Gray (Resident at London, England Office)
Marshall J. Langer (P.A.) (Resident at London, England Office)
Stephen L. Perrone (P.A.)
Preston L. Prevatt
Rosemarie N. Sanderson Schade (P.A.) (Resident at Amsterdam, The Netherlands Office)

CONSULTING ATTORNEY

Patrick L. Murray (Not admitted in the United States)

For full biographical listings, see the Martindale-Hubbell Law Directory

SPENCER AND KLEIN, PROFESSIONAL ASSOCIATION (AV)

Suite 1901, 801 Brickell Avenue, 33131
Telephone: 305-374-7700
Telecopier: 305-374-4890
Email: SandK@primenet.com

Thomas R. Spencer, Jr.
Brent D. Klein

(See Next Column)

SPENCER AND KLEIN PROFESSIONAL ASSOCIATION—*Continued*

Paul D. Breitner
Steven W. Simon
David M. Tarlow
Kevin Spencer
Edelberto Farres

OF COUNSEL

M. Christina Del-Valle (P.A.)

Representative Clients: America Publishing Group; American Association of Physicians and Surgeons; Chrysler Corporation; Coldwell Banker; Editorial Televisa; Grupo Anaya, S.A.; Independent Living Care, Inc.; Managed Care of America, Inc.; New Times, Inc.; Winn-Dixie Stores.

For full biographical listings, see the Martindale-Hubbell Law Directory

SQUIRE, SANDERS & DEMPSEY L.L.P. (AV)

201 South Biscayne Boulevard, 2900 Miami Center, 33131-4330
Telephone: 305-577-8700
Fax: 305-358-1425
URL: http://www.ssd.com
Cincinnati, Ohio Office: PNC Center, 201 East Fifth Street, Suite 1700, Cincinnati, Ohio 45202.
Telephone: 513-361-1200.
Fax: 513-361-1201.
Cleveland, Ohio Office: 4900 Key Tower, 127 Public Square, Cleveland, Ohio 44114-1304.
Telephone: 216-479-8500.
Fax: 216-479-8780.
Columbus, Ohio Office: 1300 Huntington Center, 41 South High Street, Columbus, Ohio 43215-6150.
Telephone: 614-365-2700.
Fax: 614-365-2499.
Houston, Texas Office: 6250 Chase Tower, 600 Travis Street, Houston, Texas 77002-3007.
Telephone: 713-546-5850.
Fax: 713-546-5830.
Miami, Florida Office: 201 South Biscayne Boulevard, 2900 Miami Center, Miami, Florida 33131-4330.
Telephone: 305-577-8700.
Fax: 305-358-1425.
New York, New York Office: 350 Park Avenue, New York, New York 10022-6002.
Telephone: 212-872-9800.
Fax: 212-872-9815.
Phoenix, Arizona Office: Two Renaissance Square, 40 North Central Avenue, Suite 2700, Phoenix, Arizona 85004-4498.
Telephone: 602-528-4000.
Fax: 602-253-8129.
Washington, D.C. Office: 1201 Pennsylvania Avenue, N.W., Suite 500, Washington, D.C. 20004-2491.
Telephone: 202-626-6600.
Fax: 202-626-6780.
Almaty, Kazakhstan Office: 141 Albay Khan Avenue, Second Floor, Almaty, Kazakhstan 480091.
Telephone: +73-27-50-11-25.
Fax: +73-27-50-11-25.
Bratislava, Slovak Republic Office: Zochova 5, 811 03 Bratislava, Slovak Republic.
Telephone: 421-7-5441-7611.
Fax: 42-1-7-6280-2212.
Brussels, Belgium Office: Avenue Louise, 165 Box 15, 1050 Brussels, Belgium.
Telephone: 32-2-627-1111.
Fax: 32-2-627-1100.
Budapest, Hungary Office: H-1062 Budapest, Andrassy ut. 64, Budapest, Hungary.
Telephone: 36-1-428-7111.
Fax: 36-1-428-7100.
Kyiv, Ukraine Office: 14A Yaroslaviv Val, Kyiv 252034, Ukraine.
Telephone: 38-044-228-8687.
Fax: 38-044-228-4938.
London, England Office: Royex House, Aldermanbury Square, London EC2V 7HR.
Telephone: 44-171-776-5200.
Fax: 44-171-776-5233.
Madrid, Spain Office: Calle Velazquez 108-110, 28006 Madrid, Spain.
Telephone: 34-91-590-2420.
Fax: 34-91-590-2421.
Moscow, Russian Federation Office: Paveletskaya Square II, 1 Valovaya Street, 5th Floor, Moscow 113054, Russian Federation.
Telephone: 7-501-258-5250.
Fax: 7-501-258-5251.
Prague, Czech Republic Office: Václavské náměst 1 57/813, 110 00 Praha 1, Czech Republic.
Telephone: 420-2-2166-2111.
Fax: 420-2-2166-2222.
Hong Kong Office: Rooms 1101-2 St. George's Building, 2 Ice House Street, Central, Hong Kong.
Telephone: 852-2509-9732.
Fax: 852-2509-9772.

(See Next Column)

Taipei, Taiwan Office: 14F, 116 Nanking East Road, Sec. 2, Taipei, Taiwan, Republic of China.
Telephone: 886-2-2531-2888.
Fax: 886-2-2571-6199.

PARTNERS

Albert A. del Castillo
Kenneth M. Myers
Luis Reiter

ASSOCIATES

David K. Jacobs
Lori Smith-Lalla

For full biographical listings, see the Martindale-Hubbell Law Directory

STEEL HECTOR & DAVIS LLP (AV)

A Registered Limited Liability Partnership
200 South Biscayne Boulevard, 33131-2398
Telephone: 305-577-7000
Fax: 305-577-7001
URL: http://www.steelhector.com
Key West, Florida Office: 309 Whitehead Street, 33040.
Telephone: 305-292-7272.
Fax: 305-292-7271.
Naples, Florida Office: 5551 Ridgewood Drive, Suite 101, 34108-2718.
Telephone: 941-593-1800.
Fax: 941-593-1801.
Tallahassee, Florida Office: 215 South Monroe, Suite 601, 32301-1804.
Telephone: 850-222-2300.
Fax: 850-222-8410.
West Palm Beach, Florida Office: 1900 Phillips Point West, 777 South Flagler Drive, 33401-6198.
Telephone: 561-650-7200.
Fax: 561-655-1509.
Caracas, Venezuela Office: Centro Seguros Sudamérica, Piso 10, Oficina 10-A, Avenida Francisco de Miranda, El Rosal Caracas 1060.
Telephone: 582-953-4006.
Fax: 582-953-4846.
London, England Office: Holborn Gate, First Floor, 26 Southampton Buildings, London, U.K. WC2A 1AN.
Telephone: 44-171-203-8425.
Fax: 44-171-203-8475.
São Paulo, Brazil Office: Moreira Lima & Royster Advogados, Av. Paulista, 1842, conj. 188, Torre Norte, São Paulo, SP 01310-923 Brasil.
Telephone: 55.11.283.2077.
Fax: 55.11.283.2078.
Rio de Janeiro, Brazil Office: Moreira Lima & Royster Advogados, Av. Rio Branco, 108-30 andar, Rio de Janeiro, RJ 20040-001 Brasil.
Telephone: 55.21.509.5782.
Fax: 55.21.509.5783.
Santo Domingo, Dominican Republic Office: Pedro Henriquez Ureña No. 157, Santo Domingo, Dominican Republic.
Telephone: 809.534.5490.
Fax: 809.534.5419.

MEMBERS OF FIRM

William C. Steel (1916-1983)
Darrey A. Davis (1910-1986)
Ron A. Adams (P.A.)
Patricia Del Pino Arias
José I. Astigarraga
Carlos A. Batlle (P.A.)
Roi E. Baugher, II (See listing at Naples)
Lawrence P. Bemis (P.A.)
Donna E. Blanton (See Listing at Tallahassee)
John T. Butler
Mark R. Cheskin (P.A.)
Matthew M. Childs (P.A.) (See listing at Tallahassee)
Barry G. Craig
Clay Craig
Denise Brody Crockett (P.A.)
Leslie J. Croland
Maria T. Currier (P.A.) (Resident at Caracas, Venezuela Office)
Alvin Bruce Davis
Norman Davis
Sonia de Cruz (P.A.)
Jorge Diaz-Silveira (P.A.)
Zena Manes Dickstein (P.A.)
Elizabeth J. du Fresne (P.A.)
Thomas V. Eagan (P.A.)
Ellen Ann Feinberg (P.A.) (See listing at West Palm Beach)
Gerry S. Gibson (P.A.) (See listing at West Palm Beach)
Harvey A. Goldman
Daniel E. Gonzalez (P.A.)
Gregory S. Grossman
George R. Harper (P.A.)
Louis J. Hector
William K. Hill (P.A.)
Timothy T. Hughes
Thomas R. Julin
Thomas M. Karr (P.A.)
Bradford D. Kaufman (P.A.) (See listing at West Palm Beach)
William B. Killian
Joseph P. Klock, Jr.
Peter M. Kramer (P.A.)
Michael A. Laing (P.A.)
Wendy S. Leavitt
Alvin F. Lindsay III
David M. Lindsey
John W. Little, III (P.A.) (See Listing at West Palm Beach)
Bruce A. McAllister (See listing at West Palm Beach)
Thomas R. McGuigan (P.A.)
Serge G. Martin
James E. Morgan, III, (P.A.)
Guy E. Motzer (P.A.)
Jeffrey I. Mullens (P.A.) (See Listing at West Palm Beach)
Edward M. Mullins
Janet T. Munn
Lewis F. Murphy (P.A.)
Thomas G. O'Brien III (See Listing at West Palm Beach)
Joseph W. Pallot (P.A.)
Eduardo Palmer
Rebekah J. Poston
Mark D. Rich
Sherwin P. Simmons (P.A.)
Edwin G. Torres
Samuel C. Ullman (P.A.)
Jose F. Valdivia, III (P.A.) (Resident, Caracas and London Offices)
Jim Watt (See Listing at West Palm Beach)

(See Next Column)

STEEL HECTOR & DAVIS LLP, *Miami—Continued*

MEMBERS OF FIRM (Continued)

Victoria L. Weber (See Listing at Tallahassee)
Carl E. Westman (See Listing at Naples)
Thomas R. Woolsey (P.A.) (See Listing at West Palm Beach)
Miguel A. Zaldívar, Jr. (P.A.) (Resident, Caracas and London Offices)
David W. Zimmerman

ASSOCIATES

Elisha L. Anagnostis
Lisa R. Askowitz
Roy J. Barquet
Jeffrey S. Bartel
Alison Bethel
Danielle Gotwols Bowser
David A. Buchsbaum
Helene Christianne Cejas
Jordan Patrick Clark
Anne Marie Estevez
Sean W. Firley
Cori Franco
Digna French
Heather L. Gatley
Carl E. Goldfarb
Eduardo W. Gonzalez
Michael Greene
M. Glenn Hamel-Smith
Brian L. Heller
Roberto P. Hernandez
Reed Herrero
Kathleen Hudson
Jay Kim
Robin Lea
Brian L. Lerner
Arthur R. Lewis, Jr.
Nikki B. Lewis
Richard C. Lorenzo
Rina Lyubkin
Margarita Martinez Miguez
Jeff T. Mihm
Gabriel Nieto
Ann Maria Pannella
Albert J. Piantini
Matthew R. Piepenburg
Robert W. Pittman
Carlotta J. Roos
Simon A. Ruan (Resident, Caracas, Venezuela Office)
Alex Rubio
Jose G. Sepulveda
Tricia A. Shackelford
Shanker Singham
Jennifer Y. Sun
Susan Torres
Angelica M. Trujillo
Robert C.L. Vaughan
Gregory C. Ward
Jessica M. Weiner
Curtis A. Wolfe
Sandra K. Wolkov

OF COUNSEL

James M. Herron
Wilson Smith (P.A.)
Harry Wiggin (Resident at London, England Office)

LEGAL SUPPORT PERSONNEL

Michael P. Harrell
James B. Krog
Sean C. Stafford (Government Relations Consultant) (Resident at Tallahassee Office)

Representative Clients: FPL Group, Inc.; John Hancock Mutual Life Insurance Co.

For full biographical listings, see the Martindale-Hubbell Law Directory

STROOCK & STROOCK & LAVAN LLP (AV)

First Union Financial Center, 200 South Biscayne Boulevard NL Suite 3300, 33131-2385
Telephone: 305-358-9900
Telecopier: 305-789-9302
Email: infomiami@stroock.com *URL:* http://www.stroock.com
New York, N.Y. Office: 180 Maiden Lane, New York, NY, 10038-4982.
Telephone: 212-806-5400.
Telecopiers: 212-806-6006; 212-806-5919; 212-806-6086; 212-425-9509; 212-806-6176. Email: info@stroock.com
New York Conference Center: 767 Third Avenue, New York, N.Y., 10017-2023.
Telephones: 212-806-5767; 5768; 5769; 5770.
Telecopier: 212-421-6234. Email: info@stroock.com
Boston, Massachusetts Office: 100 Federal Street, Boston, MA, 02110-1813.
Telephone: 617-482-6800.
Fax: 617-330-5111. Email: infoboston@stroock.com
Los Angeles, California Office: 2029 Century Park East, Suite 1800, Los Angeles, CA., 90067-3086.
Telephone: 310-556-5800.
Telecopier: 310-556-5959. Email: infola@stroock.com
Washington, D.C. Office: 1150 Seventeenth Street, N.W., Suite 600, Washington, D.C., 20036-4652.
Telephone: 202-452-9250.
Telecopier: 202-293-2293. Email: infodc@stroock.com

RESIDENT PARTNERS

Scott L. Baena
Michael Basile
Manuel A. Fernandez
Mindy A. Mora
Carey A. Stiss
Robert W. Turken

OF COUNSEL

Richard S. Savitt

SPECIAL COUNSEL

Robert M. Siegel

(See Next Column)

Marcello A. Benedetto (Not admitted in FL)
Richard J. Bernard
Brandon A. Block
Sean M. Cleary
Monica Cunill-Fals
Brent A. Friedman
Daniel R. Green
Karen S. Harkness
Jason Z. Jones
Marina Kievsky
Elena M. Marquez
Mary E. Moulton
Kevin S. Neiman
Jay M. Sakalo
George S. Savage
Richard B. Simring
Marchèlle A. Wiley

For full biographical listings, see the Martindale-Hubbell Law Directory

TRALINS AND ASSOCIATES, P.A. (AV)

Suite 3310 2 South Biscayne Boulevard, 33131
Telephone: 305-374-3300
Telefax: 305-374-4933

Myles J. Tralins

For full biographical listings, see the Martindale-Hubbell Law Directory

WALTON LANTAFF SCHROEDER & CARSON (AV)

A Partnership including Professional Associations
9350 Financial Centre, 9350 South Dixie Highway, 33156
Telephone: 305-379-6411; 305-671-1300
Telecopier: 305-670-7065
Email: dtharp@waltonlantaff.com *URL:* http://www.waltonlantaff.com
West Palm Beach, Florida Office: United National Bank Tower, Suite 800, 1645 Palm Beach Lakes Boulevard.
Telephone: 561-689-6700.
Telecopier: 561-689-2647.
Fort Lauderdale, Florida Office: Blackstone Building, Third Floor, 707 Southeast Third Avenue.
Telephone: 954-463-8456.
Telecopier: 954-763-6294.

MEMBERS OF FIRM

Miller Walton (1901-1987)
William C. Lantaff (1913-1970)
Laurence A. Schroeder (1907-1995)
Samuel O. Carson (1912-1997)
Michael R. Jenks (P.A.)
David K. Tharp (P.A.)
Wayne T. Gill (P.A.) (West Palm Beach Office)
Charles Brown Mirman (P.A.)
Jonathan J. Davis (Ft. Lauderdale Office)
Bernard I. Probst
Lawrence D. Smith, Jr.
Beth J. Leahy (Ft. Lauderdale Office)
Henry Suarez
Richard G. Rosenblum (Ft. Lauderdale Office)
Robert J. Strunin
Deborah Poore Knight (Ft. Lauderdale Office)
Robert L. Teitler
Allison Chittem Hartnett
Amy L. Smith (P.A.) (West Palm Beach Office)
William G. Hersman
Kurt A. Wyland (West Palm Beach Office)
David S. Tadros (P.A.) (West Palm Beach Office)
Warren Brown (Resident, Fort Lauderdale Office)

OF COUNSEL

John P. Joy
Garth A. Webster (P.A.)
Stuart A. Goldstein
Rhett P. Dove, III
William J. Gray

ASSOCIATES

Kenneth L. Valentini
Steven E. Foor (West Palm Beach Office)
Gregg R. Margre (West Palm Beach Office)
Jane Anderson (West Palm Beach Office)
Leroy G. Lee
Michele E. Ready
Danilo J. Iglesias (Resident, Fort Lauderdale Office)
Eric D. Sachs
Gerald K. McKim (West Palm Beach Office)
Thomas J. Caldwell
Ann H. Park
Lazaro C. Rodriguez
Thomas E. Falcon
Michael H. Galex
Antonino G. Hernandez
Daniel G. Williams (West Palm Beach Office)
Gabriel Bellon
M. Cristina Brodermann
William T. Abel (West Palm Beach Office)
Sandra M. Ferrera
Edward M. Harvey, Jr. (Fort Lauderdale Office)

For full biographical listings, see the Martindale-Hubbell Law Directory

WELBAUM, GUERNSEY, HINGSTON, GREENLEAF & GREGORY, L.L.P. (AV)

Penthouse Suite, 901 Ponce de Leon Boulevard (Coral Gables), 33134-3009
Telephone: 305-441-8900
Fax: 305-441-2255
Email: wghgglaw@bellsouth.net

MEMBERS OF FIRM

R. Earl Welbaum
Dan B. Guernsey
Robert A. Hingston
W. Frank Greenleaf
John H. Gregory

ASSOCIATES

Michael Yates
Michael Jay Rune, II

(See Next Column)

WELBAUM, GUERNSEY, HINGSTON, GREENLEAF & GREGORY L.L.P.—*Continued*

OF COUNSEL

René Sacasas

For full biographical listings, see the Martindale-Hubbell Law Directory

*MILTON,** Santa Rosa Co.

JOHNSON, GREEN, MILLER & GIBSON, P.A. (AV)

6850 Caroline Street, P.O. Box 605, 32572-0605
Telephone: 850-623-3841
Fax: 850-623-3555

T. Sol Johnson
Paul R. Green
Johnny L. Miller, Jr.
Michael Gibson

Representative Client: School Board of Santa Rosa County.

For full biographical listings, see the Martindale-Hubbell Law Directory

*NAPLES,** Collier Co.

GRANT, FRIDKIN, PEARSON, ATHAN & CROWN, P.A. (AV)

Pelican Bay Corporate Centre, 5551 Ridgewood Drive, Suite 501, 34108
Telephone: 941-514-1000
Fax: 941-514-0377
Email: info@gfpac.com *URL:* http://www.gfpac.com
Key West, Florida Office: 422 Fleming Street, 33040.
Telephone: 305-296-4553.
Fax: 305-296-7049.

SHAREHOLDERS

G. Helen Athan
Todd L. Bradley
Howard L. Crown
Jeffrey D. Fridkin
Richard C. Grant
William M. Pearson

Mark W. McFall
Thomas G. Norsworthy
D. Keith Wickenden

For full biographical listings, see the Martindale-Hubbell Law Directory

PORTER WRIGHT MORRIS & ARTHUR LLP (AV)

5801 Pelican Bay Boulevard Suite 300, 34108-2709
Telephone: 941-593-2900; (800-876-7962)
FAX: 941-593-2990
Email: apf@porterwright.com *URL:* http://www.porterwright.com
Columbus, Ohio Office: 41 South High Street, 43215-6194.
Telephones: 614-227-2000; (800-533-2794).
Fax: 614-227-2100. Internet: cmh@porterwright.com.
Dayton, Ohio Office: One Dayton Centre, One South Main Street, Suite 1600, 45402-2028.
Telephones: 937-449-6810; (800-533-4434).
Fax: 937-449-6820. Internet: day@porterwright.com.
Cincinnati, Ohio Office: 250 E. Fifth Street, Suite 2200, 45202-4199.
Telephones: 513-381-4700; (800-582-5813).
Fax: 513-421-0991. Internet: cvg@porterwright.com.
Cleveland, Ohio Office: 925 Euclid Avenue, Suite 1700, 44115-1483.
Telephones: 216-443-9000; (800-824-1980).
Fax: 216-443-9011. Internet: cle@porterwright.com.
Washington, D.C. Office: 1667 K Street, N.W., Suite 1100, 20006-1605.
Telephones: 202-778-3000; (800-456-7962).
Fax: 202-778-3063. Internet: dca@porterwright.com.

MEMBERS OF FIRM

Robert M. Buckel
W. Jeffrey Cecil
Mary Beth Clary
Robert C. Gebhardt
Harry L. Henning
Jeffrey S. Kannensohn
Dixon F. Miller
Gary K. Wilson

RESIDENT ASSOCIATES

S. Dresden Brunner
Margaret Castellana
Jeanette Martinez Lombardi

For full biographical listings, see the Martindale-Hubbell Law Directory

QUARLES & BRADY LLP (AV)

Barnett Center, 4501 Tamiami Trail North Suite 300, 34103-3060
Telephone: 941-262-5959
Fax: 941-434-4999
URL: http://www.quarles.com
Milwaukee, Wisconsin Office: 411 East Wisconsin Avenue, 53202-4497.
Telephone: 414-277-5000.
Fax: 414-271-3552.
Madison, Wisconsin Office: Firstar Plaza, One South Pinckney Street, P.O. Box 2113, 53701-2113.
Telephone: 608-251-5000.
Fax: 608-251-9166.
West Palm Beach, Florida Office: 222 Lakeview Avenue, 4th Floor, 33401.
Telephone: 561-653-5000.
Fax: 561-653-5333.

(See Next Column)

Phoenix, Arizona Office: One Camelback Building, One East Camelback Road, Suite 400, 85012-1649.
Telephone: 602-230-5500.
Fax: 602-230-5598.
Chicago, Illinois Office: Quarles & Brady LLC, Citicorp Center, 500 West Madison Street, Suite 3700.
Telephone: 312-715-5000.
Fax: 312-715-5155.

PARTNERS

Thomas E. Maloney
David L. Petersen
F. Joseph McMackin, III
Timothy G. Hains
Robert E. Doyle, Jr.
Leo J. Salvatori
Kimberly Leach Johnson
John D. Humphreville

ASSOCIATES

Samara S. Holland
Mark Hubert Muller
Lisa Carozza Lottes
James T. Demarest
Susan Kubar
Edmond E. Koester
C. Lane Wood
Judith T. Beckler
Nicole M. Marginian

BUSINESS MANAGEMENT SUPPORT PERSONNEL

ADMINISTRATOR

Charryl A. Youman

LEGAL ASSISTANT

Tianna Johnson
Barbara Roller

For full biographical listings, see the Martindale-Hubbell Law Directory

*ORLANDO,** Orange Co.

BAKER & HOSTETLER LLP (AV)

SunBank Center, Suite 2300, 200 South Orange Avenue, 32802-3432
Telephone: 407-649-4000
Fax: 407-841-0168
To contact an attorney on the Internet use first initial and surname followed by @baker-hostetler.com
URL: http://www.bakerlaw.com
In Cleveland, Ohio: 3200 National City Center, 1900 East Ninth Street.
Telephone: 216-621-0200.
In Cincinnati, Ohio: 312 Walnut Street, Suite 2650.
Telephone: 513-929-3400.
In Columbus, Ohio: Capitol Square, Suite 2100, 65 East State Street.
Telephone: 614-228-1541.
In Denver, Colorado: 303 East 17th Avenue, Suite 1100.
Telephone: 303-861-0600.
In Houston, Texas: 1000 Louisiana, Suite 2000.
Telephone: 713-751-1600.
In Long Beach, California: 300 Oceangate, Suite 620.
Telephone: 362-432-2827.
In Los Angeles, California: 600 Wilshire Boulevard.
Telephone: 213-624-2400.
In Washington, D. C.: Washington Square, Suite 1100, 1050 Connecticut Avenue, N.W.
Telephone: 202-861-1500.

OFFICE MANAGING PARTNER

G. Thomas Ball (Managing Partner-Orlando Office)

PARTNERS

Wendy R. Anderson
Thomas R. deRosa (Not admitted in FL)
Jeffrey E. Decker
Denis L. Durkin
James V. Etscorn
John W. Foster, Sr.
Richard T. Fulton
Kurt P. Gruber
Jeffery Q. Jonasen
Jerry R. Linscott
John Melicharek, Jr.
Frank M. Mock
Rosemary O'Shea
Hector A. Perez
Richard D. Robinson
Joel H. Sharp, Jr.
Robert W. Thielhelm, Jr.
Robert J. Webb
Karen Whitehead
David S. Wood
Kenneth C. Wright

ASSOCIATES

Odiator Arugu
Daniel Bachrach
John Y. Benford
Allison L. Bickel
Lynn E. Burnsed
Scott E. Damon
Jorge de la Osa
Barbara A. Egolf
Christopher N. Fountas
Jason C. Gamel
Eric S. Golden
William C. Guthrie
Michael N. Hutter
Bonnie J. Jackson
Kirk D. Johnson
Matthew P. Julian
Mark S. Lieblich
Mark D. Scheinblum
Ben W. Subin
Christine A. Wasula

OF COUNSEL

Laurie J. Levin

RETIRED PARTNER

V. Keith Young

For full biographical listings, see the Martindale-Hubbell Law Directory

Orlando—Continued

BROAD AND CASSEL (AV)

A Partnership including Professional Associations
390 N. Orange Avenue, Suite 1100, 32801
Telephone: 407-839-4200
Telecopier: 407-425-8377
URL: http:www.broadandcassel.com
Boca Raton, Florida Office: Corporate Centre at Boca Raton, Suite 300, 7777 Glades Road, 33434.
Telephone: 561-483-7000.
Fort Lauderdale, Florida Office: Suite 1130, Broward Financial Centre, 500 E. Broward Boulevard, 33394.
Telephone: 954-764-7060.
Miami, Florida Office: Miami Center, 201 South Biscayne Boulevard, Suite 3000, 33131.
Telephone: 305-373-9400.
Tallahassee, Florida Office: 215 South Monroe Street, Suite 400, 32302.
Telephone: 850-681-6810.
Tampa, Florida Office: 100 North Tampa, Suite 3500, 33602.
Telephone: 813-225-3020.
West Palm Beach, Florida Office: The Reflections Office Center, Fifth Floor, 400 Australian Avenue, South, 33401.
Telephone: 561-832-3300.

RESIDENT PARTNERS

C. Ken Bishop (P.A.)
Robert D. Gatton (P.A.)
C. David Brown, II, (P.A.)
F. Vernon Bennett
Anthony W. Palma (P.A.)
James E. Slater (P.A.)
Robert T. Rosen (P.A.)
Randal M. Alligood (P.A.)
Andrew B. Thomas (P.A.)
Jack R. Elliott (P.A.)
Richard N. Milian (P.A.)
Gary W. Johnson (P.A.)
Christopher D. Rolle (P.A.)
Marian Wossum Schlow (P.A.)
Roy S. Kobert (P.A.)
Douglas E. Starcher (P.A.)

RESIDENT ASSOCIATES

Gene E. Crick, Jr.
Scott G. Miller
Keith F. White
Robert Alfert, Jr.
Robert F. Mallett
Leigh Ann Murvin
H. Scott Dulaney
John J. Senical, Jr.
David F. Leon
Haylee Alison Albert
Nathan L. Townsend
Juli L. Simas
Heather M. Conger
Holly L. Haworth
Michael P. Devoe
Stuart Sloan
Todd W. Watson

OF COUNSEL

Donna M. More
I. Burton Spraker
Wanda L. Brown
Alan M. Gerlach

General Counsel for: Bank of Central Florida; Trammell Crow Residential; CED, Inc.; Quality Factory Outlet Centers; Orlando-Orange County Expressway Authority; Orange County School Board.
Approved Attorneys for: Attorneys' Title Insurance Fund; Chicago Title Insurance Co.; Commonwealth Land Title Insurance Co.; Ticor Title Insurance Co.

For full biographical listings, see the Martindale-Hubbell Law Directory

CARLTON, FIELDS, WARD, EMMANUEL, SMITH & CUTLER, P.A. (AV)

Citrus Center, 255 South Orange Avenue, Suite 1600 (32801-3488), P.O. Box 1171, 32802-1171
Telephone: 407-849-0300
Fax: (407) 648-9099
URL: http://www.carltonfields.com
Miami, Florida Office: 4000 International Place, 100 S.E. Second Street, 33131-9101, P.O. Box 019101, 33131-9101.
Telephone: 305-530-0050.
Pensacola, Florida Office: Harbourview Building, 25 West Cedar Street, 4th Floor, 32501-5974, P.O. Box 12426, 32582-2426.
Telephone: 850-434-0142.
St. Petersburg, Florida Office: One Progress Plaza, 200 Central Avenue, Suite 2300, 33701-4352, P.O. Box 2861, 33731-2861.
Telephone: 727-821-7000.
Tallahassee, Florida Office: 215 South Monroe Street, Suite 500, 32301-1866, P.O. Drawer 190, 32302-0190.
Telephone: 850-224-1585.
Tampa, Florida Office: One Harbour Place, 777 South Harbour Island Boulevard, 33602-5799, P.O. Box 3239, 33601-3239.
Telephone: 813-223-7000.
West Palm Beach, Florida Office: Esperanté, 222 Lakeview Avenue, Suite 1400, 33401-6149, P.O. Box 150, 33402-0150.
Telephone: 561-659-7070.

Charles J. Cacciabeve
Vivian P. Cocotas
Philip A. Diamond
Keith J. Hesse
Daniel C. Johnson
Jeffry R. Jontz
Thomas D. Scanlon
Vernon Swartsel
Robert L. Young

Howard A. Cohen
Arthur D. Sims, II
Charlotte L. Warren
Thomas P. Wert

For full biographical listings, see the Martindale-Hubbell Law Directory

DECUBELLIS & MEEKS, P.A. (AV)

Suite 801, Citrus Center, 255 South Orange Avenue, P.O. Box 4976, 32802-4976
Telephone: 407-872-2200
Telecopier: 407-423-1038

Daniel L. DeCubellis
Mary B. Meeks
John A. Shughart, Jr.
Jennifer C. Carter
Brett M. Wendt

Representative Clients: Design Professional Insurance Corp.; Florida Lawyers Mutual Insurance Corp.; International Game Technology, Inc.; Jennings Environmental Services, Inc.; Mader Southeast, Inc.; Orange County; PGA Tour, Inc.; SouthTrust Bank, N.A.

For full biographical listings, see the Martindale-Hubbell Law Directory

EUBANKS, HILYARD & BOGAN, P.A. (AV)

Suite 600 First Union Building, 20 North Orange Avenue, P.O. Box 4973, 32802-4973
Telephone: 407-425-4251
Telecopier: 407-841-8431

Ernest H. Eubanks
Rodney G. Ross (1934-1982)
Sutton G. Hilyard, Jr.
Bruce R. Bogan

Bobby G. Palmer, Jr.
W. Gregory Lockeby

Representative Clients: AIG Aviation, Inc.; AVEMCO Insurance Co.; Phoenix Aviation Managers, Inc.; Ranger Insurance Co.; Old Republic Insurance Co.; Signal Aviation Underwriters; Underwriters at Lloyds; Orange County Sheriff's Office; United Technologies Corp.; Reliance Insurance Co.

For full biographical listings, see the Martindale-Hubbell Law Directory

FOLEY & LARDNER (AV)

Suite 1800, 111 North Orange Avenue, P.O. Box 2193, 32802-2193
Telephone: 407-423-7656
Facsimile: 407-648-1743
Email: foleylardner@worldnet.att.net *URL:* http://www.foleylardner.com
Los Angeles, California Office: 2029 Century Park East, 35th Floor.
Telephone: 310-277-2223.
Fax: 310-557-8475.
Sacramento, California Office: 300 Capitol Mall, Suite 1125.
Telephone: 916-443-8005.
Fax: 916-443-2240.
San Diego, California Office: 402 West Broadway, 23rd Floor.
Telephone: 619-234-6655.
Fax: 619-234-3510.
San Francisco, California Office: One Maritime Plaza, Sixth Floor.
Telephone: 415-434-4484.
Fax: 415-434-4507.
Denver, Colorado Office: 1999 Broadway, Suite 2560.
Telephone: 303-297-0260.
Fax: 303-297-0266.
Washington, D.C. Office: Washington Harbour, Suite 500, 3000 K Street, N.W.
Telephone: 202-672-5300.
Telex: 904136 (Foley Lard Wash).
Facsimile: 202-672-5399.
Jacksonville, Florida Office: The Greenleaf Building, 200 Laura Street. P.O. Box 240.
Telephone: 904-359-2000.
Facsimile: 904-359-8700.
Tallahassee, Florida Office: 300 East Park Avenue, P.O. Box 1454.
Telephone: 850-222-6100.
Facsimile: 850-561-6475.
Tampa, Florida Offices: Suite 2700, One Hundred N. Tampa Street, P.O. Box 3391.
Telephones: 813-229-2300; Pinellas County: 813-442-3296.
Facsimile: 813-221-4210.
West Palm Beach, Florida Office: Suite 200, Phillips Point East Tower, 777 South Flagler Drive.
Telephone: 561-655-5050.
Facsimile: 561-655-6925.
Chicago, Illinois Office: Suite 3300, One IBM Plaza, 330 N. Wabash Avenue.
Telephone: 312-755-1900.
Facsimile: 312-755-1925.
Annapolis, Maryland Office: Suite 102, 175 Admiral Cochrane Drive.
Telephone: 410-266-8077.
Telex: 899149 (Oldtownpat).
Facsimile: 410-266-8664.
Madison, Wisconsin Office: Verex Plaza, 150 East Gilman Street, P.O. Box 1497.
Telephone: 608-257-5035.
Facsimile: 608-258-4258.
Milwaukee, Wisconsin Office: Firstar Center, 777 East Wisconsin Avenue.
Telephone: 414-271-2400.
Telex: 26-819 (Foley Lard Mil).
Facsimile: 414-297-4900.

(See Next Column)

FOLEY & LARDNER—*Continued*

Brussels, Belgium Office: Avenue Louise, 283.
Telephone: 32-2-646-2777.
Facsimile: 32-2-646-7574.

RESIDENT PARTNERS

J. Gordon Arkin	John P. Horan
Edmund T. Baxa, Jr.	Thomas K. Maurer
Jennifer S. Brown	K. Rodney May
Terence J. Delahunty, Jr.	Sybil Meloy
Mary A. Doty	Paul E. Rosenthal
Richard A. DuRose	John A. Sanders
Mark C. Extein	Ronald M. Schirtzer
Michael Gay	Kathleen L. Maloney Skambis
James S. Grodin	J. Walter Spiva
John R. Hamilton	Christi L. Underwood
Richard A. Heinle	Jon M. Wilson

R. Duke Woodson

RETIRED PARTNERS

Norman F. Burke	Francis V. Gay

Egerton K. van den Berg

SPECIAL COUNSEL

Lili C. Metcalf

RESIDENT ASSOCIATES

Ellen Avery-Smith	Christina Kennedy
Scott M. Clements	John S. Lord, Jr.
Scott A. Cookson	Michael W. McNatt
Michael D. Crosbie	Cindy L. Rodgers
Martha H. Formella	Jason A. Rosenthal
Kevin D. Fowler	Debi Vanessa Rumph
J. Andrew Hagan	Jennifer L. Slone
Michele A. Hipp	Jeffrey A. Yost

General Counsel for: The Greater Orlando Aviation Authority.
Attorneys for: Citrus Central, Inc.

For full biographical listings, see the Martindale-Hubbell Law Directory

GURNEY & HANDLEY, P.A. (AV)

225 East Robinson Street, Suite 450, 32801
Telephone: 407-843-9500
Facsimile: 407-649-4941
Email: gurney-handley@worldnet.att.net

Leon H. Handley	Ronald L. Harrop
John L. Sewell	Francis E. Pierce, III
Robert S. Green	Peter N. Smith
W. Marvin Hardy, III	Richard E. Dunegan

David Brian Falstad

Steven H. Preston	Paul D. Rang

OF COUNSEL

Richard W. Lassiter	David W. Roquemore, Jr.

Ley H. Smith

Representative Clients: Beneficial Mortgage Corp.; John Hancock Mutual Life Insurance Co.; University of Florida; Crown Bank, FSB; Colonial Bank; Empire Fire & Marine Insurance Co.

For full biographical listings, see the Martindale-Hubbell Law Directory

HILL, REIS, ADAMS, HALL & SCHIEFFELIN, P.A. (AV)

1417 East Concord Street, 32803
Telephone: 407-896-0425
Fax: 407-896-9236
Email: mainbox@hrahs.com

G. Bruce Hill	Larry D. Hall
Gregory F. Reis	Thomas L. Schieffelin, Jr.
Janet W. Adams	William W. Large

Matthew P. Bartolomei

David O Doyle, Jr	Andrew Vlahos

Heidi Jo Haycook

Representative Clients: The Florida Hospital Trust Fund; The Florida Hospital Excess Trust Fund; Florida Hospital Workers Compensation/Self Insurance Trust Fund; Bartow Memorial Hospital; Bay Medical Center; Brooksville Regional Hospital; Cape Canaveral Hospital; Cape Coral Hospital; Desoto Memorial Hospital.

For full biographical listings, see the Martindale-Hubbell Law Directory

HOLLAND & KNIGHT LLP (AV)

200 South Orange Avenue, Suite 2600, 32801
Telephone: 407-425-8500
Fax: 407-244-5288
Mailing Address: P.O. Box 1526, 32802-1526
Email: hklaw.com *URL:* http://www.hklaw.com
Atlanta, Georgia Office: 1201 West Peachtree Street, N.E., Suite 2000.
Telephone: 404-817-8500.
Fax: 404-881-0470. 34200ston, Massachusetts Office: One Beacon Street.
Telephone: 617-523-2700.
Fax: 617-523-6850.
Bradenton, Florida Office: 1001 3rd Avenue West, Suite 600.
Telephone: 941-748-7076.
Fax: 941-747-9774.
Falls, Church, Virginia Office: 3110 Fairview Park Drive, Suite 900.
Telephone: 703-645-8600.
Fax: 703-645-8610.
Fort Lauderdale, Florida Office: One East Broward Boulevard, Suite 1300.
Telephone: 954-525-1000.
Fax: 954-463-2030.
Jacksonville, Florida Office: 50 North Laura Street, Suite 3900.
Telephone: 904-353-2000.
Fax: 904-358-1872.
Lakeland, Florida Office: 92 Lake Wire Drive.
Telephone: 941-682-1161.
Fax: 941-688-1186.
Melbourne, Florida Office: 1499 South Harbor City Boulevard, Suite 201.
Telephone: 407-951-1776.
Fax: 407-951-1849.
Miami, Florida Office: 701 Brickell Avenue, Suite 3000.
Telephone: 305-374-8500.
Fax: 305-789-7799.
New York, New York Office: 195 Broadway, 24th Floor.
Telephone: 212-513-3200.
Fax: 212-385-9010.
Providence, Rhode Island Office: 50 Exchange Terrace, Suite 300, Union Station Plaza.
Telephone: 401-751-8500.
Fax: 401-553-6850.
San Francisco, California Office: 44 Montgomery Street, Suite 4050.
Telephone: 415-743-6900.
Fax: 415-743-6910.
St. Petersburg, Florida Office: 200 Central Avenue, Suite 1600.
Telephone: 727-896-7171.
Fax: 727-822-8048.
Tallahassee, Florida Office: 315 South Calhoun Street, Suite 600.
Telephone: 850-224-7000.
Fax: 850-224-8832.
Tampa, Florida Office: 400 North Ashley Drive, Suite 2300.
Telephone: 813-227-8500.
Fax: 813-229-0134.
Washington, D.C. Office: 2100 Pennsylvania Avenue, N.W., Suite 400.
Telephone: 202-955-3000.
Fax: 202-955-5564.
West Palm Beach, Florida Office: 625 North Flagler Drive, Suite 700.
Telephone: 561-833-2000.
Fax: 561-650-8399.
Mexico City, Mexico Office: HOLLAND & KNIGHT-GALLÁSTEGUI Y LOZANO, S.C. (Joint Venture Office) Avenida Paseo de los Tamarindos No. 400, Torre "B" - 2° Piso, Col. Bosques d las Lomas, C.P. 05120 Mexico, D.F.
Telephone: 011-525-261-1866.
Fax: 011-525-261-1867.
Tel Aviv, Israel Office: Holland & Knight LTD, 23 Derech Petach-Tikva, 18th Floor.
Telephone: +011-972-3-566-7666.
Fax: +011-972-3-566-7667.
Buenos Aires, Argentina Office: San Martin 323--Piso 18, 1004.
Telephone: +54-11 4324-7600.
Fax: +54-11 4324-7601.

ORLANDO MEMBERS AND ASSOCIATES

Charles W. Abbott	John W. Howell
Glenn Arthur Adams	Gregory J. Johansen
David J. Akins	Scott J. Johnson
Stephen T. Ball	David A. Jones
James H. Beusse	Kevin P. Kelly
Robert N. Blackford	Chris N. Kolos
Thomas Boroughs	Stephen R. Looney
David S. Bralow	Raymer F. Maguire, Jr.
Terence F. Brennan	C. Parkhill Mays, Jr.
Christopher C. Brockman	James M. McCrae
Mark J. Buhler	Brian A. McDowell
Thomas M. Burke	Jack C. McElroy
Mary Beth Cantrell	Howell W. Melton, Jr.
David E. Cardwell	A. Guy Neff
Randall C. Clement	Leslie King O'Neal
Louis T. M. Conti	James A. Park, III
John H. Dannecker	Mark P. Rabinowitz
Robert W. Duckworth	Jonathan D. Rich
James L. Fly	Kenneth R. Richie
William L. Grant	Rory C. Ryan
William O. E. Henry	Michael P. Sampson
J. Fraser Himes	Bradley M. Saxton

(See Next Column)

HOLLAND & KNIGHT LLP, *Orlando—Continued*

ORLANDO MEMBERS AND ASSOCIATES (Continued)

Steven R. Schooley
James E. L. Seay
Erik P. Shuman
Roger W. Sims
Lee Stuart Smith
Thomas B. Smith
Stephen W. Snively
Richard L. Stockton
Eli H. Subin
Robin L. Uricchio
Joseph J. Van Heyde, II
Christopher J. Weiss
Gary A. Whitlock
Jeffrey P. Wieland
William B. Wilson
Scott E. Wilt
Robert L. Wolter
Leighton D. Yates, Jr.
Samuel J. Zusmann, Jr.

SENIOR COUNSEL

David G. Maire
Harry H. Marvel
Enrique J. Mora

Christopher Annunziato
Brent C. Bell
Cynthia J. Brennan
Sacha M. Brown
William E. Clague
Alison Danaceau
John R. Dierking
Phillip C. Dozier
Suzanne E. Gilbert
James A. Hattaway
Scott A. Justice
Douglas A. Kelly
Todd F. Kobrin
Margaret "Amie" Kozan
Eduardo S. Lombard
L. Christian Marlin
Tom McAleavey
Robert E. McFadden
James H. McNeil, Jr.
Michael Gerard Murphy
Terry M. Sanks
Kathy Ann Webb-Harris
Kathryn B. Williams

OF COUNSEL

Richard L. Fletcher, Jr.

For full biographical listings, see the Martindale-Hubbell Law Directory

LITCHFORD & CHRISTOPHER, PROFESSIONAL ASSOCIATION (AV)

NationsBank Center, Suite 2200, 390 North Orange Avenue, P.O. Box 1549, 32802
Telephone: 407-422-6600
Telecopier: 407-841-0325
Email: lawfirm@litchris.com *URL:* http://www.litchris.com

Hal K. Litchford
Donald E. Christopher
Mark Lang
Brian D. DeGailler
David G. Lerner
Alan B. Taylor

Scott K. Lippman
G. Steven Fender
Jill Barron Dugger
Susan E. Sewell
Joanne Reed Day

Reference: Citrus Bank.

For full biographical listings, see the Martindale-Hubbell Law Directory

SHUTTS & BOWEN LLP (AV)

A Partnership including Professional Associations
20 North Orange Avenue, Suite 1000, 32801
Telephone: 407-423-3200
Telefax: 407-425-8316
URL: HTTP://WWW.SHUTTS-LAW.COM
Miami, Florida Office: 1500 Miami Center, 201 South Biscayne Boulevard.
Telephone: 305-358-6300.
Telefax: 305-381-9982.
West Palm Beach, Florida Office: One Clearlake Centre, 250 Australian Avenue, Suite 500.
Telephone: 561-835-8500.
Fax: 561-650-8530.
Tallahassee, Florida Office: 215 South Monroe Street, Suite 804.
Telephone: 850-521-0600.
Fax: 850-521-0604.
Fort Lauderdale, Florida Office: First Union Center, Suite 2000, 200 East Broward Boulevard.
Telephone: 954-524-5505.
Fax: 954-524-5506.
Amsterdam, The Netherlands Office: Shutts & Bowen, B.V., Europa Boulevard 59, 1083 AD, Amsterdam.
Telephone: (31 20) 661-0969.
Fax: (31 20) 642-1475.
London, England Office: 43 Grosvenor Street, London W1X 9PG.
Telephone: 441-71-493-4840.
Telefax: 441-71-493-4299.

MEMBERS OF FIRM

Andrew M. Brumby (Resident)
Charles Robinson Fawsett (P.A.)
Robert A. Freyer (Resident)
Scott A. Glass
Michael L. Gore (Resident)
Michael J. Grindstaff (P.A.)
Mary Ruth Houston
J. Gregory Humphries
Brian M. Jones
Rod Jones (Resident)
Patrick M. Muldowney
I. Ed Pantaleon
Robert A. Savill (Resident)
Mark D. Thomson
James G. Willard (Resident)
Kenneth W. Wright (Resident)

(See Next Column)

RESIDENT ASSOCIATES

Leann M. Brezinsky
Meredith A. Harper
Daniel T. O'Keefe
Jennifer L. Perry
Angela D. Shaw
Scott K. Spivack
David Tetrick, Jr.

For full biographical listings, see the Martindale-Hubbell Law Directory

CRAIG B. WARD, P.A. (AV)

Suite 501, 105 East Robinson Street, 32801-1601
Telephone: 407-843-6000
Fax: 407-839-0577
Email: CBWardlaw@aol.com

Craig B. Ward

OF COUNSEL

Charles D. Miner

Representative Clients: Gladco, Inc. (American Gladiators); Lake of the Woods Homeowners Association, Inc.; Metro One, Inc. (Real Estate); National Ambulance Builders, Inc.; Poole Construction Co., Inc.; Power Concrete Products Co.; Richard Sibley Associates, Inc. (Advertising); Scientific-Atlanta, Inc.
Approved Agent for: First American Title Insurance Co.; Attorneys' Title Insurance Fund.

For full biographical listings, see the Martindale-Hubbell Law Directory

ORMOND BEACH, Volusia Co.

KOREY, SWEET, MCKINNON, SIMPSON & VUKELJA (AV)

Granada Oaks Professional Building, 595 West Granada Boulevard, Suite A, 32174-9448
Telephone: 904-677-3431
Fax: 904-673-0748

MEMBERS OF FIRM

Edward F. Simpson, Jr.
Robert Kit Korey
Noah C. McKinnon, Jr. (Also Of Counsel, Coble & Simpson, Daytona Beach)
Jeffrey C. Sweet
David A. Vukelja

OF COUNSEL

Scott E. Simpson (Also Member, Coble & Simpson, Daytona Beach)

For full biographical listings, see the Martindale-Hubbell Law Directory

PALM BEACH, Palm Beach Co.

CALDWELL & PACETTI (AV)

324 Royal Palm Way, Suite #300, P.O. Box 2775, 33480-2775
Telephone: 561-655-0620
Fax: 561-655-3775
Email: floridalaw@earthlink.net

MEMBERS OF FIRM

Manley P. Caldwell (1901-1971)
Madison F. Pacetti (1914-1994)
Manley P. Caldwell, Jr.
Kenneth W. Edwards
Mary M. Viator
Charles F. Schoech
Elizabeth S. (Betsy) Burden
John A. Weig
Leonard G. Rubin

OF COUNSEL

Paul A. Turk, Jr.

Representative Clients: Estero Fire Protection District; Everglades Agricultural Area Environmental Protection District; Indian Trail Improvement District; Northern Palm Beach County Improvement District; Troup-Indiantown Water Control District; City of Belle Glade; Town of Hypoluxo; Town of Lake Clarke Shores; Village of Wellington.
Approved Attorneys For: Attorneys' Title Insurance Fund.

For full biographical listings, see the Martindale-Hubbell Law Directory

DUANE, MORRIS & HECKSCHER LLP (AV)

249 Royal Palm Way, Suite 403, 33480
Telephone: 561-366-5400
Fax: 561-366-5401
Philadelphia, Pennsylvania Office: Suite 4200, One Liberty Place.
Telephone: 215-979-1000.
Fax: 215-979-1020.
New York, New York Office: 380 Lexington Avenue.
Telephone: 212-692-1000.
Fax: 212-692-1020.
Chicago, Illinois Office: 227 West Monroe Street, Suite 3400.
Telephone: 312-499-6700.
Fax: 312-499-6701.
Washington, D.C. Office: 1667 K Street, N.W., Suite 700.
Telephone: 202-776-7800.
Fax: 202-776-7801.
San Francisco, California Office: 100 Spear Street.
Telephone: 415-371-2200.
Fax: 415-371-2201.

(See Next Column)

DUANE, MORRIS & HECKSCHER LLP—*Continued*

Boston, Massachusetts Office: One International Place, 14th Floor.
Telephone: 617-598-3100.
Fax: 617-598-3101.
Miami, Florida Office: 200 South Biscayne Boulevard, Suite 3410.
Telephone: 305-960-2200.
Fax: 305-960-2201.
Wilmington, Delaware Office: 1201 Market Street, Suite 1500.
Telephone: 302-571-5550.
Fax: 302-571-5560.
Harrisburg, Pennsylvania Office: 305 North Front Street, 5th Floor, P.O. Box 1003.
Telephone: 717-237-5500.
Fax: 717-232-4015.
Wayne, Pennsylvania Office: 735 Chesterbrook Boulevard, Suite 300.
Telephone: 610-647-3555.
Fax: 610-640-2619.
Cherry Hill, New Jersey Office: 51 Haddonfield Road, Suite 340.
Telephone: 856-488-7300.
Fax: 856-488-7021.
Newark, New Jersey Office: One Riverfront Plaza.
Telephone: 973-424-2000.
Fax: 973-424-2001.
Allentown, Pennsylvania Office: 968 Postal Road, Suite 200, P.O. Box 90400.
Telephone: 610-266-3650.
Fax: 610-266-3651.
Houston, Texas Office: One Greenway Plaza, Suite 500.
Telephone: 713-552-9900.
Fax: 713-552-0109.
Dover, Delaware Office: 314 S. State Street.
Telephone: 302-736-0156.
Fax: 302-736-0336.
Bangor, Maine Office: 15 Columbia Street, 4th Floor.
Telephone: 207-990-4800.
Fax: 207-990-4804.
Princeton, New Jersey Office: Princeton Forrestal Village, 116 Village Boulevard, Suite 200.
Telephone: 609-734-4323.
Fax: 609-734-4387.

John Harrison Hough

ASSOCIATE

Lenora J. Fowler (Not admitted in FL)

For full biographical listings, see the Martindale-Hubbell Law Directory

MURPHY, REID, PILOTTE, ORD & AUSTIN (AV)

A Partnership of Professional Associations
Suite 100, 340 Royal Palm Way, 33480
Telephone: 561-655-4060
Facsimile: 561-832-5436
Vero Beach, Florida Office: Plantation Plaza, 6606-20th Street, 32966-7902.
Telephone: 561-567-6480.
Facsimile: 561-562-0220.

Eugene W. Murphy Jr. (P.A.) — George P. Ord (P.A.)
Frank T. Pilotte (P.A.) — Keith C. Austin, Jr. (P.A.)

OF COUNSEL

Philip H. Reid

For full biographical listings, see the Martindale-Hubbell Law Directory

WINTHROP, STIMSON, PUTNAM & ROBERTS (AV)

125 Worth Avenue, Suite 310, 33480
Telephone: 561-655-7297
Telefax: 561-833-6726
URL: http://www.winstim.com
New York, N.Y. Office: One Battery Park Plaza, 10004.
Telephone: 212-858-1000.
Fax: 212-858-1500.
Stamford, Connecticut Office: Financial Centre, 695 East Main Street, P.O. Box 6760, 06904-6760.
Telephone: 203-348-2300.
Fax: 203-965-8226.
Washington, D.C. Office: 1133 Connecticut Avenue, N.W., 20036.
Telephone: 202-775-9800.
Fax: 202-833-8491.
London, England Office: 54 Lombardo Street, London, EC3V 9DH, England.
Telephone: 011-44207-648-9200.
Fax: 011-44207-283-1656.
Tokyo, Japan Office: 608 Atagoyama Bengoshi Building 6-7, Atago 1-chome, Minato-ku, Tokyo 105 Japan.
Telephone: 011-813-3437-9740.
Fax: 011-813-3437-9261.
Hong Kong, China Office: 2505 Asia Pacific Finance Tower, Citibank Plaza, 3 Garden Road, Central.
Telephone: 011-852-2530-3400.
Fax: 011-852-2530-3355.

(See Next Column)

Singapore Office: 6 Battery Road #38-01/B, Singapore 049909.
Telephone: 65-227-4700.
Fax: 65-227-4711.

MEMBERS OF FIRM

William D. McEachern — Michael V. Sterlacci

COUNSEL

John C. Dotterrer

SENIOR COUNSEL

Howard J. Falcon, Jr. — Philip G. Hull
Douglas F. Williamson, Jr.

RESIDENT ASSOCIATES

John M. McDivitt — Guy Rabideau
Pamela J. Waldorf

For full biographical listings, see the Martindale-Hubbell Law Directory

*PANAMA CITY,** Bay Co.

BRYANT AND HIGBY, CHARTERED (AV)

833 Harrison Avenue, P.O. Drawer 860, 32402-0860
Telephone: 850-763-1787
Fax: 850-785-1533

Lynn C. Higby (1938-1992) — Rowlett W. Bryant
Clifford C. Higby

Cecilia Redding Boyd

Representative Clients: Regions Bank of New Florida; City of Panama City, Florida; Panama City Port Authority; Corrections Corporation of America; Fireman's Fund Insurance Company; Auto-Owners Insurance Co.

For full biographical listings, see the Martindale-Hubbell Law Directory

RICHARD SMOAK (AV)

103 West 5th Street, P.O. Box 1006, 32402-1006
Telephone: 904-747-1900
Fax: 904-747-1910

Representative Clients: Panama City - Bay County Airport & Industrial District; Florida Physicians Insurance Co.; National Casualty Co.; Church Mutual Insurance Co.; Arizona Chemical Co.; Bay Bank & Trust Co.; Mutual of Omaha Insurance Co.; Ranger Insurance Co.; St. Paul Fire & Marine Insurance Co.; Stone Container Corp.

For full biographical listings, see the Martindale-Hubbell Law Directory

*PENSACOLA,** Escambia Co.

BEGGS & LANE (AV)

Seventh Floor, Blount Building, 3 West Garden Street, P.O. Box 12950, 32576-2950
Telephone: 850-432-2451
Telecopier: 850-469-3330
URL: http://www.beggslane.com

MEMBERS OF FIRM

E. Dixie Beggs (Retired) — Ralph A. Peterson
Bert H. Lane (1917-1981) — Gary B. Leuchtman
Robert P. Gaines — John P. Daniel
W. Spencer Mitchem — Jeffrey A. Stone
James M. Weber — James S. Campbell
John F. Windham — David L. McGee
J. Nixon Daniel, III — Russell F. Van Sickle

ASSOCIATES

Russell A. Badders — Mary Jane Thies
Charles T. Wiggins

OF COUNSEL

Robert L. Crongeyer

For full biographical listings, see the Martindale-Hubbell Law Directory

CARLTON, FIELDS, WARD, EMMANUEL, SMITH & CUTLER, P.A. (AV)

Harbourview Building, 25 West Cedar Street, 4th Floor (32501-5974), P.O. Box 12426, 32582-2426
Telephone: 850-434-0142
Fax: (850) 434-5366
URL: http://wwwcarltonfields.com
Miami, Florida Office: 4000 International Place, 100 S.E. Second Street, 33131-9101, P.O. Box 019101, 33131-9101.
Telephone: 305-530-0050.
Orlando, Florida Office: Citrus Center, 255 South Orange Avenue, Suite 1600, 32801-3488, P.O. Box 1171, 32802-1171.
Telephone: 407-849-0300.
St. Petersburg, Florida Office: One Progress Plaza, 200 Central Avenue, Suite 2300, 33701-4352, P.O. Box 2861, 33731-2861.
Telephone: 727-821-7000.
Tallahassee, Florida Office: 215 South Monroe Street, Suite 500, 32301-1866, P.O. Drawer 190, 32302-0190.
Telephone: 850-224-1585.

(See Next Column)

CARLTON, FIELDS, WARD, EMMANUEL, SMITH & CUTLER P.A., *Pensacola—Continued*

Tampa, Florida Office: One Harbour Place, 777 South Harbour Island Boulevard, 33602-5799, P.O. Box 3239, 33601-3239.
Telephone: 813-223-7000.
West Palm Beach, Florida Office: Esperanté, 222 Lakeview Avenue, Suite 1400, 33401-6149, P.O. Box 150, 33402-0150.
Telephone: 561-659-7070.

Millard Lane Fretland
Bill B. McEachern, Jr.
Wright Moulton
Stephen L. Walker

Carol A. Ruebsamen
Lawrence C. Schill

For full biographical listings, see the Martindale-Hubbell Law Directory

SHELL, FLEMING, DAVIS & MENGE, P.A. (AV)

Ninth Floor Seville Tower, P.O. Box 1831, 32598-1831
Telephone: 850-434-2411
Fax: 850-435-1074
Email: info@shellfleming-law.com *URL:* http://www.shellfleming-law.com

Thurston A. Shell
Fletcher Fleming
Rollin D. Davis, Jr.
M. J. Menge
Danny L. Kepner
Charles L. Hoffman, Jr.
Stephen B. Shell
Maureen Duignan
Jan Shackelford
Paul W. Groom II
John B. Trawick
Braden K. Ball, Jr.
Thomas J. Gilliam, Jr.

For full biographical listings, see the Martindale-Hubbell Law Directory

SMITH, SAUER & DEMARIA (AV)

510 East Zaragoza, P.O. Box 12446, 32582-2446
Telephone: 850-434-2761
Fax: 850-438-8860
Email: 76666.3265@COMPUSERVE.COM

G. Thomas Smith
Jeffrey T. Sauer
Kathleen K. DeMaria

Representative Clients: Exxon Corp.; Amerada Hess; EastGroup Properties; American General.

For full biographical listings, see the Martindale-Hubbell Law Directory

PLANT CITY, Hillsborough Co.

TRINKLE, REDMAN, SWANSON, BYRD & COTON, P.A. (AV)

121 North Collins, P.O. Box P.O.Drawer TT, 33566
Telephone: 813-752-6133
Fax: 813-754-8957

John R. Trinkle (1901-1969)
Robert S. Trinkle
James L. Redman
Conrad Swanson
Johnnie B. Byrd, Jr.
Daniel M. Coton

Deborah R. Tracy
James C. Davis, II

General Counsel for: Sunshine State Federal Savings and Loan Assn.; Withlacoochee River Electric Cooperative, Inc.

For full biographical listings, see the Martindale-Hubbell Law Directory

PORT CHARLOTTE, Charlotte Co.

WILKINS, FROHLICH, JONES, HEVIA, RUSSELL & SUTTER, P.A. (AV)

18501 Murdock Circle, Sixth Floor, 33948
Telephone: 941-625-0700
Telecopier: 941-625-9540
Email: wilkins@wilkinslaw.com

Gary L. Wilkins
W. Cort Frohlich
Phillip J. Jones
Jesus M. Hevia
W. Kevin Russell
Brian O. Sutter
Louise O. Hanaoka
Victor G. Santiago

For full biographical listings, see the Martindale-Hubbell Law Directory

*PUNTA GORDA,** Charlotte Co.

FARR, FARR, EMERICH, SIFRIT, HACKETT AND CARR, P.A. (AV)

115 West Olympia Avenue, P.O. Drawer 1447, 33951
Telephone: 941-639-1158
Telecopier: 941-639-0028
Port Charlotte, Florida Office: 2315 Aaron Street, P.O. Box 2159, 33949.
Telephone: 941-625-6171.
Telecopier: 941-624-4557.

Earl D. Farr (1900-1988)
Guy S. Emerich
Jack O. Hackett II
Michael P. Haymans
Connie M. Schider
Mark A. Draper
Robert C. Sifrit (Resident, Port Charlotte Office)

(See Next Column)

Charles T. Boyle (Resident, Port Charlotte Office)
Darol H. M. Carr (Resident, Port Charlotte Office)
Cynthia S. Murphy (Resident, Port Charlotte Office)
David A. Holmes (Resident, Port Charlotte Office)

Jennifer R. Howell

OF COUNSEL

Earl Drayton Farr, Jr.

Representative Clients: Babcock Florida Co.; Sunset Realty Corp.
Approved Attorneys for: Chicago Title Insurance Co.

For full biographical listings, see the Martindale-Hubbell Law Directory

*QUINCY,** Gadsden Co.

LINES, HINSON AND LINES (AV)

121 North Madison Street, P.O. Box 550, 32353-0550
Telephone: 850-875-1300
Telecopier: 850-875-1350
Email: blines@net360.com

MEMBERS OF FIRM

William D. Lines (1914-1992)
Alexander L. Hinson
Blucher B. Lines

Representative Clients: Talquin Electric Cooperative, Inc.; The Quincy State Bank; Quincy Telephone Co.; Georgia Pacific Corp.; Capital City Bank.

For full biographical listings, see the Martindale-Hubbell Law Directory

*ST. AUGUSTINE,** St. Johns Co.

UPCHURCH, BAILEY & UPCHURCH, P.A. (AV)

780 North Ponce de Leon Boulevard, P.O. Drawer 3007, 32085-3007
Telephone: 904-829-9066
Facsimile: 904-825-4862
Email: info@ubulaw.com

John D. Bailey, Jr.
Frank D. Upchurch, III
Tracy Wilson Upchurch
Sidney F. Ansbacher
Katherine Gaertner Jones
Michael A. Siragusa
Stephen A. Faustini

OF COUNSEL

Frank D. Upchurch, Sr. (1894-1987)
Frank D. Upchurch, Jr.
Hamilton D. Upchurch

Representative Clients: Aero Sport, Inc.; American Culinary Federation, Inc.; Penney Retirement Community, Inc.; St. Augustine Alligator Farm, Inc.; St. Augustine-St. Johns County Board of Realtors, Inc.; Shriners Hospitals for Children; Mobro Marine, Inc.; Florida Rock & Tank Lines, Inc.; Hercules, Inc.

For full biographical listings, see the Martindale-Hubbell Law Directory

ST. PETERSBURG, Pinellas Co.

ALLAN & SHIPP, P.A. (AV)

6675 Thirteenth Avenue North, Suite 2C, 33710
Telephone: 813-381-9800
Fax: 813-381-1155
Email: law@allan-shipp.com
Clearwater, Florida Office: 2633 McCormick Drive, Suite 101, 34619.
Telephone: 813-799-7000.
Fax: 813-381-1155.

Linda R. Allan
Wayne E. Shipp

Stephen A. Baker
Terry J. Deeb
Jeffrey L. Hinds

For full biographical listings, see the Martindale-Hubbell Law Directory

CARLTON, FIELDS, WARD, EMMANUEL, SMITH & CUTLER, P.A. (AV)

One Progress Plaza, 200 Central Avenue, Suite 2300 (33701-4352), P.O. Box 2861, 33731-2861
Telephone: 727-821-7000
Fax: 727-822-3768
URL: http://www.carltonfields.com
Miami, Florida Office: 4000 International Place, 100 S.E. Second Street, 33131-9101, P.O. Box 019101, 33131-9101.
Telephone: 305-530-0050.
Orlando, Florida Office: Citrus Center, 255 South Orange Avenue, Suite 1600, 32801-3488, P.O. Box 1171, 32802-1171.
Telephone: 407-849-0300.
Pensacola, Florida Office: Harbourview Building, 25 West Cedar Street, 4th Floor, 32501-5974, P.O. Box 12426, 32582-2426.
Telephone: 850-434-0142.
Tallahassee, Florida Office: 215 South Monroe Street, Suite 500, 32301-1866, P.O. Drawer 190, 32302-0190.
Telephone: 850-224-1585.
Tampa, Florida Office: One Harbour Place, 777 South Harbour Island Boulevard, 33602-5799, P.O. Box 3239, 33601-3239.
Telephone: 813-223-7000.

(See Next Column)

CARLTON, FIELDS, WARD, EMMANUEL, SMITH & CUTLER P.A.—*Continued*

West Palm Beach, Florida Office: Esperanté, 222 Lakeview Avenue, Suite 1400, 33401-6149, P.O. Box 150, 33402-0150.
Telephone: 561-659-7070.

Steven C. Dupré
Joel B. Giles
David G. Mulock
David R. Punzak
Lee H. Rightmyer
Gary L. Sasso
Ronald L. Stephenson
Sylvia H. Walbolt
J. Michael Walls

Robert E. Biasotti
Jill H. Bowman
Matthew J. Conigliaro
Joseph Hagedorn Lang, Jr
Scott J. Sternberg

For full biographical listings, see the Martindale-Hubbell Law Directory

HOLLAND & KNIGHT LLP (AV)

200 Central Avenue, Suite 1600, 33701-3845
Telephone: 727-896-7171
Fax: 727-822-8048
Mailing Address: P.O. Box 3542, 33731-3542
Email: hklaw.com *URL:* http://www.hklaw.com
Atlanta, Georgia Office: 1201 West Peachtree Street, N.E., Suite 2000.
Telephone: 404-817-8500.
Fax: 404-881-0470.
Boston, Massachusetts Office: One Beacon Street.
Telephone: 617-523-2700.
Fax: 617-523-6850.
Bradenton, Florida Office: 1001 3rd Avenue West, Suite 600.
Telephone: 941-748-7076.
Fax: 941-747-9774.
Falls Church, Florida Office: 3110 Fairview Park Drive, Suite 900.
Telephone: 703-645-8600.
Fax: 703-645-8610.
Fort Lauderdale, Florida Office: One East Broward Boulevard, Suite 1300.
Telephone: 954-525-1000.
Fax: 954-463-2030.
Jacksonville, Florida Office: 50 North Laura Street, Suite 3900.
Telephone: 904-353-2000.
Fax: 904-358-1872.
Lakeland, Florida Office: 92 Lake Wire Drive.
Telephone: 941-682-1161.
Fax: 941-688-1186.
Melbourne, Florida Office: 1499 South Harbor City Boulevard, Suite 201.
Telephone: 407-951-1776.
Fax: 407-951-1849.
Miami, Florida Office: 701 Brickell Avenue, Suite 3000.
Telephone: 305-374-8500.
Fax: 305-789-7799.
New York, New York Office: 195 Broadway, 24th Floor.
Telephone: 212-513-3200.
Fax: 212-385-9010.
Orlando, Florida Office: 200 South Orange Avenue, Suite 2600.
Telephone: 407-425-8500.
Fax: 407-244-5288.
Providence, Rhode Island Office: 50 Exchange Terrace, Suite 300, Union Station Plaza.
Telephone: 401-751-8500.
Fax: 401-553-6850.
San Francisco, California Office: 44 Montgomery Street, Suite 4050.
Telephone: 415-743-6900.
Fax: 415-743-6910.
Tallahassee, Florida Office: 315 South Calhoun Street, Suite 600.
Telephone: 850-224-7000.
Fax: 850-224-8832.
Tampa, Florida Office: 400 North Ashley Drive, Suite 2300.
Telephone: 813-227-8500.
Fax: 813-229-0134.
Washington, D.C. Office: 2100 Pennsylvania Avenue, N.W., Suite 400.
Telephone: 202-955-3000.
Fax: 202-955-5564.
West Palm Beach, Florida Office: 625 North Flagler Drive, Suite 700.
Telephone: 561-833-2000.
Fax: 561-650-8399.
Mexico City, Mexico Office: HOLLAND & KNIGHT-GALLÁSTEGUI Y LOZANO, S.C. (Joint Venture Office) Avenida Paseo de los Tamarindos No. 400, Torre "B" - 2° Piso, Col. Bosques d las Lomas, C.P. 05120 Mexico, D.F.
Telephone: 011-525-261-1866.
Fax: 011-525-261-1867.
Tel Aviv, Israel Office: Holland & Knight LTD, 23 Derech Petach-Tikva, 18th Floor.
Telephone: +011-972-3-566-7666.
Fax: +011-972-3-566-7667.
Buenos Aires, Argentina Office: San Martin 323--Piso 18, 1004.
Telephone: +54-11 4324-7600.
Fax: +54-11 4324-7601.

(See Next Column)

William H. Bartlett
Allan B. Davis
Gerald D. Davis
Homer Duvall, III
Joseph W. Fleece
Joseph W. Fleece, III
Michael D. D. Geldart
Roy G. Harrell, Jr.
Richard O. Jacobs
S. Curtis Kiser
William R. Lane, Jr.
G. Dennis Lynn, Jr.
Bruce Marger
R. Donald Mastry
Charles W. Ross

SENIOR COUNSEL

Stephen C. Chumbris

Lisa B. Dodge
Karen M. Kelly
David M. King
Cynthia A. Mikos
Augustine S. Weekley, Jr.
Doreen Stone Young

OF COUNSEL

John P. Higgins

For full biographical listings, see the Martindale-Hubbell Law Directory

*SANFORD,** Seminole Co.

STENSTROM, MCINTOSH, COLBERT, WHIGHAM & SIMMONS, P.A. (AV)

200 West First, Suite 22, P.O. Box 4848, 32772-4848
Telephone: 407-322-2171
Fax: 407-330-2379
Orlando/Winterpark Telephone: 407-834-5119
DeLand/DeBary Telephone: 407-668-1479
URL: http://www.stenstrom.com

Thomas E. Whigham (1952-1988)
Douglas Stenstrom (Retired)
William L. Colbert
Franklin C. Whigham
Clayton D. Simmons
Robert K. McIntosh
Donna L. Surratt-McIntosh
William E. Reischmann, Jr.

Catherine D. Reischmann
James J. Partlow
Dawn M. Harrison

OF COUNSEL

Kenneth W. McIntosh
S. Kirby Moncrief

Representative Clients: City of Sanford; City of Oviedo; City of Casselberry; Seminole Community College; City of Lake Mary; Sanford Housing Authority; City of DeBary; Seminole Soccer Club, Inc.; Tuskawilla Homeowners' Association; South Seminole-North Orange Wastewater Transmission Authority.

For full biographical listings, see the Martindale-Hubbell Law Directory

*SARASOTA,** Sarasota Co.

BOWMAN, GEORGE, SCHEB, TOALE & ROBINSON, P.A. (AV)

22 South Tuttle Avenue, Suite 3, 34237
Telephone: 941-366-5510
FAX: 941-951-0839

John F. Burket (1875-1947)
John F. Burket, Jr. (1915-1984)
V. Morris Smith (1921-1996)
James J. Drymon (Retired)
I. W. Whitesell, Jr. (Retired)
David G. Bowman, Sr.
Eugene O. George
Robert P. Scheb
James E. Toale
David G. Bowman, Jr.
Robert K. Robinson
Charles D. Bailey, III

For full biographical listings, see the Martindale-Hubbell Law Directory

DICKINSON & GIBBONS, P.A. (AV)

1750 Ringling Boulevard, P.O. Box 3979, 34230
Telephone: 941-366-4680
FAX: 941-953-3136
URL: http://dglawyers.com

Francis C. Dart (1902-1972)
Gary H. Larsen
Camden T. French
Ralph L. Marchbank, Jr.
A. James Rolfes
Burwell J. Jones
Richard R. Garland
Stephen G. Brannan
Deborah J. Blue
Jeffrey D. Peairs
David S. Preston
Michael P. Murphy
Kelly S. Weaver
S. Mathew Whyte

OF COUNSEL

Patrick H. Dickinson
G. Hunter Gibbons
Ward E. Dahlgren

LEGAL SUPPORT PERSONNEL

Janet E. Gadoury (Certified Legal Assistant)
Karin M. Turner (Certified Legal Assistant)
Carol A. Owsianka (Legal Assistant)
Susanne B. Bailey (Legal Assistant)
Cathy Webster (Paralegal)
Rachel A. Brown (Paralegal)
Ron Selby
William Henley
Katherine Lloyd (Paralegal)

Representative Clients: Ford Motor Co.; Florida Power & Light Co.; Squibb Corp.

(See Next Column)

DICKINSON & GIBBONS P.A., *Sarasota—Continued*

Insurance Clients: Liberty Mutual Insurance Co.; Allstate Insurance Co.; Nationwide Insurance Group; Ohio Casualty Insurance Co.; United States Fidelity & Guaranty Co.; State Farm Insurance Company.

For full biographical listings, see the Martindale-Hubbell Law Directory

NELSON • HESSE (AV)

2070 Ringling Boulevard, P.O. Box 2524, 34230
Telephone: 941-366-7550
Fax: 941-955-3708

MEMBERS OF FIRM

Richard E. Nelson
Ronald Alexander Cyril (1938-1988)
Richard L. Smith
F. Steven Herb
Omer S. Causey
William A. Dooley
Michael S. Drews
Frederick J. Elbrecht
Gary W. Peal

ASSOCIATES

J. Neal Mobley
J. Corey Feist
Alison Hosmer

General Counsel for: Provident Bank; Dooley Mack Construction Co.
Representative Clients: Wellcraft Marine; American Marine Holdings; Vanliner Insurance; Time Warner Cable; SMH Radiology, Inc.; The Carlton Ranch, Inc.
References: Southtrust Bank; Provident Bank.

For full biographical listings, see the Martindale-Hubbell Law Directory

WILLIAMS, PARKER, HARRISON, DIETZ & GETZEN, PROFESSIONAL ASSOCIATION (AV)

200 South Orange Avenue, 34236-6749
Telephone: 941-366-4800
Telecopier: 941-366-5109
Mailing Address: P.O. Box 3258, Sarasota, Florida, 34230-3258
Email: infodesk@williamsparker.com *URL:* http://www.williamsparker.com

J.J. Williams, Jr. (1886-1968)
W. Davis Parker (1920-1982)
William T. Harrison, Jr.
George A. Dietz
Monte K. Marshall
James L. Ritchey
Hugh McPheeters, Jr.
William G. Lambrecht
John T. Berteau
John V. Cannon, III
Charles D. Bailey, Jr.
J. Michael Hartenstine
Michele B. Grimes
James L. Turner
William M. Seider
Elizabeth C. Marshall
Robert W. Benjamin
Frank Strelec
Terri Salt Costa
David A. Wallace
Mark A. Schwartz
Ric Gregoria
M. Lewis Hall, III
Jeffrey A. Grebe
John L. Moore
Linda R. Getzen
Morgan R. Bentley
Elvin W. Phillips
Susan Barrett Hecker
Carol Ann Kalish
Kimberly Page Walker
J. Hugh Middlebrooks
R. David Bustard
R. Scott Collins
Joan Bradbury Kayser
Patrick W. Ryskamp
E. John Wagner, II

OF COUNSEL

William E. Getzen
Frazer F. Hilder

LEGAL SUPPORT PERSONNEL

Mark Loveridge (Land Planner)

General Counsel for: Sarasota County Public Hospital Board; Sarasota-Manatee Airport Authority; Taylor Woodrow Homes Ltd.; FCCI Mutual Insurance Co.
Local Counsel for: Bank of America; Northern Trust Bank of Florida; SunTrust Bank, Gulfcoast.

For full biographical listings, see the Martindale-Hubbell Law Directory

*SEBRING,** Highlands Co.

SWAINE, HARRIS, SHEEHAN & McCLURE, P.A. (AV)

425 South Commerce Avenue, 33870
Telephone: 941-385-1549
Fax: 941-471-0008
Email: shsmlaw@ct.net *URL:* http://www.lawyers.com/shsmlaw
Lake Placid, Florida Office: 212 Interlake Boulevard, P.O. Box 548.
Telephone: 813-465-2811.
Fax: 813-465-6999. E-Mail: lplaw@ct.net.

J. Michael Swaine
Bert J. Harris, III
John K. McClure
J. Timothy Sheehan

Kimberly L. Sapp

Representative Clients: Barnett Bank; Lykes Bros., Inc.; City of Sebring; City of Lake Placid; Lakeshore Mall.
Approved Attorneys for: Attorneys' Title Insurance Fund.

For full biographical listings, see the Martindale-Hubbell Law Directory

*STUART,** Martin Co.

McCARTHY, SUMMERS, BOBKO, McKEY, WOOD & SAWYER, P.A. (AV)

2081 East Ocean Boulevard, Second Floor, 34996
Telephone: 561-286-1700
Fax: 561-283-1803
URL: http://www.mcsumm.com

Terence P. McCarthy
Robert P. Summers
Noel A. Bobko
John D. McKey, Jr.
Steven J. Wood
Thomas R. Sawyer
Nicola J. Boone
Steven L. Perry

Kathryn C. Bass
Robert N. Maitland, II

Representative Clients: First National Bank and Trust Company of the Treasure Coast; Hydratech Utilities; Lost Lake at Hobe Sound; Gary Player Design Group; YMCA of Martin County; Shadow Lakes Groves, Inc.; Merrill Lynch Trust Co., (Florida); Wilmington Trust, FSB; The Huntington National Bank, N.A.; WSTU-Radio, WTCN-TV.

For full biographical listings, see the Martindale-Hubbell Law Directory

*TALLAHASSEE,** Leon Co.

AUSLEY & McMULLEN, P.A. (AV)

Washington Square Building, 227 South Calhoun Street, P.O. Box 391, 32302
Telephone: 850-224-9115
Fax: 850-222-7560

John K. Aurell
DuBose Ausley
Margaret B. Ausley
James D. Beasley
John R. Beranek
C. Graham Carothers
Kevin J. Carroll
Robert N. Clarke, Jr.
J. Marshall Conrad
Timothy B. Elliott
Stephen C. Emmanuel
John P. Fons
Michael J. Glazer
Kenneth R. Hart
David J. Hull
Deborah Stephens Minnis
Robert A. Pierce
M. Julian Proctor, Jr.
H. Palmer Proctor
Steven P. Seymoe
James Harold Thompson
J. Jeffry Wahlen
Emily S. Waugh
C. Gary Williams
Lee L. Willis

Jason B. Gonzalez
William H. Hollimon
Martin B. Sipple
Craig D. Varn

LEGAL SUPPORT PERSONNEL

GOVERNMENTAL LIAISON

Stephen D. Dyal

ADMINISTRATOR

Ronald C. Callen

Representative Clients: BellSouth Telecommunications, Inc.; Capital City Bank Group, Inc.; CSX Transportation, Inc.; Tenet Healthcare Corporation; Sprint Corp./United Telephone; Tampa Electric Co.

For full biographical listings, see the Martindale-Hubbell Law Directory

BROAD AND CASSEL (AV)

A Partnership including Professional Associations
215 South Monroe Street, Suite 400, P.O. Box 11300, 32301
Telephone: 850-681-6810
Telecopier: 850-681-9792
URL: http://www.broadandcassel.com
Boca Raton, Florida Office: Corporate Centre at Boca Raton, Suite 300, 7777 Glades Road, 33434.
Telephone: 561-483-7000.
Fort Lauderdale, Florida Office: Suite 1130, Broward Financial Centre, 500 E. Broward Boulevard, 33394.
Telephone: 954-764-7060.
Miami, Florida Office: Miami Center, 201 South Biscayne Boulevard, Suite 3000, 33131.
Telephone: 305-373-9400.
Orlando, Florida Office: 390 N. Orange Avenue, Suite 1100, 32801.
Telephone: 407-839-4200.
Tampa, Florida Office: 100 North Tampa, Suite 3500, 33602.
Telephone: 813-225-3020.
West Palm Beach, Florida Office: The Reflections Office Centre, 400 Australian Avenue, South, Fifth Floor, 33401.
Telephone: 561-832-3300.

(See Next Column)

BROAD AND CASSEL—*Continued*

RESIDENT ATTORNEYS

M. Stephen Turner (P.A.)	Jay Adams (P.A.)
Ralph C. Datillio	Jodi L. Chase
Douglas L. Mannheimer (P.A.)	Donna H. Stinson
Charles S. Stratton (P.A.)	Gail E. Ferguson
David K. Miller (P.A.)	Jennifer A. Winegardner
Kelly Overstreet Johnson (P.A.)	R. Davis Thomas, Jr. (Not admitted in FL)
Mark D. Tucker	

Craig S. Farringer

For full biographical listings, see the Martindale-Hubbell Law Directory

CARLTON, FIELDS, WARD, EMMANUEL, SMITH & CUTLER, P.A. (AV)

215 South Monroe Street, Suite 500 (32301-1866), P.O. Drawer 190, 32302-0190
Telephone: 850-224-1585
Fax: (850) 222-0398
URL: http://www.carltonfields.com
Miami, Florida Office: 4000 International Place, 100 S.E. Second Street, 33131-9101, P.O. Box 019101, 33131-9101.
Telephone: 305-530-0050.
Orlando, Florida Office: Citrus Center, 255 South Orange Avenue, Suite 1600, 32801-3488, P.O Box 1171, 32802-1171.
Telephone: 407-849-0300.
Pensacola, Florida Office: Harbourview Building, 25 West Cedar Street, 4th Floor, 32501-5974, P. O. Box 12426, 32582-2426.
Telephone: 850-434-0142.
St. Petersburg, Florida Office: One Progress Plaza, 200 Lakeview Avenue, Suite 2300, 33701-4352, P.O. Box 2861, 33731-2861.
Telephone: 727-821-7000.
Tampa, Florida Office: One Harbour Place, 777 South Harbour Island Boulevard, 33602-5799, P.O. Box 3239, 33601-3239.
Telephone: 813-223-7000.
West Palm Beach, Florida Office: Esperanté, 222 Lakeview Avenue, Suite 1400, 33401-6149, P.O. Box 150, 33402-0150.
Telephone: 561-659-7070.

Martha Harrell Chumbler	F. Townsend Hawkes
Davisson F. Dunlap, Jr.	Nancy G. Linnan
W. Douglas Hall	Steven M. Malono

Robert W. Pass

Kelly A. Cruz-Brown	Cristin C. Gieser
Michael Patrick Donaldson	Lannie D. Hough, Jr.

For full biographical listings, see the Martindale-Hubbell Law Directory

FOLEY & LARDNER (AV)

300 East Park Avenue, P.O. Box 1454, 32302-0508
Telephone: 850-222-6100
Facsimile: 850-561-6475
Email: foleylardner@worldnet.att.net *URL:* http://www.foleylardner.com
Los Angeles, California Office: 2029 Century Park East, 35th Floor.
Telephone: 310-277-2223.
Fax: 310-557-8475.
Sacramento, California Office: 300 Capitol Mall, Suite 1125.
Telephone: 916-443-8005.
Fax: 916-443-2240.
San Diego, California Office: 402 West Broadway, 23rd Floor.
Telephone: 619-234-6655.
Fax: 619-234-3510.
San Francisco, California Office: One Maritime Plaza, Sixth Floor.
Telephone: 415-434-4484.
Fax: 415-434-4507.
Denver, Colorado Office: 1999 Broadway, Suite 2560.
Telephone: 303-297-0260.
Fax: 303-297-0266.
Washington, D.C. Office: Washington Harbour, Suite 500, 3000 K Street, N.W.
Telephone: 202-672-5300.
Telex: 904136 (Foley Lard Wash).
Facsimile: 202-672-5399.
Jacksonville, Florida Office: The Greenleaf Building, 200 Laura Street. P.O. Box 240.
Telephone: 904-359-2000.
Facsimile: 904-359-8700.
Orlando, Florida Office: Suite 1800, 111 North Orange Avenue, P.O. Box 2193.
Telephone: 407-423-7656.
Facsimile: 407-648-1743.
Tampa, Florida Offices: Suite 2700, One Hundred N. Tampa Street, P.O. Box 3391.
Telephones: 813-229-2300; Pinellas County: 813-442-3296.
Facsimile: 813-221-4210.
West Palm Beach, Florida Office: Suite 200, Phillips Point East Tower, 777 South Flagler Drive.
Telephone: 561-655-5050.
Facsimile: 561-655-6925.

(See Next Column)

Chicago, Illinois Office: Suite 3300, One IBM Plaza, 330 N. Wabash Avenue.
Telephone: 312-755-1900.
Facsimile: 312-755-1925.
Annapolis, Maryland Office: Suite 102, 175 Admiral Cochrane Drive.
Telephone: 410-266-8077.
Telex: 899149 (Oldtownpat).
Facsimile: 410-266-8664.
Madison, Wisconsin Office: Verex Plaza, 150 East Gilman Street, P.O. Box 1497.
Telephone: 608-257-5035.
Facsimile: 608-258-4258.
Milwaukee, Wisconsin Office: Firstar Center, 777 East Wisconsin Avenue.
Telephone: 414-271-2400.
Telex: 26-819 (Foley Lard Mil).
Facsimile: 414-297-4900.
Brussels, Belgium Office: Avenue Louise, 283.
Telephone: 32-2-646-2777.
Facsimile: 32-2-646-7574.

RESIDENT PARTNERS

Frederick L. Bateman, Jr.	Thomas J. Maida
Guy O. Farmer II	Austin B. Neal
Kevin G. Fitzgerald	Charles J. Schreiber, Jr.
Clyde W. (Billy) Galloway, Jr.	Glenda L. Thornton
Kevin E. Hyde	Walter H. Wolfe, Jr.

RESIDENT OF COUNSEL

Joseph W. Jacobs

ASSOCIATES

Wendy D. Brewer	Mari M. Presley
Michael E. Kinney	N. Wes Strickland

For full biographical listings, see the Martindale-Hubbell Law Directory

HENRY, BUCHANAN, HUDSON, SUBER & CARTER, P.A. (AV)

117 South Gadsden Street P.O. Drawer 1049, 32302
Telephone: 850-222-2920
Telecopier: 850-224-0034
Affiliated with Henry, Buchanan, Hudson, Suber, Carter & Kaywell, L.C., 201 West Marion Avenue, Suite 207, Punta Gorda, Florida, 33950.
Telephone: 941-639-4343.
Fax: 941-639-7121.

Bryan W. Henry (1925-1986)	Jesse F. Suber
John D. Buchanan, Jr.	J. Steven Carter
Edwin R. Hudson	Laura Beth Faragasso

SPECIAL COUNSEL

James W. Kaywell

Reference: Barnett Bank of Tallahassee, Inc.

For full biographical listings, see the Martindale-Hubbell Law Directory

HOLLAND & KNIGHT LLP (AV)

315 South Calhoun Street, Suite 600, 32301
Telephone: 850-224-7000
Fax: 850-224-8832
Mailing Address: P.O. Drawer 810, 32302
Email: hklaw.com *URL:* http://www.hklaw.com
Atlanta, Georgia Office: 1201 West Peachtree Street, N.E., Suite 2000.
Telephone: 404-817-8500.
Fax: 404-881-0470.
Boston, Massachusetts Office: One Beacon Street.
Telephone: 617-523-2700.
Fax: 617-523-6850.
Bradenton, Florida Office: 1001 3rd Avenue West, Suite 600.
Telephone: 941-941-748-7076.
Fax: 941-747-9774.
Falls Church, Virginia Office: 3110 Fairview Park Drive, Suite 900.
Telephone: 703-645-8600.
Fax: 703-645-8610.
Fort Lauderdale, Florida Office: One East Broward Boulevard, Suite 1300.
Telephone: 954-525-1000.
Fax: 954-463-2030.
Jacksonville, Florida Office: 50 North Laura Street, Suite 3900.
Telephone: 904-353-2000.
Fax: 904-358-1872.
Lakeland, Florida Office: 92 Lake Wire Drive.
Telephone: 941-682-1161.
Fax: 941-688-1186.
Melbourne, Florida Office: 1499 South Harbor City Boulevard, Suite 201.
Telephone: 407-951-1776.
Fax: 407-951-1849.
Miami, Florida Office: 701 Brickell Avenue, Suite 3000.
Telephone: 305-374-8500.
Fax: 305-789-7799.
New York, New York Office: 195 Broadway, 24th Floor.
Telephone: 212-513-3200.
Fax: 212-385-9010.
Orlando, Florida Office: 200 South Orange Avenue, Suite 2600.
Telephone: 407-425-8500.
Fax: 407-244-5288.

(See Next Column)

HOLLAND & KNIGHT LLP, *Tallahassee—Continued*

San Francisco, California Office: 44 Montgomery Street.
Telephone: 415-743-6900.
Fax: 415-743-6910.
St. Petersburg, Florida: 200 Central Avenue Suite 1600.
Telephone: 813-896-7171.
Fax: 813-822-8048.
Tampa, Florida Office: 400 North Ashley Drive, Suite 2300.
Telephone: 813-227-8500.
Fax: 813-229-0134.
Washington, D.C. Office: 2100 Pennsylvania Avenue, N.W., Suite 400.
Telephone: 202-922-3000.
Fax: 202-955-5564.
West Palm Beach, Florida Office: 625 North Flagler Drive, Suite 700.
Telephone: 561-833-2000.
Fax: 561-650-8399.
Providence, Rhode Island Office: 50 Exchange Terrace, Suite 300, Union Station Plaza.
Telephone: 401-751-8500.
Fax: 401-553-6850.
Mexico City, Mexico Office: HOLLAND & KNIGHT-GALLÁSTEGUI Y LOZANO, S.C. (Joint Venture Office) Avenida Paseo de los Tamarindos No. 400, Torre "B" - 2° Piso, Col. Bosques d las Lomas, C.P. 05120 Mexico, D.F.
Telephone: 011-525-261-1866.
Fax: 011-525-261-1867.
Tel Aviv, Israel Office: 23 Derech Petach-Tikva, 18th Floor.
Telephone: +011 972 (3) 566-7666.
Fax: +011 972 (3) 566-7667.
Buenos Aires, Argentina Office: San Martin 323--Piso 18, 1004.
Telephone: +54-11 4324-7600.
Fax: +54-11 4324-7601.

TALLAHASSEE MEMBERS AND ASSOCIATES

Martha W. Barnett
Elizabeth Bevington
Hume F. Coleman
Lawrence N. Curtin
Harry R. Detwiler, Jr.
James Mann Ervin, Jr.
Robert R. Feagin, III
Stephen H. Grimes
Stephen F. Hanlon
Jerome W. Hoffman
Mark E. Holcomb
Thomas J. Jones
S. Curtis Kiser
David Bruce May, Jr.
Morris H. Miller
Samuel J. Morley
Lawrence E. Sellers, Jr.
William D. Townsend
Susan L. Turner
Steven J. Uhlfelder
Nina M. Zollo

James R. Daughton Jr.
Shannon B. Hartsfield
Jennifer P. LaVia
Merideth C. Nagel
Susan L. Stephens
Karen D. Walker
Eddie Williams, III (Not admitted in FL)

For full biographical listings, see the Martindale-Hubbell Law Directory

MARILYN J. MARSHALL (AV)

254 East Sixth Avenue, 32303
Telephone: 850-561-0707
Fax: 850-561-0708
Email: mjmarshall@aol.com

For full biographical listings, see the Martindale-Hubbell Law Directory

PENNINGTON, MOORE, WILKINSON, BELL & DUNBAR, P.A. (AV)

215 South Monroe Street - 2nd Floor, 32301
Telephone: 850-222-3533
FAX: 850-222-2126
Email: email@penningtonlawfirm.com *URL:* http://www.penningtonlawfirm.com

Samuel P. Bell, III
Kevin X. Crowley
Mark K. Delegal
Marc W. Dunbar
Peter M. Dunbar
Martha J. Edenfield
Rogelio J. Fontela
William H. Hughes, III
A. Kenneth Levine
E. Murray Moore, Jr.
Edgar M. Moore
Brian A. Newman
John C. Pelham, Jr.
Carl R. Pennington, Jr.
C. Edwin Rude, Jr.
Gary A. Shipman
Cynthia S. Tunnicliff
William E. Whitney
Ben H. Wilkinson
Cathi C. Wilkinson

Douglas S. Bell
Frederick L. Busack
Karen M. Camechis
Jan Johnson Gorrie
Robert H. Hosay
John J. Matthews
Julius F. Parker III

OF COUNSEL

Robert Cintron, Jr.
R. Stuart Huff (P.A.)
Christopher W. Kanaga (Not admitted in FL)
Barbara J. Staros

Representative Clients: Time-Warner Communications; First South Bank, Florida Association of Property Appraisers; Associated Industries of Florida; State of Florida, Department of Insurance; Tallahassee Memorial Health Systems; Gulf Atlantic Insurance Company; ITT Hartford Insurance Company; Healthplan Southeast; State of Florida West Coast Regional Water Supply.

(See Next Column)

For full biographical listings, see the Martindale-Hubbell Law Directory

*TAMPA,** Hillsborough Co.

ALLEN, DELL, FRANK & TRINKLE, P.A. (AV)

1240 Barnett Plaza, 101 East Kennedy Boulevard, P.O. Box 2111, 33601
Telephone: 813-223-5351
Telecopier: 813-229-6682

Stewart C. Eggert
Joseph G. Heyck, Jr.
Michael N. Brown
Marian P. McCulloch
Robert A. Mora
Benjamin G. Morris
A. Christopher Kasten, II
Richard A. Harrison
James S. Eggert
Donald W. Stanley, Jr.
John W. Wilcox
William L. Yanger
M. David Linton
Tabatha A. Liebert
J. Bert Grandoff

Tamlyn Sbar
Craig A. Jorgensen

OF COUNSEL

Ralph C. Dell

Representative Clients: Tampa International Airport; Bank of Tampa; Seminole Electric Cooperative Inc.; Tampa General Healthcare; Tampa Greyhound Track; Tampa Bay Water, A Regional Water Supply Authority.

For full biographical listings, see the Martindale-Hubbell Law Directory

ALPERT, BARKER & RODEMS, P.A. (AV)

First Union Center, Suite 2000, 100 South Ashley Drive (33602), P.O. Box 3270, 33601-3270
Telephone: 813-223-4131
Fax: 813-228-9612
Email: Alpertfirm@Aol.com

Jonathan L. Alpert
Chris A. Barker
Ryan Christopher Rodems
David D. Ferrentino
William J. Cook

Scott J. Flint
Natalie Pedregal

For full biographical listings, see the Martindale-Hubbell Law Directory

BROAD AND CASSEL (AV)

A Partnership including Professional Associations
100 North Tampa, Suite 3500, 33602
Telephone: 813-225-3020
Fax: 813-225-3039
URL: http://www.broadandcassel.com
Boca Raton, Florida Office: Corporate Centre at Boca Raton, Suite 300, 7777 Glades Road, 33434.
Telephone: 561-483-7000.
Fort Lauderdale, Florida Office: Suite 1130, Broward Financial Centre, 500 E. Broward Boulevard, 33394.
Telephone: 954-764-7060.
Miami, Florida Office: Miami Center, 201 South Biscayne Boulevard, Suite 3000, 33131.
Telephone: 305-373-9400.
Orlando, Florida Office: 390 N. Orange Avenue, Suite 1100, 32801.
Telephone: 407-839-4200.
Tallahassee, Florida Office: 215 South Monroe Street, Suite 400, 32302.
Telephone: 850-681-6810.
West Palm Beach, Florida Office: The Reflections Office Center, Fifth Floor, 400 Australian Avenue, South, 33401.
Telephone: 561-832-3300.

RESIDENT PARTNERS

Theodore C. Taub (P.A.)
Robert E. Johnson (P.A.)
Debra K. Smietanski (P.A.)
Russell S. Thomas (P.A.)

RESIDENT ASSOCIATES

Jonathan J. Ellis
Katherine Castor
Jennifer M. Tobin
Melissa G. Thorn

OF COUNSEL

William Kent Ihrig

For full biographical listings, see the Martindale-Hubbell Law Directory

CARLTON, FIELDS, WARD, EMMANUEL, SMITH & CUTLER, P.A. (AV)

One Harbour Place, 777 South Harbour Island Boulevard (33602-5799), P.O. Box 3239, 33601-3239
Telephone: 813-223-7000
Telex: Carfield 52-2520
Fax: (813) 229-4133
URL: http://www.carltonfields.com
Miami, Florida Office: 4000 International Place, 100 S.E. Second Street, 33131-9101, P.O. Box 019101, 33131-9101.
Telephone: 305-530-0050.

(See Next Column)

CARLTON, FIELDS, WARD, EMMANUEL, SMITH & CUTLER P.A.—*Continued*

Orlando, Florida Office: Citrus Center, 255 South Orange Avenue, Suite 1600, 32801-3488, P.O. Box 1171, 32802-1171.
Telephone: 407-849-0300.
Pensacola, Florida Office: Harbourview Building, 25 West Cedar Street, 4th Floor, 32501-5974, P.O. Box 12426, 32582-2426.
Telephone: 850-434-0142.
St. Petersburg, Florida Office: One Progress Plaza, 200 Central Avenue, Suite 2300, 33701-4352, P.O. Box 2861, 33731-2861.
Telephone: 727-821-7000.
Tallahassee, Florida Office: 215 South Monroe Street, Suite 500, 32301-1866, P.O Drawer 190, 32302-0190.
Telephone: 850-224-1585.
West Palm Beach, Florida Office: Esperanté, 222 Lakeview Avenue, Suite 1400, 33401-6149, P.O. Box 150, 33402-0150.
Telephone: 561-659-7070.

David Matthew Allen
W. Patrick Ayers
George Barford
Cathleen G. Bell
E. Kelly Bittick, Jr.
Mark A. Brown
David P. Burke
Richard B. Campbell
J. Kevin Carey
Doyle E. Carlton (1887-1972)
Robert L. Ciotti
Michael G. Cooke
Chris S. Coutroulis
Edward I. Cutler
Paul C. Davis
Richard A. Denmon
Nathaniel L. Doliner
Michel G. Emmanuel (1918-1992)
Nancy J. Faggianelli
D. Wallace Fields (1910-1991)
Jeanette M. Flores
Robert S. Freedman
Edward W. Gerecke
Kenneth E. Graves
Marvin Green (1904-1986)
Donald E. Hemke
Laurence E. Kinsolving
Ruth Barnes Kinsolving
John J. Lamoureux
D. Hywel Leonard
Edgel C. Lester, Jr.
A. Broaddus Livingston
Laurel E. Lockett
Giddings E. Mabry (1877-1968)
John P. McAdams
C. Douglas McDonald, Jr.
Kathleen S. McLeroy
George J. Meyer
Kevin Jon Napper
Michael F. Nuechterlein
Sandra G. Porter
Luis Prats
Robert M. Quinn
O. K. Reaves (1877-1970)
Paula McDonald Rhodes
Donald R. Schmidt
Roger D. Schwenke
Wm. Reece Smith, Jr.
Thomas A. Snow
Robert A. Soriano
Steven L. Sparkman
Paul J. Ullom
Robert R. Vawter, Jr.
Michael J. Virgadamo
David E. Ward (1909-1995)
James R. Wiley
Peter J. Winders
Wm. Cary Wright
Gwynne A. Young

OF COUNSEL

Kenneth G. Protonentis

Eric S. Adams
Hunter J. Brownlee
Constancio B. Cater
John C. Clark
Theodore A. Corless
Joseph P. Covelli
L. Joe Davis, Jr.
Donna Brookes DeVaney
Suzanne M. Elinger
Cristin C. Geiser
Sharon P. Greenaway
Andrew Clifford Greenberg
Amanda (Amy) K. Hill
Joette Stambaugh Keen
Michelle Morgan Ketchum
Edward Kuchinski
Rachel S. Peterkin
Jennifer A. Powers
Nicole D. Quinn
Hardy L. Roberts, III
Brian F. Stayton
Adam S. Tanenbaum
Emily J. Taylor
Lavinia James Vaughn
Edmund S. Whitson, III
Stephanie J. Young

For full biographical listings, see the Martindale-Hubbell Law Directory

CUNNINGHAM, CLARK & GREIWE, P.A. (AV)

100 Ashley Drive, South, Suite 100, 33602
Telephone: 813-228-0505
Telefax: 813-229-7982

Anthony W. Cunningham
Donald G. Greiwe
James D. Clark
D. Frank Winkles

For full biographical listings, see the Martindale-Hubbell Law Directory

FOLEY & LARDNER (AV)

Suite 2700, One Hundred N. Tampa Street, P.O. Box 3391, 33601-3391
Telephone: 813-229-2300;
Pinellas County: 813-442-3296
Facsimile: 813-221-4210
Email: foleylardner@worldnet.att.net *URL:* http://www.foleylardner.com
Los Angeles, California Office: 2029 Century Park East, 35th Floor.
Telephone: 310-277-2223.
Fax: 310-557-8475.
Sacramento, California Office: 300 Capitol Mall, Suite 1125.
Telephone: 916-443-8005.
Fax: 916-443-2240.
San Diego, California Office: 402 West Broadway, 23rd Floor.
Telephone: 619-234-6655.
Fax: 619-234-3510.

(See Next Column)

San Francisco, California Office: One Maritime Plaza, Sixth Floor.
Telephone: 415-434-4484.
Fax: 415-434-4507.
Denver, Colorado Office: 1999 Broadway, Suite 2560.
Telephone: 303-297-0260.
Fax: 303-297-0266.
Washington, D.C. Office: Washington Harbour, Suite 500, 3000 K Street, N.W.
Telephone: 202-672-5300.
Telex: 904136 (Foley Lard Wash).
Facsimile: 202-672-5399.
Jacksonville, Florida Office: The Greenleaf Building, 200 Laura Street. P.O. Box 240.
Telephone: 904-359-2000.
Facsimile: 904-359-8700.
Orlando, Florida Office: Suite 1800, 111 North Orange Avenue, P.O. Box 2193.
Telephone: 407-423-7656.
Facsimile: 407-648-1743.
Tallahassee, Florida Office: 300 East Park Avenue, P.O. Box 1454.
Telephone: 850-222-6100.
Facsimile: 850-561-6475.
West Palm Beach, Florida Office: Suite 200, Phillips Point East Tower, 777 South Flagler Drive.
Telephone: 561-655-5050.
Facsimile: 561-655-6925.
Chicago, Illinois Office: Suite 3300, One IBM Plaza, 330 N. Wabash Avenue.
Telephone: 312-755-1900.
Facsimile: 312-755-1925.
Annapolis, Maryland Office: Suite 102, 175 Admiral Cochrane Drive.
Telephone: 410-266-8077.
Telex: 899149 (Oldtownpat).
Facsimile: 410-266-8664.
Madison, Wisconsin Office: Verex Plaza, 150 East Gilman Street, P.O. Box 1497.
Telephone: 608-257-5035.
Facsimile: 608-258-4258.
Milwaukee, Wisconsin Office: Firstar Center, 777 East Wisconsin Avenue.
Telephone: 414-271-2400.
Telex: 26-819 (Foley Lard Mil).
Facsimile: 414-297-4900.
Brussels, Belgium Office: Avenue Louise, 283.
Telephone: 32-2-646-2777.
Facsimile: 32-2-646-7574.

PARTNERS

Kenneth A. Beytin
Daniel N. Burton
Stephen A. Crane
Guy O. Farmer II
Matthew J. Foster
Kevin E. Hyde
Gary D. Koch
James M. Landis
Sybil Meloy
Richard Thomas Petitt
Todd B. Pfister
David M. Rieth
David L. Robbins
Marsha Griffin Rydberg
Nathan B. Simpson
Martin A. Traber
Mark J. Wolfson

OF COUNSEL

Vitauts M. Gulbis
Lewis H. Hill, III

SPECIAL COUNSEL

Bruce M. Rodgers
Susan Greco Tuttle

RETIRED PARTNERS

William J. Kiernan, Jr.

RESIDENT ASSOCIATES

Andrew J. Bohlmann
Christopher E. Butler
Marina A. Choundas
Scott T. Farrell
Brad S. Fischer
Andrew M. Fussner
Karl C. Gwynne
Heather P. Haufler
Paul A. Leighton
Troy M. Lovell
Kathryn L. Ritchie
Jon P. Tasso
Steven W. Vazquez
Lori V. Vaughan
Donald Alan Workman

For full biographical listings, see the Martindale-Hubbell Law Directory

GIBBONS, SMITH, COHN & ARNETT, A PROFESSIONAL ASSOCIATION (AV)

3321 Henderson Boulevard, P.O. Box 2177, 33601
Telephone: 813-877-9222
Fax: 813-877-9290
URL: http://www.gscalaw.com

Arthur S. Gibbons (1908-1986)
Armin H. Smith, Jr. (Retired)
Gary A. Gibbons
Kirk M. Gibbons
Roy W. Cohn
Patricia Arnett
John R. Bello, Jr.
Larry M. Segall
Rod B. Neuman
Elizabeth A. Pereira
Patti W. Woodruff
Donald Steven Burwell
Jeffrey C. Hakanson

For full biographical listings, see the Martindale-Hubbell Law Directory

Tampa—Continued

HOLLAND & KNIGHT LLP (AV)

400 North Ashley Drive, Suite 2300, 33602
Telephone: 813-227-8500
Fax: 813-229-0134
Mailing Address: P.O. Box 1288, 33601-1288
Email: hklaw.com *URL:* http://www.hklaw.com
Atlanta, Georgia Office: 1201 West Peachtree Street, N.E., Suite 2000.
Telephone: 404-817-8500.
Fax: 404-881-0470.
Boston, Massachusetts Office: One Beacon Street.
Telephone: 617-523-2700.
Fax: 617-523-6850.
Bradenton, Florida Office: 1001 3rd Avenue West, Suite 600.
Telephone: 941- 748-7076.
Fax: 941-747-9774.
Falls Church, Virginia: 3110 Fairview Park Drive, Suite 900.
Telephone: 703-645-8600.
Fax: 703-645-8610.
Fort Lauderdale, Florida Office: One East Broward Boulevard, Suite 1300.
Telephone: 954-525-1000.
Fax: 954-463-2030.
Jacksonville, Florida Office: 50 North Laura Street, Suite 3900.
Telephone: 904-353-2000.
Fax: 904-358-1872.
Lakeland, Florida Office: 92 Lake Wire Drive.
Telephone: 941-682-1161.
Fax: 941-688-1186.
Melbourne, Florida Office: 1499 South Harbor City Boulevard, Suite 201.
Telephone: 407-951-1776.
Fax: 407-951-1849.
Miami, Florida Office: 701 Brickell Avenue, Suite 3000.
Telephone: 305-374-8500.
Fax: 305-789-7799.
New York, New York Office: 195 Broadway, 24th Floor.
Telephone: 212-513-3200.
Fax: 212-385-9010.
Orlando, Florida Office: 200 South Orange Avenue, Suite 2600.
Telephone: 407-425-8500.
Fax: 407-244-5288.
Providence, Rhode Island Office: 50 Exchange Terrace, Suite 300, Union Station Plaza.
Telephone: 401-751-8500.
Fax: 401-553-6850.
San Francisco, California Office: 44 Montgomery Street, Suite 4050.
Telephone: 415-743-6900.
Fax: 415-743-6910.
St. Petersburg, Florida Office: 200 Central Avenue, Suite 1600.
Telephone: 727-896-7171.
Fax: 727-822-8048.
Tallahassee, Florida Office: 315 South Calhoun Street, Suite 600.
Telephone: 850-224-7000.
Fax: 850-224-8832.
Washington, D.C. Office: 2100 Pennsylvania Avenue, N.W., Suite 400.
Telephone: 202-955-3000.
Fax: 202-955-5564.
West Palm Beach, Florida Office: 625 North Flagler Drive, Suite 700.
Telephone: 561-833-2000.
Fax: 561-650-8399.
Mexico City, Mexico Office: HOLLAND & KNIGHT-GALLÁSTEGUI Y LOZANO, S.C. (Joint Venture Office) Avenida Paseo de los Tamarindos No. 400, Torre "B" - 2° Piso, Col. Bosques d las Lomas, C.P. 05120 Mexico, D.F.
Telephone: 011-525-261-1866.
Fax: 011-525-261-1867.
Tel Aviv, Israel Office: Holland & Knight LTD, 23 Derech Petach-Tikva, 18th Floor.
Telephone: +011-972-3-566-7666.
Fax: +011-972-3-566-7667.
Buenos Aires, Argentina Office: San Martin 323--Piso 18, 1004.
Telephone: +54-11 4324-7600.
Fax: +54-11 4324-7601.

TAMPA MEMBERS AND ASSOCIATES

A. Brian Albritton
Rod Anderson
Chester E. Bacheller
Anderson L. Baldy III
Bernard A. Barton, Jr.
Stacy D. Blank
Richard M. Blau
Karl J. Brandes
Steven L. Brannock
Warren M. Cason
Michael L. Chapman
William B. deMeza, Jr.
Richard D. Eckhard
John Germany
Leonard H. Gilbert
Frederick J. Grady
Robert J. Grammig
William F. Hamilton
G. Calvin Hayes
J. Fraser Himes
George B. Howell, III
Michael L. Jamieson
Elizabeth Belsom Johnson
Douglas S. Jones
John Arthur Jones
Robert E. V. Kelley, Jr.
D. Burke Kibler, III
Edward F. Koren
William R. Lane, Jr.
Jack A. Levine
Byrne Litschgi
Carol J. LoCicero
Bill McBride (Managing Partner)
Fredrick H. L. McClure
K. Patrick Meehan
Susan Tillotson Mills
Jack S. Newsome
Paul E. Parrish
John E. Phillips
Samuel P. Queirolo

(See Next Column)

TAMPA MEMBERS AND ASSOCIATES (Continued)

Bruce H. Roberson
Frederick M. Rothenberg
Frederick S. Schrils
James H. Shimberg, Jr.
David R. Singleton
Patrick W. Skelton
Sheryl L. Sklorman
Brian C. Sparks
Guy W. Spicola
Charles L. Stutts
Gregg Darrow Thomas
Joseph H. Varner, III
Robert H. Waltuch
Douglas A. Wright
Barbara M. Yadley

SENIOR COUNSEL

Leonard L. Kleinman
Robert J. Shapiro

Lisa M. Anguillo
Noel Boeke
David C. Borucke
Blake D. Bringgold
Lana R. Chiariello
Bradley S. Cole (Not admitted in FL)
Francis M. Curran
Elizabeth A. DeConti
Kimberly Lee Franklin
Rachel E. Fugate
Michael S. Goetz
Shane A. Hart
Christine A. Hearn
Bradford D. Kimbro
James B. Lake
Jolee Land
Mark N. Lontchar, Jr
John T. Marshall
John G. Maynard
Dennis M. McClelland
James J. McGuire (Not admitted in FL)
Maria E. Lasso Morejon
Marni M. Morgan
Louis Justin Najmy
Todd A. Nelson
Melissa E. Podolsky
Robin L. Rosenberg
Seth M. Schimmel
Peter A. Schoemann
Lester E. Segal
Keith S. Shotzberger
Robert A. Warram
Joseph J. Weissman
Carolyn T. Woods
Grace H. Yang

OF COUNSEL

Charles M. Elson (Not admitted in FL)

For full biographical listings, see the Martindale-Hubbell Law Directory

---

JOHNSON, BLAKELY, POPE, BOKOR, RUPPEL & BURNS, P.A. (AV)

100 North Tampa Street Suite 1800, P.O. Box 1100, 33602
Telephone: 813-225-2500
Telecopier: 813-223-7118
Clearwater, Florida Office: 911 Chestnut Street, P.O. Box 1368.
Telephone: 813-461-1818.
Telecopier: 813-441-8617.
Naples, Florida Office: 975 Sixth Avenue South.
Telephone: 941-435-0035.
Telecopier: 941-435-9992.

John T. Blakely
Bruce H. Bokor
Guy M. Burns
Robert M. Daisley
James W. Humann
Scott C. Ilgenfritz
Frank R. Jakes
John R. Lawson, Jr.
Michael C. Markham
F. Wallace Pope, Jr.
Darryl R. Richards
Dennis G. Ruppel
Philip M. Shasteen

Jonathan Strickland Coleman

For full biographical listings, see the Martindale-Hubbell Law Directory

---

TRENAM, KEMKER, SCHARF, BARKIN, FRYE, O'NEILL & MULLIS, PROFESSIONAL ASSOCIATION (AV)

2700 Barnett Plaza, 101 East Kennedy Boulevard, P.O. Box 1102, 33602
Telephone: 813-223-7474
FAX: 813-229-6553
Telex: 6502251910 MCI
ABA/net 1574
St. Petersburg, Florida Office: 450 Carillon Parkway, Suite 120.
Telephone: 727-898-7474.
Fax: 813-229-6553.

John J. Trenam (1912-1978)
Harry Kemker (1930-1984)
Marvin E. Barkin
William C. Frye
Albert C. O'Neill, Jr.
Harold W. Mullis, Jr.
William Knight Zewadski
Richard M. Leisner
Keith E. Rounsaville
Richard H. Sollner
Robert H. Buesing
William G. Scott, III
Stanley H. Eleff
Gary I. Teblum
Nelson D. Blank
John Sebastian Vento
Don B. Weinbren
Mary H. Quinlan
David R. Brittain
George E. Nader
Edward C. LaRose
Roberta A. Colton
Roberta Casper Watson
J. Alan Asendorf
John Daniel Goldsmith
Karen E. Lewis
John E. Johnson
D. Michael O'Leary
Richard M. Hanchett
Lansing C. Scriven
J. Cary Ross, Jr.
Marie Tomassi
Michael K. Green
Elizabeth Pascale Francis
Wendolyn S. Busch
H. Wayne Porter

(See Next Column)

TRENAM, KEMKER, SCHARF, BARKIN, FRYE, O'NEILL & MULLIS
PROFESSIONAL ASSOCIATION—*Continued*

Dinita L. James
Laura E. Prather
Robert G. Stern
Stephen Tabano
Kevin M. Smith

Nelson T. Castellano
William H. Harrell, Jr.
Charles M. Harris, Jr.
Richard J. McIntyre
Randall C. McGeorge
John F. Panzarella
Thomas D. Aitken
Kelley C. Howard
Carlos A. Rodriguez
Kevin J. Darken
David J. Rice
Joann M. Kronzer
Julie S. Sneed
Phillip G. Day
Paul B. Thanasides
Emily P. Jenkins
Becky Ferrell Anton
Spurgeon Martin D. Stamps, III
J. Eric Taylor
Steven D. Singleton
Carrie L. Freeman
Imogene L. Cathey
Phyllis C. Hogue

OF COUNSEL

Leslie D. Scharf
James V. Carideo

For full biographical listings, see the Martindale-Hubbell Law Directory

ZINOBER & MCCREA, P.A. (AV)

SouthTrust Plaza, 201 East Kennedy Boulevard Suite 850, P.O. Box 1378, 33602
Telephone: 813-224-9004
Telecopier: 813-223-4881
Email: Info@zmlaw.com

Peter W. Zinober
Richard C. McCrea, Jr.
Frank E. Brown
Karen Meyer Buesing

Shane T. Muñoz
Nancy A. Chad
Cynthia L. May
Scott T. Silverman
Melanie J. LaFond
Danielle R. May
M. Sean Moyles
Luisette Gierbolini
Jennifer M. Fowler
Ryan D. Barack
Charles M. Deal
Erich Y. Schultz

LEGAL SUPPORT PERSONNEL

Debra A. Douglas (Administrator)

For full biographical listings, see the Martindale-Hubbell Law Directory

*VERO BEACH,** Indian River Co.

COLLINS, BROWN, CALDWELL, BARKETT & GARAVAGLIA, CHARTERED (AV)

756 Beachland Boulevard, P.O. Box 3686, 32964
Telephone: 561-231-4343
FAX: 561-234-5213
Email: cbc@verolaw.com

George G. Collins, Jr.
Calvin B. Brown
William W. Caldwell
Bruce D. Barkett
Michael J. Garavaglia
Lisa N. Thompson
Susan A. Calistri

Reference: First Union Bank of Indian River County, Vero Beach, Florida.

For full biographical listings, see the Martindale-Hubbell Law Directory

GOULD, COOKSEY, FENNELL, O'NEILL, MARINE & CARTER, PROFESSIONAL ASSOCIATION (AV)

979 Beachland Boulevard, 32963
Telephone: 561-231-1100
Fax: 561-231-2020

John R. Gould (1921-1988)
Byron T. Cooksey
Darrell Fennell
Eugene J. O'Neill
Christopher H. Marine
David M. Carter
Todd W. Fennell
Susan L. Chenault
Elsbeth T. Peshel
(Not admitted in FL)

Counsel for: Indian River National Bank; Island Hopper Boats International, Inc.; Northern Trust Bank of Florida.
Approved Attorneys for: Attorneys' Title Insurance Fund; Commonwealth Land Title Insurance Company.

For full biographical listings, see the Martindale-Hubbell Law Directory

MOSS, HENDERSON, BLANTON & LANIER, P.A. (AV)

817 Beachland Boulevard, P.O. Box 3406, 32964-3406
Telephone: 561-231-1900
Fax: 561-231-4387

George H. Moss, II
Steve L. Henderson
Robin A. Blanton
Clinton W. Lanier
Fred L. Kretschmer, Jr.
Lewis W. Murphy, Jr.

(See Next Column)

Lawrence Y. Leonard
Casey Walker
Jennifer J. Huber
Anthony M. Amelio
David C. Chafin

OF COUNSEL

Charles E. Garris
Ford J. Fegert

Representative Clients: Aetna Life & Casualty; Alcoa Florida, Inc.; Florida Power & Light Co.; Insurance Company of North America; Liberty Mutual Insurance Co.; Sears, Roebuck & Co.; Sugar Cane Growers Cooperative of Florida; Norfolk Southern Corporation/North American Van Lines, Inc.

For full biographical listings, see the Martindale-Hubbell Law Directory

SMITH & SMITH (AV)

Citrus Financial Center, Suite 301, 1717 Indian River Boulevard, 32960
Telephone: 561-567-4351
Fax: 561-567-4298

MEMBERS OF FIRM

Sherman N. Smith, Jr. (1914-1998)
Sherman N. Smith, III
Anthony T. Golden

References: Citrus Bank, N.A.; Northern Trust Bank of Vero Beach.

For full biographical listings, see the Martindale-Hubbell Law Directory

*WEST PALM BEACH,** Palm Beach Co.

BROAD AND CASSEL (AV)

A Partnership including Professional Associations
The Reflections Office Centre, 400 Australian Avenue, South, Fifth Floor, 33401
Telephone: 561-832-3300
Telecopier: 561-655-1109
URL: http://www.broadandcassel.com
Boca Raton, Florida Office: Corporate Centre at Boca Raton, Suite 300, 7777 Glades Road, 33434.
Telephone: 561-483-7000.
Fort Lauderdale, Florida Office: Suite 1130, Broward Financial Centre, 500 E. Broward Boulevard, 33394.
Telephone: 954-764-7060.
Miami, Florida Office: Miami Center, 201 South Biscayne Boulevard, Suite 3000, 33131.
Telephone: 305-373-9400.
Orlando, Florida Office: 390 N. Orange Avenue, Suite 1100, 32801.
Telephone: 407-839-4200.
Tallahassee, Florida Office: 215 South Monroe Street, Suite 400, 32302.
Telephone: 850-681-6810.
Tampa, Florida Office: 100 North Tampa, Suite 3500, 33602.
Telephone: 813-225-3020.

PARTNERS

Patricia Lebow (P.A.)
Clifford I. Hertz (P.A.)
Andrew D. Rafkin
Jeffrey F. Gordon
Steven Ellison
Ronald M. Gaché(P.A.)
Edward J. Hopkins (P.A.)

ASSOCIATES

Joyce L. Elden
Donald P. Dufresne
Kristin Ahr Koch
Steven M. Parrish
Benjamin R. Alvarez

For full biographical listings, see the Martindale-Hubbell Law Directory

CARLTON, FIELDS, WARD, EMMANUEL, SMITH & CUTLER, P.A. (AV)

Esperanté, 222 Lakeview Avenue, Suite 1400 (33401-6149), P.O. Box 150, 33402-0150
Telephone: 561-659-7070
Fax: 561-659-7368
URL: http://www.carltonfields.com
Miami, Florida Office: 4000 International Place, 100 S.E. Second Street, 33131-9101, P.O. Box 019101, 33131-9101.
Telephone: 305-530-0050.
Orlando, Florida Office: Citrus Center, 255 South Orange Avenue, Suite 1600, 32801-3488, P.O. Box 1171, 32802-1171.
Telephone: 407-849-0300.
Pensacola, Florida Office: Harbourview Building, 25 West Cedar Street, 4th Floor, 32501-5974, P.O. Box 12426, 32582-2426.
Telephone: 850-434-0142.
St. Petersburg, Florida Office: One Progress Plaza, 200 Central Avenue, Suite 2300, 33701-4352, P.O. Box 2861, 33731-2861.
Telephone: 727-821-7000.
Tallahassee, Florida Office: 215 South Monroe Street, Suite 500, 32301-1866, P.O. Drawer 190, 32302-0190.
Telephone: 850-224-1585.
Tampa, Florida Office: One Harbour Place, 777 South Harbour Island Boulevard, 33602-5799, P.O. Box 3239, 33601-3239.
Telephone: 813-223-7000.

(See Next Column)

CARLTON, FIELDS, WARD, EMMANUEL, SMITH & CUTLER P.A., *West Palm Beach—Continued*

Kevin C. Beuttenmuller
Gary M. Brandenburg
Michael J. Compagno
Richard R. Ellington
Robert N. Gilbert
Thomas A. Hanson
Lynda J. Harris
John R. Hart
Joseph Ianno, Jr.
Diana Lewis
Patrick J. Rooney, Jr.
M. Richard Sapir
Michael S. Tammaro

Theodore C. Miloch, II
Saara J. Pekale (Not admitted in FL)
Michael Keith Winston
Henry S. Wulf
Garth Thomas Yearick

For full biographical listings, see the Martindale-Hubbell Law Directory

FOLEY & LARDNER (AV)

Suite 200, Phillips Point East Tower, 777 South Flagler Drive, 33401-6163
Telephone: 561-655-5050
Facsimile: 561-655-6925
Email: foleylardner@worldnet.att.net *URL:* http://www.foleylardner.com
Los Angeles, California Office: 2029 Century Park East, 35th Floor.
Telephone: 310-277-2223.
Fax: 310-557-8475.
Sacramento, California Office: 300 Capitol Mall, Suite 1125.
Telephone: 916-443-8005.
Fax: 916-443-2240.
San Diego, California Office: 402 West Broadway, 23rd Floor.
Telephone: 619-234-6655.
Fax: 619-234-3510.
San Francisco, California Office: One Maritime Plaza, Sixth Floor.
Telephone: 415-434-4484.
Fax: 415-434-4507.
Denver, Colorado Office: 1999 Broadway, Suite 2560.
Telephone: 303-297-0260.
Fax: 303-297-0266.
Washington, D.C. Office: Washington Harbour, Suite 500, 3000 K Street, N.W.
Telephone: 202-672-5300.
Telex: 904136 (Foley Lard Wash).
Facsimile: 202-672-5399.
Jacksonville, Florida Office: The Greenleaf Building, 200 Laura Street. P.O. Box 240.
Telephone: 904-359-2000.
Facsimile: 904-359-8700.
Orlando, Florida Office: Suite 1800, 111 North Orange Avenue, P.O. Box 2193.
Telephone: 407-423-7656.
Facsimile: 407-648-1743.
Tallahassee, Florida Office: 300 East Park Avenue, P.O. Box 1454.
Telephone: 850-222-6100.
Facsimile: 850-561-6475.
Tampa, Florida Offices: Suite 2700, One Hundred N. Tampa Street, P.O. Box 3391.
Telephones: 813-229-2300; Pinellas County: 813-442-3296.
Facsimile: 813-221-4210.
Chicago, Illinois Office: Suite 3300, One IBM Plaza, 330 N. Wabash Avenue.
Telephone: 312-755-1900.
Facsimile: 312-755-1925.
Annapolis, Maryland Office: Suite 102, 175 Admiral Cochrane Drive.
Telephone: 410-266-8077.
Telex: 899149 (Oldtownpat).
Facsimile: 410-266-8664.
Madison, Wisconsin Office: Verex Plaza, 150 East Gilman Street, P.O. Box 1497.
Telephone: 608-257-5035.
Facsimile: 608-258-4258.
Milwaukee, Wisconsin Office: Firstar Center, 777 East Wisconsin Avenue.
Telephone: 414-271-2400.
Telex: 26-819 (Foley Lard Mil).
Facsimile: 414-297-4900.
Brussels, Belgium Office: Avenue Louise, 283.
Telephone: 32-2-646-2777.
Facsimile: 32-2-646-7574.

PARTNERS

Richard S. Davis
Guy O. Farmer II
Kevin E. Hyde
Ellen S. Malasky
Sybil Meloy
Thomas F. Munro, II
Jack A. Porter
William P. Sklar

SPECIAL COUNSEL

Marilyn A. Moore

OF COUNSEL

William J. Dick (Not admitted in FL)

RESIDENT ASSOCIATES

Charles L. Pickett, Jr.
Mark A. Salzberg

For full biographical listings, see the Martindale-Hubbell Law Directory

GUNSTER, YOAKLEY, VALDES-FAULI & STEWART, P.A. (AV)

Phillips Point, Suite 500 East, 777 South Flagler Drive, 33401-6194
Telephone: 561-655-1980
Fax: 561-655-5677
Email: clientservices@gunster.com *URL:* http://www.gunster.com
Fort Lauderdale, Florida Office: Broward Financial Centre, Suite 1400, 500 East Broward Boulevard.
Telephone: 954-462-2000.
Fax: 954-523-1722.
Miami, Florida Office: Suite 3400, One Biscayne Tower, 2 South Biscayne Boulevard.
Telephone: 305-376-6000.
Fax: 305-376-6010.
Palm Beach, Florida Office: 151 Royal Palm Way.
Telephone: 561-833-1970.
Fax: 561-650-0655.
Stuart, Florida Office: Suite 200, 800 S.E. Monterey Commons Boulevard.
Telephone: 561-288-1980.
Fax: 561-288-0610.
Tallahassee, Florida Office: 215 South Monroe Street, Suite 830.
Telephone: 904-222-6660.
Fax: 904-222-1002.
Vero Beach, Florida Office: Suite 301, 3055 Cardinal Drive.
Telephone: 561-234-1040.
Fax: 561-234-1518.

John Kenneth Williamson (1892-1964)
Joseph F. Gunster (1894-1979)
David S. Yoakley (1917-1994)

Jerry E. Aron
David R. Atkinson, Jr.
Bernard R. Baker, III
David G. Bates
Kenneth S. Beall, Jr.
Donald J. Beuttenmuller, Jr.
Sheila Biehl
James R. Brindell
Connis O. Brown, III
Rick J. Burgess
John T. Carmody, Jr.
Bette Kester Conrad
Paul W. A. Courtnell, Jr.
Ernest A. Cox, III
Lewis F. Crippen
G. Joseph Curley
C. Craig Eller
Guillermo J. Fernández-Quincoces
Roy E. Fitzgerald
Robert S. Hackleman
Donald R. Hall
Daniel A. Hanley
Jeremy J. Hart
Kenneth M. Hart
James Stuart Higgins
Richard D. Holt
Phillip M. Hudson, III
Thomas P. Hunt
William L. Hyde
John P. Kelly
Ronald A. Kriss
Daniel M. Mackler
Michael V. Mitrione
L. Louis Mrachek
Stephen C. Page
Hugh W. Perry
Michael G. Platner
Andrew S. Robins
Mark J. Scheer
Juan E. Serralles, Jr.
Michael D. Simon
Robert S. Turk
Raúl J. Valdés-Fauli
Clemente L. Vázquez-Bello
Stephen G. Vogelsang
Julie A. S. Williamson

Jack J. Aiello
Laurie B. Aiello
Lisa W. Aiello
Mark Aaron Albright
Gregory K. Bader
Paul Bances
Osmer D. Batcheller
Courtney A. Callahan
Rebecca Cavendish
Dana A. Clayton
Susan Lawton Copeland
Heidi E. Davis
Kip A. Davis
Danielle DeVito
Jose O. Diaz
Randy R. Dow
Charles J. Duffy, III (Not admitted in FL)
Elysse A. Elder
Karen D. Geller
Michael R. Goldstein
Robert M. Graham
William T. Hennessey, III
Virginia Herrero
Susan E. Howsmon
Pamela Kristen Kay
Ansley Kennedy-Bowden
Scott Konopka
Elizabeth A. Leffert-Heise
George S. LeMieux
Patricia A. Leonard
Andrew M. Litvak
Clinton R. Losego
Kimberly K. Lunsford
Patrick W. Maraist
Michael W. Marcil
Doug Marek
Kenneth A. Norman
Nicole K. Nugan
Michelle Oms
Jason W. Owsley
Harvey E. Oyer, III
Walter W. Palmer
Ana C. Percival
J. Coleman Prewitt, Jr.
Jennifer B. Ramach
Robert S. Raynes, Jr.
Kelly L. Reagan
Hillary Rodriguez
Alan B. Rose
Wendy R. St. Charles
Meenu T. Sasser
Gregor J. Schwinghammer
Sonia Savariego Silverman
Rico M. Sogocio
Cynthia C. Spall
Lissette S. Stancioff
Gigi J. Tanghe
Aaron W. Tandy (Not admitted in FL)
Patrick M. Whitehead
Alexandra M. Woodfield
Darin I. Zenov

OF COUNSEL

William P. Burns
Janis K. Cheezem
Russell M. Gardner
David C. Goodwin
Luiz Ernesto R. Gozzoli (Not admitted in United States)
William G. Hall, Jr.
Mahesh H. Nanwani
Juan Lopez Palmer
Avron C. Rifkin
Lisa A. Schneider
Robert T. Scott

(See Next Column)

GUNSTER, YOAKLEY, VALDES-FAULI & STEWART P.A.—*Continued*

OF COUNSEL (Continued)

Steven J. Serling
Brian M. Seymour
A. Obie Stewart
Sarah Lea Tobocman
Raúl E. Valdés-Fauli
Peter Van Andel

Counsel for: City Savings Bank; Sun Bank/South Florida, N/A.

For full biographical listings, see the Martindale-Hubbell Law Directory

HOLLAND & KNIGHT LLP (AV)

625 North Flagler Drive Suite 700, 33401
Telephone: 561-833-2000
Fax: 561-650-8399
Mailing Address: P.O. Box 3208, 33402
Email: hklaw.com *URL:* http://www.hklaw.com
Atlanta, Georgia Office: 1201 West Peachtree Street, N.E., Suite 2000.
Telephone: 404-817-8500.
Fax: 404-881-0470.
Boston, Massachusetts Office: One Beacon Street.
Telephone: 617-523-2700.
Fax: 617-523-6850.
Bradenton, Florida Office: 1001 3rd Avenue West, Suite 600.
Telephone: 941-748-7076.
Fax: 941-747-9774.
Falls Church, Virginia: 3110 Fairview Park Drive, Suite 900.
Telephone: 703-645-8600.
Fax: 703-645-8610.
Fort Lauderdale, Florida Office: One East Broward Boulevard, Suite 1300.
Telephone: 954-525-1000.
Fax: 954-463-2030.
Jacksonville, Florida Office: 50 North Laura Street, Suite 3900.
Telephone: 904-353-2000.
Fax: 904-358-1872.
Lakeland, Florida Office: 92 Lake Wire Drive.
Telephone: 941-682-1161.
Fax: 941-688-1186.
Melbourne, Florida Office: 1499 South Harbor City Boulevard, Suite 201.
Telephone: 407-951-1776.
Fax: 407-951-1849.
Miami, Florida Office: 701 Brickell Avenue, Suite 3000.
Telephone: 305-374-8500.
Fax: 305-789-7799.
New York, New York Office: 195 Broadway, 24th Floor.
Telephone: 212-513-3200.
Fax: 212-385-9010.
Orlando, Florida Office: 200 South Orange Avenue, Suite 2600.
Telephone: 407-425-8500.
Fax: 407-244-5288.
Providence, Rhode Island Office: 50 Exchange Terrace, Suite 300, Union Station Plaza.
Telephone: 401-751-8500.
Fax: 401-553-6850.
San Francisco, California Office: 44 Montgomery Street, Suite 4050.
Telephone: 415-743-6900.
Fax: 415-743-6910.
St. Petersburg, Florida Office: 200 Central Avenue, Suite 1600.
Telephone: 727-896-7171.
Fax: 727-822-8048.
Tallahassee, Florida Office: 315 South Calhoun Street, Suite 600.
Telephone: 850-224-7000.
Fax: 850-224-8832.
Tampa, Florida Office: 400 North Ashley Drive, Suite 2300.
Telephone: 813-227-8500.
Fax: 813-229-0134.
Washington, D.C. Office: 2100 Pennsylvania Avenue, N.W., Suite 400.
Telephone: 202-955-3000.
Fax: 202-955-5564.
Mexico City, Mexico Office: HOLLAND & KNIGHT-GALLÁSTEGUI Y LOZANO, S.C. (Joint Venture Office) Avenida Paseo de los Tamarindos No. 400, Torre "B" - 2° Piso, Col. Bosques d las Lomas, C.P. 05120 Mexico, D.F.
Telephone: 011-525-261-1866.
Fax: 011-525-261-1867.
Tel Aviv, Israel Office: Holland & Knight LTD, 23 Derech Petach-Tikva, 18th Floor.
Telephone: +011-972-3-566-7666.
Fax: +011-972-3-566-7667.
Buenos Aires, Argentina Office: San Martin 323--Piso 18, 1004.
Telephone: +54-11 4324-7600.
Fax: +54-11 4324-7601.

MEMBERS AND ASSOCIATES

Martin J. Alexander
J. Michael Haygood
Hank Jackson
Charles W. Littell
Peter Matwiczyk
Scott B. Newman
David L. Perry, Jr.
D. Culver Smith, III

SENIOR COUNSEL

Richard L. Abedon
Eunice Tall Baros

(See Next Column)

Carrie Beth Lesser Baris
Edward Diaz
Lynn K. Gefen
William P. Gray, III
Christopher D. Scott
Jennifer Shasha
Elizabeth Stone Shavitz
Dawn Schiller Williams

OF COUNSEL

Richard S. Weinstein

For full biographical listings, see the Martindale-Hubbell Law Directory

PETERS ROBERTSON DEMAHY PARSONS MOWERS PASSARO & DRAKE P.A. (AV)

Galleria International Building, 301 Clematis Street, Suite 3000, 33401-4381
Telephone: 407-832-9698
Fax: 407-832-8355
Miami, Florida Office: Suite 600, Ingraham Building, 25 Southeast 2nd Avenue.
Telephone: 305-374-3103.
Fax: 305-377-9805.
Fort Lauderdale, Florida Office: 506 South East B Street.
Telephone: 954-761-8999.
Fax: 954-761-8990.
Fort Myers, Florida Office: Key West Professional Centre, 1342 Colonial Boulevard, Suite 45.
Telephone: 941-936-1129.
Fax: 941-936-4036.

Neil P. Robertson

Representative Clients: Auto-Owners Insurance Co.; Dade County School Board; Employers Reinsurance Group; Gallagher Bassett Insurance Service; Maryland Casualty Co.

For full biographical listings, see the Martindale-Hubbell Law Directory

QUARLES & BRADY LLP (AV)

222 Lakeview Avenue, 4th Floor, 33401
Telephone: 561-653-5000
Fax: 561-653-5333
URL: http://www.quarles.com
Milwaukee, Wisconsin Office: 411 East Wisconsin Avenue, 53202-4497.
Telephone: 414-277-5000.
Fax: 414-271-3552.
Madison, Wisconsin Office: Firstar Plaza, One South Pinckney Street, P.O. Box 2113, 53701-2113.
Telephone: 608-251-5000.
Fax: 608-251-9166.
Naples, Florida Office: Barnett Center, 4501 Tamiami Trail North, Suite 300, 34103-3060.
Telephone: 941-262-5959.
Fax: 941-434-4999.
Phoenix, Arizona Office: One Camelback Building, One East Camelback Road, Suite 400, 85012-1649.
Telephone: 602-230-5500.
Fax: 602-230-5598.
Chicago, Illinois Office: Quarles & Brady LLC, Citicorp Center, 500 West Madison Street, Suite 3700.
Telephone: 312-715-5000.
Fax: 312-715-5155.

PARTNERS

J. Rodman Steele, Jr.
Ned R. Nashban
Gregory A. Nelson
Nancy Berz Colman
Joseph W. Bain
Robert J. Sacco

OF COUNSEL

John S. Sammond

ASSOCIATES

Mark D. Passler
Stanley A. Kim
Scott D. Paul
Steven M. Greenberg

BUSINESS MANAGEMENT SUPPORT PERSONNEL

OFFICE MANAGER

Nadean R. Stone

LEGAL ASSISTANTS

Jacquelyn Brookings
Carol Cavallerano
Linda C. Clemons
Leneah R. Davis
Susan Hess
Janet E. Townsend

For full biographical listings, see the Martindale-Hubbell Law Directory

SASSER, CESTERO & SASSER, P.A. (AV)

1800 Australian Avenue, South, Suite 203, P.O. Box 2907, 33402
Telephone: 561-689-4378
Fax: 561-689-4652
URL: http://www.sasserlaw.com

Donald J. Sasser
Jorge M. Cestero
Thomas J. Sasser

Reference: First Union National Bank of Florida.

For full biographical listings, see the Martindale-Hubbell Law Directory

West Palm Beach—Continued

SEARCY DENNEY SCAROLA BARNHART & SHIPLEY, PROFESSIONAL ASSOCIATION (AV)

2139 Palm Beach Lakes Boulevard, P.O. Drawer 3626, 33402-3626
Telephone: 561-686-6300
800-780-8607
800-220-7006 (Spanish)
Fax: 561-478-0754
Email: CDS@SEARCYLAW.COM *URL:* http://www.searcylaw.com

Christian D. Searcy, Sr.
Earl L. Denney, Jr.
John Scarola
F. Gregory Barnhart
John A. Shipley
David K. Kelley, Jr.
Lance J. Block, Jr.
C. Calvin Warriner, III
William A. Norton
David J. Sales
Christopher K. Speed
William B. King
David J. White

Karen E. Terry
Sean C. Domnick
Harry A. Shevin
Patrick E. Quinlan
Darryl L. Lewis
Ellen F. Brandt

LEGAL SUPPORT PERSONNEL

Laurie J. Briggs (Paralegal)
Deane L. Cady (Paralegal/Investigator)
Daniel J. Calloway (Paralegal/Investigator)
Emilio Diamantis (Paralegal/Investigator)
David W. Gilmore (Paralegal/Investigator)
John C. Hopkins (Paralegal/Investigator)
Thaddeus E. Kulesa (Paralegal/Investigator)
J. Peter Love (Paralegal/Investigator)
William H. Seabold (Paralegal/Investigator)
Kathleen Simon (Paralegal)
Steve M. Smith (Paralegal/Investigator)
Kevin J. Walsh (Paralegal/Investigator)
Judson Whitehorn (Paralegal/Investigator)
Samantha M. Johansen (Paralegal/Investigator)

For full biographical listings, see the Martindale-Hubbell Law Directory

SHUTTS & BOWEN LLP (AV)

A Partnership including Professional Associations
One Clearlake Centre, 250 Australian Avenue Suite 500, 33401
Telephone: 561-835-8500
Fax: 561-650-8530
URL: HTTP://WWW.SHUTTS-LAW.COM
Miami, Florida Office: 1500 Miami Center, 201 South Biscayne Boulevard.
Telephone: 305-358-6300.
Telefax: 305-381-9982.
Orlando, Florida Office: 20 North Orange Avenue, Suite 1000.
Telephone: 407-423-3200.
Fax: 407-425-8316.
Tallahassee, Florida Office: 215 South Monroe Street, Suite 804.
Telephone: 850-521-0600.
Fax: 850-521-0604.
Fort Lauderdale, Florida Office: First Union Center, Suite 2000, 200 East Broward Boulevard.
Telephone: 954-524-5505.
Fax: 954-524-5506.
Amsterdam, The Netherlands Office: Shutts & Bowen, B.V., Europa Boulevard 59, 1083 AD, Amsterdam.
Telephone: (31 20) 661-0969.
Fax: (31 20) 642-1475.
London, England Office: 43 Grosvenor Street, London W1X 9PG.
Telephone: 441-71-493-4840.
Telefax: 441-71-493-4299.

MEMBERS OF FIRM

Arnold L. Berman (Resident)
James A. Farrell
Charles Robinson Fawsett (P.A.)
David A. Gart
Robert E. Gunn (P.A.) (Resident)
Joseph F. McSorley (Resident)
Arthur J. Menor (Resident)
Robert C. Sommerville (P.A.)
John B. White (P.A.)
Scott G. Williams (Resident)

RESIDENT ASSOCIATES

Michael R. Ansay
Jonathan D. Gerber
Robert B. Goldman
Mark L. Pateman
Neil B. Shoter

OF COUNSEL

John R. Day (P.A.)

For full biographical listings, see the Martindale-Hubbell Law Directory

WALTON LANTAFF SCHROEDER & CARSON (AV)

A Partnership including Professional Associations
United National Bank Tower, Suite 800, 1645 Palm Beach Lakes Boulevard, P.O. Box 2966, 33401
Telephone: 561-689-6700
Telecopier: 561-689-2647
Email: dtharp@waltonlantaff.com *URL:* http://www.waltonlantaff.com
Miami, Florida Office: 9350 Financial Centre, 9350 South Dixie Highway.
Telephone: 305-379-6411 and 305-671-1300.
Telecopier: 305-670-7065.
Fort Lauderdale, Florida Office: Third Floor, Blackstone Building, 707 Southeast Third Avenue.
Telephone: 954-463-8456.
Telecopier: 954-763-6294.

RESIDENT PARTNERS

Wayne T. Gill (P.A.)
Amy L. Smith (P.A.)
Kurt A. Wyland
David S. Tadros (P.A.)

RESIDENT ASSOCIATES

Steven E. Foor
Gregg R. Margre
Jane Anderson
Gerald K. McKim
Daniel G. Williams
William T. Abel

For full biographical listings, see the Martindale-Hubbell Law Directory

JAMES MCCARTNEY WEARN, P.A. (AV)

2023 North Flagler Drive, 33407
Telephone: 561-659-0655
Fax: 561-659-0685

James McCartney Wearn

For full biographical listings, see the Martindale-Hubbell Law Directory

WINTER HAVEN, Polk Co.

CRITTENDEN & CRITTENDEN, P.A. (AV)

103 Avenue A., N.W., P.O. Drawer 152, 33882-0152
Telephone: 941-293-2161
Fax: 941-299-3207

H. C. Crittenden (1898-1969)
Robert R. Crittenden

LEGAL SUPPORT PERSONNEL

Peggy L. Thompson
Freida G. Hart

Counsel for: City of Lake Alfred, Florida; 400 and 402 Avenue K Prof. Partnerships; Town of Dundee; Town of Lake Hamilton.
Approved Attorney for: Lawyers Title Insurance Corp.; Federal Land Bank of Columbia, South Carolina; Attorneys' Title Insurance Fund.

PETERSON & MYERS, P.A. (AV)

Lake Region Plaza, 141 5th Street N.W., P.O. Drawer 7608, 33883-7608
Telephone: 941-294-3360
Lake Wales, Florida Office: 130 East Central Avenue, P.O. Box 1079.
Telephones: 941-676-7611; 683-8942.
Lakeland, Florida Office: 100 East Main Street, P.O. Box 24628.
Telephones: 941-683-6511; 676-6934.

M. David Alexander, III
Philip O. Allen
Jack P. Brandon
Kristen Marie Buzzanca
Debra Leigh Cline
J. Davis Connor
Dennis G. Corrick
Roy A. Craig, Jr.
Clinton A. Curtis
Jacob C. Dykxhoorn
Joseph A. Geary
Maria "Mia" Gerber
Jonn D. Hoppe
Dennis P. Johnson
Kevin C. Knowlton
Douglas A. Lockwood, III
Corneal B. Myers
E. Blake Paul
Robert E. Puterbaugh
Thomas B. Putnam, Jr.
Deborah A. Ruster
Stephen R. Senn
Andrea Teves Smith
Keith H. Wadsworth
Kerry M. Wilson

General Counsel for: SunTrust Bank Mid-Florida, N.A.; Lakeland Regional Medical Center, Inc.; Housing Finance Authority of Polk County.
Representative Clients: NationsBank, N.A.; First Union National Bank; Mutual Wholesale Co.; Ben Hill Griffin, Inc.; E. R. Jahna Industries, Inc.
Approved Attorneys for: Attorneys' Title Insurance Fund; Equitable Life Assurance Society of the United States.

For full biographical listings, see the Martindale-Hubbell Law Directory

WINTER PARK, Orange Co.

TROUTMAN, WILLIAMS, IRVIN, GREEN & HELMS, PROFESSIONAL ASSOCIATION (AV)

311 West Fairbanks Avenue, 32789-5001
Telephone: 407-647-2277
Toll Free: 1-800-432-5106
Telefax: 407-628-2986
Oviedo, Florida Office: 1757 West Broadway Street, Suite 4, 32765.
Telephone: 407-359-7848.
Fax: 407-358-7849.

(See Next Column)

TROUTMAN, WILLIAMS, IRVIN, GREEN & HELMS PROFESSIONAL ASSOCIATION—*Continued*

Russell Troutman	Robert F. Green
Joseph H. Williams	Roger D. Helms
Paul B. Irvin	Joseph J. Polich, Jr.

Robert N. Hemphill

For full biographical listings, see the Martindale-Hubbell Law Directory

GEORGIA

*ALBANY,** Dougherty Co.

DONALDSON, BELL & PICKETT, P.C. (AV)

127 North Westover Boulevard, P.O. Box 1607, 31708-0639
Telephone: 912-439-8987
Facsimile: 912-439-0150
Email: DoBePi@worldnet.att.net

George P. Donaldson, III	R. Ripley Bell, Jr.

Mark L. Pickett

For full biographical listings, see the Martindale-Hubbell Law Directory

W. EDWARD MEEKS, JR. (AV)

2410 Westgate Drive, Suite 105, P.O. Drawer 71525, 31708-1525
Telephone: 912-439-9234
Fax: 912-439-9175

Representative Clients: Pritchett Ford; Tri-County Aq.; Alarm Services, Inc.; Lee County Board of Education; BESCO Steel.

For full biographical listings, see the Martindale-Hubbell Law Directory

*ATHENS,** Clarke Co.

BLASINGAME, BURCH, GARRARD, BRYANT & ASHLEY, P.C. (AV)

440 College Avenue North, P.O. Box 832, 30603
Telephone: 706-354-4000
Telecopier: 706-353-0673
Greensboro, Georgia Office: 122 N. Main Street, P.O. Box 67, 30642.
Telephone: 706-453-7139.
Fax: 706-453-7842.

J. Ralph Beaird	Andrew J. Hill, III
Gary B. Blasingame	Michael A. Morris
E. Davison Burch	Thomas H. Rogers, Jr.
Henry G. Garrard, III	William D. Harvard
Everett Clay Bryant	Rikard L. Bridges
W. Seaborn Ashley, Jr.	Ivan A. Gustafson
M. Steven Heath	David S. Thomson

Richard W. Schmidt

Matthew N. Padgett	Sean P. Dolan
Christopher G. Conley	Carter A. Lawson
Pamela Lohr Hendrix	Matthew Allen Moseley
Amy Lou Reynolds	Molly K. O'Steen

Josh B. Wages

Representative Clients: NationsBank; Georgia Power Co.; Atlanta Gas Light Company; Pittsburgh Corning Corp.; Downtown Athens Development Authority; Fowler Products Co., Inc.; Athens Newspapers, Inc.; First National Bank of Commerce; Athens First Bank & Trust Co.; Reynolds Plantation.

For full biographical listings, see the Martindale-Hubbell Law Directory

*ATLANTA,** Fulton Co.

ALTMAN, KRITZER & LEVICK, P.C. (AV)

Powers Ferry Landing, Suite 224, 6400 Powers Ferry Road, N.W., 30339
Telephone: 770-955-3555
Fax: 770-952-7821, 955-2866, 955-0038, 955-3697
Email: akl@akl.com
New York, N.Y. Office: 730 Fifth Avenue, Suite 1805, 10019.
Telephone: 212-489-3745.
Fax: 212-489-3729.
Schaumburg, Illinois Affiliate: Altman, Kritzer & Levick, Ltd., Suite 700, 1101 Perimeter Drive, 60173.
Telephone: 847-240-0340.
Fax: 847-240-0344.

Allen D. Altman	Benno G. Rothschild, Jr.
Mark J. Levick	Theodore H. Sandler
D. Charles Houk	Frank Slover
Charles L. Wood	W. Daniel Hicks, Jr.
Ephraim Spielman	Robert D. Simons
Emily Sanford Bair	Peter M. Hartman

(See Next Column)

Duane D. Sitar	Christian D. Shields
Debra M. Thompson	Theodore I. Blum
John E. Taylor	Joseph D. Wargo
John H. Lewis	J. Scott Carr
Steven J. Roberts	Michael S. French
Keith N. Wilson	Constance E. Rodts

OF COUNSEL

Craig H. Kritzer	Kevin M. Walsh
Richard P. Rubenoff	Mitchell S. Block (Not admitted in GA)
James R. Harland, Jr.	
Jack M. Martin	Ilene H. Ferenczy (Not admitted in GA)
Lori E. Kilberg	
Mark V. Benveniste	Gary L. Simpson

Andrew P. Grant

Jeremy D. Cohen	Ashley C. Stanley
Craig P. Colburn, Jr.	Kristen D. A. Carpenter
Thomas D. White	Ajay K. Jindia
Karen M. Edwards	Angela Hsu
Beth McRae Mayfield	Christen Civiletto Carey
Gil Y. Burstiner	Mary Suzanne Causey
Jack D. Pappalardo (Not admitted in GA)	David L. Pardue
	Robert A. Chubb
Michael R. Deming	Samuel R. Arden
Kristen A. Yadlosky	C. Celeste Creswell
Jeanine L. Gibbs	Stephanie D. Ratcliffe

Susan M. Gordon

LEGAL SUPPORT PERSONNEL

Cynthia A. Groszkiewicz

Representative Clients: Home Depot U.S.A., Inc.; Atlantic Southeast Airlines, Inc.; Ingles Markets, Inc.; Zartic, Inc.; Pacesetter Steel Service, Inc.; Sears, Roebuck and Co.

For full biographical listings, see the Martindale-Hubbell Law Directory

FRANCIS M. BIRD, JR. (AV)

400 Colony Square, Suite 1750, 1201 Peachtree Street, N.E., 30361
Telephone: 404-875-7990
Fax: 404-892-8560
Email: fmbirdjr@mindspring.com
Email: fmbirdjr@aol.com *URL:* http://members.aol.com/FMBIRDJR/index.html

For full biographical listings, see the Martindale-Hubbell Law Directory

BOVIS, KYLE & BURCH, LLC (AV)

A Limited Liability Corporation including Professional Corporations
Third Floor, 53 Perimeter Center East, 30346
Telephone: 770-391-9100
Telecopier: 770-668-0878
Email: bkb@boviskyle.com *URL:* http://www.boviskyle.com

John M. Bovis (P.C.)	J. Wesley Skinner
Steven J. Kyle (P.C.)	Gregory R. Veal
John V. Burch (P.C.)	Timothy J. Burson
C. Sam Thomas (P.C.)	Charles M. Medlin
James E. Singer	John H. Peavy Jr.

J.S. Scott Busby	Jana B. Tabor
Christina A. Craddock	Carl A. Hassler
Timothy A. Hickey, Jr.	John David Etheriedge

Everett A. Kliphouse

For full biographical listings, see the Martindale-Hubbell Law Directory

CHOREY, TAYLOR & FEIL, A PROFESSIONAL CORPORATION (AV)

Suite 1700, The Lenox Building, 3399 Peachtree Road, N.E., 30326
Telephone: 404-841-3200
Facsimile: 404-841-3221
Email: ctf@ctflegal.com

Thomas V. Chorey, Jr.	Celeste McCollough
John L. Taylor, Jr.	Matthew L. Hess
Otto F. Feil III	David A. Flanigan, Jr.

Jeffery T. Coleman	C. David Lumsden
Lisa Fivars Harper	John E. Brenneis

OF COUNSEL

Zack D. Cravey, Jr.	Stephen S. Ritchey

For full biographical listings, see the Martindale-Hubbell Law Directory

Atlanta—Continued

Dennis, Corry & Porter, L.L.P. (AV)

3300 One Atlanta Plaza, 950 East Paces Ferry Road, P.O. Box 18640, 30326
Telephone: 404-816-2800
Wats: 800-735-0838
Fax: 404-816-5656
URL: http://www.dcplaw.com

MEMBERS OF FIRM

Robert E. Corry, Jr.
R. Clay Porter
James S. Strawinski
Grant B. Smith
Matthew J. Jewell
Raymond J. Kurey
Ronald Ray Coleman, Jr.
Scott W. McMickle

OF COUNSEL

Douglas Dennis

ASSOCIATES

Thomas D. Trask
Christopher D. Pixley
John D. Dixon
Stephanie F. Goff
Kerry A. Quinn
George A. Koenig
Michael Goldberg
Michael F. Coogan
Todd M. Yates
Nicole L. Wolfe
Alisa W. Terry
Stephanie Collings Patel
Michael A. Prieto

Representative Clients: Schneider National, Inc.; Roadway Express, Inc.; Caliber System, Inc.

For full biographical listings, see the Martindale-Hubbell Law Directory

Fain, Major, Wiley & Brennan, P.C. (AV)

100 Glenridge Point Parkway Suite 500, 30342-1440
Telephone: 404-688-6633
Telecopier: 404-420-1544

Donald M. Fain (1931-1999)
Gene A. Major
Charles A. Wiley, Jr.
Thomas E. Brennan
John K. Miles, Jr.
Darryl G. Haynes

Brian Alligood
Kim Monroe Jackson
Robert L. Jones
James A. Rice, Jr.
James Curry
Brian M. Leepson
Stephen Anthony Fern
Michael K. Watson

Representative Clients: Allstate Insurance Co.; Budget Rent-A-Car; Arkansas Best Corp.; Chrysler Insurance Co.; Georgia Farm Bureau Mutual Insurance Co.; Hertz Corp.; Universal Underwriters Insurance Co.; Westfield Insurance Co.; Winn-Dixie Stores, Inc.

For full biographical listings, see the Martindale-Hubbell Law Directory

Gambrell & Stolz, L.L.P. (AV)

SunTrust Plaza, 303 Peachtree Street Suite 4300, 30308
Telephone: 404-577-6000
FAX: 404-221-6501
Email: lawfirm@gambrell.com *URL:* http://www.gambrell.com
Northpark Office: Suite 1230, Northpark 400 Tower, 1000 Abernathy Road, N.E., Atlanta, 30328.
Telephone: 404-577-6000.
FAX: 404-589-3400.

David H. Gambrell
Irwin W. Stolz, Jr.
Bryan M. Cavan
James R. McGuone
Nedom A. Haley
Robert G. Brazier
Tobin N. Watt
George M. Bobo
Henry B. Levi
Leo J. Fogarty
Linda A. Klein
Gary A. Barnes
Nancy E. Gordon
Michael M. Smith
Andrew H. Prussack
Robert E. DeWitt
Jennifer Grandoff Cooper

ASSOCIATES

Seaton D. Purdom
Michelle Kenyon
Allison P. Coplein
Adam L. Smith
Daniel M. Epstein
Gregory G. Schultz
Jessica A. Ryan
Joshua Tropper
(Not admitted in GA)
Steven G. Hall

For full biographical listings, see the Martindale-Hubbell Law Directory

Goldner, Sommers, Scrudder & Bass (AV)

900 Circle 75 Parkway Suite 850, 30339
Telephone: 770-612-9200
Facsimile: 770-612-9201

MEMBERS OF FIRM

Stephen L. Goldner
Susan V. Sommers
Henry E. Scrudder, Jr.
Glenn S. Bass
Alfred A. Quillian, Jr.
Sandra G. Chase
Linda Jacobsen Pollock
Benjamin David Ladner
William W. Horlock, Jr.

(See Next Column)

ASSOCIATES

Tammy Spivack Skinner
Jane Carol Taylor
Pat M. Anagnostakis

For full biographical listings, see the Martindale-Hubbell Law Directory

Hawkins & Parnell, LLP (AV)

4000 SunTrust Plaza, 303 Peachtree Street, N.E., 30308-3243
Telephone: 404-614-7400
Fax: 404-614-7500
Email: relliott@hplegal.com *URL:* http://www.hawkinsparnell.com

MEMBERS OF FIRM

Paul M. Hawkins
J. Bruce Welch
Albert H. Parnell
A. Timothy Jones
Alan F. Herman
Michael J. Goldman
H. Lane Young, II
Frank C. Bedinger, III
William H. Major, III
T. Ryan Mock, Jr.
Jack N. Sibley
Warner S. Fox
Robert U. Wright
Michael E. Hutchins
Ollie M. Harton
Kimberly Houston
Kevin J. Bahr
Charles R. Beans
Cullen Christie Wilkerson, Jr.
Peter R. York
Kristine Berry Morain
Roger M. Goode
Dennis J. Manganiello
Christine Lupo Mast
Blanche Rose Miller
Thomas G. Tidwell
Frederick A. Bading

ASSOCIATES

Allen L. Broughton
Debra E. LeVorse
Anita Wallace Thomas
Andrew A. Davenport
David H. Wilson
Stephen Michael Bowers
E. Elaine Shofner
Robert S. Thompson
Matthew F. Barr
W. Harrison Coleman, Jr.
Gina C. Marshall
Michael J. Crist
Carl H. Anderson, Jr.
Sam L. Brannen, Jr.
Margaret A. Droppleman
(Not admitted in GA)
Gregory J. Parent
Evelyn M. Fletcher
Alycen G. Adams
Angela Dixon
Michelle D. Coburn
Brian M. Weiss
Chandler W. Mason
Michael W. Kitchens

For full biographical listings, see the Martindale-Hubbell Law Directory

The Hishon Firm, LLC (AV)

999 Peachtree Street N.E. Suite 1900, 30309
Telephone: 404-817-7791
Fax: 404-817-2486

Elizabeth Anderson Hishon
(1944-1999)
Robert H. Hishon

Nancy R. Daspit

For full biographical listings, see the Martindale-Hubbell Law Directory

Holland & Knight LLP (AV)

1201 West Peachtree Street, N.E., Suite 2000, 30309-3400
Telephone: 404-817-8500
Telecopier: 404-881-0470
Email: webmaster@hklaw.com *URL:* http://www.hklaw.com
Boston, Massachusetts Office: One Beacon Street.
Telephone: 617-523-2700.
Fax: 617-523-6850.
Falls Church, Virginia Office: 3110 Fairview Park Drive, Suite 900.
Telephone: 703-645-8600.
Fax: 703-645-8610.
Fort Lauderdale, Florida Office: One East Broward Boulevard, Suite 1300.
Telephone: 954-525-1000.
Fax: 954-463-2030.
Jacksonville, Florida Office: 50 North Laura Street, Suite 3900.
Telephone: 904-353-2000.
Fax: 904-358-1872.
Lakeland, Florida Office: 92 Lake Wire Drive.
Telephone: 941-682-1161.
Fax: 941-688-1186.
Melbourne, Florida Offices: 1499 South Harbor City Boulevard, Suite 303.
Telephone: 407-951-1776.
Fax: 407-951-1849 and 700 S. Babcock Street, Suite 400.
Telephone: 407-984-2700.
Fax: 407-723-4092.
Miami, Florida Office: 701 Brickell Avenue, Suite 3000.
Telephone: 305-374-8500.
Fax: 305-789-7799.
New York, New York Office: 195 Broadway, 24th Floor.
Telephone: 212-513-3200.
Fax: 212-385-9010.
Orlando, Florida Office: 200 South Orange Avenue, Suite 2600.
Telephone: 407-425-8500.
Fax: 407-244-5288.
Providence, Rhode Island Office: One Park Row, Suite 300.
Telephone: 401-751-4545.
Fax: 401-453-6411.

(See Next Column)

HOLLAND & KNIGHT LLP—*Continued*

San Francisco, California Office: 44 Montgomery Street, Suite 4050.
Telephone: 415-743-6900.
Fax: 415-743-6910.
St. Petersburg, Florida Office: 200 Central Avenue, Suite 1600.
Telephone: 813-896-7171.
Fax: 813-822-8048.
Tallahassee, Florida Office: 315 South Calhoun Street, Suite 600.
Telephone: 850-224-7000.
Fax: 850-224-8832.
Tampa, Florida Office: 400 North Ashley Drive, Suite 2300.
Telephone: 813-227-8500.
Fax: 813-229-0134.
Washington, D.C. Office: 2100 Pennsylvania Avenue, N.W., Suite 400.
Telephone: 202-955-3000.
Fax: 202-955-5564.
West Palm Beach, Florida Office: 625 North Flagler Drive, Suite 700.
Telephone: 561-833-2000.
Fax: 561-650-8399.
Mexico City, Mexico Office: HOLLAND & KNIGHT-GALLÁSTEGUI Y LOZANO, S.C. (Joint Venture Office) Avenida Paseo de los Tamarindos No. 400, Torre "B" - 2° Piso, Col. Bosques d las Lomas, C.P. 05120 Mexico, D.F.
Telephone: 011-525-261-1866.
Fax: 011-525-261-1867.

ATLANTA MEMBERS AND ASSOCIATES

Alfred B. Adams III
Robert J. Augustine
Thomas B. Branch, III
Frank O. Brown, Jr.
Raymond P. Carpenter
Daryl G. Clarida
Eileen Crowley
Harold T. Daniel, Jr.
Laurie Webb Daniel
Preston C. Delashmit
Gregory J. Digel
W. Reeder Glass
Elizabeth C. Helm
Sherie Shortridge Holmes
Susan W. Housen
Charles S. Johnson, III
Donald Kennicott
Martha J. Kuckleburg
Caroline C. Kresky
C. Edward Kuntz
Jeffrey Y. Lewis
Mary Ann B. Oakley
A. Summey Orr III
Larry S. Pike
Stanley H. Pollock
Regina Benton Reid
Keith J. Reisman
William M. Rich
Donald L. Rickertsen
James H. Rollins
R. Phillip Shinall, III
William H. Venema
Allison Wade
Paul Webb, Jr.
Lisha A. Wheeler
Keith M. Wiener
R. Douglas Wright

SENIOR COUNSEL

Timothy W. Boyd
Robert S. Highsmith, Jr.
Leighton W. Lang
Thomas O. Marshall, Jr.
Gretchen E. Nagy
James H. Watson

ASSOCIATES

Scott L. Bonder
Rachel C. Boring
Courtney Chanin Camp
Ana C. Davis (Not admitted in GA)
Jeremy Emanuel Citron
Susan Eichler Edlein
Andrew B. Goldberger
Steven W. Hardy
C. Andrew Head
Howard S. Hirsch (Not admitted in GA)
Tanya M. Lawson
J Martin Lett
Kenneth M. Neighbors
Gregory Jack Newman
Michael K. Rafter
Mary Jo Schrade
Sharon E. Smith
Caroline Johnson Tanner
Jennifer Beth Tourial

OF COUNSEL

Harry Downs

For full biographical listings, see the Martindale-Hubbell Law Directory

HOLT NEY ZATCOFF & WASSERMAN, LLP (AV)

A Partnership including Professional Corporations
100 Galleria Parkway, Suite 600, 30339
Telephone: 770-956-9600
Facsimile: 770-956-1490
Email: mthomas@hnzw.com

MEMBERS OF FIRM

Robert G. Holt (P.C.)
James M. Ney (P.C.)
Sanford H. Zatcoff (P.C.)
Michael G. Wasserman (P.C.)
J. Scott Jacobson
Stephen C. Greenberg
Richard P. Vornholt
Brian P. Cain
Jay Frank Castle

OF COUNSEL

Penni A. Dudley

ASSOCIATES

Gregory A. Randall (Not admitted in GA)
Thomas K. Anderson
Scott E. Morris

Representative Clients: American Realty Trust, Inc.; Citibank, N.A.; Cummins South, Inc.; First American Title Insurance Co.; First Union National Bank of Georgia; Gables Residential Trust; Primavera Financial Services; The University Financing Foundation, Inc.; Nations Bank, N.A.; Safety-Kleen Corp.

(See Next Column)

For full biographical listings, see the Martindale-Hubbell Law Directory

JOHNSON & WARD (AV)

2100 The Equitable Building, 100 Peachtree Street N.W., 30303-1962
Telephone: 404-524-5626
Facsimile: 404-524-1769
Email: postmaster@johnsonward.com

MEMBERS OF FIRM

William C. Lanham
Clark H. McGehee
John C. Dabney, Jr.
Baxter P. Jones
William D. deGolian
Bruce A. Maxwell

OF COUNSEL

James E. Goodman

For full biographical listings, see the Martindale-Hubbell Law Directory

JONES, DAY, REAVIS & POGUE (AV)

3500 SunTrust Plaza, 303 Peachtree Street, 30308-3242
Telephone: 404-521-3939
Telecopier: 404-581-8330
Email: counsel@jonesday.com *URL:* http://www.jonesday.com
In Brussels, Belgium: Avenue Louise 480, 7th Floor, B-1050 Brussels.
Telephone: 32-2-645-14-11.
Telecopier: 32-2-645-14-45.
In Chicago, Illinois: 77 West Wacker.
Telephone: 312-782-3939.
Telecopier: 312-782-8585.
In Cleveland, Ohio: North Point. 901 Lakeside Avenue.
Telephone: 216-586-3939.
Telecopier: 216-579-0212.
In Columbus, Ohio: 1900 Huntington Center.
Telephone: 614-469-3939.
Telecopier: 614-461-4198.
In Dallas, Texas: 2727 North Harwood Street.
Telephone: 214-220-3939.
Telecopier: 214-969-5100.
In Frankfurt, Germany: Hochhaus am Park, Grüneburgweg 102, 60323 Frankfurt am Main.
Telephone: 49-69-9726-3939.
Telecopier: 49-69-9726-3993.
In Geneva, Switzerland: 20, rue de Candolle.
Telephone: 41-22-320-2339.
Telecopier: 41-22-320-1232.
In Hong Kong: 29th Floor, Entertainment Building, 30 Queen's Road Central.
Telephone: 852-2526-6895.
Telecopier: 852-2868-5871 or 852-2868-5699.
In Irvine, California: 5 Park Plaza, Suite 1100.
Telephone: 949-851-3939.
Telecopier: 949-553-7539.
In London, England: Bucklersbury House, 3 Queen Victoria Street.
Telephone: 44-171-236-3939.
Telecopier: 44-171-236-1113.
In Los Angeles, California: 555 West Fifth Street, Suite 4600.
Telephone: 213-489-3939.
Telecopier: 213-243-2539.
In New Delhi, India (Associate Office): Pathak & Associates (an associate firm of Jones, Day, Reavis & Pogue), 1st Floor, Dr. Gopal Das Bhaven, 28 Barakhamba Road.
Telephone: 91-11-373-8793; 91-11-335-7345.
Telecopier: 91-11-335-3761.
In New York, New York: 599 Lexington Avenue.
Telephone: 212-326-3939.
Telecopier: 212-755-7306.
In Paris, France: 120, rue du Faubourg Saint-Honoré.
Telephone: 33-1-56-59-39-39.
Telecopier: 33-1-56-59-39-38
In Pittsburgh, Pennsylvania: 500 Grant Street, 31st Floor.
Telephone: 412-391-3939.
Telecopier: 412-394-7959.
In Riyadh, Saudi Arabia: The International Law Firm (In Association with Jones, Day, Reavis & Pogue), Sulaymaniyah, Prince Mishari IBN, Abdulaziz Street, P.O. Box 22166.
Telephone: (966-1) 462-8866.
Telecopier: (966-1) 462-9001.
In Shanghai, China: 2805 Kerry Centre, 1515 Nanjing Road West.
Telephone: 86-21-5298-6568.
Telecopier: 86-21-5298-6569.
In Sydney, Australia: Governor Phillip Tower, Level 38, 1 Farrer Place.
Telephone: 61-2-9210-6921.
Telecopier: 61-2-9210-6926.
In Taipei, Taiwan: 8th Floor, 2 Tun Hwa South Road, Section 2.
Telephone: (886-2) 2704-6808.
Telecopier: (886-2) 2704-6791.
In Tokyo, Japan: Toranomon MT Building, 4th Floor, 10-3, Toranomon 3-Chome, Minato-ku, Tokyo 105, Japan.
Telephone: 81-3-3433-3939.
Telecopier: 81-3-5401-2725.
In Washington, D.C.: 51 Louisiana Avenue, N.W.
Telephone: 202-879-3939.
Telecopier: 202-626-1700.

(See Next Column)

JONES, DAY, REAVIS & POGUE, *Atlanta—Continued*

MEMBERS OF FIRM IN ATLANTA

Robert W. Smith
Girard E. Boudreau, Jr.
Russell S. Grove, Jr.
Christopher L. Carson
Alvis E. Campbell
John R. Cornell (Not admitted in GA)
William S. Paddock
John M. Edwards, Jr.
James H. Landon
David J. Bailey
R. Mason Cargill
Milford B. Hatcher, Jr.
Richard M. Kirby
G. Lee Garrett, Jr.
J. Lawrence Manning, Jr. (Not admitted in GA)
Barry J. Stein
James R. Johnson
John E. Zamer
Dan T. Carter
Scott A. Specht
William B. B. Smith
Lisa Anne Stater
R. Matthew Martin
Lizanne Thomas
Deborah A. Sudbury
Sidney R. Brown
Gregory Russell Hanthorn
Rory D. Lyons
Ralph R. Morrison
Stephanie E. Parker
Matthew J. Toddy
Michael Joseph McConnell
Samuel J. Najim (Not admitted in GA)
William Baxter Rowland
David M. Monde
Edgar C. Snow, Jr.
Elaine Rogers Walsh
Mark L. Hanson

OF COUNSEL

Ruth H. Gershon
Charles W. Whitney
John H. Grady, III

COUNSEL

L. Trammell Newton, Jr.
Arthur G. Kent
Lisa E. Chang
Robert N. Johnson

ASSOCIATES

Wade R. Wright
Elizabeth Bolton Davis
Paul Greco
Janine Cone Metcalf
Brad A. Baldwin
Diane G. Pulley
Michael P. Bruyere
Maria F. Farall
Kim Purcell Pike
Douglas M. Towns
Julie A. Fleming
Wendy Y. Hennessey
Michelle A. Hickerson
Shahram A. Eslami
S. Jefferson Greenway
Joseph E. Finley
Jeana Girard
Megan A. Kelly
M. Todd King
Edward M. Manigault
Theresia M. Moser
William N. Smith
Dean A. Calloway
John M. Lee
Mona P. März (Not admitted in United States)
David Phillips
Robin A. Schmähl
Catherine B. Stevens
Jeong-Hwa Lee Towery
Donald M. Woodard
Katherine A. Alberts
Wendy Butler
Anne M. Johnson
A. Michael Lee
Jeanne L. Shingleton
Neil M. Simon
Diana D. Suber
Shannon A. Singleton
Luke W. Andrews
Elizabeth M. Baumgarten
Bridgette M. Cooper
Deborah M. Franz
J. Elizabeth Grabowski
Kim Potter
Charmaine L. Slack
John F. Yarber

For full biographical listings, see the Martindale-Hubbell Law Directory

---

KUTAK ROCK (AV)

Suite 2100, 225 Peachtree Street, N.E., 30303-1731
Telephone: 404-222-4600
Fax: 404-222-4654
URL: http://www.kutakrock.com
Denver, Colorado Office: Suite 2900, 717 Seventeenth Street, 80202-3329.
Telephone: 303-297-2400.
Facsimile: 303-292-7799.
Kansas City, Missouri Office: One Main Plaza, Suite 810, 4435 Main Street, 64111-7727.
Telephone: 816-960-0090.
Telefax: 816-960-0041.
Little Rock, Arkansas Office: Suite 1100, 425 West Capitol Avenue, 72201-3409.
Telephone: 501-975-3000.
Facsimile: 501-975-3001.
New York, New York Office: 650 Fifth Avenue, 10019-6108.
Telephone: 212-713-6480.
Facsimile: 212-713-6481.
Oklahoma City, Oklahoma Office: Suite 475, 6305 Waterford Boulevard, 73118-1116.
Telephone: 405-848-2475.
Facsimile: 405-842-5748.
Omaha, Nebraska Office: The Omaha Building, 1650 Farnam Street, 68102-2186.
Telephone: 402-346-6000.
Facsimile: 402-346-1148.
Phoenix, Arizona Office: 16th Floor, 3300 North Central Avenue, 85012-2516.
Telephone: 602-285-1700.
Facsimile: 602-285-1868.

(See Next Column)

Pittsburgh, Pennsylvania Office: 1214 Frick Building, 437 Grant Street, 15219-6002.
Telephone: 412-261-6720.
Facsimile: 412-261-6717.
Washington, D.C. Office: Suite 1000, 1101 Connecticut Avenue, NW, 20036-4374.
Telephone: 202-828-2400.
Facsimile: 202-828-2488.
Newport Beach, California Office: Suite 450, 620 Newport Center Drive, 92660-8019.
Telephone: 949-718-6700.
Facsimile: 949-718-6708.

MEMBERS OF FIRM

Lawrence L. Thompson
Michael K. Wolensky
Edward M. Ford
Paul M. Smith
David A. Nix
David L. Amsden
William F. Clark
Robert G. Brunton
Gregory R. Crochet
Michael A. Kazamias
Angela Gottsche Miele

OF COUNSEL

Robert E. Altenbach

ASSOCIATES

David J. Gellen
Ethan H. Cohen
Elizabeth M. Davis
Donald E. Peterson
Shannon C. Baxter
Shannon L. Bizzell
Elena Kaplan

For full biographical listings, see the Martindale-Hubbell Law Directory

---

LIPSHUTZ, GREENBLATT & KING (AV)

2300 Harris Tower-Peachtree Center, 233 Peachtree Street, N.E., 30303
Telephone: 404-688-2300
Fax: 404-588-0648
Email: rmllgk@aol.com

MEMBERS OF FIRM

Robert J. Lipshutz
Edward L. Greenblatt
Randall M. Lipshutz
James V. Zito

OF COUNSEL

William R. King
Tito Mazzetta

ASSOCIATE

Paula B. Smith
Mindy C. Waitsman

For full biographical listings, see the Martindale-Hubbell Law Directory

---

LONG ALDRIDGE & NORMAN LLP (AV)

A Limited Liability Partnership including Professional Corporations
Suite 5300, 303 Peachtree Street, 30308
Telephone: 404-527-4000
Telecopier: 404-527-4198
Email: atlanta@lanlaw.com *URL:* http://www.lanlaw.com
Washington, D.C. Office: Suite 600, 701 Pennsylvania Avenue, N.W., 20004.
Telephone: 202-624-1200.
FAX: 202-624-1298.

MEMBERS OF FIRM

John G. Aldridge
Evan Appel
David L. Balser
James L. Barkin
Robert A. Bartlett
Philip D. Bartz (Resident, Washington, D.C. Office)
Steven K. Bender
Douglas L. Beresford (Resident, Washington, D.C. Office)
Gaspare J. Bono (Resident, Washington, D.C. Office)
Michael S. Bradley
Phillip A. Bradley
Wayne N. Bradley
Bruce P. Brown
David M. Calhoun
Charles E. Campbell
Clyde E. Click
J. David Dantzler, Jr.
George (Buddy) Darden
Dennis A. Davison (Resident, Washington, D.C. Office)
L. Craig Dowdy
Kevin M. Downey (Resident, Washington, D.C. Office)
Deborah S. Ebel
William L. Floyd
Barbara H. Gallo
Jeffrey K. Haidet
Thomas D. Hall
Robert D. Hancock, Jr.
Edward D. Hirsch
Frank W. Hunger (Resident, Washington, D.C. Office)
David M. Ivey
J. James Johnson
Margaret M. Joslin
Mark S. Kaufman
Steven B. Kelber (Resident, Washington, D.C. Office)
Marc R. Labgold (Resident, Washington, D.C. Office)
Steven J. Labovitz
Mark S. Lange
Thomas P. Lauth, III
H. Franklin Layson
J. Michael Levengood
James D. Levine
Clay C. Long
Maurice Ted Maloof
Gary W. Marsh
Keith W. Mason
Patrick M. McGeehan
Barbara A. McIntyre
Carl W. Mullis, III
Laura Fink Nix
Albert G. Norman, Jr.
C. Randall Nuckolls (Resident, Washington, D.C. Office)
W. Gregory Null
Ian K. Portnoy (Resident, Washington, D.C. Office)
H. Carol Saul
Douglas D. Selph
Henry F. Sewell, Jr.

(See Next Column)

LONG ALDRIDGE & NORMAN LLP—*Continued*

MEMBERS OF FIRM (Continued)

Leonard A. Silverstein
Jacolyn A. Simmons (Resident, Washington, D.C. Office)
Edgar H. Sims, Jr. (P.C.)
Jesse J. Spikes
William F. Stevens
John T. Stough, Jr. (Resident, Washington, D.C. Office)
Patricia E. Tate
John E. Theberge (Resident, Washington, D.C. Office)
James J. Thomas II
William F. Timmons
Briggs L. Tobin
Russell A. Tolley
Robert E. Tritt
Lisa W. Wannamaker
Thomas R. B. Wardell
John L. Watkins
Charles D. Weiss
Terry R. Weiss
Charles E. Wilson, III
Charles T. Zink

SENIOR COUNSEL

F. T. Davis, Jr., (P.C.)
Robert E. Hicks
W. Stell Huie

ASSOCIATES

Claire Alison Addlestone
Barry J. Armstrong
Chris Gregory Baugher
R. Daniel Beale
Erik Belenky
Kevin M. Bell (Resident, Washington, D.C. Office)
Karen L. Bernstein
L. Briley Brisendine, Jr.
Conrad D. Brooks
Gregory S. Brow
Jeffery W. Cavender
Philip A. Cooper
Lesley E. Daigle
Donna M. Donlon (Resident, Washington, D.C. Office)
Karl J. Forrest
Christine E. Frey
Jennifer Froneberger
James A. Graves
Mark R. Heilbrun (Resident, Washington, D.C. Office)
James M. Heintz (Resident, Washington, D.C. Office)
Terri Annette Herron
George F. Hobday, Jr. (Resident, Washington, D.C. Office)
John P. Hutchins
Nicole M. Imamshah (Not admitted in GA)
John N. Ingram
Doreen M Jackson (Resident, Washington, D.C. Office)
Alan R. Jenkins
Sheridan Bracken Johnson
William Henry Johnson
M. Graham Loomis
Kelly Ann Luongo
Joanna Penland Love Mangum
S. Jill Marion (Not admitted in GA)
J. Timothy Mast
Sheryl McCalla
Ann-Marie M. McGaughey
Adam G. Mersereau
Jess A. Pinkerton
Rebekah N. Plowman
Kristen M. Pollock
Julie Sonenshine Porter
Thadd A. Prisco (Resident, Washington, D.C. Office)
G. Scott Rafshoon
Rayne Rasty
M. Lee Reeves (Not admitted in GA)
Russell J. Rogers
Melissa A. Schnell
Daniel H. Sherman IV
Johnathan H. Short
Robert Todd Silliman
Jeremy C. Silverman
Stacy C. Sins
Lawrence A. Slovensky
Amy Elizabeth Smith
Steven Paul Smith
Gabriel Stephen Sterling, III (Resident, Washington, D.C. Office)
David N. Stern
Elizabeth C. Stone
Andrew J. Surdykowski
James Angel Tabb
Michael R. Tippett
Constance Ann Walters
James A. Washburn
Anna W. Nicol
Richard R. Willis
Douglas J. Witten
Angelyn M. Wright

OF COUNSEL

Juan Carlos Benitez (Resident, Washington, D.C. Office)
Theodore Brown, Jr.
Cameron Cohick (Resident, Washington, D.C. Office)
Sharon E. Crane (Resident, Washington, D.C. Office)
James W. Culbreth
Sharon A. Gay
Emily Gail Gunnells
Kirkland A. McGhee
J. Michell Philpott
Mindy S. Planer
Catherine Bax Richardson (Resident, Washington, D.C. Office)
Janice N. Smith
Gerald D. Walling

For full biographical listings, see the Martindale-Hubbell Law Directory

LORD, BISSELL & BROOK (AV)

One Atlantic Center, 1201 West Peachtree Street, N.W., Suite 3700, 30309
Telephone: 404-870-4600
Telecopy: 404-872-5547
Email: info@lordbissell.com *URL:* http://www.lordbissell.com
Chicago, Illinois Office: Suites 2600-3600 Harris Bank Building, 115 South LaSalle Street, 60603.
Telephone: 312-443-0700.
Telecopy: 312-443-0336.
Cable Address: "Lowirco."
Telex: 25-0336.
Los Angeles, California Office: 300 South Grand Avenue, 90071-3200.
Telephone: 213-485-1500.
Telecopy: 213-485-1200.
Telex: 18-1135.
Rockford, Illinois Office: 120 West State Street, Suite 200, 61101.
Telephone: 815-963-8050.
New York, N.Y. Office: One Penn Plaza, Suite 3435, 10119.
Telephone: 212-947-4700.
Facsimile: 212-947-1202.

(See Next Column)

RESIDENT PARTNERS

Michael J. Athans
Paul L. Fields, Jr.
David G. Greene
Terry R. Howell
David M. Leonard
Robert E. McLaughlin
Prescott L. Nottingham
Walton N. Smith
Thomas J. Strueber
Richard M. Watson
Corliss L. Worford

RESIDENT ASSOCIATES

Robert M. Bennison
Donald J. Chenevert
Richard E. Dolder, Jr.
Ellie A. Doyle
Kristen K. Duggan
Christopher B. Hall
Robert D. Howell
William Thomas Lacy, Jr.
Kevin A. Maxim
Steven D. Moore (Not admitted in GA)
Ugo N. Okafor

OF COUNSEL

Marsha Kellman Klevickis

For full biographical listings, see the Martindale-Hubbell Law Directory

MACEY, WILENSKY, COHEN, WITTNER & KESSLER, LLP (AV)

285 Peachtree Center Avenue, Suite 600, 30303-1229
Telephone: 404-584-1200
Telecopier: 404-681-4355
Email: Lawyers@MaceyWilensky.com

MEMBERS OF FIRM

Morris W. Macey
Frank B. Wilensky
H. William Cohen
Sheldon R. Wittner (1943-1988)
Richard P. Kessler, Jr.
Neil C. Gordon
Susan L. Howick
M. Todd Westfall
James R. Sacca
David B. Kurzweil
Robert A. Winter
Richard C. Litwin

ASSOCIATES

Pamela Gronauer Hill
Rachel Anderson Snider
Todd E. Hennings
Kristine M. Shryock
Michael C. Kaplan
Michael R. Wing
Louis G. McBryan

OF COUNSEL

Bruce L. Whitmer

For full biographical listings, see the Martindale-Hubbell Law Directory

MCCULLOUGH SHERRILL, LLP (AV)

1409 Peachtree Street, N.E., 30309
Telephone: 404-885-1500
Telecopier: 404-892-1801
Email: info@mslegal.com *URL:* http://www.mslegal.com

MEMBERS OF FIRM

Kenneth R. McCullough
John A. Sherrill
Paul M. Baisier
Mark A. Block
William D. Brunstad
Patrick J. Clarke
Michael D. Crisp
Kirk R. Fjelstul
Allen W. Groves
D. Lynn Holliday
C. Walker Ingraham
William M. Joseph
James H. Kaminer, Jr.
James W. King
Paul P. Mattingly
George L. Murphy, Jr.
Chester G. Rosenberg
Jerry A. Shaifer
Bradley C. Skidmore
W. Clayton Sparrow, Jr.
Bradley J. Taylor
Robert M. Trusty
Kathryn M. Zickert

ASSOCIATES

Susan T. Craighead
Victor A. Ellis
Gale G. Evans
Jana L. Evans
C. Clay Haden
M. Hakim Hilliard
Loren E. Kalish
Corin M. McCarthy
Kamyar Molavi
Joseph V. Myers, III
Michael S. Rodgers
Steven M. Staes
Lawrence A. Thrower
Newton Jasper Wardlaw, IV
Philip E. West

OF COUNSEL

Lawrence E. Abbott (Not admitted in GA)
Lawrence M. Gold
Deborah D. Kuchler (Not admitted in GA)
Ron D. Talley

For full biographical listings, see the Martindale-Hubbell Law Directory

MIDDLETON, MATHIS, ADAMS & TATE, P.C. (AV)

Suite 1400 The Equitable Building, 100 Peachtree Street, 30303
Telephone: 404-523-5000
Fax: 404-527-9894
Savannah, Georgia Office: 622 Drayton Street, P.O. Box 1006.
Telephone: 912-234-1133.
Fax: 912-234-8818.
Milledgeville, Georgia Office: 425 South Wayne Street.
Telephone: 912-453-9387.
Fax: 912-453-1393.

(See Next Column)

MIDDLETON, MATHIS, ADAMS & TATE P.C., *Atlanta—Continued*

Richard H. Middleton, Jr. (Resident, Savannah Office)
Charles A. Mathis, Jr. (P.C.)
Peter C. Adams (Resident, Savannah Office)
Mark A. Tate (Resident, Savannah Office)

Timothy R. Walmsley (Resident, Savannah Office)
Derek J. White (Resident, Savannah Office)
Douglas P. McManamy (Resident, Savannah Office)
Andrew B. Cash
David Krugler
Leslie S. Pickett (Resident, Savannah Office)
Stephen G. Lowry (Resident, Savannah Office)
Linda G. Bass (Resident, Milledgeville Office)
Alwyn R. Fredericks

OF COUNSEL

Maryellen C. Griffin

Reference: SunTrust Bank.

For full biographical listings, see the Martindale-Hubbell Law Directory

PAUL, HASTINGS, JANOFSKY & WALKER LLP (AV)

A Limited Liability Partnership including Professional Corporations
Firm Established in 1951; Office in 1980.
24th Floor, 600 Peachtree Street, N.E., 30308-2222
Telephone: 404-815-2400
Fax: 404-815-2424
URL: http://www.phjw.com
Los Angeles, California Office: 555 South Flower Street.
Telephone: 213-683-6000.
New York, New York Office: 399 Park Avenue.
Telephone: 212-318-6000.
Orange County, California Office: 695 Town Center Drive, Costa Mesa.
Telephone: 714-668-6200.
San Francisco, California Office: 345 California Street.
Telephone: 415-835-1600.
Stamford, Connecticut Office: 1055 Washington Boulevard.
Telephone: 203-961-7400.
Washington, D.C. Office: 1299 Pennsylvania Avenue, N.W.
Telephone: 202-508-9500.
Tokyo, Japan Office: Ark Mori Building, 12-32 Akasaka, P.O. Box 577, 1-Chome, Minato-Ku.
Telephone: (03) 3586-4711.
London, England Office: The International Financial Centre, 25 Old Broad Street.
Telephone: (011) 44-171-562-4000.
ATTORNEY E-MAIL ADDRESSES: first initial middle initial last name @phjw.com (e.g. rmasbill@phjw.com)

MEMBERS OF FIRM

Richard M. Asbill
R. Lawrence Ashe, Jr., (P.C.)
Jesse H. Austin, III
Daryl R. Buffenstein
Thomas G. Burch, Jr.
Ronald T. Coleman, Jr.
Kevin Conboy
Paul J. Connell
James H. Cox
Leslie A. Dent
William B. Hill, Jr.
Weyman T. Johnson, Jr.
Walter E. Jospin
J. Allen Maines
Philip J. Marzetti
Chris D. Molen
Julian D. Nealy
John G. Parker
W. Andrew Scott
Charles T. Sharbaugh
Wayne H. Shortridge
C. Geoffrey Weirich

SENIOR COUNSEL

William E. Eason, Jr.

OF COUNSEL

Eric W. Anderson
Tracey T. Barbaree
Cindy J.K. Davis
Kelly J. Koelker
Eric Charles Lang
Bruce R. Larson
Deborah A. Marlowe
Elizabeth Hardy Noe
Craig K. Pendergrast
Eric Jon Taylor
Michael T. Voytek
Crystal L. Williams (Not admitted in GA)

ASSOCIATES

Matthew A. Block
Stephanie A. Bohm
Samantha Brooks (Not admitted in GA)
Kristin L. Burns
David S. Cartee
Veronica J. Cherniak
G. Mark Cole
Bradley L. Cooper
Kathleen O. Currey
Michael W. Dubus
Brittany M. Elkins
Yvette Fallone
Rebecca D. Farber
David E. Gevertz
Elise Whitaker Googe
Regan McCarty Greene
Suzanne A. Harrison (Not admitted in GA)
Michael D. Haun (Not admitted in GA)
Susan E. Himmer
Edward S. Johnson, Jr.
Sarah K. Keech
Karen B. Koenig
J. Alexander Lawrence
Rebecca Gunn McCabe
Latonya S. Moore
Jeffrey C. Narvil
Robert C. Newcomer
Maureen E. O'Neill
Teresa Brazzel Pernini
Tracy S. Plott
Louis H. Pugh

(See Next Column)

ASSOCIATES (Continued)

Nancy E. Rafuse
M. Kasim Reed
T. Robert Reid
Melissa Cales Schwartz
Joseph C. Sharp
Kyle D. Sherman
Christopher S. Strickland
Brian D. Sullivan
Eric J. Taylor (Not admitted in GA)
Stanley F. Wasowski
William K. Whitner
Karen Jorik Wickliffe
John F. Woodham

For full biographical listings, see the Martindale-Hubbell Law Directory

POPE, MCGLAMRY, KILPATRICK & MORRISON, LLP (AV)

A Partnership including Professional Corporations
The Pinnacle, 3455 Peachtree Road, N.E., 30326-3243
Telephone: 404-523-7706
Fax: 404-524-1648
Phenix City, Alabama: 334-298-7354
Mailing Address: P.O. Box 191625, Atlanta, GA, 31119-1625
Email: pmkm@pmkm.com
Columbus, Georgia Office: 318 11th Street, 2nd Floor, P.O. Box 2128, 31902-2128.
Telephone: 706-324-0050.
Fax: 706-327-1536.

MEMBERS OF FIRM

C. Neal Pope (P.C.)
Max R. McGlamry (P.C.) (Resident, Columbus, Georgia Office)
Paul V. Kilpatrick, Jr. (Resident, Columbus, Georgia Office)
R. Timothy Morrison
Michael L. McGlamry
Earle F. Lasseter
William Usher Norwood, III
Jay F. Hirsch
Wade H. Tomlinson, III
Teresa Pike Tomlinson

RESIDENT ASSOCIATE

C. Elizabeth Pope

Reference: Columbus Bank & Trust Co.

For full biographical listings, see the Martindale-Hubbell Law Directory

POWELL, GOLDSTEIN, FRAZER & MURPHY LLP (AV)

191 Peachtree Street, N.E., Sixteenth Floor, 30303
Telephone: 404-572-6600
Telecopier: 404-572-6999
URL: http://www.pgfm.com
Washington, D.C. Office: Sixth Floor, 1001 Pennsylvania Avenue, N.W., 20004.
Telephone: 202-347-0066.

MEMBERS OF FIRM

Richard L. Arenburg
David M. Armitage
David R. Aufdenspring
David S. Baker
Eric P. Berezin
Thomas J. Biafore
Jerry B. Blackstock
Larry I. Bogart
Anthony R. Boggs
Mary Williams Bondurant
Cindy A. Brazell
Armin G. Brecher
William Bard Brockman
Edmund B. Burke
Gregory Marshall Chait
Timothy F. Coen
Paul F. Concannon
Frank A. Crisafi
William V. Custer, IV
V. Robert Denham, Jr.
Gabriel Dumitrescu
Marilyn M. Fish
Christopher P. Galanek
Jace C. Gatewood
Elliott Goldstein
Douglas S. Gosden
C. Scott Greene
John M. Gross
Wilbur Gordon Hamlin, Jr.
John W. Harbin
Robert R. Harlin
Hilary Harp
James W. Hawkins
Riccarda Heising
John H. Horne
Randall L. Hughes
LeeAnn Jones
Todd E. Jones
Jeffrey W. Kelley
Cynthia D. Kennedy
V. Scott Killingsworth
William L. Kinzer
Kathryn L. Knudson
Katherine M. Koops
Jay J. Levin
Robert C. Lewinson
William Joseph Linkous, Jr.
Mark A. Loeffler
Frank Love, Jr.
Rhett Wade Marionneaux, Jr.
John T. Marshall
Adrienne E. Marting
Samuel M. Matchett
James J. McAlpin, Jr.
Frank S. McGaughey, III
Charlene L. McGinty
Thomas R. McNeill
Rick Miller
Walter G. Moeling, IV
Charles Eugene Murphy, Jr.
Lesly Gaynor Murray
Carol D. Newman
E. Penn Nicholson
John R. Parks
William M. Ragland, Jr.
James C. Rawls
Thomas S. Richey
Suzanne J. Roberts
Eliot William Robinson
Kim H. Roeder
David G. Ross
Joan Boilen Sasine
Steven G. Schaffer
Stephen B. Schrock
William B. Shearer, Jr.
Jonathan R. Shils
E. A. Simpson, Jr.
Scott D. Smith
W. Scott Sorrels
G. William Speer
Ronald D. Stallings
William J. Thompson
Robert M. Travis
Rex R. Veal
James A. Walker, Jr.
G. Patrick Watson

(See Next Column)

POWELL, GOLDSTEIN, FRAZER & MURPHY LLP—*Continued*

MEMBERS OF FIRM (Continued)

Carl E. Westmoreland, Jr.
Karen Wildau
Joel C. Williams, Jr.
Gregory H. Worthy
John F. Wymer, III

COUNSEL

Linda G. Birchall
W. Scott Creasman
Wendy L. Hagenau
Beth Lanier
Rebecca L. Sigmund

ASSOCIATES

Michelle Rose Appelrouth
Joshua Berman
John R. Bielema, Jr.
Simon H. Bloom
Derek W. Bottoms
Kathlynn Lea Butler
Richard J. Carter, Jr.
Lance A. Chernow
Charlotte A. Combre
Tracy M. Culver
G. Bruce Cunningham
Michael James Delaney
Susan Langley Elliott
Michelle Ellison
Kevin B. Fischer
Maureen A. Fitzgerald
Richard Ellett Green
Jason K. Greene
Thomas M. Greene (Not admitted in GA)
Bradley W. Grout
B. Lyn Gunter
Anne H. Hicks
Matthew P. Holley
Castles R. Hollis
Michel V. Hurley
Glenn E. Johnson
Voris E. Johnson, Jr.
Joann Gallagher Jones
Jacqueline E. Kalk
Leslie S. Kehoe
Elizabeth Thompson Kertscher
Tricia Ann Kinney
Naho Kobayashi
Deborah Fleischer Kurzweil
Anne Maher LaMastra
T. Shawn Lanier
Marlo Orlin Leach
Sarah A. Lewis
Deborah J. Livesay
S. Ross Mansbach
Shawn Martin
Summer H. Martin
Stephen P. McAllister
Rick D. McMurtry
Jona J. Miller
Jennifer L. Murphy
Robin Catherine Murray-Gill Patton
Shannon Lowry Nagle
Linda C. Odom
Holly A. Pierson
Mark R. Pronk (Not admitted in GA)
Anthony Provenzano (Not admitted in GA)
John D. ReVeal (Not admitted in GA)
David D. Robinson
Eric P. Schroeder
Lars O. Scofield
Linzy O. Scott, III
Jeffrey A. Sherman
Jeffrey B. Sladkus
Louis C. Spelios
Lynn Murrell Sumlin
David S. Thomas (Not admitted in GA)
Christopher A. Thompson
Carrie G. Tolbert (Not admitted in GA)
David R. Tricker
Kathryn B. Vargo
Nicole Jennings Wade
James K. Wagner, Jr.
Steffanie F. Walke
Bruce Z. Walker
Sara Kay Wheeler
Richard W. White

For full biographical listings, see the Martindale-Hubbell Law Directory

SUTHERLAND ASBILL & BRENNAN LLP (AV)

999 Peachtree Street, N.E., 30309-3996
Telephone: 404-853-8000
Facsimile: 404-853-8806
URL: http://www.sablaw.com
Washington, D.C. Office: 1275 Pennsylvania Avenue, N.W., 20004-2415.
Telephone: 202-383-0100.
Austin, Texas Office: 816 Congress Avenue, Suite 1100, 78701-2443.
Telephone: 512-473-3622.
New York, N.Y. Office: 350 Park Avenue, 25th Floor, 10022.
Telephone: 212-616-7580.
Tallahassee, Florida Office: 2282 Killearn Center Boulevard, 32308-3561.
Telephone: 850-894-0015.

MEMBERS OF THE FIRM IN ATLANTA, GEORGIA

William A. Sutherland (1896-1987)
Alfred G. Adams, Jr.
F. Louise Adams
David I. Adelman
Peter J. Anderson
Kenneth F. Antley
William D. Barwick
John W. Bonds, Jr.
Elizabeth W. Boswell
William H. Bradley
Thomas M. Byrne
John A. Chandler
Reginald J. Clark
George L. Cohen
Katherine Meyers Cohen
N. Jerold Cohen
Thomas A. Cox
Patricia Bayer Cunningham
Peter H. Dean
Carey P. DeDeyn
B. Knox Dobbins
Eric R. Fenichel
Mac Asbill, Sr. (1893-1992)
Joseph B. Brennan (1903-1991)
J. D. Fleming, Jr.
John H. Fleming
Lisa Combs Foster
Peter A. Fozzard
Charles D. Ganz
James P. Groton
H. Edward Hales, Jr.
Victor P. Haley
James K. Hasson, Jr.
Barrett K. Hawks
James L. Henderson, III
Thomas C. Herman
Charles D. Hurt, Jr.
Thomas B. Hyman, Jr.
James B. Jordan
Edward W. Kallal, Jr.
Mark D. Kaufman
Michael G. Kerman
Bennett L. Kight
Cada T. Kilgore, III
Charles T. Lester, Jr.

(See Next Column)

MEMBERS OF THE FIRM IN ATLANTA, GEORGIA (Continued)

Alfred A. Lindseth
James M. May, III
James R. McGibbon
Daniel R. McKeithen
John H. Mobley, II
John R. Munich (Not admitted in GA)
Richard G. Murphy, Jr.
Alice Murtos
John L. North
Judith A. O'Brien
James A. Orr
William R. Patterson
James R. Paulk, Jr.
M. Celeste Pickron
S. Lawrence Polk
Richard L. Robbins
Haynes R. Roberts
Teresa Wynn Roseborough
William G. Rothschild
Herbert J. Short, Jr.
George Anthony Smith
Elizabeth Vranicar Tanis
Randolph W. Thrower
Mark D. Wasserman
Larry J. White
William R. Wildman
James H. Wilson, Jr.
Walter H. Wingfield

OF COUNSEL OF THE FIRM IN ATLANTA, GEORGIA

Michael J. Egan
William M. Hames

COUNSEL OF THE FIRM IN ATLANTA, GEORGIA

Deena R. Bernstein
Bruce A. Denning
Teresa P. Finister
Charles M. Flickinger
Carol Ann Kann Fowler
Dorothy B. Franzoni
Patricia A. Gorham
Walter T. Henderson, Jr.
V. Richard Hoyt
Susan Kalus
Alexa R. Ross
S. Perry Thomas, Jr.
Robert B. Smith

For full biographical listings, see the Martindale-Hubbell Law Directory

WEINBERG, WHEELER, HUDGINS, GUNN & DIAL, LLC (AV)

999 Peachtree Street, N.E. Suite 2700, 30309
Telephone: 404-876-2700
Facsimile: 404-875-9433
Email: firm@wwhgd.com

MEMBERS OF FIRM

Ben L. Weinberg, Jr.
Sidney F. Wheeler
J. Kenneth Moorman
John M. Hudgins, IV, (P.C.)
Robert G. Tanner
Patrick A. Thompson
Earl W. Gunn
David A. Dial
D. Lee Roberts, Jr.
Frederick N. Sager, Jr.
Carol P. Michel
John K. Train, IV
Johnathan T. Krawcheck
John C. Bonnie

ASSOCIATES

Anandhi S. Rajan
Alan M. Maxwell
Molly Prichitt Lee
Ashley P. Nichols
Beth E. Weitzman
Patrick Moore
Chloe E. Dallaire
Michael R. Boorman
Anna C. Palazzolo

Representative Clients: Chrysler Motors Corp.; Emory University; Ford Motor Co.; Merck; Otis Elevator Co.; St. Paul Fire & Marine Insurance Co.

For full biographical listings, see the Martindale-Hubbell Law Directory

*AUGUSTA,** Richmond Co.

RICHARD E. ALLEN (AV)

440 Greene Street, 30901
Telephone: 706-724-4466
Fax: 706-722-1677
Email: RALLENLAW@AOL.COM

For full biographical listings, see the Martindale-Hubbell Law Directory

BURNSIDE, WALL, DANIEL, ELLISON & REVELL (AV)

A Partnership including Professional Corporations
454 Greene Street, P.O. Box 2125, 30903
Telephone: 706-722-0768
Fax: 706-722-5984

MEMBERS OF FIRM

Robert C. Daniel, Jr. (1943-1993)
Thomas R. Burnside, Jr. (P.C.)
James B. Wall (P.C.)
James W. Ellison
Harry D. Revell
Thomas R. Burnside, III

Representative Clients: Augusta-Richmond County Commission; National Science Center Foundation, Inc.; CSRA Regional Development Center; City of Harlem, Georgia; Liquid Carbonic Corp.; Southeastern Equipment Co.; SECO Aviation, Inc.; SECO Parts & Equipment, Inc.

For full biographical listings, see the Martindale-Hubbell Law Directory

DYE, TUCKER, EVERITT, LONG & BREWTON, A PROFESSIONAL ASSOCIATION (AV)

453 Greene Street, P.O. Box 2426, 30903-2426
Telephone: 706-722-0771
Fax: 706-722-7028

(See Next Column)

DYE, TUCKER, EVERITT, LONG & BREWTON A PROFESSIONAL ASSOCIATION, *Augusta—Continued*

A. Rowland Dye
Thomas W. Tucker
A. Zachry Everitt
John B. Long
Benjamin H. Brewton
Troy A. Lanier

OF COUNSEL

A. Montague Miller

Jon E. Ingram, Jr.

Representative Clients: State Farm Insurance Cos.; Travelers-Aetna Insurance Cos.; Georgia Power Co.; Wachovia National Bank (Augusta Division); Chubb Group; MAG Mutual Insurance Company; Augusta Board of Realtors; Canal Insurance Company; St. Paul Fire and Marine Insurance Company.

For full biographical listings, see the Martindale-Hubbell Law Directory

FLETCHER, HARLEY & FLETCHER (AV)

429 Walker Street, P.O. Box 2084, 30903-2084
Telephone: 706-724-0558
Fax: 706-724-4730
URL: http://www.lawyers.com/fletcherharley&fletcher

MEMBERS OF FIRM

Leonard O. Fletcher, Jr.
C. Thompson Harley
W. Lawrence Fletcher

For full biographical listings, see the Martindale-Hubbell Law Directory

FULCHER, HAGLER, REED, HANKS & HARPER, LLP (AV)

A Partnership including Professional Corporations
520 Greene Street, 30901-1499
Telephone: 706-724-0171
Telecopier: 706-724-4573
Mailing Address: P.O. Box 1477, Augusta, Georgia, 30903-1477
Email: Fulcherlaw@AOL.com *URL:* http://www.fulcherlaw.com

MEMBERS OF FIRM

William M. Fulcher (1902-1993)
Gould B. Hagler (Retired)
William C. Reed (Retired)
Ronald C. Griffeth (1935-1998)
David H. Hanks (P.C.)
John I. Harper (P.C.)
Robert C. Hagler (P.C.)
Michael B. Hagler (P.C.)
James W. Purcell (P.C.)
J. Arthur Davison (P.C.)
Mark C. Wilby (P.C.)
N. Staten Bitting, Jr. (P.C.)
David P. Dekle (P.C.)
Scott W. Kelly (P.C.)
Elizabeth A. McLeod (P.C.)
Barry A. Fleming (P.C.)
Russell V. Mobley (P.C.)

ASSOCIATES

Stephen H. Brown
L. Dean Best
Susan Carter Lovett
Mary Bryan Murphy
Sonja R. Tate

Representative Insurance Clients: Travelers Property Casualty Corp.; American International Group; CNA Insurance Group; The Cincinnati Insurance Co.; Liberty Mutual Insurance Co.; Georgia Farm Bureau Insurance Cos.; Government Employees Insurance Co.; Safeco Insurance Co.; CIGNA Group.

For full biographical listings, see the Martindale-Hubbell Law Directory

HULL, TOWILL, NORMAN, BARRETT & SALLEY, A PROFESSIONAL CORPORATION (AV)

801 Broad Street, Suite 700, 30901
Telephone: 706-722-4481
Fax: 706-722-9779
Email: hullfirm@groupz.net *URL:* http://www.groupz.net/~advocate
Aiken, South Carolina Office: 111 Park Avenue, 29801.
Telephone: 803-648-4213.
Fax: 803-648-2601.

James M. Hull (1885-1975)
George B. Barrett (1894-1942)
Julian J. Willingham (1887-1963)
John Bell Towill (1907-1991)
Robert C. Norman (Retired, 1991)
W. Hale Barrett
Lawton Jordan, Jr.
Patrick J. Rice
Douglas D. Batchelor, Jr.
David E. Hudson
William H. Tucker (Not admitted in GA)
William F. Hammond
Mark S. Burgreen
George R. Hall
James B. Ellington
F. Michael Taylor
William J. Keogh, III
Edward J. Tarver
J. Noel Schweers, III
Susan D. Barrett
Ralph Emerson Hanna, III

James M. Holly (Not admitted in GA)
Timothy E. Moses
N. Shannon Gentry Lanier
Tara R. Simkins
Charles H. Weigle
Natalie A. Dopson
David C. Smith

(See Next Column)

OF COUNSEL

Julian B. Salley, Jr. (Not admitted in GA)

Counsel for: Morris Communications Corporation; Merry Land & Investment Company, Inc.; Castleberry/Snow's Brands, Inc.; Sun Trust Bank Augusta, N.A.; Georgia Power Co.; St. Joseph Hospital, Augusta, Georgia, Inc.; Norfolk Southern Corp.; Housing Authority of the City of Augusta; Georgia Press Association; Columbia County, Georgia.

For full biographical listings, see the Martindale-Hubbell Law Directory

SURRETT & COLEMAN, P.A. (AV)

901 Suntrust Bank Building, P.O. Box 1497, 30903
Telephone: 706-722-3301
Telecopier: 706-722-3318
Email: ecoleman@groupz.net

Carl J. Surrett
Edward J. Coleman, III

Representative Clients: Sears, Roebuck & Co.; American Home Assurance Co.; Great Southwest Fire Insurance Co.; Duke Buick, Inc.; American Southern Insurance Co.; Scottsdale Insurance Co.; Providence Washington Insurance Co.; Nautilus Insurance Co.

For full biographical listings, see the Martindale-Hubbell Law Directory

THOMPSON & SMITH, P.C. (AV)

2909-A Professional Parkway, 30907
Telephone: 706-855-5600
Telecopier: 706-855-7020

James M. Thompson
Larry I. Smith

For full biographical listings, see the Martindale-Hubbell Law Directory

WARLICK, TRITT & STEBBINS, L.L.P. (AV)

15th Floor, First Union Bank Building, 699 Broad Street, 30901-1454
Telephone: 706-722-7543
Fax: 706-722-1822
Email: wts@wts-lawfirm.com
Columbia County Office: 119 Davis Road, Martinez, Georgia 30907.
Telephone: 706-860-7595.
Fax: 706-860-7597.

MEMBERS OF FIRM

William Byrd Warlick
Roy D. Tritt (Resident, Martinez Office)
Charles C. Stebbins, III
E. L. Clark Speese
C. Gregory Bryan

OF COUNSEL

Richard E. Miley

For full biographical listings, see the Martindale-Hubbell Law Directory

*BRUNSWICK,** Glynn Co.

LAW OFFICES OF JAMES A. BISHOP (AV)

Suite 401, 777 Gloucester Street, P.O. Box 1396, 31521-1396
Telephone: 912-264-2390
Fax: 912-264-5859
Email: jbishop746@aol.com

ASSOCIATE

James A. Bishop, Jr.

For full biographical listings, see the Martindale-Hubbell Law Directory

FENDIG, MCLEMORE, TAYLOR, WHITWORTH & DURHAM, P.C. (AV)

Suite 200 Suntrust Bank Building, P.O. Box 1996, 31521
Telephone: 912-264-4126
Telecopier: 912-264-0591

Albert Fendig, Jr.
Gilbert C. McLemore, Jr.
Philip R. Taylor
David T. Whitworth
James B. Durham
Donna L. Crossland
Beth M. Duncan

For full biographical listings, see the Martindale-Hubbell Law Directory

GILBERT, HARRELL, GILBERT, SUMERFORD & MARTIN, P.C. (AV)

Suite 200 NationsBank Plaza, 31521
Telephone: 912-265-6700
Fax: 912-264-3917
Email: gilbharr@gate.net

Wallace E. Harrell
James B. Gilbert, Jr.
Rees M. Sumerford
M. Fleming Martin, III
Jameson L. Gregg
Wallace E. Harrell, III
Charles G. Spalding
Lisa Godbey Wood
Mark D. Johnson
J. Benedict Hartman
Carlton A. DeVooght
Kathryn Hackney Smith

(See Next Column)

GILBERT, HARRELL, GILBERT, SUMERFORD & MARTIN P.C.—*Continued*

OF COUNSEL

James B. Gilbert
Joseph A. Whittle
H. Hall Ware, III

Attorneys for: Sea Island Co.; Georgia-Pacific Corp.; Atlanta Gas Light Co.; Sea Harvest Packing Co.; Zurich General Accident & Liability Insurance Co.; Lumbermens Mutual Casualty Co.
Counsel for: Hercules Inc.

For full biographical listings, see the Martindale-Hubbell Law Directory

WHELCHEL, BROWN, READDICK & BUMGARTNER (AV)

5 Glynn Avenue, P.O. Box 220, 31521-0220
Telephone: 912-264-8544
Telecopier: 912-264-9667

MEMBERS OF FIRM

J. Thomas Whelchel
Richard A. Brown, Jr.
Terry L. Readdick
John E. Bumgartner
B. Kaye Katz

ASSOCIATES

G. Todd Carter
Richard K. Strickland
Bradley J. Watkins

Representative Clients: Georgia Power Co.; Sears, Roebuck & Co.; Allstate Insurance Co.; Commercial Union Insurance Co.; Georgia Farm Bureau Mutual Insurance Co.; Government Employees Insurance Co.; Nationwide Insurance Co.; State Farm Insurance Cos.; Wausau Insurance Cos.

For full biographical listings, see the Martindale-Hubbell Law Directory

BUFORD, Gwinnett Co.

CHANDLER & BRITT, LLC (AV)

A Firm of Professional Corporations
4350 South Lee Street, 30518
Telephone: 770-271-2991
Fax: 770-271-2986
Email: chandlerbrittllc@mindspring.com

MEMBERS OF FIRM

Richard B. Chandler, Jr. (P.C.)
Walt M. Britt (P.C.)
Gregory D. Jay (P.C.)
W. Wade Beavers (P.C.)
Luther H. Beck, Jr.

Deborah F. Weiss

For full biographical listings, see the Martindale-Hubbell Law Directory

*CALHOUN,** Gordon Co.

CHANCE & MADDOX (AV)

204 North Wall Street, P.O. Box 577, 30703-0577
Telephone: 706-629-4407
Fax: 706-625-2488
Email: Tomleemad@nwga.com

MEMBERS OF FIRM

Ronald F. Chance (1908-1995)
J. C. Maddox
Tommy Lee Maddox

Representative Clients: Bowater, Inc.; Basic Materials, Inc.; Willcan, Inc.
Approved Attorneys for: Lawyers Title Insurance Corp. (Policy Issuing Agent); Farmers Home Administration; The Federal Land Bank of Columbia; Astro Dye Works, Inc.; Superior Manufactor Group; Atlanta Gas Light Co.; Georgia Power Company.

For full biographical listings, see the Martindale-Hubbell Law Directory

*CAMILLA,** Mitchell Co.

VANN LAW FIRM (AV)

47 East Oakland Avenue, P.O. Box 387, 31730
Telephone: 912-336-8231
Fax: 912-336-8542
Email: frankvannlaw@mindspring.com

Frank C. Vann
Joe H. Kimmel, III

OF COUNSEL

Christopher R. Kelley (Not admitted in GA)

For full biographical listings, see the Martindale-Hubbell Law Directory

*CARTERSVILLE,** Bartow Co.

JENKINS & NELSON, P.C. (AV)

15 South Public Square, 30120
Telephone: 770-387-1373
Fax: 770-387-2396
URL: http://www.jnlaw.com

Frank E. Jenkins, III
G. Carey Nelson, P.C.

(See Next Column)

Peter R. Olson
Robert W. Lamb
John W. Nichols

For full biographical listings, see the Martindale-Hubbell Law Directory

*CEDARTOWN,** Polk Co.

MUNDY & GAMMAGE, P.C. (AV)

216 Main Street, P.O. Box 930, 30125-0930
Telephone: 770-748-3870
Fax: 770-748-2489
Rome, Georgia Office: The Carnegie Building, 607 Broad Street.
Telephone: 706-290-5180.

Emil Lamar Gammage, Jr.
William D. Sparks
Miles L. Gammage
John S. Husser
B. Jean Crane
G. Brian McWhorter

For full biographical listings, see the Martindale-Hubbell Law Directory

YORK & YORK, P.C. (AV)

York Building, 117 E. Woodland Street, P.O. Box 246, 30125
Telephone: 770-748-3780
Fax: 770-748-1175

Glenn T. York, Jr.
Michael H. York, Sr.

Local Counsel for: Bowater North American Corp.
Representative Clients: First Federal Bank of Northwest Georgia; Polk School District; City of Cedartown; Cedartown-Polk County Hospital Authority; Cedartown Industrial Development Corp.; Rockmart Development Authority.

For full biographical listings, see the Martindale-Hubbell Law Directory

*COLUMBUS,** Muscogee Co.

HATCHER, STUBBS, LAND, HOLLIS & ROTHSCHILD (AV)

A Limited Liability Partnership
Suite 500 The Corporate Center, 233 12th Street, P.O. Box 2707, 31902-2707
Telephone: 706-324-0201
Telecopier: 706-322-7747
Email: mailman@hatcherstubbs.com

MEMBERS OF FIRM

A. Edward Smith (1902-1962)
S. B. Hatcher (1887-1968)
J. Madden Hatcher (1897-1975)
Howell Hollis (1919-1991)
Aaron J. Land (1911-Retired)
Albert W. Stubbs (1913-Retired)
Alan F. Rothschild
William B. Hardegree
Morton A. Harris
J. Barrington Vaught
Charles T. Staples
James E. Humes, II
Joseph L. Waldrep
Robert C. Martin, Jr.
George W. Mize, Jr.
John M. Tanzine, III
John McKay Sheftall
Alan F. Rothschild, Jr.
William C. Pound
Teri Yancey Callahan

ASSOCIATES

Neal J. Callahan
Gregory S. Ellington
Bradley R. Coppedge
Alan G. Snipes
Carter R. Page

OF COUNSEL

Forrest L. Champion, Jr.

General Counsel for: SunTrust Bank, West Georgia, N.A.; TOM'S Foods Inc.; Muscogee County Board of Education; Board of Water Commissioners of Columbus, Georgia; St. Francis Hospital, Inc.; Georgia Crown Distributing Co.; The Jordan Company.
Local Counsel for: AFLAC, Inc.; MAG Mutual Insurance Co.

For full biographical listings, see the Martindale-Hubbell Law Directory

POPE, McGLAMRY, KILPATRICK & MORRISON, LLP (AV)

A Partnership including Professional Corporations
318 11th Street, 2nd Floor, P.O. Box 2128, 31902-2128
Telephone: 706-324-0050
Phenix City, Alabama: 334-298-7354
Fax: 706-327-1536
Email: pmkm@pmkm.com
Atlanta, Georgia Office: The Pinnacle, 3455 Peachtree Road, N.E. (30326-3243), P.O. Box 191625 (31119-1625).
Telephone: 404-523-7706.
Fax: 404-524-1648.

MEMBERS OF FIRM

C. Neal Pope (P.C.)
Max R. McGlamry (P.C.) (Resident)
Paul V. Kilpatrick, Jr. (Resident)
R. Timothy Morrison
Michael L. McGlamry
Earle F. Lasseter
William Usher Norwood, III (Resident, Atlanta Office)
Jay F. Hirsch
Wade H. Tomlinson, III
Teresa Pike Tomlinson

(See Next Column)

POPE, MCGLAMRY, KILPATRICK & MORRISON LLP, *Columbus—Continued*

RESIDENT ASSOCIATE

Matthew N. Pope

Reference: Columbus Bank & Trust Co.

For full biographical listings, see the Martindale-Hubbell Law Directory

ROTHSCHILD, MORGAN & BROWN (AV)

A Limited Liability Partnership
1025 First Avenue, P.O. Box 2788, 31902-2788
Telephone: 706-324-4167
Fax: 706-324-1969
Email: rothmor@mindspring.com

MEMBERS OF FIRM

Jerome M. Rothschild
W. Donald Morgan, Jr.
Jeffrey A. Brown

ASSOCIATE

Jeffrey H. Kight

OF COUNSEL

J. Quentin Davidson, Jr.

Reference: Columbus Bank and Trust Company.

For full biographical listings, see the Martindale-Hubbell Law Directory

COMMERCE, Jackson Co.

GREGORY M. PERRY (AV)

1774 North Broad Street, P.O. Box 299, 30529
Telephone: 706-335-3500
Fax: 706-335-5299
Email: gperry@negia.net

Representative Clients: Community Bank & Trust.
Local Counsel for: J.M. Huber Corp.

For full biographical listings, see the Martindale-Hubbell Law Directory

*CONYERS,** Rockdale Co.

TALLEY & SHARP, P.C. (AV)

1892 GA Highway 138, S.E., 30013
Telephone: 770-483-1431
Fax: 770-483-4912
Email: TASHPC@bellsouth.net

Robert E. Talley
Janice C. Sharp

Laura Jones French

LEGAL SUPPORT PERSONNEL

Kimberly A. Rowe

Attorneys for: City of Conyers; Trust Company Bank; Snapping Shoals Electric Membership Corp.; Housing Authority of Conyers, Georgia; Rockdale Hospital, Inc.

For full biographical listings, see the Martindale-Hubbell Law Directory

*DALTON,** Whitfield Co.

MITCHELL & MITCHELL, P.C. (AV)

101 North Thornton Avenue, 30722
Telephone: 706-278-2040
Fax: 706-278-3040
Email: mandm@ocsonline.com

D. Wright Mitchell (1895-1970)
Douglas W. Mitchell (1921-1984)
Erwin Mitchell
Neil Wester
Terry L. Miller
William J. Kimsey
G. Gargandi Vaughn

Counsel for: The City of Dalton, Georgia; First Bank of Dalton, Inc.
Local Counsel for: NationsBank of Dalton, Georgia.
Reference: Nations Bank of Dalton, Georgia; First Bank of Dalton, Inc.

For full biographical listings, see the Martindale-Hubbell Law Directory

*DECATUR,** De Kalb Co.

HYATT & HYATT, P.C. (AV)

Suite 201, Trust Building, 545 North McDonough Street, 30030
Telephone: 404-378-3635
Fax: 404-377-8304
Email: jhyatt@mindspring.com *URL:* http://www.lawyers.com/hyattlaw

Charles H. Hyatt (1924-1995)
John M. Hyatt

For full biographical listings, see the Martindale-Hubbell Law Directory

MCCURDY & CANDLER, L.L.C. (AV)

Suite 600, 250 East Ponce de Leon Avenue, 30030
Telephone: 404-373-1612
Telecopier: 404-378-3892
Mailing Address: P.O. Box 57, Decatur, Georgia, 30031

Scott Candler, Jr. (1926-1994)
John Walter Drake
Alan E. Rauber
John C. Sammon
Anthony DeMarlo
George Scott Candler, III
Clark E. Candler
Sidney A. Gelernter
Edna E. Hawes
Donald C. Suessmith, Jr.
Rebecca L. Collins
Lynn Wood

OF COUNSEL

R. Theodore Smith
H. Raiford Hodges, Jr.
R. Douglas Lloyd

Representative Clients: Fairfield Mortgage Association of Atlanta; SunTrust Co. Bank; Embry National Bank, Wachovia; Columbia Theological Seminary; Label America, Inc.; DeKalb Apartments, Inc.; First Union National Bank of Ga.; First Union Mortgage Co.

For full biographical listings, see the Martindale-Hubbell Law Directory

DORAVILLE, De Kalb Co.

CHESNUT, LIVINGSTON & PYE, P.C. (AV)

6485 Peachtree Industrial Boulevard, 30360
Telephone: 770-458-7606
Fax: 770-457-6082

J. David Chesnut
Richard F. Livingston, Jr.
Tom Pye

Christopher M. Kunkel
Charles A. Krawczyk
Bonnie M. Youn

For full biographical listings, see the Martindale-Hubbell Law Directory

JOE W. GERSTEIN, P.C. (AV)

6485 Peachtree Industrial Boulevard, 30360-2112
Telephone: 770-458-7606
Fax: 770-457-6082

Joe W. Gerstein

For full biographical listings, see the Martindale-Hubbell Law Directory

*DOUGLAS,** Coffee Co.

COTTINGHAM & PORTER, P.C. (AV)

319 East Ashley Street, 31533-3810
Telephone: 912-384-1616
Fax: 912-384-1775
Email: cnp@accessatc.net *URL:* http://www.lawyers.com/cottingham&porter

Sidney L. Cottingham
Robert L. Porter, Jr.
William L. Thompson

For full biographical listings, see the Martindale-Hubbell Law Directory

PRESTON & PRESTON, P.C. (AV)

250 East Ward Street, 31533
Telephone: 912-384-4700
Fax: 912-384-5839

Montgomery L. Preston (1910-1991)
Robert H. Preston

Edward L. Bagwell, III
William W. Preston

Attorneys for: Georgia Power Co.; SunTrust Bank, South Georgia, N.A. (Douglas Office); Lott Builders Supply Co.; Allstate Insurance Co.; Woodmen of the World Life Insurance Society; Atlantic Coast Federal Credit Union.
Issuing Agents for: Lawyers Title Insurance Corp.; First American Title Insurance Co.

For full biographical listings, see the Martindale-Hubbell Law Directory

*EASTMAN,** Dodge Co.

HARRISON & WALL (AV)

202 Norman Avenue, P.O. Box 0967, 31023
Telephone: 912-374-4346
Fax: 912-374-0168

MEMBERS OF FIRM

Milton Harrison
Sarah F. Wall

Attorneys for: City of Eastman; City of Chester.
Approved Attorneys for: Lawyers Title Insurance Corp.; Ticor Title Insurance Co.; Kansas City Title Insurance Co.; Federal Land Bank of Columbia, S.C.; Central Georgia Federal Land Bank; Georgia Development Authority.

For full biographical listings, see the Martindale-Hubbell Law Directory

*ELBERTON,** Elbert Co.

Hodges & Leverett, L.L.C. (AV)

25 Thomas Street, P.O. Drawer 399, 30635
Telephone: 706-283-2651
Fax: 706-283-2670
Email: hlatty@negia.net

Thomas L. Hodges, III — Robert F. Leverett

OF COUNSEL

Robert M. Heard

Counsel for: Development Authority of Elbert County, Elberton and Bowman; Elbert County Board of Education; Georgia Association of Educational Leaders; City of Hartwell.
Approved Attorneys for: First American Title Ins.

For full biographical listings, see the Martindale-Hubbell Law Directory

*FORSYTH,** Monroe Co.

Haygood, Lynch, Harris & Melton (AV)

A Limited Liability Partnership
87 North Lee Street, P.O. Box 657, 31029-0657
Telephone: 912-994-5171
Fax: 912-994-4588
Email: hlhm@mindspring.com
Monticello, Georgia Office: 311 B Forsyth Street, 31064.
Telephone: 706-468-8846.

MEMBERS OF FIRM

Charles B. Haygood, Jr.
Larry Persons Lynch
Robert L. Harris
C. Robert Melton

ASSOCIATE

Molly M. Hudson

Representative Clients: John Hancock Mutual Life Ins. Co.; City of Forsyth; Central Georgia E.M.C.
Local Counsel for: First Liberty Bank.

For full biographical listings, see the Martindale-Hubbell Law Directory

*GAINESVILLE,** Hall Co.

Smith, Gilliam and Williams (AV)

200 Old Coca-Cola Building, 301 Green Street, N.W., P.O. Box 1098, 30503
Telephone: 770-536-3381
Fax: 770-531-1481
Email: SGWFirm@Applied.net

MEMBERS OF FIRM

R. Wilson Smith, Jr. (1906-1983)
John H. Smith
Steven P. Gilliam
Jerry A. Williams
Kelly Anne Miles
Bradley J. Patten
M. Tyler Smith

ASSOCIATE

Robert A. Weber, Jr.

General Counsel for: Gainesville Industrial Electric Co.; Georgia Mutual Insurance, a Stock Company; L & R Farms; H. Wilson Manufacturing Co.; Goforth Electrical Supply; North Georgia Petroleum Co.; Gibbs Management Group, Inc.

For full biographical listings, see the Martindale-Hubbell Law Directory

Stewart, Melvin & Frost, LLP (AV)

200 Main Street, Suite 600, P.O. Box 3280, 30503
Telephone: 770-536-0101
Fax: 770-532-2171; 532-5071

MEMBERS OF FIRM

J. Douglas Stewart
W. Woodrow Stewart
John M. Melvin
Frank W. Armstrong
William H. Blalock, Jr.
J. Randall Frost
T. Treadwell Syfan
Steven A. Cornelison
D. Thomas LeFevre
J. C. Highsmith, Jr.
Mark W. Alexander

Scott Arthur Ball — Adam Stone Hicks

OF COUNSEL

Nancy L. Richardson

Representative Clients: Regions Bank of Georgia; Gainesville & Hall County Development Authority; Georgia Chair Co.; McKibbon Bros., Inc.; Nationwide Mutual Insurance Cos.; The Travelers Insurance Cos.

For full biographical listings, see the Martindale-Hubbell Law Directory

Whelchel & Dunlap, LLP (AV)

(Successors to Dunlap & Dunlap and Whelchel, Dunlap & Gignilliat)
405 Washington Street, N.E., P.O. Box 1, 30501
Telephone: 770-532-7211
Telecopier: 770-532-7361

MEMBERS OF FIRM

Edgar B. Dunlap (1892-1955)
William P. Whelchel (1895-1975)
William A. Bagwell
Wright Willingham
William L. Rogers, Jr.
John A. Gram
Edgar B. Dunlap, II
Thomas M. Cole
Thomas S. Bishop
Madeline S. Wirt

OF COUNSEL

James A. Dunlap

General Counsel for: SunTrust Bank Northeast Georgia; Housing Authority of City of Gainesville; Northeast Georgia Medical Center, Inc.
Counsel for: Georgia Power Co.; Milliken & Co.; Johnson & Johnson; Atlanta Gas Light Co.; CSX Transportation Inc.; CIGNA Property and Casualty Cos.

For full biographical listings, see the Martindale-Hubbell Law Directory

*GRIFFIN,** Spalding Co.

Robert H. Smalley, Jr., P.C. (AV)

115 North Sixth Street, P.O. Box 907, 30224
Telephone: 770-228-2125
Telecopier: 770-228-5018

Robert H. Smalley, Jr. — Thomas E. Baynham, III

Representative Clients: Premier Bank (Local Counsel); Griffin Spalding County Development Authority.

For full biographical listings, see the Martindale-Hubbell Law Directory

*HARTWELL,** Hart Co.

The Gordon Law Firm (AV)

Gordon Building, P.O. Box 870, 30643
Telephone: 706-376-5418
Fax: 706-376-5416
Email: wgordon@hartcom.net

Walter James Gordon

Kimberly A. Wilkerson

References: NationsBank of Georgia, N.A.; The Bank of Hartwell; Athens First Bank & Trust Company.

For full biographical listings, see the Martindale-Hubbell Law Directory

*HINESVILLE,** Liberty Co.

Jones, Osteen, Jones & Arnold (AV)

206 East Court Street, P.O. Box 800, 31310
Telephone: 912-876-0111
Fax: 912-368-2979
Email: JOJAl@clds.net

MEMBERS OF FIRM

Charles M. Jones
J. Noel Osteen
Billy N. Jones
Jeffery L. Arnold

ASSOCIATES

G. Brinson Williams, Jr.
Linnie L. Darden, III
Mark W. Nickerson
L. Kelly Davis

General Counsel for: The Heritage Bank; The Coastal Bank; Coastal Electric Membership Corp.; Liberty County Hospital Authority; Hinesville Area Board of Realtors; Liberty County Industrial Authority; Liberty County, Georgia; City of Hinesville.

For full biographical listings, see the Martindale-Hubbell Law Directory

*JASPER,** Pickens Co.

Landrum & Landrum (AV)

95 Stegall Drive, P.O. Box 400, 30143
Telephone: 706-692-6464; 692-6465
Fax: 706-692-6656

MEMBERS OF FIRM

Phil M. Landrum (1907-1990)
Phil M. Landrum, Jr.
Susan Landrum
Phillip M. Landrum, III

ASSOCIATE

David Lindsey

Representative Clients: Jasper Banking Co.; Pickens County, Georgia; Pickens County Board of Education; Amicalola Electric Membership Corp.; Nelson-Ball Ground Telephone Co., Inc.
Approved Attorneys for: Lawyers Title Insurance Corp.

For full biographical listings, see the Martindale-Hubbell Law Directory

*JESUP,** Wayne Co.

Howard, Carswell & Bennett, P.C. (AV)

Lawyers Building, 145 North Brunswick Street, P.O. Box 543, 31598-0543
Telephone: 912-427-4268
Fax: 912-427-0330

Joseph H. Thomas (1909-1984)
Kenneth R. Carswell
Hubert H. Howard
R. Violet Bennett

Representative Clients: Graward General Companies; Independent Fire Insurance Companies; Georgia Insurers Insolvency Pool; The Seibels Bruce Insurance Company; Cigna; Rayonier, Inc.; Georgia Power Co.; Southern Trust Insurance Co.; Cotton States Insurance Co.; Lawyers Title Insurance Corp.;

For full biographical listings, see the Martindale-Hubbell Law Directory

*JONESBORO,** Clayton Co.

Oliver, Duckworth, Sparger & Winkle, P.C. (AV)

146 N. McDonough Street, P.O. Box 37, 30236
Telephone: 770-478-8883
Fax: 770-473-0872
Email: ODSWPC@AOL.COM

G. Robert Oliver
Kevin W. Sparger
David P. Winkle

Kathy Brown Valencia
Jason E. Bring

OF COUNSEL

William H. Duckworth, Jr.

Local Counsel for: Atlanta Gas Light Co.
Representative Clients: Clayton County Hospital Authority; Southern Regional Medical Center; Clayton College and State University Foundation, Inc.; Clayton County Development Authority; Low Temp Industries, Inc.; City of Fayetteville.

For full biographical listings, see the Martindale-Hubbell Law Directory

*LA FAYETTE,** Walker Co.

The Womack Law Firm (AV)

109 East Patton Avenue, P.O. Box 549, 30728
Telephone: 706-638-2234
Fax: 706-638-3173

MEMBER OF FIRM

Ronald R. Womack

ASSOCIATE

John T. Siess

Counsel for: City of LaFayette; Housing Authority of the City of LaFayette; Walker County Board of Education; City of Trenton; State of Georgia Department of Transportation; Radix Broadcasting, Inc.; Bank of Dade.

For full biographical listings, see the Martindale-Hubbell Law Directory

*LA GRANGE,** Troup Co.

Duncan, Thomasson, Leonard & Shattuck (AV)

18 North LaFayette Square, P.O. Box 1168, 30241
Telephone: 706-882-7731
FAX: 706-845-1717
Email: duncan-thomasson@mindspring.com *URL:* http://www.lawyers.com/duncanthom

MEMBERS OF FIRM

Thurman E. Duncan
Wesley T. Leonard
James T. Thomasson, Jr.
Jeffery B. Shattuck

LEGAL SUPPORT PERSONNEL

Jane Kibby

General Counsel for: Mountville Mills, Inc.; Daniel Realty & Insurance Co., Inc.; Woodbury Business Forms, Inc.; Southern Center for Orthopedics, P.C.; Tire Pro, Inc.
Approved Attorneys for: Lawyers Title Insurance Corp.; Chicago Title Insurance Co.

For full biographical listings, see the Martindale-Hubbell Law Directory

Lewis, Taylor, Todd & Dixon, P.C. (AV)

304 Church Street, 30241
Telephone: 706-882-2501
Fax: 706-882-4905

George E. Sims, Jr. (1917-1967)
John M. Taylor
James R. Lewis (1928-1996)
Jeffrey M. Todd
Alex L. Dixon

Counsel for: The City of La Grange; West Georgia Medical Center; Troup County Board of Education; Harris County Board of Education.
Local Counsel for: State Farm Mutual Automobile Insurance Co.; Liberty Mutual Insurance Co.

(See Next Column)

Approved Attorneys for: Ticor Title Insurance Co.; Lawyers Title Insurance Corp.

For full biographical listings, see the Martindale-Hubbell Law Directory

*LAWRENCEVILLE,** Gwinnett Co.

Andersen, Davidson & Tate, P.C. (AV)

1505 Lakes Parkway, Suite 100, P.O. Box 2000, 30043
Telephone: 770-822-0900
Telecopier: 770-822-9680
Email: a-dt@mindspring.com

Thomas J. Andersen
Jeffrey R. Mahaffey
Gerald Davidson, Jr.
William M. Ray, II
Thomas T. Tate
Kathleen B. Guy
R. Bradley Carr

Tracey D. Mason
Michael J. Hay
Stephen J. Tyde, Jr.

OF COUNSEL

Ethel D. Andersen
Tanya Andrews Eades

References: Sun Trust Bank; The Bank of Gwinnett County; Chicago Title Insurance Co.; Title Insurance Company of Minnesota.

For full biographical listings, see the Martindale-Hubbell Law Directory

Thompson & Sweeny, P.C. (AV)

690 Longleaf Drive, P.O. Drawer 1250, 30046
Telephone: 770-963-1997
Telecopier: 770-822-2913
Email: thompsonsweeny@mindspring.com

Virgil Lee Thompson, Jr.
Victoria Sweeny
Melanie D. Williams

Jeffrey H. Petree
Melissa K. Stewart

Representative Clients: Gwinnett County Board of Education; City of Sugar Hill, Georgia; City of Duluth, Georgia; City of Grayson, Georgia; Downtown Development Authority of Lawrenceville, Georgia; Hayes, James & Associates, Inc.

For full biographical listings, see the Martindale-Hubbell Law Directory

*LOUISVILLE,** Jefferson Co.

Abbot, Murphy and Harvey, P.C. (AV)

190 East 7th Street, P.O. Box 31, 30434
Telephone: 912-625-7281
Facsimile: 912-625-8200

W. Wright Abbot (1892-1969)
John R. Murphy, III
James C. Abbot (1926-1997)
Fred K. Harvey, Jr.

Representative Clients: First National Bank & Trust Co., Louisville, Georgia; City of Louisville; J. M. Huber Corp.; Jefferson E.M.C.; Town of Bartow; Bank of Wadley; Forstmann and Company, Inc.; Fulghum Industries, Inc.; Hospital Authority of Jefferson County.

For full biographical listings, see the Martindale-Hubbell Law Directory

*MACON,** Bibb Co.

Anderson, Walker & Reichert, LLP (AV)

Suite 404 SunTrust Bank Building, P.O. Box 6497, 31208-6497
Telephone: 912-743-8651
Telecopier: 912-743-9636

R. Lanier Anderson (1871-1959)
Thomas L. Bass
R. Lanier Anderson, Jr. (1899-1984)
Albert P. Reichert, Jr.
Eugene S. Hatcher
Charles W. Walker (1905-1984)
Robert A. B. Reichert
Mallory C. Atkinson, Jr. (1939-1990)
Jonathan A. Alderman

Travis M. Trimble
Laura H. Wanamaker
Jeanna G. Fennell

OF COUNSEL

Albert P. Reichert

Representative Clients: Riverwood International Corporation; Radiology Associates of Macon, P.C.; Thiele Kaolin Company; SunTrust Bank, Middle Georgia, N.A.
General Insurance Clients: Liberty Mutual Insurance Co.

For full biographical listings, see the Martindale-Hubbell Law Directory

Macon—Continued

Hall, Bloch, Garland & Meyer (AV)

1500 Charter Medical Building, P.O. Box 5088, 31208-5088
Telephone: 912-745-1625
Facsimile: 912-741-8822
Email: hbgm@hbgm.com
Midtown Macon, Georgia Office: 2452 Vineville Avenue.
Telephone: 912-745-1625.
Facsimile: 912-741-3544.

MEMBERS OF FIRM

F. Kennedy Hall
Benjamin M. Garland
J. Patrick Meyer, Jr.
J. Steven Stewart
J. Burton Wilkerson, Jr.
Duncan D. Walker, III
Mark E. Toth
John Flanders Kennedy
Todd C. Brooks

ASSOCIATES

Kimberly Cofer Harris
J. Ellsworth Hall, IV

OF COUNSEL

Ellsworth Hall, III

F. Kennedy Hall, Division Counsel (Georgia): Norfolk Southern Railway Company.
Counsel for: Wachovia Bank of Georgia, N.A.; Helena Chemical Corp.; BellSouth Mobility, Inc.; Fickling & Co.; Navistar International Corporation.

For full biographical listings, see the Martindale-Hubbell Law Directory

Jones, Cork & Miller, LLP (AV)

435 Second Street, Fifth Floor, P.O. Box 6437, 31208-6437
Telephone: 912-745-2821
Telecopier: 912-743-9609
Email: lawyer@jonescork.com

MEMBERS OF FIRM

C. Baxter Jones (1895-1968)
Charles M. Cork (1908-1982)
Charles M. Cork, Jr.
Carr G. Dodson
Timothy K. Adams
John C. Cork
H. Jerome Strickland
Hubert C. Lovein, Jr.
W. Warren Plowden, Jr.
Rufus D. Sams, III
Thomas C. James, III
Steve L. Wilson
Thomas C. Alexander
C. Ashley Royal
Robert C. Norman, Jr.
Jerry A. Lumley
John T. Mitchell, Jr.
W. Carter Bates III
Howard J. Strickland, Jr.
Timothy Harden III
Cater C. Thompson
Thomas W. Joyce
Brandon A. Oren
W. Kerry Howell
David A. Pope

ASSOCIATES

Scott W. Spivey
Sharon Hurt Reeves
Bryan D. Scott
Matthew T. Strickland

General Counsel for: SunTrust Bank, Middle Georgia, N.A.; First Liberty Bank; Wesleyan College; Bibb County Board of Education.
Division Counsel for: Georgia Power Co.
Represent Locally: Bell South Communications, Inc.; The Bibb Co.; Allstate Insurance Co.; The City of Macon; St. Paul Fire & Marine Insurance Co.

For full biographical listings, see the Martindale-Hubbell Law Directory

O'Neal, Brown & Sizemore, A Professional Corporation (AV)

Suite 1001, American Federal Building, 544 Mulberry Street, 31201
Telephone: 912-742-8981
Telecopier: 912-743-5035
Email: obs@mindspring.com
Atlanta, Georgia Office: Suite 2600, One Atlanta Plaza, 950 East Paces Ferry Road, N.E.
Telephone: 404-237-6701.
Telecopier: 404-233-1267.

H. T. O'Neal, Jr. (1924-1983)
Manley F. Brown
Lamar W. Sizemore, Jr.
John C. Clark

Philip M. Brown

OF COUNSEL

James M. Wootan

For full biographical listings, see the Martindale-Hubbell Law Directory

Sell & Melton, L.L.P. (AV)

A Limited Liability Partnership including a Professional Corporation
14th Floor, 577 Mulberry Street, P.O. Box 229, 31202-0229
Telephone: 912-746-8521
Telecopier: 912-745-6426

(See Next Column)

Andrew W. McKenna (1918-1981)
John D. Comer
Mitchel P. House, Jr.
Doye E. Green
Edward S. Sell, III
John A. Draughon
R. (Chix) Miller (Managing Partner)
Russell M. Boston (P.C.)
Brian J. Passante
Jeffrey B. Hanson
Robert D. McCullers

ASSOCIATES

David M. Cusson
Lauren L. Benedict
Kevin T. Brown
Tilman E. Self, III
Michele E. Person
Shanda C. Galloway
Neil A. Halvorson

OF COUNSEL

E. S. Sell, Jr.
Buckner F. Melton
Joseph W. Popper, Jr.

LEGAL SUPPORT PERSONNEL

Linda Luck

General Counsel for: Macon Telegraph Publishing Co. (The Macon Telegraph); Macon-Bibb County Hospital Authority; County of Bibb; Smith & Sons Foods, Inc. (S & S Cafeterias); Macon Bibb County Industrial Authority; Burgess Pigment Co.
Local Counsel For: United States Aircraft Insurance Group (USAIG); United States Aviation Underwriters, Inc. (USAU).

For full biographical listings, see the Martindale-Hubbell Law Directory

*MADISON,** Morgan Co.

Lambert & Roffman, L.L.C. (AV)

126 East Washington Street, 30650
Telephone: 706-342-3566
Telecopier: 706-342-9683

MEMBERS OF FIRM

E. R. Lambert
Allan R. Roffman
M. Joseph Reitman, Jr.

George William Brown III

Representative Clients: Corporate: Walton Electric Membership Corp.; Wellington-Puritan, Inc.; Bank of Madison. Local Governments: Morgan County Board of Commissioners; City of Madison; City of Social Circle; Walton County Water and Sewage Authority; Morgan County Hospital Authority.
Local Counsel: SunTrust Bank, Northeast Georgia, N.A.; Evergreen Timberlands Corp.

For full biographical listings, see the Martindale-Hubbell Law Directory

*MARIETTA,** Cobb Co.

Custer & Hill, P.C. (AV)

324 Cherokee Street, P.O. Box 1224, 30061
Telephone: 770-429-8300
Fax: 770-429-8338
Email: custerhill@mindspring.com

Lawrence B. Custer
Douglas A. Hill

Vic Brown Hill

Reference: Nations Bank.

For full biographical listings, see the Martindale-Hubbell Law Directory

Downey & Cleveland, LLP (AV)

288 Washington Avenue, 30060
Telephone: 770-422-3233
Fax: 770-423-4199
Email: downey-cleveland@email.msn.com

OF COUNSEL

Lynn A. Downey

MEMBERS OF FIRM

Robert H. Cleveland (1940-1989)
Joseph C. Parker
Y. Kevin Williams
Russell B. Davis
G. Lee Welborn
Rodney S. Shockley
W. Curtis Anderson

ASSOCIATES

Richard A. Griggs
Tara Waller Scullion
Robert A. De Metz, Jr.
Kevin Salisbury
Sean L. Hynes

Representative Clients: Allstate Insurance Co.; St. Paul Insurance Cos.; Georgia Farm Bureau Mutual Insurance Co.; State Farm Insurance Cos.; Cotton States Mutual Insurance Co.; Colonial Insurance Co. of California; Progressive Insurance Company; Auto Owners Insurance Company; Deep South Surplus, Inc.; Ed Voyles Oldsmobile, Honda and Chrysler-Plymouth.

For full biographical listings, see the Martindale-Hubbell Law Directory

*MCDONOUGH,** Henry Co.

SMITH, WELCH & BRITTAIN (AV)

200 The Commerce Building, 235 Keys Ferry Street, P.O. Box 31, 30253
Telephone: 770-957-3937
Fax: 770-957-9165
Stockbridge, Georgia Office: 1239 Eagle's Landing Parkway.
Telephone: 770-389-4864.
Fax: 770-389-5157.

MEMBERS OF FIRM

Ernest M. Smith (1911-1992)
A. J. Welch, Jr.
J. Mark Brittain (Resident, Stockbridge Office)
E. Gilmore Maxwell

ASSOCIATES

Thomas Bruce McFarland
John P. Webb (Resident, Stockbridge Office)
Katharyne Clark Johnson
Tricia B. Smith
Bruce R. Vail

Representative Clients: Atlanta Motor Speedway, Inc.; Bellamy-Strickland Chevrolet, Inc.; Columbia/HCA Healthcare Corp.; Ceramic and Metal Coatings Corp.; Cities of Hampton, Locust Grove and Stockbridge; Georgia Farm Bureau Mutual Insurance; Killearn Properties, Inc. of Georgia; RSKCO, Inc.

For full biographical listings, see the Martindale-Hubbell Law Directory

*MILLEDGEVILLE,** Baldwin Co.

MIDDLETON, MATHIS, ADAMS & TATE, P.C. (AV)

425 South Wayne Street, 31061
Telephone: 912-453-9387
Fax: 912-453-1393
Savannah, Georgia Office: 622 Drayton Street, P.O. Box 1006.
Telephone: 912-234-1133.
Fax: 912-234-8818.
Atlanta, Georgia Office: The Equitable Building, Suite 1400, 100 Peachtree Street.
Telephone: 404-523-5000.
Fax: 404-527-9894.

Richard H. Middleton, Jr. (Resident, Savannah Office)
Charles A. Mathis, Jr. (P.C.) (Resident, Atlanta Office)
Peter C. Adams (Resident, Savannah Office)
Mark A. Tate (Resident, Savannah Office)

Timothy R. Walmsley (Resident, Savannah Office)
Derek J. White (Resident, Savannah Office)
Douglas P. McManamy (Resident, Savannah Office)
Andrew B. Cash (Resident, Atlanta Office)
David Krugler (Resident, Atlanta Office)
Leslie S. Pickett (Resident, Savannah Office)
Stephen G. Lowry (Resident, Savannah Office)
Linda G. Bass
Alwyn R. Fredericks

OF COUNSEL

Maryellen C. Griffin (Resident, Atlanta Office) 1317545

References: SunTrust Bank.

For full biographical listings, see the Martindale-Hubbell Law Directory

*MONTICELLO,** Jasper Co.

HAYGOOD, LYNCH, HARRIS & MELTON (AV)

A Limited Liability Partnership
311 B Forsyth Street, 31064
Telephone: 706-468-8846
Forsyth, Georgia Office: 87 North Lee Street, 31029-0657.
Telephone: 912-994-5171.
Fax: 912-994-4588.

Larry Persons Lynch

Representative Clients: Fairfield Financial; PL Industries, Inc.; Shadydele Farms.
Local Counsel for: McIntosh State Bank; Poly Tech Industries, Inc.; John Hancock Mutual Life Insurance Co.

For full biographical listings, see the Martindale-Hubbell Law Directory

*MOULTRIE,** Colquitt Co.

R. LAMAR MOORE, P.C. (AV)

700 South Main Street, P.O. Box 190, 31776
Telephone: 912-985-1213
Fax: 912-890-1314

L. L. Moore (1880-1962)
R. Lamar Moore

For full biographical listings, see the Martindale-Hubbell Law Directory

WHELCHEL, WHELCHEL & CARLTON (AV)

26 Second Avenue, S.W., P.O. Box 758, 31776-0758
Telephone: 912-985-1590
Fax: 912-985-0946

MEMBERS OF FIRM

Hoyt H. Whelchel (1893-1960)
Hoyt H. Whelchel, Jr.
James C. Whelchel
John M. Carlton, Jr.

ASSOCIATE

Mickey E. Waller

Representative Clients: Holman Supply Co.; Great American Indemnity Co.; City of Moultrie; Colquitt County Board of Education; Universal Underwriters Group; Riverside Manufacturing Company; Hospital Authority of Colquitt County; Georgia Interlocal Risk Management Agency; The Seibels Bruce Group Insurance; Beadles Lumber Company.

For full biographical listings, see the Martindale-Hubbell Law Directory

*NEWNAN,** Coweta Co.

GLOVER & DAVIS, P.A. (AV)

10 Brown Street, P.O. Box 1038, 30264
Telephone: 770-683-6000
Fax: 770-683-6010
Peachtree City, Georgia Office: Suite 130, 200 Westpark Drive.
Telephone: 770-487-5834.
Fax: 770-487-3492.

J. Littleton Glover
Welborn B. Davis, Jr. (1922-1974)
J. Littleton Glover, Jr.
Alan W. Jackson
Randy E. Connell
W. Robert Hancock, Jr. (Resident, Peachtree Office)
Asa M. Powell, Jr.
Jerry Ann Conner

Peter A. Durham
Mark E. Dacy (Resident, Peachtree City Office)

Representative Clients: First Citizens Corporation and Banking Subsidiaries; Putnam-Greene Financial Corporation and Banking Subsidiaries; Peachtree National Bank; Coweta County, Georgia; Georgia Baptist Children's Homes and Family Ministries, Inc.
Local Counsel for: International Playtex Corp; West Georgia Farm Credit, ACA; The William L. Bonnell Company, Inc., a division of Tredegar Industries; W. S. Badcock Corp.

For full biographical listings, see the Martindale-Hubbell Law Directory

MANN & WOOLDRIDGE, P.C. (AV)

28 Jackson Street, P.O. Box 310, 30264
Telephone: 770-253-2222
FAX: 770-253-8333
URL: http://www.lawyers.com/mann&wooldridge

Theo D. Mann
Robert B. Wooldridge
Heather A. Dognazzi

Seay Van Patten-Poulakos

OF COUNSEL

Charles Van S. Mottola

For full biographical listings, see the Martindale-Hubbell Law Directory

ROSENZWEIG, JONES & MACNABB, P.C. (AV)

32 South Court Square, P.O. Box 220, 30264
Telephone: 770-253-3282
Fax: 770-251-7262

George C. Rosenzweig
Sidney Pope Jones, Jr.
Joseph P. MacNabb

Charles C. Witcher
Douglas L. Dreyer
Jonathan W. Hickman

Approved Attorneys for: Lawyers Title Insurance Corp.; Chicago Title Insurance Co.

For full biographical listings, see the Martindale-Hubbell Law Directory

SANDERS, HAUGEN & SEARS, P.C. (AV)

11 Perry Street, P.O. Box 1177, 30263
Telephone: 770-253-3880
Fax: 770-254-0093

Walter D. Sanders (1909-1989)
Willis G. Haugen
C. Bradford Sears, Jr.
Walter S. Haugen
Theodore P. Meeker, III

OF COUNSEL

Robin Goff Mayer

Attorneys for: Southern Railway System; City of Newnan; City of Fairburn; The Bibb Co.; Bell South; Brown Steel Contractors; Coweta-Fayette EMC.

For full biographical listings, see the Martindale-Hubbell Law Directory

Newnan—Continued

WOOD, ODOM AND EDGE, P.A. (AV)

15 Jefferson Street, P.O. Drawer 1608, 30264
Telephone: 770-253-9885; 1-800-346-5357
Fax: 770-253-9896
Email: woe@bellsouth.net

Gus L. Wood
H. Parnell Odom
Arthur B. Edge, IV

Jacquelyn L. Kneidel
Walter W. Arnall

LEGAL SUPPORT PERSONNEL

Laura MacBean

For full biographical listings, see the Martindale-Hubbell Law Directory

*OCILLA,** Irwin Co.

WALTERS, DAVIS & PUJADAS, P.C. (AV)

South Cherry Street, P.O. Box 247, 31774
Telephone: 912-468-7472; 468-9433
Fax: 912-468-9022

W. Emory Walters
Thomas E. Pujadas
J. Harvey Davis
C. Vinson Walters, II

LEGAL SUPPORT PERSONNEL

Larry P. Harper

Attorneys for: Irwin County Board of Education; First State Bank of Ocilla; Irwin County; Wilcox County.
Local Counsel for: Georgia Farm Bureau Mutual Insurance Co.
Approved Attorneys for: Kaiser Aluminum & Chemical Sales, Inc.; Lawyers Title Insurance Corp.; Ticor Title Insurance Co.; Farmers Home Administration; Federal Land Bank of Columbia.

For full biographical listings, see the Martindale-Hubbell Law Directory

*PERRY,** Houston Co.

DANIEL, LAWSON, TUGGLE & JERLES, L.L.P. (AV)

912 Main Street, P.O. Box 89, 31069
Telephone: 912-987-2622
Fax: 912-987-7037
Email: dltj@alltel.net

Hubert A. Aultman (1920-1977)
Hugh Lawson, Jr. (1941-1998)

OF COUNSEL

David P. Hulbert

MEMBERS OF FIRM

Tom W. Daniel
Robert T. Tuggle, III
William R. Jerles, Jr.

Representative Clients: Flint Electric Membership Corp.; Houston County Board of Education; Tri-County Electric Membership Corp.; Agricultural Investment Management Corp.; The Bank of Perry.
Approved Attorneys for: Lawyers Title Insurance Corp.; Chicago Title Insurance Co.; Ticor Title Insurance Co.; Federal Land Bank of Columbia; Farmers Home Administration.

For full biographical listings, see the Martindale-Hubbell Law Directory

WALKER, HULBERT, GRAY & BYRD, L.L.P. (AV)

909 Ball Street, P.O. Box 1234, 31069
Telephone: 912-987-1415
Fax: 912-987-1077
Email: whgb@accucomm.net

MEMBERS OF FIRM

Larry Walker
Michael G. Gray
David G. Walker
Charles W. Byrd
David P. Hulbert, Jr.
John D. Christy

ASSOCIATE

Kellye C. Moore

Representative Clients: City of Perry; City of Reynolds; Houston County Hospital Authority; Crossroads Bank of Georgia; World Acceptance Corporation; NavCom Defense Electronics, Inc.; Brown and Williamson Tobacco Corp.; E.C.I.; Embeco; Constitution States.

For full biographical listings, see the Martindale-Hubbell Law Directory

*REIDSVILLE,** Tattnall Co.

CHENEY & CHENEY, P.C. (AV)

130 South Main Street, P.O. Box 1100, 30453-1100
Telephone: 912-557-4768
Fax: 912-557-1885
Email: cheneyandcheney@cybersouth.com

(See Next Column)

Curtis V. Cheney, Jr.
Sharon G. Cheney

For full biographical listings, see the Martindale-Hubbell Law Directory

*ROME,** Floyd Co.

BRINSON, ASKEW, BERRY, SEIGLER, RICHARDSON & DAVIS, LLP (AV)

Omberg House, 615 West First Street, P.O. Box 5513, 30162-5513
Telephone: 706-291-8853;
Atlanta: 404-521-0908
Telecopier: 706-234-3574
Email: law@brinson-askew.com *URL:* http://www.brinson-askew.com

MEMBERS OF FIRM

Robert M. Brinson (P.C.)
C. King Askew (P.C.)
Robert L. Berry
Joseph M. Seigler, Jr.
Thomas D. Richardson
J. Anderson Davis
Hendrick L. Cromartie, III
Wright W. Smith
Mark M. J. Webb
Joseph B. Atkins
I. Stewart Duggan

ASSOCIATES

James Daniel Blitch, IV
Stephen B. Moseley

Representative Clients: City of Rome; Georgia Power Co.; Unilever; General Electric Company; News Publishing Company (Rome News Tribune); Columbia Redmond Regional Medical Center; Suhner Manufacturing, Inc.; Shaw Industries, Inc.; United States Fidelity & Guaranty Co.; ConAgra, Inc.

For full biographical listings, see the Martindale-Hubbell Law Directory

SHAW, MADDOX, GRAHAM, MONK & BOLING, LLP (AV)

SunTrust Bank Building, P.O. Box 29, 30162-0029
Telephone: 706-291-6223
Toll Free: 888-291-6223
Telecopier: 706-291-7429
Email: law@shawmaddox.com *URL:* http://www.shawmaddox.com
Cedartown, Georgia Office: 223 South College Street, 30125.
Telephone: 770-749-6723.
Telecopier: 770-749-6729.

MEMBERS OF FIRM

Charles C. Shaw
John M. Graham, III
C. Wade Monk
William H. Boling, Jr.
Jo H. Stegall, III
David F. Guldenschuh
Daniel M. Roper
Jule W. Peek, Jr.
Virginia B. Harman
Scott M. Smith
Thomas H. Manning
Mather D. Graham

ASSOCIATE

Preston W. Smith

OF COUNSEL

Oscar M. Smith
James D. Maddox

LEGAL SUPPORT PERSONNEL

Christopher S. Rainwater (Senior Paralegal)
Debra A. Thwaites

Representative Clients: SunTrust Bank, Northwest Georgia N.A.; Inland Paperboard and Packaging, Inc.; Norfolk Southern Railway Co.; Aetna Casualty & Surety Co.; American Mutual Liability Insurance; Commercial Union Insurance Cos.; Hartford Accident & Indemnity Co.; St. Paul Insurance Cos.; Zurich-American Insurance Co.

For full biographical listings, see the Martindale-Hubbell Law Directory

*SAVANNAH,** Chatham Co.

BOUHAN, WILLIAMS & LEVY LLP (AV)

The Armstrong House, 447 Bull Street, P.O. Box 2139, 31402-2139
Telephone: 912-236-2491
Fax: 912-233-0811
Email: bouhan@bellsouth.net

MEMBERS OF FIRM

John J. Bouhan (1886-1971)
B. H. Levy (1912-1988)
Frank W. Seiler
Walter C. Hartridge
Edgar Pomeroy Williams
Edwin D. Robb, Jr.
Leamon R. Holliday, III
Lawrence Michael Donovan, Jr.
B. H. Levy, Jr.
John G. Lientz
M. Tyus Butler, Jr.
Roy E. Paul
Joseph A. Mulherin, III
Wilbur D. Owens, III
Peter D. Muller
Melanie L. Marks
Carlton E. Joyce
Ann Marie Stack

OF COUNSEL

George W. Williams
Alan S. Gaynor
John Michael Brennan
Samuel A. Cann

ASSOCIATES

D. Michael Conner
Patricia Ann Sharkey

General Counsel for: Savannah Electric and Power Co.; Wachovia Bank of Georgia, N.A.; Southeastern Maritime Co.; Solomons Co.; Fiduciary Services Corp.; Peeples Industry, Inc.; Board of Education of the City of Savannah and County of Chatham; The Branigar Organization, Inc.

For full biographical listings, see the Martindale-Hubbell Law Directory

Savannah—Continued

HUNTER, MACLEAN, EXLEY & DUNN, P.C. (AV)

200 East St. Julian Street, P.O. Box 9848, 31412
Telephone: 912-236-0261
Cable Address: "Ancan"
Telecopier: 912-236-4936
Telex: 54-6483
Email: hmed.com *URL:* http://www.bobbs@hmed.com
Atlanta, Georgia Office: The Peachtree, 1355 Peachtree Street, N.E., Suite 640.
Telephone: 404-876-3611.
Fax: 404-870-2025.

Malcolm R. Maclean
John B. Miller
William M. Exley, Jr.
Henry M. Dunn, Jr.
John M. Tatum
John M. Hewson, III
Arnold C. Young
M. Lane Morrison
W. Brooks Stillwell, III
Saunders Aldridge
Robert S. Glenn, Jr.
Lee C. Mundell
Andrew H. Ernst
Roland B. Williams
Leonard J. Panzitta
Dorothea Summerell Costrini
Craig S. Bonnell (Not admitted in GA)
Harold B. Yellin
Wade W. Herring, II
J. Reid Williamson, III
Glen M. Darbyshire
William E. Dillard, III
Christopher Weis Phillips
David M. Hirsberg
Robert Alvin Lewallen, Jr.
Kirby Gould Mason
Christine H. Tsai Cheng
Thomas Mills Fleming
George M. Earle
Sarah H. Lamar
Michael Jonas Thomerson
Lee Ann M. Williams, Jr
Cindy Leigh McAfee
Edward O. Henneman
Thomas Sean Cullen
Michael D. Robl
Frank S. Macgill
Triece Gignilliat Ziblut
Seslee S. Smith
Nancy Perry
Halsey G. Knapp, Jr. (Resident, Atlanta Office)
Marc G. Marling
Kenneth R. Schwartz
Jennifer A. Hartley
Benjamin R. Gross
Dennis B. Keene

SPECIAL COUNSEL

Robert A. Mullins

OF COUNSEL

Don L. Waters

Representative Clients: Great Dane Trailers; Fort Howard Corp.; West of England; Atlantic Wood Industries, Inc.; Home Insurance Co.

For full biographical listings, see the Martindale-Hubbell Law Directory

LEE, BLACK, SCHEER & HART, P.C. (AV)

10th Floor, 24 Drayton Street, P.O. Box 8205, 31412
Telephone: 912-233-1271
Telecopier: 912-232-7344
Other Savannah Office: 6555 Abercorn Street, Suite 121, P.O. Box 14477.
Telephone: 912-355-1131.

Edward H. Lee
W. Jerrold Black
Steven E. Scheer
R. Jonathan Hart

Christopher L. Rouse
John D. Lange

For full biographical listings, see the Martindale-Hubbell Law Directory

MCCORKLE, PEDIGO & JOHNSON, LLP (AV)

319 Tattnall Street, 31401
Telephone: 912-232-6000
Fax: 912-232-4080

MEMBERS OF FIRM

Phillip R. McCorkle
Carl S. Pedigo, Jr.
David H. Johnson

ASSOCIATE

K. Paul Johnson

References: Ameribank; The Savannah Bank.

For full biographical listings, see the Martindale-Hubbell Law Directory

MIDDLETON, MATHIS, ADAMS & TATE, P.C. (AV)

622 Drayton Street, P.O. Box 1006, 31412
Telephone: 912-234-1133
Fax: 912-234-8818
Atlanta, Georgia Office: The Equitable Building, Suite 1400, 100 Peachtree Street.
Telephone: 404-523-5000.
Fax: 404-527-9894.
Milledgeville, Georgia Office: 425 South Wayne Street.
Telephone: 912-453-9387.
Fax: 912-453-1393.

(See Next Column)

Richard H. Middleton, Jr.
Charles A. Mathis, Jr. (P.C.) (Resident, Atlanta Office)
Peter C. Adams
Mark A. Tate

Timothy R. Walmsley
Derek J. White
Douglas P. McManamy
David Krugler (Resident, Atlanta Office)
Andrew B. Cash (Resident, Atlanta Office)
Leslie S. Pickett
Stephen G. Lowry
Linda G. Bass (Resident, Milledgeville Office)
Alwyn R. Fredericks

OF COUNSEL

Maryellen C. Griffin (Resident, Atlanta Office)

References: SunTrust Bank.

For full biographical listings, see the Martindale-Hubbell Law Directory

*THOMASTON,** Upson Co.

ADAMS, BARFIELD, DUNAWAY & HANKINSON, LLP (AV)

Atwater Building, P.O. Drawer 671, 30286-0009
Telephone: 706-647-5466
Fax: 706-647-6434
Email: abdh@alltel.net

MEMBERS OF FIRM

Dickson Adams (1919-1975)
Ronald Barfield
David B. Dunaway
Tommy R. Hankinson
Catherine B. Evans
Ben J. Miller, Jr.

General Counsel for: City of Thomason; Thomaston Federal Savings Bank; Upson County Hospital Authority.
Representative Clients: Thomaston Mills, Inc.; Cincinnati Insurance Co.; City of Thomaston; West Georgia Farm Credit Service, ACA.
Approved Attorneys for: Lawyers Title Insurance Corp.; Chicago Title Insurance Co.

For full biographical listings, see the Martindale-Hubbell Law Directory

*THOMASVILLE,** Thomas Co.

ALEXANDER & VANN, LLP (AV)

218 East Jackson Street, P.O. Box 1479, 31799
Telephone: 912-226-2565
Fax: 912-228-0444

MEMBERS OF FIRM

Thomas H. Vann, Jr.
Charles H. Watt, III
John T. Holt
William C. Sanders
George R. Lilly, II
James H. Smith

ASSOCIATES

Dale S. Davidson (Not admitted in GA)
Raleigh W. Rollins, Jr.
Marcus R. Todd

Counsel for: Commercial Bank; Archbold Medical Center.
District Counsel for: CSX Transportation Inc.
Local Counsel for: State Farm Mutual Automobile Insurance Co.; Insurance Company of North America; Auto-Owners Insurance Co.

For full biographical listings, see the Martindale-Hubbell Law Directory

*THOMSON,** McDuffie Co.

KNOX AND SWAN (AV)

Knox Building, P.O. Box 539, 30824
Telephone: 706-595-1841
Fax: 706-595-2404

MEMBERS OF FIRM

Robert E. Knox (1916-1994)
Robert E. Knox, Jr.
W. Bryant Swan, Jr.

Representative Clients: Regions Bank; Regions Mortgage Co.; Kingsley Mill Corp.; Hardware Mutual Casualty Co.; General Accident & Assurance Corp.; Employers Mutual of Wausau; Hartford Accident & Indemnity Co.; Sentry Insurance Group; Hoover Treated Wood Products Co.

For full biographical listings, see the Martindale-Hubbell Law Directory

*TIFTON,** Tift Co.

SIMS, FLEMING & SPURLIN, P.C. (AV)

823 Love Avenue, P.O. Box 1165, 31793
Telephone: 912-386-0964
Fax: 912-386-1452
Email: jsims@planttel.net

John S. Sims, Jr.
Carlton A. Fleming, Jr.
John C. Spurlin
James M. Walker, III
Lea G. Hazel

Representative Clients: First Community Bank of Tifton; Trust Company Bank; Thomson Newspapers, Inc. (The Tifton Gazette); South Central Farm Credit Service; State Farm Mutual Automobile Insurance Co.; State Farm Fire and Casualty Insurance Co.; Tift General Hospital; TriState Outdoor Media Group; Selective Insurance; Reeves Construction Co.

(See Next Column)

SIMS, FLEMING & SPURLIN P.C.—*Continued*

For full biographical listings, see the Martindale-Hubbell Law Directory

*TOCCOA,** Stephens Co.

CLIFTON, SANDERS & SMITH, P.C. (AV)

311 S. Big A Road, P.O. Box 1005, 30577
Telephone: 706-886-7533
Fax: 706-886-0617
Email: csspc@alltel.net

Cecil L. Clifton, Jr.
Janney E. Sanders
Russell W. Smith
Marie K. Evans

Counsel for: Bank of Toccoa; Toccoa Insurance Agency, Inc.; Stephens County; Stephens County Development Authority; Pruitt Corporation.
Approved Attorneys for: Lawyers Title Insurance Corp.; Old Republic National Title Insurance Company; Lawyers Title Guaranty Fund, Inc.

For full biographical listings, see the Martindale-Hubbell Law Directory

*VALDOSTA,** Lowndes Co.

COLEMAN, TALLEY, NEWBERN, KURRIE, PRESTON & HOLLAND, LLP (AV)

910 North Patterson Street, P.O. Box 5437, 31603-5437
Telephone: 912-242-7562
Fax: 912-333-0885
Email: clf@datasys.net

Henry T. Brice (1925-1976)
B. Lamar Tillman (1912-1990)

MEMBERS OF FIRM

Wade H. Coleman
George T. Talley
C. George Newbern
Thompson Kurrie, Jr.
Richard L. Coleman
Edward F. Preston
William E. Holland
R. Clay Powell
Gregory T. Talley

Russell D. Henry

OF COUNSEL

John T. McTier

Attorneys for: Georgia Power Co.; Liberty Mutual Insurance Co.; USF&G Co.; Georgia Casualty & Surety Co.; City of Valdosta; American Turpentine Farmers Assn.

For full biographical listings, see the Martindale-Hubbell Law Directory

ELLIOTT & BLACKBURN (AV)

First Liberty Bank Building, 509 North Patterson Street Suite 201, P.O. Box 579, 31603-0579
Telephone: 912-247-0800
912-242-3333
Telecopier: 912-242-0696
Email: eblaw@surfsouth.com

W. Gus Elliott
Oris D. Blackburn, Jr.
Walter G. Elliott, II
James L. Elliott

Representative Clients: Hospital Authority of Valdosta and Lowndes County d/b/a South Georgia Medical Center; Lowndes County; The Valdosta Daily Times; Bell South Telecommunications, Inc.; Sears, Roebuck & Company; Levi Strauss & Co.; John Deere & Co.; E. I. DuPont de Nemours & Company; BP Exploration & Oil, Inc.; National Indemnity Company.

For full biographical listings, see the Martindale-Hubbell Law Directory

WARNER ROBINS, Houston Co.

ROY N. COWART, P.C. (AV)

233 N. Houston Road Houston Mall Suite 114, P.O. Box 818, 31093
Telephone: 912-922-8515
Fax: 912-922-3184
Email: cowartpc@aol.com

Roy N. Cowart

Representative Clients: Shaheen Office Supply, Inc.; Maria H. Bartlett, M.D.; Surgical Associates, P.C.; Golden Key Realty, Inc.; Houston County Associates for Exceptional Children.

For full biographical listings, see the Martindale-Hubbell Law Directory

HAWAII

*HILO,** Hawaii Co.

CARLSMITH BALL (AV)

A Partnership including Law Corporations
121 Waianuenue Avenue, P.O. Box 686, 96721-0686
Telephone: 808-935-6644
Fax: 808-935-7975
Email: execdirector@carlsmith.com *URL:* http://www.carlsmith.com
Honolulu, Hawaii Office: Suite 2200, Pacific Tower, 1001 Bishop Street. P.O. Box 656, 96809-3402.
Telephone: 808-523-2500.
Fax: 808-523-0842.
Kapolei, Hawaii Office: Suite 318, Kapolei Building, 1001 Kamokila Boulevard, 96707.
Telephone: 808-523-2500.
Fax: 808-674-0850.
Wailuku, Maui, Hawaii Office: Suite 400, One Main Plaza, 2200 Main Street, P.O. Box 1086, 96793-1086.
Telephone: 808-242-4535.
Fax: 808-244-4974.
Kailua-Kona, Hawaii Office: Suite 209, 75-1000 Henry Street, 96740.
Telephone: 808-329-6464.
Fax: 808-329-9450.
Hagatna, Guam Office: Suite 401, Bank of Hawaii Building, 134 West Soledad Avenue, P.O. Box BF, 96932-5027.
Telephone: 671-472-6813.
Fax: 671-477-4375.
Telex: 721-6445 CWCMI GM.
Saipan, Commonwealth of the Northern Mariana Islands Office: Carlsmith Building, Capitol Hill, P.O. Box 5241, 96950-5241.
Telephone: 670-322-3455.
Fax: 670-322-3368.
Los Angeles, California Office: 9th Floor, 444 South Flower Street, 90071-2901.
Telephone: 213-955-1200.
Fax: 213-623-0032.
Washington, D.C. Office: Suite 300, 1201 Pennsylvania Avenue, N.W., 20004-2401.
Telephone: 202-628-2228.
Fax: 202-628-2071.
Mexico City, Mexico Office: Carlsmith Ball, Sierra Nevada 119, Lomas de Chapultepec, 11000 Mexico, D.F.
Telephone: 52-5-520-8514, 52-5-520-8757.
Fax: 52-5-540-1545.
Mexico, D.F. Office of Carlsmith Ball, S.C. (Authorized to practice as foreign consultants in Mexico): Sierra Nevada 119, Lomas de Chapultepec, 11000 Mexico, D.F.
Telephone: 52-5-520-8514, 52-5-520-8757.
Fax: 52-5-540-1545.

RESIDENT PARTNER

Steven S. C. Lim

RESIDENT ASSOCIATE

Sherrill A. Atwood

For full biographical listings, see the Martindale-Hubbell Law Directory

*HONOLULU,** Honolulu Co.

CADES SCHUTTE FLEMING & WRIGHT (AV)

Formerly Smith, Wild, Beebe & Cades
Cades Schutte Fleming & Wright Building, 1000 Bishop Street, Suite 1200, P.O. Box 939, 96808
Telephone: 808-521-9200
Telecopier: 808-521-9210
Email: cades@cades.com
Kailua-Kona, Hawaii Office: Hualalai Center, Suite B-303, 75-170 Hualalai Road.
Telephone: 808-329-5811.
Telecopier: 808-326-1175.

MEMBERS OF FIRM

Robert B. Bunn
E. Gunner Schull
Donald E. Scearce
Richard A. Hicks
Roger H. Epstein
Jeffrey S. Portnoy
Bernice Littman
Nicholas C. Dreher
Mark A. Hazlett
Philip J. Leas
David C. Larsen
Larry T. Takumi
William A. Cardwell
C. Michael Hare
Richard R. Clifton
Roy A. Vitousek, III (Resident Partner, Kona Office)
Nelson N. S. Chun
Darryl H. W. Johnston
Vito Galati
Cary S. Matsushige
David Schulmeister
Milton M. Yasunaga
Gino L. Gabrio
Colin O. Miwa
Martin E. Hsia
Peter W. Olson
Stewart J. Martin
Rhonda L. Griswold
Gail M. Tamashiro
Grace Nihei Kido
Donna Y. L. Leong
David F.E. Banks
Dennis J. Gaughan
Patricia J. McHenry
K. James Steiner, Jr.

(See Next Column)

CADES SCHUTTE FLEMING & WRIGHT, *Honolulu—Continued*

MEMBERS OF FIRM (Continued)

Jeffrey D. Watts
James H. Ashford
Michele S. Loudermilk
Dennis W. Chong Kee
Laurie A. Kuribayashi
Catherine Carey

ASSOCIATES

Daniel H. Devaney IV
Michael H. Shikuma
Lynn H. Higashi (Resident, Kona Office)
Patrick W. Hanifin
Mitchell C. Sockett
Theodore D.C. Young
Dean T. Yamamoto
Kelly G. LaPorte
Johnnel L. Nakamura
Marc E. Rousseau
Kimberly A. Jackson (Resident, Kona Office)
Alexander Woody
Christopher T. Harrison
Jodi Shin Yamamoto
Charles K. Djou
Chris S. Mashiba
Sarah J. Lee
Stephen J. Rafferty
Mark A. Funaki
Madeleine M.V. Young
Michael L. Chun
Kristin S. Shigemura
Duane J. Young
Duke T. Fujiyama
Arthur G. Smith (1882-1966)
Urban Earl Wild (1891-1952)
Eugene H. Beebe (1889-1966)
Charles A. Gregory (1902-1972)
C. Frederick Schutte (1921-1988)
Milton Cades (1903-1992)
A. Singleton Cagle (1923-1994)
Edward deL. Boyle (1942-1994)
Douglas E. Prior (1936-1995)
William L. Fleming (1918-1997)

OF COUNSEL

J. Russell Cades
Harold S. Wright
James S. Campbell
Thomas P. Huber
William M. Swope

Counsel for: First Hawaiian Bank; Alexander & Baldwin, Inc.; Theo. H. Davies & Co., Ltd.; C. Brewer & Company, Ltd.; Bank of America, FSB; Bank of America NT&SA; The Bank of Tokyo, Ltd.; Haseko (Hawaii), Inc.; The Industrial Bank of Japan, Ltd.

For full biographical listings, see the Martindale-Hubbell Law Directory

CARLSMITH BALL (AV)

A Partnership including Law Corporations
Suite 2200, Pacific Tower, 1001 Bishop Street, P.O. Box 656, 96809-3402
Telephone: 808-523-2500
Fax: 808-523-0842
Email: execdirector@carlsmith.com *URL:* http://www.carlsmith.com
Kapolei, Hawaii Office: Suite 318, Kapolei Building, 1001 Kamokila Boulevard, 96707.
Telephone: 808-523-2500.
Fax: 808-674-0850.
Wailuku, Maui Hawaii Office: Suite 400, One Main Plaza, 2200 Main Street, P.O. Box 1086, 96793-1086.
Telephone: 808-242-4535.
Fax: 808-244-4974.
Kailua-Kona, Hawaii Office: Suite 209, 75-1000 Henry Street, 96740.
Telephone: 808-329-6464.
Fax: 808-329-9450.
Hilo, Hawaii Office: 121 Waianuenue Avenue, P.O. Box 686, 96721-0686.
Telephone: 808-935-6644.
Fax: 808-935-7975.
Hagatna, Guam Office: Suite 401, Bank of Hawaii Building, 134 West Soledad Avenue, P.O. Box BF, 96932-5027.
Telephone: 671-472-6813.
Fax: 671-477-4375.
Telex: 721-6445 CWCMI GM.
Saipan, Commonwealth of the Northern Mariana Islands Office: Carlsmith Building, Capitol Hill, P.O. Box 5241, 96950-5241.
Telephone: 670-322-3455.
Fax: 670-322-3368.
Los Angeles, California Office: 9th Floor, 444 South Flower Street, 90071-2901.
Telephone: 213-955-1200.
Fax: 213-623-0032.
Washington, D.C. Office: Suite 300, 1201 Pennsylvania Avenue, N.W., 20004-2401.
Telephone: 202-628-2228.
Fax: 202-628-2071.
Mexico City, Mexico Office: Carlsmith Ball, Sierra Nevada 119, Lomas de Chapultepec, 11000 Mexico, D.F.
Telephone: 52-5-520-8514, 52-5-520-8757.
Fax: 52-5-540-1545.
Mexico, D.F. Office of Carlsmith Ball, S.C. (Authorized to practice as foreign legal consultants in Mexico): Sierra Nevada 119, Lomas de Chapultepec, 11000 Mexico, D.F.
Telephone: 52-5-520-8514, 52-5-520-8757.
Fax: 52-5-540-1545.

MEMBERS OF FIRM

Annie Kun Baker (Partner, Resident at Los Angeles, California Office)
Joseph A. Ball (Resident at Los Angeles, California Office)
Roger B. Baymiller (Resident at Los Angeles, California Office)
Nancy M. Beckner (Resident at Washington, DC Office)
Daniel A. Bent
John F. Biehl (Resident at Saipan Office)
Michael I. Blaylock (Not admitted in HI; Resident at Los Angeles, California Office)
Stephen L. Bradford (Resident at Los Angeles, California Office)

(See Next Column)

MEMBERS OF FIRM (Continued)

Edward E. Case
James H. Case (A Law Corporation)
Mary Jane Connell
Ruth D. Davis (Resident at Hagatna, Guam Office)
Patricia Devlin
Albert H. Ebright (Resident at Los Angeles, California Office)
Steven M. Egesdal
Anna M. Elento-Sneed
Randall H. Endo (Resident at Maui, Hawaii Office)
Terrence A. Everett (Resident at Los Angeles, California Office)
Paul Mullin Ganley (A Law Corporation)
Alfonso García Cacho (Resident at Mexico Office)
Gary G. Grimmer
Michelle C. Imata
Philip D. Isaac (Resident at Hagatna, Guam Office)
Eric A. James
John C. Khil
Richard Kiefer
Karl K. Kobayashi
Nenad Krek
Robert F. Kull (Resident at Los Angeles, California Office)
David Patrick Ledger (Resident at Hagatna, Guam Office)
Katherine G. Leonard
Tom C. Leuteneker (Resident at Maui, Hawaii Office)
Steven S. C. Lim (Resident at Hilo, Hawaii Office)
Tim Lui-Kwan
B. Martin Luna (Resident at Maui, Hawaii Office)
John P. Manaut
Matthew M. Matsunaga
Randolph G. Muhlestein (Resident at Los Angeles, California Office)
Mark K. Murakami (Resident at Kapolei, Hawaii Office)
Craig G. Nakamura (Resident at Maui, Hawaii Office)
David R. Nevitt (Resident at Saipan Office)
Harry Y. Oda
Lawrence S. Okinaga (A Law Corporation)
David S. Olson (Resident at Los Angeles, California Office)
John D. Osborn (Resident at Saipan Office)
James Polish (Resident at Los Angeles, California Office)
Dean H. Robb
Tom E. Roesser
John E. Rogers (Resident at Mexico Office)
Ian L. Sandison
Meredith M. Sayre (Resident at Hagatna, Guam Office)
Marcia K. Schultz (Resident at Saipan Office)
Jonathan L. Smoller (Resident at Los Angeles, California Office)
James L. Starshak
Robert E. Strand
Thomas R. Sylvester
Lance F. Taniguchi
Terry E. Thomason
Sinforoso M. Tolentino (Resident at Hagatna, Guam Office)
Robert D. Triantos (Resident at Kailua-Kona, Hawaii Office)
Paul M. Ueoka (Resident at Maui, Hawaii Office)
J. Thomas Van Winkle (A Law Corporation)
Charles R. Wichman
Donald C. Williams (Resident at Los Angeles, California Office)
William C. Williams, Jr. (Not admitted in HI)
Allen R. Wolff
David W. K. Wong
Jon T. Yamamura
Adrián Zubikarai Arriola (Resident at Mexico Office)

ASSOCIATES

Sherrill A. Atwood (Resident at Hilo, Hawaii Office)
Deborah Elise Barack (Resident at Los Angeles, California Office)
Bruce A. Bradley (Not admitted in HI; Resident at Hagatna, Guam Office)
Patricia Cymerman (Resident at Los Angeles, California Office)
Leopoldo Galvan Mendez (Resident at Mexico Office)
Francisco A. Gil-Elorduy (Resident at Mexico Office)
Ana Laura Gordoa Lopez (Resident at Mexico Office)
Joanne L. Grimes
Dana A. Gutierrez (Resident at Hagatna, Guam Office)
Edmund W.K. Haitsuka (Resident at Kailua-Kona, Hawaii Office)
Grace E. Jo (Resident, Los Angeles, California Office)
Kevin E. Moore
Julia M. Morgan (Not admitted in HI)
Alton A. Murakami
David B. Rosen
Keiichi Sato
Jonathan A. Swanson
Kimilyn C. Tomita
Carol A. Uyeno
Kai Wang
Brent K. Yamashita
Sergio Yarritu Gonzalez (Resident at Mexico Office)

OF COUNSEL

Herbert G. Baerwitz (Resident at Los Angeles, California Office)
Donn W. Carlsmith
Roger P. Crouthamel (Resident at Hagatna, Guam Office)
Robert B. Dunlap, II (Resident at Saipan office)
Susan Lloyd Harrison Evans (Resident at Kailua-Kona, Hawaii Office)
George G. Grubb (A Law Corporation)
Tom K. Houston (Resident at Los Angeles, California Office)
Robert N. Katayama
Lorraine S. Klevansky
Herman T. F. Lum
John R. McDonough (Resident at Los Angeles, California Office)
Edward M. Ranger (Resident at Mexico Office)
Ole R. Sandberg (Not admitted in HI; Resident at Los Angeles, California Office)
Robert R. Thornton (Resident at Los Angeles, California Office)

For full biographical listings, see the Martindale-Hubbell Law Directory

CHUN, KERR, DODD, BEAMAN & WONG (AV)

Suite 900, 745 Fort Street Mall, 96813
Telephone: 808-528-8200
Telecopier: 808-536-5869

(See Next Column)

CHUN, KERR, DODD, BEAMAN & WONG—*Continued*

MEMBERS OF FIRM

Edward Y. C. Chun
William H. Dodd
Andrew V. Beaman
Danton S. Wong
Leroy E. Colombe
Trudy Burns Stone

ASSOCIATES

Andrew R. Bunn
Trevor A. Brown
Tracy D. Tanaka
John S. Nitao

References: Bank of Hawaii; First Hawaiian Bank.

For full biographical listings, see the Martindale-Hubbell Law Directory

DAMON KEY LEONG KUPCHAK HASTERT ATTORNEYS AT LAW, A LAW CORPORATION (AV)

1600 Pauahi Tower, 1001 Bishop Street, 96813-3480
Telephone: 808-531-8031
Facsimile: 808-533-2242
Email: info@hawaiilawyer.com *URL:* http://www.hawaiilawyer.com

Nelson B. Befitel
Clinton K. L. Ching
C. F. Damon, Jr.
Gerhard Frohlich
Brad K. Gushiken
Diane Deskins Hastert
Charles W. Key
Christine A. Kubota
Gregory W. Kugle
Kenneth R. Kupchak
Shannon M.I. Lau
Denis C. H. Leong
David P. McCauley
James C. McWhinnie
Anna H. Oshiro
Michelle M. Shin
Douglas C. Smith
Mark Garrett Valencia
Alan Van Etten
Michael A. Yoshida

OF COUNSEL

R. Charles Bocken
Robert H. Thomas
Harry A. Inman (Not admitted in HI)

Representative Clients: American Express Travel Related Services Company, Inc.; AIG Aviation Inc.; C. Brewer & Company, Ltd.; Odakyu Electric Co., Ltd. Fletcher Pacific Construction Co., Ltd.; The Travelers Companies; Kintetsu International Express; Microsoft Corporation; The Sumitomo Bank Limited. Ltd.

For full biographical listings, see the Martindale-Hubbell Law Directory

FUJIYAMA, DUFFY & FUJIYAMA ATTORNEYS AT LAW, A LAW CORPORATION (AV)

2700 Pauahi Tower, Bishop Square, 1001 Bishop Street, 96813
Telephone: 808-536-0802
Telecopier: 808-536-5117

Wallace S. Fujiyama (1925-1994)
James E. Duffy, Jr.
Rodney M. Fujiyama
Archie T. Ikehara

Lee T. Nakamura
Ward F. N. Fujimoto
Gregg M. Ushiroda
Danielle Noel Degele-Mathews
Deborah S. Jackson
Duane R. Miyashiro

OF COUNSEL

Davis D. Higa
Robert P. Richards (A Law Corporation)
Michele-Lynn E. Luke

Representative Clients: The Dow Chemical Company; Johnson & Johnson; Harley-Davidson; Wyeth-Ayerst Laboratories; Tokio Marine & Fire Insurance Co., Ltd.; Clark Material Handling Company; State of Hawaii Office of Hawaiian Affairs; Smithkline Beecham Corporation; Merck & Co.; Sears Roebuck.

For full biographical listings, see the Martindale-Hubbell Law Directory

GOODSILL ANDERSON QUINN & STIFEL (AV)

Alii Place, Suite 1800, 1099 Alakea Street, P.O. Box 3196, 96801-3196
Telephone: 808-547-5600
FAX: 808-547-5880
Email: info@goodsill.com *URL:* http://www.goodsill.com

MEMBERS OF FIRM

Martin Anderson
Conrad M. Weiser
David J. Dezzani
Ronald H. W. Lum
David J. Reber
John R. Lacy
Raymond S. Iwamoto
Thomas W. Williams, Jr.
William S. Miller
Jacqueline L. S. Earle
Lani L. Ewart
Randall K. Steverson
Patricia Y. Lee
Gary M. Slovin
Lisa Woods Munger
Ernest J. T. Loo
Bruce L. Lamon
Peter T. Kashiwa
Russell S. Kato
Lant A. Johnson
Vincent A. Piekarski
Mark B. Desmarais
Leighton J. H. S. Yuen
Corlis J. Chang
Carl J. Schlack, Jr.
Barbara A. Petrus
Patricia Mathias NaPier
Miki Okumura
Mark F. Ito
Wayne H. Muraoka
Audrey E. J. Ng
Gregory R. Kim
Alan S. Fujimoto
Walter C. Davison
Raymond K. Okada
Gail Otsuka Ayabe

(See Next Column)

MEMBERS OF FIRM (Continued)

Dale Edward F.T. Zane
LindaLee K. Farm
Margaret Jenkins Leong
Carol Ann Eblen
Jeffrey Scott Piper
Roy John Tjioe
Kellie M. N. Sekiya
Judy Y. Lee
A. Richard Philpott
Lennes N. Omuro
Derek R. Kobayashi
Peter Y. Kikuta

COUNSEL

Randall W. Roth
E. Laurence Gay
Alan W. C. Ma
Eric H. Sonnenberg

ASSOCIATES

Kurt K. Kawafuchi
Mary A. Renfer
Thomas L. Benedict
Edmund K. Saffery
Russell K. Kaupu
Lisa A. Bail
Carolyn K. Gugelyk
Normand R. Lezy
Darcy L. Endo-Omoto
KahBo Dye-Chiew
Eric A. Elkind
Elizabeth Haemi Lee
Kathleen A. Kelly
Tonya C. Kong
J. Denice von Gnechten
Adrienne Y. Shimonishi
David P. Cornell
Teresa R. Favilla
M. Elizabeth Raxter
Anne T. Horiuchi

OF COUNSEL

Marshall M. Goodsill
William F. Quinn
Genro Kashiwa

Representative Clients: Amfac/JMB Hawaii, Inc.; Bank of Hawaii; Chevron USA Products Co.; CNA Insurance Co.; Hawaiian Electric Industries, Inc.; Kapi'olani Health; MEDMARC; PrimeCo Personal Communications, L.P.; State Farm Insurance Companies; United States Aviation Underwriters, Inc.

For full biographical listings, see the Martindale-Hubbell Law Directory

HAMILTON, GIBSON, NICKELSEN, RUSH & MOORE

(See Rush Moore Craven Sutton Morry & Beh)

KOBAYASHI, SUGITA & GODA (AV)

A Partnership including Professional Corporations
999 Bishop Street, Suite 2600, 96813
Telephone: 808-539-8700
Telecopier: 808-539-8799
Telex: 6502396585 MCI
MCI Mail: 23 96585
ABA/Net: ABA2281
Email: ksg@aloha.net

MEMBERS OF FIRM

Bert T. Kobayashi, Jr., (Atty. At Law, A Law Corp.)
Kenneth Y. Sugita (Atty. At Law, A Law Corp.)
Alan M. Goda (Atty. At Law, A Law Corp.)
Dale W. Lee (Atty. At Law, A Law Corp.)
Lex R. Smith (Atty. At Law, A Law Corp.)
David L. Monroy (Atty. At Law, A Law Corp.)
Wendell H. Fuji (Atty. At Law, A Law Corp.)
Robert K. Ichikawa (Atty. At Law, A Law Corp.)
Janeen-Ann A. Olds (Atty. At Law, A Law Corp.)
Clifford K. Higa (Atty. At Law, A Law Corp.)
Charles W. Gall (Atty. At Law, A Law Corp.)
John F. Lezak (Atty. At Law, A Law Corp.)
Larry L. Myers (Atty. At Law, A Law Corp.)
Ernest H. Nomura (Atty. At Law, A Law Corp.)
Craig K. Shikuma (Atty. At Law, A Law Corp.)
Rod S. Aoki (Atty. At Law, A Law Corp.)

ASSOCIATES

Burt T. Lau
Christopher T. Kobayashi
Nathan H. Yoshimoto
Jonathan A. Kobayashi
Bruce A. Nakamura
Gary K. Nakata
Ruth K. Oh
David B. Tongg
Matthew H. Kobayashi
Vivian Tsoi
Ronald T. Ogomori
Elena J. Onaga
Curtis Saiki
William S. Bailey
Paul S. Kawai
Kenneth M. Nakasone
Duane C. Seabolt

OF COUNSEL

Bert T. Kobayashi, Sr.
Michael J. McGivern (Not admitted in HI)

Reference: First Hawaiian Bank.

For full biographical listings, see the Martindale-Hubbell Law Directory

McCORRISTON MIHO MILLER MUKAI (AV)

Five Waterfront Plaza, 4th Floor, 500 Ala Moana Boulevard, 96813
Telephone: 808-529-7300
Facsimile: 808-524-8293
Cable: Attorneys, Honolulu
Mailing Address: P.O. Box 2800, Honolulu, Hawaii, 96803-2800
Email: info@m4Law.com

(See Next Column)

McCorriston Miho Miller Mukai, *Honolulu—Continued*

PARTNERS

William C. McCorriston
Clifford J. Miller
Franklin K. Mukai
Stanley Y. Mukai
Donald K. O. Wong
D. Scott MacKinnon
Kenneth B. Marcus
Kenneth G. K. Hoo
Patrick K. Lau
Mark J. Bennett
Brian T. Hirai
Nadine Y. Ando
Darolyn Hatsuko Lendio
David N. Kuriyama
Michael J. O'Malley
Eric T. Kawatani
Randall K. Schmitt
John Y. Yamano
Edward T. Schorr
Michael Rosenthal
Sharon H. Nishi
David J. Minkin
Randall F. Sakumoto
Lisa M. Ginoza
Andrew W. Char
Alexander R. Jampel
Kimberly Rae McCorkle
Peter J. Hamasaki
Carrie K. S. Okinaga
Christopher J. Cole

COUNSEL

R. John Seibert
Charles E. Pear, Jr.

ASSOCIATES

Trisha M. Kimura
Stewart Pressman
Reese R. Nakamura
Maria B. Mazzeo
Jonathan H. Steiner
Stacey M. Robinson
Candace J. Park
Kevin A. Souza
Kenneth J. Mansfield
Deborah L. P. Mueller
Shaun M. Mukai
Daniel James Kunkel
Stacey C. G. Hee
Kara B. Moran

STAFF ATTORNEY

Asako Shimazu

Representative Clients: Phillip Morris USA; Hawaii Dental Service; Mandarin Oriental Hotel Group; Sports Shinko Co., Ltd.; Boyd Gaming Corporation; Gallo Winery; Pacific Basin Economic Council.

For full biographical listings, see the Martindale-Hubbell Law Directory

Paul, Johnson, Park & Niles Attorneys At Law, A Law Corporation (AV)

Suite 1300 Pacific Tower, 1001 Bishop Street, 96813
Telephone: 808-524-1212
Telecopier: 808-528-1654
Email: info@pjpn.com
Wailuku, Maui, Hawaii Office: 203 H.G.E.A. Building, 2145 Kaohu Street, P.O. Box 870. 96793-0870.
Telephone: 808-242-6644.
Fax: 808-244-9775.

James T. Paul
David Arthur Johnson
Corey Y. S. Park
Sheryl L. Nicholson
Robyn B. Chun
Judy A. Tanaka
Sheila L. Y. Sakashita

Lori A. Osmundsen
Leanne A. N. Nikaido
Jonathan R. Peterson
Pamela W. Bunn
Robert N.E. Piper

OF COUNSEL

Wayne K. T. Mau

For full biographical listings, see the Martindale-Hubbell Law Directory

Rush Moore Craven Sutton Morry & Beh (AV)

A Partnership including Law Corporations.
20th Floor, Hawaii Tower Amfac Center, 745 Fort Street, 96813-3862
Telephone: 808-521-0400
Facsimile: 808-521-0597
Cable Address: "Lawyers Honolulu"
Email: rmcsmb@lava.net *URL:* http://www.rmcsmb.com
Wailuku, Maui, Hawaii Office: One Main Plaza, Suite 650, 2200 Main Street.
Telephone: 808-244-3332.
Facsimile: 808-244-5322.

MEMBERS OF FIRM

Marshall B. Henshaw (1889-1970)
William R. Loomis (1939-1980)
Don C. Hamilton (1914-1984)
Harold W. Nickelsen (1924-1985)
Frank D. Gibson, Jr. (1920-1990)
Harold W. Conroy (Retired)
Dwight M. Rush (Retired)
Willson C. Moore, Jr. (Retired)
Anthony B. Craven (Retired)
Richard C. Sutton, Jr.
Walter Beh, II
Edward M. Sanpei
Stephen K. C. Mau (A Law Corporation)
Earl T. Sato
J. Stephen Street
Jennifer M. Yusi
David Shibata
Susan Tius
Cheryl A. Nakamura
Irene A. Anzai
Ray P. Wimberley (Resident at Maui Office)
Tracy G. Chinen
Douglas A. Crosier
Lisa K. Strandtman
Caroline S. Otani

(See Next Column)

ASSOCIATES

Ann K. Kuwaye
Denise P. Balanay
Linda N. Monden (Resident at Maui Office)
Toni M. Nelson
Glenn T. Melchinger

OF COUNSEL

G. Richard Morry

COUNSEL

Frank P. Richardson

Representative Clients: Bank of Hawaii; American Savings Bank; Hyatt Corporation; Kamehameha Schools Bernice Pauahi Bishop Estate; Travelers Insurance Co.; Underwriters at Lloyds.

For full biographical listings, see the Martindale-Hubbell Law Directory

Torkildson, Katz, Fonseca, Jaffe, Moore & Hetherington Attorneys At Law, A Law Corporation (AV)

Amfac Building, 15th Floor, 700 Bishop Street, 96813-4187
Telephone: 808-523-6000
Cable Address: "Counsel"
Telex: RCA 723-8185
Telecopier: 808-523-6001
Email: info@torkildson.com
Hilo, Hawaii Office: 100 Pauahi Street, Suite 206.
Telephone: 808-961-0406.
Telecopier: 808-935-6725.

Ernest C. Moore, Jr. (1913-1972)
Robert S. Katz
Roger W. Fonseca
Edward A. Jaffe
Ernest C. Moore, III
J. George Hetherington
Richard M. Rand
Jeffrey S. Harris
Craig K. Hirai
Gregory M. Sato
John L. Knorek
Ronald I. Heller
Wilson M. N. Loo
Steven B. Jacobson
Sabrina R. Toma
Perry W. Confalone
Oren T. Chikamoto
Phillip A. Li
Wayne S. Yoshigai
Steven L. F. Ho
Matt A. Tsukazaki
Steven V. Torkildson
Newton J. Chu (Resident, Hilo Office)
Stephanie Anne Chin

Timothy A. Walker
Clayton A. Kamida
Roman F. Amaguin, Jr.
Paul M. Saito
Daniel G. Mueller
Tamara M. Gerrard
Karen R. Tashima
Christine S.Y. Chun
Shirley M. Cheung
Ellen T. Nomura

For full biographical listings, see the Martindale-Hubbell Law Directory

Watanabe, Ing & Kawashima (AV)

A Partnership including Professional Corporations
First Hawaiian Center, 999 Bishop Street, 23rd Floor, 96813
Telephone: 808-544-8300
Facsimile: 808-544-8399
Email: allwik@wik.com

MEMBERS OF FIRM

Jeffrey N. Watanabe (Atty. At Law, A Law Corp.)
James Kawashima (Atty. At Law, A Law Corp.)
J. Douglas Ing (Atty. At Law, A Law Corp.)
Wray H. Kondo (Atty. At Law, A Law Corp.)
John T. Komeiji (Atty. At Law, A Law Corp.)
Ronald Y. K. Leong (Atty. At Law, A Law Corp.)
Robert T. Takamatsu (Atty. At Law, A Law Corp.)
Cynthia Winegar (Atty. at Law, A Law Corp.)
Randall Y. Yamamoto (Atty. At Law, A Law Corp.)
Lyle Y. Harada (Atty. At Law, A Law Corp.)
Michael A. Lorusso (Atty. At Law, A Law Corp.)
Pamela J. Larson (Atty. At Law, A Law Corp.)
John R. Aube (Atty. At Law, A Law Corp.)
Jan M.L.Y. Amii (Atty. At Law, A Law Corp.)
Edward B. Rogin (Atty. at Law, A Law Corp.)
Seth M. Reiss (Atty. At Law, A Law Corp.)
Curtis C. Kim
Lani Narikiyo (Atty. at Law, A Law Corp.)

ASSOCIATES

Donna Y. Kanemaru
Peter L. Fritz
Beth K. Fujimoto
Patsy H. Kirio
Kevin H. Oda
Michael C. Bird
Brian Y. Hiyane
Dennis J. Hwang
Teri Y. Kondo
Gregory Y.P. Tom
Jonathan W. Y. Lai
Lester M. H. Goo
Cara M. K. Ching
Brian A. Kang
Eric H. Kunisaki
Toby M. Tonaki
Edric M. Ching
Peter A. Horovitz
Diane F. Imamura
Brandon Davidson
R.Scott Simon

(See Next Column)

WATANABE, ING & KAWASHIMA—*Continued*

ASIA PACIFIC CONSULTANTS

George R. Ariyoshi — Victor Hao Li (Not admitted in HI)

LEGAL SUPPORT PERSONNEL

GOVERNMENT AFFAIRS ADVISORS

Millicent M. Y. H. Kim — Lori Ann C. Lum

References: First Hawaiian Bank; American Savings Bank.

For full biographical listings, see the Martindale-Hubbell Law Directory

MICHAEL J. Y. WONG (AV)

2222 Central Pacific Plaza, 220 South King Street, 96813
Telephone: 808-536-1855
Fax: 808-536-1857

For full biographical listings, see the Martindale-Hubbell Law Directory

RENEE M. L. YUEN ATTORNEY AT LAW, A LAW CORPORATION (AV)

Haseko Center, 820 Mililani Street, Suite 702A, 96813-2937
Telephone: 808-523-0125
Facsimile: 808-523-0127
Email: yuenlaw@hawaii.rr.com

Renee M. L. Yuen

For full biographical listings, see the Martindale-Hubbell Law Directory

KAILUA-KONA, Hawaii Co.

CADES SCHUTTE FLEMING & WRIGHT (AV)

Hualalai Center, Suite B-303, 75-170 Hualalai Road, 96740
Telephone: 808-329-5811
Telecopier: 808-326-1175
Email: cades@cades.com
Honolulu, Hawaii Office: Cades Schutte Fleming & Wright Building, 1000 Bishop Street, Suite 1200, P. O. Box 939.
Telephone: 808-521-9200.

RESIDENT PARTNER

Roy A. Vitousek, III

RESIDENT ASSOCIATES

Lynn H. Higashi — Kimberly A. Jackson

For full biographical listings, see the Martindale-Hubbell Law Directory

CARLSMITH BALL (AV)

A Partnership including Law Corporations
Suite 209 75-1000 Henry Street, 96740
Telephone: 808-329-6464
Fax: 808-329-9450
Email: execdirector@carlsmith.com *URL:* http://www.carlsmith.com
Honolulu, Hawaii Office: Suite 2200, Pacific Tower, 1001 Bishop Street. P.O. Box 656, 96809-3402.
Telephone: 808-523-2500.
Fax: 808-523-0842.
Kapolei, Hawaii Office: Suite 318, Kapolei Building, 1001 Kamokila Boulevard, 96707.
Telephone: 808-523-2500.
Fax: 808-674-0850.
Wailuku, Maui, Hawaii Office: Suite 400, One Main Plaza, 2200 Main Street, P.O. Box 1086, 96793-1086.
Telephone: 808-242-4535.
Fax: 808-244-4974.
Hilo, Hawaii Office: 121 Waianuenue Avenue, P.O. Box 686, 96721-0686.
Telephone: 808-935-6644.
Fax: 808-935-7975.
Hagatna, Guam Office: Suite 401, Bank of Hawaii Building, 134 West Soledad Avenue, P.O. Box BF, 96932-5027.
Telephone: 671-472-6813.
Fax: 671-477-4375.
Telex: 721-6445 CWCMI GM.
Saipan, Commonwealth of the Northern Mariana Islands Office: Carlsmith Building, Capitol Hill, P.O. Box 5241, 96950-5241.
Telephone: 670-322-3455.
Fax: 670-322-3368.
Los Angeles, California Office: 9th Floor, 444 South Flower Street, 90071-2901.
Telephone: 213-955-1200.
Fax: 213-623-0032.
Washington, D.C. Office: Suite 300, 1201 Pennsylvania Avenue, N.W., 20004-2401.
Telephone: 202-628-2228.
Fax: 202-628-2071.
Mexico City, Mexico Office: Carlsmith Ball, Sierra Nevada 119, Lomas de Chapultepec, 11000 Mexico, D.F.
Telephone: 52-5-520-8514, 52-5-520-8757.
Fax: 52-5-540-1545.

(See Next Column)

Mexico, D.F. Office of Carlsmith Ball, S.C. (Authorized to practice as foreign legal consultants in Mexico): Sierra Nevada 119, Lomas de Chapultepec, 11000 Mexico, D.F.
Telephone: 52-5-520-8514, 52-5-520-8757.
Fax: 52-5-540-1545.

RESIDENT PARTNER

Robert D. Triantos

ASSOCIATE

Edmund W.K. Haitsuka

OF COUNSEL

Susan Lloyd Harrison Evans

For full biographical listings, see the Martindale-Hubbell Law Directory

*WAILUKU,** Maui Co.

CARLSMITH BALL (AV)

A Partnership including Law Corporations
Suite 400, One Main Plaza, 2200 Main Street, P.O. Box 1086, 96793-1086
Telephone: 808-242-4535
Telecopier: 808-244-4974
Email: execdirector@carlsmith.com *URL:* http://www.carlsmith.com
Honolulu, Hawaii Office: Suite 2200, Pacific Tower, 1001 Bishop Street. P.O. Box 656, 96809-3402.
Telephone: 808-523-2500.
Fax: 808-523-0842.
Kapolei, Hawaii Office: Suite 318, Kapolei Building, 1001 Kamokila Boulevard, 96707.
Telephone: 808-523-2500.
Fax: 808-674-0850.
Kailua-Kona, Hawaii Office: Suite 209, 75-1000 Henry Street, 96740.
Telephone: 808-329-6464.
Fax: 808-329-9450.
Hilo, Hawaii Office: 121 Waianuenue Avenue, P.O. Box 686, 96721-0686.
Telephone: 808-935-6644.
Fax: 808-935-7975.
Hagatna, Guam Office: Suite 401, Bank of Hawaii Building, 134 West Soledad Avenue, P.O. Box BF, 96932-5027.
Telephone: 671-472-6813.
Fax: 671-477-4375.
Telex: 721-6445 CWCMI GM.
Saipan, Commonwealth of the Northern Mariana Islands Office: Carlsmith Building, Capitol Hill, P.O. Box 5241, 96950-5241.
Telephone: 670-322-3455.
Fax: 670-322-3368.
Los Angeles, California Office: 9th Floor, 444 South Flower Street, 90071-2901.
Telephone: 213-955-1200.
Fax: 213-623-0032.
Washington, D.C. Office: Suite 300, 1201 Pennsylvania Avenue, N.W., 20004-2401.
Telephone: 202-628-2228.
Fax: 202-628-2071.
Mexico City, Mexico Office: Carlsmith Ball, Sierra Nevada 119, Lomas de Chapultepec, 11000 Mexico, D.F.
Telephone: 52-5-520-8514, 52-5-520-8757.
Fax: 52-5-540-1545.
Mexico, D.F. Office of Carlsmith Ball, S.C. (Authorized to practice as foreign legal consultants in Mexico): Sierra Nevada 119, Lomas de Chapultepec, 11000 Mexico D.F.
Telephone: 52-5-520-8514, 52-5-520-8757.
Fax: 52-5-540-1545.

RESIDENT PARTNERS

Randall H. Endo — B. Martin Luna
Tom C. Leuteneker — Craig G. Nakamura
Paul M. Ueoka

For full biographical listings, see the Martindale-Hubbell Law Directory

PAUL, JOHNSON, PARK & NILES ATTORNEYS AT LAW, A LAW CORPORATION (AV)

203 H.G.E.A. Building, 2145 Kaohu Street, P.O. Box 870, 96793-0870
Telephone: 808-242-6644
Fax: 808-244-9775
Email: info@pjpn.com
Honolulu, Hawaii Office: Suite 1300 Pacific Tower, 1001 Bishop Street, 96813.
Telephone: 808-524-1212.
Telecopier: 808-528-1654.

Dennis James Niles — William M. McKeon

Carla M. Nakata — Tom Pierce

For full biographical listings, see the Martindale-Hubbell Law Directory

IDAHO

*BOISE,** Ada Co.

CANTRILL, SKINNER, SULLIVAN & KING (AV)

1423 Tyrell Lane, P.O. Box 359, 83701
Telephone: 208-344-8035
Fax: 208-345-7212
Email: csskslaw@ibm.net

MEMBERS OF FIRM

David W. Cantrill
Gardner W. Skinner, Jr.
Willis E. Sullivan, III
John L. King
Robert D. Lewis
Frank P. Kotyk

ASSOCIATES

Tyra H. Stubbs
Clinton O. Casey

Representative Clients: Safeco Insurance Companies; Prudential Property and Casualty Insurance Co.; State Insurance Fund; Farmers Insurance Co.; Jordan-Wilcomb Company; Nature Conservancy; Independent School District of Boise City; Hartford Insurance Group; Mutual of Eunumclaw Insurance Co.
Reference: Key Bank.

For full biographical listings, see the Martindale-Hubbell Law Directory

EBERLE, BERLIN, KADING, TURNBOW & MCKLVEEN, CHARTERED (AV)

Capitol Park Plaza, 300 North Sixth Street, P.O. Box 1368, 83701-1368
Telephone: 208-344-8535
Facsimile: 208-344-8542

J. Louis Eberle (1890-1964)
T.H. Eberle (1922-1977)
R.B. Kading, Jr.
R.M. Turnbow
William J. McKlveen
Warren Eugene Jones
Mark S. Geston
Thomas R. Linville
Joseph H. Uberuaga, II
Neil D. McFeeley
Kimbell D. Gourley
Steven E. Alkire
Ann K. Shepard
Stanley J. Tharp
Kimberly J. Blas

Samuel A. Diddle
Sarah E. Scott
Candice M. McHugh (Not admitted in ID)

Representative Clients: Key Bank of Idaho; Key Bank Nat'l Assn.; Key Corp Leasing Ltd.; Agribeef Co.; Cessna Aircraft Co.; Energy Release Products Corp.; Ada County Highway Dist.

For full biographical listings, see the Martindale-Hubbell Law Directory

ELAM & BURKE, A PROFESSIONAL ASSOCIATION (AV)

Key Financial Center, 702 West Idaho Street, P.O. Box 1539, 83701
Telephone: 208-343-5454
Telecopier: 208-384-5844
Email: eblaw@elamburke.com

Laurel E. Elam (1888-1974)
Carl A. Burke (1898-1961)
Carl P. Burke
M. Allyn Dingel, Jr.
John Magel
David B. Lincoln
James D. LaRue
Randall A. Peterman
Ryan P. Armbruster
William G. Dryden
Trudy Hanson Fouser
Scott L. Campbell
Bobbi Killian Dominick
Jeffery J. Ventrella
James A. Ford
Jeffrey A. Thomson
Sandra L. Clapp

J. Ray Durtschi
Rebecca A. Broadbent
Geoffrey M. Baker
Angela D. Schaer
Casey C. Robertson
Jayne Tracy Davis
Theodore C. Peters

Representative Clients: Morrison-Knudsen, Inc; Prudential Securities, Inc.; Pechiney Corp.; U.S. BanCorp; US West Communications, Inc.; State Farm Insurance Cos.; Sinclair Oil Co. d/b/a/ Sun Valley Co.; Farmers Insurance Group; Thompson Creek Mining Co.

For full biographical listings, see the Martindale-Hubbell Law Directory

EVANS, KEANE LLP (AV)

Suite 200, 1101 West River Street, P.O. Box 959, 83701-0959
Telephone: 208-384-1800
Facsimile: 208-345-3514
Email: firm@ekidalaw.com
Kellogg, Idaho Office: 111 Main Street, P.O. Box 659.
Telephone: 208-784-1105.

MEMBERS OF FIRM

Rex Blackburn
Bruce C. Jones
Jed W. Manwaring
James D. Hovren
David W. Gratton

OF COUNSEL

Blaine F. Evans

(See Next Column)

Thomas B. Humphrey
Paul J. Augustine
Patrick E. Mahoney
Monica Moen

KELLOGG OFFICE

James P. Keane (1925-1988)
Fred M. Gibler
Charles L. A. Cox
Justin W. Julian

Representative Clients: American Cyanamid Co.; Chrysler Corp.; Coeur d'Alene Mines Corp.; Crum & Forster; Ford Motor Co.; Hecla Mining Co.; Idaho Power Co.; State Farm Mutual Automobile Insurance Co.; Sunshine Mining and Refining Company,

For full biographical listings, see the Martindale-Hubbell Law Directory

JAMES R. GILLESPIE, P.A. (AV)

512 West Bannock, P.O. Box 2337, 83701
Telephone: 208-344-8400
Fax: 208-344-7100
Email: jrglaw@micron.net

James R. Gillespie

For full biographical listings, see the Martindale-Hubbell Law Directory

GREEN LAW OFFICES (AV)

P.O. Box 2597, 83701-2597
Telephone: 208-342-8915
Fax: 208-342-2718
Email: cumergreen@aol.com *URL:* http://www.greenedlaw.com

Cumer L. Green

ASSOCIATE

Debra A. Silk

LEGAL SUPPORT PERSONNEL

Gary W. Shaw (Chief, Legal Support Group)

Representative Clients: Idaho School Boards Association, Inc.; Potlatch Corporation; Bell Helmets, Inc.; R.C. Bigelow, Inc.; Fleetwood Enterprises, Inc.; United Airlines; Pacific Crown Timber; Croman Corp.; Ida-West Energy Co.; LJD Holdings, Inc.; Ram International; VFP VC Ltd.; Developers Diversified Realty Corporation; Dakota Company, Inc.

For full biographical listings, see the Martindale-Hubbell Law Directory

HOPKINS RODEN CROCKETT HANSEN & HOOPES, PLLC (AV)

802 West Bannock, Suite 900, P.O. Box 2110, 83701-2110
Telephone: 208-336-7930
Fax: 208-336-9154
Email: BoiseLaw@hrchh.com *URL:* http://www.hrchh.com
Idaho Falls, Idaho Office: 428 Park Avenue, P.O. Box 51219, 83405-1219.
Telephone: 208-523-4445.
Fax: 208-523-4474.
Washington, D.C. Office: 8 East Street, S.E., 20003.
Telephone: 202-546-0360 .
Fax: 202-546-6294.

RESIDENT PARTNER

William C. Roden

OF COUNSEL

John Michael Brassey

Representative Clients: Wells Fargo Bank; The Idaho Nature Conservancy; Basic American, Inc.; U S West Communications Inc.; Busch Agricultural Resources, Inc.; Wal-Mart, Inc.; Eastern Idaho Economic Development Council, Inc.; Mutual of Enumclaw; Reliance Insurance Co.; Wausau Insurance Cos.

For full biographical listings, see the Martindale-Hubbell Law Directory

LYNCH & ASSOCIATES, P.L.L.C. (AV)

Ninth and Idaho Center, 225 N. 9th Street, Suite 600, P.O. Box 739, 83701
Telephone: 208-331-5088
Fax: 208-331-0088
Email: Lynchassoc@lesbois.com *URL:* http://www.lawyers.com/lynch&associates

James B. Lynch

Katherine M. Lynch

For full biographical listings, see the Martindale-Hubbell Law Directory

MOORE, BASKIN & PARKER (AV)

Washington Federal Plaza, 1001 West Idaho Street, Suite 400, P.O. Box 6756, 83707
Telephone: 208-336-6900
Facsimile: 208-336-7031
Email: mail@MBPLAW.com *URL:* http://www.lawyers.com/moorebaskin&parker

(See Next Column)

MOORE, BASKIN & PARKER—*Continued*

MEMBERS OF FIRM

Michael W. Moore
Thomas P. Baskin, III
Paige Alan Parker
Richard Hansen
Wendy Cox Dvorak

ASSOCIATE

Martin C. Hendrickson

Representative Clients: Travelers Insurance Co./Aetna Casualty & Surety, Co.; Capitol Indemnity Co.; Clarendon Insurance Co.; Crawford & Co.; Empire Fire & Marine Insurance Co.; Fireman's Fund Insurance Cos.; Idaho Counties Reciprocal Management Program; Idaho State Insurance Fund; Insurance Company of the West; Protective Insurance Co.

For full biographical listings, see the Martindale-Hubbell Law Directory

*IDAHO FALLS,** Bonneville Co.

HOPKINS RODEN CROCKETT HANSEN & HOOPES, PLLC (AV)

428 Park Avenue, P.O. Box 51219, 83405-1219
Telephone: 208-523-4445
Fax: 208-523-4474
Email: IFLaw@hrchh.com *URL:* http://www.hrchh.com
Boise, Idaho Office: 802 West Bannock, Suite 900, P.O. Box 2110, 83701-2110.
Telephone: 208-336-7930.
Fax: 208-336-9154. Email: BoiseLaw@hrchh.com.
Washington, D.C. Office: 8 East Street, S.E., 20003.
Telephone: 202-546-0360.
Fax: 202-546-6294.

MEMBERS OF FIRM

Seward H. French, III (1941-1984)
Ted C. Springer (1943-1984)
C. Timothy Hopkins
William C. Roden (Resident, Boise Office)
Gregory L. Crockett
John D. Hansen
D. Fredrick Hoopes
Lary S. Larson
Paul B. Rippel
Teresa L. Sturm
Steven K. Brown
David H. Shipman
Katherine S. Moriarty

Reed E. Andrus
Curtis Reed Smith
Lance J. Schuster
Jeremy P. Pisca (Resident, Boise Office)

OF COUNSEL

John Michael Brassey (Resident, Boise Office)
Willis B. Benjamin
Orval Hansen (Resident, Washington, D.C. Office)
George L. Denison (Not admitted in ID; Resident, Washington, D.C. Office)

REGISTERED PATENT AGENT

Robert A. deGroot

Representative Clients: Wells Fargo Bank; The Idaho Nature Conservancy; Basic American, Inc.; U S West Communications Inc.; Busch Agricultural Resources, Inc.; Wal-Mart, Inc.; Eastern Idaho Economic Development Council, Inc.; Mutual of Enumclaw; Reliance Insurance Co.; Wausau Insurance Cos.

For full biographical listings, see the Martindale-Hubbell Law Directory

KELLOGG, Shoshone Co.

EVANS, KEANE LLP (AV)

111 Main Street, P.O. Box 659, 83837
Telephone: 208-784-1105
Facsimile: 208-783-7601
Email: evanskeane@nidlink.com
Boise, Idaho Office: Suite 200, 1101 West River Street, P.O. Box 959.
Telephone: 208-384-1800

James P. Keane (1925-1988)
Fred M. Gibler
Charles L. A. Cox
Justin W. Julian

Representative Clients: City of Kellogg; Coeur d Alene Mines Corp.; Crown Pacific Limited Partnership; Hecla Mining Co.; Lawyers Title Insurance Corp.; Kellogg School District No. 391; Silver Mountain Corp.; Silver Valley Resources Corporation; Sunshine Mining and Refining Company; Sunshine Precious Metals, Inc.; S.V.L. Analytical, Inc.; U.S. Bank.

For full biographical listings, see the Martindale-Hubbell Law Directory

*POCATELLO,** Bannock Co.

JONES, CHARTERED (AV)

415 South Arthur Avenue, P.O. Box 967, 83204-0967
Telephone: 208-232-5911
FAX: 208-232-5962
Email: joneslaw@poky.srv.net

Lamont Jones
Jack H. Robison
Thomas J. Holmes
Jesse C. Robison

(See Next Column)

Brett P. Allison

Representative Clients: First Security Bank of Idaho; Ireland Bank; Idaho State University; Idaho Power Co.; Alliance Title and Escrow Corp.; City of Chubbuck; I.H.C. Hospitals, Inc.; Pocatello Board of Realtors; North Pacific Insurance; Houston General Insurance.

For full biographical listings, see the Martindale-Hubbell Law Directory

MERRILL & MERRILL, CHARTERED (AV)

Key Bank Building, P.O. Box 991, 83204
Telephone: 208-232-2286
Fax: 208-232-2499
Email: mmlaw@ida.net

A. L. Merrill (1886-1961)
R. D. Merrill (1893-1972)
Wesley F. Merrill (Retired)
Dave R. Gallafent
Stephen S. Dunn
D. Russell Wight
David C. Nye
Kent L. Hawkins
Thomas W. Clark
Thomas J. Lyons
Gary L. Longmore

Representative Clients: Key Bank of Idaho; Bannock Regional Medical Center; The Travelers Insurance Co.; Aetna Casualty & Surety Co.; Hartford Accident & Indemnity Co.; Equitable Life Assurance Society; Utah Power & Light Co.; Pacific Corp.; Portneuf-Marsh Valley Canal Co.; Farm Bureau Mutual Insurance Co. of Idaho.

For full biographical listings, see the Martindale-Hubbell Law Directory

*REXBURG,** Madison Co.

RIGBY, THATCHER, ANDRUS, RIGBY, KAM & MOELLER, CHARTERED (AV)

25 North Second East, P.O. Box 250, 83440
Telephone: 208-356-3633
Fax: 208-356-0768
Email: rexlaw@srv.net

Ray W. Rigby
Gordon S. Thatcher
G. Rich Andrus
Jerry R. Rigby
Michael S. Kam
Gregory W. Moeller

Attorneys for: North Fork Reservoir Co.; Class "A" School Districts 321 & 322; Fall River, Raft River and Lost River Electric Cooperatives; Ultimate Director, Inc.; Madison Cooperative Association, Inc.; W.R. Henderson Construction, Inc.; Committee of Nine of Water District 01.
Representative Clients: Taylor Chevrolet Co.; Madison Cooperative Assn., Inc.; Valley Bank (Headquarter Office).

For full biographical listings, see the Martindale-Hubbell Law Directory

ILLINOIS

ARLINGTON HEIGHTS, Cook Co.

DALEIDEN & TREMAINE, LTD. (AV)

2815 North Douglas Avenue, 60004
Telephone: 847-577-7438
Fax: 847-577-7458

Norbert A. Daleiden
Arthur J. Tremaine

For full biographical listings, see the Martindale-Hubbell Law Directory

AURORA, Kane Co.

MICKEY, WILSON, WEILER & RENZI, P.C. (AV)

2111 Plum Street, 2nd Floor, P.O. Box 787, 60507-0787
Telephone: 630-801-9699
Fax: 630-801-9715
Email: office@mwwr.com *URL:* http://www.mwwr.com

Gary K. Mickey
Peter K. Wilson, Jr.
Bernard K. Weiler
Constance Burnett Renzi
Steven A. Andersson

For full biographical listings, see the Martindale-Hubbell Law Directory

MURPHY, HUPP, FOOTE, MIELKE AND KINNALLY (AV)

North Island Center, P.O. Box 5030, 60507
Telephone: 630-844-0056
Fax: 630-844-1905
Email: mhfmk@insnet.com

MEMBERS OF FIRM

William C. Murphy
Robert B. Hupp
Robert M. Foote
Craig S. Mielke
Patrick M. Kinnally
Paul G. Krentz
Joseph C. Loran
Gerald K. Hodge

(See Next Column)

MURPHY, HUPP, FOOTE, MIELKE AND KINNALLY, *Aurora—Continued*

Timothy D. O'Neil — Matthew J. Herman

Representative Clients: American Telephone & Telegraph Co.; Fox Valley Park District; Lyon Metal Products; Kane County Forest Preserve District; Hollywood Casino; Employers Mutual Insurance Co.; Forty-Eight Insulations, Inc.; UNR Asbestos Disease Trust; Richards-Wilcox Co.; National Bank & Trust Company of Syracuse.

For full biographical listings, see the Martindale-Hubbell Law Directory

BATAVIA, Kane Co.

DRENDEL TATNALL, A PROFESSIONAL CORPORATION (AV)

201 Houston Street, Suite 300, P.O. Box 1808, 60510-6808
Telephone: 630-406-5440
Fax: 630-406-6179

Gilbert X. Drendel, Jr. — Kevin G. Drendel
Susan B. Tatnall — Charles V. Muscarello

LEGAL SUPPORT PERSONNEL

Sheila Persinger (Legal Assistant)

Reference: Old Second National Bank of Aurora, Aurora, Illinois.

For full biographical listings, see the Martindale-Hubbell Law Directory

*BELLEVILLE,** St. Clair Co.

DUNHAM, BOMAN & LESKERA (AV)

208 N. High, 62220
Telephone: 618-235-7222
Telecopier: 618-236-2800; 618-236-1899
Collinsville Office: 300 West Clay Street.
Telephone: 618-344-7734.
Telecopier: 618-344-3853.

M.F. Oehmke (1887-1963) — William L. Berry
Wm. C. Dunham (1893-1975) — Eric C. Young
Howard Boman (1917-1985) — Robert D. Francis
John W. Leskera — John L. Bitzer

Attorneys for: Collinsville School District #10; Hanover Insurance Co.; Hartford Insurance Group; State Farm Insurance Cos.; Transamerica Insurance Group; The Travelers Indemnity Co.; Wausau Insurance Cos.; Nationwide Insurance Co.; RLI Insurance Group.

For full biographical listings, see the Martindale-Hubbell Law Directory

GUNDLACH, LEE, EGGMANN, BOYLE & ROESSLER (AV)

A Partnership including a Professional Corporation
5000 West Main Street, P.O. Box 23560, 62223-0560
Telephone: 618-277-9000; East St. Louis: 271-8000
Telecopier: 618-277-4594
St. Louis, Mo.
Email: glebr@aol.com
St. Louis, Missouri Office: 1010 Market Street, Suite 1640.
Telephone: 314-231-2084.
Telecopier: 314-231-1960.

PARTNERS

Norman J. Gundlach (1907-1996) — Kenneth L. Halvachs
Carl W. Lee — Thomas R. Peters
Richard E. Boyle — Charles J. Swartwout
Richard M. Roessler — Charlene A. Cremeens, P.C.
Robert D. Andrekanic

ASSOCIATES

Karen E. Mason — Brad G. Pelc
Curtis R. Picou — Carrie N. Oliver
Mary G. Sullivan — Thomas J. Cynor
Mark R. Kurz — James R. Garrison

Division Counsel for: Norfolk-Southern Railway Company.
Attorneys for: Illinois Central Railroad; Illinois Power Co.; Metropolitan, Prudential, Equitable, John Hancock, Northwestern Mutual and General American Life Insurance Cos.

For full biographical listings, see the Martindale-Hubbell Law Directory

NEVILLE, RICHARDS, DEFRANCO & WULLER (AV)

5 Park Place, 62226
Telephone: 618-277-0900
Facsimile: 618-277-0970
Email: nrdw@nrdw-law.com *URL:* http://www.nrdw-law.com

MEMBERS OF FIRM

James E. Neville — James E. DeFranco
Timothy S. Richards — Robert G. Wuller, Jr.

ASSOCIATES

Shari M. Brunton — Daniel L. Bradley
Ellen M. Edmonds — Matthew Charles Zittel

For full biographical listings, see the Martindale-Hubbell Law Directory

THOMPSON COBURN LLP (AV)

525 West Main Street, 62222-0730
Telephone: 618-277-4700; 314-271-1800
Telecopier: 618-236-3434
Email: info@thompsoncoburn.com *URL:* http://www.thompsoncoburn.com
St. Louis, Missouri Office: One Mercantile Center.
Telephone: 314-552-6000.
Telecopier: 314-552-7000.
Washington, D.C. Office: 700 14th Street, N.W., Suite 900.
Telephone: 202-508-1000.
Telecopier: 202-508-1010.
Billings, Montana Office: Norwest Center, 175 North 27th Street, Suite 903, 59101.
Telephone: 406-896-4100.
Fax: 406-896-4199.

PARTNERS

Thomas W. Alvey, Jr. — Joseph R. Lowery
Edward S. Bott, Jr. — Joseph C. Orlet
W. Thomas Coghill, Jr. — Kurt E. Reitz
Karl D. Dexheimer — Garrett C. Reuter
Thomas F. Hennessy, III — William A. Schmitt
Kurt S. Schroeder

OF COUNSEL

Robert L. Broderick — James R. Parham

ASSOCIATES

Ann C. Barron — Eric R. Riess
Aaron A. Buckley — Kaori Horikawa Smith
Erick E. VanDorn

Representative Clients: First Illinois Bank; General Motors Corp.; Harcros Pigments, Inc.; Illinois-American Water Co.; Marsh Co.; Memorial Hospital of Belleville; Norfolk Southern Corp.; Peabody Coal Co.

For full biographical listings, see the Martindale-Hubbell Law Directory

*BENTON,** Franklin Co.

HART AND HART (AV)

602 West Public Square, P.O. Box 937, 62812-0937
Telephone: 618-435-8123
Telecopier: 618-435-2962
URL: http://news2.intrnet.net/~hart/index.html

William H. Hart (1862-1941) — Richard O. Hart
William W. Hart (1894-1968) — Murphy C. Hart
Marion M. Hart (1896-1964) — A. Courtney Cox
William W. Hart, Jr. (1925-1996) — Pamela Sue Lacey

ASSOCIATE

Jeffrey M. Feltman

Representative Clients: NationsBank; Illinois Central Railroad; State Bankof Whittington; Healthcare Revenue Management, Inc.; Credit Bureau Systems, Inc.; Lloyd's of London, England; Hospital & Physician Publishing, Inc.; Players International, Inc.; Laidlaw Corporation; Walgreen Distribution Centers.

For full biographical listings, see the Martindale-Hubbell Law Directory

*BLOOMINGTON,** McLean Co.

DUNN, STANCZAK & WILLARD (AV)

1001 North Main Street, P.O. Box 3488, 61702-3488
Telephone: 309-828-6241
Fax: 309-828-8321
Email: Dunnlaw@aol.com

MEMBERS OF FIRM

Richard F. Dunn (1888-1963) — David L. Stanczak
Mark T. Dunn — Donald A. Willard

ASSOCIATE

Thomas J. Arkell

OF COUNSEL

Louis F. Ulbrich — Richard T. Dunn

Representative Clients: Northeastern Illinois University; Governors State University; Western Illinois University; Chicago State University; First Federal Savings & Loan Association of Bloomington; Illinois Wesleyan University; Metropolitan Life Insurance Co., Agricultural Investments and Commercial Investments; Commerce Bank; Bluestem National Bank.

For full biographical listings, see the Martindale-Hubbell Law Directory

CARBONDALE, Jackson Co.

FEIRICH/MAGER/GREEN/RYAN (AV)

2001 West Main Street, P.O. Box 1570, 62903-1570
Telephone: 618-529-3000
Telecopier: 618-529-3008
Email: fmgr@intrnet.net

(See Next Column)

FEIRICH/MAGER/GREEN/RYAN—*Continued*

MEMBERS OF FIRM

John K. Feirich (1909-1998)
T. Richard Mager
Richard A. Green
John C. Ryan
Michael F. Dahlen
Kevin L. Mechler
John S. Rendleman, III
Pieter N. Schmidt
Gary B. Nelson
Edward E. Renshaw

ASSOCIATES

Jeffrey S. Berkbigler
Kara L. Jones
David R. Tracy

Representative Clients: Country Mutual Insurance Co.; Sentry Insurance Co.; Great Central Insurance Co.; Consolidation Coal Co.; Heitman Properties, Ltd.; Southern Illinois Hospital Services; Electric Energy, Inc.; Gilster Mary Lee Corp.; Downstate National Banks.

For full biographical listings, see the Martindale-Hubbell Law Directory

*CARLINVILLE,** Macoupin Co.

PHELPS, KASTEN, RUYLE, BURNS, CARMODY & SIMS (AV)

130 East Main Street, P.O. Box 587, 62626
Telephone: 217-854-3283
FAX: 217-854-9527
Email: pkrb@accunet.net

MEMBERS OF FIRM

Edward R. Phelps (1904-1985)
John W. Russell (Retired)
Carl E. Kasten
Nancy L. Ruyle
Thomas P. Burns
Stephen R. Carmody
Byron J. Sims

Representative Clients: Carlinville National Bank; Blackburn University; Area Diesel Service, Inc.; H & H Construction Services, Inc.

For full biographical listings, see the Martindale-Hubbell Law Directory

*CARTHAGE,** Hancock Co.

HARTZELL, GLIDDEN, TUCKER AND HARTZELL (AV)

Williams Building, P.O. Box 70, 62321
Telephone: 217-357-3121
FAX: 217-357-2027
Email: hgthattys@adams.net
Macomb, Illinois Office: Old Bailey House, 100 South Campbell Street.
Telephone: 309-833-3121.

MEMBERS OF FIRM

Homer H. Williams (1894-1965)
Franklin M. Hartzell
John R. Glidden
Stanley L. Tucker
Thomas F. Hartzell

Counsel for: Marine Trust Company of Carthage; Bowen State Bank; Pioneer Lumber Co.; City of Carthage; Memorial Hospital Assn.
Local Counsel for: State Farm Mutual Insurance Co.; The Prudential Insurance Company of America; American States Insurance Co.

For full biographical listings, see the Martindale-Hubbell Law Directory

CENTRALIA, Marion Co.

WHAM & WHAM (AV)

212 East Broadway, 62801
Telephone: 618-532-5621
Fax: 618-532-5055
URL: http://www.lawyers.com/wham&wham

Charles Wham (1887-1963)
John P. Wham (1902-1992)

MEMBERS OF FIRM

James B. Wham
Richard A. Cary
Janie F. Smith
Jennifer W. Price
Daniel R. Price

OF COUNSEL

William B. Wham

Counsel for: State Farm Mutual Insurance Cos.; Auto-Owners Insurance Co; Pekin Insurance; MMI Cos; West American Ins. Co; Ohio Casualty Ins. Co.

For full biographical listings, see the Martindale-Hubbell Law Directory

CHAMPAIGN, Champaign Co.

FLYNN, PALMER & TAGUE (AV)

402 West Church Street, P.O. Box 1517, 61824-1517
Telephone: 217-352-5181
Telecopier: 217-352-7964
Email: fpt5law@aol.com

MEMBERS OF FIRM

Leonard T. Flynn
Michael J. Tague
James D. Green
Jerome P. Lyke

(See Next Column)

OF COUNSEL

Charles L. Palmer

Representative Clients: Bituminous Insurance Co.; Standard Mutual Insurance Co.; Universal Underwriters Co.; BankChampaign N.A.; BankIllinois; Champaign Asphalt Co.; Champaign Board of Education; University of Illinois; American Drug Stores, Inc.; Landaut Heyman, Inc.

For full biographical listings, see the Martindale-Hubbell Law Directory

MEYER, CAPEL, HIRSCHFELD, MUNCY, JAHN & ALDEEN, P.C. (AV)

306 West Church Street, P.O. Box 6750, 61826-6750
Telephone: 217-352-1800
Telecopier: 217-352-1083
Email: attorneys@meyercapel.com *URL:* http://www.meyercapel.com

James L. Capel, Jr. (1933-1991)
John C. Hirschfeld
Dennis K. Muncy
Francis J. Jahn
Donald R. Aldeen
John H. Elder
David B. Sholem
Mark D. Lipton
Tracy J. Nugent
Richard T. West
Rusty W. Freeland
Lorna K. Geiler
Patrick T. Fitzgerald
Todd J. Black
Joseph D. Murphy
Neil R. Rafferty
James M. Mullady
William B. Moore
Evan D. Coobs
John J. Powers
Rochelle A. Funderburg

Matt C. Deering
Jeffrey M. Davis
Marjorie A. Harris
Gregory T. Mizen
Brian C. Lawlyes

OF COUNSEL

August C. Meyer, Jr.
Richard J. Winkel, Jr.
John H. McCord

Representative Clients: BankIllinois in Champaign; Bell Foods, Inc.; Christie Clinic; Illini Cablevision, Inc.; Kuck & Associates, Inc.; Midwest Television, Inc.; Parkland College.

For full biographical listings, see the Martindale-Hubbell Law Directory

RAWLES, O'BYRNE, STANKO & KEPLEY, P.C. (AV)

501 West Church Street, P.O. Box 800, 61824-0800
Telephone: 217-352-7661
Telecopier: 217-352-2169
URL: http://www.rosklaw.com

Donald M. Reno (1906-1987)
J. Michael O'Byrne
Vance I. Kepley (Retired)
Edward H. Rawles
Stephen M. O'Byrne
Glenn A. Stanko
Brett A. Kepley
Timothy S. Jefferson

LEGAL SUPPORT PERSONNEL

Rose M. Lanter (Legal Assistant)
Karen B. Judd (Legal Assistant)

Local Counsel for: Bank One of Champaign, Urbana; Covenant Medical Center; Gibson Community Hospital; Frances Nelson Health Center; University of Illinois; Pekin Insurance Company; Union Insurance Group; New Hampshire Insurance Group; Construction Industry Welfare Fund of Central Illinois; Terra International Inc.

For full biographical listings, see the Martindale-Hubbell Law Directory

THOMAS, MAMER & HAUGHEY (AV)

Fifth Floor, National City Bank Building, 30 Main Street, 61820-3629
Telephone: 217-351-1500
Fax: 217-355-0087; 217-351-2017
217-351-2169
Mailing Address: P.O. Box 560, Champaign, Illinois, 61824-0560
Email: tmh@tmh-law.com

James G. Thomas (1901-1990)

MEMBERS OF FIRM

Stuart M. Mamer
Roger E. Haughey
Lott H. Thomas
William J. Brinkmann
Howard W. Small
David A. Bailie
Craig J. Causeman
Michael R. Cornyn
Richard R. Harden
Robert A. Hoffman
David E. Krchak
Bruce E. Warren

ASSOCIATES

Linda L. Laugges
John M. Sturmanis
Bianca Truitt Green
Kenneth D. Reifsteck

Representative Clients: American States Insurance Co.; Auto Owners Insurance Co.; Bituminous Insurance Co.; Capitol Indemnity Co.; Cannon Cochran Management Services Inc.; Chicago Motor Insurance Co.; Ecomony Fire & Casualty Co.; Federated Insurance; Hanover Insurance Co.; Hartford Insurance Co.

For full biographical listings, see the Martindale-Hubbell Law Directory

*CHARLESTON,** Coles Co.

THE BRAINARD LAW OFFICES (AV)

Brainard Building, 600 Jackson Avenue, 61920
Telephone: 217-345-3929
Fax: 217-345-6501

MEMBERS OF FIRM

H. Ogden Brainard (1905-1992)
William A. Sunderman
Henry E. Kramer
Brian L. Bower
William J. Warmoth
Mark R. Karpus
Kristin L. Wilson

OF COUNSEL

J. Leeds Bower

Representative Clients: Community Bank & Trust Savings Bank; Agri Bank FCB; Coles-Moultrie Electric Cooperative; Sarah Bush Lincoln Health Center.

For full biographical listings, see the Martindale-Hubbell Law Directory

*CHICAGO,** Cook Co.

ALTHEIMER & GRAY (AV)

Suite 4000, 10 South Wacker Drive, 60606
Telephone: 312-715-4000
Fax: 312-715-4800
Telex: RCA 297102 A G UR
URL: http://www.altheimer.com
Washington, D.C. Office: 1350 Eye Street, N.W., 20005.
Telephone: 202-312-8420.
Fax: 202-289-1408.
Springfield, Illinois, Office: 600 S. Second Street, 62704-2542.
Telephone: 217-789-1040.
Fax: 217-789-1077.
Warsaw, Poland Office: Warsaw Financial Center, ul. Emilii Plater 53, 00-113 Warsaw, Poland.
Telephone: 011-48-22-520-5000.
Fax: 011-48-22-520-5001.
Prague, Czech Republic Office: Platnerska 4, 110 00 Prague 1.
Telephone: 420-2 2481-2782.
Fax: 420-2 2481-0125.
Kyiv, Ukraine Office: 11 Mykhailivska Street, 4th Floor, 252001 Kyiv.
Telephone: 38-044-230-2534, Within Kyiv: 464-0204.
Fax: 38-044-230-2535. Fax within Kyiv: 464-0231.
Bratislava, Slovakia Office: Nam. SNP 15, 811-06 Bratislava.
Telephone: 421-7-5293-2144.
Fax: 421-7-361-566.
Istanbul, Turkey Office: Büyükdere Plaza, Büyükdere Cad No. 195, Kat 6, Levent, Istanbul 80620.
Telephone: 90 212 324-2040.
Fax: 90 212 324-2032.
Shanghai, China Office: Shanghai Kerry Centre, 1515 Nanjing West Road, Shanghai 200040 China.
Telephone: 86 21-6289-0990.
Fax: 86 21-6289-9911.
Bucharest, Romania Office: 5 Pitar Moş, Sector 1, 70151 Bucharest.
Telephone: 401-212-3791.
Fax: 401-212-3796.
London, U.K. Office: 7 Bishopsgate, London, U.K. Tel: 44-207-786-5700.
Fax: 44-207-786-1000.

Alan J. Altheimer (1903-1999)
Marlene R. Abrams
Rolando R. Acosta
Cathleen Hainer Albrecht
Rita M. Alliss
Mark H. Berens
Robert I. Berger
Myles D. (Mush) Berman
Sean W. Bezark
Bruce A. Bonjour
Scott A. Bremer
Laurence R. Bronska
Robert E. Browne
John J. Buttita
Curtis R. Calvert
Richard M. Carbonara
Gery J. Chico
Terence J. Cloney
Melanie Rovner Cohen
Alexandra R. Cole
George I. Cowell
James R. Cruger
Susan J. Daley
Jeffrey P. De Jong
Laurence B. Dobkin
Stephen M. Dorfman
Michael M. Eidelman
Bradley M. Falk
Faye B. Feinstein
Kenneth R. Gaines
Mark R. Galis
John F. Gibbons
Donald A. Gillies
Norman M. Gold
Louis B. Goldman
Phillip Gordon
James S. Gray
Milton H. Gray
Roger B. Harris
Patrick J. Head
Wm. Bruce Hoff, Jr.
Robert M. Horwitch
Peter M. Howard
Robert A. Janoski
Jaroslawa Zelinsky Johnson
David V. Kahn
Nancy L. Kasko
Mark Thomas Kindelin
Kenneth K. Kneubuhler
Jeffrey T. Kraus
Janet M. Kyte
Richard F. Levy (P.C.)
Myron Lieberman
Peter H. Lieberman
Corey E. Light
Melvin K. Lippe
Theodore J. Low
John E. Lowe
C. Vincent Maloney
Jeremy D. Margolis
Andrew W. McCune
Thomas C. McDonough

(See Next Column)

F. John McGinnis
Edward E. McNally
John W. Morrison
Barry B. Nekritz
Bridget M. O'Keefe
Stephen R. Otis
Michael L. Owen
S. Michael Peck
Richard E. Peterson
Daniel M. Pierce
Michael S. Pinsky
Anita J. Ponder
John F. Prusiecki
David B. Ritter
John E. Rogers
David C. Roston
Maria N. Saldaña
Terry M. Schlade
Robert L. Schlossberg
David W. Schoenberg
Benjamin D. Schwartz
Audrey E. Selin
Brian C. Shea
Kenneth C. Shepro
Jeffrey Norman Smith
Gary L. Specks
John C. Stiefel
Angelo F. Tiesi
S. Raymond Tillett
Jeffrey S. Torf
William F. Tueting
Darren B. Watts
Richard A. Wendy
Edward E. Wicks
Roger Wilen

RETIRED PARTNERS

David L. Fargo
Jacob Logan Fox
Lionel G. Gross
Samuel T. Lawton, Jr.
Sherwin J. Stone

ASSOCIATES

Philip Ackerman
Matthew H. Ahrens
Michael H. Altman
Robert M. Andalman
Alexis Andrews
Dirk W. Andringa
Jonathan Baird (Not admitted in IL)
Kim M. Barker
Sonia Gupta Barros
Tianne Bataille
Robert E. Blacher
Brian D. Bryant
Dina Bukhman
Leslie Carey
Michael A. Carrillo
James J. Caserio
Pawel Chudzicki
Christopher Combest
Ted A. Donner
Nathan J. Feltman
Barry Fischer
Gregory A. Fishman
Joseph P. Gattuso
Caroline R. Geraci (Not admitted in IL)
Andrew R. Greene
Kendy M. Hess
Kathleen L. Hobbins
John E. Hyatt
Marlene J. Igel
Theodore C. Jennings
Howard K. Jeruchimowitz
LaVon M. Johns-Harris
R. Scott Johnson
Iain D. Johnston
Michael G. Kelber
Renee F. Kessel
Susan M. Kortokrax
Brian K. Kozminski
Erika L. Kruse
Deborah L. Kuhn
Peter G. Lawrence
Tan H. Le (Not admitted in IL)
Julie K. Leskinen
Dorothea Lidd
Mark Maciasz
Paula C. Maggio
Lesli L. Mann (Not admitted in IL)
Daniel G.M. Marre
Jane B. McCullough
Jeffrey E. Michael
John Adam Mikowski
John W. Newlin
John M. O'Bryan
John A. O'Donohue
Catherine A. O'Malley
Angela Ortiz
Andrew E. Packer
Michael A. Peil
Dawn M. Phillips
Jay E. Presser
James F. Roberts
Andrew P. Scott
Gelene M. Stanton
John A. Strye
Tracy L. Treger
Mario M. Tricoci
Feng Xue
Aihong Yu (Not admitted in IL)
Marjorie J. Zessar

OF COUNSEL

Charles F. Adler, Jr.
Paula Kaplan Berger
Jonathan G. Harrison
Maurice Jacobs
David J. Lester
Richard A. Prince
Don H. Reuben
Jack M. Siegel

For full biographical listings, see the Martindale-Hubbell Law Directory

ARONBERG GOLDGEHN DAVIS & GARMISA (AV)

Suite 3000 One IBM Plaza, 60611
Telephone: 312-828-9600
Telecopier: 312-828-9635
Email: agdglaw@aol.com
Schaumberg, Illinois Office: 1901 North Roselle Road, Suite 800, 60195.
Telephone: 847-985-4060.

MEMBERS OF FIRM

Christopher J. Bannon
Jay A. Frank
William J. Garmisa
Mitchell S. Goldgehn
James J. Hickey
James S. Jarvis
Nathan H. Lichtenstein
Mitchell J. Melamed
Marc W. O'Brien
Tami J. Reding-Brubaker
John M. Riccione
Ned S. Robertson
David H. Sachs
James A. Smith
Robert N. Sodikoff
Andrew S. Williams

OF COUNSEL

Ronald J. Aronberg
Melvin A. Blum
Steven P. Davis
Steven H. Nemerovski
Charles E. Zeitlin

(See Next Column)

ARONBERG GOLDGEHN DAVIS & GARMISA—*Continued*

ASSOCIATES

Lisa J. Brodsky
Eric M. Brown
Howard J. Fishman
Paul A. Greenberg
Mary Vidal Hays
Elizabeth Olen Lazzara
William J. Serritella, Jr.

For full biographical listings, see the Martindale-Hubbell Law Directory

BAKER & MCKENZIE (AV)

One Prudential Plaza, 130 East Randolph Drive, 60601
Telephone: (312) 861-8000
Intn'l. Dialing: (1-312) 861-8000
Facsimiles: (1-312) 861-2899;
861-8080 (Operator)
URL: http://www.bakerinfo.com
Associated Offices of Baker & McKenzie in: Almaty, Amsterdam, Bahrain, Baku, Bangkok, Barcelona, Beijing, Berlin, Bogotá, Brasília, Brussels, Budapest, Buenos Aires, Cairo, Caracas, Dallas, Düsseldorf, Frankfurt, Geneva, Hanoi, Ho Chi Minh City, Hong Kong, Houston, Hsinchu, Juárez, Kiev, London, Madrid, Manila, Melbourne, México City, Miami, Milan, Monterrey, Moscow, Münich, New York, Palo Alto, Paris, Prague, Rio de Janeiro, Riyadh, Rome, St. Petersburg, San Diego, San Francisco, Santiago, São Paulo, Singapore, Stockholm, Sydney, Taipei, Tijuana, Tokyo, Toronto, Valencia, Warsaw, Washington, D.C. and Zürich.
Correspondent Law Firms: Hadiputranto, Hadinoto & Partners, Jakarta; Wong & Partners, Kuala Lumpur.

MEMBERS OF FIRM

Robert H. Aland
Russell Baker (1901-1979)
James G. Barnes
Peter J. H. Bentley
Robert L. Berner, Jr.
Leslie A. Bertagnolli
Neal J. Block
Andrew J. Boling
Michael L. Coleman
John J. Conroy, Jr.
Robert J. Cunningham
Robert E. Deignan
Thomas A. Doyle
Edwin R. Dunn
David W. Ellis
John C. Filosa
Richard M. Franklin
Pablo A. Garcia-Moreno
Robert J. Gareis
Michael J. Garvey
Arthur L. George
David P. Hackett
Thomas M. Haderlein
Frederick E. Henry
J. Patrick Herald
Akira Ito
Jerome W. Jakubik
Thomas E. Johnson
Sidney M. Kaplan
Mark L. Karasik
Neal A. Klegerman
Robert C. Knuepfer, Jr.
Gregg D. Lemein
Charles B. Lewis
William Joseph Linklater
Gerald L. Maatman, Jr.
Jaime F. Malagón (Not admitted in United States)
Sebastiao de Souza Mattos Neto
Maura Ann McBreen
Paul McCarthy
William S. McDowell, Jr.
John C. McKenzie (1913-1962)
John A. McLees
Michael S. Mensik
Marcel J. Molins
Peter J. Mone
John E. Morrow
John M. Murphy
Francisco Miguel Noyola
Mark A. Oates
James M. O'Brien
James P. O'Brien
Michael P. O'Brien
Daniel J. O'Connor
Nam H. Paik
Michael A. Pollard
David I. Roche
William Lynch Schaller
Dieter A. Schmitz
Paul D. Slocomb
Steven M. Surdell
Philip F. Suse
Preston M. Torbert
Michael J. Wagner
David A. Waimon
Friedrich J. Weinkopf
Jia Zhao
Edward J. Zulkey

NATIONAL PARTNERS

Patrick J. Ahern
Gerald K. Bolkema
Barrie L. Brejcha
Lisa Sopata Brogan
Martin R. Castro
David J. Davis
Hugo Dubovoy (Not admitted in United States)
Lawrence F. Haas
Paula J. Krasny
John M. McGarry
Creighton R. Meland, Jr.
Pamela J. Mills
Michael L. Morkin
Ronald L. Ohren
Vincent S. Oleszkiewicz
Lynn S. Preece
James Lee Stetson
Kerry R. Weinger
Jonathan M. Wilson
Bruce A. Zivian

SENIOR COUNSEL

Jack D. Beem
David S. Ruder
Premjit Singh

COUNSEL

Betsy Stelle Morgan

ASSOCIATES

Jonathan E. Adams
Matthew G. Allison
Brian S. Arbetter
John A. Bacon
Donna L. Bade
Torsten Bartsch (Not admitted in United States)
Adriane W. Burkland
J. Russell Carr
Jaime A. Vargas Cifuentes (Not admitted in United States)
Eli D. Cohen
Regine W. Corrado (Not admitted in IL)

(See Next Column)

ASSOCIATES (Continued)

Andrew B. Cripe
Julie D. Cromer
Jennifer N. DeLisle
Isabelle Demenge (Not admitted in United States)
David J. Dicker
Carrie J. DiSanto
Patrick D. Dolan
Jodi G. Eisenstadt
Sarah E. Fandell
Patricia C. Gallagher
Peter R. George
Peter J. Gillespie
Amy Dickman Gray
Jeffrey C. Groulx
Charles Salem Hallab
Jeffrey L. Hamera
Brent A. Hannafan
Marc A. Horwitz
Jonathan E. Hyun
Eileen McChesney Kelly
Thomas J. Kinzler
Samuel G. Kramer
Igor L. Krivoshekov
Robert S. Lawrence
Thomas V. M. Linguanti
William M. Link
Julie Sherman Lucht
David J. Malliband (Not admitted in United States)
Thomas Y. Man (Not admitted in IL)
Samuel A. Mandarino
Victor M. Marroquin
Paul Holmes Masters
Holly Klus McClellan
John D. McDonald
Richard B. Meamber
J. F. Hannes Meckel (Not admitted in United States)
José A. Morán (Not admitted in United States)
Steven J. Nagy
Ben A. Neiburger
Susan D. Newman
Michael P. Palmer
Heidi Pemberton (Not admitted in IL)
Maria S. Pugliese
Mark P. Ramsey
Esteban Raventós (Not admitted in United States)
Harun Admana Reksodiputro (Not admitted in United States)
Joan M. Richman
Phillip Rosenblatt (Not admitted in IL)
Shima S. Roy
Lavesh Samtani
Sanjiv D. Sarwate
Erika Schafer Schechter
Paul E. Schick
Mark F. Schultz
David M. Serwer
Xiaokui "Katie" Shan
Cheryl L. Slusarchuk (Not admitted in IL)
Robert J. Smetana
Maureen R. Smith
Carole A. Spink
Philip S. Stamatakos
Anthony G. Stamato
Andrew K. Strimaitis
Mark C. Swords
William J. Tarnow
Kenneth J. Vanko
Robert S. Walton
Bradley R. Weissenberger
Kathryn D. Weston-Overbey
Donna J. Williams
David G. Wix
Richard M. Wolfson
Xiong Yin

For full biographical listings, see the Martindale-Hubbell Law Directory

BARNES & THORNBURG (AV)

2600 Chase Plaza, 10 South La Salle Street, 60603
Telephone: 312-357-1313
FAX: 312-759-5646
URL: http://www.btlaw.com
Indianapolis, Indiana Office: 11 South Meridian Street, 46204.
Telephone: 317-236-1313.
FAX: 317-231-7433.
Fort Wayne, Indiana Office: Suite 600, One Summit Square, 46802.
Telephone: 219-423-9440.
FAX: 219-424-8316.
South Bend, Indiana Office: 600 1st Source Bank Center, 100 North Michigan, 46601-1632.
Telephone: 219-233-1171.
FAX: 219-237-1125.
Elkhart, Indiana Office: 121 West Franklin Street, Suite 200, 46516.
Telephone: 219-293-0681.
FAX: 219-296-2535.
Washington, D.C. Office: 1401 Eye Street, N.W., Suite 500, 20005.
Telephone: 202-289-1313.
FAX: 202-289-1330.

MEMBERS OF FIRM

Sidney G. Saltz
Richard M. Brown
William I. Kohn
John A. Rupp
Daniel P. Albers
Mark E. Rust
Bradley B. Falkof

OF COUNSEL

Eugene H. Bernstein
Charles J. Schultz
Alice O. Martin
Fredric P. Andes

ASSOCIATES

Scott T. Longman
Kathryn R. Howell (Not admitted in IL)
Melissa A. Vallone
Marc S. Silver
Mary K. Samsa
Jonathan P. Froemel
Kristan Quinn Laden
Ellen L. Luepke

Representative Clients: AMPRO, Inc.; Chicago Football, LLC; Citizens Commercial Leasing Corporation; Commonwealth Edison Company; Harley-Davidson Motor Company; International Facilities Group, LLC; Marchesan Implementos E. Maquinas Agricoles Tatu SA; Ron Weber & Associates of Illinois, Inc.; Transtech Products Corporation; Whirlpool Corporation.

For full biographical listings, see the Martindale-Hubbell Law Directory

Chicago—Continued

BRINKS HOFER GILSON & LIONE, A PROFESSIONAL CORPORATION (AV)

NBC Tower, 455 North Cityfront Plaza Drive, Suite 3600, 60611-5599
Telephone: 312-321-4200
Cable Address: "Judicature Chicago"
Telex: 254300
Facsimile: 312-321-4299
Email: iplaw@brinkshofer.com *URL:* http://www.brinkshofer.com
Toledo, Ohio Office: 1130 Edison Plaza.
Telephone: 419-244-6578.
Telex: 140342.
Facsimile: 419-244-8862.
Indianapolis, Indiana Office: One Indiana Square, Suite 2425.
Telephone: 317-636-0886.
Telex: 469632.
Facsimile: 317-634-6701. E-mail: 75471.352@compuserve.com.
Detroit, Michigan Office: 211 West Fort, Suite 1100.
Telephone: 313-967-9375.
Facsimile: 313-967-9378.
Arlington, Virginia Office: Crystal Plaza One, 2001 Jefferson Davis Highway, Suite 208.
Telephone: 703-415-0303.
Telex: 140994.
Facsimile: 703-415-0304.
San Jose, California Office: 160 West Santa Clara Street, Suite 975.
Telephone: 408-971-0627.
Fax: 408-971-0941.

Henry L. Brinks
Roy E. Hofer
Richard G. Lione
Jerome Gilson
Melvin F. Jager
David A. Anderson
Jack C. Berenzweig
Jerold A. Jacover
Gary M. Ropski
William A. Webb
Joel W. Benson
John K. Lucas
Raymond W. Green
Cynthia A. Homan
James R. Sobieraj
Richard A. Kaplan
Allan J. Sternstein
Steven P. Shurtz
Jeffery M. Duncan
Jeffery A. Handelman
Harold V. Johnson
Rodney A. Daniel
Glen P. Belvis
Doris Loew
Thomas J. Filarski
William H. Frankel
Gustavo Siller, Jr.
James P. Naughton
Timothy Q. Delaney
Bradley G. Lane
Ralph J. Gabric
Mary M. Squyres
Barbara A. Larsen (Not admitted in IL)
G. Peter Nichols
Jonathan E. Retsky
Michael E. Milz
Dominic P. Zanfardino
Robert S. Mallin
William F. Prendergast
John C. Freeman
David S. Fleming
Laura Beth Miller
Michael P. Chu

Colleen Connors Butler
Meredith Martin Addy
Kent E. Genin
Craig A. Summerfield
Philip A. Jones
Marc V. Richards
Nanette M. Norton
Andrew D. Stover
Joseph V. Norvell
Katherine L. Tabor
Stephanie S. Conis
K. Shannon Mrksich
Eric W. Gallender
Jason C. White
Emilia Francesca Cannella
Thomas M. Williams
Joseph F. Hetz
John G. Rauch
Kevin L. Leffel (Not admitted in IL)
Charles Rieck
LaTonya T. Washington
Vineet Gauri
Carmen T. Matos
Mark H. Remus
Vitaliana G. Conforti
Tadashi Horie
Janet A. Pioli
Daniel B. Burg
Jasper W. Dockrey
Steven A. Maynard (Not admitted in IL)
Christopher A. Harkins
Keith M. Stolte
James L. Katz
Kelly J. Eberspecher
Linda D. Kennedy
Donna E. Becker
Elaine K. Lee
Howard S. Michael
Scott J. Slavick
Michael G. Bennett
Vincent J. Gnoffo
Christopher N. Bolinger
Richard E. Stanley, Jr.
David Rozenblat
Matthew Joseph Kelly
Donna S. Hennessy

COUNSEL

F. David AuBuchon
Helen A. Odar
John T. Gabrielides

DETROIT OFFICE

David D. Murray

TOLEDO OFFICE

David D. Murray

INDIANAPOLIS OFFICE

OF COUNSEL

David H. Badger

COUNSEL

Lawrence A. Steward (Managing Attorney, Indianapolis Office)

(See Next Column)

Dean E. McConnell
Sanders N. Hillis

SAN JOSE OFFICE

COUNSEL

Guy W. Shoup
Charles E. Quarton

For full biographical listings, see the Martindale-Hubbell Law Directory

CASSIDAY, SCHADE & GLOOR (AV)

Suite 1040, 20 North Wacker Drive, 60606-2903
Telephone: 312-641-3100
Fax: 312-444-1669
URL: http://www.cassiday.com
Waukegan, Illinois Office: 415 Washington Street, Suite 214.
Telephone: 847-249-0700.
Fax: 847-249-8029.
Wheaton, Illinois Office: 2100 Manchester Road, Suite 615.
Telephone: 630-682-9800.
Fax: 630-682-9893.

MEMBERS OF FIRM

James D. Ahern
Timothy J. Ashe
Richard A. Barrett, Jr. (Resident Partner, Wheaton, Illinois Office)
Marc F. Benjoya (Resident Partner, Waukegan, Illinois Office)
Thomas P. Boylan
Robert S. Burtker
Joseph A. Camarra
John D. Cassiday
Susan E. Seiwert Conner
Michael J. Cucco
John R. Davis (Resident Partner, Waukegan, Illinois Office)
James A. Foster
William J. Furey
Catherine L. Garvey
Joseph A. Giannelli
D. Patterson Gloor
Jean M. Golden
John D. Hackett
Michael J. Hennig
Brian J. Hickey
Patricia J. Hogan
Richard C. Huettel
Donald F. Ivansek
David A. Johnson
Jennifer Ann Keller
James W. Kopriva
Kathleen M. McCabe
Michael J. Morrissey
Constance R. O'Neill
Kimberly L. Robinson
Bradford D. Roth
Rudolf G. Schade, Jr.
Therese S. Seeley (Resident Partner, Wheaton, Illinois Office)
John N. Seibel
A. Jeffrey Seidman
Brian C. Sundheim
Julie A. Teuscher
David C. Van Dyke
Bruce M. Wall
Sally Jo Zimmerman

ASSOCIATES

Philip M. Abellera
Edward J. Aucoin, Jr. (Resident, Waukegan, Illinois Office)
Mark M. Brennan
Scott J. Brown
Kyle R. Burkhardt
Deborah Caldwell-Stone
Jon Michael Casadont
Gawain Charlton-Perrin
John Cleary (Resident, Waukegan, Illinois Office)
Christina Conlin
Christopher J. Dalki
Thomas A. Dohrer
William M. Dunn
Michael J. Hayes, Jr.
Michael B. Jawgiel (Resident, Waukegan, Illinois Office)
Michael S. Komoll
Richard B. Korn
Sandra E. Kupelian
Mary N. Lillios
Deborah B. Lyons
Deborah A. Martin-Sheridan
Nicole Nocera
Alison E. O'Hara
Henry Z. Persons
K. Kristann Pitakskul
Thomas S. Reed
Derrick B. Reese
John J. Reid (Resident, Waukegan, Illinois Office)
Patricia A. Ryan
Jeffrey R. Sandler
Daniel R. Shaffer
Linda B. Stefani
Stephanie R. Stomberg
Douglas S. Strohm (Resident, Wheaton, Illinois Office)
James P. Sullivan
Robert D. Sweeney
Steven P. Taub (Resident, Waukegan, Illinois Office)
Hanson L. Williams
Patrick John Woytek

OF COUNSEL

Sarah G. Cronan
Jeanne M. Lamar
Thomas F. Lucas
Martha A. Pagliari
Thomas A. Reed
Anne R. Rempe

A list of Representative Clients will be made available upon request.

For full biographical listings, see the Martindale-Hubbell Law Directory

CHAPMAN AND CUTLER (AV)

111 West Monroe Street, 60603
Telephone: 312-845-3000
Fax: 312-701-2361
Email: postmaster@chapman.com *URL:* http://chapman.com
Salt Lake City, Utah Office: Suite 900, Key Bank Tower, 50 South Main Street.
Telephone: 801-533-0066.
Fax: 801-533-9595.
Phoenix, Arizona Office: Suite 1100, One Renaissance Square, 2 North Central Avenue.
Telephone: 602-256-4060.
Fax: 602-256-4099.

(See Next Column)

CHAPMAN AND CUTLER—*Continued*

Ann E. Acker
Bruce D. Agin
Leah F. Arner
David T. B. Audley
Andrea G. Bacon
Michael P. Barrett
David S. Barritt
Walter P. Begley
Michael T. Benz
Jeffrey D. Berry
Matthew C. Boba
Deborah T. Boye
Lee A. Boye
James M. Breen
Edwin S. Brown
Jeffrey A. Burger
Nancy A. Burke
James C. Burr (Resident, Salt Lake City Office)
Timothy J. Carey
Theodore S. Chapman (1877-1943)
David J. Cholst
Steven L. Clark
Rafael L. Cook
Richard A. Cosgrove
John R. Crossan
David S. Crossett
Patricia M. Curtner
Henry E. Cutler (1879-1959)
Robert P. Davis
William R. DeHaan (Resident, Phoenix Office)
John M. Dixon
Daniel J. Favero
Eric F. Fess
J. Richard Fisher, Jr.
C. Robert Foltz
Felice R. Foundos
Marc P. Franson
Steven G. Frost
Lynda K. Given
Warren F. Grienenberger
Ronald J. Hacker
Heather L. Hansche
Steven G. Hastings
John C. Hitt, Jr.
Charles S. Hughes
Charles L. Jarik
James E. Jenz
Daniel L. Johnson
Kevin P. Kalinich
Charles A. Kelly
Richard F. Klein
Mark J. Kneedy
Jonathan A. Koff
Paul C. Kosin
Kelly K. Kost
Daniel J. Kucera
Darrell R. Larsen, Jr.
Edward L. Lembitz, Jr.
Matthew R. Lewin
William M. Libit
Frederick V. Lochbihler
Robert E. Lockner
James E. Luebchow
David A. Lullo
Sean T. Maloney
Neil R. Mann
Steven C. Mason
Michael G. McGee
Timothy V. McGree
Terry A. McIlroy
David B. McMullen
Timothy P. Mohan
Robert C. Nash
Robert W. Ollis, Jr.
Lisa A. Olsen
Terence T. O'Meara
John S. Overdorff (Resident, Phoenix Office)
Thomas G. Park
Stacy K. Pike
Gary R. Polega
James R. Richardson
Ronald E. Rokosz
Anthony R. Rosso
Aron H. Routman
David S. Schaffer, Jr.
Robert J. Schneider
Richard J. Scott (Resident, Salt Lake City Office)
Edward V. Sommer
James E. Spiotto
Mark A. Sternberg
George P. Sullivan, Jr.
Ross D. Taylor
James R. Theiss, Jr.
Carol K. Thompson
Kenneth R. M. Thompson
Franklin H. Top III
M. John Trofa
John L. Tuohy
Roy M. Van Cleave (P.C.)
Terrence M. Walsh
Daniel W. Weil
Lawrence E. White
David G. Williams
Karl T. Williams
Steven N. Wohl
Richard A. Wohlleber
David E. Worsley
Anthony D. Yager
Steven N. Zaris

Kimberly L. Ahlgrim
Scott R. Anderson
Susan D. Appel
Anne N. Arbuckle
Daniel W. Baker
Mark A. Banks-Golub
Scott B. Barnett
Erin P. Bartholomy
Zulfiqar Bokhari
Peter A. Clark
S. Todd Cubbage
Keith M. Cyzen
Stathy Darcy
Liza G. Diaz
Jong Sook Divino
Christopher J. Duba
Cherie Duve
David A. Ebroon
Kelly A. Fetzer
August J. Francis
Brian D. Free
David S. Golden
Stephanie L. Grauerholz-Lofton
Madhu M. Gupta
H. Richard Hagen
Erin M. Hardtke
R. William Hunter
Mel R. Jiganti
Benjamin J. Juergens (Resident, Salt Lake City Office)
Safia Khan
Joanna C. Kitto
Gregory A. Klamrzynski
Kevin C. Knohl
Colleen A. Kushner
David J. LaSota
Michael C. Lee
Kristi A. Maher
Moira K. Metzger
Lisa Montez
Matthew M. Murphy
James R. Nelson
Brigitte T. Nuss
Cristin M. Obsitnik
Edward J. Pelican
Stacey L. Prange
Thomas M. Quirk
Mark D. Rasmussen
Dianne E. Rist
Eric M. Roberson
Susan E. Rollins
Robert C. Rubenstein
Rebecca Schmucker
Shelly A. Scinto
Susan Shallenberger
Todd N. Sheldon
Suzanne L. Shier
Jeffrey M. Smith
Frederick M. Snow
Lance R. Staker
Peter G. Swenson
Tedd T. Termunde
Jeffrey C. Torres
Robert G. Tucker
Demetria E. Vong-Spillan
Gregory W. Walker

(See Next Column)

Christopher F. Walrath
Morrison C. Warren
Glenn E. Weinstein
Rodney G. Wendt (Not admitted in IL; Resident, Salt Lake City Office)
Jamie L. Zelvin

OF COUNSEL

Peter V. Fazio
F. B. Hubachek, Jr.
Kenneth J. Vaughan

For full biographical listings, see the Martindale-Hubbell Law Directory

---

CLARK & DEGRAND (AV)

One South Wacker Drive, Suite 1495, 60606-4616
Telephone: 312-425-0500
Fax: 312-425-0501
Email: CandDeG@aol.com

MEMBERS OF FIRM

Donald C. Clark, Jr.
Luke DeGrand
Jennifer S. Holloway

ASSOCIATE

Tracey L. Wolfe

For full biographical listings, see the Martindale-Hubbell Law Directory

---

DYKEMA GOSSETT PLLC (AV)

55 East Monroe Street, Suite 3050, 60603-5709
Telephone: 312-551-4900
FAX: 312-551-4919
Email: mstarrs@dykema.com *URL:* http://www.dykema.com
Ann Arbor, Michigan Office: Suite 100, 315 East Eisenhower Parkway, 48108-3306.
Telephone: 734-214-7660.
Fax: 734-214-7696.
Bloomfield Hills, Michigan Office: 1577 North Woodward Avenue, Suite 300, 48304-2820.
Telephone: 248-203-0700.
Fax: 248-203-0763.
Detroit, Michigan Office: 400 Renaissance Center, 48243-1668.
Telephone: 313-568-6800.
Fax: 313-568-6545.
Grand Rapids, Michigan Office: Suite 700, 300 Ottawa Avenue, N.W., 49503-2304.
Telephone: 616-776-7500.
Fax: 616-776-7573.
Lansing, Michigan Office: 800 Michigan National Tower, 48933-1707.
Telephone: 517-374-9100.
Fax: 517-374-9191.
Washington, D.C. Office: Franklin Square, Suite 300 West, 1300 I Street N.W., 20005-3306.
Telephone: 202-522-8600.
Fax: 202-522-8669.
Affiliated Office: Via Matconi, 3, 40122 Bologna, Italy.
Telephone: 011-39-51-228222.
Fax: 011-39-51-6593580.

RESIDENT MEMBERS

Charles R. Bernardini
Jerome I. Maynard
Arthur F. Radke
Pierre C. Talbert, Jr.

RESIDENT OF COUNSEL

Paul G. Neilan
Darrell W. Pierce

RESIDENT ASSOCIATES

Jennifer J. Howe
Sharon A. Salinas

For full biographical listings, see the Martindale-Hubbell Law Directory

---

FOLEY & LARDNER (AV)

Suite 3300, One IBM Plaza, 330 N. Wabash Avenue, 60611-3608
Telephone: 312-755-1900
Facsimile: 312-755-1925
Email: foleylardner@worldnet.att.net *URL:* http://www.foleylardner.com
Los Angeles, California Office: 2029 Century Park East, 35th Floor.
Telephone: 310-277-2223.
Fax: 310-557-8475.
Sacramento, California Office: 300 Capitol Mall, Suite 1125.
Telephone: 916-443-8005.
Fax: 916-443-2240.
San Diego, California Office: 402 West Broadway, 23rd Floor.
Telephone: 619-234-6655.
Fax: 619-234-3510.
San Francisco, California Office: One Maritime Plaza, Sixth Floor.
Telephone: 415-434-4484.
Fax: 415-434-4507.
Denver, Colorado Office: 1999 Broadway, Suite 2560.
Telephone: 303-297-0260.
Fax: 303-297-0266.
Washington, D.C. Office: Washington Harbour, Suite 500, 3000 K Street, N.W.
Telephone: 202-672-5300.
Telex: 904136 (Foley Lard Wash).
Facsimile: 202-672-5399.

(See Next Column)

FOLEY & LARDNER, *Chicago—Continued*

Jacksonville, Florida Office: The Greenleaf Building, 200 Laura Street. P.O. Box 240.
Telephone: 904-359-2000.
Facsimile: 904-359-8700.
Orlando, Florida Office: Suite 1800, 111 North Orange Avenue, P.O. Box 2193.
Telephone: 407-423-7656.
Facsimile: 407-648-1743.
Tallahassee, Florida Office: 300 East Park Avenue, P.O. Box 1454.
Telephone: 850-222-6100.
Facsimile: 850-561-6475.
Tampa, Florida Offices: Suite 2700, One Hundred N. Tampa Street, P.O. Box 3391.
Telephones: 813-229-2300; Pinellas County: 813-442-3296.
Facsimile: 813-221-4210.
West Palm Beach, Florida Office: Suite 200, Phillips Point East Tower, 777 South Flagler Drive.
Telephone: 561-655-5050.
Facsimile: 561-655-6925.
Annapolis, Maryland Office: Suite 102, 175 Admiral Cochrane Drive.
Telephone: 410-266-8077.
Telex: 899149 (Oldtownpat).
Facsimile: 410-266-8664.
Madison, Wisconsin Office: Verex Plaza, 150 East Gilman Street, P.O. Box 1497.
Telephone: 608-257-5035.
Facsimile: 608-258-4258.
Milwaukee, Wisconsin Office: Firstar Center, 777 East Wisconsin Avenue.
Telephone: 414-271-2400.
Telex: 26-819 (Foley Lard Mil).
Facsimile: 414-297-4900.
Brussels, Belgium Office: Avenue Louise, 283.
Telephone: 32-2-646-2777.
Facsimile: 32-2-646-7574.

PARTNERS

Kevin D. Anderson	Joan M. Kubalanza
Evelyn C. Arkebauer	John R. Landis
Michael G. Bailey	John D. Lien
Salvatore A. Barbatano	J. Craig Long
Sharon R. Barner	Sean B.W. Martin
Wesley N. Becker	Edwin D. Mason
Francis A. Citera	David M. Matteson
Elizabeth L. Corey	Malcolm McCaleb, Jr.
Paul Damm (Not admitted in IL)	Gerald J. Neal
	Robert E. Neiman
James D. Dasso	Nehad S. Othman
Scott E. Early	Jefferson Perkins
Kevin J. Egan	Richard J. Phelan
Fredric J. Entin	Mark L. Prager
Frederick L. Feldkamp	Randall S. Rapp
Richard X. Fischer	Michael D. Rechtin
Phillip M. Goldberg	Hoken S. Seki
Douglas M. Hagerman	George T. Simon
Dean M. Jeske	Stephen M. Slavin
C. Richard Johnson	James R. Vogler
Bryan T. D. Jung	James A. Winkler

Robert J. Zimmerman

RETIRED PARTNER

David S. Lott

OF COUNSEL

Michael K. Cavanaugh (P.C.)	Frank J. McGarr
Sheldon Karon	Kai Allen Nebel
Jay Jung Heum Kim	Donald P. Reynolds

Larry Selander

SPECIAL COUNSEL

Becky Brueckel	Annette M. McGarry
Marianne Craigmile Holzhall	James A. Sprowl

ASSOCIATES

Ruth A. Bahe-Jachna	Joseph M. Klauke
Paul H. Beattie	Jennifer J. Kleynenberg
Marshall J. Brown	Carolyn E. Knecht
Holly Weston Bull	Thomas P. Krebs
Michelle L. Bushore	Triste N. Lieteau
Christopher M. Cahill	Urooj Mahmud
Kirsten M. Carlson	Alison E. Murphy-Kinsler
Colleen M. Conway	Randall L. Oyler
Jessica L. Davis	Mollie M. Pawlosky
Frank W. DiCastri	Andrew L. Reisman
Marisol G. Ejercito	David T. Rusoff
Greg H. Gardella	Michael J. Small
LaDale K. George	Michael S. Smith
Steven Gerenraich	Jeffrey A. Soble
Jeanne Marie Gills	Michelle A. Splude
Michael A. Glackin	Lisa L. Tharpe
Russell W. Hahn	Jason C. Turner
Charles R. Haywood	Alice J. Um
Dianne L. Hicklen	Jill L. Uylaki
Heidi Houghton	Tejal R. Vakharia

(See Next Column)

ASSOCIATES (Continued)

Randi L. Valerious	Ellen M. Wheeler
Robert J. Vechiola	Amy L. Yindrick
Peter T. Wall	Janet E. Ziegler

For full biographical listings, see the Martindale-Hubbell Law Directory

GARDNER, CARTON & DOUGLAS (AV)

Quaker Tower, Suite 3400, 321 North Clark Street, 60610-4795
Telephone: 312-644-3000
Telex: 25-3628
Telecopier: 312-644-3381
Email: postmaster@gcd.com
Email: gcdlawchgo@gcd.com
Washington, D.C. Office: Suite 900, East Tower, 1301 K Street, N.W. 20005-3317.
Telephone: 202-408-7100.
Facsimile: 202-289-1504.

MEMBERS OF FIRM

Henry A. Gardner (1883-1968)	Charles L. Byrum
Alfred T. Carton (1884-1968)	Sherrie Travis
James H. Douglas, Jr. (1899-1988)	Richard W. Young
	Michael J. Hayes, Sr.
Dale Park, Jr.	Warren von Credo Baker
George C. McKann	James D. McDonough
John T. Cusack	David A. Rubenstein
L. Edward Bryant, Jr.	William J. Barrett
Paul H. Dykstra	Patrick S. Coffey
Dewey B. Crawford	Gary W. Howell
Robert J. Wilczek	David N. Kay
Thomas Campbell	Helen J. McSweeney
Dennis J. Carlin	Peter J. Meyer
Gordon B. Nash, Jr.	Luis A. Berrones
Geoffrey B. Shields	Edwin A. Getz
William H. Roach, Jr.	Timothy R. Casey
Charles A. Freeman	Karin Jagel Flynn
Peter D. Clarke	Bart Thomas Murphy
Donna S. Wetzler	Michael D. Rosenbaum
Quin R. Frazer	Roxane C. Busey
David L. Wolfe	Gary W. Garner
Michael J. Koenigsknecht	D. Louis Glaser II
Stephen M. Gatlin (1953-1997)	Robert J. Joseph
James D. Parsons	Alan S. King
Priscilla A. (Pam) Walter	John A. Simon
Glenn E. Ferencz	John W. Watson III
Michael E. Barry	Robert L. Capizzi
David G. Strom	Edward F. Dobbins, Jr.
Steven B. Kite	Edward J. Tabaczyk
Thomas E. Lanctot	Mark A. Latham
Edward Spacapan, Jr.	Joseph H. Greenberg
Mark E. Furlane	Timothy G. McDermott
Bernadette Muller Broccolo	Stephen A. Tsoris
Michael W. Peregrine	William E. Corbin, Jr.
Stephen P. Bedell	Frances P. LaFleur
W. David Braun	Tracey L. Mihelic
W. Edward Webb	Kenneth Michael Sullivan
Debra J. Schnebel	Douglas B. Swill
Richard J. Kissel	Howard P. Zweig (P.C.)
Roy M. Harsch	Burton H. Litwin
Crystal Pruess Bush	Michael F. Csar
Nancy M. Borders	Harold L. Kaplan
Michael P. Padden	Troy M. Calkins
Frederick L. White	John P. Goebel
Michael Duffy	Terry M. Hackett
Deborah H. Bornstein	Charles R. Manzoni, Jr.
Ralph E. De Jong	Nicola Fiordalisi
Alex W. Zabrosky	Maureen A. Miller

MEMBERS OF FIRM - WASHINGTON, D.C.

Francis E. Fletcher, Jr.	James M. Jorling
M. Scott Johnson	Christopher L. White
E. Michael Flanagan	Laura C. Mow
Peter H. Wyckoff	Thomas J. Dougherty, Jr.
John E. Fiorini III	T. J. Sullivan
W. N. Harrell Smith IV	Kathleen M. Nilles
Donna K. Thiel	Attison L. Barnes III
Patrick C. Rock	George N. Grammas
Russell H. Fox	Philip G. Hampton, II
Rodney H. Glover	James M. Jacobson
Ballard Jamieson, Jr.	Carin J. Sigel

OF COUNSEL

Tom Arthur	Peter H. Merlin

William L. Morrison

COUNSEL

Joseph J. Bogdan	Raymond T. Goetz
Barbara A. Cronin	Robert M. Grossman
Mary Beth Cyze	Brian C. Rupp

COUNSEL - WASHINGTON, D.C.

James M. Jacobson	Rita Grant Ndirika

(See Next Column)

GARDNER, CARTON & DOUGLAS—*Continued*

ASSOCIATES

Kathleen M. Allen
Simon B. Anolick
Cathy Kiselyak Austin
Earl J. Barnes II
Mona L. Bentz
Greg L. Berenstein
Maja A. Berlin
Deborah F. Birndorf
Jennifer R. Breuer
Gregory L. Brown
Darren S. Cahr
Lisa M. Chavez
John C. Corrigan
John J. D'Attomo
Antonio DeBlasio
Mary E. Dicig
Mary M. Donners
Ann M. Donohue
Noelle C. Dye
William M. Ejzak
Karen A. Erikson
Christian W. Fabian (Not admitted in IL)
William P. Farrell, Jr.
Andre R. Fiebig
Scott J. Fisher
Rodrigo D. Floro, Jr.
Michael T. Foley
Angela Foster-Rice
Kevin L. Freeman
Irene F. Gallagher
William L. Goldbeck
Heidemarie Gregoriev
Gary Hall
Valerie A. Haugh
Carol M. Hines
Patrick J. Hughes
Steven Louis Johnston
Patrick J. Kelleher
Peter C. Koch
Tina D. Kourasis
Nancy L. Laethem
Marielle V. Lifshitz
Salvador M. Llach
Katherine Kendall Lobo
Lisa Anne Martin
S. Patrick McKey
Alfonso McMillian, Jr.
Mark S. Melickian
Joyce L. Meyer
Scott M. Murray
Deena S. Newlander
Michael A. Nicolas
Katherine N. O'Connell
Paulita A. Pike-Bokhari
Tracy L. Prosser
William John Quinlan
Catherine A. Redinbo
Michael P. Rhoades
Sarah Foreman Rivera
John T. Roache
Katherine O. Robinson
Kimberly K. Rubel
Jesse H. Ruiz
Roberta M. Saielli
Richard M. Saines
Arthur M. Scheller III
Jeffrey S. Shamberg
Lori L. Shannon
Steven S. Shonder
Wallace C. Solberg
Michael J. Staab
Timothy J. Stanton
Andrea Stulgies-Clauss
Connie M. Tameling
Liisa M. Thomas
Catherine M. Thomson
Linn M. Visscher
Christopher T. Waack
Evan S. Williams
Mary G. Wilson
Elaine C. Zacharakis

For full biographical listings, see the Martindale-Hubbell Law Directory

HINSHAW & CULBERTSON (AV)

A Partnership including Professional Corporations
222 North La Salle Street, Suite 300, 60601-1081
Telephone: 312-704-3000
Telex: 880-248
Facsimile: 312-704-3001
URL: http://www.hinshawculbertson.com
Other Office Locations: Appleton, Wisconsin; Belleville, Illinois; Brookfield, Wisconsin; Champaign, Illinois; Crystal Lake, Illinois; Fort Lauderdale, Florida; Jacksonville, Florida; Joliet, Illinois; Lisle, Illinois; Miami, Florida; Milwaukee, Wisconsin; Minneapolis, Minnesota; Munster, Indiana; Peoria, Illinois; Phoenix, Arizona; Rockford, Illinois; St. Louis, Missouri; San Francisco, California; Springfield, Illinois; Tampa, Florida; Waukegan, Illinois.

RESIDENT MEMBERS

Dan L. Boho
Steven R. Bonanno
Roy M. Bossen
Thomas L. Browne
Kevin Joseph Burke
Lisa M. Burman
Julian C. Campbell, Jr.
Paul J. Clementi
Shawn P. Clifford
William J. Connelly
Clare E. Connor
David R. Creagh
Stanley J. Davidson
Katherine Smith Dedrick
John W. Dubbs, III
Darrell S. Dudzik
Carlton D. Fisher
Lyndon M. Flosi
Allyn J. Franke
Thomas F. Ging
John P. Goggin
Philip L. Goldberg
Karen R. Goodman
Ilene S. Grant
Edmund Gronkiewicz
Thomas M. Hamilton, Jr.
James Harbert
Julie A. Harms
Thomas B. Hart, Jr.
Mary J. Hess
Susan M. Hickman
James M. Hofert
William J. Holloway (P.C.)
Charles A. Hornewer
Kurt L. Hudson
Fritz K. Huszagh
E. Michael Kelly
Philip Reed Kujawa
John G. Langhenry, Jr., (P.C.) (Retired)
Michael J. Leech
David H. Levitt
Alan R. Lipton
Nancy G. Lischer
Tom H. Luetkemeyer
Stephen A. Malato
Stephen H. Malato
Thomas S. Malciauskas
Terrence P. McAvoy
Thomas P. McGarry
Daniel W. McGrath
Gary E. Medler
Mark C. Metzger
Lawrence R. Moelmann
Douglas H. Momeyer
Caroline A. Mondschean
Thomas A. Morris, Jr., (P.C.)
Adria East Mossing
Donald L. Mrozek
Scott E. Nemanich
Robert E. Nord
Mark R. Olander

(See Next Column)

RESIDENT MEMBERS (Continued)

Donald J. O'Meara (P.C.)
Dean E. Parker
Philip L. Pomerance
Carol Proctor
Edward G. Proctor
Steven M. Puiszis
Marcos Reilly
J. William Roberts
Daniel K. Ryan
David M. Schultz
Kevin R. Sido
Laurie A. Siwek
Peter D. Sullivan
Timothy M. Sullivan
Robert H. Summers, Jr.
Stephen R. Swofford
Paula Fuller Tobin
Jerome R. Vainisi
Joshua G. Vincent
Peter A. Walsh
Todd M. Young
Joseph H. Hinshaw (1934-1973)
James G. Culbertson (1934-1969)
John M. Moelmann (1934-1974)
Thomas J. Weithers (1953-1982)
Ward Dunphy (1961-1979)
Dennis J. Horan (1963-1988)

RESIDENT ASSOCIATES

Joseph W. Balesteri
David John Bradford
Matthew G. Burke
Scott F. Burns
Peter Herbert Carlson
Jean G. Cleveland
Monica J. Conrad
Colleen M. Danaher Contreras
Richard M. Craig
Kent J. Cummings
Michael J. Cunningham
Anthony Ficarelli
John M. Foley
Alicia E. Fuentes
JuliAnn Y. Geldner
Liza Shawn Graham
Matthew R. Henderson
Cecilia Anne Horan
Linda K. Horras
Larry C. Jurgens
Sarah A. Kennedy
Craig T. Liljestrand
Monica F. MacNamara
Frances Wiet Makuch
Paul M. Markese
Janet L. Marren
Newton C. Marshall, II
Kathleen D. Mathewson
Daniel C. Mills
Thomas R. Mulroy, III
Robert H. Muriel
Michael S. Nardulli
Brendan A. O'Brien
Christine L. Olson
Cynthia M. Peterson
Richard B. Polony
Nicholas S. Preservati
Victoria C. Priola
David J. Richards
Jennifer M. Sender
Robert T. Shannon
Timothy G. Shelton
Karen Elaine Tinglin
James Constantine Vlahakis
Charles Henry Wahtola, III

RESIDENT COUNSEL

Richard S. Borland
Robert E. Ellis
James L. Fletcher
Jerome A. Frazel, Jr.
Perry L. Fuller
William P. Grogan
John L. Kirkland
James Tod Miles
Timothy J. O'Brien
Paul L. Pawlowski (P.C.)
Patricia J. Prange
Alan H. Swanson
Clive M. Topol
Kathryn S. Vander Broek
Darrell Widen

RESIDENT OF COUNSEL

D. Kendall Griffith (P.C.) (Retired)

Representative Clients: Aetna Life & Casualty Co.; Allstate Insurance Co.; Argonaut Insurance Co.; Continental Insurance; Farmers Insurance Group; Fireman's Fund American; Hartford Insurance Group; Maryland Casualty Co.; Unigard Security; U.S. Fidelity & Guaranty Co.

For full biographical listings, see the Martindale-Hubbell Law Directory

HOPKINS & SUTTER (AV)

A Partnership including Professional Corporations
Three First National Plaza, Suite 4100, 60602-4205
Telephone: 312-558-6600
Fax: 312-558-6538
Email: postmaster@hopsut.com *URL:* http://www.hopsut.com
Washington, D.C. Office: 888 Sixteenth Street, N.W.
Telephone: 202-835-8000.
Fax: 202-835-8136.
Troy, Michigan Office: 2800 Livernois, Suite 220.
Telephone: 248-740-6600.
Fax: 248-740-6613.

MEMBERS OF FIRM

Bryan S. Anderson
Laura L. Bilas
Jonathan P. Biller
Richard Bromley
John T. Brooks
Thomas Buranosky
Antony S. Burt
R. Lee Christie
Michael M. Conway
Mark Crane (P.C.)
Jane Gorham Ditelberg
Bruce W. Doughty
Scott A. Drane
Lawrence M. Dubin (P.C.)
Bennett L. Epstein
Jay Erens
Robert C. Feldmeier
Michael A. Ficaro
Marilyn D. Franson
Michael J. Gamsky
Stephen E. Garcia
John N. Gavin (P.C.)
Diane Gianos
Lynn H. Goldschmidt
George R. Goodman
David B. Goroff
Paul F. Hanzlik
F. Thomas Hecht
Patrick A. Heffernan
James R. Hellige
Wm. Carlisle Herbert
Van E. Holkeboer
Glen H. Kanwit
Christopher N. Knight
Dennis G. LaGory
Kenneth M. Lodge
Jeremiah Marsh (P.C.)
Mary Kay McCalla Martire
John W. McCaffrey
Mark A. McDermott
William J. McKenna, Jr.
William G. McMaster, Jr.

(See Next Column)

HOPKINS & SUTTER, *Chicago—Continued*

MEMBERS OF FIRM (Continued)

S. Kay McNab
Claudette P. Miller
Joel L. Miller
Michael P. Morrison
Emily Koenig Neuberger
Marie C. Oldham
Wayne F. Osoba
James D. Ossyra
Joe Ourth
Cordell J. Overgaard (P.C.)
John B. Palmer III
Kathleen R. Pasulka-Brown
Robert W. Patterson (P.C.)
Michael E. Phenner (P.C.)
John P. Ratnaswamy
William E. Rattner
E. Glenn Rippie
John L. Rogers, III
John E. Rooney
Dan W. Schneider
Michael Schneiderman
Samuel K. Skinner
Michael B. Solow
David M. Spector
Sam Vinson
William C. Weinsheimer
Michael H. Woolever (P.C.)
John F. Zabriskie
Christopher W. Zibart
Albert L. Hopkins (1908-1978)
Harry B. Sutter (1919-1957)

SENIOR COUNSEL

Thomas R. Mulroy (1905-1989)
Frederic W. Hickman (P.C.)

OF COUNSEL

William C. Childs (1916-1996)
William P. Sutter (P.C.)
Anderson A. Owen (1899-1983)
William A. Cromartie (1919-1985)
Charles W. Davis (1916-1987)

COUNSEL

Jay A. Steinberg

ASSOCIATES

Ethan A. Berghoff
Jennifer A. Blickenstaff
Douglas S. Buck
Thomas J. Cunningham
Kathleen M. Eggers
J. Scott England
Joel H. Feldman
Cynthia A. Fonner
John C. Ford
Andrea L. Hillier
Shalina M. Hubert
Heather Jackson
Ross E. Kimbarovsky
Karen Kremer Mahoney
Stephanie L. Matthews
Catherine B. Nelson
D. Tyler Nurnberg
Dennis A. Peterson
Eric Phillips
Reagen C. Robbins
Matthew A. Shebuski
Kevin S. Simon
Gregory L. Stelzer
Laura Levin Ulrich
Miki Vucic
Samantha Weissbluth
Tracy D. Williams

STAFF ATTORNEYS

Richard M. Fogel
Thomas E. Sweeney

For full biographical listings, see the Martindale-Hubbell Law Directory

JENNER & BLOCK (AV)

A Partnership including Professional Corporations
One IBM Plaza, 60611
Telephone: 312-222-9350
FAX: 312-527-0484
Telex: 270469
TWX: 9102215409
Cable Address: "Jenblock"
URL: http://www.jenner.com
Washington, D.C. Office: 601 Thirteenth Street, N.W., Twelfth Floor.
Telephone: 202-639-6000.
FAX: 202-639-6066.
Cable Address: "Jenblock."
Lake Forest, Illinois Office: One Westminster Place.
Telephone: 847-295-9200.
FAX: 847-295-7810.

CO-CHAIRMAN OF THE FIRM

Jerold S. Solovy

CO-CHAIRMAN OF THE FIRM

Theodore R. Tetzlaff

MEMBERS OF FIRM

Joel J. Africk
Jacqueline C. Bares (Resident, Washington, D.C. Office)
Royce R. Bedward
James D. Benak
Steven N. Berk (Resident, Washington, D.C. Office)
Debbie L. Berman
Joseph G. Bisceglia
Samuel W. Block (1911-1970)
Larry D. Blust
Richard C. Bollow
Darryl M. Bradford
David J. Bradford
Ross B. Bricker
John H. Broadley (Resident, Washington, D.C. Office)
Michael T. Brody
Patricia A. Bronte
Jerry J. Burgdoerfer
Robert L. Byman
Richard A. Campbell
Julia M. Carpenter (Resident, Washington, D.C. Office)
Neil E. Cass
Donald R. Cassling
Theresa Chmara (Resident, Washington, D.C. Office)
Timothy J. Chorvat
Jeffrey D. Colman
Deirdre E. Connell
Joseph P. Covington (Resident, Washington, D.C. Office)
Craig R. Culbertson
David W. DeBruin (Resident, Washington, D.C. Office)
Maureen F. Del Duca (Resident, Washington, D.C. Office)
Robert L. Denby
Christopher C. Dickinson
Kenneth R. Dolin
Timothy R. Donovan
Joseph E. Doyle
Jeffrey L. Elegant

(See Next Column)

MEMBERS OF FIRM (Continued)

Bruce J. Ennis, Jr. (Resident, Washington, D.C. Office)
Jerome L. Epstein (Resident, Washington, D.C. Office)
William H. Farley, Jr.
James H. Feldman
Nicole Finitzo (Resident, Lake Forest, Illinois Office)
Bill S. Forcade
Richard T. Franch
Peter B. Freeman
Gregory S. Gallopoulos
Frances Gecker
Jay S. Geller
Jefferson C. Glassie (Resident, Washington, D.C. Office)
Paula Cozzi Goedert
Robert L. Graham
Richard J. Gray
E. Lynn Grayson
David M. Greenwald
David K. Haase
Kelly A. Hackett
Joan M. Hall (Ltd.)
David A. Handzo (Resident, Washington, D.C. Office)
Donald R. Harris (Ltd.)
Kenneth L. Harris
William D. Heinz
Norman M. Hirsch
Russell J. Hoover
Donald S. Horvath
Jerald A. Jacobs (Resident, Washington, D.C. Office)
Albert E. Jenner, Jr. (1907-1988)
Richard C. Johnson (Resident, Washington, D.C. Office)
Horace W. Jordan, Jr. (Resident, Lake Forest, Illinois Office)
Rodney D. Joslin
Chester T. Kamin
Laura K. Kennedy (Resident, Washington, D.C. Office)
Carter H. Klein
C. John Koch
David M. Kroeger
Kenneth A. Kroot
Vincent E. Lazar
Leslie H. Lepow (Resident, Washington, D.C. Office)
Barry Levenstam
Charles E. Levin
Katherine J. Levy (Resident, Lake Forest, Illinois Office)
Susan C. Levy
Christopher D. Liguori
Linda L. Listrom
Alexander Lourie
Daniel Lynch
James M. Lynch
Shelley Malinowski
Edward F. Malone
Michael Z. Margolies
Robert S. Markin
Robert T. Markowski
Ronald L. Marmer
Thomas A. Marrinson
Arthur Mead Martin
Craig C. Martin
Terri L. Mascherin
John H. Mathias, Jr.
Deanne E. Maynard (Resident, Washington, D.C. Office)
J. Kevin McCall
Charles J. McCarthy (Ltd.)
Thomas J. McCarthy
Mark J. McGuire (Resident, Washington, D.C. Office)
James A. McKenna
Thomas K. McQueen
Randall E. Mehrberg
Louis Milicich
Nory Miller (Resident, Washington, D.C. Office)
John B. Morris, Jr. (Resident, Washington, D.C. Office)
Gail H. Morse
Thomas R. Mulroy, Jr.
Daniel R. Murray
Carl S. Nadler (Resident, Washington, D.C. Office)
David M. Neff
Matthew M. Neumeier
Thomas S. O'Neill
Dean N. Panos
Thomas G. Pasternak
Joel T. Pelz
Randolph M. Perkins (Resident, Lake Forest, Illinois Office)
Ronald R. Peterson
Jeff S. Pitzer
Susan R. Podolsky (Resident, Washington, D.C. Office)
Mark D. Pollack
Robert M. Portman (Resident, Washington, D.C. Office)
Rebecca L. Raftery
R. Douglas Rees
Ronald Ian Reicin
Raymond T. Reott
Donald I. Resnick
Jeffrey L. Richman
Craig A. Roeder (Resident, Washington, D.C. Office)
Carey S. Rosemarin
Carla J. Rozycki
William J. Ryan
David P. Sanders
Gregory J. Scandaglia
Lawrence S. Schaner
Stephanie A. Scharf
Stanley A. Schlitter
Marshall John Schmitt
Mark D. Schneider (Resident, Washington, D.C. Office)
William L. Scogland
Donald P. Seberger (Resident, Lake Forest, Illinois Office)
Jeffrey T. Shaw
John D. Shugrue
Gabrielle Sigel
John B. Simon
Charles B. Sklarsky
Rochelle Price Slater
Paul M. Smith (Resident, Washington, D.C. Office)
Lise T. Spacapan
Robert R. Stauffer
Catherine L. Steege
Barbara S. Steiner
Richard P. Steinken
Avidan J. Stern
Brent D. Stratton
Russ M. Strobel
Thomas P. Sullivan (Ltd.)
Mark K. Suri
Howard S. Suskin
James L. Thompson
C. Steven Tomashefsky
Terrence J. Truax
Anton R. Valukas
Richard L. Verkler (Ltd.) (Resident, Lake Forest, Illinois Office)
Donald B. Verrilli, Jr. (Resident, Washington, D.C. Office)
William A. Von Hoene, Jr.
James A. Vroman
Michael S. Walsh
Ronald L. Wanke
John F. Ward, Jr.
Maryann A. Waryjas
Eric H. Weimers
Bruce G. Wilson
Francis J. Wirtz
Larry M. Wolfson
Stephen L. Wood
Robert Alan Wynbrandt
David B. Yelin
J. Jeffrey Zimmerman

ASSOCIATES

Imad D. Abyad (Resident, Washington, D.C. Office)
Deborah R. Alexander
James D. Anderson
Johna G. Anderson
Sean M. Anderson
Thomas E. Arend, Jr. (Resident, Washington, D.C. Office)
Regina C. Ashley
Kathleen M. Banar

(See Next Column)

JENNER & BLOCK—*Continued*

ASSOCIATES (Continued)

Geoffrey A. Barrow (Resident, Washington, D.C. Office)
David C. Belt (Resident, Washington, D.C. Office)
Julie L. Bentz
Mark A. Berggren
Andrew Byerly Birge
Elizabeth E. Appel Blue (Resident, Washington, D.C. Office)
David C. Blum
Gregory M. Boyle
Traci M. Braun
Terri L. Brieske
Kara Novaco Brockmeyer
Elena N. Broder (Resident, Washington, D.C. Office)
David D. Brown
Melissa C. Brown
Karen C. Bruntrager
Alan M. Buie (Resident, Washington, D.C. Office)
Jennifer A. Burke
Timothy W. Burns
Elizabeth A. Cavanagh (Resident, Washington, D.C. Office)
Vincent E. Ceccacci, Jr.
Richard S. Chase
Karen L. Cipriani (Resident, Washington, D.C. Office)
Paul W. "Whit" Cobb, Jr. (Resident, Washington, D.C. Office)
Elizabeth Abbene Coleman
Kendra S. Collier
Neal A. Cooper
Michael B. DeSanctis (Resident, Washington, D.C. Office)
Pamela S. DiCarlantonio
Michael C. Diedrich
Michael A. Doornweerd
Eric Dorkin
Steven L. Drickey
Christopher D. Dwyer
Catherine E. Dyar
Theodore T. Eidukas
Kristina M. Entner
Katherine A. Fallow (Resident, Washington, D.C. Office)
David Feinberg
James P. Fieweger
Gabriella Filisko
M. Katherine Fischer
Felicia Franco-Feinberg
Joseph D. Frank
Gabriel A. Fuentes
Lee P. Garner
Fred R. Garzino
Heather Gerken (Resident, Washington, D.C. Office)
Ian Heath Gershengorn (Resident, Washington, D.C. Office)
Arthur Gollwitzer, III
Robert W. Gustafson
Todd W. Haigh
John J. Hamill
Sarah C. Hardgrove
John R. Harrington
William J. Haynes II (Resident, Washington, D.C. Office)
William A. Hohengarten (Resident, Washington, D.C. Office)
Douglas H. Hsiao (Resident, Washington, D.C. Office)
Daniel J. Hurtado
Kevin Jack
Andrew M. Jacobs
Andrew A. Jacobson
Stasha Jain
John C. Jaye
David Jiménez-Ekman
Clark C. Johnson
Nathan P. Judish (Resident, Washington, D.C. Office)
Jodie L. Kelley (Resident, Washington, D.C. Office)
David P. Kelly
Michael E. Kernan
Janis C. Kestenbaum (Resident, Washington, D.C. Office)
Brent E. Kidwell
F. Scott Kieff (Not admitted in IL)
Margot Klein
Jeffrey A. Koppy
Kevin M. Kordziel (Resident, Washington, D.C. Office)
Rudy Kratz
Kristin L. Kruska
Ileana H. Kutler
Andrew F. Lampert
Christina M. Landgraf
Eric K. Laumann
David C. Layden
Jorge M. Leon
S. Tony Ling
Agostino Lorenzini
Olga A. Loy
Darren H. Lubetzky
Daniel Mach (Resident, Washington, D.C. Office)
David S. Makarski
Julie Montz Mandanas
Eric P. McAlpine
Timothy P. McGrory
Gerard A. McInnis
Jennifer L. McManus
Matthew H. Metcalf
Ellen C. Meyer
Matthew S. Miller
Samuel S. Miller
Michelle D. Mills
Christopher S. Moore
Molly J. Moran
Aaron M. Muhly
Darren M. Mungerson
Nadia A. Nagib
Edward J. Neveril
Alan W. Nicgorski
Jennifer S. Oosterbaan
Michelle L. Patail
Patrick L. Patras
Bridget R. Penick
Julia H. Perkins
Aaron R. Pettit
Christine A. Picker
Megan B. Poetzel
Anthony C. Porcelli
Suzanne J. Prysak
Sherry L. Reading
Matthew J. Renaud
Meg M. Reynolds
Brian P. Rigonan
Cynthia J. Robertson (Resident, Washington, D.C. Office)
Sidney A. Rosenzweig (Resident, Washington, D.C. Office)
Scott V. Rozmus
John T. Ruskusky
Jeffrey Ryen (Resident, Washington, D.C. Office)
Eric A. Sacks
Yusuf H. Safdari (Resident, Lake Forest, Illinois Office)
Douglas B. Sanders
Shilpa S. Satoskar (Resident, Washington, D.C. Office)
Scott T. Schutte
Daniel J. Schwartz
David R. Seligman
Jon Shepard (Resident, Washington, D.C. Office)
John F. Shonkwiler
Jodi Ann Simala
Margaret J. Simpson
Steven M. Siros
Daniel W. Smith
David Z. Smith
Maile H. Solis
Andrew M. Spangler
Bruce Spiva (Resident, Washington, D.C. Office)
Richard I. Stamm
Tanya J. Stanish
Kristal S. Otto Stanley
Aaron H. Stanton
Ryan P. Stiles

ASSOCIATES (Continued)

(See Next Column)

Tanya M. Stippich
Katherine J. Strandburg
David L. Streck
Jerry L. Switzer, Jr.
Mary C. Talarico
Jeremy M. Taylor
Laura A. Tenbroeck
Matthew J. Thomas
Seth A. Travis
Therese Tully
Marc Van Allen
John M. Vande Walle
Mark P. Vrla
Charlotte L. Wager
Paul R. Walker-Bright
David E. Walters
J. Alex Ward (Resident, Washington, D.C. Office)
Christine R. Weber (Not admitted in IL)
Robert C. Weber
Benjamin C. Weinberg
Daniel J. Weiss
Wendy M. Wells
Rachel F. Williams
Daniel J. Winters
Kial S. Young (Resident, Washington, D.C. Office)

OF COUNSEL

Gerhard E. Seidel (Resident, Lake Forest, Illinois Office)

For full biographical listings, see the Martindale-Hubbell Law Directory

---

JONES, DAY, REAVIS & POGUE (AV)

77 West Wacker, 60601-1692
Telephone: 312-782-3939
Telecopier: 312-782-8585
Email: counsel@jonesday.com *URL:* http://www.jonesday.com
In Atlanta, Georgia: 3500 SunTrust Plaza, 303 Peachtree Street.
Telephone: 404-521-3939.
Telecopier: 404-581-8330. 34000 Brussels, Belgium: Avenue Louise 480, 7th Floor, B-1050 Brussels.
Telephone: 32-2-645-14-11.
Telecopier: 32-2-645-14-45.
In Cleveland, Ohio: North Point, 901 Lakeside Avenue.
Telephone: 216-586-3939.
Telecopier: 216-579-0212.
In Columbus, Ohio: 1900 Huntington Center.
Telephone: 614-469-3939.
Telecopier: 614-461-4198.
In Dallas, Texas: 2727 North Harwood Street.
Telephone: 214-220-3939.
Telecopier: 214-969-5100.
In Frankfurt, Germany: Hochhaus am Park, Grüneburgweg 102, 60323 Frankfurt am Main.
Telephone: 49-69-9726-3939.
Telecopier: 49-69-9726-3993.
In Geneva, Switzerland: 20, rue de Candolle.
Telephone: 41-22-320-2339.
Telecopier: 41-22-320-1232.
In Hong Kong: 29th Floor, Entertainment Building, 30 Queen's Road Central.
Telephone: 852-2526-6895.
Telecopier: 852-2868-5871 or 852-2868-5699.
In Irvine, California: 5 Park Plaza, Suite 1100.
Telephone: 949-851-3939.
Telecopier: 949-553-7539.
In London, England: Bucklersbury House, 3 Queen Victoria Street.
Telephone: 44-171-236-3939.
Telecopier: 44-171-236-1113.
In Los Angeles, California: 555 West Fifth Street, Suite 4600.
Telephone: 213-489-3939.
Telecopier: 213-243-2539.
In New Delhi, India (Associate Office): Pathak & Associates (an associate firm of Jones, Day, Reavis & Pogue), 1st Floor, Dr. Gopal Das Bhaven, 28 Barakhamba Road.
Telephone: 91-11-373-8793; 91-11-335-7345.
Telecopier: 91-11-335-3761.
In New York, New York: 599 Lexington Avenue.
Telephone: 212-326-3939.
Telecopier: 212-755-7306.
In Paris, France: 120, rue du Faubourg Saint-Honoré.
Telephone: 33-1-56-59-39-39.
Telecopier: 33-1-56-59-39-38
In Pittsburgh, Pennsylvania: 500 Grant Street, 31st Floor.
Telephone: 412-391-3939.
Telecopier: 412-394-7959.
In Riyadh, Saudi Arabia: The International Law Firm (In Association with Jones, Day, Reavis & Pogue), Sulaymaniyah, Prince Mishari IBN, Abdulaziz Street, P.O. Box 22166.
Telephone: (966-1) 462-8866.
Telecopier: (966-1) 462-9001.
In Shanghai, China: 2805 Kerry Centre, 1515 Nanjing Road West.
Telephone: 86-21-5298-6568.
Telecopier: 86-21-5298-6569.
In Sydney, Australia: Governor Phillip Tower, Level 38, 1 Farrer Place.
Telephone: 61-2-9210-6921.
Telecopier: 61-2-9210-6926.
In Taipei, Taiwan: 8th Floor, 2 Tun Hwa South Road, Section 2.
Telephone: (886-2) 2704-6808.
Telecopier: (886-2) 2704-6791.
In Tokyo, Japan: Toranomon MT Building, 4th Floor, 10-3, Toranomon 3-Chome, 34200o-ku, Tokyo 105, Japan.
Telephone: 81-3-3433-3939.
Telecopier: 81-3-5401-2725.

(See Next Column)

JONES, DAY, REAVIS & POGUE, *Chicago—Continued*

In Washington, D.C.: 51 Louisiana Avenue, N.W.
Telephone: 202-879-3939.
Telecopier: 202-626-1700.

MEMBERS OF FIRM IN CHICAGO

David J. Rosso
Dan B. Miller
Ronald S. Rizzo
Robert A. Yolles
Ronald A. Sandler
Douglas H. Walter
Dennis R. Homerin
Paul T. Ruxin
Thomas F. Gardner
Robert Dean Avery (Not admitted in IL)
William P. Ritchie
Lynn Leland Coe
Paul W. Schroeder
John P.C. Duncan
Daniel E. Reidy
David L. Carden
Gary T. Johnson
Michael J. Mitchell
James C. Hagy
Boyd J. Springer
Harold C. Sutter
James R. Daly
Lee Ann Russo
S. Louise Rankin
Lester J. Savit
Michael F. Dolan
Elizabeth Clough Kitslaar
David L. Witcoff
Susan Elliott
June K. Ghezzi
Thomas P. McNulty
Christopher W. Flynn
Robert J. Graves
Irene Savanis
Richard Alan Chesley
Robert C. Lee
James A. White
Steven T. Catlett (Not admitted in IL)
Stephanie Balcerzak Graves
Charles T. Wehland
Joni L. Andrioff
Timothy J. Melton
Richard K. Tomei
Robert C. Micheletto
Carol A. Ahern
Julie O. Ehrlich

OF COUNSEL

Joseph H. Golant (Not admitted in IL)
James B. Raden
William S. McKay, Jr.
William J. Harmon
Karl B. Anderson
Daniel J. Bacastow

COUNSEL

John B. Carothers III
Russell L. McIlwain
Sandra Byster Weiss
Linda A. Heban
Susan I. Matejcak

ASSOCIATES

Karen Kazel Poulos
Daniel E. White
John F. Bibby, Jr.
R. Christopher Cook
Brian W. Easley (Not admitted in IL)
Jane K. Murphy
Arlene Boxerman Rosenberg
Michael J. Gray
Tina M. Tabacchi
Eric P. Berlin
Kathleen M. Curran
John E. Hebert, IV (Not admitted in IL)
Thomas N. Molins
Brian L. Sedlak
Susan M. Solomon
Michael B. Willian
Jeffrey G. Close
Stephen E. Hall
Kendra L. Morrill
Mark P. Rotatori
Anne C. Auten
Thomas D. Brooks
David J. Kates
Anastasia Katinas
John A. Marlott
Edward B. Winslow
Michael A. Witt
Marc S. Blackman
Toni-Ann Citera
Mark A. Cody
Holly L. Dalman
James A. Francque
Mario F. Greco
Michael P. Manly
Mark J. Meyers
John T. Perugini
Andrew P. Pillsbury
Kathryn A. Stieber (Not admitted in IL)
Jason G. Winchester
Susan L. Winders
Howard A. Adelstein
Kaci L. Barnes
Charles N. Bensinger, III
Cyri K. Carifa
Timothy J. Heverin
S. Mark Sproat
Stacy A. Berman
Amelia A. Cottrell
Andrew J. Kim
Brent D. Knight
Phuong T. Lam
Beth A. O'Connor
Kelly C. Prout
Eric A. Reeves
Ray C. Schrock
Susan E. Schwartz
Joseph P. Shereda
Sabrina C. Turner
Matt Volkert

STAFF ATTORNEY

Kristine Voelker

For full biographical listings, see the Martindale-Hubbell Law Directory

KATTEN MUCHIN & ZAVIS (AV)

A Partnership including Professional Corporations
525 West Monroe Street, Suite 1600, 60661-3693
Telephone: 312-902-5200
Telecopier: 312-902-1061
URL: http://www.kmz.com
Los Angeles, California Office: 1999 Avenue of the Stars, Suite 1400.
Telephone: 310-788-4400.
Telecopier: 310-788-4471.
New York, New York Office: 1133 Avenue of the Americas, Suite 2820.
Telephone: 212-764-6886.
Telecopier: 212-382-3395.

(See Next Column)

Washington, D.C. Office: 1025 Thomas Jefferson Street, N.W., East Lobby, Suite 700.
Telephone: 202-625-3500.
Telecopier: 202-298-7570.

CHICAGO, ILLINOIS OFFICE
MEMBERS OF FIRM

Kristin J. Achterhof
Robert D. Aicher
Vincent M. Aquilino
Steven F. Banghart
Sheldon I. Banoff (P.C.)
Kevin L. Barney
Steven L. Bashwiner (P.C.)
Jonathan K. Baum
Alan M. Berry (P.C.)
Ronald S. Betman
Victor H. Bezman (P.C.)
Robert J. Brantman
James M. Broeking
David A. Bronner (P.C.)
Edwin E. Brooks
Matthew S. Brown
David J. Bryant
Denise S. Burn
James A. Burns, Jr.
Michael R. Callahan
Dawn M. Canty
Joel G. Chefitz
Debra S. Clark
Barry A. Comin
Steven D. Conlon
W. Kenneth Davis, Jr.
David R. Dlugie
William M. Doyle, Jr.
John J. Durso
Donald E. Egan (1936-1996)
Marguerite M. Elias
John E. Farrell
Jonathan S. Feld (Not admitted in IL)
Leonard A. Ferber
Laurel L. Fleming
Kurt W. Florian, Jr.
Gary J. Fox
Raymond C. Fricke
Renée M. Friedman
Gerald H. Galler (1934-1987)
Carla F. Garfinkle
James M. Gecker
Richard E. Ginsberg
Steven F. "Sonny" Ginsberg
Susan L. Goldenberg
Michael P. Goldman
Julie Helenbrook Gottshall
Stuart E. Grass
Bryan J. Green
Lewis Greenbaum
Stuart N. Greenberger (1932-1986)
Russell E. Greenblatt (P.C.)
Arthur W. Hahn
James E. Hanlon, Jr.
Charles Harris
Arnold S. Harrison (P.C.)
Kirk T. Hartley
Michael O. Hartz
Robin Heiss
Ted S. Helwig
Mary Ellen Hennessy
Amy A. Hijjawi
Janet Goelz Hoffman
Samuel B. Isaacson
Kenneth M. Jacobson
Thomas A. Karet (Not admitted in IL)
Leslie R. Karp
Melvin L. Katten (P.C.)
David J. Kaufman
Kenneth M. Kliebard
Marla J. Kreindler
William R. Kucera (1944-1989)
Julie A. Kunetka
Stewart T. Kusper
Patrick J. Lamb
Howard S. Lanznar
Jeffery Larry
Lawrence D. Levin
Stephen D. Libowsky
Seth R. Madorsky
Reid A. Mandel
Floyd A. Mandell (P.C.)
Lawrence A. Manson
Laura Keidan Martin
Jeff J. Marwil
Nina B. Matis (P.C.)
William E. Mattingly (P.C.)
John R. McElyea
Thomas J. McFadden
Todd L. McLawhorn
Antony J. McShane
Adam M. Meek
David M. Meister (1946-1991)
Kenneth W. Miller
Michael L. Molinaro
Allan B. Muchin (P.C.)
Arthur B. Muir (P.C.)
Kathleen M. Murphy
James C. Murray, Jr.
Steven V. Napolitano
Stephen M. Neumer
Terry E. Newman (P.C.)
Wesley G. Nissen
Vickie L. Norman
J. Phillip O'Brien
Laura A. O'Connell
Steven R. Olson
Keith D. Pascus
Timothy J. Patenode
Jeffrey R. Patt
Melvin E. Pearl (P.C.)
Gerald M. Penner (P.C.)
Daniel J. Perlman
Ellen P. Pesch
Michael M. Philipp
Gregory P. L. Pierce
Nancy J. Rich
Howard M. Richard (P.C.)
Saul E. Rudo
Suzanne M. Russell
Barnett P. Ruttenberg (P.C.)
David K. Schmitt
David B. Schulman (P.C.)
Richard M. Seligman (P.C.)
Russell B. Selman
Vincent A. F. Sergi (P.C.)
Steven A. Shapiro (P.C.)
David R. Shevitz (P.C.)
Stuart P. Shulruff
Perry J. Shwachman
Harvey M. Silets
Ross O. Silverman
Steven B. Silverman
Ann Marie Sink
Andrew D. Small
Robert Y. Sperling (P.C.)
Robert M. Star
Bonita L. Stone
Jude M. Sullivan
Marcia W. Sullivan (P.C.)
Ira J. Swidler
Mark K. Thomas
James D. Van De Graaff
Zachary D. Wagman
Milton S. Wakschlag
Jerry B. Wallack
Herbert S. Wander (P.C.)
Elizabeth Fleming Weber
Walter S. Weinberg
Mark S. Weisberg
Linda J. Wight
Mark D. Wood
Kenneth R. Wylie
Michael Wm. Zavis (P.C.)
Sheldon T. Zenner
Mark S. Zolno

ASSOCIATES

Brent E. Adams
Philip P. Adler
Aaron R. Allred
James Craig Anderson
Nancy C. Andrade
Brian D. Annulis (Not admitted in IL)
Nicole Nehama Auerbach
John L. Babala
Darrin S. Baim

(See Next Column)

KATTEN MUCHIN & ZAVIS—*Continued*

ASSOCIATES (Continued)

Tracy G. Barnett
Karl Barnickol
Jeffrey J. Becker
Darren R. Bertram
Jan C. Bishop
John M. Blim
Andrew A. Block
Steven P. Blonder
Fran R. Boris (Not admitted in IL)
Milton K. Buckingham
Jennifer S. Canel
Matthew J. Cannon
David C. Carlet
Michele R. Chaffee
Elizabeth E. Cibula
Daniel C. Cole
S. Keith Collins
Robert S. Collins
Denise E. Conklin
Courtney B. Cooke
Kelly L. Costello
Tanya L. Curtis
Hadar R. Danieli
Elizabeth A. Davidson
Leslie Dawn Dent
Beth A. Deverman
Richard L. DiNardo
David M. Dunbar
Phillip M. Estaver
Lee J. Eulgen (Not admitted in IL)
Valentina Famparska
Joseph T. Fernim
Richard A. Fingard
Timothy G. Franzen
Lawrence M. Gail
Ferdinand J. Gallo, III
Evan R. Gartenlaub
Amy Moor Gaylord
Kurt R. Gearhart
René Ghadimi
Steven D. Ginsburg
Adam J. Glazer
Sarah A. Goddard
Basil V. Godellas
Tara Kamradt Goff
Harley J. Goldstein (Not admitted in IL)
Scott J. Goldstein
Todd D. Golub
Lisa A. Gomez
Brian M. Graham
Stephen M. Griesemer
Mark Richard Grossmann
Christopher M. Handy
Patricia M. Hanson
Megan Hardiman
Erica Tina Helfer
Janile S. Hill
Patricia A. Holland
Rena M. Honorow
Linda Lemel Hoseman
James Wellington Hutchison
Eric M. Israel
Joni S. Jacobsen
Michael A. Jacobson
Rebecca Janovsky (Not admitted in IL)
Stephanie D. Jones
Peter B. Jurgeleit
Christian T. Kemnitz (Not admitted in IL)
Alan L. Kennard
Sean M. Keyvan
Robert C. Kimmeth
Adam R. Klein
Kristine L. Kramer
Therese P. Kuffel
Amy C. Kurson
David M. Kushnir
Joseph H. Kye
Sharron C. Lamoreaux
Mark E. Laughman
Ryan J. J. Lee (Not admitted in IL)
Jeffrey A. Levick
Lisa K. Liou
Margaret E. Lomenzo (Not admitted in IL)
Michael F. Lutz
Scott E. Lyons
Brian E. Maier
Dawn M. Manoff
Julie A. Martin
R. Gibson Masters
Ryan D. Meade
Christopher S. Mehring
Thomas J. Meier
Chad R. Michael
Linda L. Miller
Rebecca A. Milliman
James E. Mitchell
Peter R. Monahan
Katherine C. Morgan
Patrick J. Morris
Warren Y. Nakatani
Kyle E. Nenninger
Carrie L. Newton
Lisa M. Noller
Shannon M. Nolley
Kevin M. Noonan
Denise M. Orlinski
Daniel L. Overbey
Samuel L. Pappas
Thomas Michael Pikarski
Kelli Chase Plotz
Lewis D. Popoff
Paul V. Possinger
Thomas S. Ratcliffe
Jason Raymond
Anthony J. Ribaudo
Brian F. Richards
Adam B. Richmond
Liat Riff
Jenifer M. Robbins
Bradley S. Rochlen
Kathryn A. Roe
Michael E. Roll
Mary-Beth Chadwick Roselle
Marianne Rowden (Not admitted in IL)
James L. Sawyer
Benay H. Schechter
Margaret M. Scholand
Melissa A. Schubert
Laurence A. Shapero
Thomas B. Shapira
Orrin S. Shifrin
Keith A. Sigale
Nina Momtazee Sitzer
Kevin E. Slaughter
Ziemowit T. Smulkowski
James F. Spatzek, Jr.
Valerie K. Sternberg
Melanie Struhar
Brian I. Swett
Risë J. Terney
Kimberly R Thompson
Ernest W. Torain, Jr.
Kathleen A. Turnbull
Marcela Uribe
Michel Vanesse
Sally L. Venverloh
Joseph A. Venzon
Kraig S. Washburn
Elizabeth Anne Williams
Peter R. Wilson
Cassondra M. Winkelman (Not admitted in IL)
Janet H. Winningham
Fauzia Zia Zaman-Malik (Not admitted in IL)
Lance A. Zinman
Steven Zoric

OF COUNSEL

Jeffrey P. Bilas
Deborah A. Giss
Cary S. Glenner
Rex A. Guest
B. Lane Hasler
Lizabeth F. Horn
Kevin S. MacKinnon

(See Next Column)

LOS ANGELES, CALIFORNIA
MEMBERS OF FIRM

Ivy Kagan Bierman
Marsha A. Boysaw
Julia W. Brand
John J. Chung
Steve Cochran
Mark A. Conley
Craig D. Crockwell
Alan D. Croll
Michele M. Desoer
Robert T. Flick
Allan B. Goldman
Robert D. Goldschein
Angel Gomez, III
Jeremy J. F. Gray
Jon S. Grizel
Susan A. Grode
Joyce S. Jun
Valerie E. Kincaid
Howard P. King (1945-1993)
Lisa Hamilton Klein
Frederick H. Kranz
Thomas J. Leanse
Thomas S. Mahr
Zia F. Modabber
Daniel M. Pelliccioni (P.C.)
Stuart M. Richter
Earl B. Slavitt (P.C.)
Charles M. Stern
M. Kenneth Suddleson
Gail Migdal Title
Joel R. Weiner

NEW YORK, NEW YORK
MEMBERS OF FIRM

Thomas F. Berner

WASHINGTON, D.C.
MEMBERS OF FIRM

Gary P. Blitz
Virginia A. Davis
Wendy L. Fields
Christopher J. Hart
Jill K. Kerxton
Bruce E. Kosub
S. Scott Morrison
David Schwinger
Andrew J. Sherman
Gloria B. Solomon
Carol R. Van Cleef
Edward E. Zughaib

For full biographical listings, see the Martindale-Hubbell Law Directory

---

KIRKLAND & ELLIS (AV)

A Partnership including Professional Corporations
200 East Randolph Drive, 60601
Telephone: 312-861-2000
Facsimile: 312-861-2200
URL: http://www.kirkland.com
Los Angeles, California Office: 300 South Grand Avenue.
Telephone: 213-680-8400.
Facsimile: 213-626-0010.
Washington, D.C. Office: 655 Fifteenth Street, N.W.
Telephone: 202-879-5000.
Facsimile: 202-879-5200.
New York, New York Office: Citicorp Center, 153 East 53rd Street.
Telephone: 212-446-4800.
Facsimile: 212-446-4900.
London, England Office: International Financial Centre, Old Broad Street.
Telephone: 171-816-8700.
Facsimile: 171-816-8800.

MEMBERS OF FIRM

Weymouth Kirkland (1877-1965)
Howard Ellis (1892-1968)
Melvin S. Adess (P.C.)
Ellen Therese Ahern
James M. Amend (P.C.)
Garland E. (Gene) Autrey
Debra Beinstein
David M. Bernick (P.C.)
Wendy L. Bloom
Andrew B. Bloomer
Michelle H. Browdy
Paul F. Brown
Christopher Butler (Not admitted in IL)
David K. Callahan
Hammond E. Chaffetz
Carole A. Cheney
Frank Cicero, Jr., (P.C.)
David A. Coulson
Keith S. Crow
James P. Cusick
Alex Dimitrief
John Donley
Thomas E. Dutton
Robert B. Ellis
David M. Elston
Carter W. Emerson
Sheri J. Engelken
David T. Erie
Lisa G. Esayian
Bruce I. Ettelson
Kevin R. Evanich
Jill Sugar Factor
R. Scott Falk
Barry E. Fields
Steven C. Florsheim
Michael P. Foradas
Scott W. Fowkes
Deirdre A. Fox
Willard G. Fraumann (P.C.)
Daniel K. Frey
Todd A. Gale
Margaret A. Gibson
Richard C. Godfrey
Laurie T. Gunther
Jeffrey C. Hammes
David A. Handler
Steven J. Harper (P.C.)
John F. Hartmann
John T. Hickey, Jr. (P.C.)
Neil S. Hirshman
Brian D. Hogan
Gary M. Holihan
Vicki Vallen Hood
George B. Javaras (P.C.)
William R. Jentes (P.C.)
Paul F. Jock, II (P.C.)
Elmer W. Johnson (P.C.)
Garrett B. Johnson
George A. Joseph
Andrew M. Kaufman
Donald G. Kempf, Jr., (P.C.)
Michael H. Kerr (P.C.)
Gregg Kirchhoefer
William S. Kirsch
Matthew N. Kleiman
Craig A. Knot
Robert J. Kopecky
Howard G. Krane (P.C.)
G. Christian Kronberg
Robert G. Krupka (P.C.)
Thomas Otman Kuhns
Douglas J. Kurtenbach
Walter R. Lancaster
James Andrew Langan
James L. Learner
Elli Leibenstein
Jack S. Levin (P.C.)
Russell E. Levine
Mark S. Lillie
Todd F. Maynes
Anne J. McClain

(See Next Column)

KIRKLAND & ELLIS, *Chicago—Continued*

MEMBERS OF FIRM (Continued)

Steven D. McCormick
M. Scott McCoy
(Not admitted in IL)
Andrew R. McGaan
Toni B. Merrick
Alexandra G. Mihalas
Jeffrey D. Mills
Kenneth P. Morrison
James C. Munson (P.C.)
Claire Perona Murphy
Dennis M. Myers
Linda K. Myers
Emily Nicklin
James N. Nowacki
Jeffrey S. O'Connor
Robert S. Osborne (P.C.)
Reed S. Oslan
Mark A. Pals
Stephen R. Patton
Sanford E. Perl
Richard W. Porter
Jeffrey S. Powell
E. Paul Quinn
James W. Rankin
Linda S. Resh
Kevin H. Rhodes
Stephen L. Ritchie
J. Robert Robertson
Donald E. Rocap
James S. Rowe
Andrew R. Running
James H. Schink (P.C.)
John A. Schoenfeld
Jeffrey Seifman
Jeffrey T. Sheffield (P.C.)
Brian D. Sieve
Gary R. Silverman
William S. Singer
Leslie M. Smith
Tefft W. Smith
Sallie G. Smylie
James D. Sonda
Gregory E. Spitzer
James H. M. Sprayregen
John H. Stassen (P.C.)
Matthew E. Steinmetz
James A. Stempel
Michael Stolarski
William A. Streff, Jr.
Edward T. Swan
Michael G. Timmers
Stephen G. Tomlinson
Hugh J. Totten
Thomas A. Tozer
Martin T. Tully
William E. Tymm
Anita Medina Tyson
Kevin T. Van Wart
H. Kurt von Moltke
John A. Weissenbach
William R. Welke
Raymond P. Wexler (P.C.)
Michael D. Whitty
Jeffrey L. Willian
Marchell M. Willian
Helen E. Witt
W. Allen Woolley
Ted H. Zook
David J. Zott

ASSOCIATES

Catherine Abbott
Jill C. Anderson
Amy H. Andrews
David J. B. Arroyo
Gabor Balassa
Donald E. Batterson
Tony Bayard De Volo
Michael E. Berg
Jack N. Bernstein
Jeff D. Blake
Joel A. Blanchet
Brian R. Boch
James J. Boland
Nader R. Boulos
Guita Bozorgi
Bruce O. Bradford
Kenneth H. Bridges
Allison I. Brown
Richard J. Campbell, Jr.
Thomas L. Campbell
John G. Caruso
Rashmi Chandra
Amy Fisher Chase
Kevin M. Chen
Wendy L. Chronister
Kevin J. Coenen
Nathanael M. Cousins
Erik Dahl
Geoffrey M. Davis
Kevin R. Davis
Sharon B. Davis
Terrence J. Dee
Michael N. Delgass
Alexandra Nicole DeNeve
William E. Devitt
Chris L. Dickerson
Nick DiCrescenzo
Gavin J. Domm
Christopher Dougherty
Michael Dennis DuBay
Timothy A. Duffy
Deborah Dunn
Daniel J. Eisner
Timothy D. Elliott
Knight Elsberry
Rebekah R. Eubanks
Heath R. Fear
Jeffrey A. Fine
Karen M. Fine
Catherine L. Fitzpatrick
Dr. James K. Fitzpatrick
Michael D. Foster
Michelle A.H. Francis
Katheryn Frierson
Angela Bonfield Frye
Gregory W. Gallagher
Karen B. Gerbosi
C. Graham Gerst
Michael R. Gervasio
Douglas C. Gessner
Daniel D. Gordon
Daniel G. Gordon
Elizabeth Gottschalk
Thomas Eliot Gottsegen
Christopher J. Greeno
Joseph P. Gromacki
Eric A. Gurry
John F. Hagan Jr.
Bryan S. Hales
Matthew P. Hammatt
Louis R. Hernandez
Jonathan E. Hinkemeyer
Jocelyn A. Hirsch
Shelly Matthew Hirschtritt
Renee D. Honigberg
Julie Marie Hood
Kristina M. Hoy
Anne M. Huber
Bart Huff
Barry F. Irwin
Geoffrey S. Irwin
Laryn Elizabeth Ivy
(Not admitted in IL)
Joseph Thomas Jaros
Garry W. Jaunal
John M. Jennings
Andrew M. Johnstone
James C. Joslin
Chris P. Kallos
James W. Kapp, III
Hariklia Karis
John M. Kasher
(Not admitted in IL)
Andrew A. Kassof
(Not admitted in IL)
Natalie Hoyer Keller
Billie A. King
Sarah E. Kirson
John Jacob Kobus, Jr.
Thies O. Kolln
Michael P. Kornak
Austin Krumpfes
Jordon L. Kruse
David C. Kung
Christopher J. Lawhorn
Garret Leach
Craig D. Leavell
David H. C. Lee
Dennis K. Lee
Adam J. Levine

(See Next Column)

ASSOCIATES (Continued)

Jason R. Lichtenstein
Michael R. Lieber
Joelle C. Luedtke
Sarah R. Marmor
Nathaniel M. Marrs
Janette A. McMahan
Scott McMillin
Adam P. Merrill
Roberto S. Miceli
(Not admitted in IL)
Rita Mirman
(Not admitted in IL)
J. Chad Mitchell
Gabriela I. Monahan
Lara S. Moynihan
Michael J. Munn
Leonard J. Nannarone, Jr.
Michael John Newman
Michael L. Newquist
Mark Nomellini
Jeffery S. Norman
Gerald T. Nowak
Kenneth M. Obel
Stephen D. Oetgen
Darcy L. O'Loughlin
John R. O'Neil
Karin Orsic
Lea M. Parent
Michael A. Parks
John F. Paschke
Francesco Penati
(Not admitted in IL)
Adam V. Petravicius
Beverly G. Petravicius
Jablanka Petrovic
Harold Francis Pfister
Tu Minh Pham
Quentin Phillips
(Not admitted in IL)
Douglas M. Poland
Robin Ann Rademacher
Greg W. Rayford
Matthew T. Regan
Geoffrey A. Richards
Jeffrey W. Richards
Bradley V. Ritter
Maria Pellegrino Rivera
Katrin K. Robb
Ilana Simone Rubel
Julie B. Ruder
Anup Sathy
Kelly A. Schell
Tim J. Schmuckal
Sarah Schrup
Steven C. Seeger
Carol Anne Sennello
Marcus E. Sernel
Michael B. Shaw
Hab M. Siam
S Jonathan Silverman
Stephanie D. Simon
Paul R. Steadman
Michael A. Stone
Domingo P. Such, III
Christopher B. Sullivan
Maureen E. Sweeney
Christian C. Taylor
Andrew J. Terry
Douglas D. Timmer
Seth Traxler
Debra J. Tucker
Christopher M.R. Turner
Alyssa R. Unikel
Peter C. Van den Dool
Keith Villmow
Robert K. Vischer
Michael H. Weed
Ross M. Weisman
Donna M. Welch
Brett E. Well
Jacqueline A. White
Angela Toscas Wilt
André L. Zafrani
Mary E. Zaug
Barton M. Zedd
Robert R. Zitko

OF COUNSEL

Terri A. Abruzzo
Kristine L. Anderson
Sheila W. Elston
Francis J. Gerlits (P.C.)
Emile Karafiol
Chaim T. Kiffel
Robert H. Kinderman
John E. Kirkpatrick (P.C.)
Karl E. Lutz (P.C.)
Karl F. Nygren
Jeffrey W. Pickard
Gwen K. Stein
Jeffrey W. Stevenson
Roger L. Taylor
William R. Theiss
Daniel W. Vittum, Jr. (P.C.)

For full biographical listings, see the Martindale-Hubbell Law Directory

LORD, BISSELL & BROOK (AV)

Suites 2600-3600 Harris Bank Building, 115 South La Salle Street, 60603
Telephone: 312-443-0700
Telecopy: 312-443-0336
Cable Address: "Lowirco"
Telex: 25-0336
URL: http://www.lordbissell.com
Los Angeles, California Office: 300 South Grand Avenue, 90071-3200.
Telephone: 213-485-1500.
Telecopy: 213-485-1200.
Telex: 18-1135.
Atlanta, Georgia Office: One Atlantic Center, 1201 West Peachtree Street, N.W., Suite 3700, 30309.
Telephone: 404-870-4600.
Telecopy: 404-872-5547.
Rockford, Illinois Office: 120 West State Street, Suite 200, 61101.
Telephone: 815-963-8050.
New York, N.Y. Office: One Penn Plaza, Suite 3435, 10119.
Telephone: 212-947-4700.
Facsimile: 212-947-1202.

MEMBERS OF FIRM

John Solon Lord (1881-1979)
Cushman Brewer Bissell
(1900-1987)
Herbert C. Brook (1910-1990)
Charles A. Adamek
(Resident, Los Angeles Office)
David J. Adams
Steven H. Adelman
David M. Agnew
Fred L. Alvarez
Margaret M. Anderson
William C. Anderson, III
Robert P. Arnold
Stephen C. Ascher
James W. Ashley, Jr.
Michael J. Athans
(Resident, Atlanta Office)
Robert B. Austin
Robert A. Badgley
Gail M. Baev
(Resident, Los Angeles Office)
Patricia J. Barker
Carey S. Barney
M. Elizabeth Bennett
R. Clay Bennett
Jon Biasetti
William P. Bila
Kirk A. Borchardt
(Resident, Los Angeles Office)
Timothy W. Brink

(See Next Column)

LORD, BISSELL & BROOK—*Continued*

MEMBERS OF FIRM (Continued)

George L. Burgett
Thomas J. Burke, Jr.
Terrence P. Canade
Chad M. Castro
John S. Chapman
Marilee Clausing
C. Guerry Collins (Resident, Los Angeles Office)
Michael P. Comiskey
R. Dean Conlin
Robert P. Conlon
Joseph E. Coughlin
Michael Davis
Donald T. De Carlo (Resident, New York Office)
Nick J. DiGiovanni
Kirk W. Dillard
Williams P. Dorr
R. Bruce Duffield
James R. Dwyer
David P. Faulkner (Resident, Rockford Office)
Paul L. Fields, Jr. (Resident, Atlanta Office)
Edward C. Fitzpatrick
Patricia J. Foltz
Bruce W. Foudree
Albert E. Fowerbaugh, Jr.
Don W. Fowler
Cynthia M. Frey (Resident, Los Angeles Office)
Lawrence M. Friedman
Roger R. Fross
Michael J. Gaertner
Edward P. Gibbons
Laura J. Ginett
Larry S. Goldberg
Laura S. Golden
Mark R. Goodman
Lawrence A. Gray
David G. Greene (Resident, Atlanta Office)
Hugh C. Griffin
John C. Gurley
John B. Haarlow
Randall A. Hack
David C. Hall
Leisa J. Hamm
Laurence A. Hansen
D. Scott Hargadon
Louis S. Harrison
Michael R. Hassan
David F. Hauge (Resident, Los Angeles Office)
Richard A. Hemmings
Colleen M. Hennessy
Joseph A. Hinkhouse
Bobbe Hirsh
Terry R. Howell (Resident, Atlanta Office)
John E. Hrebec
John M. Hughes
John A. Jeffries
Thomas W. Jenkins
Diane I. Jennings
Richard F. Johnson
Laura A. Kane
William J. Kelty, III
David L. Kendall
Camille N. Khodadad
Celeste M. King
Jacqueline Redin Klein (Resident, Los Angeles Office)
Robert A. Knuti
Karen J. Kowal
Jeffrey S. Kravitz (Resident, Los Angeles Office)
Mark A. Kreger
Susan K. Laing
Forrest B. Lammiman
Paul H. LaRue, Jr.
LouCinda Laughlin (Resident, Los Angeles Office)
L. Anthony Lehr
David M. Leonard (Resident, Atlanta Office)
Ronald M. Lepinskas
Harvey S. Lichterman
John S. Lindemann
Gary L. Lockwood
Janet Otsuka Love
Mark J. Lura
Timothy M. Maggio
Donald J. Manikas
Paul F. Matousek
Susan Magee McColgan
Kay W. McCurdy
David C. McLauchlan
Robert E. McLaughlin (Resident, Atlanta Office)
R. R. McMahan
Dale T. Miller
Hugh L. Moore
Kathryn Montgomery Moran
Thomas J. Murnighan
Stephen M. Murray
Prescott L. Nottingham (Resident, Atlanta Office)
John N. Oest
Keith D. Parr
Jason A. Parson
Judy Platt Perlman
Mitchell J. Popham (Resident, Los Angeles Office)
Michael E. Prangle
J. Brett Pritchard
Robert J. Pugliese
Robert D. Rasor
David R. Reed
Robert B. Robinson
Victoria A. Rohner
Douglass F. Rohrman
Steven C. Roper
Louis E. Rosen
Cary Brian Samowitz (Resident, New York Office)
Eric P. Schoonveld
Daniel I. Schlessinger
David R. Schmidt
David M. Seghetti
Amy E. Shappert (Resident, Rockford Office)
Anthony B. Sherman
Bruce C. Shulan (Resident, New York Office)
David J. Slawkowski
Walter T. Slezak
Walton N. Smith (Resident, Atlanta Office)
Rowe W. Snider
Lyle Wayne Sparks
Maynerd I. Steinberg
Molly McGinnis Stine
Thomas J. Strueber (Resident, Atlanta Office)
Catalina J. Sugayan
Gerald O. Sweeney, Jr.
Robert E. Sweeney, Jr.
Bedell A. Tippins
Michael P. Trier
John B. Truskowski
Jane H. Veldman
Damon N. Vocke
Eugene H. Wachtel
David E. Walker
Ann Marie Walsh
Thomas C. Walsh
Wesley S. Walton
Richard M. Watson (Resident, Atlanta Office)
William T. Weaver
Frederic W. Weber
Gary W. Westerberg
Richard L. Wexler
Mark D. Wilcox
Keith G. Wileman (Resident, Los Angeles Office)
John T. Williams
Dennis M. Wilson
Corliss L. Worford (Resident, Atlanta Office)
Canella Gekas Woyar
John M. Wulfers
Mary Jane Yardley
Daniel J. Zollner

(See Next Column)

OF COUNSEL

Christopher R. Barth
Glen R. Bernfield
Brenda Adams Bissett (Resident, Los Angeles Office)
Paul C. Blume, Sr.
Dennis J. Fox
David M. Gooder
Sarah J. Hewitt
Marsha Kellman Klevickis (Resident, Atlanta Office)
Clarence Owen Redman
Angelo G. Savino (Resident, New York Office)
John S. Shapira
John G. Smith
Forrest L. Tozer
Patrick T. Walsh
James R. Wimmer

ASSOCIATES

Jonathan E. Aberman
Michele C. Anderson
Hugh S. Balsam
David B. Barlow
Amy B. Bellman
Robert M. Bennison (Resident, Atlanta, Georgia Office)
Gregory W. Black
Michael S. Blanton (Resident, Los Angeles, California Office)
Cynthia L. Bordelon
Joseph J. Borders
Michelle D. Bowers
Christopher M. Brainard (Resident, Los Angeles Office)
Michael T. Burnett
Mary Ellen Busch
Lisa Sawyer Cadet
Cynthia J. Cappello
Jennifer L. Carow
Donald J. Chenevert (Resident, Atlanta Office)
S.J. Robin Choi
Thomas J. Clark
Joyce F. Clough
Stephen L. Cope (Resident, Los Angeles Office)
Krista L. Cosner
Robert S. Crowder (Resident, Los Angeles Office)
Gardenia P. Cucci
Thomas D. Cunningham
Richard E. Dolder, Jr. (Resident, Atlanta Office)
Charissa Dorian (Resident, Los Angeles Office)
Ellie A. Doyle (Resident, Atlanta, Georgia Office)
Kristen K. Duggan (Resident, Atlanta Office)
Franklin T. Dunn (Resident, Los Angeles Office)
Daniel W. Eck
Charles A. Egner (Resident, Rockford Office)
William D. Ellison
Allison M. Engel
Mario A. Esposito
Mark S. Fall (Resident, Los Angeles Office)
Scott B. Feder
Sean C. Fifield
Ann Kettelson Ford
Charlene R. Fisher Foss
Jennifer A. Gallagher
Anne R. Garr-Kraemer
Jannis E. Goodnow
James B. Green (Resident, Los Angeles Office)
Christopher B. Hall (Resident, Atlanta Office)
John C. Hansen
Brian I. Hays
Robert S. Held
John M. Hochhausler (Resident, Los Angeles Office)
Jeffery K. Hoelzel
Teri Holt-Charles
Vincent I. Holzhall
Robert D. Howell (Resident, Atlanta Office)
James J. Huberty
Gerald W. Huston
Allegra Hyte
Susan P. Jordan
Cynthia A. Kaufman
Jennifer A. Kenedy
Matthew S. Klepper
David S. Klevatt
Elizabeth Klippi (Resident, Los Angeles Office)
John F. Kloecker
Christine M. Koman
David L. Koury
Emily J. Kuo
William Thomas Lacy, Jr. (Resident, Atlanta Office)
Daniel S. Lambert
Sal Lele
Jeff H. Liebling
Kristin L. Lingren
Jennifer L. Long
Jeri Rouse Looney (Resident, Los Angeles Office)
George D. Lozano (Resident, Los Angeles Office)
Rita E. Luce
Kevin A. Maxim (Resident, Atlanta Office)
C. Kevin McCabe
Arthur J. McColgan, II
Richard O. McDermott
John J. McGuirk
Kevin P. McJessy
Patrick John McLaughlin
Paul J. Molino
Steven D. Moore (Resident, Atlanta Office)
Brian D. Mulqueen
Sergei Mytko
Jane E. Nagle
Lisa A. Navarro
Jeffrey J. Neuenschwander
Debra M. Newton
Mai Lin P. Noffke
William D. Nolen
Eric B. Noyes
Susan O'Brien (Resident, Rockford, Illinois Office)
Jeffrey S. O'Dwyer
Ugo N. Okafor (Resident, Atlanta Office)
Ryan M. Opria
Debra A. Osmond
Scott R. Ostericher
Matthew J. Pagano
Diane E. Pappas
Benjamin E. Patterson
Karen N. Pavia (Resident, Los Angeles Office)
John M. Phelan
Dov J. Pinchot
William A. Rakoczy
Lori A. Renetzky
Michael K. Renetzky
Jennifer Ries
Leslie J. Rosen
Marsha L. Ross-Jackson
Nicole A. Roth
Jennifer Kaplan Schott
Christopher D. Schuering
Stacey Rubin Silver
Linda J. Simon
Karen A. Soomekh (Resident, Los Angeles Office)
Kristine M. Sorenson
Lisa Marie Starcevich
Richard P. Stowell
Denean K. Sturino
Martha Conlin Sweeney
Joseph M. Talarico
Ann Caroline Taylor
A. Kelly Turner
Jennifer G. Tuvlin
Amy S. Van Gorp
Kerry A. Vyverberg
Sarah Marion Weil
Steven T. Whitmer
Cheryl L. Wilson
James H. Wynn (Resident, Los Angeles Office)
Cara E. Zemenak

(See Next Column)

LORD, BISSELL & BROOK, *Chicago—Continued*

ATTORNEY

Susan J. G. Alexander

For full biographical listings, see the Martindale-Hubbell Law Directory

MANDEL, LIPTON AND STEVENSON LIMITED (AV)

Suite 2900, 120 North La Salle Street, 60602
Telephone: 312-236-7080
Facsimile: 312-236-0781

Alfred R. Lipton
Leonard M. Malkin
R. Peter Carey
Henry A. Waller
Kathleen Roseborough
Richard A. Lifshitz
Terry Yale Feiertag
Uve R. Jerzy
Carolyn E. Winter
Leo G. Aubel

Andrés J. Gallegos
Jennifer R. Shapiro
Joan Comiskey

OF COUNSEL

Richard L. Mandel
Nicholas Stevenson

LEGAL SUPPORT PERSONNEL

Jacqueline Steffens (Paralegal)

References: Northern Trust Co.; American National Bank of Chicago; La Salle Bank FSB.

For full biographical listings, see the Martindale-Hubbell Law Directory

MAYER, BROWN & PLATT (AV)

190 South La Salle Street, 60603-3441
Telephone: (312) 782-0600
Facsimile: (312) 701-7711
Telex: 190404
Cable: LEMAY
URL: http://www.mayerbrown.com
Berlin, Germany Office: Spreeufer 5, 10178.
Telephone: 011-49-30-247-3800.
Facsimile: 011-49-30-247-38044.
Charlotte, North Carolina Office: 100 North Tryon Street, Suite 2400.
Telephone: (704) 444-3500.
Fax: (704) 377-2033.
Cologne, Germany Office: Kaiser-Wilhelm-Ring 27-29, 50672.
Telephone: 011-49-221-5771-100.
Facsimile: 011-49-221-5771-199.
Houston, Texas Office: 700 Louisiana Street, Suite 3600, 77002-2730.
Telephone: (713) 221-1651.
Facsimile: (713) 224-6410.
Telex: 775809.
Cable: LEMAYHOU.
London, England Office: Bucklersbury House, 3 Queen Victoria Street, London, EC4N 8EL, England.
Telephone: 011-44-171-246-6200.
Facsimile: 011-44-171-329-4465.
Telex: 8811095.
Cable: LEMAYLDN.
Los Angeles, California Office: 350 South Grand Avenue, 25th Floor, 90071-1503.
Telephone: (213) 229-9500.
Facsimile: (213) 625-0248.
Telex: 188089.
Cable: LEMAYLA.
New York, New York Office: 1675 Broadway, 10019-5820.
Telephone: (212) 506-2500.
Facsimile: (212) 262-1910.
Telex: 701842.
Cable: LEMAYEN.
Washington, D.C. Office: 1909 K Street, N.W., 20006-1101.
Telephone: (202) 263-3000.
Facsimile: (202) 263-3300.
Telex: 892603.
Cable: LEMAYDC.
Representative Offices:
Ashgabat, Turkmenistan: 28 Gogol Street, 744000.
Telephone: 011-99-312-355247.
Facsimile: 011-99-312-510074.
Bishkek, Kyrgyz Republic: 66 Kalyka Akieva Str. 720001.
Telephone: 011-996-312-65-02-56.
Facsimile: 011-996-312-65-09-80.
Moscow: Paveletskaya Square II, 1 Valovaya Street, 5th Floor, 113054.
Telephone: 011-7-502-937-0500.
Facsimile: 011-7-502-937-0501.
Tashkent, Republic of Uzbekistan: 3rd Floor, 1 Turab Tula Street, 700003.
Telephones: 011-998-71-1206-627; 7371-1206-017/8.
Facsimile: 011-998-71-1206-329.
Mexico City, Mexico, D.F., Independent Mexico Correspondent: Jáuregui, Navarrete, Nader y Rojas, S.C., Torre Arcos, Paseo de los Tamarindos No. 400-B. Col. Bosques de las Lomas, 05120.
Telephone: 011-525-267-45-00.
Facsimile: 011-525-267-45-98.

(See Next Column)

Paris, France, Independent Paris Correspondent: Lambert & Lee, 13 Avenue Hoche, 75008.
Telephone: 011-33-1-53-53-43-43.
Facsimile: 011-33-1-53-96-03-83.

MEMBERS OF FIRM

David F. Abbott
Lee N. Abrams
Diane E. Ambler (Washington, D.C. Office)
J. Trent Anderson
Percy L. Angelo
Jean-Marie L. Atamian (New York, N.Y. Office)
Robert C. Baptista, Jr.
Robert N. Barnard
James R. Barry
Gregory L. Barton
Teresa A. Beaudet (Los Angeles, California Office)
Robert M. Berger
John C. Berghoff, Jr.
Nicole V.F. Bergman Fong (New York, N.Y. Office)
Edward S. Best
Michael E. Bieniek
Barry P. Biggar (New York, N.Y. Office)
Christian F. Binnig
Timothy S. Bishop
Michael T. Blair
Francis J. Blanchfield, Jr. (Charlotte, North Carolina Office)
Robert E. Bloch (Washington, D.C. Office)
David I. Bloom (Washington, D.C. Office)
Fern C. Bomchill
Kim Marie Kozaczek Boylan (Washington, D.C. Office)
Richard S. Brennan
Robert I. Bressman (New York, N.Y. Office)
Ronald S. Brody (New York, N.Y. Office)
Joan Edmonds Brophy
Hayden D. Brown (Charlotte, North Carolina Office)
Kimberlee S. Cagle (Houston, Texas Office)
Timothy P. Callahan
Michael A. Campbell
Jeffrey P. Cantrell (Charlotte, North Carolina Office)
James B. Carlson (New York, N.Y. Office)
John M. Carroll
Jean S. Chin (New York, N.Y. Office)
C. Cabell Chinnis, Jr. (Washington, D.C. Office)
Diane Citron (New York, N.Y. Office)
Paul B. Clemenceau (Houston, Texas Office)
Richard A. Cole (London, England Office)
Ian R. Coles (London, England Office)
Joseph P. Collins
Vincent J. Connelly
Robert B. Cordle (Charlotte, North Carolina Office)
George W. Craven
Paul M. Crimmins
Robert E. Curley
David S. Curry
Peter V. Darrow (New York, N.Y. Office)
Robert P. Davis (Washington, D.C. Office)
Scott J. Davis
John J. Dedyo (New York, N.Y. Office)
Laura A. DeFelice (New York, N.Y. Office)
Debora de Hoyos
William E. Deitrick
Daniel J. Delaney
Julian C. D'Esposito, Jr.
Douglas A. Doetsch
Ralph P. Dudziak
David K. Duffee (New York, N.Y. Office)
Robert T. Duffy (Charlotte, North Carolina Office)
Daniel Dumezich
Thomas C. Durham
Thomas M. Durkin
Louis P. Eatman (Los Angeles, California Office)
Kerry Lynn Edwards (Washington, D.C. Office)
Russell R. Eggert
Timothy B. Ellwood (Houston, Texas Office)
Roy T. Englert, Jr. (Washington, D.C. Office)
Tyrone C. Fahner
Donald M. Falk (Washington, D.C. Office)
Richard J. Favretto (Washington, D.C. Office)
Michael R. Feagley
Robert F. Finke
L. Bruce Fischer (Los Angeles, California Office)
Robert V. Fitzsimmons
Delilah B. Flaum
Mary C. Fontaine
J. Paul Forrester
Douglas B. Frank (Los Angeles, California Office)
Andrew L. Frey
Dennis G. Friedman
Gary D. Friedman (New York, N.Y. Office)
Marc Gary (Washington, D.C. Office)
John J. Gearen
Kenneth S. Geller (Washington, D.C. Office)
Bettina Getz
Steven R. Gilford
Michael J. Gill
Mark H. Gitenstein (Washington, D.C. Office)
Ronald B. Given
James W. Gladden, Jr.
Joseph R. Goeke
Marcia E. Goodman
Robert E. Gordon
William A. Gordon
Maureen J. Gorman
David W. Grawemeyer
Lorie Soares Griffen (Los Angeles, California Office)
Terri Truitt Griffiths (Houston, Texas Office)
Salvatore Guerrera (New York, N.Y. Office)
Frederic L. Hahn
John F. Halbleib
Marshall E. Hanbury (Not admitted in IL)
R. Douglas Harmon (Charlotte, North Carolina Office)
Kevin P. Hawken
Werner J. Hein (Washington, D.C. and Cologne, Germany Offices)
Robert A. Helman
Michael L. Hermsen
Thomas P. Hester
Carol A. Hitselberger
Debra B. Hoffman
James D. Holzhauer
Thomas R. Hood (New York, N.Y. Office)
Charles M. Horn (Washington, D.C. Office)
Carrie Kiger Huff
Robert F. Hugi
Harley Hutchins
Caryn L. Jacobs
John A. Janicik
Robert M. Jenkins, III (Washington, D.C. Office)
Thomas N. Jersild
Erika Z. Jones (Washington, D.C. Office)
Roger J. Jones
James J. Junewicz

(See Next Column)

MAYER, BROWN & PLATT—*Continued*

MEMBERS OF FIRM (Continued)

Ivan P. Kane
Michael Kantor (Washington, D.C. Office)
Wayne S. Kaplan
Alvin Charles Katz
M. Marvin Katz (Houston, Texas Office)
Timothy E. Keehan (Washington, D.C. Office)
Robert A. Kelman
Michael F. Kerr (Los Angeles, California Office)
Stanton A. Kessler
Nabil L. Khodadad (London, England Office)
Roger J. Kiley, Jr.
Thomas S. Kiriakos
Thomas L. Kittle-Kamp
Marc L. Klyman
William H. Knull, III (Houston, Texas Office)
Kenneth E. Kohler (Los Angeles, California Office)
Jason H. P. Kravitt
Simeon M. Kriesberg (Washington, D.C. Office)
Robert J. Kriss
Herbert W. Krueger
Kathryn A. Kusske (Washington, D.C. Office)
Philip Allen Lacovara (Washington, D.C. and New York, N.Y. Offices)
Paul L. Langer
Bennett W. Lasko
John F. Lawlor
Fredrick S. Levin (Los Angeles, California Office)
William A. Levy
Stuart M. Litwin
Theodore A. Livingston, Jr.
Wayne R. Luepker
George A. Luscombe, II
Christine Lutgens
Daniel W. Luther
Barry N. Machlin (Not admitted in IL)
Cary J. Malkin
Mary K. Mandeville (Charlotte, North Carolina Office)
Andrew S. Marovitz
John D. Marshall
Alan J. Martin
Daniel A. Masur (Washington, D.C. Office)
Andrew Mattei (New York, N.Y. Office)
Stephen J. Mattson
Frank D. Mayer, Jr.
Terri A. Mazur
Gregory R. McClintock (Los Angeles, California Office)
Hugh R. McCombs
Howard M. McCue, III
T. Mark McLaughlin
Jonathan C. Medow
Robert L. Mendenhall (Charlotte, North Carolina Office)
Paul Meyer
Jay Parry Monge (New York, N.Y. Office)
Myron L. Moore, III (Charlotte, North Carolina Office)
Donna Evensen Morgan
Louis P. Moritz
John E. Muench
J. Thomas Mullen
Lucia Nale
David Narefsky
Alec G. Nedelman (Los Angeles, California Office)
Brian E. Newhouse (Los Angeles, California Office)
C. Mark Nicolaides
Michael E. Niebruegge (Houston, Texas Office)
Philip J. Niehoff
John W. Noell
Lennine Occhino
Michele L. Odorizzi
Anna M. O'Meara
Jerry L. Oppenheimer (Washington, D.C. Office)
Joseph B. Organ
Dennis P. Orr (New York, N.Y. Office)
Gary A. Orseck (Washington, D.C. Office)
Carolyn P. Osolinik (Washington, D.C. Office)
Danuta Bembenista Panich
Stanley J. Parzen
George A. Pecoulas
Stuart P. Pergament (Washington, D.C. Office)
Scott P. Perlman (Washington, D.C. Office)
Brad L. Peterson
Denis Petkovic (London, England Office)
George A. Ranney, Jr.
Mitchell D. Raup (Washington, D.C. Office)
Elizabeth A. Raymond
Philip R. Recht (Los Angeles, California Office)
Phillip S. Reed
N. Neville Reid
Laura D. Richman
Michael P. Richman (New York, N.Y. Office)
Robert S. Rigg
Michael P. Rissman
Lawrence S. Robbins (Washington, D.C. Office)
William J. Robinson (Los Angeles, California Office)
Howard J. Roin
Diane J. Romza-Kutz
Matthew A. Rooney
Michael F. Rosenblum
Martin G. Rosenstein
Kenneth M. Rosenzweig
Paul J. N. Roy
Stuart M. Rozen
Javier H. Rubinstein
Deborah Schavey Ruff
George Ruhlen
Donald W. Rupert
Mark W. Ryan (Washington, D.C. Office)
John R. Sagan
Alan N. Salpeter
Gail C. Saracco
Julia R. Sarron
John M. Satalic
William A. Schmalzl
John R. Schmidt
John P. Schmitz
Edward J. Schneidman
James C. Schroeder
David A. Schuette
Stephen M. Shapiro
Kevin L. Shaw (Los Angeles, California Office)
Richard W. Shepro
Timothy C. Sherck
Ronald M. Shoss (Houston, Texas Office)
Michael N. Sloyer (New York, N.Y. Office)
Brian W. Smith (Washington, D.C. Office)
Kerry T. Smith
Lawrence K. Snider
Neil M. Soltman (Los Angeles, California Office)
Richard A. Spehr (New York, N.Y. Office)
James S. Stanhaus
Todd Evan Stark (Los Angeles, California Office)
Adrian L. Steel, Jr. (Washington, D.C. Office)
Ellyn Steuer-Miller (New York, N.Y. Office)
Scott M. Stewart
J. Robert Stoll
Jeffrey M. Strauss

MEMBERS OF FIRM (Continued)

(See Next Column)

John J. Sullivan (Washington, D.C. Office)
Robert H. Swart (Washington, D.C. Office)
Evan M. Tager (Washington, D.C. Office)
James E. Tancula (Houston, Texas Office)
Eileen McDermott Taylor (Charlotte, North Carolina Office)
Mark R. Taylor
Mark R. Ter Molen
John J. Tharp, Jr.
Paul W. Theiss
Frederick B. Thomas
William C. Tompsett
John M. Touhy
Charles S. Triplett (Washington, D.C. Office)
George J. Tzanetopoulos
Mark R. Uhrynuk (London, England Office)
Alan E. Untereiner (Washington, D.C. Office)
Jeffrey A. Usow
Barry Alan Van Dyke
Terry Otero Vilardo (Houston, Texas Office)
Thomas M. Vitale (New York, N.Y. Office)
Pierre Vogelenzang (Los Angeles, California Office)
Kathleen Walsh (New York, N.Y. Office)
James R. Walther (Los Angeles, California Office)
Robert J. Ward (New York, N.Y. Office)
Michael O. Warnecke
Neil A. Wasserstrom (Houston, Texas Office)
Don L. Weaver (Los Angeles, California Office)
Priscilla P. Weaver
Seth J. Weinberger
Barry A. White
Joel V. Williamson
Richard S. Williamson
Douglas L. Wisner (New York, N.Y. Office)
Keith J. Willner (Washington, D.C. Office)
Mark S. Wojciechowski (New York, N.Y. Office)
Steven Wolowitz (New York, N.Y. Office)
Nigel A. Wright (London, England Office)
Herbert L. Zarov
Michael I. Zinder (New York, N.Y. Office)

SENIOR COUNSEL

Roger W. Barrett
Stuart Bernstein
Jerome F. Donohoe
Albert I. Edelman (New York, N.Y. Office)
David B. Finnegan (Washington, D.C. Office)
Leo Herzel
Harvey Nixon
Patrick W. O'Brien
Wolfgang Pfletschinger (Cologne, Germany Office)
Robert L. Stern

SPECIAL CONSULTANT

Michael W. McConnell (Not admitted in IL)

SPECIAL COUNSEL

David Hyman (Washington, D.C. Office)
Charles Rothfeld (Washington, D.C. Office)

COUNSEL

Bradley J. Andreozzi
Carol J. Bilzi (Washington, D.C. Office)
Thomas B. Burnside (Washington, D.C. Office)
Michael P. Cannon
Marla Chernof Cohen
Victoria R. Collado
Richard C. Cummings, Jr.
Ronald R. Dietrich
Linda H. Earle (Houston, Texas Office)
Jack Edelbrock
Patricia V. Gentry
Graham C. Grady
Marian C. Haney
Andrea Lodahl Henneman (New York, N.Y. Office)
John R. Hewitt (New York, N.Y. Office)
Catherine W. Hoeg (Houston, Texas Office)
Diane M. Huff
John Chafer Huff
Kathy Kresch Ingber (Washington, D.C. Office)
Gary A. Isaac
Dean Alan Isaacs
Nancy S. Jacobson
Warren L. Jervey (New York, N. Y. Office)
Sultana Kaldis (Houston, Texas Office)
Andrew T. Karp (Not admitted in IL)
Michael C. Kelcy (Los Angeles, California Office)
Jeffrey S. Kinsler
Beth R. Kramer (New York, N. Y. Office)
Kim A. Leffert
Jeri Lindahl-Garcia
Robert M. Lyons (London, England Office)
Marjorie M. Margolies
Philip H. Martin
Kevin C. McDonald
Patrick J. McNerney
David R. Melton
Lillian Miller
Deborah Alfred Monson
Robert L. Morgan (Houston, Texas Office)
Andrew J. Morris (Washington, D.C. Office)
Donald C. Morris
John P. Morrison
Thomas M. Mueller (New York, N.Y. Office)
Christopher P. Murphy (Los Angeles, California Office)
Werner M. Nikowitz (New York, N.Y. Office)
Donald L. Norman, Jr.
Rex A. Palmer
Howard A. Parelskin (Washington, D.C. Office)
Ross Pazzol
Frank A. Perrone (Houston, Texas Office)
Edward R. Rabe, Jr.
Charles F. Regan, Jr.
Thomas S. Reif
Clisson S. Rexford
Carol S. Rivers
Marc E. Rosenthal
Cecilia A. Roth
Patricia F. Sharkey
Richard A. Speer (Not admitted in IL)
Andrew J. Starrels (Los Angeles, California Office)
Michael J. Sussman (London, England Office)
Oliver Ott Trumbo, II (New York, N.Y. Office)
Stephen Van Dolsen (New York, N.Y. Office)
Duncan John Walls (London, England Office)
Kimberly S. Winick (Los Angeles, California Office)
Craig A. Wolson (New York, N.Y. Office)

(See Next Column)

MAYER, BROWN & PLATT, *Chicago—Continued*

ASSOCIATES

Asheesh Agarwal
Douglas A. Albritton
DeAnna D. Allen-Bass
Michael J. Alter (Washington, D.C. Office)
Lisa M. An
James A. Andrus (Houston, Texas Office)
Stephen J. Angelson (New York, N.Y. Office)
Brian Aronson (Los Angeles, California Office)
Susan W. Ausman
Laura E. Bader
Andrei A. Baev (Los Angeles, California Office)
Jeffrey J. Bakker
Lesa A. Barkowsky-Starkins (New York, N.Y. Office)
Mary R. Barry
James E. Barz
Deborah L. Bencik
Audrey I. Bender (New York, N.Y. Office)
Joanne E. Benisch (New York, N.Y. Office)
Marc S. Berger (Washington, D.C. Office)
Andrew J. Bettwy (New York, N.Y. Office)
Howard Alan Blaustein (New York, N.Y. Office)
Bruce C. Bloomingdale
Kathryn A. Bogdanowicz (Not admitted in IL)
David C. Bolstad (Los Angeles, California Office)
Susan J. Booth (Los Angeles, California Office)
Francis R. Bradley, III (Houston, Texas Office)
Addison D. Braendel
Philip O. Brandes (New York, N.Y. Office)
Susan Brice
Maria A. Bries
Patricia Ann Brito (Houston, Texas Office)
Jennifer L. Brockett (Los Angeles, California Office)
Robert L. Bronston (Washington, D.C. Office)
Beth Y. Brotz (Los Angeles, California Office)
Gerald (Geff) Brown
Jay S. Brown (Washington, D.C. Office)
Stephen J. Brown
Vaughn J. Buffalo (New York, N.Y. Office)
Richard F. Bulger
Alison M. Butler
Kelley E. Campbell (Washington, D.C. Office)
Theresa A. Canaday
Craig W. Canetti (Washington, D.C. Office)
Shant H. Chalian (New York, N.Y. Office)
Paul Chandler
Kirsten A. Chappell
Leslie Chebli (New York, N.Y. Office)
Robert Chernoff
Peter C. Choharis (Washington, D.C. Office)
David W. Chowins
David A. Ciancuillo
Elizabeth A. Clark (Washington, D.C. Office)
Katherine M. Clark
Eric N. Cohen (New York, N.Y. Office)
Thomas B. Colby (Washington, D.C. Office)
Martin J. Collins (New York, N.Y. Office)
Gary S. Colton, Jr.,
John M. Conlon (New York, N.Y. Office)
John C. Connery, Jr.
Michael D. Coppin
Robert L. Cordell, II (New York, N.Y. Office)
J. Tyson Covey
Kristen W. Crosby
Raniero D'Aversa, Jr. (New York, N.Y. Office)
Diana L. Davis (Houston, Texas Office)
Edward A. Davis (New York, N.Y. Office)
Lynn E. Delzell
Kevin G. Desharnais
Sharon L. De Vault
Anthony J. Diana (New York, N.Y. Office)
Thomas W. Dimond
Boise A. Ding (Los Angeles, California Office)
Courtney A. Dinsmore (New York, N.Y. Office)
Michelle V. Dohra
Sean O. Dougherty (New York, N.Y. Office)
Robert M. Dow, Jr.
Kira E. Druyan
Alyssa A. Dudkowski
Lisa A. Dunsky
Christina Egan
Rebecca S. Eisner
Gayle L. Elsner
Grant J. Esposito (New York, N.Y. Office)
Douglas M. Eveleigh
Ryan P. Farley (New York, N.Y. Office)
Vince D. Feder
Deann Kay Feece (Houston, Texas Office)
Gary Feinerman
James E. Ferraioli
Ron D. Franklin (New York, N.Y. Office)
Karen P. Fredericks (New York, N.Y. Office)
Beth Freemal
Gail S. Freeman
Kristin Frey (New York, N.Y. Office)
Leigh Zeising Frishman
Katy Kendall Furton
Francis A. Fuselier (New York, N.Y. Office)
Armando M. Gamboa
Julian P. Gehman (Washington, D.C. Office)
Jennifer Geier
Bruce L. Gelman
Margaret S. Giles (Los Angeles, California Office)
Thomas N. Glushko (New York, N.Y. Office)
Scott B. Golant
Jennifer B. Gold (New York, N.Y. Office)
David M. Goldman (New York, N.Y. Office)
Jeffrey A. Goldman
Sophia Gordon (London, England Office)
Ronald P. Gould
Anthony G. Graham (Los Angeles, California Office)
Carolyn Greenwald (New York, N.Y. Office)
Richard Greta (Los Angeles, California Office)
Eric P. Grossman (Houston, Texas Office)
David S. Gualtieri
Thomas P. Hallinan (New York, N.Y. Office)
Lawrence R. Hamilton
Aaron L. Hammer
Jennifer A. Handa
Mei-Ying Hao
Gayle C. Hanz (Houston, Texas Office)
Donald F. Harmon

ASSOCIATES (Continued)

(See Next Column)

James D. Harrington
George R. Hatzmann (New York, N.Y. Office)
Neville S. Hedley
William R. Herochik
Catherine J. Hertzig (New York, N.Y. Office)
Mark F. Herzinger (New York, N.Y. Office)
Timothy B. Higginson
Daniel G. Hildebrand
David M. Hillman (New York, N.Y. Office)
Matthew B. Hinerfeld
Natalie M. Hiott-Levine (New York, N.Y. Office)
Adam K. Hollander
Christopher B. Horn
Joanna K. Horsnail
Terri L. Hoskins
Matthew C. Houchens
Chadwick A. Hoyt
Brian F. Hynes
Doug E. Ibendahl
Matthew D. Ingber (New York, N.Y. Office)
Tarek Ismail
Valerie-Leila Jaber (New York, N.Y. Office)
Nicola Jackson
William V. Jacobsen, Jr.
Miriam B. Jaffe (Los Angeles, California Office)
John W. Jarrell, Jr. (Washington, D.C. Office)
Jerome M.F. Jauffret (Los Angeles, California Office)
C. Brendan Johnson
Maureen G. Johnson (Los Angeles, California Office)
Steffen N. Johnson
Laura H. Jones (Washington, D.C. Office)
Paul A. Jorissen
Maritoni D. Kane
Jason Kanner (New York, N.Y. Office)
Loan Anh Tran Kao (Houston, Texas Office)
Michael M. Kaplan
Joshua P. Kaufman (New York, N.Y. Office)
Neil T. Kawashima
J. Bradley Keck
Jennifer L. Keegan
Charles S. Kelley (Houston, Texas Office)
Terry D. Kernell (Houston, Texas Office)
Christine A. Kexel
Kimberly B. Kiefer (Washington, D.C. Office)
Jenny Ae-Ru Ko (Los Angeles, California Office)
Carl Richard Kolbet (New York, N.Y. Office)
Anne Marie Konopack
James M. Kunick
Karen L. Kupetz (New York, N.Y. Office)
Michael E. Lackey, Jr. (Washington, D.C. Office)
Chris D. Landgraff
Kelli Lester Lash (Charlotte, North Carolina Office)
Nicholas A. Laveris (New York, N.Y. Office)
Fred Lawson
Brian Kenneth Lee (Washington, D.C. Office)
Edward S. Lee (Washington, D.C. Office)
Stacey N. Lefont (New York, N.Y. Office)
Mary B. Lemuth (Houston, Texas Office)
Bruce H. Levine (Los Angeles, California Office)
Jaimy M. Levine
Lisa L. Levine (Washington, D.C. Office)
James T. Lidbury
Thomas A. Lidbury
Susanne J. Lieu
Marc R. Lisker
Michael A. Loftis (Not admitted in IL)
Joan L. Long
Susan J. Luken (Washington, D.C. Office)
David N. Malinger
Anne Keyes MacIver
Jennifer C. Maloney (Washington, D.C. Office)
Raffi K. Mansourian (Los Angeles, California Office)
Emily W. Mao (Washington, D.C. Office)
Brian J. Massengill
Jennifer May (New York, N.Y. Office)
Douglas E. McCormack (New York, N.Y. Office)
Nerissa A. McGinn
Mark A. Mears (Los Angeles, California Office)
Kenneth J. Merlino
Demetrios G. Metropoulos
Warren Mondschein
Rita W. Morales (Washington, D.C. Office)
Scott A. Morehouse (Washington, D.C. Office)
Allen D. Moreland (New York, N.Y. Office)
Wendy L. Morris (Washington, D.C. Office)
Richard T. Morrison
Scott Mortman (New York, N.Y. Office)
Donna Mulvihill (New York, N.Y. Office)
Trent M. Murch
Sean K. Murphy (Charlotte, North Carolina Office)
D. Michael Murray
John Nadolenco (Los Angeles, California Office)
Miriam R. Nemetz (Washington, D.C. Office)
Jason Neumark
Amy E. Newman
Andrew A. Nicely (Washington, D.C. Office)
Joanna C. Nicholas
Marjorie C. Nicol (Houston, Texas Office)
Nancy V. Nieto (Not admitted in IL)
Kenneth E. Noble
Susan B. Nystrom
Keith F. Oberkfell
Ger P. O'Donnell
Heather L. O'Farrell
Christopher J. Oliver
Michael A. Olsen
Rosaria Vivo Owen
Melanie L. Oxhorn
Mark R. Pacioni
Michael G. Palek (Washington, D.C. Office)
Ronald D. Parisotto (Washington, D.C. Office)
Erick S. Parker
James A. Parker
Trupti S. Patel (New York, N.Y. Office)
James P. Patti
Eileen Penner (Washington, D.C. Office)
Bruce F. Perce
C. Dirk Peterson (Washington, D.C. Office)
Michael C. Petronio (New York, N.Y. Office)
Vytas A. Petrulis (Houston, Texas Office)
Jessica M. Pfeiffer
Kent A. Pflederer
Antonio N. Piccirillo (New York, N.Y. Office)
Jeffrey S. Piell
Julianne M. Plumb
Matthew A. Posthuma
Ashish S. Prasad
Karen L. Prena

ASSOCIATES (Continued)

(See Next Column)

MAYER, BROWN & PLATT—*Continued*

Susan R. Proffitt
Tristan E. Propst (Houston, Texas Office)
Susan Ehrmann Provenzano
Edmund L. Quatmann, Jr.
Maria M. Rabassa (Los Angeles, California Office)
Jeffrey A. Rackow (Washington, D.C. Office)
Christopher M. Read (New York, N.Y. Office)
Michael D. Rechtin, Jr.
Craig E. Reimer
Gary W. Reinbold
Erich G. Rhynhart
Daniel L. Ring
Mark J. Robertson (New York, N.Y. Office)
Sara Ann Rodriguez (Houston, Texas Office)
Walter M. Rogers
Leonard X Rosenberg
Andrew S. Rosenman
Lee H. Rubin (Washington, D.C. Office)
Abigail L. Rudoff
Timothy R. Ryan (Washington, D.C. Office)
Wladek Rzycki
Christina Saber (New York, N.Y. Office)
Adam Sanitt (London, England Office)
Jeffrey W. Sarles
Scott V. Scarpelli
Steven Scesa
Andrew H. Schapiro (New York, N.Y. Office)
Terry Schiff
Curtis W. Schuhmacher (Not admitted in IL)
Peter Schultz
Andrea J. Schwartzman (New York, N.Y. Office)
Drasan R. Scranton (Los Angeles, California Office)
Matthew P. Seeberger (Los Angeles, California Office)
Julie A. Sennello
Alpita A. Shah
Joshua M. Silverstein
Adam C. Sloane (Washington, D.C. Office)
Gilda M. Smart (New York, N.Y. Office)
Diane Green Smith
James R. Smith
Mara Shapiro Smith
Kristin Hart Smith (Washington, D.C. Office)
Robin Whitlock Smith
S. Hayes Smith (New York, N.Y. Office)
Kristin J. Staffanson
Steven G. Steger
Steven Jay Stewart
Nikki Stitt
Kaspar J. Stoffelmayr
James K. Stovall
Kenneth Suh (New York, N.Y. Office)
Michael T. Sullivan
Lily Fu Swenson (Washington, D.C. Office)
Sharon Swingle (Washington, D.C. Office)
Jeffrey P. Taft (Washington, D.C. Office)
Wayne L. Tang
Sonya J. Teague
Stuart E. Thiel
David M. Thimmig
Caroline F. Thomas (New York, N.Y. Office)
Richard J. Timmel
Michael J. Tobak, III
David A. Trapani (New York, N.Y. Office)
Christopher N. Travers (New York, N.Y. Office)
Timothy J. Tyler (Houston, Texas Office)
Angela M. Ulum
Jodi L. Valeri (Washington, D.C. Office)
Lane W. Vanderslice
Jon D. Van Gorp
Aditi Vilswanathan (New York, N.Y. Office)
John J. Voorhees
Hoang Quan Vu (Houston, Texas Office)
Rebecca E. Wacaser
Kyle F. Waldinger
Arthur C. Walker, Jr. (Washington, D.C. Office)
Barbara S. Wang (New York, N.Y. Office)
Guy G. Ward
Jeffrey L. Wasserman (New York, N.Y. Office)
Joseph P. Weber
Lyman C. Welch
David M. Well
Samantha B. Whitehouse
Daniel P. Whitmore
Janet R. Widmaier
Robert J. Wild
Edward H. Williams
Norman R. Williams, II (New York, N.Y. Office)
Gary A. Winters (Washington, D.C. Office)
Craig A. Woods
John Yatchisin, Jr. (New York, N.Y. Office)
Joseph E. Yesutis (Washington, D.C. Office)
Russell R. Young
Veronica L. Young
Patricia Anne Yurchak
Donald P. Zeithaml, Jr.
Scott M. Zemser (New York, N.Y. Office)
Richard G. Ziegler
Alexander B. Zolfaghari (New York, N.Y. Office)
Margarita Zubkus (New York, N.Y. Office)
Rebecca L. Zucker

For full biographical listings, see the Martindale-Hubbell Law Directory

MAYER, FRIEDLICH, SPIESS, TIERNEY, BROWN & PLATT

(See Mayer, Brown & Platt)

MCBRIDE BAKER & COLES (AV)

500 West Madison Street 40th Floor, 60661-2511
Telephone: 312-715-5700
Cable Address: "Chilaw"
Telex: 270258
Telecopier: 312-993-9350
Email: lastname@mbc.com *URL:* http://www.mbc.com
Oakbrook Terrace, Illinois Office: Suite 1000, One Mid America Plaza, 60181-4710.
Telephone: 630-954-2100.
Telecopier: 630-954-2112.

(See Next Column)

MEMBERS OF FIRM

David Ackerman
Henry S. Allen, Jr.
Thomas P. Arden
Andrew R. Basile
Michael J. Boland
Malcolm H. Brooks
Martin J. Campanella
John J. Cresto
Nina J. Fain
Paul D. Frenz
Anthony L. Frink
Andrew R. Gelman
Lola Miranda Hale
Kenneth A. Jenero
Francis L. Keldermans
Thomas J. Kinasz
Patrick W. Kocian
Clifton A. Lake
Richard S. Lauter
Theodore T. Lemberis
Steven R. Lifson
David S. Mann
Elias N. Matsakis
Donald G. Mulack
Carolyn O'Connor Ferry
Morgan J. Ordman
Elizabeth S. Perdue
Robert W. Queeney
Richard A. Redmond
Anne Hamblin Schiave
Robert C. Schnitz
Robert I. Schwimmer
David Shayne
Mark A. Spognardi
Mark J. Steger
William M. Stevens
Steven B. Varick
Michael L. Weissman
Alan S. Wernick
Richard R. Winter
Larry M. Zanger

SENIOR COUNSEL

Lawrence A. Coles, Jr.

OF COUNSEL

Robert O. Case
William J. Cooney
N. A. Jim Giambalvo
Geoffrey G. Gilbert
Evan M. Kjellenberg
G. Gale Roberson, Jr.
Thomas P. Ward
Joseph S. Wright, Jr.

ASSOCIATES

Naomi R. Angel
Marc L. Fogelberg
André C. Frieden
Hillary Ann Frommer
Steffanie N. Garrett
Brian D. Hector
Jerald Holisky
Staci L. Ketay
Mark A. Kromkowski
Rachel N. Lokken
Michael P. Lusk
Micah E. Marcus
Kathleen F. O'Connor
Sarah E. Pace
Charles L. Philbrick
Christopher J. Rosette
George M. Sanders
Todd J. Schneider
Phillip Michael Schreiber
Michele E. Sibley
Paul R. Simons
Peter J. Strand
Jonathan E. Strouse
Jeffrey M. Teske

For full biographical listings, see the Martindale-Hubbell Law Directory

MCFADDEN & DILLON, A PROFESSIONAL CORPORATION (AV)

135 South La Salle Street, Suite 2110, 60603-4402
Telephone: 312-201-8300
Facsimile: 312-201-0535
Email: mcfaddendillonlaw@ameritech.net

Roger J. McFadden
Thomas J. Dillon

Tyrrel J. Penn

For full biographical listings, see the Martindale-Hubbell Law Directory

PETERSON & ROSS (AV)

200 East Randolph Drive, Suite 7300, 60601-6969
Telephone: 312-861-1400
Telecopy: 312-565-0832
Email: www.petersonross.com *URL:* http://www.petersonross.com
New York, N.Y. Office: 33 Whitehall Street, 27th Floor, 10004.
Telephone: 212-820-7700.
Los Angeles, California Office: 333 South Grand Avenue, Suite 1600, 90071-1520.
Telephone: 213-625-3500.
Austin, Texas Office: 101 East Ninth Street, Suite 1000, 78701.
Telephone: 512-472-5587.
London, England Office: 37-39 Lime Street, Fifth Floor, EC3M 7AY.
Telephone: 44-207-929-2411.
San Juan, Puerto Rico Office: Capital Center, Building 1, Penthouse 1, Suite 1206, Arterial Hostos (Hato Rey), 00918.
Telephone: 787-751-8000.
Associated Independent Offices:
A.A. Amador Associates: 1803 Wheelock House, 20 Pedder Street, Central, Hong Kong, C.P.O. Box 468, Hong Kong.
Telephone: 852-2524-2230.
A.A. Amador Associates: 18th Floor Pacific Star Building, Gil Puyat Corner Makati Avenue, Makati City, Philippines.
Telephone: 632-811-5969.

MEMBERS OF FIRM

Walter Henry Eckert (1923-1944)
Walter W. Ross, Jr. (1934-1972)
Abe R. Peterson (1923-1983)
Owen Rall (1933-1985)
Theodore A. Boundas
Norbert J. Wegerzyn
Daniel B. Hales
Joseph J. Hasman
John K. Silk
Walter M. Piecewicz
Geoffrey L. Isaac
Charles D. Thomas
David J. Novotny
Regina K. McCabe
William A. Chittenden, III
Anne Fiedler
John E. Black, Jr.

(See Next Column)

PETERSON & ROSS, *Chicago—Continued*

MEMBERS OF FIRM (Continued)

Larry A. Hoellwarth
Roderick T. Dunne
Donald A. Murday
David T. Burrowes
Michael J. Rosen
R. Nathan Randall
Sean Patrick MacCarthy
Clinton J. Wesolik
Peter F. Lovato, III
Mary Cannon Veed
John Collen

OF COUNSEL

Theodore Joseph Tsoumas
Robert G. Schloerb
J. Robert Geiman
Lawrence X. Pusateri
Robert S. Milnikel
Christopher J. Graham

ASSOCIATES

Serge Adam, Jr.
Rene Robertson Campe
Janice L. Cleary
Dennis B. Condon
Carrie E. Cope
Stefan Roane Dandelles
Laura A. Derouin
Elizabeth Gwynn Doolin
Lee Ann S. Galowich
Adam Goodman
Ellen D. Jenkins
Georgia L. Joyce
Tracy K. Jurusik
Gina L. Macari
Kent Maynard, Jr.
Ross I. Molho
Andrew J. Palmer
Christine K. Pecha
Jill M. Ruby
David F. Schmidt
Heather J. Shields
Jennifer S. Stegmaier
Jennifer L. Sykora
Daniel Walsh Tarpey
Jessica Tovrov

RESIDENT PARTNERS AT LOS ANGELES, CALIFORNIA OFFICE

Robert L. Suomala
Vivian Rigdon Bloomberg
Robert H. Berkes
Barbara S. Hodous
James W. McCord

RESIDENT PARTNERS AT NEW YORK, N.Y. OFFICE

James A. Skarzynski
Alexis J. Rogoski
T. David Ackerman
William M. Billings
John J. Richardson
Ivan J. Dolowich
Karen L. Stuttman

RESIDENT OF COUNSEL AT AUSTIN, TEXAS OFFICE

James L. Nelson

RESIDENT OF COUNSEL AT SAN JUAN, PUERTO RICO

Hector Cuebas Tañon
Harold D. Vicente Colon
Mario R. Oronoz

RESIDENT ASSOCIATES AT LOS ANGELES, CALIFORNIA OFFICE

Katharine M. Arthur
Karl W. Kime
Mark W. Lau
Christine M. Macfarlane
Carmen Santana
Gayle L. Wilder

RESIDENT ASSOCIATES AT NEW YORK, N.Y. OFFICE

Rachel L. Freedman
Christopher J. Keller
Evan Shapiro
Stephanie L. Solomon

For full biographical listings, see the Martindale-Hubbell Law Directory

QUARLES & BRADY LLC (AV)

Citicorp Center, 500 West Madison Street, Suite 3700, 60661-2511
Telephone: 312-715-5000
Fax: 312-715-5155
URL: http://www.quarles.com
Milwaukee, Wisconsin Office: Quarles & Brady LLP, 411 East Wisconsin Avenue, 53202-4497.
Telephone: 414-277-5000.
Fax: 414-271-3552.
Madison, Wisconsin Office: Quarles & Brady LLP, Firstar Plaza, One South Pinckney Street, P.O. Box 2113, 53701-2113.
Telephone: 608-251-5000.
Fax: 608-251-9166.
West Palm Beach, Florida Office: Quarles & Brady LLP, 222 Lakeview Avenue, 4th Floor, 33401.
Telephone: 561-653-5000.
Fax: 561-653-5333.
Naples, Florida Office: Quarles & Brady LLP, Barnett Center, 4501 Tamiami Trail North, Suite 300, 34103-3060.
Telephone: 941-262-5959.
Fax: 941-434-4999.
Phoenix, Arizona Office: Quarles & Brady LLP, One Camelback Building, One East Camelback Road, Suite 400, 85012-1649.
Telephone: 602-230-5500.
Fax: 602-230-5598.

John A. McDonald
Richard L. Horn
Gary H. Kline
Kendall R. Meyer
Thomas A. Polachek
Thomas E. Chomicz
Robert F. Forrer
James J. Gatziolis
Peter A. Sarasek
Leonard S. Shifflett
Janice E. Rodgers
Thomas J. Magill
Alexander Terras
John P. Vail
Douglas R. Hoffman
Stephanie B. Shellenback
Sarah M. Linsley
Richard P. Blessen
John A. Klages
Marie K. Eitrheim
Timothy S. Harris
Todd A. Rowden
Patrick J. Bitterman

(See Next Column)

David B. Altman
Kurt T. Temple
Panna P. Patel
Joel A. Brodsky
Jason N. Kaplan
D. Scott Watson
James Y. Wu
Jessamyn L. Bagley

For full biographical listings, see the Martindale-Hubbell Law Directory

ROOKS, PITTS AND POUST (AV)

10 South Wacker Drive, Suite 2300, 60606
Telephone: 312-876-1700
Fax: 312-876-1155
Lisle, Illinois Office: 4200 Commerce Court, Suite 300.
Telephone: 630-245-0400.
Facsimile: 630-245-0140.
Joliet, Illinois Office: 111 North Ottawa Street.
Telephone: 815-727-4511.
Facsimile: 815-727-1586.
Winnetka, Illinois Office: 560 Green Bay Road.
Telephone: 847-441-5615.
Fax: 847-441-9367.

MEMBERS OF FIRM

Jay A. Lipe
Ray F. Drexler
Arthur I. Gould
Robert J. Baron
Stephen E. Sward
David R. Abell
John J. Blasi
James H. Ihrke
Wayne F. Plaza
Terrence E. Kiwala
George N. Gilkerson, Jr.
Terrence J. Madden
John J. Mangan
Frank C. Rowland
Fred R. McMorris
James D. Grumley
Ian M. Sherman
Jeffrey M. Dalebroux
Michael C. Borders
Geoffrey A. Bryce
Terrence M. Burns
Richard J. Kavanagh
Lee T. Hettinger
Mark W. Weisbard
David J. Bressler
Thomas R. Hill
Thomas B. Cassidy
Patricia Cari Nowak
Marc D. Ginsberg
Robert R. Gorbold
Michael F. Sexton
Clyde O. Bowles, Jr.
Bruce L. Goldsmith
Daniel V. Kinsella
Marc A. Primack
Glenn Z. Hering
Michael Gahan
George J. Vosicky
Janet A. Stiven
Richard W. Schumacher
Charles A. Le Moine
J. Barrett Long
Karen Wilson Howard
Joan D. Lindauer
Harry N. Arger
Paul A. Michalik
Michael R. Stiff
Edward P. Dismukes
Scott M. Hardek
Nick Marsico

Laura Marie Callahan
Matthew W. Campbell
Christopher F. Dekker
Gwen M. Geraghty
Pamela Davis Gorcowski
Maureen J. Hanlon
Ellen D. Holzman
Carolyn J. Jones
Lisa S. Kass
Bryan Kopman
Lynn K. Landman
John Lipinsky
James W. McConkey
David L. Miller
Daniel M. Noland
Stephanie J. Simmons
Kathy M. Sons
Cheryl A. Warzynski
Richard L. Williams

COUNSEL

Eugene H. Ruark

OF COUNSEL

Henry L. Pitts
William W. Fullagar
John G. Poust
D. Glenn Ofsthun
Jerome N. Groark
Timothy J. Groark
Arnold A. Silvestri
James L. Donnelly
John P. Hanna
H. Sam Onoda
Mark S. Anderson
Jung Y. Lowe

For full biographical listings, see the Martindale-Hubbell Law Directory

ROSENTHAL AND SCHANFIELD, PROFESSIONAL CORPORATION (AV)

Suite 4620, 55 East Monroe Street, 60603
Telephone: 312-236-5622
Telecopier: 312-236-7274

David M. Alin
Francis A. Beninati
Martin K. Blonder
Marvin Cohn
Cheryl J. Colston
James M. Dash
I. Walter Deitch
James A. Field
Barbara A. Gimbel
Jay Russell Goldberg
David A. Golin
Meanith Huon
William H. Kelly, Jr.
Stephen P. Kikoler
Ira M. Levin
Joel C. Levin
David Manjarres
Gregory R. Meeder
Howard L. Mocerf
Henry M. Morris
Gerald B. Mullin
Joseph R. Podlewski, Jr.
Lester Rosen
Robert O. Rosenman
William P. Rosenthal
Leonard Schanfield (1921-1990)
Barry E. Semer
Mark L. Shapiro

(See Next Column)

ROSENTHAL AND SCHANFIELD PROFESSIONAL CORPORATION—*Continued*

Charles R. Staley	Mary Prus Wasik
Blooma Stark	Stanley R. Weinberger
Michael B. Viner	Thomas M. White

OF COUNSEL

Richard E. Friedman	Monte Viner

For full biographical listings, see the Martindale-Hubbell Law Directory

ROSS & HARDIES (AV)

A Partnership including Professional Corporations
Suite 2500, 150 North Michigan Avenue, 60601
Telephone: 312-558-1000
Telecopier: 312-750-8600
URL: http://www.rosshardies.com
New York, N.Y. Office: 65 East 55th Street, 10022.
Telephone: 212-421-5555.
Telecopier: 212-421-5682.
Washington, D.C. Office: 888 - 16th Street, N.W., 20006.
Telephone: 202-296-8600.
Telecopier: 202-296-8791.

MEMBERS OF FIRM

CHICAGO OFFICE

William P. O'Keefe (1929-1979)	Larry R. Goldstein
Clarence H. Ross (1950-1981)	Leslie D. Locke
Richard F. Babcock (1957-1993)	Susan Grob Lichtenfeld
Melvin A. Hardies (1950-1994)	Monica A. Carroll
Keith I. Parsons (1965-1996)	Elizabeth West Speidel
David F. Sterling	Susan M. Mongillo
Robert J. Pristave *	Daniel P. Hogan
Duane A. Feurer	Robert T. Zielinski
Richard J. Rappaport	Jeffrey E. Rogers
Robert E. Wangard	Jacquelyn F. Kidder
Michael H. King *	Patrick E. Brady
James K. Toohey	Arnold E. Grant
William D. Serritella	Kurt H. Feuer
Richard E. Lieberman	Ira P. Goldberg
Robert W. Kleinman	David L. Rieser
Keith Philip Schoeneberger	Sean M. Sullivan
Paul A. Lutter	Keith A. Dorman
Lawrence R. Samuels	Patricia K. Smoots
James T. Harrington	Jeffrey A. Berman
Barbara Baran	Janice K. Hamblin
Carol Berlin Manzoni	Brian A. Sher
James B. Riley, Jr.	Gail Chaney Kalinich
Richard J. Mason *	Michael C. Cook
Scott Hodes	Steven R. Smith
Gary L. Starkman	Darryl R. Davidson
Timothy C. Klenk	David S. Guin
C. Frederick LeBaron, Jr.	Jerome K. Bowman
Donald C. Pasulka	John P. McCabe
Jonathan G. Bunge *	Darren J. Hunter
Richard T. Greenberg	John L. Senica
James J. Casey	Ginger G. Mayer
Jules I. Crystal	Joel H. Spitz
Peter J. Valeta	Beth A. Sansiper
Scott Becker	Mary Clare Bonaccorsi
Richard A. Sirus	George J. Spathis

Kimberly J. Kannensohn

OF COUNSEL

Joann Tansey Angarola	David N. McBride
Karl Berolzheimer	Bruce J. McWhirter
Jerome T. Burke	William J. Winger
Steve Lawrence	Walker Winter
Louis W. Levit *	Maurice P. Wolk

ASSOCIATES

Tammy L. Adkins	Stephen B. Mead
Cintra D. Bentley	Peter A. Milianti
Elizabeth A. Birt	Mary Margaret Moore
Elizabeth M. Bradshaw	Andrew F. Nelson
Robert L. Carter	Helmer J. Nelson
Christopher T. Considine (Not admitted in IL)	Katherine Ann Nino
	Michael R. Phillips
Marcelo N. Corpuz, III	Christian M. Poland
Scott P. Downing	Mark R. Raymond
Thomas D. Drescher	Mari Yamamoto Regnier
Audra L. Dulksnys	Sharon P. Riley
Matthew S. Elvin	Wendy L. Rubas
Jonathan I. Flaum	Edward W. Schwartz
Kara M. Friedman	Joshua B. Silverman
Lisa Allen Golant	Kelly S. Simenson
Cara M. Houck	Caroline S. Soodek
Byoung Soo Kim	Anne T. Stinneford
James A. Lawson	Eric J. Tanquilut
Emily H. Liebers	Jason M. Torf
Mary Therese Link	Katie Watson
Amy B. Manning	Charles W. Wesselhoft
Joseph A. McQuade	Peter N. Witty

(See Next Column)

ASSOCIATES (Continued)

Spencer R. Wood	Jay A. Yalowitz
William J. Wortel	Paul C. Ziebert

William F. Zieske

*Professional Corporation

For full biographical listings, see the Martindale-Hubbell Law Directory

ROTHSCHILD, BARRY & MYERS (AV)

A Partnership including Professional Corporations
Suite 3900, 55 West Monroe Street, 60603-5012
Telephone: 312-372-2345
FAX: 312-372-2350
Email: rbm01@wwa.com

MEMBERS OF FIRM

Norman J. Barry (P.C.) (1921-1998)	Roger J. Guerin
	Michael J. Wall
Edward I. Rothschild (P.C.)	Daniel Cummings
William G. Myers (P.C.)	Christopher G. Walsh, Jr.
Melvin I. Mishkin	Kenneth P. Taube
John J. Coffey, III	Jonathan E. Rothschild
Joseph P. Della Maria, Jr.	Alan S. Madans

Kevin J. Moore

ASSOCIATES

Mary T. Meegan	Robin K. Powers

John D. Silk

For full biographical listings, see the Martindale-Hubbell Law Directory

SACHNOFF & WEAVER, LTD. (AV)

30 South Wacker Drive, 29th Floor, 60606
Telephone: 312-207-1000
Telecopier: 312-207-6400
URL: http://www.sachnoff.com

J. Todd Arkebauer	Arnold A. Pagniucci
Frank D. Ballantine	Jonathan S. Quinn
Jack L. Block	Michael D. Richman
David C. Bohan	Brian D. Roche
Gary S. Caplan	Lance R. Rodgers
Paul D. Carman	James A. Rolfes
Stuart J. Chanen	Barry S. Rosen
Michael H. Cramer	Carolyn Hope Rosenberg
Charles E. Dobrusin	Harry B. Rosenberg
Stewart Dolin	Ellis B. Rosenzweig
William E. Doran	Robert A. Roth
Joel S. Feldman	Lowell E. Sachnoff
Roselyn L. Friedman	Joel R. Schaider
Jeffrey T. Gilbert	Bradley S. Schmarak
Neil Greenbaum	Charles P. Schulman
Misty S. Gruber	Jeffrey A. Schumacher
Andrew Hartman	Marshall Seeder
Seth M. Hemming	Clifford J. Shapiro
Austin L. Hirsch	Duane F. Sigelko
Cynthia Jared	Richard G. Smolev
Marc Kieselstein	Susan D. Snyder
Jeffrey L. London	Sheldon L. Solow
Michael A. LoVallo	Abraham J. Stern
Michael S. Mandell	J. Samuel Tenenbaum
Frances Meehan	Edward V. Walsh, III
Steven A. Miller	William N. Weaver, Jr.
Douglas R. Newkirk	Jeffrey B. Whitt
William A. O'Connor	Sarah R. Wolff

Richard K. Wray

Carey L. Bartell	Siobhan McCambridge
Sharon M. Buccino	James S. Montague
H. Brian Centeno	John W. Moynihan
Melissa A. Coughlin	Rachelle M. Niedzwiecki
David C. Fuechtman	Matthew J. O'Hara
W. Robert Gold	Margaret M. Pasulka
Michelle Moore Jackson	Matthew J. Petersen
Kristin R. James	Henry Pietrkowski
Jonathan T. Kamin	Neil B. Posner
Andrew Kornreich	Marie R. Quinn
Lisa J. Krasberg	Genita C. Robinson
Michael P. Lee	Bina Sanghavi
Lisa M. Madigan	Mary Lou Zwick

OF COUNSEL

Jeffrey E. Altshul	Judith Rea Heck
Jules G. Cogan	Ernest D. Simon
Clarke M. Gillespie, III	George A. Vinyard

For full biographical listings, see the Martindale-Hubbell Law Directory

Chicago—Continued

SCHIFF HARDIN & WAITE (AV)

A Partnership including Professional Corporations
Attorneys Serving Business Since 1864
6600 Sears Tower, 60606
Telephone: 312-258-5500; Facsimile: 312-258-5600.
URL: http://www.schiffhardin.com
Washington, D.C. Office: 1101 Connecticut Avenue, N.W.
Telephone: 202-778-6400.
Facsimile: 202-778-6460.
Merrillville, Indiana Office: 8585 Broadway, Suite 842.
Telephone: 219-738-3820.
Facsimile: 219-738-3826.
Dublin, Ireland Office: 34 Fitzwilliam Square.
Telephone: +353-1-662-8080.
Facsimile: +353-1-661-1053.

MEMBERS OF FIRM

Thomas W. Abendroth
John F. Adams
Barry S. Alberts
David F. Allen (P.C.)
John A. Bannon
Lauralyn G. Bengel
Katharine L. Bensen
Jill B. Berkeley
Scott Bieber
Lawrence Block (P.C.)
Stephen J. Bonebrake
Daniel S. Brennan
Felice M. Bressler
Harmon A. Brown
James E. Brown
Kevin J. Byrne
Robert D. Campbell
Joseph A. Cancila, Jr.
Heidi Dalenberg
Paul E. Dengel
Patricia Dondanville
Stephen J. Dragich
Marci A. Eisenstein
James F. X. Fahy (Resident at Dublin, Ireland Office)
Peter V. Fazio, Jr.
J. Mark Fisher
Charles D. Fox, IV
Steven D. Friedland
Mark C. Friedlander
James P. Gaughan
Eugene J. Geekie, Jr.
Lawrence M. Gill
Patricia N. Gillman
Stuart L. Goodman
Walter C. Greenough
Paul Edwin Greenwalt, III
David A. Grossberg
William M. Hannay
Frederick L. Hartmann, Jr.
Carrie Jankauer Hightman
David R. Hodgman
Andrea L. Horne
Allan Horwich
Richard J. Hoskins
Lawrence H. Jacobson
Janet M. Johnson
James M. Kane
Andrew A. Kling
Brian D. Kluever
Aphrodite Kokolis
Robert E. Kolek
Kevin L. Kolton
Aaron J. Kramer
Joseph J. Krasovec, III
Daniel L. Kraus
Donald J. Kreger
Ruth E. Krugly
Ty D. Laurie
Shirley M. Lukitsch
Thomas P. Luning
Paul M. Lurie
Owen E. MacBride
Neal A. Mancoff
Paul C. Marengo
Catherine M. Masters
Wayne A. McCoy
James R. McDaniel
Michael L. Meyer
William E. Meyer, Jr.
Robert J. Minkus
Jane Ellen Montgomery
Paula J. Morency
Ralph A. Morris
Gary L. Mowder (P.C.)
Wendy L. Nutt
Paul B. O'Flaherty (P.C.)
Joseph J. O'Hara, Jr.
Roger Pascal
Thomas J. Pauloski
Charles H.R. Peters
Guenther M. Philipp (P.C.)
Scott E. Pickens
Robert R. Pluth, Jr.
Lori Ann Prokes
Carol R. Prygrosky
Thomas B. Quinn
Robert John Regan
Robert H. Riley
Burton R. Rissman (P.C.)
Robert S. Rivkin
Kenneth M. Roberts
Gabriel M. Rodriguez
Lynn E. Rzonca
Ronald S. Safer
Henry W. Sledz, Jr.
Patricia Costello Slovak
Frederick J. Sperling
Debra L. Stetter
Linda K. Stevens
Patricia J. Thompson
Clay A. Tillack
Scott C. Tomassi
Darren M. R. Van Puymbrouck
James M. Van Vliet, Jr.
John J. Voortman (P.C.)
Thomas R. Wechter
Bruce P. Weisenthal
Robert B. Wilcox, Jr.
Ronald Wilder
Jay Williams
Helen T. Wilson
James B. Wilson (P.C.)
Lisa Winger
Mark C. Zaander
Sheldon A. Zabel
Jason A. Zellers
Christopher J. Zinski

SENIOR COUNSEL

Dean C. Cameron
Milton H. Cohen
W. Donald McSweeney
Mitchell S. Rieger
Keith Shay
Norman Waite

OF COUNSEL

Sokyoung Kevin An (Not admitted in IL)
Bruce Jay Baker
Howard R. Barron
James A. Clark
John T. Hayes
Lael F. Johnson
Robert A. Monk
Paul K. Rhoads

STAFF ATTORNEY

Brenda N. Broderick
Theodora P. Karnegis
Margaret A. Nagela

(See Next Column)

ASSOCIATES

William Macy Aguiar
David H. Anderson
Lawrence C. Bachman
Darren C. Baker
Svetlana V. Bekman
Steven C. Benz
David C. Blickenstaff
Chris L. Bollinger
Kristen E Brown
Lisa A. Brown
Jeffrey J. Bushofsky
Jennifer M. Cerven
Christine Chang
Patricia M. De Simone
Alison M. Duffy
Gregory M. Duhl
Matthew J. Fischer
Eric L. Fletcher
Jonathan P. Friedland
Julie J. Furer
Matthew G. Galo
Leslie R. Goldberg
Caroline Goodson
Miriam Hallbauer
Michael J. Hanahan
Stacie R. Hartman
Alana L. Helverson
Thomas J. Henehan
David A. Howard
Michael J. Huft
Kevin B. Hynes
Steve E. Isaacs
David Jacobs
Andrew Jarzyna
Jason W. Joseph
Kim A. Kamin
Paula M. Ketcham
Susan C. Kim
Susan Kurzydlo Koci
Mark J. Kosminskas
George C. Koutouras
Melissa J. Krasnow
Neil Lloyd
Michael D. Lurie
Susan J. Lynch
John C. Martin
David P. McHugh
Richard T. Miller
Francis P. Morrissey
Kathy Hoffmann Murphy
Olufemi F. Nicoli
Kevin P. O'Brien
Micah R. Onixt
Scott T. Piering (Not admitted in IL)
Paul A. Rahe (Not admitted in IL)
Laura M. Ricketts
Lauren G. Robinson
Christopher B. Schneider
Neil B. Solomon
Robin M. Spencer
Brenna Binns Stotter
Michael F. Tomasek
Christine Greener Uhlig
Robert W. Unikel
Sean Venden
Carlos Manuel Vigil
Jennifer S. Vollen
James D. Weier, Jr.
Laura B. Weinberg
Kathryn D. Zalewski (Not admitted in IL)

WASHINGTON, D.C. OFFICE
RESIDENT PARTNERS

Edward J. Finn
Barbara K. Heffernan
Andrew M. Klein
Drexel D. Journey
Gearold L. Knowles
Howard L. Kramer
André E. Owens

RESIDENT OF COUNSEL

John W. Glendening, Jr.
Edwin S. Rockefeller
John S. Schmid

RESIDENT ASSOCIATE

Debra Ann Palmer

RESIDENT COUNSEL

M. Thompson Rattray

MERRILLVILLE, INDIANA OFFICE
RESIDENT PARTNER

Peter L. Hatton

SENIOR STAFF ATTORNEY

Gary A. Kruse

For full biographical listings, see the Martindale-Hubbell Law Directory

---

SCHWARTZBERG, BARNETT & COHEN (AV)

55 West Monroe Street, 2400 Xerox Centre, 60603-5040
Telephone: 312-726-3555
Fax: 312-726-6299
Cable Address: "Justice"
Email: sb&c@twty.chi.il.us

MEMBERS OF FIRM

Ralph M. Schwartzberg (1939-1975)
Mark T. Barnett (1939-1970)
Hugh J. Schwartzberg
Benjamin H. Cohen

For full biographical listings, see the Martindale-Hubbell Law Directory

---

SEYFARTH, SHAW, FAIRWEATHER & GERALDSON (AV)

55 E. Monroe Street, Suite 4200, 60603-5803
Telephone: 312-346-8000
Facsimile: 312-269-8869
Cable Address: "Interlex"
International Telex: 25222
Email: mailbox@seyfarth.com *URL:* http://www.seyfarth.com
Washington, D.C. Office: 815 Connecticut Avenue, N.W.
Telephone: 202-463-2400.
Facsimile: 202-828-5393.
Los Angeles, California Office: 2029 Century Park East.
Telephone: 310-277-7200.
Facsimile: 310-201-5219.
New York, N.Y. Office: 1270 Avenue of the Americas, Suite 2500.
Telephone: 212-218-5500.
Facsimile: 212-218-5526.

(See Next Column)

SEYFARTH, SHAW, FAIRWEATHER & GERALDSON—*Continued*

San Francisco, California Office: Suite 2900, 101 California Street.
Telephone: 415-397-2823.
Facsimile: 415-397-8549.
Sacramento, California Office: 400 Capitol Mall, Suite 2350.
Telephone: 916-448-0159.
Facsimile: 916-558-4839.
Houston, Texas Office: 700 Louisiana Street, Suite 3850.
Telephone: 713-225-2300.
Facsimile: 713-225-2340.
Atlanta, Georgia Office: One Atlantic Center, 1201 West Peachtree Street, Suite 5050.
Telephone: 404-892-6412.
Facsimile: 404-892-7056.
Boston, Massachusetts Office: 101 Federal Street, Suite 2500.
Telephone: 617-737-1900.
Facsimile: 617-737-6139.
Brussels, Belgium Office: Avenue Louise 500, Box 8.
Telephone: (32) (2) 647. 60. 25.
Fax: (32) (2) 640. 70. 71.
Affiliated Law Firm:
Matray, Matray et Hallet, 34/24, Boulevard Frère-Orban, 4000, Liege, Belgium. Telephone: (32) (41) 52 70 68.
Telex: macoha 42330.
Telecopier: (32) (41) 52 08 57.

MEMBERS OF FIRM

John H. Anderson
James Baird
Edward W. Bergmann
Rody P. Biggert
Daniel M. Blouin
Michael E. Blount
Eric E. Boyd
Gregory K. Brown
Jerome F. Buch
James A. Burstein
Philip V. Carter (Retired)
Mark A. Casciari
Rose Marie J. Chidichimo
Brent I. Clark
R. Theodore Clark, Jr.
Theodore E. Cornell III
Douglas A. Darch
Thomas G. Dent
Lawrence C. DiNardo
Paul F. Donahue
William J. Fairbanks
Owen Fairweather (1913-1987)
Brenda Hofman Feis
Fredric H. Fischer
Elizabeth Pfeiler Foley
Joan E. Gale
Raymond I. Geraldson (Retired)
Jay A. Gitles
Timothy F. Haley
Amy Hartman
Valerie J. Hoffman
Charles C. Jackson
Eugene Jacobs
Jeffrey Jahns
Carl E. Johnson
Robert H. Joyce (Retired)
Frederick M. Kaplan
Gary S. Kaplan
Joel H. Kaplan
Edward J. Karlin
Jeffrey C. Kauffman
Raymond J. Kelly, Jr.
Young Kim
Carl R. Klein
Alvin L. Kruse
Andrew R. Laidlaw
Richard B. Lapp
Dixie L. Laswell
Christopher A. Lause
Bart A. Lazar
Howard J. Levine
Michael R. Levinson
Mark A. Lies, II
Ronald L. Lipinski
Bradford L. Livingston
Robert C. Long
Walter P. Loomis (Retired)
Thomas D. Lupo
Richard M. Lyon (Retired)
Robert E. Maciorowski
Marcia Andersen Mahoney
Condon A. McGlothlen
Ellen E. McLaughlin
Kristin Edell Michaels
Robert J. Mignin
Philip A. Miscimarra
Camille A. Olson
Jeryl Olson
John J. O'Malley
James P. Osick
Robert J. Paley
Gus A. Paloian
Thomas H. Peckham
Andrew H. Perellis
Thomas J. Piskorski
J. Stephen Poor
John W. Powers
Keith A. Reed
Burton X. Rosenberg
Jeffrey K. Ross
David J. Rowland
Michael J. Rybicki
Jeremy P. Sackmann
David A. Saunders
John S. Schauer
Ray J. Schoonhoven (Retired)
James A. Schraidt
William P. Schurgin
Kathleen R. Schwappach
Henry E. Seyfarth (1908-1991)
Lee C. Shaw (Retired)
Jeremy P. Sherman
Gerald D. Skoning
Robert J. Smith, Jr.
Theodore C. Stamatakos
David S. Stone
Joseph S. Turner
Robert B. Ulrich
Alan L. Unikel
Alexander S. Vesselinovitch
Michael A. Warner
Robert F. Weber
David M. Weiner
John T. Weise (Retired)
Thomas A. Witt
Peter C. Woodford
Joseph E. Wyse (Retired)
Richard Demarest Yant
Sandra P. Zemm

OF COUNSEL

Frank L. Butler
Philip L. Comella
Carrie H. Clark
Diane V. Dygert
James B. Fadim
Kathryn Hamilton Fink
R. Thomas Howell, Jr.
Peter J. Kelly
Andi S. Kenney
Daniel A. Lukas
Barbara K. Lundergan
Carol M. Merchasin (Not admitted in IL)
Edward B. Miller
Cynthia C. Mooney
Richard D. Ostrow
Eugene L. Resnick
James C. Shanley
Kimberly A. Sipes-Early
Mark H. Sokolsky

(See Next Column)

ASSOCIATES

Donald L. Abraham
Sari M. Alamuddin
David S. Baffa
Deborah A. Borst
Paul R. Brockmeyer
Jennifer L. Browning
Anthony B. Byergo
Rachel F. Calabro
Danielle M. Calucchia
Scott A. Carlson
Stephen A. Carter
James A. Casey
Stacey Loftus Cohen
Cassandra L. Curry
James L. Curtis
Deborah S. Davidson
Gregory M. Davis
Christopher J. DeGroff
Joshua L. Ditelberg
Paul S. Drizner
William F. Dugan
Hillary A. Ebach
Anamaria Elejalde
William J. Factor
Jennifer Kelly Fardy
Raymond M. Fernando
Noah Finkel
Robert P. Flanagan
Ana M. Flynn
Kyle G. French
Jeffrey D. Friedman
Susan F. Gallagher
Timothy J. Gerend
Beth T. Golub
Michael R. Gotzler
James Patrick Hanlon
Yvette Heintzelman
Patricia L. Hubbard
Robert L. Jackson III
Sheldon Leigh Jeter
Mary Kay Klimesh
John J. Koenigsknecht
Deborah A. Kop
Ronald J. Kramer
Julie E. La Eace
Daniel F. Lanciloti
Kenneth R. Landis, Jr.
Jill Leka
Laura A. Lindner
Michelle K. Mellinger
Angela Mersch
David E. Metz
Peter C. Miller
Steve Allen Miller
Ian H. Morrison
Elizabeth Nau
Stephen C. Newman
Michael Ted Novy
Christopher E. Paetsch
Gerald L. Pauling, II
Jonathan A. Pearl
James J. Powers
Allegra R. Rich
Theresa A. Robbins-Shea
Marya Savich
Rhiannon E. Schmieg
Robert J. Sell
Dawn E. Sellstrom
Joy Sellstrom
Margaret A. Sewell
John P. Sieger
William G. Skalitzky
Susannah A. Smetana
Jeffrey Srulovitz
David G. Stejkowski
Phillip B. Straub
Michele S. Suggs
Elaine M. Taussig
Shawn Van Asdale
Joshua Reed Van Kampen
Thomas A. Volz
Jill S. Vorobiev
Michael D. Wexler
Jean M. Wilson
James M. Wyman
Miles A. Zvi

For full biographical listings, see the Martindale-Hubbell Law Directory

SIDLEY & AUSTIN (AV)

A Partnership including Professional Corporations
One First National Plaza, 60603
Telephone: 312-853-7000
Telecopier: 312-853-7036
URL: http://www.sidley.com/
Dallas, Texas Office: 717 North Harwood, Suite 3400, 75201.
Telephone: 214-981-3300.
Telecopier: 214-981-3400.
London, England Office: 1 Threadneedle Street, EC2R 8AW.
Telephone: 011-44-171-360-3600.
Telecopier: 011-44-171-626-7937.
Los Angeles, California Office: 555 W. Fifth Street, 90013.
Telephone: 213-896-6000.
Telecopier: 213-896-6600.
New York, New York Office: 875 Third Avenue, 10022.
Telephone: 212-906-2000.
Telecopier: 212-906-2021.
Singapore Office: 6 Battery Road, #38-01A, Singapore 049909.
Telephone: 011-65-230-3900.
Facsimile: 011-65-230-3939.
Tokyo, Japan Office: Taisho Seimei Hibiya Building, 7th Floor, 9-1, Yurakucho, 1-Chome, Chiyoda-Ku, 100.
Telephone: 011-81-3-3218-5900.
Facsimile: 011-891-3-3218-5922.
Washington, D.C. Office: 1722 Eye Street, N.W., 20006.
Telephone: 202-736-8000.
Telecopier: 202-736-8711.
Shanghai, China Office: Room F2-G, 19/F Jiushi, Renaissance Mansion, 918 Middle Huai Hai Road, Shanghai 200020.
Telephone: 86.21.6415.6269.
Fax: 86.21.6415.6270.
Hong Kong Office: Two Exchange Square, Suite 3403-5, Central Hong Kong.
Telephone: 852.2901.3800.
Fax: 852.2901.3850.

PARTNERS

Hugh A. Abrams
Anthony J. Aiello
Thomas W. Albrecht
Geraldine M. Alexis
Julie O'Donnell Allen
Gerald A. Ambrose
Gerald L. Angst
Virginia L. Aronson
Frederic J. Artwick
Richard W. Astle
Larry A. Barden
J. Robert Barr
Susan T. Bart
Sara Elizabeth Bartlett
Frank V. Battle, Jr.
William H. Baumgartner, Jr.

(See Next Column)

SIDLEY & AUSTIN, *Chicago—Continued*

PARTNERS (Continued)

Larry D. Berning
H. Bruce Bernstein
Stephan V. Beyer
Alan P. Bielawski
Jack R. Bierig
Kevin F. Blatchford
Mark B. Blocker
John R. Box
David J. Boyd
Thomas P. Brown
Willis R. Buck, Jr.
James B. Burns
James N. Cahan
Stephen C. Carlson
Walter C. Carlson
David W. Carpenter
Patrick S. Casey
Thomas K. Cauley, Jr.
Richard A. Cederoth
Linton J. Childs
Paul L. Choi
James E. Clark
Michael A. Clark
Richard G. Clemens
Thomas A. Cole
James F. Conlan
William F. Conlon
Philip J. Crihfield
Michael W. Davis
Tracy D. Daw
William S. DeCarlo
James C. Dechene
Wilbur C. Delp, Jr. *
William G. Dickett
Beth J. Dickstein
J. Douglas Donenfeld
Michael P. Doss
Charles W. Douglas
Lory Barsdate Easton
Maja Campbell Eaton
Joseph S. Ehrman *
Nathan P. Eimer
Steven J. Ellison
Mary Beth Fahrney
Robert A. Ferencz
Bradford L. Ferguson
D. Cameron Findlay
Stephen P. Fitzell
Mary Patricia Flood
Robert P. Freeman
Todd D. Freer
Gregory H. Furda
John N. Gallo
John M. George, Jr.
Brian J. Gold
Michael L. Gold
William C. Golden
Alan L. Goldman
Andrew L. Goldstein
Sara J. Gourley
David F. Graham
Mark I. Greenberg
Jon M. Gregg
Craig A. Griffith
Scott E. Gross
Pamela R. Hanebutt
James A. Hardgrove
Holly A. Harrison
Joseph H. Harrison, Jr.
Janet E. Henderson
Scott J. Heyman
James W. Hitzeman
Kevin J. Hochberg
Michael G. Hron
Lawrence H. Hunt, Jr.
DeVerille A. Huston
Rick L. Jett
Pran Jha
David B. Johnson
Matthew E. Johnson
Linzey D. Jones, Jr.
Richard B. Kapnick
Timothy E. Kapshandy
Jim L. Kaput
Mark L. Kaufmann
Gerard D. Kelly
Gina B. Kennedy
William D. Kerr
Michael J. Kinn
Lawrence I. Kipperman
Jordan A. Klein
Andrew G. Klevorn
Shalom L. Kohn
Kiplund R. Kolkmeier
Jeffrey G. Kraft
Bryan Krakauer
Laurence D. Lasky
Brandon D. Lawniczak
Christine A. Leahy
Laura L. Leonard
John G. Levi
William F. Lloyd
James R. Looman
Frederick C. Lowinger
Robert J. Maganuco
Robert A. Malstrom
James L. Marovitz
Prentice H. Marshall, Jr.
R. Eden Martin
Henry L. Mason III
Elizabeth K. McCloy
John M. McDonough
Thomas M. McMahon
Scott Mendeloff
Michael I. Miller
Paul D. Monson
George L. Mullin
Jodie L. Nedeau
Joseph H. Nesler
Mary C. Niehaus
William J. Nissen
Lawrence J. Nyhan
Richard J. O'Brien, Jr.
John M. O'Hare
Robert M. Olian
Richard F. O'Malley, Jr.
Bridget R. O'Neill
Dennis V. Osimitz
Anastasia Polek O'Brien
David T. Pritikin
Imad I. Qasim
John M. Rafkin
Richard D. Raskin
Marc E. Raven
Anne E. Rea
Sarah J. Read
Thomas D. Rein
Albert Ritchie
Kathleen L. Roach
Ellen S. Robbins
Richard E. Robbins
Thomas A. Roberts
Martin F. Robinson
Jeffrey S. Rothstein
Priscilla E. Ryan
Thomas F. Ryan
Alfred N. Sacha
David R. Sawyier
David M. Schiffman
Michael R. Schlessinger
J. Andrew Schlickman
Eugene A. Schoon
Charles E. Schrank
Andrew H. Shaw
Stewart R. Shepherd
Michael S. Sigal
John P. Simon
Mary Jacobs Skinner
Lee M. Smolen
William M. Sneed
Scott C. Solberg
Sharp Sorensen
David M. Stahl
Stanley B. Stallworth
Debra J. Stanek
Jeffrey C. Steen
Philip P. Steptoe III
Gary B. Stern
James R. Stinehart
James R. Stinson
Susan A. Stone
Sheila A. Sundvall
Steven Sutherland
Paul A. Svoboda
Thomas E. Swaney
Michael J. Sweeney
Byron F. Taylor
Nancy A. Temple
Dale E. Thomas
Stephen P. Thomas

PARTNERS (Continued)

(See Next Column)

Jeffrey R. Tone
John W. Treece
Constantine L. Trela, Jr.
Sherry S. Treston
Howard J. Trienens *
Frank B. Vanker
Paul E. Veith
R. Todd Vieregg *
Deirdre M. Von Moltke
Roger A. Vree
James F. Warchall
Melville W. Washburn
Robert R. Watson
Susan A. Weber
Lyman W. Welch
James S. Whitehead
Douglas H. Williams
Latham Williams
Clyde F. Willian
Robert R. Wootton
David J. Zampa
Bruce M. Zessar
Jay H. Zimbler

COUNSEL

Frank L. Bixby *
James J. Carroll
Katherine J. D'Amaro
Carol A. Doyle
Neil Flanagin
Lynn D. Fleisher
Douglas F. Fuson
Alan Gabbay
Donald J. Gralen
Lisa A. Hausten
John A. Heller
David R. Hill
Edward P. Kenney
Sharon L. King
Roger F. Lewis
Thomas W. Merrill
Newton N. Minow *
Thomas H. Morsch *
Jean Marie R. Pechette
Jules M. Perlberg *
Randal C. Picker
William P. Richmond *
John C. Williams *

ASSOCIATES

Chris E. Abbinante
Richard E. Aderman
Suresh T. Advani
Gabriel Aizenberg
Frank E. Arado
Laurice Z.B. Arroyo
Jon A. Ballis
Janet E. Bauman
Michael D. Belsley
Kristen M. Benson
Sandip K. Beri
Michael D. Bess
James B. Biery
Donald E. Bingham
Suzanne M. Bish
Matthew C. Blickensderfer
Rachel M. Blum
Ann Marie Bredin
Robert E. Bull
James L. Carey
Mary Vozzola Carroll
Paul S. Caruso
Russell E. Cass
Marc A. Cavan
Mark J. Cavanaugh
Denise M. Chan
Edmond E. Chang
Nancy Y. Chu
Lisa M. Cipriano
Matthew A. Clemente
James G. Clessuras
Dennis M. Coghlan
Laura J. Cole
Erica J. Conlon
David E. Corbitt
Chadwick M. Cornell
Carrie W. Cotter
Eva S. Daniel
Adam Deutsch
Stephen Q. Dooley (Not admitted in United States)
Gregory P. Drescher
James W. Ducayet
Karen O. Dunlop
Brad B. Erens
Brian J. Fahrney
Lynn M. Feder
Sharon R. Flanagan
Jason K. Francl
Kelly K. Frazier
Amy B. Gendleman
Gary D. Gerstman
David C. Giardina
Asheesh Goel
David A. Goldberg
Robert B. Goldberg
Michael A. Gordon
Christine H. Grahl
Vanessa L. Greenwood
Heidi P. Groulx
Ralph J. Gundrum
Joel M. Hammerman
Teresa Wilton Harmon
Susan V. Harris
Brendan J. Healey
Colleen M. Helmer
John M. Heyde
Cynthia A. Hickey
Arthur F. Hickok
Allison J. Himelfarb
Kevin T. Hoffmeyer
Bradley D. Howard
Erick C. Howard
David T. Howton
Christopher E. Humber
Linda T. Ieleja
Carol A. Jones
Diane Katz
Steven F. Katz
Tamar B. Kelber
Russell Keller
Amy B. Kelley
Erin E. Kelly
John P. Kelsh
Colleen M. Kenney
Soo Y. Kim
Mark R. Kirsons
Michael J. Klein
Melissa E. Lamfalusi
Randall D. Lehner
Lori J. LePar
Douglas I. Lewis
Robert J. Lewis
Carol M. Lind
Robert M. Linden
Eileen M. Liu
Jonathan D. Lotsoff
Sarah R. Lyke
Shona M. MacIntyre
Andrew P. Massmann
Eric S. Mattson
Brian A. McAleenan
Michael E. McCann
Susan L. McKeever
Matthew F. McNamara
Matthew G. McQueen
Cheryl L. Meier
Christopher J. Menting
Lisa S. Meyer
Jason H. Miller
Scott M. Montpas
Michelle K. Moritz
Betsy J. Mukamal
John J. Muller III
Kathleen M. Mulligan
Joseph C. Mullin
Jason G. New
Tracey A. Nicastro
Kristin A. Nichols
Christopher S. Niewoehner
Darin V. Osmond
Timothy G. Payne
Joseph W. Pietrzyk
Todd R. Plotner
Melissa K. Polich
Kevin R. Pryor
Joan Radovich
Rick A. Raguse
Lisa J. Reategui
Kyle D. Rettberg
Catherine A. Ricca
David M. Richardson
Sheri Roberts
Jason M. Romick

(See Next Column)

SIDLEY & AUSTIN—*Continued*

ASSOCIATES (Continued)

Courtney A. Rosen
Kim K. W. Rucker
Abby F. Rudzin
Michele I. Ruiz
Scott E. Saef
Theodore R. Scarborough
Stefanie I. Schenk
David F. Schink
Lisa A. Schneider
Joel M. Schoenmeyer
Jeffrey C. Sharer
Kari B. Sheinfeld
Hille R. Sheppard
Ann K. Shuman
David J. Siegel
Robert M. Spalding
Karen M. Stanton
Scott D. Stein
Danielle M. Streber
Robert B. Stutz
Colleen H. Sullivan
Peter J. Tarsney
Shannon A. Toolis
Harit U. Trivedi
Mark E. Vainisi
John K. VanDeWeert
Robert C. Varnell
WeiDong Wang (Not admitted in United States)
Scott L. Warner
James D. Weiss
Evan B. Westerfield
Elissa G. Wittenberg
Michelle L. Woollen
Neil D. Wyland
Todd S. Young
Steven Yovits

STAFF ATTORNEYS

Deborah L. Cotton
Nancy K. DuCharme
Catherine L. Fletcher
Julie A. Larson
Laura J. Lazarczyk
Mitchel A. Mick
Shannon L. Race

*Denotes a lawyer employed by a Professional Corporation which is a member of the Firm.

For full biographical listings, see the Martindale-Hubbell Law Directory

SONNENSCHEIN NATH & ROSENTHAL (AV)

Suite 8000 Sears Tower, 233 South Wacker Drive, 60606
Telephone: 312-876-8000
Cable Address: "Sonberk"
Telex: 25-3526
Telecopier: 312-876-7934
URL: http://www.sonnenschein.com
New York, N.Y. Office: 1221 Avenue of the Americas, 24th Floor.
Telephone: 212-768-6700.
Facsimile: 212-391-1247.
Washington, D.C. Office: 1301 K Street, N.W., Suite 600 East Tower.
Telephone: 202-408-6400.
Fax: 202-408-6399.
San Francisco, California Office: 685 Market Street, 6th Floor.
Telephone: 415-882-5000.
Facsimile: 415-543-5472.
Los Angeles, California Office: 601 South Figueroa Street, Suite 1500.
Telephone: 213-623-9300.
Facsimile: 213-623-9924.
St. Louis, Missouri Office: One Metropolitan Square, Suite 3000.
Telephone: 314-241-1800.
Facsimile: 314-259-5959.
Kansas City, Missouri Office: Suite 1100, 4520 Main Street, 64111.
Telephone: 816-932-4400.
Facsimile: 816-531-7545.
London, England Office: Sonnenscheins, Royex House, Aldermanbury Square, EC2V 7HR.
Telephone: 0207-600-2222.
Facsimile: 0207-600-2221.

Edward Sonnenschein (1881-1935)
Hugo Sonnenschein (1883-1956)

MEMBERS OF FIRM

Neal I. Aizenstein
David Albenda (Not admitted in IL; Resident, New York, N.Y. Office)
John J. Allen (Not admitted in IL; Resident, Los Angeles, California Office)
Percy Anderson (Not admitted in IL; Resident, Los Angeles, California Office)
Reid L. Ashinoff (Not admitted in IL; Resident, New York, N.Y. Office)
Gayle M. Athanacio (Not admitted in IL; Resident, San Francisco, California Office)
Pamela Baker
Michael A. Bamberger (Not admitted in IL; Resident, New York, N.Y. Office)
William T. Barker
Michael A. Barnes (Not admitted in IL; Resident, San Francisco, California Office)
James E. Barnett (Resident, Los Angeles, California Office)
Michael H. Barr (Not admitted in IL; Resident, New York, N.Y. Office)
Michael J. Bayard (Not admitted in IL; Resident, Los Angeles, California Office)
Carol Anne Been
Susan M. Benton-Powers
Dennis N. Berman (Not admitted in IL; Resident, New York, N.Y. Office)
Amy L. Bess (Resident, Washington, D.C. Office)
Jana Cohen Blackman
Lori L. Bockman (Not admitted in IL; Resident, St. Louis, Missouri Office)
Alan B. Bornstein (Not admitted in IL; Resident, St. Louis, Missouri Office)
Peter E. M. Borrowdale (Not admitted in IL; Resident, London, England Office)
Roger T. Brice
Edward J. Buchholz (Resident, St. Louis, Missouri Office)

(See Next Column)

MEMBERS OF FIRM (Continued)

Charles R. Campbell, Jr. (Not admitted in IL; Resident, Los Angeles, California Office)
Anthony Capobianco (Not admitted in IL; Resident, Los Angeles, California Office)
Leo J. Carlin (Deceased, 1988)
Lorie A. Chaiten
Richard J. Cunningham (Resident, New York, N.Y. Office)
Robert E. Curry, Jr. (Not admitted in IL; Resident, New York, N.Y. Office)
Steven R. Davidson
Dennis S. Diaz (Not admitted in IL; Resident, Los Angeles, California Office)
J. Ross Docksey
Jeffrey L. Dorman
Mark L. Dosier
Robin M. Edwards (Not admitted in IL; Resident, San Francisco, California Office)
Todd R. Eskelsen (Not admitted in IL; Resident, Washington, D.C. Office)
Phyllis A. Ewer
Richard L. Fenton
James R. Ferguson
Elizabeth A. Ferrell (Not admitted in IL; Resident, Washington, D.C. Office)
Samuel Fifer
Sheldon I. Fink
Amy H. Fisher (Not admitted in IL; Resident, New York, N.Y. Office)
G. Robert Fisher (Not admitted in IL; Resident, Kansas City, Missouri Office)
Mark G. Flaherty (Not admitted in IL; Resident, Kansas City, Missouri Office)
Karen H. Flax
Martin J. Foley (Not admitted in IL; Resident, Los Angeles, California Office)
Jeffrey C. Fort
Gerald E. Fradin
Matthew C. Fragner (Not admitted in IL; Resident, Los Angeles, California Office)
Steven H. Frankel (Resident, San Francisco, California Office)
Linda E. Friedman (Not admitted in IL; Resident, New York, N.Y. Office)
Jacqueline A. Frome (Not admitted in IL; Resident, New York, N.Y. Office)
Michael M. Froy
Brent Matthew Giddens (Not admitted in IL; Resident, Los Angeles, California Office)
Alan S. Gilbert
Lisa J. Gilden (Not admitted in IL; Resident, Washington, D.C. Office)
Robert D. Girard (Not admitted in IL; Resident, Los Angeles, California Office)
Paul E. B. Glad (Not admitted in IL; Resident, San Francisco, California Office)
Robert N. Grant
David M. Greenbaum (Not admitted in IL; Resident, New York, N.Y. Office)
Jonathan M. Griffiths (Not admitted in IL; Resident, London, England Office)
John I. Grossbart
Peter J. Gurfein (Not admitted in IL; Resident, Los Angeles, California Office)
Philip A. Haber (Resident, New York, N.Y. Office)
Frank H. Hackmann (Resident, St. Louis, Missouri Office)
John S. Hahn (Not admitted in IL; Resident, Washington, D.C. Office)
Wayne R. Hannah, Jr.
Mark T. Hansen (Not admitted in IL; Resident, Los Angeles, California Office)
Linda Chaplik Harris
James A. Heeter (Not admitted in IL; Resident, Kansas City, Missouri Office)
Roger K. Heidenreich (Resident, St. Louis, Missouri Office)
Jan P. Helder, Jr. (Not admitted in IL; Resident, Kansas City, Missouri Office)
Marc B. Heller (Not admitted in IL; Resident, New York, N.Y. Office)
Gary A. Hernandez (Not admitted in IL; Resident, San Francisco, California Office)
Carl B. Hillemann III (Resident, St. Louis, Missouri Office)
Harold C. Hirshman
Kenneth H. Hoch
Mitchell L. Hollins
Oliver L. Holmes (Not admitted in IL; Resident, San Francisco, California Office)
Charles W. Hokanson (Not admitted in IL; Resident, Los Angeles, California Office)
Joseph P. Hornyak (Not admitted in IL; Resident, Washington, D.C. Office)
Donald P. Horwitz
Stuart E. Hunt (Not admitted in IL; Resident, Washington, D.C. Office)
Benjamin B. Iselin (Not admitted in IL; Resident, New York, N.Y., Office)
David C. Jacobson
Fruman Jacobson
Marian S. Jacobson
Robert C. Johnson
Mark P. Johnson (Not admitted in IL; Resident, Kansas City, Missouri Office)
Rupert J. L. Jones (Not admitted in IL; Resident, London, England Office)
Scott L. Jones (Not admitted in IL; Resident, Los Angeles, California Office)
Robert T. Joseph
Antoinette M. Jucker (Not admitted in IL; Resident, London, England Office)
Kevin P. Kamraczewski (Resident, Los Angeles, California Office)
Gregory S. Karawan (Not admitted in IL; Resident, New York, N.Y. Office)
Curtis E. A. Karnow (Not admitted in IL; Resident, San Francisco, California Office)
Arthur S. Katz (Not admitted in IL; Resident, New York, N.Y. Office)
Michelle Stark Kaufman (Not admitted in IL; Resident, Kansas City, Missouri Office)
Louis C. Keiler
Ronald D. Kent (Not admitted in IL; Resident, Los Angeles, California Office)
H. Sinclair Kerr, Jr. (Not admitted in IL; Resident, San Francisco, California Office)
Christopher Q. King
Robert H. King, Jr.
Leslie A. Klein
James A. Klenk
Kenneth G. Kolmin
Frederic S. Lane
David A. Lapins
John J. Lawlor

(See Next Column)

SONNENSCHEIN NATH & ROSENTHAL, *Chicago—Continued*

MEMBERS OF FIRM (Continued)

Mark R. Lehrer (Not admitted in IL; Resident, New York, N.Y. Office)
J. Bradley Leitch (Not admitted in IL; Resident, Kansas City, Missouri Office)
Jeffrey Lennard
Marc Levenstein
William G. Levi (Resident, Kansas City, Missouri Office)
Fred L. Levy (Not admitted in IL; Resident, Washington, D.C. Office)
Steven M. Levy
Julius Lewis
Mark J. Linderman (Not admitted in IL; Resident, San Francisco, California Office)
Scott A. Lindquist
Matthew F. Lintner (Not admitted in IL; Resident, San Francisco, California Office)
Richard M. Lipton
Lawrence Z. Lorber (Not admitted in IL; Resident, Washington, D.C. Office)
Donald G. Lubin
David W. Maher
Richard L. Marcus
Neal R. Marder (Not admitted in IL; Resident, Los Angeles, California Office)
John F. Marvin (Not admitted in IL; Resident, Kansas City, Missouri Office)
Michael R. Maryn (Not admitted in IL; Resident, Washington, D.C. Office)
Sandra R. McCandless (Not admitted in IL; Resident, San Francisco, California Office)
Jacques K. Meguire
Mark F. Mehlman
Cynthia L. Mellema (Not admitted in IL; Resident, San Francisco, California Office)
Robert F. Messerly
Paul J. Miller
Robert B. Millner
Martin J. Moderson (Not admitted in IL; Resident, Kansas City, Missouri Office)
James L. Moeller (Not admitted in IL; Resident, Kansas City, Missouri Office)
Patrick G. Moran
Stacey L. Murphy (Resident, St. Louis, Missouri Office)
Lisa Reilly Nadler
Bernard Nath (1899-1996)
Marlene D. Nations
Dennis Nathan Newman
Charles F. Newlin
Bernard J. Nussbaum
Philip A. O'Connell, Jr. (Resident, San Francisco, California Office)
Mary Denise O'Connor
Eric A. Oesterle
Thomas G. Opferman
Sanford M. Pastroff
Lee T. Paterson (Not admitted in IL; Resident, Los Angeles, California Office)
Roger W. Patrick (Not admitted in IL; Resident, Washington, D.C. Office)
Sidney M. Perlstadt
Laura R. Petroff (Resident, Los Angeles, California Office)
Kenneth J. Pfaehler (Not admitted in IL; Resident, Washington, D.C. Office)
Alan M. Posner
Caryl A. Potter, III (Not admitted in IL; Resident, Washington, D.C. Office)
Pamela K. Prickett (Not admitted in IL; Resident, Los Angeles, California Office)
Duane C. Quaini
Charles A. Redd (Resident, St. Louis, Missouri Office)
Kurtis B. Reeg (Resident, St. Louis, Missouri Office)
Edwin B. Reeser, III (Not admitted in IL; Resident, Los Angeles, California Office)
C. Harker Rhodes, Jr. (Retired)
Robert E. Richards
Michael W. Ring (Not admitted in IL; Resident, Los Angeles, California Office)
Steven L. Rist (Not admitted in IL; Resident, Kansas City, Missouri Office)
Howard B. Rockman
David G. Rosenbaum
Michael D. Rosenthal
Samuel R. Rosenthal (1899-1994)
Mark S. Ross (Resident, San Francisco, California Office)
Stephen H. Rovak (Resident, St. Louis, Missouri Office)
Kirk R. Ruthenberg (Resident, Washington, D.C. Office)
Ivor E. Samson (Not admitted in IL; Resident, San Francisco, California Office)
Lawrence R. Sandak (Not admitted in IL; Resident, New York, N.Y. Office)
Charles D. Satinover (1906-1998)
David L. Schiavone
Eric M. Schiller
Donald M. Schindel
Michael A. Schlanger (Not admitted in IL; Resident, Washington, D.C. Office)
Robert L. Schuchard (Not admitted in IL; Resident, Los Angeles, California Office)
Arnold P. Schuster (Not admitted in IL; Resident, San Francisco, California Office)
Robert F. Scoular (Not admitted in IL; Resident, Los Angeles, California Office)
Gary Senner
J. A. Shafran (Not admitted in IL; Resident, Los Angeles, California Office)
Harold D. Shapiro
Gerald J. Sherman
Alan H. Silberman
Arthur J. Simon
Mark C. Simon
Roger C. Siske
Peter A. Smalbach (Not admitted in IL; Resident, San Francisco, California Office)
Jane Snoddy Smith (Not admitted in IL; Resident, St. Louis, Missouri Office)
Charles Spiegel (Not admitted in IL; Resident, San Francisco, California Office)
Ronald E. Stauffer (Not admitted in IL; Resident, Washington, D.C. Office)
Thomas M. Stephens
Errol L. Stone
Leslie Chambers Strohm (Not admitted in IL; Resident, St. Louis, Missouri Office)
Daniel R. Swett
Marc D. Teitelbaum (Not admitted in IL; Resident, New York, N.Y. Office)
Eileen Bannon Trost
Scott Turow
Thomas K. Vandiver (Resident, St. Louis, Missouri Office)
Jacqueline M. Vidmar
Donna J. Vobornik
David L. Volk (Not admitted in IL; Resident, Los Angeles, California Office)

MEMBERS OF FIRM (Continued)

(See Next Column)

Susan M. Walker (Not admitted in IL; Resident, Los Angeles, California Office)
Andrew L. Weil
Margo Weinstein
Jerome P. Weiss (1934-1996)
Linda D. White
James G. Wiehl (Not admitted in IL; Resident, St. Louis, Missouri Office)
Michael S. Wien (Not admitted in IL; Resident, New York, N.Y. Office)
John Leland Williams (Not admitted in IL; Resident, San Francisco, California Office)
Daniel R. Wofsey (Not admitted in IL; Resident, St. Louis, Missouri Office)
Jerome T. Wolf (Not admitted in IL; Resident, Kansas City, Missouri Office)
Curtis E. Woods (Resident, Kansas City, Missouri Office)
Nicholas C. Yost (Not admitted in IL; Resident, San Francisco, California Office)
Andrea L. Zopp

OF COUNSEL

Jon K. Adams (Not admitted in IL; Resident, San Francisco, California Office)
Jean Allard
Donald P. Arnavas (Not admitted in IL; Resident, Washington, D.C. Office)
John R. F. Baer
Glenn Ian Becker
Karen L. Bizzini (Not admitted in IL; Resident, Los Angeles, California Office)
Andrew L. DaSilva (Not admitted in IL; Resident, New York, N.Y. Office)
Wayne H. Davis (Not admitted in IL; Resident, New York, N.Y. Office)
Eric R. Decator
David D. Gatchell (Not admitted in IL; Resident, Kansas City, Missouri Office)
Douglas David Hacking (Not admitted in IL; Resident, London, England Office)
Bryan C. Jackson (Not admitted in IL; Resident, Los Angeles, California Office)
Arnold B. Kanter
Brian N. Kaufman (Not admitted in IL; Resident, Kansas City, Missouri Office)
Mary Kay Lacey (Not admitted in IL; Resident, San Francisco, California Office)
Wendy Byers Marvin (Not admitted in IL; Resident, Kansas City, Missouri Office)
Jane Wells May
Grace Ellen Mueller (Not admitted in IL; Resident, Los Angeles, California Office)
Kara S. Navarro (Resident, San Francisco, California Office)
L. John Osborn (Not admitted in IL; Resident, Washington, D.C. Office)
Jonathan Piper
Carlos Guillermo Rizowy
Marshall S. Shapo
Frank P. VanderPloeg
Charles M. Yablon (Not admitted in IL; Resident, New York, N.Y. Office)
Shelby Yastrow
Mark L. Yates
Henry S. Zangwill (Not admitted in IL; Resident, Los Angeles, California Office)

ASSOCIATES

A. Bradford Aaron
Terence M. Abad (Not admitted in IL; Resident, San Francisco, California Office)
Wendy J. Abbott
Kimberlee C. Abraham (Not admitted in IL; Resident, New York, N.Y. Office)
JoLee M. Adamich (Not admitted in IL; Resident, Los Angeles, California Office)
Mitchell Edward Albert (Not admitted in IL; Resident, Kansas City, Missouri Office)
Christine Comer Alfaro (Resident, St. Louis, Missouri Office)
David S. Alverson (Not admitted in IL; Resident, Los Angeles, California Office)
Steven K. Barentzen (Not admitted in IL; Resident, New York, New York Office)
S. Todd Barfield (Not admitted in IL; Resident, Kansas City, Missouri Office)
Daniel D. Barnowski (Not admitted in IL; Resident, Washington, D.C. Office)
Amy E. Bauman (Not admitted in IL; Resident, Kansas City, Missouri Office)
Katharina E. Beal (Not admitted in IL; Resident, Kansas City, Missouri Office)
Joseph E. Bender
Camille E. Bennett
Keith J. Berets
Cheryl Dyer Berg (Not admitted in IL; Resident, San Francisco, California Office)
Imanta M. Bergmanis (Not admitted in IL; Resident, Washington, D.C. Office)
Kirsten K. Bergin
Melanie H. Berkowitz
Anne M. Bertsch (Resident, Washington, D.C. Office)
Susan E. Bloch (Not admitted in IL; Resident, San Francisco, California Office)
Brook Bernard Bond (Not admitted in IL; Resident, San Francisco, California Office)
Diane M. Bono (Not admitted in IL; Resident, Kansas City, Missouri Office)
Kerry E. Branch (Not admitted in IL; Resident, Los Angeles, California Office)
Michaelene Broniecki Burke
Jeffry Butler (Not admitted in IL; Resident, Los Angeles, California Office)
John J. Calkins (Not admitted in IL; Resident, Washington, D.C. Office)
Georgina Calvert-Lee (Not admitted in IL)
Stacey A. Campbell (Resident, Kansas City, Missouri Office)
Clarissa Cerda
Caryn L. Chalmers
Kevin M. Christensen (Not admitted in IL; Resident, San Francisco, California Office)
Amanda M. Coco
Kimberly L. Cofman (Not admitted in IL; Resident, St. Louis, Missouri Office)

(See Next Column)

SONNENSCHEIN NATH & ROSENTHAL—*Continued*

ASSOCIATES (Continued)

Theodore Correl (Not admitted in IL; Resident, San Francisco, California Office)
Lisa C. Creighton (Not admitted in IL; Resident, Kansas City, Missouri Office)
Timothy A. Davis (Not admitted in IL; Resident, Kansas City, Missouri Office)
Kenneth Drake (Not admitted in IL; Resident, New York, New York Office)
Stephan L. Eberle (Not admitted in IL; Resident, San Francisco, California Office)
Terri Marie Esparza (Not admitted in IL; Resident, San Francisco, California Office)
Weston A. Edwards (Not admitted in IL; Resident, Los Angeles, California Office)
Cynthia A. Faur
Megan Rebecca Flaskamper (Resident, St. Louis, Missouri Office)
Monica A. Fennell
Gretchen M. Fleischut (Not admitted in IL; Resident, Kansas City, Missouri Office)
Christy L. Forth (Resident, New York, N.Y. Office)
Gary A. Francesconi (Resident, St. Louis, Missouri Office)
Tamara L. Frantzen (Resident, Kansas City, Missouri Office)
David J. Friedman
Ann Ferguson Frolik
Catherine B. Gardner (Resident, Washington, D.C. Office)
John T. Gilbertson (Not admitted in IL; Resident, Washington, D.C. Office)
Elena B. Gobeyn
Bryce P. Goeking (Not admitted in IL; Resident, San Francisco, California Office)
Daniel A. Goldberger (Not admitted in IL; Resident, New York, N.Y. Office)
David A. Goldstein (Not admitted in IL; Resident, New York, N.Y. Office)
Wendy B. Goodman (Not admitted in IL; Resident, Washington, D.C. Office)
Michael S. Gould (Not admitted in IL; Resident, Los Angeles, California Office)
Lisa R. Green (Not admitted in IL; Resident, New York, N.Y. Office)
Jen Greenwood (Not admitted in IL; Resident, London, England Office)
K. Scott Gronowski (Not admitted in IL; Resident, St. Louis, Missouri Office)
Daniel R. Guggenheim (Resident, San Francisco, California Office)
Michael S. Gugig (Resident, New York, N.Y. Office)
Rosemary L.L. Gullikson
Kevin D. Gunn (Resident, St. Louis, Missouri Office)
Jennifer A. Hammond (Not admitted in IL; Resident, Kansas City, Missouri Office)
Allyson B. Handler (Resident, Washington, D.C. Office)
Garrett Handley-Dee
Mark L. Hanover
Thomas M. Hanson (Not admitted in IL; Resident, San Francisco, California Office)
Brett J. Hart
Kendra Kekelis Hartman
Colin D. Harvey (Not admitted in IL; Resident, London, England Office)
Sandra D. Hauser (Not admitted in IL; Resident, New York, N.Y. Office)
Aliza F. Herzberg (Resident, New York, N.Y. Office)
John F. Hirschman
Charles W. Hokanson (Not admitted in IL; Resident, Los Angeles, California Office)
Paul J. Housey (Not admitted in IL; Resident, New York, New York Office)
Susan M. Hughes
Keith J. Hwang (Not admitted in IL; Resident, Washington, D.C. Office)
Margaret A. Jacobs (Not admitted in IL; Resident, New York, N.Y. Office)
Robert J. Jakubeck (Not admitted in IL; Resident, St. Louis, Missouri Office)
John Grayson Johnson
Stephanie K. Joiner (Not admitted in IL; Resident, Los Angeles, California Office)
Laurie K. Jones (Not admitted in IL; Resident, Los Angeles, California Office)
Katherine Jough (Not admitted in IL; Resident, St. Louis, Missouri Office)
Leonard W. Jurden (Not admitted in IL; Resident, Kansas City, Missouri Office)
Steven M. Kahaner (Not admitted in IL; Resident, New York, New York Office)
Matthew I. Kaplan (Resident, Los Angeles, California Office)
Steven R. Karl (Resident, St. Louis, Missouri Office)
Deborah Kaufman (Not admitted in IL; Resident, New York, N.Y. Office)
Edward S. Kim (Not admitted in IL; Resident, Los Angeles, California Office)
Helen B. Kim (Not admitted in IL; Resident, New York, N.Y. Office)
Shaun M. Klein (Not admitted in IL; Resident, Kansas City, Missouri Office)
Lana M. Knedlik (Not admitted in IL; Resident, Kansas City, Missouri Office)
Jessie A. Kohler (Not admitted in IL; Resident, Los Angeles, California Office)
John C. Koski
Timothy J. Kuester (Not admitted in IL; Resident, Kansas City, Missouri Office)
Thomas A. Labuda, Jr.
David S. Ladwig (Not admitted in IL; Resident, Kansas City, Missouri Office)
Raymond Victor Lee (Resident, Washington, D.C. Office)
Sandra Leibow (Resident, New York, N.Y. Office)
Marci Rose Levine (Not admitted in IL; Resident, Washington, D.C. Office)
David E. Lieberman
Lisa A. MacVittie (Not admitted in IL; Resident, Washington, D.C. Office)
Joseph A. Mahoney (Not admitted in IL)
Julie A. Manning
Drew W. Marrocco (Not admitted in IL; Resident, Washington, D.C. Office)
Amy E. Mathews (Not admitted in IL; Resident, Kansas City, Missouri Office)

ASSOCIATES (Continued)

(See Next Column)

Sean McEneaney (Not admitted in IL; Resident, San Francisco, California Office)
James D. McMullen (Not admitted in IL; Resident, Kansas City, Missouri Office)
James K. McMurray (Not admitted in IL; Resident, Kansas City, Missouri Office)
Rowdy B. Meeks (Not admitted in IL; Resident, Kansas City, Missouri Office)
Steven L. Merouse
Timothy M. Metzger
Gary Meyerhoff (Not admitted in IL; Resident, New York, N.Y. Office)
John R. Miller (Not admitted in IL; Resident, Los Angeles, California Office)
Mary L. Mills
Nicole Rozsman Mills (Not admitted in IL; Resident, Los Angeles, California Office)
Matthew Minor
Maria J. Morga (Not admitted in IL; Resident, San Francisco, California Office)
Evan R. Moses (Not admitted in IL; Resident, Los Angeles, California Office)
James R. Moss, Jr. (Not admitted in IL; Resident, Los Angeles, California Office)
Robert M. Motes (Resident, St. Louis, Missouri Office)
Kevin G. Mruk
Erin O'Neal Muilenburg (Resident, San Francisco, California Office)
Gregory R. Naron
Lorena S. Neal
Dean A. Newton (Resident, Kansas City, Missouri Office)
Jeffrey E. Nimz
Emily S. Nozick (Resident, San Francisco, California Office)
Nathan C. Nudelman (Resident, New York, N.Y. Office)
Stephen J. O'Brien (Not admitted in IL; Resident, St. Louis, Missouri Office)
Michael M. O'Hear
Gregory M. Otto (Not admitted in IL; Resident, St. Louis, Missouri Office)
Terrence R. Pace (Not admitted in IL; Resident, Los Angeles, California Office)
Mark W. Page
S. Jonathan Passman (Not admitted in IL; Resident, London, England Office)
Kali S. Plomin
Julie Anna Potts (Not admitted in IL; Resident, Washington, D.C. Office)
Erika K. Powers
Alicia A. Prather (Resident, Kansas City, Missouri Office)
Timothy J. Prosser (Resident, St. Louis, Missouri Office)
Teresa Dale Pupillo (Not admitted in IL; Resident, St. Louis, Missouri Office)
James R. Ravitz
Laurence Relton (Not admitted in IL; Resident, London, England Office)
Edward H. Rice (Resident, St. Louis, Missouri Office)
Henry S. Robles (Not admitted in IL; Resident, Los Angeles, California Office)
Elena Ro (Not admitted in IL; Resident, San Francisco, California Office)
Jason L. Rubin
Francisco A. Rubio-Campos
W. Michael Ryan
Michael B. Sachs
Frank Saidara (Resident, Los Angeles, California Office)
Arjun S. Sanga (Not admitted in IL; Resident, Kansas City, Missouri Office)
Donna L. Scheidt
David I. Schrodt
Marc L. Schultz
Jonathan Schwartz (Resident, Los Angeles, California Office)
Tracy Tatnall Segal
Tamara Seyler-James (Not admitted in IL; Resident, Kansas City, Missouri Office)
David J. Shapiro (Resident, New York, N.Y. Office)
Norman E. Siegel (Not admitted in IL; Resident, Kansas City, Missouri Office)
Jordan A. Sigale
Juliet M. Simpson
Markus Sleuwen Guerrero (Not admitted in IL)
Barbara Lee Smith
Steven R. Smith (Not admitted in IL; Resident, Los Angeles, California Office)
T. Mark Smith (Not admitted in IL; Resident, Los Angeles, California Office)
Amanda C. Sommerfeld (Resident, Los Angeles, California Office)
Hilary A. Sokolowski (Not admitted in IL; Resident, New York, N.Y. Office)
Nancy A. Solotkin (Not admitted in IL; Resident, San Francisco, California Office)
Diane Sovereign (Not admitted in IL; Resident, San Francisco, California Office)
Kathryn C. Spann (Resident, New York, N.Y. Office)
Natalie J. Spears
Peter C. Spier
David J. Stagman
Todd M. Stennes
Brian R. St. James (Not admitted in IL; Resident, St. Louis, Missouri Office)
David P. Stoeberl (Resident, St. Louis, Missouri Office)
Daniela P. Stoutenburg (Not admitted in IL; Resident, Los Angeles, California Office)
Scott B. Tandy
David J. Tess (Resident, Washington, D.C. Office)
Gillian W. Thackray (Not admitted in IL; Resident, San Francisco, California Office)
Scott B. Toban
Letitia Rei Todd (Resident, San Francisco, California Office)
Elizabeth A. Tosaris (Not admitted in IL; Resident, San Francisco, California Office)
Candace Tillman Tyndall
Kelly B. Valen (Not admitted in IL; Resident, San Francisco, California Office)
Kevin Vilke (Not admitted in IL; Resident, San Francisco, California Office)
D. Mark von Waaden (Not admitted in IL; Resident, Kansas City, Missouri Office)
John E. Walker (Not admitted in IL; Resident, Los Angeles, California Office)
Lori Anne Ward
Anne Nicholson Weber
Aron G. Weber (Not admitted in IL; Resident, New York, N.Y. Office)
Wendy S. Weingart (Not admitted in IL; Resident, New York, N.Y. Office)
Sarah Weinstein (Not admitted in IL; Resident, San Francisco, California Office)
Katherine A. Wyman

ASSOCIATES (Continued)

(See Next Column)

SONNENSCHEIN NATH & ROSENTHAL, *Chicago—Continued*

Laura Ann Wytsma (Not admitted in IL; Resident, Los Angeles, California Office)
Debra B. Yale
Paula M. Yost (Not admitted in IL; Resident, San Francisco, California Office)
Virginia K. Young (Not admitted in IL; Resident, San Francisco, California Office)
Ellen Prince Zivitz

For full biographical listings, see the Martindale-Hubbell Law Directory

SPRINGER, CASEY & DIENSTAG, P.C. (AV)

100 West Monroe Street, 60603
Telephone: 312-372-0800
Fax: 312-372-0842
Email: SCDDChgo@aol.com
Barrington, Illinois Office: 509 West Old Northwest Highway 60010.
Telephone: 847-382-9797; 847-382-4213.

Wyatt Jacobs (1906-1994)
Joseph E. Springer (1937-1983)
Donald E. Casey
Gary E. Dienstag
Edward M. Springer

Kathryn M. Cochran
Jason Orleans

For full biographical listings, see the Martindale-Hubbell Law Directory

TAYLOR, MILLER, SPROWL, HOFFNAGLE & MERLETTI (AV)

33 North La Salle Street, Suite 2222, 60602-2691
Telephone: 312-782-6070
Fax: 312-782-6081
Wheaton, Illinois Office: 620 West Roosevelt Road, 60187.
Telephone: 630-665-0178.
Fax: 630-682-3690.

Orville Taylor (1885-1969)
John S. Miller (1888-1965)
Roger A. Merletti (1927-1998)
Ralph W. F. Lustgarten
Richard W. Oloffson
Frank C. Stevens
Robert W. Rohm

OF COUNSEL

Charles R. Sprowl
James J. Hoffnagle

ASSOCIATES

John R. Adams
Jack Bruce Batten
Andrew Anthony Boros
Hugh J. Doyle
Daniel K. Fritz
Adam Keith Hanna
Charlotte S. Kormendy
Christina L. Mack

For full biographical listings, see the Martindale-Hubbell Law Directory

VEDDER, PRICE, KAUFMAN & KAMMHOLZ (AV)

A Partnership including Vedder, Price, Kaufman & Kammholz, P.C.
222 North La Salle Street, 60601-1003
Telephone: 312-609-7500
Fax: 312-609-5005
Email: See addresses for individual attorneys
URL: http://www.vedderprice.com
New York, New York Office: 805 Third Avenue.
Telephone: 212-407-7700.
Facsimile: 212-407-7799.
Livingston, New Jersey Office: 354 Eisenhower Parkway, Plaza II.
Telephone: 973-579-1100.
Facsimile: 973-579-9607.

MEMBERS OF FIRM

Beverly B. Vedder (1887-1955)
William F. Price (1909-1973)
Charles R. Kaufman (1908-1990)
Theophil C. Kammholz (1909-1992)
Stanley B. Block
James T. FitzGibbon
James S. Petrie
George P. Blake
Michael G. Beemer
Richard H. Schnadig
John Jacoby
Paul F. Gleeson
Charles H. Wiggins, Jr.
Theodore J. Tierney
Michael E. Reed
Richard H. Sanders
Michael L. Igoe, Jr.
Richard L. Williams III
Allan E. Lapidus
Robert J. Stucker
Thomas L. O'Brien (1941-1996)
Richard C. Robin
Robert J. Moran
David E. Bennett
Daniel O'Rourke
William F. Walsh
Richard A. Zachar
Nina Gidden Stillman
Christine M. Rhode
Paul F. Russell
Lawrence L. Summers
Thomas G. Abram
Michael G. Cleveland
Lawrence J. Casazza
Thomas A. Baker
Rene A. Torrado, Jr.
John J. Jacobsen, Jr.
Charles B. Wolf
David L. Doyle
Ludwig E. Kolman
Byron F. Bowman
Barry A. Hartstein
E. Wayne Robinson (1952-1997)
Douglas J. Polk
John T. McEnroe
James M. Kane
Margaret A. Arnold
John R. Obiala
Cathy G. O'Kelly
Gregory G. Wrobel
James A. Spizzo
Benjamin J. Baker (1954-1995)
Pearl A. Zager

(See Next Column)

MEMBERS OF FIRM (Continued)

Douglas J. Lipke
Guy E. Snyder
Angelo J. Bufalino
Edward C. Jepson, Jr.
Dalius F. Vasys
Norman B. Julius
Bruce R. Alper
Thomas P. Desmond
Douglas M. Hambleton
Daniel T. Sherlock
Igor Potym
Jonathan H. Bogaard
John M. Wolff, Jr. (1956-1998)
Edward A. Cohen
Thomas David Paulius
Gabriel J. Minc
Mark I. Bogart
Jennifer R. Evans
Daniel C. McKay, II
Diane M. Kehl
Dean N. Gerber
Janet M. Hedrick
David A. Sturms
Joseph A. Strubbe
Thomas E. Schnur
Karen P. Layng
Thomas P. Cimino, Jr.
Steven J. Gray
Ann E. Oglanian
Randall Marc Lending
Philip L. Mowery
Michael A. Nemeroff
Timothy W. O'Donnell
Lane R. Moyer
Thomas G. Hancuch
Jeffrey C. Davis
Geoffrey R. Kass
James A. Arpaia
Wayne S. Karbal
Andrew M. Gardner
William J. Bettman
Jeffrey T. Veber

ASSOCIATES

Jean M. Langie
Lynne A. Gochanour
Paul R. Hoffman
Dena Economou
Nancy M. Gerrity
Dana Simaitis Armagno
James E. Bayles, Jr.
Steven R. Apel
Anthony J. Ashley
Barbara C. Klabacha
Thomas R. Dee
Shawn S. Magee
Thomas M. Wilde
Susan F. Lifvendahl
Courtney A. Wilson
James V. Garvey
Matthew T. O'Connor
Kevin J. Kuhn
Thomas W. Snyder
Dimitrios G. Christopoulos
Stephen D. Merwise
Bruce A. Radke
Eric J. Rietz
Douglas W. Bax
Kelly A. Starr
Theresa M. Peyton
Mark L. Winget
Aaron R. Gelb
Kathleen R. White (Not admitted in IL)
Justin L. Weisberg
John T. Bycraft
Amy Pope Brock
Gerald E. Ziebell
Chad A. Schiefelbein
Christine A. Scheel
Adriana I. Reyes-Villanueva
Andrew J. Broccolo
Brian C. Booker (Not admitted in IL)
Peter J. Bedard
Mary C. Waghorne
John M. O'Connor
Kevin C. Lane
Joshua D. Gentner
Maxwell N. Barnes
Eileen B. Berner
Gary A. Jungels
Michael R. Mulcahy
Michael D. Burstein
Wendy E. Verkler
David P. Kaminski
Allison A. Gross
James H. Goodrich
Nathan D. Koch
Keri B. Halperin
Adam S. Lewis
Elizabeth L. Clark
Jennifer Durham King
Timothy D.A. O'Hara
Stan B. Stec
Michael Derek Zolner (Not admitted in IL)
Daniel F. Cullen (Not admitted in IL)
Matthew P. Pasulka (Not admitted in IL)
Megan E. Groves

OF COUNSEL IN CHICAGO

Paul H. LaRue
John J. Cassidy, Jr.
William L. Conaghan
William O. Petersen
Catherine A. Lemmer
Frank G. Reeder
Carol L. Browne

For full biographical listings, see the Martindale-Hubbell Law Directory

WILLIAMS & MONTGOMERY LTD. (AV)

20 North Wacker Drive Suite 2100, 60606
Telephone: 312-443-3200
Facsimile: 312-443-1323
Email: SERVICES@WILLMONT.COM
Waukegan, Illinois Office: 20 S. Utica.
Telephone: 847-360-1220.
Wheaton, Illinois Office: 310 S. County Farm Road.
Telephone: 630-690-3200.
Joliet, Illinois Office: 81 North Chicago Avenue.
Telephone: 815-727-2653.
Miami, Florida Office: Clarke, Silverglate, Williams and Montgomery, 100 North Biscayne Boulevard.
Telephone: 305-377-0700.
Facsimile: 305-377-3001.

Lloyd E. Williams, Jr.
C. Barry Montgomery
Thomas H. Neuckranz
William O. Shank
Barry L. Kroll
Anthony P. Katauskas
David E. Morgans
Edward J. Murphy
Alton C. Haynes
Patrick F. Klunder
David E. Stevenson
Lawrence K. Rynning
Jeffrey H. Lipe
Lawrence A. Szymanski
Gregory J. Bird
Hall Adams, III
Mary Anne Sliwinski
Thomas J. Pontikis
Mark R. Misiorowski
Raymond Lyons, Jr.

(See Next Column)

WILLIAMS & MONTGOMERY LTD.—*Continued*

Brigid E. Kennedy
Douglas A. Miller
Edward O. Pacer
James R. Studnicka
Gregory W. Beihl

David E. Neumeister
Shimon B. Kahan
Brian J. Hunt
Bradley C. Nahrstadt
Douglas W. Lohmar, Jr.
Todd E. Carlson
Brian P. O'Neill
Summer E. Heil
Daniel H. Fogel
Peter A. Donahue
Martin D. Snyder
Howard J. Pikel
Anthony A. Enrietti
Alyssa M. Campbell
Michael R. Grabill
Frank J. Olavarria
David E. Kravitz
Kurt E. Hanson
Bruce D. Paynter
Bethany L. Hengsbach
Mark G. Poulakidas
Susan J. Ganbarg
Erica L. Harris
Rhonda K. Jokisch
Christina D. Ketcham
Matthew L. Williams
Michael L. Williams
Manuel J. Placencia, Jr.
Cherisse M. Messina

Representative Clients: Black & Decker; Columbus-Cabrini Medical Center; Federal Express; Fisher-Price; Ford Motor Company; General Electric; Goodyear Tire and Rubber; Kimberly-Clark Corp.; Waste Management; Zenith Electronics.

For full biographical listings, see the Martindale-Hubbell Law Directory

WINSTON & STRAWN (AV)

35 West Wacker Drive, 60601
Telephone: 312-558-5600
Cable Address: "Winston Chicago"
Facsimile: 312-558-5700
Email: postmaster@winston.com *URL:* http://www.winston.com
Washington, D.C. Office: 1400 L Street, N.W., 20005-3502.
Telephone: 202-371-5700.
Telecopier: 202-371-5950.
Telex: 440574 INTLAW UI.
New York, N.Y. Office: 200 Park Avenue, 10166-4193.
Telephone: 212-294-6700.
Telecopier: 212-294-4700.
Cable Address: "Coledeitz, NYK".
Telex: (RCA) 232459.
Geneva, Switzerland Office: 43 Rue du Rhone, 1204.
Telephone: (4122) 7810506.
Fax: (4122) 7810361.
Paris, France Office: 21 Avenue Victor Hugo. 75116.
Telephone: 331-5364-8282.
Fax: 331-5364-8220.

Frederick H. Winston (1853-1886)
Frederick S. Winston (1878-1909)
Silas Hardy Strawn (1891-1946)

MEMBERS OF FIRM

George B. Christensen (1905-1997)
Calvin P. Sawyier
Thomas A. Reynolds, Jr.
Edward L. Foote
Bruce L. Bower
M. Finley Maxson
Robert G. Lane
Stephen C. Bruner
Terry M. Grimm
Dean L. Overman (Washington, D.C. Office)
Scott M. Feldman
Duane M. Kelley
Albert Milstein
Kurt L. Schultz
Paul H. Hensel
Columbus R. Gangemi, Jr.
Christopher D. Murtaugh
Robert F. Denvir
Hurd Baruch
Gary A. Goodman
John R. Keys, Jr. (Washington, D.C. Office)
Gregory S. Murray
James M. Neis
Michael V. Hasten (1946-1997)
Susan E. Cremin
Robert W. Ericson (New York, N.Y. Office)
Neil E. Holmen
Gerald C. Peterson
Kimball R. Anderson
Jerome W. Pope
Thomas A. Reynolds, III
Robert F. Wall
Dan K. Webb
Wayne D. Boberg
Mark G. Henning
Gregory J. Malovance
Scott J. Szala
Charles E. Stahl (1944-1998)
James H. Russell
Thomas P. Fitzgerald
Deborah Gage Haude
Timothy J. Rivelli
Stephen C. Schulte
Edward F. Gerwin, Jr. (Washington, D.C. Office)
Jim L. Blanco
F. Ellen Duff
W. Kirk Grimm
Terry John Malik
Bruce A. Toth
Robert W. Tarun
Arnold G. Gough, Jr.
Dennis J. Kelly
R. Mark McCareins
William J. Ralph
Stephen P. Durchslag
Richard B. Teiman (New York, N.Y. Office)
Anthony J. D'Auria (New York, N.Y. Office)
Jonathan Goldstein (New York, N.Y. Office)
Joseph A. DiBenedetto (New York, N.Y. Office)
Jeffrey H. Elkin (New York, N.Y. Office)
Robert Scott Edmonds (New York, N.Y. Office)
James J. Terry (New York, N.Y. Office)
Susan Berkwitt-Malefakis (New York, N.Y. Office)
Joseph A. Walsh, Jr.
Steven F. Molo

(See Next Column)

MEMBERS OF FIRM (Continued)

Michael G. Robinson
Timothy J. Rooney
Mark M. Heatwole
Robert S. Fischler (New York, N.Y. Office)
John C. Phelan (New York, N.Y. Office)
Leonard W. Belter (Washington, D.C. Office)
Richard C. Browne (Washington, D.C. Office)
Thomas M. Buchanan (Washington, D.C. Office)
Donald K. Dankner (Washington, D.C. Office)
Peter N. Hiebert (Washington, D.C. Office)
Eric L. Hirschhorn (Washington, D.C. Office)
Frederick J. Killion (Washington, D.C. Office)
John C. Kirtland (Washington, D.C. Office)
Michael R. Lemov (Washington, D.C. Office)
William J. Madden, Jr. (Washington, D.C. Office)
J. Michael McGarry, III (Washington, D.C. Office)
Malcolm H. Philips, Jr. (Washington, D.C. Office)
John P. Proctor (Washington, D.C. Office)
Robert M. Rader (Washington, D.C. Office)
Nicholas S. Reynolds (Washington, D.C. Office)
Daniel F. Stenger (Washington, D.C. Office)
Mark J. Wetterhahn (Washington, D.C. Office)
John E. Williams (Washington, D.C. Office)
Howard M. Pearl
Lawrence R. Desideri
Thomas J. Quigley (New York, N.Y. Office)
David A. Repka (Washington, D.C. Office)
Norman Newman (1952-1998)
Anthony F. LoFrisco (New York, N.Y. Office)
James R. Thompson, Jr.
Thomas F. Blakemore
Thomas J. Frederick
George C. Lombardi
Rex L. Sessions
Margaret A. Hill (Washington, D.C. Office)
John A. Waits, II (Washington, D.C. Office)
James H. Burnley IV (Washington, D.C. Office)
Beryl F. Anthony, Jr. (Washington, D.C. Office)
Christine L. Albright
Norman R. Vander Clute (Washington, D.C. Office)
Marc S. Palay (Geneva, Switzerland Office)
Benjamin P. Fishburne, III (Washington, D.C. Office)
Barry J. Hart (Washington, D.C. Office)
Jane DiRenzo Pigott
Charles L. Kinney (Washington, D.C. Office)
James R. Curtiss (Washington, D.C. Office)
Charles C. Adams, Jr. (Geneva, Switzerland Office)
Nicolas C. Ulmer (Geneva, Switzerland Office)
Julie A. Bauer
Charles B. Boehrer
Deborah K. Boling
Terrence R. Brady
Steven J. Gavin
John L. MacCarthy
Peter C. McCabe, III
William G. Miossi
Louis J. Weber III
Sheldon L. Trubatch (Washington, D.C. Office)
Bruce Baker
John C. Lorentzen
James M. Reum
Robert A. Mangrum (Washington, D.C. Office)
William D. Brewer (New York, N.Y. Office)
James D. Burton
Christina Karcher Corsiglia
W. Gordon Dobie
Patrick O. Doyle
Gemia McDearmon Jonscher
Kenneth T. Kristl
Andrew J. McDonough
Richard E. Morgan
Michael L. Mulhern
Richard W. Pearse
Helen D. Shapiro
Charles P. Sheets
Kevin E. White
Andrea L. Flink (New York, N.Y. Office)
Derek G. P. Mackenzie (New York, N.Y. Office)
Lori J. Van Auken (New York, N.Y. Office)
James T. Pitts (Washington, D.C. Office)
John Albert Whittaker, IV (Washington, D.C. Office)
Susan Schenkel-Savitt (New York, N.Y. Office)
Gordon Alan Coffee (Washington, D.C. Office)
Patrick F. Murray (Paris, France Office)
Timothy M. Broas (Washington, D.C. Office)
Leland E. Hutchinson
M. David Galainena
William A. Carmell (New York, N.Y. Office)
Matthias A. Lydon
Mark L. Rotert
Richard A. Hibey (Washington, D.C. Office)
Christopher C. McIsaac (Washington, D.C. Office)
Eric W. Bloom (Washington, D.C. Office)
Oscar A. David
Anthony DiSarro (New York, N.Y. Office)
William J. Fellerhoff
Brian S. Hart
Eleni Skoulikas Kouimelis
R. Cabell Morris, Jr.
Jennifer T. Nijman
Andrew W. Ratts
Perry D. Robinson (Washington, D.C. Office)
Michael L. Sibarium (Washington, D.C. Office)
Thomas J. Wiegand
Daniel C. Bird, Jr.
Vincent Sol (Paris, France Office)
Thomas L. Mills (Washington, D.C. Office)
Constantine G. Papavizas (Washington, D.C. Office)
Jeffrey G. Berman (Washington, D.C. Office)
Robert C. Miller (New York, N.Y. Office)
Alan B. Howard (New York, N.Y. Office)
Edmund D. Cooke, Jr. (Washington, D.C. Office)
Peter M. Kirby (Washington, D.C. Office)
John Fehrenbach (Washington, D.C. Office)
William N. Hall (Washington, D.C. Office)
Younghee J. Ottley
Robert Everett Bostrom (New York, N.Y. Office)
William A. Anderson, II (Washington, D.C. Office)

(See Next Column)

WINSTON & STRAWN, *Chicago—Continued*

MEMBERS OF FIRM (Continued)

Patrick L. Schmidt (Washington, D.C. Office)
Daniel R. Murdock (New York, N.Y. Office)
Guy A. Morley (Washington, D.C. Office)
Rocco J. deGrasse
Joan B. Tucker Fife (Washington, D.C. Office)
Michael I. Raschid (Washington, D.C. Office)
Kathryn M. Sutton (Washington, D.C. Office)
Steven H. Epstein (New York, N.Y. Office)
William A. Kapell (New York, N.Y. Office)
Catherine Wozniak Joyce
Brant C. Weidner
W. Paul Bishop (Paris, France Office)
Nelson Kyunam Ahn (New York, N.Y. Office)
Philip Lee Harris
John W. Kaufmann (New York, N.Y. Office)
Howard L. Kruse
Carol A. Joffe (Washington, D.C. Office)
Charles B. Molster, III (Washington, D.C. Office)
Daniel G. Grove (Washington, D.C. Office)
Stanford J. Goldblatt
Michael S. Melbinger
Bruce R. Braun
Ronald H. Jacobson
Donn C. Meindertsma (Washington, D.C. Office)
Robert L. Michels
Timothy P. O'Connor
Thomas C. Poindexter (Washington, D.C. Office)
Ronald J. Nye
Patrick M. Hardiman
Vincent D. Salvatore, Jr. (Washington, D.C. Office)
Lisa D. Colling
Brian T. Black
Todd J. Ehlman (Paris, France Office)
James F. Hurst
David E. Koropp
Brian M. Montgomery
Kathleen Ann Swien
Michael J. Stepek (Geneva, Switzerland Office)
Eric J. Marcotte (Washington, D.C. Office)
Robert M. Buschmann (New York, N.Y. Office)
Bradley E. Lerman
Christoph C. Heisenberg (New York, N.Y. Office)
Daniel A. Ninivaggi (New York, N.Y. Office)
James P. Corcoran (New York, N.Y. Office)
Dale B. Tauke
David B. Love
Mary E. Wall (Washington, D.C. Office)
Robert Linn Draper (Washington, D.C. Office)
Jack Crowe
Susan W. Drewke
Bradley C. Graveline
Alexis MacDowall
Don Joseph Mizerk
Kevin J. Narko
Peter L. O'Reilly
Anita Sarafa Williams
Cheryl R. Tama
Joseph James Torres
Thomas J. Vega-Byrnes
Louise Rembar Radin (New York, N.Y. Office)
Loren A. Weil
Matthew J. Botica
William J. Cook
Michael L. Brody
Susan F. Klein (New York, N.Y. Office)
Joël Alquezar (Paris, France Office)
James A. Beha II (New York, N.Y. Office)
Peter E. Calamari (New York, N.Y. Office)
Edward G. H. Chin (New York, N.Y. Office)
Jay A. Dorsch (New York, N.Y. Office)
David B. Hertzog (New York, N.Y. Office)
Angelo P. Lopresti (New York, N.Y. Office)
David E. Mollón (New York, N.Y. Office)
Anthony L. Paccione (New York, N.Y. Office)
Steven M. Schwartz (New York, N.Y. Office)
David C. Romm (Washington, D.C. Office)
Garry R. Boehlert (Washington, D.C. Office)
James E. Sharp (Washington, D.C. Office)
Joseph A. Adams (New York, N.Y. Office)
Manes M. Merrit (New York, N.Y. Office)

OF COUNSEL

Robert M. Bor (Washington, D.C. Office)
Wendy W. Durkin
Robert E. Lesser (New York, N.Y. Office)
Carl J. Peckinpaugh (Washington, D.C. Office)
Mary Hutchings Reed
John L. Napier (Washington, D.C. Office)
Ivan O. Kline (New York, N.Y. Office)
David W. Raymond (Washington, D.C. Office)
Morris N. Simkin (New York, N.Y. Office)
Joseph B. Knotts, Jr. (Washington, D.C. Office)
Kenneth L. Spangler (New York, N.Y. Office)
Lawrence I. Kiern (Washington, D.C. Office)
Stuart Altschuler
David R. Hambourger
Kathleen A. Drapeau (New York, N.Y. Office)

SENIOR ATTORNEYS

Timothy J. Oxley
Anne W. Cottingham (Washington, D.C. Office)
E. King Poor
Barry L. Salkin (New York, N.Y. Office)
William A. Horin (Washington, D.C. Office)
Chuncheng Lian (Washington, D.C. Office)
J. David Reich, Jr. (New York, N.Y. Office)
Alan V. Lindquist

ASSOCIATES

Jennifer Perry Adams (Not admitted in IL)
Karl M. Ahlm
Aïda M. Alaka
Jon T. Alexander
Rachel Allen (Not admitted in IL)
Jose A. Auffant

(See Next Column)

ASSOCIATES (Continued)

Kevin A. Banasik (Not admitted in IL)
Derek G. Barella
Norman K. Beck
Valerie S. Beck
Lesley A. Benn
Robert L. Beranek
Matthew F. Bergmann
Mary S. Bernard
Ilene Lin Bloom
Jason L. Booth
Lester G. Bovia, Jr.
Valerie L. Bovich
Cardelle Bratton
Laura M. Brinkman
Jon Michael Brown, Jr.
Gregory J. Bynan
Christopher S. Canning
Rachel M. Cannon
Nancy L. Carey
Eric J. Carlson
John P. Carreon
Christine M. Carroll
John A. Cashman
John W. Christopher
Gary R. Clark (Not admitted in IL; Resident)
Jared Ryckoff Cloud
Catherine A. Cook
Matthew D. Costigan
Jeffrey E. Crane
Marianne W. Culver
Ken Cunningham
Timothy J. Dable
Stephen V. D'Amore
Timothy J. Dart
Damon DiCastri
John M. Dickman
Craig O. Donaldson
Peter F. Donati
David J. Doyle
George M. Doyle
Dane Drobny
Paul A. Duffy
Gregory G. Dugard
Emilie A. Duhl
Matthew I. Farmer
Linda K. Finkel
James M. Foss
Daniel P. Fowler
Joseph P. Franklin (Not admitted in IL)
Jeffrey B. Frishman
Rodger Lee Gardy, Jr.
Marcia R. Gelman (Not admitted in IL)
Greer A. Gilson
Lisa M. Golzar
Jennifer H. Gong
Jessica L. Gonzalez
Patrick F. Gordon
Taras A. Gracey
M. Christine Graff
John R. Grier
Ankur Gupta (Not admitted in IL)
J. Eric Guth
Blake T. Hannafan
Katherine L. Harenza
Douglas P. Hardy (Not admitted in IL)
Eric D. Hargan
Brendan P. Head
Brian L. Heidelberger
Eve Heidenry
Diana Juliet Hsu
Karoline E. Jackson
Fred B. Jacobsen
Shawna M. Jahn
Rachel M. Janutis
Sandra L. Jenkins
Michael Brian Johnson
Amit Kalra
Peggy M. Kane
Sonja L. Kassebaum
Betsy L. Katten
Nancy M. Kim
John C. Kocoras
Peter J. Kocoras
Cynthia M. Kostelecky
Brian J. Kozlowski
Julie A. LaBunski
Sherri Renee Lamb
Charles A. Lande
Jeffrey A. Leon
Alison A. Lester
Arlene Lim
Marie A. Lona
Michael J. Lotus
Erik B. Lundgren
Lynn C. MacDonald
Katherine A. McAvoy
Timothy J. McCaffrey
Robert J. McCormack
Shannon Kay McDaniel
Daniel J. McGuire (Not admitted in IL)
Susan Barbara McInerney
Thomas McLeay
Rebecca M. Means
Samuel Mendenhall
Hal B. Merck
Greg J. Miarecki
Raymond W. Mitchell
Paul N. Monnin
Andrea Monroe
John E. Mooney
John W. Moss
Michael T. Mullins
Cornelius M. Murphy
Pamela Whitney Myers (Not admitted in IL)
Elizabeth Anne Nemeth
Brian E. Neuffer
Jennifer McCracken New
John D. Nicolay
Lisa C. Noblett
Matthew D. O'Meara
Nicole J. Ottmer
Sarah M. Padgitt
Kevin Y. Pak
Luke Allan Palese (Not admitted in IL)
Robert J. Palmersheim
Lisa Janice Parker
Raymond Perkins
Laurette Petersen
Tracy A. Peterson
Timothy M. Pinto (Not admitted in IL)
Susan A. Pipal
James R. Pittacora
Adrienne Banks Pitts
Kevin M. Plunkett
Peter W. Poulos
Kenneth P. Purcell
Karen Caraher Quirk
Edgar Bourke Reilly
Jennifer Reiter
Michael P. Roche
B. Ballard Rogers
Michael Patrick Rohan
Ronald Y. Rothstein
Kevin M. Ryan
Derek J. Sarafa
Andrew J. Schaefer
Brian M. Schafer
John M. Schloerb
Helaine A. Scholnick
Grace L. Shaff
Colleen T. Shaughnessy
Christopher Shearer
Christine J. Siwik
Stephanie C. Slatkin
Timothy W. Smith
Erik W. A. Snapp
Julie L. Soloway
Joseph A. Spiegler
Eryk J. Spytek
Victoria F. Stach
Allison Wisk Starmann
John Stinneford
Susan A. Swingle
Janet L. Tarkoff (Not admitted in IL)
Deborah H. Telman
Robert K. Temple
Michael J. Towne
John J. Tully, Jr.
Ricardo E. Ugarte
Jeffrey M. Wagner
Andrew D. Wang
Peter C. Warman
Steven R. Worth
Edward G. Zaknoen
Joseph J. Zaknoen

(See Next Column)

WINSTON & STRAWN—*Continued*

STAFF ATTORNEYS

Edward Clancy
Monica L. David
Sean M. McCumber
Michael R. Osterhoff
Angele Robinson-Gaylord
Alene M. Shafnisky
Stephen N. Sher

For full biographical listings, see the Martindale-Hubbell Law Directory

COLLINSVILLE, Madison Co.

DUNHAM, BOMAN & LESKERA (AV)

300 West Clay Street, 62234
Telephone: 618-344-7734
Telecopier: 618-344-3853
Belleville Office: 208 N. High.
Telephone: 618-235-7222.
Telecopier: 618-236-2800; 618-236-1899.

John W. Leskera
William L. Berry
Eric C. Young
Robert D. Francis
John L. Bitzer

Attorneys for: Collinsville School District #10; Hanover Insurance Co.; Hartford Insurance Group; State Farm Insurance Cos.; Transamerica Insurance Group; The Travelers Indemnity Co.; Wausau Insurance Cos.; Nationwide Insurance Co.

For full biographical listings, see the Martindale-Hubbell Law Directory

CRYSTAL LAKE, McHenry Co.

MILITELLO, ZANCK & COEN, P.C. (AV)

40 Brink Street, 60014
Telephone: 815-459-8800
FAX: 815-459-8429

James G. Militello
Thomas C. Zanck
Patrick D. Coen
James L. Wright

Mark S. Saladin
James G. Militello, III
Barbara H. Switzer
D. Chad Mihevc
Nancy A. Stingle
David G. Phoenix

OF COUNSEL

Michael A. Ungvarsky, Jr.

References: Home State Bank of Crystal Lake; First National Bank of Crystal Lake; McHenry State Bank; Amcore Bank N.A., Woodstock.

For full biographical listings, see the Martindale-Hubbell Law Directory

ZUKOWSKI, ROGERS, FLOOD & McARDLE (AV)

50 Virginia Street, 60014-4126
Telephone: 815-459-2050
Facsimile: 815-459-9057
Email: zrfm@stans.com *URL:* http://www.zrfmlaw.com
Chicago, Illinois Office: 100 South Wacker Drive, Suite 1502.
Telephone: 312-407-7700.
Facsimile: 312-332-1901.

PARTNERS

H. David Rogers
Richard G. Flood
David W. McArdle
Jeannine A. Thoms
Stuart D. Gordon
Kevin J. O'Brien
Michael J. Chmiel
Kathleen Field Orr

ASSOCIATES

Melissa J. Cooney
Kelly A. Cahill
Michael J. Smoron
E. Regan Daniels Shepley
Michael S. Drella
Timothy P. Dwyer
Paul A. Zukowski
Tracey Anne Wertman
Jenette M Schwemler

OF COUNSEL

Timothy J. Curran
Francis S. Lorenz

For full biographical listings, see the Martindale-Hubbell Law Directory

*DANVILLE,** Vermilion Co.

HUTTON, LAURY, YOUNG & LIETZ (AV)

16 West Madison Street, P.O. Box 1128, 61832
Telephone: 217-446-9436
FAX: 217-446-9462

MEMBERS OF FIRM

Jackson R. Hutton (1914-1991)
Everett L. Laury
Austin W. Buchanan (1928-1973)
Frank R. Young
Gregory G. Lietz

LEGAL SUPPORT PERSONNEL

Bonnie Bowles (Legal Secretary)
Windy French (Legal Secretary)

Representative Clients: Employers Reinsurance Corporation; Pro National Insurance Company; Pekin Insurance Company; Illinois State Medical Insurance Services, Inc.; Sentry Insurance; Rockford Mutual Insurance Company;

(See Next Column)

The Equitable Life Assurance Society; Vermilion County Airport Authority; Westville-Belgium Sanitary District; Danville Election Commission.

For full biographical listings, see the Martindale-Hubbell Law Directory

*DECATUR,** Macon Co.

KEHART, SHAFTER & WEBBER, P.C. (AV)

One Main Place, 101 South Main Street, Suite 200, P.O. Box 860, 62525-0860
Telephone: 217-428-4689
Telecopier: 217-422-7950
Email: kswlaw@fgi.net

Michael J. Kehart
A. James Shafter
Albert G. Webber IV
Mark D. Gibson
James E. Peckert
Heidi R. Balsley
Julie C. Keller

OF COUNSEL

Albert G. Webber III
T. G. Bolen

Representative Clients: Archer-Daniels-Midland Co.; A.E. Staley Manufacturing Co.; Mueller Co.; Illinova Resource Recovery, Inc.; ; Aetna Casualty & Surety Co.; Illinois State Medical Insurance Services; Richland Sales Corp.; Lincoln Diagnostics; Hickory Point Bank & Trust.

For full biographical listings, see the Martindale-Hubbell Law Directory

DE KALB, De Kalb Co.

BOYLE, CORDES & BROWN (AV)

301 East Lincoln Highway, 60115-3307
Telephone: 815-756-6328
Fax: 815-756-8842

MEMBERS OF FIRM

John G. Boyle (1907-1996)
Gary W. Cordes
Charles G. Brown

Representative Clients: DeKalb Park District; First of America, N.A. DeKalb, Il; First National Bank in Dekalb.
References: First of America Bank-DeKalb; First National Bank in DeKalb.

For full biographical listings, see the Martindale-Hubbell Law Directory

ELGIN, Cook & Kane Cos.

ARIANO, ANDERSON, HARDY & CASTILLO, P.C. A PROFESSIONAL CORPORATION (AV)

474 Summit Street, 60120
Telephone: 847-695-2400
Telecopy: 847-695-8397
Email: aah@ariand.com *URL:* http://www.ARIAND.com
Huntley, Illinois Office: 10604 North Vine Street, 60142.
Telephone: 847-669-5020.

Frank V. Ariano
Allen M. Anderson
Ralph C. Hardy
William F. Castillo (1949-1997)
Brett E. Anderson

Scott Richmond
Karrsten Goettel
Julio C. Valdez

For full biographical listings, see the Martindale-Hubbell Law Directory

*GALESBURG,** Knox Co.

BARASH & STOERZBACH, P.C. (AV)

139 South Cherry Street, P.O. Box 1328, 61402-1328
Telephone: 309-341-6000
Telecopier: 309-343-7500
Email: galesburg@barashlaw.com
Galva, Illinois Office: 110 Exchange Street, P.O. Box 165, 61434.
Telephone: 309-932-2001.
Telefax: 309-932-3151. Email: galva@barashlaw.com.

Burrel Barash (1906-1993)
Robert C. Stoerzbach
Barry M. Barash
Dwayne I. Morrison
Daniel B. Stoerzbach
John W. Robertson
Pamela S. Wilcox
Reynolds M. Everett, Jr. (Resident, Galva Office)
Daniel S. Alcorn
John R. Rehn
Jeremy S. Karlin
Keith A. Luymes (Resident, Galva Office)

Representative Clients: Auto-Owners Insurance Co.; Farmers and Mechanics Bank; General Casualty Co.; Knox College; Medical Protective Co.; Pekin Farmers Insurance Co.; Jet Air, Inc.; State Farm Insurance; Gateway Coop.

For full biographical listings, see the Martindale-Hubbell Law Directory

Galesburg—Continued

HATTERY, SIMPSON & WEST (AV)

Suite 402 Hill Arcade, 61401
Telephone: 309-343-6152
Telecopier: 309-343-5103
Email: 5lawyers@galesburg.net *URL:* http://www.misslink.net/hsw/aprose.htm
Monmouth, Illinois Office: 1025 East Broadway.
Telephone: 309-734-3150.
Telefax: 309-734-7043.
Roseville, Illinois Office: 130 North Main Street.
Telephone: 309-426-2176.
Telefax: 309-426-2177.

MEMBERS OF FIRM

John J. Hattery
Roger L. Williamson
S. David Simpson
Thomas G. West
Ronald D. Stombaugh (Resident at Monmouth Office)
Timothy E. Sullivan
Carol Masden Simpson
George M. Hennenfent (Resident, Roseville Office)

ASSOCIATE

Patricia A. Hattery

LEGAL SUPPORT PERSONNEL

Bridget Arthur (Litigation Paralegal)
Mary Lewis (Probate Paralegal)

For full biographical listings, see the Martindale-Hubbell Law Directory

KAVANAGH, SCULLY, SUDOW, WHITE & FREDERICK, P.C.

(See Peoria)

GRANITE CITY, Madison Co.

LUEDERS, ROBERTSON & KONZEN (AV)

1939 Delmar Avenue, 62040
Telephone: 618-876-8500
Telecopier: 618-876-4534
Email: lrk.il@worldnet.att.net
Danville, Illinois Office: 809 1/2 North Gilbert, 61832.
Telephone: 217-443-0304.
Fax: 217-443-0375.

MEMBERS OF FIRM

Wesley Lueders (1896-1957)
Randall Robertson
Leo H. Konzen
R. Eric Robertson
Edward C. Fitzhenry, Jr.
Brian E. Konzen
Paul G. Foran

ASSOCIATE

Anthony R. Garavalia

Representative Clients: Ameritech; Mercantile Bank (Trust Division); Granite City Steel Division of National Steel Corporation; Allied Waste Industries, Inc.; Illinois Industrial Energy Consumers (IIEC) including Olin Corporation; Archers-Daniels-Midland Company; General Motors Corporation.

For full biographical listings, see the Martindale-Hubbell Law Directory

*HARRISBURG,** Saline Co.

JELLIFFE, FERRELL, MORRIS, DOERGE & FOSTER (AV)

108 East Walnut Street, P.O. Box 406, 62946
Telephone: 618-253-7153; 253-7647
Telecopier: 618-252-1843

OF COUNSEL

Charles R. Jelliffe

MEMBERS OF FIRM

DeWitt Twente (1904-1976)
Donald V. Ferrell
Walden E. Morris
Michal Doerge
Thomas J. Foster

Representative Clients: Auto-Owners Insurance; Country Cos; Metropolitan Life Insurance; Ohio Casualty Group; Standard Mutual Insurance Co.; State Farm Cos.; Aetna Casualty & Surety Co.; Sahara Coal Co.

For full biographical listings, see the Martindale-Hubbell Law Directory

HARVARD, McHenry Co.

ELMAN & EHARDT, LTD. (AV)

205 East Front Street, 60033-2900
Telephone: 815-943-4051
Fax: 815-943-4086

William Elman

For full biographical listings, see the Martindale-Hubbell Law Directory

*JACKSONVILLE,** Morgan Co.

BELLATTI, FAY, BELLATTI & BEARD (AV)

333 West State Street, P.O. Box 696, 62651
Telephone: 217-245-7111
Fax: 217-245-2832
Email: bellatti@csj.net
Office also at Ashland, Illinois. Telephone: 217-476-3318.

OF COUNSEL

William L. Fay
John E. Bellatti

MEMBERS OF FIRM

Walter R. Bellatti
Daniel J. Beard
Timothy E. Ruppel
Thomas L. Veith
Jeffrey L. Soltermann
C Matthew A. Smith

General Counsel for: City of Jacksonville; Bound to Stay Bound Books, Inc.
District Counsel for: Illinois Power Company; Norfolk Southern Railroad.
Representative Clients: Mercantile Bank of Illinois; First Bank; CB Accounts, Inc.; Equitable Life Assurance Society; Prudential Insurance Co.; Allstate Insurance Co.; Travelers Insurance Co.

For full biographical listings, see the Martindale-Hubbell Law Directory

RAMMELKAMP, BRADNEY, KUSTER, KEATON, FRITSCHE & LINDSAY, P.C. (AV)

232 West State Street, P.O. Box 550, 62651
Telephone: 217-245-6177
Fax: 217-243-7322
Email: ramlkamp@fgi.net

L.O. Vaught (1865-1955)
Carl E. Robinson (1886-1964)
Orville N. Foreman (1904-1972)
Albert W. Hall (1912-1986)
Theodore C. Rammelkamp (Retired)
Larry D. Kuster
Forrest G. Keaton
Barbara Fritsche
Nancy Lindsay
Maria M. Gonzalez
Richard R. Freman
H. Allen Yow

Bradley W. Wilson

OF COUNSEL

Robert E. Bradney

Representative Clients: Country Mutual Insurance Co.; State Farm Mutual Auto Insurance Co.; American States Insurance; Pekin Insurance Co.; Pleasant Plains State Bank; EMI Manufacturing; Tenneco Packaging; Soyland Power Cooperative, Inc.

For full biographical listings, see the Martindale-Hubbell Law Directory

*JOLIET,** Will Co.

MCKEOWN, FITZGERALD, ZOLLNER, BUCK, HUTCHISON & RUTTLE (AV)

2455 Glenwood Avenue, 60435
Telephone: 815-729-4800
Fax: 815-729-4711
Frankfort Office: 28 Kansas Street.
Telephone: 815-469-2176.
FAX: 815-469-0295.

MEMBERS OF FIRM

Charles J. McKeown (1908-1985)
Paul O. McKeown (1913-1982)
Richard T. Buck (1936-1992)
Douglas P. Hutchison (1939-1998)
Joseph C. Fitzgerald (Retired)
Max E. Zollner
David L. Ruttle
Theodore J. Jarz
Douglas J. McKeown
James B. Harvey
Kenneth A. Grey
Michael R. Lucas
Christopher N. Wise
Gary S. Mueller
John C. Roth
Arthur J. Wilhelmi
Thomas M. Carney

ASSOCIATE

Christopher S. Ward (Resident)

OF COUNSEL

George E. Sangmeister
Stewart C. Hutchison

Representative Clients: First Midwest Bank, N.A.; Silver Cross Hospital; Villages of: Plainfield and Mokena; Southwest Agency for Risk Management; Joliet Junior College Foundation; Cornerstone Services, Inc.; Nicor Inc.; Express Riverboat Casino, Joliet, Inc.; Joliet Valves, Inc.

For full biographical listings, see the Martindale-Hubbell Law Directory

SPESIA, AYERS & ARDAUGH (AV)

Two Rialto Square, 116 North Chicago Street, Suite 200, 60432
Telephone: 815-726-4311
Fax: 815-726-6828

MEMBERS OF FIRM

Douglas F. Spesia
E. Kent Ayers
John R. Ardaugh

(See Next Column)

SPESIA, AYERS & ARDAUGH—*Continued*

ASSOCIATES

John G. Foreman
John M. Spesia
Christian G. Spesia
Elizabeth Hoskins Dow
Barbara N. Petrungaro

OF COUNSEL

Ralph C. Murphy
Kenneth E. Timm
Arthur T. Lennon (1923-1988)

Counsel for: American Telephone & Telegraph Co.; Amoco Oil Co.; Ameritech; Caterpillar Tractor Co.; Commonwealth Edison Co.; IBM Corp.; Indiana Consolidated Ins. Co.; Lakehead Pipeline Co.; Liberty Mutual Ins. Co.; Northern Illinois Gas Co.

For full biographical listings, see the Martindale-Hubbell Law Directory

*KANKAKEE,** Kankakee Co.

BARMANN, KRAMER & BOHLEN, P.C. (AV)

Suite 502, 200 East Court Street, P.O. Box 1787, 60901
Telephone: 815-939-1133
Fax: 815-939-0994

Glen R. Barmann
Christopher W. Bohlen
Michael D. Kramer
Deborah A. Woodruff

For full biographical listings, see the Martindale-Hubbell Law Directory

LA SALLE, La Salle Co.

HERBOLSHEIMER, LANNON, HENSON, DUNCAN AND REAGAN, P.C. (AV)

State Bank Building, Suite 400, 654 First Street, P.O. Box 539, 61301
Telephone: 815-223-0111
Fax: 815-223-5829
Ottawa, Illinois Office: First Federal Savings Bank Building, 633 LaSalle Street, Suite 409.
Telephone: 815-434-1400.
Fax: 815-434-2423.

George L. Herbolsheimer (1911-1992)
R. James Lannon, Jr.
T. Donald Henson
John S. Duncan, III
Michael T. Reagan (Resident, Ottawa Office)
Douglas A. Gift
Gary R. Eiten

Karen C. Eiten
Michael C. Jansz (Resident, Ottawa Office)
Jill W. Klein
Lawrence M. Kaschak

Attorneys for: Aetna Insurance Group; St. Paul Fire and Marine Insurance Co.; State Farm Insurance Co.; La Salle State Bank; The Daily News Tribune Company, La Salle; Eureka Savings Bank; Illinois Valley Community Hospital; Community Hospital of Ottawa; Commonwealth Edison, Co.; United States Fidelity & Guaranty, Co.

For full biographical listings, see the Martindale-Hubbell Law Directory

*LINCOLN,** Logan Co.

WOODS & BATES (AV)

306 Clinton Street, 62656
Telephone: 217-735-1234
Fax: 217-735-1236
Email: bilbates@ccaonline.com

William B. Bates

Representative Clients: Illico Incorporated; The Abraham Lincoln Memorial Hospital; Lincoln Firemen's Pension Fund; Mt. Pulaski Products; Lincoln Christian College and Seminary; C.B. Accounts; Lincoln Police Pension Fund; Construction Equipment Federal Credit Union.

For full biographical listings, see the Martindale-Hubbell Law Directory

MARENGO, McHenry Co.

POLLOCK, MEYERS, EICKSTEADT & WEECH, LTD. (AV)

Harris Bank/Marengo, 100 West Washington Street, 60152
Telephone: 815-568-8071
FAX: 815-568-0003
Email: pmew@owc.net *URL:* http://www.marengolaw.com

Norman J. Pollock
Harvey A. Meyers
Richard W. Eicksteadt
Charles P. Weech

Jason E. Hunter

LEGAL SUPPORT PERSONNEL

Carolyn I. Haverly

Representative Clients: Harris Bank/Marengo; The State Bank of Woodstock; Woodstone Co.; Marengo Steel Co.; Marengo Disposal Co.; Key Development Co.; Agrinetics, Inc.; Compost Enterprises; McGill Metal Products Co.; Cardinal Savings and Loan Association.

(See Next Column)

For full biographical listings, see the Martindale-Hubbell Law Directory

*MARION,** Williamson Co.

MITCHELL, MITCHELL & BRADLEY (AV)

404 North Monroe, P.O. Box 488, 62959-2328
Telephone: 618-993-2134
Telecopier: 618-993-8702
Email: mmb@midwest.net *URL:* http://www.lawyers.com/mmb

J. C. Mitchell
Bruce W. Mitchell
John E. Bradley

OF COUNSEL

James E. Hopkins

Representative Clients: St. Paul Fire & Casualty Insurance Company; Liberty Mutual Insurance Company; Shelter Insurance Company; Atlantic Mutual Insurance Company; Farmer's Insurance Exchange; United States Fidelity and Guarantee Company; Horace Mann Insurance.

For full biographical listings, see the Martindale-Hubbell Law Directory

WINTERS, BREWSTER, CROSBY & PATCHETT (AV)

111 West Main, P.O. Box 700, 62959
Telephone: 618-997-5611
Fax: 618-997-6522
Email: winlaw@midwest.net

MEMBERS OF FIRM

Charles D. Winters (1917-1992)
John S. Brewster
Thomas F. Crosby, III
John R. (Randy) Patchett

ASSOCIATES

Rick Wayne Aeilts
Paul Jason Schafer

For full biographical listings, see the Martindale-Hubbell Law Directory

MATTOON, Coles Co.

CRAIG & CRAIG (AV)

1807 Broadway, P.O. Box 689, 61938-0689
Telephone: 217-234-6481
Telecopier: 217-234-6486; 258-8292
Email: craiglaw@advant.com
Mount Vernon, Illinois Office: 115 North 7th Street.
Telephone: 618-244-7511.

MEMBERS OF FIRM

Craig Van Meter (1895-1981)
Fred H. Kelly (1894-1971)
Robert M. Werden (1908-1969)
George N. Gilkerson (1911-1985)
John P. Ewart
Richard F. Record, Jr.
Stephen L. Corn
Robert G. Grierson
Gregory C. Ray
Paul R. Lynch (Resident, Mount Vernon Office)
Kenneth F. Werts (Resident, Mount Vernon Office)
John L. Barger

ASSOCIATES

Kathleen M. Stockwell
Kristine M. Tuttle
Julie A. Webb (Resident, Mount Vernon Office)
John M. O'Driscoll
Duane A. Deters
Katy C. Fain (Resident, Mount Vernon Office)
Erin E. Wisner
John F. Watson

OF COUNSEL

Jack E. Horsley

Representative Clients: Marathon Oil Company; Illinois Central R.R. Co.; Okaw Building & Loan, s.b., Mattoon, Illinois; The Medical Protective Co.; Consolidated Communications Inc.; D-CO Laundry Villages, Inc.; Mattoon Enterprise Park, L.L.C.; Lake Land College; Mattoon Township Park District of Coles County.

For full biographical listings, see the Martindale-Hubbell Law Directory

*MORRISON,** Whiteside Co.

LUDENS, POTTER & BURCH (AV)

409 North Cherry, P.O. Box 360, 61270-0360
Telephone: 815-772-2161
Telecopier: 815-772-7440
Email: ludenspb@essex1.com

MEMBERS OF FIRM

Lawrence A. Ludens (1912-1990)
Robert H. Potter
William A. Burch
Thomas J. Potter
Stanley B. Steines
M. Tod Melton

ASSOCIATE

Frank S. Martinez

Representative Clients: Smith Trust & Savings Bank, Morrison, Illinois; Fulton State Bank, Fulton, Illinois; Farmers State Bank, Chadwick and Mount Carroll; First Illinois National Bank, Savanna, Ill.; Country Mutual Insurance Co.; Fulton Flood Control District; Farmers Savings Bank, Preston, Iowa; Miles Savings Bank, Miles, Iowa; Iowa Mutual Insurance Company.

For full biographical listings, see the Martindale-Hubbell Law Directory

*MOUNT VERNON,** Jefferson Co.

CAMPBELL, BLACK, CARNINE, HEDIN, BALLARD & MCDONALD, P.C. (AV)

P.O. Drawer C, 62864
Telephone: 618-242-3310
Fax: 618-242-3735
Email: cbch@midwest.net *URL:* http://www.cbch.com

David A. Campbell
Terry R. Black
Roy L. Carnine
Craig R. Hedin
Mark J. Ballard
Jerome E. McDonald
Howard W. Campbell (1911-1980)
John E. Jacobsen (1922-1985)
Glenn E. Moore (1911-1991)
David E. Furnall (1905-1993)

Fred R. Mann
Charles L.P. Flynn
Matthew K. Wollin
Aaron S. Carnine

Representative Clients: Kerr-McGee Coal Corp.; Good Samaritan Hospital; Country Mutual Insurance Co.; Southern Illinois Stone Co; Rend Lake Conservancy District; Consolidation Coal Co.; Illinois State Medical Insurance Services; State Farm Automobile Insurance Co.; John Hancock Mutual Life Insurance Co.

For full biographical listings, see the Martindale-Hubbell Law Directory

HOWARD, LEGGANS, PIERCY & HOWARD (AV)

1008 Main, P.O. Drawer U, 62864
Telephone: 618-242-6594
Fax: 618-244-7197

MEMBERS OF FIRM

George W. Howard, Jr. (1907-1994)
G. W. Howard, III
David R. Leggans
David L. Piercy
Jeffrey G. Howard

Representative Clients: Bank of Illinois in Mt. Vernon; First State Bank of Dix; Tri-County Electric Cooperative; Hamilton County Telephone Co-op., City of Mt. Vernon; Mt. Vernon Township; Texico State Bank.

For full biographical listings, see the Martindale-Hubbell Law Directory

MITCHELL, NEUBAUER & HANSON, P.C. (AV)

123 South 10th Street, Mercantile Bank Building, 6th Floor, P.O. Box 1088, 62864
Telephone: 618-242-0705
Telecopier: 618-242-4820
Mailing Address: P.O. Box 1088,
Email: MNHPC@Midwest.net

A. Ben Mitchell
Timothy R. Neubauer
Leslie James Hanson

T. David Purcell
David K. Overstreet
Henry P. Villani

Attorneys for: Mercantile Bank of Southern Illinois; Mt. Vernon Grade School District #80; Stewart Brothers Oil Producers; Mt. Vernon Airport Authority; J. M. Behimer Enterprises; Marion Ford-Mercury, Inc.

For full biographical listings, see the Martindale-Hubbell Law Directory

OAK BROOK, DuPage Co.

E. LAWRENCE OLDFIELD & ASSOCIATES (AV)

Suite 201, 2021 Midwest Road, 60523
Telephone: 630-495-3377
Facsimile: 630-495-2774
Email: eloesq@ix.netcom.com *URL:* http://www.lawyers.com/eloesq
Chicago, Illinois Office: 30 North La Salle Street, Suite 1524, 60602.
Telephone: 312-782-0933.
Fax: 312-782-4474.
Inverness, Illinois Office: 1622 Colonial Parkway, Suite 201, 60067.
Telephone: 847-358-5757.
Fax: 847-358-7706.

E. Lawrence Oldfield

ASSOCIATE

Jonathan J. Fox

OF COUNSEL

Michael R. Panter
Robert J. Ross

Representative Clients: Hartford Fire Insurance Co.; Fireman's Fund; Star Insurance Co.; Mid-Way Supply, Inc.; Midwest Operating Engineers Credit Union; LTM Group, Inc.; INNOTEK Medical Products, Inc.; Northern Baptist Theological Seminary; Rose Exterminators, Inc.; Great Lakes Aquastore Systems, Inc.

For full biographical listings, see the Martindale-Hubbell Law Directory

OAKBROOK TERRACE, DuPage Co.

MCBRIDE BAKER & COLES (AV)

Suite 1000, One Mid America Plaza, 60181-4710
Telephone: 630-954-2100
Telecopier: 630-954-2112
URL: http://www.mbc.com
Chicago, Illinois Office: 500 West Madison Street, 40th Floor, 60661-2511.
Telephone: 312-715-5700.
Telecopier: 312-993-9350.

MEMBERS OF FIRM

Robert C. Aument
Steven B. Bashaw
David H. Hight
James A. Kohlstedt
Carl A. Neumann
Eric L. Singer
Douglas C. Tibble
Jacqueline W. Vlaming
David E. Zajicek

OF COUNSEL

John T. Huntington

ASSOCIATES

Daniel P. Duffy
Eric D. Filkin
Robert E. Harig
Maureen Calabrese Strauts

For full biographical listings, see the Martindale-Hubbell Law Directory

*OREGON,** Ogle Co.

WILLIAMS & MCCARTHY, A PROFESSIONAL CORPORATION (AV)

607 Washington Street, P.O. Box 339, 61061
Telephone: 815-732-2101
Fax: 815-732-2289
Rockford, Illinois Office: 321 West State Street, P.O. Box 219.
Telephone: 815-987-8900.
Fax: 815-968-0019.

Kim D. Krahenbuhl
Clayton L. Lindsey
Wendy S. Howarter
Kari A. Vanderzyl

Representative Clients: Aircraft Gear Corp.; Anderson Industries, Inc.; Gallagher Bassett Insurance Co.; Liberty Mutual Insurance Co.; Atwood Industries, Inc.; The Travelers; American Mutual Insurance Co.; Rockford Health Systems; Chrysler Corp.; USF&G, West Bend.

For full biographical listings, see the Martindale-Hubbell Law Directory

*OTTAWA,** La Salle Co.

MYERS, DAUGHERITY, BERRY, O'CONOR & KUZMA, LTD. (AV)

130 East Madison Street, 61350
Telephone: 815-434-6206
Fax: 815-434-6203
Email: mdboc@TheRamp.net
Streator, Illinois Office: 7 Northpoint Drive.
Telephone: 815-672-3116.
Fax: 815-672-0738.

John A. Berry (1912-1986)
Andrew J. O'Conor (1919-1998)
Stephen C. Myers
Eugene P. Daugherity
Richard J. Berry
Sheryl H. Kuzma

Representative Clients: Auto Owners Insurance, Co.; Union Bank; First National Bank of Ottawa, Illinois; Union Bancorp Inc.; First State Bank; First Midwest Bank; Allied Ins. Group; St. Mary's Hospital; General Casualty Insurance, Co.

For full biographical listings, see the Martindale-Hubbell Law Directory

*PEORIA,** Peoria Co.

CASSIDY & MUELLER (AV)

323 Commerce Bank Building, 416 Main Street, 61602
Telephone: 309-676-0591
Fax: 309-676-8036

MEMBERS OF FIRM

John E. Cassidy (1896-1984)
John E. Cassidy, Jr.
David B. Mueller
John E. Cassidy, III
Timothy J. Cassidy
Andrew D. Cassidy
Christopher F. Cassidy
Timothy J. Cusack
Michael W. Powell
John D. Moses
Robert M. McBride

Representative Clients: Aetna Casualty & Surety Co.; Atchison, Topeka & Santa Fe Railroad Co.; Chicago Motor Club Ins. Co.; Continental Oil Company; E.I. DuPont-DeNemours & Company; Hartford Accident & Indemnity Company; Illinois-American Water Company; Lake States Insurance Company; John P. Pearl & Associates, Ltd.; Liberty Mutual Insurance Co.

For full biographical listings, see the Martindale-Hubbell Law Directory

Peoria—Continued

HOWARD & HOWARD ATTORNEYS, P.C. (AV)

The Creve Coeur Building, Suite 200, 321 Liberty Street, 61602-1403
Telephone: 309-672-1483
Telecopier: 309-672-1568
Kalamazoo, Michigan Office: The Michigan Building, Suite 200, 100 Portage Street.
Telephone: 616-382-1483.
Telecopier: 616-382-1568.
Bloomfield Hills, Michigan Office: The Pinehurst Office Center, Suite 101, 1400 North Woodward Avenue.
Telephone: 248-645-1483.
Telecopier: 248-645-1568.
Lansing, Michigan Office: Suite 500, The Phoenix Building, 222 Washington Square, North.
Telephone: 517-485-1483.
Telecopier: 517-485-1568.

Theodore L. Eissfeldt
Jon S. Faletto
Frederick G. Hoffman
Timothy J. Howard
Diana M. Jagiella
Michael R. Lied
Scott R. Paulsen
Janice M. Powell
Leonard W. Sachs
Jeffrey G. Sorenson
Gina M. Torielli
(Not admitted in IL)
Sandra M. Traicoff

Representative Clients: National City Bank; Marion Memorial Hospital; Kmart Corp.; Greater Peoria Airport Authority; Central Illinois Light Co.; Daimler Chrysler Corporation; Princeton National Bancorp, Inc.; First Decatur Bancshares, Inc.

For full biographical listings, see the Martindale-Hubbell Law Directory

JOHNSON, BUNCE & NOBLE, P.C. (AV)

Formerly Swain, Johnson & Gard
Associated Bank Plaza, 411 Hamilton Boulevard, Suite 1900, 61602
Telephone: 309-673-0741
Facsimile: 309-673-0751
Email: info@peorialawyers.com *URL:* http://www.peorialawyers.com

Arber Johnson (1915-1982)
Mishael O. Gard (1918-1996)
James H. Bunce
Kent A. Noble
Frederick A. Johnson
James P. Johnson
Michael A. Hall

Louis P. Milot
Kathleen E. Weeks

OF COUNSEL

Ronald B. Schertz
Mark D. Howard
Frederick D. Johnson

Representative Clients: LaSalle Bank, F.S.B.; The Greater Peoria Sanitary District.

For full biographical listings, see the Martindale-Hubbell Law Directory

KAVANAGH, SCULLY, SUDOW, WHITE & FREDERICK, P.C. (AV)

301 S.W. Adams Street, Suite 700, 61602
Telephone: 309-676-1381
FAX: 309-676-0324
Email: KSSWF@aol.com
East Peoria, Illinois Office: 111 West Washington Street, Suite 206B.
Telephone: 309-694-3707.
Fax: 309-676-0324.

Jay T. Hunter (1873-1953)
Eugene Davis McLaughlin (1894-1958)
Richard J. Kavanagh (1894-1963)
J. Chase Scully, Jr. (1907-1969)
William McDowell Frederick (1907-1991)
Donald G. Beste (1905-1996)
Joseph Z. Sudow
Richard C. Kavanagh
Julian E. Cannell
David J. Walvoord
Charles G. Roth
David J. Dubicki
Phillip B. Lenzini
Karen M. Stumpe
Brian D. Mooty
James W. Springer
Gary E. Schmidt
Beth M. Wellenraiter
Robert B. Becker

OF COUNSEL

Eugene L. White
Julian B. Venezky
Jordan A. Fifield

Counsel for: First of America Bank - Illinois, N.A.; AgriBank, FCB; Construction Equipment Federal Credit Union; Travelers Insurance Co.; Phoenix Mutual Life Insurance Co.; United States Fidelity & Guaranty Co.; Equitable Life Assurance Society of the U.S.; Board of Education of the City of Peoria School District, 150; Anderson State Bank.

For full biographical listings, see the Martindale-Hubbell Law Directory

KINGERY DURREE WAKEMAN & RYAN, ASSOC. (AV)

Commerce Bank Building, 416 Main Street, Suite 915, 61602
Telephone: 309-676-3612
FAX: 309-676-1329
Email: KDWRyan@aol.com

(See Next Column)

Arthur R. Kingery
Edward R. Durree
Steven A. Wakeman
Christopher P. Ryan
Philip M. O'Donnell
James P. Lawson
Michael S. McKinley

Reference: Commerce Bank of Peoria.

For full biographical listings, see the Martindale-Hubbell Law Directory

QUINN, JOHNSTON, HENDERSON & PRETORIUS, CHARTERED (AV)

(Formerly McConnell, Kennedy, Quinn & Johnston)
227 N. E. Jefferson Street, 61602
Telephone: 309-674-1133
Telecopier: 309-674-6503
Email: quinnlaw@qjhp.com *URL:* http://www.qjhp.com
Springfield, Illinois Office: Three North, Old State Capitol Plaza, 62701.
Telephone: 217-753-1133.

Lowell R. McConnell (1911-1971)
Golden A. McConnell (1914-1974)
Joseph A. Leimkuehler (1931-1974)
Thomas B. Kennedy, Sr. (1912-1988)
R. Michael Henderson
Murvel Pretorius, Jr.
Bradley W. Dunham
Robert H. Jennetten
Gregory A. Cerulo
Paul P. Gilfillan
Mary W. McDade
Laurie M. Judd
Stanley L. Morris (Resident, Springfield Office)
James Andrew Borland (Resident, Springfield Office)
Julie A. Ward
David Blair Collins
John F. Kamin
Michael J. Holt (Resident, Springfield Office)
Matthew B. Smith
Laura Marie Donahue
Peter R. Jennetten
Michael A. Kraft
Jo Tewes Wetherill
Laura A. Sallmann
Jonathan A. Stump

OF COUNSEL

Richard E. Quinn
W. Thomas Johnston

Representative Clients: Allstate Insurance Co.; American International Insurance Co.; Bituminous Casualty Corp.; General Motors; Illinois State Medical Insurance Services, Inc.; Pekin Insurance; Peoria Journal Star, Inc.; St. Paul Insurance Co.

For full biographical listings, see the Martindale-Hubbell Law Directory

ROBERT C. STRODEL, LTD. (AV)

927 Commerce Bank Building, 61602
Telephone: 309-676-4500
Fax: 309-676-4566

Robert C. Strodel

For full biographical listings, see the Martindale-Hubbell Law Directory

SUTKOWSKI & WASHKUHN LTD. (AV)

124 Southwest Adams Street, Suite 560, 61602
Telephone: 309-680-8000
Facsimile: 309-680-8001

Edward F. Sutkowski
Wilson C. Washkuhn
Dean B. Rhoads
Robert H. Rhode
Steven P. Oates

For full biographical listings, see the Martindale-Hubbell Law Directory

WESTERVELT, JOHNSON, NICOLL & KELLER (AV)

14th Floor, Associated Bank Plaza, 411 Hamilton Boulevard, 61602
Telephone: 309-671-3550
Fax: 309-671-3588
Email: westervelt@westerveltlaw.com

MEMBERS OF FIRM

Frank T. Miller (1873-1948)
O. P. Westervelt (1887-1970)
Eugene R. Johnson (1899-1981)
David A. Nicoll (1913-1993)
Homer W. Keller
Robert D. Jackson
Wayne L. Hanold
Ross E. Canterbury
James D. Broadway
Thomas M. Hayes
Thomas G. Harvel
Roger E. Holzgrafe
Daniel L. Johns
Kevin D. Schneider
James R. Morrison
L. Lee Smith
Thomas W. O'Neal
Charles Couri
Thomas A. McConnaughay
J. Phillip Krajewski
Timothy S. Flaherty

ASSOCIATES

Bradly M. Butler
Joseph J. Bembenek
Alan L. Hellman
Denise Koehler Green

Representative Clients: Allstate Insurance Cos.; ASARCO, Inc.; Caterpillar Inc.; The Firestone Tire & Rubber Co.; John Deere Co.; The Methodist Medical Center of Illinois; Metropolitan Life Insurance Co.; Peoria and Pekin Union Ry. Co.; Sears, Roebuck and Co.; State Farm Insurance Cos.

For full biographical listings, see the Martindale-Hubbell Law Directory

*QUINCY,** Adams Co.

SCHOLZ, LOOS, PALMER, SIEBERS & DUESTERHAUS (AV)

625 Vermont Street, 62301
Telephone: 217-223-3444; 217-222-7620
FAX: 217-223-3450

MEMBERS OF FIRM

Richard F. Scholz, Sr. (1901-1975)
Delbert Loos (1909-1993)
Charles A. Scholz
James L. Palmer
Steven E. Siebers
Joseph A. Duesterhaus
Christopher G. Scholz

ASSOCIATE

Jennifer A. Winking

Representative Clients: Heintz Electric Co.; Sunset Home; Quincy Notre Dame Foundation; First Bankers Trust Company, N.A.; Merchants Wholesale, Inc.; Quincy Newspapers, Inc.; Niemann Foods, Inc.
Local Counsel: NationsBank.

For full biographical listings, see the Martindale-Hubbell Law Directory

ROCHELLE, Ogle Co.

FEARER, NYE, AHLBERG & CHADWICK (AV)

420 Fourth Avenue, P.O. Box 117, 61068
Telephone: 815-562-2156
Fax: 815-562-2158
Email: philnye@rochelle.net
Oregon, Illinois Office: 209 South Fifth Street, P.O. Box 256, 61061.
Telephone: 815-732-6113.
Fax: 815-732-3193.

MEMBERS OF FIRM

Philip H. Nye, Jr.
James G. Ahlberg
Robert T. Chadwick

Represent: Del Monte Corp.; John Hancock Mutual Life Insurance Co.; Blackhawk State Bank; Kishwaukee College; Kemper Insurance Group; First National Bank & Trust Co. of Rochelle; Flagg-Rochelle Community Park District; Rochelle Community Hospital Association.

For full biographical listings, see the Martindale-Hubbell Law Directory

*ROCKFORD,** Winnebago Co.

HOLMSTROM & KENNEDY, P.C. (AV)

800 North Church Street, P.O. Box 589, 61105
Telephone: 815-962-7071
Fax: 815-962-7181
Email: mail@holmstrom-kennedy.com *URL:* http://www.holmstrom-kennedy.com

John Holmstrom, Jr.
Richard D. Gaines
Norman E. Lindstedt
Philip R. Frankfort
Donald L. Moore
Bradley T. Koch
Gregory P. Guth
Kim M. Casey
Roberta L. Holzwarth
Michael J. Schappert
Michael Jon Shalbrack
Eugene G. Doherty
Alexander J. Mezny

Aaron W. Brooks
Kathryn A. Honecker

For full biographical listings, see the Martindale-Hubbell Law Directory

LORD, BISSELL & BROOK (AV)

120 West State Street, Suite 200, 61101
Telephone: 815-963-8050
Email: info@lordbissell.com *URL:* http://www.lordbissell.com
Chicago, Illinois Office: Suites 2600-3600 Harris Bank Building, 115 South LaSalle Street, 60603.
Telephone: 312-443-0700.
Telecopy: 312-443-0336.
Cable Address: "Lowirco."
Telex: 25-0336.
Los Angeles, California Office: 300 South Grand Avenue, 90071-3200.
Telephone: 213-485-1500.
Telecopy: 213-485-1200.
Telex: 18-1135.
Atlanta, Georgia Office: One Atlantic Center, 1201 West Peachtree Street, N.W., Suite 3700, 30309.
Telephone: 404-870-4600.
Telecopy: 404-872-5547.
New York, N.Y. Office: One Penn Plaza, Suite 3435, 10119.
Telephone: 212-947-4700.
Facsimile: 212-947-1202.

RESIDENT PARTNERS

David P. Faulkner
Amy E. Shappert

RESIDENT ASSOCIATES

Charles A. Egner
Susan O'Brien

For full biographical listings, see the Martindale-Hubbell Law Directory

WILLIAMS & MCCARTHY, A PROFESSIONAL CORPORATION (AV)

321 West State Street, P.O. Box 219, 61105-0219
Telephone: 815-987-8900
Fax: 815-968-0019
Email: mail@wilmac.com *URL:* http://www.wilmac.com
Oregon, Illinois Office: 607 Washington Street. P.O. Box 339.
Telephone: 815-732-2101.
Fax: 815-732-2289.

Thomas S. Johnson (President, Williams & McCarthy)
Edward R. Telling, III
Russell D. Anderson
John E. Pfau
Richard A. Berman
John L. Shepherd
Terry D. Anderson
Kim D. Krahenbuhl (Resident Partner, Oregon, Illinois Office)
Scott C. Sullivan
Carol N. Bailey
James P. Devine
John J. Holevas
Timothy J. Rollins
Clayton L. Lindsey (Resident Partner, Oregon, Illinois Office)
Stephen E. Balogh
Marc C. Gravino
Thomas P. Sandquist
Carl A. Ecklund

Wendy S. Howarter (Resident, Oregon, Illinois Office)
Michael T. Cyrs
Troy E. Haggestad
Kari A. Vanderzyl (Resident, Oregon, Illinois Office)
Brendan A. Maher
Daniel Andrew Dunn, Jr

Representative Clients: Aircraft Gear Corp.; Anderson Industries, Inc.; Gallagher Bassett Insurance Co.; Liberty Mutual Insurance Co.; Atwood Industries, Inc.; The Travelers; American Mutual Insurance Co.; Rockford Health Systems; Chrysler Corp.; USF&G, West Bend.

For full biographical listings, see the Martindale-Hubbell Law Directory

*ROCK ISLAND,** Rock Island Co.

LANE & WATERMAN (AV)

224 18th Street, Suite 500, 61201
Telephone: 309-786-1600
Fax: 309-786-1794
URL: http://www.l-wlaw.com
Davenport, Iowa Office: 220 North Main Street, Suite 600.
Telephone: 319-324-3246.
Fax: 319-324-1616.

Robert A. Van Vooren
Charles E. Miller
Dana M. Craig
Robert V. P. Waterman, Jr.
Peter J. Benson
John D. Telleen
Richard A. Davidson

ASSOCIATES

Jason J. O'Rourke
Courtney M. Kay-Decker

For full biographical listings, see the Martindale-Hubbell Law Directory

WESSELS, STOJAN & STEPHENS P.C. (AV)

423 Seventeenth Street, Suite 101, P.O. Box 4300, 61204-4300
Telephone: 309-794-9400
Telecopier: 309-794-9386
Waterloo, Iowa Office: Suite 2, 227 East San Marnan Drive.
Telephone: 319-232-5904.
Fax: 319-232-7181.

Pete M. Wessels
Clark J. Stojan
B. Douglas Stephens

Representative Clients: Financial Institutions: Norwest Ag Credit; Norwest Business Credit, Inc.; Banc-Boston Mortgage Corp. Insurance Companies: American Family Insurance Group; International Claim Association; Design Professionals Insurance Co. General: Missman, Stanley & Associates Professional Corp.; IBP, Inc.; Hogan's Video, Inc.; Armstrong-Curtis Foundation.

*SPRINGFIELD,** Sangamon Co.

BROWN, HAY & STEPHENS (AV)

700 Mercantile Bank Building, P.O. Box 2459, 62701-1489
Telephone: 217-544-8491
Fax: 217-544-9609

MEMBERS OF FIRM

Harvey B. Stephens
Edward J. Cunningham
Robert A. Stuart, Jr.
J. Patrick Joyce, Jr.
Eric L. Grenzebach
Jeffery M. Wilday
William F. Trapp
Paul Bown
Almon A. Manson, Jr.
Dwight H. O'Keefe, III
Donald R. Tracy
Emmet A. Fairfield
Denise M. Druhot
Harvey M. Stephens
John E. Childress
James W. Bruner
Lorilea Buerkett

COUNSEL

Elizabeth W. Anderson

ASSOCIATES

Michael J. Drake
Catherine A. DeGenova-Carter
Ronald J. Giacone, II
Rudolph M. Braud, Jr.

(See Next Column)

BROWN, HAY & STEPHENS—*Continued*

OF COUNSEL

Norman P. Jones
Ben L. DeBoice
Simon L. Friedman
Robert M. Magill

For full biographical listings, see the Martindale-Hubbell Law Directory

GIFFIN, WINNING, COHEN & BODEWES, P.C. (AV)

1 West Old State Capitol Plaza, Suite 600 Myers Building, P.O. Box 2117, 62705
Telephone: 217-525-1571
Facsimile: 217-525-1710
Email: gifwinlaw@eosinc.com

D. Logan Giffin (1890-1980)
Montgomery S. Winning (1892-1966)
C. Terry Lindner (1903-1987)
Alfred F. Newkirk (1904-1980)
James M. Winning (Retired)
Robert S. Cohen
Herman G. Bodewes
John L. Swartz
Carol Hansen Posegate
R. Mark Mifflin
Thomas P. Schanzle-Haskins, III
Gregory K. Harris
David A. Herman
Michael Joseph Mannion
Stephan J. Roth

Jane N. Denes
David O. Edwards
M. Kyle Rominger

Representative Clients: Illinois State University; Union Planters Bank; Grinnell Mutual Reinsurance Co.; Illinois League of Financial Institutions; Southern Illinois University School of Medicine; Central Illinois Builders of A.G.C.; Great Central Insurance Cos.

For full biographical listings, see the Martindale-Hubbell Law Directory

GRAHAM AND GRAHAM, LTD. (AV)

1201 South Eighth Street, 62703
Telephone: 217-523-4569
Fax: 217-523-4656
Email: GandG@Dave-World.net

James M. Graham (1851-1945)
James J. Graham (1880-1965)
Hugh J. Graham (1877-1972)
Hugh J. Graham, Jr. (1910-1994)
Hugh J. Graham, III

Richard J. Wilderson
Nancy Eckert Martin
Bradley E. Huff
April Gowdy Troemper

Counsel for: Hospital Sisters Health System.
Representative Clients: Illinois and Midland Railway; SPCSL Railway; St. Anthony's Memorial Hospital, Effingham; St. Mary's Hospital, Decatur; St. John's Hospital, Springfield.

For full biographical listings, see the Martindale-Hubbell Law Directory

SORLING, NORTHRUP, HANNA, CULLEN AND COCHRAN, LTD. (AV)

Formerly Sorling, Catron and Hardin
800 Illinois Building, 607 East Adams Street, P.O. Box 5131, 62705
Telephone: 217-544-1144
Telecopier: 217-522-3173

Carl A. Sorling (1896-1991)
B. Lacey Catron, Jr. (1912-1959)
John H. Hardin (1909-1978)
George William Cullen (1917-1986)
Thomas L. Cochran (1916-1994)
Patrick V. Reilly
William S. Hanley
R. Gerald Barris
Stephen A. Tagge
Michael A. Myers
Carl Clark Germann
Gary A. Brown
Stephen R. Kaufmann
Frederick B. Hoffmann
William R. Enlow
Craig S. Burkhardt
Michael C. Connelly
Scott C. Helmholz
John A. Kauerauf
James M. Morphew
Stephen J. Bochenek
David A. Rolf
Margaret (Peggy) J. Ryan
Mark K. Cullen
Thomas H. Wilson
Todd Michael Turner
Charles J. Northrup
R. Lee Allen

Michael T. Kokal
Elizabeth A. Urbance
Mark O. Stern
W. Jason Rankin
Melanie K. Impastato
John W. Morse
Julie B. Cox

OF COUNSEL

Charles H. Northrup
Philip E. Hanna
William B. Bates

Counsel for: AmerenCIPS; Bank One Illinois, NA; Doctors Hospital, Springfield, Ill; Illini Dairy Queen, Inc.; Springfield Airport Authority.
Representative Clients: CIGNA Insurance; WICS-TV, Inc.

For full biographical listings, see the Martindale-Hubbell Law Directory

STREATOR, La Salle Co.

MYERS, DAUGHERITY, BERRY, O'CONOR & KUZMA, LTD. (AV)

7 Northpoint Drive, 61364
Telephone: 815-672-3116
Fax: 815-672-0738
Ottawa, Illinois Office: 130 East Madison Street.
Telephone: 815-434-6206.

John A. Berry (1912-1986)
Stephen C. Myers
Eugene P. Daugherity
Richard J. Berry
Andrew J. O'Conor
Sheryl H. Kuzma

For full biographical listings, see the Martindale-Hubbell Law Directory

*WATSEKA,** Iroquois Co.

ACKMAN, MAREK & BOYD, LTD. (AV)

223 East Mulberry Street, 60970
Telephone: 815-432-5215
Kankakee, Illinois Office: Suite 400, One Dearborn Square.
Telephone: 815-933-6681.

James A. Devine

Representative Clients: American States Insurance Co.; Consumers Illinois Water Co.; Country Mutual Insurance Co.; Farmers Insurance Group; Martin Boyer Co. Inc.; Medical Protective Co.; Union Insurance Co.

For full biographical listings, see the Martindale-Hubbell Law Directory

SUNDERLAND, MURPHY, SPENN, JOHNSON AND LUEBCHOW (AV)

130 West Cherry Street, 60970
Telephone: 815-432-3936
Fax: 815-432-3112
Milford, Illinois Office: 7 South Axtel.
Telephone: 815-889-4928.
Danforth, Illinois Office: 100 South Front Street.
Telephone: 815-269-2744.
Cissna Park, Illinois Office: 102 East Firelane Avenue.
Telephone: 815-457-2136.

MEMBERS OF FIRM

Louis B. Sunderland
Patrick J. Murphy
Theodore R. Spenn
Kay Lawfer Johnson
Kevin H. Luebchow

Representative Clients: Central Bank, Ashkum, Illinois; Cissna Park State Bank; Citizens State Bank of Milford; Farmers State Bank of Danforth; Iroquois Title Co.; Iroquois Farmers State Bank; Iroquois Federal Savings and Loan Assn.; Milford Building & Loan Assn.; Watseka Farmers Grain Co.

For full biographical listings, see the Martindale-Hubbell Law Directory

*WHEATON,** DuPage Co.

DONOVAN AND ROBERTS, P.C. (AV)

104 East Roosevelt Road, Suite 202, 60187
Telephone: 630-668-4211
Fax: 630-668-2076

Keith E. Roberts, Sr.
Keith E. (Chuck) Roberts, Jr.
Henry B. Vess, III

Marie F. Leach
Robert S. Marcott
Eric A. Burgeson
Kevin H. Saville

For full biographical listings, see the Martindale-Hubbell Law Directory

PICCIONE, KEELEY & ASSOCIATES, LTD. (AV)

County Farm Professional Park, 122 South County Farm Road, 60187-4523
Telephone: 630-653-8000
Telefax: 630-653-8029
Email: info@pkalaw.com *URL:* http://www.pkalaw.com

John J. Piccione
Patrick C. Keeley
Mark W. Tader
Lynn R. Conrad
Alison S. Franklin
Thomas A. Jackson
Timothy J. Shanley

For full biographical listings, see the Martindale-Hubbell Law Directory

RATHJE, WOODWARD, DYER & BURT (AV)

300 East Roosevelt Road, Suite 300, 60187
Telephone: 630-668-8500
Fax: 630-668-9218
Email: mwdmwd@msn.com *URL:* http://www.rathjewoodward.com

(See Next Column)

RATHJE, WOODWARD, DYER & BURT, *Wheaton—Continued*

MEMBERS OF FIRM

R. Terence Kalina
Henry S. Stillwell, III
Gary L. Taylor
John F. Garrow
Reese J. Peck
Tracy D. Kasson
Mark W. Daniel

ASSOCIATES

John R. Zemenak

OF COUNSEL

Peter A. Zamis
Henry J. Burt, Jr.

For full biographical listings, see the Martindale-Hubbell Law Directory

*WOODSTOCK,** McHenry Co.

CALDWELL, BERNER & CALDWELL (AV)

100 1/2 Cass Street, P.O. Box 1289, 60098
Telephone: 815-338-3300
Fax: 815-338-0015

MEMBERS OF FIRM

William I. Caldwell (1908-1971)
James E. Berner
William I. Caldwell, Jr.
Jeffrey A. Rouhandeh

OF COUNSEL

Louis A. Bianchi

Representative Clients: Amcore Bank N.A., Woodstock; Allstate Insurance Co.; American States Insurance Co.; Capitol Indemnity Corp.; Maryland Casualty Co.; Kemper Insurance Group; Northwestern National Insurance Group; C.N.A. Group; Universal Underwriters Insurance Co.; American Home Group.

For full biographical listings, see the Martindale-Hubbell Law Directory

INDIANA

*BEDFORD,** Lawrence Co.

STEELE, STEELE, McSOLEY & McSOLEY (AV)

Bank One Building, Suite One, 1602 I Street, 47421
Telephone: 812-279-3513
Fax: 812-275-3504
URL: http://www.steele-mcsoley.com

MEMBERS OF FIRM

Ruel W. Steele (1908-1992)
Byron W. Steele
Brent E. Steele
Patrick S. McSoley
Darlene Steele McSoley

Representative Clients: Bank One, Bloomington, NA, Bedford Branch; The First National Bank of Mitchell; The Times Mail (newspaper); Ralph Rogers & Co., Inc.; Indiana Bell Telephone Co.; Texas Gas Transmission Corporation; U.S. Gypsum Company.

For full biographical listings, see the Martindale-Hubbell Law Directory

*BLOOMINGTON,** Monroe Co.

BUNGER & ROBERTSON (AV)

226 South College Square, P.O. Box 910, 47402-0910
Telephone: 812-332-9295
Fax: 812-331-8808
Email: bunrob@iquest.net

MEMBERS OF FIRM

Len E. Bunger, Jr. (1921-1993)
Don M Robertson
Thomas Bunger
Joseph D. O'Connor
James L. Whitlatch
Samuel R. Ardery
Margaret M. Frisbie
William J. Beggs
John W. Richards

ASSOCIATES

Stephen G. Miller
Holly M. Harvey

Representative Clients: Aetna Insurance Companies; Bloomington Hospital; Commercial Union Group; Indiana Insurance Co.; Liberty Mutual Insurance; Medical Protective Co.; Monroe County Community School Corp.; Professional Golf Car, Inc.; Prudential Insurance Company of America; State Farm Automobile Insurance Co.

For full biographical listings, see the Martindale-Hubbell Law Directory

BREMEN, Marshall Co.

KIZER & NEU (AV)

1406 West Plymouth Street, P.O. Box 158, 46506
Telephone: 219-546-2626
FAX: 219-546-2608
Plymouth, Indiana Office: 319 West Jefferson Street. P.O. Box 158.
Telephone: 219-936-2169.
FAX: 219-936-2642.

(See Next Column)

James H. Neu (1917-1991)
Mark E. Wagner

Counsel for: The First State Bank, Bourbon, Indiana; Bremen Castings, Inc.; Bornemann Products, Inc., all of Bremen, Indiana.

For full biographical listings, see the Martindale-Hubbell Law Directory

CHESTERTON, Porter Co.

HARRIS, WELSH & LUKMANN (AV)

107 Broadway, 46304
Telephone: 219-926-2114
Fax: 219-926-1503
Email: hwl@netnitco.net

MEMBERS OF FIRM

Michael C. Harris
Robert A. Welsh
L. Charles Lukmann, III

Representative Clients: Northern Indiana Commuter Transportation District; Duneland School Corp.; Town of Burns Harbor, Indiana; Town of Chesterton; Paulson Oil Co.; Steel & Machinery Transport, Inc.; Porter Memorial Hospital; Centier Bank; Porter County Sheriffs Merit Board.

For full biographical listings, see the Martindale-Hubbell Law Directory

*COLUMBUS,** Bartholomew Co.

SHARPNACK, BIGLEY, DAVID & RUMPLE (AV)

321 Washington Street, P.O. Box 310, 47202-0310
Telephone: 812-372-1553
Fax: 812-372-1567
Email: sbdr@hsonline.net

MEMBERS OF FIRM

Julian Sharpnack (1879-1968)
Lew G. Sharpnack (1905-1968)
Thomas C. Bigley (1912-1978)
Maurice A. David (Retired)
Thomas C. Bigley, Jr.
John R. Rumple
Timothy J. Vrana
John A. Stroh
Jeffrey S. Washburn
Joan Tupin Crites

Representative Clients: Irwin Union Bank and Trust Co.; Ameritech; State Farm Mutual Insurance Cos.; Home News Enterprises; Centra Credit Union; Richards Elevator, Inc.; GRE Insurance Group; Indiana Farmers Insurance; Glick Farms, Inc.

For full biographical listings, see the Martindale-Hubbell Law Directory

ELKHART, Elkhart Co.

BAKER & DANIELS (AV)

301 B South Main Street, Suite 307, 46516
Telephone: 219-296-6000
Fax: 219-296-6001
URL: http://www.bakerdaniels.com
Indianapolis, Indiana Office: 300 North Meridian Street, 46204.
Telephone: 317-237-0300.
South Bend, Indiana Office: First Bank Building, 205 West Jefferson Boulevard, 46601.
Telephone: 219-234-4149.
Fort Wayne, Indiana Office: 111 East Wayne Street, Suite 800, 46802.
Telephone: 219-424-8000.
Washington, D.C. Office: 805 15th Street, Suite 700, 20005.
Telephone: 202-312-7440.
Qingdao, China Office: Room C, 13th Floor, Qingdao Beer Building, May 4th Square, 35 Donghai Road, 266071.
Telephone: +011-86-532-575-1051.
Fax: +011-86-532-575-1055.

MEMBERS OF FIRM

M. Angella Castille (Resident)
George T. Dodd
Peter G. Trybula
Kennard R. Weaver (Resident)

OF COUNSEL

Paul D. Borghesani

ASSOCIATES

Daniel G. Areaux
David W. Barrett (Resident)

Representative Clients: Central Soya Co., Inc.; The Lutheran Hospital of Indiana, Inc.; Tokheim Corp.; General Motors Corp.; Eli Lilly and Co.

For full biographical listings, see the Martindale-Hubbell Law Directory

BARNES & THORNBURG (AV)

121 West Franklin Street, Suite 200, 46516
Telephone: 219-293-0681
FAX: 219-296-2535
URL: http://www.btlaw.com
Indianapolis, Indiana Office: 11 South Meridian Street, 46204.
Telephone: 317-236-1313.
FAX: 317-231-7433.
Fort Wayne, Indiana Office: Suite 600, One Summit Square, 46802.
Telephone: 219-423-9440.
FAX: 219-424-8316.

(See Next Column)

BARNES & THORNBURG—*Continued*

South Bend, Indiana Office: 600 1st Source Bank Center, 100 North Michigan, 46601-1632.
Telephone: 219-233-1171.
FAX: 219-237-1125.
Chicago, Illinois Office: 2600 Chase Plaza, 10 South La Salle Street, 60603.
Telephone: 312-357-1313.
FAX: 312-759-5646.
Washington, D.C. Office: 1401 Eye Street, N.W., Suite 500, 20005.
Telephone: 202-289-1313.
FAX: 202-289-1330.

MEMBERS OF FIRM

Geoffrey K. Church
Samuel S. Thompson
Rand W. Nilsson
Richard W. Paulen
Paul E. Becher
J. Scott Troeger
Brian J. Clark

OF COUNSEL

John R. Harman
Richard M. Treckelo

ASSOCIATES

Tracy D. Knox
Christopher M. Kelly
Jennifer A. Bickley

Representative Clients: Bank One; Elkhart Community Schools; Elkhart General Hospital; Heywood Williams Group PLC; KeyBank National Association; Partners National Health Plans of Indiana, Inc.; Rieth-Riley Construction Co., Inc.; Skyline Corporation; Whirlpool Corporation.

For full biographical listings, see the Martindale-Hubbell Law Directory

*EVANSVILLE,** Vanderburgh Co.

BARBER, HAMILTON & SHOULDERS (AV)

123 N.W. Fourth Street, Suite 402, 47708
Telephone: 812-425-9211
Fax: 812-425-9216
Email: bhslegal@evansville.net

Steve Barber
John A. Hamilton
Jeffrey T. Shoulders

For full biographical listings, see the Martindale-Hubbell Law Directory

BOWERS, HARRISON, KENT & MILLER, LLP (AV)

25 N.W. Riverside Drive, P.O. Box 1287, 47706-1287
Telephone: 812-426-1231
Fax: 812-464-3676
Email: BOWERS,HARRISON,KENT&MILLER,LLP@BHKM.COM
URL: http://WWW.BHKM.COM

MEMBERS OF FIRM

F. Wesley Bowers
Joseph H. Harrison
David V. Miller
Paul E. Black
Gary R. Case
Arthur D. Rutkowski
George C. Barnett, Jr.
Terry Noffsinger
Paul J. Wallace
David E. Gray
Gregory A. Kahre
Timothy J. Hubert
Thomas A. Massey
Greg A. Granger
Joseph H. Harrison, Jr.
Lawrence L. Grimes
Sara Harrison Zeidler
Christopher L. Lucas

ASSOCIATES

Cedric Hustace
Sean M. Georges
Douglas K. Briody
Holly H. Wilhelmus
Stacy Kerns Harris
Keith William Vonderahe

OF COUNSEL

K. Wayne Kent
William G. Greif

LEGAL SUPPORT PERSONNEL

Victor J. Ippoliti (Law Clerk)

Division Counsel in Indiana for: Southern Railway Co.
Representative Clients: Permanent Federal Savings Bank; Citizens Realty & Insurance, Inc.

For full biographical listings, see the Martindale-Hubbell Law Directory

KAHN, DEES, DONOVAN & KAHN, LLP (AV)

Fifth Main Financial Plaza, Suite 305, P.O. Box 3646, 47735-3646
Telephone: 812-423-3183
Fax: 812-423-3841
Email: evvlaw@k2d2.com

MEMBERS OF FIRM

Isidor Kahn (1887-1963)
Robert Kahn (Retired)
Arthur R. Donovan (Retired)
Harry P. Dees (Retired)
Alan N. Shovers
Thomas O. Magan
Larry R. Downs
Jon D. Goldman
Brian P. Williams
G. Michael Schopmeyer
John E. Hegeman
Jeffrey K. Helfrich
Jeffrey W. Ahlers
Marjorie J. Scharpf
Kent A. Brasseale II
Christopher D. Lee

(See Next Column)

ASSOCIATES

Mark A. McAnulty
Allison K. Comstock
Robert F. "Ted" Barron II
Mark S. Samila
Steven S. Hoar
Jason H. Guthrie
Scott F. Hill
Todd C. Barsumian
Lee F. Baker

Counsel for: Deaconess Hospital, Inc.; Keller Crescent Co., Inc.; Guardian Automotive Trim, Inc.; Atlas Van Lines, Inc.; Champion Laboratories, Inc.; Cresline Plastic Pipe Co., Inc.; University of Southern Indiana; Toyota Motor Corporate Services of North America, Inc.; AK Steel Corporation; North Park Cinemas, Inc.

For full biographical listings, see the Martindale-Hubbell Law Directory

*FORT WAYNE,** Allen Co.

BAKER & DANIELS (AV)

111 East Wayne Street, Suite 800, 46802
Telephone: 219-424-8000
Fax: 219-460-1700
URL: http://www.bakerdaniels.com
Indianapolis, Indiana Office: 300 North Meridian Street, 46204.
Telephone: 317-237-0300.
South Bend, Indiana Office: First Bank Building, 205 West Jefferson Boulevard, 46601.
Telephone: 219-234-4149.
Elkhart, Indiana Office: 301 B South Main Street, Suite 307, 46516.
Telephone: 219-296-6000.
Washington, D.C. Office: 805 15th Street, Suite 700, 20005.
Telephone: 202-312-7440.
Qingdao, China Office: Room C, 13th Floor, Qingdao Beer Building, May 4th Square, 35 Donghai Road, 266071.
Telephone: +011-86-532-575-1051.
Fax: +011-86-532-575-1055.

MEMBERS OF FIRM

Jon A. Bomberger (Resident)
John R. Burns, III (Resident)
Albert J. Dahm (Resident)
Jeffrey O. Davidson (Resident)
George T. Dodd
Kevin R. Erdman (Resident)
Timothy J. Haffner (Resident)
Steven H. Hazelrigg (Resident)
John F. Hoffman (Resident)
Robert T. Hoover (Resident)
David P. Irmscher (Resident)
Steven L. Jackson (Resident)
Michael L. James (Resident)
Joseph W. Kimmell, II (Resident)
Jeanne E. Longsworth (Resident)
Robert D. Moreland (Resident)
Michael J. Nader
Anthony Niewyk (Resident)
H. John Okeson (Resident)
Maclyn T. Parker (Resident)
Douglas Dormire Powers (Resident)
David A. Scott (Resident)
Lawrence E. Shine (Resident)
Thomas M. Shoaff (Resident)
N. Reed Silliman (Resident)
Keith E. White (Resident)

RESIDENT OF COUNSEL

John W. Porter

RESIDENT ASSOCIATES

Thomas A. Adams
Kathryn Hillebrands Burroughs
David P. Durm
Michael S. Elvin (Not admitted in IN)
Meg A. Gallmeyer
Gary D. Johnson
David J. Kuker
Scott M. Lohnes
Karen T. Moses
Laura C. O'Donnell
David N. Royster
Michael Dallas Smith
Andrew J. Welborn
Mark A. Werling

Representative Clients: Anthem Insurance Companies, Inc.; Central Soya Co., Inc.; Conseco, Inc.; Eli Lilly & Co.; Essex Group, Inc.; ITT Corp. (Aerospace/Opitical Division); Shambaugh & Son, Inc.; United Airlines; Weaver Popcorn, Inc.; Wells Fargo.

For full biographical listings, see the Martindale-Hubbell Law Directory

BARNES & THORNBURG (AV)

Suite 600, One Summit Square, 46802
Telephone: 219-423-9440
FAX: 219-424-8316
URL: http://www.btlaw.com
Indianapolis, Indiana Office: 11 South Meridian Street, 46204.
Telephone: 317-236-1313.
FAX: 317-231-7433.
South Bend, Indiana Office: 600 1st Source Bank Center, 100 North Michigan, 46601-1632.
Telephone: 219-233-1171.
FAX: 219-237-1125.
Elkhart, Indiana Office: 121 West Franklin Street, Suite 200, 46516.
Telephone: 219-293-0681.
FAX: 219-296-2535.
Chicago, Illinois Office: 2600 Chase Plaza, 10 South La Salle Street, 60603.
Telephone: 312-357-1313.
FAX: 312-759-5646.
Washington, D.C. Office: 1401 Eye Street, N.W., Suite 500, 20005.
Telephone: 202-289-1313.
FAX: 202-289-1330.

(See Next Column)

Barnes & Thornburg, *Fort Wayne—Continued*

MEMBERS OF FIRM

William T. Hopkins, Jr.
John C. Theisen
Bobby Brian Gillenwater
Mark Alan Garvin
Stephen L. Fink
John C. Barce
D. Randall Brown

OF COUNSEL

Miles C. Gerberding
Herbert C. Snyder, Jr.
Richard E. Steinbronn
Frank L. Gallucci (Not admitted in IN)
Mark D. Levick
Michael S. Gzybowski
M. Scott Hall
Michael A. Scheer
Cindy Ann Wolfer

ASSOCIATES

Kathleen M. Anderson
Mark S. Kittaka
Thomas N. O'Malley
Eric H.J. Stahlhut
Tonya S. Shea
Daniel B. Starr
Holly A. Brady
Karen A. Festa
Dawn R. Westfield
Gary C. Furst
Shaun E. Graham
Matthew M. Hohman
Gregory S. Cooper
Maci M. Doden

Representative Clients: Demeter; Do it Best Corp.; EP Graphics, Inc.; Frick Services, Inc.; General Motors Corporation; Group Dekko International; Liberty Homes, Inc.; Lincoln National Corporation; Norwest Bank Indiana, N.A.; Zollner Pistons, L.L.C.

For full biographical listings, see the Martindale-Hubbell Law Directory

Beckman Lawson, LLP (AV)

800 Standard Federal Plaza, 46802
Telephone: 219-422-0800
Facsimile: 219-420-1013
Syracuse, Indiana Office: 200 West Main Street.
Telephone: 219-457-5727.
Facsimile: 219-457-2056.

MEMBERS OF FIRM

Jack W. Lawson
Frank J. Gray
Howard B. Sandler
Stephen R. Snyder
James A. Federoff
William L. Sweet, Jr.
Richard H. Blaich
John H. Brandt
Jon A. Bragalone
Brian J. T'Kindt
Douglas R. Adelsperger
Travis S. Friend
Robert L. Nicholson
David D. Cornwell
James A. Butz
Jack C. Birch
Craig R. Patterson

ASSOCIATES

John M. Ketcham
Wendy W. Davis
Jeffrey B. Harding
Martha M. Kinder
Edward J. Ormsby
Randall L. Morgan
Daniel J. Deeb
Patrick R. Hess
Georgia L. Hartman
Brian M. Simpson
James E. Rossow, Jr.
Sarah A. Hiestand
Tandra S. Johnson
Jason M. Kuchmay
Matthew J. Elliott

OF COUNSEL

Frederick A. Beckman
Neil F. Sandler
Douglas E. Miller
Loren K. Allison

Reference: National City Bank.

For full biographical listings, see the Martindale-Hubbell Law Directory

Helmke, Beams, Boyer & Wagner (AV)

300 Metro Building, Berry & Harrison Streets, 46802-2242
Telephone: 219-422-7422
Telecopier: 219-422-6764
Email: hbbwdjb@aol.com
Email: rdboyer1@fortwayne.infi.net

MEMBERS OF FIRM

Walter E. Helmke (1901-1976)
Walter P. Helmke
R. David Boyer
Robert A. Wagner
J. Timothy McCaulay
Daniel J. Borgmann
Trina Glusenkamp Gould

ASSOCIATES

Payne D. Brown
R. David Boyer, II

OF COUNSEL

Glen J. Beams
William A. Berning

Representative Clients: Aalco Distributing Co., Inc.; Brotherhood Mutual Insurance Co.; Fremont Community Schools; Air-O-Mat, Inc.; Leo Distributors, Inc.; The City of Fort Wayne, Indiana; Foellinger Foundation, Inc.

For full biographical listings, see the Martindale-Hubbell Law Directory

Rothberg & Logan (AV)

(Formerly, Rothberg, Gallmeyer, Fruechtenicht & Logan)
2100 National City Center, 110 West Berry Street, P.O. Box 11647, 46859-1647
Telephone: 219-422-9454
Telefax: 219-422-1622

MEMBERS OF FIRM

Sol Rothberg (1910-1993)
Thomas A. Gallmeyer (1922-1981)
George E. Fruechtenicht (1925-1996)
Thomas D. Logan
Martin T. Fletcher, Sr.
F. L. Dennis Logan
David R. Smelko
Dennis F. Dykhuizen
Anne Carney
Gregory Martin Cole
Michael T. Deam
Brian L. Nehrig
Daniel G. McNamara

ASSOCIATES

J. Rickard Donovan
Christine M. Stach
Susan E. Eckart
Alisa L. Rude

OF COUNSEL

John H. Heiney

Counsel for: Parkview Hospital; Cameron Memorial Community Hospital; Norwest Bank Indiana, N.A.; Parkview Health System; Azar's, Incorporated; Fort Wayne-Allen County Airport Authority; Fort Wayne Public Transportation Corporation; Avis Industrial Corp.; Farm Credit Services of Mid-America, ASA; Slater Fort Wayne Federal Credit Union.

For full biographical listings, see the Martindale-Hubbell Law Directory

Shambaugh, Kast, Beck & Williams, LLP (AV)

600 Standard Federal Plaza, 46802-2405
Telephone: 219-423-1430
Fax: 219-422-9038
Email: skbwlawyers@skbw.com *URL:* http://www.skbw.com

MEMBERS OF FIRM

Willard Shambaugh (1897-1976)
Michael H. Kast
Edward E. Beck
Stephen J. Williams
Daniel E. Serban
John B. Powell
Ronald D. Felger
James D. Streit
Paul R. Sturm

LEGAL SUPPORT PERSONNEL

CERTIFIED PUBLIC ACCOUNTANT

David A. Fee

Counsel for: Hagerman Construction Corp.; Rogers Markets, Inc.; K & H Realty Corp.; Olive B. Cole Foundation; M. E. Raker Foundation, Inc.; Associates Financial Services Co., of Indiana, Inc.; Professional Federal Credit Union; Fort Wayne Education Association; CBT Credit Services, Inc.; Ian & Miriam Rolland Foundation, Inc.

For full biographical listings, see the Martindale-Hubbell Law Directory

*GOSHEN,** Elkhart Co.

Yoder, Ainlay, Ulmer & Buckingham (AV)

130 North Main Street, P.O. Box 575, 46527-0575
Telephone: 219-533-1171
Telecopier: 219-534-4174
Email: info@yaub.com

MEMBERS OF FIRM

George L. Pepple (1907-1963)
Frank E. Yoder (1917-1996)
John D. Ulmer
George E. Buckingham
Gregory A. Hartzler
R. Gordon Lord
Craig M. Buche
Michael F. DeBoni
Alan L. Weldy
B. Douglas Hayes
Mark A. Matthes

ASSOCIATES

Denise C. Davis
Bodie J. Stegelmann
David E. Swihart

OF COUNSEL

Charles W. Ainlay

Counsel for: CTB, Inc.; Elkhart County Farm Bureau Credit Union; Elkhart County Government; First State Bank of Middlebury; Goshen College; Goshen General Hospital; Goshen Rubber Co.; State Farm Insurance Cos.; Town of Middlebury, IN.

For full biographical listings, see the Martindale-Hubbell Law Directory

HAMMOND, Lake Co.

McHie, Myers, McHie & Enslen (AV)

53 Muenich Court, 46320
Telephone: 219-931-1707
Telecopier: 219-932-2417

MEMBERS OF FIRM

G. Edward McHie
Charles A. Myers
James E. McHie
Charles Endicott Enslen
Carol M. Green

(See Next Column)

McHie, Myers, McHie & Enslen—*Continued*

Representative Clients: USX Corporation; Ronwal Transportation, Inc.; Hammond Redevelopment Commission; Hammond Economic Development Commission; Hammond Redevelopment Authority; Highland Redevelopment Commission; Whiting Redevelopment Commission; Raytrans, Inc.; La Salle Steel Co.; Emro Marketing Co., A Division of Marathon Oil; Combined Transport Systems, Inc.; Smith Motors, Inc. of Hammond d/b/a/ Smith Cheverolet; Smith Ford of Lowell, Inc.

For full biographical listings, see the Martindale-Hubbell Law Directory

*INDIANAPOLIS,** Marion Co.

Baker & Daniels (AV)

300 North Meridian Street, 46204
Telephone: 317-237-0300
Fax: 317-237-1000
URL: http://www.bakerdaniels.com
Fort Wayne, Indiana Office: 111 East Wayne Street, Suite 800, 46802.
Telephone: 219-424-8000.
South Bend, Indiana Office: First Bank Building, 205 West Jefferson Boulevard, 46601.
Telephone: 219-234-4149.
Elkhart, Indiana Office: 301 B South Main Street, Suite 307, 46516.
Telephone: 219-296-6000.
Washington, D.C. Office: 805 15th Street, Suite 700, 20005.
Telephone: 202-312-7440.
Qingdao, China Office: Room C, 13th Floor, Qingdao Beer Building, May 4th Square, 35 Donghai Road, 266071.
Telephone: +011-86-532-575-1051.
Fax: +011-86-532-575-1055.

MEMBERS OF FIRM

Irene T. Adamczyk
Terrill D. Albright
Anne Slaughter Andrew
James A. Aschleman
Phillip E. Bainbridge
Deborah Rae Beck
Michael D. Beck
Lewis D. Beckwith
Donald P. Bennett
Ben W. Blanton
Daniel L. Boeglin
J. Jeffrey Brown
Brian K. Burke
H. Patrick Callahan
James M. Carr
Stephen A. Claffey
James W. Clark
Gregory N. Dale
Miriam Smulevitz Dant
Francina A. Dlouhy
Robert W. Elzer
Theodore J. Esping
Daniel F. Evans, Jr.
Brian S. Fennerty
Richard T. Freije, Jr.
Thomas C. Froehle Jr.
Brant O. Gardner
John A. Gardner
Nancy J. Gargula
Ronald D. Gifford
David A. Given
G. Frederick Glass
Kevin P. Griffith
Matthew R. Gutwein
Paul Lowell Haines
James H. Ham, III
David R. Hamer
David K. Herzog
Scott D. Himsel
Michael J. Huston
Jay Jaffe
Jerry R. Jenkins
Robert L. Jessup
David Lawther Johnson
John S. Keeler
Tibor D. Klopfer
Scott M. Kosnoff
Mary Katherine Lisher
Michael J. MacLean
Michael R. Maine
Mitzi Harris Martin
Byron K. Mason
Alan L. McLaughlin
Jeffrey A. Michael
David W. Miller
John T. Neighbours
Todd Murray Nierman
J. Daniel Ogren
Stephen H. Paul
Hudnall A. Pfeiffer
Thomas A. Pitman
Wendy Wright Ponader
John W. Purcell
Roberta Sabin Recker
Charles T. Richardson
Rebecca A. Richardson
Norman P. Rowe
Christopher G. Scanlon
John R. Schaibley, III
Fred E. Schlegel
Joseph M. Scimia
Gayle L. Skolnik
Andrew Z. Soshnick
Robert Kirk Stanley
Richard C. Starkey
Jeffrey M. Stautz
Thomas G. Stayton
John B. Swarbrick, Jr.
John Joseph Tanner
Brent D. Taylor
Bradley Merrill Thompson
Nancy G. Tinsley
Kevin M. Toner
Gregory J. Utken
Thomas A. Vogtner
Mark A. Voigtmann
David C. Worrell
Mark E. Wright
Robert S. Wynne
Joseph H. Yeager, Jr.

COUNSEL

Virgil L. Beeler
Henry B. Blackwell, II
Joseph B. Carney
John D. Cochran
J. B. King
William F. Landers
Thomas M. Lofton
Merrill S. Thompson
Arthur R. Whale
Dan R. Winchell

ASSOCIATES

Thaddeus R. Ailes
Michael E. Allen
James J. Ammeen, Jr.
David A. Arrensen
Michael C. Bartol
Suzette E. Bewley
James S. Birge
Robert M. Bond
Mark L. Boos
Ellen E. Boshkoff
Jennifer K. Bowman
Joseph C. Bowman
Todd N. Bundrant
Nicole Jones Cail
Janet Madden Charles
Elizabeth Kelley Cierzniak

(See Next Column)

ASSOCIATES (Continued)

Carolyn M. Coleman
Carol Warren Collins
Patrick S. Cross
Brian A. Dahl
(Not admitted in IN)
Emily F. Duck
Troy D. Farmer
Thomas M. Fisher
David A. Foster
Brenda Hacker Freije
Frederick H. Garver
Philip J. Gibbons, Jr.
Dee Dee Gowan
David L. Hanselman, Jr.
David E. Harris
David L. Hatchett
John P. Hatter, Jr.
Susan Brenneman Hawkins
Sharon A. Hilmes
Debra L. Hinshaw
Edward E. Hollis, III
Thomas F. Hurka
Thomas A. Jensen
Amy E. Kosnoff
Jennifer L. Kremp
Dennis P. Lager
Ji-Qing Liu
Christine Graffis Long
Suzann Weber Lupton
Thomas Major, Jr.
Danelle Miller Marks
Jan Michelsen
Joseph E. Miller, Jr.
Cathleen L. Nevin
Shaun Healy O'Brien
Carl R. Pebworth
Stacy L. Prall
Edward J. Prein
Cynthia Pearson Purvis
Courtney F. Ren
Andrea M. Roberts
Kent A. Rollison
MaryAnn Schlegel Ruegger
Mark C. Sausser
April E. Sellers
Brandon M. Shelton
Patricia Cowan Skelton
Melissa J. Smith
Cynthia K. Springer
Brad Sugarman
(Not admitted in IN)
Gregory L. Taylor
Jonathan T. Tempel
Michael J. Valaik
Xiang Wang
Michael R. Watters
Christine B. Zoccola
Kerry E. Zook

Representative Clients: Anthem Insurance Companies, Inc.; AT&T Corp.; Bank One, Indianapolis, N.A.; Bindley Western Industries, Inc.; City of Indianapolis; Conseco, Inc.; Cummins Engine Co., Inc.; Eli Lilly & Co.; Paul Harris Stores, Inc.; United Airlines.

For full biographical listings, see the Martindale-Hubbell Law Directory

Barnes & Thornburg (AV)

11 South Meridian Street, 46204
Telephone: 317-236-1313
FAX: 317-231-7433; 317-231-7452
URL: http://www.btlaw.com
Fort Wayne, Indiana Office: Suite 600, One Summit Square, 46802.
Telephone: 219-423-9440.
FAX: 219-424-8316.
South Bend, Indiana Office: 600 1st Source Bank Center, 100 North Michigan, 46601-1632.
Telephone: 219-233-1171.
FAX: 219-237-1125.
Elkhart, Indiana Office: 121 West Franklin Street, Suite 200, 46516.
Telephone: 219-293-0681.
FAX: 219-296-2535.
Chicago, Illinois Office: 2600 Chase Plaza, 10 South La Salle Street, 60603.
Telephone: 312-357-1313.
FAX: 312-759-5646.
Washington, D.C. Office: 1401 Eye Street, N.W., Suite 500, 20005.
Telephone: 202-289-1313.
FAX: 202-289-1330.

Earl B. Barnes (1881-1966)

MEMBERS OF FIRM

Richard E. Deer
Jack H. Rogers
Robert H. Reynolds
William R. Coffey
D. Reed Scism
Robert P. Johnstone
Tom Charles Huston
Sydney F. Arak
Daniel H. FitzGibbon
Stephen Kendall Smith
Michael R. Fruehwald
Edward O. DeLaney
Donald E. Knebel
Wayne C. Kreuscher
Kristin G. Fruehwald
Daniel W. McGill
Kent E. Agness
Michael R. Conner
Claudia V. Swhier
Catherine L. Bridge
Richard D. Conard
Larry J. Stroble
Michael Rosiello
Peter J. Rusthoven
Larry A. Mackey
Stephen W. Lee
Stanley C. Fickle
Steven R. Lammert
David M. Powlen
Michael P. Lucas
John M. Kyle III
Michael K. McCrory
Anne N. DePrez
Robert D. MacGill
Robert T. Grand
Mark D. Stuaan
Alan A. Levin
Kenneth H. Inskeep
Alan K. Mills
Douglas J. Heckler
Timothy J. Riffle
Steven W. Thornton
Howard E. Kochell
Kenneth J. Yerkes
Neal W. Steinbart
Richard A. Rezek
Lynn C. Tyler
Eric R. Moy
Jan M. Carroll
Marcie R. Horowitz
Michael G. Paton
Anne C. McGown
James M. Gutting
Margaret Best Burlingame
John R. Maley
Teresa E. Morton
Dean T. Barnhard
Dwight D. Lueck
J. Michael Grubbs
Timothy E. Niednagel
Anthony C. Sullivan
Joseph C. Chapelle

(See Next Column)

BARNES & THORNBURG, *Indianapolis—Continued*

MEMBERS OF FIRM (Continued)

Joseph E. Loftus
Andrew J. Detherage
Terry W. Dawson
Nicholas K. Kile

OF COUNSEL

Thomas M. Scanlon
Jerry P. Belknap
John W. Houghton
Lester M. Ponder
William E. Roberts
Henry C. Ryder
Robert E. Highfield
Shirley A. Shideler
Jerry E. Hyland
Edward A. Keirn
Guinn P. Doyle
Mariana Richmond
Nancy J. Harrison
Michiharu Homma
Linda K. Todd
Dilip Kulkarni
David B. Quick
William D. Hammel

ASSOCIATES

Joseph G. Eaton
Jeffery J. Qualkinbush
Donald E. Williams
Richard J. Hall
Bart A. Karwath
Michael A. Moffatt
Karen L. Kovalsky
Barbara J. Meier
Peter A. Morse, Jr.
Victoria A. Gorczyca
John T. Bailey
Edward Sean Griggs
Nicholas E. Mathioudakis
Blake J. Burgan
Christine K. Jacobson
Elaine Waterhouse Wilson
Thomas M. Maxwell
Charles P. Edwards
William E. Padgett
R. Trevor Carter
Brian L. Burdick
Derek D. Murphy
Mark J. Dinsmore
Thomas F. Shea
Michael T. Scanlon
Kenneth J. Waite
Manotti Lemorris Jenkins
Patricia L. Ogden
Kepten D. Carmichael
Amy H. Joliet
Keila M. Selders
Mark A. Lindsey
Susan M. Zoeller
Michael D. Moon, Jr.
Jill Tabor Powlick
Julie O. Farris
James R. Sweeney II
Thomas H. Engle
Jeffrey A. Hopper
Joseph J. Jacobi
Randal J. Kaltenmark
Nathan A. Baker
Jennifer C. Lee-Crist
Julie A. Russell
Susan C. Wiggington
John P. Fischer
Thomas S. Reynolds II
Thomas F. O'Gara
Jill Bracken-Emerson
Christian P. Jones
(Not admitted in IN)
Elena Pantel Anastasiou
(Not admitted in IN)
James M. Hauck
Norman J. Hedges
Angela Diane Marek
Jonathan D. Mattingly
Terri L. Bruksch
Kimberly Williams Blanchet
LaChelle D. Stepp
Dennis P. Stolle
Leslie G. Love
Andrew B. Dzeguze
Julia L. Spoor

Representative Clients: Ameritech; DePuy Orthopaedics, Inc.; Dow AgroSciences; Eli Lilly and Company; Hillenbrand Industries; The Lincoln National Life Insurance Company; Purdue Research Foundation; Roche Diagnostics Corporation; Toyota Motor Corporation; Whirlpool Corporation.

For full biographical listings, see the Martindale-Hubbell Law Directory

BOSE MCKINNEY & EVANS LLP (AV)

2700 First Indiana Plaza, 135 North Pennsylvania Street, 46204
Telephone: 317-684-5000
Facsimile: 317-684-5173
URL: http://www.boselaw.com
Indianapolis North Office: Suite 1500, 8888 Keystone Crossing, 46240.
Telephone: 317-574-3700.
Facsimile: 317-574-3716.

MEMBERS OF FIRM

William M. Evans (1923-1991)
Robert H. McKinney (Retired)
John W. Wynne (Retired)
Lewis C. Bose (Retired)
Wayne C. Ponader (Retired)
James P. Seidensticker, Jr.
(Retired)
Jon M. Bailey
Alan W. Becker
Debra Linn Burns
David A. Butcher
James E. Carlberg
James C. Carlino
Gary L. Chapman
Robert B. Clemens
James A. Coles
Kendall C. Crook
Donald K. Densborn
Ronald E. Elberger
Daniel C. Emerson
Kirk E. Grable
E. Victor Indiano
Robert K. Johnson
Robert P. Kassing
Amy Rankin Kennelly
V. Samuel Laurin III
Kathleen G. Lucas
R. J. McConnell
Daniel P. McInerny
Donald M. Meyer
Dwight L. Miller
Margaret Bannon Miller
Roderick H. Morgan
Philip A. Nicely
Theodore J. Nowacki
George Thomas Patton, Jr.
L. Parvin Price
George E. Purdy
Charles R. Rubright
Steven G. Rudolf
C. Joseph Russell
David Williams Russell
Daniel B. Seitz
John K. Smeltzer
G. Pearson Smith, Jr.
Ronald M. Soskin
Natalie J. Stucky
Karl R. Sturbaum
David L. Swider
David A. Travelstead
Michael A. Trentadue
Thomas E. Wheeler II
David L. Wills
Elizabeth Theobald Young

(See Next Column)

OF COUNSEL

Arthur W. DePrez
Phyllis J. Garrison
Peter Lynn Goerges
Rodger K. Hendershot
Judy L. Woods

ASSOCIATES

Jonathan Taggart Birge
Mary E. Browne
Cathy Elliott
Anthony P. Filomena
Temple L. Garner
Lisa McKinney Goldner
Tammy K. Haney
Stephanie Franco Holtzlander
J. Christopher Janak
Bernie W. Keller
Kathleen I. Lee
Andrew M. McNeil
John A. Millspaugh
Mary Beth Plummer
Jeffrey M. Reed
Melinda R. Shapiro
Karen Glasser Sharp
J. Gregory Shelley
Kevin S. Smith
Alan S. Townsend
Susan E. Traynor
Shilpa Mehta Upadhye
Jeffrey D. Weinstein
Monique C. Winkler

LEGAL SUPPORT PERSONNEL

Steven B. Granner
(Zoning Consultant)
Patricia H. McGuffey
(Public Affairs Consultant)
Donald Blinzinger
(Public Affairs Consultant)

Representative Clients: Association of Indiana Life Insurance Cos.; Duke Realty Limited Partnership; Emmis Communications Corp.; First Indiana Bank; Indianapolis Colts, Inc.; Indiana League of Savings Institutions, Inc.; Prudential Life Insurance Co.; Metropolitan Life Insurance Co.; USX Corp.

For full biographical listings, see the Martindale-Hubbell Law Directory

BRATTAIN & MINNIX (AV)

151 North Delaware Street Suite 760, 46204
Telephone: 317-231-1750
Facsimile: 317-231-1760

Bruce D. Brattain
Larry A. Minnix

For full biographical listings, see the Martindale-Hubbell Law Directory

HACKMAN HULETT & CRACRAFT, LLP (AV)

2400 One Indiana Square, 46204
Telephone: 317-636-5401
Facsimile: 317-686-3288

MEMBERS OF FIRM

Marvin L. Hackman
Robert S. Hulett
Michael B. Cracraft
Timothy K. Ryan
Philip B. McKiernan
Vicki L. Anderson
John D. Cochran, Jr.
Mark S. Alderfer

Marci A. Reddick
Sherri A.B. Elder
Steven W. Krohne
Ellen J. Morrison

Representative Clients: Citizens Gas & Coke Utility; F.C. Tucker Company, Inc.; Texas Eastern Products Pipeline Co.; Indiana Municipal Power Agency; Indiana Municipal Electric Association, Inc.; St. Paul Fire and Marine Insurance Co.; State Farm Mutual Automobile Insurance Co.; Allstate Insurance Co.; Walker Information, Inc.; I.V.C. Industrial Coatings, Inc.

For full biographical listings, see the Martindale-Hubbell Law Directory

ICE MILLER DONADIO & RYAN (AV)

One American Square Box 82001, 46282-0002
Telephone: 317-236-2100
Fax: 317-236-2219
Email: info@imdr.com *URL:* http://www.imdr.com
South Bend, Indiana Office: 211 West Washington Street, Suite 2420.
Telephone: 219-234-7933.
Fax: 219-234-7965. Internet E-mail: info@imdr.com. Web Site Address: http://www.imdr.com.
Chicago, Illinois Office: 135 South LaSalle Street, Suite 4100.
Telephone: 312-726-1567.
Fax: 312-641-6263. Internet E-mail: info@imdr.com. Web Site Address: http://www.imdr.com.

MEMBERS OF FIRM

Jim A. O'Neal
Berkley W. Duck
William R. Riggs
Ralph A. Cohen
Jack R. Snyder
Charles E. Wilson
Arthur P. Kalleres
Bruce A. Polizotto
Jay G. Taylor
G. Daniel Kelley, Jr.
Gordon D. Wishard
S. R. Born
David M. Mattingly
James D. Kemper
Martin J. Klaper
James R. Fisher
Richard E. Parker
Cory Brundage
Harry L. Gonso
Terry A. M. Mumford
Michael H. Boldt
David J. Mallon, Jr.
Thomas H. Ristine
Phillip R. Scaletta, III
Barton T. Sprunger
Susan B. Tabler
James L. Petersen
James S. Cunning
Gary J. Dankert
Philip C. Genetos
Byron L. Myers
James A. Shanahan
Michael A. Blickman
Philip A. Whistler
Joseph E. DeGroff
Jeffrey O. Lewis

(See Next Column)

ICE MILLER DONADIO & RYAN—*Continued*

MEMBERS OF FIRM (Continued)

John F. Prescott, Jr.
Phillip L. Bayt
Thomas K. Downs
Mary Nold Larimore
E. Van Olson
Lisa A. Stone
Marc W. Sciscoe
Richard A. Smikle
John R. Thornburgh
Mary Beth Braitman
Brenda S. Horn
Gregory L. Pemberton
L. Alan Whaley
Robert B. Bush
Bonnie L. Gallivan
Richard J. Thrapp
Zeff A. Weiss
Stephen J. Hackman
Steven K. Humke
Debra Hanley Miller
Todd W. Ponder
Michael A. Wukmer
Lucy A. Emison
Michael J. Lewinski
Melissa Proffitt Reese
Mark J. Richards
Elizabeth A. Smith
Thomas W. Peterson
Patricia A. Zelmer
Lacy M. Johnson
Michael D. Marine
Henry A. Efroymson
Terri Ann Czajka
Donald M. Snemis
Dale E. Stackhouse
Michael A. Wilkins
Sherry A. Fabina-Abney
Jane Neuhauser Herndon
Susan Barnhizer Rivas
Joseph E. Whitsett, Jr.
Kevin C. Woodhouse
Dominic F. Polizzotto
Alan H. Goldstein
Thomas C. Smith
Kevin R. Knight
Judy Starobin Okenfuss
Michael L. Tooley
Dean T. Burger
Karen Ann P. Lloyd
Curtis W. McCauley
Antje C. Petersen
Doreen J. Gridley
Mark B. Barnes

RETIRED PARTNERS

Leonard J. Betley
Leland B. Cross, Jr.
Donald F. Elliott, Jr.
Kenneth Foster
John A. Grayson
Alan H. Lobley
Robert D. McCord
Alan T. Nolan
Edward J. Ohleyer
Robert D. Risch
Geoffrey Segar
Evan E. Steger
Donald G. Sutherland

SENIOR COUNSEL

Timothy W. Sullivan
Gene E. Wilkins
Mark S. Moore
Charles R. Hug
(Not admitted in IN)
William P. Diener
Chester L. Davis, Jr.
Bradley L. Williams
Mark D. Grant
Fred H. Cate

OF COUNSEL

Nancy Menard Riddle
James B. Burroughs
Karen L. Arland
John T. Murphy
Kathleen K. Shortridge
Diana L. Wann
Daniel E. Fisher
Kelly Bauman Pitcher
Peggy J. Naile
Catherine R. Reese
Susan Rogers Brooke
Laure V. Flaniken
Ellen Davies Gregory
James L. Bebley
(Not admitted in IN)
Anita M. Hodgson
Heather K. Olinger
Stephanie Alden Smithey
C. Joseph Miller
Edward P. Steegmann
George H. Abel, II
Gary L. Stage
Mary Kay Fleming
Susan R. Scott
Karen A. Dutcher

STAFF ATTORNEYS

Sandra K. Bickel
Dana G. Meier
Mikio Nishizu
Raymond J. Schoettle
Nathan B. Maudlin

ASSOCIATES

Robert A. Anderson
John J. Morse
Thomas E. Mixdorf
Adam Arceneaux
Paul H. Sinclair
Craig C. Burke
Sarah K. Funke
Gareth W. Kuhl
Tara L. Schulstad
Rebecca J. Seamands
Christopher S. Sears
Lynn M. Gagel
Gina M. Giacone
John M. Hakes
Pamela V. Keller
Amy M. Corsaro
Gretchen W. Snelling
Michael A. Swift
Franklin E. Breckenridge, Jr.
Timothy E. Ochs
Gordon A. Hendry
Trent J. Taylor
Susanne M. Spisak
Marilee J. Springer
Russell E. Fowler, II
Veronica L. Jarnagin
Lisa Erb Harrison
P. James Schumacher
Robert L. Gauss
Angel Fleetwood Shelton
A. Richard M. Blaiklock
Lisa A. Lee
James H. Smith
Brian T. Ster
Constance Baker Phillips
Kristine Camron Gerard
Katherine A. Hunter
Sherri K. Miller
Brent W. Huber
Lynn Kantor
Carrie L. Wagner
Kathleen A. DeLaney
Denise Y. Barkdull
Adel J. Chareq
John Farina
James D. Wood
Yeiena Fertman
Michael Griffin
Casey J. Henderson
Thea E. Kelly-Bundle
Daniel L. Kim
Michael E. Millikan
Jonathan A. Napier
Brian S. Short
Jason Ty Sibbitt
Steven D. Stennett
Janice C. Whiteside
Kristine J. Bouaichi

(See Next Column)

ASSOCIATES (Continued)

Christine Mayewski Orich
Kathleen Marie Sheil Scheidt
Dennis H. Long
Ryan M. Poor
Jennifer Weflen
Dennis H. Otten
Angela M. Fifelski
Thomas A. Walsh
Michael E. Kondoudis
(Not admitted in IN)
Bradley L. Wilson
Kyle J. Hupfer
Phillip J. Fowler
Julie E. Ragsdale
Michael Buker
Michelle M. Molin
Maria Paula Poggio
(Not admitted in IN)

LEGAL SUPPORT PERSONNEL

Karen L. Stein-Ferguson

Counsel for: American United Life Insurance Co.; Chrysler Corp.; Ford Motor Company; General Electric Company; Indiana Bankers Assn.

For full biographical listings, see the Martindale-Hubbell Law Directory

JOHNSON SMITH PENCE & HEATH LLP (AV)

One Indiana Square Suite 1800, 46204
Telephone: 317-634-9777
Telecopier: 317-636-9061
Email: firm@jsplaw.com *URL:* http://www.jsplaw.com
Washington, D.C. Office: 555 Twelfth Street, N.W., Suite 650.
Telephone: 202-737-5410.
Fax: 202-737-5411.

MEMBERS OF FIRM

Wayne O Adams, III
Joseph J. Andrew
Robert M. Baker III
Thomas A. Barnard
David G. Blachly
John W. Boyd
David J. Carr
Sean Michael Clapp
James T. Crawford, Jr.
David R. Day
Mark W. Ford
John R. Hammond, III
G. Ronald Heath
Robert B. Hebert
Michael W. Hile
John David Hoover
Andrew W. Hull
Dennis A. Johnson
Richard L. Johnson
Michael J. Kaye
John R. Kirkwood
Bradley C. Morris
Mark A. Palmer
Linda L. Pence
David D. Robinson
Sally Franklin Zweig

ASSOCIATES

Kirstie D. Andersen
(Not admitted in IN)
Maureen F. Barnard
John B. Baxter
Julie Coldren Bolling
Julie Meredith Conrad
Thomas A. Dickey
John C. Erickson, III
James Scott Fanzini
Jane Ann Himsel
Melina Maniatis Kennedy
Kelly M. Lamm
Lynne M. McMahan
Alice McKenzie Morical
Steven J. Moss
Steven F. Pockrass
Michael D. Ramsey
Robert S. Schein
Ronald G. Sentman
Gregory G. Taylor
William C. Wagner
Jill S. Walschlager
Sean T. White

For full biographical listings, see the Martindale-Hubbell Law Directory

LEWIS & KAPPES, PROFESSIONAL CORPORATION (AV)

Suite 1700 One American Square, P.O. Box 82053, 46282-0003
Telephone: 317-639-1210
Telecopier: 317-639-4882
Email: Office@Lewis-Kappes.com *URL:* http://www.Lewis-Kappes.com

Ted B. Lewis (1919-1991)
Philip S. Kappes
David W. Gray
John F. Wickes, Jr.
Gary P. Price
Steven L. Tuchman
Thomas R. Ruge
M. Kent Newton
C. Duane O'Neal
Brett James Miller
Todd A. Richardson
Bette J. Dodd
Peter S. French

Brian Andrew Statz
John A. Broyles
Megan J. Kight
Christopher C. Earle
Jennifer Wheeler Terry
Stephanie Schankerman Forrest

OF COUNSEL

Samuel A. Fuller
Leslie Duvall
Lori Kyle Endris

For full biographical listings, see the Martindale-Hubbell Law Directory

LOCKE REYNOLDS LLP (AV)

1000 Capital Center South, 201 North Illinois Street, 46204-4210
Telephone: 317-237-3800
Telecopier: 317-237-3900
Email: attys@locke.com *URL:* http://www.locke.com

Theodore L. Locke (1891-1981)
Hugh E. Reynolds (1900-1968)
Emerson Boyd (1914-1986)
Hugh E. Reynolds, Jr.
Lloyd H. Milliken, Jr.
William V. Hutchens
David S. Allen
David M. Haskett

(See Next Column)

LOCKE REYNOLDS LLP, *Indianapolis—Continued*

Michael A. Bergin
David T. Kasper
Steven J. Strawbridge
Thomas L. Davis
Robert A. Fanning
Randall R. Riggs
Alan S. Brown
Michael D. Moriarty
Glenn T. Troyer
Mark J. Roberts
Kevin Charles Murray
Julia Blackwell Gelinas
Michael T. Bindner
Michael J. Schneider
Kim F. Ebert
David Elliott Jose
Terrence L. Brookie
Richard A. Huser
Thomas J. Campbell
Diane Parsons Emswiller
Howard R. Cohen
Charles B. Baldwin
Andrew James Richardson
Thomas W. Farlow
Jeffrey R. Gaither
Karl M. Koons, III
James Dimos
Kristen K. Rollison
Thomas R. Schultz
Todd J. Kaiser
Eric A. Riegner
Kevin C. Schiferl
Ariane Schallwig Johnson
Peter H. Pogue
John H. Daerr
John K. McDavid
Jeffrey S. Dible
Jeffrey J. Mortier
Nicholas C. Pappas
Brian L. McDermott

Stephen L. Vaughan
Deanna A. Dean-Webster
David S. Klinestiver
Kenneth B. Siepman
Jon M. Pinnick
Mary A. Schopper
Susan E. Cline
Bruce J. Alvarado
James D. Masur II
Mary Margaret Ruth Feldhake
Nelson D. Alexander
Donald B. Kite, Sr.
Thomas F. Bedsole
David A. Sorensen
Shannon Stewart
Derek S. Burrell
Dean R. Brackenridge
T. Joseph Wendt
Michael T. Crowley
Michelle Davis Carmichael
John D. Papageorge
Roland R. Schindler, II
Heather L. Wilson
Vincent J. Wong
Daniel G. Foote
Dionne Carroll McCoy
Daniel M. Long
Brian K. Beeler
Kristin B. Keltner
Carol M. Wyatt
Camille T. Wiggins
Joel E. Tragesser
Tricia L. Thompson
Allison Southgate Avery (Not admitted in IN)

OF COUNSEL

William B. Weisell
William H. Vobach
Robert C. Riddell
Rodney E. Corson
Paul G. Reis

Counsel for: Honda North America Motor Co., Inc.; CNA Insurance Cos.; General Motors Corp.; Kroger Co.; Navistar International Transportation Corp.; Resort Condominiums International, Inc.

For full biographical listings, see the Martindale-Hubbell Law Directory

---

ROCAP, WITCHGER & THRELKELD (AV)

One Indiana Square, Suite 2300, 46204
Telephone: 317-639-6281
FAX: 317-637-9056
Email: rocap@iquest.net

James E. Rocap, Sr. (1881-1969)
John T. Rocap (1909-1980)
Keith C. Reese (1920-1993)

MEMBERS OF FIRM

James D. Witchger
W. Brent Threlkeld
Richard A. Rocap
Thomas Todd Reynolds

ASSOCIATES

Robert A. Durham
Kandi K. Hidde
Robert F. Ahlgrim, Jr.
Kelley Bertoux Creveling
Tracy A. Arney
Edward A.B. Castaldo
Mark S. Maxwell

OF COUNSEL

James E. Rocap, Jr.
Joseph F. Quill
William C. Moore

Counsel for: Phillips Petroleum Co.; State Farm Mutual Auto Insurance Co.; Cessna Finance Corp.; American Family Insurance Group; The Travelers Insurance Co.

For full biographical listings, see the Martindale-Hubbell Law Directory

---

SOMMER & BARNARD, ATTORNEYS AT LAW, PC (AV)

4000 Bank One Tower, 111 Monument Circle, 46204
Telephone: 317-630-4000
FAX: 317-236-9802
Email: sandb@sommerbarnard.com
North Office: 8900 Keystone Crossing, Suite 1150, Indianapolis, Indiana, 46240-2134.
Telephone: 317-630-4000.
FAX: 317-844-4780.

James K. Sommer
William C. Barnard
Dan G. Sterner
James E. Hughes
Edward W. Harris, III
Frederick M. King
Jerald I. Ancel
James A. Strain

(See Next Column)

Eric R. Johnson
Gordon L. Pittenger
Frank J. Deveau
John Taylor
Robert R. Clark
Michael C. Terrell
Marlene Reich
Richard C. Richmond, III
Julianne S. Lis-Milam
Steven C. Shockley
Erick D. Ponader
Lawrence A. Vanore
Donald C. Biggs
Gayle A. Reindl
Philip L. McCool
Ann Carr Mackey
Edwin J. Broecker

Thomas R. DeVoe
Mary T. Doherty
Scott R. Alexander
Pamela H. Sherwood
Regina M. Sharrow
Julia E. Dimick
Ralph A. Caruso II
Lanae M. Harden
Craig M. Carpenter
F. Anthony Paganelli
Maggie L. Smith
Michael J. Alerding
Jill E. Reese
Michael D. Chambers (Not admitted in IN)
Bryan W. Aydelotte
Valerie C. Horvath

OF COUNSEL

Jerry Williams
Debra McVicker Lynch
Charles E. Valliere
Michael P. O'Neil
Robert B. Bennett, Jr.

Representative Clients: Comerica Bank; Federal Express; Kimball International; Monsanto; TRW, Inc.

For full biographical listings, see the Martindale-Hubbell Law Directory

---

STARK DONINGER & SMITH (AV)

Suite 700, 50 South Meridian Street, 46204
Telephone: 317-638-2400
Fax: 317-633-6618; 633-6619

MEMBERS OF FIRM

John C. Stark
Bruce E. Smith
John W. Van Buskirk
Richard W. Dyar
Patricia Seasor Bailey
Brian J. Tuohy
Mark A. Bailey
Lewis E. Willis, Jr.
Thomas A. Brodnik

ASSOCIATES

Richard B. Kaufman
Paul T. Belch
John J. Moore
Dennis R. Tyler

COUNSEL

Clarence H. Doninger
Gregory S. Fehribach
Robert D. Maas
William K. Byrum

Reference: National Bank of Indianapolis.

For full biographical listings, see the Martindale-Hubbell Law Directory

---

WOODEN & MCLAUGHLIN LLP (AV)

1600 Capital Center South, 201 North Illinois Street, 46204
Telephone: 317-639-6151
Fax: 317-639-6444

MEMBERS OF FIRM

William P. Wooden
Robert L. McLaughlin
Michael C. Cook
Ronald G. Salatich
Thomas W. Dinwiddie
John D. Nell
Douglas B. King
Dale W. Eikenberry
Andrew C. Charnstrom
Daniel D. Trachtman
Julie L. Michaelis
Thomas M. Hanahan
Mary Titsworth Chandler
Kent M. Broach
Jeffrey L. McKean

ASSOCIATES

Holly Hapak Betz
Caroline Lingelbach Young
Michael Rabinowitch
Joseph R. Alberts
John W. Hamilton
John D. Waller
David D. Thompson
Jennifer Hayes Langston
R. David Emerick
James M. Boyers

Representative Clients: AT&T; Amoco Oil Co.; Civitas Bank; Eaton & Lauth Real Estate Services, Inc.; Exxon Corp.; Hospital Corporation of America; Huntington National Bank; Merrell Dow Pharmaceutical, Inc.; Metropolitan Life Insurance Co.; Peabody Coal Company; Playtex Family Products, Inc.

For full biographical listings, see the Martindale-Hubbell Law Directory

---

*JEFFERSONVILLE,** Clark Co.

SMITH, BARTLETT, HEEKE, CARPENTER, LEWIS & THOMPSON (AV)

Holzbog House, 209 East Chestnut Street, P.O. Box 98, 47131-0098
Telephone: 812-282-7736
FAX: 812-284-8388

MEMBERS OF FIRM

Wilmer T. Fox (1881-1946)
Charles C. Fox (1912-1975)
Ernest W. Smith
Rick E. Bartlett
Sandra L. Heeke
Cheryl A. Carpenter
Sandra Winnett Lewis
Pamela K. Thompson
Mary E. Fondrisi

(See Next Column)

SMITH, BARTLETT, HEEKE, CARPENTER, LEWIS & THOMPSON—*Continued*

Representative Clients: NBD Bank, N.A.; Liberty Mutual Insurance Co.; Geo. Pfau's Sons Co., Inc.; American Family Insurance; PSI Energy; American States Insurance Co.; Greater Clark County School Corporation.

For full biographical listings, see the Martindale-Hubbell Law Directory

*LAFAYETTE,** Tippecanoe Co.

BALL, EGGLESTON, BUMBLEBURG, MCBRIDE, WALKEY & STAPLETON, PC (AV)

810 Bank One Building, P.O. Box 1535, 47902-1535
Telephone: 765-742-9046
Fax: 765-742-1966
Email: info@ball-law.com

Cable G. Ball (1904-1981)
Owen Crook (1908-1977)
Warren N. Eggleston (1923-1991)
Joseph T. Bumbleburg
John K. McBride
Jack L. Walkey
Michael J. Stapleton
Jeffrey J. Newell
James T. Hodson
Brian Wade Walker
Cheryl M. Knodle
Randy J. Williams
Brenda Mithoefer Clapper

General Counsel for: The Lafayette Union Railway Co.
Representative Clients: Farmers Insurance Group; General Accident Fire & Life Assurance Corp.; City of Lafayette Board of Parks and Recreation; West Lafayette Community School Corp.; Travelers Insurance Co.; Trustees, West Lafayette Public Library; Town of Dayton, Indiana.

For full biographical listings, see the Martindale-Hubbell Law Directory

BENNETT, BOEHNING & CLARY (AV)

6th Floor, Lafayette Bank & Trust Building, 133 North Fourth Street, P.O. Box 469, 47902-0469
Telephone: 765-742-9066
Telecopier: 765-742-7641
Email: info@Bennettlaw.com

MEMBERS OF FIRM

Richard A. Boehning
Brent E Clary
Roger Wm. Bennett
Christine A. DeSanctis
James A. Gothard

ASSOCIATES

Andrew S. Gutwein
Stuart P. Boehning

General Counsel for: Fred Gutwein & Sons Inc.; Pizza King, Inc.; Lafayette Bank and Trust Company; Journal and Courier.
Area and County Counsel for: ALCOA; Landis & Gyr.
Approved Title Attorneys for: Lawyers Title Insurance Co.

For full biographical listings, see the Martindale-Hubbell Law Directory

LAYDEN & LAYDEN (AV)

Suite 712, Bank One Building, 201 Main Street, P.O. Box 909, 47902-0909
Telephone: 765-742-7646
Fax: 765-742-0983
Email: cmlayden@iquest.net

MEMBERS OF FIRM

Charles Max Layden
Lynn M. Layden

For full biographical listings, see the Martindale-Hubbell Law Directory

STUART & BRANIGIN (AV)

The Life Building, 300 Main Street, Suite 800, P.O. Box 1010, 47902-1010
Telephone: 765-423-1561
Telecopier: 765-742-8175
Email: sb@stuartlaw.com *URL:* http://www.stuartlaw.com
Indianapolis, Indiana Office: Suite 1401, 8888 Keystone Crossing, 46240.
Telephone: 317-574-7245.
Fax: 317-574-7050.

MEMBERS OF FIRM

Allison Ellsworth Stuart (1886-1950)
Roger D. Branigin (1902-1975)
Roger D. Branigin, Jr.
Thomas L. Ryan
Thomas R. McCully
Larry R. Fisher
Nina B. Kirkpatrick
Mark Lillianfeld
Stephen R. Pennell
Anthony S. Benton
Erik D. Spykman
William E. Emerick
John C. Duffey
Bruce McSpadden
Mark E. DeYoung
Thomas B. Parent
Laura L. Bowker
Kevin D. Nicoson
Susan K. Roberts
John M. Stuckey
Deborah B. Trice
William P. Kealey
David A. Starkweather
Geoffrey L. Blazi

SENIOR COUNSEL

Russell H. Hart

COUNSEL

John F. Bodle
James V. McGlone

(See Next Column)

ASSOCIATES

Elizabeth B. Searle
Marianne Mitten Owen
David A. Locke
Karen Orr McClure
Ann Marie Waldron
Barry L. Loftus

General Counsel for: The Lafayette Life Insurance Co.; INB National Bank, N.W.; Lafayette Home Hospital, Inc.
State Counsel for: Norfolk & Western Railway Co.
Mr. Ryan is Counsel to: The Trustees of Purdue University.
Representative Clients: Aluminum Company of America; Liberty Mutual Insurance Group.

For full biographical listings, see the Martindale-Hubbell Law Directory

*LA PORTE,** La Porte Co.

NEWBY, LEWIS, KAMINSKI & JONES (AV)

916 Lincoln Way, 46350
Telephone: 219-362-1577
Direct Line Michigan City: 219-879-6300
Fax: 219-362-2106
Mailing Address: P.O. Box 1816, La Porte, Indiana, 46352-1816
Email: nlkj@nlkj.com

MEMBERS OF FIRM

John E. Newby (1916-1990)
Daniel E. Lewis (1910-1997)
Daniel E. Lewis, Jr.
Gene M. Jones
Perry F. Stump, Jr.
Edward L. Volk
Mark L. Phillips
Martin W. Kus
Marsha Schatz Volk
Mark A. Lienhoop
James W. Kaminski
William S. Kaminski
David P. Jones

ASSOCIATES

Douglas L. Biege
Andrea Nicole Kurek

SENIOR COUNSEL

Leon R. Kaminski

Counsel for: U. S. F. & G. Co.; State Farm Mutual Insurance Co.; Auto Owners Insurance Co.; Liberty Mutual Insurance Co.; Sullair Corp.; United Farm Bureau Mutual Insurance Co.; Physicians Insurance of Indiana; La Porte Hospital, Inc.; Norwest Bank.

For full biographical listings, see the Martindale-Hubbell Law Directory

*MADISON,** Jefferson Co.

KEMPER & BARLOW (AV)

201 East Main Street, 47250-3493
Telephone: 812-265-3311; 273-4440
FAX: 812-265-5748; 273-2329

MEMBERS OF FIRM

Gary K. Kemper
Robert L. Barlow, II

ASSOCIATE

Susan E. Sparks

OF COUNSEL

Joe E. Cox

Representative Clients: Indiana Gas Co.; Madison Bank & Trust Co.; Farmers Bank of Milton; United Farm Bureau Mutual Ins. Co.; Hanover College; Hartford Insurance.

For full biographical listings, see the Martindale-Hubbell Law Directory

*MARTINSVILLE,** Morgan Co.

PHILLIP R. SMITH, P.C. (AV)

359 East Morgan Street, P.O. Box 1452, 46151
Telephone: 765-342-7148
Fax: 765-342-0739
URL: http://www.lawyers.com/smith&gettelfinger

Phillip R. Smith

OF COUNSEL

William H. Wehrle

For full biographical listings, see the Martindale-Hubbell Law Directory

MERRILLVILLE, Lake Co.

BURKE COSTANZA & CUPPY LLP (AV)

Suite 600 8585 Broadway, 46410-7064
Telephone: 219-769-1313
Telecopier: 219-769-6806
Email: BCC@NETNITCO.NET
East Chicago, Indiana Office: First National Bank Building, 720 West Chicago Avenue.
Telephone: 219-397-2401.
Telecopier: 219-397-0508.
Valparaiso, Indiana Office: 15 North Franklin Street, Suite 200.
Telephone: 219-531-0134.
Telecopier: 219-531-0507.

(See Next Column)

BURKE COSTANZA & CUPPY LLP, *Merrillville—Continued*

PARTNERS

Edward L. Burke
Joseph E. Costanza
Frederick M. Cuppy
George W. Carberry
David K. Ranich
Kathryn D. Schmidt
David Cerven
Elizabeth P. Moenning
Lily M. Schaefer
Paula E. Neff
Todd A. Etzler

ASSOCIATES

Kevin E. Steele
Victor H. Prasco
Andrew L. Kraemer
Joseph Pearman
Natalie V. Shrader
Alan D. Naggatz

OF COUNSEL

Donald J. Dreyfus
T. Clifford Fleming
Gregory R. Lyman
John G. Donner

Representative Clients: Lehigh Portland Cement Company; Continental Machine & Engineering Co., Inc.; Gary Steel Products Corp.; Superior Construction Co., Inc.; Federal National Mortgage Association; St. Catherine Hospital of East Chicago, Indiana; Simon DeBartolo Property Group; The Travelers Insurance Companies (Panel Counsel); Guide One Insurance Companies; The City of East Chicago (Contract Counsel).

For full biographical listings, see the Martindale-Hubbell Law Directory

HODGES & DAVIS, P.C. (AV)

8700 Broadway, 46410
Telephone: 219-641-8700
Fax: 219-641-8710
URL: http://www.hodgesdavis.com
Portage, Indiana Office: 6082 Lute Road. P.O. Box 1037.
Telephone: 219-762-9129.
Fax: 219-762-2826.

William F. Hodges (1877-1954)
Claude V. Ridgely (1881-1963)
Thomas M. Hodges (1906-1969)
Herschel B. Davis (1901-1990)
Gilbert Gruenberg (1902-1989)
Bruce E. Sayers (1939-1990)
Clyde D. Compton
William B. Davis
Earle F. Hites
R. Lawrence Steele
Gregory A. Sobkowski
Bonnie C. Coleman
Jill M. Madajczyk
Laura B. Frost
David H. Kreider
Jeanne B. Blumenthal

OF COUNSEL

Edward J. Hussey

Representative Clients: The Methodist Hospitals, Inc.; City of Portage, Indiana; Jewel Cos., Inc.; Osco Drug, Inc.; Porter County Plan Commission; Portage Township Schools; Northwest Indiana Water Company.

For full biographical listings, see the Martindale-Hubbell Law Directory

HOEPPNER WAGNER & EVANS LLP (AV)

Twin Towers, Suite 606 South, 1000 East 80th Place, P.O. Box 10627, 46410-0627
Telephone: 219-769-6552; 800-263-1466 (IN, IL)
Fax: 219-738-2349
Email: hwe@hwelaw.com *URL:* http://www.hwelaw.com
Valparaiso, Indiana Office: 103 East Lincolnway, P.O. Box 2357, 46384-2357.
Telephone: 219-464-4961; 800-879-2246 (IN, IL).
Fax: 219-465-0603. Email: hwe@hwelaw.com

RESIDENT MEMBERS

John E. Hughes
F. Joseph Jaskowiak
Richard M. Davis
J. Brian Hittinger

RESIDENT ASSOCIATES

Jack A. Kramer
Galen A. Bradley
Jay S. Patheja

For full biographical listings, see the Martindale-Hubbell Law Directory

LUCAS, HOLCOMB & MEDREA (AV)

300 East 90th Drive, 46410
Telephone: 219-769-3561
Fax: 219-756-7409
Email: lhm@mail.icongrp.com *URL:* http://www.expage.com/page/lhm

MEMBERS OF FIRM

James A. Holcomb
John O. Stiles
Daniel A. Medrea
Robert F. Peters
Stephen R. Place
Nick Katich
Mary Linda Casey
Mark S. Lucas
David E. Woodward
Joseph M. Skozen
Louis M. Casale

ASSOCIATES

David A. Buls
Sarah M. Fischer
David M. Blaskovich

(See Next Column)

OF COUNSEL

Robert A. Lucas

Representative Clients: Bank One, Merrillville, N.A.; American States Insurance Co.; Meridian Insurance Co.; Montgomery Ward Co.; Calumet Securities Corp. (Mortgage Bankers); Indiana University; The Trustees of Indiana University; Munster Medical Research Foundation, Inc. (Operating "The Community Hospital"); Hammond Clinic.

For full biographical listings, see the Martindale-Hubbell Law Directory

SPANGLER, JENNINGS & DOUGHERTY, P.C. (AV)

8396 Mississippi Street, 46410-6398
Telephone: 219-769-2323
Facsimile: 219-769-5007
Email: spangler@sjdlaw.com
Valparaiso, Indiana Office: 150 Lincolnway, Suite 3001.
Telephone: 219-462-6151.
FAX: 219-477-4935.

Harry J. Jennings
Richard A. Mayer
Jay A. Charon
John P. McQuillan
Samuel J. Bernardi, Jr. (Valparaiso Office)
Jon F. Schmoll
Robert D. Hawk
Peter G. Koransky
David J. Hanson
Robert P. Kennedy
Allen B. Zaremba
James T. McNiece
Daniel A. Gioia
James D. McQuillan
David L. Abel, II
Harold G. Hagberg
Lawrence A. Kalina
Robert P. Stoner (Valparaiso Office)
Gregory J. Tonner
Kathleen M. Maicher
Paul B. Poracky
Robert D. Brown
Robert J. Dignam

ASSOCIATES

Anthony F. Tavitas
Lloyd P. Mullen
Kisti Good Risse
Mark D. Geheb
Greg A. Bouwer
James M. Portelli
Edward W. Hearn (Valparaiso Office)
Robert D. Hawk, Jr.
Ricardo A. Hall
Sharon L. Stanzione
Jeffrey S. Sturm
Christopher Grabarek (Valparaiso Office)
J. Brian Steele
Michael T. Terwilliger
Teresa Muth Mysliwy
Crystal Sharp Bauer
John A. Link
James L. Hough
Adam Tavitas
Ketaki Sircar

OF COUNSEL

Patrick J. Dougherty (Valparaiso Office)
Clarence Borns

Representative Clients: Allstate Insurance Company; Civitas Bank; CNA Insurance: Farmers Insurance Group; Ford Motor Credit Co.; Inland Steel Co.; School Town of Munster; St. Paul Insurance Cos.; State Farm Cos.

For full biographical listings, see the Martindale-Hubbell Law Directory

MICHIGAN CITY, La Porte Co.

SWEENEY, DABAGIA, THORNE, JANES & PAGOS, L.L.P. (AV)

An Indiana Registered Limited Liability Partnership
709 Franklin Square, P.O. Box 769, 46360
Telephone: 219-879-5321
Fax: 219-879-2942
Email: dpagos@netnitco.com *URL:* http://www.sweeney-dabagia.com

MEMBERS OF FIRM

Clarence T. Sweeney (1899-1980)
John H. Sweeney (Retired)
Jeffrey L. Thorne
William Janes
Donald W. Pagos

SENIOR COUNSEL

Lee W. Dabagia

Reference: Horizon Bank, N.A.

For full biographical listings, see the Martindale-Hubbell Law Directory

MUNSTER, Lake Co.

LAW OFFICES OF EUGENE M. FEINGOLD (AV)

625 Ridge Road, Suite A, 46321
Telephone: 219-836-8800
Fax: 219-836-8944

ASSOCIATE

Steven P. Kennedy

For full biographical listings, see the Martindale-Hubbell Law Directory

LAW OFFICES OF TIMOTHY F. KELLY (AV)

Suite 2A, 9250 Columbia Avenue, 46321
Telephone: 219-836-4062
Telecopier: 219-836-0167
Email: tfklaw@tfklaw.net

MEMBERS OF FIRM

Timothy F. Kelly
Karl K. Vanzo

(See Next Column)

LAW OFFICES OF TIMOTHY F. KELLY—*Continued*

ASSOCIATES

Steven J. Sersic | Kathleen E. Peek

LEGAL SUPPORT PERSONNEL
LEGAL ASSISTANTS

Kristen Cook Faso | Kerry E. Kelly
Lynn M. Hochstetler

For full biographical listings, see the Martindale-Hubbell Law Directory

*NEW ALBANY,** Floyd Co.

MATTOX & MATTOX (AV)

Suite 420 Elsby Building, P.O. Box 1203, 47151-1203
Telephone: 812-944-8005
Facsimile: 812-944-2255
Email: mmlaw@win.net

MEMBERS OF FIRM

Richard L. Mattox | S. Frank Mattox

ASSOCIATES

Linda A. Mattox | Derrick H. Wilson
Karen R. Goodwell

Representative Clients: AAOMS National Insurance; Cablelink, Inc.; Floyd Memorial Hospital; John Deere Co.; Kimball International, Inc.; The Medical Protective Co.; Papa Johns Intl., Inc.; PHICO Insurance Co.; Physicians Group, Inc.; Robinson Nugent, Inc.

For full biographical listings, see the Martindale-Hubbell Law Directory

WYATT, TARRANT & COMBS (AV)

(Formerly Orbison, O'Connor, MacGregor & Mattox)
The Elsby Building, 117 East Spring Street, 47150-3440
Telephone: 812-945-3561
Telecopier: 812-949-2524
URL: http://www.wyattfirm.com
Louisville, Kentucky Office: Citizens Plaza.
Telephone: 502-589-5235.
Telecopier: 502-589-0309.
Lexington, Kentucky Office: 1700 Lexington Financial Center.
Telephone: 606-233-2012.
Telecopier: 606-259-0649.
Frankfort, Kentucky Office: The Taylor-Scott Building, 311 West Main Street, P.O. Box 495.
Telephone: 502-223-2104.
Telecopier: 502-227-7681.
Nashville, Tennessee Office: 1500 Nashville City Center, 511 Union Street.
Telephone: 615-244-0020.
Telecopier: 615-256-1726.
Music Row, Nashville Office: 29 Music Square East.
Telephone: 615-255-6161.
Telecopier: 615-254-4490.
Memphis, Tennessee Office: Crescent Center, Suite 650, 6075 Poplar Avenue.
Telephone: 901-537-1000.
Telecopier: 901-537-1010.
Hendersonville, Tennessee Office: 313 E. Main Street, Suite 1.
Telephone: 615-822-8822.
Telecopier: 615-824-4684.
Tri-Cities, Tennessee Office: Northeast Tennessee Business Park, 10368 Wallace Alley Street, Suite 6, Kingsport.
Telephone: 423-279-1825.
Telecopier: 423-279-9357.

MEMBERS OF FIRM

Telford B. Orbison (1901-1990) | James E. Bourne
Richard C. O'Connor (1918-1997) | Thomas W. Sinex
J. Spencer Harmon
Charles E. MacGregor | Richard A. Bierly
John W. Woodard, Jr.

COUNSEL

Larry R. Church

Representative Clients: Allstate Insurance Co.; Amoco Oil Co.; Ford Motor Credit Corp.; Green Banner Publications, Inc.; Gettelfinger Popcorn Co., Inc.; Joe Huber Farms, Inc.; Indiana Bell Telephone Co.; Province of Our Lady of Consolation, Inc.; Public Service Indiana; United Farm Bureau Mutual Insurance Co.

For full biographical listings, see the Martindale-Hubbell Law Directory

*NOBLESVILLE,** Hamilton Co.

CHURCH, CHURCH, HITTLE & ANTRIM (AV)

938 Conner Street, P.O. Box 10, 46061-0010
Telephone: 317-773-2190
Telecopier: 317-773-5320
Email: cchadoug@msn.com

(See Next Column)

MEMBERS OF FIRM

Douglas D. Church | Bruce M. Bittner
Jack G. Hittle | Brian J. Zaiger
J. Michael Antrim | Leslie Craig Henderzahs
Martin E. Risacher | Jordan D. Church

OF COUNSEL

Manson E. Church

Representative Clients: Noblesville Schools; Westfield-Washington Schools; Community Bank; Metrobank; Towns of Westfield, Fishers and Pendleton; Reynolds Farm Equipment Co.; Weihe Engineering; Historic Railroad Multijurisdictional Port Authority.

For full biographical listings, see the Martindale-Hubbell Law Directory

NORTH VERNON, Jennings Co.

McCONNELL AND FINNERTY (AV)

38 North 5th Street, P.O. Box 90, 47265
Telephone: 812-346-5201
FAX: 812-346-8470

MEMBERS OF FIRM

Ira B. Hamilton (1899-1982) | Harold H. McConnell
Corinne R. Finnerty

ASSOCIATE

Alan L. Marshall

Representative Clients: Union Bank & Trust Co.; Farm Bureau Mutual Insurance Co.; Home Federal Savings Bank; Rose Acre Farms, Inc.; Pekin Insurance; CPX, Inc.; North Vernon Industry Corp.; NAC, Inc.; The Tribune.

For full biographical listings, see the Martindale-Hubbell Law Directory

*PAOLI,** Orange Co.

TUCKER AND TUCKER, P.C. (AV)

188 South Court Street, 47454
Telephone: 812-723-2313
Fax: 812-723-3789
Email: jctucker@kiva.net

James C. Tucker | Jennifer A. Tucker

Counsel For: Orange County Bank; Citizens Bank, Orleans; Springs Valley Bank and Trust Co.; Bank of Mitchell, Paoli; Town of West Baden Springs; The Orleans Community Schools; The Springs Valley Community Schools; Paoli Community Schools; West Washington School Corporation; Reynolds, Inc.

For full biographical listings, see the Martindale-Hubbell Law Directory

*PLYMOUTH,** Marshall Co.

KIZER & NEU (AV)

319 West Jefferson Street, P.O. Box 158, 46563
Telephone: 219-936-2169
FAX: 219-936-2642
Bremen, Indiana Office: 1406 West Plymouth Street, P.O. Box 158.
Telephone: 219-546-2626.
FAX: 219-546-2608.

MEMBERS OF FIRM

Marshall F. Kizer (1907-1988) | Mark E. Wagner (Resident at Bremen)
James H. Neu (1917-1991)
Richard F. Joyce (Retired) | Ronald D. Gifford
Harold L. Wyland | James N. Clevenger
Jere L. Humphrey | Joseph R. Morris

Counsel for: 1st Source Bank of Marshall County; Prudential Insurance Company of America; Bremen Castings, Inc.; Bornemann Products, Inc., all of Bremen, Indiana; 4th District Farm Credit Services.

For full biographical listings, see the Martindale-Hubbell Law Directory

PORTAGE, Porter Co.

HODGES & DAVIS, P.C. (AV)

6082 Lute Road, P.O. Box 1037, 46368
Telephone: 219-762-9129
Fax: 219-762-2826
URL: http://www.hodgesdavis.com
Merrillville, Indiana Office: 8700 Broadway.
Telephone: 219-641-8700.
Fax: 219-641-8710.

Clyde D. Compton | Gregory A. Sobkowski
Earle F. Hites | Bonnie C. Coleman
R. Lawrence Steele | Laura B. Frost

Representative Clients: The Methodist Hospitals, Inc.; City of Portage, Indiana; Jewel Cos., Inc.; Osco Drug, Inc.; Porter County Plan Commission; Portage Township Schools; Northwest Indiana Water Co.

For full biographical listings, see the Martindale-Hubbell Law Directory

*PRINCETON,** Gibson Co.

HALL, PARTENHEIMER & KINKLE (AV)

219 North Hart Street, P.O. Box 13, 47670
Telephone: 812-386-0050
FAX: 812-385-2575
Email: hpk@hpk-law.com

MEMBERS OF FIRM

Verner P. Partenheimer
J. Robert Kinkle
R. Scott Partenheimer

Representative Clients: Interlake Inc.; Civitas National Bank; East Gibson School Corporation; Union Planters National Bank; United Federal Savings Bank; Amax Minerals.
Approved Attorneys for: Lawyers Title Insurance; National Attorneys Title Fund and Stewart Title.

For full biographical listings, see the Martindale-Hubbell Law Directory

*SOUTH BEND,** St. Joseph Co.

BAKER & DANIELS (AV)

First Bank Building, 205 West Jefferson Boulevard, 46601
Telephone: 219-234-4149
Fax: 219-239-1900
URL: http://www.bakerdaniels.com
Indianapolis, Indiana Office: 300 North Meridian Street, 46204.
Telephone: 317-237-0300.
Fort Wayne, Indiana Office: 111 East Wayne Street, Suite 800, 46802.
Telephone: 219-424-8000.
Elkhart, Indiana Office: 301 B South Main Street, Suite 307, 46516.
Telephone: 219-296-6000.
Washington, D.C. Office: 805 15th Street, Suite 700, 20005.
Telephone: 202-312-7440.
Qingdao, China Office: Room C, 13th Floor, Qingdao Beer Building, May 4th Square, 35 Donghai Road, 266071.
Telephone: +011-86-532-575-1051.
Fax: +011-86-532-575-1055.

MEMBERS OF FIRM

Robert H. Brown
Thomas J. Brunner, Jr. (Resident)
Eric J. Groen (Not admitted in IN)
Richard L. Hill (Resident)
James M. Matthews (Resident)
Paul J. Peralta (Resident)
Peter G. Trybula

OF COUNSEL

Paul D. Borghesani
James D. Hall (Resident)
Robert A. Wade (Resident)

ASSOCIATES

Daniel G. Areaux
Anne E. Bruneel (Resident)
Kari A. Gallagher (Resident)
Carl A. Greci (Resident)
Jeff R. Heck (Resident)
Kevin D. O'Rear (Resident)
D. Lucetta Pope (Resident)
Randolph R. Rompola (Resident)
Edward A. Sullivan, III (Resident)
Daniel Tychonievich (Resident)
Lawrence R. Williams, II (Resident)
Susan M. Wilson (Resident)
Stanley F. Wruble, III (Resident)

Representative Clients: 1st Source Bank; Anthem Insurance Companies, Inc.; AT&T Corp.; City of South Bend; Conseco, Inc.; Holy Cross Health System; Quality Dining, Inc.; Society Corp.; United Airlines; WSBT, Inc.

For full biographical listings, see the Martindale-Hubbell Law Directory

BARNES & THORNBURG (AV)

600 1st Source Bank Center, 100 North Michigan, 46601-1632
Telephone: 219-233-1171
FAX: 219-237-1125
URL: http://www.btlaw.com
Indianapolis, Indiana Office: 11 South Meridian Street, 46204.
Telephone: 317-236-1313.
FAX: 317-231-7433.
Fort Wayne, Indiana Office: Suite 600, One Summit Square, 46802.
Telephone: 219-423-9440.
FAX: 219-424-8316.
Elkhart, Indiana Office: 121 West Franklin Street, Suite 200, 46516.
Telephone: 219-293-0681.
FAX: 219-296-2535.
Chicago, Illinois Office: 2600 Chase Plaza, 10 South La Salle Street, 60603.
Telephone: 312-357-1313.
FAX: 312-759-5646.
Washington, D.C. Office: 1401 Eye Street, N.W., Suite 500, 20005.
Telephone: 202-289-1313.
FAX: 202-289-1330.

James F. Thornburg (1911-1998)

MEMBERS OF FIRM

Bruce R. Bancroft
Stephen A. Seall
John A. Burgess
Nelson J. Vogel, Jr.
Roger W. Benko
Brian J. Lake
Laurence A. McHugh
Douglas K. Dieterly
Alan B. Feldbaum
Jon E. DeGuilio

(See Next Column)

MEMBERS OF FIRM (Continued)

Gerald F. Lutkus
Nancy L. Ickler
Kathleen K. Brickley
Seth D. Linfield
Michael B. Watkins
Timothy D. Hernly
Mark D. Boveri
Scott M. Keller
Joseph R. Fullenkamp
Martha B. Moo
Michael D. Hardy
Paul B. Hunt

OF COUNSEL

Warren E. McGill
Warren A. Deahl
John L. Carey
William J. Reinke
Edward J. Gray
Daniel W. Rudy
John T. Mulvihill
Franklin A. (Steve) Morse, II (Retired)
Philip J. Faccenda, Sr.
Michael P. Barnes

ASSOCIATES

Janilyn Brouwer Daub
James M. Lewis
Gerard T. Gallagher
Patrick D. Murphy
Mark J. Adey
M. Patricia Hackett
George E. Horn
John D. LaDue
S. Renee Applegarth
Jody H. Odell
Robert D. Null
Philip J. Faccenda, Jr.
Kimberly C. Metzger
John C. Smarrella
Richard J. Deahl
Adrianne L. Hoehner
D. Michael Anderson

Representative Clients: 1st Source Bank; AM General Corp.; Cadence Environmental Energy; Crowe, Chizek and Company L.L.P.; Gast Manufacturing Corporation; Memorial Hospital of South Bend; National Steel Corporation; University of Notre Dame; Whirlpool Corporation; Whiteford, Inc.

For full biographical listings, see the Martindale-Hubbell Law Directory

JONES OBENCHAIN, LLP (AV)

1800 City Center, 211 West Washington Street, P.O. Box 4577, 46634
Telephone: 219-233-1194
Fax: 233-8957
Email: firm@jonesobenchain.com

MEMBERS OF FIRM

Thomas F. Lewis, Jr.
Timothy W. Woods
John R. Obenchain
Robert W. Mysliwiec
Robert M. Edwards, Jr.
John B. Ford
Mark J. Phillipoff
John W. Van Laere
Edward P. Benchik
Thomas F. Lewis, III

Attorneys for: American Family Insurance; Ohio Casualty Co.; Koontz-Wagner Electric Co.; The Travelers Insurance Co.; H.G. Christman Construction Co., Inc.

For full biographical listings, see the Martindale-Hubbell Law Directory

ROWE & ROWE (AV)

Suite 900 Keybank Building, 46601
Telephone: 219-233-8200
Fax: 219-234-5987

R. Kent Rowe
R. Kent Rowe, III

ASSOCIATES

Robert D. Truitt
Gregory J. Haines
Marie Anne Hendrie

For full biographical listings, see the Martindale-Hubbell Law Directory

*TERRE HAUTE,** Vigo Co.

COX, ZWERNER, GAMBILL & SULLIVAN (AV)

511 Wabash Avenue, P.O. Box 1625, 47808-1625
Telephone: 812-232-6003
Fax: 812-232-6567

MEMBERS OF FIRM

Ernest J. Zwerner (1918-1980)
Benjamin G. Cox (1915-1988)
Gilbert W. Gambill, Jr.
James E. Sullivan
Benjamin G. Cox, Jr.
David W. Sullivan
Robert L. Gowdy
Louis F. Britton
Carroll D. Smeltzer
Jeffry A. Lind
Ronald E. Jumps
Scott Craig
Elizabeth A. Lewis

OF COUNSEL

Robert D. Hepburn

Counsel for: Terre Haute First National Bank; Farmers Insurance Group; Indiana-American Water Co.; Indiana State University; Merchants National Bank of Terre Haute; Rose-Hulman Institute of Technology; Tribune-Star Publishing Co., Inc.

For full biographical listings, see the Martindale-Hubbell Law Directory

*VALPARAISO,** Porter Co.

BLACHLY, TABOR, BOZIK & HARTMAN (AV)

56 South Washington Street Suite 401, 46383
Telephone: 219-464-1041
Fax: 219-464-0927
Fort Wayne, Indiana Office: 4656 West Jefferson. Suite 120. 46804.

(See Next Column)

BLACHLY, TABOR, BOZIK & HARTMAN—*Continued*

MEMBERS OF FIRM

Quentin A. Blachly (1934-1997)
James S. Bozik
Duane W. Hartman
David L. Hollenbeck
Thomas F. Macke
Randall J. Zromkoski
Richard J. Rupcich
Craig R. Van Schouwen

ASSOCIATES

Patrick A. Lyp
John C. Drier

OF COUNSEL

Glenn J. Tabor

Reference: First National Bank.

For full biographical listings, see the Martindale-Hubbell Law Directory

DOUGLAS, ALEXA, KOEPPEN & HURLEY (AV)

14 Indiana Avenue, P.O. Box 209, 46384-0209
Telephone: 219-462-2126
Fax: 219-477-4408
Email: dakh@netnitco.net

MEMBERS OF FIRM

Herbert K. Douglas
William E. Alexa
R. Bradley Koeppen
Brian J. Hurley
Mark A. Gland

Attorneys for: Urschel Laboratories, Inc.; Northern Indiana Public Service Co.; Park District, City of Valparaiso; Emerson Electric; First National Bank, Valparaiso.

For full biographical listings, see the Martindale-Hubbell Law Directory

HOEPPNER WAGNER & EVANS LLP (AV)

103 East Lincolnway, P.O. Box 2357, 46384-2357
Telephone: 219-464-4961; 800-879-2246 (IN, IL)
Fax: 219-465-0603
Email: hwe@hwelaw.com *URL:* http://www.hwelaw.com
Merrillville, Indiana Office: Twin Towers, Suite 606 South, 1000 East 80th Place, P.O. Box 10627, 46419-0627.
Telephone: 219-769-6552; 800-263-1466 (IN, IL).
Fax: 219-738-2349. Email: hwe@hwelaw.com

RETIRED

Delmar R. Hoeppner

MEMBERS OF FIRM

William H. Wagner
Larry G. Evans
William F. Satterlee, III
Gordon A. Etzler
John E. Hughes (Resident, Merrillville Office)
Morris A. Sunkel
James L. Jorgensen
Ronald P. Kuker
Richard A. Browne
F. Joseph Jaskowiak (Resident, Merrillville Office)
Richard M. Davis (Resident, Merrillville Office)
Mark E. Schmidtke
Todd A. Leeth
Michael P. Blaize
J. Brian Hittinger (Resident, Merrillville Office)

ASSOCIATES

Robert L. Clark
Lauren K. Kroeger
Jeffrey W. Clymer
Jack A. Kramer (Resident, Merrillville Office)
Galen A. Bradley (Resident, Merrillville Office)
Tina M. Bengs
Kevin G. Kerr
Karen M. Read
Jay S. Patheja (Resident, Merrillville Office)

Representative Clients: Aldi Inc.; American Family Insurance Group; American National Property & Casualty; American States Insurance Co.; Babcock & Wilcox; Bank One; Bethlehem Steel Corp.; CGU Insurance Co.; Chester, Inc.; CIGNA Property & Casualty; Citizens Financial Services, FSB; Civitas Bank; CNA Insurance Co.; Coldwell First American, Inc.; Continental Loss Adjusting Services; East Porter County Schools; First National Bank; G.A.B. Business Services; Illinois State Medical Insurance Services; Indiana Insurance Co.; JWP Hyre Electric; MB Manufacturing; Meridian Mutual Ins. Co.; National Steel Corp.; Okaya Electric America, Inc.; Owens-Corning Fiberglass Corp.; Porter-Starke Services, Inc.; Royal Insurance Co.; Security Life of Denver; State Farm Insurance Cos.; Task Force Tips, Inc.; The Travelers; Town of Kouts; Toys R Us Corp.; Tri-State Coach Lines, Inc.; United States Fidelity and Guaranty Co.; Unitrin Insurance Co.; Valparaiso University; Whiteco Industries, Inc.; Worldwide Services Co.

For full biographical listings, see the Martindale-Hubbell Law Directory

SPANGLER, JENNINGS & DOUGHERTY, P.C. (AV)

150 Lincolnway, Suite 3001, 46383
Telephone: 219-462-6151
FAX: 219-477-4935
Email: spangler@sjdlaw.com
Merrillville, Indiana Office: 8396 Mississippi Street.
Telephone: 219-769-2323.

RESIDENT PERSONNEL

Samuel J. Bernardi, Jr.
Robert P. Stoner

Edward W. Hearn
Christopher Grabarek

(See Next Column)

OF COUNSEL

Patrick J. Dougherty

Representative Clients: Ancilla; Allstate Insurance Cos.; American International Group; American National Property and Casualty Company (ANPAC); American States; Associates Financial; Auto Owners; Bank One; Beneficial Finance; Church Mutual Insurance.

For full biographical listings, see the Martindale-Hubbell Law Directory

*VINCENNES,** Knox Co.

EMISON, DOOLITTLE, KOLB & ROELLGEN (AV)

Eighth & Busseron Streets, P.O. Box 215, 47591
Telephone: 812-882-2280
FAX: 812-885-2308
Email: emison@vin.wvc.net

MEMBERS OF FIRM

Rabb Emison
Robert P. Doolittle, Jr.
Jeffrey B. Kolb
J. David Roellgen
Brian C. Dickerson

Clients Include: Security Bank & Trust Co.; Sun-Commercial Newspaper; Amoco Pipeline; El Paso Energy; Cincinnati Insurance Co.

For full biographical listings, see the Martindale-Hubbell Law Directory

IOWA

*CEDAR RAPIDS,** Linn Co.

LYNCH, DALLAS, SMITH & HARMAN, P.C. (AV)

526 Second Avenue SE, P.O. Box 2457, 52406-2457
Telephone: 319-365-9101
Facsimile: 319-365-9512
Email: attorneys@lynchdallas.com

Charles J. Lynch (1905-1983)
William M. Dallas (1905-1981)
Ralph V. Harman (Retired)
Donald E. Smith (1909-1999)
Donald G. Ribble
H. Edward Beatty
Scott E. McLeod
Robert R. Rush
Wilford H. Stone
Sean W. McPartland
Matthew J. Nagle
Elizabeth D. Jacobi
Janet Hong

Andrew W. Martin
Susan H. Sibert
Corinne R. Butkowski

Representative Clients: American States Insurance Co.; Deere & Co.; Rockwell International Corp.; State Farm Insurance Cos.; The Travelers Insurance Cos.

For full biographical listings, see the Martindale-Hubbell Law Directory

SHUTTLEWORTH & INGERSOLL, P.C. (AV)

115 Third Street S.E., Suite 500, P.O. Box 2107, 52406-2107
Telephone: 319-365-9461
Fax: 319-365-8443
URL: http://www.shuttleworthlaw.com

James C. Nemmers
Michael O. McDermott
John M. Bickel
Robert D. Houghton
Richard S. Fry
Richard C. Garberson
Gary J. Streit
Carroll J. Reasoner
Steven J. Pace
Glenn L. Johnson
Thomas P. Peffer
Dennis J. McMenimen
Kevin H. Collins
William P. Prowell
Diane Kutzko
Mark L. Zaiger
Douglas R. Oelschlaeger
Wesley B. Huisinga
Dean R. Einck
Linda M. Kirsch
Constance M. Alt
William S. Hochstetler
Kurt L. Kratovil
Brian D. Bergstrom
Gilda L. Boyer
Dean D. Carrington

Nancy J. Penner
Kevin J. Caster
Theresa C. Davis
David T. Hayes
Sarah J. Gayer
Laurie L. Dawley
Jennifer Rinden Clark
Dana L. Oxley

OF COUNSEL

Thomas M. Collins
William R. Shuttleworth

COUNSEL

Joan Lipsky
Laurie Bergren

Representative Clients: Amana Society; Archer-Daniels-Midland Co.; Cargill, Inc.; Cryovac, Inc., a Division of W. R. Grace & Co.; Firstar Bank, N.A.; General Mills, Inc.; General Motors Corp.; MCI; PMX Industries, Inc.; Goss Graphic Systems, Inc.

For full biographical listings, see the Martindale-Hubbell Law Directory

CHARLES CITY, Floyd Co.*

ELWOOD, O'DONOHOE, O'CONNOR & STOCHL (AV)

116 North Main Street, P.O. Box 307, 50616
Telephone: 515-228-8054
Fax: 515-228-8057
Cresco, Iowa Office: 217 North Elm Street. P.O. Box 377.
Telephone: 319-547-3321.
Fax: 319-547-3189.
New Hampton, Iowa Office: 101 North Locust Avenue, P.O. Box 310.
Telephone: 515-394-5943.
Fax: 515-394-5945.

MEMBERS OF FIRM

Henry L. Elwood
James E. O'Donohoe (1921-1998)
Christopher F. O'Donohoe
Richard D. Stochl
Judith Mack O'Donohoe
Joseph Patrick Braun

ASSOCIATES

Lewis M. Churbuck
Patrick Wegman

Representative Clients: Grinnell Mutual Reinsurance Co.; Security State Bank, New Hampton, Iowa; United Fire & Casualty Insurance Co.; Board of Trustees, New Hampton Municipal Light Plant; First Citizens National Bank, New Hampton, Iowa; Alliance Pipeline; Cresco Union Savings Bank, Cresco, Iowa; City of Cresco, Iowa; Featherlite Mfg., Inc.; Community First National Bank, Protivin, Iowa.

CLARINDA, Page Co.*

TURNER, JONES & BITTING (AV)

301 East Main Street, P.O. Box 231, 51632
Telephone: 712-542-2151
Fax: 712-542-2031

MEMBERS OF FIRM

Clinton H. Turner (1909-1969)
Sanford A. Turner
Paul W. Jones
Ronny M. Bitting

Representative Clients: Citizens State Bank, Clarinda, Iowa; City of Clarinda; Cities of Coin, Braddyville, Shambaugh, Blanchard and Northboro, Iowa; Lisle Corp., Clarinda, Iowa; Page County Federal Savings; Oxley Farms, Inc.
References: Citizens State Bank; Page County State Bank of Clarinda, Iowa.

For full biographical listings, see the Martindale-Hubbell Law Directory

COUNCIL BLUFFS, Pottawattamie Co.*

PETERS LAW FIRM, P.C. (AV)

233 Pearl Street, P.O. Box 1078, 51502-1078
Telephone: 712-328-3157
FAX: 712-328-9092
Email: peterslawfirm@msn.com

James A. Campbell
Dennis Leu
Dennis M. Gray
James A. Thomas
Lyle W. Ditmars
Scott H. Peters
John M. McHale
Jacob J. Peters
Leo P. Martin
Scott J. Rogers
Jon E. Heisterkamp
John M. French
Matthew G. Woods

Edward D. Jorgensen
John C. Rasmussen

Representative Clients: Bluffs Run Casino; Mercantile Bank, Council Bluffs, IA; Grinnell Mutual Reinsurance Co.; Iowa West Racing Association; Rockwell International; Shelter Insurance; State Farm Insurance; Kemper Group; The Pillsbury Co.; The Cities of Crescent, Glenwood, Treynor, McClelland, Underwood.

For full biographical listings, see the Martindale-Hubbell Law Directory

REILLY, PETERSEN & HANNAN, P.L.C. (AV)

215 South Main Street, P.O. Box 1016, 51502-1016
Telephone: 712-328-1575
Fax: 712-328-1562

C. R. Hannan
Michael G. Reilly
Deborah L. Petersen

Craig M. Dreismeier

References: Peoples National Bank of Council Bluffs.

For full biographical listings, see the Martindale-Hubbell Law Directory

TELPNER, PETERSON, SMITH & RUESCH (AV)

25 Main Place, Suite 200, P.O. Box 248, 51502-0248
Telephone: 712-325-9000
Fax: 712-328-1946
Email: telpnerlaw@aol.com

MEMBERS OF FIRM

Richard W. Peterson
Charles L. Smith
Jack E. Ruesch

(See Next Column)

ASSOCIATES

Walter P. Thomas
Shannon Dell'Orfano

OF COUNSEL

Maynard S. Telpner

Reference: Firstar Bank, Council Bluffs, Iowa.

For full biographical listings, see the Martindale-Hubbell Law Directory

CRESCO, Howard Co.*

ELWOOD, O'DONOHOE, O'CONNOR & STOCHL (AV)

217 North Elm Street, P.O. Box 377, 52136
Telephone: 319-547-3321
Fax: 319-547-3189
New Hampton, Iowa Office: 101 North Locust Avenue, P.O. Box 310.
Telephone: 515-394-5943.
Fax: 515-394-5945.
Charles City, Iowa Office: 116 Main Street. P.O. Box 307. 50616.
Telephone: 515-228-8054.
Fax: 515-228-8057.

MEMBERS OF FIRM

Henry L. Elwood
James E. O'Donohoe (1921-1998)
Christopher F. O'Donohoe
Richard D. Stochl
Judith Mack O'Donohoe
Joseph Patrick Braun

ASSOCIATES

Lewis M. Churbuck
Patrick Wegman

Representative Clients: Grinnell Mutual Reinsurance Co.; Security State Bank, New Hampton, Iowa; United Fire & Casualty Insurance Co.; Board of Trustees, New Hampton Municipal Light Plant; First Citizens National Bank, New Hampton, Iowa; Alliance Pipeline; Cresco Union Savings Bank, Cresco, Iowa; City of Cresco, Iowa; Featherlite Mfg., Inc.; Community First National Bank, Protivin, Iowa.

DALLAS CENTER, Dallas Co.

McDONALD, BROWN & FAGEN (AV)

502-15th Street, P.O. Box 250, 50063-0250
Telephone: 515-992-3728
Fax: 515-992-3971
Email: dalctlaw@mindspring.com
Grimes, Iowa Office: 306 South First Street.
Telephone: 515-986-9888.
Fax: 515-986-9876.

OF COUNSEL

John C. McDonald

MEMBERS OF FIRM

Ralph R. Brown
Charles H. Fagen

ASSOCIATE

Douglas A. Flanders

Representative Clients: Brenton Bank-Dallas Center; Dallas Mutual Insurance Co.; City of Dallas Center; City of Granger; Dallas Center-Grimes Community School District; Spurgeon Manor, Inc.; DCI Companies, Inc.; DCI Group, L.L.C.

For full biographical listings, see the Martindale-Hubbell Law Directory

DAVENPORT, Scott Co.*

CARLIN, HELLSTROM & BITTNER (AV)

A Partnership including Professional Corporations
1000 Firstar Center, 52801
Telephone: 319-328-3333
Fax: 319-328-3352

John A. Hellstrom (1921-1992)
John J. Carlin (Retired, 1993)
R. Richard Bittner (P.C.)
Robert D. Lambert (P.C.)
Michael J. Motto
Michael K. Bush
Jeffrey S. Bittner

ASSOCIATES

William J. Bush
James T. Carlin
Sara Schroeder

Representative Clients: Mercantile Bank, FSB; Firstar Bank Iowa; Lawyers Title Insurance Co.; Iowa Mutual Insurance Co.; Palmer Communications, Inc.; Palmer College Foundation; Allied Mutual Insurance Co.; Farm & City Insurance Co.; Pekin Insurance Co.; The Connelly Group, L.P.

For full biographical listings, see the Martindale-Hubbell Law Directory

GOSMA & GALLAGHER, P.L.C. (AV)

Quad City Bank Building, 4500 North Brady Street, Suite 200, 52806
Telephone: 319-388-8417
Fax: 319-388-9240
Email: lawfirm@gosma-gallagher.com
Bettendorf Office: 1989 Spruce Hills Drive.
Telephone: 319-355-5304.
Fax: 319-359-7711.

(See Next Column)

GOSMA & GALLAGHER P.L.C.—*Continued*

MEMBERS OF FIRM

Robert D. Wells (1904-1990)
Robert H. Gallagher
John S. Gosma
James G. Noth
Marie R. Rolling-Tarbox
David A. Millage
Robert S. Gallagher
Jane E. Zimmer

OF COUNSEL

Clay LeGrand
Nicholas W. LeGrand (Not admitted in IA)

References: American Bank and Trust Company, Rock Island; Great River Bank and Trust, Princeton.

For full biographical listings, see the Martindale-Hubbell Law Directory

HENINGER AND HENINGER, PROFESSIONAL CORPORATION (AV)

Suite 501, 101 West Second Street, 52801
Telephone: 319-324-0418
Fax: 319-324-5808
Email: RHenin5382@aol.com *URL:* http://www.lawyers.com/heningerlaw

Ralph U. Heninger (1908-1993)
Ralph H. Heninger
Ralph W. Heninger

For full biographical listings, see the Martindale-Hubbell Law Directory

LANE & WATERMAN (AV)

220 North Main Street, Suite 600, 52801
Telephone: 319-324-3246
Fax: 319-324-1616
URL: http://www.l-wlaw.com
Rock Island, Illinois Office: 224 18th Street, Suite 500.
Telephone: 309-786-1600.
Fax: 309-786-1794.

MEMBERS OF FIRM

Joe R. Lane (1902-1931)
Charles M. Waterman (1902-1924)
Robert A. Van Vooren
William C. Davidson
C. Dana Waterman, III
Charles E. Miller
Thomas J. Shields
James A. Mezvinsky
David A. Dettmann
Dana M. Craig
Terry M. Giebelstein
Rand S. Wonio
Curtis E. Beason
Robert V. P. Waterman, Jr.
Peter J. Benson
Michael L. Noyes
R. Scott Van Vooren
Thomas D. Waterman
John D. Telleen
Richard A. Davidson
Carole J. Anderson
Michael P. Byrne
Edmund H. Carroll, Jr.
Maria Mihalakis Waterman
John D. DeDoncker
Jeffrey W. Paul

ASSOCIATES

Theodore F. Olt III
Cameron A. Davidson
Judith L. Herrmann
Monique C. Gorsline
Jed E. Brokaw
Robert Blake McMonagle
Christopher J. Curran
Mark A. Pihart
Joseph C. Judge
Troy D. Venner

OF COUNSEL

Donald H. Sitz
Robert V. P. Waterman
Thomas N. Kamp

Representative Clients: MidAmerican Energy Co.; Lee Enterprises, Inc.; Iowa-American Water Co.; Aluminum Company of America; ANR Pipeline Co.; Hartford Insurance Group; Genesis Health System; Davenport Community School District; Commercial Union Insurance Co.

For full biographical listings, see the Martindale-Hubbell Law Directory

*DECORAH,** Winneshiek Co.

MILLER, PEARSON, GLOE, BURNS, BEATTY & COWIE, P.C. (AV)

301 West Broadway, 52101
Telephone: 319-382-4226
Fax: 319-382-3783
Email: millerlaw@salamander.com

Frank R. Miller (1915-1977)
Donald H. Gloe
James Burns
Marion L. Beatty
Robert J. Cowie, Jr.

Bradley Douglas Shidler

OF COUNSEL

Floyd S. Pearson

Counsel for: Luther College; Decorah Community School District; Winneshiek County Memorial Hospital; Community First National Bank.
Local Counsel for: Iowa Mutual Insurance Cos.; Employers Mutual Liability Insurance Co. of Wisconsin; Continental Casualty Co.; Employers Mutual Casualty Co.; Grinnell Mutual Insurance Co.; Allied Mutual Insurance Co.

For full biographical listings, see the Martindale-Hubbell Law Directory

*DES MOINES,** Polk Co.

AHLERS, COONEY, DORWEILER, HAYNIE, SMITH & ALLBEE, P.C. (AV)

100 Court Avenue, Suite 600, 50309-2231
Telephone: 515-243-7611
Fax: 515-243-2149
URL: http://www.ahlerslaw.com

Kenneth H. Haynie
H. Richard Smith
John F. McKinney, Jr.
L. W. Rosebrook
Richard G. Santi
Edgar H. Bittle
Ronald L. Sutphin
Terry L. Monson
Lance A. Coppock
David H. Luginbill
Mark W. Beerman
Edward W. Remsburg
Randall H. Stefani
Elizabeth Gregg Kennedy
Wade R. Hauser III
William J. Noth
David M. Swinton
Linda L. Kniep
John D. Hintze
Peter L. J. Pashler
Ivan T. Webber
Serge H. Garrison
Jane B. McAllister
James C. Hanks
R. Mark Cory
Ronald L. Peeler
Andrew J. Bracken
Steven L. Serck
Michael J. Eason
Steven Michael Nadel

OF COUNSEL

Paul F. Ahlers
Philip J. Dorweiler
Robert G. Allbee

Elizabeth A. Grob
Jennifer A. Clendenin
Patricia A. Westemeyer

For full biographical listings, see the Martindale-Hubbell Law Directory

BELIN LAMSON MCCORMICK ZUMBACH FLYNN, A PROFESSIONAL CORPORATION (AV)

The Financial Center, 666 Walnut Street, Suite 2000, 50309-3989
Telephone: 515-243-7100
Fax: 515-282-7615

David W. Belin (1928-1999)
Jeffrey E. Lamson
Mark McCormick
Steven E. Zumbach
Thomas L. Flynn
Roger T. Stetson
Jon L. Staudt
James L. Krambeck
Richard W. Lozier, Jr.
James V. Sarcone, Jr.
James R. Swanger
Jeffrey A. Krausman
Jeremy C. Sharpe
John T. Seitz
Robert A. Mullen
David L. Charles
William D. Bartine
Quentin R. Boyken
Charles F. Becker
Mark E. Weinhardt
Dennis P. Ogden
Edward M. Mansfield
Margaret C. Callahan
Robert D. Sharp
Garth D Adams
Michael R. Reck
Roger S. Lucas (Not admitted in IA)
Jennifer J. Lucas (Not admitted in IA)
David K. Basler

Danielle Marie Shelton

OF COUNSEL

Sue Luettjohann Seitz

For full biographical listings, see the Martindale-Hubbell Law Directory

BROWN, WINICK, GRAVES, GROSS, BASKERVILLE AND SCHOENEBAUM, P.L.C. (AV)

Two Ruan Center, Suite 1100, 601 Locust Street, 50309
Telephone: 515-242-2400
Fax: 515-283-0231
Pella, Iowa Office: 616 Franklin Place, 50219.
Telephone: 515-628-4513.
Fax: 515-628-8494.

Marvin Winick
Richard W. Baskerville
Bruce Graves
Steven C. Schoenebaum
Harold N. Schneebeck
Paul D. Hietbrink
William C. Brown
Richard K. Updegraff
Jill Thompson Hansen
Paul E. Carey
Douglas E. Gross
John D. Hunter
James H. Gilliam
Robert D. Andeweg
Alice Eastman Helle
Daniel L. Stockdale
Thomas D. Johnson
Charles J. Krogmeier
Christopher R. Sackett
Sean P. Moore
Nancy Shimanek Boyd
James L. Pray
Brenton D. Soderstrum
Brett J. Trout
Fred L. Morris
Michael D. Treinen

Miranda L. Hughes
Duane P. Hagerty
Deborah J. Schmudlach
Timothy J. Fox
William E. Hanigan
William R. Gustoff
Sean P. Conboy
Danielle K. Dixon
Christine B. Long

(See Next Column)

BROWN, WINICK, GRAVES, GROSS, BASKERVILLE AND SCHOENEBAUM, P.L.C., *Des Moines—Continued*

OF COUNSEL

John G. Fletcher
Walter R. Brown

For full biographical listings, see the Martindale-Hubbell Law Directory

CONNOLLY, O'MALLEY, LILLIS, HANSEN & OLSON, L.L.P. (AV)

300 NationsBank Building, 317 Sixth Avenue, 50309-4127
Telephone: 515-243-8157
Fax: 515-243-3919
Email: clawfirm@aol.com

MEMBERS OF FIRM

William J. Lillis
Russell J. Hansen
Michael W. O'Malley
Eugene E. Olson
Streetar Cameron
Douglas A. Fulton
Daniel L. Manning
Christopher R. Pose
Patrick T. Burk
David I. Hansen

A list of Representative Clients will be furnished upon request.
References will be furnished upon request.

For full biographical listings, see the Martindale-Hubbell Law Directory

DAVIS, BROWN, KOEHN, SHORS & ROBERTS, P.C. (AV)

(Formerly Davis, Hockenberg, Wine, Brown, Koehn & Shors, P.C.)
The Financial Center, 666 Walnut Street, Suite 2500, 50309-3993
Telephone: 515-288-2500
Cable: Davis Law
Facsimile: 515-243-0654
Email: info@lawiowa.com *URL:* http://www.lawiowa.com

Donald J. Brown
William J. Koehn
John D. Shors
Stephen W. Roberts
William R. King
Robert F. Holz, Jr.
Dennis D. Jerde
Robert A. Gamble
Michael G. Kulik
Richard E. Ramsay
F. Richard Thornton
Thomas E. Salsbery
Frank J. Carroll
Bruce I. Campbell
Jonathan C. Wilson
Patricia A. Shoff
Steven L. Nelson
David B. VanSickel
Gene R. La Suer
Deborah M. Tharnish
Brian L. Wirt
Kent A. Herink
Robert J. Douglas, Jr.
Nicholas H. Roby
Mark D. Walz
Gary M. Myers
Stanley J. Thompson
David A. Tank
David M. Erickson
Lori Torgerson Chesser
Jo Ellen Whitney
Becky S. Knutson
Julie Johnson McLean
David D. Nelson
Beverly Evans
M. Daniel Waters
Christopher P. Jannes
Sharon K. Malheiro
Kris Holub Smith
William A. Boatwright
Thomas J. Houser
Kendall R. Watkins
Scott M. Brennan

Debra Rectenbaugh Pettit
Denise R. Claton
Matthew E. Laughlin
Mark L. Stember
Judith R. "Lynn" Boes
Daniel A. Rosenberg
Alla R. Zaprudsky
Amy C. Churchill
Daniel M. Weddle

OF COUNSEL

Neal E. Smith
Donald A. Wine
A. J. Greffenius
C. Carleton Frederici
Sally A. Reavely
William D. Thomas
David W. Dunn

For full biographical listings, see the Martindale-Hubbell Law Directory

DUNCAN, GREEN, BROWN, LANGENESS & ECKLEY, A PROFESSIONAL CORPORATION (AV)

380 Capital Square, 400 Locust Street, 50309-2331
Telephone: 515-288-6440
Fax: 515-288-6448

Hearst R. (Randy) Duncan, Jr.
Brent B. (Chris) Green
Gregory R. Brown
James B. Langeness
Stephen R. Eckley
Randolph Mathieson (Matt) Duncan
Mariclare Thinnes Culver

Scott P. Duncan
Bradley C. Obermeier
Timothy S. Eckley
Lisa M. Lann
Martin J. Kenworthy

Representative Clients: American Republic Insurance Co.; Charles Gabus Ford, Inc.; Fruehauf Trailer Corp.; Bridgestone/Firestone, Inc.; The Coleman Co.; The Goodyear Co.; City of Des Moines; Federated Rural Electric Insurance Cooperative; Heller Financial, Inc.; Coca Cola Corp.

For full biographical listings, see the Martindale-Hubbell Law Directory

FINLEY, ALT, SMITH, SCHARNBERG, CRAIG, HILMES & GAFFNEY, P.C. (AV)

604 Locust Street, Fourth Floor Equitable Building, 50309
Telephone: 515-288-0145
Telecopier: 515-288-2724

Thomas A. Finley
Jerry P. Alt
Glenn L. Smith
Steven K. Scharnberg
David C. Craig
John D. (Jack) Hilmes
R. Todd Gaffney
Kerry A. Finley
Pamela J. Prager
Kevin J. Driscoll
Steven K. Huff
V. Glenn Goodwin, Jr.

Representative Clients: ALAS; American Society of Composers, Authors and Publishers; Equitable Life Assurance Society of the U.S.; Federated Insurance Co.; Meredith Corp.
Iowa Attorneys for: Midwest Medical Insurance Co.
District Attorneys for: Norfolk & Southern Railroad; Soo Line Railroad Company.

For full biographical listings, see the Martindale-Hubbell Law Directory

GREFE & SIDNEY, P.L.C. (AV)

2222 Grand Avenue, P.O. Box 10434, 50306
Telephone: 515-245-4300
Fax: 515-245-4452
Email: grandfirm@aol.com
Pella, Iowa Office: 725 Franklin Street, 50219.
Telephone: 515-628-9343.
Fax: 515-628-7252.

Rolland E. Grefe
Thomas W. Carpenter
Henry A. Harmon
Claude H. Freeman
Stephen D. Hardy
Robert C. Thomson
Craig S. Shannon
John Werner
Patrick J. McNulty
Mark W. Thomas
Guy R. Cook
Mary E. Kiener
Andrew D. Hall

Stephanie Glenn Techau
Mark A. Schultheis
Marcy A. O'Brien
Timothy N. Tripp
Donna R. Miller
Marc D. McKay

OF COUNSEL

Ross H. Sidney

Representative Clients: Adventurelands of America; Caseys General Stores, Inc.; Cincinnati Insurance Companies; Easter Enterprises, Inc.; Freeman Decorating Co.; Liberty Mutual Insurance Co.; Otis Elevator; Pella Corp.; State Farm Mutual Insurance Company; The St. Paul Companies; State Industries.

For full biographical listings, see the Martindale-Hubbell Law Directory

HANSEN, MCCLINTOCK & RILEY (AV)

Eighth Floor - Fleming Building, 218 Sixth Avenue, 50309
Telephone: 515-244-2141
Fax: 515-244-2931
Email: hmrlaw@aol.com

MEMBERS OF FIRM

Haemer Wheatcraft (1904-1983)
J. Rudolph Hansen (1904-1995)
John A. McClintock
Ronald A. Riley
Chester C. Woodburn, III
William D. Scherle
David L. Brown
John E. Swanson

ASSOCIATES

James M. Ballard
Aaron T. Oliver

Representative Clients: The St. Paul Companies; Bituminous Insurance Companies; Northwestern National Insurance Co.; The Travelers Insurance Companies; United States Aviation Insurance Group; American International Companies; Iowa Credit Union League; The McAninch Corp.; R. J. Reynolds Tobacco Co.; Brown Bros., Inc. Electrical Contractors.

For full biographical listings, see the Martindale-Hubbell Law Directory

NYEMASTER, GOODE, VOIGTS, WEST, HANSELL & O'BRIEN, A PROFESSIONAL CORPORATION (AV)

700 Walnut, Suite 1600, 50309
Telephone: 515-283-3100
Telecopier: 515-283-3108
Ames, Iowa Office: 1416 Buckeye Avenue, Ames, Iowa 50010.
Telephone: 515-233-3000.
Telecopier: 515-232-3846.

LeRoy R. Voigts
James B. West
Edgar F. Hansell
W. Don Brittin, Jr.
Don Muyskens
R. Craig Shives
Roger L. Ferris
Lawrence E. Myers
Keith E. Luchtel
Gerald J. Newbrough
Robert A. VanOrsdel
Richard J. Sapp
G. R. Neumann
Russell E. Schrage
Carlton T. King
Gregory P. Page
Randall G. Horstmann
Jay Eaton

(See Next Column)

NYEMASTER, GOODE, VOIGTS, WEST, HANSELL & O'BRIEN A PROFESSIONAL CORPORATION—*Continued*

Bradford L. Austin
Burns Mossman
Phyllis E. Pearson
Hayward L. Draper
Sara J. Sersland
James E. Gritzner
Michael W. Thrall
Mark C. Dickinson
Gregory B. Wilcox
John F. Lorentzen
Rod Kubat
Steven J. Roy
Frank B. Harty
James C. Wine
Bruce W. Baker
Thomas W. Foley
Steven H. Lytle
Terry C. Hancock
Anthony A. Longnecker
Wade H. Schut
Mark D. Aljets
G. Thomas Sullivan
Joseph A. Quinn
Joan Fletcher
Thomas H. Walton
Willard L. Boyd III
Lisette Sell
Jeffrey William Courter
Hallie E. Still-Caris
Brian J. Humke
Deborah S. Krauth

Paula S. Dierenfeld
John B. Tuffnell
Jill M. Stevenson
Angel West
Kathryn Atkinson Overberg
Angela L. Watson
Jennifer L. Vergilii
Debra L. Dalton
Amy L. VanDuyn
Neal K. Westin
John T. Clendenin
Stephanie L. Marett

OF COUNSEL

Samuel G. O'Brien
John J. McLaughlin
Drew R. Tillotson
Frank B. Comfort
Luther L. Hill, Jr.
Barry Nadler

Representative Clients: Burlington Northern and Santa Fe Railway Company; East Des Moines National Bank; Northwestern Bell Telephone Co.; Amoco Oil Co.; Inter-State Assurance Co.; Central Life Assurance Co.; Montgomery Ward; Deere & Co.

For full biographical listings, see the Martindale-Hubbell Law Directory

---

PATTERSON, LORENTZEN, DUFFIELD, TIMMONS, IRISH, BECKER & ORDWAY, L.L.P. (AV)

729 Insurance Exchange Building, 50309
Telephone: 515-283-2147
Fax: 515-283-1002
Email: mail@pattersonfirm.com *URL:* http://www.pattersonfirm.com

MEMBERS OF FIRM

G. O. Patterson (1914-1982)
James A. Lorentzen (Retired)
Theodore T. Duffield
William E. Timmons (Retired)
Roy M. Irish
F. H. Becker (Retired)
Gary D. Ordway
Robin L. Hermann
Harry Perkins, III
Michael F. Lacey, Jr.
Gregory J. Wilson
Jeffrey A. Boehlert
Douglas A. Haag
Charles E. Cutler
Michael D. Huppert
Martin C. Sprock
William A. Wickett
Frederick M. Haskins
Jeffrey A. Baker
Janice M. Herfkens
Coreen K. Bezdicek
Patrick V. Waldron

ASSOCIATE

Michael S. Jones

General Counsel for: Iowa Insurance Institute.
Representative Clients: Allied Mutual Insurance Company; CNA Insurance Company; Chubb Insurance Group; Continental Western Insurance Co.; Farmers Insurance Group; Farmland Insurance Company; Grinnell Mutual Reinsurance Company; Hawkeye Security Insurance Company; Iowa Insurance Institute, St. Paul Fire & Marine Insurance Company.

For full biographical listings, see the Martindale-Hubbell Law Directory

---

PINGEL & TEMPLER, P.C. (AV)

Suite 437 3737 Woodland Avenue (West Des Moines), P.O. Box 1991, 50309
Telephone: 515-225-3737
Fax: 515-225-9510

Ronni F. Begleiter
John C. Conger
Thomas M. Cunningham
Michael A. Dee
Robert K. DuPuy
Brad Epperly
Keri K. Farrell-Kolb
Michael J. Green
Jeffrey L. Goodman
Lawrence L. Marcucci
Greg A. Naylor
Jon R. Pearce
C. Jean Pendleton
John R. Perkins
Kurt S. Peterson
G. Brian Pingel
Jeffrey D. Stone
Barbara M. Tapscott (Not admitted in IA)
John A. Templer, Jr.

For full biographical listings, see the Martindale-Hubbell Law Directory

---

THE ROSENBERG LAW FIRM (AV)

1010 Insurance Exchange Building, 505 Fifth Avenue, 50309
Telephone: 515-243-7600
Email: bdr@worldnet.att.net

(See Next Column)

MEMBERS OF FIRM

Raymond Rosenberg
Dean A. Stowers
Brent D. Rosenberg

Reference: Firstar Bank, Des Moines, Iowa.

For full biographical listings, see the Martindale-Hubbell Law Directory

---

SULLIVAN & WARD, P.C. (AV)

801 Grand, Suite 3500, 50309-2719
Telephone: 515-244-3500
Telecopier: 515-244-3599
Email: swpc@netins.net

John T. Ward
Harlan (Bud) Hockenberg
Michael P. Joynt
Louis R. Hockenberg
Richard R. Chabot
Robert M. Holliday
Mark Landa
John V. Donnelly
Dennis L. Puckett
James G. Sawtelle

OF COUNSEL

Lawrence F. Scalise

Jill Mataya Corry
Jason D. Walke
Matthew D. Gardner

Representative Clients: Iowa Association of Electric Cooperatives; Central Iowa Power Cooperative; Prudential Insurance Company of America; National Rural Utilities Cooperative Finance Corp.; Norwest Bank Des Moines, N.A.; First Union Mortgage Corp.; Travelers Insurance Co.; Siegwerk, Inc.

For full biographical listings, see the Martindale-Hubbell Law Directory

---

WHITFIELD & EDDY, P.L.C. (AV)

317 6th Avenue, Suite 1200 Locust at 6th, 50309-4195
Telephone: 515-288-6041
Fax: 515-246-1474
Email: info@whitfieldlaw.com *URL:* http://www.whitfieldlaw.com

Gary Gately
Timothy J. Walker
David L. Phipps
Benjamin B. Ullem
Robert L. Fanter
Bernard L. "Jerry" Spaeth
William L. Fairbank
Robert G. Bridges
Jaki K. Samuelson
Kevin M. Reynolds
Thomas H. Burke
Thomas Henderson
George H. Frampton
Megan Manning Antenucci
Wendy L. Carlson
Thomas S. Reavely
Gary A. Norton
Frank M. Grenard (Not admitted in IA)
Mark V. Hanson
Maureen Roach Tobin
August B. Landis
Richard J. Kirschman
John F. Fatino

Jason M. Casini
Roscoe A. Ries, Jr.
Lisa A. Nelson
J. Campbell Helton
Anjela A. Shutts
Danette L. Kennedy
Stephen E. Doohen
Sean A. Pelletier
Matthew C. Ahmann

OF COUNSEL

John C. Eddy
Harley A. Whitfield
A. Roger Witke

General Counsel for: Hawkeye-Security Insurance Co.; Iowa Funeral Directors Assn.; Tom Fairweather Trust Farms; Townsend Engineering Co.; United Security Insurance Co.
Representative Clients: Brenton Bank; Crum & Forster Commercial Insurance; Decker Truck Line, Inc.; General Motors Co.

For full biographical listings, see the Martindale-Hubbell Law Directory

---

*DUBUQUE,** Dubuque Co.

O'CONNOR & THOMAS, P.C. (AV)

700 Locust Street, Suite 200, CyCare Plaza, 52001-6874
Telephone: 319-557-8400
Telecopier: 319-556-1867
Email: othomaspc@mwci.net

John C. O'Connor
Brendan T. Quann
A. John Arenz
Chad C. Leitch
Richard K. Whitty
Stephen C. Krumpe
James E. Goodman, Jr.

Davin C. Curtiss
Paul J. Sigwarth
Thomas S. Collins
Amy Collins White
George A. Davis

OF COUNSEL

Robert M. Bertsch

Representative Clients: American Trust & Savings Bank; Dubuque Bank & Trust Company; Firstar Bank; Mercantile Bank Midwest; The Archdiocese of Dubuque; A.Y. McDonald Industries, Inc.

For full biographical listings, see the Martindale-Hubbell Law Directory

*ELDORA,** Hardin Co.

WILSON & CRAIG, PROFESSIONAL CORPORATION (AV)

1305 Twelfth Street, P.O. Box 431, 50627-0431
Telephone: 515-939-5475
Fax: 515-939-3157
Email: wel@netins.net
Hubbard, Iowa Office: 213 East Maple.
Telephone: 515-864-3338. Tuesday and Thursday A.M. only.

Donald C. Wilson
Patrick J. Craig

William J. Coarts

Representative Clients: Hardin County Savings Bank, Eldora, Iowa; Security State Bank, Hubbard, Iowa; City Union Union, Iowa; Harold H. Luiken & Sons, Inc., Steamboat Rock, Iowa; Dodger Industries, Inc., Eldora, Iowa; Whink Products Co., Eldora, Iowa; Heart of Iowa Telecommunications Co-operative, Union, Iowa; Eldora-New Providence School District, Eldora, Iowa; BCLUW School District, Conrad, Iowa; Praire Land Cooperative, Hubbard, Iowa.

*ESTHERVILLE,** Emmet Co.

FITZGIBBONS BROTHERS (AV)

A Partnership including a Professional Corporation
108 North 7th Street, P.O. Box 496, 51334
Telephone: 712-362-7215
Fax: 712-362-3526

MEMBERS OF FIRM

Leo E. Fitzgibbons
Francis Fitzgibbons
Joseph L. Fitzgibbons
Harold W. White (P.C.)
Ned A. Stockdale
Scot Bauermeister

For full biographical listings, see the Martindale-Hubbell Law Directory

GRINNELL, Poweshiek Co.

BIERMAN & BIERMAN, P.C. (AV)

920 Main Street, P.O. Box 713, 50112
Telephone: 515-236-6128
Email: bb@pcpartner.net
Pella, Iowa Office: 702 Liberty Street, 50219.
Telephone: 515-628-3283.

John F. (Rick) Bierman, III

OF COUNSEL

John F. Bierman

Representative Clients: Altemeier Farms, Inc.; John Campbell Charitable Trust; ASI Signs; Cargill, Inc.; Donaldson Co., Inc.; Grinnell Day Care Center, Inc.; Grinnell College; Grinnell State Bank; Ramsey-Weeks, Inc.; State Farm Insurance.

For full biographical listings, see the Martindale-Hubbell Law Directory

*HAMPTON,** Franklin Co.

HOBSON, CADY & CADY (AV)

9 First Street S.W., P.O. Box 456, 50441
Telephone: 515-456-2555
Fax: 515-456-3315
Email: cadyart@rconnect.com

MEMBERS OF FIRM

A. J. Hobson (1903-1972)
G. Arthur Cady
G. A. Cady, III

General Counsel for: Ag Services of America, Inc.
A list of Representative Clients will be furnished upon request.
References: First National Bank of Hampton; Liberty Bank & Trust.

For full biographical listings, see the Martindale-Hubbell Law Directory

*IOWA CITY,** Johnson Co.

MEARDON, SUEPPEL, DOWNER & HAYES P.L.C. (AV)

122 South Linn Street, 52240
Telephone: 319-338-9222
Fax: 319-338-7250

William L. Meardon (1919-1997)
William F. Sueppel
Robert N. Downer
James D. McCarragher
Mark T. Hamer
Thomas D. Hobart
Margaret T. Lainson
Douglas D. Ruppert
Timothy J. Krumm
William J. Sueppel
Charles A. Meardon

Dawn Barker Anderson

Representative Clients: United Technologies-Automotive; Perpetual Savings Bank; Economy Advertising Company; Metro Pavers, Inc.; League of Iowa Municipalities; Hills Bank and Trust Co.; J.M. Swank Co.; City of Muscatine; McComas-Lacina Construction Co., Inc.; Diamond Dave's Taco Company, Inc.

(See Next Column)

For full biographical listings, see the Martindale-Hubbell Law Directory

*MARSHALLTOWN,** Marshall Co.

CARTWRIGHT, DRUKER & RYDEN (AV)

112 West Church Street, P.O. Box 496, 50158
Telephone: 515-752-5467
Fax: 515-752-4370

MEMBERS OF FIRM

H. G. Cartwright (1902-1982)
Rex J. Ryden
John B. Grier
John F. Veldey
Joel T. S. Greer
Sharon Soorholtz Greer

ASSOCIATE

Merrill C. Swartz

OF COUNSEL

Harry Druker

Representative Clients: Mercantile Bank; Marshalltown Trowel Co.; Travelers Insurance Co.; Lennox Industries Inc.; State Farm Mutual Insurance Co., Bloomington, Ill.; Farm Bureau Mutual Insurance Co.; Allied Group; Employers Group.

For full biographical listings, see the Martindale-Hubbell Law Directory

HARRISON, BRENNECKE, MOORE, SMAHA & MCKIBBEN (AV)

302 Masonic Temple Building, P.O. Box 618, 50158
Telephone: 515-752-4271
Fax: 515-752-5266
Email: MWW@MTNIA.COM

MEMBERS OF FIRM

G. A. Mote (1874-1965)
Arley J. Wilson (1913-1982)
William L. Welp (1920-1997)
Allen E. Brennecke
James R. Moore
Leslie E. Smaha
Larry E. McKibben
James L. Goodman
William J. Lorenz
James C. Ellefson
Douglas W. Beals
Michael R. Horn
Norma J. Meade

OF COUNSEL

Roger E. Harrison

A List of Representatve Clients will be furnished upon request.

For full biographical listings, see the Martindale-Hubbell Law Directory

*MASON CITY,** Cerro Gordo Co.

BROWN, KINSEY & FUNKHOUSER, P.L.C. (AV)

214 North Adams, P.O. Box 679, 50402-0679
Telephone: 515-423-6223
Fax: 515-423-9995

MEMBERS OF FIRM

David E. Funkhouser
Robert S. Kinsey, III
Scott D. Brown
John P. Lander

ASSOCIATE

Jackie D. Armstrong

Representative Clients: Allstate Insurance Co.; The St. Paul Companies; Continental Western Ins. Co.; Home Ins. Co.; American Family Ins. Co.

For full biographical listings, see the Martindale-Hubbell Law Directory

WINSTON & BYRNE, LAWYERS, A PROFESSIONAL CORPORATION (AV)

119 Second Street, N.W., 50401
Telephone: 515-423-1913
Fax: 515-423-8998
Email: winston.byrne@mach3ww.com

Harold R. Winston
Michael G. Byrne
Patrick B. Byrne

Representative Clients: Woodharbor Molding & Millworks, Inc.; Winkleman Farms, Inc.; Sparboe Iowa Corporation; Schmidt Family Farms, Inc.; First Citizen's National Bank of Mason City; Norwest Bank Iowa, N.A.

For full biographical listings, see the Martindale-Hubbell Law Directory

*NEVADA,** Story Co.

CAHILL LAW OFFICES (AV)

1015 Fifth Street, 50201
Telephone: 515-382-6571
Fax: 515-382-4338

MEMBERS OF FIRM

Donald L. Nelson (1922-1984)
Thomas J. Cahill
Joseph R. Cahill

General Counsel for: Community Bank.
Representative Clients: Colo Telephone Co.; Allied Group; Iowa Mutual Insurance Co.

For full biographical listings, see the Martindale-Hubbell Law Directory

*NEW HAMPTON,** Chickasaw Co.

ELWOOD, O'DONOHOE, O'CONNOR & STOCHL (AV)

101 North Locust Avenue, P.O. Box 310, 50659
Telephone: 515-394-5943
Fax: 515-394-5945
Cresco, Iowa Office: 217 North Elm Street. P.O. Box 377.
Telephone: 319-547-3321.
Fax: 319-547-3189.
Charles City, Iowa Office: 116 North Main Street. P.O. Box 307. 50616.
Telephone: 515-228-8054.
Fax: 515-228-8057.

MEMBERS OF FIRM

Henry L. Elwood
James E. O'Donohoe (1921-1998)
Christopher F. O'Donohoe
Richard D. Stochl
Judith Mack O'Donohoe
Joseph Patrick Braun

ASSOCIATES

Lewis M. Churbuck
Patrick Wegman

Representative Clients: Grinnell Mutual Reinsurance Co.; Security State Bank, New Hampton, Iowa; United Fire & Casualty Insurance Co.; Board of Trustees, New Hampton Municipal Light Plant; First Citizens National Bank, New Hampton, Iowa; Alliance Pipeline; Cresco Union Savings Bank, Cresco, Iowa; Featherlite Mfg., Inc.; Community First National Bank, Protivin, Iowa; City of Cresco, Iowa.

*NEWTON,** Jasper Co.

BRIERLY LAW OFFICE, L.L.P. (AV)

211 First Avenue West, 50208
Telephone: 515-792-4160
Fax: 515-792-2410
Email: brierly@netins.ins
Grinnell, Iowa Office: 717 Fifth Avenue.
Telephone: 515-236-8622.
Sully, Iowa Office: 618 4th Street.
Telephone: 515-594-4420.
Affiliated with Dale A. Lamb, 717 5th Avenue, Grinnell, Iowa, 50112-1600.
Telephone: 515-236-3610.

MEMBERS OF FIRM

Laurence L. Brierly (1903-1984)
Ennis McCall (1912-1987)
Lewis M. Girdner (1925-1997)
Dennis F. Chalupa
Bradley McCall
Mark A. Otto
John H. Terpstra
DuWayne J. Dalen
Terri J. Rekemeyer

Representative Clients: Thombert, Inc. (Plastics); Edwards Publications, Inc.; Pyramid, Inc.; Mid-Iowa Savings Bank, FSB; Pleasantville State Bank; J. H. McKlveen and Co.; Midwest Manufacturing Co.; Cities of Mitchellville, Kellogg and Lynnville.

For full biographical listings, see the Martindale-Hubbell Law Directory

*OTTUMWA,** Wapello Co.

JOHNSON, HESTER, WALTER & BRECKENRIDGE, L.L.P. (AV)

111 West Second Street, P.O. Box 716, 52501-0716
Telephone: 515-684-5481
Telecopier: 515-684-5487
Email: jhwb@lisco.com

MEMBERS OF FIRM

David J. Hester
Thomas M. Walter
Robert E. Breckenridge, II

ASSOCIATE

Kenneth A. Duker

OF COUNSEL

Walter F. Johnson

Representative Clients: Firstar Bank Ottumwa; Deere and Co.; Lee Enterprises Inc.; Liberty Mutual Insurance Co.; Auto-owners Ins. Group; John Deere Ottumwa Works; Cardinal Community School District; Farmers Bank of Northern Missouri.

For full biographical listings, see the Martindale-Hubbell Law Directory

KIPLE, KIPLE, DENEFE, BEAVER & GARDNER, L.L.P. (AV)

104 South Court Street, P.O. Box 493, 52501
Telephone: 515-683-1626
Fax: 515-683-3597
Email: KIPLELAW@PCSIA.COM

MEMBERS OF FIRM

Charles M. Kiple
J. Terrence Denefe
Jerome M. Beaver
Steven Gardner

ASSOCIATE

Paul Zingg

General Counsel for: Winger Contracting Co.; Ideal Ready-Mix Co., Inc.; Wapello Rural Water Association, Inc.; Norris Asphalt Paving Co; J & J Steel, Inc.; Home Oil Stations, Inc.; Elliott Oil, Inc.

(See Next Column)

Representative Clients: Crawford & Company; Farm Bureau Mutual Insurance Co.

For full biographical listings, see the Martindale-Hubbell Law Directory

PERRY, Dallas Co.

WILLIS & SACKETT (AV)

1212 Second Street, P.O. Box 310, 50220
Telephone: 515-465-5331
Telecopier: 515-465-5333

MEMBERS OF FIRM

Blake Willis (1892-1961)
George H. Sackett (1900-1983)
Ned Willis (1921-1998)
G. Robert Sackett

Counsel for: Perry State Bank; City of Perry Water Dept.
Local Counsel: Farm Credit Services.

SHELDON, O'Brien Co.

WOLFF, WHORLEY, DE HOOGH & THOMPSON (AV)

218 9th Street, P.O. Box 309, 51201
Telephone: 712-324-4385
FAX: 712-324-5106

MEMBERS OF FIRM

Paul Wolff (1909-1987)
Thomas J. Whorley
John F. De Hoogh
Keith G. Thompson

References: Citizens State Bank, Sheldon, Iowa; Security State Bank, Sheldon, Iowa.

For full biographical listings, see the Martindale-Hubbell Law Directory

*SIOUX CITY,** Woodbury Co.

BARON, SAR, GOODWIN, GILL & LOHR (AV)

750 Pierce Street, P.O. Box 717, 51102
Telephone: 712-277-1015
FAX: 712-277-3067

MEMBERS OF FIRM

A. Frank Baron
Jeffrey A. Sar
F. Lee Goodwin
David L. Gill
Gregory N. Lohr

For full biographical listings, see the Martindale-Hubbell Law Directory

BERENSTEIN, MOORE, BERENSTEIN, HEFFERNAN & MOELLER, L.L.P. (AV)

Firstar Bank Building, 501 Pierce Street, Suite 300, P.O. Box 3207, 51102
Telephone: 712-252-0020
Fax: 712-252-0656
Email: BMBHMLAW@aol.com

MEMBERS OF FIRM

Marvin S. Berenstein
Dan A. Moore
Craig S. Berenstein
Maureen Brown Heffernan
Richard H. Moeller
Jeffrey A. Johnson
Mitchell A. Herigstad

ASSOCIATES

Dawn E. Mastalir
Tina Marie Sabag-Hodne
Kimberly K. Wolff
Kelly Kay Salker
Robert B. Weinberg

Representative Clients: Aalfs Mfg., Inc.; Beef Products, Inc.; Briar Cliff College; Canal Capital Corporation - Sioux City Stockyards; Dakota Dunes Development Co.; First American Bank; Firstar Bank Iowa, N.A.; Mercy Medical Center - Sioux City; Sioux City Community School District; Wells Dairy & Blue Bunny Ice Cream.

For full biographical listings, see the Martindale-Hubbell Law Directory

CRARY, HUFF, INKSTER, HECHT & SHEEHAN, P.C. (AV)

614 Pierce Street, P.O. Box 27, 51102-0027
Telephone: 712-277-4561
Fax: 712-277-4605
URL: http://www.craryhuff.com
South Sioux City, Nebraska Office: 1419 Dakota Avenue 68776.
Telephone: 402-494-2052.
Fax: 402-494-3231. E-Mail: mschmied@craryhuff.com
Dakota Dunes, South Dakota Office: 600 Stevens Port Drive, Suite 105, 57049.
Telephone: 605-232-3340.
Fax: 605-232-8931. E-Mail: djesse@craryhuff.com

S. D. Crary (1875-1969)
Wallace W. Huff (1910-1973)
Ralph W. Crary (1898-1992)
Robert J. Crary (Retired)
Bruce A. Crary
David R. Crary
Stewart A. Huff
Sandra K. Inkster Ehrich (Resident, South Sioux City, Nebraska Office)
Daryl L. Hecht
Rosemary F. Sheehan (Resident, Dakota Dunes Office)
Dennis R. Ringgenberg

(See Next Column)

CRARY, HUFF, INKSTER, HECHT & SHEEHAN P.C., *Sioux City—Continued*

Daniel L. Hartnett (Resident, South Sioux City, Nebraska Office)
Larry A. Storm
Steven R. Jensen
Michael P. Schmiedt (Resident, South Sioux City, Nebraska Office)
Molly Martin Williams
Darrell A. Jesse (Resident, Dakota Dunes, South Dakota Office)

Cody M. McCullough
Laura Denise-Marie Schmitt

General Counsel for: Nutra-Flo Co.; Iowa Meat Processing Co.; Floyd Valley Packing Co.; Marx Truck Line; Mopar, Inc.

For full biographical listings, see the Martindale-Hubbell Law Directory

GILDEMEISTER, WILLIA, KEANE, STAHLE & ANDREASEN, L.L.P. (AV)

Suite 400 Firstar Bank Building, 501 Pierce, P.O. Box 1768, 51102
Telephone: 712-277-0686
Fax: 712-277-0687

Frank J. Margolin (1901-1989)
G. Daniel Gildemeister
N. Richard Willia, Jr.
Edward J. Keane
Robert J. Stahle
Steven J. Andreasen

Rosanne Lienhard

Representative Clients: Continental Insurance Companies; Empire Fire & Marine Insurance Co.

For full biographical listings, see the Martindale-Hubbell Law Directory

HEIDMAN, REDMOND, FREDREGILL, PATTERSON, PLAZA & DYKSTRA, L.L.P. (AV)

A Registered Limited Liability Partnership including Professional Corporations
701 Pierce Street, Suite 200, P.O. Box 3086, 51102
Telephone: 712-255-8838
Fax: 712-258-6714
Email: lawyers@pionet.net

MEMBERS OF FIRM

Marvin F. Heidman
James W. Redmond
Alan E. Fredregill (P.C.)
Charles T. Patterson
Thomas M. Plaza
Daniel D. Dykstra
Lance D. Ehmcke
Margaret M. Prahl
Gregg E. Williams
Cynthia C. Moser
Judith A. Higgs
John C. Gray
Daniel B. Shuck
Rita C. Grimm
Edward C."Ted" Poulsen
Patrick L. Sealey

ASSOCIATES

Jeff W. Wright
Sarah J. Kuehl
Kathleen M. Deegan (Not admitted in IA)

OF COUNSEL

John W. Gleysteen (Retired)
Robert R. Eidsmoe (Retired)
Jacob C. Gleysteen (1883-1943)
H. Clifford Harper (1891-1959)

Representative Clients: Mercy Medical Center; Allied Insurance Group; Irving F. Jensen, Co.; Terra International, Inc.; P.I.C. International Group, P.L.C.; Grinnell Mutual Reinsurance Co.; Travelers Insurance Co.; United Fire & Casualty; Kemper Insurance Group; American Family Insurance.

For full biographical listings, see the Martindale-Hubbell Law Directory

MARKS, MADSEN & HIRSCHBACH (AV)

Suite 303, Piper-Jaffrey Building, P.O. Box 3226, 51102
Telephone: 712-258-1200
Fax: 712-258-2012

MEMBERS OF FIRM

George F. Madsen
George L. Hirschbach

OF COUNSEL

Bernard B. Marks

Representative Clients: Briar Cliff College; First Federal Savings Bank of Siouxland; First National Bank in Le Mars; The Security National Bank of Sioux City, Iowa; The Security National Bank of South Dakota; Sioux City Brick and Tile Co.; Siouxland Oncology-Hematology Associates; Valley Bank & Trust, Mapleton, Iowa; Western Iowa Tech. Community College.

For full biographical listings, see the Martindale-Hubbell Law Directory

RAWLINGS, NIELAND, PROBASCO, KILLINGER, ELLWANGER, JACOBS & MOHRHAUSER (AV)

522 Fourth Street, Suite 300, 51101
Telephone: 712-277-2373
FAX: 712-277-3304

(See Next Column)

James W. Kindig (1879-1950)
Lowell C. Kindig (1913-1992)
Robert E. Beebe (1913-1988)
Gene A. Probasco (Retired)

MEMBERS OF FIRM

Maurice B. Nieland
Sam S. Killinger
Michael W. Ellwanger
Michael P. Jacobs
Jeffrey R. Mohrhauser
Jeffrey D. Garreans
Rebecca A. Nelson

ASSOCIATE

Matthew T.E. Early

OF COUNSEL

William J. Rawlings

Representative Clients: Arnold Motor Supply; Chesterman Co.; CNA Insurance Co.; Farmers Savings Bank, Remsen, Iowa; Farm Bureau Insurance Co.; Maryland Casualty Co.; Norwest Bank Iowa, National Association; NWIP, Inc.; St. Paul Fire and Marine Insurance Co.; United Fire and Casualty Co.

For full biographical listings, see the Martindale-Hubbell Law Directory

*WATERLOO,** Black Hawk Co.

DUTTON, BRAUN, STAACK & HELLMAN, P.L.C. (AV)

3151 Brockway Road, P.O. Box 810, 50704
Telephone: 319-234-4471
Fax: 319-234-8029
Email: dbsh@wloolaw.com

David J. Dutton
Robert W. Braun
Thomas L. Staack
James R. Hellman
Michael A. Mc Enroe
Cheryl L. Weber
Steven K. Daniels
Bruce L. Braley
John J. Hines
James F. Kalkhoff

Kevin D. Ahrenholz
Carolyn A. Rafferty
Chad A. Swanson
Lynn M. Smith
James H. Cook

Representative Clients: Kemper Insurance Group; Reliance National Insurance Co.; CNA Insurance Cos.; The Travers Insurance Co.; Hawkeye Community College; Crossroads Ford, Ltd.; Black Hawk County Solid Waste Management Commission; Allen Memorial Hospital; Tri/Mark, Inc.; Heartland Inns of America, L.L.C.

For full biographical listings, see the Martindale-Hubbell Law Directory

KANSAS

*DODGE CITY,** Ford Co.

FOULSTON & SIEFKIN L.L.P. (AV)

810 Frontview, P.O. Box 1147, 67801
Telephone: 316-227-8126
Fax: 316-227-8451
URL: http://www.foulston.com
Wichita, Kansas Office: 100 North Broadway, 700 NationsBank Financial Center, 67202.
Telephone: 316-267-6371.
FAX: 316-267-6345.
Topeka, Kansas Office: 1515 NationsBank Tower, 534 Kansas Avenue, 66603.
Telephone: 785-233-3600.
FAX: 785-233-1610.
Member: Lex Mundi, The World's Leading Association of Independent Law Firms.

MEMBERS OF FIRM

William P. Trenkle, Jr.
David J. Rebein
R. Douglas Reagan
D. Shane Bangerter
Thomas W. Young

ASSOCIATES

Tamara L. Davis
Patricia A. Voth

For full biographical listings, see the Martindale-Hubbell Law Directory

WILLIAMS, STROBEL, MALONE, MASON & RALPH, P.A. (AV)

Second Floor, Nations Bank Building, P.O. Box 39, 67801
Telephone: 316-225-4168
FAX: 316-225-7261
Email: wsmmr@pld.com

Carl Van Riper (1879-1950)
C. W. Hughes (1910-1960)
James A. Williams (Retired)
Ken W. Strobel
Terry J. Malone
Ronald C. Mason
Bradley C. Ralph

Representative Clients: Roto-Mix, Inc.; Hartford Accident & Indemnity Co.; Travelers Insurance Co.; Farmers State Bank, Bucklin; Dodge City Board of Education; City of Dodge City; Western Plains Medical Complex; Farmers Ins. Group; ConAgra Refrigerated Foods Companies; Shelter Ins.

(See Next Column)

WILLIAMS, STROBEL, MALONE, MASON & RALPH P.A.—*Continued*

For full biographical listings, see the Martindale-Hubbell Law Directory

*EMPORIA,** Lyon Co.

ATHERTON & HUTH (AV)

527 Commercial, Suite 304, P.O. Box 624, 66801
Telephone: 316-342-1277; 342-1278
FAX: 316-342-2343
Email: atlaw@valu_line.net

MEMBERS OF FIRM

John G. Atherton
Stephen J. Atherton
Deborah A. Huth

Representative Clients: NationsBank, Emporia, Kansas; Great West Casualty Co.; American States Insurance Cos.; Manufacturers and Wholesalers Indemnity Co.; American Casualty Cos.; Universal Underwriters Insurance Co.; Travelers Insurance Co.; Maryland Casualty Co.; Shelter Insurance Companies; American Family Insurance.

For full biographical listings, see the Martindale-Hubbell Law Directory

*GARNETT,** Anderson Co.

STEVEN B. DOERING (AV)

111 East Fourth Street, P.O. Box 345, 66032
Telephone: 785-448-5493
FAX: 785-448-5458

Reference: Kansas State Bank.

For full biographical listings, see the Martindale-Hubbell Law Directory

*GREAT BEND,** Barton Co.

GLENN E. OPIE (AV)

Suite 102, 2015 Forest Avenue, Drawer E, 67530
Telephone: 316-793-5455
FAX: 316-793-5456
Email: glenn.opie@greatbend.com

General Counsel for: Straub International; Trethar Farms.
Local Counsel for: Atchison, Topeka & Santa Fe Railway Co.; Continental Oil Co.; Texaco, Inc.; The Prudential Insurance Co. of America; Natural Gas Pipeline Company of America; General Motots Corp.; Coachman Industries; John Hancock Mutual Life Insurance Company.

For full biographical listings, see the Martindale-Hubbell Law Directory

*HAYS,** Ellis Co.

DREILING, BIEKER & HOFFMAN, LLP (AV)

111 West 13th Street, P.O. Box 579, 67601
Telephone: 785-625-3537
FAX: 785-625-8129

MEMBERS OF FIRM

Norbert R. Dreiling
Dennis L. Bieker
Donald F. Hoffman

ASSOCIATES

Melvin J. Sauer, Jr.
Robert E. Diehl

General Counsel: Dreiling Oil Company, Hays, Kansas; Golden Belt Bank, FSA, Ellis, Kansas; Midland Marketing, Inc., Hays, Kansas; St. John's Rest Home, Victoria & Hays, Kansas.
Representative Clients: Farm Bureau Mutual Insurance Company of Kansas; Midwest Energy of Hays, Kansas.

For full biographical listings, see the Martindale-Hubbell Law Directory

*HUTCHINSON,** Reno Co.

GILLILAND & HAYES, P.A. A PROFESSIONAL ASSOCIATION (AV)

20 West 2nd Avenue, 2nd Floor, P.O. Box 2977, 67504-2977
Telephone: 316-662-0537
Facsimile: 316-669-9426
URL: http://www.gillilandhayes.com
Wichita, Kansas Office: The Orpheum Centre, Suite 300, 200 North Broadway, P.O. Box 49406.
Telephone: 316-262-2266.
Facsimile: 316-263-2202.
Kansas City, Missouri Office: 12th Floor, 3100 Broadway.
Telephone: 816-753-3100.
Facsimile: 816-753-2271.

Robert J. Gilliland
John F. Hayes
James R. Gilliland
John S. Schmidt
Bruce B. Waugh (Not admitted in KS; Resident, Kansas City, Missouri Office)
Michael R. O'Neal
Bradley D. Dillon
Gerald L. Green
David N. Zimmerman (Not admitted in KS; Resident, Kansas City, Missouri Office)
Scott J. Mann
Carol Z. Smith (Resident, Kansas City, Missouri Office)

(See Next Column)

Kathleen A. Hardee (Resident, Kansas City, Missouri Office)
Kendall R. Cunningham (Resident, Wichita Office)
Mark R. Maloney (Resident, Wichita Office)

Thomas A. Dower
Tracy Applegate Cole
Laura A. Hederstedt
Terri Roberts Munsell (Resident, Kansas City, Missouri Office)
Lisa M. Ward
Kimberly Breda Bushek (Resident, Kansas City, Missouri Office)
E. Thomas Pyle, III
Tara L. Bragg

OF COUNSEL

Robert P. Reams (Not admitted in KS; Resident, Kansas City, Missouri Office)

Representative Clients: Allied Group; CNA Insurance; Dillon Companies; Farm Bureau Mutual Insurance Co.; Fidelity Deposit Co. of Maryland; Kansas Medical Mutual Insurance Co.; Hutchinson Clinic; Hutchinson Hospital Corp.; Central Bank & Trust; U.S. Fidelity Corp.

For full biographical listings, see the Martindale-Hubbell Law Directory

*JUNCTION CITY,** Geary Co.

WEARY, DAVIS, HENRY, STRUEBING, TROUP, KAUS & RYAN, L.C. (AV)

819 North Washington Street, P.O. Box 187, 66441
Telephone: 785-762-2210
Telefax: 785-238-3880
Email: wearylaw@wearylaw.com *URL:* http://www.wearylaw.com
Manhattan, Kansas Office: Colony Square Office Building, 555 Poyntz Avenue.
Telephone: 785-539-2208.
Telefax: 785-539-4882.

MEMBERS OF FIRM

Victor A. Davis, Jr.
Keith R. Henry
Steven R. Struebing
David P. Troup
Wendy L. Kaus
Tim W. Ryan

OF COUNSEL

Robert K. Weary

Representative Clients: Central National Bank; Unified School District #475; First State Bank of Junction City; Mid-America & Kansas Cable Telecommunications Assns.; Matlock-Johnson Developers; Kansas State Bank of Manhattan; Steel & Pipe Supply Co., Inc.; Icon Enterprises.
Local Counsel for: Sprint-United Telephone Company of Kansas; First Savings Bank of Manhattan.

For full biographical listings, see the Martindale-Hubbell Law Directory

*KANSAS CITY,** Wyandotte Co.

BODDINGTON & BROWN, CHARTERED (AV)

Suite 100 Security Bank Building, Minnesota Avenue at 7th Street, 66101
Telephone: 913-371-1272; Toll Free 888-371-1272
FAX: 913-371-5726
Email: BB19@idt.net

N. Jack Brown
Kenneth E. Holm
Leo L. Logan
David W. Hauber
D. Scott Brown
Stephen P. Doherty
Christopher J. Eaton

OF COUNSEL

Lisa R. Wetzler
Edward M. Boddington, Jr. (Retired)
Albert M. Ross (Retired)

Reference: Security Bank of Kansas City.

For full biographical listings, see the Martindale-Hubbell Law Directory

HOLBROOK, HEAVEN & OSBORN, P.A. (AV)

757 Armstrong, P.O. Box 171927, 66117
Telephone: 913-342-2500
Fax: 913-342-0603
Merriam, Kansas Office: 6700 Antioch Street.
Telephone: 913-677-1717.
Fax: 913-677-0403.

Reid F. Holbrook
Lewis A. Heaven, Jr. (Resident, Merriam Office)
Thomas E. Osborn
Robert L. Kennedy
Janet M. Simpson
John D. Tongier (Resident, Merriam Office)
Thomas M. Sutherland
Thomas S. Busch (Resident, Merriam Office)
Henry F. Sonday, Jr.
Kurt S. Brack (Resident, Merriam Office)
Joy D. Hays (Resident, Merriam Office)
Douglas G. Peterson
Daniel W. Peters

(See Next Column)

HOLBROOK, HEAVEN & OSBORN P.A., *Kansas City—Continued*

Lynaia M. Holsapple
Diane L. Waters
Richard J. Plouff (Resident, Merriam Office)
Shawn L. Stogsdill (Resident, Merriam Office)

For full biographical listings, see the Martindale-Hubbell Law Directory

*LAWRENCE,** Douglas Co.

ALLEN, COOLEY & ALLEN (AV)

201 Mercantile Bank Tower, 900 Massachusetts, 66044-2868
Telephone: 785-843-0222
Fax: 785-843-0254

MEMBERS OF FIRM

Milton P. Allen, Sr. (1914-1988)
Gerald L. Cooley
Milton P. Allen, Jr.

ASSOCIATES

Michelle Ann Davis
Randall F. Larkin

Representative Clients: LRM Industries, Inc.; Shelter Insurance Cos.; National Casualty Insurance Co.; B.A. Green Construction Co.; The World Co., Inc.; Sunflower Cable TV; City of Lawrence; City of Eudora; Scottsdale Insurance Co.; Lawrence Journal World.

For full biographical listings, see the Martindale-Hubbell Law Directory

BARBER, EMERSON, SPRINGER, ZINN & MURRAY, L.C. (AV)

1211 Massachusetts Street, P.O. Box 667, 66044
Telephone: 785-843-6600
Fax: 785-843-8405
Email: beszm@aol.com

John A. Emerson
Byron E. Springer
Richard L. Zinn
Thomas V. Murray
Calvin J. Karlin
Jane M. Eldredge
Mark A. Andersen
William N. Fleming

Charles F. Blaser
Cheryl L. Jackson
Terence E. Leibold

COUNSEL

Richard A. Barber (1911-1998)
Martin B. Dickinson, Jr.
Glee S. Smith, Jr.

Representative Clients: Mercantile Bank of Lawrence; University National Bank of Lawrence; Douglas County Bank; FMC Corp.; Mine Safety Appliances Co.; Equitable Life Assurance Society of the U.S.; The Travelers Insurance Co.; American Family Insurance Co.

For full biographical listings, see the Martindale-Hubbell Law Directory

*MCPHERSON,** McPherson Co.

BREMYER & WISE, P.A. (AV)

The Bremyer Building, 120 W. Kansas Avenue, P.O. Box 1146, 67460
Telephone: 316-241-0554
Telefax: 316-241-7692
Email: bwlaw@bwisecounsel.com

Robert W. Wise
Brett A. Reber
Casey R. Law
Randee Koger
Jill Bremyer-Archer
David N. Harger
Jeffrey A. Houston

OF COUNSEL

John K. Bremyer
Jay K. Bremyer

For full biographical listings, see the Martindale-Hubbell Law Directory

WILLIAM S. MILLS (AV)

900 North Main Street, P.O. Box 1244, 67460
Telephone: 316-241-7333
FAX: 316-241-7335

OVERLAND PARK, Johnson Co.

SHUGHART THOMSON & KILROY, A PROFESSIONAL CORPORATION (AV)

Suite 1100, 32 Corporate Woods, 9225 Indian Creek Parkway, 66210
Telephone: 913-451-3355
Email: Solutions@STKLAW.COM *URL:* http://www.stklaw.com
Kansas City, Missouri Office: Twelve Wyandotte Plaza, 120 West 12th Street, 64105.
Telephone: 816-421-3355.
Springfield, Missouri Office: Suite 1200, Hammons Tower, 901 St. Louis, 65806.
Telephone: 417-869-3353.
Denver, Colorado Office: 1050 17th Street, Suite 2350. 80265.
Telephone: 303-572-9300.
Fax: 303-572-7883.

(See Next Column)

KANSAS OFFICE ATTORNEYS

Steven D. Ruse
James P. O'Hara
Anthony F. Rupp
Gregory L. Musil
Lawrence A. Swain
Christine M. Graham
Andrew M. DeMarea
Daniel D. Owen
Eric F. Broucek
Amy E. Patton

For full biographical listings, see the Martindale-Hubbell Law Directory

WALLACE, SAUNDERS, AUSTIN, BROWN & ENOCHS, CHARTERED (AV)

10111 West 87th Street, P.O. Box 12290, 66282-2290
Telephone: 913-888-1000
Fax: 913-888-1065
Email: info@op.wsabe.com *URL:* http://www.wsabe.com
Wichita, Kansas Office: 600 Epic Center, 301 North Main Street, 67202-4806.
Telephone: 316-269-2100.
Fqx: 316-269-2479.
Springfield, Missouri Office: 1702 Hammons Tower, 901 St. Louis Street, 65806-2505.
Telephone: 417-866-2300.
Fax: 417-866-2444.
Kansas City, Missouri Office: 2405 Grand Boulevard, Suite 500, 64108.
Telephone: 913-888-1000.
Fax: 913-888-1065.

Frank Saunders, Jr.
Barton Brown
Richmond M. Enochs
James G. Butler, Jr.
James O. Schwinn
Richard T. Merker
H. Wayne Powers
Rod L. Richardson
Paul Hasty, Jr.
Barry E. Warren
Sally H. Harris
Mark W. McKinzie
Michael P. Oliver
James L. Sanders
Rudolf H. Beese
Michael J. Dutton
Thomas D. Billam
Kevin L. Bennett
Gary R. Terrill
Timothy G. Lutz
Mark V. Bodine
Norman I. Reichel, Jr.
Kirby A. Vernon (Resident, Wichita Office)
Douglas C. Hobbs (Resident, Wichita Office)
Patrick E. McGrath
Robert A. Mintz
D'Ambra Howard
J. Philip Davidson (Resident, Wichita Office)
D. Steven Marsh (Resident, Wichita Office)
Stephen H. Snead (Resident, Springfield, Missouri Office)
Karl Kuckelman
John M. Ross
Michael D. Streit (Resident, Wichita Office)
Timothy J. Finnerty (Resident, Wichita Office)
Eric A. Van Beber
Kurt W. Ratzlaff (Resident, Wichita Office)

OF COUNSEL

Rick E. Bailey (Resident, Wichita Office)
James K. McMurray (Resident, Wichita Office)
Barry D. Martin
Richard D. Simpson
Nicholas Nagrich (Resident, Springfield Office)
Teresa J. James (Resident, Wichita Office)
William R. Smith (Resident, Wichita Office)
Gary A. Schafersman

Larry J. Austin (Retired)
Kenneth B. Wallace (1912-1982)

Derrick A. Pearce
Arlen L Tanner
Christopher John McCurdy (Resident, Wichita Office)
Donald J. Fritschie
Tristram E. Felix (Resident, Wichita Office)
James L. Mowbray
Patrick T. Smith
Deena M. Hyson-Glenn (Resident, Wichita Office)
Debra A. Vermillion
Janell J. Foster (Resident, Wichita Office)
Kenneth R. Fenley, Jr.
Jason L. Bush
Michael A. Smoots, Jr.
David R. Frye
Gregory S. Young (Resident, Wichita Office)
Joel I. Krieger
Glenn S. Grayson
Chris R. Pace
Derron D. Gunderman
Russell Todd King (Resident, Wichita Office)
David Curotto
Michael H. Stang
James R. Redeker
Jeffrey W. Deane
Todd E. Gonyer
Steven T. Shanholtzer (Resident, Springfield Office)
Patrick J. Murphy (Resident, Wichita Office)
Susan F. Colburn (Resident, Springfield Office)
Anthony M. Singer (Resident, Wichita Office)

For full biographical listings, see the Martindale-Hubbell Law Directory

PARSONS, Labette Co.

DEARTH, MARKHAM & JACK, CHARTERED (AV)

1712 Broadway, P.O. Box 1034, 67357
Telephone: 316-421-1970; 421-3650
Fax: 316-421-8846
Email: dmj@par1.net *URL:* http://www.par1.net/users/dmj

(See Next Column)

DEARTH, MARKHAM & JACK CHARTERED—*Continued*

Glenn Jones (1911-1985) David K. Markham
Richard C. Dearth Jeffry L. Jack

OF COUNSEL

John B. Markham

Representative Clients: First National Bank and Trust Co.; Commercial Bank; Labette County State Bank; Day & Zimmerman International, Inc.; Liberty Mutual Insurance Co.; American States Insurance Co.; Federated Insurance Co.

For full biographical listings, see the Martindale-Hubbell Law Directory

*ST. JOHN,** Stafford Co.

SHIELDS LAW OFFICE, P.A. (AV)

106 East Third Street, P.O. Box 427, 67576
Telephone: 316-549-3212
Fax: 316-549-3268

Emerson H. Shields

Representative Client: First National Bank & Trust of St. John.

*SALINA,** Saline Co.

CLARK, MIZE & LINVILLE, CHARTERED (AV)

129 South Eighth, P.O. Box 380, 67402-0380
Telephone: 785-823-6325
Fax: 785-823-1868
URL: http://www.cml-law.com
Lindsborg, Kansas Office: 128 North Main, 67456.
Telephone: 785-227-2010.

James P. Mize (1910-1988) Lawton M. Nuss
Peter L. Peterson Mickey W. Mosier
John W. Mize Paula J. Wright
Greg A. Bengtson Eric N. Anderson
Donald G. Reinsch

SPECIAL COUNSEL

Ilene Munk Gaekwad

OF COUNSEL

L. O. Bengtson C. L. Clark (Retired)
Aubrey G. Linville (Retired)

Representative Clients: Salina Regional Health Center; City of Salina; Salina Airport Authority; Solomon State Bank; Unified School District 305; Tony's Pizza Service; Sunflower Bank, N.A.; Wilson & Company Engineers & Architects; Exide Corporation; Sunflower Health Network.

For full biographical listings, see the Martindale-Hubbell Law Directory

HAMPTON & ROYCE, L.C. (AV)

Ninth Floor United Building, 119 West Iron, P.O. Box 1247, 67401
Telephone: 785-827-7251
Fax: 785-827-2815
Email: hren@hamptonlaw.com

Howard Engleman (Retired) Jack N. Stewart (Retired)

MEMBERS OF FIRM

C. Stanley Nelson J. Stan Sexton
W. Dean Owens Debra Egli James
N. Royce Nelson Jeffrey E. King
Sidney A. Reitz Terry D. Criss
David D. Moshier John Andrew O'Leary
Brian Wilson Wood

SPECIAL COUNSEL

Clarence L. King, Jr.

ASSOCIATES

Tisha S. Morrical Todd W. Davidson

Representative Clients: Blue Beacon International, Inc.; First Bank Kansas; First National Bank of Beloit; Great Plains Manufacturing, Inc.; Kansas Grain & Feed Assn.; Morrison Enterprises; St. Francis Academy, Inc.; Salina Journal, Inc.; Salina Supply Co.; Sellers Tractor Co., Inc.

For full biographical listings, see the Martindale-Hubbell Law Directory

*TOPEKA,** Shawnee Co.

FAIRCHILD, HANEY & BUCK, P.A. (AV)

5851 SW 29th Street, 66614
Telephone: 785-235-2200
Facsimile: 785-235-8950
Email: markbuck@networksplus.net *URL:* http://www.lawyers.com/topeka_insurance

Ronald W. Fairchild Thomas D. Haney
Mark A. Buck

James Phillip Gragson Lisa E. Janati

For full biographical listings, see the Martindale-Hubbell Law Directory

FISHER, PATTERSON, SAYLER & SMITH, L.L.P. (AV)

3550 S.W. 5th Street, P.O. Box 949, 66601
Telephone: 785-232-7761
Fax: 785-232-6604
Email: fpss@cjnetworks.com
Overland Park, Kansas Office: 11050 Roe Avenue, Suite 210, 66211.
Telephone: 913-339-6757.
Fax: 913-339-6187.

MEMBERS OF FIRM

Donald Patterson Steve R. Fabert
Edwin Dudley Smith (Resident, Overland Park Office) Ronald J. Laskowski
Larry G. Pepperdine Michael K. Seck (Resident, Overland Park Office)
James P. Nordstrom David P. Madden (Resident, Overland Park Office)
Justice B. King Steven K. Johnson
J. Steven Pigg
Kristine A. Larscheid

ASSOCIATES

Billy E. Newman Jennifer R. Rose (Resident, Overland Park Office)
David R. Cooper
Kelly A. Feyh (Resident, Overland Park Office)

OF COUNSEL

David H. Fisher

RETIRED

Charles Keith Sayler (Retired)

Representative Clients: Gage Shopping Center, Inc.; Fireman's Fund-American Insurance Cos.; United States Fidelity and Guaranty Co.; The Procter & Gamble Company; Commercial Union Insurance Companies; National Casualty; The Hartford; Berkshire Hathaway Companies.

For full biographical listings, see the Martindale-Hubbell Law Directory

GOODELL, STRATTON, EDMONDS & PALMER, L.L.P. (AV)

515 South Kansas Avenue, 66603-3999
Telephone: 785-233-0593
Fax: 785-233-8870
Email: GSEP@CJNETWORKS.COM *URL:* http://www.cjnetworks.com/~gsep
Kansas City, Missouri Office: 10401 Holmes Road, Suite 280.
Telephone: 816-943-8577.

MEMBERS OF FIRM

Gerald L. Goodell Patrick M. Salsbury
Wayne T. Stratton John H. Stauffer, Jr.
Arthur E. Palmer Les E. Diehl
H. Philip Elwood David E. Bruns
Harold S. Youngentob N. Larry Bork
Gerald J. Letourneau Catherine M. Walberg
Charles R. Hay Steve A. Schwarm

OF COUNSEL

Robert E. Edmonds (Retired) John A. Bausch
Robert A. McClure Richard W. Holmes

ASSOCIATES

Anne M. Kindling Scott C. Palecki
Laura B. Lawson

SPECIAL COUNSEL

Joseph E. McKinney Marta Fisher Linenberger
Curtis J. Waugh

Counsel for: Columbian National Title Insurance Co.; Central Regional Dental Testing Service, Inc.; Heartland Community Bankers Association; The Menninger Foundation; Topeka Chamber of Commerce; Washburn University of Topeka; Reser's Fine Foods; ConAgra; Monfort, Inc.

For full biographical listings, see the Martindale-Hubbell Law Directory

WRIGHT, HENSON, SOMERS, SEBELIUS, CLARK & BAKER, LLP (AV)

Commerce Bank Building, 100 Southeast Ninth Street, 2nd Floor, P.O. Box 3555, 66601-3555
Telephone: 785-232-2200
FAX: 785-232-3344
Email: wrighthenson@wrighthenson.com *URL:* http://www.wrighthenson.com

MEMBERS OF FIRM

Thomas E. Wright K. Gary Sebelius
Charles N. Henson Bruce J. Clark
Dale L. Somers Anne Lamborn Baker
Evelyn Zabel Wilson

ASSOCIATES

Michael M. Walker John H. Hutton

SPECIAL COUNSEL

David P. Mudrick

(See Next Column)

WRIGHT, HENSON, SOMERS, SEBELIUS, CLARK & BAKER LLP, *Topeka—Continued*

OF COUNSEL

John H. Wachter
Scott S. Sumpter

For full biographical listings, see the Martindale-Hubbell Law Directory

*WICHITA,** Sedgwick Co.

DEPEW AND GILLEN, L.L.C. (AV)

151 North Main, Suite 800, 67202-1409
Telephone: 316-262-4000
Facsimile: 316-265-3819
Email: DG@DEPEWGILLEN.COM *URL:* HTTP://WWW.DEPEWGILLEN.COM

Spencer L. Depew
Dennis L. Gillen
Jack Scott McInteer
Randall K. Rathbun
David W. Nickel
Nicholas S. Daily
Charles C. Steincamp

For full biographical listings, see the Martindale-Hubbell Law Directory

FOULSTON & SIEFKIN L.L.P. (AV)

700 NationsBank Financial Center, 67202
Telephone: 316-267-6371
Facsimile: 316-267-6345
URL: http://www.foulston.com
Topeka, Kansas Office: 1515 NationsBank Tower, 534 Kansas Avenue, 66603.
Telephone: 785-233-3600.
Fax: 785-233-1610.
Dodge City, Kansas Office: 810 Frontview, P.O. Box 1147, 67801.
Telephone: 316-227-8126.
Fax: 316-227-8451.
Member: Lex Mundi, The World's Leading Association of Independent Law Firms.

MEMBERS OF FIRM

Robert L. Howard
Charles J. Woodin
Mikel L. Stout
Benjamin C. Langel
Phillip S. Frick
Stanley G. Andeel
Frederick L. Haag
Richard D. Ewy
Darrell L. Warta
Harvey R. Sorensen
James M. Armstrong
Mary Kathleen Babcock
Charles P. Efflandt
James D. Oliver
Gary L. Ayers
Gloria G. Farha Flentje
Larry G. Rapp
R. Douglas Reagan (Resident, Dodge City Office)
Jay F. Fowler
Stephen M. Kerwick
Gary E. Knight
Christopher M. Hurst
Vaughn Burkholder
Terry C. Cupps
Wyatt M. Wright
Jim H. Goering
Wyatt A. Hoch
Amy S. Lemley
James P. Rankin (Resident, Topeka Office)
Douglas L. Hanisch
Douglas L. Stanley
J. Steven Massoni
Timothy B. Mustaine
Jeffery A. Jordan
Trisha A. Thelen
William R. Wood, II
Eric F. Melgren
Kevin J. Arnel
Craig W. West
Carol A. Beier
William P. Trenkle, Jr. (Resident, Dodge City Office)
David J. Rebein (Resident, Dodge City Office)
Eric K. Kuhn
Jay M. Rector
Stewart T. Weaver
Thomas W. Young (Resident, Dodge City Office)
Mark A. Biberstein
Jeff P. DeGraffenreid
Martha Aaron Ross

SPECIAL COUNSEL

Gaye B. Tibbets
James L. Grimes, Jr. (Resident, Topeka Office)
David M. Traster
John C. Peck
A. J. "Jack" Focht
Robert A. Fox (Resident, Topeka Office)
David E. Rogers
Thomas L. Theis (Resident, Topeka Office)

ASSOCIATES

William M. Anderson
Donald D. Berner
Boyd A. Byers
Holly A. Dyer
Aaron L. Kite
William P. Matthews
Jay M. McGrath
Andrew J. Nolan
Michael J. Norton
Todd N. Tedesco
Jamie L. Wagle
Shannon D. Wead

Representative Clients: The Boeing Company; The Coleman Co.; Koch Industries, Inc.; State Farm Mutual Insurance Co.; Shelter Insurance Company; Atlantic Richfield Co.; Via Christi Health System; The Wichita Clinic.

For full biographical listings, see the Martindale-Hubbell Law Directory

GOTT, YOUNG & BOGLE, P.A.

(See Young, Bogle, McCausland, Wells & Blanchard, P.A.)

JOHNSON, KENNEDY, DAHL & WILLIS (AV)

River Park Place, 727 North Waco, Suite 585, 67203-3596
Telephone: 316-263-4921
Fax: 316-263-0045

MEMBERS OF FIRM

Douglas D. Johnson
E. Craig Kennedy
David L. Dahl
Jeffrey L. Willis
Harold T. Pickler

Representative Clients: Kansas Electric Power Cooperative, Inc.; Liberty Mutual Insurance Co.

For full biographical listings, see the Martindale-Hubbell Law Directory

KAHRS, NELSON, FANNING, HITE & KELLOGG L.L.P. (AV)

200 W. Douglas, Suite 600, 67202
Telephone: 316-265-7761
Telecopier: 316-267-7803
URL: http://www.kahrsnelson.com

MEMBERS OF FIRM

William A. Kahrs (1904-1989)
Robert H. Nelson (1904-1977)
Darrell D. Kellogg (1931-1992)
Richard C. Hite
Richard L. Honeyman
Larry A. Withers
Gary A. Winfrey
Clark R. Nelson
Steven D. Gough
Scott J. Gunderson
Randy Troutt
Arthur S. Chalmers
Kim R. Martens
Linda S. Parks
Forrest James Robinson, Jr.
Don D. Gribble, II
John G. Pike
Alan R. Pfaff
Dennis V. Lacey
Donald N. Peterson, II
Lisa Adrian McPherson

ASSOCIATES

Jerry D. Hawkins
Jon E. Newman
Scott R. Schillings
Richard D. Crowder

OF COUNSEL

H. W. Fanning
Vince P. Wheeler

Representative Clients: Advance Chemical Dist., Inc.; Learjet Corp.; Hahner, Foreman & Harness, Contractors; New York Life Insurance Co.; General Motors Corp.; St. Paul Insurance Cos.

For full biographical listings, see the Martindale-Hubbell Law Directory

KLENDA, MITCHELL, AUSTERMAN & ZUERCHER, L.L.C. (AV)

1600 Epic Center, 301 North Main Street, 67202-4888
Telephone: 316-267-0331
Telecopier: 316-267-0333
Email: info@kmazlaw.com

L. D. Klenda (1937-1996)
Alexander B. Mitchell, II
Gary M. Austerman
Michael R. Biggs
Alan D. Herman
John V. Wachtel
J. Michael Morris
David D. Broomfield
Jeffrey D. Peier
Scott A. Eads
Mark J. Lazzo
John B. Gilliam
Gregory B. Klenda
Christopher A. McElgunn

Mary T. Malicoat
Robert L. Omer
Todd E. Shadid
Erin E. Syring
Kimberly A. Wingate
Todd M. Allison
Laura Diane Fent

OF COUNSEL

Vincent L. Bogart
Ronald M. Gott
Bruce W. Zuercher

Representative Clients: Bombardier Capital Inc.; Kansas Newman College; National Cooperative Refinery Assn.; New York Bagel Enterprises, Inc.; Petroleum, Inc.; Play By Play Toys & Novelties, Inc.; THORN Americas, Inc. d/b/a Rent-A-Center of America, Inc.; Sterling House Corporation.
Franchise Client: ALCF, Inc. (Association of Little Caesars Franchisees); Olsten Staffing Service Franchisees.

For full biographical listings, see the Martindale-Hubbell Law Directory

MORRIS, LAING, EVANS, BROCK & KENNEDY, CHARTERED (AV)

Fourth Floor, 200 West Douglas, 67202-3084
Telephone: 316-262-2671
Fax: 316-262-6226; 262-5991
Topeka, Kansas Office: 800 S.W. Jackson, Suite 914, 66612-2214.
Telephone: 913-232-2662.
Fax: 913-232-9983.

Lester L. Morris (1901-1966)
Verne M. Laing (Retired)
Ferd E. Evans, Jr. (1919-1991)
Robert B. Morton (Retired)
Ralph R. Brock
Joseph W. Kennedy
Robert I. Guenthner
Ken M. Peterson
Robert D. Overman
Richard D. Greene
A. J. Schwartz, Jr.
Donald E. Schrag
William B. Sorensen, Jr.
Dennis M. Feeney
Jeffery L. Carmichael
Robert W. Coykendall
Robert K. Anderson
Susan R. Schrag

(See Next Column)

MORRIS, LAING, EVANS, BROCK & KENNEDY CHARTERED—*Continued*

Robert E. Nugent
Michael Lennen
Karl R. Swartz
Roger L. Theis
Jana Deines Abbott
Richard F. Hayse
(Resident, Topeka Office)
Thomas R. Docking
Diane S. Worth
Tim J. Moore
Janet Huck Ward
Carlos J. Nolla-Corretjer

James D. Young
Brian J. Christensen

OF COUNSEL

Marvin W. Maydew
(Resident, Topeka Office)
T. Lynn Ward
Roger N. Walter

References: The Emprise Banks of Kansas; Mercantile Bank of Topeka; Southwest National Bank; Twin Lakes National Bank.

For full biographical listings, see the Martindale-Hubbell Law Directory

TRIPLETT, WOOLF & GARRETSON, LLC (AV)

2959 North Rock Road, Suite 300, 67226
Telephone: 316-630-8100
Fax: 316-630-8101
Email: twg@twgfirm.com

MEMBERS OF FIRM

Thomas C. Triplett
John P. Woolf
Thomas P. Garretson
James A. Walker
Timothy E. McKee
Theron E. Fry
Eric B. Metz
Ron H. Harnden
Lee Thompson
Eric S. Strickler
Tad Patton
Bradley A. Stout
Rachael K. Pirner
Jeffrey D. Leonard

ASSOCIATES

Jeffery C. Dahlgren
Jeffrey E. Goering
Jerald W. Rogers
Christopher C. Swyers
Kent G. Voth

Representative Clients: Anheuser-Busch Companies, Inc.; Brite Voice Systems, Inc.; Coleman Company, Inc.; Dow Chemical Co.; Friends University; KPMG Peat Marwick; National Plastics Color, Inc.; Total Petroleum, Inc.; Travelers Insurance Co.; Willis Corroon of Kansas, Inc.

For full biographical listings, see the Martindale-Hubbell Law Directory

YOUNG, BOGLE, MCCAUSLAND, WELLS & BLANCHARD, P.A. (AV)

106 West Douglas, Suite 923, 67202
Telephone: 316-265-7841
Facsimile: 316-265-3956
Email: ybmwblaw@aol.com

Glenn D. Young, Jr.
Jerry D. Bogle
Paul S. McCausland
William A. Wells
Patrick C. Blanchard

J. Michael Peters

OF COUNSEL

Orlin L. Wagner
Barry L. Arbuckle

Representative Clients: Bridgestone/Firestone Inc.; Deere & Co.; Citibank; Metropolitan Life Insurance Co.; Equitable Life Assurance Society of the United States; New York Life Insurance Co.

For full biographical listings, see the Martindale-Hubbell Law Directory

*WINFIELD,** Cowley Co.

HERLOCKER, ROBERTS & ST. PETER, L.L.C. (AV)

115 East Ninth Avenue, P.O. Box 754, 67156
Telephone: 316-221-4600
FAX: 316-221-7504

Charles W. Roberts (1867-1941)
Lloyd S. Roberts (1900-1968)
Harry O. Janicke (1902-1978)
John A. Herlocker (1911-1984)
Kay Roberts
Thomas D. Herlocker
J. Dennis Herlocker
Nicholas M. St. Peter

Representative Clients: Risk Counselors, Inc.; Sidwell Charitable Trust; H. L. Snyder Memorial Research Foundation; Cover-rite Construction Services, Inc.; Sumner Regional Medical Center.

For full biographical listings, see the Martindale-Hubbell Law Directory

KENTUCKY

ASHLAND, Boyd Co.

MARTIN, JUSTICE & VINCENT (AV)

431 Sixteenth Street, P.O. Box 2528, 41105-2528
Telephone: 606-329-8338
Fax: 606-325-8199
Email: mjvlaw@zoomnet.net

Richard W. Martin
David Justice
John F. Vincent
Thomas Wade Lavender, II

ASSOCIATE

Charles D. Oppenheimer

Representative Clients: City of Ashland; FIVCO Area Development District; Boyd County Sanitation District No. 2.
Insurance Counsel for: State Farm Mutual Automobile Insurance Co.; State Farm Fire and Casualty Co.; Travelers Insurance Co.; Grange Mutual Insurance Co.; Great American Insurance Co.

For full biographical listings, see the Martindale-Hubbell Law Directory

*BOWLING GREEN,** Warren Co.

BRODERICK & THORNTON (AV)

921 College Street, Phoenix Place, P.O. Box 3100, 42102-3100
Telephone: 270-782-6700
Facsimile: 270-782-3110

David F. Broderick
Steven O. Thornton

ASSOCIATES

Kenneth P. O'Brien
Andrew A. Stanford

Representative Clients: Allstate Insurance Co.; National City Bank, Kentucky; American States Insurance Co.; Capital Enterprise Insurance; Fireman's Fund Insurance Co.; Imperial Casualty & Indemnity; Indiana Lumbermen's Mutual Insurance; Kentucky Medical Insurance Co.; Scotty's Contracting & Stone, Inc.; St. Paul Insurance Co.

For full biographical listings, see the Martindale-Hubbell Law Directory

COLE, MOORE & BAKER (AV)

921 College Street-Phoenix Place, P.O. Box 10240, 42102-7240
Telephone: 270-782-6666
FAX: 270-782-8666
Email: CMB@Premiernet.net

MEMBERS OF FIRM

John David Cole
Frank Hampton Moore, Jr.
Matthew J. Baker
Dov Moore

ASSOCIATES

John David Cole, Jr.
Stefan R. Hughes
Matthew P. Cook

OF COUNSEL

Frank R. Goad

Counsel for: Western Kentucky Cola-Cola Bottling Co.; Clark Distributing Co., Inc.; Scotty's Contracting & Stone Co.
Local Counsel for: General Electric Co.; Bucyrus-Erie Company; Wal-Mart Stores, Inc.; Kroger/Country Oven.
Representative Insurance Clients: Liberty Mutual Insurance Co.; Travelers Insurance Co.; Wausau Insurance Co.

For full biographical listings, see the Martindale-Hubbell Law Directory

HARLIN, PARKER, ALCOTT & CHAUDOIN, P.S.C. (AV)

519 East Tenth Street, P.O. Box 390, 42102-0390
Telephone: 502-842-5611
Telefax: 502-842-2607
Email: hpac@premiernet.net *URL:* http://www.lawyers.com/hp

William Jerry Parker
James David Bryant
Mark D. Alcott
Robert C. Chaudoin

Robert Shannon Morgan

OF COUNSEL

Jo T. Orendorf

Insurance Clients: Government Employees Insurance Co.; American International Group; CIGNA/ESIS.
Railroad and Utilities Clients: District Attorneys for BellSouth Telecommunications, Inc.; CSX Transportation, Inc.
Local Counsel for: General Motors Corp.; Ford Motor Co.; Chrysler Corp.; Holley Performance Products, Inc.

For full biographical listings, see the Martindale-Hubbell Law Directory

Bowling Green—Continued

KERRICK, GRISE & STIVERS (AV)

1025 State Street, P.O. Box 9547, 42102-9547
Telephone: 502-782-8160
Fax: 502-782-5856
Email: kgs@kgslaw.com
Elizabethtown, Kentucky Office: 2935 Dolphin Drive, Suite 102.
Telephone: 502-769-5788.
Fax: 502-737-9285.

MEMBERS OF FIRM

Thomas N. Kerrick
John R. Grise
Gregory N. Stivers
H. Brent Brennenstuhl
Laura M. Hagan

ASSOCIATES

Karl N. Crandall
Shawn Rosso Alcott
Jason B. Bell

OF COUNSEL

Jeffrey R. O'Grody

LEGAL SUPPORT PERSONNEL

Patricia Logsdon
Laura Lockhart Lico
Allison Lusk

Representative Clients: Dollar General Corp.; Columbia Greenview Regional Hospital; Hospital Corporation of America; Hardin Memorial Hospital; Fir-Star Bank; TKR Cable.

For full biographical listings, see the Martindale-Hubbell Law Directory

CORBIN, Knox & Whitley Cos.

LEICK, HAMMONS AND BRITTAIN (AV)

First National Bank & Trust Company Building, P.O. Box 1388, 40702
Telephone: 606-528-5252; 528-2442
Fax: 606-528-2491

MEMBERS OF FIRM

Herman E. Leick
Robert P. Hammons
Gary W. Brittain
Paul K. Winchester

LEGAL SUPPORT PERSONNEL

Flora M. McFadden

Counsel for: The First National Bank & Trust Company of Corbin; Pepsi-Cola Bottling Company of Corbin; Corbin Board of Education.

For full biographical listings, see the Martindale-Hubbell Law Directory

COVINGTON, Kenton Co.

STRAUSS & TROY A LEGAL PROFESSIONAL ASSOCIATION (AV)

Suite 1400, 50 East Rivercenter Boulevard, 41011
Telephone: 513-621-8900; 513-621-2120
Telecopier: 513-629-9444
URL: http://www.strauss-troy.com
Cincinnati, Ohio Office: The Federal Reserve Building, 150 East Fourth Street, 45202-4018.
Telephone: 513-621-2120.
Telecopier: 513-241-8259.

Martin C. Butler (Resident)
Timothy B. Theissen (Resident)
Marshall K. Dosker (Resident)

Pete A. Smith (Resident)
Daniel J. Whalen (Resident)

OF COUNSEL

Samuel M. Allen (Resident)
Paul J. Theissen (Resident)
Gordon H. Hood (Resident)

For full biographical listings, see the Martindale-Hubbell Law Directory

TAFT, STETTINIUS & HOLLISTER LLP (AV)

Thomas More Centre Suite 400, 2670 Chancellor Drive, 41017-3491
Telephone: 606-331-2838; 513-381-2838
Facsimile: 513-381-6613
URL: http://www.taftlaw.com
Cincinnati, Ohio Office: 1800 Firstar Tower, 425 Walnut Street.
Telephone: 513-381-2838.
Columbus, Ohio Office: Twelfth Floor, 21 East State Street.
Telephone: 614-221-2838.
Cleveland, Ohio Office: Sixth Floor, Bond Court Building, 1300 East Ninth Street.
Telephone: 216-241-2838.

RESIDENT MEMBERS

Robert B. Craig

RESIDENT ASSOCIATES

John C. Middleton
Thomas P. Vergamini

Counsel for: Cordant Technologies; The David J. Joseph Company; Duro Bag; Frank Messer & Sons Construction; G & J Pepsi Cola Bottlers, Inc.; Gibson Greetings, Inc.; James Graham Brown Foundation; Morton International.

For full biographical listings, see the Martindale-Hubbell Law Directory

WARE, BRYSON, WEST & KUMMER (AV)

157 Barnwood Drive, 41017
Telephone: 606-341-0255
Fax: 606-341-1876

MEMBERS OF FIRM

Rodney S. Bryson
Larry C. West
John R. Kummer
Mark W. Howard
Greg D. Voss
Robert B. Cetrulo
Susanne M. Cetrulo
David W. Martin

ASSOCIATE

James M. West
Orie S. Ware (1882-1974)
William O. Ware (1908-1961)
James C. Ware (1913-1991)

Attorneys For: First National Bank of Northern Ky.; State Farm Insurance Co.; Reliance Insurance Group; Maryland Casualty Insurance Co.; Kemper Insurance Co.; State Farm Fire & Casualty Insurance Co.; Cincinnati Insurance Co.; Northern Ky. Title; Harper Construction Co.; Norfolk Southern Railway.

For full biographical listings, see the Martindale-Hubbell Law Directory

*ELIZABETHTOWN,** Hardin Co.

COLEMAN, EASTON, LOCHMILLER & HALL (AV)

(Formerly Reford H. Coleman and Associates)
2907 Ring Road, P.O. Box 1177, 42702-1177
Telephone: 502-737-0600
Fax: 502-737-0488
Email: celh@ne.infi.net

Reford H. Coleman
Kelly Mark Easton
Beth Ann Lochmiller
M. Brent Hall

ASSOCIATE

Matthew C. Hess

Representative Clients: American States Insurance Cos.; Federated Rural Elec. Insurance Co.; General Motors Corp.; The Hartford; Indiana Insurance Co.; Kentucky Association of Counties All-Lines Fund; Kentucky Farm Bureau Mutual Insurance Co.; Liberty Mutual Insurance Co.; State Auto Insurance Co.; United Services Automobile Association (State Counsel).

For full biographical listings, see the Martindale-Hubbell Law Directory

LEWIS & PRESTON (AV)

102 West Dixie Avenue, 42701
Telephone: 502-765-4106
Fax: 502-737-0443

MEMBERS OF FIRM

Paul M. Lewis
Dwight Preston

Approved Attorneys for: Commonwealth Land Title.
Reference: Cecilian Bank.
Agents for: First American Title Insurance; Midland First American.

*FRANKFORT,** Franklin Co.

STITES & HARBISON (AV)

Formerly Stites, McElwain & Fowler and Harbison, Kessinger, Lisle & Bush
421 West Main Street, 40601
Telephone: 502-223-3477
Fax: 502-223-4124
Louisville, Kentucky Office: 400 West Market Street, Suite 1800.
Telephone: 502-587-3400.
Fax: 502-587-6391.
Lexington, Kentucky Office: 250 West Main Street, Suite 2300.
Telephone: 606-226-2300.
Fax: 606-253-9144.
Hyden, Kentucky Office: 21976 Main Street, Farmer Campbell Building, Second Floor.
Telephone: 606-672-4200.
Fax: 606-672-4100
Jeffersonville, Indiana Office: 323 East Court Avenue.
Telephone: 812-282-7566.
Fax: 812-284-5519.
Atlanta, Georgia Office: 3350 Cumberland Circle, Suite 1700, Riverwood.
Telephone: 770-850-7000.
Fax: 770-850-7070.
Washington, D.C. Office: 1200 G Street, N.W., Suite 800.

MEMBERS OF FIRM

Ben B. Fowler (1916-1990)
Bruce F. Clark
Mark R. Overstreet
Judith A. Villines

Michele Whittington
W. Brian Burnette

COUNSEL

Jennifer S. Smart

For full biographical listings, see the Martindale-Hubbell Law Directory

Frankfort—Continued

STOLL, KEENON & PARK, LLP (AV)

307 Washington Street, 40601
Telephone: 502-875-6220
Telecopier: 502-875-6235
URL: http://www.skp.com
Henderson, Kentucky Office: 201 C North Main Street, 42420-3103.
Telephone: 270-831-1900.
Facsimile: 270-827-4060.
Lexington, Kentucky Office: 201 E. Main Street, Suite 1000, 40507-1380.
Telephone: 606-231-3000.
Telecopier: 606-253-1093; 606-253-1027.
Louisville, Kentucky Office: 400 West Market Street, Suite 2650, 40202.
Telephone: 502-568-9100.
Telecopier: 502-568-5700.

Robert W. Kellerman

ASSOCIATE

Boyd Tristan Cloern

Representative Clients: Kentucky State University; Kentucky Press Assn.; Plantmix Asphalt Industry of Kentucky, Inc.; Kentucky Optometric Assn.; Kentucky Podiatry Assn.; Frankfort Scrap Metal Co.; Lexington Scrap Metal Co.; Lowes, Inc. (Retail Stores); Farmers Bank and Capital Trust Co.; Kentucky Retirement Systems.

For full biographical listings, see the Martindale-Hubbell Law Directory

WYATT, TARRANT & COMBS (AV)

The Taylor-Scott Building, 311 West Main Street, 40601-1807
Telephone: 502-223-2104
Telecopier: 502-227-7681
URL: http://www.wyattfirm.com
Louisville, Kentucky Office: Citizens Plaza.
Telephone: 502-589-5235.
Telecopier: 502-589-0309.
Lexington, Kentucky Office: 1700 Lexington Financial Center.
Telephone: 606-233-2012.
Telecopier: 606-259-0649.
New Albany, Indiana Office: The Elsby Building, 117 East Spring Street.
Telephone: 812-945-3561.
Telecopier: 812-949-2524.
Memphis, Tennessee Office: Crescent Center, Suite 650, 6075 Poplar Avenue.
Telephone: 901-537-1000.
Telecopier: 901-537-1010.
Nashville, Tennessee Office: 1500 Nashville City Center, 511 Union Street.
Telephone: 615-244-0020.
Telecopier: 615-256-1726.
Music Row, Nashville Office: 29 Music Square East.
Telephone: 615-255-6161.
Telecopier: 615-254-4490.
Hendersonville, Tennessee Office: 313 E. Main Street, Suite 1.
Telephone: 615-822-8822.
Telecopier: 615-824-4684.
Tri-Cities, Tennessee Office: Northeast Tennessee Business Park, 10368 Wallace Alley Street, Suite 6, Kingsport.
Telephone: 423-279-1825.
Telecopier: 423-279-9357.

MEMBERS OF FIRM

George L. Seay, Jr. — Joseph J. Zaluski

ASSOCIATE

Lesly Ann Reisenfeld-Davis

Representative Clients: Arch Coal, Inc.; Centran Corp.; David J. Joseph Co.; Goodyear; Huscoal, Inc.; Hillshire Farms & Kahn's; Kentucky Criterion Coal; Nutone, Inc.; Sara Lee Corp.; Zeigler Coal Holding Co., Inc.

For full biographical listings, see the Martindale-Hubbell Law Directory

*GEORGETOWN,** Scott Co.

E. DURWARD WELDON (AV)

217 East Main Street, 40324
Telephone: 502-863-1285

Approved Attorney for: Lawyers Title Insurance Corporation of Richmond, Virginia; Louisville Title Division of Commonwealth Land Title Insurance Co. (Binder Agent); The Equitable Life Assurance Society of the United States.

For full biographical listings, see the Martindale-Hubbell Law Directory

*GLASGOW,** Barren Co.

GARMON & GOODMAN (AV)

139 North Public Square, P.O. Box 663, 42142-0663
Telephone: 270-651-8812
Telecopier: 270-651-8846

(See Next Column)

MEMBERS OF FIRM

Larry D. Garmon — Charles A. Goodman III

Representative Clients: James N. Gray Company (construction); Pedigo-Lessenberry Insurance Agency, Inc.; Lyons Company, Inc. (construction); Commonwealth Relocation Services; Glasgow Radiology, P.S.C.; Cardiology Associates of Southern Kentucky, P.S.C.; Green Tree Financial Services, Inc.
Approved Attorneys for: Chicago Title Insurance Co.; Commonwealth Land Title Insurance Co. (Agent).
Reference: The New Farmers National Bank of Glasgow, Glasgow, KY.

For full biographical listings, see the Martindale-Hubbell Law Directory

HERBERT & HERBERT (AV)

135 North Public Square, P.O. Box 1000, 42141
Telephone: 502-651-9000
Fax: 502-651-3317
Email: h&hlaw@glasgow-ky.com

MEMBERS OF FIRM

H. Jefferson Herbert, Jr. — Betty Reece Herbert

ASSOCIATES

Brian K. Pack — Wesley W. Stephens

Representative Clients: Alliance Corp. (Construction); Eaton Corp.; Pan-Osten, Inc.; Supreme Mills, Inc.; T.J. Samson Community Hospital.
Approved Attorneys for: Fireman's Fund Insurance Companies; Indiana Insurance Co.; Agway Insurance Co.; Travelers Insurance Co.
Reference: South Central Bank, Glasgow, Kentucky.

For full biographical listings, see the Martindale-Hubbell Law Directory

*HARLAN,** Harlan Co.

HUFF LAW OFFICES (AV)

417 East Mound Street, Drawer 151, 40831
Telephone: 606-573-4466
Fax: 606-573-7078

Gayle G. Huff

ASSOCIATES

Antony L. Saragas — Elizabeth Ann Huff
William Stacy Huff

Representative Clients: Old Republic Insurance Co.; Underwriters Safety & Claims; Manalapan Mining Co.; R.B. Coal Co.; Eastover Mining Co., a division of Duke Power Co.; American Mining Insurance Co.; Employers Risk Services; Forest Industry Workers Compensation Fund.

For full biographical listings, see the Martindale-Hubbell Law Directory

RICE & HENDRICKSON (AV)

398 Woodland Hills, P.O. Box 980, 40831
Telephone: 606-573-3955
Fax: 606-573-3956

MEMBERS OF FIRM

William A. Rice — H. Kent Hendrickson

Representative Clients: USX Corp.; Navistar International Transportation Corp.; Bituminous Casualty Corp.; Kentucky Utilities Co.; Aetna Casualty & Surety Co.; The Hartford Insurance Group; Benham Coal, Inc.; Maytag Corporation; Harlan Cumberland Coal Co.; Pafco General Insurance.

For full biographical listings, see the Martindale-Hubbell Law Directory

*HAZARD,** Perry Co.

BARRET, HAYNES, MAY, CARTER AND ROARK, P.S.C. (AV)

113 Lovern Street, P.O. Box 1017, 41701
Telephone: 606-436-2165; 436-4824
Fax: 606-439-1450
Email: bhmer@mis.net

Maxwell P. Barret (1918-1988) — Randall Scott May
Hoover Haynes (Retired) — Ralph D. Carter
J. L. Roark

Denise Moore Davidson — Timothy C. Bates

Representative Clients: Citizens State Bank; Virginia Iron, Coal & Coke Co.; Blue Diamond Coal Co.; Kentucky Power Co.; Royal Globe Insurance Co.; Firemen's Fund; American Insurance Group; Old Republic Insurance Co.; Nationwide Insurance Co.; Kentucky Farm Bureau Mutual Insurance Co.

For full biographical listings, see the Martindale-Hubbell Law Directory

GULLETT, COMBS, REED & BOWLING (AV)

109 Broadway, Second Floor, P.O. Box 1039, 41702-1039
Telephone: 606-439-1373; 1-800-949-8812
Fax: 606-439-4450
Email: apgullet@mis.net
Email: 1234rong@tgtel.com

(See Next Column)

GULLETT, COMBS, REED & BOWLING, *Hazard—Continued*

MEMBERS OF FIRM

Asa P. Gullett, III
Teresa G. Combs Reed
Ronald G. Combs
Matthew Lawton Bowling

ASSOCIATE

Jameson D. Combs

LEGAL SUPPORT PERSONNEL

Jacqueline E. Goodin
Jimmie Lynn Jones

Reference: Peoples Bank and Trust Co.

For full biographical listings, see the Martindale-Hubbell Law Directory

*HENDERSON,** Henderson Co.

DEEP & WOMACK (AV)

790 Bob Posey Street, P.O. Box 50, 42419-0050
Telephone: 502-827-2522
Fax: 502-826-2870
Email: deep@henderson.net
Louisville, Kentucky Office: 1228 Starks Building, 455 South Fourth Avenue. P.O. Box 70033, 40270-0033.
Telephone: 502-589-2530.
Fax: 502-589-9297. E-Mail: Deep_Womack@msn.com

MEMBERS OF FIRM

Charles David Deep
Zack N. Womack

ASSOCIATES

Toni Cline Renfro (Resident, Louisville Office)
Carol Schureck Petitt (Resident, Louisville Office)
Jacqueline Chauvin (Resident, Louisville Office)

For full biographical listings, see the Martindale-Hubbell Law Directory

SHEFFER • HUTCHINSON • KINNEY (AV)

145 North Main Street, 42420
Telephone: 270-826-3300
Telecopier: 270-827-5070
URL: http://www.kylaw.com
Bowling Green, Kentucky Office: Fountain Square, 400 E. Main Street, Suite 300.
Telephone: 270-745-0000.
Telecopier: 270-842-9399.
Evansville, Indiana Office: One Riverfront Place, 20 N.W. First Street, Suite 700.
Telephone: 812-425-5200.
Telecopier: 812-425-2464.
Frankfort, Kentucky Office: 124 West Todd Street.
Telephone: 502-227-1500.
Telecopier: 502-875-7059.
Lexington, Kentucky Office: 250 West Main Street, Suite 1810.
Telephone: 606-381-1250.
Telecopier: 606-381-8250.
Louisville, Kentucky Office: 1600 National City Tower, 101 South First Street.
Telephone: 502-582-1600.
Telecopier: 502-582-1193.
Owensboro, Kentucky Office: 115 E. Second Street.
Telephone: 270-684-3700.
Telecopier: 270-684-3881.
Paducah, Kentucky Office: Citizens Bank Building, 333 Broadway, Suite 1001. 333 Broadway, Suite 1001.
Telephone: 270-443-9401.
Telecopier: 270-443-3624.

MEMBERS OF FIRM

Ronald G. Sheffer
Charles B. West
Peter B. Lewis (Resident, Owensboro Office)
James A. Sigler (Resident, Paducah Office)
John A. Sheffer (Resident, Owensboro Office)
Edwin A. Jones
Dawn S. Kelsey
Donna M. Sauer
Anne D. Watkins
John S. Harrison

OF COUNSEL

Robert A. Marshall

For full biographical listings, see the Martindale-Hubbell Law Directory

*LEXINGTON,** Fayette Co.

BOEHL STOPHER & GRAVES (AV)

444 West Second Street, 40508
Telephone: 606-252-6721
FAX: 606-253-1445
Louisville, Kentucky Office: Suite 2300, Aegon Center, 400 West Market Street.
Telephone: 502-589-5980.
Fax: 502-561-9400.

(See Next Column)

Paducah, Kentucky Office: Suite 340 Executive Inn Riverfront, One Executive Boulevard.
Telephone: 270-442-4369.
Fax: 270-442-4689.
Prestonsburg, Kentucky Office: 105 West Court Street.
Telephone: 606-886-8004.
Fax: 606-886-9579.
New Albany, Indiana Office: Elsby East, Suite 204, 400 Pearl Street.
Telephone: 812-948-5053.
Fax: 812-948-9233.

RESIDENT PARTNERS

W. T. Adkins
Nolan Carter, Jr.
Ronald L. Green
Kim Martin Wilkie
Guillermo A. Carlos
James B. Cooper
Steven R. Armstrong

RESIDENT ASSOCIATES

Brennen C. Ragone
William E. Brown, II
Ronald E. Thornsberry

Counsel for: Ford Motor Co.; Texas Eastern Transmission Corp.; Coca-Cola Bottling Co.; National Collegiate Athletic Assn.; Hartford Accident and Indemnity Co.; Continental Insurance Group; St. Paul Fire & Marine Insurance Co.; Lloyds of London; Old Republic Insurance Co.

For full biographical listings, see the Martindale-Hubbell Law Directory

GERALDS, JONES, SHERROW, SCHRADER & RICE, P.S.C. (AV)

259 West Short Street, 40507
Telephone: 606-255-7946
Fax: 606-233-4099

Oscar H. Geralds, Jr.
Ernest H. Jones, II
Billy W. Sherrow
John P. Schrader
John G. Rice

Robert L. Swisher
Patsey Ely Yewell
Cheryl D. Morgan

OF COUNSEL

Frances Geralds Rohlfing

Representative Clients: Allstate Insurance Co.; State Farm Mutual Automobile Insurance Co.; State Farm Fire and Casualty Co.; Colonial Insurance Company of California; Horace Mann; North American Specialty Insurance Co.; Pennsylvania National Insurance Company.
Reference: Bank of the Bluegrass & Trust Co.

For full biographical listings, see the Martindale-Hubbell Law Directory

HARBISON, KESSINGER, LISLE & BUSH

(See Stites & Harbison)

JACKSON & KELLY (AV)

175 East Main Street, Suite 500, P.O. Box 2150, 40595
Telephone: 606-255-9500
Fax: 606-281-6478
Charleston, West Virginia Office: 1600 Laidley Tower, P.O. Box 553.
Telephone: 304-340-1000.
Fax: 304-340-1130.
Washington, D.C. Office: 2401 Pennsylvania Avenue, N.W., Suite 400.
Telephone: 202-973-0200.
Fax: 202-973-0232.
Denver, Colorado Office: Suite 2710, 1660 Lincoln Street.
Telephone: 303-390-0003.
Fax: 303-390-0040.
Martinsburg, West Virginia Office: 300 Foxcroft Avenue, P.O. Box 1068.
Telephone: 304-263-8800.
Fax: 304-263-7110.
Morgantown, West Virginia Office: 6000 Hampton Center, P.O. Box 619.
Telephone: 304-599-3000.
Fax: 304-285-2040.
New Martinsville, West Virginia Office: 256 Russell Avenue, P.O. Box 68.
Telephone: 304-455-1751.
Fax: 304-455-6314.
Parkersburg, West Virginia Office: 800 Garfield Avenue, P.O. Box 718, 26102.
Telephone: 304-422-1419.
Fax: 304-422-1422.
Fairmont, West Virginia Office: 1000 Technology Drive, Suite 1310, 26554.
Telephone: 304-368-2000.
Fax: 304-368-2020.
Wheeling, West Virginia Office: 1144 Market Street, 26003.
Telephone: 304-233-4000.
Fax: 304-233-4077.

MEMBERS OF FIRM

William A. Hoskins, III (Administrative Manager)
Jeffrey J. Yost
A. Stuart Bennett
William E. Doll, Jr.
Martin E. Hall
Kevin M. McGuire
W. Rodes Brown
Natalie D. Brown
Stanton L. Cave

(See Next Column)

JACKSON & KELLY—*Continued*

ASSOCIATES

Jacqueline Syers Duncan	Jay E. Ingle
Sannie Overly	Thomas J. Hodge
Robert F. Duncan	Victoria J. Sopranik (Not admitted in KY)
David B. Mattingly	

LEGAL SUPPORT PERSONNEL

Lana H. Thomas (Office Manager)

Representative Clients: Bank One; Consol of Kentucky; Cyprus Amax Minerals Co.; Electric Fuels Corp.; GTE Mobilnet; Kentucky Association of Counties and the Kentucky Municipal League; Kentucky Medical Assn.; Lane's End Farm; St. Joseph Hospital; TECO Energy, Inc.

For full biographical listings, see the Martindale-Hubbell Law Directory

LANDRUM & SHOUSE (AV)

106 West Vine Street, P.O. Box 951, 40588-0951
Telephone: 606-255-2424
Facsimile: 606-233-0308
Louisville, Kentucky Office: Suite 1900, 220 West Main Street, 40202-2119.
Telephone: 502-589-7616.
Facsimile: 502-589-2119.

MEMBERS OF FIRM

John H. Burrus	Mark J. Hinkel
William C. Shouse	John Garry McNeill
Pierce W. Hamblin	R. Kent Westberry (Resident, Louisville Office)
Mark L. Moseley	Jane Durkin Samuel
Leslie Patterson Vose	Douglas L. Hoots, CPCU
John R. Martin, Jr. (Resident, Louisville Office)	Dave Whalin (Resident, Louisville Office)
Larry C. Deener	Daniel E. Murner
Sandra Mendez Dawahare	

ASSOCIATES

Stephen R. Chappell	Carolyn C. Zerga
Estill D. Banks, II	David W. Zahniser
Robert Thaddeus (Thad) Keal (Resident, Louisville Office)	Kathleen Campbell Deskins
Sun S. Choy (Resident, Louisville Office)	Rheanne Dodson Falkner (Resident, Louisville Office)
Melanie Lee Straw-Boone (Resident, Louisville Office)	Shannon M. Naish
	Bradley C. Hooks
	Alex L. Scutchfield

OF COUNSEL

Weldon Shouse	Thomas M. Cooper

Representative Clients: State Auto Insurance Co.; Northland Insurance Co.; Ohio Casualty Insurance; Safeco Insurance; Scottsdale Insurance Co.; Cincinnati Insurance Co.; Crawford & Co.; CSX Transportation, Inc.; Lexington-Fayette Urban County Airport; American States Insurance Co.

For full biographical listings, see the Martindale-Hubbell Law Directory

JAMES R. ODELL, P.S.C. (AV)

171 North Upper Street, P.O. Box 2258, 40588-2258
Telephone: 606-231-0210
Fax: 606-252-2917
Email: odelllaw@aol.com

James R. Odell

For full biographical listings, see the Martindale-Hubbell Law Directory

GEORGE F. RABE (AV)

Suite 1004 First National Building, 167 West Main Street, 40507-1708
Telephone: 606-255-2313

ASSOCIATE

Steven M. McCauley

For full biographical listings, see the Martindale-Hubbell Law Directory

ROBERTS & SMITH (AV)

167 West Main Street Suite 200, 40507-1701
Telephone: 606-233-1104
Fax: 606-255-6438
Email: LRob70165@aol.com

MEMBERS OF FIRM

Larry S. Roberts	Kenneth W. Smith

For full biographical listings, see the Martindale-Hubbell Law Directory

STITES & HARBISON (AV)

Formerly Stites, McElwain & Fowler and Harbison, Kessinger, Lisle & Bush
250 West Main Street, Suite 2300, 40507-1758
Telephone: 606-226-2300
Fax: 606-253-9144
Louisville, Kentucky Office: 400 West Market Street, Suite 1800.
Telephone: 502-587-3400.
Fax: 502-587-6391.

(See Next Column)

Frankfort, Kentucky Office: 421 West Main Street.
Telephone: 502-223-3477.
Fax: 502-223-4124. Hyden, Kentucky Office: 21976 Main Street, Farmer Campbell Building, Second Floor.
Telephone: 606-672-4200.
Fax: 606-672-4100.
Jeffersonville, Indiana Office: 323 East Court Avenue.
Telephone: 812-282-7566.
Fax: 812-284-5519.
Atlanta, Georgia Office: 3350 Cumberland Circle, Suite 1700 Riverwood.
Telephone: 770-850-7000.
Fax: 770-850-7070.
Washington, D.C. Office: 1200 G Street, N.W., Suite 800.

MEMBERS OF FIRM

James W. Stites (1897-1975)	Thomas E. Meng
Clinton M. Harbison (1886-1975)	Walter R. Byrne, Jr.
	Janet A. Craig
Ben B. Fowler (1916-1990)	Gregory P. Parsons
Richard Bush, Jr. (1915-1991)	Kenneth R. Sagan
Kent McElwain (1927-1992)	Richard G. Griffith
Rufus Lisle (1909-1997)	J. Clarke Keller
Nathan Elliott, Jr. (1914-1998)	Laura D. Keller
Sidney C. Kinkead, Jr.	James W. Taylor
George W. Mills	Ashley W. Ward
Steven L. Beshear	W. Bradford Boone
Joe B. Campbell	Cheryl Ulene Lewis
Bruce M. Reynolds	Lynn C. Stidham
Buckner Hinkle, Jr.	William T. Gorton III
J. David Porter	Benjamin Lee Kessinger, III
Stephen M. Ruschell	Lissa Wathen
Robert M. Beck, Jr.	Andrew R. Jacobs
Charles J. Lisle	Elizabeth Lee Thompson
John M. Famularo	Erica L. Horn

Don A. Pisacano	Jane Brannon
Anne E. Gorham	Jeffrey J. Chapuran
Lisa K. Ramsey	Dustan Chad McCoy
Rebecca B. Stephenson	Daniel E. Danford
Darren J. Duzyk	W. Blaine Early, III
Amanda Pope Thompson	Laura A. D'Angelo

Mary Gay Whitmer

OF COUNSEL

Ralph F. Kessinger	Charles E. Palmer, Jr.

COUNSEL

Ben L. Kessinger, Jr.	Calvert T. Roszell

Thomas J. Stipanowich

For full biographical listings, see the Martindale-Hubbell Law Directory

STOLL, KEENON & PARK, LLP (AV)

201 E. Main Street, Suite 1000, 40507-1380
Telephone: 606-231-3000
Telecopier: 606-253-1093; 606-253-1027
URL: http://www.skp.com
Frankfort, Kentucky Office: 307 Washington Street, 40601.
Telephone: 502-875-6220.
Telecopier: 502-875-6235.
Henderson, Kentucky Office: 201 C North Main Street, 42420-3103.
Telephone: 270-831-1900.
Telecopier: 270-827-4060.
Louisville, Kentucky Office: 400 West Market Street, Suite 2650, 40202-3377.
Telephone: 502-568-9100.
Telecopier: 502-568-5700.

MEMBERS OF FIRM

Wallace Muir (1878-1947)	William M. Lear, Jr.
Richard C. Stoll (1876-1949)	Gary W. Barr
Rodman W. Keenon (1883-1966)	Donald P. Wagner
William H. Townsend (1890-1964)	Frank L. Wilford
	Harvie B. Wilkinson
James Park (1892-1970)	Robert W. Kellerman
John L. Davis (1913-1970)	Lizbeth Ann Tully
Gladney Harville (1921-1978)	J. David Smith, Jr.
Gayle A. Mohney (1906-1980)	Eileen M. O'Brien
G. Lee Langston (1942-1983)	David C. Schwetschenau
C. William Swinford (1921-1986)	Anita M. Britton
Robert F. Houlihan	Rena Gardner Wiseman
Leslie W. Morris II	Denise Kirk Ash
Lindsey W. Ingram, Jr.	Bonnie Hoskins
William L. Montague	C. Joseph Beavin
Bennett Clark	Diane M. Carlton
William T. Bishop, III	Larry A. Sykes
John Stanley Hoffman	P. Douglas Barr
Richard C. Stephenson	Perry M. Bentley
Charles E. Shivel, Jr.	Dan M. Rose
Robert M. Watt, III	Gregory D. Pavey
J. Peter Cassidy, Jr.	J. Mel Camenisch, Jr.
David H. Thomason	David E. Fleenor
Samuel D. Hinkle IV	Lea Pauley Goff
R. David Lester	Laura Day DelCotto
Robert F. Houlihan, Jr.	Culver V. Halliday

(See Next Column)

STOLL, KEENON & PARK LLP, *Lexington—Continued*

MEMBERS OF FIRM (Continued)

James D. Allen
Richard A. Nunnelley
John Browning Park
Palmer G. Vance, II
William L. Montague, Jr.

ASSOCIATES

Mary Beth Griffith
Susan Beverly Jones
Todd S. Page
Melissa Anne Stewart
Kymberly T. Wellons
Charles R. Baesler, Jr.
Patricia Kirkwood Burgess
Steven B. Loy
Richard B. Warne
John H. Henderson
Lindsey W. Ingram, III
Jeffery T. Barnett
Elizabeth Friend Bird
Amy C. Liebermann
Della M. Justice
Molly J. Cue
Crystal Lynn Osborne
John A. Thomason
Boyd Tristan Cloern
Donnie E. Martin
David T. Royse

OF COUNSEL

James G. Stephenson
Douglas P. Romaine
George D. Smith

Representative Clients: Bank One, Lexington, NA; Farmers Capital Bank Corp.; The Tokai Bank Ltd.; Link Belt Construction Equipment Co.; General Motors Corp.; International Business Machines Corp.; Rockwell International Corp.; Square D Co.

For full biographical listings, see the Martindale-Hubbell Law Directory

WILSON, DECAMP & TALBOTT, P.S.C. (AV)

National City Plaza, 301 East Main Street, Suite 1000, 40507-1586
Telephone: 606-225-1191
Fax: 606-225-5176
Email: wdtlaw@gte.net

Philip E. Wilson
Earl S. Wilson, Jr.
Patterson A. DeCamp
John S. Talbott, III

Authorized Agent for: Commonwealth Land Title Insurance Company.

For full biographical listings, see the Martindale-Hubbell Law Directory

WYATT, TARRANT & COMBS (AV)

1700 Lexington Financial Center, 40507-1746
Telephone: 606-233-2012
Telecopier: 606-259-0649
URL: http://www.wyattfirm.com
Louisville, Kentucky Office: Citizens Plaza.
Telephone: 502-589-5235.
Telecopier: 502-589-0309.
Frankfort, Kentucky Office: The Taylor-Scott Building, 311 West Main Street.
Telephone: 502-223-2104.
Telecopier: 502-227-7681.
New Albany, Indiana Office: The Elsby Building, 117 East Spring Street.
Telephone: 812-945-3561.
Telecopier: 812-949-2524.
Memphis, Tennessee Office: Crescent Center, Suite 650, 6075 Poplar Avenue.
Telephone: 901-537-1000.
Telecopier: 901-537-1010.
Nashville, Tennessee Office: 1500 Nashville City Center, 511 Union Street.
Telephone: 615-244-0020.
Telecopier: 615-256-1726.
Music Row, Nashville Office: 29 Music Square East.
Telephone: 615-255-6161.
Telecopier: 615-254-4490.
Hendersonville, Tennessee Office: 313 E. Main Street, Suite 1.
Telephone: 615-822-8822.
Telecopier: 615-824-4684.
Tri-Cities, Tennessee Office: Northeast Tennessee Business Park, 10368 Wallace Alley Street, Suite 6, Kingsport.
Telephone: 423-279-1825.
Telecopier: 423-279-9357.

MEMBERS OF FIRM

Bert T. Combs (1911-1991)
William H. McCann
Herbert D. Sledd
H. Foster Pettit
Richard C. Ward
Stewart E. Conner
James T. Hodge
Henry E. Kinser
Jeff A. Woods
Thomas J. Luber
Bradford L. Cowgill
Mark T. MacDonald
J. Mark Burton
Paul J. Cox
Judge B. Wilson II
Bruce B. McElvein
Gayle B. McGrath
Debra H. Dawahare
George J. Miller
David A. Smart
Karen J. Greenwell
William B. Owsley
Marco M. Rajkovich, Jr.
John M. Williams

(See Next Column)

ASSOCIATES

Cheryl K. Harris
Charles D. Webb, Jr.
William Craig Robertson III
Bruce R. Smith
Preston S. Cecil
Pamela R. Goodwine
Julie M. O'Daniel
Melanie J. Kilpatrick
Robert H. Eardley
M. Elizabeth Henderson
Vonda K. Tolliver

COUNSEL

Edward T. Breathitt
Scotty Baesler
Jack G. Jones, Jr.
Robert J. Brown
Penny R. Warren
Philip D. Kessack
James H. Newberry, Jr.
Forrest W. Ragsdale III
Mary L. Fullington

Representative Clients: Arch Coal, Inc.; Ashland Inc.; Baptist Healthcare System, Inc.; Berwind Corp.; Design Professional Insurance Co.; Fasig-Tipton Co., Inc.; GRW Engineers, Inc.; Kentucky Coal Assn.; Lexington-Fayette Urban County Government; PNC Bank, National Association.

For full biographical listings, see the Martindale-Hubbell Law Directory

*LONDON,** Laurel Co.

FARMER, KELLEY, BROWN AND WILLIAMS (AV)

502 West Fifth Street, Drawer 490, 40741
Telephone: 606-878-7640
Fax: 606-878-2364
Email: fpfarmer@farmerlaw.com
Lexington, Kentucky Office: 1082 Griffin Gate Drive, 40511-1384.
Telephone: 606: 263-2567.
Facsimile: 606: 878-2364.

MEMBERS OF FIRM

F. Preston Farmer
John F. Kelley, Jr.
Michael P. Farmer
Martha L. Brown
Jason E. Williams

ASSOCIATES

Suzanne S. Farmer
Jennifer S. Nicholson

Representative Clients: The Aetna Casualty and Surety Co.; American States Insurance Co.; Auto-Owner's Insurance Co.; Bituminous Insurance Co.; Canadian Universal Insurance Co.; Chubb Insurance Co.; Cotton States Insurance Co.; Crum & Forster Underwriters Group; Eagle Insurance Co.; Equity Mutual Insurance Co.

For full biographical listings, see the Martindale-Hubbell Law Directory

HAMM, MILBY & RIDINGS (AV)

120 North Main Street, 40741
Telephone: 606-864-4126
Fax: 606-878-8144
Email: hmrlaw@kih.net

MEMBERS OF FIRM

Robert L. Milby
Marcia Milby Ridings

James A. Ridings
Gregory A. Lay
R. Aaron Hostettler

Representative Clients: Acceleration National; Aetna Life & Casualty Ins. Co.; All Risk Claims Service, Inc.; Allstate Insurance Co.; Alexis; American Automobile Mutual Ins.; American Bankers; American Hardware Ins. Co.

For full biographical listings, see the Martindale-Hubbell Law Directory

*LOUISVILLE,** Jefferson Co.

BOEHL STOPHER & GRAVES (AV)

Suite 2300 Aegon Center, 400 West Market Street, 40202-3354
Telephone: 502-589-5980
FAX: 502-561-9400
Lexington, Kentucky Office: 444 West Second Street.
Telephone: 606-252-6721.
Fax: 606-253-1445.
Paducah, Kentucky Office: Suite 340 Executive Inn Riverfront, One Executive Boulevard.
Telephone: 270-442-4369.
Fax: 270-442-4689.
Prestonsburg, Kentucky Office: 105 West Court Street.
Telephone: 606-886-8004.
Fax: 606-886-9579.
New Albany, Indiana Office: Elsby East, Suite 204, 400 Pearl Street.
Telephone: 812-948-5053.
Fax: 812-948-9233.

OF COUNSEL

Joseph E. Stopher
George R. Effinger (Resident at Paducah)
Galen J. White, Jr.

MEMBERS OF FIRM

Herbert F. Boehl (1894-1986)
Arthur J. Deindoerfer (1907-1990)
Raymond O. Harmon (1918-1990)
James M. Graves (1912-1994)
William M. Newman, Jr. (1949-1995)
William O. Guethlein
Larry L. Johnson

(See Next Column)

BOEHL STOPHER & GRAVES—*Continued*

MEMBERS OF FIRM (Continued)

W. T. Adkins (Resident at Lexington)
Edward H. Stopher
Nolan Carter, Jr. (Resident at Lexington)
Jefferson K. Streepey
Wesley G. Gatlin
George R. Carter
Robert E. Stopher
Philip J. Reverman, Jr.
Peter J. Glauber
Raymond G. Smith
Walter E. Harding
Robert M. Brooks
Ronald L. Green (Resident at Lexington)
Richard L. Walter (Resident at Paducah)
Douglas A. U'Sellis
Kim Martin Wilkie (Resident at Lexington)
John Harlan Callis, III (Resident at Prestonsburg)
Charles D. Walter (Resident at Paducah)
Janie McKenzie Wells (Resident at Prestonsburg)
Guillermo A. Carlos (Resident at Lexington)
Jeffrey L. Hansford (Resident at New Albany, Indiana)
Matthew Hunter Jones (Resident at New Albany, Indiana)
James B. Cooper (Resident at Lexington)
Martin H. Kinney, Jr.
Bayard V. Collier (Resident at Prestonsburg)
Richard W. Edwards
David T. Klapheke
Daniel S. Stratemeyer (Resident at Paducah)
Steven R. Armstrong (Resident at Lexington)

ASSOCIATES

Mary Ann Kiwala
Bruce D. Atherton
William J. Crowe
Denise Basford Askin
Deron L. Johnson (Resident at Prestonsburg)
Brennen C. Ragone (Resident at Lexington)
Gretchen Nunn Gullett (Resident at Prestonsburg)
C. Tom Anderson (Resident at Prestonsburg)
Timothy L. Gray
Richard Vernon Evans
George T. T. Kitchen III
Elizabeth A. Schott (Resident at New Albany, Indiana)
James L. Fischer, Jr. (Resident at Albany, Indiana)
Ronald E. Thornsberry (Resident at Lexington)
Scott A. Davidson
Kurt A. Scharfenberger
P. Kevin Moore

Counsel for: Ford Motor Co.; Texas Eastern Transmission Corp.; Coca-Cola Bottling Co.; Hartford Accident and Indemnity Co.; Continental Insurance Group; St. Paul Fire & Marine Insurance Co.; Lloyds of London; Old Republic Insurance Co.

For full biographical listings, see the Martindale-Hubbell Law Directory

FORE, MILLER & SCHWARTZ (AV)

First Trust Centre, Suite 700 North, 200 South Fifth Street, 40202
Telephone: 502-589-5250
Fax: 502-589-1637

MEMBERS OF FIRM

F. Larkin Fore
Dan T. Schwartz
Stephen H. Miller
Bryan J. Dillon
Donald J. LaDuke

ASSOCIATES

Louis I. Waterman
Joseph C. Spalding

OF COUNSEL

Karl M. Walz

References: American States Insurance Co.; Crawford & Company; Paragon Group, Inc.; Queens Group; Southeastern Dairies, Inc.; Ticor Title Co.; First National Bank of Louisville; Stockyards Bank; Arrow Electric Co.

For full biographical listings, see the Martindale-Hubbell Law Directory

JOSEPH G. GLASS (AV)

Suite 200, 235 South Fifth Street, 40202
Telephone: 502-584-7288
FAX: 502-584-0208

For full biographical listings, see the Martindale-Hubbell Law Directory

GREENEBAUM DOLL & McDONALD PLLC (AV)

3300 National City Tower, 40202
Telephone: 502-589-4200
Fax: 502-587-3695
Email: pad@gdm.com *URL:* http://www.gdm.com
Lexington, Kentucky Office: 1400 Vine Center Tower.
Telephone: 606-231-8500.
Fax: 606-255-2742.
Covington, Kentucky Office: 50 East RiverCenter Boulevard, P.O. Box 2673.
Telephone: 606-655-4200.
Fax: 606-655-4239.
Frankfort, Kentucky Office: Suite 101, 229 West Main Street.
Telephone: 502-875-0050.
Fax: 502-875-0850.
Cincinnati, Ohio Office: 2800 Chemed Center, 255 East Fifth Street.
Telephone: 513-455-7600.
Fax: 513-455-8500.

(See Next Column)

Nashville, Tennessee Office: 700 Two American Center, 3102 West End Avenue.
Telephone: 615-760-7100.
Fax: 615-760-7300.

S. L. Greenebaum (1902-1973)
Edward L. McDonald (1870-1961)
Angus W. McDonald (1912-1980)
W. VanMeter Alford (1916-1981)
Laramie L. Leatherman (1932-1994)
P. Richard Anderson, Jr.
Thomas A. Brown
Edwin H. Perry
Michael G. Shaikun *
Martin S. Weinberg *
Ivan M. Diamond
Michael M. Fleishman *
Wm. T. (Bill) Robinson III
Edward B. Weinberg *
Charles Fassler
W. Plumer Wiseman, Jr.
Eric L. Ison
John H. Stites, III
John R. Cummins
Lloyd R. Cress
James L. Beckner (Not admitted in KY)
Charles J. Lavelle
Mark S. Ament
Hiram Ely, III
Peggy B. Lyndrup
June Nalley King
John W. Ames
Barbara Reid Hartung
Richard S. Cleary
David B. Sandler
Janet P. Jakubowicz
Margaret E. Keane
Tandy C. Patrick
Holland N. McTyeire, V
Mary G. Eaves
Mark S. Riddle
Philip C. Eschels
Jeffrey A. Savarise
Jeffrey A. McKenzie
Patrick J. Welsh
Glenn A. Price, Jr.
Bradley E. Dillon
Daniel E. Fisher
Mark F. Sommer
Michael de León Hawthorne
Patrick R. Northam
J. Mark Grundy
Jerrold R. Perchik
Vickie Yates Brown
Thomas J. Birchfield
Robert D. Hudson
Mark H. Oppenheimer
John S. Lueken
John K. Bush
Amy B. Berge
James C. Eaves, Jr.
Daniel P. Cherry
Paul E. Porter
Brent R. Baughman
Laurel S. Banks

ASSOCIATES

Craig P. Siegenthaler
Katherine A. Hessenbruch
Thomas E. Powell, II
Carolyn J. Wheatley
D. Bryan Wickens
Erin N. O'Daniel
Melissa S. Norman
Elizabeth Kaplan
Emily C. Moore
Lynda C. Bannister
Christopher J. Rusek
Ann Toni Kereiakes
Eric A. Braun
James J. G. Dimas
Andrew M. Fleischman
Christie A. Moore
David J. Herzig
Sean P. Gallagher
Johna Howard Casey
Alison J. Brehm
Elisabeth Summers Gray
W. Ashley Hess
Andrew James Murray
Stacy Charlotte Kula
B. Dale Hamblin, Jr.

OF COUNSEL

A. Robert Doll
R. Van Young
William C. Ballard, Jr.
Kimberly Jenci Hawthorne
Paul B. Whitty
Robert L. Brown
Henry L. Smith, Jr. (Not admitted in KY)
Lori B. Sullivan

LEGAL SUPPORT PERSONNEL

Nancy L. Fritz (Research Specialist)

Representative Clients: Ashland Inc.; Brown-Forman Corp.; Humana Inc.
*A Professional Service Corporation

For full biographical listings, see the Martindale-Hubbell Law Directory

FRANK P. HILLIARD (AV)

The Starks Building, Suite 380, 455 South 4th Avenue, 40202
Telephone: 502-583-0380
Fax: 502-583-9089
Email: fphil380@bellsouth.net

ASSOCIATE

Charles Edward Monarch

For full biographical listings, see the Martindale-Hubbell Law Directory

MIDDLETON & REUTLINGER, P.S.C. (AV)

2500 Brown and Williamson Tower, 40202-3410
Telephone: 502-584-1135
Fax: 502-561-0442
URL: http://middreut.com
Jeffersonville, Indiana Office: 530 East Court Avenue, 47130.
Telephone: 812-282-1132.
Fax: 812-282-3188.

O. Grant Bruton
Kenneth S. Handmaker
Ian Y. Henderson
James N. Williams, Jr.
Charles G. Middleton, III
Charles D. Greenwell
Brooks Alexander
John W. Bilby
C. Kent Hatfield
Timothy P. O'Mara
D. Randall Gibson
G. Kennedy Hall, Jr.
James R. Higgins, Jr.
Mark S. Fenzel

(See Next Column)

MIDDLETON & REUTLINGER P.S.C., *Louisville—Continued*

Kathiejane Oehler
Charles G. Lamb
Thomas W. Frentz
William Jay Hunter, Jr.
James E. Milliman
David J. Kellerman
Kipley J. McNally
Julie A. Gregory
Dennis D. Murrell
Henry S. Alford

Augustus S. Herbert
Dana L. Collins
Thomas P. O'Brien III
John F. Salazar
Nancy J. Schook
Clayton R. Hume
Scot A. Duvall
Terri Elms Phelps
Laura D. Robertson
James R. Robinson
Jason P. K. Underwood
Jeffrey A. Haeberlin

OF COUNSEL

Henry Meigs, II
J. Paul Keith, III

For full biographical listings, see the Martindale-Hubbell Law Directory

J. BRUCE MILLER LAW GROUP (AV)

One Riverfront Plaza, Suite 1800, 40202-2927
Telephone: 502-587-0900
Telecopier: 502-587-9008
Email: jbm@jbmlg.com *URL:* http://www.jbmlg.com

J. Bruce Miller
Norma C. Miller
Katherine G. Kitchen
Angela Lee Summers
David Scott Dupps
Ashley N. Blacketer
Jason A. Kron
Nicholas Garrett Hawkins

OF COUNSEL

Michael J. Kitchen
Denis B. Fleming, Jr.

Representative Clients: Advance Machinery Co., Inc.; Anson Machine Mfg. Co.; Biddinger Investment Capital Corp. (Indiana); Carneal Enterprises, Inc. (Kentucky/Florida); MPD Inc. (Owensboro, Kentucky); Motion Picture Association of America; Packaging Unlimited Group (Kentucky/North Carolina); Paducah Medical Supply, Inc. (Kentucky/Tennessee/Florida); Sun Group Broadcasting, Inc. (Indiana/Tennessee); Louisville Gas & Electric Co.

For full biographical listings, see the Martindale-Hubbell Law Directory

MORGAN & POTTINGER, P.S.C. (AV)

601 West Main Street, 40202
Telephone: 502-589-2780
Telecopier: 502-585-3498
URL: http://www.morganandpottinger.com
Lexington, Kentucky Office: 133 West Short Street.
Telephone: 606-253-1900.
Telecopier: 606-255-2038.
New Albany, Indiana Office: 120 East Market Street.
Telephone: 812-948-0008.
Telecopier: 812-944-6215.

Patrick E. Morgan
John T. McGarvey
C. Edward Hastie (Resident, Lexington Office)
M. Deane Stewart
James I. Murray (Resident, Lexington Office)
Douglas Gene Sharp
John A. Majors
Mark J. Sandlin
Scott T. Rickman (Resident, Lexington Office)
M. Thurman Senn
Hal D. Friedman

Thomas C. Fenton
Ruthanne Q. Whitt
Garret B. Hannegan (Resident, New Albany, Indiana Office)
Diane E. Bluhm (Not admitted in KY)
Laura Kincheloe (Resident, Lexington Office)
Drayer L. Bott
John Allan Combs (Resident, Lexington Office)
Jean T. Harrod

SENIOR COUNSEL

David C. Pottinger

COUNSEL

Elmer E. Morgan
J. Jeffrey Cooke

For full biographical listings, see the Martindale-Hubbell Law Directory

ROTH FOLEY BRYANT & COOPER, PLLC (AV)

First Trust Centre, Suite 300S, 200 South Fifth Street, 40202-3236
Telephone: 502-569-7550
Fax: 502-540-0123
Email: RFBC.com

Irvin D. Foley
David M. Roth
David H. Cooper
Lisa Koch Bryant
K. Gail Russell
Christian L. Juckett

OF COUNSEL

James E. Fahey
David W. Gray

Representative Clients: Bank One, Kentucky, N.A.; Huntington National Bank; Commonwealth Bank & Trust Co.; Farm Credit Services of Mid-America; Century Indemnity Co.; Travelers Casualty and Insurance Co.; Tumbleweed, LLC; John R. Gains Thoroughbreds, LLC; ARM Financial Group, Inc.; Osborn Enterprises.

(See Next Column)

For full biographical listings, see the Martindale-Hubbell Law Directory

SHEFFER • HUTCHINSON • KINNEY (AV)

1600 National City Tower, 101 South Fifth Street, 40202
Telephone: 502-582-1600
Telecopier: 502-582-1193
URL: http://www.kylaw.com
Bowling Green, Kentucky Office: Fountain Square, 400 E. Main Street, Suite 300.
Telephone: 270-745-0000.
Telecopier: 270-842-9399.
Evansville, Indiana Office: One Riverfront Place, 20 N.W. First Street, Suite 700.
Telephone: 812-425-5200.
Telecopier: 812-425-2464.
Frankfort, Kentucky Office: 124 West Todd Street.
Telephone: 502-227-1500.
Telecopier: 502-875-7059.
Henderson, Kentucky Office: 145 North Main Street.
Telephone: 270-826-3300.
Telecopier: 270-827-5070.
Lexington, Kentucky Office: 250 West Main Street, Suite 1810.
Telephone: 606-381-1250.
Telecopier: 606-381-8250.
Owensboro, Kentucky Office: 115 E. Second Street.
Telephone: 270-684-3700.
Telecopier: 270-684-3881.
Paducah, Kentucky Office: Citizens Bank Building, 33 Broadway, Suite 1001.
Telephone: 270-443-9401.
Telecopier: 270-443-3624.

MEMBERS OF FIRM

Ronald G. Sheffer
F. Chris Gorman
John A. Sheffer (Resident, Owensboro Office)
C. Thomas Miller (Resident)
Brian F. Haara
William H. May
Anne D. Watkins
Tara Beckwith
Laura Cheatham Elliott
David W. Tandy

OF COUNSEL

Robert A. Marshall

For full biographical listings, see the Martindale-Hubbell Law Directory

STITES & HARBISON (AV)

Formerly Stites, McElwain & Fowler and Harbison, Kessinger, Lisle & Bush
400 West Market Street, Suite 1800, 40202
Telephone: 502-587-3400
Fax: 502-587-6391
URL: http://www.stites.com
Frankfort, Kentucky Office: 421 West Main Street.
Telephone: 502-223-3477.
Fax: 502-223-4124.
Lexington, Kentucky Office: 250 West Main Street, Suite 2300.
Telephone: 606-226-2300.
Fax: 606-253-9144.
Hyden, Kentucky Office: 21976 Main Street, Farmer Campbell Building, Second Floor.
Telephone: 606-672-4200.
Jeffersonville, Indiana Office: 323 East Court Avenue.
Telephone: 812-282-7566.
Fax: 812-284-5519.
Atlanta, Georgia Office: 3350 Cumberland Circle, Suite 1700 Riverwood.
Telephone: 770-850-7000.
Fax: 770-850-7070.
Washington, D.C. Office: 1200 G Street, N.W., Suite 800.
Telephone: 202-434-8968.

MEMBERS OF FIRM

James W. Stites (1897-1975)
Clinton M. Harbison (1886-1980)
S. Lloyd Cardwell (1909-1987)
Ben B. Fowler (1916-1990)
Richard Bush, Jr. (1915-1991)
Kent McElwain (1927-1992)
Rufus Lisle (1909-1997)
Nathan Elliott, Jr. (1914-1998)
James Timothy White (P.C.) (Atlanta, Georgia Office)
David C. Brown
Sidney C. Kinkead, Jr. (Lexington, Kentucky Office)
George W. Mills (Lexington, Kentucky Office)
C. Dant Kearns
W. Robinson Beard
Ralston W. Steenrod
Robert W. Lanum (Jeffersonville, Indiana Office)
K. Morgan Varner, III, (P.C.) (Atlanta, Georgia Office)
Richard W. Stephens (P.C.) (Atlanta, Georgia Office)
Steven L. Beshear (Lexington, Kentucky Office)
Joe B. Campbell (Lexington, Kentucky Office)
J. Bissell Roberts
Bruce M. Reynolds (Lexington, Kentucky Office)
Charles J. Cronan, IV
T. Kennedy Helm, III
Buckner Hinkle, Jr. (Lexington, Kentucky Office)
J. D. Humphries, III, (P.C.) (Atlanta, Georgia Office)
William H. Haden, Jr.
J. David Porter (Lexington, Kentucky Office)

(See Next Column)

STITES & HARBISON—*Continued*

MEMBERS OF FIRM (Continued)

Stephen M. Ruschell (Lexington, Kentucky Office)
David B. Ratterman
Robert M. Beck, Jr. (Lexington, Kentucky Office)
Charles J. Lisle (Lexington, Kentucky Office)
Bruce F. Clark (Frankfort, Kentucky Office)
William E. Hellmann
James R. Williamson
John M. Famularo (Lexington, Kentucky Office)
Thomas E. Meng (Lexington, Kentucky Office)
Douglass C. E. Farnsley
Robert W. Griffith
Walter R. Byrne, Jr. (Lexington, Kentucky Office)
W. Kennedy Simpson
Philip W. Collier
C. Craig Bradley, Jr.
Mark R. Overstreet (Frankfort, Kentucky Office)
W. Patrick Stallard
John A. Bartlett
Robert M. Connolly
John L. Tate
Jefferey M. Yussman
Joseph L. Hamilton
Janet A. Craig (Lexington, Kentucky Office)
James C. Seiffert
Gregory P. Parsons (Lexington, Kentucky Office)
Judith A. Villines (Frankfort, Kentucky Office)
Kenneth R. Sagan (Lexington, Kentucky Office)
Richard G. Griffith (Lexington, Kentucky Office)
Michael D. Risley
J. Clarke Keller (Lexington, Kentucky Office)
John P. Gallagher (P.C.) (Atlanta, Georgia Office)
William Wimberly Hopson (Atlanta, Georgia Office)
Laura D. Keller (Lexington, Kentucky Office)
James W. Taylor (Lexington, Kentucky Office)
Alex P. Herrington, Jr.
R. Daniel Douglass (P.C.) (Atlanta, Georgia Office)
Richard A. Vance
Ashley W. Ward (Lexington, Kentucky Office)
W. Bradford Boone (Lexington, Kentucky Office)
Allen L. Morris (Jeffersonville, Indiana Office)
T. Matthew Mashburn (P.C.) (Atlanta, Georgia Office)
Carol Dan Browning
Cynthia L. Coffee
Cheryl Ulene Lewis (Lexington and Hyden, Kentucky Offices)
Rebecca F. Schupbach
Lynn C. Stidham (Lexington, Kentucky Office)
William T. Gorton III (Lexington, Kentucky Office)
Shannon Antle Hamilton
Brooks D. Kubik
Kathleen O. McKune
Benjamin Lee Kessinger, III (Lexington, Kentucky Office)
T. Morgan Ward, Jr.
Lissa Wathen (Lexington, Kentucky Office)
Erica L. Horn
Brian A. Cromer
Andrew R. Jacobs (Lexington, Kentucky Office)
Brenda J. Runner
W. Thomas Halbleib, Jr.
Elizabeth Lee Thompson (Lexington, Kentucky Office)
Marc S. Murphy

Michele Whittington (Frankfort, Kentucky Office)
Don A. Pisacano (Lexington, Kentucky Office)
Catharine C. Young
Jacqueline K. Armstrong
Anne E. Gorham (Lexington, Kentucky Office)
Catherine Murr Young
Robin S. Craddock
Mauritia G. Kamer
Douglas B. Bates (Jeffersonville, Indiana Office)
Lisa M. Ramsey (Lexington, Kentucky Office)
Rebecca B. Stephenson (Lexington, Kentucky Office)
Darren J. Duzyk (Lexington, Kentucky Office)
Barry A. Hines
Cynthia S. Buttorff
Bethany A. Breetz
Matthew W. Breetz
Amanda Pope Thompson (Lexington, Kentucky Office)
Jason P. Thomas
Holly M. Everett
Jane Brannon (Lexington, Kentucky Office)
Jeffrey J. Chapuran (Lexington, Kentucky Office)
Gregory L. Davis
Marjorie A. Farris
Dustan C. McCoy (Lexington, Kentucky Office)
Nancy E. McElwain
Jennifer Robinson Proud
Angela L. Stinebruner
John Patrick Hamm
William A. Green, III
Daniel E. Danford (Lexington, Kentucky Office)
Woodrow A. Jones, Jr.
Kristin L. Ray
Tyler B. Ross
W. Blaine Early, III (Lexington, Kentucky Office)
Laura A. D'Angelo (Lexington, Kentucky Office)
C. Lewis Borders
Mark D. Fridy
Margaret Appenfelder
W. Brian Burnette (Frankfort, Kentucky Office)
Padma G. Hinrichs
T. Caice Lee (Jeffersonville, Indiana Office)

OF COUNSEL

T. Kennedy Helm, Jr.
Ralph F. Kessinger (Lexington, Kentucky Office)
James W. Stites, Jr.
Jamieson G. McPherson
Charles E. Palmer, Jr. (Lexington, Kentucky Office)

COUNSEL

Ben L. Kessinger, Jr. (Lexington, Kentucky Office)
Calvert T. Roszell (Lexington, Kentucky Office)
Lively M. Wilson
Romano L. Mazzoli
Alfred S. Joseph, III
Thomas J. Stipanowich (Lexington, Kentucky Office)
John A. Johnson
Kenneth G. Lee (Washington, D.C. Office)

(See Next Column)

COUNSEL (Continued)

Paul J. Houk
James A. Nitsche
Eric P. Sloter (Not admitted in KY)
Joseph L. Hardesty
Jennifer S. Smart (Frankfort, Kentucky Office)
Mary Gay Whitmer (Lexington, Kentucky Office)
Bryan C. Pierce

For full biographical listings, see the Martindale-Hubbell Law Directory

STITES, MCELWAIN & FOWLER

(See Stites & Harbison)

STOLL, KEENON & PARK, LLP (AV)

400 West Market Street Suite 2650, 40202-3377
Telephone: 502-568-9100
Telecopier: 502-568-5700
URL: http://www.skp.com
Frankfort, Kentucky Office: 307 Washington Street, 40601.
Telephone: 502-875-6220.
Telecopier: 502-875-6235.
Henderson, Kentucky Office: 201 C North Main Street, 42420-3103.
Telephone: 270-831-1900.
Telecopier: 270-827-4060.
Lexington, Kentucky Office: 210 E. Main Street, Suite 1000, 40507-1380.
Telephone: 606-231-3000.
Telecopier: 606-253-1093; 606-253-1380.

MEMBERS OF FIRM

Samuel D. Hinkle, IV
Robert W. Kellerman
Lea Pauley Goff
Culver V. Halliday

For full biographical listings, see the Martindale-Hubbell Law Directory

TILFORD, DOBBINS, ALEXANDER, BUCKAWAY & BLACK (AV)

Suite 1400, One Riverfront Plaza, 40202
Telephone: 502-584-6137
Fax: 502-584-2318

MEMBERS OF FIRM

Charles W. Dobbins (1916-1992)
Henry J. Tilford (1880-1968)
George S. Wetherby (1905-1954)
Lawrence W. Wetherby (1908-1994)
John T. Metcalf (1890-1974)
Stuart E. Alexander
William A. Buckaway, Jr.
Charles W. Dobbins, Jr.
Terrell L. Black
Mark Wesley Dobbins
Stuart E. Alexander, III
John M. Nader

ASSOCIATES

John A. Wilmes
Sandra F. Keene
Patrick T. Schmidt
Thomas J.B. Hurst
H. Kevin Eddins
William J. Walsh, IV
Dana M. Taylor

OF COUNSEL

Randolph Noe
Carolyn K. Balleisen
Michael G. Karem

For full biographical listings, see the Martindale-Hubbell Law Directory

WOODWARD, HOBSON & FULTON (AV)

2500 National City Tower, 101 South Fifth Street, 40202
Telephone: 502-581-8000
Fax: 502-581-8111
Email: WHF@IGLOU.COM
Lexington, Kentucky Office: PNC Bank Plaza, 200 West Vine Street, Suite 500.
Telephone: 606-244-7100.
Telecopier: 606-244-7111.

MEMBERS OF FIRM

Ernest Woodward (1877-1968)
Robert P. Hobson (1893-1966)
Will H. Fulton (1888-1953)
John P. Sandidge
Ernest Woodward II (1917-1990)
John A. Fulton (1919-1987)
Robert C. Hobson (1918-1999)
William D. Grubbs
Lionel A. Hawse (Resident, Lexington, Kentucky Office)
Harry K. Herren
Glen S. Bagby (Resident, Lexington, Kentucky Office)
David R. Monohan
Will H. Fulton
Robert L. Hallenberg
Richard H. C. Clay
Thomas A. Hoy
John F. Gleason
J. Robert Lyons, Jr. (Resident, Lexington, Kentucky Office)
J. Michael Dalton
Elizabeth Ullmer Mendel
Michael A. Luvisi
Alice Barns Herrington
Jann B. Logsdon
Linsey W. West (Resident, Lexington, Kentucky Office)
David T. Schaefer
Patrick Michael
D. Craig York
Donna King Perry

ASSOCIATES

Christopher R. Fitzpatrick
Eric M. Jensen
Bruce A. Rector (Resident, Lexington, Kentucky Office)
Kathryn A. Quesenberry
Christopher R. Cashen (Resident, Lexington, Kentucky Office)
D. Sean Nilsen
Jill F. Lowenbraun

(See Next Column)

WOODWARD, HOBSON & FULTON, *Louisville—Continued*

ASSOCIATES (Continued)

Jeffrey D. Thompson
Angela Logan Edwards
Laurie Goetz Kemp
Christopher L. Rhoads (Resident, Lexington Office)
Kristin M. Lomond
John D. Kermode (Resident, Lexington Office)
Anne W. Miller
Robert D. Walker, II
James T. Blaine Lewis
Lisa Clephas Hester
Stephen D. Weisskopf
W. William Cegelka (Resident, Lexington, Kentucky Office)
Sheila M. Donovan (Resident, Lexington, Kentucky Office)
Mary E. Schaffner
Jennifer Kincaid Adams
Alexander M. Say
Katherine A. Wolfe (Not admitted in KY)

OF COUNSEL

Fielden Woodward
Daniel N. Brock (Resident, Lexington, Kentucky Office)
Kenneth L. Anderson

Representative Clients: American Home Insurance Co.; Brown-Forman Corp.; CARITAS Health Services, Inc.; CSX Transportation, Inc.; Fischer Packing Company; Ford Motor Co.; Nationwide Insurance Co., Inc.; Ralston Purina Co.; Toyota Motor Corp.; Wal-Mart Stores, Inc.

For full biographical listings, see the Martindale-Hubbell Law Directory

WYATT, TARRANT & COMBS (AV)

Citizens Plaza, 40202-2898
Telephone: 502-589-5235
Telecopier: 502-589-0309
URL: http://www.wyattfirm.com
Lexington, Kentucky Office: 1700 Lexington Financial Center.
Telephone: 606-233-2012.
Telecopier: 606-259-0649.
Frankfort, Kentucky Office: The Taylor-Scott Building, 311 West Main Street.
Telephone: 502-223-2104.
Telecopier: 502-227-7681.
New Albany, Indiana Office: The Elsby Building, 117 East Spring Street,
Telephone: 812-945-3561.
Telecopier: 812-949-2524.
Memphis, Tennessee Office: Crescent Center, Suite 650, 6075 Poplar Avenue.
Telephone: 901-537-1000.
Telecopier: 901-537-1010.
Nashville, Tennessee Office: 1500 Nashville City Center, 511 Union Street.
Telephone: 615-244-0020.
Telecopier: 615-256-1726.
Music Row, Nashville Office: 29 Music Square East.
Telephone: 615-255-6161.
Telecopier: 615-254-4490.
Hendersonville, Tennessee Office: 313 E. Main Street, Suite 1.
Telephone: 615-822-8822.
Telecopier: 615-824-4684.
Tri-Cities, Tennessee Office: Northeast Tennessee Business Park, 10368 Wallace Alley Street, Suite 6, Kingsport.
Telephone: 423-279-1825.
Telecopier: 423-279-9357.

MEMBERS OF FIRM

Wilson W. Wyatt, Sr. (1905-1996)
John E. Tarrant (1898-1990)
Bert T. Combs (1911-1991)
Telford B. Orbison (1901-1990)
Richard C. O'Connor (1918-1997)
Stuart E. Lampe (1906-1994)
John S. Osborn, Jr.
Robert L. Maddox
Edgar A. Zingman
Lawrence L. Jones, III
Richard W. Iler
Russell H. Riggs
Robert C. Ewald
A. Wallace Grafton, Jr.
Samuel G. Bridge, Jr.
H. Alexander Campbell
Stewart E. Conner
R. Lawrence Baird
J. Larry Cashen
Parker W. Duncan, Jr.
Martin Rockwell
Robert I. Cusick
Edwin S. Hopson
Grover C. Potts, Jr.
John P. Reisz
K. Gregory Haynes
M. Stephen Pitt
Stephen D. Berger
Francis J. Mellen, Jr.
Martin P. Duffy
Walter M. Jones
Michael B. Vincenti
Mark C. Blackwell
Frank F. Chuppe, Jr.
Thomas J. Luber
Allison Joseph Maggiolo
Richard Northern
Merrill S. Schell
Kevin J. Hable
J. Michael Brown
Paul J. Cox
G. Alexander Hamilton
Patrick W. Mattingly
Parker W. Eads
David W. Seewer
Virginia Hamilton Snell
Arthur Adams Rouse
Gordon B. Wright
Cynthia W. Young
Byron E. Leet
Caryn F. Price
Leo F. Camp
J. Anthony Goebel
Robert A. Heath
William H. Hollander
Michael K. Kirk
Joan Lloyd Cooper
Stephen R. Price, Sr.
Mark A. Robinson
Rita L. Fadell
Norman W. Graham
Michelle Turner
Cornelius E. Coryell, II
Clinton J Elliott
Jeffrey E. Wallace
Carole Douglas Christian

(See Next Column)

MEMBERS OF FIRM (Continued)

Denise St. Clair Kaiser
Donald J. Kelly
Jean W. Bird
Barbara Wetzel Gernert

ASSOCIATES

Jane C. Fousheé
Clara M. Passafiume
Franklin K. Jelsma
Kevin P. Crooks
Cynthia Blevins Doll
Paul J. Dyar
Timothy G. Hatfield
Deborah H. Patterson
Steven L. Snyder
Michelle D. Wyrick
Mitzi D. Wyrick
Gregory S. Berman
Myka L. Hopgood
Bobby C. Simpson
Sandra Hinojosa Hubbard
Laura Hodges Theilmann
Daniel G. Brown
David E. Saffer
Dana Cosby Williams
Kenneth W. Brown
David A. Calhoun
Courtney Townes Good
C. Tyson Gorman
Gordon A. Rowe, Jr.
Pamela J. Ledford
Rick G. Alsip
Wendi Johnson
Angela C. McCorkle
Jennifer R. Rawert
Kenneth Todd Veirs

COUNSEL

Frank W. Burke, Sr.
Martin R. Snyder
Douglas W. Becker
Karen L. Hale

OF COUNSEL

Gordon B. Davidson

Representative Clients: Ashland Inc.; Churchill Downs, Inc.; E.I. du Pont de Nemours and Company; Ford Motor Co.; General Electric Co.; Henry Vogt Machine Co.; Norton Healthcare, Inc.; PNC Bank, National Association; United Catalysts Inc.

For full biographical listings, see the Martindale-Hubbell Law Directory

*MANCHESTER,** Clay Co.

LAW FIRM OF NEVILLE SMITH (AV)

110 Lawyer Street, P.O. Box 447, 40962
Telephone: 606-598-2113
Fax: 606-598-8029

MEMBERS OF FIRM

Chas. C. Smith (1903-1975)
Neville Smith
Harold Rader

Counsel for: Red Bird Hospital; Clay County Board of Education; Mid South Electrics, Inc.; Elk River Resources, Inc.
Local Counsel for: Kentucky Farm Bureau Insurance Cos.
Approved Attorneys for: Louisville Title Division of Commonwealth Land Title Insurance Co.; Title Insurance Company of Minnesota.

For full biographical listings, see the Martindale-Hubbell Law Directory

*MOUNT VERNON,** Rockcastle Co.

CLONTZ & COX (AV)

Courthouse, 115 Richmond, P.O. Box 1350, 40456
Telephone: 606-256-5111
Fax: 606-256-2036

MEMBERS OF FIRM

Carl R. Clontz
Jerry J. Cox
John E. Clontz

ASSOCIATES

Jerome S. Fish, II

Representative Clients: The Bank of Mt. Vernon; Citizens Bank, Brodhead, Kentucky; Kentucky Farm Bureau Mutual Insurance Co.; Louisville Title Division of Commonwealth Land Title Insurance Co.
Reference: The Bank of Mt. Vernon, Mt. Vernon, Kentucky.

For full biographical listings, see the Martindale-Hubbell Law Directory

*MURRAY,** Calloway Co.

GREGORY, EASLEY AND COURTNEY (AV)

204 South Sixth Street, P.O. Box 230, 42071
Telephone: 502-753-2633
Fax: 502-753-1825

MEMBERS OF FIRM

Nat R. Hughes (1906-1981)
John A. Gregory, Jr.
R. Sidney Easley
Dennis J. Courtney

Representative Clients: Kentucky Farm Bureau Mutual Insurance Co.; State Farm Mutual Automobile Insurance; R. T. Vanderbilt Co.; Briggs and Stratton Corp.; State Auto Insurance; Meridian Insurance Co.; Peoples Bank of Murray; Murray State University Credit Union.

For full biographical listings, see the Martindale-Hubbell Law Directory

*OWENSBORO,** Daviess Co.

McCARROLL, NUNLEY & HARTZ (AV)

111 East Third Street, P.O. Box 925, 42302-0925
Telephone: 502-683-3535
FAX: 502-926-6056

(See Next Column)

McCarroll, Nunley & Hartz—*Continued*

MEMBERS OF FIRM

Clarence McCarroll (1916-1989)
Marvin P. Nunley
Max S. Hartz

Representative Clients: Aetna Casualty & Surety Company; Allstate Insurance Company; American Hardware Mutual Insurance Company; American Motorists Insurance Company; Automobile Club Insurance Company; Celina Mutual Insurance Company; Chubb Group of Insurance Companies; CIGNA Insurance Companies; Citizens Insurance Company of America; CNA Insurance Company.

For full biographical listings, see the Martindale-Hubbell Law Directory

Sheffer • Hutchinson • Kinney (AV)

115 East Second Street, 42301
Telephone: 270-684-3700
Telecopier: 270-684-3881
URL: http://www.kylaw.com
Bowling Green, Kentucky Office: Fountain Square, 400 E. Main Street, Suite 300.
Telephone: 270-745-0000.
Telecopier: 270-842-9399.
Evansville, Indiana Office: One Riverfront Place, 20 N.W. First Street, Suite 700.
Telephone: 812-425-5200.
Telecopier: 812-425-2464.
Frankfort, Kentucky Office: 124 West Todd Street.
Telephone: 502-227-1500.
Telecopier: 502-875-7059.
Henderson, Kentucky Office: 145 North Main Street.
Telephone: 270-826-3300.
Telecopier: 270-827-5070.
Lexington, Kentucky Office: 250 West Main Street, Suite 1810.
Telephone: 606-381-1250.
Telecopier: 606-381-8250.
Louisville, Kentucky Office: 1600 National City Tower, 101 South Fifth Street.
Telephone: 502-582-1600.
Telecopier: 502-582-1193.
Paducah, Kentucky Office: Citizens Bank Building, 333 Broadway, Suite 1001.
Telephone: 270-443-9401.
Telecopier: 270-443-3624.

MEMBERS OF FIRM

Ronald G. Sheffer
Mark R. Hutchinson (Resident)
Peter B. Lewis (Resident)
Howard E. Frasier, Jr. (Resident, Bowling Green Office)
John A. Sheffer (Resident)
Christopher C. Wischer
Anne D. Watkins
Melanie Ann Kennedy

OF COUNSEL

Robert A. Marshall

For full biographical listings, see the Martindale-Hubbell Law Directory

*PADUCAH,** McCracken Co.

Boehl Stopher & Graves (AV)

Suite 340 Executive Inn Riverfront, One Executive Boulevard, 42001
Telephone: 270-442-4369
FAX: 270-442-4689
Louisville, Kentucky Office: Aegon Center, Suite 2300, 400 West Market Street.
Telephone: 502-589-5980.
Fax: 502-561-9400.
Lexington, Kentucky Office: 444 West Second Street.
Telephone: 606-252-6721.
Fax: 606-253-1445.
Prestonsburg, Kentucky Office: 105 West Court Street.
Telephone: 606-886-8004.
Fax: 606-886-9579.
New Albany, Indiana Office: Elsby East, Suite 204, 400 Pearl Street.
Telephone: 812-948-5053.
Fax: 812-948-9233.

RESIDENT OF COUNSEL

George R. Effinger

RESIDENT PARTNERS

Richard L. Walter
Charles D. Walter
Daniel S. Stratemeyer

Counsel for: Ford Motor Co.; Texas Eastern Transmission Corp.; Coca-Cola Bottling Co.; National Collegiate Athletic Assn.; Hartford Accident and Indemnity Co.; Continental Insurance Group; St. Paul Fire & Marine Insurance Co.; Lloyds of London; Old Republic Insurance Co.

For full biographical listings, see the Martindale-Hubbell Law Directory

Denton & Keuler (AV)

Paducah Bank & Trust Company Building, 555 Jefferson Street, P.O. Box 929, 42001
Telephone: 502-443-8253
Fax: 502-442-6000
Email: dk@dklaw.com *URL:* http://www.dklaw.com

MEMBERS OF FIRM

W. David Denton
Thomas J. Keuler
William E. Pinkston
Lisa Hayden Emmons
David L. Kelly
Theodore S. Hutchins

ASSOCIATES

Glenn D. Denton
Stacey Ann Blankenship
Joanne M. Talbott

OF COUNSEL

Samuel Carlick

LEGAL SUPPORT PERSONNEL

PARALEGALS

Janet S. Burnett CPS
Douglas W. Painter
Sonja F. Skibinski
Samuel P. Watson

Reference: The Paducah Bank & Trust Co.

For full biographical listings, see the Martindale-Hubbell Law Directory

McMurry & Livingston (AV)

7th Floor, Citizens Bank Building, 333 Broadway, P.O. Box 1700, 42002-1700
Telephone: 502-443-6511
Telefax: 502-443-6548
Email: mcmurry@vci.net

W. Pelham McMurry
W. Fletcher McMurry Schrock
David C. Booth
Stephen E. Smith, Jr.
Phillip L. Little
G. Kent Price
Kerry D. Smith

ASSOCIATES

Julie Howard Price

OF COUNSEL

Milton M. Livingston, Jr.

Counsel for: Citizens Bank & Trust Co. of Paducah; Paducah Power System.
Representative Clients: Reliance Insurance Co.; Home Insurance Co.; Lowes Companies, Inc.

For full biographical listings, see the Martindale-Hubbell Law Directory

Sheffer • Hutchinson • Kinney (AV)

Citizens Bank Building, 333 Broadway, Suite 1001, 42001
Telephone: 270-443-9401
Telecopier: 270-443-3624
URL: http://www.kylaw.com
Bowling Green, Kentucky Office: Fountain Square, 400 E. Main Street, Suite 300.
Telephone: 270-745-0000.
Telecopier: 270-842-9399.
Evansville, Indiana Office: One Riverfront Place, 20 N.W. First Street, Suite 700.
Telephone: 812-425-5200.
Telecopier: 812-425-2464.
Frankfort, Kentucky Office: 124 West Todd Street.
Telephone: 502-227-1500.
Telecopier: 502-875-7059.
Henderson, Kentucky Office: 145 North Main Street.
Telephone: 270-826-3300.
Telecopier: 270-827-5070.
Lexington, Kentucky Office: 250 West Main Street, Suite 1810.
Telephone: 606-381-1250.
Telecopier: 606-381-8250.
Louisville, Kentucky Office: 1600 National City Tower, 101 South Fifth Street.
Telephone: 502-582-1600.
Telecopier: 502-582-1193.
Owensboro, Kentucky Office: 115 E. Second Street.
Telephone: 270-684-3700.
Telecopier: 270-684-3881.

MEMBERS OF FIRM

Ronald G. Sheffer
Burke B. Terrell
James A. Sigler
C. Thomas Miller (Resident, Louisville Office)
Scott A. Hoover
Amy Jo Harwood

OF COUNSEL

Robert A. Marshall

For full biographical listings, see the Martindale-Hubbell Law Directory

*PAINTSVILLE,** Johnson Co.

WELLS, PORTER, SCHMITT & JONES (AV)

327 Main Street, 41240
Telephone: 606-789-3747; 789-3749; 789-3775
Fax: 606-789-3790
URL: http://www.wpsj.com

MEMBERS OF FIRM

John V. Porter, Jr.
Michael J. Schmitt
Donald L. Jones

ASSOCIATES

Johnny L. Griffith
Kimberly E. Colley
Darrin W. Banks
Jeffrey M. Baldwin
Johnny Ray Harris

LEGAL SUPPORT PERSONNEL

Crystal Tucker
Tamara R. McMonigle (Paralegal)

Representative Clients: Columbia Gas Transmission Corp.; Columbia Gas of Kentucky; C. & O. Railway Co.; Ashland Oil, Inc.; Travelers Insurance Co.; United States Fidelity & Guaranty Co.; Fireman's Fund-American Insurance Co.

For full biographical listings, see the Martindale-Hubbell Law Directory

*PIKEVILLE,** Pike Co.

BAIRD, BAIRD, BAIRD AND JONES, P.S.C. (AV)

415 Second Street, P.O. Box 351, 41502
Telephone: 606-437-6276
Fax: 606-437-6383
Lexington, Kentucky Office: 841 Corporate Drive, Suite 101, 40503.
Telephone: 606-224-7750.
Fax: 606-224-1031.

William J. Baird (1913-1987)
William J. Baird, III
John H. Baird
Charles J. Baird
Paul Edward Jones
James B. Ratliff
Russell H. Davis, Jr.
Billy R. Shelton
Sam A. Carter
Lois A. Kitts
Virginia Baird Gannon
M. Kathryn Manis

Representative Clients: James River Coal Co.; American International Companies; Old Republic Insurance Co.; Pittston Coal Group; Community Trust Bancorp, Inc.; Accordia; AT Massey Coal Co., Inc.; Teco Coal Corp.; Kentucky Farm Bureau Mutual Insurance Co.; GAB, Business's Services, Inc.
Approved Attorneys for: Lawyers Title Insurance Corp.

For full biographical listings, see the Martindale-Hubbell Law Directory

*PRESTONSBURG,** Floyd Co.

KAZEE, KINNER & CHAFIN (AV)

119 East Court Street, P.O. Box 700, 41653
Telephone: 606-886-2361; 886-2362
FAX: 606-886-9603
Email: dbkazee@pcc-uky.campus.mci.net
Paintsville, Kentucky Office: Family Federal Building, Suite 202, P.O. Box 1275.
Telephone: 606-789-3059.

MEMBERS OF FIRM

D. B. Kazee
Mitchell D. Kinner
John T. Chafin
P. Franklin Heaberlin
Robert J. Patton
William C. Mullins

Representative Clients: Island Creek Coal Co.; The Elk Horn Coal Corp.; First Commonwealth Bank; Old Republic Insurance Co.; Zurich American Insurance Co.; Maryland Casualty Co.; Bituminous Casualty Corp.; Mack Financial Corp.; Nationwide Insurance; Kentucky May Coal Co., Inc.

For full biographical listings, see the Martindale-Hubbell Law Directory

*RICHMOND,** Madison Co.

COY, GILBERT & GILBERT (AV)

212 North Second Street, P.O. Box 1178, 40476-1178
Telephone: 606-623-3877
Fax: 606-624-5435
Email: cgg@mail.iclub.org *URL:* http://www.lawyers.com/cgglawfirm

MEMBERS OF FIRM

Charles R. Coy
James T. Gilbert
Jerry W. Gilbert
Mark A. Shepherd

General Counsel: Peoples Bank and Trust Co. of Madison County.

For full biographical listings, see the Martindale-Hubbell Law Directory

*SOMERSET,** Pulaski Co.

THE FIRM OF JOHN G. PRATHER (AV)

48 Public Square, P.O. Box 616, 42502-0616
Telephone: 606-679-1626; 679-4838; 678-5604
Fax: 606-679-8204
Email: pratherlaw@som-uky.campuscwix.net

MEMBERS OF FIRM

John G. Prather
John G. Prather, Jr.
Winter R. Huff (Ms.)

ASSOCIATE

Michelle Ross Altobella

Representative Clients: First & Farmers Bank of Somerset; Sentry-Dairyland Insurance; Hartford Accident & Indemnity; Cracker Barrel Old Country Store, Inc.; Somerset Independent Board of Education; Kentucky School Boards Insurance Trust; Kentucky Medical Insurance Company; Southern Belle Dairy; Norfolk Southern Railway; FDIC.

For full biographical listings, see the Martindale-Hubbell Law Directory

LOUISIANA

*ABBEVILLE,** Vermilion Parish

COOPER & WOODRUFF, A LAW CORPORATION (AV)

121 East St. Victor Street, P.O. Box 1213, 70510
Telephone: 318-893-8810
Fax: 318-893-9872
Email: coopwood@acadian.net

Silas B. Cooper, Jr.
Calvin E. Woodruff, Jr.
Carl W. Robicheaux

Representative Clients: Vermilion Bank & Trust Co., Kaplan, La.; First Commercial Bank of Abbeville; South Central Bell Telephone Co.; City of Kaplan; State Farm Insurance Co.; The Travelers Insurance Co.; United States Fidelity & Guaranty Co.; The Rice Millers Assn. (U.S.A.); National Audubon Society (Rainey Sanctuary); Liberty Rice Mill.

For full biographical listings, see the Martindale-Hubbell Law Directory

*ALEXANDRIA,** Rapides Parish

GOLD, WEEMS, BRUSER, SUES & RUNDELL, A PROFESSIONAL LAW CORPORATION (AV)

2001 MacArthur Drive, P.O. Box 6118, 71307-6118
Telephone: 318-445-6471
Facsimile: 318-445-6476

Leo Gold (1907-1987)
George B. Hall (1924-1971)
Charles S. Weems, III
Henry B. Bruser, III
Eugene J. Sues
Edward E. Rundell
Robert G. Nida
Dee D. Drell
Sam N. Poole, Jr.
Peggy Dean St. John
Kenneth O. Ortego
Raymond L. Brown, Jr.
James Ogden Middleton, II
Randall L. Wilmore
Dorrell J. Brister
Gregory B. Upton
Randall M. Seeser
J. Kendall Rathburn
Charles D. Elliott
G. Trippe Hawthorne
John J. Zachary
Amanda Wood Barnett
Rebecca Alexander
E. June Wells-Foster
Valerie Martinez Thompson
Michael J. O'Shee
R. Steven Calhoun

OF COUNSEL

Camille F. Gravel

Representative Clients: Automated Prescription Systems, Inc.; Roy O. Martin Lumber Co., Inc.; Rapides Bank & Trust Company in Alexandria; Aetna Casualty Group; Allstate Insurance Co.; Texas Industries, Inc.; International Paper Company; Louisiana-Pacific Corporation.

For full biographical listings, see the Martindale-Hubbell Law Directory

*BATON ROUGE,** East Baton Rouge Parish

BREAZEALE, SACHSE & WILSON, L.L.P. (AV)

Twenty-Third Floor, One American Place, P.O. Box 3197, 70821-3197
Telephone: 225-387-4000
Fax: 225-387-5397
URL: http://www.bswllp.com
New Orleans, Louisiana Office: LL&E Tower, Suite 1500, 909 Poydras Street.
Telephone: 504-584-5454.
Fax: 504-584-5452.
Covington, Louisiana Office: 2255 Highway 190 North, Suite 200.
Telephone: 504-871-9444.
Fax: 504-871-9666.

(See Next Column)

BREAZEALE, SACHSE & WILSON L.L.P.—*Continued*

MEMBERS OF FIRM

H. Payne Breazeale (1886-1990)
Victor A. Sachse, Jr. (1903-1979)
Maurice J. Wilson (1919-1990)
H. Payne Breazeale, Jr. (1920-1979)
Gordon A. Pugh
James E. Toups, Jr.
Paul M. Hebert, Jr.
Van R. Mayhall, Jr.
Leonard R. Nachman, II
Claude F. Reynaud, Jr.
Murphy J. Foster, III
David R. Cassidy
Robert T. Bowsher
Christine Lipsey
David R. Kelly
Robert L. Atkinson
David M. Charlton
Douglas K. Williams
Stephen F. Chiccarelli
Emile C. Rolfs, III
John E. Heinrich
Richard D. Leibowitz
Michael R. Hubbell
John W. Barton, Jr.
Jude C. Bursavich
Joseph E. Friend (Resident, New Orleans Office)
Peter J. Butler, Jr. (Resident, New Orleans Office)
Steven B. Loeb
James R. Chastain, Jr.
Frank S. Craig, III
L. Linton Morgan (Resident, Covington Office)
Michael R. Marget (Not admitted in LA)
Deborah Duplechin Harkins
Leo C. Hamilton
J. Mark Robinson
Linda Perez Clark
Trenton J. Oubre
Jerry L. Stovall, Jr.
Luis A. Leitzelar
James R. Austin
Richard G. Passler (Resident, New Orleans Office)
W. Christopher Beary (Resident, New Orleans Office)
James L. Williams, IV (Resident, Covington Office)
Warner J. Delaune, Jr.

ASSOCIATES

Jeanne C. Comeaux
Michael A. Crawford
Stephen R. Whalen
Andrew T. McMains
Cullen J. Dupuy
Joseph P. Titone
Juliet T. Rizzo
Michael C. Luquet (Resident, New Orleans Office)
David C. Voss
Ralph T. Rabalais (Resident, New Orleans Office)
W. Brett Mason
Donna Bramlett Wood
R. Charles Ellis
Cynthia Doiron Pugh
Rajini Sharma
Walter R. Wellenreiter (Resident, New Orleans Office)
Scott N. Hensgens
Melissa M. Shirley
J. Alan Harrell
Lance J. Kinchen
William Bowen McRae, Jr.
A. Todd Caruso
Tara L. Foto (Resident, New Orleans Office)
Martin L. Morgan (Resident, Covington Office)
Ben B. Hu
Thomas R. Temple, Jr.

OF COUNSEL

Victor A. Sachse, III
Gary L. Laborde

SPECIAL COUNSEL

Peter J. Butler (Resident, New Orleans Office)
Robert W. Fenet

Counsel for: Allied-Signal Corp.; Reynolds Metal Co.; Illinois Central Railroad Co.

For full biographical listings, see the Martindale-Hubbell Law Directory

KANTROW, SPAHT, WEAVER & BLITZER, A PROFESSIONAL LAW CORPORATION (AV)

Suite 300, City Plaza, 445 North Boulevard, P.O. Box 2997, 70821-2997
Telephone: 225-383-4703
Fax: 225-343-0630; 343-0637

Byron R. Kantrow (1909-1997)
Carlos G. Spaht
Geraldine B. Weaver
Sidney M. Blitzer, Jr.
Paul H. Spaht
Lee C. Kantrow
John C. Miller
Vincent P. Fornias
David S. Rubin
Diane L. Crochet
Richard F. Zimmerman, Jr.
Bob D. Tucker
Martin E. Golden
J. Michael Robinson, Jr.
Connell L. Archey
Randal J. Robert

C. William Belsom, Jr.
Linda Orlansky Posner

Representative Clients: CNA Insurance Cos.; Federal Deposit Insurance Corp.; Hartford Insurance Group; Air Products and Chemicals, Inc.; CF Industries, Inc.; AT&T; United Companies Financial Corp.

For full biographical listings, see the Martindale-Hubbell Law Directory

PHELPS DUNBAR, L.L.P. (AV)

Suite 701, 445 North Boulevard, P.O. Box 4412, 70821-4412
Telephone: 225-346-0285
Telecopier: 225-381-9197
Email: info@phelps.com
New Orleans, Louisiana Office: Texaco Center, 400 Poydras Street.
Telephone 504-566-1311.
Telecopier: 504-568-9130; 504-568-9007.
Cable Address: "Howspencer."
Telex: 584125 WU.
Telex: 6821155 WUI.

(See Next Column)

Jackson, Mississippi Office: Suite 500, SkyTel Centre, 200 South Lamar Street, P.O. Box 23066.
Telephone: 601-352-2300.
Telecopier: 601-360-9777.
Tupelo, Mississippi Office: Seventh Floor, One Mississippi Plaza, P.O. Box 1220.
Telephone: 662-842-7907.
Telecopier: 662-842-3873.
Houston, Texas Office: Suite 900, 3040 Post Oak Boulevard.
Telephone: 713-626-1386.
Telecopier: 713-626-1388.
London, England Office: Suite 731, Level 7, Lloyd's, 1 Lime Street, London EC3M 7DQ England.
Telephone: 011-44-207-929-4765.
Telecopier: 011-44-207-929-0046.
Telex: 987321.

OF COUNSEL

Frank S. Craig, Jr.

RESIDENT PARTNERS

Jonathan C. Benda
Allen D. Darden
Susan W. Furr
Michael D. Hunt
H. Alston Johnson, III
F. Scott Kaiser
Thomas H. Kiggans
Steven J. Levine
Richard E. Matheny
Freddie Pitcher, Jr.
Marshall M. Redmon (Also at London, England Office)
Randy P. Roussel

COUNSEL

J. Michael Cutshaw
Jane A. Robert

RESIDENT ASSOCIATES

Jeffrey M. Barbin
Jane H. Barney
Rebecca Bellows Crawford
Christine S. Goldberg
Gwen P. Harmon
Kimberly L. Hood
Clinton D. Howie
Karleen Joseph
Kelsey B. Kornick
Patrick O'Hara
Rebecca Fariss Penniman
Patrick Ragan Richard
William S. Robbins
Clinton Ryan Stuart
Virginia Yoder Trainor

Representative Clients: Bank One; Great Southern Life Insurance Company; Hibernia National Bank; Louisiana Companies; Louisiana Farm Bureau Casualty Company; Louisiana Lottery Corporation; Louisiana Public Facilities Authority; Louisiana Workers' Compensation Corporation; Union Pacific Railroad Company; Uniroyal Chemical Company.

For full biographical listings, see the Martindale-Hubbell Law Directory

POWERS & WILLARD, L.L.P. (AV)

7967 Office Park Boulevard, P.O. Box 15948, 70895
Telephone: 225-928-1951
Fax: 225-929-9834

MEMBERS OF FIRM

John Dale Powers
William E. Willard

ASSOCIATES

Neil H. Mixon
Lindsey J. Leavoy
Edwin L. Hightower
Andrew P. Sellers, Jr.
Suzanne K. Sasser
Kyle C. Marionneaux

General Counsel for: Audubon Insurance Co.
Louisiana Counsel for: Hancock Bank & Trust Co.; Hertz Corp.; Ciba-Geigy Corp.; Utica Mutual Insurance Co.

For full biographical listings, see the Martindale-Hubbell Law Directory

TAYLOR, PORTER, BROOKS & PHILLIPS, L.L.P. (AV)

Bank One Centre, 8th Floor, 451 Florida Street, P.O. Box 2471, 70821
Telephone: 225-387-3221
Telecopier: 225-346-8049
New Orleans, Louisiana Office: Pan-American Life Center, 601 Poydras Street, Suite 2655.
Telephone: 504-524-1956.
Fax: 504-522-1810.

William H. McClendon, III
William Shelby McKenzie
John S. Campbell, Jr.
Robert H. Hodges
John R. Tharp
W. Luther Wilson
Gerald L. Walter, Jr.
J. Clayton Johnson
G. Michael Pharis
Eugene R. Groves
A. Michael Dufilho
W. Arthur Abercrombie, Jr.
Fredrick R. Tulley
Vernon P. Middleton
James L. Ellis
John Michael Parker
Nancy C. Dougherty
Mary E. Tharp
J. Ashley Moore
Edwin W. Fleshman
Vicki M. Crochet
Harry J. ("Skip") Philips, Jr.
Lloyd J. Lunceford
Thomas R. Peak
C. Michael Hart
John F. McDermott
Brett P. Furr
M. Lenore Feeney
Marc S. Whitfield
John H. Runnels
David J. Messina (Resident, New Orleans Office)
Gregory E. Bodin
James C. Carver
Margaret L. Tooke
Deborah E. Lamb
T. MacDougall Womack
David M. Bienvenu, Jr.

(See Next Column)

TAYLOR, PORTER, BROOKS & PHILLIPS L.L.P., *Baton Rouge—Continued*

Matthew J. Randazzo, III (Resident, New Orleans Office)
Kathleen C. Mason
David J. Shelby, II
Erick Y. Miyagi
William E. Hodgkins
Anne J. Crochet
Jayne L. Middleton
Robert W. Barton
Preston J. Castille, Jr.
Eleanor Owen Kerr
John Stewart Tharp
John S. Campbell, III
John P. Murrill
Bonnie J. Davis
Mary Dougherty Jackson
Andree Matherne Cullens (Resident, New Orleans Office)
Brandon K. Black
Amy Groves Lowe
Katherine B. Muslow (Resident, New Orleans Office)
Wm. Alan Miller
John B. Noland, Jr
Todd S. Manuel
Phillip E. Foco
Timothy J. Poché

OF COUNSEL

Tom F. Phillips
Frank M. Coates, Jr.
John L. Glover
William A. Norfolk

General Counsel for: Baton Rouge Water Works Company; Capital City Press; Hollingsworth-Richards Automobile Group; Louisiana Home Builders Self Insurers Fund; Louisiana State University and A. and M. College; Louisiana Television Broadcasting Co.; Pennington Biomedical Research Foundation; Stanocola Medical Center; The Newton Group, Inc.

For full biographical listings, see the Martindale-Hubbell Law Directory

*CROWLEY,** Acadia Parish

BAROUSSE & CRATON (AV)

211 North Parkerson Avenue, P.O. Drawer 1305, 70527-1305
Telephone: 318-785-1000
Facsimile: 318-785-2000
Email: barcra@juno.com

MEMBERS OF FIRM

Homer Ed Barousse, Jr.
John F. Craton

Representative Clients: First Bank, N.A. of Crowley and Lake Charles; Francis Drilling Fluids, Ltd.; Farm Credit Bank of Texas; First South Production Credit Association; J.I. Case Credit Corporation; Louisiana Sheriffs' Association; Broussard Rice Mill, Inc.; Mermentau River Harbor and Terminal District; Farm Service Agency.

For full biographical listings, see the Martindale-Hubbell Law Directory

*FRANKLIN,** St. Mary Parish

AYCOCK, HORNE & COLEMAN (AV)

519 Main Street, P.O. Box 592, 70538
Telephone: 318-828-1880
Fax: 318-828-2232
Morgan City, Louisiana Office: 1304 Victor II Boulevard, P.O. Box 1700.
Telephone: 504-384-4523.

MEMBERS OF FIRM

Clarence C. Aycock (1916-1987)
John E. Coleman, Jr.
James R. McClelland
Andrew Reed

ASSOCIATE

Margaret E. Judice

OF COUNSEL

Tom Lee Horne, Jr.

Representative Clients: St. Mary Bank & Trust Co.; M.C. Bank & Trust Co.; South Central Bell Telephone Co.; Cotten Land Corp.; Bayou Bouillon Corp.; St. Mary Galvanizing Corp.; St. Mary Parish Government; City of Franklin.

For full biographical listings, see the Martindale-Hubbell Law Directory

HAMMOND, Tangipahoa Parish

CURET & BARRON (AV)

106 North Oak Street, 70401
Telephone: 504-345-1820
Fax: 504-345-6563

Ronald A. Curet
Sharon B. Barron

General Counsel for: Hancock Bank of Louisiana.

*LAFAYETTE,** Lafayette Parish

DAVIDSON, MEAUX, SONNIER, MCELLIGOTT & SWIFT (AV)

810 South Buchanan Street, P.O. Drawer 2908, 70502
Telephone: 318-237-1660
Fax: 318-237-3676

MEMBERS OF FIRM

James J. Davidson, Jr. (1904-1990)
V. Farley Sonnier (1942-1988)
Richard C. Meaux, Sr.
James J. Davidson, III
John E. McElligott, Jr.
John G. Swift
Jeffrey A. Rhoades
Philip A. Fontenot
Kyle L. Gideon
Theodore G. Edwards, IV
Mark C. Andrus

(See Next Column)

ASSOCIATES

John T. Andrishok
Christopher J. Piasecki
Nicholas J. Zeringue

OF COUNSEL

Jan Whitehead Swift

General Counsel: Southwest Louisiana Electric Membership Corp., Inc.; Macro Oil Co., Inc.; Dwight W. Andrus Insurance Agency; Lafayette Airport Commission.
Local Counsel: Southern Pacific Transportation Co.
Representative Clients: Highlands Insurance Co.; Wal-Mart Stores, Inc.; USAA.

For full biographical listings, see the Martindale-Hubbell Law Directory

ONEBANE, BERNARD, TORIAN, DIAZ, MCNAMARA & ABELL (AV)

Suite 600, Versailles Centre, 102 Versailles Boulevard, P.O. Box 3507, 70502
Telephone: 318-237-2660
Telecopier: 318-266-1232
Email: info@onebane.com
Monroe, Louisiana Office: 1900 N. 18th Street, Suite 420, P.O. Box 2255, 71207.
Telephone: 318-340-0220.
Fax: 318-340-0110.

Joseph Onebane (1917-1987)
John G. Torian, II (1936-1991)
James E. Diaz
Timothy J. McNamara
Edward C. Abell, Jr.
Lawrence L. Lewis, III
Robert M. Mahony
Daniel G. Fournerat
Douglas W. Truxillo
Randall C. Songy
Michael G. Durand
Greg Guidry
Joseph L. Lemoine, Jr.
Mark L. Riley
Graham N. Smith
Gordon T. Whitman
Gary P. Kraus
Richard J. Petre, Jr.
Charles J. Boudreaux, Jr.
James R. Shelton
Thomas G. Smart
Roger E. Ishee
Jennifer M. Kleinpeter
Steven C. Lanza
Joel P. Babineaux

Alison M. Brumley
Jesse D. Lambert
Brent G. Sonnier
Cary B. Bryson
Maria F. Manuel
Greg R. Mier
Jennifer L. Smith
Janice Church Reeves
Mark B. Oliver
Chanelle T. Delahoussaye
Aimee L. Williams
A.G. "Alec" Alexander, III
Terry J. Blanchard
William E. Bourgeois (Resident, Monroe, Louisiana Office)

OF COUNSEL

William E. Kellner

Representative Clients: Commercial Union Insurance Co.; Enron Corp.; First National Bank of Lafayette; Highlands Insurance Co.; Marathon Oil Co.; Ocean Energy, Inc.; Pizza Hut, Inc.; Schering-Plough Corp.; Tenneco, Inc.; Whitney National Bank.

For full biographical listings, see the Martindale-Hubbell Law Directory

PREIS KRAFT & ROY, A PROFESSIONAL LAW CORPORATION (AV)

Suite 400, Versailles CentrÉ, 102 Versailles Boulevard, P.O. Drawer 94-C, 70509
Telephone: 318-237-6062
Fax: 318-237-9129
Email: pkr@pkrlaw.com
NewOrleans Office: Pan American Life Center, 601 Poydras Street, Suite 1855.
Telephone: 504-581-6062.
Fax: 504-522-9129.
Houston, Texas Office: 520 Post Oak Boulevard, Suite 800.
Telephone: 713-355-6062.
Telefax: 713-572-9129.

Edwin G. Preis, Jr.
Ralph E. Kraft
L. Lane Roy
Ward F. Lafleur
F. Douglas Gatz, Jr.
Charles A. Mouton
Kay A. Theunissen
Jennifer E. Beyer
Richard J. Hymel
George Caflisch (Not admitted in LA; Resident, Houston, Texas Office)

David R. Rabalais
Marc D. Moroux
Edward King Alexander, Jr.
G. Edward Williams, Jr.
Timothy W. Basden
Larry A. Wallace, Jr.
L. Marika Steele
Jeff R. Rytlewski
Angella R. Hebert
Alison Ann Darsey
Jean Ann Billeaud

Approved Counsel for: American Gulf Group; American International Group; American Oilfield Divers, Inc.; American P & I Club; American United Life Insurance Company; Association of Diving Contractors, Inc.; Assuranceforeningen Gard; Assuranceforeningen Skuld, Automation Communica-

(See Next Column)

PREIS KRAFT & ROY A PROFESSIONAL LAW CORPORATION—*Continued*

tion Engineering Corporation; Cal Dive International, Inc.; CBI Industries, Inc.

For full biographical listings, see the Martindale-Hubbell Law Directory

*LAKE CHARLES,** Calcasieu Parish

BERGSTEDT & MOUNT (AV)

Second Floor, Magnolia Life Building, P.O. Drawer 3004, 70602-3004
Telephone: 318-433-3004
Facsimile: 318-433-8080

MEMBERS OF FIRM

Thomas M. Bergstedt
Benjamin W. Mount
Van C. Seneca

ASSOCIATE

Annette N. Peltier

OF COUNSEL

Charles S. Ware

Representative Clients: ARCO Chemical Company; Ashland Oil Co.; CIGNA Property & Casualty Companies; Columbia Women's & Children's Hospital; The Hartford Steam Boiler Inspection & Insurance Company; Leach Company; Olin Corporation; Occidental Chemical Corporation; Terra Corporation; R. D. Werner Company.

For full biographical listings, see the Martindale-Hubbell Law Directory

PLAUCHÉ SMITH & NIESET, A PROFESSIONAL LAW CORPORATION (AV)

1123 Pithon Street, P.O. Drawer 1705, 70602
Telephone: 318-436-0522
Facsimile: 318-436-9637

S. W. Plauché (1889-1952)
S. W. Plauché, Jr. (1915-1966)
A. Lane Plauché
Allen L. Smith, Jr.
James R. Nieset
Frank M. Walker, Jr.
Michael J. McNulty, III
Jeffrey M. Cole
Andrew R. Johnson, IV
Charles V. Musso, Jr.
Christopher P. Ieyoub
H. David Vaughan, II
Joseph R. Pousson, Jr.
Rebecca S. Young
V. Ed McGuire, III

Representative Clients: CIGNA; CNA Insurance Cos.; Commercial Union Insurance Cos.; Crum & Forster; Reliance Insurance Cos.; Royal Insurance Group; State Farm; U.S. Insurance Group.

For full biographical listings, see the Martindale-Hubbell Law Directory

RAGGIO, CAPPEL, CHOZEN & BERNIARD (AV)

500 Magnolia Life Building, P.O. Box 820, 70601
Telephone: 318-436-9481
Fax: 318-436-9499
Email: RCCB@RaggioCappel.com

MEMBERS OF FIRM

Alvin O. King (1890-1958)
Thomas C. Hall (1919-1973)
Thomas L. Raggio (Retired)
Richard B. Cappel
Frederick L. Cappel
Richard A. Chozen
Stephen A. Berniard, Jr.
Christopher M. Trahan
L. Paul Foreman
Kevin J. Koenig

ASSOCIATE

Eric W. Roan

Counsel for: Aetna Casualty & Surety Co.; Allstate Insurance Co.; United States Fidelity and Guaranty Co.; ABB Lummus Global, Inc.; The St. Paul Companies; Windsor Insurance Group; Coregis Insurance Co.; Government Employees Insurance Co.; Calcasieu Parish Police Jury.

For full biographical listings, see the Martindale-Hubbell Law Directory

SCOFIELD, GERARD, VERON, SINGLETARY & POHORELSKY, A PROFESSIONAL LAW CORPORATION (AV)

1114 Ryan Street, P.O. Drawer 3028, 70601
Telephone: 318-433-9436
Telefax: 318-436-0306
URL: http://www.sgvsp.com

John B. Scofield
Richard E. Gerard, Jr.
J. Michael Veron
C. Eston Singletary
John R. Pohorelsky
Scott J. Scofield
Patrick D. Gallaugher, Jr.
Robert E. Landry
Russell J. Stutes, Jr.
W. Todd Fontenot
David W. Clark

Representative Clients: Admiral Insurance Co.; Amoco Production Co.; Banc One; Browning-Ferris Industries, Inc.; Brown & Root Construction Co.; Cosmos Broadcasting Corp.; Dresser Industries, Inc.; Kansas City Southern Railway Co.; Mobil Oil Corp.; Phillips Petroleum Co.

For full biographical listings, see the Martindale-Hubbell Law Directory

STOCKWELL, SIEVERT, VICCELLIO, CLEMENTS & SHADDOCK, L.L.P. (AV)

One Lakeside Plaza, P.O. Box 2900, 70601
Telephone: 318-436-9491
Fax: 318-493-7210; 493-2709

MEMBERS OF FIRM

Oliver P. Stockwell (1907-1993)
Fred H. Sievert, Jr. (1923-1988)
Charles D. Viccellio
Robert W. Clements
William E. Shaddock
Emmett C. Sole
John Stanton Bradford
Stephen C. Polito
Robert S. Dampf
William B. Monk
H. Alan McCall
Brian L. Coody
Paul L. Veazey, Jr.
James Anthony Blanco
Andrew D. McGlathery, III
Susan Gay Viccellio
Benjamin J. Guilbeau, Jr.
H. Aubrey White, III

OF COUNSEL

Thomas G. Henning
Randy J. Fuerst

ASSOCIATES

Lee W. Boyer
Allen J. Mitchell, II
Todd M. Ammons

Representative Clients: The Continental Insurance Cos.; State Farm Insurance Cos.; PPG Industries, Inc.; Entergy Gulf States Inc.; Lakeside National Bank of Lake Charles; Lake Charles Memorial Hospital; Texaco, Inc.; St. Patrick Hospital of Lake Charles; Firestone-Bridgestone, Inc.; Reliance Insurance Co.

For full biographical listings, see the Martindale-Hubbell Law Directory

METAIRIE, Jefferson Parish

BERNARD, CASSISA, ELLIOTT & DAVIS, A PROFESSIONAL LAW CORPORATION (AV)

1615 Metairie Road, P.O. Box 55490, 70055-5490
Telephone: 504-834-2612
Telecopier: 504-838-9438
Email: bcande@communique.net
Oxford, Mississippi Office: 1727 East University Avenue, Suite E, 38655.
Telephone: 601-234-7236.
Fax: 601-234-7691.

Peter L. Bernard, Jr. (1920-1991)
Frank L. Micholet (1913-1972)
Paul V. Cassisa, Sr.
Stephen N. Elliott
Benjamin Franklin Davis, Jr.
Eugene M. McEachin, Jr.
Robert A. McMahon, Jr.
Carl J. Giffin, Jr.
Paul V. Cassisa, Jr.
Howard B. Kaplan
William L. Brockman
Robert A. Knight
Ann M. Sico

OF COUNSEL

Robert H. Wood, Jr.

Representative Clients: Royal Insurance Group; General Motors Corp.; Hartford Insurance Group; Nissan Motor Corp.; Honda North America, Inc.

For full biographical listings, see the Martindale-Hubbell Law Directory

CHEHARDY, SHERMAN, ELLIS, BRESLIN & MURRAY, L.L.P. (AV)

A Limited Liability Partnership of Professional Law Corporations and Individuals
One Galleria Boulevard, Suite 1100, 70001
Telephone: 504-833-5600
Fax: 504-833-8080
Email: staff@chehardy.com
Baton Rouge, Louisiana Office: 6513 Perkins Road, 70808.
Telephone: 225-763-9220.
Telefax: 225-766-9143.

Lawrence E. Chehardy (Professional Law Corporation)
David R. Sherman (Professional Law Corporation)
Michael H. Ellis (Professional Law Corporation)
T. Peter Breslin, Jr. (Professional Law Corporation)
Julian R. Murray, Jr.
Robert G. Stassi
P.J. Stakelum III, (Professional Corporation)
George B. Recile
Steven E. Hayes
Alvin A. LeBlanc, Jr.(Professional Law Corporation)
Stephen D. Marx
Paula Perrone
John C. Anderson
Elizabeth O. Rome
Joseph L. Alphonse

OF COUNSEL

Patricia E. Pannell

Representative Clients: American Express Financial Planners; City of Kenner; Columbus Metairie Properties, L.L.C.; Fair Grounds Corp.; First American Bank and Trust; First American Title Insurance Co.; Gibbs Construction Company, Inc.; Grimaldi Construction Company, Inc.; Kostmayer Construction Company, Inc.; L & L Oil Company, Inc.

For full biographical listings, see the Martindale-Hubbell Law Directory

Metairie—Continued

CHOPIN, WAGAR, COLE, RICHARD, REBOUL & KUTCHER, LLP (AV)

Two Lakeway Center, Suite 900, 3850 North Causeway Boulevard, 70009-6983
Telephone: 504-830-3838
Telefax: 504-830-3840
URL: http://www.chopin.com
Mandeville, Louisiana Office: Two Sanctuary Boulevard, Suite 201, 70471. *Telephone:* 504-674-6680.

Richard A. Chopin (P.L.C.)
Nelson W. Wagar, III, (P.L.C.)
Kevin L. Cole
Thomas M. Richard
Brian Reboul
Robert A. Kutcher
Elizabeth Smyth Sirgo
Nicole Sophia Tygier

Michael L. Cohen
John I. Goodwin, III
Vicki A. Turko
Diana L. Tonagel
Leah R. Simpson
Patricia Diane Tunmer
Judith Armshaw Miller
John S. Bair
Elia Diaz-Yaeger
Raymond R. Egan, III
Patrick E. Moore
Matthew D. Monson

OF COUNSEL
John B. Krentel

For full biographical listings, see the Martindale-Hubbell Law Directory

HAILEY, MCNAMARA, HALL, LARMANN & PAPALE, L.L.P. (AV)

A Limited Liability Partnership including Professional Law Corporations
Suite 1400, One Galleria Boulevard, P.O. Box 8288, 70011
Telephone: 504-836-6500
Fax: 504-836-6565
URL: http://www.haileymcnamara.com

MEMBERS OF FIRM

James W. Hailey, Jr., (P.L.C.)
W. Marvin Hall (P.L.C.)
Antonio E. Papale, Jr., (P.L.C.)
Laurence E. Larmann (P.L.C.)
Michael P. Mentz
Richard T. Simmons, Jr.,(P.L.C.)
Michael J. Vondenstein
David K. Persons
Dominic J. Ovella
C. Kelly Lightfoot
John T. Culotta (P.L.C.)
John E. Unsworth, Jr.
Julie DiFulco Robles
Claude A. Greco
Valerie T. Schexnayder
W. Evan Plauche
Kurt D. Engelhardt

ASSOCIATES

William R. Seay, Jr.
W. Glenn Burns
James W. Hailey, III
Frederic Theodore Le Clercq
Barbara Bourdonnay O'Donnell
Kathryn T. Wiedorn
Joseph L. Spilman, III
Caroline D. Ibos
Robert D. Ford
Lynnette Hall-Lewis
Kevin O. Larmann
Tammy M. Stewart
Danny N. Bowz
Edward C. Vocke, IV
C. Angelle Goudeau
Alayne R. Corcoran
David K. Groome, Jr.
Kristen M. Baumer
Gabriel J. Veninata

OF COUNSEL
Henry D. McNamara, Jr., (P.L.C.)

Representative Clients: Diamond Offshore Drilling Inc.; The Flintkote Co.; Lockheed Martin Corporation; Rheem Manufacturing Co.; State Farm Fire & Casualty Co.; Textron, Inc; Travelers Companies; Coca-Cola Enterprises, Inc.

For full biographical listings, see the Martindale-Hubbell Law Directory

*MINDEN,** Webster Parish

KITCHENS, BENTON, KITCHENS & WARREN, A PROFESSIONAL LAW CORPORATION (AV)

420 Broadway, P.O. Box 740, 71055
Telephone: 318-377-5331
Fax: 318-377-5361

Graydon K. Kitchens, Sr. (1903-1988)
John B. Benton, Jr. (Semi Retired)
Paul E. Kitchens
William Rick Warren
Graydon K. Kitchens, III
Graydon K. Kitchens, Jr.

Representative Clients: State Farm Insurance Co.; Howard Lumber & Supply Co., Inc.; Minden Building & Loan Assn.; Mister Twister, Inc.; Minden Housing Authority.
Reference: Minden Bank & Trust Co.

For full biographical listings, see the Martindale-Hubbell Law Directory

*MONROE,** Ouachita Parish

DAVENPORT, FILES & KELLY, L.L.P. (AV)

1509 Lamy Lane, P.O. Box 4787, 71211-4787
Telephone: 318-387-6453
FAX: 318-323-6533
Email: dfk@dfklaw.com

Thos. W. Davenport (1909-1962)
Wm. G. Kelly, Jr.
Thomas W. Davenport, Jr.
Jack B. Files
Mike C. Sanders
Ramsey L. Ogg
Michael J. Fontenot
M. Shane Craighead

W. David Hammett
Carey B. Underwood

STAFF ATTORNEY
Stacy L. Guice

Representative Clients: CHUBB Group; Crum & Forster Group; GAINSCO County Mutual Insurance Company; Government Employees Insurance Company; Highlands Insurance Company; Trinity Universal Insurance Company; Zurich American Insurance Companies.

For full biographical listings, see the Martindale-Hubbell Law Directory

HAYES, HARKEY, SMITH & CASCIO, L.L.P. (AV)

2811 Kilpatrick Boulevard, P.O. Box 8032, 71211-8032
Telephone: 318-387-2422
FAX: 318-388-5809

Thomas M. Hayes, Jr. (1915-1994)
Louis D. Smith (Retired)
Joseph D. Cascio, Jr.
Charles S. Smith
Thomas M. Hayes, III
Bruce McKamy Mintz
C. Joseph Roberts, III
John B. Saye

OF COUNSEL
Haynes L. Harkey, Jr.

Karen L. Hayes
Harry McClellan Moffett, IV

Representative Clients: Cigna, Inc.; CNA; St. Francis Medical Center, Inc.; St. Paul Insurance Group; Cooper Industries; Riverwood International Corp.; Scott Truck and Tractor.

For full biographical listings, see the Martindale-Hubbell Law Directory

SNELLINGS, BREARD, SARTOR, INABNETT & TRASCHER, LLP (AV)

1503 North 19th Street, P.O. Box 2055, 71207-2055
Telephone: 318-387-8000
Fax: 318-387-8200
Email: sbsit@bayou.com *URL:* http://www.bayou.com/sbsit

MEMBERS OF FIRM

George M. Snellings, Jr. (1910-1984)
Daniel Ryan Sartor, Jr.
Carrick R. Inabnett
Charles C. Trascher, III
L. Kent Breard, Jr.
Clara Moss Sartor
William Brooks Watson
David C. McMillin
Jon Keith Guice

ASSOCIATES

Wendy E. W. Giovingo
William Michael Street

OF COUNSEL
Kent Breard

Representative Clients: Bank One; Cross Keys Bank; Delta Air Lines, Inc.; Federal Deposit Insurance Co.; Glenwood Regional Medical Center; John Hancock Mutual Life Insurance Company; Kemper Insurance Group; Horace Mann Insurance Cos.; Louisiana Association of Educators; Midland Mortgage Company.

For full biographical listings, see the Martindale-Hubbell Law Directory

MORGAN CITY, St. Mary Parish

LIPPMAN, MAHFOUZ & MARTIN (AV)

Inglewood Mall, 1025 Victor II Boulevard, P.O. Box 2526, 70381
Telephone: 504-384-1833
Fax: 504-385-4632

MEMBERS OF FIRM

Alfred S. Lippman
Thomas L. Mahfouz
Dale P. Martin

ASSOCIATES

Brian M. Tranchina
David M. Thorguson

For full biographical listings, see the Martindale-Hubbell Law Directory

*NATCHITOCHES,** Natchitoches Parish

McCoy Roberts Begnaud & Friedman, A Law Corporation (AV)

300 St. Denis Street, P.O. Box 1369, 71458-1369
Telephone: 318-352-6495
Telecopier: 318-352-9982
Email: mccoylaw@cp-tel.net

Kenneth D. McCoy, Jr.
Mark L. Roberts
Mark A. Begnaud
Gregory D. Friedman

Representative Clients: Central Bank; Farm Credit Bank of Texas; First South PCA; Natchitoches Parish Port Commission; Peoples State Bank; Red River Waterway District; Reserve Life Insurance Co.; Riverwood International Corp.

For full biographical listings, see the Martindale-Hubbell Law Directory

*NEW IBERIA,** Iberia Parish

Landry & Watkins (AV)

211 East Main Street, P.O. Box 12040, 70562-2040
Telephone: 318-364-7626; Lafayette: 318-234-5921
Telecopier: 318-367-2715
Email: LanWat@aol.com

MEMBERS OF FIRM

Alfred Smith Landry
Edward P. Landry
William A. Repaske
Kreig A. Breaux

OF COUNSEL

Jacob S. Landry
Guyton H. Watkins

ASSOCIATE

Charles Benjamin Landry

Representative Clients: Entex, a Division of NorAm Energy Corp.; Iberia Sugar Co-operative, Inc.; Hartford Accident & Indemnity Co.; Iberia Savings Bank; Liberty Mutual Insurance Co.; Premier Bank, N.A.

For full biographical listings, see the Martindale-Hubbell Law Directory

*NEW ORLEANS,** Orleans Parish

Adams and Reese LLP (AV)

Attorneys and Counselors at Law
4500 One Shell Square, 70139
Telephone: 504-581-3234
Telefax: 504-566-0210
Email: info@arlaw.com *URL:* http://www.arlaw.com
Baton Rouge, Louisiana Office: Bank One Centre, 19th Floor, North Tower, 451 Florida Street.
Telephone: 225-336-5200.
Fax: 225-336-5220.
Mobile, Alabama Office: 4500 One St. Louis Centre.
Telephone: 334-433-3234.
Fax: 334-438-7733.
Washington, D.C. Office: 1455 Pennsylvania Avenue, N.W., Suite 200
Telephone: 202-737-3234.
Fax: 202-737-0264.
Houston, Texas Office: 4400 One Houston Center, 1221 McKinney.
Telephone: 713-652-5151.
Fax: 713-652-5152.
Jackson, Mississippi Office: 111 Capital Building, Suite 350, 111 Capital Street.
Telephone: 601-353-3234.
Fax: 601-355-9708.

MEMBERS OF FIRM

St. Clair Adams, Jr. (1906-1963)
W. Ford Reese (1917-1971)
Sam A. LeBlanc, III
James E. Blazek
Lawrence L. McNamara
Edward J. Rice, Jr.
Robert A. Vosbein
Louis A. Wilson, Jr.
Robert B. Nolan
Michael G. Crow
Robert E. Couhig, Jr.
Eddy M. Quijano (Resident, Baton Rouge Office)
Mark C. Surprenant
Philip A. Franco
Mark J. Spansel
Joseph W. Looney
Albert S. Dittmann, Jr.
Paul G. Pastorek
Thomas G. O'Brien
Charles F. Gay, Jr.
Rebecca A. Bush
John M. Duck
Philip O. Bergeron
Richard B. Eason, II
F. Lee Butler (Resident, Houston, Texas)
Paul O. Dicharry
Luis A. Perez
Mark S. Embree
Joseph P. Gordon, Jr.
William B. Gaudet
Scott E. Delacroix
Glen M. Pilie
Deborah B. Rouen
Robin B. Cheatham
Louis C. LaCour, Jr.
Donald C. Massey
Richard O. Kingrea (Resident, Mobile, Alabama Office)
Edwin C. Laizer
Martin A. Stern
Leslie A. Lanusse
Harry M. Zimmerman, Jr.
A. Kirk Gasperecz
T. Semmes Favrot
Deborah Cunningham Foshee
Jane C. Raiford
Kathleen F. Drew
Margaret M. Joffe

(See Next Column)

MEMBERS OF FIRM (Continued)

James G. Perdigao
E. Paige Sensenbrenner
Brooke Duncan III
Edward H. Arnold, III
Rodi W. Culotta
Francis V. Liantonio, Jr.
Mark R. Beebe
Alex E. Cosculluela (Resident, Houston, Texas Office)
E. Gregg Barrios
B. Troy Villa
Sean D. Moore
Jeffrey W. Bennett
Kenneth F. Tamplain, Jr.
Sharon R. Rodi
Tyson B. Shofstahl
Lisa Lemaire Maher
Jefferson D. Stewart
Arthur F. Hickham, Jr.
Michael N. Mire
William J. Kelly III
James T. Rogers III
Richard J. Kernion, Jr.
Ralph H. Wall
Donna M. Borrello
Janis van Meerveld
Laurie Briggs Young
Ronald J. Sholes

ASSOCIATES

Roy A. Perrin, III
Gregory A. Grefer
Jeffrey E. Richardson
Douglas H. Edwards
Robert N. Markle
Valeria M. Sercovich
Robert A. Vosbein, Jr.
Johnny L. Domiano, Jr.
Whitney L. Cole
Tara E. Bell
C. Byron Berry
Robert L. Bonnaffons
Shannan L. Boudreaux
B. Jeffrey Brooks (Resident, District of Columbia Office)
Nicolas S. Dufour
Kirk P. Groh
Christy F. Kane
Melissa S. LaBauve
Jennifer Reilly Cook
Rusty J. Savoie
Wanda L. Theriot
Raymond J. Turcotte, Jr
Roland M. Vandenweghe, Jr.
Dale D. Smith
Chauntis T. Jenkins
William Scarth Clark

OF COUNSEL

Henry B. Alsobrook, Jr.
Joel L. Borrello
Robert J. Conrad
Joseph H. Kavanaugh
Thomas J. Wyllie

SPECIAL COUNSEL

Julian P. Brignac
Karen Lewis Wilkins
Edward M. Morris
James A. Hayes (Resident, District of Columbia Office)

Representative Clients: American International Group, Inc.; Shell Oil Co.; Underwriters at Lloyds of London; Reichhold Chemicals, Inc.; Rollins Environmental Services, Inc.; Oschner Medical Center; Merrell Dow Pharmaceuticals, Inc.; Louisiana Medical Mutual Insurance Co. (LAMMICO); Reading & Bates Drilling Co.

For full biographical listings, see the Martindale-Hubbell Law Directory

Ates & Associates, A Professional Law Corporation (AV)

4004 Magazine Street, Suite A, 70115
Telephone: 504-899-9969
Telefax: 504-764-9686
Destrehan, Louisiana Office: 13726 River Road, Suite A, 70047.
Telephone: 504-764-9911.
Telefax: 504-764-9686.

J. Robert Ates

For full biographical listings, see the Martindale-Hubbell Law Directory

Best Koeppel, A Professional Law Corporation (AV)

LL & E Tower, 909 Poydras Street Suite 2200, 70112
Telephone: 504-593-2400
Telecopier: 504-593-2401
Email: bstkpplesq@aol.com
Houston, Texas Office: 1900 West Loop South, Suite 300, 77027.
Telephone: 713-964-4072.
Telecopier: 713-963-2503.

Laurence E. Best
Peter S. Koeppel
R. Jeffrey Bridger
James H. Daigle, Jr.
M. Davis Ready
Suzanne M. Risey

LEGAL SUPPORT PERSONNEL

PARALEGAL

Debora N. Dufrene

Representative Clients: Lexington Insurance Co.; Rowan Companies, Inc.; Rowandrill, Inc.; Rowan International, Inc.; Atlantic Maritime Services, Inc.; Rowan Drilling (U.K.), Ltd.; Hartford Insurance Co.; Trinity Marine Group; Elevating Boats, Inc.; CITGO Petroleum Corp.

For full biographical listings, see the Martindale-Hubbell Law Directory

Breazeale, Sachse & Wilson, L.L.P. (AV)

LL&E Tower, Suite 1500, 909 Poydras Street, 70112
Telephone: 504-584-5454
Fax: 504-584-5452
URL: http://www.bswllp.com
Baton Rouge, Louisiana Office: Twenty-Third Floor, One American Place, P.O. Box 3197.
Telephone: 225-387-4000.
Fax: 225-387-5397.

(See Next Column)

BREAZEALE, SACHSE & WILSON L.L.P., *New Orleans—Continued*

Covington, Louisiana Office: 2255 Highway 190 North, Suite 200.
Telephone: 504-871-9444.
Fax: 504-871-9666.

MEMBERS OF FIRM

Gordon A. Pugh
Van R. Mayhall, Jr.
Joseph E. Friend (Resident)
Peter J. Butler, Jr.
Deborah Duplechin Harkins
Richard G. Passler
W. Christopher Beary

RESIDENT ASSOCIATES

Michael C. Luquet
Ralph T. Rabalais
Walter R. Wellenreiter
Tara L. Foto

OF COUNSEL

Gary L. Laborde

SPECIAL COUNSEL

Peter J. Butler

For full biographical listings, see the Martindale-Hubbell Law Directory

CHAFFE, MCCALL, PHILLIPS, TOLER & SARPY, L.L.P. (AV)

A Partnership including a Professional Law Corporation
2300 Energy Centre, 1100 Poydras Street, 70163-2300
Telephone: 504-585-7000
Telecopier: 504-585-7075
Cable Address: "Denegre"
Telex: (AT&T) 460122 CMPTS
Email: cmptsno%chaffe@mcimail.com *URL:* http://www.chaffe.com
Baton Rouge, Louisiana Office: 202 Two United Plaza, 8550 United Plaza Boulevard.
Telephone: 504-922-4300.
Fax: 504-922-4304.
Caracas, Venezuela Office: Edificio Exa, Piso 10, Oficina PH-10, Avenida Venezuela entre Calles EL Retiro y Alameda, El Rosal.
Telephone: 011-582-953-4136.
Fax: 011-582-953-6518.

MEMBERS OF FIRM

Robert B. Deane
Peter A. Feringa, Jr.
J. Dwight LeBlanc, Jr.
Charles L. Chassaignac
G. Phillip Shuler, III
Robert B. Fisher, Jr.
Corinne Ann Morrison
William F. Grace, Jr.
Robert S. Rooth
Harry R. Holladay
Marc G. Shachat
Derek Anthony Walker
Jonathan C. McCall
Kathleen S. Plemer
Thomas D. Forbes
Julie D. Livaudais
John F. Olinde
Carmelite M. Bertaut
E. Howell Crosby
Keith Eric Gisleson
Henry D. Salassi, Jr. (Resident Partner, Baton Rouge)
W. Anthony Toups, III
Douglas L. Grundmeyer
J. Gregory Wyrick
Charles P. Blanchard
Robert B. Landry, III
Brent A. Talbot
Betty F. Mullin
Merle F. Shoughrue
James C. Young
Andrew C. Partee, Jr.
Mary L. Meyer
L. Kenneth Krogstad (Resident Partner, Baton Rouge)
Ronald L. Naquin
Scott C. Barney
Daniel A. Tadros
D. Scott Landry (Resident Partner, Baton Rouge)
Kellye L. Walker

SPECIAL PARTNERS

H. Evans Scobee (Resident Special Partner, Baton Rouge)
John C. Saunders, Jr.

ASSOCIATES

Keith C. Armstrong (Resident Associate, Baton Rouge)
Julie D. Savage
Richard B. Ramirez
Keith E. Andrews
Jena Smith-Malfatti
Earl F. Sundmaker, III
Lou Anne Milliman
Peter J. Rotolo, III
Gregory J. Walsh
H. Michael Bush
Justin B. Schmidt
Ivan Mauricio Rodriguez
Alexandra M. Lamothe
Nicole M. Alexander (Not admitted in LA)

OF COUNSEL

George W. Pigman, Jr.
Paul A. Nalty
Andrew Rinker, Jr.
Bernardo Bentata (Resident Associate, Caracas)
Suzanne Haik Terrell

Representative Clients: Associated Builders and Contractors, Inc.; Brown & Williamson Tobacco Corporation; CSX Transportation, Inc.; Liverpool and London Steamship Protection and Indemnity Assn. Ltd.; Resolution Trust Corporation; The Allstate Insurance Co.; The Equitable Life Assurance Society of the United States; The West of England Steam Ship Owners Mutual Insurance Assn. (Luxembourg).

For full biographical listings, see the Martindale-Hubbell Law Directory

CHRISTOVICH AND KEARNEY, L.L.P. (AV)

Suite 2300 Pan American Life Center, 601 Poydras Street, 70130-6078
Telephone: 504-561-5700
Fax: 504-561-5743
Email: c&k@christovich.com

(See Next Column)

MEMBERS OF FIRM

Alvin R. Christovich, Jr.
William K. Christovich
J. Walter Ward, Jr.
Lawrence J. Ernst
James F. Holmes
Robert E. Peyton
C. Edgar Cloutier
Charles W. Schmidt, III
Richard K. Christovich
Terry Christovich Gay
E. Phelps Gay
J. Warren Gardner, Jr.
Kevin R. Tully
Lance R. Rydberg
Elizabeth S. Cordes
Charles M. Lanier, Jr.
Philip J. Borne
James A. Holmes

ASSOCIATES

Robert D. Peyton
Craig B. Mitchell
Joseph M. Guillot
Scott J. Sonnier
John K. Nieset
Janet L. White
Mary Beth Meyer
Kory J. Ickler

OF COUNSEL

John A. Stassi II

Representative Clients: Highlands Insurance Co.; Progressive Insurance Company; AIG Group; Liberty Mutual Insurance Co.; Sofamor-Danek Group, Inc.; Brown & Root, Inc.; Otis Elevator Co.; Dillard Department Stores, Inc.; A.C.& S.

For full biographical listings, see the Martindale-Hubbell Law Directory

FAVRET, DEMAREST, RUSSO & LUTKEWITTE, A PROFESSIONAL LAW CORPORATION (AV)

Suite 1400, 1515 Poydras Building, 1515 Poydras Street, 70112
Telephone: 504-561-1006
Telecopier: 504-523-0699
Email: favret@bellsouth.net

Clarence F. Favret, Sr. (1896-1988)
Marshall J. Favret
J. Paul Demarest
Anthony J. Russo
Thomas J. Lutkewitte
Clarence F. Favret, III

Angela C. Imbornone
Dean Joseph Favret
Michael W. Boleware
Seth H. Schaumburg

Reference: Hibernia National Bank.

For full biographical listings, see the Martindale-Hubbell Law Directory

FEINGERTS & ASSOCIATES, A PROFESSIONAL LAW CORPORATION (AV)

Poydras Center, Suite 26th Floor, 650 Poydras Street, 70130-6161
Telephone: 504-568-1515
Fax: 504-568-1521

Bruce L. Feingerts
Gary S. Brown
A. Elizabeth Tarver

For full biographical listings, see the Martindale-Hubbell Law Directory

FRILOT, PARTRIDGE, KOHNKE & CLEMENTS, L.C. (AV)

3600 Energy Centre, 1100 Poydras Street, 70163-3600
Telephone: 504-599-8000
Telecopier: 504-599-8100
Email: postmaster@fpkc.com *URL:* http://www.fpkc.com

Francis H. Brown, III
James H. Brown, Jr.
George E. Cain, Jr.
Michael T. Cali
Miles P. Clements
Andrew S. de Klerk
George A. Frilot, III (A Professional Law Corp.)
John J. Hainkel, III
Edward F. Kohnke, IV
Allen J. Krouse, III
J. Dwight LeBlanc, III
Douglas P. Matthews
Kenneth A. Mayeaux
Robert B. McNeal
Wayne K. McNeil
Patrick J. McShane
Joseph N. Mole
David A. Olson
Scott S. Partridge
Greg A. Pellegrini
Michael R. Phillips
James F. Shuey
James R. Silverstein
Peter E. Sperling
Patrick A. Talley (P.C.)
Patricia E. Weeks

Sidney A. Backstrom
Joel Edwin Cape (Not admitted in LA)
Nairda T. Lesa Colón
Bruce Arne Cranner
Frederick T. Greschner, Jr.
Brant David Imperatore
Stephanie Ann May
Michael B. North

For full biographical listings, see the Martindale-Hubbell Law Directory

GAINSBURGH, BENJAMIN, DAVID, MEUNIER & WARSHAUER (AV)

2800 Energy Centre, 1100 Poydras, 70163-2800
Telephone: 504-522-2304
Telecopier: 504-528-9973
Email: DPHILLIPS@GAINSBEN.COM

(See Next Column)

GAINSBURGH, BENJAMIN, DAVID, MEUNIER & WARSHAUER—*Continued*

OF COUNSEL

Samuel C. Gainsburgh
Jack C. Benjamin

MEMBERS OF FIRM

Robert J. David
Gerald E. Meunier
Irving J. Warshauer
Stevan C. Dittman
Madeleine M. Landrieu
Darryl M. Phillips
Jeffrey A. Mitchell

ASSOCIATE

Gary B. Roth

For full biographical listings, see the Martindale-Hubbell Law Directory

THE GODFREY FIRM A PROFESSIONAL LAW CORPORATION (AV)

2500 Energy Centre, 1100 Poydras Street, 70163-2500
Telephone: 504-585-7538
Fax: 504-585-7535
Email: godfryfirm@aol.com

Jarrell E. Godfrey, Jr.
Cloyd F. Van Hook
Patrick M. Files
Elizabeth Earnest

For full biographical listings, see the Martindale-Hubbell Law Directory

GORDON, ARATA, MCCOLLAM, DUPLANTIS & EAGAN, L.L.P. (AV)

A Registered Limited Liability Partnership including Professional Law Corporations
201 St. Charles Avenue, Suite 4000, 70170-4000
Telephone: 504-582-1111
Fax: 504-582-1121
Lafayette, Louisiana Office: 625 East Kaliste Saloom Road.
Telephone: 318-237-0132.
Fax: 318-237-3451.
Baton Rouge, Louisiana Office: 1400 One American Place.
Telephone: 225-381-9643.
Fax: 225-336-9763.

MEMBERS OF FIRM

John A. Gordon (A P.L.C.)
Blake G. Arata (A P.L.C.)
John M. McCollam (A P.L.C.)
Ewell E. (Tim) Eagan Jr., (A P.L.C.)
Guy E. Wall
Cynthia A. Nicholson
Cathy E. Chessin
Paul E. Bullington
Steven W. Copley
Jason A. T. Jumonville
Marion D. Welborn Weinstock
Ernest E. Svenson
Martin E. Landrieu
A. Gregory Grimsal
Donna Phillips Currault
Scott A. O'Connor
C. Peck Hayne Jr.
Marcy V. Massengale
Howard E. Sinor, Jr.

ASSOCIATES

Tina Crawford Santopadre
Ginger Johnson Guichet
Martin P. Averill
J. Nicholas Graydon
Andrée M. Braud
Fernand L. Laudumiey, IV

LAFAYETTE OFFICE
RESIDENT MEMBERS OF FIRM

B. J. Duplantis (A P.L.C.)
William F. Bailey
Samuel E. Masur

RESIDENT ASSOCIATES

Denis C. Swords
Gregory G. Duplantis

BATON ROUGE OFFICE
RESIDENT MEMBERS OF FIRM

James J. Brady
Teanna West Neskora

Representative Clients: Bank One, LA, N.A.; Charles Schwab & Co., Inc.; Chevron, USA, Inc.; Cox Communications, Inc.; Duke Energy Corp.; Entergy Corp.; First National Bank of Commerce; Lorillard Tobacco Co.; Union Oil Company of California; Universal Health Services, Inc.

For full biographical listings, see the Martindale-Hubbell Law Directory

HERMAN, HERMAN, KATZ & COTLAR, L.L.P. (AV)

A Partnership including Professional Law Corporations
Formerly Herman & Herman
820 O'Keefe Avenue, 70113
Telephone: 504-581-4892
Telecopier: 504-561-6024
Email: HHKC@HHKC.COM

Harry Herman (1914-1987)
Russ M. Herman (A Professional Law Corporation)
Maury A. Herman (A Professional Law Corporation)
Morton H. Katz (A Professional Law Corporation)
Sidney A. Cotlar (A Professional Law Corporation)
Steven J. Lane
Leonard A. Davis (A Professional Law Corporation)
James C. Klick
Steve Herman
Brian D. Katz
Richard E. King
David K. Fox

(See Next Column)

OF COUNSEL

Joseph A. Kott
Warren A. Goldstein

For full biographical listings, see the Martindale-Hubbell Law Directory

JONES, WALKER, WAECHTER, POITEVENT, CARRÈRE & DENÈGRE, L.L.P. (AV)

201 St. Charles Avenue, 70170-5100
Telephone: 504-582-8000
Telecopiers: Xerox 7033, 504-582-8549; 504-582-8574; 504-582-8583
Email: marketing@jwlaw.com
Baton Rouge, Louisiana Office: Fifth Floor, Four United Plaza, 8555 United Plaza Boulevard.
Telephone: 225-231-2000.
Telecopier: 225-231-2010.
Lafayette, Louisiana Office: Suite 120, 500 Dover Boulevard.
Telephone: 318-406-5610.
Telecopier: Xerox 7021, 318-406-5620.
Washington, D.C. Office: 499 South Capitol Street, S.W., Suite 600.
Telephone: 202-828-8363.
Telecopier: Xerox 7021, 202-828-6907.

MEMBERS OF FIRM

Joseph Merrick Jones (1903-1963)
J. Mort Walker, Jr. (1904-1983)
Edward B. Poitevent (1913-1996)
Ernest A. Carrère, Jr. (1915-1997)
Arthur J. Waechter, Jr.
George Denègre
John V. Baus
Robert B. Acomb, Jr.
Edward B. Benjamin, Jr.
Patrick W. Browne, Jr.
Charles W. Lane, III
John J. Weigel
Donald L. King
James Larkin Selman, II
John R. Peters, Jr.
Donald O. Collins
John C. Combe, Jr.
R. Henry Sarpy, Jr.
Edward F. Martin
Carl C. Hanemann
Raymond J. Salassi, Jr.
Stewart E. Niles, Jr.
John D. Kitchen
Janice M. Foster
Harry S. Hardin, III
John J. Broders
Glenn G. Goodier
Robert R. Casey (See Baton Rouge, Louisiana listing)
Edward J. Koehl, Jr.
Thomas M. Nosewicz
David F. Edwards
L. Richards McMillan, II
R. Patrick Vance
John G. Gomila, Jr.
Robert B. Bieck, Jr.
Rudolph R. Ramelli
Madeleine Fischer
David G. Radlauer
John C. Blackman (See Baton Rouge, Louisiana listing)
J. Kelly Duncan
Stanhope B. Denègre
Edward H. Bergin
Grady S. Hurley
Edward Dirk Wegmann
William M. Backstrom, Jr.
Alex P. Trostorff
James E. Wright, III
Joseph J. Lowenthal, Jr.
Margaret F. Murphy
Alton E. Bayard, III (See Baton Rouge, Louisiana listing)
Robert T. Lemon, II
H. Mark Adams
Elizabeth Jones Futrell
Michael A. Chernekoff
Richard J. Tyler
William H. Hines
W. Philip Clinton
William B. Masters
Thomas A. Casey, Jr.
R. Lewis McHenry
Curtis R. Hearn
Gary H. Miller
Carl D. Rosenblum
Covert J. Geary
Pauline F. Hardin
R. Christian Johnsen (See Washington, D.C. listing)
Kenneth J. Najder
Thomas K. Potter, III
Jefferson R. Tillery
Patrick J. Veters
John L. Duvieilh
Richard D. Bertram
Lisa Manget Buchanan
Wayne G. Zeringue, Jr.
Robert L. Walsh
Leon Gary Jr. (See Baton Rouge, Louisiana listing)
Charles A. Landry (See Baton Rouge, Louisiana listing)
Donald E. Bradford (See Baton Rouge, Louisiana listing)
Michael T. Perry (See Baton Rouge, Louisiana listing)
Robert W. Scheffy, Jr. (See Baton Rouge, Louisiana listing)
B. Michael Mauldin (See Baton Rouge, Louisiana listing)
Davis B. Allgood (See Baton Rouge, Louisiana listing)
Louis S. Quinn, Jr. (See Baton Rouge, Louisiana listing)
John C. Reynolds
M. Richard Schroeder
J. Marshall Page, III
Thomas Y. Roberson, Jr.
William J. Joyce
Susan K. Chambers
Robin D. McGuire (See Lafayette, Louisiana listing)
Richard P. Wolfe
Brad J. Axelrod (See Baton Rouge, Louisiana listing)
Jeffry W. Gray (See Baton Rouge, Louisiana listing)
Judith V. Windhorst
William L. Schuette, Jr. (See Baton Rouge, Louisiana listing)
Douglas N. Currault II
Donna Thompson Mueller
A. Justin Ourso III (See Baton Rouge, Louisiana listing)
Nan Roberts Eitel
F. Rivers Lelong, Jr.
Dionne M. Rousseau
Andrew R. Lee
T. Michael Twomey
Michael C. Herbert (See Baton Rouge, Louisiana listing)
H. Hughes Grehan
Louis S. Nunes III
Katy W. Kimbell
Jennifer Hantel Traina

(See Next Column)

JONES, WALKER, WAECHTER, POITEVENT, CARRÈRE & DENÈGRE L.L.P., *New Orleans—Continued*

SPECIAL COUNSEL

John Clark Boyce (See Baton Rouge, Louisiana listing)
Thomas A. Casey (See Baton Rouge, Louisiana listing)
John J. Jaskot (Not admitted in LA; See Washington, D.C. listing)
Stanley A. Millan
Mark G. Otts
William H. Strait
Fred L. Chevalier (See Baton Rouge, Louisiana listing)
John M. Girault
Virginia W. Gundlach
Mary Ellen Jordan
Michele Whitesell Crosby (See Baton Rouge, Louisiana listing)
Scott T. Zander
Corinne B. Viso
Robert B. Worley, Jr.
Thomas P. Hubert
Sidney F. Lewis, V.
Clyde H. Jacob, III
Cornelius R. Heusel

ASSOCIATES

S. Michele Ray
Laura Leigh Blackston
Michelle A. Bourque
Timothy S. Cragin
Jennifer L. Anderson
Amy M. Winters
Mary Hassinger Schmidt
Mark W. Mercante
Alida C. Hainkel
Stephen G. Charbonnet
Richard T. Gallagher, Jr.
Keith M. Landry
Jonathan H. Sandoz
Charles L. Rice, Jr.
Karen M. Fontana
William P. Barnette
James D. Canafax
Mark A. Cunningham
R. Scott Jenkins
Elizabeth S. Robins
Erika R. Schwarz
James Meza, III
Ann Allen Arceneaux
Laurie M. Chess
Genevieve Hartel Salassi
David M. Kerth (See Baton Rouge, Louisiana listing)
Regina N. Hamilton (See Baton Rouge, Louisiana listing)
Amy L. Landry
Michael A.G. Korengold
Joseph S. Piacun
Sarah K. Mills
Kelly C. Simoneaux
Margaret M. Landry
L. Etienne Balart
Tina M. Boudreaux
Matthew T. Brown
Norman E. Anseman, III
Miriam W. Henry
Timothy P. Brechtel
Antonio D. Robinson (See Baton Rouge, Louisiana listing)
Corey Christopher DuFresne
Rebecca G. Moore
Gregory M. Carpenter
William B. Lackey (Not admitted in LA)
Gregory D. Latham

Representative Clients: Freeport-McMoRan, Inc.; Freeport-McMoRan Copper & Gold, Inc.; International Shipholding, Inc.; Avondale Industries; Tulane Medical Center; Texaco, Inc.; McDonald's Corp.; Wal-Mart Stores, Inc.; National Marine, Inc.; State of Louisiana.

For full biographical listings, see the Martindale-Hubbell Law Directory

LEAKE, ANDERSSON & MANN, L.L.P. (AV)

1700 Energy Centre, 1100 Poydras Street, 70163-1701
Telephone: 504-585-7500
Facsimile: 504-585-7775

W. Paul Andersson
Lawrence A. Mann
Kevin Cramer O'Bryon
George D. Fagan
Donald E. McKay, Jr.
Stanton E. Shuler, Jr.
Guy D. Perrier

OF COUNSEL

Robert E. Leake, Jr.

ASSOCIATES

J. Ronald Ward, Jr.
Louis P. Bonnaffons
Ellen Heidingsfelder Manning
Dean M. Arruebarrena
Craig M. Cousins
Charles R. Daniel, II

Representative Clients: Commercial Credit Services Corp.; Government Employees Insurance Co.; National Food Processors, Inc.; National Union Fire Insurance Co.; Nationwide Insurance Co.; Professional Construction Services, Inc.

For full biographical listings, see the Martindale-Hubbell Law Directory

LEE, FUTRELL & PERLES, L.L.P. (AV)

Suite 2409, 201 St. Charles Avenue, 70170-2409
Telephone: 504-569-1725
Fax: 504-569-1726
Email: mgr@leefutrell.com *URL:* http://www.lawyers.com/lf&plaw

Gary A. Lee
John Maurice Futrell
Richard M. Perles

Representative Clients: Certain Underwriters at Lloyd's, London; Institute of London Underwriters Companies.

For full biographical listings, see the Martindale-Hubbell Law Directory

LOWE, STEIN, HOFFMAN, ALLWEISS & HAUVER, L.L.P. (AV)

One Shell Square, 701 Poydras Street Suite 3600, 70139-7735
Telephone: 504-581-2450
Telecopier: 504-581-2461

(See Next Column)

MEMBERS OF FIRM

Robert C. Lowe
Mark S. Stein
Mitchell J. Hoffman
Michael R. Allweiss
Terence L. Hauver
Ellen Widen Kessler
Max J. Cohen
Suzette Marie Smith
David M. Prados
Marynell L. Piglia

Kermit L. Roux, III
Charlton D. Hunley
Barbara H. Weiss
Paula H. Lee
Stanley Dale Broome

OF COUNSEL

Mark S. Goldstein
Alicia M. Bendana

For full biographical listings, see the Martindale-Hubbell Law Directory

MCCALLA, THOMPSON, PYBURN, HYMOWITZ & SHAPIRO (AV)

A Limited Liability Partnership including Professional Corporations
Suite 2800, Poydras Center, 650 Poydras Street, 70130
Telephone: 504-524-2499
Fax: 504-523-8679
Email: mtphs@mtphs.com *URL:* http://www.mtphs.com
Gulfport, Mississippi Office: The Markham Building, 2301 14th Street, Suite 507, 39501.
Telephone: 228-868-2774.
Fax: 228-865-3911.

MEMBERS OF FIRM

Christopher P. Charlton (1956-1993)
Robert K. McCalla (P.C.)
Horace A. Thompson III (P.C.)
Keith M. Pyburn, Jr., (P.C.)
Steven Hymowitz (P.C.)
Howard Shapiro (P.C.)
Stefanie Band Allweiss
James M. McGrew (P.C.)
Steven R. Cupp (P.C.)

ASSOCIATES

Heather G. Magier
Taryn S. Southon
Megan Shemwell Nash
Edward F. Harold
Robert Rachal
David P. Bendana
René E. Thorne
Larry E. Demmons
Stacey C. S. Cerrone
Charlotte S. Marquez
Lawrence J. Sorohan II
Cecilia C. Woodley

For full biographical listings, see the Martindale-Hubbell Law Directory

MILLING BENSON WOODWARD L.L.P. (AV)

A Partnership including Professional Law Corporations
Suite Twenty-Three Hundred, 909 Poydras Street, 70112-1017
Telephone: 504-569-7000
Telecopier: 504-569-7001
ABA net: 15656
MCI Mail: "Milling"
Email: milling@millinglaw.com
Lafayette, Louisiana Office: 101 La Rue France, Suite 200.
Telephone: 318-232-3929.
Telecopier: 318-233-4957.
Mandeville (North Shore), Louisiana Office: 2140 8th Street.
Telephone: 504-867-9622.
Telecopier: 504-867-8364.

MEMBERS OF FIRM

David Conroy (P.C.)
Neal D. Hobson (P.C.)
F. Frank Fontenot (P.C.)
William C. Gambel (P.C.)
Charles A. Snyder (P.C.)
Richard A. Whann (P.C.)
Emile A. Wagner, III, (P.C.)
Charles D. Marshall, Jr. (P.C.)
James K. Irvin (P.C.)
Hilton S. Bell (P.C.)
Robert L. Clayton (P.C.)
David N. Schell, Jr. (P.C.)
Jean M. Sweeney (P.C.)
Peter M. Meisner (P.C.)
Timothy T. Roniger (P.C.)
Roselyn B. Koretzky (P.C.)
Michael M. Duran (P.C.)
Jay Corenswet (P.C.)
Alanna S. Arnold (P.C.)
Benjamin O. Schupp (P.C.)
J. Timothy Betbeze (P.C.)

PARTNERS EMERITUS

G. Henry Pierson, Jr., (P.C.)
Joseph B. Miller

OF COUNSEL

Wilson S. Shirley, Jr., (P.C.)
Guy C. Lyman, Jr., (P.C.)

SPECIAL COUNSEL

Roger C. Linde
George M. Papale

ASSOCIATES

Sherry L. Tew
Sergio J. Alarcon
Murphy S. Christina
Sheila L. Moragas
Rodrick E. Anderson
Stacie M. Hollis

LAFAYETTE OFFICE
RESIDENT MEMBERS OF FIRM

Robert L. Cabes (P.C.)
C. Randall Loewen
Daniel A. Rees (L.L.C.)

ASSOCIATE

Gregory M. Attrep

MANDEVILLE (NORTH SHORE) OFFICE
RESIDENT MEMBER OF FIRM

McChord Carrico (P.C.)

(See Next Column)

MILLING BENSON WOODWARD L.L.P.—*Continued*

SPECIAL COUNSEL

Julia M. Pearce

For full biographical listings, see the Martindale-Hubbell Law Directory

PHELPS DUNBAR, L.L.P. (AV)

Texaco Center, 400 Poydras Street, 70130-3245
Telephone: 504-566-1311
Telecopier: 504-568-9130, 504-568-9007
Cable Address: "Howspencer"
Telex: 584125 WU
Telex: 6821155 WUI
Email: info@phelps.com
Baton Rouge, Louisiana Office: Suite 701, 445 North Boulevard, P.O. Box 4412.
Telephone: 225-346-0285.
Telecopier: 225-381-9197.
Jackson, Mississippi Office: Suite 500, SkyTel Centre, 200 South Lamar Street, P.O. Box 23066.
Telephone: 601-352-2300.
Telecopier: 601-360-9777.
Tupelo, Mississippi Office: Seventh Floor, One Mississippi Plaza, P.O. Box 1220.
Telephone: 662-842-7907.
Telecopier: 662-842-3873.
Houston, Texas Office: Suite 900, 3040 Post Oak Boulevard.
Telephone: 713-626-1386.
Telecopier: 713-626-1388.
London, England Office: Suite 731, Level 7, Lloyd's, 1 Lime Street, London EC3M 7DQ England.
Telephone: 011-44-207-929-4765.
Telecopier: 011-44-207-929-0046.
Telex: 987321.

OF COUNSEL

Fred M. Bush, Jr. (Not admitted in LA; Resident, Tupelo, Mississippi Office)
Frank S. Craig, Jr. (Resident, Baton Rouge, Louisiana Office)
George W. Healy, III
James Bradley Kemp, Jr.
Harry S. Redmon, Jr.
John W. Sims
John G. Weinmann
J. Barbee Winston

RESIDENT PARTNERS

William D. Aaron, Jr.
Neil C. Abramson
Julia Marie Adams (Not admitted in LA; Resident, Houston, Texas Office)
Lee R. Adler
M. Nan Alessandra
Reuben V. Anderson (Not admitted in LA; Resident, Jackson, Mississippi Office)
Jane E. Armstrong
Barbara L. Arras
Brent B. Barriere
Gerardo R. Barrios
Ross F. Bass, Jr. (Not admitted in LA; Resident, Jackson, Mississippi Office)
William M. Beasley (Not admitted in LA; Resident, Tupelo, Mississippi Office)
Jonathan C. Benda (Resident, Baton Rouge, Louisiana Office)
Virginia Boulet
William C. Brabec (Not admitted in LA; Resident, Jackson, Mississippi Office)
F. M. Bush, III (Not admitted in LA; Resident, Tupelo, Mississippi Office)
Patrick J. Butler, Jr.
Roy C. Cheatwood
Philip deV. Claverie
Robert C. Clotworthy
James W. Craig (Not admitted in LA; Resident, Jackson, Mississippi Office)
David Lee Crawford (Not admitted in LA; Resident, Houston, Texas Office)
R. Pepper Crutcher, Jr. (Resident, Jackson, Mississippi Office)
Allen D. Darden (Resident, Baton Rouge, Louisiana Office)
Christopher O. Davis
Deborah Shelby Dees (Not admitted in LA; Resident, Jackson, Mississippi Office)
Nancy Scott Degan
Susan Fahey Desmond
Richard N. Dicharry (Also at London, England Office)
Mark C. Dodart (Also at London, England Office)
Gary E. Friedman (Not admitted in LA; Resident, Jackson, Mississippi Office)
Mark A. Fullmer
Susan W. Furr (Resident, Baton Rouge, Louisiana Office)
George M. Gilly
George B. Hall, Jr.
J. Clifton Hall III (Houston, Texas and London, England Offices)
Stephen P. Hall (Also at London, England Office)
E. Clifton Hodge, Jr. (Not admitted in LA; Resident, Jackson, Mississippi Office)
Jean Magee Hogan (Not admitted in LA; Resident, Tupelo, Mississippi Office)
Sessions Ault Hootsell III
C. Delbert Hosemann, Jr. (Not admitted in LA; Resident, Jackson, Mississippi Office)
William H. Howard, III (Also at London, England Office)
Michael D. Hunt (Resident, Baton Rouge, Louisiana Office)
David M. Hunter
H. Alston Johnson, III (Resident, Baton Rouge, Louisiana Office)
F. Scott Kaiser (Resident, Baton Rouge, Louisiana Office)
Thomas H. Kiggans (Resident, Baton Rouge, Louisiana Office)
Stephen H. Leech, Jr. (Not admitted in LA; Resident, Jackson, Mississippi Office)
Steven J. Levine (Resident, Baton Rouge, Louisiana Office)
John P. Manard, Jr.

(See Next Column)

RESIDENT PARTNERS (Continued)

Richard E. Matheny (Resident, Baton Rouge, Louisiana Office)
Robert P. McCleskey, Jr. (Also at London, England Office)
Dan M. McDaniel, Jr. (Not admitted in LA; Resident, Jackson, Mississippi Office)
Pamela G. Michiels (Also at London, England Office)
Paul O. Miller, III (Not admitted in LA; Resident, Jackson, Mississippi Office)
Armin J. Moeller, Jr. (Resident, Jackson, Mississippi Office)
Luther T. Munford (Not admitted in LA; Resident, Jackson, Mississippi Office)
Matthew R. Muth (Not admitted in LA; Resident, Houston, Texas Office)
Deborah A. Newman (Not admitted in LA; Resident, Houston, Texas Office)
Dinetia M. Newman (Not admitted in LA; Resident, Tupelo, Mississippi Office)
Robert W. Nuzum
James W. O'Mara (Not admitted in LA; Resident, Jackson, Mississippi Office)
Paul L. Peyronnin
Gregory D. Pirkle (Not admitted in LA; Resident, Tupelo, Mississippi Office)
Freddie Pitcher, Jr. (Resident, Baton Rouge, Louisiana Office)
Edward B. Poitevent, II
Marshall M. Redmon (Baton Rouge, Louisiana and London, England Offices)
William J. Riviere
John W. Robinson, III (Not admitted in LA; Resident, Jackson, Mississippi Office)
Harry Rosenberg
James H. Roussel (Also at London, England Office)
Randy P. Roussel (Resident, Baton Rouge, Louisiana Office)
Mary Ellen Roy
Glover A. Russell, Jr. (Not admitted in LA; Resident, Jackson, Mississippi Office)
Bruce V. Schewe
Danny G. Shaw
W. Thomas Siler, Jr. (Not admitted in LA; Resident, Jackson, Mississippi Office)
John P. Sneed (Resident, Jackson, Mississippi Office)
David P. Steiner
Claude LeRoy Stuart, III (Not admitted in LA; Resident, Houston, Texas Office)
James A. Stuckey
David M. Thomas, II (Not admitted in LA; Resident, Jackson, Mississippi Office)
Frank W. Trapp (Not admitted in LA; Resident, Jackson, Mississippi Office)
Harvey D. Wagar, III
Brian D. Wallace
Michael B. Wallace (Not admitted in LA; Resident, Jackson, Mississippi Office)
David P. Webb (Not admitted in LA; Resident, Jackson, Mississippi Office)
Kent E. Westmoreland (Not admitted in LA; Houston, Texas and London, England Offices)
Stephen M. Wilson (Not admitted in LA; Resident, Jackson, Mississippi Office)
Alan C. Wolf
Joseph A. Ziemianski (Not admitted in LA; Resident, Houston, Texas Office)

COUNSEL

Alissa J. Allison
J. Michael Cutshaw (Resident, Baton Rouge, Louisiana Office)
Edwin K. Legnon
Peter B. Magnuson (Not admitted in LA; Resident, Houston, Texas Office)
Jeffrey S. Moore (Not admitted in LA; Resident, Tupelo, Mississippi Office)
Jane A. Robert (Resident, Baton Rouge, Louisiana Office)
Linda Bounds Sherman (Not admitted in LA; Resident, Jackson, Mississippi Office)
G. Kay L. Trapp (Not admitted in LA; Resident, Tupelo, Mississippi Office)

RESIDENT ASSOCIATES

Dawn Amber Abuso
Joseph Lee Adams (Not admitted in LA; Resident, Jackson, Mississippi Office)
Jeffrey M. Barbin (Resident, Baton Rouge, Louisiana Office)
Jane H. Barney (Resident, Baton Rouge, Louisiana Office)
Martin K. Bech
Thomas M. Beh
Jennifer M. Benson (Resident, Houston, Texas Office)
Ashley S. Bergeron
Wendy T. Blanchard (Resident, Houston, Texas Office)
Nora T. Bolling
Peggy Eileen Bordelon
Maurice E. Bostick
Debra M. Brown (Not admitted in LA; Resident, Jackson, Mississippi Office)
Stratton Bull (Not admitted in LA; Resident, Jackson, Mississippi Office)
Jennifer L. Burrows
Evan T. Caffrey
Heather J. Camp (Not admitted in LA; Resident, Jackson, Mississippi Office)
Mary A. Cazes (Resident, Houston, Texas Office)
Rebecca Y. Cooper
S. Michael Cooper
Rebecca Bellows Crawford (Resident, Baton Rouge, Louisiana Office)
Scott M. Cullen
Lawrence W. DaGate
Christine McCue Daly
Daniel E. Davillier
Katherine Miller Determan
Caroline McS. Dolan
Patrick W. Drouilhet (Resident, Houston, Texas Office)
Scott Ellzey (Not admitted in LA; Resident, Tupelo, Mississippi Office)
Ken Fairly (Not admitted in LA; Resident, Jackson, Mississippi Office)
Laura Schuler Favaloro (Not admitted in LA; Resident, Houston, Texas Office)
Mark Fijman (Not admitted in LA; Resident, Jackson, Mississippi Office)
Tracey E. Flemings
Kari L. Foster (Not admitted in LA; Resident, Jackson, Mississippi Office)
Christine S. Goldberg (Resident, Baton Rouge, Louisiana Office)

(See Next Column)

PHELPS DUNBAR L.L.P., *New Orleans—Continued*

RESIDENT ASSOCIATES (Continued)

Kevin M. Grace
Christopher R. Green (Not admitted in LA; Resident, Jackson, Mississippi Office)
Eric T. Hamer (Not admitted in LA; Resident, Jackson, Mississippi Office)
Hansel M. Harlan
Gwen P. Harmon (Resident, Baton Rouge Office)
Rebecca Hawkins (Not admitted in LA; Resident, Jackson, Mississippi Office)
Stacy S. Head
Christopher L. Hewitt (Not admitted in LA)
Kimberly L. Hood (Resident, Baton Rouge, Louisiana Office)
Clinton D. Howie (Resident, Baton Rouge, Louisiana Office)
Gregory M. Hunsucker (Not admitted in LA; Resident, Tupelo, Mississippi Office)
Mark Stewart Johnson (Not admitted in LA; Resident, Tupelo, Mississippi Office)
R. Hayes Johnson, Jr. (Not admitted in LA; Resident, Jackson, Mississippi Office)
Amanda Jones (Not admitted in LA; Resident, Jackson, Mississippi Office)
Karleen Joseph (Resident, Baton Rouge, Louisiana Office)
Marilee R. Kainer (Not admitted in LA; Resident, Houston, Texas Office)
David M. Korn
Kelsey B. Kornick (Resident, Baton Rouge, Louisiana Office)
M. David Kurtz
Kent A. Lambert
Candice L. Leonard (Not admitted in LA; Resident, Houston, Texas Office)
Mark C. Lewis (Not admitted in LA; Resident, Tupelo, Mississippi Office)
Tricia A. Martinez
Barry L. McGraw (Not admitted in LA; Resident, Tupelo, Mississippi Office)
Mark L. McNamara
Karen Klaas Milhollin (Not admitted in LA; Resident, Houston, Texas Office)
J. Douglas Minor, Jr. (Not admitted in LA; Resident, Jackson, Mississippi Office)
Thomas Kent Ledyard Morrison
Wendy Russell Mullins (Not admitted in LA; Resident, Jackson, Mississippi Office)
W. Spencer Murphy
Douglas C. Noble (Not admitted in LA; Resident, Jackson, Mississippi Office)
Debra S. Noll (Not admitted in LA; Resident, Houston, Texas Office)
Leah E. Nunn
Sheryl A. Odems (Not admitted in LA)
Patrick O'Hara (Resident, Baton Rouge, Louisiana Office)
W. Sean O'Neil
Daniel T. Pancamo
David L. Patrón
Rebecca Fariss Penniman (Resident, Baton Rouge, Louisiana Office)
A. Matt Pesnell (Not admitted in LA; Resident, Jackson, Mississippi Office)
Chelye E. Prichard (Not admitted in LA; Resident, Jackson, Mississippi Office)
Stanley T. Proctor (Not admitted in LA; Resident, Houston, Texas Office)
Katherine Karam Quirk
Dawn M. Rawls
Patrick Ragan Richard (Resident, Baton Rouge, Louisiana Office)
Joanne Rinardo
William S. Robbins (Resident, Baton Rouge, Louisiana Office)
Mary Frances Lindquist Rosamond
Owen Bennett St. Amant
Mark B. Schaffer (Not admitted in LA; Resident, Houston, Texas Office)
William G. Schlotthauer
John L. Schouest (Resident, Houston, Texas Office)
William A. Schreiner, Jr. (Not admitted in LA)
Eric M. Schroeder
Jay Russell Sever
James W. Shelson (Not admitted in LA; Resident, Jackson, Mississippi Office)
Robert S. Stassi
Clinton Ryan Stuart (Resident, Baton Rouge, Louisiana Office)
Tania Tetlow
Cynthia J. Thomas
Elizabeth E. Thomas (Not admitted in LA; Resident, Tupelo, Mississippi Office)
Virginia Yoder Trainor (Resident, Baton Rouge, Louisiana Office)
E. Russell Turner (Not admitted in LA; Resident, Jackson, Mississippi Office)
Kara Van de Carr (Not admitted in LA)
Anne Magee Vaughan
Bryan P. Vezey (Not admitted in LA; Resident, Houston, Texas Office)
Sheila T. Walet
Alistair M. Ward
G. Benjamin Ward
Michael F. Weiner
Lara E. White
Ronald J. White
Robert L. Wollfarth, Jr.
Dawei Zhang
April M. Zubizarreta (Not admitted in LA; Resident, Houston, Texas Office)

Representative Clients: The Britannia Steamship Insurance Assn., Ltd.; Cleco Corporation; Edison Chouest Offshore, L.L.C.; Entergy Enterprises, Inc.; Hibernia National Bank; North Mississippi Health Services, Inc. (and affiliated entities); The Travelers Insurance Company; Underwriters at Lloyd's, London; Union Pacific Railroad Company; Uniroyal Chemical Company.

For full biographical listings, see the Martindale-Hubbell Law Directory

PLAUCHÉ MASELLI LANDRY & PARKERSON L.L.P. (AV)

Bank One Center, Suite 4240, 201 St. Charles Avenue, 70170-4240
Telephone: 504-582-1142
Fax: 504-582-1172
URL: http://www.pmlpnola.com

(See Next Column)

MEMBERS OF FIRM

Andrew L. Plauché, Jr.
Joseph Maselli, Jr.
Arthur W. Landry
G. Bruce Parkerson
Robert E Caraway, III

ASSOCIATES

Mark E. Young
Thomas L. Hutchinson
Cherie T. Burlett
Kenan S. Rand, Jr.
Elizabeth Salzer Schell
J. Marie Rudd
Wendy K. Lappenga
Deborah F. Malveaux
Diane S. Mitnik
Lori P. Moser

Reference: Bank One of Louisiana.

For full biographical listings, see the Martindale-Hubbell Law Directory

SESSIONS & FISHMAN, L.L.P. (AV)

A Registered Limited Liability Partnership including Professional Corporations
201 St. Charles Avenue, Suite 3500, 70170-3500
Telephone: 504-582-1500
Telex: 58364NLN
Fax: 504-582-1555
Email: counsel@sessions-law.com
Metairie, Louisiana Office: Lakeway Two, 3850 North Causeway Boulevard, Suite 350.
Telephone: 504-828-3700.
Fax: 504-828-3737.

MEMBERS OF FIRM

Max Nathan, Jr. (P.C.)
Robert E. Winn
L. K. Clement, Jr.
William M. Lucas, Jr.
Michael J. Molony, Jr. (P.C.)
Jack M. Alltmont
J. David Forsyth
James Ryan, III
Peter S. Title
Carole Cukell Neff
Camilo K. Salas, III
Dorothy S. Jacobs (P.C.)
Joy Goldberg Braun
Andrew A. Braun
Joyce M. Dombourian (P.C.)
Alan D. Ezkovich
John William Hite, III
Sharon Cormack Mize
David H. Bernstein
David P. Salley
Raymond P. Ward
Michael A. Berenson
Brian D. Roth
Edward J. Rivera

SPECIAL COUNSEL

David Israel (Resident Manager, Metairie Office)

ASSOCIATES

Maria N. Rabieh
Glen E. Mercer
Deana D. Palmisano
Leslie N. Ladner
Theresa Urban Guill
Suzanne Lacey Wisdom

Representative Clients: Air Products & Chemicals, Inc.; Bethlehem Steel Corp.; Brown & Williamson Tobacco Corporation; The Equitable Life Assurance Society of the United States; Holiday Inns, Inc.; J.C. Penney Co., Inc.; State Farm Insurance Cos.; United Services Automobile Assn.; Volkswagen of America, Inc.

For full biographical listings, see the Martindale-Hubbell Law Directory

SHER GARNER CAHILL RICHTER KLEIN MCALISTER & HILBERT, L.L.C. (AV)

909 Poydras Street Twenty-Eighth Floor, 70112-1033
Telephone: 504-299-2100
Fax: 504-299-2300
URL: http://www.shergarner.com

Leopold Z. Sher (P.C.)
James M. Garner
Elwood F. Cahill, Jr.
Richard P. Richter
Steven I. Klein (P.C.)
Thomas P. McAlister
Peter L. Hilbert, Jr., (P.C.)
Marie A. Moore
Debra Fischman Cottrell
Robert P. Thibeaux
Darnell Bludworth
Martha Y. Curtis
Neal J. Kling
Karen T. Holzenthal
Dorothy S. Watkins Lawrence
Keith A. Kornman
John Thomas Balhoff, II
William J. Furnish, Jr.
Deborah M. Aymé
Michael H. Pinkerton
Edward J. Rantz, Jr.
Alvin C. Miester, III
Brandon A. Brown
J. Michael Monahan, II

OF COUNSEL

Timothy B. Francis

For full biographical listings, see the Martindale-Hubbell Law Directory

STONE, PIGMAN, WALTHER, WITTMANN & HUTCHINSON, L.L.P. (AV)

A Partnership including Professional Corporations
546 Carondelet Street, 70130-3588
Telephone: 504-581-3200
Fax: 504-581-3361
Email: info@stonepigman.com

(See Next Column)

STONE, PIGMAN, WALTHER, WITTMANN & HUTCHINSON L.L.P.—*Continued*

MEMBERS OF FIRM

Saul Stone
Ewell P. Walther, Jr. (1932-1990)
Phillip A. Wittmann
William D. Treeby (P.C.)
Hirschel T. Abbott, Jr., (P.C.)
Michael R. Fontham (P.C.)
Anthony M. DiLeo (P.C.)
Wayne J. Lee (P.C.)
James C. Gulotta, Jr., (P.C.)
Paul L. Zimmering
John M. Landis
Stephen H. Kupperman (P.C.)
Stephen G. Bullock
Steven W. Usdin (P.C.)
Judy Y. Barrasso (P.C.)
Susan Gayle Talley (P.C.)
Douglas D. Dodd
John W. Colbert
Noel J. Darce
C. Lawrence Orlansky (P.C.)
Michael R. Schneider (P.C.)
Scott T. Whittaker
Barry W. Ashe (P.C.)
George C. Freeman, III
Joseph L. Caverly (P.C.)
Richard E. Sarver
Michael D. Landry
Mary L. Dumestre (P.C.)
Karen H. Freese (P.C.)
John P. Cerise (P.C.)
Paul J. Masinter
Dorothy Hudson Wimberly (P.C.)
Rachel Wendt Wisdom

SPECIAL COUNSEL

Paul O. H. Pigman (P.C.)
Campbell C. Hutchinson (P.C.)
David L. Stone (P.C.)
Denise M. Pilié

ASSOCIATES

Mary Modenbach White
Stephanie D. Shuler
C. Joyce Hall
Michael Q. Walshe, Jr.
H. Minor Pipes, III
Keith B. Hall
Leon J. Reymond, III
Christopher A. Colvin
John P. Farnsworth
April D. Dulaney
Dana M. Shelton
Scott B. Arceneaux
Linda A. Verlander
Jennifer D. Rogers
Celeste R. Coco-Ewing
Sandra Diggs-Miller
Shelley L. Poore

For full biographical listings, see the Martindale-Hubbell Law Directory

TERRIBERRY, CARROLL & YANCEY, L.L.P. (AV)

3100 Energy Centre, 1100 Poydras Street, 70163-3100
Telephone: 504-523-6451
Cable Address: "Terrib"
Telex: 6821224 (WUI)
Fax: 504-524-3257
Email: info@terriberry.com

Benjamin W. Yancey (1906-1991)
Walter Carroll, Jr. (Retired)

MEMBERS OF FIRM

G. Edward Merritt
John A. Bolles
Charles F. Lozes
Robert J. Barbier
Hugh Ramsay Straub
David B. Lawton
Janet Wessler Marshall
D. Kirk Boswell
Gary A. Hemphill
Laurence R. De Buys, IV
Kevin J. LaVie
Stephen E. Mattesky
Gerald M. Baca
Michael M. Butterworth
John A. Scialdone

COUNSEL

Andrew T. Martinez
Cynthia Anne Wegmann

ASSOCIATES

Evans Martin Mcleod
Kenneth J. Gelpi, Jr.

OF COUNSEL

James L. Schupp, Jr.

Representative Clients: Assuranceforeningen Gard; Assuranceforeningen Skuld; The Britannia Club; Certain Underwriters at Lloyd's; The London Steam-Ship Owners' Mutual Insurance Assn. Ltd.; New Orleans Steamship Assn.; Nordisk Skibsrederforening (Northern Shipowners Defence Club); Scandinavian Marine Claims Office, Inc.; Steamship Mutual Underwriting Assn. Ltd.; United Kingdom Mutual Steam Ship Assurance Assn. Ltd.

For full biographical listings, see the Martindale-Hubbell Law Directory

*PLAQUEMINE,** Iberville Parish

BORRON & DELAHAYE, A PROFESSIONAL LAW CORPORATION (AV)

58065 Meriam Street, P.O. Box 679, 70765-0679
Telephone: 225-687-3571; 343-3148
Fax: 225-687-9695

Paul G. Borron (1874-1960)
J. Evan Delahaye (1910-1997)
Paul G. Borron, Jr. (1908-1997)
Paul G. Borron, III
John L. Delahaye

Representative Clients: American Sugar Cane League; Iberville Trust & Savings Bank; A. Wilbert's Sons Limited Partnership; Nadler, Inc.; Harry L. Laws & Co., Inc.; J. Supple's Sons Planting Co., Ltd.; Hebert Brothers Engineers; River Valley Services, Inc.; Graugnard Brothers, Inc.; Iberville Building & Loan Assn.

For full biographical listings, see the Martindale-Hubbell Law Directory

*SHREVEPORT,** Caddo Parish

BARLOW AND HARDTNER L.C. (AV)

Tenth Floor, Louisiana Tower, 401 Edwards Street, 71101-3289
Telephone: 318-227-1131
Telecopier: 318-227-1141
Mailing Address: P.O. Box 8, Shreveport, Louisiana, 71161-0008

Ray A. Barlow (1931-1995)
Quintin T. Hardtner, III
Malcolm S. Murchison
Kay Cowden Medlin
Joseph L. Shea, Jr.
David R. Taggart
Stephen E. Ramey
Michael B. Donald
Jay A. Greenleaf

OF COUNSEL

Cecil E. Ramey, Jr.
Paula Hazelrig Hickman
Jerald N. Jones

Gail Bowen McCulloch
Jonathan D. Baughman
Sarah A. Kirkpatrick
David A. Barlow
William T. Gates

Representative Clients: NorAm Energy Corp. (formerly Arkla, Inc.); The Magale Foundation; Central and South West Corporation; Panhandle Eastern Corp.; Pennzoil Producing Co.; Ashland Oil, Inc.; The Daughters of the Cross; Southwestern Electric Power Company; The Centex Construction Group; General Electric Co.

For full biographical listings, see the Martindale-Hubbell Law Directory

BLANCHARD, WALKER, O'QUIN & ROBERTS, A PROFESSIONAL LAW CORPORATION (AV)

Fourteenth Floor, Premier Bank Tower, 400 Texas Street, P.O. Drawer 1126, 71101
Telephone: 318-221-6858
Fax: 318-227-2967
Email: BWOR@BWOR.com
Bossier City, Louisiana Office: 2285 Benton Road, Suite B-201.
Telephone: 318-742-9255.
Fax: 318-742-9210.

Gilbert L. Hetherwick
Robert Roberts III
Neilson S. Jacobs
John T. Cox, Jr.
J. Edgerton Pierson, Jr., (P.C.)
W. Michael Adams
Wm. Timothy Allen, III
Reginald E. Cassibry
J. David Garrett
Cecil W. Talley
Robert W. Johnson
Michael E. Riddick
Edward Keith Carter
Paul M. Adkins
A. M. Stroud, III
Leslie Idom Kalmbach
Gary H. Love
Pamela G. Nathan
Julie Van Thof
Stacey D. Williams

OF COUNSEL

Pike Hall, Jr.
Marlin Risinger, Jr.

For full biographical listings, see the Martindale-Hubbell Law Directory

MAYER, SMITH & ROBERTS, L.L.P. (AV)

1550 Creswell, 71101
Telephone: 318-222-2135, 222-2268
Fax: 318-222-6420
Email: (Attorney's First Name)@MSRLAW.COM

MEMBERS OF FIRM

Caldwell Roberts
Walter O. Hunter, Jr.
Mark A. Goodwin
Ben Marshall, Jr.
Alexander S. Lyons
Kim Purdy Thomas
David Butterfield
Henry N. Bellamy
John C. Turnage
Paul R. Mayer, Jr.
Steven E. Soileau
Deborah Shea Baukman
Caldwell Roberts, Jr.
Frank K. Carroll
Dalton Roberts Ross

OF COUNSEL

Paul R. Mayer

Representative Clients: CNA Insurance Companies; Liberty Mutual Insurance Company; United States Fidelity and Guaranty Company; Schumpert Medical Center; Travelers Insurance Company; Great American Insurance Company; Insurance Corporation of America; Highlands Insurance Company.

For full biographical listings, see the Martindale-Hubbell Law Directory

SIMON, FITZGERALD, COOKE, REED & WELCH (AV)

Suite 200, 4700 Line Avenue, 71106
Telephone: 318-868-2600
Telecopier: 318-868-8966

MEMBERS OF FIRM

Fred Simon (1904-1993)
Archie M. Simon (1909-1997)
Thomas P. Fitzgerald (1914-1993)
Paul M. Cooke
Chatham H. Reed
Keith M. Welch
Kevin R. Molloy

(See Next Column)

SIMON, FITZGERALD, COOKE, REED & WELCH, *Shreveport—Continued*

A list of Representative Clients will be furnished upon request.

For full biographical listings, see the Martindale-Hubbell Law Directory

WILKINSON, CARMODY & GILLIAM (AV)

1700 Beck Building, 400 Travis Street, P.O. Box 1707, 71166
Telephone: 318-221-4196
Telecopier: 318-221-3705
Email: wcg1895@aol.com

MEMBERS OF FIRM

John D. Wilkinson (1867-1929)
William Scott Wilkinson (1895-1985)
Arthur R. Carmody, Jr.
Bobby S. Gilliam
Mark E. Gilliam
William Allen Haynes

Representative Clients: Farmers Insurance Group; Home Federal Savings & Loan Association of Shreveport; The Kansas City Southern Railway Co.; KTAL-TV; Lincoln National Life Insurance Co.; Mobil Oil Co.; Schumpert Medical Center; Sears, Roebuck & Co.; Southern Pacific Transportation Co.; Southwestern Electric Power Co.

For full biographical listings, see the Martindale-Hubbell Law Directory

*WINNFIELD,** Winn Parish

SIMMONS AND DERR (AV)

Simmons Building, Church Street, P.O. Box 525, 71483
Telephone: 318-628-3951
Fax: 318-648-0644

MEMBERS OF FIRM

Kermit M. Simmons
Jacque D. Derr

Reference: Bank of Winnfield & Trust Co.

For full biographical listings, see the Martindale-Hubbell Law Directory

MAINE

*AUBURN,** Androscoggin Co.

SKELTON, TAINTOR & ABBOTT, A PROFESSIONAL CORPORATION (AV)

95 Main Street, P.O. Box 3200, 04212-3200
Telephone: 207-784-3200
Fax: 207-784-3345

Charles H. Abbott
Stephen P. Beale
Jill A. Checkoway
John B. Cole
Bryan M. Dench
Peter M. Garcia
Ronald P. Lebel
Michael R. Poulin
Norman J. Rattey
Stephen B. Wade

James E. Belleau
Harold N. Skelton
William Holton Stiles
William K. Skelton

OF COUNSEL

William B. Skelton, II

General Counsel for: Androscoggin Savings Bank; Bates College; Central Maine Medical Center; Auburn Savings & Loan Association; Auburn Housing Authority; Maine School Administrative District No. 52; Lewiston Sun-Journal; Geiger Bros.; White Rock Distilleries, Inc.

For full biographical listings, see the Martindale-Hubbell Law Directory

*AUGUSTA,** Kennebec Co.

PIERCE ATWOOD (AV)

77 Winthrop Street, 04330
Telephone: 207-622-6311
Fax: 207-623-9367
Email: info@PierceAtwood.com *URL:* http://www.pierceatwood.com
Portland, Maine Office: One Monument Square.
Telephone: 207-791-1100.
Fax: 207-791-1350.
Newburyport, Massachusetts Office: 6 Harris Street.
Telephone: 978-465-9599.
Fax: 978-465-9945.

MEMBERS OF FIRM

Warren E. Winslow, Jr.
Malcolm L. Lyons
Michael D. Seitzinger
John C. Nivison

ASSOCIATES

Helen L. Edmonds
Ann M. St. Peter-Griffith

COUNSEL

Daniel J. Stevens

For full biographical listings, see the Martindale-Hubbell Law Directory

PRETI, FLAHERTY, BELIVEAU, PACHIOS & HALEY, LLC (AV)

45 Memorial Circle, P.O. Box 1058, 04332-1058
Telephone: 207-623-5300
Telecopier: 207-623-2914
Email: admin@preti.com *URL:* http://www.preti.com
Portland, Maine Office: One City Center, P.O. Box 9546, 04112-9546.
Telephone: 207-791-3000.
Telefax: 207-791-3111.
Bath, Maine Office: Thirty Front Street, P.O. Box 665, 04530-0665.
Telephone: 207-443-5576.
Telefax: 207-443-6665.

RESIDENT MEMBERS OF FIRM

Severin M. Beliveau
Michael J. Gentile
Bruce C. Gerrity
Anthony W. Buxton
James C. Pitney, Jr.
Virginia E. Davis
Joseph G. Donahue
Ann R. Robinson
Stephen E. F. Langsdorf
Charles F. Dingman
Mark B. LeDuc

RESIDENT ASSOCIATE

Donald J. Sipe

For full biographical listings, see the Martindale-Hubbell Law Directory

*BANGOR,** Penobscot Co.

EATON, PEABODY, BRADFORD & VEAGUE, P.A. (AV)

Fleet Center-Exchange Street, P.O. Box 1210, 04402-1210
Telephone: 207-947-0111
Telecopier: 207-942-3040
Email: eaton@eatonpeabody.com *URL:* http://www.eatonpeabody.com
Augusta, Maine Office: 77 Sewall Street, Suite 3000.
Telephone: 207-622-3747.
Telecopier: 207-622-9732.
Blue Hill, Maine Office: One East Blue Hill Road.
Telephone: 207-374-2812.
Telecopier: 207-374-2548.
Brunswick, Maine Office: 167 Park Row.
Telephone: 207-729-1144.
Telecopier: 207-729-1140.
Dover-Foxcroft, Maine Office: 30 East Main Street.
Telephone: 207-564-8378.
Telecopier: 207-564-7059.

George F. Eaton (1892-1956)
Malcolm E. Morrell, Jr.
Thomas M. Brown
Edward D. Leonard, III
Calvin E. True
Bernard J. Kubetz
Thomas C. Johnston
Clarissa B. Edelston
Douglas M. Smith (Dover-Foxcroft and Augusta Offices)
Daniel G. McKay
Stephen G. Morrell (Resident, Brunswick Office)
Glen L. Porter
Gordon H. S. Scott (Resident, Augusta Office)
Clare Hudson Payne
Michael B. Trainor
John A. Cunningham (Resident, Brunswick Office)
William B. Devoe
Karen A. Huber
P. Andrew Hamilton
Laurie A. Dart
Judy A.S. Metcalf (Resident, Brunswick Office)
Jonathan B. Huntington (Resident, Dover-Foxcroft Office)
Thad B. Zmistowski
Lorena R. Rush
Dorisann B. W. Wagner (Resident, Augusta Office)
Roger L. Huber

OF COUNSEL

George F. Peabody
Martin L. Wilk (Resident, Brunswick Office)
Dorrance Sexton, Jr. (Resident, Blue Hill Office)

William V. Ferdinand, Jr. (Resident, Augusta Office)
Nathaniel S. Putnam
David M. Austin
Darin G. Haugen
Stephen C. Smith
Matthew S. Raynes

For full biographical listings, see the Martindale-Hubbell Law Directory

GROSS, MINSKY, MOGUL & SINGAL, P.A. (AV)

Key Plaza, 23 Water Street, P.O. Box 917, 04402-0917
Telephone: 207-942-4644; 800-274-7124
Telecopier: 207-942-3699
Email: law@gmms.com

Edward I. Gross (1912-1999)
Jules L. Mogul (1930-1994)
George Z. Singal
Louis H. Kornreich
George C. Schelling
Edward W. Gould
Steven J. Mogul
James R. Wholly
Daniel A. Pileggi
Philip K. Clarke

Wayne P. Libhart (Retired)
Sandra L. Rothera
James S. Nixon

(See Next Column)

GROSS, MINSKY, MOGUL & SINGAL P.A.—*Continued*

OF COUNSEL

Norman Minsky

Representative Client: Dahl Chase Pathology Associates.
Local Counsel for: The St. Paul Insurance Cos.; Aetna Life & Casualty Co.; Imperial Casualty & Indemnity Co.

For full biographical listings, see the Martindale-Hubbell Law Directory

BAR HARBOR, Hancock Co.

FENTON, CHAPMAN, FENTON, SMITH & KANE, P.A. (AV)

109 Main Street, P.O. Box B, 04609
Telephone: 207-288-3331
Fax: 207-288-9326
Email: fentonlawfirm@acadia.net *URL:* http://www.lawyers.com/fcfs&klaw

William Fenton
Douglas B. Chapman
Nathaniel R. Fenton
Chadbourn H. Smith
Daniel H. Kane (1940-1995)
Hancock Griffin, Jr. (1912-1980)

Margaret T. Jeffery

Reference: Bar Harbor Banking and Trust Co.

For full biographical listings, see the Martindale-Hubbell Law Directory

*BATH,** Sagadahoc Co.

PRETI, FLAHERTY, BELIVEAU, PACHIOS & HALEY, LLC (AV)

Thirty Front Street, P.O. Box 665, 04530-0665
Telephone: 207-443-5576
Telefax: 207-443-6665
Email: admin@preti.com *URL:* http://www.preti.com
Portland, Maine Office: One City Center, P.O. Box 9546, 04112-9546.
Telephone: 207-791-3000.
Telefax: 207-791-3111.
Augusta, Maine Office: 45 Memorial Circle, P.O. Box 1058, 04332-1058.
Telephone: 207-623-5300.
Telefax: 207-623-2914.

RESIDENT MEMBERS OF FIRM

Mark L. Haley
Brian L. Champion

RESIDENT ASSOCIATES

Tracey G. Burton
Jon A. Fitzgerald
Jeffrey W. Peters

For full biographical listings, see the Martindale-Hubbell Law Directory

KENNEBUNK, York Co.

JENSEN BAIRD GARDNER & HENRY (AV)

(Successor to Walker, Bradford & LaBrique)
11 Main Street, Suite 4, 04043
Telephone: 207-985-4676
Telecopier: 207-985-4932
Email: info@jbgh.com *URL:* http://www.jbgh.com
Portland, Maine Office: Ten Free Street, P.O. Box 4510, 04112-4510.
Telephone: 207-775-7271.
Telecopier: 207-775-7935.

OF COUNSEL

John D. Bradford

RESIDENT MEMBER OF FIRM

David J. Jones

Representative Clients: General Motors Acceptance Corp.; Sedgwick James.

For full biographical listings, see the Martindale-Hubbell Law Directory

*PORTLAND,** Cumberland Co.

BENNETT BENNETT AND TROIANO, P.A. (AV)

Suite 300, 121 Middle Street, P.O. Box 7799, 04112-7799
Telephone: 207-773-4775
Telecopier: 207-774-2366
Email: lawyers@bennettlegal.com *URL:* http://www.bennettlegal.com

Herbert H. Bennett (1928-1992)
Peter Bennett
Jeffrey Bennett
Joseph A. Troiano
Frederick B. Finberg

Julie A. Boesky

OF COUNSEL

Jonathan M. Dunitz

Counsel for: Associated Grocers of New England; General Star Indemnity Company; Coca Cola Bottling Company of Northern New England, Inc.; Northern Utilities/Bay State Gas; Pratt & Whitney (Division of United Technologies); Primerica Financial Services (Citigroup); Sprague Energy (C.H. Sprague & Son); Perrier Group of America, Inc.; Lepage Bakeries, Inc. (Country Kitchen); Texaco, Inc.

(See Next Column)

For full biographical listings, see the Martindale-Hubbell Law Directory

BERNSTEIN, SHUR, SAWYER & NELSON, A PROFESSIONAL CORPORATION (AV)

100 Middle Street, P.O. Box 9729, 04104-5029
Telephone: 207-774-1200
Telecopier: 207-774-1127
Email: lawyers@mainelaw.com
Email: lawyers@bernsteinshur.com *URL:* http://www.mainelaw.com
Augusta, Maine Office: 146 Capitol Street, Box 5057, 04330.
Telephone: 207-623-1596.
Telecopier: 207-626-0200.

Leonard M. Nelson
William W. Willard
Gregory A. Tselikis
F. Paul Frinsko
Peter J. Rubin
Eric F. Saunders
Gordon F. Grimes
Philip H. Gleason
Geoffrey H. Hole
Mary L. Schendel
John M. R. Paterson
Charles E. Miller
Richard M. Schade
Lee K. Bragg
John H. Montgomery, III
Christopher L. Vaniotis
Nathan H. Smith
Robert J. Keach
Jeffrey A. Thaler
James A. Houle
John L. Carpenter
Patrick J. Scully
Anthony E. Perkins
Joseph J. Hahn
Diane S. Lukac
Nelson A. Toner
David A. Soley
Lester F. Wilkinson, Jr.
Kenneth W. Lehman
Kate S. Debevoise
Patricia A. Peard
Karen B. Lovell
Robert F. Macdonald, Jr.
Robert J. Crawford
Jaimie Paul Schwartz
Scott E. Schul
Christopher J. Devlin
Eliza M. Cope Nolan

Kenneth L. Jordan, Jr.
Todd S. Holbrook
Wayne E. Tumlin
Daniel P. Riley, Jr.
Glenn Israel
William M. Welch
Tom S. Hanson
Gregory M. Cunningham
Deborah Shelles Cameron
Wendy J. Harlan
Linda J. Cohen
Daniel J. Mitchell
Katherine D. Clark
Kurt W. Adams
Joan M. Fortin
Michael A. Fagone
James A. Clifford
James F. Keenan, Jr.

OF COUNSEL

Sumner Thurman Bernstein
Herbert H. Sawyer

SPECIAL COUNSEL

Daniel E. Harris (Not admitted in ME)

Representative Clients: UNUM; Georgia-Pacific Corp.; University of Maine; Sebago, Inc.; Greater Portland Transit District; Pharmacia, Inc.; Rite Aid; Northwest Airlines.

For full biographical listings, see the Martindale-Hubbell Law Directory

BURNS RAY & DELANO, PROFESSIONAL ASSOCIATION (AV)

193 Middle Street, 04101-4062
Telephone: 207-775-3581
Facsimile: 207-775-3814
Email: mailcenter@brdlaw.com

George F. Burns
David P. Ray
Arnold C. Macdonald
Mary DeLano
Elizabeth A. Burns
Carrie A. Green

OF COUNSEL

Joanne F. Cole

Representative Clients: Maine Yankee Atomic Power Company; Tractebel Power, Inc.; Hancock Lumber Co., Inc.; Jackson Laboratory; Hague International (engineering); Aetna Life & Casualty Co.; The Hartford; Great American Insurance Co.; Wausau Insurance Co.

For full biographical listings, see the Martindale-Hubbell Law Directory

DOUGLAS, DENHAM, ROGERS & HOOD (AV)

103 Exchange Street, P.O. Box 7108, 04112-7108
Telephone: 207-774-1486
Facsimile: 207-774-3147
Email: info@dougden.com *URL:* http://www.dougden.com

MEMBERS OF FIRM

Martica S. Douglas
Alison A. Denham
Deborah Buccina Rogers
Elizabeth Ernst Hood
James E. Fortin
Sheilah R. McLaughlin
James F. Martemucci
Theodore H. Irwin, Jr.

Representative Clients: Allstate Insurance Co.; Metropolitan Property and Casualty Insurance Co.; AMICA Mutual Insurance Co.; National Grange Mutual; Continental/CNA; General Accident Group; Sentry Insurance Co.'s; The Travelers; Yasuda Fire & Mutual; Zurich-American Insurance Co.

For full biographical listings, see the Martindale-Hubbell Law Directory

Portland—Continued

DRUMMOND & DRUMMOND, LLP (AV)

One Monument Way, 04101
Telephone: 207-774-0317
Telefax: 207-761-4690
Email: info@ddlaw.com

MEMBERS OF FIRM

David N. Fisher, Jr.
Horace W. Horton
Arthur A. Cerullo
Robert C. Santomenna
Andrew W. Sparks
Alexandra E. Caulfield

ASSOCIATES

Paul E. Peck
Jennifer I. Richard
Douglas F Britton
J. Daniel Hoffman
Wadleigh B. Drummond (1885-1979)
Josiah H. Drummond (1914-1991)

Representative Clients: Forest City Chevrolet; Keeley Construction Co., Inc.; Maine Surgical Supply Co.; Olympia Sport Center, Inc.; Fleet Bank of Maine; Gorham Savings Bank; Key Bank of Maine; Peoples Heritage Bank; Metropolitan Life Insurance Co.; John Hancock Life Insurance Co.

For full biographical listings, see the Martindale-Hubbell Law Directory

JENSEN BAIRD GARDNER & HENRY (AV)

Ten Free Street, P.O. Box 4510, 04112-4510
Telephone: 207-775-7271
Telecopier: 207-775-7935
Email: info@jbgh.com *URL:* http://www.jbgh.com
York County Office: 11 Main Street, Suite 4, Kennebunk, Maine, 04043.
Telephone: 207-985-4676.
Telecopier: 207-985-4932.

MEMBERS OF FIRM

Kenneth Baird (1914-1987)
N. B. Walker (1851-1935)
Thomas B. Walker (1882-1968)
Walter E. Webber
Kenneth M. Cole, III
Nicholas S. Nadzo
Frank H. Frye
David J. Jones (Resident, York County Office)
Michael A. Nelson
Ronald A. Epstein
William H. Dale
Joseph H. Groff III
F. Bruce Sleeper
Deborah M. Mann
Leslie E. Lowry, III
Patricia McDonough Dunn
Michael J. Quinlan
R. Lee Ivy
Richard H. Spencer, Jr.

OF COUNSEL

Raymond E. Jensen
M. Donald Gardner
Merton G. Henry
John D. Bradford (Resident, York County Office)
James E. Kaplan

ASSOCIATES

Natalie L. Burns
Sally J. Daggett
Brendan P. Rielly
Suzanne R. Scott

Representative Clients: General Motors Acceptance Corp.; IBM; Federal National Mortgage Co.

For full biographical listings, see the Martindale-Hubbell Law Directory

MARCUS, GRYGIEL & CLEGG, P.A. (AV)

100 Middle Street, East Tower, 04101-4102
Telephone: 207-828-8000
Fax: 207-773-3210
Email: firm@mgc-law.com

George J. Marcus
Jennie L. Clegg
Marilyn E. Mistretta
Lee H. Bals

Sean P. Joyce
Barbara G. Shaw
Michael J. Gartland
Regan M. Hornney

OF COUNSEL

Stephen G. Grygiel
Andrew Jeffrey Zulieve

For full biographical listings, see the Martindale-Hubbell Law Directory

MURRAY, PLUMB & MURRAY (AV)

75 Pearl Street, P.O. Box 9785, 04104-5085
Telephone: 207-773-5651
Telefax: 207-773-8023
Email: info@mpmlaw.com *URL:* http://www.mpmlaw.com

MEMBERS OF FIRM

E. Stephen Murray
Peter S. Plumb
John C. Lightbody
Thomas C. Newman
John C. Bannon
Susan D. Thomas
Drew A. Anderson
Richard L. O'Meara
Christopher B. Branson

ASSOCIATES

Barbara T. Schneider
Charles P. Piacentini, Jr.
Michael D. Traister
Rita S. Saliba

(See Next Column)

COUNSEL

Richard H. Field (1903-1978)
Peter L. Murray
Charlton S. Smith

For full biographical listings, see the Martindale-Hubbell Law Directory

NORMAN, HANSON & DETROY, LLC (AV)

Fifth Floor, 415 Congress Street, P.O. Box 4600, 04112
Telephone: 207-774-7000
Telecopier: 207-775-0806
Email: info@nhdlaw.com *URL:* http://www.nhdlaw.com

MEMBERS OF FIRM

David C. Norman
Robert F. Hanson
Peter J. DeTroy, III
Stephen Hessert
Roderick R. Rovzar
Theodore H. Kirchner
Mark G. Lavoie
Stephen W. Moriarty
James D. Poliquin
John H. King, Jr.
Paul F. Driscoll
William O. LaCasse
Mark E. Dunlap
Robert W. Bower, Jr.
Jonathan W. Brogan
Christopher C. Taintor
David P. Very
Daniel L. Cummings
Alexander F. McCann

ASSOCIATES

Russell B. Pierce, Jr.
Anne M. Carney
David L. Herzer, Jr.
Thomas S. Marjerison
Adrian P. Kendall
Emily A. Bloch
Anne H. Jordan

Representative Clients: Allstate Insurance Co.; Bath Iron Works Corp.; Boise Cascade Corp.; Commercial Union Insurance Co.; Home Insurance Co.; Hanover Insurance Co.; Hartford Insurance Co.; Mead Paper Corp.; Medical Mutual Insurance Co.; Peerless Insurance Co.

For full biographical listings, see the Martindale-Hubbell Law Directory

PEABODY & ARNOLD LLP (AV)

One City Center, 04101
Telephone: 207-773-6300
Fax: 207-773-0609
URL: http://www.peabodyarnold.com
Boston, Massachusetts Office: 50 Rowes Wharf.
Telephone: 617-951-2100.
Telecopier: 617-951-2125.
Providence, Rhode Island Office: One Citizens Plaza, Suite 1100.
Telephone: 401-831-8330.
Fax: 401-831-8359.

MEMBERS OF FIRM

Jonathan Bangs
Ripley E. Hastings

ASSOCIATE

Jonathan L. Goldberg

COUNSEL

John K. Dineen

For full biographical listings, see the Martindale-Hubbell Law Directory

PERKINS, THOMPSON, HINCKLEY & KEDDY, P.A. (AV)

One Canal Plaza, P.O. Box 426, 04112-0426
Telephone: 207-774-2635
Fax: 207-871-8026
Email: admin@pthklaw.com *URL:* http://www.pthklaw.com

Thomas Schulten
Bruce E. Leddy
Douglas S. Carr
Andrew A. Cadot
Philip C. Hunt
John S. Upton
Peggy L. McGehee
Melissa Hanley Murphy
John H. Rich III
John A. Ciraldo
John A. Hobson
Timothy P. Benoit
Fred W. Bopp III
Craig N. Denekas
Mark P. Snow
William J. Sheils

David B. McConnell
Paul D. Pietropaoli
Aaron D. Julien
Gregory B. Poitras
Jennifer L. Sanders
John G. Osborn

OF COUNSEL

Owen W. Wells

For full biographical listings, see the Martindale-Hubbell Law Directory

PIERCE ATWOOD (AV)

One Monument Square, 04101
Telephone: 207-791-1100
Fax: 207-791-1350
Email: info@PierceAtwood.com *URL:* http://www.pierceatwood.com
Augusta, Maine Office: 77 Winthrop Street.
Telephone: 207-622-6311.
Fax: 207-623-9367.
Newburyport, Massachusetts Office: 6 Harris Street.
Telephone: 978-465-9599.
Fax: 978-465-9945.

(See Next Column)

PIERCE ATWOOD—*Continued*

MEMBERS OF FIRM

Leonard A. Pierce (1885-1960)
Edward W. Atwood (1897-1977)
Jotham D. Pierce (1918-1990)
Fred C. Scribner, Jr. (1908-1994)
Ralph I. Lancaster, Jr.
Gerald M. Amero
Bruce A. Coggeshall
S. Mason Pratt, Jr.
Jotham D. Pierce, Jr.
Warren E. Winslow, Jr. (Resident, Augusta Office)
Everett P. Ingalls, III
Malcolm L. Lyons (Resident, Augusta Office)
James B. Zimpritch
James G. Good
Peter W. Culley
Jeffrey M. White
Louise K. Thomas
John W. Gulliver
John D. Delahanty
Charles S. Einsiedler, Jr.
Peter H. Jacobs
Michael D. Seitzinger (Resident, Augusta Office)
Daniel M. Snow
Richard P. Hackett
William J. Kayatta, Jr.
Thomas R. Doyle
Dennis C. Keeler
Philip F. W. Ahrens, III
James R. Erwin
Robert H. Stier, Jr.
Kevin F. Gordon
Jacob A. Manheimer
Elaine S. Falender
John C. Nivison (Resident, Augusta Office)
Margaret Coughlin LePage
Kenneth Fairbanks Gray
John J. Aromando
David J. Champoux
Gloria A. Pinza
William E. Taylor
Catherine R. Connors
David E. Barry
Dixon P. Pike
Sarah H. Beard
Anthony R. Derosby
Barbara K. Wheaton
Matthew D. Manahan
Judith A. Fletcher Woodbury
Robert H. Ravenelle
Ryan S. Stinneford
Elizabeth R. Butler

OF COUNSEL

Charles W. Allen
Vincent L. McKusick
Sigrid E. Tompkins
William C. Smith
Jeremiah D. Newbury

ASSOCIATES

Kate L. Geoffroy
Deborah L. Shaw
James M. Saffian
David P. Littell
Jonathan A. Block
Jared S. des Rosiers
Allan M. Muir
William L. Worden
Debra L. Brown
Geraldine G. Sanchez
K. Douglas Erdmann
Keith J. Cunningham
Byrne J. Decker
Helen L. Edmonds (Resident, Augusta Office)
William D. Hewitt
Christopher T. Roach
Daniel H. Roberts
James H. Douglass
Margaret K. Minister
Ande A. Smith
Larissa S. Pratt
Ann L. Rudisill
Chris A. Caseiro
Patrick R. Scanlon (Not admitted in ME)
Mitchell R. Kops (Not admitted in ME)
Nathan V. Gemmiti
Thomas A. Loureiro
Steven J. Scott
Ann M. St. Peter-Griffith (Resident, Augusta Office)
Peter S. Black
Ella L. Brown (Not admitted in ME)

COUNSEL

Daniel J. Stevens (Resident, Augusta Office)
Michael S. Wilson
Jacquelyn M. Kurz
Elizabeth Eddy Griffin

For full biographical listings, see the Martindale-Hubbell Law Directory

PRETI, FLAHERTY, BELIVEAU, PACHIOS & HALEY, LLC (AV)

One City Center, P.O. Box 9546, 04112-9546
Telephone: 207-791-3000
Telecopier: 207-791-3111
Email: admin@preti.com *URL:* http://www.preti.com
Augusta, Maine Office: 45 Memorial Circle, P.O. Box 1058, 04332-1058.
Telephone: 207-623-5300.
Telefax: 207-623-2914.
Bath, Maine Office: Thirty Front Street, P.O. Box 665, 04530-0665.
Telephone: 207-443-5576.
Telefax: 207-443-6665.

John J. Flaherty (1929-1995)

MEMBERS OF FIRM

Severin M. Beliveau (Augusta Office)
Harold C. Pachios
Mark L. Haley (Bath Office)
Michael J. Gentile (Augusta Office)
Christopher D. Nyhan
Eric P. Stauffer
Jonathan S. Piper
Daniel Rapaport
John P. Doyle, Jr.
Bruce C. Gerrity (Augusta Office)
Anthony W. Buxton (Augusta Office)
Alfred C. Frawley, III
Jeffrey T. Edwards
Michael G. Messerschmidt
Randall B. Weill
James C. Pitney, Jr. (Augusta Office)
Evan M. Hansen
Virginia E. Davis (Augusta Office)
Leonard M. Gulino
Dennis C. Sbrega
Geoffrey K. Cummings
Estelle A. Lavoie
Judith Sapp (Not admitted in ME)
Susan E. LoGiudice
Michael Kaplan
Michael L. Sheehan

(See Next Column)

MEMBERS OF FIRM (Continued)

Joseph G. Donahue (Augusta Office)
David B. Van Slyke
Ann R. Robinson (Augusta Office)
Stephen E. F. Langsdorf (Augusta Office)
John P. McVeigh
Elizabeth A. Olivier
Charles F. Dingman (Augusta Office)
Mark B. LeDuc (Augusta Office)
Nelson J Larkins
Jeanne T. Cohn-Connor
Robert O. Newton
John S. Rudd
Timothy J. Bryant
Brian L. Champion (Bath Office)

SENIOR COUNSEL

George J. Mitchell

COUNSEL

Robert F. Preti
Albert J. Beliveau, Jr.
Robert W. Smith
Gregory P. Hansel
Naomi Sakamoto
Peter S. Carlisle

ASSOCIATES

James E. Phipps
Kevin J. Beal
Bonnie L. Martinolich
Tracey G. Burton (Bath Office)
Donald J. Sipe (Augusta Office)
Roy T. Pierce
Elizabeth A. Campbell
Jon A. Fitzgerald (Bath Office)
Jeffrey W. Peters (Bath Office)
Matthew J. LaMourie
Sigmund D. Schutz
Susan Pereira
Joel H. Thompson
Sharon G. Newman (Not admitted in ME)

Representative Clients: The St. Paul Companies; KeyBank National Assn.; Maine Municipal Assn.; Blethen-Maine Newspapers, Inc.; Maine Turnpike Authority; American International Group; Maine Automobile Dealers Assn.; Hannaford Brothers Co.; L.L. Bean; Maine Health Care Assn.

For full biographical listings, see the Martindale-Hubbell Law Directory

TROUBH, HEISLER & PIAMPIANO, P.C. (AV)

511 Congress Street, P.O. Box 9711, 04104-5011
Telephone: 207-780-6789
Fax: 207-774-2339
Email: info@thplaw.com

William B. Troubh
Edwin A. Heisler
Robert J. Piampiano
Kevin M. Gillis
Michael P. Boyd
Thomas E. Getchell
Michael Richards
William K. McKinley
Daniel F. Gilligan
Paul S. Bulger
John G. Richardson

Daniel R. Felkel
Ann Brandt
John P. Flynn, III

For full biographical listings, see the Martindale-Hubbell Law Directory

VERRILL & DANA, LLP (AV)

One Portland Square, P.O. Box 586, 04112-0586
Telephone: 207-774-4000
Fax: 207-774-7499
Email: advice@verdan.com *URL:* http://www.verdan.com
Augusta, Maine Office: 45 Memorial Circle, P.O. Box 957.
Telephone: 207-623-3889.
Fax: 207-622-3117.
Kennebunk, Maine Office: 403-404 Lafayette Center, P.O. Box 147.
Telephone: 207-985-7193.
Fax: 207-985-3957.
Washington, D.C. Office: 400 North Capitol Street, Suite 585.
Telephone: 202-624-9733.
Fax: 202-393-5218.

OF COUNSEL

Roger A. Putnam
Robert B. Williamson, Jr.
Louis A. Wood
Marianne McGettigan
Linda A. Monica
Carolyn S. Wollen
W. John Amerling
A. Robert Ruesch
Barbara E. Merrill (Resident Of Counsel, Augusta Office)
Peter B. Bickerman (Resident Of Counsel, Augusta Office)

MEMBERS OF FIRM

Peter B. Webster
Charles R. Oestreicher
Michael T. Healy
Christopher J. W. Coggeshall
Robert B. Patterson, Jr.
Judith M. Coburn
Christopher S. Neagle
David C. Hillman
James T. Kilbreth, III
John D. Duncan
Andrew M. Horton
William S. Harwood
James G. Goggin
Beth Dobson
Gregory S. Fryer
Gregory L. Foster
Gregg H. Ginn
David E. Warren
William C. Knowles
Gene R. Libby (Resident Partner, Kennebunk Office)
James C. Palmer
Mark K. Googins
David C. Boyer, Jr.
Keith C. Jones
Douglas P. Currier
Timothy J. O'Brien
Kimberly S. Couch
James A. McCormack
Alan D. MacEwan
Charles C. Soltan (Resident Partner, Augusta Office)
Robert E. Cleaves, IV
Claudia D. Raessler
Lisa S. Boehm
Suzanne E. Meeker

(See Next Column)

VERRILL & DANA LLP, *Portland—Continued*

MEMBERS OF FIRM (Continued)

Raymond A. Pelletier, Jr.
Michael J. Donlan (Resident Partner, Kennebunk Office)
Roger A. Clement, Jr.
Eric D. Altholz
David L. Galgay, Jr.
Seth W. Brewster
Robert C. Brooks
James I. Cohen
Juliet T. Browne
Charles P. Bacall

ASSOCIATES

Kevin G. Anderson
Anthony M. Calcagni
Elizabeth Connellan
Hope K. Creal
Jonathan R. Doolittle
Kristen Potter Farnham
Brent G.T. Geraty
Kenneth F. Ginder
Charles C. Hedrick (Resident Associate, Augusta Office)
Stephen C. Jordan
Janet P. Judge
Kurt E. Klebe
Karin L. Larson
Rita H. Logan (Not admitted in ME)
Sean M. Mahoney
Christopher B. McLaughlin
Jeffrey A. Meyers
Jacqueline W. Rider
Daniel L. Rosenthal
Laurie A. Williamson

Counsel for: ASCAP; Bowdoin College; Fleet Bank; Hannaford Bros. Co.; Maine Blue Cross and Blue Shield; Maine Public Service Co.; Peoples Heritage Bank; Portland Water District.

For full biographical listings, see the Martindale-Hubbell Law Directory

*ROCKLAND,** Knox Co.

STROUT & PAYSON, P.A. (AV)

10 Masonic Street, P.O. Box 248, 04841-0248
Telephone: 207-594-8400
Fax: 207-594-2724
Email: splaw@midcoast.com

Arthur E. Strout
Joseph B. Pellicani (1936-1988)
Robert J. Levine
Esther R. Barnhart
Carol Ann Lundquist
Randal E. Watkinson
Elizabeth E. Biddle
James Davidson

OF COUNSEL

Curtis M. Payson
John Knight

Approved Attorneys for: First American Title Insurance Co.; Chicago Title Insurance Co.

For full biographical listings, see the Martindale-Hubbell Law Directory

SACO, York Co.

SMITH ELLIOTT SMITH & GARMEY, P.A. (AV)

199 Main Street, P.O. Box 1179, 04072
Telephone: 207-774-3199
Telefax: 207-774-2235
Email: info@sesgattorneys.com *URL:* http://www.sesgattorneys.com

Charles W. Smith (1915-1983)
Randall E. Smith
Charles W. Smith, Jr.
Terrence D. Garmey
Peter W. Schroeter
Richard P. Romeo
Robert H. Furbish
William S. Kany
Keith R. Jacques
John H. O'Neil, Jr.
Harry B. Center, II
David S. Abramson
Daniel F. Driscoll

Mark T. Kremzner
Seth D. Harrow
Sarah Kent Hall

OF COUNSEL

Roger S. Elliott
J. Michael Conley

Representative Clients: City of Biddeford; Saco and Biddeford Savings Institution; Ocean Communities Federal Credit Union.
Local Counsel for: East Guard Insurance Co.
Reference: Saco & Biddeford Savings Institution.

For full biographical listings, see the Martindale-Hubbell Law Directory

MARYLAND

*ANNAPOLIS,** Anne Arundel Co.

FOLEY & LARDNER (AV)

Suite 102, 175 Admiral Cochrane Drive, 21401-7367
Telephone: 410-266-8077
Telex: 899149 (Oldtownpat)
Facsimile: 410-266-8664
Email: www.foleylardner.com *URL:* http://www.foleylardner.com
Los Angeles, California Office: 2029 Century Park East, 35th Floor.
Telephone: 310-277-2223.
Fax: 310-557-8475.

(See Next Column)

Sacramento, California Office: 300 Capitol Mall, Suite 1125.
Telephone: 916-443-8005.
Fax: 916-443-2240.
San Diego, California Office: 402 West Broadway, 23rd Floor.
Telephone: 619-234-6655.
Fax: 619-234-3510.
San Francisco, California Office: One Maritime Plaza, Sixth Floor.
Telephone: 415-434-4484.
Fax: 415-434-4507.
Denver, Colorado Office: 1999 Broadway, Suite 2560.
Telephone: 303-297-0260.
Fax: 303-297-0266.
Washington, D.C. Office: Washington Harbour, Suite 500, 3000 K Street, N.W.
Telephone: 202-672-5300.
Telex: 904136 (Foley Lard Wash).
Facsimile: 202-672-5399.
Jacksonville, Florida Office: The Greenleaf Building, 200 Laura Street. P.O. Box 240.
Telephone: 904-359-2000.
Facsimile: 904-359-8700.
Orlando, Florida Office: Suite 1800, 111 North Orange Avenue, P.O. Box 2193.
Telephone: 407-423-7656.
Facsimile: 407-648-1743.
Tallahassee, Florida Office: 300 East Park Avenue, P.O. Box 1454.
Telephone: 850-222-6100.
Facsimile: 850-561-6475.
Tampa, Florida Offices: Suite 2700, One Hundred N. Tampa Street, P.O. Box 3391.
Telephones: 813-229-2300; Pinellas County: 813-442-3296.
Facsimile: 813-221-4210.
West Palm Beach, Florida Office: Suite 200, Phillips Point East Tower, 777 South Flagler Drive.
Telephone: 561-655-5050.
Facsimile: 561-655-6925.
Chicago, Illinois Office: Suite 3300, One IBM Plaza, 330 N. Wabash Avenue.
Telephone: 312-755-1900.
Facsimile: 312-755-1925.
Madison, Wisconsin Office: Verex Plaza, 150 East Gilman Street, P.O. Box 1497.
Telephone: 608-257-5035.
Facsimile: 608-258-4258.
Milwaukee, Wisconsin Office: Firstar Center, 777 East Wisconsin Avenue.
Telephone: 414-271-2400.
Telex: 26-819 (Foley Lard Mil).
Facsimile: 414-297-4900.
Brussels, Belgium Office: Avenue Louise, 283.
Telephone: 32-2-646-2777.
Facsimile: 32-2-646-7574.

PARTNER

Brian J. McNamara

For full biographical listings, see the Martindale-Hubbell Law Directory

*BALTIMORE,** (Independent City)

ALLEN, JOHNSON, ALEXANDER & KARP, P.A. (AV)

Suite 1540, 100 East Pratt Street, 21202
Telephone: 410-727-5000
Fax: 410-727-0861
Email: ajakmd@aol.com
Washington, D.C. Office: 1707 L Street, N.W., Suite 1050.
Telephone: 202-828-4141.

Daniel Karp
D'Ana E. Johnson (Resident, Washington, D.C. Office)
Yvette M. Bryant
George B. Breen (Resident, Washington, D.C. Office)

OF COUNSEL

Donald C. Allen

Kevin Bock Karpinski
Lisa M. Sifford
Michelle Lee Seidleck
J. Christopher Boucher

Representative Clients: Scottsdale Insurance Co.; Nautilus Insurance Co.; Jefferson Insurance Co.; Liberty Mutual Insurance Co.; Avis Rent-A-Car; Otis Elevator Co.; Montgomery Elevator Co.; Admiral Insurance Co.; Local Government Insurance Trust; Penn National Insurance Co.

For full biographical listings, see the Martindale-Hubbell Law Directory

HOGAN & HARTSON L.L.P. (AV)

111 South Calvert Street, 21202
Telephone: 410-659-2700
Fax: 410-539-6981
Washington, D.C. Office: Columbia Square, 555 13th Street, N.W.
Telephone: 202-637-5600.
Telex: 89-2757.
Cable Address: "Hogander Washington".
Fax: 202-637-5910.

(See Next Column)

HOGAN & HARTSON L.L.P.—*Continued*

Brussels, Belgium Office: Avenue des Arts 41, 1040.
Telephone: (32.2) 505.09.11.
Fax: (32.2) 505.09.96.
Budapest, Hungary Office: Bank Center, Granite Tower, 9th Floor, Budapest V., Szabadsag ter 7, 1944 Hungary.
Telephone: (36-1) 302-9050.
Fax: (36-1) 302-9060.
London, England Office: 21 Garlick Hill, EC4V 2AU.
Telephone: (44 171) 815 1200.
Fax: (44 171) 329 0299.
Moscow, Russia Office: 33/2 Usacheva Street, Building 3, 119048.
Telephone: (7095) 245-5190. Int'l
Telephone: (7501) 907-0451.
Fax: (7095) 245-5192. Int'l
Fax: (7501) 907-0462.
Paris, France (Affiliated Office): Cariddi, Mee, Rué, Avocats Associés à la Cour de Paris, 12, rue de la Paix, 75002.
Telephone: (33-1) 42.61.57.71.
Fax: (33-1) 42.61.79.21.
Prague, Czech Republic (Affiliated Office): Hogan & Hartson, Advokátní Kanceláře, v.o.s., Opletalova 37, 110 00.
Telephone: (420-2) 2211-7111.
Fax: (420-2) 2421-5105.
Warsaw, Poland Office: Hogan & Hartson Sp.zo.o, Atrium Tower, Al. Jana Pawla II 25, 00-854.
Telephone: (48-22) 653-4200.
Fax: (48-22) 653-4250.
Rockville, Maryland Office: 600 Jefferson Plaza, Suite 203.
Telephone: 301-315-2206.
Fax: 301-315-9046.
Colorado Springs, Colorado Office: Two North Cascade Avenue, Suite 1300.
Telephone: 719-448-5900.
Fax: 719-448-5922.
Denver, Colorado Office: One Tabor Center, Suite 1500, 1200 Seventeenth Street.
Telephone: 303-899-7300.
Fax: 303-899-7333.
Los Angeles, California Office: Biltmore Tower, 500 S. Grand Avenue, Suite 1900.
Telephone: 213-337-6700.
Fax: 213-337-6701.
McLean, Virginia Office: 8300 Greensboro Drive.
Telephone: 703-610-6100.
Fax: 703-610-6200.
New York, New York Office: 885 Third Avenue, 26th Floor.
Telephone: 212-409-9800.
Fax: 212-409-9801.

PARTNERS

Gil A. Abramson
George Beall
Michael D. Colglazier
Amy Bowerman Freed
James A. Gede, Jr.
Kevin G. Gralley
Stephen J. Immelt
J. Clinton Kelly
David P. King
Walter G. Lohr, Jr.
Thene M. Martin
Nancy Doerr O'Neil (Also at Washington, D.C. Office)
Michael J. Silver
Edward C. Sledge
Ralph S. Tyler
Joseph H. Young

RESIDENT ASSOCIATES

Maura L. DeMouy
Felicia A. Emry
David F. Hannan
Kamil Ismail
Lisa J. Lenderman
Stephanie D. Marks
Douglas R. M. Nazarian
Mark S. Saudek
Nicholas G. Stavlas
Heather H. P. Vovakes
Edith F. Webster

For full biographical listings, see the Martindale-Hubbell Law Directory

KRAMON & GRAHAM, P.A. (AV)

One South Street, Suite 2600, 21202-3201
Telephone: 410-752-6030
Facsimile: 410-539-1269

Andrew Jay Graham
James M. Kramon
Lee H. Ogburn
Jeffrey H. Scherr
Nancy E. Gregor
James P. Ulwick
Philip M. Andrews
Gertrude C. Bartel
Marilyn Hope Fisher
Max H. Lauten
Kathleen A. Birrane
Kevin F. Arthur
Aron U. Raskas
Geoffrey H. Genth
Karl J. Nelson

John Augustine Bourgeois
Herbert Burgunder, III
John F. Dougherty
Michael E. Blumenfeld

Representative Clients: Georgia-Pacific Corp.; Sacred Heart Hospital; Toll Brothers, Inc.

For full biographical listings, see the Martindale-Hubbell Law Directory

LORD & WHIP, A PROFESSIONAL ASSOCIATION (AV)

800 One Center Plaza, 120 West Fayette Street, 21201-3700
Telephone: 410-539-5881
Fax: 410-685-6726
URL: http://www.lordwhip.com

George W. P. Whip (1884-1961)
Robert E. Coughlan, Jr. (1899-1971)
Frederick J. Green, Jr. (1919-1988)
George L. Huber, Jr.
Edward M. Ranier
J. Paul Mullen
Robert C. Erlandson
John J. Boyd
Frank F. Daily
W. John Vernon
Pamela Thomas Broache

OF COUNSEL

Robert P. Schlenger

Michael S. DeBaugh
Michelle J. Abrams
Christopher M. Erwin
Kathleen M. Bustraan
Michael H. Daney
Cynthia M. Dietz
J. Daniel Vorsteg

Representative Clients: Associated Aviation Underwriters; CIGNA; CNA; General Star Management; Government Employees Insurance Companies; Great American Insurance Companies; Harbison-Walker Refactories; Lockheed Martin Corp.; Reliance Insurance Company; Unilever, Inc.

For full biographical listings, see the Martindale-Hubbell Law Directory

MICHAEL P. MAY (AV)

7305 Harford Road, 21234
Telephone: 410-444-7606
Fax: 410-444-7609
Email: m.may@quixmail.com *URL:* http://www.lawyers.com/michaelmaylaw

For full biographical listings, see the Martindale-Hubbell Law Directory

NEUBERGER, QUINN, GIELEN, RUBIN & GIBBER, P.A. (AV)

27th Floor, One South Street, 21202-3282
Telephone: 410-332-8550
Fax: 410-332-8594

Isaac M. Neuberger
Michael L. Quinn
Price O. Gielen
Richard Rubin
Allan J. Gibber
Robert M. Ercole
Thomas M. Wood, IV
Deborah Hunt Devan
Allan P. Hillman
Cynthia L. Leppert
Robert P. Legg

Susan M. Wilkins
Sonya F. Lorge
Dennis J. Reinhold (Not admitted in MD)
Hillary J. Michaud
Nathan D. Adler
Hugh M. Bernstein
Cindy L. Burgess
Alison J. Julio
Michaela L. Cavanaugh (Not admitted in MD)
Hilarie E. Snyder

Representative Clients: Bank of Glen Burnie; Blue Cross-Blue Shield of Maryland; Circuit City Stores; Grass Family Investments; Koons Automotive Dealerships; Merry-Go-Round Bankruptcy Trustee; Rite-Aid Corporation; Sterling Capital, LTD; Struever Bros., Eccles & Rouse; TESSCO Technologies.

For full biographical listings, see the Martindale-Hubbell Law Directory

NILES, BARTON & WILMER (AV)

Suite 1400, 111 S. Calvert Street, 21202-6185
Telephone: 410-783-6300
Cable Address: "Nilwo"
Telecopier: 410-783-6363

MEMBERS OF FIRM

A. Adgate Duer
John Gill Wharton
Forrest F. Bramble, Jr.
Patrick J. B. Donnelly
Larry J. Albert
V. Timothy Bambrick
Robert F. Scholz
Robert P. O'Brien
John L. Wood
Steven E. Leder
Matthew L. Kimball
R. Wayne Pierce
David D. Gilliss
Paul McDermott Finamore
George E. Reede, Jr.
Jeffrey A. Wothers
Craig D. Roswell

OF COUNSEL

Carlyle Barton, Jr.

ASSOCIATES

Susan D. Baker
Susan B. Austin
Kevin J. Willging
Jason C. Brino
Donald L. Speidel
John R. Glassburn, III
Joel P. Williams
Eric A. Frechtel
Brian L. Moffet
Matthew G. Hjortsberg
Bambi L. Wilson
Thomas P. Turgeon
Julie A. Furst
Ronald E. Council, Jr

(See Next Column)

NILES, BARTON & WILMER, *Baltimore—Continued*

ASSOCIATES (Continued)

Ranji Martelli Garrett
Ann M. Grillo
Susan S. Muller
Robert S. Reverski, Jr.

For full biographical listings, see the Martindale-Hubbell Law Directory

PHILLIPS P. O'SHAUGHNESSY, P.A. (AV)

1102 Terrace Glen, 21210
Telephone: 410-532-0300
FAX: 410-532-2220
URL: http://www.oshaughnessy.wld.com
Ft. Lauderdale, Florida Office: One East Broward Boulevard, Suite 700, 33301.
Telephone: 800-882-3133.

Phillips P. O'Shaughnessy
Robin Frazier Kandel

For full biographical listings, see the Martindale-Hubbell Law Directory

PIERSON, PIERSON & NOLAN (AV)

Suite 2020 Redwood Tower, 217 East Redwood Street, 21202
Telephone: 410-727-7733
Fax: 410-625-0253
Email: piernol@ibm.net

MEMBERS OF FIRM

Leon H. A. Pierson (1901-1981)
Edward Pierson (1906-1990)
W. Michel Pierson
James J. Nolan, Jr.
Robert L. Pierson

For full biographical listings, see the Martindale-Hubbell Law Directory

PIPER & MARBURY L.L.P. (AV)

36 South Charles Street, 21201-3018
Telephone: 410-539-2530
FAX: 410-539-0489
Email: lawfirm@pipermar.com *URL:* http://www.pipermar.com
Washington, D.C. Office: 1200 Nineteenth Street, N.W., 20036-2430.
Telephone: 202-861-3900.
FAX: 202-223-2085.
New York, N.Y. Office: 1251 Avenue of the Americas, 10020-1104.
Telephone: 212-835-6000.
FAX: 212-835-6001.
Philadelphia, Pennsylvania Office: 3400 Two Logan Square, 18th & Arch Streets, 19103-2762.
Telephone: 215-656-3300.
FAX: 215-656-3301.
Easton, Maryland Office: 117 Bay Street, 21601-2703.
Telephone: 410-820-4460.
FAX: 410-820-4463.
Princeton, N.J. Office: 116 Village Boulevard, Suite 200, Princeton Forrestal Village, 08540.
Telephone: 609-951-2252.
FAX: 609-951-2216.
Reston, Virginia Office: 1850 Centennial Park Drive, Suite 610, Commerce Executive Park III, 20191.
Telephone: 703-391-7100.
Fax: 703-309-5299.

MEMBERS OF FIRM

George L. Russell, Jr.
Earl J. Silbert
Shale D. Stiller
Leonard E. Cohen
John E. Corette, III (Resident, Washington, D.C. Office)
Wilbert H. Sirota
Sheldon Krantz (Resident, Washington, D.C. Office)
Robert A. Meister (Resident, New York, N.Y. Office)
Lewis A. Noonberg (Resident, Washington, D.C. Office)
Joseph G. Finnerty, Jr.
Henry Robbins Lord
Donald E. Sharpe
Richard K. White, Jr.
Carl L. Vacketta (Resident, Washington, D.C. Office)
Michael A. Varet (Resident, New York, N.Y. Office)
William R. Weissman (Resident, Washington, D.C. Office)
Mitchell Fenton (Resident, New York, N.Y. Office)
Edwin M. Martin, Jr. (Resident, Washington, D.C. Office)
Philip L. Cohan (Resident, Washington, D.C. Office)
Lawrence M. Katz
George A. Nilson
Broughton M. Earnest (Resident, Easton Office)
Russell H. Gardner
Steven D. Shattuck
Robert F. Fink (Resident, New York, N.Y. Office)
John E. Kratz, Jr.
David P. Langlois
Ronald L. Plesser (Resident, Washington, D.C. Office)
James J. Winn, Jr.
Jayne M. Kurzman (Resident, New York, N.Y. Office)
J. Brian Molloy (Resident, Washington, D.C. Office)
Jay I. Morstein
Michael Esher Yaggy
E. Leslie Hoffman III (Resident, Washington, D.C. Office)
Stanard T. Klinefelter
John E. McKeever (Resident, Philadelphia, PA Office)
Norman J. Resnicow (Resident, New York, N.Y. Office)
Gregory A. Smith (Resident, Washington, D.C. Office)
Neil J. Dilloff
Jeffrey D. Herschman
Michael Hirschberg (Resident, New York, N.Y. Office)
Leo G. Kailas (Resident, New York, N.Y. Office)
Richard M. Kremen
Joseph H. Langhirt

(See Next Column)

MEMBERS OF FIRM (Continued)

Randall B. Lowe (Washington, D.C. and New York, N.Y. Office)
Kenneth G. Starling (Resident, Washington, D.C. Office)
Mark J. Tauber (Resident, Washington, D.C. Office)
Thomas C. Wheeler (Resident, Washington, D.C. Office)
Anthony L. Young (Resident, Washington. D.C. Office)
Francis B. Burch, Jr.
Deborah E. Jennings
John T. Westermeier, Jr. (Resident, Washington, D.C. Office)
Larry D. Harris (Resident, Washington, D.C. Office)
Jeffrey F. Liss (Resident, Washington, D.C. Office)
Stephen R. Mysliwiec (Resident, Washington, D.C. Office)
Ernest M. Stern (Resident, Reston, Virginia Office)
Richard C. Tilghman, Jr.
Earl S. Wellschlager
Daniel J. Carrigan (Resident, Washington, D.C. Office)
Richard J. Hafets
William F. Kiniry, Jr. (Resident, Philadelphia, Pennsylvania Office)
Edward J. Levin
Alan C. Porter (Resident, Washington, D.C. Office)
Kenneth L. Thompson
Charles B. Wayne
William D. Blakely (Resident, Washington, D.C. Office)
Michael F. Brockmeyer
David B. Dempsey (Resident, Washington, D.C. Office)
Andrew L. Deutsch (Resident, New York, N.Y. Office)
Mark J. Friedman
Elizabeth Grieb
John P. Machen
Stanley McDermott III (Resident, New York, N.Y. Office)
Stephen L. Owen
Robert W. Smith, Jr.
Stewart K. Diana
Jay Gary Finkelstein (Resident, Washington, D.C. Office)
John E. Griffith, Jr.
Lee A. Sheller
Sandra P. Gohn
William L. Henn, Jr.
Elizabeth A. McKennon
Joel A. Dewey
Marianne Schmitt Hellauer
Robert J. Mathias
Mark Muedeking
David S. Musgrave
Jonathan D. Smith
Paul A. Tiburzi
Kenneth C. H. Willig (Resident, New York, N.Y. Office)
David H. Bamberger (Resident, Washington, D.C. Office)
David Clarke, Jr. (Resident, Washington, D.C. Office)
Garry P. McCormack
Deborah R. Meshulam (Resident, Washington, D.C. Office)
Cynthia J. Morris (Resident, Washington, D.C. Office)
Anthony H. Rickert (Resident, Washington, D.C. Office)
Charles P. Scheeler
Cindy V. Schlaefer (Resident, New York, N.Y. Office)
Paul D. Shelton
Koren Blair (Resident, New York, N.Y. Office)
Kurt J. Fischer
Adam S. Hoffinger
James P. Rathvon (Resident, Washington, D.C. Office)
Stanley R. Soya (Resident, Washington, D.C. Office)
Wm. Roger Truitt
Robert A. Assuncao
Nora E. Garrote (Resident, Washington, D.C. Office)
Douglas H. Green (Resident, Washington, D.C. Office)
Sandra Jarva Weiss (Resident, Washington, D.C. Office)
Steven J. Mandell
Raymond G. Mullady, Jr.
Richard J. Vacura (Resident, Washington, D.C. Office)
David J. Fisher
Emmett F. McGee, Jr.
Paul Stanley Novak
Ronald P. Schiller (Resident, Philadelphia, Pennsylvania Office)
Theodore D. Segal
Kristin H. R. Franceschi
Eric B. Miller
Paul J. Pollock (Resident, New York, N.Y. Office)
Gina Monath Zawitoski
David B. Buss (Resident, New York, N.Y. Office)
Robert C. Douglas
O. Daniel Ansa (Resident, Philadelphia, Pennsylvania Office)
Benjamin S. Boyd (Resident, Washington, D.C. Office)
John D. Corse
Joseph G. Finnerty III (Resident, New York, N.Y. Office)
Eric Paltell
Richard P. Rector (Resident, Washington, D.C. Office)
Stephen M. Sharkey
Herbert D. Frerichs, Jr.
Mary E. Gately (Resident, Washington, D.C. Office)
Leonard L. Gordon (Resident, Washington, D.C. Office)
Katrina C. Kamantauskas-Holder
James D. Mathias
Anthony L. Meagher
Kevin P. Mullen (Resident, Washington, D.C. Office)
Marta D. Harting
Joseph Kernen
Amy W. Schulman (Resident, New York, N.Y. Office)
Nancy A. Spangler (Resident, Reston, Virginia Office)
C. Kevin Kobbe

SENIOR COUNSEL

Thomas A. Melfe
L. P. Scriggins

OF COUNSEL

M. Peter Moser
Robert M. Goldman
Donald P. McPherson, III
William L. Reynolds
Cary M. Feldman
Evelyn W. Pasquier
Lucinda J. Bach
Robert P. Rothman
Emilio W. Cividanes (Resident, Washington, D.C. Office)
Stuart Mendelsohn
John F. Kaufman
Monica P. McCabe (Resident, New York, N.Y. Office)
Richard J. Oparil
Barbara Rowland (Resident, Washington, D.C. Office)
Julie Ronder Domike (Resident, Washington, D.C. Office)
Kathleen A. Ellis
Nicolai J. Sarad (Resident, New York, NY Office)
Glen K. Allen
Susan K. Datesman

(See Next Column)

PIPER & MARBURY L.L.P.—*Continued*

OF COUNSEL (Continued)

Thomas L. Totten
Jane A. Wilson
Carville B. Collins
E. Ashton Johnston (Resident, Washington, D.C. Office)
Cynthia K. Nicholson (Resident, Washington, DC Office)

PARTNER EMERITUS

Andre W. Brewster
Frank T. Gray
Charles T. Albert
Edward Owen Clarke, Jr.
Decatur H. Miller
Roger D. Redden
Toni K. Allen (Resident, Washington, D.C. Office)
Nathan B. Feinstein (Resident, Washington, D.C. Office)
Robert W. Ogren (Resident, Washington, D.C. Office)

ASSOCIATES

William F. Tilghman (Resident, Washington, D.C. Office)
Ray L. Earnest (Resident, Easton Office)
Michael R. Hepworth (Resident, New York, N.Y. Office)
Mary L. Porter
Carolyn M. Bamberger (Resident, Washington, D.C. Office)
John L. Moore, Jr. (Resident, Washington, D.C. Office)
Carol M. Fischer (Resident, New York, N.Y. Office)
Timothy P. Branigan (Resident, Washington, D.C. Office)
JoAnn E. Levin
Brigit McCann Macksey
Sheila Stark (Resident, Washington, D.C. Office)
James J. Halpert (Resident, Washington, D.C. Office)
Susan S. Maher
Deborah P. Nason
Jane Kwok Ping Tam (Resident, Washington, D.C. Office)
Tracey Gann Turner
Anne Therese Bechamps
Theresa M. Connolly
Peter M. Corrigan
Edward F. Maluf (Resident, New York, N.Y. Office)
Robert A. Salerno
Jordan I. Bailowitz
R. Timothy Bryan (Resident, Washington, D.C. Office)
Eric S. Connuck (Resident, New York, N.Y. Office)
John Caleb Dougherty
Douglas A. Rappaport (Resident, N.Y., N.Y. Office)
Marianne Mancino Thiede
Linda Marotta Thomas
Joanne F. Weil (Resident, New York, N.Y. Office)
Loren H. Brown (Resident, New York, N.Y. Office)
Bruce T. Carton (Resident, Washington, D.C. Office)
Wm. David Chalk
Paul J. Day
H. Bruce Dorsey
Daniel M. Horrigan (Resident, Washington, D.C. Office)
Janice W. Housey (Resident, Washington, D.C. Office)
Carla G. Pennington-Cross (Resident, Philadelphia, PA Office)
George Faulkner Ritchie IV
Keith E. Smith
Stacie E. Tobin
Eugene A. Arbaugh, Jr.
Rita C. Burghardt (Resident, New York, N.Y. Office)
Karen Detling
Elizabeth R. Dewey (Resident, Washington, D.C. Office)
Jonathan David Eisner
Guy E. Flynn
Monica Derbes Gibson
Carol Guy-Jackson (Resident, Washington, D.C. Office)
Martin T. Hillery (Resident, New York, N.Y. Office)
Julie Ann Kaminski
Heather Anne Klink
Cheryl Lardieri
Richard J. Marks
Stephen P. McLaughlin (Resident, New York, N.Y. Office)
Keara M. Gordon (Resident, Washington, D.C. Office)
Chuong H. Pham (Not admitted in MD)
Christian E. Plaza (Resident, Reston, Virginia Office)
Howard S. Schwartz
Steven P. Steinberg
Holly Emrick Svetz (Resident, Washington, D.C. Office)
William Taylor IV
Marisa C. Terrenzi (Resident, Washington, D.C. Office)
Alycia M. Vivona (Not admitted in MD; Resident, New York, N.Y. Office)
Thomas G. Walsh
Neal Walters
Jennifer B. Bernheim (Resident, New York, N.Y. Office)
Michelle Farren Blain (Not admitted in MD)
Kris O. Carter (Resident, Washington, D.C. Office)
Maria Ellena Chavez-Ruark
Quincy M. Crawford, III
Renée Crittendon
Joel M. Eads
Chandra Emery (Resident, Washington, D.C. Office)
Debra McPipkin Enderle (Not admitted in MD)
Heather E. Gange (Resident, Washington, D.C. Office)
Jeffrey E. Gordon
Steven J. Groseclose (Resident, Washington, D.C. Office)
Carol W. Gustavson (Not admitted in MD)
Brett Ingerman
Brian R. Kennedy (Resident, Washington, D.C. Office)
Charles J. Kresslein
Rachel B. Mandell
Anant S. Narayanan (Resident, Washington, DC Office)
George J. Nemphos
Susan B. Ross
Anthony J. Rosso
Larry Robert Seegull
Beth A. Winograd
Paul D. Ackerman
J. Darrel Barros
Kimberly C. Betterton
Robert L. Bourguignon (Resident, New York, NY Office)
Shari-Ellen Bourque (Not admitted in MD)
Michael S. Caplan
Eric M. Falkenberry (Resident, New York, N.Y. Office)
Elizabeth J. Feeney
Stefanie J. Fogel (Resident, Philadelphia, Pennsylvania Office)
Lorrie A. Giventer
Marion Kristal Goldberg
Steven F. Gooby
Leeann K. Kelly-Judd

(See Next Column)

ASSOCIATES (Continued)

Heidi L. Levine
Hugh J. Marbury
Bradley McConnell (Resident, Washington, D.C. Office)
Wendy I. Norris (Resident, New York, N.Y. Office)
Andrew M. Price (Resident, Washington, D.C. Office)
Tilghman Earle Price
William F. Reynolds, Jr. (Resident, Washington, D.C. Office)
Stephanie L. Shack
Anoop G. Shroff (Resident, Washington, D.C. Office)
Eric S. Wechselblatt
Natalie F. Zaidman
Kenneth S. Aneckstein
William J. Crowley
Erik M. Feig (Resident, Washington, D.C. Office)
Daina Beth Garonzik
Barbara Shatz Goldstein (Resident, New York, NY Office)
David P. Handler (Resident, Washington, D.C. Office)
Kelly Tubman Hardy
Jason C. Harmon
Andrew Marc Herscowitz (Resident, Washington, D.C. Office)
Tashir J. Lee (Resident, Washington, D.C. Office)
Robye Shaw Margolius
J. Todd Metcalf
Eric S. Namrow
Tacey J. Nusbaum
Susan H. Pope (Resident, Washington, D.C. Office)
Kevin Michael Robertson
David E. Singer
Amy L. Schaner Stanley (Resident, Washington, D.C. Office)
Laura Lynn Swartz
John R. Wellschlager
Geoffrey T. Willard (Resident, Washington, D.C. Office)
Jeffrey M. Yeatman
Anthony P. Ashton
Jason Edward Balog
Robin K. Bohnenstengel
Emily Cann
Mark Wayne Carmean (Resident, Washington, D.C. Office)
Matthew Cheney
Sulee J. Clay (Resident, Washington, D.C. Office)
Holly Lynn Drumheller
Palmina M. Fava-Pastilha
Tashina Gauhar
Laura A. Giantris
Tami J. Howie (Resident, Washington, D.C. Office)
Keli B.C. Isaacson
Nicole P. Kangas (Resident, Philadelphia, Pennsylvania Office)
Elisha A. King
Daniel J. Layden (Resident, Philadelphia, PA Office)
Amy Susan Leavens (Resident, Philadelphia, PA Office)
Cameron J. Macdonald
Joy M. Napier-Joyce (Not admitted in MD)
Christina Jessica Pappas
Jayne Anderson Risk (Not admitted in MD; Resident, Philadelphia, Pennsylvania Office)
Virginia Rowthorn
Joseph M. Stella (Resident, New York, NY Office)
James Michael Sullivan (Resident, Washington, D.C. Office)
Shaun Leland Terrill
Janice L. Weiner (Resident, Washington, D.C. Office)
Madeleine Boyer Kadas (Resident, Washington, D.C. Office)
Alisa M. Bergman (Resident, Washington, D.C. Office)
Marylou Brown
Nicole Lefcourt Campbell
Kimberleigh Criswell
Brett D. Feldman (Resident, Philadelphia, Pennsylvania Office)
Paul A. Fenn
Ada Fernandez (Resident, Washington, D.C. Office)
Lisa Wong Fitch (Resident, Washington, D.C. Office)
Jordan C. Frame
Dina S. Glassman (Resident, New York, N.Y. Office)
Scott N. Godes (Resident, Washington, D.C. Office)
David M. Hryck (Resident, New York, N.Y. Office)
Michelle J. Hummer
Kimberly A. Jones
Brian S. Kestenbaum (Resident, Philadelphia, PA Office)
Kay Lee Kim (Resident, New York, N.Y. Office)
Michael G. Langan (Resident, Washington, D.C. Office)
Paul Alexander Mallos
Laurie Ann Martino (Resident, New York, N.Y. Office)
Sara Z. Moghadam (Resident, Washington, D.C. Office)
Michell Mayer Motsko
Jonathan S. Nash
Edward S. Scheideman (Resident, Washington, D.C. Office)
Willie W. Williams
Alec Zacaroli (Resident, Washington, D.C. Office)
Dana C. Lumsden (Resident, New York, N.Y. Office)
Annmarie Palermo Smits (Resident, New York, N.Y. Office)
Robert L. McKay, Jr. (Resident, Washington, D.C. Office)

For full biographical listings, see the Martindale-Hubbell Law Directory

---

REDMOND, BURGIN & GUTIERREZ, P.A. (AV)

1301, The Fidelity Building, 210 North Charles Street, 21202
Telephone: 410-752-1555
Fax: 410-752-1064
URL: http://www.RBGLAW.com
Upper Marlboro, Maryland Office: 14746 Main Street.
Telephone: 301-952-1555.

Leonard C. Redmond, III
Harold L. Burgin
Maria Cristina Gutierrez

Mark B. Martin
Joseph I. Tivvis, Jr.
Bambi Glenn
Rita Pazniokas
Jeffrey P. Schomig

For full biographical listings, see the Martindale-Hubbell Law Directory

Baltimore—Continued

SEMMES, BOWEN & SEMMES, A PROFESSIONAL CORPORATION (AV)

250 West Pratt Street, 21201
Telephone: 410-539-5040
Facsimile: 410-539-5223
URL: http://www.semmes.com
Washington D.C. Office: Suite 900, 1025 Connecticut Avenue, N.W.
Telephone: 202-822-8250.
Towson, Maryland Office: Eleventh Floor, 401 Washington Avenue.
Telephone: 410-296-4400.
Hagerstown, Maryland Office: 322 East Antietam Street.
Telephone: 301-739-4558.
Salisbury, Maryland Office: 231 West Main Street.
Telephone: 410-749-1710.
McLean, Virginia Office: Suite 410, 6862 Elm Street.
Telephone: 703-760-9473.

PRINCIPALS

John E. Semmes (1851-1925)
Jesse N. Bowen (1879-1938)
John E. Semmes, Jr. (1881-1967)
Franklin Goldstein
Cleaveland D. Miller
Alan N. Gamse
J. Snowden Stanley, Jr.,
Robert E. Scott, Jr.
Richard T. Sampson (Resident, Washington, D.C. Office)
Rudolph L. Rose
William J. Jackson
Daniel J. Moore (Resident, Towson, Maryland Office)
JoAnne Zawitoski
Thomas G. Hagerty (Resident, Washington, D.C. Office)
Richard W. Scheiner
Maxine Adler
Perry E. Darby
Scott D. Goetsch
James A. Johnson
Stan M. Haynes
Robert W. Hesselbacher, Jr.
William H. Kable
Joanne M. Dicus
Stephen S. McCloskey
Kevin M. Soper (Resident, Towson, Maryland Office)
Margaret Fonshell Ward (Resident, Towson, Maryland Office)
Paul N. Farquharson
Heather Holt Kraus
Ralph L. Arnsdorf (Resident, Towson, Maryland Office)
Brian A. Balenson
Joseph F. Giordano (Resident, McLean, Virginia Office)
Joel D. Newport (Resident, Towson, Maryland Office)
Robert E. Rockwell (Resident, Hagerstown, Maryland Office)
Jonathan R. Topazian (Resident, Washington, D.C. Office)
Thomas V. McCarron
Anthony Jackson Zaccagnini

OF COUNSEL

Jonathan ILsong Ahn
Thomas E. Cinnamond
William R. Dorsey, III
Richard H. Gimer (Resident, Washington, D.C. Office)
L. Stephen Hess
David R. Owen

COUNSEL

James Bremer (Resident, McLean, Virginia Office)
Thomas L. Lilly (Resident, Salisbury, Maryland Office)
Diana P. Nowezki (Resident, Washington, D.C. Office)
William C. Stifler
William C. Trimble, Jr.
Christopher R. West

SENIOR ASSOCIATES

Lori L. Blair (Resident, Towson, Maryland Office)

ASSOCIATES

Christine Affleck Basham (Resident, Towson, Maryland Office)
Eric S. Belk
Shannon O. Colvin (Resident, Towson, Maryland Office)
Christopher G. Cwalina
Ami C. Dwyer (Resident, Towson, Maryland Office)
Natalie Stroud Fenner (Resident, Towson, Maryland Office)
Lawrence G. Giambelluca
Alexander McKenzie Giles
Alison E. Goldenberg
Diarmuid F. Gorham
Robert L. Hebb
Dana L. Jelinski (Resident, McLean, Virginia Office)
Kenneth S. Knuckey
William A. Kress
Dominic A. Lancelotta
Anthony G. Lardieri
Stuart M. Lesser
Susannah I. Maxwell (Resident, Towson, Maryland Office)
Jennifer T. Mix
Scott Hamilton Phillips
Theresa J. Withers

Representative Clients of Semmes, Bowen & Semmes: Bethlehem Steel Corp.; General MotorsCorp.; Liberty Mutual Insurance Co.; Mack Trucks, Inc.; Marriott Corp.

For full biographical listings, see the Martindale-Hubbell Law Directory

---

VENABLE ATTORNEYS AT LAW VENABLE, BAETJER AND HOWARD, LLP (AV)

A Partnership including Professional Corporations
1800 Mercantile Bank & Trust Building, 2 Hopkins Plaza, 21201
Telephone: 410-244-7400
Fax: 410-244-7742
URL: http://www.venable.com
Washington, D.C. Office: Venable, Baetjer, Howard & Civiletti LLP, Suite 1000, 1201 New York Avenue, N.W.
Telephone: 202-962-4800.
Fax: 202-962-8300.

(See Next Column)

McLean, Virginia Office: Suite 400, 2010 Corporate Ridge.
Telephone: 703-760-1600.
Fax: 703-821-8949.
Rockville, Maryland Office: Suite 500, One Church Street, P. O. Box 1906.
Telephone: 301-217-5600.
Fax: 301-217-5617.
Towson, Maryland Office: 210 Allegheny Avenue, P. O. Box 5517.
Telephone: 410-494-6200.
Fax: 410-821-0147.

MEMBERS OF FIRM

Richard M. Venable (1839-1910)
Edwin G. Baetjer (1868-1945)
Charles McH. Howard (1870-1942)
Jacques T. Schlenger (P.C.)
George H. Spencer (Not admitted in MD; Resident, Washington, D.C. Office)
William J. McCarthy (P.C.)
Russell Ronald Reno, Jr. (P.C.)
Thomas P. Perkins, III (P.C.)
James A. Cole
Robert J. Frank (Not admitted in MD; Resident, Washington, D.C. Office)
Benjamin R. Civiletti (P.C.) (Also at Washington, D.C. and Towson, Maryland Offices)
John B. Howard (Resident, Towson, Maryland Office)
Norman N. Kunitz (Not admitted in MD; Resident, Washington, D.C. Office)
Anthony M. Carey (Also at Washington, D.C. Office)
David E. Belcher
George Cochran Doub (P.C.)
John Henry Lewin, Jr. (P.C.)
Stanley Mazaroff (P.C.)
Lee M. Miller (P.C.)
Neal D. Borden (Also at Washington, D.C. Office)
Robert A. Shelton
Thomas J. Kenney, Jr. (P.C.)
Roger W. Titus (Resident, Rockville, Maryland Office)
Jan K. Guben (Also at Washington, D. C Office)
Ian D. Volner (Not admitted in MD; Resident, Washington, D.C. Office)
Thomas W. W. Haines
Thomas J. Madden (Not admitted in MD; Resident, Washington, D.C. Office)
William L. Walsh, Jr. (P.C.) (Not admitted in MD; Resident, McLean, Virginia Office)
Ronald R. Glancz (Not admitted in MD; Resident, Washington, D.C. Office)
Robert G. Smith (P.C.)
James D. Wright (P.C.)
Joe A. Shull (Resident, Washington, D.C. Office)
David M. Malone (Resident, Washington, D.C. Office)
Gerard Treanor (Not admitted in MD; Resident, Washington, D.C. Office)
Kenneth C. Bass, III (Not admitted in MD; Washington, D.C. and McLean, Virginia Offices)
John H. Zink, III (Resident, Towson, Maryland Office)
Lars E. Anderson (Not admitted in MD; Resident, McLean, Virginia Office)
John G. Milliken (Not admitted in MD; Resident, McLean, Virginia Office)
Paul F. Strain (P.C.)
Alexander I. Lewis, III (P.C.) (Also at Towson, Maryland Office)
William D. Dolan, III (P.C.) (Not admitted in MD; Resident, McLean, Virginia Office)
Paul T. Glasgow (Resident, Rockville, Maryland Office)
Joseph C. Wich, Jr. (Resident, Towson, Maryland Office)
Joseph G. Block (Not admitted in MD; Resident, Washington, D.C. Office)
Sondra Harans Block (Resident, Rockville, Maryland Office)
Jeffrey J. Radowich
Edward F. Glynn, Jr. (Resident, Washington, D.C. Office)
Marina V. Schneller (Not admitted in MD; Resident, Washington, D.C. Office)
Gabor J. Kelemen (Not admitted in MD; Resident, Washington, D.C. Office)
Craig E. Smith
Robert G. Ames (Also at Washington, D.C. Office)
Michael Schatzow (Also at Washington, D.C. Office)
John F. Cooney (Not admitted in MD; Resident, Washington, D.C. Office)
Lawrence B. Bernard (Resident, Washington, D.C. Office)
John W. Schneller (Not admitted in MD; Resident, Washington, D.C. Office)
Bryson L. Cook (P.C.) (Also at Washington, D.C. Office)
Nell B. Strachan
Barbara E. Schlaff
David G. Lane (Resident, McLean, Virginia Office)
N. Frank Wiggins (Not admitted in MD; Resident, Washington, D.C. Office)
A. Wayne Lalle, Jr. (Not admitted in MD; Resident, McLean, Virginia Office)
Brock R. Landry (Not admitted in MD; Resident, Washington, D.C. Office)
Richard L. Wasserman (P.C.)
G. Stewart Webb, Jr.
James K. Archibald (Also at Washington, D.C. Office)
George W. Johnston (P.C.)
Constance H. Baker
Judson W. Starr (Not admitted in MD; Also at Washington, D.C. and Towson, Maryland Offices)
Robert Kinberg (Not admitted in MD; Resident, Washington, D.C. Office)
Allen Wood (Not admitted in MD; Resident, Washington, D.C. Office)
Edward L. Wender (P.C.)
David M. Fleishman
Jana Howard Carey (P.C.)
Jeffrey D. Knowles (Not admitted in MD; Resident, Washington, D.C. Office)
Jeffrey A. Dunn (Also at Washington, D.C. Office)
Mitchell Kolkin
George F. Pappas (Also at Washington, D.C. Office)
William D. Coston (Not admitted in MD; Resident, Washington, D.C. Office)
Kenneth S. Slaughter (Not admitted in MD; Resident, Washington, D.C. Office)
Kenneth G. Hurwitz (Also at Washington, D.C. Office)
Peter P. Parvis
James L. Shea (Also at Washington, D.C. Office)
Jeffrey P. Ayres (P.C.)
Brigid E. Kenney

(See Next Column)

VENABLE ATTORNEYS AT LAW VENABLE, BAETJER AND HOWARD, LLP—*Continued*

MEMBERS OF FIRM (Continued)

Kenneth R. Hoffman (Also at Washington, D.C. Office)
David G. Adams (Not admitted in MD; Resident, Washington, D.C. Office)
Mark B. Harrison (Not admitted in MD; Resident, Washington, D.C. Office)
Elizabeth C. Honeywell
Ellen F. Dyke (Not admitted in MD; Resident, McLean, Virginia Office)
Maurice Baskin (Resident, Washington, D.C. Office)
John J. Pavlick, Jr. (Not admitted in MD; Resident, Washington, D.C. Office)
John B. Beaty (Resident, Washington, D.C. Office)
Amy Berman Jackson (Not admitted in MD; Resident, Washington, D.C. Office)
C. Carey Deeley, Jr. (Also at Towson, Maryland Office)
George William Lewis (Not admitted in MD; Resident, Washington, D.C. Office)
Christopher R. Mellott
Robert Zinkham
David Eugene Rice
John L. Sullivan, III (Not admitted in MD; Resident, McLean, Virginia Office)
Robert Charles Hill (Not admitted in MD; Resident, Washington, D.C. Office)
Ashley J. Wells (Not admitted in MD; Resident, Washington, D.C. Office)
M. King Hill, III (Resident, Towson, Maryland Office)
James A. Dunbar (Resident, Towson, Maryland Office)
Elizabeth R. Hughes
Ronald W. Taylor
Robert L. Waldman
Thomas J. Kelly, Jr. (Not admitted in MD; Resident, Washington, D.C. Office)
John A. Roberts (Also at Rockville, Maryland Office)
Geoffrey M. Levitt (Not admitted in MD; Resident, Washington, D.C. Office)
Thomas D. Washburne, Jr.
Robert A. Hoffman (Resident, Towson, Maryland Office)
Robert J. Bolger, Jr. (Also at Washington, D.C. Office)
Anita J. Finkelstein (Not admitted in MD; Resident, Washington, D.C. Office)
Mary Jane Saunders (Not admitted in MD; Resident, Washington, D.C. Office)
John A. Wilhelm (Not admitted in MD; Resident, McLean, Virginia Office)
Charles R. "Rod" Marvin, Jr. (Not admitted in MD; Resident, Washington, D.C. Office)
David J. Heubeck
J. Michael Brennan (Resident, Towson, Maryland Office)
Walter R. Calvert
John M. Bredehoft (Not admitted in MD; Resident, McLean, Virginia Office)
Andrew Fois (Not admitted in MD; Resident, Washington, D.C. Office)
Julie A. Petruzzelli (Not admitted in MD; Resident, Washington, D.C. Office)
Herbert G. Smith, II (Not admitted in MD; Resident, Washington, D.C. Office)
Patrick J. Stewart (Also at Washington, D.C. Office)
David C. Mancini (Resident, McLean, Virginia Office)
James R. Burdett (Not admitted in MD; Resident, Washington, D.C. Office)
Douglas B. McDonald (Not admitted in MD; Resident, McLean, Virginia Office)
Gary M. Hnath (Resident, Washington, D.C. Office)
Kevin L. Shepherd
James E. Cumbie
Newton B. Fowler, III
Michael J. Baader
Davis V. R. Sherman
Mitchell Y. Mirviss
Geoffrey R. Garinther (Also at Towson, Maryland Office)
Wallace E. Christner (Also at Washington, D.C. Office)
Elizabeth Corr Smedley (Not admitted in MD; Resident, McLean, Virginia Office)
Michael A. Gollin (Resident, Washington, D.C. Office)
Thomas M. Lingan
Terri L. Turner
Michael W. Robinson (Resident, McLean, Virginia Office)
Jeffrey K. Gonya
M. Jay Yurow (Not admitted in MD; Resident, McLean, Virginia Office)
Courtney G. Capute
Todd J. Horn
Patrick L. Clancy (Resident, Rockville, Maryland Office)
David W. Goewey (Not admitted in MD; Resident, Washington, D.C. Office)
Lindsay Beardsworth Meyer (Not admitted in MD; Resident, Washington, D.C. Office)
J. Scott Hommer, III (Not admitted in MD; Resident, McLean, Virginia Office)
Gregory A. Cross
John A. McCauley
John T. Prisbe
Elizabeth Marzo Borinsky
Joseph C. Schmelter (Also at McLean, Virginia Office)
John P. Sarbanes
Sandra L. Howard
Robert H. Geis, Jr.
Fernand A. Lavallee (Not admitted in MD; Resident, Washington, D. C. Office)
Vicki Margolis (Also at Washington, D.C. Office)
Judith L. Wheat (Not admitted in MD; Resident, Washington, D.C. Office)
Christine M. McAnney (Not admitted in MD; Resident, McLean, Virginia Office)
Wm. Craig Dubishar (Not admitted in MD; Resident, McLean, Virginia Office)
Maria F. Howell
Dino S. Sangiamo
Marina Lolley Sabett
Connie N. Bertram (Not admitted in MD; Resident, Washington, D.C. Office)

(See Next Column)

OF COUNSEL

A. Samuel Cook (P.C.) (Resident, Towson, Maryland Office)
Arthur W. Machen, Jr. (P.C.)
Robert M. Thomas (P.C.)
Robert R. Bair (P.C.)
Frank Horton (Not admitted in MD; Resident, Washington, D.C. Office)
Emried D. Cole, Jr.
Judith A. Armold (Also at Washington, D.C. Office)
Thomas J. Cooper (Not admitted in MD; Resident, Washington, D.C. Office)
David R. Lasso (Not admitted in MD; Resident, McLean, Virginia Office)
Gary D. Hailey (Not admitted in MD; Resident, Washington, D.C. Office)
Gary L. Shaffer (Not admitted in MD; Resident, Washington, D.C. Office)
Timmy F. Ruppersberger (Resident, Towson, Maryland Office)
Robert G. Rathbun (Not admitted in MD; Resident, Washington, D.C. Office)
Ariel Vannier (Also at Washington, D.C. Office)
Barbara L. Waite (Resident, Washington, D.C. Office)
Robin L. Zimelman
Janet F. Satterthwaite (Not admitted in MD; Resident, Washington, D.C. Office)
David G. Dickman (Not admitted in MD; Resident, Washington, D.C. Office)
Lisa Harris Dean (Not admitted in MD; Resident, McLean, Virginia Office)
Rebecca E. Pearson (Not admitted in MD; Resident, Washington, D.C. Office)
John B. Howard, Jr.
Jeffrey S. Tenenbaum (Not admitted in MD; Resident, Washington, D.C. Office)

ASSOCIATES

Ariana W. Arnold (Resident, Rockville, Maryland Office)
Theodore W. Atkinson (Not admitted in MD; Resident, Washington, D.C. Office)
Marcia A. Auberger (Not admitted in MD; Resident, Washington, D.C. Office)
Scharon L. Ball
Paul D. Barker, Jr.
Jeffrey A. Barnes
Louis B. Barr
Nathan A. Beaver (Not admitted in MD; Resident, Washington, D.C. Office)
John B. Beckman
Robin B. Bowerfind
Gregory S. Braker (Resident, Washington, D.C. Office)
Gail Brashers-Krug (Resident, Towson, Maryland Office)
Patricia Russell Brown (Resident, Washington, D.C. Office)
Darek S. Bushnaq
Daniel William China (Resident, Towson, Maryland Office)
Kevin B. Collins (Also at Rockville, Maryland Office)
Michael W. Conron
Jeffrey W. Cottle
Patricia Gillis Cousins (Resident, Rockville, Maryland Office)
Carla Draluck Craft (Resident, Washington, D.C. Office)
Donald P. Creston (Not admitted in MD; Resident, Washington, D.C. Office)
Peter J. Curtin (Not admitted in MD; Also at Washington, D.C. Office)
James Nicholas Czaban (Not admitted in MD; Resident, Washington, D.C. Office)
Rosemary E. Dailey (Resident, Washington, D.C. Office)
Kosha K. Dalal
Laurie Curry Daugherty (Resident, McLean, Virginia Office)
Paul A. Debolt (Not admitted in MD; Resident, Washington, D.C. Office)
Kathleen S. Dolan (Not admitted in MD; Resident, Washington, D.C. Office)
Maureen E. Donahue (Resident, Washington, D.C. Office)
Charles W. Durant (Not admitted in MD; Resident, McLean, Virginia Office)
James P. Dvorak, Jr. (Not admitted in MD; Resident, McLean, Virginia Office)
John P. Edgar
Jeffrey B. Elikan (Not admitted in MD)
Edward S. Evans, III
Patricia A. Exposito (Resident, Washington, D.C. Office)
Catherine A. Ferguson (Resident, Washington, D.C. Office)
Heather Deans Foley
Stephanie A. Goldfine (Resident, Washington, D.C. Office)
Rebecca L. Goldsmith (Resident, Washington, D.C. Office)
Therese M. Goldsmith
Matthew B. Greiner (Not admitted in MD; Resident, Washington, D.C. Office)
Keith G. Haddaway (Resident, Washington, D.C. Office)
E. Anne Hamel
John C. Hardwick, Jr. (Resident, Washington, D.C. Office)
Andrew M. Herzig (Not admitted in MD; Resident, Washington, D.C. Office)
Lara L. Hjortsberg
Jeremy K. Huffman (Not admitted in MD; Resident, Washington, D.C. Office)
Davida H. Isaacs (Not admitted in MD; Resident, Washington, D.C. Office)
Linda M. Jackson (Not admitted in MD; Resident, McLean, Virginia Office)
Thora A. Johnson
Matthew F. Kadish (Not admitted in MD; Resident, Washington, D.C. Office)
Elizabeth C. Keenan
Melissa E. Lamb (Resident, Washington, D.C. Office)
Michael P. Leary (Not admitted in MD; Resident, Washington, D.C. Office)
Norman Lencz
Erik J. Lichter
Patricia A. Malone (Resident, Towson, Maryland Office)
Mark Darius Robert Maneche
Gilda S. Mann
Anne W. Marculewicz
William A. McComas
Heather L. McDowell (Resident, Washington, D.C. Office)

(See Next Column)

VENABLE ATTORNEYS AT LAW VENABLE, BAETJER AND HOWARD, LLP, *Baltimore—Continued*

ASSOCIATES (Continued)

Jeannette C. Meacham (Not admitted in MD; Resident, Washington, D.C. Office)
Emily A. Miller (Not admitted in MD; Resident, Washington, D.C. Office)
Daniel P. Moylan (Resident, Towson, Maryland Office)
Thomas V. Mulrine (Resident, Washington, D.C. Office)
John G. Nahajzer (Resident, Washington, D.C. Office)
Chellis E. Neal (Resident, Washington, D.C. Office)
William T. Nesbitt (Resident, Washington, D.C. Office)
Brian J. O'Connor
Andrew Douglas Price (Not admitted in MD; Resident, Washington, D.C. Office)
W. Joseph Price (Not admitted in MD; Resident, Washington, D.C. Office)
John M. Ramirez
L. Eric Ranieri
Johana A. Reed (Resident, Washington, D.C. Office)
Maria E. Rodriguez
Christina L. Romeres
Martin L. Saad (Resident, Washington, D.C. Office)
Michael A. Sartori (Not admitted in MD; Resident, Washington, D.C. Office)
Jason R. Scherr
Joshua N. Schopf (Resident, Washington, D.C. Office)
Sara T. Schumacher (Resident, Washington, D.C. Office)
Jagpreet Singh (Not admitted in MD; Resident, Washington, D.C. Office)
J. Linwood Smith
Melissa Landau Steinman (Resident, Washington, D.C. Office)
Thomas H. Strong
Neal H. Strum
Michael S. Swanenburg (Resident, Towson, Maryland Office)
Lisa Bittle Tancredi
Catherine M. Voorhees (Not admitted in MD; Resident, Washington, D.C. Office)
Gregory L. Waddoups (Not admitted in MD; Resident, Washington, D.C. Office)
David R. Warner (Resident, Rockville, Maryland Office)
James E. Weaver
Rita L. Wecker (Resident, Washington, D.C. Office)
Paul N. Wengert (Not admitted in MD; Resident, McLean, Virginia Office)
Kathleen E. Wherthey (Resident, Rockville, Maryland Office)
Sally R. Wiest
Katherine D. Williams (Resident, Towson, Maryland Office)
Samantha M. Williams (Not admitted in MD; Resident, Washington, D.C. Office)
Kristin K. Woody (Not admitted in MD; Resident, Washington, D.C. Office)
Damon W. D. Wright (Not admitted in MD; Resident, Washington, D.C. Office)
George Abe Zachariah (Resident, Washington, D.C. Office)
Scott A. Zebrak (Resident, Washington, D.C. Office)

For full biographical listings, see the Martindale-Hubbell Law Directory

WHITEFORD, TAYLOR & PRESTON L.L.P. (AV)

7 Saint Paul Street, 21202-1626
Telephone: 410-347-8700
Telex: 5101012334
Fax: 410-752-7092
Email: wt&pllp@wtplaw.com *URL:* http://www.wtplaw.com
Towson, Maryland Office: 210 West Pennsylvania Avenue.
Telephone: 410-832-2000.
Fax: 410-832-2015.
Washington, D.C. Office: 1025 Connecticut Avenue, N.W.
Telephone: 202-659-6800.
Fax: 202-331-0573.
Columbia, Maryland Office: 10440 Little Patuxent Parkway.
Telephone: 410-884-0700.
Fax: 410-884-0719.
Alexandria, Virginia Office: 1317 King Street.
Telephone: 703-836-5742.
Fax: 703-836-0265.

MEMBERS OF FIRM

Paul F. Due (1896-1972)
Palmer R. Nickerson (1898-1969)
W. Hamilton Whiteford (1903-1992)
B. Conway Taylor, Jr. (1918-1993)

Barbara Lee Ayres (Resident Towson Office)
George J. Bachrach
Thomas C. Barbuti
G. Scott Barhight (Resident Towson Office)
Philip B. Barnes (Resident Towson Office)
Thomas C. Beach, III
Steven E. Bers
Ascanio S. Boccuti (Resident Towson Office)
Glenn R. Bonard (Resident Washington, D.C. Office)
Anne Talbot Brennan (Resident Towson Office)
Edward M. Buxbaum
Stephen B. Caplis
John F. Carlton
Robert F. Carney
Priscilla C. Caskey
James R. Chason (Resident Towson Office)
John V. Church
Jonathan E. Claiborne (Resident Towson Office)
Ward B. Coe, III (Managing Partner)
Robert B. Curran
William M. Davidow, Jr.
B. Ford Davis
Deborah H. Diehl
Joseph D. Douglass (Resident Washington, D.C. Office)
Gardner M. Duvall
Judith C. Ensor (Resident Towson Office)

(See Next Column)

(Continued)

John P. Evans (Resident Towson Office)
Howard R. Feldman
Martin T. Fletcher
D. Scott Freed
Stephen F. Fruin
Dale B. Garbutt
Peter D. Guattery
John J. Hathway (Columbia, Maryland and Washington, D.C. Offices)
John A. Hayden, III (Resident Towson Office)
Eva H. Hill
James C. Holman
Daniel H. Honemann
Kenneth J. Ingram (Resident Washington, D.C. Office)
Harry S. Johnson
Frank S. Jones, Jr.
Lisa A. Kershner
Thomas P. Kimmitt, Jr. (Resident Towson Office)
Frederick Singley Koontz
George S. Lawler (Resident Towson Office)
Paul W. Madden
Natalie C. Magdeburger (Resident Towson Office)
Richard J. Magid
Jonathan Z. May
Kevin C. McCormick
M. Natalie McSherry
Albert J. Mezzanotte, Jr.
Joseph J. Mezzanotte
Douglas F. Murray
Paul M. Nussbaum
Kenneth Oestreicher
Dana C. Petersen
Jeanne M. Phelan
Joseph K. Pokempner
Gary S. Posner
Wilbur D. Preston, Jr.
Arthur P. Rogers (Resident Washington, D.C. Office)
Herman B. Rosenthal
James F. Rosner (Resident Towson Office)
William F. Ryan, Jr.
Joseph N. Schaller
Robert Sloan, III
Gail M. Stern
Gerard P. Sunderland
Andrew J. Terrell (Resident Washington, D.C. Office)
Lisa L. Walker
Warren N. Weaver
William B. Whiteford
Larry M. Wolf
Robert M. Wright
Thurman W. Zollicoffer, Jr.

OF COUNSEL

Edward S. Cogen (Resident Washington, D.C. Office)
Robert S. Hillman
Edward A. Johnston (Resident Towson Office)
Fenton L. Martin
Lee A. Satterfield (Resident Washington, D.C. Office)
Paul A. Serini
George D. Solter (Resident Towson Office)
John H. Somerville
C. William Tayler (Resident Washington, D.C. Office)
Ernest C. Trimble (Resident Towson Office)
Richard C. Whiteford

ASSOCIATES

Sandra Harlen Benzer
Tracy A. Cannon
Mary Claire Chesshire
Allison B. Colgan
Pamela M. Conover
Stuart W. Cox
Elise R. Davison
Julie Alyssa DiGrigolis
Christopher R. Dollase
Karen A. Doner (Resident, Washington, D.C. Office)
Gail K. Donovan
Warren B. Duckett, III
Jane Saindon Dudley (Resident, Washington, DC Office)
Julianne Erin Dymowski (Resident Washington, D.C. Office)
Robert Dennis Earle
Edwin G. Fee, Jr. (Resident Towson Office)
Beth A. Gasiorowski (Resident, Towson Office)
David K. Gildea (Resident Towson Office)
Eric R. Harlan
Scott K. Intner
Kim Y. Johnson
Kathy P. Kerrigan
Melanie J. Kirwin
Mark C. Kopec
Gary W. Kuc
Dana O. Lynch
Deirdre M. MacCarthy
Pinelopi Makrodimitris
Frank J. Mastro
Roseanne M. Matricciani
Mary Kaitlin McSally (Resident Washington D.C. Office)
Melissa L. Menkel
Margaret R. Miller (Resident Towson Office)
Diane Preston Moore (Resident Washington, D.C. Office)
Padraic McSherry Morton
S. Keith Moulsdale
Carmina Pérez-Fowler
Cynthia E. Rodgers-Waire
Elizabeth Sarah Rudnick
James B. Rutledge, III
Jennifer M. Ryan (Resident Towson Office)
Leora R. Simantov (Resident Towson Office)
Catherine Whitehurst Steiner
Michael A. Stodghill
Dwight W. Stone, II
Michael A. Stover
Brent C. Strickland
Ilana Subar
Valerie L. Tetro (Resident, Washington, DC Office)
Steven E. Tiller
Stephanie L. Wagner
Thomas J. Whiteford (Resident Towson Office)

For full biographical listings, see the Martindale-Hubbell Law Directory

WRIGHT, CONSTABLE & SKEEN, LLP (AV)

One Charles Center, 16th Floor, 100 N. Charles Street, 21201
Telephone: 410-659-1300
Telex: 710 234-2383 CALDAS
Fax: 410-659-1350

MEMBERS OF FIRM

Wm. Pepper Constable (1882-1976)
John D. Wright (1903-1976)
George W. Constable (Retired)
Read A. McCaffrey (1913-1995)
William A. Skeen (Retired)
John Brentnall Powell, Jr.
Michael J. Abromaitis
Monte Fried
James W. Constable
David W. Skeen
James D. Skeen
Douglas G. Worrall
Kenneth F. Davies

(See Next Column)

WRIGHT, CONSTABLE & SKEEN LLP—*Continued*

MEMBERS OF FIRM (Continued)

Stephen F. White
Brian S. Goodman
Frederick L. Kobb
Paul F. Evelius
Lois A. Fenner McBride
Charles J. Morton, Jr.

ASSOCIATES

Mary Alice Smolarek
Catherine H. Bellinger
Carol J. Glover
Tracey D. King
David J. Shuster
Howard S. Stevens

COUNSEL

Francis N. Iglehart, Jr.
P. McEvoy Cromwell
C. Gordon Haines

Representative Clients: Conowingo Power Co.; Weyerhaeuser Co.; Commercial Credit Corp.; Noxell Corp.; Consolidated Rail Corp.; Murray Corp.; Atlantic Mutual Insurance Co.; Sea Containers, Ltd.; Great Atlantic & Pacific Tea Co.; Tyson Foods, Inc.

For full biographical listings, see the Martindale-Hubbell Law Directory

*BEL AIR,** Harford Co.

STARK & KEENAN, A PROFESSIONAL ASSOCIATION (AV)

30 Office Street, 21014
Telephone: 410-838-5522
Baltimore: 410-879-2222
Fax: 410-879-0688
Email: wstarkee@aol.com
Havre de Grace Office: "The Old Ordinary" 100 St. John Street, 21078.
Telephone: 410-939-0100.

Elwood V. Stark, Jr.
Charles B. Keenan, Jr.
Edwin G. Carson
Judith Cline-Silverstein
Gregory A. Szoka
Robert S. Lynch
Paul W. Ishak

Claire Prin Blomquist
Lawrence F. Kreis, Jr.
Craig H. DeRan

For full biographical listings, see the Martindale-Hubbell Law Directory

BETHESDA, Montgomery Co.

CAPLAN, BUCKNER, ROHRBAUGH & KOSTECKA, CHTD. (AV)

Three Bethesda Metro, 20814-3324
Telephone: 301-718-1900
Fax: 301-718-8359

Donald M. Caplan
Steven R. Buckner
Robert A. Rohrbaugh
Robert C. Kostecka

Daryl Sue Caplan
Mimi Leigh Magyar
David P. Korteling

For full biographical listings, see the Martindale-Hubbell Law Directory

PALEY, ROTHMAN, GOLDSTEIN, ROSENBERG & COOPER, CHARTERED (AV)

Seventh Floor, One Bethesda Center, 4800 Hampden Lane, 20814
Telephone: 301-656-7603
Telecopier: 301-654-7354
Email: prg@paleyrothman.com

Glenn M. Cooper
Victor J. Rosenberg
Mark S. Goldstein
Mark S. Rothman
Stephen H. Paley
Paula A. Calimafde
Ronald A. Dweck
Arthur H. Blitz
Robert H. Maclay
Steven A. Widdes
Hope Eastman
Dennis L. Sharp
Albert D. Pailet
Diane A. Fox
Theodore P. Stein
Jeffrey A. Kolender
Wendelin I. Lipp
Mark A. Binstock
Patricia M. Weaver

Alan D. Eisler
David M. Rothenstein
Brent M. Goldstein
Kathleen M. Dumais
James R. Hammerschmidt
Deborah A. Cohn

SENIOR COUNSEL

Alan S. Mark
Daniel S. Koch
Daniel P. Hodin

For full biographical listings, see the Martindale-Hubbell Law Directory

COLLEGE PARK, Prince Georges Co.

WILLONER, CALABRESE & ROSEN, P.A. (AV)

4603 Calvert Road, 20740-3421
Telephone: 301-699-1400
Fax: 301-779-2213
Email: willoner@wilcalros.com

(See Next Column)

Ronald A. Willoner
John F. Calabrese
Steven Rosen
Stephen F. Shea

Reference: F&M Bank-Allegiance, Bethesda, Maryland.

For full biographical listings, see the Martindale-Hubbell Law Directory

*EASTON,** Talbot Co.

EWING, DIETZ, TURNER & KEHOE, PROFESSIONAL ASSOCIATION (AV)

16 South Washington Street, P.O. Box 1146, 21601
Telephone: 410-822-1988
Fax: 410-820-5053
URL: http://www.edtklaw.com

L. Clark Ewing (1919-1998)
Philip E. L. Dietz, Jr.
Christopher B. Kehoe
John F. Hall
Karen M. Kaludis
Stephen H. Kehoe

Sharon M. Shilling

OF COUNSEL

Henry P. Turner

References: The Talbot Bank of Easton, Maryland; St. Michaels Bank.

For full biographical listings, see the Martindale-Hubbell Law Directory

WHEELER, THOMPSON, PARKER & COUNTS, LLP (AV)

129 North Washington Street, P.O. Box 1209, 21601
Telephone: 410-822-1122
Fax: 410-822-3635
Email: wtpc@dmv.com

MEMBERS OF FIRM

Edward T. Miller (1895-1968)
Ernest M. Thompson (1921-1989)
Charles E. Wheeler
Dorothy H. Thompson
Willard C. Parker, II
Richard L. Counts, III
Douglas A. Collison

OF COUNSEL

Donald H. Olson

Representative Clients: Chicago Title Insurance Company of Maryland; State Farm Mutual Insurance Co.; Chesapeake College; Habitat for Humanity of Talbot County; Talbot County Board of Education; Fuller Motor Sales, Inc.; St. Michaels Housing Authority.
References: Nationsbank, Easton Branch; Talbot Bank, Easton, Maryland; St. Michaels Bank, Eston, Maryland.

For full biographical listings, see the Martindale-Hubbell Law Directory

*FREDERICK,** Frederick Co.

OFFUTT, HORMAN, BURDETTE & FREY, P.A. (AV)

Offutt Building, 22 West Second Street, 21701
Telephone: 301-662-8248;
Hagerstown: 301-293-6032;
Montgomery Co., D.C./Va. line: 301-948-5633
Fax: 301-663-8968

W. Jerome Offutt
Amos A. Holter
John N. Burdette
George T. Horman
Charles Burton Frey

Lisa Anne Rudy
Chris M. May

Representative Clients: Donald B. Rice Tire Co., Inc.; Meadows Van and Storage Co.; Central Maryland Farm Credit, ACA; QUADS Trust Co.; Frederick Aviation, Inc.
Local Counsel: St. James Servicing Corp.; First National Bank of Maryland.
Co-Counsel for: Central Maryland Farm Credit, ACA.
Reference: Frederick Branch of First National Bank of Maryland.

For full biographical listings, see the Martindale-Hubbell Law Directory

GREENBELT, Prince Georges Co.

STANLEY S. PICKETT (AV)

Suite 414 Capital Office Park, 6411 Ivy Lane, 20770
Telephone: 301-513-0613
Fax: 301-513-0618
Email: lossp@intr.net

Stanley Sinclair Pickett

ASSOCIATES

Gordon J. Brumback
Stacy S. Pickett Trimble

LEGAL SUPPORT PERSONNEL

Vivian A. Wolfe (Paralegal)

Representative Clients: B.F. Saul Co.; McDonald and Eudy Printers, Inc.; Condominium Management, Inc.; Long & Foster Realtors; Mitron Systems Corp.; Glenanden Housing Authority; Community Associations, Inc.; Hagmer Management, Inc.; Quantum Management, Inc.

For full biographical listings, see the Martindale-Hubbell Law Directory

LANHAM, Prince Georges Co.

McCarthy & Costello, L.L.P. (AV)
Washington Business Park, Suite 300, 4640 Forbes Boulevard, 20706-4323
Telephone: 301-306-1900
Fax: 301-306-1988
Email: mbc@erols.com *URL:* http://home.erols.com/mbc

MEMBERS OF FIRM

Kevin J. McCarthy
John F. X. Costello
Charles E. Channing, Jr.
Timothy Altemus
Michael J. Winkelman

For full biographical listings, see the Martindale-Hubbell Law Directory

*LA PLATA,** Charles Co.

Thomas C. Hayden, Jr., P.A. (AV)
105 La Grange Avenue, P.O. Box 1039, 20646
Telephone: 301-934-9531; 301-870-3477
Fax: 301-934-5473

Thomas C. Hayden, Jr.
H. A. Turner, IV
Thomas R. Simpson, Jr.

Representative Client: County First Bank.
Reference: County First Bank, La Plata, Maryland.

For full biographical listings, see the Martindale-Hubbell Law Directory

LEXINGTON PARK, St. Marys Co.

Sparling, Densford and Reynolds, P.A. (AV)
22335 Exploration Drive, Suite 2030, 20653
Telephone: 301-863-7054
Fax: 301-863-7112

George R. Sparling
Edward Kim Reynolds
Joseph R. Densford

Jacquelyn V. Raley

Representative Clients: The Wildewood Group; Shah Associates, M.D., P.A.; Maryland Automobile Insurance Fund.
Approved Attorneys for: Chicago Title Company of Maryland; Lawyers Title Insurance Corporation of Richmond, Virginia.

For full biographical listings, see the Martindale-Hubbell Law Directory

RIVERDALE, Prince Georges Co.

Meyers, Billingsley, Rodbell & Rosenbaum, P.A. (AV)
Suite 400 Berkshire Building, 6801 Kenilworth Avenue, 20737-1385
Telephone: 301-699-5800
Fax: 301-779-5746
Email: mbrrlaw@martindalemail.com
Annapolis, Maryland Office: 95 Cathedral Street, Suite 100, 21401.
Telephone: 410-267-6670.
Fax: 410-267-8222.

William V. Meyers
Lance W. Billingsley
Paul B. Rodbell
Robert H. Rosenbaum
Russell E. Warfel
Linda C. Carter
Joseph B. Chazen
Michele LaRocca
Paul A. Turkheimer
David A. Carter

Frederick Stichnoth
Bud Stephen Tayman
M. Andree Green
Gina Marie Smith
Mindy Sue Kursban
M. Evan Meyers
Douglas C. Meister
David J. Martin

Reference: First National Bank of Maryland.

For full biographical listings, see the Martindale-Hubbell Law Directory

*ROCKVILLE,** Montgomery Co.

Anderson & Quinn (AV)
The Adams Law Center, 25 Wood Lane, 20850
Telephone: 301-762-3303
Fax: 301-762-3776
Email: rscanlon@andersonquinn.com

MEMBERS OF FIRM

Charles C. Collins (1900-1973)
Robert E. Anderson (Retired)
Francis X. Quinn
Donald P. Maiberger
Robert P. Scanlon
John A. Rego
Alice Kelley Scanlon

ASSOCIATES

Kerry S. McGeever
Timothy J. Mulreany
Todd P. Maiberger
Jennifer D. Burke
Marc N. Steren

Representative Clients: C & P Telephone; Allstate Insurance Co.; State Farm Mutual Automobile Insurance Co.; Liberty Mutual Insurance Co.; American International Adjustment Co.; Marriott Corp.

(See Next Column)

For full biographical listings, see the Martindale-Hubbell Law Directory

Brault, Graham, Scott & Brault, LLC (AV)
101 South Washington Street, 20850
Telephone: 301-424-1060
Fax: 301-424-7991
Email: bgsb@earthlink.net
Washington, D.C. Office: Brault, Graham, Scott & Brault, PLLC, 1140 Connecticut Avenue, N.W., Suite 250.
Telephone: 202-785-1200.
FAX: 202-785-4301.
Fairfax, Virginia Office: Suite 500, 11350 Random Hills Road, Fair Oaks Plaza, 22030-7429.
Telephone: 202-785-1200.

OF COUNSEL

Laurence T. Scott
James Robert Miller

MEMBERS OF FIRM

Denver H. Graham (1922-1987)
Albert E. Brault (Retired)
Albert D. Brault (Resident)
Leo A. Roth, Jr.
James S. Wilson (Resident)
Ronald G. Guziak
Daniel L. Shea (Resident)
M. Kathleen Parker (Resident)
David G. Mulquin (Resident)
James M. Brault (Resident)
Regina Ann Casey (Resident)

ASSOCIATES

Rhonda Ann Hurwitz (Resident)
Joan F. Brault (Resident)

Representative Clients: American Oil Co.; Crum & Forster Group; Fireman's Fund American Insurance Cos.; Kemper Group; Reliance Insurance Cos.; Safeco Group; Government Employees Insurance Co.; Medical Mutual Insurance Society of Maryland; Legal Mutual Liability Insurance Society of Maryland.

For full biographical listings, see the Martindale-Hubbell Law Directory

Bromberg, Rosenthal, Siegel & Goodman (AV)
110 North Washington Street Suite 405, 20850-2223
Telephone: 301-251-6200
Fax: 301-309-9436
Email: brsg@brsglaw.com *URL:* http://www.lawyers.com/brs&glaw
Washington, D.C. Office: Suite 536, 1522 K Street, N.W.

MEMBERS OF FIRM

Jonathan R. Bromberg
Barry J. Rosenthal
Gary Siegel
Leonard S. Goodman

ASSOCIATE

Audra J. Small

Representative Clients: Agriculture Federal Credit Union; GEICOS Federal Credit Union; Dexall Biomedical Labs; N.R.L. Federal Credit Union; OBA Federal S&L; Dept. of Commerce FCU; Allen & Associates Int'l, Ltd.; Medserv International, Inc.; ImageCorp, Inc.

For full biographical listings, see the Martindale-Hubbell Law Directory

Chen, Walsh, Tecler & McCabe, L.L.P. (AV)
Suite 300, 200-A Monroe Street, 20850
Telephone: 301-279-9500
Fax: 301-294-5195
Email: cwtm@radix.net

MEMBERS OF FIRM

William James Chen, Jr.
John Burgess Walsh, Jr.
Kenneth B. Tecler
John F. McCabe, Jr.

ASSOCIATE

Teresa Kenney

For full biographical listings, see the Martindale-Hubbell Law Directory

Hogan & Hartson L.L.P. (AV)
600 Jefferson Plaza, Suite 203, 20852
Telephone: 301-315-2206
Fax: 301-315-9046
Washington, D.C. Office: Columbia Square, 555 13th Street, N.W.
Telephone: 206-637-5600.
Telex: 89-2757.
Cable Address: "Hogander Washington".
Fax: 202-637-5910.
Brussels, Belgium Office: Avenue des Arts 41, 1040.
Telephone: (32.2) 505.09.11.
Fax: (32.2) 505.09.96.
Budapest, Hungary Office: Bank Center, Granite Tower, 9th Floor, Budapest V., Szabadsag ter 7, 1944 Hungary.
Telephone: (36-1) 302-9050.
Fax: (36-1) 302-9060.
London, England Office: 21 Garlick Hill, EC4V 2AU.
Telephone: (44 171) 815 1200.
Fax: (44 171) 329 0299.

(See Next Column)

HOGAN & HARTSON L.L.P.—*Continued*

Moscow, Russia Office: 33/2 Usacheva Street, Building 3, 119048.
Telephone: (7095) 245-5190. Int'l
Telephone: (7501) 907-0451.
Fax: (7095) 245-5192. Int'l
Fax: (7501) 907-0462.
Paris, France (Affiliated Office): Cariddi, Mee, Rué, Avocats Associés à la Cour de Paris, 12, rue de la Paix, 75002.
Telephone: (33-1) 42.61.57.71.
Fax: (33-1) 42.61.79.21.
Prague, Czech Republic (Affiliated Office): Hogan & Hartson, Advokátní Kanceláře, v.o.s., Opletalova 37, 110 00.
Telephone: (420-2) 2211-7111.
Fax: (420-2) 2421-5105.
Warsaw, Poland Office: Hogan & Hartson Sp.zo.o, Atrium Tower, Al. Jana Pawla II 25, 00-854.
Telephone: (48-22) 653-4200.
Fax: (48-22) 653-4250.
Baltimore, Maryland Office: 111 South Calvert Street.
Telephone: 410-659-2700.
Fax: 410-539-6981.
Colorado Springs, Colorado Office: Two North Cascade Avenue, Suite 1300.
Telephone: 719-448-5900.
Fax: 719-448-5922.
Denver, Colorado Office: One Tabor Center, Suite 1500, 1200 Seventeenth Street.
Telephone: 303-899-7300.
Fax: 303-899-7333.
Los Angeles, California Office: Biltmore Tower, 500 S. Grand Avenue, Suite 1900.
Telephone: 213-337-6700.
Fax: 213-337-6701.
McLean, Virginia Office: 8300 Greensboro Drive.
Telephone: 703-610-6100.
Fax: 703-610-6200.
New York, New York Office: 885 Third Avenue, 26th Floor.
Telephone: 212-409-9800.
Fax: 212-409-9801.

PARTNERS

Stanley J. Brown
Steven A. Robins
Clyde H. Sorrell, Jr.

For full biographical listings, see the Martindale-Hubbell Law Directory

---

MILLER, MILLER & CANBY, CHARTERED (AV)

200-B Monroe Street, 20850
Telephone: 301-762-5212
Fax: 301-762-6044

William M. Canby (1930-1994)
Patrick C. McKeever
James L. Thompson
Lewis R. Schumann
Joel S. Kline
Joseph P. Suntum
Maury S. Epner

OF COUNSEL

Robert L. Burchett
James R. Miller, Jr.

Ellen S. Walker
Susan W. Carter
Suzanne Levant Rotbert
Michael Gert Campbell
Robert E. Gough

Representative Clients: Asbury Methodist Home Inc.; Sandy Spring National Bank of Maryland.

For full biographical listings, see the Martindale-Hubbell Law Directory

---

THOMAS D. MURPHY, P.C. (AV)

Suite 2 Adams Law Center, 31 Wood Lane, 20850
Telephone: 301-424-0400
Email: murphyslaw@erols.com

Thomas D. Murphy

James A. Mood, Jr.

For full biographical listings, see the Martindale-Hubbell Law Directory

---

STEIN, SPERLING, BENNETT, DE JONG, DRISCOLL, GREENFEIG & METRO, P.C. (AV)

25 West Middle Lane, 20850-2204
Telephone: 301-340-2020; 800-435-5230
Telecopier: 301-340-8217
Email: lawfirm@steinsperling.com
Falls Church, Virginia Office: 6245 Leesburg Pike, Suite 140, 22044.
Telephone: 703-237-0500.
Telecopier: 703-534-2899.

(See Next Column)

Fred A. Balkin
Millard S. Bennett
David S. De Jong
David C. Driscoll, Jr.
Stuart S. Greenfeig
Ann G. Jakabcin
A. Howard Metro
Jeffrey M. Schwaber
Donald N. Sperling
Paul T. Stein

Jeffrey D. Goldstein
Jolie S. Deutschman
Karen Plave Goldstein
David W. Lease
Edward D. McGuire, Jr.
William J. Scott
Darcy A. Shoop
Marc J. Smith
Joseph D. Grandinetti, Jr. (Not admitted in MD)
Debra Sue Grimes

OF COUNSEL

Alan S. Kerxton

For full biographical listings, see the Martindale-Hubbell Law Directory

---

VENABLE ATTORNEYS AT LAW VENABLE, BAETJER AND HOWARD, LLP (AV)

A Partnership including Professional Corporations
Suite 500, One Church Street, P.O. Box 1906, 20850-4129
Telephone: 301-217-5600
Fax: 301-217-5617
URL: http://www.venable.com
Baltimore, Maryland Office: 1800 Mercantile Bank & Trust Building, 2 Hopkins Plaza.
Telephone: 410-244-7400.
Fax: 410-244-7742.
Washington, D.C. Office: Venable, Baetjer, Howard & Civiletti LLP, Suite 1000, 1201 New York Avenue, N.W.
Telephone: 202-962-4800.
Fax: 202-962-8300.
McLean, Virginia Office: Suite 400, 2010 Corporate Ridge.
Telephone: 703-760-1600.
Fax: 703-821-8949.
Towson, Maryland, Office: 210 Allegheny Avenue, P. O. Box 5517.
Telephone: 410-494-6200.
Fax: 410-821-0147.

MEMBERS OF FIRM

Roger W. Titus
Paul T. Glasgow
Sondra Harans Block
John A. Roberts (Also at Baltimore, Maryland Office)
Patrick L. Clancy

ASSOCIATES

Ariana W. Arnold
Kevin B. Collins (Also at Baltimore, Maryland Office)
Patricia Gillis Cousins
David R. Warner
Kathleen E. Wherthey

For full biographical listings, see the Martindale-Hubbell Law Directory

---

*SALISBURY,** Wicomico Co.

DUVALL & DUVALL, L.L.P. (AV)

108 East Market Street, P.O. Box 4077, 21803-4077
Telephone: 410-548-1010
Fax: 410-548-1045
Email: billduva@shore.intercom.net

MEMBERS OF FIRM

William G. Duvall
Richard M. Duvall

Reference: Nations Bank.

For full biographical listings, see the Martindale-Hubbell Law Directory

---

SILVER SPRING, Montgomery Co.

GINGELL & JENKINS, P.C. (AV)

Suite 506 Wheaton Plaza South, 11160 Veirs Mill Road, 20902
Telephone: 301-949-0100
Telecopier: 301-949-0467
Email: rgingdjen@aol.com *URL:* http://www.lawyers.com/gingelljenkins

Robert A. Gingell
Donn K. Jenkins

LEGAL SUPPORT PERSONNEL

Karen Thompson
Paula Brock (Real Estate Paralegal)

Representative Clients: Air Flow Co. (Industrial Air Conditioning); Bethesda Realty Co.; Photo Science, Inc.
References: Sovran Bank; First National Bank of Maryland (Rockville, Maryland, Branch); Signet Bank Maryland.

For full biographical listings, see the Martindale-Hubbell Law Directory

Silver Spring—Continued

LINOWES AND BLOCHER LLP (AV)

Suite 1000, 1010 Wayne Avenue, 20910-5600
Telephone: 301-588-8580
Telecopier: 301-495-9044
TTY/TDD: 301-588-3380
Email: inbox@linowes-law.com *URL:* http://www.linowes-law.com
Washington, D.C. Office: Suite 302, 1150 17th Street, N.W.
Telephone: 202-293-8510.
Telecopier: 202-293-8513.
Greenbelt, Maryland Office: Suite 202, 6411 Ivy Lane.
Telephone: 301-982-3382.
Telecopier: 301-982-0595.
Annapolis, Maryland Office: 145 Main Street.
Telephone: 410-268-0881.
Telecopier: 301-261-2603.
Frederick, Maryland Office: 228 West Patrick Street.
Telephone: 301-695-0244.
Telecopier: 301-663-6656.
Columbia, Maryland Office: Suite B215, 10015 Old Columbia Road.
Telephone: 410-312-5457.
Fax: 410-290-5285.

MEMBERS OF FIRM

Joseph P. Blocher
Todd D. Brown
Walter S. B. Childs (Resident Partner, Annapolis, Maryland office)
David M. Cohen
Kathryn J. Dahl (Resident Partner, Annapolis, Maryland office)
C. Robert Dalrymple
John J. Delaney
Stephen P. Elmendorf
Bradford F. Englander
Andrew M. Goldstein
Myles Hannan
Gerald W. Heller
William M. Hoffman, Jr.
John L. Hollingshead
Douglas M. Irvin
Andrew L. Isaacson
Stephen Z. Kaufman
Lawrence R. Liebesman
Robert H. Metz
Maurice J. Montaldi (Not admitted in MD)
John R. Orrick, Jr.
Robert C. Park, Jr.
Midgett S. Parker, Jr. (Resident Partner, Greenbelt, Maryland office)
David M. Plott (Resident Partner, Annapolis, Maryland office)
Leslie Moore Romine (Resident Partner, Greenbelt, Maryland office)
Barbara A. Sears
Paul-Michael Sweeney
Raymond B. Via, Jr.
James A. Vidmar, Jr.
Roger D. Winston
James B. Witkin
Richard M. Zeidman

PARTNERS EMERITUS

Charles G. Dalrymple
R. Robert Linowes

OF COUNSEL

David L. Cahoon
Cynthia A. Giordano (Resident, Washington, D.C. office)
Renee B. Loren

ASSOCIATES

Andrew Wycoff Crocker
Jessica N. Drexler
John A. Elmendorf
Michelle F. Giannini (Not admitted in MD)
James E. Gilbert
Bruce C. Johnson
John Edward Lucian
Timothy P. Martin
Dorothy H. Moore (Not admitted in MD)
Lella Amiss E. Pape (Not admitted in MD)
Rafe Petersen
Dana Deisinger Resnik
William W. Riggins III
Joel W. Ruderman
Martin L. Schnider, Jr.
Garland H. Stillwell (Resident, Greenbelt, Maryland office)
Emily J. Vaias
Mark Michael Viani
Scott C. Wallace
Earl Edward Wise III

For full biographical listings, see the Martindale-Hubbell Law Directory

SAUNDERS & SCHMIELER (AV)

8737 Colesville Road, Suite L-200, 20910-3921
Telephone: 301-588-7717
Facsimile: 301-588-5073
Email: admin@sslawfirm.com *URL:* http://www.sslawfirm.com
Washington, D.C. Office: 1050 17th Street, N.W., #600
Telephone: 202-833-2999.
Baltimore, Maryland Office: Suite 2700, 111 South Calvert Street.
Telephone: 410-235-7558.
Arlington, Virginia Office: 2111 Wilson Boulevard, Suite 700.
Telephone: 703-243-1100.
Richmond, Virginia Office: 4900 Cutshaw Avenue.
Telephone: 804-353-9800.

MEMBER OF FIRM

Jeffrey R. Schmieler

ASSOCIATES

Nicole E. Ames
A. Benjamin Horton
Lucas F. Webster

(See Next Column)

OF COUNSEL

Vincent D. Thomas, Jr.

For full biographical listings, see the Martindale-Hubbell Law Directory

*TOWSON,** Baltimore Co.

LAW OFFICE OF MICHAEL H. BURGOYNE, P.A. (AV)

305 Washington Avenue, Suite 501, 21204
Telephone: 410-847-9600
Fax: 410-847-9689
Email: MHBoffice@AOL.com *URL:* http://www.lawyers.com/mhboffice

Michael H. Burgoyne

Maureen L. Rowland

For full biographical listings, see the Martindale-Hubbell Law Directory

NOLAN, PLUMHOFF & WILLIAMS, CHARTERED (AV)

Suite 700, Nottingham Centre, 502 Washington Avenue, 21204-4528
Telephone: 410-823-7800
Fax: 410-296-2765
Email: npw@nolanplumhoff.com

James D. Nolan (Retired, 1980)
J. Earle Plumhoff (1940-1988)
Newton A. Williams
Thomas J. Renner
William P. Englehart, Jr.
Stephen J. Nolan
Robert L. Hanley, Jr.
Robert S. Glushakow
Douglas L. Burgess
Robert E. Cahill, Jr.
C. William Clark
Catherine A. Potthast
E. Bruce Jones
Melinda A. Kimmitt

Representative Clients: Baltimore County, Maryland; Bituminous Insurance Companies; Board of Education of Anne Arundel County; Carolina Freight Carriers Corporation; Humane Society of Baltimore County, Inc.; Patapsco Federal Savings & Loan Association; Pulte Home Corporation; Royal Oak Federal Savings Bank, F.S.B.; Shelter Development Corporation; Summit Broadcasting Corporation.

For full biographical listings, see the Martindale-Hubbell Law Directory

ROYSTON, MUELLER, MCLEAN & REID, LLP (AV)

Suite 600, 102 West Pennsylvania Avenue, 21204
Telephone: 410-823-1800
Fax: 410-828-7859
Email: mail@rmmr.com

MEMBERS OF FIRM

R. Taylor McLean
E. Harrison Stone
Thomas F. McDonough
Laurel Paretta Evans
Keith R. Truffer
Robert S. Handzo
Edward J. Gilliss
John W. Browning

ASSOCIATES

Edward U. Lee III
Timothy J. Oursler
Craig P. Ward

OF COUNSEL

Richard A. Reid
Eugene W. Cunningham, Jr.
Bradford G. Y. Carney
Charles F. Stein III
H. Emslie Parks

Representative Clients: Bell Atlantic-MD; The Reuben H. Donnelley Corporation; Mercantile-Safe Deposit and Trust Co.; Ruby Tuesday, Inc.; Redland Genstar, Inc.; Rosedale Federal Savings and Loan Assn.; Royal Insurance Co.; The Williams Companies, Inc.

For full biographical listings, see the Martindale-Hubbell Law Directory

VENABLE ATTORNEYS AT LAW VENABLE, BAETJER AND HOWARD, LLP (AV)

A Partnership including Professional Corporations
210 Allegheny Avenue, P.O. Box 5517, 21204
Telephone: 410-494-6200
Fax: 410-821-0147
URL: http://www.venable.com
Baltimore, Maryland Office: 1800 Mercantile Bank & Trust Building, 2 Hopkins Plaza.
Telephone: 410-244-7400.
Fax: 410-244-7742.
Washington, D.C. Office: Venable, Baetjer, Howard & Civiletti LLP, Suite 1000, 1201 New York Avenue, N.W.
Telephone: 202-962-4800.
Fax: 202-962-8300.
McLean, Virginia Office: Suite 400, 2010 Corporate Ridge.
Telephone: 703-760-1600.
Fax: 703-821-8949.
Rockville, Maryland Office: Suite 500, One Church Street, P. O. Box 1906.
Telephone: 301-217-5600.
Fax: 301-217-5617.

(See Next Column)

VENABLE ATTORNEYS AT LAW VENABLE, BAETJER AND HOWARD, LLP—*Continued*

PARTNERS

James D. C. Downes (1906-1979)
James H. Cook (1918-1993)
Benjamin R. Civiletti (P.C.) (Also at Washington, D.C. and Baltimore, Maryland Offices)
John B. Howard
John H. Zink, III
Alexander I. Lewis, III (P.C.) (Also at Baltimore, Maryland Office)
Joseph C. Wich, Jr.
Judson W. Starr (Not admitted in MD; Also at Washington, D.C. and Baltimore, Maryland Offices)
C. Carey Deeley, Jr. (Also at Baltimore, Maryland Office)
M. King Hill, III
James A. Dunbar
Robert A. Hoffman
J. Michael Brennan
Geoffrey R. Garinther (Also at Baltimore, Maryland Office)

OF COUNSEL

A. Samuel Cook (P.C.)
Timmy F. Ruppersberger

ASSOCIATES

Gail Brashers-Krug
Daniel William China
Patricia A. Malone
Daniel P. Moylan
Michael S. Swanenburg
Katherine D. Williams

For full biographical listings, see the Martindale-Hubbell Law Directory

WHITEFORD, TAYLOR & PRESTON L.L.P. (AV)

210 West Pennsylvania Avenue, 21204-4515
Telephone: 410-832-2000
Fax: 410-832-2015
Email: wt&pllp@wtplaw.com *URL:* http://www.wtplaw.com
Baltimore, Maryland Office: 7 Saint Paul Street.
Telephone: 410-347-8700.
Telex: 5101012334.
Fax: 410-752-7092.
Washington, D.C. Office: 1025 Connecticut Avenue, N.W.
Telephone: 202-659-6800.
Fax: 202-331-0573.
Columbia, Maryland Office: 10440 Little Patuxent Parkway.
Telephone: 410-884-0700.
Fax: 410-884-0719.
Alexandria, Virginia Office: 1317 King Street.
Telephone: 703-836-5742.
Fax: 703-836-0265.

PARTNERS

Barbara Lee Ayres
G. Scott Barhight
Philip B. Barnes
Ascanio S. Boccuti
Anne Talbot Brennan
James R. Chason
Jonathan E. Claiborne
Judith C. Ensor
John P. Evans
John A. Hayden, III
Thomas P. Kimmitt, Jr.
George S. Lawler
Natalie C. Magdeburger
James F. Rosner

OF COUNSEL

Edward A. Johnston
George D. Solter
Ernest C. Trimble

RESIDENT ASSOCIATES

Julie Alyssa DiGrigolis
Edwin G. Fee, Jr.
Beth A. Gasiorowski
David K. Gildea
Margaret R. Miller
Jennifer M. Ryan
Leora R. Simantov
Thomas J. Whiteford

For full biographical listings, see the Martindale-Hubbell Law Directory

WHITNEY & BOGRIS, LLP (AV)

401 Washington Avenue, Twelfth Floor, 21204
Telephone: 410-583-8000
Fax: 410-583-8031
Email: HGWC@worldnet.att.net

MEMBERS OF FIRM

Daniel W. Whitney
George D. Bogris

ASSOCIATES

Kathleen D. Leslie
Henry Russell
Sandra A. Tofte
Michael A. Giacomazza
Arlene L. Sew
Gerald S. Gaetano (Not admitted in MD)
Scott A. McCabe (Not admitted in MD)
Jeffrey C. Shipley

OF COUNSEL

Joseph E. Dever
David L. Feldstein
Ronald V. Miller, Jr.

For full biographical listings, see the Martindale-Hubbell Law Directory

*UPPER MARLBORO,** Prince Georges Co.

KNIGHT, MANZI, NUSSBAUM & LAPLACA, P.C. (AV)

14440 Old Mill Road, 20772
Telephone: 301-952-0100
Annapolis/Baltimore: 410-792-3786
Fax: 301-952-0221

(See Next Column)

William E. Knight
Robert A. Manzi
Ronald M. Miller
William C. Brennan, Jr.
Harry J. Trainor, Jr.
Andrew W. Nussbaum
Raymond G. LaPlaca
John F. Shay, Jr.
Sheldon L. Gnatt
Daniel A. LaPlaca
Gail Borjeson Viens
Roger C. Thomas
Monica M. Haley-Pierson
Daniel F. Lynch III
Norman D. Rivera

Robert L. Lombardo
Amy B. Glaser
Brent M. Ahalt
Terry L. Bell

For full biographical listings, see the Martindale-Hubbell Law Directory

*WESTMINSTER,** Carroll Co.

WESLEY D. BLAKESLEE (AV)

104 East Main Street, 21157
Telephone: 410-848-6655; 876-6660
Fax: 410-876-9257
Email: blakesleew@aol.com *URL:* http://www.lawyers.com/blakeslee

For full biographical listings, see the Martindale-Hubbell Law Directory

DULANY & LEAHY, LLP (AV)

127 East Main Street, 21157-5012
Telephone: 410-848-3333; Baltimore Line: 410-876-2117
FAX: 410-876-0747
Email: dulany@dulany.com

MEMBERS OF FIRM

William B. Dulany
J. Brooks Leahy
Amber Dahlgreen Curtis
Kenneth Michael Williams

Representative Clients: Lehigh Portland Cement Co.; Pizza Hut of Maryland, Inc.; McGregor Printing Corporation; Mutual Fire Insurance Company of Carroll County; Carroll Lutheran Village, Inc.; Western Maryland College.
Reference: Carroll County Bank and Trust Co.

For full biographical listings, see the Martindale-Hubbell Law Directory

WALSH & FISHER, A PROFESSIONAL ASSOCIATION (AV)

179 East Main Street, 21157
Telephone: 410-848-9200; 876-2135
Telecopier: 410-848-9313
Email: wandf@qis.net

D. Eugene Walsh (1895-1980)
Charles O. Fisher
Charles O. Fisher, Jr.
David B. Weisgerber

Representative Clients: Genstar Stone Products Co., Conewago Contractors, Inc.; Westminster Bank and Trust Co.; Carroll County General Hospital, Inc.; Adams County National Bank.

For full biographical listings, see the Martindale-Hubbell Law Directory

MASSACHUSETTS

AMESBURY, Essex Co.

THE HAMEL LAW FIRM (AV)

Five Market Square, P.O. Box 198, 01913-0398
Telephone: 978-388-3558
Telecopier: 978-388-0441
Email: hamellaw@excelr8.net
Email: hamellaw@lawyers.com *URL:* http://www.lawyers.com/hamellaw

MEMBER OF FIRM

Richard P. Hamel

ASSOCIATES

H. Scott Haskell
Peter R. Ayer, Jr.
Roger D. Turgeon

Representative Clients: First and Ocean National Bank, Newburyport, MA.
Approved Attorneys for: Chicago Title Insurance; Old Republic Title Insurance Co.

For full biographical listings, see the Martindale-Hubbell Law Directory

*BOSTON,** Suffolk Co.

BARRON & STADFELD, P.C. (AV)

50 Staniford Street, Suite 200, 02114
Telephone: 617-723-9800
Telecopier: 617-523-8359
Email: barron@barronstad.com *URL:* HTTP://WWW.BARRONSTAD.COM
Hyannis, Massachusetts Office: 258 Winter Street.
Telephone: 617-778-6622.

(See Next Column)

BARRON & STADFELD P.C., *Boston—Continued*

Bernard A. Dwork
Enid M. Starr
Thomas V. Bennett
Edward E. Kelly
Kevin F. Moloney
David P. Dwork
Julie Taylor Moran
Robert J. Hoffer
Joseph G. Butler
Denise L. Page
Rosemary Purtell
Kerry Paul Choi
John K. Britt

Roger T. Manwaring
Shawn P. O'Rourke
Kevin P. Scanlon
Kathleen M. Morrissey
Edward J. Fallman
Teresa C. Scibelli

OF COUNSEL

Hertz N. Henkoff
Elliott J. Mahler

For full biographical listings, see the Martindale-Hubbell Law Directory

BERNKOPF, GOODMAN & BASEMAN LLP (AV)

125 Summer Street, 02110-1621
Telephone: 617-790-3000
Telecopier: 617-790-3300
URL: http://www.bgblaw.com

MEMBERS OF FIRM

Abraham K. Cohen (1891-1957)
Max E. Bernkopf (1919-1967)
Sylvan A. Goodman (1935-1981)
Kenneth M. Goldberg
Alan J. Grace
Marvin N. Geller
Neil R. Markson
Gary P. Lilienthal
James B. Fox
Peter B. McGlynn
Sheryl C. Starr
Richard B. Michaud
Lydia G. Chesnick
Martin C. Pomeroy
Eric R. Allon
David L. Doyle
John B. Harkavy
James D. Friedman

OF COUNSEL

Harris I. Baseman

ASSOCIATES

Bruce D. Levin
Richard P. Bennett
Michael J. Radin
John F. Farraher, Jr.
Todd D. Goldberg
Jason A. Manekas
Elizabeth A. Long
Richard D. Vetstein

For full biographical listings, see the Martindale-Hubbell Law Directory

BINGHAM DANA LLP (AV)

150 Federal Street, 02110
Telephone: 617-951-8000
Telecopy: 617-951-8736
Email: info@bingham.com *URL:* http://www.bingham.com
Hartford, Connecticut Office: One State Street.
Telephone: 860-240-2700.
Fax: 860-240-2800.
London, England Office: 39 Victoria Street, SWIH 0EE.
Telephone: 011-44-71-799-2646.
Telecopy: 011-44-71-799-2654.
Washington, D.C. Office: 1120 20th Street, N.W.
Telephone: 202-778-6150.
Fax: 202-778-6155.
Los Angeles, California Office: The Wells Fargo Center, 333 South Grand Avenue, Suite 1570.
Telephone: 213-687-2700.
Fax: 213-617-9109.
New York, New York Office: 399 Park Avenue.
Telephone: 212-318-7700.
Fax: 212-752-5378.
Singapore Office: Level 15 Prudential Tower, 30 Cecil Street, 049712.
Telephone: 011.65.232.2768.
Fax: 011.65.232.2888.

MEMBERS OF FIRM

Donald-Bruce Abrams
John F. Adkins
Jonathan M. Albano
Marion Giliberti Barish
Cynthia Faye Barnett
Robert A. J. Barry
Mark W. Batten
Alan W. Beloff
Wayne D. Bennett
William N. Berkowitz
Jonathan K. Bernstein
David C. Boch
Jeremiah J. Bresnahan, Jr.
Johan Van't Hul Brigham
John S. Brown
Marijane Benner Browne
Robert A. Buhlman
David C. Casey
John J. Concannon, III
Lea Anne Copenhefer
Sherry L. Countryman
John J. Curtin, Jr.
Neal J. Curtin
James S. Davis
Louis J. Duval
M. Gordon Ehrlich
Frederick F. Eisenbiegler
David L. Engel
Randal A. Farrar
Roger D. Feldman
Sula R. Fiszman
Francis H. Fox
Daniel L. Goldberg
Linda J. Groves
Steven W. Hansen
Richard M. Harter
Henry S. Healy
Thomas J. Hennessey
Joe H. Hicks
Patricia J. Hill
Thomas John Holton
Janice W. Howe
Russell E. Isaia
Charles L. Janes

(See Next Column)

MEMBERS OF FIRM (Continued)

David O. Johanson
Roger P. Joseph
Brian Keeler
Gerald J. Kehoe
William D. Kirchick
Joseph L. Kociubes
Amy L. Kyle
George P. Mair
Colin S. Marshall
S. Elaine McChesney
William A. McCormack
Robert E. McDonnell
Stephen M. Miklus
Henry T. A. Moniz
Scott Carson Moriearty
Justin P. Morreale
Guy B. Moss
David J. Murphy
Martin F. Murphy
Michael P. O'Brien
Victor J. Paci
Martin J. Pasqualini
Thomas E. Peckham
Victor H. Polk, Jr.
Gerald F. Rath
Marc A. Reardon
Marcia Robinson
Neal A. Rosen
Vincent M. Sacchetti
T. Malcolm Sandilands
Daniel S. Savrin
Edward A. Saxe
Julie A. Scallen
James G. Scantling
(Not admitted in MA)
Toby R. Serkin
Norman J. Shachoy
Leslie H. Shapiro
Lawrence I. Silverstein
John R. Skelton
Edwin E. Smith
John R. Snyder
Charles L. Solomont
William G. Southard
James C. Stokes
E. Clothier Tepper
Richard A. Toelke
John R. Utzschneider
Peter Van
Paul M. Vaughn
Julio E. Vega
Thomas H. Walsh, Jr.
Sabin Willett
Robert M. Wolf
Jay S. Zimmerman
(Managing Partner)
Peter F. Zupcofska

OF COUNSEL

Austin S. Ashley
Hugh J. Ault
Sumner H. Babcock
Natalie B. Choate
Joseph H. B. Edwards
Beth A. Frothingham
(Not admitted in MA)
Gordon B. Greer
Burton M. Harris
Joseph F. Hunt
Richard H. Johnson
John R. Kirk
Richard D. Leggat
William J. McNally
James F. Monahan
Francis S. Moulton, Jr.
Andrew C. Phelan
James N. Rice
Mark E. Robinson
Donna M. White
James M. White, Jr.
Mari Anne Wilson

ASSOCIATES

Rebecca Federman Alperin
Susan M.N. Antonio
Lisa M. Asiaf
Elizabeth L. Belanger
James L. Black, Jr.
Evelyn M. Bonn
Melanie J. Brockway
Stephen D. Brook
Timothy P. Burke
James P. Carrigan
Theresa R. Cline
Matthew J. Cohen
Mary P. Cohn
Christopher C. Cooper
Deidre E. Corkery
William S. D. Cravens
Matthew J. Cushing
Joshua M. Dalton
Maria E. Damico
Susan Walsh Davis
Mary DeNevi
Erika De La Rosa De La Fuente
(Not admitted in the United States)
Richard S. Denhup
Barbara Ann Dirsa
Jenelle Celine Dodds
Deidre A. Doherty
Michael G. Donovan
Alicia L. Downey
Judith G. Edington
Stephen H. Faberman
Richard M. Filosa
Joanne D.C. Foley
(Not admitted in MA)
Jason D. Frank
Julia Frost-Davies
Anthony Edward Fuller
Matthew F. Furlong
Sarah K. Gagan
Natascha Suzanne George
Jennifer K. Godsil
Cristina E. Gonzalez
Sandra E. Grandison
Allison R. Handel
Joseph Michael Hiffa
Robert R. Hindman
David B. Hobbie
Jennifer H. Hurford
Barry N. Hurwitz
Bellenden Rand Hutcheson
Daniel James Jackson
Richard A. Johnson, Jr.
Meerie M. Joung
Sandra E. Kahn
Matthew J. Kelly
Joseph Kim
(Not admitted in MA)
Megan H. Lawrence
Eunice E. Lee
Andrea Orr LeFebvre
Dennis C. Liu
Angelique M.S. Magliulo
Prem N. Malali
Colleen Ann Manning
A. Scott Marra
Sarah E. Marston
Joseph R. Martinez
Cameron S. Matheson
Maura McCaffery
James C. McGrath
T. Joseph McNabb, Jr.
Siobhan Elizabeth Mee
Garfield A. Miller
Michael K. Murphy
Mary Beth Murrane
Heidi A. Nadel
Daniel A. Nelson
Jennifer E. Newton
James E. O'Connell, III
Glen R. Openshaw
William S. Perkins
Kathleen M. Phelps
Martha F. Phelps
Nicole Andraya Raucher
Stuart M. Rees
Paul M. Robertson
Lucas Rogers
Juan O. Rossello
Rheba Rutkowski
Darcy A. Ryding
Jonathan M. Sachs
Donald J. Savery
Matthew D. Schnall
Peter B. Schoch
Arnold D. Scott, Jr.
Emily L. Sebert
(Not admitted in MA)
David P. Sharrow
David L. Silvian

(See Next Column)

BINGHAM DANA LLP—*Continued*

ASSOCIATES (Continued)

Sabita Singh
Raymond Francis Skoglund
Christopher R. Smith
Shaun B. Spencer
Tycho H. E. Stahl
(Not admitted in MA)
Suzanne M. Suppa
Steven M. Taibl
Fiona S. Trevelyan
Ian M. de Buy Wenniger
Frans Christopher Wethly
Andrew B. White
David Yamin
Seth M. Yurdin

LEGAL SUPPORT PERSONNEL

William A. Bachman

For full biographical listings, see the Martindale-Hubbell Law Directory

BLOOM & BUELL (AV)

1340 Soldiers Field Road, 02135-1020
Telephone: 617-254-4400; 800-354-6004
Telecopier: 617-254-7610
Email: office@bloombuell.com *URL:* http://www.bloombuell.com

MEMBERS OF FIRM

Laurence J. Bloom
Barbara Hayes Buell
William J. Davenport
Marc J. Gervais
Richard M. Haley

ASSOCIATES

Barry T. Putterman
Barbara D. Weninger

For full biographical listings, see the Martindale-Hubbell Law Directory

BURNS & LEVINSON LLP (AV)

125 Summer Street, 02110-1624
Telephone: 617-345-3000
Telecopier: 617-345-3299
URL: http://www.burnslevinson.com
Hingham, Massachusetts Office: 175 Derby Street.
Telephone: 781-749-3810.
Telecopier: 781-749-3980.
Wellesley, Massachusetts Office: 60 Walnut Street.
Telephone: 781-235-1034.
Telecopier: 781-235-5975.

MEMBERS OF FIRM

Lawrence M. Levinson
Thomas D. Burns

Jeffrey L. Alitz
Victor Bass
Raymond E. Baxter
Brian D. Bixby
Paul G. Boylan
William H. Clancy
Clifford R. Cohen
John A. Donovan, Jr.
Steven C. Goodwin
Michael H. Goshko
Maura A. Greene
Jay S. Gregory
David E. Grossman
Evelyn A. Haralampu
David J. Hatem
Warren D. Hutchison
Kenneth A. Johnson
Dennis J. Kelly
Kevin G. Kenneally
Mark J. Levinson
Jeffrey R. Martin
Steven J. Marullo
Michael J. Meagher
Howard D. Medwed
William E. Moderi
Darrell Mook
Robert J. O'Regan
Frederick S. Paulsen
Maria-Eugenia Recalde
Nancy M. Reimer
Robert C. Rives, Jr.
David P. Rosenblatt
Richard A. Savrann
Frank A. Segall
Gary W. Smith
Traver Clinton Smith, Jr.
Barry L. Solar
Norman C. Spector
Paul E. Stanzler
Richard J. Tetrault
George N. Tobia, Jr.
Michael G. Tracy
Nancy R. Van Tine
Stuart M. Van Tine
(Resident, Hingham Office)
Mark Ventola
Josef B. Volman
Cheryl A. Waterhouse
Michael Weinberg
Robert W. Weinstein
Richard L. Wulsin

ASSOCIATES

Joseph Alexander, Jr.
Janet R. Barringer
Andrew P. Botti
Dwight T. Burns, III
Romeo G. Camba
Victoria A. Crawshaw
William H. DiAdamo
Laura Beth Foster
Ann Connell Fox
Lisa A. Furnald
Michael P. Giunta
Christopher D. Guerin
Michael D. Healan
Kathleen A. Hunter
Renee Inomata
Andrew D. Kang
John Joseph Kenney, Jr.
Garrett Jorgen Lee
Luigi Leo
David M. Losier
Lyn M. Lustig
Robin M. Lynch
Gregg M. Lysko
Mark W. Manning
Paul R. Mastrocola
Jennifer F. McNally
Lawrence J. McNally, Jr.
YeWon Min
Lesa S. Muccini
Leslie B. Muldowney
Mark F. Murphy
Christina M. Murray
Robert T. Norton
John G. O'Neill
Michael P. Roche
Michelle F. Rosenberg
(Resident, Hingham Office)
Farnaz Sadeghi
James J. Scanlon
Ingrid C. Schroffner
James K. Schwartz
Pamela G. Smith

(See Next Column)

ASSOCIATES (Continued)

Ronald J. Snyder
Kenneth B. Walton
Virginia L. Wondolowski
Adam Michael Zaiger

OF COUNSEL

Edmund J. O'Brien
Harry A. Pierce
David M. Thomas
Herbert M. Weiss

For full biographical listings, see the Martindale-Hubbell Law Directory

CASNER & EDWARDS, LLP (AV)

1 Federal Street, 27th Floor, 02110-2003
Telephone: 617-426-5900
Telecopier: 617-426-8810
Email: ce@thecia.net

MEMBERS OF FIRM

Thomas D. Edwards (1931-1987)
Andrew J. Casner, Jr.
(1931-1999)
Haskell A. Kassler
Walter H. Mayo, III
Martin E. Greenblatt
Charles M. Hamann
Robert A. Murphy
Robert E. Cowden, III
John H. Ashby
Douglas K. Mansfield
Andrew M. Higgins
Terrance J. Hamilton
Robert S. Kutner
David J. Chavolla
Stephen M. Perry
Gary L. Hoff
Anita W. Robboy
Peter A. Caro
Gregg S. Blackburn
Linda A. Ouellette
Joan M. Griffin

ASSOCIATES

Donna Brewer MacKenna
Gary L. Kemp
Matthew T. Murphy
Mark W. Williamson
William F. McSweeny, III
Elizabeth L. Desmond
Martha A. Coravos

For full biographical listings, see the Martindale-Hubbell Law Directory

CHERWIN, GLICKMAN & THEISE, LLP (AV)

A Limited Liability Partnership including Professional Corporations
One International Place, 02110-2622
Telephone: 617-330-1625
Fax: 617-330-1642
Email: cgandt@cgandt.com

Joel I. Cherwin (P.C.)
Jay F. Theise
Marshall D. Stein
David K. Wanger
William O. Rizzo
Lisa Lee Foster
Julie A. Koshgarian

LEGAL SUPPORT PERSONNEL

Beverly Twomey (Administrator)

For full biographical listings, see the Martindale-Hubbell Law Directory

CHOATE, HALL & STEWART (AV)

A Partnership Including Professional Corporations
Exchange Place, 02109-2891
Telephone: 617-248-5000
Cable Address: "Chohalste".
Telecopier: 617-248-4000
Telex: 49615860.
Email: info@choate.com *URL:* http://www.choate.com
Manchester, New Hampshire Office: 1155 Elm Street.
Telephone: 603-629-9300.
Telecopier: 603-634-0063.

MEMBERS OF FIRM

Pamela E. Berman (P.C.)
Allen M. Bornheimer (P.C.)
David J. Brown (P.C.)
Samuel B. Bruskin (P.C.)
Robert M. Buchanan, Jr. (P.C.)
Lyman G. Bullard, Jr. (P.C.)
Mark D. Cahill (P.C.)
Karen L. Cartotto (P.C.)
Jonathan Chiel (P.C.)
Stephen M. L. Cohen (P.C.)
Sarah Chapin Columbia (P.C.)
John M. Cornish (P.C.)
F. Davis Dassori (P.C.)
Roslyn G. Daum (P.C.)
Brian A. Davis (P.C.)
Ailsa DePrada Deitemeyer (P.C.)
Stephen K. Fogg (P.C.)
Robert S. Frank, Jr. (P.C.)
William P. Gelnaw, Jr. (P.C.)
Frank Giso III (P.C.)
Charles L. Glerum (P.C.)
Kenneth A. Glusman (P.C.)
Laura C. Glynn (P.C.)
Myra J. Green (P.C.)
Andrew C. Griesinger (P.C.)
Harry A. Hanson, III (P.C.)
Jeffrey L. Heidt (P.C.)
Carla B. Herwitz (P.C.)
Edward F. Hines, Jr. (P.C.)
Richard N. Hoehn (P.C.)
Jeffrey R. Howard (P.C.)
(Not admitted in MA)
Anne Rickard Jackowitz
Robert V. Jahrling, III (P.C.)
Christopher M. Jedrey (P.C.)
Michael G. Jones (P.C.)
James R. Kane (P.C.)
Mitchell H. Kaplan (P.C.)
Dennis J. Kearney (P.C.)
Alicia M. Colarte Kelly (P.C.)
Larry C. Kenna (P.C.)
W. Brewster Lee (P.C.)
Kevin J. Lesinski (P.C.)
Kevin P. Light (P.C.)
William A. Lowell (P.C.)
Thomas F. Maffei (P.C.)
James A. McDaniel (P.C.)
Arnold P. Messing (P.C.)
Mark A. Michelson (P.C.)
Louis C. Miller (P.C.)
John A. Nadas (P.C.)
Andrew L. Nichols (P.C.)
Jeremiah T. O'Sullivan (P.C.)
Peter M. Palladino (P.C.)
Sam Pasternack (P.C.)
Frank B. Porter, Jr. (P.C.)

(See Next Column)

CHOATE, HALL & STEWART, *Boston—Continued*

MEMBERS OF FIRM (Continued)

Cameron Read (P.C.)
William C. Rogers (P.C.)
A. Hugh Scott (P.C.)
Thomas E. Shirley (P.C.)
M. James Shumaker (P.C.)
Michael S. Sophocles (P.C.)
John R. Walkey (P.C.)
Michael Arthur Walsh (P.C.)
Willie J. Washington (P.C.)
Thomas H. P. Whitney, Jr. (P.C.)
Eric W. Wodlinger (P.C.)

SENIOR COUNSEL

Marion R. Fremont-Smith (P.C.)

OF COUNSEL

Richard C. Allen
Mark A. Borreliz
James P. Hawkins
Patricia A. Hennessy
Judith A. Johnson
Kathleen King Parker
Laurence D. Pierce
David J. Powsner
Henry M. Rosen
Nora J. Schneider

SPECIAL COUNSEL

Heidi A. Schiller

ASSOCIATES

E. Kenly Ames
Oliver F. Ames, Jr.
David A. Attisani
James M. Atwood
John R. Baraniak, Jr.
Ingrid M. Bologovsky
Michael Henry Bunis
Frederick P. Callori
Jerry Canada
Joseph M. Centofanti
Andrea M. Cezeaux
Steven L. Charlip
Katherine A. Chaurette
Charles Augustus Cheever
Ann Chiga (Not admitted in MA)
David B. Colleran
Christine A. Conley
Nolly Elisabeth Corley
Andrea L. Crowley
Paul G. Cushing
Keith A. Custis
Denise W. DeFranco
Michelle L. Dineen
Jeffrey C. Doherty
Valerie M. Doty
Joshua A. Engel
Lawrence Friedman
John J. Goldrosen
Douglas R. Gooding
James W. Hackett, Jr.
H. Hamilton Hackney, III
Kurt Wm. Hemr (Not admitted in MA)
Eric Bradford Hermanson
William S. Hewitt, Jr. (Resident, Manchester, New Hampshire Office)
Andrew J. Hickey
Megan C. Holding
Sarah G. Hunt
David P. Hutchinson
Sarah E. Idelson
Michael A. Jacobs (Not admitted in MA)
Brenda H. Jarrell
Michael I. Joachim
Anthony Donghun Kang
Gregory C. Keating
Brian J. King
Robert Kole
David C. Kurtz
Karen D. Lane
David H. London
Katrine Benedict MacGregor
Cynthia Thomas MacLean
Nick Malhotra
Eric J. Marandett
Elizabeth M. McCarron
Scott L. McConchie
Carla E. Munroe
Thomas J. Murphy
Raymond A. O'Brien
Rachel Krongrad Pemstein
Carlos Perez-Albuerne
Paul D. Popeo
Alison C. Reif
Tricia A. Rice
Kathleen M. Sablone
Michael B. Sandler
Larry W. Schwartz
Laura M. Scott
Gregg D. Shapiro
Leigh Earls Slayne
Carlton S. Smith, Jr.
Steven M. Smith
Christine G. Solt
Andrew J. Synnott
Reginald F. Thors
Stephen J. Tonkovich
Kevin M. Tormey
William D. Troyka
John S. Tuohy
Chad Vella
John F. Ventola
Lisa Fishbone Wallack
Christopher M. Waterman
Christine J. Wichers
Alyssa S. Wiener
David B. Zanger

For full biographical listings, see the Martindale-Hubbell Law Directory

CORNELL & GOLLUB (AV)

75 Federal Street, 02110
Telephone: 617-482-8100
Telecopier: 617-482-3917
Email: CornellGollub@worldnet.att.net
Wakefield, Rhode Island Office: 146 Main Street, 02879.
Telephone: 401-782-2072.
Telecopier: 401-782-4941.

MEMBERS OF FIRM

Robert W. Cornell (1910-1988)
Karl L. Gollub (1934-1985)
David H. Sempert
Peter M. Durney
Paul F. Lynch
Jane Treen Brand
Janet J. Bobit
David W. McGough

ASSOCIATES

Thomas A. Pursley
Susan Donaldson Novins
Marie Chadeayne Chafe
Kelly L. Wilkins
James P. Kerr
Patricia A. Hartnett
David G. Braithwaite
Jennifer L. Davis
Matthew J. Ginsburg
Kenneth M. Robbins

OF COUNSEL

Philip J. Foley

For full biographical listings, see the Martindale-Hubbell Law Directory

CRAIG AND MACAULEY, PROFESSIONAL CORPORATION (AV)

Federal Reserve Plaza, 600 Atlantic Avenue, 02210-2211
Telephone: 617-367-9500
Telecopier: 617-742-1788; 617-248-0886
URL: http://prospex.com/craig-macauley/

Charles C. Craig (1904-1996)
William F. Macauley
David F. Hannon
Mary P. Brody
A. Van C. Lanckton
Richard E. Quinby
Stephen Wald
William R. Moorman, Jr.
John G. Snyder
Martin P. Desmery
Christopher J. Panos
Christopher S. Dalton

OF COUNSEL

John C. Craig
Donald W. Suchma

Joseph A. Brear, Jr.

Alan D. Hoch
Janice O'Neill Fahey
Christopher J. Currier
Alex M. Rodolakis
Daniel C. Reiser
Karen E. Romito
Luke W. Schemmel
David M. Shamberger

Mark A. Metcalf

For full biographical listings, see the Martindale-Hubbell Law Directory

CURLEY & CURLEY, P.C. (AV)

27 School Street, 02108-4391
Telephone: 617-523-2990
Fax: 617-523-7602

Robert A. Curley
Robert A. Curley, Jr.
Eugene F. Nowell
David D. Dowd
Martin J. Rooney
Lisabeth Ryan Kundert
Stephen J. Gill
Charles Mark Furcolo

Joni Katz Mackler

For full biographical listings, see the Martindale-Hubbell Law Directory

DAY, BERRY & HOWARD LLP (AV)

Twenty First Floor, 260 Franklin Street, 02110
Telephone: 617-345-4600
Telecopier: 617-345-4745
Email: Postmaster@dbh.com *URL:* http://www.dbh.com
Greenwich, Connecticut Office: One East Putnam Avenue.
Telephone: 203-862-7800.
Hartford, Connecticut Office: CityPlace I.
Telephone: 860-275-0100.
Telecopier: 860-275-0343.
Stamford, Connecticut Office: One Canterbury Green.
Telephone: 203-977-7300.
Telecopier: 203-977-7301.

MEMBERS OF FIRM IN BOSTON

David B. Broughel
Lewis A. Burleigh
Daniel J. Carragher
Jeffrey A. Clopeck
Nancy M. Cullen
George L. Cushing
Charles Donelan
Bruce D. Hickey
William A. Hunter
James A. McGraw
J. Charles Mokriski
Francis H. Morrison III
Ross A. Pascal
William Shields
H. Lawrence Tafe III
Kenneth E. Werner

Cynthia J. Williams

ASSOCIATES OF FIRM IN BOSTON

Scott C. Altonian
John G. Balboni
Bonnie J. Crowley (Not admitted in MA)
Tricia F. Deraska
Andrea Falcione
Jonathan I. Handler
Louise A. Handler
Rahul A. Kalke
John P. McLafferty
Kathleen S. Moore
Mary Theresa Moran
Jason W. Morgan
Faith B. Nirenstein
John J. Phillips
Kenneth C. Pickering
Anton Richard Reinert
Kent D.B. Sinclair

Maura D. Sullivan

COUNSEL

Stephen G. Howard
Frank A. Libby, Jr.
Richard S. Novak
Eric K. Runge

For full biographical listings, see the Martindale-Hubbell Law Directory

DECHERT PRICE & RHOADS (AV)

Ten Post Office Square South, 02109-4603
Telephone: 617-728-7100
Telefax: 617-426-6567
URL: http://www.dechert.com
Philadelphia, Pennsylvania: 4000 Bell Atlantic Tower, 1717 Arch Street, 19103-2793.
Telephone: 215-994-4000.
New York, New York: 30 Rockefeller Plaza, 10112.
Telephone: 212-698-3500.
Washington, D.C.: 1775 Eye Street, N.W., 20006.
Telephone: 202-261-3300.

(See Next Column)

DECHERT PRICE & RHOADS—*Continued*

Harrisburg, Pennsylvania: Thirty North Third Street, 17101-1603.
Telephone: 717-237-2000.
Princeton, New Jersey: Princeton Pike Corporate Center, P.O. Box 5218, 08543-5218.
Telephone: 609-620-3200.
Hartford, Connecticut: 90 State House Square, 16103-3702.
Telephone: 860-524-3999.
London, England: 2 Serjeants' Inn, EC4Y 1LT.
Telephone: (0171) 583-5353. (Also see Titmuss Sainer Dechert).
Brussels, Belgium: 65 Avenue Louise, 1050.
Telephone: (02) 535-5411.
Paris, France: 55, avenue Kléber, 75116.
Telephone: 33-(0) 1-53 65 05 00.

RESIDENT PARTNERS

Adrienne M. Baker
Timothy C. Blank
Bernard J. Bonn III
Susan M. Camillo
Joseph R. Fleming
Sheldon A. Jones

RESIDENT OF COUNSEL

Alan L. Lefkowitz

RESIDENT ASSOCIATES

Katherine T. Alen
Allison R. First
Thomas A. Gormley III
Mark K. Loughman
John V. O'Hanlon (Not admitted in MA)
Barry S. Pollack (Not admitted in MA)
Matthew A. Porter
William E. Schwartz (Not admitted in MA)
Tracy Morse Soehle
Kara W. Swanson
Oleg A. Vyadro
Anthony H. Zacharski

For full biographical listings, see the Martindale-Hubbell Law Directory

DUANE, MORRIS & HECKSCHER LLP (AV)

One International Place, 14th Floor, 02110-2600
Telephone: 617-598-3100
Fax: 617-598-3101
URL: http://www.duanemorris.com
Philadelphia, Pennsylvania Office: Suite 4200, One Liberty Place.
Telephone: 215-979-1000.
Fax: 215-979-1020.
New York, New York Office: 380 Lexington Avenue.
Telephone: 212-692-1000.
Fax: 212-692-1020.
Chicago, Illinois Office: 227 West Monroe Street, Suite 3400.
Telephone: 312-499-6700.
Fax: 312-499-6701.
Washington, D.C. Office: 1667 K Street, N.W., Suite 700.
Telephone: 202-776-7800.
Fax: 202-776-7801.
San Francisco, California Office: 100 Spear Street.
Telephone: 415-371-2200.
Fax: 415-371-2201.
Miami, Florida Office: 200 South Biscayne Boulevard, Suite 3410.
Telephone: 305-960-2200.
Fax: 305-960-2201.
Wilmington, Delaware Office: 1201 Market Street, Suite 1500.
Telephone: 302-571-5550.
Fax: 302-571-5560.
Harrisburg, Pennsylvania Office: 305 North Front Street, 5th Floor, P.O. Box 1003.
Telephone: 717-237-5500.
Fax: 717-232-4015.
Wayne, Pennsylvania Office: 735 Chesterbrook Boulevard, Suite 300.
Telephone: 610-647-3555.
Fax: 610-640-2619.
Cherry Hill, New Jersey Office: 51 Haddonfield Road, Suite 340.
Telephone: 856-488-7300.
Fax: 856-488-7021. P Newark, New Jersey Office: One Riverfront Plaza.
Telephone: 973-424-2000.
Fax: 973-424-2001.
Newark, New Jersey Office: One Riverfront Plaza.
Telephone: 973-733-9880.
Fax: 973-733-9881.
Palm Beach, Florida Office: 249 Royal Palm Way, Suite 403.
Telephone: 561-366-5400.
Fax: 561-366-5401.
Allentown, Pennsylvania Office: 968 Postal Road, Suite 200, P.O. Box 90400.
Telephone: 610-266-3650.
Fax: 610-266-3651.
Houston, Texas Office: One Greenway Plaza, Suite 500.
Telephone: 713-552-9900.
Fax: 713-552-0109.
Dover, Delaware Office: 314 S. State Street.
Telephone: 302-736-0156.
Fax: 302-736-0336.

(See Next Column)

RESIDENT PARTNERS

Dana C. Blakslee
Joel S. Freedman
Michael R. Gottfried
Paul D. Moore
Terry Philip Segal
Martin B. Shulkin (Partner-in-Charge, Boston, Massachusetts Office)
Jeffrey D. Sternklar

RESIDENT ASSOCIATES

Kathaleen K. Cutone
Wayne J. Martorelli (Not admitted in MA)
Gwen Philips May (Not admitted in MA)
Anthony J. Fitzpatrick
Richard M. Wong

OF COUNSEL

D. Dennis Allegretti

For full biographical listings, see the Martindale-Hubbell Law Directory

ESDAILE, BARRETT & ESDAILE (AV)

75 Federal Street, 02110
Telephone: 617-482-0333
Fax: 617-426-2978
Email: Esdaile@AOL.COM

MEMBERS OF FIRM

J. Newton Esdaile
Charles W. Barrett, Jr.
James N. Esdaile, Jr.
Norman I. Jacobs
Michael E. Mone
Patricia L. Kelly
Robert J. Rutecki

ASSOCIATES

Shaun Spencer Forsyth
Rhonda Traver Maloney
Steven J. Ryan
C. William Barrett
Mary Moynihan Conneely
Jon M. Jacobs
Kathryn E. Hand

OF COUNSEL

Charles J. Murray

For full biographical listings, see the Martindale-Hubbell Law Directory

FOLEY, HOAG & ELIOT LLP (AV)

One Post Office Square, 02109
Telephone: 617-832-1000
Telecopier: 617-832-7000
Email: fhe@fhe.com *URL:* http://www.fhe.com
Washington, D.C. Office: 1747 Pennsylvania Avenue, N.W.
Telephone: 202-223-1200.
Telecopier: 202-785-6687.

MEMBERS OF FIRM

David L. Weltman
Verne W. Vance, Jr.
David B. Ellis
David W. Walker
Mark F. Clark
John D. Patterson, Jr.
James K. Brown
Robert L. Birnbaum
William J. Cheeseman
Christian M. Hoffman
Michael B. Keating
Adam Sonnenschein
Leonard Schneidman
Edward N. Gadsby, Jr.
Peter B. Ellis
John H. Henn
Barry B. White
Arnold M. Zaff
Louis P. Georgantas
Philip Burling
John M. Stevens, Jr.
Peter W. Coogan
Sandra Shapiro
Paul V. Lyons
Nick Littlefield
Kenneth L. Grinnell
Deborah A. Willard
John L. Burke, Jr. (Resident, Washington, D.C. Office)
Charles J. Beard
Deborah B. Breznay
Richard W. Benka
Arthur G. Telegen
Thomas M. S. Hemnes
Stephen B. Deutsch
Donald R. Ware
Peter M. Rosenblum
Paul R. Murphy
Marc K. Temin
Toni G. Wolfman
Jacob N. Polatin
Joseph C. Maher, Jr.
Steven W. Phillips
Paul S. Reichler (Resident at Washington, D.C. Office)
Laurie Burt
William B. Koffel
Kevin J. Fitzgerald
David R. Pierson
Dean F. Hanley
Stefanie D. Cantor
Robert W. Sweet, Jr.
Brandon F. White
David R. Geiger
Bruce A. Kinn
Robert S. Sanoff
James A. Smith
Wendy B. Jacobs
Gary C. Crossen
Richard d'A. Belin
James T. Montgomery, Jr. (Resident at Washington, D.C. Office)
Andrew Z. Schwartz
Arlene L. Bender
Bruce R. Parker
Mark L. Johnson
Jonathan H. Hulbert
David A. Broadwin
Carol Hempfling Pratt
Michael N. Glanz
Philip C. Swain
Nicholas C. Theodorou
Richard R. Schaul-Yoder
Susan Barbieri Montgomery
Seth D. Jaffe
Douglas M. McGarrah
David H. Feinberg
William R. Kolb
Anthony D. Mirenda
Teresa A. Martland
Mary Beth Gentleman
Michele A. Whitham
Jonathan M. Ettinger
Peter M. Casey
Claire Laporte
Dan Danielsen
Donald W. Muirhead
Edward G. Black
Beth E. Arnold

(See Next Column)

FOLEY, HOAG & ELIOT LLP, *Boston—Continued*

OF COUNSEL

John F. Bok
Dennis R. Kanin
Gloria Cordes Larson

COUNSEL

Michael A. Albert
Diane E. Bissonnette
Janis H. Brennan (Resident at Washington, D.C. Office)
Richard M. Brunell
Paula A. Campbell
Robert L. Cowdrey
Stephanie Cutler (Resident at Washington, D.C. Office)
Deborah Drosnin
Marie Beatrice Grause (Resident at Washington, D.C. Office)
Traci Duvall Humes (Resident at Washington, D.C. Office)
Alima Joned (Resident at Washington, D.C. Office)
Paul V. Kelly
Alexander H. Pyle
Todd H. Shuster
Charles E. Weinstein

ASSOCIATES

David A. Anderson
Gil Arie (Not admitted in MA)
Matthew C. Baltay
Wayne Barnett
Justin Yale Bernold
Pamela B. Blatte
Robert L. Bocchino, Jr.
Jonathan E. Book
Michael Parker Boudett
Jill L. Bradford
James W. Bucking
Vincent J. Canzoneri
Charles H. Cella
Pat A. Cerundolo
Jeffrey D. Collins
Monica E. Conyngham
Sarah Cooleybeck
Andrew J. Cordner
Richard G. Costello (Not admitted in MA)
Melissa E. Crow (Resident at Washington, D.C. Office)
Eric P. Damon (Not admitted in MA)
Kathleen O'Loughlin Dias
Karen B. Dietrich
Michael V. Dowd
Benjamin J. Ericson
Emily L. Fantasia
Barbara A. Fiacco
Nora E. Field
Jeffrey S. Follett
Sarah A. Forster
Andrew D. Friedman
Evan Georgopoulos
Deborah L. Giambanco
Tamara Greeman (Not admitted in the United States)
Nicole R. Hadas
Daniel H. Haines
Katherine M. Hamill
John D. Hancock
Malcolm G. Henderson (Not admitted in MA)
Vickie L. Henry
Kenneth A. Itrato
Adam P. Kahn
Edward J. Kelly
Jonathan A. Keselenko
Randall E. Kromm
T. Maria Lam
Kenneth S. Leonetti
George N. Lester, IV
Daniel M. Malabonga (Resident at Washington, D.C. Office)
Linda P. Marglous
Lawrence H. Martin
Robert A. Mazzarese
Eileen M. McGettigan
Earl W. Mellott, II
Vijay Moses
Jeffrey B. Mullan
Gerard P. O'Connor
Daniele M. Ouellette
Danell Palladine Dean (Resident at Washington, D.C. Office)
Chinh H. Pham
Shirin Philipp
Jack W. Pirozzolo
Hal L. Poret
Hilary Ames Poret
Jeffrey L. Quillen
Keith M. Rodda
Jeffrey L. Roelofs
Michael L. Rosen
Anne E. Saturnelli
Kristine Sheehy
John A. Shope
Brian A. Silikovitz
Tracey E. Spruce
Paul G. Sweeney
Kingsley L. Taft
Anita Varma (Not admitted in MA)
Matthew P. Vincent
Karen L. Vossler
Stephen C. Warneck
M. Sharon Webb
Michael J. Webber
Xinhua (Howard) Zhang
Colin J. Zick

For full biographical listings, see the Martindale-Hubbell Law Directory

FRIEDMAN & ATHERTON (AV)

(Formerly Friedman, Atherton, King & Turner)
(Formerly Friedman, Atherton, Sisson & Kozol)
Exchange Place, 53 State Street, 02109-2803
Telephone: 617-227-5540
Telecopier: 617-523-1559

Lee M. Friedman (1897-1957)
Percy A. Atherton (1903-1940)
Frank L. Kozol (1927-1993)
Robert D. Kozol (1938-1999)

OF COUNSEL

Frank H. Shapiro

MEMBERS OF FIRM

Joel A. Kozol
Lee H. Kozol
William I. Cowin
Richard M. Zinner
Matthew S. Kozol
David M. Kozol

ASSOCIATES

Christine P. Deshler
Angela M. Kalivas
Janet Kenton-Walker
Olive E. Larson
David A. Rich
Meredith Anne Rosenthal
Herbert Weinberg

(See Next Column)

COUNSEL

Paul S. Alpert
Thomas C. Bailey
Michael P. Morizio

For full biographical listings, see the Martindale-Hubbell Law Directory

GADSBY & HANNAH LLP (AV)

225 Franklin Street, 02110-2811
Telephone: 617-345-7000
Telefax: 617-345-7050
Email: gadsby@ghlaw.com *URL:* http://www.ghlaw.com
Washington, D.C. Office: 1747 Pennsylvania Avenue, N.W.
Telephone: 202-429-9600.

PARTNERS

Richard K. Allen
Ronald G. Busconi
Wendell Robert Carr, Jr.
Harold J. Carroll
Jeffrey P. Cleven
Paul E. Clifford
Thomas G. Collins
Peter M. Coppinger
Allan R. Curhan
Charles A. Dale, III
Lawrence H. Gennari
Marianne Gilleran
Leigh A. Gilligan
John R. Hallal
Harry R. Hauser
Peter S. Johnson
Robert J. Kaler
Lawrence R. Katz
Cynthia B. Keliher
Daniel J. Kelly
Stanley A. Martin
Diane M. McDermott
John M. McKelway, Jr.
James J. Myers
Olivia A. O'Neill
Michael N. Sheetz
Steven M. Shishko
Evan Slavitt
Jeffrey M. Stoler (Not admitted in MA)
Kevin J. Toomey
Patrick C. Toomey
Robert A. Trevisani
Walter D. Wekstein
Burton Winnick
William A. Zucker

OF COUNSEL

Douglas A. Fineberg (Not admitted in MA)

ASSOCIATES

Pamela J. Attardo
M. Carolina Avellaneda
Joseph A. Barra
Michael J. Cashton
Matthew R. Caton
Thomas H. Dolan
Michael B. Donahue
Michael J. Epstein
John P. Giffune
Paul Marshall Harris
Daniel C. Hohler
Andrew A. Honegger
Laura A. Huber
David A. Kelly
Barbara J. Kroncke
Marc D. Lazar
Edward W. Little, Jr.
Susan J. Matthew
Lisa T. McElroy
Kimberly M. Parker
Mark S. Resnick
Lisa M. Rico
Elizabeth R. Sahatjian
Elisabeth Schreuer
Stephanie A. Shaw
Scott Aron Silverman
Risa G. Sorkin
Marta B. van Dam
Susanne M. Walsh
David M. Watson
Andrew S. White

WASHINGTON, D.C. OFFICE

RESIDENT PARTNERS

Brian A. Darst (Not admitted in MA)
Michael A. Hordell
Paul F. Kilmer (Not admitted in MA)
Carol L. B. Matthews (Not admitted in MA)
Lawrence G. Meyer (Not admitted in MA)
Paralee White (Not admitted in MA)

RESIDENT ASSOCIATES

Thomas W. Brooke (Not admitted in MA)
Laura L. Hoffman (Not admitted in MA)
Stephen J. Jeffries (Not admitted in MA)
Anthony R. Masiello
Lisa K. Miller (Not admitted in MA)

For full biographical listings, see the Martindale-Hubbell Law Directory

GILMAN, MCLAUGHLIN & HANRAHAN, LLP (AV)

A Partnership including a Professional Corporation
Harbor Plaza, 470 Atlantic Avenue, 02210
Telephone: 617-482-1900
Fax: 617-338-8079

Walter H. McLaughlin, Sr. (1907-1994)

MEMBERS OF FIRM

Walter H. McLaughlin, Jr.
Robert E. McLaughlin
David G. Hanrahan
John B. Shevlin, Jr.
William F. York
Michael Eby
David L. Klebanoff

COUNSEL

Arthur M. Gilman
Donna E. Cohen

ASSOCIATES

James R. Peluso
Leigh A. McLaughlin
Ross D. Ginsberg
Robert E. McLaughlin, Jr.
Brenda A. Buan
Rakel M. Meir

For full biographical listings, see the Martindale-Hubbell Law Directory

Boston—Continued

Goodwin, Procter & Hoar LLP (AV)

A Partnership including Professional Corporations
Exchange Place, 02109-2881
Telephone: 617-570-1000
Telecopier: 617-523-1231
URL: http://www.gph.com
Washington, D.C. Office: 1717 Pennsylvania Avenue, N.W.
Telephone: 202-974-1000.
Telecopier: 202-331-9330.
New York, N.Y. Office: 599 Lexington Avenue.
Telephone: 212-813-8800.
Telecopier: 212-355-3333.

MEMBERS OF FIRM

Robert E. Goodwin (1878-1971)
Joseph O. Procter (1880-1932)
Samuel Hoar (1877-1952)
Marshall Simonds (P.C.)
Edward T. O'Dell (P.C.)
Joseph W. Haley (P.C.)
George W. Butterworth, III
David P. Ries (P.C.)
Richard E. Floor (P.C.)
Jerome H. Somers (P.C.)
Shepard M. Remis (P.C.)
Steven J. Comen
Jeremiah S. Buckley (Resident, Washington D.C. Office)
Jon D. Schneider (P.C.)
Robert C. Pomeroy (P.C.)
Stephen W. Carr (P.C.)
Paul F. Ware, Jr., (P.C.)
Don M. Kennedy (P.C.)
Richard A. Soden
Edward L. Glazer (P.C.)
William V. Buccella
Raymond P. Boulanger (P.C.)
Thomas J. Griffin, Jr.
Paul F. McDonough, Jr.
Robert F. Houser (P.C.)
Howard A. Cubell
Kenneth A. Cohen (P.C.)
John J. Cleary (P.C.)
Michael H. Glazer (P.C.)
Anthony M. Feeherry
F. Beirne Lovely, Jr., (P.C.)
Paul R. Gauron (P.C.)
James J. Dillon (P.C.)
John Kenneth Felter (P.C.)
Lawrence R. Cahill (P.C.)
Lawrence E. Kaplan (P.C.)
Martin R. Healy
David F. Dietz (P.C.)
Paul W. Lee (P.C.)
Edward Matson Sibble, Jr., (P.C.)
William P. Mayer
Daniel M. Glosband (P.C.)
Donna Sherry
Henry C. Dinger (P.C.)
Stuart M. Cable
Susan Hall Mygatt
Paul D. Schwartz (P.C.)
Diane L. Currier (P.C.)
Thomas P. Storer (P.C.)
James W. Nagle
Lynne B. Barr
Michael J. Pappone (P.C.)
Paul E. Nemser
Marian A. Tse
Martin Carmichael III (P.C.)
Raymond C. Zemlin (P.C.)
Christopher P. Davis
Stephen D. Poss (P.C.)
Laura C. Hodges Taylor (P.C.)
John R. LeClaire (P.C.)
Regina M. Pisa (P.C.)
William H. Whitledge (P.C.)
Richard A. Oetheimer
Philip H. Newman
Alexander A. Randall
Kevin M. Dennis
Geoffrey R. T. Kenyon
Gilbert G. Menna (P.C.)
Adam N. Weisenberg (P.C.)
Nancer H. Ballard
Wilfred J. Benoit, Jr.
Trudy A. Ernst
Daniel P. Condon
Robert M. Hale
F. Dennis Saylor, IV
John C. Englander
Christopher B. Barker
Ettore A. Santucci (P.C.)
Gregory A. Bibler
R. Todd Cronan
H. David Henken
Joseph L. Johnson III
Joseph M. Kolar (Resident, Washington, D.C. Office)
Cerise H. Lim-Epstein
Matthew T. Giuliani
Elizabeth McDermott
Minta E. Kay (P.C.)
Ross D. Gillman (Resident, New York, N.Y. Office)
J. Anthony Downs
Steven M. Ellis
Jeffrey C. Hadden
H. Neal Sandford
Bradford J. Smith
Mark E. Tully
Keith D. Shugarman (Resident, Washington, D.C. Office)
Thomas M. Hefferon (Resident, Washington, D.C. Office)
Margaret B. Crockett
Kenneth J. Parsigian
David W. Watson
Robert P. Whalen, Jr.
Eileen M. Herlihy
Elizabeth Shea Fries
Mary-Kathleen O'Connell
Kim M. Rubin
Andrew C. Sucoff
James M. Broderick
John B. Daukas
Gregory J. Lyons
Kathryn I. Murtagh
Brenda Ruel Sharton
Robert S. Insolia (Resident, New York, N.Y. Office)
Jennifer H. Weiss
Richard J. Holmstrom (Resident, New York, N.Y. Office)
Janet B. Korins (Resident, New York, N.Y. Office)
James C. Rehnquist
Peter T. Fariel
Anthony S. Fiotto
John G. Loughnane
Neil McLaughlin
Maura Griffith Moffatt
Joseph A. Piacquad
David J. Apfel
Ralph F. Boyd, Jr.
Scott F. Duggan
Robert G. Kester
Rebecca A. Lee
James A. Matarese
Jeffrey P. Naimon (Washington, D.C. Office)
Jeremy M. Sternberg
Andrew F. Viles

SENIOR COUNSEL

Theresa A. Cook
Alan Dankner
Michael J. Litchman
John O. Newell
Kristina Hansen Wardwell

(See Next Column)

COUNSEL

Rosemary Chun Dodek
Lori Epstein-Plaut (Not admitted in MA)
N. Linda Goldstein (Resident, Washington, D.C. Office)
Christopher W. Hornig (Resident, Washington, D.C. Office)
Evan Jones
R. Jeffrey Lyman
Joanne A. Robbins
David W. Roderer (Resident, Washington, D.C. Office)
Daniel E. Willert

RETIRED COUNSEL

Henry B. Shepard, Jr., (P.C.)

OF COUNSEL RETIRED

Samuel L. Batchelder, Jr.
Robert B. Fraser (P.C.)
William H. Gorham (P.C.)
Donald B. Gould
William B. King (P.C.)
William J. Pechilis (P.C.)
Charles D. Post
Frederick J. Robbins (P.C.)
Russell G. Simpson (P.C.)
Arthur L. Stevenson

ASSOCIATES

Jonathan D. Jerison (Resident, Washington, D.C. Office)
Marsha Weinerman
Gordon H. Piper
Toby B. Richard
Claire M. Holland
Donna Stoehr Hanlon
James A. Bunta
Patricia D. Popov
James J. Berriman
Josefina R. Childress
Jackie L. Segel
Bruce I. Tribush
Elise N. Zoli
Frederick W. Backus
Carla Folz Brigham
Victoria C. DeMaret
David R. Zipps
Giles A. Birch
Douglas C. Doskocil
Jay Todd Hahn (Resident, New York, N.Y. Office)
Jennifer Locke
Patricia S. Mugavero (Resident, Washington, D.C. Office)
Gregory G. Patchen (Resident, New York, N.Y. Office)
Ellen S. Winer
John Hunt
Stephen G. Charkoudian
Peter M. Green
Michael K. Murray
Samuel L. Richardson
Margo H.K. Tank (Resident, Washington, D.C. Office)
Kathleen R. Browne
Robert N. Driscoll
Janet M. Dunlap
Jennifer Merrigan Fay
John P. Feeney
Dori Chadbourne Gouin
Jennifer A.T. Grace
James H. Hammons, Jr.
Donald C. Hancock
Thomas E. Joaquin
Michael J. Kendall
Jonathan S. Klavens
James W. McGarry
David L. Permut (Resident, Washington, D.C. Office)
Amy Silverstein
Kevin F. Slayne
Christopher W. Thome
Andrew J. Weidhaas
U. Gwyn Williams
Roberto M. Braceras
Karen B. Clark
Gus P. Coldebella
Howard W. Davis
Anthony H. Dowling
Barbara J. Ellis
Melissa Fang
Raymond C. Garrigan (Resident, New York, N.Y. Office)
John T. Haggerty
Michael K. Harrington
Andrew E. Lelling
Charles N. LeRay
David P. Lewis
Francis N. Mastroianni
Paige H. Pease
Bernard J. Podurgiel
Walter S. Pollard, Jr.
Heidi Goldstein Shepherd
Mark C. Solakian
Will Todd
R. David Hosp
Christopher T. Holding
Thomas J. LaFond
Thomas I. Benda
Diane Boissonneault
Andrew J. Boyd
Douglas E. Cornelius
Daniel P. Dain
Jackson B.R. Galloway
Leeann Ghazil Gaunt
Kimberly B. Herman
Bradley A. Jacobson
Erika B. Johnson (Not admitted in MA)
Jennifer Keravuori
Eric G. Kevorkian
Andrew R. Levin
Jeremy A. Litt (Resident, New York, N.Y. Office)
Graham N. Luce
Mark R. Mansoor
William R. Matthews
John Barry McDonald
Eric P. Meyerowitz (Resident, New York, N.Y. Office)
Christopher D. Moore
Colleen A. Murphy
Diane M. Musi
Dana Ng
Michael J. O'Connor
Charles H. Sturdy
Reed Sussman
Joan E. Tagliareni
Lisa M. Weisglass (Resident, New York, N.Y. Office)
Gina Lynn Ziccolella (Not admitted in MA)
Daniel P. Bradford
Brett M. Goldberg
Joshua S. Goodman
Jeanine L.G. Grachuk
Christopher Okumura
Stephen T. Adams
Jennifer Backes Brown
Rajeev Balakrishna
Roman A. Bejger (Resident, New York, N.Y. Office)
Eugenia B. Bettencourt
Robert E. Bishop
Erica Blake
David L. Bohan
Stephen A. Boyko (Resident, New York, N.Y. Office)
Brooks R. Brown
Christopher E. Brown
Allison V. Buck
Amy R. Doherty
Kerry A. Doherty
Heather V. Edes
David A. Elchoness (Not admitted in MA)
Nancy Nearing Go
Lisa R. Haddad
Wisla C. Heneghan
Weiyen M. Jonas
Jeffrey I. Klein

(See Next Column)

GOODWIN, PROCTER & HOAR LLP, *Boston—Continued*

ASSOCIATES (Continued)

Peter N. Koufos (Resident, Washington, D.C. Office)
Donald L. Lancaster
Kerri E. Lawlor (Resident, New York, N.Y. Office)
Kathryn L. Link
Matthew M. McWhorter (Not admitted in MA)
Cindy S. Oh
Sarah C. Peck
Jeffrey Alan Simes
Jonathan P. Skinner
Kristen P. Sosnosky
William E. Stern
Alexander B. Temel
Scott A. Webster
Nicholas J. Arena
Daryl L. Wiesen
Catherine C. Adams
Leslie S. Blickenstaff
Peter G. Brassard
Douglas S. Brooks
Ernest W. Cloutier
Kelly M. Corbett
Sean Edman (Not admitted in MA)
Daniel M. Forman
Tammie C. Garner
Eric J. Graham
Susan Sullivan Grinblatas
Lynn D. Holdsworth
Jennifer E. Inker
Avani Kherdekar (Not admitted in MA)
Dana C. Lanzillo
Suzanne Lecaroz
Jan-Yung Lin
David Loh
Lauree Elisa Mansour
Christine McManus
Jennifer G. Mihalich
Hugh Miller, III
John C. Molloy
Kambo F. Mwangi
Avani S. Nayak
Cymier Payne
Kathryn A. Peterson
Rita M. Schwantes
Greer Shaw
Michael Stawasz
Tenley Stephenson
Peter M. Sullivan
Shannon Sweeney
Kristine E. Terhune
Elisabeth M. Todaro
Christopher Torres
Christine Venezia
Sarah E. Walters
Jaren D. Wilcoxson
Mary E. Windham Jones
Kelli A. Ayers
Pamela Zimlin Baker
Marc E. Brown
Diana C. Corbin
Jonathan M. Cosco
Jonathan Crowley
Mark F. Daly
Kevin M. Davis
John M. Ferguson (Resident, New York, N.Y. Office)
James D. Filpi (Resident, Washington, D.C. Office)
David Gerard Fromm
Carol M. Gilchrist
Stuart M. Glass
Mark E. Harrison
Julie C. Jones
Thomas Kesoglou (Resident, New York, N.Y. Office)
Kai W. Lyman
James McDonald
Katherine M. McGaugh
Adam B. Michaels
Steven M. Moheban
Robin J. Olson
Kathleen W. Orejuela
Stephanie F. Paré (Resident, New York, N.Y. Office)
Stephany Phelps
Shawn P. Reddington
Julie A. Richmond
Stuart L. Rosenthal
Gregg A. Rubenstein
Dena M. Sarke
Sharon J. Schlesinger
David G. Seibel
Robert W. Shields
Christopher J. Signorello
Andrea L. Studley
Christine C. Sullivan
Jacob G. Thiessen (Resident, Washington, D.C. Office)
Michael S. Turner
Paul J. Verbesey
Bradford K. Watts
Kenneth F. Whittaker
Jodi L. Walker
Christopher M. Witeck (Resident, Washington, D.C. Office)
Dana Zakarian

For full biographical listings, see the Martindale-Hubbell Law Directory

HALE AND DORR LLP (AV)

A Partnership including Professional Corporations
60 State Street, 02109
Telephone: 617-526-6000
Cable Address: "Hafis."
Telex: 94-0472
Telecopier: Domestic 617-526-5000; 617-742-9108
URL: http://www.haledorr.com
Washington, D.C. Office: 1455 Pennsylvania Avenue, N.W.
Telephone: 202-942-8400.
Cable Address: "Hafis Wsh."
Telecopier: 202-942-8484.

RETIRED PARTNERS

Samuel S. Dennis, 3rd, (P.C.)
James D. St. Clair (P.C.)
Herbert W. Vaughan

MEMBERS OF FIRM

John F. Cogan, Jr. (P.C.)
Jerome P. Facher
James A. Brink
Paul P. Brountas
John D. Hamilton, Jr.
Robert E. Fast
Harold Hestnes
Ernest V. Klein
John K. P. Stone, III
S. Donald Gonson
John C. Christie, Jr. (Resident, Washington, D.C. Office)
Martin S. Kaplan (P.C.)
Hugh R. Jones, Jr.
Philip D. Stevenson
Alexander A. Bernhard
James B. Lampert
John W. Delaney
Vincent P. McCarthy
John G. Fabiano
C. Hall Swaim
John H. Morton
John M. Westcott, Jr.
Richard W. Giuliani
Stephen H. Oleskey
Richard L. Berkman
Thomas E. Neely
Robert Tuchmann
Harry T. Daniels
Robert W. Mahoney

(See Next Column)

MEMBERS OF FIRM (Continued)

Joseph P. Barri
Paul P. Daley
Richard J. Innis
Richard V. Wiebusch
Linda K. Sherman
James L. Quarles III (Resident, Washington, D.C. Office)
Joel H. Sirkin
Mark A. Heller (Resident, Washington, D.C. Office)
Joan A. Lukey
Robert D. Keefe
Jay P. Urwitz (Resident, Washington, D.C. Office)
Jeffrey B. Rudman
David E. Redlick
Edward Young
John A. Burgess
William F. Lee
Roger M. Ritt
Mark G. Borden
Neil H. Jacobs
Michael L. Fay
Gilbert B. Kaplan (Resident, Washington, D.C. Office)
Richard A. Johnston
John J. Regan
James C. Burling
Andrew H. Cohn
William H. Schmidt
Peter B. Tarr
Katharine E. Bachman
Mark N. Polebaum
Allen H. Fox (Resident, Washington, D.C. Office)
William C. Benjamin
Steven D. Singer
David H. Erichsen
Paul G. Wallach (Resident, Washington, D.C. Office)
Robert D. Burke
Joseph J. Christian
William R. O'Reilly, Jr.
John D. Sigel
Thomas N. O'Connor
Steven S. Snider (Resident, Washington, D.C. Office)
Geoffrey S. Stewart (Resident, Washington, D.C. Office)
Michael D. Esch (Resident, Washington, D.C. Office)
Michelle D. Miller
Merriann M. Panarella
Jay E. Bothwick
Sarah Rothermel
Jeffrey N. Carp
Philip P. Rossetti
David Sylvester (Resident, Washington, D.C. Office)
Jeffrey J. Davidson (Resident, Washington, D.C. Office)
Kenneth H. Slade
Pamela J. Wilson
Jennifer C. Snyder
Wayne M. Kennard
Thomas L. Barrette, Jr.
William G. McElwain (Resident, Washington, D.C. Office)
John F. Batter III
Karen F. Green
Melvin R. Shuman
Michael R. Heyison
Christopher J. Perry
Michael J. Bevilacqua
David A. Westenberg
Stephen A. Jonas
Robert C. Kirsch
Peter J. Macdonald
Mark G. Matuschak
Patrick J. Rondeau
Richard M. Tardiff
Jeffrey A. Stein
Hollie L. Baker
Jeffrey A. Hermanson
Hal J. Leibowitz
Paul V. Rogers (Resident, Washington, D.C. Office)
A. Silvana Giner
Christopher P. Harvey
Louise Nicholson Howe (Resident, Washington, D.C. Office)
William F. Leahy (Resident, Washington, D.C. Office)
Susan W. Murley
Brent B. Siler (Resident, Washington, D.C. Office)
A. William Caporizzo
Kenneth R. Meade (Resident, Washington, D.C. Office)
William H. Paine
David C. Phelan
Andrea J. Robinson
Jonathan D. Rosenfeld
Wayne L. Stoner
Henry N. Wixon (Resident, Washington, D.C. Office)
David B. Bassett
John H. Chory
James W. Prendergast
Brenda J. Fingold
Mary Jo Johnson
Paul Jakubowski
Donald R. Steinberg
Virginia Kingsley Kapner
Thomas S. Ward
Jonathan Wolfman
Stuart M. Falber
Daniel W. Halston
Kenneth A. Hoxsie
Wayne A. Keown
Dimitri P. Racklin
Gabrielle R. Wolohojian
David A. Wilson (Resident, Washington, D.C. Office)
James R. Burke
Jorge L. Contreras, Jr.
Shann Kerner
Michael J. LaCascia
Michael J. Nathanson
Kathleen M. Weinstein (Resident, Washington, D.C. Office)
Charles P. Kindregan
S. Tara Miller
Daniel P. Tighe
Scott M. Alter (Resident, Washington, D.C. Office)
Mitchel Appelbaum
Keith R. Barnett
Michael G. Bongiorno
William S. Gehrke
Richard N. Kimball
Leonard A. Pierce
Sean P. Sherman (Resident, Washington, D.C. Office)
Susan McWhan Tobin
Cynthia D. Vreeland
Wendy E. Anderson (Resident, Washington, D.C. Office)
Jane A. Bell
Sean T. Boulger
Jamie N. Class
Michael A. Diener
Robert F. Fitzpatrick Jr.
Marc N. Henschke
Joseph E. Mullaney III
Lisa J. Pirozzolo
Laura E. Schneider
Joseph L. Stanganelli
Beth E. Turetsky
Michael D. Bain
Jonathan C. Black
Lisa Stephanian Burton
Anne G. Depew
Richard A. Goldenberg
Mark C. Kalpin
Susan Valente Marandett
Dominic E. Massa
James J. Nicklaus
Scott E. Pueschel
M. Kathryn Rickards
Mark Daniel Selwyn
Jason Tate Sherwood
Colleen Superko
Cynthia T. Mazareas
Anne Marie Towle
Kathleen F. Burke
Marc F. Dupré
Stephen M. Edwards
John Theodore Gutkoski
Peter N. Handrinos
Joseph C. Hogan, III

(See Next Column)

HALE AND DORR LLP—*Continued*

MEMBERS OF FIRM (Continued)

Barry J. Hurewitz (Resident, Washington, D.C. Office)
Jane A. Kalinski (Resident, Washington, D.C. Office)
Christine A. Maglione
Melisa Moonan (Resident, Washington, D.C. Office)
Gretchen A. Rice
Richard J. Rosensweig
Sara J. Shanahan
Mary E. Tenn
J. Patrick Toher
Christopher Umana
Danielle Y. Vanderzanden
James G. Votaw (Resident, Washington, D.C. Office)

COUNSEL

Norman B. Asher
Louis H. Hamel, Jr.
Peter A. Spaeth
Miriam R. Gamson (Resident, Washington, D.C. Office)
William F. Winslow (Resident, Washington, D.C. Office)
Robyn B. Klinger
Alfred Server
Gary P. Brady
William J. Salisbury
Pamela Coravos
Rajesh Vallabh (Not admitted in MA)
Paul W. Jameson (Resident, Washington, D.C. Office)
Cris R. Revaz (Resident, Washington, D.C. Office)

ASSOCIATES

Andrea Alexander
Devin J. Anderson
Eric S. Andreas (Resident, Washington, D.C. Office)
Alexander D. Baldwin (Resident, Washington, D.C. Office)
P. Michael Baratta
Steven D. Barrett
Denise Marie Barton
C. Tama Benson
Rhonda L. Bergel
Lisa L. Bonner
Karen E. Bravo (Not admitted in MA)
Ethan J. Brown
Michael S. Buckner (Resident, Washington, D.C. Office)
Erika J. S. Buell
Kerry Burke (Resident, Washington, D.C. Office)
Eric C. Burnett
Amy C. Burns
Douglas L. Burton
Sally L. Byrne
Lisa M. Cameron
Sean T. Carnathan
Melinda P. Carnes (Not admitted in MA)
David J. Cerveny
Mona Chandra (Not admitted in MA)
Anne Clark
Monica K. Cloherty
Robert P. Clower III
Kimberly E. Cohen
Matthew T. Connolly
Timothy J. Corbett
Lia Der Marderosian
Peter M. Dichiara
Kristine L. Dimitrova
Jeffrey C. Dorsey (Resident, Washington, D.C. Office)
James M. Dowd (Not admitted in MA; Resident, Washington, D.C. Office)
Zachary D. Drench
Christian M. Ehrbar
Betsy Facher
Shiva Falsafi
Vinita Chopra Ferrera
Daniel W. Finegold
Jessica A. Foster
Matthew J. Gardella
Jason S. Gerlach
Charles V. Ghoorah (Resident, Washington, D.C. Office)
Nicole R. Gill
Ahaviah Diane Glaser
Philip J. Gordon
Edward D. Grieff (Resident, Washington, D.C. Office)
Dimitry S. Herman
Michael Q. Hyde (Resident, Washington, D.C. Office)
Adam D. Janoff
Dennis L. Jenkins
Richard E. Johnston
Belinda M. Juran
Kristin R. Kaldor
Marianne F. K. Kane
Matthew N. Kane
Benjamin A. Kaplan
Lance A. Kawesch
Michael J. Kelly
Ilran Kim
Peter J. Kolovos
Jeremy S. Kream
Karin J. Kysilka (Resident, Washington, D.C. Office)
Kenneth R. Lepage
Karen Lowy Tinsky (Resident, Washington, D.C. Office)
Martin F. Mahoney II
Michael K. Mahoney
Amanda P. Masselam
Charles F. McCain, II
Daniel D. McCawley (Resident, Washington, D.C. Office)
C. Stanley McGee
Pamela D. Meekins
David C. Megan
Paula H. Mercer (Not admitted in MA)
Aaron W. Moore
Jeffrey C. Morgan
Marisa A. Murtagh
Douglas J. Nash
Peter C. Necheles
Christina Nicolosi
Peter D. Ocko
Richard W. O'Neill
Jonathan H. Owsley
Paige Parisi
Keum J. Park
Claire L. Patton
Stephanie Philbin (Resident, Washington, D.C. Office)
Ian J. Platt
Linda E. Podheiser
Natalie L. Reed (Resident, Washington, D.C. Office)
Jay G. Reilly
Jason A. Reyes
Michelle H. Rhee
Jeanette Camara Richmond
Sean Roche
Thomas B. Rosedale
Elizabeth A. Rowe
Lawrence J. Rowe
Kerry Pyle Rubin (Resident, Washington, D.C. Office)
Rachel Sands
Karen E. Schneck
Andrew P. Schoeffler (Resident, Washington, D.C. Office)
Jonathan A. Shapiro
Timothy F. Silva
Kara Cline Sims
Jan M. Siok
Maria D. Stahl
Mary B. Strother
Michael J. Summersgill
David A. Suski (Resident, Washington, D.C. Office)
Gavin A. Symes
Thomas A. Tak
Wendell C. Taylor
Jamey L. Tesler
Basilios E. Tsingos
Nikos D. Tsonis

(See Next Column)

ASSOCIATES (Continued)

Kimberly Boyle Wethly
Donald W. Wiest (Not admitted in MA)
Jane K. Williamson
G. Perry Wu

Barbara A. Barakat
William A. Caldwell
Hy David Rubenstein (Resident, Washington, D.C. Office)
David J. Shapiro
Laurence D. Shind
Patricia Anne Whalen

For full biographical listings, see the Martindale-Hubbell Law Directory

---

HEMENWAY & BARNES (AV)

60 State Street, 02109
Telephone: 617-227-7940
Fax: 617-227-0781

MEMBERS OF FIRM

Alfred Hemenway (1863-1927)
Charles B. Barnes (1893-1956)
Roy A. Hammer
Lawrence T. Perera
John J. Madden
George T. Shaw
Timothy F. Fidgeon
Michael B. Elefante
Michael J. Puzo
Thomas L. Guidi
Edward Notis-McConarty
Diane C. Tillotson
Stephen W. Kidder
Susan Hughes Banning
Frederic J. Marx
Deborah J. Hall
Kurt F. Somerville
Teresa A. Belmonte
Brian C. Broderick
Charles Fayerweather

ASSOCIATES

Andrea H. Maislen
Maureen E. Curran
Joseph L. Bierwirth, Jr.
J. David Gibbs
Dennis R. Delaney
Kendra Chencus

OF COUNSEL

George H. Kidder
David H. Morse

For full biographical listings, see the Martindale-Hubbell Law Directory

---

HILL & BARLOW, A PROFESSIONAL CORPORATION (AV)

One International Place, 02110-2600
Telephone: 617-428-3000
Fax: 617-428-3500
URL: http://www.hillbarlow.com

Arthur Dehon Hill (1869-1947)
Robert Shaw Barlow (1869-1943)
Richard L. Alfred
Martin S. Allen
James A. Aloisi, Jr.
R. Hale Andrews, Jr.
Valerie L. Andrews
Charles A. Baker III
Peter E. Ball
Thomas H. Belknap
Robert A. Bertsche
Gregory P. Bialecki
Martha Born
Thomas C. Chase
Richard S. Chute
Frances Cohen
Timothy J. Dacey, III
Charles R. Dougherty
Bruce E. Falby
William B. Forbush III
John G. Gillis
John A. D. Gilmore
Michael J. Goldberg
Lisa C. Goodheart
Michael S. Greco
David A. Hoffman
Peter Katz
Richard L. Levine
Winifred I. Li
Terrence W. Mahoney
Neil V. McKittrick
Wayne H. Miller
Alexander W. Moore
Christopher L. Noble
Stephen M. Nolan
Gregory D. Peterson
Richard W. Renehan
Richard D. Rudman
Miriam Vock Sheehan
Joseph D. Steinfield
Jonathan Strong
John L. Sullivan
Elliot M. Surkin
Daniel A. Taylor
Andrea M. Teichman
Dennis W. Townley
William A. Truslow
E. Randolph Tucker
John C. Vincent, Jr.
Barbara Freedman Wand
Audrey K. Wang
Richard M. Zielinski

SENIOR COUNSEL

Gael Mahony

OF COUNSEL

Kingsbury Browne, Jr.
James R. Repetti
Carl M. Sapers
Richard A. Wiley

ASSOCIATES AND OTHER ATTORNEYS

Matthew S. Axelrod
Patrick J. Bannon
Jarrett Tomás Barrios
Kirsten Nelson Callahan
Edward S. Cheng
Jennifer L. Chiasson
Susan J. Cole
Joshua M. Davis
Susan C. Dawson
Nancy E. Dempze
Deborah Hesford DosSantos
Eleanor A. Evans
Thanda A. Fields
Magda L. Fleckner
Donna Frankel
David Samuel Friedman
Stuart J. Hamilton
David P. Horne
Geoffrey A. Howell
Renée M. Jones
Brian S. Kaplan
Hannah Laws Kilson
Seth Barney Kosto
Monica P. LaFond
John D. Lawrence
Brian P. Lenihan

(See Next Column)

HILL & BARLOW A PROFESSIONAL CORPORATION, *Boston—Continued*

ASSOCIATES AND OTHER ATTORNEYS (Continued)

Adam N. Lewis
Joseph S. Lieber
Frank G. Lowenstein
Jonathan T. Mann
Heather G. Merrill
Richelle A. Nessralla
Robert J. O'Connor, Jr.
Karen A. Pickett
Adam B. Price
Michael A. Rauch
Marjory D. Robertson
Carol V. Rose
Ellen J. Rubin
Robert D. Ryan
C. Dylan Sanders
Kimberly H. Scheckner
Robert F. Schwartz
Haeryung A. Shin
Anne L. Showalter
Melissa J. Solomon
Debra A. Squires-Lee
Catherine M. (Kay) Stockwell
Cornelia R. Tenney
Karen Tosh
Liza Vertinsky
Michael D. Vhay
Janet A. Viggiani
Bruce Wickersham
Daniel C. Winston

For full biographical listings, see the Martindale-Hubbell Law Directory

HINCKLEY, ALLEN & SNYDER LLP (AV)

28 State Street, 30th Floor, 02109-1775
Telephone: 617-345-9000
Email: firm@haslaw.com *URL:* http://www.haslaw.com
Providence, Rhode Island Office: 1500 Fleet Center.
Telephone: 401-274-2000.
Fax: 401-277-9600. URL: http://www.hawlaw.com.

MEMBERS OF FIRM

Paula K. Andrews
David D. Barricelli
(Not admitted in MA)
E. Jerome Batty
(Not admitted in MA)
Jonathan Bell
Deborah L. Benson
Leon C. Boghossian III
Paul Bork
Stephen J. Carlotti
(Not admitted in MA)
David Barry Connolly
Michael J. Connolly
Robert Corrente
Joseph P. Curran
(Not admitted in MA)
Michael P. DeFanti
Eric F. Eisenberg
Malcolm Farmer, III
Margaret D. Farrell
(Not admitted in MA)
Noel M. Field, Jr.
(Not admitted in MA)
Pasco Gasbarro Jr.
Bruce G. Goodman
Hugh J. Gorman, III
Alan P. Gottlieb
Gerard R. Goulet
William R. Grimm
Paul A. Hedstrom
Richard L. E. Jocelyn
(Not admitted in MA)
Michael J. Kelly
Joel Lewin
Doris Jami Licht
Kevin F. Long
Sandra Matrone Mack
(Not admitted in MA)
Matthew T. Marcello, III
(Not admitted in MA)
Frederick P. McClure
Elizabeth Murdock Myers
Paul F. O'Donnell, III
H. Peter Olsen
(Not admitted in MA)
Julianne Palumbo
John J. Pendergast, III
(Not admitted in MA)
Gerald J. Petros
Richard H. Pierce
James O. Reavis
James P. Redding
(Not admitted in MA)
Jeremy Ritzenberg
Ralph J. Rivkind
Lawrence R. Robins
David J. Rubin
Charles E. Schaub, Jr.
Douglas F. Seaver
Scott E. Sheridan
Paul A. Silver
Herman Snyder
David R. Sullivan
Robert F. Sylvia
Christopher C. Tsouros
Howard E. Walker
(Not admitted in MA)
Richard D. Wayne
Doreen M. Zankowski
John R. Allen (Retired)
Richard W. Billings (Retired)
Thomas J. Hogan (Retired)
Jacques V. Hopkins (Retired)
James A. Jackson (Retired)
James E. Keeley (Retired)
Robert F. Pickard (Retired)
Robert W. Shadd (Retired)
Richard F. Staples (Retired)
Edwin G. Torrance (Retired)

ASSOCIATES

Jessica M. Bettencourt
(Not admitted in MA)
Mark Bianchi
Charles D. Blackman
Gail Bonner
(Not admitted in MA)
Alyssa V. Boss
Neil L. Brodsky
Christopher R. Bush
Alexandra K. Callam
Brent R. Canning
(Not admitted in MA)
Jane E. Cohen
Andrew D. Cummings
June E. Daniel
(Not admitted in MA)
Kristine L. Donabedian
Josephine A. Giuffre
Kim Herman Goslant
Veronica A. Greenbaum
Gloria Maria Gutierrez
Christopher P. Hamilton
Kelley Jordan-Price
Catherine S. Kim
John P. Martin
Christopher W. Morog
Katharine Carter Noble
Amy Page Oberg
(Not admitted in MA)
Elena B. Olson
Timothy J. Perry
Michael J. Pisaturo
Michael T. Renaud
Lynn E. Riley
Leah A. Rochwarg
Andrew F. Shure
Michael G. Tauber
Lauren Timoney Upton
Lawrence W. Vernaglia
Joseph D. Whelan
(Not admitted in MA)

(See Next Column)

OF COUNSEL

Willard Krasnow
Debra Dyleski Najjar
Willard R. Pope
Bentley Tobin
Joachim A. Weissfeld
(Not admitted in MA)

For full biographical listings, see the Martindale-Hubbell Law Directory

HUTCHINS, WHEELER & DITTMAR, A PROFESSIONAL CORPORATION (AV)

101 Federal Street, 02110
Telephone: 617-951-6600
Facsimile: 617-951-1295
URL: http://www.hutch.com

STOCKHOLDERS/MEMBERS

Katherine L. Babson, Jr.
Robert G. Bannish
Mark N. Berman
Laura L. Carroll
Cornelius J. Chapman, Jr.
John H. Clymer
Donald D. Cooper
David T. Dinwoodey
James S. Dittmar
Alan H. Einhorn
Jack H. Fainberg
Francis J. Feeney, Jr.
Robert M. Finkel
David A. Forman
Marilyn French
Carolyn Jacoby Gabbay
Ronald Garmey
Frederick H. Grein, Jr.
John J. Griffin, Jr.
William E. Halmkin
John D. Hughes
Franklin C. Huntington, IV
Steven R. Kanes
Jonathan R. Karis
Deborah S. Kay
Robert L. Kirby, Jr.
David P. Kreisler
David A. Martland
Anthony J. Medaglia, Jr. (P.C.)
James L. Messenger
Patricia Ann Metzer (Miss)
Arthur S. Meyers, Jr.
John D. Mitchell, Jr.
(Not admitted in MA)
Evelyn Venables Moreno
Joseph H. Newberg
Mary Ellen O'Mara
Steven M. Peck
Sanford F. Remz
Sander A. Rikleen
Charles W. Robins
Regina Strazulla Rockefeller
David S. Rosenthal
Robert P. Sherman
Richard M. Stein
Joseph C. Tanski
Craig M. Tateronis
Robert A. Thompson
John C. Thomson
Richard L. Trembowicz
Andrew M. Troop
Susan Tribble Valente
James R. Westra

ASSOCIATES

Sean D. Abbott
Richard L. Alcock
David M. Barbash
(Not admitted in MA)
Meredith Anne Benedict
Seth A. Berry
Anthony J. Bravo, Jr.
P. Monique Byrne
Steven J. Cagnetta
Susan Jane Chester
Thomas M. Ciampa
Sarah Thiemann Connally
William J. Connolly, III
Alan Jay Cooke
Patricia K. Dolan
Errol M. Dominguez
Laura E. Doyle
Anastasia M. Fernands
Steven M. Giordano
Shelly B. Goldstone
Marc G. Guggenheim
Lori E. Harris
(Not admitted in MA)
John F. Hemenway
Kyle Reid Hofmann
Richard W. Holtz
Frank F. Huang
Gordon M. Jones, III
Sanjit S. Korde
Denise L. Kosineski
Wanda A. Luettgen
David B. Mack
Ellen M. Majdloch
Joseph C. Marrow
Daniel M. McCarthy
Nygina T. Mills
(Not admitted in MA)
Christopher R. Mirick
Francis C. Morrissey
Patrick J. O'Toole, Jr.
Lisa A. Paolillo
Alison Smith Piasecki
Jennifer C. Platt
R. Robert Popeo, Jr.
Steven Y. Quintero
Mark D. Robins
Andrew S. Rogovin
Laura S. Sarah
Shefali A. Shah
Dorothy R. Simboli
Sandra A. Smith
Ricardo Manuel Sousa
Friedrich von Krusentiern

OF COUNSEL

Nicholas U. Sommerfeld

For full biographical listings, see the Martindale-Hubbell Law Directory

KOPELMAN AND PAIGE, P.C. (AV)

Park Square Building, 31 St. James Avenue, 7th Floor, 02116
Telephone: 617-556-0007
Fax: 617-654-1735

Leonard Kopelman
Donald G. Paige
Elizabeth A. Lane
Joyce F. Frank
John W. Giorgio
Barbara J. Saint Andre
Joel B. Bard
Everett Joseph Marder
Patrick J. Costello
Joseph L. Tehan, Jr.
Anne-Marie M. Hyland
Theresa M. Dowdy
Deborah Eliason
Richard Bowen

(See Next Column)

KOPELMAN AND PAIGE P.C.—*Continued*

Edward M. Reilly
William Hewig, III
Jeanne S. McKnight
Judith Chanoux Cutler
David J. Doneski
Sandra M. Charton
Ilana Marie Quirk
Patricia A. Cantor
Robert Patten
Mark R. Reich
Brian W. Riley
Thomas P. Lane, Jr.
Mary L. Giorgio
Kathleen Elisabeth Connolly
Christopher J. Groll
Michele E. Randazzo
John R. Hucksam Jr.
Kathleen M. O'Donnell
Darren Robert Klein

For full biographical listings, see the Martindale-Hubbell Law Directory

LOONEY & GROSSMAN LLP (AV)

101 Arch Street, 02110-1112
Telephone: 617-951-2800
Fax: 617-951-2819
URL: http://www.lgllp.com

Stewart F. Grossman (P.C.)
Richard J. Grahn
Bertram E. Snyder
Robert Cushman Barber
Joseph H. Matzkin
Wesley S. Chused
Melvin S. Hoffman

SENIOR COUNSEL

William F. Looney, Jr.

OF COUNSEL

Sherman H. Starr, Jr.
Elizabeth M. Adler
Maria Galvagna Mesinger

ASSOCIATES

Adam J. Ruttenberg
Pamela A. Harbeson
Mary E. Corbett
Benjamin D. Stevenson
Edward V. Colbert, III

For full biographical listings, see the Martindale-Hubbell Law Directory

MARTIN, MAGNUSON, MCCARTHY & KENNEY (AV)

101 Merrimac Street, 02114-4716
Telephone: 617-227-3240
Telecopier: 617-227-3346

MEMBERS OF FIRM

Ephraim Martin (1900-1988)
Clement McCarthy (1921-1985)
Harold E. Magnuson (1912-1999)
Raymond J. Kenney, Jr. *
Charles P. Reidy, III *
Daniel J. Griffin, Jr. *
Philip E. Murray, Jr. *
Joseph L. Doherty, Jr. *
Paul R. Keane *
John P. Mulvey *
Paul M. McTague *
Carol A. Kelly *
Edward F. Mahoney *
Douglas A. Robertson *

COUNSEL

Edward F. Hennessey

Joan L. Atlas *
Joseph B. Bertrand *
Teresa J. Farris *
Kevin C. Reidy *
Stephen M. O'Shea *
Christopher J. Maley *
Jennifer A. Brennan *
Sean M. Ennis *
Katharine S. Perry *
Amato J. Bocchino, Jr. *
Darlene Dawson *

Representative Clients: Allstate Insurance Co.; American International Adjustment Co.; Browning - Ferris Industries, Inc.; Fireman's Fund Insurance Cos.; Medical Professional Mutual Insurance Co.; Multi Systems Agency LTD.; Risk Management Foundation; St. Paul ProMutual Insurance Cos.; Wausau Insurance Cos.
Reference: Fleet Bank.
*Employees of The Professional Corporation of McCarthy, Kenney & Reidy.

For full biographical listings, see the Martindale-Hubbell Law Directory

MINTZ, LEVIN, COHN, FERRIS, GLOVSKY AND POPEO, P.C. (AV)

One Financial Center, 02111
Telephone: 617-542-6000
FAX: 617-542-2241
Internet: Each Attorney's Internet Address takes the following form: first initial last name @mintz.com (e.g., rmintz@mintz.com)
URL: http://www.mintz.com
Washington, D.C. Office: 701 Pennsylvania Avenue, N.W. Suite 900.
Telephone: 202-434-7300.
Fax: 202-434-7400.
Reston, Virginia Office: 12021 Sunset Hills Road, Suite 310.
Telephone: 703-464-4800.
Fax: 703-464-4895.

Richard G. Mintz
Jerome Gotkin
Francis X. Meaney
R. Robert Popeo
Stanford N. Goldman, Jr.
Peter M. Saparoff
Thomas J. Kelly
Stephen M. Weiner

(See Next Column)

David A. Gilbert
Thomas R. Murtagh
Frederick J. Pittaro
Irwin M. Heller
Stephen M. Leonard
Robert M. Gault
David H. Halpert
Martha J. Koster
Michael P. Last
Thomas M. Reardon
Jeffrey M. Wiesen
Joel R. Bloom
Robert Duggan
Richard E. Mikels
Dennis I. Greene
Richard R. Kelly
John K. Markey
Christopher H. Milton
A. Jason Mirabito
Gregory A. Sandomirsky
Maxwell D. Solet
Michael S. Gardener
C. Stephen Parker, Jr.
Michael J. Lieberman
John R. Regier
David G. Spackman
Andrew R. Urban
Ellen L. Janos
Stuart A. Offner
Cameron F. Kerry
Patrick J. Sharkey
Stanley A. Twarog
Douglas A. Zingale
Elizabeth B. Burnett
Charles E. Carey
Jonathan L. Kravetz
Ann-Ellen Marcus Hornidge
Kenneth M. Bello
Peter A. Biagetti
Rachael Macindoe Dorr
H. Joseph Hameline
Stephen T. Langer
Paul D. Wilson
Neil H. Aronson
Joseph G. Blute
Mary Lee Moore
Paul J. Ricotta
Jeffrey S. Robbins
Samuel M. Starr
Leocadia Irine Zak
R. Mark Chamberlin (Not admitted in MA)
Thomas S. Crane
Timothy J. Langella
David S. Lintz
John R. Pomerance
Steven P. Rosenthal
William T. Whelan
Leonard Weiser-Varon
Joshua Davis
Henry A. Sullivan
Kim V. Marrkand
Susan J. Cohen
William M. Hill
William W. Kannel
Tracy A. Miner
Richard H. Moche
Rosemary M. Allen
Daniel O. Gaquin
David B. Bernstein
Michael F. Connolly
Lewis J. Geffen
Susan P. Phillips
Anne L. Bruno
Beth I. Z. Boland
Michael L. Fantozzi (Not admitted in MA)
Shari A. Levitan
Jeffrey R. Porter
Ivor R. Elrifi
Mary-Laura Greely
Peter S. Lawrence
Howard J. Susser
John F. Sylvia
Joseph P. Curtin
Kevin M. McGinty
Stephen T. Murray
Meghan B. Burke
Susan M. Finegan
Charles D. Ferris (Resident, Washington, D.C. Office)
Frank W. Lloyd (Resident, Washington, D.C. Office)
Bruce D. Sokler (Resident, Washington, D.C. Office)
Charles Alan Samuels (Resident, Washington, D.C. Office)
Howard J. Symons (Resident, Washington, D.C. Office)
Christopher J. Harvie (Resident, Washington, D.C. Office)

OF COUNSEL

Francis X. Bellotti
Kenneth J. Novack
Eve T. Horwitz
Linda D. Bentley

SPECIAL COUNSEL

Judith Lidsky
Maryann Civitello

John Paul Sullivan
Robert J. Ryan
Marilyn Newman
William P. McDermott
Marie Lefton
Peter M. Miller
Kathleen C. Tulloh Brink
Meryl J. Epstein
Roberta Fitzpatrick
Judith Slovin
Paul C. Levites
Cynthia J. Larose
Linda B. Port
Seni M. Adio
Navjeet K. Bal
John J. Cheney, III
Donna M. Evans
Allen H. Forbes
Carolyn B. Sullivan
John A. Sym
Sally E. Williamson
Gail Eagan
John W. Hawkins
Michael R. B. Balfe
Peter T. Butterfield
Patrick T. Clendenen
Brett N. Dorny
Allan M. Green
Pamela B. Greene
Judith I. Jacobs
Joseph P. Messina
Jill M.E. Sullivan
Nancy D. Adams
Elizabeth Brody Gluck
Ann E. Drobot
Edward P. Gonzales
Julie E. Korostoff
Scott A. Lively
Andrew J. Merken
A. W. Phinney, III
Bram Shapiro
Suzanne D. Abair (Not admitted in MA)
Joan E. Cirillo
Ron I. Honig
Bernard K. Hooper (Not admitted in MA)
Neil K. Sherring
Kimberly H. Kelley
Kevin J. Walsh
Susan M. Basham
Sarah S. Cabot
William M. ("Mo") Cowan
Samuel E. Feigin
Mark D. Flaherty
John A. Harre (Not admitted in MA)
William C. Hicks
Peter J. Marathas, Jr.
Kelly A. McEnaney
John Miller
Michel Morency
Nancy D. Prior
Darin P. Smith
Thomas M. Sullivan
Wendy Lynne Weber
Daniel M. Carroll
Deborah A. Daccord

(See Next Column)

MINTZ, LEVIN, COHN, FERRIS, GLOVSKY AND POPEO P.C., *Boston—Continued*

Scott C. Ford
Matthew S. Forsyth
Joanne S. Sturrock (Not admitted in United States)
Cristina D. Hernandez-Malaby
Benjamin L. Hincks
Brian P. Keane
John P. Kelleher
Christopher Kovach (Not admitted in MA)
Gabriela V. Lambert
William A. Marino
Colleen P. McElhinney
Reena I. Thadhani
Josiah M. Black
Thomas R. Burton, III
Robert Y. Chow
William C. Coffey
William L. Coffman (Not admitted in MA)
David F. Crosby
Rufina C. Garay
Benjamin S. Harshbarger
Matthew C. Hurley (Not admitted in MA)
Marion K. Odence-Ford
Leslie Meyer-Leon
Scott Alan Samuels
Laurence A. Schoen
Grant Sovern
Michael M. Suga (Not admitted in MA)
Nancy F. Trodden
Joseph Vittiglio
Stefan J. Vounessea
Scott A. Whitaker (Not admitted in MA)
Beverly Armstrong
Tyler Chapman
Katherine M. Comer
Samuel F. Davenport
Mark I. Davies (Not admitted in MA)
Enoh T. DeGraff
Geri L. Haight
Michael R. Harrington
Michelle E. Leinbach
John T. Prince
Brian E. Lewis (Not admitted in MA)
Jeffrey L. Salinger
P. Miyoko Sato
Adam L. Sisitsky
Garfield B. Simms
Virginia Tsai
Steven D. Weatherhead
Mark J. Gallagher
Christopher J. Hunter
Christopher H. Kallaher
James J. Skeffington, Jr
Francine D. Wachtmann
Carolyn A. Waldmann

For full biographical listings, see the Martindale-Hubbell Law Directory

NUTTER, MCCLENNEN & FISH, LLP (AV)

A Partnership including a Professional Corporation
One International Place, 02110-2699
Telephone: 617-439-2000
Telex: 94-0790
Facsimile: 617-973-9748
URL: http://www.nutter.com
Hyannis, Massachusetts Office: Route 132, 1513 Iyannough Road, P.O. Box 1630.
Telephone: 508-790-5400.
Facsimile: 508-771-8079.

MEMBERS OF FIRM

John P. Driscoll, Jr.
Charles B. Abbott
Duane R. Batista
Constantine Alexander
James W. Hackett
Augustus F. Wagner, Jr.
Gene A. Blumenreich
Michael E. Mooney
Andrew J. McElaney, Jr.
Daniel J. Gleason
William T. Sherry, Jr.
Michael J. Bohnen
Charles A. Rosebrock
Robert A. Fishman
Edward P. Leibensperger
Stephen M. Andress
Kenneth R. Berman
Karl P. Fryzel
Thomas P. Jalkut
Neil P. Motenko
Anne S. Rogers
Mary K. Ryan
David E. Watson
Gary D. Zanercik
Thomas J. Engellenner
Peter Nils Baylor
Sharon R. Burger
Patrick M. Butler
Paul R. Eklund
Michael A. Leon
James H. Simon
Michael T. Cetrone
David C. Henderson
Arthur R Hofmann, Jr.
David R. Schmahmann
David S. Szabo
Nelson G. Apjohn
Peter R. Brown
Dianne Hobbs
Marianne Ajemian
Martin C. Pentz
Philip R. Rosenblatt
Robert L. Ullmann
William C. Geary, III
James G. Ward
Stephen J. Brake
Michael K. Krebs
Lisa Cameron Wood
James E. Dawson
Thomas O. Bean
Beth H. Mitchell
Deborah J. Manus
Diane Rosse
Richard P. Schwartz
Timothy M. Smith
Nancy A. McGuire
Hugh A. O'Reilly
Joseph F. Shea
Suzanne L. Glassburn

OF COUNSEL

Irving J. Helman (P.C.)
Norman T. Byrnes
William H. MacCrellish, Jr.
Frederick D. Herberich
Dana C. Coggins
Bancroft R. Wheeler
John Larkin Thompson
Charles R. Parrott
Frances H. Miller
Michael I. Falkoff
Teresa M. Patten
Susan Leonard Repetti
Geoffrey Hargreaves-Heald
Maria D. Buckley
Carl M. DeFranco, Jr. (Not admitted in MA)

(See Next Column)

JUNIOR PARTNERS

Robert D. Webb
Julia Satti Cosentino
Susan C. Murphy
John C. Fitzpatrick
John Christopher
Andrée M. Saulnier
John P. Dougherty
Gary L. Gill-Austern
Ronald E. Cahill

ASSOCIATES

Angela C. Ahn
Thomas W. Aylesworth
Erik P. Bartenhagen
Michelle L. Basil
Steven Reid Bourne
Vanessa L. Carnes
Patrick J. Cassidy
Tia Chapman
Kathryn Childs
Christine R. Collins (Not admitted in MA)
Kathryn Keough Conde
Lisa Dickstein (Not admitted in MA)
Anne Marie Duffy
Ellen M. Dunham
Peter I. Dunn
Paul D. Durkee
Scott E. Erlich
Willie Evans
David L. Ferrera
Daniel L. Fiedler (Not admitted in MA)
Marcia R. Ginsberg
Alexander S. Glovsky
Andrea F. Grable
Elizabeth M. Harvey
Brian W. Hicks
Neil C. Higgins
Kelly Lane Hiller
Lisa T. Johnson-Firth (Not admitted in MA)
Daniel J. Mahoney
Amy J. Mastrobattista
Dianne McCarthy
Douglas B. McLaughlin
Scott A. McQuilkin
Mobina F. Mohsin
Indranil "Indy" Mukerji
Thomas W. Muldoon
Margaret L. Oliver
Daniel P. Olohan
Mary Kate Olohan
Stephen J. Patterson
Marc A. Polk
Francis R. Powell
David M. Rogers
Richard J. Roos
Michelle B. Rosenberg
Scott D. Rothenberger
Patricia B. Siefer
Daniel S. Shore
David Thomas
Dylan Tyson Tonry
Carol Meyerdierks Tsao
Christa von der Luft
Barbara A. Walsh
Kenneth T. Willis
Nadia A. Yassa

HYANNIS, MASSACHUSETTS OFFICE
PARTNERS

Augustus F. Wagner, Jr.
Patrick M. Butler

OF COUNSEL

Edward F. McLaughlin, Jr.

JUNIOR PARTNER

Sarah M. Manning

ASSOCIATES

Shari L. Lobe
Cathleen J. Cinella

For full biographical listings, see the Martindale-Hubbell Law Directory

PALMER & DODGE LLP (AV)

One Beacon Street, 02108
Telephone: 617-573-0100
Facsimile: 617-227-4420
URL: http://www.palmerdodge.com

MEMBERS OF FIRM

Moorfield Storey (1887-1929)
John L. Thorndike (1887-1920)
Bradley W. Palmer (1893-1946)
Robert G. Dodge (1910-1964)
F. Andrew Anderson
Neil P. Arkuss
James T. Barrett
Michael R. Brown
Lawrence B. Cohen
Norman P. Cohen
Matthew C. Dallett
Jeanne P. Darcey
Jean M. DeLuca
Charles E. DeWitt, Jr.
Andrew L. Eisenberg
Lynnette C. Fallon
Steven N. Farber
Mark A. Fischer
Ruth E. Fitch
Christopher M. Flanagan
Nathaniel S. Gardiner
Michael T. Gass
Laurie S. Gill
Robert H. Hale
Laurie J. Hall
Richard Hiersteiner
Malcolm E. Hindin
Jeffrey F. Jones
Stanley Keller
Michael J. Lacek
William L. Lahey
Daryl J. Lapp
Scott P. Lewis
Francis C. Lynch
Michael Lytton
Judith A. Malone
Maureen P. Manning
Eric F. Menoyo
Thomas W. Merrill
Raymond M. Murphy
Arthur B. Page
Steven L. Paul
David R. Pokross, Jr.
John E. Rattigan, Jr.
John A. Rissman (Not admitted in MA)
David R. Rodgers
Marc A. Rubenstein
Kenneth W. Salinger
Yvonne E. Schlaeppi (Not admitted in MA)
Thomas G. Schnorr
Steven L. Schreckinger
Mark E. Schreiber
Thane D. Scott
Elizabeth P. Seaman
James R. Shea, Jr.
Thomas M. Spera
Craig E. Stewart
Walter J. St. Onge III
Russell B. Swapp
Jeffrey Swope
Peter S. Terris
John M. Thomas
George Ticknor
Roger P. Vacco
James M. Whalen
John L. Whitlock

(See Next Column)

PALMER & DODGE LLP—*Continued*

MEMBERS OF FIRM (Continued)

John Taylor Williams
Donald F. Winter
Tamara S. Wolfson
R. Robert Woodburn, Jr.
Jackson W. Wright, Jr.

SENIOR COUNSEL

Joan Garrity Flynn
Jay E. Gruber
Rhonda G. Hollander
Ann C. King
Mary S. Tracy
Pamela M. Veasy
Cassandra Warshowsky

COUNSEL

Susanna C. Burgett
Jonathan T. Foot
Akiyo Fujii
Jane M. Guevremont
John C. Kacoyannakis
Kathryn Cochrane Murphy
Harvey Nosowitz
Caroline W. O'Leary (Not admitted in MA)
Marianna C. Pierce
Anne Robbins
Zick Rubin
David L. Ruediger
Francisco X. Stork
Jane B. Thomassen

ASSOCIATES

Stacie Sawchak Aarestad
Sally L. Adams
Anita S. Agajanian
Marcia H. Anderegg
Carol J. Anguilla (Not admitted in MA)
Constantine Athanas
LeeAnn Baker
Kevin D. Batt
Thomas W. Beetham
Evan B. Berg
James E. Boudreau
Caroline R. Broderick
Julie A. Brogan
Katherine Keeton Carter
David J. Chused
Judith K. Crosby
Kimberly S. Davis
Dyann DelVecchio
Celeste K. DeMarco
Francesco A. De Vito
R. Lisa Di Luna
Marc Dohan
Emily R. Donovan
Ruth T. Dowling (Not admitted in MA)
Eddirland Duncan
Emily C. Ehl
Ronald S. Eppen
Jordana B. Glasgow
Marc J. Goldstein
Alexis Obolensky Goltra
Jay Gonzalez
Catherine Herrin Gorecki
Joseph F. Hardcastle
Beth J. Hermanson
John J. Hitt
M. Jennifer Hopeman
Edith C. Howe
Scott H. Kapilian
Laura Anne Kelly
Paul M. Kinsella
Aras Lapinskas
Paul Laurino
Joshua W. Leichter
Betty Lo Cualio
Antonio D. Martini
Stephanie H. Massey
Matthew V. P. McTygue
Brenda M. Mercurio
Eileen F. Morrison
Sarah J. Moskowitz
Kris A. Moussette
Stephen M. Muniz
Suzanne Nam
Matthew J. Nevins
Suzette Rodriguez O'Connor
Erin L. O'Donnell
George E. Olson
Katharine A. Pacella
Sandra Park
John W. Pickett
Gregory J. Ploussios
Eric P. Raciti
Sarah M. Richards
David Rios (Not admitted in MA)
Elaine M. Rogers
Jay D. Rosenbaum
Mark C. Rosenthal
Christian J. Rowley
Laurie M. Ruskin
Matthew P. Schaefer
Eileen P. Seman
Tarrant L. Sibley
Lori Silver
Richard B. Smith
Dawn Reddy Solowey
Kim I. Stollar (Not admitted in MA)
G. Thacher Storm
Joshua M. Thayer
Kerry John Tomasevich
Vasiliki L. Tripodis
Joanne M. Vasily-Cioffi
Senta L. Wong
Janet M. Zipin

OF COUNSEL

Virginia Aldrich
Theodore Chase
Casimir de Rham, Jr.
Robert J. McGee
Robert P. Moncreiff
James W. Perkins
John A. Perkins
Mary G. Sullivan
James L. Terry
John P. Weitzel
William Williams II
Peter Wirth
John M. Woolsey, Jr.

For full biographical listings, see the Martindale-Hubbell Law Directory

PEABODY & ARNOLD LLP (AV)

50 Rowes Wharf, 02110-3342
Telephone: 617-951-2100
Telecopier: 617-951-2125
URL: http://www.peabodyarnold.com
Providence, Rhode Island Office: One Citizens Plaza, Suite 1100.
Telephone: 401-831-8330.
Fax: 401-831-8359.
Portland, Maine Office: One City Center.
Telephone: 207-773-6300.
Fax: 207-773-0609.

(See Next Column)

MEMBERS OF FIRM

Francis Peabody (1899-1938)
Edward K. Arnold (1899-1937)
Samuel H. Batchelder (1909-1966)
Willard B. Luther (1909-1962)
Vincent M. Amoroso
Joseph S. Ayoub, Jr.
Paul J. Ayoub
Jonathan Bangs (Resident, Portland, Maine Office)
James H. Belanger
Michael F. Burke
Donald S. Burnham
Philip H. Cahalin
Kevin C. Cain
Amelia M. Charamba
Sean O. Coffey (Resident, Providence, Rhode Island Office)
Frederick E. Connelly, Jr.
John P. Connelly
William A. Cotter, Jr., (P.C.)
Jason M. Cotton
Robert J. Coughlin
Philip M. Cronin
Linda S. Dalby
Amanda D. Darwin
Allen N. David
Paul R. Devin
Michael P. Duffy
David W. Fitts
Robert Payne Fox, Jr.
Thomas Frisardi
R. Alan Fryer
Robert T. Gill
Michael J. Glazerman
John R. Gowell, Jr. (Resident, Providence, Rhode Island Office)
Deborah S. Griffin
Frank S. Hamblett
Christine Hasiotis
Ripley E. Hastings
Joseph D. S. Hinkley
William E. Kelly
Susan Fay Kendall
John A. Kessler, Jr.
Anil Khosla
Maynard M. Kirpalani
Jennifer L. Lauro
Peter J. Martin
Sam A. Mawn-Mahlau
Robert A. McCall
John J. O'Connor
E. Joseph O'Neil
Jeffrey B. Pine (Resident, Providence, Rhode Island Office)
Alexander H. Pratt, Jr.
Frank N. Ray (Resident, Providence, Rhode Island Office)
Douglas C. Reynolds
George C. Rockas
E. Macey Russell
Suanne C. St. Charles
Peter M. Shapland
Molly Haynes Sherden
Joseph M. Smick
Randolph L. Smith
John T. Smolak
Vincent M. Tentindo
Donald E. Vaughan
Robert A. Vigoda
Edward E. Watts, III
Harvey Weiner
Rebecca J. Wilson
Mark E. Young
Stephen Ziobrowski

OF COUNSEL

Dale A. Coggins
Robert DeN. Cope
Kenneth F. Ehrlich
Paul C. Kelly
Lark Jurev Palermo
Berj A. Terzian
Kent A. Willever (Resident, Providence, Rhode Island Office)

COUNSEL

John G. Brooks
John K. Dineen
James A. P. Homans (Retired)
Samuel S. Robinson
Peter B. Seamans

ASSOCIATES

Glenn B. Asch
Charles D. Blackburn (Not admitted in MA)
Andrew H. Butler
Mark J.T. Caggiano
John J. Canniff
Edward T. Canuel
Laura Cormier Capshaw
Anthony C. Chang
Kathleen M. Colbert
Sandra P. Criss
Kim L. Crockett
Timothy J. Culver
Patrick J. Dolan
Robin A. Dumas
Timothy O. Egan
Thomas C. Farrell
Christine M. Filosa
Linda Kelliher Fisher
Heather W. Gebbia
Darren I. Goldberg
Jonathan L. Goldberg (Resident, Portland, Maine Office)
Kristin Garner Griffin
Marc M. Groman
Elsie Bennett Kappler
John F. Keefe
Robert D. Keough
Kristin M. Kraeger
Tobias M. Lederberg (Resident, Providence, Rhode Island Office)
Andrew H. Lee
Rita D. Lu
Joanne T. Marchi
Robert E. Mazow
Tristan McCann
Mark W. McCarthy
Mark A. Merante
Benedict A. Monachino
David G. O'Brien
Julie Gearty O'Neill (Not admitted in MA)
Stephen L. Pike
Jennifer A. Post
Barry D. Ramsdell
Ana M. Rivera
Adam D. Rogoff
Ingrid Sorensen
Kelly J. Stringham
Mark E. Swirbalus
Daniel B. Trinkle
Andrea L. Truppa (Resident, Providence, Rhode Island Office)
Joseph B. White (Resident, Providence, Rhode Island Office)

For full biographical listings, see the Martindale-Hubbell Law Directory

PRINCE, LOBEL & TYE LLP (AV)

585 Commercial Street, 02109-1024
Telephone: 617-367-2202
Fax: 617-523-0977

(See Next Column)

PRINCE, LOBEL & TYE LLP, *Boston—Continued*

MEMBERS OF FIRM

Elliot D. Lobel, P.C.
Donald G. Tye
Walter B. Prince
Martin E. Fishkin
William A. Worth
Nancy A. Freed
Robert P. Maloney
Samuel C. Sichko
Lawrence A. Kletter
Patricia M. Annino

ASSOCIATES

Stephen K. Fischer
Linda M. Medonis
Pasquale DeSantis
Linda R. Bosse
Nancy A. Dolberg
Thomas A. Bockhorst
Laurie F. Rubin
Andrew D. Ashe
Kathryn Dowling Silveria
Angela L. Lackard

OF COUNSEL

Dennis P. Crimmins
Richard C. Heidlage
Richard E. Kaplan
Geoffrey H. Lewis (P.C.)
Lenore Zug Lobel
Susan M. Miller
Neil R. Schauer

For full biographical listings, see the Martindale-Hubbell Law Directory

ROCHE, CARENS & DEGIACOMO, P.C. (AV)

99 High Street, 02110
Telephone: 617-457-4000
Facsimile: 617-482-3868
Email: firm@rcdpc.com *URL:* http://www.rcdpc.com
Woburn, Massachusetts Office: 600 Unicorn Park Drive.
Telephone: 781-933-5505.

Frederick W. Roche (1914-1971)
James R. DeGiacomo
Michael T. Putziger
Judith K. Wyman
John C. Wyman
Richard J. Saletta
John W. Gahan, III
Frank M. Capezzera
Loring A. Cook, III
John J. O'Connor, Jr.
Susan J. Baronoff
Anne Hanford
Mark G. DeGiacomo
Joseph R. Tarby III (Resident, Woburn Office)
Joan P. Armstrong
Tracie L. Longman
Francis A. DiLuna (Resident, Woburn Office)
Thomas S. Vangel
Howard J. Castleman

Elizabeth B. Ornstein
Maureen McGahan-Supple
Laurie Alexander-Krom
Jacqueline F. Walsh
Deirdre M. Robinson
Jonathan Lee Mezrich
Rebecca Borden Lapham
Michael P. Connolly
Christopher L. Brown
Beth L. Powers

OF COUNSEL

Thomas J. Carens
Robert J. Sherer
Lynne Callahan DeGiacomo
Joel Z. Eigerman
Newton H. Levee

For full biographical listings, see the Martindale-Hubbell Law Directory

ROPES & GRAY (AV)

One International Place, 02110
Telephone: 617-951-7000
Fax: 617-951-7050
Email: postmaster@ropesgray.com *URL:* http://www.ropesgray.com
Washington, D.C. Office: One Franklin Square, 1301 K Street, NW, Suite 800 East.
Telephone: 202-626-3900.
Telecopy: 202-626-3961.
Providence, Rhode Island Office: 30 Kennedy Plaza.
Telephone: 401-455-4400.
Telecopy: 401-455-4401.

MEMBERS OF FIRM

John E. Beard
Truman S. Casner
John A. Ritsher
Arthur G. Siler
Fred R. Becker
Michael Nussbaum (Washington, D.C. Office)
C. Dean Dusseault
Howard K. Fuguet
David J. Blattner, Jr.
Nicholas A. Grace
Thomas G. Dignan, Jr.
Paul B. Galvani
Nelson G. Ross
Robert F. Hayes
William G. Meserve
Susan R. Shapiro
Ronald L. Groves
Carolyn M. Osteen
Philip J. Smith
Francis X. Hanlon
Edward P. Lawrence
Robert H. Morse (Washington, D.C. Office)
Thomas M. Susman (Washington, D.C. Office)
Richard P. Ward
Peter H. Dodson
Russell A. Gaudreau, Jr.
G. Marshall Moriarty
William L. Patton
Ronald B. Schram
Ivor Cary Armistead III
Virginia F. Coleman
Martin E. Lybecker (Washington, D.C. Office)
William F. McCarthy
Claire R. McGuire
Robert L. Nutt
Stephen B. Perlman
Samuel J. Buffone (Washington, D.C. Office)
Francis L. Coolidge
Robert D. Guiod
John C. Kane, Jr.
Douglas N. Ellis, Jr.
Robert K. Gad, III
Stephen P. Lindsay

(See Next Column)

MEMBERS OF FIRM (Continued)

Steven J. Simons
John H. Mason
David L. Raish
Mary E. Weber
Lawrence D. Bragg, III
Colburn T. Cherney (Washington, D.C. Office)
William S. Eggeling (Providence, Rhode Island Office)
Edward J. Joyce
Richard J. Lettieri
R. Hardin Matthews
Nancy R. Rice
Roscoe Trimmier, Jr.
Deborah J. Weiss
Kenneth W. Erickson
John W. Gerstmayr
Steven T. Hoort
John T. Montgomery
Daniel T. Roble
Harvey J. Wolkoff
Nancy E. Forbes
David M. Mandel
Gregory E. Moore
Stephen E. Shay (Not admitted in MA)
Jeffrey B. Storer
J. Daniel Berry (Washington, D.C. Office)
Christopher A. Klem
James L. Sigel
Dennis M. Coleman (Providence, Rhode Island Office)
Mark A. Greenwood (Washington, D.C. Office)
Susan A. Johnston
Dwight W. Quayle
Robert N. Shapiro
David O. Stewart (Washington, D.C. Office)
Geoffrey B. Davis (Providence, Rhode Island Office)
Don S. DeAmicis
Thomas B. Draper
Thomas H. Hannigan, Jr.
Joseph B. Kittredge, Jr.
R. Bradford Malt
Winthrop G. Minot
Alan G. Priest (Washington, D.C. Office)
John C. Bartenstein
David C. Chapin
Eric M. Elfman
Douglas H. Meal
Diane B. Patrick
Gregory D. Sheehan
David B. Walek
Steven A. Wilcox
John D. Donovan, Jr.
David A. Fine
Steven A. Kaufman
Brett A. Robbins
Adelbert L. Spitzer
Keith F. Higgins
William A. Knowlton
Alfred O. Rose
Jonathan M. Zorn
Timothy W. Diggins
Karen Kemper Henson
John M. Loder
Mark V. Nuccio
Rom P. Watson
Peter M. Brody (Washington, D.C. Office)
Hemmie Chang
John O. Chesley, II
Michael K. Fee
Susan M. Galli
Joan McPhee (Providence, Rhode Island Office)
Martin J. Newhouse
Anne Phillips Ogilby
Peter N. Rosenberg
Larry J. Rowe
R. Newcomb Stillwell
Mark P. Szpak
Randall W. Bodner
Daniel S. Evans
David A. McKay
Lauren I. Norton
Lee Rubin-Collins
Robert B. Gordon
Martin Hall
Walter R. McCabe, III
Ann L. Milner
Thomas B. Smith (Washington, D.C. Office)
Bryan Chegwidden
Christopher M. Leich
Alyson B.G. Allen
Marc J. Bloostein
Brenda Sweeny Diana
Patrick Diaz
Michele M. Garvin
Raj Marphatia
Loretta R. Richard
Diana L. Cooper
Joel F. Freedman
Jane D. Goldstein
Timothy M. McCrystal
Patrick O'Brien
Lisa M. Ropple

COUNSEL

Daniel Steiner
Samuel Frankenheim
Daniel I. Halperin (Not admitted in MA)
William W. Park
Clayton S. Marsh
Renée M. Landers
Brien T. O'Connor

ASSOCIATES

Arthur W. Hughes, III
W. Thomas Moulton, Jr.
Robert C. Macaulay, Jr.
Susan T. Nicholson
Richard A. Szczebak
Dina L. Michels (Washington, D.C. Office)
Peter A. Alpert
Mary C. Hennessey (Washington, D.C. Office)
Richard D. Batchelder, Jr.
Collin J. Beecroft
Matthew M. Burke
Deborah J. Coleman
Peter L. Ebb
Howard S. Glazer
Timothy J. Hinkle
Karen A. Johnson
Richard A. Manley, Jr.
James M. Wilton
James R. Brown, Jr.
James S. DeGraw
Colleen M. Granahan
Nancy T. Hegarty
Dacia A. Rubel
Debra Brown Allen
Michael P. Allen
Christopher J. Austin
David R. Baron
Darca L. Boom
Katrin Borland de Marneffe (Not admitted in MA)
Luke T. Cadigan
Josephine M. Greaves
Edward J. Hudson
Brigid K. Hurley
Joann S. Nestor
Anthony D. Rizzotti
Michael F. Sexton
Paul F. Van Houten (Not admitted in MA)
J. Steven Baughman (Washington, D.C. Office)
C. Todd Boes
Ana M. Francisco
Suzanne M. Lambert
Vivian E. Lee
Alexander Manganiello
Brian D. McCabe
Moira T. Roberts (Washington, D.C. Office)
Peter E. Schwartz
Aaron S. Ahola
Bridget M. Bettigole
Kyle A. Bettigole
Alison T. Bomberg
Jennifer Cabranes Braceras
Joan M. Guckert
Thomas R. Hiller
Julie Haggerty Jones

(See Next Column)

ROPES & GRAY—*Continued*

ASSOCIATES (Continued)

Philip C. Koski
John B. Livingston
Laura J. McCollum
Ann R. Parker
E. David Pemstein
Robert A. Skinner
David C. Sullivan
Jane E. Willis
Alyssa Albertelli (Washington, D.C. Office)
Katharine S. Bolland
Eve M. Brunts
Byung W. Choi
Lisa M. Fairfax
Daniel J. Harding
Rachel E. Hershfang
Jillian B. Johnston
Robert G. Jones
Robert R. Leveille
Jennifer S. Lobel-Schneider
D. Ross Martin
Colleen H. McDuffie (Washington, D.C. Office)
Sueyoung Min
Joseph P. Mingolla
Elizabeth Madden Mirabile
Jennifer T. Peppet
Michele T. Perillo
Michael J. Stick
Bryan A. Supran
Charles E. D. Thorland
Richard S. Weitzel
Shari H. Wolkon
R. Bryan Woodard
Nicholas T. Antoun
Brian R. Bassett
David J. Baum (Washington, D.C. Office)
Andrew P. Borggaard
Jennifer M. Borggaard
Catherine Carroll (Washington, D.C. Office)
Tanya Cluff
Ryan D. Darrah
Gregory C. Davis
Michelle M. Davis
Mark B. Elefante
Therese M. Flynn
Leigh R. Fraser (Not admitted in MA)
Alexandra Glazier
Richard E. Gordet
Trent A. Hankins
Amanda F. Henshon
Amanda C. Holt
Kenneth L. Horton
Marc L. Kesselman (Washington, D.C. Office)
Van P.T. Le
David C. Lodemore
Craig E. Marcus
Maxine L. Mauricio
Jennifer D. McNasby (Washington, D.C. Office)
Mark D. Meredith
Melissa B. Mostow
Jennifer N. Nelson
R. Daniel O'Connor
Kimberly A. Petersen
Andrea Geiger Re
W. Jane Rogers
Amy E. Samsel
Kevin J. Sullivan
Crystal D. Talley
Stephen M. Welles
Dalila Argaez Wendlandt
Elizabeth Rover Bailey
Ellen V. Benson
John Bueker
Audrey Price DiMarzo
Jeffrey A. Doctoroff
Michael G. Doherty
Sean Doherty
Helen H. Dorini
Jason E. Dunn
Taline Festekjian
Amy K. Campin Goebel
Scott C. Goebel
Jeffrey B. Hawkins
Christopher C. Henry
Robert L. Kilroy
Kelly B. Kramer (Washington, D.C. Office)
Deborah L. Levi
Jessica Lind
David M. McIntosh
Sheila A. Mikhail
Anne Oh
Keith E. Plaster
Gregory T. Pusch
Elizabeth J. Reza
Todd M. Richman (Washington, D.C. Office)
Megan M. Rose
March Sadowitz
William M. Shields
Joseph J. Sklansky
Christopher M. Taylor
James E. Thomas
Eric L. Tracy
Daniel H. Weintraub
Owen L. Wilcox
Sean M. Becker
David R. Boschetto
Jason Brown
C. Lewis Collins
Tricia Hwang Connerly
David L. Coombs
Douglas M. Demay
Peter Fratangelo
Alexandra D. Furth
Jodi R. Goldstein (Washington, D.C. Office)
Kari K. Harris
Christopher E. Houston
Scott S. Jones
Jon S. Liland
Sarah B. Lowman
John B. McGinty, Jr.
Matthew W. McNamee
Catherine A. Mondell
Mona R. Patel
Sharon Remmer
Claudette Robertson
John R. Samia
C. William Thomas, Jr.
Stacy L. Vezina
Deidre J. Waz

OF COUNSEL

H. Brian Holland
Warren E. Carley
Allen O. Eaton
James B. Ames
Edward B. Hanify
Francis H. Burr
Andrew H. Cox
Harry K. Mansfield
Ernest J. Sargeant
Oscar W. Haussermann, Jr.
Paul F. Perkins
John M. Harrington, Jr.
Thomas L. P. O'Donnell
Henry S. Streeter
George C. Caner, Jr.
Jerome M. Leonard
George H. Lewald
A. Lane McGovern
George T. Finnegan
Alfred W. Fuller
Joan D. Fuller
Richard W. Southgate
Peter Leffingwell Albrecht
Champe A. Fisher
Ruth R. O'Brien
W. Lincoln Boyden
John A. Pike
Edward A. Benjamin
Henry L. Hall, Jr.
Charles P. Normandin
Thomas W. Taylor

For full biographical listings, see the Martindale-Hubbell Law Directory

SHERIN AND LODGEN LLP (AV)

100 Summer Street, 02110
Telephone: 617-426-5720
Fax: 617-542-5186
Email: lawyers@sherin.com *URL:* http://www.sherin.com
Los Angeles, California Office: 11300 W. Olympic Boulevard, Suite 700.
Telephone: 310-914-7891.
Fax: 310-552-5327.

MEMBERS OF FIRM

Arthur L. Sherin (1946-1964)
George E. Lodgen (1946-1971)
Morton B. Brown
George Waldstein
John M. Reed
Robert J. Muldoon, Jr.
Alette E. Reed
Edward M. Bloom
Joshua M. Alper
Gary M. Markoff
Bryan G. Killian
David A. Guberman
Frank J. Bailey
Kenneth J. Mickiewicz
Craig M. Brown
Thomas A. Hippler
Ronald W. Ruth
Mark A. Nowak
Thomas P. Gorman
Steven D. Eimert
Andrew Royce
John J. Slater III
John C. La Liberte
C. Forbes Sargent III
David A. Brown
Michael S. Strauss
Christopher A. Kenney

ASSOCIATES

Robert M. Carney
Caroline Woodward
Michael S. Bloom
Kenneth D. Small
Margaret H. Paget
Michael J. Ostroskey
James M. Wodarski
Jessica R. Yaffie
William P. Keefe
Amy D. Porter
Thomas F. Dunn
Brian G. Luneau
Michael P. Sams
Erin M. McNamara
James W. Matthews
Thomas S. Dean

OF COUNSEL

Janet E. Bostwick
Kurt A. James

For full biographical listings, see the Martindale-Hubbell Law Directory

STROOCK & STROOCK & LAVAN LLP (AV)

100 Federal Street, 02110-1813
Telephone: 617-482-6800
Fax: 617-330-5111
Email: infoboston@stroock.com *URL:* http://www.stroock.com
New York, N.Y. Office: 180 Maiden Lane, New York, NY, 10038.
Telephone: 212-806-5400.
Telecopiers: 212-806-6006; 212-806-5919; 212-806-6086; 212-425-9509; 212-806-6176. Email: info@stroock.com
New York Conference Center: 767 Third Avenue, New York, N.Y., 10017-2023.
Telephones: 212-806-5767; 5768; 5769; 5770.
Telecopier: 212-421-6234. Email: info@stroock.com
Budapest, Hungary Office: East-West Business Center, Rákóczi út 1-3, H-1088 Budapest, Hungary.
Telephone: 011-36-1-266-9520; 011-36-1-266-7770.
Telecopier: 011-36-1-266-9279. Email: stroock@stroock.hu
Los Angeles, California Office: 2029 Century Park East, Suite 1800, Los Angeles, Ca., 90067-3086.
Telephone: 310-556-5800.
Telecopier: 310-556-5959. Email: infola@stroock.com
Miami, Florida Office: First Union Financial Center, 200 South Biscayne Boulevard, Suite 3300, Miami, Fl., 33131-2385.
Telephone: 305-358-9900.
Telecopier: 305-789-9302. Email: infomiami@stroock.com
Washington, D.C. Office: 1150 Seventeenth Street, N.W., Suite 600, Washington, D.C., 20036-4652.
Telephone: 202-452-9250.
Telecopier: 202-293-2293. Email: infodc@stroock.com

MEMBERS OF FIRM

Peter J. Antoszyk
Siri F. Boreske
Paul D. Broude
Howard M. Gitten (Not admitted in MA)
Jeffrey S. Lowenthal
Stephen M. Richmond
Peter Wittenborg

OF COUNSEL

Stephen M. Sheehy

ASSOCIATES

Bruce H. Bagdasarian
Joel G. Beckman
Ann C. Bonis
Kyle S. Chase
John R. Condon
Christine R. Fitzgerald
Leslie Anne Hawes
David Kantaros

For full biographical listings, see the Martindale-Hubbell Law Directory

TAYLOR, DUANE, BARTON & GILMAN, LLP (AV)

111 Devonshire Street, 02109
Telephone: 617-654-8200
Fax: 617-482-5350
Providence, Rhode Island Office: 10 Dorrance Street, Suite 700, 02903.
Telephone: 401-273-7171.
Fax: 401-273-2904.

(See Next Column)

TAYLOR, DUANE, BARTON & GILMAN LLP, *Boston—Continued*

MEMBERS OF FIRM

Allan E. Taylor
James J. Duane, III
John J. Barton
Pamela Slater Gilman
Edward D. Shoulkin
Jennifer Ellis Burke
Francis A. Connor, III
Gina Witalec Verdi

ASSOCIATES

Robert C. Shindell
Craig R. Waksler
Stephen Adams
Christine A. Kelly
Andria Coletta
Sheri L. Pizzi
Tryntje I. Houghton
Robert M. Elmer
Tamara J. Smith
Jennifer L. Buckley

For full biographical listings, see the Martindale-Hubbell Law Directory

TESTA, HURWITZ & THIBEAULT, LLP (AV)

125 High Street, 02110
Telephone: 617-248-7000
Telecopier: 617-248-7100
Email: postmaster@tht.com *URL:* http://www.tht.com

MEMBERS OF FIRM

Donald L. Anglehart
Jocelyn M. Arel
William B. Asher Jr.
Kevin M. Barry
Steven M. Bauer
Thomas A. Beaudoin
David C. Berry
Scott A. Birnbaum
Mitchell S. Bloom
Steven C. Browne
Mark H. Burnett
David J. Byer
E. Michael Collins
Henry W. Comstock Jr.
Michael A. Conza
Karen Faulds Copenhaver
William J. Corcoran
John J. Cotter
Leslie E. Davis
F. George Davitt
Linda DeRenzo
Eric A. Deutsch
Daniel P. Finkelman
Adam P. Forman
David S. Godkin
Brian D. Goldstein
Dean C. Gordanier Jr.
Gordon H. Hayes Jr.
Jordan D. Hershman
John M. Hession
Joseph A. Hugg
Stephen A. Hurwitz
Erin E. Karzmer
Jin-Kyung (Kay) Kim
Rufus C. King
Douglas J. Kline
Kevin T. Lamb
Roger A. Lane
Laurence E. Lewis
George W. Lloyd
Mark J. Macenka
Timothy C. Maguire
Louis J. Marett
John A. Meltaus
Edwin L. Miller Jr.
Jonathan M. Moulton
Robin A. Painter
Brian E. Pastuszenski
Edmund R. Pitcher
William L. Prickett
Howard S. Rosenblum
Joseph F. Savage, Jr.
William J. Schnoor Jr.
William B. Simmons Jr.
Mark D. Smith
Andrew E. Taylor Jr.
David W. Tegeler
Richard J. Testa
George W. Thibeault
Thomas A. Turano
John F. Welsh
Lawrence S. Wittenberg

COUNSEL

Alan J. Applebaum
Daniel J. Bernstein
Kimberly M. Collins
Margaret M. Holland (Not admitted in MA)
Anne G. Plimpton
Robert M. Thomas, Jr. (Not admitted in MA)

ASSOCIATES

Erica B. Abate
Todd S. Anderson
Christian A. Aviza
John R. Bauer
Laurier W. Beaupre
Howard J. Beber
Serge O. Bechade
Marc E. Betinsky
Mark T. Bettencourt
Deborah S. Birnbach
Michael H. Bison
Isabelle A.S. Blundell
Jean M. Boyle
Maureen A. Bresnahan
Michael H. Brodowski
Alfred L. Browne
Carson G. Burnham
Debra A. Buxbaum
Jennifer A. Camacho
Anthony J. Canata
Joseph A. Capraro, Jr.
Patricia Cashman
Laurie A. Cerveny
Victor I. Chang
Jerrie L. Chiu
Dina M. Ciarimboli
Paul T. Citardi
Rebecca A. Connolly
Monique Cormier
Eleanor R. Cornish
Katherine M. Criniti
Michael J. Crowley (Not admitted in MA)
Elisa T. Deener-Agus
Carol E. Didget
Christopher J. Dole
Carrie Dolmat-Connell
Esther B. Dominguez
Deborah B. Dong
Jennifer L. Dupre
Jason A. Duva
Roy D. Edelstein
Jennifer A. Fago
Joseph L. Farmer
Burt M. Fealing
Karen L. Febeo
Robert N. Feldman
Lillian Feng
Kathy A. Fields
John V. Forcier
Richard D. Forrest
Edward D. Freedman
Inez H. Friedman
Daniel L. Furman
Elizabeth A. Garner
Michel F. Généreux
Garrett G. Gillespie (Not admitted in MA)
Jennifer M. Goddard
Todd C. Goffman
Lawrence A. Gold
Antonio G. Gomes

(See Next Column)

ASSOCIATES (Continued)

Kenneth J. Gordon
Duncan A. Greenhalgh
Tracey M. Greenwald
Gregg A. Griner
Gary M. Grossman
William G. Guerin
Elizabeth Harmer-Dionne
Kirstan Brooks Harris (Not admitted in MA)
John F. Harvey
Kristie P. Hathaway
Ira Heffan
Jeffrey M. Held
Sara Hinchey
Michael D. Hochberg
Mary T. Hornby
Robert V. Housley
Jeffrey A. Huebschmann
Elaine M. Hughes
Michael D. Innes
Barbara M. Johnson
Kristina E. Johnson
David T. Jones
Gregory A. Jones
Minnie P. Joung
Kimberley J. Kaplan-Gross
James R. Kasinger
Wendy A. Kelley
Patrick J. Kennedy
Elizabeth E. Kim
Mi K. Kim
Sandy M. Kim
Mary B. Kuusisto
John D. Lanza
Ann M. Laquerre
Connie Lee
Timothy P. Linkkila
Florence R. Liu
Kurt W. Lockwood
Bryan P. Lord
Robert B. Lovett
Eva Maija Marceau
Peter E. Markman
Matthew A. Martel
Arnold P. May
John T. McCarthy
Kevin M. McKenna
Marianne M. McLaughlin
Robert C. McNamec
Stephen T. Mears
Carl E. Metzger
Thomas C. Meyers (Not admitted in MA)
Lori Ann Mihalich
Anne T. Mitchell
Lisel M. Mittelholzer
Audranne Mixon
Brenda A. Moffitt
Alexis Mokotoff
Ronda P. Moore
John M. Mutkoski
Jennifer C. Muto
Richard Myrus
Laurence P. Naughton
Malcolm B. Nicholls III
Susan J. Nock
Kimberly C. Nuzum
Kevin J. O'Connor
Thomas P. Olivier
Andrew P. O'Meara, III
Erika Leigh Ozer
Eric S. Palace
Edwin C. Pease
Deborah J. Peckham
Justin M. Perrotta
Theodore J. Petrakos
Scott J. Pinarchick
John R. Pitfield
Jamiel E. Poindexter
Mark D. Pomfret
Joel T. Pond
Robert E. Puopolo
Amy R. Ratner
Kurt Rauschenbach
Patricia R. Ray
Gustavo Resendiz
George E. (Jed) Rice
David A. Rines
Nicholas W. Robbins
Christopher F. Robertson (Not admitted in MA)
James M. Rock
Arthur M. Rogers III
Joseph S. Rosen
Meredith J. Ross
Richard S. Sanders
Christopher W. Sanzone
Michael J. Schmelzer
Craig T. Smith
Jane I. Song
Lauren A. Stagnone
Christopher W. Stamos
John W. Steinmetz
Debbi R. Stern
Christopher R. Stone
Geoffrey M. Stone
Heather M. Stone
Walter H. Stowell III
Joseph P. Sullivan
Jacqueline G. Taylor
Debra B. Thomas
Joseph R. Torpy
Robert J. Tosti
Paul D. Tutun
Michael J. Twomey
Allan B. Urgent
Miguel J. Vega
Christine C. Vito
Sarah A. Wasserman
Jean Weidemier
Stephen D. Whetstone
Kelly R. Whiting
Charles F. Willson
Daniel A. Wilson
Matthew A. Wolfman

LEGAL SUPPORT PERSONNEL
REGISTERED PATENT AGENTS
TECHNOLOGY SPECIALISTS

Elias C. Behrakis
Brian A. Fairchild
Danielle L. Herritt
Joseph B. Milstein
Dianne Mary Rees
Michael A. Rodriguez
J. Scott Southworth
Patrick Robert Henson Waller

For full biographical listings, see the Martindale-Hubbell Law Directory

WILLCOX, PIROZZOLO AND MCCARTHY, PROFESSIONAL CORPORATION (AV)

50 Federal Street, 02110
Telephone: 617-482-5470
Telecopier: 617-423-1572

Harold M. Willcox (1925-1975)
Jack R. Pirozzolo
Richard F. McCarthy

Richard L. Binder
Richard E. Bennett
Judith Seplowitz Ziss
Christopher R. Goddu
Katherine L. Young

OF COUNSEL

Richard P. Crowley

For full biographical listings, see the Martindale-Hubbell Law Directory

BRAINTREE, Norfolk Co.

LANE, LANE AND KELLY (AV)

836 Washington Street, P.O. Box 850270, 02185
Telephone: 781-848-0040
Fax: 781-380-4136
URL: http://www.lawyers.com/lanelaneandkelly

Myron N. Lane (1907-1972)
Richard B. Lane
Robert P. Kelly

ASSOCIATES

Evelyn V. Henry
Edward D. McDonald
Elizabeth M. Sullivan

Representative Client: The Braintree Cooperative Bank; First Federal Savings Bank of America; Salem Five Cents Savings Bank; Wellesley Co-operative Bank; PNC Mortgage Corp. of America; Gale Associates, Inc.; Garaventa U.S.A. Inc.

For full biographical listings, see the Martindale-Hubbell Law Directory

*CAMBRIDGE,** Middlesex Co.

WILLIAM M. O'BRIEN (AV)

185 Alewife Brook Parkway, Suite 400, 02138
Telephone: 617-661-2600
Fax: 617-868-8040

For full biographical listings, see the Martindale-Hubbell Law Directory

*DEDHAM,** Norfolk Co.

GELERMAN, CASHMAN & DONAHUE (AV)

270 Bridge Street, 02026-1764
Telephone: 617-329-8300
Telecopier: 781-329-0387
URL: http://www.lawyers.com/gelerman_cashman_donahue

MEMBERS OF FIRM

Michael C. Donahue
Daniel F. Cashman
Richard A. Gelerman
Gail M. Buschmann
John M. Lovely
Robert Nichols
M. Christine Breslin
Michael C. Bainum

OF COUNSEL

Richard A. Feigenbaum

For full biographical listings, see the Martindale-Hubbell Law Directory

HINGHAM, Plymouth Co.

GILLIS & ANGLEY (AV)

Suite 227, 160 Old Derby Street, 02043
Telephone: 781-749-2432
Telecopier: 781-740-0768
Email: galaw@ici.net

MEMBERS OF FIRM

Ralph J. Gillis
Edward T. Angley

ASSOCIATE

Philip H. Barthel

For full biographical listings, see the Martindale-Hubbell Law Directory

HOLYOKE, Hampden Co.

LYON, FERRITER & FITZPATRICK, LLP (AV)

Whitney Place, 14 Bobala Road, 01040
Telephone: 413-536-4000
Fax: 413-536-3773
Email: lyonferr@aol.com

MEMBERS OF FIRM

Maurice J. Ferriter
Clarke S. Lyon
William D. Fitzpatrick
James F. Donnelly
Peter C. Connor
John J. Ferriter
Priscilla Fifield Chesky
Robert C. Sacco

ASSOCIATE

Robyn Andrea Porter

OF COUNSEL

William E. Begley

Representative Clients: Mount Holyoke College; Newspapers of New England, Inc.; Loomis House Retirement Community; Atlas Copco Compressors Inc.; Hazen Paper Company.

For full biographical listings, see the Martindale-Hubbell Law Directory

HYANNIS, Barnstable Co.

MURPHY AND MURPHY (AV)

243 South Street, P.O. Box M, 02601
Telephone: 508-775-3116
Telecopier: 508-775-3720
Email: murphmurph@capecod.net

(See Next Column)

MEMBERS OF FIRM

Henry L. Murphy, Jr.
J. Douglas Murphy

ASSOCIATES

G. Arthur Hyland, Jr.
Susan Merritt-Glenny

For full biographical listings, see the Martindale-Hubbell Law Directory

LOWELL, Middlesex Co.

DONAHUE & DONAHUE, ATTORNEYS, P.C. (AV)

21 George Street, 01852
Telephone: 978-458-6887
Fax: 978-458-3424

Daniel J. Donahue (1860-1939)
Joseph P. Donahue (1889-1973)
Charles A. Donahue (1891-1964)
Richard K. Donahue
Joseph P. Donahue, Jr.
Joseph D. Regan
Michael W. Gallagher
Richard K. Donahue, Jr.
Andrea S. Barisano
Matthew C. Donahue
Richard E. Cavanaugh
Kelly R. Spencer
Alicia A. Donahue

Kelly M. Quigley

Representative Clients: The Travelers Insurance Co.; Ciro's Restaurants; Black & Decker; Burger King Corp.; White Consolidated, Inc.

For full biographical listings, see the Martindale-Hubbell Law Directory

GOLDMAN & CURTIS, P.C. (AV)

Lowell Place, 144 Merrimack Street, 01852
Telephone: 978-454-8804; 729-2625
Fax: 978-459-2730

Frank Goldman (1890-1965)
Robert H. Goldman (1918-1991)
James T. Curtis
Cornelia C. Adams
Gregory T. Curtis
Carolyn L. Greenberg
James T. Curtis, Jr.

OF COUNSEL

Efthemios J. Bentas
Matthew P. Demaras

For full biographical listings, see the Martindale-Hubbell Law Directory

*SPRINGFIELD,** Hampden Co.

DOHERTY, WALLACE, PILLSBURY AND MURPHY, P.C. (AV)

19th Floor, One Monarch Place, 1414 Main Street, 01144
Telephone: 413-733-3111
Telecopier: 413-734-3910
Email: DWPM@DWPM.com *URL:* http://www.dwpm.com

Dudley B. Wallace (1900-1987)
Louis W. Doherty (1898-1990)
Frederick S. Pillsbury (1919-1996)
Paul S. Doherty
Samuel A. Marsella
Philip J. Callan, Jr.
Gary P. Shannon
Robert L. Leonard
A. Craig Brown
L. Jeffrey Meehan
David J. Martel
John James McCarthy
William P. Hadley
Barry M. Ryan
Deborah A. Basile
Paul M. Maleck
Claire L. Thompson
W. Garth Janes
Gregory A. Schmidt

Michael K. Callan
Steven M. Coyle
Michael D. Sweet
James J. Bregianes
Grace M. Calamita

OF COUNSEL

Robert E. Murphy
Matthew J. Ryan, Jr.

Local Counsel for: Nationwide Mutual Insurance Co.; Liberty Mutual Insurance Co.; General Motors Corp.; Wausau Insurance Cos.; Royal Insurance; Metropolitan Property & Liability Insurance Co.
Representative Clients: Fontaine Bros.; F.L. Roberts and Company Inc.; Town of Longmeadow.

For full biographical listings, see the Martindale-Hubbell Law Directory

EGAN, FLANAGAN AND COHEN, P.C. (AV)

67 Market Street, P.O. Box 9035, 01102-9035
Telephone: 413-737-0260
Fax: 413-737-0121
Email: efc@eganflanagan.com

James F. Egan (1896-1986)
Edward T. Collins (1902-1995)
William C. Flanagan
Mary Egan Boland
John J. Egan
Theodore C. Brown
Edward J. McDonough, Jr.
Maurice M. Cahillane
John G. Bagley
Robert L. Quinn
Eileen Z. Sorrentino

Joseph A. Pacella
Kevin D. Withers
Paula C. Tredeau (Not admitted in MA)
Joseph M. Pacella

(See Next Column)

EGAN, FLANAGAN AND COHEN P.C., *Springfield—Continued*

OF COUNSEL

J. David Keaney
Charles S. Cohen
David G. Cohen

Counsel for: Mercy Hospital; Roman Catholic Diocese of Springfield; McKinstry, Incorporated; Sheriff of Hampden County; ProMutual Insurance.

For full biographical listings, see the Martindale-Hubbell Law Directory

WALTHAM, Middlesex Co.

HARNISH, JENNEY, MITCHELL AND RESH (AV)

564 Main Street, 02154
Telephone: 781-894-0000
Telecopier: 781-893-8357

MEMBERS OF FIRM

Francis E. Jenney
David L. Mitchell
Harvey J. Resh
Joseph Melone
Robert C. Mann
Margaret Manzon Skinner

ASSOCIATE

Rhonda B. Fogel

For full biographical listings, see the Martindale-Hubbell Law Directory

*WORCESTER,** Worcester Co.

FLETCHER, TILTON & WHIPPLE, P.C. (AV)

370 Main Street, 01608
Telephone: 508-798-8621
Telecopier: 508-791-1201
Email: ftw@ftwlaw.com *URL:* http://www.ftwlaw.com

Sumner B. Tilton (1904-1981)
Paris Fletcher (1903-1989)
Robert J. Whipple (1912-1997)
Henry C. Horner
John E. Hodgson
Sumner B. Tilton, Jr.
Phillips S. Davis
Robert R. Kimball
Douglas Q. Meystre
Alexander E. Drapos
Warner S. Fletcher
Robert F. Dore, Jr.
Arthur H. Miller
(Not admitted in MA)
James M. Burgoyne
William D. Jalkut
Mark L. Donahue
Lucille B. Brennan
Kirk A. Carter
Dennis F. Gorman
Frederick M. Misilo, Jr.
Brian J. Buckley
David J. Officer
Richard C. Barry, Jr.
Emanuel N. Bardanis
Vincent W. Lau
Allison R. Quinn

OF COUNSEL

Ralph F. Sbrogna
Diane M. Wittenberg

For full biographical listings, see the Martindale-Hubbell Law Directory

GLICKMAN, SUGARMAN, KNEELAND & GRIBOUSKI (AV)

11 Harvard Street, P.O. Box 2917, 01613
Telephone: 508-756-6206
Fax: 508-831-0443

MEMBERS OF FIRM

Melvyn Glickman
David W. Sugarman
David J. Kneeland, Jr.
James Gribouski

ASSOCIATES

Joe Boynton
Wayne M. LeBlanc
James F. Scola

For full biographical listings, see the Martindale-Hubbell Law Directory

MACCARTHY, POJANI & HURLEY, LLP (AV)

Worcester Plaza, 446 Main Street, 01608
Telephone: 508-798-2480
Fax: 508-797-9561

RETIRED PARTNER

Philip J. MacCarthy

MEMBERS OF FIRM

John Macuga, Jr. (1949-1998)
Dennis Pojani
John F. Hurley, Jr.
William J. Ritter

Representative Clients: American Polymers, Inc.; Bay Finance Company, Inc.; Commerce Insurance Company; E.J. Cross, Inc.; E. Stanley Wright Museum Foundation, Inc.; Fleet National Bank; Liberty Mutual Insurance Company; Melville Corporation; The Talbots, Inc.

For full biographical listings, see the Martindale-Hubbell Law Directory

MIRICK, O'CONNELL, DEMALLIE & LOUGEE, LLP (AV)

100 Front Street, 01608-1477
Telephone: 508-791-8500
Fax: 508-791-8502
Email: general@modl.com *URL:* http://www.modl.com

(See Next Column)

MEMBERS OF FIRM

Robert J. Martin
David L. Lougee
Robert V. Deiana
John O. Mirick
Demitrios M. Moschos
Robert P. Lombardi
Edward C. Bassett, Jr.
James C. Donnelly, Jr.
Andrew B. O'Donnell
Michael R. Mosher
Robert L. Hamer
David E. Surprenant
Paul J. D'Onfro
Richard C. Van Nostrand
Jeffrey L. Donaldson
Alden J. Bianchi
Peter J. Dawson
Joseph H. Baldiga
Janet Wilson Moore
Joseph M. Hamilton
William S. Rogers, Jr.
Joan O. Vorster

OF COUNSEL

Richard W. Mirick
John H. Budd
Charles B. Straus, III

ASSOCIATES

Robert S. Heppe, Jr.
Michele P. Rosano
Kimberly A. Rozak
Arthur S. Wells
Christopher J. Alessandro
Patricia L. Davidson
Margaret J. Hurley
David L. Renauld
Elizabeth L. B. Greene
Glen M. Mair
Sheila G. Lehto
Matthew P. McCue
Robert N. Meltzer
Sharon P. Siegel
Michael D. Badger
Paul W. Carey
Christine E. Devine
Jeffrey E. Swaim
Robert B. Gibbons
Todd K. Helwig
Kristine M. Canepa
Jay P. Symonds
Kevin J. Bourque
Adam D. Page
Adrienne Walker Kotowski
Melissa A. O'Neill

References: Flagship Bank & Trust Co.; Fleet National Bank.

For full biographical listings, see the Martindale-Hubbell Law Directory

MOUNTAIN, DEARBORN & WHITING LLP (AV)

370 Main Street, 01608
Telephone: 508-756-2423
Fax: 508-755-6640

MEMBERS OF FIRM

Alfred N. Whiting (1920-1989)
Thomas R. Mountain
Richard W. Dearborn
Samuel R. DeSimone
Henry W. Beth
Stuart A. Hammer
Francis J. Russell
Dale R. Harger
Mark W. Bloom
Donald J. O'Neil
Lawrence S. Delaney
Ann K. Molloy
Lisa D. Tingue

For full biographical listings, see the Martindale-Hubbell Law Directory

MICHIGAN

*ADRIAN,** Lenawee Co.

WALKER, WATTS, JACKSON & MCFARLAND (AV)

160 North Winter Street, 49221
Telephone: 517-265-8138
Fax: 517-265-8286
URL: http://www.lawyers.com/wwj&m

MEMBERS OF FIRM

William H. Walker
Prosser M. Watts, Jr.
Mark A. Jackson
Michael McFarland

ASSOCIATE

David Christopher McFarland

Attorneys for: Bank of Lenawee; Consumers Power Co.; Norfolk & Western Railway Co.; Citizens Gas Fuel Co.; Auto Owners Insurance Co.; Amerisure Co.; Blissfield Manufacturing Co.; Adrian College.

For full biographical listings, see the Martindale-Hubbell Law Directory

*ALLEGAN,** Allegan Co.

ORTON, TOOMAN, HALE, MCKOWN AND KIEL, P.C. (AV)

314 Trowbridge Street, P.O. Box 239, 49010
Telephone: 616-673-2136
Fax: 616-673-2898

Rex W. Orton (1914-1988)
Lester J. Tooman
Gregory D. Hale
Stephen B. McKown
David F. Kiel

Representative Clients: Allegan Public Schools; Dorr Township; Allegan General Hospital; Allegan Medical Clinic, P.C.; Kalamazoo Ferry Co.; Allegan Foundation.

For full biographical listings, see the Martindale-Hubbell Law Directory

ALMA, Gratiot Co.

FORTINO, PLAXTON, MOSKAL & COSTANZO, P.C. (AV)

Warwick Professional Center, 175 Warwick Drive, P.O. Box 578, 48801
Telephone: 517-463-2101
Fax: 517-463-2104

John J. Moskal (1932-1997) | Charles M. Fortino
Anthony G. Costanzo

OF COUNSEL

Alfred J. Fortino | Kenneth D. Plaxton

LEGAL SUPPORT PERSONNEL

PARALEGALS

Gillene M. Weller

Attorneys for: Farmers State Bank, Breckenridge; State Farm Mutual Insurance Co.; Auto Owners Insurance Co.; The Ohio Casualty Ins. Co.; Commercial Bank; Bear Truss and Components Co.; Alma Iron and Metal; Powell Fabrication & Mfg.; City of Alma.

For full biographical listings, see the Martindale-Hubbell Law Directory

*ANN ARBOR,** Washtenaw Co.

BRAUN KENDRICK FINKBEINER PLC (AV)

First National Building, 210 S. Main, Suite 700, 48104
Telephone: 313-995-4100
Telecopier: 313-995-4798
Email: ALBFIE@BKF-LAW.COM *URL:* http://www.bkf-law.com
Bay City, Michigan Office: 201 Phoenix Building, P.O. Box 2039.
Telephone: 517-895-8505.
Telecopier: 517-895-8437.
Saginaw, Michigan Office: 101 N. Washington, Suite 812.
Telephone: 517-753-3461.
Telecopier: 517-753-3951.
Saginaw Township, Michigan Office: 5800 Gratiot Road, Suite 107, P.O. Box 5169.
Telephone: 517-799-8692.
Fax: 517-799-4666.
Mt. Pleasant, Michigan Office: 805 North Brown.
Telephone: 517-775-7404.
Telecopier: 517-775-3764.

Barry M. Levine

Bridgette B. Skaff

Representative Clients: The Dow Chemical Co.; General Motors Corp.; Merrill, Lynch, Inc.; Saginaw General Hospital; Saginaw News; The Wickes Foundation; City of Ypsilanti.

For full biographical listings, see the Martindale-Hubbell Law Directory

DYKEMA GOSSETT PLLC (AV)

315 East Eisenhower Parkway, Suite 100, 48108-3306
Telephone: 734-214-7660
Fax: 734-214-7696
Email: mstarrs@dykema.com *URL:* http://www.dykema.com
Bloomfield Hills, Michigan Office: 1577 North Woodward Avenue, Suite 300, 48304-2820.
Telephone: 248-203-0700.
Fax: 248-203-0763.
Chicago, Illinois Office: 55 East Monroe Street, Suite 3050, 60603-5709.
Telephone: 312-551-4900.
Fax: 312-551-4919.
Detroit, Michigan Office: 400 Renaissance Center, 48243-1668.
Telephone: 313-568-6800.
Fax: 313-568-6545.
Grand Rapids, Michigan Office: Suite 700, 300 Ottawa Avenue, N.W., 49503-2304.
Telephone: 616-776-7500.
Fax: 616-776-7573.
Lansing, Michigan Office: 800 Michigan National Tower, 48933-1707.
Telephone: 517-374-9100.
Fax: 517-374-9191.
Washington, D.C. Office: Franklin Square, Suite 300 West, 1300 I Street, N.W.. 20005-3306.
Telephone: 202-522-8600.
Fax: 202-522-8669.
Affiliated Office: Via Matconi, 3, 40122 Bologna, Italy, Telephone; 011-39-51-228222.
Fax: 011-39-51-6593580.

RESIDENT MEMBERS

James C. Adams | Sharon M. Kelly
James M. Cameron, Jr. | Richard J. Landau
Marie R. Deveney | Andrew J. McGuinness
Phyllis Donaldson-Adams | Janet L. Neary
James P. Greene | Daniel J. Stephenson
E. Edward Hood (Member in Charge) | Kent P. Talcott

RETIRED MEMBER

Raymond T. Huetteman, Jr.

(See Next Column)

RESIDENT ASSOCIATES

Jennifer G. Anderson | Bradley L. Smith
Krista L. Lenart | Steven A. Susswein
Allison L. Mann | William M. Thacker
Claire S. Pouget | Lisa M. Waits
Jeffrey N. Silveri | Angela R. White

For full biographical listings, see the Martindale-Hubbell Law Directory

GARAN, LUCOW, MILLER & SEWARD, P.C. (AV)

101 North Main Street, Suite 460, 48104-1400
Telephone: 734-930-5600
Fax: 734-930-0043
URL: http://www.garanlucow.com
Detroit, Michigan Office: 1000 Woodbridge Place.
Telephone: 313-446-1530.
Fax: 313-259-0450.
Port Huron, Michigan Office: Port Huron Office Center, 511 Fort Street, Suite 505.
Telephone: 810-985-4400.
Fax: 810-985-4107.
Grand Blanc, Michigan Office: 8332 Office Park Drive.
Telephone: 810-695-3700.
Fax: 810-695-6488.
Troy, Michigan Office: 1111 West Long Lake Road, Suite 300.
Telephone: 248-641-7600.
Fax: 248-641-0222.
Mount Clemens, Michigan Office: Towne Square Development, 10 South Main Street, Suite 307.
Telephone: 810-954-3800:
Fax: 810-954-3803.
Grand Rapids, Michigan Office: First of America Center, 171 Monroe Avenue, N.W., Suite 950.
Telephone: 616-742-5500.
Fax: 616-742-5566.
Lansing, Michigan Office: 530 Creyts Road, Suite A.
Telephone: 517-327-0300.
Fax: 517-327-0309.
Traverse City, Michigan Office: 1131 East Eighth Street, P.O. Box 3150.
Telephone: 231-941-1611.
Fax: 231-941-4420.
Marquette, Michigan Office: 228 West Washington Street, Suite 4,
Telephone: 906-228-7772.
Fax: 906-228-5999.

Judith A. Moskus (Resident) | John W. Whitman

John J. Koselka | Suzanne R. Fanning

For full biographical listings, see the Martindale-Hubbell Law Directory

HOOPER, HATHAWAY, PRICE, BEUCHE & WALLACE (AV)

126 South Main Street, 48104
Telephone: 313-662-4426
Fax: 313-662-9559
Email: hhpbw@voyager.net

Joseph C. Hooper (1899-1980) | Mark R. Daane
John R. Hathaway (Retired) | Gregory A. Spaly
Alan E. Price | William J. Stapleton
James R. Beuche | Anthony P. Patti
Bruce T. Wallace | Angela L. Jackson
Charles W. Borgsdorf | Susan T. Cannell
Kurtis R. Dumaw

OF COUNSEL

James A. Evashevski

Representative Clients: Avfuel Corporation; Bank of Ann Arbor; Castrol North America; Chem-Trend Incorporated; Ervin Industries, Inc.; First Martin Corporation; Glacier Hills, Inc.; Prestolite Electric, Inc.; Southern States Cooperative; E.B. Eddy Forest Products, Ltd.

For full biographical listings, see the Martindale-Hubbell Law Directory

JOSCELYN, MCNAIR AND JEFFREY, P.C. (AV)

110 Miller Avenue Suite 100, P.O. Box 130589, 48113-0589
Telephone: 734-662-7904
Fax: 734-662-1030
Email: jmjpc@msn.com

Kent B. Joscelyn | John W. McNair
M. Sheila Jeffrey

For full biographical listings, see the Martindale-Hubbell Law Directory

Ann Arbor—Continued

KITCH DRUTCHAS WAGNER DENARDIS & VALITUTTI, A PROFESSIONAL CORPORATION (AV)

303 Detroit Street, Suite 400, P.O. Box 8610, 48107-8610
Telephone: 734-994-7600
Fax: 734-994-7626
URL: http://www.kitch.com
Detroit, Michigan Office: One Woodward, Tenth Floor, 48226-3499.
Telephone: 313-965-7900.
Fax: 313-965-7403.
Lansing, Michigan Office: 120 Washington Square, North, Suite 280, One Michigan Avenue, 48933-1609.
Telephone: 517-372-6430.
Fax: 517-372-0441.
Macomb County Office: Towne Square Development, 10 South Main Street, Suite 301, Mount Clemens, 48043-7903.
Telephone: 810-463-9770.
Fax: 810-463-8994.
Marquette, Michigan Office: Old City Hall, 220 West Washington, Suite 500, 49855-4344.
Telephone: 906-228-0001.
Fax: 906-228-0003.
Toledo, Ohio Office: 405 Madison Avenue, Suite 1500, 43604-1235.
Telephone: 419-243-4006.
Fax: 419-243-7333.
Grand Rapids, Michigan Office: 300 Ottawa, NW, Suite 210, 49503.
Telephone: 616-456-8384.
Fax: 616-456-8795.

Clyde M. Metzger, III (Principal)
Daniel J. Niemann (Associate Principal)
Carole S. Empey (Principal)
Richard J. Joppich (Associate Principal)
Ellen M. Keefe-Garner (Associate Principal)

Judith A. Sherman
Frank A. Misuraca

For full biographical listings, see the Martindale-Hubbell Law Directory

MILLER, CANFIELD, PADDOCK AND STONE, P.L.C. (AV)

A Professional Limited Liability Company
Founded in 1852 by Sidney Davy Miller
101 North Main Street, Seventh Floor, 48104-1400
Telephone: 734-663-2445
Fax: 734-747-7147
URL: http://www.millercanfield.com
Detroit, Michigan Office: 150 West Jefferson, Suite 2500, 48226-4415.
Telephone: 313-963-6420.
Fax: 313-496-7500.
Cable Address: "Stem Detroit."
Troy, Michigan Office: 840 West Long Lake Road, Suite 200, 48098.
Telephone: 248-879-2000.
Fax: 248-879-2001.
Grand Rapids, Michigan Office: 99 Monroe, N.W., Suite 1200, 49503-2639.
Telephone: 616-454-8656.
Fax: 616-776-6322.
Howell, Michigan Office: 121 South Barnard Street, Suite 4, 48843-2305.
Telephone: 517-546-7600.
Telecopier: 517-546-6974.
Kalamazoo, Michigan Office: 444 West Michigan Avenue, 49007-3752.
Telephone: 616-381-7030.
Fax: 616-382-0244.
Lansing, Michigan Office: One Michigan Avenue, Suite 900, 48933-1609.
Telephone: 517-487-2070.
Fax: 517-374-6304.
Monroe, Michigan Office: 214 East Elm Avenue, Suite 100, 48162-2682.
Telephone: 734-243-2000.
Fax: 734-243-0901.
Washington, D.C. Office: 1900 K Street, N.W., Suite 1150. 20006.
Telephone: 202-429-5575; 785-0600.
Fax: 202-331-1118; 785-1234.
Pensacola, Florida Office: 25 West Cedar, 32501.
Telephone: 850-469-1088.
Fax: 850-432-0677.
New York, New York Office: 1450 Broadway, 41st Floor, 10018.
Telephone: 212-704-4400.
Fax: 212-704-4410.
Gdynia, Poland Office: UL. Slaska 21, 81-319.
Telephone: 011-485-831-2808.
Fax: 011-48-58-628 6411.
Warsaw, Poland Office: UL. Nowogrodzkall, 5th Floor, 00-513.
Telephone: 011-4822 529 0200.
Fax: 011-4822 529 0201.
Katowice, Poland Office: UL. Francuska 35/37, 40-027.
Telephone: 011 (48-32) 757-2414.
Fax: 011 (48-32) 757-2483.

(See Next Column)

PRINCIPALS OF FIRM

Robert E. Gilbert
Erik H. Serr
Allyn D. Kantor
Gregory L. Curtner
Bettye S. Elkins
Timothy D. Sochocki
David A. French
J. David Reck
David N. Parsigian
Charles A. Duerr, Jr.
Marta A. Manildi
Douglas M. Kilbourne
Roselyn R. Parmenter
John O. Renken

OF COUNSEL/SENIOR COUNSEL

Edmond F. DeVine
John B. DeVine
Paul R. Dimond

RESIDENT SENIOR ATTORNEY

Linda O. Goldberg

RESIDENT ASSOCIATES

Suzanne L. DeVine
Alice Censoplano Elkin
David L. Freedman

Representative Firm Clients: Chrysler Corporation; Comerica, Incorporated; City of Detroit, Michigan; Detroit Tigers, Inc.; First of Michigan; Ford Motor Company; Ford Motor Credit Company; Great Lakes Bancorp; Henry Ford Hospital; INVETECH Company.

For full biographical listings, see the Martindale-Hubbell Law Directory

PEAR SPERLING EGGAN & MUSKOVITZ, P.C. (AV)

Domino's Farms, 24 Frank Lloyd Wright Drive, 48105
Telephone: 734-665-4441
Fax: 734-665-8788
Email: peare@dominos.com
Ypsilanti, Michigan Offices: 5 South Washington Street.
Telephone: 734-483-3626 and 2164 Bellevue at Washtenaw.
Telephone: 734-483-7177.

Edwin L. Pear
Lawrence W. Sperling
Andrew M. Eggan
Melvin J. Muskovitz
Thomas E. Daniels
Joel F. Graziani
Paul R. Fransway
Francyne Stacey
Karl V. Fink
Scott H. Mandel
David E. Kempner
Jeffrey P. Thennisch

Counsel for: Domino's Pizza, Inc.; Townsend and Bottum, Inc.; Cleary College; Victory Lane Quick Oil Change Inc.; Citizens Banking Corp.; Washtenaw News Co., Inc.; Ann Arbor Transportation Authority; Meadowbrook Insurance Group; Michigan Municipal Liability & Property Pool.
Approved Attorneys for: Lawyers Title Insurance Corp.

For full biographical listings, see the Martindale-Hubbell Law Directory

BATTLE CREEK, Calhoun Co.

KREIS, ENDERLE, CALLANDER & HUDGINS, A PROFESSIONAL CORPORATION (AV)

One West Michigan Avenue, 49017
Telephone: 616-966-3000
Facsimile: 616-966-3022
Email: kech@kech.com *URL:* http://www.kech.com
Kalamazoo, Michigan Office: One Moorsbridge, P.O. Box 4010, 49003-4010.
Telephone: 616-324-3000.
Fax: 616-324-3010.

Russell A. Kreis (Resident, Kalamazoo Office)
Alan G. Enderle (Resident, Kalamazoo Office)
Douglas L. Callander (Resident, Kalamazoo Office)
C. Reid Hudgins III (Resident, Kalamazoo Office)
Robert B. Borsos (Resident, Kalamazoo Office)
Jeffrey C. O'Brien (Resident, Kalamazoo Office)
Stephen J. Hessen (Resident, Kalamazoo Office)
Jeffery S. Rubel (Resident, Kalamazoo Office)
Thomas G. King (Resident, Kalamazoo Office)
Stephen L. Simons
Mark E. Kreter
Daniel P. McGlinn (Resident, Kalamazoo Office)
Raymond C. Schultz (Resident, Kalamazoo Office)
Jeffrey D. Swenarton (Resident, Kalamazoo Office)
James C. Boerigter (Resident, Kalamazoo Office)
John F. Koryto (Resident, Kalamazoo Office)
Janice Roark Peters (Resident, Kalamazoo Office)
Matthew S. DePerno (Resident, Kalamazoo Office)
Annette D. Nickel (Resident, Kalamazoo Office)
Peter F. Davis (Resident, Kalamazoo Office)
Manuel R. Rupe (Resident, Kalamazoo Office)
Floyd E. Gates, Jr.

OF COUNSEL

James M. Sullivan

For full biographical listings, see the Martindale-Hubbell Law Directory

*BAY CITY,** Bay Co.

Braun Kendrick Finkbeiner PLC (AV)

201 Phoenix Building, P.O. Box 2039, 48708
Telephone: 517-895-8505
Telecopier: 517-895-8437
Email: ALBFIE@BKF-LAW.COM *URL:* http://www.bkf-law.com
Saginaw, Michigan Office: 101 N. Washington, Suite 812. 8th Floor Second National Bank Building.
Telephone: 517-753-3461.
Telecopier: 517-753-3951.
Saginaw Township, Michigan Office: 5800 Gratiot Road, Suite 107, P.O. Box 5169.
Telephone: 517-799-8692.
Fax: 517-799-4666.
Ann Arbor, Michigan Office: First National Building. 201 S. Main, Suite 700.
Telephone: 313-995-4100.
Telecopier: 313-995-4798.
Mt. Pleasant, Michigan Office: 805 North Brown.
Telephone: 517-775-7404.
Telecopier: 517-775-3764.

Ralph J. Isackson
Frank M. Quinn
Gregory E. Meter
Daniel S. Opperman
Gregory T. Demers
Jeffrey C. Wilson

Michael E. Wooley

Representative Clients: Bay Health Systems; Catholic Federal Credit Union; City of Saginaw; City of Vassar; City of Zilwaukee; Corporate Service; Cox Cable.

For full biographical listings, see the Martindale-Hubbell Law Directory

BIRMINGHAM, Oakland Co.

Hyman Lippitt, P.C. (AV)

185 Oakland Avenue, Suite 300, 48009
Telephone: 248-646-8292
Facsimile: 248-646-8375
Email: hymalipp@tir.com

J. Leonard Hyman
Norman L. Lippitt
Douglas A. Hyman
Brian D. O'Keefe
H. Joel Newman
Nazli G. Sater
Kenneth F. Neuman
Terry S. Givens
Paul J. Fischer
John A. Sellers
Robert H. Lippitt
Roger L. Myers
Sally A. Rutledge
Joseph Pia
John P. Gonway
Leif K. Anderson
Jennifer S. Gold
Julie Lyons Kosovec
Dawn S. Spratley
Michael T. Price

For full biographical listings, see the Martindale-Hubbell Law Directory

David A. Sebastian (AV)

401 South Old Woodward Avenue, Suite 430, 48009
Telephone: 248-433-1444
Fax: 248-594-4477
Email: sebastlaw@aol.com *URL:* http://www.lawyers.com/sebastian

For full biographical listings, see the Martindale-Hubbell Law Directory

BLOOMFIELD HILLS, Oakland Co.

Adkison, Need, Green & Allen (AV)

1533 North Woodward Avenue, Suite 210, 48304
Telephone: 248-540-7400
Fax: 248-540-7401
URL: http://www.adkisonneed.com

MEMBERS OF FIRM

Phillip G. Adkison
Gregory K. Need
Paul Green
Kelly A. Allen

ASSOCIATES

Annette J. Benson
Miriam Blanks-Smart
Kevin M. Chudler
Richard D. Kuhn, Jr.

Nicki L. Weisberger

OF COUNSEL

John M. Fuleras
Thomas R. Curran, Jr.

For full biographical listings, see the Martindale-Hubbell Law Directory

Buesser, Buesser, Black, Lynch, Fryhoff & Graham, P.C. (AV)

505 North Woodward Avenue, Suite 1000, 48304
Telephone: 248-642-7880
Telecopier: 248-642-9319
Email: jimw@buesserlaw.com *URL:* http://www.buesserlaw.com

(See Next Column)

Frederick G. Buesser, Jr. (1916-1993)
William R. Buesser
Michael J. Black
William O. Lynch
Timothy T. Fryhoff
Ronald F. Graham
L. James Wilson

Neil K. Disney
Ronald C. Paul

Diane M. Buettner

OF COUNSEL

Charles E. Blank
Susan E. Cohen

Representative Clients: Wayne County Medical Society; Frances P. Rhoades Memorial Foundation; Detroit Country Day School; Air-Way Manufacturing Co.; American States University Co.; Holiday Inns, Inc.; The Promus Companies Incorporated; Premo Pharmaceutical Co.; Citizens Insurance Co. of America; Michigan River Corp.

For full biographical listings, see the Martindale-Hubbell Law Directory

Dickinson Wright PLLC (AV)

525 North Woodward Avenue, Suite 2000, 48304-2970
Telephone: 248-433-7200
Facsimile: 248-433-7274
URL: http://www.dickinson-wright.com
Detroit, Michigan Office: 500 Woodward Avenue, Suite 4000.
Telephone: 313-223-3500.
Facsimile: 313-223-3598.
Grand Rapids, Michigan Office: 200 Ottawa Avenue, N.W., Suite 900.
Telephone: 616-458-1300.
Facsimile: 616-458-6753.
Lansing, Michigan Office: Suite 200, 215 South Washington Square.
Telephone: 517-371-1730.
Facsimile: 517-487-4700.
Washington, D.C. Office: Suite 800, 1901 L Street, N.W.
Telephone: 202-457-0160.
Facsimile: 202-659-1559.

MEMBERS

Maureen H. Burke
Charles F. Clippert
Roger H. Cummings
Stephen E. Dawson
Joseph W. DeLave
Sara Anne Engle
Judith E. Gowing
Deborah L. Grace
Henry M. Grix
Charles T. Harris
Robert B. Hotchkiss
Robert P. Hurlbert
Thomas H. Kosik
John A. Krsul, Jr.
Robert A. LaBelle
Elise S. Levasseur
Cynthia A. Moore
John H. Norris
Edward H. Pappas
Gregory J. Parry
Richard W. Paul
Robert V. Peterson
Elizabeth M. Pezzetti
Amy A. Stawski

Larry J. Stringer

CONSULTING MEMBER

Ward Randol, Jr.

OF COUNSEL

Nancy A. Downie
Paul T. Fitzpatrick
Hanley M. Gurwin
Bethany E. Hawkins
Douglas L. Mann
Thomas D. McLennan
Zan M. Nicolli
Michele Kozlowicz Reilly
John D. Stout
John A. Ziegler, Jr.

RESIDENT ASSOCIATES

Karen B. Benjamin
Liza Cheuk May Chan
Linda Kuiper Ford
Judith Fertel Layne
Ashley E. Lowe
Suzanne T. Orlowski

Daniel D. Quick

LEGAL SUPPORT PERSONNEL

JAPANESE CLIENT SUPPORT

Yukiko Sato (Director, Japanese Business)

For full biographical listings, see the Martindale-Hubbell Law Directory

Dykema Gossett PLLC (AV)

1577 North Woodward Avenue Suite 300, 48304-2820
Telephone: 248-203-0700
Fax: 248-203-0763
Email: mstarrs@dykema.com *URL:* http://www.dykema.com
Ann Arbor, Michigan Office: 315 East Eisenhower Parkway, Suite 100, 48108-3306.
Telephone: 734-214-7660.
Fax: 734-214-7696.
Chicago, Illinois Office: 55 East Monroe Street, Suite 3050, 60603-5709.
Telephone: 312-551-4900.
Fax: 312-551-4919.
Detroit, Michigan Office: 400 Renaissance Center, 48243-1668.
Telephone: 313-568-6800.
Fax: 313-568-6545.
Grand Rapids, Michigan Office: Suite 700, 300 Ottawa Avenue, N.W., 49503-2304.
Telephone: 616-776-7500.
Fax: 616-776-7573.
Lansing, Michigan Office: 800 Michigan National Tower, 48933-1707.
Telephone: 517-374-9100.
Fax: 517-374-9191.

(See Next Column)

DYKEMA GOSSETT PLLC, *Bloomfield Hills—Continued*

Washington, D.C. Office: Franklin Square, Suite 300 West, 1300 I Street, N.W., 20005-3306.
Telephone: 202-522-8600.
Fax: 202-522-8669.
Affiliated Office: Via Matconi, 3, 40122 Bologna, Italy.
Telephone: 011-39-51-228222.
Fax: 011-39-51-6593580.

RESIDENT MEMBERS

Maria B. Abrahamsen
Robert A. Berlow
Bowden V. Brown
B. Kingsley Buhl
Donald M. Crawford
Michael G. Cumming
Robert L. Duty
Fred J. Fechheimer
Alan M. Greene
Dennis M. Haffey (Member in Charge)
Joseph H. Hickey
Kevin M. Hinman
Craig L. John
Louis W. Kasischke
Robert L. Kelly
Gregory M. Kopacz
Gerald T. Lievois
Stuart D. Logan
Howard N. Luckoff
Barbara Goldman Mandell
D. Richard McDonald
James D. Obermanns
Marilyn A. Peters
Ronald L. Rose
Charles R. Rutherford
Rex E. Schlaybaugh, Jr.
Thomas B. Spillane, Jr.
Mark H. Sutton

RETIRED MEMBER

Donald E. Shely

OF COUNSEL

Anthony Ilardi, Jr.

RESIDENT ASSOCIATES

David A. Antonelli
Kimberly A. Bickersteth
John F. Buckert
Brendan J. Cahill
Amy Lynn Carson
Jennifer M. Crawford
Douglas J. Fryer
Kyle R. Hauberg
William L. Huebner
William F. Kolakowski III
Andrew J. Lusk
Michael M. Metz
Douglas S. Parker
Maryann Pierce Perttunen
Karen R. Pifer
Stephen L. Tupper
Melanie Mayo West

For full biographical listings, see the Martindale-Hubbell Law Directory

HOWARD & HOWARD ATTORNEYS, P.C. (AV)

The Pinehurst Office Center, Suite 101, 1400 North Woodward Avenue, 48304-2855
Telephone: 248-645-1483
Telecopier: 248-645-1568
Kalamazoo, Michigan Office: The Michigan Building, Suite 200, 100 Portage Street.
Telephone: 616-382-1483.
Telecopier: 616-382-1568.
Lansing, Michigan Office: The Phoenix Building, Suite 500, 222 Washington Square, North.
Telephone: 517-485-1483.
Telecopier: 517-485-1568.
Peoria, Illinois Office: One Technology Plaza, Suite 600, 211 Fulton Street.
Telephone: 309-672-1483.
Telecopier: 309-672-1568.

John J. Andler
Brian R. Balow
James T. Bork
John E. Carlson
Philip T. Carter
Carlene A. Caudill
Anthony P. Cho
Ronald R. Cook
Michael G. Cruse
Chris T. Danikolas
Mark A. Davis
Charles E. Dunn
Gregory L. Epstein
Carol A. Friend
Kirkland W. Garey
David J. Gaskey
William S. Gottschalk
Samuel J. Haidle
John G. Hayward
Christopher R. Herter
William H. Honaker
Shannon A. Hunt
Melanye K. Johnson
Robert B. Johnston
Douglas R. Kelly
Daniel N. King
Jon H. Kingsepp
Steven C. Kohl
Timothy E. Kraepel
Kerrie A. Laba
David B. Lipski
Patrick M. McCarthy
Rhonda L. McCoy-Pfau
Harold W. Milton, Jr.
Robert D. Mollhagen
C. Douglas Moran
Bruce N. Moss
Mahesh K. Nayak
Theodore W. Olds III
Susan E. Padley
Gary A. Peters
Brad A. Rayle
Brian J. Renaud
Rhonda L. Ross
Jeffrey A. Sadowski
Lee A. Sartori
Paula L. Schneider
Robert L. Schwartz
Raymond E. Scott
Randall L. Shoemaker
Jon Robert Steiger
Gina M. Torielli
Donald F. Tucker
Thomas H. Walters
James C. Wickens
David L. Wisz
Timothy M. Wittebort
John E. Young
Marla Gottlieb Zwas

Representative Clients: National City Corp.; Kmart Corp.; Daimler Chrysler Corporation; Indian Head Industries; Meritor, Inc.; Coopers & Lybrand; Champion International.

(See Next Column)

For full biographical listings, see the Martindale-Hubbell Law Directory

*DETROIT,** Wayne Co.

BODMAN, LONGLEY & DAHLING LLP (AV)

34th Floor 100 Renaissance Center, 48243
Telephone: 313-259-7777
Fax: 313-393-7579
Email: info@bodmanlongley.com *URL:* http://www.bodmanlongley.com
Troy, Michigan Office: Suite 2020, 755 West Big Beaver Road.
Telephone: 248-362-2110.
Fax: 248-244-0780.
Ann Arbor, Michigan Office: 110 Miller, Suite 300.
Telephone: 734-761-3780.
Fax: 734-930-2494.
Northern Michigan Office: 229 Court Street, P.O. Box 405, Cheboygan.
Telephone: 231-627-4351.
Fax: 231-627-2802.

MEMBERS OF FIRM

Henry E. Bodman (1874-1963)
Clifford B. Longley (1888-1954)
Louis F. Dahling (1892-1992)
Richard D. Rohr
Carson C. Grunewald
Walter O. Koch (Troy Office)
Michael B. Lewiston
George D. Miller, Jr.
Mark W. Griffin (Ann Arbor Office)
Thomas A. Roach (Ann Arbor Office)
Kenneth R. Lango (Troy Office)
James T. Heimbuch
Herold McC. Deason
James A. Smith
James R. Buschmann
George G. Kemsley
Joseph N. Brown
David M. Hempstead
Joseph J. Kochanek
Randolph S. Perry
James J. Walsh
David G. Chardavoyne
David W. Hipp
Robert G. Brower
Larry R. Shulman
Charles N. Raimi
Terrence B. Larkin (Troy Office)
Thomas Van Dusen (Troy Office)
Fredrick J. Dindoffer
Robert J. Diehl, Jr.
John C. Cashen (Troy Office)
Lloyd C. Fell (Cheboygan Office)
F. Thomas Lewand
Michael A. Stack (Cheboygan Office)
Kathleen A. Lieder (Cheboygan Office)
Karen L. Piper
Harvey W. Berman (Ann Arbor Office)
Barbara A. Bowman
R. Craig Hupp
Lawrence P. Hanson (Cheboygan Office)
Christopher J. Dine
Jerold Lax (Ann Arbor Office)
Diane L. Akers
Ralph E. McDowell
Susan M. Kornfield (Ann Arbor Office)
Stephen I. Greenhalgh
Kathleen O'Callaghan Hickey
Thomas J. Tallerico
Dennis J. Levasseur
David P. Larsen
Gary D. Reeves (Troy Office)
Barnett Jay Colvin
David W. Barton (Cheboygan Office)
Sandra L. Sorini (Ann Arbor Office)
Stephen K. Postema (Ann Arbor Office)
Bonnie S. Sherr
Marc M. Bakst
Nicholas P. Scavone, Jr.
Carl F. Stafford
Sol M. Friedman
Jeffrey G. Raphelson

COUNSEL

Alfred C. Wortley, Jr.
Robert A. Nitschke
John S. Dobson (Ann Arbor Office)
Lewis A. Rockwell
James C. Conboy, Jr. (Cheboygan Office)
David J. Dykhouse

SENIOR ATTORNEYS

Anthony T. Finn
Richard Barr West (Cheboygan Office)

ASSOCIATES

Deanna L. Dixon
Timothy R. Damschroder (Ann Arbor Office)
David A. Shand (Ann Arbor Office)
Laurie E. Phelan
Andrew Z. Spilkin
Sarah Heisler Gidley
Michael J. Laramie (Troy Office)
David L. Kasper (Troy Office)
Cortney E. Goldberg
Amy J. Durant (Cheboygan Office)
Andrew H. Curoe
Courtland W. Anderson (Ann Arbor Office)
Alan N. Harris (Ann Arbor Office)
Rachelle Propson Tyshka
Melissa A. Lewis
Thomas G. Cecil
Christene M. Devitt (Cheboygan Office)
Robert P. Tiplady
Gene P. Bowen (Troy Office)
Scott P. Gyorke
Margaret M. Wood
Brian R. Trumbauer
Forrest O. Dillon
Christopher P. Mazzoli (Troy Office)
Charles S. Hegarty
Emily M. Kellndorfer (Ann Arbor Office)
Kimberley R. Crouch
David M. Walker
Kurt M. Brauer
J. Adam Behrendt
Erik S. Prater
David C. Reese
Ursula A. Petrozzi

Representative Clients: Archdiocese of Detroit; Comerica Bank; The Detroit Lions, Inc.; Ford Estates; Lear Corp.; Charles Stewart Mott Foundation; Norfolk Southern Corporation; Panhandle Eastern Corporation; State Farm Insurance Companies.

(See Next Column)

BODMAN, LONGLEY & DAHLING LLP—*Continued*

For full biographical listings, see the Martindale-Hubbell Law Directory

BOOTHMAN, HEBERT & ELLER, P.C. (AV)

Marquette Building, 243 West Congress, Suite 950, 48226
Telephone: 313-964-0150
Fax: 313-964-2226
Email: boothman@mail.mich.com

Dale L. Hebert
Richard C. Boothman
Gary S. Eller

Edward C. Reynolds, Jr.
Marta J. Hoffman

Representative Clients: University of Michigan; Mutual Insurance Corporation of America; Emergency Physicians Medical Group; Pronational; HCR Manor Care, Inc.
Reference: Comerica Bank-Detroit.

For full biographical listings, see the Martindale-Hubbell Law Directory

BRADY, HATHAWAY, BRADY & BRETZ, PROFESSIONAL CORPORATION (AV)

1330 Buhl Building, 48226-3602
Telephone: 313-965-3700
Telecopier: 313-965-2830
Email: brady@bradyhathaway.com

John F. Brady
Thomas M. J. Hathaway
Thomas P. Brady
Daniel J. Bretz
Connie M. Cessante
David A. Hardesty
Paul W. Coughenour
Jeffrey A. Steele
Tracy A. Leahy

David M. Cessante

Representative Clients: Beam Stream, Inc.; Bundy Corporation; Energy Conversion Devices, Inc.; Schering Corporation; Warner-Lambert; Wolverine Technologies; ABB Environmental Services.

For full biographical listings, see the Martindale-Hubbell Law Directory

CLARK HILL PLC (AV)

500 Woodward Avenue, Suite 3500, 48226-3435
Telephone: 313-965-8300
Facsimile: 313-965-8252
Email: email@clarkhill.com *URL:* http://www.clarkhill.com
Birmingham, Michigan Office: 255 S. Old Woodward Avenue, Third Floor 48009-6179.
Telephone: 248-642-9692.
Facsimile: 248-642-2174.
Okemos, Michigan Office: 2455 Woodlake Circle, 48864-5941.
Telephone: 517-381-9193.
Facsimile: 517-381-0268.

Robert B. Webster (Resident, Birmingham Office)
George N. Bashara, Jr.
John F. Burns
William B. Dunn
J. Walker Henry
D. Kerry Crenshaw
Timothy W. Mast (Resident, Birmingham Office)
Douglas J. Rasmussen
Douglas H. West (Resident, Birmingham Office)
Timothy D. Wittlinger
Frederick R. Damm
David M. Hayes
J. Thomas Lenga
Thomas F. Sweeney (Resident, Birmingham Office)
David E. Nims, III
Roderick S. Coy (Resident, Lansing Office)
James E. Brenner
P. Robert Brown, Jr.
Robert L. Weyhing
Thomas S. Nowinski
Richard C. Sanders
Dennis G. Bonucchi (Resident, Birmingham Office)
Peter D. Holmes
David M. Lawson (Resident, Birmingham Office)
Frank T. Mamat
Robert R. Cleary
Robert A. W. Strong (Resident, Birmingham Office)
Mark W. McInerney
Judith Greenstone Miller (Resident, Birmingham Office)
Kevin S. Hendrick
William A. Moore
Charles H. Polzin (Resident, Birmingham Office)
Daniel J. Scully, Jr.
Duane L. Tarnacki
Kevin M. Bernys (Resident, Birmingham Office)
Joseph A. Bonventre (Resident, Birmingham Office)
Peter A. Jackson
Ada Snyder Kerwin (Resident, Birmingham Office)
Cynthia L.M. Johnson
Timothy M. Koltun
Rachelle G. Silberberg
Michael J. Sullivan
Reginald G. Dozier
Daniel H. Minkus (Resident, Birmingham Office)
Dorothy Hanigan Basmaji (Resident, Birmingham Office)
Charles G. Goedert (Resident, Birmingham Office)
John J. Hern, Jr.
John E. Berg
Edward C. Hammond (Resident, Birmingham Office)
Andrea M. Kanski
J. Thomas MacFarlane (Resident, Birmingham Office)
Paul E. Scheidemantel
Thomas M. Dixon
Elizabeth Jolliffe Basten

(See Next Column)

Edward J. Hood
Kevin H. Breck (Resident, Birmingham Office)
Joseph E. Turner
Barbara A. Van Zanten
David A. Breuch

OF COUNSEL

John C. Donnelly
Charles M. Bayer
Martin C. Oetting
David P. Wood
Dwight H. Vincent
Leonard W. Smith
Ralph H. Houghton, Jr. (Resident, Birmingham Office)
Richard C. Marsh

SENIOR ASSOCIATE

Thomas E. Maier (Resident, Lansing Office)

Mary Ray Brophy (Resident, Birmingham Office)
Mary C. Dirkes
George M. Mesrey
Randi P. Glanz (Resident, Birmingham Office)
David Scott Mendelson (Resident, Birmingham Office)
John T. Clappison
Lira A. Johnson
Paul J. Smothers (Resident, Birmingham Office)
John P. Hensien
Christopher A. McMican (Resident, Birmingham Office)
Danon D. Goodrum
Julie A. Lawson
Louise B. Sable (Resident, Birmingham Office)
Evelyn L. Sullen
Gerald E. Szpotek, Jr. (Resident, Birmingham Office)
Catherine H. Finn
Anthony A. Agosta
Susan M. Bisio
Sean P. Byrne
David C. Kocab
Daniel H. Serlin (Resident, Birmingham Office)
Yvette Mari VanRiper
Brian M. Ziff
Robert A. LeFevre (Resident, Lansing Office)
Haran C. Rashes (Resident, Lansing Office)
C. J. Keller Smith
Aaron Craig Thomas
Jack Vanhoorelbeke

For full biographical listings, see the Martindale-Hubbell Law Directory

DICKINSON WRIGHT PLLC (AV)

500 Woodward Avenue, Suite 4000, 48226-3425
Telephone: 313-223-3500
Facsimile: 313-223-3598
URL: http://www.dickinson-wright.com
Bloomfield Hills, Michigan Office: 525 North Woodward Avenue, Suite 2000.
Telephone: 248-433-7200.
Facsimile: 248-433-7274.
Grand Rapids, Michigan Office: 200 Ottawa Avenue, N.W., Suite 900.
Telephone: 616-458-1300.
Facsimile: 616-458-6753.
Lansing, Michigan Office: Suite 200, 215 South Washington Square.
Telephone: 517-371-1730.
Facsimile: 517-487-4700.
Washington, D.C. Office: Suite 800, 1901 L Street, N.W.
Telephone: 202-457-0160.
Facsimile: 202-659-1559.

Selden S. Dickinson (1892-1964)
Edward P. Wright (1894-1962)
Richard C. Van Dusen (1925-1991)

MEMBERS OF FIRM

Harolyn D. Beverly
Richard M. Bolton
Andrew S. Boyce
Richard L. Braun, II
William T. Burgess
Lawrence G. Campbell
James N. Candler, Jr.
Margaret A. Coughlin
Julia Donovan Darlow
Bernadette M. Dennehy
Mark Alan Densmore
David R. Deromedi
Terence M. Donnelly
Barbara Hughes Erard
John A. Everhardus
K. Scott Hamilton
Michael C. Hammer
Thomas D. Hammerschmidt, Jr.
Craig W. Hammond
Verne C. Hampton, II
Mark R. High
Steven H. Hilfinger
Edgar C. Howbert
Timothy H. Howlett
Maurice G. Jenkins
W. Anthony Jenkins
Robert S. Krause
Monica J. Labe
Kathleen A. Lang
John K. Lawrence
Keith J. Lerminiaux
Joseph C. Marshall, III
Kenneth J. McIntyre
Thomas G. McNeill
David L. Morrow (Not admitted in MI)
Sharon R. Newlon
Francis R. Ortiz
James A. Plemmons
Claudia Rast
Mark K. Riashi
Douglas D. Roche
Jeffrey S. Ruprich
James A. Samborn
Jerome M. Schwartz
John E. S. Scott
Colleen M. Shevnock
William P. Shield, Jr.
Herbert G. Sparrow, III
Bruce C. Thelen
Louis Theros
Michelle V. Thurber
Michael Gary Vartanian
Richard A. Wilhelm
J. Bryan Williams
Paul M. Wyzgoski
Thomas V. Yates

CONSULTING MEMBERS

Fred W. Freeman
Charles R. Kinnaird
Patrick J. Ledwidge
Russell A. McNair, Jr.
Charles R. Moon

OF COUNSEL

Thomas G. Peck

(See Next Column)

DICKINSON WRIGHT PLLC, *Detroit—Continued*

ASSOCIATES

Patricia M. Adler
Brian M. Akkashian
Paul R. Bernard
Robert F. Boesiger
Shari M. Borsini
Michael G. Brady
Bruce R. Byrd
Dawn R. Copley
Ann-Jeannine Foeller
Rick A. Haberman
Matthew F. Hiser
Scott A. MacGriff
Leah H. Maguire
Brian Martinuzzi
Amy E. Metz
Jodi M. Schebel
Scott T. Seabolt
Rachele L. Szot
Andrew J. Tavi
Joseph P. Tocco
David F. Viviano
Peter H. Webster
Rhonda D. Welburn
Kathryn S. Wood

LEGAL SUPPORT PERSONNEL

CHIEF INFORMATION OFFICER

Michael W. Harnish

JAPANESE CLIENT SUPPORT

Yukiko Sato (Director, Japanese Business) (Bloomfield Hills Office)

Representative Client: Mich Con.

For full biographical listings, see the Martindale-Hubbell Law Directory

DYKEMA GOSSETT PLLC (AV)

400 Renaissance Center, 48243-1668
Telephone: 313-568-6800
Fax: 313-568-6545
Email: mstarrs@dykema.com *URL:* http://www.dykema.com
Ann Arbor, Michigan Office: 315 East Eisenhower Parkway, Suite 100, 48108-3306.
Telephone: 734-214-7660.
Fax: 734-214-7696.
Bloomfield Hills, Michigan Office: 1577 North Woodward Avenue, Suite 300, 48304-2820.
Telephone: 248-203-0700.
Fax: 248-203-0763.
Chicago, Illinois Office: 55 East Monroe Street, Suite 3050, 60603-5709.
Telephone: 312-551-4900.
Fax: 312-551-4919.
Grand Rapids, Michigan Office: Suite 700, 300 Ottawa Avenue, N.W., 49503-2304.
Telephone: 616-776-7500.
Fax: 616-776-7573.
Lansing, Michigan Office: 800 Michigan National Tower, 48933-1707.
Telephone: 517-374-9100.
Fax: 517-374-9191.
Washington, D.C. Office: Franklin Square, Suite 300 West, 1300 I Street, N.W., 20005-3306.
Telephone: 202-522-8600.
Fax: 202-522-8669.
Affiliated Office: Via Matconi, 3, 40122 Bologna, Italy.
Telephone: 011-39-51-228222.
Fax: 011-39-51-6593580.

MEMBERS OF FIRM

Maria B. Abrahamsen (Resident at Bloomfield Hills Office)
James C. Adams (Resident at Ann Arbor Office)
Ted T. Amsden
Susan Artinian
George W. Ash
Joseph C. Basta
Robert A. Berlow (Resident at Bloomfield Hills Office)
J. Michael Bernard
Charles R. Bernardini (Not admitted in MI; Resident at Washington, D.C. and Chicago Offices)
Bowden V. Brown (Resident at Bloomfield Hills Office)
B. Kingsley Buhl (Resident at Bloomfield Hills Office)
James M. Cameron, Jr. (Resident at Ann Arbor Office)
Timothy K. Carroll
William H. Carroll (Not admitted in MI; Resident at Washington, D.C. Office)
James W. Collier
Laurence D. Connor
Michael P. Cooney
Margaret A. Costello
Sandra M. Cotter (Resident at Lansing Office)
Donald M. Crawford (Resident at Bloomfield Hills Office)
Michael G. Cumming (Resident at Bloomfield Hills Office)
Bruce G. Davis (Resident at Lansing Office)
Marie R. Deveney (Resident at Ann Arbor Office)
Steven A. Diaz (Not admitted in MI; Resident at Washington, D.C. Office)
Dennis M. Doherty
Alan R. Dominick (Resident at Lansing Office)
Phyllis Donaldson-Adams (Resident at Ann Arbor Office)
David E. Doran (Resident at Grand Rapids Office)
Robert L. Duty (Resident at Bloomfield Hills Office)
Laura J. Eisele
James M. Elsworth
John A. Entenman
Joseph K. Erhardt
Albert Ernst (Resident at Lansing Office)
Fred J. Fechheimer (Resident at Bloomfield Hills Office)
J. Kay Felt
John A. Ferroli (Resident at Grand Rapids Office)
William E. Fisher
Jane Forbes
Robert J. Franzinger
Martin Jay Galvin

(See Next Column)

MEMBERS OF FIRM (Continued)

Grant P. Gilezan
Julia A. Goatley (Resident at Lansing Office)
Alan M. Greene (Resident at Bloomfield Hills Office)
James P. Greene (Resident at Ann Arbor Office)
Steven E. Grob
Edward A. Groobert (Not admitted in MI; Resident at Washington, D.C. Office)
Dennis M. Haffey (Member in Charge of Bloomfield Hills Office)
Mark E. Hauck
Joseph H. Hickey (Resident at Bloomfield Hills Office)
Patrick F. Hickey
Kevin M. Hinman (Resident at Bloomfield Hills Office)
J. Timothy Hobbs (Not admitted in MI; Resident at Washington, D.C. Office)
E. Edward Hood (Member in Charge of Ann Arbor Office)
Kathryn J. Humphrey
Margaret Adams Hunter
Mark D. Jacobs
Craig L. John (Resident at Bloomfield Hills Office)
Zora E. Johnson
Louis W. Kasischke (Resident at Bloomfield Hills Office)
Barbara A. Kaye
Joel D. Kellman
Robert L. Kelly (Resident at Bloomfield Hills Office)
Sharon M. Kelly (Resident at Ann Arbor Office)
Mary Steck Kershner
James P. Kiefer (Resident at Lansing Office)
Gregory M. Kopacz (Resident at Bloomfield Hills Office)
Kathrin E. Kudner
Nicole Yvette Lamb-Hale
Richard J. Landau (Resident at Ann Arbor Office)
Mark C. Larson
Michael A. Lesha
Kathleen McCree Lewis
Gerald T. Lievois (Resident at Bloomfield Hills Office)
Seth M. Lloyd
Stuart D. Logan (Resident at Bloomfield Hills Office)
Howard N. Luckoff (Resident at Bloomfield Hills Office)
D. Biard MacGuineas (Not admitted in MI; Resident at Washington, D.C. Office)
Barbara Goldman Mandell (Resident at Bloomfield Hills Office)
Stewart L. Mandell
Richard M. Matthews
Bonnie L. Mayfield
Jerome I. Maynard (Member in Charge of Chicago Office)
Richard J. McClear
Debra M. McCulloch
Bruce A. McDonald (Not admitted in MI; Resident at Washington, D.C. Office)
D. Richard McDonald (Resident at Bloomfield Hills Office)
Thomas J. McGraw
Andrew J. McGuinness (Resident at Ann Arbor Office)
Richard D. McLellan
Patrick E. Mears (Resident at Grand Rapids Office)
Derek I. Meier
Mark A. Metz
Fredrick M. Miller
Aleksandra A. Miziolek
Stephen S. Muhich (Resident at Grand Rapids Office)
Janet L. Neary (Resident at Ann Arbor Office)
James D. Obermanns (Resident at Bloomfield Hills Office)
Theodore H. Oldham
Howard E. O'Leary, Jr. (Resident at Washington, D.C. Office)
Judy A. O'Neill
Brian J. Page (Resident at Grand Rapids Office)
William J. Perrone (Resident at Lansing Office)
Marilyn A. Peters (Resident at Bloomfield Hills Office)
Cameron H. Piggott
Richard E. Rabbideau
Arthur F. Radke (Resident at Chicago Office)
Paul R. Rentenbach
Joseph A. Ritok, Jr.
Ronald L. Rose (Resident at Bloomfield Hills Office)
Charles R. Rutherford (Resident at Bloomfield Hills Office)
Suzanne Sahakian
Ronald J. Santo
Rosemary G. Schikora
Rex E. Schlaybaugh, Jr. (Resident at Bloomfield Hills Office)
Lloyd A. Semple (Chairman of the Firm)
Todd J. Shoudy
Lori M. Silsbury (Resident at Lansing Office)
Thomas B. Spillane, Jr. (Resident at Bloomfield Hills Office)
Wilfred A. Steiner, Jr.
Daniel J. Stephenson (Resident at Ann Arbor Office)
Mark H. Sutton (Resident at Bloomfield Hills Office)
Pierre C. Talbert, Jr. (Not admitted in MI; Resident at Chicago Office)
Kent P. Talcott (Resident at Ann Arbor Office)
Roger K. Timm
Ronald J. Torbert
David L. Tripp
Thomas Stephen Vaughn
Jill M. Wheaton
Sherrill D. Wolford
Fred L. Woodworth (Member in Charge of Washington, D.C. Office)
Daniel G. Wyllie
Donald S. Young
Stephen H. Zimmerman (Resident at Lansing and Washington, D.C. Offices)
Frank K. Zinn

OF COUNSEL

Hilary Stephen Cairnie (Not admitted in MI; Resident at Washington, D.C. Office)
Anthony Ilardi, Jr. (Resident at Bloomfield Hills Office)
Paul G. Neilan (Resident at Chicago Office)
Darrell W. Pierce (Resident at Chicago Office)

RETIRED MEMBERS

James T. Blake
Earl R. Boonstra
James W. Draper
Raymond T. Huetteman, Jr. (Resident at Ann Arbor Office)
Donald E. Shely (Resident at Bloomfield Hills Office)
Paul H. Townsend, Jr.
James D. Tracy
Paul R. Trigg, Jr.

(See Next Column)

DYKEMA GOSSETT PLLC—*Continued*

Raymond K. Dykema (1889-1971)
Elroy O. Jones (1889-1973)
Renville Wheat (1893-1968)
James H. Spencer (1908-1970)
Nathan B. Goodnow (1906-1985)
William T. Gossett (1904-1998)

ASSOCIATES

Jennifer G. Anderson (Resident at Ann Arbor Office)
Peter M. Angelini, Jr.
David A. Antonelli (Resident at Bloomfield Hills Office)
Kimberly A. Bickersteth (Resident at Bloomfield Hills Office)
John F. Birmingham, Jr.
Thomas S. Bishoff
Deric J. Bomar
Scott D. Broekstra (Resident at Grand Rapids Office)
John M. Brown (Resident at Lansing Office)
John F. Buckert (Resident at Bloomfield Hills Office)
Brendan J. Cahill (Resident at Bloomfield Hills Office)
Amy Lynn Carson (Resident at Bloomfield Hills Office)
Eric Thomas Carver
Jennifer M. Crawford (Resident at Bloomfield Hills Office)
Joi M. Cunningham
Christopher T. Dement (Resident at Grand Rapids Office)
Mark E. Derwent (Resident at Grand Rapids Office)
Michael P. Farrell (Resident at Grand Rapids Office)
Sherrie L. Farrell
Kara Lynn S. Ferrara
Adam M. Fishkind
Cheryl Anne Fletcher
Douglas J. Fryer (Resident at Bloomfield Hills Office)
Kevin P. Fularczyk
David W. Geiss
Gail A. Goldfarb
David G. Hagens (Resident at Grand Rapids Office)
Ronald E. Hall, Jr.
Mariam M. Harb
Melissa Davis Hartranft
Kyle R. Hauberg (Resident at Bloomfield Office)
James F. Hermon
Robert M. Horwitz
Jennifer J. Howe (Resident at Chicago Office)
William L. Huebner (Resident at Bloomfield Hills Office)
Benjamin W. Jeffers
Judy Parker Jenkins (Not admitted in MI; Resident at Washington, D.C. Office)
Christopher Kelly (Not admitted in MI; Resident at Washington, D.C. Office)
David C. Koelsch
Jin-Kyu Koh
William F. Kolakowski III (Resident at Bloomfield Hills Office)
Jeffrey S. Kopp
Joanne R. Lax
Krista L. Lenart (Resident at Ann Arbor Office)
Michelle A. LeVeque (Resident at Grand Rapids Office)
Steven C. Liedel (Resident at Lansing Office)
William Lee Logan, III (Resident at Lansing Office)
Eric C. Lund (Not admitted in MI; Resident at Grand Rapids Office)
Andrew J. Lusk (Resident at Bloomfield Hills Office)
Mary T. Malpass
Allison L. Mann (Resident at Ann Arbor Office)
Michael M. Metz (Resident at Bloomfield Hills Office)
Heidi A. Naasko
James D. Oegema (Resident at Lansing Office)
Christopher S. Olson
Douglas S. Parker (Resident at Bloomfield Hills Office)
Maryann Pierce Perttunen (Resident at Bloomfield Hills Office)
Mark W. Peters
Karen R. Pifer (Resident at Bloomfield Hills Office)
Claire S. Pouget (Resident at Ann Arbor Office)
Kathleen A. Reed
Kristan L. Richardson (Resident at Lansing Office)
Sharon A. Salinas (Not admitted in MI; Resident at Chicago Office)
William R. Schikora
James A. Shepherd (Resident at Grand Rapids Office)
Jeffrey N. Silveri (Resident at Ann Arbor Office)
Bradley L. Smith (Resident at Ann Arbor Office)
Christine Mason Soneral (Resident at Lansing Office)
Sharon S. Spungen (Resident at Grand Rapids Office)
Steven A. Susswein (Resident at Ann Arbor Office)
Andrea L. Szymanski
William M. Thacker (Resident at Ann Arbor Office)
Stephen L. Tupper (Resident at Bloomfield Hills Office)
Marina P. Vandenbrink
Mark David van der Laan (Resident at Grand Rapids Office)
Lisa M. Waits (Resident at Ann Arbor Office)
Melanie Mayo West (Resident at Bloomfield Hills Office)
Angela R. White (Resident at Ann Arbor Office)
Katherine M. White
Marvin Douglas Wilder
Tiffany N. Wilder
Wendell Alan Wilk (Resident at Lansing Office)
Leonard C. Wolfe (Resident at Lansing Office)
Kevin M. Zielke
Nicholas G. Zotos

For full biographical listings, see the Martindale-Hubbell Law Directory

FILDEW HINKS, P.L.L.C. (AV)

3600 Penobscot Building, 645 Griswold Street, 48226-4291
Telephone: 313-961-9700
Facsimile: 313-961-0754

(See Next Column)

MEMBERS OF FIRM

Stanley L. Fildew (1896-1978)
Frank T. Hinks (1887-1974)
Richard E. Hinks (1916-1990)
John H. Fildew
Alan C. Miller
Randall S. Wangen
Mary Jane Ruffley
Robert D. Welchli
William P. Thorpe
Colleen A. Kramer
Stephen J. Pokoj
Charles S. Kennedy III

ASSOCIATE

Walter B. Fisher Jr.

References: First of America Bank-Detroit, N.A.; Comerica Bank-Detroit; National Bank of Detroit.

For full biographical listings, see the Martindale-Hubbell Law Directory

GARAN, LUCOW, MILLER & SEWARD, P.C. (AV)

1000 Woodbridge Place, 48207-3192
Telephone: 313-446-1530
Fax: 313-259-0450
URL: http://www.garanlucow.com
Grand Blanc, Michigan Office: 8332 Office Park Drive.
Telephone: 810-695-3700.
Fax: 810-695-6488.
Port Huron, Michigan Office: Port Huron Office Center, 511 Fort Street, Suite 505.
Telephone: 810-985-4400.
Fax: 810-985-4107.
Ann Arbor, Michigan Office: 101 North Main Street, Suite 460.
Telephone: 734-930-5600.
Fax: 734-930-0043.
Troy, Michigan Office: 1111 West Long Lake Road, Suite 300.
Telephone: 248-641-7600.
Fax: 248-641-0222.
Mount Clemens, Michigan Office: Towne Square Development, 10 S. Main Street, Suite 307.
Telephone: 810-954-3800.
Fax: 810-954-3803.
Grand Rapids, Michigan Office: First of America Center, 171 Monroe Avenue, N.W., Suite 950.
Telephone: 616-742-5500.
Fax: 616-742-5566.
Lansing, Michigan Office: 530 Creyts Road, Suite A.
Telephone: 517-327-0300.
Fax: 517-327-0309.
Traverse City, Michigan Office: 1131 East Eighth Street, P.O. Box 3150.
Telephone: 231-941-1611.
Fax: 231-941-4420.
Marquette, Michigan Office: 228 West Washington Street, Suite 4,
Telephone: 906-228-7772.
Fax: 906-228-5999.

Daniel L. Garan (1922-1997)
Thomas F. Myers
Dennis P. Partridge
John E. McSorley
Lamont E. Buffington
Thomas L. Misuraca
Rosalind Rochkind
James J. Hayes, Jr.
Thomas W. Emery
Boyd E. Chapin, Jr.
Frederick B. Plumb
James S. Goulding
John J. Gillooly
Timothy E. O'Neill
Robert D. Goldstein
Michael J. DePolo
Thomas R. Paxton
Daniel S. Saylor
David M. Shafer
C. David Miller, II
Robert A. Obringer

Steven E. Nurenberg
Lynn E. Geist
Mark T. Rajt
Jami E. Leach
Allison L. Hoff
Charles A. Harrison, III
Erik Stamell
David M. Saperstein
Clare M. Cylkowski
Timothy James Jordan
David Allan Couch
Stacey Lynn King
Stephen Hudak

OF COUNSEL

Milton Lucow
Albert A. Miller
Matthew A. Seward
Jon P. Desenberg
Nancy J. Bourget

Counsel for: Allstate Insurance Co.; Sears, Roebuck & Co.; Liberty Mutual Insurance Co.; Continental Insurance Companies.

For full biographical listings, see the Martindale-Hubbell Law Directory

HONIGMAN MILLER SCHWARTZ AND COHN (AV)

2290 First National Building, 660 Woodward Avenue, 48226
Telephone: 313-465-7000
Telecopier: 313-465-8000
Telex: 235705
Email: mvg@honigman.com *URL:* http://law.honigman.com
Lansing, Michigan Office: Phoenix Building, 222 North Washington Square, Suite 400, 48933-1800.
Telephone: 517-484-8282.

(See Next Column)

HONIGMAN MILLER SCHWARTZ AND COHN, *Detroit—Continued*

MEMBERS OF FIRM

Richard J. Aaron (Lansing, Michigan Office)
Jean-Vierre Adams
Joel S. Adelman
Peter M. Alter
Ann L. Andrews (Lansing, Michigan Office)
Norman C. Ankers
Joseph T. Aoun
Frederick M. Baker, Jr. (Lansing, Michigan Office)
C. Leslie Banas
Donald F. Baty, Jr.
Thomas J. Beale
Norman H. Beitner
Maurice S. Binkow
Richard Bisio
Jonathan R. Borenstein
Richard J. Burstein
Judy B. Calton
William M. Cassetta
Carol A. Clark
Gerald S. Cook
Roger Cook
Gregory J. DeMars
Daniel J. Demlow (Lansing, Michigan Office)
Patrick T. Duerr
Christopher J. Dunsky
John H. Eggertsen
David A. Ettinger
Cameron J. Evans
Herschel P. Fink
David Foltyn
Frederick J. Frank
William F. Frey
Michael J. Friedman
Kenneth C. Gold
Mark A. Goldsmith
Margaret E. Greene
Gerald M. Griffith
Andrea Hansen (Lansing, Michigan Office)
Daniel G. Helton
Raymond W. Henney
Carl W. Herstein
William O. Hochkammer
Steven G. Howell
Alan M. Hurvitz
Jeffrey A. Hyman
Norman Hyman
Linn A. Hynds
Howard B. Iwrey
Robert M. Jackson
Sandra L. Jasinski (Lansing, Michigan Office)
S. Lee Johnson
Carey F. Kalmowitz
John M. Kamins
John S. Kane (Lansing, Michigan Office)
Timothy Sawyer Knowlton (Lansing, Michigan Office)
Walter J. Kramarz
Jeffrey R. Kravitz
Robert J. Krueger, Jr.
Donald J. Kunz
Mary Jo Larson
Marguerite Munson Lentz
Denise J. Lewis
Russell S. Linden
Stuart M. Lockman
Ronald S. Longhofer
Lawrence D. McLaughlin
Mitchell R. Meisner
Cyril Moscow
Lawrence J. Murphy
Steven C. Nadeau
Brian J. Negele
Charles Nida
James H. Novis
Joseph G. Nuyen, Jr.
Nancy M. Omichinski
David K. Page
Lisa M. Panepucci
Alex L. Parrish
John D. Pirich (Lansing, Michigan Office)
Joseph M. Polito
Julie E. Robertson
G. Scott Romney
Linda S. Ross
Chris E. Rossman
J. Adam Rothstein
Phyllis G. Rozof
Roberta R. Russ
William D. Sargent
Laurence J. Schiff
Steven P. Schneider
Alan E. Schwartz
Alan Stuart Schwartz
Mark Shaevsky
Michael B. Shapiro
Sherill Siebert
Tracy E. Silverman
Richard S. Soble
Samuel T. Stahl
Mark A. Stern
Theodore B. Sylwestrzak
Stuart H. Teger
Cynthia G. Thomas
Sheryl L. Toby
Sheldon S. Toll
Brad M. Tomtishen
Grant R. Trigger
Alan M. Valade (Lansing, Michigan Office)
Margaret Van Meter
Patrick R. Van Tiflin (Lansing, Michigan Office)
Robert B. Weiss
Mark R. Werder
Randall P. Whately
William A. Wichers II
Sheldon P. Winkelman
I. W. Winsten
Jeffrey L. Woolstrum
Ruth E. Zimmerman (Lansing, Michigan Office)
William J. Zousmer
Richard E. Zuckerman

ASSOCIATES

David E. Barnes
Jonathan David Block
Peter C. Bolton
John Michael Breza
Amy M. Brooks
James T. Carroll, III
Jason Schian Conti
Andrew S. Doctoroff
Gail A. Eynon
Steven D. Feenstra
Amy B. Folbe
Andrew J. Gerdes (Lansing, Michigan Office)
Dean Googasian
Frank L. Gorman
William S. Hammond
John P. Kanan
Richard T. Karcher
Raymond M. Kethledge
Dawn R. Kreysar
Jennifer L. Kushner
Johann Lee
Patrick G. LePine
Stefanie K. Longhofer
Liesl A. Maloney
Tina McCree Orr
Denise Stellmach Owczarek
Richard W. Paige
Kristine McKimson Renke
Anthony Rivera
Jeanne M. Scherlinck
Tricia A. Sherick (Not admitted in MI)
Scott A. Small
Stephanie L. Speranza
Alison M. Stanley (Lansing, Michigan Office)
Daniel L. Stanley (Lansing, Michigan Office)
Michelle Epstein Taigman
Michael David Warren, Jr.
Michelle Weaver

(See Next Column)

ASSOCIATES (Continued)

Stuart J. Weiss
Michelle M. Wezner
Scott A. Wolfson
Lisa B. Zimmer
Jennifer S. Zbytowski

OF COUNSEL

Milton J. Miller
Rodman N. Myers
Margaret Shannon
Harry Christopher Goplerud (P.A.)
Jason L. Honigman (1904-1990)
Irwin I. Cohn (1896-1984)

General Counsel for: The Detroit Free Press; The Detroit Medical Center; Handleman Co.; Pulte Corporation; William C. Roney & Co.
Local or Special Counsel for: American Society of Composers, Authors and Publishers (ASCAP); AutoAlliance International Inc. (formerly Mazda Motor Manufacturing (USA) Corporation); Bank One; The Taubman Company, Inc.

For full biographical listings, see the Martindale-Hubbell Law Directory

JAFFE, RAITT, HEUER & WEISS, PROFESSIONAL CORPORATION (AV)

One Woodward Avenue, Suite 2400, 48226
Telephone: 313-961-8380
Telecopier: 313-961-8358
Cable Address: "Jafsni"
Southfield,Michigan Office: Travelers Tower, Suite 1520.
Telephone: 313-961-8380.

Derek S. Adolf
Gail A. Anderson
Christopher A. Andreoff
Robert S. Bolton
R. Christopher Cataldo
Thomas E. Coughlin
Jeffrey L. Forman
Wallace H. Glendening
Gary R. Glenn
Joel S. Golden
Robert J. Gordon
Larry K. Griffis
Karen F. R. Grotberg (Not admitted in MI)
Jeffrey G. Heuer
Blair B. Hysni
Ira J. Jaffe
Shirley A. Powers Kaigler
Robin H. Krueger
Mark P. Krysinski
Sharon J. LaDuke
Melanie LaFave
Robert E. Lewis
Susan S. Lichterman
Eric A. Linden
Ralph R. Margulis
Joel J. Morris
William S. Noakes
Lawrence C. Patrick, Jr.
Harold D. Pope, III
Victor F. Ptasznik
Jane Derse Quasarano
Mark K. Rabidoux
Cecil G. Raitt
David H. Raitt
Michael A. Rajt
Louis P. Rochkind
Mark D. Rubenfire
Stephen G. Schafer
Linda C. Scheuerman
Brian G. Shannon
Joseph J. Shannon
Lawrence R. Shoffner
William E. Sider
Arthur H. Siegal
Elliot A. Spoon
Peter Sugar
George A. Sumnik
Susan M. Sutton
Holli Hart Targan
David D. Warner
Arthur A. Weiss
Jeffrey M. Weiss
Jeffrey D. Weisserman
Jay L. Welford
Thomas H. Williams
Wendy L. Zabriskie
Richard A. Zussman

Patrice S. Arend
Lise Anne Barrera
Traci Kemp Brocks
Eric S. Bronstein
Ian M. Burnstein
Christopher A. Chekan
Michelle L. Coakley
Jill H. Collins
Karen J. Craft
Liam E. Hart
Kirk D. Hornburg
Milton I. Kovinsky
Sara M. Kruse
Stephen S. Laplante
Alicia S. McGinnis
Matthew J. Murphy (Not admitted in MI)
Carla Mecoli Kamp
Joshua F. Opperer
Julia A. Perkins
Brian S. Raznick
Eric D. Scheible
Thomas L. Shaevsky
Jordan H. Smith
Kirk I. Tousaw
Henry Wineman, III
Laith L. Yaldoo

OF COUNSEL

David Griem
Carolyn Slasinski-Griem

Representative Clients: Michigan State Hospital Finance Auth.; The Stroh Brewery Co.; Unisys Corp.; Weiss Construction Co.

For full biographical listings, see the Martindale-Hubbell Law Directory

KELLER, THOMA, SCHWARZE, SCHWARZE, DUBAY & KATZ, P.C. (AV)

440 East Congress, 5th Floor, 48226
Telephone: 313-965-7610
Fax: 313-965-4480
Bingham Farms, Michigan Office: 30150 Telegraph Road, Suite 444, 48025.
Telephone: 248-642-5218.

(See Next Column)

KELLER, THOMA, SCHWARZE, SCHWARZE, DUBAY & KATZ P.C.—*Continued*

Leonard A. Keller (1906-1970)
Thomas H. Schwarze (1943-1998)
Richard J. Thoma (Retired)
Frederick B. Schwarze
Dennis B. DuBay
James R. Miller
Stewart J. Katz
Anthony J. Heckemeyer
Thomas L. Fleury
Terrence J. Miglio
Gary P. King
Robert A. Lusk
Linda M. Foster
Bruce M. Bagdady
Carl F. Schwarze
Brian A. Kreucher
Christopher M. Murray
Mark C. Knoth
John J. Rabaut
Martha A. Proctor
Joseph R. Furton, Jr.

Karin M. Young
Richard W. Fanning, Jr.
Cara L. Brott
Jonathon A. Rabin
Priscilla L. Schwarze
Susan D. Koval

Counsel for: Livonia Public Schools; Ludington News Co., Inc.
Representative Clients: Borg-Warner Corp.; E & L Transport Co.; The Kroger Co.; Holnam, Inc.
Public Employer Clients: City of Farmington Hills; City of Flint; City of Grosse Pointe Woods; Saginaw Public Schools.

For full biographical listings, see the Martindale-Hubbell Law Directory

KITCH DRUTCHAS WAGNER DENARDIS & VALITUTTI, A PROFESSIONAL CORPORATION (AV)

One Woodward, Tenth Floor, 48226-3499
Telephone: 313-965-7900
Fax: 313-965-7403
URL: http://www.kitch.com
Lansing, Michigan Office: 120 Washington Square, North, Suite 280, One Michigan Avenue, 48933-1609.
Telephone: 517-372-6430.
Fax: 517-372-0441.
Macomb County Office: Towne Square Development, 10 South Main Street, Suite 301, Mount Clemens, 48043-7903.
Telephone: 810-463-9770.
Fax: 810-463-8994.
Toledo, Ohio Office: 405 Madison Avenue, Suite 1500, 43604-1235.
Telephone: 419-243-4006.
Fax: 419-243-7333.
Marquette, Michigan Office: Old City Hall, 220 West Washington, Suite 500, 49855-4344.
Telephone: 906-228-0001.
Fax: 906-228-0003.
Ann Arbor, Michigan Office: 303 Detroit Street, Suite 400, P.O. Box 8610, 48107-8610.
Telephone: 734-994-7600.
Fax: 734-994-7626.
Grand Rapids, Michigan Office: 300 Ottawa, NW, Suite 210, 49503.
Telephone: 616-456-8384.
Fax: 616-456-8795.

FIRM PRINCIPALS

Richard A. Kitch
Gregory G. Drutchas
Ronald E. Wagner (Managing Principal)
Ralph F. Valitutti, Jr.
Richard R. DeNardis
Mona K. Majzoub
Harry J. Sherbrook
Anthony G. Arnone
Charles W. Fisher
Clyde M. Metzger, III (Principal, Ann Arbor Office)
Thomas J. Foley
Victor J. Abela
James H. Hughesian
John P. Ryan (Principal, Lansing Office)
William D. Chaklos
Steve N. Cheolas (Principal, Macomb County Office)
Richard S. Baron
Susan Healy Zitterman
John S. Wasung (Principal, Toledo, Ohio Office)
William W. Vertes
John Paul Hessburg
Karen Bernard Berkery
R. Michael O'Boyle
Daniel R. Shirey
John M. Sier
Richard T. Counsman
Steven M. Waclawski
Stephen R. Brzezinski
Michael P. McCasey (Grand Rapids Office)
Thomas R. Shimmel
Carole S. Empey (Ann Arbor)
Carol Ann Tarnowsky
Michael J. Watza
Sara Mae Gerbitz
Linda M. Garbarino
Susan Marie Beutel
Mark A. Wisniewski
Frederick H. Hoops, III

FIRM ASSOCIATE PRINCIPALS

Susan M. Ramage (Grand Rapids Office)
Daniel J. Niemann (Ann Arbor Office)
Sharon A. DeWaele
Richard J. Joppich (Ann Arbor Office)
Ellen M. Keefe-Garner (Ann Arbor Office)
Kenneth M. Essad
Kim J. Sveska
Verlin R. Nafziger
Dean A. Etsios
Barbara A. Martin
Cheryl A. Cardelli
Paula M. Burgess (Toledo, Ohio Office)
Lauri A. Read
Cullen B. McKinney
Anthony J. Nellis
Jeffrey T. Gorcyca
Timothy R. Ward

(See Next Column)

FIRM SENIOR ASSOCIATES

Robert A. Fehniger
Antonio Mauti
Joseph P. McGill
Richard P. Cuneo (Toledo, Ohio Office)
Richard M. Mitchell
Mary Catherine Storen
Van P. Andres (Toledo, Ohio Office)
Laura L. Witty
Marcia L. Malouin (Lansing Office)
Ellen C. Padesky
Jeffrey A. Magid
Joyce A. Reynolds
Donald B. Lenderman
Dennis W. Fliehman (Lansing Office)
Eric O. Husby
Richard J. Suhrheinrich
Daniel S. Hoops
Sheley L. DeGraw
Laura L. Selzer
R. Lisa Panah
Christina A. Ginter
Terese L. Farhat

FIRM ASSOCIATES

Amy B. Fagan
Nancie S. Merlino (Toledo, Ohio Office)
Judith A. Sherman (Ann Arbor Office)
Frank A. Misuraca (Ann Arbor Office)
Eric M. St. Onge (Lansing Office)
Dina M. Ferrar
Kenneth John Pocius
Heather A. Betts
Anne E. Lawter
Brian Michael Brown
Christa Sarafa
Christine E. Rice (Grand Rapids Office)

For full biographical listings, see the Martindale-Hubbell Law Directory

MILLER, CANFIELD, PADDOCK AND STONE, P.L.C. (AV)

A Professional Limited Liability Company
Founded in 1852 by Sidney Davy Miller
150 West Jefferson, Suite 2500, 48226-4415
Telephone: 313-963-6420
Fax: 313-496-7500
Cable Address: "Stem Detroit"
URL: http://www.millercanfield.com
Ann Arbor, Michigan Office: 101 North Main Street, 7th Floor, 48104-1400.
Telephone: 734-663-2445.
Fax: 734-747-7147.
Troy, Michigan Office: 840 West Long Lake Road, Suite 200, 48098.
Telephone: 248-879-2000.
Fax: 248-879-2001.
Grand Rapids, Michigan Office: 99 Monroe, N.W., Suite 1200, 49503-2639.
Telephone: 616-454-8656.
Fax: 616-776-6322.
Howell, Michigan Office: 121 South Barnard Street, Suite 4, 48843-2305.
Telephone: 517-546-7600.
Telecopier: 517-546-6974.
Kalamazoo, Michigan Office: 444 West Michigan Avenue, 49007-3752.
Telephone: 616-381-7030.
Fax: 616-382-0244.
Lansing, Michigan Office: One Michigan Avenue, Suite 900, 48933-1609.
Telephone: 517-487-2070.
Fax: 517-374-6304.
Monroe, Michigan Office: 214 East Elm Avenue, Suite 100, 48162-2682.
Telephone: 734-243-2000.
Fax: 734-243-0901.
Washington, D.C. Office: 1900 K Street, N.W., Suite 1150. 20006.
Telephone: 202-429-5575; 785-0600.
Fax: 202-331-1118; 785-1234.
Pensacola, Florida Office: 25 West Cedar, 32501.
Telephone: 850-469-1088.
Fax: 850-432-0677.
New York, New York Office: 1450 Broadway, 41st Floor, 10018.
Telephone: 212-704-4400.
Fax: 212-704-4410.
Gdynia, Poland Office: UL. Slaska 21, 81-319.
Telephone: 011-485-831-2808.
Fax: 011-48-58-628 6411.
Warsaw, Poland Office: UL. Nowogrodzkall, 5th Floor, 00-513.
Telephone: 011-4822 529 0200.
Fax: 011-4822 529 0201.
Katowice, Poland Office: UL. Francuska 35/37, 40-027.
Telephone: 011 (48-32) 757-2414.
Fax: 011 (48-32) 757-2483.

PRINCIPALS OF FIRM

John W. Gelder (Troy Office)
Stevan Uzelac (P.C.)
Robert L. DeJong (Grand Rapids Office)
Robert S. Ketchum
Samuel J. McKim, III, (P.C.)
Rocque E. Lipford (P.C.) (Monroe Office)
Joel L. Piell
Robert E. Gilbert (Ann Arbor Office)
Eric V. Brown, Jr. (Kalamazoo Office)
Bruce D. Birgbauer
John A. Thurber (P.C.) (Troy Office)
Orin D. Brustad
Carl H. von Ende
Erik H. Serr (Ann Arbor Office)
Allyn D. Kantor (Ann Arbor Office)
Charles E. Ritter (Kalamazoo Office)
Thomas G. Parachini
John A. Campbell (Kalamazoo Office)
David D. Joswick (P.C.)

(See Next Column)

MILLER, CANFIELD, PADDOCK AND STONE P.L.C., *Detroit—Continued*

PRINCIPALS OF FIRM (Continued)

John A. Marxer (P.C.) (Troy Office)
Gregory L. Curtner (Ann Arbor and New York, N.Y. Offices)
Dennis R. Neiman
Kenneth E. Konop (Troy Office)
Leonard D. Givens
Bettye S. Elkins (Ann Arbor Office)
W. Mack Faison
Joseph F. Galvin
Ronald H. Riback (Troy Office)
James W. Williams (Troy Office)
Thomas P. Hustoles (Kalamazoo Office)
William J. Danhof (Lansing Office)
Clarence L. Pozza, Jr.
Jerry T. Rupley
Michael W. Hartmann
Kent E. Shafer
James C. Foresman
John R. Cook (Kalamazoo Office)
Thomas W. Linn
Stephen G. Palms (Troy Office)
Jerome R. Watson
Frank L. Andrews (Troy Office)
Donna J. Donati
Donald W. Keim
Larry J. Saylor
Mark E. Putney (Grand Rapids Office)
James G. Vantine, Jr. (Kalamazoo Office)
Richard J. Seryak
Michael R. Atkins (Lansing Office)
Leland D. Barringer
Timothy D. Sochocki (Ann Arbor Office)
Thomas C. Phillips (Lansing Office)
Christopher J. Dembowski (Lansing Office)
Marjory G. Basile
Terrence M. Crawford
Michael J. Hodge (Lansing Office)
J. Kevin Trimmer (Troy Office)
Richard A. Gaffin (Grand Rapids Office)
Kevin M. McCarthy (Kalamazoo Office)
Ronald E. Baylor (Kalamazoo Office)
Beverly Hall Burns
Charles S. Mishkind
Stephen J. Ott (Troy Office)
Amanda Van Dusen
Peter W. Waldmeir
Thomas G. Appleman (Troy Office)
Thomas H. Van Dis (Kalamazoo Office)
Walter Briggs Connolly, Jr.
Michael P. Coakley
Cynthia B. Faulhaber (Lansing Office)
Jeffrey M. McHugh
Robert F. Rhoades
James E. Spurr (Kalamazoo Office)
Gregory V. Di Censo (Troy Office)
Brad B. Arbuckle (Bloomfield Hills Office)
Mark T. Boonstra
Harold W. Bulger, Jr.
Michael G. Campbell (Grand Rapids Office)
David A. French (Ann Arbor Office)
Karen A. McCoy
Kevin J. Moody (Lansing Office)
Steven M. Stankewicz (Kalamazoo Office)
Robert E. Lee Wright (Grand Rapids Offices)
Michael A. Indenbaum
J. David Reck (Ann Arbor and Howell Offices)
Michael H. Traison
Jonathan S. Green
Le Roy L. Asher, Jr.
Vernon Bennett III (Kalamazoo and Grand Rapids Offices)
Douglas W. Crim (Grand Rapids Office)
Pamela Chapman Enslen (Kalamazoo Office)
Michael P. McGee
David N. Parsigian (Ann Arbor Office)
Jay B. Rising (Lansing Office)
Deborah W. Thompson
Richard T. Urbis
Steven A. Roach
Richard A. Walawender
Brian J. Doren
Irene Bruce Hathaway
Megan P. Norris
Lawrence M. Dudek
Charles A. Duerr, Jr. (Ann Arbor Office)
Ronald E. Hodess (Troy Office)
Donald J. Hutchinson
Marta A. Manildi (Ann Arbor Office)
Kathryn L. Ossian
Don M. Schmidt (Kalamazoo Office)
Kurt N. Sherwood (Kalamazoo Office)
Michael A. Alaimo
David K. McLeod
George D. Mesritz
Dawn M. Schluter (Troy Office)
Ballard Jay Yelton III (Kalamazoo Office)
Steven E. Chester (Lansing Office)
Thomas R. Cox
Joanne B. Faycurry
Robert J. Haddad (Troy Office)
Sherry Katz-Crank (Lansing Office)
Douglas M. Kilbourne (Ann Arbor Office)
James R. Lancaster, Jr. (Lansing Office)
Roselyn R. Parmenter (Ann Arbor Office)
Lori L. Purkey (Kalamazoo Office)
John O. Renken (Washington, D.C. and Ann Arbor Offices)
John G. VanSlambrouck (Kalamazoo Office)
John H. Willems
Raymond J. Carey
Frederick A. Acomb
Brant A. Freer
Sally A. Hamby (Troy Office)
Erich H. Hintzen (Troy Office)
Richard I. Loebl
Stanley J. Stek (Grand Rapids Office)

OF COUNSEL/SENIOR COUNSEL

Eric V. Brown, Sr. (Kalamazoo Office)
Edmond F. DeVine (Ann Arbor Office)
James E. Tobin
John B. DeVine (Ann Arbor Office)
Stratton S. Brown
Richard B. Gushée
Peter P. Thurber
Lawrence A. King (P.C.) (Troy Office)
Robert E. Hammell
Joseph F. Maycock, Jr.
Allen Schwartz
George E. Parker, III
Richard A. Jones (P.C.) (Troy Office)
Gilbert E. Gove

(See Next Column)

OF COUNSEL/SENIOR COUNSEL (Continued)

David E. Hathaway (Grand Rapids Office)
Gerard Thomas (Kalamazoo Office)
George E. Bushnell, Jr.
Henry R. Nolte, Jr. (Troy Office)
Richard I. Lott (Pensacola, Florida Office)
Patricia D. Lott (Pensacola Office)
Tillman L. Lay (Washington, D.C. Office)
David L. Kaser (Principal)
Geoffrey M. Chinn (New York Office)
Walter A. Payne, III
Paul R. Dimond (Ann Arbor Office)
Anne Saad McAlpine
Michael B. Peterman
Jamir R. Couch (Washington, D.C. Office)

SENIOR ATTORNEYS

Leo P. Goddeyne (Kalamazoo Office)
William B. Beach
Robert J. Sandler
David J. Hasper (Grand Rapids Office)
Steven C. Kahn (Washington, D.C. Office)
Stephen L. Elkins (Grand Rapids Office)
Clifford T. Flood (Lansing Office)
Linda O. Goldberg (Ann Arbor Office)
Louis B. Reinwasser (Lansing Office)

ASSOCIATES

Brian S. Westenberg (Troy Office)
Amy S. Davis
A. Michael Palizzi
Patrick F. McGow
Lisa D. Pick (Troy Office)
Michael C. Fayz
Anna M. Maiuri (Troy Office)
Thomas D. Colis
Dean M. Altobelli
Derek T. Montgomery
Mark K. Schrupp
Terence A. Thomas
Clara G. Dequick
Jason S. Rose (Troy Office)
Jeffrey D. Adelman
Loyal A. Eldridge III (Kalamazoo Office)
Kurt P. McCamman (Kalamazoo Office)
Scott R. Sikkenga (Kalamazoo Office)
Anthony J. Mavrinac
John T. Stecco (Grand Rapids Office)
Suzanne L. DeVine (Ann Arbor Office)
Michael V. Camarota (Kalamazoo Office)
Alice Censoplano Elkin (Ann Arbor Office)
Thomas A. Norton
Lindsay L. Bray
Holly E. Dolbey
Jennifer A. Bielfield
Martin C. Brook
Sherylle A. O. Gordon (Troy Office)
Kristin A. Hermann
William A. Phillips
Sarah S. Swallow (Kalamazoo Office)
James B. Thelen (Kalamazoo Office)
Vincent E. Woltjer (Grand Rapids Office)
Oren R. Griffin (Kalamazoo Office)
Robert J. Nolan (Grand Rapids Office)
David L. Freedman (Ann Arbor Office)
Joanna Zakalik Totsky
Philip B. Phillips
Daljit S. Doogal (Troy Office)
Kimberly A. Paulson
Freeman L. Farrow
Valarie Tatem Bomar
Adam S. Forman
Todd A. Miller
Kevin A. Smith
Stuart M. Heath (Kalamazoo Office)
James M. Pelland
Andrew T. Blum (Grand Rapids Office)
Susan I. Robbins (New York Office)
Anna H. Benson (Pensacola Office)
Nancy Gerarda Itnyre
Nancy E. Vettorello

Representative Firm Clients: Chrysler Corporation; Comerica, Incorporated; City of Detroit, Michigan; Detroit Tigers, Inc.; First of Michigan; Ford Motor Company; Ford Motor Credit Company; Great Lakes Bancorp; Henry Ford Hospital; INVETECH Company.

For full biographical listings, see the Martindale-Hubbell Law Directory

PEPPER HAMILTON LLP (AV)

100 Renaissance Center, 36th Floor, 48243-1157
Telephone: 313-259-7110
Telecopy: 313-259-7926
Email: phinfo@pepperlaw.com *URL:* http://www.pepperlaw.com
Philadelphia, Pennsylvania Office: 3000 Two Logan Square, Eighteenth and Arch Streets, 19103-2799.
Telephone: 215-981-4000.
Fax: 215-981-4750.
Washington, D.C. Office: Hamilton Square, 600 Fourteenth Street, N.W. 20005-2004.
Telephone: 202-220-1200.
Fax: 202-220-1665.
New York, New York Office: 750 Lexington Avenue, Suite 600, 10022-1200.
Telephone: 212-813-9668.
Fax: 212-813-9802.
Wilmington, Delaware Office: 1201 Market Street, Suite 1600, P.O. Box 1709, 19899-1709.
Telephone: 302-777-6500.
Fax: 302-656-8865.
Pittsburgh, Pennsylvania Office: 500 Grant Street, 50th Floor, 15219-2502.
Telephone: 412-454-5000.
Fax: 412-281-0717.

(See Next Column)

PEPPER HAMILTON LLP—*Continued*

Harrisburg, Pennsylvania Office: 200 One Keystone Plaza, North Front and Market Streets, P.O. Box 1181, 17108-1181.
Telephone: 717-255-1155.
Fax: 717-238-0575.
Berwyn, Pennsylvania Office: 1235 Westlakes Drive, Suite 400, 19312-2401.
Telephone: 610-640-7800.
Fax: 610-640-7835.
Cherry Hill, New Jersey Office: LibertyView Building, Suite 420, 457 Haddonfield Road, 08002-2220.
Telephone: 856-910-7200.
Fax: 856-665-7743.

PARTNERS

Abraham Singer (Managing Partner, Detroit Office)
Joel D. Applebaum
Hugh Douglas Camitta
I. William Cohen
Michael A. Fleming
Scott L. Gorland
Lisa Sommers Gretchko
René M. L. Hansemann
Vicki R. Harding
Stuart E. Hertzberg
Dennis S. Kayes
Kay Standridge Kress
Robert C. Ludolph
David L. Maurer
David Murphy
Barbara Rom
Michael B. Staebler
Thomas P. Wilczak

OF COUNSEL

Mark E. Schlussel

ASSOCIATES

James P. Allen
Rachel Grossman Baxter
Barbara Eckert Buchanan
Judith E. Caliman
Ciara M. Comerford
P. Casey Coston
Andrew J. Currie
Matthew J. Lund
Michelle Motowski
Todd A. Richards
Kelly L. Schadel
Fara L. Shimek

For full biographical listings, see the Martindale-Hubbell Law Directory

RILEY AND ROUMELL, P.C. (AV)

7th Floor, Ford Building, 48226-3986
Telephone: 313-962-8255
Telefax: 313-962-2937

Wallace D. Riley
George T. Roumell, Jr.
William F. Dennis
Steven M. Zarowny
Allen J. Lippitt
Alfred John Eppens
Wilber M. Brucker III
Gregory T. Schultz

OF COUNSEL

D. Michael Cherry
William D. Cohan
Emmet E. Tracy, Jr.

Representative Clients: First of Chicago NBD Corp.; Comerica Bank-Detroit; Federal National Mortgage Assn.; Federal Home Loan Mortgage Corp.; SCOR S.A.; Chas. Verheyden, Inc.; Detroit Board of Education; County of Wayne; City of Livonia.

For full biographical listings, see the Martindale-Hubbell Law Directory

TIMMIS & INMAN L.L.P. (AV)

300 Talon Centre, 48207
Telephone: 313-396-4200
Facsimile: 313-396-4228
Email: info@timmis-inman.com *URL:* http://www.timmis-inman.com

Michael T. Timmis
Robert E. Graziani
George A. Peck
Henry J. Brennan, III
Mark W. Peyser
Richard M. Miettinen
Bradley J. Knickerbocker
George M. Malis

Michael F. Wais
Erich J. D'Andrea
Shannon M. Nichols
Anthony J. Long
Alex N. Saleh
Michael J. Sheehan
Andrew D. Kehagiaras
John E.F. Gerlach
Jennifer A. Bourgoin

OF COUNSEL

Richard L. Levin
William B. Fitzgerald
David E. Costa

LEGAL SUPPORT PERSONNEL

PARALEGALS

Linda M. Bierl
Leslie A. Reaser

Representative Clients: Detroit Mortgage & Realty; DMR Fiancial Services, Inc.; J. Levin Sons Co.; Green Tree Financial Servicing Corp.; Hematology-Oncology Associates East, PC; Lakeshore Ear, Nose & Throat Center, PC; Micromanagement Systems, Inc.; Phoenix Crystal Corp.; Talon Surfaces LLC; Talon Automated Equipment Company.

For full biographical listings, see the Martindale-Hubbell Law Directory

EAST LANSING, Ingham Co.

SMITH HAUGHEY RICE & ROEGGE, P.C. (AV)

1400 Abbott Road, Suite 410, 48823-1902
Telephone: 517-332-3030
Facsimile: 517-332-3468
Grand Rapids, Michigan Office: 200 Calder Plaza Building, 250 Monroe Avenue, N.W., 49503-2251.
Telephone: 616-774-8000.
Facsimile: 616-774-2461.
Traverse City, Michigan Office: City Centre Plaza, Suite 100, 202 East State Street, P.O. Box 848, 49685-0848.
Telephone: 231-929-4878.
Facsimile: 231-929-4182.

Douglas G. Powe
Richard C. Kraus

Veronica A. Marsich
Mary K. Robbins-Kralapp
Brian E. Madar
Margaret A. Chamberlain

Representative Clients: Chevron; Cincinnati Insurance Co.; General Motors Corp.; Kemper Insurance Group; Michigan Hospital Assn.; Navistar International; St. Paul Insurance Cos.; Steelcase, Inc.; Dow Elanco.

For full biographical listings, see the Martindale-Hubbell Law Directory

FARMINGTON HILLS, Oakland Co.

COUZENS, LANSKY, FEALK, ELLIS, ROEDER & LAZAR, P.C. (AV)

39395 West 12 Mile Road, Suite 200, 48331-2913
Telephone: 248-489-8600
Facsimile: 248-489-4156
Email: info@couzens.com *URL:* http://www.couzens.com

Sheldon A. Fealk
Jack S. Couzens, II
Jerry M. Ellis
Donald M. Lansky
Bruce J. Lazar
Alan C. Roeder
Renard J. Kolasa
Kathryn Gilson Sussman
Jeffrey A. Levine
Phillip L. Sternberg
Marc L. Prey
Lisa J. Walters
Stephen Scapelliti
Donald A. Wagner
Michael P. Witzke
Cyrus Raamin Kashef
Gregg A. Nathanson
David B. Deutsch
Mark S. Frankel

Roger E. Winkelman
Alisa A. Kwang
Turkia Awada Mullin
Raoul K. Maitra

Representative Clients: Provided upon request.
Reference: Michigan National Bank.

For full biographical listings, see the Martindale-Hubbell Law Directory

*FLINT,** Genesee Co.

PATRICK M. KIRBY (AV)

1335 South Linden Road, Suite G, 48532-3420
Telephone: 810-230-0833
Fax: 810-230-8222

For full biographical listings, see the Martindale-Hubbell Law Directory

MACDONALD, FITZGERALD & MACDONALD, P.C. (AV)

200 McKinnon Building, 48502
Telephone: 810-232-3184; 234-2204
Fax: 810-232-9632

Robert J. MacDonald (1914-1987)
John J. FitzGerald (1919-1995)
R. Duncan MacDonald
Timothy J. MacDonald
Robert J MacDonald

References: Michigan National Bank; NBD Bank, N.A.; Citizen's Bank.

For full biographical listings, see the Martindale-Hubbell Law Directory

GRAND BLANC, Genesee Co.

GARAN, LUCOW, MILLER & SEWARD, P.C. (AV)

8332 Office Park Drive, 48439
Telephone: 810-695-3700
Fax: 810-695-6488
URL: http://www.garanlucow.com
Detroit, Michigan Office: 1000 Woodbridge Place.
Telephone: 313-446-1530.
Fax: 313-259-0450.
Port Huron, Michigan Office: Port Huron Office Center, 511 Fort Street, Suite 505.
Telephone: 810-985-4400.
Fax: 810-985-4187.
Ann Arbor, Michigan Office: 101 North Main Street, Suite 460.
Telephone: 734-930-5600.
Fax: 734-930-0043.

(See Next Column)

GARAN, LUCOW, MILLER & SEWARD P.C., *Grand Blanc—Continued*

Troy, Michigan Office: 1111 West Long Lake Road, Suite 300.
Telephone: 248-641-7600.
Fax: 248-641-0222.
Mount Clemens, Michigan Office: Towne Square Development, 10 S. Main Street, Suite 307.
Telephone: 810-954-3800.
Fax: 810-954-3803.
Grand Rapids, Michigan Office: First of America Center, 171 Monroe Avenue, N.W., Suite 950.
Telephone: 616-742-5500.
Fax: 616-742-5566.
Lansing, Michigan Office: 530 Creyts Road, Suite A.
Telephone: 517-327-0300.
Fax: 517-327-0309.
Traverse City, Michigan Office: 1131 East Eighth Street, P.O. Box 3150.
Telephone: 231-941-1611.
Fax: 231-941-4420.
Marquette, Michigan Office: 228 West Washington Street, Suite 4,
Telephone: 906-228-7772.
Fax: 906-228-5999.

Joseph Kochis (Resident) — William J. Brickley (Resident)

Peter L. Diesel — John B. Farrell
Robert H. Shannon

For full biographical listings, see the Martindale-Hubbell Law Directory

*GRAND RAPIDS,** Kent Co.

BORRE, PETERSON, FOWLER & REENS, P.C. (AV)

300 Ottawa N.W., Suite 500, P.O. Box 1767, 49501-1767
Telephone: 616-459-1971
Fax: 616-459-2393
Email: 105162.1531@compuserve.com

Glen V. Borre
James B. Peterson
Ben A. Fowler
William C. Reens
Frank H. Johnson
Mark D. Sevald
Harold E. Nelson
William R. Vander Sluis
William G. Krupar
John C. Arndts

Michelle H. Anthes

References: Old Kent Bank; NBD Bank/First Chicago Bank; The Huntington Bank.

For full biographical listings, see the Martindale-Hubbell Law Directory

DICKINSON WRIGHT PLLC (AV)

200 Ottawa Avenue, N.W., Suite 900, 49503-2423
Telephone: 616-458-1300
Facsimile: 616-458-6753
URL: http://www.dickinson-wright.com
Detroit, Michigan Office: 500 Woodward Avenue, Suite 4000.
Telephone: 313-223-3500.
Facsimile: 313-223-3598.
Bloomfield Hills, Michigan Office: 525 North Woodward Avenue, Suite 2000.
Telephone: 248-433-7200.
Facsimile: 248-433-7274.
Lansing, Michigan Office: Suite 200, 215 South Washington Square.
Telephone: 517-371-1730.
Facsimile: 517-487-4700.
Washington, D.C. Office: Suite 800, 1901 L Street, N.W.
Telephone: 202-457-0160.
Facsimile: 202-659-1559.

RESIDENT MEMBERS

Geoffrey A. Fields
William J. Fisher, III
Richard A. Glaser
Daniel F. Gosch
Erin E. Gravelyn
Kathryn Kraus Nunzio
James Gavan O'Connor
Gregory M. Palmer
John L. Teeples
Richard A. Wendt
Rock A. Wood

OF COUNSEL

Stuart F. Cheney — Kevin J. O'Dowd
Philip F. Wood

RESIDENT ASSOCIATES

Juan R. Balboa
Keith J. Brodie
Scott A. Dienes
Leslee M. Lewis
Edward P. Perdue

For full biographical listings, see the Martindale-Hubbell Law Directory

DYKEMA GOSSETT PLLC (AV)

Suite 700, 300 Ottawa Avenue, N.W., 49503-2304
Telephone: 616-776-7500
Fax: 616-776-7573
Email: mstarrs@dykema.com *URL:* http://www.dykema.com
Ann Arbor, Michigan Office: 315 East Eisenhower Parkway, Suite 100, 48108-3306.
Telephone: 734-214-7660.
Fax: 734-214-7696.
Bloomfield Hills, Michigan Office: 1577 North Woodward Avenue, Suite 300, 48304-2820.
Telephone: 248-203-0700.
Fax: 248-203-0763.
Chicago, Illinois Office: 55 East Monroe Street, Suite 3050, 60603-5709.
Telephone: 312-551-4900.
Fax: 312-551-4919.
Detroit, Michigan Office: 400 Renaissance Center, 48243-1668.
Telephone: 313-568-6800.
Fax: 313-568-6545.
Lansing, Michigan Office: 800 Michigan National Tower, 48933-1707.
Telephone: 517-374-9100.
Fax: 517-374-9191.
Washington, D.C. Office: Franklin Square, Suite 300 West, 1300 I Street, N.W., 20005-3306.
Telephone: 202-522-8600.
Fax: 202-522-8669.
Affiliated Office: Via Matconi, 3, 40122 Bologna, Italy,
Telephone: 011-39-51-228222.
Fax: 011-39-51-6593580.

RESIDENT MEMBERS

David E. Doran
John A. Ferroli
Patrick E. Mears
Stephen S. Muhich
Brian J. Page

RESIDENT ASSOCIATES

Scott D. Broekstra
Christopher T. Dement
Mark E. Derwent
Michael P. Farrell
David G. Hagens
Michelle A. LeVeque
Eric C. Lund (Not admitted in MI)
James A. Shepherd
Sharon S. Spungen
Mark David van der Laan

For full biographical listings, see the Martindale-Hubbell Law Directory

GARAN, LUCOW, MILLER & SEWARD, P.C. (AV)

First of America Center, 171 Monroe Avenue, N.W., Suite 950, 49503
Telephone: 616-742-5500
Fax: 616-742-5566
URL: http://www.garanlucow.com
Detroit, Michigan Office: 10000 Woodbridge Place.
Telephone: 313-446-1530.
Fax: 313-259-0450.
Grand Blanc, Michigan Office: 8332 Office Park Drive.
Telephone: 810-695-3700.
Fax: 810-695-6488.
Port Huron, Michigan Office: Port Huron Office Center, 511 Fort Street, Suite 505.
Telephone: 810-985-4400.
Fax: 810-985-4107.
Ann Arbor, Michigan Office: 101 North Main Street, Suite 460.
Telephone: 734-930-5600.
Fax: 734-930-0043.
Troy, Michigan Office: 1111 West Long Lake Road, Suite 300.
Telephone: 248-641-7600.
Fax: 248-641-0222.
Mount Clemens, Michigan Office: Towne Square Development, 10 S. Main Street, Suite 307.
Telephone: 810-954-3800.
Fax: 810-954-3803.
Lansing, Michigan Office: 530 Creyts Road, Suite A.
Telephone: 517-327-0300.
Fax: 517-327-0309.
Traverse City, Michigan Office: 1131 East Eighth Street, P.O. Box 3150.
Telephone: 231-941-1611.
Fax: 231-941-4420.
Marquette, Michigan Office: 228 West Washington Street, Suite 4,
Telephone: 906-228-7772.
Fax: 906-228-5999.

David N. Campos — Richard E. Holmes, Jr.

Thomas R. TerMaat
Matthew P. Venema
Michael D. Wade
Lori A. Ittner
Jill S Mulder

Counsel for: Allstate Insurance Co.; Sears, Roebuck & Co.; Liberty Mutual Insurance Co.; Continental Insurance Companies.

For full biographical listings, see the Martindale-Hubbell Law Directory

Grand Rapids—Continued

GRUEL, MILLS, NIMS AND PYLMAN (AV)

50 Monroe Place, Suite 700 West, 49503
Telephone: 616-235-5500
Fax: 616-235-5550

MEMBERS OF FIRM

Grant J. Gruel
William F. Mills
J. Clarke Nims
Norman H. Pylman, II
Scott R. Melton
Brion J. Brooks
Thomas R. Behm
J. Paul Janes

Representative Clients: Aquinas College; Bell Helmet Co.; Blodgett Memorial Medical Center; Chem Central, Inc.; Cook Pump Co.; Grove, Inc.; NBDC; Heim Corp.

For full biographical listings, see the Martindale-Hubbell Law Directory

KITCH DRUTCHAS WAGNER DENARDIS & VALITUTTI, A PROFESSIONAL CORPORATION (AV)

300 Ottawa, NW, Suite 210, 49503
Telephone: 616-456-8384
Fax: 616-456-8795
URL: http://www.kitch.com
Detroit, Michigan Office: One Woodward, Tenth Floor, 48226-3499.
Telephone: 313-965-7900.
Fax: 313-965-7403.
Lansing, Michigan Office: 120 Washington Square, North, Suite 280, One Michigan Avenue, 48933-1609.
Telephone: 517-372-6430.
Fax: 517-372-0441.
Marquette, Michigan Office: Old City Hall, 220 West Washington, Suite 500, 49855-4344.
Telephone: 906-228-0001.
Fax: 906-228-0003.
Toledo, Ohio Office: 405 Madison Avenue, Suite 1500, 43604-1235.
Telephone: 419-243-4006.
Fax: 419-243-7333.
Ann Arbor, Michigan Office: 303 Detroit Street, Suite 400, P.O. Box 8610, 48107-8610.
Telephone: 734-994-7600.
Fax: 734-994-7626.

Michael P. McCasey (Principal)
Susan M. Ramage (Associate Principal)
Christine E. Rice

For full biographical listings, see the Martindale-Hubbell Law Directory

MCSHANE & BOWIE, P.L.C. (AV)

1100 Campau Square Plaza, 99 Monroe Avenue, N.W., P.O. Box 360, 49501-0360
Telephone: 616-732-5000
Fax: 616-732-5099

OF COUNSEL

Jack M. Bowie (Retired)

MEMBERS OF FIRM

T. Gerald McShane (1902-1982)
David L. Smith
William H. Bowie
Keith P. Walker
Terry J. Mroz
Dan M. Challa
John F. Shape
Wayne P. Bryan
Richard A. Durell
Steven E. Bratschie
John R. Grant
Judy L. Walton

ASSOCIATES

Michael D. DeVries
Laura J. Luyendyk
Ruth Ann Skidmore

Representative Clients: Old Kent Bank; Amway Hotel Corp.; BETA Design Group, Inc.; Wolverine Gas & Oil Co., Inc.; M. W. VanderVeen Co.; Betten Imports, Inc.

For full biographical listings, see the Martindale-Hubbell Law Directory

MILLER, CANFIELD, PADDOCK AND STONE, P.L.C. (AV)

A Professional Limited Liability Company
Founded in 1852 by Sidney Davy Miller
99 Monroe, N.W. Suite 1200, 49503-2639
Telephone: 616-454-8656
Fax: 616-776-6322
URL: http://www.millercanfield.com
Detroit, Michigan Office: 150 West Jefferson, Suite 2500, 48226-4415.
Telephone: 313-963-6420.
Fax: 313-496-7500.
Cable Address: "Stem Detroit."
Ann Arbor, Michigan Office: 101 North Main Street, 7th Floor, 48104-1400.
Telephone: 734-663-2445.
Fax: 734-747-7147.
Troy, Michigan Office: 840 West Long Lake Road, Suite 200, 48098.
Telephone: 248-879-2000.
Fax: 248-879-2001.

(See Next Column)

Howell, Michigan Office: 121 South Barnard Street, Suite 4, 48843-2305.
Telephone: 517-546-7600.
Telecopier: 517-546-6974.
Kalamazoo, Michigan Office: 444 West Michigan Avenue, 49007-3752.
Telephone: 616-381-7030.
Fax: 616-382-0244.
Lansing, Michigan Office: One Michigan Avenue, Suite 900, 48933-1609.
Telephone: 517-487-2070.
Fax: 517-374-6304.
Monroe, Michigan Office: 214 East Elm Avenue, Suite 100, 48162-2682.
Telephone: 734-243-2000.
Fax: 734-243-0901.
Washington, D.C. Office: 1900 K Street, N.W., Suite 1150. 20006.
Telephone: 202-429-5575; 785-0600.
Fax: 202-331-1118; 785-1234.
Pensacola, Florida Office: 25 West Cedar, 32501.
Telephone: 850-469-1088.
Fax: 850-432-0677.
New York, New York Office: 1450 Broadway, 41st Floor, 10018.
Telephone: 212-704-4400.
Fax: 212-704-4410.
Gdynia, Poland Office: UL. Slaska 21, 81-319.
Telephone: 011-485-831-2808.
Fax: 011-48-58-628 6411.
Warsaw, Poland Office: UL. Nowogrodzkall, 5th Floor, 00-513.
Telephone: 011-4822 529 0200.
Fax: 011-4822 529 0201.
Katowice, Poland Office: UL. Francuska 35/37, 40-027.
Telephone: 011 (48-32) 757-2414.
Fax: 011 (48-32) 757-2483.

PRINCIPALS

Robert L. DeJong
Mark E. Putney
Richard A. Gaffin
Charles S. Mishkind
Michael G. Campbell
Robert E. Lee Wright
Douglas W. Crim
Stanley J. Stek
Vernon Bennett III

OF COUNSEL/SENIOR COUNSEL

David E. Hathaway

RESIDENT SENIOR ATTORNEYS

David J. Hasper
Stephen L. Elkins

RESIDENT ASSOCIATES

John T. Stecco
Vincent E. Woltjer
Andrew T. Blum
Robert J. Nolan

Representative Firm Clients: Chrysler Corporation; Comerica, Incorporated; City of Detroit, Michigan; Detroit Tigers, Inc.; First of Michigan; Ford Motor Company; Ford Motor Credit Company; Great Lakes Bancorp; Henry Ford Hospital; INVETECH Company.

For full biographical listings, see the Martindale-Hubbell Law Directory

SMITH HAUGHEY RICE & ROEGGE, P.C. (AV)

200 Calder Plaza Building, 250 Monroe Avenue, N.W., 49503-2251
Telephone: 616-774-8000
Facsimile: 616-774-2461
East Lansing, Michigan Office: 1400 Abbott Rd., Suite 410, 48823-1902.
Telephone: 517-332-3030.
Facsimile: 517-332-3468.
Traverse City, Michigan Office: City Centre Plaza, Suite 100, 202 East State Street, P.O. Box 848, 49685-0848.
Telephone: 231-929-4878.
Facsimile: 231-929-4182.

Clifford A. Mitts (1902-1962)
Laurence D. Smith (1913-1980)
Robert V.V. Rice (1899-1982)
Michael S. Barnes (1944-1989)
L. Roland Roegge
Thomas F. Blackwell
P. Laurence Mulvihill
Lawrence P. Mulligan
Thomas R. Tasker
Paul H. Reinhardt
Lance R. Mather
Charles F. Behler
John R. Sparks
Gary A. Rowe
William W. Jack, Jr.
William J. Hondorp
Thomas M. Weibel
James G. Black
E. Thomas Mc Carthy, Jr.
Glenn W. House, Jr.
Craig R. Noland
Paul M. Oleniczak
Craig S. Neckers
John C. O'Loughlin
Anthony J. Quarto
John M. Kruis
Paul Van Oostenburg
Dale Ann Iverson
William R. Jewell
Jon D. Vander Ploeg
Patrick F. Geary
Terence J. Ackert
Brian J. Kilbane
Robert C. Stone
Albert J. Engel, III
Phillip K. Mowers
Carol D. Carlson
Christopher R. Genther
Marilyn S. Nickell Tyree
Beth Suzanne Kromer
Robert M. Kruse
Aileen M. Leipprandt
David J. DeGraw
Matthew L. Meyer

Martha P. Forman
Karl Werner Butterer, Jr.
Garrett J. Tenhave-Chapman
J. Joseph Rossi
Stacie R. Seitz
William A. Sikkel IV
James J. Rosloniec
Angela T. Ross

(See Next Column)

SMITH HAUGHEY RICE & ROEGGE P.C., *Grand Rapids—Continued*

OF COUNSEL

A. B. Smith, Jr. David O. Haughey

Representative Clients: Chevron; Cincinnati Insurance Co.; General Motors Corp.; Kemper Insurance Group; Michigan Hospital Assn.; Navistar International; St. Paul Insurance Cos.; Steelcase, Inc.; Dow Elanco.

For full biographical listings, see the Martindale-Hubbell Law Directory

*HILLSDALE,** Hillsdale Co.

PARKER, HAYES & LOVINGER, P.C. (AV)

14-16 South Howell Street, P.O. Box 358, 49242
Telephone: 517-437-7210
Fax: 517-437-0260

James B. Parker
Lawrence L. Hayes, Jr.
John P. Lovinger

Representative Clients: Hillsdale County National Bank; Villages of Jonesville and Camden; Hillsdale County (Labor Counsel); Hillsdale College; Powell Petroleum Co.; Foulke Construction Co.; Somerset Township; Hillsdale Tool & Mfg. Co.

For full biographical listings, see the Martindale-Hubbell Law Directory

HOLLAND, Ottawa Co.

CUNNINGHAM DALMAN, P.C. (AV)

321 Settlers Road, P.O. Box 1767, 49422-1767
Telephone: 616-392-1821
Fax: 616-392-4769
Email: cunndalm@crossover.net *URL:* http://www.holland-law.com

Gordon H. Cunningham
Ronald L. Dalman
Max R. Murphy
James A. Bidol
Andrew J. Mulder
Kenneth B. Breese
Jeffrey K. Helder
Ronald J. Vander Veen
David M. Zessin
Mark H. Zietlow
Randall S. Schipper
Susan E. Vroegop
Joel G. Bouwens

Gregory J. McCoy
Jason M. Milstone
Aaron Leal
Dawn J. Ward

Representative Clients: Huntington National Bank; First of America Bank-Holland, N.A.; Ameribank; City of Holland; Auto Club Insurance Assn. (AAA); American States Insurance Co.; Holland Economic Development Corp.; Hope College; Western Theological Seminary.
Reference: Huntington National Bank.

For full biographical listings, see the Martindale-Hubbell Law Directory

*HOUGHTON,** Houghton Co.

VAIRO, MECHLIN, TOMASI, JOHNSON & MANCHESTER (AV)

400 East Houghton Avenue, 49931
Telephone: 906-482-0770
Fax: 906-482-2938
Calumet, Michigan Office: 1175 Calumet Avenue, Suite K. 44913.
Telephone: 906-337-0312.

MEMBERS OF FIRM

Gerald G. Vairo
David R. Mechlin
Paul J. Tomasi
Frederick N. Johnson
Jeryl A. Manchester

Representative Clients: City of Houghton; Elm River Township; First National Bank of Calumet-Lake Linden; Lake Linden-Hubbell School District; Portage Charter Township; Portage View Hospital; Superior National Bank and Trust Company; Michigan Technological University; North County Bank; Upper Peninsula Power Co.

For full biographical listings, see the Martindale-Hubbell Law Directory

*JACKSON,** Jackson Co.

MARCOUX, ALLEN, ABBOTT, SCHOMER & BOWER, P.C. (AV)

145 South Jackson Street, P.O. Box 787, 49204-0787
Telephone: 517-787-4100
Fax: 517-787-9455
Email: marcoux@jacksonmi.com

William J. Marcoux (Retired)
William O. Allen
William M. Abbott
John H. Schomer
Diane Y. Bower
William B. Nichols, Jr.
Robert T. Kendall, III
Timothy R. Allen
Richard C. Lindsey, Jr.

OF COUNSEL

Walter R. Boris
Lawrence L. Bullen
Philip M. Moilanen
Terry J. Klaasen
T. Harrison Stanton

For full biographical listings, see the Martindale-Hubbell Law Directory

*KALAMAZOO,** Kalamazoo Co.

EARLY, LENNON, PETERS & CROCKER, P.C. (AV)

900 Comerica Building, 49007-4752
Telephone: 616-381-8844
Fax: 616-349-8525
Email: elpc@michbar.org

George H. Lennon, III
John T. Peters, Jr.
David G. Crocker
Harold E. Fischer, Jr.
Lawrence M. Brenton
Gordon C. Miller
Blake D. Crocker
Robert M. Taylor
Patrick D. Crocker
Andrew J. Vorbrich
Nicolette G. Hahn
Robert G Lennon

OF COUNSEL

Vincent T. Early
C. H. Mullen
Thompson Bennett

Attorneys for: Aetna Insurance; Kemper Group; Medical Protective Co.; Zurich Insurance; Liberty Mutual; Home Insurance.

For full biographical listings, see the Martindale-Hubbell Law Directory

HOWARD & HOWARD ATTORNEYS, P.C. (AV)

The Michigan Building, Suite 200, 100 Portage Street, 49007-4802
Telephone: 616-382-1483
Telecopier: 616-382-1568
Bloomfield Hills, Michigan Office: The Pinehurst Office Center, Suite 101, 1400 North Woodward Avenue.
Telephone: 248-645-1483.
Telecopier: 248-645-1568.
Lansing, Michigan Office: The Phoenix Building, Suite 500, 222 Washington Square North.
Telephone: 517-485-1483.
Telecopier: 517-485-1568.
Peoria, Illinois Office: One Technology Plaza, Suite 600, 211 Fulton Street.
Telephone: 309-672-1483.
Telecopier: 309-672-1568.

Jeffrey P. Chalmers
Richard M. Clark
William A. Dornbos
James H. Geary
Joseph B. Hemker
Gina M. Torielli

Representative Clients: National City Corp.; Kmart Corp.; Stryker Corp.; DaimlerChrysler Corporation.

For full biographical listings, see the Martindale-Hubbell Law Directory

KREIS, ENDERLE, CALLANDER & HUDGINS, A PROFESSIONAL CORPORATION (AV)

One Moorsbridge, P.O. Box 4010, 49003-4010
Telephone: 616-324-3000
Facsimile: 616-324-3010
Email: kech@kech.com *URL:* http://www.kech.com
Battle Creek, Michigan Office: One West Michigan Avenue, 49017.
Telephone: 616-966-3000.
Fax: 616-966-3022.

Russell A. Kreis
Alan G. Enderle
Douglas L. Callander
C. Reid Hudgins III
Robert B. Borsos
Jeffrey C. O'Brien
Stephen J. Hessen
Jeffery S. Rubel
Thomas G. King
Stephen L. Simons (Resident, Battle Creek Office)
Mark E. Kreter (Resident, Battle Creek Office)
Daniel P. McGlinn
Raymond C. Schultz
Jeffrey D. Swenarton
James C. Boerigter
John F. Koryto
Janice Roark Peters
Matthew S. DePerno
Annette D. Nickel
Peter F. Davis
Manuel R. Rupe
Floyd E. Gates, Jr. (Resident, Battle Creek Office)

OF COUNSEL

James M. Sullivan (Resident, Battle Creek Office)

For full biographical listings, see the Martindale-Hubbell Law Directory

LEWIS & ALLEN, P.C. (AV)

Old Kent Bank Building, Suite 800, 136 East Michigan Avenue, 49007-3946
Telephone: 616-388-7600
Fax: 616-349-3831

Dean S. Lewis
W. Fred Allen, Jr.
Barry R. Smith
William A. Redmond
Stephen M. Denenfeld
Anne McGregor Fries
Gregory G. St. Arnauld
James M. Marquardt
Christopher T. Haenicke
Winfield J. Hollander (1906-1996)

LEGAL SUPPORT PERSONNEL

Dorothy B. Kelly

For full biographical listings, see the Martindale-Hubbell Law Directory

Kalamazoo—Continued

MILLER, CANFIELD, PADDOCK AND STONE, P.L.C. (AV)

A Professional Limited Liability Company
Founded in 1852 by Sidney Davy Miller
444 West Michigan Avenue, 49007-3752
Telephone: 616-381-7030
Fax: 616-382-0244
URL: http://www.millercanfield.com
Detroit, Michigan Office: 150 West Jefferson, Suite 2500, 48226-4415.
Telephone: 313-963-6420.
Fax: 313-496-7500.
Cable Address: "Stem Detroit."
Ann Arbor, Michigan Office: 101 North Main Street, 7th Floor, 48104-1400.
Telephone: 734-663-2445.
Fax: 734-747-7147.
Troy, Michigan Office: 840 West Long Lake Road, Suite 200, 48098.
Telephone: 248-879-2000.
Fax: 248-879-2001.
Grand Rapids, Michigan Office: 99 Monroe, N.W., Suite 1200, 49503-2639.
Telephone: 616-454-8656.
Fax: 616-776-6322.
Howell, Michigan Office: 121 South Barnard Street, Suite 4, 48843-2305.
Telephone: 517-546-7600.
Telecopier: 517-546-6974.
Lansing, Michigan Office: One Michigan Avenue, Suite 900, 48933-1609.
Telephone: 517-487-2070.
Fax: 517-374-6304.
Monroe, Michigan Office: 214 East Elm Avenue, Suite 100, 48162-2682.
Telephone: 734-243-2000.
Fax: 734-243-0901.
Washington, D.C. Office: 1900 K Street, N.W., Suite 1150. 20006.
Telephone: 202-429-5575; 785-0600.
Fax: 202-331-1118; 785-1234.
Pensacola, Florida Office: 25 West Cedar, 32501.
Telephone: 850-469-1088.
Fax: 850-432-0677.
New York, New York Office: 1450 Broadway, 41st Floor, 10018.
Telephone: 212-704-4400.
Fax: 212-704-4410.
Gdynia, Poland Office: UL. Slaska 21, 81-319.
Telephone: 011-485-831-2808.
Fax: 011-48-58-628 6411.
Warsaw, Poland Office: UL. Nowogrodzkall, 5th Floor, 00-513.
Telephone: 011-4822 529 0200.
Fax: 011-4822 529 0201.
Katowice, Poland Office: UL. Francuska 35/37, 40-027.
Telephone: 011 (48-32) 757-2414.
Fax: 011 (48-32) 757-2483.

PRINCIPALS

Eric V. Brown, Jr.
Charles E. Ritter
John A. Campbell
Thomas P. Hustoles
John R. Cook
James G. Vantine, Jr.
Kevin M. McCarthy
Ronald E. Baylor
Thomas H. Van Dis
James E. Spurr
Steven M. Stankewicz
Vernon Bennett III
Pamela Chapman Enslen
Don M. Schmidt
Kurt N. Sherwood
Ballard Jay Yelton, III
John G. VanSlambrouck
Lori L. Purkey

OF COUNSEL/SENIOR COUNSEL

Eric V. Brown, Sr.
Gerard Thomas

RESIDENT SENIOR ATTORNEYS

Leo P. Goddeyne

RESIDENT ASSOCIATES

Loyal A. Eldridge III
Kurt P. McCamman
Scott R. Sikkenga
James B. Thelen
Michael V. Camarota
Sarah S. Swallow
Oren R. Griffin
Stuart M. Heath

Representative Firm Clients: Chrysler Corporation; Comerica, Incorporated; City of Detroit, Michigan; Detroit Tigers, Inc.; First of Michigan; Ford Motor Company; Ford Motor Credit Company; Great Lakes Bancorp; Henry Ford Hospital; INVETECH Company.

For full biographical listings, see the Martindale-Hubbell Law Directory

LANSING, Ingham Co.

DICKINSON WRIGHT PLLC (AV)

Suite 200, 215 South Washington Square, 48933-1816
Telephone: 517-371-1730
Facsimile: 517-487-4700
URL: http://www.dickinson-wright.com
Detroit, Michigan Office: 500 Woodward Avenue, Suite 4000.
Telephone: 313-223-3500.
Facsimile: 313-223-3598.
Bloomfield Hills, Michigan Office: 525 North Woodward Avenue, Suite 2000.
Telephone: 248-433-7200.
Facsimile: 248-433-7274.

(See Next Column)

Grand Rapids, Michigan Office: 200 Ottawa Avenue, N.W., Suite 900.
Telephone: 616-458-1300. Facsimile 616-458-6753.
Washington, D.C. Office: Suite 800, 1901 L Street, N.W.
Telephone: 202-457-0160.
Facsimile: 202-659-1559.

RESIDENT MEMBERS

James W. Bliss
John M. Dempsey
Dwight D. Ebaugh
Peter H. Ellsworth
Joseph A. Fink
James E. Lozier
Peter S. Sheldon
Kester K. So
Jeffery V. Stuckey

CONSULTING MEMBER

Judson Werbelow

OF COUNSEL

David C. Coey

RESIDENT ASSOCIATES

Sara Allswede Arons
Jennifer L. Frye
Ann K. Johannes
Tina K. Speagle (Not admitted in MI)
Todd A. Svanda
Jennifer L. Uetz

For full biographical listings, see the Martindale-Hubbell Law Directory

DYKEMA GOSSETT PLLC (AV)

800 Michigan National Tower, 48933-1707
Telephone: 517-374-9100
Fax: 517-374-9191
Email: mstarrs@dykema.com *URL:* http://www.dykema.com
Ann Arbor, Michigan Office: 315 East Eisenhower Parkway, Suite 100, 49108-3306.
Telephone: 734-214-7660.
Fax: 734-214-7696.
Bloomfield Hills, Michigan Office: 1577 North Woodward Avenue, Suite 300, 48304-2820.
Telephone: 248-203-0700.
Fax: 248-203-0763.
Chicago, Illinois Office: 55 East Monroe Street, Suite 3050, 60603-5709.
Telephone: 312-551-4900.
Fax: 312-551-4919.
Detroit, Michigan Office: 400 Renaissance Center, 48243-1668.
Telephone: 313-568-6800.
Fax: 313-568-6545.
Grand Rapids, Michigan Office: Suite 700, 300 Ottawa Avenue, N.W., 49503-2304.
Telephone: 616-776-7500.
Fax: 616-776-7573.
Washington, D.C. Office: Franklin Square, Suite 300 West, 1300 I Street, N.W., 20005-3306.
Telephone: 202-522-8600.
Fax: 202-522-8669.
Affiliated Office: Via Matconi, 3, 40122 Bologna, Italy.
Telephone: 011-39-51-228222.
Fax: 011-39-51-6593580.

RESIDENT MEMBERS

Bruce G. Davis
Sandra M. Cotter
Alan R. Dominick
Albert Ernst
Julia A. Goatley
James P. Kiefer
Richard D. McLellan (Member in Charge)
William J. Perrone
Lori M. Silsbury
Stephen H. Zimmerman

RESIDENT ASSOCIATES

John M. Brown
Steven C. Liedel
William Lee Logan, III
James D. Oegema
Kristan L. Richardson
Christine Mason Soneral
Wendell Alan Wilk
Leonard C. Wolfe

For full biographical listings, see the Martindale-Hubbell Law Directory

FOSTER, SWIFT, COLLINS & SMITH, P.C. (AV)

313 South Washington Square, 48933-2193
Telephone: 517-371-8100
Telecopier: 517-371-8200
URL: http://www.fosterswift.com
Farmington Hills, Michigan Office: 32300 Northwestern Highway, Suite 230.
Telephone: 248-539-9900.
Fax: 248-851-7504.

Walter S. Foster (1877-1961)
Richard B. Foster (1908-1996)
Theodore W. Swift
John L. Collins
Webb A. Smith
Allan J. Claypool
Gary J. McRay
Robert J. McCullen
Stephen I. Jurmu
William K. Fahey
Stephen O. Schultz
William R. Schulz
David H. Aldrich
Scott A. Storey
Charles A. Janssen
Charles E. Barbieri
James B. Jensen, Jr.
Scott L. Mandel
Robert E. McFarland
James B. Croom
Michael D. Sanders
David J. Houston

(See Next Column)

FOSTER, SWIFT, COLLINS & SMITH P.C., *Lansing—Continued*

Brian A. Kaser
Sherry A. Stein
Brent A. Titus
Stephen J. Lowney
Kenneth T. Brooks
Louis K. Nigg
Glen A. Schmiege
Patricia A. Calore
Kevin T. McGraw
Michael J. Bommarito
Deanna Swisher
Jean G. Schtokal
Mark H. Canady
Eric E. Doster
Michael W. Puerner
Stephen J. Rhodes
Matt G. Hrebec
Brian G. Goodenough
Melissa J. Jackson
Steven H. Lasher
Nancy L. Kahn
Mark J. Burzych
Thomas R. Meagher
Douglas A. Mielock
Scott R. Forbush
Peter R. Albertins
Scott A. Chernich
Matthew W. Collins
Christopher A. Ballard
Rebecca S. Davies
Andrea J. Roe
Jennifer M. Van Horn
Anne M. Skilton
Toree S. Randall
John C. Schlinker
Barbara J. Oyer
Michael R. Huber
Nicole M. Bowman
Geoffrey D. Harrison
Thomas J. Byrne
Claire V. Groen
Joel W. Baar
Jennifer A. Kildea
John P. Nicolucci

OF COUNSEL

Lawrence B. Lindemer
David VanderHaagen
John W. Ester
Donald E. Martin
Norman D. Hawkins
Paul J. Millenbach

LEGAL SUPPORT PERSONNEL

LEGAL ASSISTANTS

Toni R. Blanken
Terri L. Bolyard
Sandra L. De Santis
Tracey C. Drumm
Ida Rose Farhat, CLA
Kelly A. LaGrave, CLA
Jerri L. Luidens
Jeanne M. Phillips, CLA
Marsha M. Pullen
Carole M. Schneider
Lisa J. Silverthorn, CLA
Theresa G. Solberg
Barbara Toleno
Janice S. Underwood, CLA
Jaxine L. Wintjen, CLA

For full biographical listings, see the Martindale-Hubbell Law Directory

GARAN, LUCOW, MILLER & SEWARD, P.C. (AV)

Office Park West, 530 Creyts Road, Suite A, 48917
Telephone: 517-327-0300
Fax: 517-327-0309
URL: http://www.garanlucow.com
Detroit, Michigan Office: 1000 Woodbridge Place.
Telephone: 313-446-1530.
Fax: 313-259-0450.
Port Huron, Michigan Office: Port Huron Office Center, 511 Fort Street, Suite 505.
Telephone: 810-985-4400.
Fax: 810-985-4187.
Ann Arbor, Michigan Office: 101 North Main Street, Suite 460.
Telephone: 734-930-5600.
Fax: 734-930-0043.
Troy, Michigan Office: 1111 West Long Lake Road, Suite 300.
Telephone: 248-641-7600.
Fax: 248-641-0222.
Mount Clemens, Michigan Office: Towne Square Development, 10 S. Main Street, Suite 307.
Telephone: 810-954-3800.
Fax: 810-954-3803.
Grand Rapids, Michigan Office: First of America Center, 171 Monroe Avenue, N.W., Suite 950.
Telephone: 616-742-5500.
Fax: 616-742-5566.
Grand Blanc, Michigan Office: 8332 Office Park Drive.
Telephone: 810-695-3700.
Fax: 810-695-6488.
Traverse City, Michigan Office: 1131 East Eighth Street, P.O. Box 3150.
Telephone: 231-941-1611.
Fax: 231-941-4420.
Marquette, Michigan Office: 228 West Washington Street, Suite 4,
Telephone: 906-228-7772.
Fax: 906-228-5999.

Kenneth V. Klaus (Resident)

Paul E. Tower (Resident)

For full biographical listings, see the Martindale-Hubbell Law Directory

HONIGMAN MILLER SCHWARTZ AND COHN (AV)

A Partnership including Professional Corporations
222 North Washington Square, Suite 400, 48933-1800
Telephone: 517-484-8282
Telecopier: 517-484-8286
Email: mvg@honigman.com *URL:* http://law.honigman.com
Detroit, Michigan Office: 2290 First National Building, 660 Woodward Avenue, 48226.
Telephone: 313-465-7000.

(See Next Column)

MEMBERS

Richard J. Aaron
Ann L. Andrews
Frederick M. Baker, Jr.
Daniel J. Demlow
Andrea Hansen
Sandra L. Jasinski
John S. Kane
Timothy Sawyer Knowlton
John D. Pirich
Alan M. Valade
Patrick R. Van Tiflin
Ruth E. Zimmerman

ASSOCIATES

Andrew J. Gerdes
Alison M. Stanley
Daniel L. Stanley

General Counsel for: Dart Container Corp; Forbes-Cohen Properties (The Lansing Mall); Michigan Hospital Association.
Legal or Special Counsel for: Champion International; Greater Detroit Resource Recovery Authority; Michigan Gas Utilities, a division of UtiliCorp United, Inc.

For full biographical listings, see the Martindale-Hubbell Law Directory

HOWARD & HOWARD ATTORNEYS, P.C. (AV)

The Phoenix Building, Suite 500, 222 Washington Square, North, 48933-1817
Telephone: 517-485-1483
Telecopier: 517-485-1568
Kalamazoo, Michigan Office: The Michigan Building, Suite 200, 100 Portage Street.
Telephone: 616-382-1483.
Telecopier: 616-382-1568.
Bloomfield Hills, Michigan Office: The Pinehurst Office Center, Suite 101, 1400 North Woodward Avenue.
Telephone: 248-645-1483.
Telecopier: 248-645-1568.
Peoria, Illinois Office: One Technology Plaza, Suite 600, 211 Fulton Street.
Telephone: 309-672-1483.
Telecopier: 309-672-1568.

Stewart A. Binke
Michael J. Brown
Todd D. Chamberlain
Ann D. Fillingham
Michele LaForest Halloran
Ellen M. House-Harvath
James R. Holcomb
Shannon A. Hunt
Robert D. Mollhagen
C. Douglas Moran
Brad S. Rutledge
Gina M. Torielli
Donald F. Tucker

Representative Clients: National City Corp.; Kmart Corp.; DaimlerChrysler Corporation; CSX Transportation, Inc.

For full biographical listings, see the Martindale-Hubbell Law Directory

KITCH DRUTCHAS WAGNER DENARDIS & VALITUTTI, A PROFESSIONAL CORPORATION (AV)

One Michigan Avenue, 120 Washington Square, North, Suite 280, 48933-1609
Telephone: 517-372-6430
Fax: 517-372-0441
URL: http://www.kitch.com
Detroit, Michigan Office: One Woodward, Tenth Floor, 48226-3499.
Telephone: 313-965-7900.
Fax: 313-965-7403.
Macomb County Office: Towne Square Development, 10 South Main Street, Suite 301, Mount Clemens, 48043-7903.
Telephone: 810-463-9770.
Fax: 810-463-8994.
Toledo, Ohio Office: 405 Madison Avenue, Suite 1500, 43604-1235.
Telephone: 419-243-4006.
Fax: 419-243-7333.
Marquette, Michigan Office: Old City Hall, 220 West Washington Street, Suite 500, 49855-4344.
Telephone: 906-228-0001.
Fax: 906-228-0003.
Ann Arbor, Michigan Office: 303 Detroit Street, Suite 400, P.O. Box 8610. 48107-8610.
Telephone: 734-994-7600.
Fax: 734-994-7626.
Grand Rapids, Michigan Office: 300 Ottawa, NW, Suite 210, 49503.
Telephone: 616-456-8384.
Fax: 616-456-8795.

Richard A. Kitch (Principal)
John P. Ryan (Principal)
Dennis W. Fliehman
Marcia L. Malouin
Eric M. St. Onge
Richard J. Suhrheinrich

For full biographical listings, see the Martindale-Hubbell Law Directory

Lansing—Continued

MILLER, CANFIELD, PADDOCK AND STONE, P.L.C. (AV)

A Professional Limited Liability Company
Founded in 1852 by Sidney Davy Miller
Suite 900, One Michigan Avenue, 48933-1609
Telephone: 517-487-2070
Fax: 517-374-6304
URL: http://www.millercanfield.com
Detroit, Michigan Office: 150 West Jefferson, Suite 2500, 48226-4415.
Telephone: 313-963-6420.
Fax: 313-496-7500.
Cable Address: "Stem Detroit."
Ann Arbor, Michigan Office: 101 North Main Street, 7th Floor, 48104-1400.
Telephone: 734-663-2445.
Fax: 734-747-7147.
Troy, Michigan Office: 840 West Long Lake Road, Suite 200, 48098.
Telephone: 248-879-2000.
Fax: 248-879-2001.
Grand Rapids, Michigan Office: 99 Monroe, N.W., Suite 1200, 49503-2639.
Telephone: 616-454-8656.
Fax: 616-776-6322.
Howell, Michigan Office: 121 South Barnard Street, Suite 4, 48843-2305.
Telephone: 517-546-7600.
Telecopier: 517-546-6974.
Kalamazoo, Michigan Office: 444 West Michigan Avenue, 49007-3752.
Telephone: 616-381-7030.
Fax: 616-382-0244.
Monroe, Michigan Office: 214 East Elm Avenue, Suite 100, 48162-2682.
Telephone: 734-243-2000.
Fax: 734-243-0901.
Washington, D.C. Office: 1900 K Street, N.W., Suite 1150. 20006.
Telephone: 202-429-5575; 785-0600.
Fax: 202-331-1118; 785-1234.
Pensacola, Florida Office: 25 West Cedar, 32501.
Telephone: 850-469-1088.
Fax: 850-432-0677.
New York, New York Office: 1450 Broadway, 41st Floor, 10018.
Telephone: 212-704-4400.
Fax: 212-704-4410.
Gdynia, Poland Office: UL. Slaska 21, 81-319.
Telephone: 011-485-831-2808.
Fax: 011-48-58-628 6411.
Warsaw, Poland Office: UL. Nowogrodzkall, 5th Floor, 00-513.
Telephone: 011-4822 529 0200.
Fax: 011-4822 529 0201.
Katowice, Poland Office: UL. Francuska 35/37, 40-027.
Telephone: 011 (48-32) 757-2414.
Fax: 011 (48-32) 757-2483.

RESIDENT PRINCIPALS

William J. Danhof
Michael R. Atkins
Thomas C. Phillips
Christopher J. Dembowski
Michael J. Hodge
Cynthia B. Faulhaber
Kevin J. Moody
Jay B. Rising
Steven E. Chester
Sherry Katz-Crank
James R. Lancaster, Jr.

RESIDENT SENIOR ATTORNEYS

Clifford T. Flood
Louis B. Reinwasser

RESIDENT ASSOCIATE

Dean M. Altobelli

Representative Firm Clients: Chrysler Corporation; Comerica, Incorporated; City of Detroit, Michigan; Detroit Tigers, Inc.; First of Michigan; Ford Motor Company; Ford Motor Credit Company; Great Lakes Bancorp; Henry Ford Hospital; INVETECH Company.

For full biographical listings, see the Martindale-Hubbell Law Directory

SMITH HAUGHEY RICE & ROEGGE, P.C.

(See East Lansing)

TIMMER, JAMO & O'LEARY (AV)

521 Seymour Avenue, 48933
Telephone: 517-371-3500
Fax: 517-371-4514
Email: TIMJAMOLOP@MICHBAR.ORG

MEMBERS OF FIRM

James A. Timmer
James S. Jamo
James S. O'Leary
Kathleen A. Lopilato

Representative Clients: Auto Owners Insurance Co.; Travelers/Aetna Insurance Co.; Western Surety Co.; Indiana Insurance Company/The Netherlands Insurance Companies; Michigan Municipal League; Meadowbrook Insurance; Citizens Insurance Company of America; Speedway SuperAmerica LLC; TIG/Nationwide Insurance Co.; Wolverine Mutual Insurance Co.

For full biographical listings, see the Martindale-Hubbell Law Directory

*MARQUETTE,** Marquette Co.

KENDRICKS BORDEAU, P.C. (AV)

128 West Spring Street, 49855
Telephone: 906-226-2543
Fax: 906-226-2819
Email: kendbord@up.net

George T. Kendricks (1918-1991)
Stephen F. Adamini
Ronald D. Keefe
William R. Smith
Dennis H. Girard
Kenneth J. Seavoy
D. Gregor MacGregor, III
Michael J. Kolasa
Tami M. Seavoy

Suzanne L. Curry
Joseph Jon Haggenmiller

OF COUNSEL

Robert M. Bordeau

For full biographical listings, see the Martindale-Hubbell Law Directory

*MIDLAND,** Midland Co.

CURRIE KENDALL POLASKY MEISEL, PLC (AV)

6024 Eastman Avenue, P.O. Box 2765, 48641-2765
Telephone: 517-839-0300
Fax: 517-832-0077
Saginaw, Michigan Office: 4800 Fashion Square Boulevard, Suite 100, 48603.
Telephone: 517-792-9300; 517-792-1111.
Fax: 517-792-7000; 517-793-6597.

Gilbert A. Currie (1882-1960)
Gilbert A. Currie (1923-1998)
Peter J. Kendall (1961-1999)
William C. Collins
Ramon F. Rolf, Jr.
Daniel J. Cline
Peter A. Poznak
Julia A. Close
Jeffrey N. Dyer
Jonathan E. Lauderbach
Amy E. Wilson
Cheryl L. Whitman
Todd M. Gambrell
Frank M. Polasky (Resident, Saginaw Office)
Robert H. Meisel (Resident, Saginaw Office)
Michael H. Allen (Resident, Saginaw Office)
Larry L. Preston (Resident, Saginaw Office)
David J. Kolat (Resident, Saginaw Office)
M. Randall Jurrens (Resident, Saginaw Office)
John E. Gannon (Resident, Saginaw Office)
Carolyn Pollock Cary (Resident, Saginaw Office)
John D. Jolley (Resident, Saginaw Office)
W. Jay Brown (Resident, Saginaw Office)

OF COUNSEL

James A. Kendall

Counsel for: Chemical Financial Corp.; Chemical Bank & Trust Co.; Saginaw Valley State University; Northwood University; The Midland Foundation; Elsa U. Pardee Foundation; Rollin M. Gerstacker Foundation; Charles J. Strosacker Foundation.

For full biographical listings, see the Martindale-Hubbell Law Directory

*MONROE,** Monroe Co.

MILLER, CANFIELD, PADDOCK AND STONE, P.L.C. (AV)

A Professional Limited Liability Company
Founded in 1852 by Sidney Davy Miller
214 East Elm Avenue, Suite 100, 48162-2682
Telephone: 734-243-2000
Fax: 734-243-0901
URL: http://www.millercanfield.com
Detroit, Michigan Office: 150 West Jefferson, Suite 2500, 48226-4415.
Telephone: 313-963-6420.
Fax: 313-496-7500.
Cable Address: "Stem Detroit."
Ann Arbor, Michigan Office: 101 North Main Street, 7th Floor, 48104-1400.
Telephone: 734-663-2445.
Fax: 734-747-7147.
Troy, Michigan Office: 840 West Long Lake Road, Suite 200, 48098.
Telephone: 248-879-2000.
Fax: 248-879-2001.
Grand Rapids, Michigan Office: 99 Monroe, N.W., Suite 1200, 49503-2639.
Telephone: 616-454-8656.
Fax: 616-776-6322.
Howell, Michigan Office: 121 South Barnard Street, Suite 4, 48843-2305.
Telephone: 517-546-7600.
Telecopier: 517-546-6974.
Kalamazoo, Michigan Office: 444 West Michigan Avenue, 49007-3752.
Telephone: 616-381-7030.
Fax: 616-382-0244.
Lansing, Michigan Office: One Michigan Avenue, Suite 900, 48933-1609.
Telephone: 517-487-2070.
Fax: 517-374-6304.

(See Next Column)

MILLER, CANFIELD, PADDOCK AND STONE P.L.C., *Monroe—Continued*

Washington, D.C. Office: 1900 K Street, N.W., Suite 1150. 20006.
Telephone: 202-429-5575; 785-0600.
Fax: 202-331-1118; 785-1234.
Pensacola, Florida Office: 25 West Cedar, 32501.
Telephone: 850-469-1088.
Fax: 850-432-0677.
New York, New York Office: 1450 Broadway, 41st Floor, 10018.
Telephone: 212-704-4400.
Fax: 212-704-4410.
Gdynia, Poland Office: UL. Slaska 21, 81-319.
Telephone: 011-485-831-2808.
Fax: 011-48-58-628 6411.
Warsaw, Poland Office: UL. Nowogrodzkall, 5th Floor, 00-513.
Telephone: 011-4822 529 0200.
Fax: 011-4822 529 0201.
Katowice, Poland Office: UL. Francuska 35/37, 40-027.
Telephone: 011 (48-32) 757-2414.
Fax: 011 (48-32) 757-2483.

RESIDENT PRINCIPALS

Rocque E. Lipford (P.C.)

Representative Firm Clients: Chrysler Corporation; Comerica, Incorporated; City of Detroit, Michigan; Detroit Tigers, Inc.; First of Michigan; Ford Motor Company; Ford Motor Credit Company; Great Lakes Bancorp; Henry Ford Hospital; INVETECH Company.

For full biographical listings, see the Martindale-Hubbell Law Directory

READY, SULLIVAN & READY, L.L.P. (AV)

204 South Macomb Street, 48161
Telephone: 734-242-7600
Fax: 734-242-0366

MEMBERS OF FIRM

Thomas D. Ready — Durward L. Hutchinson
Michael L. Heller — John F. Ready

ASSOCIATES

Conly K. Crossley — Christina D. Hills
Frank L. Arnold

Representative Client: Motorists Insurance Cos.

For full biographical listings, see the Martindale-Hubbell Law Directory

*MOUNT CLEMENS,** Macomb Co.

GARAN, LUCOW, MILLER & SEWARD, P.C. (AV)

Towne Square Development, 10 S. Main Street Suite 307, 48043-2370
Telephone: 810-954-3800
Fax: 810-954-3803
URL: http://www.garanlucow.com
Detroit, Michigan Office: 1000 Woodbridge Place.
Telephone: 313-446-1530.
Fax: 313-259-0450.
Grand Blanc, Michigan Office: 8332 Office Park Drive.
Telephone: 810-695-3700.
Fax: 810-695-6488.
Ann Arbor, Michigan Office: 101 North Main Street, Suite 460.
Telephone: 734-930-5600.
Fax: 734-930-0043.
Troy, Michigan Office: 1111 West Long Lake Road, Suite 300.
Telephone: 248-641-7600.
Fax: 248-641-0222.
Port Huron, Michigan Office: Port Huron Office Center, 511 Fort Street, Suite 505.
Telephone: 810-985-4400.
Fax: 810-985-4107.
Grand Rapids, Michigan Office: First of America Center, 171 Monroe Avenue, N.W., Suite 950.
Telephone: 616-742-5500.
Fax: 616-742-5566.
Lansing, Michigan Office: 530 Creyts Road, Suite A.
Telephone: 517-327-0300.
Fax: 517-327-0309.
Traverse City, Michigan Office: 1131 East Eighth Street, P.O. Box 3150.
Telephone: 231-941-1611.
Fax: 231-941-4420.
Marquette, Michigan Office: 228 West Washington Street, Suite 4,
Telephone: 906-228-7772.
Fax: 906-228-5999.

Richard E. Eaton (Resident) — Robert F. MacAlpine

For full biographical listings, see the Martindale-Hubbell Law Directory

KITCH DRUTCHAS WAGNER DENARDIS & VALITUTTI, A PROFESSIONAL CORPORATION (AV)

Towne Square Development, 10 South Main Street, Suite 301, 48043-7903
Telephone: 810-463-9770
Fax: 810-463-8994
URL: http://www.kitch.com
Detroit, Michigan Office: One Woodward, Tenth Floor, 48226-3499.
Telephone: 313-965-7900.
Fax: 313-965-7403.
Lansing, Michigan Office: 120 Washington Square, North, Suite 280, One Michigan Avenue, 48933-1609.
Telephone: 517-372-6430.
Fax: 517-372-0441.
Marquette, Michigan Office: Old City Hall, 220 West Washington, Suite 500, 49855-4344.
Telephone: 906-228-0001.
Fax: 906-228-0003.
Toledo, Ohio Office: 405 Madison Avenue, Suite 1500, 43604-1235.
Telephone: 419-243-4006.
Fax: 419-243-7333.
Ann Arbor, Michigan Office: 303 Detroit Street, Suite 400, P.O. Box 8610, 48107-8610.
Telephone: 734-994-7600.
Fax: 734-994-7626.
Grand Rapids, Michigan Office: 300 Ottawa, NW, Suite 210, 49503.
Telephone: 616-456-8384.
Fax: 616-456-8795.

Ralph F. Valitutti, Jr. (Principal) — Steve N. Cheolas (Principal)

For full biographical listings, see the Martindale-Hubbell Law Directory

*MOUNT PLEASANT,** Isabella Co.

HALL AND LEWIS, P.C. (AV)

300 South University Avenue, 48858
Telephone: 517-773-0004
Fax: 517-772-1512

Thomas W. Hall, Jr. — John W. Lewis

Becky J. Bolles

Representative Clients: Blodgett Oil Co., Inc.; Clark's Manufactured Homes, Inc.; DeWitt Lumber Co.; The Embers, Inc.; Family Home Health Care; Isabella Community Credit Union; JEFCO Investments, Ltd.; Keystone Property Management, Inc.; Lincoln Hill, Inc.; Midland Area Credit Union.

For full biographical listings, see the Martindale-Hubbell Law Directory

LYNCH, GALLAGHER, LYNCH & MARTINEAU, P.L.L.C. (AV)

555 North Main Street, P.O. Box 446, 48858
Telephone: 517-773-9961
Fax: 517-773-2107
Email: lglm@power-net.net
Lansing, Michigan Office: 2400 Lake Lansing Road, Suite B.
Telephone: 517-485-0400.
Fax: 517-485-0402.

MEMBERS OF FIRM

Edward N. Lynch (1908-1984) — Michael J. Hackett
Byron P. Gallagher — Richard J. Garcia
John J. Lynch — Nancy E. Gallagher
Steven W. Martineau — Jennifer M. Galloway
Paula K. Manis (Resident at Lansing Office)

Representative Clients: Amoco Production, Co.; Liquid Transport, Inc.; Central Concrete Products; Central Michigan University; Northern Michigan Oil and Gas Corp.

For full biographical listings, see the Martindale-Hubbell Law Directory

*MUSKEGON,** Muskegon Co.

CULVER, SHERIDAN, KNOWLTON, EVEN & FRANKS, P.C. (AV)

250 Terrace Plaza, P.O. Box 629, 49443
Telephone: 231-724-4320
Telecopier: 231-724-4330
Email: cskef@novagate.com

Fred C. Culver, Jr. — Michael M. Knowlton
James M. Sheridan — Kevin B. Even
Eugene A. Franks

David E. Waterstradt — Douglas Poland
Foster D. Potter — Scott Knowlton
Joseph S. Bush

Representative Clients: SPX Corp.; National City Bank of Michigan/Illinois; Old Kent Bank of Grand Haven; Comerica Bank; NBD Bank; East Shore Chemical Company; Muskegon County Association of Realtors; Midland Groceries.

For full biographical listings, see the Martindale-Hubbell Law Directory

Muskegon—Continued

LAGUE, NEWMAN & IRISH, A PROFESSIONAL CORPORATION (AV)

600 Terrace Plaza, P.O. Box 389, 49443
Telephone: 231-725-8148
Telecopier: 231-726-3404
Email: firm@lnilaw.com

Eric R. Gielow
Charyn K. Hain
Todd L. Helle
Karen L. Kayes
Richard C. Lague
William M. Newman
Michael J. Philbrick
Bruce P. Rissi
J. Scott Timmer
Alvin D. Treado

LEGAL SUPPORT PERSONNEL

Rebecca A. McCroskey
Lynette E. Reichert
Deborah K. Kendra
Cindy S. Thielman

General Counsel: Hackley Hospital & Medical Center; Kaydon Corp.; Cole's Quality Foods; Kurdziel Industries.
Local Counsel: SPX Corp.; Booth Newspapers Inc.; National City Bank; Neway Anchorlok International.

For full biographical listings, see the Martindale-Hubbell Law Directory

PLYMOUTH, Wayne Co.

DRAUGELIS & ASHTON, L.L.P. (AV)

843 Penniman Avenue, 48170-1690
Telephone: 734-453-4044
Fax: 734-453-2011
Clawson, Michigan Office: 380 North Main Street.
Telephone: 248-588-7704.

MEMBERS OF FIRM

Edward F. Draugelis
John A. Ashton
Donald S. Scully
Richard T. Haynes
Lamberto DiStefano
David T. Rogers
Joseph R. Conte
Steven O. Ashton

ASSOCIATES

Floyd C. Virant
Taras P. Jarema
Timothy M. McKercher
Joel B. Ashton
Donald E. Walker
Heather A. Jefferson
Roger D. Ajluni
Margaret L. Browning

Representative Client: State Farm Mutual Automobile Insurance Co.
Reference: National Bank of Detroit, Plymouth Branch.

For full biographical listings, see the Martindale-Hubbell Law Directory

*PORT HURON,** St. Clair Co.

GARAN, LUCOW, MILLER & SEWARD, P.C. (AV)

Port Huron Office Center, 511 Fort Street, Suite 505, 48060-3922
Telephone: 810-985-4400
Fax: 810-985-4107
URL: http://www.garanlucow.com
Detroit, Michigan Office: 1000 Woodbridge Place.
Telephone: 313-446-1530.
Fax: 313-259-0450.
Grand Blanc, Michigan Office: 8332 Office Park Drive.
Telephone: 810-695-3700.
Fax: 810-695-6488.
Ann Arbor, Michigan Office: 101 North Main Street, Suite 460.
Telephone: 734-930-5600.
Fax: 734-930-0043.
Troy, Michigan Office: 1111 West Long Lake Road, Suite 300.
Telephone: 248-641-7600.
Fax: 248-641-0222.
Mount Clemens, Michigan Office: Towne Square Development, 10 S. Main Street, Suite 307.
Telephone: 810-954-3800.
Fax: 810-954-3803.
Grand Rapids, Michigan Office: First of America Center, 171 Monroe Avenue, N.W., Suite 950.
Telephone: 616-742-5500.
Fax: 616-742-5566.
Lansing, Michigan Office: 530 Creyts Road, Suite A.
Telephone: 517-327-0300.
Fax: 517-327-0309.
Traverse City, Michigan Office: 1131 East Eighth Street, P.O. Box 3150.
Telephone: 231-941-1611.
Fax: 231-941-4420.
Marquette, Michigan Office: 228 West Washington Street, Suite 4,
Telephone: 906-228-7772.
Fax: 906-228-5999.

Randolph J. Martinek

Robert L. Goldenbogen
Meghan A. McGlynn

For full biographical listings, see the Martindale-Hubbell Law Directory

*SAGINAW,** Saginaw Co.

BRAUN KENDRICK FINKBEINER PLC (AV)

101 N. Washington Suite 812, 48607-1297
Telephone: 517-753-3461
Telecopier: 517-753-3951
Email: ALBFIE@BKF-LAW.COM *URL:* http://www.bkf-law.com
Saginaw Township Office, Michigan Office: 5800 Gratiot Road, Suite 107, P.O. Box 5169. Telephone 517-799-8692.
Fax: 517-799-4666.
Bay City, Michigan Office: 201 Phoenix Building, P.O. Box 2039.
Telephone: 517-895-8505.
Telecopier: 517-895-8437.
Ann Arbor, Michigan Office: First National Building. 201 S. Main, Suite 700.
Telephone: 313-995-4100.
Telecopier: 313-995-4798.
Mt. Pleasant, Michigan Office: 805 North Brown.
Telephone: 517-775-7404.
Telecopier: 517-775-3764.

Hugo E. Braun (1894-1973)
Russell A. Schafer (1906-1982)
James V. Finkbeiner
Hugo E. Braun, Jr.
Edward J. McArdle (1938-1989)
Thomas F James (1940-1990)
John W. Wolf
C. Patrick Kaltenbach
Harold J. Blanchet, Jr.
David L. Turner
Kenneth W. Kable
E. Louis Ognisanti
Bruce L. Dalrymple
Jeffrey J. Endean
Robert A. Kendrick
Charles A. Gilfeather
Thomas R. Luplow
John A. Decker
Michael J. Sauer
Timothy L Curtiss
Scott C. Strattard
Craig W. Horn
Phillip J. Stahle
Francis J. Keating
Barry M. Levine
Brian F. Bauer
Judith A. Lincoln
Glenn L. Fitkin
Brian S. Makaric

Jamie C. Hecht Nisidis
Ellen E. Crane
David J. Klippert
Lorraine S. Paskiewicz
Frederick C. Overdier
R. Paul Larsen
Brian K. Elder

OF COUNSEL

J. Richard Kendrick

Representative Clients: The Dow Chemical Co.; General Motors Corp.; Merrill, Lynch, Inc.; Saginaw General Hospital; Saginaw News; The Wickes Foundation.

For full biographical listings, see the Martindale-Hubbell Law Directory

CURRIE KENDALL POLASKY MEISEL, PLC (AV)

4800 Fashion Square Boulevard, Suite 100, 48603
Telephone: 517-792-1111; 517-792-9300
Fax: 517-793-6597; 517-792-7000
Midland, Michigan Office: 6024 Eastman Avenue, P.O. Box, 2765.
Telephone: 517-839-0300.
Fax: 517-832-0077.

Frank M. Polasky
Robert H. Meisel
Michael H. Allen
Larry L. Preston
David J. Kolat
M. Randall Jurrens
John E. Gannon
Carolyn Pollock Cary
John D. Jolley
W. Jay Brown
William C. Collins (Resident, Midland Office)
Ramon F. Rolf, Jr. (Resident, Midland Office)
Daniel J. Cline (Resident, Midland Office)
Peter A. Poznak (Resident, Midland Office)
Julia A. Close (Resident, Midland Office)
Jeffrey N. Dyer (Resident, Midland Office)
Jonathan E. Lauderbach (Resident, Midland Office)
Amy E. Wilson (Resident, Midland Office)
Cheryl L. Whitman (Resident, Midland Office)
Todd M. Gambrell (Resident, Midland Office)

OF COUNSEL

James A. Kendall (Resident, Midland Office)

Counsel for: Chemical Financial Corp.; Chemical Bank & Trust Co.; Saginaw Valley State University; Northwood University; The Midland Foundation; Elsa U. Pardee Foundation; Rollin M. Gerstacker Foundation; Charles J. Strosacker Foundation.

For full biographical listings, see the Martindale-Hubbell Law Directory

O'NEILL, WALLACE & DOYLE, P.C. (AV)

300 St. Andrews Road, Suite 302, P.O. Box 1966, 48605
Telephone: 517-790-0960
Fax: 517-790-6902
Flint, Michigan Office: 2483 South Linden Road.
Telephone: 810-732-7079.
Fax: 810-732-5889.

(See Next Column)

O'NEILL, WALLACE & DOYLE P.C., *Saginaw—Continued*

Terence J. O'Neill	Thomas J. Doyle
David A. Wallace	Charles F. Filipiak

David Carbajal	John J. Danieleski, Jr.
James E. O'Neill, III	Darrin L. Nichols

Representative Clients: Home Insurance Co.; Great American Insurance Co.; Farmers Insurance Co.; Cincinnati Insurance Co.; Ohio Casualty Insurance Co.; Safeco Insurance Co.; Liberty Mutual Insurance Co.; CUNA Mutual Insurance.; Pioneer State Mutual Insurance Co.; Auto Owners Insurance Co.

For full biographical listings, see the Martindale-Hubbell Law Directory

*ST. IGNACE,** Mackinac Co.

BROWN AND BROWN (AV)

First National Bank Building, 49781
Telephone: 906-643-7800; 800-643-7840
Fax: 906-643-7157
Email: bblaw@sault.com

MEMBERS OF FIRM

James J. Brown (1839-1920)	Prentiss M. Brown, Jr.
Prentiss M. Brown (1889-1973)	Charles M. Brown
James J. Brown (Retired)	Tom H. Evashevski

Counsel for: Union Terminal and Piers, Mackinac Island, Michigan; First National Bank, St. Ignace; Mackinac Island Carriage Tours; McGregor Oil Co.; City of St. Ignace.

For full biographical listings, see the Martindale-Hubbell Law Directory

*ST. JOSEPH,** Berrien Co.

TAGLIA, FETTE, DUMKE, PASSARO & KAHNE, P.C. (AV)

720 State Street, P.O. Box 890, 49085
Telephone: 616-983-0755
Fax: 616-983-0774

Paul A. Taglia	T. J. (Tim) Passaro
Thomas R. Fette	Howard H. Kahne
Michael E. Dumke	L. A. White

Amy L. Judd

For full biographical listings, see the Martindale-Hubbell Law Directory

SOUTHFIELD, Oakland Co.

JAFFE, RAITT, HEUER & WEISS, PROFESSIONAL CORPORATION (AV)

Travelers Tower, Suite 1520, 48076
Telephone: 313-961-8380
Detroit, Michigan Office: One Woodward Avenue, Suite 2400.
Telephone: 313-961-8380.
Telecopier: 313-961-8358.

Ira J. Jaffe

Representative Clients: Edgemere Enterprises; Frankel Associates; Unisys Corp.

For full biographical listings, see the Martindale-Hubbell Law Directory

MASON STEINHARDT JACOBS PERLMAN & PESICK, PROFESSIONAL CORPORATION (AV)

Suite 1500, 4000 Town Center, 48075-1415
Telephone: 248-358-2090
Fax: 248-358-3599
Email: admin@msjp.com *URL:* http://www.msjp.com

Gordon I. Ginsberg	Jerome P. Pesick
Irving I. Boigon	Richard A. Polk
Jack Schon	Neil S. Silver
Frederick D. Steinhardt	L. Jeffrey Zauberman
John E. Jacobs	Howard A. Lax
Michael B. Perlman	H. Adam Cohen

Diane Flagg Goldstein

Jeffrey B. Linden	David E. Nykanen

Jacquelyn L. Lane

OF COUNSEL

Walter B. Mason, Jr.	Walter J. Goldsmith
Erwin B. Ellmann	Randolph J. Friedman

Marvin C. Daitch

Representative Clients: Citibank, N.A.; City of Dearborn; DeMattia Development Co.; Forest City Enterprises; Michigan Wholesale Drug Assn.; Mortgage Bankers Association of Michigan; Nationwide Insurance Co.; City of Taylor; Union Labor Life Insurance Co.; Yellow Freight Systems, Inc.

For full biographical listings, see the Martindale-Hubbell Law Directory

SOMMERS, SCHWARTZ, SILVER & SCHWARTZ, P.C. (AV)

2000 Town Center, Suite 900, 48075
Telephone: 248-355-0300
Telecopier: 248-746-4001
Plymouth, Michigan Office: 747 South Main Street.
Telephone: 313-455-4250.

Stanley S. Schwartz	Richard L. Groffsky
Leonard B. Schwartz	David J. Winter
Lawrence Warren	Joseph E. Grinnan
Steven J. Schwartz	David M. Black
John F. Vos, III	B. A. Tyler
Jeffrey N. Shillman	Robert B. Sickels
David R. Getto	Daniel D. Swanson
Norman D. Tucker	Michael J. Cunningham
Robert H. Darling	Steven L. Schwartz
Paul W. Hines	J. Lee Tilson
Donald J. Gasiorek	James D. Ledbetter
Patrick B. McCauley	Patrick J. Burkett
Justin C. Ravitz	David A. Kotzian
Kenneth V. Cockrel (1938-1988)	Matthew G. Curtis
Gary A. Taback	Charles R. Ash, III
Allen J. Kovinsky	Helen K. Joyner
David L. Nelson	Robert J. Schwartz
Joseph A. Golden	John L. Runco
William M. Brukoff	Patricia A. Stamler
Richard D. Toth	Susanne Pryce
Allen J. Wall	Lisa K. Pernick
Richard D. Fox	Joseph H. Bourgon
Frank Mafrice	Tracy L. Allen
James J. Vlasic	Sam G. Morgan
Leon M. Schurgin	Andrew Kochanowski
Victor A. Coen	Anne M. Schoepfle

Kenneth T. Watkins

Gerald D. Keller	Marcy B. Spitz
Murray C. Slomovitz	Richard H. McDermott
Carl B. Downing	Randall M. Blau
Jabran G. Yasso	Marc C. Tucker
David J. Szymanski	Jennifer M. Grieco
David F. Greco	Cameron R. Getto
Peter L. Schwartz	Matthew A. Fraiberg
Lena Agree	Ericka M. Jackson

OF COUNSEL

Norman S. Sommers	Jeremy L. Winer
Howard Silver	H. Rollin Allen
Paul Groffsky	Charles S. Farmer
Donald R. Epstein	Marvin R. Stempien

General Counsel for: City of Taylor; Foodland Distributors; C.A. Muer Corporation; Vlasic & Company; Nederlander Corporation; Midwest Health Centers, P.C.
Representative Clients: Michigan National Bank; Universal Underwriters Insurance Co.; Rite-Aid of Michigan; Don Lee Distributors.

For full biographical listings, see the Martindale-Hubbell Law Directory

STURGIS, St. Joseph Co.

BIRD, SVENDSEN, BROTHERS, SCHESKE & PATTISON, P.C. (AV)

227 West Chicago Road, P.O. Box 7158, 49091
Telephone: 616-651-2445
Fax: 616-651-4044
Email: bsbs@2mm.com

Roger A. Bird	Eric J. Scheske
Robert P. Brothers	Robert K. Pattison

OF COUNSEL

John T. Svendsen

For full biographical listings, see the Martindale-Hubbell Law Directory

DRESSER, DRESSER, GILBERT & HAAS, P.C. (AV)

112 South Monroe Street, 49091
Telephone: 616-651-3281
Fax: 616-651-3261
Email: law@voyager.net

Raymond H. Dresser (1901-1968)	John R. Dresser
	Walter H. Gilbert
John E. Oster (1948-1981)	Patrick Joseph Haas, Jr.
Raymond H. Dresser, Jr.	Michael J. Caywood (Not admitted in MI)

LEGAL SUPPORT PERSONNEL

Mary G. Dresser (Legal Assistant)

Attorneys for: Freeman Manufacturing Co.; Burr Oak Tool and Gauge, Inc.; Citizens Bank; Michigan; Sturgis Bank & Trust Company; Federal Savings Bank; Midwest Tool & Cutlery, Co.

For full biographical listings, see the Martindale-Hubbell Law Directory

*TRAVERSE CITY,** Grand Traverse Co.

GARAN, LUCOW, MILLER & SEWARD, P.C. (AV)
1131 East Eighth Street, P.O. Box 3150, 49685-3150
Telephone: 231-941-1611
Fax: 231-941-4420
URL: http://www.garanlucow.com
Detroit, Michigan Office: 1000 Woodbridge Place.
Telephone: 313-446-1530.
Fax: 313-259-0450.
Port Huron, Michigan Office: Port Huron Office Center, 511 Fort Street, Suite 505.
Telephone: 810-985-4400.
Fax: 810-985-4187.
Ann Arbor, Michigan Office: 101 North Main Street, Suite 460.
Telephone: 734-930-5600.
Fax: 734-930-0043.
Troy, Michigan Office: 1111 West Long Lake Road, Suite 300.
Telephone: 248-641-7600.
Fax: 248-641-0222.
Mount Clemens, Michigan Office: Towne Square Development, 10 S. Main Street, Suite 307.
Telephone: 810-954-3800.
Fax: 810-954-3803.
Grand Rapids, Michigan Office: First of America Center, 171 Monroe Avenue, N.W., Suite 950.
Telephone: 616-742-5500.
Fax: 616-742-5566.
Grand Blanc, Michigan Office: 8332 Office Park Drive.
Telephone: 810-695-3700.
Fax: 810-695-6488.
Lansing, Michigan Office: 530 Creyts Road, Suite A.
Telephone: 517-327-0300.
Fax: 517-327-0309.
Marquette, Michigan Office: 228 West Washington Street, Suite 4,
Telephone: 906-228-7772.
Fax: 906-228-5999.

Peter B. Worden, Jr.
Douglas J. Read
John W. Sharp
Michael J. Swogger

Linda Marsh-Raetz

For full biographical listings, see the Martindale-Hubbell Law Directory

SMITH HAUGHEY RICE & ROEGGE, P.C. (AV)
City Centre Plaza, Suite 100, 202 East State Street, P.O. Box 848, 49685-0848
Telephone: 231-929-4878
Facsimile: 231-929-4182
Grand Rapids, Michigan Office: 200 Calder Plaza Building, 250 Monroe Avenue, N.W., 49503-2251.
Telephone: 616-774-8000.
Facsimile: 616-774-2461.
East Lansing, Michigan Office: 1400 Abbott Rd., Suite 410, 48823-1902.
Telephone: 517-332-3030.
Facsimile: 517-332-3468.

George Frederick Bearup
Mark P. Bickel
R. Jay Hardin
Charles B. Judson
Robert W. Tubbs
Jeffrey R. Wonacott
Robert W. Parker
Paul T. Jarboe
Jeffrey E. Gwillim

Todd W. Millar
Erin Eileen Gerrity
Peter J. Boyles
Rachel Y. Brochert
Eric W. Phelps

Representative Clients: Chevron; Cincinnati Insurance Co.; General Motors Corp.; Kemper Insurance Group; Michigan Hospital Assn.; Navistar International; St. Paul Insurance Cos.; Steelcase, Inc.; Dow Elanco.

For full biographical listings, see the Martindale-Hubbell Law Directory

TROY, Oakland Co.

CAMPBELL, O'BRIEN & MISTELE, P.C. (AV)
850 Stephenson Highway Suite 410, 48083-1163
Telephone: 248-588-5800
Fax: 248-588-6669; 1-888-647-8353
Email: COMLAW@ADVDATA.NET *URL:* http://www.lawyers.com/comlaw

Edwin G. O'Brien (1907-1983)
Dale C. Campbell
Henry E. Mistele
Paul W. Loock
Robert J. Figa
Curtis H. Mistele

References: First Federal of Michigan; Comerica Bank.

For full biographical listings, see the Martindale-Hubbell Law Directory

CHARTERS, HECK, O'DONNELL, PETRULIS & ZORZA, P.C. (AV)
888 West Big Beaver, Suite 1490, 48084
Telephone: 248-362-4700
Fax: 248-362-1030
URL: http://www.lawyers.com/chartersheckopz

John P. Charters
Michael A. Heck
Margaret A. O'Donnell
Donald L. Petrulis
John L. Zorza, II

Allan R. Gurvitz

For full biographical listings, see the Martindale-Hubbell Law Directory

GARAN, LUCOW, MILLER & SEWARD, P.C. (AV)
1111 West Long Lake Road, Suite 300, 48098-6333
Telephone: 248-641-7600
Fax: 248-641-0222
URL: http://www.garanlucow.com
Detroit, Michigan Office: 10000 Woodbridge Place.
Telephone: 313-446-1530.
Fax: 313-259-0450.
Grand Blanc, Michigan Office: 8332 Office Park Drive.
Telephone: 810-695-3700.
Fax: 810-695-6488.
Port Huron, Michigan Office: Port Huron Office Center, 511 Fort Street, Suite 505.
Telephone: 810-985-4400.
Fax: 810-985-4107.
Ann Arbor, Michigan Office: 101 North Main Street, Suite 460.
Telephone: 734-930-5600.
Fax: 734-930-0043.
Mount Clemens, Michigan Office: Suite 307, Towne Square Development, 10 South Main Street.
Telephone: 810-954-3800.
Fax: 810-954-3803.
Grand Rapids, Michigan Office: First of America Center, 171 Monroe Avenue, N.W., Suite 950.
Telephone: 616-742-5500.
Fax: 616-742-5566.
Lansing, Michigan Office: 530 Creyts Road, Suite A.
Telephone: 517-327-0300.
Fax: 517-327-0309.
Traverse City, Michigan Office: 1131 East Eighth Street, P.O. Box 3150.
Telephone: 231-941-1611.
Fax: 231-941-4420.
Marquette, Michigan Office: 228 West Washington Street, Suite 4,
Telephone: 906-228-7772.
Fax: 906-228-5999.

James L. Borin
Roger A. Smith
Mark Shreve
John P. Seyfried (Resident)
Edward M. Freeland
Steven A. Matta
Ian C. Simpson
Susan M. Williams

David J. Lankford
Brian E. Etzel
Dawn M. Patterson
Kristin Stiles Smolek
Monia (Monica) C. Gregor
Beth A. Andrews
Darryl Keenan Segars
Adam K. Gordon

Counsel for: Allstate Insurance Co.; Sears, Roebuck & Co.; Liberty Mutual Insurance Co.; Continental Insurance Companies.

For full biographical listings, see the Martindale-Hubbell Law Directory

HACKETT & MAXWELL, P.C. (AV)
City Center Building, Suite 1470, 888 West Big Beaver Road, 48084
Telephone: 810-362-2600
Fax: 810-362-3610
Email: hackmax@voyager.net

Patrick E. Hackett
Phillip B. Maxwell

Dennis W. Krakow
Mireille Leruth Phillips

For full biographical listings, see the Martindale-Hubbell Law Directory

AUSTIN HIRSCHHORN, P.C. (AV)
Suite 710 Columbia Center, 201 West Big Beaver Road, 48084-4152
Telephone: 248-680-1660
Fax: 248-680-1671
Email: austinh@ix.netcom.com

Austin Hirschhorn

For full biographical listings, see the Martindale-Hubbell Law Directory

Troy—Continued

MILLER, CANFIELD, PADDOCK AND STONE, P.L.C. (AV)

A Professional Limited Liability Company
Founded in 1852 by Sidney Davy Miller
840 West Long Lake Road Suite 200, 48098
Telephone: 248-879-2000
Fax: 248-879-2001
URL: http://www.millercanfield.com
Detroit, Michigan Office: 150 West Jefferson, Suite 2500, 48226-4415.
Telephone: 313-963-6420.
Fax: 313-496-7500.
Cable Address: "Stem Detroit."
Ann Arbor, Michigan Office: 101 North Main Street, 7th Floor, 48104-1400.
Telephone: 734-663-2445.
Fax: 734-747-7147.
Grand Rapids, Michigan Office: 99 Monroe, N.W., Suite 1200, 49503-2639.
Telephone: 616-454-8656.
Fax: 616-776-6322.
Howell, Michigan Office: 121 South Barnard Street, Suite 4, 48843-2305.
Telephone: 517-546-7600.
Telecopier: 517-546-6974.
Kalamazoo, Michigan Office: 444 West Michigan Avenue, 49007-3752.
Telephone: 616-381-7030.
Fax: 616-382-0244.
Lansing, Michigan Office: One Michigan Avenue, Suite 900, 48933-1609.
Telephone: 517-487-2070.
Fax: 517-374-6304.
Monroe, Michigan Office: 214 East Elm Avenue, Suite 100, 48162-2682.
Telephone: 734-243-2000.
Fax: 734-243-0901.
Washington, D.C. Office: 1900 K Street, N.W., Suite 1150. 20006.
Telephone: 202-429-5575; 785-0600.
Fax: 202-331-1118; 785-1234.
Pensacola, Florida Office: 25 West Cedar, 32501.
Telephone: 850-469-1088.
Fax: 850-432-0677.
New York, New York Office: 1450 Broadway, 41st Floor, 10018.
Telephone: 212-704-4400.
Fax: 212-704-4410.
Gdynia, Poland Office: UL. Slaska 21, 81-319.
Telephone: 011-485-831-2808.
Fax: 011-48-58-628 6411.
Warsaw, Poland Office: UL. Nowogrodzkall, 5th Floor, 00-513.
Telephone: 011-4822 529 0200.
Fax: 011-4822 529 0201.
Katowice, Poland Office: UL. Francuska 35/37, 40-027.
Telephone: 011 (48-32) 757-2414.
Fax: 011 (48-32) 757-2483.

RESIDENT PRINCIPALS

John W. Gelder
John A. Thurber (P.C.)
John A. Marxer (P.C.)
Kenneth E. Konop
Ronald H. Riback
James W. Williams
Stephen G. Palms
Frank L. Andrews
J. Kevin Trimmer
Stephen J. Ott
Thomas G. Appleman
Gregory V. Di Censo
Brad B. Arbuckle
Ronald E. Hodess
Dawn M. Schluter
Robert J. Haddad
Sally A. Hamby
Erich H. Hintzen

OF COUNSEL/SENIOR COUNSEL

Lawrence A. King (P.C.)
Richard A. Jones (P.C.)
Henry R. Nolte, Jr.

RESIDENT ASSOCIATES

Brian S. Westenberg
Lisa D. Pick
Anna M. Maiuri
Daljit S. Doogal
Sherylle A. O. Gordon
Jason S. Rose

CONTRACT ATTORNEYS

Ronald P. Weitzman

Representative Firm Clients: Chrysler Corporation; Comerica, Incorporated; City of Detroit, Michigan; Detroit Tigers, Inc.; First of Michigan; Ford Motor Company; Ford Motor Credit Company; Great Lakes Bancorp; Henry Ford Hospital; INVETECH Company.

For full biographical listings, see the Martindale-Hubbell Law Directory

POLING, MCGAW & POLING, P.C. (AV)

Suite 275, 5435 Corporate Drive, 48098
Telephone: 248-641-0500
Telecopier: 248-641-0506
URL: http://www.lawyers.com/polingmcgaw&poling

Benson T. Buck (1926-1989)
Richard B. Poling
D. Douglas McGaw
Richard B. Poling, Jr.
Gregory C. Hamilton
Veronica B. O'Hara
James R. Parker
Shannon M. Acton

(See Next Column)

OF COUNSEL

Ralph S. Moore

Representative Clients: City of Troy; United States Fidelity & Guaranty Co.; Sentry Insurance Co.; Admiral Insurance; DeMaria Construction Co.; Leo Corporation; Aetna Casualty and Surety Co.; Concord Design; Pneumo-Abex.

For full biographical listings, see the Martindale-Hubbell Law Directory

YPSILANTI, Washtenaw Co.

PEAR SPERLING EGGAN & MUSKOVITZ, P.C. (AV)

5 South Washington Street, 48197
Telephone: 734-483-3626
Fax: 734-483-1107
Email: ameggan@ameritech.net
Ann Arbor, Michigan Office: Domino's Farms, 24 Frank Lloyd Wright Drive.
Telephone: 734-665-4441
Other Ypsilanti, Michigan Office: 2164 Bellevue at Washtenaw.
Telephone: 734-483-7177.

Lawrence W. Sperling
Andrew M. Eggan
Thomas E. Daniels

Counsel for: Domino's Pizza, Inc.; Citizens Banking Corp.; Townsend and Bottum, Inc.; The Credit Bureau of Ypsilanti; City of Ypsilanti (Labor Counsel); Michigan Municipal Worker's Compensation; Self-Insurance Fund.
Approved Attorneys for: Lawyers Title Insurance Corp.

For full biographical listings, see the Martindale-Hubbell Law Directory

GUAM

HAGATÑA, Hagåtña Dist.

CARLSMITH BALL

A Partnership including Law Corporations
Suite 401, Bank of Hawaii Building, 134 West Soledad Avenue, P.O. Box BF, 96932-5027
Telephone: 671-472-6813
Fax: 671-477-4375
Telex: 721-6445 CWCMI GM
Email: execdirector@carlsmith.com *URL:* http://www.carlsmith.com
Honolulu, Hawaii Office: Suite 2200, Pacific Tower, 1001 Bishop Street. P.O. Box 656, 96809-3402.
Telephone: 808-523-2500.
Fax: 808-523-0842.
Kapolei, Hawaii Office: Suite 318, Kapolei Building, 1001 Kamokila Boulevard, 96707.
Telephone: 808-523-2500.
Fax: 808-674-0850.
Wailuku, Maui Hawaii Office: Suite 400, One Main Plaza, 2200 Main Street, P.O. Box 1086, 96793-1086.
Telephone: 808-242-4535.
Fax: 808-244-4974.
Kailua-Kona, Hawaii Office: Suite 209, 75-1000 Henry Street, 96740.
Telephone: 808-329-6464.
Fax: 808-329-9450.
Hilo, Hawaii Office: 121 Waianuenue Avenue, P.O. Box 686, 96721-0686.
Telephone: 808-935-6644.
Fax: 808-935-7975.
Saipan, Commonwealth of the Northern Mariana Islands Office: Carlsmith Building, Capitol Hill, P.O. Box 5241, 96950-5241.
Telephone: 670-322-3455.
Fax: 670-322-3368.
Los Angeles, California Office: 9th Floor, 444 South Flower Street, 90071-2901.
Telephone: 213-955-1200.
Fax: 213-623-0032.
Washington, D.C. Office: Suite 300, 1201 Pennsylvania Avenue, N.W., 20004-2401.
Telephone: 202-628-2228.
Fax: 202-628-2071.
Mexico City, Mexico Office: Sierra Nevada 119, Lomas de Chapultepec 11000 Mexico, D.F.
Telephone: 52-5-520-8514, 52-5-520-8757.
Fax: 52-5-540-1545.
Mexico, D.F. Office of Carlsmith Ball, S.C. (Authorized to practice as foreign legal consultants in Mexico): Sierra Nevada 119, Lomas de Chapultepec 11000 Mexico, D.F.
Telephone: 52-5-520-8514, 52-5-520-8757.
Fax: 52-5-540-1545.

RESIDENT PARTNERS

Ruth D. Davis
Philip D. Isaac
David Patrick Ledger
Meredith M. Sayre
Sinforoso M. Tolentino

(See Next Column)

CARLSMITH BALL—*Continued*

RESIDENT ASSOCIATES

Bruce A. Bradley
Stacy Sachiko Fukuhara
Dana A. Gutierrez

OF COUNSEL

Roger P. Crouthamel

For full biographical listings, see the Martindale-Hubbell Law Directory

---

TIMOTHY A. STEWART

162 Archbishop Felixberto Camacho Flores Street, 96910
Telephone: +671-472-6978
Telecopier: +671-472-8782
URL: http://www.lawpac.com
Email: tas@lawpac.com *URL:*
http://www.lawyers.com/timothystewartlaw

Representative Agency Clients: American Bureau of Collections; National Association of Credit Management; United Mercantile Agencies; Financial Collection Agencies.
Representative Subrogation Clients: CIGNA/AFIA Cos.; AIG/AIU Cos.; Chung Kuo Insurance Co., Ltd.

For full biographical listings, see the Martindale-Hubbell Law Directory

BASTIANELLI, BROWN & KELLEY CHARTERED, *Washington—Continued*

OF COUNSEL

H. Clayton Cook, Jr. Marcus W. Sisk, Jr.

For full biographical listings, see the Martindale-Hubbell Law Directory

CHARAPP, DEESE & WEISS, LLP (AV)

1901 Pennsylvania Avenue, N.W., Suite 1001, 20006
Telephone: 202-463-9100
Fax: 202-463-2091
Vienna, Virginia Office: 8300 Boone Boulevard, Suite 500, 22182.
Telephone 703-714-9576.
Bethesda, Maryland Office: 3 Bethesda Metro Center, Suite 700, 20814.
Telephone: 301-657-6258.
Richmond, Virginia Office: 2201 West Broad Street, Suite 201, 23220.
Telephone: 804-358-8680.
Fax: 804-358-3889.

Michael G. Charapp

OF COUNSEL

Edward H. Kim

For full biographical listings, see the Martindale-Hubbell Law Directory

COHEN MOHR LLP (AV)

Suite 504, 1055 Thomas Jefferson Street, N.W., 20007
Telephone: 202-342-2550
Facsimile: 202-342-6147
URL: http://www.cohenmohr.com
McLean, Virginia Office: 1420 Beverly Road, Suite 380, 22101.
Telephone: 703-761-1100.
Telecopier: 703-761-0180.

David S. Cohen
Andrew J. Mohr
Victor G. Klingelhofer
William F. Savarino
Russell J. Gaspar
Daniel H. DuVal (Resident, McLean, VA Office)

OF COUNSEL

Brian L. Longest (Not admitted in DC)
Laurel Ann Hockey
Andrew B. Katz

ASSOCIATES

John J. O'Brien
Alex D. Kondé
Rowena E. Laxa

For full biographical listings, see the Martindale-Hubbell Law Directory

THE FALK LAW FIRM PLLC (AV)

A Professional Limited Liability Corporation
Suite 260 One Westin Center, 2445 M Street, N.W., 20037
Telephone: 202-833-8700
Telecopier: 202-872-1725
Email: FalkLaw@erols.com *URL:* http://www.falklawfirm.com

James H. Falk, Sr.
James H. Falk, Jr.
Stephen A. Best
John M. Falk

OF COUNSEL

Pierre E. Murphy
Elizabeth C. Collins

For full biographical listings, see the Martindale-Hubbell Law Directory

KILCULLEN, WILSON AND KILCULLEN, CHARTERED (AV)

Suite 300, 1800 K Street, N.W., 20006
Telephone: 202-296-5700
Telecopier: 202-296-5706
Email: kwk@attny.com *URL:* http://www.attny.com

John L. Kilcullen (1916-1994)

MEMBERS

William H. Butterfield
Ronald E. Gilbertson
Christopher M. Johnson
Peter M. Kilcullen
Cyrus E. Phillips, IV
Walter A. I. Wilson

OF COUNSEL

Robert J. Gomez
Douglas K. Olson

For full biographical listings, see the Martindale-Hubbell Law Directory

FLORIDA

*FORT LAUDERDALE,** Broward Co.

CUMMINGS & SNYDER, P.A. (AV)

1600 Southeast 17th Street Causeway, P.O. Box 460327, 33346-1116
Telephone: 954-761-8700
Telecopier: 954-524-6927
Email: administrator@cummingslaw.com *URL:* http://www.cummingslaw.com
Tallahassee, Florida Office: 1004 DeSoto Park Drive, P.O. Box 589, 32302-0589.
Telephone: 850-878-3700.
Telecopier: 850-656-0329.

F. Alan Cummings

Bradley S. Copenhaver
Alejandro Espino

OF COUNSEL

James E. Glass

Representative Clients: American Bridge Company; American International Group; Dillingham Construction Holdings, Inc.; Hubbard Construction Company; Odebrecht Construction, Inc.; Reliance Surety Company; Traylor Bros., Inc.; Condotte America, Inc.; Seaboard Surety Company; Alabama Department of Transportation.

For full biographical listings, see the Martindale-Hubbell Law Directory

LEIBY CONSTRUCTION LAW FIRM, PROFESSIONAL ASSOCIATION (AV)

Pine Island Commons, 8551 West Sunrise Boulevard, Suite 304, 33322
Telephone: 954-382-9199
Fax: 954-382-9063
URL: http://www.lawyers.com/leibylaw
Email: info@leibylaw.com *URL:* http://www.leibylaw.com

Larry R. Leiby
Salvatore H. Fasulo
Richard Eric Guttentag
Adam C. Linkhorst
Douglas J. Roberts
Michael E. Stearns
Kevin J. Taylor

For full biographical listings, see the Martindale-Hubbell Law Directory

*ORLANDO,** Orange Co.

BROWN, WARD, SALZMAN & WEISS, P.A. (AV)

111 North Orange Avenue, Suite 875, P.O. Box 2873, 32802-2873
Telephone: 407-425-9566
Fax: 407-425-9596; Email: firm@orlandolaw.net
Email: brownu@osceola.k12.fl.us *URL:* http://www.orlandolaw.net

Usher Larry Brown
John H. Ward
Gary S. Salzman
Jeffrey S. Weiss
Suzanne D'Agresta

Scott D. Danahy
James G. Vickaryous
Robert L. Butterfield, Jr.
Allison Carmine McDonald

Representative Clients: The School Board of Osceola County; The School Board of Indian River County; The School Board of Putnam County; Osceola County; Osceola Sheriff (Osceola County Investigative Bureau); Orange County Comptroller; General Electric Capital Modular Space; Honeywell, Inc.

For full biographical listings, see the Martindale-Hubbell Law Directory

*TALLAHASSEE,** Leon Co.

CUMMINGS & SNYDER, P.A. (AV)

1004 DeSoto Park Drive, P.O. Box 589, 32302-0589
Telephone: 850-878-3700
Telecopier: 850-656-0329
Email: administrator@cummingslaw.com *URL:* http://www.cummingslaw.com
Fort Lauderdale, Florida Office: 1600 Southeast 17th Street Causeway, P.O. Box 460327, 33346-1116.
Telephone: 954-761-8700.
Telecopier: 954-524-6927.

F. Alan Cummings
Patricia Anne Hamilton Snyder

W. Guy McKenzie, Jr.
Daniel Te Young

Representative Clients: American Bridge Company; American International Group; Dillingham Construction Holdings, Inc.; Hubbard Construction Company; Odebrecht Construction, Inc.; Reliance Surety Company; Traylor Bros., Inc.; Condotte America, Inc.; Seaboard Surety Company; Alabama Department of Transportation.

For full biographical listings, see the Martindale-Hubbell Law Directory

*TAMPA,** Hillsborough Co.

JOHN W. BAKAS, JR. (AV)

201 East Kennedy Boulevard, Suite 400, 33602-5823
Telephone: 813-228-8015
Fax: 813-228-8208
Email: jbakas@aol.com *URL:* http://www.bakas.com

For full biographical listings, see the Martindale-Hubbell Law Directory

WINTER PARK, Orange Co.

LYON KIRWIN, P.A. (AV㊉)

338 Morse Boulevard, Suite 150, 32789
Telephone: 407-740-6600
Facsimile: 407-740-6363

V. Frederic Lyon
Brian P. Kirwin
Bruce Alan Norris
Brian W. Bennett

James C. Washburn
Michelle B. Kane
Michael D. Chiumento, III

Representative Clients: American Express; Centex-Rooney; City of St. Petersburg; Clancy & Theys Construction Co.; Duke Engineering & Services; Florida Power Corp.; Sea World of Florida; Seminole County, Florida; Seminole County Public Schools; South Florida Water Management District; U.S. Steel.

For full biographical listings, see the Martindale-Hubbell Law Directory

GEORGIA

*ATLANTA,** Fulton Co.

SMITH, CURRIE & HANCOCK LLP (AV)

2600 Harris Tower-Peachtree Center, 233 Peachtree Street, N.E., 30303-1530
Telephone: 404-521-3800
Telecopier: 404-688-0671
Email: smith-currie-hancock@worldnet.att.net *URL:* http://www.smithcurrie.com

MEMBERS OF FIRM

Overton A. Currie (Retired)
Luther P. House, Jr. (Retired)
Glower W. Jones (Retired)
Robert B. Ansley, Jr. (Retired)
Bert R. Oastler (Retired)
Aubrey L. Coleman, Jr.
Thomas E. Abernathy, IV
Philip L. Fortune
Thomas J. Kelleher, Jr.
Frank E. Riggs, Jr.
Ronald G. Robey
John T. Flynn
James F. Butler, III
Joseph C. Staak
Hubert J. Bell, Jr.
Philip E. Beck
James K. Bidgood, Jr.
S. Gregory Joy
Robert C. Chambers
Karl Dix, Jr.
John E. Menechino, Jr.
William L. Baggett, Jr.

ASSOCIATES

Mark V. Hanrahan
Eugene J. Heady
David A. Roberts
Deborah R. Murphey
Stacey L. Robinson
Eric L. Nelson
Anthony D. Lehman
Edward J. McNaughton

Construction Clients: Jacobs Engineering; Caddell Construction Co., Inc.; Turner Construction Co.; Martin K. Eby Construction Co., Inc.; Danis Industries Corp.; Georgia Chapter of Associated General Contractors; Georgia Highway Contractors Association; Massachusetts Water Resources Authority; City of Amarillo; S. P. McCarl's & Co.

For full biographical listings, see the Martindale-Hubbell Law Directory

*AUGUSTA,** Richmond Co.

FLETCHER, HARLEY & FLETCHER (AV)

429 Walker Street, P.O. Box 2084, 30903-2084
Telephone: 706-724-0558
Fax: 706-724-4730
URL: http://www.lawyers.com/fletcherharley&fletcher

MEMBERS OF FIRM

Leonard O. Fletcher, Jr.
C. Thompson Harley
W. Lawrence Fletcher

For full biographical listings, see the Martindale-Hubbell Law Directory

HAWAII

*HONOLULU,** Honolulu Co.

CARLSMITH BALL (AV)

A Partnership including Law Corporations
Suite 2200, Pacific Tower, 1001 Bishop Street, P.O. Box 656, 96809-3402
Telephone: 808-523-2500
Fax: 808-523-0842
Email: execdirector@carlsmith.com *URL:* http://www.carlsmith.com
Kapolei, Hawaii Office: Suite 318, Kapolei Building, 1001 Kamokila Boulevard, 96707.
Telephone: 808-523-2500.
Fax: 808-674-0850.
Wailuku, Maui Hawaii Office: Suite 400, One Main Plaza, 2200 Main Street, P.O. Box 1086, 96793-1086.
Telephone: 808-242-4535.
Fax: 808-244-4974.
Kailua-Kona, Hawaii Office: Suite 209, 75-1000 Henry Street, 96740.
Telephone: 808-329-6464.
Fax: 808-329-9450.
Hilo, Hawaii Office: 121 Waianuenue Avenue, P.O. Box 686, 96721-0686.
Telephone: 808-935-6644.
Fax: 808-935-7975.
Hagatna, Guam Office: Suite 401, Bank of Hawaii Building, 134 West Soledad Avenue, P.O. Box BF, 96932-5027.
Telephone: 671-472-6813.
Fax: 671-477-4375.
Telex: 721-6445 CWCMI GM.
Saipan, Commonwealth of the Northern Mariana Islands Office: Carlsmith Building, Capitol Hill, P.O. Box 5241, 96950-5241.
Telephone: 670-322-3455.
Fax: 670-322-3368.
Los Angeles, California Office: 9th Floor, 444 South Flower Street, 90071-2901.
Telephone: 213-955-1200.
Fax: 213-623-0032.
Washington, D.C. Office: Suite 300, 1201 Pennsylvania Avenue, N.W., 20004-2401.
Telephone: 202-628-2228.
Fax: 202-628-2071.
Mexico City, Mexico Office: Carlsmith Ball, Sierra Nevada 119, Lomas de Chapultepec, 11000 Mexico, D.F.
Telephone: 52-5-520-8514, 52-5-520-8757.
Fax: 52-5-540-1545.
Mexico, D.F. Office of Carlsmith Ball, S.C. (Authorized to practice as foreign legal consultants in Mexico): Sierra Nevada 119, Lomas de Chapultepec, 11000 Mexico, D.F.
Telephone: 52-5-520-8514, 52-5-520-8757.
Fax: 52-5-540-1545.

MEMBERS OF FIRM

Anna M. Elento-Sneed
Terry E. Thomason
William C. Williams, Jr. (Not admitted in HI)

ASSOCIATES

Jonathan A. Swanson
Carol A. Uyeno

For Complete List of Firm Personnel, See General Section

For full biographical listings, see the Martindale-Hubbell Law Directory

ILLINOIS

*CHICAGO,** Cook Co.

BLATT, HAMMESFAHR & EATON (AV)

333 W. Wacker Drive, Suite 1900, 60606
Telephone: 312-849-8000
FAX: 312-357-0198
Email: BHE@BHELAW.COM *URL:* HTTP://WWW.BHELAW.COM
New York, New York Office: 45 Broadway, 12th Floor.
Telephone: 212-363-1900.
Fax: 212-363-2600. Email: bhe@bhelaw.com.

MEMBER OF FIRM

Richard L. Blatt

For full biographical listings, see the Martindale-Hubbell Law Directory

WILDMAN, HARROLD, ALLEN & DIXON (AV)

225 West Wacker Drive, 30th Floor, 60606-1229
Telephone: 312-201-2000
Fax: 312-201-2555
Email: hennessy@whad.com *URL:* http://www.whad.com
Aurora, Illinois Office: 1961 W. Downer Place.
Telephone: 630-892-7021.
Fax: 630-892-7158.

(See Next Column)

WILDMAN, HARROLD, ALLEN & DIXON, *Chicago—Continued*

Waukegan, Illinois Office: 404 West Water, P. O. Box 890.
Telephone: 847-625-5550.
Fax: 847-625-5555.
Lisle, Illinois Office: 4300 Commerce Court, Suite 320.
Telephone: 630-955-0555.
Fax: 630-955-0662
Toronto, Ontario correspondent Office: Keel Cottrelle. 36 Toronto Street, Suite 920.
Telephone: 416-367-2900.
Telefax: 416-367-2791.
Telex: 062-18660.

MEMBERS OF FIRM

Paul S. Chervin (Waukegan Office)
Roger G. Fein
Anthony G. Hopp
Mark J. McCombs
James R. Morrin
Linda E. Spring (Waukegan Office)
Sanford M. Stein
Louis P. Vitullo

OF COUNSEL

John Alden Fritchey IV
Lee B. McClain

Judith A. El-Amin

For full biographical listings, see the Martindale-Hubbell Law Directory

INDIANA

*INDIANAPOLIS,** Marion Co.

HOFFMAN DREWRY HANCOCK & SIMMONS (AV)

9100 Keystone Crossing, Suite 350, 46240
Telephone: 317-580-4848
Telecopier: 317-580-4855

Robert J. Hoffman
Michael F. Drewry
William J. Hancock
David L. Simmons
Richard S. Pitts
David B. Vornehm
Joseph M. Leone
Richard W. McMinn

OF COUNSEL

S. Douglas Trolson

For full biographical listings, see the Martindale-Hubbell Law Directory

LOUISIANA

*NEW ORLEANS,** Orleans Parish

FEINGERTS & ASSOCIATES, A PROFESSIONAL LAW CORPORATION (AV)

Poydras Center, Suite 26th Floor, 650 Poydras Street, 70130-6161
Telephone: 504-568-1515
Fax: 504-568-1521

Bruce L. Feingerts
Gary S. Brown
A. Elizabeth Tarver

For full biographical listings, see the Martindale-Hubbell Law Directory

HEALTH CARE LAW

ALABAMA

*BIRMINGHAM,** Jefferson Co.

Berkowitz, Lefkovits, Isom & Kushner, A Professional Corporation (AV)

SouthTrust Tower, 420 North Twentieth Street, Suite 1600, 35203-5202
Telephone: 205-328-0480
Telecopier: 205-322-8007
URL: http://www.blik.com

Harold B. Kushner
B. G. Minisman, Jr.
D. J. Simonetti
Thomas O. Kolb
Walton E. Williams III

Matthew W. Barnes
Alane A. Phillips

For Complete List of Firm Personnel, See General Section

For full biographical listings, see the Martindale-Hubbell Law Directory

Bradley Arant Rose & White LLP (AV)

2001 Park Place, Suite 1400, P.O. Box 830709, 35283-0709
Telephone: 205-521-8000
Facsimile: 205-521-8800
Facsimile (SouthTrust Tower Office): 205-521-8500
URL: http://www.barw.com
Huntsville, Alabama Office: 200 Clinton Avenue West, Suite 900, 35801.
Telephone: 205-517-5100.
Facsimile: 205-533-5069.
Washington, D.C. Office: 801 Pennsylvania Avenue, NW, Suite 230, 20004.
Telephone: 202-347-8893.
Facsimile: 202-347-1684.

MEMBERS OF FIRM

James S. Christie Jr.
Deane K. Corliss
Scott E. Ludwig (Resident, Huntsville Office)
John K. Molen
Robert C. Walthall

OF COUNSEL

S. Revelle Gwyn (Resident, Huntsville Office)

ASSOCIATES

Jolee Hancock Bollinger
K. Wood Herren
David E. Roth
Richard L. Sharff Jr.

For Complete List of Firm Personnel, See General Section

For full biographical listings, see the Martindale-Hubbell Law Directory

Haskell Slaughter & Young, L.L.C. (AV)

1200 AmSouth/Harbert Plaza, 1901 Sixth Avenue North, 35203
Telephone: 205-251-1000
Facsimile: 205-324-1133
Email: hsy@hsy.com
Montgomery, Alabama Office: 305 South Lawrence Street, P.O. Box 4660. 36103-4660.
Telephone: 334-265-8573.
Facsimile: 334-264-7945.

William M. Slaughter
E. Alston Ray
Mark Edward Ezell
Ross N. Cohen
Gwen L. Windle

Representative Clients: HEALTHSOUTH Corporation/HEALTHSOUTH Medical Centers; Northeast Alabama Regional Medical Center; Pickens County (Alabama) Medical Center.

For Complete List of Firm Personnel, See General Section

For full biographical listings, see the Martindale-Hubbell Law Directory

Johnston Barton Proctor & Powell LLP (AV)

2900 AmSouth/Harbert Plaza, 1901 Sixth Avenue North, 35203-2618
Telephone: 205-458-9400
Telecopier: 205-458-9500
Email: Law@JBPP.com

MEMBERS OF FIRM

Don B. Long, Jr.
J. William Rose, Jr.
Ralph H. Smith II
William D. Jones III
Oscar M. Price III
W. Hill Sewell
William G. Somerville III
R. Marcus Givhan
David M. Hunt
Haskins W. Jones
Russell L. Irby, III

COUNSEL

Richard J. Brockman

(See Next Column)

OF COUNSEL

Jerome K. Lanning

ASSOCIATES

Debra Lee Mackey
Karen M. Ross
Randall D. McClanahan
Bradley C. Mayhew
W. Jonathan Daniel
James F. Henry
Gina Pearson Hunter

General Counsel for: Ball HealthCare, Inc.; Baptist Health System, Inc.; Carecorps Management Corporation; Health Partners Southeast, Inc.; Lakeshore Foundation; Southern Medical Assn.; U.S.A. Healthcare, Inc.
Counsel for: Alabama Hospital Assn.; Alabama Nursing Home Assn.; Northport Health Services, Inc.

For full biographical listings, see the Martindale-Hubbell Law Directory

Parsons, Lee & Juliano, P.C. (AV)

2200 AmSouth/Harbert Plaza, 1901 Sixth Avenue, North, P.O. Box 371088, 35237-1088
Telephone: 205-326-6600
Fax: 205-324-7097

Robert E. Parsons
Jasper P. Juliano
Marcus W. Lee
Marda W. Sydnor
David A. Lee
John M. Bergquist
Paul J. DeMarco
Deborah Ann Payne
Dorothy A. Powell
David Samuel Snoddy

For full biographical listings, see the Martindale-Hubbell Law Directory

Smith, Spires & Peddy, P.C. (AV)

2015 Second Avenue North Suite 200, 35203
Telephone: 205-251-5885
Fax: 205-251-8642

Paul G. Smith

Representative Clients: Cigna Insurance; St. Paul; CNA Health Pro; U.S. Liability Ins. Co.; Diversicare, Inc.; The Huie Group.

For full biographical listings, see the Martindale-Hubbell Law Directory

*MOBILE,** Mobile Co.

Carr, Alford, Clausen & McDonald, L.L.C. (AV)

One St. Louis Centre, Suite 5000, P.O. Drawer C, 36601
Telephone: 334-432-1600
Facsimile: 334-432-1700
URL: http://www.cacm.com

Davis Carr
Helen Johnson Alford
Andrew C. Clausen
James H. McDonald, Jr.
James W. Lampkin, II
Jean M. Powers

Annette McDermott Carwie
M. Lauren Lemmon
Thomas M. Rockwell
Pamela Ann Moore
W. Ben. Broadwater
Paul V. Lagarde
Frank L. Parker, Jr.
Christina M. Adcock
Kathleen Cobb Kaufman
Joseph Anthony Zarzaur, Jr.

For full biographical listings, see the Martindale-Hubbell Law Directory

Johnstone, Adams, Bailey, Gordon and Harris, L.L.C. (AV)

Royal St. Francis Building, 104 St. Francis Street, 8th Floor, P.O. Box 1988, 36633
Telephone: 334-432-7682
Facsimile: 334-432-0712 or 334-432-2800
Email: attorneys@JohnstoneAdams.com *URL:* http://www.JohnstoneAdams.com
Bay Minette, Alabama Office: Dahlberg Building, 107 Hand Avenue, P.O. Box 729, 36507.
Telephone: 334-937-9473.
Facsimile: 334-937-9475.

MEMBERS OF FIRM

E. Watson Smith
Wade B. Perry, Jr.
R. Gregory Watts

For Complete List of Firm Personnel, See General Section

For full biographical listings, see the Martindale-Hubbell Law Directory

*MONTGOMERY,** Montgomery Co.

Brantley & Wilkerson, P.C. (AV)

405 South Hull Street, P.O. Box 830, 36101-0830
Telephone: 334-265-1500
Fax: 334-265-0319
Email: ashley@brantleywilkerson.com *URL:* http://www.brantleywilkerson.com

Mark D. Wilkerson

(See Next Column)

BRANTLEY & WILKERSON P.C., *Montgomery—Continued*

R. Winston Lee

Representative Clients: Alabama Board of Nursing (Hearing Officer); State Health Planning and Development Agency.
Reference: South Trust Bank, N.A.

For full biographical listings, see the Martindale-Hubbell Law Directory

KAUFMAN & ROTHFEDER, P.C. (AV)

2740 Zelda Road, Drawer 4540, 36103-4540
Telephone: 334-244-1111
Fax: 334-244-1969
Email: firm@krlegal.com *URL:* http://www.krlegal.com

John Ward Weiss
Carla Cole Gilmore
Jo Claudia Mitchum

OF COUNSEL

Gregg Brantley Everett

Counsel for: Dale Medical Center; Evergreen Medical Center; Community Health Systems, Inc.; The Russell Hospital Corporation.

For full biographical listings, see the Martindale-Hubbell Law Directory

ALASKA

*ANCHORAGE,** Third Judicial District

BLISS & WILKENS, LLC (AV)

431 West Seventh Avenue Suite 202, 99501-3583
Telephone: 907-276-2999
Facsimile: 907-276-2956

MEMBERS OF FIRM

Ronald L. Bliss
James K. Wilkens

ASSOCIATE

Alfred Clayton, Jr.

OF COUNSEL

Jean E. Kizer
Deborah K. Periman

LEGAL SUPPORT PERSONNEL

Nanette Shearer

For full biographical listings, see the Martindale-Hubbell Law Directory

ARIZONA

*PHOENIX,** Maricopa Co.

ALLEN & PRICE, P.L.C. (AV)

2850 East Camelback Road, Suite 170, 85016-4380
Telephone: 602-381-0500
Fax: 602-381-8899
Email: allen@aplaw.com
Email: price@aplaw.com
Email: schacter@aplaw.com
Email: sanders@aplaw.com

Robert E. B. Allen
Charles S. Price

Scott A. Shacter
Barry R. Sanders

For full biographical listings, see the Martindale-Hubbell Law Directory

BARCLAY & GOERING, P.C. (AV)

1001 North Central, Suite 600, 85004
Telephone: 602-340-1010
Fax: 602-340-1515
Email: bag1001@aol.com

Steven C. Barclay

For full biographical listings, see the Martindale-Hubbell Law Directory

BONN, LUSCHER, PADDEN & WILKINS, CHARTERED (AV)

805 North Second Street, 85004
Telephone: 602-254-5557
Fax: 602-254-0656
Email: firm@blpw.com

Jeff C. Padden

OF COUNSEL

Brian A. Luscher

For full biographical listings, see the Martindale-Hubbell Law Directory

DAVID G. DERICKSON, P.C. (AV)

3636 North Central, Suite 1050, 85012
Telephone: 602-277-6072
Fax: 602-277-6078
Email: david.derickson@azbar.org

David G. Derickson

For full biographical listings, see the Martindale-Hubbell Law Directory

DOYLE & WINTHROP, P.C. (AV)

2800 North Central Avenue Suite 1550, P.O. Box 10417, 85004
Telephone: 602-240-6711
Fax: 602-240-6951
Mailing Address: P.O. Box 10417, Phoenix, Arizona, 85064-0417
Las Vegas, Nevada Office: Edward D. Boyack, Esq., 2626 S. Rainbow Blvd., Suite 101, 89146.
Telephone: 702-873-1622.
Fax: 702-873-2280.

Lawrence F. Winthrop
William H. Doyle
Judith A. Berman

For full biographical listings, see the Martindale-Hubbell Law Directory

FENNEMORE CRAIG, A PROFESSIONAL CORPORATION (AV)

3003 North Central Avenue, Suite 2600, 85012-2913
Telephone: 602-916-5000
Fax: 602-916-5999
Tucson, Arizona Office: One South Church Avenue, Suite 1000, 85701-1620.
Telephone: 520-879-6800.
Fax: 520-879-6899.

Jay S. Ruffner
Jordan Green
Timothy J. Burke
Phillip F. Fargotstein
Scott M. Finical
Andrew M. Federhar
J. Barry Shelley
Jean Marie Sullivan

Kenneth J. Lee

LEGAL SUPPORT PERSONNEL

LEGAL ASSISTANTS

Claudia L. Parks

For Complete List of Firm Personnel, See General Section

For full biographical listings, see the Martindale-Hubbell Law Directory

JENNINGS, STROUSS & SALMON, P.L.C. (AV)

A Professional Limited Liability Company
One Renaissance Square, Two North Central Avenue, 85004-2393
Telephone: 602-262-5911
Fax: 602-253-3255
Email: info@jsslaw.com *URL:* http://www.jsslaw.com
Arrowhead Office: 16150 North Arrowhead Fountains Center Drive, Suite 250, Peoria, Arizona.
Telephone: 623-878-2222.
Fax: 623-878-1333.

George C. Spilsbury
Rita A. Meiser
Anne L. Kleindienst
John C. West
Joen M. Schaefer
Robert J. Werner
Ernest Calderón
Richard K. Delo

ASSOCIATES

Gordon Lewis
Johnny J. Sorenson

For Complete List of Firm Personnel, See General Section

For full biographical listings, see the Martindale-Hubbell Law Directory

JOHNSTON & DODD, P.L.C. (AV)

One North First Street, Suite 700, 85004
Telephone: 602-452-0600
Facsimile: 602-716-5997
Email: johnston-doddlaw@uswest.net

Logan T. Johnston, III
Catherine M. Dodd
Anne C. Longo
Kenneth M. Rudisill, Jr.

For full biographical listings, see the Martindale-Hubbell Law Directory

LEWIS AND ROCA, LLP (AV)

A Limited Liability Partnership including a Professional Corporation
40 North Central Avenue, 85004-4429
Telephone: 602-262-5311
Fax: 602-262-5747
Email: clientservice@lrlaw.com *URL:* http://www.lrlaw.com
Tucson, Arizona Office: One South Church Avenue, Suite 700, 86701-1620.
Telephone: 520-622-2090.
Fax: 520-622-3088. E-Mail: clientservice@lrlaw.com.

(See Next Column)

LEWIS AND ROCA LLP—*Continued*

Las Vegas, Nevada Affiliated Office: Ashcraft and Heinz LLP, 3960 Howard Hughes Parkway, 89109.
Telephone: 702-990-3570.
Fax: 702-990-3571.

MEMBERS OF FIRM

Merton E. Marks (P.C.)
Foster Robberson

ASSOCIATES

Bruce E. Samuels
Leanne Dodds-Eastman

OF COUNSEL

Joseph A. Mislove

Representative Clients: Arizona Hospital Assn.; Blood Systems, Inc.; Mutual Insurance Company of Arizona; Phoenix Memorial Hospital; St. Joseph's; Samaritan Health System; Scottsdale Memorial Hospitals.

For Complete List of Firm Personnel, See General Section

For full biographical listings, see the Martindale-Hubbell Law Directory

MYERS & JENKINS, A PROFESSIONAL CORPORATION (AV)

Phoenix Corporate Center, 3003 North Central Avenue, Suite 1900, 85012
Telephone: 602-200-7900
Facsimile: 602-200-7910
Email: firm@mjlegal.com

Stephen W. Myers
William Scott Jenkins
Teresa Dawn Farrison

Gregory D. Honig

Reference: Wells Fargo Bank.

For full biographical listings, see the Martindale-Hubbell Law Directory

QUARLES & BRADY LLP (AV)

One Camelback Building, One East Camelback Road, Suite 400, 85012-1649
Telephone: 602-230-5500
Fax: 602-230-5598
URL: http://www.quarles.com
Milwaukee, Wisconsin Office: 411 East Wisconsin Avenue.
Telephone: 414-277-5000.
Fax: 414-271-3552.
Madison, Wisconsin Office: First Wisconsin Plaza, One South Pinckney Street, P.O. Box 2113.
Telephone: 608-251-5000.
Fax: 608-251-9166.
West Palm Beach, Florida Office: 222 Lakeview Avenue, 4th Floor.
Telephone: 407-653-5000.
Fax: 407-653-5333.
Naples, Florida Office: Barnett Center, 4501 Tamiami Trail North, Suite 300.
Telephone: 813-262-5959.
Fax: 813-434-4999.
Chicago, Illinois Office: Quarles & Brady LLC, Citicorp Center, 500 West Madison Street, Suite 3700.
Telephone: 312-715-5000.
Fax: 312-715-5155.

MEMBER OF THE FIRM

P. Robert Fannin

ASSOCIATES

Wendy Gerlach Briggs
Jeffrey A. Sandquist

For full biographical listings, see the Martindale-Hubbell Law Directory

SNELL & WILMER L.L.P. (AV)

One Arizona Center, 85004-2202
Telephone: 602-382-6000
Fax: 602-382-6070
Email: postmaster@snellwilmer.com *URL:* http://www.swlaw.com
Tucson, Arizona Office: One South Church Avenue, Suite 1500, 85701-1612.
Telephone: 520-882-1200.
Fax: 520-884-1294.
Orange County Office: 1920 Main Street, Suite 1200, Irvine, California 92614-7230.
Telephone: 949-253-2700.
Fax: 949-955-2507.
Salt Lake City, Utah Office: 111 East Broadway, Suite 900, 84111-1004.
Telephone: 801-237-1900.
Fax: 801-237-1950.

MEMBERS OF FIRM

Gerard Morales
Richard W. Sheffield
Donald H. Smith
Paul J. Giancola
Barry D. Halpern
Terry Morris Roman
GinaMarie Rossano
Maria Nutile

OF COUNSEL

Edward Jacobson

(See Next Column)

ASSOCIATES

Terri N.A. Buccino
Elizabeth A. Guth
Dora Fitzpatrick
Amy L. Leinen

Representative Clients: For list of Representative Clients, see end of biographical listings in the Martindale-Hubbell Law Directory.

For Complete List of Firm Personnel, See General Section

For full biographical listings, see the Martindale-Hubbell Law Directory

ULRICH, KESSLER & ANGER, P.C. (AV)

3707 North Seventh Street, Suite 250, 85014-5059
Telephone: 602-248-9465
Fax: 602-248-0165
Email: ukapc@aol.com

Paul G. Ulrich
Donn G. Kessler
William H. Anger

For full biographical listings, see the Martindale-Hubbell Law Directory

SCOTTSDALE, Maricopa Co.

SACKS TIERNEY P.A. (AV)

4250 North Civic Center Boulevard, 85251
Telephone: 480-425-2600
Facsimile: 480-970-4610
Email: ST@sackstierney.com
Phoenix, Arizona Office: Two North Central Avenue, Suite 1960. 85004.
Telephone: 480-435-2600.
Fax: 480-970-4610.

Seymour Sacks
Marvin S. Cohen
David C. Tierney
Stephen Aron Benson
Michael R. Rooney
Robert G. Kimball
Stephen P. Linzer
Marcia J. Busching
Randall S. Yavitz
Sharon Brook Shively
James W. Armstrong
Steven M. Goldstein
Judith M. Dworkin
Robert J. Lord
Sharon S. Moyer
Candess J. Hunter
Lori R. Miller
Brian E. Ditsch

Sharyl Poulson Speaker
Steven W. Bienstock
Andrew Lane de Mars
Scott B. Cohen
Mark D. Dillon
John L. Habib
W. Kevin Bell
Isabel M. Humphrey
Julie A. Inderlied
Laura G. Meyer
Stephen A. Wolf

Reference: M&I Thunderbird Bank.

For full biographical listings, see the Martindale-Hubbell Law Directory

ARKANSAS

*LITTLE ROCK,** Pulaski Co.

BARBER, MCCASKILL, JONES & HALE, P.A. (AV)

2700 Regions Center, 400 West Capitol Avenue, 72201-3414
Telephone: 501-372-6175
Telecopier: 501-375-2802

Azro L. Barber (1885-1979)
Elbert A. Henry (1889-1966)
John B. Thurman (1912-1971)
Austin McCaskill, Sr.
Glenn W. Jones
Michael E. Hale
John S. Cherry, Jr.
Robert L. Henry, III
Micheal L. Alexander
William H. Edwards, Jr.
G. Spence Fricke
Gail Ponder Gaines
Michael J. Emerson
R. Kenny McCulloch
Tim A. Cheatham
Joseph F. Kolb
Scott Michael Strauss
Baucum Fulk
D. Keith Fortner
Wendy Scholtens Wood
Morris L. Williams, III
Michelle Bass Miller

Attorneys for: Baptist Health Corp.; CIGNA Insurance Companies; CNA Insurance; Connecticut General Insurance Company; Fireman's Fund Insurance Co.; General Motors Acceptance Corp.; Hanover Insurance Co.; Insurance Company of North America; Minnesota Mining & Manufacturing; Royal Insurance.

For full biographical listings, see the Martindale-Hubbell Law Directory

THE HEALTH LAW FIRM (AV)

Pavilion in the Park, 8201 Cantrell Road, Suite 255, 72227-2448
Telephone: 501-221-7100
Telefax: 501-224-8787
URL: http://www.lawyers.com/healthlaw
URL: http://www.healthlawfirm.com

(See Next Column)

THE HEALTH LAW FIRM, *Little Rock—Continued*

Harold H. Simpson | Lynne Trulock Ravellette
Sara Fairbanks Israel

Representative Clients: Arkansas Pharmacists Association; Baptist Health; Carroll Regional Medical Center; Central Health Corporation; North Arkansas Regional Medical Center; Ouachita County Medical Center; White River Medical Center.
Reference: Regions Bank.

For full biographical listings, see the Martindale-Hubbell Law Directory

CALIFORNIA

*BAKERSFIELD,** Kern Co.

BORTON, PETRINI & CONRON, LLP (AV)

The Borton, Petrini & Conron Building, 1600 Truxtun Avenue, 93301
Telephone: 661-322-3051
Voice Mail: 661-395-6700
Fax: 661-322-4628
Mailing Address: P.O. Box 2026, Bakersfield, California, 93303
Email: bpcbak@bpclaw.com *URL:* http://www.bpclaw.com
Other City Locations: Fresno, Los Angeles, Modesto, Redding, Sacramento, San Bernardino, San Diego, San Francisco, San Jose, San Luis Obispo, Santa Ana and Ventura.

MEMBER OF FIRM
George F. Martin

ASSOCIATES
Stephen M. Crane | Raymond G. Robinson

For Complete List of Firm Personnel, See General Section

For full biographical listings, see the Martindale-Hubbell Law Directory

BEVERLY HILLS, Los Angeles Co.

HERZOG, FISHER, GRAYSON & WOLFE, A LAW CORPORATION (AV)

9460 Wilshire Boulevard Fifth Floor, 90212
Telephone: 310-278-4300
Fax: 310-278-5430

James P. Herzog | Michael A. Grayson
David R. Fisher | Herbert N. Wolfe

Doreen W. Shenfeld | Jerry R. Sparks
Bree Arlyn-Pessin

OF COUNSEL
Todd I. Grayson

For full biographical listings, see the Martindale-Hubbell Law Directory

EMERYVILLE, Alameda Co.

CHILVERS & TAYLOR, PC (AV)

Baybridge Office Plaza, 5801 Christie Avenue, Suite 590, 94608
Telephone: 510-923-6230
Fax: 510-923-6236
Email: counsel@chilvers-taylor.com *URL:* http://www.chilvers-taylor.com

Robert M. Chilvers | William "Zak" Taylor

Leila Clark-Riddell | Aviva Cuyler

OF COUNSEL
Kathy L. Hensley

Representative Clients: Omni Healthcare, Inc.; San Francisco IPA; Saatchi & Saatchi Advertising, N.A., Inc.; United Broadcasting Co.any.

For full biographical listings, see the Martindale-Hubbell Law Directory

JAMES JAY SELTZER (AV)

Watergate Towers, Tenth Floor, 2200 Powell Street, Suite 1035, 94608
Telephone: 510-596-2500
Telecopier: 510-596-2519
URL: http://www.secureadvise.com
Email: lawoffices@jjseltzer.com *URL:* http://www.lawyers.com/jamesjayseltzer

For full biographical listings, see the Martindale-Hubbell Law Directory

*FRESNO,** Fresno Co.

DOWLING, AARON & KEELER, INCORPORATED (AV)

6051 North Fresno Street, Suite 200, 93710
Telephone: 559-432-4500
Fax: 559-432-4590
Email: dak@daklaw.com *URL:* http://www.daklaw.com
Bakersfield, California Office: 110 South Mt. Claire, Suite 203. 93309.
Telephone: 661-396-0451. Web Site: http://www.daklaw.com.

Michael D. Dowling | Richard M. Aaron
John C. Ganahl

Larry B. Lindenau | Justin D. Harris

Reference: Wells Fargo Bank (Main).

For Complete List of Firm Personnel, See General Section

For full biographical listings, see the Martindale-Hubbell Law Directory

*LOS ANGELES,** Los Angeles Co.

DEMETRIOU, DEL GUERCIO, SPRINGER & MOYER, LLP (AV)

801 South Grand Avenue, 10th Floor, 90017
Telephone: 213-624-8407
Telecopy: 213-624-0174
Email: ddsm@juno.com

MEMBERS OF FIRM
Angela Shanahan | Stephen A. Del Guercio

OF COUNSEL
Ronald J. Del Guercio

Reference: Bank of America, L.A. Main Office, Los Angeles, Calif.

For full biographical listings, see the Martindale-Hubbell Law Directory

FOLEY & LARDNER (AV)

35th Floor, One Century Plaza, 2029 Century Park East (Century City), 90067-3021
Telephone: 310-277-2223
Facsimile: 310-557-8475
Email: foleylardner@worldnet.att.net *URL:* http://www.foleylardner.com
Sacramento, California Office: 300 Capitol Mall, Suite 1125.
Telephone: 916-443-8005.
Fax: 916-443-2240.
San Diego, California Office: 402 West Broadway, 23rd Floor.
Telephone: 619-234-6655.
Fax: 619-234-3510.
San Francisco, California Office: One Maritime Plaza, Sixth Floor.
Telephone: 415-434-4484.
Fax: 415-434-4507.
Denver, Colorado Office: 1999 Broadway, Suite 2560.
Telephone: 303-297-0260.
Fax: 303-297-0266.
Washington, D.C. Office: Washington Harbour, Suite 500, 3000 K Street, N.W.
Telephone: 202-672-5300.
Telex: 904136 (Foley Lard Wash).
Facsimile: 202-672-5399.
Jacksonville, Florida Office: The Greenleaf Building, 200 Laura Street. P.O. Box 240.
Telephone: 904-359-2000.
Facsimile: 904-359-8700.
Orlando, Florida Office: Suite 1800, 111 North Orange Avenue, P.O. Box 2193.
Telephone: 407-423-7656.
Facsimile: 407-648-1743.
Tallahassee, Florida Office: 300 East Park Avenue, P.O. Box 1454.
Telephone: 850-222-6100.
Facsimile: 850-561-6475.
Tampa, Florida Offices: Suite 2700, One Hundred N. Tampa Street, P.O. Box 3391.
Telephones: 813-229-2300; Pinellas County: 813-442-3296.
Facsimile: 813-221-4210.
West Palm Beach, Florida Office: Suite 200, Phillips Point East Tower, 777 South Flagler Drive.
Telephone: 561-655-5050.
Facsimile: 561-655-6925.
Chicago, Illinois Office: Suite 3300, One IBM Plaza, 330 N. Wabash Avenue.
Telephone: 312-755-1900.
Facsimile: 312-755-1925.
Annapolis, Maryland Office: Suite 102, 175 Admiral Cochrane Drive.
Telephone: 410-266-8077.
Telex: 899149 (Oldtownpat).
Facsimile: 410-266-8664.
Madison, Wisconsin Office: Verex Plaza, 150 East Gilman Street, P.O. Box 1497.
Telephone: 608-257-5035.
Facsimile: 608-258-4258.

(See Next Column)

FOLEY & LARDNER—*Continued*

Milwaukee, Wisconsin Office: Firstar Center, 777 East Wisconsin Avenue.
Telephone: 414-271-2400.
Telex: 26-819 (Foley Lard Mil).
Facsimile: 414-297-4900.
Brussels, Belgium Office: Avenue Louise, 283.
Telephone: 32-2-646-2777.
Facsimile: 32-2-646-7574.

PARTNERS

Richard M. Albert
Peter Aronson
Salvatore A. Barbatano (Not admitted in CA)
Richard A. Blacker
David A. Blumenthal (Resident also at Foley & Lardner, Washington, D.C. Office)
Lowell C. Brown
Douglas L. Carden
Jonathon E. Cohn
C. Darryl Cordero
Edsell M. Eady, Jr.
James N. Godes
James R. Kalyvas
Ralph B. Kostant
Anita D. Lee
Robert C. Leventhal
Robyn A. Meinhardt
Charles B. Oppenheim
Michael R. Overly
Clare Richardson
Ted R. Rittmaster
Denise Rios Rodriguez
Richard F. Seiden
Robert D. Sevell
Mitchell S. Shapiro
Tami S. Smason
Rochelle Buchsbaum Spandorf
Terri Wagner Cammarano
J. Mark Waxman (Also at Washington, D.C.)
Carl Weissburg
Jon M. Wilson
Mark S. Windisch

OF COUNSEL

Lawrence C. Conn
Robert J. Enders
Robert A. Klein

SPECIAL COUNSEL

Jeffrey R. Bates
Thomas L. Blasdell
Howard W. Cohen
Greg R. Miller

ASSOCIATES

Hema Rao Anwar
Kimberly F. Applequist
Kristin K. Bear
Devon W. Block
Catherine J. Carter
Shirley S. Cho
Elizabeth S. Elson
Doaa A. Fathallah
Michael A. Graham
Amy B. Hafey
Susanna E. Hathaway
Lorna D. Hennington
Mir Saied Kashani
Frederick D. Kim
Glenn M. Kubota
Holly R. Lake
Mark Tae Lee
Sara Mars
Pauline Scheinberg Maxwell
Clint McCord
Heather D. McNeill
Rhonda H. Mehlman
Jerilyn López Mendoza
Shana Torem Mintz
Muira K. Mishra
James D. Nguyen
Leila Nourani
Lisa A. Palombo
Nicholas J. Pauley
T. Joshua Ritz
Damon Rubin
William O. Stein
Martha Stulman
Amy D. Tichenor
Diane Ung
Karen R. Weinstein
Jennifer C. Yang

For full biographical listings, see the Martindale-Hubbell Law Directory

GALTON & HELM LLP (AV)

500 South Grand Avenue Suite 1200, 90071
Telephone: 213-629-8800
Telecopier: 213-629-0037
Email: GaltonHelm@GaltonHelm.usa.com
Palm Desert, California Office: 73-929 Larrea.
Telephone: 760-776-5600.
Fax: 760-776-5602.

MEMBERS OF FIRM

Stephen H. Galton
Hugh H. Helm
Michael F. Bell
Daniel W. Maguire (Resident at Palm Desert)
David A. Lingenbrink
Robert F. Keehn

ASSOCIATES

Melissa M. Cowan
Joanna M. Todd
Michael B. Bernacchi
David J. Weinman
Nicole Blohm Pomerantz
Jennifer L. Kurzon
Eduardo A. Brito
Deanna E. McCray
Ann C. Schneider
Edith S. Shea

LEGAL SUPPORT PERSONNEL

Lana Banks (Paralegal)
Mardi Walsh (Paralegal)
Lynne M. Koss (Paralegal)
Toni Quigley (Paralegal)

For full biographical listings, see the Martindale-Hubbell Law Directory

HOOPER, LUNDY & BOOKMAN, INC. (AV)

Watt Plaza, Suite 1600, 1875 Century Park East, 90067-2517
Telephone: 310-551-8111
Telecopier: 310-551-8181

(See Next Column)

Robert W. Lundy, Jr.
Patric Hooper
Lloyd A. Bookman
W. Bradley Tully
John R. Hellow
Angela A. Mickelson
Laurence D. Getzoff
Jay N. Hartz
Byron J. Gross
David P. Henninger
Todd E. Swanson
Mark Jeffry Dicks
Linda Randlett Kollar

Gina Reese
Jonathan P. Neustadter
Julia Schollenberger
Betty J. Levine
William A. Larkin
Stacy L. Dull
Robert R. Valencia
Daron L. Tooch
Glenn E. Solomon

Representative Clients: Tenet Healthcare Corp.; Kaiser Foundation Health Plan; City of Hope National Medical Center; County of Los Angeles; Queen of Angels/Hollywood Presbyterian Medical Center; Beach Cities Health District; Kauai Medical Group; Vista Health Plans.
Reference: City National Bank.

For full biographical listings, see the Martindale-Hubbell Law Directory

HORVITZ & LEVY, LLP (AV)

A Partnership including Professional Corporations
18th Floor, 15760 Ventura Boulevard (Encino), 91436
Telephone: 818-995-0800
Fax: 818-995-3157

Ellis J. Horvitz (A P.C.)
Barry R. Levy (A P.C.)
Peter Abrahams
David M. Axelrad
Frederic D. Cohen
S. Thomas Todd
David S. Ettinger
Daniel J. Gonzalez
Mitchell C. Tilner
Christina J. Imre
Lisa Perrochet
Stephen E. Norris
Sandra J. Smith
John A. Taylor, Jr.
Julie L. Woods
Lisa R. Jaskol
H. Thomas Watson

Mary F. Dant
Holly R. Paul
Andrea M. Gauthier
Judith E. Gordon
Patricia Lofton
L. Rachel Lerman Helyar
Mary-Christine (M.C.) Sungaila
Stephanie Rae Williams
Curt Cutting
Wendy S. Albers
Robert H. Wright
Nina E. Scholtz
Orly Degani

OF COUNSEL

Jon B. Eisenberg

Representative Clients: California Medical Association; California Association of Hospitals and Health Systems; Truck Insurance Exchange; Cedars-Sinai Medical Center; Southern California Physicians Insurance Exchange; Truck Insurance Exchange; Physicians & Surgeons Division of Fremont Indemnity; NORCAL Mutual Insurance Company; Kaiser Foundation Health Plan, Inc.; CHD Insurance Services.

For full biographical listings, see the Martindale-Hubbell Law Directory

KONOWIECKI & RANK LLP (AV)

A Partnership including a Professional Corporation
Library Tower, 633 West 5th Street, Suite 3500, 90071-2007
Telephone: 213-229-0990
Telefax: 213-229-0992

Peter C. Rank
Joseph S. Konowiecki
Michael C. Foster
Jon N. Manzanares
Kevin B. Kroeker
Peter Roan
Peter R. Mason
Denise E. Hanna
Edna M. Chism
Scott J. Moore
Robert C. Hayden
Gail D. Schubert

ASSOCIATES

Cynthia J. Billey
Michael J. Blake
Ana Castillo
Ronan Cohen
Richard A. Cross
Rosa Kwon Easton
I-Fan C. Go
Melinda A. Hess
Sandra Lee Hitt
Lynn E. Iba
Robert M. Kessler
Harry H.W. Kim
Thomas C. Knego
Stephen J. Krause
Phillip R. Maltin
John A. Mueller
Jeffrey D. Olster
Leslie Overfelt
Gary S. Pancer
Tallien Perry
Payman Pezhman
Harold C. Pope
Robin M. Prendergast
Ira L. Robinson
Michael B. Spencer
India S. Thompson
Keith A. Weaver
John A. Zrnich

Representative Clients: PacifiCare Health Systems, Inc.; Henry Mayo Newhall Memorial Hospital; Santa Clarita Health Care Assoc.; College Health Enterprises; Granada Hills Community Hospital; Redlands Community Hospital; Health Care Partners.
Reference: Bank of America.

For full biographical listings, see the Martindale-Hubbell Law Directory

*OAKLAND,** Alameda Co.

HAIMS, MACGOWAN, VALENTINO & PEEBLES, L.L.P. (AV)

490 Grand Avenue, 94610
Telephone: 510-835-0500
Facsimile: 510-835-2833

MEMBERS OF FIRM

Arnold B. Haims — Caroline N. Valentino
Clyde L. MacGowan — Dianne D. Peebles

For full biographical listings, see the Martindale-Hubbell Law Directory

PASADENA, Los Angeles Co.

CHRISTENSEN & AUER (AV)

225 South Lake, Ninth Floor, 91101
Telephone: 626-568-2900
Fax: 626-568-1566
Email: jdc@jdclaw.com

Jay D. Christensen — Stephen G. Auer

ASSOCIATES

Anna M. Suda — Lisa Case

For full biographical listings, see the Martindale-Hubbell Law Directory

*SACRAMENTO,** Sacramento Co.

HUNTER RICHEY DI BENEDETTO & BREWER, LLP (AV)

A Limited Liability Partnership
Renaissance Tower, 801 K Street, 23rd Floor, 95814-3525
Telephone: 916-491-3000
Facsimile: 916-491-3080
Email: hrdb@hrdb.com *URL:* http://www.hrdb.com

MEMBERS OF FIRM

William S. Hunter — James F. Geary
Win R. Richey — Janet C. Eisenbeis
Florence L. Di Benedetto — Stephen C. Ruehmann
Roy E. Brewer — Sharon K. Sandeen
Anne E. Ferguson — Jack V. Lovell
Patricia J. Hartman

OF COUNSEL

Laurie E. Davis

LEGAL SUPPORT PERSONNEL

Lori J. Moody (Paralegal) — Jennifer E. Mueller (Legal Assistant)
Deborah M. Johnson (Paralegal) — Michele L. Nickell (Legal Assistant)
Linda Jane Hall (Executive Assistant)
Lynetta G. Goodwin

For full biographical listings, see the Martindale-Hubbell Law Directory

LIVINGSTON & MATTESICH, LAW CORPORATION (AV)

1201 K Street, Suite 1100, 95814
Telephone: 916-442-1111
Fax: 916-448-1709
Email: l&m@lmlaw.net *URL:* http://www.lmlaw.net

Gene Livingston — Emilio E. Varanini, III
James M. Mattesich — Kenneth M. Malovos
Carol Livingston — Kathleen E. Finnerty
Rebecca M. Ceniceros — Joanna R. Mendoza

Steven P. Belzer — Baldassaro (Bill) Di Capo
Jeffrey Leacox — John McKinsey
Randy Pollack — Timothy E. Naccarato
Alice H. Choi — Craig N. Lundgren
Stephen Craig Hunter — Mary Farrell Taylor
Matthew J. Goldman — Brian Crone
Joel C. Baiocchi — Gay L. Carroll
Steven G. Churchwell

Representative Clients: Bayer Corporation; BioMedical Disposal; Health Industry Manufacturers Association; Novartis Pharmaceuticals Corporation.

For full biographical listings, see the Martindale-Hubbell Law Directory

*SAN DIEGO,** San Diego Co.

HAIGHT, BROWN & BONESTEEL, L.L.P. (AV)

A Partnership including Professional Corporations
101 West Broadway, Suite 1000, 92101-3544
Telephone: 619-595-5583
Telecopier: 619-595-7873
URL: http://www.hbblaw.com
Santa Monica, California Office: 1620 26th Street, Suite 4000 North, P.O. Box 680.
Telephone: 310-449-6000.
Telecopier: 310-829-5117.
Telex: 705837.

(See Next Column)

Santa Ana, California Office: Suite 900, 5 Hutton Centre Drive.
Telephone: 714-754-1100.
Telecopier: 714-754-0826.
Riverside, California Office: California Tower, 3737 Main Street, Suite 800.
Telephone: 909-341-8300.
Fax: 909-341-8309.
San Francisco, California Office: 101 Bush Street, 27th Floor.
Telephone: 415-986-7700.
Fax: 415-986-6945.

RESIDENT ASSOCIATE

Siobhan A. Cullen

For full biographical listings, see the Martindale-Hubbell Law Directory

LINDLEY, SCALES & CORBETT, A PROFESSIONAL CORPORATION (AV)

550 West C Street, Suite 1800, 92101
Telephone: 619-234-9181
Fax: 619-234-8475
Email: lsc@adnc.com

Robert M. McLeod

Representative Clients: San Diego Hospital Association; San Diego Blood Bank; Donald N. Sharp Memorial Hospital.

For full biographical listings, see the Martindale-Hubbell Law Directory

*SAN FRANCISCO,** San Francisco Co.

HAIGHT, BROWN & BONESTEEL, L.L.P. (AV)

A Partnership including Professional Corporations
100 Bush Street, 27th Floor, 94104-3902
Telephone: 415-986-7700
Telecopier: 415-986-6945
URL: http://www.hbblaw.com
Santa Monica, California Office: 1620 26th Street, Suite 4000 North, P.O. Box 680.
Telephone: 310-449-6000.
Telecopier: 310-829-5117.
Telex: 705837.
Santa Ana, California Office: Suite 900, 5 Hutton Centre Drive.
Telephone: 714-754-1100.
Telecopier: 714-754-0826.
Riverside, California Office: California Tower, 3737 Main Street, Suite 800.
Telephone: 909-341-8300.
Fax: 909-341-8309.
San Diego, California Office: 101 West Broadway, Suite 1000.
Telephone: 619-595-5583.
Fax: 619-595-7873.

RESIDENT MEMBER

Patricia H. Perry

For full biographical listings, see the Martindale-Hubbell Law Directory

*SANTA ANA,** Orange Co.

MCNEIL, SUSSON, PARRETT & TROPP, A PROFESSIONAL CORPORATION (AV)

2100 North Broadway, Suite 103, 92706-2624
Telephone: 714-835-1922
Facsimile: 714-835-2720
Email: info@msplawyers.com

Joseph D. McNeil — James R. Parrett
Dana E. Susson — Deborah S. Tropp

Maxine M. Morisaki-Price — Alison J. Vitacolonna

For full biographical listings, see the Martindale-Hubbell Law Directory

SANTA MONICA, Los Angeles Co.

HAIGHT, BROWN & BONESTEEL, L.L.P. (AV)

A Partnership including Professional Corporations
1620 26th Street, Suite 4000 North, P.O. Box 680, 90404
Telephone: 310-449-6000
Telecopier: 310-829-5117
Telex: 705837
URL: http://www.hbblaw.com
Santa Ana, California Office: Suite 900, 5 Hutton Centre Drive.
Telephone: 714-754-1100.
Telecopier: 714-754-0826.
Riverside, California Office: California Tower, 3737 Main Street, Suite 800.
Telephone: 909-341-8300.
Fax: 909-341-8309.
San Francisco, California Office: 101 Bush Street, 27th Floor.
Telephone: 415-986-7700.
Fax: 415-986-6945.
San Diego, California Office: 101 West Broadway, Suite 1000.
Telephone: 619-595-5583.
Fax: 619-595-7873.

(See Next Column)

HAIGHT, BROWN & BONESTEEL L.L.P.—*Continued*

MEMBERS OF FIRM

Michael J. Bonesteel (A Professional Corporation)
Dennis K. Wheeler (A Professional Corporation)
Thomas M. Moore
David J. Fleming
David C. McGovern
Lisa J. Golden
Mario Horwitz
William A. Hanssen
Cary D. Glassner

ASSOCIATES

Carolyn L. Trokey
Suzanne V. Stouder
Shanna R. Davis
Joseph M. Elguindy
Ronald T. Labriola
Jayme C. Quick

OF COUNSEL

Kathryn M. Forgie
Caroline Kelley Moore

For full biographical listings, see the Martindale-Hubbell Law Directory

COLORADO

*DENVER,** Denver Co.

BERENBAUM, WEINSHIENK & EASON, P.C. (AV)

Suite 2600 Republic Plaza, 370 17th Street, 80202
Telephone: 303-825-0800
Facsimile: 303-629-7610
Email: berenbaum1@aol.com *URL:* http://www.BWELaw.com

M. Frances Cetrulo
Edwin G. Perlmutter

Representative Clients: Home Depot; Sprint Spectrum, L.P.; Town of Vail, Colorado; First Union Corporation; City of Englewood, Colorado; Oakwood Homes; Karman, Inc.; Wells Fargo Bank, N.A.; Berkshire Life Insurance Co.; Trinity Ventures.

For full biographical listings, see the Martindale-Hubbell Law Directory

MARLIN W. BURKE, P.C. (AV)

Mile High Center, 1700 Broadway, Suite 1800, 80290
Telephone: 303-863-7036
Fax: 303-832-6947
Email: mwburke@uswest.net

Marlin W. Burke

For full biographical listings, see the Martindale-Hubbell Law Directory

GORSUCH KIRGIS LLP (AV)

Tower 1, Suite 1000, 1515 Arapahoe Street, 80202
Telephone: 303-376-5000
Fax: 303-376-5001

PARTNER

Ellen E. Stewart

ASSOCIATE

Barbara A. Kakenmaster

For full biographical listings, see the Martindale-Hubbell Law Directory

HOLME ROBERTS & OWEN LLP (AV)

Suite 4100, 1700 Lincoln, 80203
Telephone: 303-861-7000
Telecopier: 303-866-0200
Email: hro@hro.com *URL:* http://www.hro.com
Boulder, Colorado Office: Suite 400, 1401 Pearl Street.
Telephone: 303-444-5955.
Telecopier: 303-444-1063.
Colorado Springs, Colorado Office: Suite 1300, 90 South Cascade Avenue.
Telephone: 719-473-3800.
Telecopier: 719-633-1518.
Salt Lake City, Utah Office: Suite 1100, 111 East Broadway.
Telephone: 801-521-5800.
Telecopier: 801-521-9639.
London, England Office: Heathcoat House, 3rd Floor, 20 Savile Row.
Telephone: 011-44-171-494-5600.
Telecopier: 011-44-171-287-9344.

PARTNERS OF FIRM

Blaine J. Benard (Salt Lake City Office)
Bruce F. Black
Susan E. Duffey Campbell (Colorado Springs Office)
Steve L. Gaines (Colorado Springs Office)
Mary L. Groves
Donald J. Hopkins
Richard L. Nagl (Colorado Springs Office)
Nick Nimmo
Mary Hurley Stuart
Gary R. Thorup (Salt Lake City Office)
John R. Wylie (Colorado Springs Office)

OF COUNSEL

Frank E. Moss (Salt Lake City Office)
Richard L. Schrepferman

(See Next Column)

ASSOCIATE

M. Mashenka Lundberg

For Complete List of Firm Personnel, See General Section

For full biographical listings, see the Martindale-Hubbell Law Directory

MONTGOMERY LITTLE & MCGREW, P.C. (AV)

The Quadrant, 5445 DTC Parkway, Suite 800 (Englewood), 80111
Telephone: 303-773-8100
Telecopier: 303-220-0412
URL: http://www.mlmpc.com

Robert R. Montgomery
Robert N. Spencer
Patrick T. O'Rourke

Representative Clients: BP Amoco; Bristol-Myers Squibb; Colorado Medical Society; Cyprus Minerals; Dillon Cos., Inc., d/b/a King Soopers; The St. Paul Insurance Cos.; University of Colorado Health Sciences Center; HealthOne; Teva Pharmaceuticals; Childrens Hospital.

For Complete List of Firm Personnel, See General Section

For full biographical listings, see the Martindale-Hubbell Law Directory

OTTEN, JOHNSON, ROBINSON, NEFF & RAGONETTI, P.C. (AV)

950 Seventeenth Street, 16th Floor, 80202
Telephone: 303-825-8400
Telecopier: 303-825-6525
URL: http://www.ojrnr.com

Karen L. Barsch
James D. Leonard

Representative Clients: Associated Surgeons M.D., P.C.; Cleo Wallace Center; Consultants in Obstetrics & Gynecology, P.C.; Coram Healthcare Corp.; GeriMed of America, Inc.; Immunological Associates of Denver, Inc.; Institute for Limb Preservation, Inc.; Johnson County Memorial Hospital; Orthopaedics of Jackson Hole, P.C.; QualMed, Inc.; ROMED Corp.; The Steadman Hawkins Clinic.

For Complete List of Firm Personnel, See General Section

For full biographical listings, see the Martindale-Hubbell Law Directory

YU STROMBERG CLEVELAND, P.C. (AV)

Suite 700, 650 South Cherry Street, 80246
Telephone: 303-388-9311
Telecopier: 303-322-3872
Email: ysc@yscpc.com *URL:* http://www.yustrombergcleveland.com

Frederick Y. Yu
Wallis S. Stromberg
Henry C. Cleveland, III
Barbara L. Crawford
Michael M. Schmidt
Allen W. Staver

Paul D. Godec
Karen L. Allison
Gregory C. Parham
Walter J. Landen, Jr.

Reference: Mountain States Bank.

For full biographical listings, see the Martindale-Hubbell Law Directory

CONNECTICUT

*BRIDGEPORT,** Fairfield Co.

KOSKOFF, KOSKOFF & BIEDER, P.C. (AV)

350 Fairfield Avenue, 06604
Telephone: 203-336-4421
Fax: 203-368-3244
Email: KKB@KOSKOFF.com
Stamford, Connecticut Office: 1172 Bedford Street.
Telephone: 203-325-3686.
Danbury, Connecticut Office: 1 Moss Avenue.
Telephone: 203-792-7100.

Joel H. Lichtenstein
Karen E. Koskoff
Michael A. Stratton

For full biographical listings, see the Martindale-Hubbell Law Directory

*HARTFORD,** Hartford Co.

O'BRIEN, TANSKI & YOUNG (AV)

CityPlace II, 06103
Telephone: 860-525-2700
Telefax: 860-247-7861

MEMBERS OF FIRM

Donald W. O'Brien
James M. Tanski
Roland F. Young, III
Robert D. Silva

OF COUNSEL

Hilary Fisher Nelson
Donna R. Zito
Richard A. O'Connor

(See Next Column)

O'BRIEN, TANSKI & YOUNG, *Hartford—Continued*

ASSOCIATES

Albert G. Danker, Jr. | Amy F. Goodusky
Agnes McDermott Alvord | Andrew S. Wildstein
Kathleen M. Nevins | Angela D. Ober

References: Shawmut National Bank; New England Bank.

For full biographical listings, see the Martindale-Hubbell Law Directory

*NEW HAVEN,** New Haven Co.

VOTRE & ASSOCIATES, P.C. (AV)

105 Court Street, Suite 302, 06511-6957
Telephone: 203-498-0065
Fax: 203-821-3595
URL: http://www.lawyers.com/votre&associates

Kenneth A. Votre

John-Henry M. Steele

OF COUNSEL

Neil K. Rutter

For full biographical listings, see the Martindale-Hubbell Law Directory

WIGGIN & DANA (AV)

One Century Tower, 06508-1832
Telephone: 203-498-4400
Telefax: 203-782-2889
URL: http://www.wiggin.com
Hartford, Connecticut Office: One CityPlace.
Telephone: 203-297-3700.
Fax: 203-525-9380.
Stamford, Connecticut Office: Three Stamford Plaza, 301 Tresser Boulevard.
Telephone: 203-363-7600.
Telefax: 203-363-7676.

MEMBERS OF FIRM

John Q. Tilson | Jeanette Carpenter Schreiber
J. Michael Eisner | Maureen Weaver (Resident, Hartford Office)
Melinda A. Agsten
Merton G. Gollaher

ASSOCIATES

Catherine P. Baatz (Resident, Hartford Office) | Charles J. Keegan (Not admitted in CT)
Tina Clark Beamon | Edward M. Kennedy, Jr.
Carolyn C. Brady | Richard H. Lugli
Michelle Wilcox DeBarge (Resident, Hartford Office) | Karen E. Overchuk (Resident, Hartford Office)

For Complete List of Firm Personnel, See General Section

For full biographical listings, see the Martindale-Hubbell Law Directory

STAMFORD, Fairfield Co.

ROSENBLUM & FILAN, L.L.C. (AV Ⓣ)

One Landmark Square, 06901
Telephone: 203-358-9200
Fax: 203-358-0687
Email: counsel@rosenblumfilan.com *URL:* http://www.rosenblumfilan.com
White Plains, New York Office: 50 Main Street.
Telephone: 914-686-6100.
Fax: 914-686-6140.
New York, New York Office: 400 Madison Avenue.
Telephone: 212-888-8001.
Fax: 212-888-3331.

MEMBERS OF FIRM

Patrick J. Filan | Alan S. Rubenstein
James B. Rosenblum | Samuel Tannenbaum
James S. Newfield

James F. Biondo | James A. Mahar

OF COUNSEL

Theodore J. Greene

For full biographical listings, see the Martindale-Hubbell Law Directory

WATERBURY, New Haven Co.

DRUBNER, HARTLEY, O'CONNOR & MENGACCI (AV)

500 Chase Parkway, 06708
Telephone: 203-753-9291
FAX: 203-753-6373
Email: drubner@dhom.com

(See Next Column)

MEMBERS OF FIRM

Norman S. Drubner | Gary B. O'Connor
James E. Hartley, Jr. | Joseph A. Mengacci
Gary D. Jones

ASSOCIATES

Linda T. Wihbey | Jayne Elser Welch

Representative Clients: American Medical Response; St. Mary's Hospital; Connecticut Hospice; Opticare Eye Health & Vision Centers.

For full biographical listings, see the Martindale-Hubbell Law Directory

WESTPORT, Fairfield Co.

LEVETT ROCKWOOD P.C. (AV)

33 Riverside Avenue, P.O. Box 5116, 06881
Telephone: 203-222-0885
Telecopier: 203-226-8025

Suzanne B. Albani | Marc J. Kurzman
Robert O. Barberi | David R. Levett
Edward B. Chansky | Judy A. Rabkin
Madeleine F. Grossman | Sharon M. Schweitzer
Dorit Schutzengel Heimer | Steven M. Siegelaub
Cheryl L. Johnson | Peter H. Struzzi
Barbara A. Young

OF COUNSEL

William O. Rockwood, Jr.

Debra R. Cardinali | Robin K. Higgins
Stephen M. Cowherd | Douglas R. Sansted
Christopher M. Graham | Rodger F. Smith, Jr.
Patricia D. Weitzman

Representative Clients: Cannondale Corp.; Caradon, Inc.; DataViz, Inc.; Dooney & Bourke, Inc.; GAF Corporation; Heyman Properties; Hospital of Saint Raphael; Marketing Corporation of America; Olin Corporation; St. Vincent's Medical Center.

For full biographical listings, see the Martindale-Hubbell Law Directory

DISTRICT OF COLUMBIA

WASHINGTON, D.C. Co.

THE FALK LAW FIRM PLLC (AV)

A Professional Limited Liability Corporation
Suite 260 One Westin Center, 2445 M Street, N.W., 20037
Telephone: 202-833-8700
Telecopier: 202-872-1725
Email: FalkLaw@erols.com *URL:* http://www.falklawfirm.com

James H. Falk, Sr. | Stephen A. Best
James H. Falk, Jr. | John M. Falk

OF COUNSEL

Pierre E. Murphy | Elizabeth C. Collins

For full biographical listings, see the Martindale-Hubbell Law Directory

FELDESMAN, TUCKER, LEIFER, FIDELL & BANK LLP (AV)

2001 L Street, N.W., 2nd Floor, 20036
Telephone: 202-466-8960
Telefax: 202-293-8103
Rockville, Maryland Office: One Church Street, Suite 800.
Telephone: 301-279-6770.
Falls Church, Virginia Office: 5661 Columbia Pike, Suite 200.
Telephone: 703-671-5800.

Margaret H. Long (1940-1990)

MEMBERS OF FIRM

James L. Feldesman | Beth Goodman
Marna S. Tucker | Edward T. Waters
Jacqueline C. Leifer | Roger A. Schwartz
Eugene R. Fidell | Michael B. Glomb
Rita M. Bank | Tanya A. Harvey
Pamela B. Forbes | Richard C. Shadyac, Jr.
Mary S. Pence | David P. Sheldon
Jonathan M. Dana | Bruce F. Hoffmeister
M. Toni Waldman

ASSOCIATES

Robin A. Clark | Mary Price
Jennifer P. Rosenberg | Savalle C. Sims
Garrett L. Lee | Alice J. Gallin-Dwyer
Marcie H. Zakheim | Elizabeth A. Greczek
Kathy S. Ghiladi | Jennifer L. Dziedzic
Daniel L. Gray | Alan J. Van Luven

For full biographical listings, see the Martindale-Hubbell Law Directory

Washington—Continued

KING, PAGANO & HARRISON (AV)

1730 Pennsylvania Avenue, N.W., 20006
Telephone: 202-371-6800
Fax: 202-371-6770
URL: http://www.kph.com
New York, New York Office: 425 Park Avenue, 10022.
Telephone: 212-223-4000.
FAX: 212-223-4134.

MEMBERS OF FIRM

Jeffrey W. King
Jeffrey W. Pagano (Resident, New York, N.Y. Office)
Keith J. Harrison
Steven Schaars
Jeffrey L. Poston

ASSOCIATE

Christopher Flynn

Representative Clients: Kaiser Permanente; Medica; Optimum Choice; Aetna-U.S. Healthcare; NYLCare; Medlantic Healthcare Group; American Association of Health Plans; George Washington University Health Plan; Health Partners of Alabama; Health Plus of Michigan.

For full biographical listings, see the Martindale-Hubbell Law Directory

MICHAELS & BONNER, P.C. (AV)

Suite 900, 1140 Connecticut Avenue, N.W., 20036
Telephone: 202-223-5000
Telecopier: 202-857-0634
Email: name@mwblegal.com *URL:* http://www.michaelsbonner.com
Reston, Virginia Office: 12021 Sunset Hills Road, Suite 310, 20190.
Telephone: 703-464-4800.
Fax: 703-464-4895.

Walter J. Bonner
John T. Brennan, Jr.
Robert S. Canterman
Mark R. Eaton
David Florin
Thomas A. Guidoboni
Arthur N. Lerner
Joel L. Michaels
Margit H. Nahra
David W. O'Brien
Michael R. Pollard
Christine Clements Rinn
Robert L. Roth
Barbara H. Ryland
Kathleen M. Stratton

Jody Goodman
Wayne D. Hettenbach
Beth M. Kramer
Alicia J. Palmer
Jessica S. Walton

For full biographical listings, see the Martindale-Hubbell Law Directory

POWERS, PYLES, SUTTER & VERVILLE, P.C. (AV)

Twelfth Floor, 1875 Eye Street, N.W., 20006-5409
Telephone: 202-466-6550
Fax: 202-785-1756
Email: ppsv@ppsv.com *URL:* http://www.ppsv.com

Galen D. Powers
James C. Pyles
Ronald N. Sutter
Richard E. Verville
Mary Susan Philp
Mark R. Fitzgerald
Robert J. Saner, II
Stanley A. Freeman
David C. Beck
Peter W. Thomas
Thomas Hylden
Marie Catherine Infante
Christopher L. Keough
Harold Damelin
Joel M. Hamme
Joel M. Rudnick

Marla P. Spindel
Ana-Maria McKessy
Karen S. Lovitch
Arthur S. DiDio
Kimberly N. Brown
C. Anthony Russo (Not admitted in DC)

OF COUNSEL

Rebecca L. Burke
Donald W. Aaronson
Douglas Benson Tesdahl
Edith S. Marshall

For full biographical listings, see the Martindale-Hubbell Law Directory

SCHMELTZER, APTAKER & SHEPARD, P.C. (AV)

The Watergate, Suite 1000, 2600 Virginia Avenue, N.W., 20037-1905
Telephone: 202-333-8800
Cable Address: "Ship"
Telex: 440517
Facsimile: 202-337-6065
Email: sas@saslaw.com *URL:* http://www.saspc.com
Los Angeles, California Office: 1999 Avenue of the Stars, Twenty-Seventh Floor, 90067-4095.
Telephone: 310-557-2966.
FAX: 310-286-6610.

Frank H. Case III

COUNSEL

Denise Bonn
Martin Jay Gaynes

For full biographical listings, see the Martindale-Hubbell Law Directory

VENABLE ATTORNEYS AT LAW VENABLE, BAETJER, HOWARD & CIVILETTI, LLP (AV)

A Partnership including Professional Corporations
Suite 1000, 1201 New York Avenue, N.W., 20005
Telephone: 202-962-4800
Fax: 202-962-8300
URL: http://www.venable.com
Baltimore, Maryland Office: Venable, Baetjer and Howard LLP, 1800 Mercantile Bank & Trust Building, 2 Hopkins Plaza.
Telephone: 410-244-7400.
Fax: 410-244-7742.
McLean, Virginia Office: Venable, Baetjer and Howard LLP, Suite 400, 2010 Corporate Ridge.
Telephone: 703-760-1600.
Fax: 703-821-8949.
Rockville, Maryland Office: Venable, Baetjer and Howard LLP, Suite 500, One Church Street, P. O. Box 1906.
Telephone: 301-217-5600.
Fax: 301-217-5617.
Towson, Maryland Office: Venable, Baetjer and Howard LLP, 210 Allegheny Avenue, P. O. Box 5517.
Telephone: 410-494-6200.
Fax: 410-821-0147.

MEMBERS OF FIRM

Robert G. Ames (Also at Baltimore, Maryland Office)
James K. Archibald (Also at Baltimore, Maryland Office)
Kenneth C. Bass, III (Also at McLean, Virginia Office)
Benjamin R. Civiletti (P.C.) (Also at Baltimore and Towson, Maryland Offices)
Jeffrey A. Dunn (Also at Baltimore, Maryland Office)
David W. Goewey
Amy Berman Jackson
George F. Pappas (Also at Baltimore, Maryland Office)
James L. Shea (also at Baltimore, Maryland Office)
Kenneth S. Slaughter

For Complete List of Firm Personnel, See General Section

For full biographical listings, see the Martindale-Hubbell Law Directory

FLORIDA

BOCA RATON, Palm Beach Co.

JOSEPH HARRISON (AV)

Crystal Corporate Center, 2500 North Military Trail, Suite 275, 33431
Telephone: 561-241-9306
Fax: 561-241-9308

For full biographical listings, see the Martindale-Hubbell Law Directory

*FORT LAUDERDALE,** Broward Co.

CONRAD & SCHERER (AV)

A Partnership of Professional Associations
Eighth Floor, 633 South Federal Highway, P.O. Box 14723, 33302
Telephone: 954-462-5500
Facsimile: 954-463-9244
Miami, Florida Office: 44 West Flagler Street, Suite 402, 33130.
Telephone: 305-856-9920.
Facsimile: 305-374-4408.

MEMBERS OF FIRM

William R. Scherer, Jr., (P.A.)
Gary S. Genovese (P.A.)
William V. Carcioppolo (P.A.)
Linda Rae Spaulding (P.A.)
Reid A. Cocalis (P.A.)
Willie Earl Hall (P.A.)
Ronald A. FitzGerald
James F. Carroll
Paul R. Larkin, Jr.
Dominic L. Brandy

OF COUNSEL

Rex Conrad

ASSOCIATES

Albert L. Frevola, Jr.
William R. Scherer, III
Vanessa A. Reynolds
Douglas Todd Marx
Janine Renee Kalagher
James A. Epstein
Angel Petti
Nicholas William Romanello
Shari L. McCartney
Catherine M. Rodriguez
Wendy A. Delvecchio

Local Counsel for: American Home Assurance Group; Caterpillar Tractor Co.; Division of Risk Management, State of Florida; Florida East Coast Railway; Fort Motor Co.; Liberty Mutual Insurance Co.; Ryder Truck Lines; Unigard Insurance Group.
Approved Attorneys for: Attorneys' Title Insurance Fund.
Reference: Barnett Bank of Fort Lauderdale.

For full biographical listings, see the Martindale-Hubbell Law Directory

*JACKSONVILLE,** Duval Co.

SMITH HULSEY & BUSEY (AV)

1800 First Union National Bank Tower, 225 Water Street, P.O. Box 53315, 32201-3315
Telephone: 904-359-7700
Facsimile: 904-359-7708; 353-9908
Email: vsharp@smithhulsey.com

Lloyd Smith (1915-1987)

MEMBERS OF FIRM

Stephen D. Busey
Earl E. Googe, Jr.
Jeanne E. Helton
Cynthia C. Jackson
G. Preston Keyes
Richard E. Klein
William E. Kuntz
Lauren P. Langham
M. Richard Lewis, Jr.
John F. MacLennan
Raymond R. Magley
E. Owen McCuller, Jr.
James H. Post
Bryan L. Putnal
E. Lanny Russell
Joel Settembrini, Jr.
Tim E. Sleeth
John R. Smith, Jr.
Harry M. Wilson, III

Brandon L. Ayscue
Brannon B. Belcastro
James A. Bolling, Jr.
Charmaine T.M. Chiu
Ryan C. Curtis
Michael R. Freed
Reynold N. Hoover
Michael J. Ivan, Jr.
Tonya L. Janney
Charles H. Keller
Bradley R. Markey
R. Leanne McKnight
Bert J. Millis
Stephen D. Moore, Jr.
Jon L. Swergold

OF COUNSEL

Mark Hulsey
John E. Thrasher

Representative Clients: ATP Tour, Inc; Baptist/St. Vincent's Health System, Inc.; Browning-Ferris Industries, Inc.; First Union National Bank of Florida; Florida Rock Industries, Inc.; PGA Tour, Inc.; KPMG Peat Marwick; The Regency Group, Inc.; The Ritz-Carlton Hotel Co.; University of Florida.

For full biographical listings, see the Martindale-Hubbell Law Directory

*MIAMI,** Dade Co.

DRESNICK & ELLSWORTH, P.A. (AV)

Suntrust Plaza, Suite 701, 201 Alhambra Circle (Coral Gables), 33134-5108
Telephone: 305-461-1975
Fax: 305-461-2292

Mark A. Dresnick
Sean M. Ellsworth

Monica L. Felder

OF COUNSEL

Deborah J. Miller

For full biographical listings, see the Martindale-Hubbell Law Directory

JEFFREY S. WEINER, P.A. (AV)

Two Datran Center Nineteenth Floor, Suite 1910, 9130 South Dadeland Boulevard, 33156-7858
Telephone: 305 670-9939
Fax: 305 670-9299
Email: lawfirm@jeffweiner.com
Boca Raton, Florida Office: Mizner Park. 327 Plaza Real, Suite 215, 33432.

Jeffrey S. Weiner

Mycki L. Ratzan
Michael B. Cohen
Jason M. Wandner

LEGAL SUPPORT PERSONNEL

Duchess Weiner (Law Office Administrator)

For full biographical listings, see the Martindale-Hubbell Law Directory

NORTH PALM BEACH, Palm Beach Co.

BOBO, SPICER, CIOTOLI, FULFORD, BOCCHINO & DEBEVOISE, P.A. (AV)

1240 U.S. Highway One, 33408
Telephone: 561-684-6600
Fax: 561-622-6288
Email: info@bobospicer.com *URL:* http://www.bobospicer.com
Orlando, Florida Office: Landmark Center One, Suite 510, 315 East Robinson Street, 32801-1949.
Telephone: 407-849-1060.
Fax: 407-843-4751.
Clearwater, Florida Office: 300 Turner Street, 33756.
Telephone: 727-443-6663.

(See Next Column)

A. Russell Bobo
David W. Spicer
Eugene L. Ciotoli
Jeffrey C. Fulford
John W. Bocchino
D. Andrew DeBevoise (Resident, Orlando Office)
Armando T. Lauritano
Raul Romaguera
Gregorio A. Francis (Resident, Orlando Office)
Michael D. Burt
Casey D. Shomo
J. Clancey Bounds (Resident, Orlando Office)

Thomas W. Poulton (Resident, Orlando Office)
Damian M. Fletcher
Michael D. Starks (Resident, Orlando Office)
Anthony P. Corsini
Ian D. Forsythe (Resident, Orlando Office)
Scott L. Reed (Resident, Orlando Office)
Amy M. Dukes
Denise L. Dawson
Deborah L. Moskowitz (Resident, Orlando Office)

For full biographical listings, see the Martindale-Hubbell Law Directory

*ORLANDO,** Orange Co.

BOBO, SPICER, CIOTOLI, FULFORD, BOCCHINO & DEBEVOISE, P.A. (AV)

Landmark Center One, Suite 510, 315 East Robinson Street, 32801-1949
Telephone: 407-849-1060
Fax: 407-843-4751
Email: info@bobospicer.com *URL:* http://www.bobospicer.com
North Palm Beach, Florida Office: 1240 U.S. Highway One, 33408.
Telephone: 561-684-6600.
FAX: 561-622-6288.
Clearwater, Florida Office: 300 Turner Street, 33756.
Telephone: 727-443-6663.

John W. Bocchino
D. Andrew DeBevoise
Armando T. Lauritano
Gregorio A. Francis
J. Clancey Bounds

Thomas W. Poulton
Michael D. Starks
Ian D. Forsythe
Scott L. Reed
Deborah L. Moskowitz

For full biographical listings, see the Martindale-Hubbell Law Directory

HILL, REIS, ADAMS, HALL & SCHIEFFELIN, P.A. (AV)

1417 East Concord Street, 32803
Telephone: 407-896-0425
Fax: 407-896-9236
Email: mainbox@hrahs.com

G. Bruce Hill
Gregory F. Reis
Janet W. Adams
Larry D. Hall
Thomas L. Schieffelin, Jr.
William W. Large
Matthew P. Bartolomei

David O Doyle, Jr
Andrew Vlahos
Heidi Jo Haycook

Representative Clients: The Florida Hospital Trust Fund; The Florida Hospital Excess Trust Fund; Florida Hospital Workers Compensation/Self Insurance Trust Fund; Bartow Memorial Hospital; Bay Medical Center; Brooksville Regional Hospital; Cape Canaveral Hospital; Cape Coral Hospital; Desoto Memorial Hospital.

For full biographical listings, see the Martindale-Hubbell Law Directory

*PENSACOLA,** Escambia Co.

BOZEMAN, JENKINS & MATTHEWS, P.A. (AV)

SunTrust Tower, 220 West Garden Street, Suite 801, P.O. Box 13105, 32501
Telephone: 850-434-6223
Fax: 850-434-5242
Email: bojema@pen.net *URL:* http://www.bojema.pen.net
Fort Walton Beach Office: 151 Mary Esther Boulevard, Suite 401.
Telephone: 850-651-2151.
Fax: 850-434-5242.
Panama City Office: 475 Harrison Avenue, Suite 203A.
Telephone: 850-872-0110.
Fax: 850-434-5242.

Frank C. Bozeman, Jr.
Thomas R. Jenkins
Larry A. Matthews
Janice K. Skievaski
Frank C. Bozeman, III

Robert T. Bleach
John B. Fricke, Jr.
J. Andrew Talbert
Raymond F. Higgins, III
Jeremiah J. Talbott
Sidney M. McCrackin

For full biographical listings, see the Martindale-Hubbell Law Directory

*SARASOTA,** Sarasota Co.

WILLIAMS, PARKER, HARRISON, DIETZ & GETZEN, PROFESSIONAL ASSOCIATION (AV)

200 South Orange Avenue, 34236-6749
Telephone: 941-366-4800
Telecopier: 941-366-5109
Mailing Address: P.O. Box 3258, Sarasota, Florida, 34230-3258
Email: infodesk@williamsparker.com *URL:* http://www.williamsparker.com

William T. Harrison, Jr.
John V. Cannon, III
Robert W. Benjamin
Frank Strelec
David A. Wallace
John L. Moore
Carol Ann Kalish
Kimberly Page Walker
J. Hugh Middlebrooks

General Counsel for: Sarasota County Public Hospital Board; Sarasota-Manatee Airport Authority; Taylor Woodrow Homes Ltd.; FCCI Mutual Insurance Co.
Local Counsel for: Bank of America; Northern Trust Bank of Florida; SunTrust Bank, Gulfcoast.

For Complete List of Firm Personnel, See General Section

For full biographical listings, see the Martindale-Hubbell Law Directory

*TALLAHASSEE,** Leon Co.

AMUNDSEN, MOORE & TORPY (AV)

502 East Park Avenue, P.O. Drawer 1759, 32302
Telephone: 850-425-2444
Facsimile: 850-425-2447
Email: ammolaw@nettally.com
Melbourne, Florida Office: Amundsen, Moore & Torpy, 202 North Harbor City Boulevard, Suite 300, 32935.
Telephone: 407-255-2332.
Facsimile: 407-253-2546.

Paul H. Amundsen
Richard W. Moore

Rodolfo Nuñez
Julia E. Smith

OF COUNSEL

Byron B. Mathews, Jr.

For full biographical listings, see the Martindale-Hubbell Law Directory

PAUL WATSON LAMBERT (AV)

1114 East Park Avenue, 32301-2651
Telephone: 850-224-9393
Email: lambertaty@aol.com *URL:* http://www.lawyers.com/lambertlawfirm

For full biographical listings, see the Martindale-Hubbell Law Directory

MCFARLAIN, WILEY, CASSEDY & JONES, PROFESSIONAL ASSOCIATION (AV)

215 South Monroe Street, Suite 600, P.O. Box 2174, 32316-2174
Telephone: 850-222-2107
Telecopier: 850-222-8475
Email: firm@mcfarlain.com *URL:* http://www.mcfarlain.com

Richard C. McFarlain
William B. Wiley
Douglas P. Jones
Charles A. Stampelos
H. Darrell White, Jr.
Christopher Barkas
Harold R. Mardenborough, Jr.
Terrell C. Madigan

Robert A. McNeely
P. David Brannon

LEGAL SUPPORT PERSONNEL

Diane L. Doll (Office Manager)

For full biographical listings, see the Martindale-Hubbell Law Directory

ROSE, SUNDSTROM & BENTLEY, LLP (AV)

2548 Blairstone Pines Drive, P.O. Box 1567, 32301-1567
Telephone: 850-877-6555
Telecopier: 850-656-4029
URL: http://www.rsbattorneys.com

MEMBERS OF FIRM

Chris H. Bentley (P.A.)
Steven T. Mindlin (P.A.)
Diane D. Tremor (P.A.)
John L. Wharton

Representative Clients: Arbor Health Care Co.; Columbia/HCA Health Care Corp.; Shands Hospital.
Reference: Capital City Bank, Tallahassee.

For full biographical listings, see the Martindale-Hubbell Law Directory

*TAMPA,** Hillsborough Co.

MORRISON & MILLS, P.A. (AV)

1200 West Platt Street Suite 100, 33606
Telephone: 813-258-3311
Telecopier: 813-258-3209
Email: mmills3@tampabay.rr.com

Thomas K. Morrison
Frederick J. Mills

Kevin A. DiTanna
Bradley Abraham Tobin

Representative Clients: Bergen Brunswig Corporation; PharMerica, Inc.; Community Care Network, Inc.; HealthDirect, Inc.; AmComp, Inc.; Pinnacle Assurance, Inc.

For full biographical listings, see the Martindale-Hubbell Law Directory

*VERO BEACH,** Indian River Co.

STEWART, EVANS & HAFNER, P.A. (AV)

3355 Ocean Drive, P.O. Box 3345, 32964-3345
Telephone: 561-231-3500
FAX: 561-231-9876
Email: firm@sneh.com

William J. Stewart
Cynthia L. Cambron

Representative Clients: Indian River Memorial Hospital, Inc.; Indian River Hospital Foundation, Inc.

For full biographical listings, see the Martindale-Hubbell Law Directory

*WEST PALM BEACH,** Palm Beach Co.

LIGGIO, BENRUBI & WILLIAMS, P.A. (AV)

1615 Forum Place, Suite 3B, 33401
Telephone: 561-616-3333
Fax: 561-616-3266
Email: liggio@aol.com *URL:* http://www.lawyers.com/liggiolaw

Jeffrey M. Liggio
Richard M. Benrubi
Jene P. Williams

LEGAL SUPPORT PERSONNEL

Yara B. Vega (Paralegal)
Kathy G. Harmon (Paralegal)
Sharon Lynn (Paralegal)

For full biographical listings, see the Martindale-Hubbell Law Directory

SEARCY DENNEY SCAROLA BARNHART & SHIPLEY, PROFESSIONAL ASSOCIATION (AV)

2139 Palm Beach Lakes Boulevard, P.O. Drawer 3626, 33402-3626
Telephone: 561-686-6300
800-780-8607
800-220-7006 (Spanish)
Fax: 561-478-0754
Email: CDS@SEARCYLAW.COM *URL:* http://www.searcylaw.com

Sean C. Domnick

LEGAL SUPPORT PERSONNEL

Samantha M. Johansen (Paralegal/Investigator)

For Complete List of Firm Personnel, See General Section

For full biographical listings, see the Martindale-Hubbell Law Directory

WIEDERHOLD, MOSES, BULFIN & RUBIN, P.A. (AV)

Northbridge Centre, Suite 800, 515 North Flagler Drive, P.O. Box 3918, 33402
Telephone: 561-659-2296;
Broward: 954-763-5630
Fax: 561-659-2865
Email: bobmoses@bellsouth.net

John P. Wiederhold
Robert D. Moses
John J. Bulfin
Kenneth M. Rubin

Lawrence I. Bass
Kay Seeber Hoff
Bruce R. Katzell

LEGAL SUPPORT PERSONNEL

Gina Truzzolino (Paralegal/Investigator)

Reference: Bank of America.

For full biographical listings, see the Martindale-Hubbell Law Directory

GEORGIA

*ATLANTA,** Fulton Co.

GOLDNER, SOMMERS, SCRUDDER & BASS (AV)

900 Circle 75 Parkway Suite 850, 30339
Telephone: 770-612-9200
Facsimile: 770-612-9201

MEMBERS OF FIRM

Stephen L. Goldner   Susan V. Sommers

ASSOCIATE

Tammy Spivack Skinner

For Complete List of Firm Personnel, See General Section

For full biographical listings, see the Martindale-Hubbell Law Directory

LONG ALDRIDGE & NORMAN LLP (AV)

A Limited Liability Partnership including Professional Corporations
Suite 5300, 303 Peachtree Street, 30308
Telephone: 404-527-4000
Telecopier: 404-527-4198
Email: atlanta@lanlaw.com *URL:* http://www.lanlaw.com
Washington, D.C. Office: Suite 600, 701 Pennsylvania Avenue, N.W., 20004.
Telephone: 202-624-1200.
FAX: 202-624-1298.

MEMBERS OF FIRM

Phillip A. Bradley
J. James Johnson
Steven J. Labovitz
Mark S. Lange
Gary W. Marsh
H. Carol Saul
Edgar H. Sims, Jr. (P.C.)
John E. Theberge (Resident, Washington, D.C. Office)
Briggs L. Tobin

ASSOCIATE

Philip A. Cooper

For Complete List of Firm Personnel, See General Section

For full biographical listings, see the Martindale-Hubbell Law Directory

PARKER, HUDSON, RAINER & DOBBS LLP (AV)

1500 Marquis Two Tower, 285 Peachtree Center Avenue, N.E., 30303
Telephone: 404-523-5300
Fax: 404-522-8409
Tallahassee, Florida Office: The Perkins House, 118 North Gadsden Street, 32301.
Telephone: 904-681-0191.
Fax: 904-681-9493.

MEMBERS OF FIRM

John H. Parker, Jr.
Paul L. Hudson, Jr.
Robert A. Weiss (Resident, Tallahassee, Florida Office)
Jonathan L. Rue
David G. Cleveland
Leo E. Reichert
Armando L. Basarrate, II

For full biographical listings, see the Martindale-Hubbell Law Directory

PIERCE & YOUNG (AV)

Building 1700, 2255 Cumberland Parkway Northwest, 30339-4575
Telephone: 770-435-0500
Telecopier: 770-435-0362

MEMBERS OF FIRM

J. Wayne Pierce   Richard M. Young
Christy A. Dunkelberger

For full biographical listings, see the Martindale-Hubbell Law Directory

*COLUMBUS,** Muscogee Co.

ROTHSCHILD, MORGAN & BROWN (AV)

A Limited Liability Partnership
1025 First Avenue, P.O. Box 2788, 31902-2788
Telephone: 706-324-4167
Fax: 706-324-1969
Email: rothmor@mindspring.com

MEMBERS OF FIRM

Jerome M. Rothschild   W. Donald Morgan, Jr.
Jeffrey A. Brown

ASSOCIATE

Jeffrey H. Kight

Reference: Columbus Bank and Trust Company.

For Complete List of Firm Personnel, See General Section

For full biographical listings, see the Martindale-Hubbell Law Directory

*MACON,** Bibb Co.

SELL & MELTON, L.L.P. (AV)

A Limited Liability Partnership including a Professional Corporation
14th Floor, 577 Mulberry Street, P.O. Box 229, 31202-0229
Telephone: 912-746-8521
Telecopier: 912-745-6426

John D. Comer   Jeffrey B. Hanson

General Counsel for: Macon Telegraph Publishing Co. (The Macon Telegraph); Macon-Bibb County Hospital Authority; County of Bibb; Smith & Sons Foods, Inc. (S & S Cafeterias); Macon Bibb County Industrial Authority; Burgess Pigment Co.
Local Counsel For: United States Aircraft Insurance Group (USAIG); United States Aviation Underwriters, Inc. (USAU).

For Complete List of Firm Personnel, See General Section

For full biographical listings, see the Martindale-Hubbell Law Directory

NORCROSS, Gwinnett Co.

PHEARS & MOLDOVAN (AV)

A Partnership of Professional Corporations
4725 Peachtree Corners Circle Suite 375, 30092
Telephone: 770-446-2116
Telecopier: 770-263-6715
Email: phearsmold@aol.com

MEMBERS OF FIRM

H. Wayne Phears (P.C.)   Victor L. Moldovan (P.C.)

Richard O. Samms

For full biographical listings, see the Martindale-Hubbell Law Directory

HAWAII

*HONOLULU,** Honolulu Co.

CARLSMITH BALL (AV)

A Partnership including Law Corporations
Suite 2200, Pacific Tower, 1001 Bishop Street, P.O. Box 656, 96809-3402
Telephone: 808-523-2500
Fax: 808-523-0842
Email: execdirector@carlsmith.com *URL:* http://www.carlsmith.com
Kapolei, Hawaii Office: Suite 318, Kapolei Building, 1001 Kamokila Boulevard, 96707.
Telephone: 808-523-2500.
Fax: 808-674-0850.
Wailuku, Maui Hawaii Office: Suite 400, One Main Plaza, 2200 Main Street, P.O. Box 1086, 96793-1086.
Telephone: 808-242-4535.
Fax: 808-244-4974.
Kailua-Kona, Hawaii Office: Suite 209, 75-1000 Henry Street, 96740.
Telephone: 808-329-6464.
Fax: 808-329-9450.
Hilo, Hawaii Office: 121 Waianuenue Avenue, P.O. Box 686, 96721-0686.
Telephone: 808-935-6644.
Fax: 808-935-7975.
Hagatna, Guam Office: Suite 401, Bank of Hawaii Building, 134 West Soledad Avenue, P.O. Box BF, 96932-5027.
Telephone: 671-472-6813.
Fax: 671-477-4375.
Telex: 721-6445 CWCMI GM.
Saipan, Commonwealth of the Northern Mariana Islands Office: Carlsmith Building, Capitol Hill, P.O. Box 5241, 96950-5241.
Telephone: 670-322-3455.
Fax: 670-322-3368.
Los Angeles, California Office: 9th Floor, 444 South Flower Street, 90071-2901.
Telephone: 213-955-1200.
Fax: 213-623-0032.
Washington, D.C. Office: Suite 300, 1201 Pennsylvania Avenue, N.W., 20004-2401.
Telephone: 202-628-2228.
Fax: 202-628-2071.
Mexico City, Mexico Office: Carlsmith Ball, Sierra Nevada 119, Lomas de Chapultepec, 11000 Mexico, D.F.
Telephone: 52-5-520-8514, 52-5-520-8757.
Fax: 52-5-540-1545.
Mexico, D.F. Office of Carlsmith Ball, S.C. (Authorized to practice as foreign legal consultants in Mexico): Sierra Nevada 119, Lomas de Chapultepec, 11000 Mexico, D.F.
Telephone: 52-5-520-8514, 52-5-520-8757.
Fax: 52-5-540-1545.

(See Next Column)

CARLSMITH BALL—*Continued*

MEMBERS OF FIRM

Nancy M. Beckner (Resident at Washington, DC Office)
James L. Starshak

OF COUNSEL

Edward M. Ranger (Resident at Mexico Office)

For Complete List of Firm Personnel, See General Section

For full biographical listings, see the Martindale-Hubbell Law Directory

GOODSILL ANDERSON QUINN & STIFEL (AV)

Alii Place, Suite 1800, 1099 Alakea Street, P.O. Box 3196, 96801-3196
Telephone: 808-547-5600
FAX: 808-547-5880
Email: info@goodsill.com *URL:* http://www.goodsill.com

MEMBERS OF FIRM

David J. Dezzani
Raymond S. Iwamoto
Jacqueline L. S. Earle
Ernest J. T. Loo
Margaret Jenkins Leong
A. Richard Philpott

ASSOCIATE

Thomas L. Benedict

Representative Clients: Kapi'olani Health; Oahu Care Facility; Pearl City Nursing Home; Wahiawa General Hospital.

For Complete List of Firm Personnel, See General Section

For full biographical listings, see the Martindale-Hubbell Law Directory

ROBBINS & RHODES ATTORNEYS AT LAW, A LAW CORPORATION (AV)

Suite 2200 Davies Pacific Center, 841 Bishop Street, 96813
Telephone: 808-524-2355
Fax: 808-526-0290
Email: robbinsrhodes@lava.net

Kenneth S. Robbins
Vincent A. Rhodes

Representative Clients: Hawaii Health Care Systems (HHSC); Kapiolani Health Care Systems, Inc.; Kona Community Hospital; Maui Memorial Hospital; North Hawaii Community Hospital; St. Francis Medical Center; State of Hawaii; Wilcox Memorial Hospital.

For full biographical listings, see the Martindale-Hubbell Law Directory

TORKILDSON, KATZ, FONSECA, JAFFE, MOORE & HETHERINGTON ATTORNEYS AT LAW, A LAW CORPORATION (AV)

Amfac Building, 15th Floor, 700 Bishop Street, 96813-4187
Telephone: 808-523-6000
Cable Address: "Counsel"
Telex: RCA 723-8185
Telecopier: 808-523-6001
Email: info@torkildson.com
Hilo, Hawaii Office: 100 Pauahi Street, Suite 206.
Telephone: 808-961-0406.
Telecopier: 808-935-6725.

J. George Hetherington

For Complete List of Firm Personnel, See General Section

For full biographical listings, see the Martindale-Hubbell Law Directory

IDAHO

*POCATELLO,** Bannock Co.

MERRILL & MERRILL, CHARTERED (AV)

Key Bank Building, P.O. Box 991, 83204
Telephone: 208-232-2286
Fax: 208-232-2499
Email: mmlaw@ida.net

D. Russell Wight

Representative Clients: Bannock Regional Medical Center; Southeastern Idaho Physician Hospital Organization, Inc.

For Complete List of Firm Personnel, See General Section

For full biographical listings, see the Martindale-Hubbell Law Directory

ILLINOIS

*CHICAGO,** Cook Co.

ARONBERG GOLDGEHN DAVIS & GARMISA (AV)

Suite 3000 One IBM Plaza, 60611
Telephone: 312-828-9600
Telecopier: 312-828-9635
Email: agdglaw@aol.com
Schaumberg, Illinois Office: 1901 North Roselle Road, Suite 800, 60195.
Telephone: 847-985-4060.

MEMBER OF FIRM

Mitchell J. Melamed

OF COUNSEL

Steven H. Nemerovski

ASSOCIATE

Lisa J. Brodsky

For Complete List of Firm Personnel, See General Section

For full biographical listings, see the Martindale-Hubbell Law Directory

BLATT, HAMMESFAHR & EATON (AV)

333 W. Wacker Drive, Suite 1900, 60606
Telephone: 312-849-8000
FAX: 312-357-0198
Email: BHE@BHELAW.COM *URL:* HTTP://WWW.BHELAW.COM
New York, New York Office: 45 Broadway, 12th Floor.
Telephone: 212-363-1900.
Fax: 212-363-2600. Email: bhe@bhelaw.com.

MEMBERS OF FIRM

Joan S. Callan
Gregory D. Hopp

For full biographical listings, see the Martindale-Hubbell Law Directory

THE ELDEN LAW FIRM (AV)

150 North Michigan Avenue, 25th Floor, 60601-7567
Telephone: 312-781-3600
Fax: 312-781-3601

Douglas L. Elden
Robbin C. Elden

OF COUNSEL

Charles M. Jacobs
Susan Weagly

For full biographical listings, see the Martindale-Hubbell Law Directory

FORAN & SCHULTZ (AV)

Suite 3000, 30 North La Salle Street, 60602
Telephone: 312-368-8330
Fax: 312-580-2600
Email: law@foran.com *URL:* http://www.Foran.com

MEMBER OF FIRM

Brooke R. Whitted

ASSOCIATES

Jessica D. Klein
Lara A. Cleary

For full biographical listings, see the Martindale-Hubbell Law Directory

GESSLER, HUGHES & SOCOL, LTD. (AV)

Three First National Plaza, Suite 2200, 60602
Telephone: 312-580-0100
Telecopy: 312-580-1994

Benjamin P. Beringer
Anjali Dayal
Mark S. Dym
George W. Gessler
John K. Hughes
Joshua Karsh
Peter M. Katsaros
Kimberley Marsh
Alex W. Miller
Terence J. Moran
Matthew J. Piers
Kalman D. Resnick
Frederick S. Rhine
Jonathan A. Rothstein
Michael P. Simkus
Donna Kaner Socol

Gary Chodorow
Ruth M. Dunning
S. Todd Neal
Mark A. Pellegrino
Steven C. Steinback
Dana H. Sukenik
J. Eric Vander Arend
Mark B. Weiner
Charles H. Wintersteen

OF COUNSEL

Darius S. Francescatti, M.D.
Susan R. Gzesh

For full biographical listings, see the Martindale-Hubbell Law Directory

SCHWARTZBERG, BARNETT & COHEN (AV)

55 West Monroe Street, 2400 Xerox Centre, 60603-5040
Telephone: 312-726-3555
Fax: 312-726-6299
Cable Address: "Justice"
Email: sb&c@twty.chi.il.us

(See Next Column)

SCHWARTZBERG, BARNETT & COHEN, *Chicago—Continued*

MEMBERS OF FIRM

Ralph M. Schwartzberg (1939-1975)
Mark T. Barnett (1939-1970)
Hugh J. Schwartzberg
Benjamin H. Cohen

For full biographical listings, see the Martindale-Hubbell Law Directory

STAMOS & TRUCCO (AV)

10 North Dearborn Street, Fifth Floor, 60602
Telephone: 312-630-7979
Telecopier: 312-630-1183

James J. Stamos
Michael T. Trucco
Peter A. Gaido

ASSOCIATES

Mary Ann O'Reilly
Julie N. Howie
Charles Bletsas
Michael T. Wierzbicki

OF COUNSEL

John J. Stamos
Keith L. Moore

For full biographical listings, see the Martindale-Hubbell Law Directory

WILDMAN, HARROLD, ALLEN & DIXON (AV)

225 West Wacker Drive, 30th Floor, 60606-1229
Telephone: 312-201-2000
Fax: 312-201-2555
Email: hennessy@whad.com *URL:* http://www.whad.com
Aurora, Illinois Office: 1961 W. Downer Place.
Telephone: 630-892-7021.
Fax: 630-892-7158.
Waukegan, Illinois Office: 404 West Water, P. O. Box 890.
Telephone: 847-625-5550.
Fax: 847-625-5555.
Lisle, Illinois Office: 4300 Commerce Court, Suite 320.
Telephone: 630-955-0555.
Fax: 630-955-0662
Toronto, Ontario correspondent Office: Keel Cottrelle. 36 Toronto Street, Suite 920.
Telephone: 416-367-2900.
Telefax: 416-367-2791.
Telex: 062-18660.

MEMBERS OF FIRM

Douglas R. Carlson
James A. Christman
Jerald P. Esrick
Helaine Wachs Heydemann
David F. Pardys (Waukegan Office)
Peter A. Tomaras
Jeanne E. Walker

OF COUNSEL

Howard Arvey

Erin L. Bishop
Karen Julie Ecanow
Dara J. Keidan
Heather Huthwaite Martin
Barbara M. Prohaska (Lisle Office)
John A. Roberts

For full biographical listings, see the Martindale-Hubbell Law Directory

*KANKAKEE,** Kankakee Co.

BARMANN, KRAMER & BOHLEN, P.C. (AV)

Suite 502, 200 East Court Street, P.O. Box 1787, 60901
Telephone: 815-939-1133
Fax: 815-939-0994

Glen R. Barmann
Christopher W. Bohlen
Michael D. Kramer

For Complete List of Firm Personnel, See General Section

For full biographical listings, see the Martindale-Hubbell Law Directory

INDIANA

*BLOOMINGTON,** Monroe Co.

BUNGER & ROBERTSON (AV)

226 South College Square, P.O. Box 910, 47402-0910
Telephone: 812-332-9295
Fax: 812-331-8808
Email: bunrob@iquest.net

MEMBERS OF FIRM

Joseph D. O'Connor
James L. Whitlatch
William J. Beggs

(See Next Column)

ASSOCIATE

Holly M. Harvey

Representative Clients: Bloomington Hospital, Inc.; Bloomington Convalescent Center; Nurse Call Plus; Hospice of Bloomington; Phico Insurance, Co.; Medical Protective Insurance Co.; Children's Organ Transplant Association.

For Complete List of Firm Personnel, See General Section

For full biographical listings, see the Martindale-Hubbell Law Directory

*EVANSVILLE,** Vanderburgh Co.

FINE & HATFIELD, A PROFESSIONAL CORPORATION (AV)

520 N.W. Second Street, P.O. Box 779, 47705-0779
Telephone: 812-425-3592
Telecopier: 812-421-4269
Email: Fine@Fine-Hatfield.com *URL:* http://www.Fine-Hatfield.com

Todd I. Glass
Thomas R. Fitzsimmons

David D. Sanders

A List of Representative Clients Furnished Upon Request.

For full biographical listings, see the Martindale-Hubbell Law Directory

KAHN, DEES, DONOVAN & KAHN, LLP (AV)

Fifth Main Financial Plaza, Suite 305, P.O. Box 3646, 47735-3646
Telephone: 812-423-3183
Fax: 812-423-3841
Email: evvlaw@k2d2.com

MEMBERS OF FIRM

Alan N. Shovers
Thomas O. Magan
Larry R. Downs
G. Michael Schopmeyer
John E. Hegeman
Jeffrey K. Helfrich
Kent A. Brasseale II

ASSOCIATE

Robert F. "Ted" Barron II

Counsel for: Deaconess Hospital, Inc.; Wabash General Hospital; The Rehabilitation Center; Healthsouth Tri-State Rehabilitation Hospital.

For Complete List of Firm Personnel, See General Section

For full biographical listings, see the Martindale-Hubbell Law Directory

RUDOLPH, FINE, PORTER & JOHNSON LLP (AV)

221 N.W. Fifth Street, Second Floor, P.O. Box 1507, 47706
Telephone: 812-422-9444
Fax: 812-421-7459
URL: http://www.rfpj@rfpj.com

MEMBERS OF FIRM

L. Montgomery Porter
Scott S. Stone

Reference: National City Bank of Evansville.

For full biographical listings, see the Martindale-Hubbell Law Directory

ZIEMER, STAYMAN, WEITZEL & SHOULDERS, LLP (AV)

(Formerly Early, Arnold & Ziemer)
One Riverfront Place, 20 N.W. First Street 9th Floor, P.O. Box 916, 47706-0916
Telephone: 812-424-7575
Telecopier: 812-421-5089

MEMBERS OF FIRM

Ted C. Ziemer, Jr.
Patrick A. Shoulders

ASSOCIATES

Robert L. Burkart
Peter Michael Castelli

Reference: Old National Bank in Evansville.

For full biographical listings, see the Martindale-Hubbell Law Directory

*INDIANAPOLIS,** Marion Co.

HALL, RENDER, KILLIAN, HEATH & LYMAN PROFESSIONAL SERVICES CORPORATION (AV)

Suite 2000, One American Square Box 82064, 46282
Telephone: 317-633-4884
Fax: 317-633-4878
Email: hrkhl@hrkhl.com *URL:* http://www.hrkhl.com
Indianapolis North Office: Suite 820, 8402 Harcourt Road, 46260.
Telephone: 317-871-6222.
Fax: 317-338-3946.
Louisville, Kentucky Office: AEGON Center, Suite 1530, 400 West Market Street, 40202.
Telephone: 502-568-1890.
Fax: 502-568-4878.

(See Next Column)

HALL, RENDER, KILLIAN, HEATH & LYMAN PROFESSIONAL SERVICES CORPORATION—*Continued*

William S. Hall
John C. Render
R. Terry Heath
Stephen W. Lyman
L. Richard Gohman
Jeffrey Peek
Clifford A. Beyler
Joseph R. Impicciche
Timothy C. Lawson
Douglas P. Long
William H. Thompson
Timothy W. Kennedy
Steven H. Pratt
N. Kent Smith
Mary C. Gaughan
Fred J. Bachmann
R. Thomas Carter (Not admitted in IN; Resident, Louisville, Kentucky Office)
Maureen O'Brien Griffin
Robert A. Hicks
Kevin P. Speer
Gregory W. Moore
Donald R. Russell
Jeffrey W. Short
Clifton E. Johnson
Gerald L. Stovall (Not admitted in IN; Resident, Louisville, Kentucky Office)
Jon F. Spadorcia
John C. Meade
Gregg M. Wallander
Samuel H. DeShazer (Not admitted in IN; Resident, Louisville, Kentucky Office)
Todd J. Selby
James B. Hogan
David M. Leonard

René Remek Savarise (Resident, Louisville, Kentucky Office)
Pamela J. Jones
James R. Willey
Christopher L. Riegler
William D. Roberts (Resident, Louisville, Kentucky Office)
Keith D. Barber
A. Courtney Guild, Jr. (Not admitted in IN; Resident, Louisville, Kentucky Office)
Mary Liatti Hill
Norris Cunningham
Susan D. Bizzell
Allison D. Wharry
Anthony J. Elpers (Not admitted in IN; Resident, Louisville, Kentucky Office)
Dave C. Bromund
Letha S. Kramer
Gregory P. Kult
Sharon K. Hager (Not admitted in IN; Resident, Louisville, Kentucky Office)
David C. Lind, II
Angela M. Smith
Matthew W. Forsythe (Not admitted in IN; Resident, Louisville, Kentucky Office)
J. Chad Killian
John P. Ryan
Rhett M. Stuard
Stephan C. Masoncup (Not admitted in IN)
Traci R. Little
Edward L. Schoenbaechler (Not admitted in IN; Resident, Louisville, Kentucky Office)

For full biographical listings, see the Martindale-Hubbell Law Directory

ICE MILLER DONADIO & RYAN (AV)

One American Square Box 82001, 46282-0002
Telephone: 317-236-2100
Fax: 317-236-2219
Email: info@imdr.com *URL:* http://www.imdr.com
South Bend, Indiana Office: 211 West Washington Street, Suite 2420.
Telephone: 219-234-7933.
Fax: 219-234-7965. Internet E-mail: info@imdr.com. Web Site Address: http://www.imdr.com.
Chicago, Illinois Office: 135 South LaSalle Street, Suite 4100.
Telephone: 312-726-1567.
Fax: 312-641-6263. Internet E-mail: info@imdr.com. Web Site Address: http://www.imdr.com.

MEMBERS OF FIRM

Ralph A. Cohen
James D. Kemper
Harry L. Gonso
David J. Mallon, Jr.
Michael A. Blickman
Mary Nold Larimore
Brenda S. Horn
Gregory L. Pemberton
L. Alan Whaley
Bonnie L. Gallivan
Richard J. Thrapp
Michael A. Wukmer
Sherry A. Fabina-Abney
Susan Barnhizer Rivas
Kevin C. Woodhouse
Kevin R. Knight
Karen Ann P. Lloyd

RETIRED PARTNERS

Leonard J. Betley
Leland B. Cross, Jr.
Geoffrey Segar

SENIOR COUNSEL

Bradley L. Williams

OF COUNSEL

Nancy Menard Riddle
Kelly Bauman Pitcher
Laure V. Flaniken

ASSOCIATES

Paul H. Sinclair
Christopher S. Sears
Amy M. Corsaro
Lynn Kantor
Kathleen A. DeLaney
John Farina

For Complete List of Firm Personnel, See General Section

For full biographical listings, see the Martindale-Hubbell Law Directory

JOHNSON SMITH PENCE & HEATH LLP (AV)

One Indiana Square Suite 1800, 46204
Telephone: 317-634-9777
Telecopier: 317-636-9061
Email: firm@jsplaw.com *URL:* http://www.jsplaw.com
Washington, D.C. Office: 555 Twelfth Street, N.W., Suite 650.
Telephone: 202-737-5410.
Fax: 202-737-5411.

MEMBERS OF FIRM

Thomas A. Barnard
David G. Blachly
David J. Carr
Sean Michael Clapp
John David Hoover
Andrew W. Hull
John R. Kirkwood
Mark A. Palmer
Linda L. Pence
Sally Franklin Zweig

ASSOCIATES

Maureen F. Barnard
James Scott Fanzini
Steven J. Moss

For Complete List of Firm Personnel, See General Section

For full biographical listings, see the Martindale-Hubbell Law Directory

LOCKE REYNOLDS LLP (AV)

1000 Capital Center South, 201 North Illinois Street, 46204-4210
Telephone: 317-237-3800
Telecopier: 317-237-3900
Email: attys@locke.com *URL:* http://www.locke.com

Glenn T. Troyer
Kevin Charles Murray
Michael T. Bindner
David Elliott Jose
Thomas W. Farlow

Brian K. Beeler
Camille T. Wiggins

Representative Clients: Behavior Corp.; Carmel Health Care Management, Inc.; Caylor-Nickel, P.C.; Columbia Women's Hospital of Indianapolis; GrandCare, Inc.; Madison County Imaging, P.C.; St. Francis Hospital Center; St. Margaret Mercy Health Center; Urology of Indiana, L.L.C.

For Complete List of Firm Personnel, See General Section

For full biographical listings, see the Martindale-Hubbell Law Directory

MCNAMAR, FEARNOW & MCSHARAR, P.C. (AV)

Bank One Center Tower, 111 Monument Circle, Suite 4500, 46204-5145
Telephone: 317-630-4500
Fax: 317-630-4501
Email: mfm@indy.net

David F. McNamar
Randall R. Fearnow
Janet A. McSharar
Alastair J. Warr
John H. Sharpe
Paul (Rick) Rauch, III
Marianna P. Moran

For full biographical listings, see the Martindale-Hubbell Law Directory

TABBERT HAHN EARNEST & WEDDLE (AV)

Suite 2100, One Indiana Square, 46204-2101
Telephone: 317-639-5444
Fax: 317-639-5232
Email: jtyrrell@tabberthahn.com *URL:* http://www.tabberthahn.com

Don A. Tabbert
Gregory F. Hahn
Lante K. Earnest
Robert G. Weddle
Mark K. Sullivan
Judy M. Tyrrell
Lara D. Engelking
Matthew W. Conner
Heather L. Fesko

OF COUNSEL

James J. Nocon
William D. Lalley
Joseph W. Hammes
Dale E. Sporleder

For full biographical listings, see the Martindale-Hubbell Law Directory

ZEIGLER COHEN & KOCH (AV)

8500 Keystone Crossing, Suite 510, 46240
Telephone: 317-254-4400
Facsimile: 317-254-4403

Robert G. Zeigler
Steven J. Cohen
Edna M. Koch
David Becsey
Roger K. Kanne

ASSOCIATES

Joseph D. McPike, II
Kathryn A. Elias
Lakshmi Reddy

OF COUNSEL

Marilyn A. Young

For full biographical listings, see the Martindale-Hubbell Law Directory

LAFAYETTE, * Tippecanoe Co.

STUART & BRANIGIN (AV)

The Life Building, 300 Main Street, Suite 800, P.O. Box 1010, 47902-1010
Telephone: 765-423-1561
Telecopier: 765-742-8175
Email: sb@stuartlaw.com *URL:* http://www.stuartlaw.com
Indianapolis, Indiana Office: Suite 1401, 8888 Keystone Crossing, 46240.
Telephone: 317-574-7245.
Fax: 317-574-7050.

MEMBERS OF FIRM

Thomas R. McCully
Larry R. Fisher
Nina B. Kirkpatrick

Representative Client: Wabash Valley Hospital, Inc.; Arnett Clinic, Inc.
General Counsel For: Lafayette Home Hospital, Inc.

For Complete List of Firm Personnel, See General Section

For full biographical listings, see the Martindale-Hubbell Law Directory

MERRILLVILLE, Lake Co.

HODGES & DAVIS, P.C. (AV)

8700 Broadway, 46410
Telephone: 219-641-8700
Fax: 219-641-8710
URL: http://www.hodgesdavis.com
Portage, Indiana Office: 6082 Lute Road. P.O. Box 1037.
Telephone: 219-762-9129.
Fax: 219-762-2826.

Clyde D. Compton
William B. Davis
Earle F. Hites
R. Lawrence Steele
Gregory A. Sobkowski
Bonnie C. Coleman
Jill M. Madajczyk
Laura B. Frost
David H. Kreider
Jeanne B. Blumenthal

OF COUNSEL

Edward J. Hussey

Representative Clients: The Methodist Hospitals, Inc.; The Lutheran Retirement Home of Northwest Indiana; Geminus Corp.; Visiting Nurse Association of Northwest Indiana, Inc.; Visiting Nurse Association of Porter County, Indiana, Inc.

For Complete List of Firm Personnel, See General Section

For full biographical listings, see the Martindale-Hubbell Law Directory

PORTAGE, Porter Co.

HODGES & DAVIS, P.C. (AV)

6082 Lute Road, P.O. Box 1037, 46368
Telephone: 219-762-9129
Fax: 219-762-2826
URL: http://www.hodgesdavis.com
Merrillville, Indiana Office: 8700 Broadway.
Telephone: 219-641-8700.
Fax: 219-641-8710.

Clyde D. Compton
Earle F. Hites
R. Lawrence Steele
Gregory A. Sobkowski
Bonnie C. Coleman
Laura B. Frost

Representative Clients: The Methodist Hospitals, Inc.; The Lutheran Retirement Home of Northwest, Indiana; Geminus Corp.; Visiting Nurse Association of Northwest Indiana, Inc.; Visiting Nurse Association of Porter County, Indiana, Inc.

For full biographical listings, see the Martindale-Hubbell Law Directory

IOWA

DES MOINES, * Polk Co.

FINLEY, ALT, SMITH, SCHARNBERG, CRAIG, HILMES & GAFFNEY, P.C. (AV)

604 Locust Street, Fourth Floor Equitable Building, 50309
Telephone: 515-288-0145
Telecopier: 515-288-2724

Thomas A. Finley
David C. Craig

Representative Clients: ALAS; American Society of Composers, Authors and Publishers; Equitable Life Assurance Society of the U.S.; Federated Insurance Co.; Meredith Corp.; Catholic Health Corp.
Iowa Attorneys for: Midwest Medical Insurance Co.

For Complete List of Firm Personnel, See General Section

For full biographical listings, see the Martindale-Hubbell Law Directory

KANSAS

HUTCHINSON, * Reno Co.

GILLILAND & HAYES, P.A. A PROFESSIONAL ASSOCIATION (AV)

20 West 2nd Avenue, 2nd Floor, P.O. Box 2977, 67504-2977
Telephone: 316-662-0537
Facsimile: 316-669-9426
URL: http://www.gillilandhayes.com
Wichita, Kansas Office: The Orpheum Centre, Suite 300, 200 North Broadway, P.O. Box 49406.
Telephone: 316-262-2266.
Facsimile: 316-263-2202.
Kansas City, Missouri Office: 12th Floor, 3100 Broadway.
Telephone: 816-753-3100.
Facsimile: 816-753-2271.

Robert J. Gilliland
John F. Hayes
James R. Gilliland
John S. Schmidt
Bruce B. Waugh (Not admitted in KS; Resident, Kansas City, Missouri Office)
Michael R. O'Neal
Bradley D. Dillon
Gerald L. Green
David N. Zimmerman (Not admitted in KS; Resident, Kansas City, Missouri Office)
Scott J. Mann
Carol Z. Smith (Resident, Kansas City, Missouri Office)
Kathleen A. Hardee (Resident, Kansas City, Missouri Office)
Kendall R. Cunningham (Resident, Wichita Office)
Mark R. Maloney (Resident, Wichita Office)

Thomas A. Dower
Tracy Applegate Cole
Laura A. Hederstedt
Terri Roberts Munsell (Resident, Kansas City, Missouri Office)
Lisa M. Ward
Kimberly Breda Bushek (Resident, Kansas City, Missouri Office)
E. Thomas Pyle, III
Tara L. Bragg

OF COUNSEL

Robert P. Reams (Not admitted in KS; Resident, Kansas City, Missouri Office)

Representative Clients: Health Care Inc.; Horizons Mental Health Center, Inc.; Hospice of Reno County, Inc.; Hutchinson Clinic, P.A.; Hutchinson Hospital Corp.; Stafford District Hospital.

For full biographical listings, see the Martindale-Hubbell Law Directory

TOPEKA, * Shawnee Co.

GOODELL, STRATTON, EDMONDS & PALMER, L.L.P. (AV)

515 South Kansas Avenue, 66603-3999
Telephone: 785-233-0593
Fax: 785-233-8870
Email: GSEP@CJNETWORKS.COM *URL:* http://www.cjnetworks.com/~gsep
Kansas City, Missouri Office: 10401 Holmes Road, Suite 280.
Telephone: 816-943-8577.

MEMBERS OF FIRM

Gerald L. Goodell
Wayne T. Stratton
Arthur E. Palmer
H. Philip Elwood
Harold S. Youngentob
Charles R. Hay
Les E. Diehl
David E. Bruns
Catherine M. Walberg
Steve A. Schwarm

ASSOCIATES

Anne M. Kindling
Scott C. Palecki

SPECIAL COUNSEL

Marta Fisher Linenberger
Curtis J. Waugh

Counsel for: The Menninger Foundation; Stormont-Vail Health Care, Inc.; St. Paul Fire & Marine Insurance Co.; Kansas Hospital Association; Heartland Health; Kansas Medical Society; Columbia HCA, Overland Park, Kansas; Pratt Regional Medical Center; Great Plains Health Alliance; Shawnee County Mental Health Center.

For Complete List of Firm Personnel, See General Section

For full biographical listings, see the Martindale-Hubbell Law Directory

WICHITA, * Sedgwick Co.

FOULSTON & SIEFKIN L.L.P. (AV)

700 NationsBank Financial Center, 67202
Telephone: 316-267-6371
Facsimile: 316-267-6345
URL: http://www.foulston.com
Topeka, Kansas Office: 1515 NationsBank Tower, 534 Kansas Avenue, 66603.
Telephone: 785-233-3600.
Fax: 785-233-1610.

(See Next Column)

FOULSTON & SIEFKIN L.L.P.—*Continued*

Dodge City, Kansas Office: 810 Frontview, P.O. Box 1147, 67801.
Telephone: 316-227-8126.
Fax: 316-227-8451.
Member: Lex Mundi, The World's Leading Association of Independent Law Firms.

MEMBERS OF FIRM

Stanley G. Andeel
Gary L. Ayers
Larry G. Rapp
Gary E. Knight

SPECIAL COUNSEL

Thomas L. Theis (Resident, Topeka Office)

For Complete List of Firm Personnel, See General Section

For full biographical listings, see the Martindale-Hubbell Law Directory

KENTUCKY

*BOWLING GREEN,** Warren Co.

KERRICK, GRISE & STIVERS (AV)

1025 State Street, P.O. Box 9547, 42102-9547
Telephone: 502-782-8160
Fax: 502-782-5856
Email: kgs@kgslaw.com
Elizabethtown, Kentucky Office: 2935 Dolphin Drive, Suite 102.
Telephone: 502-769-5788.
Fax: 502-737-9285.

MEMBERS OF FIRM

Thomas N. Kerrick
John R. Grise
Gregory N. Stivers
H. Brent Brennenstuhl
Laura M. Hagan

ASSOCIATES

Karl N. Crandall
Shawn Rosso Alcott
Jason B. Bell

OF COUNSEL

Jeffrey R. O'Grody

LEGAL SUPPORT PERSONNEL

Patricia Logsdon
Laura Lockhart Lico
Allison Lusk

Representative Clients: Columbia Greenview Regional Hospital; Rivendell Hospital Corporation of America; Russell County Hospital; Wayne County Hospital; Hardin Memorial Hospital; Kentucky Hospital Association Trust.

For full biographical listings, see the Martindale-Hubbell Law Directory

COVINGTON, Kenton Co.

GILLILAND & ASSOCIATES (AV)

211 Grandview Suite 205, 41017
Telephone: 606-344-8515
Fax: 606-344-8516
Email: thefirm@gilliland.com *URL:* http://www.gilliland.com
Columbus, Ohio Office: 1335 Dublin Road, Suite 200A, 43215.
Telephone: 614-481-5984.
Fax: 614-481-5985. E-mail: columbusfirm@gilliland.com.
Indianapolis, Indiana Office: 8888 Keystone Crossing, Suite 1300, 46420.
Telephone: 317-581-8585.
Fax: 317-575-4180. E-mail: indyfirm@gilliland.com.

John C. Gilliland, II

Rudy A. Bisciotti
Ursula M. McDonnell (Not admitted in KY)
Randy S. Jackson, Jr.

For full biographical listings, see the Martindale-Hubbell Law Directory

*LEXINGTON,** Fayette Co.

PIPER, WELLMAN & BOWERS (AV)

200 North Upper Street, 40507
Telephone: 606-231-1012
Fax: 606-231-1015
Email: pwb200@uky.campus.mci.net

MEMBERS OF FIRM

George C. Piper
Dean T. Wellman
Barbara J. Bowers

ASSOCIATE

Johann F. Herklotz

Representative Clients: The Virginia Insurance Reciprocal; Woodford Hospital; Clark Regional Medical Center; Garrard Memorial Hospital; Century American Insurance Co.; Central Kentucky Physicians, Inc.; Nazareth Health, Inc. d/b/a/ St. Josephs Hospital, a division of Sisters of Charity of Nazareth Health Corp.; Kentucky River Medical Center; Appalachian Regional Healthcare, Inc.; Mary Chiles Hospital.

(See Next Column)

For full biographical listings, see the Martindale-Hubbell Law Directory

STOLL, KEENON & PARK, LLP (AV)

201 E. Main Street, Suite 1000, 40507-1380
Telephone: 606-231-3000
Telecopier: 606-253-1093; 606-253-1027
URL: http://www.skp.com
Frankfort, Kentucky Office: 307 Washington Street, 40601.
Telephone: 502-875-6220.
Telecopier: 502-875-6235.
Henderson, Kentucky Office: 201 C North Main Street, 42420-3103.
Telephone: 270-831-1900.
Telecopier: 270-827-4060.
Louisville, Kentucky Office: 400 West Market Street, Suite 2650, 40202-3377.
Telephone: 502-568-9100.
Telecopier: 502-568-5700.

MEMBERS OF FIRM

J. Peter Cassidy, Jr.
Samuel D. Hinkle IV
R. David Lester
J. David Smith, Jr.
Dan M. Rose

Representative Clients: Kentucky Medical Services Foundation, Inc.; Louden & Co., Inc.; Louisville Pathology Foundation, Inc.; Medical Rehabilitation Centers, Inc.; Pathology & Cytology Laboratories, Inc.; Sisters of Charity of Nazareth Health Corp.; University Pathologists, P.S.C.; Women's Care Center, PLLC.

For Complete List of Firm Personnel, See General Section

For full biographical listings, see the Martindale-Hubbell Law Directory

*LOUISVILLE,** Jefferson Co.

HALL, RENDER, KILLIAN, HEATH & LYMAN PROFESSIONAL SERVICES CORPORATION (AV)

AEGON Center, Suite 1530, 400 West Market Street, 40202
Telephone: 502-568-1890
Fax: 502-568-4878
Email: hrkhl@hrkhl.com
Indianapolis, Indiana Office: Suite 2000, One American Square, Box 82064, 46282.
Telephone: 317-633-4884.
Fax: 317-633-4878.
Indianapolis North Office: Suite 820, 8402 Harcourt Road, 46260.
Telephone: 317-871-6222.
Fax: 317-338-3946.

R. Thomas Carter
Gerald L. Stovall
Samuel H. DeShazer

René Remek Savarise
William D. Roberts
A. Courtney Guild, Jr.
Matthew W. Forsythe
Sharon K. Hager
Edward L. Schoenbaechler

For full biographical listings, see the Martindale-Hubbell Law Directory

WOODWARD, HOBSON & FULTON (AV)

2500 National City Tower, 101 South Fifth Street, 40202
Telephone: 502-581-8000
Fax: 502-581-8111
Email: WHF@IGLOU.COM
Lexington, Kentucky Office: PNC Bank Plaza, 200 West Vine Street, Suite 500.
Telephone: 606-244-7100.
Telecopier: 606-244-7111.

MEMBERS OF FIRM

David R. Monohan
Thomas A. Hoy
Jann B. Logsdon

ASSOCIATES

Eric M. Jensen
Stephen D. Weisskopf
Alexander M. Say
Katherine A. Wolfe (Not admitted in KY)

Representative Clients: CARITAS Health Services, Inc.; Catholic Health Initiatives; Flaget Memorial Hospital; Marymount Medical Center, Inc.

For Complete List of Firm Personnel, See General Section

For full biographical listings, see the Martindale-Hubbell Law Directory

LOUISIANA

*BATON ROUGE,** East Baton Rouge Parish

KEAN, MILLER, HAWTHORNE, D'ARMOND, MCCOWAN & JARMAN, L.L.P. (AV)

22nd Floor, One American Place, 70825
Telephone: 225-387-0999
Fax: 225-388-9133
Mailing Address: P.O. Box 3513, Baton Rouge, Louisiana, 70821
URL: http://WWW.KMLAW.COM
New Orleans, Louisiana Office: Energy Centre, Suite 1560, 1100 Poydras Street, 70163.
Telephone: 504-585-3050.
Fax: 504-585-3051.
Plaquemine, Louisiana Office: Suite 10, 23425 Railroad Avenue, 70764.
Telephone: 225-687-9845.
Fax: 225-382-3445.
Lake Charles, Louisiana Office: One Lakeshore Drive, Suite 1220, 70629.
Telephone: 318-430-0350.
Fax: 318-436-5566.
Covington, Louisiana Office: 503 North New Hampshire Street, P.O. Box 3096, 70433.
Telephone: 504-875-0400.
Fax: 504-875-0500.

MEMBERS OF FIRM

Vance A. Gibbs
G. Blane Clark, Jr.
Bradley C. Myers
James P. Doré
Cynthia M. Chemay
Gregg R. Kronenberger
Linda G. Rodrigue
John F. Jakuback

Kevin C. Curry

Representative Clients: Baton Rouge Clinic, Baton Rouge, LA; Louisiana Medical Malpractice Insurance Co., Metairie, LA; Surgical Associates of Baton Rouge, Baton Rouge, LA; Vascular Surgery Associates, Baton Rouge, LA.

For full biographical listings, see the Martindale-Hubbell Law Directory

WATSON, BLANCHE, WILSON & POSNER (AV)

Registered Limited Liability Partnership
505 North Boulevard, P.O. Drawer 2995, 70821-2995
Telephone: 225-387-5511
Fax: 225-387-5972

Robert L. Roland
Peter T. Dazzio
Felix R. Weill
William E. Scott, III
Michael M. Remson
P. Chauvin Wilkinson, Jr.
Randall L. Champagne
René J. Pfefferle
P. Scott Jolly

Representative Clients: Baton Rouge General Health System; Louisiana Hospital Association Trust Funds; Willis-Knighton Medical Centers.

For full biographical listings, see the Martindale-Hubbell Law Directory

*GRETNA,** Jefferson Parish

WINDHORST, GAUDRY, RANSON, HIGGINS & GREMILLION, L.L.C. (AV)

Oakwood Corporate Center, 401 Whitney Avenue Suite 500, P.O. Box 1910, 70056
Telephone: 504-362-2466; 367-9247
Telcopier: 504-362-5938
Email: wgrhg@gs.verio.net

Thomas L. Gaudry, Jr.
Daniel A. Ranson
Daryl A. Higgins
Gregory G. Gremillion
Wade A. Langlois, III
Michael D. Peytavin

OF COUNSEL

Fritz H. Windhorst (Retired)

Steven Dow Oliver
Thomas W. Darling
David J. Dowell, Jr.
John A Leslie
Walter Patrick Maestri
B. Wesley Pitts

Reference: Hibernia National Bank.

For full biographical listings, see the Martindale-Hubbell Law Directory

*MONROE,** Ouachita Parish

MCLEOD VERLANDER (AV)

A Partnership including Professional Law Corporations
1900 North 18th Street, Suite 610, P.O. Box 2270, 71207-2270
Telephone: 318-325-7000
Telecopier: 318-324-0580
Email: mv@mv-law.com *URL:* http://www.lawyers.com/mvlaw

MEMBERS OF FIRM

Robert P. McLeod (P.L.C.)
David E. Verlander, III (P.L.C.)

(See Next Column)

Rick W. Duplissey
Donald C. Douglas, Jr.
Laurie J. Burkett

Representative Clients: Columbia North Monroe Hospital; Columbia Health Systems; The Orthopaedic Clinic of Monroe, Inc.; Louisiana Medical Mutual Insurance Co.; Extracorporeal Technologies, Inc.; Daig Corporation; Western Indemnity Company; Evanston Insurance Company; Shand Morahan.

For full biographical listings, see the Martindale-Hubbell Law Directory

*NEW ORLEANS,** Orleans Parish

BEAHM AND GREEN (AV)

145 Robert E. Lee Boulevard Suite 408, 70124-2552
Telephone: 504-288-2000
Fax: 504-288-2099
Email: Frank@Beahm.com *URL:* http://www.Beahm.com

Franklin D. Beahm
Charles S. Green, Jr.

ASSOCIATES

Julie G. Hamner
Candice V. Bates

For full biographical listings, see the Martindale-Hubbell Law Directory

BOGGS, LOEHN & RODRIGUE (AV)

A Partnership including Law Corporations
Suite 1850, Entergy Building, 639 Loyola Avenue, 70130-3597
Telephone: 504-523-7090
Fax: 504-581-6822
Email: BLAR@bellsouth.net

Charles A. Boggs (A Law Corporation)
Thomas E. Loehn (A Law Corporation)
Edward A. Rodrigue, Jr., (A Law Corporation)

Anne E. Medo
Matthew B. Moreland

Reference: First National Bank of Commerce, New Orleans, La.

For full biographical listings, see the Martindale-Hubbell Law Directory

BUCKLEY & HAYES, L.L.P. (AV)

A Partnership including a Professional Corporation
1555 Poydras Street Suite 1700, 70112
Telephone: 504-523-5100
Fax: 504-523-5698
Covington, Louisiana Office: 2301 North HIghway 190, Suite 3, 70433.
Telephone: 504-871-7005.
Fax: 504-871-7051.

MEMBERS OF FIRM

Lloyd W. Hayes
E. Ross Buckley, Jr., (A Professional Law Corp.)
Marianne S. Pensa
William H. Voigt

ASSOCIATES

Michele D. Ahlers
Ernest Philip Legier, Jr.
Elton A. Foster

OF COUNSEL

Harold A. Thomas

For full biographical listings, see the Martindale-Hubbell Law Directory

MCGLINCHEY STAFFORD (AV)

A Professional Limited Liability Company
643 Magazine Street, 70130-3477
Telephone: 504-586-1200
Fax: 504-596-2800
TDD: (504) 596-2728
Telex: 584327
Cable Address: "MACSTAC"
Mailing Address: P.O. Box 60643, New Orleans, Louisiana, 70160-0643
Email: @mcglinchey.com *URL:* http://www.mcglinchey.com
Dallas, Texas Office: 2777 Stemmons Freeway, Suite 925, 75207-2401.
Telephone: 214-860-9700.
Fax: 214-860-9750.
Houston, Texas Office: 2727 Allen Parkway, Suite 1900, 77019.
Telephone: 713-520-1900.
Fax: 713-520-1025.
Baton Rouge, Louisiana Office: Ninth Floor, One American Place, 70825-0001.
Telephone: 504-383-9000.
Fax: 504-343-3076.
Jackson, Mississippi Office: Suite 1200, SkyTel Centre, 200 South Lamar Street, 39201.
Telephone: 601-960-8400.
Fax: 601-960-8406.
Lake Providence, Louisiana Office: 405 Morgan Street, 71254-2691.
Telephone: 318-559-1200.
Fax: 318-559-0609.

(See Next Column)

McGLINCHEY STAFFORD—*Continued*

Monroe, Louisiana Office: Dean ONB Tower, 130 Desiard Street, Suite 807, 71201.
Telephone: 318-651-0807.
Fax: 318-651-0809.

MEMBERS OF FIRM

Donna Guinn Klein
Eve B. Masinter
Robin Spencer Palmisano
Monica A. Frois
Louis J. Lupin

ASSOCIATES

Deborah A. Van Meter
Joan Marie Canny
B. Aven Bruser

OF COUNSEL

Joe Giarrusso, Jr.

MEMBER OF FIRM

Errol J. King (Resident, Baton Rouge Office)

ASSOCIATE

Ashley Byrd Lowe (Resident, Baton Rouge Office)

For full biographical listings, see the Martindale-Hubbell Law Directory

MILLING BENSON WOODWARD L.L.P. (AV)

A Partnership including Professional Law Corporations
Suite Twenty-Three Hundred, 909 Poydras Street, 70112-1017
Telephone: 504-569-7000
Telecopier: 504-569-7001
ABA net: 15656
MCI Mail: "Milling"
Email: milling@millinglaw.com
Lafayette, Louisiana Office: 101 La Rue France, Suite 200.
Telephone: 318-232-3929.
Telecopier: 318-233-4957.
Mandeville (North Shore), Louisiana Office: 2140 8th Street.
Telephone: 504-867-9622.
Telecopier: 504-867-8364.

MEMBER OF FIRM

Roselyn B. Koretzky (P.C.)

SPECIAL COUNSEL

George M. Papale

See General Section for list of Representative Clients

For Complete List of Firm Personnel, See General Section

For full biographical listings, see the Martindale-Hubbell Law Directory

WARD NELSON, LLC (AV)

1539 Jackson Avenue, 6th Floor, 70130
Telephone: 504-561-5000
Fax: 504-588-1334

MEMBERS OF FIRM

Joseph R. Ward, Jr.
Craig R. Nelson
Lisa A. Condrey

ASSOCIATES

Lynn H. Frank
James Everet Brouillette

OF COUNSEL

Christina Papastavros Fay

Representative Clients: Associated Aviation Underwriters; Associated International Underwriters; Colonial Penn Insurance; Fidelity & Casualty of New York; Fireman's Insurance of Newark; Gulf Ins. Co.; Prudential Property and Cas. Ins. Co.; State Farm Fire & Casualty Co.; State Farms Mutual Automobile Insurance Co.; The Weitz Company.

For full biographical listings, see the Martindale-Hubbell Law Directory

WILSON & BOWLING (AV)

A Partnership including Professional Law Corporations
Suite 2411, Bank One Center, 201 St. Charles Avenue, 70170
Telephone: 504-586-5200
Facsimile: 504-586-5201
Email: wilsbowl@gs.net
Gulfport, Mississippi Office: 715 Markham Building, 2301 14th Street, 39501.
Telephone: 228-575-6202.
Fax: 228-864-6227.

Gordon F. Wilson, Jr., (P.L.C.)
David A. Bowling (P.L.C.)

Jeanne B. Roques
Susannah Ross Cooley
John D. Acomb

For full biographical listings, see the Martindale-Hubbell Law Directory

MAINE

*BANGOR,** Penobscot Co.

EATON, PEABODY, BRADFORD & VEAGUE, P.A. (AV)

Fleet Center-Exchange Street, P.O. Box 1210, 04402-1210
Telephone: 207-947-0111
Telecopier: 207-942-3040
Email: eaton@eatonpeabody.com *URL:* http://www.eatonpeabody.com
Augusta, Maine Office: 77 Sewall Street, Suite 3000.
Telephone: 207-622-3747.
Telecopier: 207-622-9732.
Blue Hill, Maine Office: One East Blue Hill Road.
Telephone: 207-374-2812.
Telecopier: 207-374-2548.
Brunswick, Maine Office: 167 Park Row.
Telephone: 207-729-1144.
Telecopier: 207-729-1140.
Dover-Foxcroft, Maine Office: 30 East Main Street.
Telephone: 207-564-8378.
Telecopier: 207-564-7059.

Malcolm E. Morrell, Jr.
Daniel G. McKay

Nathaniel S. Putnam

For Complete List of Firm Personnel, See General Section

For full biographical listings, see the Martindale-Hubbell Law Directory

GROSS, MINSKY, MOGUL & SINGAL, P.A. (AV)

Key Plaza, 23 Water Street, P.O. Box 917, 04402-0917
Telephone: 207-942-4644; 800-274-7124
Telecopier: 207-942-3699
Email: law@gmms.com

Edward I. Gross (1912-1999)
Jules L. Mogul (1930-1994)
George Z. Singal
Louis H. Kornreich
George C. Schelling
Edward W. Gould
Steven J. Mogul
James R. Wholly
Daniel A. Pileggi
Philip K. Clarke

Wayne P. Libhart (Retired)
Sandra L. Rothera
James S. Nixon

OF COUNSEL

Norman Minsky

Representative Client: Dahl Chase Pathology Associates.
Local Counsel for: The St. Paul Insurance Cos.; Aetna Life & Casualty Co.; Imperial Casualty & Indemnity Co.

For full biographical listings, see the Martindale-Hubbell Law Directory

*PORTLAND,** Cumberland Co.

FRIEDMAN BABCOCK & GAYTHWAITE (AV)

Suite 400, Six City Center, P.O. Box 4726, 04112-4726
Telephone: 207-761-0900
Telecopier: 207-761-0186
Email: info@fbg-law.com *URL:* http://www.fbg-law.com

MEMBERS OF FIRM

Harold J. Friedman
Ernest J. Babcock
Martha C. Gaythwaite
Karen Frink Wolf
Jennifer S. Riggle
Laurence H. Leavitt
Elizabeth A. Germani
Michelle Allott
Tracy D. Hill

ASSOCIATES

Susan J. Guerette
L. John Topchik
Sally A. Morris
Catherine C. Miller
Kieran N. Shields
Evan Smith

For full biographical listings, see the Martindale-Hubbell Law Directory

MARCUS, GRYGIEL & CLEGG, P.A. (AV)

100 Middle Street, East Tower, 04101-4102
Telephone: 207-828-8000
Fax: 207-773-3210
Email: firm@mgc-law.com

George J. Marcus
Jennie L. Clegg
Marilyn E. Mistretta
Lee H. Bals

Sean P. Joyce
Barbara G. Shaw
Michael J. Gartland
Regan M. Hornney

OF COUNSEL

Stephen G. Grygiel
Andrew Jeffrey Zulieve

For full biographical listings, see the Martindale-Hubbell Law Directory

Portland—Continued

PRETI, FLAHERTY, BELIVEAU, PACHIOS & HALEY, LLC (AV)

One City Center, P.O. Box 9546, 04112-9546
Telephone: 207-791-3000
Telecopier: 207-791-3111
Email: admin@preti.com *URL:* http://www.preti.com
Augusta, Maine Office: 45 Memorial Circle, P.O. Box 1058, 04332-1058.
Telephone: 207-623-5300.
Telefax: 207-623-2914.
Bath, Maine Office: Thirty Front Street, P.O. Box 665, 04530-0665.
Telephone: 207-443-5576.
Telefax: 207-443-6665.

MEMBERS OF FIRM

Christopher D. Nyhan
Eric P. Stauffer
John P. Doyle, Jr.
Michael G. Messerschmidt
Susan E. LoGiudice
Charles F. Dingman (Augusta Office)

ASSOCIATE

James E. Phipps

Representative Clients: Stephens Memorial Hospital; Rumford Community Hospital; Maine Health Care Assn.; The Aroostook Medical Center; Blue Hill Memorial Hospital; Maine Coast Memorial Hospital; Mount St. Joseph; Olympus Healthcare, Inc.; NYLCare Health Plans of Maine, Inc.; Tufts Associated Health Plans.

For Complete List of Firm Personnel, See General Section

For full biographical listings, see the Martindale-Hubbell Law Directory

VERRILL & DANA, LLP (AV)

One Portland Square, P.O. Box 586, 04112-0586
Telephone: 207-774-4000
Fax: 207-774-7499
Email: advice@verdan.com *URL:* http://www.verdan.com
Augusta, Maine Office: 45 Memorial Circle, P.O. Box 957.
Telephone: 207-623-3889.
Fax: 207-622-3117.
Kennebunk, Maine Office: 403-404 Lafayette Center, P.O. Box 147.
Telephone: 207-985-7193.
Fax: 207-985-3957.
Washington, D.C. Office: 400 North Capitol Street, Suite 585.
Telephone: 202-624-9733.
Fax: 202-393-5218.

MEMBERS OF FIRM

David C. Hillman
Beth Dobson
Claudia D. Raessler

ASSOCIATE

Laurie A. Williamson

For Complete List of Firm Personnel, See General Section

For full biographical listings, see the Martindale-Hubbell Law Directory

SOUTH PORTLAND, Cumberland Co.

VAN MEER & BELANGER, P.A. (AV)

25 Long Creek Drive, 04106
Telephone: 207-871-7500
Fax: 207-871-7505
Email: VBLAW@GWI.NET

Thomas J. Van Meer
Norman R. Belanger
D. Kelley Young
Richard N. Bryant

Betts J. Gorsky
Mary McQuillen

For full biographical listings, see the Martindale-Hubbell Law Directory

MARYLAND

*BALTIMORE,** (Independent City)

GALLAGHER, EVELIUS & JONES, LLP (AV)

Park Charles Suite 400, 218 North Charles Street, 21201
Telephone: 410-727-7702
Facsimile: 410-468-2786
URL: http://www.gejlaw.com

MEMBERS OF FIRM

Francis X. Gallagher (1928-1972)
C. Edward Jones (1908-1999)
John C. Evelius (Retired)
Richard O. Berndt
Thomas N. Biddison, Jr.
Robert R. Kern, Jr.
Saul E. Gilstein
Thomas B. Lewis
Bonnie Abrams Travieso
Stephen A. Goldberg
Linda H. Jones
Jack C. Tranter
Leslie B. Speed
Christopher J. Fritz
David E. Raderman
Peter E. Keith
Nita L. Schultz

(See Next Column)

MEMBERS OF FIRM (Continued)

Michael W. Skojec
Kathryn Kelley Hoskins
Mark P. Keener
Kevin J. Davidson
Eileen M. Lunga
Lori A. Nicolle
Kenneth S. Gross
Thomas C. Dame

ASSOCIATES

Valarie K. Oulds
Margaret Stevens Jacks
Matthew W. Oakey
Rebecca A. Weaver
Michael J. Henigan
David W. Kinkopf
Paul S. Caiola
Jason W. Gaarder
M. Kirsten Andrews

LEGAL ASSISTANTS

Patricia C. Quayle
Iris T. H. Heath
Connie L. Ennis
Margaret Graff
Margo Gibson Hughes
Jonathan T. Gillis
Brenda J. Heacock
Dwayne L. Rodeheaver

Representative Clients: Mercy Medical Center, Inc.; Bon Secours Hospital of Baltimore, Inc.; Cardinal Shehan Center for the Aging, Inc.; Civista Health, Inc.

For full biographical listings, see the Martindale-Hubbell Law Directory

VENABLE ATTORNEYS AT LAW VENABLE, BAETJER AND HOWARD, LLP (AV)

A Partnership including Professional Corporations
1800 Mercantile Bank & Trust Building, 2 Hopkins Plaza, 21201
Telephone: 410-244-7400
Fax: 410-244-7742
URL: http://www.venable.com
Washington, D.C. Office: Venable, Baetjer, Howard & Civiletti LLP, Suite 1000, 1201 New York Avenue, N.W.
Telephone: 202-962-4800.
Fax: 202-962-8300.
McLean, Virginia Office: Suite 400, 2010 Corporate Ridge.
Telephone: 703-760-1600.
Fax: 703-821-8949.
Rockville, Maryland Office: Suite 500, One Church Street, P. O. Box 1906.
Telephone: 301-217-5600.
Fax: 301-217-5617.
Towson, Maryland Office: 210 Allegheny Avenue, P. O. Box 5517.
Telephone: 410-494-6200.
Fax: 410-821-0147.

MEMBERS OF FIRM

Benjamin R. Civiletti (P.C.) (Also at Washington, D.C. and Towson, Maryland Offices)
Robert A. Shelton
Thomas J. Kenney, Jr. (P.C.)
Kenneth C. Bass, III (Not admitted in MD; Washington, D.C. and McLean, Virginia Offices)
Paul F. Strain (P.C.)
William D. Dolan, III (P.C.) (Not admitted in MD; Resident, McLean, Virginia Office)
Joseph C. Wich, Jr. (Resident, Towson, Maryland Office)
Robert G. Ames (Also at Washington, D.C. Office)
Nell B. Strachan
Barbara E. Schlaff
G. Stewart Webb, Jr.
James K. Archibald (Also at Washington, D.C. Office)
George W. Johnston (P.C.)
Constance H. Baker
Edward L. Wender (P.C.)
David M. Fleishman
Jana Howard Carey (P.C.)
Jeffrey A. Dunn (Also at Washington, D.C. Office)
George F. Pappas (Also at Washington, D.C. Office)
Kenneth S. Slaughter (Not admitted in MD; Resident, Washington, D.C. Office)
Peter P. Parvis
James L. Shea (Also at Washington, D.C. Office)
Amy Berman Jackson (Not admitted in MD; Resident, Washington, D.C. Office)
Robert Zinkham
M. King Hill, III (Resident, Towson, Maryland Office)
James A. Dunbar (Resident, Towson, Maryland Office)
Robert L. Waldman
David J. Heubeck
Davis V. R. Sherman
Geoffrey R. Garinther (Also at Towson, Maryland Office)
Terri L. Turner
Michael W. Robinson (Resident, McLean, Virginia Office)
Todd J. Horn
David W. Goewey (Not admitted in MD; Resident, Washington, D.C. Office)
John T. Prisbe
John P. Sarbanes
Vicki Margolis (Also at Washington, D.C. Office)

OF COUNSEL

A. Samuel Cook (P.C.) (Resident, Towson, Maryland Office)

ASSOCIATE

Elizabeth C. Keenan

For Complete List of Firm Personnel, See General Section

For full biographical listings, see the Martindale-Hubbell Law Directory

*SALISBURY,** Wicomico Co.

DUVALL & DUVALL, L.L.P. (AV)

108 East Market Street, P.O. Box 4077, 21803-4077
Telephone: 410-548-1010
Fax: 410-548-1045
Email: billduva@shore.intercom.net

(See Next Column)

DUVALL & DUVALL L.L.P.—*Continued*

MEMBERS OF FIRM

William G. Duvall
Richard M. Duvall

Reference: Nations Bank.

For full biographical listings, see the Martindale-Hubbell Law Directory

MASSACHUSETTS

*BOSTON,** Suffolk Co.

BLOOM & BUELL (AV)

1340 Soldiers Field Road, 02135-1020
Telephone: 617-254-4400; 800-354-6004
Telecopier: 617-254-7610
Email: office@bloombuell.com *URL:* http://www.bloombuell.com

MEMBERS OF FIRM

Laurence J. Bloom
Barbara Hayes Buell
William J. Davenport
Marc J. Gervais
Richard M. Haley

ASSOCIATES

Barry T. Putterman
Barbara D. Weninger

For full biographical listings, see the Martindale-Hubbell Law Directory

HINCKLEY, ALLEN & SNYDER LLP (AV)

28 State Street, 30th Floor, 02109-1775
Telephone: 617-345-9000
Email: firm@haslaw.com *URL:* http://www.haslaw.com
Providence, Rhode Island Office: 1500 Fleet Center.
Telephone: 401-274-2000.
Fax: 401-277-9600. URL: http://www.hawlaw.com.

MEMBERS OF FIRM

E. Jerome Batty (Not admitted in MA)
Jonathan Bell
Leon C. Boghossian III
Paul Bork
Stephen J. Carlotti (Not admitted in MA)
Michael P. DeFanti
Eric F. Eisenberg
Pasco Gasbarro Jr.
Bruce G. Goodman
Alan P. Gottlieb
Gerard R. Goulet
William R. Grimm
Paul A. Hedstrom
Richard L. E. Jocelyn (Not admitted in MA)
Michael J. Kelly
Frederick P. McClure
H. Peter Olsen (Not admitted in MA)
Julianne Palumbo
John J. Pendergast, III (Not admitted in MA)
James O. Reavis
Douglas F. Seaver
Robert F. Sylvia
Howard E. Walker (Not admitted in MA)
Richard D. Wayne

ASSOCIATES

Brent R. Canning (Not admitted in MA)
Michael G. Tauber
Lawrence W. Vernaglia

OF COUNSEL

Willard Krasnow

For Complete List of Firm Personnel, See General Section

For full biographical listings, see the Martindale-Hubbell Law Directory

*SPRINGFIELD,** Hampden Co.

ANNINO, DRAPER & MOORE, P.C. (AV)

1500 Main Street, Suite 1818, P.O. Box 15428, 01115
Telephone: 413-732-6400
Fax: 413-732-3339
Email: admatlaw@aol.com
Westfield, Massachusetts Office: 52 Court Street.
Telephone: 413-562-9829.

Calvin W. Annino, Jr.
Mark E. Draper
Louis S. Moore
Michael R. Siddall

For full biographical listings, see the Martindale-Hubbell Law Directory

MICHIGAN

*ANN ARBOR,** Washtenaw Co.

MILLER, CANFIELD, PADDOCK AND STONE, P.L.C. (AV)

A Professional Limited Liability Company
Founded in 1852 by Sidney Davy Miller
101 North Main Street, Seventh Floor, 48104-1400
Telephone: 734-663-2445
Fax: 734-747-7147
URL: http://www.millercanfield.com
Detroit, Michigan Office: 150 West Jefferson, Suite 2500, 48226-4415.
Telephone: 313-963-6420.
Fax: 313-496-7500.
Cable Address: "Stem Detroit."
Troy, Michigan Office: 840 West Long Lake Road, Suite 200, 48098.
Telephone: 248-879-2000.
Fax: 248-879-2001.
Grand Rapids, Michigan Office: 99 Monroe, N.W., Suite 1200, 49503-2639.
Telephone: 616-454-8656.
Fax: 616-776-6322.
Howell, Michigan Office: 121 South Barnard Street, Suite 4, 48843-2305.
Telephone: 517-546-7600.
Telecopier: 517-546-6974.
Kalamazoo, Michigan Office: 444 West Michigan Avenue, 49007-3752.
Telephone: 616-381-7030.
Fax: 616-382-0244.
Lansing, Michigan Office: One Michigan Avenue, Suite 900, 48933-1609.
Telephone: 517-487-2070.
Fax: 517-374-6304.
Monroe, Michigan Office: 214 East Elm Avenue, Suite 100, 48162-2682.
Telephone: 734-243-2000.
Fax: 734-243-0901.
Washington, D.C. Office: 1900 K Street, N.W., Suite 1150. 20006.
Telephone: 202-429-5575; 785-0600.
Fax: 202-331-1118; 785-1234.
Pensacola, Florida Office: 25 West Cedar, 32501.
Telephone: 850-469-1088.
Fax: 850-432-0677.
New York, New York Office: 1450 Broadway, 41st Floor, 10018.
Telephone: 212-704-4400.
Fax: 212-704-4410.
Gdynia, Poland Office: UL. Slaska 21, 81-319.
Telephone: 011-485-831-2808.
Fax: 011-48-58-628 6411.
Warsaw, Poland Office: UL. Nowogrodzkall, 5th Floor, 00-513.
Telephone: 011-4822 529 0200.
Fax: 011-4822 529 0201.
Katowice, Poland Office: UL. Francuska 35/37, 40-027.
Telephone: 011 (48-32) 757-2414.
Fax: 011 (48-32) 757-2483.

PRINCIPALS OF FIRM

Robert E. Gilbert
Bettye S. Elkins
Roselyn R. Parmenter

OF COUNSEL/SENIOR COUNSEL

John B. DeVine

Representative Firm Clients: Chrysler Corporation; Comerica, Incorporated; City of Detroit, Michigan; Detroit Tigers, Inc.; First of Michigan; Ford Motor Company; Ford Motor Credit Company; Great Lakes Bancorp; Henry Ford Hospital; INVETECH Company.

For Complete List of Firm Personnel, See General Section

For full biographical listings, see the Martindale-Hubbell Law Directory

BATTLE CREEK, Calhoun Co.

KREIS, ENDERLE, CALLANDER & HUDGINS, A PROFESSIONAL CORPORATION (AV)

One West Michigan Avenue, 49017
Telephone: 616-966-3000
Facsimile: 616-966-3022
Email: kech@kech.com *URL:* http://www.kech.com
Kalamazoo, Michigan Office: One Moorsbridge, P.O. Box 4010, 49003-4010.
Telephone: 616-324-3000.
Fax: 616-324-3010.

Russell A. Kreis (Resident, Kalamazoo Office)
C. Reid Hudgins III (Resident, Kalamazoo Office)
Daniel P. McGlinn (Resident, Kalamazoo Office)

For Complete List of Firm Personnel, See General Section

For full biographical listings, see the Martindale-Hubbell Law Directory

BINGHAM FARMS, Oakland Co.

SMALL, TOTH, BALDRIDGE & VAN BELKUM, P.C. (AV)

30100 Telegraph Road Suite 250, 48025-4516
Telephone: 248-647-9595
Facsimile: 248-647-9599

Richard L. Small
John M. Toth
David M. Baldridge
Thomas G. Van Belkum
Keith P. Felty

Stephanie A. Griz-Kochkodan
Kristin Allen

Representative Clients: The Medical Protective Co.; Michigan Physicians Mutual Liability Insurance Co.; Physicians Insurance Company of Michigan; Michigan Society of Oral and Maxillofacial Surgeons; Michigan Association of Orthodontists; Michigan Association of Endodontists; AAMOS National; California Association of Oral and Maxillofacial Surgeons; Oakwood United Hospitals; The Detroit Medical Center Affiliated Hospitals.

For full biographical listings, see the Martindale-Hubbell Law Directory

BLOOMFIELD HILLS, Oakland Co.

DAVID D. PATTON & ASSOCIATES, P.C. (AV)

44 East Long Lake Road, Suite 100, P.O. Box 829, 48303-0829
Telephone: 248-258-6020
Fax: 248-258-6052
Email: litigation@aol.com *URL:* http://www.lawyers.com/dpattonlaw

David D. Patton

Ellen Bartman Jannette
Patricia C. White
Humma S. Siddiqi
Kelly P. Bekolay
David H. Patton (1912-1993)

OF COUNSEL

Lawrence J. Acker

For full biographical listings, see the Martindale-Hubbell Law Directory

PORTNOY, PIDGEON & ROTH, P.C. (AV)

3883 Telegraph, Suite 103, 48302
Telephone: 248-647-4242
Fax: 248-647-8251
Email: DWINNIE103@AOL.COM *URL:* http://www.lawyers.com/portnoypidgeon&roth

Bernard N. Portnoy (Retired)
James M. Pidgeon
Robert P. Roth
Marc S. Berlin
Sheila Connor-Heath
Anne Loridas Randall
Joseph M. LaBella
Melinda A. Davis

Representative Clients: North Oakland Medical Center, Pontiac General Hospital Division; Hurly Medical Center, Flint, Michigan; McLaren Regional Medical Center, Flint, Michigan; William Beaumont Hospital, Royal Oak, Michigan; Horizon Health Systems; Lapeer Regional Hospital; OUM Group; Oakwood Health Care & Co, Inc.

For full biographical listings, see the Martindale-Hubbell Law Directory

PROVIZER & PHILLIPS, P.C. (AV)

6785 Telegraph Road, Suite 400, 48301
Telephone: 248-642-0444
Facsimile: 248-642-6661
Toll Free: 1-800-288-9080
URL: http://www.lawyers.com/provizer&phillips

Harold M. Provizer
Randall E. Phillips
Marilyn A. Madorsky
Evan A. Zagoria
Noel F. Beck
Mark S. Baumkel

Constance S. Hall
Ellen C. Busch
Donald J. Parthum, Jr.
Keith A. Castora
Gregory A. Nave

For full biographical listings, see the Martindale-Hubbell Law Directory

*DETROIT,** Wayne Co.

BODMAN, LONGLEY & DAHLING LLP (AV)

34th Floor 100 Renaissance Center, 48243
Telephone: 313-259-7777
Fax: 313-393-7579
Email: info@bodmanlongley.com *URL:* http://www.bodmanlongley.com
Troy, Michigan Office: Suite 2020, 755 West Big Beaver Road.
Telephone: 248-362-2110.
Fax: 248-244-0780.
Ann Arbor, Michigan Office: 110 Miller, Suite 300.
Telephone: 734-761-3780.
Fax: 734-930-2494.
Northern Michigan Office: 229 Court Street, P.O. Box 405, Cheboygan.
Telephone: 231-627-4351.
Fax: 231-627-2802.

(See Next Column)

MEMBERS OF FIRM

Mark W. Griffin (Ann Arbor Office)
Randolph S. Perry
Charles N. Raimi
Lloyd C. Fell (Cheboygan Office)
F. Thomas Lewand
Kathleen A. Lieder (Cheboygan Office)
Karen L. Piper
Barbara A. Bowman
Lawrence P. Hanson (Cheboygan Office)
Sandra L. Sorini (Ann Arbor Office)

ASSOCIATE

Deanna L. Dixon

For Representative Client List, See General Section

For Complete List of Firm Personnel, See General Section

For full biographical listings, see the Martindale-Hubbell Law Directory

BUTZEL LONG, A PROFESSIONAL CORPORATION (AV)

Suite 900, 150 West Jefferson, 48226
Telephone: 313-225-7000
Telecopier: 313-225-7080
Email: melnick@butzel.com *URL:* http://www.butzel.com
Birmingham, Michigan Office: Suite 200, 32270 Telegraph Road.
Telephone: 810-258-1616.
Telecopier: 810-258-1439.
Okemos, Michigan Office: Suite 300, 2127 University Park Drive.
Telephone: 517-372-6622.
Telecopier: 517-372-6672.
Ann Arbor, Michigan Office: Suite 300, 350 South Main Street.
Telephone: 313-995-3110.
Telecopier: 313-995-1777.
Grosse Pointe Farms, Michigan Office: Suite 260, 21 Kercheval.
Telephone: 313-886-5446.
Telecopier: 313-886-2114.
Boca Raton, Florida Office: Suite 411, 1200 North Federal Highway.
Telephone: 561-368-2151.
Telecopier: 561-368-4668.
Palm Beach Gardens, Florida Office: Suite 227, 11382 Prosperity Farms Road.
Telephone: 561-625-4442.
Telecopier: 561-625-6901.
Naples, Florida Office: Suite 705, 801 Laurel Oak Drive.
Telephone: 941-597-4500.
Telecopier: 941-597-5623.

Philip J. Kessler
John P. Hancock, Jr.
Alexander B. Bragdon
D. Stewart Green (Birmingham)
Keefe A. Brooks
Gordon J. Walker (Birmingham)
James L. Hughes
E. William S. Shipman
Carey A. DeWitt
Andrea Roumell Dickson
Clara DeMatteis Mager
Jordan S. Schreier (Ann Arbor)

SENIOR ATTORNEYS

Eric R. Wapnick
Max R. Hoffman, Jr. (Okemos)
Thomas L. Sparks (Okemos)

Representative Clients: Blue Care Network; Blue Cross and Blue Shield of Michigan; Chelsea Community Hospital; Complete Business Solutions, Inc.; Memorial Health Care; Mercy Health Services; Mt. Clemens General Hospital; University of Michigan; William Beaumont Hospital.

For full biographical listings, see the Martindale-Hubbell Law Directory

DYKEMA GOSSETT PLLC (AV)

400 Renaissance Center, 48243-1668
Telephone: 313-568-6800
Fax: 313-568-6545
Email: mstarrs@dykema.com *URL:* http://www.dykema.com
Ann Arbor, Michigan Office: 315 East Eisenhower Parkway, Suite 100, 48108-3306.
Telephone: 734-214-7660.
Fax: 734-214-7696.
Bloomfield Hills, Michigan Office: 1577 North Woodward Avenue, Suite 300, 48304-2820.
Telephone: 248-203-0700.
Fax: 248-203-0763.
Chicago, Illinois Office: 55 East Monroe Street, Suite 3050, 60603-5709.
Telephone: 312-551-4900.
Fax: 312-551-4919.
Grand Rapids, Michigan Office: Suite 700, 300 Ottawa Avenue, N.W., 49503-2304.
Telephone: 616-776-7500.
Fax: 616-776-7573.
Lansing, Michigan Office: 800 Michigan National Tower, 48933-1707.
Telephone: 517-374-9100.
Fax: 517-374-9191.
Washington, D.C. Office: Franklin Square, Suite 300 West, 1300 I Street, N.W., 20005-3306.
Telephone: 202-522-8600.
Fax: 202-522-8669.
Affiliated Office: Via Matconi, 3, 40122 Bologna, Italy.
Telephone: 011-39-51-228222.
Fax: 011-39-51-6593580.

(See Next Column)

DYKEMA GOSSETT PLLC—*Continued*

MEMBERS OF FIRM

Maria B. Abrahamsen (Resident at Bloomfield Hills Office)
Phyllis Donaldson-Adams (Resident at Ann Arbor Office)
J. Kay Felt
Jane Forbes
Kathrin E. Kudner
Seth M. Lloyd
Thomas J. McGraw

ASSOCIATES

Joanne R. Lax
Kathleen A. Reed

For Complete List of Firm Personnel, See General Section

For full biographical listings, see the Martindale-Hubbell Law Directory

---

GLEICHER & PATEK, P.C. (AV)

1500 Buhl Building, 48226
Telephone: 313-964-6900
Fax: 313-964-6976
URL: http://www.lawyers.com/gplaw

Elizabeth Gleicher
Barbara A. Patek

LEGAL SUPPORT PERSONNEL

Laura Bocchini (Legal Coordinator)

For full biographical listings, see the Martindale-Hubbell Law Directory

---

HONIGMAN MILLER SCHWARTZ AND COHN (AV)

2290 First National Building, 660 Woodward Avenue, 48226
Telephone: 313-465-7000
Telecopier: 313-465-8000
Telex: 235705
Email: mvg@honigman.com *URL:* http://law.honigman.com
Lansing, Michigan Office: Phoenix Building, 222 North Washington Square, Suite 400, 48933-1800.
Telephone: 517-484-8282.

MEMBERS OF FIRM

Joseph T. Aoun
William M. Cassetta
John H. Eggertsen
David A. Ettinger
Gerald M. Griffith
William O. Hochkammer
Linn A. Hynds
Carey F. Kalmowitz
Stuart M. Lockman
Joseph G. Nuyen, Jr.
Julie E. Robertson
Linda S. Ross
Chris E. Rossman
Tracy E. Silverman
Brad M. Tomtishen

ASSOCIATES

James T. Carroll, III
William S. Hammond
Dawn R. Kreysar

OF COUNSEL

Margaret Shannon

Counsel to: CoreSource, Inc. (Northbrook, Illinois); The Detroit Medical Center (Detroit, MI); Mercy Health Services (Farmington Hills, MI); Intracoastal Health Systems (West Palm Beach, FL); Michigan Health and Hospital Association (Lansing, MI); Home Medical Equipment Association of Michigan (Lansing, MI); Florida Health Choice (Delray Beach, FL); Holy Cross Hospital (Ft. Lauderdale, FL); Texas Health Resources (Dallas, TX); Alegent Health (Omaha, NE).

For Complete List of Firm Personnel, See General Section

For full biographical listings, see the Martindale-Hubbell Law Directory

---

JAFFE, RAITT, HEUER & WEISS, PROFESSIONAL CORPORATION (AV)

One Woodward Avenue, Suite 2400, 48226
Telephone: 313-961-8380
Telecopier: 313-961-8358
Cable Address: "Jafsni"
Southfield,Michigan Office: Travelers Tower, Suite 1520.
Telephone: 313-961-8380.

Linda C. Scheuerman
Arthur A. Weiss

For Complete List of Firm Personnel, See General Section

For full biographical listings, see the Martindale-Hubbell Law Directory

---

KITCH DRUTCHAS WAGNER DENARDIS & VALITUTTI, A PROFESSIONAL CORPORATION (AV)

One Woodward, Tenth Floor, 48226-3499
Telephone: 313-965-7900
Fax: 313-965-7403
URL: http://www.kitch.com
Lansing, Michigan Office: 120 Washington Square, North, Suite 280, One Michigan Avenue, 48933-1609.
Telephone: 517-372-6430.
Fax: 517-372-0441.
Macomb County Office: Towne Square Development, 10 South Main Street, Suite 301, Mount Clemens, 48043-7903.
Telephone: 810-463-9770.
Fax: 810-463-8994.

(See Next Column)

Toledo, Ohio Office: 405 Madison Avenue, Suite 1500, 43604-1235.
Telephone: 419-243-4006.
Fax: 419-243-7333.
Marquette, Michigan Office: Old City Hall, 220 West Washington, Suite 500, 49855-4344.
Telephone: 906-228-0001.
Fax: 906-228-0003.
Ann Arbor, Michigan Office: 303 Detroit Street, Suite 400, P.O. Box 8610, 48107-8610.
Telephone: 734-994-7600.
Fax: 734-994-7626.
Grand Rapids, Michigan Office: 300 Ottawa, NW, Suite 210, 49503.
Telephone: 616-456-8384.
Fax: 616-456-8795.

FIRM PRINCIPALS

Richard A. Kitch
Karen Bernard Berkery
John M. Sier
Carol Ann Tarnowsky

For Complete List of Firm Personnel, See General Section

For full biographical listings, see the Martindale-Hubbell Law Directory

---

LEWIS & MUNDAY, A PROFESSIONAL CORPORATION (AV)

(Formerly Lewis, Clay & Munday, P.C.)
1300 First National Building, 660 Woodward Avenue, 48226-3531
Telephone: 313-961-2550
Fax: 313-961-1270
Email: camille.miller@lewis-pc.com *URL:* http://www.lewis-pc.com
Washington, D.C. Office: 1120 Connecticut Avenue, Suite 280. 20036.
Telephone: 202-835-0616.
Fax: 202-833-3316.
Boston, Massachusetts Office: 101 Federal Street, Suite 1900. 02110.
Telephone: 617-478-0553.
Fax: 617-478-0543.

David Baker Lewis
Reuben A. Munday
Camille Stearns Miller
Jacqueline H. Sellers
David N. Zacks
Thomas J. Guyer
Blair A. Person
Karen Kendrick Brown (Resident, Washington, D.C. Office)
Susan D. Hoffman
Hans J. Massaquoi, Jr.

Althea Lynn Simpson
Donica Thomas Varner
Kris W. Krueger
Cylenthia LaToye Miller
Joseph N. Ejbeh
Yolanda R. Bates
Caroletta L. Edgar-Sprinkle
Derek G. McBride
Ayanna Weber
Deborah Jean Williamson
Darice Elizabeth Weber
Krystal M. Gardner
Syeda Taqi

COUNSEL

G. Allen Bass (Resident, Boston, Massachusetts Office)
Leamon R. Sowell, Jr.
Gail Pabarue Bennett
Roger M. Groves
Carol H. Rodriguez
Linda M. Bruton
Brian J. Kott

OF COUNSEL

Otis M. Smith (1922-1994)
Herbert O. Reid, Sr. (1915-1991)

Representative Clients: Aetna Life & Casualty Co.; Chrysler Motors Corp.; Chrysler Financial Corp.; MCI Communications Corp.; City of Detroit; City of Detroit Building Authority; City of Detroit Downtown Development Authority; Consolidated Rail Corp. (Conrail); Equitable Life Assurance Society of the United States.

For full biographical listings, see the Martindale-Hubbell Law Directory

---

MILLER, CANFIELD, PADDOCK AND STONE, P.L.C. (AV)

A Professional Limited Liability Company
Founded in 1852 by Sidney Davy Miller
150 West Jefferson, Suite 2500, 48226-4415
Telephone: 313-963-6420
Fax: 313-496-7500
Cable Address: "Stem Detroit"
URL: http://www.millercanfield.com
Ann Arbor, Michigan Office: 101 North Main Street, 7th Floor, 48104-1400.
Telephone: 734-663-2445.
Fax: 734-747-7147.
Troy, Michigan Office: 840 West Long Lake Road, Suite 200, 48098.
Telephone: 248-879-2000.
Fax: 248-879-2001.
Grand Rapids, Michigan Office: 99 Monroe, N.W., Suite 1200, 49503-2639.
Telephone: 616-454-8656.
Fax: 616-776-6322.
Howell, Michigan Office: 121 South Barnard Street, Suite 4, 48843-2305.
Telephone: 517-546-7600.
Telecopier: 517-546-6974.
Kalamazoo, Michigan Office: 444 West Michigan Avenue, 49007-3752.
Telephone: 616-381-7030.
Fax: 616-382-0244.

(See Next Column)

MILLER, CANFIELD, PADDOCK AND STONE P.L.C., *Detroit—Continued*

Lansing, Michigan Office: One Michigan Avenue, Suite 900, 48933-1609.
Telephone: 517-487-2070.
Fax: 517-374-6304.
Monroe, Michigan Office: 214 East Elm Avenue, Suite 100, 48162-2682.
Telephone: 734-243-2000.
Fax: 734-243-0901.
Washington, D.C. Office: 1900 K Street, N.W., Suite 1150. 20006.
Telephone: 202-429-5575; 785-0600.
Fax: 202-331-1118; 785-1234.
Pensacola, Florida Office: 25 West Cedar, 32501.
Telephone: 850-469-1088.
Fax: 850-432-0677.
New York, New York Office: 1450 Broadway, 41st Floor, 10018.
Telephone: 212-704-4400.
Fax: 212-704-4410.
Gdynia, Poland Office: UL. Slaska 21, 81-319.
Telephone: 011-485-831-2808.
Fax: 011-48-58-628 6411.
Warsaw, Poland Office: UL. Nowogrodzkall, 5th Floor, 00-513.
Telephone: 011-4822 529 0200.
Fax: 011-4822 529 0201.
Katowice, Poland Office: UL. Francuska 35/37, 40-027.
Telephone: 011 (48-32) 757-2414.
Fax: 011 (48-32) 757-2483.

PRINCIPALS OF FIRM

Bettye S. Elkins (Ann Arbor Office)
James C. Foresman
Roselyn R. Parmenter (Ann Arbor Office)

OF COUNSEL/SENIOR COUNSEL

John B. DeVine (Ann Arbor Office)
David L. Kaser (Principal)

SENIOR ATTORNEY

Robert J. Sandler

ASSOCIATES

David L. Freedman (Ann Arbor Office)
Nancy E. Vettorello

Representative Firm Clients: Chrysler Corporation; Comerica, Incorporated; City of Detroit, Michigan; Detroit Tigers, Inc.; First of Michigan; Ford Motor Company; Ford Motor Credit Company; Great Lakes Bancorp; Henry Ford Hospital; INVETECH Company.

For Complete List of Firm Personnel, See General Section

For full biographical listings, see the Martindale-Hubbell Law Directory

TIMMIS & INMAN L.L.P. (AV)

300 Talon Centre, 48207
Telephone: 313-396-4200
Facsimile: 313-396-4228
Email: info@timmis-inman.com *URL:* http://www.timmis-inman.com

George A. Peck
Richard M. Miettinen

Erich J. D'Andrea
Shannon M. Nichols
Anthony J. Long

OF COUNSEL

William B. Fitzgerald

Representative Client: Eastpointe Radiologists, P.C.; Harper Hospital; Bixy Medical Center; Omnicare Health Plan; Institute of Pathology; Bone & Joint Medical Center; Health Care Associates Insurance Fund; Surgical Group Services; Kalamazoo Radiology, P.C.; Holy Cross Radiologists, P.L.C.

For Complete List of Firm Personnel, See General Section

For full biographical listings, see the Martindale-Hubbell Law Directory

VANDER MALE, BELLAMY, GILCHRIST, VANDE VUSSE & CAFFERTY (AV)

333 West Fort, Suite 1100, 48226
Telephone: 313-964-3070
Fax: 313-628-4701
Email: HEALTHLAWYERS@wwnet.net

MEMBERS OF FIRM

Frederick B. Bellamy
Bruce A. Vande Vusse
Alan G. Gilchrist
Michael S. Cafferty
Keith J. Soltis

ASSOCIATES

Joseph E. Kozely, Jr.
Michael P. Risko
Lawrence David Rosenstock

For full biographical listings, see the Martindale-Hubbell Law Directory

WILLMARTH, TANOURY, RAMAR, CORBET, GARVES & SHAW (AV)

535 Griswold, Suite 1730, 48226-3602
Telephone: 313-964-6300
Fax: 313-964-6310
Email: mdwillth@home.net

MEMBERS OF FIRM

Daniel R. Corbet
John M. Perrin
Brian R. Garves
John J. Ramar
David R. Nauts
Bruce R. Shaw
Anthony J. Paradiso
William A. Tanoury
Mark D. Willmarth

ASSOCIATES

Marie C. Kennedy
Frank Hamidi
Wayne Walker
Kristen E. Skaff
Elizabeth L. Sokol
Steven J. Bonasso
Robert S. Silverman
Colleen P. O'Connor
Carmine G. Paterra
Lara R. Stutz
Joseph J. Ceglarek, II
Eric G. Tucciarone
Derek Steven Wilczynski
Michael P. Robach

For full biographical listings, see the Martindale-Hubbell Law Directory

*GRAND RAPIDS,** Kent Co.

GRUEL, MILLS, NIMS AND PYLMAN (AV)

50 Monroe Place, Suite 700 West, 49503
Telephone: 616-235-5500
Fax: 616-235-5550

MEMBERS OF FIRM

Grant J. Gruel
Scott R. Melton
William F. Mills
Brion J. Brooks
J. Clarke Nims
Thomas R. Behm
Norman H. Pylman, II
J. Paul Janes

Representative Clients: Aquinas College; Bell Helmet Co.; Blodgett Memorial Medical Center; Chem Central, Inc.; Cook Pump Co.; Grove, Inc.; NBDC; Heim Corp.

For full biographical listings, see the Martindale-Hubbell Law Directory

WARNER NORCROSS & JUDD LLP (AV)

900 Old Kent Building, 111 Lyon Street, N.W., 49503-2489
Telephone: 616-752-2000
Fax: 616-752-2500
URL: http://www.wnj.com
Muskegon, Michigan Office: 400 Terrace Plaza, P.O. Box 900.
Telephone: 231-727-2600.
Fax: 231-727-2699.
Holland, Michigan Office: Curtis Center, Suite 300, 170 College Avenue.
Telephone: 616-396-9800.
Fax: 616-396-3656.
Southfield, Michigan Office: 1000 Town Center, Suite 650.
Telephone: 248-223-5000.
Fax: 248-223-5005.

MEMBERS OF FIRM

George L. Whitfield
Stephen R. Kretschman
Charles E. McCallum
Richard E. Cassard
John H. Logie
Kathleen M. Hanenburg
John R. Marquis (Resident Member, Holland Office)
Sue O. Conway
Cameron S. DeLong
Ernest M. Sharpe
Richard L. Bouma
Peter L. Gustafson
Valerie Pierre Simmons
Susan Gell Meyers

For full biographical listings, see the Martindale-Hubbell Law Directory

*KALAMAZOO,** Kalamazoo Co.

KREIS, ENDERLE, CALLANDER & HUDGINS, A PROFESSIONAL CORPORATION (AV)

One Moorsbridge, P.O. Box 4010, 49003-4010
Telephone: 616-324-3000
Facsimile: 616-324-3010
Email: kech@kech.com *URL:* http://www.kech.com
Battle Creek, Michigan Office: One West Michigan Avenue, 49017.
Telephone: 616-966-3000.
Fax: 616-966-3022.

Russell A. Kreis
C. Reid Hudgins III
Daniel P. McGlinn

For Complete List of Firm Personnel, See General Section

For full biographical listings, see the Martindale-Hubbell Law Directory

LANSING, Ingham Co.

FOSTER, SWIFT, COLLINS & SMITH, P.C. (AV)

313 South Washington Square, 48933-2193
Telephone: 517-371-8100
Telecopier: 517-371-8200
URL: http://www.fosterswift.com
Farmington Hills, Michigan Office: 32300 Northwestern Highway, Suite 230.
Telephone: 248-539-9900.
Fax: 248-851-7504.

Gary J. McRay
Stephen I. Jurmu
James B. Jensen, Jr.
Brian A. Kaser
Louis K. Nigg
Eric E. Doster
Andrea J. Roe

For Complete List of Firm Personnel, See General Section

For full biographical listings, see the Martindale-Hubbell Law Directory

FRASER TREBILCOCK DAVIS & FOSTER, P.C. (AV)

1000 Michigan National Tower, 48933
Telephone: 517-482-5800
Fax: 517-482-0887
URL: http://WWW.FTDF.COM
Detroit, Michigan Office: One Woodward Avenue, Suite 1550.
Telephone: 313-237-7300.
Fax: 313-961-1651.

Robert W. Stocker, II
Stephen L. Burlingame
Iris K. Linder
Michael C. Levine

Counsel for: Beverly Enterprises; Ingham Regional Medical Center; Timberview Village, Inc.; Paragon Health Network, Inc.

For full biographical listings, see the Martindale-Hubbell Law Directory

*MUSKEGON,** Muskegon Co.

LAGUE, NEWMAN & IRISH, A PROFESSIONAL CORPORATION (AV)

600 Terrace Plaza, P.O. Box 389, 49443
Telephone: 231-725-8148
Telecopier: 231-726-3404
Email: firm@lnilaw.com

Eric R. Gielow
Todd L. Helle
Richard C. Lague
William M. Newman
Michael J. Philbrick
J. Scott Timmer

General Counsel: Hackley Hospital & Medical Center; Zeeland Community Hospital; Mecosta County General Hospital; Lakeland Regional Health Systems; Memorial Medical Center; Suburban Heights Medical Center; Kelsey Memorial Hospital; Three Rivers Area Hospital.

For Complete List of Firm Personnel, See General Section

For full biographical listings, see the Martindale-Hubbell Law Directory

ST. CLAIR SHORES, Macomb Co.

SAURBIER, SIEGAN & SANFIELD, P.C. (AV)

Suite 402, 400 Maple Park Boulevard, 48081
Telephone: 810-447-3700
Fax: 810-447-3755
Email: scott@saurbier.com
Detroit Office: 1028 Buhl Building.
Telephone: 313-965-2220.

SHAREHOLDERS

Scott A. Saurbier
Renée S. Siegan
Joel A. Sanfield

Marc D. Saurbier
Lawrence T. Garcia
John C. Valenti
Sara B. Keough
David C. Wiegel
Matthew J. Nagaj
Valerie Henning Mock

For full biographical listings, see the Martindale-Hubbell Law Directory

SOUTHFIELD, Oakland Co.

SOMMERS, SCHWARTZ, SILVER & SCHWARTZ, P.C. (AV)

2000 Town Center, Suite 900, 48075
Telephone: 248-355-0300
Telecopier: 248-746-4001
Plymouth, Michigan Office: 747 South Main Street.
Telephone: 313-455-4250.

Steven J. Schwartz
James J. Vlasic

General Counsel for: City of Taylor; Foodland Distributors; C.A. Muer Corporation; Vlasic & Company; Nederlander Corporation; Midwest Health Centers, P.C.
Representative Clients: Michigan National Bank; Universal Underwriters Insurance Co.; Don Lee Distributors; Rite-Aid of Michigan.

For Complete List of Firm Personnel, See General Section

For full biographical listings, see the Martindale-Hubbell Law Directory

*TRAVERSE CITY,** Grand Traverse Co.

DINGEMAN, DANCER & CHRISTOPHERSON, P.L.C. (AV)

100 Park Street, 49684
Telephone: 231-929-0500
Fax: 231-929-0504
Email: dingeman@dingemandancer.com *URL:* http://www.Dingemandancer.com

James A. Christopherson

Representative Clients: Bay Eye Associates, P.C.; Cardiothoracic Surgeons of Grand Traverse, P.C.; Northern Physicians Insurance Company, Ltd.; Northern Physicians Organization, Inc.; Physicians Management Service Organization, Inc.; Pulmonary & Critical Care of Northwest Michigan, P.C.; Medysis, Inc.; Contact, Inc.; Northern Michigan Surgery Center, L.L.C.; Bay Area Urology, P.C.

For full biographical listings, see the Martindale-Hubbell Law Directory

TROY, Oakland Co.

BARLOW & DERBY (AV)

1450 West Long Lake Road Suite 365, 48098
Telephone: 248-641-3300
Facsimile: 248-641-3305
Email: barlowlan@aol.com

Thomas W. H. Barlow
Matthew S. Derby

ASSOCIATES

Holly Christine Beatty
Christine R. Essique

For full biographical listings, see the Martindale-Hubbell Law Directory

POLING, MCGAW & POLING, P.C. (AV)

Suite 275, 5435 Corporate Drive, 48098
Telephone: 248-641-0500
Telecopier: 248-641-0506
URL: http://www.lawyers.com/polingmcgaw&poling

Benson T. Buck (1926-1989)
Richard B. Poling
D. Douglas McGaw
Richard B. Poling, Jr.
Gregory C. Hamilton
Veronica B. O'Hara
James R. Parker
Shannon M. Acton

OF COUNSEL

Ralph S. Moore

Representative Clients: City of Troy; United States Fidelity & Guaranty Co.; Sentry Insurance Co.; Admiral Insurance; DeMaria Construction Co.; Leo Corporation; Aetna Casualty and Surety Co.; Concord Design; Pneumo-Abex.

For full biographical listings, see the Martindale-Hubbell Law Directory

IMMIGRATION AND NATURALIZATION

ALABAMA

*BIRMINGHAM,** Jefferson Co.

BRADLEY ARANT ROSE & WHITE LLP (AV)

2001 Park Place, Suite 1400, P.O. Box 830709, 35283-0709
Telephone: 205-521-8000
Facsimile: 205-521-8800
Facsimile (SouthTrust Tower Office): 205-521-8500
URL: http://www.barw.com
Huntsville, Alabama Office: 200 Clinton Avenue West, Suite 900, 35801.
Telephone: 205-517-5100.
Facsimile: 205-533-5069.
Washington, D.C. Office: 801 Pennsylvania Avenue, NW, Suite 230, 20004.
Telephone: 202-347-8893.
Facsimile: 202-347-1684.

MEMBER OF FIRM

G. Edward Cassady III

For Complete List of Firm Personnel, See General Section

For full biographical listings, see the Martindale-Hubbell Law Directory

ARIZONA

MESA, Maricopa Co.

BRENT M. GUNDERSON, P.C. (AV)

123 North Centennial Way, Suite 122, 85201
Telephone: 602-655-7440
Fax: 602-655-7099
Email: Brent.Gunderson@azbar.org *URL:* http://www.lawyers.com/gundersonlaw

Brent M. Gunderson

For full biographical listings, see the Martindale-Hubbell Law Directory

*PHOENIX,** Maricopa Co.

BACON & DEAR, PLC (AV)

340 East Palm Lane, Suite 240, 85004
Telephone: 602-256-6700
Fax: 602-257-0600

MEMBERS

Roxana C. Bacon — Diane M. Dear

ASSOCIATES

Eric R. Bowman (Not admitted in AZ) — Danielle L. Ventura

For full biographical listings, see the Martindale-Hubbell Law Directory

FENNEMORE CRAIG, A PROFESSIONAL CORPORATION (AV)

3003 North Central Avenue, Suite 2600, 85012-2913
Telephone: 602-916-5000
Fax: 602-916-5999
Tucson, Arizona Office: One South Church Avenue, Suite 1000, 85701-1620.
Telephone: 520-879-6800.
Fax: 520-879-6899.

Christopher P. Staring

Jeffrey S. Silvyn

For Complete List of Firm Personnel, See General Section

For full biographical listings, see the Martindale-Hubbell Law Directory

VLASSIS & VLASSIS (AV)

1545 West Thomas Road, 85015
Telephone: 602-248-8811
Fax: 602-274-8983
Email: vlassis@compuserve.com *URL:* http://www.lawyers.com/vlassis&vlassis

George P. Vlassis — Elizabeth D. Vlassis

References: Bank One; First Star Metropolitan Bank & Trust.

For full biographical listings, see the Martindale-Hubbell Law Directory

CALIFORNIA

IRVINE, Orange Co.

LAW OFFICES OF JOHN R. ALCORN (AV)

2010 Main, Suite 840, 92614
Telephone: 949-553-8LAW
Fax: 949-553-8550
Email: immigration-usa@jr-alcorn.com *URL:* http://www.jr-alcorn.com
Chicago, Illinois Office: 203 North La Salle Street, Suite 2100, 60601.
Telephone: 312-558-1788.
Fax: 312-558-3106.

LEGAL SUPPORT PERSONNEL

Audrey T. Ishibashi (Paralegal) — Amy Lauren Gettys

For full biographical listings, see the Martindale-Hubbell Law Directory

OSWALD & YAP, A PROFESSIONAL CORPORATION (AV)

16148 Sand Canyon Avenue, 92618
Telephone: 949-788-8900
Telefax: 949-788-8980
URL: http://www.oswald-yap.com

Michael A. Oswald — Niall Sweetnam
Calvin C.S. Yap — Mark D. Holmes

Tzong-Bing Tsai — Edward W. Russey, III
Joseph A. Weber — Richard T. Hsueh
Carol A. Gefis

OF COUNSEL

John W. Allured — Reed M. Williams

For full biographical listings, see the Martindale-Hubbell Law Directory

PAPARELLI & PARTNERS LLP (AV)

4 Park Plaza, Suite 200, 92614-8560
Telephone: 949-955-5555
Fax: 949-955-5599
Email: kmo@entertheusa.com

Angelo A. Paparelli — Monica E. Lukoschek
J. Ira Burkemper

ASSOCIATES

Suzanne G. Brummett — Yoshiko I. Robertson
Martine Pigeaud (Not admitted in CA) — Theresa A. Fisher

For full biographical listings, see the Martindale-Hubbell Law Directory

*LOS ANGELES,** Los Angeles Co.

BONAPARTE & MIYAMOTO, A PROFESSIONAL LAW CORPORATION (AV)

11911 San Vicente Boulevard, Suite 355, 90049
Telephone: 310-471-3481
FAX: 310-471-1686
Email: 73344.441@Compuserve.com *URL:* http://www.lawyers.com/bonapartelaw
Other Los Angeles Office: 919 South Grand Avenue, Suite 208E.
Telephone: 213-688-8872.
FAX: 213-688-8887.
Newport Beach, California Office: 5030 Campus Drive.
Telephone: 949-955-2012.
FAX: 949-833-1423.

Ronald H. Bonaparte — Lynn Miyamoto

Thomas E. Cummings

For full biographical listings, see the Martindale-Hubbell Law Directory

RALPH EHRENPREIS A PROFESSIONAL LAW CORPORATION (AV)

Suite 450, 1801 Century Park East, 90067
Telephone: 310-553-6600
Telefax: 310-553-2616
Cable Address: "Immlaw"
Email: ehrenpreis@earthlink.net *URL:* http://www.lawyers.com/ehrenpreis

Ralph Ehrenpreis

Bernard J. Lurie

References: City National Bank (Beverly Hills Office, Beverly Hills, California); Great American Bank (Century City Office, Los Angeles, California).

For full biographical listings, see the Martindale-Hubbell Law Directory

Los Angeles—Continued

IVENER & HOLT LLP (AV)

11601 Wilshire Boulevard, Suite 1430, 90025
Telephone: 310-477-3000
Fax: 310-477-2652
Email: mark@ivener.com *URL:* http://www.ilw.com/ivener
Canadian Associate Office: 1300-808 Nelson Street, Vancouver, British Columbia V6Z 2H2.
Telephone: 604-688-0558.
FAX: 604-685-8972.
Japanese Associate Office: 13th Floor Urbannet Otemachi Building, 2-2-2 Otemachi, Chiyoda-Ku, Tokyo 100-0004, Japan.
Telephone: 813-3231-8888.
Fax: 813-3231-8881.

Mark A. Ivener
Rebecca L. Holt

OF COUNSEL

Lawrence F. Liebenbaum

For full biographical listings, see the Martindale-Hubbell Law Directory

JOHN A. JOANNES A PROFESSIONAL CORPORATION (AV)

11911 San Vicente Boulevard Suite 375, 90049
Telephone: 310-440-4240
Facsimile: 310-471-2862
Email: jjoannespc@aol.com *URL:* http://www.usvisa.cjb.net

John A. Joannes

OF COUNSEL

Stephen L. Teller

For full biographical listings, see the Martindale-Hubbell Law Directory

O'MELVENY & MYERS LLP (AV)

400 South Hope Street, 90071-2899
Telephone: 213-430-6000
Facsimile: 213-430-6407
Cable: MOMS
Telex: 674122
Email: omminfo@omm.com *URL:* http://www.omm.com
Century City, CA Office: 1999 Avenue of the Stars, Los Angeles, 90067-6035.
Telex: 674097. Tel: 310-553-6700.
Fax: 310-246-6779.
Newport Beach, CA Office: 610 Newport Center Drive, 92660-6429.
Telex: 4722088. Tel: 949-760-9600.
Fax: 949-823-6994.
San Francisco, CA Office: Embarcadero Center West, 275 Battery Street, 94111-3305. Tel: 415-984-8700.
Fax: 415-984-8701.
New York, NY Office: Citicorp Center, 153 East 53rd Street, 10022-4611.
Telex: 129165. Tel: 212-326-2000.
Fax: 212-326-2061.
Washington, DC Office: 555 13th Street, N.W., 20004-1109.
Cable: MOMSWSH.
Telex: 89622. Tel: 202-383-5300.
Fax: 202-383-5414.
London Office: O'Melveny & Myers, 3 Finsbury Square, London, EC2A 1LA, England. Tel: 44-171-256-8451. Fax 44-171-638-8205.
Tokyo Office: Akasaka Twin Tower, East 14F, 2-17-23, Akasaka, Minato-ku, Tokyo 107-0052, Japan. Tel: 03-5562-2800.
Fax: 03-5575-3840.
Hong Kong Office: O'Melveny & Myers, Suite 1905, Tower Two, Lippo Centre, 89 Queensway, Central, Hong Kong. Tel: 852-2523-8266.
Fax: 852-2522-1760.
Shanghai Office: Kerry Centre, 20F, 1515 Nanjing Road West, Shanghai, 200040 People's Republic of China. Tel: 86-21-5298-5600.
Fax: 86-21-5298-5500.

OF COUNSEL

Lowell C. Martindale, Jr. (Newport Beach and San Francisco, CA Offices)

For Complete List of Firm Personnel, See General Section

For full biographical listings, see the Martindale-Hubbell Law Directory

LAW OFFICES OF CARL SHUSTERMAN (AV)

One Wilshire Building, 624 South Grand Avenue, Suite 1608, 90017
Telephone: 213-623-4592
Fax: 213-623-3720
Email: carl@shusterman.com *URL:* http://www.shusterman.com

ASSOCIATES

Elahe Najfabadi
Ellen Ma Lee
Elif Keles (Not admitted in CA)

For full biographical listings, see the Martindale-Hubbell Law Directory

BERNARD P. WOLFSDORF A PROFESSIONAL CORPORATION (AV)

17383 Sunset Boulevard, Suite 120 (Pacific Palisades), 90272
Telephone: 310-573-4242
FAX: 310-573-5093
Email: visalaw@wolfsdorf.com *URL:* http://www.wolfsdorf.com

Bernard P. Wolfsdorf

Michele A. Buchanan
Stephen M. Dewar (Not admitted in CA)
Michael S. Greenbaum (Not admitted in CA)
Avi Friedman
Rita Kushner (Not admitted in CA)
Ilana Smith
Tien-Li Loke Walsh

OF COUNSEL

C. Daniel Levy

Representative Clients: Twentieth Century Fox Film Corp.; Sony Corp.; Teradyne, Inc.; Bax Global, Inc.; Cedars Sinai Medical Center; UCLA-School of Medicine; No Fear, Inc.; LA Models; Klasky-Csupo, Inc.; Jose-Eber Hair Salons.

For full biographical listings, see the Martindale-Hubbell Law Directory

NEWPORT BEACH, Orange Co.

HIRSON WEXLER PERL & STARK, A PROFESSIONAL CORPORATION (AV)

4685 MacArthur Court, Suite 400, 92660
Telephone: 949-251-8844
Fax: 949-251-1545
Email: hwps@hwps.com *URL:* http://www.hwps.com
Los Angeles Office: 6310 San Vicente Boulevard, Suite 415.
Telephone: 323-936-0200.
Fax: 323-936-4488. Email: hwps-la@hwps.com.
San Diego Office: 8899 University Center Lane, Suite 310.
Telephone: 858-452-5700.
Fax: 858-452-1911. Email: hwps-sd@hwps.com.
Phoenix, Arizona Office: 3443 North Central Avenue, Suite 706.
Telephone: 602-266-4700.
Fax: 602-265-8108. Email: hwps-az@hwps.com.
Las Vegas, Nevada Office: 3753 Howard Hughes Parkway, 200 Las Vegas.
Telephone: 702-737-5414.
Fax: 702-792-5107. Email: hwps-lv@hwps.com.
New York, New York Office: 140 Broadway, Forty-Sixth Floor.
Telephone: 212-509-4921.
Fax: 212-509-4923. Email: hwps-ny@hwps.com.

David Hirson
Mitchell L. Wexler
Gary B. Perl (Resident, San Diego Office)
Joanne Trifilo Stark (Resident, Phoenix, Arizona and Las Vegas, Nevada Offices)
David T. Huang (Not admitted in CA)

David B. Raft
Catherine I. Mayou
Thomas J. Joy (Resident, Los Angeles Office)
Dare F. Delano
Marlene Z. Stanger

OF COUNSEL

Lance Kaplan

For full biographical listings, see the Martindale-Hubbell Law Directory

*SAN DIEGO,** San Diego Co.

NANCY FULLER-JACOBS & ASSOCIATES (AV)

11512 El Camino Real, Suite 200, 92130
Telephone: 619-259-4875
Fax: 619-259-4752
Email: nfjlaw@cts.com *URL:* http://www.lawyers.com/nfj&alaw

ASSOCIATES

Karine Faure
E. Franklin Haignere

For full biographical listings, see the Martindale-Hubbell Law Directory

*SAN FRANCISCO,** San Francisco Co.

LAW OFFICES JACK I. KAISER (AV)

633 Battery Street, Sixth Floor, 94111-1809
Telephone: 415-986-4444
Facsimile: 415-986-7224

ASSOCIATE

Nancy J. Kubasek

For full biographical listings, see the Martindale-Hubbell Law Directory

*SAN JOSE,** Santa Clara Co.

MARGARET ANN REDMOND (AV)

Suite 318, 95 South Market Street, 95113
Telephone: 408-977-7730
Fax: 408-977-7731
Email: redmondatty@earthlink.net *URL:* http://www.lawyers.com/margaretannredmond

For full biographical listings, see the Martindale-Hubbell Law Directory

STUDIO CITY, Los Angeles Co.

THE MILLER LAW OFFICES (AV)

12441 Ventura Boulevard, 91604
Telephone: 818-508-9005
Fax: 818-508-9458
Email: info@millerlawoffices.com *URL:* http://www.millerlawoffices.com

Charles M. Miller
Terri Senesac Miller

John M. Levant

For full biographical listings, see the Martindale-Hubbell Law Directory

COLORADO

*DENVER,** Denver Co.

ANN ALLOTT A PROFESSIONAL CORPORATION (AV)

Suite 260, 2305 East Arapahoe Road (Littleton), 80122
Telephone: 303-797-8055
Fax: 303-797-6136
Email: usimmlaw@allott.com *URL:* http://www.allott.com

Ann Allott

Barbara L. Widick

LEGAL SUPPORT PERSONNEL

Todd Irwin (Associate Paralegal)
Cindy Conti (Paralegal)
Barbara Mathews (Paralegal)
Kerry Paolillo (Legal Assistant)
Adrianne Pachedras (Legal Assistant)

For full biographical listings, see the Martindale-Hubbell Law Directory

C. JAMES COOPER (AV)

Citywide Bank Building, 12075 East 45th Avenue, Suite 315, 80239-3128
Telephone: 303-371-1822
Fax: 303-373-1822
Email: 73344.77@compuserve.com *URL:* http://www.lawyers.com/cjcooper
References: First Interstate Bank of Denver; City Wide Bank of Denver.

For full biographical listings, see the Martindale-Hubbell Law Directory

LAW OFFICES OF RUMI ENGINEER (AV)

333 W. Hampden Avenue, Suite 703 (Englewood), 80110
Telephone: 303-781-4855
Fax: 303-789-5329
Email: rengineer@compuserve.com

For full biographical listings, see the Martindale-Hubbell Law Directory

ROBERT G. HEISERMAN, P.C. (AV)

Suite 2280, World Trade Center, 1675 Broadway, 80202
Telephone: 303-629-1065
Toll Free: 800-873-3302
Fax: 303-623-1710
Email: 73032.61@compuserve.com
Aspen, Colorado Office: 950 Matchless Drive, P.O. Box 10630.
Telephone: 970-925-2702.

Robert G. Heiserman

Barbara H. Lutes
Douglas R. Penn

Reference: Norwest Bank, Denver, N.A.

For full biographical listings, see the Martindale-Hubbell Law Directory

DISTRICT OF COLUMBIA

WASHINGTON, D.C. Co.

CARLINER, REMES AND MIRBAGHERI-SMITH, P.C. (AV)

Suite 903, 1700 K Street, N.W., 20006
Telephone: 202-223-0050
Fax: 202-223-0052
Email: info@carliner-remes.com *URL:* http://www.carliner-remes.com

David Carliner
Robert A. Remes
Ladan Mirbagheri Smith

Panravee Vongjaroenrat (Not admitted in DC)

For full biographical listings, see the Martindale-Hubbell Law Directory

KRUPIN GREENBAUM & O'BRIEN, LLC (AV)

1156 15th Street, NW Suite 200, 20005
Telephone: 202-530-0700
Fax: 202-530-0703
URL: http://www.KGOLaw.com

Jay P. Krupin
Jonathan W. Greenbaum
James J. O'Brien
Caryn G. Pass
Alison J. Hurewitz
Adrian Van Nelson II (Not admitted in DC)

COUNSEL

Jeffrey A. Spector

Kimberley Ann Best (Not admitted in DC)
Erica D. Brown
Scott V. Kamins (Not admitted in DC)
Sidney E. Lebowitz (Not admitted in DC)
Manesh K. Rath
D. Jay Sumner (Not admitted in DC)
Monique A. van Stiphout (Not admitted in DC)
Hollie R. Vona (Not admitted in DC)
Teresa Burke Wright

For full biographical listings, see the Martindale-Hubbell Law Directory

MAGGIO & KATTAR, P.C. (AV)

Eleven Dupont Circle, N.W., Suite 775, 20036
Telephone: 202-483-0053
FAX: 202-483-6801
Email: inquire@maggio-kattar.com *URL:* http://www.maggio-kattar.com

Michael Maggio

Alison J. Brown (Not admitted in DC)
Elizabeth A. Quinn (Not admitted in DC)
Atessa Chehrazi (Not admitted in DC)
James Alexander (Not admitted in DC)

For full biographical listings, see the Martindale-Hubbell Law Directory

WASSERMAN, MANCINI & CHANG (AV)

1915 Eye Street, N.W., Suite 400, 20006
Telephone: 202-783-8905
Fax: 202-333-1688
URL: http://www.lawyers.com/wassermanmancini&chang

MEMBERS OF FIRM

Jack Wasserman (1913-1980)
Mark A. Mancini
Sam Hsien-Cheng Chang

ASSOCIATES

Joan Jacqueline Karaganis (Not admitted in DC)
Richard W. Chang
Sonal J. Mehta (Not admitted in DC)

Reference: First American Bank, Washington, D.C.

For full biographical listings, see the Martindale-Hubbell Law Directory

PALMA R. YANNI (AV)

2612 P Street, N.W., 20007
Telephone: 202-338-1995
Fax: 202-338-1994
Email: palma-yanni@mindspring.com *URL:* http://www.palma-yanni.com

LEGAL SUPPORT PERSONNEL

Ninoska Herrera

For full biographical listings, see the Martindale-Hubbell Law Directory

FLORIDA

*FORT LAUDERDALE,** Broward Co.

HARRY D. POLATSEK, P.A. (AV⊕)

Suite 1216 The International Building, 2455 East Sunrise Boulevard, 33304
Telephone: 954-566-0377
Telefax: 954-566-0526
Email: polatsek@compuserve.com *URL:* http://ilw.com/polatsek
Coral Gables, Florida Office: 220 Alhambra Circle, Suite 810.
Telephone: 954-566-0377.
Lake Worth, Florida Office: 508 Lucerne Avenue.
Telephone: 561-585-7353.

Harry D. Polatsek
Christopher A. Wilburn
Franklin A. Blanco
(Not admitted in FL)
Stephen R. Kain
Frederick A. Polatsek

For full biographical listings, see the Martindale-Hubbell Law Directory

HOLLYWOOD, Broward Co.

MAZEN M. SUKKAR, P.A. (AV)

2432 Hollywood Boulevard, 33020
Telephone: 954-922-2836
Fax: 954-923-1990

Mazen M. Sukkar

*MIAMI,** Dade Co.

BANDER, FOX-ISICOFF & ASSOCIATES, P.A. (AV)

Rivergate Plaza, Suite 300, 444 Brickell Avenue, 33131
Telephone: Dade: 305-358-5800
Fax: 305-374-6593
Email: banderfox@banderfox.com

Michael A. Bander
Tammy Fox-Isicoff

Leonard Storchevoy
Joshua Bratter

For full biographical listings, see the Martindale-Hubbell Law Directory

BRAUWERMAN & ASSOCIATES, P.A. (AV)

1000 Brickell Avenue, Suite 1040, 33131
Telephone: 305-758-1234
Telecopier: 305-576-6251
Mailing Address: 1776 North Pine Island Road, Suite 208, Fort Lauderdale, 33322
Email: visas@brauwermanlaw.com *URL:* http://www.brauwermanlaw.com
Fort Lauderdale, Florida Office: Suite 208, 1776 North Pine Island Road, 33322.
Telephone: 954-527-1234.
Telecopier: 954-424-8935.

Jeffrey N. Brauwerman
Suzan C. Brauwerman

Bradley O. June
Mildred Morgado

For full biographical listings, see the Martindale-Hubbell Law Directory

RIFKIN AND ASSOCIATES, P.A. (AV)

1110 Brickell Avenue, Suite 210, 33131
Telephone: 305-371-2777
Facsimile: 305-375-9517
Email: lsrifkin@bellsouth.net
Orlando, Florida Office: Day Building, Suite 100, 605 East Robinson Street, 32801.
Telephone: 407-425-8472.
Fax: 407-426-8440.

Larry S. Rifkin

Cecilia M. Olavarria
Rosemary Lopez

LEGAL SUPPORT PERSONNEL

Michelle M. Ramos, Director, Immigration Practice Group

For full biographical listings, see the Martindale-Hubbell Law Directory

*TAMPA,** Hillsborough Co.

MANEY & GORDON, P.A. (AV)

Nationsbank Plaza, 101 East Kennedy Boulevard, Suite 3170, 33602-5152
Telephone: 813-221-1366
Fax: 813-223-5920
Email: rhmaney@gte.net *URL:* http://www.richardmaney.com
Other Tampa Office: Immigration Center, 5509 W. Gray Street, Suite 211, 33609.

(See Next Column)

Orlando, Florida Office: 9415 Tradeport Drive, 32827.
Telephone: 407-851-4083.
Fax: 407-851-4083.

Richard Henry Maney
Jeffrey Lee Gordon

Alexander A. Caviedes

For full biographical listings, see the Martindale-Hubbell Law Directory

WINTER PARK, Orange Co.

EDWARD C. BESHARA, P.A. (AV)

Lee World Center, 1850 Lee Road, Suite 300, 32789
Telephone: 407-629-6455
Fax: 407-629-4569
URL: http://www.visaentryusa.com
Email: ebesh@worldnet.att.net *URL:* http://www.lawyers.com/visaentryusa

Edward Charles Beshara

Representative Clients: Sunshine Seven Tours; Grande Journeys; Laser Photonics Inc.; Walter Lorens Surgical; AmSouth Bank; Impro Data Technology; Visa Entry USA Foundation.

For full biographical listings, see the Martindale-Hubbell Law Directory

GEORGIA

*ATLANTA,** Fulton Co.

ELARBEE, THOMPSON & TRAPNELL, LLP (AV)

800 International Tower, 229 Peachtree Street, N.E., 30303
Telephone: 404-659-6700
Fax: 404-222-9718
Email: info@elarbeethompson.com *URL:* http://www.elarbeethompson.com

MEMBERS OF FIRM

Fred W. Elarbee, Jr. (1925-1986)
Robert L. Thompson
John R. Trapnell
David M. Vaughan
John Lewis Sapp
William M. Earnest
Walter O. Lambeth, Jr.
Joseph M. Freeman
Stanford G. Wilson
Brent L. Wilson
Victor A. Cavanaugh
Nancy F. Reynolds
Sharon Parker Morgan
Mark D. Halverson
R. Read Gignilliat
Douglas H. Duerr
Victor J. Maya
William Drummond Deveney
Kelly Michael Hundley

ASSOCIATES

Patrick L. Lail
Kenneth N. Winkler
Laura K. Johnson
G. Cornelius Nevitt
Scott E. Atwood
Alisa L. Pittman
Richard M. Escoffery
C. Shawn Jones
Jeffrey B. Kent
Lance P. McMillian
Annette A. Idalski
Nicole A. Richardson

Representative Clients: Cox Communications, Inc.; Dunlop Tire Corp.; National Service Industries; Atlanta Gas Light Co.; Brown & Williamson Tobacco Corp.; Engelhard Corp.; Louisiana-Pacific Corp.; MCI WorldCom; Florida Power and Light Co.; Southwire Co.

For full biographical listings, see the Martindale-Hubbell Law Directory

LONG ALDRIDGE & NORMAN LLP (AV)

A Limited Liability Partnership including Professional Corporations
Suite 5300, 303 Peachtree Street, 30308
Telephone: 404-527-4000
Telecopier: 404-527-4198
Email: atlanta@lanlaw.com *URL:* http://www.lanlaw.com
Washington, D.C. Office: Suite 600, 701 Pennsylvania Avenue, N.W., 20004.
Telephone: 202-624-1200.
FAX: 202-624-1298.

MEMBERS OF FIRM

James D. Levine
Henry F. Sewell, Jr.

ASSOCIATES

Daniel H. Sherman IV
Robert Todd Silliman

For Complete List of Firm Personnel, See General Section

For full biographical listings, see the Martindale-Hubbell Law Directory

McCULLOUGH SHERRILL, LLP (AV)

1409 Peachtree Street, N.E., 30309
Telephone: 404-885-1500
Telecopier: 404-892-1801
Email: info@mslegal.com *URL:* http://www.mslegal.com

(See Next Column)

McCullough Sherrill LLP—*Continued*

MEMBER OF FIRM

James W. King

ASSOCIATE

Susan T. Craighead

For Complete List of Firm Personnel, See General Section

For full biographical listings, see the Martindale-Hubbell Law Directory

Powell, Goldstein, Frazer & Murphy LLP (AV)

191 Peachtree Street, N.E., Sixteenth Floor, 30303
Telephone: 404-572-6600
Telecopier: 404-572-6999
URL: http://www.pgfm.com
Washington, D.C. Office: Sixth Floor, 1001 Pennsylvania Avenue, N.W., 20004.
Telephone: 202-347-0066.

COUNSEL

Rebecca L. Sigmund

Representative Clients: Nedlloyd Lines (USA), Inc.; CSR America, Inc.; Miescor (USA), Inc.; The Fuji Bank-Atlanta, Limited; Kubota Manufacturing Corporation of America, Inc.

For Complete List of Firm Personnel, See General Section

For full biographical listings, see the Martindale-Hubbell Law Directory

Schwartz Kuck & Associates LLP (AV)

Suite 450 - RiverEdge One, 5500 Interstate North Parkway, 30328-4662
Telephone: 770-951-1100
Facsimile: 770-951-1113
Email: dale@immlawfirm.com; ckuck@immlawfirm.com
URL: http://www.lawyers.com/schwartzkuck&associates
URL: http://www.immlawfirm.com

Dale M. Schwartz
Charles H. Kuck

ASSOCIATE

Andrea F. Rahal

LEGAL SUPPORT PERSONNEL

Katherine M. Griffin (Paralegal)
Elaine M. Stice (Paralegal)
Deborah Haven (Paralegal Assistant)
Susan Oross (Paralegal)
Lauren Karseboom (Paralegal)
Susan Anderson (Paralegal)
Patricia Lamoreau (Office Manager/Paralegal)

For full biographical listings, see the Martindale-Hubbell Law Directory

HAWAII

*HONOLULU,** Honolulu Co.

Carlsmith Ball (AV)

A Partnership including Law Corporations
Suite 2200, Pacific Tower, 1001 Bishop Street, P.O. Box 656, 96809-3402
Telephone: 808-523-2500
Fax: 808-523-0842
Email: execdirector@carlsmith.com *URL:* http://www.carlsmith.com
Kapolei, Hawaii Office: Suite 318, Kapolei Building, 1001 Kamokila Boulevard, 96707.
Telephone: 808-523-2500.
Fax: 808-674-0850.
Wailuku, Maui Hawaii Office: Suite 400, One Main Plaza, 2200 Main Street, P.O. Box 1086, 96793-1086.
Telephone: 808-242-4535.
Fax: 808-244-4974.
Kailua-Kona, Hawaii Office: Suite 209, 75-1000 Henry Street, 96740.
Telephone: 808-329-6464.
Fax: 808-329-9450.
Hilo, Hawaii Office: 121 Waianuenue Avenue, P.O. Box 686, 96721-0686.
Telephone: 808-935-6644.
Fax: 808-935-7975.
Hagatna, Guam Office: Suite 401, Bank of Hawaii Building, 134 West Soledad Avenue, P.O. Box BF, 96932-5027.
Telephone: 671-472-6813.
Fax: 671-477-4375.
Telex: 721-6445 CWCMI GM.
Saipan, Commonwealth of the Northern Mariana Islands Office: Carlsmith Building, Capitol Hill, P.O. Box 5241, 96950-5241.
Telephone: 670-322-3455.
Fax: 670-322-3368.
Los Angeles, California Office: 9th Floor, 444 South Flower Street, 90071-2901.
Telephone: 213-955-1200.
Fax: 213-623-0032.

(See Next Column)

Washington, D.C. Office: Suite 300, 1201 Pennsylvania Avenue, N.W., 20004-2401.
Telephone: 202-628-2228.
Fax: 202-628-2071.
Mexico City, Mexico Office: Carlsmith Ball, Sierra Nevada 119, Lomas de Chapultepec, 11000 Mexico, D.F.
Telephone: 52-5-520-8514, 52-5-520-8757.
Fax: 52-5-540-1545.
Mexico, D.F. Office of Carlsmith Ball, S.C. (Authorized to practice as foreign legal consultants in Mexico): Sierra Nevada 119, Lomas de Chapultepec, 11000 Mexico, D.F.
Telephone: 52-5-520-8514, 52-5-520-8757.
Fax: 52-5-540-1545.

MEMBERS OF FIRM

Lance F. Taniguchi
Sinforoso M. Tolentino (Resident at Hagatna, Guam Office)

For Complete List of Firm Personnel, See General Section

For full biographical listings, see the Martindale-Hubbell Law Directory

Goodsill Anderson Quinn & Stifel (AV)

Alii Place, Suite 1800, 1099 Alakea Street, P.O. Box 3196, 96801-3196
Telephone: 808-547-5600
FAX: 808-547-5880
Email: info@goodsill.com *URL:* http://www.goodsill.com

MEMBERS OF FIRM

Peter T. Kashiwa
Alan S. Fujimoto

COUNSEL

Alan W. C. Ma

ASSOCIATE

KahBo Dye-Chiew

For Complete List of Firm Personnel, See General Section

For full biographical listings, see the Martindale-Hubbell Law Directory

ILLINOIS

AURORA, Kane Co.

Murphy, Hupp, Foote, Mielke and Kinnally (AV)

North Island Center, P.O. Box 5030, 60507
Telephone: 630-844-0056
Fax: 630-844-1905
Email: mhfmk@insnet.com

MEMBERS OF FIRM

Robert B. Hupp
Patrick M. Kinnally

Representative Clients: American Telephone & Telegraph Co.; Fox Valley Park District; Lyon Metal Products; Kane County Forest Preserve District; Hollywood Casino; Employers Mutual Insurance Co.; Forty-Eight Insulations, Inc.; UNR Asbestos Disease Trust; Richards-Wilcox Co.; National Bank & Trust Company of Syracuse.

For Complete List of Firm Personnel, See General Section

For full biographical listings, see the Martindale-Hubbell Law Directory

*CHICAGO,** Cook Co.

Douglas Bristol (AV)

321 South Plymouth Court, Suite 1525, 60604-3912
Telephone: 312-663-4466
Fax: 312-663-5252

For full biographical listings, see the Martindale-Hubbell Law Directory

Gessler, Hughes & Socol, Ltd. (AV)

Three First National Plaza, Suite 2200, 60602
Telephone: 312-580-0100
Telecopy: 312-580-1994

Benjamin P. Beringer
Anjali Dayal
Mark S. Dym
George W. Gessler
John K. Hughes
Joshua Karsh
Peter M. Katsaros
Kimberley Marsh
Alex W. Miller
Terence J. Moran
Matthew J. Piers
Kalman D. Resnick
Frederick S. Rhine
Jonathan A. Rothstein
Michael P. Simkus
Donna Kaner Socol

Gary Chodorow
Ruth M. Dunning
S. Todd Neal
Mark A. Pellegrino
Steven C. Steinback
Dana H. Sukenik
J. Eric Vander Arend
Mark B. Weiner
Charles H. Wintersteen

(See Next Column)

GESSLER, HUGHES & SOCOL LTD., *Chicago—Continued*

OF COUNSEL

Darius S. Francescatti, M.D. Susan R. Gzesh

For full biographical listings, see the Martindale-Hubbell Law Directory

MANDEL, LIPTON AND STEVENSON LIMITED (AV)

Suite 2900, 120 North La Salle Street, 60602
Telephone: 312-236-7080
Facsimile: 312-236-0781

Alfred R. Lipton
Leonard M. Malkin
R. Peter Carey
Henry A. Waller
Kathleen Roseborough
Richard A. Lifshitz
Terry Yale Feiertag
Uve R. Jerzy
Carolyn E. Winter
Leo G. Aubel

Andrés J. Gallegos
Jennifer R. Shapiro
Joan Comiskey

OF COUNSEL

Richard L. Mandel Nicholas Stevenson

LEGAL SUPPORT PERSONNEL

Jacqueline Steffens (Paralegal)

References: Northern Trust Co.; American National Bank of Chicago; La Salle Bank FSB.

For full biographical listings, see the Martindale-Hubbell Law Directory

MINSKY, MCCORMICK & HALLAGAN, P.C. (AV)

122 South Michigan Avenue, Suite 1800, 60603
Telephone: 312-427-6163
Fax: 312-427-6513

Joseph Minsky (1925-1992)
Margaret H. McCormick
James Hallagan
Carlina Tapia-Ruano

Sandra Valenzuela
Patricia S. Davis
Stephen J. Navarre
Kathy Ko

INDIANA

*INDIANAPOLIS,** Marion Co.

ICE MILLER DONADIO & RYAN (AV)

One American Square Box 82001, 46282-0002
Telephone: 317-236-2100
Fax: 317-236-2219
Email: info@imdr.com *URL:* http://www.imdr.com
South Bend, Indiana Office: 211 West Washington Street, Suite 2420.
Telephone: 219-234-7933.
Fax: 219-234-7965. Internet E-mail: info@imdr.com. Web Site Address: http://www.imdr.com.
Chicago, Illinois Office: 135 South LaSalle Street, Suite 4100.
Telephone: 312-726-1567.
Fax: 312-641-6263. Internet E-mail: info@imdr.com. Web Site Address: http://www.imdr.com.

MEMBERS OF FIRM

Richard E. Parker
Thomas H. Ristine
Dale E. Stackhouse

STAFF ATTORNEY

Mikio Nishizu

ASSOCIATE

Maria Paula Poggio (Not admitted in IN)

Representative Clients: Aisin Seiki; Allegiant Technology; Delco Remy America; Indiana Precision Technology; Newcourt Credit Group, Inc.; Ontario Corp; Pac West Racing; Technisource; Thomson Consumer Electronics; Wavetek Wandel & Goltermann.

For Complete List of Firm Personnel, See General Section

For full biographical listings, see the Martindale-Hubbell Law Directory

LEWIS & KAPPES, PROFESSIONAL CORPORATION (AV)

Suite 1700 One American Square, P.O. Box 82053, 46282-0003
Telephone: 317-639-1210
Telecopier: 317-639-4882
Email: Office@Lewis-Kappes.com *URL:* http://www.Lewis-Kappes.com

(See Next Column)

Ted B. Lewis (1919-1991)
Philip S. Kappes
David W. Gray
John F. Wickes, Jr.
Gary P. Price
Steven L. Tuchman
Thomas R. Ruge
M. Kent Newton
C. Duane O'Neal
Brett James Miller
Todd A. Richardson
Bette J. Dodd
Peter S. French

Brian Andrew Statz
John A. Broyles
Megan J. Kight
Christopher C. Earle
Jennifer Wheeler Terry
Stephanie Schankerman Forrest

OF COUNSEL

Samuel A. Fuller
Leslie Duvall
Lori Kyle Endris

For full biographical listings, see the Martindale-Hubbell Law Directory

LOUISIANA

METAIRIE, Jefferson Parish

DAVID A. M. WARE & ASSOCIATES (AV)

Two Lakeway Center, 3850 North Causeway Boulevard, Suite 1555, 70002-1752
Telephone: 504-830-5900
Toll Free: 1-800-537-0179
After hours: 504-893-3943
Telefax: 504-830-5909
Email: davware@bellsouth.net *URL:* http://www.David-Ware.com
Baton Rouge, Louisiana Office: Suite C, 11750 Bricksome Avenue.
Telephone: 225-292-9091.
Telefax: 225-296-5401.
Pensacola, Florida Office: 224 E. Government Street.
Telephone: 850-434-6868.
Fax: 850-434-6850.

ASSOCIATE

Marvic Gonzalez Thompson

Representative Clients: Woodward-Clyde; Dover Elevator.

For full biographical listings, see the Martindale-Hubbell Law Directory

*NEW ORLEANS,** Orleans Parish

MCGLINCHEY STAFFORD (AV)

A Professional Limited Liability Company
643 Magazine Street, 70130-3477
Telephone: 504-586-1200
Fax: 504-596-2800
TDD: (504) 596-2728
Telex: 584327
Cable Address: "MACSTAC"
Mailing Address: P.O. Box 60643, New Orleans, Louisiana, 70160-0643
Email: @mcglinchey.com *URL:* http://www.mcglinchey.com
Dallas, Texas Office: 2777 Stemmons Freeway, Suite 925, 75207-2401.
Telephone: 214-860-9700.
Fax: 214-860-9750.
Houston, Texas Office: 2727 Allen Parkway, Suite 1900, 77019.
Telephone: 713-520-1900.
Fax: 713-520-1025.
Baton Rouge, Louisiana Office: Ninth Floor, One American Place, 70825-0001.
Telephone: 504-383-9000.
Fax: 504-343-3076.
Jackson, Mississippi Office: Suite 1200, SkyTel Centre, 200 South Lamar Street, 39201.
Telephone: 601-960-8400.
Fax: 601-960-8406.
Lake Providence, Louisiana Office: 405 Morgan Street, 71254-2691.
Telephone: 318-559-1200.
Fax: 318-559-0609.
Monroe, Louisiana Office: Dean ONB Tower, 130 Desiard Street, Suite 807, 71201.
Telephone: 318-651-0807.
Fax: 318-651-0809.

MEMBERS OF FIRM

Dermot S. McGlinchey (1933-1993)
Graham Stafford (1940-1987)
Samuel Lang (1909-1989)
Colvin G. Norwood, Jr., (P.C.)
David S. Willenzik (P.C.)
Frank Voelker, Jr., (P.C.)
B. Franklin Martin, III, (P.C.)
E. Fredrick Preis, Jr.
Henri Wolbrette, III, (P.C.)
William V. Dalferes, Jr., (P.C.)
Constance Charles Willems
Bennet Scott Koren
James M. Fantaci
Kathleen A. Manning
Kenneth A. Weiss
Donna Guinn Klein
Michael M. Noonan
J. Patrick Beauchamp
Rudy J. Cerone
Anthony Rollo
Craig Lewis Caesar
Eve B. Masinter
Stephen W. Rider

(See Next Column)

McGlinchey Stafford—*Continued*

MEMBERS OF FIRM (Continued)

Eric A. Shuman
Kathleen Krail Charvet
Laura Hobson Brown
Robin Spencer Palmisano
Charles R. Penot, Jr.
Lauren A. Welch
Thomas A. Roberts
Arthur H. Leith
Stephen P. Beiser
Joseph F. Clark, Jr.
Michael J. de Blanc, Jr.
Katherine Conklin
Kevin L. O'Dea
Mark N. Bodin
Richard A. Aguilar
Lisa E. Maurer
Mark N. Mallery
Monica A. Frois
Louis J. Lupin
Anita Lechner Bosch
Susan M. Tyler
John H. Clegg
Daphne McNutt
R. Keith Colvin
Joyce L. Schenewerk

ASSOCIATES

Margaret Woolverton Triebes
Elizabeth P. Blitch
Patrick J. O'Cain
Daniel T. Plunkett
Erin Fury Parkinson
Lauren L. Zimmermann
Deborah A. Van Meter
David Ball
Eliska Marie Plunkett
Deirdre C. McGlinchey
Ann D. Levine
Dwayne C. Jefferson
Sarah Suzanne Wommack Mahoney
Edward L. Fenasci
Joan Marie Canny
Stephanie G. John
Gary G. Hebert
Mindy Brickman Patrón
Denise Langlois Brown
Lance Andrew Bowling
Jonas P. Baker
David S. Landry
Stephanie M. Sisson
John A. Marzullo
Christopher E. Moore (Not admitted in LA)
Eric J. Simonson
Gina M. Venezia
James E. Swinnen
Jaye Andras Caffrey
A. Kelton Longwell
B. Aven Bruser
Julia Haynes Terry (Not admitted in LA)

OF COUNSEL

Joe Giarrusso, Jr.
Margaret G. Diamond
Mary Lynne Friedman

MEMBERS OF FIRM

Michael David Ferachi (Resident, Baton Rouge Office)
Michael H. Rubin (Resident, Baton Rouge Office)
William H. Leech, Sr. (Resident, Jackson Office)
Sue Hicks Fairbank (Resident, Jackson Office)
Robert Marshall Grodner (Resident, Baton Rouge Office)
J. Scott Sheehan (Resident, Houston Office)
Stephen P. Strohschein (Resident, Baton Rouge Office)
Rodolfo J. Aguilar, Jr. (Resident, Baton Rouge Office)
Wilton J. Johnson, III (Resident, Jackson Office)
Mary Terrell Joseph (Resident, Baton Rouge Office)
William S. Mendenhall (Resident, Jackson Office)
Samuel E. Scott (Resident, Jackson Office)
Richard A. Curry (Resident, Baton Rouge Office)
Jennifer Lynn Davis (Resident, Houston Office)
Mark D. Herbert (Resident, Jackson Office)
Joel W. Mohrman (Resident, Houston Office)
Paul S. West (Resident, Baton Rouge Office)
Samuel A. Bacot (Resident, Baton Rouge Office)
Stephen C. Edds (Resident, Jackson Office)
Richard A. Fogel (Resident, Dallas Office)
Mark A. Sanders (Resident, Houston Office)
Errol J. King (Resident, Baton Rouge Office)
James C. Crigler, Jr. (Resident, Lake Providence Office)
Wesson H. Tribble (Resident, Houston Office)
Dan E. West (Resident, Baton Rouge Office)
Deborah J. Bullion-Gascoyne (Resident, Houston Office)
S. Jess Sperry (Resident, Baton Rouge Office)

ASSOCIATES

Jolie S. Lenz (Resident, Houston Office)
Jon Ann H. Giblin (Resident, Baton Rouge Office)
Derrick B. Carson (Resident, Houston Office)
Kathleen H. Eiler (Resident, Jackson Office)
Amy Kebert Elder (Resident, Jackson Office)
Pamela L. Hancock (Resident, Jackson Office)
Jean-Paul Perrault (Resident, Baton Rouge Office)
Claude B. Anello (Resident, Houston Office)
Vincent J. Bodin (Resident, Houston Office)
Donald Ray Cravins, Jr. (Resident, Baton Rouge Office)
David E. Harrell, Jr. (Resident, Houston Office)
Danice L. McKeehan (Resident, Dallas Office)
D. Jeffrey Wagner
Ashley Byrd Lowe (Resident, Baton Rouge Office)
Lisa C. Bingham (Resident, Houston Office)
Renee Gluth (Resident, Baton Rouge Office)
Craig A. Horton (Resident, Houston Office)
Shannon Richards (Resident, Houston Office)

(See Next Column)

ASSOCIATES (Continued)

Virginia M. Todd (Resident, Jackson Office)
Mark H. Tyson (Resident, Jackson Office)
Lindsay Patterson (Resident, Jackson Office)
Amanda K. Bishop
F. Sherman Boughton, Jr. (Resident, Lake Providence Office)

For full biographical listings, see the Martindale-Hubbell Law Directory

Murov & Ward, L.L.C. (AV)

615 Baronne Street Suite 150, 70113
Telephone: 504-523-6100
Fax: 504-524-5240
Email: mail@murov.com *URL:* http://www.ilw.com/murov

Mark G. Murov
Rita K. Ward
Jeremy Scott Zollinger
Jay C. Ruby

Reference: Whitney National Bank, New Orleans, La.

For full biographical listings, see the Martindale-Hubbell Law Directory

MAINE

*PORTLAND,** Cumberland Co.

Pierce Atwood (AV)

One Monument Square, 04101
Telephone: 207-791-1100
Fax: 207-791-1350
Email: info@PierceAtwood.com *URL:* http://www.pierceatwood.com
Augusta, Maine Office: 77 Winthrop Street.
Telephone: 207-622-6311.
Fax: 207-623-9367.
Newburyport, Massachusetts Office: 6 Harris Street.
Telephone: 978-465-9599.
Fax: 978-465-9945.

MEMBERS OF FIRM

Charles S. Einsiedler, Jr.
Anthony R. Derosby

For Complete List of Firm Personnel, See General Section

For full biographical listings, see the Martindale-Hubbell Law Directory

MARYLAND

*BALTIMORE,** (Independent City)

Venable Attorneys at Law Venable, Baetjer and Howard, LLP (AV)

A Partnership including Professional Corporations
1800 Mercantile Bank & Trust Building, 2 Hopkins Plaza, 21201
Telephone: 410-244-7400
Fax: 410-244-7742
URL: http://www.venable.com
Washington, D.C. Office: Venable, Baetjer, Howard & Civiletti LLP, Suite 1000, 1201 New York Avenue, N.W.
Telephone: 202-962-4800.
Fax: 202-962-8300.
McLean, Virginia Office: Suite 400, 2010 Corporate Ridge.
Telephone: 703-760-1600.
Fax: 703-821-8949.
Rockville, Maryland Office: Suite 500, One Church Street, P. O. Box 1906.
Telephone: 301-217-5600.
Fax: 301-217-5617.
Towson, Maryland Office: 210 Allegheny Avenue, P. O. Box 5517.
Telephone: 410-494-6200.
Fax: 410-821-0147.

MEMBERS OF FIRM

Alexander I. Lewis, III (P.C.) (Also at Towson, Maryland Office)
Jana Howard Carey (P.C.)
Maurice Baskin (Resident, Washington, D.C. Office)
Robert Charles Hill (Not admitted in MD; Resident, Washington, D.C. Office)

For Complete List of Firm Personnel, See General Section

For full biographical listings, see the Martindale-Hubbell Law Directory

WHEATON, Montgomery Co.

Johnson & Yang, P.C. (AV)

2730 University Boulevard West, Suite 500, 20902
Telephone: 301-949-0800
Fax: 301-949-6057
Email: ljohnson@hake.com *URL:* http://www.ilw.com/johnson

(See Next Column)

JOHNSON & YANG P.C., *Wheaton—Continued*

Laurence F. Johnson
Yun Jung Yang

Norma Briscoe Hoffpauir
Laura M. Dawkins

LEGAL SUPPORT PERSONNEL

Cesar O. Granados (Legal Assistant)
Jin Joo Kim (Legal Assistant)
Lisa M. Puertas (Office Administrator)

For full biographical listings, see the Martindale-Hubbell Law Directory

MASSACHUSETTS

*BOSTON,** Suffolk Co.

BASTONE ASSOCIATES (AV)

85 Devonshire Street, 02109
Telephone: 617-BAS-TONE; 617-227-3535
Telecopier: 617-720-4927

Lawrence D. Bastone

For full biographical listings, see the Martindale-Hubbell Law Directory

PALMER & DODGE LLP (AV)

One Beacon Street, 02108
Telephone: 617-573-0100
Facsimile: 617-227-4420
URL: http://www.palmerdodge.com

MEMBER OF FIRM

Russell B. Swapp

ASSOCIATES

Dyann DelVecchio
Eileen F. Morrison

For Complete List of Firm Personnel, See General Section

For full biographical listings, see the Martindale-Hubbell Law Directory

GERALD C. ROVNER (AV)

50 Congress Street Suite 500, 02109-4001
Telephone: 617-523-3330
Fax: 617-523-7324
Email: RovnerEsq@AOL.COM

ASSOCIATE

Joy Anne Cahaly

For full biographical listings, see the Martindale-Hubbell Law Directory

WELLESLEY, Norfolk Co.

WHITE & MCDERMOTT, P.C. (AV)

65 William Street, 02481
Telephone: 781-431-1700
Fax: 781-237-8120
Email: mail@WhiteMcD.com

Kevin R. McNamara

LEGAL SUPPORT PERSONNEL

Hilary R. McGregor
Richard L. Pitter

For full biographical listings, see the Martindale-Hubbell Law Directory

MICHIGAN

*ANN ARBOR,** Washtenaw Co.

PIERCE AND HAHN (AV)

An Association of Professional Corporations
709 West Huron Street, Suite 200, 48103
Telephone: 734-769-9191
Fax: 734-747-7450
Email: piercehahn@aol.com

Richard W. Pierce, P.C.
Gary L. Hahn, P.C.

References: Comerica Bank; Key Bank.

For full biographical listings, see the Martindale-Hubbell Law Directory

BATTLE CREEK, Calhoun Co.

KREIS, ENDERLE, CALLANDER & HUDGINS, A PROFESSIONAL CORPORATION (AV)

One West Michigan Avenue, 49017
Telephone: 616-966-3000
Facsimile: 616-966-3022
Email: kech@kech.com *URL:* http://www.kech.com
Kalamazoo, Michigan Office: One Moorsbridge, P.O. Box 4010, 49003-4010.
Telephone: 616-324-3000.
Fax: 616-324-3010.

Douglas L. Callander (Resident, Kalamazoo Office)
John F. Koryto (Resident, Kalamazoo Office)

For Complete List of Firm Personnel, See General Section

For full biographical listings, see the Martindale-Hubbell Law Directory

BLOOMFIELD HILLS, Oakland Co.

HOWARD & HOWARD ATTORNEYS, P.C. (AV)

The Pinehurst Office Center, Suite 101, 1400 North Woodward Avenue, 48304-2855
Telephone: 248-645-1483
Telecopier: 248-645-1568
Kalamazoo, Michigan Office: The Michigan Building, Suite 200, 100 Portage Street.
Telephone: 616-382-1483.
Telecopier: 616-382-1568.
Lansing, Michigan Office: The Phoenix Building, Suite 500, 222 Washington Square, North.
Telephone: 517-485-1483.
Telecopier: 517-485-1568.
Peoria, Illinois Office: One Technology Plaza, Suite 600, 211 Fulton Street.
Telephone: 309-672-1483.
Telecopier: 309-672-1568.

Carol A. Friend
C. Douglas Moran
Jon Robert Steiger
James C. Wickens

Representative Clients: For Representative Client list, see General Practice, Bloomfield Hills, MI.

For Complete List of Firm Personnel, See General Section

For full biographical listings, see the Martindale-Hubbell Law Directory

*DETROIT,** Wayne Co.

BUTZEL LONG, A PROFESSIONAL CORPORATION (AV)

Suite 900, 150 West Jefferson, 48226
Telephone: 313-225-7000
Telecopier: 313-225-7080
Email: melnick@butzel.com *URL:* http://www.butzel.com
Birmingham, Michigan Office: Suite 200, 32270 Telegraph Road.
Telephone: 810-258-1616.
Telecopier: 810-258-1439.
Okemos, Michigan Office: Suite 300, 2127 University Park Drive.
Telephone: 517-372-6622.
Telecopier: 517-372-6672.
Ann Arbor, Michigan Office: Suite 300, 350 South Main Street.
Telephone: 313-995-3110.
Telecopier: 313-995-1777.
Grosse Pointe Farms, Michigan Office: Suite 260, 21 Kercheval.
Telephone: 313-886-5446.
Telecopier: 313-886-2114.
Boca Raton, Florida Office: Suite 411, 1200 North Federal Highway.
Telephone: 561-368-2151.
Telecopier: 561-368-4668.
Palm Beach Gardens, Florida Office: Suite 227, 11382 Prosperity Farms Road.
Telephone: 561-625-4442.
Telecopier: 561-625-6901.
Naples, Florida Office: Suite 705, 801 Laurel Oak Drive.
Telephone: 941-597-4500.
Telecopier: 941-597-5623.

James C. Bruno
Clara DeMatteis Mager
Nicholas J. Stasevich

Debra Auerbach Clephane
Elizabeth A. DuMouchelle
Linda J. Truitt
Christopher L. Wendt

Representative Clients: ABB Robotics; Complete Business Solutions, Inc.; Detroit Diesel Corp.; Kajima International, Inc.; Kelly Services; Michigan National Bank; Takata Corp.; TRW Automotive; The University of Michigan; William Beaumont Hospital.

For full biographical listings, see the Martindale-Hubbell Law Directory

Detroit—Continued

ENGLISH & VAN HORNE, P.C. (AV)

4472 Penobscot Building, 48226
Telephone: 313-961-5100
Email: 73344.1363@compuserve.com

John E. English — Pieter H. van Horne (Retired)

Michael Patrick Nowlan — Lolita Dimovski

OF COUNSEL

Richard W. Pierce, P.C.

Reference: First of America Bank (Main Office Branch), Detroit.

For full biographical listings, see the Martindale-Hubbell Law Directory

*GRAND RAPIDS,** Kent Co.

WARDROP & WARDROP, P.C. (AV)

Suite 150 The Frey Building, 300 Ottawa Avenue, N.W., 49503
Telephone: 616-459-1225
Fax: 616-459-7273
Email: wardrop@wardroplaw.com

Robert F. Wardrop II — Thomas M. Wardrop

Mary Saur Cohn — Brian L. Groen

For full biographical listings, see the Martindale-Hubbell Law Directory

WARNER NORCROSS & JUDD LLP (AV)

900 Old Kent Building, 111 Lyon Street, N.W., 49503-2489
Telephone: 616-752-2000
Fax: 616-752-2500
URL: http://www.wnj.com
Muskegon, Michigan Office: 400 Terrace Plaza, P.O. Box 900.
Telephone: 231-727-2600.
Fax: 231-727-2699.
Holland, Michigan Office: Curtis Center, Suite 300, 170 College Avenue.
Telephone: 616-396-9800.
Fax: 616-396-3656.
Southfield, Michigan Office: 1000 Town Center, Suite 650.
Telephone: 248-223-5000.
Fax: 248-223-5005.

MEMBERS OF FIRM

Janet Percy Knaus — Kathleen M. Hanenburg

ASSOCIATE

Andrea J. Bernard

For full biographical listings, see the Martindale-Hubbell Law Directory

*KALAMAZOO,** Kalamazoo Co.

KREIS, ENDERLE, CALLANDER & HUDGINS, A PROFESSIONAL CORPORATION (AV)

One Moorsbridge, P.O. Box 4010, 49003-4010
Telephone: 616-324-3000
Facsimile: 616-324-3010
Email: kech@kech.com *URL:* http://www.kech.com
Battle Creek, Michigan Office: One West Michigan Avenue, 49017.
Telephone: 616-966-3000.
Fax: 616-966-3022.

Douglas L. Callander — John F. Koryto

For Complete List of Firm Personnel, See General Section

For full biographical listings, see the Martindale-Hubbell Law Directory

LANSING, Ingham Co.

FOSTER, SWIFT, COLLINS & SMITH, P.C. (AV)

313 South Washington Square, 48933-2193
Telephone: 517-371-8100
Telecopier: 517-371-8200
URL: http://www.fosterswift.com
Farmington Hills, Michigan Office: 32300 Northwestern Highway, Suite 230.
Telephone: 248-539-9900.
Fax: 248-851-7504.

Gary J. McRay — Jean G. Schtokal

For Complete List of Firm Personnel, See General Section

For full biographical listings, see the Martindale-Hubbell Law Directory

INSURANCE DEFENSE

ALABAMA

*ANDALUSIA,** Covington Co.

ALBRITTONS, CLIFTON, ALVERSON & MOODY, P.C. (AV)

(Powell, Albritton & Albritton)
(Albrittons & Rankin)
(Albrittons, Givhan, Clifton & Alverson)
(Albrittons & Givhan)
109 Opp Avenue, P.O. Box 880, 36420
Telephone: 334-222-3177
Telecopier: 334-222-2696

Ed. T. Albritton (1857-1925)
Wm. Harold Albritton, Sr. (1881-1929)
Dempsey M. Powell (1863-1949)
Albert L. Rankin (1909-1970)
Robert Bynum Albritton (1905-1983)
William H. Albritton, Jr. (1907-1983)
James Marvin Albritton (1915-1987)
James R. Clifton
William Harold Albritton, IV
William B. Alverson, Jr.
Thomas B. Albritton
Julie S. Moody

Benjamin M. Bowden

General Counsel for: Coca-Cola Bottling Co. of Andalusia; Opp-Micolas Cotton Mills.
Attorneys for: First Alabama Bank; Alabama Power Co.; The Travelers; Liberty Mutual Ins. Co; Kemper Insurance; Crum & Forster Insurance Cos; CSX Transporation.

For full biographical listings, see the Martindale-Hubbell Law Directory

POWELL, PEEK & WEAVER (AV)

201 East Troy Street, Drawer 969, 36420
Telephone: 334-222-4103
Facsimile: 334-222-4105
Email: ppw@alaweb.com

MEMBERS OF FIRM

Abner R. Powell (1875-1940)
Abner R. Powell, Jr. (1916-1987)
Abner R. Powell, III
John M. Peek
Gary L. Weaver
Abner Riley Powell, IV

Representative Clients: State Farm Insurance Group; ALFA Insurance Companies; U.S.F.& G. Co.; CNA Insurance; Auto Owners Insurance Co.; Southern Guaranty Co.; Covington County Bank; Colonial Bank of Opp, Alabama.

For full biographical listings, see the Martindale-Hubbell Law Directory

*ATHENS,** Limestone Co.

PATTON, LATHAM, LEGGE & COLE (AV)

Professional Building, 315 West Market Street, P.O. Box 470, 35612
Telephone: 256-232-2010
Fax: 256-230-0610
Email: pllclaw@hiwaay.net

MEMBERS OF FIRM

Roy B. Patton (1885-1954)
David U. Patton (Retired)
Byrd R. Latham
Winston V. Legge, Jr.
P. Michael Cole
Claire Jones Tinney

Local Counsel for: Auto-Owners Insurance Co.; Avis; Blue Cross and Blue Shield of Alabama; State Farm Life Insurance Co.; State Farm Mutual Automobile Insurance Co.; State Farm Fire and Casualty Co.; Travelers Insurance Co.; The St. Paul Companies; Wausau Insurance Company.

For full biographical listings, see the Martindale-Hubbell Law Directory

*BIRMINGHAM,** Jefferson Co.

BRADLEY ARANT ROSE & WHITE LLP (AV)

2001 Park Place, Suite 1400, P.O. Box 830709, 35283-0709
Telephone: 205-521-8000
Facsimile: 205-521-8800
Facsimile (SouthTrust Tower Office): 205-521-8500
URL: http://www.barw.com
Huntsville, Alabama Office: 200 Clinton Avenue West, Suite 900, 35801.
Telephone: 205-517-5100.
Facsimile: 205-533-5069.
Washington, D.C. Office: 801 Pennsylvania Avenue, NW, Suite 230, 20004.
Telephone: 202-347-8893.
Facsimile: 202-347-1684.

(See Next Column)

MEMBERS OF FIRM

Joseph S. Bird III
Philip J. Carroll III
James S. Christie Jr.
Brittin Turner Coleman
James W. Gewin
Norman Jetmundsen Jr.
Hobart A. McWhorter Jr.
John H. Morrow
Michael R. Pennington
John D. Watson III

COUNSEL

Amy K. Myers

For Complete List of Firm Personnel, See General Section

For full biographical listings, see the Martindale-Hubbell Law Directory

CARR, ALLISON, PUGH, HOWARD, OLIVER & SISSON, P.C. (AV)

400 Vestavia Parkway, Suite 400, 35216
Telephone: 205-822-2006
Fax: 205-822-2057
Email: CFC@caphos.com
Florence, Alabama Office: 212 South Cedar Street, 35630.
Telephone: 256-718-6040.
Fax: 256-718-2150.
Mobile, Alabama Office: P.O. Box 781,36601-0781.
Telephone: 334-621-4340.
Fax: 334-626-8928.

Charles F. Carr (Resident, Daphne Office)
Russell Q. Allison
Bennett L. Pugh
David K. Howard (Resident, Florence Office)
Thomas L. Oliver, II
William H. Sisson (Resident, Daphne Office)
Glenn E. Ireland
Thomas C. Logan
Donald B. Kirkpatrick, II
Sarah J. Carlisle
Craig W. Goolsby (Resident, Daphne Office)

Gregg L. Smith
Joseph H. Driver
Brett A. Ross
Thomas S. Thornton, III
W. Bradford Kittrell
Jeffrey B. Carr
Joseph H. Hilley
Jeremy N. Trousdale
Ryan G. Brake
Caroline T. Pryor (Resident, Daphne Office)

For full biographical listings, see the Martindale-Hubbell Law Directory

CLARK & SCOTT, P.C. (AV)

3500 Blue Lake Drive, Suite 350, P.O. Box 380548, 35238-0548
Telephone: 205-967-9675
Telecopier: 205-967-7563
WATS: 800-955-8678
Mobile, Alabama Office: Clark, Scott & Sullivan, P.C., 10th Floor, Regions Bank Building, 56 St. Joseph Street, P.O. Box 1034.
Telephone: 205-433-1346.
Telecopier: 205-433-1086. WATS: 800-239-6733.
Jackson, Mississippi Office: Clark, Scott & Streetman, P.A., 447 Northpark Drive, Ridgeland, 39157.
Telephone: 601-977-0102.
Telecopier: 601-957-0690.

William A. Scott, Jr.
John W. Clark, Jr.
G. Steven Henry
Anthony N. Fox
Judith E. Dolan
Wayne Morse
James C. Ayers, Jr.
Kelly W. Otto
David Whittington McDowell
Joseph E. Stott
Shane M. Oncale

Cynthia A. Martin
Tommy C. Ritter, Jr.
J. Craig Lewis
Rosemary Sizemore Moore
Freddie N. Harrington, Jr.

Representative Clients: American International Group; ITT Hartford; Fireman's Fund Insurance Company; American Medical Systems, Inc.; Crum & Forster Companies; MEDMARC Insurance Company; Parke Davis/Warner Lambert Co.; Pfizer, Inc.; GAINSCO; Southern Heritage Insurance Company.

For full biographical listings, see the Martindale-Hubbell Law Directory

CORLEY, MONCUS & WARD, P.C. (AV)

400 Shades Creek Parkway, Suite 100, P.O. Box 59807, 35259
Telephone: 205-879-5959
Telecopier: 205-871-4411

Claude McCain Moncus
James S. Ward
Ezra B. Perry, Jr.
F. Lane Finch, Jr.

For Complete List of Firm Personnel, See General Section

For full biographical listings, see the Martindale-Hubbell Law Directory

Birmingham—Continued

FRIEDMAN, LEAK & BLOOM, P.C. (AV)

3800 Colonnade Parkway, Suite 650, 35243
Telephone: 205-278-7000
Fax: 205-278-7001
Email: Info@FLB-law.com *URL:* http://www.FLB-law.com

E. Martin Bloom
Jeffrey E. Friedman
Joe L. Leak
P. Thomas Dazzio, Jr.
Christopher J. Zulanas
J. Michael Bowling
C. Mark Bain
Robert R. Bedwell III

For full biographical listings, see the Martindale-Hubbell Law Directory

HALL, CONERLY, MUDD & BOLVIG, P.C. (AV)

1400 Financial Center, 505 North 20th Street, 35203-2626
Telephone: 205-251-8143

Jack J. Hall
Edward O. Conerly
William A. Mudd
C. Peter Bolvig
Jack J. Hall, Jr.

Christy Lynn Campbell Osborne
Paul C. Garrison
Kerry Phillip Luke
Sia Marie Kantargis
Linda Hinson Ambrose
P. Ted Colquett
Jerry D. Redmond, Jr.
David R. Wells

Counsel for: ALFA Insurance Cos.; Allstate Insurance Co.; Insurance Company of North America; Crum & Forster Insurance Co.; Canal Insurance Co.; Argonaut Insurance Co.; Chubb Pacific Indemnity Group; Commercial Union Cos.; General Accident Group.

For full biographical listings, see the Martindale-Hubbell Law Directory

HARRIS, CLECKLER & HOLLIS (AV)

Historic 2007 Building, 2007 Third Avenue North, 35203-2366
Telephone: 205-328-2366
Telecopier: 205-328-0013
Email: hcbr@mindspring.com *URL:* http://www.harriscleckler.com

Lyman H. Harris
Michael H. Cleckler
Jeffrey K. Hollis

ASSOCIATE

Jason A. Shamblin

For full biographical listings, see the Martindale-Hubbell Law Directory

LLOYD, SCHREIBER & GRAY, P.C. (AV)

Two Perimeter Park South Suite 100, 35243
Telephone: 205-967-8822
Telecopier: 205-967-2380
Email: lsgpc@aol.com

James S. Lloyd
Joseph Allen Schreiber
James C. Gray, III
Mark C. Peterson
Gerald Alan Templeton
Stephen Errol Whitehead

Legrand H. Amberson, Jr.
Thomas J. Skinner, IV
Laura C. Nettles
Howard Yeilding Downey
E. Britton Monroe
Ashley T. Robinson
Brock G. Murphy
Jennifer A. McCammon
Kathy R. Davis
Heidi Wells
Michael J. Clemmer

For full biographical listings, see the Martindale-Hubbell Law Directory

LUSK, FRALEY, MCALISTER & SIMMS, P.C. (AV)

Suite 1700 AmSouth/Harbert Plaza, 1901 Sixth Avenue North, 35203
Telephone: 205-323-7100
Fax: 205-323-7050
Email: Lusk-Fraley.com

Donald D. Lusk
John M. Fraley
David L. McAlister
Keri Donald Simms
Kenneth A. Dowdy
David Lawrence Dean
David Thurston White, III
Susan Gilman McAlister
Payton Caldwell Lusk
Leslie Ann Caldwell

For full biographical listings, see the Martindale-Hubbell Law Directory

PARSONS, LEE & JULIANO, P.C. (AV)

2200 AmSouth/Harbert Plaza, 1901 Sixth Avenue, North, P.O. Box 371088, 35237-1088
Telephone: 205-326-6600
Fax: 205-324-7097

(See Next Column)

Robert E. Parsons
Jasper P. Juliano
Marcus W. Lee
Marda W. Sydnor
David A. Lee
John M. Bergquist
Paul J. DeMarco
Deborah Ann Payne
Dorothy A. Powell
David Samuel Snoddy

For full biographical listings, see the Martindale-Hubbell Law Directory

PORTERFIELD, HARPER & MILLS, P.A. (AV)

22 Inverness Center Parkway, Suite 600, P.O. Box 530790, 35242-4821
Telephone: 205-980-5000
Fax: 205-980-5001

Neal D. Moore, III
J. Paul Sizemore
C. Jeffery Ash

Representative Clients: CIGNA; St. Paul Insurance Co.; The Travelers; Figgie International; White Consolidated Industries; Terex Corp.; Wausau Insurance; Baptist Health Systems, Inc.; Bruno's, Inc.; Harley Davidson, Inc.

For full biographical listings, see the Martindale-Hubbell Law Directory

SMITH & ELY, LLP (AV)

2000-A Southbridge Parkway Suite 405, 35209
Telephone: 205-802-2214
Fax: 205-879-4445

MEMBERS OF FIRM

Carol Ann Smith
Brenen G. Ely

ASSOCIATES

Susan Rogers
Susan Caroline Haygood
Toby Dykes

OF COUNSEL

Lisa B. Singer

For full biographical listings, see the Martindale-Hubbell Law Directory

SMITH, SPIRES & PEDDY, P.C. (AV)

2015 Second Avenue North Suite 200, 35203
Telephone: 205-251-5885
Fax: 205-251-8642

Paul G. Smith
Thomas S. Spires
A. Joe Peddy
Todd Hamilton
Thomas Coleman, Jr.

B. Scott Tyra
James L. Sanders, II
Julie L. Jenkins
Matthew C. Williams
Clarence "Chip" Rivers, IV
Jason M. Langley
R. Timothy Estes

Representative Clients: John Deere Insurance Company; Safeco Insurance Company; Tokio Fire & MarineInc.; St. Paul Insurance Co.; CNA Ins. Co.; Chubb & Son s, Inc.; Axa Global Risks; Royal Insurance Company; Zurich Insurance Company; Cincinnati Ins. Co.

For full biographical listings, see the Martindale-Hubbell Law Directory

SPAIN & GILLON, L.L.C. (AV)

The Zinszer Building, 2117 2nd Avenue North, 35203
Telephone: 205-328-4100
Telecopier: 205-324-8866
Email: ddh@spain-gillon.com *URL:* http://lawlinks.com:80/atty/al/sggbn.html

MEMBERS OF FIRM

Ollie L. Blan, Jr.
Eugene P. Stutts
Charles D. Stewart
Elizabeth Ann McMahan
Paul L. Sotherland
Robert L. Williams
Gary A. Parker
W. Gregory Smith
Steve R. Burford
Earl H. Lawson, Jr.

General Counsel for: Alabama Insurance Guaranty Association; Alabama Life and Disability Insurance Guaranty Association; Liberty Mutual Insurance Co.; Federated Mutual Insurance Co.; Factory Mutual Insurance Co.
Counsel for: The Minnesota Life Insurance Co.; Government Employees Insurance Co.; Massachusetts Mutual Life Insurance Co.; Liberty National Life Insurance Co.; The Guardian Life Insurance Company of America.

For Complete List of Firm Personnel, See General Section

For full biographical listings, see the Martindale-Hubbell Law Directory

STARNES & ATCHISON LLP (AV)

100 Brookwood Place, 35209
Telephone: 205-868-6000
Telecopier: 205-868-6099
Mailing Address: P.O. Box 598512, 35259-8512
Email: information@starneslaw.com
Mobile, Alabama Office: Riverview Plaza, Suite 1106, 63 South Royal Street, 36602.
Telephone: 334-433-6049.

(See Next Column)

STARNES & ATCHISON LLP—*Continued*

MEMBERS OF FIRM

W. Stancil Starnes
W. Michael Atchison
William Anthony Davis, III
John P. Scott, Jr.
L. Graves Stiff, III
Chris N. Galanos
J. Bentley Owens, III
Michael K. Wright
Robert P. Mackenzie, III
Allan R. Wheeler

ASSOCIATES

Jeannie Bugg Walston
Anthony Cameron Harlow
Rik S. Tozzi
Reed R. Bates
Bryan Oxford Balogh
W. Christian Hines, III
James M. Terrell

Representative Clients: Mutual Assurance, Inc.; CNA Insurance Co.; United States Fidelity & Guaranty Co.; Zurich Insurance Company; AIG Adjustment Aviation; Travelers Ins. Co.; Aetna Casualty & Surety Co.; Hartford Insurance Company; State Farm Mutual Auto Co.; American Medical International.

For full biographical listings, see the Martindale-Hubbell Law Directory

*BREWTON,** Escambia Co.

OTTS, MOORE & JORDAN (AV)

401 Evergreen Avenue, P.O. Box 467, 36427
Telephone: 334-867-7724
Fax: 334-867-2624

MEMBERS OF FIRM

John Thaddeus Moore
J. David Jordan

OF COUNSEL

Lee M. Otts

ASSOCIATE

James Eric Coale

Representative Clients: Container Corporation of America; First National Bank, Brewton; Southern Pine Electric Cooperative; Exxon Corp.; Mobil-GC Corp.; Pennzoil Exploration & Production Co.; T.R. Miller Mill Co., Inc.; Texaco, Inc.
Approved Attorneys for: Mississippi Valley Title Insurance Co.; Auto Owners Insurance Co.

For full biographical listings, see the Martindale-Hubbell Law Directory

*CULLMAN,** Cullman Co.

ST. JOHN & ST. JOHN, L.L.C. (AV)

108 Third Street South East, P.O. Drawer K, 35056-3542
Telephone: 256-734-3542
Fax: 256-734-3544

MEMBERS OF FIRM

F. E. St. John (1874-1943)
Finis E. St. John (1909-1984)
Finis E. St. John, III (1933-1984)
Finis E. St. John, IV
Gaynor L. St. John

ASSOCIATE

Rita P. Farris

OF COUNSEL

Juliet G. St. John

Attorneys for: U.S. Fidelity & Guaranty Co.; Travelers Insurance Co.; Liberty Mutual Insurance Co.; ALFA Mutual Insurance Co.; First Federal Savings & Loan; The Atlanta Casualty Companies; Auto-Owners Insurance Co.; Golden-Rod Broilers, Inc.; Cullman Products, Inc.; McGriff Industries, Inc.

For full biographical listings, see the Martindale-Hubbell Law Directory

*DECATUR,** Morgan Co.

EYSTER, KEY, TUBB, WEAVER & ROTH (AV)

Eyster Building, 402 East Moulton Street, S.E., P.O. Box 1607, 35602
Telephone: 256-353-6761
Fax: 256-353-6767

John C. Eyster (1863-1926)
Charles H. Eyster, Sr. (1888-1964)
Wm. B. Eyster (1921-1995)

MEMBERS OF FIRM

John S. Key
J. Glynn Tubb
Lawrence C. Weaver
Nicholas B. Roth
J. Witty Allen
William L. Middleton, III
James G. Adams, Jr.
John R. Baggette, Jr.
Jenny L. Mcleroy

General Counsel for: Alabama Farmers Cooperative.
Regional Counsel for: AmSouth Bank.
Local Counsel for: Allstate Insurance Co.; Champion International Corp; Goodyear; General Electric; Liberty Mutual Insurance Co.; Nationwide; Saginaw Steering Gear Division, General Motors Corp.; Sedgwick James; Sheffield Risk; State Farm Mutual Automobile Insurance Co.; 3M; The Travelers.

For full biographical listings, see the Martindale-Hubbell Law Directory

HARRIS, CADDELL & SHANKS, P.C. (AV)

214 Johnston Street, S.E., P.O. Box 2688, 35602-2688
Telephone: 256-340-8000
Telecopier: 256-340-8040
Email: hcs@ala-net.com

Julian Harris (1904-1994)
Norman W. Harris (1907-1998)
Philip T. Shanks (Retired)
Charles L. Murphree (Retired)
John A. Caddell
Robert H. Harris
Jon H. Moores
Thomas A. Caddell
William E. Shinn, Jr.
Gary A. Phillips
Dow M. Perry, Jr.
Barnes F. Lovelace, Jr.
Jeffrey S. Brown
David W. Langston
Huel Harris

Attorneys for: Acceptance Insurance Co.; Auto-Owners Insurance Co.; ALFA Insurance Cos.; American General Life & Accident Insurance Co.; Amerisure Ins. Co.; Canal Ins. Co.; Michigan Mutual Ins. Co.; Southern Guaranty Ins. Co.; U.S.F. & G. Co.; Utica Mutual Ins. Co.

For full biographical listings, see the Martindale-Hubbell Law Directory

*DOTHAN,** Houston Co.

COBB & SHEALY, P.A. (AV)

206 North Lena Street, P.O. Box 6346, 36302
Telephone: 334-794-8526
Fax: 334-677-0030
URL: http://www.cobb-shealy.com

Herman W. Cobb
Steadman S. Shealy, Jr.
Raymond Todd Derrick
Richard Elder Crum
James H. Pike
Joseph A. Morris
Brian T. Mosholder
Joseph D. Talmadge, Jr.

Representative Clients: Travelers Insurance; Nationwide Insurance; Auto-Owners Insurance; Employers Casualty of Texas; Safeco Insurance; Federated Insurance; Universal Underwriters; National Security Insurance; Great Central Insurance.
Approved Title Attorneys for: Mississippi Valley Title Ins. Co.

For full biographical listings, see the Martindale-Hubbell Law Directory

HARDWICK, HAUSE & SEGREST (AV)

212 North Lena Street, P.O. Box 1469, 36302
Telephone: 334-794-4144
Fax: 334-671-9330
URL: http://www.lawyers.com/hhslawfirm

W. G. Hardwick (1910-1993)
William G. Hause (Retired)

MEMBERS OF FIRM

Jere C. Segrest
Kevin Walding
Tina Whitehead Stamps

Counsel for: Dothan City Board of Education; American General Life & Accident Ins. Co.; General Motors Acceptance Corp.; Alabama Power Co.; Liberty National Life Ins. Co.; CBI-Equifax, Inc.; Houston County Board of Education; Cincinnati Insurance Companies.

For full biographical listings, see the Martindale-Hubbell Law Directory

LEE & MCINISH (AV)

238 West Main Street, P.O. Box 1665, 36302
Telephone: 334-792-4156
Facsimile: 334-794-8342
Email: leemc@graceba.net

MEMBERS OF FIRM

W. L. Lee (1873-1944)
Alto V. Lee, III (1915-1987)
William L. Lee, III
Alan C. Livingston
William C. Carn, III
Peter A. McInish
Jerry M. White

ASSOCIATES

William L. Lee, IV
William W. Nichols
William C. White, II

OF COUNSEL

H. Dwight McInish

Counsel for: Seaboard Coast Line Railroad Co.; Atlanta & St. Andrews Bay Railroad Co.; ALFA; U. S. F. & G. Co.; Maryland Casualty Co.; Continental Insurance Cos.; Royal-Globe Group; Slocomb National Bank; GTE South.

For full biographical listings, see the Martindale-Hubbell Law Directory

*ELBA,** Coffee Co.

L. MERRILL SHIRLEY (AV)

431 North Court Street, P.O. Box 408, 36323
Telephone: 334-897-5775
Fax: 334-897-2304

Representative Clients: National Security Insurance Co.; Peoples Bank of Elba; ALFA Mutual Insurance Co.; Fireman's Fund Insurance Group; Southern Guaranty Insurance Co.; Elba General Hospital and Nursing Home.

(See Next Column)

L. MERRILL SHIRLEY, *Elba—Continued*

References: Peoples Bank; National Security Insurance Co.

For full biographical listings, see the Martindale-Hubbell Law Directory

ENTERPRISE, Coffee Co.

CASSADY, FULLER & MARSH, LLP (AV)

203 East Lee Avenue, P.O. Box 310910, 36331
Telephone: 334-347-2626
Telecopier: 334-393-1396

MEMBERS OF FIRM

Joe C. Cassady
Kenneth T. Fuller
M. Dale Marsh
Joe C. Cassady, Jr.
R. Rainer Cotter, III

Representative Clients: RegionsBank; Enterprise Health Care Authority; Sessions Co., Inc.; Allstate; State Farm Mutual Insurance Co.; Community Bank & Trust Co.; Conagra, Inc.
Approved Attorneys for: First American Title Insurance Co.

For full biographical listings, see the Martindale-Hubbell Law Directory

*FLORENCE,** Lauderdale Co.

JONES & TROUSDALE (AV)

115 Helton Court, Suite B, P.O. Box 367, 35631-0367
Telephone: 256-767-0333
Telefax: 256-767-0331
Email: JTAttys@aol.com

MEMBERS OF FIRM

Robert E. Jones, III
Preston S. Trousdale, Jr.
A. DeLoach Stewart

For full biographical listings, see the Martindale-Hubbell Law Directory

*FORT PAYNE,** De Kalb Co.

SCRUGGS, JORDAN, DODD & DODD (AV)

207 Alabama Avenue, South, P.O. Box 681109, 35967
Telephone: 256-845-5932
Fax: 256-845-4325
Email: scruggs@peop.tdsnet.com *URL:* http://www.lawyers.com/scruggsjordandodd&dodd

William D. Scruggs, Jr.
Robert K. Jordan
J. David Dodd
E. Allen Dodd, Jr.
Holly Hendrickson

Representative Clients: State Farm Insurance Company; Allstate Insurance Co., Inc.; USF&G Insurance Co.; Nucor, Inc.; Ladd Engineering, Inc.; ALABAMA Band; First Federal Bank; Fritz Structural Steel, Inc.; Williamson Oil Co., Inc.

For full biographical listings, see the Martindale-Hubbell Law Directory

*GADSDEN,** Etowah Co.

FORD AND HOWARD, P.C. (AV)

(Formerly Ford & Associates)
The Lancaster Building, 645 Walnut Street, Suite 5, P.O. Box 388, 35902
Telephone: 256-546-5432
Fax: 256-546-5435
Email: fordfirm@aol.com

George P. Ford
H. Edgar Howard

Bradley Williams Cornett
Vann Allan Spray

OF COUNSEL

Elizabeth R. Howard

Reference: AmSouth Bank, N.A.

For full biographical listings, see the Martindale-Hubbell Law Directory

TORBERT & TORBERT, P.A. (AV)

1024 Forrest Avenue, 35901
Telephone: 256-547-7551
Fax: 256-547-7553
Email: torbert@microxl.com

Jack W. Torbert
Jack W. Torbert, Jr.

References: South Trust Bank of Etowah County, N.A.; First Alabama Bank of Gadsden, N.A.

For full biographical listings, see the Martindale-Hubbell Law Directory

*GUNTERSVILLE,** Marshall Co.

LUSK & LUSK (AV)

452 Gunter Avenue, P.O. Box 609, 35976
Telephone: 256-582-3248
Fax: 256-582-3215

(See Next Column)

MEMBERS OF FIRM

Marion F. Lusk (1896-1986)
Louis B. Lusk

Representative Clients: AmSouth Bank of Alabama, Guntersville; United States Fidelity & Guaranty Co.; The Travelers Insurance Co.; St. Paul Cos.; ALFA Mutual Insurance Cos.; Hartford Group; Liberty Mutual Insurance Co.; Allstate Insurance Co.; Home of New York Group.

For full biographical listings, see the Martindale-Hubbell Law Directory

HALEYVILLE, Winston Co.

LOWE, MOBLEY & LOWE (AV)

1210-21st Street, P.O. Box 576, 35565
Telephone: 205-486-5296
Fax: 205-486-4531
Email: lml@lowemobleylowe.com *URL:* http://www.lowemobleylowe.com

MEMBERS OF FIRM

Walter Joe James, Jr. (1923-1990)
John W. Lowe
Jeffery A. Mobley
Jonathan B. Lowe

Representative Clients: Traders & Farmers Bank; Burdick-West Memorial Hospital.
Approved Attorneys for: Lawyers Title Insurance Corp.

For full biographical listings, see the Martindale-Hubbell Law Directory

*HUNTSVILLE,** Madison Co.

BRADLEY ARANT ROSE & WHITE LLP (AV)

200 Clinton Avenue West, Suite 900, 35801
Telephone: 205-517-5100
Facsimile: 205-517-5200
URL: http://www.barw.com
Birmingham, Alabama Office: 2001 Park Place, Suite 1400, P.O. Box 830709.
Telephone: 205-521-8000.
Facsimile: 205-521-8800. Facsimile (SouthTrust Tower Office): 205-521-8500.
Washington, D.C. Office: 801 Pennsylvania Avenue, NW, Suite 230, 20004.
Telephone: 202-347-8893.
Facsimile: 202-347-1684.

RESIDENT PARTNERS

Patrick H Graves Jr.
Warne S. Heath
Gary C. Huckaby
E. Cutter Hughes Jr.

RESIDENT ASSOCIATE

Kimberly B. Martin

For Complete List of Firm Personnel, See General Section

For full biographical listings, see the Martindale-Hubbell Law Directory

HENDERSON & BUTLER (AV)

200 West Court Square Suite 972, 35801
Telephone: 205-536-4457
Fax: 205-536-4484
Email: henders@ro.com

Danny D. Henderson
Clint W. Butler

ASSOCIATE

Larry O. Daniel, Jr.

For full biographical listings, see the Martindale-Hubbell Law Directory

SPURRIER, RICE, WOOD & HALL (AV)

3226 Bob Wallace Avenue, 35805
Telephone: 256-533-5015
Fax: 256-536-0105
Email: srwhlaw@hiwaay.net

MEMBERS OF FIRM

Donald N. Spurrier
Benjamin R. Rice
Robert V. Wood, Jr.
Ruth Ann Hall

ASSOCIATES

Earl Thomas Forbes
Deborah S. Hensley
Jonathan B. Medlock
Richard L. Morris
Craig A. Bardell

Representative Clients: Alfa Mutual Insurance Co.; Allstate Insurance Co.; American Indemnity Group; Harleyville Insurance Co.; State Farm Insurance Cos.; Risk Co.; CNA Maryland Casualty Co.; Farmers Insurance Group; Guidant Insurance Co.

For full biographical listings, see the Martindale-Hubbell Law Directory

*MOBILE,** Mobile Co.

ARMBRECHT, JACKSON, DEMOUY, CROWE, HOLMES & REEVES, L.L.C. (AV)

1300 Riverview Plaza, P.O. Box 290, 36601
Telephone: 334-405-1300
Facsimile: 334-432-6843; 433-3821
Email: adc@ajlaw.com

(See Next Column)

ARMBRECHT, JACKSON, DEMOUY, CROWE, HOLMES & REEVES L.L.C.—*Continued*

MEMBERS OF FIRM

Rae M. Crowe
Broox G. Holmes
W. Boyd Reeves
Kirk C. Shaw
Norman E. Waldrop, Jr.
Grover E. Asmus II
Douglas L. Brown
Donald C. Radcliff
M. Kathleen Miller
Edward A. Dean
Wm. Steele Holman II
James E. Robertson, Jr.
Scott G. Brown
Clifford C. Brady
Richard W. Franklin
Rodney R. Cate

ASSOCIATES

A. Edwin Stuardi, III
J. Walton Jackson
Sam David Knight

Representative Clients: American Security Group (Regional Counsel); Burlington Northern Santa Fe Railroad Co. (District Counsel); Kimberly-Clark Corp.; Loyal American Life Insurance Co.; Mutual Assurance, Inc.; Travelers Insurance Co.; Wausau Insurance Companies.

For Complete List of Firm Personnel, See General Section

For full biographical listings, see the Martindale-Hubbell Law Directory

---

BRISKMAN & BINION, P.C. (AV)

205 Church Street, P.O. Box 43, 36601
Telephone: 334-433-7600
Fax: 334-433-4485
Email: briskman@zebra.net

Donald M. Briskman
Mack B. Binion
Christ N. Coumanis
Kimberly C. Hodgson

A List of Representative Clients will be furnished upon request.
References: Regions Bank; AmSouth Bank, N.A.; Southtrust Bank of Mobile.

For full biographical listings, see the Martindale-Hubbell Law Directory

---

CARR, ALFORD, CLAUSEN & MCDONALD, L.L.C. (AV)

One St. Louis Centre, Suite 5000, P.O. Drawer C, 36601
Telephone: 334-432-1600
Facsimile: 334-432-1700
URL: http://www.cacm.com

Davis Carr
Helen Johnson Alford
Andrew C. Clausen
James H. McDonald, Jr.
James W. Lampkin, II
Jean M. Powers

Annette McDermott Carwie
M. Lauren Lemmon
Thomas M. Rockwell
Pamela Ann Moore
W. Ben. Broadwater
Paul V. Lagarde
Frank L. Parker, Jr.
Christina M. Adcock
Kathleen Cobb Kaufman
Joseph Anthony Zarzaur, Jr.

For full biographical listings, see the Martindale-Hubbell Law Directory

---

FRAZER, GREENE, UPCHURCH & BAKER, L.L.C. (AV)

First National Bank Building, Suite 2206 107 Saint Francis Street, 36602
Telephone: 334-431-6020
Facsimile: 334-431-6030
URL: http://www.frazergreene.com

MEMBERS OF FIRM

A. Danner Frazer, Jr.
Edward C. Greene
Michael E. Upchurch
D. Brent Baker

Bruce M. Westbrook
W. Austin Mulherin, III
Marcus Edward McDowell

For full biographical listings, see the Martindale-Hubbell Law Directory

---

GALLOWAY, SMITH, WETTERMARK & EVEREST, LLP (AV)

3263 Cottage Hill Road, P.O. Box 16629, 36616-0629
Telephone: 334-476-4493
Fax: 334-479-5566
Email: GSWE@GSWELAW.COM

MEMBERS OF FIRM

Thomas M. Galloway
Robert H. Smith
Thomas M. Galloway, Jr.
Lawrence M. Wettermark
Robert M. Galloway
Mark J. Everest

ASSOCIATES

Andrew J. Rutens
Theodore L. Greenspan
Thomas O. Gaillard, III

General Counsel for: Mobile Greyhound Park.
Counsel for: Alfa Mutual Insurance Co.; American States Ins. Co.; Cigna Ins. Co.; County of Mobile.

For full biographical listings, see the Martindale-Hubbell Law Directory

---

GARDNER, MIDDLEBROOKS, FLEMING, GIBBONS & KITTRELL, P.C. (AV)

64 North Royal Street, Drawer 3103, 36652
Telephone: 334-433-8100
Telecopier: 334-433-8181
Email: GMFH@WORLDNET.ATT.NET
Birmingham, Alabama Office: Suite 450, 2013 1st Avenue, North.
Telephone: 205-250-7776.
Telecopier: 205-250-7675.
Washington, D.C. Office: 1919 S Street NW, Washington, D.C.
Telephone: 202-667-8278.
Telecopier: 202-234-1003.

J. Cecil Gardner
Sherwood C. Middlebrooks, III
Charles J. Fleming
John D. Gibbons
Braxton L. Kittrell, Jr.

Mary Elizabeth Olsen
Kimberly J. Calametti
Walter G. (Stoney) Chavers

Representative Clients: CNA Insurance Cos.; Canal Insurance Co.; Safeway Insurance Company of Alabama; Honda Motor Co.; Toyota Motor Co., U.S.A.; Bay Equipment Co.; Lyon Properties, Inc.; Southside Storage, Inc.

For full biographical listings, see the Martindale-Hubbell Law Directory

---

HELMSING, SIMS & LEACH, P.C. (AV)

The Laclede Building, 150 Government Street, Suite 2000, P.O. Box 2767, 36652
Telephone: 334-432-5521
Telecopy: 334-432-0633

Larry U. Sims
Frederick G. Helmsing
John N. Leach, Jr.
Warren C. Herlong, Jr.
James B. Newman
Robert H. Rouse
Charles H. Dodson, Jr.
Joseph P. H. Babington
R. Alan Alexander
John J. Crowley, Jr.
Joseph D. Steadman
Todd S. Strohmeyer

William R. Lancaster
Robin Kilpatrick Fincher
John Townsend Dukes
John Casey Pipes
James Bradford Pittman, Jr.

For full biographical listings, see the Martindale-Hubbell Law Directory

---

INGE, TWITTY & DUFFY (AV)

1410 Regions Bank Building, 56 St. Joseph Street, P.O. Box 1109, 36633
Telephone: 334-433-3200
Facsimile: 334-433-3444

MEMBERS OF FIRM

James J. Duffy, Jr.
James J. Duffy, III

Francis H. Inge (1902-1959)
Thos. E. Twitty (1901-1975)
Richard H. Inge (1912-1980)

For full biographical listings, see the Martindale-Hubbell Law Directory

---

JOHNSTONE, ADAMS, BAILEY, GORDON AND HARRIS, L.L.C. (AV)

Royal St. Francis Building, 104 St. Francis Street, 8th Floor, P.O. Box 1988, 36633
Telephone: 334-432-7682
Facsimile: 334-432-0712 or 334-432-2800
Email: attorneys@JohnstoneAdams.com *URL:* http://www.JohnstoneAdams.com
Bay Minette, Alabama Office: Dahlberg Building, 107 Hand Avenue, P.O. Box 729, 36507.
Telephone: 334-937-9473.
Facsimile: 334-937-9475.

MEMBERS OF FIRM

Ben H. Harris, Jr.
William H. Hardie, Jr.
Joseph M. Allen, Jr.
I. David Cherniak
David C. Hannan
Wade B. Perry, Jr.
Celia J. Collins
Tracy P. Turner
Lawrence J. Seiter

For Complete List of Firm Personnel, See General Section

For full biographical listings, see the Martindale-Hubbell Law Directory

---

PIERCE, LEDYARD, LATTA & WASDEN, P.C. (AV)

Colonial Bank Centre Suite 400, 41 North Beltline, 36608
Telephone: 334-344-5151
Facsimile: 334-344-9696
Mailing Address: P.O. Box 16046, Mobile, AL, 36616
URL: http://www.pllaw.com

(See Next Column)

PIERCE, LEDYARD, LATTA & WASDEN P.C., *Mobile—Continued*

Donald F. Pierce
Goodman G. Ledyard
Forrest S. Latta
H. William Wasden
Edward G. Isaacs Bowron
John Charles S. Pierce
W. Pemble DeLashmet
C. William Daniels, Jr.

David P. York
Mark Pickett Eiland
James Robert Turnipseed
Michael A. Montgomery
Jeffrey U. Beaverstock

Representative Clients: Admiral Insurance Co.; Auto Owners Insurance Co.; Blue Cross and Blue Shield; Connecticut Mutual Life Insurance Co.; Electric Insurance; The Hartford Insurance Co.; Mid-West National Life Insurance Co.; The Prudential Insurance Co.; Royal Insurance Co.; United Insurance Co.

For full biographical listings, see the Martindale-Hubbell Law Directory

SINTZ, CAMPBELL, DUKE & TAYLOR (AV)

3763 Professional Parkway, 36609
Telephone: 334-344-7241
Fax: 334-344-7400

MEMBERS OF FIRM

Peter V. Sintz (1940-1997)
Robert C. Campbell, III
Frank G. Taylor
Steven L. Terry

ASSOCIATES

Wm. Kyle Morris
Kathryn W. Petersen
Barry C. Prine

OF COUNSEL

Leon G. Duke

LEGAL SUPPORT PERSONEL

James A. Koblas

Representative Clients: Aetna C & S Insurance Co.; Mobile County School Board; Auto-Owners Insurance Co.; Argonaut Insurance Co.; Mostellar Medical Clinic; Scottsdale Insurance Co.; American International Group; Alabama School of Math and Science; Mobile County Sheriff's Office.

For full biographical listings, see the Martindale-Hubbell Law Directory

*MONTGOMERY,** Montgomery Co.

BALL, BALL, MATTHEWS & NOVAK, P.A. (AV)

2000 Interstate Park Drive, Suite 204, 36109
Telephone: 334-387-7680
Fax: 334-387-3222
Email: Firm@Ball-Ball.com

Fred S. Ball (1866-1942)
Charles A. Ball (1904-1969)
Fred S. Ball, Jr. (1896-1974)
Richard A. Ball (1906-1983)
John R. Matthews, Jr.
Richard A. Ball, Jr.
Tabor R. Novak, Jr.
Clyde C. Owen, Jr.
C. Winston Sheehan, Jr.
William H. Brittain II
E. Hamilton Wilson, Jr.
Richard E. Broughton
T. Cowin Knowles
Gerald C. Swann, Jr.
Mark T. Davis
James A. Rives

Fred B. Matthews
Allison L. Alford
Michael L. White
Emily C. Marks
Brandy A. Adkins
George R. Parker

LEGAL SUPPORT PERSONNEL

Lon Worley (Office Manager)

Counsel for: Beech Aircraft Corporation; Bell Helicopter Co.; John Deere Co.; Government Employees Insurance Co.; Chubb & Son; Cigna Co.; Chrysler Corp.; Associated Aviation Underwriters.

For full biographical listings, see the Martindale-Hubbell Law Directory

BRANTLEY & WILKERSON, P.C. (AV)

405 South Hull Street, P.O. Box 830, 36101-0830
Telephone: 334-265-1500
Fax: 334-265-0319
Email: ashley@brantleywilkerson.com *URL:* http://www.brantleywilkerson.com

Paul A. Brantley

Amanda C. Carter

Representative Clients: Associated Resources, Inc.; Construction Claims Management, Inc.; Southern Risk Services, Inc.
Reference: South Trust Bank, N.A.

For full biographical listings, see the Martindale-Hubbell Law Directory

MOOTY & ASSOCIATES, P.C. (AV)

Colonial Bank Building, 4th Floor, 671 South Perry Street, Suite 400, 36104
Telephone: 334-264-0400
Fax: 334-264-0380
Email: hdm@mooty-assoc.com

H. Dean Mooty, Jr.

Paul P. Telehany
Michael A. Fritz, Sr.

Representative Clients: Alabama Oilmen's Association/Alabama Association of Convenience Stores; Five Star Insurance Group, Ltd.; AlaComp; Price Oil, Inc.; Major Oil Company, Inc.; Royal Insurance Company.
References: SouthTrust Bank; Sterling Bank.

For full biographical listings, see the Martindale-Hubbell Law Directory

MORROW, ROMINE & PEARSON, P.C. (AV)

122 South Hull Street, P.O. Box 4804, 36103-4804
Telephone: 334-262-7707
Fax: 334-262-7742
Email: MRP@MRPLAW.COM

Roger S. Morrow
Wesley Romine
Joel H. Pearson

Chandra C. Wright

Representative Clients: Auto Owner's Insurance Company; Owner's Insurance Company; Universal Underwriters Insurance Company; Universal Underwriters Life Insurance Company; Universal Underwriters Service Corp.; Ranger Insurance Company; Armed Forces Insurance; State Automobile Mutual Insurance Company; The Travelers Indemnity Company of Illinois; Construction Materials Limited, Inc.

For full biographical listings, see the Martindale-Hubbell Law Directory

NIX, HOLTSFORD & VERCELLI, P.C. (AV)

300 A Water Street, Suite 300, P.O. Box 4128, 36103
Telephone: 334-262-2006
Fax: 334-834-3616
Email: NHV@JUNO.COM

H. E. Nix, Jr.
Alex L. Holtsford, Jr.
Charles E. Vercelli, Jr.
Floyd R. Gilliland, Jr.
T. Randall Lyons
Steven A. Higgins
Kenneth A. Hitson, Jr.

David P. Stevens
Todd E. Hughes
Rick A. Howard
Stacy Anne Linn
Jay S. Tuley

LEGAL SUPPORT PERSONNEL

Richard M. Seibert (Firm Manager)
Ashley Collins (Paralegal)
Monica E. Jayroe (Paralegal)
Suzanne H. Long (Legal Assistant)
Kelley S. Tracy (Paralegal)

Representative Clients: Auto-Owners Insurance Co.; Alfa Insurance Companies; Crum & Forster; Gay & Taylor; Kemper Group; Ranger Insurance Co.; State Farm Mutual Insurance Companies; United States Fidelity & Guaranty Co.; Wal-Mart Stores; Wausau Insurance Co.

For full biographical listings, see the Martindale-Hubbell Law Directory

ROBISON & BELSER, P.A. (AV)

200 Coosa Street, 36104
Telephone: 334-834-7000
Telecopier: 334-834-7011
Mailing Address: Drawer 1470, Montgomery, AL, 36102
Email: tsides@mont.mindspring.com

Philip H. Butler
Robert F. Northcutt
Martha Ann Miller
Terry A. Sides
Charles B. Haigler, III

General Counsel for: Montgomery County Board of Education.
Representative Clients: Union Bank & Trust Co.; Liberty National Life Insurance Co.; State Farm Mutual Fire & Casualty Co.

For full biographical listings, see the Martindale-Hubbell Law Directory

WEBB & ELEY, P.C. (AV)

166 Commerce Street, Suite 300, P.O. Box 238, 36101-0238
Telephone: 334-262-1850
Fax: 334-262-1772
Email: webbeley1@mindspring.com

James W. Webb
Michael M. Eley
Kendrick E. Webb
Craig S. Dillard
Bart Harmon
William R. Chandler

(See Next Column)

WEBB & ELEY P.C.—*Continued*

Frank E. Bankston, Jr.
Pamela Robinson Higgins
Shawn Junkins Cole
Michael J. Cohan
Lisa D. Van Wagner

LEGAL SUPPORT PERSONNEL

Janice B. Miller (Business Manager)

Representative Clients: American Amicable Life Insurance Co.; Association of County Commissioners of Alabama; CIGNA Insurance Co.; First Union Mortgage Corp.; ITT Hartford; Meadowbrook Insurance Group; Nationwide Insurance Co.; Titan Indemnity Co.; United States Fidelity & Guaranty Co.; Wausau Insurance Co.

For full biographical listings, see the Martindale-Hubbell Law Directory

PELL CITY, St. Clair Co.

BLAIR AND PARSONS (AV)

St. Clair Land Title Building, 1711 Cogswell Avenue, 35125
Telephone: 205-884-3440
Fax: 205-884-3442

MEMBERS OF FIRM

A. Dwight Blair
Elizabeth S. Parsons

Representative Clients: Colonial Bank; Metro Bank; Am South Bank; State Farm Mutual Insurance Cos; ALFA Mutual Insurance Co.; Allstate Insurance Co.; St. Paul Insurance Cos.; Auto Owners Insurance Co.; Reliance Insurance Cos.; National Bank of Commerce.

For full biographical listings, see the Martindale-Hubbell Law Directory

*RUSSELLVILLE,** Franklin Co.

MCDOWELL & BEASON (AV)

(Formerly McDowell, Beason & Pilati)
507 North Jackson, P.O. Box 818, 35653
Telephone: 256-332-1660
Fax: 256-332-0318
Email: Legal@Getaway.Com

Daniel G. McDowell
Eddie Beason

OF COUNSEL

Joe Fine

Representative Clients: Citizens Bank & Savings Co. of Russellville; City of Phil Campbell; Russellville City Board of Education; Franklin County Board of Education; Mutual Savings Life Insurance Co.; State Farm Fire & Casualty Co.; State Farm Mutual Automobile Ins. Co.; Marshall Durbin Co.

For full biographical listings, see the Martindale-Hubbell Law Directory

*SELMA,** Dallas Co.

REEVES & STEWART, P.C. (AV)

Regions Bank Building, 101 Church Street, P.O. Box 457, 36702-0457
Telephone: 334-875-7236
Fax: 334-875-7625

Archie T. Reeves, Jr.
B. Kincey Green, Jr.
Robert E. Armstrong, III
Allen S. Reeves

Local Attorneys for: State Farm Mutual Automobile Insurance Cos.; St. Paul Insurance Cos.; International Paper Co.; Regions Bank; Alabama Power Co.; South Central Bell Telephone; Alabama Gas Corp.; Columbia-HCA, Inc.; CSX Transportation.
Assistant Division Counsel for: Norfolk Southern Corp.

For full biographical listings, see the Martindale-Hubbell Law Directory

*TROY,** Pike Co.

CALHOUN, FAULK, WATKINS & FAIRCLOTH, L.L.C. (AV)

78 South Court Square, P.O. Box 489, 36081
Telephone: 334-566-7200
Fax: 334-566-7584

Richard F. Calhoun
Joseph E. Faulk
William Keith Watkins
Robert Curry Faircloth
James G. Clower (Retired)

Representative Clients: State Farm Mutual Automobile, Insurance Co.; Hartford Insurance Group; United States Fidelity & Guaranty Co.; Aetna Insurance Co.; Travelers Insurance Co.; Allstate Insurance Co.; Liberty National Life Insurance Co.

For full biographical listings, see the Martindale-Hubbell Law Directory

*TUSCALOOSA,** Tuscaloosa Co.

DAVIDSON, WIGGINS, JONES & COLEMAN, P.C. (AV)

2625 Eighth Street, P.O. Box 1939, 35403
Telephone: 205-759-5771
Fax: 205-752-8259
Email: wiggins@dbtech.net
Email: tj@dbtech.net

(See Next Column)

G. Stephen Wiggins
Thomas R. Jones, Jr.
Charles M. Coleman

Randal Kevin Davis
J. Paul Zimmerman
Roman Ashley Shaul

OF COUNSEL

M. McCoy Davidson

Representative Clients: Peco Foods, Inc.; St. Paul Companies, Inc.; Illinois-Central Railroad Co.; The Travelers Group; Mutual Assurance, Inc.; Cigna Insurance Companies; Zenith Insurance Company; Industrial Development Board of the City of Tuscaloosa, Alabama; Nationwide Insurance Company; Blue Cross and Blue Shield of Alabama.

For full biographical listings, see the Martindale-Hubbell Law Directory

DONALD, RANDALL, DONALD & TIPTON (AV)

Ninth Floor, AmSouth Building, 2330 University Boulevard, P.O. Box 2155, 35403
Telephone: 205-758-2585
Fax: 205-758-2593
Email: drdtlaw@bellsouth.net

MEMBERS OF FIRM

William J. Donald
B. Wayne Randall
William J. Donald, III
Ritchie L. Tipton

ASSOCIATES

Laurie K. Pratt
Elizabeth Utsey Sadler
John R. Franks, Jr.

References: AmSouth Bank; The Bank of Vernon.

For full biographical listings, see the Martindale-Hubbell Law Directory

PHELPS, JENKINS, GIBSON & FOWLER, L.L.P. (AV)

1201 Greensboro Avenue, P.O. Box 020848, 35402-0848
Telephone: 205-345-5100
Fax: 205-758-4394
Fax: 205-391-6658
Fax: 205-391-6663

MEMBERS OF FIRM

Sam M. Phelps
James J. Jenkins
Johnson Russell Gibson, III
Randolph M. Fowler
C. Barton Adcox
Farley A. Poellnitz
A. Courtney Crowder

ASSOCIATES

Karen C. Welborn
Stephen E. Snow
W. David Ryan
Bryan Patrick Winter
John M. Compton
Charles T. Grimes
Jenny B. Compton
(Not admitted in AL)
Laura C. Karns

LEGAL SUPPORT PERSONNEL

Christine Holt (Paralegal)
Lori R. Woodard (Paralegal)
Melissa D. Harvey (Paralegal)

Attorneys for: Aetna Insurance Co.; Allstate Insurance Co.; Carolina Casualty Insurance Co.; Continental Insurance Cos.; Fireman's Fund-American Insurance Cos.; Great American Insurance Co.; Hanover Insurance Co.

For full biographical listings, see the Martindale-Hubbell Law Directory

ZEANAH, HUST, SUMMERFORD, DAVIS, JONES & WILLIAMSON, L.L.C. (AV)

Seventh Floor, AmSouth Bank Building, P.O. Box 1310, 35403
Telephone: 205-349-1383
Fax: 205-391-1319
Email: ZHSDJ@mail.dbtech.net

MEMBERS OF FIRM

Olin W. Zeanah (1922-1987)
Wilbor J. Hust, Jr.
E. Clark Summerford
Kenneth D. Davis
Christopher H. Jones
Beverly Smith Williamson

OF COUNSEL

Marvin T. Ormond

Representative Clients: Alfa Insurance Cos.; Hartford Insurance Group; Home Insurance Co.; Nationwide Insurance Co.; Alabama Power Co.; Liberty Mutual Insurance Co.; The Uniroyal Goodrich Tire Co.

For full biographical listings, see the Martindale-Hubbell Law Directory

*TUSCUMBIA,** Colbert Co.

ASHE, TANNER, WRIGHT & KELLEY, P.C. (AV)

105 West Second Street, P.O. Box 899, 35674
Telephone: 256-383-6357
Telecopier: 256-381-4612

Braxton W. Ashe
J. Michael Tanner
Grant A. Wright
Charles J. Kelley (Resident)

(See Next Column)

ASHE, TANNER, WRIGHT & KELLEY P.C., *Tuscumbia—Continued*

Nickolas J. Steles

For full biographical listings, see the Martindale-Hubbell Law Directory

ALASKA

*ANCHORAGE,** Third Judicial District

DELANEY, WILES, HAYES, GERETY, ELLIS & YOUNG, INC. (AV)

1007 West Third Avenue, Suite 400, 99501
Telephone: 907-279-3581
Fax: 907-277-1331
Email: dwhge@alaska.net

Daniel A. Gerety
Clay A. Young
William E. Moseley
James B. Friderici
Howard A. Lazar
Donald C. Thomas
Timothy J. Lamb

Representative Clients: Continental Insurance Co.; Liberty Northwest; Maryland Insurance Group; Royal Insurance Co.; The Doctors Company; Norcal Mutual Insurance Co.; HealthCare Indemnity Co.; Medical Insurance Exchange of California; Lutheran Health Systems; Great American Insurance Company.

For Complete List of Firm Personnel, See General Section

For full biographical listings, see the Martindale-Hubbell Law Directory

DELISIO MORAN GERAGHTY & ZOBEL, P.C. (AV)

943 West Sixth Avenue, 99501-2033
Telephone: 907-279-9574
Facsimile: 907-276-4231
Email: delisiomoran@dmgz.com

Joseph M. Moran
Michael C. Geraghty
Patricia L. Zobel
Gregory L. Youngmun
David D. Floerchinger
Deirdre D. Ford

Kevin J. Anderson
John D. Harjehausen

OF COUNSEL

Stephen S. DeLisio

LEGAL SUPPORT PERSONNEL

Candace M. Holliday (Paralegal)
Patrick G. Carnahan (Paralegal)
Heather R. Kegley (Paralegal)

For full biographical listings, see the Martindale-Hubbell Law Directory

LAW OFFICES OF ROBERT H. WAGSTAFF (AV)

First National Bank Building, 425 G Street, Suite 610, 99501
Telephone: 907-277-8611
Facsimile: 907-258-7329

For full biographical listings, see the Martindale-Hubbell Law Directory

ARIZONA

*FLAGSTAFF,** Coconino Co.

MANGUM, WALL, STOOPS & WARDEN, P.L.L.C. (AV)

100 North Elden, P.O. Box 10, 86002
Telephone: 520-779-6951
Fax: 520-773-1312

H. Karl Mangum (1908-1993)

OF COUNSEL

Douglas J. Wall
Robert W. Warden
Daniel J. Stoops

MEMBERS OF FIRM

A. Dean Pickett
Stephen K. Smith
Melinda L. Garrahan
Michael H. Hinson

ASSOCIATES

Annette Star Lustgarten
Rebecca Smith Currey
R. Scott Currey
Melinda K. Jacquez
Franklin Hoover

Representative Clients: Northern Arizona University; Flagstaff Unified School District; Museum of Northern Arizona; Arizona School Board Association.
Local Counsel for: Bank of America-Arizona; Arizona Public Service; U.S.A.A.; State Farm Fire & Casualty Insurance Co.; Insurance Company of the West.

(See Next Column)

For Complete List of Firm Personnel, See General Section

For full biographical listings, see the Martindale-Hubbell Law Directory

MESA, Maricopa Co.

UDALL, SHUMWAY, BLACKHURST, ALLEN & LYONS, P.C. (AV)

30 West First Street, 85201-1446
Telephone: 480-461-5300
Facsimile: 480-461-5398
Email: usbalsea@vtc.net
Willcox, Arizona Office: 135 East Maley.
Telephone: 602-384-3389.
Fax: 602-384-2280.

David K. Udall
Dale R. Shumway
Dennis P. Blackhurst
John H. Lyons
Barry C. Dickerson
Steven H. Everts
Clark R. Richter
Roger C. Decker
Peter W. Taylor
Denise Lowell-Britt
Stephen L. West

David R. Schwartz
Robert M. Jarrett, Jr. (Resident, Willcox Office)
Brian T. Allen
Curtis M. Chipman
April A. Speelmon

Representative Clients: Arizona Property and Casualty Insurance Guaranty Fund, Inc.; Wal-Mart Stores, Inc.; Lexington Insurance Co.; Farmers Insurance Co.; Coronet Insurance Co.

For full biographical listings, see the Martindale-Hubbell Law Directory

*PHOENIX,** Maricopa Co.

BEER & TOONE, P.C. (AV)

76 East Mitchell, 85012
Telephone: 602-263-0900
Fax: 602-263-0917
Email: law@beer-toone.com

Paul Beer
Thomas L. Toone
Michael C. Sheedy

Matthew F. Winter

LEGAL SUPPORT PERSONNEL

Adrienne D. Hogate (Legal Assistant)
Sandra Alcumbrac (Legal Assistant)

Representative Clients: AIG Aviation, Inc.; AVEMCO Insurance Company; Beech Aircraft Corporation; Cessna Aircraft Company; Loss Management Services, Inc.; Mercury Insurance Group; The Southland Corporation dba 7-Eleven Food Stores; State of Arizona; Underwriters at Lloyds, London; Thrifty Car Rental.

For full biographical listings, see the Martindale-Hubbell Law Directory

BESS KUNZ, A PROFESSIONAL CORPORATION (AV)

7210 North 16th Street, 85020-5201
Telephone: 602-331-4600
Telecopier: 602-331-8600

Leon D. Bess
Donald R. Kunz
Timothy R. Hyland
William M. Demlong
Matthew D. Kleifield

Thomas P. Liddy
Connie Totorica Gould
Elliot H. Wernick
Beth H. Schneider

Representative Clients: John Alden Life Insurance Co.; John Hancock Mutual Insurance Co.; Lincoln National Life Insurance Co.; MassMutual; Metropolitan Life Insurance Co.; New York Life Insurance Co.; The Paul Revere Life Insurance Co.; Safeco Insurance Company of America; The Equitable Life Assurance Society of the United States; The Travelers Insurance.

For full biographical listings, see the Martindale-Hubbell Law Directory

BONNETT, FAIRBOURN, FRIEDMAN & BALINT, P.C. (AV)

4041 North Central Avenue Suite 1100, 85012
Telephone: 602-274-1100
Fax: 602-274-1199

William G. Fairbourn
Robert J. Spurlock
C. Kevin Dykstra
Guy A. Hanson
Robert D. Ryan

Jason Ebe

For full biographical listings, see the Martindale-Hubbell Law Directory

LAW OFFICES OF MICHAEL E. BRADFORD (AV)

4131 North 24th Street Building C Suite 201, 85016
Telephone: 602-955-0088
Fax: 602-955-6445
Email: meblaw@primenet.com

(See Next Column)

LAW OFFICES OF MICHAEL E. BRADFORD—*Continued*

ASSOCIATE

Jeffrey L. Bradford

OF COUNSEL

Jerry Steele

For full biographical listings, see the Martindale-Hubbell Law Directory

BURCH & CRACCHIOLO, P.A. (AV)

702 East Osborn Road, Suite 200, 85014
Telephone: 602-274-7611
Fax: 602-234-0341
Mailing Address: P.O. Box 16882, Phoenix, AZ, 85011
Email: library@bcattorneys.com

Brian Kaven
Ian Neale
F. Michael Carroll
Daniel R. Malinski

Theodore (Todd) Julian
Steven J. Lippman

Representative Clients: Bashas' Inc.; Farmers Insurance Group; U-Haul International, Inc.

For Complete List of Firm Personnel, See General Section

For full biographical listings, see the Martindale-Hubbell Law Directory

CHARLES T. CARSON (AV)

3200 North Central Avenue Suite 1130, 85012
Telephone: 602-230-8819
Fax: 602-230-1335
Email: CTCarso@aol.com

For full biographical listings, see the Martindale-Hubbell Law Directory

COPPLE, CHAMBERLIN, BOEHM & MURPHY, P.C. (AV)

Suite 300 The Brookstone, 2025 North Third Street, 85004
Telephone: 602-528-4700
Fax: 602-253-4909
Tucson, Arizona Office: 127 West Franklin.
Telephone: 520-622-8855.
Fax: 520-628-7988.

Steven D. Copple
Thomas J. Chamberlin
Scott E. Boehm
Robert S. Murphy

OF COUNSEL

Frederick O. Robertshaw

Representative Clients: Aetna Casualty & Surety Co.; Aetna Life Insurance Co.; CIGNA; First State Insurance Co.; National Farmers Union Insurance Co.; Vrum & Forster Insurance Co.; World Service Life Insurance Co.; St. Paul Fire & Marine Insurance Co.; Transamerica Insurance Group; Auto Owners Insurance Co.

For full biographical listings, see the Martindale-Hubbell Law Directory

CRONIN & STANEWICH (AV)

One Columbus Plaza, 3636 North Central Avenue, Suite 560, 85012
Telephone: 602-222-4646
Fax: 602-222-4656
Email: cslaw@msn.com

MEMBERS OF FIRM

Robert S. Cronin, Jr.
Robert B. Stanewich

Representative Client: Liberty Mutual Insurance Co.

For full biographical listings, see the Martindale-Hubbell Law Directory

DOHERTY & VENEZIA, A PROFESSIONAL CORPORATION (AV)

100 West Clarendon, Suite 1720, 85013
Telephone: 602-277-1585
Fax: 602-277-1182

Julie A. Doherty
Stephen M. Venezia

Representative Clients: Cigna Property and Casualty Insurance; Colorado Western Insurance Co.; Concord General Corp.; Classic Fire & Marine Insurance Co.; Crawford & Co.; The Country Cos.; Insurance Company of the West; Intel; ITT Hartford; Kemper Risk Management.

For full biographical listings, see the Martindale-Hubbell Law Directory

WILLIAM J. DOWNEY, P.C. (AV)

3636 North Central Avenue, Suite 1150, 85012
Telephone: 602-222-4350
Facsimile: 602-222-4353
Email: downey@primenet.com *URL:* http://www.lawyers.com/williamjdowney

William J. Downey

(See Next Column)

Dane London Wood
Patrick B. Sigl
Elan Shai Mizrahi

For full biographical listings, see the Martindale-Hubbell Law Directory

DOYLE & WINTHROP, P.C. (AV)

2800 North Central Avenue Suite 1550, P.O. Box 10417, 85004
Telephone: 602-240-6711
Fax: 602-240-6951
Mailing Address: P.O. Box 10417, Phoenix, Arizona, 85064-0417
Las Vegas, Nevada Office: Edward D. Boyack, Esq., 2626 S. Rainbow Blvd., Suite 101, 89146.
Telephone: 702-873-1622.
Fax: 702-873-2280.

William H. Doyle
Angila L. Gallenstein

For full biographical listings, see the Martindale-Hubbell Law Directory

FENNEMORE CRAIG, A PROFESSIONAL CORPORATION (AV)

3003 North Central Avenue, Suite 2600, 85012-2913
Telephone: 602-916-5000
Fax: 602-916-5999
Tucson, Arizona Office: One South Church Avenue, Suite 1000, 85701-1620.
Telephone: 520-879-6800.
Fax: 520-879-6899.

Kenneth J. Sherk
John D. Everroad
William L. Thorpe
Phillip F. Fargotstein
Andrew M. Federhar
James J. Trimble
Jean Marie Sullivan
Douglas C. Northup
Marc H. Lamber

Mark H. Brain
James D. Burgess

LEGAL SUPPORT PERSONNEL

LEGAL ASSISTANTS

Beverly Cooper
Ann V. Kooi
Claudia L. Parks

For Complete List of Firm Personnel, See General Section

For full biographical listings, see the Martindale-Hubbell Law Directory

HARRIS, PALUMBO, POWERS & CUNNINGHAM, P.L.L.C. (AV)

361 East Coronado, Suite 101, P.O. Box 13568, 85002-3568
Telephone: 602-271-9344
Fax: 602-252-2099
Email: harrispalumbo@worldnet.att.net

John David Harris
Frank I. Powers
Shawn M. Cunningham

OF COUNSEL

Anthony J. Palumbo

For full biographical listings, see the Martindale-Hubbell Law Directory

HERZOG AND O'CONNOR, P.C. (AV)

5353 North 16th Street, Suite 175, 85016
Telephone: 602-277-5710
Fax: 602-277-6124

Michael W. Herzog
Mark S. O'Connor

Kirk A. Barberich

For full biographical listings, see the Martindale-Hubbell Law Directory

HOLLOWAY ODEGARD & SWEENEY, P.C. (AV)

3101 North Central Avenue, Suite 1200, 85012
Telephone: 602-240-6670
Telefax: 602-240-6677
Email: hos-law@primenet.com

Paul W. Holloway
Sally A. Odegard
Kevin B. Sweeney
Peter C. Kelly, II

Steven Ray Beeghley
Diana L. Clarke
Charles M. Callahan
Kenneth J. Januszewski

OF COUNSEL

Joseph C. Dolan

Representative Clients: Capitol Indemnity Ins. Co.; Carl Warren Co.; City of Scottsdale, AZ; Employers Reinsurance Corp.; Farmers Insurance Group; Guaranty National Ins. Co.; L.M.I. Insurance Co.; Safeco Ins. Co.; Southwest Risk Services, Inc.

For full biographical listings, see the Martindale-Hubbell Law Directory

Phoenix—Continued

JENNINGS, STROUSS & SALMON, P.L.C. (AV)

A Professional Limited Liability Company
One Renaissance Square, Two North Central Avenue, 85004-2393
Telephone: 602-262-5911
Fax: 602-253-3255
Email: info@jsslaw.com *URL:* http://www.jsslaw.com
Arrowhead Office: 16150 North Arrowhead Fountains Center Drive, Suite 250, Peoria, Arizona.
Telephone: 623-878-2222.
Fax: 623-878-1333.

T. Patrick Flood
W. Michael Flood
Michael G. Helms
David Brnilovich
John C. West
Jay A. Fradkin
H. Christian Bode
Michael J. O'Connor
Jennifer M. Bligh
Kim D. Steinmetz
Cody M. Hall
Richard K. Delo

OF COUNSEL

Gary L. Stuart

ASSOCIATES

Cynthia A. Coates
Andrew B. Turk
Bryan S. VanMeveren
John P. Robertson, II
Johnny J. Sorenson
C. David Martinez
Kevin R. Robling

For Complete List of Firm Personnel, See General Section

For full biographical listings, see the Martindale-Hubbell Law Directory

MARK & PEARLSTEIN, P.A. (AV)

Suite 150 The Brookstone, 2025 North Third Street, 85004
Telephone: 602-257-0200
Fax: 602-271-4711
Email: mplaw@primenet.com

Leonard J. Mark
Mr. Lynn M. Pearlstein

OF COUNSEL

Stephen G. Campbell

For full biographical listings, see the Martindale-Hubbell Law Directory

MCALLISTER & ABROMOVITZ (AV)

2025 North Third Street Suite 100, 85004
Telephone: 602-253-8840
Telefax: 602-253-5526
Email: manda@primenet.com

Michael L. McAllister

Representative Clients: Allianz Insurance Group; Arizona State Compensation Fund; The Tokio Marine and Fire Insurance Group; Liberty Mutual Company; Republic Insurance.

For full biographical listings, see the Martindale-Hubbell Law Directory

MUCHMORE & WALLWORK, A PROFESSIONAL CORPORATION (AV)

2700 North Central Avenue, Suite 1225, 85004-1165
Telephone: 602-240-6699
Data: 602-240-6698
Facsimile: 602-240-6697
Email: muchwork@mmww.com *URL:* http://www.mmww.com

Charles J. Muchmore
Nicholas J. Wallwork
Fredric D. Bellamy

SENIOR COUNSEL

Steve Owens

COUNSEL

Bridget S. Bade

Christopher D. Payne
Carolina L. Carver
Margaret Benny Hurst
Mindy K. Brinker

OF COUNSEL

Leslie Kyman Cooper
George H. King

LEGAL SUPPORT PERSONNEL

Gloria A. Torres (Administrator)
James R. Potts (Systems Administrator and Litigation Support Manager)
Gale James (Finance Manager)

Representative Clients: AgrEvo USA Company; BHP Copper, Inc.; Chevron U.S.A., Inc.; Cyprus Amax Minerals Company; Homes by Dave Brown, Inc.; National Indemnity Insurance Company; Standard Insurance Company; Washington Mills Electro Minerals Corporation; Cadbury Beverages, Inc.; Eisenberg Company.

For full biographical listings, see the Martindale-Hubbell Law Directory

RAYMOND, GREER & SASSAMAN, P.C. (AV)

3636 North Central Avenue, Suite 1070, 85012-1940
Telephone: 602-274-0500
Fax: 602-265-7560
Email: rgslaw@syspac.com

Randy L. Sassaman
Leonard D. Greer
Michael J. Raymond

OF COUNSEL

Mark J. Moryl

For full biographical listings, see the Martindale-Hubbell Law Directory

RHEES, HOPKINS & KREAMER (AV)

100 West Clarendon Suite 700, 85013
Telephone: 602-263-6010
Fax: 602-263-6016
Email: rhk@primenet.com

MEMBERS OF FIRM

Michael L. Rhees
Stephen M. Hopkins
Joseph C. Kreamer
Kelly Brown

For full biographical listings, see the Martindale-Hubbell Law Directory

ROBBINS & GREEN, A PROFESSIONAL ASSOCIATION (AV)

1800 Norwest Tower, 3300 North Central Avenue, 85012-2578
Telephone: 602-248-7600
Fax: 602-266-5369
Email: @RGLaw.com

Philip A. Robbins
Richard W. Abbuhl
William H. Sandweg III
Brian Imbornoni
Dwayne Ross

For full biographical listings, see the Martindale-Hubbell Law Directory

SHIMMEL, HILL, BISHOP & GRUENDER, P.C. (AV)

3700 North 24th Street, 85016
Telephone: 602-224-9500
Telecopier: 602-955-6176
URL: http://www.shimmelhill.com

Daniel F. Gruender
Scott J. Richardson

OF COUNSEL

Charles A. Finch

Representative Clients: AZ Property & Casualty Guaranty Fund; GAB Business Services; Liberty Mutual Insurance Co.; Rushmore National Life Insurance Co.; Prairie State Life Insurance Co.

For full biographical listings, see the Martindale-Hubbell Law Directory

SHORALL & STEVENS, P.C. (AV)

2828 North Central Avenue, Suite 1210, 85004-1022
Telephone: 602-230-5400
Fax: 602-230-5432

Thomas J. Shorall, Jr.
Don C. Stevens, II
Paul J. McGoldrick

Michael R. Golder
Scott M. Zerlaut
D. Andrew Bell

Representative Clients: Great American; State of Arizona; American Contractors Insurance Group.

For full biographical listings, see the Martindale-Hubbell Law Directory

SMOCK AND WEINBERGER (AV)

2700 North Central Avenue Suite 1125, 85004
Telephone: 602-230-5150
Telecopier: 602-230-5155

MEMBERS OF FIRM

Timothy R. Smock
Brian A. Weinberger

ASSOCIATE

Frank W. Moskowitz

For full biographical listings, see the Martindale-Hubbell Law Directory

STRUCKMEYER AND WILSON (AV)

910 East Osborn Road, 85014
Telephone: 602-248-9222
Fax: 602-263-0464
Email: drwilson@struckmeyerandwilson.com *URL:* http://www.struckmeyerandwilson.com

Donald R. Wilson
Fred C. Struckmeyer, Jr. (1912-1992)

(See Next Column)

STRUCKMEYER AND WILSON—*Continued*

ASSOCIATES

John P. Kaites
Stephen D. Hoffman
Anthony S. Coss
Timothy J. Watson
Karl A Fazio
Michele S. Coss
Scott Brian Humble

Representative Clients: American International Group; Commercial Union Cos.; Fireman's Fund American Insurance Cos.; Granite States Insurance Co.; Horace Mann Insurance Cos.; United States Fidelity and Guaranty Co.; Zurich Insurance Co.; Ohio Casualty; Jewelers Mutual Insurance; National Union Fire Insurance Co.

For full biographical listings, see the Martindale-Hubbell Law Directory

THOMAS & ELARDO, P.C. (AV)

2700 North Central Avenue, Suite 1500, 85004
Telephone: 602-274-8289
Fax: 602-285-4482

Benjamin C. Thomas
John A. Elardo
Neal B. Thomas

Jeffrey W. Brecher
Susan E. Irwin
Reed R. Johnson
Kenneth J. Peace
Jeffrey J. Spamer
Christina W. Kelly

Representative Clients: Alexsis Risk Management Services; Allied Group Ins.; Allstate Ins. Co.; American States Ins. Co.; Atlanta Casualty Ins. Co.; California Casualty Ins. Co.; CIGNA; CNA; Constitution State Management Co.; Continental Loss Adjustment Co.

For full biographical listings, see the Martindale-Hubbell Law Directory

SCOTTSDALE, Maricopa Co.

HERMAN, GOLDSTEIN & FORSYTH, P.C. (AV)

(Formerly Grossman, Goldstein & Forsyth, P.C.)
5040 East Shea Boulevard Suite 168, 85254
Telephone: 602-948-9424
Fax: 602-948-9425

Jill A. Herman
Evan S. Goldstein
Keith B. Forsyth

Pari K. Scroggin
Sanford K. Gerber

For full biographical listings, see the Martindale-Hubbell Law Directory

*TUCSON,** Pima Co.

CHANDLER, TULLAR, UDALL & REDHAIR, L.L.P. (AV)

1700 Bank of America Plaza, 33 North Stone Avenue, 85701-1415
Telephone: 520-623-4353
Telefax: 520-792-3426

MEMBERS OF FIRM

Thomas Chandler
D. B. Udall
Jack Redhair
Steven Weatherspoon
Edwin M. Gaines, Jr.
Dwight M. Whitley, Jr.
E. Hardy Smith
John J. Brady
Charles V. Harrington
Kurt Kroese

ASSOCIATES

Lori A. Petersen
Elizabeth D. Bushell
Christopher R. Pennison
Charles Alexander Davis
Michael Scott Redhair
Sue Ann Welch
Stephen L. Wetherell
Edward Moomjian, II

Representative Clients: CNA Insurance; Farmers Insurance Exchange; Mutual Insurance Company of Arizona; The Travelers Insurance Co.; Transamerica Insurance Co.; Chubb Group of Insurance Co.; National Aviation Underwriters; St. Paul Insurance Co.; State Farm Mutual Insurance Cos.; Allstate Insurance.

For full biographical listings, see the Martindale-Hubbell Law Directory

GOERING, ROBERTS, BERKMAN, RUBIN & BROGNA, P.C. (AV)

Suite 302, 1840 East River Road, 85718
Telephone: 520-577-9300
Fax: 520-577-0848
Email: grbrb@aol.com

Scott Goering
Howard T. Roberts, Jr.
David L. Berkman
William L. Rubin
Carmine A. Brogna
Christopher L. Enos

Representative Clients: Fireman's Fund Insurance; Safeco Insurance; Royal Insurance; Sentry Insurance; American International Group; Farmers Insurance; USAA; Country Companies; Cigna; Arizona Municipal Risk Retention Pool.
Reference: Bank One.

For full biographical listings, see the Martindale-Hubbell Law Directory

HAZLETT & WILKES (AV)

310 South Williams Boulevard, Suite 305, 85711
Telephone: 520-790-9663
Fax: 520-790-9616
Email: hazlettwilkes@juno.com

MEMBERS OF FIRM

Carl E. Hazlett
James M. Wilkes

ASSOCIATE

Thomas M. Bayham

For full biographical listings, see the Martindale-Hubbell Law Directory

KIMBLE, NELSON, AUDILETT, MCDONOUGH & MOLLA, P.C. (AV)

335 North Wilmot Road, Suite 500, 85711
Telephone: 520-748-2440
Fax: 520-748-2469

Darwin J. Nelson
Daryl A. Audilett
Lawrence McDonough
Negatu Molla

OF COUNSEL

William Kimble

Representative Clients: State of Arizona; General Motors Corp.; Procter & Gamble Co.; St. Paul Fire and Marine Insurance Co.; City of Tucson; Tucson Electric Power Co.; United States Fidelity & Guaranty Co.; Coriegis Co.; Allstate Insurance Co.

For full biographical listings, see the Martindale-Hubbell Law Directory

RABINOVITZ & ASSOCIATES, P.C. (AV)

721 North 4th Avenue, P.O. Box 41600, 85717
Telephone: 520-624-5526
Toll Free: 1-800-365-0821
Fax: 520-622-3776

Bernard I. Rabinovitz

John D. Ellis

LEGAL SUPPORT PERSONNEL

Michael Nielson (Paralegal)
Lisa Busciglio (Paralegal)
Ruth Polizzi (Paralegal)

Representative Client: Firemans Fund Insurance Co.

For full biographical listings, see the Martindale-Hubbell Law Directory

*YUMA,** Yuma Co.

CLARK AND ASSOCIATES (AV)

256 South Second Avenue, 85364
Telephone: 520-783-6233
Fax: 520-783-0533
Email: jasclark@yahoo.com *URL:* http://www.lawyers.com/j_clark&assoc

MEMBER OF FIRM

A. James Clark

ASSOCIATE

Heather D. Moore

Representative Clients: Viking Insurance Co.; Ryder Truck Rentals, Inc.; Federated Insurance; The Millers Group.

For full biographical listings, see the Martindale-Hubbell Law Directory

ARKANSAS

*BATESVILLE,** Independence Co.

GREGG & FARRIS (AV)

262 Boswell Street, P.O. Box 2496, 72501
Telephone: 870-793-7556
Fax: 870-793-6921

MEMBERS OF FIRM

John C. Gregg
Phillip B. Farris

For full biographical listings, see the Martindale-Hubbell Law Directory

*BENTON,** Saline Co.

BAXTER, JENSEN, PAYNE, YOUNG & SMITH (AV)

A Partnership including a Professional Association
310 West Conway Street, P.O. Drawer 1038, 72018-1038
Telephone: 501-315-0600
Fax: 501-315-0088
URL: http://www.baxterlaw.com

(See Next Column)

BAXTER, JENSEN, PAYNE, YOUNG & SMITH, *Benton—Continued*

MEMBERS OF FIRM

Ray Baxter (P.A.)
Terence C. Jensen
John Payne
Perry Y. Young
David E. Smith

LEGAL SUPPORT PERSONNEL

Meleah Carter

Representative CLients: American States Insurance Co.; Farm Bureau Insurance; General Accident Insurance Co.; Arkansas School Board Assn. (self-insurance program); Harleysville Insurance Co.; Nationwide Insurance Co.; Travelers Insurance Co.

For full biographical listings, see the Martindale-Hubbell Law Directory

ELLIS LAW FIRM (AV)

126 North Main Street, P.O. Box 1259, 72018
Telephone: 501-315-1000
Fax: 501-315-4222
Email: gdellis@aristotle.net

MEMBER OF FIRM

George D. Ellis

LEGAL SUPPORT PERSONNEL

Rhonda Beck Malone (Paralegal)

References: The Union Bank of Benton; Benton State Bank.

For full biographical listings, see the Martindale-Hubbell Law Directory

*BLYTHEVILLE,** Mississippi Co.

REID, BURGE, PREVALLET & COLEMAN (AV)

417 North Broadway, P.O. Box 107, 72316-0107
Telephone: 870-763-4586
Fax: 870-763-4642
URL: http://www.lawyers.com/rbpclaw

MEMBERS OF FIRM

Max B. Reid (1895-1959)
Dan M. Burge
Richard A. Reid
Donald E. Prevallet
Robert Lynn Coleman

Counsel for: Farmers Bank and Trust Co.; Arkansas Power & Light Co.; Bush Canning Co.; Allstate Insurance Cos.; Farmers Insurance Group; Wausau Insurance Cos.; United States Fidelity & Guaranty Co.; State Farm Cos.; Hartford Group.

For full biographical listings, see the Martindale-Hubbell Law Directory

*FAYETTEVILLE,** Washington Co.

DAVIS, COX & WRIGHT, PLC (AV)

19 East Mountain Street, P.O. Drawer 1688, 72702-1688
Telephone: 501-521-7600
Fax: 501-521-7661
Email: daviscoxwright@dcw-plc.com *URL:* http://www.dcw-plc.com

Sidney P. Davis, Jr.
Walter B. Cox
Tilden P. Wright, III
Constance G. Clark
William Jackson Butt, II
Kelly P. Carithers
Don A. Taylor
Paul H. Taylor
John G. Trice
Laura J. Andress

Mark W. Dossett
S. Lance Cox
Robin Miller

Representative Clients: Arkansas Farm Bureau Insurance Companies; Fireman's Fund Insurance Group; St. Paul Insurance Cos.; Kemper Insurance Group; Employers Mutual Companies; Foremont Insurance Company; Colonia Ins. Cos.; CNA Insurance Cos.

For full biographical listings, see the Martindale-Hubbell Law Directory

GREENHAW & GREENHAW (AV)

P.O. Box 4276, 72702
Telephone: 501-442-2562
Fax: 501-442-8479

Karl Greenhaw (1892-1967)
Leonard F. Greenhaw
William K. Greenhaw
John F. Greenhaw

Representative Clients: Southwestern Electric Power Co.; Commonwealth Theatres, Inc.; Federal Deposit Insurance Corp.; Foremost Dairies, Inc.; Pillsbury Mills, Inc.; Burlington Northern Railroad; Royal-Globe Insurance Group; St. Paul-Mercury Indemnity Co.; Government Employees Insurance Co.; General Electric Co.

For full biographical listings, see the Martindale-Hubbell Law Directory

JONES, JONES & LUSHBAUGH, PLC (AV)

112 South East Street, 72701
Telephone: 501-443-4313, 443-2021
Fax: 501-575-0528
Email: jjl@ar-attorneys.com

(See Next Column)

Lewis D. Jones
Gregory D. Jones
Bradley H. Lushbaugh

Representative Clients: Allstate Insurance Co.; The Home Insurance Co.; Horace Mann Insurance Co.; Miller's Mutual Fire Insurance Co.; The Firemen's Insurance Companies; Countrywide Insurance Group; AM Family Insurance Co.; Boatman's National Bank of Northwest Arkansas.
Approved Attorneys for: Lawyers Title Insurance Co.
Reference: Boatman's National Bank of Northwest Arkansas.

For full biographical listings, see the Martindale-Hubbell Law Directory

*FORREST CITY,** St. Francis Co.

BUTLER, HICKY & LONG (AV)

A Partnership of Professional Corporations
2216 North Washington Street, P.O. Box 989, 72335
Telephone: 870-633-4611
FAX: 870-633-6848
Email: bhlfirm@IPA.NET

MEMBERS OF FIRM

Philip Hicky (Ltd.)
Fletcher Long, Jr. (P.A.)

ASSOCIATE

Rita Reed Harris

Representative Clients: First National Bank of Eastern Arkansas; Southern Farm Bureau Insurance Cos.; United States Aviation Underwriters Group; National Aviation Underwriters; Hartford Accident and Indemnity Co.; Peoples Implement Co.; Virginia Insurance Reciprocal.

For full biographical listings, see the Martindale-Hubbell Law Directory

*FORT SMITH,** Sebastian Co.

DAILY & WOODS, P.L.L.C. (AV)

Stephens Office Building, 623 Garrison Avenue, P.O. Box 1446, 72902
Telephone: 501-782-0361
Fax: 501-782-6160
Email: DailyWoods@aol.com

MEMBERS OF FIRM

Ben Core
Jerry L. Canfield
Thomas A. Daily
Wyman R. Wade, Jr.
Stanley A. Leasure
Douglas M. Carson

ASSOCIATES

Todd Patrick Lewis
Barry D. Neal
Leigh M. Chiles

OF COUNSEL

James E. West

Representative Clients: Metropolitan Property and Liability Insurance Co.; Metropolitan Life Insurance Co.; Claims Management, Inc. (Wal-Mart); Mutual of Omaha; AEGON Insurance Group; United Services Automobile Association; American International Adjustment Co.; American Professional Insurance Co.; Commercial Union Insurance Cos.; General Accident Insurance Co.

For full biographical listings, see the Martindale-Hubbell Law Directory

JONES, JACKSON & MOLL, PLC (AV)

401 North Seventh Street, P.O. Box 2023, 72902-2023
Telephone: 501-782-7203
Fax: 501-782-9460
Email: jjmlaw@aol.com

MEMBERS OF FIRM

Robert L. Jones, Jr.
Randolph C. Jackson
Mark A. Moll
J. Scott Hardin

M. Chad Trammell
Jay William Kutchka

Insurance Counsel for: Farmers Insurance Group; State Farm Insurance Cos.; Maryland Insurance Cos.; Shelter Insurance Cos.; Travelers Insurance Co.; CNA Insurance Co.; Automobile Club Insurance Cos.
Counsel for: Merchants National Bank, Fort Smith, Arkansas; Beverly Enterprises, Inc.; Austin Powder Co.

For full biographical listings, see the Martindale-Hubbell Law Directory

LEDBETTER, COGBILL, ARNOLD & HARRISON, LLP (AV)

622 Parker Avenue, P.O. Box 185, 72902-0185
Telephone: 501-782-7294
Fax: 501-782-1493

MEMBERS OF FIRM

Charles R. Ledbetter
J. Michael Cogbill
James A. Arnold, II
Ronald D. Harrison
E. Diane Graham
R. Ray Fulmer, II

ASSOCIATES

Rebecca D. Hattabaugh
Virginia C. Trammell
Daniel A. Stewart

Representative Clients: First National Bank of Fort Smith; Bank of Mansfield; Commercial Bank at Alma.

(See Next Column)

LEDBETTER, COGBILL, ARNOLD & HARRISON LLP—*Continued*

Local Attorneys for: Liberty Mutual Insurance Co.; St. Paul Insurance Cos.; Fireman's Fund Ins. Co.; American Physicians Insurance Exchange; CIGNA Ins. Co.; Canal Insurance Co.

For full biographical listings, see the Martindale-Hubbell Law Directory

PRYOR, BARRY, SMITH, KARBER AND ALFORD P.L.C. (AV)

315 North 7th Street, P.O. Drawer 848, 72902-0848
Telephone: 501-782-8813
Fax: 501-785-0254
Email: pbska@ipa.net

MEMBERS OF FIRM

G. Byron Dobbs (1907-1976)
Owen C. Pearce (1917-1976)
Thomas B. Pryor (1869-1952)
Thomas B. Pryor, Jr. (1904-1953)
Thomas B. Pryor
Ben T. Barry
Gregory G. Smith
Gregory T. Karber
John D. Alford

ASSOCIATE

Jacqueline J. Johnston

Representative Clients: State Farm Insurance Co.; Allstate Government Employees Insurance Co.; National Security Fire & Casualty Co.; Nationwide Insurance Co.; Scottish and York International Insurance Group; Brown-Hiller-Clark & Associates; Progressive Insurance Co.; National General Insurance; American Excel Corp.; American National Property and Casualty Insurance Co.

For full biographical listings, see the Martindale-Hubbell Law Directory

WARNER, SMITH & HARRIS, PLC (AV)

214 North Sixth Street, P.O. Box 1626, 72901
Telephone: 501-782-6041
Fax: 501-782-0841

Harry Preston Warner (1885-1969)
Cecil Randolph Warner (1890-1955)
Thomas G. Graves (1939-1971)
Douglas O. Smith, Jr.
C. Wayne Harris
Gerald L. DeLung
Patrick Neill Moore
Lillard Cody Hayes
G. Alan Wooten
James Melvin Dunn
John Alan Lewis
Joel D. Johnson
J. Randall McGinnis
Kathryn Stocks Campbell
R. Gregory Aclin

Jason Trevor Browning
Matthew C. Carter

OF COUNSEL

C. R. Warner, Jr.

Local Counsel for: Continental National American Group; Crum & Forster Insurance Group; Fireman's Fund-American Insurance Cos.; Home Insurance Group; Safeco Insurance Group; Maryland Casualty Co.; Reliance Insurance Cos.; Highlands Insurance Co.; Ohio Casualty Co.; St. Paul Fire and Marine Insurance Co.

For full biographical listings, see the Martindale-Hubbell Law Directory

*JONESBORO,** Craighead Co.

BARRETT & DEACON, A PROFESSIONAL ASSOCIATION (AV)

Union Planters Bank Building, 300 South Church Street, P.O. Box 1700, 72403
Telephone: 870-931-1700
Fax: 870-931-1800

Joe C. Barrett (1897-1980)
John C. Deacon
J. Barry Deacon
Ralph W. Waddell
Paul D. Waddell
D. Price Marshall, Jr.
James D. Bradbury

Kevin W. Cole
Robert S. Jones
Jennifer S. Cameron
James F. Gramling, Jr

For full biographical listings, see the Martindale-Hubbell Law Directory

SNELLGROVE, LANGLEY, LOVETT & CULPEPPER (AV)

Second Floor, 111 East Huntington, P.O. Box 1346, 72403-1346
Telephone: 870-932-8357
Fax: 870-932-5488

MEMBERS OF FIRM

G. D. Walker (1910-1989)
Frank Snellgrove, Jr.
Stanley R. Langley
Glenn Lovett, Jr.
Malcolm Culpepper
D. Todd Williams
Michael E. Mullally

ASSOCIATE

Anita Perkins Leonard

Representative Clients: Union Planters Bank, N.A. (formerly Mercantile Bank); Regions Bank; Travelers Insurance Co.; Aetna Insurance Co.; ITT Hartford Insurance Co.; Commercial Union Insurance Co.; CNA Insurance Group; State Farm Insurance Cos.; Columbia Mutual Insurance Co.; Bituminous Insurance Co.

(See Next Column)

For full biographical listings, see the Martindale-Hubbell Law Directory

WOMACK, LANDIS, PHELPS, MCNEILL & MCDANIEL, A PROFESSIONAL ASSOCIATION (AV)

Century Center, 301 West Washington, P.O. Box 3077, 72403
Telephone: 870-932-0900
Fax: 870-932-2553
URL: http//www.wlpmm-firm.com

Tom D. Womack
Carl David Landis
John V. Phelps
Paul D. McNeill
Lucinda McDaniel
Richard A. Lusby
Jeffrey W. Puryear

Mark Alan Mayfield
David Christopher Gardner
Dan Clark Young
Jeffrey L. Singleton

Representative Clients: American General Insurance Co.; CNA Insurance Cos.; Farmland Insurance Co.; Federated Insurance Co.; Home Indemnity Company of N.Y.; St. Paul Insurance Cos.; Shelter Insurance Co.; United States Fidelity & Guaranty Co.

For full biographical listings, see the Martindale-Hubbell Law Directory

*LITTLE ROCK,** Pulaski Co.

ALLEN LAW FIRM, A PROFESSIONAL CORPORATION (AV)

950 Centre Place, 212 Center Street, 72201
Telephone: 501-374-7100
Telecopier: 501-374-1611
Email: hwallen@cei.net *URL:* http://www.lawyers.com/allenlawfirm

H. William Allen

Representative Clients: Garlock, Inc.; St. Paul Insurance Co.; Central Arkansas Risk Management Association.

For full biographical listings, see the Martindale-Hubbell Law Directory

ANDERSON, MURPHY & HOPKINS, L.L.P. (AV)

400 West Capitol Avenue, Suite 2640, 72201
Telephone: 501-372-1887
Fax: 501-372-7706
Email: ande@att.net

MEMBERS OF FIRM

Overton S. Anderson, II
Randy P. Murphy
Mariam T. Hopkins

ASSOCIATES

Michael P. Vanderford
Penny Brown Wilbourn
David A. Littleton
Scott D. Provencher

For full biographical listings, see the Martindale-Hubbell Law Directory

BARBER, MCCASKILL, JONES & HALE, P.A. (AV)

2700 Regions Center, 400 West Capitol Avenue, 72201-3414
Telephone: 501-372-6175
Telecopier: 501-375-2802

Azro L. Barber (1885-1979)
Elbert A. Henry (1889-1966)
John B. Thurman (1912-1971)
Austin McCaskill, Sr.
Glenn W. Jones
Michael E. Hale
John S. Cherry, Jr.
Robert L. Henry, III
Micheal L. Alexander
William H. Edwards, Jr.
G. Spence Fricke
Gail Ponder Gaines
Michael J. Emerson
R. Kenny McCulloch
Tim A. Cheatham
Joseph F. Kolb
Scott Michael Strauss
Baucum Fulk
D. Keith Fortner
Wendy Scholtens Wood
Morris L. Williams, III
Michelle Bass Miller

Attorneys for: Associated Aviation Underwriters; CNA Insurance Companies; Fireman's Fund Insurance Co.; GAB Robins; Hanover Insurance Co.; Royal Insurance; State Farm Automobile Insurance, Co.; Tokio Marine & Fire Insurance Group; United States Fidelity & Guaranty Co.; Universal Underwriters Insurance Co.

For full biographical listings, see the Martindale-Hubbell Law Directory

FRIDAY, ELDREDGE & CLARK (AV)

A Limited Liability Partnership of Individuals and Professional Associations
Formerly, Smith, Williams, Friday, Eldredge & Clark
2000 Regions Center, 400 West Capitol Avenue, 72201-3493
Telephone: 501-376-2011
Telecopier: 501-376-2147
Email: fecmh@fec.net

MEMBERS OF FIRM

William H. Sutton (P.A.)
Frederick S. Ursery (P.A.)
John Dewey Watson (P.A.)
J. Phillip Malcom (P.A.)
James M. Simpson, Jr. (P.A.)
Donald H. Bacon (P.A.)
Barry E. Coplin (P.A.)
Elizabeth Robben Murray (P.A.)
Laura Hensley Smith (P.A.)
William Mell Griffin III (P.A.)

(See Next Column)

FRIDAY, ELDREDGE & CLARK, *Little Rock—Continued*

MEMBERS OF FIRM (Continued)

Kevin A. Crass (P.A.)
William A. Waddell, Jr. (P.A.)
Scott J. Lancaster (P.A.)
James C. Baker (P.A.)
Scott H. Tucker (P.A.)
Guy Alton Wade (P.A.)
Tonia P. Jones (P.A.)
David D. Wilson (P.A.)
R. Christopher Lawson (P.A.)
Gregory D. Taylor (P.A.)
Fran C. Hickman (P.A.)
Betty J. Demory (P.A.)

ASSOCIATES

Clifford W. Plunkett
Jason B. Hendren
Susan N. Childers
Christopher A. Averitt
Joseph P. McKay

Counsel for: Union Pacific System; St. Paul Insurance Co.; Liberty Mutual Insurance Co.; Cigna Property & Casualty Co.; Entergy Arkansas, Inc.; Dillard's, Inc.; Browning Arms Co.; Phillips Petroleum Co.; Aetna Casualty & Surety Co.

For Complete List of Firm Personnel, See General Section

For full biographical listings, see the Martindale-Hubbell Law Directory

HUCKABAY, MUNSON, ROWLETT & TILLEY, P.A. (AV)

Regions Center, Suite 1900, 400 West Capitol, 72201
Telephone: 501-374-6535
Fax: 501-374-5906

Mike Huckabay
Bruce E. Munson
Beverly A. Rowlett
James W. Tilley
John E. Moore
Tim Boone
Rick Runnells
Sarah Ann Presson
D. Michael Huckabay, Jr.
Carol Lockard Worley
Mark S. Breeding

Elizabeth Fletcher Rogers
Julia L. Busfield
Jane M. Yocum
Terry D. Dugger

Representative Clients: Allstate Insurance Company; American International Group; American National Property and Casualty; Farmers Insurance Group; General Electric Company; Nationwide Insurance Company; St. Vincent Infirmary Medical Center; State Farm Mutual Automobile Insurance Company; State Farm Fire and Casualty Company; Tenet Healthcare Corp.; Travelers Insurance Co.

For full biographical listings, see the Martindale-Hubbell Law Directory

KILPATRICK, AUD & WILLIAMS, L.L.P. (AV)

Regions Center, 400 West Capitol Avenue, Suite 1910, 72201-4849
Telephone: 501-372-0401
Facsimile: 501-372-5277

Joseph E. Kilpatrick, Jr.
Michael E. Aud
Aylmer Gene Williams

For full biographical listings, see the Martindale-Hubbell Law Directory

LASER, WILSON, BUFFORD & WATTS, P.A. (AV)

101 South Spring Street, Suite 300, 72201-2488
Telephone: 501-376-2981
Telecopier: 501-376-2417
Email: laser@laserlaw.com

Sam Laser
Dan F. Bufford
Richard N. Watts
Frank B. Newell
J. Kendal "Ken" Cook
Alfred F. Angulo, Jr.
David M. Donovan
Kevin J. Staten

Brian A. Brown
Karen J. Hughes
Thomas J. Diaz
Keith Martin McPherson
Deborah S. Denton
Andy L. Turner
Donna L. Gay
Sara A. Farris

OF COUNSEL

Ralph R. Wilson

Representative Clients: Allstate Insurance Co.; American International Insurance Group; Continental Insurance Cos.; Farm Bureau Insurance Cos. (Casualty & Fire); Farmers Insurance Group; GAB Business Services, Inc.; St. Paul Insurance Cos.; Scottsdale Insurance Co.; State Farm Auto (Fire) Insurance Cos.

For full biographical listings, see the Martindale-Hubbell Law Directory

ROSE LAW FIRM, A PROFESSIONAL ASSOCIATION (AV)

120 East Fourth Street, 72201
Telephone: 501-375-9131
Telecopy: 501-375-1309

David L. Williams
Richard T. Donovan
Amy Lee Stewart
David P. Martin
Michael G. Smith
Michael N. Shannon

COUNSEL

Phillip Carroll

(See Next Column)

Jennifer B. Hendren
John D. Coulter

Representative Clients: The Equitable Life Assurance Society of the United States; Bridgestone/Firestone, Inc.; CIGNA Companies; Georgia-Pacific Corp.; General Motors Corp.; John Hancock Mutual Life Insurance Co.; Kemper Insurance Group; New York Life Insurance Co.; The Prudential Insurance Company of America; USX Corp.

For Complete List of Firm Personnel, See General Section

For full biographical listings, see the Martindale-Hubbell Law Directory

SPRINGDALE, Washington Co.

CYPERT, CROUCH, CLARK & HARWELL (AV)

111 Holcomb Street, P.O. Box 1400, 72765-4496
Telephone: 501-751-5222
Fax: 501-751-5777
Email: nwark.com

James E. Crouch
Charles L. Harwell

General Counsel for: First National Bank of Springdale; Northwest Health Systems; Springdale School District.
Representative Clients: Purina Mills, Inc.; Swift-Eckrich, Inc.; Arkansas and Missouri RRCO.
Insurance Clients: American National Property and Casualty Co.; Liberty Mutual; Fireman's Fund; Chicago Title.

For Complete List of Firm Personnel, See General Section

For full biographical listings, see the Martindale-Hubbell Law Directory

WEST MEMPHIS, Crittenden Co.

RIEVES & MAYTON (AV)

304 East Broadway, P.O. Box 1359, 72303
Telephone: 870-735-3420
Telecopier: 870-735-4678
Email: rieves.mayton@worldnet.att.net
Little Rock, Arkansas Office: Suite 1719, First Commercial Building, 400 West Capitol.
Telephone: 501-376-0504.
Telecopier: 501-372-3482.

MEMBERS OF FIRM

Elton A. Rieves, Jr. (1909-1984)
Elton A. Rieves, III
Michael R. Mayton
Elton A. Rieves, IV

ASSOCIATES

David S. Wilson, III
Eric Newkirk

For full biographical listings, see the Martindale-Hubbell Law Directory

CALIFORNIA

*AUBURN,** Placer Co.

LEUPP, WACHOB & WOODALL (AV)

149 Court Street, 95603
Telephone: 530-888-1100
Fax: 530-888-1821
URL: http://www.lawyers.com/lwwlaw

MEMBERS OF FIRM

Thomas A. Leupp
Charles D. Wachob
Timothy S. Woodall

For full biographical listings, see the Martindale-Hubbell Law Directory

*BAKERSFIELD,** Kern Co.

BORTON, PETRINI & CONRON, LLP (AV)

The Borton, Petrini & Conron Building, 1600 Truxtun Avenue, 93301
Telephone: 661-322-3051
Voice Mail: 661-395-6700
Fax: 661-322-4628
Mailing Address: P.O. Box 2026, Bakersfield, California, 93303
Email: bpcbak@bpclaw.com *URL:* http://www.bpclaw.com
Other City Locations: Fresno, Los Angeles, Modesto, Redding, Sacramento, San Bernardino, San Diego, San Francisco, San Jose, San Luis Obispo, Santa Ana and Ventura.

MEMBERS OF FIRM

George F. Martin
Richard E. Hitchcock
John F. Petrini
Stephen M. Dake
Paul Lafranchise
Richard E. Morton
Calvin R. Stead
Steve Karcher
Victoria R. Allard-Bernhardt

(See Next Column)

BORTON, PETRINI & CONRON LLP—*Continued*

ASSOCIATES

William G. Welzenbach
Stephen M. Crane
Brian Jensen Stowell
Richard D. Brown
Raymond G. Robinson
Dee H. Stasnopolis
Randall Steven Joyce
John W. Fox
Timothy B. Liebaert
Clayton A. Mack
Michael J. Stump

OF COUNSEL

Roy J. Gargano
Jere N. Sullivan, Sr.

For Complete List of Firm Personnel, See General Section

For full biographical listings, see the Martindale-Hubbell Law Directory

ROBINSON, PALMER & LOGAN (AV)

Suite 150, 3434 Truxtun Avenue, 93301
Telephone: 805-323-8277
Fax: 805-323-4205
Email: RPLLAW@AOL.COM

MEMBERS OF FIRM

Oliver U. Robinson
William D. Palmer
Gary L. Logan

ASSOCIATES

Marshall S. Fontes
David T. Ungar

For full biographical listings, see the Martindale-Hubbell Law Directory

BERKELEY, Alameda Co.

BURESH, KAPLAN, JANG & FELLER (AV)

2298 Durant Avenue, 94704
Telephone: 510-548-7474
Fax: 510-548-7488

Scott Buresh
Ann S. Kaplan
Alan J. Jang
Fred M. Feller
Gina Dashman Boer
Peggy Chang

ASSOCIATES

Noël S. Plummer
Charles A. Alfonzo
Leticia Gonzaléz
Edward C. Schroeder, Jr.

OF COUNSEL

Lawrence A. Baker

For full biographical listings, see the Martindale-Hubbell Law Directory

BEVERLY HILLS, Los Angeles Co.

HERZOG, FISHER, GRAYSON & WOLFE, A LAW CORPORATION (AV)

9460 Wilshire Boulevard Fifth Floor, 90212
Telephone: 310-278-4300
Fax: 310-278-5430

James P. Herzog
David R. Fisher
Michael A. Grayson
Herbert N. Wolfe

Doreen W. Shenfeld
Jerry R. Sparks
Bree Arlyn-Pessin

OF COUNSEL

Todd I. Grayson

For full biographical listings, see the Martindale-Hubbell Law Directory

WILNER, KLEIN & SIEGEL, A PROFESSIONAL CORPORATION (AV)

Suite 700, 9601 Wilshire Boulevard, 90210
Telephone: 310-550-4595
Facsimile: 310-275-3509
Brea, California Office: 3230 East Imperial Highway, Suite 309.
Telephone: 714-579-2600.
Facsimile: 714-579-2549.

Walter Klein
Samuel Wilner
Leonard Siegel
Laura J. Snoke
Jodi Zucker Taksar
Edward E. Wallace
Joseph R. Serpico

Floyd W. Cranmore
Edwin J. Howard
Thomas M. Ware, II
Joshua B. Bereny
Mitchell S. Brachman
Stephen Coopersmith
Steven J. Parker (Resident, Brea Office)
Darrell J. Mariz
Alison M. Walz
Robert D. Moore (Resident, Brea Office)
Allen Donald MacNeil (Resident, Brea Office)
Steven M. Hepps (Resident, Brea Office)

(See Next Column)

OF COUNSEL

Richard B. Kott (Resident, Brea Office)

Reference: City National Bank.

For full biographical listings, see the Martindale-Hubbell Law Directory

BURBANK, Los Angeles Co.

MARRONE ROBINSON FREDERICK & FOSTER, PROFESSIONAL CORPORATION (AV)

111 North First Street, Suite 300, 91502-1851
Telephone: 818-841-1144
Fax: 818-841-0746

Phillip R. Marrone
Jay Robinson
J. Alan Frederick
Thomas A. Foster
Robert Boon

Dennis P. De Franzo
Gary D. Ellington
Scot G. Sandoval
Douglas Fee
Phillip H. Howard
Ann Katherine Shell
Sue-Ann A. Peterson
Lucy G. Mendoza
Peter W. Dye

Representative Clients: Collier-Keyworth Co.; Columbia Pictures Industries, Inc.; Fireman's Insurance of Washington, D.C.; Holiday Inn, Inc.; MCA; Inc.; National Continental Insurance Co.; Textron, Inc.

For full biographical listings, see the Martindale-Hubbell Law Directory

BURLINGAME, San Mateo Co.

WINTERS, KRUG, DELBON & NASTARI (AV)

345 Lorton Avenue, Suite 101, 94010-4116
Telephone: 650-579-1422
Fax: 650-579-1852
Email: wkdlaw@aol.com *URL:* http://www.wkdlaw@aol.com

MEMBERS OF FIRM

Daniel W. Winters
John S. Krug
David A. Delbon
Jerry E. Nastari
David F. Zucca
Michelle A. Ward

Representative Clients: California State Automobile Association; City of Burlingame; City of San Carlos; Fireman's Fund; Great American Insurance Company; State Farm Mutual Automobile Insurance Company; Tokio Marine Management Company; Town of Hillsborough; Town of Woodside; USAA Property and Casualty Insurance; Zurich Commercial.

For full biographical listings, see the Martindale-Hubbell Law Directory

CHICO, Butte Co.

PETERS, RUSH, HABIB & MCKENNA (AV)

414 Salem Street, P.O. Box 3509, 95928
Telephone: 530-342-3593
FAX: 530-342-4272
Email: prhmlaw@dcsi.net

Guy R. Kennedy (1871-1933)
Jerome D. Peters (1891-1953)
James C. Farnsworth (1957-1997)
Jerome D. Peters, Jr. (Retired)
David R. Fuller (Retired)

MEMBERS OF FIRM

David H. Rush
Mark A. Habib
James P. McKenna

ASSOCIATE

Carmen M. Palomo

Representative Clients: Pacific Gas & Electric Co.; Gregory Bragg & Associates; Helena Chemical Co.; Wells Fargo Bank; Church Mutual Insurance Co.; AEGON Insurance Group; John Deere Insurance Co.; Harco National Insurance Co.; Milwaukee Insurance Co.; Progressive Insurance Co.

For full biographical listings, see the Martindale-Hubbell Law Directory

SHEPHERD & CRABTREE (AV)

Suite 1, 1367 East Lassen Avenue, 95973
Telephone: 530-893-3700
Fax: 530-893-1579

MEMBERS OF FIRM

Michael T. Shepherd
Richard L. Crabtree

ASSOCIATES

Lindsey A. Holmes
Ron S. Chaplin

For full biographical listings, see the Martindale-Hubbell Law Directory

COSTA MESA, Orange Co.

MORROW & WHITE (AV)

535 Anton Boulevard, Suite 1150, 92626-1977
Telephone: 949-979-7999
Fax: 949-979-7779

(See Next Column)

MORROW & WHITE, *Costa Mesa—Continued*

William D. Morrow
Christopher A. White
David A. Gerlt
Robert D. Bills, Jr.
Anthony C. Edwards

For full biographical listings, see the Martindale-Hubbell Law Directory

DANVILLE, Contra Costa Co.

CRADDICK, CANDLAND & CONTI, PROFESSIONAL CORPORATION (AV)

Danville-San Ramon Medical Center, 915 San Ramon Valley Boulevard, Suite 260, 94526-0810
Telephone: 925-838-1100
Fax: 925-743-0729

Marrs A. Craddick (1928-1996)
D. Stuart Candland
Richard J. Conti
Robert W. Hodges
W. David Walker
Andrew S. Miller
Thomas G. Manning
Steven L. Brown, Jr.

Jean Louise Perry
Kristine Keala Meredith
Matthew C. Mani
Emily C. Millar
Michael E. Gatto

Representative Clients: Kaiser Foundation Hospitals; Medical Insurance Exchange of California; The Doctor's Co.; County of Contra Costa; Farmers Insurance Group (Truck Insurance Exchange); Professional Risk Management of California, Inc.; Claremont Liability Insurance Company; Program Beta.

For full biographical listings, see the Martindale-Hubbell Law Directory

*EL CENTRO,** Imperial Co.

HORTON, KNOX, CARTER & FOOTE (AV)

Law Building, 895 Broadway, 92243
Telephone: 760-352-2821
Telefax: 760-352-8540
Email: hkcf@earthlink.net
Brawley Office: 195 South Second Street.
Telephone: 760-344-2360.
Fax: 760-344-9778.

MEMBERS OF FIRM

Harry W. Horton (1892-1966)
James H. Carter (1918-1978)
Reginald L. Knox, Jr. (1916-1996)
Orlando B. Foote, III
John Penn Carter, III
Frank A. Oswalt, III
Dennis H. Morita
Philip J. Krum, Jr.
Mercedes Z. Wheeler (Resident, Brawley Office)

ASSOCIATES

Patrick M. Pace (Resident, Brawley Office)
Ruth Bermudez Montenegro
Jeffrey M. Garber
Steve Escalera
Mark V. Santa-Romana

OF COUNSEL

Paul D. Engstrand

Representative Clients: Automobile Club of Southern Calif.; Imperial Irrigation District; Union Pacific Co.; Reliance Insurance Cos.; Pioneer Memorial Hospital District; City of Imperial; San Diego Gas & Electric Co.; Chevron U.S.A.; Bixby Land Co.

For full biographical listings, see the Martindale-Hubbell Law Directory

EMERYVILLE, Alameda Co.

BISHOP, BARRY, HOWE, HANEY & RYDER, A PROFESSIONAL CORPORATION (AV)

Watergate Tower III, 2000 Powell Street, Suite 1425, 94608
Telephone: 510-596-0888
Fax: 510-596-0899
Email: FirmGeneral@BBHHR.com
San Francisco Office: 44 Montgomery Street, Suite 1300, 94104.
Telephone: 415-421-8550.

Ross R. Ryder (1940-1989)
Nelson C. Barry
Drayton F. Howe, Jr.
Jeffrey N. Haney
Thomas O. Haran
Rebecca B. Aherne
Michael W. Bolechowski
Mark C. Raskoff
Patricia S. Lakner
Gregory R. de la Peña

J. Scott Wood
Mitchell J. Alward
Marco R. Sumarriva
Jane E. Carey
Carol L. Healey
Mary Margaret Ryan
Thomas Edward Foran
John F. Cooke
Jean H. Hurricane
Daniel M. O'Connell
Lisa S. Wiggins
Edward M. Lai

(See Next Column)

OF COUNSEL

Lawrence S. Molton
David P. Osako

Representative Clients: American Excess & Surplus Ins. Co. (AESIC); Argonaut Ins. Co.; CGU Insurance; Farmers Insurance; Firemans Fund Ins. Co.; General Reinsurance Co.; Gerling American Ins. Co.; Great American Ins. Company; Royal/SunAlliance; TIG.

For full biographical listings, see the Martindale-Hubbell Law Directory

ENCINO, Los Angeles Co.

LAW OFFICES OF KRISTI WEILER DEAN (AV)

Suite 230, 6345 Balboa Boulevard, 91316
Telephone: 818-774-2131
FAX: 818-774-2141
Email: kwdlaw@mindspring.com *URL:* http://www.kwdlaw.com

ASSOCIATES

Raymond J. Feinberg
Leslie A. Blozan
John J. Cariati

OF COUNSEL

Stuart E. Rissman

Representative Clients: Topa Insurance; JMB Realty Corp.; The Bekins Co.; AMFAC Resorts; Schifrin, Gagnon and Dickey; AIMS; Alexsis Risk Management, Inc.; Golden Bear Insurance Co.

For full biographical listings, see the Martindale-Hubbell Law Directory

STAITMAN SNYDER TANNENBAUM & DORENFELD, LLP (AV)

Suite 1401, 16633 Ventura Boulevard, 91436-1840
Telephone: 818-981-5300; 213-872-3530
FAX: 818-981-7104

Bradley A. Snyder
Jack J. Tannenbaum
David K. Dorenfeld

Rodger S. Greiner
Deborah K. Galer
Peter A. Mittenthal

For full biographical listings, see the Martindale-Hubbell Law Directory

STONE & ROSENBLATT, A LAW CORPORATION (AV)

16133 Ventura Boulevard Suite 855, 91436
Telephone: 818-789-2232
Fax: 818-789-2269
Email: info@stone-rosenblatt.com

Ira H. Rosenblatt
Gregory E. Stone
John S. Cha

Richard S. McGuire
Adam J. Soibelman
Gregory S. Miller
Richard A. Phillips
Suzanne R. Feffer
Gregg S. Garfinkel

For full biographical listings, see the Martindale-Hubbell Law Directory

*EUREKA,** Humboldt Co.

MITCHELL, BRISSO, DELANEY & VRIEZE (AV)

814 Seventh Street, P.O. Drawer 1008, 95502
Telephone: 707-443-5643
Fax: 707-444-9586
Email: mitchlaw@humboldt1.com

MEMBERS OF FIRM

Clifford B. Mitchell
Nancy K. Delaney
Paul A. Brisso
John M. Vrieze
William F. Mitchell

ASSOCIATES

Russell Scott Gans
Nicholas R. Kloeppel

RETIRED PARTNER

Robert C. Dedekam

Representative Clients: California Automobile Assn.; State Farm; Allstate; Fireman's Fund; Hartford; Travelers; Wausau; Viking; Nationwide; Redwood Empire Municipal Insurance Fund.

For full biographical listings, see the Martindale-Hubbell Law Directory

*FRESNO,** Fresno Co.

DOWLING, AARON & KEELER, INCORPORATED (AV)

6051 North Fresno Street, Suite 200, 93710
Telephone: 559-432-4500
Fax: 559-432-4590
Email: dak@daklaw.com *URL:* http://www.daklaw.com
Bakersfield, California Office: 110 South Mt. Claire, Suite 203. 93309.
Telephone: 661-396-0451. Web Site: http://www.daklaw.com.

(See Next Column)

DOWLING, AARON & KEELER INCORPORATED—*Continued*

Stephen M. Blumberg
Philip David Kopp
Dale Ikeda
Adolfo M. Corona
Gary M. Fachin
Francine Marie Kanne
James C. Sherwood
David J. Weiland

Leigh W. Burnside

Reference: Wells Fargo Bank (Main).

For Complete List of Firm Personnel, See General Section

For full biographical listings, see the Martindale-Hubbell Law Directory

MARDEROSIAN, OREN & PABOOJIAN, A PROFESSIONAL CORPORATION (AV)

1260 Fulton Mall, 93721-1783
Telephone: 559-441-7991
Facsimilie: 559-441-8170

C. Sam Titus (1957-1990)
Michael G. Marderosian
Eric P. Oren
Warren R. Paboojian
Brett L. Runyon
Alan M. Simpson
Sue Ann Cercone

Michael E. Lehman
David J. Frankenberger, Jr.
Lance E. Armo
Stephen T. Knudsen

For full biographical listings, see the Martindale-Hubbell Law Directory

GARDENA, Los Angeles Co.

McGARRY & LAUFENBERG (AV)

1125 West 190th Street, Suite 230, 90248
Telephone: 310-380-1650
Fax: 310-380-1662
Email: jjmjjlaw@aol.com

MEMBERS OF FIRM

James J. McGarry
Jeffrey J. Laufenberg
William Leamon Cummings
John E. Zegel

For full biographical listings, see the Martindale-Hubbell Law Directory

IRVINE, Orange Co.

ANDRADE & ASSOCIATES (AV)

First Security Bank Building, 18401 Von Karman, Suite 350, 92612
Telephone: 949-553-1951
Telecopier: 949-553-0655
Email: andrade@andradelaw.com
San Diego, California Office: Tokia Bank Building, 3111 Camino Del Rio North, Suite 1100.
Telephone: 619-291-2481.
Las Vegas, Nevada Office: 3753 Howard Hughes Parkway, Suite 200.
Telephone: 888-553-1951.

MEMBER OF FIRM

Richard B. Andrade

ASSOCIATES

Frank A. Satalino
Lori A. McClaskey
Eric Rans
Deborah J. Taddeucci

Representative Clients: American International Cos.; American Home Assurance; Insurance Company of North America (INA); National Union Fire Insurance of Pittsburgh, PA.; Aetna Insurance Co.; Fremont Insurance Co.; Maryland Casualty; Commercial Union Insurance Co.; Superior National Insurance Co.; Lloyds of London; Wausau Insurance.

For full biographical listings, see the Martindale-Hubbell Law Directory

CARL J. KLUNDER (AV)

108 Pacifica, Suite 340, P.O. Box 19799, 92623-9799
Telephone: 714-727-2099
Fax: 714-727-3057

For full biographical listings, see the Martindale-Hubbell Law Directory

MOWER, KOELLER, NEBEKER, CARLSON & HALUCK, LLP (AV)

108 Pacifica, P.O. Box 19799, 92623-9799
Telephone: 714-753-1229
Fax: 714-753-1413
Email: infoir@mknch.com *URL:* http://www.mknch.com
San Bernardino, California Office: 412 West Hospitality Lane, Suite 300, 92408.
Telephone: 909-381-3334.
Fax: 909-889-2007.
San Diego, California Office: 225 Broadway, 21st Floor.
Telephone: 619-233-1600.
Fax: 619-236-0527.
Yuma, Arizona Office: P.O. Box 10969, 85366.
Telephone: 520-782-2531.

(See Next Column)

Phoenix, Arizona Office: 3200 North Central Avenue, Suite 2300, 85012-2443.
Telephone: 602-256-0000.
Fax: 602-256-2488.

MEMBERS OF FIRM

Jon R. Mower
Keith D. Koeller
William L. Haluck
Joseph J. Cullen
Patrick A. Carreon
Edward W. Schmitt
Ellen E. Hunter

Mark D. Newcomb
Terrence J. Giannone
Eric W. Smith
Aashish Y. Desai
Daniel Gavin
Erik R. Musurlian
John R. Armstrong

For full biographical listings, see the Martindale-Hubbell Law Directory

STEVENS & KRAMER, A PROFESSIONAL CORPORATION (AV)

18022 Cowan, Suite 200D, 92614-6808
Telephone: 949-253-9553
Fax: 949-253-9643
Agoura Hills, California Office: 30401 W. Agoura Road, Suite 102.
Telephone: 818-879-1699.
Fax: 818-879-1673.

Carl R. Stevens
Jeffrey S. Kramer

Angela M. Rossi
Lee E. Burrows
Andrea Felice Parke
Phillip M. Hayes
Javier H. Van Oordt
Curtis M. King
Addison K. Adams
César H. Nava

LEGAL SUPPORT PERSONNEL

Hanna M. Weiss (Paralegal)
Stephanie R. Ramirez

Representataive Clients: American State Insurance Co.; Gulf Insurance Group; Hartford Insurance Co.; Infinity Insurance Group; Motors Insurance Co.; State Farm Fire and Casualty; Reliance Insurance Co.; AIG; VestaInsurance.

For full biographical listings, see the Martindale-Hubbell Law Directory

WESIERSKI & ZUREK, LLP (AV)

One Corporate Park Drive Second Floor, 92606
Telephone: 949-975-1000
Telecopier: 949-756-0517
Email: Lawyers@wzllp.com
Los Angeles, California Office: 777 South Figueroa, Suite 850, 90017.
Telephone: 213-627-2300.
Telecopier: 213-629-2725.

PARTNERS

Christopher P. Wesierski
Ronald Zurek (Resident, Los Angeles Office)
Terence P. Carney
Thomas G. Wianecki

JUNIOR PARTNER

Paul J. Lipman (Resident, Los Angeles Office)

Mark J. Giannamore (Resident, Los Angeles Office)
Bruce Vail Rorty
Regina A. Leago (Resident, Los Angeles Office)
Thomas E. Martin
G. Brent Sims
Lisa M. Dale
Kevin T. Meade
Jonyson Allen Pierce
Raymond E. Brown
Brett G. Hampton (Resident, Los Angeles Office)
Jeffrey N. Gesell

OF COUNSEL

Daniel J. Ford, Jr.

For full biographical listings, see the Martindale-Hubbell Law Directory

LARKSPUR, Marin Co.

WEINBERG, HOFFMAN, CASEY & ROPERS (AV)

A Partnership including a Professional Corporation
900 Larkspur Landing Circle, Suite 155, 94939
Telephone: 415-461-9666
Fax: 415-461-9681

Ivan Weinberg
Joseph Hoffman
A. Michael Casey
Mark Ropers

For full biographical listings, see the Martindale-Hubbell Law Directory

LONG BEACH, Los Angeles Co.

FLYNN, DELICH & WISE (AV)

One World Trade Center, Suite 1800, 90831-1800
Telephone: 562-435-2626
Fax: 562-437-7555
Email: NicholasP@FDW-LAW.COM
San Francisco, California Office: One California Street, Suite 350.
Telephone: 415-693-5566.
Fax: 415-693-0410. Email: SAMD@FDW-LAW.COM

(See Next Column)

FLYNN, DELICH & WISE, *Long Beach—Continued*

Erich P. Wise
Nicholas S. Politis

Sook H. Lee

LEGAL SUPPORT PERSONNEL

Denise C. Orr (Legal Assistant)

Representative Clients: American Hawaii Cruises; American President Lines; Through Transport Mutual Insurance Association, Ltd.; The Britannia Steam Ship Insurance Association Limited; The Steamship Mutual Underwriting Association (Bermuda) Ltd.; General Steamship Corp., Ltd.; Commodore Cruise Line, Ltd.; Interocean Steamship Corporation; Sea-Land Service, Inc.; Hatteras Yachts.

For full biographical listings, see the Martindale-Hubbell Law Directory

FORD, WALKER, HAGGERTY & BEHAR, PROFESSIONAL LAW CORPORATION (AV)

One World Trade Center, Twenty Seventh Floor, 90831
Telephone: 562-983-2500
Telecopier: 562-983-2555
Email: FWHB@FWHB.COM

G. Richard Ford
Timothy L. Walker
William C. Haggerty
Jeffrey S. Behar
Mark Steven Hennings
Donna Rogers Kirby
Tina Ivankovic Mangarpan
Joseph A. Heath
Robert J. Chavez
James D. Savage
Patrick J. Gibbs
Robert Reisinger

Arthur W. Schultz
Jon T. Moseley
Maxine J. Lebowitz
Timothy P. McDonald
K. Michele Williams
Stephen Ward Moore
James O. Miller
Stanley L. Scarlett
Scott A. Ritsema
Colleen A. Deziel
Thomas L. Gourdé
Patrick J. Stark
Shayne L. Wulterin
Charles J. Schmitt
John A. Haughton
Kristen C. Vine
Joel E. D. Odou
Christopher L. Mass
Robert Montes, Jr.
Alison S. Mathews
Tatia M. Tokunaga
Mark F. Wendorff
Anneke Joan Stewart
Pamela J. Paluga

OF COUNSEL

Theodore P. Shield, P.L.C.

For full biographical listings, see the Martindale-Hubbell Law Directory

MOORE, RUTTER & EVANS (AV)

A Partnership including a Professional Corporation
555 East Ocean Boulevard, Suite 500, 90802-5090
Telephone: 562-435-4499
Facsimile: 562-495-4299
Email: mrelaw@gte.net *URL:* http://www.lawyers.com/moorerutter&evans
Huntington Beach, California Office: 2120 Main Street, Suite 250, 92648.
Telephone: 714-374-3333.
Fax: 714-374-9395

RESIDENT PARTNERS

Neal Moore
Mark D. Rutter
William D. Evans (P.C.)

OF COUNSEL

Michael J. Emling

For full biographical listings, see the Martindale-Hubbell Law Directory

WISE, WIEZOREK, TIMMONS & WISE, A PROFESSIONAL CORPORATION (AV)

3700 Santa Fe Avenue, Suite 300, P.O. Box 2190, 90801-2190
Telephone: 310-834-5028; 562-595-5318
Fax: 310-834-8018
URL: http://www.wwtw.com
Redding, California Office: 292 Hemsted Drive, Suite 101.
Telephone: 530-221-7632.
Fax: 530-221-8832.

George E. Wise
Duane H. Timmons
Anthony F. Wiezorek
Susan E. Anderson Wise
Michael J. Pearce
Mark C. Allen, III
Richard P. Dieffenbach
Steven C. Rice
Stephen M. Smith
Thomas J. Yocis
James M. Cox
Mathew J. Vande Wydeven

Susan Graham

For full biographical listings, see the Martindale-Hubbell Law Directory

*LOS ANGELES,** Los Angeles Co.

ANDERSON, ABLON, LEWIS & GALE, LLP (AV)

Suite 2000 Equitable Plaza Building, 3435 Wilshire Boulevard, 90010-2006
Telephone: 213-388-3385
Fax: 213-388-8432
URL: http://www.aalg.com
San Juan Capistrano, California Office: 30240 Rancho Viejo Road, Suite F, 92675.
Telephone: 949-248-8040.
Fax: 949-248-8044.
Thousand Oaks, California Office: 220-H Briarwood Building, 299 West Hillcrest Drive, 91360.
Telephone: 805-373-5273.
Fax: 805-495-1456.

MEMBERS OF FIRM

Robert E. Lewis
Jerald E. Gale
Harris D. Bass

OF COUNSEL

Lawrence Jay Poteet
Charles R. Anderson
Herman Ablon

ASSOCIATES

Farhad Kazemzadeh
Candace Connart Bleifer
Ronald A. Gorrie
Michael D. Anderson

For full biographical listings, see the Martindale-Hubbell Law Directory

BACON & MILLS, LLP (AV)

800 Wilshire Boulevard, Suite 950, 90017
Telephone: 213-486-6500
Fax: 213-486-6552
Email: baconmills@earthlink.net *URL:* http://www.baconmills.com
Brea, California Office: Three Pointe Drive, Suite 308.
Telephone: 714-257-2100.
Fax: 714-257-2101.

Robert Parker Mills
Robert L. Bacon (Resident, Brea Office)
Theodore E. Bacon (Resident, Brea Office)
John F. Norris (Resident, Brea Office)
James W. Colfer
Patrick A. Connolly, III
Jill L. Johnson
Melissa Lee Mello

Representative Clients: Nationwide/Wausau Insurance Company.

For full biographical listings, see the Martindale-Hubbell Law Directory

BELCHER, HENZIE & BIEGENZAHN, A PROFESSIONAL CORPORATION (AV)

333 South Hope Street, Suite 3650, 90071-1479
Telephone: 213-624-8293
Telecopier: 213-576-9964

Frank B. Belcher (1891-1979)
Leo J. Biegenzahn (1926-1996)
David Bernard (1931-1978)
John S. Curtis
E. Lee Horton
William T. DelHagen
Julia Azrael
Jeffrey L. Horwith
Raymond E. Hane, III

Georgette Renata Herget
John Erin McOsker
Paul R. Flaherty
Ian C. Fusselman
Jeffrey D. Wolf
Debby Lynne Zajac

OF COUNSEL

George M. Henzie

Reference: Bank of America (Los Angeles Main Office).

For full biographical listings, see the Martindale-Hubbell Law Directory

BLACK, COMPEAN & HALL A LIMITED LIABILITY PARTNERSHIP (AV)

445 South Figueroa Street, Suite 2800, 90071-1632
Telephone: 213-629-9500
FAX: 213-629-4868
Email: bchinsurlaw@earthlink.com

MEMBERS OF FIRM

Robert H. Black
Michael D. Compean
Frederick G. Hall

ASSOCIATES

Vicente Valencia, Jr.
Daniel Eli
Lisa Jennifer Martin

Reference: The Pacific Bank.

For full biographical listings, see the Martindale-Hubbell Law Directory

Los Angeles—Continued

BOOTH, MITCHEL & STRANGE (AV)

30th Floor-Equitable Plaza, 3435 Wilshire Boulevard, 90010-2050
Telephone: 213-738-0100
Fax: 213-380-3308
Email: BMSLEGAL@AOL.COM
Costa Mesa, California Office: 3080 Bristol Street, Suite 550.
Telephone: 714-641-0217.
Fax: 714-957-0411. Email: bmslaw2@aol.com.
San Diego, California Office: 550 West "C" Street, Suite 1060, 92101-3532.
Telephone: 619-238-7620.
Fax: 619-238-7625.

MEMBERS OF FIRM

Bates Booth (1903-1967)
Norman R. Willian (1917-1968)
Michael D. Kellogg (1949-1996)
William F. Rummler (Los Angeles Office)
Michael T. Lowe (Costa Mesa Office)
Seth W. Whitaker (Los Angeles Office)
Walter B. Hill, Jr. (Costa Mesa Office)
Robert H. Briggs (Costa Mesa Office)
David R. Kipper
Marla Lamedman Kelley (Costa Mesa Office)
Paul R. Howell
Craig E. Guenther (Costa Mesa Office)
David L. Hughes (Costa Mesa Office)
Daniel M. Crowley (Los Angeles Office)
Steven M. Mitchel (Los Angeles Office)
James G. Stanley (Costa Mesa Office)
Thomas T. Johnson (Los Angeles Office)

OF COUNSEL

George C. Mitchel (Los Angeles Office)
Owen W. Strange (Los Angeles Office)

ASSOCIATES

Robert W. Huston (Los Angeles Office)
Christopher C. Lewi (Los Angeles Office)
Norma Pedroza Chavez

RESIDENT ASSOCIATES COSTA MESA OFFICE

Elizabeth Currin Bonn
Stacie L. Brandt
Scott S. Mizen
Sean T. Osborn
Laila Morcos Santana

RESIDENT ASSOCIATE SAN DIEGO OFFICE

Derek J. Emge

Representative Clients: Southern California Gas Co.; Southern Counties Title Insurance Co.

For full biographical listings, see the Martindale-Hubbell Law Directory

CHAPMAN, GLUCKSMAN & DEAN, A PROFESSIONAL CORPORATION (AV)

11900 West Olympic Boulevard, Suite 800, 90064-0704
Telephone: 310-207-7722
Facsimile: 310-207-6550
Email: administrator@cgdlawyers.com *URL:* http://www.cgdlawyers.com

Richard H. Glucksman
Arthur J. Chapman
Randall J. Dean
Craig A. Roeb
Dominic J. Fote
Glenn T. Barger

Thomas L. Halliwell
Christopher R. Kent
Jeffrey A. Cohen
Gregory K. Sabo
Jon A. Turigliatto
A. Allen Mescobi
Myrna Linett Strapp
Brad D. Citron
L. Heather Carlo
Eileen J. Gaisford
Felix M. Martin
Marla B. Shah
Wendy L. Pietrek
Jeffrey W. Korn

OF COUNSEL

Wendy M. Housman
Thomas J. Pabst

Reference: First Professional Bank, Santa Monica.

For full biographical listings, see the Martindale-Hubbell Law Directory

CLARK & TREVITHICK, A PROFESSIONAL CORPORATION (AV)

800 Wilshire Boulevard, 12th Floor, 90017
Telephone: 213-629-5700
Telecopier: 213-624-9441
Email: postmaster@clarktrev.com
San Francisco, California Office: 456 Montgomery Street, 20th Floor.
Telephone: 415-288-6520.
Fax: 415-398-2820.

Philip W. Bartenetti
Vincent Tricarico
Leonard Brazil
Arturo Santana Jr.

OF COUNSEL

Dolores Cordell
Raimund Freihube

For Complete List of Firm Personnel, See General Section

For full biographical listings, see the Martindale-Hubbell Law Directory

DAAR & NEWMAN, PROFESSIONAL CORPORATION (AV)

Suite 2500, 865 South Figueroa Street, 90017-2567
Telephone: 213-892-0999
FAX: 213-892-1066
Email: lawyers@daarnewman.com *URL:* http://www.daarnewman.com

David Daar
Michael R. Newman
Jeffery J. Daar
Marsha McLean-Utley
Michael J. White

OF COUNSEL

Rodney W. Loeb
William F. White, Jr.
Samuel T. Rees
Leo S. Rich

LEGAL SUPPORT PERSONNEL

Joe A. Morton
Frank E. Raab

Representative Clients: Allianz Insurance Co.; American Income Life Insurance Co.; American Life and Casualty Insurance Co.; Balboa Insurance Co.; California Casualty Insurance Co.; National Benefit Life Insurance Co.; Capital Life Insurance Co.; Charter National Life; Columbian Mutual Life; Connecticut Mutual Life Insurance Co.

For full biographical listings, see the Martindale-Hubbell Law Directory

DANIELS, FINE, ISRAEL & SCHONBUCH, LLP (AV)

A Partnership including a Professional Corporation
1801 Century Park East, 9th Floor, 90067
Telephone: 310-556-7900
Telecopier: 310-556-2807

MEMBERS OF FIRM

John P. Daniels (Inc.)
Paul R. Fine
Mark R. Israel
Michael N. Schonbuch
Scott M. Leavitt
Michelle R. Press

ASSOCIATES

Scott Ashford Brooks
Spencer A. Schneider
Erin B. Hallissy
Maureen M. Michail
Shell Duncan Grimes

OF COUNSEL

Mary Hulett
Timothy J. Hughes

For full biographical listings, see the Martindale-Hubbell Law Directory

DAVIS & FOX (AV)

1901 Avenue of the Stars, Suite 400, 90067
Telephone: 310-286-2915
Fax: 310-286-2916

Calvin E. Davis
Steven A. Fox
Elizabeth A. Kooyman
John J. Stumreiter
Amy L. Freisleben
Barbara Kekich
Gregory M. Sinderbrand

For full biographical listings, see the Martindale-Hubbell Law Directory

FONDA, HILBERMAN & FRASER LLP (AV)

1925 Century Park East, Suite 2250, 90067-2273
Telephone: 310-553-3320
FAX: 310-553-4232
URL: http://www.FHFLAW.com
Glendale, California Office: 1000 N. Central Avenue, Suite 310, 91202.
Telephone: 818-543-1380.
Fax: 818-543-1389.

Peter M. Fonda
Joe W. Hilberman
Stephen C. Fraser
Amy W. Lyons
Patrick W. Mayer

Laurie DeYoung
Stephen Diamond
Thomas E. Donahue
Nancy E. Dunne
Marley S. Fox
Cecille L. Hester
Frederick James
James A. Keens (Resident, Glendale Office)
Mara Margulies
Kristina M. Pedro (Resident, Glendale Office)

Representative Clients: Truck Insurance Exchange; Allstate Ins. Co.; Regents of California.
Reference: Sanwa Bank of California (Los Angeles Headquarters Corporate Office).

For full biographical listings, see the Martindale-Hubbell Law Directory

GALTON & HELM LLP (AV)

500 South Grand Avenue Suite 1200, 90071
Telephone: 213-629-8800
Telecopier: 213-629-0037
Email: GaltonHelm@GaltonHelm.usa.com
Palm Desert, California Office: 73-929 Larrea.
Telephone: 760-776-5600.
Fax: 760-776-5602.

(See Next Column)

GALTON & HELM LLP, *Los Angeles—Continued*

MEMBERS OF FIRM

Stephen H. Galton
Hugh H. Helm
Michael F. Bell
Daniel W. Maguire (Resident at Palm Desert)
David A. Lingenbrink
Robert F. Keehn

ASSOCIATES

Melissa M. Cowan
Joanna M. Todd
Michael B. Bernacchi
David J. Weinman
Nicole Blohm Pomerantz
Jennifer L. Kurzon
Eduardo A. Brito
Deanna E. McCray
Ann C. Schneider
Edith S. Shea

LEGAL SUPPORT PERSONNEL

Lana Banks (Paralegal)
Mardi Walsh (Paralegal)
Lynne M. Koss (Paralegal)
Toni Quigley (Paralegal)

For full biographical listings, see the Martindale-Hubbell Law Directory

GOLDSMITH & BURNS (AV)

A Partnership including a Professional Corporation
18425 Burbank Boulevard, Suite 615 (Tarzana), 91356-2800
Telephone: 818-708-2585
Telecopier: 818-996-4537
Email: info@goldsmithcalaw.com

William I. Goldsmith (A Professional Corporation)
Jack D. Hull

ASSOCIATES

Howard D. Myers
Stuart D. Meyers

Representative Clients: Safeco Insurance; Farmers Insurance; General Insurance Co.; Hartford Insurance; Royal Insurance; Cigna Insurance; Travellers Insurance; Scottsdale Insurance; Fireman's Fund; Allstate Insurance.

For full biographical listings, see the Martindale-Hubbell Law Directory

GRAY, YORK & DUFFY LLP (AV)

15760 Ventura Boulevard, 16th Floor (Encino), 91436
Telephone: 818-907-4000; 310-553-0445
Fax: 818-783-4551
Email: gydlaw@pacbell.net
Redwood City, California Office: 702 Marshall Street, Suite 500, 94063.
Telephone: 650-365-7343.
Fax: 650-365-6225.
San Francisco, California Office: 660 Market Street, Suite 490, 94105.
Telephone: 415-908-1300.
Fax: 415-974-6199.

MEMBERS OF FIRM

Gary S. Gray
James R. York
John J. Duffy
Arlene A. Colman
Barry D. Brown
William F. Flahavan

Reference: Marathon National Bank, Los Angeles, California.

For full biographical listings, see the Martindale-Hubbell Law Directory

HAWKINS, SCHNABEL, LINDAHL & BECK, LLP (AV)

660 South Figueroa Street, Suite 1500, 90017
Telephone: 213-488-3900
Telecopier: 213-486-9883
Email: hslb@hslblaw.com

MEMBERS OF FIRM

Roger E. Hawkins
Laurence H. Schnabel
George M. Lindahl
Kelley K. Beck
Jon P. Kardassakis
William E. Keitel
Rena Denton Stone
Timothy A. Gonzales
Ram F. Cogan
Kurt G. Gresenz
David C. Moore

For full biographical listings, see the Martindale-Hubbell Law Directory

HORVITZ & LEVY, LLP (AV)

A Partnership including Professional Corporations
18th Floor, 15760 Ventura Boulevard (Encino), 91436
Telephone: 818-995-0800
Fax: 818-995-3157

Ellis J. Horvitz (A P.C.)
Barry R. Levy (A P.C.)
Peter Abrahams
David M. Axelrad
Frederic D. Cohen
S. Thomas Todd
David S. Ettinger
Daniel J. Gonzalez
Mitchell C. Tilner
Christina J. Imre
Lisa Perrochet
Stephen E. Norris
Sandra J. Smith
John A. Taylor, Jr.
Julie L. Woods
Lisa R. Jaskol
H. Thomas Watson

(See Next Column)

Mary F. Dant
Holly R. Paul
Andrea M. Gauthier
Judith E. Gordon
Patricia Lofton
L. Rachel Lerman Helyar
Mary-Christine (M.C.) Sungaila
Stephanie Rae Williams
Curt Cutting
Wendy S. Albers
Robert H. Wright
Nina E. Scholtz
Orly Degani

OF COUNSEL

Jon B. Eisenberg

Representative Clients: State Farm Insurance Company; Farmers Insurance Group of Companies; AIG Risk Management; CNA Insurance; Home Insurance Company; Allstate Insurance Company; Transamerica Insurance Company; California Insurance Guarantee Association; 20th Century Insurance Company.

For full biographical listings, see the Martindale-Hubbell Law Directory

JONES, DAY, REAVIS & POGUE (AV)

555 West Fifth Street Suite 4600, 90013-1025
Telephone: 213-489-3939
Telecopier: 213-243-2539
Email: counsel@jonesday.com *URL:* http://www.jonesday.com
In Irvine, California: 5 Park Plaza, Suite 1100.
Telephone: 949-851-3939.
Telecopier: 949-553-7539.
In Atlanta, Georgia: 3500 SunTrust Plaza, 303 Peachtree Street.
Telephone: 404-521-3939.
Telecopier: 404-581-8330.
In Brussels, Belgium: Avenue Louise 480, 7th Floor, B-1050 Brussels.
Telephone: 32-2-645-14-11.
Telecopier: 32-2-645-14-45.
In Chicago, Illinois: 77 West Wacker.
Telephone: 312-782-3939.
Telecopier: 312-782-8585.
In Cleveland, Ohio: North Point, 901 Lakeside Avenue.
Telephone: 216-586-3939.
Telecopier: 216-579-0212.
In Columbus, Ohio: 1900 Huntington Center.
Telephone: 614-469-3939.
Telecopier: 614-461-4198.
In Dallas, Texas: 2727 North Harwood Street.
Telephone: 214-220-3939.
Telecopier: 214-969-5100.
In Frankfurt, Germany: Hochhaus am Park, Grüneburgweg 102, 60323 Frankfurt am Main.
Telephone: 49-69-9726-3939.
Telecopier: 49-69-9726-3993.
In Geneva, Switzerland: 20, rue de Candolle.
Telephone: 41-22-320-2339.
Telecopier: 41-22-320-1232.
In Hong Kong: 29th Floor, Entertainment Building, 30 Queen's Road Central.
Telephone: 852-2526-6895.
Telecopier: 852-2868-5871.
In London England: Bucklersbury House, 3 Queen Victoria Street.
Telephone: 44-20-7236-3939.
Telecopier: 44-20-7236-1113.
In New York, New York: 599 Lexington Avenue.
Telephone: 212-326-3939.
Telecopier: 212-755-7306.
In Paris, France: 120, rue du Faubourg Saint-Honoré.
Telephone: 33-1-56-59-3939.
Telecopier: 33-1-56-59-3938
In Pittsburgh, Pennsylvania: 500 Grant Street, 31st Floor.
Telephone: 412-391-3939.
Telecopier: 412-394-7959.
In Riyadh, Saudi Arabia: The International Law Firm (In Association with Jones, Day, Reavis & Pogue), Sulaymaniyah, Prince Mishari IBN, Abdulaziz Street, P.O. Box 22166.
Telephone: (966-1) 462-8866.
Telecopier: (966-1) 462-9001.
In Shanghai, China: 2805 Kerry Centre, 1515 Nanjing Road West.
Telephone: 86-21-5298-6568.
Telecopier: 86-21-5298-6569.
In Sydney, Australia: Governor Phillip Tower, Level 38, 1 Farrer Place.
Telephone: 61-2-9210-6921.
Telecopier: 61-2-9210-6926.
In Taipei, Taiwan: 8th Floor, 2 Tun Hwa South Road, Section 2.
Telephone: (886-2) 2704-6808.
Telecopier: (886-2) 2704-6791.
In Tokyo, Japan: Toranomon 45 Mori Building, 3th Floor, 1-5, Toranomon 5-Chome, Minato-ku, Tokyo 105, Japan.
Telephone: 81-3-3433-3939.
Telecopier: 81-3-5401-2725.
In Washington, D.C.: 51 Louisiana Avenue, N.W.
Telephone: 202-879-3939.
Telecopier: 202-626-1700.

(See Next Column)

JONES, DAY, REAVIS & POGUE—*Continued*

MEMBER OF FIRM IN LOS ANGELES

Lester O. Brown

For Complete List of Firm Personnel, See General Section

For full biographical listings, see the Martindale-Hubbell Law Directory

KERN & GONZALEZ, A PROFESSIONAL CORPORATION (AV)

601 West 5th Street, Suite 1100, 90071
Telephone: 213-629-8100
Facsimile: 213-627-8765
URL: http://www.kernlaw.net

René J. Kern, Jr.
Michael D. Gonzalez
Tina L. Gentile

Christina L. Young
Angela J. Armitage
Michele Marsh
Cynthia L. Filla
David G. Hoiles, Jr.
Michele Sherer Ancheta
Sue S. Kim
Gail S. Taningco

Representative Clients: 20th Century Insurance Company; TM Claims Service, Inc.; United States Fidelity and Guaranty Company.

For full biographical listings, see the Martindale-Hubbell Law Directory

LOVICH & PENN (AV)

777 South Figueroa, Suite 1507, 90017
Telephone: 213-689-3625
Fax: 213-689-3653

STAFF COUNSEL
AMERICAN INTERNATIONAL COMPANIES
MANAGING ATTORNEY

Richard A. Lovich

For full biographical listings, see the Martindale-Hubbell Law Directory

McKAY, BYRNE & GRAHAM (AV)

3250 Wilshire Boulevard, Suite 603, 90010
Telephone: 213-386-6900
Fax: 213-381-1762
Email: mbg@mbglaw.com

John P. McKay
Michael A. Byrne
Robert L. Graham
Mark G. Cunningham
Paul A. de Lorimier

Jeffrey Cabot Myers
Debra Ellwood Meppen
Dawn M. Flores-Oster
April Paradise
Gabriela Escudero Goldberg
Nancy A. Ramsey

OF COUNSEL

Gail D. Solo (A Professional Corporation)

For full biographical listings, see the Martindale-Hubbell Law Directory

NEUMEYER & BOYD, LLP (AV)

2029 Century Park East, Suite 1100, 90067
Telephone: 310-553-9393
Fax: 310-553-8437

MEMBERS OF FIRM

Richard A. Neumeyer
Carol Boyd
Lydia E. Hachmeister

OF COUNSEL

Eugene R. Grace

ASSOCIATES

Katherine Tatikian
Daniel F. Sanchez
Reid L. Denham
Katy A. Nelson
Larry P. Nathenson

For full biographical listings, see the Martindale-Hubbell Law Directory

OCHOA & SILLAS (AV)

444 South Flower Street, 18th Floor, 90071
Telephone: 213-362-1400
Fax: 213-622-0162
Email: sillasla@aol.com
Sacramento Office: Wells Fargo Center, 400 Capitol Mall, Suite 1850.
Telephone: 916-447-3383.
FAX: 916-447-3495. Email: OchoaSac@aol.com
Mexico City, Mexico Office: Los Cormoran No. 73, Lomas De Las Aquilas, Deleg. Alvaro Obregon, 01730, Mexico, D.F.C.F.
Telephone: 011-525-635-1145.
Fax: 011-525-53401454.

MEMBERS OF FIRM

Ralph M. Ochoa (Resident, Sacramento Office)
Herman Sillas
Jacqueline Rich Moore (Resident, Sacramento Office)
Tomás R. Lopez

(See Next Column)

ASSOCIATES

Jack T. Molodanof (Resident, Sacramento Office)
Francisco Valles Lopez (Not admitted in the United States)
Rita A. Reyes
Christopher Eric Ochoa (Resident, Sacramento Office)
Cirina A. K. Rose
M. Eric Parkan

OF COUNSEL

Daniel P. Aguilera
Cochran & Lotkin, Washington, D.C.

Representative Clients: American Golf; BKK Corp. (Toxic substance treatment); Chrysler; Department of Water and Power of Los Angeles; Sacramento Municipal Utility District; Department of Insurance; Metropolitan Water District, Los Angeles; General Motors; Hughes Aircraft; ICN Laboratories.

For full biographical listings, see the Martindale-Hubbell Law Directory

O'MELVENY & MYERS LLP (AV)

400 South Hope Street, 90071-2899
Telephone: 213-430-6000
Facsimile: 213-430-6407
Cable: MOMS
Telex: 674122
Email: omminfo@omm.com *URL:* http://www.omm.com
Century City, CA Office: 1999 Avenue of the Stars, Los Angeles, 90067-6035.
Telex: 674097. Tel: 310-553-6700.
Fax: 310-246-6779.
Newport Beach, CA Office: 610 Newport Center Drive, 92660-6429.
Telex: 4722088. Tel: 949-760-9600.
Fax: 949-823-6994.
San Francisco, CA Office: Embarcadero Center West, 275 Battery Street, 94111-3305. Tel: 415-984-8700.
Fax: 415-984-8701.
New York, NY Office: Citicorp Center, 153 East 53rd Street, 10022-4611.
Telex: 129165. Tel: 212-326-2000.
Fax: 212-326-2061.
Washington, DC Office: 555 13th Street, N.W., 20004-1109.
Cable: MOMSWSH.
Telex: 89622. Tel: 202-383-5300.
Fax: 202-383-5414.
London Office: O'Melveny & Myers, 3 Finsbury Square, London, EC2A 1LA, England. Tel: 44-171-256-8451. Fax 44-171-638-8205.
Tokyo Office: Akasaka Twin Tower, East 14F, 2-17-23, Akasaka, Minato-ku, Tokyo 107-0052, Japan. Tel: 03-5562-2800.
Fax: 03-5575-3840.
Hong Kong Office: O'Melveny & Myers, Suite 1905, Tower Two, Lippo Centre, 89 Queensway, Central, Hong Kong. Tel: 852-2523-8266.
Fax: 852-2522-1760.
Shanghai Office: Kerry Centre, 20F, 1515 Nanjing Road West, Shanghai, 200040 People's Republic of China. Tel: 86-21-5298-5600.
Fax: 86-21-5298-5500.

PARTNER

Richard B. Goetz

For Complete List of Firm Personnel, See General Section

For full biographical listings, see the Martindale-Hubbell Law Directory

OSTROVE, KRANTZ & OSTROVE, A PROFESSIONAL CORPORATION (AV)

(Successor To: Ostrove and Lancer, A Professional Corporation; David Ostrove, A Professional Corporation)
5757 Wilshire Boulevard, Suite 535, 90036-3600
Telephone: 323-939-3400
Fax: 323-939-3500
Email: OSTROVE@AOL.COM *URL:* http://www.lawyers.com/ok&olaw

David Ostrove
David S. Krantz
Kenneth E. Ostrove

Reference: First Business Bank.

For full biographical listings, see the Martindale-Hubbell Law Directory

PRESTHOLT, KLEEGER, FIDONE & VILLASENOR (AV)

Suite 1600, 1055 West 7th Street, 90017
Telephone: 213-895-4811
FAX: 213-895-4817
San Francisco, California Office: 989 Market Street, 6th Floor.
Telephone: 415-267-6362.
Fax: 415-267-6275.

MEMBERS OF FIRM

David A. Prestholt
Gary P. Fidone
Lisa A. Villasenor
Brian D. Holmberg
David Crawford, III
Archie Chin
Avigal Horrow
Marjorie E. Motooka

For full biographical listings, see the Martindale-Hubbell Law Directory

Los Angeles—Continued

ROBINSON, DI LANDO & WHITAKER, A PROFESSIONAL LAW CORPORATION (AV)

800 Wilshire Boulevard Suite 1100, 90017-2687
Telephone: 213-229-0100
Facsimile: 213-229-0114
Email: rdwlaw@gte.net
San Francisco, California Office: 417 Montgomery Street, Suite 910. 94104.
Telephone: 415-391-9475.
Fax: 415-391-3799.

Michael C. Robinson, Jr.
Michael A. Di Lando
Ronald S. Whitaker
Jack M. Liebhaber
Timothy L. Salazar

Steve H. Yu
Mark Kane
Cynthia A. Goodman
Bradley R. Blamires
Farzad Tabatabai
Martin J. Mendoza
David K. Stewart
Michelle B. Dykstra
Charles H. Brown, II
Michael B. Wilk

For full biographical listings, see the Martindale-Hubbell Law Directory

SELMAN ● BREITMAN (AV)

11766 Wilshire Boulevard, Sixth Floor, 90025-6538
Telephone: 310-445-0800
Fax: 310-473-2525
San Diego, California Office: Wyndham Emerald Plaza, 402 W. Broadway, Suite 400, 92101.
Telephone: 619-595-4880.
Facsimile: 619-595-4890.
San Francisco, California Office: Citicorp Center, One Sansome Street, Suite 1900, 94104.
Telephone: 415-951-4646.
Fax: 415-951-4676.
Santa Ana, California Office: 450 4th Street, Suite 250, 92701.
Telephone: 714-647-9700.
Fax: 714-647-9200.

MEMBERS OF FIRM

Sterling Tao (1961-1998)
Neil Selman
Craig R. Breitman
Robert A. Steller
Alan B. Yuter
Nancy W. Shokohi
Jeffrey C. Segal
A. Scott Goldberg
Elaine K. Fresch
Nicholas Banko (Partner, San Francisco Office)
Brad D. Bleichner
Monica Cruz Thornton
John S. Knowlton
Jerry C. Popovich (Partner, Santa Ana Office)

OF COUNSEL

Jan Long Pocaterra
Jacqueline F. Stein (Resident, San Diego Office)
Paul Edmond Stephan (Resident, San Francisco Office)

Lynette Klawon
Anthony L. Cione
Sheryl W. Leichenger
Lisa H. Kahn
David H. Oken
Pauline A. New
Eldon S. Edson
Sarah F. Burke (Resident, San Francisco Office)
Linda Wendell Hsu (Resident, San Francisco Office)
Jack M. Zakariaie
Jean Dettmann Fisher (Resident, San Diego Office)
Lincoln V. Horton
Nichelle D. Frelix
Albert T. Liou (Resident, Santa Ana Office)
Viiu Spangler
Meka Moore
Richard T. Breen
Christopher R. Aker (Resident, San Francisco Office)
Mindi C. Grant
Ben M. Llaneta (Resident, San Diego Office)
Richard Scott
Craig R. Maki
Jennifer J. Capabianco (Resident, San Francisco Office)
Michelle L. Koskella (Resident, San Francisco Office)
Kelly M. Lynch
Kimberly S. Poese (Resident, Santa Ana Office)
Veronica E. Aitken
Roger G. Honey
Shereef Moharram
Kiera Berkley
Gregory J. Newman
Tamara Madenlian
Michelle E. Davis
Josh I. Keane
Michael Robert Hoffman
Natalie A. Barbanell
Kirk J. Retz
Paul A. Herp (Resident, San Francisco Office)
Greg M. Whaling (Resident, San Francisco Office)

Reference: City National Bank (Beverly Hills Branch).

For full biographical listings, see the Martindale-Hubbell Law Directory

*MODESTO,** Stanislaus Co.

BRUNN & FLYNN, A PROFESSIONAL CORPORATION (AV)

928 12th Street, P.O. Box 3366, 95353
Telephone: 209-521-2133
Fax: 209-521-7584
Email: brunnfly@ix.netcom.com

(See Next Column)

Charles K. Brunn
Timothy T. Flynn
Gerald E. Brunn
Roger S. Matzkind

Michael G. Donovan
Andrew N. Eshoo

Representative Clients: ACWA-Joint Powers Insurance Authority; Basic Resources, Inc.; CIGNA Insurance Cos.; City of Merced; City of Turlock; CNA Insurance Cos.; Colonial Insurance Co.; County of Mariposa; County of Merced; USAA Insurance Co.

For full biographical listings, see the Martindale-Hubbell Law Directory

MONTEREY, Monterey Co.

HARRAY & LINKER (AV)

80 Garden Court, Suite 260, 93940
Telephone: 831-373-3101
Fax: 831-373-6712
Email: general@harray-linker.com

Richard K. Harray
Stan L. Linker

ASSOCIATES

Christine Balbo Reed
J. Kenneth Gorman
Debra Gemgnani Tipton

Representative Clients: The Travelers Insurance Co.; OPTIMA HEALTHCARE/CHIC; State Farm; Beta Healthcare; CNA/RSKCE; DPIC; Sequoia Insurance Co.; Midstate Insurance Co.; Community Hospital of Monterey Peninsula; Kmart; Salinas Valley Memorial Hospital; Allstate; John Deere Co.

For full biographical listings, see the Martindale-Hubbell Law Directory

*OAKLAND,** Alameda Co.

ANTHONY & CARLSON, LLP (AV)

1999 Harrison Street, Suite 2000, 94612-3517
Telephone: 510-835-8400
Fax: 510-835-5566

MEMBERS OF FIRM

Steven R. Anthony
Richard H. Carlson

Felicia C. Strankman

OF COUNSEL

Jane L. Trigero

For full biographical listings, see the Martindale-Hubbell Law Directory

BENNETT, SAMUELSEN, REYNOLDS AND ALLARD, A PROFESSIONAL CORPORATION (AV)

1951 Webster Street, Suite 200, 94612-2909
Telephone: 510-444-7688; 510-987-8001
Fax: 510-444-5849
Email: BSRALIT@AOL.COM

Bryant M. Bennett (Retired)
David J. Samuelsen
Richard L. Reynolds
Anthony J. Allard
John G. Cowperthwaite

Roger Blake Hohnsbeen
Thomas S. Gelini
Frederick W. Gatt
Candace Dabney-Smith
David L. Dees
Roderick D. Hill

Representative Clients: Allstate Insurance Co.; California State Automobile Assn.; The Continental Insurance Cos.; County of Alameda.

For full biographical listings, see the Martindale-Hubbell Law Directory

HAIMS, MACGOWAN, VALENTINO & PEEBLES, L.L.P. (AV)

490 Grand Avenue, 94610
Telephone: 510-835-0500
Facsimile: 510-835-2833

MEMBERS OF FIRM

Arnold B. Haims
Clyde L. MacGowan
Caroline N. Valentino
Dianne D. Peebles

For full biographical listings, see the Martindale-Hubbell Law Directory

LOMBARDI, LOPER & CONANT, LLP (AV)

1999 Harrison Street, Suite 1950, 94612
Telephone: 510-433-2600
Fax: 510-433-2699

Ralph A. Lombardi
Bruce P. Loper
Matthew S. Conant
Chris P. Lavdiotis
Peter O. Glaessner
Timothy J. McCaffery
GayLynn Renee Kirn

Jeffrey D Hosking
Joseph Blaise Adams
Paul S. Lecky

(See Next Column)

LOMBARDI, LOPER & CONANT LLP—*Continued*

OF COUNSEL

George S. Peyton, Jr.
Linda C. Roodhouse
Lori A. Sebransky

For full biographical listings, see the Martindale-Hubbell Law Directory

ORANGE, Orange Co.

BRADY, VORWERCK & RYDER (AV)

790 The City Drive, Suite 450, 92868-4941
Telephone: 714-703-2111
Facsimile: 714-703-2121
Email: mail@bvrlaw.com *URL:* http://www.bvrlaw.com
Walnut Creek Office: Station Plaza, 3100 Oak Road, Suite 230, 94596.
Telephone: 925-274-9500.
Fax: 925-274-9501.
Las Vegas, Nevada Office: Ryder & Caspino, 2755 East Desert Inn Road, Suite 230, 89121.
Telephone: 702-697-6500.
Fax: 702-697-6505.

MEMBERS OF FIRM

James Brady
Gregg Vorwerck
Robert B. Ryder
Michael W. Caspino

ASSOCIATES

Richard G. Arneal
Steven R. Bartell
Edward B. Batista
Holly C. Beal
David G. Bebb
Robert N. Bershin
David A. Brewster
Kevin J. Broerman
Robert T. Bryson
Joseph A. Cardella
Raj K. Dixit
Jerold M. Gorski
Susan B. Grabarsky
Leonard S. Jensen
Michael D. Lind
Wilfred A. Llaurado
Carol L. Meedon
James H. Millane
Grant R. Mullen
Janet C. Pancoast (Not admitted in CA)
Kenneth E. Pollock
Robert W. Pritchard
Kevin M. Razban
Elizabeth Ashley Rosebrock
Steven D. Sperling
Ravi Sudan
John G. Wilcoxson III

For full biographical listings, see the Martindale-Hubbell Law Directory

HOLLINS, SCHECHTER, FEINSTEIN & CONDAS, A PROFESSIONAL CORPORATION (AV)

12th Floor, 505 South Main Street, P.O. Box 11021, 92856-8121
Telephone: 714-558-9119
Fax: 714-558-9091
San Diego, California Office: 12526 High Bluff Drive, Suite 300, 92130-2067.
Telephone: 858-792-3502.
Palm Springs, California Office: 1111 Tahquitz Canyon Way, Suite 121, 92262-0102.
Telephone: 760-416-0288.

Andrew S. Hollins
Bruce Lee Schechter
Thomas M. Condas
Jack H. Snyder
Kenneth C. Jones
Richard T. Collins
Bryan R. Bush

Mary Ann Schiller
Jodie P. Filkins
Helen M. Luetto
Scott T. Jelensky
James D. Norris
Steven M. Hingst
Limor Lehavi
Gene A. McKenzie, Jr.
Michael J. Eyre
Danny C. Soong
Heather M. Brown-Smith

OF COUNSEL

Marc J. Feinstein

Representative Clients: Acceptance Risk Managers; Admiral Insurance Co.; American States Insurance Co.; California Compensation Co.; Colonial Penn Insurance Co.; Commercial Union Insurance Cos.; Farmers Insurance Exchange; Farmers Insurance Group of Companies; Fire Insurance Exchange; Garden Insurance Services; Home Base; Hull & Company, Inc.; Investors Insurance Group; K&K Insurance Group, Inc.; Lexington Insurance Company; Mercury Insurance Company; Mid-Century Insurance Co.; Ryder Services Corp.; St. Paul Fire and Marine Insurance Co.; The Regents of the University of California; Truck Insurance Exchange; U.S. Rentals; Utica Mutual Insurance Co.; Viking Insurance Co.

For full biographical listings, see the Martindale-Hubbell Law Directory

PASADENA, Los Angeles Co.

COLLINS, COLLINS, MUIR & TRAVER LLP (AV)

Successor to Collins & Collins
Suite 300, 265 North Euclid, 91101
Telephone: 626-793-1163
FAX: 626-793-5982
Newport Beach, California Office: 333 Bayside Drive, 92660.
Telephone: 949-723-7700.
Fax: 949-723-7701.

(See Next Column)

Affiliated Offices: Drage, Olson & Tiet, LLP, 810 S. Casino Center Boulevard, Las Vegas, Nevada, 89101.
Telephone: 702-384-1600.
Fax: 702-384-1664.

MEMBERS OF FIRM

James E. Collins (1910-1987)
Robert J. Traver (Retired)
Paul L. Rupard (Retired)
John J. Collins
Samuel J. Muir
Frank J. D'Oro
Brian K. Stewart

ASSOCIATES

Robert H. Stellwagen, Jr.
Tomas A. Guterres
Christine E. Drage
Stephen W. Olson
Peter L. Stacy
Kien C. Tiet
Martha L. Cazeneuve
Howard Franco, Jr.
Jeffrey M. Hall
Michael M. Bergfeld
Jennifer M. Gregg

For full biographical listings, see the Martindale-Hubbell Law Directory

FREEBURG, JUDY & NETTELS (AV)

600 South Lake Avenue, Suite 500, 91106
Telephone: 626-585-4150
Fax: 626-585-0718
Tustin, California Office: 440 West First Street, Suite 102, 92780-3047.
Telephone: 714-508-1800.
Facsimile: 714-508-1809.

Steven J. Freeburg
J. Lawrence Judy
Charles F. Nettels

ASSOCIATES

Ingall W. Bull, Jr.
Richard B. Castle
Cynthia B. Schaldenbrand (Resident, Tustin Office)
Holly A. McNulty
Karen S. Freeburg
Jennifer D. Helsel
Carla Lynn Crochet (Resident, Tustin Office)
Edward William Burns

For full biographical listings, see the Martindale-Hubbell Law Directory

*REDDING,** Shasta Co.

HALKIDES & MORGAN, A PROFESSIONAL CORPORATION (AV)

833 Mistletoe Lane, P.O. Drawer 492170, 96049-2170
Telephone: 530-221-8150
Fax: 530-221-7963

G. Dennis Halkides
Arthur L. Morgan, Jr.
William D. Ayres
John P. Kelley
Richard W. Clopine
Ryan M. Lee

Representative Clients: Anheuser-Busch, Inc.; Cessna Aircraft Co.; County of Shasta; Gallagher Bassett Insurance Service; Great American Insurance Co.; Northern California Schools Insurance Group; Novastar International; Simpson Timber Co.; Standard Oil Company of California; The Times-Mirror Co.

For full biographical listings, see the Martindale-Hubbell Law Directory

MAIRE, MANSELL & BEASLEY, A LAW CORPORATION (AV)

2851 Park Marina Drive Suite 300, P.O. Drawer 994607, 96099-4607
Telephone: 916-246-6050
Fax: 916-246-6060
Email: mmblaw@maire-law.com

Wayne H. Maire
Patrick R. Beasley
Eric R. Maire

Tamara L. Wood
Eric A. Omstead
Gary E. Haslerud

For full biographical listings, see the Martindale-Hubbell Law Directory

DOUGLAS H. NEWLAN (AV)

434 Redcliff Drive, Suite B, P.O. Box 491736, 96049-1736
Telephone: 530-221-0184
Fax: 530-221-8744

For full biographical listings, see the Martindale-Hubbell Law Directory

*REDWOOD CITY,** San Mateo Co.

BRANSON BRINKOP GRIFFITH & STRONG LLP (AV)

643 Bair Island Road, Suite 400, 94063
Telephone: 650-365-7710
Fax: 650-365-7981

Thomas A. Branson
Fred R. Brinkop
David L. Strong
Harry A. Griffith
John R. Campo
John H. Podesta

(See Next Column)

BRANSON BRINKOP GRIFFITH & STRONG LLP, *Redwood City—Continued*

Gillian A. Sward
Christopher P. Kiely
Elizabeth F. Von Emster
John E. Meerchaum
Linda J. Moin
Matthew S. Foy
Christopher C. Knowdell
Brett T. Moroney
Birte Susanne Scholz
Dermot J. Fitzgerald

Reference: Union Bank.

For full biographical listings, see the Martindale-Hubbell Law Directory

HOWARD ROME MARTIN & RIDLEY LLP (AV)

643 Bair Island Road, Suite 400, P.O. Box 2189, 94064-2189
Telephone: 650-365-7715
Facsimile: 650-364-5297

MEMBERS OF FIRM

Joseph C. Howard, Jr.
Henry D. Rome
Glenn D. Martin
Shawn M. Ridley

Beth Clare Hopwood
Scott L. Johnson
James M. Harrington

OF COUNSEL

Kristi L. Curtis

Representative Clients: Kemper Insurance Company; CGU Insurance Company; AIG Technical Services, Inc.; Fireman's Fund Insurance Company; Superior National Insurance Company; CNA Insurance; Crum & Forster Group; CALCO Medical Management Corporation; Crawford & Company; Lexington Insurance Company.

For full biographical listings, see the Martindale-Hubbell Law Directory

*RIVERSIDE,** Riverside Co.

BELL, ORROCK & WATASE, LLP (AV)

2001 Iowa Avenue, Suite 115, 92507
Telephone: 909-683-6014
Fax: 909-683-0314
Email: bellorrockwa@earthlink.net

Michael A. Bell
Stanley O. Orrock
Kenneth D. Watase

David A. Williams
Micheal A. Fortino
Dana M. Smith

For full biographical listings, see the Martindale-Hubbell Law Directory

*SACRAMENTO,** Sacramento Co.

ABBOTT & NOLEN (AV)

350 University Avenue, Suite 280, 95825
Telephone: 916-564-9990
Fax: 916-564-9991
Email: abbott_nolen@compuserve.com *URL:* http://www.lawyers.com/abbottandnolen

David W. Abbott
Rhudolph Nolen, Jr.

ASSOCIATE

Bruce M. Timm

Representative Clients: National Chiropractic Mutual Ins. Co.; Pi Omega Delta Ins. Co.; Travelers Ins. Co.

For full biographical listings, see the Martindale-Hubbell Law Directory

ANWYL, SCOFFIELD, STEPP & UNIVERSAL (AV)

2180 Harvard Street, Suite 200, 95815-3318
Telephone: 916-565-1800
Fax: 916-565-2374
Email: postmaster@anwylaw.com

MEMBERS OF FIRM

James T. Anwyl
Lindy H. Scoffield
Leigh A. Stepp
Jon D. Universal

ASSOCIATES

Lynn A. Garcia
Robert Matthew Lovein
Daniela F. Alneida

Representative Clients: Allstate Insurance Company; Cendant Mobility Services, Inc.; CNA Insurance; Coors Brewing Co.; DaimlerChrysler Corporation; GTE Data Services; Kemper Insurance Group; Pizza Hut of America, Inc.; Sears Roebuck & Co.; St. Paul Fire & Marine Insurance Company.

For full biographical listings, see the Martindale-Hubbell Law Directory

BAILEY & BROWN (AV)

1419 Twenty-First Street, 95814
Telephone: 916-447-2451
Fax: 916-447-8066
Email: BANDB001@JPS.NET

(See Next Column)

MEMBERS OF FIRM

F. Eugene Bailey (1921-1996)
David I. Brown
William J. Schmidt

ASSOCIATE

Diana L. Penny

OF COUNSEL

Robert B. Walker

Representative Clients: American States Insurance; CIGNA; Coregis; Crawford & Co.; Mercury Insurance; VFIS; Philadelphia Insurance Co.; American Equity Insurance Co.; St. Paul Insurance; Westport Insurance.

For full biographical listings, see the Martindale-Hubbell Law Directory

CAULFIELD, DAVIES & DONAHUE (AV)

3500 American River Drive, Suite 100, 95864
Telephone: 916-487-7700
Fax: 916-487-7091
Fairfield, California Office: Fairfield West Plaza, 1455 Oliver Road, Suite 130.
Telephone: 707-426-0223.

MEMBERS OF FIRM

Richard Hyland Caulfield
Robert E. Davies
James R. Donahue
Bruce E. Leonard
Matthew Paul Donahue
Brian C. Haydon

ASSOCIATES

Chance L. Trimm
Shawn C. Moore
Catherine A.J. Woodbridge

For full biographical listings, see the Martindale-Hubbell Law Directory

DIEPENBROCK & COSTA (AV)

455 University Avenue, Suite 300, 95825
Telephone: 916-565-6222
Fax: 916-565-6220
Email: dpc@diepcos.com

MEMBERS OF FIRM

Anthony C. Diepenbrock
Daniel P. Costa

ASSOCIATES

John P. Cotter
Nora E. Dwyer
Evan D. Williams
Scott W. DePeel
Paul R. Cotter
Jean M. O'Sullivan

Representative Clients: Allstate; CNA Insurance Co.; Century Surety Co.; Clarendon/North American; Federated Mutual; Great American Insurance Cos.; Midland Risk; Progressive; Safeco; Sequoia Insurance Co.

For full biographical listings, see the Martindale-Hubbell Law Directory

DONAHUE, WOOD, LOVING & VOGEL (AV)

83 Scripps Drive, Suite 200, 95825
Telephone: 916-648-7444
Fax: 916-648-7447

MEMBERS OF FIRM

James E. Donahue
Gerrit W. Wood
Walter H. Loving, III
Barry Vogel
William K. Blakemore
Stephen J. Mackey
Mark A. Bates
Thomas P. Connolly III

Douglas P. Winter
Aleshia M. White
Luke A. Foster
Judith Clark Martin
Brian J. O'Connor
Catherine L. Manske

For full biographical listings, see the Martindale-Hubbell Law Directory

EDSON, LAPLANTE & SPINELLI (AV)

400 Capitol Mall, 20th Floor, 95814
Telephone: 916-448-7888
Fax: 916-448-6888

MEMBERS OF FIRM

Richard J. Edson
John M. Laplante
Domenic D. Spinelli
Lynette T. Brannan

ASSOCIATES

J. Scott Donald
Ross R. Nott
John W. Ranucci
M. Teresa Abad Levenfeld
Jill S. Picone
Gregory J. Fisher
Peter J. Hirsig

Representative Clients: Allstate Ins.; Firemans Fund Ins.; Nationwide Insu.; CNA Ins.; The Travelers Insurance Co.; Northbrook Property and Casualty Ins.; St. Paul Insurance; The Maryland Ins. Group; ITT Hartford; Wausau Ins. Co.

For full biographical listings, see the Martindale-Hubbell Law Directory

Sacramento—Continued

GALLAWA • BROWN • KROESCH, A PROFESSIONAL CORPORATION (AV)

2207 J Street, 95816
Telephone: 916-444-9364
Fax: 916-444-5921
Email: gbk@gbklawoffices.com

Walter E. Gallawa	Douglas A. Kroesch

Gary Gallawa

Robert Browning Miller

For full biographical listings, see the Martindale-Hubbell Law Directory

GREVE, CLIFFORD, WENGEL & PARAS, LLP (AV)

980 Ninth Street, Suite 1900, 95814-2739
Telephone: 916-443-2011
Telecopier: 916-441-7457
Email: greveclifford.com *URL:* http://www.greveclifford.com

MEMBERS OF FIRM

Edward T. Clifford	Robert L. Collins
Lawrence A. Wengel	Scott E. Cofer
Gary L. Vinson	William J. Barcellona
Bradley R. Larson	Bradley W. Kragel
William L. Baker	Craig L. Scott

ASSOCIATES

John D. Broghammer	Terry A. German

OF COUNSEL

Irving H. Perluss

RETIRED

Claire H. Greve	George E. Paras

PARALEGALS

Claudia Cross	H. Gregory Vitaich

Representative Clients: Allstate Insurance Co.; CNA; Commercial Union Insurance Co.; Design Professionals Insurance Co.; Foremost Insurance Group; Republic Insurance Co.; Underwriters, at Lloyds; E&O Professionals; Zurich American Insurance Co.; RA & MCO.

For full biographical listings, see the Martindale-Hubbell Law Directory

HARDY ERICH BROWN & WILSON, A PROFESSIONAL CORPORATION (AV)

1000 G Street, 95814
Telephone: 916-449-3800
Fax: 916-449-3888
Mailing Address: P.O. Box 13530, Sacramento, California, 95853-4530
Email: hebw@hebw.com *URL:* http://www.hebw.com

John Quincy Brown, Jr.	L. Kent Wyatt
Anthony D. Osmundson	Bruce E. Salenko
Thomas C. Richards	Brian H. Charter
L. Thomas Wagner	Richard L. Alley
David L. Perrault	Glenda N. Reager
Sara A. Clark	Whitney A. Davis
John Quincy Brown, III	John C. Miller, Jr.
David S. Worthington	Michael J. Nelson

OF COUNSEL

Cavan Hardy	William A. Wilson
Norwood R. Erich	Richard M. Cunha

Kelly F. Watson	Karin G. Shine
Kristine E. Balogh	Reginald A. Dunn

Representative Clients: AIG Aviation, Inc.; The Chubb Insurance Company; Fireman's Fund Insurance Company; Government Employees Insurance Company; Great West Casualty Insurance Company; Liberty Mutual Insurance Company; Royal Insurance Company; Travelers Insurance Company; Twentieth Century Insurance Company; Zurich American Insurance Company.

For full biographical listings, see the Martindale-Hubbell Law Directory

JOHNSON, SCHACHTER & COLLINS, A PROFESSIONAL CORPORATION (AV)

California Plaza, 2180 Harvard Street, #560, 95815
Telephone: 916-921-5800
Telecopier: 916-921-0247
Email: law@jscattorneys.com

Robert H. Johnson	George W. Holt
Alesa M. Schachter	Kellie M. Murphy
Kim H. Collins	Alvin Gittisriboongul

Susan E. Slager

(See Next Column)

OF COUNSEL

Ford R. Smith	Carolyn M. Wood

Susanne M. Shelley

Representative Clients: CAMICO; Chicago Insurance; Fireman's Fund Insurance Cos.; Insurance Company of the West; Interstate National; NAVISTAR; Sears, Roebuck and Co.; Shand Morahan; Westport Insurance Corp.
Reference: U.S. Bank, Sacramento.

For full biographical listings, see the Martindale-Hubbell Law Directory

KEITGES & BANGLE, A PROFESSIONAL LAW CORPORATION (AV)

3620 American River Drive Suite 218, 95864
Telephone: 916-568-3400
Fax: 916-568-3404
Email: saclaw@keitgesbangle.com *URL:* http://www.lawyers.com/keitgesbangle
Fairfield, California Office: 2300 Boynton Avenue, Suite 203. 94533.
Telephone: 707-422-1301.
Fax: 707-427-6677.

Cyril A. Keitges, Jr.	Jill H. Latchaw
Raymond Bangle, III	James E. Gingrich

For full biographical listings, see the Martindale-Hubbell Law Directory

MASON & THOMAS (AV)

2151 River Plaza Drive, Suite 100, 95833
Telephone: 916-567-8211
Fax: 916-567-8212
Email: M&T@MasonThomas.com

MEMBERS OF FIRM

Stephen A. Mason	Bradley S. Thomas

ASSOCIATES

Douglas W. Brown	Patrick J. Hehir
Robert G. Kruse	Kevin L. Elder
David S. Yost	Michele Raley

For full biographical listings, see the Martindale-Hubbell Law Directory

MATHENY SEARS LINKERT & LONG, LLP (AV)

3638 American River Drive, P.O. Box 13711, 95853-4711
Telephone: 916-978-3434
Fax: 916-978-3430
Email: info@msll.com *URL:* http://www.msll.com

MEMBERS OF FIRM

Henry G. Matheny (1933-1984)	Kent M. Luckey
Douglas A. Sears	Matthew C. Jaime
Richard S. Linkert	Michael A. Bishop
Ernest A. Long	Robert B. Berrigan
Joann Georgallis	Ronald E. Enabnit

Eric R. Wiesel

ASSOCIATES

Andrea Croak Christensen	Paul Richard Baleria
Michael G. Jones	James F. Curran
Eric M. Bonzell	Andreas C. Rockas
Mary Elizabeth Wood	Timothy P. Chang

OF COUNSEL

James C. Damir

LEGAL SUPPORT PERSONNEL

PARALEGALS

Frances Studer	Lynell Rae Steed

Jennifer Bachman

Representative Clients: AIG; Granite States Insurance Co.; National Union Fire Insurance Co.; Old Republic Insurance Co.; Prudential Property & Casualty Insurance Co.; State Farm Mutual Automobile Insurance Co.; State Farm Fire and Casualty Co.; T.I.G. Insurance; United Services Automobile Assn.

For full biographical listings, see the Martindale-Hubbell Law Directory

MCDONALD, SAELTZER, MORRIS, CREEGGAN & WADDOCK (AV)

555 Capitol Mall, Suite 700, 95814
Telephone: 916-444-5706
Fax: 916-444-8529

MEMBERS OF FIRM

Richard C. Creeggan	Thomas P. Waddock

Gregory R. Madsen

ASSOCIATES

Jennifer Hammond-Carroll	Lance J Curtis
Patricia M. Keegan	Greg T. Mino

OF COUNSEL

William O. Morris

Reference: Wells Fargo Bank.

For full biographical listings, see the Martindale-Hubbell Law Directory

Sacramento—Continued

Nageley, Meredith & Miller, Inc. (AV)

8001 Folsom Boulevard, Suite 100, 95826
Telephone: 916-386-8282
Fax: 916-386-8952
Email: mail@mnlawfirm.com

Sam R. Nageley
Gregory A. Meredith
Andrea M. Miller
Lawrence N. Hensley
Craig S. MacGlashan
Janet M. Meredith
Carole Hansen Sharples
L. Alan Warwick
Drew M. Johnson
James C. Keowen
Duane S. Oliveira

For full biographical listings, see the Martindale-Hubbell Law Directory

Porter, Scott, Weiberg & Delehant, A Professional Corporation (AV)

350 University Avenue, Suite 200, 95825
Telephone: 916-929-1481
Fax: 916-927-3706
Email: pswdlaw@aol.com

Russell G. Porter
A. Irving Scott, Jr.
Edwin T. Weiberg
John W. Delehant
Anthony S. Warburg
Ned P. Telford
James K. Mirabell
Craig A. Caldwell
Terence J. Cassidy
Tom H. Bailey
Carl J. Calnero
Russ J. Wunderli
Nancy J. Sheehan
Norman V. Prior
Timothy M. Blaine
Stephen E. Horan
Carl L. Fessenden

Elisa Ungerman
Michael J. Baytosh
David A. Melton
Jennifer E. Duggan
Vanessa W. Whang
Dennis C. Huie
Michael W. Pott
Kellianne Akbar
Daniel M. Steinberg
Jack Woodside
Jonathan A. Corr
Kristina M. Hall
Alden J. Parker
Avery E. Dority
Robin Weideman
Denise A. Carnaroli
Lara S. Hilley
Sean Allen
Ralph R. Nevis
Darrin M. Menezes
Shane Singh

For full biographical listings, see the Martindale-Hubbell Law Directory

Riegels Campos & Kenyon LLP (AV)

2500 Venture Oaks Way, Suite 220, 95833-4222
Telephone: 916-779-7100
Fax: 916-779-7120
Email: rckrecpt@rcklaw.com *URL:* http://www.rcklaw.com

MEMBERS OF FIRM

Dennis M. Campos
John E. Fischer
Cyrus A. Johnson
Charity Kenyon
Jeffery Owensby
David A. Riegels
Sue Ellen Wooldridge

Representative Clients: Allstate Life Insurance Company; Blue Cross of California; Farmers Insurance Group; Prudential Insurance Companies of America; Sutter Health.

For full biographical listings, see the Martindale-Hubbell Law Directory

Rushford & Bonotto, LLP (AV)

2277 Fair Oaks Boulevard, Suite 495, 95825
Telephone: 916-565-0590
Facsimile: 916-565-0599
Mailing Address: P.O. Box 255689, Sacramento, CA, 95865
Email: Rushford-BonottoLLP@worldnet.att.net

MEMBERS OF FIRM

James W. Rushford
Phillip R. Bonotto
Brett Rosenthal
Curtis W. Cable

Jennifer R. Porter

Representative Clients: Allstate Insurance Company; Bayer Corporation (formerly Miles, Inc.); California Builders Supply; Dravo Corporation; Federated Insurance Company; Federated Department Stores; GLC Carbon Corporation; General Mills, Inc.; Government Employees Insurance Company (GEICO); Grange Insurance Group; Liberty Mutual Insurance Company; Hopeman Brothers, Inc.

For full biographical listings, see the Martindale-Hubbell Law Directory

Rust, Armenis, Schwartz, Lamb & Bills, A Professional Corporation (AV)

4330 Auburn Boulevard, Suite 2500, 95841-0958
Telephone: 916-972-8300
FAX: 916-972-7878
Email: mail@raslblaw.com
San Francisco, California Office: 350 California Street, Suite 1900.
Telephone: 415-765-5910.
FAX: 415-765-5914.

David C. Rust (1924-1980)
Michael P. Armenis (1919-1988)
Fred A. Schwartz
David J. Bills
Ronald R. Lamb
Scott D. Schwartz
Brian S. Turner

R. Duane Skelton
W. David Corrick
Carl E. Kadlic (Resident, San Francisco Office)

Reference: Imperial Bank (Main Office, 455 Capitol Mall, Sacramento).

For full biographical listings, see the Martindale-Hubbell Law Directory

Schuering Zimmerman & Scully, LLP (AV)

400 University Avenue, 95825
Telephone: 916-567-0400
Fax: 916-568-0400
Email: szs@szs.com

MEMBERS OF FIRM

Steven T. Scully (1948-1994)
Leo H. Schuering, Jr.
Robert H. Zimmerman
Thomas J. Doyle
Lawrence S. Giardina
Anthony D. Lauria
Keith D. Chidlaw
John J. Sillis
Scott A. Linn
Donna W. Low
Raymond R. Gates

Christian Koster
Michael W. McCall
Dominique A. Pollara
Theodore D. Poppinga
John P. Rhode
Stephen L. Ramazzini
Jonathan A. Saul
Jeffrey J. Whitelaw

For full biographical listings, see the Martindale-Hubbell Law Directory

Trimble, Sherinian, & Varanini (AV)

1001 G Street, Suite 200, 95814
Telephone: 916-444-8271
Fax: 916-443-7372
Mailing Address: P.O. Box 590, Sacramento, CA, 95812-0590
Email: varanin@ns.net *URL:* http://www.lawyers.com/trimblesherinian&varanini

MEMBERS OF FIRM

Jerome M. Varanini
Suzanne M. Trimble
Suzanne A. Sherinian
Heather R. Chubb
Linda L. Bunce

Representative Clients: A.I.A.C.; American International Adjusting Co.; Auto Club of Southern California; Canadian Indemnity; Chubb Group of Insurance Cos.; Civil Service Insurance Co.; Deans & Homer; Guaranty National Insurance Co.; ITT Hartford; K & K Claims Service.

For full biographical listings, see the Martindale-Hubbell Law Directory

*SAN BERNARDINO,** San Bernardino Co.

Middlebrook, Kaiser & Popka, A Professional Corporation (AV)

1411 North "D" Street, P.O. Box 1319, 92402-1319
Telephone: 909-888-5751
Fax: 909-888-7360
Email: MKPSB2@PacBell.net
Palm Springs Office: 3001 East Tahquitz Canyon Way, Suite 109.
Telephone: 619-322-0806.
Fax: 619-322-8979.

Greg C. Middlebrook
Michael R. Kaiser (Resident, Palm Springs Office)
Dennis G. Popka

Jeffrey Mark Yoss (Resident, Palm Springs Office)
Sandra A. Shoupe-Gorga (Resident, Palm Springs Office)
Dennis R. Stout
Julie A. Sohnlein
Daren E. Hengesbach

OF COUNSEL

John W. Furness

Reference: Wells Fargo Bank.

For full biographical listings, see the Martindale-Hubbell Law Directory

THORNTON, TAYLOR, DOWNS, BECKER, TOLSON & DOHERTY—*Continued*

ASSOCIATES

Sandra E. Stone
Stephan T. Pastis
J. Edward Kerley
Michael T. Richmond
Gail S. Greenwood
Karen A. Braje
Marysia S. Okreglak

OF COUNSEL

Jerome F. Downs
James F. Thornton
Andrean L. Kalemis

For full biographical listings, see the Martindale-Hubbell Law Directory

VOGL & MEREDITH (AV)

456 Montgomery Street, 20th Floor, 94104
Telephone: 415-398-0200
Facsimile: 415-398-2820

Samuel E. Meredith
David R. Vogl
John P. Walovich
Jean N. Yeh
Thomas S. Clifton

Nicole L. Meredith
Dennis Gildea
Michael S. Burke
Martin Ross Sances
Joshua A. Ridless
David G. Valdez

For full biographical listings, see the Martindale-Hubbell Law Directory

WUERFEL & CHOLAKIAN, A PROFESSIONAL CORPORATION (AV)

555 Montgomery Street, Ninth Floor, 94111
Telephone: 415-398-1551; 800-992-5990
FAX: 415-398-3301
Email: sos@sflaw.net *URL:* http://www.sflaw.net
Santa Rosa, California Office: 131-A Stony Circle, Suite 515, 95401.
Telephones: 415-398-1551; 800-992-5990.
FAX: 415-398-1551.
Costa Mesa, California Office: Avenue of the Arts.
Telephone: 714-825-3590; 800-992-5990.

Mark D. Wuerfel
Kevin K. Cholakian
Julian J. Pardini
Nan R. Hooven
Sherri K. McElroy

SPECIAL COUNSEL

Dean C. Burnick
Charlene P. Rosack
Jonathan Gross
Michael A. Topp

Aaron D. Bigby
D. Clark Burton
Anthony J. Calero
Elizabeth A. Doyle
Linda L. Duiven
Jay E. Framson
Stephen D. Geist
Andrew A. Goode
David J. Heilman
Timothy S. Kirk
Stephen J. Liberatore
Anne Marie Master
Thomas A. Moore
Julianne Pinter

LEGAL SUPPORT PERSONNEL

Marla J. Kuresa (Legal Administrator)

For full biographical listings, see the Martindale-Hubbell Law Directory

*SAN JOSE,** Santa Clara Co.

ROBINSON & WOOD, INC. (AV)

227 North First Street, 95113
Telephone: 408-298-7120
Fax: 408-298-0477
Email: rw@r-winc.com

Archie S. Robinson
Weldon S. Wood
Thomas R. Fellows
David S. Henningsen
Hugh F. Lennon
Jesse F. Ruiz
Christian B. Nielsen
Jonathan L. Lee
Jon B. Zimmerman
Mark B. Schellerup
Andrew W. Olsson
Arthur J. Casey
Joseph C. Balestrieri
John L. Winchester, III
Robert A. Nakamae

Rebecca L. Moon
Ann A. Nguyen
Kenneth I. Schumaker
Anne C. Bailey
Stephen D. Bays
Jill K. Ernst
Colin G. McCarthy
Bonnie M. Ross
Mario Alvarado
Christopher K. Karic
Alison M. Hershberger
Camille L. Acayan
Valerie M. Drogus
Jennifer L. Bautista

For full biographical listings, see the Martindale-Hubbell Law Directory

SIMONCINI & ASSOCIATES (AV)

1694 The Alameda, 95126
Telephone: 408-280-7711
Facsimile: 408-280-1330
Email: kds@simoncini-law.com *URL:* http://www.simoncini-law.com

(See Next Column)

Kenneth D. Simoncini
Melanie D. Roberts
Marilynn J. Winters
Kerri A. Ridley

LEGAL SUPPORT PERSONNEL

Pamela A. Bauer (Paralegal - Case Manager)

For full biographical listings, see the Martindale-Hubbell Law Directory

SAN MATEO, San Mateo Co.

McDOWALL, COTTER, DUNN, VALE & BRACCO, A PROFESSIONAL CORPORATION (AV)

2070 Pioneer Court, P.O. Box 937, 94403
Telephone: 650-572-7933
Fax: 650-572-0834
Email: lawyers@mcdowalllaw.com
Palo Alto, California Office: 425 Sherman Avenue, Suite 100.
Telephone: 408-244-8755; Other Areas: 415-326-8410.
Fax: 415-326-3911.

William D. McDowall
Bernard T. Cotter
Thomas G. Dunn
Robert D. Vale
Michael A. Bracco
Richard M. Kelly

Representative Clients: State Farm Mutual Automobile Insurance Co.; State Farm Fire & Casualty Co.; California State Automobile Assn.; Allegiance Insurance Co.; Argonaut Insurance Cos.

For full biographical listings, see the Martindale-Hubbell Law Directory

*SAN RAFAEL,** Marin Co.

FREITAS, McCARTHY, MacMAHON & KEATING, LLP (AV)

Westamerica Building, Third Floor, 1108 Fifth Avenue, 94901
Telephone: 415-456-7500
Fax: 415-456-0266
Email: inquiry@freitaslaw.com
Point Reyes, California Office: 11150 Sir Francis Drake Boulevard.
Telephone: 415-663-1333.

MEMBERS OF FIRM

Thomas F. Keating, Jr.
Neil J. Moran
Richard P. Murray
Peter A. Kleinbrodt

ASSOCIATES

Beverly Wood
H. Shaina Goldman

Representative Clients: Westamerica Bank; Fireman's Fund American; Atlantic Mutual Insurance Co.; Allstate Insurance Co.; Commerce Clearing House; Pacific Telesis; Industrial Indemnity Co.; Atlantic Mutual Insurance Companies; City of San Rafael; Martin Municipal Water District.

For full biographical listings, see the Martindale-Hubbell Law Directory

JOHNS & CHRISTENSEN, A PROFESSIONAL CORPORATION (AV)

135 Paul Drive, Suite 100, 94903
Telephone: 415-459-5223
Facsimile: 415-453-2555
Email: info@johnsandchristensen.com *URL:* http://www.johnsandchristensen.com

Christopher Johns
Robert C. Christensen

David Gray Douglas
Jennifer A.D. Lehman
Farimah Faiz

OF COUNSEL

Mark J. Helmueller
Burton C. "Skip" Allyn, IV

For full biographical listings, see the Martindale-Hubbell Law Directory

PLASTIRAS & TERRIZZI (AV)

24 Professional Center Parkway, Suite 150, 94903
Telephone: 415-472-8100
Fax: 415-472-8110
Email: plastir@ix.netcom.com *URL:* http://www.attorneyliability.com

Basil Plastiras
Michael P. Terrizzi

Lynnette Brawer

For full biographical listings, see the Martindale-Hubbell Law Directory

*SANTA ANA,** Orange Co.

BEAM, BROBECK & WEST (AV)

600 West Santa Ana Boulevard, Suite 1000, 92701
Telephone: 714-558-3944
Fax: 714-568-0129

MEMBERS OF FIRM

Byron J. Beam
David J. Brobeck, Jr.
John E. West
Kirk H. Nakamura
Daniel R. Sullivan
Charles W. Matheis, Jr.

(See Next Column)

BEAM, BROBECK & WEST, *Santa Ana—Continued*

ASSOCIATES

Gregory L. Rippetoe
Jennifer J. Miller
Donald S. Zalewski
David R. Rosenberg
Louise M. Douville
Kermit D. Marsh
Kelly A. Fortin
Barbara J. Salvini
Lil G. Delcampo
Michael J. Peffer
L. Steven Hattendorf

Representative Clients: Aetna Insurance Co.; American General Life Insurance Co.; American Hospital Supply; Carl Warren & Co.; Casualty Insurance Co.; City of Anaheim; City of Fullerton; City of Newport Beach; Empire Insurance Cos.; Physicians Interindemnity.

For full biographical listings, see the Martindale-Hubbell Law Directory

CASSIDY, WARNER, LANE & WINSTEAD, A PROFESSIONAL CORPORATION (AV)

600 West Santa Ana Boulevard, Suite 700, 92701
Telephone: 714-835-9431
Fax: 714-835-5264
Email: cdaly@cassidywarner.com

B. Kent Warner
Timothy X. Lane
Bruce A. Winstead

David C. Olson
Glen A. Stebens

OF COUNSEL

Alvin M. Cassidy

For full biographical listings, see the Martindale-Hubbell Law Directory

GARRETT & JENSEN (AV)

433 Civic Center Drive, West, P.O. Box 22002, 92702-2002
Telephone: 714-550-0100
Fax: 714-550-0471
URL: http://www.lawyers.com/garrettjensen
Riverside, California Office: 3403 10th Street, Suite 700.
Telephone: 909-781-0222.

MEMBERS OF FIRM

Boyd F. Jensen, II
Betty L. Fracisco
Mark S. Armijo
Douglas M. Borthwick

OF COUNSEL

Kenneth R. Garrett

Representative Clients: Automobile Club of Southern California; Ward North America; All Risk Claims Services; St. Paul Insurance Co.; John Deere Insurance Co.; Knott's Berry Farm; Global Van Lines; C.R. England, Inc.; Premier Parks Inc.; Falken Tire Corporation.

For full biographical listings, see the Martindale-Hubbell Law Directory

HAIGHT, BROWN & BONESTEEL, L.L.P. (AV)

A Partnership including Professional Corporations
Suite 900, 5 Hutton Centre Drive, 92707
Telephone: 714-754-1100
Telecopier: 714-754-0826
URL: http://www.hbblaw.com
Santa Monica, California Office: 1620 26th Street, Suite 4000 North, P.O. Box 680.
Telephone: 310-449-6000.
Telecopier: 310-829-5117.
Telex: 705837.
Riverside, California Office: California Tower, 3737 Maine Street, Suite 800.
Telephone: 909-341-8300.
Fax: 909-341-8309.
San Francisco, California Office: 100 Bush Street, 27th Floor.
Telephone: 415-986-7700.
Fax: 415-986-6945.
San Diego, California Office: 101 West Broadway, Suite 1000.
Telephone: 619-595-5583.
Fax: 619-595-7873.

RESIDENT MEMBERS

Bruce L. Cleeland
Mark R. VonderHaar
Jeffrey S. Gerardo
Richard O. Knapp

ASSOCIATES

Laura M. Knox
Wendy J. Schmitt
Steven M. Dailey
Antoinette P. Hewitt

Counsel for: Orange County: Aetna Casualty and Surety Co.; Zurich-American Insurance Cos.; Industrial Indemnity Co.; Professional Liability Claims Managers; Maryland Casualty Insurance Co.; Royal Insurance Company of America.

For full biographical listings, see the Martindale-Hubbell Law Directory

LONG & WILLIAMSON, A PROFESSIONAL CORPORATION (AV)

5 Hutton Centre Drive, Suite 1000, 92707
Telephone: 714-668-1400
Fax: 714-668-1411
Email: palong@long-williamson.com *URL:* http://www.long-williamson.com
San Diego, California Office: 12770 High Bluff Drive, #380, 92130.
Telephone: 858-350-4614.
Fax: 858-481-3703.

Patrick A. Long
John S. Williamson

John A. Delis
Thomas Patrick Long
Lori R. Simon
Abraham H. Tang

Reference: Orange National Bank.

For full biographical listings, see the Martindale-Hubbell Law Directory

MARLIN & SALTZMAN, A PROFESSIONAL LAW CORPORATION (AV)

203 North Golden Circle Drive, Suite 310, 92705
Telephone: 714-560-9300
Fax: 714-560-9313
URL: http://www.marlinandsaltzman.com
Woodland Hills, California Office: Westhills Plaza, 20700 Ventura Boulevard, Suite 227, 91364.
Telephone: 818-702-0600.
Fax: 818-702-6555.

Louis M. Marlin
Stanley D. Saltzman

Thomas F. Hozduk
Stephen P. O'Dell
Sven D. Buncher
Alan S. Lazar

For full biographical listings, see the Martindale-Hubbell Law Directory

SHUPE, REAGAN & WYNE (AV)

A Partnership including a Professional Corporation
Shupe Law Building, 333 Civic Center Drive West, 92701-4518
Telephone: 714-558-4898
Telecopier: 714-558-9060
Email: shupelaw@aol.com *URL:* http://www.shupelaw.com

R. Q. Shupe (A Professional Corporation)
Elaine W. Reagan
Julie Ellen Wyne

Wendy Diane Wayland
Joseph M. Geis
Kim Kitzi

For full biographical listings, see the Martindale-Hubbell Law Directory

WALSH & DECLUES, LLP (AV)

6 Hutton Centre Drive Suite 1050, P.O. Box 22021, 92702-2021
Telephone: 714-436-1776
Facsimile: 714-436-1771
Email: sao@wd-law.com
Encino, California Office: 15821 Ventura Boulevard, Suite 625, P.O. Box 20087, 91416.
Telephone: 818-986-1776.
Facsimile: 818-382-2071.
Walnut Creek, California Office: 2125 Oak Grove Road, Suite 110, 94598.
Telephone: 925-686-1776.
Facsimile: 925-906-1773.

MEMBERS OF FIRM

J. Michael Declues (Managing Partner, Santa Ana Office)
Dennis J. Walsh (Managing Partner, Encino Office)
Michael E. Burkett (Founding Partner, Resident, Santa Ana Office)
Glenn S. Goldby (Partner, Resident, Santa Ana Office)
Jeffrey P. Thompson

Joanne C. Schwartz
Jeffrey A. Smith
Judith D. Anderson
Gregory A. Wille
Cary K. Quan
Jennifer K. Berneking
Shari S. Daneshrad (Resident, Encino Office)
Kathleen G. Maylin (Resident, Walnut Creek Office)
Karen R. Shulman
Michelle R. Walker (Resident, Encino Office)
George E. Ordonez (Resident, Encino Office)
Gayle C. Heirshberg
James L. Armstrong, Jr. (Resident, Walnut Creek Office)

Representative Clients: Regents of the University of California; University of California at Los Angeles; Home Depot U.S.A., Inc.; Ralph's Grocery Co.; Farmers Insurance Group; Alliance of Schools for Cooperative Insurance Programs; Carl Warren & Co.; Weyerhaeuser Co.; U-Haul, Inc.; GAB Ropins of North America, Inc.

For full biographical listings, see the Martindale-Hubbell Law Directory

WALNUT CREEK, Contra Costa Co.

ANDERSON, GALLOWAY & LUCCHESE, A PROFESSIONAL CORPORATION (AV)

1676 North California Boulevard Suite 500, 94596-4183
Telephone: 925-943-6383
Facsimile: 925-943-7542

Robert L. Anderson
George Patrick Galloway
David R. Lucchese
Martin J. Everson
Thomas J. Donnelly
Ralph J. Smith
James M. Nelson
Scott E. Murray
David A. Depolo
Karen A. Sparks
Stephen J. Brooks
Joseph S. Picchi
Erin Ruddy Sabey
Lea K. Baldacci
Michael E. Brewer
Sonja M. Dahl
Patricia A. Timm
Jeffrey S. Mitchell

Martha J. James
Shelton L. Smith
Steven M. McKinley
William L. Brelsford, Jr.

For full biographical listings, see the Martindale-Hubbell Law Directory

WESTLAKE VILLAGE, Ventura Co.

MICHAELIS, MONTANARI & JOHNSON, A PROFESSIONAL LAW CORPORATION (AV)

31255 Cedar Valley Drive, Suite 217, 91361
Telephone: 805-371-4611
Fax: 818-865-8444
Mailing Address: P.O. Box 7507, Thousand Oaks, CA, 91359-7507
Email: mmj@vc.net

James I. Michaelis
James P. Johnson
Garry L. Montanari
Gary J. LaPook

Miriam Piwoz Goodman
Wesley S. Wenig

Representative Clients: AIG Aviation, Inc.; Associated Aviation Underwriters; Certain Underwriters at Lloyd's of London; Certain Underwriters at the Institute of London Underwriters; CIGNA; Phoenix Aviation Managers, Inc.; Universal Loss Management, Inc.

For full biographical listings, see the Martindale-Hubbell Law Directory

COLORADO

*BOULDER,** Boulder Co.

MARTIN & MEHAFFY, LLC (AV)

1655 Walnut Street, Suite 300, P.O. Box 1260, 80302
Telephone: 303-442-3375
Fax: 303-444-8398
Email: mmllc@aol.com *URL:* http://www.planetnetwork.com/law/index.htm/

MEMBERS OF FIRM

John R. Mehaffy
Lawrence C. Rider
Donald James Humphrey
Joel C. Maguire
Matthew S. Humphrey

Jonathan L. Miller
Laura S. Moore
Christopher M. Ernst

SPECIAL COUNSEL

Margaret R. Brubaker

Approved Attorneys for: Attorneys Title Guaranty Fund, Inc.

For full biographical listings, see the Martindale-Hubbell Law Directory

*COLORADO SPRINGS,** El Paso Co.

KANE, DONLEY & JOHNSON, P.C. (AV)

90 South Cascade Avenue, Suite 830, 80903
Telephone: 719-471-1650
Fax: 719-471-1663
Mailing Address: P.O. Box 1119, Colorado Springs, CO, 80901
Email: kdandjpc@earthlink.net

Jerry A. Donley
Mark H. Kane
Jack E. Donley
David M. Johnson
Hayden W. Kane, II

William A. Palmer
Katherine L. Hays

OF COUNSEL

Hayden W. Kane

Representative Clients: American International Companies; Shelter Insurance Co.; Metropolitan Insurance Co.

(See Next Column)

Reference: State Bank & Trust and Bank One.

For full biographical listings, see the Martindale-Hubbell Law Directory

RETHERFORD, MULLEN, JOHNSON & BRUCE, L.L.C. (AV)

415 South Sahwatch, P.O. Box 1580, 80901
Telephone: 719-475-2014
Toll Free: 1-800-281-2014
Fax: 719-630-1267
Email: info@rmjblaw.com

MEMBERS OF FIRM

Jerry A. Retherford
J. Stephen Mullen
Anthony A. Johnson
Neil C. Bruce
Patrick R. Salt
Lori M. Moore

ASSOCIATES

Timothy E. Reilly
Debra P. DeRee

OF COUNSEL

Marilyn Brock Doig
Patricia L. Peterson

Representative Clients: Allstate Insurance Company; American Continental Insurance Company; American National Property & Casualty Insurance Company; American States Insurance Company; EMC Insurance Companies; Farmers Alliance Insurance Company; Farmers Insurance Exchange; Fireman's Fund Insurance Company; GEICO; Hawkeye-Security Insurance Company; Interstate Insurance Company; ITT Hartford; Omaha Property and Casualty; Progressive Insurance Company; State Farm Fire Insurance Company; State Farm Mutual Automobile Insurance Company; Union Insurance Company.

For full biographical listings, see the Martindale-Hubbell Law Directory

WITTMAN & McCORD (AV)

A Partnership including a Professional Corporation
Suite 320 UMB Bank Building, 5825 Delmonico Drive, 80919
Telephone: 719-590-9899
Fax: 719-590-9984
Email: wittcord-law@pcisys.net
Denver, Colorado Office: 10630 East Bethany Drive (Aurora), 80014.
Telephone: 303-337-4952.
Fax: 303-337-6165.

MEMBERS OF FIRM

Sherwin V. "Bud" Wittman, II, (P.C.)
Edward M. McCord, P.C.

ASSOCIATES

J. Bradley Hardman
Keith D. Vance

Representative Clients: Allstate Insurance Co.; Carolina Casualty Insurance Co.; E & O Professionals Insurance Co.; John Deere Transportation Insurance Co.; Motor Cargo Co.; Providian Auto & Home Insurance Co.; Safeco Insurance Co.; USAA Insurance Co.; USF & G Insurance Co.; Utica Mutual Insurance Co.

For full biographical listings, see the Martindale-Hubbell Law Directory

*DENVER,** Denver Co.

BYRNE, KIELY & WHITE, LLP (AV)

The Chancery, Suite 1300, 1120 Lincoln Street, 80203
Telephone: 303-861-5511
Fax: 303-861-0304

MEMBERS OF FIRM

Thomas J. Byrne
Joseph A. Kiely (1944-1992)
William White

OF COUNSEL

Michael L. Poindexter

John C. Knudsen
Laynie B. Gilida

For full biographical listings, see the Martindale-Hubbell Law Directory

COOPER & CLOUGH, P.C. (AV)

Suite 600 Writer Square, 1512 Larimer Street, 80202
Telephone: 303-607-0077
Fax: 303-607-0472
Email: cooper-clough@plinet.com

Paul D. Cooper
Kay J. Rice
John E. Clough
Larry S. McClung

Paul A. Faraci
Gary W. Flanagan
Nicholas Ghiselli
Deanne Potestio
Christopher L. Ingold

For full biographical listings, see the Martindale-Hubbell Law Directory

GORSUCH KIRGIS LLP (AV)

Tower 1, Suite 1000, 1515 Arapahoe Street, 80202
Telephone: 303-376-5000
Fax: 303-376-5001

(See Next Column)

*SANTA BARBARA,** Santa Barbara Co.

MULLEN & HENZELL, L.L.P. (AV)

A California registered limited liability partnership
112 East Victoria Street, Post Office Drawer 789, 93102-0789
Telephone: 805-966-1501
FAX: 805-966-9204
Email: mh@mullenlaw.com

MEMBERS OF FIRM

Mack S. Staton
Edward C. Thoits
Lawrence T. Sorensen
William E. Degen
Michael E. Cage

OF COUNSEL

Charles S. Bargiel

ASSOCIATE

Paul K. Wilcox

Representative Clients: California State Auto Association (No. Calif. Auto Club); Interinsurance Exchange of the Automobile Club of Southern California; Fireman's Fund Insurance Co.; State Farm Fire & Casualty Co.; State Farm Mutual Automobile Insurance Co.

For full biographical listings, see the Martindale-Hubbell Law Directory

*SANTA CRUZ,** Santa Cruz Co.

BURTON, VOLKMANN & SCHMAL, LLP (AV)

133 Mission Street, Suite 102, 95060
Telephone: 831-425-5023
FAX: 831-427-3159

PARTNERS

John S. Burton
Timothy R. Volkmann
Timothy J. Schmal

ASSOCIATES

Thomas P. Dwyer
Karen E. Lintott
Brandt R. Stickel
Todd A. James
Christopher B. Dort

For full biographical listings, see the Martindale-Hubbell Law Directory

SANTA MONICA, Los Angeles Co.

HAIGHT, BROWN & BONESTEEL, L.L.P. (AV)

A Partnership including Professional Corporations
1620 26th Street, Suite 4000 North, P.O. Box 680, 90404
Telephone: 310-449-6000
Telecopier: 310-829-5117
Telex: 705837
URL: http://www.hbblaw.com
Santa Ana, California Office: Suite 900, 5 Hutton Centre Drive.
Telephone: 714-754-1100.
Telecopier: 714-754-0826.
Riverside, California Office: California Tower, 3737 Main Street, Suite 800.
Telephone: 909-341-8300.
Fax: 909-341-8309.
San Francisco, California Office: 101 Bush Street, 27th Floor.
Telephone: 415-986-7700.
Fax: 415-986-6945.
San Diego, California Office: 101 West Broadway, Suite 1000.
Telephone: 619-595-5583.
Fax: 619-595-7873.

MEMBERS OF FIRM

Roy G. Weatherup
Denis J. Moriarty
Michael J. Leahy
Victor Anderson III
Robert L. Kaufman
Valerie A. Moore
Gary A. Bague
Richard E. Wirick

ASSOCIATES

Birgit Sale
Christopher V. Kendrick
Robin Zukin
Cynthia Siegal Hizami
Teresa M. Wainman
Eugenie A. Gifford
Yu-Feng (Frances) Chou
Antonia M. Chan

For full biographical listings, see the Martindale-Hubbell Law Directory

KOHRS & FISKE (AV)

3250 Ocean Park Boulevard, 90405
Telephone: 310-452-5524
Telecopier: 310-452-6115

MEMBERS OF FIRM

Conrad Kohrs
Luciana Perinetti O'Brien
J. Peter Fiske
Michael M. Amir

OF COUNSEL

Kim F. Cassulo

LEGAL SUPPORT PERSONNEL

Jane Watson
Jomana Asi

For full biographical listings, see the Martindale-Hubbell Law Directory

WATERS, MCCLUSKEY & BOEHLE (AV)

3250 Ocean Park Boulevard, Suite 300, 90405-3220
Telephone: 310-396-3411
Facsimile: 310-450-0925
Email: wmb@wmboehle.com
Santa Ana, California Office: Suite 1000, 200 West Santa Ana Boulevard.
Telephone: 714-953-4407.
Facsimile: 714-953-2118.

MEMBERS OF FIRM

William W. Waters (1898-1979)
Timothy R. Lee
Laurence R. Corcoran (1927-1987)
Gregg W. Brugger
Kevin G. McCluskey
Fritz B. Hax
Stacey B. Spurlock (Resident, Santa Ana Office)
Wayne J. Boehle
Richard A. Wall (Resident, Santa Ana Office)
Michael T. Montgomery

ASSOCIATES

Quyen H. Khuong (Resident, Santa Ana)
Julie C. Chang-Lee (Resident, Santa Ana Office)
Christine Y. Chien (Resident, Santa Ana Office)
Joseph C. Graven
Kirk Michael Olson (Resident, Santa Ana Office)
Portasha R. Moore
Brett C. Drouet

References: Bank of America; Santa Monica Business Park, Santa Monica; California National Bank, Los Angeles; First Republic, Los Angeles.

For full biographical listings, see the Martindale-Hubbell Law Directory

*SANTA ROSA,** Sonoma Co.

BABIN, SEEGER, CROW & MANWELL, LLP (AV)

100 Stony Point Road, Suite 125, 95401
Telephone: 707-526-7370
Fax: 707-526-0307

MEMBERS OF FIRM

Norbert C. Babin
Debra Crow
Martin L. Seeger, IV
Malcolm T. Manwell
Susan H. Rapp

ASSOCIATES

Constance F. Morrison
Frank E. Preston
Max R. Breall

For full biographical listings, see the Martindale-Hubbell Law Directory

*STOCKTON,** San Joaquin Co.

MAYALL, HURLEY, KNUTSEN, SMITH & GREEN, A PROFESSIONAL CORPORATION (AV)

2453 Grand Canal Boulevard, Second Floor, 95207-8253
Telephone: 209-477-3833
Fax: 209-473-4818

Dennis J. Green
Kristen M. Hegge
William W. Hale
Vladimir F. Kozina
Mark Stephen Adams
Steven A. Malcoun
J. Anthony Abbott
Mark E. Berry
Peter J. Whipple
William J. Gorham, III
Joseph A. Salazar, Jr.

William L. Anderson
Kim D. Jennings
Robert E. Laubengayer
Jennifer K. Doherty
Kimberly P. Willy
Christine H. Long
Patrick Lin

Representative Clients: Allstate Insurance Co.; California State Automobile Assn.; The Maryland; Scottsdale; State Farm Mutual Insurance Cos.; Beck Development, Inc; HD Arnaiz, Ltd; Vito Transporation; Stockton Unified School District; San Joaquin County Rapid Transit District.

For full biographical listings, see the Martindale-Hubbell Law Directory

VALLEJO, Solano Co.

DUNN, ROGASKI, PREOVOLOS & WEBER (AV)

241 Georgia Street, P.O. Box 1072, 94590
Telephone: 707-553-1555
Fax: 707-553-9043

MEMBERS OF FIRM

Robert C. Dunn
Michael J. Preovolos
Chester A. Rogaski, Jr.
Howard R. Weber

ASSOCIATES

Jill Noonan
Jon A.C. Vonder Haar
Jeffrey S. Olds
Leeanne Y. Patterson

Representative Clients: Norcal Mutual Insurance Co.; Nationwide Insurance Co.; Medical Insurance Exchange of California; California Insurance Guarantee Assn.; Scottsdale Insurance Co.; CAP/MPT; Kaiser Foundation Hospitals.
Reference: Bank of America, NT & SA.

For full biographical listings, see the Martindale-Hubbell Law Directory

GORSUCH KIRGIS LLP—*Continued*

PARTNERS

James A. Jablonski
Peter R. Nadel
Dudley P. Spiller
Stuart Pack
Charles F. McVay

ASSOCIATES

Heather Anne Hawker
Julie Leamon Rosen

For full biographical listings, see the Martindale-Hubbell Law Directory

GRUND & BRESLAU, P.C. (AV)

303 East Seventeenth Avenue, Suite 303, 80203-1263
Telephone: 303-830-7770
Facsimile: 303-830-2313
Email: g&b@grundbreslau.com

John W. Grund
Richard R. Rardin
Brad W. Breslau
Julie J. Noonan
Della S. Nelson
Graden P. Jackson

Representative Clients: Admiral Insurance Co.; Allstate Insurance Co.; American Family Insurance Co.; CGU/Hawkeye-Security Insurance Co.; Custard Insurance Adjusters, Inc.; Essex Insurance Co.; Homestead Insurance Co.; Horace Mann Insurance Co.; PAFCO General Insurance Co.; St. Paul Insurance Cos.

For full biographical listings, see the Martindale-Hubbell Law Directory

HALABY CROSS & SCHLUTER (AV)

Suite 1400, 1873 South Bellaire Street, 80222
Telephone: 303-691-5300
Fax: 303-691-5307

Theodore S. Halaby
Jonathan A. Cross
Leslie L. Schluter

ASSOCIATES

Andrew J. Carafelli
Matthew A. Samuelson
E. James Wilder, IV
Sue Ann Haskell
Marc C. Diamant

For full biographical listings, see the Martindale-Hubbell Law Directory

THE HUSTEAD LAW FIRM A PROFESSIONAL CORPORATION (AV)

Regency Plaza One, 4643 South Ulster Street, Suite 1250, 80237
Telephone: 303-721-5000
Facsimile: 303-721-5001
URL: http://www.thlf.com

Patrick Q. Hustead

Stephen C. Larson
Benton J. Barton (Not admitted in CO)
Duane E. Bolin
Janlynn R. Fleener

Representative Clients: Acceptance Group Insurance Companies; Amwest Insurance Company; Colorado Western Insurance Company; Connecticut Surety; Contractors Bonding and Insurance Company; Insurance Company of the West; Merchants Bonding Company; Underwriters at Lloyd's London; Odyssey Re London; The St. Paul Surety Group.

For full biographical listings, see the Martindale-Hubbell Law Directory

LEVY & LAMBDIN, P.C. (AV)

Plaza Tower One, Suite 900, 6400 South Fiddlers Green Circle (Englewood), 80111
Telephone: 303-796-2900
Telecopier: 303-796-2081

Marc R. Levy
Stuart D. Morse
Suzanne J. Lambdin
Karen Hannah Wheeler

Martha C. Ferris
Stephanie Ann Montague
Gerald D. Pratt
Brian J. Waters
Michael S. Power
Ivan A. Sarkissian
Janet S. Bouffard
Lelia Kathleen Chaney
Jane E. Hershey

For full biographical listings, see the Martindale-Hubbell Law Directory

LONG & JAUDON, P.C. (AV)

The Bailey Mansion, 1600 Ogden Street, 80218-1414
Telephone: 303-832-1122
FAX: 303-832-1348

Lawrence A. Long (1908-1992)
Michael T. McConnell
Joseph C. Jaudon, Jr.
Stephen P. Hopkins
David B. Higgins
Alan D. Avery
Frederick W. Long
Cecelia A. Fleischner
Gary B. Blum
Walter N. Houghtaling
Christine Anne Craigmile

(See Next Column)

Sheri Hood Roswell
David H. Yun

Representative Clients: Travelers Property Casualty Company; The Doctors Company; Home Insurance Company; Baxter Healthcare; CNA.

For Complete List of Firm Personnel, See General Section

For full biographical listings, see the Martindale-Hubbell Law Directory

MARKUSSON, GREEN & JARVIS, P.C. (AV)

Suite 2300, 1050 Seventeenth Street, 80265
Telephone: 303-572-4200
Fax: 303-595-3780

James K. Green
Dennis H. Markusson
H. Keith Jarvis
Thomas E. Napp

Kirstin G. Lindberg
William B. Stanton
Jason L. Romero
William T. Webb
Ashley E. Moller

Representative Clients: CGU; Medmarc; Ohio Casualty Group; Reliance Insurance Co.; Republic Insurance Co.; Traveler's Insurance Companies; Utah Home Fire Insurance Co.; General Star Management Co.; The Terracon Companies; Dow Elanco.

For full biographical listings, see the Martindale-Hubbell Law Directory

MONTGOMERY LITTLE & MCGREW, P.C. (AV)

The Quadrant, 5445 DTC Parkway, Suite 800 (Englewood), 80111
Telephone: 303-773-8100
Telecopier: 303-220-0412
URL: http://www.mlmpc.com

Robert R. Montgomery
John R. Riley
David C. Little
Christopher B. Little
Richard L. Murray, Jr.
Karen B. Best
Kevin J. Kuhn
Timothy M. Schulte
William H. Knapp
Carole Salamaha
Daniel P. Murphy
Patrick T. O'Rourke
Robert N. Spencer
Julie J. Collett

OF COUNSEL

J. Bayard Young

Representative Clients: Colorado Physicians Insurance; The St. Paul Insurance Cos.; University of Colorado Health Sciences Center; HealthOne; Westport Insurance Corp.; CNA; Dentists Professional Liablity Trust; Design Professionals Insurance Corp.; Farmers Insurance Co.; State Volunteer Mutual Insurance Co.

For Complete List of Firm Personnel, See General Section

For full biographical listings, see the Martindale-Hubbell Law Directory

SENTER GOLDFARB & RICE, L.L.C. (AV)

Suite 700, 400 South Colorado Boulevard, P.O. Box 22833, 80222
Telephone: 303-320-0509
FAX: 303-320-0210
Email: SGRLLC.com

MEMBERS OF FIRM

William Lee Senter
Joel S. Babcock
James E. Goldfarb
Arthur J. Kutzer
Thomas Sullivan Rice
Peter H. Doherty
Steven Jay Dawes
John D. Hayes

Sonja S. McKenzie
Eric M. Ziporin
Alenka Jana Han
Craig R. Anderson
Pamela Lewis Mosher
Peter J. Morgan
Tiffaney A. Norton
James S. Simko
Brian R. Reynolds
Karen F. Hubler

References: Norwest Bank of Denver; Bank of Cherry Creek; The Byers State Bank.

For full biographical listings, see the Martindale-Hubbell Law Directory

WELLS, ANDERSON & RACE, LLC (AV)

1700 Broadway, Suite 1850, 80290
Telephone: 303-830-1212
Fax: 303-830-0898

Mary A. Wells
Geoffrey S. Race
Sheryl L. Anderson
Suanne M. Dell

William Strohmeyer
L. Michael Brooks, Jr.
Nathalia S. A. Hardy

Representative Clients: Allied Group Insurance; Chubb/Pacific Indemnity Group; Great American Insurance Cos.; American States Ins. Co.; Royal Insurance Co.; State Farm Fire and Casualty Co.; The St. Paul Insurance Cos.; United Fire and Casualty Co.; Insurance Company of the West.

For full biographical listings, see the Martindale-Hubbell Law Directory

Denver—Continued

WITTMAN & MCCORD (AV)

A Partnership including a Professional Corporation
10630 East Bethany Drive (Aurora), 80014
Telephone: 303-337-4952
Fax: 303-337-6165
Email: wittcord-law@pcisys.net
Colorado Springs, Colorado Office: Suite 320 UMB Bank Building, 5825 Delmonico Drive.
Telephone: 719-590-9899.
Fax: 719-590-9984.

MEMBERS OF FIRM

Sherwin V. "Bud" Wittman, II, (P.C.)
Edward M. McCord, P.C.

ASSOCIATES

J. Bradley Hardman
Keith D. Vance

Representative Clients: Allstate Insurance Co.; Carolina Casualty Insurance Co.; E & O Professionals Insurance Co.; John Deere Transportation Insurance Co.; Motor Cargo Co.; Providian Auto & Home Insurance Co.; Safeco Insurance Co.; USAA Insurance Co.; USF & G Insurance Co.; Utica Mutual Insurance Co.

For full biographical listings, see the Martindale-Hubbell Law Directory

WOOD, RIS & HAMES, PROFESSIONAL CORPORATION (AV)

1775 Sherman Street, Suite 1600, 80203-4313
Telephone: 303-863-7700
Telecopier: 303-830-8772

Edward L. Wood (1899-1974)
F. Michael Ludwig
Charles E. Weaver
Clayton B. Russell
Mark R. Davis
Dennis A. Hanson
Michel P. Williams
Jennifer L. Veiga
Barbara L. Brundin
William A. Rogers, III
Robert G. Wheeler

OF COUNSEL

William K. Ris
Eugene S. Hames
Stephen E. Connor
Donald L. Cook

SPECIAL COUNSEL

Donald B. Gentry

Counsel for: American Family Insurance Co.; American International Companies; Canal Insurance Company; Equitable Life Assurance Society of the United States; Fireman's Fund Insurance Co.; Home Insurance Co.; Liberty Mutual Insurance Group; Metropolitan Life Insurance Co.; Prudential Insurance Company of America; Safeco Insurance Co.

For full biographical listings, see the Martindale-Hubbell Law Directory

ENGLEWOOD, Arapahoe Co.

BURG SIMPSON ELDREDGE & HERSH, P.C. (AV)

40 Inverness Drive East, 80112
Telephone: 303-792-5595
Fax: 303-708-0527
URL: http://www.burgsimpson.com
Cody, Wyoming Office: 1135 14th Street.
Telephone: 307-527-7891.
Fax: 307-527-7897.
Sterling, Colorado Office: 131 Hamilton Street.
Telephone: 970-521-1010.

Michael S. Burg
Peter W. Burg
Alan K. Simpson (Not admitted in CO)
Scott J. Eldredge
David P. Hersh
Thomas W. Henderson
Matthew R. Giacomini
Kerry N. Jardine
William L. Simpson (Not admitted in CO)
Colin M. Simpson (Not admitted in CO)

Kieth Van Doren
Matthew S. McElhiney
Rosemary Orsini
Robb A. Nelson
Holly S. Baer
Diane Vaksdal Smith
Joseph M. Kiple
Douglas J. Kotarek
David K. Te Selle
Tiffanie D. Stasiak

OF COUNSEL

Dale J. Coplan

Representative Clients: Allied Group Insurance; Budget Rent-A-Car; CNA Insurance Companies; Continental Divide Insurance Co.; Crum & Forster Commercial Insurance Co.; Hartford Insurance Cos.; National Farmers Union Insurance; Progressive Insurance Co.; Royal Insurance; TIG Insurance Company.

For full biographical listings, see the Martindale-Hubbell Law Directory

CONNECTICUT

*BRIDGEPORT,** Fairfield Co.

BAI, POLLOCK AND COYNE, P.C. (AV)

Park City Plaza, 10 Middle Street, P.O. Box 1978, 06604
Telephone: 203-366-7991
Fax: 203-366-4723
Email: bpc@snet.net

Arnold J. Bai (1931-1992)
Paul E. Pollock
James E. Coyne
Jeffrey A. Blueweiss
Garie J. Mulcahey
Raymond J. Plouffe, Jr.
Philip F. von Kuhn
Madonna A. Sacco
Michael S. Lynch
David J. Robertson
Edward P. Brady III

Gaileen A. Kaufman
Kevin S. Coyne
Colleen D. Fries
Neal P. Rogan
Louis A. Annecchino
Robert J. Weber, III
Heidi Marie Priwall
Anthony D. Sutton
Kevin J. Curseaden

For full biographical listings, see the Martindale-Hubbell Law Directory

COTTER, COTTER AND SOHON, P.C. (AV)

P.O. Box 5660 Bayview Station, 06610
Telephone: 203-335-3131
Fax: 203-874-1983
Email: tcotter@cottercottersohon.com
Milford, Connecticut Office: 500 Boston Post Road, 06460.
Telephone: 203-882-7143.
Fax: 203-874-1983.

D. Harold Cotter (1893-1961)
Thomas H. Cotter
John J. Cotter
Thomas Galvin Cotter
Catherine N. Anderson
Kevin M. Blake
James F. Mullen
Catherine A. Stewart
Michael V. Vocalina
Bryan L. LeClerc
Brian W. Smith

Gina M. Hall

Representative Clients: Royal Globe Indemnity Co.; Covenant Group; United States Fidelity & Guaranty Co.; Commercial Union Insurance Co.; Transport Insurance Co.; Metropolitan Insurance Co.; CNA; Nationwide Insurance Co.; Employers of Wassau Insurance Co.; Peerless Insurance Co.

For full biographical listings, see the Martindale-Hubbell Law Directory

WILLIAMS, COONEY & SHEEHY (AV)

One Lafayette Circle, 06604
Telephone: 203-331-0888
Telecopier: 203-331-0896
Email: wilcooshee@aol.com

MEMBERS OF FIRM

Ronald D. Williams
Robert J. Cooney
Edward Maum Sheehy
Dion W. Moore
Ronald D. Williams, Jr.
Francis A. Smith, Jr. (1951-1989)

Suzannah Kim Nigro
Michael Richard Brandt

Representative Clients: Connecticut Medical Insurance Co.; Utica Mutual Insurance Co.; Pennsylvania National Insurance; Podiatry Insurance Company of America; Preferred Physicians Mutual; Medical Liability Mutual Insurance Company.

For full biographical listings, see the Martindale-Hubbell Law Directory

GLASTONBURY, Hartford Co.

TROWBRIDGE & BASINE, P.C. (AV)

45 Glastonbury Boulevard, 06033
Telephone: 860-633-3995
FAX: 860-633-3449

Robert L. Trowbridge
Robert B. Basine

For full biographical listings, see the Martindale-Hubbell Law Directory

*HARTFORD,** Hartford Co.

DANAHER, TEDFORD, LAGNESE & NEAL, P.C. (AV)

Capitol Place, 21 Oak Street, 06106
Telephone: 860-247-3666
Telecopier: 860-547-1321
New York, N.Y. Office: 20 Exchange Place.
Telephone: 212-269-7100.
Baltimore, Maryland Office: 201 North Charles Street, Suite 2402.
Telephone: 410-385-1088.

(See Next Column)

DANAHER, TEDFORD, LAGNESE & NEAL P.C.—*Continued*

R. Cornelius Danaher, Jr.
Frederick B. Tedford
Joyce A. Lagnese
Kenneth R. Neal
Peter J. Ponziani
Frank H. Santoro
Catherine Ann Mohan
Craig A. Fontaine
Paul F. Slater (Resident, New York, N.Y. Office)
Kathleen F. Munroe
Calum B. Anderson
Matthew G. Conway
Charles E. Vermette, Jr.
Paul T. Edwards
Donald S. Meringer (Not admitted in CT; Resident, Baltimore, Maryland Office)

Christopher Coxon
Michael J. Dugan
Vincent A. Errante, Jr.
Charles F. Gfeller
M. Karen Noble
Theodore F. Roberts (Not admitted in CT; Resident, Baltimore, Maryland Office)
Lucy Romeo
Christopher J. Sochacki
Christine S. Synodi
Maureen Elizabeth Townsend
Brian Alain Zemil (Resident, Baltimore, Maryland Office)

OF COUNSEL

Robert C. Danaher
Marissa Banez (Not admitted in CT; Resident, New York, N.Y. Office)

For full biographical listings, see the Martindale-Hubbell Law Directory

GORDON, MUIR AND FOLEY, LLP (AV)

Hartford Square North, Ten Columbus Boulevard, 06106-5123
Telephone: 860-525-5361
Telecopier: 860-525-4849
Email: admin@gmflaw.com *URL:* http://www.gmflaw.com

MEMBERS OF FIRM

William S. Gordon, Jr. (1946-1956)
George Muir (1939-1976)
Edward J. Foley (1955-1983)
Peter C. Schwartz
John J. Reid
John H. Goodrich, Jr.
R. Bradley Wolfe
Jon Stephen Berk
William J. Gallitto
Gerald R. Swirsky
Robert J. O'Brien
Philip J. O'Connor
Kenneth G. Williams
Mary Ann Santacroce
Mary Anne Alicia Charron
Andrew J. Hern
Reneé W. Dwyer
Patty G. Swan

ASSOCIATES

Doreen West Amata
Howard A. Steinman
Erik E. Roberts
Christopher J. Casciani

Reference: People's Bank.

For full biographical listings, see the Martindale-Hubbell Law Directory

GOULD, KILLIAN & WYNNE (AV)

280 Trumbull Street, 25th Floor, 06103-3595
Telephone: 860-278-1270
Telecopier: 860-244-9290

MEMBERS OF FIRM

Samuel Gould (1905-1994)
Robert K. Killian
Francis J. Wynne
Martin A. Gould
Mark W. Baronas
William F. Healey
Nancy E. Gould
Robert O. Wynne

For full biographical listings, see the Martindale-Hubbell Law Directory

HOWD & LUDORF (AV)

65 Wethersfield Avenue, 06114
Telephone: 860-249-1361
Fax: 860-522-9549
Email: handl@ix.netcom.com

MEMBERS OF FIRM

John R. Lilliendahl, III
John J. Bogdanski
Philip T. Newbury, Jr.
Thomas R. Gerarde
Mark J. Claflin
Christopher M. Vossler
William F. Corrigan
David S. Monastersky
Michael J. Rose
Michael T. McCormack
Colette S. Griffin
Elizabeth Fitzsimmons Mucci
Elissa A. Flanagan
Melinda P. Frechette
Keith E. Marquis
Paul Erickson
Daniel C. DeMerchant

RETIRED

Edward S. Ludorf

Representative Clients: CIGNA; Reliance; Safeco/American States Insurance Co.; Allstate; Windsor Insurance Co.; Infinity Insurance Co.; Atlantic Mutual Insurance Co.; Geico.

For full biographical listings, see the Martindale-Hubbell Law Directory

JACKSON, O'KEEFE AND PHELAN (AV)

36 Russ Street, 06106-1571
Telephone: 860-278-4040
Fax: 860-527-2500
West Hartford, Connecticut Office: 62 LaSalle Road.
Telephone: 860-521-7500.
Fax: 860-561-5399.
Bethlehem, Connecticut Office: 423 Munger Lane. Telephone/
Fax: 203-266-5255.

MEMBERS OF FIRM

Jay W. Jackson
Andrew J. O'Keefe
Denise Martino Phelan
Matthew J. O'Keefe
Michael E. Riley
Peter K. O'Keefe
Philip R. Dunn, Jr.
Kathryn M. Cunningham
Joseph M. Busher, Jr.
Kristen E. Scholhamer

Representative Clients: Travelers Aetna Property Casualty Co.; ITT Hartford; Liberty Mutual Insurance Co.; Connecticut Medical Insurance Co.

For full biographical listings, see the Martindale-Hubbell Law Directory

KENNY, BRIMMER, MELLEY & MAHONEY (AV)

5 Grand Street, 06106
Telephone: 860-527-4226
FAX: 860-527-0214

Joseph P. Kenny (1920-1993)

MEMBERS OF FIRM

William J. Melley, III
Richard C. Mahoney
Anita M. Varunes
Dennis F. McCarthy

ASSOCIATES

Shannon K. McCarthy
Flora Pizzoferrato

OF COUNSEL

Leslie R. Brimmer

Representative Clients: Allstate Insurance Co.; Peerless Insurance Co.; Berkshire Mutual Fire Insurance Co.; Dorchester Mutual Fire Insurance Co.; Abington Mutual Fire Insurance Co.

For full biographical listings, see the Martindale-Hubbell Law Directory

O'BRIEN, TANSKI & YOUNG (AV)

CityPlace II, 06103
Telephone: 860-525-2700
Telefax: 860-247-7861

MEMBERS OF FIRM

Donald W. O'Brien
James M. Tanski
Roland F. Young, III
Robert D. Silva

OF COUNSEL

Hilary Fisher Nelson
Donna R. Zito
Richard A. O'Connor

ASSOCIATES

Albert G. Danker, Jr.
Agnes McDermott Alvord
Kathleen M. Nevins
Amy F. Goodusky
Andrew S. Wildstein
Angela D. Ober

References: Shawmut National Bank; New England Bank.

For full biographical listings, see the Martindale-Hubbell Law Directory

SKELLEY ROTTNER P.C. (AV)

P.O. Box 340890, 06134-0890
Telephone: 860-561-7077
Telecopier: 860-561-7088
Email: postmaster@skelleyrottner.com *URL:* http://www.skelleyrottner.com

Joseph F. Skelley, Jr. (1927-1995)
Joel J. Rottner
Susan L. Miller
James G. Geanuracos
Randall M. Hayes
Elizabeth M. Cristofaro
Kirby G. Huget
Matthew Dallas Gordon
Carl F. Yeich

Laura Ondrush
Robyn Sondak
Deborah Lynn Bucklan
Steven Greg Howe

OF COUNSEL

Susan E. Malliet

References: Fleet Bank; Liberty Bank.

For full biographical listings, see the Martindale-Hubbell Law Directory

SOROKIN, GROSS & HYDE, P.C. (AV)

One Corporate Center, 06103
Telephone: 860-525-6645
Fax: 860-522-1781
Email: sorokin@sorokinlaw.com
Simsbury, Connecticut Office: 720 Hopmeadow Street.
Telephone: 860-651-9348.

(See Next Column)

SOROKIN, GROSS & HYDE P.C., *Hartford—Continued*

Rocky Hill, Connecticut Office: 2360 Main Street.
Telephone: 860-563-9305.
Fax: 860-529-6931.

Jeffery P. Apuzzo
Jeffrey R. Martin
Richard C. Robinson

Jeffrey R. Neidle
Gwen P. Weisberg

For Complete List of Firm Personnel, See General Section

For full biographical listings, see the Martindale-Hubbell Law Directory

NORTH HAVEN, New Haven Co.

CELLA, MCKEON & WILLIAMS, P.C. (AV)

Suite A, 21 Washington Avenue, P.O. Box 221, 06473
Telephone: 203-239-5851
Fax: 203-234-2974
Email: cella.mckeon@snet.net

Carl E. Cella
Thomas P. McKeon
James G. Williams
Kevin P. Walsh
Michael F. O'Connor
Lisa D. Galati
Gerald T. Giaimo
Robert J. Flanagan, Jr.

For full biographical listings, see the Martindale-Hubbell Law Directory

STAMFORD, Fairfield Co.

LAW OFFICES OF MICHAEL GENE CLEAR (AV)

184 Atlantic Street, P.O. Box 3292, 06905
Telephone: 203-973-0240
Facsimile: 203-973-0244
Email: MCLEAR9948@aol.com

For full biographical listings, see the Martindale-Hubbell Law Directory

DELAWARE

*WILMINGTON,** New Castle Co.

CASARINO, CHRISTMAN & SHALK (AV)

Suite 1220, 222 Delaware Avenue, P.O. Box 1276, 19899
Telephone: 302-594-4500
Telecopier: 302-594-4509
URL: http://www.casarino.com

MEMBERS OF FIRM

Stephen P. Casarino
Colin M. Shalk
Beth H. Christman
Donald M. Ransom

Kenneth M. Doss
Diane M. Willette
Stacey L. Cummings
Thomas P. Leff

For full biographical listings, see the Martindale-Hubbell Law Directory

ROBERT W. RALSTON (AV)

10 East 13th Street, P.O. Box 1396, 19899
Telephone: 302-429-0758
Fax: 302-429-0193

For full biographical listings, see the Martindale-Hubbell Law Directory

SMITH, KATZENSTEIN & FURLOW LLP (AV)

The Corporate Plaza, 800 Delaware Avenue, P.O. Box 410, 19899
Telephone: 302-652-8400
Fax: 302-652-8405
Email: info@skfdelaware.com *URL:* http://www.SKFDelaware.com

MEMBERS OF FIRM

Robert J. Katzenstein
Laurence V. Cronin
Brett D. Fallon
Charles E. Butler

Kathleen M. Miller

For Complete List of Firm Personnel, See General Section

For full biographical listings, see the Martindale-Hubbell Law Directory

DISTRICT OF COLUMBIA

WASHINGTON, D.C. Co.

ALLEN, JOHNSON, ALEXANDER & KARP, P.A. (AV)

1707 L Street, N.W., Suite 1050, 20036
Telephone: 202-828-4141
Fax: 202-429-8798
Email: ajakdc@aol.com
Baltimore, Maryland Office: Suite 1540, 100 East Pratt Street.
Telephone: 410-727-5000.

D'Ana E. Johnson

Representative Clients: Scottsdale Insurance Co.; Nautilus Insurance Co.; Jefferson Insurance Co.; Liberty Mutual Insurance Co.; Avis Rent-A-Car; Otis Elevator Co.; Montgomery Elevator Co.; Admiral Insurance Co.; Local Government Insurance Trust; Penn National Insurance Co.

For Complete List of Firm Personnel, See General Section

For full biographical listings, see the Martindale-Hubbell Law Directory

CARR GOODSON WARNER, A PROFESSIONAL CORPORATION (AV)

1301 K Street, N.W., Suite 400, East Tower, 20005-3300
Telephone: 202-310-5500
Telecopier: 202-310-5555
Email: (attorney initials)@cgw-law.com *URL:* http://www.carrgoodsonwarner.com
Vienna, Virginia Office: Tycon Towers, 8000 Towers Crescent Drive, Suite 1350, 22182.
Telephone: 703-691-8818.
Baltimore, Maryland Office: 401 East Pratt Street, Suite 1622, The World Trade Center, 21202.
Telephone: 410-752-1570.
Rockville, Maryland Office: 31 Wood Lane, 20850.
Telephone: 301-424-7024.

Robert W. Goodson
David H. Jacobs
(Not admitted in DC)
Paul J. Maloney
Thomas L. McCally
Kevin M. Murphy
Jan E. Simonsen

Janette M. Blee
(Not admitted in DC)
Maureen A. Delaney
James P. Steele

For Complete List of Firm Personnel, See General Section

For full biographical listings, see the Martindale-Hubbell Law Directory

THE FALK LAW FIRM PLLC (AV)

A Professional Limited Liability Corporation
Suite 260 One Westin Center, 2445 M Street, N.W., 20037
Telephone: 202-833-8700
Telecopier: 202-872-1725
Email: FalkLaw@erols.com *URL:* http://www.falklawfirm.com

James H. Falk, Sr.
James H. Falk, Jr.
Stephen A. Best
John M. Falk

OF COUNSEL

Pierre E. Murphy
Elizabeth C. Collins

For full biographical listings, see the Martindale-Hubbell Law Directory

THE FEINBERG GROUP, LLP (AV)

1120 20th Street, N.W. Suite 740 South, 20036-3437
Telephone: 202-371-1110
Fax: 202-962-9290
Email: kfeinberg@thefeinberggroup.com *URL:* http://www.krfassociates.com
New York, N.Y. Office: 780 3rd Avenue, Suite 2202.
Telephone: 212-527-9600.
Fax: 212-527-9611. Email: kfeinberg@thefeinberggroup.com.

PARTNERS

Kenneth R. Feinberg
Deborah E. Greenspan
Michael K. Rozen
(Resident, New York Office)
Peter H. Woodin
(Resident, New York Office)

ASSOCIATE

Fredric M. Brooks (Not admitted in DC)

SENIOR COUNSEL

Jacqueline E. Zins

For full biographical listings, see the Martindale-Hubbell Law Directory

Washington—Continued

MACLEAY, LYNCH, GREGG & LYNCH, P.C. (AV)

Suite 1150, 1629 K Street, N.W., 20006
Telephone: 202-785-0123
FAX: 202-393-3390
Email: maclmac@aol.com

Donald Macleay (1908-1994)
Hugh Lynch, Jr. (1913-1994)
John C. Lynch
Michael Maloney
Robert P. Lynch
Robert G. McGinley
James C. Gregg

Jack David Lapidus
David C. Numrych

For full biographical listings, see the Martindale-Hubbell Law Directory

VENABLE ATTORNEYS AT LAW VENABLE, BAETJER, HOWARD & CIVILETTI, LLP (AV)

A Partnership including Professional Corporations
Suite 1000, 1201 New York Avenue, N.W., 20005
Telephone: 202-962-4800
Fax: 202-962-8300
URL: http://www.venable.com
Baltimore, Maryland Office: Venable, Baetjer and Howard LLP, 1800 Mercantile Bank & Trust Building, 2 Hopkins Plaza.
Telephone: 410-244-7400.
Fax: 410-244-7742.
McLean, Virginia Office: Venable, Baetjer and Howard LLP, Suite 400, 2010 Corporate Ridge.
Telephone: 703-760-1600.
Fax: 703-821-8949.
Rockville, Maryland Office: Venable, Baetjer and Howard LLP, Suite 500, One Church Street, P. O. Box 1906.
Telephone: 301-217-5600.
Fax: 301-217-5617.
Towson, Maryland Office: Venable, Baetjer and Howard LLP, 210 Allegheny Avenue, P. O. Box 5517.
Telephone: 410-494-6200.
Fax: 410-821-0147.

MEMBERS OF FIRM

James K. Archibald (Also at Baltimore, Maryland Office)
Benjamin R. Civiletti (P.C.) (Also at Baltimore and Towson, Maryland Offices)
Jeffrey A. Dunn (Also at Baltimore, Maryland Office)
Ronald R. Glancz
George F. Pappas (Also at Baltimore, Maryland Office)
James L. Shea (also at Baltimore, Maryland Office)

For Complete List of Firm Personnel, See General Section

For full biographical listings, see the Martindale-Hubbell Law Directory

WILMER, CUTLER & PICKERING (AV)

2445 M Street, N.W., 20037-1420
Telephone: 202-663-6000
Fax: 202-663-6363
Email: Law@Wilmer.Com *URL:* http://www.wilmer.com
Baltimore, Maryland Office: 100 Light Street, 21202.
Telephone: 410-986-2800.
Fax: 410-986-2828.
New York, New York Office: 520 Madison Avenue, 10022.
Telephone: 212-230-8800.
Fax: 212-230-8888.
European Offices:
4 Carlton Gardens, London, SW1Y 5AA, England. Telephone: +44 (20) 7 872 1000.
Fax: +44 (20) 7 839 3537.
Rue de la Loi 15# Wetstraat, B-1040 Brussels, Belgium. Telephone: +32 (2) 285 49 00.
Fax: +32 (2) 285 49 49.
Friedrichstrasse 95, D-10117 Berlin, Germany. Telephone: +49 (30) 20 22 64 00.
Fax: +49 (30) 20 22 65 00.

MEMBERS OF FIRM

A. Stephen Hut, Jr.
Lynn Bregman
John Payton
Thomas F. Connell
W. Scott Blackmer
Philip D. Anker
Joseph K. Brenner
David P. Donovan
Roger W. Yoerges
Denise Esposito

COUNSEL

Carol H. Fishman
Joseph E. Killory, Jr.

For Complete List of Firm Personnel, See General Section

For full biographical listings, see the Martindale-Hubbell Law Directory

FLORIDA

BOCA RATON, Palm Beach Co.

MICHAUD, BUSCHMANN, FOX, FERRARA & MITTELMARK, P.A. (AV)

33 Southeast 8th Street, 33432
Telephone: 561-392-0540
Fax: 561-392-0582
Email: Bocalaw@MBFFM.com *URL:* http://www.MBFFM.com

Scott H. Michaud
Paul Buschmann
Brian S. Fox
James T. Ferrara
Michael K. Mittelmark
Marc T. Millian

Marcy G. Blitz
Linda A. McCullough
Kimberly M. Hall

For full biographical listings, see the Martindale-Hubbell Law Directory

BRANDON, Hillsborough Co.

PILKA & ASSOCIATES, P.A. (AV)

213 Providence Road, 33511
Telephone: 813-653-3800
Facsimile: 813-651-0710
Mailing Address: P.O. Box 3470, Brandon, Florida, 33509-3470
Email: law@pilka.com

Daniel F. Pilka
John N. Jenkins

David A. Finlay
Mark E. Hager
Russell E. Klemm

OF COUNSEL

Robert A. Fraser
Scott F. Barnett
Joseph B. Donnelly
Veronica E. Donnelly

For full biographical listings, see the Martindale-Hubbell Law Directory

CORAL GABLES, Dade Co.

LANE, REESE, AULICK, SUMMERS & FIELD, P.A. (AV)

Suite 304 Douglas Centre, 2600 Douglas Road, 33134
Telephone: 305-444-4418
Fax: 305-444-5504
Email: LRASF-Miami@MSN.COM

Frank A. Lane
William S. Reese
Cecilia Aulick
William L. Summers
Paul H. Field

C. Page Lane
Lorenzo Jackson, Jr.
Luis J. Perdomo

For full biographical listings, see the Martindale-Hubbell Law Directory

PARENTI, FALK, WAAS, HERNANDEZ & CORTINA, P.A. (AV)

113 Almeria Avenue, 33134
Telephone: 305-447-6500
Fax: 305-447-1777
Email: pfw@gate.net

Michael J. Parenti, III
Glenn P. Falk
Norman M. Waas
Edward Hernandez
Armando Cortina
Gail Leverett Parenti
Scott Solomon
Michael Patrick Bonner

Gonzalo Barr
Cheryl Lynn Potter

For full biographical listings, see the Martindale-Hubbell Law Directory

DEERFIELD BEACH, Broward Co.

CARMAN, BEAUCHAMP, SANG & TOPKIN, P.A. (AV)

600 West Hillsboro Boulevard, Suite 400, 33441
Telephone: 954-426-4401
Fax: 954-426-4630
URL: http://www.carmanbeauchamp.com
Orlando, Florida Office: 600 East Colonial Drive, Suite 310.
Telephone: 407-423-4848.
Fax: 407-423-4804.
Stuart, Florida Office: Suite 232, 900 East Ocean Boulevard.
Telephone: 561-287-7005.

Kenneth P. Carman
J. Frank Beauchamp, III
Allen C. Sang
Sanford R. Topkin

Michael Kraft
Rikki Winters
Michael Goldstein

For full biographical listings, see the Martindale-Hubbell Law Directory

*FORT LAUDERDALE,** Broward Co.

BILLING, COCHRAN, HEATH, LYLES & MAURO, P.A. (AV)

Suite 301, 888 S.E. 3rd Avenue, 33316
Telephone: 954-764-7150
Fax: 954-764-7279
Email: bchlm@bchlm-pa.com *URL:* http://www.bchlm-pa.com
West Palm Beach, Florida Office: Reflections Office Centre, 400 Australian Avenue, Suite 801.
Telephones: 561-659-5970.
Fax: 561-659-6173.
Tampa, Florida Office: 3001 N. Rocky Point Drive East, Suite 200.
Telephone: 813-281-4671.
Fax: 813-289-7748.

Steven F. Billing (1947-1998)
Clark J. Cochran, Jr.
Thomas C. Heath
Dennis E. Lyles
John W. Mauro
Gregory T. Anderson (Resident, West Palm Beach Office)
William Tucker Craig
Kenneth W. Morgan, Jr.
Aline O. Marcantonio
Shawn B. McKamey
Kevin M. Vannatta
Vivian Hattem Fazio
Michael A. Weiss
T. Christine Perez
Hal B. Anderson
Carol J. Healy Glasgow

Representative Clients: City of Fort Lauderdale; The St. Paul Insurance Co.; Caduceus Self Insurance Fund; Government Employees Insurance Co.; Prudential Insurance Co.; The Travelers; Shelby Mutual Insurance Co.; Guardian Life Insurance Company of America; State Farm Fire & Casualty Co.; Holy Cross Hospital.

For full biographical listings, see the Martindale-Hubbell Law Directory

BLACKMORE & BLACKMORE (AV)

320 Southeast 10th Court, 33316
Telephone: 954-522-0418; 1-800-646-2786
Fax: 954-522-4974
Email: adelelaw@bellsouth.net *URL:* http://www.lawyers.com/blackmore

MEMBERS OF FIRM

Robert W. Blackmore
Adele M. Blackmore

For full biographical listings, see the Martindale-Hubbell Law Directory

CATRI, HOLTON, KESSLER & KESSLER, P.A. (AV)

The Litigation Building, 3rd Floor, 633 S. Andrews Avenue, 33302
Telephone: 954-463-8593
Fax: 954-462-1303

Charles T. Kessler (1930-1997)
Wesley L. Catri
Raymond O. Holton, Jr.
Paula C. Kessler
Andrea L. Kessler

Gerard A. Tuzzio
Edwina V. Kessler

For full biographical listings, see the Martindale-Hubbell Law Directory

CONRAD & SCHERER (AV)

A Partnership of Professional Associations
Eighth Floor, 633 South Federal Highway, P.O. Box 14723, 33302
Telephone: 954-462-5500
Facsimile: 954-463-9244
Miami, Florida Office: 44 West Flagler Street, Suite 402, 33130.
Telephone: 305-856-9920.
Facsimile: 305-374-4408.

MEMBERS OF FIRM

William R. Scherer, Jr., (P.A.)
Gary S. Genovese (P.A.)
William V. Carcioppolo (P.A.)
Linda Rae Spaulding (P.A.)
Reid A. Cocalis (P.A.)

OF COUNSEL

Rex Conrad

ASSOCIATE

Albert L. Frevola, Jr.

Local Counsel for: American Home Assurance Group; Caterpillar Tractor Co.; Division of Risk Management, State of Florida; Florida East Coast Railway; Fort Motor Co.; Liberty Mutual Insurance Co.; Ryder Truck Lines; Unigard Insurance Group.
Approved Attorneys for: Attorneys' Title Insurance Fund.
Reference: Barnett Bank of Fort Lauderdale.

For Complete List of Firm Personnel, See General Section

For full biographical listings, see the Martindale-Hubbell Law Directory

DONAHOE, PECARO & VOLLENDER, P.A. (AV)

Trial Lawyers Building, 633 Southeast 3rd Avenue, Suite 301, 33301-3151
Telephone: 954-761-3800
1-800-761-3801
FAX: 954-761-1855
Email: donpecvol@aol.com

(See Next Column)

John E. Donahoe
Paul R. Pecaro
Donald W. Vollender

Representative Clients: Allstate Insurance Co.

For full biographical listings, see the Martindale-Hubbell Law Directory

ESLER & LINDIE, P.A. (AV)

Suite 300 The Advocate Building, 315 S.E. Seventh Street, 33301
Telephone: 954-764-5400
FAX: 954-764-5408
Email: eslerandlindie@martindalemail.com *URL:* http://www.lawyers.com/esler&lindie

Gary A. Esler
Beth G. Lindie

Representative Clients: The Chubb Group of Insurance Cos.; Fireman's Fund Insurance Co.; Infinity Insurance Co.; Fortune Insurance Co.; State of Florida-Department of Risk Management; Ohio Casualty Insurance Co.; Midland Risk Insurance Co.; Commercial Casualty Insurance Company of Georgia.
References: Capital Bank.

For full biographical listings, see the Martindale-Hubbell Law Directory

LAW OFFICES OF JAMES J. GALLAGHER (AV)

200 East Broward Boulevard, Suite 2020, 33301
Telephone: 954-462-1117
Fax: 954-763-3316

STAFF COUNSEL
AMERICAN INTERNATIONAL COMPANIES

MANAGING ATTORNEY

James J. Gallagher

SENIOR TRIAL SPECIALIST

David L. Perkins

TRIAL ATTORNEY

Donald E. Mates

SENIOR WORKERS' COMPENSATION TRIAL ATTORNEY

Manuel A. Fernandez

For full biographical listings, see the Martindale-Hubbell Law Directory

HALICZER, PETTIS & WHITE, P.A. (AV)

101 Northeast Third Avenue, Sixth Floor, 33301
Telephone: 954-523-9922
Fax: 954-522-2512
Orlando, Florida Office: NationsBank Building, Suite 1275, 111 North Orange Avenue. 32801.
Telephone: 407-841-9866.
Fax: 407-841-9915.

James S. Haliczer
Eugene K. Pettis
Kenneth E. White

Amy B. Talisman
Anthony K. Goodman
Anthony V. Scalese
Debra B. Potter
William Bassett, Jr.
Frank J. Taddeo

For full biographical listings, see the Martindale-Hubbell Law Directory

KELLEY, KRONENBERG, KELLEY, GILMARTIN, FICHTEL & WANDER, P.A. (AV)

Suite 4000 8201 Peters Road, 33324
Telephone: 954-370-9970
Dade Line: 305-940-2701
West Palm Beach Line: 561-687-4224
Fax: 954-382-1988
Miami Lakes, Florida Office: Suite 204, 15600 NW 67th Avenue, 33014.
Telephone: 305-826-7260. Broward Line: 954-522-5991.
Fax: 305-826-0936.
West Palm Beach, Florida Office: 1400 Centrepark Boulevard. Suite 200. 33401.
Telephone: 561-684-5956. Broward Line: 954-761-8554.
Fax: 561-684-5753.
Orlando, Florida Office: 20 North Orange Avenue, Suite 807, First Union Tower, 32801.
Telephone: 407-648-9450.
Fax: 407-648-4167.

W. L. Adams (1924-1984)
Steven P. Kronenberg (Miami Office)
John M. Kelley (Fort Lauderdale Office)
Karen Baust Gilmartin (Miami Office)
Michael J. Fichtel (Fort Lauderdale Office)
Howard L. Wander (West Palm Beach Office)
Vivianne A. Wicker (Liability Dept., Ft. Lauderdale Office)
Robert L. Bamdas (Longshore Dept., West Palm Beach Office)

OF COUNSEL

Charles E. Kelley

For full biographical listings, see the Martindale-Hubbell Law Directory

Fort Lauderdale—Continued

KUBICKI DRAPER (AV)

One East Broward Boulevard Suite 1600, 33301
Telephone: 954-768-0011
Fax: 954-768-0514
Miami, Florida Office: Penthouse City National Bank Building, 25 West Flagler Street, 33130.
Telephone: 305-374-1212.
Fax: 305-374-7846.
West Palm Beach, Florida Office: Mellon United National Bank, Suite 1100, 1645 Palm Beach Lakes Boulevard, 33401.
Telephone: 561-640-0303.
Fax: 561-640-0524.

Earleen H. Cote
Clifford Gorman
Kenneth M. Oliver
Jorge A. Peña
Jane Carlene Rankin
Harold A. Saul

Edmund M. Aristone, Jr.
Michael J. Carney
Melinda L. Chmielarz
Paul Raymond James
Beth R. Leboff
Michael G. Moore

For full biographical listings, see the Martindale-Hubbell Law Directory

SISTARE & ASSOCIATES (AV)

600 South Andrews Avenue, Suite 600, 33301
Telephone: 954-522-2320
Fax: 954-522-2223
Email: sistare@gate.net *URL:* http://www.sistare.com

MEMBER OF FIRM

Susan P. Sistare

ASSOCIATE

Jahna Y. (Jay) Hoyte

For full biographical listings, see the Martindale-Hubbell Law Directory

*FORT MYERS,** Lee Co.

HENDERSON, FRANKLIN, STARNES & HOLT, PROFESSIONAL ASSOCIATION (AV)

1715 Monroe Street, P.O. Box 280, 33902-0280
Telephone: 941-334-4121
Telecopier: 941-332-4494

Albert M. Frierson
Stephen L. Helgemo
John A. Noland
Gerald W. Pierce
J. Terrence Porter
Michael J. Corso
Vicki L. Sproat
John W. Lewis
Craig Ferrante
James L. Nulman
Harold N. Hume, Jr.
Bruce M. Stanley Sr.
Daniel W. Sheppard
Chad J. Motes
Steven G. Koeppel
Douglas B. Szabo
Randal H. Thomas
Robert C. Shearman
Andrew L. Ringers, Jr.
John F. Potanovic, Jr.
Paula F. Kelley
Jeffrey D. Kottkamp
J. Eric Stiffler
Cora Cisneros Molloy
Keith R. Kyle
Danni Lynn Germano
Elizabeth Wolt
Alane C. Laboda
Laurie Hannan-Anton
Neil R. Jetter

Representative Clients: CIGNA Group; CSX Transportation, Inc.; Fireman's Fund Insurance Cos.; The Hartford Insurance Group; Huntington National Bank, N.A.; NationsBank, N.A.; Travelers/Aetna Insurance Group; Sprint-Florida, Inc.

For Complete List of Firm Personnel, See General Section

For full biographical listings, see the Martindale-Hubbell Law Directory

FORT WALTON BEACH, Okaloosa Co.

LAW OFFICES OF ARDEN J. LEA (AV(T))

29-B Miracle Strip Parkway S.W., 32548
Telephone: 850-302-0666; 850-302-0667
Telecopy: 850-302-0668
Email: AJL@Emeraldsurf.net
(Also Of Counsel to Barton, Richardson, Conseco & Whitney, New Orleans, Louisiana)

For full biographical listings, see the Martindale-Hubbell Law Directory

*GAINESVILLE,** Alachua Co.

MONACO, MONACO & BIRDER (AV)

Second Floor, 901 N.W. 57th Street, P.O. Box 15508, 32604-5508
Telephone: 352-331-3333
Fax: 352-332-7519

(See Next Column)

Toby S. Monaco
Lynn Erickson Monaco
Dudley D. Birder, Jr.
Jennifer C. Lester
Bennett A. Hutson

For full biographical listings, see the Martindale-Hubbell Law Directory

*JACKSONVILLE,** Duval Co.

BULLOCK, CHILDS, PENDLEY, REED, HERZFELD & RUBIN (AV)

711 Blackstone Building, 233 East Bay Street, 32202
Telephone: 904-354-0286; 800-940-5299
Fax: 904-354-2778
Email: dchilds@bellsouth.net

Bruce S. Bullock
W. Douglas Childs
Michael C. Pendley
Ronald E. Reed

ASSOCIATE

Tyler F. Tygart

Representative Clients: A List of Representative Clients will be furnished upon request.
Reference: First Union National Bank.

For full biographical listings, see the Martindale-Hubbell Law Directory

COKER, MYERS, SCHICKEL, SORENSON, HIGGINBOTHAM & GREEN, P.A. (AV)

136 East Bay Street, P.O. Box 1860, 32201
Telephone: 904-356-6071
Fax: 904-353-2425

Howard C. Coker
M. Wayne Myers
John J. Schickel
Charles A. Sorenson
Wm. Earl Higginbotham
Samuel H. Lanier
J. Thomas McKeel
Mark M. Green
R. Daniel Noey
Ronald M. Owen
John Moffitt Howell
James H. Daniel
Richard R. Alexander

For full biographical listings, see the Martindale-Hubbell Law Directory

THE CRAMER LAW FIRM (AV)

1 Independent Drive, Suite 3300, 32202
Telephone: 904-632-2211
Fax: 904-632-2324
Email: cramerjax@worldnet.att.net

Jeffrey A. Cramer

Leonard S. Magid
Richard L. Ruth

Reference: Suntrust Bank.

For full biographical listings, see the Martindale-Hubbell Law Directory

MOSELEY, WARREN, PRICHARD & PARRISH, P.A. (AV)

501 West Bay Street, 32202
Telephone: 904-356-1306
Telecopier: 904-354-0194
Cable Address: "Ragland"
Email: firm@mwpplaw.com

Reuben Ragland (1882-1954)
Louis Kurz (1891-1965)
E. Dale Joyner (1943-1993)
James F. Moseley
Robert E. Warren
Joseph W. Prichard, Jr.
Robert B. Parrish
Andrew J. Knight II
Richard K. Jones
James F. Moseley, Jr.
Phillip A. Buhler

Stanley M. Weston
Kimberly Held Israel
Tracy A. Chesser
Michael A. Garfield
Eric Lee Hearn
Samuel Allen Maroon

OF COUNSEL

James E. Williams
Neil C. Taylor

Counsel for: CSX Transportation; Britannia Steam Ship Insurance Assn., Ltd.; The West of England Protection & Indemnity Assn. (Luxembourg); Crowley American Transport Services, Inc.; United Kingdom Mutual Steamship Assurance Assn., Ltd. (Bermuda); The London Steam-Ship Owners' Mutual Insurance Assn., Ltd.

For full biographical listings, see the Martindale-Hubbell Law Directory

SAALFIELD, COULSON, SHAD & JAY, P.A. (AV)

225 Water Street, Suite 1000, 32202-4458
Telephone: 904-355-4401
Fax: 904-355-3503
Email: SCJ4401@BellSouth.net

John R. Saalfield
Michael I. Coulson
Charles Thomas Shad
Harvey L. Jay, III
Joseph B. Stokes, III

(See Next Column)

SAALFIELD, COULSON, SHAD & JAY P.A., *Jacksonville—Continued*

Gail A Stafford
Brett Q. Lucas
Carl Scott Schuler

Representative Clients: American Continental Ins. Co.; Baptist/St. Vincent's Health System; Century Products; CNA Ins. Co.; Cosco, Inc.; Crawford & Co.; Dependable Protective Mutual; Dillard Dept. Stores, Inc.; First Floridian Ins. Co.; Florida Podiatrist Trust.

For full biographical listings, see the Martindale-Hubbell Law Directory

*MIAMI,** Dade Co.

ANGONES, HUNTER, MCCLURE, LYNCH & WILLIAMS, P.A. (AV)

Ninth Floor-Concord Building, 66 West Flagler Street, 33130-1805
Telephone: 305-371-5000
Fort Lauderdale: 954-728-9112
Fax: 305-371-3948
Fort Lauderdale, Florida Office: Suite 203N Justice Building, 524 South Andrews Avenue.
Telephone: 954-779-3456.
Fax: 954-832-0037.

Frank R. Angones
Steven Kent Hunter
John McClure
Christopher J. Lynch
Stewart D. Williams
B. Scott Hunter
Leopoldo Garcia, Jr.

Thomas W. Paradise (Resident, Fort Lauderdale Office)
Donna Joy Hunter
Lourdes Alfonsin Ruiz
Kara D. Phinney
C. David Durkee

Insurance Clients: Allstate Insurance Co.; Prudential Property & Casualty Insurance Co.; Travelers Insurance Co.; Rollins Hudig Hall Healthcare Risk, Inc.

For Complete List of Firm Personnel, See General Section

For full biographical listings, see the Martindale-Hubbell Law Directory

ANDREW J. ANTHONY, P.A. (AV)

999 Ponce de Leon Boulevard (Coral Gables) Suite 1035, 33134-5822
Telephone: 305-444-8927
Fax: 305-529-1072

Andrew J. Anthony

Bradley Allan Silverman

OF COUNSEL

Neal Gary Rosensweig

For full biographical listings, see the Martindale-Hubbell Law Directory

ARMSTRONG & MEJER, P.A. (AV)

Suite 1111 Douglas Centre, 2600 Douglas Road (Coral Gables), 33134
Telephone: 305-444-3355
Fax: 305-442-4300
Email: Amesq@Aol.com

Timothy J. Armstrong
Alvaro L. Mejer

M. Emelina Mejer-Kondla

Reference: First Union National Bank.

For full biographical listings, see the Martindale-Hubbell Law Directory

BUTLER BURNETTE PAPPAS (AV)

Alfred I. DuPont Building, 169 East Flagler Street, Suite 1300, 33131
Telephone: 305-416-9998
Telecopier: 305-416-6848
URL: http://www.bbplaw.com
Tampa, Florida Office: Suite 1100, Bayport Plaza, 6200 Courtney Campbell Causeway, 33607-5946.
Telephone: 813-281-1900.
Telecopier: 813-281-0900.
Tallahassee, Florida Office: 3520 Thomasville Road, Suite 102, 32308.
Telephone: 850-894-4111.
Telecopier: 850-894-4999.

John J. Pappas

ASSOCIATES

Marc J. Gutterman
Eric M. Zivitz
Mark A. Greenberg

For full biographical listings, see the Martindale-Hubbell Law Directory

GEORGE, HARTZ, LUNDEEN, FLAGG & FULMER (AV)

4800 LeJeune Road (Coral Gables), 33146
Telephone: 305-662-4800
Fax: 305-667-8015
Fort Lauderdale, Florida Office: Suite 300 Justice Building East, 524 South Andrews Avenue, 33301.
Telephone: 954-462-1620.
Fax: 954-524-3810.
Fort Myers, Florida Office: Suite 402, Huntington Plaza, 2000 Main Street, 33901.
Telephone: 941-337-7787.
Fax: 941-337-4303.
Tallahassee, Florida Office: 800 N. Calhoun Street, 32303.
Telephone: 850-224-5252.
Fax: 850-222-3082.
West Palm Beach, Florida Office: 312 Clematis Street, Anthony Building, Suite 301, 33401.
Telephone: 561-366-9772.
Fax: 561-366-9783.
Orlando, Florida Office: Winter Park Plaza, Suite 150, 1560 Orange Avenue (Winter Park), 32789.
Telephone: 407-539-0700.
Fax: 407-539-0890.

Charles K. George
Charles Michael Hartz
Mitchell L. Lundeen
Clinton D. Flagg
Liana C. Silsby (Resident, Fort Lauderdale Office)
C. Richard Fulmer, Jr. (Resident, Fort Lauderdale Office)
A. Scott Lundeen
David V. King (Resident, West Palm Beach Office)
Crane A. Johnstone (Resident, Fort Lauderdale Office)
Douglas W. Barnes (Resident, Fort Lauderdale Office)
Craig R. Stevens (Resident at Ft. Myers Office)
Lynne E. Denneler (Resident, Fort Myers Office)
John R. Buchholz
Esther E. Galicia (Resident, Fort Lauderdale Office)
R. David de Armas (Resident, Orlando Office)
Maria A. Santoro (Resident, Tallahassee Office)
Michael H. Imber (Resident, West Palm Beach Office)

ASSOCIATES

Peter K. Spillis
Susan Bernhardt Rogers (Resident at Ft. Lauderdale Office)
Misty Merri Catherine Taylor
Michael W. LeRoy (Resident, Orlando Office)
Jack R. Simmons
Scott B. Albee (Resident, Fort Myers Office)
Merrilee A. Jobes (Resident, Fort Lauderdale Office)
Kristin Heller Woolam (Resident, Fort Myers Office)
Daniel D. Dolan, II
Paul C. Buckley (Resident, Fort Lauderdale Office)
James B. Birmingham (Resident, Orlando Office)
Joel Elizabeth Marano (Resident, Orlando Office)
Cesar A. Sastre
Stacey Z. Margulies
K. Mitch Espat (Resident, Orlando Office)
Christopher W. Royer (Resident, Fort Lauderdale Office)
Gary F. Baumann (Resident, Fort Lauderdale Office)
Brian J. Huott (Resident, West Palm Beach Office)
Michael L. Glass
H. Lawrence Hardy (Resident, Tallahassee Office)
Melissa A. Schlutow (Resident, Fort Lauderdale Office)
Jason S. Robbins (Resident, Fort Lauderdale Office)
Jack C. Morgan III (Resident, Fort Myers Office)
Sean A. Clarke (Resident, West Palm Beach Office)
Neal C. Falk (Resident, West Palm Beach Office)

OF COUNSEL

A. Blackwell Stieglitz

For full biographical listings, see the Martindale-Hubbell Law Directory

ROLAND H. GOMEZ (AV)

Suite 400, 8100 Oak Lane (Miami Lakes), 33016
Telephone: 305-825-5506
URL: http://www.lawyers.com/rolandhgomez

ASSOCIATES

Doreen E. Lasch
Richard M. Gomez
John Edward Korf

Reference: United National Bank.

For full biographical listings, see the Martindale-Hubbell Law Directory

HARDY, BISSETT & TEICHNER, P.A. (AV)

501 Northeast First Avenue, 33132
Telephone: 305-358-6200
Broward: 954-462-6377
Fax: 305-577-8230

G. Jack Hardy
G. William Bissett
Lee Philip Teichner

Lyle E. Shapiro

Representative Clients: International Paper Co.; Bridgestone/Firestone, Inc.; American International Underwriters; American International Group, Inc.; Crown Equipment Corp.; The Budd Company; Loewen Group International,

(See Next Column)

HARDY, BISSETT & TEICHNER P.A.—*Continued*

Inc.; St. Paul Insurance Company; Titan International, Inc.; Sunstate Manufactured Homes of Georgia, Inc. d/b/a Peach State Homes, Inc.

For full biographical listings, see the Martindale-Hubbell Law Directory

HAYDEN AND MILLIKEN, P.A. (AV)

Suite 63, 5915 Ponce de Leon Boulevard, 33146-2477
Telephone: 305-662-1523
Fax: 305-663-1358
Tampa, Florida Office: 615 De Leon Street 33606-2719.
Telephone: 813-251-1770.
Fax: 813-254-5436.
Cape Canaveral, Florida Office: 101 George King Boulevard, Suite 5, 32920,
Telephone: 407-868-0022.
Fax: 407-868-5060.

Reginald M. Hayden, Jr.
William Barry Milliken
William R. Boeringer
Timothy P. Shusta (Resident, Tampa, Florida Office)

Patrick M. Talbot

Representative Clients: Seaboard Marine, Ltd.; Tropical Shipping and Construction Co., Ltd.; Great American Insurance Co.; Marine Office of America Corp.; St. Paul Fire and Marine Insurance Co.; Britannia P & I; Newcastle P & I; Steamship Mutual; The Swedish Club.

For full biographical listings, see the Martindale-Hubbell Law Directory

LAW OFFICES OF DAVID R. HOWLAND (AV)

145 Almeria Avenue (Coral Gables), 33134
Telephone: 305-446-1200
Fax: 305-444-9249

ASSOCIATE

Philip E. Glatzer

Reference: Barnett Bank.

For full biographical listings, see the Martindale-Hubbell Law Directory

JOSEPHS, JACK & GAEBE, P.A. (AV)

Grove Professional Building, 2950 S.W. 27th Avenue, Suite 100, 33133-3765
Telephone: Dade County: 305-445-3800
Telecopier: 305-448-5800
Email: TheFirm@FloridaAttorneys.com *URL:* http://www.Florida-Attorneys.com

Michael R. Josephs
Lewis N. Jack, Jr.
John S. Gaebe

Elisabeth M. Allen
Helen Leen Miranda
Scott A. Cole
Stephanie E. Demos
Scott T. McCullough
Tamara D. McKeown
Christopher T. Lemos

Representative Clients: U-Haul Corporation; ITT Sheraton; Zurich-American Insurance Company; Republic Claims Service Company; Southern Fire Insurance Adjusters.

For full biographical listings, see the Martindale-Hubbell Law Directory

KATZ, BARRON, SQUITERO, FAUST & BERMAN, P.A. (AV)

Seventh Floor, 2699 South Bayshore Drive, 33133-5408
Telephone: 305-856-2444; North Broward/Boca Raton: 954-781-4720; *Broward:* 954-522-3636; North Broward: 954-781-0637
Facsimile: 305-285-9227
URL: http://www.kbsfb.com
Fort Lauderdale, Florida Office: 100 Northeast 3rd Avenue, Suite 280, 33301.
Telephone: 305-860-2599.
Fax: 954-522-5119.

Michael D. Katz
Ronald M. Barron (1945-1994)
John R. Squitero
Marc L. Faust
Richard E. Berman
Anthony H. Pelle
Howard L. Friedberg
Robert C. Grady
Erica L. English
William D. Rohrer
Richard B. Ivans
Bernard Allen
W. Todd Boyd
David S. Drobner
Charles D. Robbins
Charles D. Brecker

OF COUNSEL

William A. Zeiher
Roger S. Goldman
Richard Morton

(See Next Column)

Michael I. Kean
Michele L. McNichol
Adam J. Lamb
William R. Trueba
Alex Espenkotter
Jill D. Levy
Jose R. Riguera
Monica A. Rey-Moran
Mathai Jacob

For full biographical listings, see the Martindale-Hubbell Law Directory

JAMES C. KELLEY, P.A. (AV)

1 Daytran Center, 9100 S. Dadeland Boulevard, Suite 1707, 33156
Telephone: 305-670-0828
Facsimile: 305-670-5077
Email: jfrank08@course.com

James C. Kelley

Jonathan Derek Franklin

SPECIAL COUNSEL

Paul R. Wallace

For full biographical listings, see the Martindale-Hubbell Law Directory

KUBICKI DRAPER (AV)

Penthouse City National Bank Building, 25 West Flagler Street, 33130
Telephone: 305-374-1212
Fax: 305-374-7846
West Palm Beach, Florida Office: Mellon United National Bank, Suite 1100, 1645 Palm Beach Lakes Boulevard, 33401.
Telephone: 561-640-0303.
Fax: 561-640-0524.
Fort Lauderdale, Florida Office: One East Broward Boulevard, Suite 1600, 33301.
Telephone: 954-768-0011.
Fax: 954-768-0514.

Gene Kubicki
Daniel Draper, Jr.
Robert Baldwin Brown, III
Rolando A. Diaz
James M. Eckhart
Angela C. Flowers
Meg G. Kerr
Elwood T. Lippincott, Jr.
Peter H. Murphy

Lynn L. Audie
Peter S. Baumberger
Caryn Bellus-Lewis
André G. Crenshaw
Roger Cruz
Jason Klein
Patrick W. Knight
Rosie M. Loy-Perez
Brad J. McCormick
Monica Medina
Dennis J. Murphy
Peter J. Oppenheimer
Elizabeth M. Rodriguez
Carol A. Scott
Anita Margaret Tamayo
Jorge E. Torres
Michael Sundance Walsh
Charles Handel Watkins

OF COUNSEL

Aubrey L. Talburt

For full biographical listings, see the Martindale-Hubbell Law Directory

LEVINE & PARTNERS, P.A. (AV)

1110 Brickell Avenue, 7th Floor, 33131
Telephone: Dade: 305-372-1350
Telefax: 305-372-1352
URL: http://www.levinelawfirm.com

I. Stanley Levine
Robert J. Levine
Suzan Jon Jacobs
Alan W. Levine
Allan S. Reiss
Judith L. Gelber

For full biographical listings, see the Martindale-Hubbell Law Directory

LIGMAN, MARTIN & EVANS, P.L. (AV)

230 Catalonia Avenue, 33134-6705
Telephone: 305-445-2682
Fax: 305-445-6571
Email: lmepl@gateway.net
Pompano Beach Office: 1280 S.W. 36th Avenue, Suite 303.
Telephone: (954) 9689922.
Fax: (954) 968-9933.
South Dade Office: Dadeland Towers North, 9200 S. Dadeland Boulevard, Suite 700, Miami Florida, 33156.
Telephone: 305-670-6000.
Fax: 305-670-6068.
West Palm Beach Office: 201 Arkana Court, West Palm Beach, Florida, 33401.
Telephone: 561-835-9809.

(See Next Column)

LIGMAN, MARTIN & EVANS P.L., *Miami—Continued*

Michael G. Martin (1935-1981)	James M. Redmond
Daniel V. Ligman (P.A.)	Donald F. Harrington
Gordon J. Evans (P.A.)	D. Brent Davis
Joseph W. Ligman (P.A.)	Richard Giardino
John J. Phillips, Jr.	George A. David
Gregory J Prusak	Michael R. Seward

For full biographical listings, see the Martindale-Hubbell Law Directory

MCGRANE & NOSICH, P.A. (AV)

2801 Ponce de Leon Boulevard Twelfth Floor, 33134
Telephone: 305-442-4800
Fax: 305-442-2339

Miles A. McGrane, III — James J. Nosich

Marc P. Ganz — Marsha B. Wharin
Rachel Alters — Rhea P. Grossman
Brian H. Adler — Ruben V. Chavez

OF COUNSEL

William R. Lemos

LEGAL SUPPORT PERSONNEL

Edward F. Gray (Legal Assistant) — Sandra Arnold (Legal Assistant)
Jill Scharaga (Legal Assistant)

For full biographical listings, see the Martindale-Hubbell Law Directory

ARTHUR C. MOLLER, P.A. (AV)

The Waterford, 5805 Blue Lagoon Drive Suite 420, 33126
Telephone: 305-260-0098
Facsimile: 305-260-7550
Email: arthurmolleriii@ms.com

Arthur C. Moller, III

Mark A. Johnson — Rogelio A. Zaldivar

Representative Clients: AIG Aviation; Phoenix Aviation Managers; London Underwriters and Companies; Loss Management Services; Reliance Insurance Companies; Denny's Restaurants; American Airlines.

For full biographical listings, see the Martindale-Hubbell Law Directory

JOHN C. MULLIN, JR., P.A. (AV)

The Biscayne Building, 19 W. Flagler Street, Suite 210, 33130-4406
Telephone: 305-375-0050
Toll-Free: 877-701-9169
Fax: 305-375-0443
Email: jcmullinjr@aol.com *URL:* http://www.fla-lawfirm.com

John C. Mullin, Jr.

For full biographical listings, see the Martindale-Hubbell Law Directory

NICKLAUS & WICKS, P.A. (AV)

2511 Ponce de Leon Boulevard, Suite 300 (Coral Gables), 33134
Telephone: 305-460-9888
Facsimile: 305-460-9889
Email: enicklaus@aol.com *URL:* http://www.lawyers.com/nicklaus&wicks

Edward R. Nicklaus — William R. Wicks, III

Ronald Pena — Michael C. Gordon

For full biographical listings, see the Martindale-Hubbell Law Directory

O'CONNOR & MEYERS, P.A. (AV)

2801 Ponce de Leon Boulevard, 9th Floor (Coral Gables), 33134
Telephone: 305-445-4090
FAX: 305-445-7728
Mailing Address: P.O. Box 14-9022, Coral Gables, Florida, 33114
Fort Lauderdale, Florida Office: 800 Southeast 3rd. Avenue, Suite 200. 33316.
Telephone: 305-463-0033.
Fax: 954-463-9562.

Kevin P. O'Connor — Jay P. Chimpoulis
Addison J. Meyers — Oscar E. Marrero
Lucie M. McAllister

Ofelia Damas-Rodriquez — Lawrence M. Siff
Henry J. Hearns — David R. Cassetty
M. Katherine Hunter — Sheri M. Zachary
Scott D. Kirschbaum

OF COUNSEL

Charles A. Curran — Peter R. Restani

Representative Clients: AAMOS National Insurance Co.; Chevron Products Co.; Florida Department of Insurance; Florida League of Cities; Frontier Healthcare; Gulf Atlantic Insurance; Imphynet Medical Management; Liberty Mutual Insurance Co.; Miami Children's Hospital; Tenet Healthsystems.

For full biographical listings, see the Martindale-Hubbell Law Directory

ROSS & ASSOCIATES (AV)

Grove Plaza, 2900 S.W. 28th Terrace, Seventh Floor, 33133
Telephone: 305-441-2470
Fax: 305-442-2559
Email: Rossport@aol.com

Timothy W. Ross

ASSOCIATE

Helenemarie Blake

For full biographical listings, see the Martindale-Hubbell Law Directory

SPARKMAN, ROBB & MASON (AV)

Suite 1003 Biscayne Building, 19 West Flagler Street, 33130
Telephone: 305-374-0033
Broward: 954-522-0045
Fax: 305-539-0767
Fort Lauderdale, Florida Office: Suite 402, 200 S.E. Sixth Street.
Telephones: 305-463-3590; Dade: 305-945-4461.

MEMBERS OF FIRM

James T. Sparkman — Michael A. Robb
Donald Edward Mason

ASSOCIATE

John William Gautier

For full biographical listings, see the Martindale-Hubbell Law Directory

LAW OFFICES OF GREGORY P. SREENAN, P.A. (AV)

One Biscayne Tower, Suite 2600, 2 South Biscayne Boulevard, 33131
Telephone: 305-374-4170
Fax: 305-374-4121
Email: sreenan@compuserve.com

Gregory P. Sreenan

For full biographical listings, see the Martindale-Hubbell Law Directory

VALLE & CRAIG, P.A. (AV)

Suite 2520 World Trade Center, 80 Southwest Eighth Street, P.O. Box 113009, 33111-3009
Telephone: 305-373-2888; 800-609-6151
Facsimile: 305-373-2889

Laurence F. Valle — Lawrance B. Craig, III
Timothy Maze Hartley

Frank J. Sioli, Jr. — Michael A. Vasquez
Michael J. Lynott — Brian M. McKell

For full biographical listings, see the Martindale-Hubbell Law Directory

MIAMI LAKES, Dade Co.

PYSZKA, BLACKMON, LEVY & SAVOLA, P.A. (AV)

14750 Northwest 77th Court, Suite 300, 33016
Telephone: 305-512-3737
Fax: 305-512-1237
Email: Pyszka_Douberley@compuserve.com

Gerard E. Pyszka — Benjamin D. Levy
Phillip D. Blackmon, Jr. — L.H. Steven Savola

Cindy J. Mishcon

For full biographical listings, see the Martindale-Hubbell Law Directory

NORTH PALM BEACH, Palm Beach Co.

BOBO, SPICER, CIOTOLI, FULFORD, BOCCHINO & DEBEVOISE, P.A. (AV)

1240 U.S. Highway One, 33408
Telephone: 561-684-6600
Fax: 561-622-6288
Email: info@bobospicer.com *URL:* http://www.bobospicer.com
Orlando, Florida Office: Landmark Center One, Suite 510, 315 East Robinson Street, 32801-1949.
Telephone: 407-849-1060.
Fax: 407-843-4751.
Clearwater, Florida Office: 300 Turner Street, 33756.
Telephone: 727-443-6663.

(See Next Column)

BOBO, SPICER, CIOTOLI, FULFORD, BOCCHINO & DEBEVOISE P.A.—*Continued*

A. Russell Bobo
David W. Spicer
Eugene L. Ciotoli
Jeffrey C. Fulford
John W. Bocchino
D. Andrew DeBevoise (Resident, Orlando Office)
Armando T. Lauritano
Raul Romaguera
Gregorio A. Francis (Resident, Orlando Office)
Michael D. Burt
Casey D. Shomo
J. Clancey Bounds (Resident, Orlando Office)

Thomas W. Poulton (Resident, Orlando Office)
Damian M. Fletcher
Michael D. Starks (Resident, Orlando Office)
Anthony P. Corsini
Ian D. Forsythe (Resident, Orlando Office)
Scott L. Reed (Resident, Orlando Office)
Amy M. Dukes
Denise L. Dawson
Deborah L. Moskowitz (Resident, Orlando Office)

For full biographical listings, see the Martindale-Hubbell Law Directory

*OCALA,** Marion Co.

WEINER & ARGO, P.A. (AV)

50 South East First Avenue, 34471-2152
Telephone: 352-732-7140
Fax: 352-732-3540
Email: wego@aiservices.com

Irwin J. Weiner
B. Wayne Argo

Representative Clients: Atlantic Mutual Cos.; CIGNA Insurance Cos.; Crum & Forster Insurance Co.; First Floridian Insurance Co.; Florida Farm Bureau Insurance Cos.; Ryder TBS, Inc.; The Travelers Cos.; Universal Underwriters Group; Windsor Group; Zurich Insurance Cos.

For full biographical listings, see the Martindale-Hubbell Law Directory

*ORLANDO,** Orange Co.

BELL, LEEPER & ROPER, P.A. (AV)

Suite 700, 135 West Central Boulevard, 32801
Telephone: 407-843-1661
Fax: 407-423-0374

Michael M. Bell
Andrew J. Leeper
Michael J. Roper

Cynthia Davis Lally
Ernest H. Kohlmyer, III
Michael Harrison Bowling
Mary Grace Dyleski

LEGAL SUPPORT PERSONNEL

Marchia Ochinero (Medical Consultant)

For full biographical listings, see the Martindale-Hubbell Law Directory

BOBO, SPICER, CIOTOLI, FULFORD, BOCCHINO & DEBEVOISE, P.A. (AV)

Landmark Center One, Suite 510, 315 East Robinson Street, 32801-1949
Telephone: 407-849-1060
Fax: 407-843-4751
Email: info@bobospicer.com *URL:* http://www.bobospicer.com
North Palm Beach, Florida Office: 1240 U.S. Highway One, 33408.
Telephone: 561-684-6600.
FAX: 561-622-6288.
Clearwater, Florida Office: 300 Turner Street, 33756.
Telephone: 727-443-6663.

John W. Bocchino
D. Andrew DeBevoise
Armando T. Lauritano
Gregorio A. Francis
J. Clancey Bounds

Thomas W. Poulton
Michael D. Starks
Ian D. Forsythe
Scott L. Reed
Deborah L. Moskowitz

For full biographical listings, see the Martindale-Hubbell Law Directory

CAMERON, MARRIOTT, WALSH, HODGES & COLEMAN, P.A. (AV)

15 West Church Street, Suite 301, 32801
Telephone: 407-841-5030
Fax: 407-843-1727
Email: cammariott@aol.com
Daytona Beach, Florida Office: 432 South Beach Street.
Telephone: 904-257-1755.
Fax: 904-252-5601.
Ocala, Florida Office: 25 East Silver Springs Boulevard.
Telephone: 904-351-1119.
Fax: 904-351-0151.

(See Next Column)

A. Craig Cameron
E. Peyton Hodges

Douglas J. LaPointe
Louis D. Kaye
Brian R. Pink
G. Yates Rumbley
Martin J. Jaffe
Richard M. Adams
Frank M. Costanzo

Representative Clients: Albertson's; AIG; All-State; Auto Owners; American Family Insurance Group; American Fire and Casualty Insurance Co.; AT&T; Automobile Club Insurance Co.; Avis; Black & Decker.

For full biographical listings, see the Martindale-Hubbell Law Directory

EUBANKS, HILYARD & BOGAN, P.A. (AV)

Suite 600 First Union Building, 20 North Orange Avenue, P.O. Box 4973, 32802-4973
Telephone: 407-425-4251
Telecopier: 407-841-8431

Ernest H. Eubanks
Rodney G. Ross (1934-1982)
Sutton G. Hilyard, Jr.
Bruce R. Bogan

Bobby G. Palmer, Jr.
W. Gregory Lockeby

Representative Clients: AIG Aviation, Inc.; AVEMCO Insurance Co.; Phoenix Aviation Managers, Inc.; Ranger Insurance Co.; Old Republic Insurance Co.; Signal Aviation Underwriters; Underwriters at Lloyds; Orange County Sheriff's Office; United Technologies Corp.; Reliance Insurance Co.; Montgomery Kone, Inc.

For full biographical listings, see the Martindale-Hubbell Law Directory

GROWER, KETCHAM, MORÉ, RUTHERFORD, NOECKER, BRONSON, SIBONI & EIDE, P.A. (AV)

390 North Orange Avenue, Suite 1900, P.O. Box 538065, 32853-8065
Telephone: 407-423-9545
Telefacsimile: 407-425-7104
Ocala, Florida Office: 307 N.W. 3rd Street.
Telephone: 352-629-7441.
Telefacsimile: 352-629-7745.

Mason H. Grower, III
Walter A. Ketcham, Jr.
Hector A. Moré
Launa K. Rutherford
A. Scott Noecker
Michael C. Siboni (Resident Partner, Ocala Office)
Jeanelle G. Bronson
Eric R. Eide
David W. Henry
Kelly Gardner Hamer (Resident Partner, Ocala Office)
David B. Blessing
Patrick H. Telan

Benjamin W. Newman
Jack Erskine Holt, III
William H. Olney
Robert B. Buchanan
John M. Crotty
Christopher R. Fay
Scot D. Warner
M. Suzanne Chistolini
Stephen P. Matzuk
Diego "Woody" Rodriguez
Michael Richard Jackson
Jeremy K. Markman
Sharon T. De Shazo

For full biographical listings, see the Martindale-Hubbell Law Directory

HILL, REIS, ADAMS, HALL & SCHIEFFELIN, P.A. (AV)

1417 East Concord Street, 32803
Telephone: 407-896-0425
Fax: 407-896-9236
Email: mainbox@hrahs.com

G. Bruce Hill
Gregory F. Reis
Janet W. Adams
Larry D. Hall
Thomas L. Schieffelin, Jr.
William W. Large
Matthew P. Bartolomei

David O Doyle, Jr
Andrew Vlahos
Heidi Jo Haycook

Representative Clients: The Florida Hospital Trust Fund; The Florida Hospital Excess Trust Fund; Florida Hospital Workers Compensation/Self Insurance Trust Fund; Bartow Memorial Hospital; Bay Medical Center; Brooksville Regional Hospital; Cape Canaveral Hospital; Cape Coral Hospital; Desoto Memorial Hospital.

For full biographical listings, see the Martindale-Hubbell Law Directory

MARYBETH MCDONALD P.A. (AV)

333 North Orange Avenue, Suite 201, 32801
Telephone: 407-540-0014
Fax: 407-540-0015

Marybeth McDonald

For full biographical listings, see the Martindale-Hubbell Law Directory

Orlando—Continued

McEwan, Martinez, Luff, Dukes & Ruffier, P.A. (AV)

108 East Central Boulevard, P.O. Box 753, 32801
Telephone: 407-423-8571
Fax: 407-423-8637

Wilson Sanders (1911-1981)
O. Beverley McEwan (1913-1995)
John S. McEwan, II
Rafael E. "Ralph" Martinez
H. David Luff
Thomas E. Dukes, III
William E. Ruffier
Tyler S. McClay

Juan A. Ruiz
Ruth C. Osborne
Susan D. Kennedy

Representative Clients: Bridgestone/Firestone, Inc.; City Cab of Orlando, Inc.; CNA Insurance Company; Dependable Protective Mutual; Florida Physicians Insurance Co.; Gulf Atlantic Insurance Co.; Marine Office of America; M.C.I. Telecommunications Corporation.

For full biographical listings, see the Martindale-Hubbell Law Directory

McGee & Powers, P.A. (AV)

201 East Pine Street, Suite 700, P.O. Box 3589, 32801
Telephone: 407-422-5742
Telecopy: 407-423-1377

Patrick A. McGee
James K. Powers
Brenda J. Newman
Donna C. Valin

For full biographical listings, see the Martindale-Hubbell Law Directory

Meier, Lengauer, Bonner, Muszynski & Doyle, P.A. (AV)

37 North Orange Avenue, Suite 1100, 32801
Telephone: 407-872-7774
Facsimile: 407-872-7997

George A. Meier III
Steven F. Lengauer
Robert E. Bonner
Alexander Muszynski III
Donna Canina Doyle
Donald L. O'Dell

Ernest J. Myers
Veronica Lee Harvey
Melinda G. Baum
Mercedes R. Wechsler
Mary Catherine Wellman
Melodie Brosious Jaffe

Representative Clients: AIG Aviation, Inc.; Auto Owners Insurance Company; Chubb & Son; City of Orlando; Federal Express Corp.; Gallagher-Bassett Insurance Service; Phoenix Avaition, Inc.; Westfield Companies; Zurich Insurance Co.; Crum and Forster Insurance.

For full biographical listings, see the Martindale-Hubbell Law Directory

O'Neill, Chapin, Liebman & Cooper (AV)

A Partnership including Professional Associations
865 Eola Park Center, 200 East Robinson Street, 32801
Telephone: 407-425-2751
Telex: 407-423-1192

Bernard C. O'Neill, Jr. (P.A.)
John B. Liebman (P.A.)
Mark O. Cooper (P.A.)

ASSOCIATE

Rod C. Lundy

OF COUNSEL

Bruce E. Chapin (P.A.)

Reference: First Union National Bank.

For full biographical listings, see the Martindale-Hubbell Law Directory

David C. Schwartz, P.A. (AV)

201 East Pine Street, Suite 700, 32801
Telephone: 407-481-8500
Fax: 407-481-9010
Email: dcschwartz@prodigy.net

David C. Schwartz

For full biographical listings, see the Martindale-Hubbell Law Directory

Shepard, Filburn & Goodblatt, P.A. (AV)

221 Northeast Ivanhoe Boulevard Suite 205, 32804
Telephone: 407-206-2020
Fax: 407-206-2021
Email: sfglaw@sfg-law.com

Clifford B. Shepard, III
Mark C. Filburn
Amy E. Goodblatt

Nicole J. Ferrara
Dani S. Theobald

Representative Clients: Cintas Corporation; Intercargo Insurance Company; Trade Insurance Services, Inc.; Heilig-Myers Furniture Co.; Danella Construction Company; Adventist Health Systems, Inc.; Titan Indemnity Company; Hersh National Painting & Roofing Company; Sysco Food Services, Inc.; American Contractors Indemnity Company; Home Depot U.S.A., Inc.

For full biographical listings, see the Martindale-Hubbell Law Directory

PALM BEACH, Palm Beach Co.

Mintmire & Associates (AV)

265 Sunrise Avenue, Suite 204, 33480
Telephone: 561-832-5696
Fax: 561-659-5371
Email: MintmireFL@aol.com

Donald F. Mintmire
Jeffrey A. Shaffer

OF COUNSEL

Paul Safran, Jr.

For full biographical listings, see the Martindale-Hubbell Law Directory

*PENSACOLA,** Escambia Co.

Bozeman, Jenkins & Matthews, P.A. (AV)

SunTrust Tower, 220 West Garden Street, Suite 801, P.O. Box 13105, 32501
Telephone: 850-434-6223
Fax: 850-434-5242
Email: bojema@pen.net *URL:* http://www.bojema.pen.net
Fort Walton Beach Office: 151 Mary Esther Boulevard, Suite 401.
Telephone: 850-651-2151.
Fax: 850-434-5242.
Panama City Office: 475 Harrison Avenue, Suite 203A.
Telephone: 850-872-0110.
Fax: 850-434-5242.

Frank C. Bozeman, Jr.
Thomas R. Jenkins
Larry A. Matthews
Janice K. Skievaski
Frank C. Bozeman, III

Robert T. Bleach
John B. Fricke, Jr.
J. Andrew Talbert
Raymond F. Higgins, III
Jeremiah J. Talbott
Sidney M. McCrackin

For full biographical listings, see the Martindale-Hubbell Law Directory

Bridgers & Gill (AV)

121 Palafox Place, Suite A, 32501
Telephone: 850-432-6484
Fax: 850-432-6383

MEMBERS OF FIRM

J. Dixon Bridgers, III (Retired)
Jeffrey P. Gill
Rachel P. Ray

ASSOCIATES

Karen L. Jordan
Brent F. Bradley

For full biographical listings, see the Martindale-Hubbell Law Directory

Young & Associates, Attorneys At Law, P.A. (AV)

Seville Tower, Seventh Floor, 226 South Palafox Place, 32501
Telephone: 850-432-2222
Fax: 850-432-1444
Tampa, Florida Office: 1517 Seventh Avenue, Suite C, 33605.
Telephone: 813-242-6262.
Fax: 813-342-6363.

B. Richard Young

Michael T. Bill
David A. Fugett
Peter S. Roumbos
B. B. Boles, III
Ricardo J. Diaz
James R. Barnes

For full biographical listings, see the Martindale-Hubbell Law Directory

ST. PETERSBURG, Pinellas Co.

Fox, Grove, Abbey, Adams, Byelick & Kiernan (AV)

A Limited Liability Partnership
Eleventh Floor, 360 Central Avenue, 33701
Telephone: 727-821-2080
FAX: 727-822-3970
Email: fgstpete@fgstpete.com
Tampa, Florida Office: 500 East Kennedy Boulevard, Suite 200.
Telephone: 813-223-7800.
Fox & Grove, Chartered Offices:
Chicago, Illinois Office: 311 South Wacker Drive, Suite 6200.
Telephone: 312-876-0500.
San Francisco, California Office: 240 Stockton Street, Suite 900.
Telephone: 415-956-1360.

OF COUNSEL

Kalvin M. Grove

(See Next Column)

FOX, GROVE, ABBEY, ADAMS, BYELICK & KIERNAN—*Continued*

MEMBERS OF FIRM

David J. Abbey
Jeffrey M. Adams
Robert P. Byelick
Michael K. Kiernan
Joseph P. Ludovici
V. Joseph Mueller
Robert J. Lancaster
John D. Kiernan

ASSOCIATES

Hillary H. Coleman
Kimberly A. Staffa
Samantha A. Brem
Christopher D. Marone
Jaime B. Eagan
Christopher L. Petruccelli
Brian C. Guenther
William Chris Demas
Kelly Morgan Fisher
John A. Cautero
Richard J. McKyton
Regina Anita Henderson
George Hunter

Reference: First Union Bank.

For full biographical listings, see the Martindale-Hubbell Law Directory

WOOD & ASSOCIATES, P.A. (AV)

5015 Fourth Street North Suite A, 33703
Telephone: 727-520-9811
Facsimile: 727-520-0628

J. Emory Wood

David M. Fernandez

Representative Clients: Casualty Indemnity Exchange; State Farm Fire & Casualty Co.; State Farm Mutual Automobile Insurance Co.; Southern Insurance Co.; Nationwide Insurance Co.; Coronet Insurance Co.; General Telephone Company of Florida; Apex Adjusting Co.; Unisource Insurance Co.

For full biographical listings, see the Martindale-Hubbell Law Directory

*SARASOTA,** Sarasota Co.

DICKINSON & GIBBONS, P.A. (AV)

1750 Ringling Boulevard, P.O. Box 3979, 34230
Telephone: 941-366-4680
FAX: 941-953-3136
URL: http://dglawyers.com

Francis C. Dart (1902-1972)
Gary H. Larsen
Camden T. French
Ralph L. Marchbank, Jr.
A. James Rolfes
Burwell J. Jones
Richard R. Garland
Stephen G. Brannan
Deborah J. Blue
Jeffrey D. Peairs
David S. Preston

OF COUNSEL

Patrick H. Dickinson
G. Hunter Gibbons
Ward E. Dahlgren

LEGAL SUPPORT PERSONNEL

Janet E. Gadoury (Certified Legal Assistant)
Karin M. Turner (Certified Legal Assistant)
Carol A. Owsianka (Legal Assistant)
Susanne B. Bailey (Legal Assistant)
Cathy Webster (Paralegal)
Rachel A. Brown (Paralegal)
Ron Selby
William Henley
Katherine Lloyd (Paralegal)

Representative Clients: Ford Motor Co.; Florida Power & Light Co.; Squibb Corp.
Insurance Clients: Liberty Mutual Insurance Co.; Allstate Insurance Co.; Nationwide Insurance Group; Ohio Casualty Insurance Co.; United States Fidelity & Guaranty Co.; State Farm Insurance Company.

For Complete List of Firm Personnel, See General Section

For full biographical listings, see the Martindale-Hubbell Law Directory

*TALLAHASSEE,** Leon Co.

BUTLER BURNETTE PAPPAS (AV)

3520 Thomasville Road, Suite 102, 32308
Telephone: 850-894-4111
Telecopier: 850-894-4999
URL: http://www.bbplaw.com
Tampa, Florida Office: Suite 1100, Bayport Plaza, 6200 Courtney Campbell Causeway, 33607-5946.
Telephone: 813-281-1900.
Telecopier: 813-281-0900.
Miami, Florida Office: Alfred I. DuPont Building, 169 East Flagler Street, Suite 1300, 33131.
Telephone: 305-416-9998.
Telecopier: 305-416-6848.

Guy E. Burnette, Jr.
William L. Wallis
Kathy Johnson Maus

(See Next Column)

ASSOCIATES

Michael Shelley
Gina G. Smith
Kim E. Wells

For full biographical listings, see the Martindale-Hubbell Law Directory

CALLAHAN LAW FIRM (AV)

433 North Magnolia Drive, 32308
Telephone: 850-877-2525
Telecopier: 850-656-1539
Email: clf@polaris.net *URL:* http://www.polaris.net/callahan

Michael T. Callahan

For full biographical listings, see the Martindale-Hubbell Law Directory

HENRY, BUCHANAN, HUDSON, SUBER & CARTER, P.A. (AV)

117 South Gadsden Street P.O. Drawer 1049, 32302
Telephone: 850-222-2920
Telecopier: 850-224-0034
Affiliated with Henry, Buchanan, Hudson, Suber, Carter & Kaywell, L.C., 201 West Marion Avenue, Suite 207, Punta Gorda, Florida, 33950.
Telephone: 941-639-4343.
Fax: 941-639-7121.

Bryan W. Henry (1925-1986)
John D. Buchanan, Jr.
Edwin R. Hudson
Jesse F. Suber
J. Steven Carter
Laura Beth Faragasso

SPECIAL COUNSEL

James W. Kaywell

Reference: Barnett Bank of Tallahassee, Inc.

For full biographical listings, see the Martindale-Hubbell Law Directory

MCFARLAIN, WILEY, CASSEDY & JONES, PROFESSIONAL ASSOCIATION (AV)

215 South Monroe Street, Suite 600, P.O. Box 2174, 32316-2174
Telephone: 850-222-2107
Telecopier: 850-222-8475
Email: firm@mcfarlain.com *URL:* http://www.mcfarlain.com

Richard C. McFarlain
William B. Wiley
Douglas P. Jones
Charles A. Stampelos
H. Darrell White, Jr.
Christopher Barkas
Harold R. Mardenborough, Jr.
Terrell C. Madigan

Robert A. McNeely
P. David Brannon

LEGAL SUPPORT PERSONNEL

Diane L. Doll (Office Manager)

For full biographical listings, see the Martindale-Hubbell Law Directory

POLSTON, DEAN & HEALY, P.A. (AV)

Suite 900, Highpoint Center, 106 East College Avenue (32301), P.O. Box 1836, 32302-1836
Telephone: 850-513-0404
Fax: 850-681-0506
Email: polston@polstonlaw.com *URL:* http://www.lawyers.com/polstonlaw

Ricky L. Polston
James J. Dean
David P. Healy

For full biographical listings, see the Martindale-Hubbell Law Directory

*TAMPA,** Hillsborough Co.

ALPERT, BARKER & RODEMS, P.A. (AV)

First Union Center, Suite 2000, 100 South Ashley Drive (33602), P.O. Box 3270, 33601-3270
Telephone: 813-223-4131
Fax: 813-228-9612
Email: Alpertfirm@Aol.com

Jonathan L. Alpert
Chris A. Barker
Ryan Christopher Rodems
David D. Ferrentino
William J. Cook

Scott J. Flint
Natalie Pedregal

For full biographical listings, see the Martindale-Hubbell Law Directory

BARR, MURMAN, TONELLI, HERZFELD & RUBIN (AV)

Suite 1750, 201 East Kennedy Boulevard, P.O. Box 172669, 33672-0669
Telephone: 813-223-3951
Fax: 813-229-2254
URL: http://www.hrfirm.com
New Port Richey, Florida Office: 7613 Little Road, 34654.
Telephone: 727-846-8646;
Fax: 727-846-8913.

(See Next Column)

BARR, MURMAN, TONELLI, HERZFELD & RUBIN, *Tampa—Continued*

James A. Murman
Michael A. Tonelli
Daniel H. Sleet
T. Gregory Slother
John W. Boult
Gregory G. Frazier
Joseph S. Silver
Clifford L. Somers

ASSOCIATES

John J. Kozak
Morris D. Purcell, Jr.
Robert J. Scanlan
Pamela A. Walton
Edward D. Friscia
James R. Wilson
Jerry A. Setchel

OF COUNSEL

Billy R. Barr

Representative Clients: Hillsborough County School Board; The Hertz Company; Royal Insurance Co.; Allstate Insurance Co.; CIGNA Insurance Co.; Werner, Co.; Burger King Corp.; Enterprise Leasing Co.; Risk Management Services (Kash 'N Karry/Food Lion, Inc.; Kenan Transport.

For full biographical listings, see the Martindale-Hubbell Law Directory

BUTLER BURNETTE PAPPAS (AV)

Suite 1100, Bayport Plaza, 6200 Courtney Campbell Causeway, 33607-5946
Telephone: 813-281-1900
Telecopier: 813-281-0900
Outside Florida: 1-800-283-1193
URL: http://www.bbplaw.com
Tallahassee, Florida Office: 3520 Thomasville Road, Suite 102, 32308.
Telephone: 850-894-4111.
Telecopier: 850-894-4999.
Miami, Florida Office: Alfred I. DuPont Building, 169 East Flagler Street, Suite 1300, 33131.
Telephone: 305-416-9998.
Telecopier: 305-416-6848.

OF COUNSEL

Paul B. Butler, Jr.

MEMBERS OF FIRM

Guy E. Burnette, Jr. (Tallahassee Office)
John J. Pappas
John W. Weihmuller
Scott S. Katz
Lee Craig
Lewis F. Collins, Jr.
W. Douglas Berry
Gerald T. Albrecht
F. Robert Radel, II
Jay I. Sinsley
Christopher J. Nicholas
William L. Wallis (Tallahassee Office)
Kathy Johnson Maus (Tallahassee Office)
R. Steven Rawls
Anthony J. Russo

ASSOCIATES

William R. Lewis
William S. Daskam, IV
Matthew L. Litsky
Lisa A. Oonk
Charles E. Reynolds, II
Paula B. Tarr
Yoniece Mitchell Dixon
Scott J. Frank
Brian D. Webb
Alan J. Nisberg
Denise Anderson Byrd
John M. Odom
David J. Pettinato
Hobart M. Hind Jr.
Leann P. Parker
Robert C. Weill
J. Kurt Kaple
Robin M. Trindel
Linc M. Benkert
Lisa M. Streater
Patricia A. McLean
Robert E. Vaughn Jr.
J. Pablo Cáceres
Michael Shelley (Tallahassee Office)
Jennifer L. Sonnenfeld
Carolyn M. Holt
Keith M. Hoffman
Jason J. Ricardo
Maureen Madigan Deskins
Lisa E. Wegrzyn
Christopher J. Konicek
Carol M. Rooney
Susan A. Byron
Alan D. Stewart
Kimberly D. Nolen
Andrew Lee Patten
Marc J. Gutterman (Miami Office)
Eric M. Zivitz (Miami Office)
Gregory T. Zele
Jeremy W. Rogers
Gina G. Smith (Tallahassee Office)
Kim E. Wells (Tallahassee Office)
Mark A. Greenberg (Miami Office)
Aaron D. Alfano
Abigail O'Brien Dressel
Lisa A. Delzotti
Gary L Lewis
Caroline A. Adams
Jennifer Lynn Cusson
Bradley T. Guldalian

Representative Clients: ACE USA; American International Group/AIG; Chubb Insurance Group; Factory Mutual Engineering; HSB/IRI; Nationwide Insurance Co.; State Farm Fire and Casualty Insurance Co.; Travelers Ins. Co.; Underwriters at Lloyd's; Zurich American.

For full biographical listings, see the Martindale-Hubbell Law Directory

THOMAS F. GRANAHAN, P.A. (AV)

1906 North Tampa Street, 33602-2133
Telephone: 813-229-1084
Fax: 813-228-6820
Email: granahan@mindspring.com

Thomas F. Granahan

For full biographical listings, see the Martindale-Hubbell Law Directory

HAYDEN AND MILLIKEN, P.A. (AV)

615 de Leon Street, 33606-2719
Telephone: 813-251-1770
Fax: 813-254-5436
Miami, Florida Office: Suite 63, 5915 Ponce de Leon Boulevard.
Telephone: 305-662-1523.
Fax: 305-663-1358.
Cape Canaveral, Florida Office: 101 George King Boulevard, Suite 5, 32920.
Telephone: 407-868-0022.
Fax: 407-868-5060.

Reginald M. Hayden, Jr.
William Barry Milliken
Timothy P. Shusta (Resident)

Matthew J. Valcourt

Representative Clients: Seaboard Marine, Ltd.; Tropical Shipping and Construction Co., Ltd.; Great American Insurance Co.; Marine Office of America Corp.; St. Paul Fire and Marine Insurance Co.; Britannia P & I; Newcastle P & I; Steamship Mutual.
Reference: Dadeland Bank.

For full biographical listings, see the Martindale-Hubbell Law Directory

MEIROSE & FRISCIA, P.A. (AV)

500 North Westshore Boulevard, Suite 635, 33609
Telephone: 813-289-8800
Fax: 813-281-2005
Email: mftampa@worldnet.att.net

Leo H. Meirose, Jr.
Francis E. Friscia

Gregory Scott R. Haney

For full biographical listings, see the Martindale-Hubbell Law Directory

RYWANT, ALVAREZ, JONES, RUSSO & GUYTON, PROFESSIONAL ASSOCIATION (AV)

Suite 500 Perry Paint & Glass Building, 109 North Brush Street, P.O. Box 3283, 33601
Telephone: 813-229-7007
Fax: 813-223-6544
Ocala, Florida Office: 3300 S.W. 34th Avenue, Suite 124C, 32674.
Telephone: 904-237-8810.
FAX: 904-237-2022.

Carmen Alpizar
Manuel J. Alvarez
Matthew R. Danahy
Matthew D. Emerson
Lisa A. Griffin
John A.C. Guyton, III
M.C. Collins Guyton
Gregory D. Jones
Burke G. Lopez
Andrew F. Russo
Michael S. Rywant

LEGAL SUPPORT PERSONNEL

Bradley Hugh Holt

Representative Clients: Peerless Insurance Co.; Gulf Insurance Group; Employers Casualty Co.; Landmark Insurance Co.

For full biographical listings, see the Martindale-Hubbell Law Directory

SANTOS, DUTTON, LYNOTT & HENRY, P.A. (AV)

One Harbour Place, Suite 950, 777 South Harbour Island Boulevard, 33602
Telephone: 813-229-1111
Fax: 813-229-3311

F. Robert Santos
Scott W. Dutton
Daniel J. Lynott
David G. Henry

Gregory Joseph Blackburn (Resident)
Harry Lee Coe, IV
Michael H. Ashy

Representative Clients: American Vehicle Insurance; Capacity Insurance Co.; Erie Insurance Co.; Fortune Insurance Group; The Hanover Insurance Co.; The Travelers Insurance Co.; The Shelby Insurance Group; State Farm Mutual Automobile Insurance Co.; Usher Insurance Co.

For full biographical listings, see the Martindale-Hubbell Law Directory

SHOFI, HENNEN, GRAMOVOT & ASSOCIATES (AV)

The Lincoln Center, Suite 560, 5401 West Kennedy Boulevard, 33609
Telephone: 813-289-7500
FAX: 813-289-5548
Mailing Address: P.O. Box 10430, Tampa, Florida, 33679-0430
Email: shglaw@gte.net

John D. Shofi
William E. Hennen
Larry I. Gramovot

Jon A. McAuliffe
Kenneth S. Takacs, Jr.
Frank Scott Williams

(See Next Column)

SHOFI, HENNEN, GRAMOVOT & ASSOCIATES—*Continued*

LEGAL SUPPORT PERSONNEL

Marianne Santucci (Legal Assistant)
Raymond Hernandez

Reference: City Bank of Tampa.

For full biographical listings, see the Martindale-Hubbell Law Directory

STEWART, JOYNER & JORDAN-HOLMES, P.A. (AV)

1112 East Kennedy Boulevard, P.O. Box 172297, 33672
Telephone: 813-229-9300
Fax: 813-229-7415
Email: cjholmes@sjjhlaw.com

Delano S. Stewart
Arthenia L. Joyner
Clark Jordan-Holmes
Eurich Z. Griffin
Karen C.D. McDonald
Steve E. Baker

For full biographical listings, see the Martindale-Hubbell Law Directory

*VERO BEACH,** Indian River Co.

MOSS, HENDERSON, BLANTON & LANIER, P.A. (AV)

817 Beachland Boulevard, P.O. Box 3406, 32964-3406
Telephone: 561-231-1900
Fax: 561-231-4387

George H. Moss, II
Robin A. Blanton
Clinton W. Lanier
Lewis W. Murphy, Jr.

Jennifer J. Huber

Representative Clients: Aetna Life & Casualty; Alcoa Florida, Inc.; Florida Power & Light Co.; Insurance Company of North America; Liberty Mutual Insurance Co.; Sears, Roebuck & Co.; Sugar Cane Growers Cooperative of Florida; Norfolk Southern Corporation/North American Van Lines, Inc.

For Complete List of Firm Personnel, See General Section

For full biographical listings, see the Martindale-Hubbell Law Directory

*WEST PALM BEACH,** Palm Beach Co.

ADAMS, COOGLER, WATSON & MERKEL, P.A. (AV)

Suite 1600, 1555 Palm Beach Lakes Boulevard, P.O. Box 2069, 33402
Telephone: 561-478-4500
Fax: 561-684-7346
Email: ACWMLAW@AOL.COM

Samuel H. Adams (1913-1981)
Roy R. Watson
Robert G. Merkel
James C. Barry
Reed W. Kellner
Catherine Lynn Kasten
Scott S. Warburton
Peter A. Cooke
Patricia A. Judge
Kathryn L. Tignor

Alexander D. Barker
Jodi G. Barrett
Stephanie Brown
James W. Flanagan
Paul L. Harwood
Thomas Hodas
Catherine M. Paris

OF COUNSEL

L. C. Shepard, Jr.

For full biographical listings, see the Martindale-Hubbell Law Directory

ALAN C. ESPY, P.A. (AV)

Commerce Pointe, Suite 420, 1818 South Australian Avenue, 33409
Telephone: 561-478-4777
Fax: 561-478-0886
Email: espy@flite.net

Alan C. Espy

OF COUNSEL

James C. Paine, Jr.

For full biographical listings, see the Martindale-Hubbell Law Directory

FLANAGAN, MANIOTIS & BERGER, P.A. (AV)

2586 Forest Hill Boulevard, 33406
Telephone: 561-964-7501
Facsimile: 561-964-8025

Patrick B. Flanagan
Nicholas Maniotis
Thomas A. Berger

Nicholas J. Ryan

Representative Clients: American Family Insurance Group; American Indemnity Insurance Co.; Auto-Owners Insurance Co.; Kemper Insurance Group; Pepsi Cola Bottling of Ft. Lauderdale-Palm Beach, Inc.; State Farm Insurance Cos.
References: Suntrust Bank; West Palm beach.

For full biographical listings, see the Martindale-Hubbell Law Directory

KUBICKI DRAPER (AV)

Mellon United National Bank, Suite 1100, 1645 Palm Beach Lakes Boulevard, 33401
Telephone: 561-640-0303
Fax: 561-640-0524
Miami, Florida Office: Penthouse City National Bank Building, 25 West Flagler Street, 33130.
Telephone: 305-374-1212.
Fax: 305-374-7846.
Fort Lauderdale, Florida Office: One East Broward Boulevard, Suite 1600, 33301.
Telephone: 954-768-0011.
Fax: 954-768-0514.

David Knight
Hubert S. McGinley
Lloyd R. Schwed
Stephen W. Schwed
Michael S. Smith

Laurie J. Adams
Rosemarie Gasparri
Jason J. Guari
Joseph Brian Landy
Matthew N. Posgay

For full biographical listings, see the Martindale-Hubbell Law Directory

ROZELLE AND CALL (AV)

470 Columbia Drive Suite E-100, 33409
Telephone: 561-689-1050
Fax: 561-689-6147

MEMBERS OF FIRM

Douglas D. Rozelle, Jr.
John S. Call, Jr.

ASSOCIATE

Glenn T. Williams

Representative Clients: Wal-Mart Stores, Inc.; Motors Insurance Corp.; American Contractors Insurance Group, Inc.; The Equitable Life Assurance Society; Connecticut General Life Insurance Co.; Safeco Insurance Co.; Phar-Mor of Florida, Inc.; World Wide Insurance Group; Chrysler Insurance Co.; United Service Automobile Association; The Hartford Insurance Company.

For full biographical listings, see the Martindale-Hubbell Law Directory

WIEDERHOLD, MOSES, BULFIN & RUBIN, P.A. (AV)

Northbridge Centre, Suite 800, 515 North Flagler Drive, P.O. Box 3918, 33402
Telephone: 561-659-2296;
Broward: 954-763-5630
Fax: 561-659-2865
Email: bobmoses@bellsouth.net

John P. Wiederhold
Robert D. Moses
John J. Bulfin
Kenneth M. Rubin

Lawrence I. Bass
Kay Seeber Hoff
Bruce R. Katzell

LEGAL SUPPORT PERSONNEL

Gina Truzzolino (Paralegal/Investigator)

Reference: Bank of America.

For full biographical listings, see the Martindale-Hubbell Law Directory

WINTER PARK, Orange Co.

SWANN, HADLEY & ALVAREZ, P.A. (AV)

1031 West Morse Boulevard, Suite 270, 32789
Telephone: 407-647-2777
Fax: 407-647-2157

Richard R. Swann
Ralph V. Hadley, III
P. Raúl Alvarez, Jr.
Thomas H. Justice III
Griffith J. Winthrop, III
Stephen B. Sambol

Stuart P. Buchanan
Mark H. Ruff
Peter Francis Carr, Jr.
Kimberly M. Reid
Jeffrey M. Thompson

OF COUNSEL

L. Pharr Abner

For full biographical listings, see the Martindale-Hubbell Law Directory

GEORGIA

*ATHENS,** Clarke Co.

BLASINGAME, BURCH, GARRARD, BRYANT & ASHLEY, P.C. (AV)

440 College Avenue North, P.O. Box 832, 30603
Telephone: 706-354-4000
Telecopier: 706-353-0673
Greensboro, Georgia Office: 122 N. Main Street, P.O. Box 67, 30642.
Telephone: 706-453-7139.
Fax: 706-453-7842.

J. Ralph Beaird
Gary B. Blasingame
E. Davison Burch
Henry G. Garrard, III
Everett Clay Bryant
W. Seaborn Ashley, Jr.
M. Steven Heath
Andrew J. Hill, III
Michael A. Morris
Thomas H. Rogers, Jr.
William D. Harvard
Rikard L. Bridges
Ivan A. Gustafson
David S. Thomson
Richard W. Schmidt

Matthew N. Padgett
Christopher G. Conley
Pamela Lohr Hendrix
Amy Lou Reynolds
Sean P. Dolan
Carter A. Lawson
Matthew Allen Moseley
Molly K. O'Steen
Josh B. Wages

Representative Clients: NationsBank; Georgia Power Co.; Atlanta Gas Light Company; Pittsburgh Corning Corp.; Downtown Athens Development Authority; Fowler Products Co., Inc.; Athens Newspapers, Inc.; First National Bank of Commerce; Athens First Bank & Trust Co.; Reynolds Plantation.

For full biographical listings, see the Martindale-Hubbell Law Directory

*ATLANTA,** Fulton Co.

BOVIS, KYLE & BURCH, LLC (AV)

A Limited Liability Corporation including Professional Corporations
Third Floor, 53 Perimeter Center East, 30346
Telephone: 770-391-9100
Telecopier: 770-668-0878
Email: bkb@boviskyle.com *URL:* http://www.boviskyle.com

John M. Bovis (P.C.)
Steven J. Kyle (P.C.)
John V. Burch (P.C.)
James E. Singer
Gregory R. Veal
Timothy J. Burson
Charles M. Medlin
John H. Peavy Jr.

J.S. Scott Busby
Christina A. Craddock
Timothy A. Hickey, Jr.
Jana B. Tabor
Carl A. Hassler
Everett A. Kliphouse

For Complete List of Firm Personnel, See General Section

For full biographical listings, see the Martindale-Hubbell Law Directory

DENNIS, CORRY & PORTER, L.L.P. (AV)

3300 One Atlanta Plaza, 950 East Paces Ferry Road, P.O. Box 18640, 30326
Telephone: 404-816-2800
Wats: 800-735-0838
Fax: 404-816-5656
URL: http://www.dcplaw.com

MEMBERS OF FIRM

Robert E. Corry, Jr.
R. Clay Porter
James S. Strawinski
Grant B. Smith
Matthew J. Jewell
Raymond J. Kurey
Ronald Ray Coleman, Jr.
Scott W. McMickle

OF COUNSEL

Douglas Dennis

ASSOCIATES

Thomas D. Trask
Christopher D. Pixley
John D. Dixon
Stephanie F. Goff
Kerry A. Quinn
George A. Koenig
Michael Goldberg
Michael F. Coogan
Todd M. Yates
Nicole L. Wolfe
Alisa W. Terry
Stephanie Collings Patel
Michael A. Prieto

Representative Clients: Schneider National, Inc.; Roadway Express, Inc.; Caliber System, Inc.

For full biographical listings, see the Martindale-Hubbell Law Directory

FAIN, MAJOR, WILEY & BRENNAN, P.C. (AV)

100 Glenridge Point Parkway Suite 500, 30342-1440
Telephone: 404-688-6633
Telecopier: 404-420-1544

(See Next Column)

Gene A. Major
Charles A. Wiley, Jr.
Thomas E. Brennan
John K. Miles, Jr.
Darryl G. Haynes

Brian Alligood
Kim Monroe Jackson
Robert L. Jones
James A. Rice, Jr.
James Curry
Brian M. Leepson
Stephen Anthony Fern
Michael K. Watson

Representative Clients: Allstate Insurance Co.; Budget Rent-A-Car; Arkansas Best Corp.; Chrysler Insurance Co.; Georgia Farm Bureau Mutual Insurance Co.; Hertz Corp.; Universal Underwriters Insurance Co.; Westfield Insurance Co.; Winn-Dixie Stores, Inc.

For Complete List of Firm Personnel, See General Section

For full biographical listings, see the Martindale-Hubbell Law Directory

FREEMAN MATHIS & GARY, LLP (AV)

100 Galleria Parkway, 16th Floor, 30339-5959
Telephone: 770-818-0000
Fax: 770-937-9960
URL: http://www.fmglaw.com

MEMBERS

Theodore Freeman
Benton J. Mathis, Jr.
T. Bart Gary
Philip Wade Savrin
Maureen M. Middleton
Matthew P. Stone

ASSOCIATES

Mary Anne Ackourey
Dana Kristin Maine
Jennifer E. Moore
Robert W. Stanley
William H. Buechner, Jr.
Robert W. Capobianco

Representative Clients: AIG; Association of County Commissioners of Georgia; General Star Indemnity; Coregis Insurance Co.; Chicago Title Insurance Co.; Scottsdale Insurance Co.; Summit Risk Services, Inc.; The St. Paul Companies; Willis Corroon; Zurich American Insurance Co.

For full biographical listings, see the Martindale-Hubbell Law Directory

GOLDNER, SOMMERS, SCRUDDER & BASS (AV)

900 Circle 75 Parkway Suite 850, 30339
Telephone: 770-612-9200
Facsimile: 770-612-9201

MEMBERS OF FIRM

Stephen L. Goldner
Susan V. Sommers
Henry E. Scrudder, Jr.
Glenn S. Bass
Alfred A. Quillian, Jr.
Sandra G. Chase
Linda Jacobsen Pollock
Benjamin David Ladner
William W. Horlock, Jr.

ASSOCIATES

Tammy Spivack Skinner
Jane Carol Taylor

For Complete List of Firm Personnel, See General Section

For full biographical listings, see the Martindale-Hubbell Law Directory

GOODMAN, MCGUFFEY, AUST & LINDSEY, LLP (AV)

2100 Tower Place, 3340 Peachtree Road, N.E., 30326-1084
Telephone: 404-264-1500
Fax: 404-264-1737
Email: gmal@atlanta.com

MEMBERS OF FIRM

William S. Goodman
C. Wade McGuffey, Jr.
Judy Farrington Aust
Edward H. Lindsey, Jr.
Joe David Jackson
Kathryn A. Cater
Debra L. Dalton
Lisa A. Wade

Michael A. Dalton
Danielle F. Forte

For full biographical listings, see the Martindale-Hubbell Law Directory

GRAY & GILLILAND, P.C. (AV)

400 Perimeter Center Terrace, Suite 1050, 30346-1239
Telephone: 770-392-4800
Telecopy: 770-392-4808

John C. Gray
T. Cullen Gilliland
Charles A. Ratz
Melissa A. Garrett
T. Jeffery Lehman
Robert W. Browning

P. Steven Kratsch

OF COUNSEL

E. Reid Garrett
David S. Currie
Mark B. Bullman

For full biographical listings, see the Martindale-Hubbell Law Directory

Atlanta—Continued

HALL, BOOTH, SMITH & SLOVER, A PROFESSIONAL CORPORATION (AV)

230 Peachtree Street, N.W., Suite 2500, 30303-1515
Telephone: 404-954-5000
Fax: 404-954-5020
Email: mail@hbss.net

John E. Hall, Jr.
Alexander H. Booth
Rush S. Smith, Jr.
Jack G. Slover, Jr.
Timothy H. Bendin
Michael A. Pannier
Roger S. Sumrall
Robert L. Shannon, Jr.
Michael G. Frick
T. Andrew Graham
Phillip E. Friduss

Karl M. Braun
Heather C. McGrotty
Deborah L. Stevenson
Sharon Davis King
Jonathan Marigliano
Roger G. Martin
Steven D. Prelutsky
Fred L. Hubbs Jr.
Steven J. Zaloudek
Ashley D. Phillips
Rob S. Register
Noel Langston Hurley
L. Clint Crosby
Cheveda D. Grier
Rebecca T. Christian
Wendy A. Weber (Not admitted in GA)

Reference: Wachovia Bank of Georgia.

For full biographical listings, see the Martindale-Hubbell Law Directory

HARMAN, OWEN, SAUNDERS & SWEENEY, A PROFESSIONAL CORPORATION (AV)

1900 Peachtree Center Tower, 230 Peachtree Street, N.W., 30303
Telephone: 404-688-2600
Telecopier: 404-525-4347

H. Andrew Owen
Frederick F. Saunders, Jr.
Timothy J. Sweeney
Perry A. Phillips
Michael W. McElroy
David C. Will
Charles J. Cole
Rolfe M. Martin

Merritt McGarrah Wofford

For full biographical listings, see the Martindale-Hubbell Law Directory

NALL, MILLER, OWENS, HOCUTT & HOWARD, LLP (AV)

Suite 200 Peachtree & Broad Building, 66 Luckie Street, 30303
Telephone: 404-522-2200
Fax: 404-522-2208

MEMBERS OF FIRM

James S. Owens, Jr.
Robert B. Hocutt
George Robert Neuhauser
Kenneth P. McDuffie
Michael D. Hostetter

ASSOCIATES

Charles Richard Carson
Paul Jay Pontrelli
Mary Anne Palma

Approved Attorneys for: Lawyers Title Insurance Corp.; Commonwealth Land Title Insurance Co.

For full biographical listings, see the Martindale-Hubbell Law Directory

PIERCE & YOUNG (AV)

Building 1700, 2255 Cumberland Parkway Northwest, 30339-4575
Telephone: 770-435-0500
Telecopier: 770-435-0362

MEMBERS OF FIRM

J. Wayne Pierce
Richard M. Young
Christy A. Dunkelberger

For full biographical listings, see the Martindale-Hubbell Law Directory

SMITH, HOWARD & AJAX, LLP (AV)

300 Atlanta Financial Center South, 3333 Peachtree Road, N.E., 30326
Telephone: 404-239-1900
Fax: 404-239-1930

MEMBERS OF FIRM

Fred W. Ajax, Jr.
Donald R. Andersen
Bruce H. Beerman
James T. Brieske
Susan Teale Couvillon
Harvey S. Gray
John A. Howard
Matthew G. Moffett
Michael J. Rust
Marion Smith, II
Michael D. St. Amand
David K. Whatley

ASSOCIATES

Mark D. Gropp
Joseph P. Hewes
Matthew L. Hilt
Meredith H. Ragains
LaXavier Patrice Reddick-Hood

(See Next Column)

OF COUNSEL

T. Michael Hurley, Jr.
Larry S. McReynolds

For full biographical listings, see the Martindale-Hubbell Law Directory

SWIFT, CURRIE, MCGHEE & HIERS (AV)

1355 Peachtree Street, N.E., 30309-3238
Telephone: 404-874-8800
Telecopier: 404-888-6199
Email: scmhlaw.com

MEMBERS OF FIRM

James T. McDonald, Jr.
John F. Sacha
Michael H. Schroder
Stephen L. Cotter
Robert R. Potter
Douglas A. Bennett
Mark T. Dietrichs
Lynn M. Roberson
Mark J. Goodman
Joseph A. Munger
R. Briggs Peery
Thomas D. Martin
Bradley S. Wolff
Frederick Owen Ferrand
John W. Campbell
Stephen M. Schatz
Richard H. Sapp, III
Charles M. McDaniel, Jr.
Michael Ryder
Susan A. Dewberry

OF COUNSEL

Frank M. Swift
Warner S. Currie
Glover McGhee
James B. Hiers, Jr.

ASSOCIATES

Michael H. Friedman
Debra Dawn Chambers
Micheal D. Watson
Thomas E. Best
Richard A. Watts
Peggy R. Goodnight
Kenneth B. Still
Michael C. Kendall
Timothy C. Lemke
Bright Kinnett Wright
Douglas W. Brown, Jr.
Christopher D. Balch
Joan Perkins Shaker
David Charles King
Willie C. Adams
W. Wright Mitchell
H. Lee Pruett
Thomas J. Mazziotti
Robert E. Jones
Kristine J. Moschella
Megan W. Grout
Kenneth A. David
J. Michael Parsons
Lloyd N. Bell
Erik S. Rodriguez
James D. Johnson
Cabell D. Townsend
Scott M. Williamson
Sharon Leah Neal
John F. Blount
Casey W. Stevens
Amy Greenstein

Representative Clients: Chubb Insurance Group; Cagle's Inc.; Gold Kist, Inc.; Kemper Insurance Group; Maryland Casualty Cos.; PHH Homequity; Sedgwick James; State Farm Fire & Casualty Co.; The Travelers Cos.; Super Valu.

For full biographical listings, see the Martindale-Hubbell Law Directory

THOMAS, KENNEDY, SAMPSON & PATTERSON (AV)

3355 Main Street, 30337
Telephone: 404-688-4503
Telecopier: 404-681-2950; Litigation Dept.
Telecopier: 404-684-9515
URL: http://www.tksp.com

MEMBERS OF FIRM

R. E. Thomas, Jr. (1911-1996)
John Loren Kennedy (1942-1994)
Thomas G. Sampson
P. Andrew Patterson
Jeffrey E. Tompkins

ASSOCIATES

Thomas G. Sampson, II
Ceasar C. Mitchell, II.
Erika Nicole Jackson

LEGAL SUPPORT PERSONNEL

Gwendolyn C.H. Dixon
Elbetha (Beth) Martin (Paralegal)
Nancy Allen-Haskell
Yvonne Torrence
Shyril E. Beck
Constance Harris (Paralegal)
Lisa Russell Johnson

For full biographical listings, see the Martindale-Hubbell Law Directory

WEBB, CARLOCK, COPELAND, SEMLER & STAIR, LLP (AV)

A Partnership including Professional Corporations
2600 Marquis Two Tower, 285 Peachtree Center Avenue, P.O. Box 56887, 30343-0887
Telephone: 404-522-8220
Fax: 404-523-2345; 404-222-9482

MEMBERS OF FIRM

Dennis J. Webb (P.C.)
Thomas S. Carlock (P.C.)
Wade K. Copeland (P.C.)
Robert C. Semler (P.C.)
Kent T. Stair (P.C.)
Douglas W. Smith
David F. Root
William E. Zschunke
Wayne D. McGrew, III
Douglas A. Wilde
E. Alan Miller
Frederick M. Valz, III
Johannes S. Kingma
Dennis G. Lovell, Jr.
Brian R. Neary
Marvin D. Dikeman
Adam L. Appel
R. Michael Ethridge
Daniel J. Huff
Scott D. Huray
Gregory H. Wheeler
Christopher A. Whitlock

(See Next Column)

WEBB, CARLOCK, COPELAND, SEMLER & STAIR LLP, *Atlanta—Continued*

ASSOCIATES

Mary Katherine Greene
Leslie B. Zacks
James R. Doyle, II
Kimberly K. Nagy
Melissa C. Duffey
Charles E. Rogers
Chad D. Graddy
Lisa Shaw Estes
Jessica D. McKinney
Jonathon A. Fligg
Lynn B. Olmert
Jerry B. McNally
Jerry W. Cain, Jr.
Austin E. Carter
Brian J. Amero
John C. Patton
James S. V. Weston
Erika K. Kohler
Katherine K. Bone
Amy H. Ferguson
James A. Collura, Jr.
Kimberly P. Murphy
Ashley E. Sexton

For full biographical listings, see the Martindale-Hubbell Law Directory

ZIRKLE AND HOFFMAN (AV)

Five Concourse Parkway, Suite 2900, 30328
Telephone: 770-551-8700
Fax: 770-512-0329
Email: zh@zirklaw.com *URL:* http://www.zirklaw.com

MEMBERS OF FIRM

Charles B. Zirkle, Jr.
G. Scott Hoffman
Eric S. Jones
Ben E. Pellegrini
Deborah G. Krotenberg

ASSOCIATES

Donnell J. Collins
Nancy C. Collins
Brian J. Mongelluzzo
Deborah S. Urbach

LEGAL SUPPORT PERSONNEL
PARALEGALS

Karen H. Jones (Paralegal)
Susan J. Millican (Paralegal)

For full biographical listings, see the Martindale-Hubbell Law Directory

*AUGUSTA,** Richmond Co.

DYE, TUCKER, EVERITT, LONG & BREWTON, A PROFESSIONAL ASSOCIATION (AV)

453 Greene Street, P.O. Box 2426, 30903-2426
Telephone: 706-722-0771
Fax: 706-722-7028

A. Rowland Dye
Thomas W. Tucker
A. Zachry Everitt
John B. Long
Benjamin H. Brewton
Troy A. Lanier

OF COUNSEL

A. Montague Miller

Jon E. Ingram, Jr.

Representative Clients: State Farm Insurance Cos.; Travelers-Aetna Insurance Cos.; Georgia Power Co.; Wachovia National Bank (Augusta Division); Chubb Group; MAG Mutual Insurance Company; Augusta Board of Realtors; Canal Insurance Company; St. Paul Fire and Marine Insurance Company.

For full biographical listings, see the Martindale-Hubbell Law Directory

HULL, TOWILL, NORMAN, BARRETT & SALLEY, A PROFESSIONAL CORPORATION (AV)

801 Broad Street, Suite 700, 30901
Telephone: 706-722-4481
Fax: 706-722-9779
Email: hullfirm@groupz.net *URL:* http://www.groupz.net/~advocate
Aiken, South Carolina Office: 111 Park Avenue, 29801.
Telephone: 803-648-4213.
Fax: 803-648-2601.

James M. Hull (1885-1975)
George B. Barrett (1894-1942)
Julian J. Willingham (1887-1963)
John Bell Towill (1907-1991)
Robert C. Norman (Retired, 1991)
W. Hale Barrett
Lawton Jordan, Jr.
Patrick J. Rice
Douglas D. Batchelor, Jr.
David E. Hudson
William H. Tucker (Not admitted in GA)
William F. Hammond
Mark S. Burgreen
George R. Hall
James B. Ellington
F. Michael Taylor
William J. Keogh, III
Edward J. Tarver
J. Noel Schweers, III
Susan D. Barrett
Ralph Emerson Hanna, III

James M. Holly (Not admitted in GA)
Timothy E. Moses
N. Shannon Gentry Lanier
Tara R. Simkins
Charles H. Weigle
Natalie A. Dopson
David C. Smith

(See Next Column)

OF COUNSEL

Julian B. Salley, Jr. (Not admitted in GA)

Counsel for: Nationwide Insurance Co.; Northbrook Property & Casualty Insurance Co.; Merastar Insurance Co.; Cotton States Insurance Co.; Medical Protective Insurance Co.; St. Joseph Hospital, Augusta, Georgia, Inc.; Norfolk Southern Corp.; Housing Authority of the City of Augusta; Georgia Press Association.

For full biographical listings, see the Martindale-Hubbell Law Directory

WILEY S. OBENSHAIN, III, P.C. (AV)

511 Court House Lane, 30904
Telephone: 706-722-1789
Fax: 706-722-3934

Wiley S. Obenshain, III

For full biographical listings, see the Martindale-Hubbell Law Directory

SURRETT & COLEMAN, P.A. (AV)

901 Suntrust Bank Building, P.O. Box 1497, 30903
Telephone: 706-722-3301
Telecopier: 706-722-3318
Email: ecoleman@groupz.net

Carl J. Surrett
Edward J. Coleman, III

Representative Clients: Sears, Roebuck & Co.; American Home Assurance Co.; Great Southwest Fire Insurance Co.; Duke Buick, Inc.; American Southern Insurance Co.; Scottsdale Insurance Co.; Providence Washington Insurance Co.; Nautilus Insurance Co.

For full biographical listings, see the Martindale-Hubbell Law Directory

THOMPSON & SMITH, P.C. (AV)

2909-A Professional Parkway, 30907
Telephone: 706-855-5600
Telecopier: 706-855-7020

James M. Thompson
Larry I. Smith

For full biographical listings, see the Martindale-Hubbell Law Directory

*BRUNSWICK,** Glynn Co.

FENDIG, MCLEMORE, TAYLOR, WHITWORTH & DURHAM, P.C. (AV)

Suite 200 Suntrust Bank Building, P.O. Box 1996, 31521
Telephone: 912-264-4126
Telecopier: 912-264-0591

Albert Fendig, Jr.
Gilbert C. McLemore, Jr.
Philip R. Taylor
David T. Whitworth
James B. Durham
Donna L. Crossland
Beth M. Duncan

Counsel For: Suntrust Bank of S.E. Georgia, N.A.; Sea Island Property Owners Assn.; Calsilite Manufacturing Co.; Crum & Forster; MMI Insurance Companies, Inc.; The Hertz Corp.; Insurance Company of North America; United States Fidelity & Guaranty Co; The St. Paul Companies, Inc.; CNA Insurance.

For full biographical listings, see the Martindale-Hubbell Law Directory

GILBERT, HARRELL, GILBERT, SUMERFORD & MARTIN, P.C. (AV)

Suite 200 NationsBank Plaza, 31521
Telephone: 912-265-6700
Fax: 912-264-3917
Email: gilbharr@gate.net

Wallace E. Harrell
James B. Gilbert, Jr.
Rees M. Sumerford
M. Fleming Martin, III
Jameson L. Gregg
Wallace E. Harrell, III
Charles G. Spalding
Lisa Godbey Wood
Mark D. Johnson
J. Benedict Hartman
Carlton A. DeVooght
Kathryn Hackney Smith

OF COUNSEL

James B. Gilbert
Joseph A. Whittle
H. Hall Ware, III

Representative Clients: Zurich General Accident & Liability Insurance Co.; Lumbermen's Mutual Casualty Co.; Metropolitan Life Insurance Co.; Jefferson Standard Life Insurance Co.; St. Paul Insurance Companies; MAG Mutual Insurance Co.; Colonial Penn Life Insurance Co.

For full biographical listings, see the Martindale-Hubbell Law Directory

JORDAN & BRISTOL (AV)

1528 Ellis Street, P.O. Box 2115, 31521
Telephone: 912-262-9200
Fax: 912-262-0277
Email: jordanod@gate.net

(See Next Column)

JORDAN & BRISTOL—*Continued*

Randall A. Jordan — Steven P. Bristol

Representative Clients: Norfolk Southern Corp.; National Foundation Life Insurance Co.; American Centennial Insurance Co.; Delta Life Insurance Co.; Cooper Industries, Inc.; McGraw-Edison Co.; Progressive Preferred Insurance Co.; Integrity Insurance Co.; AllState Insurance Co.; Occidental Fire & Casualty of North Carolina.

For full biographical listings, see the Martindale-Hubbell Law Directory

WHELCHEL, BROWN, READDICK & BUMGARTNER (AV)

5 Glynn Avenue, P.O. Box 220, 31521-0220
Telephone: 912-264-8544
Telecopier: 912-264-9667

MEMBERS OF FIRM

J. Thomas Whelchel
Richard A. Brown, Jr.
Terry L. Readdick
John E. Bumgartner
B. Kaye Katz

ASSOCIATES

G. Todd Carter
Richard K. Strickland
Bradley J. Watkins

Representative Clients: Georgia Power Co.; Sears, Roebuck & Co.; Allstate Insurance Co.; Commercial Union Insurance Co.; Georgia Farm Bureau Mutual Insurance Co.; Government Employees Insurance Co.; Nationwide Insurance Co.; State Farm Insurance Cos.; Wausau Insurance Cos.

For full biographical listings, see the Martindale-Hubbell Law Directory

*COLUMBUS,** Muscogee Co.

HATCHER, STUBBS, LAND, HOLLIS & ROTHSCHILD (AV)

A Limited Liability Partnership
Suite 500 The Corporate Center, 233 12th Street, P.O. Box 2707, 31902-2707
Telephone: 706-324-0201
Telecopier: 706-322-7747
Email: mailman@hatcherstubbs.com

MEMBERS OF FIRM

William B. Hardegree
James E. Humes, II
Joseph L. Waldrep
Robert C. Martin, Jr.
Teri Yancey Callahan

ASSOCIATE

Gregory S. Ellington

Local Counsel for: Liberty Mutual Insurance Co.; Home Insurance Co.; Kemper Insurance Co.; MAG Mutual Insurance Co.; Southern Guaranty Insurance Co.; Safeco Insurance Company; Ryder Systems, Inc.; Central Mutual Insurance Co.; Southern Mutual Insurance Co.

For Complete List of Firm Personnel, See General Section

For full biographical listings, see the Martindale-Hubbell Law Directory

ROTHSCHILD, MORGAN & BROWN (AV)

A Limited Liability Partnership
1025 First Avenue, P.O. Box 2788, 31902-2788
Telephone: 706-324-4167
Fax: 706-324-1969
Email: rothmor@mindspring.com

MEMBERS OF FIRM

Jerome M. Rothschild
W. Donald Morgan, Jr.
Jeffrey A. Brown

ASSOCIATE

Jeffrey H. Kight

Reference: Columbus Bank and Trust Company.

For Complete List of Firm Personnel, See General Section

For full biographical listings, see the Martindale-Hubbell Law Directory

*DALTON,** Whitfield Co.

KINNEY, KEMP, SPONCLER, JOINER & THARPE (AV)

A Partnership including a Professional Corporation
225 West King Street, P.O. Box 398, 30722-0398
Telephone: 706-278-5211
Fax: 706-275-6566
Email: attorney@kinneyandkemp.com

MEMBERS OF FIRM

R. Carter Pittman (1898-1972)
Hinton Eugene Kinney (1913-1996)
L. Hugh Kemp (P.C.)
Maurice M. Sponcler, Jr.
Horace Greely Joiner, Jr.
Henry C. Tharpe, Jr.
F. Gregory Melton
Richard W. Andrews
Timothy H. Allred
Mark D. Newberry
Robert Adam Cowan

ASSOCIATE

Chad D. Plumley

(See Next Column)

OF COUNSEL

Susan W. Bisson
William J. Kimsey
J. Tracy Ward

General Counsel for: North Georgia Electric Membership Corporation; Queen Carpet Corp.; Hardwick Bank & Trust Company.
Representative Clients: Allstate Insurance Co.; Liberty Mutual Insurance Co.; State Farm Mutual Automobile Insurance Co.; Norfolk Southern Railway Company; General Motors Corporation; Dalton Board of Education.

For full biographical listings, see the Martindale-Hubbell Law Directory

*GAINESVILLE,** Hall Co.

SMITH, GILLIAM AND WILLIAMS (AV)

200 Old Coca-Cola Building, 301 Green Street, N.W., P.O. Box 1098, 30503
Telephone: 770-536-3381
Fax: 770-531-1481
Email: SGWFirm@Applied.net

MEMBERS OF FIRM

R. Wilson Smith, Jr. (1906-1983)
John H. Smith
Steven P. Gilliam
Jerry A. Williams
Kelly Anne Miles
Bradley J. Patten
M. Tyler Smith

ASSOCIATE

Robert A. Weber, Jr.

General Counsel for: Gainesville Industrial Electric Co.; Georgia Mutual Insurance, a Stock Company; L & R Farms; H. Wilson Manufacturing Co.; Goforth Electrical Supply; North Georgia Petroleum Co.; Gibbs Management Group, Inc.

For full biographical listings, see the Martindale-Hubbell Law Directory

*JESUP,** Wayne Co.

HOWARD, CARSWELL & BENNETT, P.C. (AV)

Lawyers Building, 145 North Brunswick Street, P.O. Box 543, 31598-0543
Telephone: 912-427-4268
Fax: 912-427-0330

Joseph H. Thomas (1909-1984)
Hubert H. Howard
Kenneth R. Carswell
R. Violet Bennett

Representative Clients: Independent Fire Insurance Cos.; Georgia Insurers Insolvency Pool; The Seibels Bruce Insurance Co.; Southern Trust Insurance Co.; CIGNA Insurance Cos.; Southern Fidelity Insurance Co.; Great Central Insurance Co.; Kemper Insurance Co.; Cotton States Insurance Co.; Liberty Mutual Insurance Co.

For full biographical listings, see the Martindale-Hubbell Law Directory

*MACON,** Bibb Co.

ANDERSON, WALKER & REICHERT, LLP (AV)

Suite 404 SunTrust Bank Building, P.O. Box 6497, 31208-6497
Telephone: 912-743-8651
Telecopier: 912-743-9636

Robert A. B. Reichert — Jonathan A. Alderman

Travis M. Trimble

OF COUNSEL

Albert P. Reichert

Representative Clients: Riverwood International Corporation; Radiology Associates of Macon, P.C.; Thiele Kaolin Company; SunTrust Bank, Middle Georgia, N.A.
General Insurance Clients: Liberty Mutual Insurance Co.

For Complete List of Firm Personnel, See General Section

For full biographical listings, see the Martindale-Hubbell Law Directory

HALL, BLOCH, GARLAND & MEYER (AV)

1500 Charter Medical Building, P.O. Box 5088, 31208-5088
Telephone: 912-745-1625
Facsimile: 912-741-8822
Email: hbgm@hbgm.com
Midtown Macon, Georgia Office: 2452 Vineville Avenue.
Telephone: 912-745-1625.
Facsimile: 912-741-3544.

MEMBERS OF FIRM

F. Kennedy Hall
Benjamin M. Garland
J. Steven Stewart
Mark E. Toth
John Flanders Kennedy
Todd C. Brooks

ASSOCIATES

Kimberly Cofer Harris
J. Ellsworth Hall, IV

Representative Clients: Norfolk Southern Railway Company; Central of Georgia Railroad Company; Railway Claims Services, Inc.; United States Fidelity & Guaranty Company; Houston General Insurance Company; Rail Tex, Inc.; Georgia Central Railway Company.

(See Next Column)

HALL, BLOCH, GARLAND & MEYER, *Macon—Continued*

For Complete List of Firm Personnel, See General Section

For full biographical listings, see the Martindale-Hubbell Law Directory

*MARIETTA,** Cobb Co.

DOWNEY & CLEVELAND, LLP (AV)

288 Washington Avenue, 30060
Telephone: 770-422-3233
Fax: 770-423-4199
Email: downey-cleveland@email.msn.com

OF COUNSEL

Lynn A. Downey

MEMBERS OF FIRM

Robert H. Cleveland (1940-1989)
Joseph C. Parker
Y. Kevin Williams
Russell B. Davis
G. Lee Welborn
Rodney S. Shockley
W. Curtis Anderson

ASSOCIATES

Richard A. Griggs
Tara Waller Scullion
Robert A. De Metz, Jr.
Kevin Salisbury
Sean L. Hynes

Representative Clients: Allstate Insurance Co.; St. Paul Insurance Cos.; Georgia Farm Bureau Mutual Insurance Co.; State Farm Insurance Cos.; Cotton States Mutual Insurance Co.; Colonial Insurance Co. of California; Progressive Insurance Company; Auto Owners Insurance Company; Deep South Surplus, Inc.

For full biographical listings, see the Martindale-Hubbell Law Directory

MOORE INGRAM JOHNSON & STEELE, LLP (AV)

A Limited Liability Company
192 Anderson Street, P.O. Box 3305, 30060-8604
Telephone: 770-429-1499
Telecopier: 770-429-8631

MEMBERS OF FIRM

John H. Moore
William R. Johnson
Robert D. Ingram
G. Phillip Beggs

ASSOCIATES

Michelle S. Davenport
Kevin B. Carlock
Alexander T. Galloway, III

Representative Clients: Crawford & Co.; The PMA Group; Scottsdale Insurance Co.; Transamerica Specialty Insurance Co.; Great Central Insurance Company; Wausau Insurance Company; Georgia Oilman's Association; Associated Risk Services, Inc.; PCA Solutions, Inc.; Coca Cola Enterprises.

For full biographical listings, see the Martindale-Hubbell Law Directory

*ROME,** Floyd Co.

BRINSON, ASKEW, BERRY, SEIGLER, RICHARDSON & DAVIS, LLP (AV)

Omberg House, 615 West First Street, P.O. Box 5513, 30162-5513
Telephone: 706-291-8853;
Atlanta: 404-521-0908
Telecopier: 706-234-3574
Email: law@brinson-askew.com *URL:* http://www.brinson-askew.com

MEMBERS OF FIRM

Robert M. Brinson (P.C.)
C. King Askew (P.C.)
Robert L. Berry
Joseph M. Seigler, Jr.
Thomas D. Richardson
J. Anderson Davis
Hendrick L. Cromartie, III
Wright W. Smith
Mark M. J. Webb
Joseph B. Atkins
I. Stewart Duggan

ASSOCIATES

James Daniel Blitch, IV
Stephen B. Moseley

Representative Clients: Georgia Power Co.; Electric Mutual Liability Insurance Co.; United States Fidelity & Guaranty Co.; Cigna Property & Casualty Cos.; Cincinnati Insurance Co.; Canal Insurance Co.; Commercial Union Assurance Co.; Georgia Farm Bureau Mutual Insurance Co.; Design Professional Insurance Co.; MAG Mutual Insurance Co.

For full biographical listings, see the Martindale-Hubbell Law Directory

*SAVANNAH,** Chatham Co.

BARROW, SIMS & LEE, A PROFESSIONAL CORPORATION (AV)

7 East Congress Street, Suite 901, P.O. Box 8185, 31412
Telephone: 912-234-7215
Fax: 912-234-7119
Email: bsmlpc@bellsouth.net

Charles W. Barrow
R. Stephen Sims
A. Mark Lee
Christine J. Bedingfield

For full biographical listings, see the Martindale-Hubbell Law Directory

BRENNAN & WASDEN LLP (AV)

33 Bull Street, Suite 590, 31401
Telephone: 912-232-6700
Fax: 912-232-0799

Joseph P. Brennan
Wiley A. Wasden III
Marvin W. McGahee
James V. Painter
Elizabeth A. White
Edward L. Newberry, Jr.
W. Andrew Bowen

For full biographical listings, see the Martindale-Hubbell Law Directory

FORBES & BOWMAN (AV)

Park South D-14, 7505 Waters Avenue, P.O. Box 13929, 31416-0929
Telephone: 912-352-1190
FAX: 912-352-1471

Morton G. Forbes
Catherine McKenzie Bowman
John A. Foster
Scot V. Pool
D. Campbell Bowman, Jr.

Representative Clients: American International Group; Atlantic Mutual Insurance Co.; Audubon Insurance Group; Cotton States Insurance Companies; Crawford & Co.; Frito-Lay, Inc.; GAB Business Services, Inc.; Minnesota Mutual Life Insurance Co.; Mutual Service Insurance Companies; OUM & Associates.

For full biographical listings, see the Martindale-Hubbell Law Directory

KARSMAN, BROOKS & CALLAWAY, P.C. (AV)

301 West Congress Street, P.O. Box 9149, 31412
Telephone: 912-238-2750
Cable Address: "Karbro"
Telecopier: 912-238-2767

Stanley M. Karsman
Charles C. Brooks
Timothy F. Callaway, III
Stanley E. Harris, Jr.
James L. Drake, Jr.
Dana F. Braun
R. Krannert Riddle
Edward M. Hughes
Timothy J. Haeussler

For full biographical listings, see the Martindale-Hubbell Law Directory

KENT, WORSHAM & SMART (AV)

18 East Bay Street, P.O. Box 9117, 31412
Telephone: 912-238-1500
FAX: 912-238-5515

MEMBERS OF FIRM

Martin Kent
Hugh M. Worsham, Jr.
Don Smart
Joseph Y. Rahimi, II

References: The Coastal Bank of Georgia.

For full biographical listings, see the Martindale-Hubbell Law Directory

*SWAINSBORO,** Emanuel Co.

SHEPHERD, GARY & MCWHORTER (AV)

SSG Building, 109 East Moring Street, Drawer 99, 30401
Telephone: 912-237-7551
Facsimile: 912-237-7514

MEMBERS OF FIRM

Felix C. Williams (1899-1972)
George L. Smith, II (1912-1973)
Sidney B. Shepherd
Loren Gary, II
William H. McWhorter, Jr.
Millard B. Shepherd, Jr.

Representative Clients: City of Swainsboro, Adrian, Garfield and Nunez; The Citizens Bank of Swainsboro; Rayonier, Inc.; Farm Bureau Insurance Co.; Yeomans Wood and Timer Co.

For full biographical listings, see the Martindale-Hubbell Law Directory

*VALDOSTA,** Lowndes Co.

CLYATT, CLYATT & DEVAUGHN, P.C. (AV)

410 North Valdosta Road, P.O. Box 5799, 31603
Telephone: 912-241-9091
Fax: 912-245-1635
Email: ccd1@surfsouth.com

Robert M. Clyatt
Melissa M. Clyatt
C. Elizabeth DeVaughn
Carl G. Fulp, III
N. Daniel Lovein
Sandra Guest Sanders

For full biographical listings, see the Martindale-Hubbell Law Directory

COLEMAN, TALLEY, NEWBERN, KURRIE, PRESTON & HOLLAND, LLP (AV)

910 North Patterson Street, P.O. Box 5437, 31603-5437
Telephone: 912-242-7562
Fax: 912-333-0885
Email: clf@datasys.net

Henry T. Brice (1925-1976)
B. Lamar Tillman (1912-1990)

(See Next Column)

COLEMAN, TALLEY, NEWBERN, KURRIE, PRESTON & HOLLAND LLP—*Continued*

MEMBERS OF FIRM

Wade H. Coleman
George T. Talley
C. George Newbern
Thompson Kurrie, Jr.
Richard L. Coleman
Edward F. Preston
William E. Holland
R. Clay Powell
Gregory T. Talley

Russell D. Henry

OF COUNSEL

John T. McTier

Representative Clients: Liberty Mutual Insurance Co.; Metropolitan Insurance Co.; USF&G Co.; American Mutual Fire Insurance Co.; Safeco Insurance Co.; American Hardware Mutual Insurance Co.; Georgia Casualty & Surety Co.; Reserve Life Insurance Co.; Grange Mutual Casualty Co.; Commercial Union Insurance Cos.

For full biographical listings, see the Martindale-Hubbell Law Directory

HAWAII

*HONOLULU,** Honolulu Co.

AYABE, CHONG, NISHIMOTO, SIA & NAKAMURA (AV)

A Partnership including a Professional Corporation
Pauahi Tower, Suite 2500, 1001 Bishop Street, 96813
Telephone: 808-537-6119
Telecopier: 808-526-3491
Email: ACNSN@pixi.com

MEMBERS OF FIRM

Sidney K. Ayabe (P.C.)
Robert A. Chong
John S. Nishimoto
Richard F. Nakamura
Jeffrey H. K. Sia
Kenneth T. Goya
Francis M. Nakamoto
Calvin E. Young
Diane W. Wong
Rodney S. Nishida
Patricia T. Fujii
Gail M. Kang
Ann H. Aratani
Philip S. Uesato
Ronald M. Shigekane
Robin R. Horner
Stephen G. Dyer
Steven L. Goto

J. Thomas Weber
Robert Y. Nakamoto, Jr.
Robert A. Mash
Gary S. Miyamoto
Jodi L. Kimura
Michael J. Van Dyke
Zale T. Okazaki

Representative Clients: Travelers Insurance Co.; St. Paul Fire and Marine Insurance Co.; The Employers Group of Insurance Companies; TIG Insurance Co.; Pacific Insurance Co.; Hartford Accident and Indemnity Co.; Continental Casualty Co.; CNA Insurance Co.; Wausau Insurance Co.

For full biographical listings, see the Martindale-Hubbell Law Directory

FUKUNAGA MATAYOSHI HERSHEY & CHING (AV)

A Partnership including a Law Corporation
841 Bishop Street, Suite 1200, 96813
Telephone: 808-533-4300
Fax: 808-531-7585

PARTNERS

Kenneth K. Fukunaga
Jerold T. Matayoshi (A Law Corporation)
James H. Hershey
Wesley H. H. Ching
Patricia Kehau Wall

ASSOCIATES

Lois H. Yamaguchi
Robert R. Sadaoka
Celia A. Urion
Sheree Kon-Herrera

OF COUNSEL

Leighton K. Chong
Kathleen M. Douglas

Representative Clients: Employers Reinsurance Corporation; First Insurance Co. of Hawaii, Ltd.; General Accident Insurance; ITT Hartford Insurance Group; RLI Insurance Co.; TIG Insurance Company; TM Claims Service, Inc.; The Travelers Indemnity Company; Wausau Underwriters Insurance Co.; Yasuda Fire & Marine.

For full biographical listings, see the Martindale-Hubbell Law Directory

GOODSILL ANDERSON QUINN & STIFEL (AV)

Alii Place, Suite 1800, 1099 Alakea Street, P.O. Box 3196, 96801-3196
Telephone: 808-547-5600
FAX: 808-547-5880
Email: info@goodsill.com *URL:* http://www.goodsill.com

(See Next Column)

MEMBERS OF FIRM

Martin Anderson
David J. Dezzani
John R. Lacy
William S. Miller
Jacqueline L. S. Earle
Lisa Woods Munger
Mark B. Desmarais
Corlis J. Chang
Barbara A. Petrus
Patricia Mathias NaPier
Wayne H. Muraoka
LindaLee K. Farm
Margaret Jenkins Leong
Carol Ann Eblen
Roy John Tjioe
A. Richard Philpott
Lennes N. Omuro
Derek R. Kobayashi

ASSOCIATES

Thomas L. Benedict
Edmund K. Saffery
Lisa A. Bail
Carolyn K. Gugelyk
Normand R. Lezy
Kathleen A. Kelly
Tonya C. Kong
J. Denice von Gnechten
Teresa R. Favilla
M. Elizabeth Raxter
Anne T. Horiuchi

Representative Clients: AIG; Argonaut Insurance Co.; CNA Insurance Co.; Farmers Insurance Group of Companies; Kemper Insurance; MEDMARC; Paul Revere Life Insurance; State Farm Insurance Companies; United States Aviation Underwriters, Inc.

For Complete List of Firm Personnel, See General Section

For full biographical listings, see the Martindale-Hubbell Law Directory

KESSNER DUCA UMEBAYASHI BAIN & MATSUNAGA ATTORNEYS AT LAW, A LAW CORPORATION (AV)

19th Floor, Central Pacific Plaza, 220 South King Street, 96813
Telephone: 808-536-1900
Telecopier: 808-529-7177
Telex: 723 8616 OPAC IIR

Robert C. Kessner
James N. Duca
Clyde S. Umebayashi
Elton John Bain
Emma S. Matsunaga
Muriel M. Taira

Beverly S. K. Tom
Jacqueline W.S. Amai
Melanie S. Matsui
Cori Ann C. Takamiya

OF COUNSEL

Kathy K. Higham

For full biographical listings, see the Martindale-Hubbell Law Directory

LYONS, BRANDT, COOK & HIRAMATSU (AV)

841 Bishop Street, Suite 1800, 96813
Telephone: 808-524-7030
Facsimile: 808-533-3011
Email: lbch@hits.net

MEMBERS OF FIRM

Samuel A. B. Lyons
George W. Brandt
Thomas E. Cook
Beverly Lynne K. Hiramatsu
Jeffrey A. Griswold
Bradford F. K. Bliss
Steven Y. Otaguro
Stefan M. Reinke
Paul R. Grable
Edquon Lee
Bonnie L. Moore

OF COUNSEL

Birney Baxter Bervar

For full biographical listings, see the Martindale-Hubbell Law Directory

MCCORRISTON MIHO MILLER MUKAI (AV)

Five Waterfront Plaza, 4th Floor, 500 Ala Moana Boulevard, 96813
Telephone: 808-529-7300
Facsimile: 808-524-8293
Cable: Attorneys, Honolulu
Mailing Address: P.O. Box 2800, Honolulu, Hawaii, 96803-2800
Email: info@m4Law.com

PARTNERS

William C. McCorriston
Mark J. Bennett
Nadine Y. Ando
Darolyn Hatsuko Lendio
Randall K. Schmitt
John Y. Yamano
Lisa M. Ginoza
Kimberly Rae McCorkle
Carrie K. S. Okinaga
Christopher J. Cole

COUNSEL

R. John Seibert

ASSOCIATES

Maria B. Mazzeo
Jonathan H. Steiner
Stacey M. Robinson
Kenneth J. Mansfield
Deborah L. P. Mueller
Kara B. Moran

Representative Clients: Allstate Insurance Company; State Farm Insurance; Scottsdale Insurance Company; American Insurance Group; Design Professional Insurance Company.

For Complete List of Firm Personnel, See General Section

For full biographical listings, see the Martindale-Hubbell Law Directory

Honolulu—Continued

MIYAGI, NOHR & MYHRE (AV)

1001 Bishop Street, Suite 1200, 96813
Telephone: 808-524-2466
Fax: 808-524-2556

Melvyn M. Miyagi
Katharine M. Nohr
James V. Myhre
Michael H. Tsuchida
John E. Drotz

OF COUNSEL

Carleton B. Reid

Representative Clients: American International Group; State Farm Insurance; TIG Insurance; Crum & Forster; ITT Specialty Risk Services; Marriott International; The Hartford; USAA; Budget Rent A Car; Crawford & Company.

For full biographical listings, see the Martindale-Hubbell Law Directory

ROBBINS & RHODES ATTORNEYS AT LAW, A LAW CORPORATION (AV)

Suite 2200 Davies Pacific Center, 841 Bishop Street, 96813
Telephone: 808-524-2355
Fax: 808-526-0290
Email: robbinsrhodes@lava.net

Kenneth S. Robbins

Representative Clients: Argonaut Insurance Co.; CNA Insurance Co.; Great American Insurance Co.; Guaranty National Insurance Co.; LLoyds of London; TIG Insurance Co.

For full biographical listings, see the Martindale-Hubbell Law Directory

TAM, O'CONNOR, HENDERSON, TAIRA & YAMAUCHI ATTORNEYS AT LAW, A LAW CORPORATION (AV)

20th Floor, Central Pacific Plaza, 220 South King Street, 96813
Telephone: 808-545-3030
Fax: 808-523-8051
Fax: 808-537-6782
Email: lawyers@50thstatelaw.com

James K. Tam
Michael F. O'Connor
Harvey E. Henderson, Jr.
Lissa H. Andrews
Robert M. Yamauchi
Darryl M. Taira
Stuart M. Kodish

Wesley H. Ikeda
Russ S. Awakuni
Kevin W. Herring
Fred I. Waki

OF COUNSEL

Paul M. Dold

Representative Clients: Western Heritage Insurance Co.; American International Companies; Burlington Insurance Co.; Federal Insurance Co.; Chubb-/Pacific Indemnity Group; United States Services Automobile Assn.; Employers Reinsurance Company; AIG Hawaii Insurance Co., Inc.; CNA Insurance Co.

For full biographical listings, see the Martindale-Hubbell Law Directory

TOM & PETRUS (AV)

212 Merchant Street Suite 200, 96813
Telephone: 808-522-0800
Fax: 808-522-0809

MEMBERS OF FIRM

Michael D. Tom
Brad S. Petrus
Richard B. Miller

ASSOCIATES

Leslie H. Kondo
Stephen M. Teves
David R. Harada-Stone
Lauren K. Rauschenburg

COUNSEL

Lyle Minoru Ishida

Representative Clients: Allstate Insurance Co.; State Farm Insurance Companies; Dai-Tokyo Royal State Insurance Co.; GRE/Albany Insurance Co.; GEICO; AIG Hawaii Insurance Co.; Hawaiian Insurance and Guar. C., Ltd.; Progressive Adjusting Co., Inc.; Travelers Property Casualty.

For full biographical listings, see the Martindale-Hubbell Law Directory

WATANABE, ING & KAWASHIMA (AV)

A Partnership including Professional Corporations
First Hawaiian Center, 999 Bishop Street, 23rd Floor, 96813
Telephone: 808-544-8300
Facsimile: 808-544-8399
Email: allwik@wik.com

MEMBERS OF FIRM

Jeffrey N. Watanabe (Atty. At Law, A Law Corp.)
James Kawashima (Atty. At Law, A Law Corp.)
J. Douglas Ing (Atty. At Law, A Law Corp.)
Wray H. Kondo (Atty. At Law, A Law Corp.)

(See Next Column)

MEMBERS OF FIRM (Continued)

John T. Komeiji (Atty. At Law, A Law Corp.)
Ronald Y. K. Leong (Atty. At Law, A Law Corp.)
Robert T. Takamatsu (Atty. At Law, A Law Corp.)
Cynthia Winegar (Atty. at Law, A Law Corp.)
Randall Y. Yamamoto (Atty. At Law, A Law Corp.)
Lyle Y. Harada (Atty. At Law, A Law Corp.)
Michael A. Lorusso (Atty. At Law, A Law Corp.)
Pamela J. Larson (Atty. At Law, A Law Corp.)
John R. Aube (Atty. At Law, A Law Corp.)
Jan M.L.Y. Amii (Atty. at Law, A Law Corp.)
Edward B. Rogin (Atty. at Law, A Law Corp.)
Seth M. Reiss (Atty. At Law, A Law Corp.)
Curtis C. Kim
Lani Narikiyo (Atty. at Law, A Law Corp.)

ASSOCIATES

Donna Y. Kanemaru
Peter L. Fritz
Beth K. Fujimoto
Patsy H. Kirio
Kevin H. Oda
Michael C. Bird
Brian Y. Hiyane
Dennis J. Hwang
Teri Y. Kondo
Gregory Y.P. Tom
R. Scott Simon

ASIA PACIFIC CONSULTANTS

George R. Ariyoshi
Victor Hao Li (Not admitted in HI)

LEGAL SUPPORT PERSONNEL

GOVERNMENT AFFAIRS ADVISORS

Millicent M. Y. H. Kim
Lori Ann C. Lum

References: First Hawaiian Bank; American Savings Bank.

For Complete List of Firm Personnel, See General Section

For full biographical listings, see the Martindale-Hubbell Law Directory

IDAHO

*BOISE,** Ada Co.

BRASSEY, WETHERELL, CRAWFORD & MCCURDY, L.L.P. (AV)

Washington Federal Plaza, 1001 West Idaho-3rd Floor, P.O. Box 1009, 83701-1009
Telephone: 208-344-7300
Facsimile: 208-344-7077
Email: bwcm@micron.net

Andrew C. Brassey
Robert T. Wetherell
J. Nick Crawford
William A. McCurdy

Michael J. Elia
Jason D. Melville

Representative Clients: Acordia Ski Resort Services; CNA Insurance Companies; Coregis; Gordon Trucking, Inc.; Houston General Insurance Company; Medical Insurance Exchange of California; Sinclair Oil Corporation; State of Idaho, Bureau of Risk Management; Sun Valley Company.

For full biographical listings, see the Martindale-Hubbell Law Directory

CANTRILL, SKINNER, SULLIVAN & KING (AV)

1423 Tyrell Lane, P.O. Box 359, 83701
Telephone: 208-344-8035
Fax: 208-345-7212
Email: cssklaw@ibm.net

MEMBERS OF FIRM

David W. Cantrill
Gardner W. Skinner, Jr.
Willis E. Sullivan, III
John L. King
Robert D. Lewis
Frank P. Kotyk

ASSOCIATES

Tyra H. Stubbs
Clinton O. Casey

Representative Clients: Safeco Insurance Companies; Prudential Property and Casualty Insurance Co.; State Insurance Fund; Farmers Insurance Co.; Jordan-Wilcomb Company; Nature Conservancy; Independent School District of Boise City; Hartford Insurance Group; Mutual of Eunumclaw Insurance Co.
Reference: Key Bank.

For full biographical listings, see the Martindale-Hubbell Law Directory

ELAM & BURKE, A PROFESSIONAL ASSOCIATION (AV)

Key Financial Center, 702 West Idaho Street, P.O. Box 1539, 83701
Telephone: 208-343-5454
Telecopier: 208-384-5844
Email: eblaw@elamburke.com

(See Next Column)

ELAM & BURKE A PROFESSIONAL ASSOCIATION—*Continued*

M. Allyn Dingel, Jr.
John Magel
James D. LaRue
William G. Dryden
Trudy Hanson Fouser
Jeffery J. Ventrella
Jeffrey A. Thomson

J. Ray Durtschi
Rebecca A. Broadbent
Casey C. Robertson

Representative Clients: State Farm Insurance; United Heritage Mutual Life Insurance; Progressive Insurance Co.; Farmers Insurance; Employers Reinsurance Corp.; Prudential Insurance Company of America; Idaho State Insurance Fund; Ohio Casualty Insurance Companies; Wausau Insurance Co.; Lincoln National Life Insurance.

For Complete List of Firm Personnel, See General Section

For full biographical listings, see the Martindale-Hubbell Law Directory

GARDNER & CHARNEY, P.L.L.P. (AV)

350 North 9th Street - Suite B-60, 83702
Telephone: 208-387-0881
Fax: 208-387-3501
Email: agboi@aol.com

Alan R. Gardner
Dennis M. Charney

Representative Clients: Safeco Insurance Cos.; Wausau Insurance Cos.; Farmers Insurance Group; St. Paul Insurance Company; Traveler's Insurance Cos.; Fremont Insurance Co.; Intermountain Health Care; Chubb Insurance Company; Reliance Insurance Co.; Albertson's, Inc.

For full biographical listings, see the Martindale-Hubbell Law Directory

LYNCH & ASSOCIATES, P.L.L.C. (AV)

Ninth and Idaho Center, 225 N. 9th Street, Suite 600, P.O. Box 739, 83701
Telephone: 208-331-5088
Fax: 208-331-0088
Email: Lynchassoc@lesbois.com *URL:* http://www.lawyers.com/lynch&associates

James B. Lynch

Katherine M. Lynch

For full biographical listings, see the Martindale-Hubbell Law Directory

MOORE, BASKIN & PARKER (AV)

Washington Federal Plaza, 1001 West Idaho Street, Suite 400, P.O. Box 6756, 83707
Telephone: 208-336-6900
Facsimile: 208-336-7031
Email: mail@MBPLAW.com *URL:* http://www.lawyers.com/moorebaskin&parker

MEMBERS OF FIRM

Michael W. Moore
Thomas P. Baskin, III
Paige Alan Parker
Richard Hansen
Wendy Cox Dvorak

ASSOCIATE

Martin C. Hendrickson

Representative Clients: Travelers Insurance Co./Aetna Casualty & Surety, Co.; Capitol Indemnity Co.; Clarendon Insurance Co.; Crawford & Co.; Empire Fire & Marine Insurance Co.; Fireman's Fund Insurance Cos.; Idaho Counties Reciprocal Management Program; Idaho State Insurance Fund; Insurance Company of the West; Protective Insurance Co.

For full biographical listings, see the Martindale-Hubbell Law Directory

*POCATELLO,** Bannock Co.

COOPER & LARSEN (AV)

151 North 3rd Avenue, Suite 210, P.O. Box 4229, 83205-4229
Telephone: 208-235-1145
Fax: 208-235-1182
URL: http://cooperlarsen.uswestdex.com
Email: gary-c@crsinternet.com *URL:* http://www.lawyers.com/cooperlarsen

Gary L. Cooper
Reed W. Larsen
James P. Price

Representative Clients: Abertsons; Allstate; Federated; Farmers; Hartford; Orion Auto; North Pacific; Safeco.

For full biographical listings, see the Martindale-Hubbell Law Directory

MAGUIRE & KRESS, P.C. (AV)

353 East Lander, P.O. Box 4758, 83205-4758
Telephone: 208-232-5167
Fax: 208-232-5181
Email: maguire@crsinternet.com *URL:* http://www.lawyers.com/maguirekresslaw

(See Next Column)

Martin R. Ward (1943-1997)
David H. Maguire
David R. Kress

Representative Clients: Farmers Insurance Group (Truck Exchange); The American Insurance Group; North Pacific Insurance; State Farm Insurance Company; Mutual Services Insurance Company; Modern Roofing & Insulation Co.; United States Fidelity & Guaranty Co.

For full biographical listings, see the Martindale-Hubbell Law Directory

MERRILL & MERRILL, CHARTERED (AV)

Key Bank Building, P.O. Box 991, 83204
Telephone: 208-232-2286
Fax: 208-232-2499
Email: mmlaw@ida.net

Stephen S. Dunn
D. Russell Wight
David C. Nye
Kent L. Hawkins

Representative Clients: Farm Bureau Mutual Insurance Co. of Idaho; Aetna Life & Casualty; St. Paul Insurance; The Travelers Insurance Co.

For Complete List of Firm Personnel, See General Section

For full biographical listings, see the Martindale-Hubbell Law Directory

RACINE, OLSON, NYE, BUDGE & BAILEY, CHARTERED (AV)

Center Plaza, Corner First and Center, Suite 2A, P.O. Box 1391, 83201-1391
Telephone: 208-232-6101
FAX: 208-232-6109
Email: racine@crsinternet.com
Associated Office: McGrath, Marotz & Smith, 414 Shoup, P.O. Box 50731, Idaho Falls, 83405.
Telephone: 208-524-0731.
Fax: 208-529-4166.

Louis F. Racine, Jr.
William D. Olson
W. Marcus W. Nye
Randall C. Budge
John A. Bailey, Jr.
John R. Goodell
John B. Ingelstrom
Daniel C. Green
Brent O. Roche
Kirk Hadley
Fred J. Lewis
Mitchell W. Brown

Eric S. Hunn
David E. Alexander
Lisa M. Christon
Richard A. Hearn
Eric L. Olsen

Representative Clients: Allstate Insurance Co.; Farmers Insurance Group of Cos.; Idaho Irrigation Pumpers Assn.; Monsanto Co.; North Pacific Insurance Co.; Safeco Insurance Co.; U.S. Bank.

For full biographical listings, see the Martindale-Hubbell Law Directory

*TWIN FALLS,** Twin Falls Co.

BENOIT, ALEXANDER, SINCLAIR, HARWOOD & HIGH, L.L.P. (AV)

126 Second Avenue North, P.O. Box 366, 83303-0366
Telephone: 208-733-5463
FAX: 208-734-1438
Email: bashh@bashh.com *URL:* http://www.bashh.com
Ketchum, Idaho Office: 160 Second Street East, Suite 218.
Telephone: 208-726-4900.
Fax: 208-726-3101.

MEMBERS OF FIRM

Harry Benoit (1893-1966)
Edward L. Benoit (1921-1998)
J. Robert Alexander
J. Walter Sinclair
Robert M. Harwood (Resident, Ketchum Office)
Thomas B. High, P.A.

ASSOCIATES

John K. Butler
Stephanie A. Fassett
Jerold W. Lee
Anthony M. Valdez

PARALEGAL

Judy S. Imlay (Paralegal)

Counsel for: College of Southern Idaho; Independent Meat Co.; Twin Falls School District #411; City of Twin Falls; City of Filer.
Local Counsel for: Home Insurance Co.; Medical Insurance Exchange of California; Mutual of Enumclaw Insurance; Safeco.

For full biographical listings, see the Martindale-Hubbell Law Directory

ILLINOIS

AURORA, Kane Co.

MURPHY, HUPP, FOOTE, MIELKE AND KINNALLY (AV)

North Island Center, P.O. Box 5030, 60507
Telephone: 630-844-0056
Fax: 630-844-1905
Email: mhfmk@insnet.com

MEMBERS OF FIRM

William C. Murphy
Robert B. Hupp
Robert M. Foote
Craig S. Mielke
Patrick M. Kinnally
Paul G. Krentz
Joseph C. Loran
Gerald K. Hodge

Timothy D. O'Neil
Matthew J. Herman

Representative Clients: American Telephone & Telegraph Co.; Fox Valley Park District; Lyon Metal Products; Kane County Forest Preserve District; Hollywood Casino; Employers Mutual Insurance Co.; Forty-Eight Insulations, Inc.; UNR Asbestos Disease Trust; Richards-Wilcox Co.; National Bank & Trust Company of Syracuse.

For full biographical listings, see the Martindale-Hubbell Law Directory

*BELLEVILLE,** St. Clair Co.

DUNHAM, BOMAN & LESKERA (AV)

208 N. High, 62220
Telephone: 618-235-7222
Telecopier: 618-236-2800; 618-236-1899
Collinsville Office: 300 West Clay Street.
Telephone: 618-344-7734.
Telecopier: 618-344-3853.

M.F. Oehmke (1887-1963)
Wm. C. Dunham (1893-1975)
Howard Boman (1917-1985)
John W. Leskera
William L. Berry
Eric C. Young
Robert D. Francis
John L. Bitzer

Attorneys for: Collinsville School District #10; Hanover Insurance Co.; Hartford Insurance Group; State Farm Insurance Cos.; Transamerica Insurance Group; The Travelers Indemnity Co.; Wausau Insurance Cos.; Nationwide Insurance Co.; RLI Insurance Group.

For full biographical listings, see the Martindale-Hubbell Law Directory

FREEARK, HARVEY, MENDILLO, DENNIS, WULLER & CAIN, P.C. (AV)

115 West Washington Street, P.O. Box 546, 62222
Telephone: 618-233-2686
Telecopier: 618-233-5677
Email: freeark@peaknet.net

Ray H. Freeark, Jr.
Ted R. Harvey, Jr.
James R. Mendillo
Ted W. Dennis
Ransom P. Wuller
Jeffery A. Cain

Michael P. Murphy
Denise Rusnack
W. Jeffrey Muskopf

Representative Clients: American Federation of Teachers, Local 434, Belleville, Illinois and 743, Granite City, Illinois.
Local Counsel for: Illinois State Medical Inter-Insurance Exchange, Chicago, Illinois; Sentry Insurance Co., Stevens Point, Wisconsin; General Casualty Cos., Springfield, Illinois and Sun Prairie, Wisconsin; Allstate Insurance Co., St. Louis, Missouri and Arlington Heights, Illinois; St. Paul Fire & Marine Insurance Co.; Travelers Insurance Co.; Northbrook Insurance Co., Arlington Heights, Illinois; Employers Insurance of Wausau, River Forest, Illinois and St. Louis, Missouri.

For full biographical listings, see the Martindale-Hubbell Law Directory

NEVILLE, RICHARDS, DEFRANCO & WULLER (AV)

5 Park Place, 62226
Telephone: 618-277-0900
Facsimile: 618-277-0970
Email: nrdw@nrdw-law.com *URL:* http://www.nrdw-law.com

MEMBERS OF FIRM

James E. Neville
Timothy S. Richards
James E. DeFranco
Robert G. Wuller, Jr.

ASSOCIATES

Shari M. Brunton
Ellen M. Edmonds
Daniel L. Bradley
Matthew Charles Zittel

For full biographical listings, see the Martindale-Hubbell Law Directory

BOLINGBROOK, Will Co.

MOSS AND BLOOMBERG, LTD. (AV)

305 West Briarcliff Road, Suite 201, P.O. Box 1158, 60440-0858
Telephone: 630-759-0800
Telecopier: 630-759-8504
Email: info@mb-lawyers.com

Barry L. Moss
Steven P. Bloomberg
George A. Marchetti
David J. Freeman
Daniel C. Shapiro

For full biographical listings, see the Martindale-Hubbell Law Directory

CARBONDALE, Jackson Co.

BRANDON, SCHMIDT, GOFFINET & SOLVERSON (AV)

916 West Main Street, P.O. Box 3898, 62902-3898
Telephone: 618-549-0777
Telecopier: 618-457-4691
Email: CdaleLaw@aol.com

MEMBERS OF FIRM

Wm. Kent Brandon
Charles E. Schmidt
Jeffrey A. Goffinet
Christy W. Solverson

ASSOCIATES

Reona J. Daly
Michelle M. Schafer
Matthew S. Wilzbach

Representative Clients: State Farm Insurance Co.; Pekin Insurance Co.; Milwaukee Insurance Company; Illinois State Medical Insurance Services; The St. Paul Insurance Co.; Indiana Insurance Co.; Madison Mutual Insirance Co.; Professional Insurance Company of Michigan (PICOM); United States Fidelity and Guarranty Co.
Reference: Fist National Bank of Carbondale.

For full biographical listings, see the Martindale-Hubbell Law Directory

CENTRALIA, Marion Co.

WHAM & WHAM (AV)

212 East Broadway, 62801
Telephone: 618-532-5621
Fax: 618-532-5055
URL: http://www.lawyers.com/wham&wham

Charles Wham (1887-1963)
John P. Wham (1902-1992)

MEMBERS OF FIRM

James B. Wham
Richard A. Cary
Janie F. Smith
Jennifer W. Price
Daniel R. Price

OF COUNSEL

William B. Wham

Counsel for: State Farm Mutual Insurance Cos.; Auto-Owners Insurance Co; Pekin Insurance; MMI Cos; West American Ins. Co; Ohio Casualty Ins. Co.

For full biographical listings, see the Martindale-Hubbell Law Directory

*CHARLESTON,** Coles Co.

THE BRAINARD LAW OFFICES (AV)

Brainard Building, 600 Jackson Avenue, 61920
Telephone: 217-345-3929
Fax: 217-345-6501

MEMBERS OF FIRM

H. Ogden Brainard (1905-1992)
William A. Sunderman
Henry E. Kramer
Brian L. Bower
William J. Warmoth
Mark R. Karpus
Kristin L. Wilson

OF COUNSEL

J. Leeds Bower

Representative Clients: Community Bank & Trust Savings Bank; Agri Bank FCB; Coles-Moultrie Electric Cooperative; Sarah Bush Lincoln Health Center; Country Companies; Prudential Insurance Co.; Protection Mutual Insurance Co.; The Hartford Insurance Companies.

For full biographical listings, see the Martindale-Hubbell Law Directory

*CHICAGO,** Cook Co.

ARONBERG GOLDGEHN DAVIS & GARMISA (AV)

Suite 3000 One IBM Plaza, 60611
Telephone: 312-828-9600
Telecopier: 312-828-9635
Email: agdglaw@aol.com
Schaumberg, Illinois Office: 1901 North Roselle Road, Suite 800, 60195.
Telephone: 847-985-4060.

MEMBERS OF FIRM

Christopher J. Bannon
Mitchell S. Goldgehn
James J. Hickey
John M. Riccione
James A. Smith

(See Next Column)

ARONBERG GOLDGEHN DAVIS & GARMISA—*Continued*

ASSOCIATES

Lisa J. Brodsky
Howard J. Fishman
Paul A. Greenberg
William J. Serritella, Jr.

For Complete List of Firm Personnel, See General Section

For full biographical listings, see the Martindale-Hubbell Law Directory

BATES MECKLER BULGER & TILSON (AV)

8300 Sears Tower, 233 South Wacker, 60606
Telephone: 312-474-7900
Facsimile: 312-474-7898
URL: http://www.bmbt.com

MEMBERS OF FIRM

Robert J. Bates, Jr.
Scott L. Carey
Catherine M. Crisham
Janet R. Davis
Maria G. Enriquez
Brent J. Graber
Maryann C. Hayes
Robert C. Heist
Kathleen H. Jensen
James H. Kallianis, Jr.
Philip R. King
Mari Henry Leigh
Michael I. Leonard
Mary F. Licari
Michael M. Marick
Steven D. Pearson
John E. Rodewald
Scott M. Seaman
Mark G. Sheridan
Brian J Williams
Timothy A. Wolfe

ASSOCIATES

Dina L. Brantman
John K. Daly
Robin I. Edelstein
Mary E. Gootjes
Christopher E. Kentra
Joseph P. Pozen
(Not admitted in IL)
Monica T. Sullivan

OF COUNSEL

Eileen King Bower
Matthew M. Murphy
Thomas J. O'Brien

For full biographical listings, see the Martindale-Hubbell Law Directory

BELGRADE AND O'DONNELL, A PROFESSIONAL CORPORATION (AV)

311 South Wacker Drive, Suite 2770, 60606
Telephone: 312-360-9500
Facsimile: 312-360-9550
Email: bodpc@aol.com

Steven B. Belgrade
John A. O'Donnell
George M. Velcich
Kim Richard Kardas

Patrick J. Cullinan
Lisa E. Nelson
James Kent Minnette
Richard P. Girzadas

For full biographical listings, see the Martindale-Hubbell Law Directory

BLATT, HAMMESFAHR & EATON (AV)

333 W. Wacker Drive, Suite 1900, 60606
Telephone: 312-849-8000
FAX: 312-357-0198
Email: BHE@BHELAW.COM *URL:* HTTP://WWW.BHELAW.COM
New York, New York Office: 45 Broadway, 12th Floor.
Telephone: 212-363-1900.
Fax: 212-363-2600. Email: bhe@bhelaw.com.

MEMBERS OF FIRM

Zacarias R. Chacon
Hugo Chaviano
Kathleen A. McQueeny

ASSOCIATES

Mary I. Babbo
Lesley A. Dable
Peggy A. Glenn
Ryan M. Henderson
Bruce M. Lichtcsien
Joseph G. Lyons
Marc A. Polansky

For full biographical listings, see the Martindale-Hubbell Law Directory

CONNELLY & SCHROEDER (AV)

One North Franklin Street, Suite 1200, 60606-3421
Telephone: 312-251-9600
Fax: 312-251-9601
Geneva, Illinois Office: 1250 Executive Place, Suite 201.
Telephone: 630-232-6440.
FAX: 630-232-6450

MEMBERS OF FIRM

Michael P. Connelly
John L. Schroeder
(Resident, Geneva Office)

ASSOCIATES

Michelle L. Adams
(Resident, Geneva Office)
Thomas W. Dillon
(Resident, Geneva Office)
Carolyn A. Schroeder
(Resident, Geneva)
Martha Swatek
(Resident, Geneva Office)

For full biographical listings, see the Martindale-Hubbell Law Directory

CRYSTAL, HEYTOW & WARNICK, P.C. (AV)

Suite 1350, 111 West Washington Street, 60602
Telephone: 312-541-1700
Facsimile: 312-541-9798
Email: offices@chwlegal.com

Frederick H. Crystal
Richard D. Heytow
Jeffrey L. Warnick

Renata Seward
Carri Ann Lausman
Timothy D. Nimrod

For full biographical listings, see the Martindale-Hubbell Law Directory

DOWD & DOWD, LTD. (AV)

Suite 1000, 55 West Wacker Drive, 60601
Telephone: 312-704-4400
Telecopier: 312-704-4500
Lake Geneva, Wisconsin Office: P.O. Box 356.
Telephone: 414-275-0057.
Telecopier: 414-275-6786.
Des Plaines Office: 575 Lee Street.
Telephone: 847-827-5117.
Telecopier: 847-827-0076.

Joseph V. Dowd
Michael E. Dowd (1957-1996)
Kenneth Gurber
Patrick C. Dowd
Robert J. Golden
Patrick J. Ruberry
John M. McAndrews
Anthony R. Rutkowski

Daniel J. Arnett
S. Robert Depke
Beth S. Dolehide
David J. Farina
William P. Heffernan
Teri L. Meade
Matthew J Murphy
Gregory M. Norgle
Michael G. Patrizio
Michael W. Van Zalingen
Karen W. Worsek

LEGAL SUPPORT PERSONNEL

Carol Barnes

OF COUNSEL

Guenther Ahlf
Tobias G. Barry
John A. Garrity, III
Peter F. Higgins
Daniel C. McKay
Sam L. Miller
Joel S. Ostrow
Norman E. Samelson

Representative Clients: Gallagher Bassett Services, Inc.; Kemper National Insurance Companies; Schneider National Carriers; Scottsdale Insurance Company; Swift Transportation; Acceptance Insurance Companies; AI Transportation; Borg Warner Protective Services; Clarendon National Insurance Company; Landstar Inway, Inc.
Reference: American National Bank in Chicago.

For full biographical listings, see the Martindale-Hubbell Law Directory

GESSLER, HUGHES & SOCOL, LTD. (AV)

Three First National Plaza, Suite 2200, 60602
Telephone: 312-580-0100
Telecopy: 312-580-1994

Benjamin P. Beringer
Anjali Dayal
Mark S. Dym
George W. Gessler
John K. Hughes
Joshua Karsh
Peter M. Katsaros
Kimberley Marsh
Alex W. Miller
Terence J. Moran
Matthew J. Piers
Kalman D. Resnick
Frederick S. Rhine
Jonathan A. Rothstein
Michael P. Simkus
Donna Kaner Socol

Gary Chodorow
Ruth M. Dunning
S. Todd Neal
Mark A. Pellegrino
Steven C. Steinback
Dana H. Sukenik
J. Eric Vander Arend
Mark B. Weiner
Charles H. Wintersteen

OF COUNSEL

Darius S. Francescatti, M.D.
Susan R. Gzesh

For full biographical listings, see the Martindale-Hubbell Law Directory

GREENE AND LETTS (AV)

30 North La Salle Street, Suite 1520, 60602
Telephone: 312-346-1100
Telefax: 312-346-4571
Email: greneletts@aol.com

MEMBERS OF FIRM

Martin P. Greene
Eileen M. Letts
Allen P. Walker

ASSOCIATES

Fernando M. Bustamante
Shirley R. Calloway
(Not admitted in IL)
Lakeisha R. Mayfield

(See Next Column)

GREENE AND LETTS, *Chicago—Continued*

OF COUNSEL

Kevin T. Lee
Ellen E. Douglass

LEGAL SUPPORT PERSONNEL

Mary Ann Alexander (Legal Assistant)
Barbara Nelson (Legal Assistant)

For full biographical listings, see the Martindale-Hubbell Law Directory

HASKELL & PERRIN (AV)

200 West Adams, Suite 2600, 60606
Telephone: 312-781-9393
Fax: 312-781-9178
Email: hasper@haskellperrin.com

MEMBERS OF FIRM

James Kirk Perrin
John J. Lynch
Mary Elizabeth Denefe

OF COUNSEL

Donald M. Haskell

ASSOCIATE

Nancy J. Robinson

For full biographical listings, see the Martindale-Hubbell Law Directory

JOHNSON & BELL, LTD. (AV)

Suite 2200, 222 North La Salle Street, 60601
Telephone: 312-372-0770
Facsimile: 312-372-9818
Waukegan, Illinois Office: Nine North County Street, Suite G-1, 60085.
Telephone: 847-662-7458.
Facsimile: 847-662-7366.
Highland, Indiana Office: 900 Indianapolis Boulevard, Suite A, 46322.
Telephone: 219-923-5250.
Facsimile: 219-923-6170.

William V. Johnson
John W. Bell
Jack T. Riley, Jr.
Brian C. Fetzer
Thomas H. Fegan
Thomas J. Andrews
William G. Beatty
John A. Childers
Margaret A. Unger
Howard Patrick Morris
Scott W. Hoyne
James S. Stickles, Jr.
Frederick S. Mueller
Joseph R. Marconi
Robert M. Burke
Kurt C. Meihofer
Glenn F. Fencl
Cornelius J. Harrington, III
David J. Loughnane
Michael P. Siavelis
William A. Geiser
Kevin G. Owens
Dennis C. Cusack
Charles P. Rantis
Robert J. Comfort
Alan Jay Goldstein
Steven B. Novy
Daniel C. Murray
William K. McVisk
Joseph F. Spitzzeri
Joseph B. Carini, III
Kathryn K. Loft
Gregory D. Conforti
Frank P. Nowicki
Frank S. Gildea
Joseph J. McNerney
Gregory E. Schiller
Howard W. Foster
William J. Anaya
Robert R. McNamara
Marilyn McCabe Reidy
William B. Bower

W. Gregory Aimonette
Michael J. Burns
Timothy R. Couture
Patrick T. Garvey
Laura B. Glaser
Stefanie R. Glover
Guy Halpern
Susan W. Horn
Mark D. Johnson
Matthew L. Johnson
Mindy L. Kallus
Mary Kenney
Andrew J. Kovarik
Richard P. Long
David M. Macksey
Steven A. Marderosian
Julie M. McClelland
Laura J. McGrath
Victor Michel
Susan V. Nordheim
Michael A. Pauletto
Lynn M. Reid
Joseph D. Ryan
Todd M. Saranecki
Charlene M. Sheridan
Ann M. Smith
Robert Spitkovsky, Jr.
Terry Takash
Kendra A. Thramann
Kelly N. Warnick
Steven D. Welhouse
David A. Wilford
David A. Wilson (Resident, Highland, Indiana Office)
Steven F. Wittman
Jennifer D. Yoder (Resident, Highland, Indiana Office)

References available upon request.

For full biographical listings, see the Martindale-Hubbell Law Directory

KAPLAN, BEGY & VON OHLEN (AV)

One First National Plaza 51st Floor, 60603
Telephone: 312-345-3000
Fax: 312-345-3119
URL: http://www.kbvlaw.com

(See Next Column)

MEMBERS OF FIRM

Fred C. Begy, III
Larry S. Kaplan
James D. Solon
Robert C. von Ohlen, Jr.
Joseph A. Bosco
Richard A. Walker
Mitchell J. Kanaan
Patrick J. Keating

ASSOCIATES

Keith S. Yamaguchi
Thomas C. Sokol
Robert K. Villa
Nicole Halpern Murphy
Telly Andrews
Tamara S. Dykstra

For full biographical listings, see the Martindale-Hubbell Law Directory

KIESLER & BERMAN (AV)

Suite 1300, 188 West Randolph Street, 60601
Telephone: 312-332-2840
FAX: 312-332-4547
Email: info@thekillerbees.com *URL:* http://www.kieslerberman.com
Wheaton Office: 2100 Manchester, Suite 605.
Telephone: 630-752-8247.
Fax: 630-752-9587.
Joliet Office: 57 West Jefferson Street.
Telephone: 815-723-2755.
Fax: 815-723-2763.
Waukegan Office: 216 Madison Street.
Telephone: 847-244-5805.
Fax: 847-244-3996.

FOUNDERS

Marvin D. Berman
Robert L. Kiesler

MEMBERS OF FIRM

Stephen B. Frew (Managing Partner)
Clinton J. Feil
Alan P. Miller
John R. Garofalo
Dale L. Schlafer
Lyle F. Koester
Mark S. Vilimek
Rory D. Cassidy
Patti Olson Deuel
David J. Kiesler
Jeffrey S. Pavlovich
John J. Piegore
Pamela K. Harman

SENIOR TRIAL COUNSEL

Edward L. Cooper

ASSOCIATES

Donna D. Ciancio
Donald E. Elder
Mary E. Haeger
Shari J. Kalik
Thomas J. Kanyock
Bryan W. Luce
William P. McElligott
Peter R. Mennella
Shannon F. O'Shea
John P. Palumbo
Jeanne M. Zeiger

SENIOR COUNSEL

Frank N. Rago

For full biographical listings, see the Martindale-Hubbell Law Directory

MACCABE & MCGUIRE (AV)

Suite 3333, 77 West Wacker Drive, 60601
Telephone: 312-357-2600
Fax: 312-357-0317
Email: MacMcLaw77@aol.com

MEMBERS OF FIRM

Edward H. MacCabe
Maureen A. McGuire

ASSOCIATES

Timothy J. Murphy
Diedre S. Dunn
Margaret T. Conway

OF COUNSEL

Brian J. Mulhern

For full biographical listings, see the Martindale-Hubbell Law Directory

MERLO, KANOFSKY & BRINKMEIER, LTD. (AV)

208 South La Salle Street, Suite 950, 60604
Telephone: 312-553-5500
Facsimile: 312-553-1586

Michael J. Merlo
Martin A. Kanofsky
Alan J. Brinkmeier
Michael R. Gregg
Linda J. Schneider

David G. Boyer
John D. Dalton
Sarah DiLorenzo
Michael J. Gilmartin
Molly A. Horrigan
Donald G. Machalinski
Anne M. O'Brien
Ross D. Roloff
Mark H. Shanberg
Sandra J. Weber
David R. Zeigler

For full biographical listings, see the Martindale-Hubbell Law Directory

QUINLAN & CRISHAM, LTD. (AV)

30 North La Salle Street, Suite 2900, 60602
Telephone: 312-263-0900
Telecopier: 312-263-5013

(See Next Column)

QUINLAN & CRISHAM LTD.—*Continued*

William R. Quinlan
Thomas M. Crisham
Thomas C. Hynes
Gino L. DiVito
Mary Patricia Benz
Michael C. Bruck
James R. Carroll
Thomas C. Hofbauer
John F. Kennedy
Jeffrey T. Kubes
Eugene E. Murphy, Jr.
Michael I Rothstein
Caesar A. Tabet
Cheryl I. Niro

Frank M. Adams, Jr.
Brian J. Alesia
Michael T. Beirne
Catherine J. Casey
Jasmine De La Torre
Karina H. DeHayes
Edward Fitzsimmons Dunne
Lisa M. Hegedus
Erin Bolan Hines
John N. Hourihane, Jr.
David M. Jenkins
J. Christopher Madden
Michelle A. Michalik
James A. Niewiara
Martin J. O'Hara
John P. O'Malley
J. Jeffrey Patton
Jean M. Prendergast
Melissa M. Riahei
John H. Scheid
Daniel L. Stanner
Michael A. Steigmann

For full biographical listings, see the Martindale-Hubbell Law Directory

RUSIN PATTON MACIOROWSKI & FRIEDMAN, LTD. (AV)

Suite 1530 10 South Riverside Plaza, 60606
Telephone: 312-454-5110
Fax: 312-454-6166
Urbana, Illinois Office: 301 West Green Street, P.O. Box 985, 61803-0985.
Telephone: 217-328-7091.
Fax: 217-328-7093.

Michael E. Rusin
Stephen J. Friedman
John W. Patton Jr.
John A. Maciorowski
Kenneth N. Marshall
Gregory G. Vacala
Daniel Arkin
Randall R. Stark

Anuradha Y Boyapati
Todd A. Bresney
Luke A. Casson
R. Mark Cosimini (Resident, Urbana Office)
Daniel R. Egan
Frederick Scott Glassman
William J. Harrington
Daniel P. Johnston
David M. Lewin
Theodore James Powers
Gregory A. Rode
Mark P. Rusin
David F. Ryan
Douglas Sullivan
Edward R. Tomkowiak
Cynthia M. Wallach
Catherine A. Zaryczny

For full biographical listings, see the Martindale-Hubbell Law Directory

SCARIANO, ELLCH, HIMES, SRAGA AND PETRARCA, CHARTERED (AV)

Two Prudential Plaza 180 North Stetson Suite 3100, 60601-6224
Telephone: 312-565-3100
Facsimile: 312-565-0000
Chicago Heights, Illinois Office: 1450 Aberdeen, 60411.
Telephone: 708-755-1900.
Facsimile: 708-755-0000.

Anthony G. Scariano
Robert H. Ellch
A. Lynn Himes
Alan T. Sraga
Justino D. Petrarca
Lawrence Jay Weiner
John M. Izzo
Raymond A. Hauser
Kathleen Roche Hirsman
Daniel M. Boyle
Teri E. Engler
Rosanne Ciambrone

Kelly A. Hayden
Todd K. Hayden
Christopher L. Petrarca
Sarah E. Joyce
Joel R. DeTella
Susan H. Walter (Resident)
Brian J. Fahey
David A. Harley
Bradley C. Coleman
Christina Sepiol
Alan M. Mullins
John E. Fester
Michael Alan DeBartolo

OF COUNSEL

John Kralovec

For full biographical listings, see the Martindale-Hubbell Law Directory

STONE & MOORE, CHARTERED (AV)

30 North La Salle Street, Suite 4300, 60602
Telephone: 312-332-5656
Fax: 312-332-5858
URL: http://www.stonemoore.com
Merrillville, Indiana Office: 500 E. 86th Avenue, 46410.
Telephone: 219-736-5959.
Fax: 219-736-5858.
Wheaton, Illinois Office: 600 W. Roosevelt Road, Suite 1A, 60187.
Telephone: 630-221-9292.
Fax: 630-221-9393.

(See Next Column)

William G. Stone
Robert Charles Moore (Also at Wheaton, Illinois Office)
Raymond R. Pesavento
Rosario Cibella
Richard M. Johnson, Jr.
J. Murray Pinkston, III
Julie Osswald Hooven

Christian D. Ambler
Jeffrey W. Henning
Erica Lewis Battaglia
Kevin Kemp Lyons
Kristin E. Rooney
Daniel S. Schulz
Matthew B. Stephens
A. Christine Svenson
Douglas W. Walker

For full biographical listings, see the Martindale-Hubbell Law Directory

SUDEKUM, ROSENBERG & CASSIDY, CHARTERED (AV)

30 West Monroe Street Suite 1450, 60603-2404
Telephone: 312-803-6250
Fax: 312-803-6260
Merrillville, Indiana Office: 1000 E. 80th Place, Suite 5055; 46410.
Telephone: 219-736-7500.
Fax: 219-736-1442.

Frederick J. Sudekum, III
Harry B. Rosenberg, Jr.
John C. Cassidy
Albert S. DeVito
Lawrence Shulruff
Florence M. Hackman
Thomas W. Hargrove

OF COUNSEL

Barbara Turotsy

For full biographical listings, see the Martindale-Hubbell Law Directory

TAYLOR, MILLER, SPROWL, HOFFNAGLE & MERLETTI (AV)

33 North La Salle Street, Suite 2222, 60602-2691
Telephone: 312-782-6070
Fax: 312-782-6081
Wheaton, Illinois Office: 620 West Roosevelt Road, 60187.
Telephone: 630-665-0178.
Fax: 630-682-3690.

Orville Taylor (1885-1969)
John S. Miller (1888-1965)
Roger A. Merletti (1927-1998)
Ralph W. F. Lustgarten
Richard W. Oloffson
Frank C. Stevens
Robert W. Rohm

OF COUNSEL

Charles R. Sprowl
James J. Hoffnagle

ASSOCIATES

John R. Adams
Jack Bruce Batten
Andrew Anthony Boros
Hugh J. Doyle
Daniel K. Fritz
Adam Keith Hanna
Charlotte S. Kormendy
Christina L. Mack

For full biographical listings, see the Martindale-Hubbell Law Directory

TRIBLER ORPETT & CRONE, A PROFESSIONAL CORPORATION (AV)

30 North La Salle Street, Suite 2200, 60602
Telephone: 312-201-6400
Fax: 312-201-6401
Email: to&c@tribler.com *URL:* http://www.tribler.com

John W. Carver
Douglas C. Crone
Steven R. McMannon
Michael J. Meyer
Mitchell A. Orpett
H. Wesley Sunu
Panos T. Topalis
Willis R. Tribler

Angela Coumas
Michael W. Donaubauer
David R. Edsey
Ana M. McNamara
Kevin A. Titus
William Yu

OF COUNSEL

Daniel D. Drew

For full biographical listings, see the Martindale-Hubbell Law Directory

WILDMAN, HARROLD, ALLEN & DIXON (AV)

225 West Wacker Drive, 30th Floor, 60606-1229
Telephone: 312-201-2000
Fax: 312-201-2555
Email: hennessy@whad.com *URL:* http://www.whad.com
Aurora, Illinois Office: 1961 W. Downer Place.
Telephone: 630-892-7021.
Fax: 630-892-7158.
Waukegan, Illinois Office: 404 West Water, P. O. Box 890.
Telephone: 847-625-5550.
Fax: 847-625-5555.
Lisle, Illinois Office: 4300 Commerce Court, Suite 320.
Telephone: 630-955-0555.
Fax: 630-955-0662

(See Next Column)

Wildman, Harrold, Allen & Dixon, *Chicago—Continued*

Toronto, Ontario correspondent Office: Keel Cottrelle. 36 Toronto Street, Suite 920.
Telephone: 416-367-2900.
Telefax: 416-367-2791.
Telex: 062-18660.

MEMBERS OF FIRM

Cal R. Burnton
Leland H. Chait
Anthony G. Hopp
Steven L. Larson (Waukegan Office)
Douglas L. Prochnow

OF COUNSEL

Bernard Harrold
Lee B. McClain

Kenneth M. Gorenberg
Michone J. Kuhlman (Waukegan Office)
Kevin B. Reid

Representative Clients: Illinois State Medical Insurance Services, Inc.; United States Aviation Underwriters; Crawford and Co.; General Casualty Co.; CIGNA Companies; Interstate Insurance Group; CNA; Illinois Provider Trust; The Doctors Company; The Travelers Cos.

For full biographical listings, see the Martindale-Hubbell Law Directory

Worker & Power (AV)

55 East Monroe Suite 4550, 60603
Telephone: 312-345-1718
Fax: 312-345-1778
Email: worker@starnetusa.com *URL:* http://www.workerandpower.com

Danny L. Worker
John M. Power
Kevin J. Glenn
Mary F. Sitko
Kimberly A. Wilkins
Miguel A. Ruiz

ASSOCIATES

Nancy S. Miller
Laura A. Caldwell
Matthew J. Ligda
Margaret M. O'Connell
Jennifer L. Green

OF COUNSEL

Gary W. Leydig
J. Timothy Lovett

For full biographical listings, see the Martindale-Hubbell Law Directory

Yelton & Kehl, Ltd. (AV)

One East Wacker Drive Suite 3720, 60601
Telephone: 312-832-9255
Fax: 312-832-9277
URL: http://www.yeltonkehl.com

Robert C. Yelton III
Jeffrey Edward Kehl

Ryan J. Harrington
Karen M. Talty

OF COUNSEL

Joel S. Ostrow

For full biographical listings, see the Martindale-Hubbell Law Directory

COLLINSVILLE, Madison Co.

Dunham, Boman & Leskera (AV)

300 West Clay Street, 62234
Telephone: 618-344-7734
Telecopier: 618-344-3853
Belleville Office: 208 N. High.
Telephone: 618-235-7222.
Telecopier: 618-236-2800; 618-236-1899.

John W. Leskera
William L. Berry
Eric C. Young
Robert D. Francis
John L. Bitzer

Attorneys for: Collinsville School District #10; Hanover Insurance Co.; Hartford Insurance Group; State Farm Insurance Cos.; Transamerica Insurance Group; The Travelers Indemnity Co.; Wausau Insurance Cos.; Nationwide Insurance Co.

For full biographical listings, see the Martindale-Hubbell Law Directory

*DANVILLE,** Vermilion Co.

Hutton, Laury, Young & Lietz (AV)

16 West Madison Street, P.O. Box 1128, 61832
Telephone: 217-446-9436
FAX: 217-446-9462

MEMBERS OF FIRM

Everett L. Laury
Frank R. Young
Gregory G. Lietz

Representative Clients: Employers Reinsurance Corporation; Pro National Insurance Company; Kentucky National Insurance Company; Pekin Insurance Company; Illinois State Medical Insurance Services, Inc.; Sentry Insurance; Rockford Mutual Insurance Company; Frankenmuth Mutual Insurance Company; Cumis Insurance Society; The Equitable Life Assurance Society.

For Complete List of Firm Personnel, See General Section

For full biographical listings, see the Martindale-Hubbell Law Directory

*DECATUR,** Macon Co.

Erickson, Davis, Murphy, Johnson, Griffith & Walsh, Ltd. (AV)

225 South Main Street, P.O. Box 25138, 62525-5138
Telephone: 217-428-0948
Fax: 217-428-0996
Email: lawyer@law225.com

Wayne E. Armstrong (1916-1977)
Frederick P. Erickson
Garry E. Davis
W. Scott Murphy
Evan H. Johnson
Thomas E. Griffith
Michael A. Walsh

Robert C. Bollinger
David T. Tanner

Representative Clients: A.E. Staley Manufacturing Company; Archer Daniels Midland Company; Cincinnati Insurance Company; Country Mutual Insurance Company; General Casualty Insurance Companies; Illinois Power Company; Illinois State Medical Insurance Exchange; Millikin University; Reliance Insurance Company; St. Paul Insurance Co.; State Farm Insurance Co.; Western States Insurance Company.

For full biographical listings, see the Martindale-Hubbell Law Directory

Kehart, Shafter & Webber, P.C. (AV)

One Main Place, 101 South Main Street, Suite 200, P.O. Box 860, 62525-0860
Telephone: 217-428-4689
Telecopier: 217-422-7950
Email: kswlaw@fgi.net

Michael J. Kehart
A. James Shafter
Albert G. Webber IV
Mark D. Gibson
James E. Peckert
Heidi R. Balsley
Julie C. Keller

OF COUNSEL

Albert G. Webber III
T. G. Bolen

Representative Clients: Aetna Casualty & Surety Co.; AIG - American International Group; American States Insurance Co.; GAB Business Services, Inc.; Countrywide Services Corp.; Illinois State Medical Insurance Services; American Continental Insurance Co. - MMI Companies.; Fireman's Fund.

For full biographical listings, see the Martindale-Hubbell Law Directory

Winters, Featherstun, Gaumer, Kenney, Postlewait & Stocks (AV)

225 N. Water Street, Suite 200, P.O. Box 1760, 62525-1760
Telephone: 217-429-4453; 429-5213
Telecopier: 217-425-8892
Email: wfgkps@fgi.net

MEMBERS OF FIRM

Robert P. Vail (1877-1964)
Walker H. Mills (1893-1962)
Thos. H. Armstrong (1897-1981)
Roswell C. Prince (1919-1994)
Robert D. Winters
Glen A. Featherstun
Daniel L. Gaumer
Frederic Lee Kenney
R. Samuel Postlewait
Jerrold H. Stocks

ASSOCIATE

Joseph N. Van Vooren

Representative Clients: Allstate Insurance Co.; Bridgestone/Firestone, Inc.; USF&G Co.; CIGNA; The Cincinnati Insurance Co.; Brotherhood Mutual Insurance Co.; Pelein Insurance Co.; Archer-Daniels-Midland Co.; Northland Insurance Cos.; Employers Mutual Cos.

For full biographical listings, see the Martindale-Hubbell Law Directory

*EDWARDSVILLE,** Madison Co.

Heyl, Royster, Voelker & Allen, Professional Corporation (AV)

Suite 100, Mark Twain Plaza II, 103 West Vandalia Street, P.O. Box 467, 62025
Telephone: 618-656-4646
Telecopier: 618-656-7940
Peoria, Illinois Office: Suite 600, Bank One Building, 124 S.W. Adams, 61602.
Telephone: 309-676-0400.
Telecopier: 309-676-3374.
Springfield, Illinois Office: Suite 575, First of America Center, P.O. Box 1687, 62705.
Telephone: 217-522-8822.
Telecopier: 217-523-3902.

(See Next Column)

HEYL, ROYSTER, VOELKER & ALLEN PROFESSIONAL CORPORATION—*Continued*

Urbana, Illinois Office: Suite 300, 102 East Main Street, P.O. Box 129, 61801.
Telephone: 217-344-0060.
Telecopier: 217-344-9295.
Rockford, Illinois Office: Suite 1015, Talcott Building, P.O. Box 1288, 61105.
Telephone: 815-963-4454.
Telecopier: 815-963-0399.

RESIDENT PERSONNEL

Robert H. Shultz, Jr. | Kent L. Plotner
John A. Ess | Robert D. Rowland

RESIDENT OF COUNSEL

William J. Becker | Edward E. Johnston

Christine M. McClimans | Joseph P. Whyte
James A. Telthorst | Robert G. Jones
Jennifer B. Johnson

For full biographical listings, see the Martindale-Hubbell Law Directory

REED, ARMSTRONG, GORMAN, COFFEY, GILBERT & MUDGE, PROFESSIONAL CORPORATION (AV)

One Mark Twain Plaza, Suite 300, P.O. Box 368, 62025
Telephone: 618-656-0257
Facsimile: 618-692-4416
Email: reed@ezl.com
Other Edwardsville Office: 125 North Buchanan, P.O. Box 247.
Telephone: 618-656-2244.
Fax: 618-658-1307.

Harry C. Armstrong | Martin K. Morrissey
James E. Gorman | Michael J. Bedesky
Stephen C. Mudge | David Laurent

Bryan L. Skelton | Katherine M. Smith
Ronald D. Robinson | Tara Inlow English

Representative Clients: State Farm Insurance Cos.; Country Companies; Standard Mutual Casualty Co.; General Casualty Co. of Wisconsin; Lloyds of London; Hawkeye Security Insurance Co.; Shelter Insurance Companies; Pekin Insurance Cos.; American International Adjusting Co.; Employers Reinsurance Corp.

For full biographical listings, see the Martindale-Hubbell Law Directory

THOMSON LAW OFFICE (AV)

A Professional Corporation
1 Sunset Hill Professional Centre Suite B, P.O. Box 538, 62025
Telephone: 618-692-0028
Telecopier: 618-692-0269
Email: firminfo@thomsonlaw.com
Springfield, Illinois Office: 1920 South Spring Street, 62703.
Telephone: 217-522-3620.
Facsimile: 217-525-6557.

Stephen W. Thomson

Danya L. Johnson | Brian L. Gifford

For full biographical listings, see the Martindale-Hubbell Law Directory

*HARRISBURG,** Saline Co.

JELLIFFE, FERRELL, MORRIS, DOERGE & FOSTER (AV)

108 East Walnut Street, P.O. Box 406, 62946
Telephone: 618-253-7153; 253-7647
Telecopier: 618-252-1843

OF COUNSEL

Charles R. Jelliffe

MEMBERS OF FIRM

DeWitt Twente (1904-1976) | Walden E. Morris
Donald V. Ferrell | Michal Doerge
Thomas J. Foster

Representative Clients: Auto-Owners Insurance; Country Cos; Metropolitan Life Insurance; Ohio Casualty Group; Standard Mutual Insurance Co.; State Farm Cos.; Aetna Casualty & Surety Co.; Sahara Coal Co.

For full biographical listings, see the Martindale-Hubbell Law Directory

*JACKSONVILLE,** Morgan Co.

RAMMELKAMP, BRADNEY, KUSTER, KEATON, FRITSCHE & LINDSAY, P.C. (AV)

232 West State Street, P.O. Box 550, 62651
Telephone: 217-245-6177
Fax: 217-243-7322
Email: ramlkamp@fgi.net

(See Next Column)

L.O. Vaught (1865-1955) | Larry D. Kuster
Carl E. Robinson (1886-1964) | Forrest G. Keaton
Orville N. Foreman (1904-1972) | Barbara Fritsche
Albert W. Hall (1912-1986) | Nancy Lindsay
Theodore C. Rammelkamp (Retired) | Maria M. Gonzalez
Richard R. Freeman
H. Allen Yow

Bradley W. Wilson

OF COUNSEL

Robert E. Bradney

Representative Clients: American States/Safeco; Auto Owners Insurance; Country Mutual Insurance; Federated Insurance; General Casualty; Grinnell Mutual Insurance; Pekin Insurance Company; State Auto of Ohio; State Farm Mutual Auto Ins.; St. Paul Fire & Casualty.

For full biographical listings, see the Martindale-Hubbell Law Directory

*KANKAKEE,** Kankakee Co.

ACKMAN, MAREK & BOYD, LTD. (AV)

Suite 400, One Dearborn Square, 60901
Telephone: 815-933-6681
Email: marek1@netcom.net
Watseka, Illinois Office: 223 East Mulberry Street.
Telephone: 815-432-5215.

Richard L. Ackman | Robert W. Boyd
J. Dennis Marek | John J. Boyd

James A. Devine | Dana M. Meyer

Representative Clients: American States Insurance Co.; Auto Owners Insurance Co.; Bituminous Insurance Co.; Consumers Illinois Water Co.; Country Mutual Insurance Co.; EMCASCO; Farmers Insurance Group; Grinnell Mutual Insurance Company; Martin Boyer Co. Inc.; Medical Protective Co.; Union Insurance Co.; Watseka First National Bank; Western States Insurance Company.

For full biographical listings, see the Martindale-Hubbell Law Directory

LA SALLE, La Salle Co.

HERBOLSHEIMER, LANNON, HENSON, DUNCAN AND REAGAN, P.C. (AV)

State Bank Building, Suite 400, 654 First Street, P.O. Box 539, 61301
Telephone: 815-223-0111
Fax: 815-223-5829
Ottawa, Illinois Office: First Federal Savings Bank Building, 633 LaSalle Street, Suite 409.
Telephone: 815-434-1400.
Fax: 815-434-2423.

George L. Herbolsheimer (1911-1992) | John S. Duncan, III
R. James Lannon, Jr. | Michael T. Reagan (Resident, Ottawa Office)
T. Donald Henson | Douglas A. Gift
Gary R. Eiten

Karen C. Eiten | Jill W. Klein
Michael C. Jansz (Resident, Ottawa Office) | Lawrence M. Kaschak

Attorneys for: Aetna Insurance Group; St. Paul Fire and Marine Insurance Co.; State Farm Insurance Co.; The La Salle National Bank; La Salle State Bank; The Daily News Tribune Company, La Salle; Eureka Savings and Loan Assn.; Illinois Valley Community Hospital; Community Hospital of Ottawa; Commonwealth Edison, Co.

For full biographical listings, see the Martindale-Hubbell Law Directory

*MARION,** Williamson Co.

MITCHELL, MITCHELL & BRADLEY (AV)

404 North Monroe, P.O. Box 488, 62959-2328
Telephone: 618-993-2134
Telecopier: 618-993-8702
Email: mmb@midwest.net *URL:* http://www.lawyers.com/mmb

J. C. Mitchell | Bruce W. Mitchell
John E. Bradley

OF COUNSEL

James E. Hopkins

Representative Clients: St. Paul Fire & Casualty Insurance Company; Liberty Mutual Insurance Company; Shelter Insurance Company; Claims Management, Inc.; Kemper Insurance; Walmart Stores, Inc.; Horace Mann Inc.; Preferred Risk Group; Waite Hill Insurance Company.

For full biographical listings, see the Martindale-Hubbell Law Directory

*MOUNT VERNON,** Jefferson Co.

CAMPBELL, BLACK, CARNINE, HEDIN, BALLARD & McDONALD, P.C. (AV)

P.O. Drawer C, 62864
Telephone: 618-242-3310
Fax: 618-242-3735
Email: cbch@midwest.net *URL:* http://www.cbch.com

David A. Campbell
Terry R. Black
Roy L. Carnine
Craig R. Hedin
Mark J. Ballard
Jerome E. McDonald
Howard W. Campbell (1911-1980)
John E. Jacobsen (1922-1985)
Glenn E. Moore (1911-1991)
David E. Furnall (1905-1993)

Fred R. Mann
Charles L.P. Flynn
Matthew K. Wollin
Aaron S. Carnine

Representative Clients: Country Mutual Insurance Co.; Illinois State Medical Insurance Services; State Farm Automobile Insurance Co.; John Hancock Mutual Life Insurance Co.; Kemper Insurance Co.; Travelers Insurance Co.; Allstate Insurance Co.; Illinois Founders Insurance Co.; Pekin Insurance Co.; St. Paul Insurance Co.

For full biographical listings, see the Martindale-Hubbell Law Directory

*OTTAWA,** La Salle Co.

MYERS, DAUGHERITY, BERRY, O'CONOR & KUZMA, LTD. (AV)

130 East Madison Street, 61350
Telephone: 815-434-6206
Fax: 815-434-6203
Email: mdboc@TheRamp.net
Streator, Illinois Office: 7 Northpoint Drive.
Telephone: 815-672-3116.
Fax: 815-672-0738.

John A. Berry (1912-1986)
Andrew J. O'Conor (1919-1998)
Stephen C. Myers
Eugene P. Daugherity
Richard J. Berry
Sheryl H. Kuzma

Representative Clients: Auto Owners Insurance, Co.; Union Bank; First National Bank of Ottawa, Illinois; Union Bancorp Inc.; First State Bank; First Midwest Bank; Allied Ins. Group; St. Mary's Hospital; General Casualty Insurance, Co.

For full biographical listings, see the Martindale-Hubbell Law Directory

*PEORIA,** Peoria Co.

CASSIDY & MUELLER (AV)

323 Commerce Bank Building, 416 Main Street, 61602
Telephone: 309-676-0591
Fax: 309-676-8036

MEMBERS OF FIRM

John E. Cassidy (1896-1984)
John E. Cassidy, Jr.
David B. Mueller
John E. Cassidy, III
Timothy J. Cassidy
Andrew D. Cassidy
Christopher F. Cassidy
Timothy J. Cusack
Michael W. Powell
John D. Moses
Robert M. McBride

Representative Clients: Aetna Casualty & Surety Co.; Atchison, Topeka & Santa Fe Railroad Co.; Chicago Motor Club Ins. Co.; Continental Oil Company; E.I. DuPont-DeNemours & Company; Hartford Accident & Indemnity Company; Illinois-American Water Company; Lake States Insurance Company; John P. Pearl & Associates, Ltd.; Liberty Mutual Insurance Co.

For full biographical listings, see the Martindale-Hubbell Law Directory

HEYL, ROYSTER, VOELKER & ALLEN, PROFESSIONAL CORPORATION (AV)

Suite 600, Bank One Building, 124 S.W. Adams, 61602
Telephone: 309-676-0400
Telecopier: 309-676-3374
Email: firm@hrva.com *URL:* http://www.hrva.com
Springfield, Illinois Office: Suite 575, First of America Center, P.O. Box 1687, 62705.
Telephone: 217-522-8822.
Telecopier: 217-523-3902.
Urbana, Illinois Office: Suite 300, 102 East Main Street, P.O. Box 129, 61801.
Telephone: 217-344-0060.
Telecopier: 217-344-9295.
Rockford, Illinois Office: Suite 1015, Talcott Building, P.O. Box 1288, 61105.
Telephone: 815-963-4454.
Telecopier: 815-963-0399.
Edwardsville, Illinois Office: Suite 100, Mark Twain Plaza II, 103 West Vandalia Street, P.O. Box 467, 62025.
Telephone: 618-656-4646.
Telecopier: 618-656-7940.

(See Next Column)

Clarence W. Heyl (1884-1968)
John H. Royster (1907-1985)
William J. Voelker, Jr. (1917-1993)
Lyle W. Allen (Of Counsel)
Richard N. Molchan (Of Counsel)
Gary M. Peplow (Of Counsel)
Robert V. Dewey, Jr. (Managing Partner)
Duncan B. Cooper III
Brent H. Gwillim
Rex K. Linder
Timothy L. Bertschy
Gary D. Nelson
David R. Sinn
Roger R. Clayton
Bradford B. Ingram
Stephen J. Heine
Karen L. Kendall
Craig S. Young
Nicholas J. Bertschy
William I. Covey
Christopher P. Larson
James M. Voelker
Joseph G. Feehan
Matthew S. Hefflefinger
David A. Perkins
Lisa A. LaConte
Brad A. Elward

RESIDENT OF COUNSEL

Timothy W. Kirk
John C. Mulgrew, Jr.
Debra Allard

Craig L. Unrath
James J. Manning
Mark D. Hansen
Patricia M. Gibson
Tobin J. Taylor
Mark A. Ludolph

For full biographical listings, see the Martindale-Hubbell Law Directory

NICOARA & STEAGALL (AV)

Commerce Bank Building, 416 Main Street, Suite 815, 61602-1103
Telephone: 309-674-6085
Fax: 309-674-6032
Email: 70754.3140@compuserve.com

MEMBERS OF FIRM

John P. Nicoara
Richard L. Steagall

Representative Clients: Farmers Insurance Group; Illinois Founders Insurance Co.; Ohio Casualty Group; Southeastern Aviation Underwriters.
Reference: Commerce Bank.

For full biographical listings, see the Martindale-Hubbell Law Directory

*QUINCY,** Adams Co.

BRENNAN & BARNARD (AV)

314 North Sixth Street, 62301
Telephone: 217-223-6000
Fax: 217-223-6072
Email: bb@bcl.net

MEMBERS OF FIRM

Jerry L. Brennan
Jonathan H. Barnard
Babette L. Brennan

For full biographical listings, see the Martindale-Hubbell Law Directory

*ROCKFORD,** Winnebago Co.

HEYL, ROYSTER, VOELKER & ALLEN, PROFESSIONAL CORPORATION (AV)

Suite 1015, Talcott Building, P.O. Box 1288, 61105
Telephone: 815-963-4454
Telecopier: 815-963-0399
Peoria, Illinois Office: Suite 600, Bank One Building, 124 S.W. Adams, 61602.
Telephone: 309-676-0400.
Telecopier: 309-676-3374.
Springfield, Illinois Office: Suite 575, First Of America Center, P.O. Box 1687, 62705.
Telephone: 217-522-8822.
Telecopier: 217-523-3902.
Urbana, Illinois Office: Suite 300, 102 East Main Street, P.O. Box 129, 61801.
Telephone: 217-344-0060.
Telecopier: 217-344-9295.
Edwardsville, Illinois Office: Suite 100, Mark Twain Plaza II, 103 West Vandalia Street, P.O. Box 467, 62025.
Telephone: 618-656-4646.
Telecopier: 618-656-7940.

RESIDENT PERSONNEL

Douglas J. Pomatto
Kevin J. Luther
Richard K. Hunsaker
Mark J. McClenathan
Charles D. McCann

Susan M. Witt
William W. Ranard
Matthew S. Morrison
Ronald D. Fiet
Keith E. Edeus, Jr.

For full biographical listings, see the Martindale-Hubbell Law Directory

*SPRINGFIELD,** Sangamon Co.

GIFFIN, WINNING, COHEN & BODEWES, P.C. (AV)

1 West Old State Capitol Plaza, Suite 600 Myers Building, P.O. Box 2117, 62705
Telephone: 217-525-1571
Facsimile: 217-525-1710
Email: gifwinlaw@eosinc.com

Carol Hansen Posegate
R. Mark Mifflin
Thomas P. Schanzle-Haskins, III
Gregory K. Harris

Representative Clients: Illinois State University Board of Trustees; Auto Owners Insurance Co.; Grinnell Mutual Reinsurance Company; Horace Mann Insurance Company; Great Central Insurance Cos.; Standard Mutual Insurance Co.; Transamerica Insurance Company; Associated Beer Distributors of Illinois Risk Management Association.

For Complete List of Firm Personnel, See General Section

For full biographical listings, see the Martindale-Hubbell Law Directory

HEYL, ROYSTER, VOELKER & ALLEN, PROFESSIONAL CORPORATION (AV)

Suite 575, First of America Center, P.O. Box 1687, 62705
Telephone: 217-522-8822
Telecopier: 217-523-3902
Peoria, Illinois Office: Suite 600, Bank One Building, 124 S.W. Adams, 61602.
Telephone: 309-676-0400.
Telecopier: 309-676-3374.
Urbana, Illinois Office: Suite 300, 102 East Main Street, P.O. Box 129, 61801.
Telephone: 217-344-0060.
Telecopier: 217-344-9295.
Rockford, Illinois Office: Suite 1015, Talcott Building, P.O. Box 1288, 61105.
Telephone: 815-963-4454.
Telecopier: 815-963-0399.
Edwardsville, Illinois Office: Suite 100, Mark Twain Plaza II, 103 West Vandalia Street, P.O. Box 467, 62025.
Telephone: 618-656-4646.
Telecopier: 618-656-7940.

RESIDENT PERSONNEL

Frederick P. Velde
Gary L. Borah
Gary S. Schwab
Adrian E. Harless
Scott D. Spooner
Daniel R. Simmons
Patrick J. Londrigan
Kurt M. Koepke

RESIDENT OF COUNSEL

James T. Dougherty (Resident)

Susan Hoffee-Hunt
Theresa M. Powell
Lori Poppe Hiltabrand

For full biographical listings, see the Martindale-Hubbell Law Directory

*URBANA,** Champaign Co.

HEYL, ROYSTER, VOELKER & ALLEN, PROFESSIONAL CORPORATION (AV)

Suite 300, 102 East Main Street, P.O. Box 129, 61801
Telephone: 217-344-0060
Telecopier: 217-344-9295
Peoria, Illinois Office: Suite 600, Bank One Building, 124 S.W. Adams, 61602.
Telephone: 309-676-0400.
Telecopier: 309-676-3374.
Springfield, Illinois Office: Suite 575, First Of America Center, P.O. Box 1687, 62705.
Telephone: 217-522-8822.
Telecopier: 217-523-3902.
Rockford, Illinois Office: Suite 1015, Talcott Building, P.O. Box 1288, 61105.
Telephone: 815-963-4454.
Telecopier: 815-963-0399.
Edwardsville, Illinois Office: Suite 100, Mark Twain Plaza II, 103 West Vandalia Street, P.O. Box 467, 62025.
Telephone: 618-656-4646.
Telecopier: 618-656-7940.

RESIDENT PERSONNEL

James C. Kearns
Edward M. Wagner
Michael E. Raub
Bruce L. Bonds
John D. Flodstrom
Bradford J. Peterson

OF COUNSEL

Daniel S. Hall (Resident)
Richard P. Klaus (Resident)

Elaine Massock
Toney J. Tomaso
Keith E. Fruehling
Jay E. Znaniecki

For full biographical listings, see the Martindale-Hubbell Law Directory

*WHEATON,** DuPage Co.

NORTON, MANCINI, ARGENTATI, WEILER & DEANO (AV)

109 North Hale Street, P.O. Box 846, 60189-0846
Telephone: 630-668-9440
Fax: 630-668-9489
Chicago, Illinois Office: 111 West Washington Street, Suite 835.
Telephone: 312-807-4999.
Fax: 312-807-4998.

John E. Norton
Lorenzo A. Mancini
Patricia L. Argentati
Thomas R. Weiler
James L. DeAno
Thomas J. Long

Denis K. Sheehan
W. Mark Sickles
Dawn C. Didier
W. Anthony Andrews
Christopher J. May
Scott D. Braun
Melissa M. Tomaska
Paul E. Brady

OF COUNSEL

Adrianna K. Liber

Representative Clients: Aetna Life & Casualty; Allstate Insurance Company; Chicago Motor Club Insurance Company; County of DuPage; Frontier Insurance Co.; CNA Insurance Company; Hartford Insurance Company; Illinois State Medical Insurance Services, Inc.; St. Paul Insurance Company; Wausau Insurance Companies.

For full biographical listings, see the Martindale-Hubbell Law Directory

INDIANA

*BLOOMINGTON,** Monroe Co.

BUNGER & ROBERTSON (AV)

226 South College Square, P.O. Box 910, 47402-0910
Telephone: 812-332-9295
Fax: 812-331-8808
Email: bunrob@iquest.net

MEMBERS OF FIRM

Don M Robertson
Joseph D. O'Connor
James L. Whitlatch
Samuel R. Ardery
William J. Beggs
John W. Richards

Representative Clients: Aetna Insurance Companies; Bloomington Hospital; Commercial Union Group; Indiana Insurance Co.; Liberty Mutual Insurance; Medical Protective Co.; Monroe County Community School Corp.; Professional Golf Car, Inc.; Prudential Insurance Company of America; State Farm Automobile Insurance Co.

For Complete List of Firm Personnel, See General Section

For full biographical listings, see the Martindale-Hubbell Law Directory

KELLEY, BELCHER & BROWN, A PROFESSIONAL CORPORATION (AV)

301 West Seventh Street, P.O. Box 3250, 47402-3250
Telephone: 812-336-9963
Telecopier: 812-336-4588

William H. Kelley
Thomas J. Belcher
Darla Sue Brown

Shannon L. Robinson
Kyle M. Baker
Michael W. Phelps

For full biographical listings, see the Martindale-Hubbell Law Directory

MILLER CARSON BOXBERGER & MURPHY, LLP (AV)

3100 John Hinkle Place, Suite 106, 47408
Telephone: 812-333-1225
Fax: 812-333-1925
Email: mcbm@kiva.net
Fort Wayne, Indiana Office: 1400 One Summit Square.
Telephone: 219-423-9411.
Telecopier: 219-423-4329. Email: counsel@mcbm.com.

MEMBERS OF FIRM

Edward J. Liptak
Douglas A. Hoffman

ASSOCIATE

Jason E. Salerno (Resident, Bloomington Office)

Representative Insurance Clients: Allstate Insurance Company; Bliss-McKnight Group; CIGNA Companies; Crum & Forster Commercial Insurance Companies; Employers Mutual of Wausau; General Accident Fire & Life Assurance Corp., LTD; Liberty Mutual Insurance Co.; Safeco/American States Insurance Co.; The Medical Protective Company; Universal Underwriters.

For full biographical listings, see the Martindale-Hubbell Law Directory

*COLUMBUS,** Bartholomew Co.

SHARPNACK, BIGLEY, DAVID & RUMPLE (AV)

321 Washington Street, P.O. Box 310, 47202-0310
Telephone: 812-372-1553
Fax: 812-372-1567
Email: sbdr@hsonline.net

MEMBERS OF FIRM

Thomas C. Bigley, Jr.
John A. Stroh
Timothy J. Vrana
Joan Tupin Crites

Representative Clients: State Farm Mutual Insurance Cos.; GRE Insurance Group; Indiana Farmers Insurance; Prudential Ins. Co.; Auto Owner Insurance Co.

For Complete List of Firm Personnel, See General Section

For full biographical listings, see the Martindale-Hubbell Law Directory

*EVANSVILLE,** Vanderburgh Co.

FINE & HATFIELD, A PROFESSIONAL CORPORATION (AV)

520 N.W. Second Street, P.O. Box 779, 47705-0779
Telephone: 812-425-3592
Telecopier: 812-421-4269
Email: Fine@Fine-Hatfield.com *URL:* http://www.Fine-Hatfield.com

Thomas H. Bryan
Todd I. Glass
Danny E. Glass
Elaine Brown Elliott

H. Linwood Shannon, III
Boyd A. Toler
Laura L. Pamplin

A List of Representative Clients Furnished Upon Request.

For full biographical listings, see the Martindale-Hubbell Law Directory

KAHN, DEES, DONOVAN & KAHN, LLP (AV)

Fifth Main Financial Plaza, Suite 305, P.O. Box 3646, 47735-3646
Telephone: 812-423-3183
Fax: 812-423-3841
Email: evvlaw@k2d2.com

MEMBERS OF FIRM

Jeffrey W. Ahlers
Christopher D. Lee

ASSOCIATES

Mark A. McAnulty
Jason H. Guthrie
Steven S. Hoar
Todd C. Barsumian
Lee F. Baker

Representative Clients: United States Fidelity & Guaranty Insurance Co.; United Farm Bureau Mutual of Indiana; I.T.T. Hartford Insurance Co.; American Family Insurance Co.; CIGNA Insurance Co.; CNA Insurance Co.; Chubb Insurance; United Services Automobile Association; Shelby Insurance Company; Hastings Mutual Insurance Company.

For Complete List of Firm Personnel, See General Section

For full biographical listings, see the Martindale-Hubbell Law Directory

RUDOLPH, FINE, PORTER & JOHNSON LLP (AV)

221 N.W. Fifth Street, Second Floor, P.O. Box 1507, 47706
Telephone: 812-422-9444
Fax: 812-421-7459
URL: http://www.rfpj@rfpj.com

MEMBERS OF FIRM

Ross E. Rudolph
James D. Johnson

ASSOCIATES

Jennifer L. Johnson
James A. Edgar

Reference: National City Bank of Evansville.

For full biographical listings, see the Martindale-Hubbell Law Directory

*FORT WAYNE,** Allen Co.

MILLER CARSON BOXBERGER & MURPHY, LLP (AV)

1400 One Summit Square, 46802-3137
Telephone: 219-423-9411
Telecopier: 219-423-4329
Email: counsel@mcbm.com
Bloomington, Indiana Office: 3100 John Hinkle Place, Suite 106.
Telephone: 812-333-1225.
Fax: 812-333-1925. E-mail: mcbm@kiva.net.

MEMBERS OF FIRM

Milford M. Miller, Jr.
Edward J. Liptak (Resident, Bloomington, Indiana Office)
Philip L. Carson
Bruce O. Boxberger
Robert T. Keen, Jr.
Edward L. Murphy, Jr.
Larry L. Barnard
Thomas W. Yoder
Arthur E. Mandelbaum
John J. Wernet
Diana C. Bauer
Richard P. Samek
James P. Buchholz
Phillip A. Renz
Douglas A. Hoffman (Resident, Bloomington Office)

(See Next Column)

ASSOCIATES

Karl J. Veracco
Monica S. Sandkuhler
M. Randall Spencer
Heidi K. Ellison
Stephen J. Harants
Tina M. Yordy
Timothy M. Pape
Jason E. Salerno (Resident, Bloomington Office)
Calvert S. Miller
Howard E. Green

Representative Clients: Allstate Insurance Company; Bliss-McKnight Group; CIGNA Companies; Crum & Forster Commercial Insurance Companies; General Accident Fire & Life Assurance Corp., LTD; Liberty Mutual Insurance Co.; Safeco/American States Insurance Co.; The Medical Protective Company; Universal Underwriters; Wausau Insurance Cos.

For full biographical listings, see the Martindale-Hubbell Law Directory

HAMMOND, Lake Co.

ABRAHAMSON, REED & ADLEY (AV)

200 Russell Street, 46320
Telephone: 219-937-1500
Fax: 219-937-3174

MEMBERS OF FIRM

Harold Abrahamson
Kenneth D. Reed
Michael C. Adley

ASSOCIATES

Scott R. Bilse
John P. Reed

References: Calumet National Bank, Hammond; Mercantile National Bank, Hammond.

For full biographical listings, see the Martindale-Hubbell Law Directory

*INDIANAPOLIS,** Marion Co.

JOHNSON SMITH PENCE & HEATH LLP (AV)

One Indiana Square Suite 1800, 46204
Telephone: 317-634-9777
Telecopier: 317-636-9061
Email: firm@jsplaw.com *URL:* http://www.jsplaw.com
Washington, D.C. Office: 555 Twelfth Street, N.W., Suite 650.
Telephone: 202-737-5410.
Fax: 202-737-5411.

MEMBERS OF FIRM

Robert M. Baker III
John David Hoover
Sean Michael Clapp
Andrew W. Hull
G. Ronald Heath
Mark A. Palmer
Linda L. Pence

ASSOCIATES

Steven J. Moss
Michael D. Ramsey
William C. Wagner

For Complete List of Firm Personnel, See General Section

For full biographical listings, see the Martindale-Hubbell Law Directory

LINDER & HOLLOWELL, A PROFESSIONAL CORPORATION (AV)

615 Russell Avenue, P.O. Box 845, 46206-0845
Telephone: 317-637-3170
Fax: Available Upon Request

Robert Hollowell (1899-1980)
Charles W. Linder, Jr.

H. Andrew Sonneborn
Sharon L. Wright
Lewis J. Gregory

For full biographical listings, see the Martindale-Hubbell Law Directory

LOCKE REYNOLDS LLP (AV)

1000 Capital Center South, 201 North Illinois Street, 46204-4210
Telephone: 317-237-3800
Telecopier: 317-237-3900
Email: attys@locke.com *URL:* http://www.locke.com

Hugh E. Reynolds, Jr.
Thomas J. Campbell
Lloyd H. Milliken, Jr.
Diane Parsons Emswiller
William V. Hutchens
Thomas W. Farlow
David S. Allen
Jeffrey R. Gaither
David M. Haskett
Karl M. Koons, III
Michael A. Bergin
James Dimos
David T. Kasper
Kristen K. Rollison
Steven J. Strawbridge
Thomas R. Schultz
Thomas L. Davis
Todd J. Kaiser
Robert A. Fanning
Eric A. Riegner
Randall R. Riggs
Kevin C. Schiferl
Mark J. Roberts
Peter H. Pogue
Kevin Charles Murray
John H. Daerr
Julia Blackwell Gelinas
John K. McDavid
Terrence L. Brookie
Jeffrey J. Mortier
Richard A. Huser
Nicholas C. Pappas

(See Next Column)

LOCKE REYNOLDS LLP—*Continued*

Stephen L. Vaughan
Deanna A. Dean-Webster
Jon M. Pinnick
Mary A. Schopper
Susan E. Cline
Bruce J. Alvarado
Mary Margaret Ruth Feldhake
Nelson D. Alexander
Donald B. Kite, Sr.
Thomas F. Bedsole
David A. Sorensen
Derek S. Burrell
Dean R. Brackenridge
T. Joseph Wendt
Michelle Davis Carmichael
John D. Papageorge
Heather L. Wilson
Vincent J. Wong
Daniel G. Foote
Dionne Carroll McCoy
Carol M. Wyatt
Joel E. Tragesser
Tricia L. Thompson

OF COUNSEL

William H. Vobach
Robert C. Riddell

Representative Clients: Associated Aviation Underwriters; Center for Claims Resolution; Citizens Insurance Co. (The Hanover Group); CNA Insurance Cos.; The Hartford Insurance Co.; The Medical Protective Co.; Nationwide Insurance Co.; PHICO Insurance Co.; Royal Insurance Cos.; U.S.F. & G. Cos.

For Complete List of Firm Personnel, See General Section

For full biographical listings, see the Martindale-Hubbell Law Directory

ROCAP, WITCHGER & THRELKELD (AV)

One Indiana Square, Suite 2300, 46204
Telephone: 317-639-6281
FAX: 317-637-9056
Email: rocap@iquest.net

James E. Rocap, Sr. (1881-1969)
John T. Rocap (1909-1980)
Keith C. Reese (1920-1993)

MEMBERS OF FIRM

James D. Witchger
W. Brent Threlkeld
Richard A. Rocap
Thomas Todd Reynolds

ASSOCIATES

Robert A. Durham
Kandi K. Hidde
Robert F. Ahlgrim, Jr.
Kelley Bertoux Creveling
Tracy A. Arney
Edward A.B. Castaldo
Mark S. Maxwell

OF COUNSEL

James E. Rocap, Jr.
Joseph F. Quill
William C. Moore

Representative Clients: Motorist Mutual Insurance Co.; American Family Insurance Group; The Travelers Insurance Co.; State Farm Fire and Casualty Insurance Co.; Reliance National Insurance Co.; Statesman Insurance Co.; USAA Insurance; State Farm Mutual Automobile Insurance Co.; Northwestern National Insurance Co.

For full biographical listings, see the Martindale-Hubbell Law Directory

SMITH & BEMENDERFER (AV)

7209 North Shadeland Avenue, 46250
Telephone: 317-578-1900
Facsimile: 317-578-1330

T. Neil Bemenderfer
Mark R. Smith
Donna H. Fisher

ASSOCIATES

Rebecca J. Maas
Kimberly E. Howard
Michael R. Bain
Jeffrey D. Hawkins

For full biographical listings, see the Martindale-Hubbell Law Directory

TABBERT HAHN EARNEST & WEDDLE (AV)

Suite 2100, One Indiana Square, 46204-2101
Telephone: 317-639-5444
Fax: 317-639-5232
Email: jtyrrell@tabberthahn.com *URL:* http://www.tabberthahn.com

Don A. Tabbert
Gregory F. Hahn
Lante K. Earnest
Robert G. Weddle
Mark K. Sullivan
Judy M. Tyrrell
Lara D. Engelking
Matthew W. Conner
William W. Mathews
Heather L. Fesko
Charles R. Whybrew

OF COUNSEL

James J. Nocon
William D. Lalley
Joseph W. Hammes
Dale E. Sporleder

For full biographical listings, see the Martindale-Hubbell Law Directory

YARLING & ROBINSON (AV)

151 North Delaware, Suite 1535, P.O. Box 44128, 46204
Telephone: 317-262-8800
Fax: 317-262-3046
Email: yrhl@yarling.com *URL:* http://www.yarling.com

(See Next Column)

MEMBERS OF FIRM

Charles F. Robinson, Jr.
John W. Hammel
Linda Y. Hammel
Douglas E. Rogers
Mark S. Gray
Matthew C. Robinson

ASSOCIATE

Jeffrey R. Mitchell

OF COUNSEL

Richard W. Yarling

Representative Clients: Allstate Insurance Co.; American Family Mutual Insurance Company; General Motors Acceptance Corporation; Monroe Guaranty Insurance Company; Northbrook Property & Casualty Company; Pafco General Insurance Company; Progressive Insurance Companies; USFG/St. Paul Insurance Company; Wausau Insurance Companies.

For full biographical listings, see the Martindale-Hubbell Law Directory

ZEIGLER COHEN & KOCH (AV)

8500 Keystone Crossing, Suite 510, 46240
Telephone: 317-254-4400
Facsimile: 317-254-4403

Robert G. Zeigler
Steven J. Cohen
Edna M. Koch
David Becsey
Roger K. Kanne

ASSOCIATES

Joseph D. McPike, II
Kathryn A. Elias
Lakshmi Reddy

OF COUNSEL

Marilyn A. Young

For full biographical listings, see the Martindale-Hubbell Law Directory

*LAFAYETTE,** Tippecanoe Co.

BALL, EGGLESTON, BUMBLEBURG, MCBRIDE, WALKEY & STAPLETON, PC (AV)

810 Bank One Building, P.O. Box 1535, 47902-1535
Telephone: 765-742-9046
Fax: 765-742-1966
Email: info@ball-law.com

Cable G. Ball (1904-1981)
Owen Crook (1908-1977)
Warren N. Eggleston (1923-1991)
Joseph T. Bumbleburg
John K. McBride
Jack L. Walkey
Michael J. Stapleton
Jeffrey J. Newell
James T. Hodson
Brian Wade Walker
Cheryl M. Knodle
Randy J. Williams
Brenda Mithoefer Clapper

Representative Clients: Travelers Insurance Co.; Grain Dealers Mutual Insurance Co.; Indiana Farmers Insurance Group; Indiana Insurance Co.; American Family Insurance Co; Town of Dayton, Indiana.

For full biographical listings, see the Martindale-Hubbell Law Directory

STUART & BRANIGIN (AV)

The Life Building, 300 Main Street, Suite 800, P.O. Box 1010, 47902-1010
Telephone: 765-423-1561
Telecopier: 765-742-8175
Email: sb@stuartlaw.com *URL:* http://www.stuartlaw.com
Indianapolis, Indiana Office: Suite 1401, 8888 Keystone Crossing, 46240.
Telephone: 317-574-7245.
Fax: 317-574-7050.

MEMBERS OF FIRM

Allison Ellsworth Stuart (1886-1950)
Roger D. Branigin (1902-1975)
Larry R. Fisher
Stephen R. Pennell
Anthony S. Benton
William E. Emerick
John C. Duffey
Thomas B. Parent
Laura L. Bowker
Kevin D. Nicoson
Susan K. Roberts
John M. Stuckey
Deborah B. Trice
William P. Kealey
David A. Starkweather
Geoffrey L. Blazi

SENIOR COUNSEL

Russell H. Hart

COUNSEL

James V. McGlone

General Counsel for: The Lafayette Life Insurance Co.; INB National Bank, N.W.; Lafayette Home Hospital, Inc.
State Counsel for: Norfolk & Western Railway Co.
Mr. Ryan is Counsel to: The Trustees of Purdue University.
Representative Clients: Aluminum Company of America; Liberty Mutual Insurance Group.

For Complete List of Firm Personnel, See General Section

For full biographical listings, see the Martindale-Hubbell Law Directory

MERRILLVILLE, Lake Co.

HOEPPNER WAGNER & EVANS LLP (AV)

Twin Towers, Suite 606 South, 1000 East 80th Place, P.O. Box 10627, 46410-0627
Telephone: 219-769-6552; 800-263-1466 (IN, IL)
Fax: 219-738-2349
Email: hwe@hwelaw.com *URL:* http://www.hwelaw.com
Valparaiso, Indiana Office: 103 East Lincolnway, P.O. Box 2357, 46384-2357.
Telephone: 219-464-4961; 800-879-2246 (IN, IL).
Fax: 219-465-0603. Email: hwe@hwelaw.com

RESIDENT MEMBERS

John E. Hughes
F. Joseph Jaskowiak
Richard M. Davis

RESIDENT ASSOCIATES

Jack A. Kramer
Galen A. Bradley

Representative Clients: American States Insurance Company; American National Property & Casualty; American Family Insurance Group; CGU Insurance Company; CIGNA Property & Casualty; CNA Insurance Company; Continental Loss Adjusting Services; Indiana Insurance Company; Meridian Mutual Insurance Company; Royal Insurance Company; State Farm Mutual Automobile Insurance Company; Travelers Insurance Company; United States Fidelity and Guaranty Company; Unitrin Insurance Company; Worldwide Services.

For Complete List of Firm Personnel, See General Section

For full biographical listings, see the Martindale-Hubbell Law Directory

SPANGLER, JENNINGS & DOUGHERTY, P.C. (AV)

8396 Mississippi Street, 46410-6398
Telephone: 219-769-2323
Facsimile: 219-769-5007
Email: spangler@sjdlaw.com
Valparaiso, Indiana Office: 150 Lincolnway, Suite 3001.
Telephone: 219-462-6151.
FAX: 219-477-4935.

John P. McQuillan
Samuel J. Bernardi, Jr. (Valparaiso Office)
Jon F. Schmoll
Robert D. Hawk
David J. Hanson
Robert P. Kennedy
James T. McNiece
James D. McQuillan
David L. Abel, II
Robert P. Stoner (Valparaiso Office)
Gregory J. Tonner
Kathleen M. Maicher
Paul B. Poracky
Robert D. Brown
Robert J. Dignam

ASSOCIATES

Kisti Good Risse
Mark D. Geheb
Robert D. Hawk, Jr.
Ricardo A. Hall
Sharon L. Stanzione

OF COUNSEL

Patrick J. Dougherty (Valparaiso Office)

Representative Clients: Allstate Insurance Cos.; American International Group; American States Insurance Co.; Associates Financial Services Co. of Indiana; Civitas Bank; Beneficial Financial Co.; Boise Cascade Corp.; CNA Insurance; Chrysler Financial Corp.

For Complete List of Firm Personnel, See General Section

For full biographical listings, see the Martindale-Hubbell Law Directory

MUNSTER, Lake Co.

LAW OFFICES OF TIMOTHY F. KELLY (AV)

Suite 2A, 9250 Columbia Avenue, 46321
Telephone: 219-836-4062
Telecopier: 219-836-0167
Email: tfklaw@tfklaw.net

MEMBERS OF FIRM

Timothy F. Kelly
Karl K. Vanzo

ASSOCIATES

Steven J. Sersic
Kathleen E. Peek

For Complete List of Firm Personnel, See General Section

For full biographical listings, see the Martindale-Hubbell Law Directory

*SOUTH BEND,** St. Joseph Co.

DORAN • BLACKMOND LLP (AV)

1700 Valley American Bank Building, 211 W. Washington Street, 46601
Telephone: 219-288-1800
Fax: 219-236-4265

MEMBERS OF FIRM

M. Edward Doran (1895-1982)
John E. Doran
Don G. Blackmond

(See Next Column)

ASSOCIATES

Don Gregory Blackmond
Peter J. Van Dyke
Lynn M. Butcher

OF COUNSEL

A. Howard Williams

For full biographical listings, see the Martindale-Hubbell Law Directory

ROWE & ROWE (AV)

Suite 900 Keybank Building, 46601
Telephone: 219-233-8200
Fax: 219-234-5987

R. Kent Rowe
R. Kent Rowe, III

ASSOCIATES

Robert D. Truitt
Gregory J. Haines
Marie Anne Hendrie

For full biographical listings, see the Martindale-Hubbell Law Directory

*TERRE HAUTE,** Vigo Co.

COX, ZWERNER, GAMBILL & SULLIVAN (AV)

511 Wabash Avenue, P.O. Box 1625, 47808-1625
Telephone: 812-232-6003
Fax: 812-232-6567

MEMBERS OF FIRM

Ernest J. Zwerner (1918-1980)
Benjamin G. Cox (1915-1988)
Gilbert W. Gambill, Jr.
James E. Sullivan
Benjamin G. Cox, Jr.
David W. Sullivan
Robert L. Gowdy
Louis F. Britton
Carroll D. Smeltzer
Jeffry A. Lind
Ronald E. Jumps
Scott Craig
Elizabeth A. Lewis

OF COUNSEL

Robert D. Hepburn

Counsel for: Terre Haute First National Bank; Farmers Insurance Group; Indiana-American Water Co.; Indiana State University; Merchants National Bank of Terre Haute; Rose-Hulman Institute of Technology; Tribune-Star Publishing Co., Inc.; Equitable Life Assurance Society of U.S.; Federated Mutual Insurance Co.; Fireman's Fund; General Accident Group; Guaranty National Insurance; Milwaukee Mutual Insurance Co.; Ohio Casualty Insurance Co.; Hartford Insurance; The Travelers Co.; United Services Auto Assn.; Vernon Insurance Co.; Hoosier Insurance Co.

For full biographical listings, see the Martindale-Hubbell Law Directory

SACOPULOS, JOHNSON, CARTER & SACOPULOS (AV)

676 Ohio Street, 47807
Telephone: 812-238-2565
FAX: 812-238-1945
Email: sjcs@gte.net

MEMBERS OF FIRM

Gus Sacopulos
R. Steven Johnson
Gregory S. Carter
Peter J. Sacopulos
Michael J. Sacopulos

Representative Clients: Bituminous Casualty; Auto-Owners Insurance Co.; Indiana Insurance Co.; Victoria Ins. Co.; American States Insurance Co.; CNA Insurance Co.; Physicians & Surgeons Insurance Co.; American Family Insurance Co.; WalMart Stores, Inc.; USF&G.

For full biographical listings, see the Martindale-Hubbell Law Directory

*VALPARAISO,** Porter Co.

HOEPPNER WAGNER & EVANS LLP (AV)

103 East Lincolnway, P.O. Box 2357, 46384-2357
Telephone: 219-464-4961; 800-879-2246 (IN, IL)
Fax: 219-465-0603
Email: hwe@hwelaw.com *URL:* http://www.hwelaw.com
Merrillville, Indiana Office: Twin Towers, Suite 606 South, 1000 East 80th Place, P.O. Box 10627, 46419-0627.
Telephone: 219-769-6552; 800-263-1466 (IN, IL).
Fax: 219-738-2349. Email: hwe@hwelaw.com

MEMBERS OF FIRM

William F. Satterlee, III
John E. Hughes (Resident, Merrillville Office)
Ronald P. Kuker
F. Joseph Jaskowiak (Resident, Merrillville Office)
Richard M. Davis (Resident, Merrillville Office)
Mark E. Schmidtke
Michael P. Blaize

ASSOCIATES

Robert L. Clark
Jeffrey W. Clymer
Jack A. Kramer (Resident, Merrillville Office)
Galen A. Bradley (Resident, Merrillville Office)
Kevin G. Kerr
Karen M. Read

Representative Clients: American States Insurance Company; American National Property & Casualty; American Family Insurance Group; CGU Insurance Company; CIGNA Property & Casualty; CNA Insurance Company;

(See Next Column)

HOEPPNER WAGNER & EVANS LLP—*Continued*

Continental Loss Adjusting Services; Indiana Insurance Company; Meridian Mutual Insurance Company; Royal Insurance Company; State Farm Mutual Automobile Insurance Company; Travelers Insurance Company; United States Fidelity and Guaranty Company; Unitrin Insurance Company; Worldwide Services.

For Complete List of Firm Personnel, See General Section

For full biographical listings, see the Martindale-Hubbell Law Directory

SPANGLER, JENNINGS & DOUGHERTY, P.C. (AV)

150 Lincolnway, Suite 3001, 46383
Telephone: 219-462-6151
FAX: 219-477-4935
Email: spangler@sjdlaw.com
Merrillville, Indiana Office: 8396 Mississippi Street.
Telephone: 219-769-2323.

RESIDENT PERSONNEL

Samuel J. Bernardi, Jr. — Robert P. Stoner

Edward W. Hearn — Christopher Grabarek

OF COUNSEL

Patrick J. Dougherty

Representative Clients: Allstate Insurance Cos.; State Farm Insurance Cos.; The Saint Paul Companies; CNA Insurance Cos.; Maryland Insurance Cos.; American Specialty Insurance Services; J&N Enterprises; Indiana Beach, Inc.; CertainTeed Corp.; Fireman's Fund.

For full biographical listings, see the Martindale-Hubbell Law Directory

*VINCENNES,** Knox Co.

EMISON, DOOLITTLE, KOLB & ROELLGEN (AV)

Eighth & Busseron Streets, P.O. Box 215, 47591
Telephone: 812-882-2280
FAX: 812-885-2308
Email: emison@vin.wvc.net

MEMBERS OF FIRM

Rabb Emison — Jeffrey B. Kolb
Robert P. Doolittle, Jr. — J. David Roellgen
Brian C. Dickerson

Clients Include: American Family Insurance, Co.; Cincinnati Insurance, Co.; Indiana Insurance, Co.; United Farm Bureau Insurance, Co.; Sentry Insurance, Co.; GRE Insurance, Co.; Prudential Insurance, Co.

For full biographical listings, see the Martindale-Hubbell Law Directory

*WARSAW,** Kosciusko Co.

ROCKHILL, PINNICK, PEQUIGNOT, HELM, LANDIS & RIGDON (AV)

105 East Main Street, 46580-2742
Telephone: 219-267-6116
Telecopier: 219-269-9264
Email: rockhill@kconline.com

MEMBERS OF FIRM

Brooks C. Pinnick — Vern K. Landis
Stanley E. Pequignot — Jay A. Rigdon
Richard K. Helm — Jamelyn E. Freeman

ASSOCIATE

Dana Leon

Representative Clients: State Farm Insurance Cos.; Motorists Mutual Insurance Co.; Brotherhood Mutual Insurance.

For full biographical listings, see the Martindale-Hubbell Law Directory

IOWA

*CEDAR RAPIDS,** Linn Co.

PICKENS, BARNES & ABERNATHY (AV)

Tenth Floor American Building, P.O. Box 74170, 52407-4170
Telephone: 319-366-7621
Fax: 319-366-3158
Email: PBAbernath@AOL.com

MEMBERS OF FIRM

Terry J. Abernathy — Matthew G. Novak

ASSOCIATES

Thad J. Collins — Stephanie L. Hinz

(See Next Column)

RETIRED

James F. Pickens — Minor Barnes

A list of Representative Clients furnished upon request.

For full biographical listings, see the Martindale-Hubbell Law Directory

SHUTTLEWORTH & INGERSOLL, P.C. (AV)

115 Third Street S.E., Suite 500, P.O. Box 2107, 52406-2107
Telephone: 319-365-9461
Fax: 319-365-8443
URL: http://www.shuttleworthlaw.com

John M. Bickel — Thomas P. Peffer
Robert D. Houghton — Kevin H. Collins
Richard S. Fry — Diane Kutzko
Richard C. Garberson — Mark L. Zaiger
Steven J. Pace — Douglas R. Oelschlaeger
Glenn L. Johnson — Constance M. Alt
Kurt L. Kratovil

Nancy J. Penner — Theresa C. Davis
Kevin J. Caster — Sarah J. Gayer
Jennifer Rinden Clark

Representative Clients: Auto-Owners Insurance; CIGNA Companies; CNA Insurance Companies; Farmers Insurance Group; Farmland Mutual Insurance Company; Fireman's Fund Insurance Companies; General Casualty Company of Wisconsin.

For Complete List of Firm Personnel, See General Section

For full biographical listings, see the Martindale-Hubbell Law Directory

*COUNCIL BLUFFS,** Pottawattamie Co.

SMITH PETERSON LAW FIRM (AV)

35 Main Place, Suite 300, P.O. Box 249, 51502
Telephone: 712-328-1833
Fax: 712-328-8320
Email: email@smithpeterson.com
Omaha, Nebraska Office: 9290 West Dodge Road, Suite 205.
Telephone: 402-397-8500.
Fax: 402-397-5519.

MEMBERS OF FIRM

Raymond A. Smith (1892-1977) — Lawrence J. Beckman
John LeRoy Peterson (1895-1969) — Gregory G. Barntsen
W. Curtis Hewett
Harold T. Beckman — Steven H. Krohn
Robert J. Laubenthal — Randy R. Ewing
Richard A. Heininger — Joseph D. Thornton
T. J. Pattermann

ASSOCIATES

Daniel L. Fretheim — Paul M. Shotkoski

Representative Clients: Redland Insurance Group; Iowa Western Community College; Farm Credit Service of The Midlands; Demma Fruit Co.; Peoples National Bank; Council Bluffs Board of Water Works Trustee.

For full biographical listings, see the Martindale-Hubbell Law Directory

*DECORAH,** Winneshiek Co.

MILLER, PEARSON, GLOE, BURNS, BEATTY & COWIE, P.C. (AV)

301 West Broadway, 52101
Telephone: 319-382-4226
Fax: 319-382-3783
Email: millerlaw@salamander.com

Frank R. Miller (1915-1977) — James Burns
Donald H. Gloe — Marion L. Beatty
Robert J. Cowie, Jr.

Bradley Douglas Shidler

OF COUNSEL

Floyd S. Pearson

Counsel for: Luther College; Decorah Community School District; Winneshiek County Memorial Hospital; Community First National Bank.
Local Counsel for: Iowa Mutual Insurance Cos.; Employers Mutual Liability Insurance Co. of Wisconsin; Continental Casualty Co.; Employers Mutual Casualty Co.; Grinnell Mutual Insurance Co.; Allied Mutual Insurance Co.

For full biographical listings, see the Martindale-Hubbell Law Directory

*DES MOINES,** Polk Co.

FINLEY, ALT, SMITH, SCHARNBERG, CRAIG, HILMES & GAFFNEY, P.C. (AV)

604 Locust Street, Fourth Floor Equitable Building, 50309
Telephone: 515-288-0145
Telecopier: 515-288-2724

(See Next Column)

FINLEY, ALT, SMITH, SCHARNBERG, CRAIG, HILMES & GAFFNEY P.C., *Des Moines—Continued*

Thomas A. Finley
Steven K. Scharnberg
Glenn L. Smith
John D. (Jack) Hilmes
Kerry A. Finley

Representative Clients: ALAS; American Society of Composers, Authors and Publishers; Equitable Life Assurance Society of the U.S.; Federated Insurance Co.; Meredith Corp.
Iowa Attorneys for: Midwest Medical Insurance Co.
District Attorneys for: Norfolk & Southern Railroad; Soo Line Railroad Company.

For Complete List of Firm Personnel, See General Section

For full biographical listings, see the Martindale-Hubbell Law Directory

GREFE & SIDNEY, P.L.C. (AV)

2222 Grand Avenue, P.O. Box 10434, 50306
Telephone: 515-245-4300
Fax: 515-245-4452
Email: grandfirm@aol.com
Pella, Iowa Office: 725 Franklin Street, 50219.
Telephone: 515-628-9343.
Fax: 515-628-7252.

Henry A. Harmon
Patrick J. McNulty
Claude H. Freeman
Mark W. Thomas
Stephen D. Hardy
Guy R. Cook
John Werner
Andrew D. Hall

Stephanie Glenn Techau
Marcy A. O'Brien
Mark A. Schultheis
Donna R. Miller
Marc D. McKay

OF COUNSEL

Ross H. Sidney

Representative Clients: Adventurelands of America; Caseys General Stores, Inc.; Cincinnati Insurance Company; Crum and Forster; Employers Mutual Insurance; Liberty Mutual Insurance Co.; Montgomery Elevator; Otis Elevator; Reliance Insurance; State Farm Insurance Companies/The St. Paul Companies.

For Complete List of Firm Personnel, See General Section

For full biographical listings, see the Martindale-Hubbell Law Directory

HANSEN, McCLINTOCK & RILEY (AV)

Eighth Floor - Fleming Building, 218 Sixth Avenue, 50309
Telephone: 515-244-2141
Fax: 515-244-2931
Email: hmrlaw@aol.com

MEMBERS OF FIRM

Haemer Wheatcraft (1904-1983)
Chester C. Woodburn, III
J. Rudolph Hansen (1904-1995)
William D. Scherle
John A. McClintock
David L. Brown
Ronald A. Riley
John E. Swanson

ASSOCIATES

James M. Ballard
Aaron T. Oliver

Representative Clients: The St. Paul Companies; Bituminous Insurance Companies; Northwestern National Insurance Co.; The Travelers Insurance Companies; United States Aviation Insurance Group; American International Companies; Iowa Credit Union League; The McAninch Corp.; R. J. Reynolds Tobacco Co.; Brown Bros., Inc. Electrical Contractors.

For full biographical listings, see the Martindale-Hubbell Law Directory

HUBER, BOOK, CORTESE, HAPPE & BROWN, P.L.C. (AV)

317 Sixth Avenue, Suite 200, 50309-4127
Telephone: 515-243-4148
Fax: 515-243-5481
Email: huber@desmoineslaw.com

MEMBERS OF FIRM

James C. Huber
Joseph S. Cortese II
Richard G. Book
Joseph A. Happe
Patrick D. Smith

Representative Clients: Atlantic Mutual Cos.; CNA Insurance Cos.; Fireman's Fund American Insurance Companies; Great West Casualty Co.; Liberty Mutual Insurance Co.; Maryland Insurance Group; Prudential Property and Casualty Insurance Co.; USF&G Company.
Reference: Bank of America.

For full biographical listings, see the Martindale-Hubbell Law Directory

PATTERSON, LORENTZEN, DUFFIELD, TIMMONS, IRISH, BECKER & ORDWAY, L.L.P. (AV)

729 Insurance Exchange Building, 50309
Telephone: 515-283-2147
Fax: 515-283-1002
Email: mail@pattersonfirm.com *URL:* http://www.pattersonfirm.com

(See Next Column)

MEMBERS OF FIRM

G. O. Patterson (1914-1982)
Jeffrey A. Boehlert
James A. Lorentzen (Retired)
Douglas A. Haag
Theodore T. Duffield
Charles E. Cutler
William E. Timmons (Retired)
Michael D. Huppert
Roy M. Irish
Martin C. Sprock
F. H. Becker (Retired)
William A. Wickett
Gary D. Ordway
Frederick M. Haskins
Robin L. Hermann
Jeffrey A. Baker
Harry Perkins, III
Janice M. Herfkens
Michael F. Lacey, Jr.
Coreen K. Bezdicek
Gregory J. Wilson
Patrick V. Waldron

ASSOCIATE

Michael S. Jones

General Counsel for: Iowa Insurance Institute.
Representative Clients: Allied Mutual Insurance Company; CNA Insurance Company; Chubb Insurance Group; Continental Western Insurance Co.; Farmers Insurance Group; Farmland Insurance Company; Grinnell Mutual Reinsurance Company; Hawkeye Security Insurance Company; Iowa Insurance Institute, St. Paul Fire & Marine Insurance Company.

For full biographical listings, see the Martindale-Hubbell Law Directory

PEDDICORD, WHARTON, THUNE AND SPENCER, A PROFESSIONAL CORPORATION (AV)

700 Des Moines Building, 405 Sixth Avenue, P.O. Box 9130, 50306-9130
Telephone: 515-243-2100
Fax: 515-243-2132
1-800-383-2100

Roland D. Peddicord
Stephen W. Spencer
John M. Wharton
Lee P. Hook
Paul C. Thune
Joseph M. Barron
Timothy W. Wegman

Michael S. Roling
Steven T. Durick
Lori Elizabeth Loftsgard

For full biographical listings, see the Martindale-Hubbell Law Directory

WHITFIELD & EDDY, P.L.C. (AV)

317 6th Avenue, Suite 1200 Locust at 6th, 50309-4195
Telephone: 515-288-6041
Fax: 515-246-1474
Email: info@whitfieldlaw.com *URL:* http://www.whitfieldlaw.com

Timothy J. Walker
George H. Frampton
David L. Phipps
Megan Manning Antenucci
Benjamin B. Ullem
Wendy L. Carlson
Robert L. Fanter
Gary A. Norton
Bernard L. "Jerry" Spaeth
Frank M. Grenard
William L. Fairbank
(Not admitted in IA)
Robert G. Bridges
Mark V. Hanson
Jaki K. Samuelson
Maureen Roach Tobin
Kevin M. Reynolds
August B. Landis
Thomas H. Burke
Richard J. Kirschman
Thomas Henderson
John F. Fatino

Jason M. Casini
Anjela A. Shutts
Roscoe A. Ries, Jr.
Stephen E. Doohen
J. Campbell Helton
Sean A. Pelletier
Matthew C. Ahmann

General Counsel for: American Equity Investment Life Co.; Hawkeye-Security Insurance Co.; United Security Insurance Co.
Representative Clients: Allied Mutual Insurance Co.; Crum & Forster Commercial Insurance; National Insurance Assn.; Royal Insurance; Scottsdale Insurance Co.; Tudor Insurance.

For Complete List of Firm Personnel, See General Section

For full biographical listings, see the Martindale-Hubbell Law Directory

*MASON CITY,** Cerro Gordo Co.

DE VRIES, PRICE & DAVENPORT, A PROFESSIONAL CORPORATION (AV)

30 Fourth Street, N.W., P.O. Box 1953, 50401
Telephone: 515-423-1173
Fax: 515-423-1731

C. Bradley Price
Rustin T. Davenport

David E. Schrock

Representative Clients: Allstate Insurance Company; Auto Owners Insurance Company; Farm Bureau Mutual Insurance Company; Federated Mutual Insurance Company; General Casualty Insurance Company of Wisconsin; Integrity Mutual Insurance Company; Iowa Mutual Insurance Company; Northwestern National Insurance Company; Scottsdale Insurance; Travelers Insurance Group.

For full biographical listings, see the Martindale-Hubbell Law Directory

*SIOUX CITY,** Woodbury Co.

Heidman, Redmond, Fredregill, Patterson, Plaza & Dykstra, L.L.P. (AV)

A Registered Limited Liability Partnership including Professional Corporations
701 Pierce Street, Suite 200, P.O. Box 3086, 51102
Telephone: 712-255-8838
Fax: 712-258-6714
Email: lawyers@pionet.net

MEMBERS OF FIRM

Marvin F. Heidman
James W. Redmond
Alan E. Fredregill (P.C.)
Charles T. Patterson
Thomas M. Plaza
Daniel D. Dykstra
Lance D. Ehmcke
Margaret M. Prahl
Gregg E. Williams
Cynthia C. Moser
Judith A. Higgs
John C. Gray
Daniel B. Shuck
Rita C. Grimm
Edward C."Ted" Poulsen
Patrick L. Sealey

ASSOCIATES

Jeff W. Wright
Sarah J. Kuehl

OF COUNSEL

John W. Gleysteen (Retired)
Robert R. Eidsmoe (Retired)
Jacob C. Gleysteen (1883-1943)
H. Clifford Harper (1891-1959)

Representative Clients: Mercy Medical Center; Allied Insurance Group; Irving F. Jensen, Co.; Terra International, Inc.; P.I.C. International Group, P.L.C.; Grinnell Mutual Reinsurance Co.; Travelers Insurance Co.; United Fire & Casualty; Kemper Insurance Group; American Family Insurance.

For Complete List of Firm Personnel, See General Section

For full biographical listings, see the Martindale-Hubbell Law Directory

Mayne & Mayne (AV)

400 Pioneer Bank Building, 701 Pierce Street, P.O. Box 5049, 51102-5049
Telephone: 712-252-3220
Fax: 712-252-1535
Email: maynelaw@aol.com

OF COUNSEL

Wiley Mayne

MEMBERS OF FIRM

John D. Mayne
Robert J. Pierson

Representative Clients: American Home Insurance Co.; American Empire Insurance Company; Capitol Indemnity Company; Chubb Insurance; Design Professionals Financial Corp.; Fremont Indemnity Company; Heritage Insurance; Podiatry Insurance Company of America; Ranger Insurance; Utica Mutual Insurance Company.

For full biographical listings, see the Martindale-Hubbell Law Directory

KANSAS

*HUTCHINSON,** Reno Co.

Gilliland & Hayes, P.A. A Professional Association (AV)

20 West 2nd Avenue, 2nd Floor, P.O. Box 2977, 67504-2977
Telephone: 316-662-0537
Facsimile: 316-669-9426
URL: http://www.gillilandhayes.com
Wichita, Kansas Office: The Orpheum Centre, Suite 300, 200 North Broadway, P.O. Box 49406.
Telephone: 316-262-2266.
Facsimile: 316-263-2202.
Kansas City, Missouri Office: 12th Floor, 3100 Broadway.
Telephone: 816-753-3100.
Facsimile: 816-753-2271.

Robert J. Gilliland
John F. Hayes
James R. Gilliland
John S. Schmidt
Bruce B. Waugh (Not admitted in KS; Resident, Kansas City, Missouri Office)
Michael R. O'Neal
Bradley D. Dillon
Gerald L. Green
David N. Zimmerman (Not admitted in KS; Resident, Kansas City, Missouri Office)
Scott J. Mann
Carol Z. Smith (Resident, Kansas City, Missouri Office)
Kathleen A. Hardee (Resident, Kansas City, Missouri Office)
Kendall R. Cunningham (Resident, Wichita Office)
Mark R. Maloney (Resident, Wichita Office)

(See Next Column)

Thomas A. Dower
Tracy Applegate Cole
Laura A. Hederstedt
Terri Roberts Munsell (Resident, Kansas City, Missouri Office)
Lisa M. Ward
Kimberly Breda Bushek (Resident, Kansas City, Missouri Office)
E. Thomas Pyle, III
Tara L. Bragg

OF COUNSEL

Robert P. Reams (Not admitted in KS; Resident, Kansas City, Missouri Office)

Representative Clients: Allied Group; CNA Insurance; CNA Health Pro; Farm Bureau Mutual Insurance Co.; Fidelity Deposit Co. of Maryland; Kansas Medical Mutual Insurance Co.; St. Paul Fire & Marine Insurance Co.; State Farm Insurance Co.; Travelers Insurance Companies; Vesta Companies.

For full biographical listings, see the Martindale-Hubbell Law Directory

*KANSAS CITY,** Wyandotte Co.

Holbrook, Heaven & Osborn, P.A. (AV)

757 Armstrong, P.O. Box 171927, 66117
Telephone: 913-342-2500
Fax: 913-342-0603
Merriam, Kansas Office: 6700 Antioch Street.
Telephone: 913-677-1717.
Fax: 913-677-0403.

Reid F. Holbrook
Lewis A. Heaven, Jr. (Resident, Merriam Office)
Thomas E. Osborn
Robert L. Kennedy
Janet M. Simpson
John D. Tongier (Resident, Merriam Office)
Thomas M. Sutherland
Thomas S. Busch (Resident, Merriam Office)
Kurt S. Brack (Resident, Merriam Office)
Daniel W. Peters

For Complete List of Firm Personnel, See General Section

For full biographical listings, see the Martindale-Hubbell Law Directory

OVERLAND PARK, Johnson Co.

Fisher, Patterson, Sayler & Smith, L.L.P. (AV)

11050 Roe Avenue, Suite 210, 66211
Telephone: 913-339-6757
FAX: 913-339-6187
Email: fpss@worldnet.att.net
Topeka, Kansas Office: 3550 S.W. 5th Street, P.O. Box 949, 66601.
Telephone: 785-232-7761.
Fax: 785-232-6604.

MEMBERS OF FIRM

Edwin Dudley Smith (Resident)
Michael K. Seck (Resident)
David P. Madden (Resident)

ASSOCIATES

Kelly A. Feyh (Resident)
Jennifer R. Rose (Resident)

For full biographical listings, see the Martindale-Hubbell Law Directory

*TOPEKA,** Shawnee Co.

Fisher, Patterson, Sayler & Smith, L.L.P. (AV)

3550 S.W. 5th Street, P.O. Box 949, 66601
Telephone: 785-232-7761
Fax: 785-232-6604
Email: fpss@cjnetworks.com
Overland Park, Kansas Office: 11050 Roe Avenue, Suite 210, 66211.
Telephone: 913-339-6757.
Fax: 913-339-6187.

MEMBERS OF FIRM

Donald Patterson
Edwin Dudley Smith (Resident, Overland Park Office)
Larry G. Pepperdine
James P. Nordstrom
Justice B. King
J. Steven Pigg
Steve R. Fabert
Ronald J. Laskowski
Michael K. Seck (Resident, Overland Park Office)
David P. Madden (Resident, Overland Park Office)
Steven K. Johnson
Kristine A. Larscheid

ASSOCIATES

Billy E. Newman
David R. Cooper
Kelly A. Feyh (Resident, Overland Park Office)
Jennifer R. Rose (Resident, Overland Park Office)

OF COUNSEL

David H. Fisher

(See Next Column)

*ELIZABETHTOWN,** Hardin Co.

COLEMAN, EASTON, LOCHMILLER & HALL (AV)
(Formerly Reford H. Coleman and Associates)
2907 Ring Road, P.O. Box 1177, 42702-1177
Telephone: 502-737-0600
Fax: 502-737-0488
Email: celh@ne.infi.net

Reford H. Coleman
Kelly Mark Easton
Beth Ann Lochmiller
M. Brent Hall

ASSOCIATE
Matthew C. Hess

Representative Clients: American States Insurance Cos.; Federated Rural Elec. Insurance Co.; General Motors Corp.; The Hartford; Indiana Insurance Co.; Kentucky Association of Counties All-Lines Fund; Kentucky Farm Bureau Mutual Insurance Co.; Liberty Mutual Insurance Co.; State Auto Insurance Co.; United Services Automobile Association (State Counsel).

For full biographical listings, see the Martindale-Hubbell Law Directory

*HARLAN,** Harlan Co.

HUFF LAW OFFICES (AV)
417 East Mound Street, Drawer 151, 40831
Telephone: 606-573-4466
Fax: 606-573-7078

Gayle G. Huff

ASSOCIATES
Antony L. Saragas
Elizabeth Ann Huff
William Stacy Huff

Representative Clients: Old Republic Insurance Co.; Underwriters Safety & Claims; Manalapan Mining Co.; R.B. Coal Co.; Eastover Mining Co., a division of Duke Power Co.; American Mining Insurance Co.; Employers Risk Services; Forest Industry Workers Compensation Fund.

For full biographical listings, see the Martindale-Hubbell Law Directory

RICE & HENDRICKSON (AV)
398 Woodland Hills, P.O. Box 980, 40831
Telephone: 606-573-3955
Fax: 606-573-3956

MEMBERS OF FIRM
William A. Rice
H. Kent Hendrickson

Representative Clients: USX Corp.; Navistar International Transportation Corp.; Bituminous Casualty Corp.; Kentucky Utilities Co.; Aetna Casualty & Surety Co.; The Hartford Insurance Group; Benham Coal, Inc.; Maytag Corporation; Harlan Cumberland Coal Co.; Pafco General Insurance.

For full biographical listings, see the Martindale-Hubbell Law Directory

*HENDERSON,** Henderson Co.

DEEP & WOMACK (AV)
790 Bob Posey Street, P.O. Box 50, 42419-0050
Telephone: 502-827-2522
Fax: 502-826-2870
Email: deep@henderson.net
Louisville, Kentucky Office: 1228 Starks Building, 455 South Fourth Avenue. P.O. Box 70033, 40270-0033.
Telephone: 502-589-2530.
Fax: 502-589-9297. E-Mail: Deep_Womack@msn.com

MEMBERS OF FIRM
Charles David Deep
Zack N. Womack

ASSOCIATES
Toni Cline Renfro (Resident, Louisville Office)
Jacqueline Chauvin (Resident, Louisville Office)
Carol Schureck Petitt (Resident, Louisville Office)

For full biographical listings, see the Martindale-Hubbell Law Directory

*LEXINGTON,** Fayette Co.

FERRERI, FOGLE & PICKLESIMER (AV)
500 Quality Place, 300 East Main Street, 40507
Telephone: 606-253-4700
Telefax: 606-253-4702
Email: fflex@pop.net
Louisville, Kentucky Office: 203 Speed Building, 333 Guthrie Green.
Telephone: 502-582-1381.
Telefax: 502-581-9887.

MEMBERS OF FIRM
Thomas L. Ferreri
Max D. Picklesimer
Joel W. Aubrey
Sherri P. Brown

(See Next Column)

ASSOCIATES
Hugh Brett Stonecipher
Stephanie Dawn Ross
Gary A. Stephens

Representative Clients: Associated Industries of Kentucky; Averitt Express; Gallagher Bassett Services; Indiana Insurance Company; Kentucky Insurance Guaranty Association; Kentucky League of Cities; Liberty Mutual Group; State Farm Insurance; Travelers Insurance Company; Underwriters Safety & Claims.

For full biographical listings, see the Martindale-Hubbell Law Directory

FOWLER, MEASLE & BELL, L.L.P. (AV)
Kincaid Towers, 300 West Vine Street, 6th Floor, 40507-1660
Telephone: 606-252-6700
Fax: 606-255-3735
Email: fmb@mis.net

MEMBERS OF FIRM
Guy R. Colson
E. Patrick Moores
James D. Ishmael, Jr.
T. Bruce Bell
Elizabeth S. Feamster
R. Craig Reinhardt
Barry M. Miller

ASSOCIATES
Susan S. Kennedy
Michael E. Liska
Katherine J. Hornback
Wesley R. Butler

OF COUNSEL
Walter C. Cox, Jr.

Representative Clients: General Electric Co.; Kentucky Farm Bureau Mutual Ins. Co.; Progressive Casualty Ins. Co; Grange Mutual Ins. Co.; Cotton States Mutual Ins. Co.; Prudential Property & Casualty Ins. Co.; Ranger Ins. Co.; Motorist Mutual Ins. Co.; Kentucky National Ins. Co.

For full biographical listings, see the Martindale-Hubbell Law Directory

GERALDS, JONES, SHERROW, SCHRADER & RICE, P.S.C. (AV)
259 West Short Street, 40507
Telephone: 606-255-7946
Fax: 606-233-4099

Oscar H. Geralds, Jr.
Ernest H. Jones, II
Billy W. Sherrow
John P. Schrader
John G. Rice

Robert L. Swisher
Patsey Ely Yewell
Cheryl D. Morgan

OF COUNSEL
Frances Geralds Rohlfing

Representative Clients: Allstate Insurance Co.; State Farm Mutual Automobile Insurance Co.; State Farm Fire and Casualty Co.; Colonial Insurance Company of California; Horace Mann; North American Specialty Insurance Co.; Pennsylvania National Insurance Company.
Reference: Bank of the Bluegrass & Trust Co.

For full biographical listings, see the Martindale-Hubbell Law Directory

LANDRUM & SHOUSE (AV)
106 West Vine Street, P.O. Box 951, 40588-0951
Telephone: 606-255-2424
Facsimile: 606-233-0308
Louisville, Kentucky Office: Suite 1900, 220 West Main Street, 40202-2119.
Telephone: 502-589-7616.
Facsimile: 502-589-2119.

MEMBERS OF FIRM
John H. Burrus
William C. Shouse
Pierce W. Hamblin
Mark L. Moseley
Leslie Patterson Vose
John R. Martin, Jr. (Resident, Louisville Office)
Larry C. Deener
Sandra Mendez Dawahare
Mark J. Hinkel
John Garry McNeill
R. Kent Westberry (Resident, Louisville Office)
Jane Durkin Samuel
Douglas L. Hoots, CPCU
Dave Whalin (Resident, Louisville Office)
Daniel E. Murner

ASSOCIATES
Stephen R. Chappell
Robert Thaddeus (Thad) Keal (Resident, Louisville Office)
Sun S. Choy (Resident, Louisville Office)
David W. Zahniser
Rheanne Dodson Falkner (Resident, Louisville Office)
Shannon M. Naish
Bradley C. Hooks

OF COUNSEL
Weldon Shouse
Thomas M. Cooper

Representative Clients: State Auto Insurance Co.; Northland Insurance Co.; Ohio Casualty Insurance; Safeco Insurance; Scottsdale Insurance Co.; Cincinnati Insurance Co.; Crawford & Co.; CSX Transportation, Inc.; Lexington-Fayette Urban County Airport; American States Insurance Co.

For Complete List of Firm Personnel, See General Section

For full biographical listings, see the Martindale-Hubbell Law Directory

Lexington—Continued

LYNN, FULKERSON, NICHOLS AND KINKEL, PLLC (AV)

267 West Short Street, 40507
Telephone: 606-253-0523
Telefax: 606-254-2098
Email: mail@LFNK.com

MEMBERS OF FIRM

Deddo G. Lynn
Calvin R. Fulkerson
Mark E. Nichols
Steven G. Kinkel

ASSOCIATES

Marshall R. Hixson
Jo Alice Van Nagell
Melanie Sublett Marrs

Representative Clients: The Kemper National Insurance Group; Maryland Casualty Corp.; St. Paul Fire and Marine Insurance Company.

For full biographical listings, see the Martindale-Hubbell Law Directory

PIPER, WELLMAN & BOWERS (AV)

200 North Upper Street, 40507
Telephone: 606-231-1012
Fax: 606-231-1015
Email: pwb200@uky.campus.mci.net

MEMBERS OF FIRM

George C. Piper
Dean T. Wellman
Barbara J. Bowers

ASSOCIATE

Johann F. Herklotz

Representative Clients: The Virginia Insurance Reciprocal; Woodford Hospital; Clark Regional Medical Center; Garrard Memorial Hospital; Century American Insurance Co.; Equity Residential Properties Trust; Nazareth Health, Inc. d/b/a/ St. Josephs Hospital, a division of Sisters of Charity of Nazareth Health Corp.; Kentucky River Medical Center; Fireman's Fund Insurance Co.; Central Kentucky Physicians, Inc. (CKPI).

For full biographical listings, see the Martindale-Hubbell Law Directory

ROBERTS & SMITH (AV)

167 West Main Street Suite 200, 40507-1701
Telephone: 606-233-1104
Fax: 606-255-6438
Email: LRob70165@aol.com

MEMBERS OF FIRM

Larry S. Roberts
Kenneth W. Smith

For full biographical listings, see the Martindale-Hubbell Law Directory

STOLL, KEENON & PARK, LLP (AV)

201 E. Main Street, Suite 1000, 40507-1380
Telephone: 606-231-3000
Telecopier: 606-253-1093; 606-253-1027
URL: http://www.skp.com
Frankfort, Kentucky Office: 307 Washington Street, 40601.
Telephone: 502-875-6220.
Telecopier: 502-875-6235.
Henderson, Kentucky Office: 201 C North Main Street, 42420-3103.
Telephone: 270-831-1900.
Telecopier: 270-827-4060.
Louisville, Kentucky Office: 400 West Market Street, Suite 2650, 40202-3377.
Telephone: 502-568-9100.
Telecopier: 502-568-5700.

MEMBERS OF FIRM

Leslie W. Morris II
J. Peter Cassidy, Jr.
Robert W. Kellerman
Eileen M. O'Brien
Perry M. Bentley
Palmer G. Vance, II

ASSOCIATES

Todd S. Page
Molly J. Cue

Representative Clients: AAA Michigan Insurance Co.; American International Group; CNA Insurance Co.; CGU Insurance Co.; Employers Reinsurance Corp.; Fireman's Fund Insurance Co.; Government Employees Insurance Co.; Grange Mutual Casualty Co.; Nationwide Insurance Cos; GRE.

For Complete List of Firm Personnel, See General Section

For full biographical listings, see the Martindale-Hubbell Law Directory

VIMONT & WILLS PLLC (AV)

Suite 300, 155 East Main Street, 40507-1317
Telephone: 606-252-2202
Telecopier: 606-259-2927
Email: vimont@lex.infi.net

Richard E. Vimont
Timothy C. Wills
Fred E. Fugazzi, Jr.
J. Stan Lee

For full biographical listings, see the Martindale-Hubbell Law Directory

*LONDON,** Laurel Co.

FARMER, KELLEY, BROWN AND WILLIAMS (AV)

502 West Fifth Street, Drawer 490, 40741
Telephone: 606-878-7640
Fax: 606-878-2364
Email: fpfarmer@farmerlaw.com
Lexington, Kentucky Office: 1082 Griffin Gate Drive, 40511-1384.
Telephone: 606: 263-2567.
Facsimile: 606: 878-2364.

MEMBERS OF FIRM

F. Preston Farmer
John F. Kelley, Jr.
Michael P. Farmer
Martha L. Brown
Jason E. Williams

ASSOCIATES

Suzanne S. Farmer
Jennifer S. Nicholson

Representative Clients: Wal-Mart Stores; Bituminous Insurance Co.; State Farm Fire & Casualty Insurance; Geico; Kentucky National Insurance Co.; Sentry Claims; Shelter Insurance Co.; Crum & Forester Underwriters Group; Omni.

For full biographical listings, see the Martindale-Hubbell Law Directory

HAMM, MILBY & RIDINGS (AV)

120 North Main Street, 40741
Telephone: 606-864-4126
Fax: 606-878-8144
Email: hmrlaw@kih.net

MEMBERS OF FIRM

Robert L. Milby
Marcia Milby Ridings

James A. Ridings
Gregory A. Lay
R. Aaron Hostettler

Representative Clients: Acceleration National; Aetna Life & Casualty Ins. Co.; All Risk Claims Service, Inc.; Allstate Insurance Co.; Alexis; American Automobile Mutual Ins.; American Bankers; American Hardware Ins. Co.; American Home Ins.; American Inter-Fidelity Exchange.

For full biographical listings, see the Martindale-Hubbell Law Directory

TOOMS & HOUSE (AV)

310 West Fifth Street, P.O. Box 520, 40743-0520
Telephone: 606-864-4145
FAX: 606-864-4279

MEMBERS OF FIRM

Murray L. Brown (1894-1980)
Roy E. Tooms (1917-1986)
R. William Tooms
Brian C. House

ASSOCIATE

Roy G. Collins

Representative Insurance Clients: State Auto Mutual Insurance Co.; Grange Mutual Casualty Co.; Kentucky Farm Bureau Mutual Insurance Co.; Canal Insurance Co.; Crawford Risk Management Services; Imperial Casualty Co.; National Union Fire Insurance Co.; Tennessee Farmers Mutual Insurance Company; National Casualty Company; Grocers Insurance Company.

For full biographical listings, see the Martindale-Hubbell Law Directory

*LOUISVILLE,** Jefferson Co.

FERRERI, FOGLE & PICKLESIMER (AV)

203 Speed Building, 333 Guthrie Green, 40202
Telephone: 502-582-1381
Telefax: 502-581-9887
Email: fflou@aye.net
Lexington, Kentucky Office: 500 Quality Place, 300 East Main Street.
Telephone: 606-253-4700.
Telefax: 606-253-4702.

MEMBERS OF FIRM

Thomas L. Ferreri
James G. Fogle
Max D. Picklesimer
Phillipe W. Rich
Walter C. Jobson
Brian Timothy Gannon

ASSOCIATES

J. D. Raine, Jr.
Allan Weiss

OF COUNSEL

William A. Miller
Glenn L. Schilling

Representative Clients: Associated Industries of Kentucky; Averitt Express; Gallagher Bassett Services; Indiana Insurance Company; Kentucky Insurance Guaranty Association; Kentucky League of Cities; Liberty Mutual Group; State Farm Insurance; Travelers Insurance Company; Underwriters Safety & Claims.

For full biographical listings, see the Martindale-Hubbell Law Directory

Louisville—Continued

GOLDBERG & SIMPSON, P.S.C. (AV)

3000 National City Tower, 40202
Telephone: 502-589-4440
Telefax: 502-581-1344
Email: mail@gsatty.com *URL:* http://www.gsatty.com

Fred M. Goldberg
Jonathan D. Goldberg
Mitchell A. Charney
Steven A. Goodman
Stephen E. Smith
Mary Alice Maple
John J. McLaughlin
Charles H. Cassis
Christopher M. George
Emily L. Lawrence

Jan M. West
Sherry P. Porter
James Michael Wells
Stephanie Lynn Morgan-White
Michael F. Lawrence
Karen L. De Haan
George Hunt Rounsavall, Jr.
Stacey A. Huse

OF COUNSEL

Ronald V. Simpson
David A. Brill

Representative Clients: National City Bank; Liberty Mutual Insurance Co.; Jewish Hospital Healthcare Services, Inc.; Louisville & Jefferson County Board of Health; Providian Corp.

For full biographical listings, see the Martindale-Hubbell Law Directory

HALL, RENDER, KILLIAN, HEATH & LYMAN PROFESSIONAL SERVICES CORPORATION (AV)

AEGON Center, Suite 1530, 400 West Market Street, 40202
Telephone: 502-568-1890
Fax: 502-568-4878
Email: hrkhl@hrkhl.com
Indianapolis, Indiana Office: Suite 2000, One American Square, Box 82064, 46282.
Telephone: 317-633-4884.
Fax: 317-633-4878.
Indianapolis North Office: Suite 820, 8402 Harcourt Road, 46260.
Telephone: 317-871-6222.
Fax: 317-338-3946.

A. Courtney Guild, Jr.
Sharon K. Hager

For full biographical listings, see the Martindale-Hubbell Law Directory

FRANK P. HILLIARD (AV)

The Starks Building, Suite 380, 455 South 4th Avenue, 40202
Telephone: 502-583-0380
Fax: 502-583-9089
Email: fphil380@bellsouth.net

ASSOCIATE

Charles Edward Monarch

For full biographical listings, see the Martindale-Hubbell Law Directory

HUMMEL & COAN (AV)

Kentucky Home Life Building, The Seventeenth Floor, 239 South Fifth Street, 40202-3268
Telephone: 502-585-3084
Fax: 502-585-3548
Email: hummelandcoan@hc-attys.com

OF COUNSEL

Rothschild Aberson Miller & Goodin

MEMBERS OF FIRM

Dennis J. Hummel
Marvin L. Coan
David L. Sage

Representative Clients: Georgia Pacific Corp.; Safeco Insurance Cos.; GRE-/Indiana Insurance Company; Tricon Global Restaurants, Inc.; Dr. Bizer's Vision World; Calvert Insurance Co.; Fabricated Metals Corporation; Western Heritage Insurance Co.; Nobel Insurance Company.

For full biographical listings, see the Martindale-Hubbell Law Directory

MIDDLETON & REUTLINGER, P.S.C. (AV)

2500 Brown and Williamson Tower, 40202-3410
Telephone: 502-584-1135
Fax: 502-561-0442
URL: http://middreut.com
Jeffersonville, Indiana Office: 530 East Court Avenue, 47130.
Telephone: 812-282-1132.
Fax: 812-282-3188.

(See Next Column)

O. Grant Bruton
Kenneth S. Handmaker
Charles G. Middleton, III
Charles D. Greenwell
John W. Bilby
Timothy P. O'Mara
D. Randall Gibson
G. Kennedy Hall, Jr.
Mark S. Fenzel
Kathiejane Oehler
William Jay Hunter, Jr.
James E. Milliman
David J. Kellerman
Julie A. Gregory
Dennis D. Murrell

Augustus S. Herbert
Dana L. Collins

Counsel for: Chevron USA; Logan Aluminum, Inc.; MCI Communications Corp.; Metropolitan Life Insurance Co.; Porcelain Metal Corp.; The Home Insurance Co.; The Kroger Co.; Demars Haka Development, Inc.

For Complete List of Firm Personnel, See General Section

For full biographical listings, see the Martindale-Hubbell Law Directory

O'BRYAN, BROWN & TONER (AV)

455 South Fourth Avenue, Suite 1500, Starks Building, 40202
Telephone: 502-585-4700
Fax: 502-585-4703
Email: mail@obtlaw.com

MEMBERS OF FIRM

Donald K. Brown, Jr.
Christopher P. O'Bryan
Gerald R. Toner
John L. Dotson
Emily A. Faith
James P. Grohmann
David Scott Strite

ASSOCIATES

Andrew N. Clooney
Tracy Sullivan Prewitt
Beth H. McMasters
Cathleen Charters Palmer
Clay Edwards
Peter D. Palmer
Charles Wayne Miller

OF COUNSEL

Joseph C. O'Bryan

For full biographical listings, see the Martindale-Hubbell Law Directory

PEDLEY ZIELKE GORDINIER OLT & PENCE, PLLC (AV)

1150 Starks Building, 455 South Fourth Avenue, 40202
Telephone: 502-589-4600
Fax: 502-584-0422
Email: pzgop@undial.com

MEMBERS OF FIRM

Lawrence L. Pedley
Laurence J. Zielke
John K. Gordinier
Joseph M. Whittle
William W. Stodghill
Stephen B. Pence
Ronald L. Gaffney
John H. Dwyer, Jr.
Ilam E. Smith

OF COUNSEL

Schuyler J. Olt
Linda Shearer Speed

Caroline George Meena
Randal K. Perkins
Michael D. Ekman
Benjamin S. Schecter
Robert Bruce Bonar
Janice M. Theriot

For full biographical listings, see the Martindale-Hubbell Law Directory

SEGAL AND SHANKS (AV)

327 Guthrie Green, 40202
Telephone: 502-583-3455
Fax: 502-583-3039
Jeffersonville, Indiana Office: 425 East 7th Street.
Telephone: 812-288-7107.

MEMBERS OF FIRM

Richard G. Segal
C. A. Dudley Shanks
Perry Adanick

For full biographical listings, see the Martindale-Hubbell Law Directory

SITLINGER, MCGLINCY, STEINER, THEILER & KAREM (AV)

Suite 370, Starks Building, 455 South Fourth Street, 40202-2508
Telephone: 502-589-2627
Fax: 502-583-3415

MEMBERS OF FIRM

Lee E. Sitlinger
Dennis R. McGlincy
Jack W. Steiner, Jr.
Charles E. Theiler, II
Edmund Pete Karem
Curt Sitlinger
Scott Edmund Karem
Tammy C. Snyder

LEGAL SUPPORT PERSONNEL

Lynn Wockenfuss

Representative Clients: State Farm Mutual Automobile Insurance Co; State Farm Fire & Casualty Co.; American International Insurance Co.; Walgreen Company.

For full biographical listings, see the Martindale-Hubbell Law Directory

Louisville—Continued

TILFORD, DOBBINS, ALEXANDER, BUCKAWAY & BLACK (AV)

Suite 1400, One Riverfront Plaza, 40202
Telephone: 502-584-6137
Fax: 502-584-2318

MEMBERS OF FIRM

Charles W. Dobbins (1916-1992)
Henry J. Tilford (1880-1968)
George S. Wetherby (1905-1954)
Lawrence W. Wetherby (1908-1994)
John T. Metcalf (1890-1974)
Stuart E. Alexander
William A. Buckaway, Jr.
Charles W. Dobbins, Jr.
Terrell L. Black
Mark Wesley Dobbins
Stuart E. Alexander, III
John M. Nader

ASSOCIATES

John A. Wilmes
Sandra F. Keene
Patrick T. Schmidt
Thomas J.B. Hurst
H. Kevin Eddins
William J. Walsh, IV
Dana M. Taylor

OF COUNSEL

Randolph Noe
Carolyn K. Balleisen
Michael G. Karem

For full biographical listings, see the Martindale-Hubbell Law Directory

WOODWARD, HOBSON & FULTON (AV)

2500 National City Tower, 101 South Fifth Street, 40202
Telephone: 502-581-8000
Fax: 502-581-8111
Email: WHF@IGLOU.COM
Lexington, Kentucky Office: PNC Bank Plaza, 200 West Vine Street, Suite 500.
Telephone: 606-244-7100.
Telecopier: 606-244-7111.

MEMBERS OF FIRM

Harry K. Herren
Elizabeth Ullmer Mendel
Alice Barns Herrington

ASSOCIATES

Jill F. Lowenbraun
Laurie Goetz Kemp
Robert D. Walker, II

Representative Clients: America Home Insurance Co.; Fireman's Fund Insurance Co.; Prudential Property and Casualty Co.; Royal Insurance Co.; Underwriters at Lloyd's London; CNA Insurance Co.; CIGNA Corp.; American International Group; Acceptance Insurance.

For Complete List of Firm Personnel, See General Section

For full biographical listings, see the Martindale-Hubbell Law Directory

*MADISONVILLE,** Hopkins Co.

FRANKLIN, GORDON & HOBGOOD (AV)

24 Court Street, P.O. Box 547, 42431
Telephone: 502-821-7252

MEMBERS OF FIRM

Charles G. Franklin (1883-1959)
Carroll S. Franklin (1919-1980)
Laurence T. Gordon
Byron L. Hobgood
Charles G. Franklin, II

ASSOCIATE

Paul H. Riley, Jr.

Representative Clients: St. Paul Insurance Cos.; Medical Protective Insurance Co.; Kentucky Medical Insurance Co.; Universal Underwriters; Progressive Casualty Insurance Co.; The Professional Insurance Co.
Approved Attorneys for: Louisville Title Division of Commonwealth Land Title Insurance Co.

*OWENSBORO,** Daviess Co.

MCCARROLL, NUNLEY & HARTZ (AV)

111 East Third Street, P.O. Box 925, 42302-0925
Telephone: 502-683-3535
FAX: 502-926-6056

MEMBERS OF FIRM

Clarence McCarroll (1916-1989)
Marvin P. Nunley
Max S. Hartz

Representative Clients: Aetna Casualty & Surety Company; Allstate Insurance Company; American Hardware Mutual Insurance Company; American Motorists Insurance Company; Automobile Club Insurance Company; Celina Mutual Insurance Company; Chubb Group of Insurance Companies; CIGNA Insurance Companies; Citizens Insurance Company of America; CNA Insurance Company.

For full biographical listings, see the Martindale-Hubbell Law Directory

*PAINTSVILLE,** Johnson Co.

WELLS, PORTER, SCHMITT & JONES (AV)

327 Main Street, 41240
Telephone: 606-789-3747; 789-3749; 789-3775
Fax: 606-789-3790
URL: http://www.wpsj.com

MEMBERS OF FIRM

Michael J. Schmitt
Donald L. Jones

ASSOCIATES

Kimberly E. Colley
Darrin W. Banks

Representative Clients: Kentucky Farm Bureau; Allstate; Grange; CNA; Fireman's Fund; Northbrook; Continental Insurance; CIGNA; Ohio Casualty; Tennessee Farmers Insurance.

For Complete List of Firm Personnel, See General Section

For full biographical listings, see the Martindale-Hubbell Law Directory

*PRESTONSBURG,** Floyd Co.

KAZEE, KINNER & CHAFIN (AV)

119 East Court Street, P.O. Box 700, 41653
Telephone: 606-886-2361; 886-2362
FAX: 606-886-9603
Email: dbkazee@pcc-uky.campus.mci.net
Paintsville, Kentucky Office: Family Federal Building, Suite 202, P.O. Box 1275.
Telephone: 606-789-3059.

MEMBERS OF FIRM

D. B. Kazee
Mitchell D. Kinner
John T. Chafin
P. Franklin Heaberlin
Robert J. Patton
William C. Mullins

Representative Clients: Maryland Casualty Co.; Old Republic Insurance Co.; St. Paul Insurance Cos.; Bituminous Casualty Corp.; Commercial Union Assurance Co.; Kentucky Central Insurance Cos.; Capital Enterprise Insurance Group; State Automobile Mutual Insurance Co.; Reliance Insurance Co.; Scottsdale Insurance Co.

For full biographical listings, see the Martindale-Hubbell Law Directory

LOUISIANA

*ALEXANDRIA,** Rapides Parish

BOLEN & ERWIN, LTD. A PROFESSIONAL LAW CORPORATION (AV)

709 Versailles Boulevard, P.O. Box 11590, 71315-1590
Telephone: 318-445-8236
Fax: 318-443-1770
Email: belaw@bolenlaw.com

James A. Bolen, Jr.
L. Lyle Parker
Daniel G. Brenner

Madeline J. Lee
Michael D. Hislop
Gregory Engelsman
Michael J. Gautier, Jr
Rodney Cabrera
Richard T. Conrad, III
Steven M. Rachal
Donna J. Duplechian

OF COUNSEL

Gregory S. Erwin

For full biographical listings, see the Martindale-Hubbell Law Directory

*BATON ROUGE,** East Baton Rouge Parish

ATKINSON, PERRY, ATKINSON & BALHOFF, L.L.C. (AV)

7520 Perkins Road, Suite 260, P.O. Box 83260, 70884-3260
Telephone: 504-767-7730
Fax: 504-767-7967
Email: apabllc@msn.com

Daniel R. Atkinson
John W. Perry, Jr.
Daniel R. Atkinson, Jr.
Daniel J. Balhoff
Joseph W. Mengis

ASSOCIATE

Barbara G. Baier

LEGAL SUPPORT PERSONNEL

Becky Bourgeois (Legal Secretary/Paralegal)
Renee Bordelon (Legal Secretary/Paralegal)
Sue Rivere (Legal Secretary)
Cindy Martrain (Paralegal)
Wendy Cotton (Legal Secretary)

For full biographical listings, see the Martindale-Hubbell Law Directory

Baton Rouge—Continued

FUNDERBURK & ANDREWS (AV)

329 St. Ferdinand Street, 70802-6146
Telephone: 504-387-2200
Fax: 504-383-0142
Email: fnalaw@bellsouth.net

MEMBERS OF FIRM

Robert C. Funderburk, Jr.
David T. Butler, Jr.
Arthur H. Andrews
Pamela Seeber Chehardy
John L. Dugas

For full biographical listings, see the Martindale-Hubbell Law Directory

LAW OFFICES OF ROBERT D. HOOVER, P.L.C. (AV)

9352 Interline Avenue, P.O. Box 40816, 70835-0816
Telephone: 225-925-2929
Fax: 225-925-2585

Robert D. Hoover

Matthew W. Tierney

For full biographical listings, see the Martindale-Hubbell Law Directory

KLEINPETER & KLEINPETER (AV)

1680 South Lobdell Avenue, Suite E, P.O. Box 66443, 70896
Telephone: 225-926-5093
Telecopier: 225-926-5318

MEMBERS OF FIRM

Robert L. Kleinpeter
R. Loren Kleinpeter

Representative Clients: Argonaut Insurance Co.; American Indemnity Co.; Allstate Insurance Co.; Consolidated American Inc. Co.; South Carolina Insurance Co.; TransAmerica Insurance Group; St. Paul Fire & Marine Insurance Co.; Scottsdale Insurance Co.; Fireman's Fund Insurance Co.; Western Heritage Insurance Co.

For full biographical listings, see the Martindale-Hubbell Law Directory

LANE, FERTITTA, JANNEY & THOMAS (AV)

435 Louisiana Avenue, P.O. Box 3335, 70821
Telephone: 225-387-0241
Fax: 225-387-1238

MEMBERS OF FIRM

Horace C. Lane (1921-1989)
William F. Janney
Frank A. Fertitta
Richard S. Thomas

Representative Clients: State Farm Mutual Automobile Insurance Co.; State Farm Fire & Casualty Co.; United States Fidelity & Guaranty Co.; Aetna Casualty & Surety Co.; Employers Liability Assurance Corp., Ltd.; Allstate Insurance Co.; St. Paul Fire and Marine Insurance Co.; The Medical Protective Co.; Safeco Insurance Co. of America; Horace Mann Insurance Co.

For full biographical listings, see the Martindale-Hubbell Law Directory

LONG LAW FIRM, L.L.P. (AV)

Suite 800 Two United Plaza, 8550 United Plaza Boulevard, 70809-7013
Telephone: 225-922-5110
Fax: 225-922-5105
Email: longlaw.com
Washington, D.C. Office: Market Square, Suite 750, 801 Pennsylvania Avenue, N.W., 20004-2167.
Telephone: 202-737-9212.
FAX: 202-624-0659.

MEMBERS OF FIRM

Russell B. Long
Joseph E. Juban
C. Kris Kirkpatrick
Albert Dale Clary
Michael A. Patterson
David L. Guerry
C. Stokes McConnell, Jr.

ASSOCIATES

Daniel D. Holliday, III
Jennifer J. Vosburg
Tracy Averett Morganti

OF COUNSEL

Melanie Peirron Patrick

For full biographical listings, see the Martindale-Hubbell Law Directory

NAVRATIL, HARDY & BOURGEOIS L.L.P. (AV)

445 North Boulevard, Suite 800, P.O. Box 3551, 70821-3551
Telephone: 225-379-7300
Fax: 225-379-7316

MEMBERS OF FIRM

Boris F. Navratil
David H. Hardy
André G. Bourgeois

ASSOCIATE

Alan P. McGlynn

(See Next Column)

OF COUNSEL

Robert L. Boese
Johnnie L. Matthews

For full biographical listings, see the Martindale-Hubbell Law Directory

SEALE, SMITH, ZUBER & BARNETTE (AV)

Two United Plaza, Suite 200, 8550 United Plaza Boulevard, 70809
Telephone: 225-924-1600
Telecopier: 225-924-6100
Email: SSZB@WORLDNET.ATT.NET

Armbrust Gordon Seale (1913-1989)
Robert W. Smith (1922-1989)
Donald S. Zuber
Kenneth E. Barnette
William C. Kaufman III
John W. L. Swanner
James H. Morgan III
Ronald A. Seale
Charles K. Watts
Brent E. Kinchen
Myron A. Walker, Jr.
Daniel A. Reed
Lawrence R. Anderson, Jr.
Catherine S. Nobile
Anthony J. Russo, Jr.
Richard T. Reed

ASSOCIATE

Michael P. Bienvenu

OF COUNSEL

William H. Brown

Representative Clients: Farmers Insurance Group; St. Paul Fire and Marine Insurance Company; United Services Automobile Association; Progressive Insurance Co.
Reference: Bank One, Louisiana, N.A., Baton Rouge, Louisiana.

For full biographical listings, see the Martindale-Hubbell Law Directory

SHOCKEY & ZIOBER, A PROFESSIONAL LAW CORPORATION (AV)

5551 Corporate Boulevard, Suite 3-A, P.O. Box 80286, 70898-0286
Telephone: 225-929-8929
Telecopier: 225-928-7694

John David Ziober
William C. Shockey

Douglas J. Cochran
James E. Moore, Jr.

For full biographical listings, see the Martindale-Hubbell Law Directory

O'NEAL WALSH & ASSOCIATES (AV)

501 Louisiana Avenue, 70802
Telephone: 225-383-8649
Fax: 225-344-1687
Mailing Address: P.O. Box 3157, Baton Rouge, Louisiana, 70821-3157
Email: onealwalsh@aol.com

O'Neal Walsh

David M. Lefeve
Matthew W. Bailey
W. Paul Wilkins
Scott E. Frazier
Steven A. DeBosier

For full biographical listings, see the Martindale-Hubbell Law Directory

*COVINGTON,** St. Tammany Parish

AUBERT & PAJARES, L.L.C. (AV)

506 East Rutland Street, 70433-3219
Telephone: 504-809-2000
Fax: 504-809-2001
Email: info@aubertpajares.com *URL:* http://www.aubertpajares.com
New Orleans, Louisiana Office: 201 St. Charles Avenue, Suite 2500, 70130.

Christopher J. Aubert
Raymond J. Pajares
David J. Schexnaydre

ASSOCIATES

Tracy E. Gold
David Michael Gold
John W. Fairless
James P. Meyer
Leo R. Hemelt, II
Elizabeth Ashley Carter
William J. Perry
Richard C. Badeaux
Suzanne M. Ganucheau
John V. Lawrence
Brett M. Bollinger
Mark W. Verret
M. Paige Freeman Rosato
Cynthia A. Langston
Richard J. Garvey, Jr.

Representative Clients: Dover Elevator Company; General Star Management Company; Macrsk, Inc.; Penske Truck Leasing Company, L.P.; PHICO Services Company; Reliance National Indemnity Company; Schindler Elevator Corporation; Tenent HealthSystem; Westinghouse Electric Cotporation; Xerox Corporation.

For full biographical listings, see the Martindale-Hubbell Law Directory

*GRETNA,** Jefferson Parish

WINDHORST, GAUDRY, RANSON, HIGGINS & GREMILLION, L.L.C. (AV)

Oakwood Corporate Center, 401 Whitney Avenue Suite 500, P.O. Box 1910, 70056
Telephone: 504-362-2466; 367-9247
Telcopier: 504-362-5938
Email: wgrhg@gs.verio.net

Thomas L. Gaudry, Jr.
Daniel A. Ranson
Daryl A. Higgins
Gregory G. Gremillion
Wade A. Langlois, III
Michael D. Peytavin

OF COUNSEL

Fritz H. Windhorst (Retired)

Steven Dow Oliver
Thomas W. Darling
David J. Dowell, Jr.
John A Leslie
Walter Patrick Maestri
B. Wesley Pitts

Reference: Hibernia National Bank.

For full biographical listings, see the Martindale-Hubbell Law Directory

*HOUMA,** Terrebonne Parish

HENDERSON, HANEMANN & MORRIS, A PROFESSIONAL LAW CORPORATION (AV)

300 Lafayette Street, 70360
Telephone: 504-868-2081
New Orleans: 504-581-1434
Telecopier: 504-868-0080

Philip E. Henderson
Charles Hanemann
Robert L. Morris (1940-1986)
J. Mark Graham
Joseph A. Reilly, Jr.
Barry J. Boudreaux

Emilie Melancon Daye

Representative Clients: Alliance Insurance Company; Applied Hydraulic Systems, Inc.; Falcon Drilling Company, Inc.; Lafayette Insurance Company; Liverpool and London Steamship Protection and Indemnity Association Limited; Louisiana Medical Mutual Insurance Company; The Steamship Mutual Underwriter Association Limited; Gray & Co., Inc.; Union Oil Company of California; Minnesota Mining and Manufacturing Co.

For full biographical listings, see the Martindale-Hubbell Law Directory

*LAFAYETTE,** Lafayette Parish

BROUSSARD, DAVID & DAIGLE, A PROFESSIONAL LAW CORPORATION (AV)

557 Jefferson Street, P.O. Drawer 3308, 70502-3308
Telephone: 318-234-7000
Fax: 318-237-0344
Email: bdandd@bdandd.com *URL:* http://www.bdandd.com

Hal J. Broussard
Susan A. Daigle
Bryan D. Scofield
Ped C. Kay, III
Todd G. Crawford

James T. Rivera
Catherine E. Hensgens

Representative Clients: Certain London Underwriters per individual approval of instructions; Lloyds of London Member Syndicates; Institute of London Underwriter Member Companies; Reliance Insurance Company of Pennsylvania; Reliance Insurance Company of Illinois; Reliance National Insurance Company; The Louisiana Insurance Guaranty Association; Louisiana Oilfield Legislative Committee, Inc. (Louisiana Association of Oilfield Casing Contractors; Association of Oilwell Servicing Contractors; Louisiana Pipeline Contractors Association; Offshore Pipeline Contractors Association; Louisiana Oilfield Contractor Association).

For full biographical listings, see the Martindale-Hubbell Law Directory

DAVIDSON, MEAUX, SONNIER, MCELLIGOTT & SWIFT (AV)

810 South Buchanan Street, P.O. Drawer 2908, 70502
Telephone: 318-237-1660
Fax: 318-237-3676

MEMBERS OF FIRM

James J. Davidson, Jr. (1904-1990)
V. Farley Sonnier (1942-1988)
Richard C. Meaux, Sr.
James J. Davidson, III
John E. McElligott, Jr.
John G. Swift
Jeffrey A. Rhoades
Philip A. Fontenot
Kyle L. Gideon
Theodore G. Edwards, IV
Mark C. Andrus

ASSOCIATES

John T. Andrishok
Christopher J. Piasecki
Nicholas J. Zeringue

(See Next Column)

OF COUNSEL

Jan Whitehead Swift

General Counsel: Southwest Louisiana Electric Membership Corp., Inc.; Macro Oil Co., Inc.; Dwight W. Andrus Insurance Agency; Lafayette Airport Commission.
Local Counsel: Southern Pacific Transportation Co.
Representative Clients: Highlands Insurance Co.; Wal-Mart Stores, Inc.; USAA.

For full biographical listings, see the Martindale-Hubbell Law Directory

JEANSONNE & REMONDET, L.L.C. (AV)

200 West Congress Street, Suite 1100, P.O. Box 91530, 70509
Telephone: 318-237-4370
Facsimile: 318-235-2011
New Orleans, Louisiana Office: 1 Canal Place, 365 Canal Street, Suite 2300.
Telephone: 504-524-7333.
Fax: 504-524-3339.
Shreveport, Louisiana Office: Harry Patterson Tower, 6007 Financial Plaza, Suite 708.
Telephone: 318-671-8102.
Fax: 318-671-8103.

John A. Jeansonne, Jr.
Michael J. Remondet, Jr.

G. Andrew Veazey
Donald W. Washington
Dona K. Renegar
Jason B. Boudreaux
Thomas H. Huval
James T. McManus
Joseph S. Cage, Jr.
Pride J. Doran
R. Royal Alexander
Mary Katherine Paine

LEGAL SUPPORT PERSONNEL

Monica L. Abshire (Paralegal, Office Manager and Notary Public)
Nancy M. Fruge (Paralegal)
Christi A. Guidry
S. Dianne Thibodeaux (Paralegal)

For full biographical listings, see the Martindale-Hubbell Law Directory

JUDICE & ADLEY, A PROFESSIONAL LAW CORPORATION (AV)

926 Coolidge Boulevard, Drawer 51769, 70505
Telephone: 318-235-2405
Fax: 318-235-0965
Email: judicadley@ibm.net

Marc W. Judice
Michael W. Adley
James J. Hautot, Jr.
Katherine A. Pavy
Jocelyn R. Guidry

Danielle M. Smith
Imelda T. Fisher
Stacy N. Amy
Michelle Regan Popp

Representative Clients: American International Cos.; Chubb Group; Electric Mutual Insurance Co.; Evanston Insurance Co.; First Horizon Insurance Co.; First State Insurance Co.; General Electric Co.; The Hartford Group; Highlands Insurance Co.; Insurance Company of North America.

For full biographical listings, see the Martindale-Hubbell Law Directory

THE JUNEAU FIRM A PROFESSIONAL LAW CORPORATION (AV)

The Harding Center, 1018 Harding Street Suite 202, 70503
Telephone: 318-269-0052
Facsimile: 318-269-0061
Mailing Address: P.O. Drawer 51268, Lafayette, Louisiana, 70505-1268

Patrick A. Juneau
Michael J. Juneau
Barry L. Domingue
Thomas R. Juneau
Sue Nations
John R. Whaley
Karen B. Levy

Representative Clients: Allianz Insurance Co.; American International Group; American Re-Insurance Co.; Audubon Insurance Group; CNA Insurance Cos.; Electric Insurance Co.; Jefferson Insurance Co.; Lexington Insurance Co.; Reliance National Insurance Co.; United National Insurance Group.

For full biographical listings, see the Martindale-Hubbell Law Directory

ONEBANE, BERNARD, TORIAN, DIAZ, MCNAMARA & ABELL (AV)

Suite 600, Versailles Centre, 102 Versailles Boulevard, P.O. Box 3507, 70502
Telephone: 318-237-2660
Telecopier: 318-266-1232
Email: info@onebane.com
Monroe, Louisiana Office: 1900 N. 18th Street, Suite 420, P.O. Box 2255, 71207.
Telephone: 318-340-0220.
Fax: 318-340-0110.

(See Next Column)

ONEBANE, BERNARD, TORIAN, DIAZ, MCNAMARA & ABELL, *Lafayette—Continued*

Joseph Onebane (1917-1987)
John G. Torian, II (1936-1991)
James E. Diaz
Timothy J. McNamara
Edward C. Abell, Jr.
Lawrence L. Lewis, III
Robert M. Mahony
Daniel G. Fournerat
Douglas W. Truxillo
Randall C. Songy
Michael G. Durand
Greg Guidry
Joseph L. Lemoine, Jr.
Mark L. Riley
Graham N. Smith
Gordon T. Whitman
Gary P. Kraus
Richard J. Petre, Jr.
Charles J. Boudreaux, Jr.
James R. Shelton
Thomas G. Smart
Roger E. Ishee
Jennifer M. Kleinpeter
Steven C. Lanza
Joel P. Babineaux

Alison M. Brumley
Jesse D. Lambert
Brent G. Sonnier
Cary B. Bryson
Maria F. Manuel
Greg R. Mier
Jennifer L. Smith
Janice Church Reeves
Mark B. Oliver
Chanelle T. Delahoussaye
Aimee L. Williams
A.G. "Alec" Alexander, III
Terry J. Blanchard
William E. Bourgeois (Resident, Monroe, Louisiana Office)

OF COUNSEL

William E. Kellner

Representative Clients: Commercial Union Insurance Co.; Enron Corp.; Highlands Insurance Co.; Marathon Oil Co.; Ocean Energy, Inc.; Pizza Hut, Inc.; St. Paul Insurance Companies; Schering-Plough Corp.; Tenneco, Inc.; Whitney National Bank.

For full biographical listings, see the Martindale-Hubbell Law Directory

PREIS KRAFT & ROY, A PROFESSIONAL LAW CORPORATION (AV)

Suite 400, Versailles CentrÉ, 102 Versailles Boulevard, P.O. Drawer 94-C, 70509
Telephone: 318-237-6062
Fax: 318-237-9129
Email: pkr@pkrlaw.com
NewOrleans Office: Pan American Life Center, 601 Poydras Street, Suite 1855.
Telephone: 504-581-6062.
Fax: 504-522-9129.
Houston, Texas Office: 520 Post Oak Boulevard, Suite 800.
Telephone: 713-355-6062.
Telefax: 713-572-9129.

Edwin G. Preis, Jr.
Ralph E. Kraft
L. Lane Roy
Ward F. Lafleur
F. Douglas Gatz, Jr.
Charles A. Mouton
Kay A. Theunissen
Jennifer E. Beyer
Richard J. Hymel
George Caflisch (Not admitted in LA; Resident, Houston, Texas Office)

David R. Rabalais
Marc D. Moroux
Edward King Alexander, Jr.
G. Edward Williams, Jr.
Timothy W. Basden
Larry A. Wallace, Jr.
L. Marika Steele
Jeff R. Rytlewski
Angella R. Hebert
Alison Ann Darsey
Jean Ann Billeaud

Approved Counsel for: American Gulf Group; American International Group; American Oilfield Divers, Inc.; American P & I Club; American United Life Insurance Company; Association of Diving Contractors, Inc.; Assuranceforeningen Gard; Assuranceforeningen Skuld, Automation Communication Engeneering Corporation; Cal Dive International, Inc.; CBI Industries, Inc.

For full biographical listings, see the Martindale-Hubbell Law Directory

VOORHIES & LABBÉ, A PROFESSIONAL LAW CORPORATION (AV)

Fourth Floor, St. John Place, 700 St. John Street, P.O. Box 3527, 70502-3527
Telephone: 318-232-9700
Fax: 318-235-4943
Email: vl@vola.com *URL:* http://www.vola.com

Bennett J. Voorhies (1901-1970)
Donald Labbé (1900-1966)
D. Mark Bienvenu (1931-1991)
Robert A. Lecky (1940-1998)
H. Edwin McGlasson, Jr.
W. Gerald Gaudet
Richard D. Chappuis, Jr.
William M. Bass
John N. Chappuis
Robert L. Ellender
Cyd Sheree Page
Robert M. Francez
Robert M. Kallam
Elizabeth L. Guglielmo
Samuel R. Aucoin
James Allen Lochridge, Jr.
Mary McCrory Hamilton
Bradley Joseph Haight
Simone Chachere Dupre
George J. Armbruster, III

Julie A. Scheib
Brent Paul Frederick

(See Next Column)

OF COUNSEL

John W. Hutchison

Representative Clients: Adams & Porter Associates; Aetna Casualty & Surety Insurance Co.; AIG Aviation, Inc.; American Home Assurance Co.; AMICA Mutual Insurance Co.; Appalachian Insurance Co.; Audubon/AIG Insurance Co.; Aviation Office of America; Bellefonte Insurance Co.; Chubb Group of Insurance Co.

For full biographical listings, see the Martindale-Hubbell Law Directory

*LAKE CHARLES,** Calcasieu Parish

BERGSTEDT & MOUNT (AV)

Second Floor, Magnolia Life Building, P.O. Drawer 3004, 70602-3004
Telephone: 318-433-3004
Facsimile: 318-433-8080

MEMBERS OF FIRM

Thomas M. Bergstedt
Benjamin W. Mount
Van C. Seneca

ASSOCIATE

Annette N. Peltier

OF COUNSEL

Charles S. Ware

Representative Clients: ARCO Chemical Company; Ashland Oil Co.; CIGNA Property & Casualty Companies; Columbia Women's & Children's Hospital; The Hartford Steam Boiler Inspection & Insurance Company; Leach Company; Olin Corporation; Occidental Chemical Corporation; Terra Corporation; R. D. Werner Company.

For full biographical listings, see the Martindale-Hubbell Law Directory

GUILLORY & MCCALL, L.L.C. (AV)

901 Lakeshore Drive, Suite 1030, P.O. Drawer 1607, 70602-1607
Telephone: 318-433-9996
Telefax: 318-433-9937

Robert E. Guillory, Jr.
William T. McCall
H. Clay Ward, III
Drury B. Cunningham

Representative Clients: American Interstate Insurance Company; American Modern Insurance Group; Cigna Property and Casualty Companies; Eagle Insurance Group (WA); Gryphon Insurance Group; ITT Hartford Insurance Group; Shelter Mutual Insurance Company; Superior National Insurance Group; Associated International Insurance Company.

For full biographical listings, see the Martindale-Hubbell Law Directory

PLAUCHÉ SMITH & NIESET, A PROFESSIONAL LAW CORPORATION (AV)

1123 Pithon Street, P.O. Drawer 1705, 70602
Telephone: 318-436-0522
Facsimile: 318-436-9637

S. W. Plauché (1889-1952)
S. W. Plauché, Jr. (1915-1966)
A. Lane Plauché
Allen L. Smith, Jr.
James R. Nieset
Frank M. Walker, Jr.
Michael J. McNulty, III
Jeffrey M. Cole
Andrew R. Johnson, IV
Charles V. Musso, Jr.
Christopher P. Ieyoub
H. David Vaughan, II
Joseph R. Pousson, Jr.
Rebecca S. Young
V. Ed McGuire, III

Representative Clients: CIGNA; CNA Insurance Cos.; Commercial Union Insurance Cos.; Crum & Forster; Reliance Insurance Cos.; Royal Insurance Group; State Farm; U.S. Insurance Group.

For full biographical listings, see the Martindale-Hubbell Law Directory

WOODLEY, WILLIAMS, BOUDREAU, NORMAN, BROWN & DOYLE (AV)

A Registered Limited Liability Company
500 Kirby Street, P.O. Box 3731, 70602-3731
Telephone: 318-433-6328
Facsimile: 318-433-7513
Email: woodley@woodleywilliams.com

MEMBERS OF FIRM

Edmund E. Woodley (1925-1989)
James E. Williams (P.C.)
Robert J. Boudreau
Rick J. Norman
Donald C. Brown
James B. Doyle
Thomas J. Solari
Darrell W. Alston
Michele S. Caballero
M. Keith Prudhomme
Matthew D. Henrich

OF COUNSEL

Milo A. Nickel

Representative Clients: Agency Management Corp.; Travelers Insurance Co.

For full biographical listings, see the Martindale-Hubbell Law Directory

METAIRIE, Jefferson Parish

HAILEY, MCNAMARA, HALL, LARMANN & PAPALE, L.L.P. (AV)

A Limited Liability Partnership including Professional Law Corporations
Suite 1400, One Galleria Boulevard, P.O. Box 8288, 70011
Telephone: 504-836-6500
Fax: 504-836-6565
URL: http://www.haileymcnamara.com

MEMBERS OF FIRM

James W. Hailey, Jr., (P.L.C.)
W. Marvin Hall (P.L.C.)
Antonio E. Papale, Jr., (P.L.C.)
Laurence E. Larmann (P.L.C.)
Michael P. Mentz
Richard T. Simmons, Jr.,(P.L.C.)
Michael J. Vondenstein
David K. Persons
Dominic J. Ovella
C. Kelly Lightfoot
John T. Culotta (P.L.C.)
John E. Unsworth, Jr.
Julie DiFulco Robles
Claude A. Greco
Valerie T. Schexnayder
W. Evan Plauche
Kurt D. Engelhardt

ASSOCIATES

William R. Seay, Jr.
W. Glenn Burns
James W. Hailey, III
Frederic Theodore Le Clercq
Barbara Bourdonnay O'Donnell
Kathryn T. Wiedorn
Joseph L. Spilman, III
Caroline D. Ibos
Robert D. Ford
Lynnette Hall-Lewis
Kevin O. Larmann
Tammy M. Stewart
Danny N. Bowz
Edward C. Vocke, IV
C. Angelle Goudeau
Alayne R. Corcoran
David K. Groome, Jr.
Kristen M. Baumer
Gabriel J. Veninata

OF COUNSEL

Henry D. McNamara, Jr., (P.L.C.)

Representative Clients: Diamond Offshore Drilling Inc.; The Flintkote Co.; Lockheed Martin Corporation; Rheem Manufacturing Co.; State Farm Fire & Casualty Co.; Textron, Inc; Travelers Companies; Coca-Cola Enterprises, Inc.

For full biographical listings, see the Martindale-Hubbell Law Directory

REICH, MEEKS & TREADAWAY, L.L.C. (AV)

Two Lakeway Center, Suite 1830, 3850 North Causeway Boulevard, 70002
Telephone: 504-830-3999
Fax: 504-830-3950
URL: http://www.rmtlaw.com

Robert S. Reich
S. Daniel Meeks
Randell E. Treadaway
Lawrence R. Plunkett, Jr.

Michelle L. Maraist
Jimmy Arthur Castex, Jr.
Mark S. Senter
Patricia Cowen Penton
Patrice W. Oppenheim
John B. Esnard, III

For full biographical listings, see the Martindale-Hubbell Law Directory

*MONROE,** Ouachita Parish

DAVENPORT, FILES & KELLY, L.L.P. (AV)

1509 Lamy Lane, P.O. Box 4787, 71211-4787
Telephone: 318-387-6453
FAX: 318-323-6533
Email: dfk@dfklaw.com

Thos. W. Davenport (1909-1962)
Wm. G. Kelly, Jr.
Thomas W. Davenport, Jr.
Jack B. Files
Mike C. Sanders
Ramsey L. Ogg
Michael J. Fontenot
M. Shane Craighead

W. David Hammett
Carey B. Underwood

STAFF ATTORNEY

Stacy L. Guice

Representative Clients: American International Group (AIG); Chubb Group; Commercial Aviation; GAINSCO; GEICO; Highlands Ins. Co.; Scottsdale Ins. Co.; Trinity Universal Ins. Co.; United States Aircraft Ins. Group; Zurich-American Ins. Cos.

For full biographical listings, see the Martindale-Hubbell Law Directory

HAYES, HARKEY, SMITH & CASCIO, L.L.P. (AV)

2811 Kilpatrick Boulevard, P.O. Box 8032, 71211-8032
Telephone: 318-387-2422
FAX: 318-388-5809

Thomas M. Hayes, Jr. (1915-1994)
Louis D. Smith (Retired)
Joseph D. Cascio, Jr.
Charles S. Smith
Thomas M. Hayes, III
Bruce McKamy Mintz
C. Joseph Roberts, III
John B. Saye

(See Next Column)

OF COUNSEL

Haynes L. Harkey, Jr.

Karen L. Hayes
Harry McClellan Moffett, IV

Representative Clients: American Indemnity Co.; Employers Reinsurance Corporation; Hanover Insurance Co.; Cigna, Inc.; CNA; Ohio Casualty Insurance Cos.; State Farm Insurance Co.; St. Francis Medical Center, Inc.; St. Paul Insurance Group; Travelers Ins. Co.

For full biographical listings, see the Martindale-Hubbell Law Directory

THEUS, GRISHAM, DAVIS & LEIGH, L.L.P. (AV)

1600 Lamy Lane, Drawer 4768, 71211-4768
Telephone: 318-388-0100
Fax: 318-322-8813
Email: tgdl@theuslaw.com *URL:* http://www.theuslaw.com

MEMBERS OF FIRM

John C. Theus, Sr. (1865-1938)
Orin M. Grisham (1866-1944)
Ronald L. Davis (1897-1959)
John C. Theus, Jr. (1901-1972)
E. K. Theus (1906-1974)
Thomas W. Leigh (1903-1983)
Ronald L. Davis, Jr. (1930-1999)
Robert Lee Curry, III
Charles H. Heck
Edwin K. Theus, Jr.
J. Michael Hart
Paul D. Spillers
Phillip D. Myers
David H. Nelson
Thomas G. Zentner, Jr.
James M. Edwards
Robert J. Bozeman
Sharon Ingram Marchman
C. Wendell Manning
F. Williams Sartor, Jr.
George M. Snellings, IV

ASSOCIATE

Charles H. Heck, Jr.

Representative Clients: Moore Oil Co., Inc.; CNA Insurance Company; American International Group, Inc.; Commercial Union Insurance Co.; Liberty Mutual Insurance Co.; Louisiana Medical Mutual Insurance Co.; Travelers Insurance Co.

For full biographical listings, see the Martindale-Hubbell Law Directory

*NATCHITOCHES,** Natchitoches Parish

CORKERN & CREWS, L.L.C. (AV)

616 Front Street, P.O. Box 1036, 71458-1036
Telephone: 318-352-2302
Telecopier: 318-352-7548
Email: recsec@cp-tel.net

MEMBERS OF FIRM

Ronald E. Corkern, Jr.
Steven D. Crews

Jason O. Methvin

Representative Clients: State Farm Mutual Auto Ins. Co.; State Farm Fire & Casualty Company; Town of Campti; City of Natchitoches; Town of Montgomery; Conagra, Inc.; Corsection Corp. of America; Edward D. Jones & Co.; Natchitoches Housing Authority; St. Paul Cos.; Ranger Ins. Co.; Louisiana Sheriff's Assn.; Colonial Life & Accident Ins. Co.; Patterson Ins. Co.; Gallagher-Bassett.

For full biographical listings, see the Martindale-Hubbell Law Directory

*NEW IBERIA,** Iberia Parish

LANDRY & WATKINS (AV)

211 East Main Street, P.O. Box 12040, 70562-2040
Telephone: 318-364-7626; Lafayette: 318-234-5921
Telecopier: 318-367-2715
Email: LanWat@aol.com

MEMBERS OF FIRM

Alfred Smith Landry
Edward P. Landry
William A. Repaske
Kreig A. Breaux

OF COUNSEL

Jacob S. Landry
Guyton H. Watkins

ASSOCIATE

Charles Benjamin Landry

Representative Clients: Entex, a Division of NorAm Energy Corp.; Iberia Sugar Co-operative, Inc.; Hartford Accident & Indemnity Co.; Iberia Savings Bank; Liberty Mutual Insurance Co.; Premier Bank, N.A.; CNA Insurance Companies; USAA; Federated Insurance Co.; Nationwide Insurance Co.

For full biographical listings, see the Martindale-Hubbell Law Directory

ROY, FORREST & LOPRESTO, LTD. (AV)

110 French Street, P.O. Box 10087, 70562-0087
Telephone: 318-364-2343
Fax: 318-364-6702
Email: rf&lattys@aisp.net
Lafayette, Louisiana Office: 714 East Kaliste Saloom Road, Suite A-2, P.O. Drawer 53569, 70508.
Telephone: 318-232-5137.
Fax: 318-232-5297.

(See Next Column)

ROY, FORREST & LOPRESTO LTD., *New Iberia—Continued*

Leon E. Roy, Jr. (1936-1988)
L. Albert Forrest
Alex A. Lopresto, III
Leon E. Roy, III

Representative Clients: State Farm Insurance Cos.; Bank One; Trinity Cos.; Insured Lloyds; U.S. Aviation Insurance Group; Universal Fabricators, Inc.; Prudential Property and Casualty Co.; National Security & Fire Insurance Co.; Rowan Companies, Inc.; Cal Dive International, Inc.

For full biographical listings, see the Martindale-Hubbell Law Directory

*NEW ORLEANS,** Orleans Parish

BAUS, HAMMOND & DALY, L.L.P. (AV)

200 Carondelet Street Suite 1600, 70130-2922
Telephone: 504-569-0380
Fax: 504-569-0386
Email: bhd@bhdlaw.com *URL:* http://www.bhdlaw.com

John V. Baus, Jr.
Peirce A. Hammond, II
David S. Daly
Jennifer Carter de Blanc

For full biographical listings, see the Martindale-Hubbell Law Directory

BEST KOEPPEL, A PROFESSIONAL LAW CORPORATION (AV)

LL & E Tower, 909 Poydras Street Suite 2200, 70112
Telephone: 504-593-2400
Telecopier: 504-593-2401
Email: bstkpplesq@aol.com
Houston, Texas Office: 1900 West Loop South, Suite 300, 77027.
Telephone: 713-964-4072.
Telecopier: 713-963-2503.

Laurence E. Best
Peter S. Koeppel
R. Jeffrey Bridger
James H. Daigle, Jr.
M. Davis Ready
Suzanne M. Risey

LEGAL SUPPORT PERSONNEL

PARALEGAL

Debora N. Dufrene

Representative Clients: Lexington Insurance Co.; Rowan Companies, Inc.; Rowandrill, Inc.; Rowan International, Inc.; Atlantic Maritime Services, Inc.; Rowan Drilling (U.K.), Ltd.; Hartford Insurance Co.; Trinity Marine Group; Elevating Boats, Inc.; CITGO Petroleum Corp.

For full biographical listings, see the Martindale-Hubbell Law Directory

BOGGS, LOEHN & RODRIGUE (AV)

A Partnership including Law Corporations
Suite 1850, Entergy Building, 639 Loyola Avenue, 70130-3597
Telephone: 504-523-7090
Fax: 504-581-6822
Email: BLAR@bellsouth.net

Charles A. Boggs (A Law Corporation)
Thomas E. Loehn (A Law Corporation)
Edward A. Rodrigue, Jr., (A Law Corporation)

Anne E. Medo
Matthew B. Moreland

Reference: First National Bank of Commerce, New Orleans, La.

For full biographical listings, see the Martindale-Hubbell Law Directory

BUCKLEY & HAYES, L.L.P. (AV)

A Partnership including a Professional Corporation
1555 Poydras Street Suite 1700, 70112
Telephone: 504-523-5100
Fax: 504-523-5698
Covington, Louisiana Office: 2301 North HIghway 190, Suite 3, 70433.
Telephone: 504-871-7005.
Fax: 504-871-7051.

MEMBERS OF FIRM

Lloyd W. Hayes
E. Ross Buckley, Jr., (A Professional Law Corp.)
Marianne S. Pensa
William H. Voigt

ASSOCIATES

Michele D. Ahlers
Ernest Philip Legier, Jr.
Elton A. Foster

OF COUNSEL

Harold A. Thomas

For full biographical listings, see the Martindale-Hubbell Law Directory

CHRISTOVICH AND KEARNEY, L.L.P. (AV)

Suite 2300 Pan American Life Center, 601 Poydras Street, 70130-6078
Telephone: 504-561-5700
Fax: 504-561-5743
Email: c&k@christovich.com

(See Next Column)

MEMBERS OF FIRM

Alvin R. Christovich, Jr.
William K. Christovich
J. Walter Ward, Jr.
Lawrence J. Ernst
James F. Holmes
Robert E. Peyton
C. Edgar Cloutier
Charles W. Schmidt, III
Richard K. Christovich
Terry Christovich Gay
E. Phelps Gay
J. Warren Gardner, Jr.
Kevin R. Tully
Lance R. Rydberg
Elizabeth S. Cordes
Charles M. Lanier, Jr.
Philip J. Borne
James A. Holmes

ASSOCIATES

Robert D. Peyton
Craig B. Mitchell
Joseph M. Guillot
Scott J. Sonnier
John K. Nieset
Janet L. White
Mary Beth Meyer
Kory J. Ickler

OF COUNSEL

John A. Stassi II

Representative Clients: Highlands Insurance Co.; Progressive Insurance Company; AIG Group; Liberty Mutual Insurance Co.; Ranger Insurance Co.; CNA Insurance Cos.; Underwriters at Lloyds; Associated Aviation Underwriters; Relaince National Risk Specialists; Zurich-American Insurance Group.

For full biographical listings, see the Martindale-Hubbell Law Directory

EVANS AND CLESI, A PROFESSIONAL LAW CORPORATION (AV)

336 Lafayette Street, Suite 200, 70130
Telephone: 504-523-8523
Fax: 504-523-8522
Email: evansandclesi@juno.com

Kenneth Randall Evans
Anthony J. Clesi, Jr.

Lane A. Schaffer
William M. McGoey
H. James Parker
Karen M. Dicke

OF COUNSEL

Jeanne Lazarre Billings

Representative Clients: State Farm Mutual Automobile Insurance Co.; State Farm Fire & Casualty Co.; International Indemnity Co.; Regional Transit Authority; Transit Management of Southeast Louisiana; State of Louisiana Office of Risk Management.

For full biographical listings, see the Martindale-Hubbell Law Directory

FRILOT, PARTRIDGE, KOHNKE & CLEMENTS, L.C. (AV)

3600 Energy Centre, 1100 Poydras Street, 70163-3600
Telephone: 504-599-8000
Telecopier: 504-599-8100
Email: postmaster@fpkc.com *URL:* http://www.fpkc.com

Francis H. Brown, III
James H. Brown, Jr.
George E. Cain, Jr.
Michael T. Cali
Miles P. Clements
Andrew S. de Klerk
George A. Frilot, III (A Professional Law Corp.)
John J. Hainkel, III
Edward F. Kohnke, IV
Allen J. Krouse, III
J. Dwight LeBlanc, III
Douglas P. Matthews
Kenneth A. Mayeaux
Robert B. McNeal
Wayne K. McNeil
Patrick J. McShane
Joseph N. Mole
David A. Olson
Scott S. Partridge
Greg A. Pellegrini
Michael R. Phillips
James F. Shuey
James R. Silverstein
Peter E. Sperling
Patrick A. Talley (P.C.)
Patricia E. Weeks

Sidney A. Backstrom
Joel Edwin Cape (Not admitted in LA)
Nairda T. Lesa Colón
Bruce Arne Cranner
Frederick T. Greschner, Jr.
Brant David Imperatore
Stephanie Ann May
Michael B. North

For full biographical listings, see the Martindale-Hubbell Law Directory

JOHNSON, JOHNSON, BARRIOS & YACOUBIAN, A PROFESSIONAL LAW CORPORATION (AV)

One Shell Square, 701 Poydras Street, Suite 4900, 70139-7701
Telephone: 504-528-3001
Facsimile: 504-528-3030
Email: jjbylaw@bellsouth.net

Ronald A. Johnson
Edward S. Johnson
Bettye A. Barrios
Alan J. Yacoubian
Salvador J. Pusateri
Rene S. Paysse, Jr.

Cindy T. Matherne
Lance E. Harwell
Salvatore A. Faso, II
Michael W. Mallory
Kevin G. Barreca
Wesley S. Alost
Thomas A. French
T. Gavin Hoppe

(See Next Column)

JOHNSON, JOHNSON, BARRIOS & YACOUBIAN A PROFESSIONAL LAW CORPORATION—*Continued*

Representative Clients: AXA Global Risks (UK) Ltd.; Canal Insurance Company; Commercial Union Assurance Company, PLC; Global Special Risks, Inc.; Institute of London Underwriters Companies; Louisiana Insurance Guaranty Association; Permanent General Assurance Corporation; RCA Syndicate #1, Ltd.; Underwriters at Lloyd's, London; Zurich Re (UK) Ltd.

For full biographical listings, see the Martindale-Hubbell Law Directory

LEAKE, ANDERSSON & MANN, L.L.P. (AV)

1700 Energy Centre, 1100 Poydras Street, 70163-1701
Telephone: 504-585-7500
Facsimile: 504-585-7775

W. Paul Andersson
Lawrence A. Mann
Kevin Cramer O'Bryon
George D. Fagan
Donald E. McKay, Jr.
Stanton E. Shuler, Jr.
Guy D. Perrier

OF COUNSEL

Robert E. Leake, Jr.

ASSOCIATES

J. Ronald Ward, Jr.
Louis P. Bonnaffons
Ellen Heidingsfelder Manning
Dean M. Arruebarrena
Craig M. Cousins
Charles R. Daniel, II

Representative Clients: GEICO; Preferred Risk Mutual Insurance Co.; National Union Fire Insurance Co.; Nationwide Insurance Co.; U.S. Fire Insurance Co.; Interstate Insurance Gp.; Kemper Insurance; Great West Casualty Company.

For full biographical listings, see the Martindale-Hubbell Law Directory

LEE, FUTRELL & PERLES, L.L.P. (AV)

Suite 2409, 201 St. Charles Avenue, 70170-2409
Telephone: 504-569-1725
Fax: 504-569-1726
Email: mgr@leefutrell.com *URL:* http://www.lawyers.com/lf&plaw

Gary A. Lee
John Maurice Futrell
Richard M. Perles

Representative Clients: Certain Underwriters at Lloyd's, London; Institute of London Underwriters Companies.

For full biographical listings, see the Martindale-Hubbell Law Directory

LOWE, STEIN, HOFFMAN, ALLWEISS & HAUVER, L.L.P. (AV)

One Shell Square, 701 Poydras Street Suite 3600, 70139-7735
Telephone: 504-581-2450
Telecopier: 504-581-2461

MEMBERS OF FIRM

Mitchell J. Hoffman
Michael R. Allweiss
Max J. Cohen
Marynell L. Piglia

Kermit L. Roux, III
Paula H. Lee
Stanley Dale Broome

For Complete List of Firm Personnel, See General Section

For full biographical listings, see the Martindale-Hubbell Law Directory

MAGINNIS & HURLEY, A PROFESSIONAL LAW CORPORATION (AV)

Suite 2040 Canal Place One, 365 Canal Street, 70130
Telephone: 504-524-5353
Fax: 504-524-5403
Email: maginnis+hurley@gs.net

Michael J. Maginnis
Timothy P. Hurley
José R. Cot
Sallye Goodwin Webb
Lisa D. Kothe

For full biographical listings, see the Martindale-Hubbell Law Directory

McGLINCHEY STAFFORD (AV)

A Professional Limited Liability Company
643 Magazine Street, 70130-3477
Telephone: 504-586-1200
Fax: 504-596-2800
TDD: (504) 596-2728
Telex: 584327
Cable Address: "MACSTAC"
Mailing Address: P.O. Box 60643, New Orleans, Louisiana, 70160-0643
Email: @mcglinchey.com *URL:* http://www.mcglinchey.com
Dallas, Texas Office: 2777 Stemmons Freeway, Suite 925, 75207-2401.
Telephone: 214-860-9700.
Fax: 214-860-9750.
Houston, Texas Office: 2727 Allen Parkway, Suite 1900, 77019.
Telephone: 713-520-1900.
Fax: 713-520-1025.

(See Next Column)

Baton Rouge, Louisiana Office: Ninth Floor, One American Place, 70825-0001.
Telephone: 504-383-9000.
Fax: 504-343-3076.
Jackson, Mississippi Office: Suite 1200, SkyTel Centre, 200 South Lamar Street, 39201.
Telephone: 601-960-8400.
Fax: 601-960-8406.
Lake Providence, Louisiana Office: 405 Morgan Street, 71254-2691.
Telephone: 318-559-1200.
Fax: 318-559-0609.
Monroe, Louisiana Office: Dean ONB Tower, 130 Desiard Street, Suite 807, 71201.
Telephone: 318-651-0807.
Fax: 318-651-0809.

MEMBERS OF FIRM

William V. Dalferes, Jr., (P.C.)
Stephen W. Rider
Lauren A. Welch
Arthur H. Leith
Michael J. de Blanc, Jr.
Monica A. Frois

ASSOCIATES

Elizabeth P. Blitch
Erin Fury Parkinson
Deirdre C. McGlinchey
Dwayne C. Jefferson

MEMBERS OF FIRM

Michael David Ferachi (Resident, Baton Rouge Office)
Samuel E. Scott (Resident, Jackson Office)
Mark A. Sanders (Resident, Houston Office)
James C. Crigler, Jr. (Resident, Lake Providence Office)
Wesson H. Tribble (Resident, Houston Office)
Dan E. West (Resident, Baton Rouge Office)

ASSOCIATES

Kathleen H. Eiler (Resident, Jackson Office)
Pamela L. Hancock (Resident, Jackson Office)
Lisa C. Bingham (Resident, Houston Office)
Renee Gluth (Resident, Baton Rouge Office)
Craig A. Horton (Resident, Houston Office)
Shannon Richards (Resident, Houston Office)
Virginia M. Todd (Resident, Jackson Office)
Mark H. Tyson (Resident, Jackson Office)

For full biographical listings, see the Martindale-Hubbell Law Directory

MIDDLEBERG, RIDDLE & GIANNA (AV)

201 St. Charles Avenue Suite 3100, 70170-3100
Telephone: 504-525-7200
Telecopier: 504-581-5983
Dallas, Texas Office: 2323 Bryan Street, Suite 1600.
Telephone: 214-220-6300;
Telecopier: 214-220-2785.
Austin, Texas Office: 1300 South Mopac Expressway, First Floor.
Telephone: 512-434-8334.
Houston, Texas Office: 7676 Woodway, Suite 325.
Telephone: 713-430-5000.
Telecopier: 713-430-5090.

MEMBERS OF FIRM

Ira Joel Middleberg
Michael Lee Riddle (Not admitted in LA)
Dominic J. Gianna

Paul J. Mirabile
John D. Person
Alan Dean Weinberger
L. Marlene Quarles
Edward T. Suffern, Jr.
Barry H. Grodsky
E. Ralph Lupin
A.J. Herbert, III
Marshall J. Simien, Jr.
Wade P. Webster
Rebecca J. King
Alvin Moon
Ernestine L. Anderson-Trahan
Steven A. Watts
R. Dean Church, Jr.
Michael M. Simpson
Michele A. Engnath

For full biographical listings, see the Martindale-Hubbell Law Directory

PLAUCHÉ MASELLI LANDRY & PARKERSON L.L.P. (AV)

Bank One Center, Suite 4240, 201 St. Charles Avenue, 70170-4240
Telephone: 504-582-1142
Fax: 504-582-1172
URL: http://www.pmlpnola.com

MEMBERS OF FIRM

Andrew L. Plauché, Jr.
Joseph Maselli, Jr.
Arthur W. Landry
G. Bruce Parkerson
Robert E Caraway, III

ASSOCIATES

Mark E. Young
Thomas L. Hutchinson
Cherie T. Burlett
Kenan S. Rand, Jr.
Elizabeth Salzer Schell
J. Marie Rudd
Wendy K. Lappenga
Deborah F. Malveaux
Diane S. Mitnik
Lori P. Moser

Reference: Bank One of Louisiana.

For full biographical listings, see the Martindale-Hubbell Law Directory

New Orleans—Continued

PULASKI, GIEGER & LABORDE, L.L.C. (AV)

Suite 4800, One Shell Square, 701 Poydras Street, 70139
Telephone: 504-561-0400
Telecopier: 504-561-1011
Covington, Louisiana Office: 434 North Columbia Street, Suite 200, 70433.
Telephone: 504-561-0400.
Telecopier: 504-809-9677.

Michael T. Pulaski
Ernest P. Gieger, Jr.
Kenneth H. Laborde
Lambert M. Laperouse
Robert W. Maxwell
Keith W. McDaniel
Sharon D. Smith
Leo R. McAloon, III
Christopher J. Wnuk
John Burke Sanders
Julianne T. Echols
Hilliard F. Kelly, III
Lorie G. DeMarcay

Marjorie Randall Brown
Gina S. Montgomery

For full biographical listings, see the Martindale-Hubbell Law Directory

SAPORITO & SLEDGE, L.L.C. (AV)

639 Loyola Avenue Suite 2100, 70113
Telephone: 504-529-5070
Fax: 504-529-5434

Jerry L. Saporito
Michael D. Sledge

Edward T. Hayes

Representative Clients: Chance Industries; Dunlop Tire Corporation; Fleetwood Enterprises; General Motors Corporation; Pacific Insurance Company; Prudential Property and Casualty Company; Royal Insurance Company; TDK Corporation; Toyota Motor Sales, USA, Inc.; TRW, Inc.

For full biographical listings, see the Martindale-Hubbell Law Directory

SUTTERFIELD & WEBB L.L.C. (AV)

650 Poydras Street, Suite 2715, 70130
Telephone: 504-598-2715
Fax: 504-529-7197
Email: info@swslaw.com

James R. Sutterfield
Daniel A. Webb

William J. Sommers, Jr.
Charmagne A. Padua
Gordon P. Serou, Jr.

OF COUNSEL

Robert A. Redwine

For full biographical listings, see the Martindale-Hubbell Law Directory

WAGNER & BAGOT (AV)

Suite 2660, Poydras Center, 650 Poydras Street, 70130-6105
Telephone: 504-525-2141
Telecopier: 504-523-1587
TWX: 5106017673
ELN: 62928850
"INCISIVE"

Thomas J. Wagner
Michael H. Bagot, Jr.

Thomas A. Rayer, Jr.
Brian P. Brancato
Thomas P. Henican
Dana A. Henderson

For full biographical listings, see the Martindale-Hubbell Law Directory

WARD NELSON, LLC (AV)

1539 Jackson Avenue, 6th Floor, 70130
Telephone: 504-561-5000
Fax: 504-588-1334

MEMBERS OF FIRM

Joseph R. Ward, Jr.
Craig R. Nelson
Lisa A. Condrey

ASSOCIATES

Lynn H. Frank
James Everet Brouillette

OF COUNSEL

Christina Papastavros Fay

Representative Clients: Associated Aviation Underwriters; Associated International Underwriters; John Deer Transportation Services; Fidelity & Casualty of New York; Fireman's Insurance of Newark; Prudential Property and Casualty Ins. Co.; State Farm Fire & Casualty Co.; State Farms Mutual Automobile Insurance Co.

For full biographical listings, see the Martindale-Hubbell Law Directory

*SHREVEPORT,** Caddo Parish

BARLOW AND HARDTNER L.C. (AV)

Tenth Floor, Louisiana Tower, 401 Edwards Street, 71101-3289
Telephone: 318-227-1131
Telecopier: 318-227-1141
Mailing Address: P.O. Box 8, Shreveport, Louisiana, 71161-0008

Joseph L. Shea, Jr.
Michael B. Donald
Jay A. Greenleaf

Representative Clients: Delonghi America, Inc.; NorAm Energy Corp. (formerly Arkla, Inc.); Central and South West Corporation; 'Abeille Compagnia Italiana de Assicurazoni, S.p.A.; Panhandle Eastern Corp.; Providence Washington Insurance Co.; Pennzoil Producing Co.; Johnson Controls, Inc.; Ashland Oil, Inc.; Southwestern Electric Power Company.

For Complete List of Firm Personnel, See General Section

For full biographical listings, see the Martindale-Hubbell Law Directory

BLANCHARD, WALKER, O'QUIN & ROBERTS, A PROFESSIONAL LAW CORPORATION (AV)

Fourteenth Floor, Premier Bank Tower, 400 Texas Street, P.O. Drawer 1126, 71101
Telephone: 318-221-6858
Fax: 318-227-2967
Email: BWOR@BWOR.com
Bossier City, Louisiana Office: 2285 Benton Road, Suite B-201.
Telephone: 318-742-9255.
Fax: 318-742-9210.

W. Michael Adams
Paul M. Adkins
A. M. Stroud, III
Pamela G. Nathan

For Complete List of Firm Personnel, See General Section

For full biographical listings, see the Martindale-Hubbell Law Directory

MAYER, SMITH & ROBERTS, L.L.P. (AV)

1550 Creswell, 71101
Telephone: 318-222-2135, 222-2268
Fax: 318-222-6420
Email: (Attorney's First Name)@MSRLAW.COM

MEMBERS OF FIRM

Caldwell Roberts
Walter O. Hunter, Jr.
Mark A. Goodwin
Ben Marshall, Jr.
Alexander S. Lyons
Kim Purdy Thomas
David Butterfield
Henry N. Bellamy
John C. Turnage
Paul R. Mayer, Jr.
Steven E. Soileau
Deborah Shea Baukman
Caldwell Roberts, Jr.
Frank K. Carroll
Dalton Roberts Ross

OF COUNSEL

Paul R. Mayer

Representative Clients: CNA Insurance Companies; Liberty Mutual Insurance Company; United States Fidelity and Guaranty Company; Schumpert Medical Center; Travelers Insurance Company; Great American Insurance Company; Insurance Corporation of America; Highlands Insurance Company.

For full biographical listings, see the Martindale-Hubbell Law Directory

WILKINSON, CARMODY & GILLIAM (AV)

1700 Beck Building, 400 Travis Street, P.O. Box 1707, 71166
Telephone: 318-221-4196
Telecopier: 318-221-3705
Email: wcg1895@aol.com

MEMBERS OF FIRM

John D. Wilkinson (1867-1929)
William Scott Wilkinson (1895-1985)
Arthur R. Carmody, Jr.
Bobby S. Gilliam
Mark E. Gilliam
William Allen Haynes

Representative Clients: Farmers Insurance Group; Home Federal Savings & Loan Association of Shreveport; The Kansas City Southern Railway Co.; KTAL-TV; Lincoln National Life Insurance Co.; Mobil Oil Co.; Schumpert Medical Center; Sears, Roebuck & Co.; Southern Pacific Transportation Co.; Southwestern Electric Power Co.

For full biographical listings, see the Martindale-Hubbell Law Directory

MAINE

*AUGUSTA,** Kennebec Co.

JOHNSON & WEBBERT, L.L.P. (AV)

160 Capitol Street, P.O. Box 29, 04332-0029
Telephone: 207-623-5110
Fax: 207-622-4160
Email: pjohnson@johnsonwebbert.com *URL:* http://www.lawyers.com/jwl-law

Phillip E. Johnson
David G. Webbert

Representative Clients: Agway, Inc.; American Eagle Insurance Co.; AVEMCO; Central Maine Power Co.; The Doctors Company; ITT/Hartford; Loss Management Services, Inc.; Shand, Morahan & Co.; Travelers Insurance Co.; Union Water Power Company; USAIG.

For full biographical listings, see the Martindale-Hubbell Law Directory

*BANGOR,** Penobscot Co.

EATON, PEABODY, BRADFORD & VEAGUE, P.A. (AV)

Fleet Center-Exchange Street, P.O. Box 1210, 04402-1210
Telephone: 207-947-0111
Telecopier: 207-942-3040
Email: eaton@eatonpeabody.com *URL:* http://www.eatonpeabody.com
Augusta, Maine Office: 77 Sewall Street, Suite 3000.
Telephone: 207-622-3747.
Telecopier: 207-622-9732.
Blue Hill, Maine Office: One East Blue Hill Road.
Telephone: 207-374-2812.
Telecopier: 207-374-2548.
Brunswick, Maine Office: 167 Park Row.
Telephone: 207-729-1144.
Telecopier: 207-729-1140.
Dover-Foxcroft, Maine Office: 30 East Main Street.
Telephone: 207-564-8378.
Telecopier: 207-564-7059.

Bernard J. Kubetz
Douglas M. Smith (Dover-Foxcroft and Augusta Offices)
Glen L. Porter
Gordon H. S. Scott (Resident, Augusta Office)
William B. Devoe
Judy A.S. Metcalf (Resident, Brunswick Office)
Jonathan B. Huntington (Resident, Dover-Foxcroft Office)

For Complete List of Firm Personnel, See General Section

For full biographical listings, see the Martindale-Hubbell Law Directory

RUDMAN & WINCHELL, LLC (AV)

84 Harlow Street, P.O. Box 1401, 04402-1401
Telephone: 207-947-4501
Telecopy: 207-941-9715
URL: http://www.rudman-winchell.com

MEMBERS OF FIRM

Abraham M. Rudman (1896-1970)
Albert H. Winchell, Jr. (1924-1992)
Gerald E. Rudman
Phillip D. Buckley
Michael P. Friedman
Winfred A. Stevens
Robert E. Sutcliffe
Paul W. Chaiken
David C. King
John W. McCarthy
Frank T. McGuire
Bruce C. Mallonee
Paul H. Sighinolfi
William H. Hanson
George F. Eaton, II
Edith A. Richardson
Michael M. McAleer
Brett D. Baber
Barbara A. Cardone
Robert E. Murray, Jr.
Edmond J. Bearor
Curtis E. Kimball
Brent A. Singer

ASSOCIATES

Jane E. Skelton
Leigh Stephens McCarthy
Virginia Kozak Putnam
Ajaz S. Fiazzuddin
Anne-Marie Storey Hamer
Hans S. Peterson
Christopher J. Austin

Counsel for: Penobscot Shoe Co.; Sherman Lumber Co.; Webber Oil Co.; Fleet Bank of Maine; Key Bank of Maine; McCain Foods, Inc.
Local Counsel for: Commercial Union York Insurance Cos.; Hanover Insurance Company; Liberty Mutual Insurance Co.

For full biographical listings, see the Martindale-Hubbell Law Directory

WEATHERBEE, WOODCOCK, BURLOCK & WOODCOCK (AV)

136 Broadway, P.O. Box 1127, 04402-1127
Telephone: 207-942-9900
Telefax: 207-942-6999
Email: info@weathwood.com

(See Next Column)

MEMBERS OF FIRM

Peter M. Weatherbee
John A. Woodcock, Jr.
Stephen J. Burlock
Timothy C. Woodcock

Representative Clients: Royal Globe Insurance Co.; Travelers Insurance Co.; Maine Bonding & Casualty Co.; Maryland Casualty Co.; Aetna Casualty & Surety Co.; Metropolitan Life Insurance Co.; John Hancock Life Insurance Co.; Massachusetts Mutual Life Insurance Co.; Prudential Life Insurance Co.

For full biographical listings, see the Martindale-Hubbell Law Directory

*PORTLAND,** Cumberland Co.

BURNS RAY & DELANO, PROFESSIONAL ASSOCIATION (AV)

193 Middle Street, 04101-4062
Telephone: 207-775-3581
Facsimile: 207-775-3814
Email: mailcenter@brdlaw.com

George F. Burns
David P. Ray
Arnold C. Macdonald
Mary DeLano
Elizabeth A. Burns
Carrie A. Green

OF COUNSEL

Joanne F. Cole

Representative Clients: Maine Yankee Atomic Power Company; Tractebel Power, Inc.; Hancock Lumber Co., Inc.; Jackson Laboratory; Hague International (engineering); Aetna Life & Casualty Co.; The Hartford; Great American Insurance Co.; Wausau Insurance Co.

For full biographical listings, see the Martindale-Hubbell Law Directory

FRIEDMAN BABCOCK & GAYTHWAITE (AV)

Suite 400, Six City Center, P.O. Box 4726, 04112-4726
Telephone: 207-761-0900
Telecopier: 207-761-0186
Email: info@fbg-law.com *URL:* http://www.fbg-law.com

MEMBERS OF FIRM

Harold J. Friedman
Ernest J. Babcock
Martha C. Gaythwaite
Karen Frink Wolf
Jennifer S. Riggle
Laurence H. Leavitt
Elizabeth A. Germani
Michelle Allott
Tracy D. Hill

ASSOCIATES

Susan J. Guerette
L. John Topchik
Sally A. Morris
Catherine C. Miller
Kieran N. Shields
Evan Smith

For full biographical listings, see the Martindale-Hubbell Law Directory

MONAGHAN, LEAHY, HOCHADEL & LIBBY, LLP (AV)

95 Exchange Street, P.O. Box 7046, 04112-7046
Telephone: 207-774-3906
Facsimile: 207-774-3965
Email: info@mlhl.com *URL:* http://www.mlhl.com

MEMBERS OF FIRM

Thomas F. Monaghan
Thomas G. Leahy
Joseph M. Hochadel
Kevin G. Libby
Christopher C. Dinan
Matthew J. Monaghan
Michael H. Hill

ASSOCIATES

Cornelia Fuchs Fisher
John J. Wall, III
Noah D. Wuesthoff
Ivy L. Frignoca
Carol G. Ford

Representative Client: Scottsdale Insurance Company.
Reference: York Insurance Group of Maine.

For full biographical listings, see the Martindale-Hubbell Law Directory

PETRUCCELLI & MARTIN, LLP (AV)

50 Monument Square, P.O. Box 9733, 04104-5033
Telephone: 207-775-0200
Telecopier: 207-775-2360
Email: info@petruccellimartin.com *URL:* http://www.petruccellimartin.com

MEMBERS OF FIRM

Gerald F. Petruccelli
Joel C. Martin
Michael K. Martin
James B. Haddow
Linda C. Russell

Thomas C. Bradley
Bruce A. McGlauflin

Representative Clients: Associated Aviation Underwriters; Bombardier, Inc.; Chicago Title Insurance Co.; Chubb Insurance Co.; Norfolk Dedham Mutual Insurance Co.; Northern Security Insurance Co.; Ticor Title Insurance Co.; Union Mutual Fire Insurance Co.; Vermont Mutual Insurance Co.

For full biographical listings, see the Martindale-Hubbell Law Directory

Portland—Continued

PIERCE ATWOOD (AV)

One Monument Square, 04101
Telephone: 207-791-1100
Fax: 207-791-1350
Email: info@PierceAtwood.com *URL:* http://www.pierceatwood.com
Augusta, Maine Office: 77 Winthrop Street.
Telephone: 207-622-6311.
Fax: 207-623-9367.
Newburyport, Massachusetts Office: 6 Harris Street.
Telephone: 978-465-9599.
Fax: 978-465-9945.

MEMBERS OF FIRM

Ralph I. Lancaster, Jr.
Malcolm L. Lyons (Resident, Augusta Office)
Peter W. Culley
Louise K. Thomas
Michael D. Seitzinger (Resident, Augusta Office)
William J. Kayatta, Jr.
John C. Nivison (Resident, Augusta Office)
John J. Aromando
David E. Barry

ASSOCIATES

Jared S. des Rosiers
Debra L. Brown
Geraldine G. Sanchez
K. Douglas Erdmann
Christopher T. Roach
Ann M. St. Peter-Griffith (Resident, Augusta Office)

COUNSEL

Daniel J. Stevens (Resident, Augusta Office)

For Complete List of Firm Personnel, See General Section

For full biographical listings, see the Martindale-Hubbell Law Directory

PRETI, FLAHERTY, BELIVEAU, PACHIOS & HALEY, LLC (AV)

One City Center, P.O. Box 9546, 04112-9546
Telephone: 207-791-3000
Telecopier: 207-791-3111
Email: admin@preti.com *URL:* http://www.preti.com
Augusta, Maine Office: 45 Memorial Circle, P.O. Box 1058, 04332-1058.
Telephone: 207-623-5300.
Telefax: 207-623-2914.
Bath, Maine Office: Thirty Front Street, P.O. Box 665, 04530-0665.
Telephone: 207-443-5576.
Telefax: 207-443-6665.

MEMBERS OF FIRM

Severin M. Beliveau (Augusta Office)
Christopher D. Nyhan
Jonathan S. Piper
Daniel Rapaport
Bruce C. Gerrity (Augusta Office)
Jeffrey T. Edwards
Michael G. Messerschmidt
Randall B. Weill
Evan M. Hansen
Geoffrey K. Cummings
Michael Kaplan
Stephen E. F. Langsdorf (Augusta Office)
John P. McVeigh
Elizabeth A. Olivier
Nelson J Larkins
Robert O. Newton
Timothy J. Bryant

ASSOCIATES

Kevin J. Beal
Elizabeth A. Campbell

Representative Clients: The St. Paul Companies; Maine Municipal Assn.; American International Group; MGA Insurance Services; Gallagher Bassett; Dunlap Corp.; Crawford and Co.; Maine Bonding Co.; The Travelers Insurance Co.

For Complete List of Firm Personnel, See General Section

For full biographical listings, see the Martindale-Hubbell Law Directory

RICHARDSON, WHITMAN, LARGE & BADGER, A PROFESSIONAL CORPORATION (AV)

465 Congress Street, 04101-3528
Telephone: 207-774-7474
Telecopier: 207-774-1343
URL: http://www.rwlb.com
Bangor, Maine Office: One Merchants Plaza, P.O. Box 2429.
Telephone: 207-945-5900.
Telecopier: 207-945-0758.

Harrison L. Richardson
John S. Whitman
Wendell G. Large
Frederick J. Badger, Jr. (Resident, Bangor Office)
Elizabeth G. Stouder
Barri Bloom
Ann M. Murray (Resident, Bangor Office)
Frederick F. Costlow (Resident, Bangor Office)
John B. Lucy (Resident, Bangor Office)

Anne H. Cressey
Thomas R. McKeon
Carol I. Eisenberg
Paul R. Johnson

For full biographical listings, see the Martindale-Hubbell Law Directory

THOMPSON & BOWIE (AV)

Three Canal Plaza, P.O. Box 4630, 04112
Telephone: 207-774-2500
Telecopier: 207-774-3591
Email: law@thompsonbowie.com

MEMBERS OF FIRM

Roy E. Thompson, Jr.
James M. Bowie
Daniel R. Mawhinney
Rebecca H. Farnum
Glenn H. Robinson
Frank W. DeLong, III
Michael E. Saucier
Mark V. Franco
Edward R. Benjamin, Jr.
Cathy S. Roberts
Paul C. Catsos

ASSOCIATES

Elizabeth Knox Peck
Thomas G. Diebold
Michael R. Bosse
Lisa M. Fitzgibbon

For full biographical listings, see the Martindale-Hubbell Law Directory

WRIGHT & COON, P.A. (AV)

Four Canal Plaza, P.O. Box 7526, 04112
Telephone: 207-775-7722
Fax: 207-772-7045
Email: lexfori@lexfori.com

Steven F. Wright
John R. Coon
Brita J. Forssberg

For full biographical listings, see the Martindale-Hubbell Law Directory

MARYLAND

*ANNAPOLIS,** Anne Arundel Co.

COUNCIL, BARADEL, KOSMERL & NOLAN, P.A. (AV)

125 West Street, Fourth Floor, P.O. Box 2289, 21404-2289
Telephone: 410-268-6600
Baltimore: 410-269-6190
Washington, D.C.: 301-261-2247
FAX: 410-269-8409
Email: cbkn@cbknlaw.com

Ronald E. Council
Ronald A. Baradel
Wayne T. Kosmerl
James P. Nolan
William F. Flood, III
Kevin M. Schaeffer
Donna McCabe Schaeffer
Frederick C. Sussman

John Naumann Strange
Susan T. Ford
Edwin H. Staples, II
Susan Stobbart Shapiro

OF COUNSEL

George N. Manis
Nicholas Goldsborough

Representative Clients: Anne Arundel County; Annapolis Bank and Trust; Bank of Maryland; State Farm Mutual Automobile Insurance Co.; Annapolis Yacht Club; Annapolis Yacht Sales, Inc.

For full biographical listings, see the Martindale-Hubbell Law Directory

HYATT, PETERS & WEBER (AV)

1919 West Street, P.O. Box 6635, 21401
Telephone: 410-266-0626
Fax: 410-841-5065
Email: info@hyatt.hpwsb.com *URL:* http://www.hpwlaw.com

Alan J. Hyatt
Paula J. Peters
Paul J. Weber

ASSOCIATES

Sara H. Arthur
Sharon M. Grosfeld
Gregg M. Weinberg
Jonathan A. Hodgson
John L. Hill
Arlette K. Bright
Bruce F. Bright (Not admitted in MD)

OF COUNSEL

Steven G. Tyler

For full biographical listings, see the Martindale-Hubbell Law Directory

*BALTIMORE,** (Independent City)

ALLEN, JOHNSON, ALEXANDER & KARP, P.A. (AV)

Suite 1540, 100 East Pratt Street, 21202
Telephone: 410-727-5000
Fax: 410-727-0861
Email: ajakmd@aol.com
Washington, D.C. Office: 1707 L Street, N.W., Suite 1050.
Telephone: 202-828-4141.

(See Next Column)

ALLEN, JOHNSON, ALEXANDER & KARP P.A.—*Continued*

Daniel Karp
Yvette M. Bryant

Representative Clients: Scottsdale Insurance Co.; Nautilus Insurance Co.; Jefferson Insurance Co.; Liberty Mutual Insurance Co.; Avis Rent-A-Car; Otis Elevator Co.; Montgomery Elevator Co.; Admiral Insurance Co.; Local Government Insurance Trust; Penn National Insurance Co.

For Complete List of Firm Personnel, See General Section

For full biographical listings, see the Martindale-Hubbell Law Directory

---

CHURCH & HOUFF, P.A. (AV)

2 North Charles Street, Suite 600, 21201
Telephone: 410-539-3900
Fax: 410-539-3987
Towson, Maryland Office: Suite 220 Nottingham Centre, 502 Washington Avenue, 21204.
Telephone: 410-427-3900.
Fax: 410-427-3914.

George M. Church
Edward F. Houff
F. Ford Loker, Jr.
Robin Silver
R. Thomas Radcliffe, Jr.
Charles E. Rosolio

Christine T. Altemus
Winslow F. Bouscaren
Michael M. Rafi
James George Koutras
Allison L. Silvain
Laura A. Cellucci

OF COUNSEL

Patrick C. Smith

For full biographical listings, see the Martindale-Hubbell Law Directory

---

CORNBLATT, BENNETT, PENHALLEGON & ROBERSON, P.A. (AV)

Suite 1800, 201 North Charles Street, 21201
Telephone: 410-752-7600
Fax: 410-752-2110
Email: mail@cbprlaw.com

Theodore B. Cornblatt
S. Woods Bennett
John R. Penhallegon
Patrick A. Roberson
Jeffrey Y. Laynor

J. Michael Harrison
Gary E. Dumer, Jr.

For full biographical listings, see the Martindale-Hubbell Law Directory

---

FERGUSON, SCHETELICH & HEFFERNAN, P.A. (AV)

1401 NationsBank Center, 100 South Charles Street, 21201-2725
Telephone: 410-837-2200
Fax: 410-837-1188
URL: http://www.FSHLaw.com

Robert L. Ferguson, Jr.
Thomas J. Schetelich
Christopher J. Heffernan
Craig F. Ballew
Michael N. Russo, Jr.

Peter J. Basile
Ann D. Ware
Tracey J. McLauchlin
Michele P. Zahner
Michael K. Hourigan

For full biographical listings, see the Martindale-Hubbell Law Directory

---

FUNK & BOLTON, A PROFESSIONAL ASSOCIATION (AV)

100 Light Street, Suite 1000, 21202
Telephone: 410-659-7700
Facsimile: 410-659-7773
Email: FBLAW@FBLAW.COM
Annapolis, Maryland Office: 191 Main Street, 21401.
Telephone: 410-269-1554.
Facsimile: 410-268-0612.
Chestertown, Maryland Office: 315 High Street, Suite 202, 21620.
Telephone: 410-810-1381.
Facsimile: 410-810-1383.

David M. Funk
Bryan D. Bolton
Derek B. Yarmis

Michael R. McCann
James F. Taylor
Eric B. Myers

For full biographical listings, see the Martindale-Hubbell Law Directory

---

GOODELL, DEVRIES, LEECH & GRAY, LLP (AV)

Suite 2000, One South Street, 21202
Telephone: 410-783-4000
Telecopy: 410-783-4040
Email: GDLG@GDLGLAW.COM

(See Next Column)

MEMBERS OF FIRM

E. Charles Dann, Jr.
David W. Allen
Linda S. Woolf

For full biographical listings, see the Martindale-Hubbell Law Directory

---

HARDWICK & HARRIS (AV)

The Fidelity Building, 210 North Charles Street, Suite 900, 21202
Telephone: 410-727-0828
FAX: 410-727-5893

Jack L. Hardwick
Edward B. Harris, Jr.
George C. Davis
Clifford L. Hardwick
Michael J. Perticone

For full biographical listings, see the Martindale-Hubbell Law Directory

---

REDMOND, BURGIN & GUTIERREZ, P.A. (AV)

1301, The Fidelity Building, 210 North Charles Street, 21202
Telephone: 410-752-1555
Fax: 410-752-1064
URL: http://www.RBGLAW.com
Upper Marlboro, Maryland Office: 14746 Main Street.
Telephone: 301-952-1555.

Leonard C. Redmond, III
Harold L. Burgin

Joseph I. Tivvis, Jr.

For Complete List of Firm Personnel, See General Section

For full biographical listings, see the Martindale-Hubbell Law Directory

---

ROLLINS, SMALKIN, RICHARDS & MACKIE, L.L.C. (AV)

401 North Charles Street, 21201
Telephone: 410-727-2443
Fax: 410-727-8390
URL: http://www.rsrm.com

MEMBERS OF FIRM

H. Beale Rollins (1898-1985)
Samuel S. Smalkin (1906-1982)
Edward C. Mackie
John F. Linsenmeyer
Thomas C. Gentner
Glenn W. Trimmer
Patrick G. Cullen
James P. O'Meara
Paul G. Donoghue
Ralph E. Wilson III

ASSOCIATES

Kenneth G. Macleay
Donna Lynn Kolakowski-Hollen
Meg Bantley Whiteford
J. James Roos
Jessica R. Di Cicco

OF COUNSEL

Raymond A. Richards (Retired)

LEGAL SUPPORT PERSONNEL

Guy M. Craig

For full biographical listings, see the Martindale-Hubbell Law Directory

---

THOMAS & LIBOWITZ, P.A. (AV)

100 Light Street, Suite 1100, 21202-1053
Telephone: 410-752-2468
Fax: 410-752-2046; 752-2049; 752-0979
Email: thomasandlibowitz.com *URL:* http://www.thomasandlibowitz.com

Michael S. Libowitz
Robert J. Lynott
Peter W. Taliaferro
Thomas C. Swiss
Michael J. Collins
David P. Chaisson

OF COUNSEL

Basil A. Thomas
Susan M. Rittenhouse

LEGAL SUPPORT PERSONNEL

PARALEGALS

Donna Janney
Angel Lavin
Kelly Nusbaum

Representative Clients: Sinclair Broadcast Group, Inc. (Television and Radio stations); Roy Kirby & Sons, Inc. (Contractor); First Mariner Bank; Scandia Manufacturing Co. Inc. (Defense Contractor); Atlantic Automotive Corp. t/a Heritgage Automotive Group; Candy Express Franchising, Inc.; Wire Spectrum Services (Contractors-Transmission Tower Sites); Acrodyne Communications, Inc.; Alexis Logic Corporation (Software Developers); Selnic Corporation (Electronis Distributors); Liberty Mutual Insurance Company.

For full biographical listings, see the Martindale-Hubbell Law Directory

Baltimore—Continued

VENABLE ATTORNEYS AT LAW VENABLE, BAETJER AND HOWARD, LLP (AV)

A Partnership including Professional Corporations
1800 Mercantile Bank & Trust Building, 2 Hopkins Plaza, 21201
Telephone: 410-244-7400
Fax: 410-244-7742
URL: http://www.venable.com
Washington, D.C. Office: Venable, Baetjer, Howard & Civiletti LLP, Suite 1000, 1201 New York Avenue, N.W.
Telephone: 202-962-4800.
Fax: 202-962-8300.
McLean, Virginia Office: Suite 400, 2010 Corporate Ridge.
Telephone: 703-760-1600.
Fax: 703-821-8949.
Rockville, Maryland Office: Suite 500, One Church Street, P. O. Box 1906.
Telephone: 301-217-5600.
Fax: 301-217-5617.
Towson, Maryland Office: 210 Allegheny Avenue, P. O. Box 5517.
Telephone: 410-494-6200.
Fax: 410-821-0147.

MEMBERS OF FIRM

Benjamin R. Civiletti (P.C.) (Also at Washington, D.C. and Towson, Maryland Offices)
John Henry Lewin, Jr. (P.C.)
Roger W. Titus (Resident, Rockville, Maryland Office)
Ronald R. Glancz (Not admitted in MD; Resident, Washington, D.C. Office)
John H. Zink, III (Resident, Towson, Maryland Office)
William D. Dolan, III (P.C.) (Not admitted in MD; Resident, McLean, Virginia Office)
Paul T. Glasgow (Resident, Rockville, Maryland Office)
Joseph C. Wich, Jr. (Resident, Towson, Maryland Office)
Nell B. Strachan
James K. Archibald (Also at Washington, D.C. Office)
Jeffrey A. Dunn (Also at Washington, D.C. Office)
George F. Pappas (Also at Washington, D.C. Office)
James L. Shea (Also at Washington, D.C. Office)
Jeffrey P. Ayres (P.C.)
C. Carey Deeley, Jr. (Also at Towson, Maryland Office)
Christopher R. Mellott
M. King Hill, III (Resident, Towson, Maryland Office)
John A. Roberts (Also at Rockville, Maryland Office)
David J. Heubeck
Herbert G. Smith, II (Not admitted in MD; Resident, Washington, D.C. Office)
John A. McCauley
John T. Prisbe
Christine M. McAnney (Not admitted in MD; Resident, McLean, Virginia Office)
Marina Lolley Sabett

ASSOCIATES

Daniel William China (Resident, Towson, Maryland Office)
Patricia A. Malone (Resident, Towson, Maryland Office)

For Complete List of Firm Personnel, See General Section

For full biographical listings, see the Martindale-Hubbell Law Directory

WARD, KERSHAW & MINTON, A PROFESSIONAL ASSOCIATION (AV)

113 West Monument Street, 21201
Telephone: 410-685-6700
Fax: 410-685-6704
Email: wkmfirm@aol.com *URL:* http://www.wkamlaw.com

John T. Ward
Robert B. Kershaw
Thomas J. Minton
April Falcon Doss
J. Dirk Schwenk

OF COUNSEL

Richard V. Falcon

For full biographical listings, see the Martindale-Hubbell Law Directory

WRIGHT, CONSTABLE & SKEEN, LLP (AV)

One Charles Center, 16th Floor, 100 N. Charles Street, 21201
Telephone: 410-659-1300
Telex: 710 234-2383 CALDAS
Fax: 410-659-1350

MEMBERS OF FIRM

Wm. Pepper Constable (1882-1976)
John D. Wright (1903-1976)
George W. Constable (Retired)
Read A. McCaffrey (1913-1995)
William A. Skeen (Retired)
John Brentnall Powell, Jr.
Michael J. Abromaitis
Monte Fried
James W. Constable
David W. Skeen
James D. Skeen
Douglas G. Worrall
Kenneth F. Davies
Stephen F. White
Brian S. Goodman
Frederick L. Kobb
Paul F. Evelius
Lois A. Fenner McBride
Charles J. Morton, Jr.

ASSOCIATES

Mary Alice Smolarek
Catherine H. Bellinger
Carol J. Glover
Tracey D. King
David J. Shuster
Howard S. Stevens

(See Next Column)

COUNSEL

Francis N. Iglehart, Jr.
P. McEvoy Cromwell
C. Gordon Haines

Representative Clients: Conowingo Power Co.; Weyerhaeuser Co.; Commercial Credit Corp.; Noxell Corp.; Consolidated Rail Corp.; Murray Corp.; Atlantic Mutual Insurance Co.; Sea Containers, Ltd.; Great Atlantic & Pacific Tea Co.; Tyson Foods, Inc.

For full biographical listings, see the Martindale-Hubbell Law Directory

YOUNG & VALKENET, L.L.C. (AV)

Suite 707 The Susquehanna Building, 29 West Susquehanna Avenue, 21204
Telephone: 410-583-2414
Telefax: 410-583-2418

Thomas G. Young, III
Thomas C. Valkenet

For full biographical listings, see the Martindale-Hubbell Law Directory

CHEVY CHASE, Montgomery Co.

PYNE & DERRY, P.C. (AV)

Chevy Chase Metro Building Suite 640, Two Wisconsin Circle, 20815
Telephone: 301-961-0240
Fax: 301-907-3920
Email: pyne-derry@juno.com

John J. Pyne
Peter E. Derry

For full biographical listings, see the Martindale-Hubbell Law Directory

*ROCKVILLE,** Montgomery Co.

ANDERSON & QUINN (AV)

The Adams Law Center, 25 Wood Lane, 20850
Telephone: 301-762-3303
Fax: 301-762-3776
Email: rscanlon@andersonquinn.com

MEMBERS OF FIRM

Charles C. Collins (1900-1973)
Robert E. Anderson (Retired)
Francis X. Quinn
Donald P. Maiberger
Robert P. Scanlon
John A. Rego
Alice Kelley Scanlon

ASSOCIATES

Kerry S. McGeever
Timothy J. Mulreany
Todd P. Maiberger
Jennifer D. Burke
Marc N. Steren

Representative Clients: C & P Telephone; Allstate Insurance Co.; State Farm Mutual Automobile Insurance Co.; Liberty Mutual Insurance Co.; American International Adjustment Co.; Marriott Corp.

For full biographical listings, see the Martindale-Hubbell Law Directory

ARMSTRONG, DONOHUE, CEPPOS & VAUGHAN, CHARTERED (AV)

Suite 101, 204 Monroe Street, 20850
Telephone: 301-251-0440
Telecopier: 301-279-5929

Larry A. Ceppos
H. Patrick Donohue
John C. Monahan
H. Kenneth Armstrong
Benjamin S. Vaughan
Pamela Barrow Kincheloe

Sharon A. Marcial
J. Eric Rhoades
Richard S. Schrager
Andrew J. Marter
Susan E. Mikorski

Representative Clients: Medical Mutual Liability Insurance Society of Maryland; Kaiser Permanente; Shady Grove Adventist Hospital; American Medical International, Inc.; Crum & Forster Commercial Insurance Cos.; Atlantic Mutual Insurance Co.; Nationwide Mutual Insurance Co.; Harleysville Mutual Insurance Co.; St. Paul Fire & Marine Insurance Co.; American Reliance Insurance Co.

For full biographical listings, see the Martindale-Hubbell Law Directory

BRAULT, GRAHAM, SCOTT & BRAULT, LLC (AV)

101 South Washington Street, 20850
Telephone: 301-424-1060
Fax: 301-424-7991
Email: bgsb@earthlink.net
Washington, D.C. Office: Brault, Graham, Scott & Brault, PLLC, 1140 Connecticut Avenue, N.W., Suite 250.
Telephone: 202-785-1200.
FAX: 202-785-4301.
Fairfax, Virginia Office: Suite 500, 11350 Random Hills Road, Fair Oaks Plaza, 22030-7429.
Telephone: 202-785-1200.

OF COUNSEL

Laurence T. Scott
James Robert Miller

(See Next Column)

BRAULT, GRAHAM, SCOTT & BRAULT LLC—*Continued*

MEMBERS OF FIRM

Denver H. Graham (1922-1987)
Albert E. Brault (Retired)
Albert D. Brault (Resident)
Leo A. Roth, Jr.
James S. Wilson (Resident)
Ronald G. Guziak
Daniel L. Shea (Resident)
M. Kathleen Parker (Resident)
David G. Mulquin (Resident)
James M. Brault (Resident)
Regina Ann Casey (Resident)

ASSOCIATES

Rhonda Ann Hurwitz (Resident)
Joan F. Brault (Resident)

Representative Clients: American Oil Co.; Crum & Forster Group; Fireman's Fund American Insurance Cos.; Kemper Group; Reliance Insurance Cos.; Safeco Group; Government Employees Insurance Co.; Medical Mutual Insurance Society of Maryland; Legal Mutual Liability Insurance Society of Maryland.

For full biographical listings, see the Martindale-Hubbell Law Directory

GLEASON, FLYNN & EMIG, CHARTERED (AV)

451 Hungerford Drive, Suite 600, 20850
Telephone: 301-294-2110
FAX: 301-294-0737
Email: lawyers@gleason-law.com

James P. Gleason, Jr.
Michael F. Flynn, Jr.
Gerard J. Emig
Christopher C. Fogleman

OF COUNSEL

Katherine S. Duyer
Laurie R. Hanig

ASSOCIATES

Byron J. Mitchell
Shelley Lynne Bagoly
M. Shannon Madden
Thomas K. McCraw, Jr.

For full biographical listings, see the Martindale-Hubbell Law Directory

SILVER SPRING, Montgomery Co.

SAUNDERS & SCHMIELER (AV)

8737 Colesville Road, Suite L-200, 20910-3921
Telephone: 301-588-7717
Facsimile: 301-588-5073
Email: admin@sslawfirm.com *URL:* http://www.sslawfirm.com
Washington, D.C. Office: 1050 17th Street, N.W., #600
Telephone: 202-833-2999.
Baltimore, Maryland Office: Suite 2700, 111 South Calvert Street.
Telephone: 410-235-7558.
Arlington, Virginia Office: 2111 Wilson Boulevard, Suite 700.
Telephone: 703-243-1100.
Richmond, Virginia Office: 4900 Cutshaw Avenue.
Telephone: 804-353-9800.

MEMBER OF FIRM

Jeffrey R. Schmieler

ASSOCIATES

Nicole E. Ames
A. Benjamin Horton
Lucas F. Webster

For Complete List of Firm Personnel, See General Section

For full biographical listings, see the Martindale-Hubbell Law Directory

*TOWSON,** Baltimore Co.

MUDD, HARRISON & BURCH (AV)

105 West Chesapeake Avenue, 300 Jefferson Building, 21204
Telephone: 410-828-1335
FAX: 410-828-1042
Email: mhb@mhblaw.com

MEMBERS OF FIRM

John E. Mudd
T. Rogers Harrison (1949-1995)
Richard C. Burch
Douglas W. Biser
H. Patrick Stringer, Jr.
Andrew Janquitto

James R. Andersen
Matthew Paul Lalumia
Nancy C. Hopkins

OF COUNSEL

Wm. T. Russell, Jr.

Representative Clients: The Maryland Insurance Group; The Ohio Insurance Group; USAA Property & Casualty Insurance; Safeco Insurance Companies; Montgomery Mutual Insurance Co.; North American Specialty Insurance Co.; Mutual Benefit Insurance Co.; Peninsula General Insurance Co.; Universal Underwriters Group; Zurich Insurance Group; The St. Paul Companies.

For full biographical listings, see the Martindale-Hubbell Law Directory

VENABLE ATTORNEYS AT LAW VENABLE, BAETJER AND HOWARD, LLP (AV)

A Partnership including Professional Corporations
210 Allegheny Avenue, P.O. Box 5517, 21204
Telephone: 410-494-6200
Fax: 410-821-0147
URL: http://www.venable.com
Baltimore, Maryland Office: 1800 Mercantile Bank & Trust Building, 2 Hopkins Plaza.
Telephone: 410-244-7400.
Fax: 410-244-7742.
Washington, D.C. Office: Venable, Baetjer, Howard & Civiletti LLP, Suite 1000, 1201 New York Avenue, N.W.
Telephone: 202-962-4800.
Fax: 202-962-8300.
McLean, Virginia Office: Suite 400, 2010 Corporate Ridge.
Telephone: 703-760-1600.
Fax: 703-821-8949.
Rockville, Maryland Office: Suite 500, One Church Street, P. O. Box 1906.
Telephone: 301-217-5600.
Fax: 301-217-5617.

PARTNERS

Benjamin R. Civiletti (P.C.) (Also at Washington, D.C. and Baltimore, Maryland Offices)
John H. Zink, III
Joseph C. Wich, Jr.
C. Carey Deeley, Jr. (Also at Baltimore, Maryland Office)
M. King Hill, III

ASSOCIATE

Patricia A. Malone

For Complete List of Firm Personnel, See General Section

For full biographical listings, see the Martindale-Hubbell Law Directory

WHITNEY & BOGRIS, LLP (AV)

401 Washington Avenue, Twelfth Floor, 21204
Telephone: 410-583-8000
Fax: 410-583-8031
Email: HGWC@worldnet.att.net

MEMBERS OF FIRM

Daniel W. Whitney
George D. Bogris

ASSOCIATES

Kathleen D. Leslie
Henry Russell
Sandra A. Tofte
Michael A. Giacomazza
Arlene L. Sew
Gerald S. Gaetano (Not admitted in MD)
Scott A. McCabe (Not admitted in MD)
Jeffrey C. Shipley

OF COUNSEL

Joseph E. Dever
David L. Feldstein
Ronald V. Miller, Jr.

For full biographical listings, see the Martindale-Hubbell Law Directory

MASSACHUSETTS

*BOSTON,** Suffolk Co.

BADGER, DOLAN, PARKER & COHEN (AV)

Formerly Badger, Sullivan, Kelley & Cole
2 Oliver Street, 02109
Telephone: 617-482-3030
Fax: 617-482-6919
Email: badger@badgerlaw.com *URL:* http://www.badgerlaw.com

MEMBERS OF FIRM

Walter I. Badger (1885-1926)
John J. Sullivan (1926-1979)
David W. Kelley (1935-1986)
George F. Parker, III
James B. Dolan, Jr.
Lawrence J. Cohen

ASSOCIATE

R. Christopher Green

OF COUNSEL

G. Mitchell Eckel, III
Dorothy M. Bickford

For full biographical listings, see the Martindale-Hubbell Law Directory

BLOOM & BUELL (AV)

1340 Soldiers Field Road, 02135-1020
Telephone: 617-254-4400; 800-354-6004
Telecopier: 617-254-7610
Email: office@bloombuell.com *URL:* http://www.bloombuell.com

MEMBERS OF FIRM

Laurence J. Bloom
Barbara Hayes Buell
William J. Davenport
Marc J. Gervais
Richard M. Haley

(See Next Column)

BLOOM & BUELL, *Boston—Continued*

ASSOCIATES

Barry T. Putterman
Barbara D. Weninger

For full biographical listings, see the Martindale-Hubbell Law Directory

COGAVIN AND WAYSTACK (AV)

2 Center Plaza, 02108
Telephone: 617-742-3340
Telecopier: 617-723-7563
Email: law@cogway.com *URL:* http://cogway.com

MEMBERS OF FIRM

John J. Cogavin
Edward W. Waystack
John P. Fitzgerald
Gerard A. Butler
Kevin J. McGinty

ASSOCIATES

David T. Donnelly
John J. Jarosak
Thomas M. Franco
Mark A. Darling
Owen Roe O'Neill
Audrey Lewchik Bradley
Daniel S. McInnis
William P. Hurley
Denis P. Bergin
Mark R. Freitas
Kevin M. Tierney

Representative Clients: Fireman's Fund Insurance Co.; The Andover Companies; The Hartford Insurance Co.; The Travelers Insurance Co.; Plymouth Rock Assurance Corporation; Maryland Casualty Insurance Co.; Chubb Insurance Company; National Grange Mutual Insurance Co.; Zurich-American Insurance Group; Commercial Union Insurance Company.

For full biographical listings, see the Martindale-Hubbell Law Directory

CORNELL & GOLLUB (AV)

75 Federal Street, 02110
Telephone: 617-482-8100
Telecopier: 617-482-3917
Email: CornellGollub@worldnet.att.net
Wakefield, Rhode Island Office: 146 Main Street, 02879.
Telephone: 401-782-2072.
Telecopier: 401-782-4941.

MEMBERS OF FIRM

Robert W. Cornell (1910-1988)
Karl L. Gollub (1934-1985)
David H. Sempert
Peter M. Durney
Paul F. Lynch
Jane Treen Brand
Janet J. Bobit
David W. McGough

ASSOCIATES

Thomas A. Pursley
Susan Donaldson Novins
Marie Chadeayne Chafe
Kelly L. Wilkins
James P. Kerr
Patricia A. Hartnett
David G. Braithwaite
Jennifer L. Davis
Matthew J. Ginsburg
Kenneth M. Robbins

OF COUNSEL

Philip J. Foley

For full biographical listings, see the Martindale-Hubbell Law Directory

CRAIG AND MACAULEY, PROFESSIONAL CORPORATION (AV)

Federal Reserve Plaza, 600 Atlantic Avenue, 02210-2211
Telephone: 617-367-9500
Telecopier: 617-742-1788; 617-248-0886
URL: http://prospex.com/craig-macauley/

William F. Macauley
A. Van C. Lanckton
Richard E. Quinby
Stephen Wald
William R. Moorman, Jr.
Martin P. Desmery
Christopher J. Panos

For Complete List of Firm Personnel, See General Section

For full biographical listings, see the Martindale-Hubbell Law Directory

CURLEY & CURLEY, P.C. (AV)

27 School Street, 02108-4391
Telephone: 617-523-2990
Fax: 617-523-7602

Robert A. Curley
Robert A. Curley, Jr.
Eugene F. Nowell
David D. Dowd
Martin J. Rooney
Lisabeth Ryan Kundert
Stephen J. Gill
Charles Mark Furcolo
Joni Katz Mackler

For full biographical listings, see the Martindale-Hubbell Law Directory

CURTIN, MURPHY & O'REILLY, P.C. (AV)

55 Summer Street, 02110
Telephone: 617-574-1700
Facsimile: 617-574-1710

(See Next Column)

William H. Murphy
Thomas P. O'Reilly
Richard N. Curtin
Linda C. Scarano
Scott E. Richardson
Linda D. Oliveira
Paul M. Moretti
Jeffrey C. McLucas

Kevin P. Jones
Chrisann Leal
Christine Lynn DeRosa

OF COUNSEL

Richard T. Corbett
Dori P. Kelly

For full biographical listings, see the Martindale-Hubbell Law Directory

FINNERTY & FINNERTY (AV)

Suite 230, 21 Custom House Street, 02110
Telephone: 617-737-3770
Fax: 617-737-0684
Email: AttysFandF@aol.com *URL:* http://www.finnertyfinnerty.baweb.com

MEMBERS OF FIRM

John F. Finnerty (1917-1994)
John F. Finnerty, Jr.
Brian P. Finnerty
Gail E. Finnerty

For full biographical listings, see the Martindale-Hubbell Law Directory

GOVERNO AND KAVANAGH LLP (AV)

99 High Street, 02110
Telephone: 617-423-4500
Fax: 617-423-4505
Email: dgoverno@counsel.com *URL:* http://www.governoandkavanagh.com

David M. Governo
Eileen P. Kavanagh

ASSOCIATES

Ann M. Collins
Lisa A. Hack
Michael D. Riseberg
Cynthia J. Stephens
Adam A. Larson

OF COUNSEL

Gregory J. Wenger
Timothy J. Dodd (Not admitted in MA)

For full biographical listings, see the Martindale-Hubbell Law Directory

GRIFFIN & GOULKA (AV)

Two Oliver Street, 02109
Telephone: 617-423-6677
Telecopier: 617-423-5755
Email: griffgoulk@aol.com

MEMBERS OF FIRM

J. Kenneth Griffin
Joanne L. Goulka
Christopher S. Williams
Robert P. La Hait

ASSOCIATES

Jon-Paul Lapointe
John B. Tewksbury
Mark E. Warren

For full biographical listings, see the Martindale-Hubbell Law Directory

KOPELMAN AND PAIGE, P.C. (AV)

Park Square Building, 31 St. James Avenue, 7th Floor, 02116
Telephone: 617-556-0007
Fax: 617-654-1735

Leonard Kopelman
Donald G. Paige
Elizabeth A. Lane
Joyce F. Frank
John W. Giorgio
Barbara J. Saint Andre
Joel B. Bard
Everett Joseph Marder
Patrick J. Costello

William Hewig, III

For Complete List of Firm Personnel, See General Section

For full biographical listings, see the Martindale-Hubbell Law Directory

MARTIN, MAGNUSON, McCARTHY & KENNEY (AV)

101 Merrimac Street, 02114-4716
Telephone: 617-227-3240
Telecopier: 617-227-3346

MEMBERS OF FIRM

Ephraim Martin (1900-1988)
Clement McCarthy (1921-1985)
Harold E. Magnuson (1912-1999)
Raymond J. Kenney, Jr. *
Charles P. Reidy, III *
Daniel J. Griffin, Jr. *
Philip E. Murray, Jr. *
Joseph L. Doherty, Jr. *
Paul R. Keane *
John P. Mulvey *
Paul M. McTague *
Carol A. Kelly *
Edward F. Mahoney *
Douglas A. Robertson *

COUNSEL

Edward F. Hennessey

(See Next Column)

MARTIN, MAGNUSON, MCCARTHY & KENNEY—*Continued*

Joan L. Atlas *
Joseph B. Bertrand *
Teresa J. Farris *
Kevin C. Reidy *
Stephen M. O'Shea *
Christopher J. Maley *
Jennifer A. Brennan *
Sean M. Ennis *
Katharine S. Perry *
Amato J. Bocchino, Jr. *
Darlene Dawson *

Representative Clients: Allstate Insurance Co.; American International Adjustment Co.; Browning - Ferris Industries, Inc.; Fireman's Fund Insurance Cos.; Medical Professional Mutual Insurance Co.; Multi Systems Agency LTD.; Risk Management Foundation; St. Paul ProMutual Insurance Cos.; Wausau Insurance Cos.
Reference: Fleet Bank.
*Employees of The Professional Corporation of McCarthy, Kenney & Reidy.

For full biographical listings, see the Martindale-Hubbell Law Directory

MCCORMACK & EPSTEIN (AV)

One International Place, 02110
Telephone: 617-951-2929
Telecopier: 617-951-2672
New York, N.Y. Office: The Empire State Building, 350 Fifth Avenue, 60th Floor, 10118-6098.
Telephone: 212-935-0881.

MEMBERS OF FIRM

Robert D. Epstein
Michael J. McCormack
Mark E. Cohen
Joseph H. Aronson

Brian C. Duffey
George X. Pucci
Marc L. LaCasse
Amy M. Soisson
Stephen D. Rosenberg
Lisa M. Solomon (Not admitted in MA)
Nicole M. Arangio
Ara J. Balikian
Anil Adyanthaya
John A. Krebs

Representative Clients: First State Insurance Co.; Crum & Forster Commercial Insurance; Liberty Mutual Insurance Co.; Massachusetts Bay Transportation Authority; Technical Aid Corporation.

For full biographical listings, see the Martindale-Hubbell Law Directory

PALMER & DODGE LLP (AV)

One Beacon Street, 02108
Telephone: 617-573-0100
Facsimile: 617-227-4420
URL: http://www.palmerdodge.com

MEMBERS OF FIRM

Michael J. Lacek
Scott P. Lewis
Steven L. Schreckinger
Thane D. Scott
Craig E. Stewart
Jeffrey Swope
Tamara S. Wolfson

COUNSEL

Jane M. Guevremont
Harvey Nosowitz

For Complete List of Firm Personnel, See General Section

For full biographical listings, see the Martindale-Hubbell Law Directory

SHAPIRO & ASSOCIATES (AV)

One Beacon Street, 24th Floor, 02108
Telephone: 617-227-8100
Fax: 617-523-8100
Email: email@ShapiroLaw.com *URL:* http://www.ShapiroLaw.com
Dedham, Massachusetts Office: 450 Washington Street, Suite 107.
Telephone: 781-329-8100.
Fax: 781-329-9800.

Daniel B. Shapiro

ASSOCIATES

N. Melina Bell
John J. Sheehan
Sharon T. Kohler
Marsha A. Kaufmann

For full biographical listings, see the Martindale-Hubbell Law Directory

TAYLOR, DUANE, BARTON & GILMAN, LLP (AV)

111 Devonshire Street, 02109
Telephone: 617-654-8200
Fax: 617-482-5350
Providence, Rhode Island Office: 10 Dorrance Street, Suite 700, 02903.
Telephone: 401-273-7171.
Fax: 401-273-2904.

MEMBERS OF FIRM

Allan E. Taylor
James J. Duane, III
John J. Barton
Pamela Slater Gilman
Edward D. Shoulkin
Jennifer Ellis Burke
Francis A. Connor, III
Gina Witalec Verdi

(See Next Column)

ASSOCIATES

Robert C. Shindell
Craig R. Waksler
Stephen Adams
Christine A. Kelly
Andria Coletta
Sheri L. Pizzi
Tryntje I. Houghton
Robert M. Elmer
Tamara J. Smith
Jennifer L. Buckley

For full biographical listings, see the Martindale-Hubbell Law Directory

BROCKTON, Plymouth Co.

VINCENT P. CAHALANE, P.C. (AV)

478 Torrey Street, Suite 12, 02301-4696
Telephone: 508-588-1222
Fax: 508-584-4748
URL: http://www.lawyers.com/cahalanelaw

Vincent P. Cahalane
Robert J. Zullas
Julie A. Cahalane Cahill
Andrew H. P. Norton
Kristopher S. Stefani

Representative Clients: Quincy Mutual Fire Insurance Co.; Admiral Insurance Co.

For full biographical listings, see the Martindale-Hubbell Law Directory

*CAMBRIDGE,** Middlesex Co.

NEVILLE & KELLEY (AV)

Bulfinch Square, 43 Thorndike Street, 02141
Telephone: 617-876-7100
Fax: 617-225-0627
Springfield, Massachusetts Office: 1350 Main Street, 10th Floor, 01103.
Telephone: 413-736-7100.
Fax: 413-739-5388.

MEMBERS OF FIRM

Constance M. Neville
Paul R. Kelley

Sara Gens Birenbaum
Patricia J. DiGiovanni
John L. Kerr
June A. Harris
Paul J. Franco
Maria Elisa Ciampa
Kimberly D. Goodman
Nina E. Kallen
Patrick J. McHugh
Lisa A. Shapiro
Jennifer A. Hylemon

OF COUNSEL

Paul M. Richardson

For full biographical listings, see the Martindale-Hubbell Law Directory

LOWELL, Middlesex Co.

DONAHUE & DONAHUE, ATTORNEYS, P.C. (AV)

21 George Street, 01852
Telephone: 978-458-6887
Fax: 978-458-3424

Daniel J. Donahue (1860-1939)
Joseph P. Donahue (1889-1973)
Charles A. Donahue (1891-1964)
Richard K. Donahue
Joseph P. Donahue, Jr.
Joseph D. Regan
Michael W. Gallagher
Richard K. Donahue, Jr.
Andrea S. Barisano
Matthew C. Donahue
Richard E. Cavanaugh
Kelly R. Spencer
Alicia A. Donahue

Kelly M. Quigley

Representative Clients: The Travelers Insurance Co.; Jefferson Insurance; Monticello Insurance; Coregis Group; Rockwell International Corp.

For full biographical listings, see the Martindale-Hubbell Law Directory

*SPRINGFIELD,** Hampden Co.

ROBINSON DONOVAN MADDEN & BARRY, P.C. (AV)

Suite 1600, Tower Square, 1500 Main Street, 01115-5609
Telephone: 413-732-2301
Fax: 413-785-4658
Email: service@robinson-donovan.com *URL:* http://www.robinson-donovan.com

Homans Robinson (1894-1973)
Lawrence M. Sinclair (1942-1986)
Milton J. Donovan (1906-1995)

RETIRED

John H. Madden, Jr.
Edward J. Barry
Richard S. Milstein

OF COUNSEL

Victor Rosenberg

SENIOR COUNSEL

Jonathan P. Rice

(See Next Column)

ROBINSON DONOVAN MADDEN & BARRY P.C., *Springfield—Continued*

Gordon H. Wentworth
James H. Tourtelotte
Ronald C. Kidd
Jeffrey W. Roberts
Jeffrey L. McCormick
James F. Martin
Robert P. Cunningham
John C. Sikorski
Nancy Frankel Pelletier
Paul S. Weinberg
Frederica H. McCarthy
Matthew J. King
Neva Kaufman Rohan
Douglas F. Boyd
James K. Bodurtha
Keith A. Minoff
Patricia M. Rapinchuk
Kimberly Davis Crear

E. Paul Amata
Lisa A. Bongiovi
(Not admitted in MA)
Edward J. Carroll, III
James D. Chadwell
John E. Garber
Patrick J. Markey
Carla W. Newton
Betsy Macmillan Stevens

Representative Clients: BankBoston, N.A.; United Cooperative Bank; Fleet National Bank; CNA; Commercial Union Insurance Co.; Hanover Insurance Group.

For full biographical listings, see the Martindale-Hubbell Law Directory

WELLESLEY, Norfolk Co.

ZIZIK, LASALLE & POWERS, A PROFESSIONAL CORPORATION (AV)

One Hollis Street, Suite 400, 02482
Telephone: 781-431-8777
Fax: 781-431-8749
Email: ZLPLAW@aol.com
Providence, Rhode Island Office: 40 Westminister Street, Suite 201, 02903.
Telephone: 401-421-7110.
Fax: 401-421-7111.
Boston, Massachusetts Office: 101 Federal Street, Suite 1900, 02110.
Telephone: 781-431-8777.
Fax: 781-431-8749.
Cape Cod, Massachusetts Office: 49 Locust Street, Falmouth, 02540.
Telephone: 508-540-1113.
Fax: 508-540-1144.

David W. Zizik
Richard E. Powers
Faith A. LaSalle
Brian A. O'Connell
Cathryn Spaulding
Donna M. LaMontagne
Karen M. Connors
William J. Fidurko
Scott A. Bell
Kimberly K. Ryan

For full biographical listings, see the Martindale-Hubbell Law Directory

*WORCESTER,** Worcester Co.

BURNS & FARREY (AV)

446 Main Street, Floor 22, 01608-2302
Telephone: 508-756-6288
Fax: 508-831-9769
Boston, Massachusetts Office: 150 Federal Street, 26th Floor, 02110.
Telephone: 617-439-4758.
Fax: 617-439-4148.

MEMBERS OF FIRM

John C. Burns (1952-1984)
Thomas B. Farrey, III

ASSOCIATES

Edward B. McGrath
James T. Huggard
Brooke P. Seliger
Janet Marie Bolger
Patricia A. O'Connor
Marco T. Bon Tempo
Thomas Peter Brady
Michael James Merriam
James P. McLarnon, Jr.
Susan M. Sherman
Anna Szeto
Richard E. McCue
Jeffrey A. Fishman
Francis J. Duggan

For full biographical listings, see the Martindale-Hubbell Law Directory

HASSETT & DONNELLY (AV)

(Formerly Healy & Rocheleau, P.C.)
Denholm Building, 484 Main Street Suite 560, 01608
Telephone: 508-791-6287
Fax: 508-791-2652
Email: davidhassett@hassettanddonnelly.com

J. Oscar Rocheleau (1906-1990)
Edward P. Healy
David F. Hassett
Gerard T. Donnelly

Anthony N. Tomasiello, Jr.
Sarah B. Christie
Julie D. McAlarney
Scott T. Ober
Jennifer E. Parker
Melanie S. Weaver
Laura L. Hancock

Representative Clients: American International Group; Amica Insurance; Commonwealth of Massavhusetts Executive Office of Communities Development; Covernant Mutual Insurance Co.; Fitchburg Mutual Insurance Co.; Guaranty Fund Management Services; MassWest Insurance Co.; Preferred Mutual Insurance Co.; National Grange Insurance Co.; Worcester/Berkshire Insurance Cos.

For full biographical listings, see the Martindale-Hubbell Law Directory

MACCARTHY, POJANI & HURLEY, LLP (AV)

Worcester Plaza, 446 Main Street, 01608
Telephone: 508-798-2480
Fax: 508-797-9561

RETIRED PARTNER

Philip J. MacCarthy

MEMBERS OF FIRM

John F. Hurley, Jr.
William J. Ritter

Representative Clients: Commerce Insurance Company; Liberty Mutual Insurance Company; Prenier Insurance Co.; Travelers Insurance Company; Western World Insurance Co.; Worcester Insurance Co.

For Complete List of Firm Personnel, See General Section

For full biographical listings, see the Martindale-Hubbell Law Directory

MILTON, LAURENCE & DIXON (AV)

100 Front Street, Suite 1020, 01608-1402
Telephone: 508-791-6386
Fax: 508-799-4879
Email: mld@chamber.worcester.ma.us

MEMBERS OF FIRM

Stanley B. Milton (1924-1992)
Robert C. Milton (1932-1977)
Gerard R. Laurence
Charles W. Dixon
Paul P. O'Connor
Karen A. Loughlin
Daniel M. Wrenn
Karyn E. Polito

OF COUNSEL

John G. Preston
Judy Eldredge

Representative Clients: American Policyholders Insurance Co.; CIGNA; Chubb & Sons; CNA Insurance; General Accident Group; Hanover Insurance Co.; Liberty Mutual Insurance Co.; Medical Professional Mutual Ins. Co. (Promutual); St. Paul Tire and Marine Insurance Co; The Travelers.

For full biographical listings, see the Martindale-Hubbell Law Directory

MICHIGAN

ALMA, Gratiot Co.

FORTINO, PLAXTON, MOSKAL & COSTANZO, P.C. (AV)

Warwick Professional Center, 175 Warwick Drive, P.O. Box 578, 48801
Telephone: 517-463-2101
Fax: 517-463-2104

John J. Moskal (1932-1997)
Charles M. Fortino
Anthony G. Costanzo

OF COUNSEL

Alfred J. Fortino
Kenneth D. Plaxton

LEGAL SUPPORT PERSONNEL

PARALEGALS

Gillene M. Weller

Attorneys for: Farmers State Bank, Breckenridge; State Farm Mutual Insurance Co.; Auto Owners Insurance Co.; The Ohio Casualty Ins. Co.; Commercial Bank; Bear Truss and Components Co.; Alma Iron and Metal; Powell Fabrication & Mfg.; City of Alma.

For full biographical listings, see the Martindale-Hubbell Law Directory

*ANN ARBOR,** Washtenaw Co.

BRAUN KENDRICK FINKBEINER PLC (AV)

First National Building, 210 S. Main, Suite 700, 48104
Telephone: 313-995-4100
Telecopier: 313-995-4798
Email: ALBFIE@BKF-LAW.COM *URL:* http://www.bkf-law.com
Bay City, Michigan Office: 201 Phoenix Building, P.O. Box 2039.
Telephone: 517-895-8505.
Telecopier: 517-895-8437.
Saginaw, Michigan Office: 101 N. Washington, Suite 812.
Telephone: 517-753-3461.
Telecopier: 517-753-3951.
Saginaw Township, Michigan Office: 5800 Gratiot Road, Suite 107, P.O. Box 5169.
Telephone: 517-799-8692.
Fax: 517-799-4666.
Mt. Pleasant, Michigan Office: 805 North Brown.
Telephone: 517-775-7404.
Telecopier: 517-775-3764.

(See Next Column)

BRAUN KENDRICK FINKBEINER PLC—*Continued*

Barry M. Levine

Representative Clients: Farm Bureau Insurance Group; Firemans Fund American Insurance; Frankenmuth Mutual Insurance Co.; Fremont Mutual Insurance Co.; Great Lakes American Life Ins. Co.; Hartford Insurance Group; Hastings Mutual Insurance Co.; Kemper Insurance Group; Michigan Mutual Liability Co.; Mutual Benefit Life Ins. Co.

For Complete List of Firm Personnel, See General Section

For full biographical listings, see the Martindale-Hubbell Law Directory

GARAN, LUCOW, MILLER & SEWARD, P.C. (AV)

101 North Main Street, Suite 460, 48104-1400
Telephone: 734-930-5600
Fax: 734-930-0043
URL: http://www.garanlucow.com
Detroit, Michigan Office: 1000 Woodbridge Place.
Telephone: 313-446-1530.
Fax: 313-259-0450.
Port Huron, Michigan Office: Port Huron Office Center, 511 Fort Street, Suite 505.
Telephone: 810-985-4400.
Fax: 810-985-4107.
Grand Blanc, Michigan Office: 8332 Office Park Drive.
Telephone: 810-695-3700.
Fax: 810-695-6488.
Troy, Michigan Office: 1111 West Long Lake Road, Suite 300.
Telephone: 248-641-7600.
Fax: 248-641-0222.
Mount Clemens, Michigan Office: Towne Square Development, 10 South Main Street, Suite 307.
Telephone: 810-954-3800:
Fax: 810-954-3803.
Grand Rapids, Michigan Office: First of America Center, 171 Monroe Avenue, N.W., Suite 950.
Telephone: 616-742-5500.
Fax: 616-742-5566.
Lansing, Michigan Office: 530 Creyts Road, Suite A.
Telephone: 517-327-0300.
Fax: 517-327-0309.
Traverse City, Michigan Office: 1131 East Eighth Street, P.O. Box 3150.
Telephone: 231-941-1611.
Fax: 231-941-4420.
Marquette, Michigan Office: 228 West Washington Street, Suite 4,
Telephone: 906-228-7772.
Fax: 906-228-5999.

Judith A. Moskus (Resident) John W. Whitman

John J. Koselka Suzanne R. Fanning

For full biographical listings, see the Martindale-Hubbell Law Directory

MILLER, CANFIELD, PADDOCK AND STONE, P.L.C. (AV)

A Professional Limited Liability Company
Founded in 1852 by Sidney Davy Miller
101 North Main Street, Seventh Floor, 48104-1400
Telephone: 734-663-2445
Fax: 734-747-7147
URL: http://www.millercanfield.com
Detroit, Michigan Office: 150 West Jefferson, Suite 2500, 48226-4415.
Telephone: 313-963-6420.
Fax: 313-496-7500.
Cable Address: "Stem Detroit."
Troy, Michigan Office: 840 West Long Lake Road, Suite 200, 48098.
Telephone: 248-879-2000.
Fax: 248-879-2001.
Grand Rapids, Michigan Office: 99 Monroe, N.W., Suite 1200, 49503-2639.
Telephone: 616-454-8656.
Fax: 616-776-6322.
Howell, Michigan Office: 121 South Barnard Street, Suite 4, 48843-2305.
Telephone: 517-546-7600.
Telecopier: 517-546-6974.
Kalamazoo, Michigan Office: 444 West Michigan Avenue, 49007-3752.
Telephone: 616-381-7030.
Fax: 616-382-0244.
Lansing, Michigan Office: One Michigan Avenue, Suite 900, 48933-1609.
Telephone: 517-487-2070.
Fax: 517-374-6304.
Monroe, Michigan Office: 214 East Elm Avenue, Suite 100, 48162-2682.
Telephone: 734-243-2000.
Fax: 734-243-0901.
Washington, D.C. Office: 1900 K Street, N.W., Suite 1150. 20006.
Telephone: 202-429-5575; 785-0600.
Fax: 202-331-1118; 785-1234.
Pensacola, Florida Office: 25 West Cedar, 32501.
Telephone: 850-469-1088.
Fax: 850-432-0677.

(See Next Column)

New York, New York Office: 1450 Broadway, 41st Floor, 10018.
Telephone: 212-704-4400.
Fax: 212-704-4410.
Gdynia, Poland Office: UL. Slaska 21, 81-319.
Telephone: 011-485-831-2808.
Fax: 011-48-58-628 6411.
Warsaw, Poland Office: UL. Nowogrodzkall, 5th Floor, 00-513.
Telephone: 011-4822 529 0200.
Fax: 011-4822 529 0201.
Katowice, Poland Office: UL. Francuska 35/37, 40-027.
Telephone: 011 (48-32) 757-2414.
Fax: 011 (48-32) 757-2483.

PRINCIPALS OF FIRM

Robert E. Gilbert David A. French
Allyn D. Kantor Marta A. Manildi

Representative Firm Clients: Chrysler Corporation; Comerica, Incorporated; City of Detroit, Michigan; Detroit Tigers, Inc.; First of Michigan; Ford Motor Company; Ford Motor Credit Company; Great Lakes Bancorp; Henry Ford Hospital; INVETECH Company.

For Complete List of Firm Personnel, See General Section

For full biographical listings, see the Martindale-Hubbell Law Directory

PEAR SPERLING EGGAN & MUSKOVITZ, P.C. (AV)

Domino's Farms, 24 Frank Lloyd Wright Drive, 48105
Telephone: 734-665-4441
Fax: 734-665-8788
Email: peare@dominos.com
Ypsilanti, Michigan Offices: 5 South Washington Street.
Telephone: 734-483-3626 and 2164 Bellevue at Washtenaw.
Telephone: 734-483-7177.

Edwin L. Pear Paul R. Franswav
Lawrence W. Sperling Francyne Stacey
Andrew M. Eggan Karl V. Fink
Melvin J. Muskovitz Scott H. Mandel
Thomas E. Daniels David E. Kempner
Joel F. Graziani Jeffrey P. Thennisch

Counsel for: Domino's Pizza, Inc.; Townsend and Bottum, Inc.; Cleary College; Victory Lane Quick Oil Change Inc.; Citizens Banking Corp.; Washtenaw News Co., Inc.; Ann Arbor Transportation Authority; Meadowbrook Insurance Group; Michigan Municipal Liability & Property Pool.
Approved Attorneys for: Lawyers Title Insurance Corp.

For full biographical listings, see the Martindale-Hubbell Law Directory

*BAY CITY,** Bay Co.

BRAUN KENDRICK FINKBEINER PLC (AV)

201 Phoenix Building, P.O. Box 2039, 48708
Telephone: 517-895-8505
Telecopier: 517-895-8437
Email: ALBFIE@BKF-LAW.COM *URL:* http://www.bkf-law.com
Saginaw, Michigan Office: 101 N. Washington, Suite 812. 8th Floor Second National Bank Building.
Telephone: 517-753-3461.
Telecopier: 517-753-3951.
Saginaw Township, Michigan Office: 5800 Gratiot Road, Suite 107, P.O. Box 5169.
Telephone: 517-799-8692.
Fax: 517-799-4666.
Ann Arbor, Michigan Office: First National Building. 201 S. Main, Suite 700.
Telephone: 313-995-4100.
Telecopier: 313-995-4798.
Mt. Pleasant, Michigan Office: 805 North Brown.
Telephone: 517-775-7404.
Telecopier: 517-775-3764.

Frank M. Quinn Gregory E. Meter
Jeffrey C. Wilson

Michael E. Wooley

Representative Clients: Bay Health Systems; Catholic Federal Credit Union; City of Saginaw; City of Vassar; City of Zilwaukee; Corporate Service; Cox Cable.

For Complete List of Firm Personnel, See General Section

For full biographical listings, see the Martindale-Hubbell Law Directory

SMITH & BROOKER, P.C. (AV)

703 Washington Avenue, P.O. Box 921, 48707-0921
Telephone: 517-892-2595
Fax: 517-893-5113
Email: sbrooker@tir.com

Glenn F. Doyle (Retired) George B. Mullison
Richard C. Sheppard Charles T. Hewitt

(See Next Column)

SMITH & BROOKER P.C., *Bay City—Continued*

OF COUNSEL

Carl H. Smith, Jr. | Albert C. Hicks
Francis B. Drinan

Representative Clients: Allen Medical Building Co.; Charter Township of Hampton; CIGNA; Medical Protective Insurance Co.; Monitor Sugar Co.; Region VII Area Agency on Aging; State Farm Mutual Automobile Insurance Co.; Sterling Area Health Center; Medical Staff of Bay Medical Center; Secura Insurance.

For full biographical listings, see the Martindale-Hubbell Law Directory

BINGHAM FARMS, Oakland Co.

SMALL, TOTH, BALDRIDGE & VAN BELKUM, P.C. (AV)

30100 Telegraph Road Suite 250, 48025-4516
Telephone: 248-647-9595
Facsimile: 248-647-9599

Richard L. Small | David M. Baldridge
John M. Toth | Thomas G. Van Belkum
Keith P. Felty

Stephanie A. Griz-Kochkodan | Kristin Allen

Representative Clients: Kemper Insurance Group; Mt. Vernon Insurance Co.; Allstate Insurance Co.; Anthem Insurance Co.; Lincoln Insurance Group; Philadelphia Insurance Cos.; Hastings Mutual Insurance Co.; General Star Management Co.; Lincoln Mutual Insurance Co.; CNA Insurance Group.

For full biographical listings, see the Martindale-Hubbell Law Directory

BIRMINGHAM, Oakland Co.

LACEY & JONES, LLP (AV)

600 South Adams Road, Suite 300, 48009-6827
Telephone: 248-433-1414
Fax: 248-433-1241
URL: http://www.laceyjones.com
Ann Arbor, Michigan Office: Suite 525, 220 East Huron, 48104.
Telephone: 734-761-8358.
Fax: 734-761-3134.
Detroit, Michigan Office: Suite 3250, Penobscot Building, 645 Griswold, 48226.
Telephone: 313-961-6474.
Fax: 313-961-5688.
Grand Rapids, Michigan Office: Suite 430, Ledyard Building, 125 Ottawa Avenue, N.W., 49503.
Telephone: 616-776-3641.
Fax: 616-776-3516.
Jackson, Michigan Office: 740 West Michigan Avenue, 49201.
Telephone: 517-782-2000.
Fax: 517-782-3917.

Ralph B. Lacey (1885-1966) | John A. Hilgendorf (Retired)
William J. Jones (1908-1991) | Theodore A. Lughezzani (Retired)
Robert B. Lacey (1912-1976)
Steve N. Yardley (Retired)

MEMBERS OF FIRM

Brian S. Ahearn (Resident, Detroit)
Kathleen McNichol Behn
Larry P. Beidelman
Mary F. Clinton (Resident, Ann Arbor)
William A. Day
David J. Duthie (Resident, Grand Rapids)
T. F. Felker, Jr.
John Hayes
Charles J. Hurbis (Resident, Ann Arbor)
Lawrence G. Kozaruk
Richard N. Lovernick (Resident, Ann Arbor)
Charles E. Mann
Gerald M. Marcinkoski
J. Patrick O'Neill
Sean J. Powers
Michael T. Reinholm
Bruce C. Roberts
Peter M. Roggenbaum
Thomas J. Sullivan (Resident, Jackson)
Dennis E. Zacharski

Carrie G. Barrett
John C. Dickinson
Dawn M. Drobnich
Timothy D. Finegan
Timothy M. McAree (Resident, Grand Rapids)
D. Michael McCann
Dallas G. Moon
Robert H. Orlowski, Jr.
Johnnie B. Rambus
Kenneth S. Wilson

OF COUNSEL

Robert L. Beardslee
Georgette E. David (Resident, Ann Arbor)
Robert G. Lewandowski
William G. Sinn

Representative Clients: Alexsis, Inc.; Ameritech; Chrysler Corporation; CIGNA; Liberty Mutual Insurance Company; Meijer, Inc.; Metropolitan Prop. & Casualty; Michigan Hospital Association; Travelers Insurance Company; University of Michigan.

For full biographical listings, see the Martindale-Hubbell Law Directory

VANDEVEER GARZIA, PROFESSIONAL CORPORATION (AV)

220 Park Street, Suite 300, 48009
Telephone: 810-645-0100
Fax: 810-645-2430
Wayne County Office: Suite 1600, 333 West Fort Street, Detroit, Michigan.
Telephone: 313-961-4880.
Fax: 313-961-3822.

John J. Lynch, III | Shelley K. Miller
James K. Thome | David B. Timmis

Christian E. Hildebrandt

Representative Clients: Aetna Casualty and Surety Co.; Chubb Insurance; CNA Group; Farmers Insurance Group; Goodyear Tire & Rubber Co.; Transamerica Insurance Group; Travelers Insurance Company.

For full biographical listings, see the Martindale-Hubbell Law Directory

BLOOMFIELD HILLS, Oakland Co.

CYNTHIA ADKISON, P.C. (AV)

1533 North Woodward Avenue Suite 210, 48304
Telephone: 248-683-1000
Fax: 248-683-1007

Cynthia Adkison

For full biographical listings, see the Martindale-Hubbell Law Directory

BEIER HOWLETT, PROFESSIONAL CORPORATION (AV)

200 East Long Lake Road, Suite 110, 48304-2361
Telephone: 248-645-9400
Fax: 248-645-9344
URL: http://www.beierhowlett.com

James L. Howlett
Daniel C. Devine
Lawrence R. Ternan
Stephen W. Jones
Frank S. Galgan
Kenneth J. Sorensen
Thomas J. Trenta
Mark W. Hafeli
Timothy J. Currier
Mary T. Schmitt Smith
Joseph F. Yamin
John D. Staran
Phyllis Aiuto Zimmerman
P. Daniel Christ
Lauren M. Underwood

Elizabeth A. Barrett Bonner
Mary M. Kucharek
Richard A. Joslin, Jr.
Michael C. Gibbons
Jon M. Midtgard
Paul L. Nystrom
Genevieve Dwaihy Hopkins
Jeffrey S. Kragt

OF COUNSEL

Dean G. Beier | Catherine J. Hulbert
Robert G. Waddell | Thomas V. Trainer

Representative Clients: City of Birmingham; Oakland County Road Commission; Examen, Inc.; Auto Club Insurance Association (AAA); Lake States Insurance Company; Michigan Millers Insurance Company; Western Indemnity Insurance Company; Secura Insurance Company; AIG Insurance Company; Michigan Municipal League.

For full biographical listings, see the Martindale-Hubbell Law Directory

FEDERLEIN & KERANEN, P.C. (AV)

6895 Telegraph Road, 48301
Telephone: 248-647-9653
Fax: 248-647-9683
Email: firm@fk-law.com *URL:* http://www.fk-law.com
Detroit, Michigan Office: 407 East Fort, Suite 350.
Telephone: 313-965-6090.
Marquette, Michigan Office: 122 West Spring Street.
Telephone: 906-225-1770.
Fax: 906-225-1764.
Sault Ste. Marie, Michigan Office: 204 East Spruce Street.
Telephone: 906-635-6286.
Fax: 906-635-5390.

Walter J. Federlein | Thomas M. Keranen

Frederick F. Butters
Maria J. Bernard (Resident, Detroit Office)
Peter J. Cavanaugh
J. Christian Hauser (Resident, Detroit Office)
Gary Quesada
Jeffrey Michael Gallant

For full biographical listings, see the Martindale-Hubbell Law Directory

HARDIG PARSONS PEDERSEN & STOUT, PLLC (AV)

74 West Long Lake Road, Suite 203, 48304
Telephone: 248-642-3500
Facsimile: 248-645-1128
URL: http://www.hpplaw.com
Charlevoix, Michigan Office: 212 Bridge Street. 49720.
Telephone: 616-547-1200.

(See Next Column)

HARDIG PARSONS PEDERSEN & STOUT PLLC—*Continued*

Pawleys Island, South Caroline Office: 216 Highway 17. P.O. Box 1607. 29585.
Telephone: 803-237-9121.
West Palm Beach, Florida Office: 1450 North Bridge Tower. 515 North Flagler. 33401.
Telephone: 561-833-1622.

MEMBERS OF FIRM

Joseph L. Hardig, Jr.
Donald H. Parsons (Resident, Charlevoix Office)
Joseph L. Hardig, III
Edward C. Pedersen
Bradley S. Stout
John C. Benso (Not admitted in MI; Resident, Pawleys Island, South Carolina Office)

OF COUNSEL

John W. Henke
Patrick T. Barone
Gordon A. Snavely
Robert J. Cucco
Edward K. Pedersen, Jr.

For full biographical listings, see the Martindale-Hubbell Law Directory

DAVID D. PATTON & ASSOCIATES, P.C. (AV)

44 East Long Lake Road, Suite 100, P.O. Box 829, 48303-0829
Telephone: 248-258-6020
Fax: 248-258-6052
Email: litigation@aol.com *URL:* http://www.lawyers.com/dpattonlaw

David D. Patton

Ellen Bartman Jannette
Patricia C. White
Humma S. Siddiqi
Kelly P. Bekolay
David H. Patton (1912-1993)

OF COUNSEL

Lawrence J. Acker

For full biographical listings, see the Martindale-Hubbell Law Directory

PORTNOY, PIDGEON & ROTH, P.C. (AV)

3883 Telegraph, Suite 103, 48302
Telephone: 248-647-4242
Fax: 248-647-8251
Email: DWINNIE103@AOL.COM *URL:* http://www.lawyers.com/portnoypidgeon&roth

Bernard N. Portnoy (Retired)
James M. Pidgeon
Robert P. Roth
Marc S. Berlin
Sheila Connor-Heath
Anne Loridas Randall
Joseph M. LaBella
Melinda A. Davis

Representative Clients: Continental Insurance Co.; Continental Health Care; OUM Group.

For full biographical listings, see the Martindale-Hubbell Law Directory

PROVIZER & PHILLIPS, P.C. (AV)

6785 Telegraph Road, Suite 400, 48301
Telephone: 248-642-0444
Facsimile: 248-642-6661
Toll Free: 1-800-288-9080
URL: http://www.lawyers.com/provizer&phillips

Harold M. Provizer
Randall E. Phillips
Marilyn A. Madorsky
Noel F. Beck

Constance S. Hall
Ellen C. Busch
Donald J. Parthum, Jr.
Gregory A. Nave

Representative Clients: Jefferson Ins. Co.; Reliance National Ins. Co.; Blackmoor Group; Thomas Howell Group; Fleming & Hall.

For full biographical listings, see the Martindale-Hubbell Law Directory

*DETROIT,** Wayne Co.

BLAKE, KIRCHNER, SYMONDS, MACFARLANE, LARSON & SMITH, P.C. (AV)

1432 Buhl Building, 535 Griswold Street, 48226
Telephone: 313-961-7321
Fax: 313-961-5972
Email: bksml@ameritech.net

F. Peter Blake
Arthur G. Kirchner
Daniel C. Symonds
Bruce F. MacFarlane
Meria E. Larson
Richard P. Smith
Kevin T. Kennedy
Jane P. Garrett
Christopher G. Manolis
David B. Klein

Rebecca S. Austin
R. Edward Boucher

Reference: Comerica Bank.

For full biographical listings, see the Martindale-Hubbell Law Directory

BOOTHMAN, HEBERT & ELLER, P.C. (AV)

Marquette Building, 243 West Congress, Suite 950, 48226
Telephone: 313-964-0150
Fax: 313-964-2226
Email: boothman@mail.mich.com

Dale L. Hebert
Richard C. Boothman
Gary S. Eller

Edward C. Reynolds, Jr.
Marta J. Hoffman

Representative Clients: University of Michigan; Mutual Insurance Corporation of America; Emergency Physicians Medical Group; Pronational; HCR Manor Care, Inc.
Reference: Comerica Bank-Detroit.

For full biographical listings, see the Martindale-Hubbell Law Directory

GARAN, LUCOW, MILLER & SEWARD, P.C. (AV)

1000 Woodbridge Place, 48207-3192
Telephone: 313-446-1530
Fax: 313-259-0450
URL: http://www.garanlucow.com
Grand Blanc, Michigan Office: 8332 Office Park Drive.
Telephone: 810-695-3700.
Fax: 810-695-6488.
Port Huron, Michigan Office: Port Huron Office Center, 511 Fort Street, Suite 505.
Telephone: 810-985-4400.
Fax: 810-985-4107.
Ann Arbor, Michigan Office: 101 North Main Street, Suite 460.
Telephone: 734-930-5600.
Fax: 734-930-0043.
Troy, Michigan Office: 1111 West Long Lake Road, Suite 300.
Telephone: 248-641-7600.
Fax: 248-641-0222.
Mount Clemens, Michigan Office: Towne Square Development, 10 S. Main Street, Suite 307.
Telephone: 810-954-3800.
Fax: 810-954-3803.
Grand Rapids, Michigan Office: First of America Center, 171 Monroe Avenue, N.W., Suite 950.
Telephone: 616-742-5500.
Fax: 616-742-5566.
Lansing, Michigan Office: 530 Creyts Road, Suite A.
Telephone: 517-327-0300.
Fax: 517-327-0309.
Traverse City, Michigan Office: 1131 East Eighth Street, P.O. Box 3150.
Telephone: 231-941-1611.
Fax: 231-941-4420.
Marquette, Michigan Office: 228 West Washington Street, Suite 4,
Telephone: 906-228-7772.
Fax: 906-228-5999.

Daniel L. Garan (1922-1997)
Thomas F. Myers
Dennis P. Partridge
John E. McSorley
Lamont E. Buffington
Thomas L. Misuraca
Rosalind Rochkind
James J. Hayes, Jr.
Thomas W. Emery
Boyd E. Chapin, Jr.
Frederick B. Plumb
James S. Goulding
John J. Gillooly
Robert D. Goldstein
Michael J. DePolo
Thomas R. Paxton
Daniel S. Saylor
David M. Shafer
C. David Miller, II
Robert A. Obringer

Steven E. Nurenberg
Lynn E. Geist
Mark T. Rajt
Jami E. Leach
Allison L. Hoff
Charles A. Harrison, III
Erik Stamell
Clare M. Cylkowski
Timothy James Jordan
David Allan Couch
Stacey Lynn King
Stephen Hudak

OF COUNSEL

Milton Lucow
Albert A. Miller
Matthew A. Seward
Jon P. Desenberg
Nancy J. Bourget

Counsel for: Allstate Insurance Co.; Sears, Roebuck & Co.; Liberty Mutual Insurance Co.; Continental Insurance Companies.

For Complete List of Firm Personnel, See General Section

For full biographical listings, see the Martindale-Hubbell Law Directory

MICHAEL A. GUNDERSON (AV)

2850 Cadillac Tower, 48226
Telephone: 313-496-8900
Telefax: 313-496-9969
Email: gunderlaw@aol.com

LEGAL SUPPORT PERSONNEL

Doreen Michaels (Paralegal)

For full biographical listings, see the Martindale-Hubbell Law Directory

Detroit—Continued

HAYDUK, ANDREWS & HYPNAR, P.C. (AV)

1700 Buhl Building, 535 Griswold, 48226
Telephone: 313-962-4500
Fax: 313-964-6577
Email: hahpc3@aol.com

Mark S. Hayduk
Robin K. Andrews
Mark A. Hypnar

Sean Angus McPhillips
Francis J. Lagrou

Representative Clients: Farmers Insurance Group; Admiral Insurance Co.; American Modern Home Insurance; Western Heritage Insurance; Northpointe Insurance; Shelby Mutual Insurance; Vik Brothers Ins.; Investors Ins. Group.

For full biographical listings, see the Martindale-Hubbell Law Directory

KELLER, THOMA, SCHWARZE, SCHWARZE, DUBAY & KATZ, P.C. (AV)

440 East Congress, 5th Floor, 48226
Telephone: 313-965-7610
Fax: 313-965-4480
Bingham Farms, Michigan Office: 30150 Telegraph Road, Suite 444, 48025.
Telephone: 248-642-5218.

Leonard A. Keller (1906-1970)
Frederick B. Schwarze
Dennis B. DuBay
James R. Miller
Stewart J. Katz
Anthony J. Heckemeyer
Thomas L. Fleury
Terrence J. Miglio
Gary P. King
Robert A. Lusk
Linda M. Foster
Bruce M. Bagdady
Carl F. Schwarze
Brian A. Kreucher
Christopher M. Murray
Mark C. Knoth
John J. Rabaut
Martha A. Proctor
Joseph R. Furton, Jr.

Counsel for: Livonia Public Schools; Ludington News Co., Inc.
Representative Clients: Borg-Warner Corp.; E & L Transport Co.; The Kroger Co.; Holnam, Inc.
Public Employer Clients: City of Farmington Hills; City of Flint; City of Grosse Pointe Woods; Saginaw Public Schools.

For Complete List of Firm Personnel, See General Section

For full biographical listings, see the Martindale-Hubbell Law Directory

KITCH DRUTCHAS WAGNER DENARDIS & VALITUTTI, A PROFESSIONAL CORPORATION (AV)

One Woodward, Tenth Floor, 48226-3499
Telephone: 313-965-7900
Fax: 313-965-7403
URL: http://www.kitch.com
Lansing, Michigan Office: 120 Washington Square, North, Suite 280, One Michigan Avenue, 48933-1609.
Telephone: 517-372-6430.
Fax: 517-372-0441.
Macomb County Office: Towne Square Development, 10 South Main Street, Suite 301, Mount Clemens, 48043-7903.
Telephone: 810-463-9770.
Fax: 810-463-8994.
Toledo, Ohio Office: 405 Madison Avenue, Suite 1500, 43604-1235.
Telephone: 419-243-4006.
Fax: 419-243-7333.
Marquette, Michigan Office: Old City Hall, 220 West Washington, Suite 500, 49855-4344.
Telephone: 906-228-0001.
Fax: 906-228-0003.
Ann Arbor, Michigan Office: 303 Detroit Street, Suite 400, P.O. Box 8610, 48107-8610.
Telephone: 734-994-7600.
Fax: 734-994-7626.
Grand Rapids, Michigan Office: 300 Ottawa, NW, Suite 210, 49503.
Telephone: 616-456-8384.
Fax: 616-456-8795.

FIRM PRINCIPALS

Richard A. Kitch
Ronald E. Wagner (Managing Principal)
Ralph F. Valitutti, Jr.
Richard R. DeNardis
Mona K. Majzoub
Harry J. Sherbrook
Anthony G. Arnone
Charles W. Fisher
Clyde M. Metzger, III (Principal, Ann Arbor Office)
Thomas J. Foley
Victor J. Abela
James H. Hughesian
John P. Ryan (Principal, Lansing Office)
William D. Chaklos
Steve N. Cheolas (Principal, Macomb County Office)
Susan Healy Zitterman
John S. Wasung (Principal, Toledo, Ohio Office)
William W. Vertes
Karen Bernard Berkery
Daniel R. Shirey
Richard T. Counsman
Steven M. Waclawski
Stephen R. Brzezinski

(See Next Column)

Thomas R. Shimmel
Carole S. Empey (Ann Arbor)
Michael J. Watza
Sara Mae Gerbitz
Linda M. Garbarino
Susan Marie Beutel
Mark A. Wisniewski

FIRM ASSOCIATE PRINCIPALS

Susan M. Ramage (Grand Rapids Office)
Daniel J. Niemann (Ann Arbor Office)
Sharon A. DeWaele
Kenneth M. Essad
Kim J. Sveska
Dean A. Etsios
Barbara A. Martin
Cheryl A. Cardelli
Paula M. Burgess (Toledo, Ohio Office)
Lauri A. Read
Cullen B. McKinney
Anthony J. Nellis
Jeffrey T. Gorcyca

FIRM SENIOR ASSOCIATES

Antonio Mauti
Joseph P. McGill
Mary Catherine Storen
Laura L. Witty
Sheley L. DeGraw
Laura L. Selzer
R. Lisa Panah
Christina A. Ginter

Representative Clients: CNA Insurance Companies; Home Insurance Co.; MHA Insurance Co.; State Farm Insurance Company; St. Paul Insurance Co.; The Travelers Insurance Company.

For Complete List of Firm Personnel, See General Section

For full biographical listings, see the Martindale-Hubbell Law Directory

LUPO & KOCZKUR, P.C. (AV)

1000 First National Building, 48226
Telephone: 313-964-0110
Fax: 313-964-3711
Email: DLupo92965@aol.com *URL:* http://www.lawyers.com/l&klaw

Dane A. Lupo
Paul S. Koczkur
Ronald E. Westen

Robert P. George
Alexander B. Jarowyj
Gabriel Orzame Jr.
Dane A. Lupo, Jr.
Bradley T. Guldalian

Representative Clients: Anheuser-Busch, Inc.; United Artists; ITT; Olsten; Thermadyne Industries; National Beverage; CIGNA/Insurance Company of North America; Michigan Millers; Walt Disney World; Vic Tanny International.

For full biographical listings, see the Martindale-Hubbell Law Directory

PATTERSON, PHIFER & PHILLIPS, P.C. (AV)

L.B. King Building, 1274 Library Street, Suite 500, 48226
Telephone: 313-964-2360
Fax: 313-964-6870
URL: http://www.lawyers.com/p3

Michael D. Patterson
Randolph D. Phifer
Dwight W. Phillips
Joseph M. White

Marvin Allen Cooke

Representative Clients: Detroit Board of Education; Fireman's Fund Insurance Co.; General Motors Corp.; Liberty Mutual Insurance Co.; Metropolitan Life Insurance Co.; Michigan Basic Property Insurance Assn.; New York Life Insurance Co.; Wayne State University.
Reference: First of American Bank-Detroit, N.A.

For full biographical listings, see the Martindale-Hubbell Law Directory

RUTLEDGE, MANION, RABAUT, TERRY & THOMAS, P.C. (AV)

2300 Buhl Building, 48226
Telephone: 313-965-6100
Telefax: 313-965-6558

Alvin A. Rutledge
Paul J. Manion
Vincent C. Rabaut, Jr.
Christopher L. Terry
David M. Thomas
Anthony J. Calati
Lisa Sabon Anstess
David A. Brauer
Patrick D. Filbin
Matthew A. Brauer

Amy Schlotterer

LEGAL SUPPORT PERSONNEL

PARALEGALS

Gloria A. Lambright
Laura A. Matheson
Lynn B. Bossler
Michelle R. Devereaux
Jacquelyn A. McClinton

For full biographical listings, see the Martindale-Hubbell Law Directory

TIMMIS & INMAN L.L.P. (AV)

300 Talon Centre, 48207
Telephone: 313-396-4200
Facsimile: 313-396-4228
Email: info@timmis-inman.com *URL:* http://www.timmis-inman.com

(See Next Column)

TIMMIS & INMAN L.L.P.—*Continued*

Robert E. Graziani
Mark W. Peyser
Bradley J. Knickerbocker

Anthony J. Long
Michael J. Sheehan

LEGAL SUPPORT PERSONNEL

PARALEGALS

Leslie A. Reaser

Representative Clients: Continental Insurance Company; Sentry Insurance Co.; Transamerica Insurance Group; Certain Underwriters at Lloyds of London; Regency Insurance Co.; Tangent Insurance Co.; Wausau Insurance Co.

For Complete List of Firm Personnel, See General Section

For full biographical listings, see the Martindale-Hubbell Law Directory

VANDEVEER GARZIA, PROFESSIONAL CORPORATION (AV)

Suite 1600, 333 West Fort Street, 48226
Telephone: 313-961-4880
Fax: 313-961-3822
Email: vg@voyager.net
Oakland County Office: 220 Park Street, Suite 300, Birmingham, Michigan.
Telephone: 810-645-0100.
Fax: 810-645-2430.

Fred L. Vandeveer (1879-1972)
James E. Haggerty, Sr. (1900-1966)
Leroy G. Vandeveer (1902-1981)
Buelle A. Doelle (1902-1985)
James E. Plastow, Jr.
Michael M. Hathaway
John J. Lynch, III (Resident, Oakland County Office)
Thomas M. Peters
James K. Thome
Gary Alan Miller
William L. Kiriazis
Daniel P. Steele
Shelley K. Miller (Resident, Oakland County Office)
Terrance P. Lynch
Dennis B. Cotter
Bruce E. Pearce
Hal O. Carroll
David B. Timmis (Resident, Oakland County Office)

Nancy A. Hensley
Dawn M. Twydell
Christian E. Hildebrandt (Resident, Oakland County Office)
Donald C. Brownell

Representative Clients: CNA Insurance Co.; Chubb Insurance; Farmers Insurance Group; Home Insurance Co.; Maryland Casualty Co.; Michigan Property & Casualty; Republic Franklin Insurance Co.; Sentry Insurance Co.; Travelers Insurance Co.; Transamerica Insurance Co.

For full biographical listings, see the Martindale-Hubbell Law Directory

WILLMARTH, TANOURY, RAMAR, CORBET, GARVES & SHAW (AV)

535 Griswold, Suite 1730, 48226-3602
Telephone: 313-964-6300
Fax: 313-964-6310
Email: mdwillth@home.net

MEMBERS OF FIRM

Daniel R. Corbet
Brian R. Garves
David R. Nauts
Anthony J. Paradiso
John M. Perrin
John J. Ramar
Bruce R. Shaw
William A. Tanoury
Mark D. Willmarth

ASSOCIATES

Marie C. Kennedy
Wayne Walker
Elizabeth L. Sokol
Robert S. Silverman
Carmine G. Paterra
Joseph J. Ceglarek, II
Derek Steven Wilczynski
Frank Hamidi
Kristen E. Skaff
Steven J. Bonasso
Colleen P. O'Connor
Lara R. Stutz
Eric G. Tucciarone
Michael P. Robach

For full biographical listings, see the Martindale-Hubbell Law Directory

WULFMEIER & OTTENWESS, PLC (AV)

The Buhl Building, 535 Griswold Suite 850, 48226
Telephone: 313-965-2121
Facsimile: 313-965-7680
Email: law@wulf-ott.com *URL:* http://www.wulf-ott.com
Ann Arbor Office: 320 N. Main Street, Suite 102, 48104.
Telephone: 734-761-1900.
Facsimile: 734-769-0433.

LeRoy H. Wulfmeier, III
David M. Ottenwess
Cheryl L. Chandler
Daniel J. Dulworth
John J. Moran
Stephanie L. Pappas

For full biographical listings, see the Martindale-Hubbell Law Directory

EAST LANSING, Ingham Co.

RAYMOND JOSEPH & ASSOCIATES (AV)

713 Applegate Lane, 48823-2109
Telephone: 517-351-5540
Fax: 517-351-8343

OF COUNSEL

George R. Sidwell (1899-1983)
Michael Bowman
Bruce C. Blanton
Mary E. Low

Representative Clients: Ashland Oil, Inc.; Complete Auto Transit, Inc.; Employers Insurance of Wausau; Evans Products Co.; Grain Dealers Mutl.; Harbor Insurance Co.; Interstate Motor Freight System; Lansing Symphony Assn., Inc.; Prudential LMI Insurance Co.

For full biographical listings, see the Martindale-Hubbell Law Directory

SMITH HAUGHEY RICE & ROEGGE, P.C. (AV)

1400 Abbott Road, Suite 410, 48823-1902
Telephone: 517-332-3030
Facsimile: 517-332-3468
Grand Rapids, Michigan Office: 200 Calder Plaza Building, 250 Monroe Avenue, N.W., 49503-2251.
Telephone: 616-774-8000.
Facsimile: 616-774-2461.
Traverse City, Michigan Office: City Centre Plaza, Suite 100, 202 East State Street, P.O. Box 848, 49685-0848.
Telephone: 231-929-4878.
Facsimile: 231-929-4182.

Douglas G. Powe
Richard C. Kraus

Veronica A. Marsich
Mary K. Robbins-Kralapp
Brian E. Madar
Margaret A. Chamberlain

Representative Clients: Chevron; Cincinnati Insurance Co.; General Motors Corp.; Kemper Insurance Group; Michigan Hospital Assn.; Navistar International; St. Paul Insurance Cos.; Steelcase, Inc.; Dow Elanco.

For full biographical listings, see the Martindale-Hubbell Law Directory

FARMINGTON HILLS, Oakland Co.

BIRNKRANT & BIRNKRANT, P.C. (AV)

Hunters Square Office Building, 31555 West Fourteen Mile Road, Suite 201, 48334
Telephone: 248-932-7500
Facsimile: 248-932-5720

Jon J. Birnkrant
Sherwin M. Birnkrant

Dana Loewenstein

Representative Clients: Insurance Company of North America; CIGNA; City of Pontiac; ESIS; RHK Technology, Inc.; The Maccabees.

For full biographical listings, see the Martindale-Hubbell Law Directory

HALIW SICILIANO AND MYCHALOWYCH (AV)

37000 Grand River, Suite 350, 48335
Telephone: 248-442-0510
Fax: 248-442-0518
Email: hsmfirm@aol.com

MEMBERS OF FIRM

Andrew J. Haliw III
Joseph A. Siciliano
Andrew W. Mychalowych
Nanette Lynn Korpi
Raymond L. Feul
John N. Kaspers
David A. Monroe
Scott A. Decius
Katherine A. Jarred
Mark Gerard Chiesa

OF COUNSEL

Frank C. Kerr
Alphonse Tabaka
David Loeffler
William W. Decker, Jr.

For full biographical listings, see the Martindale-Hubbell Law Directory

KAUFMAN AND PAYTON (AV)

200 Kaufman Financial Center, 30833 Northwestern Highway, 48334-2551
Telephone: 248-626-5000
Telefacsimile: 248-626-2843
Email: kaufman200@aol.com *URL:* http://www.KAUFMANLAW.com
Grand Rapids, Michigan Office: 146 Monroe Center, Suite 210.
Telephone: 616-459-4200.
Fax: 616-459-4929.

Alan Jay Kaufman
Donald L. Payton
Ralph C. Chapa, Jr.
Raymond I. Foley, II
Jeffrey K. Van Hattum
John Eric Franceschi
Eric J. Smith

ASSOCIATE

Lawrence C. Atorthy

(See Next Column)

KAUFMAN AND PAYTON, *Farmington Hills—Continued*

OF COUNSEL

Thomas D. Van Hattum

Representative Clients: A.I.G.; Amway; Burns & Wilcox; Colony Ins.; Markel Companies; Gainsco; St. Paul; Scottsdale Ins. Co.; Pioneer Mutual Ins. Co.; Underwriters at Lloyds.

For full biographical listings, see the Martindale-Hubbell Law Directory

NEMIER, TOLARI, LANDRY, MAZZEO & JOHNSON, P.C. (AV)

37000 Grand River, Suite 300, 48335
Telephone: 248-476-6900
Fax: 248-476-6564
Email: firm@ntlmj.com

Craig L. Nemier
David B. Landry
Jeffrey L. Tolari
Rik Mazzeo
Mark R. Johnson

Michelle E. Mathieu
Katharine R. Shishkovsky
Kathy Contos Nash
Carol J. Surma

OF COUNSEL

William R. Still
Terry E. Pietryga

LEGAL SUPPORT PERSONNEL

Nancy Vayda Dembinski (Paralegal)

Representative Clients: Amerisure/Michigan Mutual Insurance Co.; Chubb Group of Insurance Cos.; Citizens Insurance Co.; Crum & Forster (U.S. Insurance Group); General Accident Insurance; State Farm Fire & Casualty; Nationwide; St. Paul Fire & Marine Insurance Co.; Westfield Insurance Cos.; PepsiCo.

For full biographical listings, see the Martindale-Hubbell Law Directory

SECREST, WARDLE, LYNCH, HAMPTON, TRUEX AND MORLEY (AV)

30903 Northwestern Highway, P.O. Box 3040, 48333-3040
Telephone: 248-851-9500
Telefacsimile: 248-851-2158
Lansing, Michigan Office: 7335 Westshire Drive, Suite 103.
Telephone: 517-627-1881.
Telefacsimile: 517-627-1887.
Mount Clemens, Michigan Office: 94 Macomb Place.
Telephone: 810-465-7180.
Telefacsimile: 810-465-0673.
Grand Rapids, Michigan Office: 833 Kenmoor, S.E.
Telephone: 616-285-0143.
Fax: 616-285-0145.

MEMBER OF FIRM

Charles E. Griffiths

For full biographical listings, see the Martindale-Hubbell Law Directory

*FLINT,** Genesee Co.

GAULT DAVISON A PROFESSIONAL SERVICE CORPORATION (AV)

Tenth Floor, Northbank Center, 432 North Saginaw Street, 48502-2032
Telephone: 810-234-3633
Fax: 810-233-3387
Email: gltdav@tir.com *URL:* http://www.gaultdavison.com

Frederick L. Schmoll, III
Edward B. Davison
Richard C. Hohenstein

Michael W. Edmunds

For full biographical listings, see the Martindale-Hubbell Law Directory

*GAYLORD,** Otsego Co.

BENSINGER, COTANT, MENKES & AARDEMA, P.C. (AV)

308 West Main Street, P.O. Box 1000, 49735
Telephone: 517-732-7536
Fax: 517-732-4922
URL: http://www.bcma.net
Grand Rapids, Michigan Office: 983 Spaulding Avenue, S.E.
Telephone: 616-949-7963.
Fax: 616-949-5264.
Marquette, Michigan Office: 122 West Bluff.
Telephone: 906-225-1000.
Fax: 906-225-0818.

Richard G. Bensinger
James C. Cotant
Michael E. Menkes
Robert Bryan Aardema (Resident, Grand Rapids Office)
Patrick J. Michaels
Kerr L. Moyer (Resident, Grand Rapids)
Brian W. Whitelaw (Resident, Grand Rapids Office)
Dale L. Arndt (Resident, Grand Rapids)

(See Next Column)

Gregory A. Elzinga (Resident, Marquette)
William J. Maynard (Resident, Marquette)
Glenn W. Smith (Resident, Marquette)
Daniel Joseph Bebble
Michael G. Summers (Resident, Marquette Office)
Lynn A. Moon (Resident, Marquette Office)
Roger W. Zappa (Resident, Marquette Office)
Scott R. Eckhold
Frank S. Spies (Resident, Grand Rapids Office)
William M. Fury

Representative Clients: Accident Fund of Michigan; Auto-Owner Insurance Co.; Citizens/Hanover Insurance Co.; Farm Bureau Mutual Insurance Co.; Employers Reinsurance Co.; Lake State Mutual Insurance Co.; Michigan Hospital Association; Michigan Licensed Beverage Association; Physicians Insurance Co. of Michigan; State Farm Mutual Insurance Co.

For full biographical listings, see the Martindale-Hubbell Law Directory

GRAND BLANC, Genesee Co.

GARAN, LUCOW, MILLER & SEWARD, P.C. (AV)

8332 Office Park Drive, 48439
Telephone: 810-695-3700
Fax: 810-695-6488
URL: http://www.garanlucow.com
Detroit, Michigan Office: 1000 Woodbridge Place.
Telephone: 313-446-1530.
Fax: 313-259-0450.
Port Huron, Michigan Office: Port Huron Office Center, 511 Fort Street, Suite 505.
Telephone: 810-985-4400.
Fax: 810-985-4187.
Ann Arbor, Michigan Office: 101 North Main Street, Suite 460.
Telephone: 734-930-5600.
Fax: 734-930-0043.
Troy, Michigan Office: 1111 West Long Lake Road, Suite 300.
Telephone: 248-641-7600.
Fax: 248-641-0222.
Mount Clemens, Michigan Office: Towne Square Development, 10 S. Main Street, Suite 307.
Telephone: 810-954-3800.
Fax: 810-954-3803.
Grand Rapids, Michigan Office: First of America Center, 171 Monroe Avenue, N.W., Suite 950.
Telephone: 616-742-5500.
Fax: 616-742-5566.
Lansing, Michigan Office: 530 Creyts Road, Suite A.
Telephone: 517-327-0300.
Fax: 517-327-0309.
Traverse City, Michigan Office: 1131 East Eighth Street, P.O. Box 3150.
Telephone: 231-941-1611.
Fax: 231-941-4420.
Marquette, Michigan Office: 228 West Washington Street, Suite 4,
Telephone: 906-228-7772.
Fax: 906-228-5999.

Joseph Kochis (Resident)
William J. Brickley (Resident)

Peter L. Diesel
John B. Farrell
Robert H. Shannon

For full biographical listings, see the Martindale-Hubbell Law Directory

*GRAND RAPIDS,** Kent Co.

BENSINGER, COTANT, MENKES & AARDEMA, P.C. (AV)

983 Spaulding Avenue, S.E., 49546
Telephone: 616-949-7963
Fax: 616-949-5264
URL: http://www.bcma.net
Gaylord, Michigan Office: 308 West Main, P.O. Box 1000.
Telephone: 517-732-7536.
Fax: 517-732-4922.
Marquette, Michigan Office: 122 West Bluff.
Telephone: 906-225-1000.
Fax: 906-225-0818.

Robert Bryan Aardema
Brian W. Whitelaw
Kerr L. Moyer
Dale L. Arndt
Frank S. Spies

Representative Clients: Allstate Insurance Co.; Physicians Insurance Co. of Michigan; State Farm Mutual Insurance Co.; Foremost Insurance Co.; Northern Mutual Insurance; Auto-Owners Insurance Co.; Insurance Equities Corp.; Osteopathic Mutual Insurance Co. Northbrook Insurance Co.; Michigan Hospital Association.

For full biographical listings, see the Martindale-Hubbell Law Directory

BOS & GLAZIER, P.L.C. (AV)

300 Ottawa N.W., Suite 800, 49503
Telephone: 616-458-6814
Fax: 616-458-0608
Email: bglazier@bosglazier.com *URL:* http://www.bosglazier.com

(See Next Column)

Bos & Glazier P.L.C.—*Continued*

Carole D. Bos | Bradley K. Glazier
Susan Wilson Keener

ASSOCIATES

Gwen E. Buday | Thomas S. Olsson

For full biographical listings, see the Martindale-Hubbell Law Directory

Garan, Lucow, Miller & Seward, P.C. (AV)

First of America Center, 171 Monroe Avenue, N.W., Suite 950, 49503
Telephone: 616-742-5500
Fax: 616-742-5566
URL: http://www.garanlucow.com
Detroit, Michigan Office: 10000 Woodbridge Place.
Telephone: 313-446-1530.
Fax: 313-259-0450.
Grand Blanc, Michigan Office: 8332 Office Park Drive.
Telephone: 810-695-3700.
Fax: 810-695-6488.
Port Huron, Michigan Office: Port Huron Office Center, 511 Fort Street, Suite 505.
Telephone: 810-985-4400.
Fax: 810-985-4107.
Ann Arbor, Michigan Office: 101 North Main Street, Suite 460.
Telephone: 734-930-5600.
Fax: 734-930-0043.
Troy, Michigan Office: 1111 West Long Lake Road, Suite 300.
Telephone: 248-641-7600.
Fax: 248-641-0222.
Mount Clemens, Michigan Office: Towne Square Development, 10 S. Main Street, Suite 307.
Telephone: 810-954-3800.
Fax: 810-954-3803.
Lansing, Michigan Office: 530 Creyts Road, Suite A.
Telephone: 517-327-0300.
Fax: 517-327-0309.
Traverse City, Michigan Office: 1131 East Eighth Street, P.O. Box 3150.
Telephone: 231-941-1611.
Fax: 231-941-4420.
Marquette, Michigan Office: 228 West Washington Street, Suite 4,
Telephone: 906-228-7772.
Fax: 906-228-5999.

David N. Campos | Richard E. Holmes, Jr.

Thomas R. TerMaat | Michael D. Wade
Matthew P. Venema | Lori A. Ittner
Jill S Mulder

Counsel for: Allstate Insurance Co.; Sears, Roebuck & Co.; Liberty Mutual Insurance Co.; Continental Insurance Companies.

For full biographical listings, see the Martindale-Hubbell Law Directory

Nelson and Kreuger, Professional Corporation (AV)

1010 McKay Tower, 146 Monroe Center, N.W., 49503
Telephone: 616-459-2112
Fax: 616-459-0657
URL: http://www.lawyers.com/nelsonkreuger

James R. Nelson | Steven L. Kreuger
Jon J. Schrotenboer

Representative Clients: Admiral Insurance Co.; Farm Bureau Insurance Group; Fireman's Fund Insurance Co.; Frankenmuth Mutual Insurance Co.; Great American Insurance Cos.; Hastings Mutual Insurance Co.; Michigan Educational Employees Insurance Co.; United States Fidelity & Guaranty; MLBA Limited Liability Pool.
Reference: Old Kent Bank.

For full biographical listings, see the Martindale-Hubbell Law Directory

Roberts, Betz & Bloss, P.C. (AV)

5005 Cascade Road SE, 49546-3724
Telephone: 616-285-8899
Telecopier: 616-285-0045

Michael J. Roberts | Gregory A. Block
Michael W. Betz | Michael T. Small
David J. Bloss | Ralph M. Reisinger
Henry S. Emrich

Connie R. Thacker

For full biographical listings, see the Martindale-Hubbell Law Directory

Smith Haughey Rice & Roegge, P.C. (AV)

200 Calder Plaza Building, 250 Monroe Avenue, N.W., 49503-2251
Telephone: 616-774-8000
Facsimile: 616-774-2461
East Lansing, Michigan Office: 1400 Abbott Rd., Suite 410, 48823-1902.
Telephone: 517-332-3030.
Facsimile: 517-332-3468.

(See Next Column)

Traverse City, Michigan Office: City Centre Plaza, Suite 100, 202 East State Street, P.O. Box 848, 49685-0848.
Telephone: 231-929-4878.
Facsimile: 231-929-4182.

Clifford A. Mitts (1902-1962) | Craig S. Neckers
Laurence D. Smith (1913-1980) | John C. O'Loughlin
Robert V.V. Rice (1899-1982) | Anthony J. Quarto
Michael S. Barnes (1944-1989) | John M. Kruis
L. Roland Roegge | Paul Van Oostenburg
Thomas F. Blackwell | Dale Ann Iverson
P. Laurence Mulvihill | William R. Jewell
Lawrence P. Mulligan | Jon D. Vander Ploeg
Thomas R. Tasker | Patrick F. Geary
Paul H. Reinhardt | Terence J. Ackert
Lance R. Mather | Brian J. Kilbane
Charles F. Behler | Robert C. Stone
John R. Sparks | Albert J. Engel, III
Gary A. Rowe | Phillip K. Mowers
William W. Jack, Jr. | Carol D. Carlson
William J. Hondorp | Christopher R. Genther
Thomas M. Weibel | Marilyn S. Nickell Tyree
James G. Black | Beth Suzanne Kromer
E. Thomas Mc Carthy, Jr. | Robert M. Kruse
Glenn W. House, Jr. | Aileen M. Leipprandt
Craig R. Noland | David J. DeGraw
Paul M. Oleniczak | Matthew L. Meyer

Martha P. Forman | Stacie R. Seitz
Karl Werner Butterer, Jr. | William A. Sikkel IV
Garrett J. Tenhave-Chapman | James J. Rosloniec
J. Joseph Rossi | Angela T. Ross

OF COUNSEL

A. B. Smith, Jr. | David O. Haughey

Representative Clients: Chevron; Cincinnati Insurance Co.; General Motors Corp.; Kemper Insurance Group; Michigan Hospital Assn.; Navistar International; St. Paul Insurance Cos.; Steelcase, Inc.

For full biographical listings, see the Martindale-Hubbell Law Directory

Tolley, VandenBosch, Walton, Korolewicz & Brengle, P.C. (AV)

1700 East Beltline, N.E., Suite 200, 49525-4512
Telephone: 616-447-1800
Fax: 616-447-1881

Peter R. Tolley | Richard J. Durden
Michael C. Walton | Robert C. Greene
Lawrence Korolewicz | Miles J. Postema
Todd R. Dickinson | James K. Schepers
James B. Doezema | Susan Jasper Stein
Mark J. Colon

Representative Clients: State Farm Insurance Co.; Sentry Insurance Co.; Fremont Mutual Insurance Co.; Phoenix Aviation; Admiral Insurance; Kemper Insurance; Northbrook Excess & Surplus Insurance Co.; St. Paul Companies; Aetna Insurance Co.; Chicago Title Insurance Co.

For full biographical listings, see the Martindale-Hubbell Law Directory

GROSSE POINTE PARK, Wayne Co.

Allan G. Meganck (AV)

1033 Bishop, 48230
Telephone: 313-881-0845
Fax: 313-881-0845
Email: lawtalk@aol.com

For full biographical listings, see the Martindale-Hubbell Law Directory

HOLLAND, Ottawa Co.

Cunningham Dalman, P.C. (AV)

321 Settlers Road, P.O. Box 1767, 49422-1767
Telephone: 616-392-1821
Fax: 616-392-4769
Email: cunndalm@crossover.net *URL:* http://www.holland-law.com

Gordon H. Cunningham | Jeffrey K. Helder
Ronald L. Dalman | Ronald J. Vander Veen
Max R. Murphy | David M. Zessin
James A. Bidol | Mark H. Zietlow
Andrew J. Mulder | Randall S. Schipper
Kenneth B. Breese | Susan E. Vroegop
Joel G. Bouwens

Gregory J. McCoy | Aaron Leal
Jason M. Milstone | Dawn J. Ward

Representative Clients: Auto Club Insurance Assn. (AAA); American States Insurance Co.; Huntington National Bank; First of America Bank - Holland, N.A.; Ameribank; City of Holland; Board of County Road Commissioners; Holland Economic Development Corp.

For full biographical listings, see the Martindale-Hubbell Law Directory

*HOUGHTON,** Houghton Co.

VAIRO, MECHLIN, TOMASI, JOHNSON & MANCHESTER (AV)

400 East Houghton Avenue, 49931
Telephone: 906-482-0770
Fax: 906-482-2938
Calumet, Michigan Office: 1175 Calumet Avenue, Suite K. 44913.
Telephone: 906-337-0312.

MEMBERS OF FIRM

Gerald G. Vairo
David R. Mechlin
Paul J. Tomasi
Frederick N. Johnson
Jeryl A. Manchester

Representative Clients: Accident Fund Co.; Aetna Life and Casualty Company; Auto Owners Insurance Company; Auto Club Insurance Assn.; Citizens Insurance Company of America; Fireman's Fund Insurance Co.; Frankenmuth Mutual Insurance Co.; Wausau Insurance Companies; Utica Mutual; U.S.F.&G Cos.

For full biographical listings, see the Martindale-Hubbell Law Directory

*JACKSON,** Jackson Co.

MARCOUX, ALLEN, ABBOTT, SCHOMER & BOWER, P.C. (AV)

145 South Jackson Street, P.O. Box 787, 49204-0787
Telephone: 517-787-4100
Fax: 517-787-9455
Email: marcoux@jacksonmi.com

William J. Marcoux (Retired)
William O. Allen
William M. Abbott
John H. Schomer
Diane Y. Bower
William B. Nichols, Jr.
Robert T. Kendall, III
Timothy R. Allen
Richard C. Lindsey, Jr.

OF COUNSEL

Walter R. Boris
Lawrence L. Bullen
Philip M. Moilanen
Terry J. Klaasen
T. Harrison Stanton

For full biographical listings, see the Martindale-Hubbell Law Directory

*KALAMAZOO,** Kalamazoo Co.

EARLY, LENNON, PETERS & CROCKER, P.C. (AV)

900 Comerica Building, 49007-4752
Telephone: 616-381-8844
Fax: 616-349-8525
Email: elpc@michbar.org

John T. Peters, Jr.
Harold E. Fischer, Jr.

Attorneys for: Aetna Insurance; Hastings Insurance; Kemper Group; Liberty Mutual; Medical Protective Co.; Scott Wetzel Services; Willis Corroon; Zurich Insurance.

For Complete List of Firm Personnel, See General Section

For full biographical listings, see the Martindale-Hubbell Law Directory

MILLER, CANFIELD, PADDOCK AND STONE, P.L.C. (AV)

A Professional Limited Liability Company
Founded in 1852 by Sidney Davy Miller
444 West Michigan Avenue, 49007-3752
Telephone: 616-381-7030
Fax: 616-382-0244
URL: http://www.millercanfield.com
Detroit, Michigan Office: 150 West Jefferson, Suite 2500, 48226-4415.
Telephone: 313-963-6420.
Fax: 313-496-7500.
Cable Address: "Stem Detroit."
Ann Arbor, Michigan Office: 101 North Main Street, 7th Floor, 48104-1400.
Telephone: 734-663-2445.
Fax: 734-747-7147.
Troy, Michigan Office: 840 West Long Lake Road, Suite 200, 48098.
Telephone: 248-879-2000.
Fax: 248-879-2001.
Grand Rapids, Michigan Office: 99 Monroe, N.W., Suite 1200, 49503-2639.
Telephone: 616-454-8656.
Fax: 616-776-6322.
Howell, Michigan Office: 121 South Barnard Street, Suite 4, 48843-2305.
Telephone: 517-546-7600.
Telecopier: 517-546-6974.
Lansing, Michigan Office: One Michigan Avenue, Suite 900, 48933-1609.
Telephone: 517-487-2070.
Fax: 517-374-6304.
Monroe, Michigan Office: 214 East Elm Avenue, Suite 100, 48162-2682.
Telephone: 734-243-2000.
Fax: 734-243-0901.
Washington, D.C. Office: 1900 K Street, N.W., Suite 1150. 20006.
Telephone: 202-429-5575; 785-0600.
Fax: 202-331-1118; 785-1234.

(See Next Column)

Pensacola, Florida Office: 25 West Cedar, 32501.
Telephone: 850-469-1088.
Fax: 850-432-0677.
New York, New York Office: 1450 Broadway, 41st Floor, 10018.
Telephone: 212-704-4400.
Fax: 212-704-4410.
Gdynia, Poland Office: UL. Slaska 21, 81-319.
Telephone: 011-485-831-2808.
Fax: 011-48-58-628 6411.
Warsaw, Poland Office: UL. Nowogrodzkall, 5th Floor, 00-513.
Telephone: 011-4822 529 0200.
Fax: 011-4822 529 0201.
Katowice, Poland Office: UL. Francuska 35/37, 40-027.
Telephone: 011 (48-32) 757-2414.
Fax: 011 (48-32) 757-2483.

PRINCIPALS

Eric V. Brown, Jr.
Charles E. Ritter
James G. Vantine, Jr.
Ronald E. Baylor
James E. Spurr
Pamela Chapman Enslen
Ballard Jay Yelton, III

RESIDENT ASSOCIATES

Kurt P. McCamman
Scott R. Sikkenga

Representative Firm Clients: Chrysler Corporation; Comerica, Incorporated; City of Detroit, Michigan; Detroit Tigers, Inc.; First of Michigan; Ford Motor Company; Ford Motor Credit Company; Great Lakes Bancorp; Henry Ford Hospital; INVETECH Company.

For Complete List of Firm Personnel, See General Section

For full biographical listings, see the Martindale-Hubbell Law Directory

RYAN, JAMIESON, MORRIS & RYAN (AV)

121 West Cedar Street, 49007
Telephone: 616-382-5143
Fax: 616-382-1896 E-Mail: ryanlaw@aol.com
Email: rjmpc@net-link.net

James D. Ryan
Daniel K. Jamieson
Christopher D. Morris
Ronald W. Ryan

Representative Clients: Auto-Owners Insurance Co.; Imperial Midwest Insurance Co.; Liberty Mutual Insurance Co.; Michigan Property and Casualty Guaranty Association.

For full biographical listings, see the Martindale-Hubbell Law Directory

LANSING, Ingham Co.

FOSTER, SWIFT, COLLINS & SMITH, P.C. (AV)

313 South Washington Square, 48933-2193
Telephone: 517-371-8100
Telecopier: 517-371-8200
URL: http://www.fosterswift.com
Farmington Hills, Michigan Office: 32300 Northwestern Highway, Suite 230.
Telephone: 248-539-9900.
Fax: 248-851-7504.

John L. Collins
Webb A. Smith
William R. Schulz
David H. Aldrich
Scott A. Storey
Charles E. Barbieri
Scott L. Mandel
Michael D. Sanders
Kevin T. McGraw
Mark H. Canady
Michael W. Puerner
Matthew W. Collins
Toree S. Randall

LEGAL SUPPORT PERSONNEL

LEGAL ASSISTANTS

Carole M. Schneider
Theresa G. Solberg

For Complete List of Firm Personnel, See General Section

For full biographical listings, see the Martindale-Hubbell Law Directory

FRASER TREBILCOCK DAVIS & FOSTER, P.C. (AV)

1000 Michigan National Tower, 48933
Telephone: 517-482-5800
Fax: 517-482-0887
URL: http://WWW.FTDF.COM
Detroit, Michigan Office: One Woodward Avenue, Suite 1550.
Telephone: 313-237-7300.
Fax: 313-961-1651.

Peter L. Dunlap
C. Mark Hoover
Brett J. Bean
Gary C. Rogers
Mark A. Bush
Brian D. Herrington

Representative Clients: Auto Owners Insurance Co.; Farm Bureau Insurance Co's; Hartford Insurance Co.; Metropolitan Life Insurance Co.; Michigan Lawyer's Mutual Insurance Company; MICOA; Pro National Insurance Co.; Prudential Insurance Company of America; State Farm Insurance Co's; Auto Club Insurance Association.

For full biographical listings, see the Martindale-Hubbell Law Directory

Lansing—Continued

GARAN, LUCOW, MILLER & SEWARD, P.C. (AV)

Office Park West, 530 Creyts Road, Suite A, 48917
Telephone: 517-327-0300
Fax: 517-327-0309
URL: http://www.garanlucow.com
Detroit, Michigan Office: 1000 Woodbridge Place.
Telephone: 313-446-1530.
Fax: 313-259-0450.
Port Huron, Michigan Office: Port Huron Office Center, 511 Fort Street, Suite 505.
Telephone: 810-985-4400.
Fax: 810-985-4187.
Ann Arbor, Michigan Office: 101 North Main Street, Suite 460.
Telephone: 734-930-5600.
Fax: 734-930-0043.
Troy, Michigan Office: 1111 West Long Lake Road, Suite 300.
Telephone: 248-641-7600.
Fax: 248-641-0222.
Mount Clemens, Michigan Office: Towne Square Development, 10 S. Main Street, Suite 307.
Telephone: 810-954-3800.
Fax: 810-954-3803.
Grand Rapids, Michigan Office: First of America Center, 171 Monroe Avenue, N.W., Suite 950.
Telephone: 616-742-5500.
Fax: 616-742-5566.
Grand Blanc, Michigan Office: 8332 Office Park Drive.
Telephone: 810-695-3700.
Fax: 810-695-6488.
Traverse City, Michigan Office: 1131 East Eighth Street, P.O. Box 3150.
Telephone: 231-941-1611.
Fax: 231-941-4420.
Marquette, Michigan Office: 228 West Washington Street, Suite 4,
Telephone: 906-228-7772.
Fax: 906-228-5999.

Kenneth V. Klaus (Resident)

Paul E. Tower (Resident)

For full biographical listings, see the Martindale-Hubbell Law Directory

HONIGMAN MILLER SCHWARTZ AND COHN (AV)

A Partnership including Professional Corporations
222 North Washington Square, Suite 400, 48933-1800
Telephone: 517-484-8282
Telecopier: 517-484-8286
Email: mvg@honigman.com *URL:* http://law.honigman.com
Detroit, Michigan Office: 2290 First National Building, 660 Woodward Avenue, 48226.
Telephone: 313-465-7000.

MEMBERS

Ann L. Andrews
Frederick M. Baker, Jr.
Daniel J. Demlow
Sandra L. Jasinski
John S. Kane
Timothy Sawyer Knowlton
John D. Pirich
Alan M. Valade
Ruth E. Zimmerman

ASSOCIATES

Andrew J. Gerdes
Daniel L. Stanley

Representative Clients: Aon Corporation; Continental Insurance.

For Complete List of Firm Personnel, See General Section

For full biographical listings, see the Martindale-Hubbell Law Directory

SMITH HAUGHEY RICE & ROEGGE, P.C.

(See East Lansing)

TIMMER, JAMO & O'LEARY (AV)

521 Seymour Avenue, 48933
Telephone: 517-371-3500
Fax: 517-371-4514
Email: TIMJAMOLOP@MICHBAR.ORG

MEMBERS OF FIRM

James A. Timmer
James S. Jamo
James S. O'Leary
Kathleen A. Lopilato

Representative Clients: Auto Owners Insurance Co.; National Indemnity Insurance Co.; Pennsylvania Insurance Co.; Travelers Insurance Co.; Ohio Farmers Insurance Co.; Bankers Life & Casualty Co.; Western Casualty & Surety Co.; Indiana Insurance Co.; Western Surety Co.; United State Aviation Underwriters.

For full biographical listings, see the Martindale-Hubbell Law Directory

*MARQUETTE,** Marquette Co.

BENSINGER, COTANT, MENKES & AARDEMA, P.C. (AV)

122 West Bluff, 49855
Telephone: 906-225-1000
Fax: 906-225-0818
URL: http://www.bcma.net
Gaylord, Michigan Office: 308 West Main, P.O. Box 1000.
Telephone: 517-732-7536.
Fax: 517-732-4922.
Grand Rapids, Michigan Office: 983 Spaulding Avenue, S.E.
Telephone: 616-949-7963.
Fax: 616-949-5264.

Gregory A. Elzinga
William J. Maynard
Glenn W. Smith
Michael G. Summers
Lynn A. Moon
Roger W. Zappa

Representative Clients: Allstate Insurance Co.; Auto-Owners Insurance Co.; Michigan Physicians Insurance Co.; Northern Mutual Insurance Co.; Federated Insurance Co.; Employers Reinsurance Co.; D & N Bank-FSB; Michigan Licensed Beverage Association; State Farm Insurance Co.; Farm Bureau Mutual Insurance Co.

For full biographical listings, see the Martindale-Hubbell Law Directory

SWANSON & DETTMANN (AV)

Marquette Professional Building, 148 West Washington Street, 49855
Telephone: 906-228-7355
Fax: 906-228-7357

MEMBERS OF FIRM

Keith E. Swanson
Darrell R. Dettmann

LEGAL SUPPORT PERSONNEL

Susan Frances Valenti

Representative Clients: Kemper Insurance Cos.; USF&G Insurance Co.; SETSEG, Inc.; Gallagher Bassett Insurance Service; North Pointe Insurance Co.; Auto Owners Insurance Co.; CoreSource, Inc.; USAA; Upper Peninsula Health Education Corp.; Travelers Insurance Co.
Reference: First of America Bank-Marquette, N.A.

For full biographical listings, see the Martindale-Hubbell Law Directory

*MONROE,** Monroe Co.

BRAUNLICH, RUSSOW & BRAUNLICH, A PROFESSIONAL CORPORATION (AV)

111 South Macomb Street, 48161
Telephone: 734-241-8300
Fax: 734-241-7715

William J. Braunlich, Jr. (1924-1992)
Thomas P. Russow
William H. Braunlich

Philip A. Costello
Ann L. Nickel
Jeffrey A. Dulany, P.C.

LEGAL SUPPORT PERSONNEL

Ruth G. Flint

Representative Clients: State Farm Mutual Insurance Co.; Auto Club Insurance Assn.; Board of Road Commissioners, Monroe County; Port of Monroe; Monroe County Community College; City of Luna Pier; City of Petersburg; Auto-Owners Insurance Co.; Fremont Mutual Insurance Co.; Citizens Insurance Co. of America.

For full biographical listings, see the Martindale-Hubbell Law Directory

*MOUNT CLEMENS,** Macomb Co.

GARAN, LUCOW, MILLER & SEWARD, P.C. (AV)

Towne Square Development, 10 S. Main Street Suite 307, 48043-2370
Telephone: 810-954-3800
Fax: 810-954-3803
URL: http://www.garanlucow.com
Detroit, Michigan Office: 1000 Woodbridge Place.
Telephone: 313-446-1530.
Fax: 313-259-0450.
Grand Blanc, Michigan Office: 8332 Office Park Drive.
Telephone: 810-695-3700.
Fax: 810-695-6488.
Ann Arbor, Michigan Office: 101 North Main Street, Suite 460.
Telephone: 734-930-5600.
Fax: 734-930-0043.
Troy, Michigan Office: 1111 West Long Lake Road, Suite 300.
Telephone: 248-641-7600.
Fax: 248-641-0222.
Port Huron, Michigan Office: Port Huron Office Center, 511 Fort Street, Suite 505.
Telephone: 810-985-4400.
Fax: 810-985-4107.

(See Next Column)

GARAN, LUCOW, MILLER & SEWARD P.C., *Mount Clemens—Continued*

Grand Rapids, Michigan Office: First of America Center, 171 Monroe Avenue, N.W., Suite 950.
Telephone: 616-742-5500.
Fax: 616-742-5566.
Lansing, Michigan Office: 530 Creyts Road, Suite A.
Telephone: 517-327-0300.
Fax: 517-327-0309.
Traverse City, Michigan Office: 1131 East Eighth Street, P.O. Box 3150.
Telephone: 231-941-1611.
Fax: 231-941-4420.
Marquette, Michigan Office: 228 West Washington Street, Suite 4,
Telephone: 906-228-7772.
Fax: 906-228-5999.

Richard E. Eaton (Resident)
Robert F. MacAlpine

For full biographical listings, see the Martindale-Hubbell Law Directory

MARTIN, BACON & MARTIN, P.C. (AV)

44 First Street, 48043
Telephone: 810-979-6500
Fax: 810-468-7016
URL: http://www.lawyers.com/martin

James N. Martin
Jonathan E. Martin
Paul R. VanTol
Michael R. Janes
Kevin L. Moffatt
John W. Crimando
Victor T. Van Camp

Patrick D. Ball
Amy M. Johnston
Sean S. Cleland

Reference: Community Central Bank - Mt. Clemens.

For full biographical listings, see the Martindale-Hubbell Law Directory

PLYMOUTH, Wayne Co.

DRAUGELIS & ASHTON, L.L.P. (AV)

843 Penniman Avenue, 48170-1690
Telephone: 734-453-4044
Fax: 734-453-2011
Clawson, Michigan Office: 380 North Main Street.
Telephone: 248-588-7704.

MEMBERS OF FIRM

Edward F. Draugelis
John A. Ashton
Donald S. Scully
Richard T. Haynes
Lamberto DiStefano
David T. Rogers
Joseph R. Conte
Steven O. Ashton

ASSOCIATES

Floyd C. Virant
Taras P. Jarema
Timothy M. McKercher
Joel B. Ashton
Donald E. Walker
Heather A. Jefferson
Roger D. Ajluni
Margaret L. Browning

Representative Clients: State Farm Automobile Insurance Co.; State Farm Fire and Casualty Co.

For full biographical listings, see the Martindale-Hubbell Law Directory

*PORT HURON,** St. Clair Co.

GARAN, LUCOW, MILLER & SEWARD, P.C. (AV)

Port Huron Office Center, 511 Fort Street, Suite 505, 48060-3922
Telephone: 810-985-4400
Fax: 810-985-4107
URL: http://www.garanlucow.com
Detroit, Michigan Office: 1000 Woodbridge Place.
Telephone: 313-446-1530.
Fax: 313-259-0450.
Grand Blanc, Michigan Office: 8332 Office Park Drive.
Telephone: 810-695-3700.
Fax: 810-695-6488.
Ann Arbor, Michigan Office: 101 North Main Street, Suite 460.
Telephone: 734-930-5600.
Fax: 734-930-0043.
Troy, Michigan Office: 1111 West Long Lake Road, Suite 300.
Telephone: 248-641-7600.
Fax: 248-641-0222.
Mount Clemens, Michigan Office: Towne Square Development, 10 S. Main Street, Suite 307.
Telephone: 810-954-3800.
Fax: 810-954-3803.
Grand Rapids, Michigan Office: First of America Center, 171 Monroe Avenue, N.W., Suite 950.
Telephone: 616-742-5500.
Fax: 616-742-5566.
Lansing, Michigan Office: 530 Creyts Road, Suite A.
Telephone: 517-327-0300.
Fax: 517-327-0309.
Traverse City, Michigan Office: 1131 East Eighth Street, P.O. Box 3150.
Telephone: 231-941-1611.
Fax: 231-941-4420.

(See Next Column)

Marquette, Michigan Office: 228 West Washington Street, Suite 4,
Telephone: 906-228-7772.
Fax: 906-228-5999.

Randolph J. Martinek

Robert L. Goldenbogen
Meghan A. McGlynn

For full biographical listings, see the Martindale-Hubbell Law Directory

ROYAL OAK, Oakland Co.

CARDELLI HEBERT, P.C. (AV)

322 West Lincoln, 48067
Telephone: 248-544-1100
Toll Free 1-800-411-7774
Telecopier: 248-544-1191
Email: cardelli.hebert@worldnet.att.net

Thomas G. Cardelli
Deborah A. Hebert

Mary Ann J. O'Neil
Nicholas S. Andrews
John L. Weston
R. Carl Lanfear, Jr.
Robert J. Lantzy
Catherine Dritsas
Mark G. Cooper
Timothy R. Noonan

Representative Clients: Allianz Insurance Company; ITT Hartford Insurance; Indiana Insurance.

For full biographical listings, see the Martindale-Hubbell Law Directory

*SAGINAW,** Saginaw Co.

BRAUN KENDRICK FINKBEINER PLC (AV)

101 N. Washington Suite 812, 48607-1297
Telephone: 517-753-3461
Telecopier: 517-753-3951
Email: ALBFIE@BKF-LAW.COM *URL:* http://www.bkf-law.com
Saginaw Township Office, Michigan Office: 5800 Gratiot Road, Suite 107, P.O. Box 5169. Telephone 517-799-8692.
Fax: 517-799-4666.
Bay City, Michigan Office: 201 Phoenix Building, P.O. Box 2039.
Telephone: 517-895-8505.
Telecopier: 517-895-8437.
Ann Arbor, Michigan Office: First National Building. 201 S. Main, Suite 700.
Telephone: 313-995-4100.
Telecopier: 313-995-4798.
Mt. Pleasant, Michigan Office: 805 North Brown.
Telephone: 517-775-7404.
Telecopier: 517-775-3764.

Harold J. Blanchet, Jr.
E. Louis Ognisanti
Bruce L. Dalrymple
Charles A. Gilfeather
Timothy L Curtiss
Scott C. Strattard
Craig W. Horn
Brian S. Makaric

Jamie C. Hecht Nisidis

Representative Clients: Farm Bureau Insurance Group; Firemans Fund American Insurance; Frankenmuth Mutual Insurance Co.; Fremont Mutual Insurance Co.; Great Lakes American Life Ins. Co.; Hartford Insurance Group; Hastings Mutual Insurance Co.; Kemper Insurance Group; Michigan Mutual Liability Co.; Mutual Benefit Life Ins. Co.

For Complete List of Firm Personnel, See General Section

For full biographical listings, see the Martindale-Hubbell Law Directory

O'NEILL, WALLACE & DOYLE, P.C. (AV)

300 St. Andrews Road, Suite 302, P.O. Box 1966, 48605
Telephone: 517-790-0960
Fax: 517-790-6902
Flint, Michigan Office: 2483 South Linden Road.
Telephone: 810-732-7079.
Fax: 810-732-5889.

Terence J. O'Neill
David A. Wallace
Thomas J. Doyle
Charles F. Filipiak

David Carbajal
James E. O'Neill, III
John J. Danieleski, Jr.
Darrin L. Nichols

Representative Clients: Home Insurance Co.; Great American Insurance Co.; Farmers Insurance Co.; Cincinnati Insurance Co.; Ohio Casualty Insurance Co.; Safeco Insurance Co.; Liberty Mutual Insurance Co.; CUNA Mutual Insurance.; Pioneer State Mutual Insurance Co.; Auto Owners Insurance Co.

For full biographical listings, see the Martindale-Hubbell Law Directory

ST. CLAIR SHORES, Macomb Co.

SAURBIER, SIEGAN & SANFIELD, P.C. (AV)

Suite 402, 400 Maple Park Boulevard, 48081
Telephone: 810-447-3700
Fax: 810-447-3755
Email: scott@saurbier.com
Detroit Office: 1028 Buhl Building.
Telephone: 313-965-2220.

SHAREHOLDERS

Scott A. Saurbier
Renée S. Siegan
Joel A. Sanfield

Marc D. Saurbier
Lawrence T. Garcia
John C. Valenti
Sara B. Keough
David C. Wiegel
Matthew J. Nagaj
Valerie Henning Mock

For full biographical listings, see the Martindale-Hubbell Law Directory

SOUTHFIELD, Oakland Co.

COLLINS, EINHORN, FARRELL & ULANOFF, A PROFESSIONAL CORPORATION (AV)

4000 Town Center, Suite 909, 48075-1473
Telephone: 248-355-4141
Facsimile: 248-355-2277

Morton H. Collins
Brian D. Einhorn
Clayton F. Farrell
Stuart A. Ulanoff
Dale J. McLellan
Kenneth C. Merritt
Noreen L. Slank
Michael J. Sullivan
Janice G. Hildenbrand
Neil W. MacCallum

Theresa M. Asoklis
Karen C. Liddle
Deborah A. Lujan
Shannon M. Kos
Kevin P. Moloughney
Susan P. Saltzman
Daniel E. Collins
J. Mark Cooney
David C. Anderson

For full biographical listings, see the Martindale-Hubbell Law Directory

ROMAIN, KUCK & EGERER, P.C. (AV)

24901 Northwestern Highway, Suite 400, 48075-2255
Telephone: 248-358-4490
Facsimile: 248-358-0761

Timothy E. Egerer
Michael Paul Daniels
John C. Brennan
Karen L. Hahn
David S. Robinson, Jr.
David A. Kanaan
Melanie T. Frazier
Claude Romain (1936-1989)
Ernst W. Kuck (Retired)

Johnny A. Ioanou
Kenneth Guinn Harlan
Mark E. Williams
Jane Kent Mills
Bonnie L. Bovee
Anthony D. Shapero
Barton C. Rachwal

For full biographical listings, see the Martindale-Hubbell Law Directory

SCHWARTZ & JALKANEN, P.C. (AV)

24400 Northwestern Highway, Suite 200, 48075-6821
Telephone: 248-352-2555
Facsimile: 248-352-5963

Melvin R. Schwartz
Arthur W. Jalkanen
Karl Eric Hannum

Gregory A. Light
David C. Dixon

For full biographical listings, see the Martindale-Hubbell Law Directory

SIEMION, HUCKABAY, BODARY, PADILLA, MORGANTI & BOWERMAN, P.C. (AV)

One Towne Square Suite 1400, P.O. Box 5068, 48086-5068
Telephone: 248-357-1400
Fax: 248-357-3343
Email: siemhuck@michbar.org

Robert P. Siemion
Charles A. Huckabay
James W. Bodary
Gerald V. Padilla
Raymond W. Morganti
Cathy Rogers Bowerman
Michael J. Rinkel
Mark A. Roberts
Arnold J. Matusz
Steven B. Sinkoff
Eugene Kelly Cullen
Karen M. Leonetti
Thomas M. Caplis

Donna Montano Severyn
Rita V. Countegan

For full biographical listings, see the Martindale-Hubbell Law Directory

SOMMERS, SCHWARTZ, SILVER & SCHWARTZ, P.C. (AV)

2000 Town Center, Suite 900, 48075
Telephone: 248-355-0300
Telecopier: 248-746-4001
Plymouth, Michigan Office: 747 South Main Street.
Telephone: 313-455-4250.

Leonard B. Schwartz
John F. Vos, III
Allen J. Wall
Joseph E. Grinnan
Lisa K. Pernick

Representative Clients: Crum & Forster Insurance Company; Great American Insurance Company; Royal Insurance Company; Michigan Mutual/Amerisure Insurance Company; Universal Underwriters Insurance Company; ESIS, Inc.; Corporate Service, Inc.

For Complete List of Firm Personnel, See General Section

For full biographical listings, see the Martindale-Hubbell Law Directory

SULLIVAN, WARD, BONE, TYLER & ASHER, P.C. (AV)

25800 Northwestern Highway, Suite 1000, 48075
Telephone: 248-746-0700
FAX: 248-746-2760
Email: swbt&a@swbta.com *URL:* http://www.swbta.com
Traverse City, Michigan Office: 12935 S. West Bay Shore Drive, Suite 310, Lake States Building.
Telephone: 231-947-1335.
Grand Rapids, Michigan Office: 2025 East Beltline S.E., Suite 406.
Telephone: 616-940-4114.
San Francisco, California Office: Citicorp Center, One Sansome Street.
Deerfield Beach, Florida Office: 665 Southeast 10th Street.

Richard G. Ward
Richard A. Bone
Lee C. Patton
Gerard J. Andree
Alan S. Helmore
Scott D. Feringa
Thomas L. Auth, Jr.
Kevin J. Gleeson
John M. Simmerer
Eric D. Geller
Dale Louis Gudenau
Jeffry G. Powers
Sharon S. Almonrode
Robert E. Sullivan, Jr.
Colin H. John, Jr.
Charles E. Randau
Michael J. Asher (Resident, San Francisco, California Office)
Ronald S. Lederman
Sheri B. Cataldo
Donald K. Warwick
William J. Ewald
Craig S. Thompson
Thaddeus E. Morgan
John W. Mulcrone
Lisa Chapman-Haase
Christopher B. McMahon

Representative Clients: Allstate Insurance Co.; American International Group; The Great Atlantic & Pacific Tea Company; William Beaumont Hospital; Beech Aircraft; Bormans, Inc. dba/Farmer Jack Supermarkets; City of Detroit; CNA Insurance Companies.

For full biographical listings, see the Martindale-Hubbell Law Directory

*TRAVERSE CITY,** Grand Traverse Co.

GARAN, LUCOW, MILLER & SEWARD, P.C. (AV)

1131 East Eighth Street, P.O. Box 3150, 49685-3150
Telephone: 231-941-1611
Fax: 231-941-4420
URL: http://www.garanlucow.com
Detroit, Michigan Office: 1000 Woodbridge Place.
Telephone: 313-446-1530.
Fax: 313-259-0450.
Port Huron, Michigan Office: Port Huron Office Center, 511 Fort Street, Suite 505.
Telephone: 810-985-4400.
Fax: 810-985-4187.
Ann Arbor, Michigan Office: 101 North Main Street, Suite 460.
Telephone: 734-930-5600.
Fax: 734-930-0043.
Troy, Michigan Office: 1111 West Long Lake Road, Suite 300.
Telephone: 248-641-7600.
Fax: 248-641-0222.
Mount Clemens, Michigan Office: Towne Square Development, 10 S. Main Street, Suite 307.
Telephone: 810-954-3800.
Fax: 810-954-3803.
Grand Rapids, Michigan Office: First of America Center, 171 Monroe Avenue, N.W., Suite 950.
Telephone: 616-742-5500.
Fax: 616-742-5566.
Grand Blanc, Michigan Office: 8332 Office Park Drive.
Telephone: 810-695-3700.
Fax: 810-695-6488.
Lansing, Michigan Office: 530 Creyts Road, Suite A.
Telephone: 517-327-0300.
Fax: 517-327-0309.
Marquette, Michigan Office: 228 West Washington Street, Suite 4,
Telephone: 906-228-7772.
Fax: 906-228-5999.

(See Next Column)

GARAN, LUCOW, MILLER & SEWARD P.C., *Traverse City—Continued*

Peter B. Worden, Jr. | John W. Sharp
Douglas J. Read | Michael J. Swogger

Linda Marsh-Raetz

For full biographical listings, see the Martindale-Hubbell Law Directory

RUNNING, WISE, FORD AND PHILLIPS, P.L.C. (AV)

326 State Street, P.O. Box 686, 49684
Telephone: 616-946-2700
Tele-Fax: 616-946-0857
Email: RWWFP@rwwfp.com

Harry T. Running (Deceased) | William L. Wise (Retired)

MEMBERS OF FIRM

Richard W. Ford | Sandra P. Howard
Thomas J. Phillips | Kent E. Gerberding
Michael I. Conlon

ASSOCIATE

Bradley L. Putney

OF COUNSEL

Douglas J. Donaldson | Miles C. Gerberding

Local Counsel For: Auto-Owners Insurance Co.; John Hancock Mutual Life Insurance Co.; Amoco Production Co.; Underwriters at Lloyds London; Bankers Multiple Line Insurance Co.; America's Insurance Company.

For full biographical listings, see the Martindale-Hubbell Law Directory

SMITH HAUGHEY RICE & ROEGGE, P.C. (AV)

City Centre Plaza, Suite 100, 202 East State Street, P.O. Box 848, 49685-0848
Telephone: 231-929-4878
Facsimile: 231-929-4182
Grand Rapids, Michigan Office: 200 Calder Plaza Building, 250 Monroe Avenue, N.W., 49503-2251.
Telephone: 616-774-8000.
Facsimile: 616-774-2461.
East Lansing, Michigan Office: 1400 Abbott Rd., Suite 410, 48823-1902.
Telephone: 517-332-3030.
Facsimile: 517-332-3468.

George Frederick Bearup | Robert W. Tubbs
Mark P. Bickel | Jeffrey R. Wonacott
R. Jay Hardin | Robert W. Parker
Charles B. Judson | Paul T. Jarboe
Jeffrey E. Gwillim

Todd W. Millar | Peter J. Boyles
Erin Eileen Gerrity | Rachel Y. Brochert
Eric W. Phelps

Representative Clients: Chevron; Cincinnati Insurance Co.; General Motors Corp.; Kemper Insurance Group; Michigan Hospital Assn.; Navistar International; St. Paul Insurance Cos.; Steelcase, Inc.; Dow Elanco.

For full biographical listings, see the Martindale-Hubbell Law Directory

TROY, Oakland Co.

BOWEN, RADABAUGH, MILTON & BROWN, P.C. (AV)

4967 Crooks Road, Suite 150, 48098
Telephone: 248-641-8000
Fax: 248-641-8219
Email: brmb@brmb.com *URL:* http://www.brmb.com

Thomas R. Bowen | Lisa T. Milton
James M. Radabaugh | Susan Leigh Brown

Geoffrey D. Marshall | Mark P. Dunn

OF COUNSEL

Meri Craver Borin

For full biographical listings, see the Martindale-Hubbell Law Directory

GARAN, LUCOW, MILLER & SEWARD, P.C. (AV)

1111 West Long Lake Road, Suite 300, 48098-6333
Telephone: 248-641-7600
Fax: 248-641-0222
URL: http://www.garanlucow.com
Detroit, Michigan Office: 10000 Woodbridge Place.
Telephone: 313-446-1530.
Fax: 313-259-0450.
Grand Blanc, Michigan Office: 8332 Office Park Drive.
Telephone: 810-695-3700.
Fax: 810-695-6488.
Port Huron, Michigan Office: Port Huron Office Center, 511 Fort Street, Suite 505.
Telephone: 810-985-4400.
Fax: 810-985-4107.
Ann Arbor, Michigan Office: 101 North Main Street, Suite 460.
Telephone: 734-930-5600.
Fax: 734-930-0043.
Mount Clemens, Michigan Office: Suite 307, Towne Square Development, 10 South Main Street.
Telephone: 810-954-3800.
Fax: 810-954-3803.
Grand Rapids, Michigan Office: First of America Center, 171 Monroe Avenue, N.W., Suite 950.
Telephone: 616-742-5500.
Fax: 616-742-5566.
Lansing, Michigan Office: 530 Creyts Road, Suite A.
Telephone: 517-327-0300.
Fax: 517-327-0309.
Traverse City, Michigan Office: 1131 East Eighth Street, P.O. Box 3150.
Telephone: 231-941-1611.
Fax: 231-941-4420.
Marquette, Michigan Office: 228 West Washington Street, Suite 4,
Telephone: 906-228-7772.
Fax: 906-228-5999.

James L. Borin | Edward M. Freeland
Roger A. Smith | Steven A. Matta
Mark Shreve | Ian C. Simpson
John P. Seyfried (Resident) | Susan M. Williams

David J. Lankford | Monia (Monica) C. Gregor
Brian E. Etzel | Beth A. Andrews
Dawn M. Patterson | Darryl Keenan Segars
Kristin Stiles Smolek | Adam K. Gordon

Counsel For: Aetna Life & Casualty Co.; Allstate Insurance Co.; American Home Insurance Co.; American International Adjustment Co.; American States Insurance Co.; Amerisure-Insurance Co.; Amsted Industries; Auto Club Insurance Assn.; Auto-Owners Insurance Co.; Buckeye Union Insurance Co.

For full biographical listings, see the Martindale-Hubbell Law Directory

HOLAHAN, MALLOY, MAYBAUGH, MONNICH & DELIE (AV)

Suite 100, 2690 Crooks Road, 48084-4700
Telephone: 248-362-4747
Fax: 248-362-4779
East Tawas, Michigan Office: 910 East Bay Street.
Telephone: 517-362-4747.
Fax: 517-362-7331.

MEMBERS OF FIRM

J. Michael Malloy, III | John R. Monnich
James D. Maybaugh | David L. Delie, Jr.

OF COUNSEL

Thomas H. O'Connor | Maureen Holahan (Retired; Resident, East Tawas Office)

Representative Clients: Chubb Companies; American States Insurance Co.; Travelers Insurance; Employers Reinsurance; Hartford Insurance Company.

For full biographical listings, see the Martindale-Hubbell Law Directory

POLING, MCGAW & POLING, P.C. (AV)

Suite 275, 5435 Corporate Drive, 48098
Telephone: 248-641-0500
Telecopier: 248-641-0506
URL: http://www.lawyers.com/polingmcgaw&poling

Benson T. Buck (1926-1989) | Gregory C. Hamilton
Richard B. Poling | Veronica B. O'Hara
D. Douglas McGaw | James R. Parker
Richard B. Poling, Jr. | Shannon M. Acton

OF COUNSEL

Ralph S. Moore

Representative Clients: City of Troy; United States Fidelity & Guaranty Co.; Sentry Insurance Co.; Admiral Insurance; DeMaria Construction Co.; Leo Corporation; Aetna Casualty and Surety Co.; Concord Design; Pneumo-Abex.

For full biographical listings, see the Martindale-Hubbell Law Directory

WEST BLOOMFIELD, Oakland Co.

CHEATHAM, ESTES & HOLLMAN, P.C. (AV)

5777 West Maple Road, Suite 130, P.O. Box 255002, 48325-5002
Telephone: 248-932-2000
Fax: 248-932-2008

Charles C. Cheatham | Lee Estes
Mary E. Hollman

Christopher P. Jelinek

COUNSEL

Lynn L. Lower

For full biographical listings, see the Martindale-Hubbell Law Directory

INTELLECTUAL PROPERTY LAW

ALABAMA

*BIRMINGHAM,** Jefferson Co.

BERKOWITZ, LEFKOVITS, ISOM & KUSHNER, A PROFESSIONAL CORPORATION (AV)

SouthTrust Tower, 420 North Twentieth Street, Suite 1600, 35203-5202
Telephone: 205-328-0480
Telecopier: 205-322-8007
URL: http://www.blik.com

David A. Larsen
J. Forrest Hinton
Patricia Clotfelter

Matthew W. Barnes

For Complete List of Firm Personnel, See General Section

For full biographical listings, see the Martindale-Hubbell Law Directory

VEAL & ASSOCIATES (AV)

200 Cahaba Park Circle Suite 125, 35242
Telephone: 205-991-0082
FAX: 205-991-8718
Email: veal@alabama.com *URL:* http://www.alabama.com/patents/

Robert J. Veal

ASSOCIATES

Kenneth M. Bush
N. Alexander Nolte (Not admitted in AL)

Representative Clients: EBSCO Industries; Electro Mechanical Corporation; Marathon Corporation; Southern Building Code Congress International; Russell Corporation; Maxxim Medical, Inc.; Kappler Safety Group; Crystal Medical Technologies.

For full biographical listings, see the Martindale-Hubbell Law Directory

ARIZONA

*PHOENIX,** Maricopa Co.

FENNEMORE CRAIG, A PROFESSIONAL CORPORATION (AV)

3003 North Central Avenue, Suite 2600, 85012-2913
Telephone: 602-916-5000
Fax: 602-916-5999
Tucson, Arizona Office: One South Church Avenue, Suite 1000, 85701-1620.
Telephone: 520-879-6800.
Fax: 520-879-6899.

C. Owen Paepke
Ray K. Harris

Paul F. Wille (Not admitted in AZ)
Stacie K. Smith
Sandra L. Etherton

LEGAL SUPPORT PERSONNEL

LEGAL ASSISTANTS

Amy Thompson

For Complete List of Firm Personnel, See General Section

For full biographical listings, see the Martindale-Hubbell Law Directory

HORNE, BISTROW & DULBERG, P.C. (AV)

Renaissance Two, 40 North Central, Suite 2800, 85004
Telephone: 602-253-9700
Fax: 602-258-4805
Email: kcorson@azlitigation.com *URL:* http://www.azlitigation.com

Michael S. Dulberg

For full biographical listings, see the Martindale-Hubbell Law Directory

SNELL & WILMER L.L.P. (AV)

One Arizona Center, 85004-2202
Telephone: 602-382-6000
Fax: 602-382-6070
Email: postmaster@snellwilmer.com *URL:* http://www.swlaw.com
Tucson, Arizona Office: One South Church Avenue, Suite 1500, 85701-1612.
Telephone: 520-882-1200.
Fax: 520-884-1294.

(See Next Column)

Orange County Office: 1920 Main Street, Suite 1200, Irvine, California 92614-7230.
Telephone: 949-253-2700.
Fax: 949-955-2507.
Salt Lake City, Utah Office: 111 East Broadway, Suite 900, 84111-1004.
Telephone: 801-237-1900.
Fax: 801-237-1950.

MEMBERS OF FIRM

George H. Lyons
Quinn Williams
Michael K. Kelly
Timothy J. Casey
Sid Leach (Not admitted in AZ)
Terry Morris Roman
Timothy G. O'Neill
Charles F. Hauff, Jr.
Shaukat A. Karjeker (Not admitted in AZ)

ASSOCIATES

Damon L. Boyd
David Caplan
Brett A. Carlson
John A. Fisher
Andrew Foster Halaby
Cynthia Pillote
Shahpar Shahpar
Mark M. Takahashi
Michael Byorick (Not admitted in AZ)
Deborah M. Chess
Robert Lee Fraley
Karen Lynn Hunnicutt
Daniel R. Pote
Howard Sobelman
Laura J. Zeman

Representative Clients: For list of Representative Clients, see end of biographical listings in the Martindale-Hubbell Law Directory.

For Complete List of Firm Personnel, See General Section

For full biographical listings, see the Martindale-Hubbell Law Directory

*TUCSON,** Pima Co.

DURANDO, BIRDWELL & JANKE, LLP (AV)

2929 East Broadway Boulevard, 85716
Telephone: 520-881-9442
Fax: 520-881-9448
Email: durando@rtd.com
Portland, Oregon Office: Birdwell, Janke & Durando, LLP, Suite 1925, 900 S.W. Fifth Avenue, 97204-1221.
Telephone: 503-228-1841.
Fax: 503-228-2635.

William A. Birdwell
Antonio R. Durando
Garth Janke

For full biographical listings, see the Martindale-Hubbell Law Directory

SNELL & WILMER L.L.P. (AV)

One South Church Avenue, Suite 1500, 85701-1612
Telephone: 520-882-1200
Fax: 520-884-1294
URL: http://www.swlaw.com
Phoenix, Arizona Office: One Arizona Center, 85004-2202.
Telephone: 602-382-6000.
Fax: 602-382-6070.
Orange County Office: 1920 Main Street, Suite 1200, Irvine, California 92614-7230.
Telephone: 949-253-2700.
Fax: 949-955-2507.
Salt Lake City, Utah Office: 111 East Broadway, Suite 900, 84111-1004.
Telephone: 801-237-1900.
Fax: 801-237-1950.

MEMBER OF FIRM

Michael S. Milroy

ASSOCIATES

Anders T. Aannestad
Lawrence R. Oremland (Not admitted in AZ)

Representative Clients: For list of Representative Clients, see end of biographical listings in the Martindale-Hubbell Law Directory.

For full biographical listings, see the Martindale-Hubbell Law Directory

ARKANSAS

*LITTLE ROCK,** Pulaski Co.

WRIGHT, LINDSEY & JENNINGS LLP (AV)

200 West Capitol Avenue, Suite 2200, 72201
Telephone: 501-371-0808
Fax: 501-376-9442
Email: info@wlj.com *URL:* http://www.wlj.com
Fayetteville, Arkansas Office: 101 West Mountain Street, Suite 206, 72701.
Telephone: 501-575-0808.
Fax: 501-575-0999.
Russellville, Arkansas Office: 1110 West "B" Street, Suite E, 72801.
Telephone: 501-968-7995.

Nancy Bellhouse May
Ray F. Cox, Jr.

(See Next Column)

WRIGHT, LINDSEY & JENNINGS LLP, *Little Rock—Continued*

ASSOCIATE

J. Charles Dougherty

Representative Clients: Acxiom Corp.; ASCAP; Entergy Corp.; J.B. Hunt Transport Services, Inc.; Mobile Process Technology, Inc.; Sisters of Mercy Health Systems, St. Louis; Stephens Inc.; SalesMark, Inc.; StaffMark, Inc.; University of Arkansas.

For full biographical listings, see the Martindale-Hubbell Law Directory

CALIFORNIA

EMERYVILLE, Alameda Co.

LEGAL STRATEGIES GROUP (AV)

5905 Christie Avenue, 94608
Telephone: 510-450-9600
Fax: 510-450-9601
URL: http://www.lsglaw.com

SHAREHOLDERS

Ralph C. Alldredge
Timothy R. Cahn
Joshua R. Floum
Karen S. Frank
Gregory S. Gilchrist
Peter H. Goldsmith
Vincent L. Johnson
Leigh A. Kirmssé
Louise E. Ma
Maureen A. Sheehy
Heather A. Young

OF COUNSEL

Robert J. Vizas

ASSOCIATE

Jeffrey N. Hyman

AFFILIATE COUNSEL

Christine A. Amatruda
Gia L. Cincone
R. Dennis Claessens (Not admitted in CA)
Gregory P. Farnham
Ariela Freed
Jennifer Connors Hayes
Daniel J. Kroll
Jonathan P. Marvin
Paul J. Neibergs
Margaret R. O'Donnell
William Michael Quinn, Jr.
Nancy Lee Tang

For full biographical listings, see the Martindale-Hubbell Law Directory

IRVINE, Orange Co.

GAUNTLETT & ASSOCIATES (AV)

18400 Von Karman, Suite 300, 92612
Telephone: 949-553-1010
Fax: 949-553-2050
Email: info@gauntlettlaw.com *URL:* http://www.gauntlettlaw.com

David A. Gauntlett

Eileen Spadoni
James A. Lowe (Not admitted in CA)
Richard Wm. Zevnik
Eric J. Schindler
Eric Robert Little
Dean H. McVay
Raymond J. Liddy
Julia C. Weissman

For full biographical listings, see the Martindale-Hubbell Law Directory

SNELL & WILMER L.L.P. (AV)

1920 Main Street, Suite 1200, 92614-7230
Telephone: 949-253-2700
FAX: 949-955-2507
URL: http://www.swlaw.com
Phoenix, Arizona Office: One Arizona Center, 85004-2202.
Telephone: 602-382-6000.
Fax: 602-382-6070.
Tucson, Arizona Office: One South Church Avenue, Suite 1500, 85701-1630.
Telephone: 520-882-1200.
Fax: 520-884-1294.
Salt Lake City, Utah Office: 111 East Broadway, Suite 900, 84111-1004.
Telephone: 801-237-1900.
Fax: 801-237-1950.

MEMBERS OF FIRM

William S. O'Hare, Jr.
William T. Gay

ASSOCIATE

Henry G. Kohlmann

Representative Clients: For list of Representative Clients, see end of biographical listings in the Martindale-Hubbell Law Directory.

For Complete List of Firm Personnel, See General Section

For full biographical listings, see the Martindale-Hubbell Law Directory

*LOS ANGELES,** Los Angeles Co.

BLANC WILLIAMS JOHNSTON & KRONSTADT, LLP (AV)

A Partnership including Professional Corporations
Suite 1700, 1900 Avenue of the Stars, 90067
Telephone: 310-552-2500
Telecopier: 310-552-1191
Email: bwjk@bwjk.com

MEMBERS OF FIRM

Ronald L. Blanc (P.C.)
Harley J. Williams (P.C.)
Ronald L. Johnston (P.C.)
John A. Kronstadt
James R. Farrand
Richard T. McCoy III
Regina A. Stagg
John C. Rawls III
Daniel M. Grigsby
Suzanne V. Wilson
Dawn Weekes Glenn

James S. Blackburn
Vivian W. Yang
Allison Binder
Jennifer M. Lloyd
Mark S. Dancsecs

OF COUNSEL

Sol Rosenthal

Reference: Santa Monica Bank (Beverly Hills Office).

For full biographical listings, see the Martindale-Hubbell Law Directory

HORVITZ & LEVY, LLP (AV)

A Partnership including Professional Corporations
18th Floor, 15760 Ventura Boulevard (Encino), 91436
Telephone: 818-995-0800
Fax: 818-995-3157

Ellis J. Horvitz (A P.C.)
Barry R. Levy (A P.C.)
Peter Abrahams
David M. Axelrad
Frederic D. Cohen
S. Thomas Todd
David S. Ettinger
Daniel J. Gonzalez
Mitchell C. Tilner
Christina J. Imre
Lisa Perrochet
Stephen E. Norris
Sandra J. Smith
John A. Taylor, Jr.
Julie L. Woods
Lisa R. Jaskol
H. Thomas Watson

Mary F. Dant
Holly R. Paul
Andrea M. Gauthier
Judith E. Gordon
Patricia Lofton
L. Rachel Lerman Helyar
Mary-Christine (M.C.) Sungaila
Stephanie Rae Williams
Curt Cutting
Wendy S. Albers
Robert H. Wright
Nina E. Scholtz
Orly Degani

OF COUNSEL

Jon B. Eisenberg

Reference: Bank of California (Los Angeles, California Office).

For full biographical listings, see the Martindale-Hubbell Law Directory

LOEB & LOEB LLP (AV)

A Limited Liability Partnership including Professional Corporations
Suite 1800, 1000 Wilshire Boulevard, 90017-2475
Telephone: 213-688-3400
Facsimile: 213-688-3460
Email: info@loeb.com *URL:* http://www.loeb.com
Century City, California Office: Suite 2200, 10100 Santa Monica Boulevard, Los Angeles, 90067-4164.
Telephone: 310-282-2000.
Facsimile: 310-282-2192.
New York, N.Y. Office: 345 Park Avenue, 10154-0037.
Telephone: 212-407-4000.
Facsimile: 212-407-4990.
Nashville, Tennessee Office: 45 Music Square West, 37203-3205.
Telephone: 615-749-8300;
Facsimile: 615-749-8308.
Rome, Italy Office: Piazza Digione 1, 00197.
Telephone: 011-3906-808-8456.
Facsimile: 011-3906-808-8288.

MEMBERS OF FIRM

David W. Grace (Century City Office)
Stuart Lubitz (Century City Office)
Stephen R. Mick (Century City Office)
Jai H. Rho (Century City Office)
William H. Wright (Century City Office)

SENIOR COUNSEL

Dorie G. Choderker (Century City Office)
Louis A. Mok (Century City Office)
Michael J. Ram (Century City Office)
John P. Scherlacher (Century City Office)

(See Next Column)

LOEB & LOEB LLP—*Continued*

ASSOCIATES

Ying Chen (Century City Office)
Amedeo F. Ferraro
Philip J. Graves
David L. Lubitz (Century City Office)
Wein-ing Yang (Century City Office)

For Complete List of Firm Personnel, See General Section

For full biographical listings, see the Martindale-Hubbell Law Directory

MENES LAW CORPORATION (AV)

1801 Century Park East, Suite 1560, 90067
Telephone: 310-286-1313
Fax: 310-556-5695
Email: mlc@meneslaw.com

Barry A. Menes
Paul I. Menes

Marc M. Messineo

OF COUNSEL

John R. Climaco (Not admitted in CA)
Edward M. Bernstein (Not admitted in CA)

For full biographical listings, see the Martindale-Hubbell Law Directory

MITCHELL, SILBERBERG & KNUPP LLP (AV)

A Partnership including Professional Corporations
11377 West Olympic Boulevard, 90064
Telephone: 310-312-2000
Fax: 310-312-3100
Email: info@msk.com *URL:* http://www.msk.com

MEMBERS OF FIRM

Miriam Claire Beezy (A Professional Corporation)
George M. Borkowski (A Professional Corporation)
Jeffrey D. Goldman (A Professional Corporation)
Steven E. Shapiro (A Professional Corporation)
David A. Steinberg (A Professional Corporation)
Robert C. Welsh (A Professional Corporation)

ASSOCIATES

Marc E. Mayer
Brent Rabowsky
Joseph G. Swan

References: Wells Fargo Bank, N.A.; Merrill, Lynch.

For Complete List of Firm Personnel, See General Section

For full biographical listings, see the Martindale-Hubbell Law Directory

OPPENHEIMER WOLFF & DONNELLY LLP (AV)

2029 Century Park East 38th Floor, 90067
Telephone: 310-788-5000
FAX: 310-277-1297
Email: oppenheimer.com
Minneapolis, Minnesota Office: 3300 Plaza VII, 45 South Seventh Street. 55402.
Telephone: 612-607-7000.
FAX: 612-607-7100.
Amsterdam, The Netherlands Office: Keizergracht 241.
Telephone: 31-20-423-4555.
FAX: 312-20-423-4545.
Brussels, Belgium Office: Avenue Louise 240, Box 5, 1050.
Telephone: 32-2-626-0500.
FAX: 32-2-626-0510.
Geneva, Switzerland Office: Rue Gabriel Eynard, 6, 1205.
Telephone: (41/22) 311-7410.
FAX: (41/22) 311-4707.
Newport Beach, California Office: 500 Newport Center Drive, Suite 700, 92660.
Telephone: 949-823-6000.
FAX: 949-823-6100.
New York, N.Y. Office: The Chrysler East Building, 19th Floor, 666 Third Avenue, 10017.
Telephone: 212-826-5000.
FAX: 212-486-0708.
Paris, France Office: 35 Boulevard des Capucines, 75002.
Telephone: (33/1) 53 45 40 00.
FAX: (33/1) 53 45 40 10.
St. Paul, Minnesota Office: 1700 First National Bank Building, 55101.
Telephone: 651-605-2000.
FAX: 651-605-2100.
Washington, D.C. Office: Oppenheimer Wolff Donnelly & Bayh LLP, 1350 Eye Street, N.W., Suite 200, 20005.
Telephone: 202-312-8000.
FAX: 202-312-8100.
Palo Alto, California Office: 3373 Hillview Avenue, Suite 200, 94304.
Telephone: 650-320-4000.
FAX: 650-320-4100.

(See Next Column)

Chicago, Illinois Office: Oppenheimer Wolff & Donnelly (Illinois), Two Prudential Plaza, 45th Floor, 180 North Stetson Avenue, 60601.
Telephone: 312-616-1800.
Fax: 312-616-5800.

RESIDENT PARTNERS

Alan C. Rose
William Poms
Guy Porter Smith
Charles Berman
Gary E. Lande
Louis J. Bovasso
Michael D. Harris
Mark P. Wine
Gregory B. Wood
Christopher Darrow
Jane Shay Wald
Douglas N. Larson
David J. Oldenkamp
Marc E. Brown
J. Patrick Weir
Charles Rosenberg
Michael B. Farber
Alan P. Block
Scott R. Hansen

RESIDENT ASSOCIATES

Sandra M. Parker
Cynthia A. Lock
Joel D. Voelzke
George L. Fountain
Barbara J. Quinn
Ronald S. Tamura
Jake A. Taylor
Sung I. Oh

Reference: City National Bank (Century Plaza Office, Century City).

For full biographical listings, see the Martindale-Hubbell Law Directory

SMALL LARKIN, LLP (AV)

10940 Wilshire Boulevard, Eighteenth Floor, 90024
Telephone: 310-209-4400
Fax: 310-209-4450
Cable Address: SLK MARK
Telex: 6502238698
Email: info@sliplaw.com *URL:* http://www.sliplaw.com

MEMBERS OF FIRM

Thomas M. Small
Joan Kupersmith Larkin
Christopher C. Larkin
Jon E. Hokanson
Kenneth L. Wilton

J. Alison Grabell
Jodi L. Sax
Jill A. Schwartz

LEGAL SUPPORT PERSONNEL

Susan Brady Blasco

For full biographical listings, see the Martindale-Hubbell Law Directory

WHITE O'CONNOR CURRY GATTI & AVANZADO LLP (AV)

10100 Santa Monica Boulevard Suite 300, 90067
Telephone: 310-712-6100
Fax: 310-712-6199

Andrew M. White
Michael J. O'Connor
James E. Curry
Melvin N.A. Avanzado
John M. Gatti

OF COUNSEL

Jonathan D. Avila
Frederick F. Mumm

Jonathan H. Anschell
David E. Fink
James W. Irey
Holly J. Sadlon
Lee S. Brenner
Katherine J. Kunberger
Sydney Arfin
Edward Muir Anderson
Marci D. Friedman
Meredith C. Hightower
J Rudy Freeman, II

For full biographical listings, see the Martindale-Hubbell Law Directory

NEWPORT BEACH, Orange Co.

DRUMMOND & DUCKWORTH (AV)

4590 MacArthur Boulevard, Suite 500, 92660
Telephone: 949-724-1255
Fax: 949-724-1139
Email: patent_lawyer@worldnet.att.net

William H. Drummond
David G. Duckworth

For full biographical listings, see the Martindale-Hubbell Law Directory

OPPENHEIMER WOLFF & DONNELLY LLP (AV)

500 Newport Center Drive, Suite 700, 92660
Telephone: 949-823-6000
FAX: 949-823-6100
Email: info@oppenheimer.com *URL:* http://www.oppenheimer.com
Minneapolis, Minnesota Office: 3300 Plaza VII, 45 South Seventh Street. 55402.
Telephone: 612-607-7000.
FAX: 612-607-7100.
Amsterdam, The Netherlands Office: Keizergracht 241.
Telephone: 31-20-423-4555.
FAX: 312-20-423-4545.
Brussels, Belgium Office: Avenue Louise 240, Box 5, 1050.
Telephone: 32-2-626-0500.
FAX: 32-2-626-0510.

(See Next Column)

OPPENHEIMER WOLFF & DONNELLY LLP, *Newport Beach—Continued*

Geneva, Switzerland Office: Rue Gabriel Eynard, 6, 1205.
Telephone: (41/22) 311-7410.
FAX: (41/22) 311-4707.
New York, N.Y. Office: The Chrysler East Building, 19th Floor, 666 Third Avenue, 10017.
Telephone: 212-826-5000.
FAX: 212-486-0708.
Paris, France Office: 35 Boulevard des Capucines, 75002.
Telephone: (33/1) 53 45 40 00.
FAX: (33/1) 53 45 40 10.
St. Paul, Minnesota Office: 1700 First National Bank Building, 55101.
Telephone: 651-605-2000.
FAX: 651-605-2100.
Washington, D.C. Office: Oppenheimer Wolff Donnelly & Bayh LLP, 1350 Eye Street, N.W., Suite 200, 20005.
Telephone: 202-312-8000.
FAX: 202-312-8100.
Los Angeles, California Office: 2029 Century Park East, 38th Floor, 90067.
Telephone: 310-788-5000.
FAX: 310-277-1297.
Palo Alto, California Office: 3373 Hillview Avenue, Suite 200, 94304.
Telephone: 650-320-4000.
FAX: 650-320-4100.
Chicago, Illinois Office: Oppenheimer Wolff & Donnelly (Illinois), Two Prudential Plaza, 45th Floor, 180 North Stetson Avenue, 60601.
Telephone: 312-616-1800.
Fax: 312-616-5800.

RESIDENT PARTNERS

Edward F. O'Connor — Bruce M. Canter
Kurt A. MacLean — James W. Inskeep

RESIDENT ASSOCIATE

Louis C. Cullman

Reference: City National Bank (Century Plaza Office, Century City).

For full biographical listings, see the Martindale-Hubbell Law Directory

LARRY K. ROBERTS, INC. (AV)

660 Newport Center Drive, Suite 710, P.O. Box 8569, 92658
Telephone: 949-640-6200
Facsimile: 949-640-1206
Email: LarryKRoberts@prodigy.net

Larry K. Roberts

For full biographical listings, see the Martindale-Hubbell Law Directory

PALO ALTO, Santa Clara Co.

BOZICEVIC, FIELD & FRANCIS, LLP (AV)

285 Hamilton Avenue, Suite 200, 94301
Telephone: 650-327-3400
Facsimile: 650-327-3231
URL: http://www.brpatent.com

Karl Bozicevic — Bret E. Field
Carol L. Francis

ASSOCIATE

Dianna L. Devore

OF COUNSEL

Renée A. Fitts

PATENT AGENTS

Pamela J. Sherwood — Paula A. Borden

TECHNICAL CONSULTANT

Donna D. Johnson (Technical Consultant)

LEGAL SUPPORT PERSONNEL

Judith A. Morrow

For full biographical listings, see the Martindale-Hubbell Law Directory

OPPENHEIMER WOLFF & DONNELLY LLP (AV)

3373 Hillview Avenue, Suite 200, 94304
Telephone: 650-320-4000
FAX: 650-320-4100
Email: oppenheimer.com
Minneapolis, Minnesota Office: 3300 Plaza VII, 45 South Seventh Street. 55402.
Telephone: 612-607-7000.
FAX: 612-607-7100.
Amsterdam, The Netherlands Office: Keizergracht 241.
Telephone: 31-20-423-4555.
FAX: 312-20-423-4545.
Brussels, Belgium Office: Avenue Louise 240, Box 5, 1050.
Telephone: 32-2-626-0500.
FAX: 32-2-626-0510.
Geneva, Switzerland Office: Rue Gabriel Eynard, 6, 1205.
Telephone: (41/22) 311-7410.
FAX: (41/22) 311-4707.

(See Next Column)

Newport Beach, California Office: 500 Newport Center Drive, Suite 700, 92660.
Telephone: 949-823-6000.
FAX: 949-823-6100.
New York, N.Y. Office: The Chrysler East Building, 19th Floor, 666 Third Avenue, 10017.
Telephone: 212-826-5000.
FAX: 212-486-0708.
Paris, France Office: 35 Boulevard des Capucines, 75002.
Telephone: (33/1) 53 45 40 00.
FAX: (33/1) 53 45 40 10.
St. Paul, Minnesota Office: 1700 First National Bank Building, 55101.
Telephone: 651-605-2000.
FAX: 651-605-2100.
Washington, D.C. Office: Oppenheimer Wolff Donnelly & Bayh LLP, 1350 Eye Street, N.W., Suite 200, 20005.
Telephone: 202-312-8000.
FAX: 202-312-8100.
Los Angeles, California Office: 2029 Century Park East, 38th Floor, 90067.
Telephone: 310-788-5000.
FAX: 310-277-1297.
Chicago, Illinois Office: Oppenheimer Wolff & Donnelly (Illinois), Two Prudential Plaza, 45th Floor, 180 North Stetson Avenue, 60601.
Telephone: 312-616-1800.
Fax: 312-616-5800.

RESIDENT PARTNERS

Michael H. Kalkstein — Timothy T. Huber
Claude A. S. Hamrick — Chris S. Graham
Robert O. Guillot — E. Patrick Ellisen
Chien (Chris) W. Chou

RESIDENT ASSOCIATES

Michael K. Bosworth — Valerie M. Wagner
Esther H. La — Michael N. Edelman
Lisa K. Roberts — Justin F. Boyce
Ben H. Bedi — Leah Sherry
Anthony B. Diepenbrock, III — Donald A. Larkin

Reference: City National Bank (Century Plaza Office, Century City).

For full biographical listings, see the Martindale-Hubbell Law Directory

*SACRAMENTO,** Sacramento Co.

LIVINGSTON & MATTESICH, LAW CORPORATION (AV)

1201 K Street, Suite 1100, 95814
Telephone: 916-442-1111
Fax: 916-448-1709
Email: l&m@lmlaw.net *URL:* http://www.lmlaw.net

Gene Livingston — Emilio E. Varanini, III
James M. Mattesich — Kenneth M. Malovos
Carol Livingston — Kathleen E. Finnerty
Rebecca M. Ceniceros — Joanna R. Mendoza

Steven P. Belzer — Baldassaro (Bill) Di Capo
Jeffrey Leacox — John McKinsey
Randy Pollack — Timothy E. Naccarato
Alice H. Choi — Craig N. Lundgren
Stephen Craig Hunter — Mary Farrell Taylor
Matthew J. Goldman — Brian Crone
Joel C. Baiocchi — Gay L. Carroll
Steven G. Churchwell

Representative Clients: 3M Company; Celldata Medical Technologies, Inc.; Hansen Information Technologies, Inc.; Hi-Voltage Wire Works, Inc.; HPT Research, Inc.; Hygiea Biological Laboratories, Inc.; Optimum Data Systems, Inc.; Salt Web, Inc.; Techosystems; Varatouch Technology, Inc.

For full biographical listings, see the Martindale-Hubbell Law Directory

*SAN DIEGO,** San Diego Co.

KENNERSON SCHWARTZ SEMERDJIAN & HAILE LLP (AV)

A Limited Liability Partnership
101 West Broadway, Suite 810, 92101
Telephone: 619-236-8821
Facsimile: 619-236-8827
URL: http://www.lawyers.com/ksshlaw

OF COUNSEL

Paul R. Kennerson

MEMBERS OF FIRM

Ross J. Schwartz — Dick A. Semerdjian
Jeffrey A. Haile

James R. Ballard — John K. Grant

For full biographical listings, see the Martindale-Hubbell Law Directory

San Diego—Continued

LUCE, FORWARD, HAMILTON & SCRIPPS LLP (AV)

A Partnership including Professional Corporations
600 West Broadway, Suite 2600, 92101
Telephone: 619-236-1414
Fax: 619-232-8311
URL: http://www.luce.com
La Jolla, California Office: 4275 Executive Square, Suite 800, 92037.
Telephone: 858-455-6611.
Fax: 858-232-8311.
Los Angeles, California Office: 777 South Figueroa, Suite 3600, 90017.
Telephone: 213-892-4992.
Fax: 213-892-7731.
San Francisco, California Office: 121 Spear Street, Suite 200, 94105.
Telephone: 415-356-4600.
Fax: 415-356-4610.
New York, N.Y. Office: Citicorp Center, 153 East 53rd Street, 26th Floor, 10022.
Telephone: 212-754-1414.
Fax: 212-644-9727.
Chicago, Illinois Office: 180 North La Salle Street, Suite 3110, 60601.
Telephone: 312-641-0580.
Fax: 312-641-0380.

Callie A. Bjurstrom
Craig R. Brown (Resident, New York, N.Y. Office)
Kevin A. Cahill
Huhnsik Chung (Resident, New York, N.Y. Office)
Sean L. Collin
Martin D. Fern (Resident, Los Angeles Office)
Jeffrey L. Fillerup (Resident, San Francisco Office)
Peter K. Hahn
Charles L. Hellerich
James B. Hicks (Resident, Los Angeles Office)
Kathy A. Jorrie (Resident, Los Angeles Office)
Kimball Ann Lane (Resident, New York, N.Y. Office)

ASSOCIATES

John T. Brooks
Aurelia E. Flores
James A. Goniea (Resident, San Francisco Office)
Lucinda Y. Quan
Edward H. Sikorski (Not admitted in CA)
Marjorie A. Stender
John D. Vaughn

For Complete List of Firm Personnel, See General Section

For full biographical listings, see the Martindale-Hubbell Law Directory

*SAN FRANCISCO,** San Francisco Co.

DILLINGHAM & MURPHY, LLP (AV)

225 Bush Street, Sixth Floor, 94104-4207
Telephone: 415-397-2700
Cable Address: "Paladin"
Fax: 415-397-3300
Email: DM@wirepaladin.com *URL:* http://www.wirepaladin.com
Washington, DC Office: 1155 Connecticut Avenue, N.W., Suite 1120.
Telephone: 202-835-9880.
Facsimile: 202-835-9885.

MEMBERS OF FIRM

William O. Dillingham
William F. Murphy
Lucy E. Bettis
John N. Dahlberg
Mitchell B. Greenberg
Patrick J. Hagan
Edward E. Hartley
Jack C. Henning
Thomas J. Klitgaard
Albert A. Foster, Jr. (Resident, Washington, DC Office)

Richard Anthony Chavez
Kathleen L. D'Armagnac
Curtis F. Dowling
James C. Jardin
Michael Y. Lateef
Charles P. Murrin
Mark J. Rogers
Pamela Winston Bertani

For full biographical listings, see the Martindale-Hubbell Law Directory

MAJESTIC, PARSONS, SIEBERT & HSUE, A PROFESSIONAL CORPORATION (AV)

Four Embarcadero Center, Suite 1100, 94111-4106
Telephone: 415-248-5500
Telecopier: 415-362-5418
URL: http://www.mpsh.com
Santa Clara, California Office: 2700 Augustine Drive, Suite 198.
Telephone: 415-248-5500.

Gerald P. Parsons
Martin F. Majestic
J. Suzanne Siebert
James S. Hsue
K. Alison deRuntz

Tom Hunter
Stephen J. Le Blanc
Nancy E. Martin
Dang M. Vo

OF COUNSEL

Keiichi Nishimura

(See Next Column)

LEGAL SUPPORT PERSONNEL

Philip Yau
Michael G. Cleveland
Steven R. Vosen (Patent Agent)

For full biographical listings, see the Martindale-Hubbell Law Directory

*SAN JOSE,** Santa Clara Co.

BERGESON & ELIOPOULOS, LLP (AV)

55 Almaden Boulevard, Suite 400, 95113
Telephone: 408-291-6200
Fax: 408-297-6000
URL: http://www.beglaw.com
Washington, D.C. Affiliate Office: Bergeson & Campbell, P.C., 1300 Eye Street, NW, Suite 100 West, 20005.
Telephone: (202)-962-8585.
Fax: (202)-962-8599. URL: www.bclaw.com.

Daniel J. Bergeson
William T. Eliopoulos
Mary Anne Rodgers
John L. Antracoli
Donald P. Gagliardi
Ina Stangenes
Marily P. Lerner

OF COUNSEL

Anthony M. Glassman

ASSOCIATES

Marc G. Van Niekerk
Eunhae Park
Mark E. Waite
Evelyn A. Peyton
William A. Hodkowski

For full biographical listings, see the Martindale-Hubbell Law Directory

McMANIS, FAULKNER & MORGAN (AV)

160 West Santa Clara Street, 10th Floor, 95113
Telephone: 408-279-8700
Fax: 408-279-3244; 408-279-0494
Email: mfm@mfmlaw.com *URL:* http://www.mfmlaw.com

James McManis
William Faulkner
Donelle Morgan
Lisa Herrick
Michael Reedy
Erica Yew

Michelle Tidalgo
Colleen Duffy Smith
Lillian Wolf
Rebecca Hughes
Kalpana Vrudhula
Ray M. Baluyot
Catherine Bechtel
Arron Nesbitt

OF COUNSEL

Mary Arand

For full biographical listings, see the Martindale-Hubbell Law Directory

SANTA MONICA, Los Angeles Co.

HAIGHT, BROWN & BONESTEEL, L.L.P. (AV)

A Partnership including Professional Corporations
1620 26th Street, Suite 4000 North, P.O. Box 680, 90404
Telephone: 310-449-6000
Telecopier: 310-829-5117
Telex: 705837
URL: http://www.hbblaw.com
Santa Ana, California Office: Suite 900, 5 Hutton Centre Drive.
Telephone: 714-754-1100.
Telecopier: 714-754-0826.
Riverside, California Office: California Tower, 3737 Main Street, Suite 800.
Telephone: 909-341-8300.
Fax: 909-341-8309.
San Francisco, California Office: 101 Bush Street, 27th Floor.
Telephone: 415-986-7700.
Fax: 415-986-6945.
San Diego, California Office: 101 West Broadway, Suite 1000.
Telephone: 619-595-5583.
Fax: 619-595-7873.

MEMBERS OF FIRM

Morton Rosen
Theresa M. Marchlewski
William E. Ireland
Christopher I. Ritter

OF COUNSEL

R. Roy Finkle

For full biographical listings, see the Martindale-Hubbell Law Directory

COLORADO

*BOULDER,** Boulder Co.

HOLME ROBERTS & OWEN LLP (AV)

Suite 400, 1401 Pearl Street, 80302
Telephone: 303-444-5955
Telecopier: 303-444-1063
Email: hro@hro.com *URL:* http://www.hro.com
Denver, Colorado Office: Suite 4100, 1700 Lincoln.
Telephone: 303-861-7000.
Telecopier: 303-866-0200.
Colorado Springs, Colorado Office: Suite 1300, 90 South Cascade Avenue.
Telephone: 719-473-3800.
Telecopier: 719-633-1518.
Salt Lake City, Utah Office: Suite 1100, 111 East Broadway.
Telephone: 801-521-5800.
Telecopier: 801-521-9639.
London, England Office: Heathcoat House, 3rd Floor, 20 Savile Row.
Telephone: 011-44-171-494-5600.
Telecopier: 011-44-171-287-9344.

PARTNERS OF FIRM

Kent A. Fischmann
Christopher J. Kulish

For Complete List of Firm Personnel, See General Section

For full biographical listings, see the Martindale-Hubbell Law Directory

*COLORADO SPRINGS,** El Paso Co.

HOLME ROBERTS & OWEN LLP (AV)

Suite 1300, 90 South Cascade Avenue, 80903
Telephone: 719-473-3800
Telecopier: 719-633-1518
Email: hro@hro.com *URL:* http://www.hro.com
Denver, Colorado Office: Suite 4100, 1700 Lincoln.
Telephone: 303-861-7000.
Telecopier: 303-866-0200.
Boulder, Colorado Office: Suite 400, 1401 Pearl Street.
Telephone: 303-444-5955.
Telecopier: 303-444-1063.
Salt Lake City, Utah Office: Suite 1100, 111 East Broadway.
Telephone: 801-521-5800.
Telecopier: 801-521-9639.
London, England Office: Heathcoat House 3rd Floor, 20 Savile Row.
Telephone: 011-44-171-494-5600.
Telecopier: 011-44-171-287-9344.

PARTNERS OF FIRM

Susan E. Duffey Campbell
Steven B. Smith

For Complete List of Firm Personnel, See General Section

For full biographical listings, see the Martindale-Hubbell Law Directory

*DENVER,** Denver Co.

GORSUCH KIRGIS LLP (AV)

Tower 1, Suite 1000, 1515 Arapahoe Street, 80202
Telephone: 303-376-5000
Fax: 303-376-5001

PARTNERS

S. Lee Terry, Jr.
Cynthia Smith Cain

ASSOCIATES

Pantea M. Garroussi
Anastasia G. Khokhryakova

LEGAL SUPPORT PERSONNEL

Lansing Wallace
Veronica Ehrenzeller

For full biographical listings, see the Martindale-Hubbell Law Directory

HOLME ROBERTS & OWEN LLP (AV)

Suite 4100, 1700 Lincoln, 80203
Telephone: 303-861-7000
Telecopier: 303-866-0200
Email: hro@hro.com *URL:* http://www.hro.com
Boulder, Colorado Office: Suite 400, 1401 Pearl Street.
Telephone: 303-444-5955.
Telecopier: 303-444-1063.
Colorado Springs, Colorado Office: Suite 1300, 90 South Cascade Avenue.
Telephone: 719-473-3800.
Telecopier: 719-633-1518.
Salt Lake City, Utah Office: Suite 1100, 111 East Broadway.
Telephone: 801-521-5800.
Telecopier: 801-521-9639.
London, England Office: Heathcoat House, 3rd Floor, 20 Savile Row.
Telephone: 011-44-171-494-5600.
Telecopier: 011-44-171-287-9344.

(See Next Column)

PARTNERS OF FIRM

Boyd N. Boland
Ross E. Breyfogle
Susan E. Duffey Campbell (Colorado Springs Office)
Kent A. Fischmann (Boulder Office)
Richard L. Gabriel
Lynn Parker Hendrix
Christopher J. Kulish (Boulder Office)
Thomas R. Marsh
George G. Matava
John R. Posthumus
Steven B. Smith (Colorado Springs Office)

SPECIAL COUNSEL

James L. Johnson

ASSOCIATES

Robert Boyd Berube
Brian A. Carpenter
Nancy L. Dempsey
Jeffrey A. Divney
Stanley J. Gradisar
Kenneth J. Johnson

For Complete List of Firm Personnel, See General Section

For full biographical listings, see the Martindale-Hubbell Law Directory

SHERIDAN ROSS, P.C. (AV)

1560 Broadway, Suite 1200, 80202
Telephone: 303-863-9700
Facsimile: 303-863-0223
Email: srlaw@sheridanross.com

David F. Zinger
Craig C. Groseth
Michael L. Tompkins
Todd P. Blakely
Gary J. Connell
Sabrina Crowley Stavish
Joseph E. Kovarik
Susan Pryor Willson
Lewis D. Hansen
Robert R. Brunelli
Douglas W. Swartz
Richard L. Hughes

Bruce A. Kugler
Dana Lynn Hartje
Paul S. Hansra
Don D. Cha
Benjamin Baughman Lieb
Bradley M. Knepper
John C. Scott
Miriam R. Drickman

OF COUNSEL

Philip H. Sheridan (P.C.)
Wannell M. Crook
Theresa A. Brown

LEGAL SUPPORT PERSONNEL

TECHNICAL SPECIALIST

Dennis J. Dupray
Angela Dallas-Pedretti

PARALEGALS

Janet E. Balent
Peggy West

Representative Clients: Ball Corporation; British Nuclear Fuels; Case Logic Inc.; COBE Laboratories; Coors Brewing Company; Heska Corporation; J.D. Edwards & Company; Maxtor Corporation; University of Colorado; Vicorp Restaurants, Inc.

For full biographical listings, see the Martindale-Hubbell Law Directory

WESTMINSTER, Adams Co.

CIANCIO & JONSEN, P.C. (AV)

12000 North Pecos Street Suite 200, 80234-2079
Telephone: 303-451-0300
Fax: 303-280-0614
Email: ciancio@csn.net
Email: jonsen@csn.net

Gene A. Ciancio
Eric R. Jonsen

Cynthia M. Ciancio

For full biographical listings, see the Martindale-Hubbell Law Directory

CONNECTICUT

FAIRFIELD, Fairfield Co.

PERMAN & GREEN, LLP (AV)

425 Post Road, 06430-6232
Telephone: 203-259-1800
Facsimile: 203-255-5170
Email: pgpatent@aol.com *URL:* http://www.pgpatent.com

MEMBER OF FIRM

Martey R. Perman (1939-1993)

MANAGING PARTNER

Clarence A. Green

PARTNERS

Harry F. Smith
Mark F. Harrington

(See Next Column)

PERMAN & GREEN LLP—*Continued*

ASSOCIATES

David M. Warren (Not admitted in CT)
Albert W. Hilburger
Thomas L. Tully
Michael J. Tully (Not admitted in CT)
John J. Goodwin (Not admitted in CT)
Ralph D. Gelling (Not admitted in CT)
Thomas P. Dowd (Not admitted in CT)
Joseph A. Fischetti
Janik Marcovici

OF COUNSEL

Donald C. Caulfield
Paul Weinstein

For full biographical listings, see the Martindale-Hubbell Law Directory

*HARTFORD,** Hartford Co.

McCORMICK, PAULDING & HUBER, LLP (AV)

CityPlace II, 185 Asylum Street, 06103-4102
Telephone: 860-549-5290
Fax: 860-527-0464
Email: MPH@IP-Lawyers.com *URL:* http://www.IP-lawyers.com
Springfield, Massachusetts Office: SIS Center, 1441 Main Street.
Telephone: 413-736-5401.
Fax: 413-733-4543.

MEMBERS OF FIRM

Theodore R. Paulding
Donald K. Huber
John C. Hilton
Frederick J. Haesche
John C. Linderman
J. Kevin Grogan (Resident, Springfield, Massachusetts Office)
Arthur F. Dionne (Resident, Springfield, Massachusetts Office)

ASSOCIATES

Richard R. Michaud
Daniel G. Mackas
Peter J. Rainville (Not admitted in CT)
Marina F. Cunningham
Susan C. Oygard (Resident, Springfield, Massachusetts Office)
Nicholas J. Tuccillo (Resident, Springfield, Massachusetts Office)
Michael T. Clorite
Daniel M. Barbieri
Wm. Tucker Griffith
Stephen P. Scuderi (Resident, Springfield, Massachusetts Office)
Marylou J. Lavoié (Resident, Springfield, Massachusetts Office)

OF COUNSEL

John J. Dempsey (Not admitted in CT)

For full biographical listings, see the Martindale-Hubbell Law Directory

DELAWARE

*WILMINGTON,** New Castle Co.

CONNOLLY BOVE LODGE & HUTZ LLP (AV)

1220 Market Street, P.O. Box 2207, 19899-2207
Telephone: 302-658-9141
Telecopier: 302-658-5614
Email: cblhlaw@cblhlaw.com *URL:* http://www.cblhlaw.com

James M. Mulligan, Jr.
Arthur G. Connolly, Jr.
Rudolf E. Hutz
Harold Pezzner
Richard M. Beck (Not admitted in DE)
Paul E. Crawford
Stanley C. Macel, III
Thomas M. Meshbesher
George Pazuniak
N. Richard Powers
Jeffrey B. Bove
Collins J. Seitz, Jr.
Patricia Smink Rogowski
Mary W. Bourke
Robert G. McMorrow, Jr. (Not admitted in DE)
R. Eric Hutz
William E. McShane (Not admitted in DE)
John D. Fairchild (Not admitted in DE)
Ashley I. Pezzner
Gerard M. O'Rourke
Thomas A. Stevens
Oleh V. Bilynsky
Allan Neal Kutzenco (Not admitted in DE)
Frank Z. Yang (Not admitted in DE)
James M. Olsen
Eric J. Evain

For Complete List of Firm Personnel, See General Section

For full biographical listings, see the Martindale-Hubbell Law Directory

MORRIS, NICHOLS, ARSHT & TUNNELL (AV)

1201 North Market Street, P.O. Box 1347, 19899-1347
Telephone: 302-658-9200
Telecopier: 302-658-3989
URL: http://www.mnat.com

(See Next Column)

MEMBERS OF FIRM

Richard L. Sutton
Johannes R. Krahmer
O. Francis Biondi
Lewis S. Black, Jr.
Paul Welsh
William O. LaMotte, III
Douglas E. Whitney
William H. Sudell, Jr.
Martin P. Tully
Thomas R. Hunt, Jr.
A. Gilchrist Sparks, III
Richard D. Allen
David Ley Hamilton
John F. Johnston
Walter C. Tuthill
Donald F. Parsons, Jr.
Jack B. Blumenfeld
Donald Nelson Isken
Donald E. Reid
Denison H. Hatch, Jr.
Thomas C. Grimm
Kenneth J. Nachbar
Andrew M. Johnston
Mary B. Graham
Michael Houghton
Matthew B. Lehr
Thomas R. Pulsifer
Jon E. Abramczyk
Alan J. Stone
Louis G. Hering
Frederick H. Alexander
R. Judson Scaggs, Jr.
William M. Lafferty
Karen Jacobs Louden
Donna L. Culver
Julia Heaney
Jonathan I. Lessner
Robert J. Dehney
Colm F. Connolly

ASSOCIATES

Rachel A. Dwares
Jeffrey R. Wolters
Maryellen Noreika
David J. Teklits
S. Mark Hurd
Rodger D. Smith
Lisa K. W. Crossland
Eric D. Schwartz
Lucinda C. Cucuzzella
Mona A. Lee
Stanford L. Stevenson, III
J. Andrew Huffman
Derek C. Abbott
Jessica Zeldin
Bradley James Enna
David A. Harris
Elizabeth A. Brown
Patricia A. O'Neill
Gregory W. Werkheiser
Wendy L. Walter
Christopher F. Carlton
Stephanie L. Nagel
Joelle E. Polesky
Richard W. Ellis
Francis X. Gorman
John D. Pirnot
Megan E. Ward

COUNSEL

Andrew B. Kirkpatrick, Jr.
David A. Drexler
Walter L. Pepperman, II

DECEASED PARTNERS

Hugh M. Morris (1878-1966)
Alexander L. Nichols (1906-1985)
James M. Tunnell, Jr. (1910-1986)
S. Samuel Arsht (1910-1999)

Representative Clients: AstraZeneca Inc.; The Chase Manhattan Bank (USA); The Coca-Cola Company; Data General Corporation; Ford Motor Company; J.P. Morgan & Co. Incorporated; McDonald's Corporation; Merck & Co., Inc.; Texaco Inc.; U S West, Inc.

For full biographical listings, see the Martindale-Hubbell Law Directory

DISTRICT OF COLUMBIA

WASHINGTON, D.C. Co.

ARENT FOX KINTNER PLOTKIN & KAHN, PLLC (AV)

1050 Connecticut Avenue, N.W., 20036-5339
Telephone: 202-857-6000
Fax: 202-857-6395
URL: http://www.arentfox.com
New York City Office: 1675 Broadway, 25th Floor.
Telephone: 212-484-3900.
Telecopier: 212-484-3990.
Budapest Office: EMKE Building, Rakoczi ut 42, 1072 Budapest, Hungary.
Telephone: (36-1) 429 2080.
Fax: (36-1) 269 0599.
Middle East Office: The Law Office of Mohammed Bin Saud Al Rasheed, P.O. Box 62982, Riyadh 11595 Kingdom of Saudi Arabia.
Telephone: (966-1) 464-3139.
Facsimile: (966-1) 464-9264.
Bucharest Office: B-dul N. Titulescu, Nr.1 B1.A7, Sc. 1, Et. 6 Apt. 16, Sector 1, Bucharest, Romania.
Telephone: 011-401-211-8797.
Fax: 011-401-211-8771.

MEMBERS OF FIRM

Douglas R. Bush
Hunter T. Carter
Michael A. Grow
David C. Gryce
Sheldon H. Klein
Paul A. Koches
Peter S. Reichertz
Lewis Rose
Stephanie Karen Wade

(See Next Column)

ARENT FOX KINTNER PLOTKIN & KAHN PLLC, *Washington—Continued*

ASSOCIATES

Sarira D. Alexander
Nancy Susan Appel
Cristina A. Carvalho (Not admitted in DC)
Elizabeth H. Cohen
James R. Davis, II
John P. Feldman
Christie L. Grymes
Anthony V. Lupo
Rita M. Odin
Kerry H. Owens (Not admitted in DC)
Bryan A. Sims
David A. Vogel

For full biographical listings, see the Martindale-Hubbell Law Directory

BARKATS & ASSOCIATES, CHARTERED, ATTORNEYS AND COUNSELORS AT LAW (AV)

1250 Eye Street, N.W., 20005
Telephone: 202-682-1396
Telecopier: 202-789-0895
URL: http://www.lawyers.com/barkatslaw
Paris, France Office: 24, Rue de Prony, 75017 Paris, France.
Telephone: 01 44 29 32 32.
Telecopier: 44 29 31 00.
Affiliated Law Firm: Robert J. Shutak, 1424 Fourth Street, Santa Monica, California 90401.
Telephone: 310-458-3343.
Telecopier: 301-451-0043.

MEMBER OF THE FIRM IN WASHINGTON, D.C.

Pierre-Philippe Barkats

ASSOCIATES

Robert Clifton Burns
Jeffrey Thomas Gutierrez (Not admitted in DC)
Pat James Kalellis (Not admitted in DC)

OF COUNSEL

Jerome K. Tankel
Jacques R. Beghain (Not admitted in the United States)

For full biographical listings, see the Martindale-Hubbell Law Directory

FISHER WAYLAND COOPER LEADER & ZARAGOZA L.L.P. (AV)

A Registered Limited Liability Partnership
Suite 400, 2001 Pennsylvania Avenue, N.W., 20006-1851
Telephone: 202-659-3494
Facsimile: 202-296-6518
Email: fwclz@fwclz.com *URL:* http://www.fwclz.com

Ben S. Fisher (1890-1954)
Charles V. Wayland (1910-1980)
Martin R. Leader
Richard R. Zaragoza
Clifford M. Harrington
Kathryn R. Schmeltzer
Douglas Woloshin
David D. Oxenford
Barry H. Gottfried
Bruce D. Jacobs
Carroll John Yung
Glenn S. Richards
Robert C. Fisher
Scott R. Flick
Lauren Lynch Flick
Miles S. Mason

OF COUNSEL

Ben C. Fisher
Grover C. Cooper

ASSOCIATES

Dawn M. Sciarrino
Colette M. Capretz
Stephen J. Berman
Veronica D. McLaughlin
Stephanie Blessey Lilley
Jaqualin Friend Peterson
Cynthia D. Greer
Lara Strayer Meisner
David S. Konczal
Susan M. Hafeli
Tina R. Reynolds
Brendan Holland
Katherine Tong-Shin Suh
Max D. Gale (Not admitted in DC)
Joan E. Masters (Not admitted in DC)
Indra Sehdev Chalk (Not admitted in DC)

For full biographical listings, see the Martindale-Hubbell Law Directory

LAW OFFICES OF GARFINKLE & ASSOCIATES (AV)

1150 Connecticut Avenue, N.W., Suite 505, 20036
Telephone: 202-457-0200
Facsimile: 202-857-0550
URL: http://www.lawyers.com/washingtonartlaw

Ann M. Garfinkle

ASSOCIATE

Laura A. Possessky

OF COUNSEL

Austin P. Frum (Retired)

For full biographical listings, see the Martindale-Hubbell Law Directory

HARNESS, DICKEY & PIERCE, P.L.C. (AV)

888 Sixteenth Street, N.W., 20006
Telephone: 202-835-7480
Email: info@hdp.com *URL:* http://www.hdp.com
Troy, Michigan Office: 5445 Corporate Drive, Suite 400.
Telephone: 248-641-1600. Telefacsimile (All Groups); 248-641-0270.

(See Next Column)

Ann Arbor, Michigan Office: 301 East Liberty Street, Suite 555.
Telephone: 734-662-8000.
Telefacsimile: 734-662-7813.

MEMBER OF FIRM

W. R. Duke Taylor

Representative Clients: Chrysler Corp.; The Black and Decker Manufacturing Co.; Monroe Auto Equipment Co.; La-Z-Boy Chair Co.; Hughes Aircraft; Budd Co.; Dow Chemical Co.; Procter & Gamble; General Motors Corporation.

For full biographical listings, see the Martindale-Hubbell Law Directory

KILE MCINTYRE HARBIN & LEE (AV)

The Evening Star Building Suite 800, 1101 Pennsylvania Avenue, N.W., 20004
Telephone: 202-639-1260; 202-783-3355; 1-800-858-9666
Fax: 202-639-1299; 202-639-1298
URL: http://www.kilemcintyre.com
Atlanta, Georgia Office: Kile McIntyre & King, Promenade Two, Suite 3775, 1230 Peachtree Street, N.E., 30309.
Telephone: 404-873-2424.
Fax: 404-876-3649.
New York, New York Office: 729 Seventh Avenue, 14th Floor, 10019.
Telephone: 212-921-9713.
Fax: 212-921-9778.

MEMBERS OF FIRM

Bradford E. Kile
Lawrence Harbin
Eugene M. Lee
Timothy F. Loomis
John C. McIntyre, Jr. (Resident, Atlanta, Georgia Office)
Paul N. King (Resident, Atlanta, Georgia and Washington, D.C. Offices)

ASSOCIATES

Anne M. Sterba
Richard A. Sterba
Richard H. Hill, II (Resident, Atlanta, Georgia Office)

OF COUNSEL

Paul M. Craig, Jr.
Charles D. Reed
Karan Singh (Resident, New York, New York Office)
Raymond E. Vickery, Jr.
Jerome D. Jackson
Bruce K. Lagerman (Not admitted in DC)

For full biographical listings, see the Martindale-Hubbell Law Directory

KING, PAGANO & HARRISON (AV)

1730 Pennsylvania Avenue, N.W., 20006
Telephone: 202-371-6800
Fax: 202-371-6770
URL: http://www.kph.com
New York, New York Office: 425 Park Avenue, 10022.
Telephone: 212-223-4000.
FAX: 212-223-4134.

MEMBERS OF FIRM

Jeffrey W. King
Jeffrey W. Pagano (Resident, New York, N.Y. Office)
Keith J. Harrison
James E. Kellett (Resident, New York, N.Y. Office)
Steven Schaars
Jeffrey L. Poston
Ira M. Saxe (Not admitted in DC; Resident, New York, N.Y. Office)

OF COUNSEL

Herbert I. Meyer (Resident, New York, N.Y. Office)

ASSOCIATES

Cheryl A. Maier
Christopher Flynn
Emily B. Zuckerman (Not admitted in DC; Resident, New York, N.Y. Office)
Thomas W. Jones, Jr.
Eric M. Carr (Not admitted in DC; Resident, New York, N.Y. Office)

Representative clients: Brink's Inc.; The Pittston Co.; BAX Global; Kaiser Permanents: Group Health Association of America; Capital Credit Corp.; Systems Engineering Services Corp.; Noel Biscare.

For full biographical listings, see the Martindale-Hubbell Law Directory

KUBOVCIK & KUBOVCIK (AV)

The Farragut Building, 900 17th Street, N.W., Suite 710, 20006
Telephone: 202-887-9023
Fax: 202-887-9093
Email: kubo@ricochet.net *URL:* http://www.lawyers.com/kubovicklaw

Ronald J. Kubovcik
Keiko Tanaka Kubovcik

For full biographical listings, see the Martindale-Hubbell Law Directory

LEVINE SULLIVAN & KOCH, L.L.P. (AV)

1050 Seventeenth Street, N.W. Suite 800, 20036
Telephone: 202-508-1100
Facsimile: 202-861-9888
Email: info@lsklaw.com

(See Next Column)

LEVINE SULLIVAN & KOCH L.L.P.—*Continued*

MEMBERS OF FIRM

Lee Levine
Michael D. Sullivan
Elizabeth C. Koch
James E. Grossberg
Celeste Phillips
(Not admitted in DC)
Seth D. Berlin

OF COUNSEL

Cameron A. Stracher

ASSOCIATES

Jay Ward Brown
Jacquelyn J. Orr
(Not admitted in DC)
Ashley I. Kissinger

For full biographical listings, see the Martindale-Hubbell Law Directory

OPPENHEIMER WOLFF DONNELLY & BAYH LLP (AV)

1350 Eye Street, N.W. Suite 200, 20005
Telephone: 202-312-8000
FAX: 202-312-8100
URL: http://www.owdlaw.com
Oppenheimer Wolff & Donnelly LLP
Minneapolis, Minnesota Office: 3300 Plaza VII, 45 South Seventh Street. 55402.
Telephone: 612-607-7000.
FAX: 612-607-7100.
Amsterdam, The Netherlands Office: Keizergracht 241.
Telephone: 31-20-423-4555.
FAX: 31-20-423-4545.
Brussels, Belgium Office: Avenue Louise 240, Box 5, 1050.
Telephone: 32-2-626-0500.
FAX: 32-2-626-0510.
Geneva, Switzerland Office: Rue Gabriel Eynard, 6, 1206.
Telephone: (41/22) 311-7410.
FAX: (41/22) 311-7407.
New York, N.Y. Office: Citicorp Center, 153 East 53rd Street, 10022.
Telephone: 212-826-5000.
FAX: 212-486-0708.
Newport Beach, California Office: 500 Newport Center Drive, Suite 700, 92660.
Telephone: 949-719-6000.
FAX: 949-719-6020.
Paris, France Office: 53 Avenue Montaigne, 75008.
Telephone: (33/1) 44 95 03 50.
FAX: (33/1) 44 95 03 40.
St. Paul, Minnesota Office: 1700 First National Bank Building, 55101.
Telephone: 651-605-2000.
FAX: 651-605-2100.
Los Angeles, California Office: 2029 Century Park East, 38th Floor, 90067.
Telephone: 310-788-5000.
FAX: 310-277-1297.
Palo Alto, California Office: 3373 Hillview Avenue, Suite 200, 94304.
Telephone: 650-320-4000.
FAX: 650-320-4100.
Chicago, Illinois Office: Oppenheimer Wolff & Donnelly (Illinois), Two Prudential Plaza, 45th Floor, 180 North Stetson Avenue, 60601.
Telephone: 312-616-1800.
Fax: 312-616-5800.

RESIDENT PARTNER

M. Peter Adler

For full biographical listings, see the Martindale-Hubbell Law Directory

RADER, FISHMAN & GRAUER PLLC (AV)

1233 20th Street, Suite 501, 20036
Telephone: 202-955-3750
Fax: 202-955-3751
Email: info@raderfishman.com *URL:* http://www.intelprop.com
Grand Rapids, Michigan Office: Rader, Fishman, Grauer & McGarry PLLC, 171 Monroe Avenue, N.W., Suite 600, 49503.
Telephone: 616-742-3500.
Fax: 616-742-1010.
Bloomfield Hills, Michigan Office: 1533 North Woodward, Suite 140, 48304.
Telephone: 248-594-0600.
Fax: 248-594-0610.
Denver, Colorado Office: 7887 East Belleview Avenue, 80111.
Telephone: 303-228-1658.
Fax: 303-228-1659.

Ronald P. Kananen
Shmuel (Sandy) Livnat

ASSOCIATES

Steven L. Nichols
(Not admitted in DC)
Christopher Mark Tanner
(Not admitted in DC)

OF COUNSEL

Paul W. Fish
William D. Stokes
Wallace G. Walter

PATENT AGENTS

Paul D. Amrozowicz
David K. Benson

For full biographical listings, see the Martindale-Hubbell Law Directory

ROTHWELL, FIGG, ERNST & KURZ, A PROFESSIONAL CORPORATION (AV)

Suite 701 East Tower, 555 Thirteenth Street, N.W., 20004
Telephone: 202-783-6040
Facsimile: 202-783-6031
Email: rfek@rfek.com *URL:* http://www.rfek.com
Omaha, Nebraska Office: 13906 Gold Circle, Suite 204, 68144.
Telephone: 402-333-1550.
Fax: 402-333-1510.

G. Franklin Rothwell
E. Anthony Figg
Barbara G. Ernst
Raymond A. Kurz
George R. Repper
Bart G. Newland
Steven Lieberman
Vincent M. De Luca
Celine Jimenez Crowson
Joseph A. Hynds
Robert J. Jondle (Resident, Omaha, Nebraska Office)

Mark I. Bowditch
Kenneth M. Fagin
Jeffrey W. Rennecker
Stephen A. Saxe
Martha Cassidy
Julie A. Nelson
Lisa A. Uldrich (Not admitted in DC; Resident, Omaha, Nebraska Office)
Elizabeth A. Leff
(Not admitted in DC)
Gregg Jansen
Nancy T. Morris
Robert H. Cameron
(Not admitted in DC)
David D. Nelson
(Not admitted in DC)
Anna J. Kurian

OF COUNSEL

Don M. Kerr
(Not admitted in DC)
Jeffrey L. Ihnen
Glenn E. Karta

For full biographical listings, see the Martindale-Hubbell Law Directory

SMITH, GAMBRELL & RUSSELL, LLP (AV)

Suite 800, 1850 M Street, N.W., 20036
Telephone: 202-659-2811
Cable Address: "Jemead".
Telex: WUI 64470; WU 89-2393.
Telecopier: 202-659-1462
Atlanta, Georgia Office: Suite 3100, Promenade II, 1230 Peachtree Street, N.E.
Telephone: 404-815-3500.
Facsimile: 404-815-3509.

MEMBERS OF FIRM

Andrew B. Beveridge (1915-1972)
Joseph A. DeGrandi (1927-1999)
Robert G. Weilacher
Richard G. Young
Michael A. Makuch
Dennis C. Rodgers
Helen Hill Minsker
William F. Rauchholz

ASSOCIATE

Michael K. Carrier (Not admitted in DC)

PATENT AGENT - CHINA ONLY

Qixia Zhang

For full biographical listings, see the Martindale-Hubbell Law Directory

VENABLE ATTORNEYS AT LAW VENABLE, BAETJER, HOWARD & CIVILETTI, LLP (AV)

A Partnership including Professional Corporations
Suite 1000, 1201 New York Avenue, N.W., 20005
Telephone: 202-962-4800
Fax: 202-962-8300
URL: http://www.venable.com
Baltimore, Maryland Office: Venable, Baetjer and Howard LLP, 1800 Mercantile Bank & Trust Building, 2 Hopkins Plaza.
Telephone: 410-244-7400.
Fax: 410-244-7742.
McLean, Virginia Office: Venable, Baetjer and Howard LLP, Suite 400, 2010 Corporate Ridge.
Telephone: 703-760-1600.
Fax: 703-821-8949.
Rockville, Maryland Office: Venable, Baetjer and Howard LLP, Suite 500, One Church Street, P. O. Box 1906.
Telephone: 301-217-5600.
Fax: 301-217-5617.
Towson, Maryland Office: Venable, Baetjer and Howard LLP, 210 Allegheny Avenue, P. O. Box 5517.
Telephone: 410-494-6200.
Fax: 410-821-0147.

MEMBERS OF FIRM

Kenneth C. Bass, III (Also at McLean, Virginia Office)
James R. Burdett
William D. Coston
Jeffrey A. Dunn (Also at Baltimore, Maryland Office)
Robert J. Frank
Michael A. Gollin
Mark B. Harrison
Gary M. Hnath
Gabor J. Kelemen
(Not admitted in DC)
Robert Kinberg
Norman N. Kunitz
Vicki Margolis (Also at Baltimore, Maryland Office)
George F. Pappas (Also at Baltimore, Maryland Office)

(See Next Column)

VENABLE ATTORNEYS AT LAW VENABLE, BAETJER, HOWARD & CIVILETTI, LLP, *Washington—Continued*

MEMBERS OF FIRM (Continued)

Julie A. Petruzzelli
Mary Jane Saunders
John W. Schneller
Marina V. Schneller
Herbert G. Smith, II
George H. Spencer
Ashley J. Wells
Allen Wood

OF COUNSEL

Janet F. Satterthwaite
Gary L. Shaffer (Not admitted in DC)
Barbara L. Waite

ASSOCIATES

Marcia A. Auberger
Patricia Russell Brown
Peter J. Curtin (Also at Baltimore, Maryland Office)
Catherine A. Ferguson
Rebecca L. Goldsmith (Not admitted in DC)
Michael P. Leary (Not admitted in DC)
Chellis E. Neal
Andrew Douglas Price
Martin L. Saad
Michael A. Sartori
Melissa Landau Steinman
Catherine M. Voorhees
George Abe Zachariah
Scott A. Zebrak

For Complete List of Firm Personnel, See General Section

For full biographical listings, see the Martindale-Hubbell Law Directory

FLORIDA

*MIAMI,** Dade Co.

MALLOY & MALLOY, P.A. (AV)

2800 S.W. Third Avenue, 33129
Telephone: 305-858-8000
Fort Lauderdale: 954-525-9611
In Florida: 800-337-7239
Facsimile: 305-858-0008
URL: http://www.MALLOYLAW.com
Fort Lauderdale, Florida Office: 2101 West Commercial Boulevard. Suite 4100. 33309.
Telephone: 954-525-9611.

Jennie S. Malloy
John Cyril Malloy, III
Peter A. Matos

Louis R. Gigliotti, Jr.
Andrew W. Ransom

OF COUNSEL

John Cyril Malloy
James E. Wetterling, Jr.

Representative Clients: Tasco Sales, Inc.; Turnberry Associates/Aventura Mall; Editorial Televisa; Cigarette Racing Team, Inc.; Sloppy Joe's (Bar) Int'l, Inc.; Hog's Breath (Saloon) Int'l, Inc.; Krieger Watch Corp.; Navarro Discount Pharmacies; Nailtiques Cosmetic Corp.; Cheeburger Cheeburger Restaurants.

For full biographical listings, see the Martindale-Hubbell Law Directory

WINSHIP & BYRNE (AV)

First Union Financial Center, 200 South Biscayne Boulevard, Suite 1870, 33131
Telephone: 305-381-8698
Fax: 305-665-0447
Email: winbyrne@aol.com

Blaine H. Winship
Karin M. Byrne

For full biographical listings, see the Martindale-Hubbell Law Directory

*ORLANDO,** Orange Co.

ALLEN, DYER, DOPPELT, MILBRATH & GILCHRIST (AV)

255 South Orange Avenue, Suite 1401, P.O. Box 3791, 32802-3791
Telephone: 407-841-2330
Fax: 407-841-2343
Email: info@addmg.com

Herbert L. Allen
Robert Dyer
Ava K. Doppelt
Stephen D. Milbrath
Brian R. Gilchrist
Christopher F. Regan
Jeffrey S. Whittle
David L. Sigalow
Richard K. Warther
Michael W. Taylor (Not admitted in FL)
Enrique G. Estevez

LEGAL SUPPORT PERSONNEL

PATENT AGENTS

Carl M. Napolitano, Ph.D.
Jacqueline E. Hartt, Ph.D.

For full biographical listings, see the Martindale-Hubbell Law Directory

MORAN & SHAMS, P.A. (AV)

111 North Orange Avenue, Suite 1200, P.O. Box 472, 32802-0472
Telephone: 407-841-4141
Fax: 407-841-4148
Email: moran-shams@moran-shams.com

Thomas P. Moran
Robert S. MacDonald

Lawrence H. Haber

Representative Clients: J.S.S. International Group, Inc.; Cruises Only, L.L.C.; All Cellular, Inc.; Fitzgerald Communications, Inc.; Ostalkiewicz Diamond Importers.

For full biographical listings, see the Martindale-Hubbell Law Directory

*TAMPA,** Hillsborough Co.

ARTHUR W. FISHER, III, P.A. (AV)

Suite 316, 5553 West Waters Avenue, 33634-0500
Telephone: 813-885-2006
Fax: Available Upon Request
Email: 74732.1301@compuserve.com

Arthur W. Fisher, III

Reference: Sun Bank of Tampa Florida.

For full biographical listings, see the Martindale-Hubbell Law Directory

STEIN, SCHIFINO & VAN DER WALL (AV)

600 North Westshore Boulevard Suite 1000, 33609
Telephone: 813-289-2966
Facsimile: 813-289-2967
Email: stein@steinpatent.com *URL:* http://www.steinpatent.com
Miami, Florida Office: First Union Financial Center, 200 South Biscayne Boulevard, Suite 4600.
Telephone: 305-358-6000. Toll Free: 800-377-0077.
Telecopier: 305-530-8880.

Stefan V. Stein
Sara Anne Schifino
Robert J. Van Der Wall

ASSOCIATE

Harvey Stuart Kauget (Resident, Tampa Office)

OF COUNSEL

Leon Chasan (Not admitted in FL)

For full biographical listings, see the Martindale-Hubbell Law Directory

HAWAII

*HONOLULU,** Honolulu Co.

CARLSMITH BALL (AV)

A Partnership including Law Corporations
Suite 2200, Pacific Tower, 1001 Bishop Street, P.O. Box 656, 96809-3402
Telephone: 808-523-2500
Fax: 808-523-0842
Email: execdirector@carlsmith.com *URL:* http://www.carlsmith.com
Kapolei, Hawaii Office: Suite 318, Kapolei Building, 1001 Kamokila Boulevard, 96707.
Telephone: 808-523-2500.
Fax: 808-674-0850.
Wailuku, Maui Hawaii Office: Suite 400, One Main Plaza, 2200 Main Street, P.O. Box 1086, 96793-1086.
Telephone: 808-242-4535.
Fax: 808-244-4974.
Kailua-Kona, Hawaii Office: Suite 209, 75-1000 Henry Street, 96740.
Telephone: 808-329-6464.
Fax: 808-329-9450.
Hilo, Hawaii Office: 121 Waianuenue Avenue, P.O. Box 686, 96721-0686.
Telephone: 808-935-6644.
Fax: 808-935-7975.
Hagatna, Guam Office: Suite 401, Bank of Hawaii Building, 134 West Soledad Avenue, P.O. Box BF, 96932-5027.
Telephone: 671-472-6813.
Fax: 671-477-4375.
Telex: 721-6445 CWCMI GM.
Saipan, Commonwealth of the Northern Mariana Islands Office: Carlsmith Building, Capitol Hill, P.O. Box 5241, 96950-5241.
Telephone: 670-322-3455.
Fax: 670-322-3368.
Los Angeles, California Office: 9th Floor, 444 South Flower Street, 90071-2901.
Telephone: 213-955-1200.
Fax: 213-623-0032.
Washington, D.C. Office: Suite 300, 1201 Pennsylvania Avenue, N.W., 20004-2401.
Telephone: 202-628-2228.
Fax: 202-628-2071.

(See Next Column)

CARLSMITH BALL—*Continued*

Mexico City, Mexico Office: Carlsmith Ball, Sierra Nevada 119, Lomas de Chapultepec, 11000 Mexico, D.F.
Telephone: 52-5-520-8514, 52-5-520-8757.
Fax: 52-5-540-1545.
Mexico, D.F. Office of Carlsmith Ball, S.C. (Authorized to practice as foreign legal consultants in Mexico): Sierra Nevada 119, Lomas de Chapultepec, 11000 Mexico, D.F.
Telephone: 52-5-520-8514, 52-5-520-8757.
Fax: 52-5-540-1545.

MEMBER OF FIRM
Daniel A. Bent
ASSOCIATE
Brent K. Yamashita
OF COUNSEL
Herbert G. Baerwitz (Resident at Los Angeles, California Office)
Robert R. Thornton (Resident at Los Angeles, California Office)

For Complete List of Firm Personnel, See General Section

For full biographical listings, see the Martindale-Hubbell Law Directory

FUKUNAGA MATAYOSHI HERSHEY & CHING (AV)

A Partnership including a Law Corporation
841 Bishop Street, Suite 1200, 96813
Telephone: 808-533-4300
Fax: 808-531-7585

PARTNERS
Kenneth K. Fukunaga
Jerold T. Matayoshi (A Law Corporation)
James H. Hershey
Wesley H. H. Ching
Patricia Kehau Wall
ASSOCIATES
Lois H. Yamaguchi
Robert R. Sadaoka
Celia A. Urion
Sheree Kon-Herrera
OF COUNSEL
Leighton K. Chong
Kathleen M. Douglas

For full biographical listings, see the Martindale-Hubbell Law Directory

GOODSILL ANDERSON QUINN & STIFEL (AV)

Alii Place, Suite 1800, 1099 Alakea Street, P.O. Box 3196, 96801-3196
Telephone: 808-547-5600
FAX: 808-547-5880
Email: info@goodsill.com *URL:* http://www.goodsill.com

MEMBERS OF FIRM
John R. Lacy
William S. Miller
Jacqueline L. S. Earle
Gregory R. Kim
LindaLee K. Farm
Roy John Tjioe
ASSOCIATE
Russell K. Kaupu

Representative Clients: Amfac/JMB Hawaii, Inc.; Bank of Hawaii; Chevron USA Products Co.; CNA Insurance Co.; Hawaiian Electric Industries, Inc.; Kapi'olani Health; MEDMARC; PrimeCo Personal Communications, L.P.; State Farm Insurance Companies; United States Aviation Underwriters, Inc.

For Complete List of Firm Personnel, See General Section

For full biographical listings, see the Martindale-Hubbell Law Directory

ILLINOIS

*CHICAGO,** Cook Co.

CAHILL, CHRISTIAN & KUNKLE, LTD. (AV)

Santa Fe Building, 224 South Michigan Avenue, Suite 1300, 60604
Telephone: 312-341-1688
Fax: 312-341-1689
URL: http://www.cck.com

William J. Kunkle, Jr.
Roseann Oliver
William T. Cahill
John M. Christian
Lorna E. Propes
Scott B. Greene
Mary Kathryn Kelly
Suzanne M. Metzel
Matthew J. Gehringer
Steven E. Nieslawski
Michael K. Bartosz
Donald Lee Homyk
OF COUNSEL
Louis B. Garippo

(See Next Column)

Daniel J. Collins
Jeanne M. Cullen
Elizabeth A. Kaveny
Frederic T. Knape
David R. Nordwall
Elisha S. Rosenblum
Melisa G. Thompson

For full biographical listings, see the Martindale-Hubbell Law Directory

COOK, ALEX, MCFARRON, MANZO, CUMMINGS & MEHLER (AV)

200 West Adams, Suite 2850, 60606
Telephone: 312-236-8500
Fax: 312-236-8176
Email: firm@cammcm.com

Granger Cook, Jr.
John L. Alex
Daniel M. Riess
Eugene M. Cummings
Gary W. McFarron
Raymond M. Mehler
Edward D. Manzo
Stephen B. Heller
David Lesht
Andrew G. Kolomayets
Mark J. Murphy
John R. Lagowski
Michael J. McGee
David Michael Mundt
Michael A. Dorfman
OF COUNSEL
Fred S. Lockwood (P.C.)
William H. Magidson

For full biographical listings, see the Martindale-Hubbell Law Directory

DICK AND HARRIS (AV)

Suite 3800, 181 West Madison Street, 60602
Telephone: 312-726-4000
Telecopier: 312-726-5834

MEMBERS OF FIRM
Richard Eugene Dick
Richard D. Harris
Howard E. Silverman
John S. Pacocha
ASSOCIATES
Douglas B. Teaney
Herbert H. Finn
Christopher Sean Clancy
James K. Cleland
Jeannette Sanniola Zimmer

For full biographical listings, see the Martindale-Hubbell Law Directory

HAMMAN & BENN (AV)

Suite 3300, 10 South La Salle Street, 60603-1002
Telephone: 312-372-2920
Facsimile: 312-372-7762

George W. Hamman
Marvin N. Benn
Dawn M. Cassie
Richard J. Superfine
Stephen J. Cassin
Jeanne M. Hoffmann
Jack Shore
OF COUNSEL
Jeffrey M. Carey
Ronald Olbrysh
Mitchell H. Saranow

For full biographical listings, see the Martindale-Hubbell Law Directory

MICHAEL T. HANNAFAN & ASSOCIATES, LTD. (AV)

One East Wacker Drive, Suite 2710, 60601
Telephone: 312-527-0055
Fax: 312-527-0220
Email: mthannafan@aol.com

Michael T. Hannafan

Cory A. Johnson

Reference: The Northern Trust Co.

For full biographical listings, see the Martindale-Hubbell Law Directory

MARSHALL, O'TOOLE, GERSTEIN, MURRAY & BORUN (AV)

6300 Sears Tower, 233 South Wacker Drive, 60606-6402
Telephone: 312-474-6300
Fax: 312-474-0448
URL: http://www.marshallotoole.com

MEMBERS OF FIRM
Richard H. Anderson
Michael F. Borun
Richard A. Brandon
David W. Clough
Madeline Henricks Devereux
Christine A. Dudzik
Patrick D. Ertel
David A. Gass
Allen H. Gerstein
Robert M. Gerstein
Roger A. Heppermann
Martin J. Hirsch
Douglass C. Hochstetler
Trevor B. Joike
Richard M. LaBarge
William E. McCracken
Carl E. Moore
James J. Napoli
Anthony Nimmo
Edward M. O'Toole
Li-Hsien Rin-Laures
Nate F. Scarpelli
Richard A. Schnurr
Jeffrey S. Sharp
Timothy J. Vezeau
Karl A. Vick
James P. Zeller

(See Next Column)

LOUISIANA

*BATON ROUGE,** East Baton Rouge Parish

KEAN, MILLER, HAWTHORNE, D'ARMOND, McCOWAN & JARMAN, L.L.P. (AV)

22nd Floor, One American Place, 70825
Telephone: 225-387-0999
Fax: 225-388-9133
Mailing Address: P.O. Box 3513, Baton Rouge, Louisiana, 70821
URL: http://WWW.KMLAW.COM
New Orleans, Louisiana Office: Energy Centre, Suite 1560, 1100 Poydras Street, 70163.
Telephone: 504-585-3050.
Fax: 504-585-3051.
Plaquemine, Louisiana Office: Suite 10, 23425 Railroad Avenue, 70764.
Telephone: 225-687-9845.
Fax: 225-382-3445.
Lake Charles, Louisiana Office: One Lakeshore Drive, Suite 1220, 70629.
Telephone: 318-430-0350.
Fax: 318-436-5566.
Covington, Louisiana Office: 503 North New Hampshire Street, P.O. Box 3096, 70433.
Telephone: 504-875-0400.
Fax: 504-875-0500.

Russel O. Primeaux — Morgan E. Malino

Representative Clients: Analytical Specialists, Inc., Baton Rouge, LA: ANCO Industries, Inc., Baton Rouge, LA; Anomeric, Inc., Baton Rouge, LA; Associated Grocers, Baton Rouge, LA; Basic Industries, Inc., Baton Rouge, LA; Lion Investbanc, Baton Rouge, LA; Piccadilly Cafeterias, Inc.; Sea Sanitizer International, L.L.C., Baton Rouge, LA.

For full biographical listings, see the Martindale-Hubbell Law Directory

*NEW ORLEANS,** Orleans Parish

McGLINCHEY STAFFORD (AV)

A Professional Limited Liability Company
643 Magazine Street, 70130-3477
Telephone: 504-586-1200
Fax: 504-596-2800
TDD: (504) 596-2728
Telex: 584327
Cable Address: "MACSTAC"
Mailing Address: P.O. Box 60643, New Orleans, Louisiana, 70160-0643
Email: @mcglinchey.com *URL:* http://www.mcglinchey.com
Dallas, Texas Office: 2777 Stemmons Freeway, Suite 925, 75207-2401.
Telephone: 214-860-9700.
Fax: 214-860-9750.
Houston, Texas Office: 2727 Allen Parkway, Suite 1900, 77019.
Telephone: 713-520-1900.
Fax: 713-520-1025.
Baton Rouge, Louisiana Office: Ninth Floor, One American Place, 70825-0001.
Telephone: 504-383-9000.
Fax: 504-343-3076.
Jackson, Mississippi Office: Suite 1200, SkyTel Centre, 200 South Lamar Street, 39201.
Telephone: 601-960-8400.
Fax: 601-960-8406.
Lake Providence, Louisiana Office: 405 Morgan Street, 71254-2691.
Telephone: 318-559-1200.
Fax: 318-559-0609.
Monroe, Louisiana Office: Dean ONB Tower, 130 Desiard Street, Suite 807, 71201.
Telephone: 318-651-0807.
Fax: 318-651-0809.

MEMBER OF FIRM

Charles R. Penot, Jr.

MEMBER OF FIRM

Michael David Ferachi (Resident, Baton Rouge Office)

For full biographical listings, see the Martindale-Hubbell Law Directory

MAINE

*PORTLAND,** Cumberland Co.

PIERCE ATWOOD (AV)

One Monument Square, 04101
Telephone: 207-791-1100
Fax: 207-791-1350
Email: info@PierceAtwood.com *URL:* http://www.pierceatwood.com
Augusta, Maine Office: 77 Winthrop Street.
Telephone: 207-622-6311.
Fax: 207-623-9367.
Newburyport, Massachusetts Office: 6 Harris Street.
Telephone: 978-465-9599.
Fax: 978-465-9945.

MEMBERS OF FIRM

Jeffrey M. White
William J. Kayatta, Jr.
James R. Erwin
Robert H. Stier, Jr.
Gloria A. Pinza

ASSOCIATES

William L. Worden
Chris A. Caseiro
Patrick R. Scanlon (Not admitted in ME)
Steven J. Scott
Peter S. Black

For Complete List of Firm Personnel, See General Section

For full biographical listings, see the Martindale-Hubbell Law Directory

PRETI, FLAHERTY, BELIVEAU, PACHIOS & HALEY, LLC (AV)

One City Center, P.O. Box 9546, 04112-9546
Telephone: 207-791-3000
Telecopier: 207-791-3111
Email: admin@preti.com *URL:* http://www.preti.com
Augusta, Maine Office: 45 Memorial Circle, P.O. Box 1058, 04332-1058.
Telephone: 207-623-5300.
Telefax: 207-623-2914.
Bath, Maine Office: Thirty Front Street, P.O. Box 665, 04530-0665.
Telephone: 207-443-5576.
Telefax: 207-443-6665.

MEMBERS OF FIRM

Jonathan S. Piper
Judith Sapp (Not admitted in ME)
Mark B. LeDuc (Augusta Office)
Timothy J. Bryant

COUNSEL

Gregory P. Hansel

ASSOCIATE

Roy T. Pierce

Representative Clients: The St. Paul Companies; KeyBank National Assn.; Maine Municipal Assn.; Blethen-Maine Newspapers, Inc.; Maine Turnpike Authority; American International Group; Maine Automobile Dealers Assn.; Hannaford Brothers Co.; L.L. Bean; Maine Health Care Assn.

For Complete List of Firm Personnel, See General Section

For full biographical listings, see the Martindale-Hubbell Law Directory

MARYLAND

*BALTIMORE,** (Independent City)

VENABLE ATTORNEYS AT LAW VENABLE, BAETJER AND HOWARD, LLP (AV)

A Partnership including Professional Corporations
1800 Mercantile Bank & Trust Building, 2 Hopkins Plaza, 21201
Telephone: 410-244-7400
Fax: 410-244-7742
URL: http://www.venable.com
Washington, D.C. Office: Venable, Baetjer, Howard & Civiletti LLP, Suite 1000, 1201 New York Avenue, N.W.
Telephone: 202-962-4800.
Fax: 202-962-8300.
McLean, Virginia Office: Suite 400, 2010 Corporate Ridge.
Telephone: 703-760-1600.
Fax: 703-821-8949.
Rockville, Maryland Office: Suite 500, One Church Street, P. O. Box 1906.
Telephone: 301-217-5600.
Fax: 301-217-5617.
Towson, Maryland Office: 210 Allegheny Avenue, P. O. Box 5517.
Telephone: 410-494-6200.
Fax: 410-821-0147.

(See Next Column)

VENABLE ATTORNEYS AT LAW VENABLE, BAETJER AND HOWARD, LLP—*Continued*

MEMBERS OF FIRM

George H. Spencer (Not admitted in MD; Resident, Washington, D.C. Office)
Robert J. Frank (Not admitted in MD; Resident, Washington, D.C. Office)
Norman N. Kunitz (Not admitted in MD; Resident, Washington, D.C. Office)
Kenneth C. Bass, III (Not admitted in MD; Washington, D.C. and McLean, Virginia Offices)
Marina V. Schneller (Not admitted in MD; Resident, Washington, D.C. Office)
Gabor J. Kelemen (Not admitted in MD; Resident, Washington, D.C. Office)
John W. Schneller (Not admitted in MD; Resident, Washington, D.C. Office)
Robert Kinberg (Not admitted in MD; Resident, Washington, D.C. Office)
Allen Wood (Not admitted in MD; Resident, Washington, D.C. Office)
Jeffrey A. Dunn (Also at Washington, D.C. Office)
George F. Pappas (Also at Washington, D.C. Office)
William D. Coston (Not admitted in MD; Resident, Washington, D.C. Office)
Mark B. Harrison (Not admitted in MD; Resident, Washington, D.C. Office)
George William Lewis (Not admitted in MD; Resident, Washington, D.C. Office)
Robert Charles Hill (Not admitted in MD; Resident, Washington, D.C. Office)
Ashley J. Wells (Not admitted in MD; Resident, Washington, D.C. Office)
Mary Jane Saunders (Not admitted in MD; Resident, Washington, D.C. Office)
David J. Heubeck
Julie A. Petruzzelli (Not admitted in MD; Resident, Washington, D.C. Office)
Herbert G. Smith, II (Not admitted in MD; Resident, Washington, D.C. Office)
James R. Burdett (Not admitted in MD; Resident, Washington, D.C. Office)
Gary M. Hnath (Resident, Washington, D.C. Office)
Michael A. Gollin (Resident, Washington, D.C. Office)
Vicki Margolis (Also at Washington, D.C. Office)

OF COUNSEL

Gary L. Shaffer (Not admitted in MD; Resident, Washington, D.C. Office)
Barbara L. Waite (Resident, Washington, D.C. Office)
Janet F. Satterthwaite (Not admitted in MD; Resident, Washington, D.C. Office)

ASSOCIATES

Marcia A. Auberger (Not admitted in MD; Resident, Washington, D.C. Office)
Patricia Russell Brown (Resident, Washington, D.C. Office)
Peter J. Curtin (Not admitted in MD; Also at Washington, D.C. Office)
Catherine A. Ferguson (Resident, Washington, D.C. Office)
Rebecca L. Goldsmith (Resident, Washington, D.C. Office)
Michael P. Leary (Not admitted in MD; Resident, Washington, D.C. Office)
Chellis E. Neal (Resident, Washington, D.C. Office)
Andrew Douglas Price (Not admitted in MD; Resident, Washington, D.C. Office)
Martin L. Saad (Resident, Washington, D.C. Office)
Michael A. Sartori (Not admitted in MD; Resident, Washington, D.C. Office)
Melissa Landau Steinman (Resident, Washington, D.C. Office)
Catherine M. Voorhees (Not admitted in MD; Resident, Washington, D.C. Office)
George Abe Zachariah (Resident, Washington, D.C. Office)
Scott A. Zebrak (Resident, Washington, D.C. Office)

For Complete List of Firm Personnel, See General Section

For full biographical listings, see the Martindale-Hubbell Law Directory

POTOMAC, Montgomery Co.

JOHN GIBSON SEMMES (AV Ⓣ)

10220 River Road, Suite 201, 20854
Telephone: 301-299-8775
Telecopier: 301-299-7486

For full biographical listings, see the Martindale-Hubbell Law Directory

SILVER SPRING, Montgomery Co.

SAUNDERS & SCHMIELER (AV)

8737 Colesville Road, Suite L-200, 20910-3921
Telephone: 301-588-7717
Facsimile: 301-588-5073
Email: admin@sslawfirm.com *URL:* http://www.sslawfirm.com
Washington, D.C. Office: 1050 17th Street, N.W., #600
Telephone: 202-833-2999.
Baltimore, Maryland Office: Suite 2700, 111 South Calvert Street.
Telephone: 410-235-7558.
Arlington, Virginia Office: 2111 Wilson Boulevard, Suite 700.
Telephone: 703-243-1100.

(See Next Column)

Richmond, Virginia Office: 4900 Cutshaw Avenue.
Telephone: 804-353-9800.

MEMBER OF FIRM

Jeffrey R. Schmieler

ASSOCIATES

Nicole E. Ames
A. Benjamin Horton
Lucas F. Webster

For Complete List of Firm Personnel, See General Section

For full biographical listings, see the Martindale-Hubbell Law Directory

MASSACHUSETTS

*BOSTON,** Suffolk Co.

GELB & GELB LLP (AV)

20 Custom House Street, 02110
Telephone: 617-345-0010
Facsimile: 617-345-0009
Email: g&g@gelbgelb.com *URL:* http://www.gelbgelb.com

MEMBERS OF FIRM

Richard M. Gelb
Gail Kleven Gelb

Aaron J. Bullwinkel
Brian G. Cafferty

For full biographical listings, see the Martindale-Hubbell Law Directory

HINCKLEY, ALLEN & SNYDER LLP (AV)

28 State Street, 30th Floor, 02109-1775
Telephone: 617-345-9000
Email: firm@haslaw.com *URL:* http://www.haslaw.com
Providence, Rhode Island Office: 1500 Fleet Center.
Telephone: 401-274-2000.
Fax: 401-277-9600. URL: http://www.hawlaw.com.

MEMBERS OF FIRM

Paula K. Andrews
David D. Barricelli (Not admitted in MA)
Jonathan Bell
Deborah L. Benson
Paul Bork
Stephen J. Carlotti (Not admitted in MA)
Michael P. DeFanti
Eric F. Eisenberg
Malcolm Farmer, III
Margaret D. Farrell (Not admitted in MA)
Pasco Gasbarro Jr.
William R. Grimm
Paul A. Hedstrom
Richard L. E. Jocelyn (Not admitted in MA)
Elizabeth Murdock Myers
Paul F. O'Donnell, III
H. Peter Olsen (Not admitted in MA)
Julianne Palumbo
John J. Pendergast, III (Not admitted in MA)
Gerald J. Petros
James O. Reavis
Lawrence R. Robins
David R. Sullivan
Robert F. Sylvia
Howard E. Walker (Not admitted in MA)
Richard D. Wayne

ASSOCIATES

Neil L. Brodsky
Jane E. Cohen
Kelley Jordan-Price
Joseph D. Whelan (Not admitted in MA)

OF COUNSEL

Willard Krasnow
Bentley Tobin
Joachim A. Weissfeld (Not admitted in MA)

For Complete List of Firm Personnel, See General Section

For full biographical listings, see the Martindale-Hubbell Law Directory

*SPRINGFIELD,** Hampden Co.

MCCORMICK, PAULDING & HUBER, LLP (AV Ⓣ)

SIS Center, 1441 Main Street, 01103
Telephone: 413-736-5401
Fax: 413-733-4543
Email: MPH@IP-Lawyers.com *URL:* http://www.IP-Lawyers.com
Hartford, Connecticut Office: CityPlace II, 185 Asylum Street.
Telephone: 860-549-5290.
Fax: 860-527-0464.

MEMBERS OF FIRM

John C. Linderman
J. Kevin Grogan
Arthur F. Dionne

ASSOCIATES

Susan C. Oygard (Not admitted in MA)
Nicholas J. Tuccillo (Not admitted in MA)
Stephen P. Scuderi
Marylou J. Lavoié (Not admitted in MA)

(See Next Column)

McCormick, Paulding & Huber LLP, *Springfield—Continued*

OF COUNSEL

John J. Dempsey

For full biographical listings, see the Martindale-Hubbell Law Directory

MICHIGAN

*ANN ARBOR,** Washtenaw Co.

Bodman, Longley & Dahling LLP (AV)

110 Miller, Suite 300, 48104
Telephone: 734-761-3780
Fax: 734-930-2494
Email: info@bodmanlongley.com *URL:* http://www.bodmanlongley.com
Detroit, Michigan Office: 34th Floor, 100 Renaissance Center.
Telephone: 313-259-7777.
Fax: 313-393-7579.
Troy, Michigan Office: Suite 2020, 755 West Big Beaver Road.
Telephone: 248-362-2110.
Fax: 248-244-0780.
Northern Michigan Office: 229 Court Street, P.O. Box 405, Cheboygan.
Telephone: 231-627-4351.
Fax: 231-627-2802.

RESIDENT PARTNERS

Susan M. Kornfield
Stephen K. Postema

RESIDENT ASSOCIATES

Timothy R. Damschroder
Courtland W. Anderson
Alan N. Harris

For full biographical listings, see the Martindale-Hubbell Law Directory

Butzel Long, A Professional Corporation (AV)

Suite 300, 350 South Main Street, 48104-2131
Telephone: 313-995-3110
Telecopier: 313-995-1777
Email: melnick@butzel.com *URL:* http://www.butzel.com
Detroit, Michigan Office: Suite 900, 150 West Jefferson.
Telephone: 313-225-7000.
Telecopier: 313-225-7080.
Birmingham, Michigan Office: Suite 200, 32270 Telegraph Road.
Telephone: 810-258-1616.
Telecopier: 810-258-1439.
Okemos, Michigan Office: Suite 300, 2127 University Park Drive.
Telephone: 517-372-6622.
Telecopier: 372-6672.
Grosse Pointe Farms, Michigan Office: Suite 260, 21 Kercheval.
Telephone: 313-886-5446.
Telecopier: 313-886-2114.
Boca Raton, Florida Office: Suite 411, 1200 North Federal Highway.
Telephone: 561-368-2151.
Telecopier: 561-368-4668.
Palm Beach Gardens, Florida Office: Suite 227, 11382 Prosperity Farms Road.
Telephone: 561-625-4442.
Telecopier: 561-625-6901.
Naples, Florida Office: Suite 705, 801 Laurel Oak Drive.
Telephone: 941-597-4500.
Telecopier: 941-597-5623.

James E. Stewart (Resident)
Leonard M. Niehoff (Resident)
J. Michael Huget (Resident)

John C. Biattner (Resident)

For full biographical listings, see the Martindale-Hubbell Law Directory

Harness, Dickey & Pierce, P.L.C. (AV)

Suite 555, 301 East Liberty Street, 48104
Telephone: 734-662-8000
Telex: 287637 HARNES UR
Telefacsimile: 734-662-7813
Email: info@hdp.com *URL:* http://www.hdp.com
Troy, Michigan Office: 5445 Corporate Drive, Suite 400.
Telephone: 248-641-1600. Telefacsimile (All Groups): 248-641-0270.
Washington, D.C. Office: 888 Sixteenth Street, N.W.
Telephone: 202-835-7480.

MEMBERS OF FIRM

James E. Stephenson (Resident)
Steven L. Oberholtzer (Resident)
Eric J. Sosenko (Resident)

(See Next Column)

RESIDENT ASSOCIATES

Scott M. Confer
Christopher DeVries
Jeffrey M. Cox (Resident at Ann Arbor Office)

Representative Clients: Chrysler Corp.; The Black and Decker Manufacturing Co.; Thermos Co.; Monroe Auto Equipment Co.; La-Z-Boy Chair Co.; Hughes Aircraft; Budd Co.; Dow Chemical Co.; Procter & Gamble; Kmart Properties; General Motors Corporation.

For full biographical listings, see the Martindale-Hubbell Law Directory

BLOOMFIELD HILLS, Oakland Co.

Lyon & Artz PLC (AV)

3883 Telegraph Road, Suite 207, 48302-1476
Telephone: 248-645-5200
Facsimile: 248-645-1016
Email: lyonpc@lyonpc.com *URL:* http://www.lyonpc.com
Southfield, Michigan Office: 28333 Telegraph Road, 48034.
Telephone: 248-223-9500.
Fax: 248-223-9522.

Lyman R. Lyon
Alexander P. Brackett (Not admitted in MI)
Laurence C. Begin

LEGAL SUPPORT PERSONNEL

Kurt Vanvoorheis

For full biographical listings, see the Martindale-Hubbell Law Directory

Rader, Fishman & Grauer PLLC (AV)

1533 North Woodward, Suite 140, 48304
Telephone: 248-594-0600
Fax: 248-594-0610
Email: info@raderfishman.com *URL:* http://www.intelprop.com
Grand Rapids, Michigan Office: Rader, Fishman, Grauer & McGarry PLLC, 171 Monroe Avenue, N.W., Suite 600, 49503.
Telephone: 616-742-3500.
Fax: 616-742-1010.
Washington D.C. Office: 1233 20th Street, Suite 501, 20036.
Telephone: 202-955-3750.
Fax: 202-955-3751.
Denver, Colorado Office: 7887 East Belleview Avenue, 80111.
Telephone: 303-228-1658.
Fax: 303-228-1659.

Ralph Terrance Rader
Michael D. Fishman
Richard D. Grauer
Joseph V. Coppola, Sr.
Michael B. Stewart
Eric M. Dobrusin
Glenn E. Forbis
James F. Kamp
Stefan V. Chmielewski
Kevin D. Rutherford
Annette R. Carrothers
Matthew J. Russo (Resident, Denver Office)
Kristin L. Murphy
William Cosnowski, Jr.
Anna M. Shih
Michelle L. Visser
John P. Guenther

OF COUNSEL

Andrew S. Walker
Jill N. Johnston

PATENT AGENT

Alexander D. Rabinovich

For full biographical listings, see the Martindale-Hubbell Law Directory

*DETROIT,** Wayne Co.

Bodman, Longley & Dahling LLP (AV)

34th Floor 100 Renaissance Center, 48243
Telephone: 313-259-7777
Fax: 313-393-7579
Email: info@bodmanlongley.com *URL:* http://www.bodmanlongley.com
Troy, Michigan Office: Suite 2020, 755 West Big Beaver Road.
Telephone: 248-362-2110.
Fax: 248-244-0780.
Ann Arbor, Michigan Office: 110 Miller, Suite 300.
Telephone: 734-761-3780.
Fax: 734-930-2494.
Northern Michigan Office: 229 Court Street, P.O. Box 405, Cheboygan.
Telephone: 231-627-4351.
Fax: 231-627-2802.

MEMBERS OF FIRM

Randolph S. Perry
James J. Walsh
David G. Chardavoyne
Susan M. Kornfield (Ann Arbor Office)
Dennis J. Levasseur
Jeffrey G. Raphelson

ASSOCIATES

Timothy R. Damschroder (Ann Arbor Office)
Courtland W. Anderson (Ann Arbor Office)
Alan N. Harris (Ann Arbor Office)

For Representative Clients list, See General Section

For Complete List of Firm Personnel, See General Section

For full biographical listings, see the Martindale-Hubbell Law Directory

Detroit—Continued

BUTZEL LONG, A PROFESSIONAL CORPORATION (AV)

Suite 900, 150 West Jefferson, 48226
Telephone: 313-225-7000
Telecopier: 313-225-7080
Email: melnick@butzel.com *URL:* http://www.butzel.com
Birmingham, Michigan Office: Suite 200, 32270 Telegraph Road.
Telephone: 810-258-1616.
Telecopier: 810-258-1439.
Okemos, Michigan Office: Suite 300, 2127 University Park Drive.
Telephone: 517-372-6622.
Telecopier: 517-372-6672.
Ann Arbor, Michigan Office: Suite 300, 350 South Main Street.
Telephone: 313-995-3110.
Telecopier: 313-995-1777.
Grosse Pointe Farms, Michigan Office: Suite 260, 21 Kercheval.
Telephone: 313-886-5446.
Telecopier: 313-886-2114.
Boca Raton, Florida Office: Suite 411, 1200 North Federal Highway.
Telephone: 561-368-2151.
Telecopier: 561-368-4668.
Palm Beach Gardens, Florida Office: Suite 227, 11382 Prosperity Farms Road.
Telephone: 561-625-4442.
Telecopier: 561-625-6901.
Naples, Florida Office: Suite 705, 801 Laurel Oak Drive.
Telephone: 941-597-4500.
Telecopier: 941-597-5623.

Richard E. Rassel
Philip J. Kessler
James E. Stewart (Ann Arbor)
Keefe A. Brooks
Leonard M. Niehoff (Ann Arbor)
J. Michael Huget (Ann Arbor)

Representative Clients: Bridgestone/Firestone, Inc.; Detroit Diesel Corp.; The Detroit News, Inc.; Kelly Services; Merrill Lynch & Co., Inc.; Stroh Companies; Takata Corp.; TRW Automotive; The University of Michigan.

For full biographical listings, see the Martindale-Hubbell Law Directory

MILLER, CANFIELD, PADDOCK AND STONE, P.L.C. (AV)

A Professional Limited Liability Company
Founded in 1852 by Sidney Davy Miller
150 West Jefferson, Suite 2500, 48226-4415
Telephone: 313-963-6420
Fax: 313-496-7500
Cable Address: "Stem Detroit"
URL: http://www.millercanfield.com
Ann Arbor, Michigan Office: 101 North Main Street, 7th Floor, 48104-1400.
Telephone: 734-663-2445.
Fax: 734-747-7147.
Troy, Michigan Office: 840 West Long Lake Road, Suite 200, 48098.
Telephone: 248-879-2000.
Fax: 248-879-2001.
Grand Rapids, Michigan Office: 99 Monroe, N.W., Suite 1200, 49503-2639.
Telephone: 616-454-8656.
Fax: 616-776-6322.
Howell, Michigan Office: 121 South Barnard Street, Suite 4, 48843-2305.
Telephone: 517-546-7600.
Telecopier: 517-546-6974.
Kalamazoo, Michigan Office: 444 West Michigan Avenue, 49007-3752.
Telephone: 616-381-7030.
Fax: 616-382-0244.
Lansing, Michigan Office: One Michigan Avenue, Suite 900, 48933-1609.
Telephone: 517-487-2070.
Fax: 517-374-6304.
Monroe, Michigan Office: 214 East Elm Avenue, Suite 100, 48162-2682.
Telephone: 734-243-2000.
Fax: 734-243-0901.
Washington, D.C. Office: 1900 K Street, N.W., Suite 1150. 20006.
Telephone: 202-429-5575; 785-0600.
Fax: 202-331-1118; 785-1234.
Pensacola, Florida Office: 25 West Cedar, 32501.
Telephone: 850-469-1088.
Fax: 850-432-0677.
New York, New York Office: 1450 Broadway, 41st Floor, 10018.
Telephone: 212-704-4400.
Fax: 212-704-4410.
Gdynia, Poland Office: UL. Slaska 21, 81-319.
Telephone: 011-485-831-2808.
Fax: 011-48-58-628 6411.
Warsaw, Poland Office: UL. Nowogrodzkall, 5th Floor, 00-513.
Telephone: 011-4822 529 0200.
Fax: 011-4822 529 0201.
Katowice, Poland Office: UL. Francuska 35/37, 40-027.
Telephone: 011 (48-32) 757-2414.
Fax: 011 (48-32) 757-2483.

(See Next Column)

PRINCIPALS OF FIRM

Mark E. Putney (Grand Rapids Office)
Marjory G. Basile
Richard A. Gaffin (Grand Rapids Office)

Representative Firm Clients: Chrysler Corporation; Comerica, Incorporated; City of Detroit, Michigan; Detroit Tigers, Inc.; First of Michigan; Ford Motor Company; Ford Motor Credit Company; Great Lakes Bancorp; Henry Ford Hospital; INVETECH Company.

For Complete List of Firm Personnel, See General Section

For full biographical listings, see the Martindale-Hubbell Law Directory

TIMMIS & INMAN L.L.P. (AV)

300 Talon Centre, 48207
Telephone: 313-396-4200
Facsimile: 313-396-4228
Email: info@timmis-inman.com *URL:* http://www.timmis-inman.com

Michael T. Timmis
Robert E. Graziani
George A. Peck
Henry J. Brennan, III
Mark W. Peyser
Richard M. Miettinen
Bradley J. Knickerbocker
George M. Malis

Michael F. Wais
Erich J. D'Andrea
Shannon M. Nichols
Anthony J. Long
Alex N. Saleh

OF COUNSEL

William B. Fitzgerald

Representative Clients: Detroit Mortgage & Realty; DMR Fiancial Services, Inc.; J. Levin Sons Co.; Green Tree Financial Servicing Corp.; Hematology-Oncology Associates East, PC; Lakeshore Ear, Nose & Throat Center, PC; Micromanagement Systems, Inc.; Phoenix Crystal Corp.; Talon Surfaces LLC; Talon Automated Equipment Company.

For Complete List of Firm Personnel, See General Section

For full biographical listings, see the Martindale-Hubbell Law Directory

*GRAND RAPIDS,** Kent Co.

MILLER, CANFIELD, PADDOCK AND STONE, P.L.C. (AV)

A Professional Limited Liability Company
Founded in 1852 by Sidney Davy Miller
99 Monroe, N.W. Suite 1200, 49503-2639
Telephone: 616-454-8656
Fax: 616-776-6322
URL: http://www.millercanfield.com
Detroit, Michigan Office: 150 West Jefferson, Suite 2500, 48226-4415.
Telephone: 313-963-6420.
Fax: 313-496-7500.
Cable Address: "Stem Detroit."
Ann Arbor, Michigan Office: 101 North Main Street, 7th Floor, 48104-1400.
Telephone: 734-663-2445.
Fax: 734-747-7147.
Troy, Michigan Office: 840 West Long Lake Road, Suite 200, 48098.
Telephone: 248-879-2000.
Fax: 248-879-2001.
Howell, Michigan Office: 121 South Barnard Street, Suite 4, 48843-2305.
Telephone: 517-546-7600.
Telecopier: 517-546-6974.
Kalamazoo, Michigan Office: 444 West Michigan Avenue, 49007-3752.
Telephone: 616-381-7030.
Fax: 616-382-0244.
Lansing, Michigan Office: One Michigan Avenue, Suite 900, 48933-1609.
Telephone: 517-487-2070.
Fax: 517-374-6304.
Monroe, Michigan Office: 214 East Elm Avenue, Suite 100, 48162-2682.
Telephone: 734-243-2000.
Fax: 734-243-0901.
Washington, D.C. Office: 1900 K Street, N.W., Suite 1150. 20006.
Telephone: 202-429-5575; 785-0600.
Fax: 202-331-1118; 785-1234.
Pensacola, Florida Office: 25 West Cedar, 32501.
Telephone: 850-469-1088.
Fax: 850-432-0677.
New York, New York Office: 1450 Broadway, 41st Floor, 10018.
Telephone: 212-704-4400.
Fax: 212-704-4410.
Gdynia, Poland Office: UL. Slaska 21, 81-319.
Telephone: 011-485-831-2808.
Fax: 011-48-58-628 6411.
Warsaw, Poland Office: UL. Nowogrodzkall, 5th Floor, 00-513.
Telephone: 011-4822 529 0200.
Fax: 011-4822 529 0201.
Katowice, Poland Office: UL. Francuska 35/37, 40-027.
Telephone: 011 (48-32) 757-2414.
Fax: 011 (48-32) 757-2483.

(See Next Column)

MILLER, CANFIELD, PADDOCK AND STONE P.L.C., *Grand Rapids—Continued*

PRINCIPALS

Richard A. Gaffin

Representative Firm Clients: Chrysler Corporation; Comerica, Incorporated; City of Detroit, Michigan; Detroit Tigers, Inc.; First of Michigan; Ford Motor Company; Ford Motor Credit Company; Great Lakes Bancorp; Henry Ford Hospital; INVETECH Company.

For Complete List of Firm Personnel, See General Section

For full biographical listings, see the Martindale-Hubbell Law Directory

RADER, FISHMAN, GRAUER & MCGARRY PLLC (AV)

171 Monroe Avenue, N.W., Suite 600, 49503
Telephone: 616-742-3500
Fax: 616-742-1010
Email: info@raderfishman.com *URL:* http://www.intelprop.com
Washington D.C. Office: Rader, Fishman & Grauer PLLC, 1233 20th Street, Suite 501, 20036.
Telephone: 202-955-3750.
Fax: 202-955-3751.
Bloomfield Hills, Michigan Office: Rader, Fishman & Grauer PLLC, 1533 North Woodward, Suite 140, 48304.
Telephone: 248-594-0600.
Fax: 248-594-0610.
Denver, Colorado Office: Rader, Fishman & Grauer PLLC, 7887 East Belleview Avenue, 80111.
Telephone: 303-228-1658.
Fax: 303-228-1659.

John E. McGarry
H. Lawrence Smith
Joel E. Bair
G. Thomas Williams, III
Mark A. Davis
Michael F. Kelly
Donald J. Wallace

For full biographical listings, see the Martindale-Hubbell Law Directory

OKEMOS, Ingham Co.

MCLEOD & MOYNE, P.C. (AV)

2190 Commons Parkway, 48864
Telephone: 517-347-4100
Telecopier: 517-347-4103
Email: ianmcleodpc@voyager.net *URL:* http://www.lawyers.com/mandmlaw

Ian C. McLeod
Mary M. Moyne

Reference: Michigan National Bank, Lansing, Michigan.

For full biographical listings, see the Martindale-Hubbell Law Directory

*SAGINAW,** Saginaw Co.

REISING, ETHINGTON, BARNES, KISSELLE, LEARMAN & MCCULLOCH, P.C. (AV)

5291 Colony Drive, North, 48603
Telephone: 517-799-5300
Telecopier: 517-792-8585
Email: postmaster@reising.com *URL:* http://www.reising.com
Troy, Michigan Office: Suite 400, 201 West Big Beaver Road. P.O. Box 4390.
Telephone: 248-689-3500.

John F. Learman
John K. McCulloch
Robert L. Stearns

Robert L. Farris

For full biographical listings, see the Martindale-Hubbell Law Directory

SOUTHFIELD, Oakland Co.

BROOKS & KUSHMAN, P.C. (AV)

1000 Town Center, Twenty Second Floor, 48075
Telephone: 248-358-4400

Ernie L. Brooks
James A. Kushman
David R. Syrowik
Mark A. Cantor
Ralph M. Burton
Robert C. J. Tuttle
Earl J. LaFontaine
Ronald M. Nabozny
Thomas A. Lewry
John E. Nemazi
Kevin J. Heinl
William G. Abbatt
Donald J. Harrington
Paul M. Schwartz
George R. Mosher
Frederick M. Ritchie
John M. Sheridan
Elizabeth F. Janda
Robert C. Brandenburg
A. Frank Duke
Timothy G. Newman
John M. Halan
Jeffrey M. Szuma
Maria Franek Angileri
James R. Ignatowski
Frank A. Angileri

(See Next Column)

William G. Conger
Sangeeta G. Shah
Christopher W. Quinn
Konstantine J. Diamond
David S. Bir
James N. Kallis
Hugo A. Delevie
Ralph Edwin Smith
Gigette Marie Bejin
Mark E. Stuenkel
Michael S. Brodbine
Seth E. Rodack
Pete N. Kiousis
Raymond J. Vivacqua
John J. Ignatowski
James Proscia
Ginta D. Kukainis

For full biographical listings, see the Martindale-Hubbell Law Directory

LYON & ARTZ PLC (AV)

28333 Telegraph Road, Suite 250, 48034
Telephone: 248-223-9500
Fax: 248-223-9522
Email: jsartz@tir.com *URL:* http://www.lyonpc.com
Bloomfield Hills, Michigan Office: 3883 Telegraph Road, Suite 207, 48302.
Telephone: 248-645-5200.
Fax: 248-645-1016.

John A. Artz
John S. Artz
Kevin G. Mierzwa
Robert P. Renke (Not admitted in MI)
Angela M. Brunetti
Franklin MacKenzie

For full biographical listings, see the Martindale-Hubbell Law Directory

TROY, Oakland Co.

HARNESS, DICKEY & PIERCE, P.L.C. (AV)

5445 Corporate Drive, Suite 400, 48098
Telephone: 248-641-1600
Cable Address: "PATENTS TROYMICHIGAN"
Telex: 287637 HARNES UR
Telefacsimile (All Groups): 248-641-0270
Email: info@hdp.com *URL:* http://www.hdp.com
Ann Arbor, Michigan Office: 301 East Liberty Street, Suite 555.
Telephone: 734-662-8000.
Telefacsimile: 734-662-7813.
Washington, D.C. Office: 888 Sixteenth Street, N.W.
Telephone: 202-835-7480.

MEMBERS OF FIRM

J. King Harness (1897-1977)
Arthur W. Dickey (1897-1964)
Hodgson S. Pierce (1896-1947)
Charles H. Blair
Joseph R. Papp
H. Keith Miller
James E. Stephenson (Resident at Ann Arbor Office)
Bernard J. Cantor
Christopher M. Brock
Richard L. Carlson
Ronald L. Hofer
Paul A. Keller
G. Gregory Schivley
Ronald W. Wangerow
Gregory A. Stobbs
Steven L. Oberholtzer (Resident at Ann Arbor Office)
Michael P. Brennan
Gordon K. Harris, Jr.
Stephen J. Foss
Gary L. Newtson
W. R. Duke Taylor (Also at Washington, D.C. Office)
Richard P. Vitek
Robert S. Nolan
Philip R. Warn
Philip E. Rettig
Mark D. Elchuk
Michael J. Schmidt
Lisabeth H. Coakley
Eric J. Sosenko (Resident at Ann Arbor Office)
Robert M. Siminski
Stephen T. Olson
Stanley M. Erjavac
Robert J. Lenihan, II
Douglas P. LaLone
David P. Utykanski
Thomas Traian Moga
Monte Lee Falcoff

ASSOCIATES

Michael R. Bascobert
John V. Biernacki
Anna M. Budde
Scott M. Confer (Resident at Ann Arbor Office)
Jeffrey M. Cox (Resident at Ann Arbor Office)
Christopher DeVries (Resident at Ann Arbor, Michigan Office)
Garrett C. Donley
Christopher A. Eusebi
Joseph M. Lafata
Timothy D. MacIntyre
Ryan W. Massey
David A. McClaughry
John A. Miller
George D. Moustakas
Douglas A. Mullen
George T. Schooff
Preston H. Smirman
Jeffrey L. Snyder
Joseph L. Stevenson
Bryant E. Wade
Donald G. Walker
Gregory A. Walters
Richard W. Warner
Michael D. Zalobsky

COUNSEL

Robert J. Wallace, Sr.
Charles R. Kiczek
Donald F. Scherer

Representative Clients: The Black and Decker Manufacturing Co.; DaimlerChrysler Corp.; Emerson Electric Co.; General Motors Corp.; Kmart Corp.; La-Z-Boy Incorporated; Matsushita Electric; Seiko Epson Co.; Standard Products Co.; Sun Microsystems Laboratories Inc.

For full biographical listings, see the Martindale-Hubbell Law Directory

Troy—Continued

REISING, ETHINGTON, BARNES, KISSELLE, LEARMAN & McCULLOCH, P.C. (AV)

Suite 400, 201 West Big Beaver, P.O. Box 4390, 48099
Telephone: 248-689-3500
Fax: 248-689-4071
Email: postmaster@reising.com *URL:* http://www.reising.com
Saginaw, Michigan Office: 5291 Colony Drive North, Saginaw, Michigan, 48603.
Telephone: 517-799-5300.
FAX: 517-792-8585.
Elk Rapids, Michigan Office: 212 River Street, P.O. Box 834, 49629.
Telephone: 616-264-9948.
FAX: 616-264-9949.

Richard P. Barnard (1924-1993)
Stuart C. Barnes (1885-1968)
John M. Kisselle (1894-1980)
Paul J. Reising (1923-1993)
Robert C. Collins
Paul J. Ethington
John C. Evans
Francis J. Fodale
William H. Francis
William H. Griffith
Richard W. Hoffmann
John F. Learman (Resident, Saginaw, Michigan Office)
Jeanne-Marie Marshall (Resident, Elk Rapids Office)
John K. McCulloch (Resident Saginaw, Michigan Office)
Steven L. Permut
William J. Schramm
Robert L. Stearns (Resident Saginaw, Michigan Office)
James D. Stevens
Andrew M. Grove
Eric T. Jones
William J. Waugaman

Edward J. Biskup
Robert L. Farris (Resident, Saginaw, Michigan Office)
John P. Moran
Matthew J. Schmidt
Charles R. White

Reference: Michigan National Bank of Detroit.

For full biographical listings, see the Martindale-Hubbell Law Directory

INTERNATIONAL BUSINESS LAW

ALABAMA

*BIRMINGHAM,** Jefferson Co.

BRADLEY ARANT ROSE & WHITE LLP (AV)

2001 Park Place, Suite 1400, P.O. Box 830709, 35283-0709
Telephone: 205-521-8000
Facsimile: 205-521-8800
Facsimile (SouthTrust Tower Office): 205-521-8500
URL: http://www.barw.com
Huntsville, Alabama Office: 200 Clinton Avenue West, Suite 900, 35801.
Telephone: 205-517-5100.
Facsimile: 205-533-5069.
Washington, D.C. Office: 801 Pennsylvania Avenue, NW, Suite 230, 20004.
Telephone: 202-347-8893.
Facsimile: 202-347-1684.

MEMBERS OF FIRM

James Patrick Alexander
Thomas Neely Carruthers Jr.
G. Edward Cassady III
A. H. Gaede Jr.
T. Barr Linton (Not admitted in AL)
Virginia Calvert Patterson
James E. Rotch

ASSOCIATES

Helena F. Barkworth
Donna M. Crowe
Douglas E. Eckert
K. Wood Herren

For Complete List of Firm Personnel, See General Section

For full biographical listings, see the Martindale-Hubbell Law Directory

ARIZONA

*PHOENIX,** Maricopa Co.

FENNEMORE CRAIG, A PROFESSIONAL CORPORATION (AV)

3003 North Central Avenue, Suite 2600, 85012-2913
Telephone: 602-916-5000
Fax: 602-916-5999
Tucson, Arizona Office: One South Church Avenue, Suite 1000, 85701-1620.
Telephone: 520-879-6800.
Fax: 520-879-6899.

Robert P. Robinson
John D. Everroad
Timothy J. Burke
Charles M. King
Michael V. Mulchay
Gregg Hanks
J. Barry Shelley

Vera E. Munoz
Sal J. Rivera

LEGAL SUPPORT PERSONNEL

LEGAL ASSISTANTS

Donna M. Horwitz

For Complete List of Firm Personnel, See General Section

For full biographical listings, see the Martindale-Hubbell Law Directory

MEYER, HENDRICKS & BIVENS, P.A. (AV)

3003 North Central Avenue Suite 1200, 85012-2915
Telephone: 602-604-2200
Facsimile: (24 Hrs.) 602-263-5333
Mailing Address: P.O. Box 2199, 85001-2199

Robert K. Rogers
Scott M. Theobald

Randall Lindsey

Reference: Northern Trust Bank of Arizona.

For full biographical listings, see the Martindale-Hubbell Law Directory

QUARLES & BRADY LLP (AV)

One Camelback Building, One East Camelback Road, Suite 400, 85012-1649
Telephone: 602-230-5500
Fax: 602-230-5598
URL: http://www.quarles.com
Milwaukee, Wisconsin Office: 411 East Wisconsin Avenue.
Telephone: 414-277-5000.
Fax: 414-271-3552.

(See Next Column)

Madison, Wisconsin Office: First Wisconsin Plaza, One South Pinckney Street, P.O. Box 2113.
Telephone: 608-251-5000.
Fax: 608-251-9166.
West Palm Beach, Florida Office: 222 Lakeview Avenue, 4th Floor.
Telephone: 407-653-5000.
Fax: 407-653-5333.
Naples, Florida Office: Barnett Center, 4501 Tamiami Trail North, Suite 300.
Telephone: 813-262-5959.
Fax: 813-434-4999.
Chicago, Illinois Office: Quarles & Brady LLC, Citicorp Center, 500 West Madison Street, Suite 3700.
Telephone: 312-715-5000.
Fax: 312-715-5155.

MEMBERS OF THE FIRM

P. Robert Moya
David G. Beauchamp

For full biographical listings, see the Martindale-Hubbell Law Directory

ARKANSAS

*LITTLE ROCK,** Pulaski Co.

ROSE LAW FIRM, A PROFESSIONAL ASSOCIATION (AV)

120 East Fourth Street, 72201
Telephone: 501-375-9131
Telecopy: 501-375-1309

Herbert C. Rule, III
W. Wilson Jones
Allen W. Bird, II
William H. Kennedy, III
Amy Lee Stewart
Kathryn Bennett Perkins
Michael N. Shannon

Counsel for: Aluminum Company of America; Bridgestone/Firestone, Inc.; The Equitable Life Assurance Society of The United States; General Motors Corp.; The Prudential Insurance Company of America; Stephens Group Inc.; TCBY Enterprises, Inc.; Tyson Foods, Inc.

For Complete List of Firm Personnel, See General Section

For full biographical listings, see the Martindale-Hubbell Law Directory

CALIFORNIA

CLAREMONT, Los Angeles Co.

JOHN W. TULAC (AV)

401 Harvard Avenue, 91711
Telephone: 909-445-1100
Fax: 909-445-1104
Email: jwtulac@ix.netcom.com *URL:* http://www.lawyers.com/jwt
Reference: Marine National Bank, Irvine.

For full biographical listings, see the Martindale-Hubbell Law Directory

COSTA MESA, Orange Co.

FELDHAKE, AUGUST & ROQUEMORE (AV)

Plaza Tower, Suite 1730, 600 Anton Boulevard, 92626-7124
Telephone: 714-438-3885
Fax: 714-438-3888
Email: farlaw@hqonline.com

Robert J. Feldhake
Kenneth S. August
Lisa A. Roquemore
Joshua M. Wolff

ASSOCIATES

Dimitri P. Gross
Supriya Kakkar
Katherine A. Slayton

OF COUNSEL

Arthur J. Swerdloff
Arthur M. Wilcox, Jr.

For full biographical listings, see the Martindale-Hubbell Law Directory

LONG BEACH, Los Angeles Co.

FLYNN, DELICH & WISE (AV)

One World Trade Center, Suite 1800, 90831-1800
Telephone: 562-435-2626
Fax: 562-437-7555
Email: NicholasP@FDW-LAW.COM
San Francisco, California Office: One California Street, Suite 350.
Telephone: 415-693-5566.
Fax: 415-693-0410. Email: SAMD@FDW-LAW.COM

Erich P. Wise
Nicholas S. Politis

(See Next Column)

FLYNN, DELICH & WISE, *Long Beach—Continued*

Sook H. Lee

LEGAL SUPPORT PERSONNEL

Denise C. Orr (Legal Assistant)

Representative Clients: American Hawaii Cruises; American President Lines; Through Transport Mutual Insurance Association, Ltd.; The Britannia Steam Ship Insurance Association Limited; The Steamship Mutual Underwriting Association (Bermuda) Ltd.; General Steamship Corp., Ltd.; Commodore Cruise Line, Ltd.; Interocean Steamship Corporation; Sea-Land Service, Inc.; Hatteras Yachts.

For full biographical listings, see the Martindale-Hubbell Law Directory

RUSSELL & MIRKOVICH (AV)

One World Trade Center, Suite 1450, 90831-1450
Telephone: 562-436-9911
FAX: 562-436-1897
Email: counsel@russell-mirkovich.com

Carlton E. Russell
Joseph N. Mirkovich

ASSOCIATE

Margaret E. Morrow
Steven Y. Otera

For full biographical listings, see the Martindale-Hubbell Law Directory

WOOLLEY RUSSELL & JOHNSON (AV)

444 West Ocean Boulevard, Suite 1700, 90802
Telephone: 562-495-6000
Telecopier: 562-435-1359
Email: mail@transportlawyers.com *URL:* http://www.transportlawyers.com
Port Hueneme, California Office: 105 East Port Hueneme Road, 93041.
Telephone: 562-495-6000.
Fax: 562-435-1359.

MEMBERS OF FIRM

David E. R. Woolley
Thomas A. Russell
Philip L. Johnson

ASSOCIATE

Thomas G. Walsh

LEGAL SUPPORT PERSONNEL

PARALEGAL

Dawn C. Breaux

For full biographical listings, see the Martindale-Hubbell Law Directory

*LOS ANGELES,** Los Angeles Co.

ALVARADO, SMITH & SANCHEZ, A PROFESSIONAL CORPORATION (AV)

611 West Sixth Street, Suite 2650, 90017
Telephone: 213-229-2400
Facsimile: 213-229-2499
URL: http://www.alvarado-smith.com
Irvine, California Office: 4 Park Plaza, Suite 1200, 92614.
Telephone: 949-955-6800.
Fax: 949-955-6899.

Raymond G. Alvarado
Ruben A. Smith
Maurice Sanchez
John M. Sorich
Raúl F. Salinas
Frances Q. Jett
Theresa Eileen Antonucci
Diane C. Barrio
Rosario M. Tobias

OF COUNSEL

Martin N. Burton

For full biographical listings, see the Martindale-Hubbell Law Directory

LAW OFFICES OF DAVID B. BLOOM A PROFESSIONAL CORPORATION (AV)

3325 Wilshire Boulevard, Ninth Floor, 90010
Telephone: 323-938-5248; 384-4088
Telecopier: 213-385-2009

David B. Bloom

Stephen S. Monroe (A Professional Corporation)
Raphael A. Rosemblat
James E. Adler
Roy A. Levun
Jonathan Udell
Susan Carole Jay
Edward Idell
Sandra Kamenir
Steven Wayne Lazarus
Andrew Edward Briseno
Shelley M. Gould
Ted L. Travis

For full biographical listings, see the Martindale-Hubbell Law Directory

BRAND FARRAR & BUXBAUM LLP (AV)

515 South Flower Street, Suite 3500, 90071-2201
Telephone: 213-228-0288
Fax: 213-426-6222
Email: bfb-la@brandfarrar.com
Beijing (Peking), China Office: Suite 2518, China World Trade Centre, 1 Jian Guo Men Wai Avenue, Beijing, China.
Telephone: 86-10-6505-2288 Ext. 2523/2518.
Fax: 86-10-6505-2638. Email: bjbfbbj@public3.bta.net.cn
Chengdu, Sichuan, China Office: Suite 11A, Sichuan International Mansion, No. 1 Zhong Xi Shun Cheng Street, Chengdu, China.
Telephone: 86-28-652-1316.
Fax: 86-28-652-0547. Email: cdbfbcd@mail.sc.cninfo.net.
Chongqing, China Office: Suite 1510, Metropolitan Tower, 68 Zourong Lu, Chongqing, China.
Telephone: 86-23-6382-8381.
Fax: 86-23-6382-8373. Email: cqbfbcq@public.cta.cq.cn.
Guangzhou (Canton), China Office: Suite 1305, Main Tower, GITIC Plaza Hotel, 339 Huanshi Dong Road, Guangzhou, China.
Telephone: 86-20-8331-1888, Ext. 71305.
Fax: 86-20-8331-2671. Email: gzbfbgz@public.guangzhou.gd.cn.
Hong Kong, China Office: Brand Farrar Buxbaum LLP, 5/F., Landmark East, 12 Ice House Street, Central, Hong Kong, China.
Telephone: 852-2523-7001.
Fax: 852-2845-0947. Email: hkbfbhk@hk.super.net.
Los Angeles, California Office: Brand Farrar & Buxbaum LLP, Suite 3500, 515 South Flower Street, Los Angeles, California, 90071-2201.
Telephone: 213-228-0288.
Fax: 213-426-6222. Email: bfb-la@brandfarrar.com.
New York, New York Office: 275 Madison Avenue, 37th Floor, New York, New York, 10097.
Telephone: 212-286-0038.
Fax: 212-573-9077. Email: martineh@aol.com
Shanghai, China Office: Brand Farrar Buxbaum LLP, Suites 2611-12, Central Plaza, 227 Huangpi Bei Lu, Shanghai, China.
Telephone: 86-21-6375-8918.
Fax: 86-21-6375-8922. Email: shbfbsh@public2.sta.net.cn
Shenzhen, China Office: Suite 2103A, Shenzhen Development Center, Renmin Nan Lu, Shenzhen, China.
Telephone: 86-755-229-8009.
Fax: 86-755-229-8011. Email: szbfbsz@public.szptt.net.cn.
Ulaanbaatar, Mongolia Office: Brand Farrar Buxbaum LLP, 4/F., Time Center, No. 50 Baga Toiruu, Ulaanbaatar, Mongolia.
Telephone: 976-1-31-0711.
Fax: 976-1-32-5102. Email: mgbfbmg@magicnet.mn.
Xiamen, China Office: Suite 1182 Jian Ye Building, 28 Hubin North Road, Xiamen, China.
Telephone: 86-592-506-3059.
Fax: 86-592-511-1044. Email: xmbfbxm@public.xm.fj.cn.
Associated Office, Mumbai, Bombay, India: Shah & Sanghavi, Advocates, Solicitors & Notary, 114-A Mittal Court, Nariman Point, Mumbai 400 021 India.
Telephone: 91-22-285-5755/56 or 91-22-285-3592/93.
Fax: 91-22-284-5040.

PRINCIPALS

Michael A. Brand
David C. Buxbaum (China Offices)
Kenneth Y. Choy (Hong Kong Office)
Robert W. Dziubla
David W. Farrar
Amy E. Freilich
Margaret G. Graf
John Masao Iino
Charles K. Kolstad
Edward H. Martin (New York Office)
Gregory D. Trimarche
Li Zhuogen (China Offices)

OTHER ATTORNEYS RESIDENT IN LOS ANGELES OFFICE

Sherry L. Geyer
Joan M. Marquardt
James H. Service
Jeffrey S. Allen
Julia Sylva
Brian J. Kim
Lisa Teng

OTHER ATTORNEYS RESIDENT IN BEIJING OFFICE

Hao Xiaodong
Bin Zhao
Luo Rongping
Zhang Chunbo

OTHER ATTORNEYS RESIDENT IN CHENGDU, SICHUAN OFFICE

Zeng Xiangyu
Wu Wen

OTHER ATTORNEY RESIDENT IN CHONGQING OFFICE

Du Fei

OTHER ATTORNEYS RESIDENT IN GUANGZHOU OFFICE

Zou Wenyan (Not admitted in United States)
Feng Ruiding
Jia Guangxi

OTHER ATTORNEYS RESIDENT IN HONG KONG OFFICE

Shane F. Weir
Cheonghar Wong
N.T.S. Kularatne
Simon Woo
David William Gunson
Arthur Burton Crook
Simon K.C. Lee
Cheng Yuen Yi
Lo Wing Cheong
Nicholas C. McGrenra
Eva Y.N. Kwok

OTHER ATTORNEYS RESIDENT IN NEW YORK OFFICE

Vincent I. S. Hsieh (Of Counsel)
Jeffrey Schall
Jonathan Chun Wang

(See Next Column)

BRAND FARRAR & BUXBAUM LLP—*Continued*

OTHER ATTORNEYS RESIDENT IN SHANGHAI OFFICE

Lin Yong | Tang Ying
Wu Hong Liang | Zhang Guoyao
Qi Zhenwen

OTHER ATTORNEYS RESIDENT IN SHENZHEN OFFICE

Zhong Wenya | Zhang He

OTHER ATTORNEYS RESIDENT IN ULAANBAATAR OFFICE

Byambaa Bayarmaa | Ajiv Enhktuya

OTHER ATTORNEY RESIDENT IN XIAMEN OFFICE

Deng Sheng

For full biographical listings, see the Martindale-Hubbell Law Directory

DAAR & NEWMAN, PROFESSIONAL CORPORATION (AV)

Suite 2500, 865 South Figueroa Street, 90017-2567
Telephone: 213-892-0999
FAX: 213-892-1066
Email: lawyers@daarnewman.com *URL:* http://www.daarnewman.com

David Daar | Jeffery J. Daar
Michael R. Newman | Marsha McLean-Utley
Michael J. White

OF COUNSEL

Rodney W. Loeb | Samuel T. Rees
William F. White, Jr. | Leo S. Rich

LEGAL SUPPORT PERSONNEL

Joe A. Morton | Frank E. Raab

Representative Clients: Allianz Insurance Co.; American Income Life Insurance Co.; American Life and Casualty Insurance Co.; Balboa Insurance Co.; California Casualty Insurance Co.; National Benefit Life Insurance Co.; Capital Life Insurance Co.; Charter National Life; Columbian Mutual Life; Connecticut Mutual Life Insurance Co.

For full biographical listings, see the Martindale-Hubbell Law Directory

PETER A. GELLES (AV)

1801 Century Park East Suite 1520, 90067
Telephone: 310-201-7900
Facsimile: 310-201-7925
Email: petergelles@msn.com

For full biographical listings, see the Martindale-Hubbell Law Directory

MATTHIAS & BERG LLP (AV)

1990 South Bundy Drive, Suite 790, 90025-5244
Telephone: 310-820-0083
Facsimile: 310-820-8313
Email: info@matthiasberg.com

MEMBERS OF FIRM

Michael R. Matthias | Jeffrey P. Berg

ASSOCIATES

Kenneth M. H. Hoff | Ari Lorin Markow

OF COUNSEL

Stuart R. Singer

Representative Clients: Am Tec, Inc.; Chatsworth Products, Inc.; Greater China Corp.; Mexalit, S.A.; National Quality Care, Inc.; Network Holdings International, Inc.; New Sea Escape Cruises, Inc.; Residential Resources, Inc.

For full biographical listings, see the Martindale-Hubbell Law Directory

O'MELVENY & MYERS LLP (AV)

400 South Hope Street, 90071-2899
Telephone: 213-430-6000
Facsimile: 213-430-6407
Cable: MOMS
Telex: 674122
Email: omminfo@omm.com *URL:* http://www.omm.com
Century City, CA Office: 1999 Avenue of the Stars, Los Angeles, 90067-6035.
Telex: 674097. Tel: 310-553-6700.
Fax: 310-246-6779.
Newport Beach, CA Office: 610 Newport Center Drive, 92660-6429.
Telex: 4722088. Tel: 949-760-9600.
Fax: 949-823-6994.
San Francisco, CA Office: Embarcadero Center West, 275 Battery Street, 94111-3305. Tel: 415-984-8700.
Fax: 415-984-8701.
New York, NY Office: Citicorp Center, 153 East 53rd Street, 10022-4611.
Telex: 129165. Tel: 212-326-2000.
Fax: 212-326-2061.
Washington, DC Office: 555 13th Street, N.W., 20004-1109.
Cable: MOMSWSH.
Telex: 89622. Tel: 202-383-5300.
Fax: 202-383-5414.
London Office: O'Melveny & Myers, 3 Finsbury Square, London, EC2A 1LA, England. Tel: 44-171-256-8451. Fax 44-171-638-8205.

(See Next Column)

Tokyo Office: Akasaka Twin Tower, East 14F, 2-17-23, Akasaka, Minato-ku, Tokyo 107-0052, Japan. Tel: 03-5562-2800.
Fax: 03-5575-3840.
Hong Kong Office: O'Melveny & Myers, Suite 1905, Tower Two, Lippo Centre, 89 Queensway, Central, Hong Kong. Tel: 852-2523-8266.
Fax: 852-2522-1760.
Shanghai Office: Kerry Centre, 20F, 1515 Nanjing Road West, Shanghai, 200040 People's Republic of China. Tel: 86-21-5298-5600.
Fax: 86-21-5298-5500.

PARTNER

Greyson Lee Bryan

For Complete List of Firm Personnel, See General Section

For full biographical listings, see the Martindale-Hubbell Law Directory

*MODESTO,** Stanislaus Co.

RICHARD DOUGLAS BREW A PROFESSIONAL LAW CORPORATION (AV)

Suite 350 / Judge Frank C. Damrell Building, 1601 I Street, 95354-1135
Telephone: 209-572-3157
Telefax: 209-572-4641
Email: rdbplc@interleg.com

Richard Douglas Brew

For full biographical listings, see the Martindale-Hubbell Law Directory

NEWPORT BEACH, Orange Co.

JEFFREY R. MATSEN & ASSOCIATES (AV)

5001 Birch Street, 92660
Telephone: 949-442-9191
Fax: 949-442-9199
Email: jmatsen@urjet.net *URL:* http://www.lawyers.com/jeffreyrmatsen

For full biographical listings, see the Martindale-Hubbell Law Directory

MYERS & FLEMING, LLP (AV)

20301 Acacia Street, Suite 150, 92660
Telephone: 949-752-2001
Facsimile: 949-553-1413
Email: myersfleming@ocba.net *URL:* http://www.lawyers.com/myersfleming

Frank B. Myers | Dawn D. Fleming

For full biographical listings, see the Martindale-Hubbell Law Directory

*SAN DIEGO,** San Diego Co.

NANCY FULLER-JACOBS & ASSOCIATES (AV)

11512 El Camino Real, Suite 200, 92130
Telephone: 619-259-4875
Fax: 619-259-4752
Email: nfjlaw@cts.com *URL:* http://www.lawyers.com/nfj&alaw

ASSOCIATES

Karine Faure | E. Franklin Haignere

For full biographical listings, see the Martindale-Hubbell Law Directory

HAIGHT, BROWN & BONESTEEL, L.L.P. (AV)

A Partnership including Professional Corporations
101 West Broadway, Suite 1000, 92101-3544
Telephone: 619-595-5583
Telecopier: 619-595-7873
URL: http://www.hbblaw.com
Santa Monica, California Office: 1620 26th Street, Suite 4000 North, P.O. Box 680.
Telephone: 310-449-6000.
Telecopier: 310-829-5117.
Telex: 705837.
Santa Ana, California Office: Suite 900, 5 Hutton Centre Drive.
Telephone: 714-754-1100.
Telecopier: 714-754-0826.
Riverside, California Office: California Tower, 3737 Main Street, Suite 800.
Telephone: 909-341-8300.
Fax: 909-341-8309.
San Francisco, California Office: 101 Bush Street, 27th Floor.
Telephone: 415-986-7700.
Fax: 415-986-6945.

RESIDENT MEMBER

George R. Gonzalez

For full biographical listings, see the Martindale-Hubbell Law Directory

LAW OFFICES OF CHARLES P. LEBEAU (AV)

Historic Hayward-Patterson Building, 1887, 2148 Broadway, 92102
Telephone: 858-456-1100
Fax: 858-455-5024
Email: lebeaulaw@worldnet.att.net *URL:* http://www.lebeaulaw.com

(See Next Column)

LAW OFFICES OF CHARLES P. LEBEAU, *San Diego—Continued*

LEGAL SUPPORT PERSONNEL

Rebecca Cisinsky (Paralegal/Secretary)
Jill Gisondo (Secretary)

For full biographical listings, see the Martindale-Hubbell Law Directory

LUCE, FORWARD, HAMILTON & SCRIPPS LLP (AV)

A Partnership including Professional Corporations
600 West Broadway, Suite 2600, 92101
Telephone: 619-236-1414
Fax: 619-232-8311
URL: http://www.luce.com
La Jolla, California Office: 4275 Executive Square, Suite 800, 92037.
Telephone: 858-455-6611.
Fax: 858-232-8311.
Los Angeles, California Office: 777 South Figueroa, Suite 3600, 90017.
Telephone: 213-892-4992.
Fax: 213-892-7731.
San Francisco, California Office: 121 Spear Street, Suite 200, 94105.
Telephone: 415-356-4600.
Fax: 415-356-4610.
New York, N.Y. Office: Citicorp Center, 153 East 53rd Street, 26th Floor, 10022.
Telephone: 212-754-1414.
Fax: 212-644-9727.
Chicago, Illinois Office: 180 North La Salle Street, Suite 3110, 60601.
Telephone: 312-641-0580.
Fax: 312-641-0380.

John W. Brooks
Craig R. Brown (Resident, New York, N.Y. Office)
Huhnsik Chung (Resident, New York, N.Y. Office)
Sean L. Collin
Peter K. Hahn
Phillip L. Jelsma
Kimball Ann Lane (Resident, New York, N.Y. Office)
John B. McNeece III

ASSOCIATES

Aurelia E. Flores
Jeanne M. Malitz
Lourdes M. Slater (Resident, New York, N.Y. Office)

For Complete List of Firm Personnel, See General Section

For full biographical listings, see the Martindale-Hubbell Law Directory

THE PAGE FIRM, A P.C. (AV)

401 B Street, Suite 2100, 92101-4244
Telephone: 619-231-1822
Fax: 619-231-1877
URL: http://www.lawyers.com/pagefirm

Richard W. Page

For full biographical listings, see the Martindale-Hubbell Law Directory

*SAN FRANCISCO,** San Francisco Co.

ERNEST BROWN & COMPANY A PROFESSIONAL CORPORATION (AV)

414 Jackson Street, Suite 401, 94111
Telephone: 415-249-0134
Fax: 415-249-0138
URL: http://www.ernestbrown.com
Email: starchris@aol.com *URL:* http://www.lawyers.com/ebrownlaw
San Diego, California Office: 4370 La Jolla Village Drive, Suite 400.
Telephone: 619-546-4368.
Fax: 619-546-9227.
Sacramento, California Office: 980 Ninth Street, 16th Floor.
Telephone: 916-449-9541.
Fax: 916-446-7104.

Ernest C. Brown

Robert C. Schneider (Resident, Phoenix, Arizona Office)
Clement K. Wong

For full biographical listings, see the Martindale-Hubbell Law Directory

LAW OFFICES OF KEVIN W. FINCK (AV)

Two Embarcadero Center, Suite 1670, 94111
Telephone: 415-296-9100
Facsimile: 415-394-6446
Email: kfinck@flash.net

OF COUNSEL

Marla Raucher Osborn

For full biographical listings, see the Martindale-Hubbell Law Directory

FLYNN, DELICH & WISE (AV)

One California Street, Suite 350, 94111
Telephone: 415-693-5566
Fax: 415-693-0410
Email: SamD@fdw-law.com
Long Beach, California Office: 1 World Trade Center, Suite 1800.
Telephone: 562-435-2626.
Fax: 562-437-7555. Email: NicholasP@FDW-LAW.COM.

John A. Flynn (1945-1997)
Sam D. Delich
James B. Nebel

OF COUNSEL

Pecos Bill Field

Faye Lee Peterson
Conte C. Cicala
Jeanine S. Tede

Representative Clients: American Hawaii Cruises; American President Lines; Through Transport Mutual Insurance Association, Ltd.; The Britannia Steam Ship Insurance Association Limited; The Steamship Mutual Underwriting Association (Bermuda) Ltd.; General Steamship Corp., Ltd.; Commodore Cruise Line, Ltd.; Interocean Steamship Corporation; Sea-Land Service, Inc.; Hatteras Yachts.

For full biographical listings, see the Martindale-Hubbell Law Directory

STIMMEL, STIMMEL & SMITH, A PROFESSIONAL CORPORATION (AV)

100 Bush Street, Suite 850, 94104
Telephone: 415-392-2018
Fax: 415-391-2124
Email: stimmelpc@stimmel-law.com *URL:* http://www.stimmel-law.com

Norman S. Stimmel (1914-1991)
Lee D. Stimmel
Andrine K. Smith

OF COUNSEL

Jeffrey S. Rosen
Joanne M. Reming
Susan B. Jordan
Darrick T. Chase

For full biographical listings, see the Martindale-Hubbell Law Directory

*VENTURA,** Ventura Co.

LASCHER & LASCHER, A PROFESSIONAL CORPORATION (AV)

605 Poli Street, P.O. Box 25540, 93002
Telephone: 805-648-3228
Fax: 805-643-7692
Email: mail@lascher.com *URL:* http://www.lascher.com

Edward L. Lascher (1928-1991)
Wendy Cole Lascher

Gabriele Mezger-Lashly
Denise Abundis Brogna

Reference: Bank of Ventura.

For full biographical listings, see the Martindale-Hubbell Law Directory

COLORADO

*COLORADO SPRINGS,** El Paso Co.

FLYNN MCKENNA WRIGHT & KARSH (AV)

limited liability company
Plaza of the Rockies 111 South Tejon, Suite 202, 80903-3300
Telephone: 719-578-8444
Fax: 719-578-8836

OF COUNSEL

James T. Flynn

MEMBERS OF FIRM

R. Tim McKenna
Bruce M. Wright
Randolph M. Karsh
Brian T. Murphy
Michael C. Potarf
Karl A. Berg, Jr.

Representative Clients: Barrers, Siqueiros y Torres Landa, S.C. (Mexico City).

For full biographical listings, see the Martindale-Hubbell Law Directory

*DENVER,** Denver Co.

ALFERS & CARVER, LLC (AV)

Equitable Building, 730 17th Street, Suite 340, 80202
Telephone: 303-592-7674
Fax: 303-592-7680
Email: ccarver@alfers-carver.com

Stephen D. Alfers
Craig R. Carver
Bruce C. Kirchhoff
Don H. Sherwood

(See Next Column)

ALFERS & CARVER LLC—*Continued*

ASSOCIATE
Michelle C. Carmody

For full biographical listings, see the Martindale-Hubbell Law Directory

HARRY L. ARKIN & ASSOCIATES, P.C. (AV)

Suite 2750 Lincoln Center, 1660 Lincoln Street, 80264
Telephone: 303-863-8400
Telefax: 303-832-4703
Email: harkin00@counsel.com
Email: hnikra@aol.com
London, England Office: Verulam Chambers, Peer House, 8-14 Verulam Street, WCIX 8LZ.
Telephone: 071 813-2400.
Fax: 071 405-3870.

Harry L. Arkin

Michael B. Levy

LEGAL SUPPORT PERSONNEL

Patricia A. Hanson
Karen R. Loveland

For full biographical listings, see the Martindale-Hubbell Law Directory

EDWARD O. BYRNE & ASSOCIATES P.C. (AV)

303 East 17th Avenue, Suite 700, 80203-1260
Telephone: 303-861-4266
Fax: 303-831-7267

Edward O. Byrne

OF COUNSEL

The Law Office of Horus L. Kai, Beijing, Shanghai and Dalian, People's Republic of China

For full biographical listings, see the Martindale-Hubbell Law Directory

COX PADMORE SKOLNIK & SHAKARCHY (AV)

Suite 2550, 1775 Sherman Street, 80203
Telephone: 303-839-9191
Fax: 303-839-9318
Email: cpss@aol.com
Palo Alto, California Office: 755 Page Mill Road, Suite A280.
Telephone: 650-424-0600.
Fax: 650-493-9408.
New York, New York Office: 630 Third Avenue.
Telephone: 212-953-6633.
Fax: 212-949-6943.

Gerald Padmore
Theresa M. Moore

OF COUNSEL
Charlotte R. Robinson

Reference: Norwest Bank.

For full biographical listings, see the Martindale-Hubbell Law Directory

HOLME ROBERTS & OWEN LLP (AV)

Suite 4100, 1700 Lincoln, 80203
Telephone: 303-861-7000
Telecopier: 303-866-0200
Email: hro@hro.com *URL:* http://www.hro.com
Boulder, Colorado Office: Suite 400, 1401 Pearl Street.
Telephone: 303-444-5955.
Telecopier: 303-444-1063.
Colorado Springs, Colorado Office: Suite 1300, 90 South Cascade Avenue.
Telephone: 719-473-3800.
Telecopier: 719-633-1518.
Salt Lake City, Utah Office: Suite 1100, 111 East Broadway.
Telephone: 801-521-5800.
Telecopier: 801-521-9639.
London, England Office: Heathcoat House, 3rd Floor, 20 Savile Row.
Telephone: 011-44-171-494-5600.
Telecopier: 011-44-171-287-9344.

PARTNERS OF FIRM

John P. Babb
Frank Erisman
Mark M. Hrenya
Garth B. Jensen
Bruce R. Kohler (Resident Managing Partner, London, England Office)
Manuel L. Martinez
Steven B. Richardson
Judith L. Roberts
Martha Traudt Collins Rolle (London, England Office)
W. Dean Salter
Paul G. Thompson (London, England Office)
Francis R. Wheeler
David B. Wilson

OF COUNSEL
Frank E. Moss (Salt Lake City Office)

(See Next Column)

SPECIAL COUNSEL
Linda K. Wackwitz

For Complete List of Firm Personnel, See General Section

For full biographical listings, see the Martindale-Hubbell Law Directory

SCHLUETER & ASSOCIATES, P.C. (AV)

1050 Seventeenth Street, Suite 1700, 80265
Telephone: 303-292-3883
Facsimile: 303-296-8880
Email: 76304.3546@compuserve.com

Henry F. Schlueter

Celia Velletri

For full biographical listings, see the Martindale-Hubbell Law Directory

WELBORN SULLIVAN MECK & TOOLEY, P.C. (AV)

1775 Sherman Street, Suite 1800, 80203-4318
Telephone: 303-376-4490
Facsimile: 303-376-4495
Email: wsmt@aol.com

John F. Welborn
John F. Meck
Scott L. Sells
Stephen A. Bain
Amy E. Mang

Representative Clients: Cameco Corporation; Cyprus Amax Minerals Corp.; Resource Development Ltd.; Western Mining Corporation (USA); WMC (Argentina) Inc.; WMC Exploration Inc.; WMC Chile S.A.; WMC Mineracao Ltda.; WMC Miniere S.A.R.L.; WMC International Limited.

For Complete List of Firm Personnel, See General Section

For full biographical listings, see the Martindale-Hubbell Law Directory

CONNECTICUT

*NEW HAVEN,** New Haven Co.

VOTRE & ASSOCIATES, P.C. (AV)

105 Court Street, Suite 302, 06511-6957
Telephone: 203-498-0065
Fax: 203-821-3595
URL: http://www.lawyers.com/votre&associates

Kenneth A. Votre

John-Henry M. Steele

OF COUNSEL
Neil K. Rutter

For full biographical listings, see the Martindale-Hubbell Law Directory

DISTRICT OF COLUMBIA

WASHINGTON, D.C. Co.

BARKATS & ASSOCIATES, CHARTERED, ATTORNEYS AND COUNSELORS AT LAW (AV)

1250 Eye Street, N.W., 20005
Telephone: 202-682-1396
Telecopier: 202-789-0895
URL: http://www.lawyers.com/barkatslaw
Paris, France Office: 24, Rue de Prony, 75017 Paris, France.
Telephone: 01 44 29 32 32.
Telecopier: 44 29 31 00.
Affiliated Law Firm: Robert J. Shutak, 1424 Fourth Street, Santa Monica, California 90401.
Telephone: 310-458-3343.
Telecopier: 301-451-0043.

MEMBER OF THE FIRM IN WASHINGTON, D.C.
Pierre-Philippe Barkats

ASSOCIATES

Robert Clifton Burns
Jeffrey Thomas Gutierrez (Not admitted in DC)
Pat James Kalellis (Not admitted in DC)

OF COUNSEL

Jerome K. Tankel
Jacques R. Beghain (Not admitted in the United States)

For full biographical listings, see the Martindale-Hubbell Law Directory

Washington—Continued

DAHLGREN AND CLOSE (AV)

1000 Connecticut Avenue, N.W., Suite 204, 20036
Telephone: 202-659-1440
Fax: 202-659-5755

MEMBERS OF FIRM

John O. Dahlgren (1913-1989) David P. Close

OF COUNSEL

Joseph D. Crumlish

For full biographical listings, see the Martindale-Hubbell Law Directory

STEWART AND STEWART (AV)

Suite 200, 2100 M Street, N.W., 20037-1207
Telephone: 202-785-4185
Telecopier: 202-466-1286; 466-1287; 466-1288
Email: general@stewartlaw.com
Moscow, Russia Office: Leninskiy Prospect, Dom 42, Corpus 1, Suite 1562, Moscow 117119.
Telephone: 011-7-95-938-7775.
Fax: 011-7-95-938-7648. Email: stewart@pol.ru
Charleroi, Belgium Office: Boulevard Dewandre 13, B6000 Charleroi.
Telephone: 011-32-7-132-5131.
Fax: 011-32-7-132-3526. Email: spinoitwese@compuserve.com

Eugene L. Stewart, Founder (1920-1998)

MEMBERS OF FIRM

Terence P. Stewart
James R. Cannon, Jr.
Wesley K. Caine
William A. Fennell
Geert De Prest
Alan M. Dunn

ASSOCIATES

David S. Johanson
Dennis R. Nuxoll
Marta Maria Prado (Not admitted in DC)

OF COUNSEL

Bernard Spinoit (Not admitted in the United States)
Lane Steven Hurewitz
Patrick John McDonough (Not admitted in DC)
Amy S. Dwyer
Eric P. Salonen
James R. Holbein (Not admitted in DC)

For full biographical listings, see the Martindale-Hubbell Law Directory

VERNER, LIIPFERT, BERNHARD, MCPHERSON AND HAND, CHARTERED (AV)

901 15th Street, N.W., 20005-2301
Telephone: 202-371-6000
Cable Address: "Verlip"
Fax: 202-371-6279
Email: verner.com *URL:* http://www.verner.com
Houston, Texas Office: 1111 Bagby, Suite 4700, 77002.
Telephone: 713-225-7200.
Fax: 713-752-2199.
Honolulu, Hawaii Office: 745 Fort Street, Suite 600, 96813.
Telephone: 808-566-0999.
Fax: 808-566-0995.
Austin, Texas Office: Suite 1440 San Jacinto Center, 98 San Jacinto Boulevard, 78701.
Telephone: 512-703-6000.
Fax: 512-703-6003.
Las Vegas, Nevada Affiliate Office: Gary C. Moss, Hughes Center, 3960 Howard Hughes Parkway, Suite 400, 89109.
Telephone: 702-737-3433.
Fax: 702-737-1612.
Miami, Florida Office: 3100 First Union Financial Center, 200 South Biscayne Boulevard, 33131.
Telephone: 305-371-8801.
Fax: 305-371-6545.

Berl Bernhard
James J. Blanchard (Not admitted in DC)
Harold I. Freilich
Andrea Jill Grant
Lloyd N. Hand
Jane Hickie (Not admitted in DC)
Lawrence E. Levinson (Not admitted in DC)
Jorge Luis Lopez (Resident, Miami, Florida Office)
Harry McPherson
Martin Mendelsohn
John A. Merrigan
John D. Waihee, III (Resident, Honolulu, Hawaii Office)
William A. Zeitler

SPECIAL COUNSEL

Robert J. Dole (Not admitted in DC)
George J. Mitchell

SENIOR COUNSEL

Wayne S. Bishop
Alvaro Cifuentes de Castro

SENIOR ADVISOR

Ann W. Richards (Resident, Austin, Texas Office)

OF COUNSEL

Frederick J. McConville
Renton L. K. Nip (Resident, Honolulu, Hawaii Office)
Steven R. Phillips

(See Next Column)

LEGAL SUPPORT PERSONNEL

Maria Fabiana Jorge (Director, Latin American Affairs)
David A. Weiss (Director of Trade Policy)

For Complete List of Firm Personnel, See General Section

For full biographical listings, see the Martindale-Hubbell Law Directory

WATT, TIEDER, HOFFAR & FITZGERALD, L.L.P. (AV)

601 Pennsylvania Avenue, N.W., Suite 900, 20004
Telephone: 703-749-1000
Telecopier: 703-893-8029
Email: contactus@wthf.com *URL:* http://www.wthf.com
McLean Virginia Office: 7929 Westpark Drive, Suite 400,
Telephone: 703-749-1000.
Telecopier: 703-893-8029.
Irvine California Office: 3 Park Plaza, Suite 1500.
Telephone: 949-852-6700.

MEMBERS OF FIRM

John B. Tieder, Jr. Robert K. Cox

For full biographical listings, see the Martindale-Hubbell Law Directory

WEADON & ASSOCIATES (AV)

1819 Pennsylvania Avenue, N.W. Suite 550, 20006
Telephone: 202-965-4100
Fax: 202-965-4252
Email: dweadon@aol.com

Donald Alford Weadon, Jr.

COUNSEL

Thomas P. Scott, III

For full biographical listings, see the Martindale-Hubbell Law Directory

WILMER, CUTLER & PICKERING (AV)

2445 M Street, N.W., 20037-1420
Telephone: 202-663-6000
Fax: 202-663-6363
Email: Law@Wilmer.Com *URL:* http://www.wilmer.com
Baltimore, Maryland Office: 100 Light Street, 21202.
Telephone: 410-986-2800.
Fax: 410-986-2828.
New York, New York Office: 520 Madison Avenue, 10022.
Telephone: 212-230-8800.
Fax: 212-230-8888.
European Offices:
4 Carlton Gardens, London, SW1Y 5AA, England. Telephone: +44 (20) 7 872 1000.
Fax: +44 (20) 7 839 3537.
Rue de la Loi 15# Wetstraat, B-1040 Brussels, Belgium. Telephone: +32 (2) 285 49 00.
Fax: +32 (2) 285 49 49.
Friedrichstrasse 95, D-10117 Berlin, Germany. Telephone: +49 (30) 20 22 64 00.
Fax: +49 (30) 20 22 65 00.

MEMBERS OF FIRM

Daniel K. Mayers
James S. Campbell
Louis R. Cohen
F. David Lake, Jr.
Jeffrey M. Lang
Paul J. Mode, Jr.
C. Loring Jetton, Jr.
William T. Lake
Dieter G. F. Lange (Not admitted in DC; Resident, European Office, London, England)
Charles S. Levy
Richard W. Cass
Kenneth W. Gideon
Robert C. Cassidy, Jr.
John D. Greenwald (Not admitted in DC)
John H. Harwood II
Roberto Dañino
Stephen P. Doyle
George P. Stamas
Russell J. Bruemmer
Robert M. Kimmitt
Paul Mitchard (Not admitted in DC; Resident, European Office, London, England)
William J. Wilkins
Andrew N. Vollmer
Jeffrey N. Shane
Matthias Wissmann (Not admitted in DC; Resident, European Office, Berlin, Germany)
James S. Venit (Not admitted in DC; Resident, European Office, Brussels, Belgium)
Dr. Andreas Weitbrecht (Not admitted in DC; Resident, European Offices, Berlin, Germany and Brussels, Belgium)
John H. Ratliff (Not admitted in DC; Resident, European Office, Brussels, Belgium)
W. Scott Blackmer
Gary B. Born (European Offices, London, England and Berlin, Germany)
John B. Watkins V
Sheila C. Cheston
Paul A. von Hehn (Not admitted in DC; Resident, European Office, Brussels, Belgium)
Marc C. Hansen (Not admitted in DC; Resident, European Office, Brussels, Belgium)
Andrew K. Parnell (Not admitted in DC; Resident, European Office, London, England)
Jorge E. Alers
Paul S. Dwyer Jr.
Robert B. Stack

(See Next Column)

WILMER, CUTLER & PICKERING—*Continued*

MEMBERS OF FIRM (Continued)

Dr. Natalie Lübben (Not admitted in DC; Resident, European Office, Berlin, Germany)
Michael R. Holter (Not admitted in DC; Resident, European Office, London, England)
Thomas Mueller (Resident, European Office, Brussels, Belgium)
Christian L. Duvernoy (Resident, European Office, Brussels, Belgium)
Timothy E. Stumpff
Dr. Roland Steinmeyer (Not admitted in DC; Resident, European Office, Berlin, Germany)

SENIOR COUNSEL

Lloyd N. Cutler

COUNSEL

Lester Nurick
Leonard M. Shambon
Patricia A. Sherman
John J. Kallaugher (Not admitted in DC; European Offices, London, England and Brussels, Belgium)
Marcia A. Wiss
Ronald I. Meltzer
Martin Seyfarth (Not admitted in DC; Resident, European Office, Berlin, Germany)

For Complete List of Firm Personnel, See General Section

For full biographical listings, see the Martindale-Hubbell Law Directory

WOLF, ARNOLD & CARDOSO, P.C. (AV)

1150 18th Street, N.W. Suite 275, 20036
Telephone: 202-857-0585
Facsimile: 202-293-2068
Email: wac@interlawyers.com *URL:* http://www.interlawyers.com
New York, N.Y. Office: Wolf, Arnold & Knoll, P.C., 590 Madison Avenue.
Telephone: 212-521-4410.
Fax: 212-465-9104.
Rio de Janeiro, Brazil Office: Cardoso, Rocha, Trindale & Lara Resende.
Bogota, Colombia Office: Arango, Nieto, Calderon & Asociados.
Caribbean Office: Dunn, Cox, Orett and Ashenheim, Kingston, Jamaica.
Other Associated offices also throughout Latin America, The Caribbean, Asia and the South Pacific.

Elting Arnold (1912-1988)
Louis T. Urbanczyk (1926-1995)
Maurice Wolf
Carlos E. Cardoso (Not admitted in the United States; Resident Rio de Janeiro, Brazil)
Lawrence I. Knoll
Gilberto Arango (Not admitted in the United States; Resident, Bogota, Columbia)
Rafael Nieto-Navia (Not admitted in the United States; Resident Bogota, Columbia Office)

For full biographical listings, see the Martindale-Hubbell Law Directory

FLORIDA

*FORT LAUDERDALE,** Broward Co.

MONTERO FINIZIO VELASQUEZ WEISSING AND REYES, P.A. (AV)

200 Southeast Ninth Street, 33316
Telephone: 954-767-6500
FAX: 954-766-2690
1-800-344-0322
Email: mfvw@worldnet.att.net *URL:* http://www.monterofinizio.com
Boca Raton, Florida Office: 2200 Corporate Boulevard, N.W., Suite 315.
Telephone: 561-982-9930.
Miami, Florida Office: 28 West Flagler Street, Suite 202.
Telephone: 305-381-9500.

Hiram M. Montero
Paul G. Finizio
Carlos A. Velasquez
Matthew D. Weissing
Carlos J. Reyes, Jr.
Jamie J. Finizio-Bascombe
Edward Montoya

Mara Shlackman
Emily DeSantis
Janet Ochoa
Marina Garcia Wood

For full biographical listings, see the Martindale-Hubbell Law Directory

*KISSIMMEE,** Osceola Co.

POHL & SHORT, P.A.

(See Winter Park)

*MIAMI,** Dade Co.

ADAMS, GALLINAR, IGLESIAS & MEYER, P.A. (AV)

Colonial Bank Center, 1200 Brickell Avenue, Ninth Floor, 33131
Telephone: 305-416-6800
Facsimile: 305-416-6811
Email: agimlaw@agimlaw.com *URL:* http://www.lawyers.com/agimlaw

Robert R. Adams
Michael D. Gallinar
Mario A. Iglesias
James M. Meyer

Marta M. Cil
Enrique N. Bascuas
Santiago Eljaiek, III

For full biographical listings, see the Martindale-Hubbell Law Directory

BIERMAN, SHOHAT, LOEWY & KLEIN, PROFESSIONAL ASSOCIATION (AV)

Penthouse Two, 800 Brickell Avenue, 33131-2944
Telephone: 305-358-7000
Facsimile: 305-358-4010

Donald I. Bierman
Edward R. Shohat
Ira N. Loewy
Theodore Klein

Michael A. Pizzi, Jr.

Reference: United National Bank of Miami.

For full biographical listings, see the Martindale-Hubbell Law Directory

MURAI, WALD, BIONDO & MORENO, P.A. (AV)

9th Floor Ingraham Building, 25 Southeast 2nd Avenue, 33131
Telephone: 305-358-5900
Fax: 305-358-9490
Email: mwbm@gate.net

Rene V. Murai
Gerald B. Wald
Gerald J. Biondo
M. Cristina Moreno
Cristina Echarte Brochin

Antonio Arzola
Maria Victoria Currais
Lynette Ebeoglu McGuinness

Reference: Union Planters Bank.

For full biographical listings, see the Martindale-Hubbell Law Directory

SPENCER AND KLEIN, PROFESSIONAL ASSOCIATION (AV)

Suite 1901, 801 Brickell Avenue, 33131
Telephone: 305-374-7700
Telecopier: 305-374-4890
Email: SandK@primenet.com

Thomas R. Spencer, Jr.
Brent D. Klein

Representative Clients: America Publishing Group; American Association of Physicians and Surgeons; Chrysler Corporation; Coldwell Banker; Editorial Televisa; Grupo Anaya, S.A.; Independent Living Care, Inc.; Managed Care of America, Inc.; New Times, Inc.; Winn-Dixie Stores.

For Complete List of Firm Personnel, See General Section

For full biographical listings, see the Martindale-Hubbell Law Directory

*ORLANDO,** Orange Co.

POHL & SHORT, P.A.

(See Winter Park)

*SARASOTA,** Sarasota Co.

WILLIAMS, PARKER, HARRISON, DIETZ & GETZEN, PROFESSIONAL ASSOCIATION (AV)

200 South Orange Avenue, 34236-6749
Telephone: 941-366-4800
Telecopier: 941-366-5109
Mailing Address: P.O. Box 3258, Sarasota, Florida, 34230-3258
Email: infodesk@williamsparker.com *URL:* http://www.williamsparker.com

William G. Lambrecht
J. Michael Hartenstine
Michele B. Grimes
James L. Turner
Robert W. Benjamin
M. Lewis Hall, III
Susan Barrett Hecker
R. David Bustard

General Counsel for: Sarasota County Public Hospital Board; Sarasota-Manatee Airport Authority; Taylor Woodrow Homes Ltd.; FCCI Mutual Insurance Co.

(See Next Column)

WILLIAMS, PARKER, HARRISON, DIETZ & GETZEN PROFESSIONAL ASSOCIATION, *Sarasota—Continued*

Local Counsel for: Bank of America; Northern Trust Bank of Florida; SunTrust Bank, Gulfcoast.

For Complete List of Firm Personnel, See General Section

For full biographical listings, see the Martindale-Hubbell Law Directory

*TAMPA,** Hillsborough Co.

SHARP, SMITH & HARRISON, P.A. (AV)

One Urban Centre, Suite 630, 4830 West Kennedy Boulevard, 33609-2574
Telephone: 813-286-4199
Fax: 813-286-4197
Email: sharpsmith@earthlink.net

William M. Sharp, Sr.
Karen R. Smith
William T. Harrison, III

For full biographical listings, see the Martindale-Hubbell Law Directory

WINTER PARK, Orange Co.

POHL & SHORT, P.A. (AV)

280 West Canton Avenue, Suite 410, P.O. Box 3208, 32790
Telephone: 407-647-7645; 407-647-POHL
Telefax: 407-647-2314
Email: ps@pohlshort.com

Dwight I. Cool
Alexander S. Douglas II
Gary A. Forster
E. Givens Goodspeed
Mark A. Grimes
Robert S. Hoofman
Roger A. Kelly
Adam O. Kirwan
David J. Kohs
Frank L. Pohl
James Everett Shepherd V
Houston E. Short
John R. Simpson, Jr.

Representative Clients: American Generator Co.; Copelco Capital, Inc.; Denim U.S.A., Inc.; Ford Motor Credit Co.; Lodestar Technology, Inc.; Lutheran Brotherhood; SunTrust, N.A.; Trax, Inc.

For full biographical listings, see the Martindale-Hubbell Law Directory

GEORGIA

*ATLANTA,** Fulton Co.

HARKLEROAD & HERMANCE, A PROFESSIONAL CORPORATION (AV)

2500 International Tower-Peachtree Center, 229 Peachtree Street, N.E., 30303
Telephone: 404-588-9211
Telecopier: 404-659-0860

Donald R. Harkleroad
James P. Hermance

For full biographical listings, see the Martindale-Hubbell Law Directory

McCULLOUGH SHERRILL, LLP (AV)

1409 Peachtree Street, N.E., 30309
Telephone: 404-885-1500
Telecopier: 404-892-1801
Email: info@mslegal.com *URL:* http://www.mslegal.com

MEMBERS OF FIRM

William M. Joseph
James W. King
W. Clayton Sparrow, Jr.

ASSOCIATES

Susan T. Craighead
Loren E. Kalish
Joseph V. Myers, III

For Complete List of Firm Personnel, See General Section

For full biographical listings, see the Martindale-Hubbell Law Directory

PIERCE & YOUNG (AV)

Building 1700, 2255 Cumberland Parkway Northwest, 30339-4575
Telephone: 770-435-0500
Telecopier: 770-435-0362

MEMBER OF FIRM

J. Wayne Pierce

For full biographical listings, see the Martindale-Hubbell Law Directory

THRASHER, WHITLEY, HAMPTON & MORGAN, A PROFESSIONAL CORPORATION (AV)

Suite 2150, Five Concourse Parkway, 30328
Telephone: 770-804-8000
Telecopier: 770-804-5555
Email: law@twhm.com
Email: main@twhm.com

Robert E. Whitley

Representative Clients: First Southeastern Securities Group, Inc.; Georgia Dental Assn.; Middle Bay Oil Company, Inc.; Perry & Co.; Smallwood, Reynolds, Stewart, Stewart & Assoc., Inc.; Sunchase Holdings, Ltd.; Touch Industries, Inc.

For full biographical listings, see the Martindale-Hubbell Law Directory

HAWAII

*HONOLULU,** Honolulu Co.

CARLSMITH BALL (AV)

A Partnership including Law Corporations
Suite 2200, Pacific Tower, 1001 Bishop Street, P.O. Box 656, 96809-3402
Telephone: 808-523-2500
Fax: 808-523-0842
Email: execdirector@carlsmith.com *URL:* http://www.carlsmith.com
Kapolei, Hawaii Office: Suite 318, Kapolei Building, 1001 Kamokila Boulevard, 96707.
Telephone: 808-523-2500.
Fax: 808-674-0850.
Wailuku, Maui Hawaii Office: Suite 400, One Main Plaza, 2200 Main Street, P.O. Box 1086, 96793-1086.
Telephone: 808-242-4535.
Fax: 808-244-4974.
Kailua-Kona, Hawaii Office: Suite 209, 75-1000 Henry Street, 96740.
Telephone: 808-329-6464.
Fax: 808-329-9450.
Hilo, Hawaii Office: 121 Waianuenue Avenue, P.O. Box 686, 96721-0686.
Telephone: 808-935-6644.
Fax: 808-935-7975.
Hagatna, Guam Office: Suite 401, Bank of Hawaii Building, 134 West Soledad Avenue, P.O. Box BF, 96932-5027.
Telephone: 671-472-6813.
Fax: 671-477-4375.
Telex: 721-6445 CWCMI GM.
Saipan, Commonwealth of the Northern Mariana Islands Office: Carlsmith Building, Capitol Hill, P.O. Box 5241, 96950-5241.
Telephone: 670-322-3455.
Fax: 670-322-3368.
Los Angeles, California Office: 9th Floor, 444 South Flower Street, 90071-2901.
Telephone: 213-955-1200.
Fax: 213-623-0032.
Washington, D.C. Office: Suite 300, 1201 Pennsylvania Avenue, N.W., 20004-2401.
Telephone: 202-628-2228.
Fax: 202-628-2071.
Mexico City, Mexico Office: Carlsmith Ball, Sierra Nevada 119, Lomas de Chapultepec, 11000 Mexico, D.F.
Telephone: 52-5-520-8514, 52-5-520-8757.
Fax: 52-5-540-1545.
Mexico, D.F. Office of Carlsmith Ball, S.C. (Authorized to practice as foreign legal consultants in Mexico): Sierra Nevada 119, Lomas de Chapultepec, 11000 Mexico, D.F.
Telephone: 52-5-520-8514, 52-5-520-8757.
Fax: 52-5-540-1545.

MEMBERS OF FIRM

Annie Kun Baker (Partner, Resident at Los Angeles, California Office)
Roger B. Baymiller (Resident at Los Angeles, California Office)
Stephen L. Bradford (Resident at Los Angeles, California Office)
Terrence A. Everett (Resident at Los Angeles, California Office)
Alfonso García Cacho (Resident at Mexico Office)
Karl K. Kobayashi
Randolph G. Muhlestein (Resident at Los Angeles, California Office)
David R. Nevitt (Resident at Saipan Office)
James Polish (Resident at Los Angeles, California Office)
John E. Rogers (Resident at Mexico Office)
Marcia K. Schultz (Resident at Saipan Office)
Lance F. Taniguchi
Donald C. Williams (Resident at Los Angeles, California Office)
William C. Williams, Jr. (Not admitted in HI)
Jon T. Yamamura
Adrián Zubikarai Arriola (Resident at Mexico Office)

OF COUNSEL

Robert N. Katayama
Edward M. Ranger (Resident at Mexico Office)

(See Next Column)

CARLSMITH BALL—*Continued*

For Complete List of Firm Personnel, See General Section

For full biographical listings, see the Martindale-Hubbell Law Directory

LAW OFFICES OF MANUEL D. GARCIA (AV)

Pacific Tower of Bishop Square, 1001 Bishop Street, Suite 2800, 96813
Telephone: 808-522-0755
Facsimile: 808-522-0760

For full biographical listings, see the Martindale-Hubbell Law Directory

GOODSILL ANDERSON QUINN & STIFEL (AV)

Alii Place, Suite 1800, 1099 Alakea Street, P.O. Box 3196, 96801-3196
Telephone: 808-547-5600
FAX: 808-547-5880
Email: info@goodsill.com *URL:* http://www.goodsill.com

MEMBERS OF FIRM

Ronald H. W. Lum
Raymond S. Iwamoto
Randall K. Steverson
Peter T. Kashiwa
Russell S. Kato
Vincent A. Piekarski
Gregory R. Kim
Alan S. Fujimoto
Kellie M. N. Sekiya

COUNSEL

Alan W. C. Ma

ASSOCIATES

KahBo Dye-Chiew
Eric A. Elkind

Representative Clients: Hilton International Co.; Japan Airlines Company, Ltd.; Kokusai Kogyo Kabushiki Kaisha; Long Term Credit Bank; Shimizu Corporation; Shinwa Golf Co., Ltd.; Suntory, Ltd.; Takenaka (U.S.A.) Corporation; Town Development Co., Ltd.; Watkins Pacific Corporation.

For Complete List of Firm Personnel, See General Section

For full biographical listings, see the Martindale-Hubbell Law Directory

MCCORRISTON MIHO MILLER MUKAI (AV)

Five Waterfront Plaza, 4th Floor, 500 Ala Moana Boulevard, 96813
Telephone: 808-529-7300
Facsimile: 808-524-8293
Cable: Attorneys, Honolulu
Mailing Address: P.O. Box 2800, Honolulu, Hawaii, 96803-2800
Email: info@m4Law.com

PARTNERS

Clifford J. Miller
Franklin K. Mukai
Stanley Y. Mukai
D. Scott MacKinnon
Kenneth B. Marcus
David N. Kuriyama
Eric T. Kawatani
Andrew W. Char
Alexander R. Jampel

COUNSEL

Charles E. Pear, Jr.

Representative Clients: TSA International Limited; Niju-Ichi Corporation; Mainami Boeki Co., Ltd.; The Daiichi Housing Co., Ltd.; Japan Leasing Corporation; Long Term Credit Bank of Japan; Seven-Eleven Japan Co., Ltd.; Oji Paper Co., Ltd.; Marubeni Corporation; Sports Shinko (Hawaii) Co., Ltd.

For Complete List of Firm Personnel, See General Section

For full biographical listings, see the Martindale-Hubbell Law Directory

ILLINOIS

*CHICAGO,** Cook Co.

ARTHUR FAKES P.C.

(See Lombard)

PATTISHALL, MCAULIFFE, NEWBURY, HILLIARD & GERALDSON (AV)

Suite 5000, 311 South Wacker Drive, 60606
Telephone: 312-554-8000
Facsimile: 312-554-8015
Washington, D.C. Office: 320 Watergate, Six Hundred, 20037.
Telephone: 202-338-1300.
Facsimile: 202-338-9349.

MEMBERS OF FIRM

Beverly W. Pattishall
Jeremiah D. McAuliffe
Robert M. Newbury
Benjamin S. Warren III (Resident Partner, Washington, D.C. Office)
Raymond I. Geraldson, Jr.
David Craig Hilliard
Edward G. Wierzbicki
Robert W. Sacoff
Mark V. B. Partridge
Joseph N. Welch II
Daniel D. Frohling
John Thompson Brown
Mary E. Innis
Douglas N. Masters

(See Next Column)

MEMBERS OF FIRM (Continued)

Brett A. August
Jonathan S. Jennings
John Michael Murphy
Kevin T. Conroy
Janet A. Marvel

OF COUNSEL

Ralph H. Lane
Diana Lee Bixler

Bradley L. Cohn
Colette A. Durst-Barkey (Resident Associate, Washington, D.C. Office)
Kathryn E. Ross
Daniel S. Goldman
Beth A. Fulkerson
Demetra Merikas
James P. Williams
Jennifer A. O'Malley
Heather F. Hines
Danielle B. Lemack
Uli Widmaier
Jennifer E. Berner
Ram Padmanabhan

For full biographical listings, see the Martindale-Hubbell Law Directory

LOMBARD, DuPage Co.

ARTHUR FAKES P.C. (AV)

929 South Main Street, Suite 109, 60148
Telephone: 630-268-0600
Telecopier: 630-268-0642
Email: ARTFAKES@AOL.COM *URL:* http://www.lawyers.com/fakeslaw

Arthur Fakes

For full biographical listings, see the Martindale-Hubbell Law Directory

INDIANA

*INDIANAPOLIS,** Marion Co.

BAMBERGER & FEIBLEMAN (AV)

1408 North Pennsylvania Street, 46202-2421
Telephone: 317-639-5151
FAX: 317-269-2030
Email: bandf@iquest.net

MEMBER OF FIRM

D. Robert Webster

Representative Clients: C.I.T. Corp.; FFI Corporation; Kipp Brothers, Inc.; BancPlus Mortgage Corp.; Hiway Parts, Inc.; NBD, Indiana; Tube Processing Corp.; Indiana Mortgage Corp.

For full biographical listings, see the Martindale-Hubbell Law Directory

STEPHEN E. PLOPPER & ASSOCIATES (AV)

Suite 3920, Bank One Tower, 111 Monument Circle, 46204
Telephone: 317-822-0800
Fax: 317-822-0808
Email: sploplaw@ameritch.net
Affiliated Firm: Klineman Rose & Wolf-Poland, Suite 115 ul. Krakowskie Przedmiescie, 00-333 Warsaw, Poland.
Telephone: +48-22 828-6060.
Fax: +48-22 828-7171.

For full biographical listings, see the Martindale-Hubbell Law Directory

TABBERT HAHN EARNEST & WEDDLE (AV)

Suite 2100, One Indiana Square, 46204-2101
Telephone: 317-639-5444
Fax: 317-639-5232
Email: jtyrrell@tabberthahn.com *URL:* http://www.tabberthahn.com

Don A. Tabbert
Gregory F. Hahn
Lante K. Earnest
Robert G. Weddle
Mark K. Sullivan
Judy M. Tyrrell
Lara D. Engelking
Matthew W. Conner
William W. Mathews
Charles R. Whybrew

OF COUNSEL

James J. Nocon
William D. Lalley
Joseph W. Hammes
Dale E. Sporleder

For full biographical listings, see the Martindale-Hubbell Law Directory

KANSAS

*WICHITA,** Sedgwick Co.

Foulston & Siefkin L.L.P. (AV)

700 NationsBank Financial Center, 67202
Telephone: 316-267-6371
Facsimile: 316-267-6345
URL: http://www.foulston.com
Topeka, Kansas Office: 1515 NationsBank Tower, 534 Kansas Avenue, 66603.
Telephone: 785-233-3600.
Fax: 785-233-1610.
Dodge City, Kansas Office: 810 Frontview, P.O. Box 1147, 67801.
Telephone: 316-227-8126.
Fax: 316-227-8451.
Member: Lex Mundi, The World's Leading Association of Independent Law Firms.

MEMBERS OF FIRM

Benjamin C. Langel
Harvey R. Sorensen
Larry G. Rapp

For Complete List of Firm Personnel, See General Section

For full biographical listings, see the Martindale-Hubbell Law Directory

LOUISIANA

*NEW ORLEANS,** Orleans Parish

Wagner & Bagot (AV)

Suite 2660, Poydras Center, 650 Poydras Street, 70130-6105
Telephone: 504-525-2141
Telecopier: 504-523-1587
TWX: 5106017673
ELN: 62928850
"INCISIVE"

Thomas J. Wagner
Michael H. Bagot, Jr.

Thomas A. Rayer, Jr.
Thomas P. Henican
Brian P. Brancato
Dana A. Henderson

For full biographical listings, see the Martindale-Hubbell Law Directory

MAINE

BAR HARBOR, Hancock Co.

Fenton, Chapman, Fenton, Smith & Kane, P.A. (AV)

109 Main Street, P.O. Box B, 04609
Telephone: 207-288-3331
Fax: 207-288-9326
Email: fentonlawfirm@acadia.net *URL:* http://www.lawyers.com/fcfs&klaw

William Fenton
Nathaniel R. Fenton
Douglas B. Chapman
Chadbourn H. Smith
Margaret T. Jeffery

Reference: Bar Harbor Banking and Trust Co.

For Complete List of Firm Personnel, See General Section

For full biographical listings, see the Martindale-Hubbell Law Directory

*PORTLAND,** Cumberland Co.

Pierce Atwood (AV)

One Monument Square, 04101
Telephone: 207-791-1100
Fax: 207-791-1350
Email: info@PierceAtwood.com *URL:* http://www.pierceatwood.com
Augusta, Maine Office: 77 Winthrop Street.
Telephone: 207-622-6311.
Fax: 207-623-9367.
Newburyport, Massachusetts Office: 6 Harris Street.
Telephone: 978-465-9599.
Fax: 978-465-9945.

MEMBERS OF FIRM

John W. Gulliver
William E. Taylor
Robert H. Stier, Jr.
Catherine R. Connors
Matthew D. Manahan

(See Next Column)

ASSOCIATES

Jonathan A. Block
William L. Worden

For Complete List of Firm Personnel, See General Section

For full biographical listings, see the Martindale-Hubbell Law Directory

Preti, Flaherty, Beliveau, Pachios & Haley, LLC (AV)

One City Center, P.O. Box 9546, 04112-9546
Telephone: 207-791-3000
Telecopier: 207-791-3111
Email: admin@preti.com *URL:* http://www.preti.com
Augusta, Maine Office: 45 Memorial Circle, P.O. Box 1058, 04332-1058.
Telephone: 207-623-5300.
Telefax: 207-623-2914.
Bath, Maine Office: Thirty Front Street, P.O. Box 665, 04530-0665.
Telephone: 207-443-5576.
Telefax: 207-443-6665.

MEMBERS OF FIRM

Severin M. Beliveau (Augusta Office)
Harold C. Pachios
Jonathan S. Piper
Randall B. Weill
Estelle A. Lavoie
Mark B. LeDuc (Augusta Office)
Timothy J. Bryant

SENIOR COUNSEL

George J. Mitchell

COUNSEL

Gregory P. Hansel
Naomi Sakamoto

Representative Clients: The St. Paul Companies; KeyBank National Assn.; Maine Municipal Assn.; Blethen-Maine Newspapers, Inc.; Maine Turnpike Authority; American International Group; Maine Automobile Dealers Assn.; Hannaford Brothers Co.; L.L. Bean; Maine Health Care Assn.

For Complete List of Firm Personnel, See General Section

For full biographical listings, see the Martindale-Hubbell Law Directory

MASSACHUSETTS

*BOSTON,** Suffolk Co.

Aresty International Law Offices, P.C. (AV)

Bay 107, Union Wharf, 02109
Telephone: 617-367-8393
Fax: 617-742-6452
Email: mail@cyberspaceattorney.com *URL:* http://www.cyberspaceattorney.com

SENIOR PARTNER

Jeffrey M. Aresty

PARTNER

Andrew S. Breines

INTERNATIONAL LAW CONSULTANT

Yi-Fu (Eve) Sun

For full biographical listings, see the Martindale-Hubbell Law Directory

Hinckley, Allen & Snyder LLP (AV)

28 State Street, 30th Floor, 02109-1775
Telephone: 617-345-9000
Email: firm@haslaw.com *URL:* http://www.haslaw.com
Providence, Rhode Island Office: 1500 Fleet Center.
Telephone: 401-274-2000.
Fax: 401-277-9600. URL: http://www.hawlaw.com.

MEMBERS OF FIRM

Jonathan Bell
Paul Bork
Stephen J. Carlotti (Not admitted in MA)
Michael P. DeFanti
Malcolm Farmer, III
Margaret D. Farrell (Not admitted in MA)
Gerard R. Goulet
William R. Grimm
Joel Lewin
Sandra Matrone Mack (Not admitted in MA)
Matthew T. Marcello, III (Not admitted in MA)
Frederick P. McClure
Paul F. O'Donnell, III
James O. Reavis
Herman Snyder
Robert F. Sylvia

OF COUNSEL

Willard Krasnow
Joachim A. Weissfeld (Not admitted in MA)

For Complete List of Firm Personnel, See General Section

For full biographical listings, see the Martindale-Hubbell Law Directory

Kopelman and Paige, P.C. (AV)

Park Square Building, 31 St. James Avenue, 7th Floor, 02116
Telephone: 617-556-0007
Fax: 617-654-1735

(See Next Column)

KOPELMAN AND PAIGE P.C.—*Continued*

Leonard Kopelman

For Complete List of Firm Personnel, See General Section

For full biographical listings, see the Martindale-Hubbell Law Directory

PALMER & DODGE LLP (AV)

One Beacon Street, 02108
Telephone: 617-573-0100
Facsimile: 617-227-4420
URL: http://www.palmerdodge.com

MEMBERS OF FIRM

F. Andrew Anderson
Mark A. Fischer
Nathaniel S. Gardiner
Stanley Keller
Michael Lytton
Yvonne E. Schlaeppi (Not admitted in MA)
Thomas M. Spera
Russell B. Swapp
John Taylor Williams

For Complete List of Firm Personnel, See General Section

For full biographical listings, see the Martindale-Hubbell Law Directory

NEWTON, Middlesex Co.

VACOVEC, MAYOTTE & SINGER (AV)

Two Newton Place, Suite 340, 255 Washington Street, 02458-1633
Telephone: 617-964-0500
Fax: 617-969-2002
Email: taxgroup@vacovec.com *URL:* http://www.vacovec.com

MEMBERS OF FIRM

Kenneth J. Vacovec
Maureen C. Mayotte
Paula N. Singer
Kenneth H. Light

ASSOCIATES

Angela M. Cox
Arthur R. Kerr, II
Tonya S. James
Scott C. Cashman
Karen J. Folb
Jay R. Krasner

OF COUNSEL

Stephen P. Koster
John G. Ganick

For full biographical listings, see the Martindale-Hubbell Law Directory

MICHIGAN

*ANN ARBOR,** Washtenaw Co.

MILLER, CANFIELD, PADDOCK AND STONE, P.L.C. (AV)

A Professional Limited Liability Company
Founded in 1852 by Sidney Davy Miller
101 North Main Street, Seventh Floor, 48104-1400
Telephone: 734-663-2445
Fax: 734-747-7147
URL: http://www.millercanfield.com
Detroit, Michigan Office: 150 West Jefferson, Suite 2500, 48226-4415.
Telephone: 313-963-6420.
Fax: 313-496-7500.
Cable Address: "Stem Detroit."
Troy, Michigan Office: 840 West Long Lake Road, Suite 200, 48098.
Telephone: 248-879-2000.
Fax: 248-879-2001.
Grand Rapids, Michigan Office: 99 Monroe, N.W., Suite 1200, 49503-2639.
Telephone: 616-454-8656.
Fax: 616-776-6322.
Howell, Michigan Office: 121 South Barnard Street, Suite 4, 48843-2305.
Telephone: 517-546-7600.
Telecopier: 517-546-6974.
Kalamazoo, Michigan Office: 444 West Michigan Avenue, 49007-3752.
Telephone: 616-381-7030.
Fax: 616-382-0244.
Lansing, Michigan Office: One Michigan Avenue, Suite 900, 48933-1609.
Telephone: 517-487-2070.
Fax: 517-374-6304.
Monroe, Michigan Office: 214 East Elm Avenue, Suite 100, 48162-2682.
Telephone: 734-243-2000.
Fax: 734-243-0901.
Washington, D.C. Office: 1900 K Street, N.W., Suite 1150. 20006.
Telephone: 202-429-5575; 785-0600.
Fax: 202-331-1118; 785-1234.
Pensacola, Florida Office: 25 West Cedar, 32501.
Telephone: 850-469-1088.
Fax: 850-432-0677.
New York, New York Office: 1450 Broadway, 41st Floor, 10018.
Telephone: 212-704-4400.
Fax: 212-704-4410.

(See Next Column)

Gdynia, Poland Office: UL. Slaska 21, 81-319.
Telephone: 011-485-831-2808.
Fax: 011-48-58-628 6411.
Warsaw, Poland Office: UL. Nowogrodzkall, 5th Floor, 00-513.
Telephone: 011-4822 529 0200.
Fax: 011-4822 529 0201.
Katowice, Poland Office: UL. Francuska 35/37, 40-027.
Telephone: 011 (48-32) 757-2414.
Fax: 011 (48-32) 757-2483.

PRINCIPALS OF FIRM

Robert E. Gilbert
Erik H. Serr
J. David Reck

Representative Firm Clients: Chrysler Corporation; Comerica, Incorporated; City of Detroit, Michigan; Detroit Tigers, Inc.; First of Michigan; Ford Motor Company; Ford Motor Credit Company; Great Lakes Bancorp; Henry Ford Hospital; INVETECH Company.

For Complete List of Firm Personnel, See General Section

For full biographical listings, see the Martindale-Hubbell Law Directory

BIRMINGHAM, Oakland Co.

HYMAN LIPPITT, P.C. (AV)

185 Oakland Avenue, Suite 300, 48009
Telephone: 248-646-8292
Facsimile: 248-646-8375
Email: hymalipp@tir.com

J. Leonard Hyman
Norman L. Lippitt
Douglas A. Hyman
Brian D. O'Keefe
H. Joel Newman
Nazli G. Sater
Kenneth F. Neuman
Terry S. Givens
Paul J. Fischer
John A. Sellers
Robert H. Lippitt
Roger L. Myers
Sally A. Rutledge
Joseph Pia
John P. Gonway
Leif K. Anderson
Jennifer S. Gold
Julie Lyons Kosovec
Dawn S. Spratley
Michael T. Price

For full biographical listings, see the Martindale-Hubbell Law Directory

CLARKSTON, Oakland Co.

BULLARD, ANDERSON & ANDERSON, PLLC (AV)

6060 Dixie Highway, Suite H, 48346-3476
Telephone: 248-623-3888
Fax: 248-623-1883
Email: firm@baalaw.com *URL:* http://www.baalaw.com

Rockwood W. Bullard III
Rae Anne Anderson
Acie G. Anderson, III

Representative Clients: ANCAR Publications, Inc.; Audio Trends, Inc.; AVC, Inc. (Advanced Visual Concepts); Clarkston Realty, Inc.; GAC Mortgage Co.; Michaelene's Granola, Inc.; Morgan Service, Inc.; Smith Disposal, Inc.; Sunview Windows, Skylights & Doors, Ltd.
Reference: NBD Bank, NA.

For full biographical listings, see the Martindale-Hubbell Law Directory

*DETROIT,** Wayne Co.

BUTZEL LONG, A PROFESSIONAL CORPORATION (AV)

Suite 900, 150 West Jefferson, 48226
Telephone: 313-225-7000
Telecopier: 313-225-7080
Email: melnick@butzel.com *URL:* http://www.butzel.com
Birmingham, Michigan Office: Suite 200, 32270 Telegraph Road.
Telephone: 810-258-1616.
Telecopier: 810-258-1439.
Okemos, Michigan Office: Suite 300, 2127 University Park Drive.
Telephone: 517-372-6622.
Telecopier: 517-372-6672.
Ann Arbor, Michigan Office: Suite 300, 350 South Main Street.
Telephone: 313-995-3110.
Telecopier: 313-995-1777.
Grosse Pointe Farms, Michigan Office: Suite 260, 21 Kercheval.
Telephone: 313-886-5446.
Telecopier: 313-886-2114.
Boca Raton, Florida Office: Suite 411, 1200 North Federal Highway.
Telephone: 561-368-2151.
Telecopier: 561-368-4668.
Palm Beach Gardens, Florida Office: Suite 227, 11382 Prosperity Farms Road.
Telephone: 561-625-4442.
Telecopier: 561-625-6901.
Naples, Florida Office: Suite 705, 801 Laurel Oak Drive.
Telephone: 941-597-4500.
Telecopier: 941-597-5623.

(See Next Column)

MILLER, CANFIELD, PADDOCK AND STONE P.L.C.—Continued

Troy, Michigan Office: 840 West Long Lake Road, Suite 200, 48098.
Telephone: 248-879-2000.
Fax: 248-879-2001.
Howell, Michigan Office: 121 South Barnard Street, Suite 4, 48843-2305.
Telephone: 517-546-7600.
Telecopier: 517-546-6974.
Kalamazoo, Michigan Office: 444 West Michigan Avenue, 49007-3752.
Telephone: 616-381-7030.
Fax: 616-382-0244.
Lansing, Michigan Office: One Michigan Avenue, Suite 900, 48933-1609.
Telephone: 517-487-2070.
Fax: 517-374-6304.
Monroe, Michigan Office: 214 East Elm Avenue, Suite 100, 48162-2682.
Telephone: 734-243-2000.
Fax: 734-243-0901.
Washington, D.C. Office: 1900 K Street, N.W., Suite 1150, 20006.
Telephone: 202-429-5575; 785-0600.
Fax: 202-331-1118; 785-1234.
Pensacola, Florida Office: 25 West Cedar, 32501.
Telephone: 850-469-1088.
Fax: 850-432-0677.
New York, New York Office: 1450 Broadway, 41st Floor, 10018.
Telephone: 212-704-4400.
Fax: 212-704-4410.
Gdynia, Poland Office: Ul. Slaska 21, 81-319.
Telephone: 011-485-831-2808.
Fax: 011-48-58-628 6411.
Warsaw, Poland Office: Ul. Nowogrodzkall, 5th Floor, 00-513.
Telephone: 011-4822 529 0200.
Fax: 011-4822 529 0201.
Katowice, Poland Office: Ul. Francuska 35/37, 40-027.
Telephone: 011 (48-32) 757-2414.
Fax: 011 (48-32) 757-2483.

PRINCIPALS

Robert L. DeJong	Michael G. Campbell
Mark E. Putney	Robert E. Lee Wright
Richard A. Gaffin	Douglas W. Crim
Charles S. Mishkind	Stanley J. Stek

Vernon Bennett III

OF COUNSEL/SENIOR COUNSEL

David E. Hathaway

RESIDENT SENIOR ATTORNEYS

David J. Hasper	Stephen L. Elkins

RESIDENT ASSOCIATES

John T. Stecco	Andrew T. Blum
Vincent E. Wolfer	Robert I. Nolan

Representative Firm Clients: Chrysler Corporation; Comerica, Incorporated; City of Detroit, Michigan; Detroit Tigers, Inc.; First of Michigan; Ford Motor Company; Ford Motor Credit Company; Great Lakes Bancorp; Henry Ford Hospital; INVETECH Company.

For full biographical listings, see the Martindale-Hubbell Law Directory

WARNER NORCROSS & JUDD L.L.P. (AV)

900 Old Kent Building, 111 Lyon Street, N.W., 49503-2489
Telephone: 616-752-2000
Fax: 616-752-2500
URL: http://www.wnj.com
Muskegon, Michigan Office: 400 Terrace Plaza, P.O. Box 900.
Telephone: 231-727-2600.
Fax: 231-727-2699.
Holland, Michigan Office: Curtis Center, Suite 300, 170 College Avenue.
Telephone: 616-396-9800.
Fax: 616-396-3656.
Southfield, Michigan Office: 1000 Town Center, Suite 650.
Telephone: 248-223-5000.
Fax: 248-223-5005.

MEMBERS OF FIRM

Charles E. McCallum	Cameron S. DeLong
James H. Breay	Michael H. Schubert (Resident Member, Muskegon Office)
Robert H. Skilton, III (Resident Member, Southfield Office)	Mark K. Harder (Resident Member, Holland Office)
Stephen C. Waterbury	Jeffrey A. Ott
Janet Percy Knaus	Judith Lowitz Adler (Resident Member, Southfield Office)
Kathleen M. Hanenburg	
Tracy T. Larsen	

COUNSEL

Jerry D. Hanscum (Resident Member, Southfield Office)

For full biographical listings, see the Martindale-Hubbell Law Directory

LANSING, Ingham Co.

FOSTER, SWIFT, COLLINS & SMITH, P.C. (AV)

313 South Washington Square, 48933-2193
Telephone: 517-371-8100
Telecopier: 517-371-8200
URL: http://www.fosterswift.com
Farmington Hills, Michigan Office: 32300 Northwestern Highway, Suite 230.
Telephone: 248-539-9900.
Fax: 248-851-7504.

Gary J. McRay	Jean G. Schtokal

For Complete List of Firm Personnel, See General Section

For full biographical listings, see the Martindale-Hubbell Law Directory

MONROE,* Monroe Co.

MILLER, CANFIELD, PADDOCK AND STONE, P.L.C. (AV)

A Professional Limited Liability Company
Founded in 1852 by Sidney Davy Miller
214 East Elm Avenue, Suite 100, 48162-2682
Telephone: 734-243-2000
Fax: 734-243-0901
URL: http://www.millercanfield.com
Detroit, Michigan Office: 150 West Jefferson, Suite 2500, 48226-4415.
Telephone: 313-963-6420.
Fax: 313-496-7500.
Cable Address: "Stem Detroit".
Ann Arbor, Michigan Office: 101 North Main Street, 7th Floor, 48104-1400.
Telephone: 734-663-2445.
Fax: 734-747-7147.
Troy, Michigan Office: 840 West Long Lake Road, Suite 200, 48098.
Telephone: 248-879-2000.
Fax: 248-879-2001.
Grand Rapids, Michigan Office: 99 Monroe, N.W., Suite 1200, 49503-2639.
Telephone: 616-454-8656.
Fax: 616-776-6322.
Howell, Michigan Office: 121 South Barnard Street, Suite 4, 48843-2305.
Telephone: 517-546-7600.
Telecopier: 517-546-6974.
Kalamazoo, Michigan Office: 444 West Michigan Avenue, 49007-3752.
Telephone: 616-381-7030.
Fax: 616-382-0244.
Lansing, Michigan Office: One Michigan Avenue, Suite 900, 48933-1609.
Telephone: 517-487-2070.
Fax: 517-374-6304.
Washington, D.C. Office: 1900 K Street, N.W., Suite 1150, 20006.
Telephone: 202-429-5575; 785-0600.
Fax: 202-331-1118; 785-1234.
Pensacola, Florida Office: 25 West Cedar, 32501.
Telephone: 850-469-1088.
Fax: 850-432-0677.
New York, New York Office: 1450 Broadway, 41st Floor, 10018.
Telephone: 212-704-4400.
Fax: 212-704-4410.
Gdynia, Poland Office: Ul. Slaska 21, 81-319.
Telephone: 011-485-831-2808.
Fax: 011-48-58-628 6411.
Warsaw, Poland Office: Ul. Nowogrodzkall, 5th Floor, 00-513.
Telephone: 011-4822 529 0200.
Fax: 011-4822 529 0201.
Katowice, Poland Office: Ul. Francuska 35/37, 40-027.
Telephone: 011 (48-32) 757-2414.
Fax: 011 (48-32) 757-2483.

RESIDENT PRINCIPALS

Roque E. Lipford (P.C.)

Representative Firm Clients: Chrysler Corporation; Comerica, Incorporated; City of Detroit, Michigan; Detroit Tigers, Inc.; First of Michigan; Ford Motor Company; Ford Motor Credit Company; Great Lakes Bancorp; Henry Ford Hospital; INVETECH Company.

For full biographical listings, see the Martindale-Hubbell Law Directory

INTERNATIONAL TRADE LAW

CALIFORNIA

CLAREMONT, Los Angeles Co.

JOHN W. TULAC (AV)

401 Harvard Avenue, 91711
Telephone: 909-445-1100
Fax: 909-445-1104
Email: jwtulac@ix.netcom.com *URL:* http://www.lawyers.com/jwt
Reference: Marine National Bank, Irvine.

For full biographical listings, see the Martindale-Hubbell Law Directory

COSTA MESA, Orange Co.

FELDHAKE, AUGUST & ROQUEMORE (AV)

Plaza Tower, Suite 1730, 600 Anton Boulevard, 92626-7124
Telephone: 714-438-3885
Fax: 714-438-3888
Email: farlaw@hqonline.com

Robert J. Feldhake
Kenneth S. August
Lisa A. Roquemore
Joshua M. Wolff

ASSOCIATES

Dimitri P. Gross
Supriya Kakkar
Katherine A. Slayton

OF COUNSEL

Arthur J. Swerdloff
Arthur M. Wilcox, Jr.

For full biographical listings, see the Martindale-Hubbell Law Directory

*LOS ANGELES,** Los Angeles Co.

STANTON P. BELLAND, P.C. (AV)

10 Universal City Plaza, Suite 2000, 91608-7806
Telephone: 818-754-3770
Telecopier: 818-754-3780
Email: stanlaw@earthlink.net

Stanton P. Belland

For full biographical listings, see the Martindale-Hubbell Law Directory

BRAND FARRAR & BUXBAUM LLP (AV)

515 South Flower Street, Suite 3500, 90071-2201
Telephone: 213-228-0288
Fax: 213-426-6222
Email: bfb-la@brandfarrar.com
Beijing (Peking), China Office: Suite 2518, China World Trade Centre, 1 Jian Guo Men Wai Avenue, Beijing, China.
Telephone: 86-10-6505-2288 Ext. 2523/2518.
Fax: 86-10-6505-2638. Email: bjbfbbj@public3.bta.net.cn
Chengdu, Sichuan, China Office: Suite 11A, Sichuan International Mansion, No. 1 Zhong Xi Shun Cheng Street, Chengdu, China.
Telephone: 86-28-652-1316.
Fax: 86-28-652-0547. Email: cdbfbcd@mail.sc.cninfo.net.
Chongqing, China Office: Suite 1510, Metropolitan Tower, 68 Zourong Lu, Chongqing, China.
Telephone: 86-23-6382-8381.
Fax: 86-23-6382-8373. Email: cqbfbcq@public.cta.cq.cn.
Guangzhou (Canton), China Office: Suite 1305, Main Tower, GITIC Plaza Hotel, 339 Huanshi Dong Road, Guangzhou, China.
Telephone: 86-20-8331-1888, Ext. 71305.
Fax: 86-20-8331-2671. Email: gzbfbgz@public.guangzhou.gd.cn.
Hong Kong, China Office: Brand Farrar Buxbaum LLP, 5/F., Landmark East, 12 Ice House Street, Central, Hong Kong, China.
Telephone: 852-2523-7001.
Fax: 852-2845-0947. Email: hkbfbhk@hk.super.net.
Los Angeles, California Office: Brand Farrar & Buxbaum LLP, Suite 3500, 515 South Flower Street, Los Angeles, California, 90071-2201.
Telephone: 213-228-0288.
Fax: 213-426-6222. Email: bfb-la@brandfarrar.com.
New York, New York Office: 275 Madison Avenue, 37th Floor, New York, New York, 10097.
Telephone: 212-286-0038.
Fax: 212-573-9077. Email: martineh@aol.com
Shanghai, China Office: Brand Farrar Buxbaum LLP, Suites 2611-12, Central Plaza, 227 Huangpi Bei Lu, Shanghai, China.
Telephone: 86-21-6375-8918.
Fax: 86-21-6375-8922. Email: shbfbsh@public2.sta.net.cn
Shenzhen, China Office: Suite 2103A, Shenzhen Development Center, Renmin Nan Lu, Shenzhen, China.
Telephone: 86-755-229-8009.
Fax: 86-755-229-8011. Email: szbfbsz@public.szptt.net.cn.

(See Next Column)

Ulaanbaatar, Mongolia Office: Brand Farrar Buxbaum LLP, 4/F., Time Center, No. 50 Baga Toiruu, Ulaanbaatar, Mongolia.
Telephone: 976-1-31-0711.
Fax: 976-1-32-5102. Email: mgbfbmg@magicnet.mn.
Xiamen, China Office: Suite 1182 Jian Ye Building, 28 Hubin North Road, Xiamen, China.
Telephone: 86-592-506-3059.
Fax: 86-592-511-1044. Email: xmbfbxm@public.xm.fj.cn.
Associated Office, Mumbai, Bombay, India: Shah & Sanghavi, Advocates, Solicitors & Notary, 114-A Mittal Court, Nariman Point, Mumbai 400 021 India.
Telephone: 91-22-285-5755/56 or 91-22-285-3592/93.
Fax: 91-22-284-5040.

PRINCIPALS

Michael A. Brand
David C. Buxbaum (China Offices)
Kenneth Y. Choy (Hong Kong Office)
Robert W. Dziubla
David W. Farrar
Amy E. Freilich
Margaret G. Graf
John Masao Iino
Charles K. Kolstad
Edward H. Martin (New York Office)
Gregory D. Trimarche
Li Zhuogen (China Offices)

OTHER ATTORNEYS RESIDENT IN LOS ANGELES OFFICE

Sherry L. Geyer
Joan M. Marquardt
James H. Service
Jeffrey S. Allen
Julia Sylva
Brian J. Kim
Lisa Teng

OTHER ATTORNEYS RESIDENT IN BEIJING OFFICE

Hao Xiaodong
Bin Zhao
Luo Rongping
Zhang Chunbo

OTHER ATTORNEYS RESIDENT IN CHENGDU, SICHUAN OFFICE

Zeng Xiangyu
Wu Wen

OTHER ATTORNEY RESIDENT IN CHONGQING OFFICE

Du Fei

OTHER ATTORNEYS RESIDENT IN GUANGZHOU OFFICE

Zou Wenyan (Not admitted in United States)
Feng Ruiding
Jia Guangxi

OTHER ATTORNEYS RESIDENT IN HONG KONG OFFICE

Shane F. Weir
Cheonghar Wong
N.T.S. Kularatne
Simon Woo
David William Gunson
Arthur Burton Crook
Simon K.C. Lee
Cheng Yuen Yi
Lo Wing Cheong
Nicholas C. McGrenra
Eva Y.N. Kwok

OTHER ATTORNEYS RESIDENT IN NEW YORK OFFICE

Vincent I. S. Hsieh (Of Counsel)
Jeffrey Schall
Jonathan Chun Wang

OTHER ATTORNEYS RESIDENT IN SHANGHAI OFFICE

Lin Yong
Wu Hong Liang
Tang Ying
Zhang Guoyao
Qi Zhenwen

OTHER ATTORNEYS RESIDENT IN SHENZHEN OFFICE

Zhong Wenya
Zhang He

OTHER ATTORNEYS RESIDENT IN ULAANBAATAR OFFICE

Byambaa Bayarmaa
Ajiv Enhktuya

OTHER ATTORNEY RESIDENT IN XIAMEN OFFICE

Deng Sheng

For full biographical listings, see the Martindale-Hubbell Law Directory

*SAN DIEGO,** San Diego Co.

NANCY FULLER-JACOBS & ASSOCIATES (AV)

11512 El Camino Real, Suite 200, 92130
Telephone: 619-259-4875
Fax: 619-259-4752
Email: nfjlaw@cts.com *URL:* http://www.lawyers.com/nfj&alaw

ASSOCIATES

Karine Faure
E. Franklin Haignere

For full biographical listings, see the Martindale-Hubbell Law Directory

DISTRICT OF COLUMBIA

WASHINGTON, D.C. Co.

ABLONDI, FOSTER, SOBIN & DAVIDOW, P.C. (AV)

1150 Eighteenth Street, N.W., Ninth Floor, 20036
Telephone: 202-296-3355
Facsimile: 202-296-3922
Email: afsd@ablondifoster.com *URL:* http://www.ablondifoster.com

(See Next Column)

ABLONDI, FOSTER, SOBIN & DAVIDOW P.C., *Washington—Continued*

Richard H. Abbey (Not admitted in DC)
Italo H. Ablondi
Gary L. Bohlke
Joel Davidow
Peter D. Ehrenhaft
F. David Foster
Peter J. Koenig (Not admitted in DC)
Will E. Leonard
Dale E. McNiel
Sturgis M. Sobin
James Taylor, Jr.

SENIOR ATTORNEY

John C. Steinberger

John C. Chiu (Not admitted in DC)
Laurent DeWinter
Sarah M. Nappi
Joel W. Rogers

COUNSEL

Michael T. Brady
Mark R. Leventhal
Mandana Parsazad

For full biographical listings, see the Martindale-Hubbell Law Directory

ADDUCI, MASTRIANI & SCHAUMBERG, L.L.P. (AV)

1200 Seventeenth Street, N.W., Fifth Floor, 20036-3006
Telephone: 202-467-6300
Telefax: 202-466-2006
Email: ams@adduci.com *URL:* http://www.adduci.com

V. James Adduci, II
Louis S. Mastriani
Tom M. Schaumberg
Barbara A. Murphy
Timothy Sullivan
David A. Guth (1953-1997)
Katherine S. Nucci
Harvey B. Fox
Gregory C. Anthes

Michael L. Doane
Steven E. Adkins
Allan J. Stevenson
Alfred M. Haas
Adam F. Bobrow

A list of Representative Clients and References will be furnished upon request.

For full biographical listings, see the Martindale-Hubbell Law Directory

MILLER & COMPANY P.C. (AV)

1825 I Street, N.W., Suite 400, 20006
Telephone: 202-429-2017
Fax: 202-659-6848
Email: intllaw@millerco.com *URL:* http://www.millerco.com
Kansas City, Missouri Office: 4929 Main Street, 64112.
Telephone: 816-561-4999.
Fax: 816-561-5999.

Marshall V. Miller (Not admitted in DC)

For full biographical listings, see the Martindale-Hubbell Law Directory

CARLOS RODRIGUEZ & ASSOCIATES (AV)

1710 Rhode Island Avenue, N.W. Tenth Floor, 20036-3007
Telephone: 202-293-3300
Facsimile: 202-293-3307
Email: rodriguez@transportlaw.com
Email: cra@intr.net *URL:* http://www.tradecompass.com/rodriguez

Carlos G. Rodriguez

ASSOCIATES

Helen M. Cousineau (Not admitted in DC)
Henry P. Gonzalez (Not admitted in DC)
Robert R. Herrell (Not admitted in DC)
Daniel W. Lenehan, III

OF COUNSEL

Todd C. Fineberg

CUSTOMS AFFAIRS COUNSEL

Donald W. Lewis

LEGAL SUPPORT PERSONNEL

Ashley W. Craig

For full biographical listings, see the Martindale-Hubbell Law Directory

THOMSEN AND BURKE, LLP (AV)

Suite 500, 1225 Eye Street, N.W., 20005
Telephone: 202-682-4741
Fax: 202-547-3713
URL: http://www.t-b.com
Baltimore, Maryland Office: Suite 400, One North Charles Street, 21201.
Telephone: 410-539-2595.
FAX: 410-783-0710.

Roszel C. Thomsen, II

Antoinette D. Paytas

For full biographical listings, see the Martindale-Hubbell Law Directory

WOLF, ARNOLD & CARDOSO, P.C. (AV)

1150 18th Street, N.W. Suite 275, 20036
Telephone: 202-857-0585
Facsimile: 202-293-2068
Email: wac@interlawyers.com *URL:* http://www.interlawyers.com
New York, N.Y. Office: Wolf, Arnold & Knoll, P.C., 590 Madison Avenue.
Telephone: 212-521-4410.
Fax: 212-465-9104.
Rio de Janeiro, Brazil Office: Cardoso, Rocha, Trindale & Lara Resende.
Bogota, Colombia Office: Arango, Nieto, Calderon & Asociados.
Caribbean Office: Dunn, Cox, Orett and Ashenheim, Kingston, Jamaica.
Other Associated offices also throughout Latin America, The Caribbean, Asia and the South Pacific.

Elting Arnold (1912-1988)
Louis T. Urbanczyk (1926-1995)
Maurice Wolf
Carlos E. Cardoso (Not admitted in the United States; Resident Rio de Janeiro, Brazil)
Lawrence I. Knoll
Gilberto Arango (Not admitted in the United States; Resident, Bogota, Columbia)
Rafael Nieto-Navia (Not admitted in the United States; Resident Bogota, Columbia Office)

For full biographical listings, see the Martindale-Hubbell Law Directory

FLORIDA

*MIAMI,** Dade Co.

SANDLER, TRAVIS & ROSENBERG, P.A. (AV)

The Waterford, 5200 Blue Lagoon Drive, Suite 600, 33126-2022
Telephone: 305-267-9200
Telecopier: 305-267-5155
Email: info@strtrade.com *URL:* http://www.strtrade.com
Washington, D.C. Office: 1300 Pennsylvania Avenue, Suite 400, 20004.
Telephone: 202-638-2230.
Fax: 202-638-2236.
New York, New York Office: 551 Fifth Avenue, Suite 605, 10176.
Telephone: 212-883-1300.
Fax: 212-883-0068.
Atlanta, Georgia Office: 1201 Peachtree Street, N.E., Suite 200, 30361-3500.
Telephone: 404-877-9197.
Fax: 404-877-9198.
Baltimore, Maryland Office: 111 South Calvert Street, Suite 2700, 21202.
Telephone: 410-385-5208.
Fax: 410-837-2441.
San Francisco, California Office: Sandler, Travis & Rosenberg and Glad & Ferguson, P.C., 1 Sutter Street, 10th Floor, 94014.
Telephone: 415-986-1088.
Fax: 415-986-2271.
Chicago, Illinois Office: 200 South Wacker Drive, Suite 3100, 60606.
Telephone: 312-674-4700.
Telecopier: 312-674-4701.

Gilbert Lee Sandler
Thomas G. Travis
Leonard L. Rosenberg
Edward M. Joffe
Jorge R. Lopez

Jorge Espinosa
Gerson M. Joseph
Larry Ordet
Carlos H. Halasz (Not admitted in FL)
Jeannette Mirabal
Francesca Russo-DiStaulo

OF COUNSEL

L. Jana Sigars

For full biographical listings, see the Martindale-Hubbell Law Directory

*ORLANDO,** Orange Co.

HENDRY, STONER, SAWICKI & BROWN, P.A. (AV)

200 East Robinson Street, Suite 500, 32801
Telephone: 407-843-5880
Fax: 407-425-7905
Email: HSSB@gdi.net

Robert R. Hendry
Richard D. Stoner
Stephen C. Sawicki
G. Steven Brown

Richard A. Barfield

OF COUNSEL

Laura A. Quigley, P.A.
Deborah J. Townsend
Carl-Christian Thier (Not admitted in FL)
Marcus R. Cigagna (Not admitted in the United States)
Jacqueline E. Danzer (Not admitted in the United States)

(See Next Column)

HENDRY, STONER, SAWICKI & BROWN P.A.—*Continued*

Counsel For: Virgin Incoming Services, Inc.; Weitnauer Trading Co. Ltd.; Dufrepex; Fairholme U.S., Inc.; Central Florida Hotel Company, L.C.; Orlando Auto Sales, Inc.; Mears Motor Leasing; Weitnauer America, Inc.; Wolf and Wolf International Inc.; New Jersey Manufacturers Insurance Co.; International Planning, Inc.

For full biographical listings, see the Martindale-Hubbell Law Directory

INDIANA

*INDIANAPOLIS,** Marion Co.

ICE MILLER DONADIO & RYAN (AV)

One American Square Box 82001, 46282-0002
Telephone: 317-236-2100
Fax: 317-236-2219
Email: info@imdr.com *URL:* http://www.imdr.com
South Bend, Indiana Office: 211 West Washington Street, Suite 2420.
Telephone: 219-234-7933.
Fax: 219-234-7965. Internet E-mail: info@imdr.com. Web Site Address: http://www.imdr.com.
Chicago, Illinois Office: 135 South LaSalle Street, Suite 4100.
Telephone: 312-726-1567.
Fax: 312-641-6263. Internet E-mail: info@imdr.com. Web Site Address: http://www.imdr.com.

MEMBERS OF FIRM

Richard E. Parker
Dale E. Stackhouse
Susan Barnhizer Rivas
Antje C. Petersen

OF COUNSEL

Daniel E. Fisher

STAFF ATTORNEY

Mikio Nishizu

Representative Clients: Avesta Sheffield; Biomet, Inc.; Reilly Industries, Inc.; Eli Lilly; Guide Corporation; Indianapolis Motor Speedway; INTAT Precision, Inc.; Delco Remy America, Inc.; Magnequench International, Inc.; Norcote International, Inc.

For Complete List of Firm Personnel, See General Section

For full biographical listings, see the Martindale-Hubbell Law Directory

LOUISIANA

*NEW ORLEANS,** Orleans Parish

MCGLINCHEY STAFFORD (AV)

A Professional Limited Liability Company
643 Magazine Street, 70130-3477
Telephone: 504-586-1200
Fax: 504-596-2800
TDD: (504) 596-2728
Telex: 584327
Cable Address: "MACSTAC"
Mailing Address: P.O. Box 60643, New Orleans, Louisiana, 70160-0643
Email: @mcglinchey.com *URL:* http://www.mcglinchey.com
Dallas, Texas Office: 2777 Stemmons Freeway, Suite 925, 75207-2401.
Telephone: 214-860-9700.
Fax: 214-860-9750.
Houston, Texas Office: 2727 Allen Parkway, Suite 1900, 77019.
Telephone: 713-520-1900.
Fax: 713-520-1025.
Baton Rouge, Louisiana Office: Ninth Floor, One American Place, 70825-0001.
Telephone: 504-383-9000.
Fax: 504-343-3076.
Jackson, Mississippi Office: Suite 1200, SkyTel Centre, 200 South Lamar Street, 39201.
Telephone: 601-960-8400.
Fax: 601-960-8406.
Lake Providence, Louisiana Office: 405 Morgan Street, 71254-2691.
Telephone: 318-559-1200.
Fax: 318-559-0609.
Monroe, Louisiana Office: Dean ONB Tower, 130 Desiard Street, Suite 807, 71201.
Telephone: 318-651-0807.
Fax: 318-651-0809.

MEMBERS OF FIRM

John H. Clegg
Daphne McNutt

ASSOCIATES

David Ball
Eric J. Simonson

For full biographical listings, see the Martindale-Hubbell Law Directory

MAINE

*PORTLAND,** Cumberland Co.

PERKINS, THOMPSON, HINCKLEY & KEDDY, P.A. (AV)

One Canal Plaza, P.O. Box 426, 04112-0426
Telephone: 207-774-2635
Fax: 207-871-8026
Email: admin@pthklaw.com *URL:* http://www.pthklaw.com

Thomas Schulten
Bruce E. Leddy
Douglas S. Carr
Andrew A. Cadot
Philip C. Hunt
John S. Upton
Peggy L. McGehee
Melissa Hanley Murphy
John H. Rich III
John A. Ciraldo
John A. Hobson
Timothy P. Benoit
Fred W. Bopp III
Craig N. Denekas
Mark P. Snow
William J. Sheils

David B. McConnell
Paul D. Pietropaoli
Aaron D. Julien
Gregory B. Poitras
Jennifer L. Sanders
John G. Osborn

OF COUNSEL

Owen W. Wells

For full biographical listings, see the Martindale-Hubbell Law Directory

MARYLAND

*BALTIMORE,** (Independent City)

THOMSEN AND BURKE, LLP (AV)

Suite 400, One North Charles Street, 21201
Telephone: 410-539-2595
Fax: 410-783-0710
URL: http://www.T-B.com
Washington, D.C. Office: Suite 500, 1225 Eye Street, N.W.
Telephone: 202-682-4741.
Fax: 202-547-3713.

MEMBER OF FIRM

Roszel C. Thomsen, II

ASSOCIATE

Antoinette D. Paytas

References: NationsBank; Mercantile-Safe Deposit & Trust Co.; Carroll County Bank and Trust Co.

For full biographical listings, see the Martindale-Hubbell Law Directory

MASSACHUSETTS

*BOSTON,** Suffolk Co.

HINCKLEY, ALLEN & SNYDER LLP (AV)

28 State Street, 30th Floor, 02109-1775
Telephone: 617-345-9000
Email: firm@haslaw.com *URL:* http://www.haslaw.com
Providence, Rhode Island Office: 1500 Fleet Center.
Telephone: 401-274-2000.
Fax: 401-277-9600. URL: http://www.hawlaw.com.

MEMBERS OF FIRM

Paula K. Andrews
E. Jerome Batty (Not admitted in MA)
Jonathan Bell
Paul Bork
Stephen J. Carlotti (Not admitted in MA)
David Barry Connolly
Joseph P. Curran (Not admitted in MA)
Michael P. DeFanti
Eric F. Eisenberg
Malcolm Farmer, III
Margaret D. Farrell (Not admitted in MA)
Pasco Gasbarro Jr.
Hugh J. Gorman, III
William R. Grimm
Michael J. Kelly
Matthew T. Marcello, III (Not admitted in MA)
Frederick P. McClure
Elizabeth Murdock Myers
Paul F. O'Donnell, III
Gerald J. Petros
Robert F. Sylvia
Howard E. Walker (Not admitted in MA)

(See Next Column)

HINCKLEY, ALLEN & SNYDER LLP, *Boston—Continued*

ASSOCIATES

Mark Bianchi
Andrew D. Cummings
June E. Daniel
(Not admitted in MA)
Gloria Maria Gutierrez
Kelley Jordan-Price

OF COUNSEL

Joachim A. Weissfeld (Not admitted in MA)

For Complete List of Firm Personnel, See General Section

For full biographical listings, see the Martindale-Hubbell Law Directory

LABOR AND EMPLOYMENT LAW

ALABAMA

*BIRMINGHAM,** Jefferson Co.

BERKOWITZ, LEFKOVITS, ISOM & KUSHNER, A PROFESSIONAL CORPORATION (AV)

SouthTrust Tower, 420 North Twentieth Street, Suite 1600, 35203-5202
Telephone: 205-328-0480
Telecopier: 205-322-8007
URL: http://www.blik.com

Frank S. James III
D. J. Simonetti
Wesley C. Redmond

Stanley W. Logan
Lee T. Clanton

For Complete List of Firm Personnel, See General Section

For full biographical listings, see the Martindale-Hubbell Law Directory

BRADLEY ARANT ROSE & WHITE LLP (AV)

2001 Park Place, Suite 1400, P.O. Box 830709, 35283-0709
Telephone: 205-521-8000
Facsimile: 205-521-8800
Facsimile (SouthTrust Tower Office): 205-521-8500
URL: http://www.barw.com
Huntsville, Alabama Office: 200 Clinton Avenue West, Suite 900, 35801.
Telephone: 205-517-5100.
Facsimile: 205-533-5069.
Washington, D.C. Office: 801 Pennsylvania Avenue, NW, Suite 230, 20004.
Telephone: 202-347-8893.
Facsimile: 202-347-1684.

MEMBERS OF FIRM

James Patrick Alexander
James S. Christie Jr.
John James Coleman Jr.
Forrest K. Covington
John E. Goodman
John William Hargrove
Warne S. Heath (Resident, Huntsville Office)
James Walker May
Robert K. Spotswood
Jay D. St. Clair
H. Harold Stephens (Resident, Huntsville Office)
Anne R. Yuengert

COUNSEL

Amy K. Myers

ASSOCIATES

Kelly Hubbard Estes
Abdul K. Kallon
Ronald H. Kent Jr.
David M. Lawson
Angus N. McFadden
T. Matthew Miller
Delores J. Simmons
Rusha C. Smith
John W. Smith T
Arnold W. Umbach III

For Complete List of Firm Personnel, See General Section

For full biographical listings, see the Martindale-Hubbell Law Directory

BURR & FORMAN LLP (AV)

3100 SouthTrust Tower, 420 North 20th Street, P.O. Box 830719, 35283-0719
Telephone: 205-251-3000
Facsimile: 205-458-5100
URL: http://www.burr.com
Huntsville, Alabama Office: Suite 204, Regency Center, 400 Meridian Street.
Telephone: 205-551-0010.
Facsimile: 205-551-0043.
Atlanta, Georgia Office: Suite 1200, One Georgia Center, 600 West Peachtree Street, 30308.
Telephone: 404-815-3000.
Facsimile: 404-817-3244.

MEMBERS OF FIRM

D. Frank Davis
J. Fredric Ingram
J. Patrick Logan
Michael L. Lucas
Dent M. Morton
Mark Taliaferro, Jr.

OF COUNSEL

Samuel H. Burr
C. V. Stelzenmuller

For Complete List of Firm Personnel, See General Section

For full biographical listings, see the Martindale-Hubbell Law Directory

CARR, ALLISON, PUGH, HOWARD, OLIVER & SISSON, P.C. (AV)

400 Vestavia Parkway, Suite 400, 35216
Telephone: 205-822-2006
Fax: 205-822-2057
Email: CFC@caphos.com
Florence, Alabama Office: 212 South Cedar Street, 35630.
Telephone: 256-718-6040.
Fax: 256-718-2150.
Mobile, Alabama Office: P.O. Box 781,36601-0781.
Telephone: 334-621-4340.
Fax: 334-626-8928.

Charles F. Carr (Resident, Daphne Office)
Russell Q. Allison
Bennett L. Pugh
David K. Howard (Resident, Florence Office)
Thomas L. Oliver, II
William H. Sisson (Resident, Daphne Office)
Glenn E. Ireland
Thomas C. Logan
Donald B. Kirkpatrick, II
Sarah J. Carlisle
Craig W. Goolsby (Resident, Daphne Office)

Gregg L. Smith
Joseph H. Driver
Brett A. Ross
Thomas S. Thornton, III
W. Bradford Kittrell
Jeffrey B. Carr
Joseph H. Hilley
Jeremy N. Trousdale
Ryan G. Brake
Caroline T. Pryor (Resident, Daphne Office)

For full biographical listings, see the Martindale-Hubbell Law Directory

GORDON, SILBERMAN, WIGGINS & CHILDS, P.C. (AV)

1400 SouthTrust Tower, 420 North 20th Street, 35203
Telephone: 205-328-0640
Facsimilie: 205-254-1500
Washington, D.C. Office: 1621 Connecticut Avenue, N.W., Suite 400.
Telephone: 202-238-0690.
Facsimile: 202-238-0968.

RESIDENT SHAREHOLDERS

Robert L. Wiggins, Jr.
Robert F. Childs, Jr.
C. Michael Quinn
James Mendelsohn
Richard J. Ebbinghouse
Ann K. Wiggins
Samuel Fisher
Ann C. Robertson
Deborah A. Mattison

RESIDENT ASSOCIATES

Byron R. Perkins
Jon C. Goldfarb
Gregory O. Wiggins
Lee Winston
Rocco Calamusa, Jr.
Joel S. Isenberg
Laura M. Hitt
Kyle T. Smith
Maury S. Weiner
Robbie Steele Martin
Abigail P. van Alstyne
Kell A. Simon
Russell W. Adams
Kimberly C. Page
Scott A. Gilliland
Eden Brown Gaines

For Complete List of Firm Personnel, See General Section

For full biographical listings, see the Martindale-Hubbell Law Directory

GORHAM & WALDREP, P.C. (AV)

2101 6th Avenue North, Suite 700, 35203
Telephone: 205-254-3216; 251-9166
Telecopier: 205-324-3802
Email: info@gorham-waldrep.com *URL:* http://www.gorham-waldrep.com
Montgomery, Alabama Office: 250 Commerce Street, P.O. Box 4837, 36103-4837.
Telephone: 334-262-0777.
Telecopier: 334-262-0742.

Thomas L. Stewart
Michael G. Kendrick
LaVeeda Morgan Battle

Victoria Franklin-Sisson

Representative Clients: Jefferson County Personnel Board; Birmingham-Jefferson Civic Center Authority; The Water Works and Sewer Board of the City of Birmingham; City of Homewood; American Federation of Government Employees Local #1945; City of Pelham; Town of Kimberly; Alabama Tire Dealers Assn.; Southern States Body Shop Assn.

For Complete List of Firm Personnel, See General Section

For full biographical listings, see the Martindale-Hubbell Law Directory

HASKELL SLAUGHTER & YOUNG, L.L.C. (AV)

1200 AmSouth/Harbert Plaza, 1901 Sixth Avenue North, 35203
Telephone: 205-251-1000
Facsimile: 205-324-1133
Email: hsy@hsy.com
Montgomery, Alabama Office: 305 South Lawrence Street, P.O. Box 4660. 36103-4660.
Telephone: 334-265-8573.
Facsimile: 334-264-7945.

(See Next Column)

HASKELL SLAUGHTER & YOUNG L.L.C., *Birmingham—Continued*

Frank M. Young, III
Richard H. Walston
Stephen L. Poer
Michael K. K. Choy
Beverly P. Baker
Carter H. Dukes

Georgia Sullivan Roberson
James A. Patton, Jr.
Joseph N. Harden

Representative Clients: The Equitable Life Assurance Society of the United States; Executive Risk; Frito-Lay, Inc.; HEALTHSOUTH Coproration; Jefferson County Racing Association; Marshall Durbin Companies; Montgomery County, Alabama; Raytheon Aircraft Company; UNUM Life Insurance Company of America; Webster Industries, Inc.

For Complete List of Firm Personnel, See General Section

For full biographical listings, see the Martindale-Hubbell Law Directory

JOHNSTON BARTON PROCTOR & POWELL LLP (AV)

2900 AmSouth/Harbert Plaza, 1901 Sixth Avenue North, 35203-2618
Telephone: 205-458-9400
Telecopier: 205-458-9500
Email: Law@JBPP.com

MEMBERS OF FIRM

Charles A. Powell, III
Anthony A. Joseph
Barry V. Frederick
William G. Somerville III
David W. Proctor
William K. Hancock
John W. Sheffield

COUNSEL

Charles Morgan, Jr.
Paul E. Toppins

ASSOCIATES

Debra Lee Mackey
Brian Roberts Bostick
M. Jefferson Starling, III
Christopher W. Deering
Jennifer Fox Swain
Donald Eugene Hayes, Jr.
Spencer A. Kinderman
William Cory Barker

General Counsel for: Baptist Health System, Inc.
Counsel for: American Color Graphics, Inc.; Beverly Enterprises, Inc.; Birmingham News Co.; Chubb Group of Insurance Companies; General Motors Corp.; Hardee's Food Systems/CKE Restuarants, Inc.; JVC America, Inc.; Southern Pride Catfish Co., Inc.; Wal-Mart Stores, Inc.

For full biographical listings, see the Martindale-Hubbell Law Directory

LEHR MIDDLEBROOKS PRICE & PROCTOR, P.C. (AV)

2021 Third Avenue North, Suite 300, 35203
Telephone: 205-326-3002
Telecopier: 205-326-3008
Email: LMPPLAW1@AOL.com
Decatur, Alabama Office: 303 Cain Street, North East, Suite 300.
Telephone: 256-308-2767.
Facsimile: 256-355-9106.

Richard I. Lehr
Albert L. Vreeland, II
David J. Middlebrooks
Brent L. Crumpton
Terry Price
Steven M. Stastny
R. David Proctor
Michael Broom
(Resident, Decatur Office)

Sally Broatch Waudby
Marcia Bull Stadeker
Kimberly Keefer Boone
Tessa M. Thrasher

For full biographical listings, see the Martindale-Hubbell Law Directory

LIGHTFOOT, FRANKLIN & WHITE, L.L.C. (AV)

The Clark Building, 400 20th Street North, 35203
Telephone: 205-581-0700
Facsimile: 205-581-0799
Email: LFWlaw@LFWlaw.com *URL:* http://www.lfwlaw.com

Warren B. Lightfoot
Mac M. Moorer
Jere F. White, Jr.
William H. King, III

Melody L. Hurdle
William H. Morrow
Anne Sikes Hornsby

For full biographical listings, see the Martindale-Hubbell Law Directory

NAKAMURA, QUINN & WALLS, LLP (AV)

(A Partnership Including Professional Corporations)
Suite 300, Landmark Center, 2100 First Avenue North, 35203-4226
Telephone: 205-323-8504
Telefax: 205-323-1102
TDD 1-800-548-2546
Email: nakquinn@scott.net
Atlanta, Georgia Office: 1800 Century Boulevard, Suite 1220.
Telephone: 404-633-5579.
Fax: 404-636-8711.

(See Next Column)

MEMBERS OF FIRM

Patrick K. Nakamura
Robert M. Weaver
John L. Quinn
George N. Davies
J. Michael Walls (P.C.)
(Resident, Atlanta, GA Office)

ASSOCIATE

Michael E. Bevers

OF COUNSEL

Claudia H. Pearson

For full biographical listings, see the Martindale-Hubbell Law Directory

REDDEN, MILLS & CLARK (AV)

940 Regions Bank Building, 417 North 20th Street, 35203
Telephone: 205-322-0457
Fax: 205-322-8481
URL: http://www.rmc-law.com

MEMBERS OF FIRM

L. Drew Redden
Gerald L. Miller
William H. Mills
Stephen W. Shaw
William N. Clark
Maxwell H. Pulliam, Jr.
Ronald J. Gault

References: SouthTrust Bank; Regions Bank.

For full biographical listings, see the Martindale-Hubbell Law Directory

JOHN D. SAXON, P.C. (AV)

1000 Financial Center, 505 North 20th Street, 35203
Telephone: 205-324-0223
Facsimile: 205-323-1583

John D. Saxon

Tammy Cecile Murphy Woolley

LEGAL SUPPORT PERSONNEL

Delilah Cole

For full biographical listings, see the Martindale-Hubbell Law Directory

SPAIN & GILLON, L.L.C. (AV)

The Zinszer Building, 2117 2nd Avenue North, 35203
Telephone: 205-328-4100
Telecopier: 205-324-8866
Email: ddh@spain-gillon.com *URL:* http://lawlinks.com:80/atty/al/sggbn.html

MEMBERS OF FIRM

Eugene P. Stutts
Alton B. Parker, Jr.
Samuel H. Frazier
Elizabeth Ann McMahan
David S. Maxey

General Counsel for: Piggly Wiggly Alabama Distributing Co.; General Corp.; Koppers Industries.
Counsel for: University of Alabama at Birmingham; Jefferson County Health Department; City of Birmingham.

For Complete List of Firm Personnel, See General Section

For full biographical listings, see the Martindale-Hubbell Law Directory

THOMAS, MEANS, GILLIS, DEVLIN, ROBINSON & SEAY, P.C. (AV)

1035 Financial Center, 505 20th Street North, 35203-2605
Telephone: 205-328-7915
Fax: 205-214-6160
Mailing Address: P.O. Box 370497, Birmingham, AL, 35237-0447
Email: tmgpc.lawfirm@tmgpc.com *URL:* http://www.tmgpc.com
Montgomery, Alabama Office: 3121 Zelda Court, P.O. Drawer 5058, 36103-5058.
Telephone: 334-270-1033.
Fax: 334-260-9396, E-mail: tmgpc.lawfirm@tmgpc.com. URL: http://www.tmgpc.com
Atlanta, Georgia Office: The Chandler Building, Suite 300, 127 Peachtree Street N.E., 30303.
Telephone: 404-222-8400.
Fax: 404-222-0080. E-Mail: tmgpc.lawfir@tmgpc.com. URL: http://www.tmgpc.com

Kenneth L. Thomas (Resident)

James L. Richey (Resident)
Lisa F. Brown (Resident)
Wendell J. Chambliss (Resident)
Valerie L. Acoff (Resident)
Edward J. Berry (Resident)

For full biographical listings, see the Martindale-Hubbell Law Directory

*CULLMAN,** Cullman Co.

ST. JOHN & ST. JOHN, L.L.C. (AV)

108 Third Street South East, P.O. Drawer K, 35056-3542
Telephone: 256-734-3542
Fax: 256-734-3544

MEMBERS OF FIRM

F. E. St. John (1874-1943)
Finis E. St. John (1909-1984)
Finis E. St. John, III (1933-1984)
Finis E. St. John, IV
Gaynor L. St. John

ASSOCIATE

Rita P. Farris

OF COUNSEL

Juliet G. St. John

Attorneys for: U.S. Fidelity & Guaranty Co.; Travelers Insurance Co.; Liberty Mutual Insurance Co.; ALFA Mutual Insurance Co.; First Federal Savings & Loan; The Atlanta Casualty Companies; Auto-Owners Insurance Co.; Golden-Rod Broilers, Inc.; Cullman Products, Inc.; McGriff Industries, Inc.

For full biographical listings, see the Martindale-Hubbell Law Directory

*HUNTSVILLE,** Madison Co.

BRADLEY ARANT ROSE & WHITE LLP (AV)

200 Clinton Avenue West, Suite 900, 35801
Telephone: 205-517-5100
Facsimile: 205-517-5200
URL: http://www.barw.com
Birmingham, Alabama Office: 2001 Park Place, Suite 1400, P.O. Box 830709.
Telephone: 205-521-8000.
Facsimile: 205-521-8800. Facsimile (SouthTrust Tower Office): 205-521-8500.
Washington, D.C. Office: 801 Pennsylvania Avenue, NW, Suite 230, 20004.
Telephone: 202-347-8893.
Facsimile: 202-347-1684.

RESIDENT PARTNERS

Warne S. Heath
E. Cutter Hughes Jr.

RESIDENT ASSOCIATE

Kimberly B. Martin

For Complete List of Firm Personnel, See General Section

For full biographical listings, see the Martindale-Hubbell Law Directory

*MOBILE,** Mobile Co.

ARMBRECHT, JACKSON, DEMOUY, CROWE, HOLMES & REEVES, L.L.C. (AV)

1300 Riverview Plaza, P.O. Box 290, 36601
Telephone: 334-405-1300
Facsimile: 334-432-6843; 433-3821
Email: adc@ajlaw.com

MEMBERS OF FIRM

Broox G. Holmes
William B. Harvey
Kirk C. Shaw
David A. Bagwell
Broox G. Holmes, Jr.

ASSOCIATE

J. Walton Jackson

Representative Clients: Automation Technology International, Inc.; Loyal American Life Insurance Co.; WKRG-TV-Channel 5; BP Oil Co.; Kimberly-Clark Corp.; David Volkert & Assoc., Inc.; Southern Chemical Formulators, Inc.; University of South Alabama.

For Complete List of Firm Personnel, See General Section

For full biographical listings, see the Martindale-Hubbell Law Directory

GARDNER, MIDDLEBROOKS, FLEMING, GIBBONS & KITTRELL, P.C. (AV)

64 North Royal Street, Drawer 3103, 36652
Telephone: 334-433-8100
Telecopier: 334-433-8181
Email: GMFH@WORLDNET.ATT.NET
Birmingham, Alabama Office: Suite 450, 2013 1st Avenue, North.
Telephone: 205-250-7776.
Telecopier: 205-250-7675.
Washington, D.C. Office: 1919 S Street NW, Washington, D.C.
Telephone: 202-667-8278.
Telecopier: 202-234-1003.

J. Cecil Gardner
Sherwood C. Middlebrooks, III
Charles J. Fleming
John D. Gibbons
Braxton L. Kittrell, Jr.

(See Next Column)

Mary Elizabeth Olsen
Kimberly J. Calametti
Walter G. (Stoney) Chavers

Representative Clients: Alabama AFL-CIO; Southwest Alabama Labor Council, AFL-CIO; Greater Mobile Port Council, AFL-CIO; Mobile/Pensacola; Building Trades Council, AFL-CIO; Paper Allied-Industrial Chemical Energy Workers International Union, AFL CIO; Oil, Chemical & Atomic Workers International Union, AFL-CIO; International Organization of Masters, Mates & Pilots, AFL-CIO; International Brotherhood of Boilermakers, AFL-CIO; International Alliance of Theatrical Stage Employees & Moving Picture Machine Operators, AFL-CIO.

For full biographical listings, see the Martindale-Hubbell Law Directory

JOHNSTONE, ADAMS, BAILEY, GORDON AND HARRIS, L.L.C. (AV)

Royal St. Francis Building, 104 St. Francis Street, 8th Floor, P.O. Box 1988, 36633
Telephone: 334-432-7682
Facsimile: 334-432-0712 or 334-432-2800
Email: attorneys@JohnstoneAdams.com *URL:* http://www.JohnstoneAdams.com
Bay Minette, Alabama Office: Dahlberg Building, 107 Hand Avenue, P.O. Box 729, 36507.
Telephone: 334-937-9473.
Facsimile: 334-937-9475.

MEMBERS OF FIRM

Wade B. Perry, Jr.
Celia J. Collins
Tracy P. Turner

OF COUNSEL

Brock B. Gordon

For Complete List of Firm Personnel, See General Section

For full biographical listings, see the Martindale-Hubbell Law Directory

LYONS, PIPES & COOK, P.C. (AV)

2 North Royal Street, P.O. Box 2727, 36652-2727
Telephone: 334-432-4481
Cable Address: "Lysea"
Telecopier: 334-433-1820
URL: http://www.LPCLaw.com

Wesley Pipes
W. David Johnson, Jr.
Joseph J. Minus, Jr.
Caroline C. McCarthy

Representative Clients: Carriers Container Council, Inc.; Crawford & Company; Inchcape Shipping Services, Inc.; INSBROK; International Systems, Inc.; Jordan Industries, Inc.; Marriott Corporation; Massachusetts Mutual Life Insurance Co.; Spectacor Management Group; United States Fidelity & Guaranty.

For Complete List of Firm Personnel, See General Section

For full biographical listings, see the Martindale-Hubbell Law Directory

SINTZ, CAMPBELL, DUKE & TAYLOR (AV)

3763 Professional Parkway, 36609
Telephone: 334-344-7241
Fax: 334-344-7400

MEMBERS OF FIRM

Peter V. Sintz (1940-1997)
Robert C. Campbell, III
Frank G. Taylor
Steven L. Terry

ASSOCIATES

Wm. Kyle Morris
Kathryn W. Petersen
Barry C. Prine

OF COUNSEL

Leon G. Duke

LEGAL SUPPORT PERSONEL

James A. Koblas

Representative Clients: Aetna C & S Insurance Co.; Mobile County School Board; Auto-Owners Insurance Co.; Argonaut Insurance Co.; Mostellar Medical Clinic; Scottsdale Insurance Co.; American International Group; Alabama School of Math and Science; Mobile County Sheriff's Office.

For full biographical listings, see the Martindale-Hubbell Law Directory

*MONTGOMERY,** Montgomery Co.

HASKELL SLAUGHTER YOUNG & GALLION, L.L.C. (AV)

305 South Lawrence Street, P.O. Box 4660, 36103-4660
Telephone: 334-265-8573
Facsimile: 334-264-7945
Email: hsymont@actworld.net
Birmingham, Alabama Office: 1200 AmSouth/Harbert Plaza, 1901 Sixth Avenue North. 35203
Telephone: 205-251-1000.
Facsimile: 205-324-1133.

(See Next Column)

HASKELL SLAUGHTER YOUNG & GALLION L.L.C., *Montgomery—Continued*

Thomas T. Gallion, III
Constance C. Walker

Representative Clients: Executive Risk; Jefferson County Racing Association; Marshall Durbin Companies; Montgomery County, Alabama; Webster Industries, Inc.

For full biographical listings, see the Martindale-Hubbell Law Directory

ROBISON & BELSER, P.A. (AV)
200 Coosa Street, 36104
Telephone: 334-834-7000
Telecopier: 334-834-7011
Mailing Address: Drawer 1470, Montgomery, AL, 36102
Email: tsides@mont.mindspring.com

David B. Byrne, Jr.
Terry A. Sides

For full biographical listings, see the Martindale-Hubbell Law Directory

THOMAS, MEANS, GILLIS, DEVLIN, ROBINSON & SEAY, P.C. (AV)
3121 Zelda Court, P.O. Drawer 5058, 36103-5058
Telephone: 334-270-1033
Fax: 334-260-9396
Email: tmgpc.lawfirm@tmgpc.com *URL:* http://www.tmgpc.com
Birmingham, Alabama Office: 1035 Financial Center, 505 20th Street North, 35203. Mailing Address: P.O. Box 370447, Birmingham, AL., 35237-0447.
Telephone: 205-328-7915.
Fax: 205-214-6160. E-mail: tmgpc.lawfirm@tmgpc.com. URL: http://www.tmgpc.com
Atlanta, Georgia Office: The Chandler Building, Suite 300, 127 Peachtree Street, N.E., 30303.
Telephone: 404-222-8400.
Fax: 404-222-0080. E-Mail: tmgpc.lawfirm@tmgpc.com. URL: http://www.tmgpc.com

Kenneth L. Thomas (Resident, Birmingham, Alabama Office)
Tyrone C. Means
H. Lewis Gillis
Marvin A. Devlin (Resident, Atlanta, Georgia Office)
Mark E. Robinson (Resident, Atlanta, Georgia Office)
Quinton S. Seay (Resident, Atlanta, Georgia Office)

James L. Richey (Resident, Birmingham, Alabama Office)
Wendell J. Chambliss (Resident, Birmingham Office)
Lisa F. Brown (Resident, Birmingham, Alabama Office)
Valerie L. Acoff (Resident, Birmingham, Alabama Office)
John W. Adams, Jr.
Paul C. Williams
Jennifer D. Odom (Resident, Atlanta, Georgia Office)
Darnell D. Coley
Edward J. Berry (Resident, Birmingham, Alabama Office)
Thaddeus L. Hamilton (Resident, Birmingham, Alabama Office)

LEGAL SUPPORT PERSONNEL

Joyce L. Lehmann
Tonya White
Bryan Palmer
Felicia Kolley
John Baker (Office Administrator)
Cathy Allen
Lakesha Baker
Larry Holmes
Linda Steele
Mary Duncan
Pamela Watkins
Paula Mosely
Rodney Barganier
Tamara Venice
Linda Stoudemier

For full biographical listings, see the Martindale-Hubbell Law Directory

VOLZ, PRESTWOOD & HANAN, P.C. (AV)
350 Adams Avenue, P.O. Box 1910, 36102-1910
Telephone: 334-264-6401
Fax: 334-834-4954

Charles H. Volz, Jr.
Alvin T. Prestwood
Charles H. Volz, III
Ellis D. Hanan
Richard D. Lively
Judy H. Barganier

For full biographical listings, see the Martindale-Hubbell Law Directory

WEBB & ELEY, P.C. (AV)
166 Commerce Street, Suite 300, P.O. Box 238, 36101-0238
Telephone: 334-262-1850
Fax: 334-262-1772
Email: webbeley1@mindspring.com

James W. Webb
Michael M. Eley
Kendrick E. Webb
Craig S. Dillard
Bart Harmon
William R. Chandler

Frank E. Bankston, Jr.
Pamela Robinson Higgins
Shawn Junkins Cole
Michael J. Cohan
Lisa D. Van Wagner

(See Next Column)

LEGAL SUPPORT PERSONNEL

Janice B. Miller (Business Manager)

Reference: Regions Bank.

For full biographical listings, see the Martindale-Hubbell Law Directory

ALASKA

*ANCHORAGE,** Third Judicial District

DELANEY, WILES, HAYES, GERETY, ELLIS & YOUNG, INC. (AV)
1007 West Third Avenue, Suite 400, 99501
Telephone: 907-279-3581
Fax: 907-277-1331
Email: dwhge@alaska.net

Howard A. Lazar
Cynthia L. Ducey
Donna M. Meyers

Amy E. Headrick

Representative Clients: Carr-Gottstein Foods Co.; City Electric; Coregis Insurance Co.; Safeway, Inc.

For Complete List of Firm Personnel, See General Section

For full biographical listings, see the Martindale-Hubbell Law Directory

OWENS & TURNER, A PROFESSIONAL CORPORATION (AV)
1500 West 33rd Avenue, Suite 200, 99503-3502
Telephone: 907-276-3963
Facsimile: 907-277-3695
Email: mail@owensturner.com *URL:* http://www.owensturner.com

Thomas P. Owens, Jr.
Terrance A. Turner
William F. Mede
Scott J. Nordstrand

Erin Rose
Patrick J McCabe
Kimberly K. Geariety
Dennis J. Efta

LEGAL SUPPORT PERSONNEL

Susan M. Lamb

Representative Clients: AT&T Alascom; Alaska Housing Finance Corporation; Alaska Railroad Corporation; Arctic Slope Regional Corporation; BP Exploration (Alaska) Inc.; Municipality of Anchorage; Petro Star, Inc.; State of Alaska; Union Oil Co. of California; University of Alaska.

For full biographical listings, see the Martindale-Hubbell Law Directory

ARIZONA

*FLAGSTAFF,** Coconino Co.

HUFFORD, HORSTMAN, MONGINI, PARNELL & MCCARTHY, P.C. (AV)
323 North Leroux Street, P.O. Box B, 86002-0808
Telephone: 520-774-1453
Fax: 520-779-3621

C. Benson Hufford
Patrice M. Horstman
Michael E.J. Mongini
Eve A. Parnell
Philip (Jay) McCarthy, Jr.

E. Duane Weston

LEGAL SUPPORT PERSONNEL

R. Gehl Tucker (Legal Assistant)
Doris Utzinger (Legal Assistant)
Vickie Belman (Legal Assistant)
Jan Blackman (Paralegal)
Dawn L. Karsten (Paralegal)

Reference: Norwest Bank Arizona, N.A.

For full biographical listings, see the Martindale-Hubbell Law Directory

MANGUM, WALL, STOOPS & WARDEN, P.L.L.C. (AV)
100 North Elden, P.O. Box 10, 86002
Telephone: 520-779-6951
Fax: 520-773-1312

H. Karl Mangum (1908-1993)

OF COUNSEL

Douglas J. Wall
Robert W. Warden
Daniel J. Stoops

MEMBERS OF FIRM

A. Dean Pickett
Stephen K. Smith
Melinda L. Garrahan
Michael H. Hinson

(See Next Column)

MANGUM, WALL, STOOPS & WARDEN P.L.L.C.—*Continued*

ASSOCIATES

Annette Star Lustgarten
Rebecca Smith Currey
R. Scott Currey
Melinda K. Jacquez
Franklin Hoover

Representative Clients: Northern Arizona University; Flagstaff Unified School District; Museum of Northern Arizona; Arizona School Board Association.
Local Counsel for: Bank of America-Arizona; Arizona Public Service; U.S.A.A.; State Farm Fire & Casualty Insurance Co.; Property Development Co.

For Complete List of Firm Personnel, See General Section

For full biographical listings, see the Martindale-Hubbell Law Directory

MESA, Maricopa Co.

JACKSON WHITE GARDNER WEECH & WALKER, P.C. (AV)

40 North Center Street, Suite 200, 85201
Telephone: 480-464-1111
Fax: 480-464-5692
Statewide: 800-243-1160
Email: firm@azmesalaw.com *URL:* http://www.azmesalaw.com
Payson, Arizona Office: 708 East Highway 260, Suite C1-E.
Telephone: 520-472-8878.

Wayne L. Gardner
Eric M. Jackson
Michael R. Pruitt
J. Grant Walker
Bradley D. Weech
Richard A. White
David L. Weed
Roger R. Foote
Otto S. Shill, III

Eric K. Macdonald
Kelly G. Black
Melody K. Seal
Patricia A. Mancabelli
Bobbie J. Rasmusson
Maureen P. Kane
James L. Tanner

For full biographical listings, see the Martindale-Hubbell Law Directory

*PHOENIX,** Maricopa Co.

FENNEMORE CRAIG, A PROFESSIONAL CORPORATION (AV)

3003 North Central Avenue, Suite 2600, 85012-2913
Telephone: 602-916-5000
Fax: 602-916-5999
Tucson, Arizona Office: One South Church Avenue, Suite 1000, 85701-1620.
Telephone: 520-879-6800.
Fax: 520-879-6899.

Donald R. Gilbert
Ronald J. Stolkin
John J. Balitis, Jr.
Janice Procter-Murphy

Jeffrey S. Silvyn
Amy Abdo Anderson
Mary Beth Phillips
Erin E. Flaharty
Sal J. Rivera
Barney M. Holtzman
Michelle G. Marshall
Lori A. Higuera
Kim S. Alvarado
Michele L. Tyler

LEGAL SUPPORT PERSONNEL

LEGAL ASSISTANTS

Jane Friedman
Ann V. Kooi

For Complete List of Firm Personnel, See General Section

For full biographical listings, see the Martindale-Hubbell Law Directory

JEROME L. FROIMSON (AV)

340 East Palm Lane, Suite 150, 85004
Telephone: 602-252-4990
Fax: 602-271-9308
URL: http://www.lawyers.com/jeromelfroimson
Email: jlflaw@aol.com *URL:* http://www.jlflaw.com

Representative Clients: Smitty's Super Value, Inc.; Fleming Foods, Inc.; Arizona Community Foundation; Jerry's Restaurants; ABC Food Service, Inc.; Logistical Support, Inc.; Quick's Music Store, Inc.; Powerscreen of Arizona, Inc.; Sierra-Sonora Enterprises, Inc. (Dominos Pizza); Respond First Aid Systems.

For full biographical listings, see the Martindale-Hubbell Law Directory

GAONA MOORE, P.C. (AV)

National Bank Plaza, 3101 North Central Avenue, Suite 720, 85012
Telephone: 602-230-2636
Facsimile: 602-230-1377

David F. Gaona
Janice H. Moore

Tracey N. Fernandes

For full biographical listings, see the Martindale-Hubbell Law Directory

AMY J. GITTLER, PLC (AV)

2633 East Indian School Road, Suite 300, 85016-6759
Telephone: 602-224-6300
Facsimile: 602-224-6020
Email: amy@cgson.com *URL:* http://www.lawyers.com/gittlerlaw

Amy J. Gittler

Tricia Brown

For full biographical listings, see the Martindale-Hubbell Law Directory

DAVID F. GOMEZ A PROFESSIONAL CORPORATION (AV)

2525 East Camelback Road Suite 860, 85016
Telephone: 602-957-8686
Telecopier: 602-956-9854
Email: DFGPC@aol.com

David F. Gomez
Michael J. Petitti, Jr.

For full biographical listings, see the Martindale-Hubbell Law Directory

JENNINGS, STROUSS & SALMON, P.L.C. (AV)

A Professional Limited Liability Company
One Renaissance Square, Two North Central Avenue, 85004-2393
Telephone: 602-262-5911
Fax: 602-253-3255
Email: info@jsslaw.com *URL:* http://www.jsslaw.com
Arrowhead Office: 16150 North Arrowhead Fountains Center Drive, Suite 250, Peoria, Arizona.
Telephone: 623-878-2222.
Fax: 623-878-1333.

Gerald W. Alston
John G. Sestak, Jr.
Rita A. Meiser
Gary L. Lassen
Glenn J. Carter
Ernest Calderón
Michael V. Perry
John J. Egbert
Robert D. Haws

ASSOCIATES

Gordon Lewis
Kimberly J. Cilke

For Complete List of Firm Personnel, See General Section

For full biographical listings, see the Martindale-Hubbell Law Directory

RODNEY G. JOHNSON, LTD. (AV)

3707 North Seventh Street, Suite 250, 85014
Telephone: 602-285-0962
Fax: 602-285-0987

Rodney G. Johnson

For full biographical listings, see the Martindale-Hubbell Law Directory

LEWIS AND ROCA, LLP (AV)

A Limited Liability Partnership including a Professional Corporation
40 North Central Avenue, 85004-4429
Telephone: 602-262-5311
Fax: 602-262-5747
Email: clientservice@lrlaw.com *URL:* http://www.lrlaw.com
Tucson, Arizona Office: One South Church Avenue, Suite 700, 86701-1620.
Telephone: 520-622-2090.
Fax: 520-622-3088. E-Mail: clientservice@lrlaw.com.
Las Vegas, Nevada Affiliated Office: Ashcraft and Heinz LLP, 3960 Howard Hughes Parkway, 89109.
Telephone: 702-990-3570.
Fax: 702-990-3571.

MEMBERS OF FIRM

Richard S. Cohen
Christopher J. Brelje
Steven J. Hulsman
Jane E. Reddin

ASSOCIATES

Todd E. Hale
Stephanie M. Cerasano

OF COUNSEL

Barbara Anstey Hoerner
David A. Kelly
Dona A. Nutini

Representative Clients: Arizona Public Service Co.; City of Phoenix; Gosnell Development Corp.; MCI Communications Corp.; Maricopa Community College District; Phoenix Memorial Hospital; Rockford Corp.; Skymall, Inc.; Southwest Risk Services; United Parcel Service, Inc.

For Complete List of Firm Personnel, See General Section

For full biographical listings, see the Martindale-Hubbell Law Directory

LUBIN & ENOCH, P.C. (AV)

2702 North Third Street Suite 3020, 85004
Telephone: 602-234-0008
Fax: 602-264-0676

Stanley Lubin
Nicholas J. Enoch

For full biographical listings, see the Martindale-Hubbell Law Directory

Phoenix—Continued

QUARLES & BRADY LLP (AV)

One Camelback Building, One East Camelback Road, Suite 400, 85012-1649
Telephone: 602-230-5500
Fax: 602-230-5598
URL: http://www.quarles.com
Milwaukee, Wisconsin Office: 411 East Wisconsin Avenue.
Telephone: 414-277-5000.
Fax: 414-271-3552.
Madison, Wisconsin Office: First Wisconsin Plaza, One South Pinckney Street, P.O. Box 2113.
Telephone: 608-251-5000.
Fax: 608-251-9166.
West Palm Beach, Florida Office: 222 Lakeview Avenue, 4th Floor.
Telephone: 407-653-5000.
Fax: 407-653-5333.
Naples, Florida Office: Barnett Center, 4501 Tamiami Trail North, Suite 300.
Telephone: 813-262-5959.
Fax: 813-434-4999.
Chicago, Illinois Office: Quarles & Brady LLC, Citicorp Center, 500 West Madison Street, Suite 3700.
Telephone: 312-715-5000.
Fax: 312-715-5155.

MEMBERS OF THE FIRM

Charles W. Herf
Jon E. Pettibone
William M. Shattuck
David A. Selden
Colleen A. Scherkenbach

ASSOCIATES

Wendy Gerlach Briggs
Gregory J. Stanton
David T. Barton
C. Christine Burns
Julie A. Pace
Leezie Kim
Kevin M. Duddlesten (Not admitted in AZ)
Mireya Castillo Martin (Not admitted in AZ)
Mark A. Torre

For full biographical listings, see the Martindale-Hubbell Law Directory

ROGERS & WHALEN, P.A. (AV)

335 East Palm Lane, 85004
Telephone: 602-253-1500
Facsimile: 602-253-0071
Email: rogers.whalen@axtek.com

Thomas M. Rogers
Donna Hylarides Whalen

For full biographical listings, see the Martindale-Hubbell Law Directory

SHIMMEL, HILL, BISHOP & GRUENDER, P.C. (AV)

3700 North 24th Street, 85016
Telephone: 602-224-9500
Telecopier: 602-955-6176
URL: http://www.shimmelhill.com

Daniel F. Gruender
Keith F. Overholt

Representative Clients: The Ashton Companies; Associated General Contractors of America; Baker Bros.; Bashas' Stores; Black Mesa Pipeline Co.; First American Health Concepts, Inc.; Klondyke, Inc.; Vastco, Inc.

For full biographical listings, see the Martindale-Hubbell Law Directory

SNELL & WILMER L.L.P. (AV)

One Arizona Center, 85004-2202
Telephone: 602-382-6000
Fax: 602-382-6070
Email: postmaster@snellwilmer.com *URL:* http://www.swlaw.com
Tucson, Arizona Office: One South Church Avenue, Suite 1500, 85701-1612.
Telephone: 520-882-1200.
Fax: 520-884-1294.
Orange County Office: 1920 Main Street, Suite 1200, Irvine, California 92614-7230.
Telephone: 949-253-2700.
Fax: 949-955-2507.
Salt Lake City, Utah Office: 111 East Broadway, Suite 900, 84111-1004.
Telephone: 801-237-1900.
Fax: 801-237-1950.

MEMBERS OF FIRM

William R. Hayden
Gerard Morales
Lonnie J. Williams, Jr.
Vaughn A. Crawford
Rebecca A. Winterscheidt
Charles P. Keller
Lisa M. Coulter

ASSOCIATES

Jennifer Abracht-Smith
Stacy Gabriel
Kristin Major
L. Drew Metcalf
Stephanie Quincy
Michelle L. Ray
Heidi J. Richter

(See Next Column)

Representative Clients: For list of Representative Clients, see end of biographical listings in the Martindale-Hubbell Law Directory.

For Complete List of Firm Personnel, See General Section

For full biographical listings, see the Martindale-Hubbell Law Directory

*TUCSON,** Pima Co.

ERNEST ALLEN COHEN (AV)

6426 Calle de Los Seris, P.O. Box 37273, 85740
Telephone: 520-297-4100
Fax: 520-297-4105

Representative Clients: International Organization of Masters, Mates & Pilots, ILA, AFL-CIO; Lawyers Mediation Service Corp.; Coast Guard Legal Aid Counsel; Masters, Mates & Pilots Health & Benefit Plan; Co-Counsel, Officers Union of International Seamen; Arizona Airlines, Inc.

For full biographical listings, see the Martindale-Hubbell Law Directory

FENNEMORE CRAIG, A PROFESSIONAL CORPORATION (AV)

Suite 1000, One South Church Avenue, 85701-1620
Telephone: 520-879-6800
Fax: 520-879-6899
Phoenix, Arizona Office: 3003 North Central Avenue, Suite 2600, 85012-2913.
Telephone: 602-916-5000.
Fax: 602-916-5999.

Ronald J. Stolkin

Jeffrey S. Silvyn
Amy Abdo Anderson

LEGAL SUPPORT PERSONNEL

LEGAL ASSISTANTS

Jane Friedman

For Complete List of Firm Personnel, See General Section

For full biographical listings, see the Martindale-Hubbell Law Directory

SNELL & WILMER L.L.P. (AV)

One South Church Avenue, Suite 1500, 85701-1612
Telephone: 520-882-1200
Fax: 520-884-1294
URL: http://www.swlaw.com
Phoenix, Arizona Office: One Arizona Center, 85004-2202.
Telephone: 602-382-6000.
Fax: 602-382-6070.
Orange County Office: 1920 Main Street, Suite 1200, Irvine, California 92614-7230.
Telephone: 949-253-2700.
Fax: 949-955-2507.
Salt Lake City, Utah Office: 111 East Broadway, Suite 900, 84111-1004.
Telephone: 801-237-1900.
Fax: 801-237-1950.

MEMBERS OF FIRM

John A. Robertson
Tibor Nagy, Jr.
James K. (Jim) Mackie

ASSOCIATE

Michael J. Massee

Representative Clients: For list of Representative Clients, see end of biographical listings in the Martindale-Hubbell Law Directory.

For full biographical listings, see the Martindale-Hubbell Law Directory

*YUMA,** Yuma Co.

CLARK AND ASSOCIATES (AV)

256 South Second Avenue, 85364
Telephone: 520-783-6233
Fax: 520-783-0533
Email: jasclark@yahoo.com *URL:* http://www.lawyers.com/j__clark&assoc

MEMBER OF FIRM

A. James Clark

ASSOCIATE

Heather D. Moore

Representative Clients: Bruce Church, Inc.; Tanimura & Antle.

For full biographical listings, see the Martindale-Hubbell Law Directory

BEVERLY HILLS, Los Angeles Co.

SWERDLOW FLORENCE SANCHEZ & RATHBUN, A LAW CORPORATION (AV)

Suite 828, 9401 Wilshire Boulevard, 90212
Telephone: 310-201-4700
Fax: 310-273-8680
URL: http://www.sfsr.com

Seymour Swerdlow
Kenneth J. Florence
Millicent N. Sanchez
Sandy K. Rathbun
Janet I. Swerdlow

Jodi L. Karpel

For full biographical listings, see the Martindale-Hubbell Law Directory

CHICO, Butte Co.

SHEPHERD & CRABTREE (AV)

Suite 1, 1367 East Lassen Avenue, 95973
Telephone: 530-893-3700
Fax: 530-893-1579

MEMBERS OF FIRM

Michael T. Shepherd
Richard L. Crabtree

ASSOCIATES

Lindsey A. Holmes
Ron S. Chaplin

For full biographical listings, see the Martindale-Hubbell Law Directory

CLAREMONT, Los Angeles Co.

JOHN C. McCARTHY (AV)

401 Harvard Avenue, 91711
Telephone: 909-621-4984
Telecopier: 909-621-5757
(Also Member, Morrisons, McCarthy & Baraban, Claremont, California and Whitefish, Montana)

For full biographical listings, see the Martindale-Hubbell Law Directory

COSTA MESA, Orange Co.

RICKS & ANDERSON, A LAW CORPORATION (AV)

3200 Park Center Drive, Suite 1155, 92626-7163
Telephone: 714-966-9190

Cecil E. Ricks, Jr.
Annette L. Anderson

For full biographical listings, see the Martindale-Hubbell Law Directory

RUTAN & TUCKER, LLP (AV)

A Partnership including Professional Corporations
611 Anton Boulevard, Fourteenth Floor, P.O. Box 1950, 92626-1998
Telephone: 714-641-5100; 213-625-7586
Telecopier: 714-546-9035
Email: rutan&tucker@rutan.com *URL:* http://www.rutan.com

MEMBERS OF FIRM

David C. Larsen (P.C.)
James L. Morris
Ernest W. Klatte III
Jeffrey Wertheimer
Lien Ski Harrison
Carol D. Carty

ASSOCIATES

Mark D. Budensiek
April L. Walter
Julie L. Drew

For Complete List of Firm Personnel, See General Section

For full biographical listings, see the Martindale-Hubbell Law Directory

ENCINO, Los Angeles Co.

WALSH & DECLUES, LLP (AV)

15821 Ventura Boulevard Suite 625, P.O. Box 20087, 91416
Telephone: 818-986-1776
Facsimile: 818-382-2071
Email: lao@wd-law.com
Santa Ana, California Office: 6 Hutton Centre Drive, Suite 1050, P.O. Box 22021, 92702-2021.
Telephone: 714-436-1776.
Facsimile: 714-436-1771.
Walnut Creek, California Office: 2125 Oak Grove Road, Suite 110, 94598.
Telephone: 925-686-1776.
Facsimile: 925-906-1773.

MEMBERS OF FIRM

Dennis J. Walsh (Managing Partner, Encino Office)
J. Michael Declues (Managing Partner, Santa Ana Office)
Michael E. Burkett (Founding Partner, Resident, Santa Ana Office)
Glenn S. Goldby (Partner, Resident, Santa Ana Office)
Jeffrey P. Thompson (Partner, Resident, Santa Ana Office)

(See Next Column)

Joanne C. Schwartz (Resident, Santa Ana Office)
Jeffrey A. Smith (Resident, Santa Ana Office)
Judith D. Anderson (Resident, Santa Ana Office)
Gregory A. Wille (Resident, Santa Ana Office)
Cary K. Quan (Resident, Santa Ana Office)
Jennifer K. Berneking (Resident, Santa Ana Office)
Shari S. Daneshrad
Kathleen G. Maylin (Resident, Walnut Creek Office)
Karen R. Shulman (Resident, Santa Ana Office)
Michelle R. Walker
George E. Ordonez
Gayle C. Heirshberg
James L. Armstrong, Jr. (Resident, Walnut Creek Office)

For full biographical listings, see the Martindale-Hubbell Law Directory

*FRESNO,** Fresno Co.

FRAMPTON, WILLIAMS & LITTLE, A PROFESSIONAL ASSOCIATION (AV)

Suite 110, Civic Center Square, 2444 Main Street, 93721-2256
Telephone: 559-486-5730
FAX: 559-486-4759

Mary Louise Frampton
Scott W. Williams
Kevin G. Little

For full biographical listings, see the Martindale-Hubbell Law Directory

JORY, PETERSON, WATKINS & SMITH (AV)

555 West Shaw, Suite C-1, P.O. Box 5394, 93755
Telephone: 559-225-6700
Telecopier: 559-225-3416
Email: jpws@jpws.com

MEMBERS OF FIRM

Jay V. Jory
John E. Peterson
Cal B. Watkins, Jr.
Michael Jens F. Smith
Marcia A. Ross
William M. Woolman
Jeffrey T. Hammerschmidt

ASSOCIATES

Carla M. McCormack
Shannon R. McFarland
Patti L. Williams
Annette A. Ballatore-Williamson

Reference: Wells Fargo Bank.

For full biographical listings, see the Martindale-Hubbell Law Directory

LANG, RICHERT & PATCH, A PROFESSIONAL CORPORATION (AV)

Fig Garden Financial Center, 5200 North Palm Avenue, 4th Floor, P.O. Box 40012, 93755
Telephone: 559-228-6700
Fax: 559-228-6727

William T. Richert (1937-1993)
Robert L. Patch, II
Val W. Saldaña
Douglas E. Noll
Michael T. Hertz
Victoria J. Salisch
Rene Lastreto, II
Charles Trudrung Taylor
Mark L. Creede
Peter N. Zeitler
Laurie L. Quigley
Tamara L. Equals
Douglas E. Griffin
Nabil E. Zumout

Christopher B. Dorian
Matthew W. Quall
Tracy E. Sagle
Julie K. Hill
Michelle Oleksa

OF COUNSEL

Frank H. Lang

References: Wells Fargo Bank (Fresno Main Office).

For full biographical listings, see the Martindale-Hubbell Law Directory

MARDEROSIAN, OREN & PABOOJIAN, A PROFESSIONAL CORPORATION (AV)

1260 Fulton Mall, 93721-1783
Telephone: 559-441-7991
Facsimilie: 559-441-8170

C. Sam Titus (1957-1990)
Michael G. Marderosian
Eric P. Oren
Warren R. Paboojian
Brett L. Runyon
Alan M. Simpson
Sue Ann Cercone

Michael E. Lehman
David J. Frankenberger, Jr.
Lance E. Armo
Stephen T. Knudsen

For full biographical listings, see the Martindale-Hubbell Law Directory

ARKANSAS

*CAMDEN,** Ouachita Co.

ALLEN P. ROBERTS, P.A. (AV)

325 Jefferson Street, S.W., P.O. Box 280, 71711-0280
Telephone: 870-836-5310
FAX: 870-836-9662
Email: aroberts@cei.net

Allen P. Roberts

Representative Clients: International Paper Co.; Camden Fairview School District; The City of Camden; Byars Oil Co.; American Fuel Cell & Coated Fabrics Co.; Star City School District; Highland Resources, Inc.; Circle B Logging Co.; First National Bank, Magnolia, Arkansas.

For full biographical listings, see the Martindale-Hubbell Law Directory

*LITTLE ROCK,** Pulaski Co.

FRIDAY, ELDREDGE & CLARK (AV)

A Limited Liability Partnership of Individuals and Professional Associations
Formerly, Smith, Williams, Friday, Eldredge & Clark
2000 Regions Center, 400 West Capitol Avenue, 72201-3493
Telephone: 501-376-2011
Telecopier: 501-376-2147
Email: fecmh@fec.net

MEMBERS OF FIRM

James W. Moore
Oscar E. Davis, Jr. (P.A.)
Elizabeth Robben Murray (P.A.)
Christopher J. Heller (P.A.)
Michael Scott Moore (P.A.)

ASSOCIATE

Daniel Lee Herrington

COUNSEL

B. S. Clark

Counsel for: Union Pacific System; St. Paul Insurance Co.; Liberty Mutual Insurance Co.; Cigna Property & Casualty Co.; Entergy Arkansas, Inc.; Dillard's, Inc.; Phillips Petroleum Co.; Aetna Casualty & Surety Co.; ALLTEL Corp.; Acxiom Corp.

For Complete List of Firm Personnel, See General Section

For full biographical listings, see the Martindale-Hubbell Law Directory

HILBURN, CALHOON, HARPER, PRUNISKI & CALHOUN, LTD. (AV)

P.O. Box 1256, 72203-1256
Telephone: 501-372-0110
Fax: 501-372-2029
Email: hilburn@aristotle.net
North Little Rock, Arkansas Office: Eighth Floor, Mercantile Bank Building, One Riverfront Place, P.O. Box 5551, 72119.
Telephone: 501-372-0110.
Fax: 501-372-2029.

David M. Fuqua
James M. McHaney, Jr.
Phil Campbell

Representative Clients: Mercantile Bank of Arkansas, N.A.; Merrill Lynch Pierce Fenner & Smith, Inc.; Central Arkansas Risk Management Association; Salomon Smith Barney, Inc.; The Kroger Co.

For Complete List of Firm Personnel, See General Section

For full biographical listings, see the Martindale-Hubbell Law Directory

ROSE LAW FIRM, A PROFESSIONAL ASSOCIATION (AV)

120 East Fourth Street, 72201
Telephone: 501-375-9131
Telecopy: 501-375-1309

Tim Boe
David P. Martin

Representative Clients: Acxiom Corporation, ALCOA; Aromatique, Inc.; Georgia-Pacific Corporation; Merico, Inc., d/b/a Colonial Bakery; Pat Salmon & Sons, Inc.; Schering-Plough Corporation; Weyerhaeuser Company.

For Complete List of Firm Personnel, See General Section

For full biographical listings, see the Martindale-Hubbell Law Directory

WRIGHT, LINDSEY & JENNINGS LLP (AV)

200 West Capitol Avenue, Suite 2200, 72201
Telephone: 501-371-0808
Fax: 501-376-9442
Email: info@wlj.com *URL:* http://www.wlj.com
Fayetteville, Arkansas Office: 101 West Mountain Street, Suite 206, 72701.
Telephone: 501-575-0808.
Fax: 501-575-0999.

(See Next Column)

Russellville, Arkansas Office: 1110 West "B" Street, Suite E, 72801.
Telephone: 501-968-7995.

John G. Lile
Kathlyn Graves
John D. Davis
William Stuart Jackson

ASSOCIATES

Don S. McKinney
Jane M. Faulkner

Representative Clients: AmTran Corp.; Meyer's Bakery Inc.; St. Joseph's Regional Health Center.

For full biographical listings, see the Martindale-Hubbell Law Directory

*PINE BLUFF,** Jefferson Co.

RAMSAY, BRIDGFORTH, HARRELSON & STARLING (AV)

11th Floor, Simmons First National Building, P.O. Drawer 8509, 71611
Telephone: 870-535-9000
Fax: 870-535-8544

MEMBER OF FIRM

Spencer F. Robinson

Representative Clients: Simmons First National Bank; Pine Bluff Sand & Gravel Co.; Stant, Inc.; McGeorge Contracting Co., Inc.; Television Station KATV.

For Complete List of Firm Personnel, See General Section

For full biographical listings, see the Martindale-Hubbell Law Directory

CALIFORNIA

ALAMEDA, Alameda Co.

WILEY PRICE & RADULOVICH, LLP (AV)

1301 Marina Village Parkway, Suite 310, 94501
Telephone: 510-337-2810
Fax: 510-337-2811
URL: http://www.wprlaw.com

Joseph E. Wiley
Suzanne I. Price
Monna R. Radulovich
Elizabeth S. Syger
Joan Pugh Newman

For full biographical listings, see the Martindale-Hubbell Law Directory

*BAKERSFIELD,** Kern Co.

BORTON, PETRINI & CONRON, LLP (AV)

The Borton, Petrini & Conron Building, 1600 Truxtun Avenue, 93301
Telephone: 661-322-3051
Voice Mail: 661-395-6700
Fax: 661-322-4628
Mailing Address: P.O. Box 2026, Bakersfield, California, 93303
Email: bpcbak@bpclaw.com *URL:* http://www.bpclaw.com
Other City Locations: Fresno, Los Angeles, Modesto, Redding, Sacramento, San Bernardino, San Diego, San Francisco, San Jose, San Luis Obispo, Santa Ana and Ventura.

MEMBER OF FIRM

Paul Lafranchise

ASSOCIATES

Randall Steven Joyce
John W. Fox

For Complete List of Firm Personnel, See General Section

For full biographical listings, see the Martindale-Hubbell Law Directory

KLEIN, DENATALE, GOLDNER, COOPER, ROSENLIEB & KIMBALL, LLP (AV)

(Formerly Di Giorgio, Davis, Klein, Wegis, Duggan & Friedman)
ARCO Tower, 4550 California Avenue, Second Floor, 93309
Telephone: 661-395-1000
Telecopier: 661-326-0418
Mailing Address: P.O. Box 11172, Bakersfield, California, 93389-1172
Email: kleinlaw@kleinlaw.com

Anthony J. Klein (Inc.)
Jay L. Rosenlieb

T. Scott Belden

Representative Clients: Smith International, Inc.; Sandrini Brothers Company; Nahama & Weagant Energy Co.; EIU of California, Inc.; Kern County Hay Growers Association, Inc.

For Complete List of Firm Personnel, See General Section

For full biographical listings, see the Martindale-Hubbell Law Directory

Fresno—Continued

SAGASER, FRANSON & JONES, A PROFESSIONAL CORPORATION (AV)

2445 Capitol Street, Second Floor, P.O. Box 1632, 93717-1632
Telephone: 559-233-4800
Fax: 559-233-9330

Howard A. Sagaser
Eric K. Hansen (1952-1996)
Donald R. Franson, Jr.
Timothy Jones
Kristi R. Culver Kapetan
Elise M. Shebelut Krause
Nancy A. Maler
W. Allen Bennett
Mark D. Kruthers
Michael S. Helsley
Jamie Katzman

For full biographical listings, see the Martindale-Hubbell Law Directory

GLENDALE, Los Angeles Co.

OTT & HOFFMAN, A PROFESSIONAL CORPORATION (AV)

700 North Central Avenue, 8th Floor, Suite 850, 91203
Telephone: 818-242-3100
Fax: 818-242-3102
Email: ohlaw@aol.com *URL:* http://www.ottlaw.com

Thomas H. Ott
Daniel E. Hoffman

Patrick Carey

Representative Clients: Alhambra Unified School District; Calif. Credit Union League; Cuna Mutual Ins. Group; Hughes Aircraft Corp.; Lockheed Federal Credit Union.

For full biographical listings, see the Martindale-Hubbell Law Directory

IRVINE, Orange Co.

ANDRADE & ASSOCIATES (AV)

First Security Bank Building, 18401 Von Karman, Suite 350, 92612
Telephone: 949-553-1951
Telecopier: 949-553-0655
Email: andrade@andradelaw.com
San Diego, California Office: Tokia Bank Building, 3111 Camino Del Rio North, Suite 1100.
Telephone: 619-291-2481.
Las Vegas, Nevada Office: 3753 Howard Hughes Parkway, Suite 200.
Telephone: 888-553-1951.

MEMBER OF FIRM

Richard B. Andrade

ASSOCIATES

Frank A. Satalino
Lori A. McClaskey
Eric Rans
Deborah J. Taddeucci

Representative Clients: Advanco Constructor's, Inc.; American Insurance Company of North America; Fireman's Fund Insurance Co.; CIGNA Insurance Co.; Gentosi Builders, Inc.; Griffith Co.; Penhall Rentals; Steve Bubalo Construction Co.; Sukut Construction, Inc.; United Rentals, Inc.; Veco International, Inc.

For full biographical listings, see the Martindale-Hubbell Law Directory

THE ENTERPRISE COUNSEL GROUP (AV)

5 Park Plaza, 92614
Telephone: 949-553-2404
Fax: 949-553-2434
URL: http://www.enterprisecounsel.com

David A. Robinson
Corey E. Taylor
Susan M. Masson
Jeffrey Lewis

For full biographical listings, see the Martindale-Hubbell Law Directory

GEORGE & SHIELDS, LLP (AV)

30 Corporate Park, Suite 300, 92606-5133
Telephone: 949-263-1085
Fax: 949-263-0585
Email: toplaw@george-shields.com *URL:* http://www.george-shields.com

MEMBERS OF FIRM

Robert K. George
Timothy F. Shields
David W. Sparks

For full biographical listings, see the Martindale-Hubbell Law Directory

OSWALD & YAP, A PROFESSIONAL CORPORATION (AV)

16148 Sand Canyon Avenue, 92618
Telephone: 949-788-8900
Telefax: 949-788-8980
URL: http://www.oswald-yap.com

Michael A. Oswald
Calvin C.S. Yap
Niall Sweetnam
Mark D. Holmes

(See Next Column)

Tzong-Bing Tsai
Joseph A. Weber
Edward W. Russey, III
Richard T. Hsueh
Carol A. Gefis

OF COUNSEL

John W. Allured
Reed M. Williams

For full biographical listings, see the Martindale-Hubbell Law Directory

SNELL & WILMER L.L.P. (AV)

1920 Main Street, Suite 1200, 92614-7230
Telephone: 949-253-2700
FAX: 949-955-2507
URL: http://www.swlaw.com
Phoenix, Arizona Office: One Arizona Center, 85004-2202.
Telephone: 602-382-6000.
Fax: 602-382-6070.
Tucson, Arizona Office: One South Church Avenue, Suite 1500, 85701-1630.
Telephone: 520-882-1200.
Fax: 520-884-1294.
Salt Lake City, Utah Office: 111 East Broadway, Suite 900, 84111-1004.
Telephone: 801-237-1900.
Fax: 801-237-1950.

MEMBERS OF FIRM

William S. O'Hare, Jr.
Frank Cronin
Christy D. Joseph

ASSOCIATE

C. Athena Roussos

Representative Clients: For list of Representative Clients, see end of biographical listings in the Martindale-Hubbell Law Directory.

For Complete List of Firm Personnel, See General Section

For full biographical listings, see the Martindale-Hubbell Law Directory

LAGUNA HILLS, Orange Co.

STANTON T. MATHEWS & ASSOCIATES, A LAW CORP. (AV)

24012 Calle de la Plata, Suite 320, 92653
Telephone: 949-586-2235
Email: Triallaw@flash.net
Email: stm@injurytriallaw.com *URL:* http://www.injurytriallaw.com

Stanton T. Mathews

Paul W. Ralph
Ronald B. Funk

LEGAL SUPPORT PERSONNEL

PARALEGAL/ADMINISTRATOR

Sharing Garrett-Anderson

LEGAL ASSISTANT

Cheri C. Wickam

For full biographical listings, see the Martindale-Hubbell Law Directory

MICHELLE A. REINGLASS (AV)

Suite 170 23161 Millcreek Road, 92653
Telephone: 949-587-0460
FAX: 949-587-1004
Email: reinglass@fea.net *URL:* http://www.lawyers.com/reinglass

ASSOCIATE

Michael E. Raabe

For full biographical listings, see the Martindale-Hubbell Law Directory

LARKSPUR, Marin Co.

MILLER LAW GROUP (AV)

Professional Corporation
Wood Island Center, 60 East Sir Francis Drake Boulevard Suite 302, 94939
Telephone: 415-464-4300
Fax: 415-464-4336
Email: mbm@millerlawgroup.com

Michele Ballard Miller
Maki Daijogo

Kathleen E. Justice
Angeline A. Covey

For full biographical listings, see the Martindale-Hubbell Law Directory

LONG BEACH, Los Angeles Co.

CAMERON, PEARLSON & GALE (AV)

One World Trade Center, Suite 1600, 90831-1600
Telephone: 562-436-3888
Telecopier: 562-437-1967
URL: http://www.cpglawyers.com
URL: http://www.lawyers.com/cmp&glaw

(See Next Column)

CAMERON, PEARLSON & GALE, *Long Beach—Continued*

MEMBERS OF FIRM

Timothy C. Cameron
Charles M. Gale
Paul R. Pearlson

ASSOCIATES

Dana K. Anderson, Jr.
Susan R. Loh

For full biographical listings, see the Martindale-Hubbell Law Directory

*LOS ANGELES,** Los Angeles Co.

BAKER & HOSTETLER LLP (AV)

600 Wilshire Boulevard, 90017-3212
Telephone: 213-624-2400
FAX: 213-975-1740
To contact an attorney on the Internet use first initial and surname followed by @baker-hostetler.com
URL: http://www.bakerlaw.com
In Cleveland, Ohio: 3200 National City Center, 1900 East Ninth Street.
Telephone: 216-621-0200.
In Cincinnati, Ohio: 312 Walnut Street, Suite 2650.
Telephone: 513-929-3400.
In Columbus, Ohio: Capitol Square, Suite 2100, 65 East State Street.
Telephone: 614-228-1541.
In Denver, Colorado: 303 East 17th Avenue, Suite 1100.
Telephone: 303-861-0600.
In Houston, Texas: 1000 Louisiana, Suite 2000.
Telephone: 713-751-1600.
In Long Beach, California: 300 Oceangate, Suite 620.
Telephone: 562-432-2827.
In Orlando, Florida: SunBank Center, Suite 2300, 200 South Orange Avenue.
Telephone: 407-649-4000.
In Washington, D. C.: Washington Square, Suite 1100, 1050 Connecticut Avenue, N.W.
Telephone: 202-861-1500.

PARTNER

Teresa R. Tracy

For Complete List of Firm Personnel, See General Section

For full biographical listings, see the Martindale-Hubbell Law Directory

BARBOSA GARCIA LLP (AV)

A Partnership including a Professional Corporation
801 South Grand Avenue Suite 300, 90017-4621
Telephone: 213-612-0800
Fax: 213-612-8085

Henry S. Barbosa (P.C.)
Lorie A. Campos
Kenneth T. Fong
Bonifacio Bonny Garcia (P.C.)
Michael L. Kadish
John F. Lagle
Peter E. Langsfeld
Benjamin D. Nieberg
Gary W. Park
Roberta R. Sistos
Jonathan B. Stone
Rajeev M. Talwani
Sylvia J. Trujillo
Thuy-Whien Vuong
John G. Yslas

OF COUNSEL

Albert A. Erkel, Jr.

SPECIAL COUNSEL

Adrienne D. Konigar
Joyce E. Paul
Melvin D. Peters

LEGAL SUPPORT PERSONNEL

Victor M. Estrada (Paralegal)
Janice H. Minamoto (Paralegal)

For full biographical listings, see the Martindale-Hubbell Law Directory

BERGMAN, WEDNER & DACEY, INC. (AV)

Suite 900, 10880 Wilshire Boulevard, 90024
Telephone: 310-470-6110
Fax: 310-474-0931
Email: ofc@bergman-wedner.com *URL:* http://www.bergman-wedner.com

Gregory M. Bergman
Gregory A. Wedner
John P. Dacey
Alan Harvey Mittelman
Robert M. Mason III
Kristi Anne Sjoholm-Sierchio
John V. Tamborelli

Lisa S. Newnan
Daphne M. Humphreys
Michele M. Goldsmith
Denise G. Godfrey
William Daryl Strickland
Pamela R. Fleming
Matthew R. Hicks
Jorge J. Luna
Paul V. Rayburn
Mark W. Waterman

OF COUNSEL

Lloyd A. Bergman (1923-1994)
Jacob A. Wedner
Marvin Goldsmith
Mark K. Kitabayashi

SPECIAL COUNSEL

Richard V. Godino

For full biographical listings, see the Martindale-Hubbell Law Directory

BLANC WILLIAMS JOHNSTON & KRONSTADT, LLP (AV)

A Partnership including Professional Corporations
Suite 1700, 1900 Avenue of the Stars, 90067
Telephone: 310-552-2500
Telecopier: 310-552-1191
Email: bwjk@bwjk.com

MEMBERS OF FIRM

Ronald L. Blanc (P.C.)
Harley J. Williams (P.C.)
Ronald L. Johnston (P.C.)
John A. Kronstadt
James R. Farrand
Richard T. McCoy III
Regina A. Stagg
John C. Rawls III
Daniel M. Grigsby
Suzanne V. Wilson
Dawn Weekes Glenn

James S. Blackburn
Vivian W. Yang
Allison Binder
Jennifer M. Lloyd
Mark S. Dancsecs

OF COUNSEL

Sol Rosenthal

Reference: Santa Monica Bank (Beverly Hills Office).

For full biographical listings, see the Martindale-Hubbell Law Directory

CLARK & TREVITHICK, A PROFESSIONAL CORPORATION (AV)

800 Wilshire Boulevard, 12th Floor, 90017
Telephone: 213-629-5700
Telecopier: 213-624-9441
Email: postmaster@clarktrev.com
San Francisco, California Office: 456 Montgomery Street, 20th Floor.
Telephone: 415-288-6520.
Fax: 415-398-2820.

Philip W. Bartenetti
Leonard Brazil

OF COUNSEL

Dolores Cordell

For Complete List of Firm Personnel, See General Section

For full biographical listings, see the Martindale-Hubbell Law Directory

CURIALE DELLAVERSON HIRSCHFELD KELLY & KRAEMER, LLP (AV)

1880 Century Park East, Suite 800, 90067-1608
Telephone: 310-203-9999
Facsimile: 310-557-1509
Email: info@cdhkk.com *URL:* http://www.cdhkk.com
San Francisco, California Office: 727 Sansome Street.
Telephone: 415-835-9000.
Facsimile: 415-834-0443.

MEMBERS OF FIRM

Joel P. Kelly (Resident)
Glen E. Kraemer (Resident)
Reed E. Schaper (Resident)

ASSOCIATES

Kathleen E. Collins (Resident)
Scott K. Liner (Resident)
Kirstin E. Muller
Leonora M. Schloss (Resident)

For full biographical listings, see the Martindale-Hubbell Law Directory

DECARLO, CONNOR & SELVO, A PROFESSIONAL CORPORATION (AV)

500 South Virgil Avenue, Fourth Floor, 90020-1430
Telephone: 213-738-7959
Fax: 213-738-1813
Email: dcs@deconsel.com
Washington, D.C. Office: 101 Constitution Avenue, N.W., Suite 322.
Telephone: 202-547-8300.
Fax: 202-547-9303.

John T. DeCarlo
Patrick T. Connor
Gerald V. Selvo

Daniel J. Hall
Lee S. Feldman
Margaret Rawls Gifford
Desmond C. Lee
Enrique Guieb Gutierrez
Daniel M. Shanley
Brian F. Quinn (Resident, Washington D.C., Office)
Willow J. Prall (Resident, Washington, D.C. Office)
Kathleen M. Jorgenson

Representative Clients: Carpenters Pension Trust for Southern California; Palm Springs Riviera Hotel & Resort; Office and Professional Employees International Union Pension Fund; United Brotherhood of Carpenters and Joiners of America; United Brotherhood of Carpenters Pension Fund.

For full biographical listings, see the Martindale-Hubbell Law Directory

Los Angeles—Continued

FORD & HARRISON LLP (AV)

333 South Grand Avenue Suite 3680, 90071
Telephone: 213-680-3410
FAX: 213-680-4161
Email: firm@fordharrison.com *URL:* http://www.fordharrison.com
Atlanta, Georgia Office: 600 Peachtree at the Circle Building, 1275 Peachtree Street, N.E. 30309.
Telephone: 404-888-3800.
Fax: 404-888-3863.
Memphis, Tennessee Office: 6750 Poplar Avenue, Suite 600, P.O. Box 171375. 38187-1375.
Telephone: 901-756-1550.
Telecopier: 901-756-1016.
Miami, Florida Office: 516 Ingraham Building, 25 S.E. 2nd Avenue. 33131.
Telephone: 305-379-3811.
Fax: 305-358-5933.
Jacksonville, Florida Office: 121 West Forsyth Street, Suite 1000. P.O. Box 41566. 32203.
Telephone: 904-356-8073.
Fax: 904-358-2319.
Tampa, Florida Office: 101 E. Kennedy Boulevard, Suite 900. 33602.
Telephone: 813-261-7800.
Fax: 813-261-7899.
Washington, D.C. Office: 1920 N Street, N.W., Suite 200. 20036.
Telephone: 202-463-6633.
Fax: 202-466-5705.

MEMBERS OF FIRM

Michael L. Lowry
Glen H. Mertens (Resident)
Kari Haugen (Resident)

ASSOCIATES

Maral Donoyan (Resident)
Brian M. Holbrook (Resident)
Wendy Suzanne Keller (Resident)

Representative Clients: Coca-Cola Enterprises; Columbia/HCA Healthcare Corp.; Delta Air Lines, Inc.; Federal Express Corporation; Kellogg Company; LIN Television Corp.; Nestle USA, Inc.; Regional Airline Assn.

For full biographical listings, see the Martindale-Hubbell Law Directory

FRIED, BIRD & CRUMPACKER, A PROFESSIONAL CORPORATION (AV)

1900 Avenue of the Stars, 25th Floor, 90067-6031
Telephone: 310-551-7400
Facsimile: 310-556-4487
Email: fbclawfirm@cs.com

Jack Fried
Brian James Bird
David W. Crumpacker, Jr.
Nikki Wolontis
Diane J. Crumpacker

David K. Johnson

OF COUNSEL

Keith T. Holmes
Madge S. Beletsky

For full biographical listings, see the Martindale-Hubbell Law Directory

GARTNER & YOUNG, A PROFESSIONAL CORPORATION (AV)

1880 Century Park East, Suite 1410, 90067
Telephone: 310-556-3576
Fax: 310-556-8459

Naomi Young
Lawrence J. Gartner

Christopher Adams Thorn
Kimberly M. Talley
John P. Lodise
Anthony S. Brill

For full biographical listings, see the Martindale-Hubbell Law Directory

GILCHRIST & RUTTER, PROFESSIONAL CORPORATION (AV)

355 South Grand Avenue, Suite 4100, 90071
Telephone: 213-617-8000
Facsimile: 213-534-8001
Email: Postmaster@grlawyers.com *URL:* http://www.grlawyers.com
Santa Monica, California Office: 1299 Ocean Avenue, Suite 900.
Telephone: 310-393-4000.
Facsimile: 310-394-4700.

Diana P. Scott

OF COUNSEL

Christine A. Page

For full biographical listings, see the Martindale-Hubbell Law Directory

GOLDSTEIN, KENNEDY & PETITO (AV)

Suite 1018, 1880 Century Park East (Century City), 90067
Telephone: 310-553-4746; 800-826-0113
Fax: 310-282-8070
URL: http://www.gkplaw.com

(See Next Column)

Charles H. Goldstein
Gregory G. Kennedy
Deborah Hanna Petito

Victor T. Fu
Douglas H. Hoang
Jonathan Manahan
Sara N. Trivedi

For full biographical listings, see the Martindale-Hubbell Law Directory

HILL, FARRER & BURRILL LLP (AV)

A Limited Liability Partnership including Professional Corporations
37th Floor, One California Plaza, 300 South Grand Avenue, 90071-3147
Telephone: 213-620-0460
Fax: 213-624-4840
URL: http://www.hfbllp.com

MEMBERS OF FIRM

Kyle D. Brown (P.C.)
Stuart H. Young, Jr., (P.C.)
Jonathan M. Brandler (P.C.)
James A. Bowles (P.C.)
Ronald W. Novotny (P.C.)
Suzanne J. Holland (P.C.)
G. Cresswell Templeton III, (P.C.)

OF COUNSEL

Stanley E. Tobin (P.C.)
James G. Johnson (P.C.)

ASSOCIATES

Karen S. Seigel
Warren J. Higgins

For Complete List of Firm Personnel, See General Section

For full biographical listings, see the Martindale-Hubbell Law Directory

IVERSON, YOAKUM, PAPIANO & HATCH (AV)

One Wilshire Building, 27th Floor 624 South Grand Avenue, 90017
Telephone: 213-624-7444
Telecopier: 213-629-4563

Paul E. Iverson (1907-1975)
Frank B. Yoakum, Jr. (1906-1991)

MEMBERS OF FIRM

Neil Papiano
Patrick M. Mc Adam
Arnold D. Larson
John M. Garrick

ASSOCIATES

Douglas C. Pease
Andrew K. Doty
Melissa A. Immel
Mary P. Lightfoot
Mark Pearson
Adam F. Burke
Scott A. Horton

OF COUNSEL

R. Noel Hatch

Representative Clients: Lockheed Corp.; International Paper; Bridgestone/-Firestone, Inc.
Reference: Bank of America (Los Angeles Head Office).

For Complete List of Firm Personnel, See General Section

For full biographical listings, see the Martindale-Hubbell Law Directory

H. ROY JEPPSON A PROFESSIONAL CORPORATION (AV)

11900 W. Olympic Boulevard Sixth Floor, 90064
Telephone: 310-826-5566
Fax: 310-826-5350
URL: http://www.lawyers.com/jeppsonlaw
Oxnard, California Office: 300 Esplanade Drive, Suite 1810.
Telephone: 805-604-1100.
Fax: 805-604-1600.

H. Roy Jeppson

Robyn F. Stalk

For full biographical listings, see the Martindale-Hubbell Law Directory

JONES, DAY, REAVIS & POGUE (AV)

555 West Fifth Street Suite 4600, 90013-1025
Telephone: 213-489-3939
Telecopier: 213-243-2539
Email: counsel@jonesday.com *URL:* http://www.jonesday.com
In Irvine, California: 5 Park Plaza, Suite 1100.
Telephone: 949-851-3939.
Telecopier: 949-553-7539.
In Atlanta, Georgia: 3500 SunTrust Plaza, 303 Peachtree Street.
Telephone: 404-521-3939.
Telecopier: 404-581-8330.
In Brussels, Belgium: Avenue Louise 480, 7th Floor, B-1050 Brussels.
Telephone: 32-2-645-14-11.
Telecopier: 32-2-645-14-45.
In Chicago, Illinois: 77 West Wacker.
Telephone: 312-782-3939.
Telecopier: 312-782-8585.
In Cleveland, Ohio: North Point, 901 Lakeside Avenue.
Telephone: 216-586-3939.
Telecopier: 216-579-0212.

(See Next Column)

JONES, DAY, REAVIS & POGUE, *Los Angeles—Continued*

In Columbus, Ohio: 1900 Huntington Center.
Telephone: 614-469-3939.
Telecopier: 614-461-4198.
In Dallas, Texas: 2727 North Harwood Street.
Telephone: 214-220-3939.
Telecopier: 214-969-5100.
In Frankfurt, Germany: Hochhaus am Park, Grüneburgweg 102, 60323 Frankfurt am Main.
Telephone: 49-69-9726-3939.
Telecopier: 49-69-9726-3993.
In Geneva, Switzerland: 20, rue de Candolle.
Telephone: 41-22-320-2339.
Telecopier: 41-22-320-1232.
In Hong Kong: 29th Floor, Entertainment Building, 30 Queen's Road Central.
Telephone: 852-2526-6895.
Telecopier: 852-2868-5871.
In London England: Bucklersbury House, 3 Queen Victoria Street.
Telephone: 44-20-7236-3939.
Telecopier: 44-20-7236-1113.
In New York, New York: 599 Lexington Avenue.
Telephone: 212-326-3939.
Telecopier: 212-755-7306.
In Paris, France: 120, rue du Faubourg Saint-Honoré.
Telephone: 33-1-56-59-3939.
Telecopier: 33-1-56-59-3938
In Pittsburgh, Pennsylvania: 500 Grant Street, 31st Floor.
Telephone: 412-391-3939.
Telecopier: 412-394-7959.
In Riyadh, Saudi Arabia: The International Law Firm (In Association with Jones, Day, Reavis & Pogue), Sulaymaniyah, Prince Mishari IBN, Abdulaziz Street, P.O. Box 22166.
Telephone: (966-1) 462-8866.
Telecopier: (966-1) 462-9001.
In Shanghai, China: 2805 Kerry Centre, 1515 Nanjing Road West.
Telephone: 86-21-5298-6568.
Telecopier: 86-21-5298-6569.
In Sydney, Australia: Governor Phillip Tower, Level 38, 1 Farrer Place.
Telephone: 61-2-9210-6921.
Telecopier: 61-2-9210-6926.
In Taipei, Taiwan: 8th Floor, 2 Tun Hwa South Road, Section 2.
Telephone: (886-2) 2704-6808.
Telecopier: (886-2) 2704-6791.
In Tokyo, Japan: Toranomon 45 Mori Building, 3th Floor, 1-5, Toranomon 5-Chome, Minato-ku, Tokyo 105, Japan.
Telephone: 81-3-3433-3939.
Telecopier: 81-3-5401-2725.
In Washington, D.C.: 51 Louisiana Avenue, N.W.
Telephone: 202-879-3939.
Telecopier: 202-626-1700.

MEMBER OF FIRM IN LOS ANGELES

William J. Emanuel

For Complete List of Firm Personnel, See General Section

For full biographical listings, see the Martindale-Hubbell Law Directory

KERN & GONZALEZ, A PROFESSIONAL CORPORATION (AV)

601 West 5th Street, Suite 1100, 90071
Telephone: 213-629-8100
Facsimile: 213-627-8765
URL: http://www.kernlaw.net

René J. Kern, Jr.
Michael D. Gonzalez
Tina L. Gentile

Christina L. Young
Angela J. Armitage
Michele Marsh
Cynthia L. Filla
David G. Hoiles, Jr.
Michele Sherer Ancheta
Sue S. Kim
Gail S. Taningco

Representative Clients: Merrill Lynch; Morgan Stanley Dean Witter; Tristar Risk Management.

For full biographical listings, see the Martindale-Hubbell Law Directory

KNEE & ROSS, LLP (AV)

A Partnership
2049 Century Park East, Suite 2050, 90067
Telephone: 310-551-0909
Fax: 310-551-2049

MEMBERS OF FIRM

Howard M. Knee
Melanie C. Ross
Lora Silverman
Lisa G. Sherman

OF COUNSEL

Ted R. Huebner
Steven M. Steese

For full biographical listings, see the Martindale-Hubbell Law Directory

KNOPFLER & ROBERTSON, LLP (AV)

Suite 500, 21650 Oxnard Street (Woodland Hills), 91367
Telephone: 818-227-0770; 213-624-1111
Telefax: 818-227-0777
Irvine, California Office: 19800 MacArthur Boulevard, Suite 270, 92612.
Telephone: 714-261-6191.
Pleasanton, California Office: 400 Main Street, Suite 204, 94566.
Telephone: 510-425-7250.
Las Vegas, Nevada Office: Knopfler & Robertson in Association with Broom & Vaisbort, LLP, 3753 Howard Hughes Parkway, Suite 200, 89109.
Telephone: 702-792-2413.
Camarillo, California Office: 1200 Paseo, Suite 170, 93010.
Telephone: 805-482-1903; 800-CONDOLAW.
Fax: 805-484-5917.

George Knopfler
Alexander Robertson, IV
Deborah Broom
Richard A. Capella
Jonathan S. Vick
Edward D. Vaisbort
William G. Kelsberg

OF COUNSEL

Scott C. Haith
James P. Lingl (Resident, Camarillo Office)
Christina S. Robertson

Janice M. Michaels
James M. Pazos
Mark Rohrer
Craig Smith
Robert Nation
William S. Dunlevy (Resident, Camarillo Office)
Scott A. Hunter

For full biographical listings, see the Martindale-Hubbell Law Directory

LOEB & LOEB LLP (AV)

A Limited Liability Partnership including Professional Corporations
Suite 1800, 1000 Wilshire Boulevard, 90017-2475
Telephone: 213-688-3400
Facsimile: 213-688-3460
Email: info@loeb.com *URL:* http://www.loeb.com
Century City, California Office: Suite 2200, 10100 Santa Monica Boulevard, Los Angeles, 90067-4164.
Telephone: 310-282-2000.
Facsimile: 310-282-2192.
New York, N.Y. Office: 345 Park Avenue, 10154-0037.
Telephone: 212-407-4000.
Facsimile: 212-407-4990.
Nashville, Tennessee Office: 45 Music Square West, 37203-3205.
Telephone: 615-749-8300;
Facsimile: 615-749-8308.
Rome, Italy Office: Piazza Digione 1, 00197.
Telephone: 011-3906-808-8456.
Facsimile: 011-3906-808-8288.

MEMBERS OF FIRM

Kevin E. Coventon
Fred B. Griffin
Sharon S. Mequet

ASSOCIATES

Victoria K. Harvey
James Urbanic

For Complete List of Firm Personnel, See General Section

For full biographical listings, see the Martindale-Hubbell Law Directory

MCNICHOLAS & MCNICHOLAS, LLP (AV)

10866 Wilshire Boulevard, Suite 1400, 90024
Telephone: 310-474-1582
FAX: 310-475-7871
URL: http://www.mcnicholaslaw.com

MEMBERS OF FIRM

John P. McNicholas
Patrick McNicholas
David M. Ring

ASSOCIATES

Eric A. Gowey
Matthew S. McNicholas
Steven G. Mehta

For full biographical listings, see the Martindale-Hubbell Law Directory

MITCHELL, SILBERBERG & KNUPP LLP (AV)

A Partnership including Professional Corporations
11377 West Olympic Boulevard, 90064
Telephone: 310-312-2000
Fax: 310-312-3100
Email: info@msk.com *URL:* http://www.msk.com

MEMBERS OF FIRM

Tracy L. Thornburg Cahill (A Professional Corporation)
William L. Cole (A Professional Corporation)
Larry C. Drapkin (A Professional Corporation)
Lawrence A. Ginsberg (A Professional Corporation)
Allen J. Gross (A Professional Corporation)
Deborah P. Koeffler (A Professional Corporation)

(See Next Column)

MITCHELL, SILBERBERG & KNUPP LLP—*Continued*

MEMBERS OF FIRM (Continued)

Adam Levin (A Professional Corporation)
Lawrence A. Michaels (A Professional Corporation)
Steven M. Schneider (A Professional Corporation)
Mark A. Wasserman (A Professional Corporation)

ASSOCIATES

Dana Anderson Childers
Daniel J. Cooper
Angelike I. Dexter
Alec Harrell
Jenny Schneider
Lee Anne Steinberg
Eric M. Steinert
Suzanne M. Steinke

References: Wells Fargo Bank, N.A.; Merrill, Lynch.

For Complete List of Firm Personnel, See General Section

For full biographical listings, see the Martindale-Hubbell Law Directory

OCHOA & SILLAS (AV)

444 South Flower Street, 18th Floor, 90071
Telephone: 213-362-1400
Fax: 213-622-0162
Email: sillasla@aol.com
Sacramento Office: Wells Fargo Center, 400 Capitol Mall, Suite 1850.
Telephone: 916-447-3383.
FAX: 916-447-3495. Email: OchoaSac@aol.com
Mexico City, Mexico Office: Los Cormoran No. 73, Lomas De Las Aquilas, Deleg. Alvaro Obregon, 01730, Mexico, D.F.C.F.
Telephone: 011-525-635-1145.
Fax: 011-525-53401454.

MEMBERS OF FIRM

Ralph M. Ochoa (Resident, Sacramento Office)
Herman Sillas
Jacqueline Rich Moore (Resident, Sacramento Office)
Tomás R. Lopez

ASSOCIATES

Jack T. Molodanof (Resident, Sacramento Office)
Francisco Valles Lopez (Not admitted in the United States)
Rita A. Reyes
Christopher Eric Ochoa (Resident, Sacramento Office)
Cirina A. K. Rose
M. Eric Parkan

OF COUNSEL

Daniel P. Aguilera
Cochran & Lotkin, Washington, D.C.

Representative Clients: American Golf; BKK Corp. (Toxic substance treatment); Chrysler; Department of Water and Power of Los Angeles; Sacramento Municipal Utility District; Department of Insurance; Metropolitan Water District, Los Angeles; General Motors; Hughes Aircraft; ICN Laboratories.

For full biographical listings, see the Martindale-Hubbell Law Directory

O'MELVENY & MYERS LLP (AV)

400 South Hope Street, 90071-2899
Telephone: 213-430-6000
Facsimile: 213-430-6407
Cable: MOMS
Telex: 674122
Email: omminfo@omm.com *URL:* http://www.omm.com
Century City, CA Office: 1999 Avenue of the Stars, Los Angeles, 90067-6035.
Telex: 674097. Tel: 310-553-6700.
Fax: 310-246-6779.
Newport Beach, CA Office: 610 Newport Center Drive, 92660-6429.
Telex: 4722088. Tel: 949-760-9600.
Fax: 949-823-6994.
San Francisco, CA Office: Embarcadero Center West, 275 Battery Street, 94111-3305. Tel: 415-984-8700.
Fax: 415-984-8701.
New York, NY Office: Citicorp Center, 153 East 53rd Street, 10022-4611.
Telex: 129165. Tel: 212-326-2000.
Fax: 212-326-2061.
Washington, DC Office: 555 13th Street, N.W., 20004-1109.
Cable: MOMSWSH.
Telex: 89622. Tel: 202-383-5300.
Fax: 202-383-5414.
London Office: O'Melveny & Myers, 3 Finsbury Square, London, EC2A 1LA, England. Tel: 44-171-256-8451. Fax 44-171-638-8205.
Tokyo Office: Akasaka Twin Tower, East 14F, 2-17-23, Akasaka, Minato-ku, Tokyo 107-0052, Japan. Tel: 03-5562-2800.
Fax: 03-5575-3840.
Hong Kong Office: O'Melveny & Myers, Suite 1905, Tower Two, Lippo Centre, 89 Queensway, Central, Hong Kong. Tel: 852-2523-8266.
Fax: 852-2522-1760.
Shanghai Office: Kerry Centre, 20F, 1515 Nanjing Road West, Shanghai, 200040 People's Republic of China. Tel: 86-21-5298-5600.
Fax: 86-21-5298-5500.

(See Next Column)

PARTNER

Gordon E. Krischer

For Complete List of Firm Personnel, See General Section

For full biographical listings, see the Martindale-Hubbell Law Directory

REXON, FREEDMAN, KLEPETAR & HAMBLETON, A PROFESSIONAL CORPORATION (AV)

12100 Wilshire Boulevard, Suite 730, 90025
Telephone: 310-826-8300
Fax: 310-826-0333
Email: rfkhlaw@aol.com

Brian L. Rexon
Jeffrey C. Freedman
Ronald J. Klepetar
Debby R. Hambleton
Wendy K. Genz

Steven J. Prough
Mara Lynn Pressman

Reference: Santa Monica Bank.

For full biographical listings, see the Martindale-Hubbell Law Directory

RINTALA, SMOOT, JAENICKE & REES (AV)

10351 Santa Monica Boulevard, Suite 400, 90025-6937
Telephone: 310-203-0935
Facsimile: 310-556-8921
Email: RSJ&R@RSJR.com

MEMBERS OF FIRM

William T. Rintala
Peter C. Smoot
J. Larson Jaenicke
Robert A. Rees
Melodie K. Larsen
Frank E. Melton
Robert W. Hodges
G. Howden Fraser

ASSOCIATES

Michael B. Garfinkel
Emily Peters
Jeffrey H. Thaler
Jaclyn A. Hoekstra

Representative Clients: William Morris Agency, Inc.; Broadcast Music, Inc.; Eaton Corp.
Reference: Santa Monica Bank.

For full biographical listings, see the Martindale-Hubbell Law Directory

ROBINSON, DI LANDO & WHITAKER, A PROFESSIONAL LAW CORPORATION (AV)

800 Wilshire Boulevard Suite 1100, 90017-2687
Telephone: 213-229-0100
Facsimile: 213-229-0114
Email: rdwlaw@gte.net
San Francisco, California Office: 417 Montgomery Street, Suite 910. 94104.
Telephone: 415-391-9475.
Fax: 415-391-3799.

Michael C. Robinson, Jr.
Michael A. Di Lando
Ronald S. Whitaker
Jack M. Liebhaber
Timothy L. Salazar

Steve H. Yu
Mark Kane
Cynthia A. Goodman
Bradley R. Blamires
Farzad Tabatabai
Martin J. Mendoza
David K. Stewart
Michelle B. Dykstra
Charles H. Brown, II
Michael B. Wilk

For full biographical listings, see the Martindale-Hubbell Law Directory

RODI, POLLOCK, PETTKER, GALBRAITH & CAHILL, A LAW CORPORATION (AV)

444 South Flower Street, Suite 1700, 90071-2901
Telephone: 213-895-4900
Telecopiers: 213-895-4921; 895-4922; 895-4750
URL: http://www.rodipollock.com

Karl B. Rodi (1908-1982)
John D. Cahill
John D. Pettker
Daniel C. Bond (1942-1977)
William R. Christian
Henry P. Pramov, Jr.
John F. Cermak, Jr.
Allan E. Ceran
Elizabeth B. Blakely
Robert C. Norton
Tim G. Ceperley
Coralie Kupfer
Cris K. O'Neall
Scott E. Adamson
Margaret Rosenthal

Sonja A. Inglin
Michael A. Abraham
Kenneth A. Franklin
Richard Nessary
Donna Yamini
Wade E. Norwood
Deepak Nanda
David J. Elbaz

OF COUNSEL

John P. Pollock
James M. Galbraith

For full biographical listings, see the Martindale-Hubbell Law Directory

Los Angeles—Continued

SCHWARTZ, STEINSAPIR, DOHRMANN & SOMMERS, LLP (AV)

6300 Wilshire Boulevard, Suite 2000, 90048
Telephone: 323-655-4700
Fax: 323-655-4488
Pittsburgh, Pennsylvania Office: 1007 Mt. Royal Boulevard, 15223.
Telephone: 412-492-8797.
Fax: 412-492-8978.

MEMBERS OF FIRM

Laurence D. Steinsapir
Robert M. Dohrmann
Richard D. Sommers
Stuart Libicki
Michael R. Feinberg
Michael D. Four
Margo A. Feinberg
Henry M. Willis
D. William Heine, Jr.
Claude Cazzulino
Dolly M. Gee

ASSOCIATES

Erika A. Zucker
Janet L. Woods

For full biographical listings, see the Martindale-Hubbell Law Directory

MENLO PARK, San Mateo Co.

DYER & WHITE LLP (AV)

Suite 200, 800 Oak Grove Avenue, 94025
Telephone: 650-325-7000
Fax: 650-325-3116
Email: cdyer@dyer-white.com

MEMBERS OF FIRM

Charles A. Dyer
Rand N. White

For full biographical listings, see the Martindale-Hubbell Law Directory

LAW OFFICE OF DENNIS LAWRENCE KENNELLY (AV)

1030 Curtis Street, Suite 200, 94025-4501
Telephone: 650-853-1291
Fax: 650-328-4715

For full biographical listings, see the Martindale-Hubbell Law Directory

SCHACHTER, KRISTOFF, ORENSTEIN & BERKOWITZ, L.L.P. (AV)

90 Middlefield Road, Suite 201, 94025
Telephone: 650-473-1400
Telecopier: 650-463-0346
San Francisco Office: 505 Montgomery Street, 14th Floor.
Telephone: 415-391-3333.
Telecopier: 415-392-6589.
Sacramento Office: 980 9th Street, Suite 1500.
Telephone: 916-442-3333.
Telecopier: 916-442-2348.

Gale Heuman Borden

For full biographical listings, see the Martindale-Hubbell Law Directory

NEWPORT BEACH, Orange Co.

FISHER & PHILLIPS LLP (AV)

A Limited Liability Partnership including Professional Corporations and Professional Associations
4675 MacArthur Court, Suite 550, 92660
Telephone: 949-851-2424
Telecopier: 949-851-0152
URL: http://www.laborlawyers.com
Atlanta, Georgia Office: 1500 Resurgens Plaza, 945 East Paces Ferry Road, N.E., 30326.
Telephone: 404-231-1400.
Telecopier: 404-240-4249.
Fort Lauderdale, Florida Office: Suite 2300 NationsBank Tower, One Financial Plaza, 33394.
Telephone: 954-525-4800.
Telecopier: 954-525-8739.
Redwood City, California Office: Suite 345, Three Lagoon Drive, 94065.
Telephone: 650-592-6160.
Telecopier: 650-592-6385.
New Orleans, Louisiana Office: 201 St. Charles Avenue, Suite 3710, 70170.
Telephone: 504-522-3303.
Telecopier: 504-529-3850.
Houston, Texas Office: 6850 Chase Tower, 600 Travis, 77002.
Telephone: 713-227-5410.
Telecopier: 713-236-6949.
Chicago, Illinois Office: 420 Marquette Building, 140 South Dearborn Street, 60603.
Telephone: 312-346-8061.
Telecopier: 312-346-3179.

RESIDENT MEMBERS

Robert J. Bekken
James J. McDonald, Jr.
Karl R. Lindegren
Robert V. Schnitz
Robert Yonowitz
John M. Polson

(See Next Column)

RESIDENT ASSOCIATES

Lyne A. Richardson
Cynthia Walker Lane
Warren Lee Nelson
Anne M. Terra
Christopher C. Hoffman
Jennifer L. Futch
John K. Skousen
John E. Lattin, IV
Christina Thuy Nguyen
Mark A. Seif
Linda J. Gulledge
Jerry D. Underwood
Amy Lynn Doherty

Representative Clients: Behr Process Corp.; California Motor Car Dealers Assn.; Marie Callendar Pie Shops, Inc.; Motor Car Dealers Association of Orange County; New Car Dealers Association of San Diego; Textron, Inc.

For full biographical listings, see the Martindale-Hubbell Law Directory

LOPEZ, HODES, RESTAINO, MILMAN & SKIKOS, A LAW CORPORATION (AV)

450 Newport Center Drive, 2nd Floor, 92660
Telephone: 949-640-8222
Fax: 949-640-8294
San Francisco, California Office: 625 Market Street, Fifteenth Floor, 94105.
Telephone: 415-956-5257.
Fax: 415-956-4416.

Ramon Rossi Lopez
Daniel M. Hodes
John M. Restaino, Jr.
Jeffrey A. Milman
Peter John Polos
Steven J. Skikos (Resident)

Christina A. Lopez Fountain
Steven B. Eggleston (Resident, San Francisco Office)
Gregory T. Skikos (Resident, San Francisco Office)
Thomas A. Schultz
Mark G. Crawford
Hilary Poulsen Gilles

OF COUNSEL

David L. Suggs (Not admitted in CA)
Jane E. Joseph (Not admitted in CA)

For full biographical listings, see the Martindale-Hubbell Law Directory

ROGER H. SCHNAPP A PROFESSIONAL CORPORATION (AV)

P.O. Box 9049, 92658-1049
Telephone: 949-752-0491
Fax: 949-752-1102
Email: RHS@SCHNAPP.COM *URL:* HTTP://WWW.SCHNAPP.COM

Roger H. Schnapp

For full biographical listings, see the Martindale-Hubbell Law Directory

*OAKLAND,** Alameda Co.

ANTHONY & CARLSON, LLP (AV)

1999 Harrison Street, Suite 2000, 94612-3517
Telephone: 510-835-8400
Fax: 510-835-5566

MEMBERS OF FIRM

Steven R. Anthony
Richard H. Carlson

Felicia C. Strankman

OF COUNSEL

Jane L. Trigero

For full biographical listings, see the Martindale-Hubbell Law Directory

ORINDA, Contra Costa Co.

GILLIN, JACOBSON, ELLIS & LARSEN (AV)

2 Theatre Square Suite 230, 94563
Telephone: 925-253-5800
Fax: 925-253-5858
Email: lawfirm@gjeld.com
San Francisco, California Office: 44 Montgomery Street, Suite 500, 94101.
Telephone: 415-986-4777.

Andrew R. Gillin
Ralph L. Jacobson
Luke Ellis
James Paul Larsen
Kristin Lucey

For full biographical listings, see the Martindale-Hubbell Law Directory

OXNARD, Ventura Co.

H. ROY JEPPSON A PROFESSIONAL CORPORATION (AV)

300 Esplanade Drive, Suite 1810, 93030
Telephone: 805-604-1100
Fax: 805-604-1600
URL: http://www.lawyers.com/jeppsonlaw
Los Angeles, California Office: 11900 West Olympic Boulevard. Sixth Floor. 90064.
Telephone: 310-826-5566.
Fax: 310-826-5350.

(See Next Column)

H. Roy Jeppson A Professional Corporation—*Continued*

H. Roy Jeppson

Robyn F. Stalk

For full biographical listings, see the Martindale-Hubbell Law Directory

PALM SPRINGS, Riverside Co.

FitzGerald & Associates (AV)

3001 Tahquitz Canyon Way, 92262
Telephone: 760-325-5055
FAX: 760-327-9262

John E. FitzGerald III

David Brian Mulé

Representative Clients: Armtec Defense Products; Association of California Hospital Districts; Big Horn Country Club; Desert Hospital; Desert Sun; Eldorado Country Club; Fantasy Springs Casino; First Community Bank; Ritz Carlton, Spa Hotel and Casino.
Reference: Palm Desert National Bank.

For full biographical listings, see the Martindale-Hubbell Law Directory

PASADENA, Los Angeles Co.

Melanie A. Calvert (AV)

Penthouse, 150 South Los Robles Avenue, Suite 930, 91101-2437
Telephone: 626-585-3555
Fax: 626-577-5219
URL: http://www.lawyers.com/mcalvertlaw

For full biographical listings, see the Martindale-Hubbell Law Directory

Lloyd C. Ownbey, Jr. (AV)

180 South Lake Avenue, Suite 510, 91101-2683
Telephone: 626-440-5960
Fax: 626-585-9669

For full biographical listings, see the Martindale-Hubbell Law Directory

*REDWOOD CITY,** San Mateo Co.

Fisher & Phillips LLP (AV)

A Limited Liability Partnership including Professional Corporations and Professional Associations
Suite 345, Three Lagoon Drive, 94065
Telephone: 650-592-6160
Telecopier: 650-592-6385
URL: http://www.laborlawyers.com
Atlanta, Georgia Office: 1500 Resurgens Plaza, 945 East Paces Ferry Road, N.E., 30326.
Telephone: 404-231-1400.
Telecopier: 404-240-4249.
Fort Lauderdale, Florida Office: Suite 2300 NationsBank Tower, One Financial Plaza, 33394.
Telephone: 954-525-4800.
Telecopier: 954-525-8739.
Newport Beach, California Office: 4675 MacArthur Court, Suite 550, 92660.
Telephone: 949-851-2424.
Telecopier: 949-851-0152.
New Orleans, Louisiana Office: 201 St. Charles Avenue, Suite 3710, 70170.
Telephone: 504-522-3303.
Telecopier: 504-529-3850.
Houston, Texas Office: 6850 Chase Tower, 600 Travis, 77002.
Telephone: 713-227-5410.
Telecopier: 713-236-6949.
Chicago, Illinois Office: 420 Marquette Building, 140 South Dearborn Street, 60603.
Telephone: 312-346-8061.
Telecopier: 312-346-3179.

RESIDENT MEMBERS

Ned A. Fine
John D. McLachlan
Lynn D. Lieber

RESIDENT ASSOCIATES

Donald E. Cope
Michael K. Perkins
John Phillip Boggs
David A. Hosilyk
David J. Reese

Representative Clients: California Motor Car Dealers Assn.; Centex Cement; Chrysler Insurance Corp.; The Limited; Nepco; Nestle Beverage Co.; Waste Management Inc.; Willamette Industries, Inc.

For full biographical listings, see the Martindale-Hubbell Law Directory

*RIVERSIDE,** Riverside Co.

Haight, Brown & Bonesteel, L.L.P. (AV)

A Partnership including Professional Corporations
California Tower, 3737 Main Street, Suite 800, 92501
Telephone: 909-341-8300
FAX: 909-341-8309
URL: http://www.hbblaw.com
Santa Monica, California Office: 1620 26th Street, Suite 4000 North, P.O. Box 680.
Telephone: 310-449-6000.
Telecopier: 310-829-5117.
Telex: 705837.
Santa Ana, California Office: Suite 900, 5 Hutton Centre Drive.
Telephone: 714-754-1100.
Telecopier: 714-754-0826.
San Francisco, California Office: 100 Bush Street, 27th Floor.
Telephone: 415-986-7700.
Fax: 415-986-6945.
San Diego, California Office: 101 West Broadway, Suite 1000.
Telephone: 619-595-5583.
Fax: 619-595-7873.

RESIDENT MEMBER

Mark S. Lester

ASSOCIATE

Bonnie B. Bailey-Jones

For full biographical listings, see the Martindale-Hubbell Law Directory

*SACRAMENTO,** Sacramento Co.

Angelo, Kilday & Kilduff (AV)

601 University Avenue, Suite 150, 95825
Telephone: 916-564-6100
Telecopier: 916-564-6263

MEMBERS OF FIRM

Laurence L. Angelo
J. Scott Smith
Bruce A. Kilday
Jeffrey S. Stone
Carolee Kilduff
Amy H. Ruggles
Christine Green Sanfilippo
Ronald J. Scholar

LEGAL SUPPORT PERSONNEL

Susan M. Jarboe (Paralegal-Law Librarian)

For full biographical listings, see the Martindale-Hubbell Law Directory

Cook, Brown & Prager, LLP (AV)

555 Capitol Mall, Suite 425, 95814-4503
Telephone: 916-442-3100
Fax: 916-442-4227
Email: cbrp@cookbrown.com
Santa Ana, California Office: 801 Civic Center Drive, Suite 450.
Telephone: 714-542-1883.
Fax: 714-542-1009.
Salinas, California Office: 450 Lincoln Avenue, Suite 202.
Telephone: 831-755-7940.
Fax: 831-755-7944.

RESIDENT PARTNERS

Dennis B. Cook
James E. Mesnier
Ronald W. Brown
Brian D. Bertossa
Terry A. Wigen

RESIDENT ASSOCIATE

Catherine M. Corfee

For full biographical listings, see the Martindale-Hubbell Law Directory

Hardy Erich Brown & Wilson, A Professional Corporation (AV)

1000 G Street, 95814
Telephone: 916-449-3800
Fax: 916-449-3888
Mailing Address: P.O. Box 13530, Sacramento, California, 95853-4530
Email: hebw@hebw.com *URL:* http://www.hebw.com

David L. Perrault
Glenda N. Reager

OF COUNSEL

Richard M. Cunha

Kelly F. Watson
Kristine E. Balogh
Lisa L. Palombo

Representative Clients: American Promotional Events, Inc.; CBM Group Inc.; Corinthian Colleges, Inc.; Foamex International, Inc.; Hines Horticulture, Inc.; The Infinity Group; Kmart Corporation; Regent of the University of California; State of California, Bureau of State Audits; United Way California Capital Region.

For full biographical listings, see the Martindale-Hubbell Law Directory

Sacramento—Continued

LIVINGSTON & MATTESICH, LAW CORPORATION (AV)

1201 K Street, Suite 1100, 95814
Telephone: 916-442-1111
Fax: 916-448-1709
Email: l&m@lmlaw.net *URL:* http://www.lmlaw.net

Gene Livingston
James M. Mattesich
Carol Livingston
Rebecca M. Ceniceros
Emilio E. Varanini, III
Kenneth M. Malovos
Kathleen E. Finnerty
Joanna R. Mendoza

Steven P. Belzer
Jeffrey Leacox
Randy Pollack
Alice H. Choi
Stephen Craig Hunter
Matthew J. Goldman
Joel C. Baiocchi
Baldassaro (Bill) Di Capo
John McKinsey
Timothy E. Naccarato
Craig N. Lundgren
Mary Farrell Taylor
Brian Crone
Gay L. Carroll
Steven G. Churchwell

Representative Clients: Fibrebond Corp.; Unilever United States, Inc.

For full biographical listings, see the Martindale-Hubbell Law Directory

MASTAGNI, HOLSTEDT & CHIURAZZI, A PROFESSIONAL CORPORATION (AV)

1912 I Street, Suite 102, 95814
Telephone: 916-446-4692
Fax: 916-447-4614
Email: mhcmailbox@mastagni.com

David P. Mastagni
John R. Holstedt
Richard J. Chiurazzi

Stephen Curtis Winter
Dennis W. Hargrave
Michael D. Amick
Barbara M. Jacobson
Kasey Christopher Clark
Brian A. Dixon
Elaine M. Cawley
Michael R. Kelly
Mark Regalbuti
Christopher W. Miller

Representative Clients: Alameda County Probation Assn.; Cannery Workers, El Dorado County Deputy Sheriffs Assn.; Folsom Police Officers Assn.; Jackson Police Officers Assn.; United Food & Commercial Workers 588, Northern California; P.O.R.A.C. Insurance Board.

For full biographical listings, see the Martindale-Hubbell Law Directory

NAGELEY, MEREDITH & MILLER, INC. (AV)

8001 Folsom Boulevard, Suite 100, 95826
Telephone: 916-386-8282
Fax: 916-386-8952
Email: mail@mnlawfirm.com

Sam R. Nageley
Gregory A. Meredith
Andrea M. Miller
Lawrence N. Hensley
Craig S. MacGlashan
Janet M. Meredith
Carole Hansen Sharples
L. Alan Warwick
Drew M. Johnson
James C. Keowen
Duane S. Oliveira

For full biographical listings, see the Martindale-Hubbell Law Directory

LAW OFFICES OF ANTHONY J. POIDMORE (AV)

400 Capitol Mall, 26th Floor, 95814
Telephone: 916-441-0636
Fax: 916-441-1858
Email: joblaw@jps.net

ASSOCIATE

Lawrence R. DeFehr

For full biographical listings, see the Martindale-Hubbell Law Directory

PORTER, SCOTT, WEIBERG & DELEHANT, A PROFESSIONAL CORPORATION (AV)

350 University Avenue, Suite 200, 95825
Telephone: 916-929-1481
Fax: 916-927-3706
Email: pswdlaw@aol.com

Russell G. Porter
A. Irving Scott, Jr.
Edwin T. Weiberg
John W. Delehant
Anthony S. Warburg
Ned P. Telford
James K. Mirabell
Craig A. Caldwell
Terence J. Cassidy
Tom H. Bailey
Carl J. Calnero
Russ J. Wunderli
Nancy J. Sheehan
Norman V. Prior
Timothy M. Blaine
Stephen E. Horan
Carl L. Fessenden

(See Next Column)

PORTER, SCOTT, WEIBERG & DELEHANT, A PROFESSIONAL CORPORATION—*Continued*

Elisa Ungerman
Michael J. Baytosh
David A. Melton
Jennifer E. Duggan
Vanessa W. Whang
Dennis C. Huie
Michael W. Pott
Kellianne Akbar
Daniel M. Steinberg
Jack Woodside
Jonathan A. Corr
Kristina M. Hall
Alden J. Parker
Avery E. Dority
Robin Weideman
Denise A. Carnaroli
Lara S. Hilley
Sean Allen
Ralph R. Nevis
Darrin M. Menezes
Shane Singh

For full biographical listings, see the Martindale-Hubbell Law Directory

SCHACHTER, KRISTOFF, ORENSTEIN & BERKOWITZ, L.L.P. (AV)

980 9th Street, Suite 1500, 95814
Telephone: 916-442-3333
Telecopier: 916-442-2348
San Francisco Office: 505 Montgomery Street, 14th Floor.
Telephone: 415-391-3333.
Telecopier: 415-392-6589.
Menlo Park Office: 90 Middlefield Road, Suite 201.
Telephone: 650-473-1400.
Telecopier: 650-463-0346.

John D. Adkisson

RESIDENT ASSOCIATES

Gail Cecchettini Whaley
Jennifer Brown Shaw
Sue Ann Van Dermyden
Charles W. Nugent

For full biographical listings, see the Martindale-Hubbell Law Directory

*SALINAS,** Monterey Co.

COOK, BROWN & PRAGER, LLP (AV)

450 Lincoln Avenue, Suite 202, 93901-2686
Telephone: 831-775-7940
Fax: 831-755-7944
Email: cbrp@cookbrown.com
Sacramento, California Office: 555 Capitol Mall, Suite 425.
Telephone: 916-442-3100.
Fax: 916-442-4227.
Santa Ana, California Office: 801 Civic Center Drive, Suite 450.
Telephone: 714-542-1883.
Fax: 714-542-1009.

RESIDENT PARTNER

Geoffrey F. Gega

For full biographical listings, see the Martindale-Hubbell Law Directory

*SAN DIEGO,** San Diego Co.

LAW OFFICES OF JOHN S. ADLER A PROFESSIONAL CORPORATION (AV)

550 West "C" Street, Suite 1500, 92101-3540
Telephone: 619-231-8825
Fax: 619-231-5899
Email: jsadleresq@aol.com

John S. Adler

For full biographical listings, see the Martindale-Hubbell Law Directory

ALHADEFF CANNON ROSE SOLAR & PARKS, LLP (AV)

550 West "C" Street, Nineteenth Floor, 92101-3540
Telephone: 619-231-8700
Facsimile: 619-231-8323
Email: ksolar@acrsp.com
Temecula, California Office: The Tower Plaza, 27555 Ynez Road, Suite 203, 92591-4677.
Telephone: 909-699-9088.
Facsimile: 909-699-9878. Email: POBERHANSLEY@ACRSP.com
Los Angeles, California Office: Olympic Center, 11150 Olympic Boulevard, Suite 860, 90064.
Telephone: 310-914-4400.
Facsimile: 310-914-0030. Email: JODONNELL@ACRSP.com
Lafayette, California Office: Lafayette Terrace, 3697 Mount Diablo Boulevard, Suite 100, 94549.
Telephone: 925-283-1599.
Facsimile: 925-283-5847. Email: GMF-CA@MSN.com

PARTNER

John L. O'Donnell, Jr. (Resident, Los Angeles, California Office)

ASSOCIATES

Genie Harrison
Traci M. Selby

References: Enefco International, Ltd.; Molding International & Engineering; Health Net.

For full biographical listings, see the Martindale-Hubbell Law Directory

San Diego—Continued

BARKER THOMAS & WALTERS, A PROFESSIONAL LAW CORPORATION (AV)

1455 Frazee Road, Suite 800, 92108
Telephone: 619-682-4040
Facsimile: 619-220-7056
Email: info@btwlaw.com *URL:* http://www.btwlaw.com

Douglas H. Barker
Anastasia E. Thomas

Catherine Petrecca
Elizabeth J. Koumas

For full biographical listings, see the Martindale-Hubbell Law Directory

FERRIS & BRITTON, A PROFESSIONAL CORPORATION (AV)

1600 First National Bank Center, 401 West A Street, 92101
Telephone: 619-233-3131
Fax: 619-232-9316
Email: manager@ferrisbritton.com *URL:* http://www.ferrisbritton.com

Alfred G. Ferris
Christopher Q. Britton
Steven J. Pynes
Michael R. Weinstein

Representative Clients: Coast Distributing Co.; Cox Communications, Inc.; Datel, Inc.; Frontier Analytics, Inc.; Jimsair Aviation Services, Inc.; Peninsula Bank; Structural Bioinformatics, Inc.; Teleport Communications Group; Southwest Airlines; Valley Independent Bank.

For Complete List of Firm Personnel, See General Section

For full biographical listings, see the Martindale-Hubbell Law Directory

FISCH, SPIEGLER, GINSBURG, LADNER & ATTARIAN, A PROFESSIONAL LAW CORPORATION (AV)

1551 Fourth Avenue, Suite 300, 92101-3184
Telephone: 619-234-1551
Telecopier: 619-234-1568
Email: FSGLA@AOL.com

Joseph J. Fisch
Mark A. Spiegler
Phillip L. Ginsburg
Karen M. Ladner
Peter J. Attarian, Jr.

For full biographical listings, see the Martindale-Hubbell Law Directory

HAIGHT, BROWN & BONESTEEL, L.L.P. (AV)

A Partnership including Professional Corporations
101 West Broadway, Suite 1000, 92101-3544
Telephone: 619-595-5583
Telecopier: 619-595-7873
URL: http://www.hbblaw.com
Santa Monica, California Office: 1620 26th Street, Suite 4000 North, P.O. Box 680.
Telephone: 310-449-6000.
Telecopier: 310-829-5117.
Telex: 705837.
Santa Ana, California Office: Suite 900, 5 Hutton Centre Drive.
Telephone: 714-754-1100.
Telecopier: 714-754-0826.
Riverside, California Office: California Tower, 3737 Main Street, Suite 800.
Telephone: 909-341-8300.
Fax: 909-341-8309.
San Francisco, California Office: 101 Bush Street, 27th Floor.
Telephone: 415-986-7700.
Fax: 415-986-6945.

RESIDENT MEMBER
DeAnn M. Salcido

For full biographical listings, see the Martindale-Hubbell Law Directory

KENNERSON SCHWARTZ SEMERDJIAN & HAILE LLP (AV)

A Limited Liability Partnership
101 West Broadway, Suite 810, 92101
Telephone: 619-236-8821
Facsimile: 619-236-8827
URL: http://www.lawyers.com/ksshlaw

OF COUNSEL
Paul R. Kennerson

MEMBERS OF FIRM
Ross J. Schwartz
Dick A. Semerdjian
Jeffrey A. Haile

James R. Ballard
John K. Grant

For full biographical listings, see the Martindale-Hubbell Law Directory

KLINEDINST, FLIEHMAN & MCKILLOP, A PROFESSIONAL CORPORATION (AV)

The Koll Center, 501 West Broadway, Suite 600, 92101-3584
Telephone: 619-239-8131
Fax: 619-238-8707
URL: http://www.kfmlaw.com
Orange County Office: Civic Center Law Building, 611 Civic Center Drive, Suite 250, Santa Ana, California, 92701.
Telephone: 714-542-1800.
Los Angeles, California Office: Wells Fargo Center, 333 South Grand Avenue, 33rd Floor, 90071.
Telephone: 213-625-8100.

SHAREHOLDERS
John D. Klinedinst
Donald R. McKillop, Sr.
G. William (Bill) Van De Weghe, Jr.
Thomas S. Ingrassia
Douglas A. Pettit
Gregory A. Garbacz
Arthur S. Moreau, III

Kendra J. Hall
Andrew N. Kohn
M. Shawn Payment
Kurt U. Campbell
G. Dale Britton
Susan S. Kohn
Heather L. Rosing
Debora A. Cappucci
Dayna Lyn Chmelka
Jennifer N. Lehman
Dennis C. Crovella
Carey L. Cooper
Kevin J. Gramling

PARALEGALS
Mary Ann Murphy-Brown
Cam B. Picano

Reference: Bank of America.

For full biographical listings, see the Martindale-Hubbell Law Directory

LUCE, FORWARD, HAMILTON & SCRIPPS LLP (AV)

A Partnership including Professional Corporations
600 West Broadway, Suite 2600, 92101
Telephone: 619-236-1414
Fax: 619-232-8311
URL: http://www.luce.com
La Jolla, California Office: 4275 Executive Square, Suite 800, 92037.
Telephone: 858-455-6611.
Fax: 858-232-8311.
Los Angeles, California Office: 777 South Figueroa, Suite 3600, 90017.
Telephone: 213-892-4992.
Fax: 213-892-7731.
San Francisco, California Office: 121 Spear Street, Suite 200, 94105.
Telephone: 415-356-4600.
Fax: 415-356-4610.
New York, N.Y. Office: Citicorp Center, 153 East 53rd Street, 26th Floor, 10022.
Telephone: 212-754-1414.
Fax: 212-644-9727.
Chicago, Illinois Office: 180 North La Salle Street, Suite 3110, 60601.
Telephone: 312-641-0580.
Fax: 312-641-0380.

Kathryn A. Bernert
William T. Earley
Michael L. Jensen
Robert A. Levy
Daniel N. Riesenberg
Mary L. Russell
Craig A. Schloss
Theodore R. Scott

ASSOCIATES
Richard J. Bergstrom
Kelly Capen Douglas
John D. Edson
Maria C. Heredia
Tami Johnson Penner
Julie A. Vogelzang

For Complete List of Firm Personnel, See General Section

For full biographical listings, see the Martindale-Hubbell Law Directory

MAXIE RHEINHEIMER STEPHENS & VREVICH, LLP (AV)

600 West Broadway, Suite 900, 92101
Telephone: 619-515-1155
Fax: 619-515-1159
Los Angeles, California Office: 555 South Flower Street, Suite 4640.
Telephone: 213-236-9878.
Fax: 213-489-7559.
Newport Beach, California Office: 110 Newport Center Drive, Suite 200.
Telephone: 714-644-8136.
Fax: 714-644-7526.
Sacramento, California Office: 400 Capital Mall, Suite 235.
Telephone: 916-444-5566.
Fax: 916-444-5494.
Las Vegas, Nevada Office: Law Office of Gary P. Sinkeldam, 4270 South Decatur Blvd., Suite B6-106.
Telephone: 702-968-8037.
Fax: 702-968-8069.

Robert C. Maxie
Jane A. Rheinheimer
Sean D. Stephens
Barry M. Vrevich

(See Next Column)

MAXIE RHEINHEIMER STEPHENS & VREVICH LLP, *San Diego—Continued*

Christine L. Cornick
Theodore Dikmen
Suzanne Lovelace Smigliani
Alison J. Barry
Ann Marie Thompson
Marie K. Peluso
Darin L. Wessel
Jason R. Bogni

OF COUNSEL

Gary P. Sinkeldam
Cheryl D. Davidson

For full biographical listings, see the Martindale-Hubbell Law Directory

MERRILL, SCHULTZ & WOLDS, LIMITED (AV)

First National Bank Building, Suite 2550, 401 West "A" Street, 92101
Telephone: 619-234-4525
Telecopier: 619-234-9740
Email: mswltd@mswltd.com

Stephen J. Schultz
David P. Wolds
Mark T. Bennett

John M. Julius, III
Laura B. Riesenberg

OF COUNSEL

Michael E. Merrill
William R. Kuntz, Jr.

Representative Clients: Associated General Contractors of America, San Diego Chapter, Inc.; Associated General Contractors Health and Welfare, Retirement, and Apprenticeship and Training Trust Funds; San Diego Opera Association; La Jolla Beach & Tennis Club; ABC Framers, Commercial and Residential Drywall Councils Health Insurance Trust Funds; Douglas E. Barnhart, Inc.; Blake Construction; United Way of San Diego County/-Health Way Trust Fund; San Diego Construction Councils; McCarthy Brothers Company.

For full biographical listings, see the Martindale-Hubbell Law Directory

OLINS, FOERSTER & HAYES (AV)

A Legal Liability Partnership including A Professional Corporation
2214 Second Avenue, 92101
Telephone: 619-238-1601
Fax: 619-238-1613
URL: http://www.ofh.com
Santa Ana, California Office: 1314 West Fifth Street, Suite C, 92703.
Telephone: 714-836-9777.
Fax: 714-954-1156.

MEMBERS OF FIRM

Douglas F. Olins
Barrett J. Foerster (A P.C.)
Dennis J. Hayes

ASSOCIATES

Laura H. Miller
Barbara J. Ginsberg
John C. Zucconi
(Resident, Santa Ana Office)

Representative Clients: United Food and Commercial Workers International Union, AFL-CIO; United Food and Commercial Workers, Locals 1036 and 588; American Federation of State, County and Municipal Employees, Local 127; American Postal Workers Union, California Area Local; American Postal Workers Union, San Diego Chapter; Association of Orange County Deputy Sheriffs; Santa Ana Firemen's Benevolent Association; San Bernardino Public Employees Association.

For full biographical listings, see the Martindale-Hubbell Law Directory

POPE & BERGER (AV)

550 West "C" Street, Seventeenth Floor, 92101
Telephone: 619-234-1222
Facsimile: 619-236-9677
Email: pope@pope-berger.com *URL:* http://www.pope-berger.com/

A. Mark Pope
Harvey C. Berger

ASSOCIATE

Timothy G. Williams

For full biographical listings, see the Martindale-Hubbell Law Directory

STOKES & MURPHY, P.C. (AV)

110 West "C" Steet, Suite 2020, 92101
Telephone: 619-702-8600
Fax: 619-702-8610
Email: mail@stokesnmurphy.com
Atlanta, Georgia Office: 3593 Hemphill Street, P.O. Box 87468.
Telephone: 404-766-0076.
Facsimile: 404-766-8823.
Pittsburgh, Pennsylvania Office: Foster Plaza X, 680 Andersen Drive.
Telephone: 412-937-3277.
Fax: 412-920-5751.
Dallas, Texas: 10127 Rita Road.
Telephone: 972-671-4350.
Fax: 972-671-4352.
Windermere, Florida: 2231 Ridgewind Way.
Telephone: 407-909-1095.
Fax: 407-909-0384.

(See Next Column)

Robert L. Murphy
Paul F. Sorrentino

RESIDENT ASSOCIATE

Regina Silva

For full biographical listings, see the Martindale-Hubbell Law Directory

*SAN FRANCISCO,** San Francisco Co.

BIANCO & MURPHY (AV)

500 Sansome Street, 8th Floor, 94111
Telephone: 415-362-3344
Telecopier: 415-986-5271
Email: LAWRLB@AOL.COM

MEMBERS OF FIRM

Robert L. Bianco
Stephen M. Murphy

ASSOCIATES

Gregory O. Bianco
Christopher M. Windle

For full biographical listings, see the Martindale-Hubbell Law Directory

LAW OFFICES OF PHILIP BOROWSKY A PROFESSIONAL CORPORATION (AV)

Steuart Street Tower, Suite 2600, One Market Plaza, 94105-1417
Telephone: 415-896-6800
Facsimile: 415-896-0600
Email: info@borowsky.com *URL:* http://www.borowsky.com
Los Angeles, California Office: 2049 Century Park East, Suite 900, 90067-3111.
Telephone: 310-551-6960.
Fax: 310-553-7237.

Philip Borowsky

Christopher J. Hayes

For full biographical listings, see the Martindale-Hubbell Law Directory

CURIALE DELLAVERSON HIRSCHFELD KELLY & KRAEMER, LLP (AV)

727 Sansome Street, 94111
Telephone: 415-835-9000
Facsimile: 415-834-0443
Email: info@cdhkk.com *URL:* http://www.cdhkk.com
Los Angeles, California Office: 1880 Century Park East, Suite 800.
Telephone: 310-203-9999.
Facsimile: 310-557-1509.

MEMBERS OF FIRM

Richard J. Curiale
Carmen Plaza de Jennings
JoAnne Dellaverson
John F. Baum
Stephen J. Hirschfeld
Joel P. Kelly
Jeffrey Sloan
(Resident, Los Angeles Office)
Glen E. Kraemer
Martin H. Kresse
(Resident, Los Angeles Office)
Reed E. Schaper
Linda A. Tripoli
(Resident, Los Angeles Office)
Donna M. Rutter
John F. Scalia

ASSOCIATES

Jayne Benz Chipman
Scott K. Liner
Kathleen E. Collins
(Resident, Los Angeles Office)
(Resident, Los Angeles Office)
Kirstin E. Muller
Dana DuFrane
(Resident, Los Angeles Office)
Karla Wolf Franklin
Alison C. Neufeld
Sarah L. Harpham
Felicia R. Reid
Brian W. Jones
Leonora M. Schloss
Harry G. Lewis
(Resident, Los Angeles Office)
Leslie A. Sprinkle

For full biographical listings, see the Martindale-Hubbell Law Directory

HAIGHT, BROWN & BONESTEEL, L.L.P. (AV)

A Partnership including Professional Corporations
100 Bush Street, 27th Floor, 94104-3902
Telephone: 415-986-7700
Telecopier: 415-986-6945
URL: http://www.hbblaw.com
Santa Monica, California Office: 1620 26th Street, Suite 4000 North, P.O. Box 680.
Telephone: 310-449-6000.
Telecopier: 310-829-5117.
Telex: 705837.
Santa Ana, California Office: Suite 900, 5 Hutton Centre Drive.
Telephone: 714-754-1100.
Telecopier: 714-754-0826.
Riverside, California Office: California Tower, 3737 Main Street, Suite 800.
Telephone: 909-341-8300.
Fax: 909-341-8309.
San Diego, California Office: 101 West Broadway, Suite 1000.
Telephone: 619-595-5583.
Fax: 619-595-7873.

(See Next Column)

HAIGHT, BROWN & BONESTEEL L.L.P.—*Continued*

RESIDENT MEMBERS

Lisa L. Oberg
Patricia H. Perry

ASSOCIATE

Felicia Y. Feng

For full biographical listings, see the Martindale-Hubbell Law Directory

LIEFF, CABRASER, HEIMANN & BERNSTEIN, LLP (AV)

Embarcadero Center West, 30th Floor, 275 Battery Street, 94111
Telephone: 415-956-1000
Telecopier: 415-956-1008
Email: mail@lchb.com *URL:* http://www.lchb.com
New York, N.Y. Office: 10 Rockefeller Plaza, 12th Floor, 10020-1903.
Telephone: 212-218-6600.
Fax: 212-218-6608.

Robert L. Lieff
Elizabeth J. Cabraser
Richard M. Heimann
William Bernstein
William B. Hirsch
James M. Finberg
Karen E. Karpen
Joseph R. Saveri
Donald C. Arbitblit
Steven E. Fineman (Resident, New York, N.Y. Office)
Robert J. Nelson
Jacqueline E. Mottek
Morris A. Ratner
Melanie M. Piech
Kelly M. Dermody
Jonathan D. Selbin
Richard M. Franco
Barry R. Himmelstein
Joshua P. Davis
Michael W. Sobol
Robert G. Eisler (Resident, New York, N.Y. Office)

Jennie L. Anderson
Lori E. Andrus
Caryn Becker
Joan T. Brown (Not admitted in CA)
Stephen H. Cassidy
Paulina do Amaral
Eric B. Fastiff
Hector D. Geribon (Resident, New York, N.Y. Office)
Pierce Gore
Rebecca M. Katz (Resident, New York, N.Y. Office)
Lisa J. Leebove
Karen J. Mandel (Resident, New York, N.Y. Office)
Scott P. Nealey
Erik L. Shawn (Resident, New York, N.Y. Office)
David S. Stellings (Resident, New York, N.Y. Office)
Steven M. Tindall
Fabrice N. Vincent
Jonathan M. Watkins
Heather A. Woodard
Yu-Yee Wu

For full biographical listings, see the Martindale-Hubbell Law Directory

THE LUCAS LAW FIRM (AV)

1700 California Street, Suite 340, 94109
Telephone: 415-434-3100
FAX: 415-434-0300
Email: lucaslaw@aol.com

Kathleen M. Lucas

For full biographical listings, see the Martindale-Hubbell Law Directory

MCGUINN, HILLSMAN & PALEFSKY, A PROFESSIONAL CORPORATION (AV)

535 Pacific Avenue, 94133
Telephone: 415-421-9292
Fax: 415-403-0202

John A. McGuinn
John R. Hillsman
Cliff Palefsky
Derek B. Jacobson
Keith A. Ehrman

Sharon R. Vinick

For full biographical listings, see the Martindale-Hubbell Law Directory

MOORE & BROWNING (AV)

100 Bush Street, Suite 225, 94104
Telephone: 415-956-6500
Fax: 415-956-6580

Michael B. Moore
Charles A. Browning

LEGAL SUPPORT PERSONNEL

Pat Medina (Paralegal)

For full biographical listings, see the Martindale-Hubbell Law Directory

MORGENSTEIN & JUBELIRER, LLP (AV)

One Market, Spear Street Tower, 32nd Floor, 94105
Telephone: 415-896-0666
Fax: 415-896-5592
Email: m&j@mj-sflaw.com

(See Next Column)

Marvin D. Morgenstein (Retired)
Eliot S. Jubelirer
Lee Ann Huntington
Jean L. Bertrand
Jeffrey R. Williams
James R. Balich
Rocky N. Unruh
James L. McGinnis
Charles W. LaGrave
William J. Carroll
John S. Worden
Wendi J. Berkowitz
Stephen M. Hankins
Bruce A. Wagman

Lewis D. Barr
David H. Bromfield
Alexander P. Catalona
Michael "Cael" S. Davis
Roberta Nicol Dempster
Laura E. Gasser
Jill L. Gillen
Natasha L. Golding
Judith A. Holiber
Shawn D. Parrish
John J. Petry

For full biographical listings, see the Martindale-Hubbell Law Directory

ROSEN, BIEN & ASARO (AV)

Eighth Floor, 155 Montgomery Street, 94104
Telephone: 415-433-6830
Fax: 415-433-7104
Email: rba@rbalaw.com

Sanford Jay Rosen
Michael W. Bien
Andrea G. Asaro

Thomas Nolan
William H. D. Fernholz
Shana J. Margolis
Ernest J. Galvan

For full biographical listings, see the Martindale-Hubbell Law Directory

LAW OFFICES OF SUSAN RUBENSTEIN (AV)

351 California Street, Suite 700, 94104
Telephone: 415-434-9800
Fax: 415-434-0513
Email: SR@REZTLAW.COM

For full biographical listings, see the Martindale-Hubbell Law Directory

SAYAD & BIREN, A PROFESSIONAL CORPORATION (AV)

Steuart Street Tower, Suite 1300, One Market, 94105-1402
Telephone: 415-281-2172
Fax: 415-281-2188
Email: saybir@pacbell.net

Pamela M. Sayad
Brenda F. Biren

For full biographical listings, see the Martindale-Hubbell Law Directory

SCHACHTER, KRISTOFF, ORENSTEIN & BERKOWITZ, L.L.P. (AV)

505 Montgomery Street, 14th Floor, 94111
Telephone: 415-391-3333
Telecopier: 415-392-6589
Sacramento Office: 980 9th Street, Suite 1500.
Telephone: 916-442-3333.
Telecopier: 916-442-2348.
Menlo Park Office: 90 Middlefield Road, Suite 201.
Telephone: 650-473-1400.
Telecopier: 650-463-0346.

MEMBERS OF FIRM

Victor Schachter
Robert P. Kristoff
Alan R. Berkowitz
Thomas E. Geidt
Ronald J. Souza
Steven R. Blackburn
Gale Heuman Borden (Resident, Menlo Park Office)
John F. Penrose
John D. Adkisson (Resident, Sacramento Office)
Daniel A. Briskin
Sharon S. Zezima

ASSOCIATES

Allen M. Kato
Gail Cecchettini Whaley (Resident, Sacramento Office)
Paul D. Warenski
Alia Samad-Salameh
Rochelle C. Holzmann
Jennifer Brown Shaw (Resident, Sacramento Office)
Sue Ann Van Dermyden (Resident, Sacramento Office)
Charles W. Nugent (Resident, Sacramento Office)
Jack S. Bailey

OF COUNSEL

Joseph D. Miller
Morton H. Orenstein

For full biographical listings, see the Martindale-Hubbell Law Directory

THE LAW OFFICES OF JON B. SIGERMAN (AV)

100 Bush Street Suite 2000, 94104
Telephone: 415-989-0715
Facsimile: 415-989-1639

For full biographical listings, see the Martindale-Hubbell Law Directory

San Francisco—Continued

TEHIN +PARTNERS, A PROFESSIONAL CORPORATION (AV)

Bank of America Center, 555 California Street, 33rd Floor, 94104-1609
Telephone: 415-951-8800
Fax: 415-951-8808
URL: http://www.tehin.com

Nikolai Tehin
Pamela J. Stevens
Reilly Atkinson, IV
Michael E. Brown
Bita Abdollahi

For full biographical listings, see the Martindale-Hubbell Law Directory

THE LOUDERBACK LAW FIRM (AV)

115 Sansome Street, Suite 1005, 94104
Telephone: 415-398-7860
Fax: 415-398-7863
Email: clouderback@louderback.org *URL:* http://www.louderback.org

Charles M. Louderback

ASSOCIATES

Elizabeth M. McQuillan
Jesse L. Miller
Stephen R. Raab

LEGAL SUPPORT PERSONNEL

Bradly M. Hamilton (Firm Administrator)
Eliza Alvarez (Secretary)

For full biographical listings, see the Martindale-Hubbell Law Directory

WALKUP, MELODIA, KELLY & ECHEVERRIA, A PROFESSIONAL CORPORATION (AV)

26th Floor, 650 California Street, 94108
Telephone: 415-981-7210
Fax: 415-391-6965

Paul V. Melodia
Daniel J. Kelly
John Echeverria
Ronald H. Wecht
Michael A. Kelly
Kevin L. Domecus
Richard H. Schoenberger

Cynthia F. Newton
Michael J. Recupero
Douglas S. Saeltzer
Khaldoun A. Baghdadi
Doris Cheng

OF COUNSEL

John D. Link
Wesley Sokolosky

Reference: Bank of California, San Francisco Main Office, 400 California Street, San Francisco, Calif. 94104.

For full biographical listings, see the Martindale-Hubbell Law Directory

WUERFEL & CHOLAKIAN, A PROFESSIONAL CORPORATION (AV)

555 Montgomery Street, Ninth Floor, 94111
Telephone: 415-398-1551; 800-992-5990
FAX: 415-398-3301
Email: sos@sflaw.net *URL:* http://www.sflaw.net
Santa Rosa, California Office: 131-A Stony Circle, Suite 515, 95401.
Telephones: 415-398-1551; 800-992-5990.
FAX: 415-398-1551.
Costa Mesa, California Office: Avenue of the Arts.
Telephone: 714-825-3590; 800-992-5990.

Mark D. Wuerfel
Kevin K. Cholakian
Julian J. Pardini
Nan R. Hooven
Sherri K. McElroy

SPECIAL COUNSEL

Dean C. Burnick
Charlene P. Rosack
Jonathan Gross
Michael A. Topp

Aaron D. Bigby
D. Clark Burton
Anthony J. Calero
Elizabeth A. Doyle
Linda L. Duiven
Jay E. Framson
Stephen D. Geist
Andrew A. Goode
David J. Heilman
Timothy S. Kirk
Stephen J. Liberatore
Anne Marie Master
Thomas A. Moore
Julianne Pinter

LEGAL SUPPORT PERSONNEL

Marla J. Kuresa (Legal Administrator)

For full biographical listings, see the Martindale-Hubbell Law Directory

*SAN JOSE,** Santa Clara Co.

MCMANIS, FAULKNER & MORGAN (AV)

160 West Santa Clara Street, 10th Floor, 95113
Telephone: 408-279-8700
Fax: 408-279-3244; 408-279-0494
Email: mfm@mfmlaw.com *URL:* http://www.mfmlaw.com

(See Next Column)

James McManis
William Faulkner
Donelle Morgan
Lisa Herrick
Michael Reedy
Erica Yew

Michelle Tidalgo
Colleen Duffy Smith
Lillian Wolf
Rebecca Hughes
Kalpana Vrudhula
Ray M. Baluyot
Catherine Bechtel
Arron Nesbitt

OF COUNSEL

Mary Arand

For full biographical listings, see the Martindale-Hubbell Law Directory

*SAN LUIS OBISPO,** San Luis Obispo Co.

ANDRE, MORRIS & BUTTERY, A PROFESSIONAL LAW CORPORATION (AV)

1102 Laurel Lane, P.O. Box 730, 93406-0730
Telephone: 805-543-4171
Fax: 805-543-0752
Email: amb@amblaw.com *URL:* http://www.amblaw.com

Dennis D. Law
J. Todd Mirolla

Kathryn M. Eppright
Kevin D. Morris

References: Bank of America National Trust and Savings Assn. (San Luis Obispo Main Branch); Mid-State Bank (San Luis Obispo).

For full biographical listings, see the Martindale-Hubbell Law Directory

SAN MATEO, San Mateo Co.

QUACKENBUSH & QUACKENBUSH (AV)

1700 South El Camino Real, Suite 408, 94402
Telephone: 650-578-8300

MEMBERS OF FIRM

William C. Quackenbush
Laura G. Quackenbush

For full biographical listings, see the Martindale-Hubbell Law Directory

*SANTA ANA,** Orange Co.

COOK, BROWN & PRAGER, LLP (AV)

801 Civic Center Drive, Suite 450, 92701-4048
Telephone: 714-542-1883
Fax: 714-542-1009
Email: cbrp@cookbrown.com
Sacramento, California Office: 555 Capitol Mall, Suite 425.
Telephone: 916-442-3100.
Fax: 916-442-4227.
Salinas, California Office: 450 Lincoln Avenue, Suite 202.
Telephone: 831-755-7940.
Fax: 831-755-7944.

RESIDENT PARTNERS

John W. Prager, Jr.
Geoffrey F. Gega

RESIDENT ASSOCIATE

Mary H. Kim

For full biographical listings, see the Martindale-Hubbell Law Directory

WALSH & DECLUES, LLP (AV)

6 Hutton Centre Drive Suite 1050, P.O. Box 22021, 92702-2021
Telephone: 714-436-1776
Facsimile: 714-436-1771
Email: sao@wd-law.com
Encino, California Office: 15821 Ventura Boulevard, Suite 625, P.O. Box 20087, 91416.
Telephone: 818-986-1776.
Facsimile: 818-382-2071.
Walnut Creek, California Office: 2125 Oak Grove Road, Suite 110, 94598.
Telephone: 925-686-1776.
Facsimile: 925-906-1773.

MEMBERS OF FIRM

J. Michael Declues (Managing Partner, Santa Ana Office)
Dennis J. Walsh (Managing Partner, Encino Office)
Michael E. Burkett (Founding Partner, Resident, Santa Ana Office)
Glenn S. Goldby (Partner, Resident, Santa Ana Office)
Jeffrey P. Thompson

Joanne C. Schwartz
Jeffrey A. Smith
Judith D. Anderson
Gregory A. Wille
Cary K. Quan
Jennifer K. Berneking
Shari S. Daneshrad (Resident, Encino Office)
Kathleen G. Maylin (Resident, Walnut Creek Office)
Karen R. Shulman

(See Next Column)

WALSH & DECLUES LLP—*Continued*

Michelle R. Walker (Resident, Encino Office)
George E. Ordonez (Resident, Encino Office)
Gayle C. Heirshberg
James L. Armstrong, Jr. (Resident, Walnut Creek Office)

Representative Clients: Regents of the University of California; University of California at Los Angeles; Home Depot U.S.A., Inc.; Ralph's Grocery Co.; Farmers Insurance Group; Alliance of Schools for Cooperative Insurance Programs; Carl Warren & Co.; Weyerhaeuser Co.; U-Haul, Inc.; GAB Ropins of North America, Inc.

For full biographical listings, see the Martindale-Hubbell Law Directory

*SANTA BARBARA,** Santa Barbara Co.

MULLEN & HENZELL, L.L.P. (AV)

A California registered limited liability partnership
112 East Victoria Street, Post Office Drawer 789, 93102-0789
Telephone: 805-966-1501
FAX: 805-966-9204
Email: mh@mullenlaw.com

MEMBERS OF FIRM

Jay L. Beckerman
Edward C. Thoits
William E. Degen

ASSOCIATES

Christine P. Roberts
Paul K. Wilcox

Representative Clients: California State Auto Association (No. Calif. Auto Club); Interinsurance Exchange of the Automobile Club of Southern California; Fireman's Fund Insurance Co.; State Farm Fire & Casualty Co.; State Farm Mutual Automobile Insurance Co.

For full biographical listings, see the Martindale-Hubbell Law Directory

SANTA MONICA, Los Angeles Co.

BAKER, KEENER & NAHRA, LLP (AV)

2850 Ocean Park Boulevard, Suite 300, 90405-2936
Telephone: 310-399-0900
Fax: 310-399-1644
Email: general@bknlawyers.com *URL:* http://www.bknlawyers.com

MEMBERS OF FIRM

Robert C. Baker
Karl A. Keener
John P. Nahra
Michael H. Bailey
Steven T. Adams
Melissa S. Fink
Jeffrey P. Nolan
Constance A. Endelicato

Brenda K. Benson
Mitchell F. Mulbarger
James D. Hepworth
Phillip A. Baker
George P. Hawley
Thomas M. Mills
R. Jeffrey Neer
Wendy Wen Yun Chang

OF COUNSEL

Daniel P. Leonard

Reference: Wells Fargo Bank (Los Angeles Head Office).

For full biographical listings, see the Martindale-Hubbell Law Directory

FOGEL, FELDMAN, OSTROV, RINGLER & KLEVENS, A LAW CORPORATION (AV)

1620 26th Street, Suite 100 South, 90404-4040
Telephone: 310-453-6711
Fax: 310-828-2191

Daniel Fogel (1923-1991)
Lester G. Ostrov
Larry R. Feldman
Joel N. Klevens
Robert M. Turner
Jerome L. Ringler
Richard L. Rosett

Thomas H. Peters
David Bricker
Stephanie Chase
Jan Greenberg Levine
Sandra L. Lepson
Lawrence C. Jones
Stacie L. Feldman
John T. Fogarty

OF COUNSEL

Carol S. May

Reference: Republic Bank of California, Beverly Hills, California.

For full biographical listings, see the Martindale-Hubbell Law Directory

HAIGHT, BROWN & BONESTEEL, L.L.P. (AV)

A Partnership including Professional Corporations
1620 26th Street, Suite 4000 North, P.O. Box 680, 90404
Telephone: 310-449-6000
Telecopier: 310-829-5117
Telex: 705837
URL: http://www.hbblaw.com
Santa Ana, California Office: Suite 900, 5 Hutton Centre Drive.
Telephone: 714-754-1100.
Telecopier: 714-754-0826.

(See Next Column)

Riverside, California Office: California Tower, 3737 Main Street, Suite 800.
Telephone: 909-341-8300.
Fax: 909-341-8309.
San Francisco, California Office: 101 Bush Street, 27th Floor.
Telephone: 415-986-7700.
Fax: 415-986-6945.
San Diego, California Office: 101 West Broadway, Suite 1000.
Telephone: 619-595-5583.
Fax: 619-595-7873.

MEMBERS OF FIRM

Neil G. McNiece
Cynthia R. Thompson

ASSOCIATES

Kristine W. Samuels
Barbara Z. Safechuck
Kara W. Lanham

OF COUNSEL

R. Roy Finkle

For full biographical listings, see the Martindale-Hubbell Law Directory

*SANTA ROSA,** Sonoma Co.

ABBEY, WEITZENBERG, HOFFMAN & EMERY, A PROFESSIONAL CORPORATION (AV)

1105 North Dutton Avenue, P.O. Box 1566, 95402
Telephone: 707-542-5050
Telecopier: 707-542-2589
Email: info@abbeylaw.com

Richard W. Abbey
Lewis R. Warren

Representative Clients: Exchange Bank of Santa Rosa; Westamerica Bank; Northwestern Title Security Co.; Geyser Peak Winery; Santa Rosa City School District; Sonoma National Bank; Arrowwood Vineyards & Winery; Friedman Bros. Hardware, Inc.; Bank of Lake County; Lasercraft, Inc.

For full biographical listings, see the Martindale-Hubbell Law Directory

UNIVERSAL CITY, Los Angeles Co.

BALLARD, ROSENBERG & GOLPER (AV)

10 Universal City Plaza, 16th Floor, 91608-1097
Telephone: 818-508-3700
FAX: 818-506-4827; 985-8167
Email: info@brglaw.com

MEMBERS OF FIRM

Kenneth R. Ballard
Richard S. Rosenberg
John B. Golper
Stephen R. Lueke
Jeffrey P. Fuchsman
Sherrie Lipsky Sheldon
Helene J. Wasserman
Jonathan S. Rosenberg

ASSOCIATES

John J. Manier
Matthew T. Wakefield
Stephen M. MacPhail
Douglas N. Silverstein
Alexander A. Molina
William D. Becker
Sherry B. Kampler
Erin Nemirovsky Medina
Edward L. Washington
Sandra A. Marciari

SENIOR COUNSEL

Elsa Bañuelos
Raquelle de la Rocha
Bruce A. Grossman

Reference: First Los Angeles Bank (Century City Office).

For full biographical listings, see the Martindale-Hubbell Law Directory

*VENTURA,** Ventura Co.

STRAUSS • URITZ A PROFESSIONAL CORPORATION (AV)

290 Maple Court, Suite 200, 93003
Telephone: 805-644-7458
Fax: 805-644-4325
Email: mail@venturalaw.com *URL:* http://www.venturalaw.com

Anthony R. Strauss

Bruce P. Crary

For full biographical listings, see the Martindale-Hubbell Law Directory

TAYLOR MCCORD, A LAW CORPORATION (AV)

721 East Main Street, P.O. Box 1477, 93002
Telephone: 805-648-4700
Email: vtafamlaw@aol.com

Richard L. Taylor
Robert L. McCord, Jr.
David L. Praver

Patrick Cherry
Susan D. Siple
Rebbecca F. Calderwood

(See Next Column)

TAYLOR MCCORD A LAW CORPORATION, *Ventura—Continued*

LEGAL SUPPORT PERSONNEL

PARALEGALS

Stephanie Gibson
Diane Lovato
Adele Rubino (Certified Legal Assistant, California Advanced Specialist)

For full biographical listings, see the Martindale-Hubbell Law Directory

WALNUT CREEK, Contra Costa Co.

LAW OFFICES OF MICHAEL J. REISER (AV)

1806 Bonanza Street, 94596
Telephone: 925-256-0400
Fax: 925-938-2279
http: //www.lawyers.com/reiserlaw
URL: http://www.reiserlaw.com

For full biographical listings, see the Martindale-Hubbell Law Directory

COLORADO

*DENVER,** Denver Co.

BERENBAUM, WEINSHIENK & EASON, P.C. (AV)

Suite 2600 Republic Plaza, 370 17th Street, 80202
Telephone: 303-825-0800
Facsimile: 303-629-7610
Email: berenbaum1@aol.com *URL:* http://www.BWELaw.com

Martin D. Buckley
I. H. Kaiser
David R. Eason
Kenneth S. Kramer

Melissa Mequi

Representative Clients: Home Depot; Sprint Spectrum, L.P.; Town of Vail, Colorado; First Union Corporation; City of Englewood, Colorado; Oakwood Homes; Karman, Inc.; Wells Fargo Bank, N.A.; Berkshire Life Insurance Co.; Trinity Ventures.

For full biographical listings, see the Martindale-Hubbell Law Directory

BROWNSTEIN HYATT & FARBER, P.C. (AV)

Twenty-Second Floor, 410 Seventeenth Street, 80202-4437
Telephone: 303-223-1100
Telecopier: 303-223-1111
Washington, D.C. Office: 1615 L Street, N.W., Suite 450, 20036.
Telephone: 202-296-7353.
Telecopier: 202-296-7009.
Glenwood Springs, Colorado Office: Box 357, 81602.
Telephone: 970-945-5302.
Telecopier: 970-945-4921.

Andrew W. Loewi
Stanley L. Garnett
Lisa Hogan

SPECIAL COUNSEL

Richard P. Barkley

Beth Doherty Quinn
A.W. Victoria Jacobs
David S. Chipman
Jennifer C. Robinson
Jeanine M. Anderson
Meghan W. Martinez

Representative Clients: Club Sports International; Columbia/HCA Healthcare Corp.; Gulf Canada Resources, Ltd.; Metro Taxi, Inc.; North American Title Company of Colorado; Pacesetter Corporation; Policy Studies Inc.; The Williams Companies; United Air Lines, Inc.; Visiting Nurse Association.

For Complete List of Firm Personnel, See General Section

For full biographical listings, see the Martindale-Hubbell Law Directory

CORTEZ MACAULAY BERNHARDT & SCHUETZE LLC (AV)

1600 Broadway, Suite 1600, 80202
Telephone: 303-864-1000
Facsimile: 303-864-1111
URL: http://www.cmblaw.com

Miles Cortez
Robert A. Schuetze
Christopher T. Macaulay
David H. Goldberg
Susan Bernhardt
Marian L. Carlson
Richard P. R. Cohn

For full biographical listings, see the Martindale-Hubbell Law Directory

DUFFORD & BROWN, P.C. (AV)

1700 Broadway, Suite 1700, 80290-1701
Telephone: 303-861-8013
Facsimile: 303-832-3804
Colorado Springs, Colorado Office: 101 N. Tejon, Suite 410.
Telephone: 719-471-0559.
Facsimile: 719-471-0583.
Affiliated Office: Solomon, Pearl, Blum & Quinn, L.L.P., New York, NY and Denver, Colorado.

Thomas G. Brown
Scott J. Mikulecky
David W. Furgason
Lawrence D. Stone
Thomas E. J. Hazard

Representative Clients: CF&I Steel, L.P.; The Colorado & Wyoming Railway Company; Colorado Permanente Medical Group, Inc.; Colorado Compensation Insurance Authority.

For Complete List of Firm Personnel, See General Section

For full biographical listings, see the Martindale-Hubbell Law Directory

GORSUCH KIRGIS LLP (AV)

Tower 1, Suite 1000, 1515 Arapahoe Street, 80202
Telephone: 303-376-5000
Fax: 303-376-5001

PARTNERS

Timothy J. Parsons
David B. Seserman
Arun Das
Dean C. Heizer

ASSOCIATE

Morgan Word

LEGAL SUPPORT PERSONNEL

Lori Kully
Anne Schuman

For full biographical listings, see the Martindale-Hubbell Law Directory

LARRY F. HOBBS, P.C. (AV)

Colorado State Bank Building, 1600 Broadway, Suite 2375, 80202
Telephone: 303-861-2300
Telecopier: 303-861-2824

Larry F. Hobbs

For full biographical listings, see the Martindale-Hubbell Law Directory

HOLME ROBERTS & OWEN LLP (AV)

Suite 4100, 1700 Lincoln, 80203
Telephone: 303-861-7000
Telecopier: 303-866-0200
Email: hro@hro.com *URL:* http://www.hro.com
Boulder, Colorado Office: Suite 400, 1401 Pearl Street.
Telephone: 303-444-5955.
Telecopier: 303-444-1063.
Colorado Springs, Colorado Office: Suite 1300, 90 South Cascade Avenue.
Telephone: 719-473-3800.
Telecopier: 719-633-1518.
Salt Lake City, Utah Office: Suite 1100, 111 East Broadway.
Telephone: 801-521-5800.
Telecopier: 801-521-9639.
London, England Office: Heathcoat House, 3rd Floor, 20 Savile Row.
Telephone: 011-44-171-494-5600.
Telecopier: 011-44-171-287-9344.

PARTNERS OF FIRM

Blaine J. Benard (Salt Lake City Office)
Susan E. Duffey Campbell (Colorado Springs Office)
Carolyn E. Daniels
Elizabeth T. Dunning (Salt Lake City Office)
Lynn Parker Hendrix
Sherri Heckel Kuhlmann
Martin D. Litt
David T. Mitzner
Richard L. Nagl (Colorado Springs Office)
K. Preston Oade, Jr.
Renée W. O'Rourke
Katherine Jean Peck
Brent E. Rychener (Colorado Springs Office)
Greggory J. Savage (Salt Lake City Office)
David S. Steefel
Mary Hurley Stuart
John R. Webb
David B. Wilson

SPECIAL COUNSEL

Carolyn Cox (Salt Lake City Office)

SENIOR COUNSEL

Steven E. Christoffersen
Lawrence M. Zavadil

ASSOCIATES

Kelly M. Condon
Denise Pino Erwin
Elizabeth A. González
Ashley Warren Jordaan (Colorado Springs Office)
Donald I. J. Kelso
Matt A. Mayer
Deborah S. Menkins (Colorado Springs Office)
Roxane J. Perruso
J. Daniel Phelan
E. Blaine Rawson (Salt Lake City Office)

For Complete List of Firm Personnel, See General Section

For full biographical listings, see the Martindale-Hubbell Law Directory

Denver—Continued

THE HUSTEAD LAW FIRM A PROFESSIONAL CORPORATION (AV)

Regency Plaza One, 4643 South Ulster Street, Suite 1250, 80237
Telephone: 303-721-5000
Facsimile: 303-721-5001
URL: http://www.thlf.com

Patrick Q. Hustead

Stephen C. Larson
Duane E. Bolin
Benton J. Barton (Not admitted in CO)
Janlynn R. Fleener

Representative Clients: Acceptance Group Insurance Companies; Amwest Insurance Company; Colorado Western Insurance Company; Connecticut Surety; Contractors Bonding and Insurance Company; Insurance Company of the West; Merchants Bonding Company; Underwriters at Lloyd's London; Odyessy Re London; The St. Paul Surety Group.

For full biographical listings, see the Martindale-Hubbell Law Directory

LONG & JAUDON, P.C. (AV)

The Bailey Mansion, 1600 Ogden Street, 80218-1414
Telephone: 303-832-1122
FAX: 303-832-1348

James A. Dierker
Gary B. Blum

Representative Clients: St. Joseph Hospital; King Soopers, Inc. (Dillon Companies, Inc.).

For Complete List of Firm Personnel, See General Section

For full biographical listings, see the Martindale-Hubbell Law Directory

FRANCES B. MCDONALD PROFESSIONAL CORPORATION (AV)

1900 Wazee Street, Suite 203, 80202-1259
Telephone: 303-297-3337
Fax: 303-297-3338
Email: fbmcd@dim.com

Frances B. McDonald

For full biographical listings, see the Martindale-Hubbell Law Directory

LAW OFFICES OF JOHN W. MCKENDREE (AV)

Creswell Mansion, 1244 Grant Street, 80203
Telephone: 303-861-8906
Fax: 303-861-7773
Email: Johnwmckendree@msn.com

ASSOCIATE

Elizabeth G. McKendree

Counsel For: Colorado-Wyoming Teamsters Construction Workers Local Union No. 13; United Brotherhood of Carpenters and Joiners of America Local 1583; International Federation of Petroleum and Chemical Workers; International Labor Relations Services, Inc.; Teamsters Local 13 Health and Welfare Trust Fund; Teamsters Local 13 Vacation Trust Fund; Colorado Centennial District Counsel of Carpenters; Boilermakers Lodge 101; Brakemans' Association of America; Boilermakers National Pension Trust.

For full biographical listings, see the Martindale-Hubbell Law Directory

TODD J. MCNAMARA, P.C. (AV)

1700 Lincoln Street, Suite 3850, 80203
Telephone: 303-830-7924
Fax: 303-830-8473
Email: bgad@idcomm.com *URL:* http://www.lawyers.com/mcnamaralaw

Todd J. McNamara

Kristina Martinez (Not admitted in CO)

LEGAL SUPPORT PERSONNEL

Bettye J. Gadison, CLA

For full biographical listings, see the Martindale-Hubbell Law Directory

MILLER & WELCH, L.L.C. (AV)

730 - 17th Street, Suite 925, 80202-3503
Telephone: 303-623-6005
Facsimile: 303-623-0311

James Rollin Miller, Jr.
Carol M. Welch
Paul R. Wood

Candace M. Dunley
Joycelyn Crucillo
Matthew D. Macy

For full biographical listings, see the Martindale-Hubbell Law Directory

OTTEN, JOHNSON, ROBINSON, NEFF & RAGONETTI, P.C. (AV)

950 Seventeenth Street, 16th Floor, 80202
Telephone: 303-825-8400
Telecopier: 303-825-6525
URL: http://www.ojrnr.com

William F. Schoeberlein
Lawrence W. Marquess
P. Kathleen Lower
Terence M. Ridley
Todd A. Fredrickson
Darin Mackender
Heidi G. Duston

Representative Clients: Allied Signal; Commercial Federal Bank; Conoco, Inc.; First Data Corp.; FMC Corp.; The Genesee Company, Inc.; Information Handling Services Group, Inc.; Dillon Cos., Inc. d/b/a King Soopers; KN Energy, Inc.; Meadow Gold Dairies; Peabody Holding Co.; Regis University; Spatial Technology, Inc.; TeleCheck Services, Inc.; TIC Holdings, Inc.; Zateca Foods, LLC.

For Complete List of Firm Personnel, See General Section

For full biographical listings, see the Martindale-Hubbell Law Directory

SEMPLE, MILLER & MOONEY, P.C. (AV)

1120 Lincoln Street, Suite 1308, 80203
Telephone: 303-595-0941
Fax: 303-861-9608
Email: smdm@relay.hcp.net

Martin Semple
Reese Miller
Patrick B. Mooney
Christopher E. Gdowski

Kathleen Marie Shannon
Frederick C. Kuhlwilm
Elizabeth J. Hyatt
Julie C. Tolleson

Representative Clients: Denver Public Schools; Adams County School District No. 50; Roaring Forks School District RE-1; City of Aurora; Denver Center for the Performing Arts; Intermountain Rural Electric Association; City of Thornton; City and County of Denver; Denver Metro Convention and Visitors Bureau; City of Englewood.

For full biographical listings, see the Martindale-Hubbell Law Directory

SHERMAN & HOWARD L.L.C. (AV)

Attorneys and Counselors at Law
633 Seventeenth Street, Suite 3000, 80202
Telephone: 303-297-2900
Telecopier: 303-298-0940
Colorado Springs, Colorado Office: Suite 1500, 90 South Cascade Avenue, 80903.
Telephone: 719-475-2440.
Las Vegas, Nevada Office: Swendseid & Stern, a member in Sherman & Howard L.L.C., 317 Sixth Street, 89101.
Telephone: 702-387-6073.
Reno, Nevada Office: Swendseid & Stern, a member in Sherman & Howard L.L.C., 50 West Liberty Street, Suite 660, 89501.
Telephone: 702-323-1980.

E. Lee Dale
Charles W. Newcom
Raymond M. Deeny (Colorado Springs Office)
W.V. Bernie Siebert
Theodore A. Olsen
N. Dawn Webber (Colorado Springs Office)
Glenn H. Schlabs (Colorado Springs Office)
Edmond F. Noel, Jr.
Andrew W. Volin
Paul J. McCue

COUNSEL

James E. Hautzinger
William L. Sasz (Colorado Springs Office)

Heather Fox Vickles
Emily F. Keimig
Jennifer M. Mardosz
Ted C. Tow, III
William A. Wright
Brenda K. (Buege) Heinicke (Colorado Springs Office)
Edward J. Butler (Colorado Springs Office)
Michael P. Gleason
Patrick R. Scully (Colorado Springs Office)
Rachel P. Dauer

Representative Clients: BACE Industries, LLC; Flatiron Structures Co. LLC; Hanifen, Imhoff Inc.; Hathaway Corp.; J.D. Edwards & Co.; Newmont Gold Company; Public Employees' Retirement Assn.; Tele-Communications, Inc.; United Artists Theatre Circuit, Inc.; U.S. West Communications, Inc.

For Complete List of Firm Personnel, See General Section

For full biographical listings, see the Martindale-Hubbell Law Directory

SLIVKA ROBINSON WATERS & O'DORISIO, A PROFESSIONAL CORPORATION (AV)

Suite 2600, 1099 18th Street, 80202-1926
Telephone: 303-297-2600
Telecopier: 303-297-2750
URL: http://www.srwo.com

(See Next Column)

SLIVKA ROBINSON WATERS & O'DORISIO A PROFESSIONAL CORPORATION, *Denver—Continued*

SHAREHOLDERS

Richard P. Slivka
Peter A. Robinson
Stephen L. Waters
John W. O'Dorisio, Jr.
Ernest J. Panasci
Chevis F. Horne, Jr.
Margaret M. McClellan
Karen Samuels Jones

Deborah A. Hogan
Kerri M. Pertcheck
Susan R. Pierson
Elizabeth E. Pinckard
Daniel A. Sweetser
Bradley S. Taylor
Jill G. VanderPloeg

SPECIAL COUNSEL

Laura J. Vogelgesang
Christine Rothe Hoth

For full biographical listings, see the Martindale-Hubbell Law Directory

STETTNER, MILLER AND COHN, P.C. (AV)
Lawrence Street Center, Suite 1000, 1380 Lawrence Street, 80204-2058
Telephone: 303-534-0273
Fax: 303-534-5036
Email: attorney@stetmill.com
Colorado Springs Office: The Woodmen Center. 1130 West Woodmen Road. 80910.
Telephone: 719-598-0590.

Kenneth R. Stettner
Robert R. Miller
Robert I. Cohn
Katherine Ann Raabe
John S. Finn
Bruce C. Anderson
William C. Berger
Brent P. Benrud

OF COUNSEL

Susan M. Schaecher

Representative Clients: Associated General Contractors of Colorado, Building Chapter, Inc.; ICG Communications; Craig Hospital; McDonald's Corp; Hensel Phelps Construction Co.; Adams County School District No. 14; John Alden Life Insurance Co.; Federal Express Corp.; McLane Co., Inc.; Health One.

For full biographical listings, see the Martindale-Hubbell Law Directory

CONNECTICUT

*HARTFORD,** Hartford Co.

SHIPMAN & GOODWIN LLP (AV)
One American Row, 06103-2819
Telephone: 860-251-5000
Telecopier: 860-251-5099
Email: www@goodwin.com *URL:* http://shipman-goodwin.com
Lakeville, Connecticut Office: 12 Porter Street.
Telephone: 203-435-2539.
Stamford, Connecticut Office: One Landmark Square.
Telephone: 203-324-8100.

MEMBERS OF FIRM

Paul W. Orth
Brian Clemow
Brenda A. Eckert
Thomas B. Mooney
Saranne P. Murray
Linda L. Yoder
Richard A. Mills, Jr.
Patrick J. McHale
Burton Kainen
Gary S. Starr
Diana Garfield
Susan M. Wright
Miguel A. Escalera, Jr.
Christine L. Chinni
Susan C. Freedman
Kimberly A. Mango

COUNSEL

Vaughan Finn
Gerald P. Stergio

ASSOCIATES

Natalie W. Welsh
Anne H. Littlefield
Henry J. Zaccardi
Jennifer Brown Mailly
Jennifer Bullock Majewski
Susan G. Fentin
Martha Watts Prestley
Sheldon D. Myers
Jennifer L. Dixon

Representative Labor Clients: American Red Cross; Bank Boston Connecticut; Caldor, Inc.; CIGNA; City of Danbury; Ensign-Bickford Industries, Inc.; Merrow Machine Company; Trinity College; Stamford Board of Education; Viacom.

For Complete List of Firm Personnel, See General Section

For full biographical listings, see the Martindale-Hubbell Law Directory

SOROKIN, GROSS & HYDE, P.C. (AV)
One Corporate Center, 06103
Telephone: 860-525-6645
Fax: 860-522-1781
Email: sorokin@sorokinlaw.com
Simsbury, Connecticut Office: 720 Hopmeadow Street.
Telephone: 860-651-9348.

(See Next Column)

Rocky Hill, Connecticut Office: 2360 Main Street.
Telephone: 860-563-9305.
Fax: 860-529-6931.

Sharon Kowal Freilich
Andrew C. Glassman
Joshua A. Hawks-Ladds
Richard C. Robinson

Jeffrey R. Neidle

For Complete List of Firm Personnel, See General Section

For full biographical listings, see the Martindale-Hubbell Law Directory

WILLIAM S. ZEMAN (AV)
44 Capitol Avenue, Suite 402, 06106
Telephone: 860-297-6505
Fax: 860-246-3727

For full biographical listings, see the Martindale-Hubbell Law Directory

MILFORD, New Haven Co.

BERCHEM, MOSES & DEVLIN, A PROFESSIONAL CORPORATION (AV)
75 Broad Street, 06460-3363
Telephone: 203-783-1200
Facsimile: 203-878-2235; 203-877-8422
URL: http://www.bmd-law.com

Robert L. Berchem
Marsha Belman Moses
Michael P. Devlin
Stephen W. Studer
Richard J. Buturla
Floyd J. Dugas
Kenneth R. Plumb
Lawrence B. Pellegrino

Brian A. Lema
Warren L. Holcomb
Michelle C. Laubin
Jonathan David Berchem
Dean R. Singewald

For full biographical listings, see the Martindale-Hubbell Law Directory

NEW BRITAIN, Hartford Co.

EISENBERG, ANDERSON, MICHALIK & LYNCH, L.L.P. (AV)
136 West Main Street, P.O. Box 2950, 06050-2950
Telephone: 860-229-4855; 225-8403
Fax: 860-223-4026
URL: http://www.eaml.com

Harold J. Eisenberg (1906-1995)

MEMBERS OF FIRM

Stephen J. Anderson
Robert A. Michalik
Edward T. Lynch, Jr.
Charles W. Bauer
Dennis G. Ciccarillo
Carl R. Ficks, Jr.
Pamela Reardon Reynolds
JoAnn Centrilla-Silvia
Kenneth R. Slater, Jr.

ASSOCIATES

Bruce A. Zawodniak
Jeffrey F. Gostyla
Alexia Cruz
Edward M. Rosenthal

Representative Clients: Apple Health Care; Berlin Steel Construction Co.; CIGNA; Connecticut Employees Union "Independent"; Fleet Bank, N.A.; Magson Uniform Corp.; TILCON Connecticut Inc.

For full biographical listings, see the Martindale-Hubbell Law Directory

*NEW HAVEN,** New Haven Co.

ROSEN & DOLAN, P.C. (AV)
400 Orange Street, 06511
Telephone: 203-787-3513
Fax: 203-789-1605
Email: davidrosen@snet.net
Email: sapincus@snet.net

David N. Rosen

Stephen M. Pincus

Reference: Peoples Bank.

For Complete List of Firm Personnel, See General Section

For full biographical listings, see the Martindale-Hubbell Law Directory

WIGGIN & DANA (AV)
One Century Tower, 06508-1832
Telephone: 203-498-4400
Telefax: 203-782-2889
URL: http://www.wiggin.com
Hartford, Connecticut Office: One CityPlace.
Telephone: 203-297-3700.
Fax: 203-525-9380.

(See Next Column)

WIGGIN & DANA—*Continued*

Stamford, Connecticut Office: Three Stamford Plaza, 301 Tresser Boulevard.
Telephone: 203-363-7600.
Telefax: 203-363-7676.

MEMBERS OF FIRM

Peter J. Lefeber
John G. Zandy
Sherry L. Dominick
Karen L. Clute
Stephen B. Harris (Resident, Hartford Office)

COUNSEL

Marcia Kenny Keegan (Resident, Hartford Office)

ASSOCIATES

Rachel B. Arnedt
Joan Allen Rowe
Alisa T. Rulnick
Jennifer B. Rubin (Resident, Stamford Office)
Peter M. Wendzel (Resident, Hartford Office)

For Complete List of Firm Personnel, See General Section

For full biographical listings, see the Martindale-Hubbell Law Directory

STAMFORD, Fairfield Co.

CASPER & DE TOLEDO LLC (AV)

1111 Summer Street, 06905
Telephone: 203-325-8600
Fax: 203-323-5970
Email: casperdetoledo.com *URL:* http://www.casperdetoledo.com

Stewart M. Casper
Victoria de Toledo

Gwendolyn Field Noto
Anastasios T. Savvaides

For full biographical listings, see the Martindale-Hubbell Law Directory

WATERBURY, New Haven Co.

SUMMA & RYAN, P.C. (AV)

19-21 Holmes Avenue, 06710
Telephone: 203-755-0390
Fax: 203-756-8746
URL: http://www.lawyers.com/summa&ryanpc

Joseph B. Summa
Mary Jane Ryan
David A. Ryan, Jr.

William A. Ryan

For full biographical listings, see the Martindale-Hubbell Law Directory

WESTPORT, Fairfield Co.

LEVETT ROCKWOOD P.C. (AV)

33 Riverside Avenue, P.O. Box 5116, 06881
Telephone: 203-222-0885
Telecopier: 203-226-8025

Suzanne B. Albani
Robert O. Barberi
Edward B. Chansky
Madeleine F. Grossman
Dorit Schutzengel Heimer
Cheryl L. Johnson
Marc J. Kurzman
David R. Levett
Judy A. Rabkin
Sharon M. Schweitzer
Steven M. Siegelaub
Peter H. Struzzi
Barbara A. Young

OF COUNSEL

William O. Rockwood, Jr.

Debra R. Cardinali
Stephen M. Cowherd
Christopher M. Graham
Robin K. Higgins
Douglas R. Sansted
Rodger F. Smith, Jr.
Patricia D. Weitzman

Representative Clients: Cannondale Corp.; Caradon, Inc.; DataViz, Inc.; Dooney & Bourke, Inc.; GAF Corporation; Heyman Properties; Hospital of Saint Raphael; Marketing Corporation of America; Olin Corporation; St. Vincent's Medical Center.

For full biographical listings, see the Martindale-Hubbell Law Directory

DELAWARE

*WILMINGTON,** New Castle Co.

SMITH, KATZENSTEIN & FURLOW LLP (AV)

The Corporate Plaza, 800 Delaware Avenue, P.O. Box 410, 19899
Telephone: 302-652-8400
Fax: 302-652-8405
Email: info@skfdelaware.com *URL:* http://www.SKFDelaware.com

(See Next Column)

MEMBERS OF FIRM

Craig B. Smith
Robert J. Katzenstein
David A. Jenkins
Laurence V. Cronin
Brett D. Fallon
Charles E. Butler

Kathleen M. Miller

For Complete List of Firm Personnel, See General Section

For full biographical listings, see the Martindale-Hubbell Law Directory

DISTRICT OF COLUMBIA

WASHINGTON, D.C. Co.

BAKER & HOSTETLER LLP (AV)

Washington Square, Suite 1100, 1050 Connecticut Avenue, N.W., 20036-5304
Telephone: 202-861-1500
Fax: 202-861-1783
To contact an attorney on the Internet use first initial and surname followed by @baker-hostetler.com
URL: http://www.bakerlaw.com
In Cleveland, Ohio: 3200 National City Center, 1900 East Ninth Street.
Telephone: 216-621-0200.
In Cincinnati, Ohio: 312 Walnut Street, Suite 2650.
Telephone: 513-929-3400.
In Columbus, Ohio: Capitol Square, Suite 2100, 65 East State Street.
Telephone: 614-228-1541.
In Denver, Colorado: 303 East 17th Avenue, Suite 1100.
Telephone: 303-861-0600.
In Houston, Texas: 1000 Louisiana, Suite 2000.
Telephone: 713-751-1600.
In Beverly Hills, California: 9150 Wilshire Boulevard, Suite 205.
Telephone: 310-385-7500.
In Long Beach, California: 300 Oceangate, Suite 620.
Telephone: 562-432-2827.
In Los Angeles, California: 600 Wilshire Boulevard.
Telephone: 213-624-2400.
In Orlando, Florida: SunBank Center, Suite 2300, 200 South Orange Avenue.
Telephone: 407-649-4000.

PARTNERS

David Alistair Grant
Brian S. Harvey
Betty Southard Murphy

For Complete List of Firm Personnel, See General Section

For full biographical listings, see the Martindale-Hubbell Law Directory

LAW OFFICES OF BERT NEIL BISGYER (AV)

1025 Thomas Jefferson Street, N.W. Suite 525 East, 20007
Telephone: 202-338-2172
Telecopier: 202-338-2447

OF COUNSEL

Carl S. Silverman

For full biographical listings, see the Martindale-Hubbell Law Directory

CARR GOODSON WARNER, A PROFESSIONAL CORPORATION (AV)

1301 K Street, N.W., Suite 400, East Tower, 20005-3300
Telephone: 202-310-5500
Telecopier: 202-310-5555
Email: (attorney initials)@cgw-law.com *URL:* http://www.carrgoodsonwarner.com
Vienna, Virginia Office: Tycon Towers, 8000 Towers Crescent Drive, Suite 1350, 22182.
Telephone: 703-691-8818.
Baltimore, Maryland Office: 401 East Pratt Street, Suite 1622, The World Trade Center, 21202.
Telephone: 410-752-1570.
Rockville, Maryland Office: 31 Wood Lane, 20850.
Telephone: 301-424-7024.

David H. Jacobs (Not admitted in DC)
Thomas L. McCally

OF COUNSEL

Edward J. Krill

Janette M. Blee (Not admitted in DC)
Tina M. Maiolo

For Complete List of Firm Personnel, See General Section

For full biographical listings, see the Martindale-Hubbell Law Directory

Washington—Continued

CHARAPP, DEESE & WEISS, LLP (AV)

1901 Pennsylvania Avenue, N.W., Suite 1001, 20006
Telephone: 202-463-9100
Fax: 202-463-2091
Vienna, Virginia Office: 8300 Boone Boulevard, Suite 500, 22182.
Telephone 703-714-9576.
Bethesda, Maryland Office: 3 Bethesda Metro Center, Suite 700, 20814.
Telephone: 301-657-6258.
Richmond, Virginia Office: 2201 West Broad Street, Suite 201, 23220.
Telephone: 804-358-8680.
Fax: 804-358-3889.

Michael G. Charapp
C. Michael Deese
Brad D. Weiss

William T. Lehner (Resident, Richmond, Virginia Office)
John J. Delaney
Sarah Daly Jackowski
Brenda Houck Harbison (Resident, Richmond, Virginia Office)
Michael C. Gartner (Not admitted in DC)
James B. St. John, III (Not admitted in DC)

OF COUNSEL

Edward H. Kim

For full biographical listings, see the Martindale-Hubbell Law Directory

---

COHEN, MILSTEIN, HAUSFELD & TOLL, P.L.L.C. (AV)

West Tower, Suite 500, 1100 New York Avenue, N.W., 20005-3964
Telephone: 202-408-4600
Facsimile: 202-408-4699
Email: lawinfo@cmht.com *URL:* http://www.CMHT.com
Seattle, Washington Office: 999 Third Avenue, Suite 3600.
Telephone: 206-521-0080.
Facsimile: 206-521-0166.

MEMBERS OF FIRM

Jerry S. Cohen (1925-1995)
Herbert E. Milstein
Michael D. Hausfeld
Steven J. Toll (Resident, Seattle, Washington Office)
Ann C. Yahner
Lisa M. Mezzetti
Andrew N. Friedman
Richard S. Lewis
Daniel S. Sommers
Daniel A. Small
Gary E. Mason
Joseph M. Sellers
Sharon A. Snyder
Mark S. Willis (Not admitted in DC)

ASSOCIATES

Lori G. Feldman (Resident, Seattle, Washington Office)
Paul T. Gallagher
Christine E. Webber
Alexander E. Barnett
Matthew James Ide (Resident, Seattle, Washington Office)
Matthew F. Pawa
Suzette M. Malveaux
Mary N. Strimel
Kristopher A. Kinkade (Resident, Seattle, Washington Office)
Agnieszka M. Fryszman
Deborah J. Vagins
Ari Karen
Charles E. Tompkins
Tamara J. Driscoll (Resident, Seattle, Washington Office)
Elizabeth Haines Cronise
Donna Solen
Lesli C. Esposito (Not admitted in DC)

OF COUNSEL

Margaret G. Farrell

For full biographical listings, see the Martindale-Hubbell Law Directory

---

THE FALK LAW FIRM PLLC (AV)

A Professional Limited Liability Corporation
Suite 260 One Westin Center, 2445 M Street, N.W., 20037
Telephone: 202-833-8700
Telecopier: 202-872-1725
Email: FalkLaw@erols.com *URL:* http://www.falklawfirm.com

James H. Falk, Sr.
James H. Falk, Jr.
Stephen A. Best
John M. Falk

OF COUNSEL

Pierre E. Murphy
Elizabeth C. Collins

For full biographical listings, see the Martindale-Hubbell Law Directory

---

THE FEINBERG GROUP, LLP (AV)

1120 20th Street, N.W. Suite 740 South, 20036-3437
Telephone: 202-371-1110
Fax: 202-962-9290
Email: kfeinberg@thefeinberggroup.com *URL:* http://www.krfassociates.com
New York, N.Y. Office: 780 3rd Avenue, Suite 2202.
Telephone: 212-527-9600.
Fax: 212-527-9611. Email: kfeinberg@thefeinberggroup.com.

(See Next Column)

PARTNERS

Kenneth R. Feinberg
Deborah E. Greenspan
Michael K. Rozen (Resident, New York Office)
Peter H. Woodin (Resident, New York Office)

ASSOCIATE

Fredric M. Brooks (Not admitted in DC)

SENIOR COUNSEL

Jacqueline E. Zins

For full biographical listings, see the Martindale-Hubbell Law Directory

---

JOSEPH D. GEBHARDT, P.C. (AV)

1101 17th Street N.W., Suite 607, 20036
Telephone: 202-496-0400
Fax: 202-496-0404

Joseph D. Gebhardt

Charles Williamson Day, Jr.

For full biographical listings, see the Martindale-Hubbell Law Directory

---

HIGHSAW, MAHONEY & CLARKE, P.C. (AV)

Suite 210, 1050 Seventeenth Street, N.W., 20036
Telephone: 202-296-8500
Fax: 202-296-7143

James L. Highsaw (1970-1992)
John O'B. Clarke, Jr.

OF COUNSEL

William G. Mahoney

For full biographical listings, see the Martindale-Hubbell Law Directory

JONES, DAY, REAVIS & POGUE (AV)

51 Louisiana Avenue, N.W., 20001-2113
Telephone: 202-879-3939
Telecopier: 202-626-1700
Email: counsel@jonesday.com *URL:* http://www.jonesday.com
In Atlanta, Georgia: 3500 SunTrust Plaza, 303 Peachtree Street.
Telephone: 404-521-3939.
Telecopier: 404-581-8330.
In Brussels, Belgium: Avenue Louise 480, 7th Floor, B-1050 Brussels.
Telephone: 32-2-645-14-11.
Telecopier: 32-2-645-14-45.
In Chicago, Illinois: 77 West Wacker.
Telephone: 312-782-3939.
Telecopier: 312-782-8585.
In Cleveland, Ohio: North Point, 901 Lakeside Avenue.
Telephone: 216-586-3939.
Telecopier: 216-579-0212.
In Columbus, Ohio: 1900 Huntington Center.
Telephone: 614-469-3939.
Telecopier: 614-461-4198.
In Dallas, Texas: 2727 North Harwood Street.
Telephone: 214-220-3939.
Telecopier: 214-969-5100.
In Frankfurt, Germany: Hochhaus am Park, Grüneburgweg 102, 60323, Frankfurt am Main.
Telephone: 49-69-9726-3939.
Telecopier: 49-69-9726-3993.
In Geneva, Switzerland: 20, rue de Candolle.
Telephone: 41-22-320-2339.
Telecopier: 41-22-320-1232.
In Hong Kong: 29th Floor, Entertainment Building, 30 Queen's Road Central.
Telephone: 852-2526-6895.
Telecopier: 852-2868-5871.
In Irvine, California: 5 Park Plaza, Suite 1100.
Telephone: 949-851-3939.
Telecopier: 949-553-7539.
In London, England: Bucklersbury House, 3 Queen Victoria Street.
Telephone: 44-171-236-3939.
Telecopier: 44-171-236-1113.
In Los Angeles, California: 555 West Fifth Street, Suite 4600.
Telephone: 213-489-3939.
Telecopier: 213-243-2539.
In New Delhi, India (Associate Office): Pathak & Associates (an associate firm of Jones, Day, Reavis & Pogue), 1st Floor, Dr. Gopal Das Bhaven, 28 Barakhamba Road.
Telephone: 91-11-373-8793.; 91-11-335-7345.
Telecopier: 91-11-335-3761.
In New York, New York: 599 Lexington Avenue.
Telephone: 212-326-3939.
Telecopier: 212-755-7306.
In Paris, France: 120, rue du Faubourg Saint-Honoré.
Telephone: 33-1-56-59-39-39.
Telecopier: 33-1-56-59-39-38
In Pittsburgh, Pennsylvania: 500 Grant Street, 31st Floor.
Telephone: 412-391-3939.
Telecopier: 412-394-7959.

(See Next Column)

JONES, DAY, REAVIS & POGUE—*Continued*

In Riyadh, Saudi Arabia: The International Law Firm (In Association with Jones, Day, Reavis & Pogue), Sulaymaniyah, Prince Mishari IBN, Abdulaziz Street, P.O. Box 22166.
Telephone: (966-1) 462-8866.
Telecopier: (966-1) 462-9001.
In Shanghai, China: 2805 Kerry Centre, 1515 Nanjing Road West.
Telephone: 86-21-5298-6568.
Telecopier: 86-21-5298-6569.
In Sydney, Australia: Governor Phillip Tower, Level 38, 1 Farrer Place.
Telephone: 61-2-9210-6921.
Telecopier: 61-2-9210-6926.
In Taipei, Taiwan: 8th Floor, 2 Tun Hwa South Road, Section 2.
Telephone: (886-2) 2704-6808.
Telecopier: (886-2) 2704-6791.
In Tokyo, Japan: Toranomon MT Building, 4th Floor, 10-3, Toranomon 3-Chome, Minato-Ku, Tokyo 105, Japan.
Telephone: 81-3-3433-3939.
Telecopier: 81-3-5401-2725.

MEMBERS OF FIRM IN WASHINGTON, D.C.

Andrew M. Kramer
Willis J. Goldsmith

COUNSEL

David A. Copus

For Complete List of Firm Personnel, See General Section

For full biographical listings, see the Martindale-Hubbell Law Directory

KING, PAGANO & HARRISON (AV)

1730 Pennsylvania Avenue, N.W., 20006
Telephone: 202-371-6800
Fax: 202-371-6770
URL: http://www.kph.com
New York, New York Office: 425 Park Avenue, 10022.
Telephone: 212-223-4000.
FAX: 212-223-4134.

MEMBERS OF FIRM

Jeffrey W. King
Jeffrey W. Pagano (Resident, New York, N.Y. Office)
Keith J. Harrison
James E. Kellett (Resident, New York, N.Y. Office)
Jeffrey L. Poston
Ira M. Saxe (Not admitted in DC; Resident, New York, N.Y. Office)

OF COUNSEL

Herbert I. Meyer (Resident, New York, N.Y. Office)

ASSOCIATES

Cheryl A. Maier
Christopher Flynn
Emily B. Zuckerman (Not admitted in DC; Resident, New York, N.Y. Office)
Eric M. Carr (Not admitted in DC; Resident, New York, N.Y. Office)

Representative Clients: Brink's, Inc.; BAX Global; GEO Logistics; COMSAT; Sharro Corp.; TNT USA Inc.; National Rehabilitation Hospital; J & B Associates; Meldisco; Metropolitan Life Insurance Company; Premium Distributors of Washington, D.C.

For full biographical listings, see the Martindale-Hubbell Law Directory

KOHN, KOHN & COLAPINTO, P.C. (AV)

3233 P Street, N.W., 20007
Telephone: 202-342-6980
Fax: 202-342-6984
Email: kkc@kkc.com *URL:* http://www.kkc.com

Stephen M. Kohn
Michael D. Kohn
David K. Colapinto

For full biographical listings, see the Martindale-Hubbell Law Directory

KRUPIN GREENBAUM & O'BRIEN, LLC (AV)

1156 15th Street, NW Suite 200, 20005
Telephone: 202-530-0700
Fax: 202-530-0703
URL: http://www.KGOLaw.com

Jay P. Krupin
Jonathan W. Greenbaum
James J. O'Brien
Caryn G. Pass
Alison J. Hurewitz
Adrian Van Nelson II (Not admitted in DC)

COUNSEL

Jeffrey A. Spector

(See Next Column)

Kimberley Ann Best (Not admitted in DC)
Erica D. Brown
Scott V. Kamins (Not admitted in DC)
Sidney E. Lebowitz (Not admitted in DC)
Manesh K. Rath
D. Jay Sumner (Not admitted in DC)
Monique A. van Stiphout (Not admitted in DC)
Hollie R. Vona (Not admitted in DC)
Teresa Burke Wright

For full biographical listings, see the Martindale-Hubbell Law Directory

MCGUINESS NORRIS & WILLIAMS, LLP (AV)

Suite 1200, 1015 Fifteenth Street, N.W., 20005
Telephone: 202-789-8600
Telecopier: 202-789-1708
Email: Info@mwlaw.com
Northern Virginia Office: 12110 Sunset Hills Road, Reston, Virginia, 22090.
Telephone: 703-476-9009.

MEMBERS OF FIRM

Jeffrey C. McGuiness
Jeffrey A. Norris
Edward E. Potter
G. John Tysse
Monte B. Lake
Robert E. Williams
Ann Elizabeth Reesman
Daniel V. Yager

SENIOR ASSOCIATE

Darryl K. Henderson (Not admitted in DC)

ASSOCIATES

Christine Cooper Block
Timothy J. Bartl (Not admitted in DC)
Corrie L. Fischel
Erin Quinn Gery
Judith A. Lampley (Not admitted in DC)
Corbett L. Anderson (Not admitted in DC)
Amy M. Habib
Heather L. MacDougall (Not admitted in DC)

OF COUNSEL

Lorence L Kessler
Lynnette Conway Jacquez
William N. LaForge

CONSULTANTS

William F. Holmes
James S. Holt
Kenneth L. Deavers
Max Lyons
Anita U. Hattiangadi
Bruce D. Kuehnl
Annie A. Blackwell

For full biographical listings, see the Martindale-Hubbell Law Directory

MILLER, CANFIELD, PADDOCK AND STONE, P.L.C. (AV)

A Professional Limited Liability Company
Founded in 1852 by Sidney Davy Miller
1900 K Street, N.W., Suite 1150, 20006
Telephone: 202-429-5575; 785-0600
Fax: 202-331-1118; 785-1234
URL: http://www.millercanfield.com
Detroit, Michigan Office: 150 West Jefferson, Suite 2500, 48226-4415.
Telephone: 313-963-6420.
Fax: 313-496-7500.
Cable Address: "Stem Detroit."
Ann Arbor, Michigan Office: 101 North Main Street, 7th Floor, 48104-1400.
Telephone: 734-663-2445.
Fax: 734-747-7147.
Troy, Michigan Office: 840 West Long Lake Road, Suite 200, 48098.
Telephone: 248-879-2000.
Fax: 248-879-2001.
Grand Rapids, Michigan Office: 99 Monroe, N.W., Suite 1200, 49503-2639.
Telephone: 616-454-8656.
Fax: 616-776-6322.
Howell, Michigan Office: 121 South Barnard Street, Suite 4, 48843-2305.
Telephone: 517-546-7600.
Telecopier: 517-546-6974.
Kalamazoo, Michigan Office: 444 West Michigan Avenue, 49007-3752.
Telephone: 616-381-7030.
Fax: 616-382-0244.
Lansing, Michigan Office: One Michigan Avenue, Suite 900, 48933-1609.
Telephone: 517-487-2070.
Fax: 517-374-6304.
Monroe, Michigan Office: 214 East Elm Avenue, Suite 100, 48162-2682.
Telephone: 734-243-2000.
Fax: 734-243-0901.
Pensacola, Florida Office: 25 West Cedar, 32501.
Telephone: 850-469-1088.
Fax: 850-432-0677.
New York, New York Office: 1450 Broadway, 41st Floor, 10018.
Telephone: 212-704-4400.
Fax: 212-704-4410.
Gdynia, Poland Office: UL. Slaska 21, 81-319.
Telephone: 011-485-831-2808.
Fax: 011-48-58-628 6411.

(See Next Column)

MILLER, CANFIELD, PADDOCK AND STONE P.L.C., *Washington—Continued*

Warsaw, Poland Office: UL. Nowogrodzkall, 5th Floor, 00-513.
Telephone: 011-4822 529 0200.
Fax: 011-4822 529 0201.
Katowice, Poland Office: UL. Francuska 35/37, 40-027.
Telephone: 011 (48-32) 757-2414.
Fax: 011 (48-32) 757-2483.

OF COUNSEL/SENIOR COUNSEL

Jamir R. Couch (Not admitted in DC)

RESIDENT SENIOR ATTORNEY

Steven C. Kahn

For full biographical listings, see the Martindale-Hubbell Law Directory

OGLETREE, DEAKINS, NASH, SMOAK & STEWART, P.C. (AV)

Fifth Floor, 2400 N Street, N.W., 20037
Telephone: 202-887-0855
Facsimile: 202-887-0866
Email: Washington@odnss.com *URL:* http://www.Ogeltreedeakins.com
Atlanta, Georgia Office: 600 Peachtree Street, N.E., Suite 2100.
Telephone: 404-881-1300.
Houston, Texas Office: One Allen Center, 500 Dallas Street, Suite 3000.
Telephone: 713-655-0855.
Chicago, Illinois Office: Twenty-Fifth Floor, Two First National Plaza, 20 South Clark Street.
Telephone: 312-558-1220.
Nashville, Tennessee Office: SunTrust Center, Suite 800, 424 Church Street.
Telephone: 615-254-1900.
Birmingham, Alabama Office: 1900 SouthTrust Tower, 420 North 20th Street.
Telephone: 205-328-1900.
Greenville, South Carolina Office: The Ogletree Building, 300 North Main Street, P.O. Box 2757.
Telephone: 864-271-1300.
Charleston, South Carolina Office: 134 Meeting Street, Suite 500, P.O. Box 1808.
Telephone: 843-853-1300.
Columbia, South Carolina Office: 1501 Main Street, Suite 600, P.O. Box 11206.
Telephone: 803-252-1300.
Raleigh, North Carolina Office: 4101 Lake Boone Trail, Suite 511, P.O. Box 31608.
Telephone: 919-787-9700.
Winston-Salem, North Carolina Office: 150 South Stratford Road, Suite 350.
Telephone: 336-725-2110.

J. Frank Ogletree, Jr. (1930-1985)
Peter G. Nash (1937-1993)
Dixie L. Atwater (1948-1992)
John A. Penello (1909-1998)
Homer L. Deakins, Jr.
Lewis Tyson Smoak
J. Hamilton Stewart, III
Peter H. Kiefer
Marshall B. Babson
David S. Fortney
Harold P. Coxson, Jr.
Bernard P. Jeweler
Joel A. Daniel
David Edward Jones (Not admitted in DC)
Michael J. Murphy
Burton J. Fishman

Yoora Kim (Not admitted in DC)
Consuela A. Pinto

OF COUNSEL

Stanley R. Strauss

Representative Clients: Chevron USA Products Co.; Deere & Co.; Eastman Chemical Company; Eastman Kodak Co.; Emery Worldwide; Fluor Corporation; General Electric Co.; John Hancock Mutual Life Insurance Co.; Michelin Tire Corporation; Nissan Motor Manufacturing Corporation U.S.A.

For full biographical listings, see the Martindale-Hubbell Law Directory

REED SMITH SHAW & MCCLAY LLP (AV)

Suite 1100 - East Tower, 1301 K Street, N.W., 20005-3317
Telephone: 202-414-9200
FAX: 202-414-9299
Email: rssm@rssm.com *URL:* http://www.rssm.com
Pittsburgh, Pennsylvania Office: 435 Sixth Avenue, 15219-1886.
Telephone: 412-288-3131.
FAX: 412-288-3063.
Philadelphia, Pennsylvania Office: 2500 One Liberty Place, 19103-7301.
Telephone: 215-851-8100.
FAX: 215-851-1420.
Harrisburg, Pennsylvania Office: 213 Market Street, 17101-2132.
Telephone: 717-234-5988.
FAX: 717-236-3777.
Princeton, New Jersey Office: 136 Main Street, Suite 250, 08540-5799.
Telephone: 609-987-0050.
FAX: 609-951-0824.
New York, N.Y. Office: 375 Park Avenue, 17th Floor, 10152.
Telephone: 212-521-5400.
FAX: 212-521-5450.

(See Next Column)

Newark, New Jersey Office: The Legal Center, One Riverfront Plaza, First Floor, 07102-5400.
Telephone: 973-621-3200.
Fax: 973-621-3199.
McLean, Virginia Office: Reed Smith Hazel & Thomas LLP, Suite 1100, 8251 Greensboro Drive, 22102-3844.
Telephone: 703-734-4600.
FAX: 703-734-4699.
Falls Church, Virginia Office: Reed Smith Hazel & Thomas LLP, Suite 1400, 3110 Fairview Park Drive, P.O. Box 12001.
Telephone: 703-641-4200.
Fax: 703-641-4340.
Leesburg, Virginia Office: Reed Smith Hazel & Thomas LLP, 44084 Riverside Parkway, Suite 300.
Telephone: 703-729-8500. Metro: 703-478-1992.
Fax: 703-478-8003.
Richmond, Virginia Office: Reed Smith Hazel & Thomas LLP, Suite 600, 411 East Franklin Street, P.O. Box 788.
Telephone: 804-344-3400.
Fax: 804-344-3410.

MEMBER OF FIRM

Michael C. Lynch

For full biographical listings, see the Martindale-Hubbell Law Directory

SCHMELTZER, APTAKER & SHEPARD, P.C. (AV)

The Watergate, Suite 1000, 2600 Virginia Avenue, N.W., 20037-1905
Telephone: 202-333-8800
Cable Address: "Ship"
Telex: 440517
Facsimile: 202-337-6065
Email: sas@saslaw.com *URL:* http://www.saspc.com
Los Angeles, California Office: 1999 Avenue of the Stars, Twenty-Seventh Floor, 90067-4095.
Telephone: 310-557-2966.
FAX: 310-286-6610.

Ira M. Shepard
Paul M. Heylman
John A. McGuinn
Gary L. Lieber
Edward R. Levin
Robert L. Duston
Henry A. Platt

Suzanne Langford Sanford
Anessa Abrams
Linda G. Hill
Trina L. Fairley (Not admitted in DC)
John R. Seewald, Jr. (Not admitted in DC)
Claudia G. Regen

COUNSEL

Don A. Zimmerman

For full biographical listings, see the Martindale-Hubbell Law Directory

SPRENGER & LANG, P.L.L.C. (AV)

1614 Twentieth Street, N.W., 20009
Telephone: 202-265-8010
Fax: 202-332-6652
Minneapolis, Minnesota Office: Sprenger & Lang, P.L.L.C., 325 Ridgewood Avenue.
Telephone: 612-871-8910.
Fax: 612-871-9270.

MEMBERS OF FIRM

Paul C. Sprenger (Resident)
Jane Lang (Resident)
Michael D. Lieder (Resident)
Lawrence P. Schaefer (Not admitted in DC; Resident, Minneapolis, Minnesota Office)
James R. Behrenbrinker (Not admitted in DC; Resident, Minneapolis, Minnesota Office)
Eli Gottesdiener (Resident)
Susan E. Stokes (Not admitted in DC; Resident, Minneapolis, Minnesota Office)
Maia R. Caplan (Resident)

Lisa C. Stratton (Resident, Minneapolis, Minnesota Office)

OF COUNSEL

Jean M. Boler (Not admitted in DC; Resident, Minneapolis, Minnesota Office)
Mara R. Thompson (Not admitted in DC; Resident, Minneapolis, Minnesota Office)

For full biographical listings, see the Martindale-Hubbell Law Directory

Washington—Continued

VENABLE ATTORNEYS AT LAW VENABLE, BAETJER, HOWARD & CIVILETTI, LLP (AV)

A Partnership including Professional Corporations
Suite 1000, 1201 New York Avenue, N.W., 20005
Telephone: 202-962-4800
Fax: 202-962-8300
URL: http://www.venable.com
Baltimore, Maryland Office: Venable, Baetjer and Howard LLP, 1800 Mercantile Bank & Trust Building, 2 Hopkins Plaza.
Telephone: 410-244-7400.
Fax: 410-244-7742.
McLean, Virginia Office: Venable, Baetjer and Howard LLP, Suite 400, 2010 Corporate Ridge.
Telephone: 703-760-1600.
Fax: 703-821-8949.
Rockville, Maryland Office: Venable, Baetjer and Howard LLP, Suite 500, One Church Street, P. O. Box 1906.
Telephone: 301-217-5600.
Fax: 301-217-5617.
Towson, Maryland Office: Venable, Baetjer and Howard LLP, 210 Allegheny Avenue, P. O. Box 5517.
Telephone: 410-494-6200.
Fax: 410-821-0147.

MEMBERS OF FIRM

Robert G. Ames (Also at Baltimore, Maryland Office)
Maurice Baskin
Kenneth C. Bass, III (Also at McLean, Virginia Office)
Connie N. Bertram
Joseph G. Block
Jeffrey A. Dunn (Also at Baltimore, Maryland Office)
David W. Goewey
Gary M. Hnath
George F. Pappas (Also at Baltimore, Maryland Office)
James L. Shea (also at Baltimore, Maryland Office)
Patrick J. Stewart (Also at Baltimore, Maryland Office)

ASSOCIATE

John C. Hardwick, Jr.

For Complete List of Firm Personnel, See General Section

For full biographical listings, see the Martindale-Hubbell Law Directory

VERNER, LIIPFERT, BERNHARD, MCPHERSON AND HAND, CHARTERED (AV)

901 15th Street, N.W., 20005-2301
Telephone: 202-371-6000
Cable Address: "Verlip"
Fax: 202-371-6279
Email: verner.com *URL:* http://www.verner.com
Houston, Texas Office: 1111 Bagby, Suite 4700, 77002.
Telephone: 713-225-7200.
Fax: 713-752-2199.
Honolulu, Hawaii Office: 745 Fort Street, Suite 600, 96813.
Telephone: 808-566-0999.
Fax: 808-566-0995.
Austin, Texas Office: Suite 1440 San Jacinto Center, 98 San Jacinto Boulevard, 78701.
Telephone: 512-703-6000.
Fax: 512-703-6003.
Las Vegas, Nevada Affiliate Office: Gary C. Moss, Hughes Center, 3960 Howard Hughes Parkway, Suite 400, 89109.
Telephone: 702-737-3433.
Fax: 702-737-1612.
Miami, Florida Office: 3100 First Union Financial Center, 200 South Biscayne Boulevard, 33131.
Telephone: 305-371-8801.
Fax: 305-371-6545.

Douglas W. Hall
Harriet Lipkin
Joseph L. Manson, III
Gary C. Moss (Resident, Las Vegas, Nevada Office)
Ronald B. Natalie
Peter S. Pantaleo
Cynthia M. Surrisi (Resident, Honolulu, Hawaii Office)

OF COUNSEL

Gregg S. Avitabile
J. Robert Kirk
Michael A. Taylor

For Complete List of Firm Personnel, See General Section

For full biographical listings, see the Martindale-Hubbell Law Directory

WEBSTER, FREDRICKSON & BRACKSHAW (AV)

Suite 300, 1819 H Street, N.W., 20006
Telephone: 202-659-8510
Telecopier: 202-659-4082
Email: firm@wf82.com

MEMBERS OF FIRM

Wendell W. Webster
Bruce A. Fredrickson
Susan L. Brackshaw
Linda M. Correia

(See Next Column)

ASSOCIATES

Jonathan C. Puth
Jeffrey E. Fallon
N. Bernard Dorsey, Jr (Not admitted in DC)

For full biographical listings, see the Martindale-Hubbell Law Directory

FLORIDA

*CLEARWATER,** Pinellas Co.

KWALL, SHOWERS & COLEMAN, P.A. (AV)

133 North Fort Harrison Avenue, 33755
Telephone: 727-441-4947
Telecopier: 727-447-3158
Email: kwall@worldnet.att.net *URL:* http://www.usalaw.com/adminlaw/

Louis Kwall
Sherwood S. (Flip) Coleman

For Complete List of Firm Personnel, See General Section

For full biographical listings, see the Martindale-Hubbell Law Directory

*FORT LAUDERDALE,** Broward Co.

AMLONG & AMLONG, P.A. (AV)

Second Floor, 500 Northeast Fourth Street, 33301-1154
Telephone: 954-462-1983
Fax: 954-523-3192

Karen Coolman Amlong
William R. Amlong

Judith M. Alexander
Randall Lane Bloom
Alain E. Boileau
Jennifer E. Daley

For full biographical listings, see the Martindale-Hubbell Law Directory

FISHER & PHILLIPS LLP (AV)

A Limited Liability Partnership including Professional Corporations and Professional Associations
Suite 2300 NationsBank Tower, One Financial Plaza, 33394
Telephone: 954-525-4800
Telecopier: 954-525-8739
URL: http://www.laborlawyers.com
Atlanta, Georgia Office: 1500 Resurgens Plaza, 945 East Paces Ferry Road, N.E., 30326.
Telephone: 404-231-1400.
Telecopier: 404-240-4249.
Redwood City, California Office: Suite 345, Three Lagoon Drive, 94065.
Telephone: 650-592-6160.
Telecopier: 650-592-6385.
Newport Beach, California Office: 4675 MacArthur Court, Suite 550, 92660.
Telephone: 949-851-2424.
Telecopier: 949-851-0152.
New Orleans, Louisiana Office: 201 St. Charles Avenue, Suite 3710, 70170.
Telephone: 504-522-3303.
Telecopier: 504-529-3850.
Houston, Texas Office: 6850 Chase Tower, 600 Travis, 77002.
Telephone: 713-227-5410.
Telecopier: 713-236-6949.
Chicago, Illinois Office: 420 Marquette Building, 140 South Dearborn Street, 60603.
Telephone: 312-346-8061.
Telecopier: 312-346-3179.

RESIDENT MEMBERS

Charles S. Caulkins (P.A.)
Christopher D. Robinson (P.A.)
James C. Polkinghorn (P.A.)
Kenneth A. Knox (P.A.)

RESIDENT ASSOCIATES

Suzanne K. Bogdan
Cathy M. Stutin
Kristen L. Sampo
Wendy J. Smith
Ashley Howell Kaplan
Karen M. Kahane
Brian A. Davis
Evan Roberts
William T. Krizner
Francisco Lopez, Jr.

Representative Clients: AutoNation USA; Boca Raton Resort & Club; Dean Foods/T.G. Lee Foods, Inc.; Hyatt Corp.; Miller Brewing Co.; Norwegian Cruise Lines; The Prudential Insurance Company of America; United States Sugar Corp.; University of Miami.

For full biographical listings, see the Martindale-Hubbell Law Directory

TRIPP SCOTT (AV)

110 S.E. 6th Street, P.O. Box 14245, 33301
Telephone: 954-525-7500
Telecopier: 954-761-8475
URL: http://www.trippscott.com

(See Next Column)

TRIPP SCOTT, *Fort Lauderdale—Continued*

Norman D. Tripp
James A. Scott
Dennis Dustin Smith
Peter G. Herman
Garry W. Johnson
Kimberly A. Gilmour
Richard D. Heller
Gregory A. McLaughlin
Steven C. Elkin
Daniel E. Taylor
Matthew Zifrony
Edward J. Pozzuoli
William J. Gross

OF COUNSEL

Welcom H. Watson, Jr.

ASSOCIATES

Laura L. Hess
Scott J. Jordan
Tammy L. Knight
Paul Octavio Lopez
Milagros (Millie) G. Muñoz
Loren K. Newman
Richard J. Simeone
Heather S. Tripp
Jeffrey S. Wood
Christine T. Yates

Representative Clients: Alamo Rent A Car, Inc.; AutoNation; Crab Pot Restaurants; Certified Tours; Florida Heat Pump, Inc.; Gehl Group, Inc.; Precision Resource, Fla. Division; Impra, Inc.

For full biographical listings, see the Martindale-Hubbell Law Directory

*FORT MYERS,** Lee Co.

KUNKEL MILLER & HAMENT (AV)

Suntrust Bank Building, 12751 New Brittany Boulevard 405, 33907
Telephone: 941-278-1600
1-800-828-7133
Telecopier: 941-278-4787
Email: KMH@laborattys.com *URL:* http://www.laborattys.com
Sarasota, Florida Office: Southtrust Bank Plaza, 1800 Second Street, Suite 970.
Telephone: 941-365-6006.
Fax: 941-365-6209.
Tampa, Florida Office: Magdalene Center, 15438 North Florida Avenue, Suite 202.
Telephone: 813-963-7736.
Telefax: 813-969-3639.

MEMBERS OF FIRM

Daniel H. Kunkel
Michael R. Miller
John M. Hament

Timothy N. Tack
Lorraine Maass Hultman
Stephanie B. Purvis
Nikhil N. Joshi

LEGAL SUPPORT PERSONNEL

Travis Campbell

Representative Clients: Bon Secours Hospitals; Century Bank; Florida Coca-Cola Enterprises, Inc.; S arasota Bank; K-Mart Corporation; National Car Rental System, Inc.; Sun Coast Media Group, Inc.; Florida Health Care Association; Manatee Memorial Hospital; Florida Aluminum and Steel Fabricators.

For full biographical listings, see the Martindale-Hubbell Law Directory

*FORT PIERCE,** St. Lucie Co.

J. DAVID RICHESON & ASSOCIATES, P.A. (AV)

317 South 2nd Street, P.O. Box 4048, 34948
Telephone: 561-465-5111
FAX: 561-466-0378
West Palm Beach, Florida Office: Suite 900 Forum III Building, 1655 Palm Beach Lakes Boulevard, 33401.
Telephone: 561-689-6660.

J. David Richeson

Elizabeth Coke
David Miklas

For full biographical listings, see the Martindale-Hubbell Law Directory

*JACKSONVILLE,** Duval Co.

BROWN, TERRELL, HOGAN, ELLIS, MCCLAMMA & YEGELWEL, P.A. (AV)

Suite 804 Blackstone Building, 233 East Bay Street, 32202-3417
Telephone: 904-632-2424
Fax: 904-632-2027
Email: mail@bthemy-law.com *URL:* http://www.bthemy-law.com

Thomas R. Brown
James T. Terrell
Wayne Hogan
Timothy D. Ellis
T. Edward McClamma
Evan J. Yegelwel
Thomas E. Duffy, Jr.
Christopher G. Burns
Anita Pryor
Alan M. Pickert

Carroll Cayer
Michael S. Sharrit
Theodore Samuel Pina, Jr.
Mark E. Calvin
Leslie A. Goller
Patricia M. Dodson
Jennifer Kolinski Millis

(See Next Column)

Reference: NCNB.

For full biographical listings, see the Martindale-Hubbell Law Directory

COFFMAN, COLEMAN, ANDREWS & GROGAN, PROFESSIONAL ASSOCIATION (AV)

2065 Herschel Street, P.O. Box 40089, 32203
Telephone: 904-389-5161
Telecopier: 904-387-9340

Patrick D. Coleman
William H. Andrews
Michael K. Grogan
Eric J. Holshouser
Mary W. Jarrett
Robert G. Riegel, Jr.
Joann M. Bricker
Michael G. Prendergast
Timothy B. Strong
Heather A. Owen

Jeffrey P. Watson
Edward H. Trent
Robert T. Devine
Allison A. Brody
Eugenia H. Donahoo
Melissa A. Dearing
Jason D. Sammis
Matthew D. Westerman

OF COUNSEL

Daniel R. Coffman, Jr.

Representative Clients: American Home Products Corp.; Anheuser-Busch Companies, Inc.; Atlantic Marine, Inc.; Baptist/St. Vincent's Health System; Blue Cross and Blue Shield of Florida, Inc.; Winn-Dixie Stores, Inc.; Xerox Corp.

For full biographical listings, see the Martindale-Hubbell Law Directory

THE CRAMER LAW FIRM (AV)

1 Independent Drive, Suite 3300, 32202
Telephone: 904-632-2211
Fax: 904-632-2324
Email: cramerjax@worldnet.att.net

Jeffrey A. Cramer

Leonard S. Magid
Richard L. Ruth

Reference: Suntrust Bank.

For full biographical listings, see the Martindale-Hubbell Law Directory

HAYNSWORTH BALDWIN JOHNSON & GREAVES LLC (AV)

1301 Riverplace Boulevard, Suite 800, P.O. Box 40593, 32203
Telephone: 904-396-3000
Facsimile: 904-396-9999
Tampa, Florida Office: 600 North Westshore Boulevard, Suite 200.
Telephone: 813-289-1247.
Greenville, South Carolina Office: 918 South Pleasantburg Drive, P.O. Box 10888.
Telephone: 864-271-7410.
Columbia, South Carolina Office: 1201 Main Street, Suite 1230.
Telephone: 803-799-5858.
Raleigh, North Carolina Office: 3605 Glenwood Avenue, Suite 210, P.O. Box 10035.
Telephone: 919-782-3340.
Greensboro, North Carolina Office: 2709 Henry Street, P.O. Box 13310.
Telephone: 336-375-9737.
Charlotte, North Carolina Office: 400 West Trade Street.
Telephone: 704-342-2588.

MEMBERS OF FIRM

Knox L. Haynsworth, Jr. (Not admitted in FL)
G. Thomas Harper (Resident)
Charles F. Henley, Jr. (Resident)

Gregg Gerlach (Not admitted in FL)
Kimberly T. Acuna (Resident)
Elizabeth A. Maas (Resident)

Representative Clients: Belk Department Stores; Citrus World, Inc.; Great Dane Trailers, Inc.; Jacksonville Urban League; Kmart Corp.; Lockheed Missiles and Space Company, Inc.; Mayo Clinic Jacksonville; Pulte Home Corp.; Sears, Roebuck and Co.; Watkins Engineers & Constructors, Inc.

For full biographical listings, see the Martindale-Hubbell Law Directory

HEDRICK, DEWBERRY & REGAN, P.A. (AV)

50 North Laura Street, Suite 2225, 32202
Telephone: 904-356-1300
Fax: 904-356-8050

Michael J. Dewberry
Alexandra Krueger Hedrick
Jeffrey C. Regan

Clinton Allen Wright III

For full biographical listings, see the Martindale-Hubbell Law Directory

Jacksonville—Continued

MALFITANO CAMPBELL & DICKINSON (AV)

300 West Adams Street, Suite 650, 32202
Telephone: 904-356-8900
Fax: 904-356-8200
Email: mcd@jax-inter.net
Tampa, Florida Office: 100 West Kennedy Boulevard, Suite 500, 33602.
Telephone: 813-222-8950.
Fax: 813-222-8951.
Lakeland, Florida Office: 500 South Florida Avenue, Suite 600, 33801.
Telephone: 941-682-0916.

Michael D. Malfitano
John W. Campbell
John F. Dickinson
F. Damon Kitchen

Angelique Groza Lyons
Margaret A. Philips
V. Ross Spano

For full biographical listings, see the Martindale-Hubbell Law Directory

LAW OFFICES OF ARCHIBALD J. THOMAS, III (AV)

Riverplace Tower, 1301 Riverplace Boulevard, Suite 1640, 32207
Telephone: 904-396-2322
Facsimile: 904-398-3271
URL: http://www.lawyers.com/employee-rights

ASSOCIATE

Philip D. Williams

For full biographical listings, see the Martindale-Hubbell Law Directory

*MIAMI,** Dade Co.

KAREN EVANS LITIGATION RESOLUTION, INC. (AV)

169 East Flagler Street, Suite 1200, 33131
Telephone: 305-371-3250
Facsimile: 305-371-3341
Email: LitResInc@aol.com

Karen Evans

For full biographical listings, see the Martindale-Hubbell Law Directory

NEIL FLAXMAN PROFESSIONAL ASSOCIATION (AV)

550 Biltmore Way, Suite 780 (Coral Gables), 33134
Telephone: 305-445-1388
Fax: 305-443-0279
URL: http://www.lawyers.com/neilflaxman

Neil Flaxman

Joseph G. Weiss, Jr.

For full biographical listings, see the Martindale-Hubbell Law Directory

JOSEPH Z. FLEMING, P.A.

(See Ford & Harrison LLP, Miami, Florida)

FORD & HARRISON LLP (AV)

516 Ingraham Building, 25 S.E. 2nd Avenue, 33131
Telephone: 305-379-3811
Fax: 305-358-5933
Email: firm@fordharrison.com *URL:* http://www.fordharrison.com
Jacksonville, Florida Office: 121 West Forsyth Street, Suite 1000. 32203.
Telephone: 904-356-8073.
Fax: 904-358-2319.
Tampa, Florida Office: 101 E. Kennedy Boulevard, Suite 900. 33602.
Telephone: 813-261-7800.
Fax: 813-261-7899.
Atlanta, Georgia Office: 600 Peachtree at the Circle Building, 1275 Peachtree Street, N.E. 30309.
Telephone: 404-888-3800.
Fax: 404-888-3863.
Los Angeles, California Office: 333 South Grand Avenue, Suite 3680. 90071.
Telephone: 213-680-3410.
Fax: 213-680-4161.
Memphis, Tennessee Office: 6750 Poplar Avenue, Suite 600, P.O. Box 171375. 38187-1375.
Telephone: 901-756-1550.
Telecopier: 901-756-1016.
Washington, D.C. Office: 1920 N Street, N.W., Suite 200. 20036.
Telephone: 202-463-6633.
Fax: 202-466-5705.

MEMBERS OF FIRM

Granville M. Alley, Jr. (1929-1976)
John-Edward Alley
Joseph Z. Fleming
Robert E. Rigrish (Not admitted in FL; Resident)

(See Next Column)

ASSOCIATES

Pedro P. Forment (Resident)
Craig J. Freger (Resident)
Jose I. Leon (Resident)
Nina Q. Smith (Resident)

Representative Clients: The Wackenhut Corporation and subsidiaries; Publix Super Markets, Inc.; Braman Motors; Biltmore Securities; Sysco Corp.; Skyline Mobile Homes, Inc.; Associated Grocers of Florida; Baxter Healthcare Corp. (Dade Div.); Edron Fixture Corp.

For full biographical listings, see the Martindale-Hubbell Law Directory

MULLER, MINTZ, KORNREICH, CALDWELL, CASEY, CROSLAND & BRAMNICK, P.A. (AV)

Suite 3600, First Union Financial Center, 200 South Biscayne Boulevard, 33131
Telephone: 305-358-5500
Broward: 954-522-0393
Facsimile: 305-379-3802
URL: http://www.mullermintz.com
Orlando Office: Suite 1525 Citrus Center, 255 South Orange Avenue.
Telephone: 407-843-1400.

David V. Kornreich
Michael W. Casey, III
James C. Crosland
James S. Bramnick
Gordon D. Rogers
Carmen S. Johnson
Jeffrey E. Mandel
Denise M. Heekin
Paul T. Ryder
Richard D. Tuschman

Teresa Adamson Herrmann
Benton N. Wood
Melissa B. Medrano
Marlene Quintana Morales
James W. Seegers
John A. Walker
James D. Stokes
David C. Miller
Jenna Rinehart Rassif
Scott S. Allen
Kelly N. Charles
Kevin J. Morris
Debra M. Leder
Steven D. Grimberg
Christi A. Shelton
Michael T. Landen
Erin A. Webb
Alexis Gonzalez

Representative Clients: Florida Power & Light Co.; Universal Studios Escape; JM Family Enterprises, Inc.; J.C. Penney Co.; Carnival Corporation; Sunbeam Television Corp.; Memorial Healthcare System; Florida East Coast Railway Company; Calder Race Course; City of Coral Gables.

For full biographical listings, see the Martindale-Hubbell Law Directory

*ORLANDO,** Orange Co.

BROWN & GREEN, P.A. (AV)

709 North Magnolia Avenue, P.O. Box 3108, 32802
Telephone: 407-425-7755
Fax: 407-422-4865
Email: brown_and_green_pa@msn.com

James G. Brown
Dorothy F. Green
Joseph E. Blitch
Deborah Lynn La Fleur (Not admitted in FL)
M. Susan Sacco

For full biographical listings, see the Martindale-Hubbell Law Directory

BROWN, WARD, SALZMAN & WEISS, P.A. (AV)

111 North Orange Avenue, Suite 875, P.O. Box 2873, 32802-2873
Telephone: 407-425-9566
Fax: 407-425-9596; Email: firm@orlandolaw.net
Email: brownu@osceola.k12.fl.us *URL:* http://www.orlandolaw.net

Usher Larry Brown
John H. Ward
Gary S. Salzman
Jeffrey S. Weiss
Suzanne D'Agresta

Scott D. Danahy
James G. Vickaryous
Robert L. Butterfield, Jr.
Allison Carmine McDonald

Representative Clients: The School Board of Osceola County; Orange County Comptroller; The School Board of Flagler County; Florida League of Cities, Inc.; Gallagher Bassett Services, Inc.; Horace Mann Companies, Inc.; Trammell Crow Company; Noble Management; Kellogg Properties; A.J. Gallagher Company.

For full biographical listings, see the Martindale-Hubbell Law Directory

DEMPSEY & SASSO (AV)

Nations Bank Building, 390 North Orange Avenue, Suite 2700, P.O. Box 1980, 32802
Telephone: 407-422-5166
Telecopier: 407-422-8556
Email: demp-sas@magicnet.net

Bernard H. Dempsey, Jr.
Michael C. Sasso

Brian D. Solomon
Barbara B. Smithers
Jeffrey K. Grant
Angelia J. Sheridan

For full biographical listings, see the Martindale-Hubbell Law Directory

Orlando—Continued

FOLEY & LARDNER (AV)

Suite 1800, 111 North Orange Avenue, P.O. Box 2193, 32802-2193
Telephone: 407-423-7656
Facsimile: 407-648-1743
Email: foleylardner@worldnet.att.net *URL:* http://www.foleylardner.com
Los Angeles, California Office: 2029 Century Park East, 35th Floor.
Telephone: 310-277-2223.
Fax: 310-557-8475.
Sacramento, California Office: 300 Capitol Mall, Suite 1125.
Telephone: 916-443-8005.
Fax: 916-443-2240.
San Diego, California Office: 402 West Broadway, 23rd Floor.
Telephone: 619-234-6655.
Fax: 619-234-3510.
San Francisco, California Office: One Maritime Plaza, Sixth Floor.
Telephone: 415-434-4484.
Fax: 415-434-4507.
Denver, Colorado Office: 1999 Broadway, Suite 2560.
Telephone: 303-297-0260.
Fax: 303-297-0266.
Washington, D.C. Office: Washington Harbour, Suite 500, 3000 K Street, N.W.
Telephone: 202-672-5300.
Telex: 904136 (Foley Lard Wash).
Facsimile: 202-672-5399.
Jacksonville, Florida Office: The Greenleaf Building, 200 Laura Street. P.O. Box 240.
Telephone: 904-359-2000.
Facsimile: 904-359-8700.
Tallahassee, Florida Office: 300 East Park Avenue, P.O. Box 1454.
Telephone: 850-222-6100.
Facsimile: 850-561-6475.
Tampa, Florida Offices: Suite 2700, One Hundred N. Tampa Street, P.O. Box 3391.
Telephones: 813-229-2300; Pinellas County: 813-442-3296.
Facsimile: 813-221-4210.
West Palm Beach, Florida Office: Suite 200, Phillips Point East Tower, 777 South Flagler Drive.
Telephone: 561-655-5050.
Facsimile: 561-655-6925.
Chicago, Illinois Office: Suite 3300, One IBM Plaza, 330 N. Wabash Avenue.
Telephone: 312-755-1900.
Facsimile: 312-755-1925.
Annapolis, Maryland Office: Suite 102, 175 Admiral Cochrane Drive.
Telephone: 410-266-8077.
Telex: 899149 (Oldtownpat).
Facsimile: 410-266-8664.
Madison, Wisconsin Office: Verex Plaza, 150 East Gilman Street, P.O. Box 1497.
Telephone: 608-257-5035.
Facsimile: 608-258-4258.
Milwaukee, Wisconsin Office: Firstar Center, 777 East Wisconsin Avenue.
Telephone: 414-271-2400.
Telex: 26-819 (Foley Lard Mil).
Facsimile: 414-297-4900.
Brussels, Belgium Office: Avenue Louise, 283.
Telephone: 32-2-646-2777.
Facsimile: 32-2-646-7574.

RETIRED PARTNER

Norman F. Burke

General Counsel for: The Greater Orlando Aviation Authority.
Attorneys for: Citrus Central, Inc.

For Complete List of Firm Personnel, See General Section

For full biographical listings, see the Martindale-Hubbell Law Directory

GARWOOD, MCKENNA, MCKENNA & WOLF, P.A. (AV)

815 North Garland Avenue, 32801
Telephone: 407-841-9496
1-800-941-9496
Telex: 407-841-0600
Email: info@gmmw.com *URL:* http://www.gmmw.com
Other Orlando, Florida Office: 731 North Garland Avenue.
Cocoa, Florida Office: 200 Brevard Avenue.

Thomas C. Garwood, Jr.
Allen J. McKenna
Susan K. McKenna
Kay L. Wolf

John M. Finnigan
John U. Biedenharn, Jr.
Arthur R. Brown, Jr.
Deborah E. Frimmel
Alfred Truesdell
Joanne Braddock Lambert
Lori R. Benton
Myrna L. Galligano
Daniel P. O'Gorman
Aaron L. Zandy

For full biographical listings, see the Martindale-Hubbell Law Directory

MORAN & SHAMS, P.A. (AV)

111 North Orange Avenue, Suite 1200, P.O. Box 472, 32802-0472
Telephone: 407-841-4141
Fax: 407-841-4148
Email: moran-shams@moran-shams.com

Thomas P. Moran
Brian J. Moran
Kelly T. Blystone
Christopher C. Skambis
James F. Kidd

Clinton C. Lyons, Jr.
Cristina Arechaga
David E. Ackley

Representative Clients: Adventist Health System Sunbelt Healthcare Corporation; China Group, Inc.; Cruises Only, LLC; Florida Hospital; Gencor Industries Inc.; MEDai, Inc.; Presbyterian Retirement Communities, Inc.; Southern Fire Protection of Orlando, Inc.; Vermont American Corporation.

For full biographical listings, see the Martindale-Hubbell Law Directory

MULLER, MINTZ, KORNREICH, CALDWELL, CASEY, CROSLAND & BRAMNICK, P.A. (AV)

Suite 1525 Citrus Center, 255 South Orange Avenue, 32801
Telephone: 407-843-1400
Facsimile: 407-843-1410
URL: http://www.mullermintz.com
Miami Office: Suite 3600 First Union Financial Center, 200 South Biscayne Boulevard.
Telephone: 305-358-5500, Broward: 954-522-0393.

David V. Kornreich
James C. Crosland
Michael W. Casey, III
James S. Bramnick
Jeffrey E. Mandel

Teresa Adamson Herrmann
Benton N. Wood
James W. Seegers

Representative Clients: Florida Power & Light Co.; Universal Studios Escape; J.C. Penney Co.; The Boeing Company; Carnival Corporation; Nabisco Foods Group; Palm Beach County; Volusia County; Seminole County; Pasco County.

For full biographical listings, see the Martindale-Hubbell Law Directory

PALM HARBOR, Pinellas Co.

FLORIN, ROEBIG, WALKER, HUDDLESTUN & ROGERS, P.A. (AV)

777 Alderman Road, 34683
Telephone: 727-786-5000
Toll Free in FL: 800-226-6581
Fax: 727-772-9833
Email: frw@gte.net *URL:* http://www.florinroebig.com

Wil H. Florin
H. Dennis Rogers
Thomas D. Roebig, Jr.
Angela E. Outten
Michael L. Walker
Wolfgang M. Florin
James E. Huddlestun
Christopher D. Gray

OF COUNSEL

Jeffrey G. Brown

For full biographical listings, see the Martindale-Hubbell Law Directory

ST. PETERSBURG, Pinellas Co.

STEIN, FORD, SCHAAF & TOWZEY, L.L.P. (AV)

501 First Avenue North, Suite 1000, 33701
Telephone: 727-894-4333
Fax: 727-894-0175

Henry A. Stein
Gary M. Schaaf
Harvey A. Ford
Phyllis J. Towzey
Paul A. Nelson
Sarah E. Williams

For full biographical listings, see the Martindale-Hubbell Law Directory

*SARASOTA,** Sarasota Co.

KUNKEL MILLER & HAMENT (AV)

Southtrust Bank Building, 1800 Second Street Suite 970, 34236
Telephone: 941-365-6006
1-800-828-7133
Telecopier: 941-365-6209
Email: KMH@laborattys.com *URL:* http://www.laborattys.com
Fort Myers, Florida Office: Suntrust Bank Building, 12751 New Brittany Boulevard, Suite 405.
Telephone: 941-278-1600.
Telecopier: 941-278-4787.
Tampa, Florida Office: Magdalene Center, 15438 North Florida Avenue, Suite 202.
Telephone: 813-963-7736.
Telefax: 813-969-3639.

(See Next Column)

KUNKEL MILLER & HAMENT—*Continued*

MEMBERS OF FIRM

Daniel H. Kunkel
Michael R. Miller
John M. Hament

Timothy N. Tack
Stephanie B. Purvis
Lorraine Maass Hultman
Nikhil N. Joshi

LEGAL SUPPORT PERSONNEL

Travis Campbell

Representative Clients: Bon Secours Hospitals; Century Bank; Florida Coca-Cola Enterprises, Inc.; S rarsota Bank; K-Mart Corporation; National Car Rental System, Inc.; Sun Coast Media Group, Inc.; Florida Health Care Association; Manatee Memorial Hospital; Florida Aluminum and Steel Fabricators.

For full biographical listings, see the Martindale-Hubbell Law Directory

WILLIAMS, PARKER, HARRISON, DIETZ & GETZEN, PROFESSIONAL ASSOCIATION (AV)

200 South Orange Avenue, 34236-6749
Telephone: 941-366-4800
Telecopier: 941-366-5109
Mailing Address: P.O. Box 3258, Sarasota, Florida, 34230-3258
Email: infodesk@williamsparker.com *URL:* http://www.williamsparker.com

John V. Cannon, III
Elvin W. Phillips
Frank Strelec
Kimberly Page Walker

General Counsel for: Sarasota County Public Hospital Board; Sarasota-Manatee Airport Authority; Taylor Woodrow Homes Ltd.; FCCI Mutual Insurance Co.
Local Counsel for: Bank of America; Northern Trust Bank of Florida; SunTrust Bank, Gulfcoast.

For Complete List of Firm Personnel, See General Section

For full biographical listings, see the Martindale-Hubbell Law Directory

*TALLAHASSEE,** Leon Co.

COOPER, COPPINS & MONROE, P.A. (AV)

1319 Thomaswood Drive P.O. Drawer 14447, 32317-4447
Telephone: 850-422-2420
Facsimile: 850-422-2730
Email: info@law-ccm.com

John C. Cooper
D. Lloyd Monroe IV
Michael F. Coppins
Gwendolyn P. Adkins

Floy M. Busby
Holly Ashby Dincman
David B. Switalski
Henry J. Graham
Dorothy Moseley Ridgway

Reference: Sun Trust Bank of Tallahassee.

For full biographical listings, see the Martindale-Hubbell Law Directory

POLSTON, DEAN & HEALY, P.A. (AV)

Suite 900, Highpoint Center, 106 East College Avenue (32301), P.O. Box 1836, 32302-1836
Telephone: 850-513-0404
Fax: 850-681-0506
Email: polston@polstonlaw.com *URL:* http://www.lawyers.com/polstonlaw

Ricky L. Polston
James J. Dean
David P. Healy

For full biographical listings, see the Martindale-Hubbell Law Directory

*TAMPA,** Hillsborough Co.

AYE LAW FIRM, P.A. (AV)

610 W. Azeele Street, 33606
Telephone: 813-221-2112
FAX: 813-254-4799
Email: WEAPA@NELA.ORG

Walter Edwards Aye

For full biographical listings, see the Martindale-Hubbell Law Directory

FECHTER & DICKSON, P.A. (AV)

1201 Swann Avenue, 33606
Telephone: 813-254-2404
Facsimile: 813-254-7750

Adrienne Fechter
Thomas W. Dickson
Luis Cabassa

For full biographical listings, see the Martindale-Hubbell Law Directory

FORD & HARRISON LLP (AV)

101 E. Kennedy Boulevard Suite 900, 33602
Telephone: 813-261-7800
Fax: 813-261-7899
Email: firm@fordharrison.com *URL:* http://www.fordharrison.com
Atlanta, Georgia Office: 600 Peachtree at the Circle Building, 1275 Peachtree Street, N.E. 30309.
Telephone: 404-888-3800.
Fax: 404-888-3863.
Los Angeles, California Office: 333 South Grand Avenue, Suite 3680. 90071.
Telephone: 213-680-3410.
Fax: 213-680-4161.
Memphis, Tennessee Office: 6750 Poplar Avenue, Suite 600, P.O. Box 171375. 38187-1375.
Telephone: 901-756-1550.
Telecopier: 901-756-1016.
Jacksonville, Florida Office: 121 West Forsyth Street, Suite 1000. 32203.
Telephone: 904-356-8073.
Fax: 904-358-2319.
Miami, Florida Office: 516 Ingraham Building, 25 S.E. 2nd Avenue. 33131.
Telephone: 305-379-3811.
Fax: 305-358-5933.
Washington, D.C. Office: 1920 N Street, N.W., Suite 200. 20036.
Telephone: 202-463-6633.
Fax: 202-466-5705.

MEMBERS OF FIRM

Granville M. Alley, Jr. (1929-1976)
Robert D. Hall, Jr. (Resident)
Tony B. Griffin (Resident)
John-Edward Alley
James M. Craig (Resident)
Joseph Z. Fleming
Edmund J. McKenna (Resident)

ASSOCIATES

Todd Sidney Aidman (Resident)
Amy Wright Littrell (Resident)
Youndy C. Cook (Resident)
Jennifer M. Monrose (Resident)
Peter H. Harutunian (Resident)
Melanie C. Parrish (Resident)
David S. Harvey, Jr (Resident)
Tammie L. Rattray (Resident)
Tracey Karen Jaensch (Resident)
Dawn Siler-Nixon (Resident)

Representative Clients: Better Business Forms; Florida Southern College; Opus South Corp.; City of Panama City, Florida; Publix Super Markets, Inc.; Santa Fe Healthcare Systems; Skyline Mobile Homes, Inc.; Southwest Florida Water Management District; Payroll Transfers, Inc.; Val-Pak Direct Marketing System.

For full biographical listings, see the Martindale-Hubbell Law Directory

HAYNSWORTH BALDWIN JOHNSON & GREAVES LLC (AV)

600 North Westshore Boulevard, Suite 200, 33609
Telephone: 813-289-1247
Facsimile: 813-289-6530
Jacksonville, Florida Office: 1301 Riverplace Boulevard, Suite 800, P.O. Box 40593.
Telephone: 904-396-3000.
Greenville, South Carolina Office: 918 South Pleasantburg Drive, P.O. Box 10888.
Telephone: 864-271-7410.
Columbia, South Carolina Office: 1201 Main Street, Suite 1230.
Telephone: 803-799-5858.
Raleigh, North Carolina Office: 3605 Glenwood Avenue, Suite 210, P.O. Box 10035.
Telephone: 919-782-3340.
Greensboro, North Carolina Office: 2709 Henry Street, P.O. Box 13310.
Telephone: 336-375-9737.
Charlotte, North Carolina Office: 400 West Trade Street.
Telephone: 704-342-2588.

MEMBERS OF FIRM

Knox L. Haynsworth, Jr. (Not admitted in FL)
Bradley R. Johnson (Resident)
Grant D. Petersen (Resident)
M. Kristen Allman (Resident)

Marc R. Edelman (Resident)
Lydia M. Nicosia (Resident)

Representative Clients: The Bank of Tampa; Burger King Corporation; Frito-Lay, Inc.; Group Technologies Corporation; Indian River Memorial Hospital, Inc.; Kmart Corp.; J.C. Penney Company, Inc.; PepsiCo, Inc.; Tropicana Products, Inc.; Wellcraft Marine Corporation.

For full biographical listings, see the Martindale-Hubbell Law Directory

KUNKEL MILLER & HAMENT (AV)

Magdalene Center, 15438 North Florida Avenue Suite 202, 33631
Telephone: 813-963-7736
1-800-828-7133
Fax: 813-969-3639
Email: KMH@laborattys.com *URL:* http://www.laborattys.com
Sarasota, Florida Office: Southtrust Bank Building, 1800 Second Street, Suite 970.
Telephone: 813-365-6006.
Telecopier: 813-365-6209.

(See Next Column)

KUNKEL MILLER & HAMENT, *Tampa—Continued*

Fort Myers, Florida Office: Suntrust Bank Building, 12751 New Brittany Boulevard, Suite 405.
Telephone: 941-278-1600.
Telecopier: 941-278-4787.

MEMBERS OF FIRM

Daniel H. Kunkel
Michael R. Miller
John M. Hament

Timothy N. Tack
Stephanie B. Purvis
Lorraine Maass Hultman
Nikhil N. Joshi

LEGAL SUPPORT PERSONNEL

Travis Campbell

Representative Clients: Bon Secours Hospitals; Century Bank; Florida Coca-Cola Enterprises, Inc.; S arasota Bank; K-Mart Corporation; National Car Rental System, Inc.; Sun Coast Media Group, Inc.; Florida Health Care Association; Manatee Memorial Hospital; Florida Aluminum and Steel Fabricators.

For full biographical listings, see the Martindale-Hubbell Law Directory

MALFITANO CAMPBELL & DICKINSON (AV)

100 West Kennedy Boulevard, Suite 500, 33602
Telephone: 813-223-7166
Fax: 813-223-2515
Mailing Address: P.O. Box 1840, Tampa, FL, 33602
Email: mcd-tpa@usa.net
Lakeland, Florida Office: 500 South Florida Avenue, Suite 600, 33801.
Telephone: 941-682-0916.
Jacksonville, Florida Office: 300 West Adams Street, Suite 650, 32202.
Telephone: 904-356-8900.
Facsimile: 904-356-8200.

Michael D. Malfitano
John F. Dickinson
John W. Campbell
F. Damon Kitchen

Angelique Groza Lyons
Margaret A. Philips
V. Ross Spano

For full biographical listings, see the Martindale-Hubbell Law Directory

ZINOBER & MCCREA, P.A. (AV)

SouthTrust Plaza, 201 East Kennedy Boulevard Suite 850, P.O. Box 1378, 33602
Telephone: 813-224-9004
Telecopier: 813-223-4881
Email: Info@zmlaw.com

Peter W. Zinober
Frank E. Brown
Richard C. McCrea, Jr.
Karen Meyer Buesing

Shane T. Muñoz
M. Sean Moyles
Nancy A. Chad
Luisette Gierbolini
Cynthia L. May
Jennifer M. Fowler
Scott T. Silverman
Ryan D. Barack
Melanie J. LaFond
Charles M. Deal
Danielle R. May
Erich Y. Schultz

LEGAL SUPPORT PERSONNEL

Debra A. Douglas (Administrator)

For full biographical listings, see the Martindale-Hubbell Law Directory

*WEST PALM BEACH,** Palm Beach Co.

CHRISTINE D. HANLEY & ASSOCIATES, P.A. (AV)

(Formerly Christine D. Wilburn & Associates, P.A.)
1000 Southern Boulevard Second Floor, 33405
Telephone: 561-659-5646
Fax: 561-659-1260
URL: http://www.cdhanley.com

Christine D. Hanley

Karen M. Nissen
Christine R. Sensenig
Donna M. DiChiara

OF COUNSEL

Diane L. Beauchesne (Not admitted in FL)
Carol A. Fulton

For full biographical listings, see the Martindale-Hubbell Law Directory

HOGG, RYCE & HUDSON (AV)

515 North Flagler Drive, 3rd Floor Pavillion, 33401
Telephone: 561-802-4155
Fax: 561-802-4156
Miami, Florida Office: 80 S.W. 8th Street. Suite 2000. 33130.
Telephone: 305-539-3787.
Fax: 305-665-5526.

(See Next Column)

Miami Beach, Florida Office: 5151 North Flagler Drive, Suite 1036. 33140.
Telephone: 305-864-1211.
Fax: 305-864-4161.

Jesse S. Hogg
Donald T. Ryce
Murray Hudson

For full biographical listings, see the Martindale-Hubbell Law Directory

QUARLES & BRADY LLP (AV)

222 Lakeview Avenue, 4th Floor, 33401
Telephone: 561-653-5000
Fax: 561-653-5333
URL: http://www.quarles.com
Milwaukee, Wisconsin Office: 411 East Wisconsin Avenue, 53202-4497.
Telephone: 414-277-5000.
Fax: 414-271-3552.
Madison, Wisconsin Office: Firstar Plaza, One South Pinckney Street, P.O. Box 2113, 53701-2113.
Telephone: 608-251-5000.
Fax: 608-251-9166.
Naples, Florida Office: Barnett Center, 4501 Tamiami Trail North, Suite 300, 34103-3060.
Telephone: 941-262-5959.
Fax: 941-434-4999.
Phoenix, Arizona Office: One Camelback Building, One East Camelback Road, Suite 400, 85012-1649.
Telephone: 602-230-5500.
Fax: 602-230-5598.
Chicago, Illinois Office: Quarles & Brady LLC, Citicorp Center, 500 West Madison Street, Suite 3700.
Telephone: 312-715-5000.
Fax: 312-715-5155.

PARTNERS

J. Rodman Steele, Jr.
Nancy Berz Colman
Ned R. Nashban
Joseph W. Bain
Gregory A. Nelson
Robert J. Sacco

OF COUNSEL

John S. Sammond

ASSOCIATES

Mark D. Passler
Scott D. Paul
Stanley A. Kim
Steven M. Greenberg

BUSINESS MANAGEMENT SUPPORT PERSONNEL

OFFICE MANAGER

Nadean R. Stone

LEGAL ASSISTANTS

Jacquelyn Brookings
Leneah R. Davis
Carol Cavallerano
Susan Hess
Linda C. Clemons
Janet E. Townsend

For full biographical listings, see the Martindale-Hubbell Law Directory

J. DAVID RICHESON & ASSOCIATES, P.A. (AV)

Suite 900 Forum III Building, 1655 Palm Beach Lakes Boulevard, 33401
Telephone: 561-689-6660
Fort Pierce, Florida Office: 317 South 2nd Street, P.O. Box 4048, 34948.
Telephone: 561-465-5111.

J. David Richeson

Elizabeth Coke
David Miklas

For full biographical listings, see the Martindale-Hubbell Law Directory

SEARCY DENNEY SCAROLA BARNHART & SHIPLEY, PROFESSIONAL ASSOCIATION (AV)

2139 Palm Beach Lakes Boulevard, P.O. Drawer 3626, 33402-3626
Telephone: 561-686-6300
800-780-8607
800-220-7006 (Spanish)
Fax: 561-478-0754
Email: CDS@SEARCYLAW.COM *URL:* http://www.searcylaw.com

Earl L. Denney, Jr.
John Scarola
William B. King

Ellen F. Brandt

LEGAL SUPPORT PERSONNEL

Deane L. Cady (Paralegal/Investigator)

For Complete List of Firm Personnel, See General Section

For full biographical listings, see the Martindale-Hubbell Law Directory

GEORGIA

*ATLANTA,** Fulton Co.

ARNOLD & ANDERSON (AV)

2500 Windy Ridge Parkway, Suite 1250, 30339-5681
Telephone: 770-541-4940
Fax: 770-541-4954

MEMBERS OF FIRM

John K. Anderson
David H. Grigereit
Kevin P. Hishta
John G. Skinner

ASSOCIATE

Holli D. (Colburn) Hidden

OF COUNSEL

John M. Arnold
James P. Swann, Jr.

LEGAL SUPPORT PERSONNEL

Deborah M. Butler (Legal Administrator)
Denise D. Lanier (Paralegal and Legal Administration)

Representative Clients: EBCO Manufacturing Co.; Flowers Bakeries, Inc.; Flowers Industries, Inc.; Golf Host Resorts, Inc. d/b/a "Tamarron Hilton Resort"; Mrs. Smith's Bakeries, Inc.; Mother's Cake & Cookie Co.; My Bread Baking Co.; Petrie Retail, Inc.; President Baking Co., Inc.

For full biographical listings, see the Martindale-Hubbell Law Directory

STEVEN D. BARNHART & ASSOCIATES, P.C. (AV)

One Georgia Center, Suite 2450, 600 West Peachtree Street, N.W., 30308-3605
Telephone: 404-874-2660
Facsimile: 404-874-2357

Steven D. Barnhart

Ken E. Jarrard
Regina T. Stamps
Michelle P. Badaruddin
Jami E. Philpott
Lara G. Cullinane

For full biographical listings, see the Martindale-Hubbell Law Directory

ELARBEE, THOMPSON & TRAPNELL, LLP (AV)

800 International Tower, 229 Peachtree Street, N.E., 30303
Telephone: 404-659-6700
Fax: 404-222-9718
Email: info@elarbeethompson.com *URL:* http://www.elarbeethompson.com

MEMBERS OF FIRM

Fred W. Elarbee, Jr. (1925-1986)
Robert L. Thompson
John R. Trapnell
David M. Vaughan
John Lewis Sapp
William M. Earnest
Walter O. Lambeth, Jr.
Joseph M. Freeman
Stanford G. Wilson
Brent L. Wilson
Victor A. Cavanaugh
Nancy F. Reynolds
Sharon Parker Morgan
Mark D. Halverson
R. Read Gignilliat
Douglas H. Duerr
Victor J. Maya
William Drummond Deveney
Kelly Michael Hundley

ASSOCIATES

Patrick L. Lail
Kenneth N. Winkler
Laura K. Johnson
G. Cornelius Nevitt
Scott E. Atwood
Alisa L. Pittman
Richard M. Escoffery
C. Shawn Jones
Jeffrey B. Kent
Lance P. McMillian
Annette A. Idalski
Nicole A. Richardson

Representative Clients: Cox Communications, Inc.; Dunlop Tire Corp.; National Service Industries; Atlanta Gas Light Co.; Brown & Williamson Tobacco Corp.; Engelhard Corp.; Louisiana-Pacific Corp.; MCI WorldCom; Florida Power and Light Co.; Southwire Co.

For full biographical listings, see the Martindale-Hubbell Law Directory

FAIN, MAJOR, WILEY & BRENNAN, P.C. (AV)

100 Glenridge Point Parkway Suite 500, 30342-1440
Telephone: 404-688-6633
Telecopier: 404-420-1544

Gene A. Major
Charles A. Wiley, Jr.
Darryl G. Haynes

Brian Alligood

Representative Clients: Allstate Insurance Co.; Budget Rent-A-Car; Arkansas Best Corp.; Chrysler Insurance Co.; Georgia Farm Bureau Mutual Insurance Co.; Hertz Corp.; Universal Underwriters Insurance Co.; Westfield Insurance Co.; Winn-Dixie Stores, Inc.

For Complete List of Firm Personnel, See General Section

For full biographical listings, see the Martindale-Hubbell Law Directory

FISHER & PHILLIPS LLP (AV)

A Limited Liability Partnership including Professional Corporations and Professional Associations
1500 Resurgens Plaza, 945 East Paces Ferry Road, N.E., 30326
Telephone: 404-231-1400
Telecopier: 404-240-4249
Email: fp@laborlawyers.com *URL:* http://www.laborlawyers.com
Fort Lauderdale, Florida Office: Suite 2300 NationsBank Tower, One Financial Plaza, 33394.
Telephone: 954-525-4800.
Telecopier: 954-525-8739.
Redwood City, California Office: Suite 345, Three Lagoon Drive, 94065.
Telephone: 650-592-6160.
Telecopier: 650-592-6385.
Newport Beach, California Office: 4675 MacArthur Court, Suite 550, 92660.
Telephone: 949-851-2424.
Telecopier: 949-851-0152.
New Orleans, Louisiana Office: 201 St. Charles Avenue, Suite 3710, 70170.
Telephone: 504-522-3303.
Telecopier: 504-529-3850.
Houston, Texas Office: 6850 Chase Tower, 600 Travis, 77002.
Telephone: 713-227-5410.
Telecopier: 713-236-6949.
Chicago, Illinois Office: 420 Marquette Building, 140 South Dearborn Street, 60603.
Telephone: 312-346-8061.
Telecopier: 312-346-3179.

MEMBERS OF FIRM

I. Walter Fisher (1914-1994)
Erle Phillips (1920-1999)
Robert J. Berghel (P.C.)
Donald E. Wright (P.C.)
Charles Kelso
Donald B. Harden (P.C.)
H. Victor Hansen (P.C.)
Robert W. Ashmore
John M. Capron
James M. Walters
Claud L. McIver, III, (P.C.)
Henry A. Huettner
Ned A. Fine (Resident Partner, Redwood City, California Office)
Griffin B. Bell, Jr.
William F. Kaspers (P.C.)
Dean E. Rice (P.C.)
Reginald J. Bell
Michael C. Towers
Robert C. Christenson
Ralph J. Zatzkis (Partner, New Orleans, Louisiana and Houston, Texas Offices)
Charles S. Caulkins (P.A.) (Resident Partner, Fort Lauderdale, Florida Office)
Robert J. Bekken (Resident Partner, Newport Beach, California Office)
Ann Margaret Pointer
Michael S. Mitchell (Resident Partner, New Orleans, Louisiana Office)
F. Kytle Frye, III
John E. Donovan
John E. Thompson
Thomas P. Rebel
Benjamin B. Culp, Jr.
Ruth W. Woodling
Douglas R. Sullenberger
Mairen C. Kelly
James D. Morgan (Resident Partner, New Orleans, Louisiana Office)
Sandra Mills Feingerts (Resident Partner, New Orleans, Louisiana Office)
James F. Hendricks, Jr. (Resident Partner, Chicago, Illinois Office)
Roger K. Quillen
John B. Gamble, Jr.
Walter J. Kruger, III
John D. McLachlan (Resident Partner, Redwood City, California Office)
Burton F. Dodd
Christopher D. Robinson (P.A.) (Resident Partner, Fort Lauderdale, Florida Office)
Lawrence S. McGoldrick
D. Albert Brannen
James J. McDonald, Jr. (Resident Partner, Newport Beach, California Office)
Howard A. Mavity
Robert P. Foster
David R. Kresser
David C. Whitlock
Keith B. Romich
Charles A. Hawkins
Andria Lure Ryan
Cynthia L. Gleason
Kurt N. Peterson
Karl R. Lindegren (Resident Partner, Newport Beach, California Office)
James C. Polkinghorn (P.A.) (Resident Partner, Fort Lauderdale, Florida Office)
Kenneth A. Knox (P.A.) (Resident Partner, Fort Lauderdale, Florida Office)
Robert V. Schnitz (Resident Partner, Newport Beach, California Office)
Lynn D. Lieber (Resident Partner, Redwood City, California Office)
Steven M. Bernstein
Joseph M. English
Stephen J. Roppolo (Resident, New Orleans, Louisiana Office)
Robert Yonowitz (Resident, Newport Beach, California Office)
Christine E. Howard
Kenneth J. Barr
Michael D. Kabat
John M. Polson (Resident, Newport Beach, California Office)
Paul T. Ryan

OF COUNSEL

Deborah R. Walworth (Resident, New Orleans, Louisiana Office)
Susan Whittington Leidner (Resident, New Orleans, Louisiana Office)

(See Next Column)

FISHER & PHILLIPS LLP, *Atlanta—Continued*

ASSOCIATES

Gary E. Thomas
Ilene Weisbard Berman
Tillman Y. Coffey
Timothy R. Maguire
Myra K. Creighton
Suzanne K. Bogdan (Resident, Fort Lauderdale, Florida Office)
Timothy H. Scott (Resident, New Orleans, Louisiana Office)
Lyne A. Richardson (Resident, Newport Beach, California Office)
Cynthia Walker Lane (Resident, Newport Beach, California Office)
Cathy M. Stutin (Resident, Fort Lauderdale, Florida Office)
C. R. Wright
Donald E. Cope (Resident, Redwood City, California Office)
Tracy L. Moon, Jr.
Kelly Lynn Kubes
Jeffrey B. Freid (Resident, Newport Beach, California Office)
Anderson B. Scott
Allison E. Thornton
Warren Lee Nelson (Resident, Newport Beach, California Office)
Howard B. Jackson
John Phillip Boggs (Resident, Redwood City, California Office)
Bryan T. White
Carlton C. Pilger
Anne M. Terra (Resident, Newport Beach, California Office)
Michelle C. Hamilton
Kristina M. Kerwin (Resident, Houston, Texas Office)
Christopher C. Hoffman (Resident, Newport Beach, California Office)
Joseph P. Shelton
Trisha M. Earls
Debbie A. Dickinson
Jennifer L. Futch (Resident, Newport Beach, California Office)
Michael K. Perkins (Resident, Redwood City, California Office)
David A. Roberts
Kristen L. Sampo (Resident, Fort Lauderdale, Florida Office)
John K. Skousen (Resident, Newport Beach, California Office)
John E. Lattin, IV (Resident, Newport Beach, California Office)
Maria C. Blanco
Daniel S. Fellner
Jason J. Stout
Wendy J. Smith (Resident, Fort Lauderdale, Florida Office)
Darren T. Horvath
Christina T. Nguyen (Resident, Newport Beach, California Office)
Ashley Howell Kaplan (Resident, Fort Lauderdale, Florida Office)
Dorian L. Lobman (Resident, New Orleans, Louisiana Office)
Maureen J. Hernandez
Kevin V. Dunphy (Resident, Chicago, Illinois Office)
Karen M. Kahane (Resident, Fort Lauderdale, Florida Office)
Kimberly N. Martin
Daniel G. Taylor
David A. Hosilyk (Resident, Redwood City, California Office)
Brian A. Davis (Resident, Fort Lauderdale, Florida Office)
Mark A. Seif (Resident, Newport Beach, California Office)
Jennifer B. Sandberg
Janel D. Ortengren
Stephen P. Gilmartin
Amanda C. Salter
Michael L. Fantaci (Resident, New Orleans, Louisiana Office)
Keith A. Watts
David J. Reese (Resident, Redwood City, California Office)
Maria Masvidal Wilson (Resident, Fort Lauderdale, Florida Office)
Christine Emerson Braugh (Resident, Houston, Texas Office)
Winston G. DeCuir, Jr. (Resident, New Orleans, Louisiana Office)
Scott D. Schneider (Resident, New Orleans, Louisiana Office)
Sheldon J. Blumling
Kayla Dye May
Evan Roberts (Resident, Fort Lauderdale, Florida Office)
Dena G. George
Erik C. Johnson
Robert J. Coursey III
Nancy H. Hasani (Resident, Newport Beach, California Office)
Jerry D. Underwood (Resident, Newport Beach, California Office)

Representative Clients: Airborne Express Corp.; Alaska International Industries, Inc.; Emory University; The Henley Group, Inc.; Miller Brewing Co.; The Prudential Insurance Company of America; United States Sugar Corp.; Yellow Freight System, Inc.

For full biographical listings, see the Martindale-Hubbell Law Directory

FORD & HARRISON LLP (AV)

600 Peachtree at the Circle Building, 1275 Peachtree Street, N.E., 30309
Telephone: 404-888-3800
FAX: 404-888-3863
Email: firm@fordharrison.com *URL:* http://www.fordharrison.com
Los Angeles, California Office: 333 South Grand Avenue, Suite 3680. 90071.
Telephone: 213-680-3410.
Fax: 213-680-4161.
Memphis, Tennessee Office: 6750 Poplar Avenue, Suite 600. P.O. Box 171375. 38187-1375.
Telephone: 901-756-1550.
Telecopier: 901-756-1016.

(See Next Column)

Miami, Florida Office: 516 Ingraham Building, 25 S.E. 2nd Avenue. 33131.
Telephone: 305-379-3811.
Fax: 305-358-5933.
Tampa, Florida Office: 101 E. Kennedy Boulevard, Suite 900. 33602.
Telephone: 813-261-7800.
Fax: 813-261-7899.
Washington, D.C. Office: 1920 N Street, N.W., Suite 200. 20036.
Telephone: 202-463-6633.
Fax: 202-466-5705.

MEMBERS OF FIRM

Robert L. McKnight (1906-1976)
Granville M. Alley, Jr. (1929-1976)
William F. Ford (1936-1990)
F. Carter Tate (1943-1999)
C. Lash Harrison
Fletcher L. Hudson (Resident, Memphis, Tennessee Office)
John-Edward Alley (At Miami and Tampa, Florida Offices)
Joseph Z. Fleming
Michael L. Lowry
Ronald C. Henson (Resident, Washington, D.C. Office)
David C. Hagaman
Ronald R. Kimzey
Herbert E. Gerson (Resident, Memphis, Tennessee Office)
Robert D. Hall, Jr. (Resident, Tampa, Florida Office)
Keith A. Warren (Resident, Memphis, Tennessee Office)
D. Gerald Coker
Jeffrey W. Bell
Tony B. Griffin (Resident, Tampa, Florida Office)
Thomas J. Kassin
Norman A. Quandt
Louis P. Britt, III (Resident, Memphis, Tennessee Office)
Bennet D. Alsher
Paula A. Hilburn
Mallory E. Phillips, III
Joshua M. Javits (Resident, Washington, D.C. Office)
Claude T. Sullivan
E. Scott Smith
Glen H. Mertens (Resident, Los Angeles, California Office)
Patricia G. Griffith
William N. Hiers, Jr.
Peter F. Munger
Karin A. Verdon
Jon M. Gumbel
Robert E. Rigrish (Resident, Miami, Florida Office)
John L. Monroe, Jr.
Frederick L. Warren, III
James M. Craig (Resident, Tampa, Florida Office)
Francis Thomas Coleman (Resident, Washington, D.C. Office)
Chad A. Shultz
Kari Haugen (Resident, Los Angeles, California Office)
Charles V. Holmes (Resident, Memphis, Tennessee Office)
Edmund J. McKenna (Resident, Tampa, Florida Office)
Robert M. Williams, Jr. (Resident, Memphis, Tennessee Office)
Devon L. Gosnell (Resident, Memphis, Tennessee Office)
Joycelyn L. Fleming
Peter J. Petesch (Resident, Washington, D.C. Office)
David A. Rosenberg (Resident, Washington, D.C. Office)

SENIOR COUNSEL

Patricia Greene Butler
Dannie B. Fogleman (Resident, Washington, D.C. Office)
Brian L. Kuhn (Resident, Memphis, Tennessee Office)
Thomas J. Walsh, Jr. (Resident, Memphis, Tennessee Office)

ASSOCIATES

Heather C. Alston
Timothy S. Bland (Resident, Memphis, Tennessee Office)
Jefferson B. Blandford
Richard E. Circeo (Resident, Memphis, Tennessee Office)
Carrie Lynn Clark (Resident, Memphis, Tennessee Office)
Patrick F. Clark
Youndy Cook (Resident, Tampa, Florida Office)
Timothy L. Covington
Caroline Wight Donaldson (Resident, Washington, D.C. Office)
Maral Donoyan (Resident, Los Angeles, California Office)
Frederick L. Douglas
A. Bradley Dozier, Jr.
Marc J. Esposito
Blair Beavers Evans (Resident, Memphis, Tennessee Office)
Carolyn K. Fisher
Pedro P. Forment (Resident, Miami, Florida Office)
Michele L. Fowler (Resident, Memphis, Tennessee Office)
Michael J. Gaugh (Resident, Washington, D.C. Office)
Ellen C. Ham
Michelle S. Harkavy (Resident, Memphis, Tennessee Office)
Peter H. Harutunian (Resident, Tampa, Florida Office)
David S. Harvey, Jr (Resident, Tampa, Florida Office)
David A. Hoffman
Brian M. Holbrook (Resident, Los Angeles, California Office)
Tracey Karen Jaensch (Resident, Tampa, Florida Office)
Wendy Suzanne Keller (Resident, Los Angeles, California Office)
Raazia A. Khan
Jose I. Leon (Resident, Miami, Florida Office)
Steven J. Lewengrub
Amy Wright Littrell (Resident, Tampa, Florida Office)
Ross E. Longood
Reagan F. McClellan
Andrew D. McClintock
Kevin J. Mencke
Leanne C. Mehrman
Jeffrey D. Mokotoff
Jennifer M. Monrose (Resident, Tampa, Florida Office)
Carl Knox Morrison (Resident, Memphis, Tennessee Office)
Ashley Swain Old (Resident, Memphis, Tennessee Office)
M. Elizabeth Ortega
Sarah B. Pierce
Tammie L. Rattray (Resident, Tampa, Florida Office)
Patrick R. Ray, Jr
Stacy M. Riley
Michele L. Sheridan (Resident, Washington, D.C. Office)
Dawn Siler-Nixon (Resident, Tampa, Florida Office)
Delaine R. Smith (Resident, Memphis, Tennessee Office)

(See Next Column)

FORD & HARRISON LLP—*Continued*

ASSOCIATES (Continued)

Nina Q. Smith (Resident, Miami, Florida Office)
Cathleen C. Sutherlin
John L. Telford, Jr
Lilia R. Urquiaga

OF COUNSEL

William B. Paul
James C. Hoover
Kenneth D. Henderson (Resident, Memphis, Tennessee Office)
F. Carlton King, Jr.
Jack B. Albanese
Steven J. Ross
Rebecca D. Cottingham
Glenn R. Bunting

Representative Clients: Carrier Corporation; Columbia/HCA Healthcare Corp.; Continental Airlines, Inc. Corrections Corporation of America; Federal Express Corporation; Knight Publishing Company; LIN Television Corp.; Nestle USA, Inc.; Publix Super Markets, Inc.; Regional Airline Assn.; Darden Restaurants, Inc.

For full biographical listings, see the Martindale-Hubbell Law Directory

FREEMAN MATHIS & GARY, LLP (AV)

100 Galleria Parkway, 16th Floor, 30339-5959
Telephone: 770-818-0000
Fax: 770-937-9960
URL: http://www.fmglaw.com

MEMBERS

Benton J. Mathis, Jr.
Christopher E. Parker
Maureen M. Middleton

ASSOCIATES

Mary Anne Ackourey
Dana Kristin Maine
Jennifer E. Moore
Robert W. Stanley
William H. Buechner, Jr.
Robert W. Capobianco
Faye R. Rosenberg

Representative Clients: AGCO Corporation; Abrams Industries, Inc.; Bill Elliot Racing Team, Inc.; Chicago Title & Trust Co.; Interstate Brands Corp; Leisure Bay Industries, Inc.; Park'N Fly; RaceTrac Petroleum, Inc.; Republic Industries; Security Capital Atlantic.

For full biographical listings, see the Martindale-Hubbell Law Directory

FREEMAN, WRIGHT & HERMAN (AV)

3060 Peachtree Road, N.W. Suite 720, 30305-2240
Telephone: 404-262-2962
Fax: 404-237-1926
Email: bhi@bellsouth.net

MEMBER OF FIRM

Joe C. Freeman, Jr.

For full biographical listings, see the Martindale-Hubbell Law Directory

GARLAND, SAMUEL & LOEB, P.C. (AV)

3151 Maple Drive, N.E., 30305
Telephone: 404-262-2225
Fax: 404-365-5041
Email: triallaw@atlanta.com

Robin N. Loeb

For full biographical listings, see the Martindale-Hubbell Law Directory

GOLDNER, SOMMERS, SCRUDDER & BASS (AV)

900 Circle 75 Parkway Suite 850, 30339
Telephone: 770-612-9200
Facsimile: 770-612-9201

MEMBERS OF FIRM

Glenn S. Bass
Linda Jacobsen Pollock

For Complete List of Firm Personnel, See General Section

For full biographical listings, see the Martindale-Hubbell Law Directory

IRVIN, STANFORD & KESSLER, LLP (AV)

One Buckhead Plaza, 3060 Peachtree Road, Suite 1050, 30305
Telephone: 404-237-1020
Fax: 404-237-1047

MEMBERS OF FIRM

Ann Hale-Smith
A. McArthur Irvin
Sandra Kaye
Gary R. Kessler
Rhonda L. Klein
Gregory S. Richters
E. Ray Stanford, Jr.

For full biographical listings, see the Martindale-Hubbell Law Directory

JACOBS AND SLAWSKY, P.A. (AV)

1950 Equitable Building, 100 Peachtree Street, N.W., 30303
Telephone: 404-522-4280
Fax: 404-527-5907
Email: lawfirm-jjd@mindspring.com

(See Next Column)

Harris Jacobs (1930-1993)
Joseph Jacobs (1908-1998)
Norman J. Slawsky
David J. Worley

Reference: First Union National Bank.

For full biographical listings, see the Martindale-Hubbell Law Directory

JONES, DAY, REAVIS & POGUE (AV)

3500 SunTrust Plaza, 303 Peachtree Street, 30308-3242
Telephone: 404-521-3939
Telecopier: 404-581-8330
Email: counsel@jonesday.com *URL:* http://www.jonesday.com
In Brussels, Belgium: Avenue Louise 480, 7th Floor, B-1050 Brussels.
Telephone: 32-2-645-14-11.
Telecopier: 32-2-645-14-45.
In Chicago, Illinois: 77 West Wacker.
Telephone: 312-782-3939.
Telecopier: 312-782-8585.
In Cleveland, Ohio: North Point. 901 Lakeside Avenue.
Telephone: 216-586-3939.
Telecopier: 216-579-0212.
In Columbus, Ohio: 1900 Huntington Center.
Telephone: 614-469-3939.
Telecopier: 614-461-4198.
In Dallas, Texas: 2727 North Harwood Street.
Telephone: 214-220-3939.
Telecopier: 214-969-5100.
In Frankfurt, Germany: Hochhaus am Park, Grüneburgweg 102, 60323 Frankfurt am Main.
Telephone: 49-69-9726-3939.
Telecopier: 49-69-9726-3993.
In Geneva, Switzerland: 20, rue de Candolle.
Telephone: 41-22-320-2339.
Telecopier: 41-22-320-1232.
In Hong Kong: 29th Floor, Entertainment Building, 30 Queen's Road Central.
Telephone: 852-2526-6895.
Telecopier: 852-2868-5871 or 852-2868-5699.
In Irvine, California: 5 Park Plaza, Suite 1100.
Telephone: 949-851-3939.
Telecopier: 949-553-7539.
In London, England: Bucklersbury House, 3 Queen Victoria Street.
Telephone: 44-171-236-3939.
Telecopier: 44-171-236-1113.
In Los Angeles, California: 555 West Fifth Street, Suite 4600.
Telephone: 213-489-3939.
Telecopier: 213-243-2539.
In New Delhi, India (Associate Office): Pathak & Associates (an associate firm of Jones, Day, Reavis & Pogue), 1st Floor, Dr. Gopal Das Bhaven, 28 Barakhamba Road.
Telephone: 91-11-373-8793; 91-11-335-7345.
Telecopier: 91-11-335-3761.
In New York, New York: 599 Lexington Avenue.
Telephone: 212-326-3939.
Telecopier: 212-755-7306.
In Paris, France: 120, rue du Faubourg Saint-Honoré.
Telephone: 33-1-56-59-39-39.
Telecopier: 33-1-56-59-39-38
In Pittsburgh, Pennsylvania: 500 Grant Street, 31st Floor.
Telephone: 412-391-3939.
Telecopier: 412-394-7959.
In Riyadh, Saudi Arabia: The International Law Firm (In Association with Jones, Day, Reavis & Pogue), Sulaymaniyah, Prince Mishari IBN, Abdulaziz Street, P.O. Box 22166.
Telephone: (966-1) 462-8866.
Telecopier: (966-1) 462-9001.
In Shanghai, China: 2805 Kerry Centre, 1515 Nanjing Road West.
Telephone: 86-21-5298-6568.
Telecopier: 86-21-5298-6569.
In Sydney, Australia: Governor Phillip Tower, Level 38, 1 Farrer Place.
Telephone: 61-2-9210-6921.
Telecopier: 61-2-9210-6926.
In Taipei, Taiwan: 8th Floor, 2 Tun Hwa South Road, Section 2.
Telephone: (886-2) 2704-6808.
Telecopier: (886-2) 2704-6791.
In Tokyo, Japan: Toranomon MT Building, 4th Floor, 10-3, Toranomon 3-Chome, Minato-ku, Tokyo 105, Japan.
Telephone: 81-3-3433-3939.
Telecopier: 81-3-5401-2725.
In Washington, D.C.: 51 Louisiana Avenue, N.W.
Telephone: 202-879-3939.
Telecopier: 202-626-1700.

MEMBER OF FIRM IN ATLANTA

Deborah A. Sudbury

For Complete List of Firm Personnel, See General Section

For full biographical listings, see the Martindale-Hubbell Law Directory

Atlanta—Continued

LONG ALDRIDGE & NORMAN LLP (AV)

A Limited Liability Partnership including Professional Corporations
Suite 5300, 303 Peachtree Street, 30308
Telephone: 404-527-4000
Telecopier: 404-527-4198
Email: atlanta@lanlaw.com *URL:* http://www.lanlaw.com
Washington, D.C. Office: Suite 600, 701 Pennsylvania Avenue, N.W., 20004.
Telephone: 202-624-1200.
FAX: 202-624-1298.

MEMBERS OF FIRM

Phillip A. Bradley
Terry R. Weiss

ASSOCIATES

R. Daniel Beale
Sheryl McCalla

OF COUNSEL

J. Michell Philpott

For Complete List of Firm Personnel, See General Section

For full biographical listings, see the Martindale-Hubbell Law Directory

MARX & MARX (AV Ⓣ)

400 Perimeter Center Terrace, N.E. Suite 900, 30346
Telephone: 404-261-9559
Email: lawmarx@aol.com
New York, New York Office: 575 Madison Avenue, 10022.
Telephone: 212-689-8516.

MEMBERS OF FIRM

Robert N. Marx
Jean Simonoff Marx (Resident)

For full biographical listings, see the Martindale-Hubbell Law Directory

McCULLOUGH SHERRILL, LLP (AV)

1409 Peachtree Street, N.E., 30309
Telephone: 404-885-1500
Telecopier: 404-892-1801
Email: info@mslegal.com *URL:* http://www.mslegal.com

MEMBER OF FIRM

Allen W. Groves

ASSOCIATES

Jana L. Evans
Steven M. Staes

For Complete List of Firm Personnel, See General Section

For full biographical listings, see the Martindale-Hubbell Law Directory

OGLETREE, DEAKINS, NASH, SMOAK & STEWART, P.C. (AV)

600 Peachtree Street, N.E., Suite 2100, 30308
Telephone: 404-881-1300
Facsimile: 404-870-1732
Email: Atlanta@odnss.com *URL:* http://www.Ogletreedeakins.com
Washington, D.C. Office: Fifth Floor, 2400 N Street, N.W.
Telephone: 202-887-0855.
Houston, Texas Office: One Allen Center, 500 Dallas Street, Suite 3000.
Telephone: 713-655-0855.
Chicago, Illinois Office: Twenty-Fifth Floor, Two First National Plaza, 20 South Clark Street.
Telephone: 312-558-1220.
Birmingham, Alabama Office: 1900 SouthTrust Tower, 420 North 20th Street.
Telephone: 205-328-1900.
Nashville, Tennessee Office: SunTrust Center, Suite 800, 424 Church Street.
Telephone: 615-254-1900.
Greenville, South Carolina Office: The Ogletree Building, 300 North Main Street, P.O. Box 2757.
Telephone: 864-271-1300.
Charleston, South Carolina Office: First Union Building, Suite 310, 177 Meeting Street, P.O. Box 1808.
Telephone: 843-853-1300.
Columbia, South Carolina Office: Palmetto Center, Suite 1820, 1426 Main Street, P.O. Box 11206.
Telephone: 803-252-1300.
Raleigh, North Carolina Office: 4101 Lake Boone Trail, Suite 511, P.O. Box 31608.
Telephone: 919-787-9700.
Winston-Salem, North Carolina Office: 150 South Stratford Road, Suite 350.
Telephone: 336-725-2110.

Homer L. Deakins, Jr.
Martha C. Perrin
Wade V. Mallard, Jr.
M. Baker Wyche III
Robert O. Sands
William A. Gray
Margaret Hutchins Campbell
Dara L. DeHaven
David Edward Jones
Jay Michael Barber
James Alfred Southerland
Phillip Lee Conner
C. Thomas Davis
Kristofer K. Strasser
Gregory J. Hare

(See Next Column)

OF COUNSEL

Joseph W. Bryan

Janet Quick Lewis
Calvin Garner Sanford, Jr.
David A. Hughes
Gail E. Farb
Andrea L. Bailey
Debra Dewar
John C. Glancy
Kevin M. Elwell
Tiffani Wedington Greene

Representative Clients: Deere & Co.; Duke Energy Corp.; Eastman Chemical Co.; Fluor Corporation; Mercedes Benz U.S. International, Inc.; Nissan Motor Manufacturing Corporation U.S.A.; R. J. Reynolds Tobacco Co.; Rockwell International; Wachovia Corporation.

For full biographical listings, see the Martindale-Hubbell Law Directory

SMITH, CURRIE & HANCOCK LLP (AV)

2600 Harris Tower-Peachtree Center, 233 Peachtree Street, N.E., 30303-1530
Telephone: 404-521-3800
Telecopier: 404-688-0671
Email: smith-currie-hancock@worldnet.att.net *URL:* http://www.smithcurrie.com

MEMBERS OF FIRM

G. Maynard Smith (1907-1992).
E. Reginald Hancock (Retired)
George K. McPherson, Jr. (Retired)
James Allan Smith (Retired)
Larry E. Forrester (Retired)
Daniel M. Shea
Marty N. Martenson
Paul R. Beshears
Catherine M. Hobart
Suzanne J. Mulliken

ASSOCIATES

Patricia S. Ruark
Robert Kendall Haderlein
Christopher S. Enloe
Matthew T. Gomes
Jennifer S. Friedman
Timothy G. Johnson (Not admitted in GA)

Labor Relations Clients: Dana Corp.; Genuine Parts Co. (NAPA); Piedmont Hospital & Health Services, Inc.; Paragon Trade Brands; Rock-Tenn Company; Lanier Worldwide; John H. Harland Co.; Oxford Industries; Piedmont Hospital Services.

For full biographical listings, see the Martindale-Hubbell Law Directory

STOKES & MURPHY, P.C. (AV)

3593 Hemphill Street, P.O. Box 87468, 30337
Telephone: 404-766-0076
Fax: 404-766-8823
Email: mail@stokesnmurphy.com
San Diego, California Office: 110 West "C" Street, Suite 2020.
Telephone: 619-702-8600.
Fax: 619-702-8610.
Pittsburgh, Pennsylvania Office: Foster Plaza X, 680 Andersen Drive.
Telephone: 412-937-3277.
Fax: 412-920-5751.
Dallas, Texas: 10127 Rita Road.
Telephone: 972-671-4350.
Fax: 972-671-4352.
Windermere, Florida: 2231 Ridgewind Way.
Telephone: 407-909-1095.
Fax: 407-909-0384.

Arch Y. Stokes
Robert L. Murphy (Resident, San Diego Office)
John R. Hunt
Margaret Mead Stokes
Karl M. Terrell
John M. O'Donnell (Not admitted in GA; Resident, Pittsburgh Office)
Paul F. Sorrentino (Not admitted in GA; Resident, San Diego Office)
Carol A. Burkett Hawkins

ASSOCIATES

Anne-Marie Mizel (Not admitted in GA; Resident, Pittsburgh Office)
H. Eric Hilton
Amelia M. Bever
Laurent R. G. Badoux
Regina Silva (Not admitted in GA; Resident, San Diego Office)
John W. Bolanovich (Resident, Atlanta Office)
A. Locke Neely (Resident, Dallas Texas)

For full biographical listings, see the Martindale-Hubbell Law Directory

*BRUNSWICK,** Glynn Co.

WHELCHEL, BROWN, READDICK & BUMGARTNER (AV)

5 Glynn Avenue, P.O. Box 220, 31521-0220
Telephone: 912-264-8544
Telecopier: 912-264-9667

MEMBERS OF FIRM

J. Thomas Whelchel
Richard A. Brown, Jr.
Terry L. Readdick
John E. Bumgartner
B. Kaye Katz

(See Next Column)

WHELCHEL, BROWN, READDICK & BUMGARTNER—*Continued*

ASSOCIATES

G. Todd Carter
Richard K. Strickland
Bradley J. Watkins

Representative Clients: Georgia Power Co.; Sears, Roebuck & Co.; Allstate Insurance Co.; Commercial Union Insurance Co.; Georgia Farm Bureau Mutual Insurance Co.; Government Employees Insurance Co.; Nationwide Insurance Co.; State Farm Insurance Cos.; Wausau Insurance Cos.

For full biographical listings, see the Martindale-Hubbell Law Directory

*CARTERSVILLE,** Bartow Co.

DAVID G. ARCHER, P.C. (AV)

336 South Tennessee Street, P.O. Box 1024, 30120
Telephone: 770-386-1116
Fax: 770-382-7484
Email: dgapc@innerx.net

David G. Archer

E. Keith Lovell
M. Faye McCord

For full biographical listings, see the Martindale-Hubbell Law Directory

*DECATUR,** De Kalb Co.

PATRICIA J. CRAFT, P.C. (AV)

P.O. Box 33765, 30033
Telephone: 404-636-6297
Fax: 404-633-1092

Patricia J. Craft

For full biographical listings, see the Martindale-Hubbell Law Directory

*LAWRENCEVILLE,** Gwinnett Co.

MICHAEL C. MURPHY (AV)

390 West Crogan Street Suite 301, 30045
Telephone: 770-682-5952
Fax: 770-682-5113
Email: michaelcmurphy@worldnet.att.net

For full biographical listings, see the Martindale-Hubbell Law Directory

*SAVANNAH,** Chatham Co.

FORBES & BOWMAN (AV)

Park South D-14, 7505 Waters Avenue, P.O. Box 13929, 31416-0929
Telephone: 912-352-1190
FAX: 912-352-1471

Morton G. Forbes
Catherine McKenzie Bowman
John A. Foster
Scot V. Pool
D. Campbell Bowman, Jr.

Representative Clients: John S. James Co.; Second Harvest Food Bank; Town & Country Extermination Co., Inc.; C.L. Futch Termite Pest Control Services; AmeriGas Propane, L.P.; Regis Corporation; Wal-Mart Stores, Inc.

For full biographical listings, see the Martindale-Hubbell Law Directory

HUNTER, MACLEAN, EXLEY & DUNN, P.C. (AV)

200 East St. Julian Street, P.O. Box 9848, 31412
Telephone: 912-236-0261
Cable Address: "Ancan"
Telecopier: 912-236-4936
Telex: 54-6483
Email: hmed.com *URL:* http://www.bobbs@hmed.com
Atlanta, Georgia Office: The Peachtree, 1355 Peachtree Street, N.E., Suite 640.
Telephone: 404-876-3611.
Fax: 404-870-2025.

Malcolm R. Maclean
Wade W. Herring, II
Kirby Gould Mason
Sarah H. Lamar
Nancy Perry

Representative Clients: CSX Intermodal, Inc.; CUMIS Insurance Society, Inc.; Great Dane Trailers, Inc.; Hershey Food Corporation; Intermarine U.S.A.; Memorial Medical Center, Inc.; Operation Management International; Sea Pines Associates, Inc.; St. Joseph's/Candler Health Systems.

For Complete List of Firm Personnel, See General Section

For full biographical listings, see the Martindale-Hubbell Law Directory

KARSMAN, BROOKS & CALLAWAY, P.C. (AV)

301 West Congress Street, P.O. Box 9149, 31412
Telephone: 912-238-2750
Cable Address: "Karbro"
Telecopier: 912-238-2767

(See Next Column)

Stanley M. Karsman
Charles C. Brooks
Timothy F. Callaway, III
Stanley E. Harris, Jr.
James L. Drake, Jr.
Dana F. Braun
R. Krannert Riddle
Edward M. Hughes
Timothy J. Haeussler

For full biographical listings, see the Martindale-Hubbell Law Directory

HAWAII

*HONOLULU,** Honolulu Co.

CARLSMITH BALL (AV)

A Partnership including Law Corporations
Suite 2200, Pacific Tower, 1001 Bishop Street, P.O. Box 656, 96809-3402
Telephone: 808-523-2500
Fax: 808-523-0842
Email: execdirector@carlsmith.com *URL:* http://www.carlsmith.com
Kapolei, Hawaii Office: Suite 318, Kapolei Building, 1001 Kamokila Boulevard, 96707.
Telephone: 808-523-2500.
Fax: 808-674-0850.
Wailuku, Maui Hawaii Office: Suite 400, One Main Plaza, 2200 Main Street, P.O. Box 1086, 96793-1086.
Telephone: 808-242-4535.
Fax: 808-244-4974.
Kailua-Kona, Hawaii Office: Suite 209, 75-1000 Henry Street, 96740.
Telephone: 808-329-6464.
Fax: 808-329-9450.
Hilo, Hawaii Office: 121 Waianuenue Avenue, P.O. Box 686, 96721-0686.
Telephone: 808-935-6644.
Fax: 808-935-7975.
Hagatna, Guam Office: Suite 401, Bank of Hawaii Building, 134 West Soledad Avenue, P.O. Box BF, 96932-5027.
Telephone: 671-472-6813.
Fax: 671-477-4375.
Telex: 721-6445 CWCMI GM.
Saipan, Commonwealth of the Northern Mariana Islands Office: Carlsmith Building, Capitol Hill, P.O. Box 5241, 96950-5241.
Telephone: 670-322-3455.
Fax: 670-322-3368.
Los Angeles, California Office: 9th Floor, 444 South Flower Street, 90071-2901.
Telephone: 213-955-1200.
Fax: 213-623-0032.
Washington, D.C. Office: Suite 300, 1201 Pennsylvania Avenue, N.W., 20004-2401.
Telephone: 202-628-2228.
Fax: 202-628-2071.
Mexico City, Mexico Office: Carlsmith Ball, Sierra Nevada 119, Lomas de Chapultepec, 11000 Mexico, D.F.
Telephone: 52-5-520-8514, 52-5-520-8757.
Fax: 52-5-540-1545.
Mexico, D.F. Office of Carlsmith Ball, S.C. (Authorized to practice as foreign legal consultants in Mexico): Sierra Nevada 119, Lomas de Chapultepec, 11000 Mexico, D.F.
Telephone: 52-5-520-8514, 52-5-520-8757.
Fax: 52-5-540-1545.

MEMBERS OF FIRM

Anna M. Elento-Sneed
Meredith M. Sayre (Resident at Hagatna, Guam Office)
Marcia K. Schultz (Resident at Saipan Office)
Terry E. Thomason

ASSOCIATES

Joanne L. Grimes
Dana A. Gutierrez (Resident at Hagatna, Guam Office)
Jonathan A. Swanson
Kimilyn C. Tomita
Carol A. Uyeno

OF COUNSEL

Susan Lloyd Harrison Evans (Resident at Kailua-Kona, Hawaii Office)
Tom K. Houston (Resident at Los Angeles, California Office)
Lorraine S. Klevansky

For Complete List of Firm Personnel, See General Section

For full biographical listings, see the Martindale-Hubbell Law Directory

GOODSILL ANDERSON QUINN & STIFEL (AV)

Alii Place, Suite 1800, 1099 Alakea Street, P.O. Box 3196, 96801-3196
Telephone: 808-547-5600
FAX: 808-547-5880
Email: info@goodsill.com *URL:* http://www.goodsill.com

MEMBERS OF FIRM

Barbara A. Petrus
Carol Ann Eblen
A. Richard Philpott

(See Next Column)

GOODSILL ANDERSON QUINN & STIFEL, *Honolulu—Continued*

ASSOCIATES

Carolyn K. Gugelyk
J. Denice von Gnechten

Representative Clients: Bank of Hawaii; Hawaii Residency Programs; Hawaii Pacific University; Hawaiian Electric Industries, Inc.; PrimeCo Personal Communications, L.P.; F. W. Woolworth Co.

For Complete List of Firm Personnel, See General Section

For full biographical listings, see the Martindale-Hubbell Law Directory

MARR HIPP JONES & PEPPER (AV)

Pauahi Tower, 1001 Bishop Street, Suite 1550, 96813
Telephone: 808-536-4900
Fax: 808-536-6700

Barry W. Marr
Kenneth B. Hipp
Patrick H. Jones
Andrew L. Pepper
Steven M. Nakashima

ASSOCIATES

Sarah O. Wang
William C.H. Jarrett
Melanie Mito May
Christopher S. Yeh
Michael W. Garrison, Jr.

For full biographical listings, see the Martindale-Hubbell Law Directory

TAM, O'CONNOR, HENDERSON, TAIRA & YAMAUCHI ATTORNEYS AT LAW, A LAW CORPORATION (AV)

20th Floor, Central Pacific Plaza, 220 South King Street, 96813
Telephone: 808-545-3030
Fax: 808-523-8051
Fax: 808-537-6782
Email: lawyers@50thstatelaw.com

James K. Tam
Michael F. O'Connor
Harvey E. Henderson, Jr.
Lissa H. Andrews
Robert M. Yamauchi
Darryl M. Taira
Stuart M. Kodish

Wesley H. Ikeda
Russ S. Awakuni
Kevin W. Herring
Fred I. Waki

OF COUNSEL

Paul M. Dold

For full biographical listings, see the Martindale-Hubbell Law Directory

TORKILDSON, KATZ, FONSECA, JAFFE, MOORE & HETHERINGTON ATTORNEYS AT LAW, A LAW CORPORATION (AV)

Amfac Building, 15th Floor, 700 Bishop Street, 96813-4187
Telephone: 808-523-6000
Cable Address: "Counsel"
Telex: RCA 723-8185
Telecopier: 808-523-6001
Email: info@torkildson.com
Hilo, Hawaii Office: 100 Pauahi Street, Suite 206.
Telephone: 808-961-0406.
Telecopier: 808-935-6725.

Robert S. Katz
Ernest C. Moore, III
Richard M. Rand
Jeffrey S. Harris
Gregory M. Sato
John L. Knorek
Sabrina R. Toma
Perry W. Confalone
Wayne S. Yoshigai

Clayton A. Kamida
Roman F. Amaguin, Jr.
Paul M. Saito
Tamara M. Gerrard
Karen R. Tashima
Christine S.Y. Chun

Representative Clients: Alexander & Baldwin, Inc.; Aloha Airlines, Inc.; Amfac, Inc.; Castle and Cooke, Inc.; Castle Medical Center; Theo H. Davies and Co., Ltd.; First Hawaiian Bank; General Motors Corp.; Council of Hawaii Hotels.

For Complete List of Firm Personnel, See General Section

For full biographical listings, see the Martindale-Hubbell Law Directory

IDAHO

*BOISE,** Ada Co.

ELAM & BURKE, A PROFESSIONAL ASSOCIATION (AV)

Key Financial Center, 702 West Idaho Street, P.O. Box 1539, 83701
Telephone: 208-343-5454
Telecopier: 208-384-5844
Email: eblaw@elamburke.com

(See Next Column)

Ryan P. Armbruster
Trudy Hanson Fouser
Bobbi Killian Dominick
James A. Ford

Rebecca A. Broadbent

Representative Clients: Morrison-Knudsen, Inc.; State Farm Insurance Cos.; United Heritage Mutual Life Insurance Co.; Con-Agra, Inc.; J.R. Simplot Co.; RiteAid.

For Complete List of Firm Personnel, See General Section

For full biographical listings, see the Martindale-Hubbell Law Directory

ILLINOIS

*CHICAGO,** Cook Co.

ALBERT, WHITEHEAD & MCGAUGH, P.C. (AV)

One South Wacker Drive, Suite 1990, 60606
Telephone: 312-357-6300
Fax: 312-357-6219

Charles G. Albert
Robert Kinchen

Allison L. Wood

For full biographical listings, see the Martindale-Hubbell Law Directory

ARONBERG GOLDGEHN DAVIS & GARMISA (AV)

Suite 3000 One IBM Plaza, 60611
Telephone: 312-828-9600
Telecopier: 312-828-9635
Email: agdglaw@aol.com
Schaumberg, Illinois Office: 1901 North Roselle Road, Suite 800, 60195.
Telephone: 847-985-4060.

MEMBERS OF FIRM

Tami J. Reding-Brubaker
John M. Riccione
Robert N. Sodikoff

For Complete List of Firm Personnel, See General Section

For full biographical listings, see the Martindale-Hubbell Law Directory

BATES MECKLER BULGER & TILSON (AV)

8300 Sears Tower, 233 South Wacker, 60606
Telephone: 312-474-7900
Facsimile: 312-474-7898
URL: http://www.bmbt.com

MEMBERS OF FIRM

Alex V. Barbour
Brian W. Bulger
J. Stuart Garbutt
Paul R. Garry
Michael I. Leonard
Joseph E. Tilson
Brian J Williams
Timothy A. Wolfe

ASSOCIATES

Eileen E. Baker
Robin I. Edelstein
Josh M. Friedman
Peter D. Lindau
Joan E. Maloney
Lisa A. Miller

For full biographical listings, see the Martindale-Hubbell Law Directory

BECKER & KAPLAN LLC (AV)

19 South La Salle Street Suite 1500, 60603
Telephone: 312-621-9500
Fax: 312-621-9011
Email: firm@beckerkaplan.com *URL:* http://www.beckerkaplan.com

Theodore M. Becker
Daniel S. Kaplan

Edward R. White
Michael J. Boxerman

For full biographical listings, see the Martindale-Hubbell Law Directory

BLATT, HAMMESFAHR & EATON (AV)

333 W. Wacker Drive, Suite 1900, 60606
Telephone: 312-849-8000
FAX: 312-357-0198
Email: BHE@BHELAW.COM *URL:* HTTP://WWW.BHELAW.COM
New York, New York Office: 45 Broadway, 12th Floor.
Telephone: 212-363-1900.
Fax: 212-363-2600. Email: bhe@bhelaw.com.

MEMBERS OF FIRM

Hugo Chaviano
Larry R. Eaton
Robert W. Hammesfahr
Kathleen A. McQueeny

(See Next Column)

BLATT, HAMMESFAHR & EATON—*Continued*

ASSOCIATES

Lesley A. Dable
Keith B. Daniels, Jr.
Leena Soni

For full biographical listings, see the Martindale-Hubbell Law Directory

FRANCZEK SULLIVAN P.C. (AV)

Suite 3400, 300 South Wacker Drive, 60606-6785
Telephone: 312-986-0300
FAX: 312-986-9192
URL: http://www.nlfpc.com

Anthony J. Crement
J. Todd Faulkner
James C. Franczek, Jr.
Ronald J. Hein, Jr.
Lisa A. Lopatka
Bruce C. Mackey
Robert E. Mann
Paul A. Millichap
David P. Radelet
John A. Relias
Michael I. Richardson
Charles P. Rose
Sally J. Scott
William R. Sullivan, Jr.
Andrea R. Waintroob
Patricia J. Whitten
James J. Zuehl

Shelli L. Boyer
Sheila M. Conroy
Terrence T. Creamer
Erika Dillon
Edward N. Druck
Gregory D. Isbell
Thomas Koutsouvas
Darcy L. Kriha
Jeffrey M. Kropp
Jeremy C. Moritz
Alec Rubenstein
Leah D. Gidron
Jennifer L. Schilling
Michael A. Warner, Jr.
Anne Elizabeth Wilson

OF COUNSEL

Michael Z. Green
Wesley A. Wildman
John L. Wren

LEGAL SUPPORT PERSONNEL

Caty E. Kearney

For full biographical listings, see the Martindale-Hubbell Law Directory

GESSLER, HUGHES & SOCOL, LTD. (AV)

Three First National Plaza, Suite 2200, 60602
Telephone: 312-580-0100
Telecopy: 312-580-1994

Benjamin P. Beringer
Anjali Dayal
Mark S. Dym
George W. Gessler
John K. Hughes
Joshua Karsh
Peter M. Katsaros
Kimberley Marsh
Alex W. Miller
Terence J. Moran
Matthew J. Piers
Kalman D. Resnick
Frederick S. Rhine
Jonathan A. Rothstein
Michael P. Simkus
Donna Kaner Socol

Gary Chodorow
Ruth M. Dunning
S. Todd Neal
Mark A. Pellegrino
Steven C. Steinback
Dana H. Sukenik
J. Eric Vander Arend
Mark B. Weiner
Charles H. Wintersteen

OF COUNSEL

Darius S. Francescatti, M.D.
Susan R. Gzesh

For full biographical listings, see the Martindale-Hubbell Law Directory

GREENE AND LETTS (AV)

30 North La Salle Street, Suite 1520, 60602
Telephone: 312-346-1100
Telefax: 312-346-4571
Email: greneletts@aol.com

MEMBERS OF FIRM

Martin P. Greene
Eileen M. Letts
Allen P. Walker

ASSOCIATES

Fernando M. Bustamante
Shirley R. Calloway (Not admitted in IL)
Lakeisha R. Mayfield

OF COUNSEL

Kevin T. Lee
Ellen E. Douglass

LEGAL SUPPORT PERSONNEL

Mary Ann Alexander (Legal Assistant)
Barbara Nelson (Legal Assistant)

For full biographical listings, see the Martindale-Hubbell Law Directory

JONES, DAY, REAVIS & POGUE (AV)

77 West Wacker, 60601-1692
Telephone: 312-782-3939
Telecopier: 312-782-8585
Email: counsel@jonesday.com *URL:* http://www.jonesday.com
In Atlanta, Georgia: 3500 SunTrust Plaza, 303 Peachtree Street.
Telephone: 404-521-3939.
Telecopier: 404-581-8330. 34000 Brussels, Belgium: Avenue Louise 480, 7th Floor, B-1050 Brussels.
Telephone: 32-2-645-14-11.
Telecopier: 32-2-645-14-45.
In Cleveland, Ohio: North Point, 901 Lakeside Avenue.
Telephone: 216-586-3939.
Telecopier: 216-579-0212.
In Columbus, Ohio: 1900 Huntington Center.
Telephone: 614-469-3939.
Telecopier: 614-461-4198.
In Dallas, Texas: 2727 North Harwood Street.
Telephone: 214-220-3939.
Telecopier: 214-969-5100.
In Frankfurt, Germany: Hochhaus am Park, Grüneburgweg 102, 60323 Frankfurt am Main.
Telephone: 49-69-9726-3939.
Telecopier: 49-69-9726-3993.
In Geneva, Switzerland: 20, rue de Candolle.
Telephone: 41-22-320-2339.
Telecopier: 41-22-320-1232.
In Hong Kong: 29th Floor, Entertainment Building, 30 Queen's Road Central.
Telephone: 852-2526-6895.
Telecopier: 852-2868-5871 or 852-2868-5699.
In Irvine, California: 5 Park Plaza, Suite 1100.
Telephone: 949-851-3939.
Telecopier: 949-553-7539.
In London, England: Bucklersbury House, 3 Queen Victoria Street.
Telephone: 44-171-236-3939.
Telecopier: 44-171-236-1113.
In Los Angeles, California: 555 West Fifth Street, Suite 4600.
Telephone: 213-489-3939.
Telecopier: 213-243-2539.
In New Delhi, India (Associate Office): Pathak & Associates (an associate firm of Jones, Day, Reavis & Pogue), 1st Floor, Dr. Gopal Das Bhaven, 28 Barakhamba Road.
Telephone: 91-11-373-8793; 91-11-335-7345.
Telecopier: 91-11-335-3761.
In New York, New York: 599 Lexington Avenue.
Telephone: 212-326-3939.
Telecopier: 212-755-7306.
In Paris, France: 120, rue du Faubourg Saint-Honoré.
Telephone: 33-1-56-59-39-39.
Telecopier: 33-1-56-59-39-38
In Pittsburgh, Pennsylvania: 500 Grant Street, 31st Floor.
Telephone: 412-391-3939.
Telecopier: 412-394-7959.
In Riyadh, Saudi Arabia: The International Law Firm (In Association with Jones, Day, Reavis & Pogue), Sulaymaniyah, Prince Mishari IBN, Abdulaziz Street, P.O. Box 22166.
Telephone: (966-1) 462-8866.
Telecopier: (966-1) 462-9001.
In Shanghai, China: 2805 Kerry Centre, 1515 Nanjing Road West.
Telephone: 86-21-5298-6568.
Telecopier: 86-21-5298-6569.
In Sydney, Australia: Governor Phillip Tower, Level 38, 1 Farrer Place.
Telephone: 61-2-9210-6921.
Telecopier: 61-2-9210-6926.
In Taipei, Taiwan: 8th Floor, 2 Tun Hwa South Road, Section 2.
Telephone: (886-2) 2704-6808.
Telecopier: (886-2) 2704-6791.
In Tokyo, Japan: Toranomon MT Building, 4th Floor, 10-3, Toranomon 3-Chome, 34200o-ku, Tokyo 105, Japan.
Telephone: 81-3-3433-3939.
Telecopier: 81-3-5401-2725.
In Washington, D.C.: 51 Louisiana Avenue, N.W.
Telephone: 202-879-3939.
Telecopier: 202-626-1700.

MEMBER OF FIRM IN CHICAGO

Dennis R. Homerin

For Complete List of Firm Personnel, See General Section

For full biographical listings, see the Martindale-Hubbell Law Directory

KAPLAN, BEGY & VON OHLEN (AV)

One First National Plaza 51st Floor, 60603
Telephone: 312-345-3000
Fax: 312-345-3119
URL: http://www.kbvlaw.com

MEMBERS OF FIRM

Fred C. Begy, III
Larry S. Kaplan
James D. Solon
Robert C. von Ohlen, Jr.
Joseph A. Bosco
Richard A. Walker
Mitchell J. Kanaan
Patrick J. Keating

(See Next Column)

KAPLAN, BEGY & VON OHLEN, *Chicago—Continued*

ASSOCIATES

Keith S. Yamaguchi
Thomas C. Sokol
Robert K. Villa
Nicole Halpern Murphy
Telly Andrews
Tamara S. Dykstra

For full biographical listings, see the Martindale-Hubbell Law Directory

LANER, MUCHIN, DOMBROW, BECKER, LEVIN AND TOMINBERG, LTD. (AV)

515 North State Street, Suite 2800, 60610
Telephone: 312-467-9800
Fax: 312-467-9479

Lawrence F. Doppelt (1935-1979)
Arthur B. Muchin
Anthony E. Dombrow
William L. Becker
Alan M. Levin
Carl S. Tominberg
Mark L. Juster
Gary Alan Wincek
Michael Klupchak
Joseph H. Yastrow
Joseph M. Gagliardo
Robert H. Brown
James J. Convery
Robert S. Letchinger
Violet M. Clark
James F. Vanek
Jeffrey P. Carren
Jane E. Shaffer
Jill P. O'Brien
Neil P. Stern
Thomas Vasiljevich
Thomas Bradley
Scott A. Gore
Jeffrey S. Fowler
Maureen A. Gorman
Clifford R. Perry, III

Mark W. Bennett
Robert T. Bernstein
Alejandro Caffarelli
Deborah Glaser Chagal
Robert S. Forman
Andrew S. Goldberg
Gregory R. James, Jr.
Jennifer A. Naber
Katherine O. Porter
Marc J. Siegel

OF COUNSEL

Isaiah S. Dorfman
Herman J. De Koven
Seymour Cohen
Richard W. Laner

References: NBD Bank Chicago; Illinois; La Salle National Bank & Trust Co.

For full biographical listings, see the Martindale-Hubbell Law Directory

LAWRENCE, KAMIN, SAUNDERS & UHLENHOP (AV)

208 South La Salle Street, Suite 1750, 60604-1188
Telephone: 312-372-1947
Telecopier: 312-372-2389
Email: LKSU@LKSU.com

MEMBER OF FIRM

Lawrence A. Rosen

ASSOCIATE

Paul M. Weltlich

OF COUNSEL

Randall B. Gold

For full biographical listings, see the Martindale-Hubbell Law Directory

LAW OFFICES OF DAVID L. LEE (AV)

Suite 660, 53 West Jackson Boulevard, 60604
Telephone: 312-347-4400
Facsimile: 312-347-3272
Email: D-lee@davidleelaw.com *URL:* http://www.davidleelaw.com

ASSOCIATE

Sarah R. Masarachia

For full biographical listings, see the Martindale-Hubbell Law Directory

MATKOV, SALZMAN, MADOFF & GUNN (AV)

Suite 2900, 55 East Monroe Street, 60603-5709
Telephone: 312-332-0777
Telecopier: 312-332-6130
URL: http://www.msmglaw.com

MEMBERS OF FIRM

George J. Matkov, Jr.
James John Salzman
Jeffrey L. Madoff
Allan Gunn
Larry G. Hall
Kenneth T. Lopatka
Michael W. Duffee
Jay G. Swardenski
John N. Raudabaugh (Not admitted in IL)
Julia A. Martin
Frank J. Saibert
Steven L. Brenneman
Deborah Lee Smith
Christopher A. Johlie
Kenneth F. Sparks
Craig R. Thorstenson
Craig T. Boggs
Beth Elaine Koch
William H. Nichols
Lisa A. Wetzel

(See Next Column)

ASSOCIATES

Jacqueline M. Damm
Thomas M. Dugard
Sang-yul Lee
Cara B. Levinson
Daniel B. Pasternak
Andrew M. Slobodien
Teri Firmiss Thompson

For full biographical listings, see the Martindale-Hubbell Law Directory

McBRIDE BAKER & COLES (AV)

500 West Madison Street 40th Floor, 60661-2511
Telephone: 312-715-5700
Cable Address: "Chilaw"
Telex: 270258
Telecopier: 312-993-9350
Email: lastname@mbc.com *URL:* http://www.mbc.com
Oakbrook Terrace, Illinois Office: Suite 1000, One Mid America Plaza, 60181-4710.
Telephone: 630-954-2100.
Telecopier: 630-954-2112.

MEMBERS OF FIRM

Kenneth A. Jenero
Patrick W. Kocian
Steven R. Lifson
Mark A. Spognardi
William M. Stevens
Steven B. Varick

OF COUNSEL

William J. Cooney

ASSOCIATES

Staci L. Ketay
Todd J. Schneider
Phillip Michael Schreiber

For Complete List of Firm Personnel, See General Section

For full biographical listings, see the Martindale-Hubbell Law Directory

McFADDEN & DILLON, A PROFESSIONAL CORPORATION (AV)

135 South La Salle Street, Suite 2110, 60603-4402
Telephone: 312-201-8300
Facsimile: 312-201-0535
Email: mcfaddendillonlaw@ameritech.net

Roger J. McFadden
Thomas J. Dillon

Tyrrel J. Penn

For full biographical listings, see the Martindale-Hubbell Law Directory

SCARIANO, ELLCH, HIMES, SRAGA AND PETRARCA, CHARTERED (AV)

Two Prudential Plaza 180 North Stetson Suite 3100, 60601-6224
Telephone: 312-565-3100
Facsimile: 312-565-0000
Chicago Heights, Illinois Office: 1450 Aberdeen, 60411.
Telephone: 708-755-1900.
Facsimile: 708-755-0000.

Anthony G. Scariano
Robert H. Ellch
A. Lynn Himes
Alan T. Sraga
Justino D. Petrarca
Lawrence Jay Weiner
John M. Izzo
Raymond A. Hauser
Kathleen Roche Hirsman
Daniel M. Boyle
Teri E. Engler
Rosanne Ciambrone

Kelly A. Hayden
Todd K. Hayden
Christopher L. Petrarca
Sarah E. Joyce
Joel R. DeTella
Susan H. Walter (Resident)
Brian J. Fahey
David A. Harley
Bradley C. Coleman
Christina Sepiol
Alan M. Mullins
John E. Fester
Michael Alan DeBartolo

OF COUNSEL

John Kralovec

For full biographical listings, see the Martindale-Hubbell Law Directory

SCHIFF & HULBERT (AV)

311 South Wacker Drive, Suite 2625, 60606
Telephone: 312-427-7570
Fax: 312-427-7560
Email: SchiffHulb@aol.com

MEMBERS OF FIRM

Matthew B. Schiff
James W. Hulbert

ASSOCIATES

Bridget A. Neuson
Linda Cecchin Kramer
Lynn M. Kreutzberg

For full biographical listings, see the Martindale-Hubbell Law Directory

Chicago—Continued

WILDMAN, HARROLD, ALLEN & DIXON (AV)

225 West Wacker Drive, 30th Floor, 60606-1229
Telephone: 312-201-2000
Fax: 312-201-2555
Email: hennessy@whad.com *URL:* http://www.whad.com
Aurora, Illinois Office: 1961 W. Downer Place.
Telephone: 630-892-7021.
Fax: 630-892-7158.
Waukegan, Illinois Office: 404 West Water, P. O. Box 890.
Telephone: 847-625-5550.
Fax: 847-625-5555.
Lisle, Illinois Office: 4300 Commerce Court, Suite 320.
Telephone: 630-955-0555.
Fax: 630-955-0662
Toronto, Ontario correspondent Office: Keel Cottrelle. 36 Toronto Street, Suite 920.
Telephone: 416-367-2900.
Telefax: 416-367-2791.
Telex: 062-18660.

MEMBERS OF FIRM

Fredrick H. Bates
James D. Fiffer
Kathy Pinkstaff Fox
Elliot H. Goldman
Charles J. Griffin, Jr.
Anne Giddings Kimball
Fred E. Schulz
Linda E. Spring (Waukegan Office)
David L. Weinstein

OF COUNSEL

Lee B. McClain

Kathie M. Contois
William C. Glynn
John F. Kuenstler
Gracelyn A. Leon
Sean Nash
Anita C. Wilson
Neil G. Wolf

For full biographical listings, see the Martindale-Hubbell Law Directory

WITWER, POLTROCK & GIAMPIETRO (AV)

Suite 2700, 125 South Wacker Drive, 60606-4546
Telephone: 312-332-6000; 236-0606
Fax: 312-332-6008
Email: wpglawyr@mcs.net *URL:* http://www.justice4you.com

MEMBERS OF FIRM

Samuel W. Witwer (1908-1998)
Lawrence A. Poltrock
Samuel W. Witwer, Jr.
Wayne B. Giampietro
Brian M. Waldron
Gregory N. Freerksen
Richard F. Sarna
James B. Dykehouse

ASSOCIATES

Jennifer K. Poltrock
James P. Popp
Michael J. Merrick
Gwendolyn D. Reeves
Julie Sparling Desierto
Daniel S. Wellner
Marla J. Haley

OF COUNSEL

Beverly Susler Parkhurst

For full biographical listings, see the Martindale-Hubbell Law Directory

LIBERTYVILLE, Lake Co.

JAMES J. DESANTO A PROFESSIONAL CORPORATION (AV)

339 North Milwaukee Avenue, 60048
Telephone: 847-816-8100
Facsimile: 847-816-8126
Email: desanto@1connect.net

James J. DeSanto

For full biographical listings, see the Martindale-Hubbell Law Directory

MATTOON, Coles Co.

CRAIG & CRAIG (AV)

1807 Broadway, P.O. Box 689, 61938-0689
Telephone: 217-234-6481
Telecopier: 217-234-6486; 258-8292
Email: craiglaw@advant.com
Mount Vernon, Illinois Office: 115 North 7th Street.
Telephone: 618-244-7511.

MEMBERS OF FIRM

Craig Van Meter (1895-1981)
Fred H. Kelly (1894-1971)
Robert M. Werden (1908-1969)
George N. Gilkerson (1911-1985)
John P. Ewart
Richard F. Record, Jr.
Stephen L. Corn
Robert G. Grierson
Gregory C. Ray
Paul R. Lynch (Resident, Mount Vernon Office)
Kenneth F. Werts (Resident, Mount Vernon Office)
John L. Barger

(See Next Column)

ASSOCIATES

Kathleen M. Stockwell
Kristine M. Tuttle
Julie A. Webb (Resident, Mount Vernon Office)
John M. O'Driscoll
Duane A. Deters
Katy C. Fain (Resident, Mount Vernon Office)
Erin E. Wisner
John F. Watson

OF COUNSEL

Jack E. Horsley

Representative Clients: Freeman United Coal Mining Co.; Howell Paving, Inc.; Consolidated Communications Inc.; R. R. Donnelley & Sons Co.; Kal Kan Foods, Inc.; Lake Land College; Trailmobile Corp.

For full biographical listings, see the Martindale-Hubbell Law Directory

*PEORIA,** Peoria Co.

HOWARD & HOWARD ATTORNEYS, P.C. (AV)

The Creve Coeur Building, Suite 200, 321 Liberty Street, 61602-1403
Telephone: 309-672-1483
Telecopier: 309-672-1568
Kalamazoo, Michigan Office: The Michigan Building, Suite 200, 100 Portage Street.
Telephone: 616-382-1483.
Telecopier: 616-382-1568.
Bloomfield Hills, Michigan Office: The Pinehurst Office Center, Suite 101, 1400 North Woodward Avenue.
Telephone: 248-645-1483.
Telecopier: 248-645-1568.
Lansing, Michigan Office: Suite 500, The Phoenix Building, 222 Washington Square, North.
Telephone: 517-485-1483.
Telecopier: 517-485-1568.

Frederick G. Hoffman
Michael R. Lied
Leonard W. Sachs

Representative Clients: For Representative Client list, see General Practice, Peoria, IL.

For Complete List of Firm Personnel, See General Section

For full biographical listings, see the Martindale-Hubbell Law Directory

KAVANAGH, SCULLY, SUDOW, WHITE & FREDERICK, P.C. (AV)

301 S.W. Adams Street, Suite 700, 61602
Telephone: 309-676-1381
FAX: 309-676-0324
Email: KSSWF@aol.com
East Peoria, Illinois Office: 111 West Washington Street, Suite 206B.
Telephone: 309-694-3707.
Fax: 309-676-0324.

Julian E. Cannell
Charles G. Roth
Phillip B. Lenzini
James W. Springer

Counsel for: First of America Bank - Illinois, N.A.; Travelers Insurance Co.; Phoenix Mutual Life Insurance Co.; Board of Education of the City of Peoria School District, 150; Anderson State Bank; Foster & Gallagher, Inc.; Champion Furnace Pipe Company; M.H. Equipment Corporation; Cohen Furniture Company; AgriBank FCB

For Complete List of Firm Personnel, See General Section

For full biographical listings, see the Martindale-Hubbell Law Directory

ST. CHARLES, Kane Co.

WESSELS & PAUTSCH, P.C. (AV)

Dunham Center, 2035 Foxfield Drive, 60174
Telephone: 630-377-1554
Fax: 630-377-1653
Email: wessels@stch.w-p.com *URL:* http://www.w-p.com
Milwaukee, Wisconsin Office: Two Plaza East, 330 East Kilbourn Avenue, Suite 1475.
Telephone: 414-291-0600.
Fax: 414-291-0200.
Chicago, Illinois Office: Chicago Bar Association Building, 321 South Plymouth Court, Suite 900.
Telephone: 312-461-0500.
Fax: 312-461-0595.
Davenport, Iowa Office: Northwest Bank Building, 101 W. Second Street, Suite 603.
Telephone: 319-333-9102.
Fax: 319-333-9105.
Minneapolis, Minnesota Office: The Colonnade, 5500 Wayzata Blvd., Suite 1230.
Telephone: 612-595-7100.
Fax: 612-595-7200.

Richard H. Wessels
Earl P. Bailey (Not admitted in IL)
Nancy E. Joerg
Gregory H. Andrews
Ronald J. Passarelli

(See Next Column)

WESSELS & PAUTSCH P.C., *St. Charles—Continued*

Joseph R. Hlavin, Jr. Laura M. Smith

Representative Clients: Ace Hardware Corp.; Allied Van Lines, Inc.; Claire's Stores, Inc.; Edward Hines Lumber Co.; Jay Foods, L.L.C.; Patten Industries, Inc.; Power Packaging Inc.; Safety-Kleen Corp; TSC Industries, Inc.; U.S. Precision Glass Co.

For full biographical listings, see the Martindale-Hubbell Law Directory

INDIANA

ELKHART, Elkhart Co.

DANIELS, SANDERS, PIANOWSKI, TODD & THOMAS (AV)

401 West High Street, 46516
Telephone: 219-294-1499
Fax: 219-294-7277

MEMBERS OF FIRM

Philip E. Byron, Jr. (1911-1977)
Robert C. Daniels (1928-1995)
Robert T. Sanders, III
Michael A. Pianowski
James L. Todd
David G. Thomas
Matthew A. Yeakey
P. Shawn Lewis

ASSOCIATE

Jason G. Ward

Representative Clients: KeyBank Corp.; Commercial Union Insurance Cos.; Aetna Casualty and Surety Co.; Ohio Casualty Insurance Co.; Yoder Oil Co., Inc.; Double Eagle Industries, Inc.; WKJG-TV; Tri-State Coach Lines, Inc.; Tom Naquin Chevrolet, Inc.

For full biographical listings, see the Martindale-Hubbell Law Directory

*EVANSVILLE,** Vanderburgh Co.

BERGER AND BERGER (AV)

313 Main Street, 47708-1485
Telephone: 812-425-8101
Outside Indiana: 800-327-0182
Fax: 812-421-5909
Email: berger@bergerlaw.com *URL:* http://www.bergerlaw.com

MEMBERS OF FIRM

Sydney L. Berger (1917-1988)
Charles L. Berger
Sheila M. Corcoran
Mark W. Rietman
David L. Clark

References: Citizens National Bank of Evansville; Old National Bank in Evansville.

For full biographical listings, see the Martindale-Hubbell Law Directory

BOWERS, HARRISON, KENT & MILLER, LLP (AV)

25 N.W. Riverside Drive, P.O. Box 1287, 47706-1287
Telephone: 812-426-1231
Fax: 812-464-3676
Email: BOWERS,HARRISON,KENT&MILLER,LLP@BHKM.COM
URL: http://WWW.BHKM.COM

MEMBER OF FIRM

Arthur D. Rutkowski

Division Counsel in Indiana for: Southern Railway Co.
Representative Clients: Permanent Federal Savings Bank; Citizens Realty & Insurance, Inc.

For Complete List of Firm Personnel, See General Section

For full biographical listings, see the Martindale-Hubbell Law Directory

FINE & HATFIELD, A PROFESSIONAL CORPORATION (AV)

520 N.W. Second Street, P.O. Box 779, 47705-0779
Telephone: 812-425-3592
Telecopier: 812-421-4269
Email: Fine@Fine-Hatfield.com *URL:* http://www.Fine-Hatfield.com

Ronald R. Allen
Danny E. Glass
H. Linwood Shannon, III

A List of Representative Clients Furnished Upon Request.

For full biographical listings, see the Martindale-Hubbell Law Directory

KAHN, DEES, DONOVAN & KAHN, LLP (AV)

Fifth Main Financial Plaza, Suite 305, P.O. Box 3646, 47735-3646
Telephone: 812-423-3183
Fax: 812-423-3841
Email: evvlaw@k2d2.com

(See Next Column)

MEMBERS OF FIRM

Arthur R. Donovan (Retired)
Thomas O. Magan
Larry R. Downs
Jon D. Goldman
Jeffrey W. Ahlers

ASSOCIATES

Mark A. McAnulty
Scott F. Hill
Todd C. Barsumian

Representative Clients: University of Evansville; University of Southern Indiana; Toyota Motor Manufacturing USA, Inc.; Lewis Bakeries, Inc.; Deaconess Hospital, Inc.; Guardian Automotive Trim, Inc.; Hella North America, Inc.; Champion Laboratories, Inc.; AK Steel Corporation.

For Complete List of Firm Personnel, See General Section

For full biographical listings, see the Martindale-Hubbell Law Directory

RUDOLPH, FINE, PORTER & JOHNSON LLP (AV)

221 N.W. Fifth Street, Second Floor, P.O. Box 1507, 47706
Telephone: 812-422-9444
Fax: 812-421-7459
URL: http://www.rfpj@rfpj.com

MEMBER OF FIRM

James D. Johnson

ASSOCIATE

Keith A. Sermersheim

Reference: National City Bank of Evansville.

For full biographical listings, see the Martindale-Hubbell Law Directory

ZIEMER, STAYMAN, WEITZEL & SHOULDERS, LLP (AV)

(Formerly Early, Arnold & Ziemer)
One Riverfront Place, 20 N.W. First Street 9th Floor, P.O. Box 916, 47706-0916
Telephone: 812-424-7575
Telecopier: 812-421-5089

MEMBERS OF FIRM

Patrick A. Shoulders
Wm. Michael Schiff
James P. Casey
Mary Lee Schiff
David A. Guerrettaz

Reference: Old National Bank in Evansville.

For full biographical listings, see the Martindale-Hubbell Law Directory

*FORT WAYNE,** Allen Co.

BECKMAN LAWSON, LLP (AV)

800 Standard Federal Plaza, 46802
Telephone: 219-422-0800
Facsimile: 219-420-1013
Syracuse, Indiana Office: 200 West Main Street.
Telephone: 219-457-5727.
Facsimile: 219-457-2056.

MEMBERS OF FIRM

Jack W. Lawson
Frank J. Gray
Howard B. Sandler
Stephen R. Snyder
James A. Federoff
William L. Sweet, Jr.
Richard H. Blaich
John H. Brandt
Jon A. Bragalone
Brian J. T'Kindt
Douglas R. Adelsperger
Travis S. Friend
Robert L. Nicholson
David D. Cornwell
James A. Butz
Jack C. Birch
Craig R. Patterson

ASSOCIATES

John M. Ketcham
Wendy W. Davis
Jeffrey B. Harding
Martha M. Kinder
Edward J. Ormsby
Randall L. Morgan
Daniel J. Deeb
Patrick R. Hess
Georgia L. Hartman
Brian M. Simpson
James E. Rossow, Jr.
Sarah A. Hiestand
Tandra S. Johnson
Jason M. Kuchmay
Matthew J. Elliott

OF COUNSEL

Frederick A. Beckman
Neil F. Sandler
Douglas E. Miller
Loren K. Allison

Reference: National City Bank.

For full biographical listings, see the Martindale-Hubbell Law Directory

*INDIANAPOLIS,** Marion Co.

BOSE MCKINNEY & EVANS LLP (AV)

2700 First Indiana Plaza, 135 North Pennsylvania Street, 46204
Telephone: 317-684-5000
Facsimile: 317-684-5173
URL: http://www.boselaw.com
Indianapolis North Office: Suite 1500, 8888 Keystone Crossing, 46240.
Telephone: 317-574-3700.
Facsimile: 317-574-3716.

(See Next Column)

BOSE MCKINNEY & EVANS LLP—*Continued*

MEMBERS OF FIRM

Jon M. Bailey
Daniel C. Emerson
Margaret Bannon Miller
Charles R. Rubright
Steven G. Rudolf
David L. Swider

ASSOCIATES

Temple L. Garner
Andrew M. McNeil
Karen Glasser Sharp
Susan E. Traynor

Representative Clients: First Indiana Bank; United Parcel Service, Inc.; Indianapolis Colts, Inc.; Pfizer, Inc.; Hyatt Regency; Marsh Super Markets, Inc.; Metropolitan School District of Pike Township; Countrymark Cooperative, Inc.; Thomson Consumer Electronics, Inc.; Yellow Freight System, Inc.

For Complete List of Firm Personnel, See General Section

For full biographical listings, see the Martindale-Hubbell Law Directory

BUSCHMANN, CARR & SHANKS, PROFESSIONAL CORPORATION (AV)

1020 Market Tower, 10 West Market Street, 46204-2963
Telephone: 317-636-5511
Fax: 317-636-3661
Email: bcs@indy.net *URL:* http://www.buschmanncarr.com

John R. Carr, III
Stephen R. Buschmann
John N. Shanks II

Representative Clients: Archer-Daniels Midland Co.; Ball Corp.; Industrial Valley Title Insurance; Creative Risk Management, Inc.; Deflecto Corporation; Glenfed Mortgage Corp.; Gates McDonald; Merchants National Bank & Trust Company of Muncie; Monumental Life Insurance Co.; National Council on Compensation Insurance.

For full biographical listings, see the Martindale-Hubbell Law Directory

ICE MILLER DONADIO & RYAN (AV)

One American Square Box 82001, 46282-0002
Telephone: 317-236-2100
Fax: 317-236-2219
Email: info@imdr.com *URL:* http://www.imdr.com
South Bend, Indiana Office: 211 West Washington Street, Suite 2420.
Telephone: 219-234-7933.
Fax: 219-234-7965. Internet E-mail: info@imdr.com. Web Site Address: http://www.imdr.com.
Chicago, Illinois Office: 135 South LaSalle Street, Suite 4100.
Telephone: 312-726-1567.
Fax: 312-641-6263. Internet E-mail: info@imdr.com. Web Site Address: http://www.imdr.com.

MEMBERS OF FIRM

William R. Riggs
S. R. Born
Martin J. Klaper
Richard E. Parker
Michael H. Boldt
David J. Mallon, Jr.
Susan B. Tabler
Byron L. Myers
Michael A. Blickman
Robert B. Bush
Melissa Proffitt Reese
Michael D. Marine
Sherry A. Fabina-Abney
Michael L. Tooley

RETIRED PARTNERS

Leland B. Cross, Jr.
Alan T. Nolan

OF COUNSEL

Karen A. Dutcher

STAFF ATTORNEY

Mikio Nishizu

ASSOCIATES

Paul H. Sinclair
Pamela V. Keller
Susanne M. Spisak
Lisa Erb Harrison
Constance Baker Phillips
Casey J. Henderson
Ryan M. Poor
Bradley L. Wilson

Counsel for: Thompson Consumer Electronics (RCA), Indianapolis; Cyprus AMAX Minerals Comapny; Associated General Contractors of Indiana, Inc.; Citizens Gas and Coke Utility; Community Hospital, Indianapolis; Cummins Engine Company, Columbus; Grote Industries, Inc., Madison; Indiana University; Ivy Tech State College.

For Complete List of Firm Personnel, See General Section

For full biographical listings, see the Martindale-Hubbell Law Directory

LOCKE REYNOLDS LLP (AV)

1000 Capital Center South, 201 North Illinois Street, 46204-4210
Telephone: 317-237-3800
Telecopier: 317-237-3900
Email: attys@locke.com *URL:* http://www.locke.com

Michael T. Bindner
Kim F. Ebert
Thomas J. Campbell
Charles B. Baldwin
James Dimos
Todd J. Kaiser
Ariane Schallwig Johnson
Brian L. McDermott

(See Next Column)

Kenneth B. Siepman
James D. Masur II
Shannon Stewart
T. Joseph Wendt
Heather L. Wilson
Vincent J. Wong
Kristin B. Keltner
Carol M. Wyatt
Camille T. Wiggins

Representative Clients: Ameritech Indiana; BMG Music; Clarian Health Partners, Inc.; Indiana State University; Kraft General Foods; The Kroger Co.; Liquid Transport Corp.; Meijer, Inc.; Navistar International Transportation Corp.; Toyota Industrial Equipment Mfg., Inc.

For Complete List of Firm Personnel, See General Section

For full biographical listings, see the Martindale-Hubbell Law Directory

MCTURNAN & TURNER (AV)

2400 Market Tower, 10 West Market Street, 46204
Telephone: 317-464-8181
Telecopier: 317-464-8131

Lee B. McTurnan
Wayne C. Turner
Jackie M. Bennett, Jr.
Jacqueline Bowman Ponder
Steven M. Badger
John F. McCauley

For full biographical listings, see the Martindale-Hubbell Law Directory

SOMMER & BARNARD, ATTORNEYS AT LAW, PC (AV)

4000 Bank One Tower, 111 Monument Circle, 46204
Telephone: 317-630-4000
FAX: 317-236-9802
Email: sandb@sommerbarnard.com
North Office: 8900 Keystone Crossing, Suite 1150, Indianapolis, Indiana, 46240-2134.
Telephone: 317-630-4000.
FAX: 317-844-4780.

Frederick M. King
Michael C. Terrell

Representative Clients: Dow Chemical Co.; Farm Bureau Insurance Co.; Wabash National Corp.; Indiana Veneers Corp.; MCL Cafeterias; MPD, Inc.; Syndicate Sales, Inc.; Woods Wire Products, Inc.;

For Complete List of Firm Personnel, See General Section

For full biographical listings, see the Martindale-Hubbell Law Directory

*LAFAYETTE,** Tippecanoe Co.

STUART & BRANIGIN (AV)

The Life Building, 300 Main Street, Suite 800, P.O. Box 1010, 47902-1010
Telephone: 765-423-1561
Telecopier: 765-742-8175
Email: sb@stuartlaw.com *URL:* http://www.stuartlaw.com
Indianapolis, Indiana Office: Suite 1401, 8888 Keystone Crossing, 46240.
Telephone: 317-574-7245.
Fax: 317-574-7050.

MEMBERS OF FIRM

Allison Ellsworth Stuart (1886-1950)
Roger D. Branigin (1902-1975)
Roger D. Branigin, Jr.
Thomas L. Ryan
Thomas R. McCully
Larry R. Fisher
Nina B. Kirkpatrick
Mark Lillianfeld
Stephen R. Pennell
Anthony S. Benton
Erik D. Spykman
William E. Emerick
John C. Duffey
Bruce McSpadden
Mark E. DeYoung
Thomas B. Parent
Laura L. Bowker
Kevin D. Nicoson
Susan K. Roberts
John M. Stuckey
Deborah B. Trice
William P. Kealey
David A. Starkweather
Geoffrey L. Blazi

SENIOR COUNSEL

Russell H. Hart

COUNSEL

John F. Bodle
James V. McGlone

ASSOCIATES

Elizabeth B. Searle
Marianne Mitten Owen
David A. Locke
Karen Orr McClure
Ann Marie Waldron
Barry L. Loftus

General Counsel for: The Lafayette Life Insurance Co.; INB National Bank, N.W.; Lafayette Home Hospital, Inc.
State Counsel for: Norfolk & Western Railway Co.
Mr. Ryan is Counsel to: The Trustees of Purdue University.
Representative Clients: Aluminum Company of America; Liberty Mutual Insurance Group.

For full biographical listings, see the Martindale-Hubbell Law Directory

MERRILLVILLE, Lake Co.

HOEPPNER WAGNER & EVANS LLP (AV)

Twin Towers, Suite 606 South, 1000 East 80th Place, P.O. Box 10627, 46410-0627
Telephone: 219-769-6552; 800-263-1466 (IN, IL)
Fax: 219-738-2349
Email: hwe@hwelaw.com *URL:* http://www.hwelaw.com
Valparaiso, Indiana Office: 103 East Lincolnway, P.O. Box 2357, 46384-2357.
Telephone: 219-464-4961; 800-879-2246 (IN, IL).
Fax: 219-465-0603. Email: hwe@hwelaw.com

RESIDENT MEMBERS

John E. Hughes
F. Joseph Jaskowiak

RESIDENT ASSOCIATE

Jack A. Kramer

Representative Clients: Bethlehem Steel Corporation; National Steel Corporation; Valparaiso University; Powdertech Industries.

For Complete List of Firm Personnel, See General Section

For full biographical listings, see the Martindale-Hubbell Law Directory

MUNSTER, Lake Co.

LAW OFFICES OF TIMOTHY F. KELLY (AV)

Suite 2A, 9250 Columbia Avenue, 46321
Telephone: 219-836-4062
Telecopier: 219-836-0167
Email: tfklaw@tfklaw.net

MEMBERS OF FIRM

Timothy F. Kelly
Karl K. Vanzo

ASSOCIATES

Steven J. Sersic
Kathleen E. Peek

For Complete List of Firm Personnel, See General Section

For full biographical listings, see the Martindale-Hubbell Law Directory

*VALPARAISO,** Porter Co.

HOEPPNER WAGNER & EVANS LLP (AV)

103 East Lincolnway, P.O. Box 2357, 46384-2357
Telephone: 219-464-4961; 800-879-2246 (IN, IL)
Fax: 219-465-0603
Email: hwe@hwelaw.com *URL:* http://www.hwelaw.com
Merrillville, Indiana Office: Twin Towers, Suite 606 South, 1000 East 80th Place, P.O. Box 10627, 46419-0627.
Telephone: 219-769-6552; 800-263-1466 (IN, IL).
Fax: 219-738-2349. Email: hwe@hwelaw.com

MEMBERS OF FIRM

William F. Satterlee, III
James L. Jorgensen
F. Joseph Jaskowiak (Resident, Merrillville Office)
Mark E. Schmidtke

ASSOCIATES

Robert L. Clark
Lauren K. Kroeger
Tina M. Bengs
Karen M. Read

Representative Clients: Bethlehem Steel Corporation; National Steel Corporation; Valparaiso University; Powdertech Industries; Ugimag.

For Complete List of Firm Personnel, See General Section

For full biographical listings, see the Martindale-Hubbell Law Directory

IOWA

*CEDAR RAPIDS,** Linn Co.

SHUTTLEWORTH & INGERSOLL, P.C. (AV)

115 Third Street S.E., Suite 500, P.O. Box 2107, 52406-2107
Telephone: 319-365-9461
Fax: 319-365-8443
URL: http://www.shuttleworthlaw.com

Glenn L. Johnson
Mark L. Zaiger
Constance M. Alt
Gilda L. Boyer

Nancy J. Penner
Sarah J. Gayer

Representative Clients: Amana Society; Archer-Daniels-Midland Co.; Cargill, Inc.; Cryovac, Inc., a Division of W. R. Grace & Co.; Firstar Bank N.A.; General Mills, Inc.; MCI; PMX Industries, Inc.; Goss Graphic Systems, Inc.

For Complete List of Firm Personnel, See General Section

For full biographical listings, see the Martindale-Hubbell Law Directory

*COUNCIL BLUFFS,** Pottawattamie Co.

SMITH PETERSON LAW FIRM (AV)

35 Main Place, Suite 300, P.O. Box 249, 51502
Telephone: 712-328-1833
Fax: 712-328-8320
Email: email@smithpeterson.com
Omaha, Nebraska Office: 9290 West Dodge Road, Suite 205.
Telephone: 402-397-8500.
Fax: 402-397-5519.

MEMBERS OF FIRM

Raymond A. Smith (1892-1977)
John LeRoy Peterson (1895-1969)
Harold T. Beckman
Robert J. Laubenthal
Richard A. Heininger
Lawrence J. Beckman
Gregory G. Barntsen
W. Curtis Hewett
Steven H. Krohn
Randy R. Ewing
Joseph D. Thornton
T. J. Pattermann

ASSOCIATES

Daniel L. Fretheim
Paul M. Shotkoski

Representative Clients: Redland Insurance Group; Iowa Western Community College; Farm Credit Service of The Midlands; Demma Fruit Co.; Peoples National Bank; Council Bluffs Board of Water Works Trustee.

For full biographical listings, see the Martindale-Hubbell Law Directory

*DES MOINES,** Polk Co.

DICKINSON, MACKAMAN, TYLER & HAGEN, P.C. (AV)

Suite 1600 Hub Tower, 699 Walnut Street, 50309-3986
Telephone: 515-244-2600
Telecopier: 515-246-4550
URL: http://www.dickinsonlaw.com

Helen C. Adams
Brent R. Appel
Kimberley K. Baer
Joseph A. Cacciatore
Rebecca Boyd Parrott
Russell L. Samson
John K. Vernon

For full biographical listings, see the Martindale-Hubbell Law Directory

FINLEY, ALT, SMITH, SCHARNBERG, CRAIG, HILMES & GAFFNEY, P.C. (AV)

604 Locust Street, Fourth Floor Equitable Building, 50309
Telephone: 515-288-0145
Telecopier: 515-288-2724

Pamela J. Prager

Representative Clients: ALAS; American Society of Composers, Authors and Publishers; Equitable Life Assurance Society of the U.S.; Federated Insurance Co.; Meredith Corp.
Iowa Attorneys for: Midwest Medical Insurance Co.
District Attorneys for: Norfolk & Southern Railroad; Soo Line Railroad Company.

For Complete List of Firm Personnel, See General Section

For full biographical listings, see the Martindale-Hubbell Law Directory

PINGEL & TEMPLER, P.C. (AV)

Suite 437 3737 Woodland Avenue (West Des Moines), P.O. Box 1991, 50309
Telephone: 515-225-3737
Fax: 515-225-9510

Thomas M. Cunningham
Greg A. Naylor

For Complete List of Firm Personnel, See General Section

For full biographical listings, see the Martindale-Hubbell Law Directory

*SIOUX CITY,** Woodbury Co.

MAYNE & MAYNE (AV)

400 Pioneer Bank Building, 701 Pierce Street, P.O. Box 5049, 51102-5049
Telephone: 712-252-3220
Fax: 712-252-1535
Email: maynelaw@aol.com

MEMBER OF FIRM

Robert J. Pierson

Representative Clients: American Telephone & Telegraph Co.; Amoco Oil Company; Central United Life Insurance Company; Century 21-Marketplace; Credit Bureau of Sioux City; Ford Motor Credit Company; Intensive Medical Services of Siouxland, P.C.; Metz Baking Company; Shell Chemical Company; U.S. West Communications Company.

For full biographical listings, see the Martindale-Hubbell Law Directory

Sioux City—Continued

SMITH & MCELWAIN (AV)

505 Fifth, Suite 530, P.O. Box 1194, 51102
Telephone: 712-255-8094
Fax: 712-255-3825
Email: smitmcel@aol.com

MEMBERS OF FIRM

MacDonald Smith
Dennis M. McElwain
Harry H. Smith (1916-1999)

Representative Clients: Iowa Federation of Labor; Iowa State Building & Construction Trades Council; Bakers' Pension Fund.
Reference: Norwest Bank, N.A.

For full biographical listings, see the Martindale-Hubbell Law Directory

KANSAS

*HUTCHINSON,** Reno Co.

GILLILAND & HAYES, P.A. A PROFESSIONAL ASSOCIATION (AV)

20 West 2nd Avenue, 2nd Floor, P.O. Box 2977, 67504-2977
Telephone: 316-662-0537
Facsimile: 316-669-9426
URL: http://www.gillilandhayes.com
Wichita, Kansas Office: The Orpheum Centre, Suite 300, 200 North Broadway, P.O. Box 49406.
Telephone: 316-262-2266.
Facsimile: 316-263-2202.
Kansas City, Missouri Office: 12th Floor, 3100 Broadway.
Telephone: 816-753-3100.
Facsimile: 816-753-2271.

Robert J. Gilliland
John F. Hayes
James R. Gilliland
John S. Schmidt
Bruce B. Waugh (Not admitted in KS; Resident, Kansas City, Missouri Office)
Michael R. O'Neal
Bradley D. Dillon
Gerald L. Green
David N. Zimmerman (Not admitted in KS; Resident, Kansas City, Missouri Office)
Scott J. Mann
Carol Z. Smith (Resident, Kansas City, Missouri Office)
Kathleen A. Hardee (Resident, Kansas City, Missouri Office)
Kendall R. Cunningham (Resident, Wichita Office)
Mark R. Maloney (Resident, Wichita Office)

Thomas A. Dower
Tracy Applegate Cole
Laura A. Hederstedt
Terri Roberts Munsell (Resident, Kansas City, Missouri Office)
Lisa M. Ward
Kimberly Breda Bushek (Resident, Kansas City, Missouri Office)
E. Thomas Pyle, III
Tara L. Bragg

OF COUNSEL

Robert P. Reams (Not admitted in KS; Resident, Kansas City, Missouri Office)

Representative Clients: CNA Insurance; Dillon Companies; Fidelity Deposit Co. of Maryland; Hutchinson Clinic; Hutchinson Hospital Corp.; Central Bank & Trust; Collins Industries; Kansas City Poster Display Co.; Sirloin Stockade International; TSW Products.

For full biographical listings, see the Martindale-Hubbell Law Directory

OVERLAND PARK, Johnson Co.

FISHER, PATTERSON, SAYLER & SMITH, L.L.P. (AV)

11050 Roe Avenue, Suite 210, 66211
Telephone: 913-339-6757
FAX: 913-339-6187
Email: fpss@worldnet.att.net
Topeka, Kansas Office: 3550 S.W. 5th Street, P.O. Box 949, 66601.
Telephone: 785-232-7761.
Fax: 785-232-6604.

MEMBERS OF FIRM

Edwin Dudley Smith (Resident)
Michael K. Seck (Resident)
David P. Madden (Resident)

ASSOCIATES

Kelly A. Feyh (Resident)
Jennifer R. Rose (Resident)

For full biographical listings, see the Martindale-Hubbell Law Directory

*TOPEKA,** Shawnee Co.

FISHER, PATTERSON, SAYLER & SMITH, L.L.P. (AV)

3550 S.W. 5th Street, P.O. Box 949, 66601
Telephone: 785-232-7761
Fax: 785-232-6604
Email: fpss@cjnetworks.com
Overland Park, Kansas Office: 11050 Roe Avenue, Suite 210, 66211.
Telephone: 913-339-6757.
Fax: 913-339-6187.

MEMBERS OF FIRM

Donald Patterson
Edwin Dudley Smith (Resident, Overland Park Office)
Larry G. Pepperdine
James P. Nordstrom
Justice B. King
J. Steven Pigg
Steve R. Fabert
Ronald J. Laskowski
Michael K. Seck (Resident, Overland Park Office)
David P. Madden (Resident, Overland Park Office)
Steven K. Johnson
Kristine A. Larscheid

ASSOCIATES

Billy E. Newman
David R. Cooper
Kelly A. Feyh (Resident, Overland Park Office)
Jennifer R. Rose (Resident, Overland Park Office)

OF COUNSEL

David H. Fisher

RETIRED

Charles Keith Sayler (Retired)

Representative Clients: Gage Shopping Center, Inc.; Fireman's Fund-American Insurance Cos.; United States Fidelity and Guaranty Co.; The Procter & Gamble Company; Commercial Union Insurance Companies; National Casualty; The Hartford; Berkshire Hathaway Companies; Hallmark Cards; Martin Marietta Corp.

For full biographical listings, see the Martindale-Hubbell Law Directory

GOODELL, STRATTON, EDMONDS & PALMER, L.L.P. (AV)

515 South Kansas Avenue, 66603-3999
Telephone: 785-233-0593
Fax: 785-233-8870
Email: GSEP@CJNETWORKS.COM *URL:* http://www.cjnetworks.com/~gsep
Kansas City, Missouri Office: 10401 Holmes Road, Suite 280.
Telephone: 816-943-8577.

MEMBERS OF FIRM

Arthur E. Palmer
Harold S. Youngentob
Les E. Diehl

SPECIAL COUNSEL

Marta Fisher Linenberger

Counsel for: Columbian National Title Insurance Co.; The Menninger Foundation; Kansas Hospital Association; Washburn University; Topeka Metropolitan Transit Authority; Hills Pet Nutrition, Inc.; City of Topeka; American Investors Life Ins. Co.; Stormont-Vail Healthcare, Inc.; Resers Fine Foods.

For Complete List of Firm Personnel, See General Section

For full biographical listings, see the Martindale-Hubbell Law Directory

WRIGHT, HENSON, SOMERS, SEBELIUS, CLARK & BAKER, LLP (AV)

Commerce Bank Building, 100 Southeast Ninth Street, 2nd Floor, P.O. Box 3555, 66601-3555
Telephone: 785-232-2200
FAX: 785-232-3344
Email: wrighthenson@wrighthenson.com *URL:* http://www.wrighthenson.com

MEMBER OF FIRM

K. Gary Sebelius

ASSOCIATE

Michael M. Walker

SPECIAL COUNSEL

David P. Mudrick

Representative Client: Western Resources, Inc.; KPL/Gas Service Company; St. Francis Hospital and Medical Center; Adams Business Forms; The May Department Stores, Inc.; Payless ShoeSource, Inc.; IBP, Inc; Jostens, Inc.; Wolf Creek Nuclear Operating Corp.

For Complete List of Firm Personnel, See General Section

For full biographical listings, see the Martindale-Hubbell Law Directory

*WICHITA,** Sedgwick Co.

FOULSTON & SIEFKIN L.L.P. (AV)

700 NationsBank Financial Center, 67202
Telephone: 316-267-6371
Facsimile: 316-267-6345
URL: http://www.foulston.com
Topeka, Kansas Office: 1515 NationsBank Tower, 534 Kansas Avenue, 66603.
Telephone: 785-233-3600.
Fax: 785-233-1610.
Dodge City, Kansas Office: 810 Frontview, P.O. Box 1147, 67801.
Telephone: 316-227-8126.
Fax: 316-227-8451.
Member: Lex Mundi, The World's Leading Association of Independent Law Firms.

MEMBERS OF FIRM

Mary Kathleen Babcock
Douglas L. Stanley
Gloria G. Farha Flentje
J. Steven Massoni

For Complete List of Firm Personnel, See General Section

For full biographical listings, see the Martindale-Hubbell Law Directory

GRACE, UNRUH & PRATT, L.C. (AV)

Suite 501, 155 North Market Street, 67202-1816
Telephone: 316-269-2006
FAX: 316-269-0437
Email: litigation@fn.net

Brian G. Grace
Gilbert L. Guthrie
Terry L. Unruh
Sharon A. Werner
Corlin J. Pratt
Kevin A. Grace

For full biographical listings, see the Martindale-Hubbell Law Directory

MARTIN, CHURCHILL, BLAIR, HILL, COLE & HOLLANDER, CHARTERED (AV)

500 North Market Street, 67214-3590
Telephone: 316-263-3200
Telecopier: 316-263-6298
Email: mclaw@martinchurchill.com

W. Stanley Churchill
Brad T. Murphree
John R. Blair
J. Michael Kennalley
Donald E. Hill
Jeffrey B. Hurt
Charles E. Cole, Jr.
Bryce A. Abbott
Ross A. Hollander
Kasey Alan Rogg

Kathleen N. Wohlgemuth
Joan M. Bowen
Michael A. Priddle

OF COUNSEL

Anthony J. Powell

RETIRED

Marvin J. Martin

Representative Clients: Labor and Employment: Coleman Company; Koch Industries, Inc.; Wescon Products Co. (Division of Latshaw Enterprises).

For full biographical listings, see the Martindale-Hubbell Law Directory

MORRIS, LAING, EVANS, BROCK & KENNEDY, CHARTERED (AV)

Fourth Floor, 200 West Douglas, 67202-3084
Telephone: 316-262-2671
Fax: 316-262-6226; 262-5991
Topeka, Kansas Office: 800 S.W. Jackson, Suite 914, 66612-2214.
Telephone: 913-232-2662.
Fax: 913-232-9983.

Robert D. Overman
Jana Deines Abbott
Dennis M. Feeney
Diane S. Worth
Susan R. Schrag
Carlos J. Nolla-Corretjer

James D. Young

References: The Emprise Banks of Kansas; Mercantile Bank of Topeka; Southwest National Bank; Twin Lakes National Bank.

For Complete List of Firm Personnel, See General Section

For full biographical listings, see the Martindale-Hubbell Law Directory

TRIPLETT, WOOLF & GARRETSON, LLC (AV)

2959 North Rock Road, Suite 300, 67226
Telephone: 316-630-8100
Fax: 316-630-8101
Email: twg@twgfirm.com

MEMBERS OF FIRM

John P. Woolf
Lee Thompson
James A. Walker
Rachael K. Pirner
Eric B. Metz
Jeffrey D. Leonard

(See Next Column)

ASSOCIATE

Jeffrey E. Goering

Representative Clients: Anheuser-Busch Companies, Inc.; Brite Voice Systems, Inc.; Coleman Company, Inc.; Dow Chemical Co.; Friends University; KPMG Peat Marwick; National Plastics Color, Inc.; Total Petroleum, Inc.; Travelers Insurance Co.; Willis Corroon of Kansas, Inc.

For Complete List of Firm Personnel, See General Section

For full biographical listings, see the Martindale-Hubbell Law Directory

KENTUCKY

*BOWLING GREEN,** Warren Co.

KERRICK, GRISE & STIVERS (AV)

1025 State Street, P.O. Box 9547, 42102-9547
Telephone: 502-782-8160
Fax: 502-782-5856
Email: kgs@kgslaw.com
Elizabethtown, Kentucky Office: 2935 Dolphin Drive, Suite 102.
Telephone: 502-769-5788.
Fax: 502-737-9285.

MEMBERS OF FIRM

Thomas N. Kerrick
Gregory N. Stivers
John R. Grise
H. Brent Brennenstuhl
Laura M. Hagan

ASSOCIATES

Karl N. Crandall
Shawn Rosso Alcott
Jason B. Bell

OF COUNSEL

Jeffrey R. O'Grody

LEGAL SUPPORT PERSONNEL

Patricia Logsdon
Laura Lockhart Lico
Allison Lusk

Representative Clients: Dollar General Corp.; Columbia Greenview Regional Hospital; Hospital Corporation of America; Hardin Memorial Hospital; FirStar Bank; TKR Cable.

For full biographical listings, see the Martindale-Hubbell Law Directory

COVINGTON, Kenton Co.

GILLILAND & ASSOCIATES (AV)

211 Grandview Suite 205, 41017
Telephone: 606-344-8515
Fax: 606-344-8516
Email: thefirm@gilliland.com *URL:* http://www.gilliland.com
Columbus, Ohio Office: 1335 Dublin Road, Suite 200A, 43215.
Telephone: 614-481-5984.
Fax: 614-481-5985. E-mail: columbusfirm@gilliland.com.
Indianapolis, Indiana Office: 8888 Keystone Crossing, Suite 1300, 46420.
Telephone: 317-581-8585.
Fax: 317-575-4180. E-mail: indyfirm@gilliland.com.

John C. Gilliland, II

Rudy A. Bisciotti
Randy S. Jackson, Jr.
Ursula M. McDonnell (Not admitted in KY)

For full biographical listings, see the Martindale-Hubbell Law Directory

TALIAFERRO, MEHLING, SHIROONI & CARRAN (AV)

1005 Madison Avenue, P.O. Box 468, 41012-0468
Telephone: 606-291-9900
Fax: 606-291-3014

MEMBERS OF FIRM

Philip Taliaferro, III
Lucinda C. Shirooni
Christopher J. Mehling
Robert W. Carran

ASSOCIATES

Howard L. Tankersley
Jerome N. Epping, Jr.
Alice G. Keys
Michelle Snodgrass-Deimling

OF COUNSEL

Norbert J. Bischoff
F. Edward Worland, Jr.

For full biographical listings, see the Martindale-Hubbell Law Directory

*HARLAN,** Harlan Co.

HUFF LAW OFFICES (AV)

417 East Mound Street, Drawer 151, 40831
Telephone: 606-573-4466
Fax: 606-573-7078

Gayle G. Huff

(See Next Column)

HUFF LAW OFFICES—*Continued*

ASSOCIATES

Antony L. Saragas
Elizabeth Ann Huff
William Stacy Huff

Representative Clients: Old Republic Insurance Co.; Underwriters Safety & Claims; Manalapan Mining Co.; R.B. Coal Co.; Eastover Mining Co., a division of Duke Power Co.; American Mining Insurance Co.; Employers Risk Services; Forest Industry Workers Compensation Fund.

For full biographical listings, see the Martindale-Hubbell Law Directory

RICE & HENDRICKSON (AV)

398 Woodland Hills, P.O. Box 980, 40831
Telephone: 606-573-3955
Fax: 606-573-3956

MEMBERS OF FIRM

William A. Rice
H. Kent Hendrickson

Representative Clients: USX Corp.; Navistar International Transportation Corp.; Bituminous Casualty Corp.; Kentucky Utilities Co.; Aetna Casualty & Surety Co.; The Hartford Insurance Group; Benham Coal, Inc.; Maytag Corporation; Harlan Cumberland Coal Co.; Pafco General Insurance.

For full biographical listings, see the Martindale-Hubbell Law Directory

*LEXINGTON,** Fayette Co.

STOLL, KEENON & PARK, LLP (AV)

201 E. Main Street, Suite 1000, 40507-1380
Telephone: 606-231-3000
Telecopier: 606-253-1093; 606-253-1027
URL: http://www.skp.com
Frankfort, Kentucky Office: 307 Washington Street, 40601.
Telephone: 502-875-6220.
Telecopier: 502-875-6235.
Henderson, Kentucky Office: 201 C North Main Street, 42420-3103.
Telephone: 270-831-1900.
Telecopier: 270-827-4060.
Louisville, Kentucky Office: 400 West Market Street, Suite 2650, 40202-3377.
Telephone: 502-568-9100.
Telecopier: 502-568-5700.

MEMBERS OF FIRM

Robert F. Houlihan
Richard C. Stephenson
Robert F. Houlihan, Jr.
Donald P. Wagner
C. Joseph Beavin
Larry A. Sykes
P. Douglas Barr
James D. Allen

ASSOCIATES

Mary Beth Griffith
Kymberly T. Wellons
Charles R. Baesler, Jr.
Elizabeth Friend Bird
Amy C. Liebermann

Representative Clients: Consolidated Freightways, Inc.; IBM Corp.; Johnson Controls, Inc.; Kentucky Utilities Co.; Lexmark International, Inc.; OSRAM Sylvania, Inc.; Parker Hannifin Corp.; Square D Co.; The Trane Co.; Transylvania University.

For Complete List of Firm Personnel, See General Section

For full biographical listings, see the Martindale-Hubbell Law Directory

VIMONT & WILLS PLLC (AV)

Suite 300, 155 East Main Street, 40507-1317
Telephone: 606-252-2202
Telecopier: 606-259-2927
Email: vimont@lex.infi.net

Timothy C. Wills

Dawn S. Logsdon

For full biographical listings, see the Martindale-Hubbell Law Directory

*LOUISVILLE,** Jefferson Co.

GREENEBAUM DOLL & MCDONALD PLLC (AV)

3300 National City Tower, 40202
Telephone: 502-589-4200
Fax: 502-587-3695
Email: pad@gdm.com *URL:* http://www.gdm.com
Lexington, Kentucky Office: 1400 Vine Center Tower.
Telephone: 606-231-8500.
Fax: 606-255-2742.
Covington, Kentucky Office: 50 East RiverCenter Boulevard, P.O. Box 2673.
Telephone: 606-655-4200.
Fax: 606-655-4239.
Frankfort, Kentucky Office: Suite 101, 229 West Main Street.
Telephone: 502-875-0050.
Fax: 502-875-0850.

(See Next Column)

Cincinnati, Ohio Office: 2800 Chemed Center, 255 East Fifth Street.
Telephone: 513-455-7600.
Fax: 513-455-8500.
Nashville, Tennessee Office: 700 Two American Center, 3102 West End Avenue.
Telephone: 615-760-7100.
Fax: 615-760-7300.

Richard S. Cleary
David B. Sandler
Margaret E. Keane
Philip C. Eschels
Jeffrey A. Savarise
Thomas J. Birchfield
Robert D. Hudson
Brent R. Baughman

ASSOCIATES

Craig P. Siegenthaler
Katherine A. Hessenbruch
Thomas E. Powell, II
Christopher J. Rusek

Representative Clients: Allied Signal, Inc.; Columbia/HCA Healthcare Corporation; Commonwealth Industries, Inc.; Dravo Lime Co.; Humana Inc.; International Paper Co.; The Kroger Co.; Shoney's, Inc.; Toyota Motor Manufacturing, North America, Inc.; Vermont American Corporation.

For Complete List of Firm Personnel, See General Section

For full biographical listings, see the Martindale-Hubbell Law Directory

HALL, RENDER, KILLIAN, HEATH & LYMAN PROFESSIONAL SERVICES CORPORATION (AV)

AEGON Center, Suite 1530, 400 West Market Street, 40202
Telephone: 502-568-1890
Fax: 502-568-4878
Email: hrkhl@hrkhl.com
Indianapolis, Indiana Office: Suite 2000, One American Square, Box 82064, 46282.
Telephone: 317-633-4884.
Fax: 317-633-4878.
Indianapolis North Office: Suite 820, 8402 Harcourt Road, 46260.
Telephone: 317-871-6222.
Fax: 317-338-3946.

Samuel H. DeShazer

A. Courtney Guild, Jr.

For full biographical listings, see the Martindale-Hubbell Law Directory

SMITH AND SMITH (AV)

400 North, First Trust Centre, 200 South Fifth Street, 40202-3204
Telephone: 502-587-0761
Fax: 502-589-5345
Email: sandsx2@couriernet.infi.net
Email: smithx2@couriernet.infi.net

James U. Smith, Jr. (1914-1977)
S. Russell Smith (1921-1973)
Joseph A. Worthington
James U. Smith, III
Andrew J. Russell
S. Russell Smith, Jr.
W. Kevin Smith
John O. Sheller
Bryan M. Cassis

LEGAL SUPPORT PERSONNEL

Amy T. Snyder, Legal Secretary
Michelle K. Crickmer, Paralegal
Jenny S. Peterson, Legal Secretary
Debra K. Hare, Office Administrator

Representative Clients: Associated Builders and Contractors, Inc.; Hall Contracting Corp.; Henry Vogt Machine Co.; Highlands Regional Medical Center; Whayne Supply Co.; W.R. Grace & Co.; The Chubb Group; Churchill Downs, Inc.

For full biographical listings, see the Martindale-Hubbell Law Directory

WOODWARD, HOBSON & FULTON (AV)

2500 National City Tower, 101 South Fifth Street, 40202
Telephone: 502-581-8000
Fax: 502-581-8111
Email: WHF@IGLOU.COM
Lexington, Kentucky Office: PNC Bank Plaza, 200 West Vine Street, Suite 500.
Telephone: 606-244-7100.
Telecopier: 606-244-7111.

MEMBERS OF FIRM

Michael A. Luvisi
Donna King Perry

ASSOCIATES

Kathryn A. Quesenberry
D. Sean Nilsen
Lisa Clephas Hester

Representative Clients: Brown-Forman Corp.; Ford Motor Co.; CSX Transportation; Field Packing Company; Fischer Packing Company; Res-Care, Inc.; Aegon Corporation; Bank One; Louisville Water Co.; CARITAS Health Services, Inc.; Wal-Mart Stores, Inc.; A. O. Smith Corp.

For Complete List of Firm Personnel, See General Section

For full biographical listings, see the Martindale-Hubbell Law Directory

LOUISIANA

*BATON ROUGE,** East Baton Rouge Parish

BREAZEALE, SACHSE & WILSON, L.L.P. (AV)

Twenty-Third Floor, One American Place, P.O. Box 3197, 70821-3197
Telephone: 225-387-4000
Fax: 225-387-5397
URL: http://www.bswllp.com
New Orleans, Louisiana Office: LL&E Tower, Suite 1500, 909 Poydras Street.
Telephone: 504-584-5454.
Fax: 504-584-5452.
Covington, Louisiana Office: 2255 Highway 190 North, Suite 200.
Telephone: 504-871-9444.
Fax: 504-871-9666.

MEMBERS OF FIRM

Gordon A. Pugh
Murphy J. Foster, III
Leo C. Hamilton
Jerry L. Stovall, Jr.

ASSOCIATES

Juliet T. Rizzo
Melissa M. Shirley
William Bowen McRae, Jr.
A. Todd Caruso

Counsel for: Allied-Signal Corp.; Reynolds Metal Co.; Illinois Central Railroad Co.

For Complete List of Firm Personnel, See General Section

For full biographical listings, see the Martindale-Hubbell Law Directory

KEAN, MILLER, HAWTHORNE, D'ARMOND, MCCOWAN & JARMAN, L.L.P. (AV)

22nd Floor, One American Place, 70825
Telephone: 225-387-0999
Fax: 225-388-9133
Mailing Address: P.O. Box 3513, Baton Rouge, Louisiana, 70821
URL: http://WWW.KMLAW.COM
New Orleans, Louisiana Office: Energy Centre, Suite 1560, 1100 Poydras Street, 70163.
Telephone: 504-585-3050.
Fax: 504-585-3051.
Plaquemine, Louisiana Office: Suite 10, 23425 Railroad Avenue, 70764.
Telephone: 225-687-9845.
Fax: 225-382-3445.
Lake Charles, Louisiana Office: One Lakeshore Drive, Suite 1220, 70629.
Telephone: 318-430-0350.
Fax: 318-436-5566.
Covington, Louisiana Office: 503 North New Hampshire Street, P.O. Box 3096, 70433.
Telephone: 504-875-0400.
Fax: 504-875-0500.

MEMBERS OF FIRM

William R. D'Armond
Michael C. Garrard
David K. Nelson
Melanie M. Hartmann
Cynthia M. Chemay
Gregg R. Kronenberger

Theresa R. Hagen
Carolyn S. Parmenter
A. Edward Hardin, Jr.

Representative Clients: Anco Industries, Inc., Baton Rouge, LA; BASF Corporation, Geismar, LA; City of Baton Rouge/Parish of East Baton Rouge; DSM Copolymer, Inc., Baton Rouge, LA; Exxon Corporation, Baton Rouge, LA; Formosa Plastics Corporation, Livingston, NJ; Lamar Advertising Co., Baton Rouge, LA; Piccadilly Cafeterias, Inc., Baton Rouge, LA; Turner Industries, Ltd., Baton Rouge, LA; Vulcan Materials Company, Geismar, LA.

For full biographical listings, see the Martindale-Hubbell Law Directory

*LAFAYETTE,** Lafayette Parish

ONEBANE, BERNARD, TORIAN, DIAZ, MCNAMARA & ABELL (AV)

Suite 600, Versailles Centre, 102 Versailles Boulevard, P.O. Box 3507, 70502
Telephone: 318-237-2660
Telecopier: 318-266-1232
Email: info@onebane.com
Monroe, Louisiana Office: 1900 N. 18th Street, Suite 420, P.O. Box 2255, 71207.
Telephone: 318-340-0220.
Fax: 318-340-0110.

Joseph Onebane (1917-1987)
John G. Torian, II (1936-1991)
James E. Diaz
Timothy J. McNamara
Edward C. Abell, Jr.
Lawrence L. Lewis, III
Robert M. Mahony
Daniel G. Fournerat
Douglas W. Truxillo
Randall C. Songy

(See Next Column)

Michael G. Durand
Greg Guidry
Joseph L. Lemoine, Jr.
Mark L. Riley
Graham N. Smith
Gordon T. Whitman
Gary P. Kraus
Richard J. Petre, Jr.
Charles J. Boudreaux, Jr.
James R. Shelton
Thomas G. Smart
Roger E. Ishee
Jennifer M. Kleinpeter
Steven C. Lanza
Joel P. Babineaux

Alison M. Brumley
Jesse D. Lambert
Brent G. Sonnier
Cary B. Bryson
Maria F. Manuel
Greg R. Mier
Jennifer L. Smith
Janice Church Reeves
Mark B. Oliver
Chanelle T. Delahoussaye
Aimee L. Williams
A.G. "Alec" Alexander, III
Terry J. Blanchard
William E. Bourgeois (Resident, Monroe, Louisiana Office)

OF COUNSEL

William E. Kellner

Representative Clients: Acadian Ambulance Service, Inc.; BellSouth Corp.; Dillard Corp.; Global Marine Drilling Co.; Marathon Oil Co.; Nike; Pennzoil; Security Finance Corp.; Union Camp Corp.; Raytheon Co.

For full biographical listings, see the Martindale-Hubbell Law Directory

METAIRIE, Jefferson Parish

ROBEIN, URANN & LURYE, A PROFESSIONAL LAW CORPORATION (AV)

2540 Severn Avenue, Suite 400, P.O. Box 6768, 70009-6768
Telephone: 504-885-9994
Fax: 504-885-9969

Louis L. Robein, Jr.
Robert H. Urann
William Lurye
Julie Richard-Spencer
Nancy Picard
Maria C. Cangemi

William Ken Hawkins
Edward K. Newman

Representative Clients: Greater New Orleans AFL-CIO; Seafarers International Union; Operating Engineers; Plumbers & Steamfitters; Operative Plasterers & Cement Masons; Carpenters Locals; Carpenters District Council; International Brotherhood of Electrical Workers; Radio Officers Union; Boilermakers.

For full biographical listings, see the Martindale-Hubbell Law Directory

MICHAEL T. TUSA, JR. (AV)

The Heritage Plaza, Suite 200, 111 Veterans Boulevard, 70005
Telephone: 504-828-1010
Telefax: 504-833-8520
Email: mtusalaw@bellsouth.net

OF COUNSEL

David E. Walker

*NEW ORLEANS,** Orleans Parish

CHAFFE, MCCALL, PHILLIPS, TOLER & SARPY, L.L.P. (AV)

A Partnership including a Professional Law Corporation
2300 Energy Centre, 1100 Poydras Street, 70163-2300
Telephone: 504-585-7000
Telecopier: 504-585-7075
Cable Address: "Denegre"
Telex: (AT&T) 460122 CMPTS
Email: cmptsno%chaffe@mcimail.com *URL:* http://www.chaffe.com
Baton Rouge, Louisiana Office: 202 Two United Plaza, 8550 United Plaza Boulevard.
Telephone: 504-922-4300.
Fax: 504-922-4304.
Caracas, Venezuela Office: Edificio Exa, Piso 10, Oficina PH-10, Avenida Venezuela entre Calles EL Retiro y Alameda, El Rosal.
Telephone: 011-582-953-4136.
Fax: 011-582-953-6518.

MEMBERS OF FIRM

G. Phillip Shuler, III
Julie D. Livaudais
Robert B. Landry, III
Andrew C. Partee, Jr.
D. Scott Landry (Resident Partner, Baton Rouge)

ASSOCIATES

Julie D. Savage
Richard B. Ramirez

OF COUNSEL

Suzanne Haik Terrell

Representative Clients: Associated Builders and Contractors, Inc.; Columbia/HCA Healthcare Corp.; Louisiana State Board of Registration for Professional Engineers and Land Surveyors; Pharmacia & Upjohn Co.; Nestle Beverage Co.; North Oaks Health System; Quorum Health Systems; Tulane University; Tulane University Hospital and Clinic; Uniroyal Chemical, Inc.

For Complete List of Firm Personnel, See General Section

For full biographical listings, see the Martindale-Hubbell Law Directory

New Orleans—Continued

VICTOR R. FARRUGIA A PROFESSIONAL LAW CORPORATION (AV)

228 St. Charles Avenue Suite 1028, 70130-2610
Telephone: 504-525-0250
Fax: 504-525-7064
Email: vrfarrugia@nela.org *URL:* http://www.lawyers.com/victorfarrugia

Victor R. Farrugia

Catherine Chauvin Cooper

For full biographical listings, see the Martindale-Hubbell Law Directory

FISHER & PHILLIPS LLP (AV)

A Limited Liability Partnership including Professional Corporations and Professional Associations
201 St. Charles Avenue, Suite 3710, 70170
Telephone: 504-522-3303
Telecopier: 504-529-3850
URL: http://www.laborlawyers.com
Atlanta, Georgia Office: 1500 Resurgens Plaza, 945 East Paces Ferry Road, N.E., 30326.
Telephone: 404-231-1400.
Telecopier: 404-240-4249.
Fort Lauderdale, Florida Office: Suite 2300 NationsBank Tower, One Financial Plaza, 33394.
Telephone: 954-525-4800.
Telecopier: 954-525-8739.
Redwood City, California Office: Suite 345, Three Lagoon Drive, 94065.
Telephone: 650-592-6160.
Telecopier: 650-592-6385.
Newport Beach, California Office: 4675 MacArthur Court, Suite 550, 92660.
Telephone: 949-851-2424.
Telecopier: 949-851-0152.
Houston, Texas Office: 6850 Chase Tower, 600 Travis, 77002.
Telephone: 713-227-5410.
Telecopier: 713-236-6949.
Chicago, Illinois Office: 420 Marquette Building, 140 South Dearborn Street, 60603.
Telephone: 312-346-8061.
Telecopier: 312-346-3179.

MEMBERS OF FIRM

Michael S. Mitchell (Resident)
Ralph J. Zatzkis
James D. Morgan (Resident)
Sandra Mills Feingerts (Resident)
Stephen J. Roppolo (Resident)

RESIDENT OF COUNSEL

Deborah R. Walworth
Susan Whittington Leidner

RESIDENT ASSOCIATES

Timothy H. Scott
Dorian L. Lobman
Michael L. Fantaci
Winston G. DeCuir, Jr.
Scott D. Schneider

Representative Clients: BASF Corp.; Blockbuster Entertainment Corp.; Ciba-Geigy Corp.; Colonial Sugars; Hormel Foods Corp.; Louisiana Land & Exploration Co.

For full biographical listings, see the Martindale-Hubbell Law Directory

LOWE, STEIN, HOFFMAN, ALLWEISS & HAUVER, L.L.P. (AV)

One Shell Square, 701 Poydras Street Suite 3600, 70139-7735
Telephone: 504-581-2450
Telecopier: 504-581-2461

MEMBERS OF FIRM

Michael R. Allweiss
Marynell L. Piglia

For Complete List of Firm Personnel, See General Section

For full biographical listings, see the Martindale-Hubbell Law Directory

MCCALLA, THOMPSON, PYBURN, HYMOWITZ & SHAPIRO (AV)

A Limited Liability Partnership including Professional Corporations
Suite 2800, Poydras Center, 650 Poydras Street, 70130
Telephone: 504-524-2499
Fax: 504-523-8679
Email: mtphs@mtphs.com *URL:* http://www.mtphs.com
Gulfport, Mississippi Office: The Markham Building, 2301 14th Street, Suite 507, 39501.
Telephone: 228-868-2774.
Fax: 228-865-3911.

MEMBERS OF FIRM

Robert K. McCalla (P.C.)
Horace A. Thompson III (P.C.)
Keith M. Pyburn, Jr., (P.C.)
Steven Hymowitz (P.C.)
Howard Shapiro (P.C.)
Stefanie Band Allweiss
James M. McGrew (P.C.)
Steven R. Cupp (P.C.)

(See Next Column)

ASSOCIATES

Heather G. Magier
Taryn S. Southon
Megan Shemwell Nash
Edward F. Harold
Robert Rachal
David P. Bendana
René E. Thorne
Larry E. Demmons
Stacey C. S. Cerrone
Charlotte S. Marquez
Lawrence J. Sorohan II

For Complete List of Firm Personnel, See General Section

For full biographical listings, see the Martindale-Hubbell Law Directory

MCGLINCHEY STAFFORD (AV)

A Professional Limited Liability Company
643 Magazine Street, 70130-3477
Telephone: 504-586-1200
Fax: 504-596-2800
TDD: (504) 596-2728
Telex: 584327
Cable Address: "MACSTAC"
Mailing Address: P.O. Box 60643, New Orleans, Louisiana, 70160-0643
Email: @mcglinchey.com *URL:* http://www.mcglinchey.com
Dallas, Texas Office: 2777 Stemmons Freeway, Suite 925, 75207-2401.
Telephone: 214-860-9700.
Fax: 214-860-9750.
Houston, Texas Office: 2727 Allen Parkway, Suite 1900, 77019.
Telephone: 713-520-1900.
Fax: 713-520-1025.
Baton Rouge, Louisiana Office: Ninth Floor, One American Place, 70825-0001.
Telephone: 504-383-9000.
Fax: 504-343-3076.
Jackson, Mississippi Office: Suite 1200, SkyTel Centre, 200 South Lamar Street, 39201.
Telephone: 601-960-8400.
Fax: 601-960-8406.
Lake Providence, Louisiana Office: 405 Morgan Street, 71254-2691.
Telephone: 318-559-1200.
Fax: 318-559-0609.
Monroe, Louisiana Office: Dean ONB Tower, 130 Desiard Street, Suite 807, 71201.
Telephone: 318-651-0807.
Fax: 318-651-0809.

MEMBERS OF FIRM

E. Fredrick Preis, Jr.
Eve B. Masinter
Stephen P. Beiser
Katherine Conklin
Kevin L. O'Dea
Mark N. Mallery
Anita Lechner Bosch

ASSOCIATES

Daniel T. Plunkett
Eliska Marie Plunkett
Joan Marie Canny
Stephanie G. John
Lance Andrew Bowling
Jonas P. Baker
Christopher E. Moore (Not admitted in LA)

MEMBER OF FIRM

Samuel E. Scott (Resident, Jackson Office)

ASSOCIATES

Vincent J. Bodin (Resident, Houston Office)
Lindsay Patterson (Resident, Jackson Office)
Amanda K. Bishop
F. Sherman Boughton, Jr. (Resident, Lake Providence Office)

For full biographical listings, see the Martindale-Hubbell Law Directory

MILLING BENSON WOODWARD L.L.P. (AV)

A Partnership including Professional Law Corporations
Suite Twenty-Three Hundred, 909 Poydras Street, 70112-1017
Telephone: 504-569-7000
Telecopier: 504-569-7001
ABA net: 15656
MCI Mail: "Milling"
Email: milling@millinglaw.com
Lafayette, Louisiana Office: 101 La Rue France, Suite 200.
Telephone: 318-232-3929.
Telecopier: 318-233-4957.
Mandeville (North Shore), Louisiana Office: 2140 8th Street.
Telephone: 504-867-9622.
Telecopier: 504-867-8364.

MEMBERS OF FIRM

Robert L. Clayton (P.C.)
Michael M. Duran (P.C.)
Alanna S. Arnold (P.C.)

ASSOCIATES

Sherry L. Tew
Murphy S. Christina

See General Section for list of Representative Clients.

For Complete List of Firm Personnel, See General Section

For full biographical listings, see the Martindale-Hubbell Law Directory

New Orleans—Continued

PHELPS DUNBAR, L.L.P. (AV)

Texaco Center, 400 Poydras Street, 70130-3245
Telephone: 504-566-1311
Telecopier: 504-568-9130, 504-568-9007
Cable Address: "Howspencer"
Telex: 584125 WU
Telex: 6821155 WUI
Email: info@phelps.com
Baton Rouge, Louisiana Office: Suite 701, 445 North Boulevard, P.O. Box 4412.
Telephone: 225-346-0285.
Telecopier: 225-381-9197.
Jackson, Mississippi Office: Suite 500, SkyTel Centre, 200 South Lamar Street, P.O. Box 23066.
Telephone: 601-352-2300.
Telecopier: 601-360-9777.
Tupelo, Mississippi Office: Seventh Floor, One Mississippi Plaza, P.O. Box 1220.
Telephone: 662-842-7907.
Telecopier: 662-842-3873.
Houston, Texas Office: Suite 900, 3040 Post Oak Boulevard.
Telephone: 713-626-1386.
Telecopier: 713-626-1388.
London, England Office: Suite 731, Level 7, Lloyd's, 1 Lime Street, London EC3M 7DQ England.
Telephone: 011-44-207-929-4765.
Telecopier: 011-44-207-929-0046.
Telex: 987321.

RESIDENT PARTNERS

William D. Aaron, Jr.
M. Nan Alessandra
Jane E. Armstrong
R. Pepper Crutcher, Jr. (Resident, Jackson, Mississippi Office)
Susan Fahey Desmond
Gary E. Friedman (Not admitted in LA; Resident, Jackson, Mississippi Office)
Susan W. Furr (Resident, Baton Rouge, Louisiana Office)
Thomas H. Kiggans (Resident, Baton Rouge, Louisiana Office)
Paul O. Miller, III (Not admitted in LA; Resident, Jackson, Mississippi Office)
Armin J. Moeller, Jr. (Resident, Jackson, Mississippi Office)
Harry Rosenberg
W. Thomas Siler, Jr. (Not admitted in LA; Resident, Jackson, Mississippi Office)
David M. Thomas, II (Not admitted in LA; Resident, Jackson, Mississippi Office)

RESIDENT ASSOCIATES

Joseph Lee Adams (Not admitted in LA; Resident, Jackson, Mississippi Office)
Christine McCue Daly
Ken Fairly (Not admitted in LA; Resident, Jackson, Mississippi Office)
Mark Fijman (Not admitted in LA; Resident, Jackson, Mississippi Office)
Christine S. Goldberg (Resident, Baton Rouge, Louisiana Office)
Karleen Joseph (Resident, Baton Rouge, Louisiana Office)
David M. Korn
Tricia A. Martinez
A. Matt Pesnell (Not admitted in LA; Resident, Jackson, Mississippi Office)
Chelye E. Prichard (Not admitted in LA; Resident, Jackson, Mississippi Office)
Joanne Rinardo
E. Russell Turner (Not admitted in LA; Resident, Jackson, Mississippi Office)
Michael F. Weiner

Representative Clients: Borg-Warner Protective Services Corp.; Citizens Utilities Company; Dow Chemical USA; General Motors Corporation; Hibernia Corporation; Louisiana Lottery Corporation; Mississippi Municipal Liability Plan; Philip Morris Incorporated; Union Pacific Railroad Company.

For Complete List of Firm Personnel, See General Section

For full biographical listings, see the Martindale-Hubbell Law Directory

WAGNER & BAGOT (AV)

Suite 2660, Poydras Center, 650 Poydras Street, 70130-6105
Telephone: 504-525-2141
Telecopier: 504-523-1587
TWX: 5106017673
ELN: 62928850
"INCISIVE"

Thomas J. Wagner
Michael H. Bagot, Jr.

Thomas A. Rayer, Jr.
Brian P. Brancato
Thomas P. Henican
Dana A. Henderson

For full biographical listings, see the Martindale-Hubbell Law Directory

*SHREVEPORT,** Caddo Parish

BLANCHARD, WALKER, O'QUIN & ROBERTS, A PROFESSIONAL LAW CORPORATION (AV)

Fourteenth Floor, Premier Bank Tower, 400 Texas Street, P.O. Drawer 1126, 71101
Telephone: 318-221-6858
Fax: 318-227-2967
Email: BWOR@BWOR.com
Bossier City, Louisiana Office: 2285 Benton Road, Suite B-201.
Telephone: 318-742-9255.
Fax: 318-742-9210.

John T. Cox, Jr.
W. Michael Adams
Pamela G. Nathan

For Complete List of Firm Personnel, See General Section

For full biographical listings, see the Martindale-Hubbell Law Directory

DAVIDSON, NIX & JONES, A PROFESSIONAL LAW CORPORATION (AV)

509 Market Street, Suite 800, 71101
Telephone: 318-424-4342
Fax: 318-226-0168

Randall S. Davidson
Ernest L. Nix, Jr.
Allison A. Jones
John S. Hodge

Grant E. Summers

For full biographical listings, see the Martindale-Hubbell Law Directory

WILKINSON, CARMODY & GILLIAM (AV)

1700 Beck Building, 400 Travis Street, P.O. Box 1707, 71166
Telephone: 318-221-4196
Telecopier: 318-221-3705
Email: wcg1895@aol.com

MEMBERS OF FIRM

John D. Wilkinson (1867-1929)
William Scott Wilkinson (1895-1985)
Arthur R. Carmody, Jr.
Bobby S. Gilliam
Mark E. Gilliam
William Allen Haynes

Representative Clients: Farmers Insurance Group; Home Federal Savings & Loan Association of Shreveport; The Kansas City Southern Railway Co.; KTAL-TV; Lincoln National Life Insurance Co.; Mobil Oil Co.; Schumpert Medical Center; Sears, Roebuck & Co.; Southern Pacific Transportation Co.; Southwestern Electric Power Co.

For full biographical listings, see the Martindale-Hubbell Law Directory

MAINE

*AUGUSTA,** Kennebec Co.

JOHNSON & WEBBERT, L.L.P. (AV)

160 Capitol Street, P.O. Box 29, 04332-0029
Telephone: 207-623-5110
Fax: 207-622-4160
Email: pjohnson@johnsonwebbert.com *URL:* http://www.lawyers.com/jwl-law

Phillip E. Johnson
David G. Webbert

Representative Clients: Agway, Inc.; AVEMCO; Central Maine Power Co.; The Doctors Company; ITT/Hartford; Loss Management Services, Inc.; Shand, Morahan & Co.; Union Water Power Company.

For full biographical listings, see the Martindale-Hubbell Law Directory

LIPMAN & KATZ, P.A. (AV)

227 Water Street, P.O. Box 1051, 04332-1051
Telephone: 207-622-3711
Telecopier: 207-622-7415
Email: lipmankatz@ibm.net

Sumner H. Lipman
David M. Lipman
Roger J. Katz
Robert J. Stolt
Keith R. Varner
Ronald E. Colby, III
Walter F. McKee

Karen E. Lipman
Tracie L. Adamson
Gregg D. Bernstein

OF COUNSEL

Joseph B. Campbell

For full biographical listings, see the Martindale-Hubbell Law Directory

*BANGOR,** Penobscot Co.

EATON, PEABODY, BRADFORD & VEAGUE, P.A. (AV)

Fleet Center-Exchange Street, P.O. Box 1210, 04402-1210
Telephone: 207-947-0111
Telecopier: 207-942-3040
Email: eaton@eatonpeabody.com *URL:* http://www.eatonpeabody.com
Augusta, Maine Office: 77 Sewall Street, Suite 3000.
Telephone: 207-622-3747.
Telecopier: 207-622-9732.
Blue Hill, Maine Office: One East Blue Hill Road.
Telephone: 207-374-2812.
Telecopier: 207-374-2548.
Brunswick, Maine Office: 167 Park Row.
Telephone: 207-729-1144.
Telecopier: 207-729-1140.
Dover-Foxcroft, Maine Office: 30 East Main Street.
Telephone: 207-564-8378.
Telecopier: 207-564-7059.

Malcolm E. Morrell, Jr.
Thomas C. Johnston
Clare Hudson Payne

Matthew S. Raynes

For Complete List of Firm Personnel, See General Section

For full biographical listings, see the Martindale-Hubbell Law Directory

RUDMAN & WINCHELL, LLC (AV)

84 Harlow Street, P.O. Box 1401, 04402-1401
Telephone: 207-947-4501
Telecopy: 207-941-9715
URL: http://www.rudman-winchell.com

MEMBERS OF FIRM

Abraham M. Rudman (1896-1970)
Albert H. Winchell, Jr. (1924-1992)
Gerald E. Rudman
Phillip D. Buckley
Michael P. Friedman
Winfred A. Stevens
Robert E. Sutcliffe
Paul W. Chaiken
David C. King
John W. McCarthy
Frank T. McGuire
Bruce C. Mallonee
Paul H. Sighinolfi
William H. Hanson
George F. Eaton, II
Edith A. Richardson
Michael M. McAleer
Brett D. Baber
Barbara A. Cardone
Robert E. Murray, Jr.
Edmond J. Bearor
Curtis E. Kimball
Brent A. Singer

ASSOCIATES

Jane E. Skelton
Leigh Stephens McCarthy
Virginia Kozak Putnam
Ajaz S. Fiazzuddin
Anne-Marie Storey Hamer
Hans S. Peterson
Christopher J. Austin

Counsel for: Penobscot Shoe Co.; Sherman Lumber Co.; Webber Oil Co.; Fleet Bank of Maine; Key Bank of Maine; McCain Foods, Inc.
Local Counsel for: Commercial Union York Insurance Cos.; Hanover Insurance Company; Liberty Mutual Insurance Co.

For full biographical listings, see the Martindale-Hubbell Law Directory

*PORTLAND,** Cumberland Co.

BENNETT BENNETT AND TROIANO, P.A. (AV)

Suite 300, 121 Middle Street, P.O. Box 7799, 04112-7799
Telephone: 207-773-4775
Telecopier: 207-774-2366
Email: lawyers@bennettlegal.com *URL:* http://www.bennettlegal.com

Herbert H. Bennett (1928-1992)
Peter Bennett
Jeffrey Bennett
Joseph A. Troiano
Frederick B. Finberg

Julie A. Boesky

OF COUNSEL

Jonathan M. Dunitz

Counsel for: Associated Grocers of New England; Coca Cola Bottling Company of Northern New England, Inc.; North American Philips Corp.; Northern Utilities/Bay State Gas; Pratt & Whitney (Division of United Technologies); Primerica Financial Services (Citigroup); Sprague Energy (C.H. Sprague & Son); Lepage Bakeries, Inc. (Country Kitchen); Texaco, Inc.

For full biographical listings, see the Martindale-Hubbell Law Directory

BURNS RAY & DELANO, PROFESSIONAL ASSOCIATION (AV)

193 Middle Street, 04101-4062
Telephone: 207-775-3581
Facsimile: 207-775-3814
Email: mailcenter@brdlaw.com

(See Next Column)

George F. Burns
David P. Ray
Arnold C. Macdonald
Mary DeLano
Elizabeth A. Burns
Carrie A. Green

OF COUNSEL

Joanne F. Cole

Representative Clients: Maine Yankee Atomic Power Company; Tractebel Power, Inc.; Hancock Lumber Co., Inc.; Jackson Laboratory; Hague International (engineering); Viking Freight, Inc.; Hancock Lumber Co., Inc.; Aetna Life & Casualty Co.; The Hartford; Great American Insurance Co.

For full biographical listings, see the Martindale-Hubbell Law Directory

PIERCE ATWOOD (AV)

One Monument Square, 04101
Telephone: 207-791-1100
Fax: 207-791-1350
Email: info@PierceAtwood.com *URL:* http://www.pierceatwood.com
Augusta, Maine Office: 77 Winthrop Street.
Telephone: 207-622-6311.
Fax: 207-623-9367.
Newburyport, Massachusetts Office: 6 Harris Street.
Telephone: 978-465-9599.
Fax: 978-465-9945.

MEMBERS OF FIRM

S. Mason Pratt, Jr.
Charles S. Einsiedler, Jr.
Peter H. Jacobs
James R. Erwin
Margaret Coughlin LePage
Anthony R. Derosby

ASSOCIATES

Allan M. Muir
Ann L. Rudisill

COUNSEL

Elizabeth Eddy Griffin

For Complete List of Firm Personnel, See General Section

For full biographical listings, see the Martindale-Hubbell Law Directory

PRETI, FLAHERTY, BELIVEAU, PACHIOS & HALEY, LLC (AV)

One City Center, P.O. Box 9546, 04112-9546
Telephone: 207-791-3000
Telecopier: 207-791-3111
Email: admin@preti.com *URL:* http://www.preti.com
Augusta, Maine Office: 45 Memorial Circle, P.O. Box 1058, 04332-1058.
Telephone: 207-623-5300.
Telefax: 207-623-2914.
Bath, Maine Office: Thirty Front Street, P.O. Box 665, 04530-0665.
Telephone: 207-443-5576.
Telefax: 207-443-6665.

MEMBERS OF FIRM

Mark L. Haley (Bath Office)
Daniel Rapaport
Michael G. Messerschmidt
Randall B. Weill
Evan M. Hansen
Geoffrey K. Cummings
Stephen E. F. Langsdorf (Augusta Office)
Elizabeth A. Olivier
Nelson J Larkins
Timothy J. Bryant

COUNSEL

Albert J. Beliveau, Jr.
Peter S. Carlisle

ASSOCIATES

Tracey G. Burton (Bath Office)
Roy T. Pierce
Elizabeth A. Campbell
Jeffrey W. Peters (Bath Office)
Matthew J. LaMourie

Representative Clients: Bronze Craft Corp.; Northern New England Benefit Trust; Maine Turnpike Authority; Maine Maritime Academy; Blethen-Maine Newspapers, Inc.; Hussey Seating Co.

For Complete List of Firm Personnel, See General Section

For full biographical listings, see the Martindale-Hubbell Law Directory

TROUBH, HEISLER & PIAMPIANO, P.C. (AV)

511 Congress Street, P.O. Box 9711, 04104-5011
Telephone: 207-780-6789
Fax: 207-774-2339
Email: info@thplaw.com

William B. Troubh
Edwin A. Heisler
Robert J. Piampiano
Kevin M. Gillis
Michael P. Boyd
Thomas E. Getchell
Michael Richards
William K. McKinley
Daniel F. Gilligan
Paul S. Bulger
John G. Richardson

Daniel R. Felkel
Ann Brandt
John P. Flynn, III

For full biographical listings, see the Martindale-Hubbell Law Directory

Portland—Continued

VERRILL & DANA, LLP (AV)

One Portland Square, P.O. Box 586, 04112-0586
Telephone: 207-774-4000
Fax: 207-774-7499
Email: advice@verdan.com *URL:* http://www.verdan.com
Augusta, Maine Office: 45 Memorial Circle, P.O. Box 957.
Telephone: 207-623-3889.
Fax: 207-622-3117.
Kennebunk, Maine Office: 403-404 Lafayette Center, P.O. Box 147.
Telephone: 207-985-7193.
Fax: 207-985-3957.
Washington, D.C. Office: 400 North Capitol Street, Suite 585.
Telephone: 202-624-9733.
Fax: 202-393-5218.

OF COUNSEL

Marianne McGettigan

MEMBERS OF FIRM

Douglas P. Currier — James A. McCormack
Timothy J. O'Brien — Robert C. Brooks

ASSOCIATES

Elizabeth Connellan — Kristen Potter Farnham
Brent G.T. Geraty

Counsel for: ASCAP; Bowdoin College; Fleet Bank; Hannaford Bros. Co.; Maine Blue Cross and Blue Shield; Maine Public Service Co.; Peoples Heritage Bank; Portland Water District.

For Complete List of Firm Personnel, See General Section

For full biographical listings, see the Martindale-Hubbell Law Directory

MARYLAND

*ANNAPOLIS,** Anne Arundel Co.

COUNCIL, BARADEL, KOSMERL & NOLAN, P.A. (AV)

125 West Street, Fourth Floor, P.O. Box 2289, 21404-2289
Telephone: 410-268-6600
Baltimore: 410-269-6190
Washington, D.C.: 301-261-2247
FAX: 410-269-8409
Email: cbkn@cbknlaw.com

Ronald E. Council — William F. Flood, III
Ronald A. Baradel — Kevin M. Schaeffer
Wayne T. Kosmerl — Donna McCabe Schaeffer
James P. Nolan — Frederick C. Sussman

John Naumann Strange — Edwin H. Staples, II
Susan T. Ford — Susan Stobbart Shapiro

OF COUNSEL

George N. Manis — Nicholas Goldsborough

Representative Clients: Anne Arundel County; Annapolis Bank and Trust; Bank of Maryland; State Farm Mutual Automobile Insurance Co.; Annapolis Yacht Club; Annapolis Yacht Sales, Inc.

For full biographical listings, see the Martindale-Hubbell Law Directory

*BALTIMORE,** (Independent City)

THE LAW OFFICES OF KATHLEEN CAHILL, LLC (AV)

15 East Chesapeake Avenue, 21286
Telephone: 410-321-6171
Fax: 410-821-7740
Email: kcahillesq@aol.com

Kathleen Cahill

For full biographical listings, see the Martindale-Hubbell Law Directory

DUBÉ & GOODGAL, P.C. (AV)

The Can Company, Suite 407, 2400 Boston Street, 21224
Telephone: 410-276-8801
Telecopier: 410-276-8807
Email: dubelaw@aol.com *URL:* http://www.dubelaw.com
Washington, D.C. Office: Suite 400, 1730 M Street, N.W.
Telephone: 202-331-2183.
Telecopier: 410-276-8807.

Lawrence E. Dubé, Jr. — Paula A. Goodgal

Reference: Merchantile Safe Deposit and Trust Co.

For full biographical listings, see the Martindale-Hubbell Law Directory

FERGUSON, SCHETELICH & HEFFERNAN, P.A. (AV)

1401 NationsBank Center, 100 South Charles Street, 21201-2725
Telephone: 410-837-2200
Fax: 410-837-1188
URL: http://www.FSHLaw.com

Robert L. Ferguson, Jr. — Christopher J. Heffernan
Thomas J. Schetelich — Craig F. Ballew
Michael N. Russo, Jr.

Peter J. Basile — Tracey J. McLauchlin
Ann D. Ware — Michele P. Zahner
Michael K. Hourigan

For full biographical listings, see the Martindale-Hubbell Law Directory

GEORGE E. GOLOMB (AV)

Suite 2700, 111 South Calvert Street, 21202
Telephone: 410-752-3866
Telefax: 410-385-5201
Email: goegle@erols.com

For full biographical listings, see the Martindale-Hubbell Law Directory

KAHN, SMITH & COLLINS, P.A. (AV)

201 North Charles Street, 10th Floor, 21201
Telephone: 410-244-1010
Fax: 410-244-8001
URL: http://www.interbit.com/ksc

Andrew H. Kahn — Francis J. Collins
Joel A. Smith — David V. Diggs
Keith J. Zimmerman

Leslie A. Pladna — Travis M. Mastroddi
Sarah Pazourek Harlan — Sabrina Willis

For full biographical listings, see the Martindale-Hubbell Law Directory

KOLLMAN & SHEEHAN, P.A. (AV)

Sun Life Building, 20 South Charles Street, 21201-3225
Telephone: 410-727-4300
Telecopier: 410-727-4391
URL: http://www.kollman-sheehan.com

Frank L. Kollman — Francis R. Laws
David M. Sheehan — Darrell R. VanDeusen
Peter S. Saucier — Clifford B. Geiger

Bruce M. Luchansky — Desmond Terrell McIlwain
Richard P. Rieman, Jr. — Joseph R. Salko
Randi Klein Hyatt — Tracy L. Knight
Jeffrey A. Trueman

For full biographical listings, see the Martindale-Hubbell Law Directory

KRUCHKO & FRIES (AV)

600 Washington Avenue, Suite 305, 21204
Telephone: 410-321-7310
Telecopier: 410-821-7918
McLean, Virginia Office: Suite 202, 7929 Westpark Drive.
Telephone: 703-734-0554.
Washington, D.C. Office: 601 Pennsylvania Avenue, Suite 900.
Telephone: 202-347-6550.

MEMBERS OF FIRM

John G. Kruchko — Jay R. Fries
Paul M. Lusky

ASSOCIATES

Kathleen A. Talty — Joan E. Book

OF COUNSEL

Frank S. Astroth

For full biographical listings, see the Martindale-Hubbell Law Directory

PIPER & MARBURY L.L.P. (AV)

36 South Charles Street, 21201-3018
Telephone: 410-539-2530
FAX: 410-539-0489
Email: lawfirm@pipermar.com *URL:* http://www.pipermar.com
Washington, D.C. Office: 1200 Nineteenth Street, N.W., 20036-2430.
Telephone: 202-861-3900.
FAX: 202-223-2085.
New York, N.Y. Office: 1251 Avenue of the Americas, 10020-1104.
Telephone: 212-835-6000.
FAX: 212-835-6001.
Philadelphia, Pennsylvania Office: 3400 Two Logan Square, 18th & Arch Streets, 19103-2762.
Telephone: 215-656-3300.
FAX: 215-656-3301.

(See Next Column)

PIPER & MARBURY L.L.P.—*Continued*

Easton, Maryland Office: 117 Bay Street, 21601-2703.
Telephone: 410-820-4460.
FAX: 410-820-4463.
Princeton, N.J. Office: 116 Village Boulevard, Suite 200, Princeton Forrestal Village, 08540.
Telephone: 609-951-2252.
FAX: 609-951-2216.
Reston, Virginia Office: 1850 Centennial Park Drive, Suite 610, Commerce Executive Park III, 20191.
Telephone: 703-391-7100.
Fax: 703-309-5299.

MEMBERS OF FIRM

Leonard E. Cohen
Russell H. Gardner
Richard J. Hafets
Emmett F. McGee, Jr.
Eric Paltell

For Complete List of Firm Personnel, See General Section

For full biographical listings, see the Martindale-Hubbell Law Directory

SEROTTE, ROCKMAN & WESCOTT, P.A. (AV)

Mercantile-Towson Building, Suite 610, 409 Washington Avenue, 21204
Telephone: 410-825-7900
Fax: 410-825-7913
Email: srwlabor@aol.com

Neal Serotte
Jeffrey E. Rockman
Lawrence S. Wescott

Elizabeth G. Jacobs
Eileen Carr Riley
Jonathan Peter Sills

For full biographical listings, see the Martindale-Hubbell Law Directory

SHAWE & ROSENTHAL (AV)

Sun Life Building, 20 South Charles Street, 21201
Telephone: 410-752-1040
Telecopier: 410-752-8861
Email: srmail@Shawe.com *URL:* http://www.shawe.com

MEMBERS OF FIRM

Earle K. Shawe
William J. Rosenthal
Carrol Hament (Retired)
Stephen D. Shawe
Arthur M. Brewer
Bruce S. Harrison
Patrick M. Pilachowski
Eric Hemmendinger
J. Michael McGuire
Mark J. Swerdlin
Gary L. Simpler
R. Michael Smith
Robert H. Ingle, III
Elizabeth I. Torphy-Donzella
Francis W. Connolly

Representative Clients: Amdahl Corp.; Baltimore Gas & Electric Co.; Bethlehem Steel Corp.; Black & Decker (U.S.) Inc.; Federal Reserve Bank of Richmond; The May Department Stores Co. (Hecht's, Washington, D.C.; Filene's); McDonald's Corp.; Thiokol Corp. (now Cordant Technologies, Inc.); United States Fidelity & Guaranty Co. (now St. Paul Cos.); Geico.

For full biographical listings, see the Martindale-Hubbell Law Directory

VENABLE ATTORNEYS AT LAW VENABLE, BAETJER AND HOWARD, LLP (AV)

A Partnership including Professional Corporations
1800 Mercantile Bank & Trust Building, 2 Hopkins Plaza, 21201
Telephone: 410-244-7400
Fax: 410-244-7742
URL: http://www.venable.com
Washington, D.C. Office: Venable, Baetjer, Howard & Civiletti LLP, Suite 1000, 1201 New York Avenue, N.W.
Telephone: 202-962-4800.
Fax: 202-962-8300.
McLean, Virginia Office: Suite 400, 2010 Corporate Ridge.
Telephone: 703-760-1600.
Fax: 703-821-8949.
Rockville, Maryland Office: Suite 500, One Church Street, P. O. Box 1906.
Telephone: 301-217-5600.
Fax: 301-217-5617.
Towson, Maryland Office: 210 Allegheny Avenue, P. O. Box 5517.
Telephone: 410-494-6200.
Fax: 410-821-0147.

MEMBERS OF FIRM

John Henry Lewin, Jr. (P.C.)
Stanley Mazaroff (P.C.)
Roger W. Titus (Resident, Rockville, Maryland Office)
Kenneth C. Bass, III (Not admitted in MD; Washington, D.C. and McLean, Virginia Offices)
John H. Zink, III (Resident, Towson, Maryland Office)
Paul T. Glasgow (Resident, Rockville, Maryland Office)
Joseph C. Wich, Jr. (Resident, Towson, Maryland Office)
Joseph G. Block (Not admitted in MD; Resident, Washington, D.C. Office)
Sondra Harans Block (Resident, Rockville, Maryland Office)
Craig E. Smith
Robert G. Ames (Also at Washington, D.C. Office)
Nell B. Strachan
Barbara E. Schlaff

(See Next Column)

MEMBERS OF FIRM (Continued)

G. Stewart Webb, Jr.
George W. Johnston (P.C.)
Jana Howard Carey (P.C.)
Jeffrey A. Dunn (Also at Washington, D.C. Office)
George F. Pappas (Also at Washington, D.C. Office)
James L. Shea (Also at Washington, D.C. Office)
Jeffrey P. Ayres (P.C.)
Maurice Baskin (Resident, Washington, D.C. Office)
C. Carey Deeley, Jr. (Also at Towson, Maryland Office)
Christopher R. Mellott
James A. Dunbar (Resident, Towson, Maryland Office)
Ronald W. Taylor
Robert L. Waldman
John A. Roberts (Also at Rockville, Maryland Office)
Patrick J. Stewart (Also at Washington, D.C. Office)
Gary M. Hnath (Resident, Washington, D.C. Office)
Mitchell Y. Mirviss
Michael W. Robinson (Resident, McLean, Virginia Office)
Todd J. Horn
Patrick L. Clancy (Resident, Rockville, Maryland Office)
David W. Goewey (Not admitted in MD; Resident, Washington, D.C. Office)
John A. McCauley
John T. Prisbe
Elizabeth Marzo Borinsky
Vicki Margolis (Also at Washington, D.C. Office)
Christine M. McAnney (Not admitted in MD; Resident, McLean, Virginia Office)
Connie N. Bertram (Not admitted in MD; Resident, Washington, D.C. Office)

OF COUNSEL

A. Samuel Cook (P.C.) (Resident, Towson, Maryland Office)

ASSOCIATES

Scharon L. Ball
Paul D. Barker, Jr.
Robin B. Bowerfind
Patricia Gillis Cousins (Resident, Rockville, Maryland Office)
E. Anne Hamel
John C. Hardwick, Jr. (Resident, Washington, D.C. Office)
Thomas H. Strong
David R. Warner (Resident, Rockville, Maryland Office)

For Complete List of Firm Personnel, See General Section

For full biographical listings, see the Martindale-Hubbell Law Directory

WHITEFORD, TAYLOR & PRESTON L.L.P. (AV)

7 Saint Paul Street, 21202-1626
Telephone: 410-347-8700
Telex: 5101012334
Fax: 410-752-7092
Email: wt&pllp@wtplaw.com *URL:* http://www.wtplaw.com
Towson, Maryland Office: 210 West Pennsylvania Avenue.
Telephone: 410-832-2000.
Fax: 410-832-2015.
Washington, D.C. Office: 1025 Connecticut Avenue, N.W.
Telephone: 202-659-6800.
Fax: 202-331-0573.
Columbia, Maryland Office: 10440 Little Patuxent Parkway.
Telephone: 410-884-0700.
Fax: 410-884-0719.
Alexandria, Virginia Office: 1317 King Street.
Telephone: 703-836-5742.
Fax: 703-836-0265.

Steven E. Bers
Peter D. Guattery
Kevin C. McCormick
Jeanne M. Phelan
Joseph K. Pokempner
Arthur P. Rogers (Resident Washington, D.C. Office)
Larry M. Wolf

OF COUNSEL

Robert S. Hillman

ASSOCIATES

Melissa L. Menkel
Elizabeth Sarah Rudnick

For Complete List of Firm Personnel, See General Section

For full biographical listings, see the Martindale-Hubbell Law Directory

BETHESDA, Montgomery Co.

PALEY, ROTHMAN, GOLDSTEIN, ROSENBERG & COOPER, CHARTERED (AV)

Seventh Floor, One Bethesda Center, 4800 Hampden Lane, 20814
Telephone: 301-656-7603
Telecopier: 301-654-7354
Email: prg@paleyrothman.com

Glenn M. Cooper
Victor J. Rosenberg
Mark S. Goldstein
Mark S. Rothman
Stephen H. Paley
Paula A. Calimafde
Ronald A. Dweck
Arthur H. Blitz
Robert H. Maclay
Steven A. Widdes
Hope Eastman
Dennis L. Sharp
Albert D. Pailet
Diane A. Fox
Theodore P. Stein
Jeffrey A. Kolender
Wendelin I. Lipp
Mark A. Binstock
Patricia M. Weaver

(See Next Column)

PALEY, ROTHMAN, GOLDSTEIN, ROSENBERG & COOPER CHARTERED, *Bethesda—Continued*

Alan D. Eisler
David M. Rothenstein
Brent M. Goldstein
Kathleen M. Dumais
James R. Hammerschmidt
Deborah A. Cohn

SENIOR COUNSEL

Alan S. Mark
Daniel S. Koch
Daniel P. Hodin

For full biographical listings, see the Martindale-Hubbell Law Directory

GARY HOWARD SIMPSON (AV)

9505 Kingsley Avenue, 20814
Telephone: 301-493-0345
Fax: 301-493-0347
Email: ghslaw@erols.com *URL:* http://www.lawyers.com/garyhsimpson

Alane Tempchin

OF COUNSEL

Krauthamer & Stahl, Chartered, Chevy Chase, Maryland

LEGAL SUPPORT PERSONNEL

Michelle Ratcliffe (Paralegal)
Joy Simpson (Paralegal)

For full biographical listings, see the Martindale-Hubbell Law Directory

*ROCKVILLE,** Montgomery Co.

STEIN, SPERLING, BENNETT, DE JONG, DRISCOLL, GREENFEIG & METRO, P.C. (AV)

25 West Middle Lane, 20850-2204
Telephone: 301-340-2020; 800-435-5230
Telecopier: 301-340-8217
Email: lawfirm@steinsperling.com
Falls Church, Virginia Office: 6245 Leesburg Pike, Suite 140, 22044.
Telephone: 703-237-0500.
Telecopier: 703-534-2899.

David C. Driscoll, Jr.
A. Howard Metro
Jeffrey M. Schwaber
Donald N. Sperling

Jeffrey D. Goldstein
Marc J. Smith

For Complete List of Firm Personnel, See General Section

For full biographical listings, see the Martindale-Hubbell Law Directory

VENABLE ATTORNEYS AT LAW VENABLE, BAETJER AND HOWARD, LLP (AV)

A Partnership including Professional Corporations
Suite 500, One Church Street, P.O. Box 1906, 20850-4129
Telephone: 301-217-5600
Fax: 301-217-5617
URL: http://www.venable.com
Baltimore, Maryland Office: 1800 Mercantile Bank & Trust Building, 2 Hopkins Plaza.
Telephone: 410-244-7400.
Fax: 410-244-7742.
Washington, D.C. Office: Venable, Baetjer, Howard & Civiletti LLP, Suite 1000, 1201 New York Avenue, N.W.
Telephone: 202-962-4800.
Fax: 202-962-8300.
McLean, Virginia Office: Suite 400, 2010 Corporate Ridge.
Telephone: 703-760-1600.
Fax: 703-821-8949.
Towson, Maryland, Office: 210 Allegheny Avenue, P. O. Box 5517.
Telephone: 410-494-6200.
Fax: 410-821-0147.

MEMBERS OF FIRM

Roger W. Titus
Paul T. Glasgow
Sondra Harans Block
John A. Roberts (Also at Baltimore, Maryland Office)
Patrick L. Clancy

ASSOCIATES

Patricia Gillis Cousins
David R. Warner

For Complete List of Firm Personnel, See General Section

For full biographical listings, see the Martindale-Hubbell Law Directory

*TOWSON,** Baltimore Co.

VENABLE ATTORNEYS AT LAW VENABLE, BAETJER AND HOWARD, LLP (AV)

A Partnership including Professional Corporations
210 Allegheny Avenue, P.O. Box 5517, 21204
Telephone: 410-494-6200
Fax: 410-821-0147
URL: http://www.venable.com
Baltimore, Maryland Office: 1800 Mercantile Bank & Trust Building, 2 Hopkins Plaza.
Telephone: 410-244-7400.
Fax: 410-244-7742.
Washington, D.C. Office: Venable, Baetjer, Howard & Civiletti LLP, Suite 1000, 1201 New York Avenue, N.W.
Telephone: 202-962-4800.
Fax: 202-962-8300.
McLean, Virginia Office: Suite 400, 2010 Corporate Ridge.
Telephone: 703-760-1600.
Fax: 703-821-8949.
Rockville, Maryland Office: Suite 500, One Church Street, P. O. Box 1906.
Telephone: 301-217-5600.
Fax: 301-217-5617.

PARTNERS

John H. Zink, III
Joseph C. Wich, Jr.
C. Carey Deeley, Jr. (Also at Baltimore, Maryland Office)

OF COUNSEL

A. Samuel Cook (P.C.)

For Complete List of Firm Personnel, See General Section

For full biographical listings, see the Martindale-Hubbell Law Directory

MASSACHUSETTS

*BOSTON,** Suffolk Co.

ANDERSON, ADLER, COHEN & HARVEY LLP (AV)

230 Congress Street, 02110
Telephone: 617-423-6674
Telefax: 617-423-7152
Email: aach@aachlaw.com *URL:* http://www.aachlaw.com

MEMBER OF FIRM

Alexandra B. Harvey

For full biographical listings, see the Martindale-Hubbell Law Directory

CARR & LISTON (AV)

294 Washington Street, Suite 506, 02108-4608
Telephone: 617-482-6355
Fax: 617-482-7197
Email: ecarr@socialaw.com *URL:* http://www.lawyers.com/carrliston

MEMBERS OF FIRM

Edwin J. Carr
Michael J. Liston

For full biographical listings, see the Martindale-Hubbell Law Directory

FOLEY, HOAG & ELIOT LLP (AV)

One Post Office Square, 02109
Telephone: 617-832-1000
Telecopier: 617-832-7000
Email: fhe@fhe.com *URL:* http://www.fhe.com
Washington, D.C. Office: 1747 Pennsylvania Avenue, N.W.
Telephone: 202-223-1200.
Telecopier: 202-785-6687.

MEMBERS OF FIRM

David B. Ellis
Philip Burling
Paul V. Lyons
Arthur G. Telegen
Stephen B. Deutsch
William B. Koffel
Kevin J. Fitzgerald
Michele A. Whitham

ASSOCIATES

Pamela B. Blatte
Michael Parker Boudett
James W. Bucking
Karen B. Dietrich
Jeffrey S. Follett
Sarah A. Forster
Jonathan A. Keselenko
Vijay Moses
Hilary Ames Poret
Michael L. Rosen
Tracey E. Spruce
Karen L. Vossler

For Complete List of Firm Personnel, See General Section

For full biographical listings, see the Martindale-Hubbell Law Directory

Boston—Continued

HINCKLEY, ALLEN & SNYDER LLP (AV)

28 State Street, 30th Floor, 02109-1775
Telephone: 617-345-9000
Email: firm@haslaw.com *URL:* http://www.haslaw.com
Providence, Rhode Island Office: 1500 Fleet Center.
Telephone: 401-274-2000.
Fax: 401-277-9600. URL: http://www.hawlaw.com.

MEMBERS OF FIRM

David D. Barricelli (Not admitted in MA)
Paul Bork
Stephen J. Carlotti (Not admitted in MA)
Michael P. DeFanti
Eric F. Eisenberg
Malcolm Farmer, III
Margaret D. Farrell (Not admitted in MA)
Pasco Gasbarro Jr.
Hugh J. Gorman, III
Gerard R. Goulet
William R. Grimm
Paul A. Hedstrom
Richard L. E. Jocelyn (Not admitted in MA)
Joel Lewin
Frederick P. McClure
H. Peter Olsen (Not admitted in MA)
Julianne Palumbo
John J. Pendergast, III (Not admitted in MA)
Gerald J. Petros
Jeremy Ritzenberg
Charles E. Schaub, Jr.
Douglas F. Seaver
Herman Snyder
David R. Sullivan
Robert F. Sylvia
Howard E. Walker (Not admitted in MA)
Richard D. Wayne

ASSOCIATES

Kelley Jordan-Price
John P. Martin

OF COUNSEL

Willard Krasnow
Debra Dyleski Najjar

For Complete List of Firm Personnel, See General Section

For full biographical listings, see the Martindale-Hubbell Law Directory

MENARD, MURPHY & WALSH LLP (AV)

One Financial Center, 02111
Telephone: 617-832-2500
Telecopier: 617-832-2550
Email: mmw@mmwlaw.com
Washington, D.C. Office: Farragut Park, 910 17th Street, NW, Suite 800, 20006.
Telephone: 202-293-3500.
Telecopier: 202-293-3596.

Arthur P. Menard
Paul J. Murphy
Joseph H. Walsh
John E. Coyne
John S. Leonard

COUNSEL

Theodore E. Daiber

ASSOCIATES

Kevin G. Mahoney
Kevin P. Sweeney
Robert S. Steinberg

For full biographical listings, see the Martindale-Hubbell Law Directory

MORGAN, BROWN & JOY, LLP (AV)

One Boston Place, 02108
Telephone: 617-523-6666
Facsimile: 617-367-3125
URL: http://www.morganbrown.com

MEMBERS OF FIRM

John W. Morgan (1898-1974)
Murray Brown (1900-1996)
William F. Joy (1918-1999)
Alan I. Kaplan
James M. Paulson
Nicholas DiGiovanni, Jr.
William F. Joy, Jr.
Robert P. Joy
Nathan L. Kaitz
Keith H. McCown
Keith B. Muntyan
Laurence J. Donoghue
Allison K. Romantz
Jaclyn L. Kugell
Philip G. Boyle
James J. Rooney
Diane M. Saunders
Joseph P. McConnell

ASSOCIATES

Brigitte M. Duffy
Patricia Lim
Maura D. McLaughlin
Stacy L. Miller

OF COUNSEL

Robert P. Morris

Representative Clients: Acushnet Company; AT&T Corp.; Boston Edison Co.; Combustion Engineering; Data General Corp.; Federated Department Stores; General Electric; John Hancock Mutual Life Insurance Co.; Kraft Foods, Inc.

For full biographical listings, see the Martindale-Hubbell Law Directory

PALMER & DODGE LLP (AV)

One Beacon Street, 02108
Telephone: 617-573-0100
Facsimile: 617-227-4420
URL: http://www.palmerdodge.com

(See Next Column)

MEMBERS OF FIRM

Michael R. Brown
Andrew L. Eisenberg
Judith A. Malone
Mark E. Schreiber
Elizabeth P. Seaman

For Complete List of Firm Personnel, See General Section

For full biographical listings, see the Martindale-Hubbell Law Directory

PRINCE, LOBEL & TYE LLP (AV)

585 Commercial Street, 02109-1024
Telephone: 617-367-2202
Fax: 617-523-0977

MEMBER OF FIRM

Walter B. Prince

ASSOCIATES

Thomas A. Bockhorst
Laurie F. Rubin

For Complete List of Firm Personnel, See General Section

For full biographical listings, see the Martindale-Hubbell Law Directory

ROCHE, CARENS & DEGIACOMO, P.C. (AV)

99 High Street, 02110
Telephone: 617-457-4000
Facsimile: 617-482-3868
Email: firm@rcdpc.com *URL:* http://www.rcdpc.com
Woburn, Massachusetts Office: 600 Unicorn Park Drive.
Telephone: 781-933-5505.

John W. Gahan, III
Susan J. Baronoff
Tracie L. Longman

Laurie Alexander-Krom

For Complete List of Firm Personnel, See General Section

For full biographical listings, see the Martindale-Hubbell Law Directory

STONEMAN, CHANDLER & MILLER LLP (AV)

99 High Street, 02110
Telephone: 617-542-6789
Telecopier: 617-556-8989

MEMBERS OF FIRM

Alan S. Miller
Robert Chandler
Carol Chandler
Kay H. Hodge
Robert G. Fraser
Macon P. Magee
Miriam K. Freedman
Rebecca Bryant

ASSOCIATES

Nancy Norfolk Nevils
Geoffrey R. Bok
Joan Lerner Stein
Karen Shaffer Levy
Sandra L. Moody
Ronald M. Jacobs
Andrew L. Rodman
John M. Simon (Not admitted in MA)

Representative Clients: Wm. Filene's Sons Co.; Beth Israel Deaconess Medical Center; Tufts Associated Health Plan; Ritz Carlton Hotel; Ocean Spray Cranberries; Citizen's Bank; Jordan's Furniture; Weston School Committee; Lexington School Committee.

For full biographical listings, see the Martindale-Hubbell Law Directory

FITCHBURG, Worcester Co.

O'CONNOR AND RYAN, P.C. (AV)

61 Academy Street, 01420
Telephone: 978-345-4166
Fax: 978-343-8416

John M. O'Connor
Edward P. Ryan, Jr.

Eugene P. O'Donnell, Jr.

For full biographical listings, see the Martindale-Hubbell Law Directory

FRAMINGHAM, Middlesex Co.

DOMESTICO & BARRY (AV)

The Meadows, 161 Worcester Road, 01701
Telephone: 508-626-9000
Fax: 508-626-9001
Email: DandBLaw@aol.com

MEMBERS OF FIRM

Charles J. Domestico
Susan Moran-Barry
James A. Kobe

For full biographical listings, see the Martindale-Hubbell Law Directory

QUINCY, Norfolk Co.

Murphy, Hesse, Toomey and Lehane (AV)

Crown Colony Plaza, 300 Crown Colony Drive, Suite 410, P.O. Box 9126, 02269-9126
Telephone: 617-479-5000
Fax: 617-479-6469
Email: lawfirm@mhtl.com

MEMBERS OF FIRM

Arthur P. Murphy
Katherine A. Hesse
James A. Toomey
Michael C. Lehane
John P. Flynn
Regina Williams Tate
Edward F. Lenox, Jr.
Mary Ellen Sowyrda
David A. DeLuca
Ann M. O'Neill
David W. Healey

ASSOCIATES

Joseph T. Bartulis, Jr.
Michael R. Bertoncini
Sreelekha Chakrabart Amoruso
Thomas W. Colomb
Michael F.X. Dolan, Jr.
Doris R. MacKenzie Ehrens
Nicola Favorito
Kevin P. Feeley, Jr.
Mary L. Gallant
Lorna M. Hebert
Robert H. Morsilli
Kathryn M. Murphy
Frank E. Rowbotham
Andrew J. Waugh
Geoffrey P. Wermuth
Donald L. Graham

COUNSEL

Paul F. Dempsey

For full biographical listings, see the Martindale-Hubbell Law Directory

*SPRINGFIELD,** Hampden Co.

Robinson Donovan Madden & Barry, P.C. (AV)

Suite 1600, Tower Square, 1500 Main Street, 01115-5609
Telephone: 413-732-2301
Fax: 413-785-4658
Email: service@robinson-donovan.com *URL:* http://www.robinson-donovan.com

Homans Robinson (1894-1973)
Lawrence M. Sinclair (1942-1986)
Milton J. Donovan (1906-1995)

RETIRED

John H. Madden, Jr.
Edward J. Barry
Richard S. Milstein

OF COUNSEL

Victor Rosenberg

SENIOR COUNSEL

Jonathan P. Rice

Gordon H. Wentworth
James H. Tourtelotte
Ronald C. Kidd
Jeffrey W. Roberts
Jeffrey L. McCormick
James F. Martin
Robert P. Cunningham
John C. Sikorski
Nancy Frankel Pelletier
Paul S. Weinberg
Frederica H. McCarthy
Matthew J. King
Neva Kaufman Rohan
Douglas F. Boyd
James K. Bodurtha
Keith A. Minoff
Patricia M. Rapinchuk
Kimberly Davis Crear

E. Paul Amata
Lisa A. Bongiovi (Not admitted in MA)
Edward J. Carroll, III
James D. Chadwell
John E. Garber
Patrick J. Markey
Carla W. Newton
Betsy Macmillan Stevens

Representative Clients: BankBoston, N.A.; United Cooperative Bank; Fleet National Bank; CNA; Commercial Union Insurance Co.; Hanover Insurance Group.

For full biographical listings, see the Martindale-Hubbell Law Directory

Skoler, Abbott & Presser, P.C. (AV)

Suite 2000, One Monarch Place, 01144
Telephone: 413-737-4753
Fax: 413-787-1941
Email: SAP@skoler-abbott.com
Worcester, Massachusetts Office: 30 Park Avenue.
Telephone: 508-757-5335.

Martin E. Skoler (1932-1991)
Ralph F. Abbott, Jr.
Jay M. Presser
John H. Glenn
Rosemary J. Nevins

Richard U. Stubbs, Jr.
Marylou Fabbo
Jo-Ann W. Davis

(See Next Column)

OF COUNSEL

Martin Fleisher

Representative Clients: Smith & Wesson Corp.; Baystate Health System; Travelers Insurance Company; Hampshire College; Proctor & Gamble Company.

For full biographical listings, see the Martindale-Hubbell Law Directory

*WORCESTER,** Worcester Co.

Mountain, Dearborn & Whiting LLP (AV)

370 Main Street, 01608
Telephone: 508-756-2423
Fax: 508-755-6640

MEMBERS OF FIRM

Alfred N. Whiting (1920-1989)
Thomas R. Mountain
Richard W. Dearborn
Samuel R. DeSimone
Henry W. Beth
Stuart A. Hammer
Francis J. Russell
Dale R. Harger
Mark W. Bloom
Donald J. O'Neil
Lawrence S. Delaney
Ann K. Molloy
Lisa D. Tingue

For full biographical listings, see the Martindale-Hubbell Law Directory

Skoler, Abbott & Presser, P.C. (AV)

30 Park Avenue, 01605
Telephone: 508-757-5335
Email: SAP@skoler-abbott.com
Springfield, Massachusetts Office: Suite 2000, One Monarch Place.
Telephone: 413-737-4753.
Fax: 413-787-1941.

Martin E. Skoler (1932-1991)
Ralph F. Abbott, Jr.
Jay M. Presser
John H. Glenn
Rosemary J. Nevins

Richard U. Stubbs, Jr.
Marylou Fabbo
Jo-Ann W. Davis

OF COUNSEL

Martin Fleisher

Representative Clients: Allegro Microsystems, Inc.; Olympus Healthcare; Baystate Medical Center; Erving Paper Mills; National Envelope Co.; Jamesbury, Inc.; Smith & Wesson; Spalding Sports Worldwide.

For full biographical listings, see the Martindale-Hubbell Law Directory

MICHIGAN

*ANN ARBOR,** Washtenaw Co.

Braun Kendrick Finkbeiner PLC (AV)

First National Building, 210 S. Main, Suite 700, 48104
Telephone: 313-995-4100
Telecopier: 313-995-4798
Email: ALBFIE@BKF-LAW.COM *URL:* http://www.bkf-law.com
Bay City, Michigan Office: 201 Phoenix Building, P.O. Box 2039.
Telephone: 517-895-8505.
Telecopier: 517-895-8437.
Saginaw, Michigan Office: 101 N. Washington, Suite 812.
Telephone: 517-753-3461.
Telecopier: 517-753-3951.
Saginaw Township, Michigan Office: 5800 Gratiot Road, Suite 107, P.O. Box 5169.
Telephone: 517-799-8692.
Fax: 517-799-4666.
Mt. Pleasant, Michigan Office: 805 North Brown.
Telephone: 517-775-7404.
Telecopier: 517-775-3764.

Barry M. Levine

Representative Clients: The Dow Chemical Co.; General Motors Corp.; Merrill, Lynch, Inc.; Saginaw General Hospital; Saginaw News; The Wickes Foundation.

For Complete List of Firm Personnel, See General Section

For full biographical listings, see the Martindale-Hubbell Law Directory

Hooper, Hathaway, Price, Beuche & Wallace (AV)

126 South Main Street, 48104
Telephone: 313-662-4426
Fax: 313-662-9559
Email: hhpbw@voyager.net

(See Next Column)

HOOPER, HATHAWAY, PRICE, BEUCHE & WALLACE—*Continued*

Bruce T. Wallace
Anthony P. Patti
Angela L. Jackson

Representative Clients: Avfuel Corporation; Bank of Ann Arbor; Castrol North America; Chem-Trend Incorporated; Ervin Industries, Inc.; First Martin Corporation; Glacier Hills, Inc.; Prestolite Electric, Inc.; Southern States Cooperative; E.B. Eddy Forest Products, Ltd.

For Complete List of Firm Personnel, See General Section

For full biographical listings, see the Martindale-Hubbell Law Directory

MILLER, CANFIELD, PADDOCK AND STONE, P.L.C. (AV)

A Professional Limited Liability Company
Founded in 1852 by Sidney Davy Miller
101 North Main Street, Seventh Floor, 48104-1400
Telephone: 734-663-2445
Fax: 734-747-7147
URL: http://www.millercanfield.com
Detroit, Michigan Office: 150 West Jefferson, Suite 2500, 48226-4415.
Telephone: 313-963-6420.
Fax: 313-496-7500.
Cable Address: "Stem Detroit."
Troy, Michigan Office: 840 West Long Lake Road, Suite 200, 48098.
Telephone: 248-879-2000.
Fax: 248-879-2001.
Grand Rapids, Michigan Office: 99 Monroe, N.W., Suite 1200, 49503-2639.
Telephone: 616-454-8656.
Fax: 616-776-6322.
Howell, Michigan Office: 121 South Barnard Street, Suite 4, 48843-2305.
Telephone: 517-546-7600.
Telecopier: 517-546-6974.
Kalamazoo, Michigan Office: 444 West Michigan Avenue, 49007-3752.
Telephone: 616-381-7030.
Fax: 616-382-0244.
Lansing, Michigan Office: One Michigan Avenue, Suite 900, 48933-1609.
Telephone: 517-487-2070.
Fax: 517-374-6304.
Monroe, Michigan Office: 214 East Elm Avenue, Suite 100, 48162-2682.
Telephone: 734-243-2000.
Fax: 734-243-0901.
Washington, D.C. Office: 1900 K Street, N.W., Suite 1150. 20006.
Telephone: 202-429-5575; 785-0600.
Fax: 202-331-1118; 785-1234.
Pensacola, Florida Office: 25 West Cedar, 32501.
Telephone: 850-469-1088.
Fax: 850-432-0677.
New York, New York Office: 1450 Broadway, 41st Floor, 10018.
Telephone: 212-704-4400.
Fax: 212-704-4410.
Gdynia, Poland Office: UL. Slaska 21, 81-319.
Telephone: 011-485-831-2808.
Fax: 011-48-58-628 6411.
Warsaw, Poland Office: UL. Nowogrodzkall, 5th Floor, 00-513.
Telephone: 011-4822 529 0200.
Fax: 011-4822 529 0201.
Katowice, Poland Office: UL. Francuska 35/37, 40-027.
Telephone: 011 (48-32) 757-2414.
Fax: 011 (48-32) 757-2483.

PRINCIPALS OF FIRM

Charles A. Duerr, Jr.

Representative Firm Clients: Chrysler Corporation; Comerica, Incorporated; City of Detroit, Michigan; Detroit Tigers, Inc.; First of Michigan; Ford Motor Company; Ford Motor Credit Company; Great Lakes Bancorp; Henry Ford Hospital; INVETECH Company.

For Complete List of Firm Personnel, See General Section

For full biographical listings, see the Martindale-Hubbell Law Directory

PEAR SPERLING EGGAN & MUSKOVITZ, P.C. (AV)

Domino's Farms, 24 Frank Lloyd Wright Drive, 48105
Telephone: 734-665-4441
Fax: 734-665-8788
Email: peare@dominos.com
Ypsilanti, Michigan Offices: 5 South Washington Street.
Telephone: 734-483-3626 and 2164 Bellevue at Washtenaw.
Telephone: 734-483-7177.

Melvin J. Muskovitz
Thomas E. Daniels
Paul R. Fransway
Francyne Stacey
David E. Kempner

Counsel for: Domino's Pizza, Inc.; Townsend and Bottum, Inc.; Dynamation, Inc.; Citizens Banking Corporation; Thomas Design and Engineering Services, Inc.; Mechanical Dynamics, Inc.; Meadowbrook Insurance Group; City of Wixom; City of Ypsilanti; Ann Arbor Transportation Authority.

For Complete List of Firm Personnel, See General Section

For full biographical listings, see the Martindale-Hubbell Law Directory

BATTLE CREEK, Calhoun Co.

KREIS, ENDERLE, CALLANDER & HUDGINS, A PROFESSIONAL CORPORATION (AV)

One West Michigan Avenue, 49017
Telephone: 616-966-3000
Facsimile: 616-966-3022
Email: kech@kech.com *URL:* http://www.kech.com
Kalamazoo, Michigan Office: One Moorsbridge, P.O. Box 4010, 49003-4010.
Telephone: 616-324-3000.
Fax: 616-324-3010.

Douglas L. Callander (Resident, Kalamazoo Office)
James C. Boerigter (Resident, Kalamazoo Office)
John F. Koryto (Resident, Kalamazoo Office)
Floyd E. Gates, Jr.

For Complete List of Firm Personnel, See General Section

For full biographical listings, see the Martindale-Hubbell Law Directory

*BAY CITY,** Bay Co.

BRAUN KENDRICK FINKBEINER PLC (AV)

201 Phoenix Building, P.O. Box 2039, 48708
Telephone: 517-895-8505
Telecopier: 517-895-8437
Email: ALBFIE@BKF-LAW.COM *URL:* http://www.bkf-law.com
Saginaw, Michigan Office: 101 N. Washington, Suite 812. 8th Floor Second National Bank Building.
Telephone: 517-753-3461.
Telecopier: 517-753-3951.
Saginaw Township, Michigan Office: 5800 Gratiot Road, Suite 107, P.O. Box 5169.
Telephone: 517-799-8692.
Fax: 517-799-4666.
Ann Arbor, Michigan Office: First National Building. 201 S. Main, Suite 700.
Telephone: 313-995-4100.
Telecopier: 313-995-4798.
Mt. Pleasant, Michigan Office: 805 North Brown.
Telephone: 517-775-7404.
Telecopier: 517-775-3764.

Ralph J. Isackson
Daniel S. Opperman
Gregory T. Demers

Representative Clients: Bay Health Systems; Catholic Federal Credit Union; City of Saginaw; City of Vassar; City of Zilwaukee; Corporate Service; Cox Cable.

For Complete List of Firm Personnel, See General Section

For full biographical listings, see the Martindale-Hubbell Law Directory

BINGHAM FARMS, Oakland Co.

VERCRUYSSE METZ & MURRAY, A PROFESSIONAL CORPORATION (AV)

Suite 200, 31780 Telegraph Road, 48025-3469
Telephone: 248-540-8019
Facsimile: 248-540-8059

Robert M. Vercruysse
Virginia F. Metz
Gregory V. Murray
David B. Calzone
Bernice McReynolds

Daniel J. Bernard
Susan Hartmus Hiser
Susan Alfred Schechter
Patricia Bordman
Ann M. Nicklas
Maria T. Harshe
James E. Roach
William E. Altman
Gary S. Fealk
Kevin B. Hirsch

For full biographical listings, see the Martindale-Hubbell Law Directory

BIRMINGHAM, Oakland Co.

HYMAN LIPPITT, P.C. (AV)

185 Oakland Avenue, Suite 300, 48009
Telephone: 248-646-8292
Facsimile: 248-646-8375
Email: hymalipp@tir.com

J. Leonard Hyman
Norman L. Lippitt
Douglas A. Hyman
Brian D. O'Keefe
H. Joel Newman
Nazli G. Sater
Kenneth F. Neuman
Terry S. Givens
Paul J. Fischer
John A. Sellers
Robert H. Lippitt
Roger L. Myers
Sally A. Rutledge
Joseph Pia
John P. Gonway
Leif K. Anderson

(See Next Column)

HYMAN LIPPITT P.C., *Birmingham—Continued*

Jennifer S. Gold
Julie Lyons Kosovec
Dawn S. Spratley
Michael T. Price

For full biographical listings, see the Martindale-Hubbell Law Directory

KIENBAUM OPPERWALL HARDY & PELTON, P.L.C. (AV)

325 South Old Woodward Avenue, 48009
Telephone: 248-645-0000
800-806-9307
Voicemail Access: 248-645-1001
Fax: 248-645-1385
Email: kohpinfo@kohp.com *URL:* http://www.kohp.com
Detroit, Michigan Office: 1037 First National Building, 48226.
Telephone: 313-961-3926.
Fax: 313-961-3945.

Thomas G. Kienbaum
Theodore R. Opperwall
Elizabeth Phelps Hardy
Eric J. Pelton

Margaret Carroll Alli
Julia Turner Baumhart
Robert Bruce Brown
Noel D. Massie
Jeffery M. Peterson

For full biographical listings, see the Martindale-Hubbell Law Directory

LACEY & JONES, LLP (AV)

600 South Adams Road, Suite 300, 48009-6827
Telephone: 248-433-1414
Fax: 248-433-1241
URL: http://www.laceyjones.com
Ann Arbor, Michigan Office: Suite 525, 220 East Huron, 48104.
Telephone: 734-761-8358.
Fax: 734-761-3134.
Detroit, Michigan Office: Suite 3250, Penobscot Building, 645 Griswold, 48226.
Telephone: 313-961-6474.
Fax: 313-961-5688.
Grand Rapids, Michigan Office: Suite 430, Ledyard Building, 125 Ottawa Avenue, N.W., 49503.
Telephone: 616-776-3641.
Fax: 616-776-3516.
Jackson, Michigan Office: 740 West Michigan Avenue, 49201.
Telephone: 517-782-2000.
Fax: 517-782-3917.

Ralph B. Lacey (1885-1966)
William J. Jones (1908-1991)
Robert B. Lacey (1912-1976)
John A. Hilgendorf (Retired)
Theodore A. Lughezzani (Retired)
Steve N. Yardley (Retired)

MEMBERS OF FIRM

Brian S. Ahearn (Resident, Detroit)
Kathleen McNichol Behn
Larry P. Beidelman
Mary F. Clinton (Resident, Ann Arbor)
William A. Day
David J. Duthie (Resident, Grand Rapids)
T. F. Felker, Jr.
John Hayes
Charles J. Hurbis (Resident, Ann Arbor)
Lawrence G. Kozaruk
Richard N. Lovernick (Resident, Ann Arbor)
Charles E. Mann
Gerald M. Marcinkoski
J. Patrick O'Neill
Sean J. Powers
Michael T. Reinholm
Bruce C. Roberts
Peter M. Roggenbaum
Thomas J. Sullivan (Resident, Jackson)
Dennis E. Zacharski

Carrie G. Barrett
John C. Dickinson
Dawn M. Drobnich
Timothy D. Finegan
Timothy M. McAree (Resident, Grand Rapids)
D. Michael McCann
Dallas G. Moon
Robert H. Orlowski, Jr.
Johnnie B. Rambus
Kenneth S. Wilson

OF COUNSEL

Robert L. Beardslee
Georgette E. David (Resident, Ann Arbor)
Robert G. Lewandowski
William G. Sinn

Representative Clients: Alexsis, Inc.; Ameritech; Chrysler Corporation; CIGNA; Liberty Mutual Insurance Company; Meijer, Inc.; Metropolitan Prop. & Casualty; Michigan Hospital Association; Travelers Insurance Company; University of Michigan.

For full biographical listings, see the Martindale-Hubbell Law Directory

BLOOMFIELD HILLS, Oakland Co.

CYNTHIA ADKISON, P.C. (AV)

1533 North Woodward Avenue Suite 210, 48304
Telephone: 248-683-1000
Fax: 248-683-1007

Cynthia Adkison

For full biographical listings, see the Martindale-Hubbell Law Directory

DAWDA, MANN, MULCAHY & SADLER, P.L.C. (AV)

1533 North Woodward Avenue Suite 200, 48304-2815
Telephone: 248-642-3700
Fax: 248-642-7791
Email: EMail@DMMS.Com

Suanne Tiberio Trimmer
John Mucha, III
Keith James

John Gerald Gleeson, Jr.

Representative Clients: Bally's Total Fitness Corp.; Burlington Coat Factory; Cardell Corp.; DSP Technology, Inc.; Dow Corning Corp.; Family Dollar Stores, Inc.; Ladbroke Racing Corp.; La-Z-Boy, Inc.; SmithGroup, Inc.; Walker Wire (ISPAT).

For full biographical listings, see the Martindale-Hubbell Law Directory

SUE ELLEN EISENBERG, P.C. (AV)

Suite 145 33 Bloomfield Hills Parkway, 48304-2945
Telephone: 248-258-6080
Fax: 248-258-9212
Email: seepc@aol.com *URL:* http://www.lawyers.com/sueelleneisenberg

Sue Ellen Eisenberg

For full biographical listings, see the Martindale-Hubbell Law Directory

GUNSBERG & BRESKIN, P.C. (AV)

The Pinehurst Building, 1400 North Woodward Avenue, Suite 200, 48304
Telephone: 248-646-9090
Facsimile: 248-647-0638

David B. Gunsberg
Marvin Breskin

Representative Clients: Autodie International; Builders Association of S.E. Michigan; Federal Broadcasting Co.; Foamade Industries; Hercules Drawn Steel Corp.; I.S.I. Manufacturing, Inc.; McKinley Properties; Masco Industries, MascoTech; Progressive Tool; Tecumseh Products, Inc.

For full biographical listings, see the Martindale-Hubbell Law Directory

ROBERT HARRISON & ASSOCIATES (AV)

Bloomfield Office Pavilion, 2550 Telegraph Road, Suite 275, 48302
Telephone: 248-253-1800
Fax: 248-253-9446
URL: http://www.lawyers.com/harrison&associates

Robert S. Harrison

ASSOCIATES

Michael J. Rex
Michael James Harrison
Rachel M. Margules

References: Comerica Bank, Southfield; Huntington Banks of Michigan, W. Bloomfield.

For full biographical listings, see the Martindale-Hubbell Law Directory

HOWARD & HOWARD ATTORNEYS, P.C. (AV)

The Pinehurst Office Center, Suite 101, 1400 North Woodward Avenue, 48304-2855
Telephone: 248-645-1483
Telecopier: 248-645-1568
Kalamazoo, Michigan Office: The Michigan Building, Suite 200, 100 Portage Street.
Telephone: 616-382-1483.
Telecopier: 616-382-1568.
Lansing, Michigan Office: The Phoenix Building, Suite 500, 222 Washington Square, North.
Telephone: 517-485-1483.
Telecopier: 517-485-1568.
Peoria, Illinois Office: One Technology Plaza, Suite 600, 211 Fulton Street.
Telephone: 309-672-1483.
Telecopier: 309-672-1568.

Carol A. Friend
Robert B. Johnston
C. Douglas Moran
Brad A. Rayle
Jon Robert Steiger
Thomas H. Walters

Representative Clients: For Representative Client list, see General Practice, Bloomfield Hills, MI.

For Complete List of Firm Personnel, See General Section

For full biographical listings, see the Martindale-Hubbell Law Directory

DAVID D. PATTON & ASSOCIATES, P.C. (AV)

44 East Long Lake Road, Suite 100, P.O. Box 829, 48303-0829
Telephone: 248-258-6020
Fax: 248-258-6052
Email: litigation@aol.com *URL:* http://www.lawyers.com/dpattonlaw

David D. Patton

(See Next Column)

DAVID D. PATTON & ASSOCIATES, P.C.—*Continued*

Ellen Bartman Jannette
Humma S. Siddiqi
Patricia C. White
Kelly P. Bekolay
David H. Patton (1912-1993)

OF COUNSEL

Lawrence J. Acker

For full biographical listings, see the Martindale-Hubbell Law Directory

DEARBORN, Wayne Co.

RILEY, HURLEY & DOLENGA, P.C. (AV)

19853 West Outer Drive, Suite 300, 48124
Telephone: 313-565-1330
Facsimile: 313-565-1318
Email: rfrpc@pop.net

Robert F. Riley
William C. Hurley
Michael D. Dolenga

Judy L. Burgard

OF COUNSEL

Mark S. Demorest
Michael J. Hainer
Leonard K. Berman

For full biographical listings, see the Martindale-Hubbell Law Directory

*DETROIT,** Wayne Co.

ABBOTT, NICHOLSON, QUILTER, ESSHAKI & YOUNGBLOOD, P.C. (AV)

300 River Place, Suite 3000, 48207-4225
Telephone: 313-566-2500
Telecopier: 313-566-2502
Email: anqey@anqey.com *URL:* http://www.anqey.com

C. Richard Abbott
John R. Nicholson
Thomas R. Quilter III
Gene J. Esshaki
John F. Youngblood
James B. Perry
Carl F. Jarboe
Jay A. Kennedy
Timothy A. Stoepker
Timothy J. Kramer
Norbert T. Madison, Jr.
William D. Gilbride, Jr.
Mary P. Nelson
Michael R. Blum
Anne Warren Bagno
Thomas J. Giachino

Eric J. Girdler
Jill A. Bankey
Daniel G. Kielczewski
George P. Butler III
Christopher P. Baker
Faith M. Gaudaen
Susan T. Rapp

OF COUNSEL

Thomas C. Shumaker
Lisa R. Gorman

For full biographical listings, see the Martindale-Hubbell Law Directory

BODMAN, LONGLEY & DAHLING LLP (AV)

34th Floor 100 Renaissance Center, 48243
Telephone: 313-259-7777
Fax: 313-393-7579
Email: info@bodmanlongley.com *URL:* http://www.bodmanlongley.com
Troy, Michigan Office: Suite 2020, 755 West Big Beaver Road.
Telephone: 248-362-2110.
Fax: 248-244-0780.
Ann Arbor, Michigan Office: 110 Miller, Suite 300.
Telephone: 734-761-3780.
Fax: 734-930-2494.
Northern Michigan Office: 229 Court Street, P.O. Box 405, Cheboygan.
Telephone: 231-627-4351.
Fax: 231-627-2802.

MEMBERS OF FIRM

James T. Heimbuch
James R. Buschmann
Robert G. Brower
John C. Cashen (Troy Office)
Lloyd C. Fell (Cheboygan Office)
Kathleen A. Lieder (Cheboygan Office)
Karen L. Piper
Jerold Lax (Ann Arbor Office)
Diane L. Akers
Stephen K. Postema (Ann Arbor Office)

ASSOCIATES

David A. Shand (Ann Arbor Office)
Courtland W. Anderson (Ann Arbor Office)
Christopher P. Mazzoli (Troy Office)
Kimberley R. Crouch

For Representative Client List, See General Section

For Complete List of Firm Personnel, See General Section

For full biographical listings, see the Martindale-Hubbell Law Directory

BRADY, HATHAWAY, BRADY & BRETZ, PROFESSIONAL CORPORATION (AV)

1330 Buhl Building, 48226-3602
Telephone: 313-965-3700
Telecopier: 313-965-2830
Email: brady@bradyhathaway.com

John F. Brady
Thomas M. J. Hathaway
Thomas P. Brady
Daniel J. Bretz
Connie M. Cessante
David A. Hardesty
Paul W. Coughenour
Jeffrey A. Steele
Tracy A. Leahy

David M. Cessante

Representative Clients: Beam Stream, Inc.; Bundy Corporation; Energy Conversion Devices, Inc.; Schering Corporation; Warner-Lambert; Wolverine Technologies; ABB Environmental Services.

For full biographical listings, see the Martindale-Hubbell Law Directory

BUTZEL LONG, A PROFESSIONAL CORPORATION (AV)

Suite 900, 150 West Jefferson, 48226
Telephone: 313-225-7000
Telecopier: 313-225-7080
Email: melnick@butzel.com *URL:* http://www.butzel.com
Birmingham, Michigan Office: Suite 200, 32270 Telegraph Road.
Telephone: 810-258-1616.
Telecopier: 810-258-1439.
Okemos, Michigan Office: Suite 300, 2127 University Park Drive.
Telephone: 517-372-6622.
Telecopier: 517-372-6672.
Ann Arbor, Michigan Office: Suite 300, 350 South Main Street.
Telephone: 313-995-3110.
Telecopier: 313-995-1777.
Grosse Pointe Farms, Michigan Office: Suite 260, 21 Kercheval.
Telephone: 313-886-5446.
Telecopier: 313-886-2114.
Boca Raton, Florida Office: Suite 411, 1200 North Federal Highway.
Telephone: 561-368-2151.
Telecopier: 561-368-4668.
Palm Beach Gardens, Florida Office: Suite 227, 11382 Prosperity Farms Road.
Telephone: 561-625-4442.
Telecopier: 561-625-6901.
Naples, Florida Office: Suite 705, 801 Laurel Oak Drive.
Telephone: 941-597-4500.
Telecopier: 941-597-5623.

William M. Saxton
Robert J. Battista
John Henry Dudley, Jr.
Donald B. Miller
John P. Hancock, Jr.
Alexander B. Bragdon
Mark T. Nelson
Michael D. Guzick (Birmingham)
Gary W. Klotz
Lynne E. Deitch
Daniel B. Tukel
Leonard M. Niehoff (Ann Arbor)
Carey A. DeWitt
David H. Oermann (Birmingham)
Robert A. Boonin
Andrea Roumell Dickson
James S. Rosenfeld
Jordan S. Schreier (Ann Arbor)
Nicholas J. Stasevich
Daniel R. W. Rustmann

OF COUNSEL

Dennis M. Devaney (Not admitted in MI)
David M. Gaskin (Grosse Pointe Farms and Birmingham)
Eugene L. Hartwig
Jerome D. Hill
Barbara T. Pichan

SENIOR ATTORNEY

Miriam R. Rosen

Debra Auerbach Clephane
Elizabeth A. DuMouchelle
Rosalie B. Harrison
Joseph M. Rogowski, II
Antoinette M. Pilzner
Regan S. Dahle
James A. Gray, III
Michael F. Smith
James Joseph Boutrous, II
Cynthia J. Haffey
Craig M. Stanley
Nicole Buonocore Porter

Representative Clients: Associated General Contractors; Detroit Diesel Corp.; Detroit Medical Center; Michigan Road Builders Assn.; Michigan Technological University; Stroh Companies; Teledyne, Inc.; Tishken Products, Inc.; The University of Michigan; William Beaumont Hospital.

For full biographical listings, see the Martindale-Hubbell Law Directory

CHARFOOS, REITER, PETERSON, HOLMQUIST & PILCHAK, P.C. (AV)

476 State of Michigan Plaza Building, 1200 Sixth Street, 48226
Telephone: 313-961-7011
Email: CRPHP@crphp.com
Farmington Hills, Michigan Office: 30500 Northwestern Highway, Suite 400.
Telephone: 248-626-7300.
Fax: 248-626-7305.

(See Next Column)

NEMETH BURWELL, P.C., *Detroit—Continued*

OF COUNSEL

Richard J. Fritz
Mary Rourke Benedetto

For full biographical listings, see the Martindale-Hubbell Law Directory

RILEY AND ROUMELL, P.C. (AV)

7th Floor, Ford Building, 48226-3986
Telephone: 313-962-8255
Telefax: 313-962-2937

Wallace D. Riley
George T. Roumell, Jr.
William F. Dennis
Steven M. Zarowny
Allen J. Lippitt
Alfred John Eppens
Wilber M. Brucker III
Gregory T. Schultz

OF COUNSEL

D. Michael Cherry
William D. Cohan
Emmet E. Tracy, Jr.

Representative Clients: Detroit Board of Education; Wayne County; City of Livonia; Lapeer County Road Commission; Manistee County Road Commission; Lake Superior State University; Village of Lake Orion; White Chapel Memorial Assn.

For full biographical listings, see the Martindale-Hubbell Law Directory

TIMMIS & INMAN L.L.P. (AV)

300 Talon Centre, 48207
Telephone: 313-396-4200
Facsimile: 313-396-4228
Email: info@timmis-inman.com *URL:* http://www.timmis-inman.com

Michael T. Timmis
Robert E. Graziani
George A. Peck
Henry J. Brennan, III
Mark W. Peyser
Richard M. Miettinen
Bradley J. Knickerbocker

Michael F. Wais
Shannon M. Nichols
Alex N. Saleh

Representative Clients: Talon, L.L.C.; Engineered Plastic Products, Inc.; Talon Automotive Group, Inc.; North American Die Casting Corp.

For Complete List of Firm Personnel, See General Section

For full biographical listings, see the Martindale-Hubbell Law Directory

VALENTINE & ASSOCIATES, P.C.

(See West Bloomfield)

WILLMARTH, TANOURY, RAMAR, CORBET, GARVES & SHAW (AV)

535 Griswold, Suite 1730, 48226-3602
Telephone: 313-964-6300
Fax: 313-964-6310
Email: mdwillth@home.net

MEMBERS OF FIRM

Daniel R. Corbet
Brian R. Garves
David R. Nauts
Anthony J. Paradiso
John M. Perrin
John J. Ramar
Bruce R. Shaw
William A. Tanoury
Mark D. Willmarth

ASSOCIATES

Marie C. Kennedy
Wayne Walker
Elizabeth L. Sokol
Robert S. Silverman
Carmine G. Paterra
Joseph J. Ceglarek, II
Derek Steven Wilczynski
Frank Hamidi
Kristen E. Skaff
Steven J. Bonasso
Colleen P. O'Connor
Lara R. Stutz
Eric G. Tucciarone
Michael P. Robach

For full biographical listings, see the Martindale-Hubbell Law Directory

WULFMEIER & OTTENWESS, PLC (AV)

The Buhl Building, 535 Griswold Suite 850, 48226
Telephone: 313-965-2121
Facsimile: 313-965-7680
Email: law@wulf-ott.com *URL:* http://www.wulf-ott.com
Ann Arbor Office: 320 N. Main Street, Suite 102, 48104.
Telephone: 734-761-1900.
Facsimile: 734-769-0433.

LeRoy H. Wulfmeier, III
David M. Ottenwess
Cheryl L. Chandler
Daniel J. Dulworth
John J. Moran
Stephanie L. Pappas

For full biographical listings, see the Martindale-Hubbell Law Directory

FARMINGTON HILLS, Oakland Co.

CHARFOOS, REITER, PETERSON, HOLMQUIST & PILCHAK, P.C. (AV)

30500 Northwestern Highway, Suite 400, 48334-3179
Telephone: 248-626-7300
Facsimile: 248-626-7305
Email: CRPHP@crphp.com
Detroit, Michigan Office: 1200 Sixth Street.
Telephone: 313-961-7011.

Myron B. Charfoos
James A. Reiter
Daniel Peterson
C. John Holmquist, Jr.
William E. Pilchak
Daniel G. Cohen

Kenneth E. Jones
Deborah S. Dorland
Danial J. Hébert
Robert C. Tice
Nedra D. Campbell

Representative Clients: Advanced Technology Laboratories, Inc.; Active Transportation Co.; Dallas & Mavis Forwarding Co.; Fabristeel Products; Fidelity Bank; Key International; Modern Engineering, Inc.; Multifastener Spring Division; Richfield Hotel Management Co.; 46th, 47th and 48th District Courts.

For full biographical listings, see the Martindale-Hubbell Law Directory

COUZENS, LANSKY, FEALK, ELLIS, ROEDER & LAZAR, P.C. (AV)

39395 West 12 Mile Road, Suite 200, 48331-2913
Telephone: 248-489-8600
Facsimile: 248-489-4156
Email: info@couzens.com *URL:* http://www.couzens.com

Sheldon A. Fealk
Bruce J. Lazar
Jeffrey A. Levine
Phillip L. Sternberg
Marc L. Prey
Stephen Scapelliti
Donald A. Wagner
Michael P. Witzke
Cyrus Raamin Kashef
Gregg A. Nathanson
David B. Deutsch
Mark S. Frankel

Roger E. Winkelman
Alisa A. Kwang
Turkia Awada Mullin
Raoul K. Maitra

Representative Clients: Provided upon request.
Reference: Michigan National Bank.

For Complete List of Firm Personnel, See General Section

For full biographical listings, see the Martindale-Hubbell Law Directory

*FLINT,** Genesee Co.

GAULT DAVISON A PROFESSIONAL SERVICE CORPORATION (AV)

Tenth Floor, Northbank Center, 432 North Saginaw Street, 48502-2032
Telephone: 810-234-3633
Fax: 810-233-3387
Email: gltdav@tir.com *URL:* http://www.gaultdavison.com

F. Robert Schmelzer
Edward B. Davison

Representative Clients: Shoney's, Inc.; City of Flint; Joseph Pontiac; Superior Pontiac Cadillac; Tuar Grimbac; Lasco Ford.

For full biographical listings, see the Martindale-Hubbell Law Directory

*GRAND RAPIDS,** Kent Co.

RHOADES, MCKEE, BOER, GOODRICH & TITTA (AV)

600 Waters Building, 161 Ottawa Avenue NW, 49503-2793
Telephone: 616-235-3500
Fax: 616-235-1639
Email: webmaster@grlaw.com *URL:* http://www.grlaw.com

Roger W. Boer
Edward B. Goodrich
Peter A. Titta
Richard G. Leonard
Arthur C. Spalding
Bruce W. Neckers
Robert J. Dugan
Terrence L. Groesser
Thomas P. Hogan
James M. Flaggert
Mary Ann Cartwright
Daniel L. Elve
Thomas L. Saxe
James L. Schipper
Laurie M. Strong
Stephen A. Hilger
Gregory G. Timmer
Mary Lynette Williams
Scott J. Steiner
Douglas P. Vanden Berge
Robert C. Shaver
John M. Lichtenberg
Dan E. Bylenga, Jr.
Mark E. Fatum

Paul A. McCarthy
Todd Allen Hendricks
Kenneth M. Horjus
Randy J. Kolar
Molly M. McNamara
Peter J. Lozicki
David E. Bevins
Mark S. Pendery
Terry L. Zabel
Mary L. Cranmer
Patrick Drueke
Anthony Allan Pearson

(See Next Column)

RHOADES, MCKEE, BOER, GOODRICH & TITTA—*Continued*

OF COUNSEL

Dale W. Rhoades
F. William McKee
Jean McKee
Charles T. Zimmerman
Robert F. Williams

Reference: First Michigan Bank.

For full biographical listings, see the Martindale-Hubbell Law Directory

WARNER NORCROSS & JUDD LLP (AV)

900 Old Kent Building, 111 Lyon Street, N.W., 49503-2489
Telephone: 616-752-2000
Fax: 616-752-2500
URL: http://www.wnj.com
Muskegon, Michigan Office: 400 Terrace Plaza, P.O. Box 900.
Telephone: 231-727-2600.
Fax: 231-727-2699.
Holland, Michigan Office: Curtis Center, Suite 300, 170 College Avenue.
Telephone: 616-396-9800.
Fax: 616-396-3656.
Southfield, Michigan Office: 1000 Town Center, Suite 650.
Telephone: 248-223-5000.
Fax: 248-223-5005.

MEMBERS OF FIRM

Donald J. Veldman (Resident Member, Muskegon Office)
Jack B. Combs
Joseph F. Martin
Robert J. Chovanec
Robert W. Sikkel (Resident Member, Holland Office)
Paul T. Sorensen
Louis C. Rabaut
Kathleen M. Hanenburg
Stephen B. Grow
Martha Walters Atwater

ASSOCIATES

Karen J. Vanderwerff
Andrea J. Bernard
Lori L. Gibson
Gerardyne M. Drozdowski
Robert A. Dubault (Resident, Muskegon Office)
Edward J. Bardelli
Daniel P. Ettinger
Dean F. Pacific

For full biographical listings, see the Martindale-Hubbell Law Directory

*JACKSON,** Jackson Co.

MARCOUX, ALLEN, ABBOTT, SCHOMER & BOWER, P.C. (AV)

145 South Jackson Street, P.O. Box 787, 49204-0787
Telephone: 517-787-4100
Fax: 517-787-9455
Email: marcoux@jacksonmi.com

William J. Marcoux (Retired)
William O. Allen
William M. Abbott
John H. Schomer
Diane Y. Bower
William B. Nichols, Jr.
Robert T. Kendall, III
Timothy R. Allen
Richard C. Lindsey, Jr.

OF COUNSEL

Walter R. Boris
Lawrence L. Bullen
Philip M. Moilanen
Terry J. Klaasen
T. Harrison Stanton

For full biographical listings, see the Martindale-Hubbell Law Directory

*KALAMAZOO,** Kalamazoo Co.

KREIS, ENDERLE, CALLANDER & HUDGINS, A PROFESSIONAL CORPORATION (AV)

One Moorsbridge, P.O. Box 4010, 49003-4010
Telephone: 616-324-3000
Facsimile: 616-324-3010
Email: kech@kech.com *URL:* http://www.kech.com
Battle Creek, Michigan Office: One West Michigan Avenue, 49017.
Telephone: 616-966-3000.
Fax: 616-966-3022.

Douglas L. Callander
James C. Boerigter
John F. Koryto
Floyd E. Gates, Jr. (Resident, Battle Creek Office)

For Complete List of Firm Personnel, See General Section

For full biographical listings, see the Martindale-Hubbell Law Directory

LEWIS & ALLEN, P.C. (AV)

Old Kent Bank Building, Suite 800, 136 East Michigan Avenue, 49007-3946
Telephone: 616-388-7600
Fax: 616-349-3831

(See Next Column)

Dean S. Lewis
W. Fred Allen, Jr.
Barry R. Smith
William A. Redmond
Stephen M. Denenfeld
Anne McGregor Fries
Gregory G. St. Arnauld
James M. Marquardt
Christopher T. Haenicke
Winfield J. Hollander (1906-1996)

LEGAL SUPPORT PERSONNEL

Dorothy B. Kelly

For full biographical listings, see the Martindale-Hubbell Law Directory

MILLER, CANFIELD, PADDOCK AND STONE, P.L.C. (AV)

A Professional Limited Liability Company
Founded in 1852 by Sidney Davy Miller
444 West Michigan Avenue, 49007-3752
Telephone: 616-381-7030
Fax: 616-382-0244
URL: http://www.millercanfield.com
Detroit, Michigan Office: 150 West Jefferson, Suite 2500, 48226-4415.
Telephone: 313-963-6420.
Fax: 313-496-7500.
Cable Address: "Stem Detroit."
Ann Arbor, Michigan Office: 101 North Main Street, 7th Floor, 48104-1400.
Telephone: 734-663-2445.
Fax: 734-747-7147.
Troy, Michigan Office: 840 West Long Lake Road, Suite 200, 48098.
Telephone: 248-879-2000.
Fax: 248-879-2001.
Grand Rapids, Michigan Office: 99 Monroe, N.W., Suite 1200, 49503-2639.
Telephone: 616-454-8656.
Fax: 616-776-6322.
Howell, Michigan Office: 121 South Barnard Street, Suite 4, 48843-2305.
Telephone: 517-546-7600.
Telecopier: 517-546-6974.
Lansing, Michigan Office: One Michigan Avenue, Suite 900, 48933-1609.
Telephone: 517-487-2070.
Fax: 517-374-6304.
Monroe, Michigan Office: 214 East Elm Avenue, Suite 100, 48162-2682.
Telephone: 734-243-2000.
Fax: 734-243-0901.
Washington, D.C. Office: 1900 K Street, N.W., Suite 1150. 20006.
Telephone: 202-429-5575; 785-0600.
Fax: 202-331-1118; 785-1234.
Pensacola, Florida Office: 25 West Cedar, 32501.
Telephone: 850-469-1088.
Fax: 850-432-0677.
New York, New York Office: 1450 Broadway, 41st Floor, 10018.
Telephone: 212-704-4400.
Fax: 212-704-4410.
Gdynia, Poland Office: UL. Slaska 21, 81-319.
Telephone: 011-485-831-2808.
Fax: 011-48-58-628 6411.
Warsaw, Poland Office: UL. Nowogrodzkall, 5th Floor, 00-513.
Telephone: 011-4822 529 0200.
Fax: 011-4822 529 0201.
Katowice, Poland Office: UL. Francuska 35/37, 40-027.
Telephone: 011 (48-32) 757-2414.
Fax: 011 (48-32) 757-2483.

PRINCIPALS

Eric V. Brown, Jr.
John A. Campbell
Thomas P. Hustoles
Kevin M. McCarthy
Pamela Chapman Enslen
Kurt N. Sherwood

RESIDENT ASSOCIATES

James B. Thelen
Oren R. Griffin

Representative Firm Clients: Chrysler Corporation; Comerica, Incorporated; City of Detroit, Michigan; Detroit Tigers, Inc.; First of Michigan; Ford Motor Company; Ford Motor Credit Company; Great Lakes Bancorp; Henry Ford Hospital; INVETECH Company.

For Complete List of Firm Personnel, See General Section

For full biographical listings, see the Martindale-Hubbell Law Directory

LANSING, Ingham Co.

FOSTER, SWIFT, COLLINS & SMITH, P.C. (AV)

313 South Washington Square, 48933-2193
Telephone: 517-371-8100
Telecopier: 517-371-8200
URL: http://www.fosterswift.com
Farmington Hills, Michigan Office: 32300 Northwestern Highway, Suite 230.
Telephone: 248-539-9900.
Fax: 248-851-7504.

(See Next Column)

FOSTER, SWIFT, COLLINS & SMITH P.C., *Lansing—Continued*

Theodore W. Swift
Stephen O. Schultz
William R. Schulz
Scott L. Mandel
Robert E. McFarland
David J. Houston
Michael J. Bommarito
Melissa J. Jackson
Peter R. Albertins
Rebecca S. Davies
John C. Schlinker

OF COUNSEL

Norman D. Hawkins

For Complete List of Firm Personnel, See General Section

For full biographical listings, see the Martindale-Hubbell Law Directory

FRASER TREBILCOCK DAVIS & FOSTER, P.C. (AV)

1000 Michigan National Tower, 48933
Telephone: 517-482-5800
Fax: 517-482-0887
URL: http://WWW.FTDF.COM
Detroit, Michigan Office: One Woodward Avenue, Suite 1550.
Telephone: 313-237-7300.
Fax: 313-961-1651.

Michael E. Cavanaugh
John J. Loose
Brandon W. Zuk
Michelyn E. Pasteur

Counsel for: Auto Owners Insurance Company; Dowley Manufacturing; Michigan Education Association; Tri-State Hospital Supply Corporation; Michigan Millers Insurance Co.; Ingham Regional Medical Center; Greater Lansing Association of Realtors.

For full biographical listings, see the Martindale-Hubbell Law Directory

HOWARD & HOWARD ATTORNEYS, P.C. (AV)

The Phoenix Building, Suite 500, 222 Washington Square, North, 48933-1817
Telephone: 517-485-1483
Telecopier: 517-485-1568
Kalamazoo, Michigan Office: The Michigan Building, Suite 200, 100 Portage Street.
Telephone: 616-382-1483.
Telecopier: 616-382-1568.
Bloomfield Hills, Michigan Office: The Pinehurst Office Center, Suite 101, 1400 North Woodward Avenue.
Telephone: 248-645-1483.
Telecopier: 248-645-1568.
Peoria, Illinois Office: One Technology Plaza, Suite 600, 211 Fulton Street.
Telephone: 309-672-1483.
Telecopier: 309-672-1568.

Todd D. Chamberlain
C. Douglas Moran

Representative Clients: For Representative Client list, see General Practice, Lansing, MI.

For Complete List of Firm Personnel, See General Section

For full biographical listings, see the Martindale-Hubbell Law Directory

*MONROE,** Monroe Co.

BRAUNLICH, RUSSOW & BRAUNLICH, A PROFESSIONAL CORPORATION (AV)

111 South Macomb Street, 48161
Telephone: 734-241-8300
Fax: 734-241-7715

William J. Braunlich, Jr. (1924-1992)
Thomas P. Russow
William H. Braunlich

Philip A. Costello
Ann L. Nickel
Jeffrey A. Dulany, P.C.

LEGAL SUPPORT PERSONNEL

Ruth G. Flint

Representative Clients: State Farm Mutual Insurance Co.; Auto Club Insurance Assn.; Board of Road Commissioners, Monroe County; Port of Monroe; Monroe County Community College; City of Luna Pier; City of Petersburg; Auto-Owners Insurance Co.; Fremont Mutual Insurance Co.; Citizens Insurance Co. of America.

For full biographical listings, see the Martindale-Hubbell Law Directory

*SAGINAW,** Saginaw Co.

BRAUN KENDRICK FINKBEINER PLC (AV)

101 N. Washington Suite 812, 48607-1297
Telephone: 517-753-3461
Telecopier: 517-753-3951
Email: ALBFIE@BKF-LAW.COM *URL:* http://www.bkf-law.com
Saginaw Township Office, Michigan Office: 5800 Gratiot Road, Suite 107, P.O. Box 5169. Telephone 517-799-8692.
Fax: 517-799-4666.

(See Next Column)

Bay City, Michigan Office: 201 Phoenix Building, P.O. Box 2039.
Telephone: 517-895-8505.
Telecopier: 517-895-8437.
Ann Arbor, Michigan Office: First National Building. 201 S. Main, Suite 700.
Telephone: 313-995-4100.
Telecopier: 313-995-4798.
Mt. Pleasant, Michigan Office: 805 North Brown.
Telephone: 517-775-7404.
Telecopier: 517-775-3764.

E. Louis Ognisanti
Robert A. Kendrick
John A. Decker

Ellen E. Crane

Representative Clients: The Dow Chemical Co.; General Motors Corp.; Merrill, Lynch, Inc.; Saginaw General Hospital; Saginaw News; The Wickes Foundation.

For Complete List of Firm Personnel, See General Section

For full biographical listings, see the Martindale-Hubbell Law Directory

MASUD, GILBERT & PATTERSON, P.C. (AV)

4449 Fashion Square Boulevard, 48603-1242
Telephone: 517-792-4499
Fax: 517-792-7725
Email: masud@journey.com

David John Masud
Donald A. Gilbert
Gary D. Patterson

Kraig M. Schutter
Paula R. Coffee
Marilyn Ann Fogelsinger

Representative Clients: Dow Corning Corp.; Bortz Health Care Facilities; Associated Builders & Contractors; Michigan Sugar Co.; Saginaw Charter Township; Saginaw Township Community School; Central Michigan Railway; St. Mary's Medical Center; Forward Corp.

For full biographical listings, see the Martindale-Hubbell Law Directory

*ST. JOSEPH,** Berrien Co.

TROFF, PETZKE & AMMESON (AV)

Law and Title Building, 811 Ship Street, P.O. Box 67, 49085
Telephone: 616-983-0161
Facsimile: 616-983-0166
Email: pnalaw@qtm.net

MEMBERS OF FIRM

Roger A. Petzke
Charles F. Ammeson

For full biographical listings, see the Martindale-Hubbell Law Directory

SOUTHFIELD, Oakland Co.

SOMMERS, SCHWARTZ, SILVER & SCHWARTZ, P.C. (AV)

2000 Town Center, Suite 900, 48075
Telephone: 248-355-0300
Telecopier: 248-746-4001
Plymouth, Michigan Office: 747 South Main Street.
Telephone: 313-455-4250.

Donald J. Gasiorek
Justin C. Ravitz
Joseph A. Golden
Daniel D. Swanson
David A. Kotzian
Patricia A. Stamler
Sam G. Morgan

David J. Szymanski
Ericka M. Jackson

OF COUNSEL

Marvin R. Stempien

Representative Clients: Automatic Data Processing; Vlasic & Co.; C. A. Muer Corp.; O/E Automation, Inc.; City of Taylor; Township of Van Buren; Vesco Oil Corp.; Royal Insurance Co.; Michigan Mutual/Amerisure Insurance Co.

For Complete List of Firm Personnel, See General Section

For full biographical listings, see the Martindale-Hubbell Law Directory

TROY, Oakland Co.

BARLOW & DERBY (AV)

1450 West Long Lake Road Suite 365, 48098
Telephone: 248-641-3300
Facsimile: 248-641-3305
Email: barlowlan@aol.com

Thomas W. H. Barlow
Matthew S. Derby

ASSOCIATES

Holly Christine Beatty
Christine R. Essique

For full biographical listings, see the Martindale-Hubbell Law Directory

Troy—Continued

BOWEN, RADABAUGH, MILTON & BROWN, P.C. (AV)

4967 Crooks Road, Suite 150, 48098
Telephone: 248-641-8000
Fax: 248-641-8219
Email: brmb@brmb.com *URL:* http://www.brmb.com

Thomas R. Bowen
James M. Radabaugh
Lisa T. Milton
Susan Leigh Brown

Geoffrey D. Marshall
Mark P. Dunn

OF COUNSEL

Meri Craver Borin

For full biographical listings, see the Martindale-Hubbell Law Directory

BROWN SCHWARTZ PATTERSON & ANKERS, P.C. (AV)

2301 West Big Beaver Road, Suite 212, 48084
Telephone: 248-816-6100
Fax: 248-816-6370

Malcolm D. Brown
Craig S. Schwartz
Scott T. Patterson
Gary C. Ankers

Jeffrey T. Harrison

For full biographical listings, see the Martindale-Hubbell Law Directory

HAINER & BERMAN, P.C. (AV)

888 West Big Beaver, Suite 1400, 48084
Telephone: 248-244-8424
Fax: 248-244-8455

Michael J. Hainer
Leonard K. Berman
Kay E. Malaney

Drew S. Norton
Paul S. Miller

OF COUNSEL

Michael A. Kus
Robert F. Riley
Mark S. Demorest

Representative Clients: American Empire Surplus Lines Insurance Co.; Biomass Energy Systems, Inc.; Bridgestone/Firestone, Inc.; Central Distributors of Beer, Inc.; Champion Enterprises, Inc.; City Management Corp.; Clarklift of Detroit, Inc.; Federal Reserve Bank of Chicago; Hotel Investment Services, Inc.; M&O Marketing, Inc.

For full biographical listings, see the Martindale-Hubbell Law Directory

POLING, McGAW & POLING, P.C. (AV)

Suite 275, 5435 Corporate Drive, 48098
Telephone: 248-641-0500
Telecopier: 248-641-0506
URL: http://www.lawyers.com/polingmcgaw&poling

Benson T. Buck (1926-1989)
Richard B. Poling
D. Douglas McGaw
Richard B. Poling, Jr.
Gregory C. Hamilton
Veronica B. O'Hara
James R. Parker
Shannon M. Acton

OF COUNSEL

Ralph S. Moore

Representative Clients: City of Troy; United States Fidelity & Guaranty Co.; Sentry Insurance Co.; Admiral Insurance; DeMaria Construction Co.; Leo Corporation; Aetna Casualty and Surety Co.; Concord Design; Pneumo-Abex.

For full biographical listings, see the Martindale-Hubbell Law Directory

STARK, REAGAN & FINNERTY, P.C. (AV)

Suite 202, 1111 West Long Lake Road, P.O. Box 7037, 48007-7037
Telephone: 248-641-9955
Facsimile: 248-641-9921
Email: @SRFPC.COM
Boca Raton, Florida Office: Suite 307B, 4800 North Federal Highway.
Telephone: 561-994-2266.
Traverse City, Michigan Office: 475 Eastwood Shores.
Telephone: 231-943-8230.
Facsimile: 231-943-8711.

Michael H. Whiting
Kenneth M. Boyer
Thomas H. Finnerty
R. Keith Stark
Joseph C. Bird
Joseph A. Ahern
Christopher E. LeVasseur
Daniel E. Chapman
William D. Girardot
James R. Waldvogel
Jeffrey J. Fleury
Michael D. FitzPatrick

OF COUNSEL

Harry S. Stark (Resident Of Counsel, Traverse City Office)
Willard M. Reagan
James E. Beall

For full biographical listings, see the Martindale-Hubbell Law Directory

VAN SUILICHEM & ASSOCIATES, P.C. (AV)

2301 West Big Beaver Road, Suite 212, 48084
Telephone: 248-816-2000
Fax: 248-816-2014

Donald A. Van Suilichem
Christina M. Brookshire
Randal Ray Cole

For full biographical listings, see the Martindale-Hubbell Law Directory

WEST BLOOMFIELD, Oakland Co.

VALENTINE & ASSOCIATES, P.C. (AV)

5767 West Maple Road, Suite 400, 48322
Telephone: 248-851-3010
Fax: 248-851-1553
Email: vallaw@umich.edu

Stephen K. Valentine, Jr.

For full biographical listings, see the Martindale-Hubbell Law Directory

LAND USE LAW

ALABAMA

*BIRMINGHAM,** Jefferson Co.

BRADLEY ARANT ROSE & WHITE LLP (AV)

2001 Park Place, Suite 1400, P.O. Box 830709, 35283-0709
Telephone: 205-521-8000
Facsimile: 205-521-8800
Facsimile (SouthTrust Tower Office): 205-521-8500
URL: http://www.barw.com
Huntsville, Alabama Office: 200 Clinton Avenue West, Suite 900, 35801.
Telephone: 205-517-5100.
Facsimile: 205-533-5069.
Washington, D.C. Office: 801 Pennsylvania Avenue, NW, Suite 230, 20004.
Telephone: 202-347-8893.
Facsimile: 202-347-1684.

MEMBER OF FIRM

Charles A. J. Beavers Jr.

For Complete List of Firm Personnel, See General Section

For full biographical listings, see the Martindale-Hubbell Law Directory

ARIZONA

*PHOENIX,** Maricopa Co.

DUSHOFF & McCALL, A PROFESSIONAL CORPORATION (AV)

Two Renaissance Square, Suite 1000, 40 North Central, 85004
Telephone: 602-254-3800
Fax: 602-258-2551
URL: http://www.dushoff@neta.com

Jay Dushoff
Michael Riikola
Jack E. McCall (1942-1995)
Leonard M. Bell

Patrick J. McGill
Robert H. Kreutzer

LEGAL SUPPORT PERSONNEL

Thomas M. Flynn

For full biographical listings, see the Martindale-Hubbell Law Directory

EARL, CURLEY & LAGARDE, P.C. (AV)

3101 N. Central Avenue, Suite 1000, 85012
Telephone: 602-265-0094
Fax: 602-265-2195
Email: ec-l@primenet.com

Stephen C. Earl
Michael J. Curley
Lynne A. Lagarde

Representative Clients: Del Webb Corporation; Desert Mountain Properties; Opus Southwest; Westcor Partners; Trammell Crow; Arizona Biltmore Hotel; The Taubman Company; Mutual of New York; Home Depot; Mark Taylor.

For full biographical listings, see the Martindale-Hubbell Law Directory

FENNEMORE CRAIG, A PROFESSIONAL CORPORATION (AV)

3003 North Central Avenue, Suite 2600, 85012-2913
Telephone: 602-916-5000
Fax: 602-916-5999
Tucson, Arizona Office: One South Church Avenue, Suite 1000, 85701-1620.
Telephone: 520-879-6800.
Fax: 520-879-6899.

Graeme Hancock
Andrew M. Federhar

Stacey A. Kelly

LEGAL SUPPORT PERSONNEL

LEGAL ASSISTANTS

Donna M. Horwitz

For Complete List of Firm Personnel, See General Section

For full biographical listings, see the Martindale-Hubbell Law Directory

LAZARUS & ASSOCIATES, A PROFESSIONAL CORPORATION (AV)

One Arizona Center, 400 East Van Buren, Suite 450, 85004
Telephone: 602-340-0900
Facsimile: 602-340-8955
Email: plazo@goodnet.com *URL:* http://www.lawyers.com/lazaruslaw

(See Next Column)

Larry S. Lazarus
Darin Ann Sender

OF COUNSEL

David K. Jones, P.C.

LEGAL SUPPORT PERSONNEL

LAND USE PLANNER

Melinda L. Schaefer

For full biographical listings, see the Martindale-Hubbell Law Directory

WITHEY & TOBIN, P.L.C. (AV)

3101 North Central Avenue, Suite 1690, 85012-2615
Telephone: 602-230-0600
Fax: 602-212-1787

Michael B. Withey
Shawn E. Tobin
Ellen Harris Hoff

For full biographical listings, see the Martindale-Hubbell Law Directory

ZEITLIN & ZEITLIN, P.C. (AV)

A Partnership including a Professional Corporation
3200 East Camelback, Suite 300, 85018-2398
Telephone: 602-648-5222
Fax: 602-648-5226
Email: zeitlin@primenet.com
Annapolis, Maryland Office: 2007 Tidewater Colony Drive, Suite 2B, 21401-8686.
Telephone: 410-266-9500.
Facsimile: 410-266-9522.
San Diego, California Office: Strauss, Asher & Zeitlin, 150 "B" Street, Suite 1950, 92101.
Telephone: 619-237-5307.
Facsimile: 619-237-5311.

Dale S. Zeitlin
Dawn Stoll Zeitlin (P.C.)

OF COUNSEL

James M. Balogh

For full biographical listings, see the Martindale-Hubbell Law Directory

CALIFORNIA

COSTA MESA, Orange Co.

RUTAN & TUCKER, LLP (AV)

A Partnership including Professional Corporations
611 Anton Boulevard, Fourteenth Floor, P.O. Box 1950, 92626-1998
Telephone: 714-641-5100; 213-625-7586
Telecopier: 714-546-9035
Email: rutan&tucker@rutan.com *URL:* http://www.rutan.com

MEMBERS OF FIRM

Leonard A. Hampel, Jr.
Michael D. Rubin
Jeffrey M. Oderman (P.C.)
David J. Aleshire
Philip D. Kohn
Joel D. Kuperberg
M. Katherine Jenson
Elizabeth L. Martyn
Kim D. Thompson
Hans Van Ligten
Robert O. Owen
Jeffrey A. Goldfarb
F. Kevin Brazil
Layne H. Melzer
A. Patrick Muñoz
S. Daniel Harbottle

SPECIAL COUNSEL

Dan Slater

ASSOCIATE

Todd O. Litfin

For Complete List of Firm Personnel, See General Section

For full biographical listings, see the Martindale-Hubbell Law Directory

HAYWARD, Alameda Co.

HALEY, PURCHIO, SAKAI & SMITH (AV)

P.O. Box 450, 22320 Foothill Boulevard, Suite 620, 94543
Telephone: 510-538-6400

MEMBERS OF FIRM

John K. Smith
Robert Sakai
Cynthia K. Birmingham

OF COUNSEL

John J. Purchio (1915-1997)
Donald A. Pearce (1898-1982)
Marlin W. Haley (1910-1993)

Representative Clients: City Center Commercial (Shopping Center); Oak Hills, Walnut Hills, Creekwood (Apartment Complexes); R. Zaballos & Sons (General Contractors); Hospital Associates; Wolf Investment Co.; Mission Valley Rock Co. (quarry); Sunol Golf & Recreation Co. (golf course).

For full biographical listings, see the Martindale-Hubbell Law Directory

LONG BEACH, Los Angeles Co.

CAMERON, PEARLSON & GALE (AV)

One World Trade Center, Suite 1600, 90831-1600
Telephone: 562-436-3888
Telecopier: 562-437-1967
URL: http://www.cpglawyers.com
URL: http://www.lawyers.com/cmp&glaw

MEMBERS OF FIRM

Timothy C. Cameron
Charles M. Gale
Paul R. Pearlson

ASSOCIATES

Dana K. Anderson, Jr.
Susan R. Loh

For full biographical listings, see the Martindale-Hubbell Law Directory

*LOS ANGELES,** Los Angeles Co.

BRAND FARRAR & BUXBAUM LLP (AV)

515 South Flower Street, Suite 3500, 90071-2201
Telephone: 213-228-0288
Fax: 213-426-6222
Email: bfb-la@brandfarrar.com
Beijing (Peking), China Office: Suite 2518, China World Trade Centre, 1 Jian Guo Men Wai Avenue, Beijing, China.
Telephone: 86-10-6505-2288 Ext. 2523/2518.
Fax: 86-10-6505-2638. Email: bjbfbbj@public3.bta.net.cn
Chengdu, Sichuan, China Office: Suite 11A, Sichuan International Mansion, No. 1 Zhong Xi Shun Cheng Street, Chengdu, China.
Telephone: 86-28-652-1316.
Fax: 86-28-652-0547. Email: cdbfbcd@mail.sc.cninfo.net.
Chongqing, China Office: Suite 1510, Metropolitan Tower, 68 Zourong Lu, Chongqing, China.
Telephone: 86-23-6382-8381.
Fax: 86-23-6382-8373. Email: cqbfbcq@public.cta.cq.cn.
Guangzhou (Canton), China Office: Suite 1305, Main Tower, GITIC Plaza Hotel, 339 Huanshi Dong Road, Guangzhou, China.
Telephone: 86-20-8331-1888, Ext. 71305.
Fax: 86-20-8331-2671. Email: gzbfbgz@public.guangzhou.gd.cn.
Hong Kong, China Office: Brand Farrar Buxbaum LLP, 5/F., Landmark East, 12 Ice House Street, Central, Hong Kong, China.
Telephone: 852-2523-7001.
Fax: 852-2845-0947. Email: hkbfbhk@hk.super.net.
Los Angeles, California Office: Brand Farrar & Buxbaum LLP, Suite 3500, 515 South Flower Street, Los Angeles, California, 90071-2201.
Telephone: 213-228-0288.
Fax: 213-426-6222. Email: bfb-la@brandfarrar.com.
New York, New York Office: 275 Madison Avenue, 37th Floor, New York, New York, 10097.
Telephone: 212-286-0038.
Fax: 212-573-9077. Email: martineh@aol.com
Shanghai, China Office: Brand Farrar Buxbaum LLP, Suites 2611-12, Central Plaza, 227 Huangpi Bei Lu, Shanghai, China.
Telephone: 86-21-6375-8918.
Fax: 86-21-6375-8922. Email: shbfbsh@public2.sta.net.cn
Shenzhen, China Office: Suite 2103A, Shenzhen Development Center, Renmin Nan Lu, Shenzhen, China.
Telephone: 86-755-229-8009.
Fax: 86-755-229-8011. Email: szbfbsz@public.szptt.net.cn.
Ulaanbaatar, Mongolia Office: Brand Farrar Buxbaum LLP, 4/F., Time Center, No. 50 Baga Toiruu, Ulaanbaatar, Mongolia.
Telephone: 976-1-31-0711.
Fax: 976-1-32-5102. Email: mgbfbmg@magicnet.mn.
Xiamen, China Office: Suite 1182 Jian Ye Building, 28 Hubin North Road, Xiamen, China.
Telephone: 86-592-506-3059.
Fax: 86-592-511-1044. Email: xmbfbxm@public.xm.fj.cn.
Associated Office, Mumbai, Bombay, India: Shah & Sanghavi, Advocates, Solicitors & Notary, 114-A Mittal Court, Nariman Point, Mumbai 400 021 India.
Telephone: 91-22-285-5755/56 or 91-22-285-3592/93.
Fax: 91-22-284-5040.

PRINCIPALS

Michael A. Brand
David C. Buxbaum (China Offices)
Kenneth Y. Choy (Hong Kong Office)
Robert W. Dziubla
David W. Farrar
Amy E. Freilich
Margaret G. Graf
John Masao Iino
Charles K. Kolstad
Edward H. Martin (New York Office)
Gregory D. Trimarche
Li Zhuogen (China Offices)

OTHER ATTORNEYS RESIDENT IN LOS ANGELES OFFICE

Sherry L. Geyer
Joan M. Marquardt
James H. Service
Jeffrey S. Allen
Julia Sylva
Brian J. Kim
Lisa Teng

OTHER ATTORNEYS RESIDENT IN BEIJING OFFICE

Hao Xiaodong
Bin Zhao
Luo Rongping
Zhang Chunbo

(See Next Column)

OTHER ATTORNEYS RESIDENT IN CHENGDU, SICHUAN OFFICE

Zeng Xiangyu
Wu Wen

OTHER ATTORNEY RESIDENT IN CHONGQING OFFICE

Du Fei

OTHER ATTORNEYS RESIDENT IN GUANGZHOU OFFICE

Zou Wenyan (Not admitted in United States)
Feng Ruiding
Jia Guangxi

OTHER ATTORNEYS RESIDENT IN HONG KONG OFFICE

Shane F. Weir
Cheonghar Wong
N.T.S. Kularatne
Simon Woo
David William Gunson
Arthur Burton Crook
Simon K.C. Lee
Cheng Yuen Yi
Lo Wing Cheong
Nicholas C. McGrenra
Eva Y.N. Kwok

OTHER ATTORNEYS RESIDENT IN NEW YORK OFFICE

Vincent I. S. Hsieh (Of Counsel)
Jeffrey Schall
Jonathan Chun Wang

OTHER ATTORNEYS RESIDENT IN SHANGHAI OFFICE

Lin Yong
Wu Hong Liang
Tang Ying
Zhang Guoyao
Qi Zhenwen

OTHER ATTORNEYS RESIDENT IN SHENZHEN OFFICE

Zhong Wenya
Zhang He

OTHER ATTORNEYS RESIDENT IN ULAANBAATAR OFFICE

Byambaa Bayarmaa
Ajiv Enhktuya

OTHER ATTORNEY RESIDENT IN XIAMEN OFFICE

Deng Sheng

For full biographical listings, see the Martindale-Hubbell Law Directory

*NAPA,** Napa Co.

GAW, VAN MALE, SMITH, MYERS & MIROGLIO, A PROFESSIONAL LAW CORPORATION (AV)

944 Main Street, 94559-3045
Telephone: 707-252-9000
Telecopier: 707-252-0792
URL: http://www.gvmsmm.com
Fairfield, California Office: Corporate Plaza. 1261 Travis Boulevard, Suite 350, 94533-4801.
Telephone: 707-425-1250.
Fax: 707-425-1255.
Redlands, California Office: 300 E. State Street, Suite 101, 92372-5200.
Telephone: 909-798-3190.
Fax: 909-798-3092.

Nicholas R. Van Male

Rhonda L. Savitch

Reference: The Vintage Bank.

For full biographical listings, see the Martindale-Hubbell Law Directory

OXNARD, Ventura Co.

ENGLAND, WHITFIELD, SCHRÖEDER & TREDWAY, L.L.P. (AV)

300 Esplanade Drive, 6th Floor, 93030
Telephone: 805-485-9627
Ventura: 647-8237
Southern California Toll Free: 800-255-3485
Fax: 805-983-0297
URL: http://www.tsurf.com/ewst/

Theodore J. England
Anson M. Whitfield
Robert W. Schröeder
David W. Tredway
Robert A. McSorley
Stuart A. Comis
Mitchel B. Kahn
Mark A. Nelson
Eric J. Kananen
Mary E. Schröeder
Oscar C. Gonzalez
Madison M. Christian
Kurt Edward Kananen

Melissa E. Cohen
Linda Kathryn Ash
Mark T. Barney
Kevin L. Dorhout
Anthony M. Ramos
Gregory J. Ramirez

Representative Clients: Dah Chong Hong (automobile dealerships); Steve thomas BMW; Vreeland Cadillac, Inc.; Willamette Industries; The Port of Hueneme; Viola, Inc. (General Contracting); Santa Clara Chemical Co.; Nakamura Berry Growers; John Taft Electric Co.; Rodgers Mortgage Co.

For full biographical listings, see the Martindale-Hubbell Law Directory

*SACRAMENTO,** Sacramento Co.

GRATTAN & GALATI (AV)

Renaissance Tower, 801 K Street, Penthouse Suite, 95814
Telephone: 916-441-6575
Fax: 916-441-6553
Email: scarey@grattangalati.com *URL:* http://www.lawyers.com/grattan&galati

(See Next Column)

GRATTAN & GALATI—*Continued*

John P. Grattan, Jr. | Scott A. Galati

LEGAL SUPPORT PERSONNEL

Sandra A. Carey

For full biographical listings, see the Martindale-Hubbell Law Directory

HUNTER RICHEY DI BENEDETTO & BREWER, LLP (AV)

A Limited Liability Partnership
Renaissance Tower, 801 K Street, 23rd Floor, 95814-3525
Telephone: 916-491-3000
Facsimile: 916-491-3080
Email: hrdb@hrdb.com *URL:* http://www.hrdb.com

MEMBERS OF FIRM

William S. Hunter
Win R. Richey
Florence L. Di Benedetto
Roy E. Brewer
Anne E. Ferguson
James F. Geary
Janet C. Eisenbeis
Stephen C. Ruehmann
Sharon K. Sandeen
Jack V. Lovell
Patricia J. Hartman

OF COUNSEL

Laurie E. Davis

LEGAL SUPPORT PERSONNEL

Lori J. Moody (Paralegal)
Deborah M. Johnson (Paralegal)
Linda Jane Hall (Executive Assistant)
Jennifer E. Mueller (Legal Assistant)
Michele L. Nickell (Legal Assistant)
Lynetta G. Goodwin

For full biographical listings, see the Martindale-Hubbell Law Directory

REMY, THOMAS AND MOOSE, LLP (AV)

455 Capitol Mall, Suite 210, 95814
Telephone: 916-443-2745
Fax: 916-443-9017
Email: RANDT@CWO.COM *URL:* http://www.cwo.com/~randt/

MEMBERS OF FIRM

Michael Helge Remy
Tina A. Thomas
James G. Moose
Whitman F. Manley

ASSOCIATES

John H. Mattox
Andrea M. Klein
Sheryl Schaffner Freeman
Erik K. Spiess
Jennifer S. Holman
Marian A. King

OF COUNSEL

Brian J. Plant

Representative Clients: Metropolitan Water District; Euron Oil and Gas; County of Butte; City of San Rafael; AKT Developments.

For full biographical listings, see the Martindale-Hubbell Law Directory

STEPHEN ROBBINS (AV)

2150 Third Avenue, 95818
Telephone: 916-455-7600
Facsimile: 916-455-7610
Email: sjmrlaw@aol.com

For full biographical listings, see the Martindale-Hubbell Law Directory

*SAN DIEGO,** San Diego Co.

HECHT, SOLBERG, ROBINSON & GOLDBERG, LLP (AV)

One America Plaza, 600 West Broadway, Eighth Floor, 92101
Telephone: 619-239-3444
Telecopier: 619-232-6828
Email: mail@hsrg.com

MEMBERS OF FIRM

Alan John Hecht (A Professional Corporation)
Darryl O. Solberg (A Professional Corporation)
Jerold H. Goldberg (A Professional Corporation)
Paul E. Robinson (A Professional Corporation)
David W. Bagley, II (A Professional Corporation)
Michael J. Maher
R. Martin Bohl
Anton Dimitroff
Susan Lee Daly

SENIOR ATTORNEYS

Richard A. Schulman
Michael A. Van Horne
Peter K. Solecki
Kenneth C. Jones

ASSOCIATES

Tricia L. Greenlee
Erik Olav Valderhaug
Nataki A. Finch

For full biographical listings, see the Martindale-Hubbell Law Directory

STEPHENSON, WORLEY, GARRATT, SCHWARTZ, GARFIELD & PRAIRIE (AV)

A Limited Liability Partnership
401 "B" Street, Suite 2400, 92101-4200
Telephone: 619-696-3500
Fax: 619-696-3555
Email: SDLAW@swgsgp.com

MEMBERS OF FIRM

Gary J. Stephenson
Donald R. Worley
Gregory C. M. Garratt
William J. Schwartz, Jr.
Michael W. Prairie
Timothy K. Garfield
Laurel Lee Hyde

OF COUNSEL

Kent H. Foster
Elaine L. Chan
Ralph E. Hughes

Reference: Bank of Commerce.

For full biographical listings, see the Martindale-Hubbell Law Directory

*SAN FRANCISCO,** San Francisco Co.

ALICE SUET YEE BARKLEY (AV)

30 Blackstone Court, 94123
Telephone: 415-775-0495
Facsimile: 415-775-6466

For full biographical listings, see the Martindale-Hubbell Law Directory

ELLMAN, BURKE, HOFFMAN & JOHNSON, A PROFESSIONAL CORPORATION (AV)

One Ecker, Suite 200, 94105
Telephone: 415-777-2727
Fax: 415-495-7587
Email: managingdirector@ellman-burke.com *URL:* http://www.ellman-burke.com

Howard N. Ellman
Michael J. Burke
Kenneth N. Burns
John D. Hoffman
Jeffrey W. Johnson
Thomas Paine
Jay L. Paxton
Thomas M. Sherwood
Leslie M. Browne
Jodi Billehus Fedor

JoAnne L. Dunec
Sarah Richards Gansa
Christina W. Chi

For full biographical listings, see the Martindale-Hubbell Law Directory

*SAN JOSE,** Santa Clara Co.

McMANIS, FAULKNER & MORGAN (AV)

160 West Santa Clara Street, 10th Floor, 95113
Telephone: 408-279-8700
Fax: 408-279-3244; 408-279-0494
Email: mfm@mfmlaw.com *URL:* http://www.mfmlaw.com

James McManis
William Faulkner
Donelle Morgan
Lisa Herrick
Michael Reedy
Erica Yew

Michelle Tidalgo
Colleen Duffy Smith
Lillian Wolf
Rebecca Hughes
Kalpana Vrudhula
Ray M. Baluyot
Catherine Bechtel
Arron Nesbitt

OF COUNSEL

Mary Arand

For full biographical listings, see the Martindale-Hubbell Law Directory

TERRA LAW LLP (AV)

60 South Market Street, Suite 200, 95113
Telephone: 408-288-7325
Fax: 408-998-4895
Burlingame, California Office: 1350 Old Bayshore Highway, Suite 760, 94010.
Telephone: 650-685-7325.
Fax: 650-685-4895.

George H. Cole, Jr.
D. D. Hughmanick
R. Prescott Jaunich
Richard O. McDonald
Breck E. Milde
William L. Myers
Jane P. Relyea
Jason R. Biggs
Joan Paul
Ronald I. Rainey

Katharine L. Hardt-Mason
Thomas E. Rossmeissl

For full biographical listings, see the Martindale-Hubbell Law Directory

*SAN LUIS OBISPO,** San Luis Obispo Co.

ANDRE, MORRIS & BUTTERY, A PROFESSIONAL LAW CORPORATION (AV)
1102 Laurel Lane, P.O. Box 730, 93406-0730
Telephone: 805-543-4171
Fax: 805-543-0752
Email: amb@amblaw.com *URL:* http://www.amblaw.com

Michael J. Morris
James C. Buttery

Kathryn M. Eppright
Kevin D. Morris

References: Bank of America National Trust and Savings Assn. (San Luis Obispo Main Branch); Mid-State Bank (San Luis Obispo).

For full biographical listings, see the Martindale-Hubbell Law Directory

*SANTA BARBARA,** Santa Barbara Co.

HATCH AND PARENT (AV)
21 East Carrillo Street, 93101-2782
Telephone: 805-963-7000
Fax: 805-965-4333
URL: http://www.HatchParent.com
Oxnard, California Office: 300 Esplanade Drive, 9th Floor, 93030-1250.
Telephone: 805-981-1818.
Fax: 805-981-1820.
South Lake Tahoe, California Office: The Summit, 96150.
Telephone: 530-542-7800.
Fax: 530-542-7802.
San Diego Office: 110 West C Street, Suite 2200, 92101.
Telephone: 619-702-6100.
Fax: 619-239-4333.

MEMBERS OF FIRM

Stanley C. Hatch
Gerald B. Parent
S. Timothy Buynak, Jr.
Susan F. Petrovich
Peter N. Brown
Stanley M. Roden
Scott S. Slater
Steven A. Amerikaner
Gary M. Kvistad
Christopher A. Jacobs
Jeffrey A. Dinkin
Jeffery H. Speich

ASSOCIATES

Lori Lewis Perry
Robert J. Saperstein
Jeanne MacCalden Kvale
Josef D. Houska
Sarah J. Knecht
Stephanie Osler Hastings
Bradley L. Lundgren
Merrilee Fellows
Deborah L. Martin
John D. Bakker
Michelle L. Pickett
Travis Pananides
Mark A. DePaco
Robin L. Lewis
Scott M. Weis
C. Anthony Boyd
Alaina M. Alexson
Timothy C. Hale

OF COUNSEL

Christine M. Frahm

For full biographical listings, see the Martindale-Hubbell Law Directory

HOLLISTER & BRACE, A PROFESSIONAL CORPORATION (AV)
1126 Santa Barbara Street, P.O. Box 630, 93101
Telephone: 805-963-6711
Fax: 805-965-0329
Email: hblaw@hbsb.com

William A. Brace (Retired)
J. James Hollister, III (Retired)
John S. Poucher
Richard C. Monk
George A. Rempe, III
Steven Evans Kirby
Bradford F. Ginder
John G. Busby
Susan H. McCollum
Robert L. Brace
Marcus Scott Bird
Charles W. Willey (P.C.)
Alexis W. Willey
Peter L. Candy

Attorneys For: Bucara Resort & Spa; Buellflat Rock Co.; Coast Rock Products; Gaviota Marine Terminal; Ian Schrager Hotels, LLC; Morehart Land Company; Santa Barbara County Rock Producers Assoc.; Santa Barbara Trust for Historic Preservation; Western States Petroleum Association.

For full biographical listings, see the Martindale-Hubbell Law Directory

SANTA MONICA, Los Angeles Co.

BERGER & NORTON, A LAW CORPORATION (AV)
1620 26th Street Suite 200 South, 90404
Telephone: 310-449-1000
Fax: 310-449-5000
URL: http://www.bergernorton.com

Michael M. Berger
Richard D. Norton
Ann E. Kelly
George M. Soneff
Edward G. Burg
Craig M. Collins
Pamela Schmidt

Kisu Shin
Sophie A. Castillo

(See Next Column)

OF COUNSEL

Gideon Kanner

For full biographical listings, see the Martindale-Hubbell Law Directory

THOUSAND OAKS, Ventura Co.

COHEN, ALEXANDER & CLAYTON, A PROFESSIONAL CORPORATION (AV)
One Boardwalk, Suite 102, 91360-5799
Telephone: 805-497-0802
Fax: 805-373-6082
Email: lawcac@ix.netcom.com

Charles W. Cohen
Leonard Alexander
Raymond C. Clayton
Ruth D. Morrow
Marguerite A. Wilson

Thomas S. Cohen

Representative Clients: Comsat General Corp.; Conejo Valley Chamber of Commerce; South Coast Area Transit.

For full biographical listings, see the Martindale-Hubbell Law Directory

COLORADO

*ASPEN,** Pitkin Co.

OATES, KNEZEVICH & GARDENSWARTZ, P.C. (AV)
Aspen Plaza Building, 3rd Floor, 533 East Hopkins Avenue, 81611
Telephone: 970-920-1700
Fax: 970-920-1121
Email: ohkg@rof.net

Leonard M. Oates
Richard A. Knezevich
Ted D. Gardenswartz
David B. Kelly

David B. Mueller

OF COUNSEL

John Thomas Kelly
Michael Feigenbaum

For full biographical listings, see the Martindale-Hubbell Law Directory

*DENVER,** Denver Co.

BROWNSTEIN HYATT & FARBER, P.C. (AV)
Twenty-Second Floor, 410 Seventeenth Street, 80202-4437
Telephone: 303-223-1100
Telecopier: 303-223-1111
Washington, D.C. Office: 1615 L Street, N.W., Suite 450, 20036.
Telephone: 202-296-7353.
Telecopier: 202-296-7009.
Glenwood Springs, Colorado Office: Box 357, 81602.
Telephone: 970-945-5302.
Telecopier: 970-945-4921.

Andrew W. Loewi
Wayne F. Forman
Bruce A. James
Cole Finegan
Mark J. Mathews

SENIOR COUNSEL

James S. Lochhead (Resident, Glenwood Springs, Colorado Office)
Gale A. Norton

Beth Doherty Quinn
Andrew L. Spielman
Chad G. Asarch

Representative Clients: Edw. C. Levy Company; Sanders Ranch Holdings, LLC; The Taubman Company, Inc.; Trammell Crow Company; Trillium Corporation; U.S. Home Corporation; Vail Associates, Inc.; Western Wireless Corp.

For Complete List of Firm Personnel, See General Section

For full biographical listings, see the Martindale-Hubbell Law Directory

GORSUCH KIRGIS LLP (AV)
Tower 1, Suite 1000, 1515 Arapahoe Street, 80202
Telephone: 303-376-5000
Fax: 303-376-5001

PARTNERS

Malcolm M. Murray
Gerald E. Dahl
Robert C. Widner

For full biographical listings, see the Martindale-Hubbell Law Directory

Denver—Continued

OTTEN, JOHNSON, ROBINSON, NEFF & RAGONETTI, P.C. (AV)

950 Seventeenth Street, 16th Floor, 80202
Telephone: 303-825-8400
Telecopier: 303-825-6525
URL: http://www.ojrnr.com

Thomas J. Ragonetti
Robert C. Fisher, Jr.
J. Thomas Macdonald
Kevin A. Gliwa
Brad W. Schacht
R. Michael Shomo
J. Bart Johnson
Munsey L. Ayers, Jr.
Nicole J. Hanak
Berkeley I. Vogelsang

OF COUNSEL

Barbara J. Green

Representative Clients: The City and County of Denver; Colorado Chapter of the APA; Denver Technological Center; Denver Television Stations--Channels 4, 6, 7, 9 and 20; Denver Union Terminal Railway Co.; Fuller & Co.; Gateway Landowners Association; Homebuilders Association of Metropolitan Denver; San Miguel Valley Corp.; Vail Associates.

For Complete List of Firm Personnel, See General Section

For full biographical listings, see the Martindale-Hubbell Law Directory

*GOLDEN,** Jefferson Co.

HOLLEY, ALBERTSON & POLK, P.C. (AV)

Suite 100, 1667 Cole Boulevard, 80401-3295
Telephone: 303-233-7838
Fax: 303-233-2860

George Alan Holley
Scott D. Albertson
Dennis B. Polk
Eric E. Torgersen
Howard R. Stone

Heather M. Davis

Reference: First Bank of Wheat Ridge.

For full biographical listings, see the Martindale-Hubbell Law Directory

CONNECTICUT

GREENWICH, Fairfield Co.

HOLLAND KAUFMANN & BARTELS, LLC (AV)

289 Greenwich Avenue, 06830-6595
Telephone: 203-869-5600
Fax: 203-869-4648

Alexander J. Holland
Charles B. Kaufmann, III
Philip H. Bartels
Harold R. Burke
Jean Mills Aranha
Lori E. Romano
John C. Fusco

OF COUNSEL

Beth K. Hansson

For full biographical listings, see the Martindale-Hubbell Law Directory

*HARTFORD,** Hartford Co.

KILLIAN, DONOHUE & SHIPMAN, LLC (AV)

363 Main Street, 06106-1885
Telephone: 860-560-1977
Telecopier: 860-249-6638
Email: lawyers@killiandonohueshipman.com
Simsbury, Connecticut Office: 141 West Street.
Telephone: 860-658-0436.
Telecopier: 860-249-6638.

Robert K. Killian, Jr.
Thomas J. Donohue, Jr.
Mark S. Shipman
Lawrence S. Shipman

For full biographical listings, see the Martindale-Hubbell Law Directory

STAMFORD, Fairfield Co.

CURTIS, BRINCKERHOFF & BARRETT, P.C. (AV)

666 Summer Street, 06901-1416
Telephone: 203-324-6777
Telecopier: 203-324-9621
Email: info@curtisbb.com

T. Ward Cleary (1916-1988)
Frederick M. Tobin
John Wayne Fox
Ward Frank Cleary
James D'Alton Murphy
Randolph T. Lovallo

OF COUNSEL

John D. Hertz
Jane F. Donovan
Richard L. Brinckerhoff
Patricia M. Gaug

(See Next Column)

Susan L. Stratton
Derek Gilman
Michael P. Murray
John J. Louizos

Counsel for: The F. A. Bartlett Tree Expert Co.; Town of Darien; Miller Automobile Corp.; Bolliger, Inc.; Titan Sports; People's Bank, Bridgeport; Fleet Bank; Federal Deposit Insurance Co.; William Pitt Foundation; Wood Logan Associates.

For full biographical listings, see the Martindale-Hubbell Law Directory

FLORIDA

*BRADENTON,** Manatee Co.

GRIMES GOEBEL GRIMES HAWKINS & GLADFELTER, P.A. (AV)

The Professional Building, 1023 Manatee Avenue West, P.O. Box 1550, 34206
Telephone: 941-748-0151
Fax: 941-748-0158
Email: ggghg@gte.net
Tampa, Florida Office: Old Hyde Park Village, 1509 West Swann Avenue, Suite 275.
Telephone: 813-258-2557.
Fax: 813-258-2327.

Caleb J. Grimes
Leslie Horton Gladfelter
William S. Galvano

Counsel for: Schroeder Manatee Inc. (Agriculture and Land Development); Lombardo & Skipper & Foley, Inc. (Civil Engineers); CCI Environmental Services, Inc. (Environmental Consultants); Creekwood Investors, Ltd.; Old Hyde Park Village Center, Ltd.; First Federal Savings & Loan Association of Florida.

Approved Attorneys for: Lawyers Title Insurance Corp.; Chicago Title Insurance Co.; Attorneys Title Insurance Fund.

For full biographical listings, see the Martindale-Hubbell Law Directory

*FORT PIERCE,** St. Lucie Co.

GONANO, HARRELL & FERGUSON (AV)

Riverside National Bank Building, 1600 South Federal Highway, Suite 200, 34950-5194
Telephone: 561-464-1032
Fax: 561-464-0282
Email: ghlaw@compuserve.com

Douglas E. Gonano
Daniel B. Harrell
Johnathan A. Ferguson

General Counsel: School Board of St. Lucie County; Reserve Community Development District; St. Lucie West Services District.

Representative Clients: East Coast Lumber & Supply Co.; Riverside National Bank of Florida; Superior Title Services, Inc.

Approved Attorneys for: Attorneys' Title Insurance Fund; Commonwealth Land Title Insurance Co.

References: Riverside National Bank of Florida; SunTrust, South Florida, N.A.

For full biographical listings, see the Martindale-Hubbell Law Directory

*JACKSONVILLE,** Duval Co.

PAPPAS METCALF JENKS MILLER & REINSCH, P.A. (AV)

200 West Forsyth Street, Suite 1400, 32202-4327
Telephone: 904-353-1980
Telecopier: 904-353-5217
Email: pmj@papmet.com

Thomas M. Jenks
Robert A. Leapley, Jr.
John G. Metcalf
Frank Estes Miller
M. Lynn Pappas
Mark A. Reinsch

Christina P. Gillam
Gary B. Davenport
G. Todd Cottrill
Thomas Ingram

LEGAL SUPPORT PERSONNEL

Mary Beth Wimmer
Glenna Thompson (Paralegal)
Donna F. Demetree (Paralegal)

For full biographical listings, see the Martindale-Hubbell Law Directory

*MIAMI,** Dade Co.

NAGIN GALLOP FIGUEREDO, P.A. (AV)

3225 Aviation Avenue - Third Floor, 33133-4741
Telephone: 305-854-5353
Facsimile: 305-854-5351

(See Next Column)

NAGIN GALLOP FIGUEREDO P.A., *Miami—Continued*

Stephen E. Nagin
Earl G. Gallop
Luis R. Figueredo
Scott L. Cagan
Eve A. Boutsis
Jeffrey B. Mallory

For full biographical listings, see the Martindale-Hubbell Law Directory

*NAPLES,** Collier Co.

QUARLES & BRADY LLP (AV)

Barnett Center, 4501 Tamiami Trail North Suite 300, 34103-3060
Telephone: 941-262-5959
Fax: 941-434-4999
URL: http://www.quarles.com
Milwaukee, Wisconsin Office: 411 East Wisconsin Avenue, 53202-4497.
Telephone: 414-277-5000.
Fax: 414-271-3552.
Madison, Wisconsin Office: Firstar Plaza, One South Pinckney Street, P.O. Box 2113, 53701-2113.
Telephone: 608-251-5000.
Fax: 608-251-9166.
West Palm Beach, Florida Office: 222 Lakeview Avenue, 4th Floor, 33401.
Telephone: 561-653-5000.
Fax: 561-653-5333.
Phoenix, Arizona Office: One Camelback Building, One East Camelback Road, Suite 400, 85012-1649.
Telephone: 602-230-5500.
Fax: 602-230-5598.
Chicago, Illinois Office: Quarles & Brady LLC, Citicorp Center, 500 West Madison Street, Suite 3700.
Telephone: 312-715-5000.
Fax: 312-715-5155.

PARTNERS

Thomas E. Maloney
David L. Petersen
F. Joseph McMackin, III
Timothy G. Hains
Leo J. Salvatori
John D. Humphreville

For Complete List of Firm Personnel, See General Section

For full biographical listings, see the Martindale-Hubbell Law Directory

*ST. AUGUSTINE,** St. Johns Co.

UPCHURCH, BAILEY & UPCHURCH, P.A. (AV)

780 North Ponce de Leon Boulevard, P.O. Drawer 3007, 32085-3007
Telephone: 904-829-9066
Facsimile: 904-825-4862
Email: info@ubulaw.com

John D. Bailey, Jr.
Frank D. Upchurch, III
Sidney F. Ansbacher
Katherine Gaertner Jones

OF COUNSEL

Hamilton D. Upchurch

General Counsel for: Flagler College; Flagler Hospital, Inc.; Prosperity Bank; St. Johns County School Board.
Representative Clients: Aero Sport, Inc.; American Culinary Federation, Inc.; Bank of St. Augustine; Penney Retirement Community, Inc.; St. Augustine Alligator Farm, Inc.; St. Augustine-St. Johns County Board of Realtors, Inc.

For Complete List of Firm Personnel, See General Section

For full biographical listings, see the Martindale-Hubbell Law Directory

*STUART,** Martin Co.

McCARTHY, SUMMERS, BOBKO, McKEY, WOOD & SAWYER, P.A. (AV)

2081 East Ocean Boulevard, Second Floor, 34996
Telephone: 561-286-1700
Fax: 561-283-1803
URL: http://www.mcsumm.com

Terence P. McCarthy
Robert P. Summers
Noel A. Bobko
John D. McKey, Jr.
Steven J. Wood
Thomas R. Sawyer
Nicola J. Boone
Steven L. Perry

Kathryn C. Bass
Robert N. Maitland, II

Representative Clients: First National Bank and Trust Company of the Treasure Coast; Hydratech Utilities; Lost Lake at Hobe Sound; Gary Player Design Group; YMCA of Martin County; Shadow Lakes Groves, Inc.; Merrill Lynch Trust Co., (Florida); Wilmington Trust, FSB; The Huntington National Bank, N.A.; WSTU-Radio, WTCN-TV.

For full biographical listings, see the Martindale-Hubbell Law Directory

*TAMPA,** Hillsborough Co.

BRICKLEMYER SMOLKER & BOLVES, P.A. (AV)

500 East Kennedy Boulevard, Suite 200, 33602-4708
Telephone: 813-223-3888
Fax: 813-228-6422
Email: bsb@bsbpropertylaw.com *URL:* http://www.bsbpropertylaw.com

Keith W. Bricklemyer
David Smolker
Brian A. Bolves
Jay J. Bartlett
Douglas C. Roland
David M. Corry
Richard A. Schlosser
Gregory J. Orcutt

R. Michael Brooks
Deborah M. Schmitt

OF COUNSEL

J.A. Jurgens

For full biographical listings, see the Martindale-Hubbell Law Directory

*VERO BEACH,** Indian River Co.

MOSS, HENDERSON, BLANTON & LANIER, P.A. (AV)

817 Beachland Boulevard, P.O. Box 3406, 32964-3406
Telephone: 561-231-1900
Fax: 561-231-4387

Steve L. Henderson

Representative Clients: Aetna Life & Casualty; Alcoa Florida, Inc.; Florida Power & Light Co.; Insurance Company of North America; Liberty Mutual Insurance Co.; Sears, Roebuck & Co.; Sugar Cane Growers Cooperative of Florida; Norfolk Southern Corporation/North American Van Lines, Inc.

For Complete List of Firm Personnel, See General Section

For full biographical listings, see the Martindale-Hubbell Law Directory

*WEST PALM BEACH,** Palm Beach Co.

QUARLES & BRADY LLP (AV)

222 Lakeview Avenue, 4th Floor, 33401
Telephone: 561-653-5000
Fax: 561-653-5333
URL: http://www.quarles.com
Milwaukee, Wisconsin Office: 411 East Wisconsin Avenue, 53202-4497.
Telephone: 414-277-5000.
Fax: 414-271-3552.
Madison, Wisconsin Office: Firstar Plaza, One South Pinckney Street, P.O. Box 2113, 53701-2113.
Telephone: 608-251-5000.
Fax: 608-251-9166.
Naples, Florida Office: Barnett Center, 4501 Tamiami Trail North, Suite 300, 34103-3060.
Telephone: 941-262-5959.
Fax: 941-434-4999.
Phoenix, Arizona Office: One Camelback Building, One East Camelback Road, Suite 400, 85012-1649.
Telephone: 602-230-5500.
Fax: 602-230-5598.
Chicago, Illinois Office: Quarles & Brady LLC, Citicorp Center, 500 West Madison Street, Suite 3700.
Telephone: 312-715-5000.
Fax: 312-715-5155.

PARTNER

Nancy Berz Colman

OF COUNSEL

John S. Sammond

For Complete List of Firm Personnel, See General Section

For full biographical listings, see the Martindale-Hubbell Law Directory

WINTER PARK, Orange Co.

VOSE, BLAU & HAYES (AV)

2705 West Fairbanks Avenue, 32789
Telephone: 407-645-3735
Fax: 407-628-5670
Email: bvose@vbh-law.com *URL:* http://www.vbh-law.com

Gretchen R. H. Vose
Leslie A. Blau
Rosemary H. Hayes

ASSOCIATES

Carolyn S. Crichton
Christina M. Page
Peter J. Meadows
Aubrey Harry Ducker, Jr.

For full biographical listings, see the Martindale-Hubbell Law Directory

GEORGIA

*ATLANTA,** Fulton Co.

GRAY & GILLILAND, P.C. (AV)

400 Perimeter Center Terrace, Suite 1050, 30346-1239
Telephone: 770-392-4800
Telecopy: 770-392-4808

John C. Gray
T. Cullen Gilliland
Charles A. Ratz
Melissa A. Garrett
T. Jeffery Lehman
Robert W. Browning

P. Steven Kratsch

OF COUNSEL

E. Reid Garrett
David S. Currie
Mark B. Bullman

For full biographical listings, see the Martindale-Hubbell Law Directory

NORCROSS, Gwinnett Co.

PHEARS & MOLDOVAN (AV)

A Partnership of Professional Corporations
4725 Peachtree Corners Circle Suite 375, 30092
Telephone: 770-446-2116
Telecopier: 770-263-6715
Email: phearsmold@aol.com

MEMBERS OF FIRM

H. Wayne Phears (P.C.)
Victor L. Moldovan (P.C.)

Richard O. Samms

For full biographical listings, see the Martindale-Hubbell Law Directory

HAWAII

*HONOLULU,** Honolulu Co.

CARLSMITH BALL (AV)

A Partnership including Law Corporations
Suite 2200, Pacific Tower, 1001 Bishop Street, P.O. Box 656, 96809-3402
Telephone: 808-523-2500
Fax: 808-523-0842
Email: execdirector@carlsmith.com *URL:* http://www.carlsmith.com
Kapolei, Hawaii Office: Suite 318, Kapolei Building, 1001 Kamokila Boulevard, 96707.
Telephone: 808-523-2500.
Fax: 808-674-0850.
Wailuku, Maui Hawaii Office: Suite 400, One Main Plaza, 2200 Main Street, P.O. Box 1086, 96793-1086.
Telephone: 808-242-4535.
Fax: 808-244-4974.
Kailua-Kona, Hawaii Office: Suite 209, 75-1000 Henry Street, 96740.
Telephone: 808-329-6464.
Fax: 808-329-9450.
Hilo, Hawaii Office: 121 Waianuenue Avenue, P.O. Box 686, 96721-0686.
Telephone: 808-935-6644.
Fax: 808-935-7975.
Hagatna, Guam Office: Suite 401, Bank of Hawaii Building, 134 West Soledad Avenue, P.O. Box BF, 96932-5027.
Telephone: 671-472-6813.
Fax: 671-477-4375.
Telex: 721-6445 CWCMI GM.
Saipan, Commonwealth of the Northern Mariana Islands Office: Carlsmith Building, Capitol Hill, P.O. Box 5241, 96950-5241.
Telephone: 670-322-3455.
Fax: 670-322-3368.
Los Angeles, California Office: 9th Floor, 444 South Flower Street, 90071-2901.
Telephone: 213-955-1200.
Fax: 213-623-0032.
Washington, D.C. Office: Suite 300, 1201 Pennsylvania Avenue, N.W., 20004-2401.
Telephone: 202-628-2228.
Fax: 202-628-2071.
Mexico City, Mexico Office: Carlsmith Ball, Sierra Nevada 119, Lomas de Chapultepec, 11000 Mexico, D.F.
Telephone: 52-5-520-8514, 52-5-520-8757.
Fax: 52-5-540-1545.
Mexico, D.F. Office of Carlsmith Ball, S.C. (Authorized to practice as foreign legal consultants in Mexico): Sierra Nevada 119, Lomas de Chapultepec, 11000 Mexico, D.F.
Telephone: 52-5-520-8514, 52-5-520-8757.
Fax: 52-5-540-1545.

(See Next Column)

MEMBERS OF FIRM

Edward E. Case
Patricia Devlin
Randall H. Endo (Resident at Maui, Hawaii Office)
Eric A. James
Richard Kiefer
Karl K. Kobayashi
Steven S. C. Lim (Resident at Hilo, Hawaii Office)
Tim Lui-Kwan
B. Martin Luna (Resident at Maui, Hawaii Office)
Mark K. Murakami (Resident at Kapolei, Hawaii Office)
Craig G. Nakamura (Resident at Maui, Hawaii Office)
David R. Nevitt (Resident at Saipan Office)
Paul M. Ueoka (Resident at Maui, Hawaii Office)

Representative Clients: Ala Moana Shopping Center; Bank of Hawaii; The Estate of James Campbell; Kaluakoi Resort; The Myers Corporation; Nippon Shinpan U.S.A. Inc.; Outrigger Hotels; Queen Emma Foundation; Servco Pacific.

For Complete List of Firm Personnel, See General Section

For full biographical listings, see the Martindale-Hubbell Law Directory

ILLINOIS

*CHICAGO,** Cook Co.

FIGLIULO & SILVERMAN, P.C. (AV)

10 South La Salle Street, Suite 3600, 60603
Telephone: 312-251-4600
Fax: 312-251-4610

James R. Figliulo
Peter A. Silverman
Carl A. Gigante
Brian P. Liston
Marc S. Porter
James H. Bowhay

James J. Sipchen, Jr.
Adam E. Bossov
Michael K. Desmond

For full biographical listings, see the Martindale-Hubbell Law Directory

MATTOON, Coles Co.

CRAIG & CRAIG (AV)

1807 Broadway, P.O. Box 689, 61938-0689
Telephone: 217-234-6481
Telecopier: 217-234-6486; 258-8292
Email: craiglaw@advant.com
Mount Vernon, Illinois Office: 115 North 7th Street.
Telephone: 618-244-7511.

MEMBERS OF FIRM

Craig Van Meter (1895-1981)
Fred H. Kelly (1894-1971)
Robert M. Werden (1908-1969)
George N. Gilkerson (1911-1985)
John P. Ewart
Richard F. Record, Jr.
Stephen L. Corn
Robert G. Grierson
Gregory C. Ray
Paul R. Lynch (Resident, Mount Vernon Office)
Kenneth F. Werts (Resident, Mount Vernon Office)
John L. Barger

ASSOCIATES

Kathleen M. Stockwell
Kristine M. Tuttle
Julie A. Webb (Resident, Mount Vernon Office)
John M. O'Driscoll
Duane A. Deters
Katy C. Fain (Resident, Mount Vernon Office)
Erin E. Wisner
John F. Watson

OF COUNSEL

Jack E. Horsley

Representative Clients: Freeman United Coal Mining Co.; Natural Gas Pipeline Company of America; Marathon Oil Company; Howell Paving, Inc.; Illinois Central R.R. Co.; Consolidated Communications Inc.; Lake Land College; Scattering Fork Drainage District of Douglas County, Illinois.

For full biographical listings, see the Martindale-Hubbell Law Directory

VERNON HILLS, Lake Co.

RICHARDS, RALPH & SCHWAB, CHARTERED (AV)

One Hawthorn Place, 175 East Hawthorn Parkway, Suite 345, 60061
Telephone: 847-367-9699
Fax: 847-367-9621
Email: dschwab@rr&s-chtd.com *URL:* http://www.lawyers.com/richardandschwab

Michael L. Ralph
Alan E. Richards
David J. Schwab

For full biographical listings, see the Martindale-Hubbell Law Directory

INDIANA

*EVANSVILLE,** Vanderburgh Co.

Bowers, Harrison, Kent & Miller, LLP (AV)

25 N.W. Riverside Drive, P.O. Box 1287, 47706-1287
Telephone: 812-426-1231
Fax: 812-464-3676
Email: BOWERS,HARRISON,KENT&MILLER,LLP@BHKM.COM
URL: http://WWW.BHKM.COM

MEMBERS OF FIRM

F. Wesley Bowers
Joseph H. Harrison
David V. Miller
Paul E. Black
Gary R. Case
Arthur D. Rutkowski
George C. Barnett, Jr.
Terry Noffsinger
Paul J. Wallace
David E. Gray
Gregory A. Kahre
Timothy J. Hubert
Thomas A. Massey
Greg A. Granger
Joseph H. Harrison, Jr.
Lawrence L. Grimes
Sara Harrison Zeidler
Christopher L. Lucas

ASSOCIATES

Cedric Hustace
Sean M. Georges
Douglas K. Briody
Holly H. Wilhelmus
Stacy Kerns Harris
Keith William Vonderahe

OF COUNSEL

K. Wayne Kent
William G. Greif

LEGAL SUPPORT PERSONNEL

Victor J. Ippoliti (Law Clerk)

Division Counsel in Indiana for: Southern Railway Co.
Representative Clients: Permanent Federal Savings Bank; Citizens Realty & Insurance, Inc.

For full biographical listings, see the Martindale-Hubbell Law Directory

*FORT WAYNE,** Allen Co.

Beckman Lawson, LLP (AV)

800 Standard Federal Plaza, 46802
Telephone: 219-422-0800
Facsimile: 219-420-1013
Syracuse, Indiana Office: 200 West Main Street.
Telephone: 219-457-5727.
Facsimile: 219-457-2056.

MEMBERS OF FIRM

Jack W. Lawson
Frank J. Gray
Howard B. Sandler
Stephen R. Snyder
James A. Federoff
William L. Sweet, Jr.
Richard H. Blaich
John H. Brandt
Jon A. Bragalone
Brian J. T'Kindt
Douglas R. Adelsperger
Travis S. Friend
Robert L. Nicholson
David D. Cornwell
James A. Butz
Jack C. Birch
Craig R. Patterson

ASSOCIATES

John M. Ketcham
Wendy W. Davis
Jeffrey B. Harding
Martha M. Kinder
Edward J. Ormsby
Randall L. Morgan
Daniel J. Deeb
Patrick R. Hess
Georgia L. Hartman
Brian M. Simpson
James E. Rossow, Jr.
Sarah A. Hiestand
Tandra S. Johnson
Jason M. Kuchmay
Matthew J. Elliott

OF COUNSEL

Frederick A. Beckman
Neil F. Sandler
Douglas E. Miller
Loren K. Allison

Reference: National City Bank.

For full biographical listings, see the Martindale-Hubbell Law Directory

*INDIANAPOLIS,** Marion Co.

Clark, Quinn, Moses & Clark (AV)

One Indiana Square, Suite 2200, 46204-2011
Telephone: 317-637-1321
Fax: 317-687-2344
Email: lawyers@cqmc-law.com

MEMBERS OF FIRM

Thomas Michael Quinn
J. Murray Clark
Matthew R. Clark

ASSOCIATES

Michael D. Keele
Cameron F. Clark
Robert V. Clutter

Representative Clients: Justus Companies; Davis Homes; Meijer Realty, Inc.; Lowe's; Marsh; MI Shottenstein; Indianapolis Colts; Fort Harrison Reuse Authority; Indianapolis Water Company; Kroger.

For full biographical listings, see the Martindale-Hubbell Law Directory

*LAFAYETTE,** Tippecanoe Co.

Stuart & Branigin (AV)

The Life Building, 300 Main Street, Suite 800, P.O. Box 1010, 47902-1010
Telephone: 765-423-1561
Telecopier: 765-742-8175
Email: sb@stuartlaw.com *URL:* http://www.stuartlaw.com
Indianapolis, Indiana Office: Suite 1401, 8888 Keystone Crossing, 46240.
Telephone: 317-574-7245.
Fax: 317-574-7050.

MEMBERS OF FIRM

Allison Ellsworth Stuart (1886-1950)
Roger D. Branigin (1902-1975)
Roger D. Branigin, Jr.
Thomas L. Ryan
Thomas R. McCully
Larry R. Fisher
Nina B. Kirkpatrick
Mark Lillianfeld
Stephen R. Pennell
Anthony S. Benton
Erik D. Spykman
William E. Emerick
John C. Duffey
Bruce McSpadden
Mark E. DeYoung
Thomas B. Parent
Laura L. Bowker
Kevin D. Nicoson
Susan K. Roberts
John M. Stuckey
Deborah B. Trice
William P. Kealey
David A. Starkweather
Geoffrey L. Blazi

SENIOR COUNSEL

Russell H. Hart

COUNSEL

John F. Bodle
James V. McGlone

ASSOCIATES

Elizabeth B. Searle
Marianne Mitten Owen
David A. Locke
Karen Orr McClure
Ann Marie Waldron
Barry L. Loftus

General Counsel for: The Lafayette Life Insurance Co.; INB National Bank, N.W.; Lafayette Home Hospital, Inc.
State Counsel for: Norfolk & Western Railway Co.
Mr. Ryan is Counsel to: The Trustees of Purdue University.
Representative Clients: Aluminum Company of America; Liberty Mutual Insurance Group.

For full biographical listings, see the Martindale-Hubbell Law Directory

KENTUCKY

*LEXINGTON,** Fayette Co.

Dunn, Franklin & Murphy (AV)

175 East Main Street Suite 300, 40507
Telephone: 606-255-9091
Fax: 606-254-4319
Email: dfmlaw@mis.net

Cecil F. Dunn
David A. Franklin
Richard V. Murphy

Rhonda E. Franklin

OF COUNSEL

C. Clinton McKinley

For full biographical listings, see the Martindale-Hubbell Law Directory

*LOUISVILLE,** Jefferson Co.

Bardenwerper & Lobb, PLLC (AV)

8311 Shelbyville Road, 40222
Telephone: 502-426-6688
Fax: 502-425-0561

William B. Bardenwerper
James T. Lobb

ASSOCIATE

Susan T. Merrill

LEGAL SUPPORT PERSONNEL

Alice Blackburn (Paralegal)
Debra Martin (Paralegal)

For full biographical listings, see the Martindale-Hubbell Law Directory

LOUISIANA

*MONROE,** Ouachita Parish

THOMPSON, SPARKS, DEAN & MORRIS (AV)

A Partnership including a Professional Corporation
1401 Royal Street, P.O. Box 2867, 71207
Telephone: 318-388-1440
Fax: 318-322-0887

MEMBERS OF FIRM

M. C. Thompson (1885-1970)
James D. Sparks (1910-1987)
George B. Dean, Jr., (P.C.)
Wood T. Sparks
John C. Morris, III

ASSOCIATE

Jennifer Allen Riley

Representative Clients: South Central Bell Telephone Co.; Greater Ouachita Water Company; PHH Homequity Corp.; Commonwealth Relocation Services, Inc.; Remax, Monroe; Bell South Advertising & Publishing Corp.; Premier Mortgage Corp.; Countrywide Funding Corp.
Approved Attorneys for: BankOne; Federal Land Bank.

For full biographical listings, see the Martindale-Hubbell Law Directory

*SHREVEPORT,** Caddo Parish

BARLOW AND HARDTNER L.C. (AV)

Tenth Floor, Louisiana Tower, 401 Edwards Street, 71101-3289
Telephone: 318-227-1131
Telecopier: 318-227-1141
Mailing Address: P.O. Box 8, Shreveport, Louisiana, 71161-0008

Quintin T. Hardtner, III
Malcolm S. Murchison
Kay Cowden Medlin
Joseph L. Shea, Jr.
David R. Taggart
Stephen E. Ramey
Michael B. Donald
Jay A. Greenleaf

OF COUNSEL

Cecil E. Ramey, Jr.
Paula Hazelrig Hickman

Representative Clients: NorAm Energy Corp. (formerly Arkla, Inc.); Central and South West Corporation; Panhandle Eastern Corp.; Pennzoil Producing Co.; Ashland Oil, Inc.; Southwestern Electric Power Company; Energy Management Corporation; TE Products Pipeline Company; Concorde Gas Marketing Company; General Electric Co.

For Complete List of Firm Personnel, See General Section

For full biographical listings, see the Martindale-Hubbell Law Directory

MAINE

*PORTLAND,** Cumberland Co.

VERRILL & DANA, LLP (AV)

One Portland Square, P.O. Box 586, 04112-0586
Telephone: 207-774-4000
Fax: 207-774-7499
Email: advice@verdan.com *URL:* http://www.verdan.com
Augusta, Maine Office: 45 Memorial Circle, P.O. Box 957.
Telephone: 207-623-3889.
Fax: 207-622-3117.
Kennebunk, Maine Office: 403-404 Lafayette Center, P.O. Box 147.
Telephone: 207-985-7193.
Fax: 207-985-3957.
Washington, D.C. Office: 400 North Capitol Street, Suite 585.
Telephone: 202-624-9733.
Fax: 202-393-5218.

MEMBERS OF FIRM

Charles R. Oestreicher
Robert E. Cleaves, IV

For Complete List of Firm Personnel, See General Section
For full biographical listings, see the Martindale-Hubbell Law Directory

MARYLAND

GREENBELT, Prince Georges Co.

FOSSETT & BRUGGER, CHARTERED (AV)

6404 Ivy Lane, Suite 720, 20770
Telephone: 301-486-1900
Telecopier: 301-486-0999
La Plata, Maryland Office: 105 LaGrange Avenue, P.O. Box F.
Telephone: 301-934-4200.

(See Next Column)

George A. Brugger
Clarence L. Fossett
Nancy L. Slepicka
William M. Shipp
John C. Fredrickson
Mary A. Zambri
Eric M. Elmore
Mark S. Petrauskas
John A. Giannetti, Jr.

LEGAL SUPPORT PERSONNEL

Dean Armstrong (Consulting Land Planner)

Representative Clients: Cafritz Companies; Citicorp Real Estate, Inc.; Coscan Brookfield Homes; Crestar Bank; The Driggs Corp.; Kettler Brothers; Kiplinger Washington Editors; The Mutual Life Insurance Company of New York; Richmond-American Homes; The Simon DeBartolo Group.

For full biographical listings, see the Martindale-Hubbell Law Directory

*LA PLATA,** Charles Co.

MUDD, MUDD & FITZGERALD, P.A. (AV)

106 St. Mary's Avenue, P.O. Box 310, 20646
Telephone: 301-934-9541
FAX: 301-934-8178

John F. Mudd (1885-1950)
F. DeSales Mudd (1909-1972)
Thomas F. Mudd
John F. Mudd
Stephen P. Fitzgerald

John E. Ray

Local Counsel for: County First Bank (La Plata); Potomac Electric Power Co.; The Hartford Insurance Group; Maryland Bank & Trust Co.; Chicago Title Insurance Co.; Peninsula Title Insurance Co.; Colonial Farm Credit Agric. Credit Assn.
Counsel for: Interstate General Corporation; SMO, Inc.

For full biographical listings, see the Martindale-Hubbell Law Directory

SILVER SPRING, Montgomery Co.

LINOWES AND BLOCHER LLP (AV)

Suite 1000, 1010 Wayne Avenue, 20910-5600
Telephone: 301-588-8580
Telecopier: 301-495-9044
TTY/TDD: 301-588-3380
Email: inbox@linowes-law.com *URL:* http://www.linowes-law.com
Washington, D.C. Office: Suite 302, 1150 17th Street, N.W.
Telephone: 202-293-8510.
Telecopier: 202-293-8513.
Greenbelt, Maryland Office: Suite 202, 6411 Ivy Lane.
Telephone: 301-982-3382.
Telecopier: 301-982-0595.
Annapolis, Maryland Office: 145 Main Street.
Telephone: 410-268-0881.
Telecopier: 301-261-2603.
Frederick, Maryland Office: 228 West Patrick Street.
Telephone: 301-695-0244.
Telecopier: 301-663-6656.
Columbia, Maryland Office: Suite B215, 10015 Old Columbia Road.
Telephone: 410-312-5457.
Fax: 410-290-5285.

MEMBERS OF FIRM

Joseph P. Blocher
Todd D. Brown
Kathryn J. Dahl (Resident Partner, Annapolis, Maryland office)
C. Robert Dalrymple
John J. Delaney
Stephen P. Elmendorf
Stephen Z. Kaufman
Robert H. Metz
Midgett S. Parker, Jr. (Resident Partner, Greenbelt, Maryland office)
David M. Plott (Resident Partner, Annapolis, Maryland office)
Leslie Moore Romine (Resident Partner, Greenbelt, Maryland office)
Barbara A. Sears

OF COUNSEL

David L. Cahoon
Cynthia A. Giordano (Resident, Washington, D.C. office)

ASSOCIATES

Andrew Wycoff Crocker
Garland H. Stillwell (Resident, Greenbelt, Maryland office)
Emily J. Vaias
Scott C. Wallace

For Complete List of Firm Personnel, See General Section

For full biographical listings, see the Martindale-Hubbell Law Directory

COLORADO

*BOULDER,** Boulder Co.

PURVIS, GRAY & GORDON, LLP (AV)

The Exeter Building, Suite 501, 1050 Walnut Street, 80302
Telephone: 303-442-3366
Fax: 303-440-3688
Email: info@pgglaw.com *URL:*
http://www.lawyers.com/purvisgrayschuetze&gordon
Denver, Colorado Office: 303 East 17th Avenue, Suite 700.
Telephone: 303-860-1888.

MEMBERS OF FIRM

William R. Gray
John A. Purvis
Glen F. Gordon

For full biographical listings, see the Martindale-Hubbell Law Directory

*DENVER,** Denver Co.

DAVIS & CERIANI, P.C. (AV)

Suite 400, Market Center, 1350 Seventeenth Street, 80202
Telephone: 303-534-9000
Telecopier: 303-534-4618
Email: davisandceriani.com

Rick G. Davis
Gary J. Ceriani
Bruce E. Rohde
Michael P. Cillo
Charles W. Bess
John W. Himmelmann

Margaret E. Peper
Patrick John Kanouff
Mark M. Osborn
Valeri Pappas

For full biographical listings, see the Martindale-Hubbell Law Directory

LONG & JAUDON, P.C. (AV)

The Bailey Mansion, 1600 Ogden Street, 80218-1414
Telephone: 303-832-1122
FAX: 303-832-1348

Lawrence A. Long (1908-1992)
Joseph C. Jaudon, Jr.
David B. Higgins
James A. Dierker
Frederick W. Long
Gary B. Blum
Michael T. McConnell
Stephen P. Hopkins
Michael T. DePinto (1956-1995)
Alan D. Avery
Cecelia A. Fleischner
Walter N. Houghtaling
Christine Anne Craigmile

Sheri Hood Roswell
David H. Yun
James Michael Miletich
Traci L. Van Pelt
Thomas J. Kresl
Michael Rosenberg
David M. McLain
Jennifer J. Gifford
Susan A. Jones (Not admitted in CO)
Christopher D. Yvars

OF COUNSEL

Linda L. Siderius

Representative Clients: Keystone Resorts, Inc.; King Soopers, Inc. (Dillon Companies, Inc.); St. Joseph Hospital; Watersaver; Travelers Property Casualty Company; The Doctors Co.; Home Insurance Co.; Baxter Healthcare; CNA.

For full biographical listings, see the Martindale-Hubbell Law Directory

PREEO, SILVERMAN & GREEN, P.C. (AV)

1401 17th Street, Suite 800, 80202
Telephone: 303-296-4440
Fax: 303-296-3330

Robert L. Preeo
Eldon E. Silverman
Jersey M. Green
Martin J. Green
Gilbert R. Egle
Marilyn W. McWilliams
Timothy Kyle Jordan
Brandon S Culter

For full biographical listings, see the Martindale-Hubbell Law Directory

PURVIS, GRAY & GORDON, LLP (AV)

303 East 17th Avenue, Suite 700, 80203
Telephone: 303-860-1888
Email: info@pgglaw.com *URL:*
http://www.lawyers.com/purvisgrayschuetze&gordon
Boulder, Colorado Office: The Exeter Building, Suite 501, 1050 Walnut Street.
Telephone: 303-442-3366.
Fax: 303-440-3688.

(See Next Column)

MEMBERS OF FIRM

William R. Gray
John A. Purvis
Glen F. Gordon

For full biographical listings, see the Martindale-Hubbell Law Directory

FLORIDA

*FORT LAUDERDALE,** Broward Co.

CONRAD & SCHERER (AV)

A Partnership of Professional Associations
Eighth Floor, 633 South Federal Highway, P.O. Box 14723, 33302
Telephone: 954-462-5500
Facsimile: 954-463-9244
Miami, Florida Office: 44 West Flagler Street, Suite 402, 33130.
Telephone: 305-856-9920.
Facsimile: 305-374-4408.

MEMBERS OF FIRM

William R. Scherer, Jr., (P.A.)
Gary S. Genovese (P.A.)
William V. Carcioppolo (P.A.)
Linda Rae Spaulding (P.A.)
Reid A. Cocalis (P.A.)
Willie Earl Hall (P.A.)
Ronald A. FitzGerald
James F. Carroll
Paul R. Larkin, Jr.
Dominic L. Brandy

OF COUNSEL

Rex Conrad

ASSOCIATES

Albert L. Frevola, Jr.
William R. Scherer, III
Vanessa A. Reynolds
Douglas Todd Marx
Janine Renee Kalagher
James A. Epstein
Angel Petti
Nicholas William Romanello
Shari L. McCartney
Catherine M. Rodriguez
Wendy A. Delvecchio

Local Counsel for: American Home Assurance Group; Caterpillar Tractor Co.; Division of Risk Management, State of Florida; Florida East Coast Railway; Fort Motor Co.; Liberty Mutual Insurance Co.; Ryder Truck Lines; Unigard Insurance Group.
Approved Attorneys for: Attorneys' Title Insurance Fund.
Reference: Barnett Bank of Fort Lauderdale.

For full biographical listings, see the Martindale-Hubbell Law Directory

PHILLIPS P. O'SHAUGHNESSY, P.A. (AV(T))

One East Broward Boulevard, Suite 700, 33301
Telephone: 800-882-3133
Email: phil.osh@worldnet.att.net *URL:* http://oshaughnessy.wld.com
Baltimore, Maryland Main Office: 1102 Terrace Glen, 21210.
Telephone: 410-532-0300.
Fax: 410-532-2220.

Phillips P. O'Shaughnessy

For full biographical listings, see the Martindale-Hubbell Law Directory

*ORLANDO,** Orange Co.

KENNETH L. MANN, P.A. (AV)

105 East Robinson Street, Suite 540, P.O. Box 551, 32802-0551
Telephone: 407-422-0006
Fax: 407-841-9516
Email: reasonablemann@worldnet.att.net *URL:*
http://www.KenMannlaw.com

Kenneth L. Mann

For full biographical listings, see the Martindale-Hubbell Law Directory

GEORGIA

*ATLANTA,** Fulton Co.

GOLDNER, SOMMERS, SCRUDDER & BASS (AV)

900 Circle 75 Parkway Suite 850, 30339
Telephone: 770-612-9200
Facsimile: 770-612-9201

MEMBERS OF FIRM

Stephen L. Goldner
Susan V. Sommers
Henry E. Scrudder, Jr.
Glenn S. Bass
Alfred A. Quillian, Jr.
Sandra G. Chase
Linda Jacobsen Pollock
Benjamin David Ladner
William W. Horlock, Jr.

(See Next Column)

GOLDNER, SOMMERS, SCRUDDER & BASS—*Continued*

ASSOCIATES

Tammy Spivack Skinner
Jane Carol Taylor
Pat M. Anagnostakis

For full biographical listings, see the Martindale-Hubbell Law Directory

PIERCE & YOUNG (AV)

Building 1700, 2255 Cumberland Parkway Northwest, 30339-4575
Telephone: 770-435-0500
Telecopier: 770-435-0362

MEMBER OF FIRM

J. Wayne Pierce

For full biographical listings, see the Martindale-Hubbell Law Directory

*BRUNSWICK,** Glynn Co.

FENDIG, MCLEMORE, TAYLOR, WHITWORTH & DURHAM, P.C. (AV)

Suite 200 Suntrust Bank Building, P.O. Box 1996, 31521
Telephone: 912-264-4126
Telecopier: 912-264-0591

Albert Fendig, Jr.
Gilbert C. McLemore, Jr.
Philip R. Taylor
David T. Whitworth
James B. Durham
Donna L. Crossland
Beth M. Duncan

For full biographical listings, see the Martindale-Hubbell Law Directory

HAWAII

*HONOLULU,** Honolulu Co.

AYABE, CHONG, NISHIMOTO, SIA & NAKAMURA (AV)

A Partnership including a Professional Corporation
Pauahi Tower, Suite 2500, 1001 Bishop Street, 96813
Telephone: 808-537-6119
Telecopier: 808-526-3491
Email: ACNSN@pixi.com

MEMBERS OF FIRM

Sidney K. Ayabe (P.C.)
John S. Nishimoto
Calvin E. Young
Gail M. Kang
Ronald M. Shigekane
Steven L. Goto

Gary S. Miyamoto

Representative Clients: CNA Insurance Company; Coregis; American National Lawyers Insurance Reciprocal; Tamarack American; Zurich-American.

For full biographical listings, see the Martindale-Hubbell Law Directory

ILLINOIS

*CHICAGO,** Cook Co.

FIGLIULO & SILVERMAN, P.C. (AV)

10 South La Salle Street, Suite 3600, 60603
Telephone: 312-251-4600
Fax: 312-251-4610

James R. Figliulo
Peter A. Silverman
Carl A. Gigante
Brian P. Liston
Marc S. Porter
James H. Bowhay

James J. Sipchen, Jr.
Adam E. Bossov
Michael K. Desmond

For full biographical listings, see the Martindale-Hubbell Law Directory

STONE & MOORE, CHARTERED (AV)

30 North La Salle Street, Suite 4300, 60602
Telephone: 312-332-5656
Fax: 312-332-5858
URL: http://www.stonemoore.com
Merrillville, Indiana Office: 500 E. 86th Avenue, 46410.
Telephone: 219-736-5959.
Fax: 219-736-5858.
Wheaton, Illinois Office: 600 W. Roosevelt Road, Suite 1A, 60187.
Telephone: 630-221-9292.
Fax: 630-221-9393.

(See Next Column)

William G. Stone
Robert Charles Moore (Also at Wheaton, Illinois Office)
Raymond R. Pesavento
Rosario Cibella
Richard M. Johnson, Jr.
J. Murray Pinkston, III
Julie Osswald Hooven

Christian D. Ambler
Jeffrey W. Henning
Erica Lewis Battaglia
Kevin Kemp Lyons
Kristin E. Rooney
Daniel S. Schulz
Matthew B. Stephens
A. Christine Svenson
Douglas W. Walker

For full biographical listings, see the Martindale-Hubbell Law Directory

IOWA

*DES MOINES,** Polk Co.

HANSEN, MCCLINTOCK & RILEY (AV)

Eighth Floor - Fleming Building, 218 Sixth Avenue, 50309
Telephone: 515-244-2141
Fax: 515-244-2931
Email: hmrlaw@aol.com

MEMBERS OF FIRM

Haemer Wheatcraft (1904-1983)
J. Rudolph Hansen (1904-1995)
John A. McClintock
Ronald A. Riley
Chester C. Woodburn, III
William D. Scherle
David L. Brown
John E. Swanson

ASSOCIATES

James M. Ballard
Aaron T. Oliver

Representative Clients: The St. Paul Companies; Bituminous Insurance Companies; Northwestern National Insurance Co.; The Travelers Insurance Companies; United States Aviation Insurance Group; American International Companies; Iowa Credit Union League; The McAninch Corp.; R. J. Reynolds Tobacco Co.; Brown Bros., Inc. Electrical Contractors.

For full biographical listings, see the Martindale-Hubbell Law Directory

HUBER, BOOK, CORTESE, HAPPE & BROWN, P.L.C. (AV)

317 Sixth Avenue, Suite 200, 50309-4127
Telephone: 515-243-4148
Fax: 515-243-5481
Email: huber@desmoineslaw.com

MEMBERS OF FIRM

James C. Huber
Richard G. Book
Joseph S. Cortese II
Joseph A. Happe
Terrence D. Brown
Patrick D. Smith

ASSOCIATES

Deborah M. Stein
William H. Grell
Jeffrey W. Lanz
R. Saffin Parrish

Representative Clients: Atlantic Mutual Cos.; CNA Insurance Cos.; Fireman's Fund American Insurance Companies; Great West Casualty Co.; Liberty Mutual Insurance Co.; Maryland Insurance Group; Prudential Property and Casualty Insurance Co.; USF&G Company.
Reference: Bank of America.

For full biographical listings, see the Martindale-Hubbell Law Directory

KANSAS

*TOPEKA,** Shawnee Co.

FISHER, PATTERSON, SAYLER & SMITH, L.L.P. (AV)

3550 S.W. 5th Street, P.O. Box 949, 66601
Telephone: 785-232-7761
Fax: 785-232-6604
Email: fpss@cjnetworks.com
Overland Park, Kansas Office: 11050 Roe Avenue, Suite 210, 66211.
Telephone: 913-339-6757.
Fax: 913-339-6187.

MEMBERS OF FIRM

Donald Patterson
Edwin Dudley Smith (Resident, Overland Park Office)
Larry G. Pepperdine
James P. Nordstrom
Justice B. King
J. Steven Pigg
Steve R. Fabert
Ronald J. Laskowski
Michael K. Seck (Resident, Overland Park Office)
David P. Madden (Resident, Overland Park Office)
Steven K. Johnson
Kristine A. Larscheid

(See Next Column)

FISHER, PATTERSON, SAYLER & SMITH L.L.P., *Topeka—Continued*

ASSOCIATES

Billy E. Newman
David R. Cooper
Kelly A. Feyh (Resident, Overland Park Office)
Jennifer R. Rose (Resident, Overland Park Office)

OF COUNSEL

David H. Fisher

RETIRED

Charles Keith Sayler (Retired)

Representative Clients: Gage Shopping Center, Inc.; Fireman's Fund-American Insurance Cos.; United States Fidelity and Guaranty Co.; The Procter & Gamble Company; Commercial Union Insurance Companies; National Casualty; The Hartford; Berkshire Hathaway Companies.

For full biographical listings, see the Martindale-Hubbell Law Directory

GOODELL, STRATTON, EDMONDS & PALMER, L.L.P. (AV)

515 South Kansas Avenue, 66603-3999
Telephone: 785-233-0593
Fax: 785-233-8870
Email: GSEP@CJNETWORKS.COM *URL:* http://www.cjnetworks.com/~gsep
Kansas City, Missouri Office: 10401 Holmes Road, Suite 280.
Telephone: 816-943-8577.

MEMBERS OF FIRM

Wayne T. Stratton
David E. Bruns

Counsel for: Columbian National Title Insurance Co.; Central Regional Dental Testing Service, Inc.; Heartland Community Bankers Association; The Menninger Foundation; Topeka Chamber of Commerce; Washburn University of Topeka; Reser's Fine Foods; ConAgra; Monfort, Inc.

For Complete List of Firm Personnel, See General Section

For full biographical listings, see the Martindale-Hubbell Law Directory

KENTUCKY

*LOUISVILLE,** Jefferson Co.

McMURRY & TALBOTT (AV)

4965 U.S. Highway 42, Suite 2800, 40222
Telephone: 502-326-9000
FAX: 502-326-9001
Email: wmcmurry@msn.com *URL:* http://www.lawyers.com/mcmurry_and_talbott

William F. McMurry
Alex F. Talbott

For full biographical listings, see the Martindale-Hubbell Law Directory

LOUISIANA

*BATON ROUGE,** East Baton Rouge Parish

POWERS & WILLARD, L.L.P. (AV)

7967 Office Park Boulevard, P.O. Box 15948, 70895
Telephone: 225-928-1951
Fax: 225-929-9834

MEMBERS OF FIRM

John Dale Powers
William E. Willard

ASSOCIATES

Neil H. Mixon
Lindsey J. Leavoy
Edwin L. Hightower
Andrew P. Sellers, Jr.
Suzanne K. Sasser
Kyle C. Marionneaux

General Counsel for: Audubon Insurance Co.
Louisiana Counsel for: Hancock Bank & Trust Co.; Hertz Corp.; Ciba-Geigy Corp.; Utica Mutual Insurance Co.

For full biographical listings, see the Martindale-Hubbell Law Directory

MAINE

*PORTLAND,** Cumberland Co.

THOMPSON & BOWIE (AV)

Three Canal Plaza, P.O. Box 4630, 04112
Telephone: 207-774-2500
Telecopier: 207-774-3591
Email: law@thompsonbowie.com

MEMBERS OF FIRM

Roy E. Thompson, Jr.
James M. Bowie
Daniel R. Mawhinney
Rebecca H. Farnum
Glenn H. Robinson
Frank W. DeLong, III
Michael E. Saucier
Mark V. Franco
Edward R. Benjamin, Jr.
Cathy S. Roberts
Paul C. Catsos

ASSOCIATES

Elizabeth Knox Peck
Thomas G. Diebold
Michael R. Bosse
Lisa M. Fitzgibbon

For full biographical listings, see the Martindale-Hubbell Law Directory

MARYLAND

*BALTIMORE,** (Independent City)

PHILLIPS P. O'SHAUGHNESSY, P.A. (AV)

1102 Terrace Glen, 21210
Telephone: 410-532-0300
FAX: 410-532-2220
URL: http://www.oshaughnessy.wld.com
Ft. Lauderdale, Florida Office: One East Broward Boulevard, Suite 700, 33301.
Telephone: 800-882-3133.

Phillips P. O'Shaughnessy

For Complete List of Firm Personnel, See General Section

For full biographical listings, see the Martindale-Hubbell Law Directory

GILBERT H. ROBINETTE (AV)

212 Washington Avenue, 21204
Telephone: 410-321-6666
Toll Free: 1-888-538-0821
Fax: 410-821-5444
Email: ghr44@aol.com *URL:* http://www.lawyers.com/gilrobinette
Charleston, West Virginia Office: 1564 Virginia Street, East, 25311.
Telephone: 304-342-1844.
Fax: 304-342-1901.

For full biographical listings, see the Martindale-Hubbell Law Directory

MICHIGAN

*DETROIT,** Wayne Co.

WILLMARTH, TANOURY, RAMAR, CORBET, GARVES & SHAW (AV)

535 Griswold, Suite 1730, 48226-3602
Telephone: 313-964-6300
Fax: 313-964-6310
Email: mdwillth@home.net

MEMBERS OF FIRM

Daniel R. Corbet
Brian R. Garves
David R. Nauts
Anthony J. Paradiso
John M. Perrin
John J. Ramar
Bruce R. Shaw
William A. Tanoury
Mark D. Willmarth

ASSOCIATES

Marie C. Kennedy
Wayne Walker
Elizabeth L. Sokol
Robert S. Silverman
Carmine G. Paterra
Joseph J. Ceglarek, II
Derek Steven Wilczynski
Frank Hamidi
Kristen E. Skaff
Steven J. Bonasso
Colleen P. O'Connor
Lara R. Stutz
Eric G. Tucciarone
Michael P. Robach

For full biographical listings, see the Martindale-Hubbell Law Directory

GAYLORD, * Otsego Co.

Bensinger, Cotant, Menkes & Aardema, P.C. (AV)
308 West Main Street, P.O. Box 1000, 49735
Telephone: 517-732-7536
Fax: 517-732-4922
URL: http://www.bcma.net
Grand Rapids, Michigan Office: 983 Spaulding Avenue, S.E.
Telephone: 616-949-7963.
Fax: 616-949-5264.
Marquette, Michigan Office: 122 West Bluff.
Telephone: 906-225-1000.
Fax: 906-225-0818.

Richard G. Bensinger James C. Cotant

Representative Clients: Michigan Lawyers Mutual.

For full biographical listings, see the Martindale-Hubbell Law Directory

GRAND RAPIDS, * Kent Co.

Bensinger, Cotant, Menkes & Aardema, P.C. (AV)
983 Spaulding Avenue, S.E., 49546
Telephone: 616-949-7963
Fax: 616-949-5264
URL: http://www.bcma.net
Gaylord, Michigan Office: 308 West Main, P.O. Box 1000.
Telephone: 517-732-7536.
Fax: 517-732-4922.
Marquette, Michigan Office: 122 West Bluff.
Telephone: 906-225-1000.
Fax: 906-225-0818.

Robert Bryan Aardema Kerr L. Moyer

Representative Clients: Michigan Lawyers Mutual.

For full biographical listings, see the Martindale-Hubbell Law Directory

MARQUETTE, * Marquette Co.

Bensinger, Cotant, Menkes & Aardema, P.C. (AV)
122 West Bluff, 49855
Telephone: 906-225-1000
Fax: 906-225-0818
URL: http://www.bcma.net
Gaylord, Michigan Office: 308 West Main, P.O. Box 1000.
Telephone: 517-732-7536.
Fax: 517-732-4922.
Grand Rapids, Michigan Office: 983 Spaulding Avenue, S.E.
Telephone: 616-949-7963.
Fax: 616-949-5264.

Gregory A. Elzinga Michael G. Summers

Representative Clients: Michigan Lawyers Mutual.

For full biographical listings, see the Martindale-Hubbell Law Directory

MEDICAL MALPRACTICE

ALABAMA

*BIRMINGHAM,** Jefferson Co.

EMOND & VINES (AV)

2200 SouthTrust Tower, 420 North 20th Street, P.O. Box 10008, 35202-0008
Telephone: 205-324-4000
Fax: 205-324-5020
Email: EmondVines@aol.com

MEMBER OF FIRM

Lanny S. Vines

ASSOCIATES

Michael Lee Allsup
Vivian D. Vines Campbell
Frank O. Hanson, Jr.

For full biographical listings, see the Martindale-Hubbell Law Directory

HARE, WYNN, NEWELL AND NEWTON (AV)

A Partnership including Professional Corporations
Suite 800 Massey Building, 290 21st Street North, 35203
Telephone: 205-328-5330
Fax: 205-324-2165

MEMBERS OF FIRM

Francis H. Hare (1904-1983)
Carlton T. Wynn
Neal C. Newell
Alex W. Newton
C. Terrell Wynn, Jr.
James J. Thompson, Jr.
Alva C. Caine
Ray O. (Ronnie) Noojin, Jr. (1945-1996)
John W. Haley (P.C.)
D. Leon Ashford (P.C.)
Scott A. Powell
James R. Pratt, III
S. Shay Samples
Bruce J. McKee
Michael D. Ermert
Nolan Edward Awbrey
James B. Gunther, Jr.
Don McKenna
Martin E. Burke

COUNSEL

Francis H. Hare, Jr., (P.C.)
James O. Haley
James K. Baker

References: AmSouth Bank of Birmingham; First Commercial Bank of Birmingham.

For full biographical listings, see the Martindale-Hubbell Law Directory

HARRIS, CLECKLER & HOLLIS (AV)

Historic 2007 Building, 2007 Third Avenue North, 35203-2366
Telephone: 205-328-2366
Telecopier: 205-328-0013
Email: hcbr@mindspring.com *URL:* http://www.harriscleckler.com

Lyman H. Harris
Michael H. Cleckler
Jeffrey K. Hollis

ASSOCIATE

Jason A. Shamblin

For full biographical listings, see the Martindale-Hubbell Law Directory

HENINGER, BURGE, VARGO AND DAVIS, LLP (AV)

1500 Financial Center, 505 North Twentieth Street, 35203
Telephone: 205-322-5153
Fax: 205-322-6706
Email: heninger@mindspring.com *URL:* http://www.lawyers.com/hbv&dlaw

MEMBERS OF FIRM

Stephen D. Heninger
S. Greg Burge
Stuart F. Vargo
Timothy C. Davis

For full biographical listings, see the Martindale-Hubbell Law Directory

HOGAN, SMITH & ALSPAUGH, P.C. (AV)

2323 Second Avenue, North, 35203
Telephone: 205-324-5635
Telecopier: 205-324-5637
Email: Chris@Hogan-Smith.com *URL:* http://www.hsa-pc.com

M. Clay Alspaugh
Ronald R. Crook
Richard D. Stratton
Jack Lee Roberts, Jr.
Benjamin E. Baker, Jr.

Reference: Regions Bank.

For full biographical listings, see the Martindale-Hubbell Law Directory

HUIE, FERNAMBUCQ AND STEWART, LLP (AV)

Suite 800, Regions Bank Building, 417 N. 20th Street, 35203
Telephone: 205-251-1193
Telecopy: 205-251-1256

MEMBERS OF FIRM

Stanley A. Cash
Robert M. Girardeau
M. Keith Gann
J. Allen Sydnor, Jr.
Walter J. Price, III
H. Lanier Brown, II

ASSOCIATES

Jennifer Devereaux Segers
Philip R. Collins

Representative Clients: Living Centers of America, Inc.; Columbia/HCA Healthcare Corp.; American International Group; MMI Companies Inc.; Quorum Health Group, Inc.; Zurich American Healthcare; CNA Pro.

For full biographical listings, see the Martindale-Hubbell Law Directory

LUSK, FRALEY, MCALISTER & SIMMS, P.C. (AV)

Suite 1700 AmSouth/Harbert Plaza, 1901 Sixth Avenue North, 35203
Telephone: 205-323-7100
Fax: 205-323-7050
Email: Lusk-Fraley.com

Donald D. Lusk
John M. Fraley
David L. McAlister
Keri Donald Simms
Kenneth A. Dowdy
David Lawrence Dean
David Thurston White, III
Susan Gilman McAlister
Payton Caldwell Lusk
Leslie Ann Caldwell

For full biographical listings, see the Martindale-Hubbell Law Directory

PITTMAN, HOOKS, DUTTON & HOLLIS, P.C. (AV)

1100 Park Place Tower, 35203
Telephone: 205-322-8880
Telecopier: 205-328-2711
Email: PHDH@4theplaintiff.com

W. Lee Pittman
Kenneth W. Hooks
Tom Dutton
L. Andrew Hollis, Jr.
Jeffrey C. Kirby
Ralph Bohanan, Jr.

Chris T. Hellums
Keith T. Belt, Jr.
Leigh King Forstman
Michael C. Bradley
Page Poerschke Liddon
Steven William Couch
J. Chris Cochran

OF COUNSEL

James H. Davis (Not admitted in AL)
Lynn A. Crosson

For full biographical listings, see the Martindale-Hubbell Law Directory

PORTERFIELD, HARPER & MILLS, P.A. (AV)

22 Inverness Center Parkway, Suite 600, P.O. Box 530790, 35242-4821
Telephone: 205-980-5000
Fax: 205-980-5001

Larry W. Harper
William T. Mills, II
William Dudley Motlow, Jr.
H. C. "Trey" Ireland, III

Representative Clients: CIGNA; St. Paul Insurance Co.; The Travelers; Figgie International; White Consolidated Industries; Terex Corp.; Wausau Insurance; Baptist Health Systems, Inc.; Bruno's, Inc.; Harley Davidson, Inc.

For full biographical listings, see the Martindale-Hubbell Law Directory

SPAIN & GILLON, L.L.C. (AV)

The Zinszer Building, 2117 2nd Avenue North, 35203
Telephone: 205-328-4100
Telecopier: 205-324-8866
Email: ddh@spain-gillon.com *URL:* http://lawlinks.com:80/atty/al/sggbn.html

MEMBERS OF FIRM

Eugene P. Stutts
Robert L. Williams
Gary A. Parker

Counsel for: University of Alabama Hospitals and Clinics; University of Alabama Health Services Foundation; Alabama Hospital Association Trust; Coastal Insurance Enterprises.

For Complete List of Firm Personnel, See General Section

For full biographical listings, see the Martindale-Hubbell Law Directory

STARNES & ATCHISON LLP (AV)

100 Brookwood Place, 35209
Telephone: 205-868-6000
Telecopier: 205-868-6099
Mailing Address: P.O. Box 598512, 35259-8512
Email: information@starneslaw.com
Mobile, Alabama Office: Riverview Plaza, Suite 1106, 63 South Royal Street, 36602.
Telephone: 334-433-6049.

(See Next Column)

STARNES & ATCHISON LLP, *Birmingham—Continued*

MEMBERS OF FIRM

W. Stancil Starnes
W. Michael Atchison
Michael A. Florie
John P. Scott, Jr.
Chris N. Galanos
Randal H. Sellers
Walter William Bates
Michael K. Wright
Robert P. Mackenzie, III
Laura Howard Peck
Mark Christopher Eagan
Sybil Vogtle Abbot

ASSOCIATES

Joseph S. Miller
Scott M. Salter
Ashley E. Watkins
Reed R. Bates
W. Christian Hines, III
Joseph L. Reese, Jr.
Geoffrey S. Bald
L. Jackson Young, Jr.

Representative Clients: Mutual Assurance, Inc.; Brookwood Medical Center; American Medical International; Medical Care International; Mobile Infirmary Medical Center; CNA Insurance Co.

For full biographical listings, see the Martindale-Hubbell Law Directory

*DECATUR,** Morgan Co.

EYSTER, KEY, TUBB, WEAVER & ROTH (AV)

Eyster Building, 402 East Moulton Street, S.E., P.O. Box 1607, 35602
Telephone: 256-353-6761
Fax: 256-353-6767

John C. Eyster (1863-1926)
Charles H. Eyster, Sr. (1888-1964)
Wm. B. Eyster (1921-1995)

MEMBERS OF FIRM

John S. Key
J. Glynn Tubb
Lawrence C. Weaver
Nicholas B. Roth
J. Witty Allen
William L. Middleton, III
James G. Adams, Jr.
John R. Baggette, Jr.
Jenny L. Mcleroy

General Counsel for: Alabama Farmers Cooperative.
Regional Counsel for: AmSouth Bank.
Local Counsel for: Allstate Insurance Co.; Champion International Corp; Goodyear; Liberty Mutual Insurance Co.; Saginaw Steering Gear Division, General Motors Corp.; State Farm Mutual Automobile Insurance Co.; 3M; The Travelers.

For full biographical listings, see the Martindale-Hubbell Law Directory

*FLORENCE,** Lauderdale Co.

JONES & TROUSDALE (AV)

115 Helton Court, Suite B, P.O. Box 367, 35631-0367
Telephone: 256-767-0333
Telefax: 256-767-0331
Email: JTAttys@aol.com

MEMBERS OF FIRM

Robert E. Jones, III
Preston S. Trousdale, Jr.
A. DeLoach Stewart

For full biographical listings, see the Martindale-Hubbell Law Directory

*HUNTSVILLE,** Madison Co.

THE LAW FIRM OF SINIARD, MCKINNEY & BRASWELL, P.C. (AV)

125 Holmes Avenue, P.O. Box 2767, 35804
Telephone: 256-536-0770
Facsimile: 256-539-0540
URL: http://www.lawyers.com/smblawfirm
URL: http://www.law-injury.com/scripts/template.cgi?index

Tommy H. Siniard
Jeffery W. McKinney
M. Roy Braswell

Michael Kenan Timberlake
James William League

For full biographical listings, see the Martindale-Hubbell Law Directory

*MOBILE,** Mobile Co.

ARMBRECHT, JACKSON, DEMOUY, CROWE, HOLMES & REEVES, L.L.C. (AV)

1300 Riverview Plaza, P.O. Box 290, 36601
Telephone: 334-405-1300
Facsimile: 334-432-6843; 433-3821
Email: adc@ajlaw.com

MEMBERS OF FIRM

Broox G. Holmes
W. Boyd Reeves
Norman E. Waldrop, Jr.
M. Kathleen Miller
Scott G. Brown
Richard W. Franklin

(See Next Column)

ASSOCIATES

Tamela E. Esham
A. Edwin Stuardi, III

Representative Clients: American Security Insurance Co. (Regional Counsel); American Security Group (Regional Counsel); Mutual Assurance, Inc.; Loyal American Life Insurance Co.; Travelers Insurance Co.; University of South Alabama Medical Center.

For Complete List of Firm Personnel, See General Section

For full biographical listings, see the Martindale-Hubbell Law Directory

BURNS, CUNNINGHAM & MACKEY, P.C. (AV)

50 St. Emanuel Street, P.O. Box 1583, 36633
Telephone: 334-432-0612
Fax: 334-432-0625
URL: http://www.bcmlawyers.com

Peter F. Burns
William M. Cunningham, Jr.
Peter S. Mackey
Gary W. Fillingim

For full biographical listings, see the Martindale-Hubbell Law Directory

CUNNINGHAM, BOUNDS, YANCE, CROWDER & BROWN, L.L.C. (AV)

1601 Dauphin Street, P.O. Box 66705, 36660
Telephone: 334-471-6191
Fax: 334-479-1031
Email: adm@cbycb.com

James A. Yance
John T. Crowder, Jr.
Robert T. Cunningham, Jr.
Joseph M. Brown, Jr.
Gregory B. Breedlove
Michael A. Worel
David G. Wirtes, Jr.
Toby D. Brown
Reggie Copeland, Jr.
Richard T. Dorman

J. Stephen Legg
George M. Dent, III

OF COUNSEL

Richard Bounds
Robert T. Cunningham
J. Kenyon Rainer, Sr., M.D., J.D.

References: Regions Bank; AmSouth Bank, N.A.

For full biographical listings, see the Martindale-Hubbell Law Directory

FRAZER, GREENE, UPCHURCH & BAKER, L.L.C. (AV)

First National Bank Building, Suite 2206 107 Saint Francis Street, 36602
Telephone: 334-431-6020
Facsimile: 334-431-6030
URL: http://www.frazergreene.com

MEMBERS OF FIRM

A. Danner Frazer, Jr.
Edward C. Greene
Michael E. Upchurch
D. Brent Baker

Bruce M. Westbrook
W. Austin Mulherin, III
Marcus Edward McDowell

For full biographical listings, see the Martindale-Hubbell Law Directory

*TUSCUMBIA,** Colbert Co.

ASHE, TANNER, WRIGHT & KELLEY, P.C. (AV)

105 West Second Street, P.O. Box 899, 35674
Telephone: 256-383-6357
Telecopier: 256-381-4612

Braxton W. Ashe
J. Michael Tanner
Grant A. Wright
Charles J. Kelley (Resident)

Nickolas J. Steles

For full biographical listings, see the Martindale-Hubbell Law Directory

ALASKA

*ANCHORAGE,** Third Judicial District

DELANEY, WILES, HAYES, GERETY, ELLIS & YOUNG, INC. (AV)

1007 West Third Avenue, Suite 400, 99501
Telephone: 907-279-3581
Fax: 907-277-1331
Email: dwhge@alaska.net

(See Next Column)

DELANEY, WILES, HAYES, GERETY, ELLIS & YOUNG INC.—*Continued*

Daniel A. Gerety
Howard A. Lazar
Timothy J. Lamb

Representative Clients: The Doctors Company; Norcal Mutual Insurance Co.; HealthCare Indemnity Co.; Medical Insurance Exchange of California; Lutheran Health Systems; Continental Insurance Co.; Liberty Northwest; Maryland Insurance Group; Royal Globe Insurance Co.

For Complete List of Firm Personnel, See General Section

For full biographical listings, see the Martindale-Hubbell Law Directory

HELM & ASSOCIATES (AV)

810 N Street, Suite 200, 99501
Telephone: 907-279-4889
Fax: 907-279-4851
Email: RicHelm@aol.com

Richard A. Helm

ASSOCIATE

Andrew D. Steiner

LEGAL SUPPORT PERSONNEL

Lynda M. Hile (Paralegal)

For full biographical listings, see the Martindale-Hubbell Law Directory

LAW OFFICES OF ROBERT H. WAGSTAFF (AV)

First National Bank Building, 425 G Street, Suite 610, 99501
Telephone: 907-277-8611
Facsimile: 907-258-7329

For full biographical listings, see the Martindale-Hubbell Law Directory

ARIZONA

*PHOENIX,** Maricopa Co.

BEGAM, LEWIS, MARKS & WOLFE (AV)

A Professional Association of Lawyers
111 West Monroe Street, Suite 1400, 85003-1787
Telephone: 602-254-6071; 1-800-285-0481
Fax: 602-252-0042
Email: blmw@aol.com

Robert G. Begam
Frank Lewis
Stanley J. Marks
Elliot G. Wolfe
Kelly J. McDonald
Daniel J. Adelman
Lisa Kurtz
Dena Rosen Epstein
Steven M. Friedman
Richard P. Traulsen
Serena C. Montague

Reference: National Bank of Arizona.

For full biographical listings, see the Martindale-Hubbell Law Directory

RICHARD A. BLACK, P.C. (AV)

125 East Coronado Road, 85004
Telephone: 602-253-4700
Fax: 602-253-8880
Email: rickb627@aol.com

Richard A. Black

For full biographical listings, see the Martindale-Hubbell Law Directory

LAW OFFICES OF MICHAEL E. BRADFORD (AV)

4131 North 24th Street Building C Suite 201, 85016
Telephone: 602-955-0088
Fax: 602-955-6445
Email: meblaw@primenet.com

ASSOCIATE

Jeffrey L. Bradford

OF COUNSEL

Jerry Steele

For full biographical listings, see the Martindale-Hubbell Law Directory

CHARLES M. BREWER, LTD. (AV)

Brewer Building, 5500 North 24th Street, P.O. Box 10720, 85064
Telephone: 602-381-8787
Fax: 602-381-1152

Charles M. Brewer

(See Next Column)

Luis Pedro Guerra
John Brian Brewer

For full biographical listings, see the Martindale-Hubbell Law Directory

JAMES F. BROOK AND ASSOCIATES (AV)

11024 North 28th Drive, Suite 200, 85029
Telephone: 602-375-0414
Toll Free: 800-322-6170
Fax: 480-874-0506
Email: JFBrook@aol.com *URL:* http://www.lawyers.com/jamesbrook
Mesa, Arizona Office: 1201 South Alma School Road, Suite 14,000. 85210.
Telephone: 480-838-5591.
Fax: 480-874-0506.
Scottsdale, Arizona Office: 7150 East Camelback Road, Suite 415, 85251.
Telephone: 480-990-0104.
Fax: 480-874-0506.
Sun City, Arizona Office: 10451 Palmeras Drive, Suite 211, 85373.
Telephone: 623-972-6824.
Fax: 480-874-0506.

Adam C. E. Davis

For full biographical listings, see the Martindale-Hubbell Law Directory

BURCH & CRACCHIOLO, P.A. (AV)

702 East Osborn Road, Suite 200, 85014
Telephone: 602-274-7611
Fax: 602-234-0341
Mailing Address: P.O. Box 16882, Phoenix, AZ, 85011
Email: library@bcattorneys.com

Daniel Cracchiolo

Representative Clients: Bashas' Inc.; Farmers Insurance Group; U-Haul International, Inc.

For Complete List of Firm Personnel, See General Section

For full biographical listings, see the Martindale-Hubbell Law Directory

COPPLE, CHAMBERLIN, BOEHM & MURPHY, P.C. (AV)

Suite 300 The Brookstone, 2025 North Third Street, 85004
Telephone: 602-528-4700
Fax: 602-253-4909
Tucson, Arizona Office: 127 West Franklin.
Telephone: 520-622-8855.
Fax: 520-628-7988.

Steven D. Copple
Thomas J. Chamberlin
Scott E. Boehm
Robert S. Murphy

OF COUNSEL

Frederick O. Robertshaw

For full biographical listings, see the Martindale-Hubbell Law Directory

CRONIN & STANEWICH (AV)

One Columbus Plaza, 3636 North Central Avenue, Suite 560, 85012
Telephone: 602-222-4646
Fax: 602-222-4656
Email: cslaw@msn.com

MEMBERS OF FIRM

Robert S. Cronin, Jr.
Robert B. Stanewich

For full biographical listings, see the Martindale-Hubbell Law Directory

DOYLE & WINTHROP, P.C. (AV)

2800 North Central Avenue Suite 1550, P.O. Box 10417, 85004
Telephone: 602-240-6711
Fax: 602-240-6951
Mailing Address: P.O. Box 10417, Phoenix, Arizona, 85064-0417
Las Vegas, Nevada Office: Edward D. Boyack, Esq., 2626 S. Rainbow Blvd., Suite 101, 89146.
Telephone: 702-873-1622.
Fax: 702-873-2280.

Lawrence F. Winthrop
William H. Doyle
Judith A. Berman
Beverly Bailey Wittekind

For full biographical listings, see the Martindale-Hubbell Law Directory

FEDER LAW OFFICE, P.A. (AV)

Biltmore Pavilion, Suite 140, 2525 E. Arizona Biltmore Circle, 85016
Telephone: 602-257-0135
Fax: 602-954-8737
Mailing Address: P.O. Box 44560, Phoenix, Arizona, 85064-4560

Harold J. Feder

For full biographical listings, see the Martindale-Hubbell Law Directory

Phoenix—Continued

FENNEMORE CRAIG, A PROFESSIONAL CORPORATION (AV)

3003 North Central Avenue, Suite 2600, 85012-2913
Telephone: 602-916-5000
Fax: 602-916-5999
Tucson, Arizona Office: One South Church Avenue, Suite 1000, 85701-1620.
Telephone: 520-879-6800.
Fax: 520-879-6899.

John D. Everroad
Phillip F. Fargotstein
Scott M. Finical
Jean Marie Sullivan

Vera E. Munoz
Tracey Ann Ager

LEGAL SUPPORT PERSONNEL

LEGAL ASSISTANTS

Claudia L. Parks

For Complete List of Firm Personnel, See General Section

For full biographical listings, see the Martindale-Hubbell Law Directory

GOLDSTEIN, MCGRODER & WOODS, LTD. A PROFESSIONAL CORPORATION (AV)

2200 East Camelback Road, Suite 221, 85016-3456
Telephone: 602-957-1500
Fax: 602-956-9294
Email: pmcgroder@aol.com

Philip T. Goldstein
Patrick J. McGroder, III
Grant Woods
Suzanne P. Clarke

Jane E. Evans

LEGAL SUPPORT PERSONNEL

Kevan S. DeWitt (Paralegal)
Karen Kay Rush

For full biographical listings, see the Martindale-Hubbell Law Directory

STUART GOLDSTEIN (AV)

2700 North Third Street, Suite 2010, 85004
Telephone: 602-279-1666
Fax: 602-285-1907
Email: stugoldstn@aol.com

Stuart W. Goldstein

Reference: Wells Fargo Bank, Park Central Office, Phoenix.

For full biographical listings, see the Martindale-Hubbell Law Directory

HARRIS, PALUMBO, POWERS & CUNNINGHAM, P.L.L.C. (AV)

361 East Coronado, Suite 101, P.O. Box 13568, 85002-3568
Telephone: 602-271-9344
Fax: 602-252-2099
Email: harrispalumbo@worldnet.att.net

John David Harris
Frank I. Powers
Shawn M. Cunningham

OF COUNSEL

Anthony J. Palumbo

For full biographical listings, see the Martindale-Hubbell Law Directory

JENNINGS, STROUSS & SALMON, P.L.C. (AV)

A Professional Limited Liability Company
One Renaissance Square, Two North Central Avenue, 85004-2393
Telephone: 602-262-5911
Fax: 602-253-3255
Email: info@jsslaw.com *URL:* http://www.jsslaw.com
Arrowhead Office: 16150 North Arrowhead Fountains Center Drive, Suite 250, Peoria, Arizona.
Telephone: 623-878-2222.
Fax: 623-878-1333.

John C. West
Jay A. Fradkin
Jennifer M. Bligh
Kim D. Steinmetz
Richard K. Delo

OF COUNSEL

Gary L. Stuart

ASSOCIATE

Bryan S. VanMeveren

For Complete List of Firm Personnel, See General Section

For full biographical listings, see the Martindale-Hubbell Law Directory

MARK & PEARLSTEIN, P.A. (AV)

Suite 150 The Brookstone, 2025 North Third Street, 85004
Telephone: 602-257-0200
Fax: 602-271-4711
Email: mplaw@primenet.com

Leonard J. Mark
Mr. Lynn M. Pearlstein

OF COUNSEL

Stephen G. Campbell

For full biographical listings, see the Martindale-Hubbell Law Directory

OLSON, JANTSCH, BAKKER & BLAKEY, P.A. (AV)

7243 North 16th Street, P.O. Box 47250, 85068-7250
Telephone: 602-861-2705
Fax: 602-371-1710
Email: ojbb@primenet.com

Duane A. Olson
Daniel P. Jantsch
Thomas G. Bakker
A. Craig Blakey, II
Byrl R. Lane
Michael L. Barth
Andrew E. Rosenzweig

Scott A. Sahlman
Susan J. Woodrow
Robert H. Feinberg

LEGAL SUPPORT PERSONNEL

NURSE CONSULTANTS

Marla Risa Cohen (R.N.)
Nancy D. Collison (R.N.)
Mary C. Foor (R.N.)

Representative Clients: Travelers Insurance Co.; St. Paul Insurance Cos.; Mutual Insurance Company of Arizona (MICA); Church Mutual Insurance Co.; Phoenix Childrens Hospital; J.C. Lincoln Hospital; Scottsdale Insurance Co.; Samaritan Health Systems; MMI Companies, Inc.; Humana, Inc.

For full biographical listings, see the Martindale-Hubbell Law Directory

STUART J. REILLY, P.C. (AV)

4647 North 32nd Street, Suite 105, 85018-3346
Telephone: 602-912-9200
Fax: 602-912-9209
Mailing Address: P.O. Box 80410, Phoenix, AZ, 85060-0410
Email: sreilly@stuartjreillypc.com *URL:* http://www.lawyers.com/stuartjreillypc

Stuart J. Reilly

For full biographical listings, see the Martindale-Hubbell Law Directory

LAW OFFICES OF RAYMOND J. SLOMSKI, P.C. (AV)

2929 North Central Avenue, Suite 1750, 85012
Telephone: 602-230-8777
Fax: 602-230-8707
Email: slomiski@earthlink.net

Raymond J. Slomski
James M. Abernethy

LEGAL SUPPORT PERSONNEL

PARALEGALS

Patti A. Hibbeler
Diana G. Weeks

For full biographical listings, see the Martindale-Hubbell Law Directory

TREON, STRICK, LUCIA & AGUIRRE A PROFESSIONAL ASSOCIATION OF LAWYERS (AV)

2700 North Central Avenue, Suite 1400, 85004-1133
Telephone: 602-285-4400
Telecopier: 602-285-4483
Email: office@TSLA.com

Richard T. Treon
Gerald J. Strick
Anthony R. Lucia
John Aguirre
Arthur G. Newman, Jr.
Michael P. Stark
Linda B. Williamson
Teri Kessel Raven
Cindy Hansel Strickland
Sharon G. Slifko

Robert C. Warnicke
Brett L Slavicek

For full biographical listings, see the Martindale-Hubbell Law Directory

TUCKER STROHM MILLER & TUCKER, P.C. (AV)

1136 East Campbell, 85014
Telephone: 602-279-3660
Fax: 602-279-2162
Email: rlslaw@worldnet.att.net

Kenneth L. Tucker
Richard L. Strohm
Daniel P. J. Miller
Kevin J. Tucker

For full biographical listings, see the Martindale-Hubbell Law Directory

Phoenix—Continued

ULRICH, KESSLER & ANGER, P.C. (AV)

3707 North Seventh Street, Suite 250, 85014-5059
Telephone: 602-248-9465
Fax: 602-248-0165
Email: ukapc@aol.com

Paul G. Ulrich
Donn G. Kessler
William H. Anger

For full biographical listings, see the Martindale-Hubbell Law Directory

SCOTTSDALE, Maricopa Co.

CAMPANA, VIEH, SHORE, OWENS & LOEB (AV)

4422 North Civic Center Plaza, Suite 101, 85251
Telephone: 480-707-5000
Fax: 480-707-5005

Richard V. Campana
James E. Vieh
William F. Shore, III
Bernard C. Owens
Donald O. Loeb

LEGAL SUPPORT PERSONNEL

Lois V. Johnson (Legal Assistant)

For full biographical listings, see the Martindale-Hubbell Law Directory

JOHN H. COTTON & ASSOCIATES, LTD. (AV)

6900 East Camelback Road, Suite 320, 85251
Telephone: 480-423-2034
Fax: 480-423-2035
Email: jhcotton1@aol.com
Las Vegas, Nevada Office: 2300 West Sahara, Suite 420, 89102.
Telephone: 702-367-9993.
Fax: 702-367-9977.

John H. Cotton

Bart J. Patterson (Resident)
Scott F. Frerichs (Resident)
Melanie Beth Bernstein (Not admitted in AZ)
Richard S. Johnson (Not admitted in AZ)
Edward R. Miley (Not admitted in AZ)

Representative Clients: American Continental/MMI Companies; Carpenter Industries; DLR Group, Inc.; KPMG Peat Marwick; Law Society of British Columbia; Opthalmic Mutual Insurance Company; The St. Paul Companies; Simula, Inc.; Tenet Health Care; The Doctors' Company.

For full biographical listings, see the Martindale-Hubbell Law Directory

*TUCSON,** Pima Co.

GOERING, ROBERTS, BERKMAN, RUBIN & BROGNA, P.C. (AV)

Suite 302, 1840 East River Road, 85718
Telephone: 520-577-9300
Fax: 520-577-0848
Email: grbrb@aol.com

Scott Goering
Howard T. Roberts, Jr.
David L. Berkman
William L. Rubin
Carmine A. Brogna
Christopher L. Enos

Representative Clients: Fireman's Fund Insurance; Safeco Insurance; Royal Insurance; Sentry Insurance; American International Group; Farmers Insurance; USAA; Country Companies; Cigna.
Reference: Bank One.

For full biographical listings, see the Martindale-Hubbell Law Directory

HARALSON, MILLER, PITT & MCANALLY, P.L.C. (AV)

One South Church Avenue Suite 900, 85701
Telephone: 520-792-3836
Telecopier: 520-624-5080
Email: mpmpc@azstarnet.com

Barry N. Akin (1939-1988)
Dale Haralson, P.C.
Janice A. Wezelman
Philip J. Hall
Grace McIlvain
Thomas G. Cotter
Armando Rivera
Gus Aragón, Jr.
Carole A. Summers

OF COUNSEL

Richard L. McAnally

Representative Clients: Bell Atlantic Metro Mobile; Farmers Investment Co.; Forest City Enterprises; Vince Granatelli Racing; KVOA Channel 4 TV; Newmont Mining Corp.; S.L. Industries, Inc.; Tucson Unified School District; University of Arizona Foundation.

For Complete List of Firm Personnel, See General Section

For full biographical listings, see the Martindale-Hubbell Law Directory

HAZLETT & WILKES (AV)

310 South Williams Boulevard, Suite 305, 85711
Telephone: 520-790-9663
Fax: 520-790-9616
Email: hazlettwilkes@juno.com

MEMBERS OF FIRM

Carl E. Hazlett
James M. Wilkes

ASSOCIATE

Thomas M. Bayham

For full biographical listings, see the Martindale-Hubbell Law Directory

HEALY & STUDWELL LAW FIRM, P.C. (AV)

5210 East Williams Circle Suite 720, 85711
Telephone: 520-790-1400
Fax: 520-790-3212

William T. Healy
James R. Studwell

Sean P. Healy

References: Bank of America; Merrill Lynch.

For full biographical listings, see the Martindale-Hubbell Law Directory

KINERK, BEAL, SCHMIDT & DYER, P.C. (AV)

Suite 6000, West Tower, 5255 East Williams Circle, 85711
Telephone: 520-790-5600
Fax: 520-790-1163
Email: kbs@azstarnet.com *URL:* http://www.azinjurylaw.com

Burton J. Kinerk
Robert L. Beal
Ted A. Schmidt
James H. Dyer
Colleen L. Kinerk

Karl R. Lautz
David W. Babcock

For full biographical listings, see the Martindale-Hubbell Law Directory

RONALD D. MERCALDO, LTD. (AV)

376 South Stone Avenue, 85701
Telephone: 520-624-1400
FAX: 520-624-1955
Email: ron@mercaldolaw.psemail.com

Ronald D. Mercaldo

Anthony J. Wiggins

For full biographical listings, see the Martindale-Hubbell Law Directory

CARTER MOREY, P.C. (AV)

Formerly Haralson, Kinerk & Morey (1978)
82 South Stone Avenue "The Citizen Building", 85701
Telephone: 520-792-4330
Fax: 520-623-9568

Carter Morey

Gregory G. Wasley
Linda S. Sherrill

For full biographical listings, see the Martindale-Hubbell Law Directory

RABINOVITZ & ASSOCIATES, P.C. (AV)

721 North 4th Avenue, P.O. Box 41600, 85717
Telephone: 520-624-5526
Toll Free: 1-800-365-0821
Fax: 520-622-3776

Bernard I. Rabinovitz

John D. Ellis

LEGAL SUPPORT PERSONNEL

Michael Nielson (Paralegal)
Lisa Busciglio (Paralegal)
Ruth Polizzi (Paralegal)

Representative Client: Firemans Fund Insurance Co.

For full biographical listings, see the Martindale-Hubbell Law Directory

SHULTZ & ROLLINS, LTD. (AV)

St. Philip's Plaza, 4280 North Campbell Avenue, Suite 214, 85718-6580
Telephone: 520-577-7777

Silas H. Shultz
Michael F. Rollins

James E. Marner

For full biographical listings, see the Martindale-Hubbell Law Directory

Tucson—Continued

STOMPOLY, STROUD, GLICKSMAN & ERICKSON, P.C. (AV)
1820 Norwest Tower, One South Church Avenue, 85702
Telephone: 520-628-8300
Telefax: 520-628-9948
Mailing Address: P.O. Box 190, Tucson, AZ, 85702-0190

John G. Stompoly

For Complete List of Firm Personnel, See General Section

For full biographical listings, see the Martindale-Hubbell Law Directory

STRICKLAND & STRICKLAND, P.C. (AV)
4400 E. Broadway, Suite 700, 85711-3517
Telephone: 520-795-8727
Fax: 520-795-5649

William E. Strickland
William E. Strickland, Jr.
Robert F. Palmquist

Representative Client: AkChin Indian Community.
Reference: Bank One (formerly Valley National Bank).

ARKANSAS

*FAYETTEVILLE,** Washington Co.

ODOM & ELLIOTT (AV)
No. 1 East Mountain Street, P.O. Drawer 1868, 72702
Telephone: 501-442-7575
FAX: 501-442-9008
Email: rzrbk63@aol.com *URL:* http://www.odomelliott.com

MEMBERS OF FIRM

Bobby Lee Odom
Don R. Elliott, Jr.
Russell B. Winburn
J. Timothy Smith
Conrad T. Odom
Jennifer Wheeler Haskins

Reference: Bank of Fayetteville, Fayetteville, Arkansas.

For full biographical listings, see the Martindale-Hubbell Law Directory

*FORREST CITY,** St. Francis Co.

BUTLER, HICKY & LONG (AV)
A Partnership of Professional Corporations
2216 North Washington Street, P.O. Box 989, 72335
Telephone: 870-633-4611
FAX: 870-633-6848
Email: bhlfirm@IPA.NET

MEMBERS OF FIRM

Philip Hicky (Ltd.)
Fletcher Long, Jr. (P.A.)

ASSOCIATE

Rita Reed Harris

Representative Clients: Baptist Memorial Hospital - Forrest City, Inc.; Baptist Memorial Hospital - Mississippi County, Inc.

For full biographical listings, see the Martindale-Hubbell Law Directory

*FORT SMITH,** Sebastian Co.

GILBREATH LAW FIRM (AV)
605 South 21st Street, 72901
Telephone: 501-782-7770
Fax: 501-782-9288
Email: attysatlaw@aol.com *URL:* http://www.lawyers.com/gilbreathlawfirm

E. C. Gilbreath
Daniel W. Gilbreath

For full biographical listings, see the Martindale-Hubbell Law Directory

LAW OFFICES OF CHARLES KARR, P.A. (AV)
First National Bank Building, 602 Garrison Avenue, Suite 650, 72901-2535
Telephone: 501-782-4028
Fax: 501-782-6410

Charles Karr

Shane Roughley

For full biographical listings, see the Martindale-Hubbell Law Directory

LEDBETTER, COGBILL, ARNOLD & HARRISON, LLP (AV)
622 Parker Avenue, P.O. Box 185, 72902-0185
Telephone: 501-782-7294
Fax: 501-782-1493

(See Next Column)

MEMBERS OF FIRM

Charles R. Ledbetter
J. Michael Cogbill
James A. Arnold, II
Ronald D. Harrison
E. Diane Graham
R. Ray Fulmer, II

ASSOCIATES

Rebecca D. Hattabaugh
Virginia C. Trammell
Daniel A. Stewart

Representative Clients: General: First National Bank of Fort Smith; Bank of Mansfield; Commercial Bank at Alma.
Local Attorneys for: St Paul Insurance Cos.; American Physician Insurance Exchange; The Medical Protective Co.

For full biographical listings, see the Martindale-Hubbell Law Directory

*LITTLE ROCK,** Pulaski Co.

ANDERSON, MURPHY & HOPKINS, L.L.P. (AV)
400 West Capitol Avenue, Suite 2640, 72201
Telephone: 501-372-1887
Fax: 501-372-7706
Email: ande@att.net

MEMBERS OF FIRM

Overton S. Anderson, II
Mariam T. Hopkins

ASSOCIATES

Michael P. Vanderford
Penny Brown Wilbourn
David A. Littleton
Scott D. Provencher

For full biographical listings, see the Martindale-Hubbell Law Directory

BARBER, MCCASKILL, JONES & HALE, P.A. (AV)
2700 Regions Center, 400 West Capitol Avenue, 72201-3414
Telephone: 501-372-6175
Telecopier: 501-375-2802

Azro L. Barber (1885-1979)
Elbert A. Henry (1889-1966)
John B. Thurman (1912-1971)
Austin McCaskill, Sr.
Glenn W. Jones
Michael E. Hale
John S. Cherry, Jr.
Robert L. Henry, III
Micheal L. Alexander
William H. Edwards, Jr.
G. Spence Fricke
Gail Ponder Gaines
Michael J. Emerson
R. Kenny McCulloch
Tim A. Cheatham
Joseph F. Kolb
Scott Michael Strauss
Baucum Fulk
D. Keith Fortner
Wendy Scholtens Wood
Morris L. Williams, III
Michelle Bass Miller

Attorneys for: CNA Insurance Companies; Fireman's Fund Insurance Co.; Hanover Insurance Co.; Royal Insurance; St. Paul Fire & Marine; United States Fidelity & Guaranty Co.; Universal Underwriters Insurance Co.

For full biographical listings, see the Martindale-Hubbell Law Directory

DUNCAN & RAINWATER TRIAL LAWYERS A PROFESSIONAL ASSOCIATION (AV)
6315 Ranch Drive, 72221-5938
Telephone: 501-228-7600
Fax: 501-228-7664
URL: http://www.lawyers.com/duncanandrainwater
Email: duncanlaw@aristotle.net *URL:* http://www.duncan-rainwater.com

Phillip J. Duncan (P.A.)
Michael R. Rainwater
Neil Ray Chamberlin
Michelle Banks Odum
J. Stephen Holt

For full biographical listings, see the Martindale-Hubbell Law Directory

HUCKABAY, MUNSON, ROWLETT & TILLEY, P.A. (AV)
Regions Center, Suite 1900, 400 West Capitol, 72201
Telephone: 501-374-6535
Fax: 501-374-5906

Mike Huckabay
Bruce E. Munson
Beverly A. Rowlett
James W. Tilley
John E. Moore
Tim Boone
Rick Runnells
Sarah Ann Presson
D. Michael Huckabay, Jr.
Carol Lockard Worley
Mark S. Breeding

Elizabeth Fletcher Rogers
Julia L. Busfield
Jane M. Yocum
Terry D. Dugger

Representative Clients: AAOMS National; Central Arkansas Hospital; Columbia/HCA Healthcare Corporation; Catholic Health Initiatives; Healthstar Ultima; Medical Park Hospital of Hope; Methodist Hospital of Jonesboro; National Park Medical Center; St. Mary's Regional Medical Center; St. Vincent Infirmary Medical Center.

For full biographical listings, see the Martindale-Hubbell Law Directory

Little Rock—Continued

KILPATRICK, AUD & WILLIAMS, L.L.P. (AV)

Regions Center, 400 West Capitol Avenue, Suite 1910, 72201-4849
Telephone: 501-372-0401
Facsimile: 501-372-5277

Joseph E. Kilpatrick, Jr. Michael E. Aud
Aylmer Gene Williams

For full biographical listings, see the Martindale-Hubbell Law Directory

LASER, WILSON, BUFFORD & WATTS, P.A. (AV)

101 South Spring Street, Suite 300, 72201-2488
Telephone: 501-376-2981
Telecopier: 501-376-2417
Email: laser@laserlaw.com

Sam Laser J. Kendal "Ken" Cook
Richard N. Watts David M. Donovan

Representative Clients: Allstate Insurance Co.; American International Insurance Group; Continental Insurance Cos.; Farm Bureau Insurance Cos. (Casualty & Fire); Farmers Insurance Group; GAB Business Services, Inc.; St. Paul Insurance Cos.; Scottsdale Insurance Co.; State Farm Auto (Fire) Insurance Cos.

For Complete List of Firm Personnel, See General Section

For full biographical listings, see the Martindale-Hubbell Law Directory

MCHENRY LAW FIRM (AV)

124 West Capitol Avenue Suite 1500, 72201
Telephone: 501-372-3425
Fax: 501-372-3428

MEMBER OF FIRM

Robert M. McHenry, Jr.

ASSOCIATES

Donna J. McHenry Monica Lee Mason
Allan L. Ward, II

References: First Commercial Bank, N.A., Little Rock, Arkansas; Boatmen's Bank & Trust, Little Rock, Ark.

For full biographical listings, see the Martindale-Hubbell Law Directory

MCMATH, VEHIK, DRUMMOND, HARRISON & LEDBETTER, P.A. (AV)

711 West Third Street, 72201
Telephone: 501-396-5400
Fax: 501-374-5118
Email: jbmcmath@aristotle.net *URL:* http://www.mvdhpa.com

Phillip H. McMath Winslow Drummond
James Bruce McMath Paul E. Harrison
Mart Vehik Sandra L. Sanders

OF COUNSEL

Sidney S. McMath

For full biographical listings, see the Martindale-Hubbell Law Directory

*MOUNTAIN HOME,** Baxter Co.

BAILEY LAW FIRM (AV)

506 Hospital Drive, 72653
Telephone: 870-425-6041
1-800-420-8260
Fax: 870-424-2543
URL: http://www.lawyers.com/bailey
URL: http://www.baileylawfirm.com

Frank H. Bailey

Representative Clients: First Federal Bank of Arkansas F.A.; The Bank of Yellville, Yellville, Arkansas.

For full biographical listings, see the Martindale-Hubbell Law Directory

*TEXARKANA,** Miller Co.

DUNN, NUTTER, MORGAN & SHAW (AV)

State Line Plaza, 6th Floor, P.O. Box 8030, 71854-5945
Telephone: 870-773-5651
Texas Telephone: 903-793-5651
Telecopier: 870-772-2037
Email: lawfirm@dnms.com *URL:* http://www.dnms.com

MEMBERS OF FIRM

Winford L. Dunn, Jr. R. Gary Nutter
W. David Carter

ASSOCIATES

Jeff M. Addison Adam O. Fellows

(See Next Column)

LEGAL SUPPORT PERSONNEL

LEGAL ASSISTANTS

Myra Conaway Wells

Representative Clients: CNA Insurance Cos.; Cigna Insurance Cos.; Christus St. Michael Health System.

For Complete List of Firm Personnel, See General Section

For full biographical listings, see the Martindale-Hubbell Law Directory

CALIFORNIA

*BAKERSFIELD,** Kern Co.

BORTON, PETRINI & CONRON, LLP (AV)

The Borton, Petrini & Conron Building, 1600 Truxtun Avenue, 93301
Telephone: 661-322-3051
Voice Mail: 661-395-6700
Fax: 661-322-4628
Mailing Address: P.O. Box 2026, Bakersfield, California, 93303
Email: bpcbak@bpclaw.com *URL:* http://www.bpclaw.com
Other City Locations: Fresno, Los Angeles, Modesto, Redding, Sacramento, San Bernardino, San Diego, San Francisco, San Jose, San Luis Obispo, Santa Ana and Ventura.

MEMBERS OF FIRM

George F. Martin Calvin R. Stead

ASSOCIATES

Stephen M. Crane Dee H. Stasnopolis
Raymond G. Robinson Randall Steven Joyce

For Complete List of Firm Personnel, See General Section

For full biographical listings, see the Martindale-Hubbell Law Directory

COSTA MESA, Orange Co.

LAW OFFICES OF W. DOUGLAS EASTON (AV)

3200 Park Center Drive, Suite 1000, 92626
Telephone: 714-850-4590
Fax: 714-427-0189
Email: lowdelaw@email.msn.com *URL:* http://www.lawyers.com/eastonlaw

Anderson L. Washburn Russel W. Jones
Brian W. Easton

For full biographical listings, see the Martindale-Hubbell Law Directory

DANVILLE, Contra Costa Co.

CRADDICK, CANDLAND & CONTI, PROFESSIONAL CORPORATION (AV)

Danville-San Ramon Medical Center, 915 San Ramon Valley Boulevard, Suite 260, 94526-0810
Telephone: 925-838-1100
Fax: 925-743-0729

Marrs A. Craddick (1928-1996) W. David Walker
D. Stuart Candland Andrew S. Miller
Richard J. Conti Thomas G. Manning
Robert W. Hodges Steven L. Brown, Jr.

Jean Louise Perry Matthew C. Mani
Kristine Keala Meredith Emily C. Millar
Michael E. Gatto

Representative Clients: Kaiser Foundation Hospitals; Medical Insurance Exchange of California; The Doctor's Co.; County of Contra Costa; Farmers Insurance Group (Truck Insurance Exchange); Professional Risk Management of California, Inc.; Claremont Liability Insurance Company; Program Beta.

For full biographical listings, see the Martindale-Hubbell Law Directory

ENCINO, Los Angeles Co.

STEPHEN H. HELLER A PROFESSIONAL CORPORATION (AV)

16830 Ventura Boulevard, Suite B, 91436-1714
Telephone: 818-995-4646
Fax: 818-995-0668
Email: stephenheller@hellerlaw.net

Stephen H. Heller

For full biographical listings, see the Martindale-Hubbell Law Directory

*FRESNO,** Fresno Co.

LANG, RICHERT & PATCH, A PROFESSIONAL CORPORATION (AV)

Fig Garden Financial Center, 5200 North Palm Avenue, 4th Floor, P.O. Box 40012, 93755
Telephone: 559-228-6700
Fax: 559-228-6727

William T. Richert (1937-1993)
Robert L. Patch, II
Val W. Saldaña
Douglas E. Noll
Michael T. Hertz
Victoria J. Salisch
Rene Lastreto, II
Charles Trudrung Taylor
Mark L. Creede
Peter N. Zeitler
Laurie L. Quigley
Tamara L. Equals
Douglas E. Griffin
Nabil E. Zumout

Christopher B. Dorian
Matthew W. Quall
Tracy E. Sagle
Julie K. Hill
Michelle Oleksa

OF COUNSEL

Frank H. Lang

References: Wells Fargo Bank (Fresno Main Office).

For full biographical listings, see the Martindale-Hubbell Law Directory

MILES, SEARS & EANNI, A PROFESSIONAL CORPORATION (AV)

2844 Fresno Street, P.O. Box 1432, 93716
Telephone: 559-486-5200
Fax: 559-486-5240
Email: mse@good.attitude.com

Wm. M. Miles (1909-1991)
Robert E. Sears (1918-1992)
Carmen A. Eanni
Richard C. Watters
William J. Seiler
Douglas L. Gordon

For full biographical listings, see the Martindale-Hubbell Law Directory

LAGUNA HILLS, Orange Co.

STANTON T. MATHEWS & ASSOCIATES, A LAW CORP. (AV)

24012 Calle de la Plata, Suite 320, 92653
Telephone: 949-586-2235
Email: Triallaw@flash.net
Email: stm@injurytriallaw.com *URL:* http://www.injurytriallaw.com

Stanton T. Mathews

Paul W. Ralph
Ronald B. Funk

LEGAL SUPPORT PERSONNEL

PARALEGAL/ADMINISTRATOR

Sharing Garrett-Anderson

LEGAL ASSISTANT

Cheri C. Wickam

For full biographical listings, see the Martindale-Hubbell Law Directory

LARKSPUR, Marin Co.

WEINBERG, HOFFMAN, CASEY & ROPERS (AV)

A Partnership including a Professional Corporation
900 Larkspur Landing Circle, Suite 155, 94939
Telephone: 415-461-9666
Fax: 415-461-9681

Ivan Weinberg
Joseph Hoffman
A. Michael Casey
Mark Ropers

For full biographical listings, see the Martindale-Hubbell Law Directory

*LOS ANGELES,** Los Angeles Co.

BONNE, BRIDGES, MUELLER, O'KEEFE & NICHOLS, PROFESSIONAL CORPORATION (AV)

3699 Wilshire Boulevard, 10th Floor, 90010-2719
Telephone: 213-480-1900
Fax: 213-738-5888
Santa Ana, California Office: 1750 East Fourth Street, Suite 450, P.O. Box 22018, 92702-2018.
Telephone: 714-835-1157.
Fax: 714-480-2585.
Santa Barbara, California Office: 801 Garden Street, Suite 300, 93101-1597.
Telephone: 805-965-2992.
Fax: 805-962-6509.
Riverside, California Office: 3403 Tenth Street, Suite 800, P.O. Box 747, 92501-0747.
Telephone: 909-788-1944.
Fax: 909-782-4666.

(See Next Column)

San Luis Obispo, California Office: 1320 Osos Street, 93401-4034.
Telephone: 805-541-8350.
Fax: 805-541-6817.
Ventura, California Office: 770 County Square Drive, Suite 200.
Telephone: 805-289-1690.
Fax: 805-289-1693.
San Francisco, California Office: Suite 1300, Steuart Street Tower, One Market Plaza, 94105-1402.
Telephone: 415-344-0425.
Fax: 415-281-2010.

Kenneth N. Mueller
David J. O'Keefe
James D. Nichols
George E. Peterson (Resident in Santa Ana Office)
Joel Bruce Douglas
Alexander B. T. Cobb
Peter R. Osinoff
Margaret Manton Holm (Resident in Santa Ana Office)
Jeffrey C. Moffat
N. Denise Taylor
Patricia K. Ramsey (Resident in Santa Barbara Office)
Theodore H. O'Leary
Michael D. Lubrani (Resident in Riverside Office)
Christopher B. Marshall (Resident in Riverside Office)
Thomas M. O'Neil
Mark B. Connely (Resident in San Luis Obispo Office)
Thomas R. Bradford
Yuk Kwong Law
Thomas G. Scully (Resident in Santa Ana Office)
Kippy L. Wroten (Resident in Santa Ana Office)
John H. Dodd (Resident in San Francisco Office)
Brian L. Hoffman

Richard J. Ryan
Louis W. Pappas
Janice B. Lee
Carmen Vigil
Steve R. Belilove
Lisa Loyola (Resident in Santa Ana Office)
Henry Yekikian
Douglas C. Smith (Resident in Riverside Office)
Julianne M. DeMarco
Frank A. Romeu, Jr. (Resident in Riverside Office)
Sara E. Hersh
Diane L. Darvey
Barbara Springe Kilroy (Resident in Santa Barbara Office)
Mary Lawrence Test
Gregory Reyna Bunch
George E. Nowotny, III
Gregory D. Werre
Kathleen M. Walker
Kevin F. Greer (Resident in Riverside Office)
Brian H. Clausen (Resident in Santa Barbara Office)
Patricia Egan Daehnke
Robert A. Mosier (Resident in Santa Ana Office)
Cynthia M. Herrera (Resident in Riverside Office)
Nancy A. Tu
Marie E. Colmey
Melanie C. Butts
Jeannette Lynne Van Horst
Raymond J. Mc Mahon (Resident in Santa Ana Office)
Nancy Lawrence Flores
Lance Alan Baer
Mitzie L. Dobson
Raymond L. Blessey
Darryl Ross (Resident in Santa Ana Office)
Melinda A. Manley
Kimberly Ann Oughton
Michael L. Bazzo (Resident in Riverside Office)
Kevin A. Duffis
Matthew A. Yarvis (Resident in Riverside Office)
Julie Beth Pollock
William R. Johnson
Mirka Brown
Juan Ramon Perez
Tara Alpin
Melissa W. Woo
Vangi M. Edmundson
Clifford A. Clancey
Nancy Charoen Eng
Georgia McCullough Mayman (Resident in Santa Ana Office)
Laura K. Sitar (Resident in Santa Ana Office)
Frank A. Alfonso
Christopher J. Boman
Staci L. Meinzer
Nhi Thuy Ngo (Resident in Riverside Office)
Kathleen Tuthill Marino
Kevin A. Roberts
Morris M. Stern
Matthew J. Sundly (Resident in Santa Ana Office)
Laura R. Mcfeaters
Martin D. Holly
Wendi K. Russell

OF COUNSEL

Bruce J. Bonne
Ried Bridges (Resident in Ventura and Santa Barbara Offices)
Harold G. Becks

Representative Clients: Southern California Physicians Insurance Exchange, Doctor's Co.; Cooperative of American Physicians; Norcal Mutual Insurance Co.

For full biographical listings, see the Martindale-Hubbell Law Directory

WILLIAM J. GARGARO, JR. A PROFESSIONAL CORPORATION (AV)

2049 Century Park East, Suite 1100, 90067
Telephone: 310-552-0633
Fax: 310-552-9760
Email: gargarolaw@email.msn.com *URL:* http://www.lawyers.com/gargarolaw

William J. Gargaro, Jr.

Reference: First Business Bank.

For full biographical listings, see the Martindale-Hubbell Law Directory

Los Angeles—Continued

GIRARDI AND KEESE (AV)

1126 Wilshire Boulevard, 90017-1904
Telephone: 213-977-0211
FAX: 213-481-1554
San Bernardino, California Office: 155 West Hospitality Lane, Suite 260.
Telephone: 909-381-1551.
FAX: 909-381-2566.

MEMBERS OF FIRM

Thomas V. Girardi
Robert M. Keese
John A. Girardi
James B. Kropff
Robert W. Finnerty
James G. O'Callahan
V. Andre Rekte (Resident, San Bernardino Office)
John K. Courtney
Amy Fisch Solomon
Thomas C. Morgan
David N. Bigelow
Carrie J. Rognlien
David R. Lira
John Alan Roberts
Shane M. Emerson Coons
Amanda L. McClintock

ASSOCIATE

Jennifer M. Ingram

References: Wells Fargo Bank (Los Angeles Head Office); Comerica Bank.

For full biographical listings, see the Martindale-Hubbell Law Directory

GORDON, EDELSTEIN, KREPACK, GRANT, FELTON & GOLDSTEIN (AV)

Suite 1800, 3580 Wilshire Boulevard, 90010
Telephone: 213-739-7000; 213-487-1520
Fax: 213-386-1671
Email: geklaw.com

Roger L. Gordon
Mark Edelstein
Howard D. Krepack
Sherry E. Grant
Richard I. Felton
Irwin L. Goldstein
Steven J. Kleifield
David A. Goldstein

OF COUNSEL

Joshua M. Merliss

ASSOCIATES

Eugenia L. Steele
Vincent F. Bennett
Adam D. Dombchik
Jennifer S. Weisman

For full biographical listings, see the Martindale-Hubbell Law Directory

KERN & GONZALEZ, A PROFESSIONAL CORPORATION (AV)

601 West 5th Street, Suite 1100, 90071
Telephone: 213-629-8100
Facsimile: 213-627-8765
URL: http://www.kernlaw.net

René J. Kern, Jr.
Michael D. Gonzalez
Tina L. Gentile

Christina L. Young
Angela J. Armitage
Michele Marsh
Cynthia L. Filla
David G. Hoiles, Jr.
Michele Sherer Ancheta
Sue S. Kim
Gail S. Taningco

Representative Clients: Norcal Mutual Insurance Company; Northwest Physicians Mutual Insurance Company; Summit Health, Ltd.; Tristar Risk Management.

For full biographical listings, see the Martindale-Hubbell Law Directory

KUSSMAN & WHITEHILL (AV)

A Partnership including a Professional Corporation
Suite 1470, 10866 Wilshire Boulevard, 90024
Telephone: 310-474-4411
Fax: 310-474-6530

Russell S. Kussman (A Professional Corporation)
Michael H. Whitehill

For full biographical listings, see the Martindale-Hubbell Law Directory

ROBERT L. LUTY A PROFESSIONAL CORPORATION (AV)

11999 San Vicente Boulevard, Suite 340, 90049
Telephone: 310-472-7166
Fax: 310-472-6229
Email: robert@robertlluty.com *URL:* http://www.lawyers.com/lutylaw

Robert L. Luty

Reference: Brentwood Savings Bank (Brentwood Branch).

For full biographical listings, see the Martindale-Hubbell Law Directory

LAW OFFICES OF CARL A. MCMAHAN (AV)

827 Moraga Drive (Bel Air), 90049
Telephone: 310-472-8078
Fax: 310-472-7014
Email: camcmahan@earthlink.net *URL:* http://www.lawyers.com/mcmahan

OF COUNSEL

Peter J. McNulty

Reference: City National Bank, Beverly Hills, California.

For full biographical listings, see the Martindale-Hubbell Law Directory

SCHLOTHAUER & COLLINS (AV)

11999 San Vicente Boulevard, Suite 340, 90049
Telephone: 310-472-1670
Fax: 310-472-5270
Affiliated San Jose California Office: Collins & Schlothauer, 60 South Market Street, Suite 1100, 95113-2204.
Telephone: 408-298-5161.
Fax: 408-297-5766.

PARTNER

Thomas L. Schlothauer

OF COUNSEL

Mark Scott Collins

For full biographical listings, see the Martindale-Hubbell Law Directory

STONE, DOLGINER & WENZEL, A LAW CORPORATION (AV)

6500 Wilshire Boulevard Suite 2060, 90048
Telephone: 323-653-2244
Fax: 323-658-1155
Email: sdwlaw@aol.com *URL:* http://www.lawyers.com/sdwfirm

Robert N. Stone
Charles I. Dolginer
Mark D. Wenzel

Henry N. Seligsohn

OF COUNSEL

A. J. Connick Doran

Reference: Union Bank (Head Office, 900 South Main Street, Los Angeles).

For full biographical listings, see the Martindale-Hubbell Law Directory

SHAN K. THÉVER & ASSOCIATES A PROFESSIONAL CORPORATION (AV)

888 South Figueroa Street, Suite 1850, 90017
Telephone: 213-489-1513
Fax: 213-896-0076

Shan K. Théver
Boyd L. Hill
Vincent McGowan

OF COUNSEL

Shirley A. Morgan
Barry E. Johnson
Marcus E. Berger

For full biographical listings, see the Martindale-Hubbell Law Directory

MONTEREY, Monterey Co.

HARRAY & LINKER (AV)

80 Garden Court, Suite 260, 93940
Telephone: 831-373-3101
Fax: 831-373-6712
Email: general@harray-linker.com

Richard K. Harray
Stan L. Linker

ASSOCIATES

Christine Balbo Reed
J. Kenneth Gorman
Debra Gemgnani Tipton

Representative Clients: Opima Health Care; Beta Healthcare Group; CNA/RSKCE; Community Hospital/Monterey Peninsula; Salinas Valley Memorial Hospital; Watsonville Community Hospital.

For full biographical listings, see the Martindale-Hubbell Law Directory

NEWPORT BEACH, Orange Co.

LOPEZ, HODES, RESTAINO, MILMAN & SKIKOS, A LAW CORPORATION (AV)

450 Newport Center Drive, 2nd Floor, 92660
Telephone: 949-640-8222
Fax: 949-640-8294
San Francisco, California Office: 625 Market Street, Fifteenth Floor, 94105.
Telephone: 415-956-5257.
Fax: 415-956-4416.

(See Next Column)

LOPEZ, HODES, RESTAINO, MILMAN & SKIKOS A LAW CORPORATION, *Newport Beach—Continued*

Ramon Rossi Lopez
Daniel M. Hodes
John M. Restaino, Jr.
Jeffrey A. Milman
Peter John Polos
Steven J. Skikos (Resident)

Christina A. Lopez Fountain
Steven B. Eggleston (Resident, San Francisco Office)
Gregory T. Skikos (Resident, San Francisco Office)
Thomas A. Schultz
Mark G. Crawford
Hilary Poulsen Gilles

OF COUNSEL

David L. Suggs (Not admitted in CA)
Jane E. Joseph (Not admitted in CA)

For full biographical listings, see the Martindale-Hubbell Law Directory

*OAKLAND,** Alameda Co.

ANTHONY & CARLSON, LLP (AV)

1999 Harrison Street, Suite 2000, 94612-3517
Telephone: 510-835-8400
Fax: 510-835-5566

MEMBERS OF FIRM

Steven R. Anthony
Richard H. Carlson

Felicia C. Strankman

OF COUNSEL

Jane L. Trigero

For full biographical listings, see the Martindale-Hubbell Law Directory

LOMBARDI, LOPER & CONANT, LLP (AV)

1999 Harrison Street, Suite 1950, 94612
Telephone: 510-433-2600
Fax: 510-433-2699

Ralph A. Lombardi
Bruce P. Loper
Matthew S. Conant
Chris P. Lavdiotis
Peter O. Glaessner
Timothy J. McCaffery
GayLynn Renee Kirn

Jeffrey D Hosking
Joseph Blaise Adams
Paul S. Lecky

OF COUNSEL

George S. Peyton, Jr.
Linda C. Roodhouse
Lori A. Sebransky

For full biographical listings, see the Martindale-Hubbell Law Directory

VAN BLOIS & ASSOCIATES (AV)

Suite 2245 Ordway Building, One Kaiser Plaza, 94612
Telephone: 510-444-1906
Contra Costa County 510-947-1055
Fax: 510-444-1294
Email: rlvblaw@mindspring.com *URL:* http://www.lawyers.com/vanblois

MEMBERS OF FIRM

R. Lewis Van Blois
Thomas C. Knowles

OF COUNSEL

Charles E. Farnsworth

For full biographical listings, see the Martindale-Hubbell Law Directory

PALM DESERT, Riverside Co.

BERMAN & WEISS (AV)

73-710 Fred Waring Drive, Suite 100, 92260
Telephone: 760-773-6677
Fax: 760-346-7779
Email: weisstrial@aol.com *URL:* http://www.lawinfo.com/law/ca/berman.html

MEMBERS OF FIRM

Richard B. Weiss
Martin M. Berman

For full biographical listings, see the Martindale-Hubbell Law Directory

PASADENA, Los Angeles Co.

JOHN C. BURTON (AV)

35 South Raymond Avenue, Suite 405, 91105
Telephone: 626-449-8300
Fax: 626-449-4417
Email: Johnburtonlaw@compuserve.com *URL:* http://www.lawyers.com/johnburtonlaw

For full biographical listings, see the Martindale-Hubbell Law Directory

FREEBURG, JUDY & NETTELS (AV)

600 South Lake Avenue, Suite 500, 91106
Telephone: 626-585-4150
Fax: 626-585-0718
Tustin, California Office: 440 West First Street, Suite 102, 92780-3047.
Telephone: 714-508-1800.
Facsimile: 714-508-1809.

Steven J. Freeburg
J. Lawrence Judy
Charles F. Nettels

ASSOCIATES

Ingall W. Bull, Jr.
Richard B. Castle
Cynthia B. Schaldenbrand (Resident, Tustin Office)
Holly A. McNulty
Karen S. Freeburg
Jennifer D. Helsel
Carla Lynn Crochet (Resident, Tustin Office)
Edward William Burns

For full biographical listings, see the Martindale-Hubbell Law Directory

MEENAN & LARIVIERE (AV)

790 East Colorado Boulevard Ninth Floor Penthouse, 91101-2113
Telephone: 626-398-0000
Fax: 626-585-0999
Email: meenlaw@msn.com *URL:* http://www.lawyers.com/meenlaw

Kevin Meenan
Denise L. Lariviere

For full biographical listings, see the Martindale-Hubbell Law Directory

GEORGE E. MOORE A PROFESSIONAL LAW CORPORATION (AV)

225 South Lake Avenue 9th Floor, 91101-3005
Telephone: 626-440-1315
Fax: 626-440-1516
Email: gemoore@pasadenatorts.com

George E. Moore

For full biographical listings, see the Martindale-Hubbell Law Directory

ZUETEL & TOMLINSON (AV)

215 North Marengo Avenue, Suite 195, 91101
Telephone: 626-577-3499
Fax: 323-684-1275

MEMBERS OF FIRM

Kenneth R. Zuetel, Jr.
Rodney G. Tomlinson

ASSOCIATE

Victoria K. Torigian

For full biographical listings, see the Martindale-Hubbell Law Directory

RANCHO SANTA FE, San Diego Co.

LAW OFFICES OF ROBERT S. KILBORNE IV (AV)

7872 Rio Senda, P.O. Box 7288, 92067
Telephone: 619-759-9050
Fax: 619-759-8020
Email: triallawyer@kilborne.com *URL:* http://www.kilborne.com

ASSOCIATE

Albert E. Cressey, III

OF COUNSEL

Russell B. Wagner

For full biographical listings, see the Martindale-Hubbell Law Directory

*SACRAMENTO,** Sacramento Co.

CLEMENT & ASSOCIATES (AV)

2209 J Street, 95816
Telephone: 916-444-9323
Fax: 916-444-9324
Email: laclaw@cwnet.com

Lesley Ann Clement

ASSOCIATES

Ronald N. Lebovits
Martha M. Stringer

For full biographical listings, see the Martindale-Hubbell Law Directory

HARDY ERICH BROWN & WILSON, A PROFESSIONAL CORPORATION (AV)

1000 G Street, 95814
Telephone: 916-449-3800
Fax: 916-449-3888
Mailing Address: P.O. Box 13530, Sacramento, California, 95853-4530
Email: hebw@hebw.com *URL:* http://www.hebw.com

John Quincy Brown, Jr.
Thomas C. Richards
L. Thomas Wagner
David L. Perrault
Sara A. Clark
John Quincy Brown, III
Bruce E. Salenko

(See Next Column)

HARDY ERICH BROWN & WILSON A PROFESSIONAL CORPORATION—*Continued*

Representative Clients: Norcal Mutual Insurance Company; Charter Behavioral Health; Mercy Healthcare; SCPIE Indemnity Company; Zurich American Insurance Company.

For full biographical listings, see the Martindale-Hubbell Law Directory

PORTER, SCOTT, WEIBERG & DELEHANT, A PROFESSIONAL CORPORATION (AV)

350 University Avenue, Suite 200, 95825
Telephone: 916-929-1481
Fax: 916-927-3706
Email: pswdlaw@aol.com

Russell G. Porter
A. Irving Scott, Jr.
Edwin T. Weiberg
John W. Delehant
Anthony S. Warburg
Ned P. Telford
James K. Mirabell
Craig A. Caldwell
Terence J. Cassidy
Tom H. Bailey
Carl J. Calnero
Russ J. Wunderli
Nancy J. Sheehan
Norman V. Prior
Timothy M. Blaine
Stephen E. Horan
Carl L. Fessenden

Elisa Ungerman
Michael J. Baytosh
David A. Melton
Jennifer E. Duggan
Vanessa W. Whang
Dennis C. Huie
Michael W. Pott
Kellianne Akbar
Daniel M. Steinberg
Jack Woodside
Jonathan A. Corr
Kristina M. Hall
Alden J. Parker
Avery E. Dority
Robin Weideman
Denise A. Carnaroli
Lara S. Hilley
Sean Allen
Ralph R. Nevis
Darrin M. Menezes
Shane Singh

For full biographical listings, see the Martindale-Hubbell Law Directory

RUST, ARMENIS, SCHWARTZ, LAMB & BILLS, A PROFESSIONAL CORPORATION (AV)

4330 Auburn Boulevard, Suite 2500, 95841-0958
Telephone: 916-972-8300
FAX: 916-972-7878
Email: mail@raslblaw.com
San Francisco, California Office: 350 California Street, Suite 1900.
Telephone: 415-765-5910.
FAX: 415-765-5914.

David C. Rust (1924-1980)
Michael P. Armenis (1919-1988)
Fred A. Schwartz
David J. Bills
Ronald R. Lamb
Scott D. Schwartz
Brian S. Turner

R. Duane Skelton
W. David Corrick
Carl E. Kadlic (Resident, San Francisco Office)

Reference: Imperial Bank (Main Office, 455 Capitol Mall, Sacramento).

For full biographical listings, see the Martindale-Hubbell Law Directory

SCHUERING ZIMMERMAN & SCULLY, LLP (AV)

400 University Avenue, 95825
Telephone: 916-567-0400
Fax: 916-568-0400
Email: szs@szs.com

MEMBERS OF FIRM

Steven T. Scully (1948-1994)
Leo H. Schuering, Jr.
Robert H. Zimmerman
Thomas J. Doyle
Lawrence S. Giardina
Anthony D. Lauria
Keith D. Chidlaw
John J. Sillis
Scott A. Linn
Donna W. Low
Raymond R. Gates

Christian Koster
Michael W. McCall
Dominique A. Pollara
Theodore D. Poppinga
John P. Rhode
Stephen L. Ramazzini
Jonathan A. Saul
Jeffrey J. Whitelaw

For full biographical listings, see the Martindale-Hubbell Law Directory

WILCOXEN, MONTGOMERY & HARBISON (AV)

A Partnership including a Professional Corporation
2114 K Street, 95816
Telephone: 916-442-2777
Email: wmh@wilcoxenlaw.com *URL:* http://www.wilcoxenlaw.com

Daniel E. Wilcoxen (Inc.)
James R. Montgomery
Joseph F. Harbison, III

(See Next Column)

Patrick L. Hinrichsen
David E. Smith
Steven H. Schultz
Michelle C. Jenni

References: SierraWest Bank; Wells Fargo Bank.

For full biographical listings, see the Martindale-Hubbell Law Directory

*SAN DIEGO,** San Diego Co.

BELSKY & ASSOCIATES (AV)

610 West Ash Street, Suite 700, 92101
Telephone: 619-232-8300
Fax: 619-338-0066
Email: Belsky1@cts.com

Daniel S. Belsky
Gabriel M. Benrubi
Vincent J. Iuliano

Bruce William Boetter

References: Centre For Health Care Medical Associates; The Doctor's Company; Grossmont Bank; Graybill Medical Group, Inc.; Kaiser Foundation HealthPlan, Inc.; Norcal Mutual Insurance Co.; Sharp Mission Park Medical Group; Sharp Rees-Stealy Medical Group; Southern California Physician Insurance Exchange; Unifirst.

For full biographical listings, see the Martindale-Hubbell Law Directory

BOUDREAU & TRENTACOSTA, A PROFESSIONAL LAW CORPORATION (AV)

401 West "A" Street, Suite 1850, 92101-9773
Telephone: 619-238-1553
Fax: 619-238-8181
Email: boutre@aol.com

Steven M. Boudreau
Robert J. Trentacosta

For full biographical listings, see the Martindale-Hubbell Law Directory

THORSNES, BARTOLOTTA, MCGUIRE & PADILLA (AV)

A Partnership including Professional Corporations
Fifth Avenue Financial Center, 11th Floor, 2550 Fifth Avenue, 92103
Telephone: 619-236-9363
Fax: 619-236-9653
Email: TBMPmail@TBMP.com *URL:* http://www.tbmp.com

Michael T. Thorsnes (A.P.C., P.C.)
Vincent J. Bartolotta, Jr., (P.C.)
John F. McGuire (P.C.)
Kevin F. Quinn (P.C.)
C. Brant Noziska (P.C.)
Mitchell S. Golub (P.C.)
Palma Cesar Hooper (P.C.)
Neal H. Rockwood (P.C.)
Daral B. Mazzarella (P.C.)
R. Christian Hulburt (P.C.)

ASSOCIATES

Catherine A. Richardson
Jodi L. Hautaluoma
Douglas J. Billings
Scott A. Kennedy
Dori K. Rybacki
James T. Atkins
Leo Bartolotta
Jill E. Cleary
James B. Drimmer
Timothy J. Tatro

OF COUNSEL

Robert S. Kennedy

For full biographical listings, see the Martindale-Hubbell Law Directory

*SAN FRANCISCO,** San Francisco Co.

BOKELMAN & BENJAMIN, A PROFESSIONAL LAW CORPORATION (AV)

Two Embarcadero Center Suite 1050, 94111-3823
Telephone: 415-398-3660
Facsimile: 415-788-0161
URL: http://www. bokelman-benjamin.com

Robert U. Bokelman
Anglia Benjamin

Amy Marie Leonard

For full biographical listings, see the Martindale-Hubbell Law Directory

COX & MOYER, A PROFESSIONAL CORPORATION (AV)

703 Market Street, Suite 1800, 94103
Telephone: 415-543-9464
Fax: 415-777-1828
Email: coxmoyer@aol.com

Ingemar E. Hoberg (1903-1971)
John H. Finger (1913-1991)
Phillip E. Brown (Retired)
Stephen T. Cox
David W. Moyer

Scott J. Allen

(See Next Column)

COX & MOYER A PROFESSIONAL CORPORATION, *San Francisco—Continued*

OF COUNSEL

Kenneth W. Rosenthal

For full biographical listings, see the Martindale-Hubbell Law Directory

LEACH, McGREEVY & BAUTISTA, LLP (AV)

2833 Laguna Street, 94123
Telephone: 415-775-4455
Telefax: 415-775-7435
Email: LMLawSF@aol.com
Southern California Office: 24752 Via San Fernando, Mission Viejo, CA 92692.
Telephone: 949-859-7464.

Theodore Tamba (1900-1973)
John T. Harmon (1928-1993)
David G. Leach
Richard E. McGreevy
A. Marquez Bautista
Robert W. Shinnick
Philip T. Kilduff
Peter C. Labrador

ASSOCIATES

John C. Connolly
Larry B. Carr
Annadel A. Almendras
David Emerson Beeby

OF COUNSEL

Lloyd F. Postel

For full biographical listings, see the Martindale-Hubbell Law Directory

MURPHY, PEARSON, BRADLEY & FEENEY, A PROFESSIONAL CORPORATION (AV)

88 Kearny Street, 10th Floor, 94108
Telephone: 415-788-1900
Telecopier: 415-393-8087
Email: IndividualsFirstInitialAndLastName@mpbf.com *URL:* http://www.mpbf.com
Sacramento, California Office: 701 University Avenue, Suite 150.
Telephone: 916-565-0300.
Fax: 916-565-1636.
San Jose, California Office: 80 South Market Street, 3rd Floor.
Telephone: 408-279-5792.
Facsimile: 408-279-5785.
Los Angeles, California Office: 11400 West Olympic Boulevard, Suite 249.
Telephone: 310-312-9565.
Fax: 310-312-9566.

Arthur V. Pearson
Gregory A. Bastian (Resident, Sacramento Office)
Timothy J. Halloran
Mark Ellis (Resident, Sacramento Office)

For Complete List of Firm Personnel, See General Section

For full biographical listings, see the Martindale-Hubbell Law Directory

TEHIN +PARTNERS, A PROFESSIONAL CORPORATION (AV)

Bank of America Center, 555 California Street, 33rd Floor, 94104-1609
Telephone: 415-951-8800
Fax: 415-951-8808
URL: http://www.tehin.com

Nikolai Tehin
Pamela J. Stevens
Reilly Atkinson, IV
Michael E. Brown
Bita Abdollahi

For full biographical listings, see the Martindale-Hubbell Law Directory

WALKUP, MELODIA, KELLY & ECHEVERRIA, A PROFESSIONAL CORPORATION (AV)

26th Floor, 650 California Street, 94108
Telephone: 415-981-7210
Fax: 415-391-6965

Paul V. Melodia
Daniel J. Kelly
John Echeverria
Ronald H. Wecht
Michael A. Kelly
Kevin L. Domecus
Richard H. Schoenberger

Cynthia F. Newton
Michael J. Recupero
Douglas S. Saeltzer
Khaldoun A. Baghdadi
Doris Cheng

OF COUNSEL

John D. Link
Wesley Sokolosky

Reference: Bank of California, San Francisco Main Office, 400 California Street, San Francisco, Calif. 94104.

For full biographical listings, see the Martindale-Hubbell Law Directory

*SAN JOSE,** Santa Clara Co.

JAN CHAMPION (AV)

Ten Almaden Boulevard, Suite 1250, 95113-2233
Telephone: 408-286-5550
Fax: 408-270-6777
URL: http://www.lawyers.com/jchampionlaw
Email: jan@championlaw.com

For full biographical listings, see the Martindale-Hubbell Law Directory

HAWKINS • BLICK (AV)

96 North Third Street, Suite 300, 95112
Telephone: 408-280-7111
Fax: 408-292-7868
URL: http://www.hawkins-law.com

MEMBERS OF FIRM

Charles F. Hawkins
Stephen L. Blick

For full biographical listings, see the Martindale-Hubbell Law Directory

SAUCEDO & CORSIGLIA, A LAW CORPORATION (AV)

50 West San Fernando Street, Suite 425, 95113
Telephone: 408-289-1417
Fax: 408-289-8127
Email: saucor@compuserve.com

Norman W. Saucedo
Bradley M. Corsiglia

For full biographical listings, see the Martindale-Hubbell Law Directory

*SANTA ANA,** Orange Co.

BEAM, BROBECK & WEST (AV)

600 West Santa Ana Boulevard, Suite 1000, 92701
Telephone: 714-558-3944
Fax: 714-568-0129

MEMBERS OF FIRM

Byron J. Beam
David J. Brobeck, Jr.
John E. West
Kirk H. Nakamura
Daniel R. Sullivan
Charles W. Matheis, Jr.

ASSOCIATES

Gregory L. Rippetoe
Jennifer J. Miller
Donald S. Zalewski
David R. Rosenberg
Louise M. Douville
Kermit D. Marsh
Kelly A. Fortin
Barbara J. Salvini
Lil G. Delcampo
Michael J. Peffer
L. Steven Hattendorf

Representative Clients: Aetna Insurance Co.; American General Life Insurance Co.; American Hospital Supply; Carl Warren & Co.; Casualty Insurance Co.; City of Anaheim; City of Fullerton; City of Newport Beach; Empire Insurance Cos.; Physicians Interindemnity.

For full biographical listings, see the Martindale-Hubbell Law Directory

McNEIL, SUSSON, PARRETT & TROPP, A PROFESSIONAL CORPORATION (AV)

2100 North Broadway, Suite 103, 92706-2624
Telephone: 714-835-1922
Facsimile: 714-835-2720
Email: info@msplawyers.com

Joseph D. McNeil
Dana E. Susson
James R. Parrett
Deborah S. Tropp

Maxine M. Morisaki-Price
Alison J. Vitacolonna

For full biographical listings, see the Martindale-Hubbell Law Directory

SANTA MONICA, Los Angeles Co.

BAKER, KEENER & NAHRA, LLP (AV)

2850 Ocean Park Boulevard, Suite 300, 90405-2936
Telephone: 310-399-0900
Fax: 310-399-1644
Email: general@bknlawyers.com *URL:* http://www.bknlawyers.com

MEMBERS OF FIRM

Robert C. Baker
Karl A. Keener
John P. Nahra
Michael H. Bailey
Steven T. Adams
Melissa S. Fink
Jeffrey P. Nolan
Constance A. Endelicato

Brenda K. Benson
Mitchell F. Mulbarger
James D. Hepworth
Phillip A. Baker
George P. Hawley
Thomas F. Mills
R. Jeffrey Neer
Wendy Wen Yun Chang

(See Next Column)

BAKER, KEENER & NAHRA LLP—*Continued*

OF COUNSEL

Daniel P. Leonard

Reference: Wells Fargo Bank (Los Angeles Head Office).

For full biographical listings, see the Martindale-Hubbell Law Directory

LAW OFFICES OF DAVID J. WEISS (AV)

1620 26th Street, Suite 3500 North, 90404-4013
Telephone: 310-449-6060
Fax: 310-449-6070
Email: dweiss@counsel.com

ASSOCIATES

David M. Hillings
Joel D. Schwartz
Pamela A. Benben
Craig S. Berman
Dania Youness
Susan M. Nichols

For full biographical listings, see the Martindale-Hubbell Law Directory

*SANTA ROSA,** Sonoma Co.

ABBEY, WEITZENBERG, HOFFMAN & EMERY, A PROFESSIONAL CORPORATION (AV)

1105 North Dutton Avenue, P.O. Box 1566, 95402
Telephone: 707-542-5050
Telecopier: 707-542-2589
Email: info@abbeylaw.com

W. Barton Weitzenberg
Patrick W. Emery

Representative Clients: Exchange Bank of Santa Rosa; Westamerica Bank; Northwestern Title Security Co.; Geyser Peak Winery; Santa Rosa City School District; Sonoma National Bank; Arrowood Vineyards & Winery; Friedman Bros. Hardware, Inc.; Bank of Lake County; Lasercraft, Inc.

For full biographical listings, see the Martindale-Hubbell Law Directory

TORRANCE, Los Angeles Co.

AGNEW & BRUSAVICH (AV)

20355 Hawthorne Boulevard, 90503
Telephone: 310-793-1400
Facsimile: 310-793-1499
Email: agnewbru@ix.netcom.com *URL:* http://www.agnew-brusavich.com

Gerald E. Agnew, Jr.
Bruce M. Brusavich

ASSOCIATES

Susan E. Hargrove
Christopher A. Kall

For full biographical listings, see the Martindale-Hubbell Law Directory

TUSTIN, Orange Co.

MADORY, ZELL AND PLEISS, A PROFESSIONAL CORPORATION (AV)

The Centre Building, Meredith Financial Centre, 17822 East 17th Street, Suite 205, 92780-2183
Telephone: 714-832-3772
Telecopier: 714-832-7163
Mailing Address: P.O. Box 11120, Santa Ana, California, 92711-1120

Richard E. Madory
Stephen H. Zell
Larry T. Pleiss
Mark G. McGrath
Stephen J. Martino

Patricia N. Scidmore
Kathryn A. Madlock
Brent S. Clemmer
Grace Morse Brumagin

Representative Clients: American Continental Insurance Co.; American Insurance Group (AIG); Eisenhower Medical Center; Optima Healthcare; County of Orange; St. Joseph Health System; Truck Insurance Exchange.

For full biographical listings, see the Martindale-Hubbell Law Directory

*VENTURA,** Ventura Co.

LAW OFFICES OF FREDERICK H. BYSSHE, JR. (AV)

10 South California Street, 93001
Telephone: 805-648-3224
Fax: 805-653-0267
Email: bysshe@west.net *URL:* http://www.lawyers.com/bysshelaw

Terence Geoghegan

For full biographical listings, see the Martindale-Hubbell Law Directory

WALNUT CREEK, Contra Costa Co.

ANDERSON, GALLOWAY & LUCCHESE, A PROFESSIONAL CORPORATION (AV)

1676 North California Boulevard Suite 500, 94596-4183
Telephone: 925-943-6383
Facsimile: 925-943-7542

Robert L. Anderson
George Patrick Galloway
David R. Lucchese
Martin J. Everson
Thomas J. Donnelly
Ralph J. Smith
James M. Nelson
Scott E. Murray
David A. Depolo
Karen A. Sparks
Stephen J. Brooks
Joseph S. Picchi
Erin Ruddy Sabey
Lea K. Baldacci
Michael E. Brewer
Sonja M. Dahl
Patricia A. Timm
Jeffrey S. Mitchell

Martha J. James
Shelton L. Smith
Steven M. McKinley
William L. Brelsford, Jr.

For full biographical listings, see the Martindale-Hubbell Law Directory

COLORADO

*BOULDER,** Boulder Co.

COOK & LEE, P.C. (AV)

5390 Manhattan Circle, 2nd Floor, 80303
Telephone: 303-543-1000
Fax: 303-543-8582
Email: cookleepc@bewellnet.com

Stephen H. Cook
Larry D. Lee

Robert K. Reimann

For full biographical listings, see the Martindale-Hubbell Law Directory

TRINE & METCALF, P.C. (AV)

1435 Arapahoe Avenue, 80302-6390
Telephone: 303-442-0173
Fax: 303-443-7677
Email: firm@trine-metcalf.com *URL:* http://www.trine-metcalf.com

William A. Trine
J. Conard Metcalf

T. Michael Kennedy

Reference: Norwest Bank of Boulder.

For full biographical listings, see the Martindale-Hubbell Law Directory

*DENVER,** Denver Co.

JOHN ASTUNO, JR. (AV)

1775 Sherman Street, Suite 1650, 80203
Telephone: 303-861-7636
Fax: 303-832-1405
Email: johnast@aol.com *URL:* http://www.lawyers.com/astonlaw

For full biographical listings, see the Martindale-Hubbell Law Directory

BOGUE KOURY & MARYLANDER LLC (AV)

1401 17th Street, Suite 320, 80202
Telephone: 303-382-1990
Fax: 303-382-1982
URL: http://www.bkmllc.com
Email: bkmlaw@bkmllc.com *URL:* http://www.lawyers.com/bkmllc

Jeffrey A. Bogue
Victoria J. Koury
Grant Marylander

For full biographical listings, see the Martindale-Hubbell Law Directory

CHALAT LAW OFFICES, P.C. (AV)

1900 Grant Street, Suite 1050, 80203
Telephone: 303-861-1042
Toll Free: 800-221-5526
Facsimile: 303-861-0506
URL: http://www.lawyers.com/chalatlawoffices
Email: Jchalat@aol.com *URL:* http://www.chalatlaw.com

James H. Chalat
Linda J. Chalat

For full biographical listings, see the Martindale-Hubbell Law Directory

Denver—Continued

COOPER & CLOUGH, P.C. (AV)

Suite 600 Writer Square, 1512 Larimer Street, 80202
Telephone: 303-607-0077
Fax: 303-607-0472
Email: cooper-clough@plinet.com

Paul D. Cooper
John E. Clough
Kay J. Rice
Larry S. McClung

Paul A. Faraci
Nicholas Ghiselli
Gary W. Flanagan
Deanne Potestio
Christopher L. Ingold

For full biographical listings, see the Martindale-Hubbell Law Directory

THE LAW FIRM OF EDWIN A. HOWE, P.C. (AV)

950 South Cherry Street, Suite 1502, 80246
Telephone: 303-756-5060
Fax: 303-756-5114
URL: http://www.lawyers.com/howelaw

Edwin A. Howe, II

LEGAL SUPPORT PERSONNEL

Julie Rotenberg (Office Administrator)

For full biographical listings, see the Martindale-Hubbell Law Directory

KENNEDY & CHRISTOPHER, P.C. (AV)

1660 Wynkoop Street, Suite 900, 80202
Telephone: 303-825-2700
Fax: 303-825-0434
Email: admn@Kennedy-Christopher.com

Frank R. Kennedy
Lisa B. Heintz
Daniel R. Christopher
Ronald H. Nemirow
Kim B. Childs
Barbara H. Glogiewicz
Elizabeth A. Starrs
Dawn E. Mitzner
Mark A. Fogg
John R. Mann
Michael T. Mihm
Daniel R. McCune
Charles R. Ledbetter
Dean A. McConnell
Edward D. Bronfin

OF COUNSEL

Paul E. Scott

Christopher K. Miller
Susan Michelle Englert
Carolyn Sprinthall Knaut
Chad K. Gillam
David B. Gelman
Benjamin Alexander Kahn
Kevin P. Perez
Steven A. Michalek
Steven H. Weigler
Jeremy A. Sitcoff
Garrison W. Kaufman
Renee E. Christian
Leslie C. Dolan
Laura M. Wassmuth

Representative Clients: American Medical International; Blue Cross/Blue Shield of Colorado; COPIC; The Doctors Co.; Hartford Insurance Co.; Home Insurance Co.; St. Paul Fire and Marine Insurance Co.; PRMS, Colorado Insurance Guaranty Association.

For full biographical listings, see the Martindale-Hubbell Law Directory

THE LEVENTHAL LAW FIRM, P.C. (AV)

950 South Cherry Street, Suite 600, 80246
Telephone: 303-759-9945
Fax: 303-759-9692
Email: office@leventhal-law.com

Jim Leventhal
Natalie Brown
Beth L. Krulewitch

James E. Puga
Timothy G. Buxton

Reference: Vectra Bank.

For full biographical listings, see the Martindale-Hubbell Law Directory

LONG & JAUDON, P.C. (AV)

The Bailey Mansion, 1600 Ogden Street, 80218-1414
Telephone: 303-832-1122
FAX: 303-832-1348

Joseph C. Jaudon, Jr.
Michael T. McConnell
Gary B. Blum
Alan D. Avery
Walter N. Houghtaling

David H. Yun

Representative Clients: St. Joseph Hospital; Travelers Property Casualty Company; The Doctors Company; Home Insurance Company; Baxter Healthcare.

For Complete List of Firm Personnel, See General Section

For full biographical listings, see the Martindale-Hubbell Law Directory

JOHN O. MARTIN, P.C. (AV)

1660 17th Street, Suite 100, 80202
Telephone: 303-892-8988
Fax: 303-820-3531
Email: jompc@worldnet.att.net

John O. Martin
Kathleen M. Shea

For full biographical listings, see the Martindale-Hubbell Law Directory

MONTGOMERY LITTLE & MCGREW, P.C. (AV)

The Quadrant, 5445 DTC Parkway, Suite 800 (Englewood), 80111
Telephone: 303-773-8100
Telecopier: 303-220-0412
URL: http://www.mlmpc.com

Robert R. Montgomery
Robert N. Spencer
Richard L. Murray, Jr.
John R. Riley
Kevin J. Kuhn
Carole Salamaha

LEGAL SUPPORT PERSONNEL

Mary Kay Ackley (Legal Assistant)
Kelly W. Roberge (Legal Assistant)
Debbie L. Kirke (Legal Assistant)

Representative Clients: Colorado Physicians Insurance; The St. Paul Insurance Cos.; University of Colorado Health Sciences Center; HealthOne; Westport Insurance Corp.; CNA; Dentists Professional Liablity Trust; Design Professionals Insurance Corp.; Interstate Insurance Co.; State Volunteer Mutual Insurance Co.

For Complete List of Firm Personnel, See General Section

For full biographical listings, see the Martindale-Hubbell Law Directory

RICHMAN & JONES, P.C. (AV)

1600 Broadway, Suite 1900, 80202
Telephone: 303-830-1717
Facsimile: 303-830-1746

Alan E. Richman
Michael W. Jones

For full biographical listings, see the Martindale-Hubbell Law Directory

TREECE, ALFREY, MUSAT & BOSWORTH, P.C. (AV)

999 18th Street, Suite 1600, 80202
Telephone: 303-292-2700
Facsimile: 303-295-0414
Email: tamb@tamblaw.com *URL:* http://www.tamblaw.com

Thomas N. Alfrey
June Baker Laird
Timothy J. Judson

Nicholas Kemp

For full biographical listings, see the Martindale-Hubbell Law Directory

ENGLEWOOD, Arapahoe Co.

SALMON, LAMPERT & CLOR, PROFESSIONAL CORPORATION (AV)

Salmon Law Building, (I-25 at East Belleview) 7450 East Progress Place, 80111
Telephone: 303-771-9900
Toll Free in Colorado: 1-800-547-9055
Fax: 303-773-6843
Breckenridge, Colorado Office: Briar Rose House, 213 Briar Rose Lane.
Telephone: 1-800-547-9055

John G. Salmon
Brian J. Lampert
Penelope Clor

Francine R. Salazar
Barbara Barrows Ezyk
S. Jane Mitchell
Martha Merrill-Hall

For full biographical listings, see the Martindale-Hubbell Law Directory

THOMAS J. TOMAZIN, P.C. (AV)

Suite 200, 5655 South Yosemite, 80111
Telephone: 303-771-1900
FAX: 303-793-0923

Thomas J. Tomazin

Representative Clients: Design Drywall Specialities; Elm Contracting; Kumpf Lincoln Mercury, Inc.; Omni Business Brokers, Inc.; Contract Design Services, Inc.; American Natural Gas Corp.; Sonex Enterprises, Inc.; Am West Energy, Inc.; Mountain States Asphalt Paving, Inc.
Reference: Guaranty Bank & Trust Co.

For full biographical listings, see the Martindale-Hubbell Law Directory

CONNECTICUT

*BRIDGEPORT,** Fairfield Co.

BAI, POLLOCK AND COYNE, P.C. (AV)

Park City Plaza, 10 Middle Street, P.O. Box 1978, 06604
Telephone: 203-366-7991
Fax: 203-366-4723
Email: bpc@snet.net

Arnold J. Bai (1931-1992)
Paul E. Pollock
James E. Coyne
Jeffrey A. Blueweiss
Garie J. Mulcahey
Raymond J. Plouffe, Jr.
Philip F. von Kuhn
Madonna A. Sacco
Michael S. Lynch
David J. Robertson
Edward P. Brady III

Gaileen A. Kaufman
Kevin S. Coyne
Colleen D. Fries
Neal P. Rogan
Louis A. Annecchino
Robert J. Weber, III
Heidi Marie Priwall
Anthony D. Sutton
Kevin J. Curseaden

For full biographical listings, see the Martindale-Hubbell Law Directory

KOSKOFF, KOSKOFF & BIEDER, P.C. (AV)

350 Fairfield Avenue, 06604
Telephone: 203-336-4421
Fax: 203-368-3244
Email: KKB@KOSKOFF.com
Stamford, Connecticut Office: 1172 Bedford Street.
Telephone: 203-325-3686.
Danbury, Connecticut Office: 1 Moss Avenue.
Telephone: 203-792-7100.

Michael P. Koskoff
Richard A. Bieder
Joel H. Lichtenstein
John D. Jessep
Christopher D. Bernard
Karen E. Koskoff
Carey B. Reilly
James D. Horwitz
Michael A. Stratton

Regina M. DeLuca
Gertrude A. Kiaunis
Joshua D. Koskoff

For full biographical listings, see the Martindale-Hubbell Law Directory

WILLIAMS, COONEY & SHEEHY (AV)

One Lafayette Circle, 06604
Telephone: 203-331-0888
Telecopier: 203-331-0896
Email: wilcooshee@aol.com

MEMBERS OF FIRM

Ronald D. Williams
Robert J. Cooney
Edward Maum Sheehy
Dion W. Moore
Ronald D. Williams, Jr.
Francis A. Smith, Jr. (1951-1989)

Suzannah Kim Nigro
Michael Richard Brandt

Representative Clients: Connecticut Medical Insurance Co.; Zimmer Manufacturing Co.; The Travelers; Preferred Physicians Mutual; Podiatry Insurance Company of America; Medical Liability Mutual Insurance Company.

For full biographical listings, see the Martindale-Hubbell Law Directory

CHESHIRE, New Haven Co.

MOORE, O'BRIEN, JACQUES & YELENAK (AV)

700 West Johnson Avenue Suite 207, 06410
Telephone: 203-272-5881
Fax: 203-272-9273

MEMBERS OF FIRM

Garrett M. Moore
Gregory E. O'Brien
Stephen L. Jacques
William P. Yelenak

For full biographical listings, see the Martindale-Hubbell Law Directory

*HARTFORD,** Hartford Co.

GORDON, MUIR AND FOLEY, LLP (AV)

Hartford Square North, Ten Columbus Boulevard, 06106-5123
Telephone: 860-525-5361
Telecopier: 860-525-4849
Email: admin@gmflaw.com *URL:* http://www.gmflaw.com

MEMBERS OF FIRM

William S. Gordon, Jr. (1946-1956)
George Muir (1939-1976)
Edward J. Foley (1955-1983)
Peter C. Schwartz
John J. Reid
John H. Goodrich, Jr.
R. Bradley Wolfe
Jon Stephen Berk
William J. Gallitto

(See Next Column)

MEMBERS OF FIRM (Continued)

Gerald R. Swirsky
Robert J. O'Brien
Philip J. O'Connor
Kenneth G. Williams
Mary Ann Santacroce
Mary Anne Alicia Charron
Andrew J. Hern
Reneé W. Dwyer
Patty G. Swan

ASSOCIATES

Doreen West Amata
Howard A. Steinman
Erik E. Roberts
Christopher J. Casciani

Reference: People's Bank.

For full biographical listings, see the Martindale-Hubbell Law Directory

JACKSON, O'KEEFE AND PHELAN (AV)

36 Russ Street, 06106-1571
Telephone: 860-278-4040
Fax: 860-527-2500
West Hartford, Connecticut Office: 62 LaSalle Road.
Telephone: 860-521-7500.
Fax: 860-561-5399.
Bethlehem, Connecticut Office: 423 Munger Lane. Telephone/
Fax: 203-266-5255.

MEMBERS OF FIRM

Jay W. Jackson
Andrew J. O'Keefe
Denise Martino Phelan
Matthew J. O'Keefe
Michael E. Riley
Peter K. O'Keefe
Philip R. Dunn, Jr.
Kathryn M. Cunningham
Joseph M. Busher, Jr.
Kristen E. Scholhamer

Representative Clients: Travelers Aetna Property Casualty Co.; ITT Hartford; Liberty Mutual Insurance Co.; Connecticut Medical Insurance Co.

For full biographical listings, see the Martindale-Hubbell Law Directory

KENNY, BRIMMER, MELLEY & MAHONEY (AV)

5 Grand Street, 06106
Telephone: 860-527-4226
FAX: 860-527-0214

Joseph P. Kenny (1920-1993)

MEMBERS OF FIRM

William J. Melley, III
Richard C. Mahoney
Anita M. Varunes
Dennis F. McCarthy

ASSOCIATES

Shannon K. McCarthy
Flora Pizzoferrato

OF COUNSEL

Leslie R. Brimmer

For full biographical listings, see the Martindale-Hubbell Law Directory

O'BRIEN, TANSKI & YOUNG (AV)

CityPlace II, 06103
Telephone: 860-525-2700
Telefax: 860-247-7861

MEMBERS OF FIRM

Donald W. O'Brien
James M. Tanski
Roland F. Young, III
Robert D. Silva

OF COUNSEL

Hilary Fisher Nelson
Donna R. Zito
Richard A. O'Connor

ASSOCIATES

Albert G. Danker, Jr.
Agnes McDermott Alvord
Kathleen M. Nevins
Amy F. Goodusky
Andrew S. Wildstein
Angela D. Ober

References: Shawmut National Bank; New England Bank.

For full biographical listings, see the Martindale-Hubbell Law Directory

*NEW HAVEN,** New Haven Co.

GALLAGHER & CALISTRO (AV)

1377 Boulevard, P.O. Box 1925, 06509
Telephone: 203-624-4165
Fax: 203-865-5598

William F. Gallagher
Roger B. Calistro
Cynthia C. Bott
Barbara L. Cox
Kurt D. Koehler
Thomas J. Airone

For full biographical listings, see the Martindale-Hubbell Law Directory

JACOBS & JACOBS (AV)

Granite Square, 700 State Street, 3rd Floor, 06511
Telephone: 203-777-2300
Fax: 203-787-5628
Email: JACOBSLAW1@AOL.com

(See Next Column)

JACOBS & JACOBS, *New Haven—Continued*

MEMBERS OF FIRM

Israel J. Jacobs (1918-1963)
Stanley A. Jacobs
Bruce D. Jacobs
Carol Wolven
Irene Prosky Jacobs
Charles R. Douthat

Kevin Ryder

Reference: BankBoston.

For full biographical listings, see the Martindale-Hubbell Law Directory

KENNEDY, JOHNSON, D'ELIA & GILLOOLY (AV)

Long Wharf Maritime Center, 545 Long Wharf Drive, 06511
Telephone: 203-865-8430
Fax: 203-865-5345
Email: kennedyjoh@aol.com

MEMBERS OF FIRM

David H. Johnson
John J. Kennedy, Jr.
John J. D'Elia
Dennis Gillooly

ASSOCIATES

Robert L. Schwab
Stephanie Z. Roberge

Reference: Bank of Boston - Connecticut.

For full biographical listings, see the Martindale-Hubbell Law Directory

NEW LONDON, New London Co.

THE REARDON LAW FIRM, P.C. (AV)

160 Hempstead Street, Drawer 1430, 06320
Telephone: 860-442-0444
Telecopier: 860-444-6445
Email: reardonlaw@aol.com *URL:* http://www.reardonlaw.com

Robert I. Reardon, Jr.
Mark A. Dubois
Scott D. Camassar
Cynthia W. Sheppard
Gary W. Huebner

LEGAL SUPPORT PERSONNEL

Bette B. Beam (Legal Administrator)
Kimberly J. Friedel (Paralegal)
Rhonda K. Bourgeois (Paralegal)
Kyle E. Wininger (Paralegal)

For full biographical listings, see the Martindale-Hubbell Law Directory

STAMFORD, Fairfield Co.

HEIDELL, PITTONI, MURPHY & BACH, LLP (AV Ⓣ)

24 Richmond Hill Avenue, 06901
Telephone: 203-327-1800
Email: hpmb@hpmb.com
New York, New York Office: 99 Park Avenue.
Telephone: 212-286-8585.
Telecopier: 212-490-8966.

Luke M. Pittoni
Elizabeth Cornacchio
John F. Costa
Daniel S. Ratner

Janice Kirsten Lunde
Geraldine Koeneke Russell
Carol L. Morris-Fox
Robert W. Finke
Paul Sean Curtin
Matthew S. Hirsch
Leah J. Terranova

For full biographical listings, see the Martindale-Hubbell Law Directory

PIAZZA & PICKEL (AV)

112 Prospect Street, P.O. Box 15390, 06901
Telephone: 203-348-2465
Fax: 203-964-9509
Email: aap@piazza-pickel.com *URL:* http://www.piazza-pickel.com

Anthony A. Piazza
Alan Scott Pickel

ASSOCIATES

Tara C.F. Ryan
Michelle M. Napoli

For full biographical listings, see the Martindale-Hubbell Law Directory

ROSENBLUM & FILAN, L.L.C. (AV Ⓣ)

One Landmark Square, 06901
Telephone: 203-358-9200
Fax: 203-358-0687
Email: counsel@rosenblumfilan.com *URL:* http://www.rosenblumfilan.com
White Plains, New York Office: 50 Main Street.
Telephone: 914-686-6100.
Fax: 914-686-6140.
New York, New York Office: 400 Madison Avenue.
Telephone: 212-888-8001.
Fax: 212-888-3331.

(See Next Column)

MEMBERS OF FIRM

Patrick J. Filan
James B. Rosenblum
Alan S. Rubenstein
Samuel Tannenbaum
James S. Newfield

James F. Biondo
James A. Mahar

OF COUNSEL

Theodore J. Greene

For full biographical listings, see the Martindale-Hubbell Law Directory

SILVER, GOLUB & TEITELL LLP (AV)

184 Atlantic Street, P.O. Box 389, 06904
Telephone: 203-325-4491
Fax: 203-325-3769
Email: silvergolubteitell.com *URL:* http://www.sgtlaw.com

MEMBERS OF FIRM

Richard A. Silver
David S. Golub
Ernest F. Teitell
Patricia M. Haugh (1942-1988)
Elaine T. Silver
John D. Josel
Mario DiNatale
Jonathan M. Levine

Marilyn J. Ramos
Richard H. Greenwood
Mary G. Curry
Kathleen L. Brandt
Paul A. Slager (Not admitted in CT)
Brad C. Gustafson

For full biographical listings, see the Martindale-Hubbell Law Directory

WESTPORT, Fairfield Co.

LAW OFFICES OF PAUL J. PACIFICO (AV)

25 Ford Road, Suite 2, 06880
Telephone: 203-221-8066
Fax: 203-222-4833

For full biographical listings, see the Martindale-Hubbell Law Directory

DELAWARE

*WILMINGTON,** New Castle Co.

SMITH, KATZENSTEIN & FURLOW LLP (AV)

The Corporate Plaza, 800 Delaware Avenue, P.O. Box 410, 19899
Telephone: 302-652-8400
Fax: 302-652-8405
Email: info@skfdelaware.com *URL:* http://www.SKFDelaware.com

MEMBER OF FIRM

Robert J. Katzenstein

Kathleen M. Miller

For Complete List of Firm Personnel, See General Section

For full biographical listings, see the Martindale-Hubbell Law Directory

DISTRICT OF COLUMBIA

WASHINGTON, D.C. Co.

THE ABELSON LAW FIRM (AV)

1814 N Street, N.W., 20036
Telephone: 202-331-0600
1-888-797-4242
Fax: 202-429-9088
URL: http://www.abelsonlaw.com
Email: maa@abelsonlaw.com *URL:* http://www.lawyers.com/abelsonlaw
Boston, Massachusetts Office: 77 North Washington Street, 02114-1908.
Pittsburgh, Pennsylvania Office: 510 Third Avenue, 15219.
Philadelphia, Pennsylvania Office: 510 Walnut Street, 19106.

Michael A. Abelson

For full biographical listings, see the Martindale-Hubbell Law Directory

CHAIKIN & SHERMAN, P.C. (AV)

The Law Building, 1232 Seventeenth Street, N.W., 20036
Telephone: 202-659-8600
Fax: 202-659-8680
Email: DCLAW@CS.COM
Rockville, Maryland Office: 51 Monroe Street, 18th Floor.
Telephone: 301-588-5151.
Fax: 202-659-8680.

(See Next Column)

CHAIKIN & SHERMAN P.C.—*Continued*

Falls Church, Virginia Office: 5673 Columbia Pike, Suite 101.
Telephone: 202-659-8600.
Fax: 202-659-8680.

Donald J. Chaikin
Ira Sherman

Joseph Cammarata
Neil Florin
Allan M. Siegel
Barry I. Buchman
Garrett V. Williams

OF COUNSEL

Silverio Coy

For full biographical listings, see the Martindale-Hubbell Law Directory

THE FEINBERG GROUP, LLP (AV)

1120 20th Street, N.W. Suite 740 South, 20036-3437
Telephone: 202-371-1110
Fax: 202-962-9290
Email: kfeinberg@thefeinberggroup.com *URL:* http://www.krfassociates.com
New York, N.Y. Office: 780 3rd Avenue, Suite 2202.
Telephone: 212-527-9600.
Fax: 212-527-9611. Email: kfeinberg@thefeinberggroup.com.

PARTNERS

Kenneth R. Feinberg
Deborah E. Greenspan
Michael K. Rozen (Resident, New York Office)
Peter H. Woodin (Resident, New York Office)

ASSOCIATE

Fredric M. Brooks (Not admitted in DC)

SENIOR COUNSEL

Jacqueline E. Zins

For full biographical listings, see the Martindale-Hubbell Law Directory

AARON M. LEVINE & ASSOCIATES (AV)

1320 - 19th Street, N.W., 20036
Telephone: 202-833-8040
Fax: 202-833-8046
Email: lawkunst@aol.com

Brandon J. Levine
Renee L. Robinson-Meyer

For full biographical listings, see the Martindale-Hubbell Law Directory

JACK H. OLENDER AND ASSOCIATES, P.C. (AV)

888 17th Street, N.W., 4th Floor, 20006
Telephone: 202-879-7777
Fax: 202-393-2245
URL: http://www.olender.com
Email: jhopc@olender.com *URL:* http://www.lawyers.com/olenderlaw

Jack H. Olender

Harlow R. Case
Gary S. Freeman
Sandra H. Robinson
Kim Keenan Solomon
Narda M. Newby
Elizabeth Jesukiewicz Frey
Melissa Rhea

OF COUNSEL

Robert S. Chabon (Not admitted in DC)

For full biographical listings, see the Martindale-Hubbell Law Directory

PANGIA & HANSEN (AV)

1717 N Street, N.W., 20036
Telephone: 202-955-6450
Fax: 202-955-9444
Email: bchansen@erols.com *URL:* http://www.lawyers.com/aviation

MEMBERS OF FIRM

Michael J. Pangia
Barry C. Hansen

ASSOCIATE

Harold E. Rambo, Jr.

For full biographical listings, see the Martindale-Hubbell Law Directory

PAULSON & NACE (AV)

1814 N Street, N.W., 20036
Telephone: 202-463-1999
Fax: 202-223-6824
Email: p&n@lawtort.com *URL:* http://www.lawyers.com/lawtort
Martinsburg, West Virginia Office: 1444 Edwin Miller Boulevard, P.O. Box 1938, 25402.
Telephone: 888-529-2628.

MEMBERS OF FIRM

Richard S. Paulson (1928-1986)
Barry J. Nace

(See Next Column)

ASSOCIATE

James A. Ferguson

OF COUNSEL

Irving R. M. Panzer

For full biographical listings, see the Martindale-Hubbell Law Directory

THE ROBINSON LAW FIRM (AV)

Market Square, 717 D Street, N.W., 4th Floor, 20004
Telephone: 202-347-6100
Fax: 202-347-0081
URL: http://www.lawyers.com/robinsonlaw

MEMBER OF FIRM

Kenneth Michael Robinson

ASSOCIATES

Cameron Robinson Kourtesis (Not admitted in DC)
Nikolaos Panagiotis Kourtesis (Not admitted in DC)

For full biographical listings, see the Martindale-Hubbell Law Directory

SWARTZ & REED (AV)

1825 Jefferson Place, 20036
Telephone: 202-429-0429
Fax: 202-429-0109
Email: swartzreed@earthlink.net

MEMBERS OF FIRM

Dean E. Swartz
Barry S. Reed

OF COUNSEL

Allan W. Steinhorn

For full biographical listings, see the Martindale-Hubbell Law Directory

FLORIDA

*BARTOW,** Polk Co.

FROST & SAUNDERS, P.A. (AV)

395 South Central Avenue, P.O. Box 2188, 33830
Telephone: 941-533-0314; 800-533-0967
Telecopier: 941-533-8985
Email: jfrost1985@aol.com

John W. Frost, II
Thomas C. Saunders
Richard E. "Rick" Dantzler
John Marc Tamayo
Mark A. Sessums
Robert J. Aranda
Peter W. Van den Boom
Nicholas D. Zorn, Jr.

Reference: Community National Bank, Bartow.

For full biographical listings, see the Martindale-Hubbell Law Directory

BOCA RATON, Palm Beach Co.

GLICK & RETAMAR (AV)

Peninsula Plaza, 2424 North Federal Highway, Suite 460, 33431
Telephone: 561-391-0448
Fax: 561-391-6449
Email: lawboca@aol.com

Brian J. Glick
Richard E. Retamar

For full biographical listings, see the Martindale-Hubbell Law Directory

MICHAUD, BUSCHMANN, FOX, FERRARA & MITTELMARK, P.A. (AV)

33 Southeast 8th Street, 33432
Telephone: 561-392-0540
Fax: 561-392-0582
Email: Bocalaw@MBFFM.com *URL:* http://www.MBFFM.com

Scott H. Michaud
Paul Buschmann
Brian S. Fox
James T. Ferrara
Michael K. Mittelmark
Marc T. Millian

Marcy G. Blitz
Linda A. McCullough
Kimberly M. Hall

For full biographical listings, see the Martindale-Hubbell Law Directory

CORAL GABLES, Dade Co.

PARENTI, FALK, WAAS, HERNANDEZ & CORTINA, P.A. (AV)

113 Almeria Avenue, 33134
Telephone: 305-447-6500
Fax: 305-447-1777
Email: pfw@gate.net

(See Next Column)

PARENTI, FALK, WAAS, HERNANDEZ & CORTINA P.A., *Coral Gables—Continued*

Michael J. Parenti, III
Glenn P. Falk
Norman M. Waas
Edward Hernandez
Armando Cortina
Gail Leverett Parenti
Scott Solomon
Michael Patrick Bonner

Gonzalo Barr
Cheryl Lynn Potter

For full biographical listings, see the Martindale-Hubbell Law Directory

CRYSTAL RIVER, Citrus Co.

BEST & ANDERSON, P.A. (AV)

Executive Center Condos, 7655 West Gulf to Lake Highway, Suite 6, 34429
Telephone: 352-795-1107
Orlando, Florida Office: 1201 East Robinson Street, 32801.
Telephone: 407-425-2985.
Melbourne, Florida Office: Healthsouth Marina Towers, 709 South Harbor City Boulevard, Suite 270, 32901.
Telephone: 407-727-9923.

David R. Best
George H. "Dutch" Anderson, III

Angela O'Neil
James William Nuebel
Lora L. Wilson
Louis Allen DeFreitas, Jr.

For full biographical listings, see the Martindale-Hubbell Law Directory

DAYTONA BEACH, Volusia Co.

CHANFRAU, CHANFRAU & BOUCK (AV)

A Partnership of Professional Associations
701 North Peninsula Drive, P.O. Box 265880, 32126-5880
Telephone: 904-258-7313
Telecopier: 904-238-1464
Email: pclaw@mindspring.com

W. M. Chanfrau (P.A.)
Philip J. Chanfrau (P.A.)
Kim E. Bouck

Elizabeth R. Chanfrau

For full biographical listings, see the Martindale-Hubbell Law Directory

KOLODINSKY, SEITZ & TRESHER (AV)

647 South Ridgewood Avenue, P.O. Box 471, 32115-0471
Telephone: 904-253-9790
Fax: 904-253-9801
Email: kbsandt@worldnet.att.net *URL:* http://www.lawyers.com/kolodinsky,seitzandtresher
New Smyrna Beach, Florida Office: 707 East Third Avenue.
Telephone: 904-427-9811.
Facsimile: 904-427-7566.

MEMBERS OF FIRM

William H. Seitz
Frederick H. Tresher, III

For full biographical listings, see the Martindale-Hubbell Law Directory

*FORT LAUDERDALE,** Broward Co.

ABRAMOWITZ & POMERANTZ, P.A. (AV)

Suite 101, 7800 West Oakland Park Boulevard (Sunrise), 33351
Telephone: 954-572-7200
Fax: 954-748-6488
Email: abrpom@aol.com

Richard Abramowitz
Howard L. Pomerantz

Marc Stuart Schiller
Gordon Lea

Reference: NCNB National Bank of Florida.

For full biographical listings, see the Martindale-Hubbell Law Directory

BILLING, COCHRAN, HEATH, LYLES & MAURO, P.A. (AV)

Suite 301, 888 S.E. 3rd Avenue, 33316
Telephone: 954-764-7150
Fax: 954-764-7279
Email: bchlm@bchlm-pa.com *URL:* http://www.bchlm-pa.com
West Palm Beach, Florida Office: Reflections Office Centre, 400 Australian Avenue, Suite 801.
Telephones: 561-659-5970.
Fax: 561-659-6173.
Tampa, Florida Office: 3001 N. Rocky Point Drive East, Suite 200.
Telephone: 813-281-4671.
Fax: 813-289-7748.

(See Next Column)

Steven F. Billing (1947-1998)
Clark J. Cochran, Jr.
Thomas C. Heath
Dennis E. Lyles
John W. Mauro
Gregory T. Anderson (Resident, West Palm Beach Office)
William Tucker Craig
Kenneth W. Morgan, Jr.
Aline O. Marcantonio
Shawn B. McKamey
Kevin M. Vannatta
Vivian Hattem Fazio
Michael A. Weiss
T. Christine Perez
Hal B. Anderson
Carol J. Healy Glasgow

Representative Clients: City of Fort Lauderdale; The St. Paul Insurance Co.; Caduceus Self Insurance Fund; Government Employees Insurance Co.; Prudential Insurance Co.; The Travelers; Shelby Mutual Insurance Co.; Guardian Life Insurance Company of America; State Farm Fire & Casualty Co.; Holy Cross Hospital.

For full biographical listings, see the Martindale-Hubbell Law Directory

CONRAD & SCHERER (AV)

A Partnership of Professional Associations
Eighth Floor, 633 South Federal Highway, P.O. Box 14723, 33302
Telephone: 954-462-5500
Facsimile: 954-463-9244
Miami, Florida Office: 44 West Flagler Street, Suite 402, 33130.
Telephone: 305-856-9920.
Facsimile: 305-374-4408.

MEMBERS OF FIRM

William R. Scherer, Jr., (P.A.)
Gary S. Genovese (P.A.)
William V. Carcioppolo (P.A.)
Linda Rae Spaulding (P.A.)
Reid A. Cocalis (P.A.)
Willie Earl Hall (P.A.)
Ronald A. FitzGerald
James F. Carroll
Paul R. Larkin, Jr.
Dominic L. Brandy

OF COUNSEL

Rex Conrad

ASSOCIATES

Albert L. Frevola, Jr.
William R. Scherer, III
Vanessa A. Reynolds
Douglas Todd Marx
Janine Renee Kalagher
James A. Epstein
Angel Petti
Nicholas William Romanello
Shari L. McCartney
Catherine M. Rodriguez
Wendy A. Delvecchio

Local Counsel for: American Home Assurance Group; Caterpillar Tractor Co.; Division of Risk Management, State of Florida; Florida East Coast Railway; Fort Motor Co.; Liberty Mutual Insurance Co.; Ryder Truck Lines; Unigard Insurance Group.
Approved Attorneys for: Attorneys' Title Insurance Fund.
Reference: Barnett Bank of Fort Lauderdale.

For full biographical listings, see the Martindale-Hubbell Law Directory

COONEY, MATTSON, LANCE, BLACKBURN, RICHARDS & O'CONNOR, P.A. (AV)

2312 Wilton Drive, P.O. Box 14546, 33302
Telephone: Telephone: 954-568-6669
WATS: 1-800-745-3864
Telecopier: 954-568-0085
Email: cooney2312@aol.com
Orlando, Florida Office: Nations Bank Tower, 111 N. Orange Avenue, Suite 1020.
Telephone: 407-843-2100.
Fax: 407-843-2061.

David F. Cooney
Michael C. Mattson
Victor Lance (1956-1995)
Ace J. Blackburn, Jr.
John H. Richards
Dennis R. O'Connor (Resident, Orlando, Florida Office)
Bruce Michael Trybus
Walter C. Wyatt
Kieran F. O'Connor (Resident, Orlando, Florida Office)
Michele McCaul Ricca
Daniel F. Tordella

Laura Douglas
Warren Kwavnick
Rochelle Bocksch
Weslee S. Arciola
Alphonso O. Peets
Robert M. Potter, III
Elizabeth Y. Foshee (Resident, Orlando Office)

Representative Clients: The Travellers; RISCORP; CIGNA Insurance Co.; Claims Center; Fiesco; Multi-Line Claims Service, Inc.; Carpenter Contractors of America; City Furniture; CNA Insurance.

For full biographical listings, see the Martindale-Hubbell Law Directory

HALICZER, PETTIS & WHITE, P.A. (AV)

101 Northeast Third Avenue, Sixth Floor, 33301
Telephone: 954-523-9922
Fax: 954-522-2512
Orlando, Florida Office: NationsBank Building, Suite 1275, 111 North Orange Avenue. 32801.
Telephone: 407-841-9866.
Fax: 407-841-9915.

(See Next Column)

HALICZER, PETTIS & WHITE P.A.—*Continued*

James S. Haliczer
Eugene K. Pettis
Kenneth E. White

Amy B. Talisman
Anthony K. Goodman
Anthony V. Scalese
Debra B. Potter
William Bassett, Jr.
Frank J. Taddeo

For full biographical listings, see the Martindale-Hubbell Law Directory

THE LAW OFFICES OF DAVID KRATHEN A PROFESSIONAL ASSOCIATION (AV)

888 East Las Olas Boulevard Suite 200, 33301
Telephone: 954-467-6400; 888-254-7066
Email: david@davidkrathen.com

David H. Krathen

Randall Rutledge
Michael Sean Freedland

For full biographical listings, see the Martindale-Hubbell Law Directory

KRUPNICK CAMPBELL MALONE ROSELLI BUSER SLAMA HANCOCK MCNELIS LIBERMAN & MCKEE, P.A. (AV)

700 Southeast 3rd Avenue, Suite 100, 33316-1186
Telephone: 954-763-8181; 877-763-8181 (Toll Free)
Fax: 954-763-8292
Email: information@krupnicklaw.com *URL:* http://www.krupnicklaw.com

Jon E. Krupnick
Walter G. Campbell, Jr.
Kevin A. Malone
Richard J. Roselli
Thomas E. Buser
Joseph J. Slama
Kelly D. Hancock
Lisa A. McNelis
Scott S. Liberman
Robert J. McKee

Carlos Acevedo (Not admitted in FL)
Louis R. Battista
Ivan F. Cabrera
Robert D. Erben
Kelley Badger Gelb
Sean J. Greene
Holly Debra Krulik
Michael J. Ryan

OF COUNSEL

Ben J. Weaver
Dianne Jay Weaver

Reference: Mellon United National Bank.

For full biographical listings, see the Martindale-Hubbell Law Directory

KUVIN & STETTIN, P.A. (AV)

888 East Las Olas Boulevard Suite 710, 33301
Telephone: 954-462-1809
Facsimile: 954-462-1830
Email: lkuvin@aol.com

Lawrence P. Kuvin
Eric L. Stettin

For full biographical listings, see the Martindale-Hubbell Law Directory

SISTARE & ASSOCIATES (AV)

600 South Andrews Avenue, Suite 600, 33301
Telephone: 954-522-2320
Fax: 954-522-2223
Email: sistare@gate.net *URL:* http://www.sistare.com

MEMBER OF FIRM

Susan P. Sistare

ASSOCIATE

Jahna Y. (Jay) Hoyte

For full biographical listings, see the Martindale-Hubbell Law Directory

WILTON L. STRICKLAND, P.A. (AV)

1401 East Broward Boulevard, Suite 303, P.O. Box 14246, 33301
Telephone: 954-760-4700; 800-760-8401
Telecopier: 954-779-7749
Email: sands@gate.net *URL:* http://www.wiltonstricklandpa.com

Wilton L. Strickland

Alexander Clark

For full biographical listings, see the Martindale-Hubbell Law Directory

*GAINESVILLE,** Alachua Co.

STRIPLING, MCMICHAEL & STRIPLING, P.A. (AV)

102 N.W. Second Avenue, P.O. Box 1287, 32602
Telephone: 352-376-8888
Fax: 352-376-4645
Email: attys@sms-pa.com *URL:* http://www.lawyers.com/smslaw

(See Next Column)

Robert O. Stripling, Jr.
Alan E. McMichael
Sylvia A. K. Stripling

For full biographical listings, see the Martindale-Hubbell Law Directory

*JACKSONVILLE,** Duval Co.

GLENN K. ALLEN A PROFESSIONAL ASSOCIATION (AV)

The Plaza Building, 353 East Forsyth Street, 32202-2822
Telephone: 904-355-7506
Facsimile: 904-353-8814
URL: http://www.glennallenpa.com
Email: GKA@glennallenpa.com *URL:* http://www.lawyers.com/glennallen

Glenn K. Allen

Jennifer Workinger Fites

For full biographical listings, see the Martindale-Hubbell Law Directory

BROWN, TERRELL, HOGAN, ELLIS, MCCLAMMA & YEGELWEL, P.A. (AV)

Suite 804 Blackstone Building, 233 East Bay Street, 32202-3417
Telephone: 904-632-2424
Fax: 904-632-2027
Email: mail@bthemy-law.com *URL:* http://www.bthemy-law.com

Thomas R. Brown
James T. Terrell
Wayne Hogan
Timothy D. Ellis
T. Edward McClamma
Evan J. Yegelwel
Thomas E. Duffy, Jr.
Christopher G. Burns
Anita Pryor
Alan M. Pickert

Carroll Cayer
Michael S. Sharrit
Theodore Samuel Pina, Jr.
Mark E. Calvin
Leslie A. Goller
Patricia M. Dodson
Jennifer Kolinski Millis

Reference: NCNB.

For full biographical listings, see the Martindale-Hubbell Law Directory

COKER, MYERS, SCHICKEL, SORENSON, HIGGINBOTHAM & GREEN, P.A. (AV)

136 East Bay Street, P.O. Box 1860, 32201
Telephone: 904-356-6071
Fax: 904-353-2425

Howard C. Coker
M. Wayne Myers
John J. Schickel
Charles A. Sorenson
Wm. Earl Higginbotham
Samuel H. Lanier
J. Thomas McKeel
Mark M. Green
R. Daniel Noey
Ronald M. Owen
John Moffitt Howell
James H. Daniel
Richard R. Alexander

For full biographical listings, see the Martindale-Hubbell Law Directory

GENTRY, PHILLIPS AND HODAK, P.A. (AV)

Suite 400, 6 East Bay Street, 32202
Telephone: 904-356-4100
Fax: 904-358-1895

William C. Gentry
Mary Kleyla Phillips
Corinne C. Hodak

Angelo M. Patacca, Jr.

For full biographical listings, see the Martindale-Hubbell Law Directory

LILES, GAVIN & COSTANTINO (AV)

One Enterprise Center, Suite 1500, 225 Water Street, 32202
Telephone: 904-634-1100
Fax: 904-634-1234
Email: triallaw@bellsouth.net

Rutledge R. Liles
R. Kyle Gavin
R. Scott Costantino

ASSOCIATES

Niels P. Murphy
Robert Bruce George

For full biographical listings, see the Martindale-Hubbell Law Directory

RICHARD L. NICHOLS (AV)

3000 Hartley Road, Suite 5, 32257
Telephone: 904-886-7010
Fax: 904-886-7282

For full biographical listings, see the Martindale-Hubbell Law Directory

Jacksonville—Continued

PAJCIC & PAJCIC, P.A. (AV)

1900 Independent Square, 32202
Telephone: 904-358-8881
Fax: 904-354-1180
Email: attorneys@pajcic.com *URL:* http://www.pajcic.com

Gary Pajcic
Stephen J. Pajcic, III
William S. Burns, Jr.
Curtis Stephen Pajcic
Robert J. Link
Lee T. Griffin
Christine A. Clark
Thomas F. Slater
Curry Gary Pajcic

Reference: Barnett Bank of Jacksonville, N.A.

For full biographical listings, see the Martindale-Hubbell Law Directory

---

SAALFIELD, COULSON, SHAD & JAY, P.A. (AV)

225 Water Street, Suite 1000, 32202-4458
Telephone: 904-355-4401
Fax: 904-355-3503
Email: SCJ4401@BellSouth.net

John R. Saalfield
Michael I. Coulson
Charles Thomas Shad
Harvey L. Jay, III
Joseph B. Stokes, III

Gail A Stafford
Brett Q. Lucas
Carl Scott Schuler

Representative Clients: American Continental Ins. Co.; Baptist/St. Vincent's Health System; Century Products; CNA Ins. Co.; Cosco, Inc.; Crawford & Co.; Dependable Protective Mutual; Dillard Dept. Stores, Inc.; First Floridian Ins. Co.; Florida Podiatrist Trust.

For full biographical listings, see the Martindale-Hubbell Law Directory

---

MATTHEW W. SOWELL, P.A. (AV)

One Independent Drive, Suite 3204, 32202
Telephone: 904-358-9000
Telecopier: 904-350-9093

Matthew W. Sowell

For full biographical listings, see the Martindale-Hubbell Law Directory

---

LARGO, Pinellas Co.

WILLIAM S. JONASSEN, P.A. (AV)

10785 Ulmerton Road, 34648
Telephone: 727-586-1484
Fax: 727-585-9818
Mailing Address: P.O. Box 366, Indian Rocks Beach, FL, 33785
Email: wjonass1@tampabayrr.com

William S. Jonassen

Representative Clients: Florida Lawyers Indemnity Group; Florida Podiatrist Trust; Gulf Atlantic Insurance Co.; Sun Coast Hospital.
General Counsel for: First National Bank of Florida.

For full biographical listings, see the Martindale-Hubbell Law Directory

---

MAITLAND, Orange Co.

BAILEY & MYERS, P.A. (AV)

100 East Sybelia Avenue Suite 375, 32751
Telephone: 407-628-2929
Fax: 407-628-3909
URL: http://www.baileymyers.com

Michael K. Bailey
Donald A. Myers, Jr.

For full biographical listings, see the Martindale-Hubbell Law Directory

---

MELBOURNE, Brevard Co.

BEST & ANDERSON, P.A. (AV)

Healthsouth Marina Towers, 709 South Harbor City Boulevard, Suite 270, 32901
Telephone: 407-727-9923
Orlando, Florida Office: 1201 East Robinson Street, 32801.
Telephone: 407-425-2985.
Crystal River, Florida Office: Executive Center Condos, 7655 West Gulf to Lake Highway, Suite 6, 34429.
Telephone: 352-795-1107.

David R. Best
George H. "Dutch" Anderson, III

Angela O'Neil
James William Nuebel
Lora L. Wilson
Louis Allen DeFreitas, Jr.

For full biographical listings, see the Martindale-Hubbell Law Directory

NANCE, CACCIATORE AND HAMILTON (AV)

525 North Harbor City Boulevard, 32935
Telephone: 321-254-8416
Fax: 321-259-8243
Email: nancacc@iu.net

MEMBERS OF FIRM

James H. Nance
S. Sammy Cacciatore
John N. Hamilton
Charles G. Barger, Jr.
James N. Nance
Sammy M. Cacciatore

Reference: The Bank.

For full biographical listings, see the Martindale-Hubbell Law Directory

---

*MIAMI,** Dade Co.

ANGONES, HUNTER, MCCLURE, LYNCH & WILLIAMS, P.A. (AV)

Ninth Floor-Concord Building, 66 West Flagler Street, 33130-1805
Telephone: 305-371-5000
Fort Lauderdale: 954-728-9112
Fax: 305-371-3948
Fort Lauderdale, Florida Office: Suite 203N Justice Building, 524 South Andrews Avenue.
Telephone: 954-779-3456.
Fax: 954-832-0037.

Frank R. Angones
Steven Kent Hunter
John McClure
Christopher J. Lynch
Stewart D. Williams
B. Scott Hunter
Leopoldo Garcia, Jr.

Thomas W. Paradise (Resident, Fort Lauderdale Office)
Donna Joy Hunter
Lourdes Alfonsin Ruiz
Kara D. Phinney

Insurance Clients: Allstate Insurance Co.; Prudential Property & Casualty Insurance Co.; Travelers Insurance Co.; Rollins Hudig Hall Healthcare Risk, Inc.

For Complete List of Firm Personnel, See General Section

For full biographical listings, see the Martindale-Hubbell Law Directory

---

DEUTSCH & BLUMBERG, P.A. (AV)

Suite 2802 New World Tower, 100 North Biscayne Boulevard, 33132
Telephone: 305-358-6329
Fax: 305-358-9304

Steven K. Deutsch
Edward R. Blumberg
James C. Blecke
Louis Thaler

For full biographical listings, see the Martindale-Hubbell Law Directory

---

FELDMAN GALE & WEBER, P.A. (AV)

201 South Biscayne Boulevard, 19th Floor, 33131-4329
Telephone: 305-358-5001
Fax: 305-358-3309
Email: fgwlaw@fgwlaw.com
Suffield, Connecticut Office: 40 Crane Hill Road, 06078.
Telephone: 860-668-0226.
Fax: 860-668-0696. Email: WCNEALON@FGWLAW.COM; WCNEALON@AOL.COM.

Jeffrey D. Feldman
James A. Gale
Michael J. Weber

Sean N. R. Wells
John C. Carey
Jennifer Johnson Watkins
Ozzie A. Farres
Nancy J. Flint
Greg Tung Nguyen

OF COUNSEL

William C. Nealon (Not admitted in FL)

For full biographical listings, see the Martindale-Hubbell Law Directory

---

FORD & SINCLAIR, P.A. (AV)

Penthouse 1-C, Two Datran Center, 9130 South Dadeland Boulevard, 33156
Telephone: 305-670-2000
Facsimile: 305-670-1353;
Toll Free-Florida only: 1-888-372-2873
Email: kip@fordsinclair.corpusa.com

T. Patrick Ford, Jr.
Charles H. Sinclair
Virginia S. Forbes

Douglas Fredric Eaton

For full biographical listings, see the Martindale-Hubbell Law Directory

Miami—Continued

FOURNARIS & SANET, P.A. (AV)

145 Almeria Avenue (Coral Gables), 33134
Telephone: 305-448-7333
Telefax: 305-448-7394
URL: http://www.lawyers.com/fournaris

Theodore J. Fournaris
Morton J. Sanet

For full biographical listings, see the Martindale-Hubbell Law Directory

FRIEDMAN AND FRIEDMAN, P.A. (AV)

Suite 1011 Barnett Bank Building, 2600 Douglas Road (S.W. 37th Avenue) (Coral Gables), 33134
Telephone: 305-446-6485; 800-446-6482
Telefax: 305-448-7636
Cable Address: "BARISTER"

Marvin Ross Friedman
Gary Alan Friedman

John Schyler Seligman

For full biographical listings, see the Martindale-Hubbell Law Directory

GEORGE, HARTZ, LUNDEEN, FLAGG & FULMER (AV)

4800 LeJeune Road (Coral Gables), 33146
Telephone: 305-662-4800
Fax: 305-667-8015
Fort Lauderdale, Florida Office: Suite 300 Justice Building East, 524 South Andrews Avenue, 33301.
Telephone: 954-462-1620.
Fax: 954-524-3810.
Fort Myers, Florida Office: Suite 402, Huntington Plaza, 2000 Main Street, 33901.
Telephone: 941-337-7787.
Fax: 941-337-4303.
Tallahassee, Florida Office: 800 N. Calhoun Street, 32303.
Telephone: 850-224-5252.
Fax: 850-222-3082.
West Palm Beach, Florida Office: 312 Clematis Street, Anthony Building, Suite 301, 33401.
Telephone: 561-366-9772.
Fax: 561-366-9783.
Orlando, Florida Office: Winter Park Plaza, Suite 150, 1560 Orange Avenue (Winter Park), 32789.
Telephone: 407-539-0700.
Fax: 407-539-0890.

Charles K. George
Charles Michael Hartz
Mitchell L. Lundeen
Clinton D. Flagg
Liana C. Silsby (Resident, Fort Lauderdale Office)
C. Richard Fulmer, Jr. (Resident, Fort Lauderdale Office)
A. Scott Lundeen
David V. King (Resident, West Palm Beach Office)
Crane A. Johnstone (Resident, Fort Lauderdale Office)
Douglas W. Barnes (Resident, Fort Lauderdale Office)
Craig R. Stevens (Resident at Ft. Myers Office)
Lynne E. Denneler (Resident, Fort Myers Office)
John R. Buchholz
Esther E. Galicia (Resident, Fort Lauderdale Office)
R. David de Armas (Resident, Orlando Office)
Maria A. Santoro (Resident, Tallahassee Office)
Michael H. Imber (Resident, West Palm Beach Office)

ASSOCIATES

Peter K. Spillis
Susan Bernhardt Rogers (Resident at Ft. Lauderdale Office)
Misty Merri Catherine Taylor
Michael W. LeRoy (Resident, Orlando Office)
Jack R. Simmons
Scott B. Albee (Resident, Fort Myers Office)
Merrilee A. Jobes (Resident, Fort Lauderdale Office)
Kristin Heller Woolam (Resident, Fort Myers Office)
Daniel D. Dolan, II
Paul C. Buckley (Resident, Fort Lauderdale Office)
James B. Birmingham (Resident, Orlando Office)
Joel Elizabeth Marano (Resident, Orlando Office)
Cesar A. Sastre
Stacey Z. Margulies
K. Mitch Espat (Resident, Orlando Office)
Christopher W. Royer (Resident, Fort Lauderdale Office)
Gary F. Baumann (Resident, Fort Lauderdale Office)
Brian J. Huott (Resident, West Palm Beach Office)
Michael L. Glass
H. Lawrence Hardy (Resident, Tallahassee Office)
Melissa A. Schlutow (Resident, Fort Lauderdale Office)
Jason S. Robbins (Resident, Fort Lauderdale Office)
Jack C. Morgan III (Resident, Fort Myers Office)
Sean A. Clarke (Resident, West Palm Beach Office)
Neal C. Falk (Resident, West Palm Beach Office)

OF COUNSEL

A. Blackwell Stieglitz

For full biographical listings, see the Martindale-Hubbell Law Directory

HILLENCAMP & ALVAREZ, P.A. (AV)

Gifford House, 2937 S.W. 27th Avenue (Coconut Grove), 33133
Telephone: 305-444-7675
Fax: 305-444-0075
Email: Trialteam@MSN.com

Ibis J. Hillencamp
Alex Alvarez

For full biographical listings, see the Martindale-Hubbell Law Directory

HOPPE & STOKES, P.A. (AV)

2nd Floor, Concord Building, 66 West Flagler Street, 33130
Telephone: 305-358-9060
Fax: 305-374-6801
URL: http://www.hoppestokes.com
Email: pilaw@hoppestokes.com *URL:* http://www.lawyers.com/hoppestokes

Bill Hoppe
Mark L. Stokes

Jacinto J. Gonzalez
Eric Matthew Ellsley
LeAnna Vasquez

For full biographical listings, see the Martindale-Hubbell Law Directory

LEVINE, BUSCH, SCHNEPPER & STEIN, P.A. (AV)

Suite 1010 One Datran Center, 9100 South Dadeland Boulevard, 33156
Telephone: 305-670-2333
Fax: 305-670-0716
Email: LEVBUSSCHS@aol.com *URL:* http://www.lawofficesoflbss.com
Broward Office: 100 South Pine Island Road, Suite 202, Plantation, Florida, 33324.
Telephone: 954-922-0800.

David H. Levine
Edward P. Busch
R. Cory Schnepper
Barry A. Stein

Sanford M. Reinstein

For full biographical listings, see the Martindale-Hubbell Law Directory

RUSSO & HEFFERNAN, P.A. (AV)

7990 Red Road, 33143
Telephone: 305-665-7171
Fax: 305-665-7146
Email: lawyers@rhpa.com *URL:* http://www.lawyers.com/russo&heffernan

Don Russo
David R. Heffernan

For full biographical listings, see the Martindale-Hubbell Law Directory

SAMS & LISTER, P.A. (AV)

73255 West 63 Avenue, Suite 201, 33143
Telephone: 305-740-5401
Fax: 305-740-5425

Murray Sams, Jr.
David P. Lister

Arthur B. Stark

For full biographical listings, see the Martindale-Hubbell Law Directory

THORNTON, MASTRUCCI & MINKIN (AV)

(Formerly Thornton, Mastrucci & Sinclair)
4699 Ponce de Leon Boulevard (Coral Gables), 33146
Telephone: 305-668-0100
Facsimile: 305-668-0400
Email: THORNTON@MSN.COM

MEMBERS OF FIRM

John W. Thornton, Sr.
Jane Thornton Mastrucci
Michael Minkin

ASSOCIATE

Cynthia Harrison Ruiz

For full biographical listings, see the Martindale-Hubbell Law Directory

MIAMI LAKES, Dade Co.

MARTIN, LIPSKY, KAUFMAN & WEINSTEIN, P.A. (AV)

7975 Northwest 154th Street Suite 230, 33016
Telephone: 305-362-6222
Fax: 305-362-0111
URL: http://www.lawyers.com/personalinjurypros

Timothy M. Martin
Joseph I. Lipsky
Daniel L. Kaufman
Mark S. Weinstein

For full biographical listings, see the Martindale-Hubbell Law Directory

NEW SMYRNA BEACH, Volusia Co.

KOLODINSKY, SEITZ & TRESHER (AV)

707 East Third Avenue, 32169
Telephone: 904-427-9811
Facsimile: 904-427-7566
Email: kbsandt@worldnet.att.net *URL:* http://www.lawyers.com/kolodinsky,seitzandtresher
Daytona Beach, Florida Office: 647 South Ridgewood Avenue, P.O. Box 471.
Telephone: 904-253-9790.
Fax: 904-253-9801.

MEMBERS OF FIRM

Rick Kolodinsky
William H. Seitz
Frederick H. Tresher, III

For full biographical listings, see the Martindale-Hubbell Law Directory

NICEVILLE, Okaloosa Co.

STANLEY BRUCE POWELL, P.A. (AV)

107 North Partin Drive, P.O. Box 400, 32588-0400
Telephone: 850-678-2118
Fax: 850-678-8336
Email: BPOWELLPA@AOL.COM

Stanley Bruce Powell
David R. Swanick III

Representative Clients: Peoples National Bank of Niceville; Destin Bank; Big Kahuna's, Inc.
References: Peoples National Bank of Niceville; Destin Bank; Vanguard Bank and Trust Co.

For full biographical listings, see the Martindale-Hubbell Law Directory

NORTH PALM BEACH, Palm Beach Co.

BOBO, SPICER, CIOTOLI, FULFORD, BOCCHINO & DEBEVOISE, P.A. (AV)

1240 U.S. Highway One, 33408
Telephone: 561-684-6600
Fax: 561-622-6288
Email: info@bobospicer.com *URL:* http://www.bobospicer.com
Orlando, Florida Office: Landmark Center One, Suite 510, 315 East Robinson Street, 32801-1949.
Telephone: 407-849-1060.
Fax: 407-843-4751.
Clearwater, Florida Office: 300 Turner Street, 33756.
Telephone: 727-443-6663.

A. Russell Bobo
David W. Spicer
Eugene L. Ciotoli
Jeffrey C. Fulford
John W. Bocchino
D. Andrew DeBevoise (Resident, Orlando Office)
Armando T. Lauritano
Raul Romaguera
Gregorio A. Francis (Resident, Orlando Office)
Michael D. Burt
Casey D. Shomo
J. Clancey Bounds (Resident, Orlando Office)

Thomas W. Poulton (Resident, Orlando Office)
Damian M. Fletcher
Michael D. Starks (Resident, Orlando Office)
Anthony P. Corsini
Ian D. Forsythe (Resident, Orlando Office)
Scott L. Reed (Resident, Orlando Office)
Amy M. Dukes
Denise L. Dawson
Deborah L. Moskowitz (Resident, Orlando Office)

For full biographical listings, see the Martindale-Hubbell Law Directory

*ORLANDO,** Orange Co.

BEST & ANDERSON, P.A. (AV)

1201 East Robinson Street, 32801
Telephone: 407-425-2985
Email: cab@bestandanderson.com *URL:* http://www.bestandanderson.com
Crystal River, Florida Office: Executive Center Condos, 7655 West Gulf to Lake Highway, Suite 6, 34429.
Telephone: 352-795-1107.
Melbourne, Florida Office: Healthsouth Marina Towers, 709 South Harbor City Boulevard, Suite 270, 32901.
Telephone: 407-727-9923.

David R. Best
George H. "Dutch" Anderson, III

Angela O'Neil
James William Nuebel
Lora L. Wilson
Louis Allen DeFreitas, Jr.

For full biographical listings, see the Martindale-Hubbell Law Directory

BILLINGS, CUNNINGHAM, MORGAN & BOATWRIGHT, PROFESSIONAL ASSOCIATION (AV)

330 East Central Boulevard, 32801
Telephone: 407-425-2000
Fax: 407-843-8274
Email: info@bcmb.com *URL:* http://www.bcmb.com

James Cunningham
Mary Ann Morgan
Joseph E. Boatwright, Jr.
Tracy L. Troutman-Cheek
Gary D. Vasquez
Randy E. Schimmelpfennig

OF COUNSEL

Jared M. Billings

For full biographical listings, see the Martindale-Hubbell Law Directory

BOBO, SPICER, CIOTOLI, FULFORD, BOCCHINO & DEBEVOISE, P.A. (AV)

Landmark Center One, Suite 510, 315 East Robinson Street, 32801-1949
Telephone: 407-849-1060
Fax: 407-843-4751
Email: info@bobospicer.com *URL:* http://www.bobospicer.com
North Palm Beach, Florida Office: 1240 U.S. Highway One, 33408.
Telephone: 561-684-6600.
FAX: 561-622-6288.
Clearwater, Florida Office: 300 Turner Street, 33756.
Telephone: 727-443-6663.

John W. Bocchino
D. Andrew DeBevoise
Armando T. Lauritano
Gregorio A. Francis
J. Clancey Bounds

Thomas W. Poulton
Michael D. Starks
Ian D. Forsythe
Scott L. Reed
Deborah L. Moskowitz

For full biographical listings, see the Martindale-Hubbell Law Directory

NOLAN CARTER, P.A. (AV)

1218 East Robinson Street, P.O. Box 2229, 32802
Telephone: 407-898-3535
Fax: 407-898-5055
Email: carmedneg@aol.com

Nolan Carter

Karen Reed Wasson

For full biographical listings, see the Martindale-Hubbell Law Directory

COONEY, MATTSON, LANCE, BLACKBURN, RICHARDS & O'CONNOR, P.A. (AV)

Nations Bank Tower, 111 North Orange Avenue Suite 1020, 32801
Telephone: 407-843-2100
Fax: 407-843-2061
Fort Lauderdale, Florida Office: 2312 Wilton Drive. P.O. Box 14546. 33302.
Telephone: 954-568-6669.
Telecopier: 954-568-0085.

Dennis R. O'Connor
Kieran F. O'Connor

Elizabeth Y. Foshee (Resident)

For full biographical listings, see the Martindale-Hubbell Law Directory

DELLECKER, WILSON & KING, P.A. (AV)

719 Vassar Street, 32804
Telephone: 407-244-3000
Fax: 407-244-3033
Email: attorneys@dwklaw.com *URL:* http://www.dwklaw.com

Robert H. "Bob" Dellecker
Brian T. Wilson
Samuel P. King
Leticia J. Marques
Kenneth J. McKenna

For full biographical listings, see the Martindale-Hubbell Law Directory

EUBANKS, HILYARD & BOGAN, P.A. (AV)

Suite 600 First Union Building, 20 North Orange Avenue, P.O. Box 4973, 32802-4973
Telephone: 407-425-4251
Telecopier: 407-841-8431

Ernest H. Eubanks
Rodney G. Ross (1934-1982)
Sutton G. Hilyard, Jr.
Bruce R. Bogan

Bobby G. Palmer, Jr.
W. Gregory Lockeby

Representative Clients: AIG Aviation, Inc.; AVEMCO Insurance Co.; Phoenix Aviation Managers, Inc.; Ranger Insurance Co.; Old Republic Insurance Co.; Signal Aviation Underwriters; Underwriters at Lloyds; Orange County Sheriff's Office; United Technologies Corp.; Reliance Insurance Co.

(See Next Column)

EUBANKS, HILYARD & BOGAN, P.A.—*Continued*

For full biographical listings, see the Martindale-Hubbell Law Directory

HILL AND PONTON, PROFESSIONAL ASSOCIATION (AV)

Suite 500, 605 East Robinson Street, P.O. Box 2673, 32802
Telephone: 407-422-4665
URL: http://www.hillponton.com

Brian D. Hill
Carol J. Ponton

Maria D. Santana (Not admitted in FL)
Silvia R. Sanders
Jeffrey D. Starker

For full biographical listings, see the Martindale-Hubbell Law Directory

HILL, REIS, ADAMS, HALL & SCHIEFFELIN, P.A. (AV)

1417 East Concord Street, 32803
Telephone: 407-896-0425
Fax: 407-896-9236
Email: mainbox@hrahs.com

G. Bruce Hill
Gregory F. Reis
Janet W. Adams
Larry D. Hall
Thomas L. Schieffelin, Jr.
William W. Large
Matthew P. Bartolomei

David O Doyle, Jr
Andrew Vlahos
Heidi Jo Haycook

Representative Clients: The Florida Hospital Trust Fund; The Florida Hospital Excess Trust Fund; Florida Hospital Workers Compensation/Self Insurance Trust Fund; Bartow Memorial Hospital; Bay Medical Center; Brooksville Regional Hospital; Cape Canaveral Hospital; Cape Coral Hospital; Desoto Memorial Hospital.

For full biographical listings, see the Martindale-Hubbell Law Directory

KELAHER LAW OFFICES, P.A. (AV)

Suite 1301, 800 North Magnolia Avenue, 32803
Telephone: 407-841-7698
Fax: 407-649-7760
Email: jim@kelaherlaw.com

James P. Kelaher

For full biographical listings, see the Martindale-Hubbell Law Directory

KARL O. KOEPKE (AV)

801 North Magnolia Avenue, Suite 107, 32803
Telephone: 407-841-0023
Fax: 407-425-4761
Email: klawfl@aol.com

ASSOCIATE

Michael H. Truax

For full biographical listings, see the Martindale-Hubbell Law Directory

MAHER, GIBSON AND GUILEY A PROFESSIONAL ASSOCIATION OF LAWYERS (AV)

Suite 200, 90 East Livingston Street, 32801
Telephone: 407-839-0866
Fax: 407-425-7958

Michael Maher
Patricia M. Gibson
David D. Guiley

Steven R. Maher
Robin Orosz Sharp
Jennifer Gentry Fernandez
Melissa H. Powers

LEGAL SUPPORT PERSONNEL

INSURANCE CLAIM COORDINATOR

Charles R. Simpson

For full biographical listings, see the Martindale-Hubbell Law Directory

MCEWAN, MARTINEZ, LUFF, DUKES & RUFFIER, P.A. (AV)

108 East Central Boulevard, P.O. Box 753, 32801
Telephone: 407-423-8571
Fax: 407-423-8637

Wilson Sanders (1911-1981)
O. Beverley McEwan (1913-1995)
John S. McEwan, II
Rafael E. "Ralph" Martinez
H. David Luff
Thomas E. Dukes, III
William E. Ruffier
Tyler S. McClay

(See Next Column)

Juan A. Ruiz
Ruth C. Osborne
Susan D. Kennedy

Representative Clients: Bridgestone/Firestone, Inc.; City Cab of Orlando, Inc.; CNA Insurance Company; Dependable Protective Mutual; Florida Physicians Insurance Co.; Gulf Atlantic Insurance Co.; Marine Office of America; M.C.I. Telecommunications Corporation.

For full biographical listings, see the Martindale-Hubbell Law Directory

MCMILLEN, REINHART & VOGHT, P.A. (AV)

20 North Orange Avenue, Suite 700, 32801
Telephone: 407-843-0126
Facsimile: 407-849-1267
URL: http://www.lawyers.com/medicalmalpractice
Email: mcmillen@floridamalpractice.com *URL:* http://www.floridamalpractice.com

Scott R. McMillen
Richard P. Reinhart
G. B. McVay Voght

For full biographical listings, see the Martindale-Hubbell Law Directory

MEYERS, MOONEY, STANLEY & HOLLINGSWORTH (AV)

(An Association of Professional Associations and Sole Proprietorships)
17 South Lake Avenue, 32801-2797
Telephone: 407-849-0940
Toll-free: 800-766-9198
Fax: 407-849-1860
Email: MeyMooMey@aol.com *URL:* http://www.lawyers.com/meyersmooney
Jacksonville Office: 2120 University Boulevard West, 32217.
Telephone: 904-367-8747; 800-951-7266.
Fax: 904-367-0650.

Irvin A. Meyers
Thomas R. Mooney
Bradley H. Hollingsworth
James A. Stanley, Jr. (Resident, Jacksonville Office)

ASSOCIATES

John V. Colvin
Thomas E. Mooney

Reference: Sun Bank & Trust of Orlando.

For full biographical listings, see the Martindale-Hubbell Law Directory

MORGAN COLLING & GILBERT, A PROFESSIONAL ASSOCIATION (AV)

20 North Orange Avenue, 16th Floor, Suite 1607, P.O. Box 4979, 32802-4979
Telephone: 407-420-1414
Fax: 407-425-8171
URL: http://www.morgancollinggilbert.com
Tampa, Florida Office: 101 East Kennedy Boulevard, Suite 1790, 33602.
Telephone: 813-223-5505.
Fax: 813-223-5402.

Michael V. Barszcz, M.D.
H. Scott Bates
Kevin J. Carden
Michael J. Carter
Alexander M. Clem
Frank F. Fernandez, III
Ronald S. Gilbert
Stephen J. Knox
Keith R. Mitnik
Michael A. Peters
Robert R. Saunders
Scott M. Whitley (Resident, Tampa Office)
John C. Willis, IV
Melvin B. Wright

Reference: Sun Bank.

For full biographical listings, see the Martindale-Hubbell Law Directory

PARKER, LANDERMAN & PARKER, P.A. (AV)

108 East Hillcrest Street, P.O. Box 2867, 32802
Telephone: 407-425-4910
Facsimile: 407-423-3140
Email: parkerpa@digital.net

E. Clay Parker
Alan J. Landerman
Henry Clay Parker, IV

For full biographical listings, see the Martindale-Hubbell Law Directory

PARRISH & FREDERICKSEN, P.A. (AV)

116 America Street, 32801
Telephone: 407-849-1776
Email: sidneyparrish@laworlando.com

Sidney H. Parrish
Kenneth S. Fredericksen

Brian F. Duckworth

For full biographical listings, see the Martindale-Hubbell Law Directory

Orlando—Continued

RICHARD B. TROUTMAN, P.A.

(See Winter Park)

WOOLFOLK, KEOUGH, DUBOSE & DEBARI, P.A. (AV)

518 East Colonial Drive, P.O. Box 1609, 32803
Telephone: 407-849-5050
Fax: 407-849-6588
Frostproof, Florida Office: 225 North Scenic Highway, 33843.
Telephone: 863-635-1155.

Edmund T. Woolfolk
Robert D. Keough
John E. DuBose, Jr.
Mary Jaye DeBari

For full biographical listings, see the Martindale-Hubbell Law Directory

PALM HARBOR, Pinellas Co.

FLORIN, ROEBIG, WALKER, HUDDLESTUN & ROGERS, P.A. (AV)

777 Alderman Road, 34683
Telephone: 727-786-5000
Toll Free in FL: 800-226-6581
Fax: 727-772-9833
Email: frw@gte.net *URL:* http://www.florinroebig.com

Wil H. Florin
Thomas D. Roebig, Jr.
Michael L. Walker
James E. Huddlestun
H. Dennis Rogers
Angela E. Outten
Wolfgang M. Florin
Christopher D. Gray

OF COUNSEL

Jeffrey G. Brown

For full biographical listings, see the Martindale-Hubbell Law Directory

*PENSACOLA,** Escambia Co.

BOZEMAN, JENKINS & MATTHEWS, P.A. (AV)

SunTrust Tower, 220 West Garden Street, Suite 801, P.O. Box 13105, 32501
Telephone: 850-434-6223
Fax: 850-434-5242
Email: bojema@pen.net *URL:* http://www.bojema.pen.net
Fort Walton Beach Office: 151 Mary Esther Boulevard, Suite 401.
Telephone: 850-651-2151.
Fax: 850-434-5242.
Panama City Office: 475 Harrison Avenue, Suite 203A.
Telephone: 850-872-0110.
Fax: 850-434-5242.

Frank C. Bozeman, Jr.
Thomas R. Jenkins
Larry A. Matthews
Janice K. Skievaski
Frank C. Bozeman, III

Robert T. Bleach
John B. Fricke, Jr.
J. Andrew Talbert
Raymond F. Higgins, III
Jeremiah J. Talbott
Sidney M. McCrackin

For full biographical listings, see the Martindale-Hubbell Law Directory

KERRIGAN, ESTESS, RANKIN & MCLEOD (AV)

400 East Government Street, 32501
Telephone: 850-444-4444
Watts No.: 1-800-444-4404
FAX: 850-444-4495
Email: lawfirm@kerrigan.com *URL:* http://www.kerrigan.com
Fort Walton Beach, Florida Office: 212 SE Eglin Parkway, Suite C.
Telephone: 850-244-1111.
Panama City, Florida Office: 836 Jenks Avenue.
Telephone: 850-871-5000.
FAX: 850-872-2148.

MEMBERS OF FIRM

Robert G. Kerrigan
George W. Estess
William Rankin
T. Michael McLeod
Randle D. Thompson
Marcus J. Michles II
Mary Ann Patti

LEGAL SUPPORT PERSONNEL

James Michael Kerrigan, Ph.D.

Reference: 1st American Bank of Pensacola.

For full biographical listings, see the Martindale-Hubbell Law Directory

ST. PETERSBURG, Pinellas Co.

CHAMBERS LAW GROUP, PROFESSIONAL ASSOCIATION (AV)

520 Fourth Street North, P.O. Box 1191, 33731-1191
Telephone: 727-896-2167
Fax: 727-822-8981
Email: CHAMLAWGRP@AOL.com

(See Next Column)

Joseph H. Chambers
Joseph W. Chambers
Jeffrey K. Chambers

John R. Mathias

Reference: NationsBank.

For full biographical listings, see the Martindale-Hubbell Law Directory

WOOD & ASSOCIATES, P.A. (AV)

5015 Fourth Street North Suite A, 33703
Telephone: 727-520-9811
Facsimile: 727-520-0628

J. Emory Wood

David M. Fernandez

Representative Clients: Casualty Indemnity Exchange; State Farm Fire & Casualty Co.; State Farm Mutual Automobile Insurance Co.; Southern Insurance Co.; Nationwide Insurance Co.; Coronet Insurance Co.; General Telephone Company of Florida; Apex Adjusting Co.; Unisource Insurance Co.

For full biographical listings, see the Martindale-Hubbell Law Directory

*SARASOTA,** Sarasota Co.

DICKINSON & GIBBONS, P.A. (AV)

1750 Ringling Boulevard, P.O. Box 3979, 34230
Telephone: 941-366-4680
FAX: 941-953-3136
URL: http://dglawyers.com

Ralph L. Marchbank, Jr.
Burwell J. Jones
Stephen G. Brannan

OF COUNSEL

G. Hunter Gibbons

Representative Clients: Venice Hospital; Physicians Protective Trust Fund; Florida Physicians Insurance Co.; Lee Memorial Hospital; Manatee Memorial Hospital; Sarasota Memorial Hospital; Columbia Hospital Corp.; Florida Physicians Trust; Alexis; Squibb Corp.

For Complete List of Firm Personnel, See General Section

For full biographical listings, see the Martindale-Hubbell Law Directory

*TALLAHASSEE,** Leon Co.

CALLAHAN LAW FIRM (AV)

433 North Magnolia Drive, 32308
Telephone: 850-877-2525
Telecopier: 850-656-1539
Email: clf@polaris.net *URL:* http://www.polaris.net/callahan

Michael T. Callahan

For full biographical listings, see the Martindale-Hubbell Law Directory

MCFARLAIN, WILEY, CASSEDY & JONES, PROFESSIONAL ASSOCIATION (AV)

215 South Monroe Street, Suite 600, P.O. Box 2174, 32316-2174
Telephone: 850-222-2107
Telecopier: 850-222-8475
Email: firm@mcfarlain.com *URL:* http://www.mcfarlain.com

Richard C. McFarlain
William B. Wiley
Douglas P. Jones
Charles A. Stampelos
H. Darrell White, Jr.
Christopher Barkas
Harold R. Mardenborough, Jr.
Terrell C. Madigan

Robert A. McNeely
P. David Brannon

LEGAL SUPPORT PERSONNEL

Diane L. Doll (Office Manager)

For full biographical listings, see the Martindale-Hubbell Law Directory

*TAMPA,** Hillsborough Co.

BARR, MURMAN, TONELLI, HERZFELD & RUBIN (AV)

Suite 1750, 201 East Kennedy Boulevard, P.O. Box 172669, 33672-0669
Telephone: 813-223-3951
Fax: 813-229-2254
URL: http://www.hrfirm.com
New Port Richey, Florida Office: 7613 Little Road, 34654.
Telephone: 727-846-8646;
Fax: 727-846-8913.

James A. Murman
Michael A. Tonelli
Daniel H. Sleet
T. Gregory Slother
John W. Boult
Gregory G. Frazier
Joseph S. Silver
Clifford L. Somers

(See Next Column)

BARR, MURMAN, TONELLI, HERZFELD & RUBIN—*Continued*

ASSOCIATES

John J. Kozak
Morris D. Purcell, Jr.
Robert J. Scanlan
Pamela A. Walton

OF COUNSEL

Billy R. Barr

Representative Clients: Tenet Healthcare Corp.; CNA HealthPro; Chicago Insurance Co.; SCPIE.

For full biographical listings, see the Martindale-Hubbell Law Directory

BAVOL, BUSH & SISCO, P.L.L.C. (AV)

100 South Ashley, Suite 2100, P.O. Box 3423, 33601-3423
Telephone: 813-228-7000
Telefax: 813-273-0091

Charles D. Bavol
Ronald E. Bush
Dale R. Sisco
Jack E. Fernandez, Jr.
Dominick J. Graziano

Robert W. Bleakley
William R. Daniel
Kevin M. Gilhool
Andrew L. Rosenkranz (On Leave)
Jay P. Dinan
Jaret J. Fuente
Kerry C. McGuinn, Jr.
Pegi Money McCabe

For full biographical listings, see the Martindale-Hubbell Law Directory

CLARK, CHARLTON, MARTINO & BORDERS, P.A. (AV)

3407 W. Kennedy Boulevard, 33609-2905
Telephone: 813-879-0700
Fax: 813-879-5498
URL: http://www.ccmb.net
Email: mail@ccmb.net *URL:* http://www.lawyers.com/ccm&b-law

Scott T. Borders
Scott Charlton
James W. Clark
Anthony T. Martino
Deborah A. Fleming

Reference: Southtrust Bank of Tampa.

For full biographical listings, see the Martindale-Hubbell Law Directory

CUNNINGHAM, CLARK & GREIWE, P.A. (AV)

100 Ashley Drive, South, Suite 100, 33602
Telephone: 813-228-0505
Telefax: 813-229-7982

Anthony W. Cunningham
Donald G. Greiwe
James D. Clark
D. Frank Winkles

For full biographical listings, see the Martindale-Hubbell Law Directory

PATRICK H. DEKLE, P.A. (AV)

808 Landmark Building, 412 Madison Street, 33602-4640
Telephone: 813-223-2300
Fax: 813-223-2659

Patrick H. Dekle

For full biographical listings, see the Martindale-Hubbell Law Directory

RYWANT, ALVAREZ, JONES, RUSSO & GUYTON, PROFESSIONAL ASSOCIATION (AV)

Suite 500 Perry Paint & Glass Building, 109 North Brush Street, P.O. Box 3283, 33601
Telephone: 813-229-7007
Fax: 813-223-6544
Ocala, Florida Office: 3300 S.W. 34th Avenue, Suite 124C, 32674.
Telephone: 904-237-8810.
FAX: 904-237-2022.

Carmen Alpizar
Manuel J. Alvarez
Matthew R. Danahy
Matthew D. Emerson
Lisa A. Griffin
John A.C. Guyton, III
M.C. Collins Guyton
Gregory D. Jones
Burke G. Lopez
Andrew F. Russo
Michael S. Rywant

LEGAL SUPPORT PERSONNEL

Bradley Hugh Holt

Representative Clients: Peerless Insurance Co.; Gulf Insurance Group; Employers Casualty Co.; Landmark Insurance Co.

For full biographical listings, see the Martindale-Hubbell Law Directory

HENRY E. VALENZUELA, P.A. (AV)

100 North Tampa Street, Suite 1825, 33602
Telephone: 813-272-1000
Fax: 813-272-1429
URL: http://www.fllawcom/valenzuela

Henry E. Valenzuela

(See Next Column)

Richard M. Mitzel
Luis Miguel Bessone

For full biographical listings, see the Martindale-Hubbell Law Directory

YERRID, KNOPIK & KRIEGER, P.A. (AV)

Barnett Plaza, Suite 2160, 101 East Kennedy Boulevard, 33602
Telephone: 813-222-8222
Fax: 813-222-8224
URL: http://www.yerridknopik.com

C. Steven Yerrid
Christopher S. Knopik
Edwin P. Krieger

Ralph L. Gonzalez
Richard C. Alvarez
Claire D. Hancock

For full biographical listings, see the Martindale-Hubbell Law Directory

*VERO BEACH,** Indian River Co.

MOSS, HENDERSON, BLANTON & LANIER, P.A. (AV)

817 Beachland Boulevard, P.O. Box 3406, 32964-3406
Telephone: 561-231-1900
Fax: 561-231-4387

George H. Moss, II

Representative Clients: Aetna Life & Casualty; Alcoa Florida, Inc.; Florida Power & Light Co.; Insurance Company of North America; Liberty Mutual Insurance Co.; Sears, Roebuck & Co.; Sugar Cane Growers Cooperative of Florida; Norfolk Southern Corporation/North American Van Lines, Inc.

For Complete List of Firm Personnel, See General Section

For full biographical listings, see the Martindale-Hubbell Law Directory

*WEST PALM BEACH,** Palm Beach Co.

ADAMS, COOGLER, WATSON & MERKEL, P.A. (AV)

Suite 1600, 1555 Palm Beach Lakes Boulevard, P.O. Box 2069, 33402
Telephone: 561-478-4500
Fax: 561-684-7346
Email: ACWMLAW@AOL.COM

Samuel H. Adams (1913-1981)
Roy R. Watson
Robert G. Merkel
James C. Barry
Reed W. Kellner
Catherine Lynn Kasten
Scott S. Warburton
Peter A. Cooke
Patricia A. Judge
Kathryn L. Tignor

Alexander D. Barker
Jodi G. Barrett
Stephanie Brown
James W. Flanagan
Paul L. Harwood
Thomas Hodas
Catherine M. Paris

OF COUNSEL

L. C. Shepard, Jr.

For full biographical listings, see the Martindale-Hubbell Law Directory

DAVIS, GORDON & DONER, P.A. (AV)

515 North Flagler Drive, 7th Floor, 33401
Telephone: 561-659-7337
Facsimile: 561-659-0143
Email: dgdc@flinet.com *URL:* http://www.dgdlaw.com

Robert E. Gordon
Adam S. Doner

Eric D. Hightower
Steven G. Calamusa

OF COUNSEL

Mikel D. Jones (Not admitted in FL)

For full biographical listings, see the Martindale-Hubbell Law Directory

FREEMAN & SUPRAN, P.A. (AV)

315 Fifth Street, 33401-3709
Telephone: 561-655-6025
Fax: 561-655-5759
Palatka, Florida Office: 415 St. Johns Avenue.
Telephone: 904-325-6239.
Fax: 904-329-9626.

Terry N. Freeman
George P. Supran
Mark D. Kairalla

For full biographical listings, see the Martindale-Hubbell Law Directory

West Palm Beach—Continued

LYTAL, REITER, CLARK, FOUNTAIN & WILLIAMS (AV)

A Limited Liability Partnership
Tenth Floor, 515 North Flagler Drive, 33401
Telephone: 561-655-1990
Broward County: 954-426-2103
Toll Free: 1-800-654-2024
Fax: 561-832-2932
Mailing Address: P.O. Box 4056, 33402
Email: lhowden@palmbeachlaw.com *URL:* http://www.palmbeachlaw.com

Lake Lytal, Jr. (P.A.)
Joseph J. Reiter (P.A.)
Mark W. Clark (P.A.)
Donald R. Fountain, Jr. (P.A.)
William S. Williams (P.A.)

David M. Gaspari
W. Hampton Keen
Nancy L. La Vista
Julie H. Littky-Rubin
Lake H. Lytal, III
Michael J. Overbeck
David C. Prather
Kevin C. Smith
Scott Bryant Smith

Reference: United National Bank.

For full biographical listings, see the Martindale-Hubbell Law Directory

SCHULER & HALVORSON, P.A. (AV)

Suite 4D Barristers Building, 1615 Forum Place, 33401-2314
Telephone: 561-689-8180
Fax: 561-684-9683
URL: http://www.sh-law.com

Richard D. Schuler
Steven W. Halvorson

Craig M. Goldenfarb

LEGAL SUPPORT PERSONNEL

Hendrik C. Van Wieringen, Jr.
Rhea D. Doran
Judith C. Spano (Certified Legal Assistant)

For full biographical listings, see the Martindale-Hubbell Law Directory

SEARCY DENNEY SCAROLA BARNHART & SHIPLEY, PROFESSIONAL ASSOCIATION (AV)

2139 Palm Beach Lakes Boulevard, P.O. Drawer 3626, 33402-3626
Telephone: 561-686-6300
800-780-8607
800-220-7006 (Spanish)
Fax: 561-478-0754
Email: CDS@SEARCYLAW.COM *URL:* http://www.searcylaw.com

Christian D. Searcy, Sr.
Earl L. Denney, Jr.
John Scarola
F. Gregory Barnhart
John A. Shipley
David K. Kelley, Jr.
Lance J. Block, Jr.
C. Calvin Warriner, III
William A. Norton
David J. Sales
Christopher K. Speed
William B. King
David J. White

Karen E. Terry
Sean C. Domnick
Harry A. Shevin
Patrick E. Quinlan
Darryl L. Lewis

LEGAL SUPPORT PERSONNEL

Laurie J. Briggs (Paralegal)
Deane L. Cady (Paralegal/Investigator)
Daniel J. Calloway (Paralegal/Investigator)
Emilio Diamantis (Paralegal/Investigator)
David W. Gilmore (Paralegal/Investigator)
John C. Hopkins (Paralegal/Investigator)
Thaddeus E. Kulesa (Paralegal/Investigator)
J. Peter Love (Paralegal/Investigator)
William H. Seabold (Paralegal/Investigator)
Kathleen Simon (Paralegal)
Steve M. Smith (Paralegal/Investigator)
Kevin J. Walsh (Paralegal/Investigator)
Judson Whitehorn (Paralegal/Investigator)
Samantha M. Johansen (Paralegal/Investigator)

For Complete List of Firm Personnel, See General Section
For full biographical listings, see the Martindale-Hubbell Law Directory

WINTER PARK, Orange Co.

RICHARD B. TROUTMAN, P.A. (AV)

Suite 500 1245 West Fairbanks Avenue, 32789
Telephone: 407-647-5002
Fax: 407-647-2050

Richard B. Troutman
Brett M. Bressler
Stephen H. McNeill

For full biographical listings, see the Martindale-Hubbell Law Directory

GEORGIA

*ALBANY,** Dougherty Co.

W. EDWARD MEEKS, JR. (AV)

2410 Westgate Drive, Suite 105, P.O. Drawer 71525, 31708-1525
Telephone: 912-439-9234
Fax: 912-439-9175
Representative Clients: Pritchett Ford; Tri-County Aq.; Alarm Services, Inc.; Lee County Board of Education; BESCO Steel.

For full biographical listings, see the Martindale-Hubbell Law Directory

*ATHENS,** Clarke Co.

COOK, NOELL, TOLLEY, BATES & MICHAEL, LLP (AV)

304 East Washington Street, P.O. Box 1927, 30603
Telephone: 706-549-6111
Fax: 706-548-0956

MEMBERS OF FIRM

J. Vincent Cook
John S. Noell, Jr.
Edward D. Tolley
Robert B. Bates
M. Kim Michael

Ronald E. Houser

For full biographical listings, see the Martindale-Hubbell Law Directory

*ATLANTA,** Fulton Co.

WILLIAM Q. BIRD AND ASSOCIATES, P.C. (AV)

14 Seventeenth Street, Suite 5, P.O. Box 7009, 30357
Telephone: 404-873-4696
Fax: 404-872-3745
Email: info@williamqbird.com *URL:* http://www.williamqbird.com

William Q. Bird

For full biographical listings, see the Martindale-Hubbell Law Directory

DAVID WM. BOONE, P.C. (AV)

3166 Mathieson Drive, 30305
Telephone: 404-239-0305
Fax: 404-239-0520

David William Boone
Simone R. Siex

For full biographical listings, see the Martindale-Hubbell Law Directory

BUTLER, WOOTEN, OVERBY, FRYHOFER, DAUGHTERY & SULLIVAN (AV)

2719 Buford Highway, 30324
Telephone: 404-321-1700
WATS 1-800-242-2962
Fax: 404-321-1713
Columbus, Georgia Office: 1500 Second Avenue, P.O. Box 2766.
Telephone: 706-322-1990; National Wats: 1-800-233-4086.
Fax: 706-323-2962.

MEMBERS OF FIRM

James E. Butler, Jr.
Joel O. Wooten, Jr.
C. Frederick Overby
George W. Fryhofer III
Peter J. Daughtery
Lee Tarte Wallace
Terrance C. Sullivan

ASSOCIATES

Jason L. Crawford
Keith A. Pittman
Joshua Sacks
Teresa Thomas Abell
Cale H. Conley

Reference: Columbus Bank and Trust, Columbus, Ga.

For full biographical listings, see the Martindale-Hubbell Law Directory

LAWRENCE A. COOPER (AV)

Resurgens Plaza, Suite 1770 945 East Paces Ferry Road, 30326
Telephone: 404-814-0000
Fax: 404-816-8900
Email: lacooperaty@mindspring.com *URL:* http://www.lawyers.com/lacooperaty

For full biographical listings, see the Martindale-Hubbell Law Directory

DOFFERMYRE, SHIELDS, CANFIELD, KNOWLES & DEVINE (AV)

Suite 1600, 1355 Peachtree Street, 30309
Telephone: 404-881-8900
Fax: 404-881-3007

(See Next Column)

DOFFERMYRE, SHIELDS, CANFIELD, KNOWLES & DEVINE—*Continued*

Foy R. Devine
Robert E. Shields
Georgiana Rizk

For full biographical listings, see the Martindale-Hubbell Law Directory

DWYER & WHITE (AV)

A Partnership including a Professional Corporation
Suite 700, 2100 Riveredge Parkway, 30328-4654
Telephone: 770-956-1984
Fax: 770-956-1381
Email: admin@dwslaw.com *URL:* http://www.dwslaw.com

MEMBERS

J. Matthew Dwyer, Jr. (P.C.)
William Woods White

For full biographical listings, see the Martindale-Hubbell Law Directory

FAIN, MAJOR, WILEY & BRENNAN, P.C. (AV)

100 Glenridge Point Parkway Suite 500, 30342-1440
Telephone: 404-688-6633
Telecopier: 404-420-1544

Gene A. Major
Charles A. Wiley, Jr.
Thomas E. Brennan
John K. Miles, Jr.
Darryl G. Haynes

Brian Alligood

Representative Clients: Allstate Insurance Co.; Budget Rent-A-Car; Arkansas Best Corp.; Chrysler Insurance Co.; Georgia Farm Bureau Mutual Insurance Co.; Hertz Corp.; Universal Underwriters Insurance Co.; Westfield Insurance Co.; Winn-Dixie Stores, Inc.

For Complete List of Firm Personnel, See General Section

For full biographical listings, see the Martindale-Hubbell Law Directory

GARLAND, SAMUEL & LOEB, P.C. (AV)

3151 Maple Drive, N.E., 30305
Telephone: 404-262-2225
Fax: 404-365-5041
Email: triallaw@atlanta.com

Edward T. M. Garland
Donald F. Samuel
Robin N. Loeb

For full biographical listings, see the Martindale-Hubbell Law Directory

GOLDNER, SOMMERS, SCRUDDER & BASS (AV)

900 Circle 75 Parkway Suite 850, 30339
Telephone: 770-612-9200
Facsimile: 770-612-9201

MEMBERS OF FIRM

Stephen L. Goldner
Susan V. Sommers
Benjamin David Ladner

ASSOCIATE

Tammy Spivack Skinner

For Complete List of Firm Personnel, See General Section

For full biographical listings, see the Martindale-Hubbell Law Directory

HALL, BOOTH, SMITH & SLOVER, A PROFESSIONAL CORPORATION (AV)

230 Peachtree Street, N.W., Suite 2500, 30303-1515
Telephone: 404-954-5000
Fax: 404-954-5020
Email: mail@hbss.net

John E. Hall, Jr.
Alexander H. Booth
Rush S. Smith, Jr.
Jack G. Slover, Jr.
Timothy H. Bendin
Michael A. Pannier
Roger S. Sumrall
Robert L. Shannon, Jr.
Michael G. Frick
T. Andrew Graham
Phillip E. Friduss

Karl M. Braun
Heather C. McGrotty
Deborah L. Stevenson
Sharon Davis King
Jonathan Marigliano
Roger G. Martin
Steven D. Prelutsky
Fred L. Hubbs Jr.
Steven J. Zaloudek
Ashley D. Phillips
Rob S. Register
Noel Langston Hurley
L. Clint Crosby
Cheveda D. Grier
Rebecca T. Christian
Wendy A. Weber
(Not admitted in GA)

Reference: Wachovia Bank of Georgia.

For full biographical listings, see the Martindale-Hubbell Law Directory

GEORGE W. HART, P.C. (AV)

Promenade Two Suite 3775, 1230 Peachtree Street, N.E., 30309-3589
Telephone: 404-876-3775
Fax: 404-873-3799

George W. Hart

Reference: SunTrust Bank.

For full biographical listings, see the Martindale-Hubbell Law Directory

HILL AND BLEIBERG (AV)

Suite 200, 47 Perimeter Center East, 30346
Telephone: 770-394-7800
Fax: 770-394-7802
Email: HBLAWFIRM@AOL.COM

MEMBERS OF FIRM

Robert P. Bleiberg
Gary Hill

ASSOCIATE

Bryan Hill

For full biographical listings, see the Martindale-Hubbell Law Directory

KIRSCHNER AND VENKER, P.C. (AV)

Suite 450, 600 West Peachtree Street, N.W., 30308
Telephone: 404-872-6646
Fax: 404-876-7168

Andrew R. Kirschner
Thomas J. Venker

For full biographical listings, see the Martindale-Hubbell Law Directory

THOMAS E. MADDOX, JR., P.C. (AV)

3521 Habersham at Northlake (Tucker), 30084-4001
Telephone: 770-414-8055
Telecopier: 770-414-8755
Email: tommylaw@worldnet.att.net

Thomas E. Maddox, Jr.

LEGAL SUPPORT PERSONNEL

Matthew K. Johnson, Jr.

For full biographical listings, see the Martindale-Hubbell Law Directory

THOMAS WILLIAM MALONE (AV)

Two Ravinia Drive Suite 300, 30346
Telephone: 770-390-7550
Fax: 770-390-7560
Email: Malonepc@aol.com *URL:* http://www.malonepc.com

J. Hoyt Young
Mark L. Stuckey
S. Bradley Houck

References: SunTrust Bank, Atlanta, Georgia; SunTrust Bank of South Georgia.

For full biographical listings, see the Martindale-Hubbell Law Directory

MATTHEWS & STEEL (AV)

462 East Paces Ferry Road, 30305
Telephone: 404-264-1292
800-776-0098
Fax: 404-264-0161
Email: postmaster@matthewssteellaw.com

MEMBERS OF FIRM

James B. Matthews, III
John D. Steel
John B. Briggs
H. Craig Stafford

For full biographical listings, see the Martindale-Hubbell Law Directory

MILLS, MORAITAKIS, KUSHEL & PEARSON (AV)

Suite 425 3445 Peachtree Road, Northeast, 30326-1276
Telephone: 404-261-0016
Facsimile: 404-261-0024

Roger Mills
Nicholas C. Moraitakis
Glenn E. Kushel
Albert M. Pearson, III

ASSOCIATE

Martha D. Turner

For full biographical listings, see the Martindale-Hubbell Law Directory

NALL, MILLER, OWENS, HOCUTT & HOWARD, LLP (AV)

Suite 200 Peachtree & Broad Building, 66 Luckie Street, 30303
Telephone: 404-522-2200
Fax: 404-522-2208

MEMBERS OF FIRM

James S. Owens, Jr.
Robert B. Hocutt
James R. Howard
George Robert Neuhauser
Robert L. Goldstucker
Kenneth P. McDuffie
Michael D. Hostetter

(See Next Column)

NALL, MILLER, OWENS, HOCUTT & HOWARD LLP, *Atlanta—Continued*

COUNSEL

Samuel A. Miller

ASSOCIATES

Charles Richard Carson
Paul Jay Pontrelli
Mary Anne Palma

LEGAL SUPPORT PERSONNEL

W. Gary Bush (Registered Nurse, Legal Assistant)
Natalie D. Summers (Paralegal)
Janice F. Clark (Paralegal)
Michelle Henderson McGhee (Paralegal)

Representative Clients: Adventist Health Systems; Charter Behavioral Health Systems of Atlanta at Peachford; Columbia HCA/Healthcare Corp.; The Doctor's Company; Em-Care, Inc.; Fisher Mangold; Georgia Osteopathic Hospital, Inc.; National Emergency Services, Inc.; Podiatry Insurance Company of America.

For full biographical listings, see the Martindale-Hubbell Law Directory

SAMUEL P. PIERCE, JR., P.C. (AV)

5064 Roswell Road Suite C-300, 30342
Telephone: 404-843-1512
Fax: 404-843-4474
URL: http://www.lawyers.com

Samuel P. Pierce, Jr.

For full biographical listings, see the Martindale-Hubbell Law Directory

PIERCE & YOUNG (AV)

Building 1700, 2255 Cumberland Parkway Northwest, 30339-4575
Telephone: 770-435-0500
Telecopier: 770-435-0362

MEMBERS OF FIRM

J. Wayne Pierce
Richard M. Young
Christy A. Dunkelberger

For full biographical listings, see the Martindale-Hubbell Law Directory

POPE, MCGLAMRY, KILPATRICK & MORRISON, LLP (AV)

A Partnership including Professional Corporations
The Pinnacle, 3455 Peachtree Road, N.E., 30326-3243
Telephone: 404-523-7706
Fax: 404-524-1648
Phenix City, Alabama: 334-298-7354
Mailing Address: P.O. Box 191625, Atlanta, GA, 31119-1625
Email: pmkm@pmkm.com
Columbus, Georgia Office: 318 11th Street, 2nd Floor, P.O. Box 2128, 31902-2128.
Telephone: 706-324-0050.
Fax: 706-327-1536.

MEMBERS OF FIRM

C. Neal Pope (P.C.)
Max R. McGlamry (P.C.) (Resident, Columbus, Georgia Office)
Paul V. Kilpatrick, Jr. (Resident, Columbus, Georgia Office)
R. Timothy Morrison
Michael L. McGlamry
Earle F. Lasseter
William Usher Norwood, III
Jay F. Hirsch
Wade H. Tomlinson, III
Teresa Pike Tomlinson

RESIDENT ASSOCIATE

C. Elizabeth Pope

Reference: Columbus Bank & Trust Co.

For full biographical listings, see the Martindale-Hubbell Law Directory

REYNOLDS & MCARTHUR (AV)

A Partnership including a Professional Corporation
Overlook II, Suite 270, 2839 Paces Ferry Rd., N.W., 30339
Telephone: 770-438-8997; 770-438-9062
Fax: 770-438-8536
Macon, Georgia Office: 850 Walnut Street, 31201.
Telephone: 912-741-6000.
Fax: 912-742-0750. Email: firm@rmtriallaw.com

MEMBERS OF FIRM

W. Carl Reynolds (P.C.)
Katherine L. McArthur
Charles M. Cork, III
O. Wendell Horne, III
Bradley J. Survant

For full biographical listings, see the Martindale-Hubbell Law Directory

SMITH, HOWARD & AJAX, LLP (AV)

300 Atlanta Financial Center South, 3333 Peachtree Road, N.E., 30326
Telephone: 404-239-1900
Fax: 404-239-1930

(See Next Column)

MEMBERS OF FIRM

Fred W. Ajax, Jr.
Susan Teale Couvillon
Harvey S. Gray
David K. Whatley

For full biographical listings, see the Martindale-Hubbell Law Directory

THOMAS, KENNEDY, SAMPSON & PATTERSON (AV)

3355 Main Street, 30337
Telephone: 404-688-4503
Telecopier: 404-681-2950; Litigation Dept.
Telecopier: 404-684-9515
URL: http://www.tksp.com

MEMBERS OF FIRM

R. E. Thomas, Jr. (1911-1996)
John Loren Kennedy (1942-1994)
Thomas G. Sampson
P. Andrew Patterson
Jeffrey E. Tompkins

ASSOCIATES

Thomas G. Sampson, II
Ceasar C. Mitchell, II.
Erika Nicole Jackson

LEGAL SUPPORT PERSONNEL

Gwendolyn C.H. Dixon
Elbetha (Beth) Martin (Paralegal)
Nancy Allen-Haskell
Yvonne Torrence
Shyril E. Beck
Constance Harris (Paralegal)
Lisa Russell Johnson

For full biographical listings, see the Martindale-Hubbell Law Directory

WEINBERG, WHEELER, HUDGINS, GUNN & DIAL, LLC (AV)

999 Peachtree Street, N.E. Suite 2700, 30309
Telephone: 404-876-2700
Facsimile: 404-875-9433
Email: firm@wwhgd.com

MEMBERS OF FIRM

Sidney F. Wheeler
John M. Hudgins, IV, (P.C.)
Robert G. Tanner
Earl W. Gunn
David A. Dial
Carol P. Michel
John K. Train, IV
Johnathan T. Krawcheck

ASSOCIATES

Alan M. Maxwell
Molly Prichitt Lee
Ashley P. Nichols
Patrick Moore

Representative Clients: American International Group; Columbia/HCA Healthcare Corp.; Emory University; Gwinnett Hospital System; Merck; St. Paul Fire & Marine Insurance Co.; Tenant Healthcare Corporation; Zurich-American Specialities Insurance Co.

For Complete List of Firm Personnel, See General Section

For full biographical listings, see the Martindale-Hubbell Law Directory

WILLIAMS & HENRY, LLP (AV)

Suite 2020, 1100 Peachtree Street, N.E., 30309-4520
Telephone: 404-873-3000
Fax: 404-873-4508
URL: http://www.whlawfirm.com

MEMBERS OF FIRM

Benjamin S. Williams
Philip C. Henry
Harvey R. Spiegel

Joseph A. Fried
Edward C. Henderson, Jr.
Gary L. Wimbish

OF COUNSEL

Robert L. Callahan, III

Reference: SunTrust Bank.

For full biographical listings, see the Martindale-Hubbell Law Directory

WOOD & GRANT (AV)

The Equitable Building Suite 2140, 100 Peachtree Street, 30303
Telephone: 404-522-1713
Fax: 404-522-1716

MEMBERS OF FIRM

L. Lin Wood
Wayne Grant

ASSOCIATE

Kimberly W. Rabren

For full biographical listings, see the Martindale-Hubbell Law Directory

*AUGUSTA,** Richmond Co.

DYE, TUCKER, EVERITT, LONG & BREWTON, A PROFESSIONAL ASSOCIATION (AV)

453 Greene Street, P.O. Box 2426, 30903-2426
Telephone: 706-722-0771
Fax: 706-722-7028

(See Next Column)

DYE, TUCKER, EVERITT, LONG & BREWTON A PROFESSIONAL ASSOCIATION—*Continued*

A. Rowland Dye
Thomas W. Tucker
A. Zachry Everitt
John B. Long
Benjamin H. Brewton
Troy A. Lanier

OF COUNSEL

A. Montague Miller

Jon E. Ingram, Jr.

Representative Clients: State Farm Insurance Cos.; Travelers-Aetna Insurance Cos.; Georgia Power Co.; Wachovia National Bank (Augusta Division); Chubb Group; MAG Mutual Insurance Company; Augusta Board of Realtors; Canal Insurance Company; St. Paul Fire and Marine Insurance Company.

For full biographical listings, see the Martindale-Hubbell Law Directory

WILEY S. OBENSHAIN, III, P.C. (AV)

511 Court House Lane, 30904
Telephone: 706-722-1789
Fax: 706-722-3934

Wiley S. Obenshain, III

For full biographical listings, see the Martindale-Hubbell Law Directory

*BRUNSWICK,** Glynn Co.

FENDIG, MCLEMORE, TAYLOR, WHITWORTH & DURHAM, P.C. (AV)

Suite 200 Suntrust Bank Building, P.O. Box 1996, 31521
Telephone: 912-264-4126
Telecopier: 912-264-0591

Albert Fendig, Jr.
Gilbert C. McLemore, Jr.
Philip R. Taylor
David T. Whitworth
James B. Durham
Donna L. Crossland
Beth M. Duncan

Counsel For: The St. Paul Companies, Inc.; CNA Insurance Co.

For full biographical listings, see the Martindale-Hubbell Law Directory

JOHN R. FERRELLE, P.C. (AV)

Suite 208 NationsBank Plaza, 777 Gloucester Street, P.O. Box 1601, 31521
Telephone: 912-264-0209
Fax: 912-264-0453
Email: rowdy@gate.net

John R. Ferrelle

For full biographical listings, see the Martindale-Hubbell Law Directory

*COLUMBUS,** Muscogee Co.

BUTLER, WOOTEN, OVERBY, FRYHOFER, DAUGHTERY & SULLIVAN (AV)

1500 Second Avenue, P.O. Box 2766, 31902
Telephone: 706-322-1990;
National Wats: 1-800-233-4086
Fax: 706-323-2962
Atlanta, Georgia Office: 2719 Buford Highway, 30324.
Telephone: 404-321-1700.
Fax: 404-321-1713. Wats Line: 1-800-242-2962.

MEMBERS OF FIRM

James E. Butler, Jr.
Joel O. Wooten, Jr.
C. Frederick Overby
George W. Fryhofer III
Peter J. Daughtery
Lee Tarte Wallace
Terrance C. Sullivan

ASSOCIATES

Jason L. Crawford
Keith A. Pittman
Joshua Sacks
Teresa Thomas Abell
Cale H. Conley

Reference: Columbus Bank and Trust, Columbus, Ga.

For full biographical listings, see the Martindale-Hubbell Law Directory

POPE, MCGLAMRY, KILPATRICK & MORRISON, LLP (AV)

A Partnership including Professional Corporations
318 11th Street, 2nd Floor, P.O. Box 2128, 31902-2128
Telephone: 706-324-0050
Phenix City, Alabama: 334-298-7354
Fax: 706-327-1536
Email: pmkm@pmkm.com
Atlanta, Georgia Office: The Pinnacle, 3455 Peachtree Road, N.E. (30326-3243), P.O. Box 191625 (31119-1625).
Telephone: 404-523-7706.
Fax: 404-524-1648.

(See Next Column)

MEMBERS OF FIRM

C. Neal Pope (P.C.)
Max R. McGlamry (P.C.) (Resident)
Paul V. Kilpatrick, Jr. (Resident)
R. Timothy Morrison
Michael L. McGlamry
Earle F. Lasseter
William Usher Norwood, III (Resident, Atlanta Office)
Jay F. Hirsch
Wade H. Tomlinson, III
Teresa Pike Tomlinson

RESIDENT ASSOCIATE

Matthew N. Pope

Reference: Columbus Bank & Trust Co.

For full biographical listings, see the Martindale-Hubbell Law Directory

*MACON,** Bibb Co.

KNIGHT & FISHER (AV)

350 Second Street, 31201-2773
Telephone: 912-741-1900
Fax: 912-742-6939
Email: AttyKnight@aol.com

MEMBERS OF FIRM

Ronald T. Knight
Joy H. Fisher

For full biographical listings, see the Martindale-Hubbell Law Directory

REYNOLDS & MCARTHUR (AV)

A Partnership including a Professional Corporation
850 Walnut Street, 31201
Telephone: 912-741-6000
Fax: 912-742-0750
Email: firm@rmtriallaw.com
Atlanta, Georgia Office: Overlook II, Suite 270, 2839 Paces Ferry Road, N.W., 30339.
Telephone: 770-438-8997; 770-438-9062.
Fax: 770-438-8536.

MEMBERS OF FIRM

W. Carl Reynolds (P.C.)
Katherine L. McArthur
Charles M. Cork, III
O. Wendell Horne, III
Bradley J. Survant

For full biographical listings, see the Martindale-Hubbell Law Directory

*MARIETTA,** Cobb Co.

STEVEN L. BEARD, P.C. (AV)

324 Cherokee Street, 30060
Telephone: 770-422-2642
Fax: 770-422-8954

Steven L. Beard

For full biographical listings, see the Martindale-Hubbell Law Directory

BROWNING & TANKSLEY, LLP (AV)

Suite 225, 166 Anderson Street, 30060
Telephone: 770-424-1500
Fax: 770-424-1740

MEMBERS OF FIRM

Thomas J. Browning
Charles B. Tanksley
Jerry A. Landers, Jr.
Benny C. Priest
Michael K. Jablonski

For full biographical listings, see the Martindale-Hubbell Law Directory

DOWNEY & CLEVELAND, LLP (AV)

288 Washington Avenue, 30060
Telephone: 770-422-3233
Fax: 770-423-4199
Email: downey-cleveland@email.msn.com

OF COUNSEL

Lynn A. Downey

MEMBERS OF FIRM

Robert H. Cleveland (1940-1989)
Joseph C. Parker
Y. Kevin Williams
Russell B. Davis
G. Lee Welborn
Rodney S. Shockley
W. Curtis Anderson

ASSOCIATES

Richard A. Griggs
Tara Waller Scullion
Robert A. De Metz, Jr.
Kevin Salisbury
Sean L. Hynes

Representative Clients: Allstate Insurance Co.; St. Paul Insurance Cos.; Georgia Farm Bureau Mutual Insurance Co.; State Farm Insurance Cos.; Cotton States Mutual Insurance Co.; Colonial Insurance Co. of California; Progressive Insurance Company; Auto Owners Insurance Company; Deep South Surplus, Inc.

For full biographical listings, see the Martindale-Hubbell Law Directory

Marietta—Continued

Jean E. Johnson, Jr., P.C. (AV)

305 Lawrence Street, 30060
Telephone: 770-427-8466
Facsimile: 770-499-2009
Email: postmaster@jejpc.com

Jean E. Johnson, Jr.

Reference: Charter Bank and Trust.

For full biographical listings, see the Martindale-Hubbell Law Directory

Richard L. Powell (AV)

142 Forest Avenue, P.O. Box 508, 30061
Telephone: 770-427-0266
Fax: 770-499-7883
Email: rpowell157@aol.com *URL:* http://www.lawyers.com/richardpowelllaw

LEGAL SUPPORT PERSONNEL

Richele L. Powell

For full biographical listings, see the Martindale-Hubbell Law Directory

*SAVANNAH,** Chatham Co.

Brennan & Wasden LLP (AV)

33 Bull Street, Suite 590, 31401
Telephone: 912-232-6700
Fax: 912-232-0799

Joseph P. Brennan
Wiley A. Wasden III
Marvin W. McGahee
James V. Painter
Elizabeth A. White
Edward L. Newberry, Jr.
W. Andrew Bowen

For full biographical listings, see the Martindale-Hubbell Law Directory

HAWAII

*HONOLULU,** Honolulu Co.

Ayabe, Chong, Nishimoto, Sia & Nakamura (AV)

A Partnership including a Professional Corporation
Pauahi Tower, Suite 2500, 1001 Bishop Street, 96813
Telephone: 808-537-6119
Telecopier: 808-526-3491
Email: ACNSN@pixi.com

MEMBERS OF FIRM

Sidney K. Ayabe (P.C.)
John S. Nishimoto
Jeffrey H. K. Sia
Stephen G. Dyer

Michael J. Van Dyke

Representative Clients: Travelers Insurance Co.; St. Paul Fire and Marine Insurance Co.; The Employers Group of Insurance Companies; TIG Insurance Co.; Pacific Insurance Co.; Hartford Accident and Indemnity Co.; Continental Casualty Co.; CNA Insurance, Medical Insurance Exchange of California; The Doctors Company; HAPI.

For full biographical listings, see the Martindale-Hubbell Law Directory

Cronin, Fried, Sekiya, Kekina & Fairbanks Attorneys at Law, A Law Corporation (AV)

1900 Davies Pacific Center, 841 Bishop Street, 96813
Telephone: 808-524-1433
Fax: 808-536-2073

Paul F. Cronin
L. Richard Fried, Jr.
Gerald Y. Sekiya
Wayne K. Kekina
David L. Fairbanks
John D. Thomas, Jr.
Stuart A. Kaneko
Bert S. Sakuda
Allen K. Williams
Keith K. H. Young

Patrick W. Border
Gregory L. Lui-Kwan
Patrick F. McTernan
Clarence S.K. Kekina
Sylvia J. Luke
Geoffrey K.S. Komeya
Frances K. Schneider

For full biographical listings, see the Martindale-Hubbell Law Directory

James Krueger Attorney at Law, A Law Corporation

(See Wailuku)

Robbins & Rhodes Attorneys At Law, A Law Corporation (AV)

Suite 2200 Davies Pacific Center, 841 Bishop Street, 96813
Telephone: 808-524-2355
Fax: 808-526-0290
Email: robbinsrhodes@lava.net

Kenneth S. Robbins
Vincent A. Rhodes

Representative Clients: Farmers Insurance Group; Hilo Medical Center; Kapiolani Health Care Systems; Kona Community Hospital; Maui Memorial Hospital; Podiatry Insurance Company of America; St. Francis Medical Center; State of Hawaii; Wilcox Memorial Hospital.

For full biographical listings, see the Martindale-Hubbell Law Directory

Law Offices of Richard Turbin A Law Corporation (AV)

Grosvenor Center, Mauka Tower, 737 Bishop Street, Suite 2730, 96813
Telephone: 808-528-4000
FAX: 808-599-1984

Richard Turbin

Rai Saint Chu
Laura Ruth Stone-Jeraj

For full biographical listings, see the Martindale-Hubbell Law Directory

KAILUA, Honolulu Co.

Winer Meheula & Devens (AV)

970 North Kalaheo Avenue, Suite A-300, 96734
Telephone: 808-254-5855
Fax: 808-254-6872
Email: winer@pacificlaw.com *URL:* http://www.pacificlaw.com

MEMBERS OF FIRM

Andrew S. Winer
William K. Meheula
Vladimir Paul Devens

OF COUNSEL

David F. Fasi

ASSOCIATE

Blue H. Kaanehe

For full biographical listings, see the Martindale-Hubbell Law Directory

*LIHUE,** Kauai Co.

James Krueger Attorney at Law, A Law Corporation

(See Wailuku)

*WAILUKU,** Maui Co.

James Krueger Attorney at Law, A Law Corporation (AV)

2065 Main Street, 96793
Telephone: 808-244-7444; Honolulu: 536-7474
Facsimile: 808-244-4177
Email: maulaw@maui.net *URL:* http://www.kruegerlaw-hawaii.org

James Krueger

Eve M. Green
Cynthia Kanoholani Wong

A List of Representative Clients and References will be furnished upon request.

For full biographical listings, see the Martindale-Hubbell Law Directory

ILLINOIS

*BELLEVILLE,** St. Clair Co.

Neville, Richards, DeFranco & Wuller (AV)

5 Park Place, 62226
Telephone: 618-277-0900
Facsimile: 618-277-0970
Email: nrdw@nrdw-law.com *URL:* http://www.nrdw-law.com

MEMBERS OF FIRM

James E. Neville
Timothy S. Richards
James E. DeFranco
Robert G. Wuller, Jr.

ASSOCIATES

Shari M. Brunton
Ellen M. Edmonds
Daniel L. Bradley
Matthew Charles Zittel

For full biographical listings, see the Martindale-Hubbell Law Directory

CARBONDALE, Jackson Co.

BRANDON, SCHMIDT, GOFFINET & SOLVERSON (AV)
916 West Main Street, P.O. Box 3898, 62902-3898
Telephone: 618-549-0777
Telecopier: 618-457-4691
Email: CdaleLaw@aol.com

MEMBERS OF FIRM

Wm. Kent Brandon
Jeffrey A. Goffinet
Charles E. Schmidt
Christy W. Solverson

ASSOCIATES

Reona J. Daly
Michelle M. Schafer
Matthew S. Wilzbach

Representative Clients: State Farm Insurance Co.; Pekin Insurance Co.; Milwaukee Insurance Company; Illinois State Medical Insurance Services; The St. Paul Insurance Co.; Indiana Insurance Co.; Madison Mutual Insirance Co.; Professional Insurance Company of Michigan (PICOM); United States Fidelity and Guarranty Co.
Reference: Fist National Bank of Carbondale.

For full biographical listings, see the Martindale-Hubbell Law Directory

*CHICAGO,** Cook Co.

BLATT, HAMMESFAHR & EATON (AV)
333 W. Wacker Drive, Suite 1900, 60606
Telephone: 312-849-8000
FAX: 312-357-0198
Email: BHE@BHELAW.COM *URL:* HTTP://WWW.BHELAW.COM
New York, New York Office: 45 Broadway, 12th Floor.
Telephone: 212-363-1900.
Fax: 212-363-2600. Email: bhe@bhelaw.com.

MEMBER OF FIRM

Joan S. Callan

For full biographical listings, see the Martindale-Hubbell Law Directory

CLIFFORD LAW OFFICES, P.C. (AV)
120 North La Salle Street, 31st Floor, 60602
Telephone: 312-899-9090
1-800-899-0410
Fax: 312-251-1160
Email: RACA@CliffordLaw.com *URL:* http://www.cliffordlaw.com

Robert A. Clifford
Kevin P. Durkin
Keith A. Hebeisen
Thomas K. Prindable

Robert P. Walsh, Jr.
Isobel S. Thomas
Susan A. Capra
Michael S. Krzak
Jeffrey J. Kroll
Timothy S. Tomasik
Richard F. Burke, Jr.
Brian Thomas Nash
Matthew I. Baker
Donald James Storino III
Timothy P. Rhatigan
Sheri L. Tarr

OF COUNSEL

Robert P. Sheridan

For full biographical listings, see the Martindale-Hubbell Law Directory

CONNELLY & SCHROEDER (AV)
One North Franklin Street, Suite 1200, 60606-3421
Telephone: 312-251-9600
Fax: 312-251-9601
Geneva, Illinois Office: 1250 Executive Place, Suite 201.
Telephone: 630-232-6440.
FAX: 630-232-6450

MEMBERS OF FIRM

Michael P. Connelly
Daniel F. Konicek (Also at Geneva Office)
John L. Schroeder (Resident, Geneva Office)
Mary Lisa Kamins

ASSOCIATES

Michelle L. Adams (Resident, Geneva Office)
Charina de los Reyes
Thomas W. Dillon (Resident, Geneva Office)
Martha Swatek (Resident, Geneva Office)

For full biographical listings, see the Martindale-Hubbell Law Directory

CORBOY & DEMETRIO, P.C. (AV)
33 North Dearborn Street 21st Floor, 60602
Telephone: 312-346-3191
FAX: 312-346-5562
TDD: 312-236-3191
Email: phc9@corboydemetrio.com *URL:* http://www.corboydemetrio.com

Philip H. Corboy
Thomas A. Demetrio

Susan J. Schwartz
Kevin G. Burke

(See Next Column)

Barry R. Chafetz
Kenneth T. Lumb
Shawn S. Kasserman
Cyril J. McIlhargie
Daniel M. Kotin
Margaret M. Power
Linda Marie Roeback

Reference: The American National Bank & Trust Company, Chicago, Illinois.

For full biographical listings, see the Martindale-Hubbell Law Directory

GESSLER, HUGHES & SOCOL, LTD. (AV)
Three First National Plaza, Suite 2200, 60602
Telephone: 312-580-0100
Telecopy: 312-580-1994

Benjamin P. Beringer
Alex W. Miller
Anjali Dayal
Terence J. Moran
Mark S. Dym
Matthew J. Piers
George W. Gessler
Kalman D. Resnick
John K. Hughes
Frederick S. Rhine
Joshua Karsh
Jonathan A. Rothstein
Peter M. Katsaros
Michael P. Simkus
Kimberley Marsh
Donna Kaner Socol

Gary Chodorow
Steven C. Steinback
Ruth M. Dunning
Dana H. Sukenik
S. Todd Neal
J. Eric Vander Arend
Mark A. Pellegrino
Mark B. Weiner
Charles H. Wintersteen

OF COUNSEL

Darius S. Francescatti, M.D.
Susan R. Gzesh

For full biographical listings, see the Martindale-Hubbell Law Directory

JEFFREY M. GOLDBERG & ASSOCIATES, LTD. (AV)
20 North Clark Street, Suite 3100, 60602
Telephone: 312-236-4146
Fax: 312-236-5913
Email: firm@goldberglaw.com

Jeffrey M. Goldberg

Michael H. Berman
Michael B. Gunzburg
Suzanne M. Bonds
Geoffrey G. Johnson
Anthony M. Goldner
Michael V. Marsh

For full biographical listings, see the Martindale-Hubbell Law Directory

HASKELL & PERRIN (AV)
200 West Adams, Suite 2600, 60606
Telephone: 312-781-9393
Fax: 312-781-9178
Email: hasper@haskellperrin.com

MEMBERS OF FIRM

James Kirk Perrin
John J. Lynch
Mary Elizabeth Denefe

OF COUNSEL

Donald M. Haskell

ASSOCIATE

Nancy J. Robinson

For full biographical listings, see the Martindale-Hubbell Law Directory

JOHNSON & BELL, LTD. (AV)
Suite 2200, 222 North La Salle Street, 60601
Telephone: 312-372-0770
Facsimile: 312-372-9818
Waukegan, Illinois Office: Nine North County Street, Suite G-1, 60085.
Telephone: 847-662-7458.
Facsimile: 847-662-7366.
Highland, Indiana Office: 900 Indianapolis Boulevard, Suite A, 46322.
Telephone: 219-923-5250.
Facsimile: 219-923-6170.

Brian C. Fetzer
Kathryn K. Loft
Marilyn McCabe Reidy

References available upon request.

For full biographical listings, see the Martindale-Hubbell Law Directory

PETER D. KASDIN, LTD. (AV)
Suite 4105, 135 South La Salle Street, 60603
Telephone: 312-630-1990
Facsimile: 312-630-1103; 212-630-9777

Peter D. Kasdin

David W. Hepplewhite
Regina Picone Etherton

(See Next Column)

PETER D. KASDIN, LTD., *Chicago—Continued*

OF COUNSEL

David W. Horan

For full biographical listings, see the Martindale-Hubbell Law Directory

LANE & LANE (AV)

33 North Dearborn Street, Suite 2300, 60602
Telephone: 312-332-1400
Fax: 312-899-8003
Email: lanelaw1@aol.com

MEMBERS OF FIRM

Fred Lane
Stephen I. Lane
Scott D. Lane

ASSOCIATE

Joseph M. Dooley III

OF COUNSEL

John F. Sandner
Daniel M. Cullan (Not admitted in IL)
Joyce Staat Lewis

MEDICAL STAFF

Cathleen Lazo-Miller (R.N.)

For full biographical listings, see the Martindale-Hubbell Law Directory

SUSAN E. LOGGANS & ASSOCIATES, P.C. (AV)

Suite 2850, 200 West Madison Street, 60606
Telephone: 312-201-8600
Telecopier: 312-201-1180
Email: loggans@logganslaw.com *URL:* http://www.logganslaw.com

Susan E. Loggans

James G. McConnell
Gregg E. Strellis
John T. Ferjak
Patrick D. Flanagan
Norman L. Rubenstein

For full biographical listings, see the Martindale-Hubbell Law Directory

THE LAW OFFICES OF MUNDAY & NATHAN (AV)

33 North Dearborn Street, Suite 2220, 60602
Telephone: 312-346-5678
Fax: 312-346-8394

John J. Munday
Thomas J. Nathan

Edward G. Proctor, Jr.
Jeffrey A. Schulkin

For full biographical listings, see the Martindale-Hubbell Law Directory

BERNARD R. NEVORAL AND ASSOCIATES LTD. (AV)

150 North Wacker Drive, Suite 2450, 60606
Telephone: 312 263-7058
FAX: 312-263-4566

Bernard R. Nevoral

Jeremy Michael West
Daniel M. Extrom
David F Szczecin

For full biographical listings, see the Martindale-Hubbell Law Directory

NOLAN LAW GROUP (AV)

One North La Salle Street, 35th Floor, 60602
Telephone: 312-372-5400
Toll Free: 888-372-3870
Facsimile: 312-372-0558
Email: dnolan1@ix.netcom.com

Donald J. Nolan
Albert E. Durkin, Jr.
William J. Jovan
Floyd A. Wisner
James H. Lawlor, III
Thomas P. Routh
James A. Santucci
Todd R. Mcquiston

Laura L. Ruhl

For full biographical listings, see the Martindale-Hubbell Law Directory

PAVALON, GIFFORD, LAATSCH & MARINO (AV)

Two North La Salle Street, Suite 1600, 60602
Telephone: 312-419-7400
Fax: 312-419-7408
Email: pavgif@aol.com
Rockford, Illinois Office: 501 Seventh Street, Suite 501, 61104.
Telephone: 815-968-5100.

(See Next Column)

MEMBERS OF FIRM

Eugene I. Pavalon
Geoffrey L. Gifford
Gary K. Laatsch
Frank C. Marino
Henry Phillip Gruss

Christine Walsh Donnelly

For full biographical listings, see the Martindale-Hubbell Law Directory

POWER ROGERS & SMITH, P.C. (AV)

35 West Wacker Drive, Suite 3700, 60601
Telephone: 312-236-9381
Fax: 312-236-0920

Joseph A. Power, Jr.
Larry R. Rogers
Todd A. Smith

Thomas G. Siracusa
Paul L. Salzetta
Thomas M. Power
Larry R. Rogers, Jr.
Ruth M. Degnan
Devon C. Bruce

For full biographical listings, see the Martindale-Hubbell Law Directory

LAW OFFICES OF EDMUND J. SCANLAN, LTD. (AV)

134 North La Salle Street, Suite 1700, 60602
Telephone: 312-372-0020
Fax: 312-372-1211
URL: http://www.lawyers.com/edmundjscanlanltd

Edmund J. Scanlan

Mario C. Palermo

For full biographical listings, see the Martindale-Hubbell Law Directory

JOHN B. SCHWARTZ & ASSOCIATES (AV)

Suite 408, Thirty-Nine South La Salle Street, 60603
Telephone: 312-332-1586
Fax: 312-332-7009
Email: JSCHW888@aol.com

John B. Schwartz

ASSOCIATE

David J. Spira

OF COUNSEL

Thomas W. Duda

For full biographical listings, see the Martindale-Hubbell Law Directory

STRIDE, CRADDOCK & STRIDE (AV)

111 West Washington Street, Suite 1837, 60602-2773
Telephone: 312-346-5800
Fax: 312-346-3870

Herbert F. Stride
J. Patrick Craddock
Herbert L. Stride

Nicholas C. Panos
Deborah A. Stride-Saran
Vickie Voukidis Blum
Michael J. Craddock
Arthur Z. Handelman

For full biographical listings, see the Martindale-Hubbell Law Directory

WILDMAN, HARROLD, ALLEN & DIXON (AV)

225 West Wacker Drive, 30th Floor, 60606-1229
Telephone: 312-201-2000
Fax: 312-201-2555
Email: hennessy@whad.com *URL:* http://www.whad.com
Aurora, Illinois Office: 1961 W. Downer Place.
Telephone: 630-892-7021.
Fax: 630-892-7158.
Waukegan, Illinois Office: 404 West Water, P. O. Box 890.
Telephone: 847-625-5550.
Fax: 847-625-5555.
Lisle, Illinois Office: 4300 Commerce Court, Suite 320.
Telephone: 630-955-0555.
Fax: 630-955-0662
Toronto, Ontario correspondent Office: Keel Cottrelle. 36 Toronto Street, Suite 920.
Telephone: 416-367-2900.
Telefax: 416-367-2791.
Telex: 062-18660.

MEMBERS OF FIRM

Richard C. Bartelt
David A. Kanter
Steven L. Larson (Waukegan Office)
Timothy G. Nickels
Robert A. Strelecky (Lisle Office)
Jeanne E. Walker

(See Next Column)

WILDMAN, HARROLD, ALLEN & DIXON—*Continued*

Paul D. Cranley
Dara J. Keidan
Martha D. Owens
John A. Roberts
John A. Terselic
(Waukegan Office)

For full biographical listings, see the Martindale-Hubbell Law Directory

JOHN C. WUNSCH, P.C. (AV)

77 West Washington Street, Suite 1420, 60602
Telephone: 312-977-9900
Fax: 312-236-2573

John C. Wunsch

Reference: The Northern Trust Co.

For full biographical listings, see the Martindale-Hubbell Law Directory

*KANKAKEE,** Kankakee Co.

ACKMAN, MAREK & BOYD, LTD. (AV)

Suite 400, One Dearborn Square, 60901
Telephone: 815-933-6681
Email: marek1@netcom.net
Watseka, Illinois Office: 223 East Mulberry Street.
Telephone: 815-432-5215.

J. Dennis Marek

Representative Clients: Frontier Insurance; Illinois State Medical Insurance Exchange; Medical Protective; Preferred Physicians Mutual.

For full biographical listings, see the Martindale-Hubbell Law Directory

LA SALLE, La Salle Co.

HERBOLSHEIMER, LANNON, HENSON, DUNCAN AND REAGAN, P.C. (AV)

State Bank Building, Suite 400, 654 First Street, P.O. Box 539, 61301
Telephone: 815-223-0111
Fax: 815-223-5829
Ottawa, Illinois Office: First Federal Savings Bank Building, 633 LaSalle Street, Suite 409.
Telephone: 815-434-1400.
Fax: 815-434-2423.

George L. Herbolsheimer (1911-1992)
R. James Lannon, Jr.
T. Donald Henson
John S. Duncan, III
Michael T. Reagan (Resident, Ottawa Office)
Douglas A. Gift
Gary R. Eiten

Karen C. Eiten
Michael C. Jansz (Resident, Ottawa Office)
Jill W. Klein
Lawrence M. Kaschak

Attorneys for: Aetna Insurance Group; St. Paul Fire and Marine Insurance Co.; State Farm Insurance Co.; La Salle State Bank; The Daily News Tribune Company, La Salle; Eureka Savings Bank; Illinois Valley Community Hospital; Community Hospital of Ottawa; Commonwealth Edison, Co.; United States Fidelity & Guaranty, Co.

For full biographical listings, see the Martindale-Hubbell Law Directory

MATTOON, Coles Co.

CRAIG & CRAIG (AV)

1807 Broadway, P.O. Box 689, 61938-0689
Telephone: 217-234-6481
Telecopier: 217-234-6486; 258-8292
Email: craiglaw@advant.com
Mount Vernon, Illinois Office: 115 North 7th Street.
Telephone: 618-244-7511.

MEMBERS OF FIRM

Craig Van Meter (1895-1981)
Fred H. Kelly (1894-1971)
Robert M. Werden (1908-1969)
George N. Gilkerson (1911-1985)
John P. Ewart
Richard F. Record, Jr.
Stephen L. Corn
Robert G. Grierson
Gregory C. Ray
Paul R. Lynch (Resident, Mount Vernon Office)
Kenneth F. Werts (Resident, Mount Vernon Office)
John L. Barger

ASSOCIATES

Kathleen M. Stockwell
Kristine M. Tuttle
Julie A. Webb (Resident, Mount Vernon Office)
John M. O'Driscoll
Duane A. Deters
Katy C. Fain (Resident, Mount Vernon Office)
Erin E. Wisner
John F. Watson

OF COUNSEL

Jack E. Horsley

Representative Clients: The Medical Protective Company; The Doctors' Company; Illinois State Medical Inter-Insurance Exchange; St. Paul Insurance Co.; Frontier Insurance Co.; Carle Risk Management.

(See Next Column)

For full biographical listings, see the Martindale-Hubbell Law Directory

NAPERVILLE, DuPage Co.

STEVEN B. LEVY, LTD. (AV)

40 Shuman Boulevard Suite 151, 60563
Telephone: 630-416-6300
Telefax: 630-416-6564
URL: http://www.lawyers.com/stevenblevy
Email: SBLEVYLTD@aol.com *URL:* http://www.sblevyltdlaw.com

Steven B. Levy

For full biographical listings, see the Martindale-Hubbell Law Directory

KATHLEEN T. ZELLNER & ASSOCIATES (AV)

1717 North Naper Boulevard Suite 203, 60563
Telephone: 630-955-1212
Facsimile: 630-955-1111
URL: http://www.lawyers.com/zellnerlaw

For full biographical listings, see the Martindale-Hubbell Law Directory

*PEORIA,** Peoria Co.

KINGERY DURREE WAKEMAN & RYAN, ASSOC. (AV)

Commerce Bank Building, 416 Main Street, Suite 915, 61602
Telephone: 309-676-3612
FAX: 309-676-1329
Email: KDWRyan@aol.com

Arthur R. Kingery
Edward R. Durree
Steven A. Wakeman
Christopher P. Ryan
Philip M. O'Donnell
James P. Lawson
Michael S. McKinley

Reference: Commerce Bank of Peoria.

For full biographical listings, see the Martindale-Hubbell Law Directory

NICOARA & STEAGALL (AV)

Commerce Bank Building, 416 Main Street, Suite 815, 61602-1103
Telephone: 309-674-6085
Fax: 309-674-6032
Email: 70754.3140@compuserve.com

MEMBERS OF FIRM

John P. Nicoara
Richard L. Steagall

Representative Clients: Farmers Insurance Group; Illinois Founders Insurance Co.
Reference: Commerce Bank.

For full biographical listings, see the Martindale-Hubbell Law Directory

ROBERT C. STRODEL, LTD. (AV)

927 Commerce Bank Building, 61602
Telephone: 309-676-4500
Fax: 309-676-4566

Robert C. Strodel

For full biographical listings, see the Martindale-Hubbell Law Directory

PERU, La Salle Co.

ANTHONY C. RACCUGLIA & ASSOCIATES (AV)

1200 Maple Drive, 61354
Telephone: 815-223-0230
Ottawa, Illinois Office: 633 La Salle Street.
Telephone: 815-434-2003.

ASSOCIATES

James A. McPhedran
Louis L. Bertrand

References: La Salle National Bank; Citizens First National Bank of Peru, Illinois.

For full biographical listings, see the Martindale-Hubbell Law Directory

*WAUKEGAN,** Lake Co.

SALVI & SCHOSTOK, P.C. (AV)

Established 1982 as Law Offices of Patrick A. Salvi, P.C.
218 North Utica Street, 60085
Telephone: 847-249-1227
Telefax: 847-249-0138
Email: salvilaw.com *URL:* http://www.salvilaw.com
Chicago, Illinois Office: 181 West Madison, Suite 3525, 60602.
Telephone: 312-372-1227.
Telefax: 312-372-3720.

Patrick A. Salvi
Michael P. Schostok
David J. Pritchard (Resident, Chicago Office)

(See Next Column)

SALVI & SCHOSTOK P.C., *Waukegan—Continued*

John Andrew Kornak
J. Matthew Dudley
Peter M. Trobe
Ellen C. Smith
Scott E. Preusen

OF COUNSEL

Bernard E. Grysen

References: First Midwest Bank, Waukegan, Illinois; Northern Trust Bank, Lake Forest, Illinois; Commercial Litigation Clients; Anderson Consulting, LLP.; Baxter Healthcare; Brunswick Corporation, Lake Forest, Illinois.

For full biographical listings, see the Martindale-Hubbell Law Directory

*WHEATON,** DuPage Co.

STEVEN B. LEVY, LTD.

(See Naperville)

O'REILLY LAW OFFICES (AV)

1776 South Naperville Road, Suite 206-A, 60187
Telephone: 630-665-4444
Telecopier: 630-665-4442

Roger Kevin O'Reilly

Molly M. O'Reilly
John F. O'Reilly

For full biographical listings, see the Martindale-Hubbell Law Directory

INDIANA

*EVANSVILLE,** Vanderburgh Co.

GERLING LAW OFFICES, PROFESSIONAL CORPORATION (AV)

519 Main Street Walkway, P.O. Box 3203, 47731
Telephone: 812-423-5251
Fax: 812-423-9928
URL: http://www.gerlinglaw.com

Gary L. Gerling
Edward B. Anderson
David G. Hatfield
Christian M. Lenn
Gayle Gerling Pettinga
Stephen Hensleigh Thomas

For full biographical listings, see the Martindale-Hubbell Law Directory

*INDIANAPOLIS,** Marion Co.

CONOUR • DOEHRMAN • STARKEY (AV)

III Meridian Plaza, Suite 100, 10333 N. Meridian Street, 46290
Telephone: 317-705-4444
Fax: 317-705-4455
Toll Free: 800-269-3443
URL: http://www.indianalaw.com

MEMBERS OF FIRM

William F. Conour
Thomas C. Doehrman

For full biographical listings, see the Martindale-Hubbell Law Directory

HALL, RENDER, KILLIAN, HEATH & LYMAN PROFESSIONAL SERVICES CORPORATION (AV)

Suite 2000, One American Square Box 82064, 46282
Telephone: 317-633-4884
Fax: 317-633-4878
Email: hrkhl@hrkhl.com *URL:* http://www.hrkhl.com
Indianapolis North Office: Suite 820, 8402 Harcourt Road, 46260.
Telephone: 317-871-6222.
Fax: 317-338-3946.
Louisville, Kentucky Office: AEGON Center, Suite 1530, 400 West Market Street, 40202.
Telephone: 502-568-1890.
Fax: 502-568-4878.

William S. Hall
Timothy W. Kennedy
N. Kent Smith

Christopher L. Riegler
A. Courtney Guild, Jr. (Not admitted in IN; Resident, Louisville, Kentucky Office)
Norris Cunningham
Letha S. Kramer
Angela M. Smith

For full biographical listings, see the Martindale-Hubbell Law Directory

HOVDE LAW FIRM (AV)

10585 North Meridian Street, Suite 345, P.O. Box 40849, 46240-0849
Telephone: 317-818-3100
Fax: 317-818-3111
Email: hovde@indy.net

(See Next Column)

F. Boyd Hovde
Frederick R. Hovde
Regina M. Poore
Robert T. Dassow

For full biographical listings, see the Martindale-Hubbell Law Directory

ICE MILLER DONADIO & RYAN (AV)

One American Square Box 82001, 46282-0002
Telephone: 317-236-2100
Fax: 317-236-2219
Email: info@imdr.com *URL:* http://www.imdr.com
South Bend, Indiana Office: 211 West Washington Street, Suite 2420.
Telephone: 219-234-7933.
Fax: 219-234-7965. Internet E-mail: info@imdr.com. Web Site Address: http://www.imdr.com.
Chicago, Illinois Office: 135 South LaSalle Street, Suite 4100.
Telephone: 312-726-1567.
Fax: 312-641-6263. Internet E-mail: info@imdr.com. Web Site Address: http://www.imdr.com.

MEMBERS OF FIRM

David J. Mallon, Jr.
Mary Nold Larimore
L. Alan Whaley
Bonnie L. Gallivan
Sherry A. Fabina-Abney
Kevin R. Knight

OF COUNSEL

Nancy Menard Riddle
Kelly Bauman Pitcher
Laure V. Flaniken
Anita M. Hodgson

ASSOCIATES

Christopher S. Sears
Kathleen A. DeLaney

Representative Clients: Indiana University; PHICO Group; Community Hospitals of Indiana, Inc.; Clarian Health Partners; MMI Cos.; Ohio Hospital Insurance Co.

For Complete List of Firm Personnel, See General Section

For full biographical listings, see the Martindale-Hubbell Law Directory

MARK C. LADENDORF & ASSOCIATES (AV)

8900 Keystone Crossing, Suite 1160, 46240
Telephone: 317-848-3700
Toll Free: 1-888-925-3700
Facsimile: 317-818-6454
URL: http://www.ladendorf.com

ASSOCIATES

Katherine H. Dimmock
Jason R. Reese

For full biographical listings, see the Martindale-Hubbell Law Directory

LOCKE REYNOLDS LLP (AV)

1000 Capital Center South, 201 North Illinois Street, 46204-4210
Telephone: 317-237-3800
Telecopier: 317-237-3900
Email: attys@locke.com *URL:* http://www.locke.com

David S. Allen
Kevin Charles Murray
Karl M. Koons, III
Todd J. Kaiser
Peter H. Pogue

Jon M. Pinnick
Susan E. Cline
Mary Margaret Ruth Feldhake
John D. Papageorge

OF COUNSEL

Robert C. Riddell
Rodney E. Corson

Representative Clients: Clarian Health Partners, Inc.; Columbia Women's Hospital of Indianapolis; MMI Companies, Inc.; The Medical Protective Co.; National Chiropractic Mutual Insurance Co.; PHICO; Medical Assurance of Indiana, Inc.; St. Francis Hospital Center; St. Vincent Hospital; Wishard Memorial Hospital.

For Complete List of Firm Personnel, See General Section

For full biographical listings, see the Martindale-Hubbell Law Directory

MILLER MULLER MENDELSON & KENNEDY (AV)

8900 Keystone Crossing Suite 1250, 46240
Telephone: 317-574-4500
1-800-394-3094
Fax: 317-574-4501
Email: mmmk@iquest.net

MEMBERS OF FIRM

Michael S. Miller
John Muller
Tilden Mendelson
Timothy J. Kennedy

ASSOCIATE

Catherine A. Kling

For full biographical listings, see the Martindale-Hubbell Law Directory

Indianapolis—Continued

MITCHELL HURST JACOBS & DICK (AV)

152 East Washington Street, 46204
Telephone: 317-636-0808
1-800-636-0808
Fax: 317-633-7680
URL: http://www.mhjd.com

MEMBERS OF FIRM

William W. Hurst
Samuel L. Jacobs
Marshall S. Hanley
Robert W. Strohmeyer, Jr.

ASSOCIATES

Danielle A. Takla
Kimberly H. Danforth
Jennifer Levin Sinder
Todd R. Ryden

For full biographical listings, see the Martindale-Hubbell Law Directory

TABBERT HAHN EARNEST & WEDDLE (AV)

Suite 2100, One Indiana Square, 46204-2101
Telephone: 317-639-5444
Fax: 317-639-5232
Email: jtyrrell@tabberthahn.com *URL:* http://www.tabberthahn.com

Don A. Tabbert
Gregory F. Hahn
Lante K. Earnest
Robert G. Weddle
Mark K. Sullivan
Judy M. Tyrrell
Lara D. Engelking
Matthew W. Conner
William W. Mathews
Heather L. Fesko
Charles R. Whybrew

OF COUNSEL

James J. Nocon
William D. Lalley
Joseph W. Hammes
Dale E. Sporleder

For full biographical listings, see the Martindale-Hubbell Law Directory

TOWNSEND & MONTROSS (AV)

230 East Ohio Street, 46204
Telephone: 317-264-4444
Fax: 317-264-2080

John F. Townsend, Jr.
W. Scott Montross

ASSOCIATE

John F. Townsend, III

Reference: N.B.D. Bank, N.A.

For full biographical listings, see the Martindale-Hubbell Law Directory

WILSON, KEHOE & WININGHAM (AV)

2859 North Meridian, 46208
Telephone: 317-920-6400
Fax: 317-920-6405
URL: http://www.wkw.com
Richmond, Indiana Office: 2901 East Main Street, 47374.
Telephone: 765-962-9113.
Connersville, Indiana Office: 118 West 30th Street, 47331.
Telephone: 765-827-1100.
Muncie, Indiana Office: 3310 West Fox Ridge Lane, 47304.
Telephone: 765-284-2474.
Fax: 765-288-8655.

MEMBERS OF FIRM

Harry A. Wilson, Jr.
D. Bruce Kehoe
William E. Winingham, Jr.

ASSOCIATES

Ralph E. Dowling
Gerald A. Griffin, M.D.
William E. Lukens

OF COUNSEL

Gerald L. Lawlis

Reference: The Indiana National Bank.

For full biographical listings, see the Martindale-Hubbell Law Directory

YOSHA KRAHULIK & LEVY (AV)

Pyramid II, First Floor, 3500 West DePauw Boulevard, Suite 2015, P.O. Box 68979, 46268
Telephone: 317-334-9200
Toll Free: 800-875-5759
Fax: 317-228-3355
URL: http://www.yoshalaw.com

MEMBERS OF FIRM

Louis Buddy Yosha
William Levy
Jon D. Krahulik

ASSOCIATES

David C. Krahulik
Jeff D. Oliphant
Julie C. Welp
Janice D. Heidt

Reference: National Bank of Indianapolis.

For full biographical listings, see the Martindale-Hubbell Law Directory

ZEIGLER COHEN & KOCH (AV)

8500 Keystone Crossing, Suite 510, 46240
Telephone: 317-254-4400
Facsimile: 317-254-4403

Robert G. Zeigler
Steven J. Cohen
Edna M. Koch
David Becsey
Roger K. Kanne

ASSOCIATES

Joseph D. McPike, II
Kathryn A. Elias
Lakshmi Reddy

OF COUNSEL

Marilyn A. Young

For full biographical listings, see the Martindale-Hubbell Law Directory

*KOKOMO,** Howard Co.

RUSSELL, MCINTYRE, HILLIGOSS & WELKE (AV)

116 North Main Street, P.O. Box 1047, 46903-1047
Telephone: 765-456-3827
Telecopier: 765-456-3839

MEMBERS OF FIRM

Richard L. Russell
James B. McIntyre
Thomas J. Hilligoss, Jr.
Curtis C. Welke
Rebecca R. McCain

For full biographical listings, see the Martindale-Hubbell Law Directory

*LAFAYETTE,** Tippecanoe Co.

STUART & BRANIGIN (AV)

The Life Building, 300 Main Street, Suite 800, P.O. Box 1010, 47902-1010
Telephone: 765-423-1561
Telecopier: 765-742-8175
Email: sb@stuartlaw.com *URL:* http://www.stuartlaw.com
Indianapolis, Indiana Office: Suite 1401, 8888 Keystone Crossing, 46240.
Telephone: 317-574-7245.
Fax: 317-574-7050.

MEMBERS OF FIRM

Allison Ellsworth Stuart (1886-1950)
Roger D. Branigin (1902-1975)
Roger D. Branigin, Jr.
Thomas L. Ryan
Thomas R. McCully
Larry R. Fisher
Nina B. Kirkpatrick
Mark Lillianfeld
Stephen R. Pennell
Anthony S. Benton
Erik D. Spykman
William E. Emerick
John C. Duffey
Bruce McSpadden
Mark E. DeYoung
Thomas B. Parent
Laura L. Bowker
Kevin D. Nicoson
Susan K. Roberts
John M. Stuckey
Deborah B. Trice
William P. Kealey
David A. Starkweather
Geoffrey L. Blazi

SENIOR COUNSEL

Russell H. Hart

COUNSEL

John F. Bodle
James V. McGlone

ASSOCIATES

Elizabeth B. Searle
Marianne Mitten Owen
David A. Locke
Karen Orr McClure
Ann Marie Waldron
Barry L. Loftus

General Counsel for: The Lafayette Life Insurance Co.; INB National Bank, N.W.; Lafayette Home Hospital, Inc.
State Counsel for: Norfolk & Western Railway Co.
Mr. Ryan is Counsel to: The Trustees of Purdue University.
Representative Clients: Aluminum Company of America; Liberty Mutual Insurance Group.

For full biographical listings, see the Martindale-Hubbell Law Directory

MUNSTER, Lake Co.

LAW OFFICES OF TIMOTHY F. KELLY (AV)

Suite 2A, 9250 Columbia Avenue, 46321
Telephone: 219-836-4062
Telecopier: 219-836-0167
Email: tfklaw@tfklaw.net

MEMBERS OF FIRM

Timothy F. Kelly
Karl K. Vanzo

ASSOCIATES

Steven J. Sersic
Kathleen E. Peek

For Complete List of Firm Personnel, See General Section

For full biographical listings, see the Martindale-Hubbell Law Directory

*NEW ALBANY,** Floyd Co.

MATTOX & MATTOX (AV)

Suite 420 Elsby Building, P.O. Box 1203, 47151-1203
Telephone: 812-944-8005
Facsimile: 812-944-2255
Email: mmlaw@win.net

MEMBERS OF FIRM

Richard L. Mattox S. Frank Mattox

ASSOCIATES

Linda A. Mattox Derrick H. Wilson
Karen R. Goodwell

Representative Clients: AAOMS National Insurance; Cablelink, Inc.; Floyd Memorial Hospital; John Deere Co.; Kimball International, Inc.; The Medical Protective Co.; Papa Johns Intl., Inc.; PHICO Insurance Co.; Physicians Group, Inc.; Robinson Nugent, Inc.

For full biographical listings, see the Martindale-Hubbell Law Directory

SEYMOUR, Jackson Co.

PARDIECK, GILL, VARGO & MACTAVISH, A PROFESSIONAL CORPORATION (AV)

100 North Chestnut Street, P.O. Box 608, 47274
Telephone: 812-523-8686
Fax: 812-522-4199
Email: pgv@pgvlaw.com
Indianapolis, Indiana Office: The Old Bailey Building, 244 North College Avenue, 46202.
Telephone: 317-639-3321.

Roger L. Pardieck John F. Vargo
W. Brent Gill (Resident, Indianapolis Office)
Bruce A. MacTavish

Thomas L. Landwerlen (Resident, Indianapolis Office) Karen J. Mellencamp Davis
Janet O. Vargo (Resident, Indianapolis Office)

OF COUNSEL

Robert C. Rothkopf (Resident, Indianapolis Office)

References: Home Federal Savings Bank, Seymour, Indiana.

For full biographical listings, see the Martindale-Hubbell Law Directory

*SOUTH BEND,** St. Joseph Co.

HARDIG, LEE AND GROVES, PROFESSIONAL ASSOCIATION (AV)

Suite 502, First Bank Building, 205 West Jefferson Boulevard, 46601
Telephone: 219-232-5923
Fax: 219-232-5942
Email: jgrovesaty@aoo.com

James F. Groves

Representative Client: South Bend-Mishawaka New Car Dealers Assn.
Reference: First Interstate Bank of South Bend.

For full biographical listings, see the Martindale-Hubbell Law Directory

ROWE & ROWE (AV)

Suite 900 Keybank Building, 46601
Telephone: 219-233-8200
Fax: 219-234-5987

R. Kent Rowe R. Kent Rowe, III

ASSOCIATES

Robert D. Truitt Gregory J. Haines
Marie Anne Hendrie

Representative Clients: Amerisure Cos.; American Family and Cigna Cos.; Central Insurance Cos.; Professional Mutual; Michigan Mutual Liability Co.; Meridian Mutual Insurance Co.; Sentry Insurance, Inc.; Standard Mutual Insurance Co.; Vernon Insurance Cos.; American States Insurance Co.

For full biographical listings, see the Martindale-Hubbell Law Directory

IOWA

*CEDAR RAPIDS,** Linn Co.

RICCOLO & BAKER, P.C. (AV)

Suite 1140, APAC Building, 425 Second Street, S.E., 52401
Telephone: 319-365-9200; Toll Free: 1-888-546-6529
Fax: 319-365-1114
Email: rb@riccolobaker.com

John L. Riccolo David L. Baker

(See Next Column)

Timothy S. Semelroth

For full biographical listings, see the Martindale-Hubbell Law Directory

*DAVENPORT,** Scott Co.

HENINGER AND HENINGER, PROFESSIONAL CORPORATION (AV)

Suite 501, 101 West Second Street, 52801
Telephone: 319-324-0418
Fax: 319-324-5808
Email: RHenin5382@aol.com *URL:* http://www.lawyers.com/heningerlaw

Ralph U. Heninger (1908-1993) Ralph H. Heninger
Ralph W. Heninger

For full biographical listings, see the Martindale-Hubbell Law Directory

*DES MOINES,** Polk Co.

ROXANNE B. CONLIN AND ASSOCIATES, P.C. (AV)

The Plaza, 300 Walnut Street - Suite 5, 50309-2239
Telephone: 515-282-3329
Fax: 515-282-0318

Roxanne B. Conlin

Thomas J. Duff Melinda Kaye Ellwanger
Tiffany B. Klosener

For full biographical listings, see the Martindale-Hubbell Law Directory

FINLEY, ALT, SMITH, SCHARNBERG, CRAIG, HILMES & GAFFNEY, P.C. (AV)

604 Locust Street, Fourth Floor Equitable Building, 50309
Telephone: 515-288-0145
Telecopier: 515-288-2724

Thomas A. Finley John D. (Jack) Hilmes
Steven K. Scharnberg Kerry A. Finley

Representative Clients: ALAS; American Society of Composers, Authors and Publishers; Equitable Life Assurance Society of the U.S.; Federated Insurance Co.; Meredith Corp.; Catholic Health Corp.; Iowa Methodist Medical Center.
Iowa Attorneys for: Midwest Medical Insurance Co.

For Complete List of Firm Personnel, See General Section

For full biographical listings, see the Martindale-Hubbell Law Directory

GALLIGAN, TULLY, DOYLE & REID, P.C. (AV)

Suite 5 The Plaza, 300 Walnut, 50309-2239
Telephone: 515-282-3333
Fax: 515-282-0318
Email: mjgalligan@aol.com

Michael J. Galligan Timm W. Reid
Robert G. Tully Richard H. Doyle

Kathleen J. Beebout

OF COUNSEL

James A. Albert

Reference: Merchantile Bank of Western Iowa.

For full biographical listings, see the Martindale-Hubbell Law Directory

PEDDICORD, WHARTON, THUNE AND SPENCER, A PROFESSIONAL CORPORATION (AV)

700 Des Moines Building, 405 Sixth Avenue, P.O. Box 9130, 50306-9130
Telephone: 515-243-2100
Fax: 515-243-2132
1-800-383-2100

Roland D. Peddicord

For full biographical listings, see the Martindale-Hubbell Law Directory

*IOWA CITY,** Johnson Co.

HAYES LORENZEN, PLC (AV)

Plaza Centre One, Suite 580, 125 Dubuque Street, 52244
Telephone: 319-887-3688

James P. Hayes Karen A. Lorenzen

For full biographical listings, see the Martindale-Hubbell Law Directory

WEST DES MOINES, Polk Co.

LaMarca & Landry, P.C. (AV)

1300 50th Street, 50266
Telephone: 515-225-2600
Fax: 515-225-8581
Islamorada, Florida Office: 202 Biscayne Boulevard, 33036.
Telephone: 305-664-8527.

George A. LaMarca — Gregory W. Landry

Gary G. Mattson — Justin E. LaVan

OF COUNSEL

Martin R. Anderson — Samuel S. Duffey

For full biographical listings, see the Martindale-Hubbell Law Directory

KANSAS

*HUTCHINSON,** Reno Co.

Gilliland & Hayes, P.A. A Professional Association (AV)

20 West 2nd Avenue, 2nd Floor, P.O. Box 2977, 67504-2977
Telephone: 316-662-0537
Facsimile: 316-669-9426
URL: http://www.gillilandhayes.com
Wichita, Kansas Office: The Orpheum Centre, Suite 300, 200 North Broadway, P.O. Box 49406.
Telephone: 316-262-2266.
Facsimile: 316-263-2202.
Kansas City, Missouri Office: 12th Floor, 3100 Broadway.
Telephone: 816-753-3100.
Facsimile: 816-753-2271.

Robert J. Gilliland
John F. Hayes
James R. Gilliland
John S. Schmidt
Bruce B. Waugh (Not admitted in KS; Resident, Kansas City, Missouri Office)
Michael R. O'Neal
Bradley D. Dillon
Gerald L. Green
David N. Zimmerman (Not admitted in KS; Resident, Kansas City, Missouri Office)
Scott J. Mann
Carol Z. Smith (Resident, Kansas City, Missouri Office)
Kathleen A. Hardee (Resident, Kansas City, Missouri Office)
Kendall R. Cunningham (Resident, Wichita Office)
Mark R. Maloney (Resident, Wichita Office)

Thomas A. Dower
Tracy Applegate Cole
Laura A. Hederstedt
Terri Roberts Munsell (Resident, Kansas City, Missouri Office)
Lisa M. Ward
Kimberly Breda Bushek (Resident, Kansas City, Missouri Office)
E. Thomas Pyle, III
Tara L. Bragg

OF COUNSEL

Robert P. Reams (Not admitted in KS; Resident, Kansas City, Missouri Office)

Representative Clients: CNA Health Pro; Kansas Medical Mutual Insurance Co.; Medical Protective; Phico; The Doctor's Company.

For full biographical listings, see the Martindale-Hubbell Law Directory

OVERLAND PARK, Johnson Co.

Fisher, Patterson, Sayler & Smith, L.L.P. (AV)

11050 Roe Avenue, Suite 210, 66211
Telephone: 913-339-6757
FAX: 913-339-6187
Email: fpss@worldnet.att.net
Topeka, Kansas Office: 3550 S.W. 5th Street, P.O. Box 949, 66601.
Telephone: 785-232-7761.
Fax: 785-232-6604.

MEMBERS OF FIRM

Edwin Dudley Smith (Resident) — Michael K. Seck (Resident)
David P. Madden (Resident)

ASSOCIATES

Kelly A. Feyh (Resident) — Jennifer R. Rose (Resident)

For full biographical listings, see the Martindale-Hubbell Law Directory

Ruben J. Krisztal (AV)

Van Eyck Building at the Renaissance, 7007 College Boulevard, Suite 405, P.O. Box 26306, 66211
Telephone: 913-451-4441
Telecopier: 913-451-1907
Email: rjknhatty@aol.com *URL:* http://www.lawyers.com/krisztallawfirm

For full biographical listings, see the Martindale-Hubbell Law Directory

Shamberg, Johnson & Bergman, Chartered (AV)

Suite 355, 4551 West 107th Street, 66207
Telephone: 913-642-0600
Fax: 913-642-9629
Email: mail@sjblaw.com *URL:* http://www.sjblaw.com
Kansas City, Kansas Office: Suite M-4, One Security Plaza.
Telephone: 913-281-1900.
Kansas City, Missouri Office: Suite 205, Scarritt Arcade Building, 819 Walnut.
Telephone: 816-556-9431.

Lynn R. Johnson — Victor A. Bergman
John M. Parisi

Steven G. Brown — Steve N. Six

OF COUNSEL

John E. Shamberg

For full biographical listings, see the Martindale-Hubbell Law Directory

*TOPEKA,** Shawnee Co.

Ralston & Pope, LLC (AV)

2913 Southwest Maupin Lane, 66614-4139
Telephone: 913-273-8002; 888-913-2783
FAX: 913-273-0744
Email: ERalston@AOL.Com

Eugene B. Ralston — Kevin L. Diehl
Ronald P. Pope

LEGAL SUPPORT PERSONNEL

PARALEGALS

Barbara Cobuluis — Colleen Wright
Corri Wecker — Ashanti Smith

For full biographical listings, see the Martindale-Hubbell Law Directory

Wright, Henson, Somers, Sebelius, Clark & Baker, LLP (AV)

Commerce Bank Building, 100 Southeast Ninth Street, 2nd Floor, P.O. Box 3555, 66601-3555
Telephone: 785-232-2200
FAX: 785-232-3344
Email: wrighthenson@wrighthenson.com *URL:* http://www.wrighthenson.com

MEMBERS OF FIRM

Thomas E. Wright — Anne Lamborn Baker
Evelyn Zabel Wilson

ASSOCIATE

Michael M. Walker

For Complete List of Firm Personnel, See General Section

For full biographical listings, see the Martindale-Hubbell Law Directory

*WICHITA,** Sedgwick Co.

Foulston & Siefkin L.L.P. (AV)

700 NationsBank Financial Center, 67202
Telephone: 316-267-6371
Facsimile: 316-267-6345
URL: http://www.foulston.com
Topeka, Kansas Office: 1515 NationsBank Tower, 534 Kansas Avenue, 66603.
Telephone: 785-233-3600.
Fax: 785-233-1610.
Dodge City, Kansas Office: 810 Frontview, P.O. Box 1147, 67801.
Telephone: 316-227-8126.
Fax: 316-227-8451.
Member: Lex Mundi, The World's Leading Association of Independent Law Firms.

MEMBERS OF FIRM

Jay F. Fowler — Amy S. Lemley
Craig W. West

For Complete List of Firm Personnel, See General Section

For full biographical listings, see the Martindale-Hubbell Law Directory

Wichita—Continued

HUTTON & HUTTON (AV)

8100 East 22nd Street North, Building 1200, 67226-2312
Telephone: 316-688-1166
Fax: 316-686-1077
Mailing Address: P.O. Box 638, Wichita, KS, 67201-0638
Email: huttnlaw@southwind.net *URL:* http://www.huttonlaw.com

Mark B. Hutton
Andrew W. Hutton

ASSOCIATES

Derek Scott Casey
Christopher P. Christian
Anne H. Pankratz
Chan P. Townsley
Deborah B. McIlhenny

OF COUNSEL

M. Prudence Hutton

For full biographical listings, see the Martindale-Hubbell Law Directory

KENTUCKY

*BOWLING GREEN,** Warren Co.

COLE, MOORE & BAKER (AV)

921 College Street-Phoenix Place, P.O. Box 10240, 42102-7240
Telephone: 270-782-6666
FAX: 270-782-8666
Email: CMB@Premiernet.net

MEMBERS OF FIRM

John David Cole
Matthew J. Baker
Frank Hampton Moore, Jr.
Dov Moore

ASSOCIATES

John David Cole, Jr.
Stefan R. Hughes
Matthew P. Cook

OF COUNSEL

Frank R. Goad

Counsel for: Western Kentucky Cola-Cola Bottling Co.; Clark Distributing Co., Inc.; Scotty's Contracting & Stone Co.
Local Counsel for: General Electric Co.; Bucyrus-Erie Company; Wal-Mart Stores, Inc.; Kroger/Country Oven.
Representative Insurance Clients: Liberty Mutual Insurance Co.; Travelers Insurance Co.; Wausau Insurance Co.

For full biographical listings, see the Martindale-Hubbell Law Directory

KERRICK, GRISE & STIVERS (AV)

1025 State Street, P.O. Box 9547, 42102-9547
Telephone: 502-782-8160
Fax: 502-782-5856
Email: kgs@kgslaw.com
Elizabethtown, Kentucky Office: 2935 Dolphin Drive, Suite 102.
Telephone: 502-769-5788.
Fax: 502-737-9285.

MEMBERS OF FIRM

Thomas N. Kerrick
Gregory N. Stivers
John R. Grise
H. Brent Brennenstuhl
Laura M. Hagan

ASSOCIATES

Karl N. Crandall
Shawn Rosso Alcott
Jason B. Bell

OF COUNSEL

Jeffrey R. O'Grody

LEGAL SUPPORT PERSONNEL

Patricia Logsdon
Laura Lockhart Lico
Allison Lusk

Representative Clients: Columbia Greenview Regional Hospital; Hospital Corporation of America; Russell County Hospital; Wayne County Hospital; Hardin Memorial Hospital; Kentucky Hospital Association Trust.

For full biographical listings, see the Martindale-Hubbell Law Directory

MILLIKEN LAW FIRM (AV)

410 East Tenth Avenue, P.O. Box 1640, 42102-1640
Telephone: 502-843-0800
Fax: 502-842-1237

W. Currie Milliken
Wesley V. Milliken

Reference: Firstar Bank, Bowling Green, Kentucky; Citizens First, Bowling Green, Kentucky.

For full biographical listings, see the Martindale-Hubbell Law Directory

COVINGTON, Kenton Co.

ROBERT E. SANDERS AND ASSOCIATES, P.S.C. (AV)

The Charles H. Fisk House, 1017 Russell Street, 41011-3052
Telephone: 606-491-3000
Fax: 606-655-4642
Email: resanders@worldnet.att.net

Robert E. Sanders

Jeffrey M. Sanders
J. Pierre Tismo
Delana S. Pierce

LEGAL SUPPORT PERSONNEL

Shirley L. Sanders
Sandra A. Sturgeon
Sheila D. Rachal

For full biographical listings, see the Martindale-Hubbell Law Directory

*ELIZABETHTOWN,** Hardin Co.

COLEMAN, EASTON, LOCHMILLER & HALL (AV)

(Formerly Reford H. Coleman and Associates)
2907 Ring Road, P.O. Box 1177, 42702-1177
Telephone: 502-737-0600
Fax: 502-737-0488
Email: celh@ne.infi.net

Reford H. Coleman
Beth Ann Lochmiller
Kelly Mark Easton
M. Brent Hall

ASSOCIATE

Matthew C. Hess

Representative Clients: American States Insurance Cos.; Federated Rural Elec. Insurance Co.; General Motors Corp.; The Hartford; Indiana Insurance Co.; Kentucky Association of Counties All-Lines Fund; Kentucky Farm Bureau Mutual Insurance Co.; Liberty Mutual Insurance Co.; State Auto Insurance Co.; United Services Automobile Association (State Counsel).

For full biographical listings, see the Martindale-Hubbell Law Directory

*LEXINGTON,** Fayette Co.

GALLION, BAKER & BRAY, P.S.C. (AV)

200 West Vine Street, Suite 710, 40507-1620
Telephone: 606-255-6885; 800-897-0837
Telecopier: 606-253-9709
Email: gbbatty@lex.infi.net

William J. Gallion
Barbara A. Kriz
Michael H. Baker
Christopher R. Jenkins
Pamela W. Bray
James R. Carpenter

H. Caywood Prewitt, Jr.
Bruce D. Gehle
David C. Jones
David L. Helmers
James M. Kennedy
Elizabeth R. Overton

For full biographical listings, see the Martindale-Hubbell Law Directory

LYNN, FULKERSON, NICHOLS AND KINKEL, PLLC (AV)

267 West Short Street, 40507
Telephone: 606-253-0523
Telefax: 606-254-2098
Email: mail@LFNK.com

MEMBERS OF FIRM

Deddo G. Lynn
Mark E. Nichols
Calvin R. Fulkerson
Steven G. Kinkel

ASSOCIATES

Marshall R. Hixson
Jo Alice Van Nagell
Melanie Sublett Marrs

OF COUNSEL

Edward R. Hays
Gordon W. Moss

Representative Clients: St. Paul Fire and Marine Insurance Co.; The Medical Protective Company; CNA.

For full biographical listings, see the Martindale-Hubbell Law Directory

SAVAGE, GARMER & ELLIOTT, P.S.C. (AV)

Opera House Office Building, 141 North Broadway, 40507
Telephone: 606-254-9351
Fax: 606-233-9769

Joe C. Savage
William R. Garmer
Robert L. Elliott

For full biographical listings, see the Martindale-Hubbell Law Directory

*LONDON,** Laurel Co.

FARMER, KELLEY, BROWN AND WILLIAMS (AV)

502 West Fifth Street, Drawer 490, 40741
Telephone: 606-878-7640
Fax: 606-878-2364
Email: fpfarmer@farmerlaw.com
Lexington, Kentucky Office: 1082 Griffin Gate Drive, 40511-1384.
Telephone: 606: 263-2567.
Facsimile: 606: 878-2364.

MEMBERS OF FIRM

F. Preston Farmer
John F. Kelley, Jr.
Michael P. Farmer
Martha L. Brown
Jason E. Williams

ASSOCIATES

Suzanne S. Farmer
Jennifer S. Nicholson

Representative Clients: The Aetna Casualty and Surety Co.; American States Insurance Co.; Auto-Owner's Insurance Co.; Bituminous Insurance Co.; Canadian Universal Insurance Co.; Chubb Insurance Co.; Cotton States Insurance Co.; Crum & Forster Underwriters Group; Eagle Insurance Co.; Equity Mutual Insurance Co.

For full biographical listings, see the Martindale-Hubbell Law Directory

*LOUISVILLE,** Jefferson Co.

FRANKLIN AND HANCE, P.S.C. (AV)

The Speed House, 505 West Ormsby Avenue, 40203
Telephone: 502-637-6000
Fax: 502-637-1413
Email: golfatty@aol.com *URL:* http://www.lawyers.com/fhlaw

Larry B. Franklin
Michael R. Hance

David B. Gray
Hope Fitzpatrick Brooks

Reference: First National Bank.

For full biographical listings, see the Martindale-Hubbell Law Directory

McMURRY & TALBOTT (AV)

4965 U.S. Highway 42, Suite 2800, 40222
Telephone: 502-326-9000
FAX: 502-326-9001
Email: wmcmurry@msn.com *URL:* http://www.lawyers.com/mcmurry_and_talbott

William F. McMurry
Alex F. Talbott

For full biographical listings, see the Martindale-Hubbell Law Directory

O'BRYAN, BROWN & TONER (AV)

455 South Fourth Avenue, Suite 1500, Starks Building, 40202
Telephone: 502-585-4700
Fax: 502-585-4703
Email: mail@obtlaw.com

MEMBERS OF FIRM

Donald K. Brown, Jr.
Christopher P. O'Bryan
Gerald R. Toner
John L. Dotson
Emily A. Faith
James P. Grohmann
David Scott Strite

ASSOCIATES

Andrew N. Clooney
Tracy Sullivan Prewitt
Beth H. McMasters
Cathleen Charters Palmer
Clay Edwards
Peter D. Palmer
Charles Wayne Miller

OF COUNSEL

Joseph C. O'Bryan

For full biographical listings, see the Martindale-Hubbell Law Directory

SITLINGER, McGLINCY, STEINER, THEILER & KAREM (AV)

Suite 370, Starks Building, 455 South Fourth Street, 40202-2508
Telephone: 502-589-2627
Fax: 502-583-3415

MEMBERS OF FIRM

Lee E. Sitlinger
Dennis R. McGlincy
Jack W. Steiner, Jr.
Charles E. Theiler, II
Edmund Pete Karem
Curt Sitlinger
Scott Edmund Karem
Tammy C. Snyder

LEGAL SUPPORT PERSONNEL

Lynn Wockenfuss

Representative Clients: State Farm Mutual Automobile Insurance Co.; State Farm Fire & Casualty Co.; American International Insurance Co.; Walgreen Company.
Reference: Commonwealth Bank & Trust Co.

For full biographical listings, see the Martindale-Hubbell Law Directory

WEISS FREDERICK WILLETT & HAYNES (AV)

1425 Citizens Plaza, 40202
Telephone: 502-583-1000
FAX: 502-583-4478

Gary M. Weiss
Carl D. Frederick
Barry Willett
William T. Haynes, Jr.
Janice M. Weiss

ASSOCIATES

Karla W. Katakis
Paul J. Hershberg
Kevin M. Adams

OF COUNSEL

Henry M. Burt

For full biographical listings, see the Martindale-Hubbell Law Directory

*MADISONVILLE,** Hopkins Co.

FRANKLIN, GORDON & HOBGOOD (AV)

24 Court Street, P.O. Box 547, 42431
Telephone: 502-821-7252

MEMBERS OF FIRM

Charles G. Franklin (1883-1959)
Carroll S. Franklin (1919-1980)
Laurence T. Gordon
Byron L. Hobgood
Charles G. Franklin, II

ASSOCIATE

Paul H. Riley, Jr.

Representative Clients: St. Paul Insurance Cos.; Medical Protective Insurance Co.; Kentucky Medical Insurance Co.; Universal Underwriters; Progressive Casualty Insurance Co.; The Professional Insurance Co.
Approved Attorneys for: Louisville Title Division of Commonwealth Land Title Insurance Co.

*SOMERSET,** Pulaski Co.

THE FIRM OF JOHN G. PRATHER (AV)

48 Public Square, P.O. Box 616, 42502-0616
Telephone: 606-679-1626; 679-4838; 678-5604
Fax: 606-679-8204
Email: pratherlaw@som-uky.campuscwix.net

MEMBERS OF FIRM

John G. Prather
John G. Prather, Jr.
Winter R. Huff (Ms.)

ASSOCIATE

Michelle Ross Altobella

Representative Clients: Kentucky Medical Insurance Company; First & Farmers Bank of Somerset; Sentry-Dairyland Insurance; Hartford Accident & Indemnity; Cracker Barrel Old Country Store, Inc.; Somerset Independent Board of Education; Kentucky School Boards Insurance Trust; Southern Belle Dairy; Norfolk Southern Railway; FDIC.

For full biographical listings, see the Martindale-Hubbell Law Directory

LOUISIANA

*BATON ROUGE,** East Baton Rouge Parish

LANE, FERTITTA, JANNEY & THOMAS (AV)

435 Louisiana Avenue, P.O. Box 3335, 70821
Telephone: 225-387-0241
Fax: 225-387-1238

MEMBERS OF FIRM

Horace C. Lane (1921-1989)
Frank A. Fertitta
William F. Janney
Richard S. Thomas

Representative Clients: State Farm Mutual Automobile Insurance Co.; State Farm Fire & Casualty Co.; United States Fidelity & Guaranty Co.; Aetna Casualty & Surety Co.; Employers Liability Assurance Corp., Ltd.; Allstate Insurance Co.; St. Paul Fire and Marine Insurance Co.; The Medical Protective Co.; Safeco Insurance Co. of America; Horace Mann Insurance Co.

For full biographical listings, see the Martindale-Hubbell Law Directory

POWERS & WILLARD, L.L.P. (AV)

7967 Office Park Boulevard, P.O. Box 15948, 70895
Telephone: 225-928-1951
Fax: 225-929-9834

MEMBERS OF FIRM

John Dale Powers
William E. Willard

ASSOCIATES

Neil H. Mixon
Lindsey J. Leavoy
Edwin L. Hightower
Andrew P. Sellers, Jr.
Suzanne K. Sasser
Kyle C. Marionneaux

(See Next Column)

POWERS & WILLARD L.L.P., *Baton Rouge—Continued*

General Counsel for: Audubon Insurance Co.
Louisiana Counsel for: Hancock Bank & Trust Co.; Hertz Corp.; Ciba-Geigy Corp.; Utica Mutual Insurance Co.

For full biographical listings, see the Martindale-Hubbell Law Directory

WATSON, BLANCHE, WILSON & POSNER (AV)

Registered Limited Liability Partnership
505 North Boulevard, P.O. Drawer 2995, 70821-2995
Telephone: 225-387-5511
Fax: 225-387-5972

Peter T. Dazzio
Felix R. Weill
William E. Scott, III
Michael M. Remson
P. Chauvin Wilkinson, Jr.
Randall L. Champagne
René J. Pfefferle
P. Scott Jolly

ASSOCIATE

Michael P. Wilson

Representative Clients: Baton Rouge General Health Center; Baton Rouge General Medical Center; Louisiana Hospital Association Malpractice and General Liability Trust Fund; Willis-Knighton Medical Centers.

For full biographical listings, see the Martindale-Hubbell Law Directory

*GRETNA,** Jefferson Parish

WINDHORST, GAUDRY, RANSON, HIGGINS & GREMILLION, L.L.C. (AV)

Oakwood Corporate Center, 401 Whitney Avenue Suite 500, P.O. Box 1910, 70056
Telephone: 504-362-2466; 367-9247
Telcopier: 504-362-5938
Email: wgrhg@gs.verio.net

Thomas L. Gaudry, Jr.
Daniel A. Ranson
Daryl A. Higgins
Gregory G. Gremillion
Wade A. Langlois, III
Michael D. Peytavin

OF COUNSEL

Fritz H. Windhorst (Retired)

Steven Dow Oliver
Thomas W. Darling
David J. Dowell, Jr.
John A Leslie
Walter Patrick Maestri
B. Wesley Pitts

Reference: Hibernia National Bank.

For full biographical listings, see the Martindale-Hubbell Law Directory

METAIRIE, Jefferson Parish

CAMPBELL, MCCRANIE, SISTRUNK, ANZELMO & HARDY, P.C. (AV)

3445 North Causeway Boulevard, Suite 800, 70002
Telephone: 504-831-0946
Fax: 504-831-2492

Frederick R. Campbell
Burgess E. McCranie, Jr.
Michael R. Sistrunk
Thomas P. Anzelmo
Sidney J. Hardy
Lance S. Ostendorf
Roy C. Beard
Mishthi Grace Ratnesar
Charles E. Sutton, Jr.
Isidro René DeRojas
Mark Emerson Hanna
Geoffrey J. Orr

Angela M. Bowlin
Catherine M. Williams
Colin D. Sherman
James H. Hunter
Richard Andrew Houston, III
Paxton K. Stelly
Michele Butler Prokop
Marty D. Parlipiano
Peter J. Wanek
Ken D. Brown

Representative Clients: Wal-Mart Stores, Inc.; Delchamps, Inc.; Greyhound Lines, Inc.; The Dial Corporation; Transport Insurance Company; Burger King Corporation; CNA Insurance Companies; The Louisiana Motor Vehicle Commission; Insbrok; Patent Scaffolding.

For full biographical listings, see the Martindale-Hubbell Law Directory

*MONROE,** Ouachita Parish

HAYES, HARKEY, SMITH & CASCIO, L.L.P. (AV)

2811 Kilpatrick Boulevard, P.O. Box 8032, 71211-8032
Telephone: 318-387-2422
FAX: 318-388-5809

Thomas M. Hayes, Jr. (1915-1994)
Louis D. Smith (Retired)
Joseph D. Cascio, Jr.
Charles S. Smith
Thomas M. Hayes, III
Bruce McKamy Mintz
C. Joseph Roberts, III
John B. Saye

OF COUNSEL

Haynes L. Harkey, Jr.

(See Next Column)

Karen L. Hayes
Harry McClellan Moffett, IV

Representative Clients: Cigna, Inc.; CNA; St. Francis Medical Center, Inc.; St. Paul Insurance Group; Travelers Ins. Co.; Northeast Louisiana Physician Hospital Organization, Inc.; Northeast Louisiana Cancer Institute, LLC; State of Louisiana Health Care Authority, through office of Rise Management.

For full biographical listings, see the Martindale-Hubbell Law Directory

MCLEOD VERLANDER (AV)

A Partnership including Professional Law Corporations
1900 North 18th Street, Suite 610, P.O. Box 2270, 71207-2270
Telephone: 318-325-7000
Telecopier: 318-324-0580
Email: mv@mv-law.com *URL:* http://www.lawyers.com/mvlaw

MEMBERS OF FIRM

Robert P. McLeod (P.L.C.)
David E. Verlander, III (P.L.C.)

Rick W. Duplissey
Donald C. Douglas, Jr.
Laurie J. Burkett

Representative Clients: Columbia Health Systems; Columbia North Monroe Hospital; Louisiana Medical Mutual Insurance Co.; The Orthopaedic Clinic of Monroe; Evanston Insurance Company; Extacorporeal Technologies, Inc.; Daig Corporation; Western Indemnity Company; Shand Morahan.

For full biographical listings, see the Martindale-Hubbell Law Directory

*NEW ORLEANS,** Orleans Parish

BEAHM AND GREEN (AV)

145 Robert E. Lee Boulevard Suite 408, 70124-2552
Telephone: 504-288-2000
Fax: 504-288-2099
Email: Frank@Beahm.com *URL:* http://www.Beahm.com

Franklin D. Beahm
Charles S. Green, Jr.

ASSOCIATES

Julie G. Hamner
Candice V. Bates

For full biographical listings, see the Martindale-Hubbell Law Directory

BOGGS, LOEHN & RODRIGUE (AV)

A Partnership including Law Corporations
Suite 1850, Entergy Building, 639 Loyola Avenue, 70130-3597
Telephone: 504-523-7090
Fax: 504-581-6822
Email: BLAR@bellsouth.net

Charles A. Boggs (A Law Corporation)
Thomas E. Loehn (A Law Corporation)
Edward A. Rodrigue, Jr., (A Law Corporation)

Anne E. Medo
Matthew B. Moreland

Reference: First National Bank of Commerce, New Orleans, La.

For full biographical listings, see the Martindale-Hubbell Law Directory

BUCKLEY & HAYES, L.L.P. (AV)

A Partnership including a Professional Corporation
1555 Poydras Street Suite 1700, 70112
Telephone: 504-523-5100
Fax: 504-523-5698
Covington, Louisiana Office: 2301 North HIghway 190, Suite 3, 70433.
Telephone: 504-871-7005.
Fax: 504-871-7051.

MEMBERS OF FIRM

Lloyd W. Hayes
E. Ross Buckley, Jr., (A Professional Law Corp.)
Marianne S. Pensa
William H. Voigt

ASSOCIATES

Michele D. Ahlers
Ernest Philip Legier, Jr.
Elton A. Foster

OF COUNSEL

Harold A. Thomas

For full biographical listings, see the Martindale-Hubbell Law Directory

CAPITELLI & WICKER (AV)

2950 Energy Centre, 1100 Poydras Street, 70163-2950
Telephone: 504-582-2425
Fax: 504-582-2422
Email: cw4law@bellsouth.net

(See Next Column)

CAPITELLI & WICKER—*Continued*

Ralph Capitelli
T. Carey Wicker, III
Paul Michael Elvir, Jr.

For full biographical listings, see the Martindale-Hubbell Law Directory

EMMETT, COBB, WAITS, KESSENICH & O'NEIL, A PROFESSIONAL LAW CORPORATION (AV)

Suite 1950, 1515 Poydras Street, 70112
Telephone: 504-581-1301
Telex: 58-4430
Telecopier: 504-581-6020
Email: ecwko@ecwko.com

Francis Emmett (Retired)
John F. Emmett
Randolph J. Waits
William E. O'Neil
J. Fredrick Kessenich
Susan E. Henning
James A. Cobb, Jr.
Michael G. Helm

OF COUNSEL

Terry A. McCall

Michael W. McMahon
William K. Terrill, II

Reference: First National Bank of Commerce, New Orleans.

For full biographical listings, see the Martindale-Hubbell Law Directory

GAINSBURGH, BENJAMIN, DAVID, MEUNIER & WARSHAUER (AV)

2800 Energy Centre, 1100 Poydras, 70163-2800
Telephone: 504-522-2304
Telecopier: 504-528-9973
Email: DPHILLIPS@GAINSBEN.COM

OF COUNSEL

Samuel C. Gainsburgh
Jack C. Benjamin

MEMBERS OF FIRM

Robert J. David
Stevan C. Dittman
Gerald E. Meunier
Madeleine M. Landrieu
Irving J. Warshauer
Darryl M. Phillips
Jeffrey A. Mitchell

ASSOCIATE

Gary B. Roth

For full biographical listings, see the Martindale-Hubbell Law Directory

LEWIS, KULLMAN & STERBCOW (AV)

2615 Pan-American Life Center, 601 Poydras Street, 70130
Telephone: 504-588-1500
Fax: 504-588-1514
Email: lewkull@bellsouth.net

MEMBERS OF FIRM

Harvey J. Lewis
Lawrence S. Kullman
Paul M. Sterbcow

ASSOCIATE

David A. Abramson

For full biographical listings, see the Martindale-Hubbell Law Directory

MARTZELL & BICKFORD (AV)

A Partnership including a Professional Corporation
338 Lafayette Street, 70130-3244
Telephone: 504-581-9065
Fax: 504-581-7635
Email: mailbox@martzellbickford.com *URL:* http://www.martzellbickford.com

John R. Martzell (P.C.)
Scott R. Bickford

Regina O. Matthews
M. Suzanne Montero
Duggan F. Ellis
Richard A. Filce
Ray L. Rhymes

LEGAL SUPPORT PERSONNEL

LITIGATION ADMINISTRATOR

Christopher H. Sherwood

PARALEGALS

Jane B. Daigle
Connie L. Cosse
Mary Wiggenhorn

FIRM ADMINISTRATOR

Stephen C. Wolf (Certified Public Accountant)

For full biographical listings, see the Martindale-Hubbell Law Directory

MCGLINCHEY STAFFORD (AV)

A Professional Limited Liability Company
643 Magazine Street, 70130-3477
Telephone: 504-586-1200
Fax: 504-596-2800
TDD: (504) 596-2728
Telex: 584327
Cable Address: "MACSTAC"
Mailing Address: P.O. Box 60643, New Orleans, Louisiana, 70160-0643
Email: @mcglinchey.com *URL:* http://www.mcglinchey.com
Dallas, Texas Office: 2777 Stemmons Freeway, Suite 925, 75207-2401.
Telephone: 214-860-9700.
Fax: 214-860-9750.
Houston, Texas Office: 2727 Allen Parkway, Suite 1900, 77019.
Telephone: 713-520-1900.
Fax: 713-520-1025.
Baton Rouge, Louisiana Office: Ninth Floor, One American Place, 70825-0001.
Telephone: 504-383-9000.
Fax: 504-343-3076.
Jackson, Mississippi Office: Suite 1200, SkyTel Centre, 200 South Lamar Street, 39201.
Telephone: 601-960-8400.
Fax: 601-960-8406.
Lake Providence, Louisiana Office: 405 Morgan Street, 71254-2691.
Telephone: 318-559-1200.
Fax: 318-559-0609.
Monroe, Louisiana Office: Dean ONB Tower, 130 Desiard Street, Suite 807, 71201.
Telephone: 318-651-0807.
Fax: 318-651-0809.

MEMBERS OF FIRM

Donna Guinn Klein
Robin Spencer Palmisano
Eric A. Shuman
Monica A. Frois

ASSOCIATE

Deborah A. Van Meter

OF COUNSEL

Joe Giarrusso, Jr.

For full biographical listings, see the Martindale-Hubbell Law Directory

WARD NELSON, LLC (AV)

1539 Jackson Avenue, 6th Floor, 70130
Telephone: 504-561-5000
Fax: 504-588-1334

MEMBERS OF FIRM

Joseph R. Ward, Jr.
Craig R. Nelson
Lisa A. Condrey

ASSOCIATES

Lynn H. Frank
James Everet Brouillette

OF COUNSEL

Christina Papastavros Fay

Representative Clients: Associated Aviation Underwriters; Associated International Underwriters; Colonial Penn Insurance; Fidelity & Casualty of New York; Fireman's Insurance of Newark; Gulf Ins. Co.; Prudential Property and Cas. Ins. Co.; State Farm Fire & Casualty Co.; State Farms Mutual Automobile Insurance Co.; The Weitz Company.

For full biographical listings, see the Martindale-Hubbell Law Directory

WILSON & BOWLING (AV)

A Partnership including Professional Law Corporations
Suite 2411, Bank One Center, 201 St. Charles Avenue, 70170
Telephone: 504-586-5200
Facsimile: 504-586-5201
Email: wilsbowl@gs.net
Gulfport, Mississippi Office: 715 Markham Building, 2301 14th Street, 39501.
Telephone: 228-575-6202.
Fax: 228-864-6227.

Gordon F. Wilson, Jr., (P.L.C.)
David A. Bowling (P.L.C.)

Jeanne B. Roques
Susannah Ross Cooley
John D. Acomb

For full biographical listings, see the Martindale-Hubbell Law Directory

*SHREVEPORT,** Caddo Parish

TROY E. BAIN (AV)

1540 Irving Place, 71101
Telephone: 318-221-0076
Fax: 318-227-8290
Reference: Commercial National Bank of Shreveport.

For full biographical listings, see the Martindale-Hubbell Law Directory

Shreveport—Continued

MAYER, SMITH & ROBERTS, L.L.P. (AV)

1550 Creswell, 71101
Telephone: 318-222-2135, 222-2268
Fax: 318-222-6420
Email: (Attorney's First Name)@MSRLAW.COM

MEMBERS OF FIRM

Caldwell Roberts
Walter O. Hunter, Jr.
Mark A. Goodwin
Ben Marshall, Jr.
Alexander S. Lyons
Kim Purdy Thomas
David Butterfield
Henry N. Bellamy
John C. Turnage
Paul R. Mayer, Jr.
Steven E. Soileau
Deborah Shea Baukman
Caldwell Roberts, Jr.
Frank K. Carroll
Dalton Roberts Ross

OF COUNSEL

Paul R. Mayer

Representative Clients: CNA Insurance Companies; Liberty Mutual Insurance Company; United States Fidelity and Guaranty Company; Schumpert Medical Center; Travelers Insurance Company; Great American Insurance Company; Insurance Corporation of America; Highlands Insurance Company.

For full biographical listings, see the Martindale-Hubbell Law Directory

SLIDELL, St. Tammany Parish

JAMES R. STRAIN, JR. (AV)

103 Galeria Boulevard, 70458
Telephone: 504-649-3662
Fax: 504-649-2462
Mailing Address: P.O. Box 2590, Slidell, LA, 70459

Representative Clients: Louisiana Medical Mutual Insurance Co.; Louisiana Patients' Compensation Fund; Medical Fitness Centers of America, Inc.; Thirstrup Medical Enterprises, Inc.; Wellness Aerobic & Sports Medicine Clinic; Jefferson Insurance Group; State of Louisiana-Dept. of Transportation and Development; State of Louisiana-Office of Risk Management.

For full biographical listings, see the Martindale-Hubbell Law Directory

MAINE

*AUGUSTA,** Kennebec Co.

PIERCE ATWOOD (AV)

77 Winthrop Street, 04330
Telephone: 207-622-6311
Fax: 207-623-9367
Email: info@PierceAtwood.com *URL:* http://www.pierceatwood.com
Portland, Maine Office: One Monument Square.
Telephone: 207-791-1100.
Fax: 207-791-1350.
Newburyport, Massachusetts Office: 6 Harris Street.
Telephone: 978-465-9599.
Fax: 978-465-9945.

MEMBERS OF FIRM

Malcolm L. Lyons
John C. Nivison

For Complete List of Firm Personnel, See General Section

For full biographical listings, see the Martindale-Hubbell Law Directory

*BANGOR,** Penobscot Co.

GROSS, MINSKY, MOGUL & SINGAL, P.A. (AV)

Key Plaza, 23 Water Street, P.O. Box 917, 04402-0917
Telephone: 207-942-4644; 800-274-7124
Telecopier: 207-942-3699
Email: law@gmms.com

Edward I. Gross (1912-1999)
Jules L. Mogul (1930-1994)
George Z. Singal
Louis H. Kornreich
George C. Schelling
Edward W. Gould
Steven J. Mogul
James R. Wholly
Daniel A. Pileggi
Philip K. Clarke

Wayne P. Libhart (Retired)
Sandra L. Rothera
James S. Nixon

OF COUNSEL

Norman Minsky

Representative Client: Dahl Chase Pathology Associates.
Local Counsel for: The St. Paul Insurance Cos.; Aetna Life & Casualty Co.; Imperial Casualty & Indemnity Co.

For full biographical listings, see the Martindale-Hubbell Law Directory

*PORTLAND,** Cumberland Co.

PRETI, FLAHERTY, BELIVEAU, PACHIOS & HALEY, LLC (AV)

One City Center, P.O. Box 9546, 04112-9546
Telephone: 207-791-3000
Telecopier: 207-791-3111
Email: admin@preti.com *URL:* http://www.preti.com
Augusta, Maine Office: 45 Memorial Circle, P.O. Box 1058, 04332-1058.
Telephone: 207-623-5300.
Telefax: 207-623-2914.
Bath, Maine Office: Thirty Front Street, P.O. Box 665, 04530-0665.
Telephone: 207-443-5576.
Telefax: 207-443-6665.

MEMBERS OF FIRM

Christopher D. Nyhan
Daniel Rapaport
Robert O. Newton

ASSOCIATE

Kevin J. Beal

Representative Clients: St. Paul Fire and Marine Insurance Co.; PHICO Insurance Co.

For Complete List of Firm Personnel, See General Section

For full biographical listings, see the Martindale-Hubbell Law Directory

THOMPSON & BOWIE (AV)

Three Canal Plaza, P.O. Box 4630, 04112
Telephone: 207-774-2500
Telecopier: 207-774-3591
Email: law@thompsonbowie.com

MEMBERS OF FIRM

Roy E. Thompson, Jr.
James M. Bowie
Daniel R. Mawhinney
Rebecca H. Farnum
Glenn H. Robinson
Frank W. DeLong, III
Michael E. Saucier
Mark V. Franco
Edward R. Benjamin, Jr.
Cathy S. Roberts
Paul C. Catsos

ASSOCIATES

Elizabeth Knox Peck
Thomas G. Diebold
Michael R. Bosse
Lisa M. Fitzgibbon

For full biographical listings, see the Martindale-Hubbell Law Directory

SACO, York Co.

SMITH ELLIOTT SMITH & GARMEY, P.A. (AV)

199 Main Street, P.O. Box 1179, 04072
Telephone: 207-774-3199
Telefax: 207-774-2235
Email: info@sesgattorneys.com *URL:* http://www.sesgattorneys.com

Randall E. Smith
Terrence D. Garmey
John H. O'Neil, Jr.

Representative Clients: City of Biddeford; Saco and Biddeford Savings Institution; Ocean Communities Federal Credit Union.
Local Counsel for: East Guard Insurance Co.
Reference: Saco & Biddeford Savings Institution.

For Complete List of Firm Personnel, See General Section

For full biographical listings, see the Martindale-Hubbell Law Directory

MARYLAND

*ANNAPOLIS,** Anne Arundel Co.

MICHAEL H. BERESTON, P.A. (AV)

8 Fleet Street, 2nd Floor, P.O. Box 2990, 21404
Telephone: 410-269-5011
Fax: 410-269-5022
Email: bereston@flash.net

Michael H. Bereston

LEGAL SUPPORT PERSONNEL

Kristina Seidel (Paralegal/Office Manager)

For full biographical listings, see the Martindale-Hubbell Law Directory

Annapolis—Continued

BRASSEL & BALDWIN, P.A. (AV)

112 West Street, 21401
Telephone: 410-216-7900
DC Metro: 301-261-2199
Fax: 410-974-6019
URL: http://www.brasselbaldwin.com
Baltimore, Maryland Office: The B & O Building, Suite 920. 2 North Charles Street, 21201-3754.
Telephone: 410-974-6000.
Fax: 410-385-2939.

Rignal W. Baldwin, Jr. | Jon W. Brassel

Jonathan P. Kagan | Mary Coale Baldwin
Alexander John May

OF COUNSEL

Richard T. Stansbury (Resident, Baltimore, Maryland Office)

For full biographical listings, see the Martindale-Hubbell Law Directory

HYATT, PETERS & WEBER (AV)

1919 West Street, P.O. Box 6635, 21401
Telephone: 410-266-0626
Fax: 410-841-5065
Email: info@hyatt.hpwsb.com *URL:* http://www.hpwlaw.com

Alan J. Hyatt | Paula J. Peters
Paul J. Weber

ASSOCIATES

Sara H. Arthur
Sharon M. Grosfeld
Gregg M. Weinberg
Jonathan A. Hodgson
John L. Hill
Arlette K. Bright
Bruce F. Bright (Not admitted in MD)

OF COUNSEL

Steven G. Tyler

For full biographical listings, see the Martindale-Hubbell Law Directory

*BALTIMORE,** (Independent City)

THE LAW OFFICES OF KATHLEEN CAHILL, LLC (AV)

15 East Chesapeake Avenue, 21286
Telephone: 410-321-6171
Fax: 410-821-7740
Email: kcahillesq@aol.com

Kathleen Cahill

For full biographical listings, see the Martindale-Hubbell Law Directory

CORNBLATT, BENNETT, PENHALLEGON & ROBERSON, P.A. (AV)

Suite 1800, 201 North Charles Street, 21201
Telephone: 410-752-7600
Fax: 410-752-2110
Email: mail@cbprlaw.com

Theodore B. Cornblatt
S. Woods Bennett
John R. Penhallegon
Patrick A. Roberson
Jeffrey Y. Laynor

J. Michael Harrison | Gary E. Dumer, Jr.

For full biographical listings, see the Martindale-Hubbell Law Directory

ELLIN AND BAKER (AV)

Second Floor, 1101 St. Paul Street, 21202
Telephone: 410-727-1787
Fax: 410-547-1787
1-800-237-1787
Email: Ellinlaw@aol.com

MEMBER OF FIRM

Marvin Ellin

For full biographical listings, see the Martindale-Hubbell Law Directory

BERTRAM M. GOLDSTEIN & ASSOCIATES, P.A. (AV)

222 Blaustein Building, One North Charles Street, 21201-3710
Telephone: 410-539-2222
Fax: 410-539-8157

Bertram M. Goldstein

Dean Kasian | Jeffrey S. Goldstein

For full biographical listings, see the Martindale-Hubbell Law Directory

GOODELL, DEVRIES, LEECH & GRAY, LLP (AV)

Suite 2000, One South Street, 21202
Telephone: 410-783-4000
Telecopy: 410-783-4040
Email: GDLG@GDLGLAW.COM

MEMBERS OF FIRM

Bruce R. Parker
Thomas V. Monahan, Jr.
Susan T. Preston
Craig B. Merkle
Bonnie J. Beavan
Amy B. Heinrich

For full biographical listings, see the Martindale-Hubbell Law Directory

ISRAELSON, SALSBURY, CLEMENTS & BEKMAN, L.L.C. (AV)

300 West Pratt Street Suite 450, 21201
Telephone: 410-539-6633
FAX: 410-625-9554

MEMBERS OF FIRM

Stuart Marshall Salsbury
Paul D. Bekman
Daniel M. Clements
Matthew Zimmerman
Laurence A. Marder

Lauren R. Calia | Leslie Hayes Russo

COUNSEL TO THE FIRM

Max R. Israelson | Michael P. Smith

OF COUNSEL

Samuel Omar Jackson, Jr. (Semi-Retired) | Wendy Lozinsky Shiff

For full biographical listings, see the Martindale-Hubbell Law Directory

JANET, WILLOUGHBY & GERSHON, LLC (AV)

Executive Centre at Hooks Lane, 8 Reservoir Circle, Suite 200, 21208-1309
Telephone: 410-653-3200
Toll Free: 888-4-MED-LAW
Fax: 410-653-9030
Email: JWG@medlawlegalteam.com

Howard Alan Janet (P.C.)
Wayne M. Willoughby (P.A.)
Zev T. Gershon
Randal D. Getz

Robin R. Smith | Denise A. Greig

LEGAL SUPPORT PERSONNEL

Joan Hunter Green (Registered Nurse/Paralegal) | Sharon Marie Schmidt (Paralegal)

For full biographical listings, see the Martindale-Hubbell Law Directory

KAHN, SMITH & COLLINS, P.A. (AV)

201 North Charles Street, 10th Floor, 21201
Telephone: 410-244-1010
Fax: 410-244-8001
URL: http://www.interbit.com/ksc

Andrew H. Kahn
Joel A. Smith
Francis J. Collins
David V. Diggs
Keith J. Zimmerman

Leslie A. Pladna
Sarah Pazourek Harlan
Travis M. Mastroddi
Sabrina Willis

For full biographical listings, see the Martindale-Hubbell Law Directory

MEHLMAN & GREENBLATT, LLC (AV)

1838 Greene Tree Road, Suite 360, 21208
Telephone: 410-486-4790
Fax: 410-486-4360
URL: http://www.lawyers.com/mehlman&greenblatt

Gerson B. Mehlman
Gary R. Greenblatt
Frederic C. Heyman
Francis X. Leary
Constance M. Hare

For full biographical listings, see the Martindale-Hubbell Law Directory

PHILLIPS P. O'SHAUGHNESSY, P.A. (AV)

1102 Terrace Glen, 21210
Telephone: 410-532-0300
FAX: 410-532-2220
URL: http://www.oshaughnessy.wld.com
Ft. Lauderdale, Florida Office: One East Broward Boulevard, Suite 700, 33301.
Telephone: 800-882-3133.

Phillips P. O'Shaughnessy | Robin Frazier Kandel

For full biographical listings, see the Martindale-Hubbell Law Directory

Baltimore—Continued

GILBERT H. ROBINETTE (AV)

212 Washington Avenue, 21204
Telephone: 410-321-6666
Toll Free: 1-888-538-0821
Fax: 410-821-5444
Email: ghr44@aol.com *URL:* http://www.lawyers.com/gilrobinette
Charleston, West Virginia Office: 1564 Virginia Street, East, 25311.
Telephone: 304-342-1844.
Fax: 304-342-1901.

For full biographical listings, see the Martindale-Hubbell Law Directory

SCANLAN, ROSEN & SHAR, LLC (AV)

26 South Street, 21202-3399
Telephone: 410-244-1155
Fax: 410-244-1157
Email: lawyers@triallaw.com *URL:* http://www.triallaw.com

Alfred L. Scanlan, Jr. Marcus Z. Shar
Marc Seldin Rosen Michael Stuart Warshaw

Timothy Cronin Lynch Neil E Duke
Kristofer P. Cubello

OF COUNSEL

Colleen A. Cavanaugh Lee H. Caplan
J. Michael McWilliams

For full biographical listings, see the Martindale-Hubbell Law Directory

SCHOCHOR, FEDERICO AND STATON, P.A. (AV)

The Paulton, 1211 St. Paul Street, 21202
Telephone: 410-234-1000
Toll Free: 888-234-0001
Facsimile: 410-234-1010
URL: http://www.sfspa.com
Washington D.C. Office: 10 G Street, N.E., Suite 650.
Telephone: 202-408-3300.

Jonathan Schochor Philip C. Federico
Kerry D. Staton

Christopher P. Kennedy Robert J. Farley
Bonnie Ardinger Winders

For full biographical listings, see the Martindale-Hubbell Law Directory

SPENCE, KOHLER, CHRISTIE & PULVER, P.A. (AV)

401 Washington Avenue, Suite 701, 21204
Telephone: 410-823-8200
Fax: 410-823-8208
Email: skcp@ix.netcom.com

Paul W. Spence Sharon A. Christie
Alison Daryl Kohler Michael A. Pulver

For full biographical listings, see the Martindale-Hubbell Law Directory

BETHESDA, Montgomery Co.

KARP, FROSH, LAPIDUS, WIGODSKY & NORWIND, P.A. (AV)

7475 Wisconsin Avenue, Suite 800, 20814
Telephone: 301-656-2111
Fax: 301-654-7748
Email: jackgold@erols.com
Washington, D.C. Office: 1150 Connecticut Avenue, N.W., Suite 900. 20036.
Telephone: 202-822-3777.
Fax: 202-828-4130.

Ronald A. Karp Jeffrey A. Wigodsky
Brian E. Frosh Edward L. Norwind
Lawrence S. Lapidus J. Philip Kessel

Jack A. Gold Donald C. Weinberg

OF COUNSEL

Douglas R. Smith Roy I. Niedermayer
Stanley A. First Maurice I. Burstein
(Not admitted in MD)

For full biographical listings, see the Martindale-Hubbell Law Directory

GREENBELT, Prince Georges Co.

HOROWITZ, FORAN & SONNTAG, P.A. (AV)

Capital Office Park, 6301 Ivy Lane, Suite 600, 20770
Telephone: 301-441-2022
Fax: 301-474-6054
Email: hofoso@aol.com

(See Next Column)

Edward S. Horowitz John R. Foran
W. Scott Sonntag

Timothy J. Driscoll Jeffrey H Horowitz
James D. Cardea

For full biographical listings, see the Martindale-Hubbell Law Directory

LARGO, Prince Georges Co.

GREGORY K. WELLS & ASSOCIATES, P.A. (AV)

1801 McCormick Drive Suite 160, 20774
Telephone: 301-925-2000
Fax: 301-925-2006
Email: gkw.associates@erols.com *URL:* http://www.lawyers.com/gregorykwells

Gregory K. Wells

Edward J. Maginnis

OF COUNSEL

Robert C. Maynard

LEGAL SUPPORT PERSONNEL

Juernine M. Wright

For full biographical listings, see the Martindale-Hubbell Law Directory

*ROCKVILLE,** Montgomery Co.

ANDERSON & QUINN (AV)

The Adams Law Center, 25 Wood Lane, 20850
Telephone: 301-762-3303
Fax: 301-762-3776
Email: rscanlon@andersonquinn.com

MEMBERS OF FIRM

Charles C. Collins (1900-1973) Donald P. Maiberger
Robert E. Anderson (Retired) Robert P. Scanlon
Francis X. Quinn John A. Rego
Alice Kelley Scanlon

ASSOCIATES

Kerry S. McGeever Todd P. Maiberger
Timothy J. Mulreany Jennifer D. Burke
Marc N. Steren

Representative Clients: C & P Telephone; Allstate Insurance Co.; State Farm Mutual Automobile Insurance Co.; Liberty Mutual Insurance Co.; American International Adjustment Co.; Marriott Corp.

For full biographical listings, see the Martindale-Hubbell Law Directory

ARMSTRONG, DONOHUE, CEPPOS & VAUGHAN, CHARTERED (AV)

Suite 101, 204 Monroe Street, 20850
Telephone: 301-251-0440
Telecopier: 301-279-5929

Larry A. Ceppos Benjamin S. Vaughan
H. Kenneth Armstrong Pamela Barrow Kincheloe

Sharon A. Marcial J. Eric Rhoades
Susan E. Mikorski

For full biographical listings, see the Martindale-Hubbell Law Directory

BRAULT, GRAHAM, SCOTT & BRAULT, LLC (AV)

101 South Washington Street, 20850
Telephone: 301-424-1060
Fax: 301-424-7991
Email: bgsb@earthlink.net
Washington, D.C. Office: Brault, Graham, Scott & Brault, PLLC, 1140 Connecticut Avenue, N.W., Suite 250.
Telephone: 202-785-1200.
FAX: 202-785-4301.
Fairfax, Virginia Office: Suite 500, 11350 Random Hills Road, Fair Oaks Plaza, 22030-7429.
Telephone: 202-785-1200.

OF COUNSEL

Laurence T. Scott James Robert Miller

MEMBERS OF FIRM

Denver H. Graham (1922-1987) Ronald G. Guziak
Albert E. Brault (Retired) Daniel L. Shea (Resident)
Albert D. Brault (Resident) M. Kathleen Parker (Resident)
Leo A. Roth, Jr. David G. Mulquin (Resident)
James S. Wilson (Resident) James M. Brault (Resident)
Regina Ann Casey (Resident)

(See Next Column)

BRAULT, GRAHAM, SCOTT & BRAULT LLC—*Continued*

ASSOCIATES

Rhonda Ann Hurwitz (Resident) Joan F. Brault (Resident)

Representative Clients: American Oil Co.; Crum & Forster Group; Fireman's Fund American Insurance Cos.; Kemper Group; Reliance Insurance Cos.; Safeco Group; Government Employees Insurance Co.; Medical Mutual Insurance Society of Maryland; Legal Mutual Liability Insurance Society of Maryland.

For full biographical listings, see the Martindale-Hubbell Law Directory

MICHAEL S. MORGENSTERN & ASSOCIATES, P.C. (AV)

51 Monroe Street, Suite 1604, 20850
Telephone: 301-217-9500
Fax: 301-217-9579
Toll Free: 1-888-888-0005
Mailing Address: P.O. Box 4690, Rockville, MD, 20850
Email: MSMlaw@erols.com
Washington, D.C. Office: 601 Pennsylvania Avenue, N.W. 20004.
Telephone: 202-393-2500.
Frederick, Maryland Office: 228 West Patrick Street. 21701.
Telephone: 301-620-7900.

Michael S. Morgenstern
Carl Morgenstern (Not admitted in MD)
Barbara L. Morgenstern (Not admitted in MD)

OF COUNSEL

W. David Allen

For full biographical listings, see the Martindale-Hubbell Law Directory

STEIN, SPERLING, BENNETT, DE JONG, DRISCOLL, GREENFEIG & METRO, P.C. (AV)

25 West Middle Lane, 20850-2204
Telephone: 301-340-2020; 800-435-5230
Telecopier: 301-340-8217
Email: lawfirm@steinsperling.com
Falls Church, Virginia Office: 6245 Leesburg Pike, Suite 140, 22044.
Telephone: 703-237-0500.
Telecopier: 703-534-2899.

Fred A. Balkin
Stuart S. Greenfeig

For Complete List of Firm Personnel, See General Section

For full biographical listings, see the Martindale-Hubbell Law Directory

TIMONIUM, Baltimore Co.

DUGAN & JAKUBOWSKI, P.A. (AV)

1966 Greenspring Drive, Suite 500, 21093-4119
Telephone: 410-308-1600
Fax: 410-308-1742

Henry E. Dugan, Jr.
Ruth A. Jakubowski

Bruce J. Babij
Pamela S. Foresman
George S. Tolley, III
Yale R. Spector
Frank W. Spector

OF COUNSEL

Marian V. Fleming

For full biographical listings, see the Martindale-Hubbell Law Directory

*TOWSON,** Baltimore Co.

WHITNEY & BOGRIS, LLP (AV)

401 Washington Avenue, Twelfth Floor, 21204
Telephone: 410-583-8000
Fax: 410-583-8031
Email: HGWC@worldnet.att.net

MEMBERS OF FIRM

Daniel W. Whitney
George D. Bogris

ASSOCIATES

Kathleen D. Leslie
Henry Russell
Sandra A. Tofte
Michael A. Giacomazza
Arlene L. Sew
Gerald S. Gaetano (Not admitted in MD)
Scott A. McCabe (Not admitted in MD)
Jeffrey C. Shipley

OF COUNSEL

Joseph E. Dever
David L. Feldstein
Ronald V. Miller, Jr.

For full biographical listings, see the Martindale-Hubbell Law Directory

MASSACHUSETTS

*BOSTON,** Suffolk Co.

ANDERSON, ADLER, COHEN & HARVEY LLP (AV)

230 Congress Street, 02110
Telephone: 617-423-6674
Telefax: 617-423-7152
Email: aach@aachlaw.com *URL:* http://www.aachlaw.com

MEMBERS OF FIRM

James H. Anderson
Sidney W. Adler
Ellen Epstein Cohen
Alexandra B. Harvey
George E. Wakeman, Jr.
A. Bernard Guekguezian

ASSOCIATES

Laura Berg Susich
Charles M. Waters
Emily Haycock Fournier
Shelley A. McNamee
Windy L. Rosebush
Michael F. Conway
J. Yasmin Tayyab
Ethan I. Davis

For full biographical listings, see the Martindale-Hubbell Law Directory

LAW OFFICES BERGSTRESSER AND ASSOCIATES, P.C. (AV)

52 Temple Place, 02111-1315
Telephone: 617-542-4365
Facsimile: 617-542-5460
Email: mmmberg@socialaw.com *URL:* http://www.bergstresser.com

Clyde D. Bergstresser
Mary M. McGoldrick

Karenina M. Darmer

For full biographical listings, see the Martindale-Hubbell Law Directory

CORNELL & GOLLUB (AV)

75 Federal Street, 02110
Telephone: 617-482-8100
Telecopier: 617-482-3917
Email: CornellGollub@worldnet.att.net
Wakefield, Rhode Island Office: 146 Main Street, 02879.
Telephone: 401-782-2072.
Telecopier: 401-782-4941.

MEMBERS OF FIRM

Robert W. Cornell (1910-1988)
Karl L. Gollub (1934-1985)
David H. Sempert
Peter M. Durney
Paul F. Lynch
Jane Treen Brand
Janet J. Bobit
David W. McGough

ASSOCIATES

Thomas A. Pursley
Susan Donaldson Novins
Marie Chadeayne Chafe
Kelly L. Wilkins
James P. Kerr
Patricia A. Hartnett
David G. Braithwaite
Jennifer L. Davis
Matthew J. Ginsburg
Kenneth M. Robbins

OF COUNSEL

Philip J. Foley

For full biographical listings, see the Martindale-Hubbell Law Directory

LANG & MORGERA, L.L.P. (AV(T))

6 Beacon Street, Suite 615, 02108
Telephone: 617-720-0176
Telecopier: 617-720-1184
URL: http://www.lawyers.com/lawdoctors
URL: http://www.lawdoctors.net
Providence, Rhode Island Office: 50 Park Row West, Suite 100.
Telephone: 401-456-0300.
Fax: 401-453-5545.

Barry D. Lang
Vincent D. Morgera

For full biographical listings, see the Martindale-Hubbell Law Directory

MEEHAN, BOYLE & COHEN, P.C. (AV)

2 Center Plaza Suite 600, 02108
Telephone: 617-523-8300
Fax: 617-523-0525

James F. Meehan
Leo V. Boyle
Cynthia J. Cohen
Warren F. Fitzgerald
Peter J. Black
John J. Carroll, Jr.
Michael B. Bogdanow
Karen R. Ristuben

Sherry Yee Mulloy
Samuel M. Furgang
Bradley Mead Henry
Jonathan E. Tobin

For full biographical listings, see the Martindale-Hubbell Law Directory

Boston—Continued

SWARTZ & SWARTZ (AV)

10 Marshall Street, 02108
Telephone: 617-742-1900
Fax: 617-367-7193
Email: Attorney@Swartzlaw.com *URL:* http://www.Swartzlaw.com

Edward M. Swartz
Alan L. Cantor
Joseph A. Swartz
Victor A. Denaro
Joan E. Swartz
James A. Swartz
David P. Angueira
Jason Mark
Lisa V. Kaprielian

OF COUNSEL

Fredric A. Swartz

For full biographical listings, see the Martindale-Hubbell Law Directory

MICHIGAN

*ANN ARBOR,** Washtenaw Co.

FERRIS & SALTER, P.C. (AV)

4158 Washtenaw Avenue, 48108
Telephone: 734-677-2020
Fax: 734-677-3277
Email: ferrissalt@aol.com *URL:* http://www.ferris-salter.com

Don Ferris
Heidi Salter-Ferris

For full biographical listings, see the Martindale-Hubbell Law Directory

HOOPER, HATHAWAY, PRICE, BEUCHE & WALLACE (AV)

126 South Main Street, 48104
Telephone: 313-662-4426
Fax: 313-662-9559
Email: hhpbw@voyager.net

Mark R. Daane
Anthony P. Patti
Angela L. Jackson

Representative Clients: Avfuel Corporation; Bank of Ann Arbor; Castrol North America; Chem-Trend Incorporated; Ervin Industries, Inc.; First Martin Corporation; Glacier Hills, Inc.; Prestolite Electric, Inc.; Southern States Cooperative; E.B. Eddy Forest Products, Ltd.

For Complete List of Firm Personnel, See General Section

For full biographical listings, see the Martindale-Hubbell Law Directory

BINGHAM FARMS, Oakland Co.

SMALL, TOTH, BALDRIDGE & VAN BELKUM, P.C. (AV)

30100 Telegraph Road Suite 250, 48025-4516
Telephone: 248-647-9595
Facsimile: 248-647-9599

Richard L. Small
John M. Toth
David M. Baldridge
Thomas G. Van Belkum
Keith P. Felty

Stephanie A. Griz-Kochkodan
Kristin Allen

Representative Clients: The Medical Protective Co.; Michigan Physicians Mutual Liability Insurance Co.; Physicians Insurance Company of Michigan; AAMOS National; CNA Insurance Group; Anthem Insurance Co.; Oakwood United Hospitals; The Detroit Medical Center Affiliated Hospital.

For full biographical listings, see the Martindale-Hubbell Law Directory

BLOOMFIELD HILLS, Oakland Co.

LAWRENCE J. ACKER, P.C. (AV)

44 East Long Lake Road, 48304
Telephone: 248-594-7277
Fax: 248-594-7280

Lawrence J. Acker

For full biographical listings, see the Martindale-Hubbell Law Directory

O'CONNOR, DEGRAZIA & TAMM, P.C. (AV)

4111 Andover Road East, 48302
Telephone: 248-433-2000
Fax: 248-433-2001
Email: odtlaw@ameritech.net

Richard M. O'Connor
James I. DeGrazia
James E. Tamm
Julie McCann O'Connor
Audrey J. Forbush

(See Next Column)

Thomas H. Schram
Timothy Mulligan
Lauri Beth Stewart
Christopher P. Kohler

Representative Clients: Regents of the University of Michigan; William Beaumont Hospital; Mutual Ins. Corp. of America; Botsford General Hospital; Michigan Municipal League; Michigan Municipal Liability and Property Pool; St. Paul Insurance Cos.; Meadowbrook Inc. Co.; National Chiropractic Mutual.

For full biographical listings, see the Martindale-Hubbell Law Directory

DAVID D. PATTON & ASSOCIATES, P.C. (AV)

44 East Long Lake Road, Suite 100, P.O. Box 829, 48303-0829
Telephone: 248-258-6020
Fax: 248-258-6052
Email: litigation@aol.com *URL:* http://www.lawyers.com/dpattonlaw

David D. Patton

Ellen Bartman Jannette
Patricia C. White
Humma S. Siddiqi
Kelly P. Bekolay
David H. Patton (1912-1993)

OF COUNSEL

Lawrence J. Acker

For full biographical listings, see the Martindale-Hubbell Law Directory

PORTNOY, PIDGEON & ROTH, P.C. (AV)

3883 Telegraph, Suite 103, 48302
Telephone: 248-647-4242
Fax: 248-647-8251
Email: DWINNIE103@AOL.COM *URL:* http://www.lawyers.com/portnoypidgeon&roth

Bernard N. Portnoy (Retired)
James M. Pidgeon
Robert P. Roth
Marc S. Berlin
Sheila Connor-Heath
Anne Loridas Randall
Joseph M. LaBella
Melinda A. Davis

Representative Clients: North Oakland Medical Center, Pontiac General Hospital Division; Hurly Medical Center, Flint, Michigan; McLaren Regional Medical Center, Flint, Michigan; William Beaumont Hospital, Royal Oak, Michigan; Lapeer Regional Hospital; Oakwood Health Care & Co., Inc.

For full biographical listings, see the Martindale-Hubbell Law Directory

PROVIZER & PHILLIPS, P.C. (AV)

6785 Telegraph Road, Suite 400, 48301
Telephone: 248-642-0444
Facsimile: 248-642-6661
Toll Free: 1-800-288-9080
URL: http://www.lawyers.com/provizer&phillips

Randall E. Phillips
Marilyn A. Madorsky
Noel F. Beck
Mark S. Baumkel

Representative Clients: Reliance National Ins. Co.; Dr. Sampson Inwald; Dr. Saul Shapiro.

For full biographical listings, see the Martindale-Hubbell Law Directory

*DETROIT,** Wayne Co.

BOOTHMAN, HEBERT & ELLER, P.C. (AV)

Marquette Building, 243 West Congress, Suite 950, 48226
Telephone: 313-964-0150
Fax: 313-964-2226
Email: boothman@mail.mich.com

Dale L. Hebert
Richard C. Boothman
Gary S. Eller

Edward C. Reynolds, Jr.
Marta J. Hoffman

Representative Clients: University of Michigan; Mutual Insurance Corporation of America; Emergency Physicians Medical Group; Pronational; HCR Manor Care, Inc.
Reference: Comerica Bank-Detroit.

For full biographical listings, see the Martindale-Hubbell Law Directory

GLEICHER & PATEK, P.C. (AV)

1500 Buhl Building, 48226
Telephone: 313-964-6900
Fax: 313-964-6976
URL: http://www.lawyers.com/gplaw

Elizabeth Gleicher
Barbara A. Patek

LEGAL SUPPORT PERSONNEL

Laura Bocchini (Legal Coordinator)

For full biographical listings, see the Martindale-Hubbell Law Directory

Detroit—Continued

KITCH DRUTCHAS WAGNER DENARDIS & VALITUTTI, A PROFESSIONAL CORPORATION (AV)

One Woodward, Tenth Floor, 48226-3499
Telephone: 313-965-7900
Fax: 313-965-7403
URL: http://www.kitch.com
Lansing, Michigan Office: 120 Washington Square, North, Suite 280, One Michigan Avenue, 48933-1609.
Telephone: 517-372-6430.
Fax: 517-372-0441.
Macomb County Office: Towne Square Development, 10 South Main Street, Suite 301, Mount Clemens, 48043-7903.
Telephone: 810-463-9770.
Fax: 810-463-8994.
Toledo, Ohio Office: 405 Madison Avenue, Suite 1500, 43604-1235.
Telephone: 419-243-4006.
Fax: 419-243-7333.
Marquette, Michigan Office: Old City Hall, 220 West Washington, Suite 500, 49855-4344.
Telephone: 906-228-0001.
Fax: 906-228-0003.
Ann Arbor, Michigan Office: 303 Detroit Street, Suite 400, P.O. Box 8610, 48107-8610.
Telephone: 734-994-7600.
Fax: 734-994-7626.
Grand Rapids, Michigan Office: 300 Ottawa, NW, Suite 210, 49503.
Telephone: 616-456-8384.
Fax: 616-456-8795.

FIRM PRINCIPALS

Richard A. Kitch
Ronald E. Wagner (Managing Principal)
Ralph F. Valitutti, Jr.
Richard R. DeNardis
Mona K. Majzoub
Harry J. Sherbrook
Anthony G. Arnone
Charles W. Fisher
Clyde M. Metzger, III (Principal, Ann Arbor Office)
Thomas J. Foley
Victor J. Abela
James H. Hughesian
John P. Ryan (Principal, Lansing Office)
William D. Chaklos
Steve N. Cheolas (Principal, Macomb County Office)
Susan Healy Zitterman
John S. Wasung (Principal, Toledo, Ohio Office)
William W. Vertes
John Paul Hessburg
Karen Bernard Berkery
Daniel R. Shirey
Richard T. Counsman
Steven M. Waclawski
Stephen R. Brzezinski
Thomas R. Shimmel
Carole S. Empey (Ann Arbor)
Carol Ann Tarnowsky
Michael J. Watza
Sara Mae Gerbitz
Linda M. Garbarino
Susan Marie Beutel
Mark A. Wisniewski

FIRM ASSOCIATE PRINCIPALS

Susan M. Ramage (Grand Rapids Office)
Daniel J. Niemann (Ann Arbor Office)
Sharon A. DeWaele
Kenneth M. Essad
Kim J. Sveska
Dean A. Etsios
Barbara A. Martin
Paula M. Burgess (Toledo, Ohio Office)
Lauri A. Read
Cullen B. McKinney
Jeffrey T. Gorcyca

FIRM SENIOR ASSOCIATES

Antonio Mauti
Joseph P. McGill
Mary Catherine Storen
Laura L. Witty
Sheley L. DeGraw
Laura L. Selzer
R. Lisa Panah
Christina A. Ginter

For Complete List of Firm Personnel, See General Section

For full biographical listings, see the Martindale-Hubbell Law Directory

MILLER, CANFIELD, PADDOCK AND STONE, P.L.C. (AV)

A Professional Limited Liability Company
Founded in 1852 by Sidney Davy Miller
150 West Jefferson, Suite 2500, 48226-4415
Telephone: 313-963-6420
Fax: 313-496-7500
Cable Address: "Stem Detroit"
URL: http://www.millercanfield.com
Ann Arbor, Michigan Office: 101 North Main Street, 7th Floor, 48104-1400.
Telephone: 734-663-2445.
Fax: 734-747-7147.
Troy, Michigan Office: 840 West Long Lake Road, Suite 200, 48098.
Telephone: 248-879-2000.
Fax: 248-879-2001.
Grand Rapids, Michigan Office: 99 Monroe, N.W., Suite 1200, 49503-2639.
Telephone: 616-454-8656.
Fax: 616-776-6322.
Howell, Michigan Office: 121 South Barnard Street, Suite 4, 48843-2305.
Telephone: 517-546-7600.
Telecopier: 517-546-6974.

(See Next Column)

Kalamazoo, Michigan Office: 444 West Michigan Avenue, 49007-3752.
Telephone: 616-381-7030.
Fax: 616-382-0244.
Lansing, Michigan Office: One Michigan Avenue, Suite 900, 48933-1609.
Telephone: 517-487-2070.
Fax: 517-374-6304.
Monroe, Michigan Office: 214 East Elm Avenue, Suite 100, 48162-2682.
Telephone: 734-243-2000.
Fax: 734-243-0901.
Washington, D.C. Office: 1900 K Street, N.W., Suite 1150. 20006.
Telephone: 202-429-5575; 785-0600.
Fax: 202-331-1118; 785-1234.
Pensacola, Florida Office: 25 West Cedar, 32501.
Telephone: 850-469-1088.
Fax: 850-432-0677.
New York, New York Office: 1450 Broadway, 41st Floor, 10018.
Telephone: 212-704-4400.
Fax: 212-704-4410.
Gdynia, Poland Office: UL. Slaska 21, 81-319.
Telephone: 011-485-831-2808.
Fax: 011-48-58-628 6411.
Warsaw, Poland Office: UL. Nowogrodzkall, 5th Floor, 00-513.
Telephone: 011-4822 529 0200.
Fax: 011-4822 529 0201.
Katowice, Poland Office: UL. Francuska 35/37, 40-027.
Telephone: 011 (48-32) 757-2414.
Fax: 011 (48-32) 757-2483.

PRINCIPALS OF FIRM

Charles E. Ritter (Kalamazoo Office)
Thomas G. Parachini
James C. Foresman
Leland D. Barringer
Brian J. Doren
Irene Bruce Hathaway

Representative Firm Clients: Chrysler Corporation; Comerica, Incorporated; City of Detroit, Michigan; Detroit Tigers, Inc.; First of Michigan; Ford Motor Company; Ford Motor Credit Company; Great Lakes Bancorp; Henry Ford Hospital; INVETECH Company.

For Complete List of Firm Personnel, See General Section

For full biographical listings, see the Martindale-Hubbell Law Directory

PYTELL & VARCHETTI, P.C. (AV)

18580 Mack Avenue, 48236
Telephone: 313-343-9200; 1-888-292-4LAW
Fax: 313-343-0207
Email: PROBATE@compuserve.com *URL:* http://www.MIprobate.com

Robert H. Pytell
Henry C. Pytell (1903-1988)
Paul E. Varchetti

For full biographical listings, see the Martindale-Hubbell Law Directory

VANDEVEER GARZIA, PROFESSIONAL CORPORATION (AV)

Suite 1600, 333 West Fort Street, 48226
Telephone: 313-961-4880
Fax: 313-961-3822
Email: vg@voyager.net
Oakland County Office: 220 Park Street, Suite 300, Birmingham, Michigan.
Telephone: 810-645-0100.
Fax: 810-645-2430.

Fred L. Vandeveer (1879-1972)
James E. Haggerty, Sr. (1900-1966)
Leroy G. Vandeveer (1902-1981)
Buelle A. Doelle (1902-1985)
James E. Plastow, Jr.
Michael M. Hathaway
John J. Lynch, III (Resident, Oakland County Office)
Thomas M. Peters
James K. Thome
Gary Alan Miller
William L. Kiriazis
Daniel P. Steele
Shelley K. Miller (Resident, Oakland County Office)
Terrance P. Lynch
Dennis B. Cotter
Bruce E. Pearce
Hal O. Carroll
David B. Timmis (Resident, Oakland County Office)

Nancy A. Hensley
Dawn M. Twydell
Christian E. Hildebrandt (Resident, Oakland County Office)
Donald C. Brownell

Representative Clients: CNA Insurance Group; Travelers Insurance Co.; J.P. Bender & Associates; Pontiac osteopathic Hospital; Mt. Clemens General Hospital; Macomb Emergency Care Physicians, P.C.

For full biographical listings, see the Martindale-Hubbell Law Directory

WILLMARTH, TANOURY, RAMAR, CORBET, GARVES & SHAW (AV)

535 Griswold, Suite 1730, 48226-3602
Telephone: 313-964-6300
Fax: 313-964-6310
Email: mdwillth@home.net

(See Next Column)

WILLMARTH, TANOURY, RAMAR, CORBET, GARVES & SHAW, *Detroit—Continued*

MEMBERS OF FIRM

Daniel R. Corbet
Brian R. Garves
David R. Nauts
Anthony J. Paradiso
John M. Perrin
John J. Ramar
Bruce R. Shaw
William A. Tanoury
Mark D. Willmarth

ASSOCIATES

Marie C. Kennedy
Wayne Walker
Elizabeth L. Sokol
Robert S. Silverman
Carmine G. Paterra
Joseph J. Ceglarek, II
Derek Steven Wilczynski
Frank Hamidi
Kristen E. Skaff
Steven J. Bonasso
Colleen P. O'Connor
Lara R. Stutz
Eric G. Tucciarone
Michael P. Robach

For full biographical listings, see the Martindale-Hubbell Law Directory

WULFMEIER & OTTENWESS, PLC (AV)

The Buhl Building, 535 Griswold Suite 850, 48226
Telephone: 313-965-2121
Facsimile: 313-965-7680
Email: law@wulf-ott.com *URL:* http://www.wulf-ott.com
Ann Arbor Office: 320 N. Main Street, Suite 102, 48104.
Telephone: 734-761-1900.
Facsimile: 734-769-0433.

LeRoy H. Wulfmeier, III
David M. Ottenwess
Cheryl L. Chandler
Daniel J. Dulworth
John J. Moran
Stephanie L. Pappas

For full biographical listings, see the Martindale-Hubbell Law Directory

EAST LANSING, Ingham Co.

SMITH HAUGHEY RICE & ROEGGE, P.C. (AV)

1400 Abbott Road, Suite 410, 48823-1902
Telephone: 517-332-3030
Facsimile: 517-332-3468
Grand Rapids, Michigan Office: 200 Calder Plaza Building, 250 Monroe Avenue, N.W., 49503-2251.
Telephone: 616-774-8000.
Facsimile: 616-774-2461.
Traverse City, Michigan Office: City Centre Plaza, Suite 100, 202 East State Street, P.O. Box 848, 49685-0848.
Telephone: 231-929-4878.
Facsimile: 231-929-4182.

Douglas G. Powe
Richard C. Kraus

Veronica A. Marsich
Mary K. Robbins-Kralapp
Brian E. Madar
Margaret A. Chamberlain

For full biographical listings, see the Martindale-Hubbell Law Directory

*GAYLORD,** Otsego Co.

BENSINGER, COTANT, MENKES & AARDEMA, P.C. (AV)

308 West Main Street, P.O. Box 1000, 49735
Telephone: 517-732-7536
Fax: 517-732-4922
URL: http://www.bcma.net
Grand Rapids, Michigan Office: 983 Spaulding Avenue, S.E.
Telephone: 616-949-7963.
Fax: 616-949-5264.
Marquette, Michigan Office: 122 West Bluff.
Telephone: 906-225-1000.
Fax: 906-225-0818.

Richard G. Bensinger
James C. Cotant
Michael E. Menkes
Robert Bryan Aardema (Resident, Grand Rapids Office)
Patrick J. Michaels
Kerr L. Moyer (Resident, Grand Rapids)
Brian W. Whitelaw (Resident, Grand Rapids Office)
Dale L. Arndt (Resident, Grand Rapids)
Gregory A. Elzinga (Resident, Marquette)
William J. Maynard (Resident, Marquette)
Glenn W. Smith (Resident, Marquette)
Daniel Joseph Bebble
Michael G. Summers (Resident, Marquette Office)
Lynn A. Moon (Resident, Marquette Office)
Roger W. Zappa (Resident, Marquette Office)
Scott R. Eckhold
Frank S. Spies (Resident, Grand Rapids Office)
William M. Fury

For full biographical listings, see the Martindale-Hubbell Law Directory

*GRAND RAPIDS,** Kent Co.

BENSINGER, COTANT, MENKES & AARDEMA, P.C. (AV)

983 Spaulding Avenue, S.E., 49546
Telephone: 616-949-7963
Fax: 616-949-5264
URL: http://www.bcma.net
Gaylord, Michigan Office: 308 West Main, P.O. Box 1000.
Telephone: 517-732-7536.
Fax: 517-732-4922.
Marquette, Michigan Office: 122 West Bluff.
Telephone: 906-225-1000.
Fax: 906-225-0818.

Brian W. Whitelaw
Dale L. Arndt

For full biographical listings, see the Martindale-Hubbell Law Directory

BUCHANAN, SILVER & BECKERING, P.L.C. (AV)

300 Ottawa N.W., Suite 800, 49503
Telephone: 616-458-2464
Fax: 616-458-0608
URL: http://www.bsblaw.com
Email: rbuchanan@bsblaw.com *URL:* http://www.lawyers.com/bsblaw

MEMBERS OF FIRM

John C. Buchanan
Lee T. Silver
Robert J. Buchanan
Jane M. Beckering

LEGAL SUPPORT PERSONNEL

Raymond E. Beckering, Jr., M.D. (Medical Consultant)

For full biographical listings, see the Martindale-Hubbell Law Directory

GRUEL, MILLS, NIMS AND PYLMAN (AV)

50 Monroe Place, Suite 700 West, 49503
Telephone: 616-235-5500
Fax: 616-235-5550

MEMBERS OF FIRM

Grant J. Gruel
William F. Mills
J. Clarke Nims
Norman H. Pylman, II
Scott R. Melton
Brion J. Brooks
Thomas R. Behm
J. Paul Janes

Representative Clients: Aquinas College; Bell Helmet Co.; Blodgett Memorial Medical Center; Chem Central, Inc.; Cook Pump Co.; Grove, Inc.; NBDC; Heim Corp.

For full biographical listings, see the Martindale-Hubbell Law Directory

SMITH HAUGHEY RICE & ROEGGE, P.C. (AV)

200 Calder Plaza Building, 250 Monroe Avenue, N.W., 49503-2251
Telephone: 616-774-8000
Facsimile: 616-774-2461
East Lansing, Michigan Office: 1400 Abbott Rd., Suite 410, 48823-1902.
Telephone: 517-332-3030.
Facsimile: 517-332-3468.
Traverse City, Michigan Office: City Centre Plaza, Suite 100, 202 East State Street, P.O. Box 848, 49685-0848.
Telephone: 231-929-4878.
Facsimile: 231-929-4182.

Clifford A. Mitts (1902-1962)
Laurence D. Smith (1913-1980)
Robert V.V. Rice (1899-1982)
Michael S. Barnes (1944-1989)
L. Roland Roegge
Thomas F. Blackwell
P. Laurence Mulvihill
Lawrence P. Mulligan
Thomas R. Tasker
Paul H. Reinhardt
Lance R. Mather
Charles F. Behler
John R. Sparks
Gary A. Rowe
William W. Jack, Jr.
William J. Hondorp
Thomas M. Weibel
James G. Black
E. Thomas Mc Carthy, Jr.
Glenn W. House, Jr.
Craig R. Noland
Paul M. Oleniczak
Craig S. Neckers
John C. O'Loughlin
Anthony J. Quarto
John M. Kruis
Paul Van Oostenburg
Dale Ann Iverson
William R. Jewell
Jon D. Vander Ploeg
Patrick F. Geary
Terence J. Ackert
Brian J. Kilbane
Robert C. Stone
Albert J. Engel, III
Phillip K. Mowers
Carol D. Carlson
Christopher R. Genther
Marilyn S. Nickell Tyree
Beth Suzanne Kromer
Robert M. Kruse
Aileen M. Leipprandt
David J. DeGraw
Matthew L. Meyer

Martha P. Forman
Karl Werner Butterer, Jr.
Garrett J. Tenhave-Chapman
J. Joseph Rossi
Stacie R. Seitz
William A. Sikkel IV
James J. Rosloniec
Angela T. Ross

OF COUNSEL

A. B. Smith, Jr.
David O. Haughey

For full biographical listings, see the Martindale-Hubbell Law Directory

GROSSE POINTE PARK, Wayne Co.

ALLAN G. MEGANCK (AV)

1033 Bishop, 48230
Telephone: 313-881-0845
Fax: 313-881-0845
Email: lawtalk@aol.com

For full biographical listings, see the Martindale-Hubbell Law Directory

*KALAMAZOO,** Kalamazoo Co.

MILLER, CANFIELD, PADDOCK AND STONE, P.L.C. (AV)

A Professional Limited Liability Company
Founded in 1852 by Sidney Davy Miller
444 West Michigan Avenue, 49007-3752
Telephone: 616-381-7030
Fax: 616-382-0244
URL: http://www.millercanfield.com
Detroit, Michigan Office: 150 West Jefferson, Suite 2500, 48226-4415.
Telephone: 313-963-6420.
Fax: 313-496-7500.
Cable Address: "Stem Detroit."
Ann Arbor, Michigan Office: 101 North Main Street, 7th Floor, 48104-1400.
Telephone: 734-663-2445.
Fax: 734-747-7147.
Troy, Michigan Office: 840 West Long Lake Road, Suite 200, 48098.
Telephone: 248-879-2000.
Fax: 248-879-2001.
Grand Rapids, Michigan Office: 99 Monroe, N.W., Suite 1200, 49503-2639.
Telephone: 616-454-8656.
Fax: 616-776-6322.
Howell, Michigan Office: 121 South Barnard Street, Suite 4, 48843-2305.
Telephone: 517-546-7600.
Telecopier: 517-546-6974.
Lansing, Michigan Office: One Michigan Avenue, Suite 900, 48933-1609.
Telephone: 517-487-2070.
Fax: 517-374-6304.
Monroe, Michigan Office: 214 East Elm Avenue, Suite 100, 48162-2682.
Telephone: 734-243-2000.
Fax: 734-243-0901.
Washington, D.C. Office: 1900 K Street, N.W., Suite 1150. 20006.
Telephone: 202-429-5575; 785-0600.
Fax: 202-331-1118; 785-1234.
Pensacola, Florida Office: 25 West Cedar, 32501.
Telephone: 850-469-1088.
Fax: 850-432-0677.
New York, New York Office: 1450 Broadway, 41st Floor, 10018.
Telephone: 212-704-4400.
Fax: 212-704-4410.
Gdynia, Poland Office: UL. Slaska 21, 81-319.
Telephone: 011-485-831-2808.
Fax: 011-48-58-628 6411.
Warsaw, Poland Office: UL. Nowogrodzkall, 5th Floor, 00-513.
Telephone: 011-4822 529 0200.
Fax: 011-4822 529 0201.
Katowice, Poland Office: UL. Francuska 35/37, 40-027.
Telephone: 011 (48-32) 757-2414.
Fax: 011 (48-32) 757-2483.

PRINCIPALS

Charles E. Ritter

Representative Firm Clients: Chrysler Corporation; Comerica, Incorporated; City of Detroit, Michigan; Detroit Tigers, Inc.; First of Michigan; Ford Motor Company; Ford Motor Credit Company; Great Lakes Bancorp; Henry Ford Hospital; INVETECH Company.

For Complete List of Firm Personnel, See General Section

For full biographical listings, see the Martindale-Hubbell Law Directory

LANSING, Ingham Co.

FRASER TREBILCOCK DAVIS & FOSTER, P.C. (AV)

1000 Michigan National Tower, 48933
Telephone: 517-482-5800
Fax: 517-482-0887
URL: http://WWW.FTDF.COM
Detroit, Michigan Office: One Woodward Avenue, Suite 1550.
Telephone: 313-237-7300.
Fax: 313-961-1651.

C. Mark Hoover
Brett J. Bean
Mark A. Bush

Marcy R. Matson
Christopher R. Royce

Representative Clients: MICOA; Pro National Insurance Co.; The Doctors Company; Michigan State University; St. Paul Insurance Company; Michigan Capital Medical Center; Frontier Insurance Company.

For full biographical listings, see the Martindale-Hubbell Law Directory

SMITH HAUGHEY RICE & ROEGGE, P.C.

(See East Lansing)

TIMMER, JAMO & O'LEARY (AV)

521 Seymour Avenue, 48933
Telephone: 517-371-3500
Fax: 517-371-4514
Email: TIMJAMOLOP@MICHBAR.ORG

MEMBERS OF FIRM

James A. Timmer
James S. Jamo
James S. O'Leary
Kathleen A. Lopilato

Representative Clients: Auto Owners Insurance Co.; Travelers/Aetna Insurance Co.; Western Surety Co.; Indiana Insurance Company/The Netherlands Insurance Companies; Michigan Municipal League; Meadowbrook Insurance; Citizens Insurance Company of America; Speedway SuperAmerica LLC; TIG/Nationwide Insurance Co.; Wolverine Mutual Insurance Co.

For full biographical listings, see the Martindale-Hubbell Law Directory

*MARQUETTE,** Marquette Co.

BENSINGER, COTANT, MENKES & AARDEMA, P.C. (AV)

122 West Bluff, 49855
Telephone: 906-225-1000
Fax: 906-225-0818
URL: http://www.bcma.net
Gaylord, Michigan Office: 308 West Main, P.O. Box 1000.
Telephone: 517-732-7536.
Fax: 517-732-4922.
Grand Rapids, Michigan Office: 983 Spaulding Avenue, S.E.
Telephone: 616-949-7963.
Fax: 616-949-5264.

Gregory A. Elzinga
Michael G. Summers
Lynn A. Moon

For full biographical listings, see the Martindale-Hubbell Law Directory

*MOUNT CLEMENS,** Macomb Co.

MARTIN, BACON & MARTIN, P.C. (AV)

44 First Street, 48043
Telephone: 810-979-6500
Fax: 810-468-7016
URL: http://www.lawyers.com/martin

James N. Martin
Jonathan E. Martin
Paul R. VanTol
Michael R. Janes
Kevin L. Moffatt
John W. Crimando
Victor T. Van Camp

Patrick D. Ball
Amy M. Johnston
Sean S. Cleland

Reference: Community Central Bank - Mt. Clemens.

For full biographical listings, see the Martindale-Hubbell Law Directory

*MOUNT PLEASANT,** Isabella Co.

GRAY, SOWLE & IACCO, A PROFESSIONAL CORPORATION (AV)

600 Broadway East, 48858
Telephone: 517-772-5932
Fax: 517-773-0538

Loren E. Gray
Donald N. Sowle
Daniel A. Iacco
Cheryl E. Gray

References: Isabella Bank & Trust; First of America of Mount Pleasant.

For full biographical listings, see the Martindale-Hubbell Law Directory

*MUSKEGON,** Muskegon Co.

LAGUE, NEWMAN & IRISH, A PROFESSIONAL CORPORATION (AV)

600 Terrace Plaza, P.O. Box 389, 49443
Telephone: 231-725-8148
Telecopier: 231-726-3404
Email: firm@lnilaw.com

Charyn K. Hain
Todd L. Helle
William M. Newman
Alvin D. Treado

General Counsel: Hackley Hospital & Medical Center.

For Complete List of Firm Personnel, See General Section

For full biographical listings, see the Martindale-Hubbell Law Directory

ST. CLAIR SHORES, Macomb Co.

MERRY, FARNEN & RYAN, A PROFESSIONAL CORPORATION (AV)

27739 Jefferson Avenue, 48081-1309
Telephone: 810-776-6700
Telecopier: 810-776-1501
URL: http://www.lawyers.com/mfr

Cynthia E. Merry
Lynda Barbat Farnen
Michael T. Ryan

For full biographical listings, see the Martindale-Hubbell Law Directory

SAURBIER, SIEGAN & SANFIELD, P.C. (AV)

Suite 402, 400 Maple Park Boulevard, 48081
Telephone: 810-447-3700
Fax: 810-447-3755
Email: scott@saurbier.com
Detroit Office: 1028 Buhl Building.
Telephone: 313-965-2220.

SHAREHOLDERS

Scott A. Saurbier
Renée S. Siegan
Joel A. Sanfield

Marc D. Saurbier
Sara B. Keough
Lawrence T. Garcia
David C. Wiegel
John C. Valenti
Matthew J. Nagaj
Valerie Henning Mock

For full biographical listings, see the Martindale-Hubbell Law Directory

SOUTHFIELD, Oakland Co.

SCHWARTZ & JALKANEN, P.C. (AV)

24400 Northwestern Highway, Suite 200, 48075-6821
Telephone: 248-352-2555
Facsimile: 248-352-5963

Melvin R. Schwartz
Arthur W. Jalkanen
Karl Eric Hannum

Gregory A. Light
David C. Dixon

For full biographical listings, see the Martindale-Hubbell Law Directory

SOMMERS, SCHWARTZ, SILVER & SCHWARTZ, P.C. (AV)

2000 Town Center, Suite 900, 48075
Telephone: 248-355-0300
Telecopier: 248-746-4001
Plymouth, Michigan Office: 747 South Main Street.
Telephone: 313-455-4250.

Stanley S. Schwartz
David J. Winter
Jeffrey N. Shillman
B. A. Tyler
David R. Getto
Michael J. Cunningham
Norman D. Tucker
Matthew G. Curtis
Paul W. Hines
Helen K. Joyner
Richard D. Fox
John L. Runco
Frank Mafrice
Susanne Pryce
Richard L. Groffsky
Anne M. Schoepfle
Kenneth T. Watkins

Jabran G. Yasso
Marc C. Tucker
Randall M. Blau
Cameron R. Getto

OF COUNSEL

Howard Silver
Jeremy L. Winer

General Counsel for: City of Taylor; Foodland Distributors; C.A. Muer Corporation; Vlasic & Company; Nederlander Corporation; Midwest Health Centers, P.C.
Representative Clients: Michigan National Bank; Don Lee Distributors; Rite-Aid of Michigan.

For Complete List of Firm Personnel, See General Section

For full biographical listings, see the Martindale-Hubbell Law Directory

*TRAVERSE CITY,** Grand Traverse Co.

SMITH HAUGHEY RICE & ROEGGE, P.C. (AV)

City Centre Plaza, Suite 100, 202 East State Street, P.O. Box 848, 49685-0848
Telephone: 231-929-4878
Facsimile: 231-929-4182
Grand Rapids, Michigan Office: 200 Calder Plaza Building, 250 Monroe Avenue, N.W., 49503-2251.
Telephone: 616-774-8000.
Facsimile: 616-774-2461.
East Lansing, Michigan Office: 1400 Abbott Rd., Suite 410, 48823-1902.
Telephone: 517-332-3030.
Facsimile: 517-332-3468.

George Frederick Bearup
Robert W. Tubbs
Mark P. Bickel
Jeffrey R. Wonacott
R. Jay Hardin
Robert W. Parker
Charles B. Judson
Paul T. Jarboe
Jeffrey E. Gwillim

Todd W. Millar
Peter J. Boyles
Erin Eileen Gerrity
Rachel Y. Brochert
Eric W. Phelps

For full biographical listings, see the Martindale-Hubbell Law Directory

THOMPSON, O'NEIL & VANDERVEEN (AV)

309 East Front Street, P.O. Box 429, 49685
Telephone: 231-929-9700; 1-800-678-1307
Fax: 231-929-7262
Email: tov@traverse.com *URL:* http://www.lawyers.com/tovtraverse

George R. Thompson
Daniel P. O'Neil
John R. VanderVeen

Jessica G. Rickard

For full biographical listings, see the Martindale-Hubbell Law Directory

TROY, Oakland Co.

HOLAHAN, MALLOY, MAYBAUGH, MONNICH & DELIE (AV)

Suite 100, 2690 Crooks Road, 48084-4700
Telephone: 248-362-4747
Fax: 248-362-4779
East Tawas, Michigan Office: 910 East Bay Street.
Telephone: 517-362-4747.
Fax: 517-362-7331.

MEMBERS OF FIRM

J. Michael Malloy, III
John R. Monnich
James D. Maybaugh
David L. Delie, Jr.

OF COUNSEL

Thomas H. O'Connor
Maureen Holahan (Retired; Resident, East Tawas Office)

For full biographical listings, see the Martindale-Hubbell Law Directory

WEST BLOOMFIELD, Oakland Co.

CHEATHAM, ESTES & HOLLMAN, P.C. (AV)

5777 West Maple Road, Suite 130, P.O. Box 255002, 48325-5002
Telephone: 248-932-2000
Fax: 248-932-2008

Charles C. Cheatham
Lee Estes
Mary E. Hollman

Christopher P. Jelinek

COUNSEL

Lynn L. Lower

For full biographical listings, see the Martindale-Hubbell Law Directory

MERGERS AND ACQUISITIONS

ALABAMA

*DOTHAN,** Houston Co.

JOHNSTON, HINESLEY, FLOWERS & CLENNEY, P.C., A PROFESSIONAL CORPORATION (AV)

291 North Oates Street, 36303
Telephone: 334-793-1115
Fax: 334-793-6603

G. David Johnston
William W. Hinesley
William T. Flowers
R. Eugene Clenney, Jr.

For full biographical listings, see the Martindale-Hubbell Law Directory

*MOBILE,** Mobile Co.

ZIEMAN, SPEEGLE, JACKSON & HOFFMAN, L.L.C. (AV)

107 St. Francis Street, Suite 3200, P.O. Box 11, 36601
Telephone: 334-694-1700
Facsimile: 334-694-1998

MEMBERS OF THE FIRM

Thomas Troy Zieman, Jr.
Jerome E. Speegle
Robert G. Jackson, Jr.
Anthony Michael Hoffman
Ben H. Harris, III

For full biographical listings, see the Martindale-Hubbell Law Directory

ARIZONA

*PHOENIX,** Maricopa Co.

FENNEMORE CRAIG, A PROFESSIONAL CORPORATION (AV)

3003 North Central Avenue, Suite 2600, 85012-2913
Telephone: 602-916-5000
Fax: 602-916-5999
Tucson, Arizona Office: One South Church Avenue, Suite 1000, 85701-1620.
Telephone: 520-879-6800.
Fax: 520-879-6899.

Arthur D. Ehrenreich
Neal Kurn
Robert P. Robinson
Robert J. Hackett
Jay S. Ruffner
Ronald L. Ballard
Stephen M. Savage
Gregg Hanks
Karen Ciupak McConnell
Jay S. Kramer
J. Barry Shelley
W. T. Eggleston, Jr.
Stephen A. Good

Thomas F. O'Malley, III
Susan M. Wissink
Paul A. Krulisky
Audrey V. Dorch (Not admitted in AZ)
Kenneth J. Lee

LEGAL SUPPORT PERSONNEL

LEGAL ASSISTANTS

Vicki Montei
Charlene Sarich

For Complete List of Firm Personnel, See General Section

For full biographical listings, see the Martindale-Hubbell Law Directory

MEYER, HENDRICKS & BIVENS, P.A. (AV)

3003 North Central Avenue Suite 1200, 85012-2915
Telephone: 602-604-2200
Facsimile: (24 Hrs.) 602-263-5333
Mailing Address: P.O. Box 2199, 85001-2199

Rand Haddock
Robert K. Rogers
Scott M. Theobald

Randall Lindsey
Salmeh K. Fodor

Reference: Northern Trust Bank of Arizona.

For full biographical listings, see the Martindale-Hubbell Law Directory

PHILIP T. PARIS (AV)

2929 North 44th Street, Suite 120, 85018
Telephone: 602-994-5813
Telecopier: 602-667-6552
Email: bkpblaw@earthlink.net *URL:* http://www.lawyers.com/philipparislaw

For full biographical listings, see the Martindale-Hubbell Law Directory

CALIFORNIA

COSTA MESA, Orange Co.

FELDHAKE, AUGUST & ROQUEMORE (AV)

Plaza Tower, Suite 1730, 600 Anton Boulevard, 92626-7124
Telephone: 714-438-3885
Fax: 714-438-3888
Email: farlaw@hqonline.com

Robert J. Feldhake
Kenneth S. August
Lisa A. Roquemore
Joshua M. Wolff

ASSOCIATES

Dimitri P. Gross
Supriya Kakkar
Katherine A. Slayton

OF COUNSEL

Arthur J. Swerdloff
Arthur M. Wilcox, Jr.

For full biographical listings, see the Martindale-Hubbell Law Directory

HERMOSA BEACH, Los Angeles Co.

NASH & EDGERTON (AV)

A Limited Liability Partnership
2615 Pacific Coast Highway, Suite 322, 90254
Telephone: 310-937-2066
Fax: 310-937-2064
Email: sedger1057@aol.com
Torrance, California Office: 3625 Del Amo Boulevard, Suite 360.
Telephone: 310-370-8272.
Fax: 310-214-9677. Email: SLN64@aol.com.

Savery L. Nash
Samuel Y. Edgerton, III
Shelley Nash
James K. Autrey
Chad Weaver
Jon C. Furgison

For full biographical listings, see the Martindale-Hubbell Law Directory

*LOS ANGELES,** Los Angeles Co.

BARBOSA GARCIA LLP (AV)

A Partnership including a Professional Corporation
801 South Grand Avenue Suite 300, 90017-4621
Telephone: 213-612-0800
Fax: 213-612-8085

Henry S. Barbosa (P.C.)
Lorie A. Campos
Kenneth T. Fong
Bonifacio Bonny Garcia (P.C.)
Michael L. Kadish
John F. Lagle
Peter E. Langsfeld
Benjamin D. Nieberg
Gary W. Park
Roberta R. Sistos
Jonathan B. Stone
Rajeev M. Talwani
Sylvia J. Trujillo
Thuy-Whien Vuong
John G. Yslas

OF COUNSEL

Albert A. Erkel, Jr.

SPECIAL COUNSEL

Adrienne D. Konigar
Joyce E. Paul
Melvin D. Peters

LEGAL SUPPORT PERSONNEL

Victor M. Estrada (Paralegal)
Janice H. Minamoto (Paralegal)

For full biographical listings, see the Martindale-Hubbell Law Directory

BRAND FARRAR & BUXBAUM LLP (AV)

515 South Flower Street, Suite 3500, 90071-2201
Telephone: 213-228-0288
Fax: 213-426-6222
Email: bfb-la@brandfarrar.com
Beijing (Peking), China Office: Suite 2518, China World Trade Centre, 1 Jian Guo Men Wai Avenue, Beijing, China.
Telephone: 86-10-6505-2288 Ext. 2523/2518.
Fax: 86-10-6505-2638. Email: bjbfbbj@public3.bta.net.cn
Chengdu, Sichuan, China Office: Suite 11A, Sichuan International Mansion, No. 1 Zhong Xi Shun Cheng Street, Chengdu, China.
Telephone: 86-28-652-1316.
Fax: 86-28-652-0547. Email: cdbfbcd@mail.sc.cninfo.net.
Chongqing, China Office: Suite 1510, Metropolitan Tower, 68 Zourong Lu, Chongqing, China.
Telephone: 86-23-6382-8381.
Fax: 86-23-6382-8373. Email: cqbfbcq@public.cta.cq.cn.
Guangzhou (Canton), China Office: Suite 1305, Main Tower, GITIC Plaza Hotel, 339 Huanshi Dong Road, Guangzhou, China.
Telephone: 86-20-8331-1888, Ext. 71305.
Fax: 86-20-8331-2671. Email: gzbfbgz@public.guangzhou.gd.cn.

(See Next Column)

BRAND FARRAR & BUXBAUM LLP, *Los Angeles—Continued*

Hong Kong, China Office: Brand Farrar Buxbaum LLP, 5/F., Landmark East, 12 Ice House Street, Central, Hong Kong, China.
Telephone: 852-2523-7001.
Fax: 852-2845-0947. Email: hkbfbhk@hk.super.net.
Los Angeles, California Office: Brand Farrar & Buxbaum LLP, Suite 3500, 515 South Flower Street, Los Angeles, California, 90071-2201.
Telephone: 213-228-0288.
Fax: 213-426-6222. Email: bfb-la@brandfarrar.com.
New York, New York Office: 275 Madison Avenue, 37th Floor, New York, New York, 10097.
Telephone: 212-286-0038.
Fax: 212-573-9077. Email: martineh@aol.com
Shanghai, China Office: Brand Farrar Buxbaum LLP, Suites 2611-12, Central Plaza, 227 Huangpi Bei Lu, Shanghai, China.
Telephone: 86-21-6375-8918.
Fax: 86-21-6375-8922. Email: shbfbsh@public2.sta.net.cn.
Shenzhen, China Office: Suite 2103A, Shenzhen Development Center, Renmin Nan Lu, Shenzhen, China.
Telephone: 86-755-229-8009.
Fax: 86-755-229-8011. Email: szbfbsz@public.szptt.net.cn.
Ulaanbaatar, Mongolia Office: Brand Farrar Buxbaum LLP, 4/F., Time Center, No. 50 Baga Toiruu, Ulaanbaatar, Mongolia.
Telephone: 976-1-31-0711.
Fax: 976-1-32-5102. Email: mgbfbmg@magicnet.mn.
Xiamen, China Office: Suite 1182 Jian Ye Building, 28 Hubin North Road, Xiamen, China.
Telephone: 86-592-506-3059.
Fax: 86-592-511-1044. Email: xmbfbxm@public.xm.fj.cn.
Associated Office, Mumbai, Bombay, India: Shah & Sanghavi, Advocates, Solicitors & Notary, 114-A Mittal Court, Nariman Point, Mumbai 400 021 India.
Telephone: 91-22-285-5755/56 or 91-22-285-3592/93.
Fax: 91-22-284-5040.

PRINCIPALS

Michael A. Brand
David C. Buxbaum (China Offices)
Kenneth Y. Choy (Hong Kong Office)
Robert W. Dziubla
David W. Farrar
Amy E. Freilich
Margaret G. Graf
John Masao Iino
Charles K. Kolstad
Edward H. Martin (New York Office)
Gregory D. Trimarche
Li Zhuogen (China Offices)

OTHER ATTORNEYS RESIDENT IN LOS ANGELES OFFICE

Sherry L. Geyer
Joan M. Marquardt
James H. Service
Jeffrey S. Allen
Julia Sylva
Brian J. Kim
Lisa Teng

OTHER ATTORNEYS RESIDENT IN BEIJING OFFICE

Hao Xiaodong
Bin Zhao
Luo Rongping
Zhang Chunbo

OTHER ATTORNEYS RESIDENT IN CHENGDU, SICHUAN OFFICE

Zeng Xiangyu
Wu Wen

OTHER ATTORNEY RESIDENT IN CHONGQING OFFICE

Du Fei

OTHER ATTORNEYS RESIDENT IN GUANGZHOU OFFICE

Zou Wenyan (Not admitted in United States)
Feng Ruiding
Jia Guangxi

OTHER ATTORNEYS RESIDENT IN HONG KONG OFFICE

Shane F. Weir
Cheonghar Wong
N.T.S. Kularatne
Simon Woo
David William Gunson
Arthur Burton Crook
Simon K.C. Lee
Cheng Yuen Yi
Lo Wing Cheong
Nicholas C. McGrenra
Eva Y.N. Kwok

OTHER ATTORNEYS RESIDENT IN NEW YORK OFFICE

Vincent I. S. Hsieh (Of Counsel)
Jeffrey Schall
Jonathan Chun Wang

OTHER ATTORNEYS RESIDENT IN SHANGHAI OFFICE

Lin Yong
Wu Hong Liang
Tang Ying
Zhang Guoyao
Qi Zhenwen

OTHER ATTORNEYS RESIDENT IN SHENZHEN OFFICE

Zhong Wenya
Zhang He

OTHER ATTORNEYS RESIDENT IN ULAANBAATAR OFFICE

Byambaa Bayarmaa
Ajiv Enhktuya

OTHER ATTORNEY RESIDENT IN XIAMEN OFFICE

Deng Sheng

For full biographical listings, see the Martindale-Hubbell Law Directory

KONOWIECKI & RANK LLP (AV)

A Partnership including a Professional Corporation
Library Tower, 633 West 5th Street, Suite 3500, 90071-2007
Telephone: 213-229-0990
Telefax: 213-229-0992

(See Next Column)

Peter C. Rank
Joseph S. Konowiecki
Michael C. Foster
Jon N. Manzanares
Kevin B. Kroeker
Peter Roan
Peter R. Mason
Denise E. Hanna
Edna M. Chism
Scott J. Moore
Robert C. Hayden
Gail D. Schubert

ASSOCIATES

Cynthia J. Billey
Michael J. Blake
Ana Castillo
Ronan Cohen
Richard A. Cross
Rosa Kwon Easton
I-Fan C. Go
Melinda A. Hess
Sandra Lee Hitt
Lynn E. Iba
Robert M. Kessler
Harry H.W. Kim
Thomas C. Knego
Stephen J. Krause
Phillip R. Maltin
John A. Mueller
Jeffrey D. Olster
Leslie Overfelt
Gary S. Pancer
Tallien Perry
Payman Pezhman
Harold C. Pope
Robin M. Prendergast
Ira L. Robinson
Michael B. Spencer
India S. Thompson
Keith A. Weaver
John A. Zrnich

Representative Clients: PacifiCare Health Systems, Inc.; Henry Mayo Newhall Memorial Hospital; Santa Clarita Health Care Assoc.; College Health Enterprises; Granada Hills Community Hospital; Redlands Community Hospital; Health Care Partners.
Reference: Bank of America.

For full biographical listings, see the Martindale-Hubbell Law Directory

MATTHIAS & BERG LLP (AV)

1990 South Bundy Drive, Suite 790, 90025-5244
Telephone: 310-820-0083
Facsimile: 310-820-8313
Email: info@matthiasberg.com

MEMBERS OF FIRM

Michael R. Matthias
Jeffrey P. Berg

ASSOCIATES

Kenneth M. H. Hoff
Ari Lorin Markow

OF COUNSEL

Stuart R. Singer

Representative Clients: Am Tec, Inc.; Chatsworth Products, Inc.; Greater China Corp.; Mexalit, S.A.; National Quality Care, Inc.; Network Holdings International, Inc.; New Sea Escape Cruises, Inc.; Residential Resources, Inc.

For full biographical listings, see the Martindale-Hubbell Law Directory

OSTROVE, KRANTZ & OSTROVE, A PROFESSIONAL CORPORATION (AV)

(Successor To: Ostrove and Lancer, A Professional Corporation; David Ostrove, A Professional Corporation)
5757 Wilshire Boulevard, Suite 535, 90036-3600
Telephone: 323-939-3400
Fax: 323-939-3500
Email: OSTROVE@AOL.COM *URL:* http://www.lawyers.com/ok&olaw

David Ostrove
David S. Krantz
Kenneth E. Ostrove

Reference: First Business Bank.

For full biographical listings, see the Martindale-Hubbell Law Directory

*SACRAMENTO,** Sacramento Co.

HUNTER RICHEY DI BENEDETTO & BREWER, LLP (AV)

A Limited Liability Partnership
Renaissance Tower, 801 K Street, 23rd Floor, 95814-3525
Telephone: 916-491-3000
Facsimile: 916-491-3080
Email: hrdb@hrdb.com *URL:* http://www.hrdb.com

MEMBERS OF FIRM

William S. Hunter
Win R. Richey
Florence L. Di Benedetto
Roy E. Brewer
Anne E. Ferguson
James F. Geary
Janet C. Eisenbeis
Stephen C. Ruehmann
Sharon K. Sandeen
Jack V. Lovell
Patricia J. Hartman

OF COUNSEL

Laurie E. Davis

LEGAL SUPPORT PERSONNEL

Lori J. Moody (Paralegal)
Deborah M. Johnson (Paralegal)
Linda Jane Hall (Executive Assistant)
Jennifer E. Mueller (Legal Assistant)
Michele L. Nickell (Legal Assistant)
Lynetta G. Goodwin

For full biographical listings, see the Martindale-Hubbell Law Directory

*SAN LUIS OBISPO,** San Luis Obispo Co.

Andre, Morris & Buttery, A Professional Law Corporation (AV)
1102 Laurel Lane, P.O. Box 730, 93406-0730
Telephone: 805-543-4171
Fax: 805-543-0752
Email: amb@amblaw.com *URL:* http://www.amblaw.com

J. Todd Mirolla

William V. Douglass

References: Bank of America National Trust and Savings Assn. (San Luis Obispo Main Branch); Mid-State Bank (San Luis Obispo).

For full biographical listings, see the Martindale-Hubbell Law Directory

COLORADO

*DENVER,** Denver Co.

Berliner Zisser Walter & Gallegos, A Professional Corporation (AV)
One Norwest Center, 1700 Lincoln Street, Suite 4700, 80203-4547
Telephone: 303-830-1700
Facsimile: 303-830-1705
Email: bzwg@bzwg.com

Martin M. Berliner
David A. Zisser
Robert W. Walter
Larry D. Gallegos

Stacey L. Bowers

OF COUNSEL

Phillip C. Gans

For full biographical listings, see the Martindale-Hubbell Law Directory

Brenman Bromberg & Tenenbaum, P.C. (AV)
Mellon Financial Center Suite 1001, 1775 Sherman Street, 80203
Telephone: 303-894-0234
Fax: 303-839-1633
Email: bbt@bbtlaw.net

Albert Brenman
Thomas R. Bromberg
A. Thomas Tenenbaum
Steven W. McDonald

Sheryl A. Johnson
Judy A. Gooch

OF COUNSEL

Duane Woodard

For full biographical listings, see the Martindale-Hubbell Law Directory

Gorsuch Kirgis LLP (AV)
Tower 1, Suite 1000, 1515 Arapahoe Street, 80202
Telephone: 303-376-5000
Fax: 303-376-5001

PARTNERS

S. Lee Terry, Jr.
Cynthia Smith Cain

ASSOCIATES

Pantea M. Garroussi
Anastasia G. Khokhryakova

LEGAL SUPPORT PERSONNEL

Lansing Wallace
Veronica Ehrenzeller

For full biographical listings, see the Martindale-Hubbell Law Directory

Schlueter & Associates, P.C. (AV)
1050 Seventeenth Street, Suite 1700, 80265
Telephone: 303-292-3883
Facsimile: 303-296-8880
Email: 76304.3546@compuserve.com

Henry F. Schlueter

Celia Velletri

For full biographical listings, see the Martindale-Hubbell Law Directory

Slivka Robinson Waters & O'Dorisio, A Professional Corporation (AV)
Suite 2600, 1099 18th Street, 80202-1926
Telephone: 303-297-2600
Telecopier: 303-297-2750
URL: http://www.srwo.com

(See Next Column)

SHAREHOLDERS

Richard P. Slivka
Peter A. Robinson
Stephen L. Waters
John W. O'Dorisio, Jr.
Ernest J. Panasci
Chevis F. Horne, Jr.
Margaret M. McClellan
Karen Samuels Jones

Deborah A. Hogan
Kerri M. Pertcheck
Susan R. Pierson
Elizabeth E. Pinckard
Daniel A. Sweetser
Bradley S. Taylor
Jill G. VanderPloeg

SPECIAL COUNSEL

Laura J. Vogelgesang
Christine Rothe Hoth

For full biographical listings, see the Martindale-Hubbell Law Directory

DISTRICT OF COLUMBIA

WASHINGTON, D.C. Co.

Silver, Freedman & Taff, L.L.P. (AV)
A Partnership including Professional Corporations
1100 New York Avenue, N.W., Suite 700, 20005-3934
Telephone: 202-414-6100
Telecopier: 202-682-0354
URL: http://www.sftlaw.com

MEMBERS OF FIRM

Sidney J. Silver (P.C.)
Robert L. Freedman (P.C.)
Barry P. Taff (P.C.)
James S. Fleischer (P.C.)
Jeffrey M. Werthan (P.C.)
Kip A. Weissman (P.C.)
Martin L. Meyrowitz (P.C.)
Richard S. Garabedian (P.C.)
Christopher R. Kelly (P.C.)
Dave M. Muchnikoff (P.C.)
Steven M. Abramson (P.C.)
Brian L. Alpert (P.C.)
Gary A. Lax (P.C.)
Michael S. Sadow (P.C.)
Nancy M. Stiles (P.C.)
Beth A. Freedman

ASSOCIATES

Craig M. Scheer
James M. Larkins, III
Matt Allen Mullins
Song A. Pak
John F. Breyer, Jr.
Michael A. Troy (Not admitted in DC)

OF COUNSEL

Howard J. Ross (P.C.)
David B. Myatt (P.C.)
John B. Selman (Not admitted in DC)
James W. Lance (Not admitted in DC)
Martin J. O'Riordan (Not admitted in DC)
Daniel C. Holdgreiwe (Not admitted in DC)
Lawrence J. Eisenberg

For full biographical listings, see the Martindale-Hubbell Law Directory

FLORIDA

*TALLAHASSEE,** Leon Co.

Robert S. Hightower (AV)
241 East Virginia Street, P.O. Box 4165, 32315-4165
Telephone: 850-222-3363
Telecopier: 850-222-0992
Email: rsh@hightowerlaw.com

Representative Clients: GTO, Inc.; Prescott Supply Company, Inc.; Southern Medical Group, P.A.; Tallahassee Mack Sales, Inc.

For full biographical listings, see the Martindale-Hubbell Law Directory

*TAMPA,** Hillsborough Co.

Fuller Holsonback & Bivins, P.A. (AV)
100 North Tampa Street, Suite 2650, 33602
Telephone: 813-229-9119
Fax: Available Upon Request
Email: jfuller521@aol.com

Jeffery M. Fuller
John P. Holsonback
Robert W. Bivins
Christina C. Young
Steven F. Thompson
William D. Mercer, Jr

For full biographical listings, see the Martindale-Hubbell Law Directory

GEORGIA

*ATLANTA,** Fulton Co.

LAWRENCE M. GOLD, P.C. (AV)

100 Galleria Parkway, Suite 695, 30339
Telephone: 770-933-9600
Facsimile: 770-933-9605
Email: lmgold1@IX.netcom.com

Lawrence M. Gold

For full biographical listings, see the Martindale-Hubbell Law Directory

HAWAII

*HONOLULU,** Honolulu Co.

CARLSMITH BALL (AV)

A Partnership including Law Corporations
Suite 2200, Pacific Tower, 1001 Bishop Street, P.O. Box 656, 96809-3402
Telephone: 808-523-2500
Fax: 808-523-0842
Email: execdirector@carlsmith.com *URL:* http://www.carlsmith.com
Kapolei, Hawaii Office: Suite 318, Kapolei Building, 1001 Kamokila Boulevard, 96707.
Telephone: 808-523-2500.
Fax: 808-674-0850.
Wailuku, Maui Hawaii Office: Suite 400, One Main Plaza, 2200 Main Street, P.O. Box 1086, 96793-1086.
Telephone: 808-242-4535.
Fax: 808-244-4974.
Kailua-Kona, Hawaii Office: Suite 209, 75-1000 Henry Street, 96740.
Telephone: 808-329-6464.
Fax: 808-329-9450.
Hilo, Hawaii Office: 121 Waianuenue Avenue, P.O. Box 686, 96721-0686.
Telephone: 808-935-6644.
Fax: 808-935-7975.
Hagatna, Guam Office: Suite 401, Bank of Hawaii Building, 134 West Soledad Avenue, P.O. Box BF, 96932-5027.
Telephone: 671-472-6813.
Fax: 671-477-4375.
Telex: 721-6445 CWCMI GM.
Saipan, Commonwealth of the Northern Mariana Islands Office: Carlsmith Building, Capitol Hill, P.O. Box 5241, 96950-5241.
Telephone: 670-322-3455.
Fax: 670-322-3368.
Los Angeles, California Office: 9th Floor, 444 South Flower Street, 90071-2901.
Telephone: 213-955-1200.
Fax: 213-623-0032.
Washington, D.C. Office: Suite 300, 1201 Pennsylvania Avenue, N.W., 20004-2401.
Telephone: 202-628-2228.
Fax: 202-628-2071.
Mexico City, Mexico Office: Carlsmith Ball, Sierra Nevada 119, Lomas de Chapultepec, 11000 Mexico, D.F.
Telephone: 52-5-520-8514, 52-5-520-8757.
Fax: 52-5-540-1545.
Mexico, D.F. Office of Carlsmith Ball, S.C. (Authorized to practice as foreign legal consultants in Mexico): Sierra Nevada 119, Lomas de Chapultepec, 11000 Mexico, D.F.
Telephone: 52-5-520-8514, 52-5-520-8757.
Fax: 52-5-540-1545.

MEMBERS OF FIRM

James H. Case (A Law Corporation)
John E. Rogers (Resident at Mexico Office)
Terrence A. Everett (Resident at Los Angeles, California Office)
William C. Williams, Jr. (Not admitted in HI)
Jon T. Yamamura

For Complete List of Firm Personnel, See General Section

For full biographical listings, see the Martindale-Hubbell Law Directory

GOODSILL ANDERSON QUINN & STIFEL (AV)

Alii Place, Suite 1800, 1099 Alakea Street, P.O. Box 3196, 96801-3196
Telephone: 808-547-5600
FAX: 808-547-5880
Email: info@goodsill.com *URL:* http://www.goodsill.com

MEMBERS OF FIRM

David J. Reber
Raymond S. Iwamoto
Miki Okumura
Gregory R. Kim
Jeffrey Scott Piper

COUNSEL

E. Laurence Gay

(See Next Column)

ASSOCIATES

Russell K. Kaupu
David P. Cornell

Representative Clients: American Savings Bank, F.S.B.; AMFAC/JMB Hawaii, Inc.; C. Brewer Homes, Inc.; Dole Food Company, Inc.; Hawaiian Electric Industries, Inc.; The MacNaughton Group; Watkins Pacific Corporation.

For Complete List of Firm Personnel, See General Section

For full biographical listings, see the Martindale-Hubbell Law Directory

ILLINOIS

*CHICAGO,** Cook Co.

FIELD & GOLAN (AV)

Three First National Plaza Suite 1500, 60602-4206
Telephone: 312-263-2300
Fax: 312-263-0939

MEMBERS OF FIRM

Robert E. Field
Stephen L. Golan
Margaret A. Christie
Donna F. Hartl

ASSOCIATES

Margaret A. Gisch
Matthew J. Cozzi
Anthony R. Taglia

OF COUNSEL

Leonard W. Golan
Stephen Edward Smith
Frank J. Dolan
John E. Vranicar

For full biographical listings, see the Martindale-Hubbell Law Directory

NISEN & ELLIOTT (AV)

200 West Adams Street, Suite 2500, 60606
Telephone: 312-346-7800
Telecopier: 312-346-9316

MEMBERS OF FIRM

Paul F. Gerbosi
Edward B. Mueller
Anthony Packard
Mark F. Zaenger
Michael J. Daley
John Foster Lesch
John K. Kneafsey
Michael H. Moirano
Robert O. Middleton
William G. Daluga, Jr.
Kenneth J. Rojc
Thomas V. McCauley
Helen M. Jensen
William A. Walker
Daniel P. Dawson
Michael J. Pavlicek

Robert Christie
Donald F. Froehlke
Thomas K. Juffernbruch
Brendan J. Kelly
Brian C. Kelly
Mary Rose C. Manczak
Bradley S. McCann
Brian D. Proctor

OF COUNSEL

Charles M. Nisen
Donald C. Shine

For full biographical listings, see the Martindale-Hubbell Law Directory

SUGAR, FRIEDBERG & FELSENTHAL (AV)

30 North La Salle Street, Suite 2600, 60602
Telephone: 312-704-9400
Telecopier: 312-372-7951
Cable: "SUGARFREE"

MEMBERS OF FIRM

Richard A. Sugar
Michael R. Friedberg
Steven A. Felsenthal
Andrew B. David
Leslie J. Weiss
Ira S. Neiman
Jonathan L. Mills
Etahn M. Cohen
Howard M. Helsinger
Robert F. Simon
Martin M. Weinstein
Charles H. Braun
Kathryn A. Erickson

ASSOCIATES

Aron L. Bornstein
Annette L. Brands
Kathryn T. Cha
Norman J. Ginsparg
William F. McGuinn
Suzanne J. Massel
Deanne Elizabeth Clarke

For full biographical listings, see the Martindale-Hubbell Law Directory

WATT & SAWYIER (AV)

The Monadnock Building, 53 West Jackson Boulevard, Suite 1120, 60604-3701
Telephone: 312-663-1440
Telecopier: 312-663-1410

OF COUNSEL

Rosalind A. Burbank

For full biographical listings, see the Martindale-Hubbell Law Directory

Chicago—Continued

WILDMAN, HARROLD, ALLEN & DIXON (AV)

225 West Wacker Drive, 30th Floor, 60606-1229
Telephone: 312-201-2000
Fax: 312-201-2555
Email: hennessy@whad.com *URL:* http://www.whad.com
Aurora, Illinois Office: 1961 W. Downer Place.
Telephone: 630-892-7021.
Fax: 630-892-7158.
Waukegan, Illinois Office: 404 West Water, P. O. Box 890.
Telephone: 847-625-5550.
Fax: 847-625-5555.
Lisle, Illinois Office: 4300 Commerce Court, Suite 320.
Telephone: 630-955-0555.
Fax: 630-955-0662
Toronto, Ontario correspondent Office: Keel Cottrelle. 36 Toronto Street, Suite 920.
Telephone: 416-367-2900.
Telefax: 416-367-2791.
Telex: 062-18660.

MEMBERS OF FIRM

John L. Eisel
Nancy J. Fuller
Carol Pegnato
Susan Wiles

For full biographical listings, see the Martindale-Hubbell Law Directory

KANSAS

*WICHITA,** Sedgwick Co.

TRIPLETT, WOOLF & GARRETSON, LLC (AV)

2959 North Rock Road, Suite 300, 67226
Telephone: 316-630-8100
Fax: 316-630-8101
Email: twg@twgfirm.com

MEMBERS OF FIRM

Thomas C. Triplett
Thomas P. Garretson
Theron E. Fry
Ron H. Harnden
Eric S. Strickler
Tad Patton

ASSOCIATES

Jeffery C. Dahlgren
Christopher C. Swyers
Kent G. Voth

Representative Clients: Anheuser-Busch Companies, Inc.; Brite Voice Systems, Inc.; Coleman Company, Inc.; Dow Chemical Co.; Friends University; KPMG Peat Marwick; National Plastics Color, Inc.; Total Petroleum, Inc.; Travelers Insurance Co.; Willis Corroon of Kansas, Inc.

For Complete List of Firm Personnel, See General Section

For full biographical listings, see the Martindale-Hubbell Law Directory

KENTUCKY

*LOUISVILLE,** Jefferson Co.

DAVID W. HARPER (AV)

2450 Meidinger Tower, 40202
Telephone: 502-583-3081
Fax: 502-583-2418
Email: dharperesq@aol.com

For full biographical listings, see the Martindale-Hubbell Law Directory

LOUISIANA

*BATON ROUGE,** East Baton Rouge Parish

PREIS, BERGERON & ATCHISON (AV)

450 Laurel Street, Suite 1000, P.O. Box 2786, 70821-2786
Telephone: 225-387-0707
Facsimile: 225-344-0510
Email: preisber@aol.com

Phillip W. Preis
Kirk A. Bergeron
Ashley C. Atchison
Charles M. Gordon, Jr.

For full biographical listings, see the Martindale-Hubbell Law Directory

METAIRIE, Jefferson Parish

HENICAN, JAMES & CLEVELAND (AV)

Suite 1200 Heritage Plaza, 111 Veterans Memorial Boulevard, 70005
Telephone: 504-837-8080
Facsimile: 504-833-0863
Mailing Address: P.O. Box 19300, New Orleans, Louisiana, 70179

MEMBERS OF FIRM

C. Ellis Henican (1905-1997)
Murray F. Cleveland (1913-1971)
Philip E. James, Jr.
Marshall G. Weaver
Edward N. George, III
Shawn M. Bridgewater

ASSOCIATES

Keith M. Benit
Jacob S. Capraro
David M. Packard

OF COUNSEL

Philip E. James
Louis V. Rand, II

Representative Clients: Better Business Bureau of New Orleans, Inc.; St. Paul Fire and Marine Insurance Co.; Stewart Enterprises, Inc.
Reference: Hibernia National Bank, New Orleans.

For full biographical listings, see the Martindale-Hubbell Law Directory

*NEW ORLEANS,** Orleans Parish

CORRERO FISHMAN HAYGOOD PHELPS WALMSLEY & CASTEIX, L.L.P. (AV)

Bank One Center, 46th Floor, 201 St. Charles Avenue, 70170-4600
Telephone: 504-586-5252
Fax: 504-586-5250

Anthony J. Correro, III
Louis Y. Fishman
Paul M. Haygood
Robert M. Walmsley, Jr.
Sterling Scott Willis

Caroline B. Blitzer

For full biographical listings, see the Martindale-Hubbell Law Directory

MICHAEL L. ECKSTEIN ATTORNEY AT LAW A PROFESSIONAL CORPORATION (AV)

1515 Poydras Street, Suite 2195, 70112
Telephone: 504-527-0701
Telecopier: 504-566-0040
VMX: 504-889-8876
Email: eck@eck-law.com

Michael L. Eckstein
David Coleman Raphael, Jr.

Representative Clients: Anserphone of New Orleans, Inc.; Dixie Web Graphic Corporations; Kencoil, Inc.; Life Point Systems, Inc.; Meeks Petroleum Company; Dan-Gulf Shipping, Inc.; Action, Inc.; TCB Industries, Inc.

For full biographical listings, see the Martindale-Hubbell Law Directory

MAINE

*PORTLAND,** Cumberland Co.

BENNETT BENNETT AND TROIANO, P.A. (AV)

Suite 300, 121 Middle Street, P.O. Box 7799, 04112-7799
Telephone: 207-773-4775
Telecopier: 207-774-2366
Email: lawyers@bennettlegal.com *URL:* http://www.bennettlegal.com

Herbert H. Bennett (1928-1992)
Peter Bennett
Jeffrey Bennett
Joseph A. Troiano
Frederick B. Finberg

Julie A. Boesky

OF COUNSEL

Jonathan M. Dunitz

Counsel for: Associated Grocers of New England; General Star Indemnity Company; Coca Cola Bottling Company of Northern New England, Inc.; Northern Utilities/Bay State Gas; Pratt & Whitney (Division of United Technologies); Primerica Financial Services (Citigroup); Sprague Energy (C.H. Sprague & Son); Perrier Group of America, Inc.; Lepage Bakeries, Inc. (Country Kitchen); Texaco, Inc.

For full biographical listings, see the Martindale-Hubbell Law Directory

MARYLAND

*BALTIMORE,** (Independent City)

RICHARD T. STANSBURY A PROFESSIONAL ASSOCIATION (AV)

Suite 920, The B & O Building, Two North Charles Street, 21201-3754
Telephone: 410-727-6200
Facsimile: 410-385-2939
Email: rts1law@aol.com *URL:* http://www.lawyers.com/richardstansburylaw
Annapolis, Maryland Office: 112 West Street, 21401.
Telephone: 410-974-6000.
Facsimile: 410-974-6019.

Richard T. Stansbury

For full biographical listings, see the Martindale-Hubbell Law Directory

THOMAS & LIBOWITZ, P.A. (AV)

100 Light Street, Suite 1100, 21202-1053
Telephone: 410-752-2468
Fax: 410-752-2046; 752-2049; 752-0979
Email: thomasandlibowitz.com *URL:* http://www.thomasandlibowitz.com

Steven Anargyros Thomas
Clinton R. Black, IV
C. Wayne Davis
Peter W. Taliaferro
James E. Myers
Charles B. Jones

OF COUNSEL

Basil A. Thomas
Susan M. Rittenhouse

LEGAL SUPPORT PERSONNEL

PARALEGALS

Melissa A. Johnson
Kelley Atkins
Kimberly Beard

Representative Clients: Sinclair Broadcast Group, Inc. (Television and Radio stations); Roy Kirby & Sons, Inc. (Contractor); First Mariner Bank; Scandia Manufacturing Co. Inc. (Defense Contractor); Atlantic Automotive Corp. t/a Heritgage Automotive Group; Candy Express Franchising, Inc.; Wire Spectrum Services (Contractors-Transmission Tower Sites); Acrodyne Communications, Inc.; Alexis Logic Corporation (Software Developers); Selnic Corporation (Electronis Distributors); Liberty Mutual Insurance Company.

For full biographical listings, see the Martindale-Hubbell Law Directory

MASSACHUSETTS

*BOSTON,** Suffolk Co.

HINCKLEY, ALLEN & SNYDER LLP (AV)

28 State Street, 30th Floor, 02109-1775
Telephone: 617-345-9000
Email: firm@haslaw.com *URL:* http://www.haslaw.com
Providence, Rhode Island Office: 1500 Fleet Center.
Telephone: 401-274-2000.
Fax: 401-277-9600. URL: http://www.hawlaw.com.

MEMBERS OF FIRM

Paula K. Andrews
David D. Barricelli (Not admitted in MA)
E. Jerome Batty (Not admitted in MA)
Jonathan Bell
Paul Bork
Stephen J. Carlotti (Not admitted in MA)
David Barry Connolly
Joseph P. Curran (Not admitted in MA)
Michael P. DeFanti
Eric F. Eisenberg
Malcolm Farmer, III
Margaret D. Farrell (Not admitted in MA)
Pasco Gasbarro Jr.
Hugh J. Gorman, III
Alan P. Gottlieb
William R. Grimm
Paul A. Hedstrom
Richard L. E. Jocelyn (Not admitted in MA)
Joel Lewin
Sandra Matrone Mack (Not admitted in MA)
Matthew T. Marcello, III (Not admitted in MA)
Frederick P. McClure
Elizabeth Murdock Myers
Paul F. O'Donnell, III
H. Peter Olsen (Not admitted in MA)
Julianne Palumbo
John J. Pendergast, III (Not admitted in MA)
Gerald J. Petros
James O. Reavis
Jeremy Ritzenberg
Ralph J. Rivkind
David J. Rubin
Charles E. Schaub, Jr.
Douglas F. Seaver
Herman Snyder
David R. Sullivan
Robert F. Sylvia
Howard E. Walker (Not admitted in MA)
Richard D. Wayne

ASSOCIATES

Jessica M. Bettencourt (Not admitted in MA)
Mark Bianchi
Alyssa V. Boss
Alexandra K. Callam
Jane E. Cohen
Andrew D. Cummings
June E. Daniel (Not admitted in MA)
Kim Herman Goslant

(See Next Column)

ASSOCIATES (Continued)

Gloria Maria Gutierrez
Kelley Jordan-Price
Catherine S. Kim
Christopher W. Morog
Elena B. Olson
Joseph D. Whelan (Not admitted in MA)

OF COUNSEL

Willard Krasnow
Willard R. Pope
Bentley Tobin
Joachim A. Weissfeld (Not admitted in MA)

For Complete List of Firm Personnel, See General Section

For full biographical listings, see the Martindale-Hubbell Law Directory

*CAMBRIDGE,** Middlesex Co.

BARRETT & ASSOCIATES (AV)

One Kendall Square, Suite 2200, 02139
Telephone: 617-621-1579
Fax: 617-621-1556
Email: barrettd@earthlink.net

Donal B. Barrett

For full biographical listings, see the Martindale-Hubbell Law Directory

WELLESLEY, Norfolk Co.

WHITE & MCDERMOTT, P.C. (AV)

65 William Street, 02481
Telephone: 781-431-1700
Fax: 781-237-8120
Email: mail@WhiteMcD.com

David A. White
Scott F. McDermott
Sharon Goddard White
John L. Koenig

John J. McCarthy, Jr.
Kathleen Gregg
Sarah C. Wickham

For full biographical listings, see the Martindale-Hubbell Law Directory

MICHIGAN

BATTLE CREEK, Calhoun Co.

KREIS, ENDERLE, CALLANDER & HUDGINS, A PROFESSIONAL CORPORATION (AV)

One West Michigan Avenue, 49017
Telephone: 616-966-3000
Facsimile: 616-966-3022
Email: kech@kech.com *URL:* http://www.kech.com
Kalamazoo, Michigan Office: One Moorsbridge, P.O. Box 4010, 49003-4010.
Telephone: 616-324-3000.
Fax: 616-324-3010.

Alan G. Enderle (Resident, Kalamazoo Office)
Matthew S. DePerno (Resident, Kalamazoo Office)

For Complete List of Firm Personnel, See General Section

For full biographical listings, see the Martindale-Hubbell Law Directory

BIRMINGHAM, Oakland Co.

HYMAN LIPPITT, P.C. (AV)

185 Oakland Avenue, Suite 300, 48009
Telephone: 248-646-8292
Facsimile: 248-646-8375
Email: hymalipp@tir.com

J. Leonard Hyman
Norman L. Lippitt
Douglas A. Hyman
Brian D. O'Keefe
H. Joel Newman
Nazli G. Sater
Kenneth F. Neuman
Terry S. Givens
Paul J. Fischer
John A. Sellers
Robert H. Lippitt
Roger L. Myers
Sally A. Rutledge
Joseph Pia
John P. Gonway
Leif K. Anderson
Jennifer S. Gold
Julie Lyons Kosovec
Dawn S. Spratley
Michael T. Price

For full biographical listings, see the Martindale-Hubbell Law Directory

BLOOMFIELD HILLS, Oakland Co.

DAWDA, MANN, MULCAHY & SADLER, P.L.C. (AV)

1533 North Woodward Avenue Suite 200, 48304-2815
Telephone: 248-642-3700
Fax: 248-642-7791
Email: EMail@DMMS.Com

(See Next Column)

DAWDA, MANN, MULCAHY & SADLER P.L.C.—*Continued*

Michael D. Mulcahy
Edward C. Dawda
Curtis J. Mann
William L. Rosin
Todd A. Schafer

Paul C. Apap
Daniel M. Israel
Wayne S. Segal
Vincent J. Wilk

OF COUNSEL

Sidney W. Smith, Jr.

Representative Clients: AMB Property, LP; Bally's Total Fitness Corp.; BASF Corp.; Cardell Corp.; Cargill, Inc.; Trammell Crow Company; Ford Motor Company.

For full biographical listings, see the Martindale-Hubbell Law Directory

*DETROIT,** Wayne Co.

BODMAN, LONGLEY & DAHLING LLP (AV)

34th Floor 100 Renaissance Center, 48243
Telephone: 313-259-7777
Fax: 313-393-7579
Email: info@bodmanlongley.com *URL:* http://www.bodmanlongley.com
Troy, Michigan Office: Suite 2020, 755 West Big Beaver Road.
Telephone: 248-362-2110.
Fax: 248-244-0780.
Ann Arbor, Michigan Office: 110 Miller, Suite 300.
Telephone: 734-761-3780.
Fax: 734-930-2494.
Northern Michigan Office: 229 Court Street, P.O. Box 405, Cheboygan.
Telephone: 231-627-4351.
Fax: 231-627-2802.

MEMBERS OF FIRM

Thomas A. Roach (Ann Arbor Office)
Kenneth R. Lango (Troy Office)
James T. Heimbuch
Herold McC. Deason
James R. Buschmann
Randolph S. Perry
Terrence B. Larkin (Troy Office)
Lloyd C. Fell (Cheboygan Office)
F. Thomas Lewand
Harvey W. Berman (Ann Arbor Office)
Barbara A. Bowman
Christopher J. Dine
Barnett Jay Colvin
Sandra L. Sorini (Ann Arbor Office)

For Representative Client list, See General Section

For Complete List of Firm Personnel, See General Section

For full biographical listings, see the Martindale-Hubbell Law Directory

BOOTHMAN, HEBERT & ELLER, P.C. (AV)

Marquette Building, 243 West Congress, Suite 950, 48226
Telephone: 313-964-0150
Fax: 313-964-2226
Email: boothman@mail.mich.com

Dale L. Hebert
Richard C. Boothman
Gary S. Eller

Edward C. Reynolds, Jr.
Marta J. Hoffman

Representative Clients: University of Michigan; Mutual Insurance Corporation of America; Emergency Physicians Medical Group; Pronational; HCR Manor Care, Inc.
Reference: Comerica Bank-Detroit.

For full biographical listings, see the Martindale-Hubbell Law Directory

BUTZEL LONG, A PROFESSIONAL CORPORATION (AV)

Suite 900, 150 West Jefferson, 48226
Telephone: 313-225-7000
Telecopier: 313-225-7080
Email: melnick@butzel.com *URL:* http://www.butzel.com
Birmingham, Michigan Office: Suite 200, 32270 Telegraph Road.
Telephone: 810-258-1616.
Telecopier: 810-258-1439.
Okemos, Michigan Office: Suite 300, 2127 University Park Drive.
Telephone: 517-372-6622.
Telecopier: 517-372-6672.
Ann Arbor, Michigan Office: Suite 300, 350 South Main Street.
Telephone: 313-995-3110.
Telecopier: 313-995-1777.
Grosse Pointe Farms, Michigan Office: Suite 260, 21 Kercheval.
Telephone: 313-886-5446.
Telecopier: 313-886-2114.
Boca Raton, Florida Office: Suite 411, 1200 North Federal Highway.
Telephone: 561-368-2151.
Telecopier: 561-368-4668.
Palm Beach Gardens, Florida Office: Suite 227, 11382 Prosperity Farms Road.
Telephone: 561-625-4442.
Telecopier: 561-625-6901.

(See Next Column)

Naples, Florida Office: Suite 705, 801 Laurel Oak Drive.
Telephone: 941-597-4500.
Telecopier: 941-597-5623.

Morris Milmet (Birmingham)
Frank B. Vecchio (Birmingham)
C. Peter Theut
Richard E. Rassel
James C. Bruno
John J. Raymond, Jr. (Boca Raton, Naples and Palm Beach Gardens, Florida and Birmingham)
Justin G. Klimko
Michael F. Golab (Birmingham)
James L. Hughes
Arthur Dudley II
Gordon W. Didier (Birmingham)
Terry O. Lang
Melvin J. Hollowell, Jr.
Nicholas J. Stasevich

SENIOR ATTORNEY

Eric R. Wapnick

David B. Braun

Representative Clients: Complete Business Solutions, Inc.; The Detroit News, Inc.; General Fasteners Co.; Infinity Broadcasting; McKechnie PLC; Ricardo Group PLC; Stroh Companies; Takata, Inc.; TRW Automotive; William Beaumont Hospital.

For full biographical listings, see the Martindale-Hubbell Law Directory

MILLER, CANFIELD, PADDOCK AND STONE, P.L.C. (AV)

A Professional Limited Liability Company
Founded in 1852 by Sidney Davy Miller
150 West Jefferson, Suite 2500, 48226-4415
Telephone: 313-963-6420
Fax: 313-496-7500
Cable Address: "Stem Detroit"
URL: http://www.millercanfield.com
Ann Arbor, Michigan Office: 101 North Main Street, 7th Floor, 48104-1400.
Telephone: 734-663-2445.
Fax: 734-747-7147.
Troy, Michigan Office: 840 West Long Lake Road, Suite 200, 48098.
Telephone: 248-879-2000.
Fax: 248-879-2001.
Grand Rapids, Michigan Office: 99 Monroe, N.W., Suite 1200, 49503-2639.
Telephone: 616-454-8656.
Fax: 616-776-6322.
Howell, Michigan Office: 121 South Barnard Street, Suite 4, 48843-2305.
Telephone: 517-546-7600.
Telecopier: 517-546-6974.
Kalamazoo, Michigan Office: 444 West Michigan Avenue, 49007-3752.
Telephone: 616-381-7030.
Fax: 616-382-0244.
Lansing, Michigan Office: One Michigan Avenue, Suite 900, 48933-1609.
Telephone: 517-487-2070.
Fax: 517-374-6304.
Monroe, Michigan Office: 214 East Elm Avenue, Suite 100, 48162-2682.
Telephone: 734-243-2000.
Fax: 734-243-0901.
Washington, D.C. Office: 1900 K Street, N.W., Suite 1150. 20006.
Telephone: 202-429-5575; 785-0600.
Fax: 202-331-1118; 785-1234.
Pensacola, Florida Office: 25 West Cedar, 32501.
Telephone: 850-469-1088.
Fax: 850-432-0677.
New York, New York Office: 1450 Broadway, 41st Floor, 10018.
Telephone: 212-704-4400.
Fax: 212-704-4410.
Gdynia, Poland Office: UL. Slaska 21, 81-319.
Telephone: 011-485-831-2808.
Fax: 011-48-58-628 6411.
Warsaw, Poland Office: UL. Nowogrodzkall, 5th Floor, 00-513.
Telephone: 011-4822 529 0200.
Fax: 011-4822 529 0201.
Katowice, Poland Office: UL. Francuska 35/37, 40-027.
Telephone: 011 (48-32) 757-2414.
Fax: 011 (48-32) 757-2483.

PRINCIPALS OF FIRM

Eric V. Brown, Jr. (Kalamazoo Office)
John R. Cook (Kalamazoo Office)
Thomas W. Linn
Thomas G. Appleman (Troy Office)
Brad B. Arbuckle (Bloomfield Hills Office)
Sally A. Hamby (Troy Office)

Representative Firm Clients: Chrysler Corporation; Comerica, Incorporated; City of Detroit, Michigan; Detroit Tigers, Inc.; First of Michigan; Ford Motor Company; Ford Motor Credit Company; Great Lakes Bancorp; Henry Ford Hospital; INVETECH Company.

For Complete List of Firm Personnel, See General Section

For full biographical listings, see the Martindale-Hubbell Law Directory

Detroit—Continued

TIMMIS & INMAN L.L.P. (AV)

300 Talon Centre, 48207
Telephone: 313-396-4200
Facsimile: 313-396-4228
Email: info@timmis-inman.com *URL:* http://www.timmis-inman.com

Michael T. Timmis
Robert E. Graziani
George A. Peck
Henry J. Brennan, III
Mark W. Peyser
Richard M. Miettinen
Bradley J. Knickerbocker
George M. Malis

Michael F. Wais
Erich J. D'Andrea
Shannon M. Nichols
Anthony J. Long
Alex N. Saleh
Jennifer A. Bourgoin

OF COUNSEL

William B. Fitzgerald
David E. Costa

LEGAL SUPPORT PERSONNEL

PARALEGALS

Linda M. Bierl

Representative Clients: Retail Resources, Inc.; Applied Process, Inc.; Insilco Corp.; Certain Underwriters at Lloyds of London; Eastpointe Radiologists, P.C.; Talon Automotive Group, Inc.; G&L Industries, Inc.; Hawthorne Metal Products Co.; Foam Rubber Products Co.; Diamond Automations, Inc.; Veltri Metal Products Co.; J&R Manufacturing, Inc.; Production Stamping, Inc.; Spiralock Corporation.

For Complete List of Firm Personnel, See General Section

For full biographical listings, see the Martindale-Hubbell Law Directory

*KALAMAZOO,** Kalamazoo Co.

KREIS, ENDERLE, CALLANDER & HUDGINS, A PROFESSIONAL CORPORATION (AV)

One Moorsbridge, P.O. Box 4010, 49003-4010
Telephone: 616-324-3000
Facsimile: 616-324-3010
Email: kech@kech.com *URL:* http://www.kech.com
Battle Creek, Michigan Office: One West Michigan Avenue, 49017.
Telephone: 616-966-3000.
Fax: 616-966-3022.

Alan G. Enderle
Matthew S. DePerno

For Complete List of Firm Personnel, See General Section

For full biographical listings, see the Martindale-Hubbell Law Directory

MILLER, CANFIELD, PADDOCK AND STONE, P.L.C. (AV)

A Professional Limited Liability Company
Founded in 1852 by Sidney Davy Miller
444 West Michigan Avenue, 49007-3752
Telephone: 616-381-7030
Fax: 616-382-0244
URL: http://www.millercanfield.com
Detroit, Michigan Office: 150 West Jefferson, Suite 2500, 48226-4415.
Telephone: 313-963-6420.
Fax: 313-496-7500.
Cable Address: "Stem Detroit."
Ann Arbor, Michigan Office: 101 North Main Street, 7th Floor, 48104-1400.
Telephone: 734-663-2445.
Fax: 734-747-7147.
Troy, Michigan Office: 840 West Long Lake Road, Suite 200, 48098.
Telephone: 248-879-2000.
Fax: 248-879-2001.
Grand Rapids, Michigan Office: 99 Monroe, N.W., Suite 1200, 49503-2639.
Telephone: 616-454-8656.
Fax: 616-776-6322.
Howell, Michigan Office: 121 South Barnard Street, Suite 4, 48843-2305.
Telephone: 517-546-7600.
Telecopier: 517-546-6974.
Lansing, Michigan Office: One Michigan Avenue, Suite 900, 48933-1609.
Telephone: 517-487-2070.
Fax: 517-374-6304.
Monroe, Michigan Office: 214 East Elm Avenue, Suite 100, 48162-2682.
Telephone: 734-243-2000.
Fax: 734-243-0901.
Washington, D.C. Office: 1900 K Street, N.W., Suite 1150. 20006.
Telephone: 202-429-5575; 785-0600.
Fax: 202-331-1118; 785-1234.
Pensacola, Florida Office: 25 West Cedar, 32501.
Telephone: 850-469-1088.
Fax: 850-432-0677.
New York, New York Office: 1450 Broadway, 41st Floor, 10018.
Telephone: 212-704-4400.
Fax: 212-704-4410.

(See Next Column)

Gdynia, Poland Office: UL. Slaska 21, 81-319.
Telephone: 011-485-831-2808.
Fax: 011-48-58-628 6411.
Warsaw, Poland Office: UL. Nowogrodzkall, 5th Floor, 00-513.
Telephone: 011-4822 529 0200.
Fax: 011-4822 529 0201.
Katowice, Poland Office: UL. Francuska 35/37, 40-027.
Telephone: 011 (48-32) 757-2414.
Fax: 011 (48-32) 757-2483.

PRINCIPALS

Eric V. Brown, Jr.
John R. Cook

Representative Firm Clients: Chrysler Corporation; Comerica, Incorporated; City of Detroit, Michigan; Detroit Tigers, Inc.; First of Michigan; Ford Motor Company; Ford Motor Credit Company; Great Lakes Bancorp; Henry Ford Hospital; INVETECH Company.

For Complete List of Firm Personnel, See General Section

For full biographical listings, see the Martindale-Hubbell Law Directory

TROY, Oakland Co.

MILLER, CANFIELD, PADDOCK AND STONE, P.L.C. (AV)

A Professional Limited Liability Company
Founded in 1852 by Sidney Davy Miller
840 West Long Lake Road Suite 200, 48098
Telephone: 248-879-2000
Fax: 248-879-2001
URL: http://www.millercanfield.com
Detroit, Michigan Office: 150 West Jefferson, Suite 2500, 48226-4415.
Telephone: 313-963-6420.
Fax: 313-496-7500.
Cable Address: "Stem Detroit."
Ann Arbor, Michigan Office: 101 North Main Street, 7th Floor, 48104-1400.
Telephone: 734-663-2445.
Fax: 734-747-7147.
Grand Rapids, Michigan Office: 99 Monroe, N.W., Suite 1200, 49503-2639.
Telephone: 616-454-8656.
Fax: 616-776-6322.
Howell, Michigan Office: 121 South Barnard Street, Suite 4, 48843-2305.
Telephone: 517-546-7600.
Telecopier: 517-546-6974.
Kalamazoo, Michigan Office: 444 West Michigan Avenue, 49007-3752.
Telephone: 616-381-7030.
Fax: 616-382-0244.
Lansing, Michigan Office: One Michigan Avenue, Suite 900, 48933-1609.
Telephone: 517-487-2070.
Fax: 517-374-6304.
Monroe, Michigan Office: 214 East Elm Avenue, Suite 100, 48162-2682.
Telephone: 734-243-2000.
Fax: 734-243-0901.
Washington, D.C. Office: 1900 K Street, N.W., Suite 1150. 20006.
Telephone: 202-429-5575; 785-0600.
Fax: 202-331-1118; 785-1234.
Pensacola, Florida Office: 25 West Cedar, 32501.
Telephone: 850-469-1088.
Fax: 850-432-0677.
New York, New York Office: 1450 Broadway, 41st Floor, 10018.
Telephone: 212-704-4400.
Fax: 212-704-4410.
Gdynia, Poland Office: UL. Slaska 21, 81-319.
Telephone: 011-485-831-2808.
Fax: 011-48-58-628 6411.
Warsaw, Poland Office: UL. Nowogrodzkall, 5th Floor, 00-513.
Telephone: 011-4822 529 0200.
Fax: 011-4822 529 0201.
Katowice, Poland Office: UL. Francuska 35/37, 40-027.
Telephone: 011 (48-32) 757-2414.
Fax: 011 (48-32) 757-2483.

RESIDENT PRINCIPALS

Thomas G. Appleman
Brad B. Arbuckle
Sally A. Hamby

Representative Firm Clients: Chrysler Corporation; Comerica, Incorporated; City of Detroit, Michigan; Detroit Tigers, Inc.; First of Michigan; Ford Motor Company; Ford Motor Credit Company; Great Lakes Bancorp; Henry Ford Hospital; INVETECH Company.

For Complete List of Firm Personnel, See General Section

For full biographical listings, see the Martindale-Hubbell Law Directory

POLING, MCGAW & POLING, P.C. (AV)

Suite 275, 5435 Corporate Drive, 48098
Telephone: 248-641-0500
Telecopier: 248-641-0506
URL: http://www.lawyers.com/polingmcgaw&poling

(See Next Column)

POLING, MCGAW & POLING P.C.—*Continued*

Benson T. Buck (1926-1989)	Gregory C. Hamilton
Richard B. Poling	Veronica B. O'Hara
D. Douglas McGaw	James R. Parker
Richard B. Poling, Jr.	Shannon M. Acton

OF COUNSEL

Ralph S. Moore

Representative Clients: City of Troy; United States Fidelity & Guaranty Co.; Sentry Insurance Co.; Admiral Insurance; DeMaria Construction Co.; Aetna Casualty and Surety Co.; Concord Design; Pneumo-Abex.

For full biographical listings, see the Martindale-Hubbell Law Directory

MUNICIPAL AND ZONING LAW

ALABAMA

*BIRMINGHAM,** Jefferson Co.

BRADLEY ARANT ROSE & WHITE LLP (AV)

2001 Park Place, Suite 1400, P.O. Box 830709, 35283-0709
Telephone: 205-521-8000
Facsimile: 205-521-8800
Facsimile (SouthTrust Tower Office): 205-521-8500
URL: http://www.barw.com
Huntsville, Alabama Office: 200 Clinton Avenue West, Suite 900, 35801.
Telephone: 205-517-5100.
Facsimile: 205-533-5069.
Washington, D.C. Office: 801 Pennsylvania Avenue, NW, Suite 230, 20004.
Telephone: 202-347-8893.
Facsimile: 202-347-1684.

MEMBERS OF FIRM

Charles A. J. Beavers Jr.
Thad Gladden Long

For Complete List of Firm Personnel, See General Section

For full biographical listings, see the Martindale-Hubbell Law Directory

GORHAM & WALDREP, P.C. (AV)

2101 6th Avenue North, Suite 700, 35203
Telephone: 205-254-3216; 251-9166
Telecopier: 205-324-3802
Email: info@gorham-waldrep.com *URL:* http://www.gorham-waldrep.com
Montgomery, Alabama Office: 250 Commerce Street, P.O. Box 4837, 36103-4837.
Telephone: 334-262-0777.
Telecopier: 334-262-0742.

Thomas L. Stewart
Michael G. Kendrick
K. Mark Parnell

Victoria Franklin-Sisson

Representative Clients: Jefferson County Personnel Board; Birmingham-Jefferson Civic Center Authority; The Water Works and Sewer Board of the City of Birmingham; City of Homewood; American Federation of Government Employees Local #1945; City of Pelham; Town of Kimberly; Alabama Tire Dealers Assn.; Southern States Body Shop Assn.

For Complete List of Firm Personnel, See General Section

For full biographical listings, see the Martindale-Hubbell Law Directory

PARSONS, LEE & JULIANO, P.C. (AV)

2200 AmSouth/Harbert Plaza, 1901 Sixth Avenue, North, P.O. Box 371088, 35237-1088
Telephone: 205-326-6600
Fax: 205-324-7097

Robert E. Parsons
Jasper P. Juliano
Marcus W. Lee
Marda W. Sydnor
David A. Lee
John M. Bergquist
Paul J. DeMarco
Deborah Ann Payne
Dorothy A. Powell
David Samuel Snoddy

For full biographical listings, see the Martindale-Hubbell Law Directory

*MOBILE,** Mobile Co.

FINKBOHNER AND LAWLER, L.L.C. (AV)

169 Dauphin Street Suite 300, P.O. Box 3085, 36652
Telephone: 334-438-5871
Fax: 334-432-8052
Email: finkbohnerlawlerllc@zebra.net

MEMBERS OF FIRM

George W. Finkbohner, Jr.
John L. Lawler
George W. Finkbohner, III
Royce A. Ray, III

For full biographical listings, see the Martindale-Hubbell Law Directory

ARIZONA

*FLAGSTAFF,** Coconino Co.

HUFFORD, HORSTMAN, MONGINI, PARNELL & MCCARTHY, P.C. (AV)

323 North Leroux Street, P.O. Box B, 86002-0808
Telephone: 520-774-1453
Fax: 520-779-3621

C. Benson Hufford
Patrice M. Horstman
Michael E.J. Mongini
Eve A. Parnell
Philip (Jay) McCarthy, Jr.

E. Duane Weston

LEGAL SUPPORT PERSONNEL

R. Gehl Tucker (Legal Assistant)
Doris Utzinger (Legal Assistant)
Vickie Belman (Legal Assistant)
Jan Blackman (Paralegal)
Dawn L. Karsten (Paralegal)

Reference: Norwest Bank Arizona, N.A.

For full biographical listings, see the Martindale-Hubbell Law Directory

MESA, Maricopa Co.

JACKSON WHITE GARDNER WEECH & WALKER, P.C. (AV)

40 North Center Street, Suite 200, 85201
Telephone: 480-464-1111
Fax: 480-464-5692
Statewide: 800-243-1160
Email: firm@azmesalaw.com *URL:* http://www.azmesalaw.com
Payson, Arizona Office: 708 East Highway 260, Suite C1-E.
Telephone: 520-472-8878.

Wayne L. Gardner
Eric M. Jackson
Michael R. Pruitt
J. Grant Walker
Bradley D. Weech
Richard A. White
David L. Weed
Roger R. Foote
Otto S. Shill, III

Eric K. Macdonald
Kelly G. Black
Melody K. Seal
Patricia A. Mancabelli
Bobbie J. Rasmusson
Maureen P. Kane
James L. Tanner

For full biographical listings, see the Martindale-Hubbell Law Directory

*PHOENIX,** Maricopa Co.

BEUS, GILBERT & DEVITT, P.L.L.C. (AV)

Suite 1000, Great American Tower, 3200 North Central Avenue, 85012-2417
Telephone: 602-274-8229
Fax: 602-234-5893

John V. Berry
Leo R. Beus
Laurie B. Craig
Michael R. Devitt
Nicholas J. DiCarlo
Paul E. Gilbert
Scott D. Larmore
Anthony H. Misseldine
Paul L. Mueller
Quinton F. Seamons (Not admitted in AZ)
Richard R. Thomas
Gordon M. Wasson

Jeffrey R. Adams
Diana Archer
Christopher A. Caserta
Craig D. Henley
Richard X. Herrera
J. Ridge Hicks
Christine N. Jones
Timothy G. Kasparek
Alan C. Kuffner
Malcolm Loeb
Michele L. Lorenzen
Daniel D. Maddy
Christopher E. Martin
Robert T. Mills
Jason Barclay Morris
Marc F. Pappalardo
Joseph B. Pierce
Wendy M. Rector

For full biographical listings, see the Martindale-Hubbell Law Directory

BONNETT, FAIRBOURN, FRIEDMAN & BALINT, P.C. (AV)

4041 North Central Avenue Suite 1100, 85012
Telephone: 602-274-1100
Fax: 602-274-1199

Jerry C. Bonnett
Michael N. Widener
Elaine A. Ryan
Tara L. Jackson
Wendy J. Harrison
Scott A. Erickson

For full biographical listings, see the Martindale-Hubbell Law Directory

DUSHOFF & MCCALL, A PROFESSIONAL CORPORATION (AV)

Two Renaissance Square, Suite 1000, 40 North Central, 85004
Telephone: 602-254-3800
Fax: 602-258-2551
URL: http://www.dushoff@neta.com

(See Next Column)

DUSHOFF & MCCALL A PROFESSIONAL CORPORATION, *Phoenix—Continued*

Jay Dushoff
Jack E. McCall (1942-1995)
Michael Riikola
Leonard M. Bell
Patrick J. McGill
Robert H. Kreutzer

LEGAL SUPPORT PERSONNEL

Thomas M. Flynn

For full biographical listings, see the Martindale-Hubbell Law Directory

EARL, CURLEY & LAGARDE, P.C. (AV)

3101 N. Central Avenue, Suite 1000, 85012
Telephone: 602-265-0094
Fax: 602-265-2195
Email: ec-1@primenet.com

Stephen C. Earl
Michael J. Curley
Lynne A. Lagarde

Representative Clients: Del Webb Corporation; Desert Mountain Properties; Opus Southwest; Westcor Partners; Trammell Crow; Arizona Biltmore Hotel; The Taubman Company; Mutual of New York; Home Depot; Mark Taylor.

For full biographical listings, see the Martindale-Hubbell Law Directory

FENNEMORE CRAIG, A PROFESSIONAL CORPORATION (AV)

3003 North Central Avenue, Suite 2600, 85012-2913
Telephone: 602-916-5000
Fax: 602-916-5999
Tucson, Arizona Office: One South Church Avenue, Suite 1000, 85701-1620.
Telephone: 520-879-6800.
Fax: 520-879-6899.

Michael Preston Green
Graeme Hancock
Andrew M. Federhar

LEGAL SUPPORT PERSONNEL

LEGAL ASSISTANTS

Donna M. Horwitz

For Complete List of Firm Personnel, See General Section

For full biographical listings, see the Martindale-Hubbell Law Directory

LAZARUS & ASSOCIATES, A PROFESSIONAL CORPORATION (AV)

One Arizona Center, 400 East Van Buren, Suite 450, 85004
Telephone: 602-340-0900
Facsimile: 602-340-8955
Email: plazo@goodnet.com *URL:* http://www.lawyers.com/lazaruslaw

Larry S. Lazarus
Darin Ann Sender

OF COUNSEL

David K. Jones, P.C.

LEGAL SUPPORT PERSONNEL

LAND USE PLANNER

Melinda L. Schaefer

For full biographical listings, see the Martindale-Hubbell Law Directory

ULRICH, KESSLER & ANGER, P.C. (AV)

3707 North Seventh Street, Suite 250, 85014-5059
Telephone: 602-248-9465
Fax: 602-248-0165
Email: ukapc@aol.com

Paul G. Ulrich
Donn G. Kessler
William H. Anger

For full biographical listings, see the Martindale-Hubbell Law Directory

WITHEY & TOBIN, P.L.C. (AV)

3101 North Central Avenue, Suite 1690, 85012-2615
Telephone: 602-230-0600
Fax: 602-212-1787

Michael B. Withey
Shawn E. Tobin
Ellen Harris Hoff

For full biographical listings, see the Martindale-Hubbell Law Directory

CALIFORNIA

*BAKERSFIELD,** Kern Co.

BORTON, PETRINI & CONRON, LLP (AV)

The Borton, Petrini & Conron Building, 1600 Truxtun Avenue, 93301
Telephone: 661-322-3051
Voice Mail: 661-395-6700
Fax: 661-322-4628
Mailing Address: P.O. Box 2026, Bakersfield, California, 93303
Email: bpcbak@bpclaw.com *URL:* http://www.bpclaw.com
Other City Locations: Fresno, Los Angeles, Modesto, Redding, Sacramento, San Bernardino, San Diego, San Francisco, San Jose, San Luis Obispo, Santa Ana and Ventura.

MEMBERS OF FIRM

George F. Martin
Richard E. Morton
Calvin R. Stead

ASSOCIATES

William G. Welzenbach
Michael S. Abril
Timothy B. Liebaert

For Complete List of Firm Personnel, See General Section

For full biographical listings, see the Martindale-Hubbell Law Directory

COSTA MESA, Orange Co.

RUTAN & TUCKER, LLP (AV)

A Partnership including Professional Corporations
611 Anton Boulevard, Fourteenth Floor, P.O. Box 1950, 92626-1998
Telephone: 714-641-5100; 213-625-7586
Telecopier: 714-546-9035
Email: rutan&tucker@rutan.com *URL:* http://www.rutan.com

MEMBERS OF FIRM

Leonard A. Hampel, Jr.
Michael D. Rubin
Jeffrey M. Oderman (P.C.)
Stan Wolcott (P.C.)
Robert S. Bower
David J. Aleshire
Philip D. Kohn
Joel D. Kuperberg
William W. Wynder
M. Katherine Jenson
Richard Montevideo
Elizabeth L. Martyn
David B. Cosgrove
Hans Van Ligten
Robert O. Owen
Jeffrey A. Goldfarb
Layne H. Melzer
Lien Ski Harrison
A. Patrick Muñoz

SPECIAL COUNSEL

Dan Slater

ASSOCIATES

Todd O. Litfin
Eric L. Dunn
Fred Galante

For Complete List of Firm Personnel, See General Section

For full biographical listings, see the Martindale-Hubbell Law Directory

LA JOLLA, San Diego Co.

MULVANEY, KAHAN & BARRY, A PROFESSIONAL CORPORATION (AV)

Suite 315, 875 Prospect Street, P.O. Box 1168, 92038-1168
Telephone: 619-454-1780
Fax: 619-454-1792
San Diego, California Office: Seventeenth Floor, First National Bank Center, 401 West "A" Street.
Telephone: 619-238-1010.
Fax: 619-238-1981.
Los Angeles, California Office: Union Bank Plaza, 445 South Figueroa Street, Suite 2600.
Telephone: 213-612-7765.
Orange, California Office: The Koll Center, 500 North State College Boulevard, Suite 440.
Telephone: 714-634-7069.
Fax: 714-939-8000.

Thomas A. Henry, Jr.

For full biographical listings, see the Martindale-Hubbell Law Directory

*LOS ANGELES,** Los Angeles Co.

BARBOSA GARCIA LLP (AV)

A Partnership including a Professional Corporation
801 South Grand Avenue Suite 300, 90017-4621
Telephone: 213-612-0800
Fax: 213-612-8085

(See Next Column)

BARBOSA GARCIA LLP—*Continued*

Henry S. Barbosa (P.C.)
Lorie A. Campos
Kenneth T. Fong
Bonifacio Bonny Garcia (P.C.)
Michael L. Kadish
John F. Lagle
Peter E. Langsfeld
Benjamin D. Nieberg
Gary W. Park
Roberta R. Sistos
Jonathan B. Stone
Rajeev M. Talwani
Sylvia J. Trujillo
Thuy-Whien Vuong
John G. Yslas

OF COUNSEL

Albert A. Erkel, Jr.

SPECIAL COUNSEL

Adrienne D. Konigar
Joyce E. Paul
Melvin D. Peters

LEGAL SUPPORT PERSONNEL

Victor M. Estrada (Paralegal)
Janice H. Minamoto (Paralegal)

For full biographical listings, see the Martindale-Hubbell Law Directory

BROWN, WINFIELD & CANZONERI, INCORPORATED (AV)

Suite 1500 California Plaza, 300 South Grand Avenue, 90071-3125
Telephone: 213-687-2100
Fax: 213-687-2149

J. Kenneth Brown
Thomas F. Winfield III
Anthony Canzoneri
Vicki E. Land
James C. Camp
Steven Abram
Dennis S. Roy
Mark Steres
Christopher Norgaard
C. Geoffrey Mitchell
Scott H. Campbell
Joshua C. Gottheim
Donald Paul Ries
Edward J. Szczepkowski
William Balderrama
Richard J. Sestak
Robert H. Badner
John H. Holloway
Anh-Bang Bill Pham
Gregg D. Freeman
Tracy M. Noonan
Richard Charles Rey II
Jeannette R. Busek
Sylvia Diana Roth
Christopher M. Pisano

Reference: Wells Fargo Bank.

For full biographical listings, see the Martindale-Hubbell Law Directory

DAPEER, ROSENBLIT & LITVAK, LLP (AV)

11500 West Olympic Boulevard, Suite 550, 90064-1524
Telephone: 310-203-8200
Fax: 310-203-8213

William Litvak
Steven H. Rosenblit
Kenneth B. Dapeer

For full biographical listings, see the Martindale-Hubbell Law Directory

OLIVER, VOSE, SANDIFER, MURPHY & LEE, A PROFESSIONAL CORPORATION (AV)

Figueroa Courtyard, Second Floor, 281 South Figueroa Street, 90012
Telephone: 213-621-2000
Telecopier: 213-621-2211

Charles S. Vose
Connie Cooke Sandifer
James Duff Murphy
Edward W. Lee
Roger W. Springer
Arthur J. Hazarabedian

Bradley E. Wohlenberg
Timothy J. Chung
Kristin L. Mendenhall

Representative Clients: Cities of Anaheim, Bell, Brea, Calabasas and Carson.
Agency Counsel Clients: Anaheim Housing Authority; Anaheim Redevelopment Agency; Brea Redevelopment Agency; Buena Park Redevelopment Authority; Compton Redevelopment Agency.

For full biographical listings, see the Martindale-Hubbell Law Directory

O'MELVENY & MYERS LLP (AV)

400 South Hope Street, 90071-2899
Telephone: 213-430-6000
Facsimile: 213-430-6407
Cable: MOMS
Telex: 674122
Email: omminfo@omm.com *URL:* http://www.omm.com
Century City, CA Office: 1999 Avenue of the Stars, Los Angeles, 90067-6035.
Telex: 674097. Tel: 310-553-6700.
Fax: 310-246-6779.
Newport Beach, CA Office: 610 Newport Center Drive, 92660-6429.
Telex: 4722088. Tel: 949-760-9600.
Fax: 949-823-6994.
San Francisco, CA Office: Embarcadero Center West, 275 Battery Street, 94111-3305. Tel: 415-984-8700.
Fax: 415-984-8701.
New York, NY Office: Citicorp Center, 153 East 53rd Street, 10022-4611.
Telex: 129165. Tel: 212-326-2000.
Fax: 212-326-2061.

(See Next Column)

Washington, DC Office: 555 13th Street, N.W., 20004-1109.
Cable: MOMSWSH.
Telex: 89622. Tel: 202-383-5300.
Fax: 202-383-5414.
London Office: O'Melveny & Myers, 3 Finsbury Square, London, EC2A 1LA, England. Tel: 44-171-256-8451. Fax 44-171-638-8205.
Tokyo Office: Akasaka Twin Tower, East 14F, 2-17-23, Akasaka, Minato-ku, Tokyo 107-0052, Japan. Tel: 03-5562-2800.
Fax: 03-5575-3840.
Hong Kong Office: O'Melveny & Myers, Suite 1905, Tower Two, Lippo Centre, 89 Queensway, Central, Hong Kong. Tel: 852-2523-8266.
Fax: 852-2522-1760.
Shanghai Office: Kerry Centre, 20F, 1515 Nanjing Road West, Shanghai, 200040 People's Republic of China. Tel: 86-21-5298-5600.
Fax: 86-21-5298-5500.

PARTNER

Richard M. Jones

For Complete List of Firm Personnel, See General Section

For full biographical listings, see the Martindale-Hubbell Law Directory

PASADENA, Los Angeles Co.

LAGERLOF, SENECAL, BRADLEY, GOSNEY & KRUSE, LLP (AV)

301 North Lake Avenue, 10th Floor, 91101-4108
Telephone: 626-793-9400
FAX: 626-793-5900
Email: mail@lagerlof.com

MEMBERS OF FIRM

Joseph J. Burris (1913-1980)
Stanley C. Lagerlof (1915-1998)
H. Jess Senecal
Jack T. Swafford
John F. Bradley
Timothy J. Gosney
William F. Kruse
Thomas S. Bunn, III
Andrew D. Turner
Rebecca J. Thyne
James D. Ciampa

ASSOCIATE

Shaun O. Kwon

Representative Clients: Gallo Glass Company; Orthopaedic Hospital; North American Chemical Company; Palmdale Water District; Public Water Agencies Group; Ventura Port District; Walnut Valley Water District; Metric Construction Co., Inc.

For full biographical listings, see the Martindale-Hubbell Law Directory

*RIVERSIDE,** Riverside Co.

HAIGHT, BROWN & BONESTEEL, L.L.P. (AV)

A Partnership including Professional Corporations
California Tower, 3737 Main Street, Suite 800, 92501
Telephone: 909-341-8300
FAX: 909-341-8309
URL: http://www.hbblaw.com
Santa Monica, California Office: 1620 26th Street, Suite 4000 North, P.O. Box 680.
Telephone: 310-449-6000.
Telecopier: 310-829-5117.
Telex: 705837.
Santa Ana, California Office: Suite 900, 5 Hutton Centre Drive.
Telephone: 714-754-1100.
Telecopier: 714-754-0826.
San Francisco, California Office: 100 Bush Street, 27th Floor.
Telephone: 415-986-7700.
Fax: 415-986-6945.
San Diego, California Office: 101 West Broadway, Suite 1000.
Telephone: 619-595-5583.
Fax: 619-595-7873.

RESIDENT MEMBERS

Mark S. Lester
Kevin M. Osterberg

ASSOCIATES

Bonnie B. Bailey-Jones
John W. Short
Jeffrey T. Gwynn

For full biographical listings, see the Martindale-Hubbell Law Directory

*SACRAMENTO,** Sacramento Co.

HYDE, MILLER, OWEN & TROST, A PROFESSIONAL CORPORATION (AV)

428 J Street, Suite 400, 95814
Telephone: 916-447-7933
Facsimile: 916-447-5195
Email: hmot@hmot.com

Richard H. Hyde
Nancy C. Miller
William L. Owen
Kirk E. Trost

Paul J. Chrisman
Matina R. Kolokotronis
Christiane E. Layton
Matthew D. Ruyak

(See Next Column)

HYDE, MILLER, OWEN & TROST A PROFESSIONAL CORPORATION, *Sacramento—Continued*

OF COUNSEL

Phillip L. Isenberg

For full biographical listings, see the Martindale-Hubbell Law Directory

*SAN DIEGO,** San Diego Co.

HOVEY & KIRBY, A PROFESSIONAL CORPORATION (AV)

402 West Broadway, Suite 1500, 92101
Telephone: 619-685-4000
Fax: 619-685-4004
Email: administrator@hoveylaw.com

Gregg B. Hovey

For full biographical listings, see the Martindale-Hubbell Law Directory

MULVANEY, KAHAN & BARRY, A PROFESSIONAL CORPORATION (AV)

Seventeenth Floor, First National Bank Center, 401 West "A" Street, 92101-7994
Telephone: 619-238-1010
Fax: 619-238-1981
Email: mkb@mkblaw.com
Los Angeles, California Office: Union Bank Plaza, 445 South Figueroa Street, Suite 2600.
Telephone: 213-612-7765.
La Jolla, California Office: Suite 315, 875 Prospect Street, P.O. Box 1168.
Telephone: 619-454-1780.
Fax: 619-454-1792.
Orange, California Office: The Koll Center, 500 North State College Boulevard, Suite 440.
Telephone: 714-634-7069.
Fax: 714-939-8000.

James F. Mulvaney
Lawrence Kahan
Everett G. Barry, Jr.
Robert A. Linn
Paula Rotenberg
Melissa A. Blackburn
Mark R. Raftery
John A. Mayers
Robin L. Cahill
Kristin L. Yokomoto
Darren John Devlin

OF COUNSEL

Rex B. Beatty
Derrick W. Samuelson (Not admitted in CA)

Representative Clients: Air Products & Chemicals, Inc.; Aoki Construction (CA) Co., Ltd.; AT&T Capital Corp.; BellSouth Communications Systems, Inc.; ITT Corp.; NationsBank; Phoenix Home Life Mutual Insurance Co.; Textron Financial Corporation; Union Bank; Wells Fargo Bank.

For full biographical listings, see the Martindale-Hubbell Law Directory

*SAN FRANCISCO,** San Francisco Co.

ELLMAN, BURKE, HOFFMAN & JOHNSON, A PROFESSIONAL CORPORATION (AV)

One Ecker, Suite 200, 94105
Telephone: 415-777-2727
Fax: 415-495-7587
Email: managingdirector@ellman-burke.com *URL:* http://www.ellman-burke.com

Howard N. Ellman
Michael J. Burke
Kenneth N. Burns
John D. Hoffman
Jeffrey W. Johnson
Thomas Paine
Jay L. Paxton
Thomas M. Sherwood
Leslie M. Browne
Jodi Billehus Fedor

JoAnne L. Dunec
Sarah Richards Gansa
Christina W. Chi

For full biographical listings, see the Martindale-Hubbell Law Directory

COLORADO

*ASPEN,** Pitkin Co.

AUSTIN, PEIRCE & SMITH, P.C. (AV)

Suite 205, 600 East Hopkins Avenue, 81611
Telephone: 970-925-2600
FAX: 970-925-4720
Email: aps_aspen@aol.com

Ronald D. Austin
Frederick F. Peirce
Thomas Fenton Smith

(See Next Column)

John M. Lassalette

Counsel for: Chase Manhattan of Colorado, Inc.; Clark's Market; Coates, Reid & Waldron Property Management, Inc.; Crystal Palace Corp.; Snowmass Shopping Center; Coldwell Banker The Aspen Brokers, Ltd.; William Poss & Assoc., Architects; Snowmass Village Resort Association; Aspen/-Pitkin County Housing Authority.

For full biographical listings, see the Martindale-Hubbell Law Directory

*CASTLE ROCK,** Douglas Co.

FOLKESTAD & FAZEKAS, P.C. (AV)

316 Wilcox Street, 80104-2495
Telephone: 303-688-3045
FAX: 303-688-3189
Email: Firm@Folkestad-Fazekas.com

James B. Folkestad
Ernest F. Fazekas, II

Aaron W. Barrick
Marc C. Patoile
James M. Hunsaker

Representative Clients: Town of Monument; Plum Creek Metropolitan District; Bell Mountain Homeowners Association, Inc.; Jackson 105 Fire Protection District; Denver Southeast Suburban Water and Sanitation District.
References: First National Bank of Castle Rock; Castle Rock Bank.

For full biographical listings, see the Martindale-Hubbell Law Directory

*DENVER,** Denver Co.

GORSUCH KIRGIS LLP (AV)

Tower 1, Suite 1000, 1515 Arapahoe Street, 80202
Telephone: 303-376-5000
Fax: 303-376-5001

PARTNERS

Roger W. Noonan
Randy D. Funk
Malcolm M. Murray
Gerald E. Dahl
Charles A. Kuechenmeister
Robert C. Widner

ASSOCIATES

Paul F. Kennebeck
Maureen Herr Juran
Kelly Elefant
Loretta P. Martinez

For full biographical listings, see the Martindale-Hubbell Law Directory

HAYES, PHILLIPS & MALONEY, P.C. (AV)

Suite 450, The Market Center, 1350 Seventeenth Street, 80202-1517
Telephone: 303-825-6444
Fax: 303-825-1269

John E. Hayes
Herbert C. Phillips
James S. Maloney
Corey Y. Hoffmann
Kendra L. Carberry

Representative Clients: City of Northglenn; City of Sheridan; Metropolitan Denver Water Authority; Parker Water and Sanitation District; Town of Winter Park; City of Black Hawk; Town of Hudson; Town of Parker; Town of Alma; City of Greenwood Village.

For full biographical listings, see the Martindale-Hubbell Law Directory

OTTEN, JOHNSON, ROBINSON, NEFF & RAGONETTI, P.C. (AV)

950 Seventeenth Street, 16th Floor, 80202
Telephone: 303-825-8400
Telecopier: 303-825-6525
URL: http://www.ojrnr.com

Thomas J. Ragonetti
J. Bart Johnson
Munsey L. Ayers, Jr.
Nicole J. Hanak
Berkeley I. Vogelsang

OF COUNSEL

Barbara J. Green

Representative Clients: CarrAmerica Realty Corp.; Carruth Sutton Co.; The City and County of Denver; Kiewit Construction Group, Inc.; Recreational Equipment, Inc. (REI); San Miguel Valley Corp.; U S WEST Real Estate, Inc.; Van Schaack Holdings, Ltd.; Village Homes; Waste Management of North America, Inc.

For Complete List of Firm Personnel, See General Section

For full biographical listings, see the Martindale-Hubbell Law Directory

GREENWOOD VILLAGE, Arapahoe Co.

ICENOGLE, NORTON & SETER, A PROFESSIONAL CORPORATION (AV)

5690 DTC Boulevard Suite 300, 80111
Telephone: 303-773-1666
Fax: 303-773-1883
Email: INS@inspc.com

(See Next Column)

ICENOGLE, NORTON & SETER A PROFESSIONAL CORPORATION—*Continued*

T. Edward Icenogle
Charles E. Norton
Kim J. Seter
Barbara K. Tenney
Erin M. Smith

Tamara K. Gilida
Shelley A. Sackett
Dawn C. Watkins
Dianne D. Miller

Representative Clients: Black Hawk - Central City Sanitation District; Bromley Park Metropolitan District; City of Cherry Hills Village, Colorado; E-470 Public Highway Authority; Fairlake Metropolitan District; Greenwood South Metropolitan District; Rocky Flats Coalition of Local Goverments; Tabernash Meadows Water & Sanitation District; Widefield Water & Sanitation District; Woodmoor Water & Sanitation District.

For full biographical listings, see the Martindale-Hubbell Law Directory

CONNECTICUT

CHESHIRE, New Haven Co.

JOHN K. KNOTT, JR. (AV)
325 South Main Street, 06410
Telephone: 203-271-3031
Fax: 203-272-5388
Email: jkkpcm@juno.com

ASSOCIATE
Priscilla C. Mulvaney

For full biographical listings, see the Martindale-Hubbell Law Directory

GREENWICH, Fairfield Co.

ALBERT, WARD & JOHNSON, P.C. (AV)
125 Mason Street, P.O. Box 1668, 06836
Telephone: 203-661-8600
Telecopier: 203-661-8051

Tom S. Ward, Jr.
Scott R. Johnson
Jane D. Hogeman
Howard R. Wolfe
Christopher A. Kristoff
Vicki K. Comberiati

OF COUNSEL
David Albert
C. Robton Perelli-Minetti

For full biographical listings, see the Martindale-Hubbell Law Directory

*HARTFORD,** Hartford Co.

KILLIAN, DONOHUE & SHIPMAN, LLC (AV)
363 Main Street, 06106-1885
Telephone: 860-560-1977
Telecopier: 860-249-6638
Email: lawyers@killiandonohueshipman.com
Simsbury, Connecticut Office: 141 West Street.
Telephone: 860-658-0436.
Telecopier: 860-249-6638.

Robert K. Killian, Jr.
Thomas J. Donohue, Jr.
Mark S. Shipman
Lawrence S. Shipman

For full biographical listings, see the Martindale-Hubbell Law Directory

NEW LONDON, New London Co.

WALLER, SMITH & PALMER, P.C. (AV)
52 Eugene O'Neill Drive, P.O. Box 88, 06320
Telephone: 860-442-0367
Telecopier: 860-447-9915
Email: wspmain@snet.net *URL:* http://www.snetyp.com/wallersmithpalmer
Old Lyme Office: 103 Halls Road.
Telephone: 860-434-8063.
Telecopier: 860-434-9452. Email: wspol@snet.net

Birdsey G. Palmer (Retired)
William W. Miner
Robert P. Anderson, Jr.
Robert W. Marrion
Hughes Griffis
Edward B. O'Connell
Frederick B. Gahagan
Tracy M. Collins
David P. Condon
Valerie Ann Votto
Charles C. Anderson

General Counsel For: Town of East Lyme.
Counsel For: Citizens Bank of Connecticut; Soneco/Northeastern, Inc.; The Nature Conservancy; Fleet Bank.
Local Counsel For: McCue Mortgage Co.; Citicorp Mortgage; U.S. Department of Housing and Urban Development.

For Complete List of Firm Personnel, See General Section

For full biographical listings, see the Martindale-Hubbell Law Directory

STAMFORD, Fairfield Co.

CACACE, TUSCH & SANTAGATA (AV)
777 Summer Street, P.O. Box 15859, 06901-0859
Telephone: 203-327-2000
Telecopier: 203-353-3392
Email: lawcts@aol.com

MEMBERS OF FIRM
Michael J. Cacace
Mark P. Santagata
Paul T. Tusch
Richard S. Fisher

OF COUNSEL
Kenneth A. DellaRocco
Eric D. Grayson

ASSOCIATES
Edward F. Nemchek
Alice Ann Fitzpatrick
Ronald E. Kowalski II
Aamina Ahmad
Demaris Page Hetrick
Patrick L. Poeschl

LEGAL SUPPORT PERSONNEL
Eva L. Chan
Cynthia L. Mammone

For full biographical listings, see the Martindale-Hubbell Law Directory

WESTPORT, Fairfield Co.

WILLIAM L. SCHEFFLER & ASSOCIATES (AV Ⓣ)
P.O. Box 2773, 06880-0773
Telephone: 203-226-6600; 1-800-429-4480
Telecopier: 203-227-1873
Email: scheff@optonline.net

For full biographical listings, see the Martindale-Hubbell Law Directory

DISTRICT OF COLUMBIA

WASHINGTON, D.C. Co.

CUTLER & STANFIELD, L.L.P. (AV)
700 Fourteenth Street, N.W. 10th Floor, 20005-2014
Telephone: 202-624-8400
Fax: 202-624-8410
Denver, Colorado Office: 1675 Broadway, 80202.
Telephone: 303-825-7000.
FAX: 303-825-7005.

MEMBERS OF FIRM
Eliot R. Cutler
Jeffrey L. Stanfield
Sheila D. Jones
Perry M. Rosen
Peter J. Kirsch
Barry Conaty
Stephen H. Kaplan (Not admitted in DC)
Sarah M. Rockwell (Not admitted in DC)
Thomas D. Roth

OF COUNSEL
Byron Keith Huffman, Jr.

ASSOCIATES
Katherine Boonin Andrus
Joel D. Armstrong (Not admitted in DC)
Françoise M. Carrier
Polly B. Jessen (Not admitted in DC)
William G. Malley
Elizabeth A. Mitchell (Resident at Denver, Colorado Office)
Dana C. Nifosi
W. Eric Pilsk
Timothy A. Pohle
John E. Putnam
Daniel S. Reimer (Not admitted in DC)
Andrew T. Swers
Sara E. Wilensky

For full biographical listings, see the Martindale-Hubbell Law Directory

FLORIDA

*FORT LAUDERDALE,** Broward Co.

JOHN M. MILLEDGE, P.A. (AV)
Republic Tower, 15th Floor, 110 Southeast 6th Street, 33301
Telephone: 954-761-8640
Fax: 954-761-8979
URL: http://www.lawyers.com/milledgelaw

John M. Milledge

Representative Clients: Florida Drive-In Theatre Management, Inc.; 3290 Sunrise Investments, Inc.; Fort Lauderdale Swap Shop; Hudson General Corp.; Medics Ambulance Services, Inc.; McKinley Financial Services, Inc.; Cumberland Farms, Inc.; Fort Lauderdale Harley Davidson, Inc.; Holmes Properties, Inc.; B & L. Communications, Inc.

For full biographical listings, see the Martindale-Hubbell Law Directory

*JACKSONVILLE,** Duval Co.

PAPPAS METCALF JENKS MILLER & REINSCH, P.A. (AV)

200 West Forsyth Street, Suite 1400, 32202-4327
Telephone: 904-353-1980
Telecopier: 904-353-5217
Email: pmj@papmet.com

Thomas M. Jenks
Robert A. Leapley, Jr.
John G. Metcalf
Frank Estes Miller
M. Lynn Pappas
Mark A. Reinsch

Christina P. Gillam
Gary B. Davenport
G. Todd Cottrill
Thomas Ingram

LEGAL SUPPORT PERSONNEL

Mary Beth Wimmer
Glenna Thompson (Paralegal)
Donna F. Demetree (Paralegal)

For full biographical listings, see the Martindale-Hubbell Law Directory

*ST. AUGUSTINE,** St. Johns Co.

UPCHURCH, BAILEY & UPCHURCH, P.A. (AV)

780 North Ponce de Leon Boulevard, P.O. Drawer 3007, 32085-3007
Telephone: 904-829-9066
Facsimile: 904-825-4862
Email: info@ubulaw.com

John D. Bailey, Jr.
Frank D. Upchurch, III
Sidney F. Ansbacher
Katherine Gaertner Jones

OF COUNSEL

Hamilton D. Upchurch

General Counsel for: Flagler College; Flagler Hospital, Inc.; Prosperity Bank; St. Johns County School Board.
Representative Clients: Bank of St. Augustine; Penney Retirement Community, Inc.; St. Augustine Alligator Farm, Inc.; St. Augustine-St. Johns County Board of Realtors, Inc.

For Complete List of Firm Personnel, See General Section

For full biographical listings, see the Martindale-Hubbell Law Directory

*TAMPA,** Hillsborough Co.

BRICKLEMYER SMOLKER & BOLVES, P.A. (AV)

500 East Kennedy Boulevard, Suite 200, 33602-4708
Telephone: 813-223-3888
Fax: 813-228-6422
Email: bsb@bsbpropertylaw.com *URL:* http://www.bsbpropertylaw.com

Keith W. Bricklemyer
David Smolker
Brian A. Bolves
Jay J. Bartlett
Douglas C. Roland
David M. Corry
Richard A. Schlosser
Gregory J. Orcutt

R. Michael Brooks
Deborah M. Schmitt

OF COUNSEL

J.A. Jurgens

For full biographical listings, see the Martindale-Hubbell Law Directory

MORRISON & MILLS, P.A. (AV)

1200 West Platt Street Suite 100, 33606
Telephone: 813-258-3311
Telecopier: 813-258-3209
Email: mmills3@tampabay.rr.com

Thomas K. Morrison
Frederick J. Mills

Kevin A. DiTanna
Bradley Abraham Tobin

Representative Clients: SouthTrust Bank of West Florida; SouthTrust Bank, National Association; NationsBank of Florida, N.A.; Mercantile Bank; Southern Commerce Bank; Regions Bank; Hillsborough County Industrial Development Authority.

For full biographical listings, see the Martindale-Hubbell Law Directory

*WEST PALM BEACH,** Palm Beach Co.

JAMES MCCARTNEY WEARN, P.A. (AV)

2023 North Flagler Drive, 33407
Telephone: 561-659-0655
Fax: 561-659-0685

James McCartney Wearn

For full biographical listings, see the Martindale-Hubbell Law Directory

GEORGIA

*ATLANTA,** Fulton Co.

DILLARD & GALLOWAY, LLC (AV)

1500 Monarch Plaza, 3414 Peachtree Road, NE, 30326
Telephone: 404-965-3680
Telecopier: 404-965-3670

MEMBERS OF FIRM

G. Douglas Dillard
William Woodson Galloway
Andrea Cantrell Jones
W. Trav Carter

For full biographical listings, see the Martindale-Hubbell Law Directory

HAWKINS & PARNELL, LLP (AV)

4000 SunTrust Plaza, 303 Peachtree Street, N.E., 30308-3243
Telephone: 404-614-7400
Fax: 404-614-7500
Email: relliott@hplegal.com *URL:* http://www.hawkinsparnell.com

MEMBERS OF FIRM

Michael J. Goldman
H. Lane Young, II
T. Ryan Mock, Jr.
Robert U. Wright
Kimberly Houston
Charles R. Beans
Cullen Christie Wilkerson, Jr.

ASSOCIATES

Allen L. Broughton
Robert S. Thompson
Carl H. Anderson, Jr.

Representative Clients: ACCG-IRMA; GIRMA; Willis Corroon Corporation of Georgia; Titan Insurance Co.; American International Group; Georgia Municipal Association.

For Complete List of Firm Personnel, See General Section

For full biographical listings, see the Martindale-Hubbell Law Directory

NATHAN V. HENDRICKS, III (AV)

6085 Lake Forrest Drive, Suite 200, 30328
Telephone: 404-255-5161
Fax: 404-255-3899

For full biographical listings, see the Martindale-Hubbell Law Directory

HOLT NEY ZATCOFF & WASSERMAN, LLP (AV)

A Partnership including Professional Corporations
100 Galleria Parkway, Suite 600, 30339
Telephone: 770-956-9600
Facsimile: 770-956-1490
Email: mthomas@hnzw.com

MEMBERS OF FIRM

James M. Ney (P.C.)
J. Scott Jacobson
Jay Frank Castle

ASSOCIATES

Thomas K. Anderson
Scott E. Morris

Representative Clients: Equitable Real Estate Investment Management, Inc.; Gables Residential Trust; Georgia Scientific & Technical Research Foundation, Inc.; NationsBank, N.A.; Trammell Crow Residential; John Weiland Homes, Inc.; Childress Klein Properties; Genuine Parts Co.

For Complete List of Firm Personnel, See General Section

For full biographical listings, see the Martindale-Hubbell Law Directory

*AUGUSTA,** Richmond Co.

BURNSIDE, WALL, DANIEL, ELLISON & REVELL (AV)

A Partnership including Professional Corporations
454 Greene Street, P.O. Box 2125, 30903
Telephone: 706-722-0768
Fax: 706-722-5984

MEMBERS OF FIRM

Robert C. Daniel, Jr. (1943-1993)
Thomas R. Burnside, Jr. (P.C.)
James B. Wall (P.C.)
James W. Ellison
Harry D. Revell
Thomas R. Burnside, III

Representative Clients: Augusta-Richmond County Commission; National Science Center Foundation, Inc.; CSRA Regional Development Center; City of Harlem, Georgia; Liquid Carbonic Corp.; Southeastern Equipment Co.; SECO Aviation, Inc.; SECO Parts & Equipment, Inc.

For full biographical listings, see the Martindale-Hubbell Law Directory

*CARTERSVILLE,** Bartow Co.

DAVID G. ARCHER, P.C. (AV)

336 South Tennessee Street, P.O. Box 1024, 30120
Telephone: 770-386-1116
Fax: 770-382-7484
Email: dgapc@innerx.net

David G. Archer

E. Keith Lovell — M. Faye McCord

For full biographical listings, see the Martindale-Hubbell Law Directory

*MCDONOUGH,** Henry Co.

SMITH, WELCH & BRITTAIN (AV)

200 The Commerce Building, 235 Keys Ferry Street, P.O. Box 31, 30253
Telephone: 770-957-3937
Fax: 770-957-9165
Stockbridge, Georgia Office: 1239 Eagle's Landing Parkway.
Telephone: 770-389-4864.
Fax: 770-389-5157.

MEMBERS OF FIRM

Ernest M. Smith (1911-1992)
A. J. Welch, Jr.
J. Mark Brittain (Resident, Stockbridge Office)
E. Gilmore Maxwell

ASSOCIATES

Thomas Bruce McFarland
John P. Webb (Resident, Stockbridge Office)
Katharyne Clark Johnson
Tricia B. Smith
Bruce R. Vail

Representative Clients: Atlanta Motor Speedway, Inc.; Alexsis, Inc.; Bellamy-Strickland Chevrolet, Inc.; Columbia/HCA Healthcare Corp.; Ceramic and Metal Coatings Corp.; Cities of Hampton, Locust Grove and Stockbridge; Georgia Farm Bureau Mutual Insurance; Killearn Properties, Inc. of Georgia.

For full biographical listings, see the Martindale-Hubbell Law Directory

*NEWNAN,** Coweta Co.

GLOVER & DAVIS, P.A. (AV)

10 Brown Street, P.O. Box 1038, 30264
Telephone: 770-683-6000
Fax: 770-683-6010
Peachtree City, Georgia Office: Suite 130, 200 Westpark Drive.
Telephone: 770-487-5834.
Fax: 770-487-3492.

J. Littleton Glover, Jr.
Randy E. Connell
W. Robert Hancock, Jr. (Resident, Peachtree Office)
Asa M. Powell, Jr.
Jerry Ann Conner

Representative Clients: Coweta County, Georgia; City of Franklin, Georgia; City of Whitesburg, Georgia; Heard County Water Authority; City of Moreland, Georgia; B-C Partners; First Citizens Corporation; Putnam-Greene Financial Corporation; Jefferson Ventures, Inc.; Landward, Inc.; Landward III, Inc..

For Complete List of Firm Personnel, See General Section

For full biographical listings, see the Martindale-Hubbell Law Directory

ILLINOIS

BOLINGBROOK, Will Co.

MOSS AND BLOOMBERG, LTD. (AV)

305 West Briarcliff Road, Suite 201, P.O. Box 1158, 60440-0858
Telephone: 630-759-0800
Telecopier: 630-759-8504
Email: info@mb-lawyers.com

Barry L. Moss
Steven P. Bloomberg
George A. Marchetti
David J. Freeman
Daniel C. Shapiro

For full biographical listings, see the Martindale-Hubbell Law Directory

*CHICAGO,** Cook Co.

FORAN & SCHULTZ (AV)

Suite 3000, 30 North La Salle Street, 60602
Telephone: 312-368-8330
Fax: 312-580-2600
Email: law@foran.com *URL:* http://www.Foran.com

MEMBERS OF FIRM

Thomas A. Foran — Richard G. Schultz

(See Next Column)

OF COUNSEL

Robert J. Weber

For full biographical listings, see the Martindale-Hubbell Law Directory

SCARIANO, ELLCH, HIMES, SRAGA AND PETRARCA, CHARTERED (AV)

Two Prudential Plaza 180 North Stetson Suite 3100, 60601-6224
Telephone: 312-565-3100
Facsimile: 312-565-0000
Chicago Heights, Illinois Office: 1450 Aberdeen, 60411.
Telephone: 708-755-1900.
Facsimile: 708-755-0000.

Anthony G. Scariano
Robert H. Ellch
A. Lynn Himes
Alan T. Sraga
Justino D. Petrarca
Lawrence Jay Weiner
John M. Izzo
Raymond A. Hauser
Kathleen Roche Hirsman
Daniel M. Boyle
Teri E. Engler
Rosanne Ciambrone

Kelly A. Hayden
Todd K. Hayden
Christopher L. Petrarca
Sarah E. Joyce
Joel R. DeTella
Susan H. Walter (Resident)
Brian J. Fahey
David A. Harley
Bradley C. Coleman
Christina Sepiol
Alan M. Mullins
John E. Fester
Michael Alan DeBartolo

OF COUNSEL

John Kralovec

For full biographical listings, see the Martindale-Hubbell Law Directory

CRYSTAL LAKE, McHenry Co.

MILITELLO, ZANCK & COEN, P.C. (AV)

40 Brink Street, 60014
Telephone: 815-459-8800
FAX: 815-459-8429

James G. Militello
Thomas C. Zanck
Patrick D. Coen
James L. Wright

Mark S. Saladin
James G. Militello, III
Barbara H. Switzer
D. Chad Mihevc
Nancy A. Stingle
David G. Phoenix

OF COUNSEL

Michael A. Ungvarsky, Jr.

References: Home State Bank of Crystal Lake; First National Bank of Crystal Lake; McHenry State Bank; Amcore Bank N.A., Woodstock.

For full biographical listings, see the Martindale-Hubbell Law Directory

ZUKOWSKI, ROGERS, FLOOD & MCARDLE (AV)

50 Virginia Street, 60014-4126
Telephone: 815-459-2050
Facsimile: 815-459-9057
Email: zrfm@stans.com *URL:* http://www.zrfmlaw.com
Chicago, Illinois Office: 100 South Wacker Drive, Suite 1502.
Telephone: 312-407-7700.
Facsimile: 312-332-1901.

PARTNERS

H. David Rogers
Richard G. Flood
David W. McArdle
Jeannine A. Thoms
Stuart D. Gordon
Kevin J. O'Brien
Michael J. Chmiel
Kathleen Field Orr

ASSOCIATES

Melissa J. Cooney
Kelly A. Cahill
Michael J. Smoron
E. Regan Daniels Shepley
Michael S. Drella
Timothy P. Dwyer
Paul A. Zukowski
Tracey Anne Wertman
Jenette M Schwemler

OF COUNSEL

Timothy J. Curran — Francis S. Lorenz

Representative Clients: Village of Algonquin; Village of Lake in the Hills; Village of Johnsburg; Village of Lakewood; Village of Bull Valley; Village of Hebron; City of Harvard; Village of Richmond; City of McHenry; Village of West Dundee; Village of Greenwood; Village of Trout Valley.

For full biographical listings, see the Martindale-Hubbell Law Directory

*PEKIN,** Tazewell Co.

ELLIFF, KEYSER, OBERLE & DANCEY, P.C. (AV)

109 South Fourth Street, P.O. Box 873, 61554
Telephone: 309-346-4148
Fax: 309-346-0633

(See Next Column)

ELLIFF, KEYSER, OBERLE & DANCEY P.C., *Pekin—Continued*

John T. Elliff (1872-1960) Patrick E. Oberle
Nathan T. Elliff (1905-1993) Burt L. Dancey
William P. Streeter

OF COUNSEL

Ronald L. Keyser

Representative Clients: City of Pekin Central Illinois Dock.
Local Counsel for: The Prudential Insurance Company of America.

For full biographical listings, see the Martindale-Hubbell Law Directory

*WAUKEGAN,** Lake Co.

DIVER, GRACH, QUADE & MASINI (AV)

Bank of Waukegan Building, 111 North County Street, 60085
Telephone: 847-662-8611
FAX: 847-662-2960

MEMBERS OF FIRM

Clarence W. Diver (1883-1962) David R. Quade
Thomas W. Diver Robert J. Masini
Brian S. Grach Sarah P. Lessman
David L. Hazan

Heidi J. Aavang Donna-Jo Rodden Vorderstrasse
Paula Vincich Randall

A list of Representative Clients will be furnished upon request.
Reference: First Midwest Bank of Waukegan.

For full biographical listings, see the Martindale-Hubbell Law Directory

INDIANA

*FORT WAYNE,** Allen Co.

HELMKE, BEAMS, BOYER & WAGNER (AV)

300 Metro Building, Berry & Harrison Streets, 46802-2242
Telephone: 219-422-7422
Telecopier: 219-422-6764
Email: hbbwdjb@aol.com
Email: rdboyer1@fortwayne.infi.net

MEMBERS OF FIRM

Walter E. Helmke (1901-1976) Robert A. Wagner
Walter P. Helmke J. Timothy McCaulay
R. David Boyer Daniel J. Borgmann
Trina Glusenkamp Gould

ASSOCIATES

Payne D. Brown R. David Boyer, II

OF COUNSEL

Glen J. Beams William A. Berning

Representative Clients: Aalco Distributing Co., Inc.; Brotherhood Mutual Insurance Co.; Fremont Community Schools; Air-O-Mat, Inc.; Leo Distributors, Inc.; The City of Fort Wayne, Indiana; Foellinger Foundation, Inc.

For full biographical listings, see the Martindale-Hubbell Law Directory

*INDIANAPOLIS,** Marion Co.

CLARK, QUINN, MOSES & CLARK (AV)

One Indiana Square, Suite 2200, 46204-2011
Telephone: 317-637-1321
Fax: 317-687-2344
Email: lawyers@cqmc-law.com

MEMBERS OF FIRM

Thomas Michael Quinn J. Murray Clark
Matthew R. Clark

ASSOCIATES

Michael D. Keele Cameron F. Clark

Representative Clients: Justus Companies; Davis Homes; Meijer Realty, Inc.; Lowe's; Marsh; MI Shottenstein; Indianapolis Colts; Fort Harrison Reuse Authority; Indianapolis Water Company; Kroger.

For full biographical listings, see the Martindale-Hubbell Law Directory

ELROD & MASCHER, P.C. (AV)

4000 East Southport Road, Suite 200, 46237
Telephone: 317-786-4929
Fax: 317-786-7899
Other Indianapolis Office: 2000 First Indiana Building, 135 North Pennsylvania Street. 46204.
Telephone: 317-264-5000.
Fax: 317-264-5400.

(See Next Column)

French M. Elrod (1906-1985) Robert G. Elrod
Gilbert E. Mascher

Jennifer Horton Mertz

Reference: National City Bank.

For full biographical listings, see the Martindale-Hubbell Law Directory

*LAFAYETTE,** Tippecanoe Co.

BALL, EGGLESTON, BUMBLEBURG, MCBRIDE, WALKEY & STAPLETON, PC (AV)

810 Bank One Building, P.O. Box 1535, 47902-1535
Telephone: 765-742-9046
Fax: 765-742-1966
Email: info@ball-law.com

Cable G. Ball (1904-1981) Michael J. Stapleton
Owen Crook (1908-1977) Jeffrey J. Newell
Warren N. Eggleston (1923-1991) James T. Hodson
Brian Wade Walker
Joseph T. Bumbleburg Cheryl M. Knodle
John K. McBride Randy J. Williams
Jack L. Walkey Brenda Mithoefer Clapper

General Counsel for: The Lafayette Union Railway Co.
Representative Clients: Farmers Insurance Group; General Accident Fire & Life Assurance Corp.; City of Lafayette Board of Parks and Recreation; West Lafayette Community School Corp.; Travelers Insurance Co.; Trustees, West Lafayette Public Library; Town of Dayton, Indiana.

For full biographical listings, see the Martindale-Hubbell Law Directory

MUNSTER, Lake Co.

LAW OFFICES OF EUGENE M. FEINGOLD (AV)

625 Ridge Road, Suite A, 46321
Telephone: 219-836-8800
Fax: 219-836-8944

ASSOCIATE

Steven P. Kennedy

For full biographical listings, see the Martindale-Hubbell Law Directory

*WARSAW,** Kosciusko Co.

ROCKHILL, PINNICK, PEQUIGNOT, HELM, LANDIS & RIGDON (AV)

105 East Main Street, 46580-2742
Telephone: 219-267-6116
Telecopier: 219-269-9264
Email: rockhill@kconline.com

MEMBERS OF FIRM

Brooks C. Pinnick Vern K. Landis
Stanley E. Pequignot Jay A. Rigdon
Richard K. Helm Jamelyn E. Freeman

ASSOCIATE

Dana Leon

Representative Clients: North Center Development, Inc.; Town of Etna Green; Town of Milford; Barbee Lakes Conservancy District; Town of Leesburg; Winona Restoration Partners, LLC.

For full biographical listings, see the Martindale-Hubbell Law Directory

IOWA

*IOWA CITY,** Johnson Co.

MEARDON, SUEPPEL, DOWNER & HAYES P.L.C. (AV)

122 South Linn Street, 52240
Telephone: 319-338-9222
Fax: 319-338-7250

William L. Meardon (1919-1997) Thomas D. Hobart
William F. Sueppel William J. Sueppel

Representative Clients: United Technologies-Automotive; Perpetual Savings Bank; Economy Advertising Company; Metro Pavers, Inc.; League of Iowa Municipalities; Hills Bank and Trust Co.; J.M. Swank Co.; City of Muscatine; McComas-Lacina Construction Co., Inc.; Diamond Dave's Taco Company, Inc.

For Complete List of Firm Personnel, See General Section

For full biographical listings, see the Martindale-Hubbell Law Directory

KENTUCKY

*LEXINGTON,** Fayette Co.

DUNN, FRANKLIN & MURPHY (AV)
175 East Main Street Suite 300, 40507
Telephone: 606-255-9091
Fax: 606-254-4319
Email: dfmlaw@mis.net

Cecil F. Dunn
David A. Franklin
Richard V. Murphy

Rhonda E. Franklin

OF COUNSEL

C. Clinton McKinley

For full biographical listings, see the Martindale-Hubbell Law Directory

STOLL, KEENON & PARK, LLP (AV)
201 E. Main Street, Suite 1000, 40507-1380
Telephone: 606-231-3000
Telecopier: 606-253-1093; 606-253-1027
URL: http://www.skp.com
Frankfort, Kentucky Office: 307 Washington Street, 40601.
Telephone: 502-875-6220.
Telecopier: 502-875-6235.
Henderson, Kentucky Office: 201 C North Main Street, 42420-3103.
Telephone: 270-831-1900.
Telecopier: 270-827-4060.
Louisville, Kentucky Office: 400 West Market Street, Suite 2650, 40202-3377.
Telephone: 502-568-9100.
Telecopier: 502-568-5700.

MEMBERS OF FIRM

Samuel D. Hinkle IV
William M. Lear, Jr.
Robert W. Kellerman
Rena Gardner Wiseman
Lea Pauley Goff

ASSOCIATE

Steven B. Loy

Representative Clients: Ball Homes, Inc.; McDonalds Corp.; National Development Council, Inc.; Super America, Inc.

For Complete List of Firm Personnel, See General Section

For full biographical listings, see the Martindale-Hubbell Law Directory

*LOUISVILLE,** Jefferson Co.

BARDENWERPER & LOBB, PLLC (AV)
8311 Shelbyville Road, 40222
Telephone: 502-426-6688
Fax: 502-425-0561

William B. Bardenwerper
James T. Lobb

ASSOCIATE

Susan T. Merrill

LEGAL SUPPORT PERSONNEL

Alice Blackburn (Paralegal)
Debra Martin (Paralegal)

For full biographical listings, see the Martindale-Hubbell Law Directory

LOUISIANA

*NEW ORLEANS,** Orleans Parish

MCGLINCHEY STAFFORD (AV)

A Professional Limited Liability Company
643 Magazine Street, 70130-3477
Telephone: 504-586-1200
Fax: 504-596-2800
TDD: (504) 596-2728
Telex: 584327
Cable Address: "MACSTAC"
Mailing Address: P.O. Box 60643, New Orleans, Louisiana, 70160-0643
Email: @mcglinchey.com *URL:* http://www.mcglinchey.com
Dallas, Texas Office: 2777 Stemmons Freeway, Suite 925, 75207-2401.
Telephone: 214-860-9700.
Fax: 214-860-9750.
Houston, Texas Office: 2727 Allen Parkway, Suite 1900, 77019.
Telephone: 713-520-1900.
Fax: 713-520-1025.
Baton Rouge, Louisiana Office: Ninth Floor, One American Place, 70825-0001.
Telephone: 504-383-9000.
Fax: 504-343-3076.

(See Next Column)

Jackson, Mississippi Office: Suite 1200, SkyTel Centre, 200 South Lamar Street, 39201.
Telephone: 601-960-8400.
Fax: 601-960-8406.
Lake Providence, Louisiana Office: 405 Morgan Street, 71254-2691.
Telephone: 318-559-1200.
Fax: 318-559-0609.
Monroe, Louisiana Office: Dean ONB Tower, 130 Desiard Street, Suite 807, 71201.
Telephone: 318-651-0807.
Fax: 318-651-0809.

MEMBERS OF FIRM

Dermot S. McGlinchey (1933-1993)
Graham Stafford (1940-1987)
Samuel Lang (1909-1989)
Colvin G. Norwood, Jr., (P.C.)
David S. Willenzik (P.C.)
Frank Voelker, Jr., (P.C.)
B. Franklin Martin, III, (P.C.)
E. Fredrick Preis, Jr.
Henri Wolbrette, III, (P.C.)
William V. Dalferes, Jr., (P.C.)
Constance Charles Willems
Bennet Scott Koren
James M. Fantaci
Kathleen A. Manning
Kenneth A. Weiss
Donna Guinn Klein
Michael M. Noonan
J. Patrick Beauchamp
Rudy J. Cerone
Anthony Rollo
Craig Lewis Caesar
Eve B. Masinter
Stephen W. Rider
Eric A. Shuman
Kathleen Krail Charvet
Laura Hobson Brown
Robin Spencer Palmisano
Charles R. Penot, Jr.
Lauren A. Welch
Thomas A. Roberts
Arthur H. Leith
Stephen P. Beiser
Joseph F. Clark, Jr.
Michael J. de Blanc, Jr.
Katherine Conklin
Kevin L. O'Dea
Mark N. Bodin
Richard A. Aguilar
Lisa E. Maurer
Mark N. Mallery
Monica A. Frois
Louis J. Lupin
Anita Lechner Bosch
Susan M. Tyler
John H. Clegg
Daphne McNutt
R. Keith Colvin
Joyce L. Schenewerk

ASSOCIATES

Margaret Woolverton Triebes
Elizabeth P. Blitch
Patrick J. O'Cain
Daniel T. Plunkett
Erin Fury Parkinson
Lauren L. Zimmermann
Deborah A. Van Meter
David Ball
Eliska Marie Plunkett
Deirdre C. McGlinchey
Ann D. Levine
Dwayne C. Jefferson
Sarah Suzanne Wommack Mahoney
Edward L. Fenasci
Joan Marie Canny
Stephanie G. John
Gary G. Hebert
Mindy Brickman Patrón
Denise Langlois Brown
Lance Andrew Bowling
Jonas P. Baker
David S. Landry
Stephanie M. Sisson
John A. Marzullo
Christopher E. Moore (Not admitted in LA)
Eric J. Simonson
Gina M. Venezia
James E. Swinnen
Jaye Andras Caffrey
A. Kelton Longwell
B. Aven Bruser
Julia Haynes Terry (Not admitted in LA)

OF COUNSEL

Joe Giarrusso, Jr.
Margaret G. Diamond
Mary Lynne Friedman

MEMBERS OF FIRM

Michael David Ferachi (Resident, Baton Rouge Office)
Michael H. Rubin (Resident, Baton Rouge Office)
William H. Leech, Sr. (Resident, Jackson Office)
Sue Hicks Fairbank (Resident, Jackson Office)
Robert Marshall Grodner (Resident, Baton Rouge Office)
J. Scott Sheehan (Resident, Houston Office)
Stephen P. Strohschein (Resident, Baton Rouge Office)
Rodolfo J. Aguilar, Jr. (Resident, Baton Rouge Office)
Wilton J. Johnson, III (Resident, Jackson Office)
Mary Terrell Joseph (Resident, Baton Rouge Office)
William S. Mendenhall (Resident, Jackson Office)
Samuel E. Scott (Resident, Jackson Office)
Richard A. Curry (Resident, Baton Rouge Office)
Jennifer Lynn Davis (Resident, Houston Office)
Mark D. Herbert (Resident, Jackson Office)
Joel W. Mohrman (Resident, Houston Office)
Paul S. West (Resident, Baton Rouge Office)
Samuel A. Bacot (Resident, Baton Rouge Office)
Stephen C. Edds (Resident, Jackson Office)
Richard A. Fogel (Resident, Dallas Office)
Mark A. Sanders (Resident, Houston Office)
Errol J. King (Resident, Baton Rouge Office)
James C. Crigler, Jr. (Resident, Lake Providence Office)
Wesson H. Tribble (Resident, Houston Office)
Dan E. West (Resident, Baton Rouge Office)
Deborah J. Bullion-Gascoyne (Resident, Houston Office)
S. Jess Sperry (Resident, Baton Rouge Office)

(See Next Column)

McGlinchey Stafford, *New Orleans—Continued*

ASSOCIATES

Jolie S. Lenz (Resident, Houston Office)
Jon Ann H. Giblin (Resident, Baton Rouge Office)
Derrick B. Carson (Resident, Houston Office)
Kathleen H. Eiler (Resident, Jackson Office)
Amy Kebert Elder (Resident, Jackson Office)
Pamela L. Hancock (Resident, Jackson Office)
Jean-Paul Perrault (Resident, Baton Rouge Office)
Claude B. Anello (Resident, Houston Office)
Vincent J. Bodin (Resident, Houston Office)
Donald Ray Cravins, Jr. (Resident, Baton Rouge Office)
David E. Harrell, Jr. (Resident, Houston Office)
Danice L. McKeehan (Resident, Dallas Office)
D. Jeffrey Wagner
Ashley Byrd Lowe (Resident, Baton Rouge Office)
Lisa C. Bingham (Resident, Houston Office)
Renee Gluth (Resident, Baton Rouge Office)
Craig A. Horton (Resident, Houston Office)
Shannon Richards (Resident, Houston Office)
Virginia M. Todd (Resident, Jackson Office)
Mark H. Tyson (Resident, Jackson Office)
Lindsay Patterson (Resident, Jackson Office)
Amanda K. Bishop
F. Sherman Boughton, Jr. (Resident, Lake Providence Office)

For full biographical listings, see the Martindale-Hubbell Law Directory

MAINE

*BANGOR,** Penobscot Co.

Eaton, Peabody, Bradford & Veague, P.A. (AV)

Fleet Center-Exchange Street, P.O. Box 1210, 04402-1210
Telephone: 207-947-0111
Telecopier: 207-942-3040
Email: eaton@eatonpeabody.com *URL:* http://www.eatonpeabody.com
Augusta, Maine Office: 77 Sewall Street, Suite 3000.
Telephone: 207-622-3747.
Telecopier: 207-622-9732.
Blue Hill, Maine Office: One East Blue Hill Road.
Telephone: 207-374-2812.
Telecopier: 207-374-2548.
Brunswick, Maine Office: 167 Park Row.
Telephone: 207-729-1144.
Telecopier: 207-729-1140.
Dover-Foxcroft, Maine Office: 30 East Main Street.
Telephone: 207-564-8378.
Telecopier: 207-564-7059.

Michael B. Trainor
P. Andrew Hamilton
Jonathan B. Huntington (Resident, Dover-Foxcroft Office)
Roger L. Huber

For Complete List of Firm Personnel, See General Section

For full biographical listings, see the Martindale-Hubbell Law Directory

*PORTLAND,** Cumberland Co.

Monaghan, Leahy, Hochadel & Libby, LLP (AV)

95 Exchange Street, P.O. Box 7046, 04112-7046
Telephone: 207-774-3906
Facsimile: 207-774-3965
Email: info@mlhl.com *URL:* http://www.mlhl.com

MEMBERS OF FIRM

Thomas F. Monaghan
Thomas G. Leahy
Joseph M. Hochadel
Kevin G. Libby
Christopher C. Dinan
Matthew J. Monaghan
Michael H. Hill

ASSOCIATES

Cornelia Fuchs Fisher
John J. Wall, III
Noah D. Wuesthoff
Ivy L. Frignoca
Carol G. Ford

For full biographical listings, see the Martindale-Hubbell Law Directory

Pierce Atwood (AV)

One Monument Square, 04101
Telephone: 207-791-1100
Fax: 207-791-1350
Email: info@PierceAtwood.com *URL:* http://www.pierceatwood.com
Augusta, Maine Office: 77 Winthrop Street.
Telephone: 207-622-6311.
Fax: 207-623-9367.

(See Next Column)

Newburyport, Massachusetts Office: 6 Harris Street.
Telephone: 978-465-9599.
Fax: 978-465-9945.

MEMBERS OF FIRM

Dennis C. Keeler
Elaine S. Falender
Matthew D. Manahan
Judith A. Fletcher Woodbury

ASSOCIATES

James M. Saffian
David P. Littell
Helen L. Edmonds (Resident, Augusta Office)
Thomas A. Loureiro

COUNSEL

Jacquelyn M. Kurz

For Complete List of Firm Personnel, See General Section

For full biographical listings, see the Martindale-Hubbell Law Directory

MARYLAND

*ANNAPOLIS,** Anne Arundel Co.

Council, Baradel, Kosmerl & Nolan, P.A. (AV)

125 West Street, Fourth Floor, P.O. Box 2289, 21404-2289
Telephone: 410-268-6600
Baltimore: 410-269-6190
Washington, D.C.: 301-261-2247
FAX: 410-269-8409
Email: cbkn@cbknlaw.com

Ronald E. Council
Ronald A. Baradel
Wayne T. Kosmerl
James P. Nolan
William F. Flood, III
Kevin M. Schaeffer
Donna McCabe Schaeffer
Frederick C. Sussman

John Naumann Strange
Susan T. Ford
Edwin H. Staples, II
Susan Stobbart Shapiro

OF COUNSEL

George N. Manis
Nicholas Goldsborough

Representative Clients: Anne Arundel County; Annapolis Bank and Trust; Bank of Maryland; State Farm Mutual Automobile Insurance Co.; Annapolis Yacht Club; Annapolis Yacht Sales, Inc.

For full biographical listings, see the Martindale-Hubbell Law Directory

*BALTIMORE,** (Independent City)

Venable Attorneys at Law Venable, Baetjer and Howard, LLP (AV)

A Partnership including Professional Corporations
1800 Mercantile Bank & Trust Building, 2 Hopkins Plaza, 21201
Telephone: 410-244-7400
Fax: 410-244-7742
URL: http://www.venable.com
Washington, D.C. Office: Venable, Baetjer, Howard & Civiletti LLP, Suite 1000, 1201 New York Avenue, N.W.
Telephone: 202-962-4800.
Fax: 202-962-8300.
McLean, Virginia Office: Suite 400, 2010 Corporate Ridge.
Telephone: 703-760-1600.
Fax: 703-821-8949.
Rockville, Maryland Office: Suite 500, One Church Street, P. O. Box 1906.
Telephone: 301-217-5600.
Fax: 301-217-5617.
Towson, Maryland Office: 210 Allegheny Avenue, P. O. Box 5517.
Telephone: 410-494-6200.
Fax: 410-821-0147.

MEMBERS OF FIRM

Thomas P. Perkins, III (P.C.)
John B. Howard (Resident, Towson, Maryland Office)
John G. Milliken (Not admitted in MD; Resident, McLean, Virginia Office)
Robert A. Hoffman (Resident, Towson, Maryland Office)

OF COUNSEL

Judith A. Armold (Also at Washington, D.C. Office)

For Complete List of Firm Personnel, See General Section

For full biographical listings, see the Martindale-Hubbell Law Directory

*BEL AIR,** Harford Co.

STARK & KEENAN, A PROFESSIONAL ASSOCIATION (AV)

30 Office Street, 21014
Telephone: 410-838-5522
Baltimore: 410-879-2222
Fax: 410-879-0688
Email: wstarkee@aol.com
Havre de Grace Office: "The Old Ordinary" 100 St. John Street, 21078.
Telephone: 410-939-0100.

Elwood V. Stark, Jr.
Charles B. Keenan, Jr.
Edwin G. Carson
Judith Cline-Silverstein
Gregory A. Szoka
Robert S. Lynch
Paul W. Ishak

Claire Prin Blomquist
Lawrence F. Kreis, Jr.
Craig H. DeRan

For full biographical listings, see the Martindale-Hubbell Law Directory

*EASTON,** Talbot Co.

EWING, DIETZ, TURNER & KEHOE, PROFESSIONAL ASSOCIATION (AV)

16 South Washington Street, P.O. Box 1146, 21601
Telephone: 410-822-1988
Fax: 410-820-5053
URL: http://www.edtklaw.com

L. Clark Ewing (1919-1998)
Philip E. L. Dietz, Jr.
Christopher B. Kehoe
John F. Hall
Karen M. Kaludis
Stephen H. Kehoe

Sharon M. Shilling

OF COUNSEL

Henry P. Turner

References: The Talbot Bank of Easton, Maryland; St. Michaels Bank.

For full biographical listings, see the Martindale-Hubbell Law Directory

*ROCKVILLE,** Montgomery Co.

MILLER, MILLER & CANBY, CHARTERED (AV)

200-B Monroe Street, 20850
Telephone: 301-762-5212
Fax: 301-762-6044

William M. Canby (1930-1994)
Patrick C. McKeever
James L. Thompson
Lewis R. Schumann
Joel S. Kline
Joseph P. Suntum
Maury S. Epner

OF COUNSEL

Robert L. Burchett
James R. Miller, Jr.

Ellen S. Walker
Susan W. Carter
Suzanne Levant Rotbert
Michael Gert Campbell
Robert E. Gough

Representative Clients: Asbury Methodist Home Inc.; Sandy Spring National Bank of Maryland.

For full biographical listings, see the Martindale-Hubbell Law Directory

*SALISBURY,** Wicomico Co.

ADKINS, POTTS & SMETHURST, L.L.P. (AV)

Suite 600, One Plaza East, P.O. Box 4247, 21803-4247
Telephone: 410-749-0161
Fax: 410-749-5021

MEMBERS OF FIRM

Raymond Stevens Smethurst, Jr.
Robert B. Taylor

Representative Clients: Bell Atlantic NYNEX Mobile; Campbell Soup Company; Delmarva Power & Light Co.; Lawyers' Title Insurance Corp.; Shopco Group; WBOC-TV.

For full biographical listings, see the Martindale-Hubbell Law Directory

SILVER SPRING, Montgomery Co.

LINOWES AND BLOCHER LLP (AV)

Suite 1000, 1010 Wayne Avenue, 20910-5600
Telephone: 301-588-8580
Telecopier: 301-495-9044
TTY/TDD: 301-588-3380
Email: inbox@linowes-law.com *URL:* http://www.linowes-law.com
Washington, D.C. Office: Suite 302, 1150 17th Street, N.W.
Telephone: 202-293-8510.
Telecopier: 202-293-8513.

(See Next Column)

Greenbelt, Maryland Office: Suite 202, 6411 Ivy Lane.
Telephone: 301-982-3382.
Telecopier: 301-982-0595.
Annapolis, Maryland Office: 145 Main Street.
Telephone: 410-268-0881.
Telecopier: 301-261-2603.
Frederick, Maryland Office: 228 West Patrick Street.
Telephone: 301-695-0244.
Telecopier: 301-663-6656.
Columbia, Maryland Office: Suite B215, 10015 Old Columbia Road.
Telephone: 410-312-5457.
Fax: 410-290-5285.

MEMBERS OF FIRM

Joseph P. Blocher
Todd D. Brown
Kathryn J. Dahl (Resident Partner, Annapolis, Maryland office)
C. Robert Dalrymple
John J. Delaney
Stephen P. Elmendorf
Stephen Z. Kaufman
Robert H. Metz
Midgett S. Parker, Jr. (Resident Partner, Greenbelt, Maryland office)
David M. Plott (Resident Partner, Annapolis, Maryland office)
Leslie Moore Romine (Resident Partner, Greenbelt, Maryland office)
Barbara A. Sears

OF COUNSEL

David L. Cahoon
Cynthia A. Giordano (Resident, Washington, D.C. office)

ASSOCIATES

Andrew Wycoff Crocker
Dorothy H. Moore (Not admitted in MD)
Garland H. Stillwell (Resident, Greenbelt, Maryland office)
Emily J. Vaias
Scott C. Wallace

For Complete List of Firm Personnel, See General Section

For full biographical listings, see the Martindale-Hubbell Law Directory

MASSACHUSETTS

*BOSTON,** Suffolk Co.

HINCKLEY, ALLEN & SNYDER LLP (AV)

28 State Street, 30th Floor, 02109-1775
Telephone: 617-345-9000
Email: firm@haslaw.com *URL:* http://www.haslaw.com
Providence, Rhode Island Office: 1500 Fleet Center.
Telephone: 401-274-2000.
Fax: 401-277-9600. URL: http://www.hawlaw.com.

MEMBERS OF FIRM

David D. Barricelli (Not admitted in MA)
E. Jerome Batty (Not admitted in MA)
Jonathan Bell
Paul Bork
Stephen J. Carlotti (Not admitted in MA)
David Barry Connolly
Michael P. DeFanti
Eric F. Eisenberg
Margaret D. Farrell (Not admitted in MA)
Pasco Gasbarro Jr.
Hugh J. Gorman, III
Alan P. Gottlieb
William R. Grimm
Paul A. Hedstrom
Richard L. E. Jocelyn (Not admitted in MA)
Joel Lewin
Sandra Matrone Mack (Not admitted in MA)
Frederick P. McClure
Elizabeth Murdock Myers
Paul F. O'Donnell, III
H. Peter Olsen (Not admitted in MA)
Julianne Palumbo
John J. Pendergast, III (Not admitted in MA)
Gerald J. Petros
James O. Reavis
Jeremy Ritzenberg
Ralph J. Rivkind
David J. Rubin
Charles E. Schaub, Jr.
Douglas F. Seaver
Herman Snyder
David R. Sullivan
Robert F. Sylvia
Howard E. Walker (Not admitted in MA)
Richard D. Wayne

ASSOCIATES

Jessica M. Bettencourt (Not admitted in MA)
Mark Bianchi
Alyssa V. Boss
Alexandra K. Callam
Jane E. Cohen
Andrew D. Cummings
June E. Daniel (Not admitted in MA)
Kim Herman Goslant
Gloria Maria Gutierrez
Kelley Jordan-Price
Catherine S. Kim
Christopher W. Morog
Elena B. Olson
Joseph D. Whelan (Not admitted in MA)

OF COUNSEL

Willard Krasnow
Willard R. Pope
Bentley Tobin
Joachim A. Weissfeld (Not admitted in MA)

(See Next Column)

HINCKLEY, ALLEN & SNYDER LLP, *Boston—Continued*

For Complete List of Firm Personnel, See General Section

For full biographical listings, see the Martindale-Hubbell Law Directory

KOPELMAN AND PAIGE, P.C. (AV)

Park Square Building, 31 St. James Avenue, 7th Floor, 02116
Telephone: 617-556-0007
Fax: 617-654-1735

Leonard Kopelman
Donald G. Paige
Elizabeth A. Lane
Joyce F. Frank
John W. Giorgio
Barbara J. Saint Andre
Joel B. Bard
Everett Joseph Marder
Patrick J. Costello
Joseph L. Tehan, Jr.
Anne-Marie M. Hyland
Theresa M. Dowdy
Deborah Eliason
Richard Bowen

Edward M. Reilly
William Hewig, III
Jeanne S. McKnight
Judith Chanoux Cutler
David J. Doneski
Sandra M. Charton
Ilana Marie Quirk
Patricia A. Cantor
Robert Patten
Mark R. Reich
Brian W. Riley
Thomas P. Lane, Jr.
Mary L. Giorgio
Kathleen Elisabeth Connolly
Christopher J. Groll
Michele E. Randazzo
John R. Hucksam Jr.
Kathleen M. O'Donnell
Darren Robert Klein

For full biographical listings, see the Martindale-Hubbell Law Directory

FRANKLIN, Norfolk Co.

ROCHE AND MURPHY (AV)

Franklin Office Park West, 38 Pond Street, Suite 308, P.O. Box 267, 02038
Telephone: 508-528-8300
FAX: 508-528-8889
Email: jroche@ncounty.net

MEMBERS OF FIRM

Neil J. Roche
Paul G. Murphy

ASSOCIATE

John J. Roche

For full biographical listings, see the Martindale-Hubbell Law Directory

MILFORD, Worcester Co.

GREENWALD, GREENWALD, POWERS & WINSOR LLP (AV)

409 Fortune Boulevard Granite Park, 01757-1746
Telephone: 508-478-8611
Fax: 508-634-3959; 478-5937
Email: ggp@ggplaw@.com *URL:* http://www.ggplaw.com

Alan Greenwald

For full biographical listings, see the Martindale-Hubbell Law Directory

*WORCESTER,** Worcester Co.

MOUNTAIN, DEARBORN & WHITING LLP (AV)

370 Main Street, 01608
Telephone: 508-756-2423
Fax: 508-755-6640

MEMBERS OF FIRM

Alfred N. Whiting (1920-1989)
Thomas R. Mountain
Richard W. Dearborn
Samuel R. DeSimone
Henry W. Beth
Stuart A. Hammer
Francis J. Russell
Dale R. Harger
Mark W. Bloom
Donald J. O'Neil
Lawrence S. Delaney
Ann K. Molloy
Lisa D. Tingue

For full biographical listings, see the Martindale-Hubbell Law Directory

MICHIGAN

BATTLE CREEK, Calhoun Co.

KREIS, ENDERLE, CALLANDER & HUDGINS, A PROFESSIONAL CORPORATION (AV)

One West Michigan Avenue, 49017
Telephone: 616-966-3000
Facsimile: 616-966-3022
Email: kech@kech.com *URL:* http://www.kech.com
Kalamazoo, Michigan Office: One Moorsbridge, P.O. Box 4010, 49003-4010.
Telephone: 616-324-3000.
Fax: 616-324-3010.

(See Next Column)

Douglas L. Callander (Resident, Kalamazoo Office)
Thomas G. King (Resident, Kalamazoo Office)

For Complete List of Firm Personnel, See General Section

For full biographical listings, see the Martindale-Hubbell Law Directory

BIRMINGHAM, Oakland Co.

BUTZEL LONG, A PROFESSIONAL CORPORATION (AV)

Suite 200, 32270 Telegraph Road, 48025
Telephone: 810-258-1616
Telecopier: 810-258-1439
Email: melnick@butzel.com *URL:* http://www.butzel.com
Detroit, Michigan Office: Suite 900, 150 West Jefferson.
Telephone: 313-225-7000.
Telecopier: 313-225-7080.
Okemos, Michigan Office: Suite 300, 2127 University Park Drive.
Telephone: 517-372-6622.
Telecopier: 517-372-6672.
Ann Arbor, Michigan Office: Suite 300, 350 South Main Street.
Telephone: 313-995-3110.
Telecopier: 313-995-1777.
Grosse Pointe Farms, Michigan Office: Suite 260, 21 Kercheval.
Telephone: 313-886-5446.
Telecopier: 313-886-2114.
Boca Raton, Florida Office: Suite 411, 1200 North Federal Highway.
Telephone: 561-368-2151.
Telecopier: 561-368-4668.
Palm Beach Gardens, Florida Office: Suite 227, 11382 Prosperity Farms Road.
Telephone: 561-625-4442.
Telecopier: 561-625-6901.
Naples, Florida Office: Suite 705, 801 Laurel Oak Drive.
Telephone: 941-597-4500.
Telecopier: 941-597-5623.

Stephen A. Bromberg (Resident)
Allan Nachman (Resident)
John J. Raymond, Jr.
David W. Berry (Resident)
D. Stewart Green (Resident)
Gordon W. Didier (Resident)
Alan S. Levine (Resident)
Anthony J. Saulino, Jr. (Resident)
Patrick A. Karbowski (Resident)
Ronald E. Reynolds (Resident)
Susan Klein Friedlaender (Resident)

Todd M. Fink (Resident)

For full biographical listings, see the Martindale-Hubbell Law Directory

HYMAN LIPPITT, P.C. (AV)

185 Oakland Avenue, Suite 300, 48009
Telephone: 248-646-8292
Facsimile: 248-646-8375
Email: hymalipp@tir.com

J. Leonard Hyman
Norman L. Lippitt
Douglas A. Hyman
Brian D. O'Keefe
H. Joel Newman
Nazli G. Sater
Kenneth F. Neuman
Terry S. Givens
Paul J. Fischer
John A. Sellers
Robert H. Lippitt
Roger L. Myers
Sally A. Rutledge
Joseph Pia
John P. Gonway
Leif K. Anderson
Jennifer S. Gold
Julie Lyons Kosovec
Dawn S. Spratley
Michael T. Price

For full biographical listings, see the Martindale-Hubbell Law Directory

BLOOMFIELD HILLS, Oakland Co.

ADKISON, NEED, GREEN & ALLEN (AV)

1533 North Woodward Avenue, Suite 210, 48304
Telephone: 248-540-7400
Fax: 248-540-7401
URL: http://www.adkisonneed.com

MEMBERS OF FIRM

Phillip G. Adkison
Gregory K. Need

ASSOCIATES

Kevin M. Chudler
Richard D. Kuhn, Jr.
Nicki L. Weisberger

For Complete List of Firm Personnel, See General Section

For full biographical listings, see the Martindale-Hubbell Law Directory

BEIER HOWLETT, PROFESSIONAL CORPORATION (AV)

200 East Long Lake Road, Suite 110, 48304-2361
Telephone: 248-645-9400
Fax: 248-645-9344
URL: http://www.beierhowlett.com

(See Next Column)

BEIER HOWLETT PROFESSIONAL CORPORATION—*Continued*

James L. Howlett
Daniel C. Devine
Lawrence R. Ternan
Stephen W. Jones
Frank S. Galgan
Kenneth J. Sorensen
Thomas J. Trenta
Mark W. Hafeli
Timothy J. Currier
Mary T. Schmitt Smith
Joseph F. Yamin
John D. Staran
Phyllis Aiuto Zimmerman
P. Daniel Christ
Lauren M. Underwood

Elizabeth A. Barrett Bonner
Mary M. Kucharek
Richard A. Joslin, Jr.
Michael C. Gibbons
Jon M. Midtgard
Paul L. Nystrom
Genevieve Dwaihy Hopkins
Jeffrey S. Kragt

OF COUNSEL

Dean G. Beier
Robert G. Waddell
Catherine J. Hulbert
Thomas V. Trainer

Representative Clients: City of Birmingham; City of Lake Angelus; City of Rochester Hills; Village of Franklin; Michigan Municipal League; Oakland University; Dundee Community Schools; Troy School District; Lincoln Consolidated Schools; Alma Public Schools.

For full biographical listings, see the Martindale-Hubbell Law Directory

O'CONNOR, DEGRAZIA & TAMM, P.C. (AV)

4111 Andover Road East, 48302
Telephone: 248-433-2000
Fax: 248-433-2001
Email: odtlaw@ameritech.net

Richard M. O'Connor
James I. DeGrazia
James E. Tamm
Julie McCann O'Connor
Audrey J. Forbush

Thomas H. Schram
Timothy Mulligan
Lauri Beth Stewart
Christopher P. Kohler

Representative Clients: Regents of the University of Michigan; William Beaumont Hospital; Mutual Ins. Corp. of America; Botsford General Hospital; Michigan Municipal League; Michigan Municipal Liability and Property Pool; St. Paul Insurance Cos.; Meadowbrook Inc. Co.; National Chiropractic Mutual.

For full biographical listings, see the Martindale-Hubbell Law Directory

*DETROIT,** Wayne Co.

ABBOTT, NICHOLSON, QUILTER, ESSHAKI & YOUNGBLOOD, P.C. (AV)

300 River Place, Suite 3000, 48207-4225
Telephone: 313-566-2500
Telecopier: 313-566-2502
Email: anqey@anqey.com *URL:* http://www.anqey.com

C. Richard Abbott
John R. Nicholson
Thomas R. Quilter III
Gene J. Esshaki
John F. Youngblood
James B. Perry
Carl F. Jarboe
Jay A. Kennedy
Timothy A. Stoepker
Timothy J. Kramer
Norbert T. Madison, Jr.
William D. Gilbride, Jr.
Mary P. Nelson
Michael R. Blum
Anne Warren Bagno
Thomas J. Giachino

Eric J. Girdler
Jill A. Bankey
Daniel G. Kielczewski
George P. Butler III
Christopher P. Baker

OF COUNSEL

Thomas C. Shumaker
Lisa R. Gorman

For full biographical listings, see the Martindale-Hubbell Law Directory

BODMAN, LONGLEY & DAHLING LLP (AV)

34th Floor 100 Renaissance Center, 48243
Telephone: 313-259-7777
Fax: 313-393-7579
Email: info@bodmanlongley.com *URL:* http://www.bodmanlongley.com
Troy, Michigan Office: Suite 2020, 755 West Big Beaver Road.
Telephone: 248-362-2110.
Fax: 248-244-0780.
Ann Arbor, Michigan Office: 110 Miller, Suite 300.
Telephone: 734-761-3780.
Fax: 734-930-2494.
Northern Michigan Office: 229 Court Street, P.O. Box 405, Cheboygan.
Telephone: 231-627-4351.
Fax: 231-627-2802.

MEMBERS OF FIRM

Thomas A. Roach (Ann Arbor Office)
Herold McC. Deason
James A. Smith
Joseph N. Brown
Randolph S. Perry
James J. Walsh
F. Thomas Lewand

(See Next Column)

MEMBERS OF FIRM (Continued)

Michael A. Stack (Cheboygan Office)
Harvey W. Berman (Ann Arbor Office)
Barbara A. Bowman
Jerold Lax (Ann Arbor Office)
Sandra L. Sorini (Ann Arbor Office)

COUNSEL

John S. Dobson (Ann Arbor Office)

ASSOCIATE

Deanna L. Dixon

Representative Clients: Archdiocese of Detroit; Comerica Bank; The Detroit Lions, Inc.; Ford Estates; Lear Corp.; Charles Stewart Mott Foundation; Norfolk Southern Corporation; Panhandle Eastern Corporation; State Farm Insurance Companies.

For Complete List of Firm Personnel, See General Section

For full biographical listings, see the Martindale-Hubbell Law Directory

JAFFE, RAITT, HEUER & WEISS, PROFESSIONAL CORPORATION (AV)

One Woodward Avenue, Suite 2400, 48226
Telephone: 313-961-8380
Telecopier: 313-961-8358
Cable Address: "Jafsni"
Southfield,Michigan Office: Travelers Tower, Suite 1520.
Telephone: 313-961-8380.

Robert S. Bolton

For Complete List of Firm Personnel, See General Section

For full biographical listings, see the Martindale-Hubbell Law Directory

MILLER, CANFIELD, PADDOCK AND STONE, P.L.C. (AV)

A Professional Limited Liability Company
Founded in 1852 by Sidney Davy Miller
150 West Jefferson, Suite 2500, 48226-4415
Telephone: 313-963-6420
Fax: 313-496-7500
Cable Address: "Stem Detroit"
URL: http://www.millercanfield.com
Ann Arbor, Michigan Office: 101 North Main Street, 7th Floor, 48104-1400.
Telephone: 734-663-2445.
Fax: 734-747-7147.
Troy, Michigan Office: 840 West Long Lake Road, Suite 200, 48098.
Telephone: 248-879-2000.
Fax: 248-879-2001.
Grand Rapids, Michigan Office: 99 Monroe, N.W., Suite 1200, 49503-2639.
Telephone: 616-454-8656.
Fax: 616-776-6322.
Howell, Michigan Office: 121 South Barnard Street, Suite 4, 48843-2305.
Telephone: 517-546-7600.
Telecopier: 517-546-6974.
Kalamazoo, Michigan Office: 444 West Michigan Avenue, 49007-3752.
Telephone: 616-381-7030.
Fax: 616-382-0244.
Lansing, Michigan Office: One Michigan Avenue, Suite 900, 48933-1609.
Telephone: 517-487-2070.
Fax: 517-374-6304.
Monroe, Michigan Office: 214 East Elm Avenue, Suite 100, 48162-2682.
Telephone: 734-243-2000.
Fax: 734-243-0901.
Washington, D.C. Office: 1900 K Street, N.W., Suite 1150. 20006.
Telephone: 202-429-5575; 785-0600.
Fax: 202-331-1118; 785-1234.
Pensacola, Florida Office: 25 West Cedar, 32501.
Telephone: 850-469-1088.
Fax: 850-432-0677.
New York, New York Office: 1450 Broadway, 41st Floor, 10018.
Telephone: 212-704-4400.
Fax: 212-704-4410.
Gdynia, Poland Office: UL. Slaska 21, 81-319.
Telephone: 011-485-831-2808.
Fax: 011-48-58-628 6411.
Warsaw, Poland Office: UL. Nowogrodzkall, 5th Floor, 00-513.
Telephone: 011-4822 529 0200.
Fax: 011-4822 529 0201.
Katowice, Poland Office: UL. Francuska 35/37, 40-027.
Telephone: 011 (48-32) 757-2414.
Fax: 011 (48-32) 757-2483.

PRINCIPALS OF FIRM

Joel L. Piell
Robert E. Gilbert (Ann Arbor Office)
Dennis R. Neiman
William J. Danhof (Lansing Office)
Jerry T. Rupley
Thomas W. Linn
Donald W. Keim
Christopher J. Dembowski (Lansing Office)
Amanda Van Dusen
Cynthia B. Faulhaber (Lansing Office)
Harold W. Bulger, Jr.
Michael P. McGee
Don M. Schmidt (Kalamazoo Office)

(See Next Column)

MILLER, CANFIELD, PADDOCK AND STONE P.L.C., *Detroit—Continued*

OF COUNSEL/SENIOR COUNSEL

Eric V. Brown, Sr. (Kalamazoo Office)
Richard B. Gushée
Robert E. Hammell
Richard I. Lott (Pensacola, Florida Office)

SENIOR ATTORNEY

William B. Beach

ASSOCIATES

Amy S. Davis
Patrick F. McGow
Thomas D. Colis
Mark K. Schrupp

Representative Firm Clients: Chrysler Corporation; Comerica, Incorporated; City of Detroit, Michigan; Detroit Tigers, Inc.; First of Michigan; Ford Motor Company; Ford Motor Credit Company; Great Lakes Bancorp; Henry Ford Hospital; INVETECH Company.

For Complete List of Firm Personnel, See General Section

For full biographical listings, see the Martindale-Hubbell Law Directory

---

VANDEVEER GARZIA, PROFESSIONAL CORPORATION (AV)

Suite 1600, 333 West Fort Street, 48226
Telephone: 313-961-4880
Fax: 313-961-3822
Email: vg@voyager.net
Oakland County Office: 220 Park Street, Suite 300, Birmingham, Michigan.
Telephone: 810-645-0100.
Fax: 810-645-2430.

Fred L. Vandeveer (1879-1972)
James E. Haggerty, Sr. (1900-1966)
Leroy G. Vandeveer (1902-1981)
Buelle A. Doelle (1902-1985)
James E. Plastow, Jr.
Michael M. Hathaway
John J. Lynch, III (Resident, Oakland County Office)
Thomas M. Peters
James K. Thome
Gary Alan Miller
William L. Kiriazis
Daniel P. Steele
Shelley K. Miller (Resident, Oakland County Office)
Terrance P. Lynch
Dennis B. Cotter
Bruce E. Pearce
Hal O. Carroll
David B. Timmis (Resident, Oakland County Office)

Nancy A. Hensley
Dawn M. Twydell
Christian E. Hildebrandt (Resident, Oakland County Office)
Donald C. Brownell

Representative Clients: Oakland County; Michigan Municipal Risk Management Association; Southeast Michigan Area Rapid Transit.

For full biographical listings, see the Martindale-Hubbell Law Directory

*KALAMAZOO,** Kalamazoo Co.

KREIS, ENDERLE, CALLANDER & HUDGINS, A PROFESSIONAL CORPORATION (AV)

One Moorsbridge, P.O. Box 4010, 49003-4010
Telephone: 616-324-3000
Facsimile: 616-324-3010
Email: kech@kech.com *URL:* http://www.kech.com
Battle Creek, Michigan Office: One West Michigan Avenue, 49017.
Telephone: 616-966-3000.
Fax: 616-966-3022.

Douglas L. Callander
Thomas G. King

For Complete List of Firm Personnel, See General Section

For full biographical listings, see the Martindale-Hubbell Law Directory

---

MILLER, CANFIELD, PADDOCK AND STONE, P.L.C. (AV)

A Professional Limited Liability Company
Founded in 1852 by Sidney Davy Miller
444 West Michigan Avenue, 49007-3752
Telephone: 616-381-7030
Fax: 616-382-0244
URL: http://www.millercanfield.com
Detroit, Michigan Office: 150 West Jefferson, Suite 2500, 48226-4415.
Telephone: 313-963-6420.
Fax: 313-496-7500.
Cable Address: "Stem Detroit."
Ann Arbor, Michigan Office: 101 North Main Street, 7th Floor, 48104-1400.
Telephone: 734-663-2445.
Fax: 734-747-7147.
Troy, Michigan Office: 840 West Long Lake Road, Suite 200, 48098.
Telephone: 248-879-2000.
Fax: 248-879-2001.
Grand Rapids, Michigan Office: 99 Monroe, N.W., Suite 1200, 49503-2639.
Telephone: 616-454-8656.
Fax: 616-776-6322.

(See Next Column)

Howell, Michigan Office: 121 South Barnard Street, Suite 4, 48843-2305.
Telephone: 517-546-7600.
Telecopier: 517-546-6974.
Lansing, Michigan Office: One Michigan Avenue, Suite 900, 48933-1609.
Telephone: 517-487-2070.
Fax: 517-374-6304.
Monroe, Michigan Office: 214 East Elm Avenue, Suite 100, 48162-2682.
Telephone: 734-243-2000.
Fax: 734-243-0901.
Washington, D.C. Office: 1900 K Street, N.W., Suite 1150. 20006.
Telephone: 202-429-5575; 785-0600.
Fax: 202-331-1118; 785-1234.
Pensacola, Florida Office: 25 West Cedar, 32501.
Telephone: 850-469-1088.
Fax: 850-432-0677.
New York, New York Office: 1450 Broadway, 41st Floor, 10018.
Telephone: 212-704-4400.
Fax: 212-704-4410.
Gdynia, Poland Office: UL. Slaska 21, 81-319.
Telephone: 011-485-831-2808.
Fax: 011-48-58-628 6411.
Warsaw, Poland Office: UL. Nowogrodzkall, 5th Floor, 00-513.
Telephone: 011-4822 529 0200.
Fax: 011-4822 529 0201.
Katowice, Poland Office: UL. Francuska 35/37, 40-027.
Telephone: 011 (48-32) 757-2414.
Fax: 011 (48-32) 757-2483.

PRINCIPALS

Don M. Schmidt

Representative Firm Clients: Chrysler Corporation; Comerica, Incorporated; City of Detroit, Michigan; Detroit Tigers, Inc.; First of Michigan; Ford Motor Company; Ford Motor Credit Company; Great Lakes Bancorp; Henry Ford Hospital; INVETECH Company.

For Complete List of Firm Personnel, See General Section

For full biographical listings, see the Martindale-Hubbell Law Directory

*MANISTEE,** Manistee Co.

GOCKERMAN, WILSON, SAYLOR & HESSLIN, P.C. (AV)

414 Water Street, P.O. Box 537, 49660-1531
Telephone: 231-723-8333
Fax: 231-723-3888
Toll Free: 1-800-748-0534
Email: gwsh@gwsh.com *URL:* http://www.gwsh.com
Grand Rapids, Michigan Office: 124 East Fulton Street. .
Telephone: 616-458-3994.
Beulah, Michigan Office: 425 N. U.S. 31,
Telephone: 231-882-7130.

Bruce C. Gockerman
Richard M. Wilson, Jr.
George V. Saylor, III
Daniel D. Hesslin
Lisa Martinuzzi
James B. Flickinger
David J. Bedells (Resident, Beulah Office)

For full biographical listings, see the Martindale-Hubbell Law Directory

*MONROE,** Monroe Co.

BRAUNLICH, RUSSOW & BRAUNLICH, A PROFESSIONAL CORPORATION (AV)

111 South Macomb Street, 48161
Telephone: 734-241-8300
Fax: 734-241-7715

William J. Braunlich, Jr. (1924-1992)
Thomas P. Russow
William H. Braunlich

Philip A. Costello
Ann L. Nickel
Jeffrey A. Dulany, P.C.

LEGAL SUPPORT PERSONNEL

Ruth G. Flint

Representative Clients: State Farm Mutual Insurance Co.; Auto Club Insurance Assn.; Board of Road Commissioners, Monroe County; Port of Monroe; Monroe County Community College; City of Luna Pier; City of Petersburg; Auto-Owners Insurance Co.; Fremont Mutual Insurance Co.; Citizens Insurance Co. of America.

For full biographical listings, see the Martindale-Hubbell Law Directory

OKEMOS, Ingham Co.

J. RICHARD ROBINSON, P.C. (AV)

2169 Jolly Road, Suite 1, P.O. Box 1430, 48805
Telephone: 517-349-3703
Fax: 517-349-4677
Email: jrobin2680@aol.com

J. Richard Robinson

For full biographical listings, see the Martindale-Hubbell Law Directory

SOUTHFIELD, Oakland Co.

MASON STEINHARDT JACOBS PERLMAN & PESICK, PROFESSIONAL CORPORATION (AV)

Suite 1500, 4000 Town Center, 48075-1415
Telephone: 248-358-2090
Fax: 248-358-3599
Email: admin@msjp.com *URL:* http://www.msjp.com

Gordon I. Ginsberg	Jerome P. Pesick
Irving I. Boigon	Richard A. Polk
Jack Schon	Neil S. Silver
Frederick D. Steinhardt	L. Jeffrey Zauberman
John E. Jacobs	H. Adam Cohen
Michael B. Perlman	Diane Flagg Goldstein

OF COUNSEL

Walter B. Mason, Jr.	Randolph J. Friedman
Erwin B. Ellmann	Marvin C. Daitch

Representative Clients: Citibank, N.A.; City of Dearborn; DeMattia Development Co.; Forest City Enterprises; Michigan Wholesale Drug Assn.; Mortgage Bankers Association of Michigan; Nationwide Insurance Co.; City of Taylor; Union Labor Life Insurance Co.; Yellow Freight Systems, Inc.

For Complete List of Firm Personnel, See General Section

For full biographical listings, see the Martindale-Hubbell Law Directory

*TAWAS CITY,** Iosco Co.

LAW OFFICES OF MYLES AND MARTIN (AV)

502 Lake Street, P.O. Box 518, 48764-0518
Telephone: 517-362-4405
Telefax: 517-362-7840

Kenneth J. Myles	Christopher P. Martin

For full biographical listings, see the Martindale-Hubbell Law Directory

*TRAVERSE CITY,** Grand Traverse Co.

OLSON, NOONAN & BZDOK, P.C. (AV)

420 East Front Street, P.O. Box 2358, 49685-2358
Telephone: 616-946-0044
Fax: 616-946-4807

James M. Olson	Christopher M. Bzdok
John D. Noonan	Karen L. Ferguson

Scott W. Howard

For full biographical listings, see the Martindale-Hubbell Law Directory

MUNICIPAL BOND/PUBLIC AUTHORITY FINANCING

ALABAMA

ALBERTVILLE, Marshall Co.

GULLAHORN & HARE, P.C. (AV)

310 West Main Street, P.O. Box 1669, 35950
Telephone: 256-878-1891
Fax: 256-878-1965
Email: g-hpc@cybertyme.com

Charles R. Hare, Jr. John C. Gullahorn

Representative Clients: First Bank of Boaz; The Home Bank; Peoples Independent Bank of Boaz; AmSouth Bank; Compass Bank; Albertville Industrial Development Board; Boaz Industrial Development Board; Marshall-Dekalb Electric Cooperative; Olympia Construction, Inc.

For full biographical listings, see the Martindale-Hubbell Law Directory

*BIRMINGHAM,** Jefferson Co.

BRADLEY ARANT ROSE & WHITE LLP (AV)

2001 Park Place, Suite 1400, P.O. Box 830709, 35283-0709
Telephone: 205-521-8000
Facsimile: 205-521-8800
Facsimile (SouthTrust Tower Office): 205-521-8500
URL: http://www.barw.com
Huntsville, Alabama Office: 200 Clinton Avenue West, Suite 900, 35801.
Telephone: 205-517-5100.
Facsimile: 205-533-5069.
Washington, D.C. Office: 801 Pennsylvania Avenue, NW, Suite 230, 20004.
Telephone: 202-347-8893.
Facsimile: 202-347-1684.

MEMBERS OF FIRM

John P. Adams
P. Nicholas Greenwood
Stephen K. Greene
John G. Harrell
Alan K. Zeigler

Representative Transactional Clients: Alabama Water Pollution Control Authority; Auburn University; City of Huntsville; City of Mobile; Decatur General Hospital; Foley Utilities Board; Huntsville-Madison County Airport Authority; Mobile Airport Authority; University of Alabama; University of Alabama at Birmingham.

For Complete List of Firm Personnel, See General Section

For full biographical listings, see the Martindale-Hubbell Law Directory

BURR & FORMAN LLP (AV)

3100 SouthTrust Tower, 420 North 20th Street, P.O. Box 830719, 35283-0719
Telephone: 205-251-3000
Facsimile: 205-458-5100
URL: http://www.burr.com
Huntsville, Alabama Office: Suite 204, Regency Center, 400 Meridian Street.
Telephone: 205-551-0010.
Facsimile: 205-551-0043.
Atlanta, Georgia Office: Suite 1200, One Georgia Center, 600 West Peachtree Street, 30308.
Telephone: 404-815-3000.
Facsimile: 404-817-3244.

MEMBERS OF FIRM

Eric L. Carlton
Joseph G. Stewart
Dwight L. Mixson, Jr.
George M. Taylor, III

For Complete List of Firm Personnel, See General Section

For full biographical listings, see the Martindale-Hubbell Law Directory

GORHAM & WALDREP, P.C. (AV)

2101 6th Avenue North, Suite 700, 35203
Telephone: 205-254-3216; 251-9166
Telecopier: 205-324-3802
Email: info@gorham-waldrep.com *URL:* http://www.gorham-waldrep.com
Montgomery, Alabama Office: 250 Commerce Street, P.O. Box 4837, 36103-4837.
Telephone: 334-262-0777.
Telecopier: 334-262-0742.

Thomas L. Stewart
Michael G. Kendrick

(See Next Column)

Leslie Miller Klasing

Representative Clients: Jefferson County Personnel Board; Birmingham-Jefferson Civic Center Authority; The Water Works and Sewer Board of the City of Birmingham; City of Homewood; American Federation of Government Employees Local #1945; City of Pelham; Town of Kimberly; Alabama Tire Dealers Assn.; Southern States Body Shop Assn.

For Complete List of Firm Personnel, See General Section

For full biographical listings, see the Martindale-Hubbell Law Directory

HASKELL SLAUGHTER & YOUNG, L.L.C. (AV)

1200 AmSouth/Harbert Plaza, 1901 Sixth Avenue North, 35203
Telephone: 205-251-1000
Facsimile: 205-324-1133
Email: hsy@hsy.com
Montgomery, Alabama Office: 305 South Lawrence Street, P.O. Box 4660. 36103-4660.
Telephone: 334-265-8573.
Facsimile: 334-264-7945.

Wyatt Rushton Haskell
Robert D. Shattuck, Jr.
William M. Slaughter
E. Alston Ray
Benjamin B. Spratling III
Mark Edward Ezell

Lynn Reynolds

For Complete List of Firm Personnel, See General Section

For full biographical listings, see the Martindale-Hubbell Law Directory

SPAIN & GILLON, L.L.C. (AV)

The Zinszer Building, 2117 2nd Avenue North, 35203
Telephone: 205-328-4100
Telecopier: 205-324-8866
Email: ddh@spain-gillon.com *URL:* http://lawlinks.com:80/atty/al/sggbn.html

MEMBERS OF FIRM

John P. McKleroy, Jr.
Glenn E. Estess, Jr.
Samuel H. Frazier
Paul S. Leonard

General Counsel for: Piggly Wiggly Alabama Distributing Co.; Auburn University Foundation.

For Complete List of Firm Personnel, See General Section

For full biographical listings, see the Martindale-Hubbell Law Directory

*MOBILE,** Mobile Co.

LYONS, PIPES & COOK, P.C. (AV)

2 North Royal Street, P.O. Box 2727, 36652-2727
Telephone: 334-432-4481
Cable Address: "Lysea"
Telecopier: 334-433-1820
URL: http://www.LPCLaw.com

Wesley Pipes
W. David Johnson, Jr.

Representative Clients: Industrial Development Board of the City of Mobile; Mobile Airport Authority.

For Complete List of Firm Personnel, See General Section

For full biographical listings, see the Martindale-Hubbell Law Directory

ARIZONA

*PHOENIX,** Maricopa Co.

JENNINGS, STROUSS & SALMON, P.L.C. (AV)

A Professional Limited Liability Company
One Renaissance Square, Two North Central Avenue, 85004-2393
Telephone: 602-262-5911
Fax: 602-253-3255
Email: info@jsslaw.com *URL:* http://www.jsslaw.com
Arrowhead Office: 16150 North Arrowhead Fountains Center Drive, Suite 250, Peoria, Arizona.
Telephone: 623-878-2222.
Fax: 623-878-1333.

George C. Spilsbury
Anne L. Kleindienst

For Complete List of Firm Personnel, See General Section

For full biographical listings, see the Martindale-Hubbell Law Directory

Phoenix—Continued

QUARLES & BRADY LLP (AV)

One Camelback Building, One East Camelback Road, Suite 400, 85012-1649
Telephone: 602-230-5500
Fax: 602-230-5598
URL: http://www.quarles.com
Milwaukee, Wisconsin Office: 411 East Wisconsin Avenue.
Telephone: 414-277-5000.
Fax: 414-271-3552.
Madison, Wisconsin Office: First Wisconsin Plaza, One South Pinckney Street, P.O. Box 2113.
Telephone: 608-251-5000.
Fax: 608-251-9166.
West Palm Beach, Florida Office: 222 Lakeview Avenue, 4th Floor.
Telephone: 407-653-5000.
Fax: 407-653-5333.
Naples, Florida Office: Barnett Center, 4501 Tamiami Trail North, Suite 300.
Telephone: 813-262-5959.
Fax: 813-434-4999.
Chicago, Illinois Office: Quarles & Brady LLC, Citicorp Center, 500 West Madison Street, Suite 3700.
Telephone: 312-715-5000.
Fax: 312-715-5155.

MEMBER OF THE FIRM

P. Robert Moya

For full biographical listings, see the Martindale-Hubbell Law Directory

SNELL & WILMER L.L.P. (AV)

One Arizona Center, 85004-2202
Telephone: 602-382-6000
Fax: 602-382-6070
Email: postmaster@snellwilmer.com *URL:* http://www.swlaw.com
Tucson, Arizona Office: One South Church Avenue, Suite 1500, 85701-1612.
Telephone: 520-882-1200.
Fax: 520-884-1294.
Orange County Office: 1920 Main Street, Suite 1200, Irvine, California 92614-7230.
Telephone: 949-253-2700.
Fax: 949-955-2507.
Salt Lake City, Utah Office: 111 East Broadway, Suite 900, 84111-1004.
Telephone: 801-237-1900.
Fax: 801-237-1950.

MEMBERS OF FIRM

William A. Hicks, III
Richard W. Sheffield
Charles E. James, Jr.

ASSOCIATE

Brigitte Finley

Representative Clients: For list of Representative Clients, see end of biographical listings in the Martindale-Hubbell Law Directory.

For Complete List of Firm Personnel, See General Section

For full biographical listings, see the Martindale-Hubbell Law Directory

*TUCSON,** Pima Co.

SNELL & WILMER L.L.P. (AV)

One South Church Avenue, Suite 1500, 85701-1612
Telephone: 520-882-1200
Fax: 520-884-1294
URL: http://www.swlaw.com
Phoenix, Arizona Office: One Arizona Center, 85004-2202.
Telephone: 602-382-6000.
Fax: 602-382-6070.
Orange County Office: 1920 Main Street, Suite 1200, Irvine, California 92614-7230.
Telephone: 949-253-2700.
Fax: 949-955-2507.
Salt Lake City, Utah Office: 111 East Broadway, Suite 900, 84111-1004.
Telephone: 801-237-1900.
Fax: 801-237-1950.

MEMBER OF FIRM

William A. Hicks, III

Representative Clients: For list of Representative Clients, see end of biographical listings in the Martindale-Hubbell Law Directory.

For full biographical listings, see the Martindale-Hubbell Law Directory

ARKANSAS

*LITTLE ROCK,** Pulaski Co.

FRIDAY, ELDREDGE & CLARK (AV)

A Limited Liability Partnership of Individuals and Professional Associations
Formerly, Smith, Williams, Friday, Eldredge & Clark
2000 Regions Center, 400 West Capitol Avenue, 72201-3493
Telephone: 501-376-2011
Telecopier: 501-376-2147
Email: fecmh@fec.net

MEMBERS OF FIRM

James A. Buttry (P.A.)
Larry W. Burks (P.A.)
Thomas P. Leggett (P.A.)
J. Shepherd Russell, III (P.A.)
Paul B. Benham, III (P.A.)
Robert S. Shafer (P.A.)
Robert B. Beach, Jr. (P.A.)

COUNSEL

William L. Patton, Jr.
John C. Echols (P.A.)

Counsel for: Union Pacific System; St. Paul Insurance Co.; Liberty Mutual Insurance Co.; Cigna Property & Casualty Co.; Entergy Arkansas, Inc.; Dillard's, Inc.; Browning Arms Co.; Phillips Petroleum Co.; Aetna Casualty & Surety Co.

For Complete List of Firm Personnel, See General Section

For full biographical listings, see the Martindale-Hubbell Law Directory

ROSE LAW FIRM, A PROFESSIONAL ASSOCIATION (AV)

120 East Fourth Street, 72201
Telephone: 501-375-9131
Telecopy: 501-375-1309

George E. Campbell
M. Jane Dickey
Kevin R. Burns

Representative Clients: Arkansas Development Finance Authority; Arkansas Department of Pollution Control and Ecology; Crews & Associates, Inc.; City of Little Rock, Arkansas Residential Housing and Public Facilities Board; Llama Co.; Morgan, Keegan & Company, Inc.; PaineWebber Incorporated; Stephens Inc.; University of Arkansas; University of Central Arkansas.

For Complete List of Firm Personnel, See General Section

For full biographical listings, see the Martindale-Hubbell Law Directory

WILLIAMS & ANDERSON (AV)

Registered Limited Liability Partnership
Twenty-Second Floor, 111 Center Street, 72201
Telephone: 501-372-0800
Fax: 501-372-6453
Email: info@williamsanderson.com *URL:* http://www.williamsanderson.com

MEMBERS OF FIRM

W. Jackson Williams
David F. Menz
James E. Hathaway III

Representative Clients: Arkansas Democrat-Gazette, Inc.; Arkansas Development Finance Authority; Entergy Corporation; Metrocentre Improvement District No. 1 of the City of Little Rock; Potlatch Corporation; Texaco, Inc.; Wal-Mart Stores, Inc.

For Complete List of Firm Personnel, See General Section

For full biographical listings, see the Martindale-Hubbell Law Directory

WRIGHT, LINDSEY & JENNINGS LLP (AV)

200 West Capitol Avenue, Suite 2200, 72201
Telephone: 501-371-0808
Fax: 501-376-9442
Email: info@wlj.com *URL:* http://www.wlj.com
Fayetteville, Arkansas Office: 101 West Mountain Street, Suite 206, 72701.
Telephone: 501-575-0808.
Fax: 501-575-0999.
Russellville, Arkansas Office: 1110 West "B" Street, Suite E, 72801.
Telephone: 501-968-7995.

John R. Tisdale
Charles C. Price
John William Spivey III
Walter McSpadden
Fred M. Perkins III

ASSOCIATES

Michele Simmons Allgood
M. Sean Hatch

Representative Clients: Arkansas Development Finance Authority; Pulaski County, Arkansas; City of Little Rock, Arkansas; Garland County Community College; University of Arkansas Community College at Hope.

For full biographical listings, see the Martindale-Hubbell Law Directory

CALIFORNIA

*BAKERSFIELD,** Kern Co.

BORTON, PETRINI & CONRON, LLP (AV)

The Borton, Petrini & Conron Building, 1600 Truxtun Avenue, 93301
Telephone: 661-322-3051
Voice Mail: 661-395-6700
Fax: 661-322-4628
Mailing Address: P.O. Box 2026, Bakersfield, California, 93303
Email: bpcbak@bpclaw.com *URL:* http://www.bpclaw.com
Other City Locations: Fresno, Los Angeles, Modesto, Redding, Sacramento, San Bernardino, San Diego, San Francisco, San Jose, San Luis Obispo, Santa Ana and Ventura.

MEMBER OF FIRM

George F. Martin

ASSOCIATES

William G. Welzenbach
Raymond G. Robinson

OF COUNSEL

Roy J. Gargano

For Complete List of Firm Personnel, See General Section

For full biographical listings, see the Martindale-Hubbell Law Directory

COSTA MESA, Orange Co.

RUTAN & TUCKER, LLP (AV)

A Partnership including Professional Corporations
611 Anton Boulevard, Fourteenth Floor, P.O. Box 1950, 92626-1998
Telephone: 714-641-5100; 213-625-7586
Telecopier: 714-546-9035
Email: rutan&tucker@rutan.com *URL:* http://www.rutan.com

MEMBERS OF FIRM

Stan Wolcott (P.C.)
William M. Marticorena

For Complete List of Firm Personnel, See General Section

For full biographical listings, see the Martindale-Hubbell Law Directory

*FRESNO,** Fresno Co.

DOWLING, AARON & KEELER, INCORPORATED (AV)

6051 North Fresno Street, Suite 200, 93710
Telephone: 559-432-4500
Fax: 559-432-4590
Email: dak@daklaw.com *URL:* http://www.daklaw.com
Bakersfield, California Office: 110 South Mt. Claire, Suite 203. 93309.
Telephone: 661-396-0451. Web Site: http://www.daklaw.com.

Dale Ikeda
David J. Weiland

Reference: Wells Fargo Bank (Main).

For Complete List of Firm Personnel, See General Section

For full biographical listings, see the Martindale-Hubbell Law Directory

*LOS ANGELES,** Los Angeles Co.

OCHOA & SILLAS (AV)

444 South Flower Street, 18th Floor, 90071
Telephone: 213-362-1400
Fax: 213-622-0162
Email: sillasla@aol.com
Sacramento Office: Wells Fargo Center, 400 Capitol Mall, Suite 1850.
Telephone: 916-447-3383.
FAX: 916-447-3495. Email: OchoaSac@aol.com
Mexico City, Mexico Office: Los Cormoran No. 73, Lomas De Las Aquilas, Deleg. Alvaro Obregon, 01730, Mexico, D.F.C.F.
Telephone: 011-525-635-1145.
Fax: 011-525-53401454.

MEMBERS OF FIRM

Ralph M. Ochoa (Resident, Sacramento Office)
Herman Sillas
Jacqueline Rich Moore (Resident, Sacramento Office)
Tomás R. Lopez

ASSOCIATES

Jack T. Molodanof (Resident, Sacramento Office)
Francisco Valles Lopez (Not admitted in the United States)
Rita A. Reyes
Christopher Eric Ochoa (Resident, Sacramento Office)
Cirina A. K. Rose
M. Eric Parkan

OF COUNSEL

Daniel P. Aguilera
Cochran & Lotkin, Washington, D.C.

Representative Clients: American Golf; BKK Corp. (Toxic substance treatment); Chrysler; Department of Water and Power of Los Angeles; Sacramento Municipal Utility District; Department of Insurance; Metropolitan Water District, Los Angeles; General Motors; Hughes Aircraft; ICN Laboratories.

(See Next Column)

For full biographical listings, see the Martindale-Hubbell Law Directory

*SAN DIEGO,** San Diego Co.

LUCE, FORWARD, HAMILTON & SCRIPPS LLP (AV)

A Partnership including Professional Corporations
600 West Broadway, Suite 2600, 92101
Telephone: 619-236-1414
Fax: 619-232-8311
URL: http://www.luce.com
La Jolla, California Office: 4275 Executive Square, Suite 800, 92037.
Telephone: 858-455-6611.
Fax: 858-232-8311.
Los Angeles, California Office: 777 South Figueroa, Suite 3600, 90017.
Telephone: 213-892-4992.
Fax: 213-892-7731.
San Francisco, California Office: 121 Spear Street, Suite 200, 94105.
Telephone: 415-356-4600.
Fax: 415-356-4610.
New York, N.Y. Office: Citicorp Center, 153 East 53rd Street, 26th Floor, 10022.
Telephone: 212-754-1414.
Fax: 212-644-9727.
Chicago, Illinois Office: 180 North La Salle Street, Suite 3110, 60601.
Telephone: 312-641-0580.
Fax: 312-641-0380.

Dennis J. Doucette
Thomas A. May

For Complete List of Firm Personnel, See General Section

For full biographical listings, see the Martindale-Hubbell Law Directory

SAN MATEO, San Mateo Co.

G. A. LASTER (AV)

630 North San Mateo Drive, P.O. Box 152, 94401-2328
Telephone: 650-342-3523
Telecopier: 650-342-6392
Email: galaster@aol.com

Gerald A. Laster

Representative Clients: Cities of Colma; King City; Mt. Shasta; Plymouth; Redwood City; Castroville Water District; Franklin County Water District; Quartz Hill Water District; Granada Sanitary District; Metropolitan Education District.

For full biographical listings, see the Martindale-Hubbell Law Directory

COLORADO

*DENVER,** Denver Co.

BALLARD SPAHR ANDREWS & INGERSOLL, LLP (AV)

Seventeenth Street Plaza Building, Suite 2300, 1225 17th Street, 80202-5596
Telephone: 303-292-2400
Fax: 303-296-3956
URL: http://www.ballardspahr.com
Baltimore, Maryland Office: 300 East Lombard Street. 19th Floor.
Telephone: 410-528-5600.
Fax: 410-528-5650.
Camden, New Jersey Office: 800 Hudson Square, 5th Floor.
Telephone: 856-541-5577.
Fax: 856-541-8272.
Philadelphia, Pennsylvania Office: 1735 Market Street, 51st Floor.
Telephone: 215-665-8500.
Fax: 215-864-8999.
Salt Lake City, Utah Office: One Utah Center, Suite 1200, 201 South Main Street.
Telephone: 801-531-3000.
Fax: 801-531-3001.
Voorhees, New Jersey Office: Suite 100, 1101 Laurel Oak Drive.
Telephone: 856-627-8555.
Fax: 856-627-1153.
Washington, D.C. Office: Suite 1000 South, 601 13th Street, N.W.
Telephone: 202-661-2200.
Fax: 202-661-2299.

Loring E. Harkness III

Matthew J. Hogan

For Complete List of Firm Personnel, See General Section

For full biographical listings, see the Martindale-Hubbell Law Directory

Denver—Continued

BROWNSTEIN HYATT & FARBER, P.C. (AV)

Twenty-Second Floor, 410 Seventeenth Street, 80202-4437
Telephone: 303-223-1100
Telecopier: 303-223-1111
Washington, D.C. Office: 1615 L Street, N.W., Suite 450, 20036.
Telephone: 202-296-7353.
Telecopier: 202-296-7009.
Glenwood Springs, Colorado Office: Box 357, 81602.
Telephone: 970-945-5302.
Telecopier: 970-945-4921.

Michael R. McGinnis
Thomas J. Mancuso
Gregory W. Berger

SPECIAL COUNSEL

Robert P. Coyne

Kent C. Veio

Representative Clients: A.G. Edwards & Sons, Inc.; Bachelor Gulch Metropolitan District; George K. Baum & Company; Beaver Creek Metropolitan District; Hanifen Imhoff, Inc.; Kirkpatrick Pettis; Lehman Brothers; Norwest Investment Services, Inc.; PaineWebber Incorporated; State of Colorado.

For Complete List of Firm Personnel, See General Section

For full biographical listings, see the Martindale-Hubbell Law Directory

HOLME ROBERTS & OWEN LLP (AV)

Suite 4100, 1700 Lincoln, 80203
Telephone: 303-861-7000
Telecopier: 303-866-0200
Email: hro@hro.com *URL:* http://www.hro.com
Boulder, Colorado Office: Suite 400, 1401 Pearl Street.
Telephone: 303-444-5955.
Telecopier: 303-444-1063.
Colorado Springs, Colorado Office: Suite 1300, 90 South Cascade Avenue.
Telephone: 719-473-3800.
Telecopier: 719-633-1518.
Salt Lake City, Utah Office: Suite 1100, 111 East Broadway.
Telephone: 801-521-5800.
Telecopier: 801-521-9639.
London, England Office: Heathcoat House, 3rd Floor, 20 Savile Row.
Telephone: 011-44-171-494-5600.
Telecopier: 011-44-171-287-9344.

PARTNERS OF FIRM

Diane S. Barrett
Steve L. Gaines (Colorado Springs Office)
Mary L. Groves
Eric E. Johnson
Lawrence L. Levin
Bruce L. Likoff
David H. Little (Salt Lake City Office)
Daniel C. Lynch
Manuel L. Martinez
Paul V. Timmins
Patricia C. Tisdale

SPECIAL COUNSEL

Charles E. Berry
Karen Schauble Leaffer

SENIOR COUNSEL

Sharon A. Thomas (Colorado Springs Office)

ASSOCIATES

Sherry A. Gonzales
Stuart J. Lark (Colorado Springs Office)
M. Mashenka Lundberg
Roxane J. Perruso
Thad W. Renaud
Richard F. Rodriguez

For Complete List of Firm Personnel, See General Section

For full biographical listings, see the Martindale-Hubbell Law Directory

SHERMAN & HOWARD L.L.C. (AV)

Attorneys and Counselors at Law
633 Seventeenth Street, Suite 3000, 80202
Telephone: 303-297-2900
Telecopier: 303-298-0940
Colorado Springs, Colorado Office: Suite 1500, 90 South Cascade Avenue, 80903.
Telephone: 719-475-2440.
Las Vegas, Nevada Office: Swendseid & Stern, a member in Sherman & Howard L.L.C., 317 Sixth Street, 89101.
Telephone: 702-387-6073.
Reno, Nevada Office: Swendseid & Stern, a member in Sherman & Howard L.L.C., 50 West Liberty Street, Suite 660, 89501.
Telephone: 702-323-1980.

Kurt A. Kaufmann
Robert P. Mitchell
John O. Swendseid (Las Vegas and Reno, Nevada Offices)
Dee P. Wisor
Stanley M. Raine
Jennifer Stern (Las Vegas and Reno, Nevada Offices)
Calvin T. Hanson
Blake T. Jordan
James P. Lane
Kendra S. Follett (Las Vegas and Reno, Nevada Offices)

COUNSEL

Michael D. Groshek

(See Next Column)

Peter J. Whitmore
Scott W. Shaver

Representative Clients: Colorado Health Facilities Authority; Colorado Student Obligation Bond Authority; Jefferson County, Colorado; Platte River Power Authority; Clark County, Nevada; Farmington, New Mexico.; City of Thornton, Colorado; Colorado Housing and Finance Authority.

For Complete List of Firm Personnel, See General Section

For full biographical listings, see the Martindale-Hubbell Law Directory

DELAWARE

*WILMINGTON,** New Castle Co.

POTTER ANDERSON & CORROON LLP (AV)

Hercules Plaza, 1313 N. Market Street, P.O. Box 951, 19899-0951
Telephone: 302-984-6000
Fax: 302-658-1192
URL: http://www.attys.pacdelaware.com

MEMBERS OF FIRM

Charles S. McDowell
Harold I. Salmons, III
Scott E. Waxman

Counsel for: The State of Delaware; Delaware Transportation Authority; Delaware Health Facilities Authority; New Castle County; Kent County; Sussex County; City of Dover; Wilmington Trust Company.

For Complete List of Firm Personnel, See General Section

For full biographical listings, see the Martindale-Hubbell Law Directory

DISTRICT OF COLUMBIA

WASHINGTON, D.C. Co.

BALLARD SPAHR ANDREWS & INGERSOLL, LLP (AV)

Suite 1000 South, 601 13th Street, N.W., 20005-3807
Telephone: 202-661-2200
Fax: 202-661-2299
URL: http://www.ballardspahr.com
Baltimore, Maryland Office: 300 East Lombard Street, 19th Floor.
Telephone: 410-528-5600.
Fax: 410-528-5650.
Camden, New Jersey Office: 800 Hudson Square, 5th Floor.
Telephone: 856-541-5577.
Fax: 856-541-8772.
Denver, Colorado Office: Seventeenth Street Plaza Building, Suite 2300, 1225 17th Street.
Telephone: 303-292-2400.
Fax: 303-296-3956.
Philadelphia, Pennsylvania Office: 1735 Market Street, 51st Floor.
Telephone: 215-665-8500.
Fax: 215-834-8999.
Salt Lake City, Utah Office: 201 South Main Street, Suite 1200.
Telephone: 801-531-3000.
Fax: 801-531-3001.
Voorhees, New Jersey Office: Suite 100, 1101 Laurel Oak Drive.
Telephone: 856-627-8555.
Fax: 856-627-1153.

Frederic L. Ballard, Jr.
Joseph A. Fanone
Charles S. Henck

John A. Washington, Jr.

For Complete List of Firm Personnel, See General Section

For full biographical listings, see the Martindale-Hubbell Law Directory

JONES, DAY, REAVIS & POGUE (AV)

51 Louisiana Avenue, N.W., 20001-2113
Telephone: 202-879-3939
Telecopier: 202-626-1700
Email: counsel@jonesday.com *URL:* http://www.jonesday.com
In Atlanta, Georgia: 3500 SunTrust Plaza, 303 Peachtree Street.
Telephone: 404-521-3939.
Telecopier: 404-581-8330.
In Brussels, Belgium: Avenue Louise 480, 7th Floor, B-1050 Brussels.
Telephone: 32-2-645-14-11.
Telecopier: 32-2-645-14-45.
In Chicago, Illinois: 77 West Wacker.
Telephone: 312-782-3939.
Telecopier: 312-782-8585.
In Cleveland, Ohio: North Point, 901 Lakeside Avenue.
Telephone: 216-586-3939.
Telecopier: 216-579-0212.

(See Next Column)

JONES, DAY, REAVIS & POGUE—*Continued*

In Columbus, Ohio: 1900 Huntington Center.
Telephone: 614-469-3939.
Telecopier: 614-461-4198.
In Dallas, Texas: 2727 North Harwood Street.
Telephone: 214-220-3939.
Telecopier: 214-969-5100.
In Frankfurt, Germany: Hochhaus am Park, Grüneburgweg 102, 60323, Frankfurt am Main.
Telephone: 49-69-9726-3939.
Telecopier: 49-69-9726-3993.
In Geneva, Switzerland: 20, rue de Candolle.
Telephone: 41-22-320-2339.
Telecopier: 41-22-320-1232.
In Hong Kong: 29th Floor, Entertainment Building, 30 Queen's Road Central.
Telephone: 852-2526-6895.
Telecopier: 852-2868-5871.
In Irvine, California: 5 Park Plaza, Suite 1100.
Telephone: 949-851-3939.
Telecopier: 949-553-7539.
In London, England: Bucklersbury House, 3 Queen Victoria Street.
Telephone: 44-171-236-3939.
Telecopier: 44-171-236-1113.
In Los Angeles, California: 555 West Fifth Street, Suite 4600.
Telephone: 213-489-3939.
Telecopier: 213-243-2539.
In New Delhi, India (Associate Office): Pathak & Associates (an associate firm of Jones, Day, Reavis & Pogue), 1st Floor, Dr. Gopal Das Bhaven, 28 Barakhamba Road.
Telephone: 91-11-373-8793.; 91-11-335-7345.
Telecopier: 91-11-335-3761.
In New York, New York: 599 Lexington Avenue.
Telephone: 212-326-3939.
Telecopier: 212-755-7306.
In Paris, France: 120, rue du Faubourg Saint-Honoré.
Telephone: 33-1-56-59-39-39.
Telecopier: 33-1-56-59-39-38
In Pittsburgh, Pennsylvania: 500 Grant Street, 31st Floor.
Telephone: 412-391-3939.
Telecopier: 412-394-7959.
In Riyadh, Saudi Arabia: The International Law Firm (In Association with Jones, Day, Reavis & Pogue), Sulaymaniyah, Prince Mishari IBN, Abdulaziz Street, P.O. Box 22166.
Telephone: (966-1) 462-8866.
Telecopier: (966-1) 462-9001.
In Shanghai, China: 2805 Kerry Centre, 1515 Nanjing Road West.
Telephone: 86-21-5298-6568.
Telecopier: 86-21-5298-6569.
In Sydney, Australia: Governor Phillip Tower, Level 38, 1 Farrer Place.
Telephone: 61-2-9210-6921.
Telecopier: 61-2-9210-6926.
In Taipei, Taiwan: 8th Floor, 2 Tun Hwa South Road, Section 2.
Telephone: (886-2) 2704-6808.
Telecopier: (886-2) 2704-6791.
In Tokyo, Japan: Toranomon MT Building, 4th Floor, 10-3, Toranomon 3-Chome, Minato-Ku, Tokyo 105, Japan.
Telephone: 81-3-3433-3939.
Telecopier: 81-3-5401-2725.

MEMBER OF FIRM IN WASHINGTON, D.C.

Mark K. Sisitsky

For Complete List of Firm Personnel, See General Section

For full biographical listings, see the Martindale-Hubbell Law Directory

LEWIS & MUNDAY, A PROFESSIONAL CORPORATION (AV)

(Formerly Lewis, Clay & Munday, P.C.)
1120 Connecticut Avenue, Suite 280, 20036
Telephone: 202-835-0616
Fax: 202-833-3316
Email: karen.brown@lewis-pc.com *URL:* http://www.lewis-pc.com
Detroit, Michigan Office: 1300 First National Building, 660 Woodward Avenue. 48226-3531.
Telephone: 313-961-2550.
Fax: 313-961-1270.
Boston, Massachusetts Office: 101 Federal Street, Suite 1900. 02110.
Telephone: 617-478-0553.
Fax: 617-478-0543.

Karen Kendrick Brown (Resident)

For full biographical listings, see the Martindale-Hubbell Law Directory

MILLER, CANFIELD, PADDOCK AND STONE, P.L.C. (AV)

A Professional Limited Liability Company
Founded in 1852 by Sidney Davy Miller
1900 K Street, N.W., Suite 1150, 20006
Telephone: 202-429-5575; 785-0600
Fax: 202-331-1118; 785-1234
URL: http://www.millercanfield.com
Detroit, Michigan Office: 150 West Jefferson, Suite 2500, 48226-4415.
Telephone: 313-963-6420.
Fax: 313-496-7500.
Cable Address: "Stem Detroit."
Ann Arbor, Michigan Office: 101 North Main Street, 7th Floor, 48104-1400.
Telephone: 734-663-2445.
Fax: 734-747-7147.
Troy, Michigan Office: 840 West Long Lake Road, Suite 200, 48098.
Telephone: 248-879-2000.
Fax: 248-879-2001.
Grand Rapids, Michigan Office: 99 Monroe, N.W., Suite 1200, 49503-2639.
Telephone: 616-454-8656.
Fax: 616-776-6322.
Howell, Michigan Office: 121 South Barnard Street, Suite 4, 48843-2305.
Telephone: 517-546-7600.
Telecopier: 517-546-6974.
Kalamazoo, Michigan Office: 444 West Michigan Avenue, 49007-3752.
Telephone: 616-381-7030.
Fax: 616-382-0244.
Lansing, Michigan Office: One Michigan Avenue, Suite 900, 48933-1609.
Telephone: 517-487-2070.
Fax: 517-374-6304.
Monroe, Michigan Office: 214 East Elm Avenue, Suite 100, 48162-2682.
Telephone: 734-243-2000.
Fax: 734-243-0901.
Pensacola, Florida Office: 25 West Cedar, 32501.
Telephone: 850-469-1088.
Fax: 850-432-0677.
New York, New York Office: 1450 Broadway, 41st Floor, 10018.
Telephone: 212-704-4400.
Fax: 212-704-4410.
Gdynia, Poland Office: UL. Slaska 21, 81-319.
Telephone: 011-485-831-2808.
Fax: 011-48-58-628 6411.
Warsaw, Poland Office: UL. Nowogrodzkall, 5th Floor, 00-513.
Telephone: 011-4822 529 0200.
Fax: 011-4822 529 0201.
Katowice, Poland Office: UL. Francuska 35/37, 40-027.
Telephone: 011 (48-32) 757-2414.
Fax: 011 (48-32) 757-2483.

PRINCIPAL OF FIRM

John O. Renken (Not admitted in DC)

For full biographical listings, see the Martindale-Hubbell Law Directory

REED SMITH SHAW & McCLAY LLP (AV)

Suite 1100 - East Tower, 1301 K Street, N.W., 20005-3317
Telephone: 202-414-9200
FAX: 202-414-9299
Email: rssm@rssm.com *URL:* http://www.rssm.com
Pittsburgh, Pennsylvania Office: 435 Sixth Avenue, 15219-1886.
Telephone: 412-288-3131.
FAX: 412-288-3063.
Philadelphia, Pennsylvania Office: 2500 One Liberty Place, 19103-7301.
Telephone: 215-851-8100.
FAX: 215-851-1420.
Harrisburg, Pennsylvania Office: 213 Market Street, 17101-2132.
Telephone: 717-234-5988.
FAX: 717-236-3777.
Princeton, New Jersey Office: 136 Main Street, Suite 250, 08540-5799.
Telephone: 609-987-0050.
FAX: 609-951-0824.
New York, N.Y. Office: 375 Park Avenue, 17th Floor, 10152.
Telephone: 212-521-5400.
FAX: 212-521-5450.
Newark, New Jersey Office: The Legal Center, One Riverfront Plaza, First Floor, 07102-5400.
Telephone: 973-621-3200.
Fax: 973-621-3199.
McLean, Virginia Office: Reed Smith Hazel & Thomas LLP, Suite 1100, 8251 Greensboro Drive, 22102-3844.
Telephone: 703-734-4600.
FAX: 703-734-4699.
Falls Church, Virginia Office: Reed Smith Hazel & Thomas LLP, Suite 1400, 3110 Fairview Park Drive, P.O. Box 12001.
Telephone: 703-641-4200.
Fax: 703-641-4340.
Leesburg, Virginia Office: Reed Smith Hazel & Thomas LLP, 44084 Riverside Parkway, Suite 300.
Telephone: 703-729-8500. Metro: 703-478-1992.
Fax: 703-478-8003.

(See Next Column)

REED SMITH SHAW & McCLAY LLP, *Washington—Continued*

Richmond, Virginia Office: Reed Smith Hazel & Thomas LLP, Suite 600, 411 East Franklin Street, P.O. Box 788.
Telephone: 804-344-3400.
Fax: 804-344-3410.

COUNSEL

Kenneth S. Barr

For full biographical listings, see the Martindale-Hubbell Law Directory

RITTER EICHNER & NORRIS, PLLC (AV)

The Jefferson Building, 1225 19th Street, N.W., 7th Floor, 20036
Telephone: 202-973-0100
Fax: 202-296-6990

ASSOCIATE

Robert A. Wrzosek

For full biographical listings, see the Martindale-Hubbell Law Directory

FLORIDA

*JACKSONVILLE,** Duval Co.

WILLIAM L. ZVARA, P.A. (AV)

4810 Arapahoe Avenue, P.O. Box 49, 32210
Telephone: 904-387-2266
Fax: 904-387-9212
Email: wzvara@wlz.com *URL:* http://www.wlz.com

William L. Zvara

*ORLANDO,** Orange Co.

BAKER & HOSTETLER LLP (AV)

SunBank Center, Suite 2300, 200 South Orange Avenue, 32802-3432
Telephone: 407-649-4000
Fax: 407-841-0168
To contact an attorney on the Internet use first initial and surname followed by @baker-hostetler.com
URL: http://www.bakerlaw.com
In Cleveland, Ohio: 3200 National City Center, 1900 East Ninth Street.
Telephone: 216-621-0200.
In Cincinnati, Ohio: 312 Walnut Street, Suite 2650.
Telephone: 513-929-3400.
In Columbus, Ohio: Capitol Square, Suite 2100, 65 East State Street.
Telephone: 614-228-1541.
In Denver, Colorado: 303 East 17th Avenue, Suite 1100.
Telephone: 303-861-0600.
In Houston, Texas: 1000 Louisiana, Suite 2000.
Telephone: 713-751-1600.
In Long Beach, California: 300 Oceangate, Suite 620.
Telephone: 362-432-2827.
In Los Angeles, California: 600 Wilshire Boulevard.
Telephone: 213-624-2400.
In Washington, D. C.: Washington Square, Suite 1100, 1050 Connecticut Avenue, N.W.
Telephone: 202-861-1500.

PARTNER

Jerry R. Linscott

For Complete List of Firm Personnel, See General Section

For full biographical listings, see the Martindale-Hubbell Law Directory

PALM BEACH, Palm Beach Co.

CALDWELL & PACETTI (AV)

324 Royal Palm Way, Suite #300, P.O. Box 2775, 33480-2775
Telephone: 561-655-0620
Fax: 561-655-3775
Email: floridalaw@earthlink.net

MEMBERS OF FIRM

Manley P. Caldwell (1901-1971)
Madison F. Pacetti (1914-1994)
Manley P. Caldwell, Jr.
Kenneth W. Edwards
Mary M. Viator
Charles F. Schoech
Elizabeth S. (Betsy) Burden
John A. Weig
Leonard G. Rubin

OF COUNSEL

Paul A. Turk, Jr.

Representative Clients: Estero Fire Protection District; Everglades Agricultural Area Environmental Protection District; Indian Trail Improvement District; Northern Palm Beach County Improvement District; Troup-Indiantown Water Control District; City of Belle Glade; Town of Hypoluxo; Town of Lake Clarke Shores; Village of Wellington.
Approved Attorneys For: Attorneys' Title Insurance Fund.

For full biographical listings, see the Martindale-Hubbell Law Directory

*SARASOTA,** Sarasota Co.

WILLIAMS, PARKER, HARRISON, DIETZ & GETZEN, PROFESSIONAL ASSOCIATION (AV)

200 South Orange Avenue, 34236-6749
Telephone: 941-366-4800
Telecopier: 941-366-5109
Mailing Address: P.O. Box 3258, Sarasota, Florida, 34230-3258
Email: infodesk@williamsparker.com *URL:* http://www.williamsparker.com

William T. Harrison, Jr.
Charles D. Bailey, Jr.
Robert W. Benjamin
Susan Barrett Hecker
J. Hugh Middlebrooks

General Counsel for: Sarasota County Public Hospital Board; Sarasota-Manatee Airport Authority; Taylor Woodrow Homes Ltd.; FCCI Mutual Insurance Co.
Local Counsel for: Bank of America; Northern Trust Bank of Florida; SunTrust Bank, Gulfcoast.

For Complete List of Firm Personnel, See General Section

For full biographical listings, see the Martindale-Hubbell Law Directory

*TAMPA,** Hillsborough Co.

MORRISON & MILLS, P.A. (AV)

1200 West Platt Street Suite 100, 33606
Telephone: 813-258-3311
Telecopier: 813-258-3209
Email: mmills3@tampabay.rr.com

Thomas K. Morrison
Frederick J. Mills

Kevin A. DiTanna
Bradley Abraham Tobin

Representative Clients: SouthTrust Bank of West Florida; SouthTrust Bank, National Association; NationsBank of Florida, N.A.; Mercantile Bank; Southern Commerce Bank; Regions Bank; Hillsborough County Industrial Development Authority; City of New Port Richey.

For full biographical listings, see the Martindale-Hubbell Law Directory

GEORGIA

*ATLANTA,** Fulton Co.

JONES, DAY, REAVIS & POGUE (AV)

3500 SunTrust Plaza, 303 Peachtree Street, 30308-3242
Telephone: 404-521-3939
Telecopier: 404-581-8330
Email: counsel@jonesday.com *URL:* http://www.jonesday.com
In Brussels, Belgium: Avenue Louise 480, 7th Floor, B-1050 Brussels.
Telephone: 32-2-645-14-11.
Telecopier: 32-2-645-14-45.
In Chicago, Illinois: 77 West Wacker.
Telephone: 312-782-3939.
Telecopier: 312-782-8585.
In Cleveland, Ohio: North Point. 901 Lakeside Avenue.
Telephone: 216-586-3939.
Telecopier: 216-579-0212.
In Columbus, Ohio: 1900 Huntington Center.
Telephone: 614-469-3939.
Telecopier: 614-461-4198.
In Dallas, Texas: 2727 North Harwood Street.
Telephone: 214-220-3939.
Telecopier: 214-969-5100.
In Frankfurt, Germany: Hochhaus am Park, Grüneburgweg 102, 60323 Frankfurt am Main.
Telephone: 49-69-9726-3939.
Telecopier: 49-69-9726-3993.
In Geneva, Switzerland: 20, rue de Candolle.
Telephone: 41-22-320-2339.
Telecopier: 41-22-320-1232.
In Hong Kong: 29th Floor, Entertainment Building, 30 Queen's Road Central.
Telephone: 852-2526-6895.
Telecopier: 852-2868-5871 or 852-2868-5699.
In Irvine, California: 5 Park Plaza, Suite 1100.
Telephone: 949-851-3939.
Telecopier: 949-553-7539.
In London, England: Bucklersbury House, 3 Queen Victoria Street.
Telephone: 44-171-236-3939.
Telecopier: 44-171-236-1113.
In Los Angeles, California: 555 West Fifth Street, Suite 4600.
Telephone: 213-489-3939.
Telecopier: 213-243-2539.

(See Next Column)

JONES, DAY, REAVIS & POGUE—*Continued*

In New Delhi, India (Associate Office): Pathak & Associates (an associate firm of Jones, Day, Reavis & Pogue), 1st Floor, Dr. Gopal Das Bhaven, 28 Barakhamba Road.
Telephone: 91-11-373-8793; 91-11-335-7345.
Telecopier: 91-11-335-3761.
In New York, New York: 599 Lexington Avenue.
Telephone: 212-326-3939.
Telecopier: 212-755-7306.
In Paris, France: 120, rue du Faubourg Saint-Honoré.
Telephone: 33-1-56-59-39-39.
Telecopier: 33-1-56-59-39-38
In Pittsburgh, Pennsylvania: 500 Grant Street, 31st Floor.
Telephone: 412-391-3939.
Telecopier: 412-394-7959.
In Riyadh, Saudi Arabia: The International Law Firm (In Association with Jones, Day, Reavis & Pogue), Sulaymaniyah, Prince Mishari IBN, Abdulaziz Street, P.O. Box 22166.
Telephone: (966-1) 462-8866.
Telecopier: (966-1) 462-9001.
In Shanghai, China: 2805 Kerry Centre, 1515 Nanjing Road West.
Telephone: 86-21-5298-6568.
Telecopier: 86-21-5298-6569.
In Sydney, Australia: Governor Phillip Tower, Level 38, 1 Farrer Place.
Telephone: 61-2-9210-6921.
Telecopier: 61-2-9210-6926.
In Taipei, Taiwan: 8th Floor, 2 Tun Hwa South Road, Section 2.
Telephone: (886-2) 2704-6808.
Telecopier: (886-2) 2704-6791.
In Tokyo, Japan: Toranomon MT Building, 4th Floor, 10-3, Toranomon 3-Chome, Minato-ku, Tokyo 105, Japan.
Telephone: 81-3-3433-3939.
Telecopier: 81-3-5401-2725.
In Washington, D.C.: 51 Louisiana Avenue, N.W.
Telephone: 202-879-3939.
Telecopier: 202-626-1700.

MEMBER OF FIRM IN ATLANTA

William S. Paddock

For Complete List of Firm Personnel, See General Section

For full biographical listings, see the Martindale-Hubbell Law Directory

LONG ALDRIDGE & NORMAN LLP (AV)

A Limited Liability Partnership including Professional Corporations
Suite 5300, 303 Peachtree Street, 30308
Telephone: 404-527-4000
Telecopier: 404-527-4198
Email: atlanta@lanlaw.com *URL:* http://www.lanlaw.com
Washington, D.C. Office: Suite 600, 701 Pennsylvania Avenue, N.W., 20004.
Telephone: 202-624-1200.
FAX: 202-624-1298.

MEMBERS OF FIRM

George (Buddy) Darden
Margaret M. Joslin
Thomas P. Lauth, III
Edgar H. Sims, Jr. (P.C.)
Jesse J. Spikes
John E. Theberge (Resident, Washington, D.C. Office)

For Complete List of Firm Personnel, See General Section

For full biographical listings, see the Martindale-Hubbell Law Directory

POWELL, GOLDSTEIN, FRAZER & MURPHY LLP (AV)

191 Peachtree Street, N.E., Sixteenth Floor, 30303
Telephone: 404-572-6600
Telecopier: 404-572-6999
URL: http://www.pgfm.com
Washington, D.C. Office: Sixth Floor, 1001 Pennsylvania Avenue, N.W., 20004.
Telephone: 202-347-0066.

MEMBERS OF FIRM

Robert C. Lewinson
Lesly Gaynor Murray
Suzanne J. Roberts
Ronald D. Stallings
Gregory H. Worthy

For Complete List of Firm Personnel, See General Section

For full biographical listings, see the Martindale-Hubbell Law Directory

THOMAS, KENNEDY, SAMPSON & PATTERSON (AV)

3355 Main Street, 30337
Telephone: 404-688-4503
Telecopier: 404-681-2950; Litigation Dept.
Telecopier: 404-684-9515
URL: http://www.tksp.com

MEMBERS OF FIRM

R. E. Thomas, Jr. (1911-1996)
John Loren Kennedy (1942-1994)
Thomas G. Sampson
P. Andrew Patterson
Jeffrey E. Tompkins

(See Next Column)

ASSOCIATES

Thomas G. Sampson, II
Ceasar C. Mitchell, II.
Erika Nicole Jackson

LEGAL SUPPORT PERSONNEL

Gwendolyn C.H. Dixon
Elbetha (Beth) Martin (Paralegal)
Nancy Allen-Haskell
Yvonne Torrence
Shyril E. Beck
Constance Harris (Paralegal)
Lisa Russell Johnson

For full biographical listings, see the Martindale-Hubbell Law Directory

*COLUMBUS,** Muscogee Co.

HATCHER, STUBBS, LAND, HOLLIS & ROTHSCHILD (AV)

A Limited Liability Partnership
Suite 500 The Corporate Center, 233 12th Street, P.O. Box 2707, 31902-2707
Telephone: 706-324-0201
Telecopier: 706-322-7747
Email: mailman@hatcherstubbs.com

MEMBERS OF FIRM

J. Barrington Vaught
James E. Humes, II
John M. Tanzine, III

General Counsel for: SunTrust Bank, West Georgia, N.A.; TOM'S Foods Inc.; Muscogee County Board of Education; Columbus Georgia Water Board; St. Francis Hospital, Inc.

For Complete List of Firm Personnel, See General Section

For full biographical listings, see the Martindale-Hubbell Law Directory

*MACON,** Bibb Co.

SELL & MELTON, L.L.P. (AV)

A Limited Liability Partnership including a Professional Corporation
14th Floor, 577 Mulberry Street, P.O. Box 229, 31202-0229
Telephone: 912-746-8521
Telecopier: 912-745-6426

R. (Chix) Miller (Managing Partner)

OF COUNSEL

Buckner F. Melton

General Counsel for: Macon Telegraph Publishing Co. (The Macon Telegraph); Macon-Bibb County Hospital Authority; County of Bibb; Smith & Sons Foods, Inc. (S & S Cafeterias); Macon Bibb County Industrial Authority; Burgess Pigment Co.
Local Counsel For: United States Aircraft Insurance Group (USAIG); United States Aviation Underwriters, Inc. (USAU).

For Complete List of Firm Personnel, See General Section

For full biographical listings, see the Martindale-Hubbell Law Directory

IDAHO

*BOISE,** Ada Co.

ELAM & BURKE, A PROFESSIONAL ASSOCIATION (AV)

Key Financial Center, 702 West Idaho Street, P.O. Box 1539, 83701
Telephone: 208-343-5454
Telecopier: 208-384-5844
Email: eblaw@elamburke.com

Ryan P. Armbruster

Representative Clients: City of Boise; Capital City Development Co.; Idaho Falls Redevelopment Agency; Ammon Urban Renewal Agency; Rigby Urban Renewal Agency; Rexburg Redevelopment Agency.

For Complete List of Firm Personnel, See General Section

For full biographical listings, see the Martindale-Hubbell Law Directory

ILLINOIS

*CHICAGO,** Cook Co.

CHAPMAN AND CUTLER (AV)

111 West Monroe Street, 60603
Telephone: 312-845-3000
Fax: 312-701-2361
Email: postmaster@chapman.com *URL:* http://chapman.com
Salt Lake City, Utah Office: Suite 900, Key Bank Tower, 50 South Main Street.
Telephone: 801-533-0066.
Fax: 801-533-9595.

(See Next Column)

CHAPMAN AND CUTLER, *Chicago—Continued*

Phoenix, Arizona Office: Suite 1100, One Renaissance Square, 2 North Central Avenue.
Telephone: 602-256-4060.
Fax: 602-256-4099.

Andrea G. Bacon
Matthew C. Boba
Deborah T. Boye
Lee A. Boye
Nancy A. Burke
James C. Burr (Resident, Salt Lake City Office)
Steven L. Clark
Richard A. Cosgrove
Patricia M. Curtner
William R. DeHaan (Resident, Phoenix Office)
C. Robert Foltz
Lynda K. Given
Charles L. Jarik
Daniel L. Johnson
Kelly K. Kost
Darrell R. Larsen, Jr.
Matthew R. Lewin
William M. Libit
James E. Luebchow
Timothy V. McGree
Robert W. Ollis, Jr.
John S. Overdorff (Resident, Phoenix Office)
Richard J. Scott (Resident, Salt Lake City Office)
M. John Trofa
John L. Tuohy
Lawrence E. White
David G. Williams
Steven N. Wohl

Susan D. Appel
Erin P. Bartholomy
Benjamin J. Juergens (Resident, Salt Lake City Office)
Lisa Montez
Susan E. Rollins
Shelly A. Scinto
Frederick M. Snow
Peter G. Swenson
Christopher F. Walrath
Rodney G. Wendt (Not admitted in IL; Resident, Salt Lake City Office)

For Complete List of Firm Personnel, See General Section

For full biographical listings, see the Martindale-Hubbell Law Directory

JONES, DAY, REAVIS & POGUE (AV)

77 West Wacker, 60601-1692
Telephone: 312-782-3939
Telecopier: 312-782-8585
Email: counsel@jonesday.com *URL:* http://www.jonesday.com
In Atlanta, Georgia: 3500 SunTrust Plaza, 303 Peachtree Street.
Telephone: 404-521-3939.
Telecopier: 404-581-8330. 34000 Brussels, Belgium: Avenue Louise 480, 7th Floor, B-1050 Brussels.
Telephone: 32-2-645-14-11.
Telecopier: 32-2-645-14-45.
In Cleveland, Ohio: North Point, 901 Lakeside Avenue.
Telephone: 216-586-3939.
Telecopier: 216-579-0212.
In Columbus, Ohio: 1900 Huntington Center.
Telephone: 614-469-3939.
Telecopier: 614-461-4198.
In Dallas, Texas: 2727 North Harwood Street.
Telephone: 214-220-3939.
Telecopier: 214-969-5100.
In Frankfurt, Germany: Hochhaus am Park, Grüneburgweg 102, 60323 Frankfurt am Main.
Telephone: 49-69-9726-3939.
Telecopier: 49-69-9726-3993.
In Geneva, Switzerland: 20, rue de Candolle.
Telephone: 41-22-320-2339.
Telecopier: 41-22-320-1232.
In Hong Kong: 29th Floor, Entertainment Building, 30 Queen's Road Central.
Telephone: 852-2526-6895.
Telecopier: 852-2868-5871 or 852-2868-5699.
In Irvine, California: 5 Park Plaza, Suite 1100.
Telephone: 949-851-3939.
Telecopier: 949-553-7539.
In London, England: Bucklersbury House, 3 Queen Victoria Street.
Telephone: 44-171-236-3939.
Telecopier: 44-171-236-1113.
In Los Angeles, California: 555 West Fifth Street, Suite 4600.
Telephone: 213-489-3939.
Telecopier: 213-243-2539.
In New Delhi, India (Associate Office): Pathak & Associates (an associate firm of Jones, Day, Reavis & Pogue), 1st Floor, Dr. Gopal Das Bhaven, 28 Barakhamba Road.
Telephone: 91-11-373-8793; 91-11-335-7345.
Telecopier: 91-11-335-3761.
In New York, New York: 599 Lexington Avenue.
Telephone: 212-326-3939.
Telecopier: 212-755-7306.
In Paris, France: 120, rue du Faubourg Saint-Honoré.
Telephone: 33-1-56-59-39-39.
Telecopier: 33-1-56-59-39-38
In Pittsburgh, Pennsylvania: 500 Grant Street, 31st Floor.
Telephone: 412-391-3939.
Telecopier: 412-394-7959.

(See Next Column)

In Riyadh, Saudi Arabia: The International Law Firm (In Association with Jones, Day, Reavis & Pogue), Sulaymaniyah, Prince Mishari IBN, Abdulaziz Street, P.O. Box 22166.
Telephone: (966-1) 462-8866.
Telecopier: (966-1) 462-9001.
In Shanghai, China: 2805 Kerry Centre, 1515 Nanjing Road West.
Telephone: 86-21-5298-6568.
Telecopier: 86-21-5298-6569.
In Sydney, Australia: Governor Phillip Tower, Level 38, 1 Farrer Place.
Telephone: 61-2-9210-6921.
Telecopier: 61-2-9210-6926.
In Taipei, Taiwan: 8th Floor, 2 Tun Hwa South Road, Section 2.
Telephone: (886-2) 2704-6808.
Telecopier: (886-2) 2704-6791.
In Tokyo, Japan: Toranomon MT Building, 4th Floor, 10-3, Toranomon 3-Chome, 34200o-ku, Tokyo 105, Japan.
Telephone: 81-3-3433-3939.
Telecopier: 81-3-5401-2725.
In Washington, D.C.: 51 Louisiana Avenue, N.W.
Telephone: 202-879-3939.
Telecopier: 202-626-1700.

MEMBERS OF FIRM IN CHICAGO

Robert A. Yolles
Robert Dean Avery (Not admitted in IL)
Lynn Leland Coe
Michael J. Mitchell
Harold C. Sutter
S. Louise Rankin
Robert J. Graves
Timothy J. Melton
Richard K. Tomei

OF COUNSEL

William J. Harmon
Daniel J. Bacastow

ASSOCIATES

John F. Bibby, Jr.
Mark J. Meyers
John T. Perugini
S. Mark Sproat

For Complete List of Firm Personnel, See General Section

For full biographical listings, see the Martindale-Hubbell Law Directory

SCARIANO, ELLCH, HIMES, SRAGA AND PETRARCA, CHARTERED (AV)

Two Prudential Plaza 180 North Stetson Suite 3100, 60601-6224
Telephone: 312-565-3100
Facsimile: 312-565-0000
Chicago Heights, Illinois Office: 1450 Aberdeen, 60411.
Telephone: 708-755-1900.
Facsimile: 708-755-0000.

Anthony G. Scariano
Robert H. Ellch
A. Lynn Himes
Alan T. Sraga
Justino D. Petrarca
Lawrence Jay Weiner
John M. Izzo
Raymond A. Hauser
Kathleen Roche Hirsman
Daniel M. Boyle
Teri E. Engler
Rosanne Ciambrone

Kelly A. Hayden
Todd K. Hayden
Christopher L. Petrarca
Sarah E. Joyce
Joel R. DeTella
Susan H. Walter (Resident)
Brian J. Fahey
David A. Harley
Bradley C. Coleman
Christina Sepiol
Alan M. Mullins
John E. Fester
Michael Alan DeBartolo

OF COUNSEL

John Kralovec

For full biographical listings, see the Martindale-Hubbell Law Directory

WATT & SAWYIER (AV)

The Monadnock Building, 53 West Jackson Boulevard, Suite 1120, 60604-3701
Telephone: 312-663-1440
Telecopier: 312-663-1410

MEMBER OF FIRM

Garland W. Watt

For full biographical listings, see the Martindale-Hubbell Law Directory

*PEORIA,** Peoria Co.

HOWARD & HOWARD ATTORNEYS, P.C. (AV)

The Creve Coeur Building, Suite 200, 321 Liberty Street, 61602-1403
Telephone: 309-672-1483
Telecopier: 309-672-1568
Kalamazoo, Michigan Office: The Michigan Building, Suite 200, 100 Portage Street.
Telephone: 616-382-1483.
Telecopier: 616-382-1568.
Bloomfield Hills, Michigan Office: The Pinehurst Office Center, Suite 101, 1400 North Woodward Avenue.
Telephone: 248-645-1483.
Telecopier: 248-645-1568.

(See Next Column)

HOWARD & HOWARD ATTORNEYS P.C.—*Continued*

Lansing, Michigan Office: Suite 500, The Phoenix Building, 222 Washington Square, North.
Telephone: 517-485-1483.
Telecopier: 517-485-1568.

Frederick G. Hoffman

Representative Clients: For Representative Client list, see General Practice, Peoria, IL.

For Complete List of Firm Personnel, See General Section

For full biographical listings, see the Martindale-Hubbell Law Directory

INDIANA

*INDIANAPOLIS,** Marion Co.

BOSE MCKINNEY & EVANS LLP (AV)

2700 First Indiana Plaza, 135 North Pennsylvania Street, 46204
Telephone: 317-684-5000
Facsimile: 317-684-5173
URL: http://www.boselaw.com
Indianapolis North Office: Suite 1500, 8888 Keystone Crossing, 46240.
Telephone: 317-574-3700.
Facsimile: 317-574-3716.

MEMBERS OF FIRM

Kirk E. Grable
Roderick H. Morgan
Ronald M. Soskin
Karl R. Sturbaum
David A. Travelstead

Representative Clients: Indiana Health Facility Financing Authority; Indiana Development Finance Authority; Indiana Bond Bank; Metropolitan School District of Wayne Township, Marion County, Indiana; Fall Creek Regional Waste District, Indiana; Johnson County, Indiana; City of Shelbyville, Indiana; Everen Securities, Inc.; J.J.B. Hilliard, W.L. Lyons, Inc.; Lehman Brothers, Inc.

For Complete List of Firm Personnel, See General Section

For full biographical listings, see the Martindale-Hubbell Law Directory

ICE MILLER DONADIO & RYAN (AV)

One American Square Box 82001, 46282-0002
Telephone: 317-236-2100
Fax: 317-236-2219
Email: info@imdr.com *URL:* http://www.imdr.com
South Bend, Indiana Office: 211 West Washington Street, Suite 2420.
Telephone: 219-234-7933.
Fax: 219-234-7965. Internet E-mail: info@imdr.com. Web Site Address: http://www.imdr.com.
Chicago, Illinois Office: 135 South LaSalle Street, Suite 4100.
Telephone: 312-726-1567.
Fax: 312-641-6263. Internet E-mail: info@imdr.com. Web Site Address: http://www.imdr.com.

MEMBERS OF FIRM

Bruce A. Polizotto
Philip C. Genetos
James A. Shanahan
Jeffrey O. Lewis
Thomas K. Downs
Brenda S. Horn
Todd W. Ponder
Lucy A. Emison
Thomas W. Peterson
Patricia A. Zelmer
Jane Neuhauser Herndon
Thomas C. Smith

SENIOR COUNSEL

Mark S. Moore
Charles R. Hug (Not admitted in IN)

OF COUNSEL

Karen L. Arland
Daniel E. Fisher
James L. Bebley (Not admitted in IN)

ASSOCIATES

Amy M. Corsaro
Lisa A. Lee
James H. Smith
Denise Y. Barkdull
Thea E. Kelly-Bundle
Daniel L. Kim
Dennis H. Otten
Michael Buker

Counsel for: Association of Indiana Counties; Indiana University; Purdue University; Indiana Bond Bank; Indiana Municipal Power Agency; Indiana Housing Finance Authority; Indiana Health Facility Financing Authority; Indiana Development Finance Authority; Citizens Gas & Coke Utility; Indianapolis International Airport Authority.

For Complete List of Firm Personnel, See General Section

For full biographical listings, see the Martindale-Hubbell Law Directory

*LAFAYETTE,** Tippecanoe Co.

STUART & BRANIGIN (AV)

The Life Building, 300 Main Street, Suite 800, P.O. Box 1010, 47902-1010
Telephone: 765-423-1561
Telecopier: 765-742-8175
Email: sb@stuartlaw.com *URL:* http://www.stuartlaw.com
Indianapolis, Indiana Office: Suite 1401, 8888 Keystone Crossing, 46240.
Telephone: 317-574-7245.
Fax: 317-574-7050.

MEMBERS OF FIRM

Allison Ellsworth Stuart (1886-1950)
Roger D. Branigin (1902-1975)
Roger D. Branigin, Jr.
Thomas L. Ryan
Thomas R. McCully
Larry R. Fisher
Nina B. Kirkpatrick
Mark Lillianfeld
Stephen R. Pennell
Anthony S. Benton
Erik D. Spykman
William E. Emerick
John C. Duffey
Bruce McSpadden
Mark E. DeYoung
Thomas B. Parent
Laura L. Bowker
Kevin D. Nicoson
Susan K. Roberts
John M. Stuckey
Deborah B. Trice
William P. Kealey
David A. Starkweather
Geoffrey L. Blazi

SENIOR COUNSEL

Russell H. Hart

COUNSEL

John F. Bodle
James V. McGlone

ASSOCIATES

Elizabeth B. Searle
Marianne Mitten Owen
David A. Locke
Karen Orr McClure
Ann Marie Waldron
Barry L. Loftus

General Counsel for: The Lafayette Life Insurance Co.; INB National Bank, N.W.; Lafayette Home Hospital, Inc.
State Counsel for: Norfolk & Western Railway Co.
Mr. Ryan is Counsel to: The Trustees of Purdue University.
Representative Clients: Aluminum Company of America; Liberty Mutual Insurance Group.

For full biographical listings, see the Martindale-Hubbell Law Directory

*NOBLESVILLE,** Hamilton Co.

CHURCH, CHURCH, HITTLE & ANTRIM (AV)

938 Conner Street, P.O. Box 10, 46061-0010
Telephone: 317-773-2190
Telecopier: 317-773-5320
Email: cchadoug@msn.com

MEMBERS OF FIRM

Douglas D. Church
Jack G. Hittle
J. Michael Antrim
Martin E. Risacher
Bruce M. Bittner
Brian J. Zaiger
Leslie Craig Henderzahs
Jordan D. Church

OF COUNSEL

Manson E. Church

Representative Clients: Noblesville Schools; Westfield-Washington Schools; Community Bank; Metrobank; Towns of Westfield, Fishers and Pendleton; Reynolds Farm Equipment Co.; Weihe Engineering; Historic Railroad Multijurisdictional Port Authority.

For full biographical listings, see the Martindale-Hubbell Law Directory

KENTUCKY

*LEXINGTON,** Fayette Co.

STOLL, KEENON & PARK, LLP (AV)

201 E. Main Street, Suite 1000, 40507-1380
Telephone: 606-231-3000
Telecopier: 606-253-1093; 606-253-1027
URL: http://www.skp.com
Frankfort, Kentucky Office: 307 Washington Street, 40601.
Telephone: 502-875-6220.
Telecopier: 502-875-6235.
Henderson, Kentucky Office: 201 C North Main Street, 42420-3103.
Telephone: 270-831-1900.
Telecopier: 270-827-4060.
Louisville, Kentucky Office: 400 West Market Street, Suite 2650, 40202-3377.
Telephone: 502-568-9100.
Telecopier: 502-568-5700.

MEMBER OF FIRM

J. David Smith, Jr.

(See Next Column)

STOLL, KEENON & PARK LLP, *Lexington—Continued*

OF COUNSEL

Douglas P. Romaine

Representative Clients: Bank One, Lexington, NA; Kentucky Association of Counties; Smith Barney, Inc.

For Complete List of Firm Personnel, See General Section

For full biographical listings, see the Martindale-Hubbell Law Directory

*LOUISVILLE,** Jefferson Co.

HARPER, FERGUSON & DAVIS (AV)

1730 Meidinger Tower, 40202
Telephone: 502-582-3871
Telecopier: 502-582-3905
Email: hfd@unidial.com

MEMBERS OF FIRM

Spencer E. Harper, Jr.
William W. Davis

OF COUNSEL

Jo M. Ferguson (Retired)

Representative Clients: Kentucky Housing Corp.; Lexington-Fayette Urban County Government; Cities of Louisville and Covington; Kenton County Airport Board (Cincinnati/No. Kentucky International Airport); Regional Airport Authority of Louisville and Jefferson County; Toyota Motor Mfg., U.S.A., Inc.; Southwire Company; Delta Air Lines, Inc.; Kentucky Utilities Co.; Louisville Gas & Electric Co.

For full biographical listings, see the Martindale-Hubbell Law Directory

PEDLEY ZIELKE GORDINIER OLT & PENCE, PLLC (AV)

1150 Starks Building, 455 South Fourth Avenue, 40202
Telephone: 502-589-4600
Fax: 502-584-0422
Email: pzgop@undial.com

MEMBERS OF FIRM

Lawrence L. Pedley
Laurence J. Zielke
John K. Gordinier
William W. Stodghill
John H. Dwyer, Jr.
Ilam E. Smith

OF COUNSEL

Schuyler J. Olt

Caroline George Meena

For full biographical listings, see the Martindale-Hubbell Law Directory

RUBIN & HAYS (AV)

First Trust Centre 200 South Fifth Street, 40202
Telephone: 502-569-7525
Telecopier: 502-569-7555
Email: rh@rubinhays.com

MEMBERS OF FIRM

Charles S. Musson
W. Randall Jones

ASSOCIATE

Christian L. Juckett

OF COUNSEL

Wm. Carl Fust

LEGAL SUPPORT PERSONNEL

Mary Embry
Kathy McKnight
Elaine Murphy

Representative Clients: Bank of Louisville; Bank One, Kentucky; First Kentucky Securities Corporation; J.C. Bradford & Co., Inc.; J.J.B. Hilliard, W.L. Lyons, Inc.; Johnston, Brown, Burnett & Knight, Inc.; National City Bank; PNC Bank; Ross, Sinclair & Associates; Stock Yards Bank and Trust Co.

For full biographical listings, see the Martindale-Hubbell Law Directory

STITES & HARBISON (AV)

Formerly Stites, McElwain & Fowler and Harbison, Kessinger, Lisle & Bush
400 West Market Street, Suite 1800, 40202
Telephone: 502-587-3400
Fax: 502-587-6391
URL: http://www.stites.com
Frankfort, Kentucky Office: 421 West Main Street.
Telephone: 502-223-3477.
Fax: 502-223-4124.
Lexington, Kentucky Office: 250 West Main Street, Suite 2300.
Telephone: 606-226-2300.
Fax: 606-253-9144.
Hyden, Kentucky Office: 21976 Main Street, Farmer Campbell Building, Second Floor.
Telephone: 606-672-4200.
Jeffersonville, Indiana Office: 323 East Court Avenue.
Telephone: 812-282-7566.
Fax: 812-284-5519.

(See Next Column)

Atlanta, Georgia Office: 3350 Cumberland Circle, Suite 1700 Riverwood.
Telephone: 770-850-7000.
Fax: 770-850-7070.
Washington, D.C. Office: 1200 G Street, N.W., Suite 800.
Telephone: 202-434-8968.

MEMBERS OF FIRM

Robert W. Lanum (Jeffersonville, Indiana Office)
William H. Haden, Jr.
William E. Hellmann
Alex P. Herrington, Jr.

For Complete List of Firm Personnel, See General Section

For full biographical listings, see the Martindale-Hubbell Law Directory

LOUISIANA

*BATON ROUGE,** East Baton Rouge Parish

BREAZEALE, SACHSE & WILSON, L.L.P. (AV)

Twenty-Third Floor, One American Place, P.O. Box 3197, 70821-3197
Telephone: 225-387-4000
Fax: 225-387-5397
URL: http://www.bswllp.com
New Orleans, Louisiana Office: LL&E Tower, Suite 1500, 909 Poydras Street.
Telephone: 504-584-5454.
Fax: 504-584-5452.
Covington, Louisiana Office: 2255 Highway 190 North, Suite 200.
Telephone: 504-871-9444.
Fax: 504-871-9666.

MEMBERS OF FIRM

Leonard R. Nachman, II
Richard D. Leibowitz
Peter J. Butler, Jr. (Resident, New Orleans Office)

SPECIAL COUNSEL

Peter J. Butler (Resident, New Orleans Office)

Counsel for: Allied-Signal Corp.; Reynolds Metal Co.; Illinois Central Railroad Co.

For Complete List of Firm Personnel, See General Section

For full biographical listings, see the Martindale-Hubbell Law Directory

*NEW ORLEANS,** Orleans Parish

FOLEY & JUDELL, L.L.P. (AV)

One Canal Place, Suite 2600, 365 Canal Street, 70130-1138
Telephone: 504-568-1249
Fax: 504-565-3900
Baton Rouge, Louisiana Office: Acadia Trace Office Building, 2237 South Acadian Thruway, Suite 610.
Telephone: 225-923-2476.
Fax: 225-923-2477.

MEMBERS OF FIRM

Harold B. Judell
Lonnie L. Bewley
J. Hugh Martin
C. Grant Schlueter
Susan Weeks
Jerry R. Osborne
O. Ray Cornelius
David M. Wolf
David E. Henderson (Resident, Baton Rouge Office)
Wayne J. Neveu
Alan L. Offner
Meredith L. Hathorn
Richard R. Storms, Jr.

OF COUNSEL

Dudley C. Foley, Jr.
John W. Cox
William H. Beck, Jr.

For full biographical listings, see the Martindale-Hubbell Law Directory

THE GODFREY FIRM A PROFESSIONAL LAW CORPORATION (AV)

2500 Energy Centre, 1100 Poydras Street, 70163-2500
Telephone: 504-585-7538
Fax: 504-585-7535
Email: godfryfirm@aol.com

Jarrell E. Godfrey, Jr.
Cloyd F. Van Hook
Patrick M. Files
Elizabeth Earnest

For full biographical listings, see the Martindale-Hubbell Law Directory

New Orleans—Continued

McGlinchey Stafford (AV)

A Professional Limited Liability Company
643 Magazine Street, 70130-3477
Telephone: 504-586-1200
Fax: 504-596-2800
TDD: (504) 596-2728
Telex: 584327
Cable Address: "MACSTAC"
Mailing Address: P.O. Box 60643, New Orleans, Louisiana, 70160-0643
Email: @mcglinchey.com *URL:* http://www.mcglinchey.com
Dallas, Texas Office: 2777 Stemmons Freeway, Suite 925, 75207-2401.
Telephone: 214-860-9700.
Fax: 214-860-9750.
Houston, Texas Office: 2727 Allen Parkway, Suite 1900, 77019.
Telephone: 713-520-1900.
Fax: 713-520-1025.
Baton Rouge, Louisiana Office: Ninth Floor, One American Place, 70825-0001.
Telephone: 504-383-9000.
Fax: 504-343-3076.
Jackson, Mississippi Office: Suite 1200, SkyTel Centre, 200 South Lamar Street, 39201.
Telephone: 601-960-8400.
Fax: 601-960-8406.
Lake Providence, Louisiana Office: 405 Morgan Street, 71254-2691.
Telephone: 318-559-1200.
Fax: 318-559-0609.
Monroe, Louisiana Office: Dean ONB Tower, 130 Desiard Street, Suite 807, 71201.
Telephone: 318-651-0807.
Fax: 318-651-0809.

MEMBERS OF FIRM

J. Patrick Beauchamp
Lisa E. Maurer
R. Keith Colvin

MEMBERS OF FIRM

Sue Hicks Fairbank (Resident, Jackson Office)
Wilton J. Johnson, III (Resident, Jackson Office)
Samuel A. Bacot (Resident, Baton Rouge Office)
Stephen C. Edds (Resident, Jackson Office)

ASSOCIATE

D. Jeffrey Wagner

For full biographical listings, see the Martindale-Hubbell Law Directory

MAINE

*BANGOR,** Penobscot Co.

Eaton, Peabody, Bradford & Veague, P.A. (AV)

Fleet Center-Exchange Street, P.O. Box 1210, 04402-1210
Telephone: 207-947-0111
Telecopier: 207-942-3040
Email: eaton@eatonpeabody.com *URL:* http://www.eatonpeabody.com
Augusta, Maine Office: 77 Sewall Street, Suite 3000.
Telephone: 207-622-3747.
Telecopier: 207-622-9732.
Blue Hill, Maine Office: One East Blue Hill Road.
Telephone: 207-374-2812.
Telecopier: 207-374-2548.
Brunswick, Maine Office: 167 Park Row.
Telephone: 207-729-1144.
Telecopier: 207-729-1140.
Dover-Foxcroft, Maine Office: 30 East Main Street.
Telephone: 207-564-8378.
Telecopier: 207-564-7059.

Michael B. Trainor

For Complete List of Firm Personnel, See General Section

For full biographical listings, see the Martindale-Hubbell Law Directory

*PORTLAND,** Cumberland Co.

Pierce Atwood (AV)

One Monument Square, 04101
Telephone: 207-791-1100
Fax: 207-791-1350
Email: info@PierceAtwood.com *URL:* http://www.pierceatwood.com
Augusta, Maine Office: 77 Winthrop Street.
Telephone: 207-622-6311.
Fax: 207-623-9367.
Newburyport, Massachusetts Office: 6 Harris Street.
Telephone: 978-465-9599.
Fax: 978-465-9945.

MEMBERS OF FIRM

Bruce A. Coggeshall
James B. Zimpritch

(See Next Column)

ASSOCIATE

James M. Saffian

COUNSEL

Michael S. Wilson

For Complete List of Firm Personnel, See General Section

For full biographical listings, see the Martindale-Hubbell Law Directory

Preti, Flaherty, Beliveau, Pachios & Haley, LLC (AV)

One City Center, P.O. Box 9546, 04112-9546
Telephone: 207-791-3000
Telecopier: 207-791-3111
Email: admin@preti.com *URL:* http://www.preti.com
Augusta, Maine Office: 45 Memorial Circle, P.O. Box 1058, 04332-1058.
Telephone: 207-623-5300.
Telefax: 207-623-2914.
Bath, Maine Office: Thirty Front Street, P.O. Box 665, 04530-0665.
Telephone: 207-443-5576.
Telefax: 207-443-6665.

MEMBERS OF FIRM

Severin M. Beliveau (Augusta Office)
Michael J. Gentile (Augusta Office)
Eric P. Stauffer
James C. Pitney, Jr. (Augusta Office)

ASSOCIATE

James E. Phipps

Representative Clients: Prudential Securities Incorporated; Kidder, Peabody & Co., Inc.; Paine Webber Incorporated; State of Maine; Towns of Dixfield, Fayette and Jay, Maine; A. G. Edwards, Inc.; Merrill Lynch & Co.; Chemical Securities Inc.; Goldman, Sachs & Co.

For Complete List of Firm Personnel, See General Section

For full biographical listings, see the Martindale-Hubbell Law Directory

MARYLAND

*BALTIMORE,** (Independent City)

Funk & Bolton, A Professional Association (AV)

100 Light Street, Suite 1000, 21202
Telephone: 410-659-7700
Facsimile: 410-659-7773
Email: FBLAW@FBLAW.COM
Annapolis, Maryland Office: 191 Main Street, 21401.
Telephone: 410-269-1554.
Facsimile: 410-268-0612.
Chestertown, Maryland Office: 315 High Street, Suite 202, 21620.
Telephone: 410-810-1381.
Facsimile: 410-810-1383.

David M. Funk
Lindsey A. Rader

Charles D. MacLeod (Resident, Chestertown Office)

For full biographical listings, see the Martindale-Hubbell Law Directory

Piper & Marbury L.L.P. (AV)

36 South Charles Street, 21201-3018
Telephone: 410-539-2530
FAX: 410-539-0489
Email: lawfirm@pipermar.com *URL:* http://www.pipermar.com
Washington, D.C. Office: 1200 Nineteenth Street, N.W., 20036-2430.
Telephone: 202-861-3900.
FAX: 202-223-2085.
New York, N.Y. Office: 1251 Avenue of the Americas, 10020-1104.
Telephone: 212-835-6000.
FAX: 212-835-6001.
Philadelphia, Pennsylvania Office: 3400 Two Logan Square, 18th & Arch Streets, 19103-2762.
Telephone: 215-656-3300.
FAX: 215-656-3301.
Easton, Maryland Office: 117 Bay Street, 21601-2703.
Telephone: 410-820-4460.
FAX: 410-820-4463.
Princeton, N.J. Office: 116 Village Boulevard, Suite 200, Princeton Forrestal Village, 08540.
Telephone: 609-951-2252.
FAX: 609-951-2216.
Reston, Virginia Office: 1850 Centennial Park Drive, Suite 610, Commerce Executive Park III, 20191.
Telephone: 703-391-7100.
Fax: 703-309-5299.

(See Next Column)

PIPER & MARBURY L.L.P., *Baltimore—Continued*

MEMBERS OF FIRM

John P. Machen
Stewart K. Diana
William L. Henn, Jr.
Elizabeth A. McKennon
Paul A. Tiburzi
Paul D. Shelton
Kurt J. Fischer
Kristin H. R. Franceschi

OF COUNSEL

Donald P. McPherson, III

For Complete List of Firm Personnel, See General Section

For full biographical listings, see the Martindale-Hubbell Law Directory

VENABLE ATTORNEYS AT LAW VENABLE, BAETJER AND HOWARD, LLP (AV)

A Partnership including Professional Corporations
1800 Mercantile Bank & Trust Building, 2 Hopkins Plaza, 21201
Telephone: 410-244-7400
Fax: 410-244-7742
URL: http://www.venable.com
Washington, D.C. Office: Venable, Baetjer, Howard & Civiletti LLP, Suite 1000, 1201 New York Avenue, N.W.
Telephone: 202-962-4800.
Fax: 202-962-8300.
McLean, Virginia Office: Suite 400, 2010 Corporate Ridge.
Telephone: 703-760-1600.
Fax: 703-821-8949.
Rockville, Maryland Office: Suite 500, One Church Street, P. O. Box 1906.
Telephone: 301-217-5600.
Fax: 301-217-5617.
Towson, Maryland Office: 210 Allegheny Avenue, P. O. Box 5517.
Telephone: 410-494-6200.
Fax: 410-821-0147.

MEMBERS OF FIRM

Thomas P. Perkins, III (P.C.)
Lee M. Miller (P.C.)
Robert A. Shelton
Thomas J. Kenney, Jr. (P.C.)
Lars E. Anderson (Not admitted in MD; Resident, McLean, Virginia Office)
Paul T. Glasgow (Resident, Rockville, Maryland Office)
Sondra Harans Block (Resident, Rockville, Maryland Office)
Edward L. Wender (P.C.)
Mitchell Kolkin
Peter P. Parvis
James E. Cumbie
Davis V. R. Sherman

For Complete List of Firm Personnel, See General Section

For full biographical listings, see the Martindale-Hubbell Law Directory

WHITEFORD, TAYLOR & PRESTON L.L.P. (AV)

7 Saint Paul Street, 21202-1626
Telephone: 410-347-8700
Telex: 5101012334
Fax: 410-752-7092
Email: wt&pllp@wtplaw.com *URL:* http://www.wtplaw.com
Towson, Maryland Office: 210 West Pennsylvania Avenue.
Telephone: 410-832-2000.
Fax: 410-832-2015.
Washington, D.C. Office: 1025 Connecticut Avenue, N.W.
Telephone: 202-659-6800.
Fax: 202-331-0573.
Columbia, Maryland Office: 10440 Little Patuxent Parkway.
Telephone: 410-884-0700.
Fax: 410-884-0719.
Alexandria, Virginia Office: 1317 King Street.
Telephone: 703-836-5742.
Fax: 703-836-0265.

William M. Davidow, Jr.
Deborah H. Diehl
D. Scott Freed
James C. Holman
Jonathan Z. May
Herman B. Rosenthal
Gail M. Stern

For Complete List of Firm Personnel, See General Section

For full biographical listings, see the Martindale-Hubbell Law Directory

RIVERDALE, Prince Georges Co.

MEYERS, BILLINGSLEY, RODBELL & ROSENBAUM, P.A. (AV)

Suite 400 Berkshire Building, 6801 Kenilworth Avenue, 20737-1385
Telephone: 301-699-5800
Fax: 301-779-5746
Email: mbrrlaw@martindalemail.com
Annapolis, Maryland Office: 95 Cathedral Street, Suite 100, 21401.
Telephone: 410-267-6670.
Fax: 410-267-8222.

Lance W. Billingsley

(See Next Column)

Frederick Stichnoth

Reference: First National Bank of Maryland.

For Complete List of Firm Personnel, See General Section

For full biographical listings, see the Martindale-Hubbell Law Directory

*TOWSON,** Baltimore Co.

VENABLE ATTORNEYS AT LAW VENABLE, BAETJER AND HOWARD, LLP (AV)

A Partnership including Professional Corporations
210 Allegheny Avenue, P.O. Box 5517, 21204
Telephone: 410-494-6200
Fax: 410-821-0147
URL: http://www.venable.com
Baltimore, Maryland Office: 1800 Mercantile Bank & Trust Building, 2 Hopkins Plaza.
Telephone: 410-244-7400.
Fax: 410-244-7742.
Washington, D.C. Office: Venable, Baetjer, Howard & Civiletti LLP, Suite 1000, 1201 New York Avenue, N.W.
Telephone: 202-962-4800.
Fax: 202-962-8300.
McLean, Virginia Office: Suite 400, 2010 Corporate Ridge.
Telephone: 703-760-1600.
Fax: 703-821-8949.
Rockville, Maryland Office: Suite 500, One Church Street, P. O. Box 1906.
Telephone: 301-217-5600.
Fax: 301-217-5617.

PARTNERS

John B. Howard
Robert A. Hoffman

For Complete List of Firm Personnel, See General Section

For full biographical listings, see the Martindale-Hubbell Law Directory

*UPPER MARLBORO,** Prince Georges Co.

KNIGHT, MANZI, NUSSBAUM & LAPLACA, P.C. (AV)

14440 Old Mill Road, 20772
Telephone: 301-952-0100
Annapolis/Baltimore: 410-792-3786
Fax: 301-952-0221

William E. Knight
Robert A. Manzi
Ronald M. Miller
William C. Brennan, Jr.
Harry J. Trainor, Jr.
Andrew W. Nussbaum
Raymond G. LaPlaca
John F. Shay, Jr.
Sheldon L. Gnatt
Daniel A. LaPlaca
Gail Borjeson Viens
Roger C. Thomas
Monica M. Haley-Pierson
Daniel F. Lynch III
Norman D. Rivera

Robert L. Lombardo
Amy B. Glaser
Brent M. Ahalt
Terry L. Bell

Representative Clients: Industrial Development Authority of Prince George's County; Prince George's County, Maryland.

For full biographical listings, see the Martindale-Hubbell Law Directory

MASSACHUSETTS

*BOSTON,** Suffolk Co.

HINCKLEY, ALLEN & SNYDER LLP (AV)

28 State Street, 30th Floor, 02109-1775
Telephone: 617-345-9000
Email: firm@haslaw.com *URL:* http://www.haslaw.com
Providence, Rhode Island Office: 1500 Fleet Center.
Telephone: 401-274-2000.
Fax: 401-277-9600. URL: http://www.hawlaw.com.

MEMBERS OF FIRM

Paula K. Andrews
David D. Barricelli (Not admitted in MA)
E. Jerome Batty (Not admitted in MA)
Jonathan Bell
Paul Bork
Stephen J. Carlotti (Not admitted in MA)
David Barry Connolly
Joseph P. Curran (Not admitted in MA)
Michael P. DeFanti
Eric F. Eisenberg
Malcolm Farmer, III
Margaret D. Farrell (Not admitted in MA)
Pasco Gasbarro Jr.
Hugh J. Gorman, III
Alan P. Gottlieb
Gerard R. Goulet
William R. Grimm
Paul A. Hedstrom
Richard L. E. Jocelyn (Not admitted in MA)
Joel Lewin
Sandra Matrone Mack (Not admitted in MA)

(See Next Column)

HINCKLEY, ALLEN & SNYDER LLP—*Continued*

MEMBERS OF FIRM (Continued)

Matthew T. Marcello, III (Not admitted in MA)
Frederick P. McClure
Elizabeth Murdock Myers
Paul F. O'Donnell, III
H. Peter Olsen (Not admitted in MA)
Julianne Palumbo
John J. Pendergast, III (Not admitted in MA)
Gerald J. Petros
James O. Reavis
Jeremy Ritzenberg
Ralph J. Rivkind
David J. Rubin
Charles E. Schaub, Jr.
Douglas F. Seaver
Herman Snyder
David R. Sullivan
Robert F. Sylvia
Howard E. Walker (Not admitted in MA)
Richard D. Wayne

ASSOCIATES

Jessica M. Bettencourt (Not admitted in MA)
Mark Bianchi
Alyssa V. Boss
Alexandra K. Callam
Jane E. Cohen
Andrew D. Cummings
June E. Daniel (Not admitted in MA)
Kim Herman Goslant
Gloria Maria Gutierrez
Kelley Jordan-Price
Catherine S. Kim
Christopher W. Morog
Elena B. Olson
Joseph D. Whelan (Not admitted in MA)

OF COUNSEL

Willard Krasnow
Willard R. Pope
Bentley Tobin
Joachim A. Weissfeld (Not admitted in MA)

For Complete List of Firm Personnel, See General Section

For full biographical listings, see the Martindale-Hubbell Law Directory

LEWIS & MUNDAY, A PROFESSIONAL CORPORATION (AV)

(Formerly Lewis, Clay & Munday, P.C.)
101 Federal Street Suite 1900, 02110
Telephone: 617-478-0553
Fax: 617-478-0543
Email: lcmlaw@aol.com *URL:* http://www.lewis-pc.com
Washington, D.C. Office: 1120 Connecticut Avenue, Suite 280. 20036.
Telephone: 202-835-0616.
Fax: 202-833-3316.
Detroit, Michigan Office: 1300 First National Building. 660 Woodward Avenue. 48226-3531.
Telephone: 313-961-2550.
Fax: 313-961-1270.

COUNSEL

G. Allen Bass (Resident)

For full biographical listings, see the Martindale-Hubbell Law Directory

MINTZ, LEVIN, COHN, FERRIS, GLOVSKY AND POPEO, P.C. (AV)

One Financial Center, 02111
Telephone: 617-542-6000
FAX: 617-542-2241
Internet: Each Attorney's Internet Address takes the following form: first initial last name @mintz.com (e.g., rmintz@mintz.com)
URL: http://www.mintz.com
Washington, D.C. Office: 701 Pennsylvania Avenue, N.W. Suite 900.
Telephone: 202-434-7300.
Fax: 202-434-7400.
Reston, Virginia Office: 12021 Sunset Hills Road, Suite 310.
Telephone: 703-464-4800.
Fax: 703-464-4895.

Francis X. Meaney
Gregory A. Sandomirsky
Maxwell D. Solet
John R. Regier
Ann-Ellen Marcus Hornidge

For Complete List of Firm Personnel, See General Section

For full biographical listings, see the Martindale-Hubbell Law Directory

PALMER & DODGE LLP (AV)

One Beacon Street, 02108
Telephone: 617-573-0100
Facsimile: 617-227-4420
URL: http://www.palmerdodge.com

MEMBERS OF FIRM

Neil P. Arkuss
Norman P. Cohen
Jean M. DeLuca
Ruth E. Fitch
Robert H. Hale
Thomas W. Merrill
Walter J. St. Onge III
John M. Thomas
Roger P. Vacco
Donald F. Winter

For Complete List of Firm Personnel, See General Section

For full biographical listings, see the Martindale-Hubbell Law Directory

MICHIGAN

*ANN ARBOR,** Washtenaw Co.

MILLER, CANFIELD, PADDOCK AND STONE, P.L.C. (AV)

A Professional Limited Liability Company
Founded in 1852 by Sidney Davy Miller
101 North Main Street, Seventh Floor, 48104-1400
Telephone: 734-663-2445
Fax: 734-747-7147
URL: http://www.millercanfield.com
Detroit, Michigan Office: 150 West Jefferson, Suite 2500, 48226-4415.
Telephone: 313-963-6420.
Fax: 313-496-7500.
Cable Address: "Stem Detroit."
Troy, Michigan Office: 840 West Long Lake Road, Suite 200, 48098.
Telephone: 248-879-2000.
Fax: 248-879-2001.
Grand Rapids, Michigan Office: 99 Monroe, N.W., Suite 1200, 49503-2639.
Telephone: 616-454-8656.
Fax: 616-776-6322.
Howell, Michigan Office: 121 South Barnard Street, Suite 4, 48843-2305.
Telephone: 517-546-7600.
Telecopier: 517-546-6974.
Kalamazoo, Michigan Office: 444 West Michigan Avenue, 49007-3752.
Telephone: 616-381-7030.
Fax: 616-382-0244.
Lansing, Michigan Office: One Michigan Avenue, Suite 900, 48933-1609.
Telephone: 517-487-2070.
Fax: 517-374-6304.
Monroe, Michigan Office: 214 East Elm Avenue, Suite 100, 48162-2682.
Telephone: 734-243-2000.
Fax: 734-243-0901.
Washington, D.C. Office: 1900 K Street, N.W., Suite 1150. 20006.
Telephone: 202-429-5575; 785-0600.
Fax: 202-331-1118; 785-1234.
Pensacola, Florida Office: 25 West Cedar, 32501.
Telephone: 850-469-1088.
Fax: 850-432-0677.
New York, New York Office: 1450 Broadway, 41st Floor, 10018.
Telephone: 212-704-4400.
Fax: 212-704-4410.
Gdynia, Poland Office: UL. Slaska 21, 81-319.
Telephone: 011-485-831-2808.
Fax: 011-48-58-628 6411.
Warsaw, Poland Office: UL. Nowogrodzkall, 5th Floor, 00-513.
Telephone: 011-4822 529 0200.
Fax: 011-4822 529 0201.
Katowice, Poland Office: UL. Francuska 35/37, 40-027.
Telephone: 011 (48-32) 757-2414.
Fax: 011 (48-32) 757-2483.

PRINCIPALS OF FIRM

Robert E. Gilbert
Timothy D. Sochocki

Representative Firm Clients: Chrysler Corporation; Comerica, Incorporated; City of Detroit, Michigan; Detroit Tigers, Inc.; First of Michigan; Ford Motor Company; Ford Motor Credit Company; Great Lakes Bancorp; Henry Ford Hospital; INVETECH Company.

For Complete List of Firm Personnel, See General Section

For full biographical listings, see the Martindale-Hubbell Law Directory

BLOOMFIELD HILLS, Oakland Co.

HOWARD & HOWARD ATTORNEYS, P.C. (AV)

The Pinehurst Office Center, Suite 101, 1400 North Woodward Avenue, 48304-2855
Telephone: 248-645-1483
Telecopier: 248-645-1568
Kalamazoo, Michigan Office: The Michigan Building, Suite 200, 100 Portage Street.
Telephone: 616-382-1483.
Telecopier: 616-382-1568.
Lansing, Michigan Office: The Phoenix Building, Suite 500, 222 Washington Square, North.
Telephone: 517-485-1483.
Telecopier: 517-485-1568.
Peoria, Illinois Office: One Technology Plaza, Suite 600, 211 Fulton Street.
Telephone: 309-672-1483.
Telecopier: 309-672-1568.

Robert L. Schwartz
Gina M. Torielli

Representative Clients: For Representative Client list, see General Practice, Bloomfield Hills, MI.

For Complete List of Firm Personnel, See General Section

For full biographical listings, see the Martindale-Hubbell Law Directory

*DETROIT,** Wayne Co.

BODMAN, LONGLEY & DAHLING LLP (AV)

34th Floor 100 Renaissance Center, 48243
Telephone: 313-259-7777
Fax: 313-393-7579
Email: info@bodmanlongley.com *URL:* http://www.bodmanlongley.com
Troy, Michigan Office: Suite 2020, 755 West Big Beaver Road.
Telephone: 248-362-2110.
Fax: 248-244-0780.
Ann Arbor, Michigan Office: 110 Miller, Suite 300.
Telephone: 734-761-3780.
Fax: 734-930-2494.
Northern Michigan Office: 229 Court Street, P.O. Box 405, Cheboygan.
Telephone: 231-627-4351.
Fax: 231-627-2802.

MEMBERS OF FIRM

Herold McC. Deason
Joseph N. Brown
F. Thomas Lewand
Barbara A. Bowman
Jerold Lax (Ann Arbor Office)
Carl F. Stafford

ASSOCIATE

Deanna L. Dixon

Representative Clients: Archdiocese of Detroit; Comerica Bank; The Detroit Lions, Inc.; Ford Estates; Lear Corp.; Charles Stewart Mott Foundation; Norfolk Southern Corporation; Panhandle Eastern Corporation; State Farm Insurance Companies.

For Complete List of Firm Personnel, See General Section

For full biographical listings, see the Martindale-Hubbell Law Directory

DICKINSON WRIGHT PLLC (AV)

500 Woodward Avenue, Suite 4000, 48226-3425
Telephone: 313-223-3500
Facsimile: 313-223-3598
URL: http://www.dickinson-wright.com
Bloomfield Hills, Michigan Office: 525 North Woodward Avenue, Suite 2000.
Telephone: 248-433-7200.
Facsimile: 248-433-7274.
Grand Rapids, Michigan Office: 200 Ottawa Avenue, N.W., Suite 900.
Telephone: 616-458-1300.
Facsimile: 616-458-6753.
Lansing, Michigan Office: Suite 200, 215 South Washington Square.
Telephone: 517-371-1730.
Facsimile: 517-487-4700.
Washington, D.C. Office: Suite 800, 1901 L Street, N.W.
Telephone: 202-457-0160.
Facsimile: 202-659-1559.

MEMBERS OF FIRM

Terence M. Donnelly
John A. Everhardus
Craig W. Hammond
W. Anthony Jenkins
Paul M. Wyzgoski
Thomas V. Yates

CONSULTING MEMBER

Charles R. Moon

ASSOCIATE

Rhonda D. Welburn

For Representative Client list, see General Section.

For Complete List of Firm Personnel, See General Section

For full biographical listings, see the Martindale-Hubbell Law Directory

DYKEMA GOSSETT PLLC (AV)

400 Renaissance Center, 48243-1668
Telephone: 313-568-6800
Fax: 313-568-6545
Email: mstarrs@dykema.com *URL:* http://www.dykema.com
Ann Arbor, Michigan Office: 315 East Eisenhower Parkway, Suite 100, 48108-3306.
Telephone: 734-214-7660.
Fax: 734-214-7696.
Bloomfield Hills, Michigan Office: 1577 North Woodward Avenue, Suite 300, 48304-2820.
Telephone: 248-203-0700.
Fax: 248-203-0763.
Chicago, Illinois Office: 55 East Monroe Street, Suite 3050, 60603-5709.
Telephone: 312-551-4900.
Fax: 312-551-4919.
Grand Rapids, Michigan Office: Suite 700, 300 Ottawa Avenue, N.W., 49503-2304.
Telephone: 616-776-7500.
Fax: 616-776-7573.
Lansing, Michigan Office: 800 Michigan National Tower, 48933-1707.
Telephone: 517-374-9100.
Fax: 517-374-9191.
Washington, D.C. Office: Franklin Square, Suite 300 West, 1300 I Street, N.W., 20005-3306.
Telephone: 202-522-8600.
Fax: 202-522-8669.

(See Next Column)

Affiliated Office: Via Matconi, 3, 40122 Bologna, Italy.
Telephone: 011-39-51-228222.
Fax: 011-39-51-6593580.

MEMBERS OF FIRM

Bowden V. Brown (Resident at Bloomfield Hills Office)
James P. Kiefer (Resident at Lansing Office)
Kathrin E. Kudner
Nicole Yvette Lamb-Hale
Stewart L. Mandell
Brian J. Page (Resident at Grand Rapids Office)

For Complete List of Firm Personnel, See General Section

For full biographical listings, see the Martindale-Hubbell Law Directory

HONIGMAN MILLER SCHWARTZ AND COHN (AV)

2290 First National Building, 660 Woodward Avenue, 48226
Telephone: 313-465-7000
Telecopier: 313-465-8000
Telex: 235705
Email: mvg@honigman.com *URL:* http://law.honigman.com
Lansing, Michigan Office: Phoenix Building, 222 North Washington Square, Suite 400, 48933-1800.
Telephone: 517-484-8282.

MEMBERS OF FIRM

John M. Kamins
Denise J. Lewis
Mitchell R. Meisner
Alex L. Parrish
Brad M. Tomtishen

Representative Clients: Michigan Municipal Bond Authority; City of Detroit, Michigan; Wayne County, Michigan; Merrill Lynch & Co.; Goldman, Sachs & Co.; PaineWebber Incorporated; Roney & Co.; Bear, Stearns & Co., Inc.; Merrill Lynch & Co.; Goldman, Sachs & Co.

For Complete List of Firm Personnel, See General Section

For full biographical listings, see the Martindale-Hubbell Law Directory

JAFFE, RAITT, HEUER & WEISS, PROFESSIONAL CORPORATION (AV)

One Woodward Avenue, Suite 2400, 48226
Telephone: 313-961-8380
Telecopier: 313-961-8358
Cable Address: "Jafsni"
Southfield,Michigan Office: Travelers Tower, Suite 1520.
Telephone: 313-961-8380.

Gail A. Anderson
Robert S. Bolton
Gary R. Glenn
Robert J. Gordon
Larry K. Griffis
Ralph R. Margulis
Lawrence C. Patrick, Jr.
Victor F. Ptasznik
David H. Raitt
Stephen G. Schafer
Susan M. Sutton
Wendy L. Zabriskie

Representative Clients: Michigan State Hospital Finance Authority.

For Complete List of Firm Personnel, See General Section

For full biographical listings, see the Martindale-Hubbell Law Directory

LEWIS & MUNDAY, A PROFESSIONAL CORPORATION (AV)

(Formerly Lewis, Clay & Munday, P.C.)
1300 First National Building, 660 Woodward Avenue, 48226-3531
Telephone: 313-961-2550
Fax: 313-961-1270
Email: camille.miller@lewis-pc.com *URL:* http://www.lewis-pc.com
Washington, D.C. Office: 1120 Connecticut Avenue, Suite 280. 20036.
Telephone: 202-835-0616.
Fax: 202-833-3316.
Boston, Massachusetts Office: 101 Federal Street, Suite 1900. 02110.
Telephone: 617-478-0553.
Fax: 617-478-0543.

David Baker Lewis
Reuben A. Munday
Camille Stearns Miller
Jacqueline H. Sellers
David N. Zacks
Thomas J. Guyer
Blair A. Person
Karen Kendrick Brown (Resident, Washington, D.C. Office)
Susan D. Hoffman
Hans J. Massaquoi, Jr.

Althea Lynn Simpson
Donica Thomas Varner
Kris W. Krueger
Cylenthia LaToye Miller
Joseph N. Ejbeh
Yolanda R. Bates
Caroletta L. Edgar-Sprinkle
Derek G. McBride
Ayanna Weber
Deborah Jean Williamson
Darice Elizabeth Weber
Krystal M. Gardner
Syeda Taqi

COUNSEL

G. Allen Bass (Resident, Boston, Massachusetts Office)
Leamon R. Sowell, Jr.
Gail Pabarue Bennett
Roger M. Groves
Carol H. Rodriguez
Linda M. Bruton
Brian J. Kott

(See Next Column)

LEWIS & MUNDAY A PROFESSIONAL CORPORATION—*Continued*

OF COUNSEL

Otis M. Smith (1922-1994) Herbert O. Reid, Sr. (1915-1991)

Representative Clients: Aetna Life & Casualty Co.; Chrysler Motors Corp.; Chrysler Financial Corp.; MCI Communications Corp.; City of Detroit; City of Detroit Building Authority; City of Detroit Downtown Development Authority; Consolidated Rail Corp. (Conrail); Equitable Life Assurance Society of the United States.

For full biographical listings, see the Martindale-Hubbell Law Directory

MILLER, CANFIELD, PADDOCK AND STONE, P.L.C. (AV)

A Professional Limited Liability Company
Founded in 1852 by Sidney Davy Miller
150 West Jefferson, Suite 2500, 48226-4415
Telephone: 313-963-6420
Fax: 313-496-7500
Cable Address: "Stem Detroit"
URL: http://www.millercanfield.com
Ann Arbor, Michigan Office: 101 North Main Street, 7th Floor, 48104-1400.
Telephone: 734-663-2445.
Fax: 734-747-7147.
Troy, Michigan Office: 840 West Long Lake Road, Suite 200, 48098.
Telephone: 248-879-2000.
Fax: 248-879-2001.
Grand Rapids, Michigan Office: 99 Monroe, N.W., Suite 1200, 49503-2639.
Telephone: 616-454-8656.
Fax: 616-776-6322.
Howell, Michigan Office: 121 South Barnard Street, Suite 4, 48843-2305.
Telephone: 517-546-7600.
Telecopier: 517-546-6974.
Kalamazoo, Michigan Office: 444 West Michigan Avenue, 49007-3752.
Telephone: 616-381-7030.
Fax: 616-382-0244.
Lansing, Michigan Office: One Michigan Avenue, Suite 900, 48933-1609.
Telephone: 517-487-2070.
Fax: 517-374-6304.
Monroe, Michigan Office: 214 East Elm Avenue, Suite 100, 48162-2682.
Telephone: 734-243-2000.
Fax: 734-243-0901.
Washington, D.C. Office: 1900 K Street, N.W., Suite 1150. 20006.
Telephone: 202-429-5575; 785-0600.
Fax: 202-331-1118; 785-1234.
Pensacola, Florida Office: 25 West Cedar, 32501.
Telephone: 850-469-1088.
Fax: 850-432-0677.
New York, New York Office: 1450 Broadway, 41st Floor, 10018.
Telephone: 212-704-4400.
Fax: 212-704-4410.
Gdynia, Poland Office: UL. Slaska 21, 81-319.
Telephone: 011-485-831-2808.
Fax: 011-48-58-628 6411.
Warsaw, Poland Office: UL. Nowogrodzkall, 5th Floor, 00-513.
Telephone: 011-4822 529 0200.
Fax: 011-4822 529 0201.
Katowice, Poland Office: UL. Francuska 35/37, 40-027.
Telephone: 011 (48-32) 757-2414.
Fax: 011 (48-32) 757-2483.

PRINCIPALS OF FIRM

Joel L. Piell
Robert E. Gilbert (Ann Arbor Office)
Dennis R. Neiman
William J. Danhof (Lansing Office)
Jerry T. Rupley
Thomas W. Linn
Donald W. Keim
Christopher J. Dembowski (Lansing Office)
Amanda Van Dusen
Cynthia B. Faulhaber (Lansing Office)
Harold W. Bulger, Jr.
Michael P. McGee

OF COUNSEL/SENIOR COUNSEL

Stratton S. Brown
Richard B. Gushée
Robert E. Hammell
Richard I. Lott (Pensacola, Florida Office)

ASSOCIATES

Amy S. Davis
Patrick F. McGow
Thomas D. Colis
Mark K. Schrupp

Representative Firm Clients: Chrysler Corporation; Comerica, Incorporated; City of Detroit, Michigan; Detroit Tigers, Inc.; First of Michigan; Ford Motor Company; Ford Motor Credit Company; Great Lakes Bancorp; Henry Ford Hospital; INVETECH Company.

For Complete List of Firm Personnel, See General Section

For full biographical listings, see the Martindale-Hubbell Law Directory

GROSSE POINTE FARMS, Wayne Co.

JOHN R. AXE AND ASSOCIATES (AV)

Suite 360, 21 Kercheval Avenue, 48236
Telephone: 313-884-1550; 1-800-383-MFCI
Fax: 313-884-0626

ASSOCIATE

Peter S. Ecklund

Reference: National City Bank.

For full biographical listings, see the Martindale-Hubbell Law Directory

LANSING, Ingham Co.

HOWARD & HOWARD ATTORNEYS, P.C. (AV)

The Phoenix Building, Suite 500, 222 Washington Square, North, 48933-1817
Telephone: 517-485-1483
Telecopier: 517-485-1568
Kalamazoo, Michigan Office: The Michigan Building, Suite 200, 100 Portage Street.
Telephone: 616-382-1483.
Telecopier: 616-382-1568.
Bloomfield Hills, Michigan Office: The Pinehurst Office Center, Suite 101, 1400 North Woodward Avenue.
Telephone: 248-645-1483.
Telecopier: 248-645-1568.
Peoria, Illinois Office: One Technology Plaza, Suite 600, 211 Fulton Street.
Telephone: 309-672-1483.
Telecopier: 309-672-1568.

Ann D. Fillingham
Brad S. Rutledge
Gina M. Torielli

Representative Clients: For Representative Client list, see General Practice, Lansing, MI.

For Complete List of Firm Personnel, See General Section

For full biographical listings, see the Martindale-Hubbell Law Directory

MILLER, CANFIELD, PADDOCK AND STONE, P.L.C. (AV)

A Professional Limited Liability Company
Founded in 1852 by Sidney Davy Miller
Suite 900, One Michigan Avenue, 48933-1609
Telephone: 517-487-2070
Fax: 517-374-6304
URL: http://www.millercanfield.com
Detroit, Michigan Office: 150 West Jefferson, Suite 2500, 48226-4415.
Telephone: 313-963-6420.
Fax: 313-496-7500.
Cable Address: "Stem Detroit."
Ann Arbor, Michigan Office: 101 North Main Street, 7th Floor, 48104-1400.
Telephone: 734-663-2445.
Fax: 734-747-7147.
Troy, Michigan Office: 840 West Long Lake Road, Suite 200, 48098.
Telephone: 248-879-2000.
Fax: 248-879-2001.
Grand Rapids, Michigan Office: 99 Monroe, N.W., Suite 1200, 49503-2639.
Telephone: 616-454-8656.
Fax: 616-776-6322.
Howell, Michigan Office: 121 South Barnard Street, Suite 4, 48843-2305.
Telephone: 517-546-7600.
Telecopier: 517-546-6974.
Kalamazoo, Michigan Office: 444 West Michigan Avenue, 49007-3752.
Telephone: 616-381-7030.
Fax: 616-382-0244.
Monroe, Michigan Office: 214 East Elm Avenue, Suite 100, 48162-2682.
Telephone: 734-243-2000.
Fax: 734-243-0901.
Washington, D.C. Office: 1900 K Street, N.W., Suite 1150. 20006.
Telephone: 202-429-5575; 785-0600.
Fax: 202-331-1118; 785-1234.
Pensacola, Florida Office: 25 West Cedar, 32501.
Telephone: 850-469-1088.
Fax: 850-432-0677.
New York, New York Office: 1450 Broadway, 41st Floor, 10018.
Telephone: 212-704-4400.
Fax: 212-704-4410.
Gdynia, Poland Office: UL. Slaska 21, 81-319.
Telephone: 011-485-831-2808.
Fax: 011-48-58-628 6411.
Warsaw, Poland Office: UL. Nowogrodzkall, 5th Floor, 00-513.
Telephone: 011-4822 529 0200.
Fax: 011-4822 529 0201.
Katowice, Poland Office: UL. Francuska 35/37, 40-027.
Telephone: 011 (48-32) 757-2414.
Fax: 011 (48-32) 757-2483.

(See Next Column)

MILLER, CANFIELD, PADDOCK AND STONE P.L.C., *Lansing—Continued*

RESIDENT PRINCIPALS

William J. Danhof
Christopher J. Dembowski
Cynthia B. Faulhaber

Representative Firm Clients: Chrysler Corporation; Comerica, Incorporated; City of Detroit, Michigan; Detroit Tigers, Inc.; First of Michigan; Ford Motor Company; Ford Motor Credit Company; Great Lakes Bancorp; Henry Ford Hospital; INVETECH Company.

For Complete List of Firm Personnel, See General Section

For full biographical listings, see the Martindale-Hubbell Law Directory

NATURAL RESOURCES LAW

ALABAMA

*BIRMINGHAM,** Jefferson Co.

BRADLEY ARANT ROSE & WHITE LLP (AV)

2001 Park Place, Suite 1400, P.O. Box 830709, 35283-0709
Telephone: 205-521-8000
Facsimile: 205-521-8800
Facsimile (SouthTrust Tower Office): 205-521-8500
URL: http://www.barw.com
Huntsville, Alabama Office: 200 Clinton Avenue West, Suite 900, 35801.
Telephone: 205-517-5100.
Facsimile: 205-533-5069.
Washington, D.C. Office: 801 Pennsylvania Avenue, NW, Suite 230, 20004.
Telephone: 202-347-8893.
Facsimile: 202-347-1684.

MEMBER OF FIRM

John E. Hagefstration Jr.

Counsel for: SouthTrust Bank of Alabama, National Association; Energen, Corporation (formerly Alagasco, Inc.); Blount, Inc.; Coca-Cola Bottling Company; United, Inc.; The New York Times Co.; Russell Corp.; Ford Motor Co.; Volkswagen of America, Inc.; Rust International Corp.

For Complete List of Firm Personnel, See General Section

For full biographical listings, see the Martindale-Hubbell Law Directory

GORHAM & WALDREP, P.C. (AV)

2101 6th Avenue North, Suite 700, 35203
Telephone: 205-254-3216; 251-9166
Telecopier: 205-324-3802
Email: info@gorham-waldrep.com *URL:* http://www.gorham-waldrep.com
Montgomery, Alabama Office: 250 Commerce Street, P.O. Box 4837, 36103-4837.
Telephone: 334-262-0777.
Telecopier: 334-262-0742.

John T. Natter — K. Mark Parnell

Representative Clients: Jefferson County Personnel Board; Birmingham-Jefferson Civic Center Authority; The Water Works and Sewer Board of the City of Birmingham; City of Homewood; American Federation of Government Employees Local #1945; City of Pelham; Town of Kimberly; Alabama Tire Dealers Assn.; Southern States Body Shop Assn.

For Complete List of Firm Personnel, See General Section

For full biographical listings, see the Martindale-Hubbell Law Directory

*MOBILE,** Mobile Co.

ARMBRECHT, JACKSON, DEMOUY, CROWE, HOLMES & REEVES, L.L.C. (AV)

1300 Riverview Plaza, P.O. Box 290, 36601
Telephone: 334-405-1300
Facsimile: 334-432-6843; 433-3821
Email: adc@ajlaw.com

MEMBERS OF FIRM

Rae M. Crowe
Conrad P. Armbrecht
David E. Hudgens
Duane A. Graham
James F. Watkins

ASSOCIATE

J. Walton Jackson

Representative Clients: Kimberly-Clark Corp.; UNOCAL; Texaco, Inc.; Mobil Oil Corp.; Pacific Enterprises Oil Co. (USA); Callon Petroleum Co.; BP Exploration, Inc.; Jim Walter Resources, Inc.; Champion International Corp.

For Complete List of Firm Personnel, See General Section

For full biographical listings, see the Martindale-Hubbell Law Directory

JOHNSTONE, ADAMS, BAILEY, GORDON AND HARRIS, L.L.C. (AV)

Royal St. Francis Building, 104 St. Francis Street, 8th Floor, P.O. Box 1988, 36633
Telephone: 334-432-7682
Facsimile: 334-432-0712 or 334-432-2800
Email: attorneys@JohnstoneAdams.com *URL:* http://www.JohnstoneAdams.com
Bay Minette, Alabama Office: Dahlberg Building, 107 Hand Avenue, P.O. Box 729, 36507.
Telephone: 334-937-9473.
Facsimile: 334-937-9475.

(See Next Column)

MEMBERS OF FIRM

Charles B. Bailey, Jr.
Ben H. Harris, Jr.
I. David Cherniak
Alan C. Christian

OF COUNSEL

Brock B. Gordon

For Complete List of Firm Personnel, See General Section

For full biographical listings, see the Martindale-Hubbell Law Directory

LYONS, PIPES & COOK, P.C. (AV)

2 North Royal Street, P.O. Box 2727, 36652-2727
Telephone: 334-432-4481
Cable Address: "Lysea"
Telecopier: 334-433-1820
URL: http://www.LPCLaw.com

Wesley Pipes — Norton W. Brooker, Jr.
Caroline C. McCarthy

Representative Clients: Champion International Corp.; Chevron U.S.A., Inc.; Coastal Corp.; Conoco, Inc.; Shell Oil Co.; Phillips Petroleum Co.; Kerr McGee Corp.; The Nature Conservancy; Atlantic Richfield Co.

For Complete List of Firm Personnel, See General Section

For full biographical listings, see the Martindale-Hubbell Law Directory

ALASKA

*ANCHORAGE,** Third Judicial District

DELANEY, WILES, HAYES, GERETY, ELLIS & YOUNG, INC. (AV)

1007 West Third Avenue, Suite 400, 99501
Telephone: 907-279-3581
Fax: 907-277-1331
Email: dwhge@alaska.net

Stephen M. Ellis — Jeffrey P. Stark

Clyde E. Sniffen, Jr.

Representative Clients: Alyeska Pipeline Service Co.; Arco Alaska Inc.; Bering Straits Native Corporation; Chevron Corporation; Mobil Oil Company; Phillips Petroleum Company; Nana Regional Corporation; Seibu Alaska Inc.

For Complete List of Firm Personnel, See General Section

For full biographical listings, see the Martindale-Hubbell Law Directory

*JUNEAU,** First Judicial District

RUDDY, BRADLEY, KOLKHORST & REGES, A PROFESSIONAL CORPORATION (AV)

Jordan Creek Center, 8800 Glacier Highway, Suite 223, P.O. Box 34338, 99801
Telephone: 907-789-0047
Fax: 907-789-0783
Email: rbklaw@alaska.net *URL:* http://www.alaska.net/~rbklaw/

William G. Ruddy — Robert K. Reges, Jr.

Representative Clients: Silver Bay Logging, Inc.; Southeast Alaska Pot Shrimp Association; State of Alaska.

For full biographical listings, see the Martindale-Hubbell Law Directory

ARIZONA

*PHOENIX,** Maricopa Co.

FENNEMORE CRAIG, A PROFESSIONAL CORPORATION (AV)

3003 North Central Avenue, Suite 2600, 85012-2913
Telephone: 602-916-5000
Fax: 602-916-5999
Tucson, Arizona Office: One South Church Avenue, Suite 1000, 85701-1620.
Telephone: 520-879-6800.
Fax: 520-879-6899.

Calvin H. Udall
James M. Bush
James W. Johnson
Lauren J. Caster
Timothy Berg
Phillip F. Fargotstein
Norman D. James
Margaret R. Gallogly
Robert J. Kramer
John M. Pearce

Jay L. Shapiro
Karen Errant
David M. Call
Lawrence E. Palles (Not admitted in AZ)

(See Next Column)

FENNEMORE CRAIG A PROFESSIONAL CORPORATION, *Phoenix—Continued*

For Complete List of Firm Personnel, See General Section

For full biographical listings, see the Martindale-Hubbell Law Directory

JENNINGS, STROUSS & SALMON, P.L.C. (AV)

A Professional Limited Liability Company
One Renaissance Square, Two North Central Avenue, 85004-2393
Telephone: 602-262-5911
Fax: 602-253-3255
Email: info@jsslaw.com *URL:* http://www.jsslaw.com
Arrowhead Office: 16150 North Arrowhead Fountains Center Drive, Suite 250, Peoria, Arizona.
Telephone: 623-878-2222.
Fax: 623-878-1333.

David J. Calverley
Richard N. Morrison
James M. Ackerman
George Esahak-Gage
Shiela B. Schmidt

ASSOCIATES

Andrew B. Turk
C. David Martinez

For Complete List of Firm Personnel, See General Section

For full biographical listings, see the Martindale-Hubbell Law Directory

MOYES STOREY (AV)

3003 North Central Avenue, Suite 1250, 85012-2915
Telephone: 602-604-2141
Facsimile: 602-274-9135

MEMBERS OF FIRM

Jay I. Moyes
Lee A. Storey
Jeffrey L. Sellers
Jeffrey C. Zimmerman

ASSOCIATE

Adrian Nathan Hansen

For full biographical listings, see the Martindale-Hubbell Law Directory

QUARLES & BRADY LLP (AV)

One Camelback Building, One East Camelback Road, Suite 400, 85012-1649
Telephone: 602-230-5500
Fax: 602-230-5598
URL: http://www.quarles.com
Milwaukee, Wisconsin Office: 411 East Wisconsin Avenue.
Telephone: 414-277-5000.
Fax: 414-271-3552.
Madison, Wisconsin Office: First Wisconsin Plaza, One South Pinckney Street, P.O. Box 2113.
Telephone: 608-251-5000.
Fax: 608-251-9166.
West Palm Beach, Florida Office: 222 Lakeview Avenue, 4th Floor.
Telephone: 407-653-5000.
Fax: 407-653-5333.
Naples, Florida Office: Barnett Center, 4501 Tamiami Trail North, Suite 300.
Telephone: 813-262-5959.
Fax: 813-434-4999.
Chicago, Illinois Office: Quarles & Brady LLC, Citicorp Center, 500 West Madison Street, Suite 3700.
Telephone: 312-715-5000.
Fax: 312-715-5155.

MEMBERS OF THE FIRM

P. Robert Fannin
James D. Vieregg
David G. Beauchamp
Daniel L. Muchow

ASSOCIATE

Jeffrey A. Sandquist

For full biographical listings, see the Martindale-Hubbell Law Directory

SNELL & WILMER L.L.P. (AV)

One Arizona Center, 85004-2202
Telephone: 602-382-6000
Fax: 602-382-6070
Email: postmaster@snellwilmer.com *URL:* http://www.swlaw.com
Tucson, Arizona Office: One South Church Avenue, Suite 1500, 85701-1612.
Telephone: 520-882-1200.
Fax: 520-884-1294.
Orange County Office: 1920 Main Street, Suite 1200, Irvine, California 92614-7230.
Telephone: 949-253-2700.
Fax: 949-955-2507.
Salt Lake City, Utah Office: 111 East Broadway, Suite 900, 84111-1004.
Telephone: 801-237-1900.
Fax: 801-237-1950.

(See Next Column)

MEMBERS OF FIRM

Steven M. Wheeler
Richard W. Shapiro
Carlos D. Ronstadt
Robert B. Hoffman
G. Van Velsor Wolf, Jr.
Jeffrey Webb Crockett

SENIOR ATTORNEY

Thomas L. Mumaw

ASSOCIATES

Robert Henry
Patrick J. Paul

Representative Clients: For list of Representative Clients, see end of biographical listings in the Martindale-Hubbell Law Directory.

For Complete List of Firm Personnel, See General Section

For full biographical listings, see the Martindale-Hubbell Law Directory

ULRICH, KESSLER & ANGER, P.C. (AV)

3707 North Seventh Street, Suite 250, 85014-5059
Telephone: 602-248-9465
Fax: 602-248-0165
Email: ukapc@aol.com

Paul G. Ulrich
Donn G. Kessler
William H. Anger

For full biographical listings, see the Martindale-Hubbell Law Directory

VLASSIS & VLASSIS (AV)

1545 West Thomas Road, 85015
Telephone: 602-248-8811
Fax: 602-274-8983
Email: vlassis@compuserve.com *URL:* http://www.lawyers.com/vlassis&vlassis

George P. Vlassis
Elizabeth D. Vlassis

References: Bank One; First Star Metropolitan Bank & Trust.

For full biographical listings, see the Martindale-Hubbell Law Directory

SCOTTSDALE, Maricopa Co.

SPARKS, TEHAN & RYLEY, P.C. (AV)

7503 First Street, 85251-4573
Telephone: 480-949-1339
Fax: 480-949-7587

Joe P. Sparks
John H. Ryley

References: Bank One, Arizona, Trust Department; Northern Trust Bank of Arizona, N.A.; Wells Fargo Bank of Arizona.

For full biographical listings, see the Martindale-Hubbell Law Directory

*TUCSON,** Pima Co.

CHANDLER, TULLAR, UDALL & REDHAIR, L.L.P. (AV)

1700 Bank of America Plaza, 33 North Stone Avenue, 85701-1415
Telephone: 520-623-4353
Telefax: 520-792-3426

MEMBERS OF FIRM

Thomas Chandler
Steven Weatherspoon
Dwight M. Whitley, Jr.
John J. Brady

ASSOCIATE

Stephen L. Wetherell

Representative Clients: Arizona Electric Power Cooperative, Inc.; Atlantic Richfield Co.; CNA Insurance; Farmers Insurance Exchange; MICA; Chubb Insurance Group; State Farm Mutual Insurance Companies.
Reference: Arizona Bank.

For Complete List of Firm Personnel, See General Section

For full biographical listings, see the Martindale-Hubbell Law Directory

STRICKLAND & STRICKLAND, P.C. (AV)

4400 E. Broadway, Suite 700, 85711-3517
Telephone: 520-795-8727
Fax: 520-795-5649

William E. Strickland
William E. Strickland, Jr.
Robert F. Palmquist

Representative Client: AkChin Indian Community.
Reference: Bank One (formerly Valley National Bank).

ARKANSAS

*TEXARKANA,** Miller Co.

DUNN, NUTTER, MORGAN & SHAW (AV)

State Line Plaza, 6th Floor, P.O. Box 8030, 71854-5945
Telephone: 870-773-5651
Texas Telephone: 903-793-5651
Telecopier: 870-772-2037
Email: lawfirm@dnms.com *URL:* http://www.dnms.com

MEMBERS OF FIRM

Charles A. Morgan
Nelson V. Shaw

OF COUNSEL

Hayes C. McClerkin

LEGAL SUPPORT PERSONNEL

LEGAL ASSISTANTS

Myra Conaway Wells
Sonja L. Oliver

Representative Clients: Reliant Energy Incorporated; Southwest Arkansas Water District; Southwest Arkansas Electric Cooperative Corp.; Red River Commission of Arkansas; Mobil Oil Co.; Oryx Energy Co.; Ethyl Corp.; Miller County Levee District No. 2; Miller County Improvement and Drainage District; Oxy, USA, Inc.

For Complete List of Firm Personnel, See General Section

For full biographical listings, see the Martindale-Hubbell Law Directory

CALIFORNIA

*BAKERSFIELD,** Kern Co.

BORTON, PETRINI & CONRON, LLP (AV)

The Borton, Petrini & Conron Building, 1600 Truxtun Avenue, 93301
Telephone: 661-322-3051
Voice Mail: 661-395-6700
Fax: 661-322-4628
Mailing Address: P.O. Box 2026, Bakersfield, California, 93303
Email: bpcbak@bpclaw.com *URL:* http://www.bpclaw.com
Other City Locations: Fresno, Los Angeles, Modesto, Redding, Sacramento, San Bernardino, San Diego, San Francisco, San Jose, San Luis Obispo, Santa Ana and Ventura.

MEMBER OF FIRM

Calvin R. Stead

ASSOCIATES

Brian Jensen Stowell
Timothy B. Liebaert
Clayton A. Mack
William R. Olson

For Complete List of Firm Personnel, See General Section

For full biographical listings, see the Martindale-Hubbell Law Directory

COSTA MESA, Orange Co.

McCORMICK, KIDMAN & BEHRENS, LLP (AV)

A Partnership of Professional Corporations
Imperial Bank Building, 695 Town Center Drive Suite 1400, 92626-7187
Telephone: 714-755-3100
Fax: 714-755-3110; 1-800-755-3125
Email: mkb1@ix.netcom.com
Sacramento, California Office: 980 Ninth Street. 16th Floor. 95814-2736.
Telephone: 916-449-9533.
Fax: 916-446-7104.
Effective April 1, 1999 the new address will be: Imperial Bank Building, 695 Town Center Drive, Suite 400.

MEMBERS OF FIRM

Homer L. (Mike) McCormick, Jr., (P.C.)
Arthur G. Kidman (P.C.)
Russell G. Behrens (P.C.)
Suzanne M. Tague (P.C.)
Janet R. Morningstar (P.C.)
Keith E. McCullough (P.C.)

ASSOCIATES

David D. Boyer
Paeter E. Garcia
Gary D. Grant
Edward L. Bertrand

For full biographical listings, see the Martindale-Hubbell Law Directory

IRVINE, Orange Co.

LAW OFFICES OF SUSAN M. TRAGER A PROFESSIONAL CORPORATION (AV)

The Landmark Building, 2100 S. E. Main Street, Suite 104, 92614
Telephone: 949-752-8971
Telefax: 949-863-9804
Email: smt@tragerlaw.com

Susan M. Trager

(See Next Column)

OF COUNSEL

Eric S. Norby

Representative Client: San Luis Rey Municipal Water District.
Reference: Sanwa Bank California.

For full biographical listings, see the Martindale-Hubbell Law Directory

*LOS ANGELES,** Los Angeles Co.

DEMETRIOU, DEL GUERCIO, SPRINGER & MOYER, LLP (AV)

801 South Grand Avenue, 10th Floor, 90017
Telephone: 213-624-8407
Telecopy: 213-624-0174
Email: ddsm@juno.com

MEMBERS OF FIRM

Craig A. Moyer
Michael A. Francis
Jennifer T. Taggart

OF COUNSEL

Ronald J. Del Guercio

Reference: Bank of America, L.A. Main Office, Los Angeles, Calif.

For full biographical listings, see the Martindale-Hubbell Law Directory

SAMUEL D. INGHAM, III (AV)

1800 Avenue of the Stars, Suite 1000, 90067-4212
Telephone: 310-556-9751
Fax: 310-556-1311
Email: singham@inghamlaw.com

ASSOCIATE

John E. Rogers, Jr.

For full biographical listings, see the Martindale-Hubbell Law Directory

O'MELVENY & MYERS LLP (AV)

400 South Hope Street, 90071-2899
Telephone: 213-430-6000
Facsimile: 213-430-6407
Cable: MOMS
Telex: 674122
Email: omminfo@omm.com *URL:* http://www.omm.com
Century City, CA Office: 1999 Avenue of the Stars, Los Angeles, 90067-6035.
Telex: 674097. Tel: 310-553-6700.
Fax: 310-246-6779.
Newport Beach, CA Office: 610 Newport Center Drive, 92660-6429.
Telex: 4722088. Tel: 949-760-9600.
Fax: 949-823-6994.
San Francisco, CA Office: Embarcadero Center West, 275 Battery Street, 94111-3305. Tel: 415-984-8700.
Fax: 415-984-8701.
New York, NY Office: Citicorp Center, 153 East 53rd Street, 10022-4611.
Telex: 129165. Tel: 212-326-2000.
Fax: 212-326-2061.
Washington, DC Office: 555 13th Street, N.W., 20004-1109.
Cable: MOMSWSH.
Telex: 89622. Tel: 202-383-5300.
Fax: 202-383-5414.
London Office: O'Melveny & Myers, 3 Finsbury Square, London, EC2A 1LA, England. Tel: 44-171-256-8451. Fax 44-171-638-8205.
Tokyo Office: Akasaka Twin Tower, East 14F, 2-17-23, Akasaka, Minato-ku, Tokyo 107-0052, Japan. Tel: 03-5562-2800.
Fax: 03-5575-3840.
Hong Kong Office: O'Melveny & Myers, Suite 1905, Tower Two, Lippo Centre, 89 Queensway, Central, Hong Kong. Tel: 852-2523-8266.
Fax: 852-2522-1760.
Shanghai Office: Kerry Centre, 20F, 1515 Nanjing Road West, Shanghai, 200040 People's Republic of China. Tel: 86-21-5298-5600.
Fax: 86-21-5298-5500.

PARTNER

Gregory B. Thorpe

For Complete List of Firm Personnel, See General Section

For full biographical listings, see the Martindale-Hubbell Law Directory

RICHMAN, LUNA, KICHAVEN & GLUSHON (AV)

1801 Century Park East, Suite 2400, 90067-2326
Telephone: 310-556-1444
Telecopier: 310-556-0444
URL: http://www.RLKG.com

MEMBERS OF FIRM

James D. Richman
Dennis R. Luna
Jeffrey G. Kichaven
Robert L. Glushon

OF COUNSEL

Hardy L. Thomas
Kurt E. Matthews

References: City National Bank (Beverly Hills, Calif.).

For full biographical listings, see the Martindale-Hubbell Law Directory

NEWPORT BEACH, Orange Co.

MYERS & FLEMING, LLP (AV)
20301 Acacia Street, Suite 150, 92660
Telephone: 949-752-2001
Facsimile: 949-553-1413
Email: myersfleming@ocba.net *URL:* http://www.lawyers.com/myersfleming

Frank B. Myers — Dawn D. Fleming

For full biographical listings, see the Martindale-Hubbell Law Directory

PASADENA, Los Angeles Co.

LAGERLOF, SENECAL, BRADLEY, GOSNEY & KRUSE, LLP (AV)
301 North Lake Avenue, 10th Floor, 91101-4108
Telephone: 626-793-9400
FAX: 626-793-5900
Email: mail@lagerlof.com

MEMBERS OF FIRM

Joseph J. Burris (1913-1980)
Stanley C. Lagerlof (1915-1998)
H. Jess Senecal
Jack T. Swafford
John F. Bradley
Timothy J. Gosney
William F. Kruse
Thomas S. Bunn, III
Andrew D. Turner
Rebecca J. Thyne
James D. Ciampa

ASSOCIATE

Shaun O. Kwon

Representative Clients: Gallo Glass Company; Orthopaedic Hospital; North American Chemical Company; Palmdale Water District; Public Water Agencies Group; Ventura Port District; Walnut Valley Water District; Metric Construction Co., Inc.

For full biographical listings, see the Martindale-Hubbell Law Directory

*SACRAMENTO,** Sacramento Co.

DOWNEY, BRAND, SEYMOUR & ROHWER LLP (AV)
Suite 1050, 555 Capitol Mall, 95814
Telephone: 916-441-0131
FAX: 916-441-4021
Email: downey@dbsr.com *URL:* http://www.dbsr.com

MEMBERS OF FIRM

James M. Day, Jr.
Kevin M. O'Brien
David E. Lindgren
Dan L. Carroll
Steven P. Saxton
Julie A. Carter
Steven H. Goldberg
Katharine E. Wagner
Patrick G. Mitchell
David R.E. Aladjem
Sean B. Murphy
Heather B. Lee
William H. Koch
Jane E. Luckhardt

COUNSEL

Taylor O. Miller

OF COUNSEL

George Basye — Philip A. Stohr

ASSOCIATES

Michael L.F. Buck
Tracy K. Hunckler
Michael N. Mills
Scott L. Shapiro
R. Bruce Steubing
Ann L. Trowbridge
Gwyn-Mohr Tully
Deborah A. Wordham

Counsel for: Las Vegas Valley Water District; East Contra Costa Irrigation District; Enron Oil and Gas Co.; Benton Oil and Gas Co.; Sacramento Municipal Utility District; Reclamation District No. 1000; Amerada Hess; General Motors Corp.; Anheuser-Busch Cos.; Mobil Oil Corp.

For Complete List of Firm Personnel, See General Section

For full biographical listings, see the Martindale-Hubbell Law Directory

GRATTAN & GALATI (AV)
Renaissance Tower, 801 K Street, Penthouse Suite, 95814
Telephone: 916-441-6575
Fax: 916-441-6553
Email: scarey@grattangalati.com *URL:* http://www.lawyers.com/grattan&galati

John P. Grattan, Jr. — Scott A. Galati

LEGAL SUPPORT PERSONNEL

Sandra A. Carey

For full biographical listings, see the Martindale-Hubbell Law Directory

LIVINGSTON & MATTESICH, LAW CORPORATION (AV)
1201 K Street, Suite 1100, 95814
Telephone: 916-442-1111
Fax: 916-448-1709
Email: l&m@lmlaw.net *URL:* http://www.lmlaw.net

(See Next Column)

Gene Livingston
James M. Mattesich
Carol Livingston
Rebecca M. Ceniceros
Emilio E. Varanini, III
Kenneth M. Malovos
Kathleen E. Finnerty
Joanna R. Mendoza

Steven P. Belzer
Jeffrey Leacox
Randy Pollack
Alice H. Choi
Stephen Craig Hunter
Matthew J. Goldman
Joel C. Baiocchi
Baldassaro (Bill) Di Capo
John McKinsey
Timothy E. Naccarato
Craig N. Lundgren
Mary Farrell Taylor
Brian Crone
Gay L. Carroll
Steven G. Churchwell

Representative Clients: NRG Energy, Inc.; Southern Energy, Inc.; Sunlaw Cogeneration Partners; Thermo Ecotek Corporation; Turlock Irrigation District.

For full biographical listings, see the Martindale-Hubbell Law Directory

*SANTA BARBARA,** Santa Barbara Co.

HOLLISTER & BRACE, A PROFESSIONAL CORPORATION (AV)
1126 Santa Barbara Street, P.O. Box 630, 93101
Telephone: 805-963-6711
Fax: 805-965-0329
Email: hblaw@hbsb.com

William A. Brace (Retired)
J. James Hollister, III (Retired)
John S. Poucher
Richard C. Monk
George A. Rempe, III
Steven Evans Kirby
Bradford F. Ginder
John G. Busby
Susan H. McCollum
Robert L. Brace
Marcus Scott Bird
Charles W. Willey (P.C.)
Alexis W. Willey
Peter L. Candy

Attorneys For: Western States Petroleum Assoc.; California Independent Petroleum Assoc.; Venoco, Inc.; Vintage Petroleum, Inc.; Torch Energy Advisors; Mobil Oil Corp.; Occidental Petroleum Corp.

For full biographical listings, see the Martindale-Hubbell Law Directory

COLORADO

*ASPEN,** Pitkin Co.

PATRICK & STOWELL, P.C. (AV)
730 East Durant Street, Suite 200, 81611
Telephone: 970-920-1028
Fax: 970-925-6847
Email: info@waterlaw.com *URL:* http://www.waterlaw.com

Kevin L. Patrick — Brian L. Stowell

Scott Carpenter Miller
Kristin L. Howse
Ramsey L. Kropf

Representative Clients: Aspcol Corp., N.V.; McCloskey Enterprises, Inc.; Snowmass Land Co., a joint venture of Heitman Financial, Ltd. and Golub & Co.; Aspen Highlands Ski Area/Hines Highlands Limited Partnership; Dallas Creek Water Co.; Fairway Pines Estates Golf Club/Loghill Village Investors, Ltd.; Telluride Regional Airport Authority; Town of Gypsum; B.C. Ziegler & Company.

For full biographical listings, see the Martindale-Hubbell Law Directory

*BOULDER,** Boulder Co.

JOSEPH ADAMS COPE (AV)
4750 Table Mesa Drive, 80303-5575
Telephone: 303-494-3000
Fax: 303-494-6309
Email: jay@Frascona.com *URL:* http://www.Frascona.com
(Also Of Counsel to Frascona, Joiner and Goodman)

For full biographical listings, see the Martindale-Hubbell Law Directory

VRANESH AND RAISCH, L.L.P. (AV)
1720 14th Street, Suite 200, P.O. Box 871, 80306-0871
Telephone: 303-443-6151
Telecopier: 303-443-9586
Email: attorneys@vraneshraisch.com

MEMBERS OF FIRM

Jerry W. Raisch
John R. Henderson
Michael D. Shimmin
Eugene J. Riordan
Paul J. Zilis
George Vranesh (1926-1997)

Richard Woodruff Curran

(See Next Column)

VRANESH AND RAISCH L.L.P.—*Continued*

OF COUNSEL

Asimakis (Maki) P. Iatridis

Representative Clients: Cyprus Climax Metals Co.; City of Fort Collins; Colorado Association of Commerce and Industry; County of Arapahoe; Eastman Kodak Company; Hendricks Mining Company; Independence Mining Co.; Metro Wastewater Reclamation District; Waste Management of North America.

For full biographical listings, see the Martindale-Hubbell Law Directory

*DENVER,** Denver Co.

ALFERS & CARVER, LLC (AV)

Equitable Building, 730 17th Street, Suite 340, 80202
Telephone: 303-592-7674
Fax: 303-592-7680
Email: ccarver@alfers-carver.com

Stephen D. Alfers
Craig R. Carver
Bruce C. Kirchhoff
Don H. Sherwood

ASSOCIATE

Michelle C. Carmody

For full biographical listings, see the Martindale-Hubbell Law Directory

BALLARD SPAHR ANDREWS & INGERSOLL, LLP (AV)

Seventeenth Street Plaza Building, Suite 2300, 1225 17th Street, 80202-5596
Telephone: 303-292-2400
Fax: 303-296-3956
URL: http://www.ballardspahr.com
Baltimore, Maryland Office: 300 East Lombard Street. 19th Floor.
Telephone: 410-528-5600.
Fax: 410-528-5650.
Camden, New Jersey Office: 800 Hudson Square, 5th Floor.
Telephone: 856-541-5577.
Fax: 856-541-8272.
Philadelphia, Pennsylvania Office: 1735 Market Street, 51st Floor.
Telephone: 215-665-8500.
Fax: 215-864-8999.
Salt Lake City, Utah Office: One Utah Center, Suite 1200, 201 South Main Street.
Telephone: 801-531-3000.
Fax: 801-531-3001.
Voorhees, New Jersey Office: Suite 100, 1101 Laurel Oak Drive.
Telephone: 856-627-8555.
Fax: 856-627-1153.
Washington, D.C. Office: Suite 1000 South, 601 13th Street, N.W.
Telephone: 202-661-2200.
Fax: 202-661-2299.

Elizabeth H. Temkin

Kristin M. Tita

For Complete List of Firm Personnel, See General Section

For full biographical listings, see the Martindale-Hubbell Law Directory

DUFFORD & BROWN, P.C. (AV)

1700 Broadway, Suite 1700, 80290-1701
Telephone: 303-861-8013
Facsimile: 303-832-3804
Colorado Springs, Colorado Office: 101 N. Tejon, Suite 410.
Telephone: 719-471-0559.
Facsimile: 719-471-0583.
Affiliated Office: Solomon, Pearl, Blum & Quinn, L.L.P., New York, NY and Denver, Colorado.

Philip G. Dufford
William C. Robb
Richard L. Fanyo
Jack F. Ross
Eugene F. Megyesy, Jr.

Joanne Herlihy

OF COUNSEL

Morris B. Hecox, Jr.

Representative Clients: Asarco, Inc.; BHP-Minerals, Inc.; CF&I Steel L.P.; Chevron Shale Oil Company; Coors Brewing Company; Cortez Pipeline Company; Cypress Climax Metals Co.; Denver Water Department; Echo Bay Mines, Ltd.-Sunnyside Gold Co.; Energy Fuels Coal, Inc.; Equitable Resources Energy Company (Balcron Oil Division); Howell Petroleum Company; McMurray Oil Company; Powderhorn Coal Co.

For Complete List of Firm Personnel, See General Section

For full biographical listings, see the Martindale-Hubbell Law Directory

FRIEDLOB SANDERSON RASKIN PAULSON & TOURTILLOTT, LLC (AV)

1400 Glenarm Place, 80202-5099
Telephone: 303-571-1400
Fax: 303-595-3159; 303-595-3970; 303-615-5472
Englewood, Colorado Office: 8400 East Prentice Avenue, 80111-2918.
Telephone: 303-571-1400.
Santa Cruz, California Office: 519 Seabright Avenue, Suite 208, 95062-3482.
Telephone: 813-460-3966.
Fax: 813-460-3968.

James W. Sanderson
Christopher R. Paulson
W. B. Tourtillott
Paul M. Seby
Brian M. Nazarenus

Carolyn Burr
Matthew G. Paulson

For full biographical listings, see the Martindale-Hubbell Law Directory

GORSUCH KIRGIS LLP (AV)

Tower 1, Suite 1000, 1515 Arapahoe Street, 80202
Telephone: 303-376-5000
Fax: 303-376-5001

PARTNERS

G. Donohue Kane
William A. Keefe

For full biographical listings, see the Martindale-Hubbell Law Directory

HOLLY I. HOLDER, P.C. (AV)

518 Seventeenth Street Suite 1500, 80202
Telephone: 303-534-3636
Fax: 303-534-6905
Email: holderpc@aol.com

Holly I. Holder

Priscilla S. Fulmer
Carmen Sower Hall

LEGAL SUPPORT PERSONNEL

Gary J. Crosby (Paralegal)
Dean C. Stalnaker (Paralegal)

For full biographical listings, see the Martindale-Hubbell Law Directory

HOLME ROBERTS & OWEN LLP (AV)

Suite 4100, 1700 Lincoln, 80203
Telephone: 303-861-7000
Telecopier: 303-866-0200
Email: hro@hro.com *URL:* http://www.hro.com
Boulder, Colorado Office: Suite 400, 1401 Pearl Street.
Telephone: 303-444-5955.
Telecopier: 303-444-1063.
Colorado Springs, Colorado Office: Suite 1300, 90 South Cascade Avenue.
Telephone: 719-473-3800.
Telecopier: 719-633-1518.
Salt Lake City, Utah Office: Suite 1100, 111 East Broadway.
Telephone: 801-521-5800.
Telecopier: 801-521-9639.
London, England Office: Heathcoat House, 3rd Floor, 20 Savile Row.
Telephone: 011-44-171-494-5600.
Telecopier: 011-44-171-287-9344.

PARTNERS OF FIRM

Phillip R. Clark
Thomas F. Cope
James F. Cress
Frank Erisman
Lynn Parker Hendrix
Paul D. Holleman
Steven B. Richardson
Martha Traudt Collins Rolle (London, England Office)
Jan N. Steiert

OF COUNSEL

Kay M. Small (Boulder Office)
Ted P. Stockmar

ASSOCIATES

Peter O. Hansen
Ann E. Lane
E. Blaine Rawson (Salt Lake City Office)
John M. Stafford

For Complete List of Firm Personnel, See General Section

For full biographical listings, see the Martindale-Hubbell Law Directory

LOHF, SHAIMAN & JACOBS, P.C. (AV)

950 South Cherry Street, Suite 900, 80246-2666
Telephone: 303-753-9000
Telecopier: 303-753-9997

David G. Ebner
J. Michael Morgan

Reference: Vectra Bank Colorado.

For full biographical listings, see the Martindale-Hubbell Law Directory

Denver—Continued

POULSON, ODELL & PETERSON, LLC (AV)

Suite 1400, 1775 Sherman Street, 80203
Telephone: 303-861-4400
Telecopier: 303-861-1225
Email: popllc@popllc.com

William G. Odell
C. M. (Pete) Peterson (Retired)
Randall M. Case
Stephen M. Thompson
Carleton L. Ekberg
Alan B. Cameron

OF COUNSEL

Robert D. Poulson
Arthur Thad Smith
Robert D. Buettner
James W. Campbell (Retired)

William F. Leonard
Scott M. Campbell
Anne A. DeWitt
Emily R. Suyat
Rebecca N. Welborn

Representative Clients: Apache Corporation; Anadarko Petroleum Corp.; Burlington Resources Oil & Gas Co.; Conoco, Inc.; Enron Oil and Gas Co.; Exxon Co., USA; Fort Collins Consolidated Royalties, Inc.; KCS Mountain Resources, Inc.; Mobil Oil Corp.; Samedan Oil Corp.

For full biographical listings, see the Martindale-Hubbell Law Directory

ROOT & SCHINDLER, P.C. (AV)

410 17th Street, Suite 460, 80202
Telephone: 303-572-1235
Fax: 303-572-1256
Email: rootschi@ix.netcom.com

Thomas E. Root
Ronald I. Schindler

For full biographical listings, see the Martindale-Hubbell Law Directory

SHERMAN & HOWARD L.L.C. (AV)

Attorneys and Counselors at Law
633 Seventeenth Street, Suite 3000, 80202
Telephone: 303-297-2900
Telecopier: 303-298-0940
Colorado Springs, Colorado Office: Suite 1500, 90 South Cascade Avenue, 80903.
Telephone: 719-475-2440.
Las Vegas, Nevada Office: Swendseid & Stern, a member in Sherman & Howard L.L.C., 317 Sixth Street, 89101.
Telephone: 702-387-6073.
Reno, Nevada Office: Swendseid & Stern, a member in Sherman & Howard L.L.C., 50 West Liberty Street, Suite 660, 89501.
Telephone: 702-323-1980.

Ronald M. Eddy
Robert A. Hykan

COUNSEL

Gary L. Greer

Representative Clients: BACE Industries, LLC; Flatiron Structures Co. LLC; Hanifen, Imhoff Inc.; Hathaway Corp.; J.D. Edwards & Co.; Newmont Gold Company; Public Employees' Retirement Assn.; Tele-Communications, Inc.; United Artists Theatre Circuit, Inc.; U.S. West Communications, Inc.

For Complete List of Firm Personnel, See General Section

For full biographical listings, see the Martindale-Hubbell Law Directory

VRANESH AND RAISCH, L.L.P.

(See Boulder)

LOUISVILLE, Boulder Co.

STEPHEN T. WILLIAMSON (AV)

813 Main, P.O. Box 850, 80027
Telephone: 303-666-4060
Fax: 303-666-4426
Email: louislaw@mindspring.com

Stephen T. Williamson

ASSOCIATE

Alan G. Hill

For full biographical listings, see the Martindale-Hubbell Law Directory

DISTRICT OF COLUMBIA

WASHINGTON, D.C. Co.

BAKER BOTTS L.L.P. (AV)

A Registered Limited Liability Partnership
The Warner, 1299 Pennsylvania Avenue, N.W., 20004-2400
Telephone: 202-639-7700
Fax: 202-639-7832
Email: postmaster@bakerbotts.com *URL:* http://www.bakerbotts.com
Houston, Texas Office: One Shell Plaza, 910 Louisiana.
Telephone: 713-229-1234.
Austin, Texas Office: 1600 San Jacinto Center, 98 San Jacinto Boulevard.
Telephone: 512-322-2500.
Dallas, Texas Office: 2001 Ross Avenue.
Telephone: 214-953-6500.
New York, New York Office: 599 Lexington Avenue.
Telephone: 212-705-5000.
Moscow, Russia Office: 10 ul. Bolshaya Dimitrovka (formerly Pushkinskaya), 103031.
Telephone: 7095/921-5300 (Local); 7501/929-7070 (International).
London, England Office: 45 Ludgate Hill.
Telephone: 0171-778-1400 (Local); 011-44-171-778-1400 (International).
Baku, Azerbaijan Office: 6-10 Vagif Mustafa-zadeh Street, Third Floor, Icheri Sheher, 370004.
Telephone: 994-12-97-63-88 (Local); 011-994-12-97-63-88 (International).

MEMBERS OF FIRM

J. Patrick Berry
William M. Bumpers
Thomas J. Eastment
Steven R. Hunsicker
Bruce F. Kiely
Mark K. Lewis
Randolph Quaile McManus

SPECIAL COUNSEL

Debra Raggio Bolton

ASSOCIATES

Joshua B. Frank
Debra J. Jezouit
Clara M. Poffenberger
Mary Ann Poirier

For Complete List of Firm Personnel, See General Section

For full biographical listings, see the Martindale-Hubbell Law Directory

BRICKFIELD, BURCHETTE & RITTS, P.C. (AV)

8th Floor, West Tower, 1025 Thomas Jefferson Street, N.W., 20007-0805
Telephone: 202-342-0800
Fax: 202-342-0807
Austin, Texas Office: Suite 1050, 1005 Congress Avenue.
Telephone: 512-472-1081.

James W. Brew
Peter J. P. Brickfield
William H. Burchette
Mark C. Davis (Not admitted in DC; Resident, Austin, Texas Office)
Michael E. Kaufmann
Peter J. Mattheis
Michael N. McCarty
Frederick H. Ritts
Fernando Rodriguez (Resident, Austin, Texas Office)
A. Hewitt Rose
Christine C. Ryan
Garrett A. Stone
Damon E. Xenopoulos

OF COUNSEL

Stephen J. Karina (Not admitted in DC)

Eric M. Devito (Not admitted in DC)
Matthew J. Jones (Not admitted in DC)
Kathleen T. Mulville (Not admitted in DC)
Frederick D. Ochsenhirt (Not admitted in DC)
Melissa Salhab (Resident, Austin, Texas Office)

For full biographical listings, see the Martindale-Hubbell Law Directory

BRUNENKANT & HASKELL, LLP (AV)

805 15th Street, N.W., Suite 1101, 20005
Telephone: 202-408-0700
Fax: 202-408-5959
Email: brunenkant@bh-law.com

Jon L. Brunenkant
Mark R. Haskell
James W. Moeller

ASSOCIATES

Cheryl J. Walker
Melissa L. Lauderdale
Christie L. Richart (Not admitted in DC)

For full biographical listings, see the Martindale-Hubbell Law Directory

Washington—Continued

COHEN, MILSTEIN, HAUSFELD & TOLL, P.L.L.C. (AV)

West Tower, Suite 500, 1100 New York Avenue, N.W., 20005-3964
Telephone: 202-408-4600
Facsimile: 202-408-4699
Email: lawinfo@cmht.com *URL:* http://www.CMHT.com
Seattle, Washington Office: 999 Third Avenue, Suite 3600.
Telephone: 206-521-0080.
Facsimile: 206-521-0166.

MEMBERS OF FIRM

Jerry S. Cohen (1925-1995)
Herbert E. Milstein
Michael D. Hausfeld
Steven J. Toll (Resident, Seattle, Washington Office)
Ann C. Yahner
Lisa M. Mezzetti
Andrew N. Friedman
Richard S. Lewis
Daniel S. Sommers
Daniel A. Small
Gary E. Mason
Joseph M. Sellers
Sharon A. Snyder
Mark S. Willis (Not admitted in DC)

ASSOCIATES

Lori G. Feldman (Resident, Seattle, Washington Office)
Paul T. Gallagher
Christine E. Webber
Alexander E. Barnett
Matthew James Ide (Resident, Seattle, Washington Office)
Matthew F. Pawa
Suzette M. Malveaux
Mary N. Strimel
Kristopher A. Kinkade (Resident, Seattle, Washington Office)
Agnieszka M. Fryszman
Deborah J. Vagins
Ari Karen
Charles E. Tompkins
Tamara J. Driscoll (Resident, Seattle, Washington Office)
Elizabeth Haines Cronise
Donna Solen
Lesli C. Esposito (Not admitted in DC)

OF COUNSEL

Margaret G. Farrell

For full biographical listings, see the Martindale-Hubbell Law Directory

CUTLER & STANFIELD, L.L.P. (AV)

700 Fourteenth Street, N.W. 10th Floor, 20005-2014
Telephone: 202-624-8400
Fax: 202-624-8410
Denver, Colorado Office: 1675 Broadway, 80202.
Telephone: 303-825-7000.
FAX: 303-825-7005.

MEMBERS OF FIRM

Eliot R. Cutler
Jeffrey L. Stanfield
Sheila D. Jones
Perry M. Rosen
Peter J. Kirsch
Barry Conaty
Stephen H. Kaplan (Not admitted in DC)
Sarah M. Rockwell (Not admitted in DC)
Thomas D. Roth

OF COUNSEL

Byron Keith Huffman, Jr.

ASSOCIATES

Katherine Boonin Andrus
Joel D. Armstrong (Not admitted in DC)
Françoise M. Carrier
Polly B. Jessen (Not admitted in DC)
William G. Malley
Elizabeth A. Mitchell (Resident at Denver, Colorado Office)
Dana C. Nifosi
W. Eric Pilsk
Timothy A. Pohle
John E. Putnam
Daniel S. Reimer (Not admitted in DC)
Andrew T. Swers
Sara E. Wilensky

For full biographical listings, see the Martindale-Hubbell Law Directory

FRANK W. FRISK, JR., P.C. (AV)

Suite 125, Canal Square, 1054 Thirty-First Street, N.W., 20007
Telephone: 202-333-8433
Fax: 202-333-8431
Email: ffrisk@gslink.com

Frank W. Frisk, Jr.

For full biographical listings, see the Martindale-Hubbell Law Directory

VENABLE ATTORNEYS AT LAW VENABLE, BAETJER, HOWARD & CIVILETTI, LLP (AV)

A Partnership including Professional Corporations
Suite 1000, 1201 New York Avenue, N.W., 20005
Telephone: 202-962-4800
Fax: 202-962-8300
URL: http://www.venable.com
Baltimore, Maryland Office: Venable, Baetjer and Howard LLP, 1800 Mercantile Bank & Trust Building, 2 Hopkins Plaza.
Telephone: 410-244-7400.
Fax: 410-244-7742.

(See Next Column)

McLean, Virginia Office: Venable, Baetjer and Howard LLP, Suite 400, 2010 Corporate Ridge.
Telephone: 703-760-1600.
Fax: 703-821-8949.
Rockville, Maryland Office: Venable, Baetjer and Howard LLP, Suite 500, One Church Street, P. O. Box 1906.
Telephone: 301-217-5600.
Fax: 301-217-5617.
Towson, Maryland Office: Venable, Baetjer and Howard LLP, 210 Allegheny Avenue, P. O. Box 5517.
Telephone: 410-494-6200.
Fax: 410-821-0147.

MEMBERS OF FIRM

James K. Archibald (Also at Baltimore, Maryland Office)
Joseph G. Block
Anthony M. Carey (Not admitted in DC; Also at Baltimore, Maryland Office)
Benjamin R. Civiletti (P.C.) (Also at Baltimore and Towson, Maryland Offices)
John F. Cooney
Jeffrey A. Dunn (Also at Baltimore, Maryland Office)
Thomas J. Kelly, Jr.
John J. Pavlick, Jr.
Michael Schatzow (Also at Baltimore, Maryland Office)
James L. Shea (also at Baltimore, Maryland Office)
Judson W. Starr (Also at Baltimore and Towson, Maryland Offices)

ASSOCIATE

Gregory S. Braker

For Complete List of Firm Personnel, See General Section

For full biographical listings, see the Martindale-Hubbell Law Directory

FLORIDA

*MIAMI,** Dade Co.

EARL, BLANK, KAVANAUGH & STOTTS, PROFESSIONAL ASSOCIATION (AV)

Suite 3760, One Biscayne Tower, Two South Biscayne Boulevard, 33131
Telephone: 305-358-3000
FAX: 305-358-5079
Email: ebkslaw.com *URL:* http://www.ebkslaw.com

William L. Earl
Robert H. Blank
Judith Smith Kavanaugh
Dennis M. Stotts
Stephen R. Verbit

Reference: NationsBank, N.A.

For full biographical listings, see the Martindale-Hubbell Law Directory

JOSEPH Z. FLEMING, P.A.

(See Ford & Harrison LLP, Miami, Florida)

*SARASOTA,** Sarasota Co.

EARL, BLANK, KAVANAUGH & STOTTS, PROFESSIONAL ASSOCIATION

(See Miami)

IDAHO

*BOISE,** Ada Co.

EBERLE, BERLIN, KADING, TURNBOW & MCKLVEEN, CHARTERED (AV)

Capitol Park Plaza, 300 North Sixth Street, P.O. Box 1368, 83701-1368
Telephone: 208-344-8535
Facsimile: 208-344-8542

William J. McKlveen

Representative Clients: Intermountain Orient; Ox Ranch.

For Complete List of Firm Personnel, See General Section

For full biographical listings, see the Martindale-Hubbell Law Directory

ELAM & BURKE, A PROFESSIONAL ASSOCIATION (AV)

Key Financial Center, 702 West Idaho Street, P.O. Box 1539, 83701
Telephone: 208-343-5454
Telecopier: 208-384-5844
Email: eblaw@elamburke.com

Carl P. Burke
John Magel
Scott L. Campbell

(See Next Column)

ELAM & BURKE A PROFESSIONAL ASSOCIATION, *Boise—Continued*

Angela D. Schaer

Representative Clients: Morrison-Knudsen, Inc.; Texas Instruments, Inc.; Pechiney Corp.; Dow Corning Corporation; State Farm Insurance Cos.; Sinclair Oil Co. d/b/a Sun Valley Co.; Farmers Insurance Group; MK Gold Co.; Thompson Creek Mining Company.

For Complete List of Firm Personnel, See General Section

For full biographical listings, see the Martindale-Hubbell Law Directory

KETCHUM, Blaine Co.

JAMES L. KENNEDY, JR. (AV)

340 Second Street East, P.O. Box 2165, 83340
Telephone: 208-726-8255
Fax: 208-726-4886

Reference: First Interstate Bank of Idaho, N.A. (Ketchum-Sun Valley Branch); First Security Bank of Idaho, N.A. (Ketchum Branch)

For full biographical listings, see the Martindale-Hubbell Law Directory

ILLINOIS

MATTOON, Coles Co.

CRAIG & CRAIG (AV)

1807 Broadway, P.O. Box 689, 61938-0689
Telephone: 217-234-6481
Telecopier: 217-234-6486; 258-8292
Email: craiglaw@advant.com
Mount Vernon, Illinois Office: 115 North 7th Street.
Telephone: 618-244-7511.

MEMBERS OF FIRM

Craig Van Meter (1895-1981)
Fred H. Kelly (1894-1971)
Robert M. Werden (1908-1969)
George N. Gilkerson (1911-1985)
John P. Ewart
Richard F. Record, Jr.
Stephen L. Corn
Robert G. Grierson
Gregory C. Ray
Paul R. Lynch (Resident, Mount Vernon Office)
Kenneth F. Werts (Resident, Mount Vernon Office)
John L. Barger

ASSOCIATES

Kathleen M. Stockwell
Kristine M. Tuttle
Julie A. Webb (Resident, Mount Vernon Office)
John M. O'Driscoll
Duane A. Deters
Katy C. Fain (Resident, Mount Vernon Office)
Erin E. Wisner
John F. Watson

OF COUNSEL

Jack E. Horsley

Representative Clients: Freeman United Coal Mining Co.; Natural Gas Pipeline Company of America; Marathon Oil Company; Illinois Central R.R. Co.; Consolidated Communications Inc.; Lake Land College; Scattering Fork Drainage District of Douglas County, Illinois.

For full biographical listings, see the Martindale-Hubbell Law Directory

INDIANA

*INDIANAPOLIS,** Marion Co.

ICE MILLER DONADIO & RYAN (AV)

One American Square Box 82001, 46282-0002
Telephone: 317-236-2100
Fax: 317-236-2219
Email: info@imdr.com *URL:* http://www.imdr.com
South Bend, Indiana Office: 211 West Washington Street, Suite 2420.
Telephone: 219-234-7933.
Fax: 219-234-7965. Internet E-mail: info@imdr.com. Web Site Address: http://www.imdr.com.
Chicago, Illinois Office: 135 South LaSalle Street, Suite 4100.
Telephone: 312-726-1567.
Fax: 312-641-6263. Internet E-mail: info@imdr.com. Web Site Address: http://www.imdr.com.

MEMBERS OF FIRM

G. Daniel Kelley, Jr.
Phillip L. Bayt

For Complete List of Firm Personnel, See General Section

For full biographical listings, see the Martindale-Hubbell Law Directory

TABBERT HAHN EARNEST & WEDDLE (AV)

Suite 2100, One Indiana Square, 46204-2101
Telephone: 317-639-5444
Fax: 317-639-5232
Email: jtyrrell@tabberthahn.com *URL:* http://www.tabberthahn.com

Mark K. Sullivan
William W. Mathews

For full biographical listings, see the Martindale-Hubbell Law Directory

*MT. VERNON,** Posey Co.

HAWLEY, HUDSON & HAWLEY (AV)

309 Main Street, P.O. Box 716, 47620
Telephone: 812-838-4495
Fax: 812-838-9445
Email: HHHLAWFIRM@MSN.COM

MEMBERS OF FIRM

K. Richard Hawley
Henry C. Hudson
Marc E. Hawley

Representative Clients: Sohio Supply Co.; Farm Bureau Oil Co.; Wade Oil Corp.; Conyers Oil Service, Inc.; Coy Oil, Inc.; Trey Exploration, Inc.; Jarvis Drilling, Inc.; K.C. Oil Corp.; Ecus Corp.; Quinn Energy Corp.

For full biographical listings, see the Martindale-Hubbell Law Directory

*PRINCETON,** Gibson Co.

HALL, PARTENHEIMER & KINKLE (AV)

219 North Hart Street, P.O. Box 13, 47670
Telephone: 812-386-0050
FAX: 812-385-2575
Email: hpk@hpk-law.com

MEMBERS OF FIRM

Verner P. Partenheimer
J. Robert Kinkle
R. Scott Partenheimer

Representative Clients: Interlake Inc.; Civitas National Bank; East Gibson School Corporation; Union Planters National Bank; United Federal Savings Bank; Amax Minerals.
Approved Attorneys for: Lawyers Title Insurance; National Attorneys Title Fund and Stewart Title.

For full biographical listings, see the Martindale-Hubbell Law Directory

KANSAS

*WICHITA,** Sedgwick Co.

DEPEW AND GILLEN, L.L.C. (AV)

151 North Main, Suite 800, 67202-1409
Telephone: 316-262-4000
Facsimile: 316-265-3819
Email: DG@DEPEWGILLEN.COM *URL:* HTTP://WWW.DEPEWGILLEN.COM

Spencer L. Depew
David W. Nickel

For Complete List of Firm Personnel, See General Section

For full biographical listings, see the Martindale-Hubbell Law Directory

FOULSTON & SIEFKIN L.L.P. (AV)

700 NationsBank Financial Center, 67202
Telephone: 316-267-6371
Facsimile: 316-267-6345
URL: http://www.foulston.com
Topeka, Kansas Office: 1515 NationsBank Tower, 534 Kansas Avenue, 66603.
Telephone: 785-233-3600.
Fax: 785-233-1610.
Dodge City, Kansas Office: 810 Frontview, P.O. Box 1147, 67801.
Telephone: 316-227-8126.
Fax: 316-227-8451.
Member: Lex Mundi, The World's Leading Association of Independent Law Firms.

MEMBERS OF FIRM

Charles J. Woodin
Jim H. Goering

For Complete List of Firm Personnel, See General Section

For full biographical listings, see the Martindale-Hubbell Law Directory

KAHRS, NELSON, FANNING, HITE & KELLOGG L.L.P. (AV)

200 W. Douglas, Suite 600, 67202
Telephone: 316-265-7761
Telecopier: 316-267-7803
URL: http://www.kahrsnelson.com

(See Next Column)

KAHRS, NELSON, FANNING, HITE & KELLOGG L.L.P.—*Continued*

MEMBERS OF FIRM

Richard C. Hite
Steven D. Gough
John G. Pike
Dennis V. Lacey
Donald N. Peterson, II

Representative Clients: Amoco Production Co.; Coastal Oil & Gas Corp.; Enron Oil & Gas Corp.; J.M. Huber Corp.; Marathon Oil Co.; Peoples Natural Gas Co.

For Complete List of Firm Personnel, See General Section

For full biographical listings, see the Martindale-Hubbell Law Directory

MORRIS, LAING, EVANS, BROCK & KENNEDY, CHARTERED (AV)

Fourth Floor, 200 West Douglas, 67202-3084
Telephone: 316-262-2671
Fax: 316-262-6226; 262-5991
Topeka, Kansas Office: 800 S.W. Jackson, Suite 914, 66612-2214.
Telephone: 913-232-2662.
Fax: 913-232-9983.

Ralph R. Brock
Joseph W. Kennedy
A. J. Schwartz, Jr.
Donald E. Schrag
Susan R. Schrag
Robert E. Nugent
Michael Lennen
Karl R. Swartz

References: The Emprise Banks of Kansas; Mercantile Bank of Topeka; Southwest National Bank; Twin Lakes National Bank.

For Complete List of Firm Personnel, See General Section

For full biographical listings, see the Martindale-Hubbell Law Directory

YOUNG, BOGLE, McCAUSLAND, WELLS & BLANCHARD, P.A. (AV)

106 West Douglas, Suite 923, 67202
Telephone: 316-265-7841
Facsimile: 316-265-3956
Email: ybmwblaw@aol.com

Glenn D. Young, Jr.
Paul S. McCausland

Representative Clients: Bridgestone/Firestone Inc.; Deere & Co.; Citibank; Metropolitan Life Insurance Co.; Equitable Life Assurance Society of the United States; New York Life Insurance Co.

For Complete List of Firm Personnel, See General Section

For full biographical listings, see the Martindale-Hubbell Law Directory

KENTUCKY

*HAZARD,** Perry Co.

GULLETT, COMBS, REED & BOWLING (AV)

109 Broadway, Second Floor, P.O. Box 1039, 41702-1039
Telephone: 606-439-1373; 1-800-949-8812
Fax: 606-439-4450
Email: apgullet@mis.net
Email: 1234rong@tgtel.com

MEMBERS OF FIRM

Asa P. Gullett, III
Ronald G. Combs
Teresa G. Combs Reed
Matthew Lawton Bowling

ASSOCIATE

Jameson D. Combs

LEGAL SUPPORT PERSONNEL

Jacqueline E. Goodin
Jimmie Lynn Jones

Reference: Peoples Bank and Trust Co.

For full biographical listings, see the Martindale-Hubbell Law Directory

*LEXINGTON,** Fayette Co.

STITES & HARBISON (AV)

Formerly Stites, McElwain & Fowler and Harbison, Kessinger, Lisle & Bush
250 West Main Street, Suite 2300, 40507-1758
Telephone: 606-226-2300
Fax: 606-253-9144
Louisville, Kentucky Office: 400 West Market Street, Suite 1800.
Telephone: 502-587-3400.
Fax: 502-587-6391.
Frankfort, Kentucky Office: 421 West Main Street.
Telephone: 502-223-3477.
Fax: 502-223-4124. Hyden, Kentucky Office: 21976 Main Street, Farmer Campbell Building, Second Floor.
Telephone: 606-672-4200.
Fax: 606-672-4100.

(See Next Column)

Jeffersonville, Indiana Office: 323 East Court Avenue.
Telephone: 812-282-7566.
Fax: 812-284-5519.
Atlanta, Georgia Office: 3350 Cumberland Circle, Suite 1700 Riverwood.
Telephone: 770-850-7000.
Fax: 770-850-7070.
Washington, D.C. Office: 1200 G Street, N.W., Suite 800.

MEMBERS OF FIRM

Thomas E. Meng
Laura D. Keller

COUNSEL

Calvert T. Roszell

For Complete List of Firm Personnel, See General Section

For full biographical listings, see the Martindale-Hubbell Law Directory

STOLL, KEENON & PARK, LLP (AV)

201 E. Main Street, Suite 1000, 40507-1380
Telephone: 606-231-3000
Telecopier: 606-253-1093; 606-253-1027
URL: http://www.skp.com
Frankfort, Kentucky Office: 307 Washington Street, 40601.
Telephone: 502-875-6220.
Telecopier: 502-875-6235.
Henderson, Kentucky Office: 201 C North Main Street, 42420-3103.
Telephone: 270-831-1900.
Telecopier: 270-827-4060.
Louisville, Kentucky Office: 400 West Market Street, Suite 2650, 40202-3377.
Telephone: 502-568-9100.
Telecopier: 502-568-5700.

MEMBERS OF FIRM

Lindsey W. Ingram, Jr.
Charles E. Shivel, Jr.
Diane M. Carlton
J. Mel Camenisch, Jr.

Representative Clients: A. T. Massey Coal Co., Inc.; Cyprus Amax Mineral Co.; Delta Natural Gas Co., Inc.; Mapco, Inc.; Peabody Coal Co.; United Coal Co.; Western Pocahontas Corp.; Ziegler Coal Holding Co.

For Complete List of Firm Personnel, See General Section

For full biographical listings, see the Martindale-Hubbell Law Directory

*PRESTONSBURG,** Floyd Co.

KAZEE, KINNER & CHAFIN (AV)

119 East Court Street, P.O. Box 700, 41653
Telephone: 606-886-2361; 886-2362
FAX: 606-886-9603
Email: dbkazee@pcc-uky.campus.mci.net
Paintsville, Kentucky Office: Family Federal Building, Suite 202, P.O. Box 1275.
Telephone: 606-789-3059.

MEMBERS OF FIRM

D. B. Kazee
Mitchell D. Kinner
John T. Chafin
P. Franklin Heaberlin
Robert J. Patton
William C. Mullins

Representative Clients: Island Creek Coal Co.; The Elk Horn Coal Corp.; First Commonwealth Bank; Old Republic Insurance Co.; Zurich American Insurance Co.; Maryland Casualty Co.; Bituminous Casualty Corp.; Mack Financial Corp.; Nationwide Insurance; Kentucky May Coal Co., Inc.

For full biographical listings, see the Martindale-Hubbell Law Directory

LOUISIANA

*BATON ROUGE,** East Baton Rouge Parish

BREAZEALE, SACHSE & WILSON, L.L.P. (AV)

Twenty-Third Floor, One American Place, P.O. Box 3197, 70821-3197
Telephone: 225-387-4000
Fax: 225-387-5397
URL: http://www.bswllp.com
New Orleans, Louisiana Office: LL&E Tower, Suite 1500, 909 Poydras Street.
Telephone: 504-584-5454.
Fax: 504-584-5452.
Covington, Louisiana Office: 2255 Highway 190 North, Suite 200.
Telephone: 504-871-9444.
Fax: 504-871-9666.

MEMBERS OF FIRM

Emile C. Rolfs, III
John W. Barton, Jr.
Jude C. Bursavich
Frank S. Craig, III
Luis A. Leitzelar

ASSOCIATE

R. Charles Ellis

(See Next Column)

BRAUN KENDRICK FINKBEINER PLC, *Bay City—Continued*

Ann Arbor, Michigan Office: First National Building. 201 S. Main, Suite 700.
Telephone: 313-995-4100.
Telecopier: 313-995-4798.
Mt. Pleasant, Michigan Office: 805 North Brown.
Telephone: 517-775-7404.
Telecopier: 517-775-3764.

Ralph J. Isackson
Frank M. Quinn
Gregory E. Meter
Daniel S. Opperman
Gregory T. Demers
Jeffrey C. Wilson

Michael E. Wooley

Representative Clients: Bay Health Systems; Catholic Federal Credit Union; City of Saginaw; City of Vassar; City of Zilwaukee; Corporate Service; Cox Cable.

For full biographical listings, see the Martindale-Hubbell Law Directory

*DETROIT,** Wayne Co.

BODMAN, LONGLEY & DAHLING LLP (AV)

34th Floor 100 Renaissance Center, 48243
Telephone: 313-259-7777
Fax: 313-393-7579
Email: info@bodmanlongley.com *URL:* http://www.bodmanlongley.com
Troy, Michigan Office: Suite 2020, 755 West Big Beaver Road.
Telephone: 248-362-2110.
Fax: 248-244-0780.
Ann Arbor, Michigan Office: 110 Miller, Suite 300.
Telephone: 734-761-3780.
Fax: 734-930-2494.
Northern Michigan Office: 229 Court Street, P.O. Box 405, Cheboygan.
Telephone: 231-627-4351.
Fax: 231-627-2802.

MEMBERS OF FIRM

Carson C. Grunewald
James A. Smith
Robert G. Brower

For Representative Client List, See General Section

For Complete List of Firm Personnel, See General Section

For full biographical listings, see the Martindale-Hubbell Law Directory

HONIGMAN MILLER SCHWARTZ AND COHN (AV)

2290 First National Building, 660 Woodward Avenue, 48226
Telephone: 313-465-7000
Telecopier: 313-465-8000
Telex: 235705
Email: mvg@honigman.com *URL:* http://law.honigman.com
Lansing, Michigan Office: Phoenix Building, 222 North Washington Square, Suite 400, 48933-1800.
Telephone: 517-484-8282.

MEMBERS OF FIRM

Christopher J. Dunsky
Kenneth C. Gold
Norman Hyman
S. Lee Johnson
Steven C. Nadeau
Brian J. Negele
John D. Pirich
(Lansing, Michigan Office)
Joseph M. Polito
Grant R. Trigger
William A. Wichers II
Jeffrey L. Woolstrum
Ruth E. Zimmerman
(Lansing, Michigan Office)

ASSOCIATE

Stuart J. Weiss

Representative Clients: Auto Alliance International Inc. (formerly Mazda Motor Manufacturing (USA) Corporation); Consumers Power Company; The Detroit Edison Company; Ford Motor Company; General Motors Corporation; Hughes Aircraft Company; Hughes Missile Systems Company; Edw. C. Levy Co.; Masco Corporation and its affiliates; Morton International, Inc.

For Complete List of Firm Personnel, See General Section

For full biographical listings, see the Martindale-Hubbell Law Directory

LANSING, Ingham Co.

HONIGMAN MILLER SCHWARTZ AND COHN (AV)

A Partnership including Professional Corporations
222 North Washington Square, Suite 400, 48933-1800
Telephone: 517-484-8282
Telecopier: 517-484-8286
Email: mvg@honigman.com *URL:* http://law.honigman.com
Detroit, Michigan Office: 2290 First National Building, 660 Woodward Avenue, 48226.
Telephone: 313-465-7000.

MEMBERS

Frederick M. Baker, Jr.
John D. Pirich

Representative Clients: Central Wayne County Sanitation Authority; City of Detroit; Landfill Management Company; Republic Waste Industries; Wayne Disposal, Inc.

For Complete List of Firm Personnel, See General Section

For full biographical listings, see the Martindale-Hubbell Law Directory

*MOUNT PLEASANT,** Isabella Co.

LYNCH, GALLAGHER, LYNCH & MARTINEAU, P.L.L.C. (AV)

555 North Main Street, P.O. Box 446, 48858
Telephone: 517-773-9961
Fax: 517-773-2107
Email: lglm@power-net.net
Lansing, Michigan Office: 2400 Lake Lansing Road, Suite B.
Telephone: 517-485-0400.
Fax: 517-485-0402.

MEMBERS OF FIRM

Edward N. Lynch (1908-1984)
Byron P. Gallagher
John J. Lynch
Steven W. Martineau
Paula K. Manis
(Resident at Lansing Office)
Michael J. Hackett
Richard J. Garcia
Nancy E. Gallagher
Jennifer M. Galloway

Representative Clients: Amoco Production Co.; Mosbacher Production Co.; Muskegon Development Co.; Lease Management, Inc.; Dow Chemical Co.; Dresser Industries, Inc.; North Michigan Oil & Gas Corp; Scanda Energy Co., Inc.

For full biographical listings, see the Martindale-Hubbell Law Directory

*SAGINAW,** Saginaw Co.

BRAUN KENDRICK FINKBEINER PLC (AV)

101 N. Washington Suite 812, 48607-1297
Telephone: 517-753-3461
Telecopier: 517-753-3951
Email: ALBFIE@BKF-LAW.COM *URL:* http://www.bkf-law.com
Saginaw Township Office, Michigan Office: 5800 Gratiot Road, Suite 107, P.O. Box 5169. Telephone 517-799-8692.
Fax: 517-799-4666.
Bay City, Michigan Office: 201 Phoenix Building, P.O. Box 2039.
Telephone: 517-895-8505.
Telecopier: 517-895-8437.
Ann Arbor, Michigan Office: First National Building. 201 S. Main, Suite 700.
Telephone: 313-995-4100.
Telecopier: 313-995-4798.
Mt. Pleasant, Michigan Office: 805 North Brown.
Telephone: 517-775-7404.
Telecopier: 517-775-3764.

Thomas R. Luplow
John A. Decker
Barry M. Levine
Glenn L. Fitkin
Brian S. Makaric

Representative Clients: The Dow Chemical Co.; General Motors Corp.; Merrill, Lynch, Inc.; Saginaw General Hospital; Saginaw News; The Wickes Foundation.

For Complete List of Firm Personnel, See General Section

For full biographical listings, see the Martindale-Hubbell Law Directory

NONPROFIT AND TAX EXEMPT ORGANIZATIONS

COLORADO

*COLORADO SPRINGS,** El Paso Co.

HOLME ROBERTS & OWEN LLP (AV)

Suite 1300, 90 South Cascade Avenue, 80903
Telephone: 719-473-3800
Telecopier: 719-633-1518
Email: hro@hro.com *URL:* http://www.hro.com
Denver, Colorado Office: Suite 4100, 1700 Lincoln.
Telephone: 303-861-7000.
Telecopier: 303-866-0200.
Boulder, Colorado Office: Suite 400, 1401 Pearl Street.
Telephone: 303-444-5955.
Telecopier: 303-444-1063.
Salt Lake City, Utah Office: Suite 1100, 111 East Broadway.
Telephone: 801-521-5800.
Telecopier: 801-521-9639.
London, England Office: Heathcoat House 3rd Floor, 20 Savile Row.
Telephone: 011-44-171-494-5600.
Telecopier: 011-44-171-287-9344.

PARTNERS OF FIRM

Steven B. Smith John R. Wylie

ASSOCIATE

Stuart J. Lark

For Complete List of Firm Personnel, See General Section

For full biographical listings, see the Martindale-Hubbell Law Directory

*DENVER,** Denver Co.

GUTHERY & RICKLES, P.C. (AV)

Cherry Creek Plaza II, 650 South Cherry Street Suite 1000, 80246-1812
Telephone: 303-320-5889
Fax: 303-320-5890

Peter C. Guthery Stephen P. Rickles

A list of Representative Clients that have provided written authorization will be furnished upon request.

For full biographical listings, see the Martindale-Hubbell Law Directory

HOLME ROBERTS & OWEN LLP (AV)

Suite 4100, 1700 Lincoln, 80203
Telephone: 303-861-7000
Telecopier: 303-866-0200
Email: hro@hro.com *URL:* http://www.hro.com
Boulder, Colorado Office: Suite 400, 1401 Pearl Street.
Telephone: 303-444-5955.
Telecopier: 303-444-1063.
Colorado Springs, Colorado Office: Suite 1300, 90 South Cascade Avenue.
Telephone: 719-473-3800.
Telecopier: 719-633-1518.
Salt Lake City, Utah Office: Suite 1100, 111 East Broadway.
Telephone: 801-521-5800.
Telecopier: 801-521-9639.
London, England Office: Heathcoat House, 3rd Floor, 20 Savile Row.
Telephone: 011-44-171-494-5600.
Telecopier: 011-44-171-287-9344.

PARTNERS OF FIRM

Donald J. Hopkins
Steven B. Smith (Colorado Springs Office)
John R. Wylie (Colorado Springs Office)

ASSOCIATE

Stuart J. Lark (Colorado Springs Office)

For Complete List of Firm Personnel, See General Section

For full biographical listings, see the Martindale-Hubbell Law Directory

FRANCES B. MCDONALD PROFESSIONAL CORPORATION (AV)

1900 Wazee Street, Suite 203, 80202-1259
Telephone: 303-297-3337
Fax: 303-297-3338
Email: fbmcd@dim.com

Frances B. McDonald

For full biographical listings, see the Martindale-Hubbell Law Directory

HAWAII

*HONOLULU,** Honolulu Co.

CARLSMITH BALL (AV)

A Partnership including Law Corporations
Suite 2200, Pacific Tower, 1001 Bishop Street, P.O. Box 656, 96809-3402
Telephone: 808-523-2500
Fax: 808-523-0842
Email: execdirector@carlsmith.com *URL:* http://www.carlsmith.com
Kapolei, Hawaii Office: Suite 318, Kapolei Building, 1001 Kamokila Boulevard, 96707.
Telephone: 808-523-2500.
Fax: 808-674-0850.
Wailuku, Maui Hawaii Office: Suite 400, One Main Plaza, 2200 Main Street, P.O. Box 1086, 96793-1086.
Telephone: 808-242-4535.
Fax: 808-244-4974.
Kailua-Kona, Hawaii Office: Suite 209, 75-1000 Henry Street, 96740.
Telephone: 808-329-6464.
Fax: 808-329-9450.
Hilo, Hawaii Office: 121 Waianuenue Avenue, P.O. Box 686, 96721-0686.
Telephone: 808-935-6644.
Fax: 808-935-7975.
Hagatna, Guam Office: Suite 401, Bank of Hawaii Building, 134 West Soledad Avenue, P.O. Box BF, 96932-5027.
Telephone: 671-472-6813.
Fax: 671-477-4375.
Telex: 721-6445 CWCMI GM.
Saipan, Commonwealth of the Northern Mariana Islands Office: Carlsmith Building, Capitol Hill, P.O. Box 5241, 96950-5241.
Telephone: 670-322-3455.
Fax: 670-322-3368.
Los Angeles, California Office: 9th Floor, 444 South Flower Street, 90071-2901.
Telephone: 213-955-1200.
Fax: 213-623-0032.
Washington, D.C. Office: Suite 300, 1201 Pennsylvania Avenue, N.W., 20004-2401.
Telephone: 202-628-2228.
Fax: 202-628-2071.
Mexico City, Mexico Office: Carlsmith Ball, Sierra Nevada 119, Lomas de Chapultepec, 11000 Mexico, D.F.
Telephone: 52-5-520-8514, 52-5-520-8757.
Fax: 52-5-540-1545.
Mexico, D.F. Office of Carlsmith Ball, S.C. (Authorized to practice as foreign legal consultants in Mexico): Sierra Nevada 119, Lomas de Chapultepec, 11000 Mexico, D.F.
Telephone: 52-5-520-8514, 52-5-520-8757.
Fax: 52-5-540-1545.

MEMBER OF FIRM

Mary Jane Connell

For Complete List of Firm Personnel, See General Section

For full biographical listings, see the Martindale-Hubbell Law Directory

KANSAS

*TOPEKA,** Shawnee Co.

GOODELL, STRATTON, EDMONDS & PALMER, L.L.P. (AV)

515 South Kansas Avenue, 66603-3999
Telephone: 785-233-0593
Fax: 785-233-8870
Email: GSEP@CJNETWORKS.COM *URL:* http://www.cjnetworks.com/~gsep
Kansas City, Missouri Office: 10401 Holmes Road, Suite 280.
Telephone: 816-943-8577.

ASSOCIATE

Scott C. Palecki

SPECIAL COUNSEL

Joseph E. McKinney

Counsel for: Columbian National Title Insurance Co.; Central Regional Dental Testing Service, Inc.; Heartland Community Bankers Association; The Menninger Foundation; Topeka Chamber of Commerce; Washburn University of Topeka; Reser's Fine Foods; ConAgra; Monfort, Inc.

For Complete List of Firm Personnel, See General Section

For full biographical listings, see the Martindale-Hubbell Law Directory

MARYLAND

*BALTIMORE,** (Independent City)

GALLAGHER, EVELIUS & JONES, LLP (AV)

Park Charles Suite 400, 218 North Charles Street, 21201
Telephone: 410-727-7702
Facsimile: 410-468-2786
URL: http://www.gejlaw.com

MEMBERS OF FIRM

Francis X. Gallagher (1928-1972)
C. Edward Jones (1908-1999)
John C. Evelius (Retired)
Richard O. Berndt
Thomas N. Biddison, Jr.
Robert R. Kern, Jr.
Saul E. Gilstein
Thomas B. Lewis
Bonnie Abrams Travieso
Stephen A. Goldberg
Linda H. Jones
Jack C. Tranter
Leslie B. Speed
Christopher J. Fritz
David E. Raderman
Peter E. Keith
Nita L. Schultz
Michael W. Skojec
Kathryn Kelley Hoskins
Mark P. Keener
Kevin J. Davidson
Eileen M. Lunga
Lori A. Nicolle
Kenneth S. Gross
Thomas C. Dame

ASSOCIATES

Valarie K. Oulds
Margaret Stevens Jacks
Matthew W. Oakey
Rebecca A. Weaver
Michael J. Henigan
David W. Kinkopf
Paul S. Caiola
Jason W. Gaarder
M. Kirsten Andrews

LEGAL ASSISTANTS

Patricia C. Quayle
Iris T. H. Heath
Connie L. Ennis
Margaret Graff
Margo Gibson Hughes
Jonathan T. Gillis
Brenda J. Heacock
Dwayne L. Rodeheaver

Representative Clients: Roman Catholic Archdiocese of Baltimore; The Shelter Group; Mercantile-Safe Deposit and Trust Co.; The Enterprise Social Investment Corp.; Mercy Medical Center, Inc.

For full biographical listings, see the Martindale-Hubbell Law Directory

OIL AND GAS LAW

ARKANSAS

*FORT SMITH,** Sebastian Co.

Daily & Woods, P.L.L.C. (AV)

Stephens Office Building, 623 Garrison Avenue, P.O. Box 1446, 72902
Telephone: 501-782-0361
Fax: 501-782-6160
Email: DailyWoods@aol.com

MEMBERS OF FIRM

Ben Core
Jerry L. Canfield
Thomas A. Daily
Wyman R. Wade, Jr.
Stanley A. Leasure
Douglas M. Carson

ASSOCIATES

Todd Patrick Lewis
Barry D. Neal
Leigh M. Chiles

OF COUNSEL

James E. West

Counsel for: Claims Management, Inc. (Wal-Mart); Arkla, Inc.; City of Fort Smith; Commercial Union Insurance Cos.; Pennzoil Exploration and Production Co.; Silvey Cos., Inc.; Metropolitan Life Insurance Co.; Chevron U.S.A., Inc.

For full biographical listings, see the Martindale-Hubbell Law Directory

CALIFORNIA

GLENDALE, Los Angeles Co.

Bright and Brown (AV)

550 North Brand Boulevard, Suite 2100, 91203
Telephone: 818-243-2121; 213-489-1414
Facsimile: 818-243-3225
Email: attorneys@brightandbrown.com

James S. Bright
Gregory C. Brown
Maureen J. Bright
John Quirk
Brian L. Becker

ASSOCIATES

PhillipaL. Altmann
Kristin L. Gamble

For full biographical listings, see the Martindale-Hubbell Law Directory

LONG BEACH, Los Angeles Co.

Taubman, Simpson, Young & Sulentor (AV)

249 East Ocean Boulevard, Suite 700, P.O. Box 22670, 90801-5670
Telephone: 562-436-9201
FAX: 562-590-9695
Email: thefirm@tsyslaw.com

E. C. Denio (1864-1952)
Geo. A. Hart (1881-1967)
Geo. P. Taubman, Jr. (1897-1970)
Matthew C. Simpson (1900-1988)
Roger W. Young
William J. Sulentor
Peter M. Williams
Maria M. Rohaidy
Stuart C. Talley

Attorneys for: Bixby Land Co.; Renick Cadillac, Inc.; Oil Operators Inc.
Local Counsel: Crown Cork & Seal Co., Inc.

For full biographical listings, see the Martindale-Hubbell Law Directory

*LOS ANGELES,** Los Angeles Co.

Knopfler & Robertson, LLP (AV)

Suite 500, 21650 Oxnard Street (Woodland Hills), 91367
Telephone: 818-227-0770; 213-624-1111
Telefax: 818-227-0777
Irvine, California Office: 19800 MacArthur Boulevard, Suite 270, 92612.
Telephone: 714-261-6191.
Pleasanton, California Office: 400 Main Street, Suite 204, 94566.
Telephone: 510-425-7250.
Las Vegas, Nevada Office: Knopfler & Robertson in Association with Broom & Vaisbort, LLP, 3753 Howard Hughes Parkway, Suite 200, 89109.
Telephone: 702-792-2413.
Camarillo, California Office: 1200 Paseo, Suite 170, 93010.
Telephone: 805-482-1903; 800-CONDOLAW.
Fax: 805-484-5917.

(See Next Column)

George Knopfler
Alexander Robertson, IV
Deborah Broom
Richard A. Capella
Jonathan S. Vick
Edward D. Vaisbort
William G. Kelsberg

OF COUNSEL

Scott C. Haith
James P. Lingl (Resident, Camarillo Office)
Christina S. Robertson

Janice M. Michaels
James M. Pazos
Mark Rohrer
Craig Smith
Robert Nation
William S. Dunlevy (Resident, Camarillo Office)
Scott A. Hunter

For full biographical listings, see the Martindale-Hubbell Law Directory

McMahon & Spiegel (AV)

355 South Grand Avenue, Suite 3290, 90071-1591
Telephone: 213-628-9800
Fax: 213-628-9813
Email: bmcmahon@pacbell.net

MEMBERS OF FIRM

M. Brian McMahon
Craig R. Spiegel

For full biographical listings, see the Martindale-Hubbell Law Directory

COLORADO

*COLORADO SPRINGS,** El Paso Co.

Wittman & McCord (AV)

A Partnership including a Professional Corporation
Suite 320 UMB Bank Building, 5825 Delmonico Drive, 80919
Telephone: 719-590-9899
Fax: 719-590-9984
Email: wittcord-law@pcisys.net
Denver, Colorado Office: 10630 East Bethany Drive (Aurora), 80014.
Telephone: 303-337-4952.
Fax: 303-337-6165.

MEMBERS OF FIRM

Sherwin V. "Bud" Wittman, II, (P.C.)
Edward M. McCord, P.C.

ASSOCIATES

J. Bradley Hardman
Keith D. Vance

Representative Clients: Allstate Insurance Co.; Carolina Casualty Insurance Co.; E & O Professionals Insurance Co.; John Deere Transportation Insurance Co.; Motor Cargo Co.; Providian Auto & Home Insurance Co.; Safeco Insurance Co.; USAA Insurance Co.; USF & G Insurance Co.; Utica Mutual Insurance Co.

For full biographical listings, see the Martindale-Hubbell Law Directory

*DENVER,** Denver Co.

Alfers & Carver, LLC (AV)

Equitable Building, 730 17th Street, Suite 340, 80202
Telephone: 303-592-7674
Fax: 303-592-7680
Email: ccarver@alfers-carver.com

Stephen D. Alfers
Craig R. Carver
Bruce C. Kirchhoff
Don H. Sherwood

ASSOCIATE

Michelle C. Carmody

For full biographical listings, see the Martindale-Hubbell Law Directory

Poulson, Odell & Peterson, LLC (AV)

Suite 1400, 1775 Sherman Street, 80203
Telephone: 303-861-4400
Telecopier: 303-861-1225
Email: popllc@popllc.com

William G. Odell
C. M. (Pete) Peterson (Retired)
Randall M. Case
Stephen M. Thompson
Carleton L. Ekberg
Alan B. Cameron

OF COUNSEL

Robert D. Poulson
Arthur Thad Smith
Robert D. Buettner
James W. Campbell (Retired)

William F. Leonard
Scott M. Campbell
Anne A. DeWitt
Emily R. Suyat
Rebecca N. Welborn

(See Next Column)

POULSON, ODELL & PETERSON LLC, *Denver—Continued*

Representative Clients: Apache Corporation; Anadarko Petroleum Corp.; Burlington Resources Oil & Gas Co.; Conoco, Inc.; Enron Oil and Gas Co.; Exxon Co., USA; Fort Collins Consolidated Royalties, Inc.; KCS Mountain Resources, Inc.; Mobil Oil Corp.; Samedan Oil Corp.

For full biographical listings, see the Martindale-Hubbell Law Directory

WELBORN SULLIVAN MECK & TOOLEY, P.C. (AV)

1775 Sherman Street, Suite 1800, 80203-4318
Telephone: 303-376-4490
Facsimile: 303-376-4495
Email: wsmt@aol.com

John F. Welborn
Stephen J. Sullivan
John F. Meck
Keith D. Tooley
Kendor P. Jones
Brian S. Tooley
Scott L. Sells
Mary V. Laitos
Molly Sommerville
Thomas C. McKee
William R. Rapson
Stephen A. Bain
Amy E. Mang
Danielle V. Smith

OF COUNSEL

Robert F. Welborn

SPECIAL COUNSEL

Jan G. Laitos

Representative Clients: BP Amoco Corporation; Evergreen Resources, Inc.; Falcon Creek Resources, Inc.; HS Resources, Inc.; Inland Resources, Inc.; J-W Operating Company; KCS Mountain Resources Inc.; Texaco Exploration & Production, Inc.; Union Pacific Resources Company; Whiting Petroleum Company.

For Complete List of Firm Personnel, See General Section

For full biographical listings, see the Martindale-Hubbell Law Directory

LOUISIANA

*BATON ROUGE,** East Baton Rouge Parish

STRAIN, DENNIS, MAYHALL & BATES, L.L.P. (AV)

318 St. Charles Street, 70802
Telephone: 225-343-0100
Fax: 225-343-0344
Email: sdmb@msn.com
Lafayette, Louisiana Office: 1018 Harding Street, Suite 104, P.O. Drawer 55319, 70505.
Telephone: 318-237-5900.
Fax: 318-233-9095.
New Orleans, Louisiana Office: 201 St. Charles Avenue, Suite 2508, 70170.
Telephone: 504-569-1649.
Fax: 504-569-1635.

MEMBERS OF FIRM

Daniel M. Barbato
James C. Bates
Don R. Beard
James L. Bullen
Howell A. Dennis, Jr.
Christopher E. Janke (Resident at New Orleans, Louisiana)
Kim G. Mayhall
Thomas C. McKowen, IV
William S. Strain

ASSOCIATE

Charles G. Blaize, Jr.

For full biographical listings, see the Martindale-Hubbell Law Directory

*LAFAYETTE,** Lafayette Parish

GORDON, ARATA, MCCOLLAM, DUPLANTIS & EAGAN, L.L.P. (AV)

A Registered Limited Liability Partnership including Professional Law Corporations
625 East Kaliste Saloom Road, 70508-2508
Telephone: 318-237-0132
Fax: 318-237-3451
New Orleans, Louisiana Office: 201 St. Charles Avenue, Suite 4000.
Telephone: 504-582-1111.
Fax: 504-582-1121.
Baton Rouge, Louisiana Office: 1400 One American Place.
Telephone: 225-381-9643.
Fax: 225-336-9763.

RESIDENT MEMBERS OF FIRM

B. J. Duplantis (A P.L.C.)
William F. Bailey
Samuel E. Masur

RESIDENT ASSOCIATES

Denis C. Swords
Gregory G. Duplantis

Representative Clients: Apache Corp.; Bass Enterprises Production Co.; BHP Petroleum (Americas), Inc.; Burlington Resources O & G; Chevron, USA, Inc.; Duke Energy Corp.; Louis Dreyfus Natural Gas; The Meridian Re-

(See Next Column)

source Corp.; Union Oil Company of California; Union Pacific Resources Co.

For full biographical listings, see the Martindale-Hubbell Law Directory

*LAKE CHARLES,** Calcasieu Parish

THE GRAY LAW FIRM A PROFESSIONAL LAW CORPORATION (AV)

Hibernia Tower, One Lakeshore Drive, Suite 900, P.O. Box 1467, 70602-1467
Telephone: 318-494-0694
Facsimile: 318-494-0697
Email: graylaw@graylawfirm.com

Andrew J. Gray, III
David L. Sigler
Anna R. Gray
Leslie Qvale Knox

Wade Thomas Visconte

For full biographical listings, see the Martindale-Hubbell Law Directory

*NEW ORLEANS,** Orleans Parish

CARVER, DARDEN, KORETZKY, TESSIER, FINN, BLOSSMAN & AREAUX, L.L.C. (AV)

1100 Poydras Street, Suite 2700, 70163
Telephone: 504-585-3800
Telecopier: 504-585-3801

M. Hampton Carver
M. Taylor Darden
I. Harold Koretzky
Frank A. Tessier
William T. Finn
Roy E. Blossman
Raymond G. Areaux
John Anthony Dunlap
Leann Opotowsky Moses
David L. Browne

OF COUNSEL

John C. Christian (P.C.)
Susan Judlin Santa Cruz
Stephen Rose
Elvige Cassard Richards
Stacy Smith Brown

J. Christopher Martin
John H. Fontham
Erin M. Hart
Shawn L. Holahan
Jonathan M. Pierce
Robert J. Nichols
Ryan E. Griffitts
Linda A. Hoffman

Representative Clients: Bass Enterprises Production Co.; CXY Energy, Inc.; CanadianOxy Offshore Production; Chevron Pipe Line Company; Chevron Chemical Co.; Clovelly Oil Co., Inc.; Computerized Processes Unlimited, Inc.; Continental Land & Fur Co., Inc.; Delta Petroleum Co., Inc.

For full biographical listings, see the Martindale-Hubbell Law Directory

GORDON, ARATA, MCCOLLAM, DUPLANTIS & EAGAN, L.L.P. (AV)

A Registered Limited Liability Partnership including Professional Law Corporations
201 St. Charles Avenue, Suite 4000, 70170-4000
Telephone: 504-582-1111
Fax: 504-582-1121
Lafayette, Louisiana Office: 625 East Kaliste Saloom Road.
Telephone: 318-237-0132.
Fax: 318-237-3451.
Baton Rouge, Louisiana Office: 1400 One American Place.
Telephone: 225-381-9643.
Fax: 225-336-9763.

MEMBERS OF FIRM

John A. Gordon (A P.L.C.)
Blake G. Arata (A P.L.C.)
John M. McCollam (A P.L.C.)
Guy E. Wall
Jason A. T. Jumonville
Martin E. Landrieu
Scott A. O'Connor
C. Peck Hayne Jr.

ASSOCIATES

Martin P. Averill
Andrée M. Braud
Fernand L. Laudumiey, IV

Representative Clients: Apache Corp.; Bass Enterprises Production Co.; BHP Petroleum (Americas), Inc.; Burlington Resources O & G; Chevron, USA, Inc.; Duke Energy Corp.; Louis Dreyfus Natural Gas; The Meridian Resource Corp.; Union Oil Company of California; Union Pacific Resources Co.

For Complete List of Firm Personnel, See General Section

For full biographical listings, see the Martindale-Hubbell Law Directory

MARTZELL & BICKFORD (AV)

A Partnership including a Professional Corporation
338 Lafayette Street, 70130-3244
Telephone: 504-581-9065
Fax: 504-581-7635
Email: mailbox@martzellbickford.com *URL:* http://www.martzellbickford.com

(See Next Column)

MARTZELL & BICKFORD—*Continued*

John R. Martzell (P.C.) | Scott R. Bickford

Regina O. Matthews
Duggan F. Ellis
M. Suzanne Montero
Richard A. Filce
Ray L. Rhymes

LEGAL SUPPORT PERSONNEL

LITIGATION ADMINISTRATOR

Christopher H. Sherwood

PARALEGALS

Jane B. Daigle
Connie L. Cosse
Mary Wiggenhorn

FIRM ADMINISTRATOR

Stephen C. Wolf (Certified Public Accountant)

For full biographical listings, see the Martindale-Hubbell Law Directory

---

PULASKI, GIEGER & LABORDE, L.L.C. (AV)

Suite 4800, One Shell Square, 701 Poydras Street, 70139
Telephone: 504-561-0400
Telecopier: 504-561-1011
Covington, Louisiana Office: 434 North Columbia Street, Suite 200, 70433.
Telephone: 504-561-0400.
Telecopier: 504-809-9677.

Michael T. Pulaski
Ernest P. Gieger, Jr.
Lambert M. Laperouse
Robert W. Maxwell
Keith W. McDaniel
Sharon D. Smith
Christopher J. Wnuk
Julianne T. Echols
Hilliard F. Kelly, III

Marjorie Randall Brown
Gina S. Montgomery

For full biographical listings, see the Martindale-Hubbell Law Directory

---

*SHREVEPORT,** Caddo Parish

DAVIDSON, NIX & JONES, A PROFESSIONAL LAW CORPORATION (AV)

509 Market Street, Suite 800, 71101
Telephone: 318-424-4342
Fax: 318-226-0168

Randall S. Davidson
Ernest L. Nix, Jr.
Allison A. Jones
John S. Hodge

Grant E. Summers

For full biographical listings, see the Martindale-Hubbell Law Directory

---

MICHIGAN

*MOUNT PLEASANT,** Isabella Co.

LYNCH, GALLAGHER, LYNCH & MARTINEAU, P.L.L.C. (AV)

555 North Main Street, P.O. Box 446, 48858
Telephone: 517-773-9961
Fax: 517-773-2107
Email: lglm@power-net.net
Lansing, Michigan Office: 2400 Lake Lansing Road, Suite B.
Telephone: 517-485-0400.
Fax: 517-485-0402.

MEMBERS OF FIRM

John J. Lynch
Paula K. Manis (Resident at Lansing Office)

Representative Clients: Amoco Production, Co.; Liquid Transport, Inc.; Central Concrete Products; Central Michigan University; Northern Michigan Oil and Gas Corp.

For Complete List of Firm Personnel, See General Section

For full biographical listings, see the Martindale-Hubbell Law Directory

PATENT, TRADEMARK, COPYRIGHT AND UNFAIR COMPETITION

(See also listings under Trademark, Copyright and Unfair Competition)

ALABAMA

*BIRMINGHAM,** Jefferson Co.

BRADLEY ARANT ROSE & WHITE LLP (AV)

2001 Park Place, Suite 1400, P.O. Box 830709, 35283-0709
Telephone: 205-521-8000
Facsimile: 205-521-8800
Facsimile (SouthTrust Tower Office): 205-521-8500
URL: http://www.barw.com
Huntsville, Alabama Office: 200 Clinton Avenue West, Suite 900, 35801.
Telephone: 205-517-5100.
Facsimile: 205-533-5069.
Washington, D.C. Office: 801 Pennsylvania Avenue, NW, Suite 230, 20004.
Telephone: 202-347-8893.
Facsimile: 202-347-1684.

MEMBERS OF FIRM

Thad Gladden Long
J. David Pugh

ASSOCIATE

John W. Smith T

Counsel for: SouthTrust Bank of Alabama, National Association; Energen, Corporation (formerly Alagasco, Inc.); Blount, Inc; Coca-Cola Bottling Company United, Inc.; The New York Times Co.; Russell Corp.; Walter Industries, Inc.; ASCAP, Auburn University.

For Complete List of Firm Personnel, See General Section

For full biographical listings, see the Martindale-Hubbell Law Directory

VEAL & ASSOCIATES (AV)

200 Cahaba Park Circle Suite 125, 35242
Telephone: 205-991-0082
FAX: 205-991-8718
Email: veal@alabama.com *URL:* http://www.alabama.com/patents/

Robert J. Veal

ASSOCIATES

Kenneth M. Bush
N. Alexander Nolte (Not admitted in AL)

For full biographical listings, see the Martindale-Hubbell Law Directory

ARIZONA

*PHOENIX,** Maricopa Co.

ALLEN & PRICE, P.L.C. (AV)

2850 East Camelback Road, Suite 170, 85016-4380
Telephone: 602-381-0500
Fax: 602-381-8899
Email: allen@aplaw.com
Email: price@aplaw.com
Email: schacter@aplaw.com
Email: sanders@aplaw.com

Robert E. B. Allen
Charles S. Price

Scott A. Shacter
Barry R. Sanders

For full biographical listings, see the Martindale-Hubbell Law Directory

FENNEMORE CRAIG, A PROFESSIONAL CORPORATION (AV)

3003 North Central Avenue, Suite 2600, 85012-2913
Telephone: 602-916-5000
Fax: 602-916-5999
Tucson, Arizona Office: One South Church Avenue, Suite 1000, 85701-1620.
Telephone: 520-879-6800.
Fax: 520-879-6899.

C. Owen Paepke
Ray K. Harris
Bryan A. Albue

Paul F. Wille (Not admitted in AZ)
Stacie K. Smith
Sandra L. Etherton

(See Next Column)

LEGAL SUPPORT PERSONNEL

LEGAL ASSISTANTS

Amy Thompson

For Complete List of Firm Personnel, See General Section

For full biographical listings, see the Martindale-Hubbell Law Directory

QUARLES & BRADY LLP (AV)

One Camelback Building, One East Camelback Road, Suite 400, 85012-1649
Telephone: 602-230-5500
Fax: 602-230-5598
URL: http://www.quarles.com
Milwaukee, Wisconsin Office: 411 East Wisconsin Avenue.
Telephone: 414-277-5000.
Fax: 414-271-3552.
Madison, Wisconsin Office: First Wisconsin Plaza, One South Pinckney Street, P.O. Box 2113.
Telephone: 608-251-5000.
Fax: 608-251-9166.
West Palm Beach, Florida Office: 222 Lakeview Avenue, 4th Floor.
Telephone: 407-653-5000.
Fax: 407-653-5333.
Naples, Florida Office: Barnett Center, 4501 Tamiami Trail North, Suite 300.
Telephone: 813-262-5959.
Fax: 813-434-4999.
Chicago, Illinois Office: Quarles & Brady LLC, Citicorp Center, 500 West Madison Street, Suite 3700.
Telephone: 312-715-5000.
Fax: 312-715-5155.

MEMBER OF THE FIRM

Glenn Spencer Bacal

ASSOCIATES

David G. Bray
Sean D. Garrison
Sherry W. Schumm
Sean D. Johnson
Allen J. Moss

For full biographical listings, see the Martindale-Hubbell Law Directory

SCOTTSDALE, Maricopa Co.

CATES & HOLLOWAY (AV)

6360 E. Thomas Road, 2-228, 85251-7051
Telephone: 602-248-0982
Fax: 602-234-3330

MEMBERS OF FIRM

Charles E. Cates
Elizabeth A. Dawn

OF COUNSEL

Frank T. Barber (Not admitted in AZ)
Richard G. Harrer (Not admitted in AZ)

Representative Clients: Albers Technologies Corporation; The Dial Corp.; Greyhound Lines, Inc.; Performance Industries, Inc.; SunCor Development Company; Tire Service Equipment Mfg. Co., Inc.; Viad Corp.

For full biographical listings, see the Martindale-Hubbell Law Directory

ARKANSAS

*LITTLE ROCK,** Pulaski Co.

ROSE LAW FIRM, A PROFESSIONAL ASSOCIATION (AV)

120 East Fourth Street, 72201
Telephone: 501-375-9131
Telecopy: 501-375-1309

William H. Kennedy, III
Amy Lee Stewart
Kathryn Bennett Perkins

Counsel for: ALLTEL Corporation; Acxiom Corporation; Aluminum Company of America; Bridgestone/Firestone, Inc.; General Motors Corp.; The Prudential Insurance Company of America; Stephens Group Inc.; TCBY Enterprises, Inc.; Tyson Foods, Inc.

For Complete List of Firm Personnel, See General Section

For full biographical listings, see the Martindale-Hubbell Law Directory

CALIFORNIA

*FRESNO,** Fresno Co.

WORREL & WORREL (AV)

St. Croix Professional Center, 2109 West Bullard Avenue, Suite 121, 93711-1258
Telephone: 209-431-4391
Fax: 209-431-4387

Richard M. Worrel (1913-1995) Rodney K. Worrel

Representative Clients: Bank of America; California State University, Fresno; California State University, Bakersfield; Duncan Enterprises; Fresno Pacific University; J. G. Boswell Co.; The Vendo Co.; City of Visalia.

For full biographical listings, see the Martindale-Hubbell Law Directory

LAGUNA HILLS, Orange Co.

STETINA BRUNDA GARRED & BRUCKER, A PROFESSIONAL CORPORATION (AV)

24221 Calle De La Louisa, 4th Floor, 92653-3642
Telephone: 949-855-1246
Facsimile: 949-855-6371; 949-855-8986
Email: stetinabrundagarred&brucker@stetinalaw.com

Kit M. Stetina (Mr.)
Bruce B. Brunda
Mark B. Garred
William J. Brucker

Matthew A. Newboles
Thomas C. Naber (Not admitted in CA)
Darren S. Rimer
Eric L. Tanezaki
Eric K. Proul

LEGAL SUPPORT PERSONNEL

Kristy Kay Moore

Representative Clients: Northrop-Grumman Corp.; No Fear, Inc.; Dunn-Edwards, Inc.; Arnette Optic Illusions, Inc.; Pick Systems; Bird Products Corp.; 3-Day Blinds, Inc.

For full biographical listings, see the Martindale-Hubbell Law Directory

LONG BEACH, Los Angeles Co.

FLYNN, DELICH & WISE (AV)

One World Trade Center, Suite 1800, 90831-1800
Telephone: 562-435-2626
Fax: 562-437-7555
Email: NicholasP@FDW-LAW.COM
San Francisco, California Office: One California Street, Suite 350.
Telephone: 415-693-5566.
Fax: 415-693-0410. Email: SAMD@FDW-LAW.COM

Erich P. Wise
Nicholas S. Politis

Sook H. Lee

LEGAL SUPPORT PERSONNEL

Denise C. Orr (Legal Assistant)

Representative Clients: American Hawaii Cruises; Neptune Orient Lines; Through Transport Mutual Insurance Association, Ltd.; The Britannia Steam Ship Insurance Association Limited; The Steamship Mutual Underwriting Association (Bermuca) Ltd.; General Steamship Corp. Ltd.; Interocean Steamship Corp.; Sea-Land Service; KVP Systems.

For full biographical listings, see the Martindale-Hubbell Law Directory

*LOS ANGELES,** Los Angeles Co.

FULWIDER PATTON LEE & UTECHT, LLP (AV)

10877 Wilshire Boulevard, 10th Floor, 90024
Telephone: 310-824-5555
FAX: 310-824-9696
Email: fulwider@fulpat.com *URL:* http:///www.fulwiderlb@fulpat.com
Long Beach, California Office: 200 Oceangate, Suite 1550.
Telephone: 562-432-0453.
Fax: 562-435-6014. Internet: fulwiderlb@fulpat.com

MEMBERS OF FIRM

Robert W. Fulwider (1903-1979)
John M. Lee (1921-1978)
Warren L. Patton (1912-1985)
Richard A. Bardin
Gilbert G. Kovelman
Vern D. Schooley (Resident Partner, Long Beach Office)
James W. Paul
Craig B. Bailey
John S. Nagy
Stephen J. Strauss
Thomas H. Majcher
Thomas A. Runk
Michael S. Elkind
Gary M. Anderson (Resident Associate, Long Beach Office)
Ronald E. Perez

ASSOCIATES

David G. Parkhurst
Gunther O. Hanke (Resident Associate, Long Beach Office)
Robert L. Kovelman
Pamela G. Maher
John V. Hanley
John K. Fitzgerald
James Juo

(See Next Column)

ASSOCIATES (Continued)

Russell C. Pangborn (Resident Associate, Long Beach Office)
Richard B. Cates
Paul Y. Feng
David J. Pitman
Susan L. Pollyea
Robert Popa
David S. Sarisky
Michael S. Doll (Resident Associate, Long Beach Office)
Paul David O'Brien
David B. Sandelands, Jr.
Samuel L. Alberstadt
Brenton G. Graham

OF COUNSEL

Francis A. Utecht (Resident, Of Counsel, Long Beach Office)
I. Morley Drucker (A Professional Corporation)
Howard N. Sommers
Ellsworth R. Roston
Leonard D. Messinger

For full biographical listings, see the Martindale-Hubbell Law Directory

HECKER & HARRIMAN (AV)

1925 Century Park East Suite 2300, 90067
Telephone: 310-286-0377
Facsimile: 310-286-0488
Email: ghecker@hh.com *URL:* http://www.hh.com
San Jose, California Office: 2055 Gateway Place, Suite 400. 95110.
Telephone: 408-467-3832.

Gary A. Hecker
J. D. Harriman II
Frank M. Weyer
Carole A. Quinn
Andrea Mast

For full biographical listings, see the Martindale-Hubbell Law Directory

JONES, DAY, REAVIS & POGUE (AV)

555 West Fifth Street Suite 4600, 90013-1025
Telephone: 213-489-3939
Telecopier: 213-243-2539
Email: counsel@jonesday.com *URL:* http://www.jonesday.com
In Irvine, California: 5 Park Plaza, Suite 1100.
Telephone: 949-851-3939.
Telecopier: 949-553-7539.
In Atlanta, Georgia: 3500 SunTrust Plaza, 303 Peachtree Street.
Telephone: 404-521-3939.
Telecopier: 404-581-8330.
In Brussels, Belgium: Avenue Louise 480, 7th Floor, B-1050 Brussels.
Telephone: 32-2-645-14-11.
Telecopier: 32-2-645-14-45.
In Chicago, Illinois: 77 West Wacker.
Telephone: 312-782-3939.
Telecopier: 312-782-8585.
In Cleveland, Ohio: North Point, 901 Lakeside Avenue.
Telephone: 216-586-3939.
Telecopier: 216-579-0212.
In Columbus, Ohio: 1900 Huntington Center.
Telephone: 614-469-3939.
Telecopier: 614-461-4198.
In Dallas, Texas: 2727 North Harwood Street.
Telephone: 214-220-3939.
Telecopier: 214-969-5100.
In Frankfurt, Germany: Hochhaus am Park, Grüneburgweg 102, 60323 Frankfurt am Main.
Telephone: 49-69-9726-3939.
Telecopier: 49-69-9726-3993.
In Geneva, Switzerland: 20, rue de Candolle.
Telephone: 41-22-320-2339.
Telecopier: 41-22-320-1232.
In Hong Kong: 29th Floor, Entertainment Building, 30 Queen's Road Central.
Telephone: 852-2526-6895.
Telecopier: 852-2868-5871.
In London England: Bucklersbury House, 3 Queen Victoria Street.
Telephone: 44-20-7236-3939.
Telecopier: 44-20-7236-1113.
In New York, New York: 599 Lexington Avenue.
Telephone: 212-326-3939.
Telecopier: 212-755-7306.
In Paris, France: 120, rue du Faubourg Saint-Honoré.
Telephone: 33-1-56-59-3939.
Telecopier: 33-1-56-59-3938
In Pittsburgh, Pennsylvania: 500 Grant Street, 31st Floor.
Telephone: 412-391-3939.
Telecopier: 412-394-7959.
In Riyadh, Saudi Arabia: The International Law Firm (In Association with Jones, Day, Reavis & Pogue), Sulaymaniyah, Prince Mishari IBN, Abdulaziz Street, P.O. Box 22166.
Telephone: (966-1) 462-8866.
Telecopier: (966-1) 462-9001.
In Shanghai, China: 2805 Kerry Centre, 1515 Nanjing Road West.
Telephone: 86-21-5298-6568.
Telecopier: 86-21-5298-6569.
In Sydney, Australia: Governor Phillip Tower, Level 38, 1 Farrer Place.
Telephone: 61-2-9210-6921.
Telecopier: 61-2-9210-6926.
In Taipei, Taiwan: 8th Floor, 2 Tun Hwa South Road, Section 2.
Telephone: (886-2) 2704-6808.
Telecopier: (886-2) 2704-6791.

(See Next Column)

JONES, DAY, REAVIS & POGUE—*Continued*

In Tokyo, Japan: Toranomon 45 Mori Building, 3th Floor, 1-5, Toranomon 5-Chome, Minato-ku, Tokyo 105, Japan.
Telephone: 81-3-3433-3939.
Telecopier: 81-3-5401-2725.
In Washington, D.C.: 51 Louisiana Avenue, N.W.
Telephone: 202-879-3939.
Telecopier: 202-626-1700.

MEMBER OF FIRM IN LOS ANGELES

Victor G. Savikas

For Complete List of Firm Personnel, See General Section

For full biographical listings, see the Martindale-Hubbell Law Directory

LYON & LYON LLP (AV)

A Limited Liability Partnership including Professional Corporations
Suite 4700, 633 West Fifth Street, 90071-2066
Telephone: 213-489-1600
Fax: 213-955-0440
Email: lyon@lyonlyon.com *URL:* http://www.lyonlyon.com
Los Angeles, California Office: Suite 4700, 633 West Fifth Street, 90071-2066.
Telephone: 213-489-1600.
Irvine, California Office: Sixth Floor, 1900 Main Street, 92614.
Telephone: 949-567-2300.
Fax: 949-567-6600.
San Jose, California Office: Suite 800, 333 West San Carlos Street, 95110.
Telephone: 408-993-1555.
Fax: 408-287-2664.
La Jolla, California Office: Suite 800, 4225 Executive Square, 92037.
Telephone: 619-552-8400.
Fax: 619-552-0159.
White Plains, New York Office: Suite 1500, 1 North Lexington Avenue, 10601.
Telephone: 914-681-8851.
Fax: 914-686-4488.
Washington, D.C. Office: Suite 1040, 1701 Pennsylvania Avenue N.W., 20006.
Telephone: 202-331-3600.
Fax: 202-331-3301.

MEMBERS OF FIRM

Roland N. Smoot
Conrad R. Solum, Jr.
James W. Geriak (A Professional Corporation) (Irvine Office)
Robert M. Taylor, Jr. (Irvine Office)
Samuel B. Stone (A Professional Corporation) (Irvine Office)
Douglas E. Olson (A Professional Corporation) (La Jolla Office)
Robert E. Lyon (A Professional Corporation)
Robert C. Weiss (A Professional Corporation)
Richard E. Lyon, Jr., (A Professional Corporation)
John D. McConaghy (A Professional Corporation)
William C. Steffin (A Professional Corporation)
Coe A. Bloomberg (A Professional Corporation)
J. Donald McCarthy
Arnold Sklar
John M. Benassi (La Jolla Office)
James H. Shalek (White Plains, N.Y. Office)
Allan W. Jansen (Irvine Office)
Robert W. Dickerson
Roy L. Anderson
David B. Murphy (Irvine Office)
James C. Brooks
Jeffrey M. Olson
Steven D. Hemminger (San Jose Office)
Jerrold B. Reilly
Paul H. Meier
John A. Rafter, Jr.
Kenneth H. Ohriner
Mary S. Consalvi (La Jolla Office)
Lois M. Kwasigroch
Lawrence R. LaPorte
Robert C. Laurenson (La Jolla Office)
Carol A. Schneider
Hope E. Melville (Irvine Office)
Michael J. Wise
Richard Warburg (La Jolla Office)
Kurt T. Mulville (Irvine Office)
Theodore S. Maceiko
Bruce G. Chapman
F.T. Alexandra Mahaney (La Jolla Office)
Stephen S. Korniczky (La Jolla Office)
James P. Brogan (Irvine Office)
David A. Randall
Christopher A. Vanderlaan
James T. Carmichael (Washington D.C. Office)

ASSOCIATES

Corrine M. Freeman (Irvine Office)
David T. Burse (San Jose Office)
Charles R. Balgenorth
Jeffrey A. Miller (San Jose Office)
Armand F. Ayazi
Jessica R. Wolff (La Jolla Office)
Jeffrey William Guise (La Jolla Office)
Charles S. Berkman (La Jolla Office)
Sheryl Rubinstein Silverstein (La Jolla Office)
David E. Wang (Irvine Office)
Kenneth S. Roberts (Irvine Office)
Brent D. Sokol
John C. Kappos (Irvine Office)
Thomas J. Brindisi
Charles Calvin Fowler (Irvine Office)
Lisa C. Ward
Vicki Gee Norton (La Jolla Office)
Michael A. Tomasulo
Charles A. Kertell
Jonathan Hallman (Irvine Office)
Lynn Y. McKernan (San Jose Office)
Michael J. Bolan (Irvine Office)

(See Next Column)

ASSOCIATES (Continued)

Gregory R. Stephenson (White Plains, N.Y. Office)
Mary Agnes Tuck
Bernard F. Rose (San Jose Office)
Daniel M. Chambers (La Jolla Office)
Yasser M. El-Gamal
Stephen C. Beuerle (La Jolla Office)
Christopher Peter Broderick
Richard San Pietro (La Jolla Office)
Kurt M. Kjelland (La Jolla Office)
Wesley B. Ames (La Jolla Office)
William Andrew English (Irvine Office)
Brian A. Schar (Irvine Office)
Carlos M. Candeloro
Peter R. Munson (La Jolla Office)
Michael S. Davidson (Irvine Office)
Todd R. Miller
Nathaniel L. Dilger (Irvine Office)
David Heskel Ben-Meir
Craig A. Neugeboren (San Jose Office)
Chad W. Miller (Irvine Office)
Manuel Federico de la Cerra (La Jolla Office)
Douglas C. Murdock (La Jolla Office)
Peter C. Mei (San Jose Office)
Alan M. Federbush (Not admitted in CA; White Plains, N.Y. Office)
Troy M. Schmelzer (La Jolla Office)
Keith Kind (La Jolla Office)
Michael D. Fabiano (La Jolla Office)
Mark A. Catan (Not admitted in CA; White Plains, N.Y. Office)
Eugene K. Hyun (Not admitted in CA; White Plains, N.Y. Office)
Mikael Havluciyan (Irvine Office)
Rahul D. Engineer (San Jose Office)
John E. Peterson (La Jolla Office)
Vincent K. Gustafson
Jon E. Maki (La Jolla Office)
Trent Edward Campione
Sarah A. Brown (Irvine Office)
Robert S. Mayer (Not admitted in CA; White Plains, N.Y. Office)
Charles M. Doyle (White Plains, N.Y. Office)
Karry W. Wang (Irvine Office)
Robert W. Prince (La Jolla Office)
Bonita L. Severy (Irvine Office)
David W. Lamb
John J. Yim (Washington D.C. Office)

OF COUNSEL

Bradford J. Duft (La Jolla Office)
Suzanne L. Biggs (La Jolla Office)
Reginald D. Greene

Representative Clients: Cedars-Sinai Medical Center; Genentech; Honda; Mag Instrument, Inc.; Mitsubishi; Panavision; Quantum Corporation; Spectra-Physics, Inc.

For full biographical listings, see the Martindale-Hubbell Law Directory

MITCHELL, SILBERBERG & KNUPP LLP (AV)

A Partnership including Professional Corporations
11377 West Olympic Boulevard, 90064
Telephone: 310-312-2000
Fax: 310-312-3100
Email: info@msk.com *URL:* http://www.msk.com

MEMBERS OF FIRM

Miriam Claire Beezy (A Professional Corporation)
George M. Borkowski (A Professional Corporation)
Jeffrey D. Goldman (A Professional Corporation)
Steven E. Shapiro (A Professional Corporation)
David A. Steinberg (A Professional Corporation)
Robert C. Welsh (A Professional Corporation)

ASSOCIATES

Marc E. Mayer
Brent Rabowsky
Joseph G. Swan

References: Wells Fargo Bank, N.A.; Merrill, Lynch.

For Complete List of Firm Personnel, See General Section

For full biographical listings, see the Martindale-Hubbell Law Directory

O'MELVENY & MYERS LLP (AV)

400 South Hope Street, 90071-2899
Telephone: 213-430-6000
Facsimile: 213-430-6407
Cable: MOMS
Telex: 674122
Email: omminfo@omm.com *URL:* http://www.omm.com
Century City, CA Office: 1999 Avenue of the Stars, Los Angeles, 90067-6035.
Telex: 674097. Tel: 310-553-6700.
Fax: 310-246-6779.
Newport Beach, CA Office: 610 Newport Center Drive, 92660-6429.
Telex: 4722088. Tel: 949-760-9600.
Fax: 949-823-6994.
San Francisco, CA Office: Embarcadero Center West, 275 Battery Street, 94111-3305. Tel: 415-984-8700.
Fax: 415-984-8701.
New York, NY Office: Citicorp Center, 153 East 53rd Street, 10022-4611.
Telex: 129165. Tel: 212-326-2000.
Fax: 212-326-2061.

(See Next Column)

O'MELVENY & MYERS LLP, *Los Angeles—Continued*

Washington, DC Office: 555 13th Street, N.W., 20004-1109.
Cable: MOMSWSH.
Telex: 89622. Tel: 202-383-5300.
Fax: 202-383-5414.
London Office: O'Melveny & Myers, 3 Finsbury Square, London, EC2A 1LA, England. Tel: 44-171-256-8451. Fax 44-171-638-8205.
Tokyo Office: Akasaka Twin Tower, East 14F, 2-17-23, Akasaka, Minato-ku, Tokyo 107-0052, Japan. Tel: 03-5562-2800.
Fax: 03-5575-3840.
Hong Kong Office: O'Melveny & Myers, Suite 1905, Tower Two, Lippo Centre, 89 Queensway, Central, Hong Kong. Tel: 852-2523-8266.
Fax: 852-2522-1760.
Shanghai Office: Kerry Centre, 20F, 1515 Nanjing Road West, Shanghai, 200040 People's Republic of China. Tel: 86-21-5298-5600.
Fax: 86-21-5298-5500.

PARTNER

Patrick Lynch

For Complete List of Firm Personnel, See General Section

For full biographical listings, see the Martindale-Hubbell Law Directory

OPPENHEIMER WOLFF & DONNELLY LLP (AV)

2029 Century Park East 38th Floor, 90067
Telephone: 310-788-5000
FAX: 310-277-1297
Email: oppenheimer.com
Minneapolis, Minnesota Office: 3300 Plaza VII, 45 South Seventh Street. 55402.
Telephone: 612-607-7000.
FAX: 612-607-7100.
Amsterdam, The Netherlands Office: Keizergracht 241.
Telephone: 31-20-423-4555.
FAX: 312-20-423-4545.
Brussels, Belgium Office: Avenue Louise 240, Box 5, 1050.
Telephone: 32-2-626-0500.
FAX: 32-2-626-0510.
Geneva, Switzerland Office: Rue Gabriel Eynard, 6, 1205.
Telephone: (41/22) 311-7410.
FAX: (41/22) 311-4707.
Newport Beach, California Office: 500 Newport Center Drive, Suite 700, 92660.
Telephone: 949-823-6000.
FAX: 949-823-6100.
New York, N.Y. Office: The Chrysler East Building, 19th Floor, 666 Third Avenue, 10017.
Telephone: 212-826-5000.
FAX: 212-486-0708.
Paris, France Office: 35 Boulevard des Capucines, 75002.
Telephone: (33/1) 53 45 40 00.
FAX: (33/1) 53 45 40 10.
St. Paul, Minnesota Office: 1700 First National Bank Building, 55101.
Telephone: 651-605-2000.
FAX: 651-605-2100.
Washington, D.C. Office: Oppenheimer Wolff Donnelly & Bayh LLP, 1350 Eye Street, N.W., Suite 200, 20005.
Telephone: 202-312-8000.
FAX: 202-312-8100.
Palo Alto, California Office: 3373 Hillview Avenue, Suite 200, 94304.
Telephone: 650-320-4000.
FAX: 650-320-4100.
Chicago, Illinois Office: Oppenheimer Wolff & Donnelly (Illinois), Two Prudential Plaza, 45th Floor, 180 North Stetson Avenue, 60601.
Telephone: 312-616-1800.
Fax: 312-616-5800.

RESIDENT PARTNERS

Alan C. Rose — Christopher Darrow
William Poms — Jane Shay Wald
Guy Porter Smith — Douglas N. Larson
Charles Berman — David J. Oldenkamp
Gary E. Lande — Marc E. Brown
Louis J. Bovasso — J. Patrick Weir
Michael D. Harris — Charles Rosenberg
Mark P. Wine — Michael B. Farber
Gregory B. Wood — Alan P. Block
Scott R. Hansen

RESIDENT ASSOCIATES

Sandra M. Parker — Barbara J. Quinn
Cynthia A. Lock — Ronald S. Tamura
Joel D. Voelzke — Jake A. Taylor
George L. Fountain — Sung I. Oh

Reference: City National Bank (Century Plaza Office, Century City).

For full biographical listings, see the Martindale-Hubbell Law Directory

PRETTY, SCHROEDER & POPLAWSKI, A PROFESSIONAL CORPORATION (AV)

19th Floor, 444 South Flower Street, 90071
Telephone: 213-622-7700
Telecopier: 213-489-4210
URL: http://www.psp-iplaw.com

Laurence H. Pretty — Michael J. MacDermott
Robert A. Schroeder — Anne Wang
Edward G. Poplawski — Paul D. Tripodi, II
Jeffrey F. Craft — Marc E. Hankin
Richard A. Wallen — Donald C. Kordich

J. Christopher James — Janene P. Bassett
Jeffrey A. Finn — William F. Mulholland, II
Gregory S. Cordrey — Carl A. Kukkonen, III
Matthew C. Lapple — Nisan A. Steinberg
Eric T. King — Denise L. McKenzie
Mark B. Mizrahi — Janaki Komandurі

COUNSEL

Daniel C. Mallery — Michael L. Crapenhoft

For full biographical listings, see the Martindale-Hubbell Law Directory

SMALL LARKIN, LLP (AV)

10940 Wilshire Boulevard, Eighteenth Floor, 90024
Telephone: 310-209-4400
Fax: 310-209-4450
Cable Address: SLK MARK
Telex: 6502238698
Email: info@sliplaw.com *URL:* http://www.sliplaw.com

MEMBERS OF FIRM

Thomas M. Small — Christopher C. Larkin
Joan Kupersmith Larkin — Jon E. Hokanson
Kenneth L. Wilton

J. Alison Grabell — Jodi L. Sax
Jill A. Schwartz

LEGAL SUPPORT PERSONNEL

Susan Brady Blasco

For full biographical listings, see the Martindale-Hubbell Law Directory

MENLO PARK, San Mateo Co.

ARNOLD WHITE & DURKEE, A PROFESSIONAL CORPORATION (AV)

155 Linfield Drive, 94025-3741
Telephone: 650-614-4500
Facsimile: 650-614-4599
Email: info@awd.com *URL:* http://www.awd.com
Houston, Texas Office: 750 Bering Drive, 77057-2198.
Telephone: 713-787-1400.
Facsimile: 713-787-1440.
Austin, Texas Office: 1900 One American Center, 600 Congress Avenue, 78701-3248.
Telephone: 512-418-3000.
Facsimile: 512-474-7577.
Washington, D.C. Office: One Franklin Square, 1301 K Street, N.W., Suite 350, East Tower, 20005.
Telephone: 202-289-0229.
Facsimile: 202-289-7535.
Chicago, Illinois Office: 800 Quaker Tower, 321 North Clark Street, 60610-4714.
Telephone: 312-744-0090.
Facsimile: 312-755-4489.
Minneapolis, Minnesota Office: 4850 U.S. Bank Place, 601 Second Avenue South, 55402-4320.
Telephone: 612-321-2800.
Facsimile: 612-321-9600.

John F. Lynch (Not admitted in CA) — Robert N. Phillips
Glenn W. Rhodes — Mark K. Dickson
David L. Bilsker
James F. Valentine

Richard J. Lutton, Jr. — Mary G. Manley
Daniel T. Shvodian — Bobby A. Ghajar
Lisa M. Martens — Mark A. Seka
Meredith M. McKenzie

OF COUNSEL

Lisa A. Garono

For full biographical listings, see the Martindale-Hubbell Law Directory

NEWPORT BEACH, Orange Co.

DRUMMOND & DUCKWORTH (AV)

4590 MacArthur Boulevard, Suite 500, 92660
Telephone: 949-724-1255
Fax: 949-724-1139
Email: patent_lawyer@worldnet.att.net

William H. Drummond David G. Duckworth

For full biographical listings, see the Martindale-Hubbell Law Directory

OPPENHEIMER WOLFF & DONNELLY LLP (AV)

500 Newport Center Drive, Suite 700, 92660
Telephone: 949-823-6000
FAX: 949-823-6100
Email: info@oppenheimer.com *URL:* http://www.oppenheimer.com
Minneapolis, Minnesota Office: 3300 Plaza VII, 45 South Seventh Street. 55402.
Telephone: 612-607-7000.
FAX: 612-607-7100.
Amsterdam, The Netherlands Office: Keizergracht 241.
Telephone: 31-20-423-4555.
FAX: 312-20-423-4545.
Brussels, Belgium Office: Avenue Louise 240, Box 5, 1050.
Telephone: 32-2-626-0500.
FAX: 32-2-626-0510.
Geneva, Switzerland Office: Rue Gabriel Eynard, 6, 1205.
Telephone: (41/22) 311-7410.
FAX: (41/22) 311-4707.
New York, N.Y. Office: The Chrysler East Building, 19th Floor, 666 Third Avenue, 10017.
Telephone: 212-826-5000.
FAX: 212-486-0708.
Paris, France Office: 35 Boulevard des Capucines, 75002.
Telephone: (33/1) 53 45 40 00.
FAX: (33/1) 53 45 40 10.
St. Paul, Minnesota Office: 1700 First National Bank Building, 55101.
Telephone: 651-605-2000.
FAX: 651-605-2100.
Washington, D.C. Office: Oppenheimer Wolff Donnelly & Bayh LLP, 1350 Eye Street, N.W., Suite 200, 20005.
Telephone: 202-312-8000.
FAX: 202-312-8100.
Los Angeles, California Office: 2029 Century Park East, 38th Floor, 90067.
Telephone: 310-788-5000.
FAX: 310-277-1297.
Palo Alto, California Office: 3373 Hillview Avenue, Suite 200, 94304.
Telephone: 650-320-4000.
FAX: 650-320-4100.
Chicago, Illinois Office: Oppenheimer Wolff & Donnelly (Illinois), Two Prudential Plaza, 45th Floor, 180 North Stetson Avenue, 60601.
Telephone: 312-616-1800.
Fax: 312-616-5800.

RESIDENT PARTNERS

Edward F. O'Connor Kurt A. MacLean
Bruce M. Canter

RESIDENT ASSOCIATE

Louis C. Cullman

Reference: City National Bank (Century Plaza Office, Century City).

For full biographical listings, see the Martindale-Hubbell Law Directory

LARRY K. ROBERTS, INC. (AV)

660 Newport Center Drive, Suite 710, P.O. Box 8569, 92658
Telephone: 949-640-6200
Facsimile: 949-640-1206
Email: LarryKRoberts@prodigy.net

Larry K. Roberts

For full biographical listings, see the Martindale-Hubbell Law Directory

SKJERVEN, MORRILL, MACPHERSON, FRANKLIN & FRIEL LLP (AV)

Suite 330, 610 Newport Center Drive, 92660
Telephone: 949-718-6780
Telecopier: 949-718-6799
San Jose, California Office: Suite 700, 25 Metro Drive.
Telephone: 408-453-9200.
Telecopier: 408-453-7979.
San Francisco, California Office: Suite 800, 601 California Street.
Telephone: 415-986-8383.
Telecopier: 415-982-7372.
Austin, Texas Office: Suite 300 West, 9600 Great Hills Trail.
Telephone: 512-794-3600.
Telecopier: 512-794-3601.

MEMBERS OF FIRM

Ken J. Koestner (Not admitted in CA; Resident) Alan H. MacPherson

(See Next Column)

ASSOCIATES

Tom Chen William L. Robinson
Theodore P. Lopez T.J. Singh

OF COUNSEL

Donald C. Lawrence

Reference: Bank of America.

For full biographical listings, see the Martindale-Hubbell Law Directory

PALO ALTO, Santa Clara Co.

FISH & NEAVE (AVⓉ)

Fish, Richardson & Neave, New York (1916-1969)
525 University Avenue Suite 300, 94301
Telephone: 650-617-4000
Telecopier: 650-617-4090
URL: http://www.fishneave.com
New York, New York Office: 1251 Avenue of the Americas.
Telephone: 212-596-9000.
Telex: 14-8367.
Cable Address: Fishneave.
Telecopier: 212-596-9090.

RESIDENT MEMBERS

Edward F. Mullowney Mark D. Rowland
Robert J. Goldman Vicki S. Veenker
Norman H. Beamer Nicola A. Pisano

RESIDENT SENIOR ATTORNEY

Gabrielle E. Higgins

RESIDENT ASSOCIATES

William H. Steinmetz (Not admitted in CA) Brian C. Cannon
Daniel M. Becker
Terrence J. P. Kearney Kurtis D. MacFerrin
Kevin P.B. Johnson David A. Makman
James E. Hopenfeld Michelle L. Finneran
William L. Leschensky Tina S. Patel
Petrina S. Hsi Steven John Cahill
James Trosino Adam P. Noah

For full biographical listings, see the Martindale-Hubbell Law Directory

BASIL P. FTHENAKIS (AV)

540 University Avenue, Suite 300, 94301-1912
Telephone: 650-326-1397
Fax: 650-326-3203
Email: basilp@fthenakis.com

For full biographical listings, see the Martindale-Hubbell Law Directory

OPPENHEIMER WOLFF & DONNELLY LLP (AV)

3373 Hillview Avenue, Suite 200, 94304
Telephone: 650-320-4000
FAX: 650-320-4100
Email: oppenheimer.com
Minneapolis, Minnesota Office: 3300 Plaza VII, 45 South Seventh Street. 55402.
Telephone: 612-607-7000.
FAX: 612-607-7100.
Amsterdam, The Netherlands Office: Keizergracht 241.
Telephone: 31-20-423-4555.
FAX: 312-20-423-4545.
Brussels, Belgium Office: Avenue Louise 240, Box 5, 1050.
Telephone: 32-2-626-0500.
FAX: 32-2-626-0510.
Geneva, Switzerland Office: Rue Gabriel Eynard, 6, 1205.
Telephone: (41/22) 311-7410.
FAX: (41/22) 311-4707.
Newport Beach, California Office: 500 Newport Center Drive, Suite 700, 92660.
Telephone: 949-823-6000.
FAX: 949-823-6100.
New York, N.Y. Office: The Chrysler East Building, 19th Floor, 666 Third Avenue, 10017.
Telephone: 212-826-5000.
FAX: 212-486-0708.
Paris, France Office: 35 Boulevard des Capucines, 75002.
Telephone: (33/1) 53 45 40 00.
FAX: (33/1) 53 45 40 10.
St. Paul, Minnesota Office: 1700 First National Bank Building, 55101.
Telephone: 651-605-2000.
FAX: 651-605-2100.
Washington, D.C. Office: Oppenheimer Wolff Donnelly & Bayh LLP, 1350 Eye Street, N.W., Suite 200, 20005.
Telephone: 202-312-8000.
FAX: 202-312-8100.
Los Angeles, California Office: 2029 Century Park East, 38th Floor, 90067.
Telephone: 310-788-5000.
FAX: 310-277-1297.

(See Next Column)

OPPENHEIMER WOLFF & DONNELLY LLP, *Palo Alto—Continued*

Chicago, Illinois Office: Oppenheimer Wolff & Donnelly (Illinois), Two Prudential Plaza, 45th Floor, 180 North Stetson Avenue, 60601.
Telephone: 312-616-1800.
Fax: 312-616-5800.

RESIDENT PARTNERS

Michael H. Kalkstein
Claude A. S. Hamrick
Robert O. Guillot
Timothy T. Huber
Chris S. Graham
E. Patrick Ellisen
Chien (Chris) W. Chou

RESIDENT ASSOCIATES

Michael K. Bosworth
Esther H. La
Lisa K. Roberts
Ben H. Bedi
Anthony B. Diepenbrock, III
Valerie M. Wagner
Michael N. Edelman
Justin F. Boyce
Leah Sherry
Donald A. Larkin

Reference: City National Bank (Century Plaza Office, Century City).

For full biographical listings, see the Martindale-Hubbell Law Directory

TOWNSEND AND TOWNSEND AND CREW LLP (AV)

A Limited Liability Partnership including a Professional Corporation
379 Lytton Avenue, 94301-1431
Telephone: 650-326-2400
Telecopier: 650-326-2422
Email: inquire@townsend.com *URL:* http://www.townsend.com
San Francisco, California Office: Two Embarcadero Center, Eighth Floor.
Telephone: 415-576-0200.
Facsimile: 415-576-0300.
Denver, Colorado Office: 1200 17th Street, Suite 2700.
Telephone: 303-571-4000.
Fax: 303-571-4321.
Seattle, Washington Office: 601 Union Street, Suite 5400.
Telephone: 206-467-9600.
Telecopier: 206-623-6793.

MEMBERS OF FIRM

Kenneth R. Allen
Robert C. Colwell
Daniel J. Furniss
David N. Slone
James F. Hann
James M. Heslin
Gary T. Aka
William M. Smith
Paul C. Haughey
Theodore G. Brown, III
William J. Bohler
Karen B. Dow
Theodore T. Herhold
Susan M. Spaeth
Joe Liebeschuetz
William L. Shaffer
Richard Takashi Ogawa
Stephen J. Akerley

OF COUNSEL

Henry K. Woodward

ASSOCIATES

Stephen Y.F. Pang
Mark D. Barrish
Melvin D. Chan
Byron W. Cooper
R. Ted Apple
Gregory Scott Bishop
Jordan Trent Jones
Paul A. Durdik
David R. Heckadon
Truong T. Dinh
James W. Soong
Sujit B. Kotwal
Rebecca E. Perez-Platt
Kim Kanzaki (Not admitted in CA)
Leonard T. Guzman
Craig P. Wong
Matthew J. Spark
Anne M. Rogaski
George B.F. Yee
Rebecca D. Fields
Igor Shoiket
James K. Okamoto
Hugh Wang
Gregory E. Stanton

For full biographical listings, see the Martindale-Hubbell Law Directory

PASADENA, Los Angeles Co.

JOSEPH E. MUETH A LAW CORPORATION (AV)

225 South Lake Avenue, Eighth Floor, 91101-1599
Telephone: 626-584-0396
Fax: 626-584-6862

Joseph E. Mueth

Reference: Bank of America, 333 South Hope Street, Los Angeles, California.

For full biographical listings, see the Martindale-Hubbell Law Directory

*SACRAMENTO,** Sacramento Co.

BOUTIN, DENTINO, GIBSON DI GIUSTO, HODELL & WEST, A PROFESSIONAL CORPORATION (AV)

455 Capitol Mall, Suite 300, 95814-4406
Telephone: 916-321-4444
Telecopier: 916-441-7597
URL: http://www.boutindentino.com
Tucson, Arizona Office: 405 West Franklin Street, 85718.
Telephone: 520-882-2944.

(See Next Column)

Stephen F. Boutin
William Dentino
Chris Gibson
John E. Di Giusto
Douglas M. Hodell
R. Michael West
Robert D. Swanson
Ned M. Gelhaar

Kimberly L. Jackson
Mark W. Owens
James R. Moore
Michael T. Sparks
Sallie-Carol Orbas
Jeffrey B. Slaton

OF COUNSEL

Robert G. West
Thomas G. Manolakas

For full biographical listings, see the Martindale-Hubbell Law Directory

HUNTER RICHEY DI BENEDETTO & BREWER, LLP (AV)

A Limited Liability Partnership
Renaissance Tower, 801 K Street, 23rd Floor, 95814-3525
Telephone: 916-491-3000
Facsimile: 916-491-3080
Email: hrdb@hrdb.com *URL:* http://www.hrdb.com

MEMBERS OF FIRM

William S. Hunter
Win R. Richey
Florence L. Di Benedetto
Roy E. Brewer
Anne E. Ferguson
James F. Geary
Janet C. Eisenbeis
Stephen C. Ruehmann
Sharon K. Sandeen
Jack V. Lovell
Patricia J. Hartman

OF COUNSEL

Laurie E. Davis

LEGAL SUPPORT PERSONNEL

Lori J. Moody (Paralegal)
Deborah M. Johnson (Paralegal)
Linda Jane Hall (Executive Assistant)
Jennifer E. Mueller (Legal Assistant)
Michele L. Nickell (Legal Assistant)
Lynetta G. Goodwin

For full biographical listings, see the Martindale-Hubbell Law Directory

LIVINGSTON & MATTESICH, LAW CORPORATION (AV)

1201 K Street, Suite 1100, 95814
Telephone: 916-442-1111
Fax: 916-448-1709
Email: l&m@lmlaw.net *URL:* http://www.lmlaw.net

Gene Livingston
James M. Mattesich
Carol Livingston
Rebecca M. Ceniceros
Emilio E. Varanini, III
Kenneth M. Malovos
Kathleen E. Finnerty
Joanna R. Mendoza

Steven P. Belzer
Jeffrey Leacox
Randy Pollack
Alice H. Choi
Stephen Craig Hunter
Matthew J. Goldman
Joel C. Baiocchi
Baldassaro (Bill) Di Capo
John McKinsey
Timothy E. Naccarato
Craig N. Lundgren
Mary Farrell Taylor
Brian Crone
Gay L. Carroll
Steven G. Churchwell

Representative Clients: 3M Company; Beterbender Manufacturing; Creative Online Computer Services, Inc.; Hansen Information Technologies, Inc.; Harrington Photography; Robot Science and Technology Magazine; Skilz Athletics.

For full biographical listings, see the Martindale-Hubbell Law Directory

O'BANION & RITCHEY LLP (AV)

400 Capitol Mall, Suite 1550, 95814
Telephone: 916-498-1010
Facsimile: 916-498-1074
Email: jpo@intellectual.com *URL:* http://www.intellectual.com

MEMBERS OF FIRM

John P. O'Banion
James M. Ritchey

For full biographical listings, see the Martindale-Hubbell Law Directory

*SAN DIEGO,** San Diego Co.

BAKER & MAXHAM, A PROFESSIONAL CORPORATION (AV)

Symphony Towers, 750 B Street, Suite 3100, 92101
Telephone: 619-233-9004
Facsimile: 619-544-1246 (Groups I, II, III)
URL: http://www.lawyers.com/bakermaxhamlaw
Email: fbaker@bakermaxham.com *URL:* http://www.bakermaxham.com

Freling E. Baker
Lawrence A. Maxham

Peter R. Martinez
Steven J. Robbins
David B. Woycechowsky

Reference: Peninsula Bank of San Diego.

For full biographical listings, see the Martindale-Hubbell Law Directory

San Diego—Continued

Fitch, Even, Tabin & Flannery (AV)

4250 Executive Square, Suite 510, 92037
Telephone: 619-552-1311
Telecopier: 619-552-0095
Email: email@fitcheven.com *URL:* http://www.fitcheven.com
Chicago, Illinois Office: 120 South La Salle, Suite 1600. 60603.
Telephone: 312-577-7000.
Fax: 312-577-7007.
Washington, D.C. Office: 1801 K Street, N.W., Suite 401L, 20006-1201.
Telephone: 202-789-4900.
Fax: 202-789-8707.

MEMBERS OF FIRM

Julius Tabin
James J. Schumann (Not admitted in CA; Resident)
Thomas F. Lebens (Resident)

Marianne S. Hamilton
Scott J. Menghini
Francis T. Kalinski II (Resident)

For full biographical listings, see the Martindale-Hubbell Law Directory

Michael H. Jester (AV)

Symphony Towers, 750 B Street, Suite 2560, 92101-8122
Telephone: 619-231-9090
Fax: 619-231-9093
Email: mjester@cts.com *URL:* http://www.lawyers.com/jesterlaw

For full biographical listings, see the Martindale-Hubbell Law Directory

*SAN FRANCISCO,** San Francisco Co.

Eckhoff & Hoppe (AV)

4 Embarcadero Center Suite 760, 94111
Telephone: 415-391-7160
Fax: 415-391-7164
Email: eckhoffho@aol.com

MEMBER OF FIRM

Bruce H. Johnsonbaugh

For full biographical listings, see the Martindale-Hubbell Law Directory

Flynn, Delich & Wise (AV)

One California Street, Suite 350, 94111
Telephone: 415-693-5566
Fax: 415-693-0410
Email: SamD@fdw-law.com
Long Beach, California Office: 1 World Trade Center, Suite 1800.
Telephone: 562-435-2626.
Fax: 562-437-7555. Email: NicholasP@FDW-LAW.COM.

John A. Flynn (1945-1997)
Sam D. Delich
James B. Nebel

OF COUNSEL

Pecos Bill Field

Faye Lee Peterson
Conte C. Cicala
Jeanine S. Tede

Representative Clients: American Hawaii Cruises; Neptune Orient Lines; Through Transport Mutual Insurance Association, Ltd.; The Britannia Steam Ship Insurance Association Limited; The Steamship Mutual Underwriting Association (Bermuda) Ltd.; General Steamship Corp, Ltd.; Commodore Cruise Line Ltd.; Interocean Steamship Corporation; Sea-Land Service, Inc.; KVP Systems, Inc.

For full biographical listings, see the Martindale-Hubbell Law Directory

Gallagher & Lathrop, A Professional Corporation (AV)

601 California Street, Suite 1111, 94108-2805
Telephone: 415-989-8080
Facsimile: 415-989-0910
Email: office@patentz.com

Thomas A. Gallagher
David N. Lathrop

Timothy Jay Lane

For full biographical listings, see the Martindale-Hubbell Law Directory

Limbach & Limbach, L.L.P. (AV)

2001 Ferry Building, 94111
Telephone: 415-433-4150
Fax: 415-433-8716
Email: inquiry@limbach.com *URL:* http://www.limbach.com
San Jose, California Office: 10 Almaden, Suite 1400.
Telephone: 408-291-5225.

(See Next Column)

MEMBERS OF FIRM

Karl A. Limbach
George C. Limbach
John K. Uilkema
Neil A. Smith
Veronica Colby Devitt
Ronald L. Yin
Gerald T. Sekimura
Michael A. Stallman
Philip A. Girard
Michael J. Pollock
Stephen M. Everett
Maria S. Cefalu
Alfred A. Equitz
Mark A. Dalla Valle
Charles P. Sammut
Mark C. Pickering
Patricia Coleman James
Kathleen A. Frost

ASSOCIATES

Alan A. Limbach
Douglas C. Limbach
Seong-Kun Oh
Cameron A. King
Kyla L. Harriel
Mayumi Maeda
Kent Tobin
Michael R. Ward
Roger S. Sampson
Tina Chen
Charles L. Hamilton
Andrew V. Smith
Eric N. Hoover
Parisa Jorjani

OF COUNSEL

J. Thomas McCarthy
Joel G. Ackerman

For full biographical listings, see the Martindale-Hubbell Law Directory

Majestic, Parsons, Siebert & Hsue, A Professional Corporation (AV)

Four Embarcadero Center, Suite 1100, 94111-4106
Telephone: 415-248-5500
Telecopier: 415-362-5418
URL: http://www.mpsh.com
Santa Clara, California Office: 2700 Augustine Drive, Suite 198.
Telephone: 415-248-5500.

Gerald P. Parsons
Martin F. Majestic
J. Suzanne Siebert
James S. Hsue
K. Alison deRuntz

Tom Hunter
Stephen J. Le Blanc
Nancy E. Martin
Dang M. Vo

OF COUNSEL

Keiichi Nishimura

LEGAL SUPPORT PERSONNEL

Philip Yau
Michael G. Cleveland
Steven R. Vosen (Patent Agent)

For full biographical listings, see the Martindale-Hubbell Law Directory

Medlen & Carroll, LLP (AV)

220 Montgomery Street, Suite 2200, 94104
Telephone: 415-705-8410
Facsimile: 415-397-8338
Email: contact@medlencarroll.com *URL:* http://www.medlencarroll.com
Cambridge, Massachusetts Office: Four Cambridge Center, Second Floor, 02142.
Telephone: 617-252-3353.
Facsimile: 617-252-3323.
Madison, Wisconsin Office: 6333 Odana Road, Second Floor, 53719.
Telephone: 608-298-3000.
Fax: 608-298-3010.

MEMBERS OF FIRM

Virginia Shaw Medlen
Peter G. Carroll
Kamrin T. MacKnight

ASSOCIATES

Lisa K. Levine
Maha Abbas Hamdan

INTERNATIONAL TRADEMARK DEPARTMENT

Daw Aye Cho (Manager)

PATENT AGENT

Emily C. Tongco

TECHNOLOGY SPECIALIST

Edward J. DesJardins, Jr.

For full biographical listings, see the Martindale-Hubbell Law Directory

Skjerven, Morrill, MacPherson, Franklin & Friel LLP (AV)

Suite 800, 601 California Street, 94108
Telephone: 415-986-8383
Telecopier: 415-982-7372
Newport Beach, California Office; Suite 330, 610 Newport Center Drive.
Telephone: 949-718-6780.
Telecopier: 949-718-6799.
San Jose, California Office: Suite 700, 25 Metro Drive.
Telephone: 408-453-9200.
Telecopier: 408-453-7979.
Austin, Texas Office: Suite 300 West, 9600 Great Hills Trail.
Telephone: 512-794-3600.
Telecopier: 512-794-3601.

(See Next Column)

HOLME ROBERTS & OWEN LLP, *Denver—Continued*

PARTNERS OF FIRM

Boyd N. Boland
Ross E. Breyfogle
Susan E. Duffey Campbell (Colorado Springs Office)
Kent A. Fischmann (Boulder Office)
Richard L. Gabriel
Lynn Parker Hendrix
Christopher J. Kulish (Boulder Office)
Thomas R. Marsh
George G. Matava
John R. Posthumus
Steven B. Smith (Colorado Springs Office)

SPECIAL COUNSEL

James L. Johnson

ASSOCIATES

Robert Boyd Berube
Brian A. Carpenter
Nancy L. Dempsey
Jeffrey A. Divney
Stanley J. Gradisar
Kenneth J. Johnson

For Complete List of Firm Personnel, See General Section

For full biographical listings, see the Martindale-Hubbell Law Directory

SHERIDAN ROSS, P.C. (AV)

1560 Broadway, Suite 1200, 80202
Telephone: 303-863-9700
Facsimile: 303-863-0223
Email: srlaw@sheridanross.com

David F. Zinger
Craig C. Groseth
Michael L. Tompkins
Todd P. Blakely
Gary J. Connell
Sabrina Crowley Stavish
Joseph E. Kovarik
Susan Pryor Willson
Lewis D. Hansen
Robert R. Brunelli
Douglas W. Swartz
Richard L. Hughes

Bruce A. Kugler
Dana Lynn Hartje
Paul S. Hansra
Don D. Cha
Benjamin Baughman Lieb
Bradley M. Knepper
John C. Scott
Miriam R. Drickman

OF COUNSEL

Philip H. Sheridan (P.C.)
Wannell M. Crook
Theresa A. Brown

LEGAL SUPPORT PERSONNEL

TECHNICAL SPECIALIST

Dennis J. Dupray
Angela Dallas-Pedretti

PARALEGALS

Janet E. Balent
Peggy West

Representative Clients: Ball Corporation; British Nuclear Fuels; Case Logic Inc.; COBE Laboratories; Coors Brewing Company; Heska Corporation; J.D. Edwards & Company; Maxtor Corporation; University of Colorado; Vicorp Restaurants, Inc.

For full biographical listings, see the Martindale-Hubbell Law Directory

CONNECTICUT

FAIRFIELD, Fairfield Co.

PERMAN & GREEN, LLP (AV)

425 Post Road, 06430-6232
Telephone: 203-259-1800
Facsimile: 203-255-5170
Email: pgpatent@aol.com *URL:* http://www.pgpatent.com

OF COUNSEL

Donald C. Caulfield
Paul Weinstein

For full biographical listings, see the Martindale-Hubbell Law Directory

MILFORD, New Haven Co.

MELVIN I. STOLTZ (AV)

51 Cherry Street, 06460
Telephone: 203-874-8183
Facsimile: 203-878-9607
Email: patlaw@ziplink.net

For full biographical listings, see the Martindale-Hubbell Law Directory

*NEW HAVEN,** New Haven Co.

BACHMAN & LAPOINTE, P.C. (AV)

900 Chapel Street, Suite 1201, 06510
Telephone: 203-777-6628
Fax: 203-865-0297
Email: iplaw@bachlap.com

(See Next Column)

Robert H. Bachman (Not admitted in CT)
Gregory P. LaPointe
Barry L. Kelmachter
George A. Coury

For full biographical listings, see the Martindale-Hubbell Law Directory

WIGGIN & DANA (AV)

One Century Tower, 06508-1832
Telephone: 203-498-4400
Telefax: 203-782-2889
URL: http://www.wiggin.com
Hartford, Connecticut Office: One CityPlace.
Telephone: 203-297-3700.
Fax: 203-525-9380.
Stamford, Connecticut Office: Three Stamford Plaza, 301 Tresser Boulevard.
Telephone: 203-363-7600.
Telefax: 203-363-7676.

MEMBERS OF FIRM

Shaun S. Sullivan
D. Terence Jones
Mary R. Norris
James F. Farrington, Jr. (Resident, Stamford Office)
Dale L. Carlson
William A. Simons (Not admitted in CT)
William A. Perrone (Resident, Stamford Office)
Merton G. Gollaher
Gregory S. Rosenblatt
Francis J. Duffin
Patricia Kavee Melick (Not admitted in CT; Resident, Stamford Office)
William J. Speranza (Resident, Stamford Office)

ASSOCIATES

Jeffrey Russell Ambroziak
Todd E. Garabedian (Not admitted in CT)
Mark W. Heaphy
Steven F. Rowell
William B. Slate (Not admitted in CT)

For Complete List of Firm Personnel, See General Section

For full biographical listings, see the Martindale-Hubbell Law Directory

SIMSBURY, Hartford Co.

LAW OFFICE OF VICTOR E. LIBERT (AV)

3 Mill Pond Lane Powder Forest Business Park, P.O. Box 538, 06070-0538
Telephone: 860-651-9321
Fax: 860-651-5735
Email: libert.i.p.law@snet.net

Victor E. Libert

ASSOCIATES

Frederick A. Spaeth
Roger C. Phillips

For full biographical listings, see the Martindale-Hubbell Law Directory

STAMFORD, Fairfield Co.

ST. ONGE STEWARD JOHNSTON & REENS, LLC (AV)

986 Bedford Street, 06905
Telephone: 203-324-6155
Telecopier: 203-327-1096
Email: info@ssjr.com *URL:* http://www.ssjr.com
New Haven, Connecticut Office: 88 Prospect Street.
Telephone: 203-562-4043.

Louis H. Reens
Thaddius J. Carvis
Gene S. Winter
James R. Cartiglia
Stephen P. McNamara
Wesley W. Whitmyer, Jr.

David W. Poirier

COUNSEL

Ronald J. St. Onge

For full biographical listings, see the Martindale-Hubbell Law Directory

WESTPORT, Fairfield Co.

LEVETT ROCKWOOD P.C. (AV)

33 Riverside Avenue, P.O. Box 5116, 06881
Telephone: 203-222-0885
Telecopier: 203-226-8025

Suzanne B. Albani
Robert O. Barberi
Edward B. Chansky
Madeleine F. Grossman
Dorit Schutzengel Heimer
Cheryl L. Johnson
Marc J. Kurzman
David R. Levett
Judy A. Rabkin
Sharon M. Schweitzer
Steven M. Siegelaub
Peter H. Struzzi
Barbara A. Young

OF COUNSEL

William O. Rockwood, Jr.

(See Next Column)

LEVETT ROCKWOOD P.C.—*Continued*

Debra R. Cardinali
Stephen M. Cowherd
Christopher M. Graham
Robin K. Higgins
Douglas R. Sansted
Rodger F. Smith, Jr.
Patricia D. Weitzman

Representative Clients: Cannondale Corp.; Caradon, Inc.; DataViz, Inc.; Dooney & Bourke, Inc.; GAF Corporation; Heyman Properties; Hospital of Saint Raphael; Marketing Corporation of America; Olin Corporation; St. Vincent's Medical Center.

For full biographical listings, see the Martindale-Hubbell Law Directory

DELAWARE

*WILMINGTON,** New Castle Co.

CONNOLLY BOVE LODGE & HUTZ LLP (AV)

1220 Market Street, P.O. Box 2207, 19899-2207
Telephone: 302-658-9141
Telecopier: 302-658-5614
Email: cblhlaw@cblhlaw.com *URL:* http://www.cblhlaw.com

James M. Mulligan, Jr.
Arthur G. Connolly, Jr.
Rudolf E. Hutz
Harold Pezzner
Richard M. Beck (Not admitted in DE)
Paul E. Crawford
Stanley C. Macel, III
Thomas M. Meshbesher
George Pazuniak
N. Richard Powers
Jeffrey B. Bove
Collins J. Seitz, Jr.
Patricia Smink Rogowski
Mary W. Bourke
Robert G. McMorrow, Jr. (Not admitted in DE)
R. Eric Hutz
William E. McShane (Not admitted in DE)
John D. Fairchild (Not admitted in DE)
Ashley I. Pezzner
Gerard M. O'Rourke
Thomas A. Stevens
Oleh V. Bilynsky
Allan Neal Kutzenco (Not admitted in DE)
Frank Z. Yang (Not admitted in DE)
James M. Olsen
Eric J. Evain

For Complete List of Firm Personnel, See General Section

For full biographical listings, see the Martindale-Hubbell Law Directory

POTTER ANDERSON & CORROON LLP (AV)

Hercules Plaza, 1313 N. Market Street, P.O. Box 951, 19899-0951
Telephone: 302-984-6000
Fax: 302-658-1192
URL: http://www.attys.pacdelaware.com

MEMBERS OF FIRM

Charles S. Crompton, Jr.
Richard L. Horwitz
Joanne Ceballos

COUNSEL

Michael B. Keehan

ASSOCIATES

Gregory J. Feulner (Not admitted in DE)
Michael A. Steinberg (Not admitted in DE)

Counsel for: E.I. duPont de Nemours & Co.; Intel Corporation; Monsanto Company; Mobil Oil Corporation; Becton Dickinson and Company; Hercules, Inc.; Hyundai Electronics Industries; University of Delaware; Henry Francis duPont Winterthur Museum, Inc.

For Complete List of Firm Personnel, See General Section

For full biographical listings, see the Martindale-Hubbell Law Directory

DISTRICT OF COLUMBIA

WASHINGTON, D.C. Co.

ADDUCI, MASTRIANI & SCHAUMBERG, L.L.P. (AV)

1200 Seventeenth Street, N.W., Fifth Floor, 20036-3006
Telephone: 202-467-6300
Telefax: 202-466-2006
Email: ams@adduci.com *URL:* http://www.adduci.com

V. James Adduci, II
Louis S. Mastriani
Tom M. Schaumberg
Barbara A. Murphy
Timothy Sullivan
David A. Guth (1953-1997)
Katherine S. Nucci
Harvey B. Fox
Gregory C. Anthes

(See Next Column)

Michael L. Doane
Steven E. Adkins
Allan J. Stevenson
Alfred M. Haas
Adam F. Bobrow

A list of Representative Clients and References will be furnished upon request.

For full biographical listings, see the Martindale-Hubbell Law Directory

ARNOLD WHITE & DURKEE, A PROFESSIONAL CORPORATION (AV)

One Franklin Square, 1301 K Street, N.W., Suite 350, East Tower, 20005
Telephone: 202-289-0229
Facsimile: 202-289-7535
Email: info@awd.com *URL:* http://www.awd.com
Houston, Texas Office: 750 Bering Drive, 77057-2198.
Telephone: 713-787-1400.
Facsimile: 713-787-1440.
Austin, Texas Office: 1900 One American Center, 600 Congress Avenue, 78701-3248.
Telephone: 512-418-3000.
Facsimile: 512-474-7577.
Chicago, Illinois Office: 800 Quaker Tower, 321 North Clark Street, 60610-4714.
Telephone: 312-744-0090.
Facsimile: 312-755-4489.
Minneapolis, Minnesota Office: 4850 U.S. Bank Place, 601 Second Avenue South, 55402-4320.
Telephone: 612-321-2800.
Facsimile: 612-321-9600.
Menlo Park, California Office: 155 Linfield Drive, 94025-3741.
Telephone: 650-614-4500.
Facsimile: 650-614-4599.

J. Paul Williamson

OF COUNSEL

Carla C. Calcagno

For full biographical listings, see the Martindale-Hubbell Law Directory

BAKER BOTTS L.L.P. (AV)

A Registered Limited Liability Partnership
The Warner, 1299 Pennsylvania Avenue, N.W., 20004-2400
Telephone: 202-639-7700
Fax: 202-639-7832
Email: postmaster@bakerbotts.com *URL:* http://www.bakerbotts.com
Houston, Texas Office: One Shell Plaza, 910 Louisiana.
Telephone: 713-229-1234.
Austin, Texas Office: 1600 San Jacinto Center, 98 San Jacinto Boulevard.
Telephone: 512-322-2500.
Dallas, Texas Office: 2001 Ross Avenue.
Telephone: 214-953-6500.
New York, New York Office: 599 Lexington Avenue.
Telephone: 212-705-5000.
Moscow, Russia Office: 10 ul. Bolshaya Dimitrovka (formerly Pushkinskaya), 103031.
Telephone: 7095/921-5300 (Local); 7501/929-7070 (International).
London, England Office: 45 Ludgate Hill.
Telephone: 0171-778-1400 (Local); 011-44-171-778-1400 (International).
Baku, Azerbaijan Office: 6-10 Vagif Mustafa-zadeh Street, Third Floor, Icheri Sheher, 370004.
Telephone: 994-12-97-63-88 (Local); 011-994-12-97-63-88 (International).

MEMBERS OF FIRM

Scott F. Partridge
James Remenick
Rodger L. Tate

SPECIAL COUNSEL

James B. Arpin

ASSOCIATES

Floyd B. Chapman
Robert A. King (Not admitted in DC)
William F. Nixon
Laurence H. Posorske
Andrew Skale (Not admitted in DC)

For Complete List of Firm Personnel, See General Section

For full biographical listings, see the Martindale-Hubbell Law Directory

BANNER & WITCOFF, LTD. (AV)

Established In 1920 - Predecessor Parent
1001 G Street, N.W., 20001-4597
Telephone: 202-508-9100
Facsimile: 202-508-9299
Email: cooperman@bannerwitcoff.com *URL:* http://www.bannerwitcoff.com
Chicago, Illinois Office: Ten South Wacker Drive.
Telephone: 312-715-1000.
Facsimile: 312-715-1234.
Boston, Massachusetts Office: 28 State Street, 28th Floor.
Telephone: 617-227-7111.
Fax: 617-227-4399.

(See Next Column)

BANNER & WITCOFF LTD., *Washington—Continued*

Portland, Oregon Office: 601 SW Second Avenue, Suite 1900.
Telephone: 503-279-6330.
Fax: 503-279-6328.

Robert F. Altherr, Jr.
Donald W. Banner
Pamela I. Banner
Gary D. Fedorochko
Daniel E. Fisher
William J. Fisher
Patricia E. Hong
Dale H. Hoscheit
Thomas H. Jackson
Sarah A. Kagan
Robert S. Katz
Christopher L. McKee
Edward F. McKie, Jr.
Nina L. Medlock
Frederic M. Meeker
Thomas L. Peterson
Joseph M. Potenza
Steven P. Schad
Joseph M. Skerpon
Susan A. Wolffe
Bradley C. Wright

OF COUNSEL

Brian E. Banner
William W. Beckett
Franklin D. Wolffe

ASSOCIATES

Steve S. Chang
Joseph P. Curtin
Thomas L. Evans
Holly M. Ford
Christopher R. Glembocki
Brian E. Hanlon
Lisa M. Hemmendinger
Lisa M. W. Hillman (Not admitted in DC)
Sumeet Magoon (Not admitted in DC)
Charles Miller (Not admitted in DC)
Ajay S. Pathak (Not admitted in DC)
Steven S. Payne (Not admitted in DC)
Paul M. Rivard
Christopher B. Roth (Not admitted in DC)
Kevin A. Wolff

For full biographical listings, see the Martindale-Hubbell Law Directory

---

BROWDY AND NEIMARK (AV)

419 Seventh Street, N.W., 20004
Telephone: 202-628-5197
Telecopier: 202-737- 3528
Mailing Address: 624 Ninth Street, N.W., Suite 300, Washington, District of Columbia, 20001-5303
Email: BRWDYNMRK@DIGIZEN.NET

Sheridan Neimark
Roger L. Browdy

Anne M. Kornbau
Norman J. Latker
Nick Bromer (Not admitted in DC)

OF COUNSEL

Iver P. Cooper

PATENT AGENT

Allen C. Yun

For full biographical listings, see the Martindale-Hubbell Law Directory

---

DICKINSON WRIGHT PLLC (AV)

Suite 800, 1901 L Street, N.W., 20036-3506
Telephone: 202-457-0160
Facsimile: 202-659-1559
URL: http://www.dickinson-wright.com
Detroit, Michigan Office: 500 Woodward Avenue, Suite 4000.
Telephone: 313-223-3500.
Facsimile: 313-223-3598.
Bloomfield Hills, Michigan Office: 525 North Woodward Avenue, Suite 2000.
Telephone: 248-433-7200.
Facsimile: 248-433-7274.
Grand Rapids, Michigan Office: 200 Ottawa Avenue, N.W., Suite 900.
Telephone: 616-458-1300.
Facsimile: 616-458-6753.
Lansing, Michigan Office: Suite 200, 215 South Washington Square.
Telephone: 517-371-1730.
Facsimile: 517-487-4700.

RESIDENT MEMBERS

Marc A. Bergsman
Conrad J. Clark
William E. Elwood
David R. Haarz
Samuel D. Littlepage
Jeffrey M. Petrash

RESIDENT OF COUNSEL

Christopher W. Brody
Laurinda L. Hicks
Lucien N. Nedzi
J. John Shimazaki

For Representative Clients, see biographical section, Detroit, Michigan.

For full biographical listings, see the Martindale-Hubbell Law Directory

THE FEINBERG GROUP, LLP (AV)

1120 20th Street, N.W. Suite 740 South, 20036-3437
Telephone: 202-371-1110
Fax: 202-962-9290
Email: kfeinberg@thefeinberggroup.com *URL:* http://www.krfassociates.com
New York, N.Y. Office: 780 3rd Avenue, Suite 2202.
Telephone: 212-527-9600.
Fax: 212-527-9611. Email: kfeinberg@thefeinberggroup.com.

PARTNERS

Kenneth R. Feinberg
Deborah E. Greenspan
Michael K. Rozen (Resident, New York Office)
Peter H. Woodin (Resident, New York Office)

ASSOCIATE

Fredric M. Brooks (Not admitted in DC)

SENIOR COUNSEL

Jacqueline E. Zins

For full biographical listings, see the Martindale-Hubbell Law Directory

---

FINNEGAN, HENDERSON, FARABOW, GARRETT & DUNNER, L.L.P. (AV)

Suite 700, 1300 I Street, N.W., 20005-3315
Telephone: 202-408-4000
Facsimile: 202-408-4400
URL: http://www.finnegan.com
Palo Alto, California Office: 700 Hansen Way.
Telephone: 650-849-6600.
Facsimile: 650-849-6666.
Atlanta, Georgia Office: 3200 SunTrust Plaza, 303 Peachtree Street, N.E.
Telephone: 404-653-6400.
Facsimile: 404-653-6444.
Tokyo, Japan Office: Toranomon No. 45 Mori Building, Third Floor, 1-5, Toranomon 5-chome Minato-Ku.
Telephone: 0081-3-3431-6943.
Facsimile: 0081-3-3431-6945.
Brussels, Belgium Office: Avenue Louise 326, Box 37, 1050.
Telephone: 011-322-646-0353.
Facsimile: 011-322-646-2135.

MEMBERS OF FIRM

Marcus B. Finnegan (1927-1979)
Douglas B. Henderson
Ford F. Farabow Jr.
Arthur S. Garrett
Donald R. Dunner
Brian G. Brunsvold
Tipton D. Jennings IV
Jerry D. Voight
Laurence R. Hefter
Kenneth E. Payne
Herbert H. Mintz
C. Larry O'Rourke (Resident Partner, Palo Alto, California Office)
Albert J. Santorelli
Michael C. Elmer (Resident Partner, Palo Alto, California Office)
Richard H. Smith
Stephen L. Peterson
John M. Romary
Bruce C. Zotter
D. Patrick O'Reilley
Allen M. Sokal
Robert D. Bajefsky
Richard Lee Stroup
David W. Hill
Thomas L. Irving
Charles E. Lipsey
Thomas W. Winland
Basil J. Lewris
Martin I. Fuchs
E. Robert Yoches
Susan Haberman Griffen
Richard B. Racine
Thomas H. Jenkins III
Robert E. Converse Jr.
Clair X. Mullen Jr.
Christopher P. Foley
John C. Paul
Griffith B. Price Jr.
John F. Hornick
Robert D. Litowitz
David M. Kelly
Kenneth John Meyers
Carol P. Einaudi
Walter Y. Boyd Jr.
Steven M. Anzalone
Darrel C. Karl
Jean Burke Fordis
Barbara Clarke McCurdy
James K. Hammond
Richard V. Burgujian
John Michael Jakes
John C. Lowe
Thomas W. Banks (Resident Partner, Palo Alto, California Office)
Christopher P. Isaac
Bryan C. Diner (Resident Partner, Brussels, Belgium Office)
M. Paul Barker (Resident Partner, Palo Alto, California Office)
Mark S. Sommers
Kenneth M. Frankel
William H. Pratt
David S. Forman
Vincent P. Kovalick
Don O. Burley
Gerson S. Panitch
James W. Edmondson
Michael R. McGurk
Cheri M. Taylor
Joann M. Neth
Linda A. Wadler
Liam O'Grady (Not admitted in DC)
Jeffrey A. Berkowitz
Michael R. Kelly (Resident Partner, Tokyo, Japan Office)
James B. Monroe (Not admitted in DC)

COUNSEL

Arthur J. Levine
George E. Hutchinson
William T. McClain
Robert F. Ziems
Robert J. Eichelburg
Ernest F. Chapman
Wayne W. Herrington

(See Next Column)

FINNEGAN, HENDERSON, FARABOW, GARRETT & DUNNER L.L.P.—*Continued*

ASSOCIATES

David Avrum Manspeizer
Lori-Ann Johnson (Resident Associate, Atlanta, Georgia Office)
R. Bruce Bower (Resident Associate, Atlanta, Georgia Office)
Lisa Peller London
Thalia V. Warnement
Michele C. Bosch
Howard Warren Levine
Leslie I. Bookoff
John R. Alison
Barbara R. Rudolph
Anthony M. Gutowski

Reference: Crestar Bank, N.A., Washington, D.C.

For full biographical listings, see the Martindale-Hubbell Law Directory

FITCH, EVEN, TABIN & FLANNERY (AV)

1801 K Street, N.W., Suite 401L, 20006-1201
Telephone: 202-789-4900
Fax: 202-789-8707
Email: email@fitcheven.com *URL:* http://www.fitcheven.com
Chicago, Illinois Office: 120 South La Salle, Suite 1600. 60603.
Telephone: 312-577-7000.
Fax: 312-577-7007.
San Diego, California Office: 4250 Executive Square, Suite 510.
Telephone: 619-552-1311.
Telecopier: 619-552-0095.

Sherri N. Blount
Edward W. Gray, Jr.

Christopher E. George

For full biographical listings, see the Martindale-Hubbell Law Directory

FITZPATRICK, CELLA, HARPER & SCINTO (AV)

1900 K Street, N.W., 20006-1110
Telephone: 202-530-1010
Facsimile: 202-530-1055
New York, N.Y. Office: 30 Rockefeller Plaza.
Telephone: 212-218-2100. International-
Telex: FCHS 236262.
Cable Address: "Fitzcel New York".
Facsimile: 212-218-2200.
Orange County, California Office: 650 Town Center Drive, Suite 1800, Costa Mesa.
Telephone: 714-540-8700.
Facsimile: 714-540-9823.

RESIDENT PARTNERS

John W. Behringer
Lawrence A. Stahl
William M. Wannisky
Warren E. Olsen
Richard P. Bauer
Scott D. Malpede
Thomas J. O'Connell
Steven E. Warner
Mark A. Williamson

COUNSEL

Robert C. Kline

RESIDENT ASSOCIATES

Christopher Philip Wrist
Gary M. Jacobs
Jack S. Cubert (Not admitted in DC; Limited to matters and proceedings before federal courts and agencies)
Jean K. Dudek
Anne M. Maher (Limited to matters and proceedings before federal courts and agencies)
Daniel S. Glueck
Brian L. Klock
T Tom C. Gellenthien
Sean W. O'Brien (Not admitted in DC; Limited to matters and proceedings before federal courts and agencies)
Natalie M. Derzko (Not admitted in DC; Limited to matters and proceedings before federal courts and agencies)
Shawn W. Fraser (Not admitted in DC; Limited to matters and proceedings before federal courts and agencies)
Edmund J. Haughey, III (Not admitted in DC; Limited to matters and proceedings before federal courts and agencies)
Justin J. Oliver (Not admitted in DC; Limited to matters and proceedings before federal courts and agencies)
Steven Wayne Stewart (Not admitted in DC; Limited to matters and proceedings before federal courts and agencies)

For full biographical listings, see the Martindale-Hubbell Law Directory

HARNESS, DICKEY & PIERCE, P.L.C. (AV)

888 Sixteenth Street, N.W., 20006
Telephone: 202-835-7480
Email: info@hdp.com *URL:* http://www.hdp.com
Troy, Michigan Office: 5445 Corporate Drive, Suite 400.
Telephone: 248-641-1600. Telefacsimile (All Groups); 248-641-0270.
Ann Arbor, Michigan Office: 301 East Liberty Street, Suite 555.
Telephone: 734-662-8000.
Telefacsimile: 734-662-7813.

(See Next Column)

MEMBER OF FIRM

W. R. Duke Taylor

Representative Clients: Chrysler Corp.; The Black and Decker Manufacturing Co.; Monroe Auto Equipment Co.; La-Z-Boy Chair Co.; Hughes Aircraft; Budd Co.; Dow Chemical Co.; Procter & Gamble; General Motors Corporation.

For full biographical listings, see the Martindale-Hubbell Law Directory

JACOBSON, PRICE, HOLMAN & STERN, PLLC (AV)

The Jenifer Building, 400 Seventh Street, N.W., 20004
Telephone: 202-638-6666
Cable Address: "Lawpat"
Telefax: 202-393-5350; 202-393-5351; 202-393-5352
Email: IP@JPHS.COM *URL:* HTTP://WWW.JPHS.COM

MEMBERS OF FIRM

Harvey B. Jacobson, Jr.
D. Douglas Price
John Clarke Holman
Simor L. Moskowitz
Michael R. Slobasky
Marsha G. Gentner
Jonathan L. Scherer
Irwin M. Aisenberg
William E. Player
Yoon S. Ham

ASSOCIATES

Leesa N. Weiss
Peter S. Weissman
Suzin C. Bailey (Not admitted in DC)
Paula L. Craig (Not admitted in DC)

LEGAL SUPPORT PERSONNEL
PATENT AGENT

Tania J. Keeble

OF COUNSEL

Marvin R. Stern
Brian B. Darville

For full biographical listings, see the Martindale-Hubbell Law Directory

KEIL & WEINKAUF (AV)

1101 Connecticut Avenue, N.W., 20036
Telephone: 202-659-0100
Telecopier: 202-659-0105

MEMBERS OF FIRM

Herbert B. Keil
Russell E. Weinkauf (Not admitted in DC)
Malcolm John MacDonald
Jason D. Voight

SPECIAL COUNSEL

Gerald H. Bjorge
Norman G. Torchin
George F. Helfrich (Not admitted in DC)
Ronald H. Smith (Not admitted in DC)

OF COUNSEL

Melvin Goldstein (Not admitted in DC)

PATENT AGENT

Henry R. Jiles

TECHNICAL AND FOREIGN PATENT ADVISOR

Barbara A. Schwalge (Not admitted in DC)

For full biographical listings, see the Martindale-Hubbell Law Directory

KENYON & KENYON (AV)

1500 K Street, N.W., 20036
Telephone: 202-220-4200
Fax: (202) 220-4201, Groups II & III
New York, N.Y. Office: One Broadway.
Telephone: 212-425-7200.
Fax: (212) 425-5288.
Frankfurt, Germany Office: Schillerstrasse 19-25, 60313 Frankfurt am Main.
Telephone: (69) 97-58-050.
Fax: (69) 97-58-05-99.
San Jose, California Office: 333 West San Carlos Street.
Telephone: 408-287-2800.
Fax: (408) 287-2800.

RESIDENT PARTNERS

John C. Altmiller
Edward T. Colbert
William K. Wells, Jr.
Frank Pietrantonio
Suzanne M. Parker
Brian S. Mudge

RESIDENT ASSOCIATES

Mark M. Supko
Judith L. Toffenetti (Not admitted in DC)
C. Kyle Musgrove (Not admitted in DC)
Gary S. Morris
William M. Merone (Not admitted in DC)
John W. Bateman (Not admitted in DC)
John McGroarty (Not admitted in DC)
Timothy M. Devlin (Not admitted in DC)
John R. Hutchins
Christopher R. Hutter
Robert L. Grabarek, Jr.
Robert L. Hails, Jr.
Karen L. Feisthamel (Not admitted in DC)

(See Next Column)

KENYON & KENYON, *Washington—Continued*

RESIDENT ASSOCIATES (Continued)

Sterlon Mason (Not admitted in DC)
Stuart D. Smolen
Brian M. Koide
Teresa A. Lavenue (Not admitted in DC)
James M. Ross
Michael N. Haynes
Kristina M. Jahns (Not admitted in DC)
Mark H. Neblett
David R. Schaffer (Not admitted in DC)
Susan A. Smith
Laurie S. Mintzer
Sinan Utku
Neil M. McCarthy (Not admitted in DC)
Paolo M. Trevisan
Fred Grasso
Clint A. Gerdine (Not admitted in DC)
Kenneth R. Corsello
Dan Salehi (Not admitted in DC)
R. Paul Zeineddin (Not admitted in DC)
Michael M. Shen (Not admitted in DC)
Anthony Dreux

For full biographical listings, see the Martindale-Hubbell Law Directory

LALOS & KEEGAN (AV)

1146 Nineteenth Street N.W., Fifth Floor, 20036-3703
Telephone: 202-887-5555
Telecopier: (202) 296-1682
Email: laloskeegan@radix.net *URL:* http://www.lawyers.com/lalos&keeganlaw

MEMBERS OF FIRM

Peter N. Lalos
Francis A. Keegan
Susan B. Flohr
Alfred A. Stadnicki (Not admitted in DC)

ASSOCIATES

Michael N. Lau (Not admitted in DC)
Nicole M. Meyer

OF COUNSEL

Snider & Chao, Washington, D.C.

For full biographical listings, see the Martindale-Hubbell Law Directory

LANE, AITKEN & MCCANN, L.L.P. (AV)

Watergate Office Building, 2600 Virginia Avenue, N.W., 20037
Telephone: 202-337-5556
Telecopier: 202-337-8073
Email: lam@washingtonpatents.com *URL:* http://www.washingtonpatents.com

MEMBERS OF FIRM

Richard L. Aitken
Clifton E. McCann
John P. Shannon, Jr.
Laurence J. Marhoefer (Not admitted in DC)
Andrew C. Aitken (Not admitted in DC)
Mark A. Wurm

ASSOCIATES

Ralph P. Albrecht
Cameron H. Tousi (Not admitted in DC)

OF COUNSEL

Joseph M. Lane

For full biographical listings, see the Martindale-Hubbell Law Directory

LEYDIG, VOIT & MAYER, LTD. (AV)

700 Thirteenth Street N.W., Suite 300, 20005-3960
Telephone: 202-737-6770
Telecopier: 202-737-6776
Email: mail@leydig.com *URL:* http://www.leydig.com
Chicago, Illinois Office: Two Prudential Plaza, Suite 4900. 180 North Stetson Avenue.
Telephone: 312-616-5600.
Telecopier: 312-616-5700.
Rockford, Illinois Office: 6815 Weaver Road, Suite 300.
Telephone: 815-963-7661.
Telecopier: 815-963-7664.

John M. Belz (Resident)
Jeffrey A. Wyand (Resident)
Jeremy M. Jay (Resident)

Xavier Pillai (Not admitted in DC; Resident)
Song Zhu (Resident)

OF COUNSEL

John P. Bundock, Jr. (Resident)
John D. Foster (Resident)

For full biographical listings, see the Martindale-Hubbell Law Directory

MORGAN & FINNEGAN, L.L.P. (AV)

A Registered Liability Partnership
1775 Eye Street, N.W., 4th Floor, 20006
Telephone: 202-857-7887
Facsimile: 202-857-7929
Email: info@morganfinnegan.com *URL:* http://www.morganfinnegan.com
New York, N.Y. Office: 345 Park Avenue, 10154.
Telephone: 212-758-4800.
Cable Address: "Findurpine".
Telecopier: (212) 751-6849.
Telex: ITT 421792.

RESIDENT PARTNERS

Edward A. Pennington
Michael S. Marcus
John E. Hoel (Not admitted in DC)

COUNSEL

Joseph C. Redmond, Jr.
John P. Moran
Stanley B. Green

ASSOCIATES

Christopher J. Hamaty
Michael A. Schwartz
Alicia A. Meros (Not admitted in DC)
Robert C. Bertin (Not admitted in DC)
J. Steven Rutt (Not admitted in DC)
Mark W. Hrozenchik (Not admitted in DC)

For full biographical listings, see the Martindale-Hubbell Law Directory

NATH & ASSOCIATES (AV)

1030 15th Street, N.W. 6th Floor, 20005
Telephone: 202-775-8383 or 202-775-9393
Facsimile: 202-775-8396 or 202-882-9409
Email: IP@NATHLAW.COM *URL:* http://www.NATHLAW.COM

MEMBERS OF FIRM

Gary M. Nath
Harold L. Novick
Suet M. Chong

ASSOCIATES

Todd L. Juneau
Lee C. Heiman (Not admitted in DC)
Paul A. Sacher (Not admitted in DC)
Michelle L. Hartland (Not admitted in DC)
Marvin C. Berkowitz (Not admitted in DC)
David R. Murphy
Gregory B. Kang (Not admitted in DC)
Scott F. Yarnell (Not admitted in DC)
Jerald L. Meyer (Not admitted in DC)
Tanya E. Jankovic (Not admitted in DC)

PATENT AGENTS

Alvin E. Tanenholtz
Joshua L. Goldberg
David H. Milligan

RETIRED

Irvin A. Lavine
Donald M. Sandler (Not admitted in DC)

For full biographical listings, see the Martindale-Hubbell Law Directory

NIKAIDO, MARMELSTEIN, MURRAY & ORAM, LLP (AV)

G Street Lobby, Metropolitan Square, 655 15th Street, N.W., Suite 330, 20005-5701
Telephone: 202-638-5000
Facsimile: 202-638-4808; 638-4810
Email: nmmo@nmmo.com *URL:* http://www.nmmo.com

MEMBERS OF FIRM

David T. Nikaido
Charles M. Marmelstein
Robert B. Murray
George E. Oram, Jr.
Ellen Marcie Emas (Not admitted in DC)
Douglas H. Goldhush

ASSOCIATES

Monica Chin Kitts (Not admitted in DC)
Richard Jason Berman
King Lit Wong
Murat Ozgu (Not admitted in DC)
Patrick D. Muir

OF COUNSEL

John H. Harman
Karen Kaechele Costantino
James A. Poulos, III (Not admitted in DC)
Herbert C. Rose

For full biographical listings, see the Martindale-Hubbell Law Directory

OPPENHEIMER WOLFF DONNELLY & BAYH LLP (AV)

1350 Eye Street, N.W. Suite 200, 20005
Telephone: 202-312-8000
FAX: 202-312-8100
URL: http://www.owdlaw.com
Oppenheimer Wolff & Donnelly LLP
Minneapolis, Minnesota Office: 3300 Plaza VII, 45 South Seventh Street. 55402.
Telephone: 612-607-7000.
FAX: 612-607-7100.

(See Next Column)

OPPENHEIMER WOLFF DONNELLY & BAYH LLP—*Continued*

Amsterdam, The Netherlands Office: Keizergracht 241.
Telephone: 31-20-423-4555.
FAX: 31-20-423-4545.
Brussels, Belgium Office: Avenue Louise 240, Box 5, 1050.
Telephone: 32-2-626-0500.
FAX: 32-2-626-0510.
Geneva, Switzerland Office: Rue Gabriel Eynard, 6, 1206.
Telephone: (41/22) 311-7410.
FAX: (41/22) 311-7407.
New York, N.Y. Office: Citicorp Center, 153 East 53rd Street, 10022.
Telephone: 212-826-5000.
FAX: 212-486-0708.
Newport Beach, California Office: 500 Newport Center Drive, Suite 700, 92660.
Telephone: 949-719-6000.
FAX: 949-719-6020.
Paris, France Office: 53 Avenue Montaigne, 75008.
Telephone: (33/1) 44 95 03 50.
FAX: (33/1) 44 95 03 40.
St. Paul, Minnesota Office: 1700 First National Bank Building, 55101.
Telephone: 651-605-2000.
FAX: 651-605-2100.
Los Angeles, California Office: 2029 Century Park East, 38th Floor, 90067.
Telephone: 310-788-5000.
FAX: 310-277-1297.
Palo Alto, California Office: 3373 Hillview Avenue, Suite 200, 94304.
Telephone: 650-320-4000.
FAX: 650-320-4100.
Chicago, Illinois Office: Oppenheimer Wolff & Donnelly (Illinois), Two Prudential Plaza, 45th Floor, 180 North Stetson Avenue, 60601.
Telephone: 312-616-1800.
Fax: 312-616-5800.

RESIDENT PARTNER

M. Peter Adler

For full biographical listings, see the Martindale-Hubbell Law Directory

PENNIE & EDMONDS LLP (AV)

1667 K Street, N.W., 20006
Telephone: 202-496-4400
Facsimile: 202-496-4444
Email: pennie.com *URL:* http://www.pennie.com
New York, New York Office: 1155 Avenue of the Americas.
Telephone: 212-790-9090.
Telex: (WUI) 66141-Pennie.
Cable Address: "Penangold."
Facsimile: GI/GII/GIII (212) 869-9741, GIII (212) 869-8864.
Palo Alto, California Office: 3300 Hillview Avenue.
Telephone: 650-493-4935.
Facsimile: 650-493-5556.

John C. Pennie (1858-1921)
Dean S. Edmonds (1879-1972)

PARTNERS

Harry C. Jones, III
Stanton T. Lawrence, III
Allan A. Fanucci
Paul J. Zegger (Not admitted in DC)
Marcia H. Sundeen

ASSOCIATES

Wilma F. Triebwasser (Not admitted in DC)
Troy R. Lester (Not admitted in DC)
H.T. Than
Nanda K. Alapati
Carl P. Bretscher (Not admitted in DC)
Greg P. Roggin
Eric J. Fues (Not admitted in DC)
Lorri W. Jones
Nancy H. Lutz
Jeffrey A. Wolfson
Granetta M. Coleman
Emil Bradley Gould
John P. Mulgrew (Not admitted in DC)
George A. Willinghan, III (Not admitted in DC)
Paul D. Bianco
Kristin A. Deming (Not admitted in DC)
Gregory J. Gonsalves (Not admitted in DC)
C. Edward Polk, Jr. (Not admitted in DC)
Anthony H. Kahng
Craig Louis Puckett (Not admitted in DC)
Max Bachrach (Not admitted in DC)
Atulya R. Agarwal (Not admitted in DC)
Vivian S. Kuo (Not admitted in DC)
Paul E. Dietze (Not admitted in DC)
Charles R. Richard (Not admitted in DC)
Gary Zhang (Not admitted in DC)

For full biographical listings, see the Martindale-Hubbell Law Directory

POLLOCK, VANDE SANDE & AMERNICK, R.L.L.P. (AV)

Eighth Floor, 1990 M Street, N.W., P.O. Box 19088, 20036
Telephone: 202-331-7111
Fax: 202-293-6229
Email: PVSP@PVSP.COM

(See Next Column)

MEMBERS OF FIRM

Elliott I. Pollock (1927-1999)
Burton A. Amernick
Richard Wiener
Morris Liss
Townsend M. Belser, Jr.
Martin Abramson
George R. Pettit
Elzbieta Chlopecka

OF COUNSEL

George Vande Sande

ASSOCIATES

Eric John Franklin
Jeffri A. Kaminski
William E. Curry (Not admitted in DC)

For full biographical listings, see the Martindale-Hubbell Law Directory

RADER, FISHMAN & GRAUER PLLC (AV)

1233 20th Street, Suite 501, 20036
Telephone: 202-955-3750
Fax: 202-955-3751
Email: info@raderfishman.com *URL:* http://www.intelprop.com
Grand Rapids, Michigan Office: Rader, Fishman, Grauer & McGarry PLLC, 171 Monroe Avenue, N.W., Suite 600, 49503.
Telephone: 616-742-3500.
Fax: 616-742-1010.
Bloomfield Hills, Michigan Office: 1533 North Woodward, Suite 140, 48304.
Telephone: 248-594-0600.
Fax: 248-594-0610.
Denver, Colorado Office: 7887 East Belleview Avenue, 80111.
Telephone: 303-228-1658.
Fax: 303-228-1659.

Ronald P. Kananen
Shmuel (Sandy) Livnat

ASSOCIATES

Steven L. Nichols (Not admitted in DC)
Christopher Mark Tanner (Not admitted in DC)

OF COUNSEL

Paul W. Fish
William D. Stokes
Wallace G. Walter

PATENT AGENTS

Paul D. Amrozowicz
David K. Benson

For full biographical listings, see the Martindale-Hubbell Law Directory

ROYLANCE, ABRAMS, BERDO & GOODMAN, L.L.P. (AV)

1225 Connecticut Avenue, N.W., 20036-2680
Telephone: 202-659-9076
Facsimile: 202-659-9344
Email: RABG@roylance.com

D. C. Roylance (1920-1995)
David S. Abrams
Robert H. Berdo
Alfred N. Goodman
Mark S. Bicks
Richard A. Flynt
John E. Holmes
Michael T. Murphy
Garrett V. Davis
Stacey J. Longanecker (Not admitted in DC)
Thomas P. Hilliard
Joseph J. Buczynski
Robert S. Green
Wayne C. Jaeschke, Jr. (Not admitted in DC)
Antigone E. Juvelis (Not admitted in DC)

SENIOR OF COUNSEL

Frank E. Robbins (Retired)

OF COUNSEL

Susan Neuberger Weller
Lance G. Johnson

For full biographical listings, see the Martindale-Hubbell Law Directory

THE M.H. SEARS LAW FIRM (AV)

910 Seventeenth Street, N.W., Suite 800, 20006
Telephone: 202-463-3892
Facsimile: 202-463-4852
Email: searshahn@aol.com *URL:* http://www.searshahn.com

MEMBERS OF FIRM

Mary Helen Sears
Thomas S. Hahn

For full biographical listings, see the Martindale-Hubbell Law Directory

SMITH, GAMBRELL & RUSSELL, LLP (AV)

Suite 800, 1850 M Street, N.W., 20036
Telephone: 202-659-2811
Cable Address: "Jemead".
Telex: WUI 64470; WU 89-2393.
Telecopier: 202-659-1462
Atlanta, Georgia Office: Suite 3100, Promenade II, 1230 Peachtree Street, N.E.
Telephone: 404-815-3500.
Facsimile: 404-815-3509.

(See Next Column)

SMITH, GAMBRELL & RUSSELL LLP, *Washington—Continued*

MEMBERS OF FIRM

Andrew B. Beveridge (1915-1972)
Joseph A. DeGrandi (1927-1999)
Robert G. Weilacher
Richard G. Young
Michael A. Makuch
Dennis C. Rodgers
Helen Hill Minsker
William F. Rauchholz

ASSOCIATE

Michael K. Carrier (Not admitted in DC)

PATENT AGENT - CHINA ONLY

Qixia Zhang

For full biographical listings, see the Martindale-Hubbell Law Directory

VENABLE ATTORNEYS AT LAW VENABLE, BAETJER, HOWARD & CIVILETTI, LLP (AV)

A Partnership including Professional Corporations
Suite 1000, 1201 New York Avenue, N.W., 20005
Telephone: 202-962-4800
Fax: 202-962-8300
URL: http://www.venable.com
Baltimore, Maryland Office: Venable, Baetjer and Howard LLP, 1800 Mercantile Bank & Trust Building, 2 Hopkins Plaza.
Telephone: 410-244-7400.
Fax: 410-244-7742.
McLean, Virginia Office: Venable, Baetjer and Howard LLP, Suite 400, 2010 Corporate Ridge.
Telephone: 703-760-1600.
Fax: 703-821-8949.
Rockville, Maryland Office: Venable, Baetjer and Howard LLP, Suite 500, One Church Street, P. O. Box 1906.
Telephone: 301-217-5600.
Fax: 301-217-5617.
Towson, Maryland Office: Venable, Baetjer and Howard LLP, 210 Allegheny Avenue, P. O. Box 5517.
Telephone: 410-494-6200.
Fax: 410-821-0147.

MEMBERS OF FIRM

Kenneth C. Bass, III (Also at McLean, Virginia Office)
Robert J. Bolger, Jr. (Also at Baltimore, Maryland Office)
William D. Coston
Jeffrey A. Dunn (Also at Baltimore, Maryland Office)
Robert J. Frank
Edward F. Glynn, Jr.
David W. Goewey
Michael A. Gollin
Gary M. Hnath
Gabor J. Kelemen (Not admitted in DC)
Robert Kinberg
Jeffrey D. Knowles
Norman N. Kunitz
Vicki Margolis (Also at Baltimore, Maryland Office)
George F. Pappas (Also at Baltimore, Maryland Office)
John W. Schneller
George H. Spencer
Ashley J. Wells
Allen Wood

OF COUNSEL

Barbara L. Waite

ASSOCIATE

James Nicholas Czaban

For Complete List of Firm Personnel, See General Section

For full biographical listings, see the Martindale-Hubbell Law Directory

WENDEROTH, LIND & PONACK, L.L.P. (AV)

2033 K Street, N.W., Suite 800, 20006
Telephone: 202-721-8200
Fax: 202-721-8250 (G-III)
202-646-1179 (G-IV)
Email: wlp@wenderoth.com

MEMBERS OF FIRM

E. F. Wenderoth (1886-1974)
John E. Lind (1892-1983)
A. Ponack (1900-1969)
Michael R. Davis
Matthew M. Jacob
Jeffrey Nolton
Warren M. Cheek, Jr.
Nils E. Pedersen
Charles R. Watts

OF COUNSEL

John T. Miller
John T. Fedigan

ASSOCIATES

Michael S. Huppert
Lee Cheng
Kaushal R. Odedra (Not admitted in DC)
Ralph H. Dean, Jr. (Not admitted in DC)
Dhiren R. Odedra (Not admitted in DC)

For full biographical listings, see the Martindale-Hubbell Law Directory

FLORIDA

CORAL SPRINGS, Broward Co.

PERSHES & SCHWARTZ, P.A. (AV)

Suite 205, 2801 University Drive, 33065
Telephone: 954-341-2801
Fax: 954-341-9801
Email: pershlaw@gate.net *URL:* http://www.lawyers.com/p&slaw

Robert E. Pershes
Jay A. Schwartz

For full biographical listings, see the Martindale-Hubbell Law Directory

*FORT LAUDERDALE,** Broward Co.

MALIN, HALEY & DIMAGGIO, P.A. (AV)

1 East Broward Boulevard Suite 1609, 33301
Telephone: 954-763-3303
Fax: 954-522-6507
Email: Patents954@aol.com *URL:* http://www.lawyers.com/mhdclaw
Miami, Florida Office: 2000 South Dixie Highway, Suite 203, 33133.
Telephone: 305-374-4082.
West Palm Beach, Florida Office: Suite 600, 500 South Australian Avenue, 33401.
Telephone: 561-832-6341.
New Address Effective February, 2000; 1936 South Andrews Avenue, Fort Lauderdale, Florida, 33316.

Eugene F. Malin (1936-1990)
Barry L. Haley
Dale Paul DiMaggio
Daniel S. Polley

Cristina Pinheiro-Palmer (Not admitted in FL)
Jeffrey H. Kamenetsky
Joanne S. Richards

OF COUNSEL

John C. Black (Not admitted in FL)

Representative Clients: IBM; Motorola; Blockbuster Entertainment; Hughes Aircraft Co.; CAE Electronics; Nova Southeastern University; Sea Ray Boats; News and Sun-Sentinel; Brunswick Corp.; Boston Whaler.

For full biographical listings, see the Martindale-Hubbell Law Directory

OLTMAN, FLYNN AND KUBLER (AV)

415 Galleria Professional Building, 915 Middle River Drive, 33304-3585
Telephone: 954-563-4814
Facsimile: 954-563-1226
Email: oltman@aksi.net *URL:* http://www.lawyers.com/oltmanflynn&kubler
Boca Raton, Florida Office: Suite 801 The Plaza, 5355 Town Center Road.
Telephone: 561-391-4900.
Miami, Florida Office: Nationsbank Tower, Suite 2750, 100 Southeast 2nd Street, 33131.
Telephone: 305-947-3888.

John H. Oltman
Frank L. Kubler

Representative Clients: Clairson International Corp.; New York Institute of Technology; Jensen Corp.; M & W Pump Corp.; Hollywood Federal Savings and Loan Assn.; Adaptive Systems, Inc.; Oki Telecom, Division of Oki America, Inc.; Security Plastics, Inc.; Eaton Oil Co.
Reference: Nations Bank, Fort Lauderdale.

For full biographical listings, see the Martindale-Hubbell Law Directory

*MIAMI,** Dade Co.

FELDMAN GALE & WEBER, P.A. (AV)

201 South Biscayne Boulevard, 19th Floor, 33131-4329
Telephone: 305-358-5001
Fax: 305-358-3309
Email: fgwlaw@fgwlaw.com
Suffield, Connecticut Office: 40 Crane Hill Road, 06078.
Telephone: 860-668-0226.
Fax: 860-668-0696. Email: WCNEALON@FGWLAW.COM; WCNEALON@AOL.COM.

Jeffrey D. Feldman
James A. Gale
Michael J. Weber

Sean N. R. Wells
John C. Carey
Jennifer Johnson Watkins
Ozzie A. Farres
Nancy J. Flint
Greg Tung Nguyen

OF COUNSEL

William C. Nealon (Not admitted in FL)

For full biographical listings, see the Martindale-Hubbell Law Directory

GEORGIA

*ATLANTA,** Fulton Co.

DEVEAU, COLTON & MARQUIS (AV)

Two Midtown Plaza Suite 1400, 1360 Peachtree Street, N.E., 30309-3209
Telephone: 404-875-3555
Facsimile: 404-875-8505
URL: http://www.patlanta.com

MEMBERS OF FIRM

Todd Deveau
Laurence P. Colton
Harold L. Marquis

ASSOCIATES

Jennifer Williams Colton
Robert J. Gorman, Jr.
Ryan A. Schneider
Dmitry Milikovsky (Not admitted in GA)
Joel D. Myers

For full biographical listings, see the Martindale-Hubbell Law Directory

SMITH, HOWARD & AJAX, LLP (AV)

300 Atlanta Financial Center South, 3333 Peachtree Road, N.E., 30326
Telephone: 404-239-1900
Fax: 404-239-1930

MEMBERS OF FIRM

Fred W. Ajax, Jr.
Donald R. Andersen
Bruce H. Beerman
James T. Brieske
Susan Teale Couvillon
Harvey S. Gray
John A. Howard
Matthew G. Moffett
Michael J. Rust
Marion Smith, II
Michael D. St. Amand
David K. Whatley

ASSOCIATES

Mark D. Gropp
Joseph P. Hewes
Matthew L. Hilt
Meredith H. Ragains
LaXavier Patrice Reddick-Hood

OF COUNSEL

T. Michael Hurley, Jr.
Larry S. McReynolds

For full biographical listings, see the Martindale-Hubbell Law Directory

THOMAS, KAYDEN, HORSTEMEYER & RISLEY, L.L.P. (AV)

100 Galleria Parkway, N.W., Suite 1500, 30339-5948
Telephone: 770-933-9500
Fax: 770-951-0933
Email: office@tkhr.com *URL:* http://www.tkhr.com

George M. Thomas
James W. Kayden
Scott A. Horstemeyer
Stephen R. Risley
Jeffrey R. Kuester
Daniel R. McClure

ASSOCIATES

Daniel J. Santos
Robert E. Stachler II (Not admitted in GA)
J. Scott Culpepper
Michael J. Tempel
Michael J. D'Aurelio
David R. Risley
Dan R. Gresham
Jon E. Holland
M. Paul Qualey, Jr.
Jennifer M. Gruber
Peter A. Nieves
Raymond W. Armentrout (Not admitted in GA)

OF COUNSEL

David P. Kelley (Not admitted in GA)
Peter V. D. Wilde (Not admitted in GA)

LEGAL SUPPORT PERSONNEL

PATENT AGENT

Robert A. Blaha

TECHNICAL ADVISOR

Cynthia J. Lee

Representative Clients: American Megatrends, Inc.; Char-Broil; General Electric Co.; Georgia Tech Research Corp.; Globespan Semiconductor, Inc.; Hewlett-Packard Co.; Lucent Technologies, Inc.; MindSpring Enterprises, Inc.; Paradyne Corp.; United Microelectronics Corp.

For full biographical listings, see the Martindale-Hubbell Law Directory

HAWAII

*HONOLULU,** Honolulu Co.

CADES SCHUTTE FLEMING & WRIGHT (AV)

Formerly Smith, Wild, Beebe & Cades
Cades Schutte Fleming & Wright Building, 1000 Bishop Street, Suite 1200, P.O. Box 939, 96808
Telephone: 808-521-9200
Telecopier: 808-521-9210
Email: cades@cades.com
Kailua-Kona, Hawaii Office: Hualalai Center, Suite B-303, 75-170 Hualalai Road.
Telephone: 808-329-5811.
Telecopier: 808-326-1175.

MEMBER OF FIRM

Martin E. Hsia

Counsel for: First Hawaiian Bank; Alexander & Baldwin, Inc.; Theo. H. Davies & Co., Ltd.; C. Brewer & Company, Ltd.; Bank of America, FSB; Bank of America NT&SA; Fun Factory, Inc.

For Complete List of Firm Personnel, See General Section

For full biographical listings, see the Martindale-Hubbell Law Directory

CARLSMITH BALL (AV)

A Partnership including Law Corporations
Suite 2200, Pacific Tower, 1001 Bishop Street, P.O. Box 656, 96809-3402
Telephone: 808-523-2500
Fax: 808-523-0842
Email: execdirector@carlsmith.com *URL:* http://www.carlsmith.com
Kapolei, Hawaii Office: Suite 318, Kapolei Building, 1001 Kamokila Boulevard, 96707.
Telephone: 808-523-2500.
Fax: 808-674-0850.
Wailuku, Maui Hawaii Office: Suite 400, One Main Plaza, 2200 Main Street, P.O. Box 1086, 96793-1086.
Telephone: 808-242-4535.
Fax: 808-244-4974.
Kailua-Kona, Hawaii Office: Suite 209, 75-1000 Henry Street, 96740.
Telephone: 808-329-6464.
Fax: 808-329-9450.
Hilo, Hawaii Office: 121 Waianuenue Avenue, P.O. Box 686, 96721-0686.
Telephone: 808-935-6644.
Fax: 808-935-7975.
Hagatna, Guam Office: Suite 401, Bank of Hawaii Building, 134 West Soledad Avenue, P.O. Box BF, 96932-5027.
Telephone: 671-472-6813.
Fax: 671-477-4375.
Telex: 721-6445 CWCMI GM.
Saipan, Commonwealth of the Northern Mariana Islands Office: Carlsmith Building, Capitol Hill, P.O. Box 5241, 96950-5241.
Telephone: 670-322-3455.
Fax: 670-322-3368.
Los Angeles, California Office: 9th Floor, 444 South Flower Street, 90071-2901.
Telephone: 213-955-1200.
Fax: 213-623-0032.
Washington, D.C. Office: Suite 300, 1201 Pennsylvania Avenue, N.W., 20004-2401.
Telephone: 202-628-2228.
Fax: 202-628-2071.
Mexico City, Mexico Office: Carlsmith Ball, Sierra Nevada 119, Lomas de Chapultepec, 11000 Mexico, D.F.
Telephone: 52-5-520-8514, 52-5-520-8757.
Fax: 52-5-540-1545.
Mexico, D.F. Office of Carlsmith Ball, S.C. (Authorized to practice as foreign legal consultants in Mexico): Sierra Nevada 119, Lomas de Chapultepec, 11000 Mexico, D.F.
Telephone: 52-5-520-8514, 52-5-520-8757.
Fax: 52-5-540-1545.

MEMBERS OF FIRM

Gary G. Grimmer
John P. Manaut

OF COUNSEL

Herbert G. Baerwitz (Resident at Los Angeles, California Office)
Robert R. Thornton (Resident at Los Angeles, California Office)

For Complete List of Firm Personnel, See General Section

For full biographical listings, see the Martindale-Hubbell Law Directory

Miami—Continued

MALIN, HALEY & DIMAGGIO, P.A. (AV)

2000 South Dixie Highway, Suite 203, 33133
Telephone: 305-374-4082
Email: Patents954@aol.com *URL:* http://www.lawyers.com/mhdclaw
Fort Lauderdale, Florida Office: 1 East Broward Boulevard, Suite 1609.
Telephone: 954-763-3303.
Fax: 954-522-6507.
West Palm Beach, Florida Office: Suite 600, 500 South Australian Avenue.
Telephone: 561-832-6341.
New Address Effective February, 2000; 1936 South Andrews Avenue, Fort Lauderdale, Florida, 33316.

Eugene F. Malin (1936-1990)
Barry L. Haley
Dale Paul DiMaggio
Daniel S. Polley

Cristina Pinheiro-Palmer (Not admitted in FL)
Jeffrey H. Kamenetsky

OF COUNSEL

John C. Black (Not admitted in FL)

Representative Clients: IBM; Motorola; Blockbuster Entertainment; Hughes Aircraft Co.; CAE Electronics; Nova Southeastern University; Sea Ray Boats; News and Sun-Sentinel; Brunswick Corp.; Boston Whaler.

For full biographical listings, see the Martindale-Hubbell Law Directory

MALLOY & MALLOY, P.A. (AV)

2800 S.W. Third Avenue, 33129
Telephone: 305-858-8000
Fort Lauderdale: 954-525-9611
In Florida: 800-337-7239
Facsimile: 305-858-0008
URL: http://www.MALLOYLAW.com
Fort Lauderdale, Florida Office: 2101 West Commercial Boulevard. Suite 4100. 33309.
Telephone: 954-525-9611.

Jennie S. Malloy
John Cyril Malloy, III
Peter A. Matos

Louis R. Gigliotti, Jr.
Andrew W. Ransom

OF COUNSEL

John Cyril Malloy
James E. Wetterling, Jr.

Representative Clients: Tasco Sales, Inc.; Turnberry Associates/Aventura Mall; Editorial Televisa; Cigarette Racing Team, Inc.; Sloppy Joe's (Bar) Int'l, Inc.; Hog's Breath (Saloon) Int'l, Inc.; Krieger Watch Corp.; Navarro Discount Pharmacies; Nailtiques Cosmetic Corp.; Cheeburger Cheeburger Restaurants.

For full biographical listings, see the Martindale-Hubbell Law Directory

NAGIN GALLOP FIGUEREDO, P.A. (AV)

3225 Aviation Avenue - Third Floor, 33133-4741
Telephone: 305-854-5353
Facsimile: 305-854-5351

Stephen E. Nagin
Earl G. Gallop
Luis R. Figueredo
Scott L. Cagan
Eve A. Boutsis
Jeffrey B. Mallory

For full biographical listings, see the Martindale-Hubbell Law Directory

*ORLANDO,** Orange Co.

ALLEN, DYER, DOPPELT, MILBRATH & GILCHRIST (AV)

255 South Orange Avenue, Suite 1401, P.O. Box 3791, 32802-3791
Telephone: 407-841-2330
Fax: 407-841-2343
Email: info@addmg.com

Herbert L. Allen
Robert Dyer
Ava K. Doppelt
Stephen D. Milbrath
Brian R. Gilchrist
Christopher F. Regan
Jeffrey S. Whittle
David L. Sigalow
Richard K. Warther
Michael W. Taylor (Not admitted in FL)
Enrique G. Estevez

LEGAL SUPPORT PERSONNEL

PATENT AGENTS

Carl M. Napolitano, Ph.D.
Jacqueline E. Hartt, Ph.D.

For full biographical listings, see the Martindale-Hubbell Law Directory

*TAMPA,** Hillsborough Co.

ARTHUR W. FISHER, III, P.A. (AV)

Suite 316, 5553 West Waters Avenue, 33634-0500
Telephone: 813-885-2006
Fax: Available Upon Request
Email: 74732.1301@compuserve.com

(See Next Column)

Arthur W. Fisher, III

Reference: Sun Bank of Tampa Florida.

For full biographical listings, see the Martindale-Hubbell Law Directory

FRIJOUF, RUST & PYLE, P.A. (AV)

201 East Davis Boulevard (Davis Islands), 33606-3787
Telephone: 813-254-5100
Telecopier: 813-254-5400
Email: Frijouf@ix.netcom.com *URL:* http://www.frijouf.com

Robert F. Frijouf
Charles R. Rust

For full biographical listings, see the Martindale-Hubbell Law Directory

PETTIS & VAN ROYEN, P.A. (AV)

Suite 700, 501 East Kennedy Boulevard, 33602-5200
Telephone: 813-226-0440
Telecopier: 813-229-8073
Email: patlaw@gate.net

David W. Pettis, Jr.
William S. (Tom) Van Royen

For full biographical listings, see the Martindale-Hubbell Law Directory

*WEST PALM BEACH,** Palm Beach Co.

MALIN, HALEY & DIMAGGIO, P.A. (AV)

Suite 600, 500 South Australian Avenue, 33401
Telephone: 561-832-6341
Email: Patents954@aol.com *URL:* http://www.lawyers.com/mhdclaw
Fort Lauderdale, Florida Office: 1 East Broward Boulevard, Suite 1609.
Telephone: 954-763-3303.
Fax: 954-522-6507.
Miami, Florida Office: 2000 South Dixie Highway, Suite 203.
Telephone: 305-374-4082.
New Address Effective February, 2000; 1936 South Andrews Avenue, Fort Lauderdale, Florida, 33316.

Eugene F. Malin (1936-1990)
Barry L. Haley
Dale Paul DiMaggio
Daniel S. Polley

Cristina Pinheiro-Palmer (Not admitted in FL)
Jeffrey H. Kamenetsky

OF COUNSEL

John C. Black (Not admitted in FL)

Representative Clients: IBM; Motorola; Blockbuster Entertainment; Hughes Aircraft Co.; CAE Electronics; Nova Southeastern University; Sea Ray Boats; News and Sun-Sentinel; Brunswick Corp.; Boston Whaler.

For full biographical listings, see the Martindale-Hubbell Law Directory

QUARLES & BRADY LLP (AV)

222 Lakeview Avenue, 4th Floor, 33401
Telephone: 561-653-5000
Fax: 561-653-5333
URL: http://www.quarles.com
Milwaukee, Wisconsin Office: 411 East Wisconsin Avenue, 53202-4497.
Telephone: 414-277-5000.
Fax: 414-271-3552.
Madison, Wisconsin Office: Firstar Plaza, One South Pinckney Street, P.O. Box 2113, 53701-2113.
Telephone: 608-251-5000.
Fax: 608-251-9166.
Naples, Florida Office: Barnett Center, 4501 Tamiami Trail North, Suite 300, 34103-3060.
Telephone: 941-262-5959.
Fax: 941-434-4999.
Phoenix, Arizona Office: One Camelback Building, One East Camelback Road, Suite 400, 85012-1649.
Telephone: 602-230-5500.
Fax: 602-230-5598.
Chicago, Illinois Office: Quarles & Brady LLC, Citicorp Center, 500 West Madison Street, Suite 3700.
Telephone: 312-715-5000.
Fax: 312-715-5155.

PARTNERS

J. Rodman Steele, Jr.
Gregory A. Nelson
Joseph W. Bain
Robert J. Sacco

For Complete List of Firm Personnel, See General Section

For full biographical listings, see the Martindale-Hubbell Law Directory

IDAHO

*BOISE,** Ada Co.

FRANK J. DYKAS, P.A. (AV)

802 West Bannock, 6th Floor, 83702
Telephone: 208-345-1122
Fax: 208-345-8370
Email: dykas@dykaslaw.com *URL:* http://www.dykaslaw.com

Frank J. Dykas

For full biographical listings, see the Martindale-Hubbell Law Directory

ILLINOIS

*CHICAGO,** Cook Co.

ARNOLD WHITE & DURKEE, A PROFESSIONAL CORPORATION (AV)

800 Quaker Tower, 321 North Clark Street, 60610-4714
Telephone: 312-744-0090
Facsimile: 312-755-4489
Email: info@awd.com *URL:* http://www.awd.com
Houston, Texas Office: 750 Bering Drive, 77057-2198.
Telephone: 713-787-1400.
Facsimile: 713-787-1440.
Austin, Texas Office: 1900 One American Center, 600 Congress Avenue, 78701-3248.
Telephone: 512-418-3000.
Facsimile: 512-474-7577.
Washington, D.C. Office: One Franklin Square, 1301 K Street, N.W. Suite 350, East Tower, 20005.
Telephone: 202-289-0229.
Facsimile: 202-289-7535.
Menlo Park, California Office: 155 Linfield Drive, 94025-3741.
Telephone: 650-614-4500.
Facsimile: 650-614-4599.
Minneapolis, Minnesota Office: 4850 U.S. Bank Place, 601 Second Avenue South, 55402-4320.
Telephone: 612-321-2800.
Facsimile: 612-321-9600.

Stephen G. Rudisill
Ronald B. Coolley
Slawomir (Steve) Z. Szczepanski

Michael J. Blankstein
Paul R. Kitch
Mary Jo Boldingh
Daniel J. Burnham
Timothy R. Baumann
Thomas V. Miller (Not admitted in IL)
Jon D. Shutter
John C. Gatz
Mark V. Campagna
Janet M. Garetto
Matthew O. Brady
Russell J. Genet
Rimas (Ray) T. Lukas
Marina N. Saito

OF COUNSEL

Harold N. Wells (Not admitted in IL)
Roger J. French

For full biographical listings, see the Martindale-Hubbell Law Directory

BANNER & WITCOFF, LTD. (AV)

Established In 1920 - Predecessor Parent
Ten South Wacker Drive, 60606-7407
Telephone: 312-715-1000
Facsimile: 312-715-1234
Email: cooperman@bannerwitcoff.com *URL:* http://www.bannerwitcoff.com
Washington, D.C. Office: 1001 G Street, N.W.
Telephone: 202-508-9100.
Facsimile: 202-508-9299.
Boston, Massachusetts Office: 28 State Street, 28th Floor.
Telephone: 617-227-7111.
Fax: 617-227-4399.
Portland, Oregon Office: 601 SW Second Avenue, 19th Floor.
Telephone: 503-279-6330.
Fax: 503-279-6328.

Mark T. Banner
James V. Callahan
Marc S. Cooperman
Laura J. DeMoor
Timothy C. Meece
Jon O. Nelson
Thomas K. Pratt
Christopher J. Renk
Robert H. Resis
John F. Rollins
Charles W. Shifley
J. Pieter van Es
Sheldon W. Witcoff

OF COUNSEL

Patricia A. Felch
Robert P. Hart
Joseph P. Krause
Darleen J. Stockley

(See Next Column)

ASSOCIATES

Matthew P. Becker
Joseph J. Berghammer (Not admitted in IL)
Scott A. Burow
Ronald C. Gorsché, Jr.
Gilberto Hernandez
William J. Klein
Janice V. Mitrius
Christopher P. Moreno
Binal J. Patel

For full biographical listings, see the Martindale-Hubbell Law Directory

DICK AND HARRIS (AV)

Suite 3800, 181 West Madison Street, 60602
Telephone: 312-726-4000
Telecopier: 312-726-5834

MEMBERS OF FIRM

Richard Eugene Dick
Richard D. Harris
Howard E. Silverman
John S. Pacocha

ASSOCIATES

Douglas B. Teaney
Herbert H. Finn
Christopher Sean Clancy
James K. Cleland
Jeannette Sanniola Zimmer

For full biographical listings, see the Martindale-Hubbell Law Directory

FITCH, EVEN, TABIN & FLANNERY (AV)

120 South La Salle, Suite 1600, 60603
Telephone: 312-577-7000
Fax: 312-577-7007
Email: email@fitcheven.com *URL:* http://www.fitcheven.com
San Diego, California Office: 4250 Executive Square, Suite 510. 92037.
Telephone: 619-552-1311.
Telecopier: 619-552-0095.
Washington, D.C. Office: Suite 1801 K Street, N.W., Suite 401L, 20006-1201.
Telephone: 202-789-4900.
Fax: 202-789-8707.

MEMBERS OF FIRM

Morgan L. Fitch, Jr.
Francis A. Even
Julius Tabin
John F. Flannery
Robert B. Jones
James J. Schumann (Resident, San Diego, California Office)
James J. Hamill
Timothy E. Levstik
Joseph E. Shipley
Robert J. Fox
Kenneth H. Samples
Philip T. Petti
John S. Paniaguas
Joseph T. Nabor
Steven C. Schroer (Not admitted in IL)
Richard A. Kaba (Not admitted in IL)
Karl R. Fink
Mark W. Hetzler
Timothy P. Maloney
Thomas F. Lebens (Resident, San Diego, California Office)
Donald A. Peterson
Bruce R. Mansfield
James L. Kurtz
Mark A. Hamill
Perry Jay Hoffman
James P. Krueger
Stephen S. Favakeh
Sherri N. Blount (Resident, Washington, D.C. Office)
Jay A. Saltzman
Edward W. Gray, Jr. (Resident, Washington, D.C. Office)

Kathleen A. Ranney
Roberta L. Hastreiter
Rebecca P. Rokos
Christopher E. George (Resident, Washington, D.C. Office)
Marianne S. Hamilton (Resident, San Diego, California Office)
Scott J. Menghini (Resident, San Diego, California Office)
Debra J. Fickler

PATENT AGENTS

Walter A. Michel
Michael Lindsey

For full biographical listings, see the Martindale-Hubbell Law Directory

LAFF, WHITESEL & SARET, LTD., A PROFESSIONAL CORPORATION (AV)

Suite 1700, 401 North Michigan Avenue, 60611-4212
Telephone: 312-661-2100
Telecopiers: 312-661-0029 312-527-3001
Email: lwcs@iplaw-today.com *URL:* http://www.iplaw-today.com

Charles A. Laff
J. Warren Whitesel
Larry L. Saret
Martin L. Stern
Louis Altman
Joseph F. Schmidt
Barry W. Sufrin
Marshall W. Sutker
Judith L. Grubner
Kevin C. Trock

William A. Meunier
G. Peter Albert, Jr.
Michael B. Allen
Lisa C. Childs
Rita A. Abbati
Jeffrey F. Canfield

OF COUNSEL

Jack R. Halvorsen
Julian J. Frazin

For full biographical listings, see the Martindale-Hubbell Law Directory

Chicago—Continued

LEYDIG, VOIT & MAYER, LTD. (AV)

Two Prudential Plaza, 180 North Stetson Avenue, Suite 4900, 60601-6780
Telephone: 312-616-5600
Telecopier: 312-616-5700
Email: mail@leydig.com *URL:* http://www.leydig.com
Rockford, Illinois Office: 6815 Weaver Road, Suite 300.
Telephone: 815-963-7661.
Telecopier: 815-963-7664.
Washington, D.C. Office: 700 Thirteenth Street, N.W., Suite 300.
Telephone: 202-737-6770.
Telecopier: 202-737-6776.

Berton Scott Sheppard
James B. Muskal
Dennis R. Schlemmer
Gordon R. Coons
John E. Rosenquist
John W. Kozak
Charles S. Oslakovic (Resident, Rockford Office)
Mark E. Phelps
H. Michael Hartmann
Bruce M. Gagala
Charles H. Mottier
John Kilyk, Jr.
Robert F. Green
John B. Conklin
James D. Zalewa
Mark J. Liss
John M. Belz (Resident, Washington, D.C. Office)
Brett A. Hesterberg
Jeffrey A. Wyand (Resident, Washington, D.C. Office)
Paul J. Korniczky
Pamela J. Ruschau
Steven P. Petersen
John M. Augustyn
Christopher T. Griffith
Wesley O. Mueller
Jeremy M. Jay (Resident, Washington, D.C. Office)
Lynn A. Sullivan
Jeffrey B. Burgan
Eley O. Thompson
Mark Joy

Allen E. Hoover
David M. Airan
Xavier Pillai (Resident, Washington, D.C. Office)
Y. Kurt Chang
Gregory C. Bays
Carol Larcher
Steven H. Sklar
Ali R. Sharifahmadian
Tamara A. Miller
M. Daniel Hefner
Thomas A. Belush
Kenneth P. Spina
Gary R. Jarosik
Thomas L. Holt
Siegmund Y. Gutman
Andrea M. Augustine
Song Zhu (Resident, Washington, D.C. Office)
Andrew J. Heinisch (Resident, Rockford Office)
Jeffery J. Makeever (Resident, Rockford Office)
Salim A. Hasan
Richard A. Wulff
Phillip M. Pippenger
Anita J. Terpstra
Anne E. Naffziger
Jamison E. Lynch
Vladan M. Vasiljevic
Lisa D. Graver
Kathryn M. Lumb
Rattan Nath
Robert M. Gould (Not admitted in IL)
Claudia M. Werner
Kevin L. Wingate (Resident, Rockford Office)

OF COUNSEL

C. Frederick Leydig
Theodore W. Anderson
John P. Bundock, Jr. (Washington, D.C. Office)
Paul L. Ahern
John D. Foster (Washington, D.C. Office)
Noel I. Smith
Harold A. Williamson (Rockford Office)

For full biographical listings, see the Martindale-Hubbell Law Directory

MARSHALL, O'TOOLE, GERSTEIN, MURRAY & BORUN (AV)

6300 Sears Tower, 233 South Wacker Drive, 60606-6402
Telephone: 312-474-6300
Fax: 312-474-0448
URL: http://www.marshallotoole.com

MEMBERS OF FIRM

Richard H. Anderson
Michael F. Borun
Richard A. Brandon
David W. Clough
Madeline Henricks Devereux
Christine A. Dudzik
Patrick D. Ertel
David A. Gass
Allen H. Gerstein
Robert M. Gerstein
Roger A. Heppermann
Martin J. Hirsch
Douglass C. Hochstetler
Trevor B. Joike
Richard M. LaBarge
William E. McCracken
Carl E. Moore
James J. Napoli
Anthony Nimmo
Edward M. O'Toole
Li-Hsien Rin-Laures
Nate F. Scarpelli
Richard A. Schnurr
Jeffrey S. Sharp
Timothy J. Vezeau
Karl A. Vick
James P. Zeller

OF COUNSEL

Owen J. Murray
Alvin D. Shulman

ASSOCIATES

Scott E. Baxendale
G. Christopher Braidwood
Thomas A. Cawley, Jr.
Jane J. Choi
Meggan F. Duffy
James A. Flight
Kevin M. Flowers
Janine M. Girzadas
Jennifer P. Goetsch
Michael R. Graham
William J. Kramer
Brent E. Matthias
Gregory C. Mayer
William K. Merkel
Thomas A. Miller
Michael Muczynski (Not admitted in IL)
Sandip H. Patel

(See Next Column)

ASSOCIATES (Continued)

David C. Read
Anthony G. Sitko
Jill E. Uhl
Lena T. Van Asdale
Andrew C. Warnecke
Michael R. Weiner

LEGAL SUPPORT PERSONNEL

PATENT AGENTS

Greta E. Noland
Joseph A. Williams, Jr.

For full biographical listings, see the Martindale-Hubbell Law Directory

McDONNELL BOEHNEN HULBERT & BERGHOFF (AV)

300 South Wacker Drive 32nd Floor, 60606
Telephone: 312-913-0001
Fax: 312-913-0002
URL: http://www.mbhb.com

MEMBERS OF FIRM

John J. McDonnell
Daniel A. Boehnen
Bradley J. Hulbert
Paul H. Berghoff
Grantland G. Drutchas
Denis A. Berntsen
James C. Gumina
David M. Frischkorn
Leif R. Sigmond, Jr.
A. Blair Hughes
Lawrence H. Aaronson
Thomas A. Fairhall
Matthew J. Sampson
Curt J. Whitenack
Michael S. Greenfield
Steven J. Sarussi
Christopher M. Cavan
Kevin E. Noonan
Robert J. Irvine, III
Amir N. Penn
George I. Lee
Joshua R. Rich

ASSOCIATES

James M. McCarthy
Thomas E. Wettermann
Audrey L. Bartnicki
Enrique Perez
Stephen Lesavich (Not admitted in IL)
Sean M. Sullivan
Roger P. Zimmerman
Vernon W. Francissen (Not admitted in IL)
Emily Miao
Richard A. Machonkin
David S. Harper
Marcus Thymian
Malcolm J. Duncan
Stephen H. Docter

For full biographical listings, see the Martindale-Hubbell Law Directory

NIRO, SCAVONE, HALLER & NIRO (AV)

181 West Madison, Suite 4600, 60602-4515
Telephone: 312-236-0733
Facsimile: 312-236-3137

Raymond P. Niro
Thomas G. Scavone
Timothy J. Haller
William L. Niro
Joseph N. Hosteny, III
Robert A. Vitale, Jr.
John C. Janka
Richard B. Megley
Paul K. Vickrey
Michael P. Mazza
Dean D. Niro
Raymond P. Niro, Jr.
Keith A. Vogt
Patrick F. Solon
Arthur A. Gasey

Christopher J. Lee
David J. Sheikh
Robert P. Greenspoon
Sally Wiggins
Richard Burns Megley, Jr.
Paul C. Gibbons
William W. Flachsbart
Gregory P. Casimer

For full biographical listings, see the Martindale-Hubbell Law Directory

PATTISHALL, McAULIFFE, NEWBURY, HILLIARD & GERALDSON (AV)

Suite 5000, 311 South Wacker Drive, 60606
Telephone: 312-554-8000
Facsimile: 312-554-8015
Washington, D.C. Office: 320 Watergate, Six Hundred, 20037.
Telephone: 202-338-1300.
Facsimile: 202-338-9349.

MEMBERS OF FIRM

Beverly W. Pattishall
Jeremiah D. McAuliffe
Robert M. Newbury
Benjamin S. Warren III (Resident Partner, Washington, D.C. Office)
Raymond I. Geraldson, Jr.
David Craig Hilliard
Edward G. Wierzbicki
Robert W. Sacoff
Mark V. B. Partridge
Joseph N. Welch II
Daniel D. Frohling
John Thompson Brown
Mary E. Innis
Douglas N. Masters
Brett A. August
Jonathan S. Jennings
John Michael Murphy
Kevin T. Conroy
Janet A. Marvel

OF COUNSEL

Ralph H. Lane
Diana Lee Bixler

(See Next Column)

PATTISHALL, MCAULIFFE, NEWBURY, HILLIARD & GERALDSON—*Continued*

Bradley L. Cohn
Colette A. Durst-Barkey (Resident Associate, Washington, D.C. Office)
Kathryn E. Ross
Daniel S. Goldman
Beth A. Fulkerson
Demetra Merikas
James P. Williams
Jennifer A. O'Malley
Heather F. Hines
Danielle B. Lemack
Uli Widmaier
Jennifer E. Berner
Ram Padmanabhan

For full biographical listings, see the Martindale-Hubbell Law Directory

PATULA & ASSOCIATES (AV)

116 South Michigan Avenue 14th Floor, 60603
Telephone: 312-201-8220
Fax: 312-372-8681
Email: patula@worldnet.ATT.NET

Timothy T. Patula

ASSOCIATES

Charles T. Riggs Jr.
Stacey P. Pappas
Adam K. Sacharoff
J. Mark Wilkinson

For full biographical listings, see the Martindale-Hubbell Law Directory

PAULEY PETERSEN KINNE & FEJER

(See Hoffman Estates)

ROCKEY, MILNAMOW & KATZ, LTD. (AV)

Two Prudential Plaza, Suite 4700, 60601
Telephone: 312-616-5400
Facsimile: 312-616-5460
Email: patent@rmklaw.com
Arlington, Virginia Office: 2001 Jefferson Davis Highway.
Telephone: 703-415-0880.
Facsimile: 703-415-0883.
Moline Office: 1630 Fifth Avenue.
Telephone: 309-797-0864.
Fax: 309-764-1485.

Lawrence J. Chapa
Thomas C. Elliott, Jr.
Randall T. Erickson
Stephen D. Geimer
Allen J. Hoover
Martin L. Katz
Kathleen A. Lyons
John P. Milnamow
Lisa von Bargen Mueller
Paul M. Odell
Robert B. Polit
Elaine M. Ramesh
Keith V. Rockey
Thomas I. Ross
Joel E. Siegel
Paul M. Vargo

OF COUNSEL

Theodore R. Scott
H. Vincent Harsha

For full biographical listings, see the Martindale-Hubbell Law Directory

ROPER & QUIGG (AV)

200 South Michigan Avenue Suite 1000, 60604
Telephone: 312-408-0855
Facsimile: 312-408-0865
URL: http://www.roperandquigg.com
Washington, D.C. Area Office: Three Crystal Park, 2231 Crystal Drive, Suite 410, Arlington, Virginia.
Telephone: 703-920-8910.

MEMBERS OF FIRM

Harry J. Roper
Donald J. Quigg (Not admitted in IL; Resident, Arlington, Virginia Office)
George S. Bosy
William P. Oberhardt
Raymond N. Nimrod
Steven R. Trybus
Aaron A. Barlow
Archie W. Umphlett (Resident, Arlington, Virginia Office)

ASSOCIATES

Sarah L. Taylor
Timothy J. Barron
John E. Titus
Anthony A. Hartmann
David R. Bennett
Deanne M. Mazzochi
Heather F. Auyang
Jason G. Harp
Jonathan Hill

OF COUNSEL

E. Eugene Innis (Not admitted in IL)

For full biographical listings, see the Martindale-Hubbell Law Directory

TREXLER, BUSHNELL, GIANGIORGI & BLACKSTONE, LTD. (AV)

105 West Adams Street 36th Floor, 60603-6299
Telephone: 312-704-1890
Fax: 312-704-8023
URL: http://www.trexlaw.com

(See Next Column)

Richard R. Trexler (1906-1995)
Richard Bushnell
Richard A. Giangiorgi
Raiford A. Blackstone, Jr.
David J. Marr
Grant H. Peters
Linda L. Palomar
James R. Foley
Thomas J. Donovan

For full biographical listings, see the Martindale-Hubbell Law Directory

WALLENSTEIN & WAGNER, LTD. (AV)

Suite 5300 311 South Wacker Drive, 60606-6622
Telephone: 312-554-3300
Facsimile: 312-554-3301
Email: iplaw@wallywag.com *URL:* http://www.wallywag.com

Robert E. Wagner
Alan L. Barry
Linda A. Kuczma
Daniel N. Christus
Thomas K. Stine
Micheal D. Lake
Roger H. Stein
Joseph A. Fuchs
Richard C. Himelhoch
Bradley F. Rademaker
Jeffrey R. Gargano

OF COUNSEL

Sidney Wallenstein

Edward L. Bishop
Robert W. Diehl
Matthew J. Gryzlo
Brent A. Hawkins
James J. Jagoda
Peter M. Klobuchar
Marc D. Machtinger
Monique Ann Morneault
James P. Muraff
Paul Joseph Nykaza
Michael K. Nutter

For full biographical listings, see the Martindale-Hubbell Law Directory

WILDMAN, HARROLD, ALLEN & DIXON (AV)

225 West Wacker Drive, 30th Floor, 60606-1229
Telephone: 312-201-2000
Fax: 312-201-2555
Email: hennessy@whad.com *URL:* http://www.whad.com
Aurora, Illinois Office: 1961 W. Downer Place.
Telephone: 630-892-7021.
Fax: 630-892-7158.
Waukegan, Illinois Office: 404 West Water, P. O. Box 890.
Telephone: 847-625-5550.
Fax: 847-625-5555.
Lisle, Illinois Office: 4300 Commerce Court, Suite 320.
Telephone: 630-955-0555.
Fax: 630-955-0662
Toronto, Ontario correspondent Office: Keel Cottrelle. 36 Toronto Street, Suite 920.
Telephone: 416-367-2900.
Telefax: 416-367-2791.
Telex: 062-18660.

MEMBERS OF FIRM

John J. Arado
Michael Dockterman
Donald Flayton
Craig Steven Fochler
Charles R. Mandly, Jr.
Carmen B. Patti
Thomas J. Ring
Lawrence S. Wick

OF COUNSEL

Diane G. Elder
Bernard Harrold
Cynthia Bushnell Stevens

Kathryn S. Bedward
David A. Copland
Gary R. Gillen
Gregory B. Gulliver
Julie M. Nichols
Kevin B. Reid
Joleen S. Willis

For full biographical listings, see the Martindale-Hubbell Law Directory

HOFFMAN ESTATES, Cook Co.

PAULEY PETERSEN KINNE & FEJER (AV)

Suite 365, 2800 West Higgins Road, 60195
Telephone: 847-490-1400
Facsimile: 847-490-1403
Email: sp-f@worldnet.att.net

MEMBERS OF FIRM

Douglas H. Pauley
Maxwell J. Petersen
Charles C. Kinne

Mark E. Fejer
Nick C. Kottis
Kevin D. Erickson

OF COUNSEL

Thomas W. Speckman
Robert C. Ryan

For full biographical listings, see the Martindale-Hubbell Law Directory

*ROCKFORD,** Winnebago Co.

LEYDIG, VOIT & MAYER, LTD. (AV)

6815 Weaver Road, Suite 300, 61114-8018
Telephone: 815-963-7661
Telecopier: 815-963-7664
Email: mail@leydig.com *URL:* http://www.leydig.com
Chicago, Illinois Office: Two Prudential Plaza, 180 North Stetson Avenue, Suite 4900.
Telephone: 312-616-5600.
Telecopier: 312-616-5700.
Washington, D.C. Office: 700 Thirteenth Street, N.W., Suite 300.
Telephone: 202-737-6770.
Telecopier: 202-737-6776.

Charles S. Oslakovic (Resident)

Andrew J. Heinisch (Resident) Jeffery J. Makeever (Resident)
Kevin L. Wingate (Resident)

OF COUNSEL

Harold A. Williamson (Resident)

For full biographical listings, see the Martindale-Hubbell Law Directory

INDIANA

*FORT WAYNE,** Allen Co.

LUNDY & ASSOCIATES, P.C. (AV)

825 Anthony Wayne Building, 203 East Berry Street, 46802-2715
Telephone: 219-422-1534
Telecopier: 219-423-1590
Email: lundylaw@worldnet.att.net
Email: LundyLaw@lawinfo.com *URL:* http://www.lawinfo.com/law/in/lundy/
Indianapolis, Indiana Office: 327 Circle Tower Building. 55 Monument Circle.
Telephone: 317-634-5552.

David A. Lundy

Reference: National City Bank.

For full biographical listings, see the Martindale-Hubbell Law Directory

*INDIANAPOLIS,** Marion Co.

LOCKE REYNOLDS LLP (AV)

1000 Capital Center South, 201 North Illinois Street, 46204-4210
Telephone: 317-237-3800
Telecopier: 317-237-3900
Email: attys@locke.com *URL:* http://www.locke.com

Richard A. Huser
Andrew James Richardson
Jeffrey R. Gaither
Jeffrey S. Dible

Stephen L. Vaughan
David S. Klinestiver
Shannon Stewart
Roland R. Schindler, II

Representative Clients: Ball Corp.; Dow AgroSciences LLC; E.S. Robbins Corporation; Electra Form, Inc.; National Wine & Spirits, Inc.; Noble Romans, Inc.; VonDuprin, Inc.; Roche Diagnostics; Ingersol Rand; ReGin Manufacturing.

For Complete List of Firm Personnel, See General Section

For full biographical listings, see the Martindale-Hubbell Law Directory

LUNDY & ASSOCIATES, P.C. (AV)

327 Circle Tower Building, 55 Monument Circle, 46204-5901
Telephone: 317-634-5552
Telecopier: 219-423-1590
Email: lundylaw@worldnet.att.net
Email: LundyLaw@lawinfo.com *URL:* http://www.lawinfo.com.law/IN/lundy/
Fort Wayne, Indiana Office: 825 Anthony Wayne Building, 203 East Berry Street.
Telephone: 219-422-1534.

David A. Lundy

Reference: National City Bank.

For full biographical listings, see the Martindale-Hubbell Law Directory

WOODARD, EMHARDT, NAUGHTON, MORIARTY & MCNETT (AV)

Bank One Center/Tower, 111 Monument Circle, Suite 3700, 46204-5137
Telephone: 317-634-3456
Telecopier: 317-637-7561

(See Next Column)

MEMBERS OF FIRM

Harold R. Woodard
C. David Emhardt
Joseph A. Naughton, Jr.
John V. Moriarty
John C. McNett
Thomas Q. Henry
James M. Durlacher
Charles R. Reeves
Vincent O. Wagner
Stephen E. Zlatos
Spiro Bereveskos
William F. Bahret
Clifford W. Browning
R. Randall Frisk
Daniel J. Lueders
Kenneth A. Gandy
Timothy N. Thomas
Kerry Pauline Sisselman
Kurt N. Jones

ASSOCIATES

John H. Allie
Holiday W. Banta
Troy J. Cole
L. Scott Paynter
J. Andrew Lowes
Charles J. Meyer
Darrin W. Harris
Matthew R. Schantz
Gregory B. Coy
Lisa A. Hiday
John V. Daniluck
Christopher A. Brown
C. John Brannon
Jason J. Schwartz
A.J. Usher, IV

STAFF ATTORNEY

Linda C. Shelby

OF COUNSEL

James L. Rowe

For full biographical listings, see the Martindale-Hubbell Law Directory

IOWA

*CEDAR RAPIDS,** Linn Co.

SHUTTLEWORTH & INGERSOLL, P.C. (AV)

115 Third Street S.E., Suite 500, P.O. Box 2107, 52406-2107
Telephone: 319-365-9461
Fax: 319-365-8443
URL: http://www.shuttleworthlaw.com

James C. Nemmers Glenn L. Johnson

Representative Clients: Aegon USA, Inc.; Alliant IES Utilities; Met-Coil Systems Corporation; Parsons Technology, Inc.

For Complete List of Firm Personnel, See General Section

For full biographical listings, see the Martindale-Hubbell Law Directory

*DES MOINES,** Polk Co.

DAVIS, BROWN, KOEHN, SHORS & ROBERTS, P.C. (AV)

(Formerly Davis, Hockenberg, Wine, Brown, Koehn & Shors, P.C.)
The Financial Center, 666 Walnut Street, Suite 2500, 50309-3993
Telephone: 515-288-2500
Cable: Davis Law
Facsimile: 515-243-0654
Email: info@lawiowa.com *URL:* http://www.lawiowa.com

Kent A. Herink

Daniel A. Rosenberg

For Complete List of Firm Personnel, See General Section

For full biographical listings, see the Martindale-Hubbell Law Directory

ZARLEY, MCKEE, THOMTE, VOORHEES & SEASE, P.L.C. (AV)

801 Grand, Suite 3200, 50309-2721
Telephone: 515-288-3667
Facsimile: 515-288-1338
Email: Patatty@Zarley.com *URL:* http://www.zarley.com
Omaha, Nebraska Office: 1111 Commercial Federal Tower, 2120 South 72nd Street.
Telephone: 402-392-2280.
Facsimile: 402-392-0734.
Toronto, Ontario, Canada Office: 40 King Street West, Suite 4300.
Telephone: 416-367-1576.
Facsimile: 416-367-6749.

MEMBERS OF FIRM

Donald H. Zarley
Bruce W. McKee
Dennis L. Thomte
Michael G. Voorhees
Edmund J. Sease
Mark D. Hansing
Kirk M. Hartung
Daniel J. Cosgrove
Heidi Sease Nebel

ASSOCIATES

Denise C. Mazour (Not admitted in IA)
Michael R. Crabb
Wendy K. Marsh
Jeffrey D. Harty
Timothy J. Zarley
James A. Napier (Not admitted in IA)
Mark Ziegelbein
Patricia L. Ades

(See Next Column)

ZARLEY, MCKEE, THOMTE, VOORHEES & SEASE P.L.C.—*Continued*

Reference: Nations Bank (Des Moines, Iowa).

For full biographical listings, see the Martindale-Hubbell Law Directory

KANSAS

*TOPEKA,** Shawnee Co.

WRIGHT, HENSON, SOMERS, SEBELIUS, CLARK & BAKER, LLP (AV)

Commerce Bank Building, 100 Southeast Ninth Street, 2nd Floor, P.O. Box 3555, 66601-3555
Telephone: 785-232-2200
FAX: 785-232-3344
Email: wrighthenson@wrighthenson.com *URL:* http://www.wrighthenson.com

MEMBER OF FIRM

Bruce J. Clark

Representative Client: Newtek, Inc.

For Complete List of Firm Personnel, See General Section

For full biographical listings, see the Martindale-Hubbell Law Directory

KENTUCKY

*LEXINGTON,** Fayette Co.

KING AND SCHICKLI (AV)

Corporate Gateway, Suite 210, 3070 Harrodsburg Road, 40503
Telephone: 606-223-4050
Facsimile: 606-224-9445
Email: iplaw1@gte.net

J. Ralph King
Warren D. Schickli

ASSOCIATES

Michael S. Hargis
Andrew D. Dorisio

OF COUNSEL

Larry M. Bauman (Not admitted in KY)
J.W. Seanor (Not admitted in KY)

Representative Clients: Addington, Inc.; DECA, Inc.; Hunter Mfg. Group, Inc.; Reese Products, Inc.; Integrity, Inc.; National Wildlife Federation; Kliklok Corporation; SerVend International; University of Kentucky Research Foundation; Link-Belt.

For full biographical listings, see the Martindale-Hubbell Law Directory

STOLL, KEENON & PARK, LLP (AV)

201 E. Main Street, Suite 1000, 40507-1380
Telephone: 606-231-3000
Telecopier: 606-253-1093; 606-253-1027
URL: http://www.skp.com
Frankfort, Kentucky Office: 307 Washington Street, 40601.
Telephone: 502-875-6220.
Telecopier: 502-875-6235.
Henderson, Kentucky Office: 201 C North Main Street, 42420-3103.
Telephone: 270-831-1900.
Telecopier: 270-827-4060.
Louisville, Kentucky Office: 400 West Market Street, Suite 2650, 40202-3377.
Telephone: 502-568-9100.
Telecopier: 502-568-5700.

MEMBERS OF FIRM

Anita M. Britton
Dan M. Rose
David E. Fleenor
William L. Montague, Jr.

Representative Clients: Bank One, Lexington, NA; Farmers Capital Bank Corp.; Link Belt Construction Equipment Co.; General Motors Corp.; International Business Machines Corp.; R.J. Reynolds Tobacco Co.; Rockwell International Corp.; Square D Co.

For Complete List of Firm Personnel, See General Section

For full biographical listings, see the Martindale-Hubbell Law Directory

*LOUISVILLE,** Jefferson Co.

MIDDLETON & REUTLINGER, P.S.C. (AV)

2500 Brown and Williamson Tower, 40202-3410
Telephone: 502-584-1135
Fax: 502-561-0442
URL: http://middreut.com
Jeffersonville, Indiana Office: 530 East Court Avenue, 47130.
Telephone: 812-282-1132.
Fax: 812-282-3188.

James R. Higgins, Jr.
Charles G. Lamb

John F. Salazar
Scot A. Duvall
Laura D. Robertson
Jeffrey A. Haeberlin

For Complete List of Firm Personnel, See General Section

For full biographical listings, see the Martindale-Hubbell Law Directory

MARYLAND

*BALTIMORE,** (Independent City)

VENABLE ATTORNEYS AT LAW VENABLE, BAETJER AND HOWARD, LLP (AV)

A Partnership including Professional Corporations
1800 Mercantile Bank & Trust Building, 2 Hopkins Plaza, 21201
Telephone: 410-244-7400
Fax: 410-244-7742
URL: http://www.venable.com
Washington, D.C. Office: Venable, Baetjer, Howard & Civiletti LLP, Suite 1000, 1201 New York Avenue, N.W.
Telephone: 202-962-4800.
Fax: 202-962-8300.
McLean, Virginia Office: Suite 400, 2010 Corporate Ridge.
Telephone: 703-760-1600.
Fax: 703-821-8949.
Rockville, Maryland Office: Suite 500, One Church Street, P. O. Box 1906.
Telephone: 301-217-5600.
Fax: 301-217-5617.
Towson, Maryland Office: 210 Allegheny Avenue, P. O. Box 5517.
Telephone: 410-494-6200.
Fax: 410-821-0147.

MEMBERS OF FIRM

George H. Spencer (Not admitted in MD; Resident, Washington, D.C. Office)
Robert J. Frank (Not admitted in MD; Resident, Washington, D.C. Office)
Norman N. Kunitz (Not admitted in MD; Resident, Washington, D.C. Office)
George Cochran Doub (P.C.)
Thomas J. Kenney, Jr. (P.C.)
Kenneth C. Bass, III (Not admitted in MD; Washington, D.C. and McLean, Virginia Offices)
Edward F. Glynn, Jr. (Resident, Washington, D.C. Office)
Gabor J. Kelemen (Not admitted in MD; Resident, Washington, D.C. Office)
John W. Schneller (Not admitted in MD; Resident, Washington, D.C. Office)
G. Stewart Webb, Jr.
Robert Kinberg (Not admitted in MD; Resident, Washington, D.C. Office)
Allen Wood (Not admitted in MD; Resident, Washington, D.C. Office)
Jeffrey D. Knowles (Not admitted in MD; Resident, Washington, D.C. Office)
Jeffrey A. Dunn (Also at Washington, D.C. Office)
George F. Pappas (Also at Washington, D.C. Office)
William D. Coston (Not admitted in MD; Resident, Washington, D.C. Office)
Ashley J. Wells (Not admitted in MD; Resident, Washington, D.C. Office)
James A. Dunbar (Resident, Towson, Maryland Office)
Robert J. Bolger, Jr. (Also at Washington, D.C. Office)
Mary Jane Saunders (Not admitted in MD; Resident, Washington, D.C. Office)
David J. Heubeck
Herbert G. Smith, II (Not admitted in MD; Resident, Washington, D.C. Office)
James R. Burdett (Not admitted in MD; Resident, Washington, D.C. Office)
Gary M. Hnath (Resident, Washington, D.C. Office)
Newton B. Fowler, III
Michael A. Gollin (Resident, Washington, D.C. Office)
David W. Goewey (Not admitted in MD; Resident, Washington, D.C. Office)
John T. Prisbe
Vicki Margolis (Also at Washington, D.C. Office)

OF COUNSEL

Barbara L. Waite (Resident, Washington, D.C. Office)

(See Next Column)

VENABLE ATTORNEYS AT LAW VENABLE, BAETJER AND HOWARD, LLP, *Baltimore—Continued*

ASSOCIATES

Marcia A. Auberger (Not admitted in MD; Resident, Washington, D.C. Office)
Paul D. Barker, Jr.
Peter J. Curtin (Not admitted in MD; Also at Washington, D.C. Office)
James Nicholas Czaban (Not admitted in MD; Resident, Washington, D.C. Office)

For Complete List of Firm Personnel, See General Section

For full biographical listings, see the Martindale-Hubbell Law Directory

BETHESDA, Montgomery Co.

LINIAK, BERENATO, LONGACRE & WHITE, LLC (AV)

Suite 240 6550 Rock Spring Drive, 20817
Telephone: 301-896-0600
Fax: 301-896-0607
Arlington, Virginia Office: 1919 South Eads Street, 22202 Virginia.
Telephone: 703-521-1827.
Leesburg, Virginia Office: 604 S. King Street, Suite 008, 20175.
Telephone: 703-737-6988.

MEMBERS OF FIRM

Thomas P. Liniak
Joseph W. Berenato, III (Not admitted in MD)

ASSOCIATES

Joseph A. Rhoa
Guillermo E. Baeza
Matthew Wade Stavish
Matthew F. Johnston

OF COUNSEL

James R. Longacre (Not admitted in MD)
John M. White

LEGAL SUPPORT PERSONNEL

George Ayvazov (Patent Agent)

For full biographical listings, see the Martindale-Hubbell Law Directory

*LA PLATA,** Charles Co.

DAVID NEWMAN CHARTERED (AV)

Centennial Square, P.O. Box 2728, 20646-2728
Telephone: 301-934-6100
Facsimile: 301-934-5782
Email: 5875616@mcimail.com *URL:* http://www.delmarlaw.com

David B. Newman, Jr.

Reference: County First Bank, La Plata, Maryland.

For full biographical listings, see the Martindale-Hubbell Law Directory

*TOWSON,** Baltimore Co.

LEONARD BLOOM & ASSOCIATES, LLC (AV)

Intellectual Property Law Offices
401 Washington Avenue, 21204
Telephone: 410-337-2295
Facsimile: 410-337-2296
Email: bkpatent@mindspring.com *URL:* http://www.lawyers.com/leonardbloom
European Associate's Office: Rue Frans Merjay, 21 B-1060, Brussels, Belgium.

Leonard Bloom

For full biographical listings, see the Martindale-Hubbell Law Directory

MASSACHUSETTS

*BOSTON,** Suffolk Co.

BANNER & WITCOFF, LTD. (AV)

Established In 1920 - Predecessor Parent
28 State Street, 28th Floor, 02109
Telephone: 617-227-7111
Fax: 617-227-4399
Email: cooperman@bannerwitcoff.com *URL:* http://www.bannerwitcoff.com
Chicago, Illinois Office: Ten South Wacker Drive.
Telephone: 312-715-1000.
Facsimile: 312-715-1234.
Washington, D.C. Office: 1001 G Street, N.W.
Telephone: 202-508-9100.
Facsimile: 202-508-9299.
Portland, Oregon Office: 601 SW Second Avenue, Suite 1900.
Telephone: 503-279-6330.
Fax: 503-279-6328.

(See Next Column)

John P. Iwanicki
Ernest V. Linek
Peter D. McDermott
Michael H. Shanahan
Kathleen M. Williams

OF COUNSEL

Dale A. Malone

ASSOCIATE

Gregory J. Cohan

For full biographical listings, see the Martindale-Hubbell Law Directory

BROMBERG & SUNSTEIN LLP (AV)

125 Summer Street, 11th Floor, 02110
Telephone: 617-443-9292
Fax: 617-443-0004
Email: IPLAW@bromsun.com *URL:* http://www.bromsun.com

MEMBERS OF FIRM

Bruce D. Sunstein
Lee Carl Bromberg
Robert L. Kann
Timothy M. Murphy
Kerry L. Timbers
Joel R. Leeman
Robert M. Asher
Thomas C. Carey
Edward J. Dailey

ASSOCIATES

Judith R.S. Stern
Lisa M. Fleming
Erik P. Belt
Theodore E. MacVeagh
Julia Huston
Jennifer G. Cramer
Steven G. Saunders
Samuel J. Petuchowski
Lisa M. Tittemore
John J. Stickevers (Not admitted in MA)
Karen L. Peterson
A. Damien Puller
Herbert Alan Newborn
R.J. Sims Preston
Jeffrey T. Klayman
Christopher D. Engebretson
Jay Sandvos
Jean M. Tibbetts

LEGAL SUPPORT PERSONNEL

Harriet Strimpel, Ph.D. (Patent Agent)

For full biographical listings, see the Martindale-Hubbell Law Directory

CESARI AND MCKENNA, L.L.P. (AV)

30 Rowes Wharf, 02110
Telephone: 617-951-2500
Fax: 617-951-3927

Robert A. Cesari
John F. McKenna
Martin J. O'Donnell
Thomas C. O'Konski
Joseph H. Born
Patricia A. Sheehan
Michael E. Attaya
Steven J. Frank
Charles J. Barbas
William A. Loginov

Michael R. Reinemann
Rita M. Rooney
Christopher K. Gagne (Not admitted in MA)
A. Sidney Johnston (Not admitted in MA)
John H. Emilian, Jr.
Joseph Stecewycz

LEGAL SUPPORT PERSONNEL

Dora V. Dodin (Patent Engineer)
Heather B. Shapiro (Technical Specialist)

For full biographical listings, see the Martindale-Hubbell Law Directory

DIKE, BRONSTEIN, ROBERTS & CUSHMAN, LLP (AV)

A Limited Liability Partnership including Professional Corporations
130 Water Street, 02109
Telephone: 617-523-3400
Telefax: 617-523-6440; 523-7318
Email: ipl@dbrc.com *URL:* http://www.dbrc.com
Marlborough, Massachusetts Office: 62 Cotting Avenue, P.O. Box 556, 01752-0556.
Telephone: 508-485-7772.
Fax: 508-485-0363.

David G. Conlin (P.C.)
George W. Neuner (P.C.)
Linda M. Buckley
Peter J. Manus
Peter F. Corless

Cara Zucker Lowen
William J. Daley, Jr.
Lisa Swiszcz Hazzard
Christine C. O'Day
Richard E. Gamache
David A. Tucker

OF COUNSEL

Sewall P. Bronstein (P.C.) (Resident, Marlborough Office)

PATENT AGENT

Robert L. Buchanan, Ph.D.

TECHNICAL SPECIALIST

Jennifer Holmes

For full biographical listings, see the Martindale-Hubbell Law Directory

Boston—Continued

HINCKLEY, ALLEN & SNYDER LLP (AV)

28 State Street, 30th Floor, 02109-1775
Telephone: 617-345-9000
Email: firm@haslaw.com *URL:* http://www.haslaw.com
Providence, Rhode Island Office: 1500 Fleet Center.
Telephone: 401-274-2000.
Fax: 401-277-9600. URL: http://www.hawlaw.com.

MEMBERS OF FIRM

Paula K. Andrews
David D. Barricelli (Not admitted in MA)
E. Jerome Batty (Not admitted in MA)
Jonathan Bell
Deborah L. Benson
Paul Bork
Stephen J. Carlotti (Not admitted in MA)
David Barry Connolly
Joseph P. Curran (Not admitted in MA)
Michael P. DeFanti
Eric F. Eisenberg
Malcolm Farmer, III
Margaret D. Farrell (Not admitted in MA)
Pasco Gasbarro Jr.
Hugh J. Gorman, III
Alan P. Gottlieb
William R. Grimm
Paul A. Hedstrom
Joel Lewin
Sandra Matrone Mack (Not admitted in MA)
Matthew T. Marcello, III (Not admitted in MA)
Elizabeth Murdock Myers
Paul F. O'Donnell, III
H. Peter Olsen (Not admitted in MA)
Gerald J. Petros
James O. Reavis
Jeremy Ritzenberg
Ralph J. Rivkind
Lawrence R. Robins
David J. Rubin
Charles E. Schaub, Jr.
Herman Snyder
David R. Sullivan
Robert F. Sylvia
Howard E. Walker (Not admitted in MA)

ASSOCIATES

Jessica M. Bettencourt (Not admitted in MA)
Mark Bianchi
Alyssa V. Boss
Alexandra K. Callam
Jane E. Cohen
Andrew D. Cummings
June E. Daniel (Not admitted in MA)
Kim Herman Goslant
Gloria Maria Gutierrez
Kelley Jordan-Price
Catherine S. Kim
Christopher W. Morog
Elena B. Olson
Joseph D. Whelan (Not admitted in MA)

OF COUNSEL

Willard R. Pope
Bentley Tobin
Joachim A. Weissfeld (Not admitted in MA)

For Complete List of Firm Personnel, See General Section

For full biographical listings, see the Martindale-Hubbell Law Directory

LAHIVE & COCKFIELD, LLP (AV)

28 State Street, 02106
Telephone: 617-227-7400
Fax: 617-742-4214
Email: LC@LAHCOC.COM *URL:* http://www.lahive.com

MEMBERS OF FIRM

John A. Lahive, Jr. (1928-1997)
Thomas V. Smurzynski
Ralph A. Loren
Giulio A. DeConti, Jr.
Ann Lamport Hammitte
Elizabeth A. Hanley
Amy B. Mandragouras
Anthony A. Laurentano
Kevin J. Canning

John V. Bianco
Jane E. Remillard
Faustino A. Lichauco
David A. Lane, Jr.
Jeanne M. DiGiorgio
Debra J. Milasincic
Nicholas P. Triano, III
Timothy J. Douros
Diana M. Collazzo

SENIOR COUNSEL

W. Hugo Liepmann
James E. Cockfield

OF COUNSEL

Jeremiah Lynch
Lawrence E. Monks
William A. Scofield, Jr.
John L. Welch

LEGAL SUPPORT PERSONNEL

PATENT AGENTS

Catherine J. Kara
Megan E. Williams
Reza Mollaaghababa

TECHNICAL SPECIALISTS

Jasbir K. Sagoo
Maria C. Laccotripe
Monica Palacios-Boyce
Cynthia M. Boroos
Peter W. Dini
Jennifer Elliott
Lauren Foster

For full biographical listings, see the Martindale-Hubbell Law Directory

LAPPIN & KUSMER LLP (AV)

200 State Street, 02109
Telephone: 617-330-1300
Telecopier: 617-330-1311

(See Next Column)

MEMBERS OF FIRM

Mark G. Lappin
Toby H. Kusmer
Elizabeth A. Levy

Steven M. Mills
Anthony P. Onello, Jr.
Carolyn G. d'Agincourt
Ronald R. Demsher
David M. Mello

OF COUNSEL

Robert J. Schiller
David Silverstein

For full biographical listings, see the Martindale-Hubbell Law Directory

LORUSSO & LOUD (AV)

440 Commercial Street, 02109
Telephone: 617-227-0700
Telefax: 617-723-4609
Telex: 286853 (RCA)
Alexandria, Virginia Office: 3137 Mt. Vernon Avenue.
Telephone: 703-739-9393.
Fax: 703-739-9391.
Portsmouth, New Hampshire Office: 249 Islington Street.
Telephone: 603-427-0070.
Fax: 603-427-5530.

MEMBERS OF FIRM

Anthony M. Lorusso (Resident at Portsmouth, New Hampshire Office)
George A. Loud (Resident, Alexandria, Virginia Office)
Thomas M. Saunders

For full biographical listings, see the Martindale-Hubbell Law Directory

MORSE & ALTMAN (AV)

85 East India Row, 02110
Telephone: 617-523-3515
FAX: 617-523-1872

Gerald Altman
Steven K. Martin

For full biographical listings, see the Martindale-Hubbell Law Directory

WILLCOX, PIROZZOLO AND MCCARTHY, PROFESSIONAL CORPORATION (AV)

50 Federal Street, 02110
Telephone: 617-482-5470
Telecopier: 617-423-1572

Harold M. Willcox (1925-1975)
Jack R. Pirozzolo
Richard F. McCarthy

Richard L. Binder
Richard E. Bennett
Judith Seplowitz Ziss
Christopher R. Goddu
Katherine L. Young

OF COUNSEL

Richard P. Crowley

For full biographical listings, see the Martindale-Hubbell Law Directory

LEXINGTON, Middlesex Co.

HAMILTON, BROOK, SMITH & REYNOLDS, P.C. (AV)

Two Militia Drive, 02421-4799
Telephone: 781-861-6240
Telecopier: 781-861-9540
URL: http://www.hbsr.com

Munroe H. Hamilton (1906-1984)
David E. Brook
James M. Smith
Leo R. Reynolds
John L. DuPré
David J. Brody
Mary Lou Wakimura
Thomas O. Hoover
Alice O. Carroll
N. Scott Pierce
Helen E. Wendler
Susan G. L. Glovsky
Doreen M. Hogle
Richard W. Wagner
Robert T. Conway
J. Grant Houston
Rodney D. Johnson

OF COUNSEL

Richard A. Wise
David J. Thibodeau, Jr.
Anne I. Craig

Gerald M. Bluhm
Raymond I. Bruttomesso, Jr.
Linda M. Chinn
Patricia L. Chisholm
Anne J. Collins
Carol A. Egner
Erik L. Ence
Antoinette G. Giugliano
Monica Grewal (Not admitted in MA)
Paul P. Kriz
Helen Lee
Elizabeth W. Mata
Timothy J. Meagher
Deirdre E. Sanders
Robert J. Sayre
Mark B. Solomon
David Suhl
C. Christina Taylor (Not admitted in MA)
Jon C. Trachtenberg
Lisa M. Treannie
Darrell L. Wong

(See Next Column)

HAMILTON, BROOK, SMITH & REYNOLDS P.C., *Lexington—Continued*

LEGAL SUPPORT PERSONNEL

SUPERVISING PATENT AGENT

Carolyn S. Elmore

PATENT AGENTS

Susan M. Abelleira
Sandra A. Brockman
Edgar W. Harlan
Joyce C. Miller

TECHNOLOGY SPECIALISTS

Mary K. Murray
Jeffrey J. Duquette
Caroline M. Fleming
C. Steven Kurlowecz
Theresa A. Devlin
Robert H. Underwood

For full biographical listings, see the Martindale-Hubbell Law Directory

*SPRINGFIELD,** Hampden Co.

DOHERTY, WALLACE, PILLSBURY AND MURPHY, P.C. (AV)

19th Floor, One Monarch Place, 1414 Main Street, 01144
Telephone: 413-733-3111
Telecopier: 413-734-3910
Email: DWPM@DWPM.com *URL:* http://www.dwpm.com

Dudley B. Wallace (1900-1987)
Louis W. Doherty (1898-1990)
Frederick S. Pillsbury (1919-1996)
Paul S. Doherty
Samuel A. Marsella
Philip J. Callan, Jr.
Gary P. Shannon
Robert L. Leonard
A. Craig Brown
L. Jeffrey Meehan
David J. Martel
John James McCarthy
William P. Hadley
Barry M. Ryan
Deborah A. Basile
Paul M. Maleck
Claire L. Thompson
W. Garth Janes
Gregory A. Schmidt

Michael K. Callan
Steven M. Coyle
Michael D. Sweet
James J. Bregianes
Grace M. Calamita

OF COUNSEL

Robert E. Murphy
Matthew J. Ryan, Jr.

Local Counsel for: Nationwide Mutual Insurance Co.; Liberty Mutual Insurance Co.; General Motors Corp.; Wausau Insurance Cos.; Royal Insurance; Metropolitan Property & Liability Insurance Co.
Representative Clients: Fontaine Bros.; F.L. Roberts and Company Inc.; Town of Longmeadow.

For full biographical listings, see the Martindale-Hubbell Law Directory

HOLLAND & BONZAGNI, P.C. (AV)

1441 Main Street, 01103
Telephone: 413-737-5524
Fax: 413-567-2079
Email: h-b@hollandlaw.com *URL:* http://www.hollandlaw.com
Longmeadow, Massachusetts Office: Longmeadow Professional Park, 171 Dwight Road, 01106.
Telephone: 413-567-2076.
Fax: 413-567-2079.

Donald S. Holland

For full biographical listings, see the Martindale-Hubbell Law Directory

MICHIGAN

*ANN ARBOR,** Washtenaw Co.

HARNESS, DICKEY & PIERCE, P.L.C. (AV)

Suite 555, 301 East Liberty Street, 48104
Telephone: 734-662-8000
Telex: 287637 HARNES UR
Telefacsimile: 734-662-7813
Email: info@hdp.com *URL:* http://www.hdp.com
Troy, Michigan Office: 5445 Corporate Drive, Suite 400.
Telephone: 248-641-1600. Telefacsimile (All Groups): 248-641-0270.
Washington, D.C. Office: 888 Sixteenth Street, N.W.
Telephone: 202-835-7480.

MEMBERS OF FIRM

James E. Stephenson (Resident)
Steven L. Oberholtzer (Resident)
Eric J. Sosenko (Resident)

RESIDENT ASSOCIATES

Scott M. Confer
Jeffrey M. Cox (Resident at Ann Arbor Office)
Christopher DeVries

Representative Clients: Chrysler Corp.; The Black and Decker Manufacturing Co.; Thermos Co.; Monroe Auto Equipment Co.; La-Z-Boy Chair Co.; Hughes Aircraft; Budd Co.; Dow Chemical Co.; Procter & Gamble; Kmart Properties; General Motors Corporation.

(See Next Column)

For full biographical listings, see the Martindale-Hubbell Law Directory

BLOOMFIELD HILLS, Oakland Co.

HOWARD & HOWARD ATTORNEYS, P.C. (AV)

The Pinehurst Office Center, Suite 101, 1400 North Woodward Avenue, 48304-2855
Telephone: 248-645-1483
Telecopier: 248-645-1568
Kalamazoo, Michigan Office: The Michigan Building, Suite 200, 100 Portage Street.
Telephone: 616-382-1483.
Telecopier: 616-382-1568.
Lansing, Michigan Office: The Phoenix Building, Suite 500, 222 Washington Square, North.
Telephone: 517-485-1483.
Telecopier: 517-485-1568.
Peoria, Illinois Office: One Technology Plaza, Suite 600, 211 Fulton Street.
Telephone: 309-672-1483.
Telecopier: 309-672-1568.

John J. Andler
John E. Carlson
Anthony P. Cho
David J. Gaskey
William S. Gottschalk
Samuel J. Haidle
William H. Honaker
Kerrie A. Laba
Rhonda L. McCoy-Pfau
Harold W. Milton, Jr.
Theodore W. Olds III
Jeffrey A. Sadowski
Paula L. Schneider
Raymond E. Scott
Randall L. Shoemaker
David L. Wisz

Representative Clients: For Representative Client list, see General Practice, Bloomfield Hills, MI.

For Complete List of Firm Personnel, See General Section

For full biographical listings, see the Martindale-Hubbell Law Directory

LYON & ARTZ PLC (AV)

3883 Telegraph Road, Suite 207, 48302-1476
Telephone: 248-645-5200
Facsimile: 248-645-1016
Email: lyonpc@lyonpc.com *URL:* http://www.lyonpc.com
Southfield, Michigan Office: 28333 Telegraph Road, 48034.
Telephone: 248-223-9500.
Fax: 248-223-9522.

Lyman R. Lyon
Laurence C. Begin
Alexander P. Brackett (Not admitted in MI)

LEGAL SUPPORT PERSONNEL

Kurt Vanvoorheis

For full biographical listings, see the Martindale-Hubbell Law Directory

RADER, FISHMAN & GRAUER PLLC (AV)

1533 North Woodward, Suite 140, 48304
Telephone: 248-594-0600
Fax: 248-594-0610
Email: info@raderfishman.com *URL:* http://www.intelprop.com
Grand Rapids, Michigan Office: Rader, Fishman, Grauer & McGarry PLLC, 171 Monroe Avenue, N.W., Suite 600, 49503.
Telephone: 616-742-3500.
Fax: 616-742-1010.
Washington D.C. Office: 1233 20th Street, Suite 501, 20036.
Telephone: 202-955-3750.
Fax: 202-955-3751.
Denver, Colorado Office: 7887 East Belleview Avenue, 80111.
Telephone: 303-228-1658.
Fax: 303-228-1659.

Ralph Terrance Rader
Michael D. Fishman
Richard D. Grauer
Joseph V. Coppola, Sr.
Michael B. Stewart
Eric M. Dobrusin
Glenn E. Forbis
James F. Kamp
Stefan V. Chmielewski
Kevin D. Rutherford
Annette R. Carrothers
Matthew J. Russo (Resident, Denver Office)
Kristin L. Murphy
William Cosnowski, Jr.
Anna M. Shih
Michelle L. Visser
John P. Guenther

OF COUNSEL

Andrew S. Walker
Jill N. Johnston

PATENT AGENT

Alexander D. Rabinovich

For full biographical listings, see the Martindale-Hubbell Law Directory

*DETROIT,** Wayne Co.

DYKEMA GOSSETT PLLC (AV)

400 Renaissance Center, 48243-1668
Telephone: 313-568-6800
Fax: 313-568-6545
Email: mstarrs@dykema.com *URL:* http://www.dykema.com
Ann Arbor, Michigan Office: 315 East Eisenhower Parkway, Suite 100, 48108-3306.
Telephone: 734-214-7660.
Fax: 734-214-7696.
Bloomfield Hills, Michigan Office: 1577 North Woodward Avenue, Suite 300, 48304-2820.
Telephone: 248-203-0700.
Fax: 248-203-0763.
Chicago, Illinois Office: 55 East Monroe Street, Suite 3050, 60603-5709.
Telephone: 312-551-4900.
Fax: 312-551-4919.
Grand Rapids, Michigan Office: Suite 700, 300 Ottawa Avenue, N.W., 49503-2304.
Telephone: 616-776-7500.
Fax: 616-776-7573.
Lansing, Michigan Office: 800 Michigan National Tower, 48933-1707.
Telephone: 517-374-9100.
Fax: 517-374-9191.
Washington, D.C. Office: Franklin Square, Suite 300 West, 1300 I Street, N.W., 20005-3306.
Telephone: 202-522-8600.
Fax: 202-522-8669.
Affiliated Office: Via Matconi, 3, 40122 Bologna, Italy.
Telephone: 011-39-51-228222.
Fax: 011-39-51-6593580.

MEMBERS OF FIRM

Joseph H. Hickey (Resident at Bloomfield Hills Office)
Kevin M. Hinman (Resident at Bloomfield Hills Office)
J. Timothy Hobbs (Not admitted in MI; Resident at Washington, D.C. Office)
Robert L. Kelly (Resident at Bloomfield Hills Office)
Barbara Goldman Mandell (Resident at Bloomfield Hills Office)
Bruce A. McDonald (Not admitted in MI; Resident at Washington, D.C. Office)
Janet L. Neary (Resident at Ann Arbor Office)
Charles R. Rutherford (Resident at Bloomfield Hills Office)
Thomas B. Spillane, Jr. (Resident at Bloomfield Hills Office)

ASSOCIATES

Christopher Kelly (Not admitted in MI; Resident at Washington, D.C. Office)
William F. Kolakowski III (Resident at Bloomfield Hills Office)

For Complete List of Firm Personnel, See General Section

For full biographical listings, see the Martindale-Hubbell Law Directory

MILLER, CANFIELD, PADDOCK AND STONE, P.L.C. (AV)

A Professional Limited Liability Company
Founded in 1852 by Sidney Davy Miller
150 West Jefferson, Suite 2500, 48226-4415
Telephone: 313-963-6420
Fax: 313-496-7500
Cable Address: "Stem Detroit"
URL: http://www.millercanfield.com
Ann Arbor, Michigan Office: 101 North Main Street, 7th Floor, 48104-1400.
Telephone: 734-663-2445.
Fax: 734-747-7147.
Troy, Michigan Office: 840 West Long Lake Road, Suite 200, 48098.
Telephone: 248-879-2000.
Fax: 248-879-2001.
Grand Rapids, Michigan Office: 99 Monroe, N.W., Suite 1200, 49503-2639.
Telephone: 616-454-8656.
Fax: 616-776-6322.
Howell, Michigan Office: 121 South Barnard Street, Suite 4, 48843-2305.
Telephone: 517-546-7600.
Telecopier: 517-546-6974.
Kalamazoo, Michigan Office: 444 West Michigan Avenue, 49007-3752.
Telephone: 616-381-7030.
Fax: 616-382-0244.
Lansing, Michigan Office: One Michigan Avenue, Suite 900, 48933-1609.
Telephone: 517-487-2070.
Fax: 517-374-6304.
Monroe, Michigan Office: 214 East Elm Avenue, Suite 100, 48162-2682.
Telephone: 734-243-2000.
Fax: 734-243-0901.
Washington, D.C. Office: 1900 K Street, N.W., Suite 1150. 20006.
Telephone: 202-429-5575; 785-0600.
Fax: 202-331-1118; 785-1234.
Pensacola, Florida Office: 25 West Cedar, 32501.
Telephone: 850-469-1088.
Fax: 850-432-0677.

(See Next Column)

New York, New York Office: 1450 Broadway, 41st Floor, 10018.
Telephone: 212-704-4400.
Fax: 212-704-4410.
Gdynia, Poland Office: UL. Slaska 21, 81-319.
Telephone: 011-485-831-2808.
Fax: 011-48-58-628 6411.
Warsaw, Poland Office: UL. Nowogrodzkall, 5th Floor, 00-513.
Telephone: 011-4822 529 0200.
Fax: 011-4822 529 0201.
Katowice, Poland Office: UL. Francuska 35/37, 40-027.
Telephone: 011 (48-32) 757-2414.
Fax: 011 (48-32) 757-2483.

PRINCIPALS OF FIRM

Marjory G. Basile
Richard A. Gaffin (Grand Rapids Office)

Representative Firm Clients: Chrysler Corporation; Comerica, Incorporated; City of Detroit, Michigan; Detroit Tigers, Inc.; First of Michigan; Ford Motor Company; Ford Motor Credit Company; Great Lakes Bancorp; Henry Ford Hospital; INVETECH Company.

For Complete List of Firm Personnel, See General Section

For full biographical listings, see the Martindale-Hubbell Law Directory

*GRAND RAPIDS,** Kent Co.

RADER, FISHMAN, GRAUER & McGARRY PLLC (AV)

171 Monroe Avenue, N.W., Suite 600, 49503
Telephone: 616-742-3500
Fax: 616-742-1010
Email: info@raderfishman.com *URL:* http://www.intelprop.com
Washington D.C. Office: Rader, Fishman & Grauer PLLC, 1233 20th Street, Suite 501, 20036.
Telephone: 202-955-3750.
Fax: 202-955-3751.
Bloomfield Hills, Michigan Office: Rader, Fishman & Grauer PLLC, 1533 North Woodward, Suite 140, 48304.
Telephone: 248-594-0600.
Fax: 248-594-0610.
Denver, Colorado Office: Rader, Fishman & Grauer PLLC, 7887 East Belleview Avenue, 80111.
Telephone: 303-228-1658.
Fax: 303-228-1659.

John E. McGarry
H. Lawrence Smith
Joel E. Bair
G. Thomas Williams, III
Mark A. Davis
Michael F. Kelly
Donald J. Wallace

For full biographical listings, see the Martindale-Hubbell Law Directory

WARNER NORCROSS & JUDD LLP (AV)

900 Old Kent Building, 111 Lyon Street, N.W., 49503-2489
Telephone: 616-752-2000
Fax: 616-752-2500
URL: http://www.wnj.com
Muskegon, Michigan Office: 400 Terrace Plaza, P.O. Box 900.
Telephone: 231-727-2600.
Fax: 231-727-2699.
Holland, Michigan Office: Curtis Center, Suite 300, 170 College Avenue.
Telephone: 616-396-9800.
Fax: 616-396-3656.
Southfield, Michigan Office: 1000 Town Center, Suite 650.
Telephone: 248-223-5000.
Fax: 248-223-5005.

MEMBERS OF FIRM

Charles E. Burpee
Douglas A. Dozeman
Janet Percy Knaus
James Moskal

ASSOCIATES

Norbert F. Kugele
William P. Dani
James L. Scott II

For full biographical listings, see the Martindale-Hubbell Law Directory

WATERS & MORSE, P.C. (AV)

400 Ledyard Building, 125 Ottawa, N.W., 49503-2898
Telephone: 616-458-7535
Fax: 616-458-7548
Email: jawaters@msn.com *URL:* http://www.lawyers.com/waters&morse

John A. Waters
James E. Bartek

For full biographical listings, see the Martindale-Hubbell Law Directory

FOSTER, SWIFT, COLLINS & SMITH, P.C.

313 South Washington Square, 48933-2193
Telephone: 517-371-8100
Telecopier: 517-371-8200
URL: http://www.fosterswift.com
Farmington Hills, Michigan Office: 32300 Northwestern Highway, Suite 230.
Telephone: 248-539-9900.
Fax: 248-851-7504.

Gary J. McRay — Steven H. Lasher
Michael R. Huber

For Complete List of Firm Personnel, See General Section

For full biographical listings, see the Martindale-Hubbell Law Directory

---

*MARQUETTE,** Marquette Co.

William … — Lynn A. …
Glenn W. … — …

For full biographical listings, see the Martindale-Hubbell Law Directory

---

McLEOD & MOYNE, P.C. (AV)

Ian C. McLeod

Representative Clients: … Hoffman … Michigan … Imperial Chemical Industries PLC … Limited, England … Nonin Corporation … Michigan.
Reference: Michigan National Bank; First of America.

For full biographical listings, see the Martindale-Hubbell Law Directory

---

*SAGINAW,** Saginaw Co.

REISING, ETHINGTON, BARNES, KISSELLE, LEARMAN & McCULLOCH, P.C. (AV)

… Colony Drive North, 48603
Telephone: 517-799-5300

John F. Learman — John K. McCulloch
Robert L. Stearns

Robert L. Farris

For full biographical listings, see the Martindale-Hubbell Law Directory

---

SOUTHFIELD, Oakland Co.

LYON & ARTZ PLC (AV)

28333 Telegraph Road, Suite 250, 48034
Telephone: 248-223-9500
Fax: 248-223-9522
Email: jsartz@tir.com *URL:* http://www.lyonpc.com
Bloomfield Hills, Michigan Office: 3583 Telegraph Road, Suite 203, 48302.
Telephone: 248-645-5200.
Fax: 248-645-1016.

(See Next Column)

John A. Artz — Robert P. …
Kevin G. Mierzwa

For full biographical listings, see the Martindale-Hubbell Law Directory

---

TRAVERSE CITY, Grand Traverse Co.

BISHOP & HEINTZ, P.C. (AV)

440 W. Front at Oak Street, P.O. Box 707, 49685
Fax: 616-946-8543
Email: info@bishop-heintz.com

For full biographical listings, see the Martindale-Hubbell Law Directory

---

TROY, Oakland Co.

HARNESS, DICKEY & PIERCE, P.L.C.

5445 Corporate Drive, …

Ronald L. Hofer — Eric J. Sosenko (Resident …
Paul A. Keller
Robert M. Siegel
Stephen T. Olson
Stanley M. Erjavac
Michael P. Brennan

ASSOCIATES

Kevin W. Mason
Jeffrey M. … (Resident at Ann Arbor Office) — George T. Schooff
Preston H. Smirman
Christopher DeVries (Resident at Ann Arbor, Michigan Office) — Jeffrey L. Snyder
Bryan K. Wheelock
Gregory A. Wagner
Joseph M. Lucas — Richard W. Warner
Timothy D. MacIntyre — Michael D. Zalobsky

COUNSEL

Robert J. Wallace, Sr. — Charles R. Kinzel
Donald F. Scherer

Representative Clients: The Black and Decker Manufacturing Co.; … Chrysler Corp.; Emerson Electric Co.; General Motors Corp.; … La-Z-Boy Incorporated; … Products Co.; …

For full biographical listings, see the Martindale-Hubbell Law Directory

PENSION AND PROFIT SHARING

ALABAMA

*MOBILE,** Mobile Co.

LYONS, PIPES & COOK, P.C. (AV)

2 North Royal Street, P.O. Box 2727, 36652-2727
Telephone: 334-432-4481
Cable Address: "Lysea"
Telecopier: 334-433-1820
URL: http://www.LPCLaw.com

Wesley Pipes
Thomas F. Garth
W. David Johnson, Jr.

General Counsel: Inchcape Shipping Services.
Counsel: The Hertz Corp.; McKenzie Tank Lines, Inc.; SCNO Barge Lines, Inc.; Scott Paper Co.; Shell Oil Corp.
Trial Counsel: Aetna Life & Casualty Co.; Chubb Group of Insurance Companies.

For Complete List of Firm Personnel, See General Section

For full biographical listings, see the Martindale-Hubbell Law Directory

ARIZONA

*PHOENIX,** Maricopa Co.

FENNEMORE CRAIG, A PROFESSIONAL CORPORATION (AV)

3003 North Central Avenue, Suite 2600, 85012-2913
Telephone: 602-916-5000
Fax: 602-916-5999
Tucson, Arizona Office: One South Church Avenue, Suite 1000, 85701-1620.
Telephone: 520-879-6800.
Fax: 520-879-6899.

Cynthia L. Shupe
David N. Heap

Joel B. Shapiro

For Complete List of Firm Personnel, See General Section

For full biographical listings, see the Martindale-Hubbell Law Directory

*TUCSON,** Pima Co.

DANIEL H. O'CONNELL, P.C. (AV)

3573 East Sunrise Drive, Suite 120, 85718-3206
Telephone: 520-615-9802
Telefax: 520-615-9789
Email: ben@dhopc.psemail.com *URL:* http://www.lawyers.com/danieloconnell-law

Daniel H. O'Connell

Benjamin J. Burnside

OF COUNSEL

Rosanne F. Lapan

Representative Clients: Empire West Cos.; Thermal Engineering, Inc.; Alban Medical Associates; Industrial Motor & Control, Inc.; Allergy Asthma Associates, P.C.
Reference: Bank of America.

For full biographical listings, see the Martindale-Hubbell Law Directory

ARKANSAS

*LITTLE ROCK,** Pulaski Co.

ROSE LAW FIRM, A PROFESSIONAL ASSOCIATION (AV)

120 East Fourth Street, 72201
Telephone: 501-375-9131
Telecopy: 501-375-1309

W. Wilson Jones
C. Brantly Buck
Ronald M. Clark
Bryant K. Cranford

(See Next Column)

Craig S. Lair
Mark Davis

Counsel for: ALLTEL Corporation; Aluminum Company of America; Bridgestone/Firestone, Inc.; The Equitable Life Assurance Society of The United States; General Motors Corp.; The Prudential Insurance Company of America; Stephens Group Inc.; Tyson Foods, Inc.

For Complete List of Firm Personnel, See General Section

For full biographical listings, see the Martindale-Hubbell Law Directory

CALIFORNIA

*FRESNO,** Fresno Co.

DIETRICH, GLASRUD, MALLEK & AUNE (AV)

An Association of Attorneys including Law Corporations
5250 North Palm Avenue, Suite 402, 93704
Telephone: 559-435-5250
Facsimile: 559-435-8776
Email: info@dgmalaw.com

Richard W. Dietrich (Inc.) (1930-1999)
Donald H. Glasrud (Inc.)
Robert A. Mallek Jr. (Inc.)
Richard E. Aune (Inc.)
Bruce A. Owdom
Thomas W. Isaac

Douglas D. Schorling
Leslie G. Miessner
Daniel J. Tekunoff

OF COUNSEL

Timothy J. Buchanan

Representative Clients: Fresno Surgery and Recovery Care Center; Helm Fertilizer, Inc.; Gragnani Farms; Wathen-Castanos, Inc.; Chicago Title Company; ABC, Inc.; The McClatchy Company; Monsanto Company; Armstrong World Industries, Inc.; Stewart Title Guaranty Company.

For full biographical listings, see the Martindale-Hubbell Law Directory

*LOS ANGELES,** Los Angeles Co.

REISH & LUFTMAN, A PROFESSIONAL CORPORATION (AV)

11755 Wilshire Boulevard 10th Floor, 90025
Telephone: 310-478-5656
Facsimile: 310-478-5831
URL: http://www.reish.com

Bruce L. Ashton
Roland M. Attenborough
Joseph C. Faucher
Martin M. Heming
James R. McDaniel
C. Frederick Reish
Mark E. Terman
Michael A. Vanic

Janine B. Jasso
Gail S. Reich
Nicholas J. White

For full biographical listings, see the Martindale-Hubbell Law Directory

*SAN DIEGO,** San Diego Co.

GARRISON ARMSTRONG LAW CORPORATION (AV)

First National Bank Center, 401 West A Street, Suite 1680, 92101-7922
Telephone: 619-232-1811

Garrison R. Armstrong

LEGAL SUPPORT PERSONNEL

Iris R. Daniel (Legal Assistant)

For full biographical listings, see the Martindale-Hubbell Law Directory

COLORADO

*DENVER,** Denver Co.

GUTHERY & RICKLES, P.C. (AV)

Cherry Creek Plaza II, 650 South Cherry Street Suite 1000, 80246-1812
Telephone: 303-320-5889
Fax: 303-320-5890

Peter C. Guthery
Stephen P. Rickles

A list of Representative Clients that have provided written authorization will be furnished upon request.

For full biographical listings, see the Martindale-Hubbell Law Directory

FLORIDA

BOCA RATON, Palm Beach Co.

RONALD T. MARTIN P.A. (AV)

Suite 200, 7000 West Palmetto Park Road, 33433
Telephone: 561-338-4100
Fax: 561-338-9086
Email: RonTMartin@aol.com

Ronald T. Martin

For full biographical listings, see the Martindale-Hubbell Law Directory

HAWAII

*HONOLULU,** Honolulu Co.

CARLSMITH BALL (AV)

A Partnership including Law Corporations
Suite 2200, Pacific Tower, 1001 Bishop Street, P.O. Box 656, 96809-3402
Telephone: 808-523-2500
Fax: 808-523-0842
Email: execdirector@carlsmith.com *URL:* http://www.carlsmith.com
Kapolei, Hawaii Office: Suite 318, Kapolei Building, 1001 Kamokila Boulevard, 96707.
Telephone: 808-523-2500.
Fax: 808-674-0850.
Wailuku, Maui Hawaii Office: Suite 400, One Main Plaza, 2200 Main Street, P.O. Box 1086, 96793-1086.
Telephone: 808-242-4535.
Fax: 808-244-4974.
Kailua-Kona, Hawaii Office: Suite 209, 75-1000 Henry Street, 96740.
Telephone: 808-329-6464.
Fax: 808-329-9450.
Hilo, Hawaii Office: 121 Waianuenue Avenue, P.O. Box 686, 96721-0686.
Telephone: 808-935-6644.
Fax: 808-935-7975.
Hagatna, Guam Office: Suite 401, Bank of Hawaii Building, 134 West Soledad Avenue, P.O. Box BF, 96932-5027.
Telephone: 671-472-6813.
Fax: 671-477-4375.
Telex: 721-6445 CWCMI GM.
Saipan, Commonwealth of the Northern Mariana Islands Office: Carlsmith Building, Capitol Hill, P.O. Box 5241, 96950-5241.
Telephone: 670-322-3455.
Fax: 670-322-3368.
Los Angeles, California Office: 9th Floor, 444 South Flower Street, 90071-2901.
Telephone: 213-955-1200.
Fax: 213-623-0032.
Washington, D.C. Office: Suite 300, 1201 Pennsylvania Avenue, N.W., 20004-2401.
Telephone: 202-628-2228.
Fax: 202-628-2071.
Mexico City, Mexico Office: Carlsmith Ball, Sierra Nevada 119, Lomas de Chapultepec, 11000 Mexico, D.F.
Telephone: 52-5-520-8514, 52-5-520-8757.
Fax: 52-5-540-1545.
Mexico, D.F. Office of Carlsmith Ball, S.C. (Authorized to practice as foreign legal consultants in Mexico): Sierra Nevada 119, Lomas de Chapultepec, 11000 Mexico, D.F.
Telephone: 52-5-520-8514, 52-5-520-8757.
Fax: 52-5-540-1545.

MEMBERS OF FIRM

John C. Khil
Harry Y. Oda
James L. Starshak

For Complete List of Firm Personnel, See General Section

For full biographical listings, see the Martindale-Hubbell Law Directory

TORKILDSON, KATZ, FONSECA, JAFFE, MOORE & HETHERINGTON ATTORNEYS AT LAW, A LAW CORPORATION (AV)

Amfac Building, 15th Floor, 700 Bishop Street, 96813-4187
Telephone: 808-523-6000
Cable Address: "Counsel"
Telex: RCA 723-8185
Telecopier: 808-523-6001
Email: info@torkildson.com
Hilo, Hawaii Office: 100 Pauahi Street, Suite 206.
Telephone: 808-961-0406.
Telecopier: 808-935-6725.

(See Next Column)

Roger W. Fonseca

For Complete List of Firm Personnel, See General Section

For full biographical listings, see the Martindale-Hubbell Law Directory

LOUISIANA

*NEW ORLEANS,** Orleans Parish

MCGLINCHEY STAFFORD (AV)

A Professional Limited Liability Company
643 Magazine Street, 70130-3477
Telephone: 504-586-1200
Fax: 504-596-2800
TDD: (504) 596-2728
Telex: 584327
Cable Address: "MACSTAC"
Mailing Address: P.O. Box 60643, New Orleans, Louisiana, 70160-0643
Email: @mcglinchey.com *URL:* http://www.mcglinchey.com
Dallas, Texas Office: 2777 Stemmons Freeway, Suite 925, 75207-2401.
Telephone: 214-860-9700.
Fax: 214-860-9750.
Houston, Texas Office: 2727 Allen Parkway, Suite 1900, 77019.
Telephone: 713-520-1900.
Fax: 713-520-1025.
Baton Rouge, Louisiana Office: Ninth Floor, One American Place, 70825-0001.
Telephone: 504-383-9000.
Fax: 504-343-3076.
Jackson, Mississippi Office: Suite 1200, SkyTel Centre, 200 South Lamar Street, 39201.
Telephone: 601-960-8400.
Fax: 601-960-8406.
Lake Providence, Louisiana Office: 405 Morgan Street, 71254-2691.
Telephone: 318-559-1200.
Fax: 318-559-0609.
Monroe, Louisiana Office: Dean ONB Tower, 130 Desiard Street, Suite 807, 71201.
Telephone: 318-651-0807.
Fax: 318-651-0809.

MEMBERS OF FIRM

Kenneth A. Weiss
Katherine Conklin

For full biographical listings, see the Martindale-Hubbell Law Directory

MASSACHUSETTS

*BOSTON,** Suffolk Co.

HINCKLEY, ALLEN & SNYDER LLP (AV)

28 State Street, 30th Floor, 02109-1775
Telephone: 617-345-9000
Email: firm@haslaw.com *URL:* http://www.haslaw.com
Providence, Rhode Island Office: 1500 Fleet Center.
Telephone: 401-274-2000.
Fax: 401-277-9600. URL: http://www.hawlaw.com.

MEMBERS OF FIRM

Paula K. Andrews
David D. Barricelli (Not admitted in MA)
E. Jerome Batty (Not admitted in MA)
Jonathan Bell
Leon C. Boghossian III
Paul Bork
Stephen J. Carlotti (Not admitted in MA)
Michael P. DeFanti
Eric F. Eisenberg
Malcolm Farmer, III
Margaret D. Farrell (Not admitted in MA)
Noel M. Field, Jr. (Not admitted in MA)
Pasco Gasbarro Jr.
Hugh J. Gorman, III
Gerard R. Goulet
William R. Grimm
Paul A. Hedstrom
Richard L. E. Jocelyn (Not admitted in MA)
Michael J. Kelly
Joel Lewin
Doris Jami Licht
Sandra Matrone Mack (Not admitted in MA)
Matthew T. Marcello, III (Not admitted in MA)
Frederick P. McClure
Elizabeth Murdock Myers
Paul F. O'Donnell, III
H. Peter Olsen (Not admitted in MA)
Julianne Palumbo
John J. Pendergast, III (Not admitted in MA)
Gerald J. Petros
Richard H. Pierce
James O. Reavis
Jeremy Ritzenberg
Ralph J. Rivkind
Charles E. Schaub, Jr.
Douglas F. Seaver
Paul A. Silver
Herman Snyder
David R. Sullivan
Robert F. Sylvia
Howard E. Walker (Not admitted in MA)
Richard D. Wayne

(See Next Column)

HINCKLEY, ALLEN & SNYDER LLP—*Continued*

ASSOCIATES

Jessica M. Bettencourt (Not admitted in MA)
Mark Bianchi
Alyssa V. Boss
Alexandra K. Callam
Jane E. Cohen
Andrew D. Cummings
June E. Daniel (Not admitted in MA)
Kelley Jordan-Price
Catherine S. Kim
Christopher W. Morog
Elena B. Olson
Joseph D. Whelan (Not admitted in MA)

OF COUNSEL

Willard Krasnow
Bentley Tobin
Joachim A. Weissfeld (Not admitted in MA)

For Complete List of Firm Personnel, See General Section

For full biographical listings, see the Martindale-Hubbell Law Directory

*CAMBRIDGE,** Middlesex Co.

MERVIN M. WILF, LTD. (AV)

2 Berkeley Place, 02138
Telephone: 617-876-5200
Email: mwilf@erols.com
Philadelphia, Pennsylvania Office: 3901 Mellon Bank Center. 1735 Market Street.
Telephone: 215-994-1430. 215-568-4842.
Facsimile: 215-994-1432.

Mervin M. Wilf

A list of Representative Clients and References will be furnished upon request.

For full biographical listings, see the Martindale-Hubbell Law Directory

MICHIGAN

*DETROIT,** Wayne Co.

BODMAN, LONGLEY & DAHLING LLP (AV)

34th Floor 100 Renaissance Center, 48243
Telephone: 313-259-7777
Fax: 313-393-7579
Email: info@bodmanlongley.com *URL:* http://www.bodmanlongley.com
Troy, Michigan Office: Suite 2020, 755 West Big Beaver Road.
Telephone: 248-362-2110.
Fax: 248-244-0780.
Ann Arbor, Michigan Office: 110 Miller, Suite 300.
Telephone: 734-761-3780.
Fax: 734-930-2494.
Northern Michigan Office: 229 Court Street, P.O. Box 405, Cheboygan.
Telephone: 231-627-4351.
Fax: 231-627-2802.

MEMBERS OF FIRM

Mark W. Griffin (Ann Arbor Office)
James R. Buschmann
Barbara A. Bowman

For Representative Clients list, See General Section

For Complete List of Firm Personnel, See General Section

For full biographical listings, see the Martindale-Hubbell Law Directory

TIMMIS & INMAN L.L.P. (AV)

300 Talon Centre, 48207
Telephone: 313-396-4200
Facsimile: 313-396-4228
Email: info@timmis-inman.com *URL:* http://www.timmis-inman.com

Michael T. Timmis
Robert E. Graziani
George A. Peck
Henry J. Brennan, III
Mark W. Peyser
Richard M. Miettinen
George M. Malis

Michael F. Wais
Erich J. D'Andrea
Shannon M. Nichols
Alex N. Saleh

OF COUNSEL

William B. Fitzgerald

LEGAL SUPPORT PERSONNEL

PARALEGALS

Linda M. Bierl

Representative Clients: Detroit Mortgage & Realty; DMR Fiancial Services, Inc.; J. Levin Sons Co.; Green Tree Financial Servicing Corp.; Hematology-Oncology Associates East, PC; Lakeshore Ear, Nose & Throat Center, PC; Micromanagement Systems, Inc.; Phoenix Crystal Corp.; Talon Surfaces LLC; Talon Automated Equipment Company.

For Complete List of Firm Personnel, See General Section

For full biographical listings, see the Martindale-Hubbell Law Directory

FARMINGTON HILLS, Oakland Co.

COUZENS, LANSKY, FEALK, ELLIS, ROEDER & LAZAR, P.C. (AV)

39395 West 12 Mile Road, Suite 200, 48331-2913
Telephone: 248-489-8600
Facsimile: 248-489-4156
Email: info@couzens.com *URL:* http://www.couzens.com

Jack S. Couzens, II
Donald M. Lansky
Bruce J. Lazar
Alan C. Roeder
Renard J. Kolasa
Kathryn Gilson Sussman
Jeffrey A. Levine
Marc L. Prey
Lisa J. Walters
Michael P. Witzke
Cyrus Raamin Kashef
David B. Deutsch

Alisa A. Kwang
Turkia Awada Mullin
Raoul K. Maitra

Representative Clients: Provided upon request.
Reference: Michigan National Bank.

For Complete List of Firm Personnel, See General Section

For full biographical listings, see the Martindale-Hubbell Law Directory

SOUTHFIELD, Oakland Co.

MADDIN, HAUSER, WARTELL, ROTH, HELLER & PESSES, P.C. (AV)

Third Floor Essex Centre, 28400 Northwestern Highway, P.O. Box 215, 48037
Telephone: 248-354-4030, 355-5200
Telefax: 248-354-1422

Milton M. Maddin (1902-1984)
Michael W. Maddin
Mark R. Hauser
C. Robert Wartell
Richard J. Maddin
Richard F. Roth
Harvey R. Heller
Ian D. Pesses
Michael S. Leib
Robert D. Kaplow
William E. Sigler
Stewart C. W. Weiner
Charles M. Lax
Stuart M. Bordman
Steven D. Sallen
Gregory J. Gamalski
Julie Chenot Mayer
Nathaniel H. Simpson
Ronald A. Sollish
Lowell D. Salesin

Mark H. Fink
Steven M. Wolock
Lori E. Talsky
Stephen E. Handelman
Ronald M. Stern
Martin Scott Frenkel
Gary M. Remer
Jennifer S. Sternberg
George V. Cassar, Jr.
Adam J. Goldstein

OF COUNSEL

Bruce N. Goldman

Reference: Comerica Bank.

For full biographical listings, see the Martindale-Hubbell Law Directory

PERSONAL INJURY

ALABAMA

ALEXANDER CITY, Tallapoosa Co.

MORRIS, HAYNES & HORNSBY (AV)

131 Main Street, P.O. Box 1660, 35011-1660
Telephone: 256-329-2000
Fax: 256-329-2015
Email: morrishayn@webshoppe.net

Larry W. Morris
Randall Stark Haynes
Clay Hornsby
Nancy L. Eady

OF COUNSEL

John F. Dillon, IV (1930-1998)
Jennie Lee Kelley

Representative Clients: Aliant Bank; City of Alexander City; Town of Wadley.
Approved Attorneys for: Lawyers Title Insurance Corp.; Mississippi Valley Title Insurance Co.

For full biographical listings, see the Martindale-Hubbell Law Directory

*ANDALUSIA,** Covington Co.

POWELL, PEEK & WEAVER (AV)

201 East Troy Street, Drawer 969, 36420
Telephone: 334-222-4103
Facsimile: 334-222-4105
Email: ppw@alaweb.com

MEMBERS OF FIRM

Abner R. Powell (1875-1940)
Abner R. Powell, Jr. (1916-1987)
Abner R. Powell, III
John M. Peek
Gary L. Weaver
Abner Riley Powell, IV

Representative Clients: State Farm Insurance Group; ALFA Insurance Companies; U.S.F.& G. Co.; CNA Insurance; Auto Owners Insurance Co.; Southern Guaranty Co.; Covington County Bank; Colonial Bank of Opp, Alabama.

For full biographical listings, see the Martindale-Hubbell Law Directory

*BIRMINGHAM,** Jefferson Co.

BAXLEY, DILLARD, DAUPHIN & MCKNIGHT (AV)

2008 3rd Avenue South, 35233
Telephone: 205-939-0995; 205-271-1100
Telecopier: 205-271-1108

MEMBERS OF FIRM

William J. Baxley
Joel E. Dillard
Charles A. Dauphin
Stewart D. McKnight, III
William C. Barclift
Betsy Palmer Collins
Donald R. James, Jr

ASSOCIATE

Elizabeth Louise Wood

For full biographical listings, see the Martindale-Hubbell Law Directory

BISHOP, COLVIN, JOHNSON & KENT (AV)

317-20th Street, North, P.O. Box 370404, 35237
Telephone: 205-251-2881
Fax: 205-254-3987
Email: BCJK@BELLSOUTH.NET

MEMBERS OF FIRM

Maurice F. Bishop (1913-1982)
Gerald D. Colvin, Jr.
Carl E. Johnson, Jr.
Burgin H. Kent
Gerald DeWitt (Whit) Colvin, III

Representative Clients: Miller Transporters, Inc.; United Van Lines, Inc.; Western Steel, Inc.; Alabama Building Products, Inc.; The City of Trussville, Alabama; Utilities Board of the City of Trussville, Alabama; Jefferson County Board of Education; University of Montevallo; Milan Express, Inc.
Reference: AmSouth Bank, N.A.

For full biographical listings, see the Martindale-Hubbell Law Directory

BRADLEY ARANT ROSE & WHITE LLP (AV)

2001 Park Place, Suite 1400, P.O. Box 830709, 35283-0709
Telephone: 205-521-8000
Facsimile: 205-521-8800
Facsimile (SouthTrust Tower Office): 205-521-8500
URL: http://www.barw.com
Huntsville, Alabama Office: 200 Clinton Avenue West, Suite 900, 35801.
Telephone: 205-517-5100.
Facsimile: 205-533-5069.

(See Next Column)

Washington, D.C. Office: 801 Pennsylvania Avenue, NW, Suite 230, 20004.
Telephone: 202-347-8893.
Facsimile: 202-347-1684.

MEMBERS OF FIRM

Joseph S. Bird III
T. Michael Brown
Philip J. Carroll III
Brittin Turner Coleman
Stewart M. Cox
Michael S. Denniston
James W. Gewin
John E. Goodman
Warne S. Heath (Resident, Huntsville Office)
Gary C. Huckaby (Resident, Huntsville Office)
E. Cutter Hughes Jr. (Resident, Huntsville Office)
David Glenn Hymer
Norman Jetmundsen Jr.
Joseph B. Mays Jr.
Michael D. McKibben
Hobart A. McWhorter Jr.
John H. Morrow
Walter J. Sears III
Sid J. Trant
John D. Watson III

ASSOCIATES

Denise Avery Dodson
Julie S. Elmer
Kenneth M. Perry

For Complete List of Firm Personnel, See General Section

For full biographical listings, see the Martindale-Hubbell Law Directory

BURGE & WETTERMARK, P.C. (AV)

2300 SouthTrust Tower, 420 North 20th Street, 35203-3204
Telephone: 205-251-9729; 800-633-3733
Fax: 205-323-0512
Email: firm@bw-law.com *URL:* http://www.bw-law.com
Atlanta, Georgia Office: 3475 Lenox Road, N.E., Suite 400, 30326.
Telephone: 404-875-2500.
Jacksonville, Florida Office: 3100 Independent Drive, 32202.
Telephone: 904-353-1555; 800-498-6657.
Fax: 904-353-3905.

Frank O. Burge, Jr.
James H. Wettermark
F. Tucker Burge
Courtney Burge Brown
Monroe Dykes Barber, Jr.
Van Kirk McCombs, II
James R. Holland, II (Not admitted in AL)

References: AmSouth Bank; First Alabama Bank, Birmingham, Alabama.

For full biographical listings, see the Martindale-Hubbell Law Directory

CAMPBELL, WALLER & MCCALLUM, L.L.C. (AV)

Suite 330, 2000-A Southbridge Parkway, 35209
Telephone: 205-803-0051
Fax: 205-803-0053

MEMBERS OF FIRM

Andrew P. Campbell
Jonathan H. Waller
Charles A. McCallum, III
David M. Loper
Martha Reeves Cook
Elizabeth Barger Anthony

For full biographical listings, see the Martindale-Hubbell Law Directory

EMOND & VINES (AV)

2200 SouthTrust Tower, 420 North 20th Street, P.O. Box 10008, 35202-0008
Telephone: 205-324-4000
Fax: 205-324-5020
Email: EmondVines@aol.com

MEMBER OF FIRM

Lanny S. Vines

ASSOCIATES

Michael Lee Allsup
Vivian D. Vines Campbell
Frank O. Hanson, Jr.

For full biographical listings, see the Martindale-Hubbell Law Directory

GORDON, SILBERMAN, WIGGINS & CHILDS, P.C. (AV)

1400 SouthTrust Tower, 420 North 20th Street, 35203
Telephone: 205-328-0640
Facsimilie: 205-254-1500
Washington, D.C. Office: 1621 Connecticut Avenue, N.W., Suite 400.
Telephone: 202-238-0690.
Facsimile: 202-238-0968.

RESIDENT SHAREHOLDERS

Bruce L. Gordon
Dennis George Pantazis

RESIDENT ASSOCIATES

Byron R. Perkins
Gregory O. Wiggins
Brian M. Clark
Craig L. Lowell
Nicole L. Gordon
Edward McFarland Johnson

For Complete List of Firm Personnel, See General Section

For full biographical listings, see the Martindale-Hubbell Law Directory

Birmingham—Continued

GORHAM & WALDREP, P.C. (AV)

2101 6th Avenue North, Suite 700, 35203
Telephone: 205-254-3216; 251-9166
Telecopier: 205-324-3802
Email: info@gorham-waldrep.com *URL:* http://www.gorham-waldrep.com
Montgomery, Alabama Office: 250 Commerce Street, P.O. Box 4837, 36103-4837.
Telephone: 334-262-0777.
Telecopier: 334-262-0742.

Charles W. Gorham
Charlie D. Waldrep
Frank G. Alfano

Representative Clients: Jefferson County Personnel Board; Birmingham-Jefferson Civic Center Authority; The Water Works and Sewer Board of the City of Birmingham; City of Homewood; American Federation of Government Employees Local #1945; City of Pelham; Town of Kimberly; Alabama Tire Dealers Assn.; Southern States Body Shop Assn.

For Complete List of Firm Personnel, See General Section

For full biographical listings, see the Martindale-Hubbell Law Directory

HARE, WYNN, NEWELL AND NEWTON (AV)

A Partnership including Professional Corporations
Suite 800 Massey Building, 290 21st Street North, 35203
Telephone: 205-328-5330
Fax: 205-324-2165

MEMBERS OF FIRM

Francis H. Hare (1904-1983)
Carlton T. Wynn
Neal C. Newell
Alex W. Newton
C. Terrell Wynn, Jr.
James J. Thompson, Jr.
Alva C. Caine
Ray O. (Ronnie) Noojin, Jr. (1945-1996)
John W. Haley (P.C.)
D. Leon Ashford (P.C.)
Scott A. Powell
James R. Pratt, III
S. Shay Samples
Bruce J. McKee
Michael D. Ermert
Nolan Edward Awbrey
James B. Gunther, Jr.
Don McKenna
Martin E. Burke

COUNSEL

Francis H. Hare, Jr., (P.C.)
James O. Haley
James K. Baker

References: AmSouth Bank of Birmingham; First Commercial Bank of Birmingham.

For full biographical listings, see the Martindale-Hubbell Law Directory

HARRIS, CLECKLER & HOLLIS (AV)

Historic 2007 Building, 2007 Third Avenue North, 35203-2366
Telephone: 205-328-2366
Telecopier: 205-328-0013
Email: hcbr@mindspring.com *URL:* http://www.harriscleckler.com

Lyman H. Harris
Michael H. Cleckler
Jeffrey K. Hollis

ASSOCIATE

Jason A. Shamblin

For full biographical listings, see the Martindale-Hubbell Law Directory

HENINGER, BURGE, VARGO AND DAVIS, LLP (AV)

1500 Financial Center, 505 North Twentieth Street, 35203
Telephone: 205-322-5153
Fax: 205-322-6706
Email: heninger@mindspring.com *URL:* http://www.lawyers.com/hbv&dlaw

MEMBERS OF FIRM

Stephen D. Heninger
S. Greg Burge
Stuart F. Vargo
Timothy C. Davis

For full biographical listings, see the Martindale-Hubbell Law Directory

HOGAN, SMITH & ALSPAUGH, P.C. (AV)

2323 Second Avenue, North, 35203
Telephone: 205-324-5635
Telecopier: 205-324-5637
Email: Chris@Hogan-Smith.com *URL:* http://www.hsa-pc.com

William W. Smith
M. Clay Alspaugh
R. Benjamin Hogan, III
Ronald R. Crook
Richard D. Stratton
Jack Lee Roberts, Jr.
Benjamin E. Baker, Jr.

Maxwell D. Carter

Reference: Regions Bank.

For full biographical listings, see the Martindale-Hubbell Law Directory

ROBERT W. LEE & ASSOCIATES, P.C. (AV)

The Landmark Center, Suite 500, 2100 First Avenue North, 35203
Telephone: 205-323-1061
Telecopier: 205-323-1066
Email: RWLEECOMP@Mindspring.com

Robert Wyeth Lee, Jr.

Wendy N. Thornton
Nancy Hahn Ippolito

OF COUNSEL

John E. Amari

For full biographical listings, see the Martindale-Hubbell Law Directory

LIGHTFOOT, FRANKLIN & WHITE, L.L.C. (AV)

The Clark Building, 400 20th Street North, 35203
Telephone: 205-581-0700
Facsimile: 205-581-0799
Email: LFWlaw@LFWlaw.com *URL:* http://www.lfwlaw.com

Warren B. Lightfoot
Samuel H. Franklin
Jere F. White, Jr.
Mac M. Moorer
John M. Johnson
M. Christian King
E. Glenn Waldrop, Jr.
Adam K. Peck
Harlan I. Prater, IV
Michael L. Bell
William S. Cox, III
William H. King, III
William H. Brooks
J. Banks Sewell, III
Lee M. Hollis

Wynn M. Shuford
John Q. Somerville
Melody L. Hurdle
J. Bradley Powell
William H. Morrow
Stephen Jackson Rowe
William Larkin Radney, IV
James F. Hughey, III

For full biographical listings, see the Martindale-Hubbell Law Directory

LUSK, FRALEY, MCALISTER & SIMMS, P.C. (AV)

Suite 1700 AmSouth/Harbert Plaza, 1901 Sixth Avenue North, 35203
Telephone: 205-323-7100
Fax: 205-323-7050
Email: Lusk-Fraley.com

Donald D. Lusk
John M. Fraley
David L. McAlister
Keri Donald Simms
Kenneth A. Dowdy
David Lawrence Dean
David Thurston White, III
Susan Gilman McAlister
Payton Caldwell Lusk
Leslie Ann Caldwell

For full biographical listings, see the Martindale-Hubbell Law Directory

MARSH, RICKARD & BRYAN, P.C. (AV)

800 Shades Creek Parkway, Suite 600, 35209-4532
Telephone: 205-879-1981
Facsimile: 205-879-1986
Email: attys@mrblaw.com

David H. Marsh
Jeffrey C. Rickard
Nat Bryan
Susan J. Silvernail
Dennis E. Goldasich, Jr.

Thomas M. Powell

OF COUNSEL

Irene T. Grubbs

For full biographical listings, see the Martindale-Hubbell Law Directory

PITTMAN, HOOKS, DUTTON & HOLLIS, P.C. (AV)

1100 Park Place Tower, 35203
Telephone: 205-322-8880
Telecopier: 205-328-2711
Email: PHDH@4theplaintiff.com

W. Lee Pittman
Kenneth W. Hooks
Tom Dutton
L. Andrew Hollis, Jr.
Jeffrey C. Kirby
Ralph Bohanan, Jr.

Chris T. Hellums
Keith T. Belt, Jr.
Leigh King Forstman
Michael C. Bradley
Page Poerschke Liddon
Steven William Couch
J. Chris Cochran

OF COUNSEL

James H. Davis (Not admitted in AL)
Lynn A. Crosson

For full biographical listings, see the Martindale-Hubbell Law Directory

SMITH & ELY, LLP (AV)

2000-A Southbridge Parkway Suite 405, 35209
Telephone: 205-802-2214
Fax: 205-879-4445

(See Next Column)

SMITH & ELY LLP—*Continued*

MEMBERS OF FIRM

Carol Ann Smith
Brenen G. Ely

ASSOCIATES

Susan Rogers
Susan Caroline Haygood
Toby Dykes

OF COUNSEL

Lisa B. Singer

For full biographical listings, see the Martindale-Hubbell Law Directory

SPAIN & GILLON, L.L.C. (AV)

The Zinszer Building, 2117 2nd Avenue North, 35203
Telephone: 205-328-4100
Telecopier: 205-324-8866
Email: ddh@spain-gillon.com *URL:* http://lawlinks.com:80/atty/al/sggbn.html

MEMBERS OF FIRM

Eugene P. Stutts
Paul L. Sotherland
Steve R. Burford
Earl H. Lawson, Jr.

General Counsel for: Alabama Insurance Guaranty Association; Alabama Life and Disability Insurance Guaranty Association; Alabama Insurance Underwriters Association.
Counsel for: Government Employees Insurance Co.; Liberty Mutual Insurance Cos.; Federated Mutual Insurance Co.; AMI Brookwood; Carraway Hospital Group; Dresser Industries; Liberty National Life Insurance Co.

For Complete List of Firm Personnel, See General Section

For full biographical listings, see the Martindale-Hubbell Law Directory

STARNES & ATCHISON LLP (AV)

100 Brookwood Place, 35209
Telephone: 205-868-6000
Telecopier: 205-868-6099
Mailing Address: P.O. Box 598512, 35259-8512
Email: information@starneslaw.com
Mobile, Alabama Office: Riverview Plaza, Suite 1106, 63 South Royal Street, 36602.
Telephone: 334-433-6049.

MEMBERS OF FIRM

W. Stancil Starnes
W. Michael Atchison
William Anthony Davis, III
Michael A. Florie
John P. Scott, Jr.
L. Graves Stiff, III
J. Bentley Owens, III
Walter William Bates
Michael K. Wright
Robert P. Mackenzie, III
Allan R. Wheeler

ASSOCIATES

Rik S. Tozzi
Bryan Oxford Balogh
Blake D. Andrews
James M. Terrell
Alfred H. Perkins, Jr.

Representative Clients: Aetna Casualty & Surety Company; Harbert Construction Co.; AMI Brookwood Medical Center; International Playtex, Inc.; Kawasaki Motors Corp.; Honda North America, Inc.; Roadway, Inc.; Cigna Corp.; Travelers Ins. Co.; United States Fidelity and Guaranty Co.

For full biographical listings, see the Martindale-Hubbell Law Directory

*CHATOM,** Washington Co.

TURNER, ONDERDONK, KIMBROUGH & HOWELL, P.A. (AV)

1021 Central Avenue, P.O. Drawer 1389, 36518
Telephone: 334-847-2237
Fax: 334-847-3115
Email: firm@tokh.com *URL:* http://www.tokh.com
Mobile, Alabama Office: 1359 Dauphin Street.
Telephone: 334-432-2855.
Fax: 334-432-2863.

Edward P. Turner, Jr.
A. Michael Onderdonk
William A. Kimbrough, Jr. (Resident, Mobile Office)
Gordon K. Howell
Marc E. Bradley (Resident, Mobile Office)
Halron W. Turner
Frank Woodson (Resident, Mobile Office)
David M. Huggins (Resident, Mobile Office)
E. Tatum Turner

LEGAL SUPPORT PERSONNEL

Thomas E. Fuller

For full biographical listings, see the Martindale-Hubbell Law Directory

*CULLMAN,** Cullman Co.

DRAKE & DRAKE (AV)

Suite A, 419 Second Avenue, S.W., P.O. Box 1165, 35055-4106
Telephone: 256-734-7602
Fax: 256-734-7696

MEMBERS OF FIRM

Tom Drake
Christine McKoy Drake

(See Next Column)

ASSOCIATE

Thomas E. Drake, II

OF COUNSEL

G. Whit Drake

Representative Clients: Cullman Electric Corp.; Shaver Poultry Breeding Farm, a Division of Cargill.
References: First National Bank of Birmingham; Peoples Bank of Cullman County.

For full biographical listings, see the Martindale-Hubbell Law Directory

*DOTHAN,** Houston Co.

FARMER, PRICE, HORNSBY & WEATHERFORD, L.L.P. (AV)

115 West Adams Street, Drawer 2228, 36302
Telephone: 334-793-2424
Fax: 334-793-6624
Email: ehornsby@ala.net; eglasgow@ala.net
Email: eprice@ala.net

MEMBERS OF FIRM

J. Hubert Farmer (1896-1976)
Edward M. Price, Jr.
Ernest H. Hornsby
Joel W. Weatherford
D. Lewis Terry, Jr.
Elizabeth B. Glasgow
J. Vincent Edge

Representative Clients: AmSouth Bank, N.A.; Pea River Electric Cooperative; Hollis & Spann, Inc.; Faulkner Construction Co., Inc.; Burnham Shoes, Inc.; Quality Inn Carousel; Sheraton Inn; Holiday Inn-Ozark; Holiday Inn-Crestview; Inn South-Montgomery.

For full biographical listings, see the Martindale-Hubbell Law Directory

*ELBA,** Coffee Co.

L. MERRILL SHIRLEY (AV)

431 North Court Street, P.O. Box 408, 36323
Telephone: 334-897-5775
Fax: 334-897-2304

Representative Clients: National Security Insurance Co.; Peoples Bank of Elba; ALFA Mutual Insurance Co.; Fireman's Fund Insurance Group; Southern Guaranty Insurance Co.; Elba General Hospital and Nursing Home.
References: Peoples Bank; National Security Insurance Co.

For full biographical listings, see the Martindale-Hubbell Law Directory

*EVERGREEN,** Conecuh Co.

WILLIAM D. MELTON (AV)

Melton Building, 100 Liberty Hill Drive, Drawer 800, 36401-0800
Telephone: 334-578-2423
Fax: 334-578-2427

References: Bank of Evergreen, Evergreen, Alabama; First National Bank of Brewton, Alabama.

For full biographical listings, see the Martindale-Hubbell Law Directory

FAIRHOPE, Baldwin Co.

MICHAEL S. MCGLOTHREN, P.C. (AV)

223 South Drive, 36532
Telephone: 334-990-3299
Fax: 334-990-3295
Mailing Address: P.O. Box 2263, Daphne, Alabama, 36526
Email: McG025@aol.com

Michael S. McGlothren

For full biographical listings, see the Martindale-Hubbell Law Directory

*FLORENCE,** Lauderdale Co.

JONES & TROUSDALE (AV)

115 Helton Court, Suite B, P.O. Box 367, 35631-0367
Telephone: 256-767-0333
Telefax: 256-767-0331
Email: JTAttys@aol.com

MEMBERS OF FIRM

Robert E. Jones, III
Preston S. Trousdale, Jr.
A. DeLoach Stewart

For full biographical listings, see the Martindale-Hubbell Law Directory

SELF & SELF (AV)

408 West Dr. Hicks Boulevard, P.O. Box 1062, 35631
Telephone: 256-767-2570; 1-800-336-2574
Fax: 256-767-2632

MEMBERS OF FIRM

Henry (Hank) H. Self, Jr.
Gilbert P. Self

(See Next Column)

SELF & SELF, *Florence—Continued*

ASSOCIATE

Missy Homan Hibbett

Reference: Bank Independent; AmSouth Bank; Compass Bank.

For full biographical listings, see the Martindale-Hubbell Law Directory

*FORT PAYNE,** De Kalb Co.

SCRUGGS, JORDAN, DODD & DODD (AV)

207 Alabama Avenue, South, P.O. Box 681109, 35967
Telephone: 256-845-5932
Fax: 256-845-4325
Email: scruggs@peop.tdsnet.com *URL:* http://www.lawyers.com/scruggsjordandodd&dodd

William D. Scruggs, Jr.
J. David Dodd
Robert K. Jordan
E. Allen Dodd, Jr.
Holly Hendrickson

Representative Clients: State Farm Insurance Company; Allstate Insurance Co., Inc.; USF&G Insurance Co.; Nucor, Inc.; Ladd Engineering, Inc.; ALABAMA Band; First Federal Bank; Fritz Structural Steel, Inc.; Williamson Oil Co., Inc.

For full biographical listings, see the Martindale-Hubbell Law Directory

*HUNTSVILLE,** Madison Co.

BRADLEY ARANT ROSE & WHITE LLP (AV)

200 Clinton Avenue West, Suite 900, 35801
Telephone: 205-517-5100
Facsimile: 205-517-5200
URL: http://www.barw.com
Birmingham, Alabama Office: 2001 Park Place, Suite 1400, P.O. Box 830709.
Telephone: 205-521-8000.
Facsimile: 205-521-8800. Facsimile (SouthTrust Tower Office): 205-521-8500.
Washington, D.C. Office: 801 Pennsylvania Avenue, NW, Suite 230, 20004.
Telephone: 202-347-8893.
Facsimile: 202-347-1684.

RESIDENT PARTNERS

Patrick H Graves Jr.
Gary C. Huckaby
Warne S. Heath
E. Cutter Hughes Jr.

For Complete List of Firm Personnel, See General Section

For full biographical listings, see the Martindale-Hubbell Law Directory

HORNSBY, WATSON & MEGINNISS (AV)

1110 Gleneagles Drive, 35801
Telephone: 256-650-5500
Fax: 256-650-5504
Email: rwhj@mindspring.com

Ralph W. Hornsby, Sr.
Ralph W. Hornsby, Jr.
S. A. "Bud" Watson, Jr.
Jeffrey G. Blackwell

OF COUNSEL

David H. Meginniss

For full biographical listings, see the Martindale-Hubbell Law Directory

MORRIS, CLOUD AND CONCHIN, P.C. (AV)

521 Madison Street, P.O. Box 248, 35804
Telephone: 256-534-0065
Fax: 256-539-0741

Harvey B. Morris (P.C.)
Joseph M. Cloud
Gary V. Conchin

Maureen "Mike" K. Cooper
Daniel B. Banks, Jr.

For full biographical listings, see the Martindale-Hubbell Law Directory

THE LAW FIRM OF SINIARD, MCKINNEY & BRASWELL, P.C. (AV)

125 Holmes Avenue, P.O. Box 2767, 35804
Telephone: 256-536-0770
Facsimile: 256-539-0540
URL: http://www.lawyers.com/smblawfirm
URL: http://www.law-injury.com/scripts/template.cgi?index

Tommy H. Siniard
Jeffery W. McKinney
M. Roy Braswell

Michael Kenan Timberlake
James William League

For full biographical listings, see the Martindale-Hubbell Law Directory

STEPHENS, MILLIRONS, HARRISON & GAMMONS, P.C. (AV)

333 Franklin Street, P.O. Box 307, 35801
Telephone: 256-533-7711
Telecopier: 256-536-9388

Paul L. Millirons
Robert C. Gammons

Douglas A. Baymiller
Steven J. Shaw

For Complete List of Firm Personnel, See General Section

For full biographical listings, see the Martindale-Hubbell Law Directory

WOLFE, JONES & BOSWELL (AV)

905 Bob Wallace Avenue Suite 100, 35801
Telephone: 205-534-2205
Fax: 205-534-0854
Email: wjb@traveller.com

MEMBERS OF FIRM

R. Wayne Wolfe
Keith S. Jones
Daniel C. Boswell

ASSOCIATES

Gary P. Wolfe
Joel R. Hamner
James Rayburn Kennamer

Representative Clients: First Union Home Equity Corp.; Norwest Financial Services; ALTUS Bank.
Approved Agents for: Stewart Title Guaranty Co.

For full biographical listings, see the Martindale-Hubbell Law Directory

*MOBILE,** Mobile Co.

ATCHISON, CROSBY, SAAD & BEEBE, P.C. (AV)

3030 Knollwood Drive, 36693
Telephone: 334-665-7200
Fax: 334-665-7250
URL: http://www.acsblaw.com

James E. Atchison
Elias J. Saad
James H. Crosby
Donald G. Beebe

Mona Ann Vivar
Jacqueline M. McConaha
Daryl A. Atchison

Representative Clients: City of Mobile; Alabama State Docks; Mobile Area Water and Sewer Board; Owens Corning, Inc.; Pilot Catastrophe Services, Inc.; Shell Oil Co.; Premdor,Inc.; Melvin Pierce Paint Co.; Commonwealth National Bank; Fiberglass Canada,Inc.

For full biographical listings, see the Martindale-Hubbell Law Directory

BRISKMAN & BINION, P.C. (AV)

205 Church Street, P.O. Box 43, 36601
Telephone: 334-433-7600
Fax: 334-433-4485
Email: briskman@zebra.net

Donald M. Briskman
Christ N. Coumanis
Mack B. Binion
Kimberly C. Hodgson

A List of Representative Clients will be furnished upon request.
References: Regions Bank; AmSouth Bank, N.A.; Southtrust Bank of Mobile.

For full biographical listings, see the Martindale-Hubbell Law Directory

BURNS, CUNNINGHAM & MACKEY, P.C. (AV)

50 St. Emanuel Street, P.O. Box 1583, 36633
Telephone: 334-432-0612
Fax: 334-432-0625
URL: http://www.bcmlawyers.com

Peter F. Burns
Peter S. Mackey
William M. Cunningham, Jr.
Gary W. Fillingim

For full biographical listings, see the Martindale-Hubbell Law Directory

CUNNINGHAM, BOUNDS, YANCE, CROWDER & BROWN, L.L.C. (AV)

1601 Dauphin Street, P.O. Box 66705, 36660
Telephone: 334-471-6191
Fax: 334-479-1031
Email: adm@cbycb.com

James A. Yance
Michael A. Worel
John T. Crowder, Jr.
David G. Wirtes, Jr.
Robert T. Cunningham, Jr.
Toby D. Brown
Joseph M. Brown, Jr.
Reggie Copeland, Jr.
Gregory B. Breedlove
Richard T. Dorman

J. Stephen Legg
George M. Dent, III

(See Next Column)

CUNNINGHAM, BOUNDS, YANCE, CROWDER & BROWN L.L.C.—*Continued*

OF COUNSEL

Richard Bounds
Robert T. Cunningham
J. Kenyon Rainer, Sr., M.D., J.D.

For full biographical listings, see the Martindale-Hubbell Law Directory

FINKBOHNER AND LAWLER, L.L.C. (AV)

169 Dauphin Street Suite 300, P.O. Box 3085, 36652
Telephone: 334-438-5871
Fax: 334-432-8052
Email: finkbohnerlawlerllc@zebra.net

MEMBERS OF FIRM

George W. Finkbohner, Jr.
John L. Lawler
George W. Finkbohner, III
Royce A. Ray, III

For full biographical listings, see the Martindale-Hubbell Law Directory

HELMSING, SIMS & LEACH, P.C. (AV)

The Laclede Building, 150 Government Street, Suite 2000, P.O. Box 2767, 36652
Telephone: 334-432-5521
Telecopy: 334-432-0633

Larry U. Sims
Frederick G. Helmsing
John N. Leach, Jr.
Warren C. Herlong, Jr.
James B. Newman
Robert H. Rouse
Charles H. Dodson, Jr.
Joseph P. H. Babington
R. Alan Alexander
John J. Crowley, Jr.
Joseph D. Steadman
Todd S. Strohmeyer

William R. Lancaster
Robin Kilpatrick Fincher
John Townsend Dukes
John Casey Pipes
James Bradford Pittman, Jr.

For full biographical listings, see the Martindale-Hubbell Law Directory

*MONTGOMERY,** Montgomery Co.

BEASLEY, ALLEN, CROW, METHVIN, PORTIS & MILES, P.C. (AV)

218 Commerce Street, P.O. Box 4160, 36104
Telephone: 334-269-2343
Fax: 334-269-2371
Mailing Address: P.O. Box 4160, 36103-4160
Email: lisa@bwamc.com

Jere Locke Beasley
J. Greg Allen
Michael J. Crow
Julia Anne Beasley
Robert L. Pittman

Edward Perry Kendall
Dana G. Taunton
Scarlette M. Tuley

For full biographical listings, see the Martindale-Hubbell Law Directory

RIGGS & NESMITH, P.A. (AV)

Lawrence Building, 472 South Lawrence Street, P.O. Box 1047, 36101
Telephone: 334-834-6990
Fax: 334-834-4796

Frank W. Riggs
Stephen M. NeSmith

LEGAL SUPPORT PERSONNEL

Patricia P. Williams (Office Manager)

For full biographical listings, see the Martindale-Hubbell Law Directory

THOMAS, MEANS, GILLIS, DEVLIN, ROBINSON & SEAY, P.C. (AV)

3121 Zelda Court, P.O. Drawer 5058, 36103-5058
Telephone: 334-270-1033
Fax: 334-260-9396
Email: tmgpc.lawfirm@tmgpc.com *URL:* http://www.tmgpc.com
Birmingham, Alabama Office: 1035 Financial Center, 505 20th Street North, 35203. Mailing Address: P.O. Box 370447, Birmingham, AL., 35237-0447.
Telephone: 205-328-7915.
Fax: 205-214-6160. E-mail: tmgpc.lawfirm@tmgpc.com. URL: http://www.tmgpc.com
Atlanta, Georgia Office: The Chandler Building, Suite 300, 127 Peachtree Street, N.E., 30303.
Telephone: 404-222-8400.
Fax: 404-222-0080. E-Mail: tmgpc.lawfirm@tmgpc.com. URL: http://www.tmgpc.com

Kenneth L. Thomas (Resident, Birmingham, Alabama Office)
Tyrone C. Means
H. Lewis Gillis
Marvin A. Devlin (Resident, Atlanta, Georgia Office)

(See Next Column)

Mark E. Robinson (Resident, Atlanta, Georgia Office)
Quinton S. Seay (Resident, Atlanta, Georgia Office)

James L. Richey (Resident, Birmingham, Alabama Office)
Wendell J. Chambliss (Resident, Birmingham Office)
Lisa F. Brown (Resident, Birmingham, Alabama Office)
Valerie L. Acoff (Resident, Birmingham, Alabama Office)
John W. Adams, Jr.
Paul C. Williams
Jennifer D. Odom (Resident, Atlanta, Georgia Office)
Darnell D. Coley
Edward J. Berry (Resident, Birmingham, Alabama Office)
Thaddeus L. Hamilton (Resident, Birmingham, Alabama Office)

LEGAL SUPPORT PERSONNEL

Joyce L. Lehmann
Tonya White
Bryan Palmer
Felicia Kolley
John Baker (Office Administrator)
Cathy Allen
Lakesha Baker
Larry Holmes
Linda Steele
Mary Duncan
Pamela Watkins
Paula Mosely
Rodney Barganier
Tamara Venice
Linda Stoudemier

For full biographical listings, see the Martindale-Hubbell Law Directory

*TUSCALOOSA,** Tuscaloosa Co.

PRINCE, POOLE & CROSS, P.C. (AV)

Suite A, Searcy Building, 2501 Sixth Street, 35401
Telephone: 205-345-1234
Fax: 205-752-6313

Robert F. Prince
Victor P. Poole, Jr.
Silas G. Cross, Jr.

Erby J. Fischer
Paul Patterson

For full biographical listings, see the Martindale-Hubbell Law Directory

*TUSCUMBIA,** Colbert Co.

ASHE, TANNER, WRIGHT & KELLEY, P.C. (AV)

105 West Second Street, P.O. Box 899, 35674
Telephone: 256-383-6357
Telecopier: 256-381-4612

Braxton W. Ashe
J. Michael Tanner
Grant A. Wright
Charles J. Kelley (Resident)

Nickolas J. Steles

For full biographical listings, see the Martindale-Hubbell Law Directory

ARIZONA

*FLAGSTAFF,** Coconino Co.

ASPEY, WATKINS & DIESEL, P.L.L.C. (AV)

123 North San Francisco, 3rd Floor, 86001
Telephone: 520-774-1478
Facsimile: 520-774-8404
Email: info@AWDLAW.com
Sedona, Arizona Office: 120 Soldier Pass Road.
Telephone: 520-282-5955.
Facsimile: 520-282-5962.
Cottonwood, Arizona Office: 2400 E. Highway 89A, Suite C.
Telephone: 520-639-1881.
Facsimile: 520-639-0272.

MEMBERS OF FIRM

Frederick M. Fritz Aspey
Harold L. Watkins
Louis M. Diesel
Bruce S. Griffen
Donald H. Bayles, Jr.
Kaign N. Christy
John J. Dempsey
Zachary J. Markham
James E. Ledbetter

Whitney Cunningham
Pernell Whynn McGuire
Stephen A. Thompson
Justin G. Vaughn
Janet Altschuler
Brett M. Hager
Mary E. Widdowson

Representative Clients: Farmer's Insurance Company of Arizona; Pepsi-Cola Bottling Company of Northern Arizona; Bill Luke's Chrysler-Plymouth, Inc.; First American Title Insurance Company; Transnation Title Insurance Co.; Page Electric Utility; Comprehensive Access Health Plan, Inc.; Northern Arizona Healthcare Corporation.
Reference: First Interstate Bank-Arizona, N.A., Flagstaff, Arizona.

For full biographical listings, see the Martindale-Hubbell Law Directory

Flagstaff—Continued

MANGUM, WALL, STOOPS & WARDEN, P.L.L.C. (AV)

100 North Elden, P.O. Box 10, 86002
Telephone: 520-779-6951
Fax: 520-773-1312

H. Karl Mangum (1908-1993)

OF COUNSEL

Douglas J. Wall
Robert W. Warden
Daniel J. Stoops

MEMBERS OF FIRM

A. Dean Pickett
Melinda L. Garrahan
Stephen K. Smith
Michael H. Hinson

ASSOCIATES

Annette Star Lustgarten
R. Scott Currey
Rebecca Smith Currey
Melinda K. Jacquez
Franklin Hoover

Representative Clients: Northern Arizona University; Flagstaff Unified School District; Museum of Northern Arizona; Arizona School Board Association.
Local Counsel for: Bank of America-Arizona; Arizona Public Service; U.S-.A.A.; State Farm Fire & Casualty Insurance Co.; Insurance Company of the West.

For Complete List of Firm Personnel, See General Section

For full biographical listings, see the Martindale-Hubbell Law Directory

*KINGMAN,** Mohave Co.

MURPHY, LUTEY, SCHMITT & BECK, P.L.L.C. (AV)

Suite H8, 2601 Stockton Hill Road, 86401
Telephone: 520-718-0888; 1-800-281-0822
Email: MLSB@GOODNET.COM
Prescott, Arizona Office: Elks Building, 117 East Gurley Street.
Telephone: 602-445-6860.
Fax: 602-445-6488.
Yuma, Arizona Office: Valley Professional Plaza, 1763 West Twenty-Fourth Street, Suite 200.
Telephone: 520-726-0314.
Fax: 520-341-1079.

Michael R. Murphy
Robert E. Schmitt

Northern Arizona Counsel for: State Farm Mutual Automobile Insurance Co.; Transamerica Title Insurance Co.; Allstate Insurance Co.
Local Counsel for: The Stockmen's Bank.
Representative Clients: Prescott College; North-Aire Aviation, Inc.; Goswick Cattle Co.; Galpin Ford, Inc.; Sedona-Oak Creek Airport Authority; Yavapai County Fair Association (Prescott Downs).

For full biographical listings, see the Martindale-Hubbell Law Directory

LAKE HAVASU CITY, Mohave Co.

WACHTEL, BIEHN & MALM (AV)

2240 McCulloch Boulevard, 86403
Telephone: 520-855-5115
Fax: 520-855-5211
Email: wbm1@ctaz.com

MEMBERS OF FIRM

Don Biehn
Denis R. Malm
Steven A. Biehn

For full biographical listings, see the Martindale-Hubbell Law Directory

MESA, Maricopa Co.

JACKSON WHITE GARDNER WEECH & WALKER, P.C. (AV)

40 North Center Street, Suite 200, 85201
Telephone: 480-464-1111
Fax: 480-464-5692
Statewide: 800-243-1160
Email: firm@azmesalaw.com *URL:* http://www.azmesalaw.com
Payson, Arizona Office: 708 East Highway 260, Suite C1-E.
Telephone: 520-472-8878.

Wayne L. Gardner
Bradley D. Weech
Eric M. Jackson
Richard A. White
Michael R. Pruitt
David L. Weed
J. Grant Walker
Roger R. Foote
Otto S. Shill, III

Eric K. Macdonald
Patricia A. Mancabelli
Kelly G. Black
Bobbie J. Rasmusson
Melody K. Seal
Maureen P. Kane
James L. Tanner

For full biographical listings, see the Martindale-Hubbell Law Directory

SKOUSEN, SKOUSEN, GULBRANDSEN & PATIENCE, P.C. (AV)

414 East Southern Avenue, 85204
Telephone: 602-833-8800
Fax: 602-833-7146

William J. Skousen
Michael J. Skousen
Richard E. Skousen
John E. Skousen
Richard M. Gulbrandsen
Gary A. Porter
Steve Patience
David L. Abney

References: Bank One, Mesa, Arizona; Bank of America, Mesa, Arizona.

For full biographical listings, see the Martindale-Hubbell Law Directory

UDALL, SHUMWAY, BLACKHURST, ALLEN & LYONS, P.C. (AV)

30 West First Street, 85201-1446
Telephone: 480-461-5300
Facsimile: 480-461-5398
Email: usbalsea@vtc.net
Willcox, Arizona Office: 135 East Maley.
Telephone: 602-384-3389.
Fax: 602-384-2280.

David K. Udall
Steven H. Everts
Dale R. Shumway
Clark R. Richter
Dennis P. Blackhurst
Roger C. Decker
John H. Lyons
Peter W. Taylor
Barry C. Dickerson
Denise Lowell-Britt
Stephen L. West

David R. Schwartz
Brian T. Allen
Robert M. Jarrett, Jr. (Resident, Willcox Office)
Curtis M. Chipman
April A. Speelmon

Representative Clients: Arizona Board of Regents; Mesa Public Schools; Grosvenor International; Church of Jesus Christ of Latter Day Saints; University of Arizona.

For full biographical listings, see the Martindale-Hubbell Law Directory

*PHOENIX,** Maricopa Co.

BEGAM, LEWIS, MARKS & WOLFE (AV)

A Professional Association of Lawyers
111 West Monroe Street, Suite 1400, 85003-1787
Telephone: 602-254-6071; 1-800-285-0481
Fax: 602-252-0042
Email: blmw@aol.com

Robert G. Begam
Daniel J. Adelman
Frank Lewis
Lisa Kurtz
Stanley J. Marks
Dena Rosen Epstein
Elliot G. Wolfe
Steven M. Friedman
Kelly J. McDonald
Richard P. Traulsen
Serena C. Montague

Reference: National Bank of Arizona.

For full biographical listings, see the Martindale-Hubbell Law Directory

BESS KUNZ, A PROFESSIONAL CORPORATION (AV)

7210 North 16th Street, 85020-5201
Telephone: 602-331-4600
Telecopier: 602-331-8600

Leon D. Bess
Timothy R. Hyland
Donald R. Kunz
William M. Demlong
Matthew D. Kleifield

Thomas P. Liddy
Elliot H. Wernick
Connie Totorica Gould
Beth H. Schneider

Representative Clients: American States Insurance Co.; Massachusetts Casualty Insurance Co.; Mercury Insurance Group; Michigan Mutual Insurance Co.; Mississippi Farm Bureau; National Casualty Co.; Risk Management Claims Service; Underwriters at Lloyds; United Services Automobile Association; Western Agricultural Insurance Co.

For full biographical listings, see the Martindale-Hubbell Law Directory

BONNETT, FAIRBOURN, FRIEDMAN & BALINT, P.C. (AV)

4041 North Central Avenue Suite 1100, 85012
Telephone: 602-274-1100
Fax: 602-274-1199

William G. Fairbourn
C. Kevin Dykstra
Robert J. Spurlock
Guy A. Hanson
Robert D. Ryan

For full biographical listings, see the Martindale-Hubbell Law Directory

Phoenix—Continued

LAW OFFICES OF MICHAEL E. BRADFORD (AV)

4131 North 24th Street Building C Suite 201, 85016
Telephone: 602-955-0088
Fax: 602-955-6445
Email: meblaw@primenet.com

ASSOCIATE
Jeffrey L. Bradford
OF COUNSEL
Jerry Steele

For full biographical listings, see the Martindale-Hubbell Law Directory

CHARLES M. BREWER, LTD. (AV)

Brewer Building, 5500 North 24th Street, P.O. Box 10720, 85064
Telephone: 602-381-8787
Fax: 602-381-1152

Charles M. Brewer

Luis Pedro Guerra
John Brian Brewer

For full biographical listings, see the Martindale-Hubbell Law Directory

JAMES F. BROOK AND ASSOCIATES (AV)

11024 North 28th Drive, Suite 200, 85029
Telephone: 602-375-0414
Toll Free: 800-322-6170
Fax: 480-874-0506
Email: JFBrook@aol.com *URL:* http://www.lawyers.com/jamesbrook
Mesa, Arizona Office: 1201 South Alma School Road, Suite 14,000. 85210.
Telephone: 480-838-5591.
Fax: 480-874-0506.
Scottsdale, Arizona Office: 7150 East Camelback Road, Suite 415, 85251.
Telephone: 480-990-0104.
Fax: 480-874-0506.
Sun City, Arizona Office: 10451 Palmeras Drive, Suite 211, 85373.
Telephone: 623-972-6824.
Fax: 480-874-0506.

Adam C. E. Davis

For full biographical listings, see the Martindale-Hubbell Law Directory

BURCH & CRACCHIOLO, P.A. (AV)

702 East Osborn Road, Suite 200, 85014
Telephone: 602-274-7611
Fax: 602-234-0341
Mailing Address: P.O. Box 16882, Phoenix, AZ, 85011
Email: library@bcattorneys.com

Daniel Cracchiolo
Brian Kaven
Ian Neale
Linda A. Finnegan
Daniel R. Malinski

Theodore (Todd) Julian
Steven J. Lippman

Representative Clients: Bashas' Inc.; Farmers Insurance Group; U-Haul International, Inc.

For Complete List of Firm Personnel, See General Section

For full biographical listings, see the Martindale-Hubbell Law Directory

CARMICHAEL & POWELL, PROFESSIONAL CORPORATION (AV)

7301 North 16th Street, Suite 103, 85020-5224
Telephone: 602-861-0777
Facsimile: 602-870-0296

Sid A. Horwitz
Richard C. Gramlich

For full biographical listings, see the Martindale-Hubbell Law Directory

COPPLE, CHAMBERLIN, BOEHM & MURPHY, P.C. (AV)

Suite 300 The Brookstone, 2025 North Third Street, 85004
Telephone: 602-528-4700
Fax: 602-253-4909
Tucson, Arizona Office: 127 West Franklin.
Telephone: 520-622-8855.
Fax: 520-628-7988.

Steven D. Copple
Thomas J. Chamberlin
Scott E. Boehm
Robert S. Murphy

OF COUNSEL
Frederick O. Robertshaw

For full biographical listings, see the Martindale-Hubbell Law Directory

CRONIN & STANEWICH (AV)

One Columbus Plaza, 3636 North Central Avenue, Suite 560, 85012
Telephone: 602-222-4646
Fax: 602-222-4656
Email: cslaw@msn.com

MEMBERS OF FIRM

Robert S. Cronin, Jr.
Robert B. Stanewich

For full biographical listings, see the Martindale-Hubbell Law Directory

CUNNINGHAM LAW FIRM (AV)

330 North Second Avenue, 85003
Telephone: 602-257-1750
Fax: 602-252-3436
Email: cunnlaw@Goodnet.com *URL:* http://www.lawyers.com/cunninghamlawfirm

James P. Cunningham
Matthew B. Cunningham

For full biographical listings, see the Martindale-Hubbell Law Directory

DEBUS KAZAN & WESTERHAUSEN, LTD. (AV)

335 East Palm Lane, 85004
Telephone: 602-257-8900
Fax: 602-257-0723
Email: debusandkazan@uswest.com

Larry L. Debus
Lawrence Ian Kazan
Tracey Westerhausen

References: Firstar Metropolitan Bank; Citibank, Arizona.

For full biographical listings, see the Martindale-Hubbell Law Directory

WILLIAM J. DOWNEY, P.C. (AV)

3636 North Central Avenue, Suite 1150, 85012
Telephone: 602-222-4350
Facsimile: 602-222-4353
Email: downey@primenet.com *URL:* http://www.lawyers.com/williamjdowney

William J. Downey

Dane London Wood
Patrick B. Sigl
Elan Shai Mizrahi

For full biographical listings, see the Martindale-Hubbell Law Directory

DOYLE & WINTHROP, P.C. (AV)

2800 North Central Avenue Suite 1550, P.O. Box 10417, 85004
Telephone: 602-240-6711
Fax: 602-240-6951
Mailing Address: P.O. Box 10417, Phoenix, Arizona, 85064-0417
Las Vegas, Nevada Office: Edward D. Boyack, Esq., 2626 S. Rainbow Blvd., Suite 101, 89146.
Telephone: 702-873-1622.
Fax: 702-873-2280.

William H. Doyle
Angila L. Gallenstein

For full biographical listings, see the Martindale-Hubbell Law Directory

FEDER LAW OFFICE, P.A. (AV)

Biltmore Pavilion, Suite 140, 2525 E. Arizona Biltmore Circle, 85016
Telephone: 602-257-0135
Fax: 602-954-8737
Mailing Address: P.O. Box 44560, Phoenix, Arizona, 85064-4560

Bruce Feder
Harold J. Feder

For full biographical listings, see the Martindale-Hubbell Law Directory

FENNEMORE CRAIG, A PROFESSIONAL CORPORATION (AV)

3003 North Central Avenue, Suite 2600, 85012-2913
Telephone: 602-916-5000
Fax: 602-916-5999
Tucson, Arizona Office: One South Church Avenue, Suite 1000, 85701-1620.
Telephone: 520-879-6800.
Fax: 520-879-6899.

John D. Everroad
Roger T. Hargrove
William L. Thorpe
Phillip F. Fargotstein
Graeme Hancock
Scott M. Finical
Christopher L. Callahan
Christopher P. Staring
Jean Marie Sullivan
Douglas C. Northup
Marc H. Lamber

Mark H. Brain
James D. Burgess

(See Next Column)

FENNEMORE CRAIG A PROFESSIONAL CORPORATION, *Phoenix—Continued*

LEGAL SUPPORT PERSONNEL

LEGAL ASSISTANTS

Nancy E. Esser

For Complete List of Firm Personnel, See General Section

For full biographical listings, see the Martindale-Hubbell Law Directory

FOGEL, LAMBER & BRONNENKANT, PROFESSIONAL ASSOCIATION (AV)

4001 North Third Street, Suite 400, 85012
Telephone: 602-264-3330
Fax: 602-274-5117

Sherman D. Fogel
Dennis M. Lamber
Rex P. Bronnenkant

Reference: Rocky Mountain Bank.

For full biographical listings, see the Martindale-Hubbell Law Directory

GOLDSTEIN, MCGRODER & WOODS, LTD. A PROFESSIONAL CORPORATION (AV)

2200 East Camelback Road, Suite 221, 85016-3456
Telephone: 602-957-1500
Fax: 602-956-9294
Email: pmcgroder@aol.com

Philip T. Goldstein
Patrick J. McGroder, III
Grant Woods
Suzanne P. Clarke

Jane E. Evans

LEGAL SUPPORT PERSONNEL

Kevan S. DeWitt (Paralegal)
Karen Kay Rush

For full biographical listings, see the Martindale-Hubbell Law Directory

STUART GOLDSTEIN (AV)

2700 North Third Street, Suite 2010, 85004
Telephone: 602-279-1666
Fax: 602-285-1907
Email: stugoldstn@aol.com

Stuart W. Goldstein

Reference: Wells Fargo Bank, Park Central Office, Phoenix.

For full biographical listings, see the Martindale-Hubbell Law Directory

JOHN PHILIP GRACE, P.C. (AV)

4500 North 32nd Street, Suite 201, 85018
Telephone: 602-954-0464
Fax: 602-954-6316

John Philip Grace

For full biographical listings, see the Martindale-Hubbell Law Directory

HARRIS, PALUMBO, POWERS & CUNNINGHAM, P.L.L.C. (AV)

361 East Coronado, Suite 101, P.O. Box 13568, 85002-3568
Telephone: 602-271-9344
Fax: 602-252-2099
Email: harrispalumbo@worldnet.att.net

John David Harris
Frank I. Powers
Shawn M. Cunningham

OF COUNSEL

Anthony J. Palumbo

For full biographical listings, see the Martindale-Hubbell Law Directory

HERZOG AND O'CONNOR, P.C. (AV)

5353 North 16th Street, Suite 175, 85016
Telephone: 602-277-5710
Fax: 602-277-6124

Michael W. Herzog
Mark S. O'Connor

Kirk A. Barberich

For full biographical listings, see the Martindale-Hubbell Law Directory

HORNE, BISTROW & DULBERG, P.C. (AV)

Renaissance Two, 40 North Central, Suite 2800, 85004
Telephone: 602-253-9700
Fax: 602-258-4805
Email: kcorson@azlitigation.com *URL:* http://www.azlitigation.com

Thomas C. Horne
Eric J. Bistrow
Michael S. Dulberg

(See Next Column)

Joel E. Sannes

For full biographical listings, see the Martindale-Hubbell Law Directory

JENNINGS, HAUG & CUNNINGHAM, L.L.P. (AV)

2800 North Central Avenue Suite Eighteen Hundred, 85004-1049
Telephone: 602-234-7800
Fax: 602-277-5595
Email: main@jhc-law.com

MEMBERS OF FIRM

Jack R. Cunningham
Larry J. Crown
Laurence R. Sharlot
Jorge Franco, Jr.

For full biographical listings, see the Martindale-Hubbell Law Directory

JENNINGS, STROUSS & SALMON, P.L.C. (AV)

A Professional Limited Liability Company
One Renaissance Square, Two North Central Avenue, 85004-2393
Telephone: 602-262-5911
Fax: 602-253-3255
Email: info@jsslaw.com *URL:* http://www.jsslaw.com
Arrowhead Office: 16150 North Arrowhead Fountains Center Drive, Suite 250, Peoria, Arizona.
Telephone: 623-878-2222.
Fax: 623-878-1333.

W. Michael Flood
David Brnilovich
Jay A. Fradkin
H. Christian Bode
Michael J. O'Connor
Jennifer M. Bligh
Kim D. Steinmetz
Cody M. Hall

OF COUNSEL

Gary L. Stuart

ASSOCIATES

Cynthia A. Coates
Andrew B. Turk
Bryan S. VanMeveren
John P. Robertson, II
Johnny J. Sorenson
C. David Martinez
Kevin R. Robling

For Complete List of Firm Personnel, See General Section

For full biographical listings, see the Martindale-Hubbell Law Directory

WILLIAM T. KEANE, P.C. (AV)

803 North 3rd Street, 85004
Telephone: 602-257-1323
Fax: 602-257-1416
Email: tyming@goodnet.com

William T. Keane

Reference: Wells Fargo Bank.

For full biographical listings, see the Martindale-Hubbell Law Directory

KIMERER & LAVELLE, P.L.C. (AV)

100 W. Clarendon Suite 2100, 85013
Telephone: 602-279-5900; 800-220-6817
Fax: 602-264-5566
Email: KimLav.com

Michael D. Kimerer
Michael J. LaVelle
Clark L. Derrick
Lori L. Voepel

Teri Dyan McCall
Matthew K. LaVelle (Not admitted in AZ)

Representative Clients: The National Basketball Association; Aetna Insurance Co.; Kaibab Industries; Centric Jones Constructors; B & B Masonry; Western Block.

For full biographical listings, see the Martindale-Hubbell Law Directory

MARK & PEARLSTEIN, P.A. (AV)

Suite 150 The Brookstone, 2025 North Third Street, 85004
Telephone: 602-257-0200
Fax: 602-271-4711
Email: mplaw@primenet.com

Leonard J. Mark
Mr. Lynn M. Pearlstein

OF COUNSEL

Stephen G. Campbell

For full biographical listings, see the Martindale-Hubbell Law Directory

TERRENCE J. MCGILLICUDDY, P.C. (AV)

5090 North 40th Street, Suite 148, 85018
Telephone: 602-957-1960
800-957-1960
Fax: 602-957-7015
Email: TJMCGILLIC@AAL.COM *URL:* http://www.lawyers.com/mcgillicuddy

(See Next Column)

TERRENCE J. MCGILLICUDDY, P.C.—*Continued*

Terrence J. McGillicuddy

For full biographical listings, see the Martindale-Hubbell Law Directory

MUCHMORE & WALLWORK, A PROFESSIONAL CORPORATION (AV)

2700 North Central Avenue, Suite 1225, 85004-1165
Telephone: 602-240-6699
Data: 602-240-6698
Facsimile: 602-240-6697
Email: muchwork@mmww.com *URL:* http://www.mmww.com

Charles J. Muchmore
Nicholas J. Wallwork
Fredric D. Bellamy

SENIOR COUNSEL

Steve Owens

COUNSEL

Bridget S. Bade

Christopher D. Payne
Carolina L. Carver
Margaret Benny Hurst
Mindy K. Brinker

OF COUNSEL

Leslie Kyman Cooper
George H. King

LEGAL SUPPORT PERSONNEL

Gloria A. Torres (Administrator)
James R. Potts (Systems Administrator and Litigation Support Manager)
Gale James (Finance Manager)

Representative Clients: AgrEvo USA Company; BHP Copper, Inc.; Chevron U.S.A., Inc.; Cyprus Amax Minerals Company; Homes by Dave Brown, Inc.; National Indemnity Insurance Company; Standard Insurance Company; Washington Mills Electro Minerals Corporation; Cadbury Beverages, Inc.; Eisenberg Company.

For full biographical listings, see the Martindale-Hubbell Law Directory

LAW OFFICES OF RAYMOND M. NORRIS (AV)

302 East Coronado Road, 85004-1524
Telephone: 602-254-9200
Fax: 602-254-7337
Email: Norrisfive@aol.com

Carolyn M. Kaluzniacki

LEGAL SUPPORT PERSONNEL

Maureen Fairbanks (Legal Assistant)

For full biographical listings, see the Martindale-Hubbell Law Directory

QUARLES & BRADY LLP (AV)

One Camelback Building, One East Camelback Road, Suite 400, 85012-1649
Telephone: 602-230-5500
Fax: 602-230-5598
URL: http://www.quarles.com
Milwaukee, Wisconsin Office: 411 East Wisconsin Avenue.
Telephone: 414-277-5000.
Fax: 414-271-3552.
Madison, Wisconsin Office: First Wisconsin Plaza, One South Pinckney Street, P.O. Box 2113.
Telephone: 608-251-5000.
Fax: 608-251-9166.
West Palm Beach, Florida Office: 222 Lakeview Avenue, 4th Floor.
Telephone: 407-653-5000.
Fax: 407-653-5333.
Naples, Florida Office: Barnett Center, 4501 Tamiami Trail North, Suite 300.
Telephone: 813-262-5959.
Fax: 813-434-4999.
Chicago, Illinois Office: Quarles & Brady LLC, Citicorp Center, 500 West Madison Street, Suite 3700.
Telephone: 312-715-5000.
Fax: 312-715-5155.

MEMBER OF THE FIRM

Colleen A. Scherkenbach

ASSOCIATE

C. Christine Burns

For full biographical listings, see the Martindale-Hubbell Law Directory

RAYMOND, GREER & SASSAMAN, P.C. (AV)

3636 North Central Avenue, Suite 1070, 85012-1940
Telephone: 602-274-0500
Fax: 602-265-7560
Email: rgslaw@syspac.com

(See Next Column)

Randy L. Sassaman
Leonard D. Greer
Michael J. Raymond

OF COUNSEL

Mark J. Moryl

For full biographical listings, see the Martindale-Hubbell Law Directory

STUART J. REILLY, P.C. (AV)

4647 North 32nd Street, Suite 105, 85018-3346
Telephone: 602-912-9200
Fax: 602-912-9209
Mailing Address: P.O. Box 80410, Phoenix, AZ, 85060-0410
Email: sreilly@stuartjreillypc.com *URL:* http://www.lawyers.com/stuartjreillypc

Stuart J. Reilly

For full biographical listings, see the Martindale-Hubbell Law Directory

ROBBINS & GREEN, A PROFESSIONAL ASSOCIATION (AV)

1800 Norwest Tower, 3300 North Central Avenue, 85012-2578
Telephone: 602-248-7600
Fax: 602-266-5369
Email: @RGLaw.com

Philip A. Robbins
Richard W. Abbuhl
William H. Sandweg III
Dwayne Ross

For full biographical listings, see the Martindale-Hubbell Law Directory

SHERWOOD, KLEIN, DUDLEY & ABRAM, P.A. (AV)

201 North Central Avenue Suite 2400, 85073
Telephone: 602-254-7041
Fax: 602-254-7540
Email: lawyers@sherwoodklein.com

Andrew G. Klein

For full biographical listings, see the Martindale-Hubbell Law Directory

LAW OFFICES OF RAYMOND J. SLOMSKI, P.C. (AV)

2929 North Central Avenue, Suite 1750, 85012
Telephone: 602-230-8777
Fax: 602-230-8707
Email: slomiski@earthlink.net

Raymond J. Slomski
James M. Abernethy

LEGAL SUPPORT PERSONNEL

PARALEGALS

Patti A. Hibbeler
Diana G. Weeks

For full biographical listings, see the Martindale-Hubbell Law Directory

TREON, STRICK, LUCIA & AGUIRRE A PROFESSIONAL ASSOCIATION OF LAWYERS (AV)

2700 North Central Avenue, Suite 1400, 85004-1133
Telephone: 602-285-4400
Telecopier: 602-285-4483
Email: office@TSLA.com

Richard T. Treon
Gerald J. Strick
Anthony R. Lucia
John Aguirre
Arthur G. Newman, Jr.
Michael P. Stark
Linda B. Williamson
Teri Kessel Raven
Cindy Hansel Strickland
Sharon G. Slifko

Robert C. Warnicke
Brett L Slavicek

For full biographical listings, see the Martindale-Hubbell Law Directory

TUCKER STROHM MILLER & TUCKER, P.C. (AV)

1136 East Campbell, 85014
Telephone: 602-279-3660
Fax: 602-279-2162
Email: rlslaw@worldnet.att.net

Kenneth L. Tucker
Richard L. Strohm
Daniel P. J. Miller
Kevin J. Tucker

Nedra J. Bates

For full biographical listings, see the Martindale-Hubbell Law Directory

WARNER ANGLE ROPER & HALLAM PLC (AV)

3550 North Central Avenue, Suite 1500, 85012
Telephone: 602-264-7101
Fax: 602-234-0419

Charles Richard Hallam
Stephen E. Jackson
Clark W. Watkin, Jr.
Jerome K. Elwell

(See Next Column)

WARNER ANGLE ROPER & HALLAM PLC, *Phoenix—Continued*

Chris R. Baniszewski

For full biographical listings, see the Martindale-Hubbell Law Directory

*PRESCOTT,** Yavapai Co.

MURPHY, LUTEY, SCHMITT & BECK, P.L.L.C. (AV)

Elks Building, 117 East Gurley Street, 86301
Telephone: 520-445-6860
Fax: 520-445-6488
Email: MLSB@GOODNET.COM
Yuma, Arizona Office: Valley Professional Plaza, 1763 West Twenty-Fourth Street, Suite 200.
Telephone: 520-726-0314.
Fax: 520-341-1079.
Kingman, Arizona Office: 2601 Stockton Hill Road, Suite H8.
Telephone: 520-718-0888; 1-800-281-0822.

MEMBERS OF FIRM

Thelton D. Beck — Robert E. Schmitt
Michael R. Murphy — Dan A. Wilson
Selmer D. Lutey — Alex B. Vakula

Scott K. Risley

Northern Arizona Counsel for: State Farm Mutual Automobile Insurance Co.; Allstate Insurance Co.
Southern Arizona Counsel for: Allstate Insurance Co.; Farmers Insurance; Western Agricultural Insurance Co.
Local Counsel for: Bank One Arizona, NA; The Stockmen's Bank.
Representative Clients: Galpin Ford, Inc.; Sedona-Oak Creek Airport Authority; Yavapai County Fair Association (Prescott Downs).

For full biographical listings, see the Martindale-Hubbell Law Directory

SCOTTSDALE, Maricopa Co.

BENNETT, CARMICHAEL & KENNEDY, L.L.P. (AV)

6991 East Camelback Road, Suite B-111, 85251
Telephone: 602-990-1133; 602-947-8303
Fax: 602-945-2149

MEMBERS OF FIRM

William F. Bennett — David H. Carmichael
Robert T. Kennedy

For full biographical listings, see the Martindale-Hubbell Law Directory

CAMPANA, VIEH, SHORE, OWENS & LOEB (AV)

4422 North Civic Center Plaza, Suite 101, 85251
Telephone: 480-707-5000
Fax: 480-707-5005

Richard V. Campana — William F. Shore, III
James E. Vieh — Bernard C. Owens
Donald O. Loeb

LEGAL SUPPORT PERSONNEL

Lois V. Johnson (Legal Assistant)

For full biographical listings, see the Martindale-Hubbell Law Directory

BRENT E. CORWIN, P.C. (AV)

5665 North Scottsdale Road Suite F-110, 85250-5959
Telephone: 480-949-0520
Fax: 480-949-2650
Email: brent.corwin@scottsdalelaw.com *URL:* http://www.scottsdalelaw.com

Brent E. Corwin

For full biographical listings, see the Martindale-Hubbell Law Directory

HERMAN, GOLDSTEIN & FORSYTH, P.C. (AV)

(Formerly Grossman, Goldstein & Forsyth, P.C.)
5040 East Shea Boulevard Suite 168, 85254
Telephone: 602-948-9424
Fax: 602-948-9425

Jill A. Herman — Evan S. Goldstein
Keith B. Forsyth

Pari K. Scroggin — Sanford K. Gerber

For full biographical listings, see the Martindale-Hubbell Law Directory

TEMPE, Maricopa Co.

LAW OFFICES OF GLYNN W. GILCREASE, JR. (AV)

1400 East Southern, Suite 425, 85282
Telephone: 602-897-0990
Fax: 602-831-5966
Email: gwgil@goodnet.com

For full biographical listings, see the Martindale-Hubbell Law Directory

*TUCSON,** Pima Co.

CHANDLER, TULLAR, UDALL & REDHAIR, L.L.P. (AV)

1700 Bank of America Plaza, 33 North Stone Avenue, 85701-1415
Telephone: 520-623-4353
Telefax: 520-792-3426

MEMBERS OF FIRM

Edwin M. Gaines, Jr. — Charles V. Harrington

Representative Clients: Arizona Electric Power Cooperative, Inc.; Atlantic Richfield Co.; CNA Insurance; Farmers Insurance Exchange; MICA; Chubb Insurance Group; State Farm Mutual Insurance Companies.
Reference: Arizona Bank.

For Complete List of Firm Personnel, See General Section

For full biographical listings, see the Martindale-Hubbell Law Directory

GABROY, ROLLMAN & BOSSÉ, P.C. (AV)

3507 North Campbell Avenue, Suite 111, 85719
Telephone: 520-320-1300
Telefax: 520-320-0717
Email: admin@gabroylaw.com

John Gabroy

For Complete List of Firm Personnel, See General Section

For full biographical listings, see the Martindale-Hubbell Law Directory

GOERING, ROBERTS, BERKMAN, RUBIN & BROGNA, P.C. (AV)

Suite 302, 1840 East River Road, 85718
Telephone: 520-577-9300
Fax: 520-577-0848
Email: grbrb@aol.com

Scott Goering — William L. Rubin
Howard T. Roberts, Jr. — Carmine A. Brogna
David L. Berkman — Christopher L. Enos

Representative Clients: Fireman's Fund Insurance; Safeco Insurance; Royal Insurance; Sentry Insurance; American International Group; Farmers Insurance; USAA; Country Companies; Cigna.
Reference: Bank One.

For full biographical listings, see the Martindale-Hubbell Law Directory

HARALSON, MILLER, PITT & MCANALLY, P.L.C. (AV)

One South Church Avenue Suite 900, 85701
Telephone: 520-792-3836
Telecopier: 520-624-5080
Email: mpmpc@azstarnet.com

Barry N. Akin (1939-1988) — Grace McIlvain
Dale Haralson, P.C. — Thomas G. Cotter
Janice A. Wezelman — Armando Rivera
Philip J. Hall — Gus Aragón, Jr.
Carole A. Summers

OF COUNSEL

Richard L. McAnally

Representative Clients available upon request.

For Complete List of Firm Personnel, See General Section

For full biographical listings, see the Martindale-Hubbell Law Directory

HEALY & STUDWELL LAW FIRM, P.C. (AV)

5210 East Williams Circle Suite 720, 85711
Telephone: 520-790-1400
Fax: 520-790-3212

William T. Healy — James R. Studwell

Sean P. Healy

References: Bank of America; Merrill Lynch.

For full biographical listings, see the Martindale-Hubbell Law Directory

Tucson—Continued

KINERK, BEAL, SCHMIDT & DYER, P.C. (AV)

Suite 6000, West Tower, 5255 East Williams Circle, 85711
Telephone: 520-790-5600
Fax: 520-790-1163
Email: kbs@azstarnet.com *URL:* http://www.azinjurylaw.com

Burton J. Kinerk
Ted A. Schmidt
Robert L. Beal
James H. Dyer
Colleen L. Kinerk

Karl R. Lautz
David W. Babcock

For full biographical listings, see the Martindale-Hubbell Law Directory

RONALD D. MERCALDO, LTD. (AV)

376 South Stone Avenue, 85701
Telephone: 520-624-1400
FAX: 520-624-1955
Email: ron@mercaldolaw.psemail.com

Ronald D. Mercaldo

Anthony J. Wiggins

For full biographical listings, see the Martindale-Hubbell Law Directory

CARTER MOREY, P.C. (AV)

Formerly Haralson, Kinerk & Morey (1978)
82 South Stone Avenue "The Citizen Building", 85701
Telephone: 520-792-4330
Fax: 520-623-9568

Carter Morey

Gregory G. Wasley
Linda S. Sherrill

For full biographical listings, see the Martindale-Hubbell Law Directory

RABINOVITZ & ASSOCIATES, P.C. (AV)

721 North 4th Avenue, P.O. Box 41600, 85717
Telephone: 520-624-5526
Toll Free: 1-800-365-0821
Fax: 520-622-3776

Bernard I. Rabinovitz

John D. Ellis

LEGAL SUPPORT PERSONNEL

Michael Nielson (Paralegal)
Lisa Busciglio (Paralegal)
Ruth Polizzi (Paralegal)

Representative Client: Firemans Fund Insurance Co.

For full biographical listings, see the Martindale-Hubbell Law Directory

DEE-DEE SAMET, P.C. (AV)

717 North Sixth Avenue, 85705
Telephone: 520-624-8595
Fax: 520-623-4560
Email: Dee-Dee.Same@azbar.org

Dee-Dee Samet

References: Bank of America; Norwest Bank.

For full biographical listings, see the Martindale-Hubbell Law Directory

SHULTZ & ROLLINS, LTD. (AV)

St. Philip's Plaza, 4280 North Campbell Avenue, Suite 214, 85718-6580
Telephone: 520-577-7777

Silas H. Shultz
Michael F. Rollins

James E. Marner

For full biographical listings, see the Martindale-Hubbell Law Directory

STOMPOLY, STROUD, GLICKSMAN & ERICKSON, P.C. (AV)

1820 Norwest Tower, One South Church Avenue, 85702
Telephone: 520-628-8300
Telefax: 520-628-9948
Mailing Address: P.O. Box 190, Tucson, AZ, 85702-0190

John G. Stompoly
Elliot A. Glicksman
George Erickson

For Complete List of Firm Personnel, See General Section

For full biographical listings, see the Martindale-Hubbell Law Directory

STRICKLAND & STRICKLAND, P.C. (AV)

4400 E. Broadway, Suite 700, 85711-3517
Telephone: 520-795-8727
Fax: 520-795-5649

William E. Strickland
William E. Strickland, Jr.
Robert F. Palmquist

Representative Client: AkChin Indian Community.
Reference: Bank One (formerly Valley National Bank).

*YUMA,** Yuma Co.

BOWMAN & SMITH, P.C. (AV)

290 South First Avenue, Suite 1, 85364
Telephone: 520-783-8879
Fax: 520-329-1816
Email: bowman@digitakdune.net *URL:* http://www.pifirm.com/bowman

Wm. Michael Smith
C. Alan Bowman

Jon R. Smith
Carol A. Bowman

Representative Clients: County of Yuma; Cocopah Indian Tribe.
Reference: County Bank.

For full biographical listings, see the Martindale-Hubbell Law Directory

CLARK AND ASSOCIATES (AV)

256 South Second Avenue, 85364
Telephone: 520-783-6233
Fax: 520-783-0533
Email: jasclark@yahoo.com *URL:* http://www.lawyers.com/j__clark&assoc

MEMBER OF FIRM

A. James Clark

ASSOCIATE

Heather D. Moore

For full biographical listings, see the Martindale-Hubbell Law Directory

MURPHY, LUTEY, SCHMITT & BECK, P.L.L.C. (AV)

Valley Professional Plaza, 1763 West Twenty-Fourth Street Suite 200, 85364
Telephone: 520-726-0314
Fax: 520-341-1079
Email: MLSB@GOODNET.COM
Prescott, Arizona Office: Elks Building, 117 East Gurley Street.
Telephone: 602-445-6860.
Fax: 602-445-6488.
Kingman, Arizona Office: 2601 Stockton Hill Road, Suite H8.
Telephone: 520-718-0888; 1-800-281-0822.

Robert E. Schmitt

Northern Arizona Counsel for: State Farm Mutual Automobile Insurance Co.; Allstate Insurance Co.
Southern Arizona Counsel for: Allstate Insurance Co.; Farmers Insurance; Western Agricultural Insurance Co.
Local Counsel for: Bank One Arizona, NA; The Stockmen's Bank.
Representative Clients: Galpin Ford, Inc.; Sedona-Oak Creek Airport Authority; Yavapai County Fair Association (Prescott Downs).

For full biographical listings, see the Martindale-Hubbell Law Directory

THE BRIAN E. SMITH LAW FIRM (AV)

The Brian Smith Building, 301 South 2nd Avenue, 85364
Telephone: 520-783-8811
Fax: 520-782-2018

Brian E. Smith
William J. Kerekes
Frank A. Fila

LEGAL SUPPORT PERSONNEL

Briget M. Marquez

Reference: Bank of America.

For full biographical listings, see the Martindale-Hubbell Law Directory

ARKANSAS

*FAYETTEVILLE,** Washington Co.

ODOM & ELLIOTT (AV)

No. 1 East Mountain Street, P.O. Drawer 1868, 72702
Telephone: 501-442-7575
FAX: 501-442-9008
Email: rzrbk63@aol.com *URL:* http://www.odomelliott.com

(See Next Column)

ODOM & ELLIOTT, *Fayetteville—Continued*

MEMBERS OF FIRM

Bobby Lee Odom
Don R. Elliott, Jr.
Russell B. Winburn
J. Timothy Smith
Conrad T. Odom
Jennifer Wheeler Haskins

Reference: Bank of Fayetteville, Fayetteville, Arkansas.

For full biographical listings, see the Martindale-Hubbell Law Directory

*JONESBORO,** Craighead Co.

MCDANIEL & WELLS, P.A. (AV)

400 South Main Street, 72401
Telephone: 870-932-5950; 1-800-954-5950
Fax: 870-932-0919
Email: pjwells1@arkansas.net *URL:* http://www.lawyers.com/mcdanielwellslaw

Bobby R. McDaniel
Phillip J. Wells

William J. Stanley

For full biographical listings, see the Martindale-Hubbell Law Directory

*LITTLE ROCK,** Pulaski Co.

THE BAKER LAW FIRM (AV)

8 Shackleford Plaza, Suite 207, P.O. Box 21220, 72221
Telephone: 501-224-3904
Fax: 501-224-3768
Email: dbaker@cei.net

Darryl E. (Chip) Baker

For full biographical listings, see the Martindale-Hubbell Law Directory

BARBER, MCCASKILL, JONES & HALE, P.A. (AV)

2700 Regions Center, 400 West Capitol Avenue, 72201-3414
Telephone: 501-372-6175
Telecopier: 501-375-2802

Azro L. Barber (1885-1979)
Elbert A. Henry (1889-1966)
John B. Thurman (1912-1971)
Austin McCaskill, Sr.
Glenn W. Jones
Michael E. Hale
John S. Cherry, Jr.
Robert L. Henry, III
Micheal L. Alexander
William H. Edwards, Jr.
G. Spence Fricke
Gail Ponder Gaines
Michael J. Emerson
R. Kenny McCulloch
Tim A. Cheatham
Joseph F. Kolb
Scott Michael Strauss
Baucum Fulk
D. Keith Fortner
Wendy Scholtens Wood
Morris L. Williams, III
Michelle Bass Miller

Attorneys for: Associated Aviation Underwriters; CNA Insurance Companies; Fireman's Fund Insurance Co.; General Motors Corp.; Hanover Insurance Co.; John Deere Insurance Co.; Royal Insurance; State Farm Automobile Insurance Company; Tokio Marine & Fire Insurance, Corp; Universal Underwriters Insurance Co.

For full biographical listings, see the Martindale-Hubbell Law Directory

DODDS, KIDD, RYAN & MOORE (AV)

313 West Second Street, 72201
Telephone: 501-375-9901
FAX: 501-376-0387
Email: dkrm@aol.com

MEMBERS OF FIRM

J. B. Dodds (1909-1964)
J. L. Kidd, Jr.
Donald S. Ryan
Judson C. Kidd
Richard N. Moore, Jr.
Charles Gregory Alagood

ASSOCIATE

Robert T. James

Reference: Pulaki Bank in Little Rock.

For full biographical listings, see the Martindale-Hubbell Law Directory

DUNCAN & RAINWATER TRIAL LAWYERS A PROFESSIONAL ASSOCIATION (AV)

6315 Ranch Drive, 72221-5938
Telephone: 501-228-7600
Fax: 501-228-7664
URL: http://www.lawyers.com/duncanandrainwater
Email: duncanlaw@aristotle.net *URL:* http://www.duncan-rainwater.com

Phillip J. Duncan (P.A.)
Michael R. Rainwater
Neil Ray Chamberlin
Michelle Banks Odum

J. Stephen Holt

For full biographical listings, see the Martindale-Hubbell Law Directory

FRIDAY, ELDREDGE & CLARK (AV)

A Limited Liability Partnership of Individuals and Professional Associations
Formerly, Smith, Williams, Friday, Eldredge & Clark
2000 Regions Center, 400 West Capitol Avenue, 72201-3493
Telephone: 501-376-2011
Telecopier: 501-376-2147
Email: fecmh@fec.net

MEMBERS OF FIRM

William H. Sutton (P.A.)
Frederick S. Ursery (P.A.)
John Dewey Watson (P.A.)
J. Phillip Malcom (P.A.)
James M. Simpson, Jr. (P.A.)
Donald H. Bacon (P.A.)
Barry E. Coplin (P.A.)
Elizabeth Robben Murray (P.A.)
Laura Hensley Smith (P.A.)
William Mell Griffin III (P.A.)
Kevin A. Crass (P.A.)
William A. Waddell, Jr. (P.A.)
Scott J. Lancaster (P.A.)
James C. Baker (P.A.)
Scott H. Tucker (P.A.)
Guy Alton Wade (P.A.)
Tonia P. Jones (P.A.)
David D. Wilson (P.A.)
Gregory D. Taylor (P.A.)
Fran C. Hickman (P.A.)

Betty J. Demory (P.A.)

ASSOCIATES

Clifford W. Plunkett
Jason B. Hendren
Susan N. Childers
Christopher A. Averitt

Joseph P. McKay

Counsel for: Union Pacific System; St. Paul Insurance Co.; Liberty Mutual Insurance Co.; Cigna Property & Casualty Co.; Entergy Arkansas, Inc.; Dillard's, Inc.; Browning Arms Co.; Brunswick Corp.; Phillips Petroleum Co.; Aetna Casualty & Surety Co.

For Complete List of Firm Personnel, See General Section

For full biographical listings, see the Martindale-Hubbell Law Directory

HUCKABAY, MUNSON, ROWLETT & TILLEY, P.A. (AV)

Regions Center, Suite 1900, 400 West Capitol, 72201
Telephone: 501-374-6535
Fax: 501-374-5906

Mike Huckabay
Bruce E. Munson
Beverly A. Rowlett
James W. Tilley
John E. Moore
Tim Boone
Rick Runnells
Sarah Ann Presson
D. Michael Huckabay, Jr.
Carol Lockard Worley

Mark S. Breeding

Elizabeth Fletcher Rogers
Julia L. Busfield
Jane M. Yocum
Terry D. Dugger

Representative Clients: Allstate Insurance Company; American International Group; American National Property and Casualty; Farmers Insurance Group; General Electric Company; Nationwide Insurance Company; State Farm Mutual Automobile Insurance Company; State Farm Fire and Casualty Company; Tenet Healthcare Corp.; Travelers Insurance Co.

For full biographical listings, see the Martindale-Hubbell Law Directory

PERRONI AND JAMES (AV)

Stewart Building, 801 West Third Street, 72201
Telephone: 501-372-6555
Fax: 501-372-6333
Email: sperroni@aol.com *URL:* http://www.lawyers.com/perroniandjames

Samuel A. Perroni
Patrick R. James (P.A.)

JaNan Arnold Davis (P.A.)
Susan L. Keller (P.A.)

LEGAL SUPPORT PERSONNEL

Sherry Joyce, CLA

References: Regions Bank, Little Rock, Ark.; Bank of Little Rock, Ark.

For full biographical listings, see the Martindale-Hubbell Law Directory

ROSE LAW FIRM, A PROFESSIONAL ASSOCIATION (AV)

120 East Fourth Street, 72201
Telephone: 501-375-9131
Telecopy: 501-375-1309

David L. Williams
Richard T. Donovan
Amy Lee Stewart
David P. Martin

Michael N. Shannon

COUNSEL

Phillip Carroll

Jennifer B. Hendren
John D. Coulter

Representative Clients: Kemper Insurance Group; Bridgestone/Firestone, Inc.; Aluminum Company of America; Baxter Healthcare Corporation; CIGNA Companies; J.A. Riggs Tractor Co.; General American Transportation Co.

(See Next Column)

ROSE LAW FIRM A PROFESSIONAL ASSOCIATION—*Continued*

For Complete List of Firm Personnel, See General Section

For full biographical listings, see the Martindale-Hubbell Law Directory

WHETSTONE LAW FIRM (AV)

First Commercial Building, 400 West Capitol, Suite 2990, 72201
Telephone: 501-376-3564
Fax: 501-376-6938

Bud B. Whetstone H. Mayo Smith

For full biographical listings, see the Martindale-Hubbell Law Directory

WEST MEMPHIS, Crittenden Co.

HALE, FOGLEMAN & ROGERS (AV)

108 Dover Road, P.O. Box 1666, 72301
Telephone: 870-735-1900
Fax: 870-735-1662

MEMBERS OF FIRM

Julian B. Fogleman Joe M. Rogers

ASSOCIATES

Timothy A. Ginn Gerald Dickinson, Jr.

General Counsel for: Drainage Districts # 2, 3 and 8 of Crittenden County; Edmondson Hotel Service, Inc.; Heath & House Construction Co.; Crittenden County, Arkansas.
Local Counsel for: Southern Farm Bureau Casualty Insurance Co.; Shelby Mutual Insurance Co.; Greyhound Lines, Inc.; American Justice Insurance Reciprocal; Graward General Companies.

For full biographical listings, see the Martindale-Hubbell Law Directory

CALIFORNIA

*BAKERSFIELD,** Kern Co.

KLEIN, DENATALE, GOLDNER, COOPER, ROSENLIEB & KIMBALL, LLP (AV)

(Formerly Di Giorgio, Davis, Klein, Wegis, Duggan & Friedman)
ARCO Tower, 4550 California Avenue, Second Floor, 93309
Telephone: 661-395-1000
Telecopier: 661-326-0418
Mailing Address: P.O. Box 11172, Bakersfield, California, 93389-1172
Email: kleinlaw@kleinlaw.com

Anthony J. Klein (Inc.)
William A. Bruce
Ned E. Dunphy
Krystyna L. Jamieson

Catherine E. Bennett

Representative Clients: Bank of America; Great Western Bank; Mojave Pipeline Co.; Transamerican Title Insurance Co.; Dean Whittier Reynolds, Inc.; California Republic Bank; San Joaquin Bank; Nahama & Weagant Energy Co.; Freymiller Trucking, Inc.; Westinghouse Electric Co.

For Complete List of Firm Personnel, See General Section

For full biographical listings, see the Martindale-Hubbell Law Directory

LAW OFFICES OF YOUNG WOOLDRIDGE (AV)

1800 30th Street, Fourth Floor, 93301
Telephone: 661-327-9661
Facsimile: 661-327-1087
Email: youngwooldridge@lightspeed.net *URL:* http://www.young.wooldridge.com

MEMBERS OF FIRM

A. Cameron Paulden (1927-1984)
Robert J. Self
G. Neil Farr
Michael R. Young
Ernest A. Conant
Steve W. Nichols
Larry R. Cox
Scott K. Kuney
Michael A. Kaia
Scott D. Howry

ASSOCIATE

Todd A. Gall

OF COUNSEL

Edward M. Carpenter John B. Young (Retired)

Representative Clients: Arvin-Edison Water Storage District; Motor City Truck Sales and Service.
References: Wells Fargo Bank; First Interstate Bank; California Republic Bank.

For Complete List of Firm Personnel, See General Section

For full biographical listings, see the Martindale-Hubbell Law Directory

COSTA MESA, Orange Co.

LAW OFFICES OF W. DOUGLAS EASTON (AV)

3200 Park Center Drive, Suite 1000, 92626
Telephone: 714-850-4590
Fax: 714-427-0189
Email: lowdelaw@email.msn.com *URL:* http://www.lawyers.com/eastonlaw

Anderson L. Washburn
Russel W. Jones
Brian W. Easton

For full biographical listings, see the Martindale-Hubbell Law Directory

ENCINO, Los Angeles Co.

STEPHEN H. HELLER A PROFESSIONAL CORPORATION (AV)

16830 Ventura Boulevard, Suite B, 91436-1714
Telephone: 818-995-4646
Fax: 818-995-0668
Email: stephenheller@hellerlaw.net

Stephen H. Heller

For full biographical listings, see the Martindale-Hubbell Law Directory

*FAIRFIELD,** Solano Co.

BARNETT • MATTICE (AV)

An Association of Sole Practitioners
712 Empire Street, 94533
Telephone: 707-425-0671
Fax: 707-425-4255
Email: bobbarnett@solano.net
Email: mikemattice@solano.net *URL:* http://www.lawyers.com/barnettmattice

Robert E. Barnett Michael C. Mattice

For full biographical listings, see the Martindale-Hubbell Law Directory

*FRESNO,** Fresno Co.

LANG, RICHERT & PATCH, A PROFESSIONAL CORPORATION (AV)

Fig Garden Financial Center, 5200 North Palm Avenue, 4th Floor, P.O. Box 40012, 93755
Telephone: 559-228-6700
Fax: 559-228-6727

William T. Richert (1937-1993)
Robert L. Patch, II
Val W. Saldaña
Douglas E. Noll
Michael T. Hertz
Victoria J. Salisch
Rene Lastreto, II
Charles Trudrung Taylor
Mark L. Creede
Peter N. Zeitler
Laurie L. Quigley
Tamara L. Equals
Douglas E. Griffin
Nabil E. Zumout

Christopher B. Dorian
Matthew W. Quall
Tracy E. Sagle
Julie K. Hill
Michelle Oleksa

OF COUNSEL

Frank H. Lang

References: Wells Fargo Bank (Fresno Main Office).

For full biographical listings, see the Martindale-Hubbell Law Directory

MILES, SEARS & EANNI, A PROFESSIONAL CORPORATION (AV)

2844 Fresno Street, P.O. Box 1432, 93716
Telephone: 559-486-5200
Fax: 559-486-5240
Email: mse@good.attitude.com

Wm. M. Miles (1909-1991)
Robert E. Sears (1918-1992)
Carmen A. Eanni
Richard C. Watters
William J. Seiler
Douglas L. Gordon

For full biographical listings, see the Martindale-Hubbell Law Directory

GARDENA, Los Angeles Co.

McGARRY & LAUFENBERG (AV)

1125 West 190th Street, Suite 230, 90248
Telephone: 310-380-1650
Fax: 310-380-1662
Email: jjmjjllaw@aol.com

MEMBERS OF FIRM

James J. McGarry
Jeffrey J. Laufenberg
William Leamon Cummings
John E. Zegel

For full biographical listings, see the Martindale-Hubbell Law Directory

GLENDALE, Los Angeles Co.

FLANAGAN, BOOTH, UNGER & MOSES (AV)
1156 North Brand Boulevard, 91202-2582
Telephone: 818-244-8694
Fax: 818-244-1852
Santa Ana, California Office: 1851 East First Street, Suite 805, 92705.
Telephone: 714-835-2607.
Fax: 714-835-4825.

MEMBERS OF FIRM
J. Michael Flanagan   Charles J. Unger

ASSOCIATES
Michael T. Danis   James A. Grover

For full biographical listings, see the Martindale-Hubbell Law Directory

O'ROURKE, ALLAN & FONG, LLP (AV)
100 West Broadway, Suite 1250, P.O. Box 10220, 91210
Telephone: 818-247-4303
Fax: 818-247-1451
Email: OAFLAW@aol.com

MEMBERS OF FIRM
Denis M. O'Rourke   Joan H. Allan
Roderick D. Fong

ASSOCIATES
Denise Michelle O'Rourke   Marina Manoukian
Toshiko Kobayashi

References: Verdugo Banking Co. (Glendale, California); Community Bank (Glendale, California).

For full biographical listings, see the Martindale-Hubbell Law Directory

IRVINE, Orange Co.

EISENBERG & FINK LLP (AV)
100 Pacifica, Suite 200, 92618
Telephone: 949-753-1500
Fax: 949-753-1516
Email: ef@ef-law.com *URL:* http://www.lawyers.com/ef-law

Lawrence S. Eisenberg   Steven A. Fink

Michael G. Mattern   Judith F. Zuckert

For full biographical listings, see the Martindale-Hubbell Law Directory

CHRISTOPHER B. MEARS, A P.C. (AV)
8001 Irvine Center Drive, Suite 1140, 92618
Telephone: 949-585-0295
Fax: 949-753-8120

Christopher B. Mears

For full biographical listings, see the Martindale-Hubbell Law Directory

STEVENS & KRAMER, A PROFESSIONAL CORPORATION (AV)
18022 Cowan, Suite 200D, 92614-6808
Telephone: 949-253-9553
Fax: 949-253-9643
Agoura Hills, California Office: 30401 W. Agoura Road, Suite 102.
Telephone: 818-879-1699.
Fax: 818-879-1673.

Carl R. Stevens

Lee E. Burrows   Javier H. Van Oordt

For full biographical listings, see the Martindale-Hubbell Law Directory

LAGUNA HILLS, Orange Co.

STANTON T. MATHEWS & ASSOCIATES, A LAW CORP. (AV)
24012 Calle de la Plata, Suite 320, 92653
Telephone: 949-586-2235
Email: Triallaw@flash.net
Email: stm@injurytriallaw.com *URL:* http://www.injurytriallaw.com

Stanton T. Mathews

Paul W. Ralph   Ronald B. Funk

LEGAL SUPPORT PERSONNEL
PARALEGAL/ADMINISTRATOR
Sharing Garrett-Anderson
LEGAL ASSISTANT
Cheri C. Wickam

For full biographical listings, see the Martindale-Hubbell Law Directory

LAGUNA NIGUEL, Orange Co.

KUHN & BELZ (AV)
28202 Cabot Road, Suite 215, 92677
Telephone: 949-364-0600
Fax: 949-364-0606
Email: kuhnbelz@ix.netcom.com *URL:* http://www.lawyers.com/kuhnbelz

MEMBERS OF FIRM
Steven R. Kuhn   David L. Belz

ASSOCIATE
Deborah L. Leifer

For full biographical listings, see the Martindale-Hubbell Law Directory

LARKSPUR, Marin Co.

WEINBERG, HOFFMAN, CASEY & ROPERS (AV)
A Partnership including a Professional Corporation
900 Larkspur Landing Circle, Suite 155, 94939
Telephone: 415-461-9666
Fax: 415-461-9681

Ivan Weinberg   A. Michael Casey
Joseph Hoffman   Mark Ropers

For full biographical listings, see the Martindale-Hubbell Law Directory

LONG BEACH, Los Angeles Co.

EDWARD P. GEORGE, JR., INC. A PROFESSIONAL CORPORATION (AV)
Suite 430, 5000 East Spring Street, 90815-1275
Telephone: 562-497-2900
Facsimile: 562-497-2904

Edward P. George, Jr.   Timothy L. O'Reilly

OF COUNSEL
Albert C. S. Ramsey

Reference: City National Bank, Long Beach.

For full biographical listings, see the Martindale-Hubbell Law Directory

REX W. JACOBS (AV)
200 Oceangate Boulevard, Suite 400, 90801-4332
Telephone: 562-491-3432
Fax: 562-491-3418
Mailing Address: 200 Oceangate, Suite 410, Long Beach, California, 90802-4332
URL: http://www.lawyers.com/rjacobs

For full biographical listings, see the Martindale-Hubbell Law Directory

PERONA, LANGER, BECK & LALLANDE, A PROFESSIONAL CORPORATION (AV)
300 East San Antonio, 90807
Telephone: 562-426-6155
Facsimile: 562-490-9823
Los Angeles, California Office: 9255 Sunset Boulevard, Suite 920.
Telephone: 562-426-6155.

James T. Perona   M. Lawrence Lallande
Major A. Langer   Ellen R. Serbin
Ronald Beck   E. Todd Trumper
Robert M. Zavidow

Michel F. Mills   Lupe G. Morales
Eric A. Hoercher   David L. Scott
Cathy A. Muller   Arnold Eisenberg

For full biographical listings, see the Martindale-Hubbell Law Directory

RUSSELL & MIRKOVICH (AV)
One World Trade Center, Suite 1450, 90831-1450
Telephone: 562-436-9911
FAX: 562-436-1897
Email: counsel@russell-mirkovich.com

Carlton E. Russell   Joseph N. Mirkovich

ASSOCIATE
Margaret E. Morrow   Steven Y. Otera

For full biographical listings, see the Martindale-Hubbell Law Directory

Long Beach—Continued

Stolpman • Krissman • Elber • Mandel & Katzman LLP (AV)

A Limited Liability Partnership
Nineteenth Floor, 111 West Ocean Boulevard, 90802-4649
Telephone: 562-435-8300
Telecopier: 562-435-8304
Email: stolpman@ix.netcom.com
Los Angeles (Westwood), California Office: Suite 1800, 10880 Wilshire Boulevard.

MEMBERS OF FIRM

Thomas G. Stolpman
Leonard H. Mandel
Bernard Katzman (Inc.)
Joel Krissman
Mary Nielsen Abbott
Donna Silver
Dennis M. Elber

ASSOCIATES

Edwin Silver
Elaine Mandel
Michael L. Luboviski

For full biographical listings, see the Martindale-Hubbell Law Directory

*LOS ANGELES,** Los Angeles Co.

Baum, Hedlund, Aristei, Guilford & Downey, A Professional Corporation (AV)

Suite 950, 12100 Wilshire Boulevard, 90025
Telephone: 310-207-3233; 800-827-0087
Facsimile: 310-820-7444
Email: bhagd@bhagd.com *URL:* http://www.bhagd.com
Washington, D.C. Office: 1250 24th Street, N.W., Suite 300.
Telephone: 202-466-0513; 800-827-0097.
Facsimile: 202-466-0527.

Michael L. Baum
Paul J. Hedlund
J. Clark Aristei
Robert E. Guilford
William J. Downey III (1947-1999)

John A. Greaves
Cara J. Luther (Resident, Washington, D.C. Office)
Robert F. Foss
Karen A. Barth

OF COUNSEL

Goerge W. Murgatroyd III
Mary F. Schiavo (Not admitted in CA)

Reference: Union Bank.

For full biographical listings, see the Martindale-Hubbell Law Directory

Biren & Katzman (AV)

815 Moraga Drive (Bel Air), 90049-1633
Telephone: 310-476-3031; 381-5609
Fax: 310-471-3165
Email: birenkatzman@biren.com *URL:* http://www.biren.com

Matthew B. F. Biren
Marc J. Katzman

Debra J. Tauger
Charles E. Koro

Reference: City National Bank (Beverly Hills Branch).

For full biographical listings, see the Martindale-Hubbell Law Directory

Law Offices of David B. Bloom A Professional Corporation (AV)

3325 Wilshire Boulevard, Ninth Floor, 90010
Telephone: 323-938-5248; 384-4088
Telecopier: 213-385-2009

David B. Bloom

Stephen S. Monroe (A Professional Corporation)
Raphael A. Rosemblat
James E. Adler
Roy A. Levun
Jonathan Udell
Susan Carole Jay
Edward Idell
Sandra Kamenir
Steven Wayne Lazarus
Andrew Edward Briseno
Shelley M. Gould
Ted L. Travis

For full biographical listings, see the Martindale-Hubbell Law Directory

Girardi and Keese (AV)

1126 Wilshire Boulevard, 90017-1904
Telephone: 213-977-0211
FAX: 213-481-1554
San Bernardino, California Office: 155 West Hospitality Lane, Suite 260.
Telephone: 909-381-1551.
FAX: 909-381-2566.

(See Next Column)

MEMBERS OF FIRM

Thomas V. Girardi
Robert M. Keese
John A. Girardi
James B. Kropff
Robert W. Finnerty
James G. O'Callahan
V. Andre Rekte (Resident, San Bernardino Office)
John K. Courtney
Amy Fisch Solomon
Thomas C. Morgan
David N. Bigelow
Carrie J. Rognlien
David R. Lira
John Alan Roberts
Shane M. Emerson Coons
Amanda L. McClintock

ASSOCIATE

Jennifer M. Ingram

References: Wells Fargo Bank (Los Angeles Head Office); Comerica Bank.

For full biographical listings, see the Martindale-Hubbell Law Directory

Gordon, Edelstein, Krepack, Grant, Felton & Goldstein (AV)

Suite 1800, 3580 Wilshire Boulevard, 90010
Telephone: 213-739-7000; 213-487-1520
Fax: 213-386-1671
Email: geklaw.com

Roger L. Gordon
Mark Edelstein
Howard D. Krepack
Sherry E. Grant
Richard I. Felton
Irwin L. Goldstein
Steven J. Kleifield
David A. Goldstein

OF COUNSEL

Joshua M. Merliss

ASSOCIATES

Eugenia L. Steele
Vincent F. Bennett
Adam D. Dombchik
Jennifer S. Weisman

For full biographical listings, see the Martindale-Hubbell Law Directory

Howard Craig Kornberg (AV)

10880 Wilshire Boulevard, Suite 1840, 90024
Telephone: 310-474-5588
Fax: 323-879-6812
http: //www.losangeles.sidewalk.msn.com/craig-kornberg
Email: hck1@ix.netcom.com *URL:* http://www.lawyers.com/hcklaw
Reference: City National Bank (Westwood Branch).

For full biographical listings, see the Martindale-Hubbell Law Directory

Kussman & Whitehill (AV)

A Partnership including a Professional Corporation
Suite 1470, 10866 Wilshire Boulevard, 90024
Telephone: 310-474-4411
Fax: 310-474-6530

Russell S. Kussman (A Professional Corporation)
Michael H. Whitehill

For full biographical listings, see the Martindale-Hubbell Law Directory

José Y. Lauchengco, Jr. (AV)

3545 Wilshire Boulevard, Suite 247, 90010
Telephone: 213-380-9897

For full biographical listings, see the Martindale-Hubbell Law Directory

Lebovits & David, A Professional Corporation (AV)

1880 Century Park East Suite 900, 90067
Telephone: 310-277-0200
Fax: 310-552-1028
Email: mlld@msn.com *URL:* http://www.lawyers.com/lebovits&david

Moses Lebovits
Deborah A. David

Kristal M. Bowman

Reference: Imperial Bank (Main Office - Beverly Hills).

For full biographical listings, see the Martindale-Hubbell Law Directory

Robert L. Luty A Professional Corporation (AV)

11999 San Vicente Boulevard, Suite 340, 90049
Telephone: 310-472-7166
Fax: 310-472-6229
Email: robert@robertlluty.com *URL:* http://www.lawyers.com/lutylaw

Robert L. Luty

Reference: Brentwood Savings Bank (Brentwood Branch).

For full biographical listings, see the Martindale-Hubbell Law Directory

Los Angeles—Continued

MAGAÑA, CATHCART & MCCARTHY (AV)

A Partnership including Professional Corporations
Suite 810 Gateway West Building, 1801 Avenue of the Stars (Century City), 90067-5899
Telephone: 310-553-6630; 213-879-2531
Fax: 310-785-9143
Email: mcmc_law@earthlink.net *URL:* http://www.mcmc-law.com

Brian R. Magaña (Professional Corporation)
Peter T. Cathcart (Professional Corporation)
William H. Wimsatt (Professional Corporation)

Richard L. Bisetti
Daniel A. Cribbs
Clay Robbins, III

OF COUNSEL

Daniel C. Cathcart (Professional Corporation)
Charles M. Finkel

RETIRED

Raoul D. Magaña
James J. McCarthy

Reference: First Los Angeles Bank (1950 Avenue of the Stars, Los Angeles (Century City), California).

For full biographical listings, see the Martindale-Hubbell Law Directory

LAW OFFICES OF CARL A. MCMAHAN (AV)

827 Moraga Drive (Bel Air), 90049
Telephone: 310-472-8078
Fax: 310-472-7014
Email: camcmahan@earthlink.net *URL:* http://www.lawyers.com/mcmahan

OF COUNSEL

Peter J. McNulty

Reference: City National Bank, Beverly Hills, California.

For full biographical listings, see the Martindale-Hubbell Law Directory

MCNICHOLAS & MCNICHOLAS, LLP (AV)

10866 Wilshire Boulevard, Suite 1400, 90024
Telephone: 310-474-1582
FAX: 310-475-7871
URL: http://www.mcnicholaslaw.com

MEMBERS OF FIRM

John P. McNicholas
Patrick McNicholas
David M. Ring

ASSOCIATES

Eric A. Gowey
Matthew S. McNicholas
Steven G. Mehta

For full biographical listings, see the Martindale-Hubbell Law Directory

PRESTHOLT, KLEEGER, FIDONE & VILLASENOR (AV)

Suite 1600, 1055 West 7th Street, 90017
Telephone: 213-895-4811
FAX: 213-895-4817
San Francisco, California Office: 989 Market Street, 6th Floor.
Telephone: 415-267-6362.
Fax: 415-267-6275.

MEMBERS OF FIRM

David A. Prestholt
Gary P. Fidone
Lisa A. Villasenor
Brian D. Holmberg
David Crawford, III
Archie Chin
Avigal Horrow
Marjorie E. Motooka

For full biographical listings, see the Martindale-Hubbell Law Directory

SELMAN • BREITMAN (AV)

11766 Wilshire Boulevard, Sixth Floor, 90025-6538
Telephone: 310-445-0800
Fax: 310-473-2525
San Diego, California Office: Wyndham Emerald Plaza, 402 W. Broadway, Suite 400, 92101.
Telephone: 619-595-4880.
Facsimile: 619-595-4890.
San Francisco, California Office: Citicorp Center, One Sansome Street, Suite 1900, 94104.
Telephone: 415-951-4646.
Fax: 415-951-4676.
Santa Ana, California Office: 450 4th Street, Suite 250, 92701.
Telephone: 714-647-9700.
Fax: 714-647-9200.

MEMBERS OF FIRM

Sterling Tao (1961-1998)
Neil Selman
Craig R. Breitman
Robert A. Steller
Alan B. Yuter
Nancy W. Shokohi
Jeffrey C. Segal
A. Scott Goldberg

(See Next Column)

MEMBERS OF FIRM (Continued)

Elaine K. Fresch
Nicholas Banko (Partner, San Francisco Office)
Brad D. Bleichner
Monica Cruz Thornton
John S. Knowlton
Jerry C. Popovich (Partner, Santa Ana Office)

OF COUNSEL

Jan Long Pocaterra
Jacqueline F. Stein (Resident, San Diego Office)
Paul Edmond Stephan (Resident, San Francisco Office)

Lynette Klawon
Anthony L. Cione
Sheryl W. Leichenger
Lisa H. Kahn
David H. Oken
Pauline A. New
Eldon S. Edson
Sarah F. Burke (Resident, San Francisco Office)
Linda Wendell Hsu (Resident, San Francisco Office)
Jack M. Zakariaie
Jean Dettmann Fisher (Resident, San Diego Office)
Lincoln V. Horton
Nichelle D. Frelix
Albert T. Liou (Resident, Santa Ana Office)
Viiu Spangler
Meka Moore
Richard T. Breen
Christopher R. Aker (Resident, San Francisco Office)
Mindi C. Grant
Ben M. Llaneta (Resident, San Diego Office)
Richard Scott
Craig R. Maki
Jennifer J. Capabianco (Resident, San Francisco Office)
Michelle L. Koskella (Resident, San Francisco Office)
Kelly M. Lynch
Kimberly S. Poese (Resident, Santa Ana Office)
Veronica E. Aitken
Roger G. Honey
Shereef Moharram
Kiera Berkley
Gregory J. Newman
Tamara Madenlian
Michelle E. Davis
Josh I. Keane
Michael Robert Hoffman
Natalie A. Barbanell
Kirk J. Retz
Paul A. Herp (Resident, San Francisco Office)
Greg M. Whaling (Resident, San Francisco Office)

Reference: City National Bank (Beverly Hills Branch).

For full biographical listings, see the Martindale-Hubbell Law Directory

STONE, DOLGINER & WENZEL, A LAW CORPORATION (AV)

6500 Wilshire Boulevard Suite 2060, 90048
Telephone: 323-653-2244
Fax: 323-658-1155
Email: sdwlaw@aol.com *URL:* http://www.lawyers.com/sdwfirm

Robert N. Stone
Charles I. Dolginer
Mark D. Wenzel

Henry N. Seligsohn

OF COUNSEL

A. J. Connick Doran

Reference: Union Bank (Head Office, 900 South Main Street, Los Angeles).

For full biographical listings, see the Martindale-Hubbell Law Directory

MENLO PARK, San Mateo Co.

DYER & WHITE LLP (AV)

Suite 200, 800 Oak Grove Avenue, 94025
Telephone: 650-325-7000
Fax: 650-325-3116
Email: cdyer@dyer-white.com

MEMBERS OF FIRM

Charles A. Dyer
Rand N. White

For full biographical listings, see the Martindale-Hubbell Law Directory

O'REILLY, COLLINS & DANKO, A PROFESSIONAL CORPORATION (AV)

2500 Sand Hill Road, Suite 201, 94025-7016
Telephone: 650-854-7700
Fax: 650-854-8350

Terry O'Reilly
James P. Collins
Michael S. Danko

Rian D. Jorgensen

For full biographical listings, see the Martindale-Hubbell Law Directory

MONTEREY, Monterey Co.

THE THOMPSON LAW OFFICE (AV)

580 Calle Principal, First Floor, 93940-2818
Telephone: 831-646-1224
Fax: 831-646-1225
URL: http://www.lawyers.com/justice-4-you
Email: rwt111@justice-4-you.com *URL:* http://www.justice-4-you.com

(See Next Column)

THE THOMPSON LAW OFFICE—*Continued*

Ralph W. Thompson III

For full biographical listings, see the Martindale-Hubbell Law Directory

NEWPORT BEACH, Orange Co.

ALLEN & FLATT INCORPORATED (AV)

Suite 370, 4400 MacArthur Boulevard, 92660
Telephone: 949-752-7474; 714-241-7474; 888-752-7474 (toll free)
Fax: 949-752-1645
Email: contactus@allen-flatt.com
Email: contactus@allaccidents.com

Robert F. Allen, Jr. | John C. Flatt

James E. Ballidis | Suzanne Boyer Leslie

Reference: Bank of America, Newport Beach.

For full biographical listings, see the Martindale-Hubbell Law Directory

LOPEZ, HODES, RESTAINO, MILMAN & SKIKOS, A LAW CORPORATION (AV)

450 Newport Center Drive, 2nd Floor, 92660
Telephone: 949-640-8222
Fax: 949-640-8294
San Francisco, California Office: 625 Market Street, Fifteenth Floor, 94105.
Telephone: 415-956-5257.
Fax: 415-956-4416.

Ramon Rossi Lopez
Daniel M. Hodes
John M. Restaino, Jr.
Jeffrey A. Milman
Peter John Polos
Steven J. Skikos (Resident)

Christina A. Lopez Fountain
Steven B. Eggleston (Resident, San Francisco Office)
Gregory T. Skikos (Resident, San Francisco Office)
Thomas A. Schultz
Mark G. Crawford
Hilary Poulsen Gilles

OF COUNSEL

David L. Suggs (Not admitted in CA)
Jane E. Joseph (Not admitted in CA)

For full biographical listings, see the Martindale-Hubbell Law Directory

ROBINSON, CALCAGNIE & ROBINSON, A PROFESSIONAL CORPORATION (AV)

Incorporated 1986
620 Newport Center Drive 7th Floor, 92660
Telephone: 949-720-1288
Fax: 949-720-1292
Email: rpc@robinson-pilaw.com
San Diego, California Office: 110 Laurel Street.
Telephone: 619-338-4060.
Fax: 619-338-0423.

Mark P. Robinson, Jr.
Kevin F. Calcagnie
Jeoffrey L. Robinson
Allan F. Davis
Joseph L. Dunn

Carlos A. Prietto, III
Stephanie M. Smith

LEGAL SUPPORT PERSONNEL

Lin Moen
Donna Hosea
Darleen Perkins
Francine Teer
Linda Baker
Erin Walker

For full biographical listings, see the Martindale-Hubbell Law Directory

WENTWORTH, PAOLI & PURDY, LLP (AV)

4631 Teller Avenue, Suite 100, 92660
Telephone: 949-752-7711
Fax: 949-752-8339
Email: oclawfirm@aol.com *URL:* http://www.lawyers.com/wentworthpaoli

Theodore S. Wentworth
William Delli Paoli
Nancy Morse Knight
Court Bryant Purdy
Edward L. Smilow

Reference: Wells Fargo Bank, Newport Beach, Calif.

For full biographical listings, see the Martindale-Hubbell Law Directory

NORWALK, Los Angeles Co.

CHARLES R. WELDON (AV)

Suite 104 Southeast Law Center, 12749 Norwalk Boulevard, P.O. Box 1110, 90651
Telephone: 562-864-3737
Fax: 562-863-9962
Email: cweldon@email.com *URL:* http://www.cweldon.com

Jerry D. Turner
E. Neal Daley
Paul R. Dixon
Paul D. Brau
Laila Havre Jacobsma

For full biographical listings, see the Martindale-Hubbell Law Directory

*OAKLAND,** Alameda Co.

ANTHONY & CARLSON, LLP (AV)

1999 Harrison Street, Suite 2000, 94612-3517
Telephone: 510-835-8400
Fax: 510-835-5566

MEMBERS OF FIRM

Steven R. Anthony | Richard H. Carlson

Felicia C. Strankman

OF COUNSEL

Jane L. Trigero

For full biographical listings, see the Martindale-Hubbell Law Directory

LAW OFFICES OF RICHARD J. BASKIN (AV)

One Kaiser Plaza, Suite 1585, 94612
Telephone: 510-444-1700
Fax: 510-444-5859
Email: rjbaskin@pacbell.net *URL:* http://www.lawyers.com/baskinlaw

For full biographical listings, see the Martindale-Hubbell Law Directory

BENNETT, SAMUELSEN, REYNOLDS AND ALLARD, A PROFESSIONAL CORPORATION (AV)

1951 Webster Street, Suite 200, 94612-2909
Telephone: 510-444-7688; 510-987-8001
Fax: 510-444-5849
Email: BSRALIT@AOL.COM

Bryant M. Bennett (Retired)
David J. Samuelsen
Richard L. Reynolds
Anthony J. Allard
John G. Cowperthwaite

Roger Blake Hohnsbeen
Thomas S. Gelini
Frederick W. Gatt
Candace Dabney-Smith
David L. Dees
Roderick D. Hill

Representative Clients: Allstate Insurance Co.; California State Automobile Assn.; The Continental Insurance Cos.; County of Alameda.

For full biographical listings, see the Martindale-Hubbell Law Directory

HAIMS, MACGOWAN, VALENTINO & PEEBLES, L.L.P. (AV)

490 Grand Avenue, 94610
Telephone: 510-835-0500
Facsimile: 510-835-2833

MEMBERS OF FIRM

Arnold B. Haims
Clyde L. MacGowan
Caroline N. Valentino
Dianne D. Peebles

For full biographical listings, see the Martindale-Hubbell Law Directory

KAZAN, MCCLAIN, EDISES, SIMON & ABRAMS, A PROFESSIONAL LAW CORPORATION (AV)

171 Twelfth Street, Suite 300, 94607
Telephone: 510-465-7728; 893-7211
TDD: (510) 763-8808
Fax: 510-835-4913
Email: postmaster@kmesa.com *URL:* http://www.KMESA.COM

Steven Kazan
David M. McClain
Aaron H. Simon
Denise Abrams
Francis E. Fernandez
Dianna J. Lyons
Simona A. Farrise

Anne Michelle Burr
Frances C. Schreiberg
Susan S. Ochi
Terry Gross
Cyrus Wadia
Gordon D. Greenwood
James L. Oberman
Andrea C. Huston
Diana Esquivel
Anthony D. Prince

OF COUNSEL

Philip A. Harley

(See Next Column)

KAZAN, MCCLAIN, EDISES, SIMON & ABRAMS A PROFESSIONAL LAW CORPORATION, *Oakland—Continued*

LEGAL SUPPORT PERSONNEL

Elizabeth C. Johnson (Director of Administration and Finance)

Reference: Union Bank (Oakland Main Branch).

For full biographical listings, see the Martindale-Hubbell Law Directory

VAN BLOIS & ASSOCIATES (AV)

Suite 2245 Ordway Building, One Kaiser Plaza, 94612
Telephone: 510-444-1906
Contra Costa County 510-947-1055
Fax: 510-444-1294
Email: rlvblaw@mindspring.com *URL:* http://www.lawyers.com/vanblois

MEMBERS OF FIRM

R. Lewis Van Blois — Thomas C. Knowles

OF COUNSEL

Charles E. Farnsworth

For full biographical listings, see the Martindale-Hubbell Law Directory

ORINDA, Contra Costa Co.

GILLIN, JACOBSON, ELLIS & LARSEN (AV)

2 Theatre Square Suite 230, 94563
Telephone: 925-253-5800
Fax: 925-253-5858
Email: lawfirm@gjeld.com
San Francisco, California Office: 44 Montgomery Street, Suite 500, 94101.
Telephone: 415-986-4777.

Andrew R. Gillin — Luke Ellis
Ralph L. Jacobson — James Paul Larsen
Kristin Lucey

For full biographical listings, see the Martindale-Hubbell Law Directory

PACIFIC PALISADES, Los Angeles Co.

WILLIAM A. SAMPSON II & ASSOCIATES (AV)

15332 Antioch Street, Suite 525, 90272-3628
Telephone: 310-472-1839
Fax: 310-472-8670

For full biographical listings, see the Martindale-Hubbell Law Directory

PALM DESERT, Riverside Co.

BERMAN & WEISS (AV)

73-710 Fred Waring Drive, Suite 100, 92260
Telephone: 760-773-6677
Fax: 760-346-7779
Email: weisstrial@aol.com *URL:* http://www.lawinfo.com/law/ca/berman.html

MEMBERS OF FIRM

Richard B. Weiss — Martin M. Berman

For full biographical listings, see the Martindale-Hubbell Law Directory

THE LAW OFFICES OF JAMES W. PARKINSON (AV)

77564 Country Club Drive, Suite B-310, 92211-0450
Telephone: 760-772-4550
Fax: 760-772-6530
Email: jwplaw1@aol.com

For full biographical listings, see the Martindale-Hubbell Law Directory

PASADENA, Los Angeles Co.

JOHN C. BURTON (AV)

35 South Raymond Avenue, Suite 405, 91105
Telephone: 626-449-8300
Fax: 626-449-4417
Email: Johnburtonlaw@compuserve.com *URL:* http://www.lawyers.com/johnburtonlaw

For full biographical listings, see the Martindale-Hubbell Law Directory

COLLINS, COLLINS, MUIR & TRAVER LLP (AV)

Successor to Collins & Collins
Suite 300, 265 North Euclid, 91101
Telephone: 626-793-1163
FAX: 626-793-5982
Newport Beach, California Office: 333 Bayside Drive, 92660.
Telephone: 949-723-7700.
Fax: 949-723-7701.
Affiliated Offices: Drage, Olson & Tiet, LLP, 810 S. Casino Center Boulevard, Las Vegas, Nevada, 89101.
Telephone: 702-384-1600.
Fax: 702-384-1664.

(See Next Column)

MEMBERS OF FIRM

James E. Collins (1910-1987) — John J. Collins
Robert J. Traver (Retired) — Samuel J. Muir
Paul L. Rupard (Retired) — Frank J. D'Oro
Brian K. Stewart

ASSOCIATES

Robert H. Stellwagen, Jr. — Kien C. Tiet
Tomas A. Guterres — Martha L. Cazeneuve
Christine E. Drage — Howard Franco, Jr.
Stephen W. Olson — Jeffrey M. Hall
Peter L. Stacy — Michael M. Bergfeld
Jennifer M. Gregg

For full biographical listings, see the Martindale-Hubbell Law Directory

MEENAN & LARIVIERE (AV)

790 East Colorado Boulevard Ninth Floor Penthouse, 91101-2113
Telephone: 626-398-0000
Fax: 626-585-0999
Email: meenlaw@msn.com *URL:* http://www.lawyers.com/meenlaw

Kevin Meenan — Denise L. Lariviere

For full biographical listings, see the Martindale-Hubbell Law Directory

GEORGE E. MOORE A PROFESSIONAL LAW CORPORATION (AV)

225 South Lake Avenue 9th Floor, 91101-3005
Telephone: 626-440-1315
Fax: 626-440-1516
Email: gemoore@pasadenatorts.com

George E. Moore

For full biographical listings, see the Martindale-Hubbell Law Directory

THON, BECK, VANNI, PHILLIPI & NUTT, A PROFESSIONAL CORPORATION (AV)

1100 East Green Street, 91106-2506
Telephone: 626-795-8333
Fax: 626-449-9933

William M. Thon — Steven V. Phillipi
Thomas P. Beck — Brian C. Nutt
Gregory R. Vanni — Kevin K. Callahan

OF COUNSEL

Anthony de los Reyes

For full biographical listings, see the Martindale-Hubbell Law Directory

RANCHO SANTA FE, San Diego Co.

LAW OFFICES OF ROBERT S. KILBORNE IV (AV)

7872 Rio Senda, P.O. Box 7288, 92067
Telephone: 619-759-9050
Fax: 619-759-8020
Email: triallawyer@kilborne.com *URL:* http://www.kilborne.com

ASSOCIATE

Albert E. Cressey, III

OF COUNSEL

Russell B. Wagner

For full biographical listings, see the Martindale-Hubbell Law Directory

*REDDING,** Shasta Co.

DUGAN BARR & ASSOCIATES (AV)

1824 Court Street, P.O. Box 994390, 96099-1648
Telephone: 530-243-8008
Fax: 530-243-1648
URL: http://www.CA-lawyer.com

Dugan Barr

ASSOCIATES

Douglas Mudford — J. Michael Favor

Representative Clients: City of Redding; Mid Valley Bank; Scott Valley Bank; 3M; Enloe Hospital.
References: Scott Valley Bank, Redding Branch; Mid Valley Bank, Redding Branch.

For full biographical listings, see the Martindale-Hubbell Law Directory

MAIRE, MANSELL & BEASLEY, A LAW CORPORATION (AV)

2851 Park Marina Drive Suite 300, P.O. Drawer 994607, 96099-4607
Telephone: 916-246-6050
Fax: 916-246-6060
Email: mmblaw@maire-law.com

Wayne H. Maire — Patrick R. Beasley
Eric R. Maire

(See Next Column)

MAIRE, MANSELL & BEASLEY A LAW CORPORATION—*Continued*

Tamara L. Wood
Eric A. Omstead
Gary E. Haslerud

For full biographical listings, see the Martindale-Hubbell Law Directory

REINER, SIMPSON & KENNEDY (AV)

2851 Park Marina Drive, Suite 200, 96001
Telephone: 530-241-1905
Fax: 530-241-0622

Russell Reiner
Robert G. Simpson
Daryl E. Kennedy

For full biographical listings, see the Martindale-Hubbell Law Directory

REDLANDS, San Bernardino Co.

WELEBIR, MCCUNE & JURE, A PROFESSIONAL LAW CORPORATION (AV)

2068 Orange Tree Lane, Suite 215, 92374
Telephone: 909-335-0444
Fax: 909-335-0452
Email: wmj@wmj-law.com *URL:* http://www.lawyers.com/wm&jlaw

Douglas F. Welebir
Richard D. McCune, Jr.
Curt W. Jure
Paul J. Burkhart
James F. Tierney, III
Melissa J. Welebir

LEGAL SUPPORT PERSONNEL

Deborah J. Marsh

For full biographical listings, see the Martindale-Hubbell Law Directory

*RIVERSIDE,** Riverside Co.

BELL, ORROCK & WATASE, LLP (AV)

2001 Iowa Avenue, Suite 115, 92507
Telephone: 909-683-6014
Fax: 909-683-0314
Email: bellorrockwa@earthlink.net

Michael A. Bell
Stanley O. Orrock
Kenneth D. Watase

David A. Williams
Micheal A. Fortino
Dana M. Smith

For full biographical listings, see the Martindale-Hubbell Law Directory

HAIGHT, BROWN & BONESTEEL, L.L.P. (AV)

A Partnership including Professional Corporations
California Tower, 3737 Main Street, Suite 800, 92501
Telephone: 909-341-8300
FAX: 909-341-8309
URL: http://www.hbblaw.com
Santa Monica, California Office: 1620 26th Street, Suite 4000 North, P.O. Box 680.
Telephone: 310-449-6000.
Telecopier: 310-829-5117.
Telex: 705837.
Santa Ana, California Office: Suite 900, 5 Hutton Centre Drive.
Telephone: 714-754-1100.
Telecopier: 714-754-0826.
San Francisco, California Office: 100 Bush Street, 27th Floor.
Telephone: 415-986-7700.
Fax: 415-986-6945.
San Diego, California Office: 101 West Broadway, Suite 1000.
Telephone: 619-595-5583.
Fax: 619-595-7873.

RESIDENT MEMBERS

Mark S. Lester
Kevin M. Osterberg

ASSOCIATES

Bonnie B. Bailey-Jones
John W. Short
Jeffrey T. Gwynn

For full biographical listings, see the Martindale-Hubbell Law Directory

*SACRAMENTO,** Sacramento Co.

CALLAHAN & DEACON (AV)

A Partnership including a Corporation
77 Cadillac Drive, Suite 240, 95825
Telephone: 916-929-1999
Fax: 916-929-1090
Email: gbc8esd@calweb.com *URL:* http://www.lawyers.com/callahan&deacon

(*See Next Column*)

Gary B. Callahan (Inc.)
Edward S. Deacon

For full biographical listings, see the Martindale-Hubbell Law Directory

CAULFIELD, DAVIES & DONAHUE (AV)

3500 American River Drive, Suite 100, 95864
Telephone: 916-487-7700
Fax: 916-487-7091
Fairfield, California Office: Fairfield West Plaza, 1455 Oliver Road, Suite 130.
Telephone: 707-426-0223.

MEMBERS OF FIRM

Richard Hyland Caulfield
Robert E. Davies
James R. Donahue
Bruce E. Leonard
Matthew Paul Donahue
Brian C. Haydon

ASSOCIATES

Chance L. Trimm
Shawn C. Moore
Catherine A.J. Woodbridge

For full biographical listings, see the Martindale-Hubbell Law Directory

DREYER, BABICH, BUCCOLA & CALLAHAM, LLP (AV)

715 University Avenue, 95825
Telephone: 916-920-2111
Fax: 916-920-5687
Email: dhunter@dbbc.com *URL:* http://www.lawyers.com/dbbc

MEMBERS OF FIRM

Roger A. Dreyer
Joseph J. Babich
Robert A. Buccola
William C. Callaham
Craig C. Sheffer
Stephen F. Davids

John W. Jefferson
Stanley P. Fleshman
Eliot M. Reiner
Hank G. Greenblatt
Timothy J. O'Connor
Mark R. Swartz
Lena L. Dalby
Christopher W. Wood
Earl "Josh" Lowery, Jr.
Michael E. Myers

For full biographical listings, see the Martindale-Hubbell Law Directory

FRIEDMAN, COLLARD, CUTTER & PANNETON, PROFESSIONAL CORPORATION (AV)

7750 College Town Drive, Suite 300, 95826
Telephone: 916-381-9011
Telecopier: 916-381-7048

Morton L. Friedman
William H. Collard
C. Brooks Cutter
John Panneton
Eric J. Ratinoff
Ron Winters

For full biographical listings, see the Martindale-Hubbell Law Directory

GALLAWA • BROWN • KROESCH, A PROFESSIONAL CORPORATION (AV)

2207 J Street, 95816
Telephone: 916-444-9364
Fax: 916-444-5921
Email: gbk@gbklawoffices.com

Walter E. Gallawa
Douglas A. Kroesch
Gary Gallawa

Robert Browning Miller

For full biographical listings, see the Martindale-Hubbell Law Directory

HARDY ERICH BROWN & WILSON, A PROFESSIONAL CORPORATION (AV)

1000 G Street, 95814
Telephone: 916-449-3800
Fax: 916-449-3888
Mailing Address: P.O. Box 13530, Sacramento, California, 95853-4530
Email: hebw@hebw.com *URL:* http://www.hebw.com

John Quincy Brown, Jr.
Anthony D. Osmundson
Thomas C. Richards
L. Thomas Wagner
David L. Perrault
Sara A. Clark
John Quincy Brown, III
David S. Worthington
Bruce E. Salenko
Brian H. Charter
Richard L. Alley
Whitney A. Davis
John C. Miller, Jr.

OF COUNSEL

Cavan Hardy
Norwood R. Erich
William A. Wilson
Richard M. Cunha

Kelly F. Watson
Kristine E. Balogh
Karin G. Shine
Reginald A. Dunn
Lisa L. Palombo

(*See Next Column*)

HARDY ERICH BROWN & WILSON A PROFESSIONAL CORPORATION, *Sacramento—Continued*

Representative Clients: Continental General Tire; The Dial Corporation; GenCorp; The Dexter Corporation; The Goodyear Tire and Rubber Company; La Z Boy, Inc.; Sacramento Municipal Utility District; Tri-Continent Scientific, Inc.; VIAD Corporation; Modesto & Empire Traction Company.

For full biographical listings, see the Martindale-Hubbell Law Directory

JOHNSON, SCHACHTER & COLLINS, A PROFESSIONAL CORPORATION (AV)

California Plaza, 2180 Harvard Street, #560, 95815
Telephone: 916-921-5800
Telecopier: 916-921-0247
Email: law@jscattorneys.com

Robert H. Johnson
Alesa M. Schachter
Kim H. Collins
George W. Holt
Kellie M. Murphy
Alvin Gittisriboongul

Susan E. Slager

OF COUNSEL

Ford R. Smith
Carolyn M. Wood
Susanne M. Shelley

Representative Clients: Big 5 Sporting Goods; Chicago Insurance; COREGIS; Fireman's Fund Insurance Cos,; Insurance Company of the West; Interstate National; NAVISTAR; Sears, Roebuck and Company; Shand Morahan.
Reference: U.S. Bank, Sacramento.

For full biographical listings, see the Martindale-Hubbell Law Directory

THOMAS F. LYTLE (AV)

1220 25th Street, 95816-5005
Telephone: 916-442-0701
Fax: 916-442-0786
Email: tomlytle@msn.com

For full biographical listings, see the Martindale-Hubbell Law Directory

MASON & THOMAS (AV)

2151 River Plaza Drive, Suite 100, 95833
Telephone: 916-567-8211
Fax: 916-567-8212
Email: M&T@MasonThomas.com

MEMBERS OF FIRM

Stephen A. Mason
Bradley S. Thomas

ASSOCIATES

Douglas W. Brown
Robert G. Kruse
David S. Yost
Patrick J. Hehir
Kevin L. Elder
Michele Raley

For full biographical listings, see the Martindale-Hubbell Law Directory

MASTAGNI, HOLSTEDT & CHIURAZZI, A PROFESSIONAL CORPORATION (AV)

1912 I Street, Suite 102, 95814
Telephone: 916-446-4692
Fax: 916-447-4614
Email: mhcmailbox@mastagni.com

David P. Mastagni
John R. Holstedt
Richard J. Chiurazzi

Stephen Curtis Winter
Dennis W. Hargrave
Michael D. Amick
Barbara M. Jacobson
Kasey Christopher Clark
Brian A. Dixon
Elaine M. Cawley
Michael R. Kelly
Mark Regalbuti
Christopher W. Miller

Representative Clients: Alameda County Probation Assn.; Cannery Workers, El Dorado County Deputy Sheriffs Assn.; Folsom Police Officers Assn.; Jackson Police Officers Assn.; United Food & Commercial Workers 588, Northern California; P.O.R.A.C. Insurance Board.

For full biographical listings, see the Martindale-Hubbell Law Directory

MATHENY SEARS LINKERT & LONG, LLP (AV)

3638 American River Drive, P.O. Box 13711, 95853-4711
Telephone: 916-978-3434
Fax: 916-978-3430
Email: info@msll.com *URL:* http://www.msll.com

MEMBERS OF FIRM

Henry G. Matheny (1933-1984)
Douglas A. Sears
Richard S. Linkert
Ernest A. Long
Joann Georgallis
Kent M. Luckey
Matthew C. Jaime
Michael A. Bishop
Robert B. Berrigan
Ronald E. Enabnit
Eric R. Wiesel

(See Next Column)

ASSOCIATES

Andrea Croak Christensen
Michael G. Jones
Eric M. Bonzell
Mary Elizabeth Wood
Paul Richard Baleria
James F. Curran
Andreas C. Rockas
Timothy P. Chang

OF COUNSEL

James C. Damir

LEGAL SUPPORT PERSONNEL

PARALEGALS

Frances Studer
Lynell Rae Steed
Jennifer Bachman

For full biographical listings, see the Martindale-Hubbell Law Directory

MEADE, BRODOVSKY, AIKEN, JACOBSEN & HINE, A LIMITED LIABILITY PARTNERSHIP (AV)

400 Capitol Mall, 26th Floor, 95814
Telephone: 916-498-7300
Fax: 916-498-7350
Email: mbsac@jps.net *URL:* http://www.lawyers.com/meade

Michael M. Meade
William B. Brodovsky
Alan A. Brodovsky
Leland J. Aiken
Allen D. Hine
Brian S. Jacobsen

Richard M. Glovin

For full biographical listings, see the Martindale-Hubbell Law Directory

WILCOXEN, MONTGOMERY & HARBISON (AV)

A Partnership including a Professional Corporation
2114 K Street, 95816
Telephone: 916-442-2777
Email: wmh@wilcoxenlaw.com *URL:* http://www.wilcoxenlaw.com

Daniel E. Wilcoxen (Inc.)
James R. Montgomery
Joseph F. Harbison, III

Patrick L. Hinrichsen
David E. Smith
Steven H. Schultz
Michelle C. Jenni

References: SierraWest Bank; Wells Fargo Bank.

For full biographical listings, see the Martindale-Hubbell Law Directory

*SAN BERNARDINO,** San Bernardino Co.

LAW OFFICES OF WILLIAM D. SHAPIRO (AV)

432 North Arrowhead Avenue, 92401
Telephone: 909-888-0102
Fax: 909-884-1767
Email: wshapiro@msn.com *URL:* http://www.lawyers.com/williamdshapiro

For full biographical listings, see the Martindale-Hubbell Law Directory

*SAN DIEGO,** San Diego Co.

THE LAW OFFICES OF BIRGER GREG BACINO, APC (AV)

3033 Fifth Avenue, Suite 301, 92103
Telephone: 800-801-4878
Fax: 619-299-0086
URL: http://www.bacinolaw.com
Washington, D.C. Office: 1201 Pennsylvania Avenue, Suite 300, 20004.
Telephone: 800-801-4878.
Houston, Texas Office: 510 Bering Street, Suite 300, 77057.
Telephone: 800-801-4878.

Birger Greg Bacino
Richard P. Verlasky
Philip Aman

OF COUNSEL

Patricia M. Sayre
Michael B. Sayre
Anthony J. DeLellis

For full biographical listings, see the Martindale-Hubbell Law Directory

BOUDREAU & TRENTACOSTA, A PROFESSIONAL LAW CORPORATION (AV)

401 West "A" Street, Suite 1850, 92101-9773
Telephone: 619-238-1553
Fax: 619-238-8181
Email: boutre@aol.com

Steven M. Boudreau
Robert J. Trentacosta

For full biographical listings, see the Martindale-Hubbell Law Directory

San Diego—Continued

CASEY, GERRY, REED & SCHENK (AV)

110 Laurel Street, 92101
Telephone: 619-238-1811
Fax: 619-544-9232
Email: cglaw@cglaw.com *URL:* http://www.CGlaw.com

MEMBERS OF FIRM

David S. Casey
Richard F. Gerry
Scott C. Cummins
David S. Casey, Jr.
T. Michael Reed
Frederick Schenk
Robert J. Francavilla
Gayle Meryl Blatt
Thomas D. Penfield
Michael P. Montgomery
Suzanne C. Etpison
Bonnie E. Kane
Thomas Luneau

Reference: San Diego National Bank.

For full biographical listings, see the Martindale-Hubbell Law Directory

DOUGHERTY, HILDRE, DUDEK & HAKLAR (AV)

2550 Fifth Avenue, Suite 600, 92103-5624
Telephone: 619-232-9131
Telefax: 619-232-7317
Email: Douhil@aol.com

William O. Dougherty
Donald F. Hildre
Frederick M. Dudek
Thomas D. Haklar

For full biographical listings, see the Martindale-Hubbell Law Directory

DUKE GERSTEL SHEARER, LLP (AV)

A Registered Limited Liability Partnership
Sixth Floor, 101 West Broadway, P.O. Box 85470, 92186-5470
Telephone: 619-232-0816
800-405-0816
Fax: 619-232-4661
Email: lawyers@dgsllp.com *URL:* http://www.dgsllp.com
Costa Mesa, California Office: 3200 Park Center Drive, Suite 1000, 92626.
Telephone: 949-551-8664, 800-405-0816.
Los Angeles, California Office: 10866 Wilshire Boulevard, Suite 1400, 90024.
Telephone: 310-475-7118, 800-405-0816.
San Francisco, California Office: 744 Montgomery Street, Fifth Floor, 94111.
Telephone: 415-773-0101.
Palm Springs, California Office: 1111 East Tahquitz Canyon Way, Suite 110, 92262.
Telephone: 760-322-7846.
Phoenix, Arizona Office: One Columbus Plaza, 3636 North Central Avenue, Suite 1200, 85012.
Telephone: 602-650-2060.
Fax: 602-650-2089.
Tucson, Arizona Office: 6969 East Sunrise Drive, Suite 102, 85750.
Telephone: 520-615-8858.
Fax: 520-615-1069.
Affiliate Las Vegas, Nevada Office: Parsons & Pursiano, LLP, City Center West, Suite 108, 7201 W. Lake Mead Boulevard, 89128.
Telephone: 702-384-9900.
Facsimile: 702-384-5900.

MEMBER OF FIRM

Ronald M. Green

ASSOCIATE

Michelle LeRoux Burton

Reference: Bank of Commerce.

For full biographical listings, see the Martindale-Hubbell Law Directory

HAIGHT, BROWN & BONESTEEL, L.L.P. (AV)

A Partnership including Professional Corporations
101 West Broadway, Suite 1000, 92101-3544
Telephone: 619-595-5583
Telecopier: 619-595-7873
URL: http://www.hbblaw.com
Santa Monica, California Office: 1620 26th Street, Suite 4000 North, P.O. Box 680.
Telephone: 310-449-6000.
Telecopier: 310-829-5117.
Telex: 705837.
Santa Ana, California Office: Suite 900, 5 Hutton Centre Drive.
Telephone: 714-754-1100.
Telecopier: 714-754-0826.
Riverside, California Office: California Tower, 3737 Main Street, Suite 800.
Telephone: 909-341-8300.
Fax: 909-341-8309.
San Francisco, California Office: 101 Bush Street, 27th Floor.
Telephone: 415-986-7700.
Fax: 415-986-6945.

RESIDENT ASSOCIATE

Scott M. Bonesteel

For full biographical listings, see the Martindale-Hubbell Law Directory

KENNERSON SCHWARTZ SEMERDJIAN & HAILE LLP (AV)

A Limited Liability Partnership
101 West Broadway, Suite 810, 92101
Telephone: 619-236-8821
Facsimile: 619-236-8827
URL: http://www.lawyers.com/ksshlaw

OF COUNSEL

Paul R. Kennerson

MEMBERS OF FIRM

Ross J. Schwartz
Dick A. Semerdjian
Jeffrey A. Haile

James R. Ballard
John K. Grant

For full biographical listings, see the Martindale-Hubbell Law Directory

LEVINE, STEINBERG & MILLER (AV)

550 West C Street, Suite 1810, 92101-8596
Telephone: 619-231-9449
Telecopier: 619-231-8638

MEMBERS OF FIRM

Harvey R. Levine
Harris I. Steinberg
Craig A. Miller
Jordan M. Cohen
Richard A. Huver

For full biographical listings, see the Martindale-Hubbell Law Directory

LUCE, FORWARD, HAMILTON & SCRIPPS LLP (AV)

A Partnership including Professional Corporations
600 West Broadway, Suite 2600, 92101
Telephone: 619-236-1414
Fax: 619-232-8311
URL: http://www.luce.com
La Jolla, California Office: 4275 Executive Square, Suite 800, 92037.
Telephone: 858-455-6611.
Fax: 858-232-8311.
Los Angeles, California Office: 777 South Figueroa, Suite 3600, 90017.
Telephone: 213-892-4992.
Fax: 213-892-7731.
San Francisco, California Office: 121 Spear Street, Suite 200, 94105.
Telephone: 415-356-4600.
Fax: 415-356-4610.
New York, N.Y. Office: Citicorp Center, 153 East 53rd Street, 26th Floor, 10022.
Telephone: 212-754-1414.
Fax: 212-644-9727.
Chicago, Illinois Office: 180 North La Salle Street, Suite 3110, 60601.
Telephone: 312-641-0580.
Fax: 312-641-0380.

OF COUNSEL

Gerald S. Davee

For Complete List of Firm Personnel, See General Section

For full biographical listings, see the Martindale-Hubbell Law Directory

MCCLELLAN & BROWN, A PROFESSIONAL CORPORATION (AV)

1144 State Street, 92101
Telephone: 619-231-0505
Fax: 619-544-0540
Email: mcclellan9@aol.com *URL:* http://www.lawyers.com/mcclellan&brown

Craig R. McClellan
LaMar B. Brown

For full biographical listings, see the Martindale-Hubbell Law Directory

OLINS, FOERSTER & HAYES (AV)

A Legal Liability Partnership including A Professional Corporation
2214 Second Avenue, 92101
Telephone: 619-238-1601
Fax: 619-238-1613
URL: http://www.ofh.com
Santa Ana, California Office: 1314 West Fifth Street, Suite C, 92703.
Telephone: 714-836-9777.
Fax: 714-954-1156.

MEMBERS OF FIRM

Douglas F. Olins
Barrett J. Foerster (A P.C.)
Dennis J. Hayes

ASSOCIATES

Laura H. Miller
John C. Zucconi
Barbara J. Ginsberg (Resident, Santa Ana Office)

For full biographical listings, see the Martindale-Hubbell Law Directory

San Diego—Continued

SELDEN LAW FIRM (AV)

1230 Columbia Street, Suite 1060, 92101
Telephone: 619-515-1111
Facsimile: 619-515-1114
Email: lseldenii@aol.com
Las Vegas, Nevada Office: Selden, Lynch & Hopper, 501 South Rancho Drive, Suite C-12, 89106.
Telephone: 702-315-1115.
Facsimile: 702-315-1114.

Lynde Selden, II

For full biographical listings, see the Martindale-Hubbell Law Directory

THORSNES, BARTOLOTTA, MCGUIRE & PADILLA (AV)

A Partnership including Professional Corporations
Fifth Avenue Financial Center, 11th Floor, 2550 Fifth Avenue, 92103
Telephone: 619-236-9363
Fax: 619-236-9653
Email: TBMPmail@TBMP.com *URL:* http://www.tbmp.com

Michael T. Thorsnes (A.P.C., P.C.)
Vincent J. Bartolotta, Jr., (P.C.)
John F. McGuire (P.C.)
Kevin F. Quinn (P.C.)
C. Brant Noziska (P.C.)
Mitchell S. Golub (P.C.)
Palma Cesar Hooper (P.C.)
Neal H. Rockwood (P.C.)
Daral B. Mazzarella (P.C.)
R. Christian Hulburt (P.C.)

ASSOCIATES

Catherine A. Richardson
Jodi L. Hautaluoma
Douglas J. Billings
Scott A. Kennedy
Dori K. Rybacki
James T. Atkins
Leo Bartolotta
Jill E. Cleary
James B. Drimmer
Timothy J. Tatro

OF COUNSEL

Robert S. Kennedy

For full biographical listings, see the Martindale-Hubbell Law Directory

*SAN FRANCISCO,** San Francisco Co.

STANLEY J. BELL A PROFESSIONAL CORPORATION (AV)

18th Floor, 505 Sansome Street, 94111
Telephone: 415-391-3700; San Jose: 408-295-1678
Fax: 415-391-3712
San Diego
San Diego, California Office: Suite 1200, 401 West A Street.
Telephone: 619-696-9445.

Stanley J. Bell

Samuel Boyd McCullagh
Sally G. Bergman
Steven J. Bell
J. Kevin Morrison
Craig William Morrison
Robert M. Dang
Frank C. Liuzzi
Hugh A. Donohoe

For full biographical listings, see the Martindale-Hubbell Law Directory

BIANCO & MURPHY (AV)

500 Sansome Street, 8th Floor, 94111
Telephone: 415-362-3344
Telecopier: 415-986-5271
Email: LAWRLB@AOL.COM

MEMBERS OF FIRM

Robert L. Bianco
Stephen M. Murphy

ASSOCIATES

Gregory O. Bianco
Christopher M. Windle

For full biographical listings, see the Martindale-Hubbell Law Directory

BLEY AND BLEY (AV)

555 Montgomery Street, Suite 605, 94111
Telephone: 415-982-7311
Fax: 415-982-7278

Bertrand A. Bley (1903-1992)
Stephen Bruce Bley

Casimir A. Wilson
Samantha Bley DeJean
Richard S. Weil

For full biographical listings, see the Martindale-Hubbell Law Directory

BOKELMAN & BENJAMIN, A PROFESSIONAL LAW CORPORATION (AV)

Two Embarcadero Center Suite 1050, 94111-3823
Telephone: 415-398-3660
Facsimile: 415-788-0161
URL: http://www. bokelman-benjamin.com

(See Next Column)

Robert U. Bokelman
Anglia Benjamin

Amy Marie Leonard

For full biographical listings, see the Martindale-Hubbell Law Directory

LAW OFFICES OF PHILIP BOROWSKY A PROFESSIONAL CORPORATION (AV)

Steuart Street Tower, Suite 2600, One Market Plaza, 94105-1417
Telephone: 415-896-6800
Facsimile: 415-896-0600
Email: info@borowsky.com *URL:* http://www.borowsky.com
Los Angeles, California Office: 2049 Century Park East, Suite 900, 90067-3111.
Telephone: 310-551-6960.
Fax: 310-553-7237.

Philip Borowsky

Christopher J. Hayes

For full biographical listings, see the Martindale-Hubbell Law Directory

ROBERT D. CARROW (AV)

One Embarcadero Center, Suite 880, 94111
Telephone: 415-981-1691
Telecopier: 415-492-8419
Telex: 470562 LAW UI
Cable Address: "JURIS"
Email: robert@carrow.com *URL:* http://www.carrow.com/
London, England Chambers: 33 Bedford Row, WC1.
Telephone: +0171 242-6476.
Telecopier: +0171 831-6065.
San Rafael, California Office: 7 Mount Lassen Drive, Suite C134. 94903.
Telephone: 415-492-1225.
Telecopier: 415-492-8419.
(Also of Counsel to Goldstein & Musto, A Professional Corporation)

For full biographical listings, see the Martindale-Hubbell Law Directory

COX & MOYER, A PROFESSIONAL CORPORATION (AV)

703 Market Street, Suite 1800, 94103
Telephone: 415-543-9464
Fax: 415-777-1828
Email: coxmoyer@aol.com

Ingemar E. Hoberg (1903-1971)
John H. Finger (1913-1991)
Phillip E. Brown (Retired)
Stephen T. Cox
David W. Moyer

Scott J. Allen

OF COUNSEL

Kenneth W. Rosenthal

For full biographical listings, see the Martindale-Hubbell Law Directory

ANTHONY P. DAVID A PROFESSIONAL CORPORATION (AV)

One Embarcadero Center, Suite 880, 94111
Telephone: 415-981-0166
Fax: 415-981-0196
URL: http://www.lawyers.com/davidlaw

Anthony P. David

For full biographical listings, see the Martindale-Hubbell Law Directory

LAW OFFICES OF CHRISTOPHER E. GRELL (AV)

The Monadnock Building, 685 Market Street, Suite 540, 94105
Telephone: 415-541-9866
Fax: 415-541-9869
URL: http://www.lawyers.com/christopheregrelllaw

ASSOCIATE

Richard F. Rescho

For full biographical listings, see the Martindale-Hubbell Law Directory

MCGUINN, HILLSMAN & PALEFSKY, A PROFESSIONAL CORPORATION (AV)

535 Pacific Avenue, 94133
Telephone: 415-421-9292
Fax: 415-403-0202

John A. McGuinn
John R. Hillsman
Cliff Palefsky
Derek B. Jacobson
Keith A. Ehrman

Sharon R. Vinick

For full biographical listings, see the Martindale-Hubbell Law Directory

San Francisco—Continued

MOORE & BROWNING (AV)

100 Bush Street, Suite 225, 94104
Telephone: 415-956-6500
Fax: 415-956-6580

Michael B. Moore
Charles A. Browning

LEGAL SUPPORT PERSONNEL

Pat Medina (Paralegal)

For full biographical listings, see the Martindale-Hubbell Law Directory

ROUDA, FEDER & TIETJEN (AV)

44 Montgomery, Suite 4000, 94104
Telephone: 415-398-5398
Fax: 415-398-8169

Ronald H. Rouda
John M. Feder
Timothy G. Tietjen

Mark J. Zanobini

LEGAL SUPPORT PERSONNEL

Cheryl Acree (Paralegal)

For full biographical listings, see the Martindale-Hubbell Law Directory

TEHIN +PARTNERS, A PROFESSIONAL CORPORATION (AV)

Bank of America Center, 555 California Street, 33rd Floor, 94104-1609
Telephone: 415-951-8800
Fax: 415-951-8808
URL: http://www.tehin.com

Nikolai Tehin
Pamela J. Stevens
Reilly Atkinson, IV
Michael E. Brown
Bita Abdollahi

For full biographical listings, see the Martindale-Hubbell Law Directory

WILLIAM L. VEEN A PROFESSIONAL CORPORATION (AV)

711 Van Ness Avenue, Suite 220, 94102
Telephone: 415-673-4800
Fax: 415-771-5845

William L. Veen
Kevin Lancaster
James G. Butler
Cynthia Bernet-McGuinn
Rebecca A. Quinn
Robert T. Ruppe
Christopher A. Viadro
Eustace de Saint Phalle
Amy M. Ratcliffe

For full biographical listings, see the Martindale-Hubbell Law Directory

WALKUP, MELODIA, KELLY & ECHEVERRIA, A PROFESSIONAL CORPORATION (AV)

26th Floor, 650 California Street, 94108
Telephone: 415-981-7210
Fax: 415-391-6965

Paul V. Melodia
Daniel J. Kelly
John Echeverria
Ronald H. Wecht
Michael A. Kelly
Kevin L. Domecus
Richard H. Schoenberger

Cynthia F. Newton
Michael J. Recupero
Douglas S. Saeltzer
Khaldoun A. Baghdadi
Doris Cheng

OF COUNSEL

John D. Link
Wesley Sokolosky

Reference: Bank of California, San Francisco Main Office, 400 California Street, San Francisco, Calif. 94104.

For full biographical listings, see the Martindale-Hubbell Law Directory

WARTNICK, CHABER, HAROWITZ, SMITH & TIGERMAN, A PROFESSIONAL CORPORATION (AV)

101 California Street, Suite 2200, 94111-5802
Telephone: 415-986-5566
Fax: 415-986-5896
Email: postoffice@wartnicklaw.com *URL:* http://www.wartnicklaw.com

Harry F. Wartnick
Madelyn J. Chaber
Steven M. Harowitz
Stephen M. Tigerman

Phillip Scott Chan
Christopher C. Lamerdin
Garry Cohen
Cheryl L. White
Gregory M. Sheffer
Martha A. H. Berman
Courtney S. Lui
Diana M. Garcia
Richard A. Brody
Leslie Shawn Kerth
Marileni (Mia) Mattis
Max Jiro Kimura
Mark L. Nissenbaum
Tod Manning
Charlene A. Jimenez

(See Next Column)

OF COUNSEL

Audrey A. Smith
Robert Brown

For full biographical listings, see the Martindale-Hubbell Law Directory

*SAN JOSE,** Santa Clara Co.

ALEXANDER, HAWES & AUDET (AV)

152 North 3rd Street, Suite 600, 95112
Telephone: 408-289-1776
Fax: 408-287-1776
URL: http://www.alexanderlaw.com
Email: access@alexanderlaw.com *URL:* http://www.lawyers.com/alexanderhawes&audet

Richard Alexander
Amanda Hawes
William M. Audet
Ann Saponara
Deborah Heller

OF COUNSEL

Michael McShane
Jana S. Stabile (Not admitted in CA)

For full biographical listings, see the Martindale-Hubbell Law Directory

JAN CHAMPION (AV)

Ten Almaden Boulevard, Suite 1250, 95113-2233
Telephone: 408-286-5550
Fax: 408-270-6777
URL: http://www.lawyers.com/jchampionlaw
Email: jan@championlaw.com

For full biographical listings, see the Martindale-Hubbell Law Directory

HAWKINS • BLICK (AV)

96 North Third Street, Suite 300, 95112
Telephone: 408-280-7111
Fax: 408-292-7868
URL: http://www.hawkins-law.com

MEMBERS OF FIRM

Charles F. Hawkins
Stephen L. Blick

ASSOCIATE

Richard E. Eichenbaum

For full biographical listings, see the Martindale-Hubbell Law Directory

LICCARDO, ROSSI, STURGES & MCNEIL, A PROFESSIONAL LAW CORPORATION (AV)

1960 The Alameda, Suite 200, 95126-1493
Telephone: 408-244-4570
Fax: 408-244-3294
URL: http://www.LRSM.com

Salvador A. Liccardo
Ronald R. Rossi
Robert S. Sturges
R. Donald McNeil
David M. Hamerslough
Susan R. Reischl
Craig Needham
Laura Liccardo
Samuel A. Chuck
Richard B. Gullen

Robert C. Colyar
Paul Salvatore Liccardo
Thomas Eamon McNeil

For full biographical listings, see the Martindale-Hubbell Law Directory

DAVID MALNICK A PROFESSIONAL CORPORATION (AV)

Ten Almaden Boulevard, Suite 500, 95113-2226
Telephone: 408-292-5900
Fax: 408-292-5995
Email: verdict@malnicklaw.com

David E. Malnick

For full biographical listings, see the Martindale-Hubbell Law Directory

LAW OFFICES OF PATRICK R. MCMAHON A PROFESSIONAL CORPORATION (AV)

485 North First Street, 95112-4041
Telephone: 408-289-1142
Fax: 408-289-9352
Email: patrickrmcmahon@patrickrmcmahonlaw.com *URL:* http://www.patrickrmcmahonlaw.com

Patrick R. McMahon

For full biographical listings, see the Martindale-Hubbell Law Directory

MCMANIS, FAULKNER & MORGAN (AV)

160 West Santa Clara Street, 10th Floor, 95113
Telephone: 408-279-8700
Fax: 408-279-3244; 408-279-0494
Email: mfm@mfmlaw.com *URL:* http://www.mfmlaw.com

(See Next Column)

McMANIS, FAULKNER & MORGAN, *San Jose—Continued*

James McManis | Lisa Herrick
William Faulkner | Michael Reedy
Donelle Morgan | Erica Yew

Michelle Tidalgo | Kalpana Vrudhula
Colleen Duffy Smith | Ray M. Baluyot
Lillian Wolf | Catherine Bechtel
Rebecca Hughes | Arron Nesbitt

OF COUNSEL
Mary Arand

For full biographical listings, see the Martindale-Hubbell Law Directory

SAUCEDO & CORSIGLIA, A LAW CORPORATION (AV)

50 West San Fernando Street, Suite 425, 95113
Telephone: 408-289-1417
Fax: 408-289-8127
Email: saucor@compuserve.com

Norman W. Saucedo | Bradley M. Corsiglia

For full biographical listings, see the Martindale-Hubbell Law Directory

SHEA & SHEA, A PROFESSIONAL LAW CORPORATION (AV)

The James Square Building, 255 North Market Street, Suite 190, 95110
Telephone: 408-292-2434
Facsimile: 408-292-1264
Email: shea-shea@worldnet.att.net *URL:* http://www.shea-shea.com

Michael M. Shea | Michael M. Shea, Jr.

For full biographical listings, see the Martindale-Hubbell Law Directory

SAN MARINO, Los Angeles Co.

JACK K. CONWAY (AV)

2460 Huntington Drive, 91108-2643
Telephone: 626-285-4333
Fax: 626-285-1526

For full biographical listings, see the Martindale-Hubbell Law Directory

SAN MATEO, San Mateo Co.

ANDERLINI, FINKELSTEIN & EMERICK, A PROFESSIONAL CORPORATION (AV)

400 South El Camino Real, Suite 700, 94402
Telephone: 650-348-0102
Fax: 650-348-0962
Email: info@afelaw.com *URL:* http://www.afelaw.com

P. Terry Anderlini | David G. Finkelstein
John J. Guheen (1944-1995) | Merrill G. Emerick
Joern-Eric W. Brugger

Paul J. Smoot | Anne Kristen Brauer

OF COUNSEL
Daniel J. Monaco | Robert M. Desky
Bruce M. Lubarsky

A list of Representative Clients will be furnished upon request.

For full biographical listings, see the Martindale-Hubbell Law Directory

*SANTA ANA,** Orange Co.

GARRETT & JENSEN (AV)

433 Civic Center Drive, West, P.O. Box 22002, 92702-2002
Telephone: 714-550-0100
Fax: 714-550-0471
URL: http://www.lawyers.com/garrettjensen
Riverside, California Office: 3403 10th Street, Suite 700.
Telephone: 909-781-0222.

MEMBERS OF FIRM
Boyd F. Jensen, II | Mark S. Armijo
Betty L. Fracisco | Douglas M. Borthwick

OF COUNSEL
Kenneth R. Garrett

Representative Clients: Automobile Club of Southern California; Ward North America; All Risk Claims Services; St. Paul Insurance Co.; John Deere Insurance Co.; Knott's Berry Farm; Global Van Lines; C.R. England, Inc.; Premier Parks Inc.; Falken Tire Corporation.

For full biographical listings, see the Martindale-Hubbell Law Directory

HAIGHT, BROWN & BONESTEEL, L.L.P. (AV)

A Partnership including Professional Corporations
Suite 900, 5 Hutton Centre Drive, 92707
Telephone: 714-754-1100
Telecopier: 714-754-0826
URL: http://www.hbblaw.com
Santa Monica, California Office: 1620 26th Street, Suite 4000 North, P.O. Box 680.
Telephone: 310-449-6000.
Telecopier: 310-829-5117.
Telex: 705837.
Riverside, California Office: California Tower, 3737 Maine Street, Suite 800.
Telephone: 909-341-8300.
Fax: 909-341-8309.
San Francisco, California Office: 100 Bush Street, 27th Floor.
Telephone: 415-986-7700.
Fax: 415-986-6945.
San Diego, California Office: 101 West Broadway, Suite 1000.
Telephone: 619-595-5583.
Fax: 619-595-7873.

RESIDENT MEMBERS
Bruce L. Cleeland | Jeffrey S. Gerardo

ASSOCIATES
Laura M. Knox | Steven M. Dailey
Jeffrey D. Farrow | S. Ann Salisbury
Wendy J. Schmitt | Antoinette P. Hewitt
D. Chad Anderton

Counsel for: Orange County: Aetna Casualty and Surety Co.; Zurich-American Insurance Cos.; Industrial Indemnity Co.; Professional Liability Claims Managers; Maryland Casualty Insurance Co.; Royal Insurance Company of America.

For full biographical listings, see the Martindale-Hubbell Law Directory

SMITH & URE (AV)

1800 North Broadway, Suite 200, 92706
Telephone: 714-550-7720
Fax: 714-550-1251
URL: http://www.smithure.com

PARTNERS
Steven C. Smith | David G. Ure
Douglas M. Campbell

F. Eugene Westhafer | Michael J. Ward
Jenous M. Langford, Jr. | John S. Clifford
Tara L. Martin

For full biographical listings, see the Martindale-Hubbell Law Directory

*SANTA BARBARA,** Santa Barbara Co.

ANGLE, CARLSON, GOLDRICK & ROBERTS (AV)

A Partnership including a Professional Corporation
200 East Carrillo Street, Suite 310, 93101
Telephone: 805-963-7400
Fax: 805-963-7610

Robert O. Angle | Miles T. Goldrick
Arthur W. Carlson (A P.C.) | Paul A. Roberts

For full biographical listings, see the Martindale-Hubbell Law Directory

*SANTA CRUZ,** Santa Cruz Co.

DUNLAP & BURDICK, A PROFESSIONAL LAW CORPORATION (AV)

Britton Jackson
121 Jewell Street, 95060
Telephone: 831-426-7040
Fax: 831-426-1095
Email: DBLawSCrz@aol.com

Michael E. Dunlap | Paul P. Burdick

For full biographical listings, see the Martindale-Hubbell Law Directory

SANTA MONICA, Los Angeles Co.

BAKER, KEENER & NAHRA, LLP (AV)

2850 Ocean Park Boulevard, Suite 300, 90405-2936
Telephone: 310-399-0900
Fax: 310-399-1644
Email: general@bknlawyers.com *URL:* http://www.bknlawyers.com

MEMBERS OF FIRM
Robert C. Baker | Steven T. Adams
Karl A. Keener | Melissa S. Fink
John P. Nahra | Jeffrey P. Nolan
Michael H. Bailey | Constance A. Endelicato

(See Next Column)

BAKER, KEENER & NAHRA LLP—*Continued*

Brenda K. Benson
Mitchell F. Mulbarger
James D. Hepworth
Phillip A. Baker
George P. Hawley
Thomas M. Mills
R. Jeffrey Neer
Wendy Wen Yun Chang

OF COUNSEL

Daniel P. Leonard

Reference: Wells Fargo Bank (Los Angeles Head Office).

For full biographical listings, see the Martindale-Hubbell Law Directory

FOGEL, FELDMAN, OSTROV, RINGLER & KLEVENS, A LAW CORPORATION (AV)

1620 26th Street, Suite 100 South, 90404-4040
Telephone: 310-453-6711
Fax: 310-828-2191

Daniel Fogel (1923-1991)
Lester G. Ostrov
Larry R. Feldman
Joel N. Klevens
Robert M. Turner
Jerome L. Ringler
Richard L. Rosett

Thomas H. Peters
David Bricker
Stephanie Chase
Jan Greenberg Levine
Sandra L. Lepson
Lawrence C. Jones
Stacie L. Feldman
John T. Fogarty

OF COUNSEL

Carol S. May

Reference: Republic Bank of California, Beverly Hills, California.

For full biographical listings, see the Martindale-Hubbell Law Directory

GREENE, BROILLET, TAYLOR, WHEELER & PANISH, LLP (AV)

100 Wilshire Boulevard, 21st Floor, P.O. Box 2131, 90407-2131
Telephone: 310-576-1200
Fax: 310-576-1220

Bruce A. Broillet
Browne Greene
Brian J. Panish
Mark T. Quigley
Christine D. Spagnoli
John C. Taylor
Timothy J. Wheeler

Scott H. Carr
Catherine M. Lena
Frank J. O'Kane Jr.
Adam K. Shea
Geoffrey S. Wells

For full biographical listings, see the Martindale-Hubbell Law Directory

HAIGHT, BROWN & BONESTEEL, L.L.P. (AV)

A Partnership including Professional Corporations
1620 26th Street, Suite 4000 North, P.O. Box 680, 90404
Telephone: 310-449-6000
Telecopier: 310-829-5117
Telex: 705837
URL: http://www.hbblaw.com
Santa Ana, California Office: Suite 900, 5 Hutton Centre Drive.
Telephone: 714-754-1100.
Telecopier: 714-754-0826.
Riverside, California Office: California Tower, 3737 Main Street, Suite 800.
Telephone: 909-341-8300.
Fax: 909-341-8309.
San Francisco, California Office: 101 Bush Street, 27th Floor.
Telephone: 415-986-7700.
Fax: 415-986-6945.
San Diego, California Office: 101 West Broadway, Suite 1000.
Telephone: 619-595-5583.
Fax: 619-595-7873.

MEMBERS OF FIRM

Peter Q. Ezzell (A Professional Corporation)
William G. Baumgaertner (A Professional Corporation)
Peter A. Dubrawski
Kevin R. Crisp
Lee Marshall
George Christensen
Kenneth G. Anderson
William O. Martin, Jr.
S. Christian Stouder

ASSOCIATES

Jeffrey A. Vinnick
Sean E. Judge
Cynthia M. Holbrook
Michael C. Martinez

For full biographical listings, see the Martindale-Hubbell Law Directory

WATERS, MCCLUSKEY & BOEHLE (AV)

3250 Ocean Park Boulevard, Suite 300, 90405-3220
Telephone: 310-396-3411
Facsimile: 310-450-0925
Email: wmb@wmboehle.com
Santa Ana, California Office: Suite 1000, 200 West Santa Ana Boulevard.
Telephone: 714-953-4407.
Facsimile: 714-953-2118.

MEMBERS OF FIRM

William W. Waters (1898-1979)
Laurence R. Corcoran (1927-1987)
Fritz B. Hax
Wayne J. Boehle
Richard A. Wall (Resident, Santa Ana Office)
Timothy R. Lee
Gregg W. Brugger
Kevin G. McCluskey
Stacey B. Spurlock (Resident, Santa Ana Office)
Michael T. Montgomery

ASSOCIATES

Quyen H. Khuong (Resident, Santa Ana)
Christine Y. Chien (Resident, Santa Ana Office)
Portasha R. Moore
Julie C. Chang-Lee (Resident, Santa Ana Office)
Joseph C. Graven
Kirk Michael Olson (Resident, Santa Ana Office)
Brett C. Drouet

References: Bank of America; Santa Monica Business Park, Santa Monica; California National Bank, Los Angeles; First Republic, Los Angeles.

For full biographical listings, see the Martindale-Hubbell Law Directory

*SANTA ROSA,** Sonoma Co.

ABBEY, WEITZENBERG, HOFFMAN & EMERY, A PROFESSIONAL CORPORATION (AV)

1105 North Dutton Avenue, P.O. Box 1566, 95402
Telephone: 707-542-5050
Telecopier: 707-542-2589
Email: info@abbeylaw.com

W. Barton Weitzenberg
Patrick W. Emery

Representative Clients: Exchange Bank of Santa Rosa; Westamerica Bank; Northwestern Title Security Co.; Geyser Peak Winery; Santa Rosa City School District; Sonoma National Bank; Arrowood Vineyards & Winery; Friedman Bros. Hardware, Inc.; Bank of Lake County; Lasercraft, Inc.

For full biographical listings, see the Martindale-Hubbell Law Directory

TORRANCE, Los Angeles Co.

AGNEW & BRUSAVICH (AV)

20355 Hawthorne Boulevard, 90503
Telephone: 310-793-1400
Facsimile: 310-793-1499
Email: agnewbru@ix.netcom.com *URL:* http://www.agnew-brusavich.com

Gerald E. Agnew, Jr.
Bruce M. Brusavich

ASSOCIATES

Susan E. Hargrove
Christopher A. Kall

For full biographical listings, see the Martindale-Hubbell Law Directory

EDWARD J. DEASON (AV)

(Formerly Martin & Deason)
Del Amo Financial Center, 21515 Hawthorne Boulevard, Suite 1000, 90503
Telephone: 310-792-2175
Fax: 310-792-2176
URL: http://www.lawyers.com/ejdlaw

For full biographical listings, see the Martindale-Hubbell Law Directory

*VENTURA,** Ventura Co.

LAW OFFICES OF FREDERICK H. BYSSHE, JR. (AV)

10 South California Street, 93001
Telephone: 805-648-3224
Fax: 805-653-0267
Email: bysshe@west.net *URL:* http://www.lawyers.com/bysshelaw

Terence Geoghegan

For full biographical listings, see the Martindale-Hubbell Law Directory

ELLISON & HINKLE, A PROFESSIONAL LAW CORPORATION (AV)

5550 Telegraph Road, P.O. Box 6130, 93006
Telephone: 805-656-4223
Fax: 805-656-4924
URL: http://www.lawyers.com/ellisonhinkle

(See Next Column)

ELLISON & HINKLE A PROFESSIONAL LAW CORPORATION, *Ventura—Continued*

David R. Ellison | Thomas L. Hinkle

For full biographical listings, see the Martindale-Hubbell Law Directory

TAYLOR McCORD, A LAW CORPORATION (AV)

721 East Main Street, P.O. Box 1477, 93002
Telephone: 805-648-4700
Email: vtafamlaw@aol.com

Richard L. Taylor | Robert L. McCord, Jr.
David L. Praver

Patrick Cherry | Susan D. Siple
Rebbecca F. Calderwood

LEGAL SUPPORT PERSONNEL
PARALEGALS

Stephanie Gibson | Diane Lovato
Adele Rubino (Certified Legal Assistant, California Advanced Specialist)

For full biographical listings, see the Martindale-Hubbell Law Directory

WHIPPLE AND VIELE, A PROFESSIONAL LAW CORPORATION (AV)

60 South California Street, 93001
Telephone: 805-643-8658; 643-8422
Fax: 805-653-6079

Edward A. Whipple

References: Wells Fargo Bank; American Commercial Bank.

For full biographical listings, see the Martindale-Hubbell Law Directory

WALNUT CREEK, Contra Costa Co.

CASPER, MEADOWS & SCHWARTZ, A PROFESSIONAL CORPORATION (AV)

California Plaza, 2121 North California Boulevard, Suite 1020, 94596
Telephone: 925-947-1147
Fax: 925-947-1131
Email: cms@cmslaw.com *URL:* http://www.cmslaw.com

Stan Casper | Michael D. Meadows
Andrew C. Schwartz | Larry E. Cook
Thomas A. Seaton

For full biographical listings, see the Martindale-Hubbell Law Directory

HINTON & ALFERT, A PROFESSIONAL CORPORATION (AV)

Suite 600, 1646 North California Boulevard, 94596-4113
Telephone: 925-932-6006
Fax: 925-932-3412
Email: ha@hintonandalfert.com *URL:* http://www.lawyers.com/hintonandalfert

Peter J. Hinton | Peter W. Alfert
Scott H. Z. Sumner

Elise Sanguinetti

For full biographical listings, see the Martindale-Hubbell Law Directory

WESTLAKE VILLAGE, Ventura Co.

R. THOMAS WIRE A PROFESSIONAL CORPORATION (AV)

4195 East Thousand Oaks Boulevard, Suite 201, 91362
Telephone: 805-497-1400
Telefax: 805-497-0101

R. Thomas Wire

For full biographical listings, see the Martindale-Hubbell Law Directory

WOODLAND HILLS, Los Angeles Co.

DIAMOND & SCHARNBERGER (AV)

5303 Comercio Way, 91364
Telephone: 818-999-2144
Fax: 818-999-6845
Email: staff@lawcase.com *URL:* http://www.staff@lawcase.com

Robert L. Diamond | Laurence M. Scharnberger
Kenneth D. Zwicker

For full biographical listings, see the Martindale-Hubbell Law Directory

COLORADO

*BOULDER,** Boulder Co.

COOK & LEE, P.C. (AV)

5390 Manhattan Circle, 2nd Floor, 80303
Telephone: 303-543-1000
Fax: 303-543-8582
Email: cookleepc@bewellnet.com

Stephen H. Cook | Larry D. Lee

Robert K. Reimann

For full biographical listings, see the Martindale-Hubbell Law Directory

FRENCH & STONE, P.C. (AV)

720 Pearl Street, 80302
Telephone: 303-449-3891
Fax: 303-449-3992

Joseph C. French | David M. Haynes
Mark M. Haynes

Reference: Bank of Boulder.

For full biographical listings, see the Martindale-Hubbell Law Directory

McCORMICK AND CHRISTOPH, P.C. (AV)

1406 Pearl Street, Suite 200, 80302-5307
Telephone: 303-443-2281
Fax: 303-443-2862

G. Paul McCormick | James R. Christoph

For full biographical listings, see the Martindale-Hubbell Law Directory

MILLER AND HARRISON, LLC (AV)

2305 Broadway, 80304-4106
Telephone: 303-449-2830
Fax: 303-449-2198

MEMBERS OF FIRM

Robert Bruce Miller | David B. Harrison

ASSOCIATE

Joan Clifford

Reference: Norwest Bank.

For full biographical listings, see the Martindale-Hubbell Law Directory

PURVIS, GRAY & GORDON, LLP (AV)

The Exeter Building, Suite 501, 1050 Walnut Street, 80302
Telephone: 303-442-3366
Fax: 303-440-3688
Email: info@pgglaw.com *URL:* http://www.lawyers.com/purvisgrayschuetze&gordon
Denver, Colorado Office: 303 East 17th Avenue, Suite 700.
Telephone: 303-860-1888.

MEMBERS OF FIRM

William R. Gray | John A. Purvis
Glen F. Gordon

For full biographical listings, see the Martindale-Hubbell Law Directory

TRINE & METCALF, P.C. (AV)

1435 Arapahoe Avenue, 80302-6390
Telephone: 303-442-0173
Fax: 303-443-7677
Email: firm@trine-metcalf.com *URL:* http://www.trine-metcalf.com

William A. Trine | J. Conard Metcalf

T. Michael Kennedy

Reference: Norwest Bank of Boulder.

For full biographical listings, see the Martindale-Hubbell Law Directory

BROOMFIELD, Boulder Co.

SCHADEN, KATZMAN, LAMPERT & McCLUNE (AV)

11870 Airport Way, 80021-2555
Telephone: 303-465-3663
Facsimile: 303-465-3884
Email: SCHKATZLAM@aol.com *URL:* http://www.lawyers.com/schadenlaw
Troy, Michigan Office; 100 West Big Beaver Road. Suite 130. 48084.
Telephone: 248-258-4800.
Fax: 248-258-2825.

(See Next Column)

SCHADEN, KATZMAN, LAMPERT & McCLUNE—*Continued*

MEMBERS OF FIRM

Richard F. Schaden
David I. Katzman (Not admitted in CO)
Bruce A. Lampert
John D. McClune (Not admitted in CO)

ASSOCIATE

Kathleen M. Schaden

OF COUNSEL

Bruce O. Wilson (Not admitted in CO)

For full biographical listings, see the Martindale-Hubbell Law Directory

*COLORADO SPRINGS,** El Paso Co.

BELTZ, EDWARDS & SABO, L.L.P. (AV)

128 South Tejon, Suite 310, 80903
Telephone: 719-634-6620
Fax: 719-634-3142
Email: BES_LLP@aol.com *URL:* http://www.lawyers.com/beslaw
Other Colorado Springs, Colorado Office: 729 South Cascade, 80903.
Telephone: 719-473-4444.
Fax: 719-444-0186.

Daniel P. Edwards
W. Thomas Beltz
John W. Sabo, III

ASSOCIATE

Daniel A. West

Representative Clients: A.M.I. Industries, Inc.; Analytical Surveys, Inc.; A.C. Israel Enterprises, Inc.; Boddington Lumber Co., Inc.; Cardiovascular Surgeons of Colorado Springs, P.C.; Colorado Springs Radiologists, P.C.; Digital, Inc.; Music Semi-Conductors, Inc.; Schlage Lock Co.; Texas Instruments.

For full biographical listings, see the Martindale-Hubbell Law Directory

MELAT, PRESSMAN, EZELL & HIGBIE, LLP (AV)

711 South Tejon Street, 80903-4054
Telephone: 719-475-0304
Fax: 719-475-0242
Email: mpeh4@aol.com

MEMBERS OF FIRM

Justin R. Melat
Glenn S. Pressman
E. Steven Ezell
Alanson Higbie

ASSOCIATES

Rebecca A. Lorenz
Judith K. Funderburg

References: U.S. Bank; Colorado Bank-Exchange.

For full biographical listings, see the Martindale-Hubbell Law Directory

TEGTMEIER LAW FIRM, P.C. (AV)

518 North Nevada, Suite 200, 80903
Telephone: 719-473-5757
Telefax: 719-473-6767
Email: richard@worldclasslaw.com

Richard L. Tegtmeier

OF COUNSEL

Stephen A. Brunette

Reference: Norwest Bank of Colorado Springs and State Bank & Trust.

For full biographical listings, see the Martindale-Hubbell Law Directory

WITTMAN & McCORD (AV)

A Partnership including a Professional Corporation
Suite 320 UMB Bank Building, 5825 Delmonico Drive, 80919
Telephone: 719-590-9899
Fax: 719-590-9984
Email: wittcord-law@pcisys.net
Denver, Colorado Office: 10630 East Bethany Drive (Aurora), 80014.
Telephone: 303-337-4952.
Fax: 303-337-6165.

MEMBERS OF FIRM

Sherwin V. "Bud" Wittman, II, (P.C.)
Edward M. McCord, P.C.

ASSOCIATES

J. Bradley Hardman
Keith D. Vance

Representative Clients: Allstate Insurance Co.; Carolina Casualty Insurance Co.; E & O Professionals Insurance Co.; John Deere Transportation Insurance Co.; Motor Cargo Co.; Providian Auto & Home Insurance Co.; Safeco Insurance Co.; USAA Insurance Co.; USF & G Insurance Co.; Utica Mutual Insurance Co.

For full biographical listings, see the Martindale-Hubbell Law Directory

*DENVER,** Denver Co.

JOHN ASTUNO, JR. (AV)

1775 Sherman Street, Suite 1650, 80203
Telephone: 303-861-7636
Fax: 303-832-1405
Email: johnast@aol.com *URL:* http://www.lawyers.com/astonlaw

For full biographical listings, see the Martindale-Hubbell Law Directory

BEEM & MANN, PROFESSIONAL CORPORATION (AV)

One Norwest Center, Suite 3901, 1700 Lincoln Street, 80203
Telephone: 303-894-8100
Fax: 303-832-5010
Email: BeemMann@aol.com

Clifford L. Beem
Stuart Mann

OF COUNSEL

Virginia Elaine Kellogg
Patrick F. Kenney

A. Mark Isley

References: Norwest Bank Denver, N.A.; The Bank of Cherry Creek

For full biographical listings, see the Martindale-Hubbell Law Directory

BOGUE KOURY & MARYLANDER LLC (AV)

1401 17th Street, Suite 320, 80202
Telephone: 303-382-1990
Fax: 303-382-1982
URL: http://www.bkmllc.com
Email: bkmlaw@bkmllc.com *URL:* http://www.lawyers.com/bkmllc

Jeffrey A. Bogue
Victoria J. Koury
Grant Marylander

For full biographical listings, see the Martindale-Hubbell Law Directory

BUCHANAN, JURDEM & ZULAUF, P.C. (AV)

Eighteenth Street Atrium, 1621 18th Street, Suite 260, 80202
Telephone: 303-297-2277
Fax: 303-297-2233

Ross B. H. Buchanan
Scott Jurdem
Karen M. Zulauf

OF COUNSEL

James W. Buchanan

For full biographical listings, see the Martindale-Hubbell Law Directory

CHALAT LAW OFFICES, P.C. (AV)

1900 Grant Street, Suite 1050, 80203
Telephone: 303-861-1042
Toll Free: 800-221-5526
Facsimile: 303-861-0506
URL: http://www.lawyers.com/chalatlawoffices
Email: Jchalat@aol.com *URL:* http://www.chalatlaw.com

James H. Chalat
Linda J. Chalat

For full biographical listings, see the Martindale-Hubbell Law Directory

CORTEZ MACAULAY BERNHARDT & SCHUETZE LLC (AV)

1600 Broadway, Suite 1600, 80202
Telephone: 303-864-1000
Facsimile: 303-864-1111
URL: http://www.cmblaw.com

Miles Cortez
Christopher T. Macaulay
Susan Bernhardt
Robert A. Schuetze
David H. Goldberg
Marian L. Carlson
Richard P. R. Cohn

For full biographical listings, see the Martindale-Hubbell Law Directory

EWING & EWING, P.C. (AV)

8400 East Prentice Avenue, Suite 1115 (Englewood), 80111
Telephone: 303-771-3300
Fax: 303-793-3321
Email: ewinglaw@aol.com

Robert Craig Ewing
Mary Ewing

Julie A. Trent

OF COUNSEL

Laurence B. James

For full biographical listings, see the Martindale-Hubbell Law Directory

Denver—Continued

THE LAW FIRM OF EDWIN A. HOWE, P.C. (AV)

950 South Cherry Street, Suite 1502, 80246
Telephone: 303-756-5060
Fax: 303-756-5114
URL: http://www.lawyers.com/howelaw

Edwin A. Howe, II

LEGAL SUPPORT PERSONNEL

Julie Rotenberg (Office Administrator)

For full biographical listings, see the Martindale-Hubbell Law Directory

KELLER, WAHLBERG & MORRATO, P.C. (AV)

1050 Seventeenth Street, Suite 1440, 80265
Telephone: 303-571-5302
Fax: 303-571-1806
Email: kwmpc@aol.com *URL:* http://www.lawyers.com/kwmlaw

Alex Stephen Keller (1928-1996) Stephen W. Wahlberg
James J. Morrato

Christopher R. Riker Daniel A. Sloane

Reference: Colorado Business Bank.

For full biographical listings, see the Martindale-Hubbell Law Directory

THE LEVENTHAL LAW FIRM, P.C. (AV)

950 South Cherry Street, Suite 600, 80246
Telephone: 303-759-9945
Fax: 303-759-9692
Email: office@leventhal-law.com

Jim Leventhal Natalie Brown
Beth L. Krulewitch

James E. Puga Timothy G. Buxton

Reference: Vectra Bank.

For full biographical listings, see the Martindale-Hubbell Law Directory

PURVIS, GRAY & GORDON, LLP (AV)

303 East 17th Avenue, Suite 700, 80203
Telephone: 303-860-1888
Email: info@pgglaw.com *URL:* http://www.lawyers.com/purvisgrayschuetze&gordon
Boulder, Colorado Office: The Exeter Building, Suite 501, 1050 Walnut Street.
Telephone: 303-442-3366.
Fax: 303-440-3688.

MEMBERS OF FIRM

William R. Gray John A. Purvis
Glen F. Gordon

For full biographical listings, see the Martindale-Hubbell Law Directory

RICHMAN & JONES, P.C. (AV)

1600 Broadway, Suite 1900, 80202
Telephone: 303-830-1717
Facsimile: 303-830-1746

Alan E. Richman Michael W. Jones

For full biographical listings, see the Martindale-Hubbell Law Directory

SAWAYA, ROSE, ROBERTS & SAWAYA, P.C. (AV)

1650 Emerson Street, 80218
Telephone: 303-839-1650
Fax: 303-832-1128
URL: http://www.sawaya-rose.com
Email: sawayarose@sawaya-rose.com *URL:* http://www.lawyers.com/sawaya-rose

Michael G. Sawaya Thomas J. Roberts
Richard B. Rose Dianne L. Sawaya

Representative Client: Sears, Roebuck and Co.
Reference: Norwest Bank Denver.

For full biographical listings, see the Martindale-Hubbell Law Directory

SPRINGER & STEINBERG, A PROFESSIONAL CORPORATION (AV)

Suite 1950, 1600 Broadway, 80202
Telephone: 303-861-2800
Fax: 303-832-7116

Jeffrey A. Springer William R. Kelso
Harvey A. Steinberg Amy Mandel Springer
Patricia J. Donahue

Reference: Norwest Bank of Denver.

For full biographical listings, see the Martindale-Hubbell Law Directory

WITTMAN & MCCORD (AV)

A Partnership including a Professional Corporation
10630 East Bethany Drive (Aurora), 80014
Telephone: 303-337-4952
Fax: 303-337-6165
Email: wittcord-law@pcisys.net
Colorado Springs, Colorado Office: Suite 320 UMB Bank Building, 5825 Delmonico Drive.
Telephone: 719-590-9899.
Fax: 719-590-9984.

MEMBERS OF FIRM

Sherwin V. "Bud" Wittman, II, (P.C.) Edward M. McCord, P.C.

ASSOCIATES

J. Bradley Hardman Keith D. Vance

Representative Clients: Allstate Insurance Co.; Carolina Casualty Insurance Co.; E & O Professionals Insurance Co.; John Deere Transportation Insurance Co.; Motor Cargo Co.; Providian Auto & Home Insurance Co.; Safeco Insurance Co.; USAA Insurance Co.; USF & G Insurance Co.; Utica Mutual Insurance Co.

For full biographical listings, see the Martindale-Hubbell Law Directory

ENGLEWOOD, Arapahoe Co.

SALMON, LAMPERT & CLOR, PROFESSIONAL CORPORATION (AV)

Salmon Law Building, (I-25 at East Belleview) 7450 East Progress Place, 80111
Telephone: 303-771-9900
Toll Free in Colorado: 1-800-547-9055
Fax: 303-773-6843
Breckenridge, Colorado Office: Briar Rose House, 213 Briar Rose Lane.
Telephone: 1-800-547-9055

John G. Salmon Brian J. Lampert
Penelope Clor

Francine R. Salazar Barbara Barrows Ezyk
S. Jane Mitchell Martha Merrill-Hall

For full biographical listings, see the Martindale-Hubbell Law Directory

THOMAS J. TOMAZIN, P.C. (AV)

Suite 200, 5655 South Yosemite, 80111
Telephone: 303-771-1900
FAX: 303-793-0923

Thomas J. Tomazin

Representative Clients: Design Drywall Specialities; Elm Contracting; Kumpf Lincoln Mercury, Inc.; Omni Business Brokers, Inc.; Contract Design Services, Inc.; American Natural Gas Corp.; Sonex Enterprises, Inc.; Am West Energy, Inc.; Mountain States Asphalt Paving, Inc.
Reference: Guaranty Bank & Trust Co.

For full biographical listings, see the Martindale-Hubbell Law Directory

*FORT COLLINS,** Larimer Co.

THE PICKERING LAW FIRM, P.C. (AV Ⓣ)

303 East Mountain Avenue Suite 201, 80524
Telephone: 970-482-1977
Fax: 970-482-1670
Email: RGPickering@msn.com *URL:* http://www.lawyers.com/pickering

Robert G. Pickering

For full biographical listings, see the Martindale-Hubbell Law Directory

LAKEWOOD, Jefferson Co.

POLIDORI, GEROME, FRANKLIN AND JACOBSON, L.L.C. (AV)

Suite 300, 550 South Wadsworth Boulevard, 80226
Telephone: 303-936-3300
Fax: 303-936-0125

Dennis J. Jacobson

For full biographical listings, see the Martindale-Hubbell Law Directory

*LAMAR,** Prowers Co.

JOHN GEHLHAUSEN, P.C. (AV)

200 South Fifth Street, Drawer 1079, 81052
Telephone: 719-336-9071
Fax: 719-336-9617
URL: http://www.tractorlaw.com

John Gehlhausen

(See Next Column)

JOHN GEHLHAUSEN, P.C.—*Continued*

Curtis L. Fleming

For full biographical listings, see the Martindale-Hubbell Law Directory

WESTMINSTER, Adams Co.

CIANCIO & JONSEN, P.C. (AV)

12000 North Pecos Street Suite 200, 80234-2079
Telephone: 303-451-0300
Fax: 303-280-0614
Email: ciancio@csn.net
Email: jonsen@csn.net

Gene A. Ciancio
Eric R. Jonsen

Cynthia M. Ciancio

For full biographical listings, see the Martindale-Hubbell Law Directory

CONNECTICUT

*BRIDGEPORT,** Fairfield Co.

BAI, POLLOCK AND COYNE, P.C. (AV)

Park City Plaza, 10 Middle Street, P.O. Box 1978, 06604
Telephone: 203-366-7991
Fax: 203-366-4723
Email: bpc@snet.net

Arnold J. Bai (1931-1992)
Paul E. Pollock
James E. Coyne
Jeffrey A. Blueweiss
Garie J. Mulcahey
Raymond J. Plouffe, Jr.
Philip F. von Kuhn
Madonna A. Sacco
Michael S. Lynch
David J. Robertson
Edward P. Brady III

Gaileen A. Kaufman
Kevin S. Coyne
Colleen D. Fries
Neal P. Rogan
Louis A. Annecchino
Robert J. Weber, III
Heidi Marie Priwall
Anthony D. Sutton
Kevin J. Curseaden

For full biographical listings, see the Martindale-Hubbell Law Directory

ELSTEIN AND ELSTEIN, P.C. (AV)

Suite 400 1087 Broad Street, 06604-4231
Telephone: 203-367-4421
Telecopier: 203-366-8615

Henry Elstein
Bruce L. Elstein

For full biographical listings, see the Martindale-Hubbell Law Directory

KOSKOFF, KOSKOFF & BIEDER, P.C. (AV)

350 Fairfield Avenue, 06604
Telephone: 203-336-4421
Fax: 203-368-3244
Email: KKB@KOSKOFF.com
Stamford, Connecticut Office: 1172 Bedford Street.
Telephone: 203-325-3686.
Danbury, Connecticut Office: 1 Moss Avenue.
Telephone: 203-792-7100.

Michael P. Koskoff
John D. Jessep
Christopher D. Bernard
Michael A. Stratton
Rosalind J. Koskoff

Joel Thomas Faxon

OF COUNSEL

James Wu

For full biographical listings, see the Martindale-Hubbell Law Directory

LESSER & SOBEL, P.C. (AV)

1000 Lafayette Boulevard, 06604
Telephone: 203-336-1811
Facsimile: 203-334-8069

Robert K. Lesser
Stanton H. Lesser
Paul A. Sobel
Neil A. Lieberthal

For full biographical listings, see the Martindale-Hubbell Law Directory

LAWRENCE J. MERLY (AV)

76 Lyon Terrace, 06604
Telephone: 203-333-1353
Fax: 203-332-7984

Reference: Peoples Savings Bank.

For full biographical listings, see the Martindale-Hubbell Law Directory

WILLIAMS, COONEY & SHEEHY (AV)

One Lafayette Circle, 06604
Telephone: 203-331-0888
Telecopier: 203-331-0896
Email: wilcooshee@aol.com

MEMBERS OF FIRM

Ronald D. Williams
Robert J. Cooney
Edward Maum Sheehy
Dion W. Moore
Ronald D. Williams, Jr.
Francis A. Smith, Jr. (1951-1989)

Suzannah Kim Nigro
Michael Richard Brandt

Representative Clients: Connecticut Medical Insurance Co.; Zimmer Manufacturing Co.; Textron-Lycoming; The Stop & Shop Companies, Inc.; Fleet Bank; Podiatry Insurance Company of America; Town of Easton, Conn.

For full biographical listings, see the Martindale-Hubbell Law Directory

GREENWICH, Fairfield Co.

WAYNE D. EFFRON, P.C. (AV)

165 West Putnam Avenue, P.O. Box 499, 06830
Telephone: 203-622-1160
Fax: 203-622-4004
Email: effronlaw@effronlaw.com

Wayne D. Effron
Brian M. Yard
Allen Gary Palmer
Kristen M. Smith

OF COUNSEL

Joel M. Kaye

For full biographical listings, see the Martindale-Hubbell Law Directory

*HARTFORD,** Hartford Co.

JACKSON, O'KEEFE AND PHELAN (AV)

36 Russ Street, 06106-1571
Telephone: 860-278-4040
Fax: 860-527-2500
West Hartford, Connecticut Office: 62 LaSalle Road.
Telephone: 860-521-7500.
Fax: 860-561-5399.
Bethlehem, Connecticut Office: 423 Munger Lane. Telephone/
Fax: 203-266-5255.

MEMBERS OF FIRM

Jay W. Jackson
Andrew J. O'Keefe
Denise Martino Phelan
Matthew J. O'Keefe
Michael E. Riley
Peter K. O'Keefe
Philip R. Dunn, Jr.
Kathryn M. Cunningham
Joseph M. Busher, Jr.
Kristen E. Scholhamer

Representative Clients: Travelers Aetna Property Casualty Co.; ITT Hartford; Liberty Mutual Insurance Co.; Connecticut Medical Insurance Co.

For full biographical listings, see the Martindale-Hubbell Law Directory

KENNY, BRIMMER, MELLEY & MAHONEY (AV)

5 Grand Street, 06106
Telephone: 860-527-4226
FAX: 860-527-0214

Joseph P. Kenny (1920-1993)

MEMBERS OF FIRM

William J. Melley, III
Richard C. Mahoney
Anita M. Varunes
Dennis F. McCarthy

ASSOCIATES

Shannon K. McCarthy
Flora Pizzoferrato

OF COUNSEL

Leslie R. Brimmer

For full biographical listings, see the Martindale-Hubbell Law Directory

*NEW HAVEN,** New Haven Co.

GALLAGHER & CALISTRO (AV)

1377 Boulevard, P.O. Box 1925, 06509
Telephone: 203-624-4165
Fax: 203-865-5598

(See Next Column)

GALLAGHER & CALISTRO, *New Haven—Continued*

William F. Gallagher
Roger B. Calistro
Cynthia C. Bott
Barbara L. Cox
Kurt D. Koehler
Thomas J. Airone

For full biographical listings, see the Martindale-Hubbell Law Directory

JACOBS & JACOBS (AV)

Granite Square, 700 State Street, 3rd Floor, 06511
Telephone: 203-777-2300
Fax: 203-787-5628
Email: JACOBSLAW1@AOL.com

MEMBERS OF FIRM

Israel J. Jacobs (1918-1963)
Stanley A. Jacobs
Bruce D. Jacobs
Carol Wolven
Irene Prosky Jacobs
Charles R. Douthat

Kevin Ryder

Reference: BankBoston.

For full biographical listings, see the Martindale-Hubbell Law Directory

KENNEDY, JOHNSON, D'ELIA & GILLOOLY (AV)

Long Wharf Maritime Center, 545 Long Wharf Drive, 06511
Telephone: 203-865-8430
Fax: 203-865-5345
Email: kennedyjoh@aol.com

MEMBERS OF FIRM

David H. Johnson
John J. Kennedy, Jr.
John J. D'Elia
Dennis Gillooly

ASSOCIATES

Robert L. Schwab
Stephanie Z. Roberge

Reference: Bank of Boston - Connecticut.

For full biographical listings, see the Martindale-Hubbell Law Directory

ROSEN & DOLAN, P.C. (AV)

400 Orange Street, 06511
Telephone: 203-787-3513
Fax: 203-789-1605
Email: davidrosen@snet.net
Email: sapincus@snet.net

David N. Rosen

Stephen M. Pincus

Reference: Peoples Bank.

For Complete List of Firm Personnel, See General Section

For full biographical listings, see the Martindale-Hubbell Law Directory

NEW LONDON, New London Co.

THE REARDON LAW FIRM, P.C. (AV)

160 Hempstead Street, Drawer 1430, 06320
Telephone: 860-442-0444
Telecopier: 860-444-6445
Email: reardonlaw@aol.com *URL:* http://www.reardonlaw.com

Robert I. Reardon, Jr.
Mark A. Dubois
Scott D. Camassar
Cynthia W. Sheppard
Gary W. Huebner

LEGAL SUPPORT PERSONNEL

Bette B. Beam (Legal Administrator)
Kimberly J. Friedel (Paralegal)
Rhonda K. Bourgeois (Paralegal)
Kyle E. Wininger (Paralegal)

For full biographical listings, see the Martindale-Hubbell Law Directory

STAMFORD, Fairfield Co.

CACACE, TUSCH & SANTAGATA (AV)

777 Summer Street, P.O. Box 15859, 06901-0859
Telephone: 203-327-2000
Telecopier: 203-353-3392
Email: lawcts@aol.com

MEMBERS OF FIRM

Michael J. Cacace
Mark P. Santagata
Paul T. Tusch
Richard S. Fisher

OF COUNSEL

Kenneth A. DellaRocco
Eric D. Grayson

ASSOCIATES

Edward F. Nemchek
Alice Ann Fitzpatrick
Ronald E. Kowalski II
Aamina Ahmad
Demaris Page Hetrick
Patrick L. Poeschl

(See Next Column)

LEGAL SUPPORT PERSONNEL

Eva L. Chan
Cynthia L. Mammone

For full biographical listings, see the Martindale-Hubbell Law Directory

CASPER & DE TOLEDO LLC (AV)

1111 Summer Street, 06905
Telephone: 203-325-8600
Fax: 203-323-5970
Email: casperdetoledo.com *URL:* http://www.casperdetoledo.com

Stewart M. Casper
Victoria de Toledo

Gwendolyn Field Noto
Anastasios T. Savvaides

For full biographical listings, see the Martindale-Hubbell Law Directory

LAW OFFICES OF MICHAEL GENE CLEAR (AV)

184 Atlantic Street, P.O. Box 3292, 06905
Telephone: 203-973-0240
Facsimile: 203-973-0244
Email: MCLEAR9948@aol.com

For full biographical listings, see the Martindale-Hubbell Law Directory

CURTIS, BRINCKERHOFF & BARRETT, P.C. (AV)

666 Summer Street, 06901-1416
Telephone: 203-324-6777
Telecopier: 203-324-9621
Email: info@curtisbb.com

T. Ward Cleary (1916-1988)
Frederick M. Tobin
John Wayne Fox
Ward Frank Cleary
James D'Alton Murphy
Randolph T. Lovallo

OF COUNSEL

John D. Hertz
Jane F. Donovan
Richard L. Brinckerhoff
Patricia M. Gaug

Susan L. Stratton
Derek Gilman
Michael P. Murray
John J. Louizos

Counsel for: The F. A. Bartlett Tree Expert Co.; Town of Darien; Miller Automobile Corp.; Bolliger, Inc.; Titan Sports; People's Bank, Bridgeport; Fleet Bank; Federal Deposit Insurance Co.; William Pitt Foundation; Wood Logan Associates.

For full biographical listings, see the Martindale-Hubbell Law Directory

PIAZZA & PICKEL (AV)

112 Prospect Street, P.O. Box 15390, 06901
Telephone: 203-348-2465
Fax: 203-964-9509
Email: aap@piazza-pickel.com *URL:* http://www.piazza-pickel.com

Anthony A. Piazza
Alan Scott Pickel

ASSOCIATES

Tara C.F. Ryan
Michelle M. Napoli

For full biographical listings, see the Martindale-Hubbell Law Directory

SILVER, GOLUB & TEITELL LLP (AV)

184 Atlantic Street, P.O. Box 389, 06904
Telephone: 203-325-4491
Fax: 203-325-3769
Email: silvergolubteitell.com *URL:* http://www.sgtlaw.com

MEMBERS OF FIRM

Richard A. Silver
David S. Golub
Ernest F. Teitell
Patricia M. Haugh (1942-1988)
Elaine T. Silver
John D. Josel
Mario DiNatale
Jonathan M. Levine

Marilyn J. Ramos
Richard H. Greenwood
Mary G. Curry
Kathleen L. Brandt
Paul A. Slager (Not admitted in CT)
Brad C. Gustafson

For full biographical listings, see the Martindale-Hubbell Law Directory

WOFSEY, ROSEN, KWESKIN & KURIANSKY, LLP (AV)

600 Summer Street, 06901
Telephone: 203-327-2300
Fax: 203-967-9273

MEMBERS OF FIRM

Abraham Wofsey (1915-1944)
Michael Wofsey (1927-1951)
David M. Rosen (1926-1967)
Julius B. Kuriansky (1952-1992)
Sydney C. Kweskin (1946-1998)
Monroe Silverman
Howard C. Kaplan
Edward M. Kweskin
David M. Cohen
Marshall Goldberg
Stephen A. Finn
Judith Rosenberg

(See Next Column)

WOFSEY, ROSEN, KWESKIN & KURIANSKY LLP—*Continued*

MEMBERS OF FIRM (Continued)

Mark H. Henderson
Matthew J. Forstadt
Steven D. Grushkin
Steven M. Frederick

OF COUNSEL

Saul Kwartin
Emanuel Margolis
Anthony R. Lorenzo

SPECIAL COUNSEL

Day R. Shields

ASSOCIATES

Joseph Brachfeld
William A. Harrison
Eric M. Higgins
Daniel M. Young
Angelo A. Ziotas

Representative Clients: Banque Paribas; Benenson Realty; Cellular Information Systems, Inc.; The Chase Manhattan Bank; First County Bank; Hartford Provision Co.; Louis Dreyfus Corp.; Norwalk Federation of Teachers; People's Bank; Ridgeway Shopping Center.

For full biographical listings, see the Martindale-Hubbell Law Directory

*VERNON,** Tolland Co.

FLAHERTY, MEISLER & COURTNEY (AV)

30 Lafayette Square, Suite 116, 06066-4554
Telephone: 860-872-7200
Fax: 860-875-6594
Email: FMACATTY@aol.com

MEMBERS OF FIRM

Leo B. Flaherty Jr. (1923-1998)
Arthur P. Meisler
Joseph D. Courtney

ASSOCIATE

Elizabeth C. Foran

Reference: Savings Bank of Rockville.

For full biographical listings, see the Martindale-Hubbell Law Directory

WESTPORT, Fairfield Co.

LAW OFFICES OF PAUL J. PACIFICO (AV)

25 Ford Road, Suite 2, 06880
Telephone: 203-221-8066
Fax: 203-222-4833

For full biographical listings, see the Martindale-Hubbell Law Directory

RUTKIN AND OLDHAM, L.L.C (AV)

321 Riverside Avenue, P.O. Box 295, 06881
Telephone: 203-227-7301
Fax: 203-222-9295
Email: aradvocate@aol.com
Greenwich Office: 125 Mason Street, 06830.
Telephone: 203-869-7277.

Arnold H. Rutkin
Sarah S. Oldham

OF COUNSEL

Kathleen A. Hogan

For full biographical listings, see the Martindale-Hubbell Law Directory

DELAWARE

*WILMINGTON,** New Castle Co.

CASARINO, CHRISTMAN & SHALK (AV)

Suite 1220, 222 Delaware Avenue, P.O. Box 1276, 19899
Telephone: 302-594-4500
Telecopier: 302-594-4509
URL: http://www.casarino.com

MEMBERS OF FIRM

Stephen P. Casarino
Beth H. Christman
Colin M. Shalk
Donald M. Ransom

Kenneth M. Doss
Stacey L. Cummings
Diane M. Willette
Thomas P. Leff

For full biographical listings, see the Martindale-Hubbell Law Directory

THE LYONS LAW FIRM (AV)

1526 Gilpin Avenue, P.O. Box 579, 19806
Telephone: 302-777-5698
Fax: 302-777-5051
Email: elyons@lyonslaw.com

(See Next Column)

Edmund Daniel Lyons
David J. Lyons

For full biographical listings, see the Martindale-Hubbell Law Directory

POTTER ANDERSON & CORROON LLP (AV)

Hercules Plaza, 1313 N. Market Street, P.O. Box 951, 19899-0951
Telephone: 302-984-6000
Fax: 302-658-1192
URL: http://www.attys.pacdelaware.com

MEMBERS OF FIRM

Daniel F. Wolcott, Jr.
Somers S. Price, Jr.
Kathleen Furey McDonough

ASSOCIATES

Todd L. Goodman
Deborah A. Cuoco

Representative Clients: Conrail; National Railroad Passenger Corp.; General Motors Corp.; Chrysler Corp.; U.S. Mineral Products Co.; Boise Cascade Corp.; Harley Davidson; Ford-New Holland, Inc.; Mazda Motor of America, Inc.

For Complete List of Firm Personnel, See General Section

For full biographical listings, see the Martindale-Hubbell Law Directory

SMITH, KATZENSTEIN & FURLOW LLP (AV)

The Corporate Plaza, 800 Delaware Avenue, P.O. Box 410, 19899
Telephone: 302-652-8400
Fax: 302-652-8405
Email: info@skfdelaware.com *URL:* http://www.SKFDelaware.com

MEMBERS OF FIRM

Robert J. Katzenstein
Laurence V. Cronin

Kathleen M. Miller

For Complete List of Firm Personnel, See General Section

For full biographical listings, see the Martindale-Hubbell Law Directory

DISTRICT OF COLUMBIA

WASHINGTON, D.C. Co.

BAUM, HEDLUND, ARISTEI, GUILFORD & DOWNEY, A PROFESSIONAL CORPORATION (AV)

1250 24th Street, N.W., Suite 300, 20037
Telephone: 202-466-0513; 800-827-0097
Fax: 202-466-0527
Email: bhagd@bhagd.com *URL:* http://www.bhagd.com
Los Angeles, California Office: Suite 950, 12100 Wilshire Boulevard.
Telephones: 310-207-3233; 800-827-0087.
Facsimile: 310-820-7444.

Cara J. Luther

OF COUNSEL

Mary F. Schiavo

For full biographical listings, see the Martindale-Hubbell Law Directory

LAW OFFICES OF NORMAN L. BLUMENFELD (AV)

Suite 901, 1001 Connecticut Avenue, N.W., 20036
Telephone: 202-223-0433
Fax: 202-835-1159

OF COUNSEL

Richard J. Byrd

For full biographical listings, see the Martindale-Hubbell Law Directory

CHAIKIN & SHERMAN, P.C. (AV)

The Law Building, 1232 Seventeenth Street, N.W., 20036
Telephone: 202-659-8600
Fax: 202-659-8680
Email: DCLAW@CS.COM
Rockville, Maryland Office: 51 Monroe Street, 18th Floor.
Telephone: 301-588-5151.
Fax: 202-659-8680.
Falls Church, Virginia Office: 5673 Columbia Pike, Suite 101.
Telephone: 202-659-8600.
Fax: 202-659-8680.

Donald J. Chaikin
Ira Sherman

Joseph Cammarata
Allan M. Siegel
Neil Florin
Barry I. Buchman
Garrett V. Williams

(See Next Column)

CHAIKIN & SHERMAN P.C., *Washington—Continued*

OF COUNSEL
Silverio Coy

For full biographical listings, see the Martindale-Hubbell Law Directory

COALE, COOLEY, LIETZ, MCINERNY & BROADUS, A PROFESSIONAL CORPORATION (AV)
818 Connecticut Avenue, N.W., Suite 857, 20006
Telephone: 202-887-4770
Facsimile: 202-887-4778

John P. Coale (A Professional Corporation)
Diane E. Cooley
David K. Lietz
Julia Wernett McInerny
Charlsa (Sandy) Broadus

Deborah St. Jean
Joseph Coale (Not admitted in DC)

For full biographical listings, see the Martindale-Hubbell Law Directory

KOONZ, MCKENNEY, JOHNSON, DEPAOLIS & LIGHTFOOT (AV)
Suite 500, 2020 K Street, N.W., 20006
Telephone: 202-659-5500
Fax: 202-785-3719
Email: dc@koonz.com *URL:* http://www.koonz.com
Greenbelt, Maryland Office: 6411 Ivy Lane, Suite 204.
Telephone: 301-345-5700.
Fax: 301-474-5578.
Falls Church, Virginia Office: Suite 400, George Mason Square, 103 W. Broad Street.
Telephone: 703-237-9300.
Fax: 703-533-5974.

Joseph H. Koonz, Jr.
Carolyn McKenney
Roger C. Johnson
Peter C. DePaolis (Resident at Falls Church, Virginia Office)
Mark J. Brice
William P. Lightfoot, Jr.
Marc Fiedler
Karen A. Crist (Resident at Falls Church, Virginia Office)
Paulette E. Chapman
David M. Schloss
Keith W. Donahoe (Resident at Greenbelt, Maryland Office)
William A. Musto (Resident at Falls Church, Virginia Office)
Julie H. Heiden (Resident at Falls Church, Virginia Office)
Harold E. Brazil
Daniel S. Kozma
Matthew H. Swyers (Resident at Falls Church, Virginia Office)
Christopher R. Banker (Resident, Greenbelt, Maryland Office)
Frank R. Kearney
Douglas K. Allston, Jr. (Resident at Greenbelt, Maryland Office)
Stephen J. Williams (Resident at Greenbelt, Maryland Office)
Kate H. Shephard
Scott M. Perry

For full biographical listings, see the Martindale-Hubbell Law Directory

AARON M. LEVINE & ASSOCIATES (AV)
1320 - 19th Street, N.W., 20036
Telephone: 202-833-8040
Fax: 202-833-8046
Email: lawkunst@aol.com

Brandon J. Levine
Renee L. Robinson-Meyer

For full biographical listings, see the Martindale-Hubbell Law Directory

JACK H. OLENDER AND ASSOCIATES, P.C. (AV)
888 17th Street, N.W., 4th Floor, 20006
Telephone: 202-879-7777
Fax: 202-393-2245
URL: http://www.olender.com
Email: jhopc@olender.com *URL:* http://www.lawyers.com/olenderlaw

Jack H. Olender

Harlow R. Case
Gary S. Freeman
Sandra H. Robinson
Kim Keenan Solomon
Narda M. Newby
Elizabeth Jesukiewicz Frey
Melissa Rhea

OF COUNSEL
Robert S. Chabon (Not admitted in DC)

For full biographical listings, see the Martindale-Hubbell Law Directory

PANGIA & HANSEN (AV)
1717 N Street, N.W., 20036
Telephone: 202-955-6450
Fax: 202-955-9444
Email: bchansen@erols.com *URL:* http://www.lawyers.com/aviation

MEMBERS OF FIRM
Michael J. Pangia
Barry C. Hansen

(See Next Column)

ASSOCIATE
Harold E. Rambo, Jr.

For full biographical listings, see the Martindale-Hubbell Law Directory

PAULSON & NACE (AV)
1814 N Street, N.W., 20036
Telephone: 202-463-1999
Fax: 202-223-6824
Email: p&n@lawtort.com *URL:* http://www.lawyers.com/lawtort
Martinsburg, West Virginia Office: 1444 Edwin Miller Boulevard, P.O. Box 1938, 25402.
Telephone: 888-529-2628.

MEMBERS OF FIRM
Richard S. Paulson (1928-1986)
Barry J. Nace

ASSOCIATE
James A. Ferguson

OF COUNSEL
Irving R. M. Panzer

For full biographical listings, see the Martindale-Hubbell Law Directory

FLORIDA

*BARTOW,** Polk Co.

FROST & SAUNDERS, P.A. (AV)
395 South Central Avenue, P.O. Box 2188, 33830
Telephone: 941-533-0314; 800-533-0967
Telecopier: 941-533-8985
Email: jfrost1985@aol.com

John W. Frost, II
Thomas C. Saunders
Richard E. "Rick" Dantzler
John Marc Tamayo
Mark A. Sessums
Robert J. Aranda
Peter W. Van den Boom
Nicholas D. Zorn, Jr.

Reference: Community National Bank, Bartow.

For full biographical listings, see the Martindale-Hubbell Law Directory

BOCA RATON, Palm Beach Co.

LAW OFFICES OF CARTER & THOMAS LLP (AV)
1200 North Federal Highway, Suite 312, 33432
Telephone: 561-368-9900
Broward 954-427-0933
Fax: 561-368-0293
Email: carterboca@aol.com

John E. Carter
Donald Joseph Thomas

Colleen M. Stiger

For full biographical listings, see the Martindale-Hubbell Law Directory

GLICK & RETAMAR (AV)
Peninsula Plaza, 2424 North Federal Highway, Suite 460, 33431
Telephone: 561-391-0448
Fax: 561-391-6449
Email: lawboca@aol.com

Brian J. Glick
Richard E. Retamar

For full biographical listings, see the Martindale-Hubbell Law Directory

WEISS & HANDLER, P.A. (AV)
Suite 218A, One Boca Place, 2255 Glades Road, 33431-7313
Telephone: 561-997-9995
Broward: 954-421-5101
Palm Beach: 561-734-8008
Telecopier: 561-997-5280
Email: weisshand@aol.com
West Palm Beach, Florida Office: 505 South Flagler Drive, Suite 1331, 33401.
Telephone: 561-655-3433.
New York, NY Office: 45 Rockefeller Plaza, Suite 1501.
Telephone: 212-332-2900.

Howard I. Weiss
Henry B. Handler

Manuel R. Comras
Donald Feldman
William M. Franz
David K. Friedman
Carol A. Kartagener
Allison L. Kay
Bruce A. Harris
Howard M. Rudolph (Resident, West Palm Beach Office)
Stacy E. Welt

(See Next Column)

WEISS & HANDLER P.A.—*Continued*

OF COUNSEL

Malcolm L. Stein (Not admitted in FL)
Harry Winderman

For full biographical listings, see the Martindale-Hubbell Law Directory

ZAPPITELL & KAPRAL, P.A. (AV)

5355 Town Center Road Penthouse 1105, 33486
Telephone: 561-367-7200
Facsimile: 561-367-1155
Email: zk@bocaratonlaw.com *URL:* http://www.bocaratonlaw.com

David J. Zappitell
Stephen M. Kapral, Jr.

OF COUNSEL

Brenda H. Rosen
Joseph P. Wagoner

For full biographical listings, see the Martindale-Hubbell Law Directory

*BRADENTON,** Manatee Co.

GRIMES GOEBEL GRIMES HAWKINS & GLADFELTER, P.A. (AV)

The Professional Building, 1023 Manatee Avenue West, P.O. Box 1550, 34206
Telephone: 941-748-0151
Fax: 941-748-0158
Email: ggghg@gte.net
Tampa, Florida Office: Old Hyde Park Village, 1509 West Swann Avenue, Suite 275.
Telephone: 813-258-2557.
Fax: 813-258-2327.

Caleb J. Grimes
John D. Hawkins
William S. Galvano
Douglas A. Peebles

For full biographical listings, see the Martindale-Hubbell Law Directory

BRANDON, Hillsborough Co.

PILKA & ASSOCIATES, P.A. (AV)

213 Providence Road, 33511
Telephone: 813-653-3800
Facsimile: 813-651-0710
Mailing Address: P.O. Box 3470, Brandon, Florida, 33509-3470
Email: law@pilka.com

Daniel F. Pilka
John N. Jenkins

David A. Finlay
Mark E. Hager
Russell E. Klemm

OF COUNSEL

Robert A. Fraser
Scott F. Barnett
Joseph B. Donnelly
Veronica E. Donnelly

For full biographical listings, see the Martindale-Hubbell Law Directory

*CLEARWATER,** Pinellas Co.

ELIHU H. BERMAN, P.A. (AV)

509 South Greenwood Avenue, 33756
Telephone: 727-465-1977
Fax: 727-465-9593
Email: elihu@gte.net

Elihu H. Berman

OF COUNSEL

Marc A. B. Silverman

References: First Union Bank; South Trust Bank; AmSouth Bank.

For full biographical listings, see the Martindale-Hubbell Law Directory

CAREY & HILBERT (AV)

622 Bypass Drive, Suite 100, 33764
Telephone: 727-799-3900
Toll Free: 800-927-0400
Fax: 727-799-8181
Email: careyandhilbert@mindspring.com *URL:* http://www.careyhilbert.com
St. Petersburg Office: 360 Central Avenue, Suite 1490.
Telephone: 727-824-0771; 800-927-0400.
Fax: 727-896-7604.
Gainesville, Florida Office: 3520 N.W. 43rd Street. 32606.
Telephone: 352-372-2000.

Thomas W. Carey
James R. Hilbert, Jr.

ASSOCIATE

Jodi Leisure

(See Next Column)

OF COUNSEL

Leonard M. Vincenti
Hugh A. Richeson, Jr. (Resident, Gainesville Office)

For full biographical listings, see the Martindale-Hubbell Law Directory

JOHN D. FERNANDEZ, P.A. (AV)

918 Drew Street, 33755
Telephone: 727-461-4441
Fax: 727-442-4423
Email: jfernand@gate.net

John D. Fernandez

For full biographical listings, see the Martindale-Hubbell Law Directory

KWALL, SHOWERS & COLEMAN, P.A. (AV)

133 North Fort Harrison Avenue, 33755
Telephone: 727-441-4947
Telecopier: 727-447-3158
Email: kwall@worldnet.att.net *URL:* http://www.usalaw.com/adminlaw/

Louis Kwall
Gregory K. Showers
Sherwood S. (Flip) Coleman
Elizabeth M. Gannon

For full biographical listings, see the Martindale-Hubbell Law Directory

CRYSTAL RIVER, Citrus Co.

BEST & ANDERSON, P.A. (AV)

Executive Center Condos, 7655 West Gulf to Lake Highway, Suite 6, 34429
Telephone: 352-795-1107
Orlando, Florida Office: 1201 East Robinson Street, 32801.
Telephone: 407-425-2985.
Melbourne, Florida Office: Healthsouth Marina Towers, 709 South Harbor City Boulevard, Suite 270, 32901.
Telephone: 407-727-9923.

David R. Best
George H. "Dutch" Anderson, III

Angela O'Neil
James William Nuebel
Lora L. Wilson
Louis Allen DeFreitas, Jr.

For full biographical listings, see the Martindale-Hubbell Law Directory

*DADE CITY,** Pasco Co.

GREENFELDER, MANDER, HANSON, MURPHY & DWYER (AV)

14217 Third Street, 33523
Telephone: 352-567-0411
Fax: 352-567-7758
Email: GMHMandD@aol.com

MEMBERS OF FIRM

Albert R. Mander, III
T. Philip Hanson, Jr.

For full biographical listings, see the Martindale-Hubbell Law Directory

DAYTONA BEACH, Volusia Co.

CHANFRAU, CHANFRAU & BOUCK (AV)

A Partnership of Professional Associations
701 North Peninsula Drive, P.O. Box 265880, 32126-5880
Telephone: 904-258-7313
Telecopier: 904-238-1464
Email: pclaw@mindspring.com

W. M. Chanfrau (P.A.)
Philip J. Chanfrau (P.A.)
Kim E. Bouck

Elizabeth R. Chanfrau

For full biographical listings, see the Martindale-Hubbell Law Directory

KOLODINSKY, SEITZ & TRESHER (AV)

647 South Ridgewood Avenue, P.O. Box 471, 32115-0471
Telephone: 904-253-9790
Fax: 904-253-9801
Email: kbsandt@worldnet.att.net *URL:* http://www.lawyers.com/kolodinsky,seitzandtresher
New Smyrna Beach, Florida Office: 707 East Third Avenue.
Telephone: 904-427-9811.
Facsimile: 904-427-7566.

MEMBERS OF FIRM

William H. Seitz
Frederick H. Tresher, III

For full biographical listings, see the Martindale-Hubbell Law Directory

Daytona Beach—Continued

LANDIS, GRAHAM, FRENCH, HUSFELD, SHERMAN & FORD, P.A. (AV)

Formerly Hull, Landis, Graham & French
543 South Ridgewood Avenue, 32114
Telephone: 904-252-4717
Fax: 904-253-7352
Email: firm@landispa.com *URL:* http://www.landispa.com
De Land, Florida Office: 145 East Rich Avenue, P.O. Box 48.
Telephone: 904-734-3451.
Deltona, Florida Office: 204 Medical Arts Center, 1555 Saxon Boulevard.
Telephone: 407-574-1461.
Fax: 407-574-0242.

Erskine W. Landis (1900-1967)
John L. Graham (1905-1978)
Thorwald J. Husfeld (1926-1995)
Richard S. Graham
William E. Sherman
Sam N. Masters

Carol Lumb Allen (Resident)
Janet M. Strickland

OF COUNSEL

J. Compton French (Retired)

Counsel for: School Board of Volusia County; Walmart Stores, Inc.; Delco Oil, Inc.; West Volusia Hospital Authority; South Florida Natural Gas Co.; Florida Public Utilities Co.; Volusia County Industrial Development Authority; Florida United Methodist Children's Home: Volusia County Educational Facilities Authority.

For full biographical listings, see the Martindale-Hubbell Law Directory

*DELAND,** Volusia Co.

LANDIS, GRAHAM, FRENCH, HUSFELD, SHERMAN & FORD, P.A. (AV)

Formerly Hull, Landis, Graham & French
145 East Rich Avenue, P.O. Box 48, 32721-0048
Telephone: 904-734-3451
Fax: 904-736-1350
Email: firm@landispa.com *URL:* http://www.landispa.com
Daytona Beach, Florida Office: 543 South Ridgewood Avenue, 32114.
Telephone: 904-252-4717.
Fax: 904-258-7352.
Deltona, Florida Office: 204 Medical Arts Center, 1555 Saxon Boulevard.
Telephone: 407-574-1461.
Fax: 407-574-0242.

Erskine W. Landis (1900-1967)
John L. Graham (1905-1978)
Thorwald J. Husfeld (1926-1995)
William E. Sherman
Richard S. Graham (Daytona Beach Office)
William A. Ottinger (Deltona Office)
Joe G. Dykes, Jr.
Frank A. Ford, Jr.
Sam N. Masters (Daytona Beach Office)

Edwin Channing Coolidge, Jr.
Carol Lumb Allen (Resident, Daytona Beach Office)
Janet M. Strickland
Steven N. Gosney

OF COUNSEL

Frank A. Ford, Sr.
J. Compton French (Daytona Beach Office; Retired)

Counsel for: School Board of Volusia County; Walmart Stores, Inc.; Delco Oil, Inc.; West Volusia Hospital Authority; South Florida Natural Gas Co.; Florida Public Utilities Co.; Volusia County Industrial Development Authority; Florida United Methodist Children's Home; Volusia County Educational Facilities Authority.

For full biographical listings, see the Martindale-Hubbell Law Directory

*FORT LAUDERDALE,** Broward Co.

ABRAMOWITZ & POMERANTZ, P.A. (AV)

Suite 101, 7800 West Oakland Park Boulevard (Sunrise), 33351
Telephone: 954-572-7200
Fax: 954-748-6488
Email: abrpom@aol.com

Richard Abramowitz
Howard L. Pomerantz

Marc Stuart Schiller
Gordon Lea

Reference: NCNB National Bank of Florida.

For full biographical listings, see the Martindale-Hubbell Law Directory

BLACKMORE & BLACKMORE (AV)

320 Southeast 10th Court, 33316
Telephone: 954-522-0418; 1-800-646-2786
Fax: 954-522-4974
Email: adelelaw@bellsouth.net *URL:* http://www.lawyers.com/blackmore

(See Next Column)

MEMBERS OF FIRM

Robert W. Blackmore
Adele M. Blackmore

For full biographical listings, see the Martindale-Hubbell Law Directory

CATRI, HOLTON, KESSLER & KESSLER, P.A. (AV)

The Litigation Building, 3rd Floor, 633 S. Andrews Avenue, 33302
Telephone: 954-463-8593
Fax: 954-462-1303

Charles T. Kessler (1930-1997)
Wesley L. Catri
Raymond O. Holton, Jr.
Paula C. Kessler
Andrea L. Kessler

Gerard A. Tuzzio
Edwina V. Kessler

For full biographical listings, see the Martindale-Hubbell Law Directory

E. HUGH CHAPPELL JR., P.A. (AV)

420 Northeast 3rd Street, 33301
Telephone: 954-467-2727
Fax: 954-523-3240
Email: ehchappell@aol.com *URL:* http://www.lawyers.com/ehchappell

E. Hugh Chappell, Jr.

Jonathan Davis Consadene

Reference: Suntrust Bank, So. Fla, N.A.; Mellon United National Bank.

For full biographical listings, see the Martindale-Hubbell Law Directory

CONRAD & SCHERER (AV)

A Partnership of Professional Associations
Eighth Floor, 633 South Federal Highway, P.O. Box 14723, 33302
Telephone: 954-462-5500
Facsimile: 954-463-9244
Miami, Florida Office: 44 West Flagler Street, Suite 402, 33130.
Telephone: 305-856-9920.
Facsimile: 305-374-4408.

MEMBERS OF FIRM

William R. Scherer, Jr., (P.A.)
Gary S. Genovese (P.A.)
William V. Carcioppolo (P.A.)
Linda Rae Spaulding (P.A.)
Reid A. Cocalis (P.A.)

OF COUNSEL

Rex Conrad

ASSOCIATE

Albert L. Frevola, Jr.

Local Counsel for: American Home Assurance Group; Caterpillar Tractor Co.; Division of Risk Management, State of Florida; Florida East Coast Railway; Fort Motor Co.; Liberty Mutual Insurance Co.; Ryder Truck Lines; Unigard Insurance Group.
Approved Attorneys for: Attorneys' Title Insurance Fund.
Reference: Barnett Bank of Fort Lauderdale.

For Complete List of Firm Personnel, See General Section

For full biographical listings, see the Martindale-Hubbell Law Directory

COONEY, MATTSON, LANCE, BLACKBURN, RICHARDS & O'CONNOR, P.A. (AV)

2312 Wilton Drive, P.O. Box 14546, 33302
Telephone: Telephone: 954-568-6669
WATS: 1-800-745-3864
Telecopier: 954-568-0085
Email: cooney2312@aol.com
Orlando, Florida Office: Nations Bank Tower, 111 N. Orange Avenue, Suite 1020.
Telephone: 407-843-2100.
Fax: 407-843-2061.

David F. Cooney
Michael C. Mattson
Victor Lance (1956-1995)
Ace J. Blackburn, Jr.
John H. Richards
Dennis R. O'Connor (Resident, Orlando, Florida Office)
Bruce Michael Trybus
Walter C. Wyatt
Kieran F. O'Connor (Resident, Orlando, Florida Office)
Michele McCaul Ricca
Daniel F. Tordella

Laura Douglas
Warren Kwavnick
Rochelle Bocksch
Weslee S. Arciola
Alphonso O. Peets
Robert M. Potter, III
Elizabeth Y. Foshee (Resident, Orlando Office)

Representative Clients: The Travellers; RISCORP; CIGNA Insurance Co.; Claims Center; Fiesco; Multi-Line Claims Service, Inc.; Carpenter Contractors of America; City Furniture; CNA Insurance.

For full biographical listings, see the Martindale-Hubbell Law Directory

Fort Lauderdale—Continued

KENNETH D. COOPER, P.A. (AV)

400 S.E. Eighth Street, 33316
Telephone: 954-522-7177
Fax: 954-764-5874
URL: http://www.lawyers.com/cooperlaw

Kenneth D. Cooper

For full biographical listings, see the Martindale-Hubbell Law Directory

DONAHOE, PECARO & VOLLENDER, P.A. (AV)

Trial Lawyers Building, 633 Southeast 3rd Avenue, Suite 301, 33301-3151
Telephone: 954-761-3800
1-800-761-3801
FAX: 954-761-1855
Email: donpecvol@aol.com

John E. Donahoe
Paul R. Pecaro
Donald W. Vollender

Representative Clients: Allstate Insurance Co.

For full biographical listings, see the Martindale-Hubbell Law Directory

ESLER & LINDIE, P.A. (AV)

Suite 300 The Advocate Building, 315 S.E. Seventh Street, 33301
Telephone: 954-764-5400
FAX: 954-764-5408
Email: eslerandlindie@martindalemail.com *URL:* http://www.lawyers.com/esler&lindie

Gary A. Esler
Beth G. Lindie

Representative Clients: The Chubb Group of Insurance Cos.; Fireman's Fund Insurance Co.; State of Florida-Department of Risk Management; Marriott Corp.; Mobile America Insurance Group, Inc.; Ohio Casualty Insurance Co.
Reference: Capital Bank.

For full biographical listings, see the Martindale-Hubbell Law Directory

GILLESPIE, GOLDMAN & KRONENGOLD (AV)

Port Royale Financial Center, 6550 North Federal Highway, 33308
Telephone: 954-771-0908
Facsimile: 954-771-9880
Email: mail@ggklaw.com *URL:* http://www.lawyers.com/ggklaw

MEMBERS OF FIRM

John R. Gillespie, Jr.
Peter R. Goldman
Jeffrey L. Kronengold

ASSOCIATE

Gary M. Farmer, Jr.

For full biographical listings, see the Martindale-Hubbell Law Directory

HEINRICH GORDON HARGROVE WEIHE & JAMES, P.A. (AV)

500 East Broward Boulevard, Suite 1000, 33394-3092
Telephone: 954-527-2800
Facsimile: 954-524-9481
Email: talexander@heinrichgordon.com *URL:* http://www.heinrichgordon.com
Orlando, Florida Office: 201 South Orange Avenue, Suite 1015.
Telephone: 407-317-9117.
Facsimile: 407-317-9114.

Elicia D. Blackwell
Mark R. Boyd
Bruce A. Chaimowitz
Richard G. Gordon
Eugene L. Heinrich
Gordon James, III
Eric L. Lundt
Jeffrey A. O'Keefe
Valerie Shea
Gilbert E. Theissen
Kenneth W. Waterway

Representative Clients: Allstate Insurance Company; Amerisure Companies; The BellSouth Companies; Miami Elevator Company; Otis Elevator Company; Schindler Elevator Corporation.

For Complete List of Firm Personnel, See General Section

For full biographical listings, see the Martindale-Hubbell Law Directory

KRUPNICK CAMPBELL MALONE ROSELLI BUSER SLAMA HANCOCK MCNELIS LIBERMAN & MCKEE, P.A. (AV)

700 Southeast 3rd Avenue, Suite 100, 33316-1186
Telephone: 954-763-8181; 877-763-8181 (Toll Free)
Fax: 954-763-8292
Email: information@krupnicklaw.com *URL:* http://www.krupnicklaw.com

Jon E. Krupnick
Walter G. Campbell, Jr.
Kevin A. Malone
Richard J. Roselli
Thomas E. Buser
Joseph J. Slama
Kelly D. Hancock
Lisa A. McNelis
Scott S. Liberman
Robert J. McKee

(See Next Column)

Carlos Acevedo (Not admitted in FL)
Louis R. Battista
Ivan F. Cabrera
Robert D. Erben
Kelley Badger Gelb
Sean J. Greene
Holly Debra Krulik
Michael J. Ryan

OF COUNSEL

Ben J. Weaver
Dianne Jay Weaver

Reference: Mellon United National Bank.

For full biographical listings, see the Martindale-Hubbell Law Directory

KUVIN & STETTIN, P.A. (AV)

888 East Las Olas Boulevard Suite 710, 33301
Telephone: 954-462-1809
Facsimile: 954-462-1830
Email: lkuvin@aol.com

Lawrence P. Kuvin
Eric L. Stettin

For full biographical listings, see the Martindale-Hubbell Law Directory

MONTERO FINIZIO VELASQUEZ WEISSING AND REYES, P.A. (AV)

200 Southeast Ninth Street, 33316
Telephone: 954-767-6500
FAX: 954-766-2690
1-800-344-0322
Email: mfvw@worldnet.att.net *URL:* http://www.monterofinizio.com
Boca Raton, Florida Office: 2200 Corporate Boulevard, N.W., Suite 315.
Telephone: 561-982-9930.
Miami, Florida Office: 28 West Flagler Street, Suite 202.
Telephone: 305-381-9500.

Hiram M. Montero
Paul G. Finizio
Carlos A. Velasquez
Matthew D. Weissing
Carlos J. Reyes, Jr.
Jamie J. Finizio-Bascombe
Edward Montoya

Mara Shlackman
Emily DeSantis
Janet Ochoa
Marina Garcia Wood

For full biographical listings, see the Martindale-Hubbell Law Directory

OPPENHEIM & PILELSKY, P.A. (AV)

1290 Weston Road, Suite 300, 33326
Telephone: 954-384-6114
Toll Free: 888-384-6114
Fax: 954-384-6115
Email: Info@oppenheimlaw.com *URL:* http://www.oppenheimlaw.com

Roy D. Oppenheim
Ellen B. Pilelsky

For full biographical listings, see the Martindale-Hubbell Law Directory

LAW OFFICES PRINCE, GLICK & MCFARLANE, P.A. (AV)

1112 Southeast 3rd Avenue, 33316
Telephone: Broward: 954-525-1112
Dade: 305-940-6414
Fax: 954-462-1243
Email: attys@pgmlaw.com *URL:* http://www.pgmlaw.com

Charles M. Prince
Joseph Glick
William J. McFarlane, III
Malcolm M. Major

OF COUNSEL

Arnold Grevior (Chartered)

For full biographical listings, see the Martindale-Hubbell Law Directory

PURDY AND FLYNN, P.A. (AV)

1107 Southeast Fourth Avenue, 33316
Telephone: 954-356-0008
Fax: 954-356-0017
Email: purdyflynn@worldnet.att.net *URL:* http://www.purdyflynn.com

H. Mark Purdy
Rose Ann Flynn

Craig Joseph Trocino

OF COUNSEL

Michael S. Insler

For full biographical listings, see the Martindale-Hubbell Law Directory

SISTARE & ASSOCIATES (AV)

600 South Andrews Avenue, Suite 600, 33301
Telephone: 954-522-2320
Fax: 954-522-2223
Email: sistare@gate.net *URL:* http://www.sistare.com

MEMBER OF FIRM

Susan P. Sistare

(See Next Column)

SISTARE & ASSOCIATES, *Fort Lauderdale—Continued*

ASSOCIATE

Jahna Y. (Jay) Hoyte

For full biographical listings, see the Martindale-Hubbell Law Directory

WILTON L. STRICKLAND, P.A. (AV)

1401 East Broward Boulevard, Suite 303, P.O. Box 14246, 33301
Telephone: 954-760-4700; 800-760-8401
Telecopier: 954-779-7749
Email: sands@gate.net *URL:* http://www.wiltonstricklandpa.com

Wilton L. Strickland

Alexander Clark

For full biographical listings, see the Martindale-Hubbell Law Directory

*FORT MYERS,** Lee Co.

BURKERT & HART (AV)

2205 McGregor Boulevard, P.O. Box 2485, 33902
Telephone: 941-337-4800
Fax: 941-337-5920
Email: burkert@burkerthart.com *URL:* http://www.burkerthart.com

MEMBERS OF FIRM

Kim Patrick Hart
Peter C. Burkert

For full biographical listings, see the Martindale-Hubbell Law Directory

GARVIN & TRIPP, A PROFESSIONAL ASSOCIATION (AV)

2532 East First Street, P.O. Drawer 2040, 33902
Telephone: 941-334-1824
FAX: 941-334-6848
Email: jgarvin@cyberstreet.com *URL:* http://www.lawyers.com/garvin&tripp

Jeffrey R. Garvin
Theodore L. Tripp, Jr.

Bruce M. Essen
Elisa S. Worthington

Reference: Northern Trust Bank, Fort Myers, Florida.

For full biographical listings, see the Martindale-Hubbell Law Directory

PATRICK E. GERAGHTY A PROFESSIONAL ASSOCIATION (AV)

The Courtney Building, Suite 100, 2069 First Street, P.O. Box 1605, 33902-1605
Telephone: 941-334-9500
Fax: 941-334-8930
URL: http://www.lawyers.com/pgeraghty

Patrick E. Geraghty
Thomas M. Dougherty

For full biographical listings, see the Martindale-Hubbell Law Directory

GOLDSTEIN, BUCKLEY, CECHMAN, RICE & PURTZ, P.A. (AV)

1515 Broadway, P.O. Box 2366, 33902-2366
Telephone: 941-334-1146
Fax: 941-334-3039
Email: info@gbclaw.com *URL:* http://www.GBClaw.com
Port Charlotte, Florida Office: Emerald Square, Suite 1, 2852 Tamiami Trail, 33952.
Telephone: 941-624-2393.
Fax: 941-624-2155.
Cape Coral, Florida Office: 1603 Hancock Bridge Parkway, 33990.
Telephone: 941-574-5575.
Fax: 941-574-9213.
Lehigh Acres, Florida Office: 1458 Lee Boulevard, Lee Boulevard Shopping Center, 33936.
Telephone: 941-368-6101.
Fax: 941-368-2461.
Naples, Florida Office: 4947 North Tamiami Trail, Suite 101, 34103.
Telephone: 941-262-4888.
Fax: 941-262-8716.

Ray Goldstein
John B. Cechman
Richard Lee Purtz
George J. Mitar
Raymond L. Racila
Luis E. Insignares
Scot D. Goldberg
Michael M. Noone
David M. Goldberg

Approved Attorneys for: Attorneys' Title Insurance Fund.

For Complete List of Firm Personnel, See General Section

For full biographical listings, see the Martindale-Hubbell Law Directory

HENDERSON, FRANKLIN, STARNES & HOLT, PROFESSIONAL ASSOCIATION (AV)

1715 Monroe Street, P.O. Box 280, 33902-0280
Telephone: 941-334-4121
Telecopier: 941-332-4494

(See Next Column)

Albert M. Frierson
Stephen L. Helgemo
John A. Noland
Gerald W. Pierce
J. Terrence Porter
Michael J. Corso
Vicki L. Sproat
John W. Lewis
Craig Ferrante
James L. Nulman
Harold N. Hume, Jr.
Bruce M. Stanley Sr.
Daniel W. Sheppard
Steven G. Koeppel
Douglas B. Szabo
Robert C. Shearman
Andrew L. Ringers, Jr.
John F. Potanovic, Jr.
Paula F. Kelley
Jeffrey D. Kottkamp
Cora Cisneros Molloy
Danni Lynn Germano

Representative Clients: CIGNA Group; CSX Transportation, Inc.; Fireman's Fund Insurance Cos.; The Hartford Insurance Group; Huntington National Bank, N.A.; NationsBank, N.A.; Travelers/Aetna Insurance Group; Sprint-Florida, Inc.

For Complete List of Firm Personnel, See General Section

For full biographical listings, see the Martindale-Hubbell Law Directory

*FORT PIERCE,** St. Lucie Co.

NEILL GRIFFIN JEFFRIES FOWLER TIERNEY & NEILL, CHARTERED (AV)

311 South Second Street, P.O. Box 1270, 34954
Telephone: 561-464-8200
Fax: 561-464-2566

Richard V. Neill
Michael Jeffries
J. Stephen Tierney, III
Richard V. Neill, Jr.

Local Counsel For: SunTrust Bank South Florida, N.A., (Commercial and Trust Departments); Chubb Group of Insurances Cos.
Approved Attorneys for: Attorneys' Title Insurance Fund; Commonwealth Land Title Insurance Co.
Reference: SunTrust Bank South Florida, N.A., Fort Pierce, Florida (Commercial and Trust Departments).

For full biographical listings, see the Martindale-Hubbell Law Directory

*GAINESVILLE,** Alachua Co.

STRIPLING, MCMICHAEL & STRIPLING, P.A. (AV)

102 N.W. Second Avenue, P.O. Box 1287, 32602
Telephone: 352-376-8888
Fax: 352-376-4645
Email: attys@sms-pa.com *URL:* http://www.lawyers.com/smslaw

Robert O. Stripling, Jr.
Alan E. McMichael
Sylvia A. K. Stripling

For full biographical listings, see the Martindale-Hubbell Law Directory

*JACKSONVILLE,** Duval Co.

GLENN K. ALLEN A PROFESSIONAL ASSOCIATION (AV)

The Plaza Building, 353 East Forsyth Street, 32202-2822
Telephone: 904-355-7506
Facsimile: 904-353-8814
URL: http://www.glennallenpa.com
Email: GKA@glennallenpa.com *URL:* http://www.lawyers.com/glennallen

Glenn K. Allen

Jennifer Workinger Fites

For full biographical listings, see the Martindale-Hubbell Law Directory

BROWN, TERRELL, HOGAN, ELLIS, MCCLAMMA & YEGELWEL, P.A. (AV)

Suite 804 Blackstone Building, 233 East Bay Street, 32202-3417
Telephone: 904-632-2424
Fax: 904-632-2027
Email: mail@bthemy-law.com *URL:* http://www.bthemy-law.com

Thomas R. Brown
James T. Terrell
Wayne Hogan
Timothy D. Ellis
T. Edward McClamma
Evan J. Yegelwel
Thomas E. Duffy, Jr.
Christopher G. Burns
Anita Pryor
Alan M. Pickert

Carroll Cayer
Michael S. Sharrit
Theodore Samuel Pina, Jr.
Mark E. Calvin
Leslie A. Goller
Patricia M. Dodson
Jennifer Kolinski Millis

Reference: NCNB.

For full biographical listings, see the Martindale-Hubbell Law Directory

Jacksonville—Continued

JOHN F. CALLENDER (AV)

1301 River Place Boulevard Suite 2105, 32207
Telephone: 904-398-8833
Fax: 904-396-4457
URL: http://www.willcontestfla.com

Reference: First Union National Bank.

For full biographical listings, see the Martindale-Hubbell Law Directory

COKER, MYERS, SCHICKEL, SORENSON, HIGGINBOTHAM & GREEN, P.A. (AV)

136 East Bay Street, P.O. Box 1860, 32201
Telephone: 904-356-6071
Fax: 904-353-2425

Howard C. Coker
M. Wayne Myers
John J. Schickel
Charles A. Sorenson
Wm. Earl Higginbotham
Samuel H. Lanier
J. Thomas McKeel
Mark M. Green
R. Daniel Noey
Ronald M. Owen
John Moffitt Howell
James H. Daniel
Richard R. Alexander

For full biographical listings, see the Martindale-Hubbell Law Directory

HUGH COTNEY, P.A. (AV)

905 Blackstone Building, 233 East Bay Street, 32202-3417
Telephone: 904-356-0162
FAX: 904-355-5170

Hugh Cotney

Representative Clients: First Insuramerica of Florida, Inc.; Deaf Services Center, Inc.

For full biographical listings, see the Martindale-Hubbell Law Directory

THE CRAMER LAW FIRM (AV)

1 Independent Drive, Suite 3300, 32202
Telephone: 904-632-2211
Fax: 904-632-2324
Email: cramerjax@worldnet.att.net

Jeffrey A. Cramer

Leonard S. Magid
Richard L. Ruth

Reference: Suntrust Bank.

For full biographical listings, see the Martindale-Hubbell Law Directory

GENTRY, PHILLIPS AND HODAK, P.A. (AV)

Suite 400, 6 East Bay Street, 32202
Telephone: 904-356-4100
Fax: 904-358-1895

William C. Gentry
Mary Kleyla Phillips
Corinne C. Hodak

Angelo M. Patacca, Jr.

For full biographical listings, see the Martindale-Hubbell Law Directory

LILES, GAVIN & COSTANTINO (AV)

One Enterprise Center, Suite 1500, 225 Water Street, 32202
Telephone: 904-634-1100
Fax: 904-634-1234
Email: triallaw@bellsouth.net

Rutledge R. Liles
R. Kyle Gavin
R. Scott Costantino

ASSOCIATES

Niels P. Murphy
Robert Bruce George

For full biographical listings, see the Martindale-Hubbell Law Directory

MAHON & FARLEY, P.A. (AV)

350 East Adams Street, 32202
Telephone: 904-354-4300
Fax: 904-354-4658

Lacy Mahon (1891-1968)
Harry B. Mahon
Joseph S. Farley, Jr.

References: First Guaranty Bank & Trust; Coastline Federal Credit Union.

For full biographical listings, see the Martindale-Hubbell Law Directory

PAJCIC & PAJCIC, P.A. (AV)

1900 Independent Square, 32202
Telephone: 904-358-8881
Fax: 904-354-1180
Email: attorneys@pajcic.com *URL:* http://www.pajcic.com

Gary Pajcic
Stephen J. Pajcic, III
William S. Burns, Jr.
Curtis Stephen Pajcic
Robert J. Link
Lee T. Griffin
Christine A. Clark
Thomas F. Slater
Curry Gary Pajcic

Reference: Barnett Bank of Jacksonville, N.A.

For full biographical listings, see the Martindale-Hubbell Law Directory

LAKELAND, Polk Co.

WILLIAM J. CORDA (AV)

Building I, 1935 East Edgewood Drive, 33803
Telephone: 941-616-1100
Fax: 941-616-1103
Email: cordalaw@aol.com

For full biographical listings, see the Martindale-Hubbell Law Directory

LAKE WORTH, Palm Beach Co.

RICHARD H. WILLITS, P.A. (AV)

2290 10th Avenue North Suite 404, 33461
Telephone: 1-800-870-0573
561-582-7600
Fax: 561-588-8819
URL: http://www.lawyers.com/willitslaw

Richard H. Willits

For full biographical listings, see the Martindale-Hubbell Law Directory

LARGO, Pinellas Co.

WILLIAM S. JONASSEN, P.A. (AV)

10785 Ulmerton Road, 34648
Telephone: 727-586-1484
Fax: 727-585-9818
Mailing Address: P.O. Box 366, Indian Rocks Beach, FL, 33785
Email: wjonass1@tampabayrr.com

William S. Jonassen

Representative Clients: Florida Lawyers Indemnity Group; Florida Podiatrist Trust; Gulf Atlantic Insurance Co.; Sun Coast Hospital.
General Counsel for: First National Bank of Florida.

For full biographical listings, see the Martindale-Hubbell Law Directory

MAITLAND, Orange Co.

BAILEY & MYERS, P.A. (AV)

100 East Sybelia Avenue Suite 375, 32751
Telephone: 407-628-2929
Fax: 407-628-3909
URL: http://www.baileymyers.com

Michael K. Bailey
Donald A. Myers, Jr.

For full biographical listings, see the Martindale-Hubbell Law Directory

MELBOURNE, Brevard Co.

BEST & ANDERSON, P.A. (AV)

Healthsouth Marina Towers, 709 South Harbor City Boulevard, Suite 270, 32901
Telephone: 407-727-9923
Orlando, Florida Office: 1201 East Robinson Street, 32801.
Telephone: 407-425-2985.
Crystal River, Florida Office: Executive Center Condos, 7655 West Gulf to Lake Highway, Suite 6, 34429.
Telephone: 352-795-1107.

David R. Best
George H. "Dutch" Anderson, III

Angela O'Neil
James William Nuebel
Lora L. Wilson
Louis Allen DeFreitas, Jr.

For full biographical listings, see the Martindale-Hubbell Law Directory

NANCE, CACCIATORE AND HAMILTON (AV)

525 North Harbor City Boulevard, 32935
Telephone: 321-254-8416
Fax: 321-259-8243
Email: nancacc@iu.net

(See Next Column)

NANCE, CACCIATORE AND HAMILTON, *Melbourne—Continued*

MEMBERS OF FIRM

James H. Nance
S. Sammy Cacciatore
John N. Hamilton
Charles G. Barger, Jr.
James N. Nance
Sammy M. Cacciatore

Reference: The Bank.

For full biographical listings, see the Martindale-Hubbell Law Directory

*MIAMI,** Dade Co.

ABRAMSON & MAGIDSON, P.A. (AV)

Suite 904, 800 Brickell Avenue, 33131
Telephone: 305-358-4400
Fax: 305-539-0477
Email: abramson@icanect.net

John M. Abramson
David L. Magidson

For full biographical listings, see the Martindale-Hubbell Law Directory

ANDREW J. ANTHONY, P.A. (AV)

999 Ponce de Leon Boulevard (Coral Gables) Suite 1035, 33134-5822
Telephone: 305-444-8927
Fax: 305-529-1072

Andrew J. Anthony

Bradley Allan Silverman

OF COUNSEL

Neal Gary Rosensweig

For full biographical listings, see the Martindale-Hubbell Law Directory

CLARKE SILVERGLATE WILLIAMS & MONTGOMERY (AV)

A Partnership of Professional Corporations
100 North Biscayne Boulevard Suite 2401, 33132
Telephone: 305-377-0700
Facsimile: 305-377-3001
Chicago, Illinois Office: Williams & Montgomery Ltd., 20 North Wacker Drive, Suite 2100.
Telephone: 312-443-3200.
Telex: 206598.
Facsimile: 312-443-1323.
Waukegan, Illinois Office: Williams & Montgomery Ltd., 20 S. Utica.
Telephone: 847-360-1220.
Wheaton, Illinois Office: Williams & Montgomery Ltd., 310 S. County Farm Road.
Telephone: 630-690-3200.
Joliet, Illinois Office: Williams & Montgomery Ltd., 81 North Chicago Avenue.
Telephone: 815-727-2653.

Mercer K. Clarke
Spencer H. Silverglate

OF COUNSEL

Henry H. Bolz, III

ASSOCIATES

Kelly Anne Luther
Richard R. Cochran
William J. Dimmig
Cynthia R. Bernard
Spencer T. Kuvin
Francisco Ramos, Jr.
Edward J. Pfister
John C. Schlesinger

For full biographical listings, see the Martindale-Hubbell Law Directory

COLSON, HICKS, EIDSON, COLSON, MATTHEWS, MARTINEZ & MENDOZA (AV)

Floor 47 First Union Financial Center, 200 South Biscayne Boulevard, 33131-2351
Telephone: 305-373-5400
Fax: 305-374-4796
URL: http://www.colson.com/

MEMBERS OF FIRM

William M. Hicks (1928-1996)
Bill Colson
Mike Eidson
Dean C. Colson
Joseph M. Matthews
Roberto Martinez
Enid Duany Mendoza
Julie Braman Kane
Robert H. Fernandez
Joseph J. Kalbac, Jr.
Daniel Uhlfelder

Reference: Northern Trust Bank of Florida.

For full biographical listings, see the Martindale-Hubbell Law Directory

DAVID L. DEEHL, P.A. (AV)

Suite 1575 Courthouse Tower, 44 West Flagler Street, 33130
Telephone: 305-358-9700
Telecopier: 305-358-4036
Email: DAVID@DEEHL.COM *URL:* http://www.lawyers.com/davidldeehl

(See Next Column)

David L. Deehl
Susan Stanfill Carlson

OF COUNSEL

Michele K. Feinzig

For full biographical listings, see the Martindale-Hubbell Law Directory

DEUTSCH & BLUMBERG, P.A. (AV)

Suite 2802 New World Tower, 100 North Biscayne Boulevard, 33132
Telephone: 305-358-6329
Fax: 305-358-9304

Steven K. Deutsch
Edward R. Blumberg
James C. Blecke
Louis Thaler

For full biographical listings, see the Martindale-Hubbell Law Directory

FERRARO & ASSOCIATES, P.A. (AV)

First Union Financial Center, 200 S. Biscayne Boulevard Suite 3800, 33131-2310
Telephone: 305-375-0111
Telefax: 305-379-6222
URL: http://www.ferrarolaw.com

James L. Ferraro

Ana M. Rivero
Dino G. Galardi
Valerie A. Conzo
O. Oliver Wragg
Kerry A. Raleigh

For full biographical listings, see the Martindale-Hubbell Law Directory

FOURNARIS & SANET, P.A. (AV)

145 Almeria Avenue (Coral Gables), 33134
Telephone: 305-448-7333
Telefax: 305-448-7394
URL: http://www.lawyers.com/fournaris

Theodore J. Fournaris
Morton J. Sanet

For full biographical listings, see the Martindale-Hubbell Law Directory

FRIEDMAN AND FRIEDMAN, P.A. (AV)

Suite 1011 Barnett Bank Building, 2600 Douglas Road (S.W. 37th Avenue) (Coral Gables), 33134
Telephone: 305-446-6485; 800-446-6482
Telefax: 305-448-7636
Cable Address: "BARISTER"

Marvin Ross Friedman
Gary Alan Friedman

John Schyler Seligman

For full biographical listings, see the Martindale-Hubbell Law Directory

ROLAND H. GOMEZ (AV)

Suite 400, 8100 Oak Lane (Miami Lakes), 33016
Telephone: 305-825-5506
URL: http://www.lawyers.com/rolandhgomez

ASSOCIATES

Doreen E. Lasch
Richard M. Gomez
John Edward Korf

Reference: United National Bank.

For full biographical listings, see the Martindale-Hubbell Law Directory

STEWART G. GREENBERG, P.A. (AV)

11440 North Kendall Drive, Suite PH-400, 33176
Telephone: 305-595-2400
Toll Free 1-888-499-9700
Fax: 305-595-5105
Email: stewart@sgglaw.com

Stewart G. Greenberg
Stuart R. Silver

For full biographical listings, see the Martindale-Hubbell Law Directory

HAGGARD, PARKS & STONE, P.A. (AV)

330 Alhambra Circle (Coral Gables), 33134
Telephone: 305-446-5700
Fax: 305-446-1154
Email: mail@haggardparksstone.com *URL:* http://www.lawyers.com/haggardparksstone

Wm. Andrew Haggard
Robert L. Parks
Mark D. Stone

Jeannete Lewis Bologna
Michael Andrew Haggard

Reference: Sun Bank of Coral Gables.

For full biographical listings, see the Martindale-Hubbell Law Directory

Miami—Continued

HALL, DAVID AND JOSEPH, P.A. (AV)

Penthouse 1428 Brickell Avenue, P.O. Box 019113, 33131-9113
Telephone: 305-374-5030
Fax: 305-374-5033

Andrew C. Hall
Christopher M. David
Allan A. Joseph

Adam S. Hall
Michael L Cotzen
Ilene Schnall
Santiago A. Cueto
Kimberly S. Rogers

For full biographical listings, see the Martindale-Hubbell Law Directory

HIGH, STACK, LAZENBY, PALAHACH & FEILER (AV)

A Partnership including Professional Associations
3929 Ponce de Leon Boulevard (Coral Gables), 33134
Telephone: 305-443-3329
Fax: 305-443-0850
Email: Highstack@aol.com
Melbourne, Florida Office: High, Stack, Lazenby, Maxwell & Platt, 525 Strawbridge Avenue.
Telephone: 407-725-5525.
FAX: 407-984-2411.

MEMBERS OF FIRM

Robert King High (1924-1967)
Charles R. Stack (P.A.)
Michael Palahach, III, (P.A.)
Michael B. Feiler

ASSOCIATES

Carlos Cruanes
Kimberly B. Bonder (Resident at Melborne Office)

OF COUNSEL

Fernando M. Palacios
Christopher M. Rundle, P.A.
Reed C. Cary
Irving J. Whitman

For full biographical listings, see the Martindale-Hubbell Law Directory

HILLENCAMP & ALVAREZ, P.A. (AV)

Gifford House, 2937 S.W. 27th Avenue (Coconut Grove), 33133
Telephone: 305-444-7675
Fax: 305-444-0075
Email: Trialteam@MSN.com

Ibis J. Hillencamp
Alex Alvarez

For full biographical listings, see the Martindale-Hubbell Law Directory

HOPPE & STOKES, P.A. (AV)

2nd Floor, Concord Building, 66 West Flagler Street, 33130
Telephone: 305-358-9060
Fax: 305-374-6801
URL: http://www.hoppestokes.com
Email: pilaw@hoppestokes.com *URL:* http://www.lawyers.com/hoppestokes

Bill Hoppe
Mark L. Stokes

Jacinto J. Gonzalez
Eric Matthew Ellsley
LeAnna Vasquez

For full biographical listings, see the Martindale-Hubbell Law Directory

JOSEPHS, JACK & GAEBE, P.A. (AV)

Grove Professional Building, 2950 S.W. 27th Avenue, Suite 100, 33133-3765
Telephone: Dade County: 305-445-3800
Telecopier: 305-448-5800
Email: TheFirm@FloridaAttorneys.com *URL:* http://www.Florida-Attorneys.com

Michael R. Josephs
Lewis N. Jack, Jr.
John S. Gaebe

Elisabeth M. Allen
Helen Leen Miranda
Scott A. Cole
Stephanie E. Demos
Scott T. McCullough
Tamara D. McKeown
Christopher T. Lemos

Representative Clients: U-Haul Corporation; ITT Sheraton; Zurich-American Insurance Company; Republic Claims Service Company; Southern Fire Insurance Adjusters.

For full biographical listings, see the Martindale-Hubbell Law Directory

LEVINE, BUSCH, SCHNEPPER & STEIN, P.A. (AV)

Suite 1010 One Datran Center, 9100 South Dadeland Boulevard, 33156
Telephone: 305-670-2333
Fax: 305-670-0716
Email: LEVBUSSCHS@aol.com *URL:* http://www.lawofficesoflbss.com
Broward Office: 100 South Pine Island Road, Suite 202, Plantation, Florida, 33324.
Telephone: 954-922-0800.

David H. Levine
Edward P. Busch
R. Cory Schnepper
Barry A. Stein

Sanford M. Reinstein

For full biographical listings, see the Martindale-Hubbell Law Directory

THE LAW OFFICES OF RONALD S. LOWY (AV)

5615 Lagorce Drive Penthouse, 33140
Telephone: 305-673-5699
Telecopier: 305-865-1809
Email: rlowyesq@bellsouth.net

Representative Clients: Tate Enterprises; British Airways, PLC; Alleghany Mutual Co.; SunTrust of Miami; Crescent Heights Companies.

For full biographical listings, see the Martindale-Hubbell Law Directory

PODHURST, ORSECK, JOSEFSBERG, EATON, MEADOW, OLIN & PERWIN, P.A. (AV)

Suite 800 City National Bank Building, 25 West Flagler Street, 33130-1780
Telephone: 305-358-2800; Fort Lauderdale: 954-463-4346
Fax: 305-358-2382
Email: Info@podhurst.com *URL:* http://www.wwdir.com/podhurst.html

Aaron Podhurst
Robert Orseck (1934-1978)
Robert C. Josefsberg
Joel D. Eaton
Barry L. Meadow
Michael S. Olin
Joel S. Perwin
Steven C. Marks
Victor M. Diaz, Jr.
Katherine W. Ezell

Xavier Martínez

OF COUNSEL

Walter H. Beckham, Jr.
Karen Podhurst Dern

References: City National Bank of Miami; Mellon United National Bank of Miami.

For full biographical listings, see the Martindale-Hubbell Law Directory

SAMS & LISTER, P.A. (AV)

73255 West 63 Avenue, Suite 201, 33143
Telephone: 305-740-5401
Fax: 305-740-5425

Murray Sams, Jr.
David P. Lister

Arthur B. Stark

For full biographical listings, see the Martindale-Hubbell Law Directory

ROBERT S. SINGER (AV)

801 Brickell Avenue, Suite 1501, 33131
Telephone: 305-381-7999
Fax: 305-381-8203
URL: http://www.lawyers.com/rssinger

For full biographical listings, see the Martindale-Hubbell Law Directory

THORNTON, MASTRUCCI & MINKIN (AV)

(Formerly Thornton, Mastrucci & Sinclair)
4699 Ponce de Leon Boulevard (Coral Gables), 33146
Telephone: 305-668-0100
Facsimile: 305-668-0400
Email: THORNTON@MSN.COM

MEMBERS OF FIRM

John W. Thornton, Sr.
Jane Thornton Mastrucci
Michael Minkin

ASSOCIATE

Cynthia Harrison Ruiz

For full biographical listings, see the Martindale-Hubbell Law Directory

MIAMI LAKES, Dade Co.

MARTIN, LIPSKY, KAUFMAN & WEINSTEIN, P.A. (AV)

7975 Northwest 154th Street Suite 230, 33016
Telephone: 305-362-6222
Fax: 305-362-0111
URL: http://www.lawyers.com/personalinjurypros

(See Next Column)

MARTIN, LIPSKY, KAUFMAN & WEINSTEIN P.A., *Miami Lakes—Continued*

Timothy M. Martin
Daniel L. Kaufman
Joseph I. Lipsky
Mark S. Weinstein

For full biographical listings, see the Martindale-Hubbell Law Directory

*NAPLES,** Collier Co.

McDONNELL TRIAL LAWYERS (AV)

1165 Eighth Street South, 34102
Telephone: 941-434-7711; 1-800-873-8060
Fax: 941-434-5629
Email: attyfirstname@mcdonnelltriallawyers. com
URL: http://www.lawyers.com/mtl

Michael McDonnell

ASSOCIATE

Gary Layne Green

For full biographical listings, see the Martindale-Hubbell Law Directory

NEW SMYRNA BEACH, Volusia Co.

KOLODINSKY, SEITZ & TRESHER (AV)

707 East Third Avenue, 32169
Telephone: 904-427-9811
Facsimile: 904-427-7566
Email: kbsandt@worldnet.att.net *URL:* http://www.lawyers.com/kolodinsky,seitzandtresher
Daytona Beach, Florida Office: 647 South Ridgewood Avenue, P.O. Box 471.
Telephone: 904-253-9790.
Fax: 904-253-9801.

MEMBERS OF FIRM

Rick Kolodinsky
William H. Seitz
Frederick H. Tresher, III

ASSOCIATE

Jason O. Brown

For full biographical listings, see the Martindale-Hubbell Law Directory

NICEVILLE, Okaloosa Co.

STANLEY BRUCE POWELL, P.A. (AV)

107 North Partin Drive, P.O. Box 400, 32588-0400
Telephone: 850-678-2118
Fax: 850-678-8336
Email: BPOWELLPA@AOL.COM

Stanley Bruce Powell
David R. Swanick III

Representative Clients: Peoples National Bank of Niceville; Destin Bank; Big Kahuna's, Inc.
References: Peoples National Bank of Niceville; Destin Bank; Vanguard Bank and Trust Co.

For full biographical listings, see the Martindale-Hubbell Law Directory

NORTH PALM BEACH, Palm Beach Co.

LAW OFFICES OF PATRICK C. MASSA, P.A. (AV)

Crystal Tree Office Centre, 1201 U.S. Highway One, Suite 400, 33408
Telephone: 561-694-1800
Facsimile: 561-694-1833
Email: pmassalaw@aol.com

Patrick C. Massa

For full biographical listings, see the Martindale-Hubbell Law Directory

*ORLANDO,** Orange Co.

BEST & ANDERSON, P.A. (AV)

1201 East Robinson Street, 32801
Telephone: 407-425-2985
Email: cab@bestandanderson.com *URL:* http://www.bestandanderson.com
Crystal River, Florida Office: Executive Center Condos, 7655 West Gulf to Lake Highway, Suite 6, 34429.
Telephone: 352-795-1107.
Melbourne, Florida Office: Healthsouth Marina Towers, 709 South Harbor City Boulevard, Suite 270, 32901.
Telephone: 407-727-9923.

David R. Best
George H. "Dutch" Anderson, III

Angela O'Neil
Lora L. Wilson
James William Nuebel
Louis Allen DeFreitas, Jr.

For full biographical listings, see the Martindale-Hubbell Law Directory

BILLINGS, CUNNINGHAM, MORGAN & BOATWRIGHT, PROFESSIONAL ASSOCIATION (AV)

330 East Central Boulevard, 32801
Telephone: 407-425-2000
Fax: 407-843-8274
Email: info@bcmb.com *URL:* http://www.bcmb.com

James Cunningham
Tracy L. Troutman-Cheek
Mary Ann Morgan
Gary D. Vasquez
Joseph E. Boatwright, Jr.
Randy E. Schimmelpfennig

OF COUNSEL

Jared M. Billings

For full biographical listings, see the Martindale-Hubbell Law Directory

NOLAN CARTER, P.A. (AV)

1218 East Robinson Street, P.O. Box 2229, 32802
Telephone: 407-898-3535
Fax: 407-898-5055
Email: carmedneg@aol.com

Nolan Carter

Karen Reed Wasson

For full biographical listings, see the Martindale-Hubbell Law Directory

COONEY, MATTSON, LANCE, BLACKBURN, RICHARDS & O'CONNOR, P.A. (AV)

Nations Bank Tower, 111 North Orange Avenue Suite 1020, 32801
Telephone: 407-843-2100
Fax: 407-843-2061
Fort Lauderdale, Florida Office: 2312 Wilton Drive. P.O. Box 14546. 33302.
Telephone: 954-568-6669.
Telecopier: 954-568-0085.

Dennis R. O'Connor
Kieran F. O'Connor

Elizabeth Y. Foshee (Resident)

For full biographical listings, see the Martindale-Hubbell Law Directory

DELLECKER, WILSON & KING, P.A. (AV)

719 Vassar Street, 32804
Telephone: 407-244-3000
Fax: 407-244-3033
Email: attorneys@dwklaw.com *URL:* http://www.dwklaw.com

Robert H. "Bob" Dellecker
Samuel P. King
Brian T. Wilson
Leticia J. Marques
Kenneth J. McKenna

For full biographical listings, see the Martindale-Hubbell Law Directory

EUBANKS, HILYARD & BOGAN, P.A. (AV)

Suite 600 First Union Building, 20 North Orange Avenue, P.O. Box 4973, 32802-4973
Telephone: 407-425-4251
Telecopier: 407-841-8431

Ernest H. Eubanks
Sutton G. Hilyard, Jr.
Rodney G. Ross (1934-1982)
Bruce R. Bogan

Bobby G. Palmer, Jr.
W. Gregory Lockeby

Representative Clients: AIG Aviation, Inc.; AVEMCO Insurance Co.; Phoenix Aviation Managers, Inc.; Ranger Insurance Co.; Old Republic Insurance Co.; Signal Aviation Underwriters; Underwriters at Lloyds; Orange County Sheriff's Office; United Technologies Corp.; Reliance Insurance Co.

For full biographical listings, see the Martindale-Hubbell Law Directory

GRIFFIN & LINDER, P.A. (AV)

28 East Washington Street, 32801-2311
Telephone: 407-425-2518
Fax: 407-841-9913

H. Terrell Griffin
Paul R. Linder

Nathan P. Carter
Dana P. Hoffman

OF COUNSEL

Elmo R. Hoffman

For full biographical listings, see the Martindale-Hubbell Law Directory

HILL AND PONTON, PROFESSIONAL ASSOCIATION (AV)

Suite 500, 605 East Robinson Street, P.O. Box 2673, 32802
Telephone: 407-422-4665
URL: http://www.hillponton.com

(See Next Column)

HILL AND PONTON PROFESSIONAL ASSOCIATION—*Continued*

Brian D. Hill
Carol J. Ponton

Maria D. Santana (Not admitted in FL)
Silvia R. Sanders
Jeffrey D. Starker

For full biographical listings, see the Martindale-Hubbell Law Directory

HILL, REIS, ADAMS, HALL & SCHIEFFELIN, P.A. (AV)

1417 East Concord Street, 32803
Telephone: 407-896-0425
Fax: 407-896-9236
Email: mainbox@hrahs.com

G. Bruce Hill
Gregory F. Reis
Janet W. Adams
Larry D. Hall
Thomas L. Schieffelin, Jr.
William W. Large
Matthew P. Bartolomei

David O Doyle, Jr
Andrew Vlahos
Heidi Jo Haycook

Representative Clients: The Florida Hospital Trust Fund; The Florida Hospital Excess Trust Fund; Florida Hospital Workers Compensation/Self Insurance Trust Fund; Bartow Memorial Hospital; Bay Medical Center; Brooksville Regional Hospital; Cape Canaveral Hospital; Cape Coral Hospital; Desoto Memorial Hospital.

For full biographical listings, see the Martindale-Hubbell Law Directory

KELAHER LAW OFFICES, P.A. (AV)

Suite 1301, 800 North Magnolia Avenue, 32803
Telephone: 407-841-7698
Fax: 407-649-7760
Email: jim@kelaherlaw.com

James P. Kelaher

For full biographical listings, see the Martindale-Hubbell Law Directory

KING, BLACKWELL & DOWNS, P.A. (AV)

25 East Pine Street, P.O. Box 1631, 32802-1631
Telephone: 407-422-2472
Fax: 407-648-0161
Email: kbdfirm@mindspring.com *URL:* http://www.kbdlaw.com

David B. King
Bruce B. Blackwell
Mayanne Downs

John F. Tannian
Thomas A. Zehnder

For full biographical listings, see the Martindale-Hubbell Law Directory

KARL O. KOEPKE (AV)

801 North Magnolia Avenue, Suite 107, 32803
Telephone: 407-841-0023
Fax: 407-425-4761
Email: klawfl@aol.com

ASSOCIATE

Michael H. Truax

For full biographical listings, see the Martindale-Hubbell Law Directory

MAHER, GIBSON AND GUILEY A PROFESSIONAL ASSOCIATION OF LAWYERS (AV)

Suite 200, 90 East Livingston Street, 32801
Telephone: 407-839-0866
Fax: 407-425-7958

Michael Maher
Patricia M. Gibson
David D. Guiley

Steven R. Maher
Robin Orosz Sharp
Jennifer Gentry Fernandez
Melissa H. Powers

LEGAL SUPPORT PERSONNEL

INSURANCE CLAIM COORDINATOR

Charles R. Simpson

For full biographical listings, see the Martindale-Hubbell Law Directory

TERRY L. MCCOLLOUGH, P.A. (AV)

400 North Ferncreek Avenue, 32803
Telephone: 407-894-8600
Fax: 407-894-8685
Email: terry131@aol.com

Terry L. McCollough

(See Next Column)

LEGAL SUPPORT PERSONNEL

Jacqueline G. Kinker (Paralegal)
Colby D. Griffin (Paralegal)

For full biographical listings, see the Martindale-Hubbell Law Directory

MEYERS, MOONEY, STANLEY & HOLLINGSWORTH (AV)

(An Association of Professional Associations and Sole Proprietorships)
17 South Lake Avenue, 32801-2797
Telephone: 407-849-0940
Toll-free: 800-766-9198
Fax: 407-849-1860
Email: MeyMooMey@aol.com *URL:* http://www.lawyers.com/meyersmooney
Jacksonville Office: 2120 University Boulevard West, 32217.
Telephone: 904-367-8747; 800-951-7266.
Fax: 904-367-0650.

Irvin A. Meyers
Thomas R. Mooney
Bradley H. Hollingsworth
James A. Stanley, Jr. (Resident, Jacksonville Office)

ASSOCIATES

John V. Colvin
Thomas E. Mooney

Reference: Sun Bank & Trust of Orlando.

For full biographical listings, see the Martindale-Hubbell Law Directory

MORGAN COLLING & GILBERT, A PROFESSIONAL ASSOCIATION (AV)

20 North Orange Avenue, 16th Floor, Suite 1607, P.O. Box 4979, 32802-4979
Telephone: 407-420-1414
Fax: 407-425-8171
URL: http://www.morgancollinggilbert.com
Tampa, Florida Office: 101 East Kennedy Boulevard, Suite 1790, 33602.
Telephone: 813-223-5505.
Fax: 813-223-5402.

Nicholas A. Buoniconti, III
Jay S. Colling
Sumeet Kaul (Resident, Tampa Office)
James J. Kelleher
Todd Long
Bryan K. McMinn
W. Clay Mitchell, Jr.
John B. Morgan
Gregory D. Prysock
Michael F. Sutton

Reference: Sun Bank.

For full biographical listings, see the Martindale-Hubbell Law Directory

WILLIAM G. OSBORNE, P.A. (AV)

538 East Washington Street, 32801-1996
Telephone: 407-422-5385
Fax: 407-422-5381

William G. Osborne

LEGAL SUPPORT PERSONNEL

Elizabeth I. Dunnigan (Office Manager)
Catherine C. Braungart (Legal Assistant)

For full biographical listings, see the Martindale-Hubbell Law Directory

OVERCHUCK, NEWSOME & SCHWERER, LLP (AV)

90 East Livingston Street, Suite 100, 32801
Telephone: 407-648-5977
Fax: 407-648-5282
Email: ons@onslaw.com *URL:* http://www.onslaw.com

John R. Overchuck
C. Richard Newsome
Alan M. Schwerer

For full biographical listings, see the Martindale-Hubbell Law Directory

PARKER, LANDERMAN & PARKER, P.A. (AV)

108 East Hillcrest Street, P.O. Box 2867, 32802
Telephone: 407-425-4910
Facsimile: 407-423-3140
Email: parkerpa@digital.net

E. Clay Parker
Alan J. Landerman
Henry Clay Parker, IV

For full biographical listings, see the Martindale-Hubbell Law Directory

PARRISH & FREDERICKSEN, P.A. (AV)

116 America Street, 32801
Telephone: 407-849-1776
Email: sidneyparrish@laworlando.com

Sidney H. Parrish
Kenneth S. Fredericksen

Brian F. Duckworth

For full biographical listings, see the Martindale-Hubbell Law Directory

Orlando—Continued

PUGH AND VAN BUREN (AV)

218 Annie Street, 32806
Telephone: 407-843-5840
Email: igpugh@aol.com *URL:* http://www.lawyers.com/pvblaw

Irby G. Pugh — Tye W. Van Buren

For full biographical listings, see the Martindale-Hubbell Law Directory

RICHARD B. TROUTMAN, P.A.

(See Winter Park)

WOOLFOLK, KEOUGH, DUBOSE & DEBARI, P.A. (AV)

518 East Colonial Drive, P.O. Box 1609, 32803
Telephone: 407-849-5050
Fax: 407-849-6588
Frostproof, Florida Office: 225 North Scenic Highway, 33843.
Telephone: 863-635-1155.

Edmund T. Woolfolk — John E. DuBose, Jr.
Robert D. Keough — Mary Jaye DeBari

For full biographical listings, see the Martindale-Hubbell Law Directory

PALM BEACH GARDENS, Palm Beach Co.

MICHAEL C. KNECHT & ASSOCIATES, P.A. (AV)

Suite 101 11380 Prosperity Farms Road, 33410
Telephone: 561-625-4110
Fax: 561-625-4115

Michael C. Knecht

SLAWSON CUNNINGHAM WHALEN & STEWART, P.L. (AV)

Harbour Financial Center, 2401 PGA Boulevard, Suite 140, 33410
Telephone: 561-625-6260
Facsimile: 561-625-6269

Richard W. Slawson (P.A.) — Jeanmarie Whalen (P.A.)
Fred A. Cunningham (P.A.) — Todd S. Stewart (P.A.)

For full biographical listings, see the Martindale-Hubbell Law Directory

PALM HARBOR, Pinellas Co.

FLORIN, ROEBIG, WALKER, HUDDLESTUN & ROGERS, P.A. (AV)

777 Alderman Road, 34683
Telephone: 727-786-5000
Toll Free in FL: 800-226-6581
Fax: 727-772-9833
Email: frw@gte.net *URL:* http://www.florinroebig.com

Wil H. Florin — H. Dennis Rogers
Thomas D. Roebig, Jr. — Angela E. Outten
Michael L. Walker — Wolfgang M. Florin
James E. Huddlestun — Christopher D. Gray

OF COUNSEL

Jeffrey G. Brown

For full biographical listings, see the Martindale-Hubbell Law Directory

*PENSACOLA,** Escambia Co.

KERRIGAN, ESTESS, RANKIN & MCLEOD (AV)

400 East Government Street, 32501
Telephone: 850-444-4444
Watts No.: 1-800-444-4404
FAX: 850-444-4495
Email: lawfirm@kerrigan.com *URL:* http://www.kerrigan.com
Fort Walton Beach, Florida Office: 212 SE Eglin Parkway, Suite C.
Telephone: 850-244-1111.
Panama City, Florida Office: 836 Jenks Avenue.
Telephone: 850-871-5000.
FAX: 850-872-2148.

MEMBERS OF FIRM

Robert G. Kerrigan — T. Michael McLeod
George W. Estess — Randle D. Thompson
William Rankin — Marcus J. Michles II
Mary Ann Patti

LEGAL SUPPORT PERSONNEL

James Michael Kerrigan, Ph.D.

Reference: 1st American Bank of Pensacola.

For full biographical listings, see the Martindale-Hubbell Law Directory

MCKENZIE & TAYLOR, P.A. (AV)

905 East Hatton Street, 32503-3931
Telephone: 850-432-2856, 1-800-343-3067
Fax: 850-432-5130
Email: jfm01@ix.netcom.com *URL:* http://www.mckenzielawfirm.com

James F. McKenzie — Stephanie A. Taylor

For full biographical listings, see the Martindale-Hubbell Law Directory

PORT CHARLOTTE, Charlotte Co.

WILKINS, FROHLICH, JONES, HEVIA, RUSSELL & SUTTER, P.A. (AV)

18501 Murdock Circle, Sixth Floor, 33948
Telephone: 941-625-0700
Telecopier: 941-625-9540
Email: wilkins@wilkinslaw.com

Gary L. Wilkins — Jesus M. Hevia
W. Cort Frohlich — Brian O. Sutter
Phillip J. Jones — Louise O. Hanaoka

For Complete List of Firm Personnel, See General Section

For full biographical listings, see the Martindale-Hubbell Law Directory

PORT RICHEY, Pasco Co.

PROLY & LAPORTE, P.A. (AV)

11914 Oak Trail Way, 34668
Telephone: 727-863-1553
Fax: 727-862-8386
Email: prolyandlaporte@micro8.com

Peter A. Proly — Craig A. Laporte

For full biographical listings, see the Martindale-Hubbell Law Directory

*PUNTA GORDA,** Charlotte Co.

WOTITZKY, WOTITZKY, MIZELL, ROSS & GOLDMAN, P.A. (AV)

223 Taylor Street, 33950
Telephone: 941-639-2171
Telecopier: 941-639-8617
Email: wwmr@sunline.net

Jason B. Goldman — Warren R. Ross
Hal F. Wotitzky

Representative Clients: Punta Gorda Corp.; Developers of Southwest Florida, Inc.; Englewood Disposal Co., Inc.; Integrated Control Systems, Inc.
Approved Attorneys for: Attorneys' Title Insurance Fund, Orlando, Florida; Chicago Title Insurance Co.

For full biographical listings, see the Martindale-Hubbell Law Directory

ST. PETERSBURG, Pinellas Co.

CHAMBERS LAW GROUP, PROFESSIONAL ASSOCIATION (AV)

520 Fourth Street North, P.O. Box 1191, 33731-1191
Telephone: 727-896-2167
Fax: 727-822-8981
Email: CHAMLAWGRP@AOL.com

Joseph H. Chambers — Joseph W. Chambers
Jeffrey K. Chambers

John R. Mathias

Reference: NationsBank.

For full biographical listings, see the Martindale-Hubbell Law Directory

*SARASOTA,** Sarasota Co.

MARTIN & GLASER, CHARTERED (AV)

2014 Fourth Street, P.O. Box 49257, 34230-6257
Telephone: 941-365-4072
FAX: 941-365-1492
Email: martinandglaser@yahoo.com *URL:* http://www.lawyers.com/peterwmartin

Peter W. Martin — Whitney C. Glaser

For full biographical listings, see the Martindale-Hubbell Law Directory

*STUART,** Martin Co.

FRIERSON & WATSON (AV)

A Partnership of Professional Associations
3601 S.E. Ocean Boulevard, Suite 4, 34996
Telephone: 561-288-1880
Fax: 561-288-1887
URL: http://www.lawyers.com/robertw,watsonlaw

(See Next Column)

FRIERSON & WATSON—*Continued*

Robert J. Watson (P.A.) Robin Wesley Frierson (P.A.)

For full biographical listings, see the Martindale-Hubbell Law Directory

*TALLAHASSEE,** Leon Co.

BROOKS, LEBOEUF, BENNETT & FOSTER, P.A. (AV)

863 East Park Avenue, 32301
Telephone: 850-222-2000
Fax: 850-222-9757

Ronald W. Brooks
Dean R. LeBoeuf
Rhonda S. Bennett
Matthew K. Foster

For full biographical listings, see the Martindale-Hubbell Law Directory

CALLAHAN LAW FIRM (AV)

433 North Magnolia Drive, 32308
Telephone: 850-877-2525
Telecopier: 850-656-1539
Email: clf@polaris.net *URL:* http://www.polaris.net/callahan

Michael T. Callahan

For full biographical listings, see the Martindale-Hubbell Law Directory

KITCHEN, JUDKINS, SIMPSON & HIGH (AV)

1102 North Gadsden Street, 32303
Telephone: 850-222-6040
Telecopier: 850-561-1471

E. C. Deeno Kitchen
James P. Judkins
Larry D. Simpson
Robert King High, Jr.

ASSOCIATE

Paul M. Villeneuve
Thomas J. Schulte, Jr.

OF COUNSEL

John R. Overchuck

For full biographical listings, see the Martindale-Hubbell Law Directory

MCFARLAIN, WILEY, CASSEDY & JONES, PROFESSIONAL ASSOCIATION (AV)

215 South Monroe Street, Suite 600, P.O. Box 2174, 32316-2174
Telephone: 850-222-2107
Telecopier: 850-222-8475
Email: firm@mcfarlain.com *URL:* http://www.mcfarlain.com

Richard C. McFarlain
William B. Wiley
Douglas P. Jones
Charles A. Stampelos
H. Darrell White, Jr.
Christopher Barkas
Harold R. Mardenborough, Jr.
Terrell C. Madigan

Robert A. McNeely
P. David Brannon

LEGAL SUPPORT PERSONNEL

Diane L. Doll (Office Manager)

For full biographical listings, see the Martindale-Hubbell Law Directory

*TAMPA,** Hillsborough Co.

TIMOTHY G. ANDERSON, P.A. (AV)

213 South Brevard Avenue, 33606
Telephone: 813-251-0072
1-800-848-3024

Timothy G. Anderson

Leslie Longshore

For full biographical listings, see the Martindale-Hubbell Law Directory

BARBAS WEED KOENIG NUÑEZ & WHEELEY (AV)

1802 West Cleveland Street, 33606
Telephone: 813-254-6575
Fax: 813-254-4690
Lakeland, Florida Office: 500 South Florida Avenue, Suite 600, 38801.
Telephone: 941-680-2712.
Palm Harbor, Florida Office: 2708 Alternate 19 North Suite 701, 34683.
Telephone: 813-443-5323.
New Port Richey, Florida Office: 6014 U.S. 19, Suite 101-4.
Telephone: 813-849-0592.

Martha-Irene Weed
Stephen M. Barbas
Matthew B. Wheeley
David F. Koenig
Kelly Barcia Nuñez
L. Gray Sanders
Nilo J. Sanchez, Jr.

ASSOCIATES

Jimmie Butler
Steven Edward Hovsepian

For full biographical listings, see the Martindale-Hubbell Law Directory

BARR, MURMAN, TONELLI, HERZFELD & RUBIN (AV)

Suite 1750, 201 East Kennedy Boulevard, P.O. Box 172669, 33672-0669
Telephone: 813-223-3951
Fax: 813-229-2254
URL: http://www.hrfirm.com
New Port Richey, Florida Office: 7613 Little Road, 34654.
Telephone: 727-846-8646;
Fax: 727-846-8913.

James A. Murman
Michael A. Tonelli
Daniel H. Sleet
T. Gregory Slother
John W. Boult
Gregory G. Frazier
Joseph S. Silver
Clifford L. Somers

ASSOCIATES

John J. Kozak
Morris D. Purcell, Jr.
Robert J. Scanlan
Pamela A. Walton
Edward D. Friscia
James R. Wilson
Jerry A. Setchel

OF COUNSEL

Billy R. Barr

Representative Client: CIGNA Insurance Co.

For full biographical listings, see the Martindale-Hubbell Law Directory

JAMES T. BUTLER & ASSOCIATES, P.A. (AV)

930 Freedom Savings Building, 220 East Madison Street, 33602
Telephone: 813-229-3232
Fax: 813-229-7943
Email: JamesButler@Ij.net

James T. Butler

For full biographical listings, see the Martindale-Hubbell Law Directory

CLARK, CHARLTON, MARTINO & BORDERS, P.A. (AV)

3407 W. Kennedy Boulevard, 33609-2905
Telephone: 813-879-0700
Fax: 813-879-5498
URL: http://www.ccmb.net
Email: mail@ccmb.net *URL:* http://www.lawyers.com/ccm&b-law

Scott T. Borders
Scott Charlton
James W. Clark
Anthony T. Martino
Deborah A. Fleming

Reference: Southtrust Bank of Tampa.

For full biographical listings, see the Martindale-Hubbell Law Directory

CUNNINGHAM, CLARK & GREIWE, P.A. (AV)

100 Ashley Drive, South, Suite 100, 33602
Telephone: 813-228-0505
Telefax: 813-229-7982

Anthony W. Cunningham
Donald G. Greiwe
James D. Clark
D. Frank Winkles

For full biographical listings, see the Martindale-Hubbell Law Directory

PATRICK H. DEKLE, P.A. (AV)

808 Landmark Building, 412 Madison Street, 33602-4640
Telephone: 813-223-2300
Fax: 813-223-2659

Patrick H. Dekle

For full biographical listings, see the Martindale-Hubbell Law Directory

CURT GENDERS, P.A. (AV)

2304 West Cleveland Street, 33609
Telephone: 813-254-4744
FAX: 813-254-5222
Email: derekba@aol.com

Curt Genders
Derek B. Alvarez

For full biographical listings, see the Martindale-Hubbell Law Directory

THOMAS F. GRANAHAN, P.A. (AV)

1906 North Tampa Street, 33602-2133
Telephone: 813-229-1084
Fax: 813-228-6820
Email: granahan@mindspring.com

Thomas F. Granahan

For full biographical listings, see the Martindale-Hubbell Law Directory

ANTHONY J. LASPADA, P.A. (AV)

1802 North Morgan Street, 33602
Telephone: 813-223-6048
Pinellas Line: 813-894-1788
Fax: 813-228-9471

(See Next Column)

ANTHONY J. LASPADA, P.A., *Tampa—Continued*

Anthony J. LaSpada

For full biographical listings, see the Martindale-Hubbell Law Directory

WILLIAM P. LEVENS (AV)

1907 West Kennedy Boulevard, 33606
Telephone: 813-251-5775
Toll Free: 1-800-395-0463
Fax: 813-251-3240
Email: watty1@tampabay.rr.com *URL:* http://www.lawyers.com/flworkcomp

For full biographical listings, see the Martindale-Hubbell Law Directory

LEVINE, HIRSCH, SEGALL & BRENNAN, P.A. (AV)

First Union Center, 100 South Ashley Drive, Suite 1600, P.O. Box 3429, 33601-3429
Telephone: 813-229-6585
Telecopier: 813-229-7210
Email: lhsb@lhsblaw.com

Arnold D. Levine
Stephen L. Segall
Richard A. Hirsch
Edward M. Brennan

For full biographical listings, see the Martindale-Hubbell Law Directory

PAUL G. MCDUFFEE, II (AV)

3907 North Boulevard, 33603-4627
Telephone: 813-229-3131
Fax: 813-221-3110

For full biographical listings, see the Martindale-Hubbell Law Directory

LAW OFFICES OF MERKLE & MAGRI, P.A. (AV)

5510 West LaSalle Street, 33607
Telephone: 813-281-9000; Clearwater, 727-441-2699
Fax: 813-281-2223

Robert W. Merkle
Ward A. Meythaler
Joseph D. Magri
David J. Plante
Gerard J. Roble

For full biographical listings, see the Martindale-Hubbell Law Directory

MURNAGHAN & FERGUSON, P.A. (AV)

Suite 2600, 100 North Tampa Street, P.O. Box 2937, 33601-2937
Telephone: 813-222-0123
Fax: 813-222-0124

Dennis R. Ferguson
Peter P. Murnaghan

Representative Clients: Alcatel Canada, Inc.; American International Group; Amerada Hess Corporation; Ashland, Inc.; APAC, Inc., E-Z Serve Convenience Stores, Inc.; The Global Group; Praxair, Inc.; The Watson Clinic.

For full biographical listings, see the Martindale-Hubbell Law Directory

RICHARD G. PIPPINGER, P.A. (AV)

13907 North Dale Mabry Highway Suite 202, 33618
Telephone: 813-265-0301
Fax: 813-265-0831
Email: attyrgp@aol.com

Richard G. Pippinger

For full biographical listings, see the Martindale-Hubbell Law Directory

CHARLES F. SANSONE (AV)

P.O. Box 18306, 33679-8306
Telephone: 813-223-9282
Fax: 813-229-0595
Email: cfsansone@aol.com

For full biographical listings, see the Martindale-Hubbell Law Directory

A LAW OFFICE OF JEFFERY L. SHIBLEY, P.A. (AV)

13902 North Dale Mabry Highway, Suite 102, 33618
Telephone: 813-264-7200
Fax: 813-960-2755
Email: tortsjd@aol.com *URL:* http://www.lawyers.com/jefferyshibley

Jeffery L. Shibley

For full biographical listings, see the Martindale-Hubbell Law Directory

SINGLETARY LAW FIRM, P.A. (AV)

P.O. Box 3354, 33601-3354
Telephone: 813-258-5959
Fax: 813-253-5784

Thomas H. Singletary

STEWART, JOYNER & JORDAN-HOLMES, P.A. (AV)

1112 East Kennedy Boulevard, P.O. Box 172297, 33672
Telephone: 813-229-9300
Fax: 813-229-7415
Email: cjholmes@sjjhlaw.com

Delano S. Stewart
Eurich Z. Griffin
Arthenia L. Joyner
Karen C.D. McDonald
Clark Jordan-Holmes
Steve E. Baker

For full biographical listings, see the Martindale-Hubbell Law Directory

SWOPE, CARDILLO, P.A. (AV)

Suite 850, 777 South Harbour Island Boulevard, 33602
Telephone: 813-273-0017
Fax: 813-223-3678
Email: dmswope@aol.com *URL:* http://www.swopelaw.com

Dale M. Swope
Matthew J. Cardillo

Angela E. Rodante
Jonathan Robert Mayes

For full biographical listings, see the Martindale-Hubbell Law Directory

VAKA, LARSON & JOHNSON, P.L. (AV)

One Harbour Place, 777 South Harbour Island Blvd., Suite 300, 33602-5729
Telephone: 813-228-6688
Fax: 813-228-6699
Email: vljlaw@idnsi.net

George A. Vaka
Daniel A. Larson
Marc D. Johnson

For full biographical listings, see the Martindale-Hubbell Law Directory

HENRY E. VALENZUELA, P.A. (AV)

100 North Tampa Street, Suite 1825, 33602
Telephone: 813-272-1000
Fax: 813-272-1429
URL: http://www.fllawcom/valenzuela

Henry E. Valenzuela

Richard M. Mitzel
Luis Miguel Bessone

For full biographical listings, see the Martindale-Hubbell Law Directory

YERRID, KNOPIK & KRIEGER, P.A. (AV)

Barnett Plaza, Suite 2160, 101 East Kennedy Boulevard, 33602
Telephone: 813-222-8222
Fax: 813-222-8224
URL: http://www.yerridknopik.com

C. Steven Yerrid
Christopher S. Knopik
Edwin P. Krieger

Ralph L. Gonzalez
Claire D. Hancock

For full biographical listings, see the Martindale-Hubbell Law Directory

*VERO BEACH,** Indian River Co.

CLEM, POLACKWICH & VOCELLE (AV)

A Partnership including Professional Associations
3333 20th Street, 32960-2469
Telephone: 561-562-8111
Fax: 561-562-2870
Email: bvocelle@cpvlaw.com *URL:* http://www.cpvlaw.com

MEMBERS OF FIRM

Chester Clem (P.A.)
Louis B. Vocelle, Jr., (P.A.)
Alan S. Polackwich, Sr. (P.A.)
Paul Richard Berg

ASSOCIATE

Janet M. Carney

OF COUNSEL

Robert Golden

References: Barnett Bank of The Treasure Coast; Northern Trust Bank of Vero Beach; Indian River National Bank; Riverside National Bank of Florida.

For full biographical listings, see the Martindale-Hubbell Law Directory

MOSS, HENDERSON, BLANTON & LANIER, P.A. (AV)

817 Beachland Boulevard, P.O. Box 3406, 32964-3406
Telephone: 561-231-1900
Fax: 561-231-4387

(See Next Column)

MOSS, HENDERSON, BLANTON & LANIER P.A.—*Continued*

Robin A. Blanton
Clinton W. Lanier
Lewis W. Murphy, Jr.

Representative Clients: Aetna Life & Casualty; Alcoa Florida, Inc.; Florida Power & Light Co.; Insurance Company of North America; Liberty Mutual Insurance Co.; Sears, Roebuck & Co.; Sugar Cane Growers Cooperative of Florida; Norfolk Southern Corporation/North American Van Lines, Inc.

For Complete List of Firm Personnel, See General Section

For full biographical listings, see the Martindale-Hubbell Law Directory

*WEST PALM BEACH,** Palm Beach Co.

ADAMS, COOGLER, WATSON & MERKEL, P.A. (AV)

Suite 1600, 1555 Palm Beach Lakes Boulevard, P.O. Box 2069, 33402
Telephone: 561-478-4500
Fax: 561-684-7346
Email: ACWMLAW@AOL.COM

Samuel H. Adams (1913-1981)
Roy R. Watson
Robert G. Merkel
James C. Barry
Reed W. Kellner
Catherine Lynn Kasten
Scott S. Warburton
Peter A. Cooke
Patricia A. Judge
Kathryn L. Tignor

Alexander D. Barker
Jodi G. Barrett
Stephanie Brown
James W. Flanagan
Paul L. Harwood
Thomas Hodas
Catherine M. Paris

OF COUNSEL

L. C. Shepard, Jr.

For full biographical listings, see the Martindale-Hubbell Law Directory

THE LAW OFFICE OF BILL BONE, P.A. (AV)

One Clearlake Centre, Suite 1404, 250 South Australian Avenue, 33401
Telephone: 561-832-9400
Fax: 561-832-9445
Email: admin@billbone.com *URL:* http://www.lawyers.com/billbone

William Dudley "Bill" Bone

OF COUNSEL

Michael A. Viscomi

LEGAL SUPPORT PERSONNEL

Jeffrey F. Chapin
Richard E. Lopez
(Paralegal and Investigator)
Tracy G. Tabb

For full biographical listings, see the Martindale-Hubbell Law Directory

DAVIS, GORDON & DONER, P.A. (AV)

515 North Flagler Drive, 7th Floor, 33401
Telephone: 561-659-7337
Facsimile: 561-659-0143
Email: dgdc@flinet.com *URL:* http://www.dgdlaw.com

Zell Davis, Jr. (Retired)
Robert E. Gordon
Adam S. Doner

Eric D. Hightower
Steven G. Calamusa

OF COUNSEL

Mikel D. Jones (Not admitted in FL)

For full biographical listings, see the Martindale-Hubbell Law Directory

THE LAW OFFICE OF TERRENCE F. DYTRYCH, P.A. (AV)

2023 North Flagler Drive, 33407
Telephone: 561-655-7808
Telecopier: 561-659-0685
Email: dytrycht@bellsouth.net

Terrence F. Dytrych

For full biographical listings, see the Martindale-Hubbell Law Directory

ALAN C. ESPY, P.A. (AV)

Commerce Pointe, Suite 420, 1818 South Australian Avenue, 33409
Telephone: 561-478-4777
Fax: 561-478-0886
Email: espy@flite.net

Alan C. Espy

OF COUNSEL

James C. Paine, Jr.

For full biographical listings, see the Martindale-Hubbell Law Directory

FARISH, FARISH & ROMANI (AV)

316 Banyan Boulevard, P.O. Box 4118, 33402
Telephone: 561-659-3500
1-800-401-4LAW
Fax: 561-655-3158
Email: farish@bellsouth.net

MEMBERS OF FIRM

Joseph D. Farish (1892-1977)
Joseph D. Farish, Jr.
Robert V. Romani

ASSOCIATES

S. Emory Rogers
Peter M. Bassaline

LEGAL SUPPORT PERSONNEL

Ken P. Beelner

References: 1st Union Bank.

For full biographical listings, see the Martindale-Hubbell Law Directory

FREEMAN & SUPRAN, P.A. (AV)

315 Fifth Street, 33401-3709
Telephone: 561-655-6025
Fax: 561-655-5759
Palatka, Florida Office: 415 St. Johns Avenue.
Telephone: 904-325-6239.
Fax: 904-329-9626.

Terry N. Freeman
George P. Supran
Mark D. Kairalla

For full biographical listings, see the Martindale-Hubbell Law Directory

PHILLIP C. HOUSTON, P.A. (AV)

Suite 1107, One Clearlake Center, 250 Australian Avenue South, 33401
Telephone: 561-835-1775
Fax: 561-835-1427
Email: houston250@aol.com

Phillip C. Houston

For full biographical listings, see the Martindale-Hubbell Law Directory

THOMAS E. KINGCADE PROFESSIONAL ASSOCIATION (AV)

209 South Olive Avenue, 33401
Telephone: 561-659-7300; 800-869-9409
Fax: 561-655-1593
Email: tekingcade@aol.com *URL:* http://www.lawyers.com/kingcade

Thomas E. Kingcade

William W. Booth

For full biographical listings, see the Martindale-Hubbell Law Directory

STEPHEN R. KOONS, P.A. (AV)

1897 Palm Beach Lakes Boulevard, Suite 219, 33409
Telephone: 561-687-2900
800-575-LAWS
FAX: 561-687-5009
URL: http://www.lawyers.com/stephenrkoons

Stephen R. Koons

For full biographical listings, see the Martindale-Hubbell Law Directory

LIGGIO, BENRUBI & WILLIAMS, P.A. (AV)

1615 Forum Place, Suite 3B, 33401
Telephone: 561-616-3333
Fax: 561-616-3266
Email: liggio@aol.com *URL:* http://www.lawyers.com/liggiolaw

Jeffrey M. Liggio
Richard M. Benrubi
Jene P. Williams

LEGAL SUPPORT PERSONNEL

Yara B. Vega (Paralegal)
Kathy G. Harmon (Paralegal)
Sharon Lynn (Paralegal)

For full biographical listings, see the Martindale-Hubbell Law Directory

LYTAL, REITER, CLARK, FOUNTAIN & WILLIAMS (AV)

A Limited Liability Partnership
Tenth Floor, 515 North Flagler Drive, 33401
Telephone: 561-655-1990
Broward County: 954-426-2103
Toll Free: 1-800-654-2024
Fax: 561-832-2932
Mailing Address: P.O. Box 4056, 33402
Email: lhowden@palmbeachlaw.com *URL:* http://www.palmbeachlaw.com

(See Next Column)

LYTAL, REITER, CLARK, FOUNTAIN & WILLIAMS, *West Palm Beach—Continued*

Lake Lytal, Jr. (P.A.)
Joseph J. Reiter (P.A.)
Mark W. Clark (P.A.)
Donald R. Fountain, Jr. (P.A.)
William S. Williams (P.A.)

David M. Gaspari
W. Hampton Keen
Nancy L. La Vista
Julie H. Littky-Rubin
Lake H. Lytal, III
Michael J. Overbeck
David C. Prather
Kevin C. Smith
Scott Bryant Smith

Reference: United National Bank.

For full biographical listings, see the Martindale-Hubbell Law Directory

PATRICK M. O'HARA, P.A. (AV)

Commerce Center, Suite 100, 324 Datura Street, 33401
Telephone: 561-659-3771
Fax: 561-659-4224

Patrick M. O'Hara

For full biographical listings, see the Martindale-Hubbell Law Directory

RICCI, HUBBARD, LEOPOLD, FRANKEL & FARMER, P.A. (AV)

1645 Palm Beach Lakes Boulevard, Suite 250, P.O. Box 2946, 33402
Telephone: 561-684-6500
Fax: 561-697-2383
Email: Ricci@bellsouth.net *URL:* http://www.riccihubbard.com

Edward M. Ricci
James R. Hubbard
Theodore J. Leopold
Lois J. Frankel
Duncan J. Farmer
Scott C. Murray
Steven G. Dell
Marina F. Parrish
Andrea D. McMillan

For full biographical listings, see the Martindale-Hubbell Law Directory

ROCA & SHARPE, P.A. (AV)

707 North Flagler Drive, 33401
Telephone: 561-659-3433
Fax: 561-659-3390
Email: rocasharpe@aol.com *URL:* http://www.roca-sharpe.com

Rafael J. Roca (P.A.)
Tracy R. Sharpe (P.A.)

For full biographical listings, see the Martindale-Hubbell Law Directory

SCHULER & HALVORSON, P.A. (AV)

Suite 4D Barristers Building, 1615 Forum Place, 33401-2314
Telephone: 561-689-8180
Fax: 561-684-9683
URL: http://www.sh-law.com

Richard D. Schuler
Steven W. Halvorson

Craig M. Goldenfarb

LEGAL SUPPORT PERSONNEL

Hendrik C. Van Wieringen, Jr.
Rhea D. Doran
Judith C. Spano (Certified Legal Assistant)

For full biographical listings, see the Martindale-Hubbell Law Directory

SEARCY DENNEY SCAROLA BARNHART & SHIPLEY, PROFESSIONAL ASSOCIATION (AV)

2139 Palm Beach Lakes Boulevard, P.O. Drawer 3626, 33402-3626
Telephone: 561-686-6300
800-780-8607
800-220-7006 (Spanish)
Fax: 561-478-0754
Email: CDS@SEARCYLAW.COM *URL:* http://www.searcylaw.com

Christian D. Searcy, Sr.
Earl L. Denney, Jr.
John Scarola
F. Gregory Barnhart
John A. Shipley
David K. Kelley, Jr.
Lance J. Block, Jr.
C. Calvin Warriner, III
William A. Norton
David J. Sales
Christopher K. Speed
William B. King
David J. White

Karen E. Terry
Sean C. Domnick
Harry A. Shevin
Patrick E. Quinlan
Darryl L. Lewis

(See Next Column)

LEGAL SUPPORT PERSONNEL

Laurie J. Briggs (Paralegal)
Deane L. Cady (Paralegal/Investigator)
Daniel J. Calloway (Paralegal/Investigator)
Emilio Diamantis (Paralegal/Investigator)
David W. Gilmore (Paralegal/Investigator)
John C. Hopkins (Paralegal/Investigator)
Thaddeus E. Kulesa (Paralegal/Investigator)
J. Peter Love (Paralegal/Investigator)
William H. Seabold (Paralegal/Investigator)
Kathleen Simon (Paralegal)
Steve M. Smith (Paralegal/Investigator)
Kevin J. Walsh (Paralegal/Investigator)
Judson Whitehorn (Paralegal/Investigator)
Samantha M. Johansen (Paralegal/Investigator)

For Complete List of Firm Personnel, See General Section

For full biographical listings, see the Martindale-Hubbell Law Directory

SILBER & VALENTE, P.A. (AV)

1801 South Australian Avenue, Suite 201, 33409
Telephone: 561-615-6200
Facsimile: 561-615-6206
Email: pvalente@parrot.telegraph.net

Louis M. Silber
Philip L. Valente, Jr.

For full biographical listings, see the Martindale-Hubbell Law Directory

WAGNER, JOHNSON, MCAFEE & BODIK, P.A. (AV)

Commerce Pointe, Suite 450, 1818 South Australian Avenue, 33409
Telephone: 561-686-5200
Fax: 561-686-6710
Email: macwjm@icanect.net

Ward Wagner, Jr.
Robert R. Johnson
Helen Wagner McAfee
William J. McAfee
Michael G. Bodik

References: SunTrust Bank, South Florida, N.A.; Fidelity Federal Savings & Loan Association of West Palm Beach.

For full biographical listings, see the Martindale-Hubbell Law Directory

WIEDERHOLD, MOSES, BULFIN & RUBIN, P.A. (AV)

Northbridge Centre, Suite 800, 515 North Flagler Drive, P.O. Box 3918, 33402
Telephone: 561-659-2296;
Broward: 954-763-5630
Fax: 561-659-2865
Email: bobmoses@bellsouth.net

John P. Wiederhold
Robert D. Moses
John J. Bulfin
Kenneth M. Rubin

Lawrence I. Bass
Kay Seeber Hoff
Bruce R. Katzell

LEGAL SUPPORT PERSONNEL

Gina Truzzolino (Paralegal/Investigator)

Reference: Bank of America.

For full biographical listings, see the Martindale-Hubbell Law Directory

WINTER PARK, Orange Co.

WENDY L. AIKIN, P.A. (AV)

288 Park Avenue North, 32789
Telephone: 407-644-4040
Fax: 407-644-4414
Email: aikinlaw@aol.com *URL:* http://www.lawyers.com/wendyaikin

Wendy L. Aikin

OF COUNSEL

Donald N. Crowell
Brenda Lee London

For full biographical listings, see the Martindale-Hubbell Law Directory

RICHARD B. TROUTMAN, P.A. (AV)

Suite 500 1245 West Fairbanks Avenue, 32789
Telephone: 407-647-5002
Fax: 407-647-2050

Richard B. Troutman
Brett M. Bressler

Stephen H. McNeill

For full biographical listings, see the Martindale-Hubbell Law Directory

GEORGIA

*ALBANY,** Dougherty Co.

CANNON, MEYER VON BREMEN & GOSS, LLP (AV)

2417 Westgate Drive, P.O. Box 70909, 31708-0909
Telephone: 912-435-1470
Telefax: 912-888-2156
Email: cmvblaw@cmvb.com

MEMBERS OF FIRM

William E. Cannon, Jr.
Michael S. Meyer von Bremen
Stephen S. Goss

ASSOCIATES

Timothy O. Davis
Toysha M. Flowers
William H. Gregory, II

For full biographical listings, see the Martindale-Hubbell Law Directory

W. EDWARD MEEKS, JR. (AV)

2410 Westgate Drive, Suite 105, P.O. Drawer 71525, 31708-1525
Telephone: 912-439-9234
Fax: 912-439-9175

Representative Clients: Pritchett Ford; Tri-County Aq.; Alarm Services, Inc.; Lee County Board of Education; BESCO Steel.

For full biographical listings, see the Martindale-Hubbell Law Directory

*ATHENS,** Clarke Co.

FOY S. HORNE, JR., P.C. (AV)

2425 West Broad Street, Suite 200, P.O. Box 706, 30603
Telephone: 706-549-6376
Fax: 706-613-2508

Foy S. Horne, Jr.

Bank Reference: NationsBank of Georgia, N.A.

For full biographical listings, see the Martindale-Hubbell Law Directory

*ATLANTA,** Fulton Co.

WILLIAM Q. BIRD AND ASSOCIATES, P.C. (AV)

14 Seventeenth Street, Suite 5, P.O. Box 7009, 30357
Telephone: 404-873-4696
Fax: 404-872-3745
Email: info@williamqbird.com *URL:* http://www.williamqbird.com

William Q. Bird

John G. Mabrey
Karin Middleton Allen

For full biographical listings, see the Martindale-Hubbell Law Directory

DAVID WM. BOONE, P.C. (AV)

3166 Mathieson Drive, 30305
Telephone: 404-239-0305
Fax: 404-239-0520

David William Boone
Simone R. Siex

For full biographical listings, see the Martindale-Hubbell Law Directory

BOVIS, KYLE & BURCH, LLC (AV)

A Limited Liability Corporation including Professional Corporations
Third Floor, 53 Perimeter Center East, 30346
Telephone: 770-391-9100
Telecopier: 770-668-0878
Email: bkb@boviskyle.com *URL:* http://www.boviskyle.com

John M. Bovis (P.C.)
Steven J. Kyle (P.C.)
John V. Burch (P.C.)
C. Sam Thomas (P.C.)
James E. Singer
J. Wesley Skinner
Gregory R. Veal
Timothy J. Burson
Charles M. Medlin
John H. Peavy Jr.

J.S. Scott Busby
Christina A. Craddock
Timothy A. Hickey, Jr.
Jana B. Tabor
Carl A. Hassler
John David Etheriedge
Everett A. Kliphouse

For full biographical listings, see the Martindale-Hubbell Law Directory

BUTLER & MACDOUGALD (AV)

152 Nassau Street, 30303
Telephone: 404-688-6100
Fax: 404-688-0711
Email: dmacd@mindspring.com
Email: lbutler@mindspring.com
Jasper, Georgia Office: The Butler-Cape House, 9205 Highway 53 West, 30143.
Telephone: 706-692-6192.
Fax: 706-692-3831.

MEMBERS OF FIRM

Larry Kent Butler
Daniel MacDougald III

OF COUNSEL

Harry W. MacDougald

For full biographical listings, see the Martindale-Hubbell Law Directory

BUTLER, WOOTEN, OVERBY, FRYHOFER, DAUGHTERY & SULLIVAN (AV)

2719 Buford Highway, 30324
Telephone: 404-321-1700
WATS 1-800-242-2962
Fax: 404-321-1713
Columbus, Georgia Office: 1500 Second Avenue, P.O. Box 2766.
Telephone: 706-322-1990; National Wats: 1-800-233-4086.
Fax: 706-323-2962.

MEMBERS OF FIRM

James E. Butler, Jr.
Joel O. Wooten, Jr.
C. Frederick Overby
George W. Fryhofer III
Peter J. Daughtery
Lee Tarte Wallace
Terrance C. Sullivan

ASSOCIATES

Jason L. Crawford
Keith A. Pittman
Joshua Sacks
Teresa Thomas Abell
Cale H. Conley

Reference: Columbus Bank and Trust, Columbus, Ga.

For full biographical listings, see the Martindale-Hubbell Law Directory

EDGAR L. CROSSETT, III, P.C. (AV)

5064 Roswell Road, Building C Suite 300, 30342-1911
Telephone: 404-843-1640
Telecopier: 404-843-4474

Edgar L. Crossett, III

Reference: Suntrust Bank.

For full biographical listings, see the Martindale-Hubbell Law Directory

DENNIS, CORRY & PORTER, L.L.P. (AV)

3300 One Atlanta Plaza, 950 East Paces Ferry Road, P.O. Box 18640, 30326
Telephone: 404-816-2800
Wats: 800-735-0838
Fax: 404-816-5656
URL: http://www.dcplaw.com

MEMBERS OF FIRM

Robert E. Corry, Jr.
R. Clay Porter
James S. Strawinski
Grant B. Smith
Matthew J. Jewell
Raymond J. Kurey
Ronald Ray Coleman, Jr.
Scott W. McMickle

OF COUNSEL

Douglas Dennis

ASSOCIATES

Thomas D. Trask
Christopher D. Pixley
John D. Dixon
Stephanie F. Goff
Kerry A. Quinn
George A. Koenig
Michael Goldberg
Michael F. Coogan
Todd M. Yates
Nicole L. Wolfe
Alisa W. Terry
Stephanie Collings Patel
Michael A. Prieto

Representative Clients: Schneider National, Inc.; Roadway Express, Inc.; Caliber System, Inc.

For full biographical listings, see the Martindale-Hubbell Law Directory

DOFFERMYRE, SHIELDS, CANFIELD, KNOWLES & DEVINE (AV)

Suite 1600, 1355 Peachtree Street, 30309
Telephone: 404-881-8900
Fax: 404-881-3007

Robert E. Shields
Kenneth S. Canfield
Ralph I. Knowles, Jr.
Leslie J. Bryan
Georgiana Rizk
Samuel W. Wethern
David S. Hagy
Bonnie L. Keith

For full biographical listings, see the Martindale-Hubbell Law Directory

Atlanta—Continued

DWYER & WHITE (AV)

A Partnership including a Professional Corporation
Suite 700, 2100 Riveredge Parkway, 30328-4654
Telephone: 770-956-1984
Fax: 770-956-1381
Email: admin@dwslaw.com *URL:* http://www.dwslaw.com

MEMBERS

J. Matthew Dwyer, Jr. (P.C.) William Woods White

For full biographical listings, see the Martindale-Hubbell Law Directory

FAIN, MAJOR, WILEY & BRENNAN, P.C. (AV)

100 Glenridge Point Parkway Suite 500, 30342-1440
Telephone: 404-688-6633
Telecopier: 404-420-1544

Gene A. Major
Thomas E. Brennan
Charles A. Wiley, Jr.
John K. Miles, Jr.
Darryl G. Haynes

Brian Alligood
James Curry
Kim Monroe Jackson
Brian M. Leepson
Robert L. Jones
Stephen Anthony Fern
James A. Rice, Jr.
Michael K. Watson

Representative Clients: Allstate Insurance Co.; Budget Rent-A-Car; Arkansas Best Corp.; Chrysler Insurance Co.; Georgia Farm Bureau Mutual Insurance Co.; Hertz Corp.; Universal Underwriters Insurance Co.; Westfield Insurance Co.; Winn-Dixie Stores, Inc.

For Complete List of Firm Personnel, See General Section

For full biographical listings, see the Martindale-Hubbell Law Directory

FREEMAN, WRIGHT & HERMAN (AV)

3060 Peachtree Road, N.W. Suite 720, 30305-2240
Telephone: 404-262-2962
Fax: 404-237-1926
Email: bhi@bellsouth.net

MEMBERS OF FIRM

Joe C. Freeman, Jr.
Arnold Wright, Jr.
Robert L. Herman

For full biographical listings, see the Martindale-Hubbell Law Directory

GARLAND, SAMUEL & LOEB, P.C. (AV)

3151 Maple Drive, N.E., 30305
Telephone: 404-262-2225
Fax: 404-365-5041
Email: triallaw@atlanta.com

Edward T. M. Garland
Donald F. Samuel
Robin N. Loeb

For full biographical listings, see the Martindale-Hubbell Law Directory

GOLDNER, SOMMERS, SCRUDDER & BASS (AV)

900 Circle 75 Parkway Suite 850, 30339
Telephone: 770-612-9200
Facsimile: 770-612-9201

MEMBERS OF FIRM

Stephen L. Goldner
Susan V. Sommers
Henry E. Scrudder, Jr.

For Complete List of Firm Personnel, See General Section

For full biographical listings, see the Martindale-Hubbell Law Directory

GEORGE W. HART, P.C. (AV)

Promenade Two Suite 3775, 1230 Peachtree Street, N.E., 30309-3589
Telephone: 404-876-3775
Fax: 404-873-3799

George W. Hart

Reference: SunTrust Bank.

For full biographical listings, see the Martindale-Hubbell Law Directory

HILL AND BLEIBERG (AV)

Suite 200, 47 Perimeter Center East, 30346
Telephone: 770-394-7800
Fax: 770-394-7802
Email: HBLAWFIRM@AOL.COM

MEMBERS OF FIRM

Robert P. Bleiberg
Gary Hill

ASSOCIATE

Bryan Hill

For full biographical listings, see the Martindale-Hubbell Law Directory

HOFFMAN & FOWLER, LLP (AV)

A Partnership of Professional Corporations
5040 Roswell Road, N.E. Suite 250, 30342
Telephone: 404-256-6464
Fax: 404-256-1422

MEMBERS OF FIRM

Clifford G. Hoffman (P.C.)
Michael C. Fowler (P.C.)

LEGAL SUPPORT PERSONNEL

Penny J. Farr (Paralegal)

For full biographical listings, see the Martindale-Hubbell Law Directory

JOHNSON & WARD (AV)

2100 The Equitable Building, 100 Peachtree Street N.W., 30303-1962
Telephone: 404-524-5626
Facsimile: 404-524-1769
Email: postmaster@johnsonward.com

MEMBERS OF FIRM

William C. Lanham
John C. Dabney, Jr.
Clark H. McGehee
William D. deGolian
Bruce A. Maxwell

For Complete List of Firm Personnel, See General Section
For full biographical listings, see the Martindale-Hubbell Law Directory

KIRSCHNER AND VENKER, P.C. (AV)

Suite 450, 600 West Peachtree Street, N.W., 30308
Telephone: 404-872-6646
Fax: 404-876-7168

Andrew R. Kirschner
Thomas J. Venker

For full biographical listings, see the Martindale-Hubbell Law Directory

KREVOLIN & HORST, LLC (AV)

Suite 2150, 100 Colony Square, 1175 Peachtree Street, N.E., 30361
Telephone: 404-888-9700
Fax: 404-888-9577

Douglas P. Krevolin
Jeffrey D. Horst

Michael G. Regas II
Michael D. Flint

For full biographical listings, see the Martindale-Hubbell Law Directory

THOMAS WILLIAM MALONE (AV)

Two Ravinia Drive Suite 300, 30346
Telephone: 770-390-7550
Fax: 770-390-7560
Email: Malonepc@aol.com *URL:* http://www.malonepc.com

J. Hoyt Young
Mark L. Stuckey
S. Bradley Houck

References: SunTrust Bank, Atlanta, Georgia; SunTrust Bank of South Georgia.

For full biographical listings, see the Martindale-Hubbell Law Directory

MATTHEWS & STEEL (AV)

462 East Paces Ferry Road, 30305
Telephone: 404-264-1292
800-776-0098
Fax: 404-264-0161
Email: postmaster@matthewssteellaw.com

MEMBERS OF FIRM

James B. Matthews, III
John B. Briggs
John D. Steel
H. Craig Stafford

For full biographical listings, see the Martindale-Hubbell Law Directory

PIERCE & YOUNG (AV)

Building 1700, 2255 Cumberland Parkway Northwest, 30339-4575
Telephone: 770-435-0500
Telecopier: 770-435-0362

MEMBERS OF FIRM

J. Wayne Pierce
Richard M. Young
Christy A. Dunkelberger

For full biographical listings, see the Martindale-Hubbell Law Directory

Atlanta—Continued

POPE, McGLAMRY, KILPATRICK & MORRISON, LLP (AV)

A Partnership including Professional Corporations
The Pinnacle, 3455 Peachtree Road, N.E., 30326-3243
Telephone: 404-523-7706
Fax: 404-524-1648
Phenix City, Alabama: 334-298-7354
Mailing Address: P.O. Box 191625, Atlanta, GA, 31119-1625
Email: pmkm@pmkm.com
Columbus, Georgia Office: 318 11th Street, 2nd Floor, P.O. Box 2128, 31902-2128.
Telephone: 706-324-0050.
Fax: 706-327-1536.

MEMBERS OF FIRM

C. Neal Pope (P.C.)
Max R. McGlamry (P.C.) (Resident, Columbus, Georgia Office)
Paul V. Kilpatrick, Jr. (Resident, Columbus, Georgia Office)
R. Timothy Morrison
Michael L. McGlamry
Earle F. Lasseter
William Usher Norwood, III
Jay F. Hirsch
Wade H. Tomlinson, III
Teresa Pike Tomlinson

RESIDENT ASSOCIATE

C. Elizabeth Pope

Reference: Columbus Bank & Trust Co.

For full biographical listings, see the Martindale-Hubbell Law Directory

REYNOLDS & McARTHUR (AV)

A Partnership including a Professional Corporation
Overlook II, Suite 270, 2839 Paces Ferry Rd., N.W., 30339
Telephone: 770-438-8997; 770-438-9062
Fax: 770-438-8536
Macon, Georgia Office: 850 Walnut Street, 31201.
Telephone: 912-741-6000.
Fax: 912-742-0750. Email: firm@rmtriallaw.com

MEMBERS OF FIRM

W. Carl Reynolds (P.C.)
Katherine L. McArthur
Charles M. Cork, III
O. Wendell Horne, III
Bradley J. Survant

For full biographical listings, see the Martindale-Hubbell Law Directory

SHIGLEY LAW FIRM, L.L.C. (AV)

3166 Mathieson Drive Suite 200, 30305
Telephone: 404-364-1999
Fax: 404-364-0880
URL: http://www.ga-law.com
Email: kshigley@mindspring.com *URL:* http://www.lawyers.com/shigleylaw

Kenneth L. Shigley

For full biographical listings, see the Martindale-Hubbell Law Directory

THOMAS, KENNEDY, SAMPSON & PATTERSON (AV)

3355 Main Street, 30337
Telephone: 404-688-4503
Telecopier: 404-681-2950; Litigation Dept.
Telecopier: 404-684-9515
URL: http://www.tksp.com

MEMBERS OF FIRM

R. E. Thomas, Jr. (1911-1996)
John Loren Kennedy (1942-1994)
Thomas G. Sampson
P. Andrew Patterson
Jeffrey E. Tompkins

ASSOCIATES

Thomas G. Sampson, II
Ceasar C. Mitchell, II.
Erika Nicole Jackson

LEGAL SUPPORT PERSONNEL

Gwendolyn C.H. Dixon
Elbetha (Beth) Martin (Paralegal)
Nancy Allen-Haskell
Yvonne Torrence
Shyril E. Beck
Constance Harris (Paralegal)
Lisa Russell Johnson

For full biographical listings, see the Martindale-Hubbell Law Directory

WILLIAMS & HENRY, LLP (AV)

Suite 2020, 1100 Peachtree Street, N.E., 30309-4520
Telephone: 404-873-3000
Fax: 404-873-4508
URL: http://www.whlawfirm.com

MEMBERS OF FIRM

Benjamin S. Williams
Philip C. Henry
Harvey R. Spiegel

Joseph A. Fried
Edward C. Henderson, Jr.
Gary L. Wimbish

(See Next Column)

OF COUNSEL

Robert L. Callahan, III

Reference: SunTrust Bank.

For full biographical listings, see the Martindale-Hubbell Law Directory

WOOD & GRANT (AV)

The Equitable Building Suite 2140, 100 Peachtree Street, 30303
Telephone: 404-522-1713
Fax: 404-522-1716

MEMBERS OF FIRM

L. Lin Wood
Wayne Grant

ASSOCIATE

Kimberly W. Rabren

For full biographical listings, see the Martindale-Hubbell Law Directory

*AUGUSTA,** Richmond Co.

BURNSIDE, WALL, DANIEL, ELLISON & REVELL (AV)

A Partnership including Professional Corporations
454 Greene Street, P.O. Box 2125, 30903
Telephone: 706-722-0768
Fax: 706-722-5984

MEMBERS OF FIRM

Robert C. Daniel, Jr. (1943-1993)
Thomas R. Burnside, Jr. (P.C.)
James B. Wall (P.C.)
James W. Ellison
Harry D. Revell
Thomas R. Burnside, III

Representative Clients: Augusta-Richmond County Commission; National Science Center Foundation, Inc.; CSRA Regional Development Center; City of Harlem, Georgia; Liquid Carbonic Corp.; Southeastern Equipment Co.; SECO Aviation, Inc.; SECO Parts & Equipment, Inc.

For full biographical listings, see the Martindale-Hubbell Law Directory

BREMEN, Haralson Co.

JACK F. WITCHER (AV)

601 Pacific Avenue, P.O. Drawer 1330, 30110
Telephone: 770-537-5848
1-800-228-6576 (Georgia only)
Fax: 770-537-3899
Email: jwitcher@mindspring

ASSOCIATES

Evan Lee Stapler
Heather Kendall Karrh

Reference: 1st National Bank of Haralson County.

For full biographical listings, see the Martindale-Hubbell Law Directory

*BRUNSWICK,** Glynn Co.

AUSTIN E. CATTS (AV)

1529 1/2 Reynolds Street, 31520
Telephone: 912-261-8448
Fax: 912-261-7919
Email: aecatts@compuserve.com *URL:* http://www.lawyers.com/austincattslaw

For full biographical listings, see the Martindale-Hubbell Law Directory

FENDIG, McLEMORE, TAYLOR, WHITWORTH & DURHAM, P.C. (AV)

Suite 200 Suntrust Bank Building, P.O. Box 1996, 31521
Telephone: 912-264-4126
Telecopier: 912-264-0591

Albert Fendig, Jr.
Gilbert C. McLemore, Jr.
Philip R. Taylor
David T. Whitworth
James B. Durham
Donna L. Crossland
Beth M. Duncan

For full biographical listings, see the Martindale-Hubbell Law Directory

*CARROLLTON,** Carroll Co.

HEAD, HEAD & HEAD (AV)

516 Newnan Street, P.O. Box 508, 30117
Telephone: 770-832-9697
Fax: 770-834-1800

MEMBERS OF FIRM

Henry C. Head
James B. Head
David C. Head

For full biographical listings, see the Martindale-Hubbell Law Directory

*NEWNAN,** Coweta Co.

GLOVER & DAVIS, P.A. (AV)

10 Brown Street, P.O. Box 1038, 30264
Telephone: 770-683-6000
Fax: 770-683-6010
Peachtree City, Georgia Office: Suite 130, 200 Westpark Drive.
Telephone: 770-487-5834.
Fax: 770-487-3492.

J. Littleton Glover
Welborn B. Davis, Jr. (1922-1974)
J. Littleton Glover, Jr.
Alan W. Jackson
Randy E. Connell
W. Robert Hancock, Jr. (Resident, Peachtree Office)
Asa M. Powell, Jr.
Jerry Ann Conner

Peter A. Durham
Mark E. Dacy (Resident, Peachtree City Office)

Representative Clients: Coweta County, Georgia; J. Smith Lanier & Co. and Insurance Subsidiaries; First Citizens Corporation and Banking Subsidiaries; Putnam-Greene Financial Corporation and Banking Subsidiaries; Batson-Cook Company, General, Corporate and Construction Divisions; Pyramid Masonry, Inc..
Local Counsel for: West Georgia Farm Credit, ACA.

For full biographical listings, see the Martindale-Hubbell Law Directory

ROSENZWEIG, JONES & MACNABB, P.C. (AV)

32 South Court Square, P.O. Box 220, 30264
Telephone: 770-253-3282
Fax: 770-251-7262

George C. Rosenzweig
Sidney Pope Jones, Jr.
Joseph P. MacNabb

Charles C. Witcher
Douglas L. Dreyer
Jonathan W. Hickman

Approved Attorneys for: Lawyers Title Insurance Corp.; Chicago Title Insurance Co.

For full biographical listings, see the Martindale-Hubbell Law Directory

NORCROSS, Gwinnett Co.

DEMING, PARKER, HOFFMAN, GREEN & CAMPBELL, P.C. (AV)

4851 Jimmy Carter Boulevard, 30093
Telephone: 770-564-2600
Fax: 770-564-2267
Covington, Georgia Office: Suite 11, 3236 Highway 278.
Telephone: 770-787-2600.
Fax: 770-564-2267.
Cumming, Georgia Office: 425 Tribble Gap Road, Suite 398, 30130.
Telephone: 770-889-2600.
Fax: 770-564-2267.

Michael D. Deming
Franklin E. Parker
Paul M. Hoffman
Jim R. Green, Jr.
Richard A. Campbell
Stephen R. Williams

OF COUNSEL

Robert E. Born

Mark L. Wells
Christopher W. T. Daly
E. Nicole Harrison
Suzanne M. Boykin

For full biographical listings, see the Martindale-Hubbell Law Directory

*REIDSVILLE,** Tattnall Co.

CHENEY & CHENEY, P.C. (AV)

130 South Main Street, P.O. Box 1100, 30453-1100
Telephone: 912-557-4768
Fax: 912-557-1885
Email: cheneyandcheney@cybersouth.com

Curtis V. Cheney, Jr.
Sharon G. Cheney

For full biographical listings, see the Martindale-Hubbell Law Directory

*VALDOSTA,** Lowndes Co.

DODD AND DENNIS, P.C. (AV)

613 N. Patterson Street, P.O. Box 1066, 31603-1066
Telephone: 912-242-4470
Telefax: 912-245-7731
URL: http://www.lawyers.com/dodd&dennis
Email: doddlaw@mail.datasys.net *URL:* http://www.doddlaw.com

Roger J. Dodd
Sam D. Dennis

References: First Union Bank; First State Bank and Trust Co.; Park Avenue Bank.

For full biographical listings, see the Martindale-Hubbell Law Directory

HAWAII

*HONOLULU,** Honolulu Co.

AYABE, CHONG, NISHIMOTO, SIA & NAKAMURA (AV)

A Partnership including a Professional Corporation
Pauahi Tower, Suite 2500, 1001 Bishop Street, 96813
Telephone: 808-537-6119
Telecopier: 808-526-3491
Email: ACNSN@pixi.com

MEMBERS OF FIRM

Sidney K. Ayabe (P.C.)
John S. Nishimoto
Richard F. Nakamura
Jeffrey H. K. Sia
Francis M. Nakamoto
Calvin E. Young
Diane W. Wong
Rodney S. Nishida
Patricia T. Fujii
Gail M. Kang
Ann H. Aratani
Ronald M. Shigekane
Robin R. Horner
Stephen G. Dyer
Steven L. Goto

J. Thomas Weber
Robert A. Mash
Gary S. Miyamoto
Jodi L. Kimura
Michael J. Van Dyke
Zale T. Okazaki

Representative Clients: Travelers Insurance Co.; St. Paul Fire and Marine Insurance Co.; The Employers Group of Insurance Companies; TIG Insurance Co.; Pacific Insurance Co.; Hartford Accident and Indemnity Co.; Continental Casualty Co.; CNA Insurance Co.; DTRIC.

For full biographical listings, see the Martindale-Hubbell Law Directory

CRONIN, FRIED, SEKIYA, KEKINA & FAIRBANKS ATTORNEYS AT LAW, A LAW CORPORATION (AV)

1900 Davies Pacific Center, 841 Bishop Street, 96813
Telephone: 808-524-1433
Fax: 808-536-2073

Paul F. Cronin
L. Richard Fried, Jr.
Gerald Y. Sekiya
Wayne K. Kekina
David L. Fairbanks
John D. Thomas, Jr.
Stuart A. Kaneko
Bert S. Sakuda
Allen K. Williams
Keith K. H. Young

Patrick W. Border
Gregory L. Lui-Kwan
Patrick F. McTernan
Clarence S.K. Kekina
Sylvia J. Luke
Geoffrey K.S. Komeya
Frances K. Schneider

For full biographical listings, see the Martindale-Hubbell Law Directory

EDMUNDS MAKI VERGA & THORN (AV)

Suite 2104, Davies Pacific Center, 841 Bishop Street, 96813
Telephone: 808-524-2000
Telecopier: 808-528-3585

John S. Edmunds
Paul Maki
Ronald J. Verga
Elise Owens Thorn
Joy S. Omonaka
Wesley D. Shimazu

Reference: Bank of Hawaii.

For full biographical listings, see the Martindale-Hubbell Law Directory

JAMES KRUEGER ATTORNEY AT LAW, A LAW CORPORATION

(See Wailuku)

LAW OFFICES OF IAN L. MATTOCH (AV)

Suite 1835, 737 Bishop Street, 96813
Telephone: 808-523-2451
Fax: 808-531-2652
Email: mattoch@mattoch.com *URL:* http://www.mattoch.com
Kaneohe, Hawaii Office: 45-781 Kamehameha Highway.
Telephone: 808-247-8598.
Waimea, Hawaii Office: Spencer House, Suite 236, Waimea Center.
Telephone: 808-885-7727.
Wailuku, Hawaii Office: Suite 523, One Main Plaza, 2200 Main Street.
Telephone: 808-244-5007.
Hilo, Hawaii Office: 688 Kanoelehua Avenue, Suite 200.
Telephone: 808-969-3302.
Fax: 808-961-5599.
Kailua-Kona, Hawaii Office: Suite D211, 75-170 Hualalai Road.
Telephone: 808-326-1516.
Fax: 808-326-7416.

Ian L. Mattoch

(See Next Column)

LAW OFFICES OF IAN L. MATTOCH—*Continued*

Bruce A. Larson
Mark F. Gallagher (Also at Wailuku, Hawaii Office)
Daniel P. Kirley
Jonathan S. Kuba
Benjamin R.C. Ignacio

Reference: First Hawaiian Bank.

For full biographical listings, see the Martindale-Hubbell Law Directory

PERKIN & HOSODA (AV)

2440 Mauka Tower, Grosvenor Center, 737 Bishop Street, 96813
Telephone: 808-523-2300
Fax: 808-531-8898

MEMBERS OF FIRM

John Francis Perkin
Lyle S. Hosoda

For full biographical listings, see the Martindale-Hubbell Law Directory

TAM, O'CONNOR, HENDERSON, TAIRA & YAMAUCHI ATTORNEYS AT LAW, A LAW CORPORATION (AV)

20th Floor, Central Pacific Plaza, 220 South King Street, 96813
Telephone: 808-545-3030
Fax: 808-523-8051
Fax: 808-537-6782
Email: lawyers@50thstatelaw.com

James K. Tam
Michael F. O'Connor
Harvey E. Henderson, Jr.
Lissa H. Andrews
Robert M. Yamauchi
Darryl M. Taira
Stuart M. Kodish

Wesley H. Ikeda
Russ S. Awakuni
Kevin W. Herring
Fred I. Waki

OF COUNSEL

Paul M. Dold

For full biographical listings, see the Martindale-Hubbell Law Directory

LAW OFFICES OF RICHARD TURBIN A LAW CORPORATION (AV)

Grosvenor Center, Mauka Tower, 737 Bishop Street, Suite 2730, 96813
Telephone: 808-528-4000
FAX: 808-599-1984

Richard Turbin

Rai Saint Chu
Laura Ruth Stone-Jeraj

For full biographical listings, see the Martindale-Hubbell Law Directory

MICHAEL J. Y. WONG (AV)

2222 Central Pacific Plaza, 220 South King Street, 96813
Telephone: 808-536-1855
Fax: 808-536-1857

For full biographical listings, see the Martindale-Hubbell Law Directory

KAILUA, Honolulu Co.

WINER MEHEULA & DEVENS (AV)

970 North Kalaheo Avenue, Suite A-300, 96734
Telephone: 808-254-5855
Fax: 808-254-6872
Email: winer@pacificlaw.com *URL:* http://www.pacificlaw.com

MEMBERS OF FIRM

Andrew S. Winer
William K. Meheula
Vladimir Paul Devens

OF COUNSEL

David F. Fasi

ASSOCIATE

Blue H. Kaanehe

For full biographical listings, see the Martindale-Hubbell Law Directory

*LIHUE,** Kauai Co.

JAMES KRUEGER ATTORNEY AT LAW, A LAW CORPORATION

(See Wailuku)

*WAILUKU,** Maui Co.

JAMES KRUEGER ATTORNEY AT LAW, A LAW CORPORATION (AV)

2065 Main Street, 96793
Telephone: 808-244-7444; Honolulu: 536-7474
Facsimile: 808-244-4177
Email: maulaw@maui.net *URL:* http://www.kruegerlaw-hawaii.org

James Krueger

(See Next Column)

Eve M. Green
Cynthia Kanoholani Wong

A List of Representative Clients and References will be furnished upon request.

For full biographical listings, see the Martindale-Hubbell Law Directory

ROST & GEIGER (AV)

610 One Main Plaza, 2200 Main Street, 96793
Telephone: 808-244-9044
Fax: 808-242-4195

Richard L. Rost
James W. Geiger

For full biographical listings, see the Martindale-Hubbell Law Directory

IDAHO

*BOISE,** Ada Co.

ALLEN DERR (AV)

Imperial Plaza, Suite 8, Ground Floor 200 N. 3rd Street, P.O. Box 1006, 83701
Telephone: 208-342-2674; 1-800-813-5169
Fax: 208-342-2676
Email: aderr@micron.net

For full biographical listings, see the Martindale-Hubbell Law Directory

ILLINOIS

AURORA, Kane Co.

MURPHY, HUPP, FOOTE, MIELKE AND KINNALLY (AV)

North Island Center, P.O. Box 5030, 60507
Telephone: 630-844-0056
Fax: 630-844-1905
Email: mhfmk@insnet.com

MEMBERS OF FIRM

William C. Murphy
Robert B. Hupp
Robert M. Foote
Craig S. Mielke
Patrick M. Kinnally
Paul G. Krentz
Joseph C. Loran
Gerald K. Hodge

Timothy D. O'Neil
Matthew J. Herman

Representative Clients: American Telephone & Telegraph Co.; Fox Valley Park District; Lyon Metal Products; Kane County Forest Preserve District; Hollywood Casino; Employers Mutual Insurance Co.; Forty-Eight Insulations, Inc.; UNR Asbestos Disease Trust; Richards-Wilcox Co.; National Bank & Trust Company of Syracuse.

For full biographical listings, see the Martindale-Hubbell Law Directory

*BELLEVILLE,** St. Clair Co.

HEILIGENSTEIN & BADGLEY, PROFESSIONAL CORPORATION (AV)

30 Public Square, 62220
Telephone: 618-235-1000
Fax: 618-235-1086

Christian E. Heiligenstein
Brad L. Badgley

Reference: Union Planters Corp.; Magna Forms; Banc Star One.

For full biographical listings, see the Martindale-Hubbell Law Directory

MCGLYNN & MCGLYNN (AV)

65 South 65th Street, 62223
Telephone: 618-398-5112; 314-381-5112
Telecopier: 618-398-5189

MEMBERS OF FIRM

Robert E. McGlynn
James McGlynn (Retired)
Michael L. McGlynn
Stephen P. McGlynn

For full biographical listings, see the Martindale-Hubbell Law Directory

*CHICAGO,** Cook Co.

ANESI, OZMON, RODIN, NOVAK & KOHEN, LTD. (AV)

161 North Clark Street, 21st Floor, 60601
Telephone: 312-372-3822
Fax: 312-372-3833

(See Next Column)

ANESI, OZMON, RODIN, NOVAK & KOHEN LTD., *Chicago—Continued*

Nat P. Ozmon
Curt N. Rodin
Mark Novak
Bruce M. Kohen
Douglas A. Colby
Joseph J. Miroballi
Marc A. Taxman
Daniel V. O'Connor

David J. Comeau
Alain Leval
Scott H. Rudin
John A. Salzeider
Telly C. Nakos
Martin J. Lucas
John M. Popelka
Edward D. D'Arcy, Jr.
Paul W. Pasche
Mark Murnane
Samantha Kavathas
Bruce D. Ogron
James G. McCarthy
Steven A. Berman
Peter J. Stavropoulos
George G. Argionis
Steven W. Burrows
Andrew M. DeLuca
Bradley Michael Arnold
Michael P. Hellman

OF COUNSEL

Noel C. Lindenmuth
Irving D. Fasman
Charles E. Anesi (1912-1995)
Richard A. Lewin (1925-1985)

For full biographical listings, see the Martindale-Hubbell Law Directory

CHARLES A. BOYLE & ASSOCIATES, LTD. (AV)

55 East Monroe Street, Suite 4520, 60603
Telephone: 312-346-4944
FAX: 312-368-1061

Charles A. Boyle

Reference: Northern Trust of Chicago.

For full biographical listings, see the Martindale-Hubbell Law Directory

CLIFFORD LAW OFFICES, P.C. (AV)

120 North La Salle Street, 31st Floor, 60602
Telephone: 312-899-9090
1-800-899-0410
Fax: 312-251-1160
Email: RACA@CliffordLaw.com *URL:* http://www.cliffordlaw.com

Robert A. Clifford
Keith A. Hebeisen
Kevin P. Durkin
Thomas K. Prindable

Robert P. Walsh, Jr.
Susan A. Capra
Jeffrey J. Kroll
Richard F. Burke, Jr.
Matthew I. Baker
Timothy P. Rhatigan
Isobel S. Thomas
Michael S. Krzak
Timothy S. Tomasik
Brian Thomas Nash
Donald James Storino III
Sheri L. Tarr

OF COUNSEL

Robert P. Sheridan

For full biographical listings, see the Martindale-Hubbell Law Directory

CONNELLY & SCHROEDER (AV)

One North Franklin Street, Suite 1200, 60606-3421
Telephone: 312-251-9600
Fax: 312-251-9601
Geneva, Illinois Office: 1250 Executive Place, Suite 201.
Telephone: 630-232-6440.
FAX: 630-232-6450

MEMBERS OF FIRM

Michael P. Connelly
John L. Schroeder (Resident, Geneva Office)

ASSOCIATES

Michelle L. Adams (Resident, Geneva Office)
Thomas W. Dillon (Resident, Geneva Office)
Carolyn A. Schroeder (Resident, Geneva)
Martha Swatek (Resident, Geneva Office)

For full biographical listings, see the Martindale-Hubbell Law Directory

CORBOY & DEMETRIO, P.C. (AV)

33 North Dearborn Street 21st Floor, 60602
Telephone: 312-346-3191
FAX: 312-346-5562
TDD: 312-236-3191
Email: phc9@corboydemetrio.com *URL:* http://www.corboydemetrio.com

Philip H. Corboy
Thomas A. Demetrio
Philip Harnett Corboy, Jr.

Robert J. Bingle
Francis Patrick Murphy
Susan J. Schwartz
Michael K. Demetrio
Kevin G. Burke
Michael G. Mahoney

(See Next Column)

Thomas F. Boleky
Barry R. Chafetz
G. Grant Dixon III
Tilden Katz
Thomas A. Killoren, Jr.
Daniel S. Kirschner
Daniel M. Kotin
Kenneth T. Lumb
Cyril J. McIlhargie
Michelle Elyse Meklir
Michael K. Muldoon
Margaret M. Power
Linda Marie Roeback
Edward G. Willer
David C. Wise

Reference: The American National Bank & Trust Company, Chicago, Illinois.

For full biographical listings, see the Martindale-Hubbell Law Directory

GESSLER, HUGHES & SOCOL, LTD. (AV)

Three First National Plaza, Suite 2200, 60602
Telephone: 312-580-0100
Telecopy: 312-580-1994

Benjamin P. Beringer
Anjali Dayal
Mark S. Dym
George W. Gessler
John K. Hughes
Joshua Karsh
Peter M. Katsaros
Kimberley Marsh
Alex W. Miller
Terence J. Moran
Matthew J. Piers
Kalman D. Resnick
Frederick S. Rhine
Jonathan A. Rothstein
Michael P. Simkus
Donna Kaner Socol

Gary Chodorow
Ruth M. Dunning
S. Todd Neal
Mark A. Pellegrino
Steven C. Steinback
Dana H. Sukenik
J. Eric Vander Arend
Mark B. Weiner
Charles H. Wintersteen

OF COUNSEL

Darius S. Francescatti, M.D.
Susan R. Gzesh

For full biographical listings, see the Martindale-Hubbell Law Directory

JEFFREY M. GOLDBERG & ASSOCIATES, LTD. (AV)

20 North Clark Street, Suite 3100, 60602
Telephone: 312-236-4146
Fax: 312-236-5913
Email: firm@goldberglaw.com

Jeffrey M. Goldberg

Michael H. Berman
Suzanne M. Bonds
Anthony M. Goldner
Michael B. Gunzburg
Geoffrey G. Johnson
Michael V. Marsh

For full biographical listings, see the Martindale-Hubbell Law Directory

HARRINGTON, THOMPSON, ACKER & HARRINGTON, LTD. (AV)

310 South Michigan Avenue, Suite 2000, 60604
Telephone: 312-922-8833

Robert E. Harrington, Jr.
Robert B. Thompson
Laurence C. Acker
Patrick J. Harrington
Kenneth J. Sophie, Jr.
Monica A. Coscia
Christy L. LeVan
James K. Schultz
Vincent B. Browne
John B. Corso
Christopher S. Crawford

Reference: American National Bank and Trust Co., Chicago, Illinois.

For full biographical listings, see the Martindale-Hubbell Law Directory

PETER D. KASDIN, LTD. (AV)

Suite 4105, 135 South La Salle Street, 60603
Telephone: 312-630-1990
Facsimile: 312-630-1103; 212-630-9777

Peter D. Kasdin

David W. Hepplewhite
Regina Picone Etherton

OF COUNSEL

David W. Horan

For full biographical listings, see the Martindale-Hubbell Law Directory

LANE & LANE (AV)

33 North Dearborn Street, Suite 2300, 60602
Telephone: 312-332-1400
Fax: 312-899-8003
Email: lanelaw1@aol.com

MEMBERS OF FIRM

Fred Lane
Stephen I. Lane
Scott D. Lane

ASSOCIATE

Joseph M. Dooley III

(See Next Column)

LANE & LANE—*Continued*

OF COUNSEL

John F. Sandner
Daniel M. Cullan
(Not admitted in IL)
Joyce Staat Lewis

MEDICAL STAFF

Cathleen Lazo-Miller (R.N.)

For full biographical listings, see the Martindale-Hubbell Law Directory

SUSAN E. LOGGANS & ASSOCIATES, P.C. (AV)

Suite 2850, 200 West Madison Street, 60606
Telephone: 312-201-8600
Telecopier: 312-201-1180
Email: loggans@logganslaw.com *URL:* http://www.logganslaw.com

Susan E. Loggans

James G. McConnell
Gregg E. Strellis
John T. Ferjak
Patrick D. Flanagan
Norman L. Rubenstein

For full biographical listings, see the Martindale-Hubbell Law Directory

THE LAW OFFICES OF MUNDAY & NATHAN (AV)

33 North Dearborn Street, Suite 2220, 60602
Telephone: 312-346-5678
Fax: 312-346-8394

John J. Munday
Thomas J. Nathan

Edward G. Proctor, Jr.
Jeffrey A. Schulkin

For full biographical listings, see the Martindale-Hubbell Law Directory

BERNARD R. NEVORAL AND ASSOCIATES LTD. (AV)

150 North Wacker Drive, Suite 2450, 60606
Telephone: 312 263-7058
FAX: 312-263-4566

Bernard R. Nevoral

Jeremy Michael West
Daniel M. Extrom
David F Szczecin

For full biographical listings, see the Martindale-Hubbell Law Directory

NOLAN LAW GROUP (AV)

One North La Salle Street, 35th Floor, 60602
Telephone: 312-372-5400
Toll Free: 888-372-3870
Facsimile: 312-372-0558
Email: dnolan1@ix.netcom.com

Donald J. Nolan
Albert E. Durkin, Jr.
William J. Jovan
Floyd A. Wisner
James H. Lawlor, III
Thomas P. Routh
James A. Santucci
Todd R. Mcquiston

Laura L. Ruhl

For full biographical listings, see the Martindale-Hubbell Law Directory

STEPHEN M. PASSEN, LTD. (AV)

Suite 2525 One IBM Plaza, 60611
Telephone: 312-527-4500
Facsimile: 312-527-4435
Email: spassen@IBM.net *URL:* http://www.lawyers.com/passenlaw

Stephen M. Passen

John J. Driscoll

For full biographical listings, see the Martindale-Hubbell Law Directory

LAW OFFICES OF ROBERT B. PATTERSON, LTD. (AV)

221 North La Salle Street, Suite 1050, 60601
Telephone: 312-236-0995
FAX: 312-984-5791
URL: http://www.lawyers.com/pattersonfirm

Robert B. Patterson

John F. Hedrich

LEGAL SUPPORT PERSONNEL

Marie E. DeRose
(Legal Assistant)
Jennifer A. Long (Paralegal)

For full biographical listings, see the Martindale-Hubbell Law Directory

PAVALON, GIFFORD, LAATSCH & MARINO (AV)

Two North La Salle Street, Suite 1600, 60602
Telephone: 312-419-7400
Fax: 312-419-7408
Email: pavgif@aol.com
Rockford, Illinois Office: 501 Seventh Street, Suite 501, 61104.
Telephone: 815-968-5100.

MEMBERS OF FIRM

Eugene I. Pavalon
Geoffrey L. Gifford
Gary K. Laatsch
Frank C. Marino
Henry Phillip Gruss

Christine Walsh Donnelly

For full biographical listings, see the Martindale-Hubbell Law Directory

POWER ROGERS & SMITH, P.C. (AV)

35 West Wacker Drive, Suite 3700, 60601
Telephone: 312-236-9381
Fax: 312-236-0920

Joseph A. Power, Jr.
Larry R. Rogers
Todd A. Smith

Thomas G. Siracusa
Paul L. Salzetta
Thomas M. Power
Larry R. Rogers, Jr.
Ruth M. Degnan
Devon C. Bruce

For full biographical listings, see the Martindale-Hubbell Law Directory

LAW OFFICES OF EDMUND J. SCANLAN, LTD. (AV)

134 North La Salle Street, Suite 1700, 60602
Telephone: 312-372-0020
Fax: 312-372-1211
URL: http://www.lawyers.com/edmundjscanlanltd

Edmund J. Scanlan

Mario C. Palermo

For full biographical listings, see the Martindale-Hubbell Law Directory

JOHN B. SCHWARTZ & ASSOCIATES (AV)

Suite 408, Thirty-Nine South La Salle Street, 60603
Telephone: 312-332-1586
Fax: 312-332-7009
Email: JSCHW888@aol.com

John B. Schwartz

ASSOCIATE

David J. Spira

OF COUNSEL

Thomas W. Duda

For full biographical listings, see the Martindale-Hubbell Law Directory

STRIDE, CRADDOCK & STRIDE (AV)

111 West Washington Street, Suite 1837, 60602-2773
Telephone: 312-346-5800
Fax: 312-346-3870

Herbert F. Stride
J. Patrick Craddock
Herbert L. Stride

Nicholas C. Panos
Deborah A. Stride-Saran
Vickie Voukidis Blum
Michael J. Craddock
Arthur Z. Handelman

For full biographical listings, see the Martindale-Hubbell Law Directory

JOHN C. WUNSCH, P.C. (AV)

77 West Washington Street, Suite 1420, 60602
Telephone: 312-977-9900
Fax: 312-236-2573

John C. Wunsch

Reference: The Northern Trust Co.

For full biographical listings, see the Martindale-Hubbell Law Directory

*EDWARDSVILLE,** Madison Co.

CARLSON WENDLER & ASSOCIATES, P.C. (AV)

90 Edwardsville Professional Park, P.O. Box 527, 62025
Telephone: 618-656-0066
Fax: 618-656-0009
Email: JCarl618@aol.com

Jon G. Carlson
Brian M. Wendler
Eric Jon Carlson

(See Next Column)

CARLSON WENDLER & ASSOCIATES P.C., *Edwardsville—Continued*

Richard W. Gibson

OF COUNSEL TO

Mullen & Minnella, Chicago, Illinois

For full biographical listings, see the Martindale-Hubbell Law Directory

*GALESBURG,** Knox Co.

HATTERY, SIMPSON & WEST (AV)

Suite 402 Hill Arcade, 61401
Telephone: 309-343-6152
Telecopier: 309-343-5103
Email: 5lawyers@galesburg.net *URL:* http://www.misslink.net/hsw/aprose.htm
Monmouth, Illinois Office: 1025 East Broadway.
Telephone: 309-734-3150.
Telefax: 309-734-7043.
Roseville, Illinois Office: 130 North Main Street.
Telephone: 309-426-2176.
Telefax: 309-426-2177.

MEMBERS OF FIRM

Roger L. Williamson
S. David Simpson
Ronald D. Stombaugh (Resident at Monmouth Office)
George M. Hennenfent (Resident, Roseville Office)

For Complete List of Firm Personnel, See General Section

For full biographical listings, see the Martindale-Hubbell Law Directory

*JOLIET,** Will Co.

MCKEOWN, FITZGERALD, ZOLLNER, BUCK, HUTCHISON & RUTTLE (AV)

2455 Glenwood Avenue, 60435
Telephone: 815-729-4800
Fax: 815-729-4711
Frankfort Office: 28 Kansas Street.
Telephone: 815-469-2176.
FAX: 815-469-0295.

MEMBERS OF FIRM

Charles J. McKeown (1908-1985)
Paul O. McKeown (1913-1982)
Richard T. Buck (1936-1992)
Douglas P. Hutchison (1939-1998)
Joseph C. Fitzgerald (Retired)
Max E. Zollner
David L. Ruttle
Theodore J. Jarz
Douglas J. McKeown
James B. Harvey
Kenneth A. Grey
Michael R. Lucas
Christopher N. Wise
Gary S. Mueller
John C. Roth
Arthur J. Wilhelmi
Thomas M. Carney

ASSOCIATE

Christopher S. Ward (Resident)

OF COUNSEL

George E. Sangmeister
Stewart C. Hutchison

Represrntative Clients: First Midwest Bank, N.A.; Silver Cross Hospital; Villages of Plainfield and Mokena; Southwest Agency for Risk Management; Joliet Junior College; Cat Scales Co.; Express Riverboat Casino, Joliet, Inc.; Nicor, Inc.

For full biographical listings, see the Martindale-Hubbell Law Directory

SPESIA, AYERS & ARDAUGH (AV)

Two Rialto Square, 116 North Chicago Street, Suite 200, 60432
Telephone: 815-726-4311
Fax: 815-726-6828

MEMBERS OF FIRM

Douglas F. Spesia
E. Kent Ayers
John R. Ardaugh

ASSOCIATES

John G. Foreman
John M. Spesia
Christian G. Spesia
Elizabeth Hoskins Dow
Barbara N. Petrungaro

OF COUNSEL

Ralph C. Murphy
Kenneth E. Timm
Arthur T. Lennon (1923-1988)

Counsel for: American Telephone & Telegraph Co.; Amoco Oil Co.; Ameritech; Caterpillar Tractor Co.; Commonwealth Edison Co.; IBM Corp.; Indiana Consolidated Ins. Co.; Lakehead Pipeline Co.; Liberty Mutual Ins. Co.; Northern Illinois Gas Co.

For full biographical listings, see the Martindale-Hubbell Law Directory

*KANKAKEE,** Kankakee Co.

BARMANN, KRAMER & BOHLEN, P.C. (AV)

Suite 502, 200 East Court Street, P.O. Box 1787, 60901
Telephone: 815-939-1133
Fax: 815-939-0994

Christopher W. Bohlen

For Complete List of Firm Personnel, See General Section

For full biographical listings, see the Martindale-Hubbell Law Directory

LIBERTYVILLE, Lake Co.

JAMES J. DESANTO A PROFESSIONAL CORPORATION (AV)

339 North Milwaukee Avenue, 60048
Telephone: 847-816-8100
Facsimile: 847-816-8126
Email: desanto@1connect.net

James J. DeSanto

For full biographical listings, see the Martindale-Hubbell Law Directory

*MARION,** Williamson Co.

HARRIS, LAMBERT, HOWERTON & DORRIS (AV)

300 West Main Street, 62959
Telephone: 618-993-2616
Fax: 618-997-1845
Email: robi8@midamer.net *URL:* http://www.lawyers.com/hlh&d

MEMBERS OF FIRM

Ralph W. Harris (1904-1982)
Richard Gordon Lambert (Retired)
Robert H. Howerton
Douglas N. Dorris

ASSOCIATES

Stephen W. Stone
Kelley Ray Phelps

For full biographical listings, see the Martindale-Hubbell Law Directory

NAPERVILLE, DuPage Co.

STEVEN B. LEVY, LTD. (AV)

40 Shuman Boulevard Suite 151, 60563
Telephone: 630-416-6300
Telefax: 630-416-6564
URL: http://www.lawyers.com/stevenblevy
Email: SBLEVYLTD@aol.com *URL:* http://www.sblevyltdlaw.com

Steven B. Levy

For full biographical listings, see the Martindale-Hubbell Law Directory

KATHLEEN T. ZELLNER & ASSOCIATES (AV)

1717 North Naper Boulevard Suite 203, 60563
Telephone: 630-955-1212
Facsimile: 630-955-1111
URL: http://www.lawyers.com/zellnerlaw

For full biographical listings, see the Martindale-Hubbell Law Directory

*PEORIA,** Peoria Co.

NICOARA & STEAGALL (AV)

Commerce Bank Building, 416 Main Street, Suite 815, 61602-1103
Telephone: 309-674-6085
Fax: 309-674-6032
Email: 70754.3140@compuserve.com

MEMBERS OF FIRM

John P. Nicoara
Richard L. Steagall

Representative Clients: Farmers Insurance Group; Illinois Founders Insurance Co.
Reference: Commerce Bank.

For full biographical listings, see the Martindale-Hubbell Law Directory

ROBERT C. STRODEL, LTD. (AV)

927 Commerce Bank Building, 61602
Telephone: 309-676-4500
Fax: 309-676-4566

Robert C. Strodel

For full biographical listings, see the Martindale-Hubbell Law Directory

PERU, La Salle Co.

ANTHONY C. RACCUGLIA & ASSOCIATES (AV)

1200 Maple Drive, 61354
Telephone: 815-223-0230
Ottawa, Illinois Office: 633 La Salle Street.
Telephone: 815-434-2003.

(See Next Column)

ANTHONY C. RACCUGLIA & ASSOCIATES—*Continued*

ASSOCIATES

James A. McPhedran | Louis L. Bertrand

References: La Salle National Bank; Citizens First National Bank of Peru, Illinois.

For full biographical listings, see the Martindale-Hubbell Law Directory

*ROCK ISLAND,** Rock Island Co.

WINSTEIN, KAVENSKY & WALLACE (AV)

4th Floor, Rock Island Bank Building, 224 18th Street, P.O. Box 4298, 61201
Telephone: 309-794-1515; 800-747-1527
Fax: 309-794-9929

MEMBERS OF FIRM

Stewart R. Winstein
Harrison H. Kavensky
Franklin S. Wallace
Craig L. Kavensky
Arthur R. Winstein
David L. Cunningham

John Allan Hartsock
Robert Kelly Leyshon
Barbara K. Wallace

Local Regional Counsel for: United Auto Workers.
Reference: First National Bank of Quad Cities.

For full biographical listings, see the Martindale-Hubbell Law Directory

*SPRINGFIELD,** Sangamon Co.

METNICK, CHERRY & FRAZIER (AV)

Second Floor, Myers Building, 1 West Old State Capitol Plaza, P.O. Box 12140, 62791
Telephone: 217-753-4242
Telefax: 217-753-4642
Email: SPRINGLAW@AOL.COM

MEMBERS OF FIRM

Michael B. Metnick
Diana N. Cherry
Richard D. Frazier

ASSOCIATES

Kathryn Saltmarsh
Scott A. Sabin

For full biographical listings, see the Martindale-Hubbell Law Directory

*WAUKEGAN,** Lake Co.

SALVI & SCHOSTOK, P.C. (AV)

Established 1982 as Law Offices of Patrick A. Salvi, P.C.
218 North Utica Street, 60085
Telephone: 847-249-1227
Telefax: 847-249-0138
Email: salvilaw.com *URL:* http://www.salvilaw.com
Chicago, Illinois Office: 181 West Madison, Suite 3525, 60602.
Telephone: 312-372-1227.
Telefax: 312-372-3720.

Patrick A. Salvi
Michael P. Schostok
David J. Pritchard (Resident, Chicago Office)

John Andrew Kornak
J. Matthew Dudley
Peter M. Trobe
Ellen C. Smith
Scott E. Preusen

OF COUNSEL

Bernard E. Grysen

References: First Midwest Bank, Waukegan, Illinois; Northern Trust Bank, Lake Forest, Illinois; Commercial Litigation Clients; Anderson Consulting, LLP.; Baxter Healthcare; Brunswick Corporation, Lake Forest, Illinois.

For full biographical listings, see the Martindale-Hubbell Law Directory

WEST FRANKFORT, Franklin Co.

SAM C. MITCHELL & ASSOCIATES (AV)

115 1/2 East Main Street, P.O. Box 280, 62896
Telephone: 618-932-2772; 937-2662
Telecopier: 618-932-3456

Sam C. Mitchell

ASSOCIATE

Bruce D. Irish

For full biographical listings, see the Martindale-Hubbell Law Directory

*WHEATON,** DuPage Co.

DONOVAN AND ROBERTS, P.C. (AV)

104 East Roosevelt Road, Suite 202, 60187
Telephone: 630-668-4211
Fax: 630-668-2076

(See Next Column)

Keith E. Roberts, Sr.
Keith E. (Chuck) Roberts, Jr.
Henry B. Vess, III

Marie F. Leach
Robert S. Marcott
Eric A. Burgeson
Kevin H. Saville

For full biographical listings, see the Martindale-Hubbell Law Directory

STEVEN B. LEVY, LTD.

(See Naperville)

O'REILLY LAW OFFICES (AV)

1776 South Naperville Road, Suite 206-A, 60187
Telephone: 630-665-4444
Telecopier: 630-665-4442

Roger Kevin O'Reilly

Molly M. O'Reilly
John F. O'Reilly

For full biographical listings, see the Martindale-Hubbell Law Directory

INDIANA

*BLOOMINGTON,** Monroe Co.

BUNGER & ROBERTSON (AV)

226 South College Square, P.O. Box 910, 47402-0910
Telephone: 812-332-9295
Fax: 812-331-8808
Email: bunrob@iquest.net

MEMBERS OF FIRM

Don M Robertson
Samuel R. Ardery
John W. Richards

Representative Clients: Aetna Insurance Companies; Bloomington Hospital; Commercial Union Group; Indiana Insurance Co.; Liberty Mutual Insurance; Medical Protective Co.; Monroe County Community School Corp.; Professional Golf Car, Inc.; Prudential Insurance Company of America; State Farm Automobile Insurance Co.

For Complete List of Firm Personnel, See General Section

For full biographical listings, see the Martindale-Hubbell Law Directory

JONES, MCGLASSON & BENCKART, P.C. (AV)

205 South Walnut Street, P.O. Box 279, 47402
Telephone: 812-332-4431
Fax: 812-332-0554
Email: jmbattys@bloomington.in.us *URL:* http://www.Bloomington.in.us/jmbattys

Robert Delano Jones
Thomas M. McGlasson
Judith Corcoran Benckart
Gregory Scott Lauer

OF COUNSEL

David Rogers

Reference: Monroe County Bank.

For full biographical listings, see the Martindale-Hubbell Law Directory

KELLEY, BELCHER & BROWN, A PROFESSIONAL CORPORATION (AV)

301 West Seventh Street, P.O. Box 3250, 47402-3250
Telephone: 812-336-9963
Telecopier: 812-336-4588

William H. Kelley
Thomas J. Belcher
Darla Sue Brown

Shannon L. Robinson
Kyle M. Baker
Michael W. Phelps

For full biographical listings, see the Martindale-Hubbell Law Directory

ELKHART, Elkhart Co.

THORNE, GRODNIK, RANSEL, DUNCAN, BYRON, HOSTETLER & TRIPPEL, LLP (AV)

228 West High Street, 46516-3176
Telephone: 219-294-7473
FAX: 219-294-5390
Mishawaka, Indiana Office: 420 Lincoln Way West, P.O. Box 1210, 46544.
Telephone: 219-256-5660.
FAX: 219-674-6835.

(See Next Column)

THORNE, GRODNIK, RANSEL, DUNCAN, BYRON, HOSTETLER & TRIPPEL LLP, *Elkhart—Continued*

MEMBERS OF FIRM

Charles H. Grodnik
J. Richard Ransel
Glenn L. Duncan
James R. Byron
Steven L. Hostetler
Michael A. Trippel

ASSOCIATES

W. Douglas Thorne
Gregg A. Hixenbaugh

OF COUNSEL

F. Richard Kramer
Joseph C. Zakas
William A. Thorne

Counsel for: Valley American Bank and Trust Co., Mishawaka, Indiana; NBD Bank.

For full biographical listings, see the Martindale-Hubbell Law Directory

*EVANSVILLE,** Vanderburgh Co.

BERGER AND BERGER (AV)

313 Main Street, 47708-1485
Telephone: 812-425-8101
Outside Indiana: 800-327-0182
Fax: 812-421-5909
Email: berger@bergerlaw.com *URL:* http://www.bergerlaw.com

MEMBERS OF FIRM

Sydney L. Berger (1917-1988)
Charles L. Berger
Sheila M. Corcoran
Mark W. Rietman
David L. Clark

References: Citizens National Bank of Evansville; Old National Bank in Evansville.

For full biographical listings, see the Martindale-Hubbell Law Directory

GERLING LAW OFFICES, PROFESSIONAL CORPORATION (AV)

519 Main Street Walkway, P.O. Box 3203, 47731
Telephone: 812-423-5251
Fax: 812-423-9928
URL: http://www.gerlinglaw.com

Gary L. Gerling
Edward B. Anderson
David G. Hatfield
Christian M. Lenn
Gayle Gerling Pettinga
Stephen Hensleigh Thomas

For full biographical listings, see the Martindale-Hubbell Law Directory

*FORT WAYNE,** Allen Co.

ROBY & HOOD (AV)

Standard Federal Plaza, 200 East Main Street, Suite 520, 46802
Telephone: 219-423-3366
Fax: 219-423-3367
Anderson, Indiana Office: One Citizens Plaza, 305 Key Bank, 46016.
Telephone: 765-642-2402.
Marion, Indiana Office: 1315 West Gillespie Street, 46952.
Telephone: 765-651-0677.

MEMBERS OF FIRM

Daniel A. Roby
G. Stanley Hood
Thomas A. Manges
David Joseph Stach

References: Norwest Bank; Bank One.

For full biographical listings, see the Martindale-Hubbell Law Directory

*INDIANAPOLIS,** Marion Co.

COHEN & MALAD, P.C. (AV)

136 North Delaware Street, P.O. Box 627, 46206-0627
Telephone: 317-636-6481
Fax: 317-636-2593
Fishers, Indiana Office: 7444 East 116th Street, Suite 200.
Telephone: 317-595-9000.
Fax: 317-841-1443.

Louis F. Cohen (1936-1992)
Richard M. Malad
Irwin B. Levin
Richard N. Bell
Eric C. Redman
John E. Bator
Paul D. Ludwig
Jarrell B. Hammond
KC Cohen (Resident, Fishers Office)
Gerald L. Williams
David J. Cutshaw

Teresa E. Dearing
Gregory L. Laker
Thomas L. Blackburn
Marilyn Ann Moores
Samuel Hodson
Deetta H. Steinmetz
John L. Stewart
Richard E. Shevitz
Richard L. Ford
Penny L. Carey
Heather V. Kimmons
Amy L. McCabe
Lisa K. Pitner Caterine
Laura S. Cohen
John M. Hauber
Maureen T. Keefe
John P. Gulyas
Mary E. Baird
Keith E. Gifford
Brian K. Zoeller
Robert E. Shive

(See Next Column)

OF COUNSEL

Stephen M. Sellmer (Resident, Fishers Office)

Reference: Bank One, Indianapolis, N.A.

For full biographical listings, see the Martindale-Hubbell Law Directory

CONOUR • DOEHRMAN • STARKEY (AV)

III Meridian Plaza, Suite 100, 10333 N. Meridian Street, 46290
Telephone: 317-705-4444
Fax: 317-705-4455
Toll Free: 800-269-3443
URL: http://www.indianalaw.com

MEMBERS OF FIRM

William F. Conour
Thomas C. Doehrman
Daniel S. Chamberlain

For full biographical listings, see the Martindale-Hubbell Law Directory

HOVDE LAW FIRM (AV)

10585 North Meridian Street, Suite 345, P.O. Box 40849, 46240-0849
Telephone: 317-818-3100
Fax: 317-818-3111
Email: hovde@indy.net

F. Boyd Hovde
Frederick R. Hovde
Regina M. Poore
Robert T. Dassow

For full biographical listings, see the Martindale-Hubbell Law Directory

ICE MILLER DONADIO & RYAN (AV)

One American Square Box 82001, 46282-0002
Telephone: 317-236-2100
Fax: 317-236-2219
Email: info@imdr.com *URL:* http://www.imdr.com
South Bend, Indiana Office: 211 West Washington Street, Suite 2420.
Telephone: 219-234-7933.
Fax: 219-234-7965. Internet E-mail: info@imdr.com. Web Site Address: http://www.imdr.com.
Chicago, Illinois Office: 135 South LaSalle Street, Suite 4100.
Telephone: 312-726-1567.
Fax: 312-641-6263. Internet E-mail: info@imdr.com. Web Site Address: http://www.imdr.com.

MEMBERS OF FIRM

James R. Fisher
Debra Hanley Miller

For Complete List of Firm Personnel, See General Section

For full biographical listings, see the Martindale-Hubbell Law Directory

MARK C. LADENDORF & ASSOCIATES (AV)

8900 Keystone Crossing, Suite 1160, 46240
Telephone: 317-848-3700
Toll Free: 1-888-925-3700
Facsimile: 317-818-6454
URL: http://www.ladendorf.com

ASSOCIATES

Katherine H. Dimmock
Jason R. Reese

For full biographical listings, see the Martindale-Hubbell Law Directory

LOCKE REYNOLDS LLP (AV)

1000 Capital Center South, 201 North Illinois Street, 46204-4210
Telephone: 317-237-3800
Telecopier: 317-237-3900
Email: attys@locke.com *URL:* http://www.locke.com

Hugh E. Reynolds, Jr.
Lloyd H. Milliken, Jr.
William V. Hutchens
David S. Allen
David M. Haskett
Michael A. Bergin
David T. Kasper
Steven J. Strawbridge
Thomas L. Davis
Robert A. Fanning
Randall R. Riggs
Mark J. Roberts
Kevin Charles Murray
Terrence L. Brookie
Richard A. Huser
Thomas J. Campbell
Diane Parsons Emswiller
Thomas W. Farlow
Karl M. Koons, III
James Dimos
Kristen K. Rollison
Thomas R. Schultz
Todd J. Kaiser
Eric A. Riegner
Kevin C. Schiferl
Peter H. Pogue
John H. Daerr
John K. McDavid
Jeffrey J. Mortier
Nicholas C. Pappas

Stephen L. Vaughan
Deanna A. Dean-Webster
Jon M. Pinnick
Mary A. Schopper
Susan E. Cline
Bruce J. Alvarado
Mary Margaret Ruth Feldhake
Nelson D. Alexander
Donald B. Kite, Sr.
Thomas F. Bedsole
David A. Sorensen
Derek S. Burrell
Dean R. Brackenridge
T. Joseph Wendt
Michelle Davis Carmichael
Heather L. Wilson

(See Next Column)

LOCKE REYNOLDS LLP—*Continued*

Vincent J. Wong
Daniel G. Foote
Carol M. Wyatt
Joel E. Tragesser
Tricia L. Thompson

OF COUNSEL

William H. Vobach
Robert C. Riddell

Representative Clients: American Honda Motor Co., Inc.; Associated Aviation Underwriters; Center for Claims Resolution; CNA Insurance Cos.; Citizens Insurance Co.; General Motors Corp.; Nationwide Insurance Co.; Siemens Corp.; St. Francis Hospital.

For Complete List of Firm Personnel, See General Section

For full biographical listings, see the Martindale-Hubbell Law Directory

MILLER MULLER MENDELSON & KENNEDY (AV)

8900 Keystone Crossing Suite 1250, 46240
Telephone: 317-574-4500
1-800-394-3094
Fax: 317-574-4501
Email: mmmk@iquest.net

MEMBERS OF FIRM

Michael S. Miller
John Muller
Tilden Mendelson
Timothy J. Kennedy

ASSOCIATE

Catherine A. Kling

For full biographical listings, see the Martindale-Hubbell Law Directory

MITCHELL HURST JACOBS & DICK (AV)

152 East Washington Street, 46204
Telephone: 317-636-0808
1-800-636-0808
Fax: 317-633-7680
URL: http://www.mhjd.com

MEMBERS OF FIRM

William W. Hurst
Samuel L. Jacobs
Richard J. Dick
Marshall S. Hanley
Robert W. Strohmeyer, Jr.

ASSOCIATES

Danielle A. Takla
Kimberly H. Danforth
Jennifer Levin Sinder
Todd R. Ryden

General Counsel For: Dr. Tavel's Vision Center; Calderon Bros. Vending Machines, Inc.; Grocers Supply Co., Inc.; Power Train Services, Inc.; Frank E. Irish, Inc.; Bedding Liquidators; Galyan's Trading Co.; Harcourt Management Co., Inc.; Kosene & Kosene Mgt. & Dev. Co., Inc.; Hasten Bancorp.

For full biographical listings, see the Martindale-Hubbell Law Directory

TOWNSEND & MONTROSS (AV)

230 East Ohio Street, 46204
Telephone: 317-264-4444
Fax: 317-264-2080

John F. Townsend, Jr.
W. Scott Montross

ASSOCIATE

John F. Townsend, III

OF COUNSEL

John F. Townsend

Reference: N.B.D. Bank, N.A.

For full biographical listings, see the Martindale-Hubbell Law Directory

THE WADDICK LAW FIRM, P.C. (AV)

9000 Keystone Crossing, Suite 1000, 46240
Telephone: 317-843-3980
FAX: 317-573-5280
Email: wwaddick@inct.net

William A. Waddick

For full biographical listings, see the Martindale-Hubbell Law Directory

WARD & WARD (AV)

1014 Circle Tower Building, 55 Monument Circle, 46204
Telephone: 317-639-9501
Fax: 317-637-1919
Email: cpw@wardlawfirm.com

MEMBERS OF FIRM

Donald W. Ward
Charles P. Ward

For full biographical listings, see the Martindale-Hubbell Law Directory

WILSON, KEHOE & WININGHAM (AV)

2859 North Meridian, 46208
Telephone: 317-920-6400
Fax: 317-920-6405
URL: http://www.wkw.com
Richmond, Indiana Office: 2901 East Main Street, 47374.
Telephone: 765-962-9113.
Connersville, Indiana Office: 118 West 30th Street, 47331.
Telephone: 765-827-1100.
Muncie, Indiana Office: 3310 West Fox Ridge Lane, 47304.
Telephone: 765-284-2474.
Fax: 765-288-8655.

MEMBERS OF FIRM

Harry A. Wilson, Jr.
D. Bruce Kehoe
William E. Winingham, Jr.

ASSOCIATES

Ralph E. Dowling
Gerald A. Griffin, M.D.
William E. Lukens

OF COUNSEL

Gerald L. Lawlis

Reference: The Indiana National Bank.

For full biographical listings, see the Martindale-Hubbell Law Directory

YARLING & ROBINSON (AV)

151 North Delaware, Suite 1535, P.O. Box 44128, 46204
Telephone: 317-262-8800
Fax: 317-262-3046
Email: yrhl@yarling.com *URL:* http://www.yarling.com

MEMBERS OF FIRM

Charles F. Robinson, Jr.
John W. Hammel
Linda Y. Hammel
Douglas E. Rogers
Mark S. Gray
Matthew C. Robinson

ASSOCIATE

Jeffrey R. Mitchell

OF COUNSEL

Richard W. Yarling

Representative Clients: Furnished upon request.

For full biographical listings, see the Martindale-Hubbell Law Directory

YOSHA KRAHULIK & LEVY (AV)

Pyramid II, First Floor, 3500 West DePauw Boulevard, Suite 2015, P.O. Box 68979, 46268
Telephone: 317-334-9200
Toll Free: 800-875-5759
Fax: 317-228-3355
URL: http://www.yoshalaw.com

MEMBERS OF FIRM

Louis Buddy Yosha
William Levy
Jon D. Krahulik

ASSOCIATES

David C. Krahulik
Jeff D. Oliphant
Julie C. Welp
Janice D. Heidt

Reference: National Bank of Indianapolis.

For full biographical listings, see the Martindale-Hubbell Law Directory

*JEFFERSONVILLE,** Clark Co.

LAW OFFICE OF EDWIN S. SEDWICK (AV)

415 East Court Avenue, 47130
Telephone: 812-282-7200
Facsimile: 812-282-7393

For full biographical listings, see the Martindale-Hubbell Law Directory

*KOKOMO,** Howard Co.

RUSSELL, MCINTYRE, HILLIGOSS & WELKE (AV)

116 North Main Street, P.O. Box 1047, 46903-1047
Telephone: 765-456-3827
Telecopier: 765-456-3839

MEMBERS OF FIRM

Richard L. Russell
James B. McIntyre
Thomas J. Hilligoss, Jr.
Curtis C. Welke
Rebecca R. McCain

For full biographical listings, see the Martindale-Hubbell Law Directory

*LAFAYETTE,** Tippecanoe Co.

BALL, EGGLESTON, BUMBLEBURG, MCBRIDE, WALKEY & STAPLETON, PC (AV)

810 Bank One Building, P.O. Box 1535, 47902-1535
Telephone: 765-742-9046
Fax: 765-742-1966
Email: info@ball-law.com

(See Next Column)

BALL, EGGLESTON, BUMBLEBURG, MCBRIDE, WALKEY & STAPLETON PC, *Lafayette—Continued*

Cable G. Ball (1904-1981)
Owen Crook (1908-1977)
Warren N. Eggleston (1923-1991)
Joseph T. Bumbleburg
John K. McBride
Jack L. Walkey
Michael J. Stapleton
Jeffrey J. Newell
James T. Hodson
Brian Wade Walker
Cheryl M. Knodle
Randy J. Williams
Brenda Mithoefer Clapper

Representative Clients: Available Upon Request.

For full biographical listings, see the Martindale-Hubbell Law Directory

WITHERED CORRIGAN & SERVICE (AV)

8 North Third Street, Suite 401, P.O. Box 499, 47902-0499
Telephone: 765-742-1988
Fax: 765-742-8774
Email: info@witheredlaw.com

Jerome L. Withered
Christopher D. Corrigan
Angela M. Service

ASSOCIATE

Michael H. Dowler

For full biographical listings, see the Martindale-Hubbell Law Directory

MERRILLVILLE, Lake Co.

MARCE GONZALEZ, JR. (AV)

Connecticut Center, 9120 Connecticut, Suite D, 46410
Telephone: 219-769-3030
FAX: 219-769-3031

For full biographical listings, see the Martindale-Hubbell Law Directory

GOUVEIA & MILLER (AV)

521 East 86th Avenue, 46410
Telephone: 219-736-6020
Fax: 219-736-2545

MEMBERS OF FIRM

Gordon E. Gouveia
Richard A. Miller

Lori D. Fisher
Mitchell A. Peters
Hilary R. Hall (Not admitted in IN; Legal Researcher)

Reference: NBD Ban, N.A.

For full biographical listings, see the Martindale-Hubbell Law Directory

SPANGLER, JENNINGS & DOUGHERTY, P.C. (AV)

8396 Mississippi Street, 46410-6398
Telephone: 219-769-2323
Facsimile: 219-769-5007
Email: spangler@sjdlaw.com
Valparaiso, Indiana Office: 150 Lincolnway, Suite 3001.
Telephone: 219-462-6151.
FAX: 219-477-4935.

Harry J. Jennings
Richard A. Mayer
Jay A. Charon
John P. McQuillan
Samuel J. Bernardi, Jr. (Valparaiso Office)
Jon F. Schmoll
Robert D. Hawk
David J. Hanson
Robert P. Kennedy
James T. McNiece
Daniel A. Gioia
James D. McQuillan
David L. Abel, II
Harold G. Hagberg
Gregory J. Tonner
Robert D. Brown
Robert J. Dignam

ASSOCIATES

Anthony F. Tavitas
Lloyd P. Mullen
Kisti Good Risse
Mark D. Geheb
James M. Portelli

Representative Clients: Allstate Insurance Company; Civitas Bank; CNA Insurance: Farmers Insurance Group; Ford Motor Credit Co.; Inland Steel Co.; School Town of Munster; St. Paul Insurance Cos.; State Farm Cos.

For Complete List of Firm Personnel, See General Section

For full biographical listings, see the Martindale-Hubbell Law Directory

MISHAWAKA, St. Joseph Co.

SCHINDLER AND OLSON (AV)

122 South Mill Street, P.O. Box 100, 46544
Telephone: 219-259-5461
Fax: 219-259-5462

OF COUNSEL

John W. Schindler (1884-1971)
John W. Schindler, Jr.

(See Next Column)

MEMBER OF FIRM

James J. Olson

A List of Representative Clients Will Be Furnished Upon Request.
Reference: 1st Source Bank of Mishawaka.

For full biographical listings, see the Martindale-Hubbell Law Directory

MUNSTER, Lake Co.

LAW OFFICES OF TIMOTHY F. KELLY (AV)

Suite 2A, 9250 Columbia Avenue, 46321
Telephone: 219-836-4062
Telecopier: 219-836-0167
Email: tfklaw@tfklaw.net

MEMBERS OF FIRM

Timothy F. Kelly
Karl K. Vanzo

ASSOCIATES

Steven J. Sersic
Kathleen E. Peek

For Complete List of Firm Personnel, See General Section

For full biographical listings, see the Martindale-Hubbell Law Directory

*NEW ALBANY,** Floyd Co.

MATTOX & MATTOX (AV)

Suite 420 Elsby Building, P.O. Box 1203, 47151-1203
Telephone: 812-944-8005
Facsimile: 812-944-2255
Email: mmlaw@win.net

MEMBERS OF FIRM

Richard L. Mattox
S. Frank Mattox

ASSOCIATES

Linda A. Mattox
Derrick H. Wilson
Karen R. Goodwell

Representative Clients: AAOMS National Insurance; Cablelink, Inc.; Floyd Memorial Hospital; John Deere Co.; Kimball International, Inc.; The Medical Protective Co.; Papa Johns Intl., Inc.; PHICO Insurance Co.; Physicians Group, Inc.; Robinson Nugent, Inc.

For full biographical listings, see the Martindale-Hubbell Law Directory

*NOBLESVILLE,** Hamilton Co.

CHURCH, CHURCH, HITTLE & ANTRIM (AV)

938 Conner Street, P.O. Box 10, 46061-0010
Telephone: 317-773-2190
Telecopier: 317-773-5320
Email: cchadoug@msn.com

MEMBERS OF FIRM

Douglas D. Church
Jack G. Hittle
J. Michael Antrim
Martin E. Risacher
Bruce M. Bittner
Brian J. Zaiger
Leslie Craig Henderzahs
Jordan D. Church

OF COUNSEL

Manson E. Church

Representative Clients: Noblesville Schools; Westfield-Washington Schools; Community Bank; Metrobank; Towns of Westfield, Fishers and Pendleton; Reynolds Farm Equipment Co.; Weihe Engineering; Historic Railroad Multijurisdictional Port Authority.

For full biographical listings, see the Martindale-Hubbell Law Directory

SEYMOUR, Jackson Co.

PARDIECK, GILL, VARGO & MACTAVISH, A PROFESSIONAL CORPORATION (AV)

100 North Chestnut Street, P.O. Box 608, 47274
Telephone: 812-523-8686
Fax: 812-522-4199
Email: pgv@pgvlaw.com
Indianapolis, Indiana Office: The Old Bailey Building, 244 North College Avenue, 46202.
Telephone: 317-639-3321.

Roger L. Pardieck
W. Brent Gill
John F. Vargo (Resident, Indianapolis Office)
Bruce A. MacTavish

Thomas L. Landwerlen (Resident, Indianapolis Office)
Karen J. Mellencamp Davis
Janet O. Vargo (Resident, Indianapolis Office)

OF COUNSEL

Robert C. Rothkopf (Resident, Indianapolis Office)

References: Home Federal Savings Bank, Seymour, Indiana.

For full biographical listings, see the Martindale-Hubbell Law Directory

*SOUTH BEND,** St. Joseph Co.

DORAN • BLACKMOND LLP (AV)

1700 Valley American Bank Building, 211 W. Washington Street, 46601
Telephone: 219-288-1800
Fax: 219-236-4265

MEMBERS OF FIRM

M. Edward Doran (1895-1982) John E. Doran
Don G. Blackmond

ASSOCIATES

Don Gregory Blackmond Peter J. Van Dyke
Lynn M. Butcher

OF COUNSEL

A. Howard Williams

For full biographical listings, see the Martindale-Hubbell Law Directory

HARDIG, LEE AND GROVES, PROFESSIONAL ASSOCIATION (AV)

Suite 502, First Bank Building, 205 West Jefferson Boulevard, 46601
Telephone: 219-232-5923
Fax: 219-232-5942
Email: jgrovesaty@aoo.com

James F. Groves

Representative Client: South Bend-Mishawaka New Car Dealers Assn.
Reference: First Interstate Bank of South Bend.

For full biographical listings, see the Martindale-Hubbell Law Directory

ROWE & ROWE (AV)

Suite 900 Keybank Building, 46601
Telephone: 219-233-8200
Fax: 219-234-5987

R. Kent Rowe R. Kent Rowe, III

ASSOCIATES

Robert D. Truitt Gregory J. Haines
Marie Anne Hendrie

For full biographical listings, see the Martindale-Hubbell Law Directory

*TERRE HAUTE,** Vigo Co.

MANN LAW FIRM (AV)

33 South Sixth Street, P.O. Box 1643, 47808-1643
Telephone: 812-232-0107
FAX: 812-232-3414
Email: mannlawfirm.com *URL:* http://www.mannlawfirm.com

MEMBERS OF FIRM

Hansford C. Mann (1911-1998) Stephen L. Williams
Max E. Goodwin Bruce D. Aukerman
John T. Roach III

References: Terre Haute First National Bank; Indiana State Bank.

For full biographical listings, see the Martindale-Hubbell Law Directory

*VALPARAISO,** Porter Co.

BLACHLY, TABOR, BOZIK & HARTMAN (AV)

56 South Washington Street Suite 401, 46383
Telephone: 219-464-1041
Fax: 219-464-0927
Fort Wayne, Indiana Office: 4656 West Jefferson. Suite 120. 46804.

MEMBERS OF FIRM

Duane W. Hartman Thomas F. Macke
Craig R. Van Schouwen

OF COUNSEL

Glenn J. Tabor

Reference: First National Bank.

For Complete List of Firm Personnel, See General Section

For full biographical listings, see the Martindale-Hubbell Law Directory

SPANGLER, JENNINGS & DOUGHERTY, P.C. (AV)

150 Lincolnway, Suite 3001, 46383
Telephone: 219-462-6151
FAX: 219-477-4935
Email: spangler@sjdlaw.com
Merrillville, Indiana Office: 8396 Mississippi Street.
Telephone: 219-769-2323.

RESIDENT PERSONNEL

Samuel J. Bernardi, Jr. Robert P. Stoner

Edward W. Hearn Christopher Grabarek

(See Next Column)

OF COUNSEL

Patrick J. Dougherty

Representative Clients: Allstate Insurance Cos.; State Farm Insurance Cos.; The Saint Paul Companies; CNA Insurance Cos.; Maryland Insurance Cos.; American Specialty Insurance Services; J&N Enterprises; Indiana Beach, Inc.; CertainTeed Corp.; Fireman's Fund.

For full biographical listings, see the Martindale-Hubbell Law Directory

IOWA

*CEDAR RAPIDS,** Linn Co.

RICCOLO & BAKER, P.C. (AV)

Suite 1140, APAC Building, 425 Second Street, S.E., 52401
Telephone: 319-365-9200; Toll Free: 1-888-546-6529
Fax: 319-365-1114
Email: rb@riccolobaker.com

John L. Riccolo David L. Baker

Timothy S. Semelroth

For full biographical listings, see the Martindale-Hubbell Law Directory

TOM RILEY LAW FIRM, P.L.C. (AV)

4040 First Avenue N.E., P.O. Box 998, 52406-0998
Telephone: 319-363-4040
FAX: 319-363-9789
Iowa City Office: 1220 Highway 6 West.
Telephone: 319-351-4996.
Fax: 319-351-7063.
Cedar Rapids, Iowa Office: Annex, 139 40th St. NE, 92402.
Fax: 319-298-2917.

Tom Riley Sara Riley
Peter C. Riley Thomas J. Currie
T. Todd Becker James E. Bennett
Mark E. Liabo Gerald J. Kucera
Hugh G. Albrecht Nestor Lobodiak

James K. Weston, II Anne Updegraff

For full biographical listings, see the Martindale-Hubbell Law Directory

*COUNCIL BLUFFS,** Pottawattamie Co.

SHELDON GALLNER, P.C. (AV)

300 West Broadway, Suite 145, P.O. Box 1588, 51503
Telephone: 712-323-0999
Fax: 712-323-0814
URL: http://www.lawyers.com/gallnerlaw

Sheldon M. Gallner Laura Laubenthal Pattermann

Eric C. Hanson

For full biographical listings, see the Martindale-Hubbell Law Directory

REILLY, PETERSEN & HANNAN, P.L.C. (AV)

215 South Main Street, P.O. Box 1016, 51502-1016
Telephone: 712-328-1575
Fax: 712-328-1562

C. R. Hannan Michael G. Reilly
Deborah L. Petersen

Craig M. Dreismeier

References: Peoples National Bank of Council Bluffs.

For full biographical listings, see the Martindale-Hubbell Law Directory

*DECORAH,** Winneshiek Co.

MILLER, PEARSON, GLOE, BURNS, BEATTY & COWIE, P.C. (AV)

301 West Broadway, 52101
Telephone: 319-382-4226
Fax: 319-382-3783
Email: millerlaw@salamander.com

Frank R. Miller (1915-1977) James Burns
Donald H. Gloe Marion L. Beatty
Robert J. Cowie, Jr.

Bradley Douglas Shidler

(See Next Column)

MILLER, PEARSON, GLOE, BURNS, BEATTY & COWIE P.C., *Decorah—Continued*

OF COUNSEL

Floyd S. Pearson

Counsel for: Luther College; Decorah Community School District; Winneshiek County Memorial Hospital; Community First National Bank.
Local Counsel for: Iowa Mutual Insurance Cos.; Employers Mutual Liability Insurance Co. of Wisconsin; Continental Casualty Co.; Employers Mutual Casualty Co.; Grinnell Mutual Insurance Co.; Allied Mutual Insurance Co.

For full biographical listings, see the Martindale-Hubbell Law Directory

*DES MOINES,** Polk Co.

ROXANNE B. CONLIN AND ASSOCIATES, P.C. (AV)

The Plaza, 300 Walnut Street - Suite 5, 50309-2239
Telephone: 515-282-3329
Fax: 515-282-0318

Roxanne B. Conlin

Thomas J. Duff
Melinda Kaye Ellwanger
Tiffany B. Klosener

For full biographical listings, see the Martindale-Hubbell Law Directory

FINLEY, ALT, SMITH, SCHARNBERG, CRAIG, HILMES & GAFFNEY, P.C. (AV)

604 Locust Street, Fourth Floor Equitable Building, 50309
Telephone: 515-288-0145
Telecopier: 515-288-2724

Steven K. Scharnberg
R. Todd Gaffney
John D. (Jack) Hilmes
Kevin J. Driscoll
V. Glenn Goodwin, Jr.

Representative Clients: ALAS; American Society of Composers, Authors and Publishers; Equitable Life Assurance Society of the U.S.; Federated Insurance Co.; Meredith Corp.
Iowa Attorneys for: Midwest Medical Insurance Co.
District Attorneys for: Norfolk & Southern Railroad; Soo Line Railroad Company.

For Complete List of Firm Personnel, See General Section

For full biographical listings, see the Martindale-Hubbell Law Directory

HAWKINS & NORRIS (AV)

2501 Grand Avenue, Suite C, 50312
Telephone: 515-288-6532
Fax: 515-288-9733

MEMBERS OF FIRM

Lex Hawkins
Glenn L. Norris

ASSOCIATES

George F. Davison, Jr.
Carla Tolbert Schemmel
David N. May

Reference: West Des Moines State Bank.

For full biographical listings, see the Martindale-Hubbell Law Directory

HUBER, BOOK, CORTESE, HAPPE & BROWN, P.L.C. (AV)

317 Sixth Avenue, Suite 200, 50309-4127
Telephone: 515-243-4148
Fax: 515-243-5481
Email: huber@desmoineslaw.com

MEMBERS OF FIRM

Joseph S. Cortese II
Joseph A. Happe
Terrence D. Brown

ASSOCIATE

Deborah M. Stein

Representative Clients: Atlantic Mutual Cos.; CNA Insurance Cos.; Fireman's Fund American Insurance Companies; Great West Casualty Co.; Liberty Mutual Insurance Co.; Maryland Insurance Group; Prudential Property and Casualty Insurance Co.; USF&G Company.
Reference: Bank of America.

For full biographical listings, see the Martindale-Hubbell Law Directory

PATTERSON, LORENTZEN, DUFFIELD, TIMMONS, IRISH, BECKER & ORDWAY, L.L.P. (AV)

729 Insurance Exchange Building, 50309
Telephone: 515-283-2147
Fax: 515-283-1002
Email: mail@pattersonfirm.com *URL:* http://www.pattersonfirm.com

MEMBERS OF FIRM

G. O. Patterson (1914-1982)
Roy M. Irish
James A. Lorentzen (Retired)
F. H. Becker (Retired)
Theodore T. Duffield
Gary D. Ordway
William E. Timmons (Retired)
Robin L. Hermann

(See Next Column)

MEMBERS OF FIRM (Continued)

Harry Perkins, III
Martin C. Sprock
Michael F. Lacey, Jr.
William A. Wickett
Gregory J. Wilson
Frederick M. Haskins
Jeffrey A. Boehlert
Jeffrey A. Baker
Douglas A. Haag
Janice M. Herfkens
Charles E. Cutler
Coreen K. Bezdicek
Michael D. Huppert
Patrick V. Waldron

ASSOCIATE

Michael S. Jones

General Counsel for: Iowa Insurance Institute.
Representative Clients: Allied Mutual Insurance Company; CNA Insurance Company; Chubb Insurance Group; Continental Western Insurance Co.; Farmers Insurance Group; Farmland Insurance Company; Grinnell Mutual Reinsurance Company; Hawkeye Security Insurance Company; Iowa Insurance Institute, St. Paul Fire & Marine Insurance Company.

For full biographical listings, see the Martindale-Hubbell Law Directory

THE ROSENBERG LAW FIRM (AV)

1010 Insurance Exchange Building, 505 Fifth Avenue, 50309
Telephone: 515-243-7600
Email: bdr@worldnet.att.net

MEMBERS OF FIRM

Raymond Rosenberg
Dean A. Stowers
Brent D. Rosenberg

Reference: Firstar Bank, Des Moines, Iowa.

For full biographical listings, see the Martindale-Hubbell Law Directory

THE WALKER LAW FIRM (AV)

2501 Grand Avenue, Suite E, 50312
Telephone: 515-281-1488
Fax: 515-281-1489
Email: ERWJK@aol.com

E. Ralph Walker
David J. Darrell
Joseph W. Fernandez

OF COUNSEL

Fred E. Rizk (Not admitted in IA)

For full biographical listings, see the Martindale-Hubbell Law Directory

*DUBUQUE,** Dubuque Co.

O'CONNOR & THOMAS, P.C. (AV)

700 Locust Street, Suite 200, CyCare Plaza, 52001-6874
Telephone: 319-557-8400
Telecopier: 319-556-1867
Email: othomaspc@mwci.net

John C. O'Connor
Chad C. Leitch
Brendan T. Quann
Richard K. Whitty
A. John Arenz
Stephen C. Krumpe
James E. Goodman, Jr.

Davin C. Curtiss
Thomas S. Collins
Paul J. Sigwarth
Amy Collins White
George A. Davis

OF COUNSEL

Robert M. Bertsch

Representative Clients: American Trust & Savings Bank; Dubuque Bank & Trust Company; Firstar Bank; Mercantile Bank Midwest; The Archdiocese of Dubuque; A.Y. McDonald Industries, Inc.

For full biographical listings, see the Martindale-Hubbell Law Directory

*IOWA CITY,** Johnson Co.

JOHNSTON, POTTERFIELD & NATHANSON, P.C. (AV)

1902 Broadway, P.O. Box 3400, 52244
Telephone: 319-354-1712
Fax: 319-354-7265
URL: http://www.lawyers.com/johnstonlaw
Cedar Rapids Office: 129 First Avenue, S.W., P.O. Box 74210.
Telephone: 319-366-1000.
Fax: 319-366-6973.
Waterloo Office: 1506 LaPorte Road, P.O. Box 2787.
Telephone: 319-235-3000.
Fax: 319-235-2108.

Joseph C. Johnston
Henry E. Nathanson
Amanda Potterfield
Cathy L. Fitzmaurice
David Burbidge

OF COUNSEL

Carl J. Goetz, Jr.

For full biographical listings, see the Martindale-Hubbell Law Directory

Iowa City—Continued

PITTON LAW OFFICES, P.A. (AV(T))

503 Iowa State Bank Building, 102 South Clinton Street, 52240
Telephone: 319-338-2508
Fax: 319-338-3334
WATS: 800-488-4430
Email: pittonlaw@iowacity.net
Minneapolis, Minnesota Office: 110 Southdale Place, 3400 West 66th Street, 55435.
Telephone: 612-925-6900.

Michael J. Pitton

For full biographical listings, see the Martindale-Hubbell Law Directory

KEOKUK, Lee Co.

LAW OFFICES OF JAMES P. HOFFMAN (AV)

Middle Road, P.O. Box 1087, 52632-1087
Telephone: 319-524-4441
Fax: 319-524-1638

For full biographical listings, see the Martindale-Hubbell Law Directory

WEST DES MOINES, Polk Co.

LAMARCA & LANDRY, P.C. (AV)

1300 50th Street, 50266
Telephone: 515-225-2600
Fax: 515-225-8581
Islamorada, Florida Office: 202 Biscayne Boulevard, 33036.
Telephone: 305-664-8527.

George A. LaMarca
Gregory W. Landry

Gary G. Mattson
Justin E. LaVan

OF COUNSEL

Martin R. Anderson
Samuel S. Duffey

For full biographical listings, see the Martindale-Hubbell Law Directory

KANSAS

OVERLAND PARK, Johnson Co.

RISJORD & JAMES, P.C. (AV)

Suite 100, 10680 Barkley, 66212
Telephone: 913-381-5151
Fax: 913-381-2569
Email: RJLaw@RisjordJames.com *URL:* http://www.risjordjames.com

Randy W. James
Aaron N. Woods

Lisa C. Beckley

RETIRED

John C. Risjord

For full biographical listings, see the Martindale-Hubbell Law Directory

SHAMBERG, JOHNSON & BERGMAN, CHARTERED (AV)

Suite 355, 4551 West 107th Street, 66207
Telephone: 913-642-0600
Fax: 913-642-9629
Email: mail@sjblaw.com *URL:* http://www.sjblaw.com
Kansas City, Kansas Office: Suite M-4, One Security Plaza.
Telephone: 913-281-1900.
Kansas City, Missouri Office: Suite 205, Scarritt Arcade Building, 819 Walnut.
Telephone: 816-556-9431.

Lynn R. Johnson
Victor A. Bergman
John M. Parisi

Steven G. Brown
Steve N. Six

OF COUNSEL

John E. Shamberg

For full biographical listings, see the Martindale-Hubbell Law Directory

*TOPEKA,** Shawnee Co.

FISHER, PATTERSON, SAYLER & SMITH, L.L.P. (AV)

3550 S.W. 5th Street, P.O. Box 949, 66601
Telephone: 785-232-7761
Fax: 785-232-6604
Email: fpss@cjnetworks.com
Overland Park, Kansas Office: 11050 Roe Avenue, Suite 210, 66211.
Telephone: 913-339-6757.
Fax: 913-339-6187.

MEMBERS OF FIRM

Donald Patterson
Edwin Dudley Smith (Resident, Overland Park Office)
Larry G. Pepperdine
James P. Nordstrom
Justice B. King
J. Steven Pigg
Steve R. Fabert
Ronald J. Laskowski
Michael K. Seck (Resident, Overland Park Office)
David P. Madden (Resident, Overland Park Office)
Steven K. Johnson
Kristine A. Larscheid

ASSOCIATES

Billy E. Newman
David R. Cooper
Kelly A. Feyh (Resident, Overland Park Office)
Jennifer R. Rose (Resident, Overland Park Office)

OF COUNSEL

David H. Fisher

RETIRED

Charles Keith Sayler (Retired)

Representative Clients: Gage Shopping Center, Inc.; Fireman's Fund-American Insurance Cos.; United States Fidelity and Guaranty Co.; The Procter & Gamble Company; Commercial Union Insurance Companies; National Casualty; The Hartford; Berkshire Hathaway Companies.

For full biographical listings, see the Martindale-Hubbell Law Directory

RALSTON & POPE, LLC (AV)

2913 Southwest Maupin Lane, 66614-4139
Telephone: 913-273-8002; 888-913-2783
FAX: 913-273-0744
Email: ERalston@AOL.Com

Eugene B. Ralston
Kevin L. Diehl
Ronald P. Pope

LEGAL SUPPORT PERSONNEL

PARALEGALS

Barbara Cobuluis
Corri Wecker
Colleen Wright
Ashanti Smith

For full biographical listings, see the Martindale-Hubbell Law Directory

WRIGHT, HENSON, SOMERS, SEBELIUS, CLARK & BAKER, LLP (AV)

Commerce Bank Building, 100 Southeast Ninth Street, 2nd Floor, P.O. Box 3555, 66601-3555
Telephone: 785-232-2200
FAX: 785-232-3344
Email: wrighthenson@wrighthenson.com *URL:* http://www.wrighthenson.com

MEMBERS OF FIRM

Thomas E. Wright
K. Gary Sebelius
Evelyn Zabel Wilson

ASSOCIATE

Michael M. Walker

SPECIAL COUNSEL

David P. Mudrick

For Complete List of Firm Personnel, See General Section

For full biographical listings, see the Martindale-Hubbell Law Directory

*WICHITA,** Sedgwick Co.

DEPEW AND GILLEN, L.L.C. (AV)

151 North Main, Suite 800, 67202-1409
Telephone: 316-262-4000
Facsimile: 316-265-3819
Email: DG@DEPEWGILLEN.COM *URL:* HTTP://WWW.DEPEWGILLEN.COM

Dennis L. Gillen
Randall K. Rathbun

For Complete List of Firm Personnel, See General Section

For full biographical listings, see the Martindale-Hubbell Law Directory

Wichita—Continued

FOULSTON & SIEFKIN L.L.P. (AV)

700 NationsBank Financial Center, 67202
Telephone: 316-267-6371
Facsimile: 316-267-6345
URL: http://www.foulston.com
Topeka, Kansas Office: 1515 NationsBank Tower, 534 Kansas Avenue, 66603.
Telephone: 785-233-3600.
Fax: 785-233-1610.
Dodge City, Kansas Office: 810 Frontview, P.O. Box 1147, 67801.
Telephone: 316-227-8126.
Fax: 316-227-8451.
Member: Lex Mundi, The World's Leading Association of Independent Law Firms.

MEMBERS OF FIRM

Mikel L. Stout
Darrell L. Warta
Jay F. Fowler
Stephen M. Kerwick
Amy S. Lemley
Craig W. West

For Complete List of Firm Personnel, See General Section

For full biographical listings, see the Martindale-Hubbell Law Directory

HUTTON & HUTTON (AV)

8100 East 22nd Street North, Building 1200, 67226-2312
Telephone: 316-688-1166
Fax: 316-686-1077
Mailing Address: P.O. Box 638, Wichita, KS, 67201-0638
Email: huttnlaw@southwind.net *URL:* http://www.huttonlaw.com

Mark B. Hutton
Andrew W. Hutton

ASSOCIATES

Derek Scott Casey
Anne H. Pankratz
Christopher P. Christian
Chan P. Townsley
Deborah B. McIlhenny

OF COUNSEL

M. Prudence Hutton

For full biographical listings, see the Martindale-Hubbell Law Directory

YOUNG, BOGLE, McCAUSLAND, WELLS & BLANCHARD, P.A. (AV)

106 West Douglas, Suite 923, 67202
Telephone: 316-265-7841
Facsimile: 316-265-3956
Email: ybmwblaw@aol.com

Glenn D. Young, Jr.
Jerry D. Bogle
Paul S. McCausland
William A. Wells

J. Michael Peters

Representative Clients: Horace Mann Ins. Co.; Deere & Co.; Bridgestone/-Firestone, Inc.; Massey-Ferguson, Inc.; Sears Roebuck & Co.; GAF Corp. (asbestos litigation).

For Complete List of Firm Personnel, See General Section

For full biographical listings, see the Martindale-Hubbell Law Directory

KENTUCKY

ASHLAND, Boyd Co.

MARTIN, JUSTICE & VINCENT (AV)

431 Sixteenth Street, P.O. Box 2528, 41105-2528
Telephone: 606-329-8338
Fax: 606-325-8199
Email: mjvlaw@zoomnet.net

Richard W. Martin
David Justice
John F. Vincent
Thomas Wade Lavender, II

ASSOCIATE

Charles D. Oppenheimer

Representative Clients: City of Ashland; FIVCO Area Development District; Boyd County Sanitation District No. 2.
Insurance Counsel for: State Farm Mutual Automobile Insurance Co.; State Farm Fire and Casualty Co.; Travelers Insurance Co.; Grange Mutual Insurance Co.; Great American Insurance Co.

For full biographical listings, see the Martindale-Hubbell Law Directory

*BOWLING GREEN,** Warren Co.

KERRICK, GRISE & STIVERS (AV)

1025 State Street, P.O. Box 9547, 42102-9547
Telephone: 502-782-8160
Fax: 502-782-5856
Email: kgs@kgslaw.com
Elizabethtown, Kentucky Office: 2935 Dolphin Drive, Suite 102.
Telephone: 502-769-5788.
Fax: 502-737-9285.

MEMBERS OF FIRM

Thomas N. Kerrick
John R. Grise
Gregory N. Stivers
H. Brent Brennenstuhl
Laura M. Hagan

ASSOCIATES

Karl N. Crandall
Shawn Rosso Alcott
Jason B. Bell

OF COUNSEL

Jeffrey R. O'Grody

LEGAL SUPPORT PERSONNEL

Patricia Logsdon
Laura Lockhart Lico
Allison Lusk

Representative Clients: Dollar General Corp.; Columbia Greenview Regional Hospital; Hospital Corporation of America; Hardin Memorial Hospital; Fir-Star Bank; TKR Cable.

For full biographical listings, see the Martindale-Hubbell Law Directory

RUDLOFF & RUDLOFF (AV)

553 East Main Street, 42101
Telephone: 270-781-7754
Fax: 270-843-0473

MEMBERS OF FIRM

William J. Rudloff
Daniel B. Rudloff

For full biographical listings, see the Martindale-Hubbell Law Directory

COVINGTON, Kenton Co.

ROBERT E. SANDERS AND ASSOCIATES, P.S.C. (AV)

The Charles H. Fisk House, 1017 Russell Street, 41011-3052
Telephone: 606-491-3000
Fax: 606-655-4642
Email: resanders@worldnet.att.net

Robert E. Sanders

Jeffrey M. Sanders
J. Pierre Tismo
Delana S. Pierce

LEGAL SUPPORT PERSONNEL

Shirley L. Sanders
Sandra A. Sturgeon
Sheila D. Rachal

For full biographical listings, see the Martindale-Hubbell Law Directory

TALIAFERRO, MEHLING, SHIROONI & CARRAN (AV)

1005 Madison Avenue, P.O. Box 468, 41012-0468
Telephone: 606-291-9900
Fax: 606-291-3014

MEMBERS OF FIRM

Philip Taliaferro, III
Christopher J. Mehling
Lucinda C. Shirooni
Robert W. Carran

ASSOCIATES

Howard L. Tankersley
Alice G. Keys
Jerome N. Epping, Jr.
Michelle Snodgrass-Deimling

OF COUNSEL

Norbert J. Bischoff
F. Edward Worland, Jr.

For full biographical listings, see the Martindale-Hubbell Law Directory

*GLASGOW,** Barren Co.

HERBERT & HERBERT (AV)

135 North Public Square, P.O. Box 1000, 42141
Telephone: 502-651-9000
Fax: 502-651-3317
Email: h&hlaw@glasgow-ky.com

MEMBERS OF FIRM

H. Jefferson Herbert, Jr.
Betty Reece Herbert

ASSOCIATES

Brian K. Pack
Wesley W. Stephens

Representative Clients: Alliance Corp. (Construction); Eaton Corp.; Pan-Osten, Inc.; Supreme Mills, Inc.; T.J. Samson Community Hospital.
Approved Attorneys for: Fireman's Fund Insurance Companies; Indiana Insurance Co.; Agway Insurance Co.; Travelers Insurance Co.

(See Next Column)

HERBERT & HERBERT—*Continued*

Reference: South Central Bank, Glasgow, Kentucky.

For full biographical listings, see the Martindale-Hubbell Law Directory

*HAZARD,** Perry Co.

GULLETT, COMBS, REED & BOWLING (AV)

109 Broadway, Second Floor, P.O. Box 1039, 41702-1039
Telephone: 606-439-1373; 1-800-949-8812
Fax: 606-439-4450
Email: apgullet@mis.net
Email: 1234rong@tgtel.com

MEMBERS OF FIRM

Asa P. Gullett, III
Ronald G. Combs
Teresa G. Combs Reed
Matthew Lawton Bowling

ASSOCIATE

Jameson D. Combs

LEGAL SUPPORT PERSONNEL

Jacqueline E. Goodin
Jimmie Lynn Jones

Reference: Peoples Bank and Trust Co.

For full biographical listings, see the Martindale-Hubbell Law Directory

*LEXINGTON,** Fayette Co.

PETER PERLMAN LAW OFFICES, P.S.C. (AV)

388 South Broadway, 40508
Telephone: 606-253-3919
Fax: 606-259-0493

Peter Perlman

Bryce D. Franklin, Jr.

OF COUNSEL

Thomas R. Hays

For full biographical listings, see the Martindale-Hubbell Law Directory

PIPER, WELLMAN & BOWERS (AV)

200 North Upper Street, 40507
Telephone: 606-231-1012
Fax: 606-231-1015
Email: pwb200@uky.campus.mci.net

MEMBERS OF FIRM

George C. Piper
Dean T. Wellman
Barbara J. Bowers

ASSOCIATE

Johann F. Herklotz

For full biographical listings, see the Martindale-Hubbell Law Directory

ROBERTS & SMITH (AV)

167 West Main Street Suite 200, 40507-1701
Telephone: 606-233-1104
Fax: 606-255-6438
Email: LRob70165@aol.com

MEMBERS OF FIRM

Larry S. Roberts
Kenneth W. Smith

For full biographical listings, see the Martindale-Hubbell Law Directory

SAVAGE, GARMER & ELLIOTT, P.S.C. (AV)

Opera House Office Building, 141 North Broadway, 40507
Telephone: 606-254-9351
Fax: 606-233-9769

Joe C. Savage
William R. Garmer
Robert L. Elliott

For full biographical listings, see the Martindale-Hubbell Law Directory

*LOUISVILLE,** Jefferson Co.

FRANKLIN AND HANCE, P.S.C. (AV)

The Speed House, 505 West Ormsby Avenue, 40203
Telephone: 502-637-6000
Fax: 502-637-1413
Email: golfatty@aol.com *URL:* http://www.lawyers.com/fhlaw

Larry B. Franklin
Michael R. Hance

David B. Gray
Hope Fitzpatrick Brooks

Reference: First National Bank.

For full biographical listings, see the Martindale-Hubbell Law Directory

HUMMEL & COAN (AV)

Kentucky Home Life Building, The Seventeenth Floor, 239 South Fifth Street, 40202-3268
Telephone: 502-585-3084
Fax: 502-585-3548
Email: hummelandcoan@hc-attys.com

OF COUNSEL

Rothschild Aberson Miller & Goodin

MEMBERS OF FIRM

Dennis J. Hummel
Marvin L. Coan
David L. Sage

Representative Clients: Georgia Pacific Corp.; Safeco Insurance Cos.; GRE-/Indiana Insurance Company; Tricon Global Restaurants, Inc.; Dr. Bizer's Vision World; Calvert Insurance Co.; Fabricated Metals Corporation; Western Heritage Insurance Co.; Nobel Insurance Company.

For full biographical listings, see the Martindale-Hubbell Law Directory

MIDDLETON & REUTLINGER, P.S.C. (AV)

2500 Brown and Williamson Tower, 40202-3410
Telephone: 502-584-1135
Fax: 502-561-0442
URL: http://middreut.com
Jeffersonville, Indiana Office: 530 East Court Avenue, 47130.
Telephone: 812-282-1132.
Fax: 812-282-3188.

O. Grant Bruton
Charles G. Middleton, III
Charles D. Greenwell
John W. Bilby
Timothy P. O'Mara
G. Kennedy Hall, Jr.
Mark S. Fenzel
Kathiejane Oehler
David J. Kellerman
Julie A. Gregory
Dennis D. Murrell

Augustus S. Herbert
Dana L. Collins

For Complete List of Firm Personnel, See General Section

For full biographical listings, see the Martindale-Hubbell Law Directory

ROTH FOLEY BRYANT & COOPER, PLLC (AV)

First Trust Centre, Suite 300S, 200 South Fifth Street, 40202-3236
Telephone: 502-569-7550
Fax: 502-540-0123
Email: RFBC.com

Irvin D. Foley
David M. Roth
David H. Cooper
Lisa Koch Bryant
K. Gail Russell
Christian L. Juckett

OF COUNSEL

James E. Fahey
David W. Gray

Representative Clients: Bank One, Kentucky, N.A.; Huntington National Bank; Commonwealth Bank & Trust Co.; Farm Credit Services of Mid-America; Century Indemnity Co.; Travelers Casualty and Insurance Co.; Tumbleweed, LLC; John R. Gains Thoroughbreds, LLC; ARM Financial Group, Inc.; Osborn Enterprises.

For full biographical listings, see the Martindale-Hubbell Law Directory

WEISS FREDERICK WILLETT & HAYNES (AV)

1425 Citizens Plaza, 40202
Telephone: 502-583-1000
FAX: 502-583-4478

Gary M. Weiss
Carl D. Frederick
Barry Willett
William T. Haynes, Jr.
Janice M. Weiss

ASSOCIATES

Karla W. Katakis
Paul J. Hershberg
Kevin M. Adams

OF COUNSEL

Henry M. Burt

For full biographical listings, see the Martindale-Hubbell Law Directory

*MADISONVILLE,** Hopkins Co.

MITCHELL, JOINER, & HARDESTY, PSC (AV)

113 East Center Street, Drawer 659, 42431-0659
Telephone: 270-825-4455
Telefax: 270-825-9600

Thomas A. Mitchell
Richard M. Joiner
Randall L. Hardesty

For full biographical listings, see the Martindale-Hubbell Law Directory

*MURRAY,** Calloway Co.

Gregory, Easley and Courtney (AV)

204 South Sixth Street, P.O. Box 230, 42071
Telephone: 502-753-2633
Fax: 502-753-1825

MEMBERS OF FIRM

John A. Gregory, Jr. R. Sidney Easley
Dennis J. Courtney

Representative Clients: Kentucky Farm Bureau Mutual Insurance Co.; State Farm Mutual Automobile Insurance; R. T. Vanderbilt Co.; Briggs and Stratton Corp.; State Auto Insurance; Meridian Insurance Co.; Peoples Bank of Murray; Murray State University Credit Union.

For Complete List of Firm Personnel, See General Section

For full biographical listings, see the Martindale-Hubbell Law Directory

NEWPORT, Campbell Co.

Johnson & Johnson, P.L.C. (AV)

20 North Grand Avenue, Suite 15, 41071
Telephone: 606-441-3900; toll free: 888-880-9311
Telecopier: 606-441-3018

Donald L. Johnson Richard G. Johnson

Representative Clients: Provident Bank of Kentucky; County Square (Super-Value) Market; Campbell Capital Development Group, Inc.; B&K Enterprises, Inc.; Yellow Cab of Newport, Inc.; Executive Transporation, Inc.; Airport Starter Systems, Inc.; Alexandria Capital Co.; M. Links Co., Inc; Hasco International Identification, Inc.

For full biographical listings, see the Martindale-Hubbell Law Directory

*PADUCAH,** McCracken Co.

Len W. Ogden, Jr. (AV)

The Sinnott House, 228 North 9th Street, 42001-1850
Telephone: 502-444-0232
Fax: 502-444-0239
Email: lenogden@apex.net

For full biographical listings, see the Martindale-Hubbell Law Directory

Saladino Law Firm (AV)

700 Clark Street, P.O. Box 1246, 42002-1246
Telephone: 502-444-0406
Fax: 502-444-0454
Email: saladino@apex.net

Charles A. Saladino

ASSOCIATES

David Vance Oakes
Kristi Saladino Schaaf
Barclay Walden Banister
Gary E. Schaaf

For full biographical listings, see the Martindale-Hubbell Law Directory

*PIKEVILLE,** Pike Co.

Gary C. Johnson, P.S.C. (AV)

104 Caroline Avenue, P.O. Box 231, 41502
Telephone: 606-437-4002
Telecopier: 606-437-0021
Hazard, Kentucky Office: 941 Memorial Drive, P.O. Box 509, 41702.
Telephone: 606-436-6059.
Fax: 606-436-4599.
Lexington, Kentucky Office: 101 Prosperous Place, Suite 100, 40509.
Telephone: 606-263-4002.
Fax: 606-263-9651.
Richmond, Kentucky Office: 128 North Second Street, 40475.
Telephone: 606-624-0505.
Fax: 606-624-5393.

Gary C. Johnson

Anita Johnson
Roy J. Downey
Julie A. Butcher (Resident, Lexington Office)
Jeffrey R. Morgan (Resident, Hazard Office)
Jeremy R. Morgan (Resident, Hazard Office)
Masten Childers, II (Resident, Richmond Office)
Rhonda Jennings Blackburn
Angela Pergrem Owens (Resident, Richmond Office)
William R. Johnson
Bryan K. Sergent

For full biographical listings, see the Martindale-Hubbell Law Directory

*SHELBYVILLE,** Shelby Co.

Neal & Davis (AV)

931 Main Street, P.O. Box 40, 40066-0040
Telephone: 502-633-6002;
Louisville: 502-589-9888
Email: tdavis@neal-davis.com
URL: http://www.neal-davis.com

Gregg Y. Neal Thomas Todd Davis

Reference: Republic Bank and Trust Co.

For full biographical listings, see the Martindale-Hubbell Law Directory

LOUISIANA

*BATON ROUGE,** East Baton Rouge Parish

Atkinson, Perry, Atkinson & Balhoff, L.L.C. (AV)

7520 Perkins Road, Suite 260, P.O. Box 83260, 70884-3260
Telephone: 504-767-7730
Fax: 504-767-7967
Email: apabllc@msn.com

Daniel R. Atkinson
John W. Perry, Jr.
Daniel R. Atkinson, Jr.
Daniel J. Balhoff
Joseph W. Mengis

ASSOCIATE

Barbara G. Baier

LEGAL SUPPORT PERSONNEL

Becky Bourgeois (Legal Secretary/Paralegal)
Renee Bordelon (Legal Secretary/Paralegal)
Sue Rivere (Legal Secretary)
Cindy Martrain (Paralegal)
Wendy Cotton (Legal Secretary)

For full biographical listings, see the Martindale-Hubbell Law Directory

deGravelles, Palmintier & Holthaus (AV)

628 St. Louis Street, 70802-0628
Telephone: 225-344-3735
Fax: 225-336-1146

MEMBERS OF FIRM

John W. deGravelles Michael C. Palmintier
Craig F. Holthaus

ASSOCIATE

Scott H. Frugé

OF COUNSEL

David W. Robinson

LEGAL SUPPORT PERSONNEL

Jimmie W. Murvin (Paralegal)

For full biographical listings, see the Martindale-Hubbell Law Directory

Dué, Caballero, Price & Guidry, (A Professional Association) (AV)

8201 Jefferson Highway, 70809
Telephone: 225-929-7481
Fax: 225-924-4519

Paul H. Dué
Rick A. Caballero
Donald W. Price
Kirk A. Guidry

Randolph A. Piedrahita Brandon Scott Andrews

OF COUNSEL

David W. Robertson

For full biographical listings, see the Martindale-Hubbell Law Directory

George and George, Ltd., A Professional Law Corporation (AV)

6767 Perkins Road, Suite 203, 70808
Telephone: 225-769-3064
Fax: 225-766-1591
Email: jimg@georgeandgeorge.com *URL:* http://www.georgeandgeorge.com

James A. George

LEGAL SUPPORT PERSONNEL

Cathy Richard (Administrative Assistant)

Reference: Hibernia National Bank of Baton Rouge.

For full biographical listings, see the Martindale-Hubbell Law Directory

Baton Rouge—Continued

LAW OFFICES OF ROBERT D. HOOVER, P.L.C. (AV)

9352 Interline Avenue, P.O. Box 40816, 70835-0816
Telephone: 225-925-2929
Fax: 225-925-2585

Robert D. Hoover

Matthew W. Tierney

For full biographical listings, see the Martindale-Hubbell Law Directory

LANE, FERTITTA, JANNEY & THOMAS (AV)

435 Louisiana Avenue, P.O. Box 3335, 70821
Telephone: 225-387-0241
Fax: 225-387-1238

MEMBERS OF FIRM

Horace C. Lane (1921-1989)
Frank A. Fertitta
William F. Janney
Richard S. Thomas

Representative Clients: State Farm Mutual Automobile Insurance Co.; State Farm Fire & Casualty Co.; United States Fidelity & Guaranty Co.; Aetna Casualty & Surety Co.; Employers Liability Assurance Corp., Ltd.; Allstate Insurance Co.; St. Paul Fire and Marine Insurance Co.; The Medical Protective Co.; Safeco Insurance Co. of America; Horace Mann Insurance Co.

For full biographical listings, see the Martindale-Hubbell Law Directory

SEALE, SMITH, ZUBER & BARNETTE (AV)

Two United Plaza, Suite 200, 8550 United Plaza Boulevard, 70809
Telephone: 225-924-1600
Telecopier: 225-924-6100
Email: SSZB@WORLDNET.ATT.NET

Armbrust Gordon Seale (1913-1989)
Robert W. Smith (1922-1989)
Donald S. Zuber
Kenneth E. Barnette
William C. Kaufman III
John W. L. Swanner
James H. Morgan III
Ronald A. Seale
Charles K. Watts
Brent E. Kinchen
Myron A. Walker, Jr.
Daniel A. Reed
Lawrence R. Anderson, Jr.
Catherine S. Nobile
Anthony J. Russo, Jr.
Richard T. Reed

ASSOCIATE

Michael P. Bienvenu

OF COUNSEL

William H. Brown

Representative Clients: Farmers Insurance Group; St. Paul Fire and Marine Insurance Company; United Services Automobile Association.
Reference: Bank One, Louisiana, N.A., Baton Rouge, Louisiana.

For full biographical listings, see the Martindale-Hubbell Law Directory

WALTER LANDRY SMITH (AV)

601 Mayflower Street, 70802
Telephone: 504-338-0700
Facsimile: 504-338-9090

For full biographical listings, see the Martindale-Hubbell Law Directory

*HOUMA,** Terrebonne Parish

ST. MARTIN & WILLIAMS, A PROFESSIONAL LAW CORPORATION (AV)

4084 Highway 311, P.O. Box 2017, 70361-2017
Telephone: 504-876-3891;
Toll Free: 1-800-256-1533
Facsimile: 504-851-2219

Michael X. St. Martin
Conrad S. P. Williams, III
Charles C. Bourque, Jr.
Joseph G. Jevic, III
Christopher J. St. Martin
Steven P. St. Martin

For full biographical listings, see the Martindale-Hubbell Law Directory

*LAFAYETTE,** Lafayette Parish

BROUSSARD, DAVID & DAIGLE, A PROFESSIONAL LAW CORPORATION (AV)

557 Jefferson Street, P.O. Drawer 3308, 70502-3308
Telephone: 318-234-7000
Fax: 318-237-0344
Email: bdandd@bdandd.com *URL:* http://www.bdandd.com

Hal J. Broussard
Susan A. Daigle
Bryan D. Scofield
Ped C. Kay, III
Todd G. Crawford

(See Next Column)

James T. Rivera
Catherine E. Hensgens

Representative Clients: Certain London Underwriters per individual approval of instructions; Lloyds of London Member Syndicates; Institute of London Underwriter Member Companies; Reliance Insurance Company of Pennsylvania; Reliance Insurance Company of Illinois; Reliance National Insurance Company; The Louisiana Insurance Guaranty Association; Louisiana Oilfield Legislative Committee, Inc. (Louisiana Association of Oilfield Casing Contractors; Association of Oilwell Servicing Contractors; Louisiana Pipeline Contractors Association; Offshore Pipeline Contractors Association; Louisiana Oilfield Contractor Association).

For full biographical listings, see the Martindale-Hubbell Law Directory

LAWRENCE K. BURLEIGH, LTD. A PROFESSIONAL LAW CORPORATION (AV)

Gordon Square, Suite 160, 100 East Vermilion Street, 70501
Telephone: 318-234-6222
Fax: 318-234-6141

Lawrence K. Burleigh, Sr.

Lawrence K. Burleigh, Jr.

For full biographical listings, see the Martindale-Hubbell Law Directory

CURTIS & LAMBERT, A PROFESSIONAL LAW CORPORATION (AV)

201 Rue Iberville, Suite 300, P.O. Box 80247, 70598-0247
Telephone: 318-235-1825
1-800-528-1825
Telefax: 318-237-0241
URL: http://www.curtis-lambertlawfirm.com

Lawrence N. Curtis
James P. Lambert

Gregory K. Klein

For full biographical listings, see the Martindale-Hubbell Law Directory

DOMENGEAUX WRIGHT & ROY, A PROFESSIONAL LAW CORPORATION (AV)

556 Jefferson Street, Suite 500, P.O. Box 3668, 70502-3668
Telephone: 318-233-3033; 1-800-375-3106
Fax: 318-232-8213
Email: info@wrightroy.com *URL:* http://www.wrightroy.com

Bob F. Wright
James Parkerson Roy
Thomas R. Edwards
James H. Domengeaux
Gilbert Hennigan Dozier
Carla Marie Perron
Michael D. Goss

ASSOCIATE

Jamie D. Parker

OF COUNSEL

Jerome E. Domengeaux

Reference: Mid-South National Bank; Advocate Financial, L.L.C.

For full biographical listings, see the Martindale-Hubbell Law Directory

RICHARD R. KENNEDY A PROFESSIONAL LAW CORPORATION (AV)

309 Polk Street, P.O. Box 3243, 70502-3243
Telephone: 318-232-1934
Fax: 318-232-9720
Email: kennedy@net-connect.net

Richard R. Kennedy

For full biographical listings, see the Martindale-Hubbell Law Directory

VOORHIES & LABBÉ, A PROFESSIONAL LAW CORPORATION (AV)

Fourth Floor, St. John Place, 700 St. John Street, P.O. Box 3527, 70502-3527
Telephone: 318-232-9700
Fax: 318-235-4943
Email: vl@vola.com *URL:* http://www.vola.com

Bennett J. Voorhies (1901-1970)
Donald Labbé (1900-1966)
D. Mark Bienvenu (1931-1991)
Robert A. Lecky (1940-1998)
H. Edwin McGlasson, Jr.
W. Gerald Gaudet
Richard D. Chappuis, Jr.
William M. Bass
John N. Chappuis
Robert L. Ellender
Cyd Sheree Page
Robert M. Francez
Robert M. Kallam
Elizabeth L. Guglielmo
Samuel R. Aucoin
James Allen Lochridge, Jr.
Mary McCrory Hamilton
Bradley Joseph Haight
Simone Chachere Dupre
George J. Armbruster, III

Julie A. Scheib
Brent Paul Frederick

(See Next Column)

VOORHIES & LABBÉ A PROFESSIONAL LAW CORPORATION, *Lafayette—Continued*

OF COUNSEL

John W. Hutchison

Representative Clients: Adams & Porter Associates; Aetna Casualty & Surety Insurance Co.; AIG Aviation, Inc.; American Home Assurance Co.; AMICA Mutual Insurance Co.; Appalachian Insurance Co.; Audubon/AIG Insurance Co.; Aviation Office of America; Bellefonte Insurance Co.; Chubb Group of Insurance Co.

For full biographical listings, see the Martindale-Hubbell Law Directory

*LAKE CHARLES,** Calcasieu Parish

BAGGETT, MCCALL & BURGESS, A PROFESSIONAL LAW CORPORATION (AV)

3006 Country Club Road, P.O. Drawer 7820, 70606-7820
Telephone: 318-478-8888
Fax: 318-478-8946
URL: http://www.baggettmccall.com
Email: bmblf@structurex.net *URL:* http://www.occupationaldisease.com

William B. Baggett
Robert C. McCall
William B. Baggett, Jr.
Roger G. Burgess
Wells T. Watson
Erin McCall Alley
Christopher C. McCall
Rebecca F. Todd
Jeffrey Thomas Gaughan
Charles Vorndran (Not admitted in LA)

For full biographical listings, see the Martindale-Hubbell Law Directory

LUNDY & DAVIS, L.L.P. (AV)

Hibernia Tower, One Lakeshore Drive, Suite 1600, P.O. Box 3010, 70602
Telephone: 318-439-0707
FAX: 318-439-1029
URL: http://www.lundydavis.com
Jackson, Mississippi Office: 405 Tombigbee Street, P.O. Box 610, 39205.
Telephone: 601-948-3010.
Facsimile: 601-948-2143.
Houston, Texas Office: 777 Walker, Suite 2500, 77002.
Telephone: 713-237-0690.
Facsimile: 713-237-0999.

MEMBERS OF FIRM

Hunter W. Lundy
Clayton A. L. Davis
Matthew E. Lundy (Resident, Houston, Texas Office)
David A. Bowers (Resident, Jackson, Mississippi Office)
Samuel B. Gabb
James D. Cain, Jr.

ASSOCIATES

Jackey W. South
Michael D. Carleton
Thomas P. LeBlanc
Charles W. Peckham (Resident, Houston, Texas Office)
Andre F. Ducote (Resident, Jackson, Mississippi Office)
David H. Hanchey

OF COUNSEL

Wayne E. Ferrell, Jr. (Resident, Jackson, Mississippi Office)

For full biographical listings, see the Martindale-Hubbell Law Directory

PLAUCHÉ SMITH & NIESET, A PROFESSIONAL LAW CORPORATION (AV)

1123 Pithon Street, P.O. Drawer 1705, 70602
Telephone: 318-436-0522
Facsimile: 318-436-9637

S. W. Plauché (1889-1952)
S. W. Plauché, Jr. (1915-1966)
A. Lane Plauché
Allen L. Smith, Jr.
James R. Nieset
Frank M. Walker, Jr.
Michael J. McNulty, III
Jeffrey M. Cole
Andrew R. Johnson, IV
Charles V. Musso, Jr.
Christopher P. Ieyoub
H. David Vaughan, II
Joseph R. Pousson, Jr.
Rebecca S. Young
V. Ed McGuire, III

Representative Clients: CIGNA; CNA Insurance Cos.; Commercial Union Insurance Cos.; Crum & Forster; Reliance Insurance Cos.; Royal Insurance Group; State Farm; U.S. Insurance Group.

For full biographical listings, see the Martindale-Hubbell Law Directory

*LEESVILLE,** Vernon Parish

THE SMITH LAW FIRM, L.L.P. (AV)

A Limited Liability Partnership including Professional Corporations
300 Courthouse Street Post Office Drawer 1528, 71496-1528
Telephone: 318-239-2244
Facsimile: 318-239-4186
Email: smithlaw@worldnetla.net

(See Next Column)

MEMBERS OF FIRM

Fern M. Wood (1877-1959)
W.C. Wood (1907-1968)
W. R. Jackson, Jr. (1920-1973)
Simeon C. Smith, III
S. Christie Smith, IV (A Professional Corporation)

For full biographical listings, see the Martindale-Hubbell Law Directory

*MINDEN,** Webster Parish

JAMES M. JOHNSON (AV)

105 Pearl Street, P.O. Box 1015, 71058-1015
Telephone: 318-377-4978
Toll Free: 877-827-4294
Fax: 318-377-9026

For full biographical listings, see the Martindale-Hubbell Law Directory

*MONROE,** Ouachita Parish

MCLEOD VERLANDER (AV)

A Partnership including Professional Law Corporations
1900 North 18th Street, Suite 610, P.O. Box 2270, 71207-2270
Telephone: 318-325-7000
Telecopier: 318-324-0580
Email: mv@mv-law.com *URL:* http://www.lawyers.com/mvlaw

MEMBERS OF FIRM

Robert P. McLeod (P.L.C.)
David E. Verlander, III (P.L.C.)

Rick W. Duplissey
Donald C. Douglas, Jr.
Laurie J. Burkett

For full biographical listings, see the Martindale-Hubbell Law Directory

MORGAN CITY, St. Mary Parish

LIPPMAN, MAHFOUZ & MARTIN (AV)

Inglewood Mall, 1025 Victor II Boulevard, P.O. Box 2526, 70381
Telephone: 504-384-1833
Fax: 504-385-4632

MEMBERS OF FIRM

Alfred S. Lippman
Thomas L. Mahfouz
Dale P. Martin

ASSOCIATES

Brian M. Tranchina
David M. Thorguson

For full biographical listings, see the Martindale-Hubbell Law Directory

*NEW ORLEANS,** Orleans Parish

BENCOMO & ASSOCIATES (AV)

Suite 2110 One Poydras Plaza, 639 Loyola Avenue, 70113
Telephone: 504-529-2929
Fax: 504-529-2018

Raul R. Bencomo

OF COUNSEL

Richard E. Anderson
Helen Hairston Babin

For full biographical listings, see the Martindale-Hubbell Law Directory

BUCKLEY & HAYES, L.L.P. (AV)

A Partnership including a Professional Corporation
1555 Poydras Street Suite 1700, 70112
Telephone: 504-523-5100
Fax: 504-523-5698
Covington, Louisiana Office: 2301 North HIghway 190, Suite 3, 70433.
Telephone: 504-871-7005.
Fax: 504-871-7051.

MEMBERS OF FIRM

Lloyd W. Hayes
E. Ross Buckley, Jr., (A Professional Law Corp.)
Marianne S. Pensa
William H. Voigt

ASSOCIATES

Michele D. Ahlers
Ernest Philip Legier, Jr.
Elton A. Foster

OF COUNSEL

Harold A. Thomas

For full biographical listings, see the Martindale-Hubbell Law Directory

CAPITELLI & WICKER (AV)

2950 Energy Centre, 1100 Poydras Street, 70163-2950
Telephone: 504-582-2425
Fax: 504-582-2422
Email: cw4law@bellsouth.net

(See Next Column)

CAPITELLI & WICKER—*Continued*

Ralph Capitelli
T. Carey Wicker, III
Paul Michael Elvir, Jr.

For full biographical listings, see the Martindale-Hubbell Law Directory

GAINSBURGH, BENJAMIN, DAVID, MEUNIER & WARSHAUER (AV)

2800 Energy Centre, 1100 Poydras, 70163-2800
Telephone: 504-522-2304
Telecopier: 504-528-9973
Email: DPHILLIPS@GAINSBEN.COM

OF COUNSEL

Samuel C. Gainsburgh
Jack C. Benjamin

MEMBERS OF FIRM

Robert J. David
Gerald E. Meunier
Irving J. Warshauer
Stevan C. Dittman
Madeleine M. Landrieu
Darryl M. Phillips
Jeffrey A. Mitchell

ASSOCIATE

Gary B. Roth

For full biographical listings, see the Martindale-Hubbell Law Directory

GEORGE W. HEALY, IV (AV)

330 Camp Street, 70130
Telephone: 504-524-3223
Fax: 504-524-3282
Email: gwhealyiv@aol.com *URL:* http://www.healyivlaw.com

Representative Clients: Bryan Chevrolet; Gilchrist Machinery; Associated Manufacturers Agents, Inc. (AMA).

For full biographical listings, see the Martindale-Hubbell Law Directory

DARLEEN M. JACOBS A PROFESSIONAL LAW CORPORATION (AV)

823 St. Louis Street, 70112
Telephone: 504-522-3287; 522-0155
Fax: 504-522-3819
Cable Address: "Darjac."

Darleen M. Jacobs
Honorable S. Sanford Levy (1902-1989)

For full biographical listings, see the Martindale-Hubbell Law Directory

LEWIS, KULLMAN & STERBCOW (AV)

2615 Pan-American Life Center, 601 Poydras Street, 70130
Telephone: 504-588-1500
Fax: 504-588-1514
Email: lewkull@bellsouth.net

MEMBERS OF FIRM

Harvey J. Lewis
Lawrence S. Kullman
Paul M. Sterbcow

ASSOCIATE

David A. Abramson

For full biographical listings, see the Martindale-Hubbell Law Directory

LOWE, STEIN, HOFFMAN, ALLWEISS & HAUVER, L.L.P. (AV)

One Shell Square, 701 Poydras Street Suite 3600, 70139-7735
Telephone: 504-581-2450
Telecopier: 504-581-2461

MEMBERS OF FIRM

Michael R. Allweiss
Max J. Cohen

OF COUNSEL

Mark S. Goldstein
Alicia M. Bendana

For Complete List of Firm Personnel, See General Section

For full biographical listings, see the Martindale-Hubbell Law Directory

MARTZELL & BICKFORD (AV)

A Partnership including a Professional Corporation
338 Lafayette Street, 70130-3244
Telephone: 504-581-9065
Fax: 504-581-7635
Email: mailbox@martzellbickford.com *URL:* http://www.martzellbickford.com

John R. Martzell (P.C.)
Scott R. Bickford

Regina O. Matthews
Duggan F. Ellis
M. Suzanne Montero
Richard A. Filce
Ray L. Rhymes

(See Next Column)

LEGAL SUPPORT PERSONNEL

LITIGATION ADMINISTRATOR

Christopher H. Sherwood

PARALEGALS

Jane B. Daigle
Connie L. Cosse
Mary Wiggenhorn

FIRM ADMINISTRATOR

Stephen C. Wolf (Certified Public Accountant)

For full biographical listings, see the Martindale-Hubbell Law Directory

MURRAY LAW FIRM (AV)

Suite 2550, LL&E Tower, 909 Poydras Street, 70112-4000
Telephone: 504-525-8100
Fax: 504-584-5249
1-800-467-8100
Email: MURRAYLF@IX.NETCOM.COM

Stephen B. Murray

Charles R. Ward, Jr.
Joseph A. Race
Perry Michael Nicosia
Linda S. Harang
Gano D. Lemoine III
Edward N. Rodriguez
Stephen B. Murray, Jr.
Julie A. Ardoin
Stephanie M. Lawrence
Robert J. Diliberto
Julie A. Jacobs

OF COUNSEL

William W. Goodell, Jr.

For full biographical listings, see the Martindale-Hubbell Law Directory

SUTTERFIELD & WEBB L.L.C. (AV)

650 Poydras Street, Suite 2715, 70130
Telephone: 504-598-2715
Fax: 504-529-7197
Email: info@swslaw.com

James R. Sutterfield
Daniel A. Webb

William J. Sommers, Jr.
Charmagne A. Padua
Gordon P. Serou, Jr.

OF COUNSEL

Robert A. Redwine

For full biographical listings, see the Martindale-Hubbell Law Directory

RALPH S. WHALEN, JR. (AV)

3170 Energy Centre, 1100 Poydras Street, 70163
Telephone: 504-582-2333
Fax: 504-582-2332
Covington, Louisiana Office: 325 North New Hampshire Street.
Telephone: 504-893-7506.

For full biographical listings, see the Martindale-Hubbell Law Directory

WILSON & BOWLING (AV)

A Partnership including Professional Law Corporations
Suite 2411, Bank One Center, 201 St. Charles Avenue, 70170
Telephone: 504-586-5200
Facsimile: 504-586-5201
Email: wilsbowl@gs.net
Gulfport, Mississippi Office: 715 Markham Building, 2301 14th Street, 39501.
Telephone: 228-575-6202.
Fax: 228-864-6227.

Gordon F. Wilson, Jr., (P.L.C.)
David A. Bowling (P.L.C.)

Jeanne B. Roques
Susannah Ross Cooley
John D. Acomb

For full biographical listings, see the Martindale-Hubbell Law Directory

*SHREVEPORT,** Caddo Parish

TROY E. BAIN (AV)

1540 Irving Place, 71101
Telephone: 318-221-0076
Fax: 318-227-8290

Reference: Commercial National Bank of Shreveport.

For full biographical listings, see the Martindale-Hubbell Law Directory

SAM N. GREGORIO A PROFESSIONAL LAW CORPORATION (AV)

1540 Irving Place, 71101
Telephone: 318-227-8282
Fax: 318-227-8290
Email: sgreg123@aol.com

(See Next Column)

SAM N. GREGORIO A PROFESSIONAL LAW CORPORATION, *Shreveport—Continued*

Sam N. Gregorio

For full biographical listings, see the Martindale-Hubbell Law Directory

SOCKRIDER, BOLIN, ANGLIN & BATTE, A PROFESSIONAL LAW CORPORATION (AV)

327 Crockett Street, 71101
Telephone: 318-221-5503
Fax: 318-221-3849

John R. Pleasant (1905-1983)
H. F. Sockrider, Jr.
James E. Bolin, Jr.
D. Rex Anglin
Gregory H. Batte

For full biographical listings, see the Martindale-Hubbell Law Directory

SLIDELL, St. Tammany Parish

JAMES R. STRAIN, JR. (AV)

103 Galeria Boulevard, 70458
Telephone: 504-649-3662
Fax: 504-649-2462
Mailing Address: P.O. Box 2590, Slidell, LA, 70459

Representative Clients: Louisiana Medical Mutual Insurance Co.; Louisiana Patients' Compensation Fund; Medical Fitness Centers of America, Inc.; Thirstrup Medical Enterprises, Inc.; Wellness Aerobic & Sports Medicine Clinic; Jefferson Insurance Group; State of Louisiana-Dept. of Transportation and Development; State of Louisiana-Office of Risk Management.

For full biographical listings, see the Martindale-Hubbell Law Directory

MAINE

*AUGUSTA,** Kennebec Co.

LIPMAN & KATZ, P.A. (AV)

227 Water Street, P.O. Box 1051, 04332-1051
Telephone: 207-622-3711
Telecopier: 207-622-7415
Email: lipmankatz@ibm.net

Sumner H. Lipman
David M. Lipman
Roger J. Katz
Robert J. Stolt
Keith R. Varner
Ronald E. Colby, III
Walter F. McKee

Karen E. Lipman
Tracie L. Adamson
Gregg D. Bernstein

OF COUNSEL

Joseph B. Campbell

For full biographical listings, see the Martindale-Hubbell Law Directory

PIERCE ATWOOD (AV)

77 Winthrop Street, 04330
Telephone: 207-622-6311
Fax: 207-623-9367
Email: info@PierceAtwood.com *URL:* http://www.pierceatwood.com
Portland, Maine Office: One Monument Square.
Telephone: 207-791-1100.
Fax: 207-791-1350.
Newburyport, Massachusetts Office: 6 Harris Street.
Telephone: 978-465-9599.
Fax: 978-465-9945.

MEMBERS OF FIRM

Malcolm L. Lyons
Michael D. Seitzinger
John C. Nivison

ASSOCIATE

Ann M. St. Peter-Griffith

COUNSEL

Daniel J. Stevens

For Complete List of Firm Personnel, See General Section

For full biographical listings, see the Martindale-Hubbell Law Directory

*BANGOR,** Penobscot Co.

EATON, PEABODY, BRADFORD & VEAGUE, P.A. (AV)

Fleet Center-Exchange Street, P.O. Box 1210, 04402-1210
Telephone: 207-947-0111
Telecopier: 207-942-3040
Email: eaton@eatonpeabody.com *URL:* http://www.eatonpeabody.com
Augusta, Maine Office: 77 Sewall Street, Suite 3000.
Telephone: 207-622-3747.
Telecopier: 207-622-9732.
Blue Hill, Maine Office: One East Blue Hill Road.
Telephone: 207-374-2812.
Telecopier: 207-374-2548.
Brunswick, Maine Office: 167 Park Row.
Telephone: 207-729-1144.
Telecopier: 207-729-1140.
Dover-Foxcroft, Maine Office: 30 East Main Street.
Telephone: 207-564-8378.
Telecopier: 207-564-7059.

Thomas M. Brown
Bernard J. Kubetz
Douglas M. Smith (Dover-Foxcroft and Augusta Offices)
Stephen G. Morrell (Resident, Brunswick Office)
Glen L. Porter
Gordon H. S. Scott (Resident, Augusta Office)
William B. Devoe
Judy A.S. Metcalf (Resident, Brunswick Office)
Jonathan B. Huntington (Resident, Dover-Foxcroft Office)
Thad B. Zmistowski

For Complete List of Firm Personnel, See General Section

For full biographical listings, see the Martindale-Hubbell Law Directory

BAR HARBOR, Hancock Co.

FENTON, CHAPMAN, FENTON, SMITH & KANE, P.A. (AV)

109 Main Street, P.O. Box B, 04609
Telephone: 207-288-3331
Fax: 207-288-9326
Email: fentonlawfirm@acadia.net *URL:* http://www.lawyers.com/fcfs&klaw

Douglas B. Chapman
Nathaniel R. Fenton

Margaret T. Jeffery

Reference: Bar Harbor Banking and Trust Co.

For Complete List of Firm Personnel, See General Section

For full biographical listings, see the Martindale-Hubbell Law Directory

*ELLSWORTH,** Hancock Co.

ROSS & FERM, LLC (AV)

204 Main Street, P.O. Box 1123, 04605
Telephone: 207-667-1373
Fax: 207-667-3427
URL: http://www.lawyers.com/ross&ferm

Michael L. Ross
William N. Ferm

ASSOCIATES

William B. Entwisle
Jessica L. Shiok

For full biographical listings, see the Martindale-Hubbell Law Directory

*PORTLAND,** Cumberland Co.

FRIEDMAN BABCOCK & GAYTHWAITE (AV)

Suite 400, Six City Center, P.O. Box 4726, 04112-4726
Telephone: 207-761-0900
Telecopier: 207-761-0186
Email: info@fbg-law.com *URL:* http://www.fbg-law.com

MEMBERS OF FIRM

Harold J. Friedman
Ernest J. Babcock
Martha C. Gaythwaite
Karen Frink Wolf
Jennifer S. Riggle
Laurence H. Leavitt
Elizabeth A. Germani
Michelle Allott
Tracy D. Hill

ASSOCIATES

Susan J. Guerette
L. John Topchik
Sally A. Morris
Catherine C. Miller
Kieran N. Shields
Evan Smith

For full biographical listings, see the Martindale-Hubbell Law Directory

Portland—Continued

PIERCE ATWOOD (AV)

One Monument Square, 04101
Telephone: 207-791-1100
Fax: 207-791-1350
Email: info@PierceAtwood.com *URL:* http://www.pierceatwood.com
Augusta, Maine Office: 77 Winthrop Street.
Telephone: 207-622-6311.
Fax: 207-623-9367.
Newburyport, Massachusetts Office: 6 Harris Street.
Telephone: 978-465-9599.
Fax: 978-465-9945.

MEMBERS OF FIRM

Ralph I. Lancaster, Jr.
Malcolm L. Lyons (Resident, Augusta Office)
Peter W. Culley
Michael D. Seitzinger (Resident, Augusta Office)
Daniel M. Snow
John C. Nivison (Resident, Augusta Office)
John J. Aromando
David E. Barry

COUNSEL

Daniel J. Stevens (Resident, Augusta Office)

For Complete List of Firm Personnel, See General Section

For full biographical listings, see the Martindale-Hubbell Law Directory

RICHARDSON, WHITMAN, LARGE & BADGER, A PROFESSIONAL CORPORATION (AV)

465 Congress Street, 04101-3528
Telephone: 207-774-7474
Telecopier: 207-774-1343
URL: http://www.rwlb.com
Bangor, Maine Office: One Merchants Plaza, P.O. Box 2429.
Telephone: 207-945-5900.
Telecopier: 207-945-0758.

Harrison L. Richardson
John S. Whitman
Wendell G. Large
Frederick J. Badger, Jr. (Resident, Bangor Office)
Elizabeth G. Stouder
Barri Bloom
Ann M. Murray (Resident, Bangor Office)
Frederick F. Costlow (Resident, Bangor Office)
John B. Lucy (Resident, Bangor Office)

Anne H. Cressey
Thomas R. McKeon
Carol I. Eisenberg
Paul R. Johnson

For full biographical listings, see the Martindale-Hubbell Law Directory

THOMPSON & BOWIE (AV)

Three Canal Plaza, P.O. Box 4630, 04112
Telephone: 207-774-2500
Telecopier: 207-774-3591
Email: law@thompsonbowie.com

MEMBERS OF FIRM

Roy E. Thompson, Jr.
James M. Bowie
Daniel R. Mawhinney
Rebecca H. Farnum
Glenn H. Robinson
Frank W. DeLong, III
Michael E. Saucier
Mark V. Franco
Edward R. Benjamin, Jr.
Cathy S. Roberts
Paul C. Catsos

ASSOCIATES

Elizabeth Knox Peck
Thomas G. Diebold
Michael R. Bosse
Lisa M. Fitzgibbon

For full biographical listings, see the Martindale-Hubbell Law Directory

TROUBH, HEISLER & PIAMPIANO, P.C. (AV)

511 Congress Street, P.O. Box 9711, 04104-5011
Telephone: 207-780-6789
Fax: 207-774-2339
Email: info@thplaw.com

William B. Troubh
Edwin A. Heisler
Robert J. Piampiano
Kevin M. Gillis
Michael P. Boyd
Thomas E. Getchell
Michael Richards
William K. McKinley
Daniel F. Gilligan
Paul S. Bulger
John G. Richardson

Daniel R. Felkel
Ann Brandt
John P. Flynn, III

For full biographical listings, see the Martindale-Hubbell Law Directory

SACO, York Co.

SMITH ELLIOTT SMITH & GARMEY, P.A. (AV)

199 Main Street, P.O. Box 1179, 04072
Telephone: 207-774-3199
Telefax: 207-774-2235
Email: info@sesgattorneys.com *URL:* http://www.sesgattorneys.com

Randall E. Smith
Charles W. Smith, Jr.
Terrence D. Garmey
Peter W. Schroeter
Robert H. Furbish
John H. O'Neil, Jr.

Reference: Saco & Biddeford Savings Institution.

For Complete List of Firm Personnel, See General Section

For full biographical listings, see the Martindale-Hubbell Law Directory

MARYLAND

*ANNAPOLIS,** Anne Arundel Co.

ALEXANDER & CLEAVER, P.A. (AV)

54 State Circle, 21401
Telephone: 410-974-9000; Toll free: 1-800-292-LAWS
Cable: "ALEXLAW"
Fax: 410-974-9002
Waldorf, MD, Fort Washington, MD & Alexandria, VA
Email: ac@alexander-cleaver.com
Ft. Washington, Maryland Office: 11414 Livingston Road.
Telephone: 301-292-3300.
Alexandria, Virginia Office: 1513 King Street.
Telephone: 703-548-7777.
Waldorf, Maryland Office: Hamilton Centre, 3200 Highway 301.
Telephone: 301-870-8080.

Gary R. Alexander
James A. Cleaver

Gerald F. Keipert
Todd K. Pounds
Denise M. Bowman
Thomas W. Kinnane
Joseph P. Hart
Jason A. Deloach
Chantel Renee Ornstein

For full biographical listings, see the Martindale-Hubbell Law Directory

COUNCIL, BARADEL, KOSMERL & NOLAN, P.A. (AV)

125 West Street, Fourth Floor, P.O. Box 2289, 21404-2289
Telephone: 410-268-6600
Baltimore: 410-269-6190
Washington, D.C.: 301-261-2247
FAX: 410-269-8409
Email: cbkn@cbknlaw.com

Ronald E. Council
Ronald A. Baradel
Wayne T. Kosmerl
James P. Nolan
William F. Flood, III
Kevin M. Schaeffer
Donna McCabe Schaeffer
Frederick C. Sussman

John Naumann Strange
Susan T. Ford
Edwin H. Staples, II
Susan Stobbart Shapiro

OF COUNSEL

George N. Manis
Nicholas Goldsborough

Representative Clients: Anne Arundel County; Annapolis Bank and Trust; Bank of Maryland; State Farm Mutual Automobile Insurance Co.; Annapolis Yacht Club; Annapolis Yacht Sales, Inc.

For full biographical listings, see the Martindale-Hubbell Law Directory

*BALTIMORE,** (Independent City)

THE LAW OFFICES OF KATHLEEN CAHILL, LLC (AV)

15 East Chesapeake Avenue, 21286
Telephone: 410-321-6171
Fax: 410-821-7740
Email: kcahillesq@aol.com

Kathleen Cahill

For full biographical listings, see the Martindale-Hubbell Law Directory

COOPER & TUERK, LLP (AV)

201 North Charles Street, Suite 2300, 21201
Telephone: 410-539-0300
Fax: 410-837-3923
Email: CANDT201@AOL.COM

MEMBERS OF FIRM

Gerald H. Cooper
Carl E. Tuerk, Jr.
Larry E. Jordan

(See Next Column)

COOPER & TUERK LLP, *Baltimore—Continued*

ASSOCIATE

Marc A. Ominsky

For full biographical listings, see the Martindale-Hubbell Law Directory

ELLIN AND BAKER (AV)

Second Floor, 1101 St. Paul Street, 21202
Telephone: 410-727-1787
Fax: 410-547-1787
1-800-237-1787
Email: Ellinlaw@aol.com

MEMBER OF FIRM

Marvin Ellin

For full biographical listings, see the Martindale-Hubbell Law Directory

INGERMAN & HORWITZ, L.L.P. (AV)

20 Park Avenue, 21201
Telephone: 410-539-1200; 1-800-776-4-LAW
Fax: 410-539-1643
Columbia, Maryland Office: 5401 Twin Knolls Road, Suite 10.
Telephone: 410-995-0800.
Frederick, Maryland Office: Patrick Center, 30 West Patrick Street, Suite 505.
Telephone: 301-694-3738.
Fax: 301-620-9517.
Hagerstown, Maryland Office: Bryan Center, 82 West Washington Street, Third Floor.
Telephone: 301-791-6328.
Cumberland, Maryland Office: Smith Building, 111 South George Street, Second Floor.
Telephone: 301-722-0860.
Salisbury, Maryland Office: 111 Baptist Street, Suite 109.
Telephone: 410-548-9919.

Bruce E. Ingerman
Alan G. Horwitz
Kenneth P. Niman

Brett Michael Schaffer
Anne E. Hoke
Robert Taylor, Jr.
Alisa Gross Cummins
Jonathan A. Kopin
M. Lisa Fleming
Lloyd A. Sarro

For full biographical listings, see the Martindale-Hubbell Law Directory

ISRAELSON, SALSBURY, CLEMENTS & BEKMAN, L.L.C. (AV)

300 West Pratt Street Suite 450, 21201
Telephone: 410-539-6633
FAX: 410-625-9554

MEMBERS OF FIRM

Stuart Marshall Salsbury
Paul D. Bekman
Daniel M. Clements
Matthew Zimmerman
Laurence A. Marder

Lauren R. Calia
Leslie Hayes Russo

COUNSEL TO THE FIRM

Max R. Israelson
Michael P. Smith

OF COUNSEL

Samuel Omar Jackson, Jr. (Semi-Retired)
Wendy Lozinsky Shiff

For full biographical listings, see the Martindale-Hubbell Law Directory

JANET, WILLOUGHBY & GERSHON, LLC (AV)

Executive Centre at Hooks Lane, 8 Reservoir Circle, Suite 200, 21208-1309
Telephone: 410-653-3200
Toll Free: 888-4-MED-LAW
Fax: 410-653-9030
Email: JWG@medlawlegalteam.com

Howard Alan Janet (P.C.)
Wayne M. Willoughby (P.A.)
Zev T. Gershon
Randal D. Getz

Robin R. Smith
Denise A. Greig

LEGAL SUPPORT PERSONNEL

Joan Hunter Green (Registered Nurse/Paralegal)
Sharon Marie Schmidt (Paralegal)

For full biographical listings, see the Martindale-Hubbell Law Directory

KAHN, SMITH & COLLINS, P.A. (AV)

201 North Charles Street, 10th Floor, 21201
Telephone: 410-244-1010
Fax: 410-244-8001
URL: http://www.interbit.com/ksc

(See Next Column)

Andrew H. Kahn
Joel A. Smith
Francis J. Collins
David V. Diggs
Keith J. Zimmerman

Leslie A. Pladna
Sarah Pazourek Harlan
Travis M. Mastroddi
Sabrina Willis

For full biographical listings, see the Martindale-Hubbell Law Directory

REDMOND, BURGIN & GUTIERREZ, P.A. (AV)

1301, The Fidelity Building, 210 North Charles Street, 21202
Telephone: 410-752-1555
Fax: 410-752-1064
URL: http://www.RBGLAW.com
Upper Marlboro, Maryland Office: 14746 Main Street.
Telephone: 301-952-1555.

Leonard C. Redmond, III
Harold L. Burgin

Joseph I. Tivvis, Jr.
Bambi Glenn

For Complete List of Firm Personnel, See General Section

For full biographical listings, see the Martindale-Hubbell Law Directory

GILBERT H. ROBINETTE (AV)

212 Washington Avenue, 21204
Telephone: 410-321-6666
Toll Free: 1-888-538-0821
Fax: 410-821-5444
Email: ghr44@aol.com *URL:* http://www.lawyers.com/gilrobinette
Charleston, West Virginia Office: 1564 Virginia Street, East, 25311.
Telephone: 304-342-1844.
Fax: 304-342-1901.

For full biographical listings, see the Martindale-Hubbell Law Directory

ROLLINS, SMALKIN, RICHARDS & MACKIE, L.L.C. (AV)

401 North Charles Street, 21201
Telephone: 410-727-2443
Fax: 410-727-8390
URL: http://www.rsrm.com

MEMBERS OF FIRM

H. Beale Rollins (1898-1985)
Samuel S. Smalkin (1906-1982)
Edward C. Mackie
John F. Linsenmeyer
Thomas C. Gentner
Glenn W. Trimmer
Patrick G. Cullen
James P. O'Meara
Paul G. Donoghue
Ralph E. Wilson III

ASSOCIATES

Kenneth G. Macleay
Donna Lynn Kolakowski-Hollen
Meg Bantley Whiteford
J. James Roos
Jessica R. Di Cicco

OF COUNSEL

Raymond A. Richards (Retired)

LEGAL SUPPORT PERSONNEL

Guy M. Craig

For full biographical listings, see the Martindale-Hubbell Law Directory

SCANLAN, ROSEN & SHAR, LLC (AV)

26 South Street, 21202-3399
Telephone: 410-244-1155
Fax: 410-244-1157
Email: lawyers@triallaw.com *URL:* http://www.triallaw.com

Alfred L. Scanlan, Jr.
Marc Seldin Rosen
Marcus Z. Shar
Michael Stuart Warshaw

Timothy Cronin Lynch
Neil E Duke
Kristofer P. Cubello

OF COUNSEL

Colleen A. Cavanaugh
Lee H. Caplan
J. Michael McWilliams

For full biographical listings, see the Martindale-Hubbell Law Directory

SCHOCHOR, FEDERICO AND STATON, P.A. (AV)

The Paulton, 1211 St. Paul Street, 21202
Telephone: 410-234-1000
Toll Free: 888-234-0001
Facsimile: 410-234-1010
URL: http://www.sfspa.com
Washington D.C. Office: 10 G Street, N.E., Suite 650.
Telephone: 202-408-3300.

Jonathan Schochor
Philip C. Federico
Kerry D. Staton

(See Next Column)

SCHOCHOR, FEDERICO AND STATON P.A.—*Continued*

Christopher P. Kennedy
Robert J. Farley
Bonnie Ardinger Winders

For full biographical listings, see the Martindale-Hubbell Law Directory

SPENCE, KOHLER, CHRISTIE & PULVER, P.A. (AV)

401 Washington Avenue, Suite 701, 21204
Telephone: 410-823-8200
Fax: 410-823-8208
Email: skcp@ix.netcom.com

Paul W. Spence
Alison Daryl Kohler
Sharon A. Christie
Michael A. Pulver

For full biographical listings, see the Martindale-Hubbell Law Directory

VENABLE ATTORNEYS AT LAW VENABLE, BAETJER AND HOWARD, LLP (AV)

A Partnership including Professional Corporations
1800 Mercantile Bank & Trust Building, 2 Hopkins Plaza, 21201
Telephone: 410-244-7400
Fax: 410-244-7742
URL: http://www.venable.com
Washington, D.C. Office: Venable, Baetjer, Howard & Civiletti LLP, Suite 1000, 1201 New York Avenue, N.W.
Telephone: 202-962-4800.
Fax: 202-962-8300.
McLean, Virginia Office: Suite 400, 2010 Corporate Ridge.
Telephone: 703-760-1600.
Fax: 703-821-8949.
Rockville, Maryland Office: Suite 500, One Church Street, P. O. Box 1906.
Telephone: 301-217-5600.
Fax: 301-217-5617.
Towson, Maryland Office: 210 Allegheny Avenue, P. O. Box 5517.
Telephone: 410-494-6200.
Fax: 410-821-0147.

MEMBERS OF FIRM

Roger W. Titus (Resident, Rockville, Maryland Office)
John H. Zink, III (Resident, Towson, Maryland Office)
William D. Dolan, III (P.C.) (Not admitted in MD; Resident, McLean, Virginia Office)
Paul T. Glasgow (Resident, Rockville, Maryland Office)
Joseph C. Wich, Jr. (Resident, Towson, Maryland Office)
James K. Archibald (Also at Washington, D.C. Office)
Jeffrey A. Dunn (Also at Washington, D.C. Office)
George F. Pappas (Also at Washington, D.C. Office)
James L. Shea (Also at Washington, D.C. Office)
Amy Berman Jackson (Not admitted in MD; Resident, Washington, D.C. Office)
C. Carey Deeley, Jr. (Also at Towson, Maryland Office)
Christopher R. Mellott
M. King Hill, III (Resident, Towson, Maryland Office)
James A. Dunbar (Resident, Towson, Maryland Office)
David J. Heubeck
Herbert G. Smith, II (Not admitted in MD; Resident, Washington, D.C. Office)
Terri L. Turner
Michael W. Robinson (Resident, McLean, Virginia Office)
David W. Goewey (Not admitted in MD; Resident, Washington, D.C. Office)
John A. McCauley
John T. Prisbe
Vicki Margolis (Also at Washington, D.C. Office)
Christine M. McAnney (Not admitted in MD; Resident, McLean, Virginia Office)
Marina Lolley Sabett

ASSOCIATES

Paul D. Barker, Jr.
Daniel William China (Resident, Towson, Maryland Office)
E. Anne Hamel

For Complete List of Firm Personnel, See General Section

For full biographical listings, see the Martindale-Hubbell Law Directory

ROBIN PAGE WEST (AV)

20 South Charles Street, Suite 703, 21201-3291
Telephone: 410-244-0400
Fax: 410-244-0402
Email: rwestn01@erols.com *URL:* http://www.lawyers.com/qui_tam

For full biographical listings, see the Martindale-Hubbell Law Directory

*BEL AIR,** Harford Co.

BROWN, BROWN & BROWN, A PROFESSIONAL ASSOCIATION (AV)

200 South Main Street, 21014
Telephone: 410-838-5500
Baltimore: 410-879-2220
Fax: 410-893-0402

(See Next Column)

A. Freeborn Brown (1915-1998)
T. Carroll Brown
Augustus F. Brown
Albert J. A. Young

Harold Douglas Norton
Christopher R. vanRoden
David E. Carey

Attorneys for: Baltimore Gas & Electric Co.; Chesapeake & Potomac Telephone Co.; Aberdeen Proving Ground Federal Credit Union; First National Bank of Maryland; Bell Atlantic Mobile Systems; First Harbor Securities; Maryland Portable Concrete, Inc.
Approved Counsel for: The Chicago Title Insurance Co. of Maryland, Inc.

For full biographical listings, see the Martindale-Hubbell Law Directory

STARK & KEENAN, A PROFESSIONAL ASSOCIATION (AV)

30 Office Street, 21014
Telephone: 410-838-5522
Baltimore: 410-879-2222
Fax: 410-879-0688
Email: wstarkee@aol.com
Havre de Grace Office: "The Old Ordinary" 100 St. John Street, 21078.
Telephone: 410-939-0100.

Elwood V. Stark, Jr.
Charles B. Keenan, Jr.
Edwin G. Carson
Judith Cline-Silverstein
Gregory A. Szoka
Robert S. Lynch
Paul W. Ishak

Claire Prin Blomquist
Lawrence F. Kreis, Jr.
Craig H. DeRan

For full biographical listings, see the Martindale-Hubbell Law Directory

BETHESDA, Montgomery Co.

KARP, FROSH, LAPIDUS, WIGODSKY & NORWIND, P.A. (AV)

7475 Wisconsin Avenue, Suite 800, 20814
Telephone: 301-656-2111
Fax: 301-654-7748
Email: jackgold@erols.com
Washington, D.C. Office: 1150 Connecticut Avenue, N.W., Suite 900. 20036.
Telephone: 202-822-3777.
Fax: 202-828-4130.

Ronald A. Karp
Brian E. Frosh
Lawrence S. Lapidus
Jeffrey A. Wigodsky
Edward L. Norwind
J. Philip Kessel

Jack A. Gold
Donald C. Weinberg

OF COUNSEL

Douglas R. Smith
Stanley A. First (Not admitted in MD)
Roy I. Niedermayer
Maurice I. Burstein

For full biographical listings, see the Martindale-Hubbell Law Directory

CHEVY CHASE, Montgomery Co.

PYNE & DERRY, P.C. (AV)

Chevy Chase Metro Building Suite 640, Two Wisconsin Circle, 20815
Telephone: 301-961-0240
Fax: 301-907-3920
Email: pyne-derry@juno.com

John J. Pyne
Peter E. Derry

For full biographical listings, see the Martindale-Hubbell Law Directory

COLUMBIA, Howard Co.

GUIDA & EAGAN, P.A. (AV)

Suite 600, Merrill Lynch Building, 10320 Little Patuxent Parkway, 21044
Telephone: 410-992-4545
FAX: 410-992-1605
Email: info@lakeviewtitle.com

Vincent M. Guida
James K. Eagan, III

Elizabeth J. Case

Reference: Taneytown Bank & Trust Co.

For full biographical listings, see the Martindale-Hubbell Law Directory

GREENBELT, Prince Georges Co.

HOROWITZ, FORAN & SONNTAG, P.A. (AV)

Capital Office Park, 6301 Ivy Lane, Suite 600, 20770
Telephone: 301-441-2022
Fax: 301-474-6054
Email: hofoso@aol.com

(See Next Column)

HOROWITZ, FORAN & SONNTAG P.A., *Greenbelt—Continued*

Edward S. Horowitz
John R. Foran

Timothy J. Driscoll
Jeffrey H Horowitz
James D. Cardea

For full biographical listings, see the Martindale-Hubbell Law Directory

LANHAM, Prince Georges Co.

McCARTHY & COSTELLO, L.L.P. (AV)

Washington Business Park, Suite 300, 4640 Forbes Boulevard, 20706-4323
Telephone: 301-306-1900
Fax: 301-306-1988
Email: mbc@erols.com *URL:* http://home.erols.com/mbc

MEMBERS OF FIRM

Kevin J. McCarthy
Charles E. Channing, Jr.
John F. X. Costello
Timothy Altemus
Michael J. Winkelman

For full biographical listings, see the Martindale-Hubbell Law Directory

*LA PLATA,** Charles Co.

MUDD, MUDD & FITZGERALD, P.A. (AV)

106 St. Mary's Avenue, P.O. Box 310, 20646
Telephone: 301-934-9541
FAX: 301-934-8178

John F. Mudd (1885-1950)
Thomas F. Mudd
F. DeSales Mudd (1909-1972)
John F. Mudd
Stephen P. Fitzgerald

John E. Ray

Local Counsel for: County First Bank (La Plata); Potomac Electric Power Co.; The Hartford Insurance Group; Maryland Bank & Trust Co.; Chicago Title Insurance Co.; Peninsula Title Insurance Co.; Colonial Farm Credit Agric. Credit Assn.
Counsel for: Interstate General Corporation; SMO, Inc.

For full biographical listings, see the Martindale-Hubbell Law Directory

LARGO, Prince Georges Co.

GREGORY K. WELLS & ASSOCIATES, P.A. (AV)

1801 McCormick Drive Suite 160, 20774
Telephone: 301-925-2000
Fax: 301-925-2006
Email: gkw.associates@erols.com *URL:* http://www.lawyers.com/gregorykwells

Gregory K. Wells

Edward J. Maginnis

OF COUNSEL

Robert C. Maynard

LEGAL SUPPORT PERSONNEL

Juernine M. Wright

For full biographical listings, see the Martindale-Hubbell Law Directory

*ROCKVILLE,** Montgomery Co.

ANDERSON & QUINN (AV)

The Adams Law Center, 25 Wood Lane, 20850
Telephone: 301-762-3303
Fax: 301-762-3776
Email: rscanlon@andersonquinn.com

MEMBERS OF FIRM

Charles C. Collins (1900-1973)
Donald P. Maiberger
Robert E. Anderson (Retired)
Robert P. Scanlon
Francis X. Quinn
John A. Rego
Alice Kelley Scanlon

ASSOCIATES

Kerry S. McGeever
Todd P. Maiberger
Timothy J. Mulreany
Jennifer D. Burke
Marc N. Steren

Representative Clients: C & P Telephone; Allstate Insurance Co.; State Farm Mutual Automobile Insurance Co.; Liberty Mutual Insurance Co.; American International Adjustment Co.; Marriott Corp.

For full biographical listings, see the Martindale-Hubbell Law Directory

ARMSTRONG, DONOHUE, CEPPOS & VAUGHAN, CHARTERED (AV)

Suite 101, 204 Monroe Street, 20850
Telephone: 301-251-0440
Telecopier: 301-279-5929

(See Next Column)

Larry A. Ceppos
H. Kenneth Armstrong
H. Patrick Donohue
Benjamin S. Vaughan
John C. Monahan
Pamela Barrow Kincheloe

Sharon A. Marcial
Andrew J. Marter
Richard S. Schrager
Susan E. Mikorski

For full biographical listings, see the Martindale-Hubbell Law Directory

BRAULT, GRAHAM, SCOTT & BRAULT, LLC (AV)

101 South Washington Street, 20850
Telephone: 301-424-1060
Fax: 301-424-7991
Email: bgsb@earthlink.net
Washington, D.C. Office: Brault, Graham, Scott & Brault, PLLC, 1140 Connecticut Avenue, N.W., Suite 250.
Telephone: 202-785-1200.
FAX: 202-785-4301.
Fairfax, Virginia Office: Suite 500, 11350 Random Hills Road, Fair Oaks Plaza, 22030-7429.
Telephone: 202-785-1200.

OF COUNSEL

Laurence T. Scott
James Robert Miller

MEMBERS OF FIRM

Denver H. Graham (1922-1987)
Ronald G. Guziak
Albert E. Brault (Retired)
Daniel L. Shea (Resident)
Albert D. Brault (Resident)
M. Kathleen Parker (Resident)
Leo A. Roth, Jr.
David G. Mulquin (Resident)
James S. Wilson (Resident)
James M. Brault (Resident)
Regina Ann Casey (Resident)

ASSOCIATES

Rhonda Ann Hurwitz (Resident)
Joan F. Brault (Resident)

Representative Clients: American Oil Co.; Crum & Forster Group; Fireman's Fund American Insurance Cos.; Kemper Group; Reliance Insurance Cos.; Safeco Group; Government Employees Insurance Co.; Medical Mutual Insurance Society of Maryland; Legal Mutual Liability Insurance Society of Maryland.

For full biographical listings, see the Martindale-Hubbell Law Directory

MICHAEL S. MORGENSTERN & ASSOCIATES, P.C. (AV)

51 Monroe Street, Suite 1604, 20850
Telephone: 301-217-9500
Fax: 301-217-9579
Toll Free: 1-888-888-0005
Mailing Address: P.O. Box 4690, Rockville, MD, 20850
Email: MSMlaw@erols.com
Washington, D.C. Office: 601 Pennsylvania Avenue, N.W. 20004.
Telephone: 202-393-2500.
Frederick, Maryland Office: 228 West Patrick Street. 21701.
Telephone: 301-620-7900.

Michael S. Morgenstern
Barbara L. Morgenstern (Not admitted in MD)
Carl Morgenstern (Not admitted in MD)

OF COUNSEL

W. David Allen

For full biographical listings, see the Martindale-Hubbell Law Directory

STEIN, SPERLING, BENNETT, DE JONG, DRISCOLL, GREENFEIG & METRO, P.C. (AV)

25 West Middle Lane, 20850-2204
Telephone: 301-340-2020; 800-435-5230
Telecopier: 301-340-8217
Email: lawfirm@steinsperling.com
Falls Church, Virginia Office: 6245 Leesburg Pike, Suite 140, 22044.
Telephone: 703-237-0500.
Telecopier: 703-534-2899.

Fred A. Balkin
Stuart S. Greenfeig
David C. Driscoll, Jr.
Donald N. Sperling
Paul T. Stein

Jeffrey D. Goldstein
Jolie S. Deutschman
Darcy A. Shoop

For Complete List of Firm Personnel, See General Section

For full biographical listings, see the Martindale-Hubbell Law Directory

*SALISBURY,** Wicomico Co.

ANTHENELLI & OTWAY (AV)

108 The Plaza, P.O. Box 4096, 21801
Telephone: 410-749-3900
Fax: 410-749-8577

MEMBERS OF FIRM

James V. Anthenelli
James L. Otway

(See Next Column)

ANTHENELLI & OTWAY—*Continued*

ASSOCIATE

John K. Phoebus

For full biographical listings, see the Martindale-Hubbell Law Directory

*TOWSON,** Baltimore Co.

NOLAN, PLUMHOFF & WILLIAMS, CHARTERED (AV)

Suite 700, Nottingham Centre, 502 Washington Avenue, 21204-4528
Telephone: 410-823-7800
Fax: 410-296-2765
Email: npw@nolanplumhoff.com

Stephen J. Nolan
Robert L. Hanley, Jr.
Robert E. Cahill, Jr.

Representative Clients: Injured Plaintiffs and Workers; Bituminous Insurance Companies; Carolina Freight Carriers Corporation; Keystone Insurance Company; Maryland Automobile Insurance Fund; Principal Casualty Insurance Company.

For Complete List of Firm Personnel, See General Section

For full biographical listings, see the Martindale-Hubbell Law Directory

VENABLE ATTORNEYS AT LAW VENABLE, BAETJER AND HOWARD, LLP (AV)

A Partnership including Professional Corporations
210 Allegheny Avenue, P.O. Box 5517, 21204
Telephone: 410-494-6200
Fax: 410-821-0147
URL: http://www.venable.com
Baltimore, Maryland Office: 1800 Mercantile Bank & Trust Building, 2 Hopkins Plaza.
Telephone: 410-244-7400.
Fax: 410-244-7742.
Washington, D.C. Office: Venable, Baetjer, Howard & Civiletti LLP, Suite 1000, 1201 New York Avenue, N.W.
Telephone: 202-962-4800.
Fax: 202-962-8300.
McLean, Virginia Office: Suite 400, 2010 Corporate Ridge.
Telephone: 703-760-1600.
Fax: 703-821-8949.
Rockville, Maryland Office: Suite 500, One Church Street, P. O. Box 1906.
Telephone: 301-217-5600.
Fax: 301-217-5617.

PARTNERS

John H. Zink, III
Joseph C. Wich, Jr.
C. Carey Deeley, Jr. (Also at Baltimore, Maryland Office)
M. King Hill, III

For Complete List of Firm Personnel, See General Section

For full biographical listings, see the Martindale-Hubbell Law Directory

WHITNEY & BOGRIS, LLP (AV)

401 Washington Avenue, Twelfth Floor, 21204
Telephone: 410-583-8000
Fax: 410-583-8031
Email: HGWC@worldnet.att.net

MEMBERS OF FIRM

Daniel W. Whitney
George D. Bogris

ASSOCIATES

Kathleen D. Leslie
Henry Russell
Sandra A. Tofte
Michael A. Giacomazza
Arlene L. Sew
Gerald S. Gaetano (Not admitted in MD)
Scott A. McCabe (Not admitted in MD)
Jeffrey C. Shipley

OF COUNSEL

Joseph E. Dever
David L. Feldstein
Ronald V. Miller, Jr.

For full biographical listings, see the Martindale-Hubbell Law Directory

*UPPER MARLBORO,** Prince Georges Co.

FISHMAN & JAKLITSCH (AV)

14350 Old Marlboro Pike, 20772
Telephone: 301-627-3333; Waldorf: 301-645-6333; Prince Frederick: 410-535-3100
Fax: 301-627-6927
Annapolis
Email: fj.llc@erols.com
Annapolis, Maryland Office: 3426 Hidden River View Road, 21403.
Telephone: 410-269-1404; 268-6333.

Jerry Fishman
Richard L. Jaklitsch

ASSOCIATE

Mark J. Palumbo
Michael A. Epstein

For full biographical listings, see the Martindale-Hubbell Law Directory

MASSACHUSETTS

AMESBURY, Essex Co.

THE HAMEL LAW FIRM (AV)

Five Market Square, P.O. Box 198, 01913-0398
Telephone: 978-388-3558
Telecopier: 978-388-0441
Email: hamellaw@excelr8.net
Email: hamellaw@lawyers.com *URL:* http://www.lawyers.com/hamellaw

MEMBER OF FIRM

Richard P. Hamel

ASSOCIATE

Roger D. Turgeon

Representative Clients: First and Ocean National Bank, Newburyport, MA.
Approved Attorneys for: Chicago Title Insurance; Old Republic Title Insurance Co.

For Complete List of Firm Personnel, See General Section

For full biographical listings, see the Martindale-Hubbell Law Directory

*BOSTON,** Suffolk Co.

BARRON & STADFELD, P.C. (AV)

50 Staniford Street, Suite 200, 02114
Telephone: 617-723-9800
Telecopier: 617-523-8359
Email: barron@barronstad.com *URL:* HTTP://WWW.BARRONSTAD.COM
Hyannis, Massachusetts Office: 258 Winter Street.
Telephone: 617-778-6622.

Bernard A. Dwork
Enid M. Starr
Edward E. Kelly
David P. Dwork
Robert J. Hoffer
Rosemary Purtell

For Complete List of Firm Personnel, See General Section

For full biographical listings, see the Martindale-Hubbell Law Directory

LAW OFFICES BERGSTRESSER AND ASSOCIATES, P.C. (AV)

52 Temple Place, 02111-1315
Telephone: 617-542-4365
Facsimile: 617-542-5460
Email: mmmberg@socialaw.com *URL:* http://www.bergstresser.com

Clyde D. Bergstresser
Mary M. McGoldrick
Karenina M. Darmer

For full biographical listings, see the Martindale-Hubbell Law Directory

DENNIS J. CURRAN (AV)

Historic City Hall, 45 School Street, 2nd Floor, 02108-3204
Telephone: 617-742-3010
Fax: 617-742-1799
URL: http://www.lawyers.com/personalinj

For full biographical listings, see the Martindale-Hubbell Law Directory

ELLIS & RAPACKI (AV)

85 Merrimac Street Suite 300, 02114
Telephone: 617-523-4800
Facsimile: 617-523-6901
Email: rellis4174@aol.com

Fredric L. Ellis
Edward D. Rapacki
Edward A. Broderick

For full biographical listings, see the Martindale-Hubbell Law Directory

ESDAILE, BARRETT & ESDAILE (AV)

75 Federal Street, 02110
Telephone: 617-482-0333
Fax: 617-426-2978
Email: Esdaile@AOL.COM

MEMBERS OF FIRM

J. Newton Esdaile
Charles W. Barrett, Jr.
James N. Esdaile, Jr.
Norman I. Jacobs
Michael E. Mone
Patricia L. Kelly
Robert J. Rutecki

ASSOCIATES

Shaun Spencer Forsyth
Rhonda Traver Maloney
Steven J. Ryan
C. William Barrett
Mary Moynihan Conneely
Jon M. Jacobs
Kathryn E. Hand

(See Next Column)

ESDAILE, BARRETT & ESDAILE, *Boston—Continued*

OF COUNSEL

Charles J. Murray

For full biographical listings, see the Martindale-Hubbell Law Directory

GRIFFIN & GOULKA (AV)

Two Oliver Street, 02109
Telephone: 617-423-6677
Telecopier: 617-423-5755
Email: griffgoulk@aol.com

MEMBERS OF FIRM

J. Kenneth Griffin
Joanne L. Goulka
Christopher S. Williams
Robert P. La Hait

ASSOCIATES

Jon-Paul Lapointe
John B. Tewksbury
Mark E. Warren

For full biographical listings, see the Martindale-Hubbell Law Directory

LAW OFFICES OF MARTIN KANTROVITZ (AV)

185 Devonshire Street, Suite 510, 02110
Telephone: 617-426-3050
Fax: 617-426-3640
Hudson, Massachusetts Office: 173 Washington Street, 01749.
Telephone: 978-562-3800.
New Bedford, Massachusetts Office: 32 William Street, 02740.
Telephone: 508-994-6010.

ASSOCIATE

Lisa Baer

For full biographical listings, see the Martindale-Hubbell Law Directory

LANG & MORGERA, L.L.P. (AV Ⓣ)

6 Beacon Street, Suite 615, 02108
Telephone: 617-720-0176
Telecopier: 617-720-1184
URL: http://www.lawyers.com/lawdoctors
URL: http://www.lawdoctors.net
Providence, Rhode Island Office: 50 Park Row West, Suite 100.
Telephone: 401-456-0300.
Fax: 401-453-5545.

Barry D. Lang
Vincent D. Morgera

For full biographical listings, see the Martindale-Hubbell Law Directory

McCORMACK & EPSTEIN (AV)

One International Place, 02110
Telephone: 617-951-2929
Telecopier: 617-951-2672
New York, N.Y. Office: The Empire State Building, 350 Fifth Avenue, 60th Floor, 10118-6098.
Telephone: 212-935-0881.

MEMBERS OF FIRM

Robert D. Epstein
Michael J. McCormack
Mark E. Cohen
Joseph H. Aronson

Brian C. Duffey
George X. Pucci
Marc L. LaCasse
Amy M. Soisson
Stephen D. Rosenberg
Lisa M. Solomon (Not admitted in MA)
Nicole M. Arangio
Ara J. Balikian
Anil Adyanthaya
John A. Krebs

Representative Clients: First State Insurance Co.; Crum & Forster Commercial Insurance; Liberty Mutual Insurance Co.; Massachusetts Bay Transportation Authority; Technical Aid Corporation.

For full biographical listings, see the Martindale-Hubbell Law Directory

MEEHAN, BOYLE & COHEN, P.C. (AV)

2 Center Plaza Suite 600, 02108
Telephone: 617-523-8300
Fax: 617-523-0525

James F. Meehan
Leo V. Boyle
Cynthia J. Cohen
Warren F. Fitzgerald
Peter J. Black
John J. Carroll, Jr.
Michael B. Bogdanow
Karen R. Ristuben

Sherry Yee Mulloy
Samuel M. Furgang
Bradley Mead Henry
Jonathan E. Tobin

For full biographical listings, see the Martindale-Hubbell Law Directory

NATHANSON & GOLDBERG, A PROFESSIONAL CORPORATION (AV)

Two Oliver Street, 8th Floor, 02109-4901
Telephone: 617-210-4800
Fax: 617-210-4824
Email: natgolaw@earthlink.net *URL:* http://www.natgolaw.com

Alvin S. Nathanson
Arthur Goldberg
Shannon M. Fitzpatrick
José Centeio
Stuart J. Frank

For full biographical listings, see the Martindale-Hubbell Law Directory

SARROUF, TARRICONE & FLEMMING (AV)

95 Commercial Wharf, 02110
Telephone: 617-227-5800
Fax: 617-227-5470
Email: Lawyers@STFLAW.COM

Camille Francis Sarrouf
Anthony Tarricone
John B. Flemming
George J. Leary, Jr.
Daniel J. Gibson
Sheryl M. Bourbeau
Camille F. Sarrouf, Jr.

For full biographical listings, see the Martindale-Hubbell Law Directory

SHAPIRO & ASSOCIATES (AV)

One Beacon Street, 24th Floor, 02108
Telephone: 617-227-8100
Fax: 617-523-8100
Email: email@ShapiroLaw.com *URL:* http://www.ShapiroLaw.com
Dedham, Massachusetts Office: 450 Washington Street, Suite 107.
Telephone: 781-329-8100.
Fax: 781-329-9800.

Daniel B. Shapiro

ASSOCIATES

N. Melina Bell
John J. Sheehan
Sharon T. Kohler
Marsha A. Kaufmann

For full biographical listings, see the Martindale-Hubbell Law Directory

SUGARMAN AND SUGARMAN, P.C. (AV)

One Beacon Street, 02108
Telephone: 617-542-1000
Telecopier: 617-542-1359
Email: info@sugarman.com

Nathan Fink (1920-1974)
Paul R. Sugarman
Neil Sugarman
W. Thomas Smith
Steven L. Hoffman
Robert W. Casby
Valerie A. Yarashus
Jodi M. Petrucelli

Kimberly Ellen Nelson Winter
Marianne Camille LeBlanc
G. Thomas Pauling
Lawrence J. Sugarman

For full biographical listings, see the Martindale-Hubbell Law Directory

SWARTZ & SWARTZ (AV)

10 Marshall Street, 02108
Telephone: 617-742-1900
Fax: 617-367-7193
Email: Attorney@Swartzlaw.com *URL:* http://www.Swartzlaw.com

Edward M. Swartz
Alan L. Cantor
Joseph A. Swartz
Victor A. Denaro
Joan E. Swartz
James A. Swartz
David P. Angueira
Jason Mark
Lisa V. Kaprielian

OF COUNSEL

Fredric A. Swartz

For full biographical listings, see the Martindale-Hubbell Law Directory

BROCKTON, Plymouth Co.

VINCENT P. CAHALANE, P.C. (AV)

478 Torrey Street, Suite 12, 02301-4696
Telephone: 508-588-1222
Fax: 508-584-4748
URL: http://www.lawyers.com/cahalanelaw

Vincent P. Cahalane
Robert J. Zullas
Julie A. Cahalane Cahill
Andrew H. P. Norton
Kristopher S. Stefani

For full biographical listings, see the Martindale-Hubbell Law Directory

FITCHBURG, Worcester Co.

O'CONNOR AND RYAN, P.C. (AV)

61 Academy Street, 01420
Telephone: 978-345-4166
Fax: 978-343-8416

(See Next Column)

O'CONNOR AND RYAN P.C.—*Continued*

John M. O'Connor　Edward P. Ryan, Jr.

Eugene P. O'Donnell, Jr.

For full biographical listings, see the Martindale-Hubbell Law Directory

FRAMINGHAM, Middlesex Co.

MORTON J. SHUMAN (AV)

The Trolley Square Building, 855 Worcester Road (Route 9 West), 01701-5248
Telephone: 508-879-4040
Fax: 508-879-4080
Boston Telephone: 617-422-0012
Email: msh7832495@aol.com *URL:* http://www.lawyers.com/mortonjshuman

For full biographical listings, see the Martindale-Hubbell Law Directory

LYNN, Essex Co.

DEMAKIS LAW OFFICES, P.C. (AV)

56 Central Avenue, 01901
Telephone: 781-595-3311
FAX: 781-592-4990

Thomas C. Demakis　Gregory C. Demakis
Sandor Rabkin

OF COUNSEL

Charles Demakis

Reference: Fleet Bank.

For full biographical listings, see the Martindale-Hubbell Law Directory

MILFORD, Worcester Co.

GREENWALD, GREENWALD, POWERS & WINSOR LLP (AV)

409 Fortune Boulevard Granite Park, 01757-1746
Telephone: 508-478-8611
Fax: 508-634-3959; 478-5937
Email: ggp@ggplaw@.com *URL:* http://www.ggplaw.com

John D. Powers

For full biographical listings, see the Martindale-Hubbell Law Directory

SOMERSET, Bristol Co.

SABRA & ASPDEN, PROFESSIONAL ASSOCIATION (AV)

1026 County Street, 02726
Telephone: 508-674-0890
Fax: 508-679-5998
Email: sabra@efortress.com

Steven P. Sabra　Matthew Mark Aspden

For full biographical listings, see the Martindale-Hubbell Law Directory

*WORCESTER,** Worcester Co.

FRANCIS A. FORD, P.C. (AV)

41 Elm Street, 01609-2514
Telephone: 508-791-7776
Fax: 508-791-4554

Francis A. Ford

For full biographical listings, see the Martindale-Hubbell Law Directory

MILTON, LAURENCE & DIXON (AV)

100 Front Street, Suite 1020, 01608-1402
Telephone: 508-791-6386
Fax: 508-799-4879
Email: mld@chamber.worcester.ma.us

MEMBERS OF FIRM

Stanley B. Milton (1924-1992)　Paul P. O'Connor
Robert C. Milton (1932-1977)　Karen A. Loughlin
Gerard R. Laurence　Daniel M. Wrenn
Charles W. Dixon　Karyn E. Polito

OF COUNSEL

John G. Preston　Judy Eldredge

Reference: Shawmut, Worcester County Bank, N.A.

For full biographical listings, see the Martindale-Hubbell Law Directory

MICHIGAN

*ANN ARBOR,** Washtenaw Co.

FERRIS & SALTER, P.C. (AV)

4158 Washtenaw Avenue, 48108
Telephone: 734-677-2020
Fax: 734-677-3277
Email: ferrissalt@aol.com *URL:* http://www.ferris-salter.com

Don Ferris　Heidi Salter-Ferris

For full biographical listings, see the Martindale-Hubbell Law Directory

HOOPER, HATHAWAY, PRICE, BEUCHE & WALLACE (AV)

126 South Main Street, 48104
Telephone: 313-662-4426
Fax: 313-662-9559
Email: hhpbw@voyager.net

Bruce T. Wallace　Anthony P. Patti
Mark R. Daane　Angela L. Jackson
Susan T. Cannell

OF COUNSEL

James A. Evashevski

Representative Clients: Avfuel Corporation; Bank of Ann Arbor; Castrol North America; Chem-Trend Incorporated; Ervin Industries, Inc.; First Martin Corporation; Glacier Hills, Inc.; Prestolite Electric, Inc.; Southern States Cooperative; E.B. Eddy Forest Products, Ltd.

For Complete List of Firm Personnel, See General Section

For full biographical listings, see the Martindale-Hubbell Law Directory

*BAY CITY,** Bay Co.

BRAUN KENDRICK FINKBEINER PLC (AV)

201 Phoenix Building, P.O. Box 2039, 48708
Telephone: 517-895-8505
Telecopier: 517-895-8437
Email: ALBFIE@BKF-LAW.COM *URL:* http://www.bkf-law.com
Saginaw, Michigan Office: 101 N. Washington, Suite 812. 8th Floor Second National Bank Building.
Telephone: 517-753-3461.
Telecopier: 517-753-3951.
Saginaw Township, Michigan Office: 5800 Gratiot Road, Suite 107, P.O. Box 5169.
Telephone: 517-799-8692.
Fax: 517-799-4666.
Ann Arbor, Michigan Office: First National Building. 201 S. Main, Suite 700.
Telephone: 313-995-4100.
Telecopier: 313-995-4798.
Mt. Pleasant, Michigan Office: 805 North Brown.
Telephone: 517-775-7404.
Telecopier: 517-775-3764.

Frank M. Quinn　Gregory E. Meter
Jeffrey C. Wilson

Michael E. Wooley

Representative Clients: Bay Health Systems; Catholic Federal Credit Union; City of Saginaw; City of Vassar; City of Zilwaukee; Corporate Service; Cox Cable.

For Complete List of Firm Personnel, See General Section

For full biographical listings, see the Martindale-Hubbell Law Directory

BIRMINGHAM, Oakland Co.

MICHAEL B. SERLING, P.C. (AV)

280 N. Old Woodward Avenue, Suite 406, 48009
Telephone: 248-647-6966
Fax: 248-647-9630

Michael B. Serling

Russell R. Beaudoen　Thomas A. Smith

OF COUNSEL

Philip J. Goodman

Reference: Comerica Bank, Birmingham, MI.

For full biographical listings, see the Martindale-Hubbell Law Directory

BLOOMFIELD HILLS, Oakland Co.

LISS AND ASSOCIATES, P.C. (AV)

The Pinehurst Building, 1400 North Woodward Avenue, Suite 200, 48304
Telephone: 248-647-9700
Facsimile: 248-647-5477; 248-647-0638

(See Next Column)

LISS AND ASSOCIATES P.C., *Bloomfield Hills—Continued*

Arthur Y. Liss
Christine S. Reiner
Ronald S. Smith

Karen E. Seder

For full biographical listings, see the Martindale-Hubbell Law Directory

DAVID D. PATTON & ASSOCIATES, P.C. (AV)

44 East Long Lake Road, Suite 100, P.O. Box 829, 48303-0829
Telephone: 248-258-6020
Fax: 248-258-6052
Email: litigation@aol.com *URL:* http://www.lawyers.com/dpattonlaw

David D. Patton

Ellen Bartman Jannette
Humma S. Siddiqi
Patricia C. White
Kelly P. Bekolay
David H. Patton (1912-1993)

OF COUNSEL

Lawrence J. Acker

For full biographical listings, see the Martindale-Hubbell Law Directory

PORTNOY, PIDGEON & ROTH, P.C. (AV)

3883 Telegraph, Suite 103, 48302
Telephone: 248-647-4242
Fax: 248-647-8251
Email: DWINNIE103@AOL.COM *URL:* http://www.lawyers.com/portnoypidgeon&roth

Bernard N. Portnoy (Retired)
Sheila Connor-Heath
James M. Pidgeon
Anne Loridas Randall
Robert P. Roth
Joseph M. LaBella
Marc S. Berlin
Melinda A. Davis

Representative Clients: McLaren Regional Medical Center; Lapeer Regional Hospital; Hurley Medical Center; North Oakland Medical Center, Pontiac General Hospital Division.

For full biographical listings, see the Martindale-Hubbell Law Directory

PROVIZER & PHILLIPS, P.C. (AV)

6785 Telegraph Road, Suite 400, 48301
Telephone: 248-642-0444
Facsimile: 248-642-6661
Toll Free: 1-800-288-9080
URL: http://www.lawyers.com/provizer&phillips

Harold M. Provizer
Evan A. Zagoria
Randall E. Phillips
Noel F. Beck
Marilyn A. Madorsky
Mark S. Baumkel

Constance S. Hall

Representative Clients: Jefferson Ins. Co.; Reliance National Ins. Co.; Blackmoor Group; Thomas Howell Group; Fleming & Hall.

For full biographical listings, see the Martindale-Hubbell Law Directory

CANNONSBURG, Kent Co.

EARDLEY LAW OFFICES, P.C. (AV)

P.O. Box 830, 49317-0830
Telephone: 616-874-2647
Facsimile: 616-874-2654

John F. Eardley
Eugenie B. Eardley

For full biographical listings, see the Martindale-Hubbell Law Directory

*DETROIT,** Wayne Co.

DYKEMA GOSSETT PLLC (AV)

400 Renaissance Center, 48243-1668
Telephone: 313-568-6800
Fax: 313-568-6545
Email: mstarrs@dykema.com *URL:* http://www.dykema.com
Ann Arbor, Michigan Office: 315 East Eisenhower Parkway, Suite 100, 48108-3306.
Telephone: 734-214-7660.
Fax: 734-214-7696.
Bloomfield Hills, Michigan Office: 1577 North Woodward Avenue, Suite 300, 48304-2820.
Telephone: 248-203-0700.
Fax: 248-203-0763.
Chicago, Illinois Office: 55 East Monroe Street, Suite 3050, 60603-5709.
Telephone: 312-551-4900.
Fax: 312-551-4919.
Grand Rapids, Michigan Office: Suite 700, 300 Ottawa Avenue, N.W., 49503-2304.
Telephone: 616-776-7500.
Fax: 616-776-7573.

(See Next Column)

Lansing, Michigan Office: 800 Michigan National Tower, 48933-1707.
Telephone: 517-374-9100.
Fax: 517-374-9191.
Washington, D.C. Office: Franklin Square, Suite 300 West, 1300 I Street, N.W., 20005-3306.
Telephone: 202-522-8600.
Fax: 202-522-8669.
Affiliated Office: Via Matconi, 3, 40122 Bologna, Italy.
Telephone: 011-39-51-228222.
Fax: 011-39-51-6593580.

MEMBERS OF FIRM

Ted T. Amsden
Susan Artinian
James M. Cameron, Jr. (Resident at Ann Arbor Office)
Laurence D. Connor
Michael P. Cooney
Margaret A. Costello
Joseph K. Erhardt
Robert J. Franzinger
Alan M. Greene (Resident at Bloomfield Hills Office)
Dennis M. Haffey (Member in Charge of Bloomfield Hills Office)
Mark E. Hauck
Joseph H. Hickey (Resident at Bloomfield Hills Office)
E. Edward Hood (Member in Charge of Ann Arbor Office)
Kathryn J. Humphrey
Craig L. John (Resident at Bloomfield Hills Office)
Zora E. Johnson
Sharon M. Kelly (Resident at Ann Arbor Office)
Gregory M. Kopacz (Resident at Bloomfield Hills Office)
Richard J. Landau (Resident at Ann Arbor Office)
Kathleen McCree Lewis
Barbara Goldman Mandell (Resident at Bloomfield Hills Office)
Bonnie L. Mayfield
Richard J. McClear
Andrew J. McGuinness (Resident at Ann Arbor Office)
Stephen S. Muhich (Resident at Grand Rapids Office)
Howard E. O'Leary, Jr. (Resident at Washington, D.C. Office)
Marilyn A. Peters (Resident at Bloomfield Hills Office)
Suzanne Sahakian
Lori M. Silsbury (Resident at Lansing Office)
Daniel J. Stephenson (Resident at Ann Arbor Office)
Mark H. Sutton (Resident at Bloomfield Hills Office)
Roger K. Timm
Ronald J. Torbert
Jill M. Wheaton
Daniel G. Wyllie
Donald S. Young

ASSOCIATES

Kimberly A. Bickersteth (Resident at Bloomfield Hills Office)
Thomas S. Bishoff
Cheryl Anne Fletcher
Douglas J. Fryer (Resident at Bloomfield Hills Office)
Kevin P. Fularczyk
David G. Hagens (Resident at Grand Rapids Office)
Robert M. Horwitz
Bradley L. Smith (Resident at Ann Arbor Office)
Steven A. Susswein (Resident at Ann Arbor Office)
Andrea L. Szymanski
Mark David van der Laan (Resident at Grand Rapids Office)
Katherine M. White
Marvin Douglas Wilder
Kevin M. Zielke

For Complete List of Firm Personnel, See General Section

For full biographical listings, see the Martindale-Hubbell Law Directory

GLEICHER & PATEK, P.C. (AV)

1500 Buhl Building, 48226
Telephone: 313-964-6900
Fax: 313-964-6976
URL: http://www.lawyers.com/gplaw

Elizabeth Gleicher
Barbara A. Patek

LEGAL SUPPORT PERSONNEL

Laura Bocchini (Legal Coordinator)

For full biographical listings, see the Martindale-Hubbell Law Directory

KITCH DRUTCHAS WAGNER DENARDIS & VALITUTTI, A PROFESSIONAL CORPORATION (AV)

One Woodward, Tenth Floor, 48226-3499
Telephone: 313-965-7900
Fax: 313-965-7403
URL: http://www.kitch.com
Lansing, Michigan Office: 120 Washington Square, North, Suite 280, One Michigan Avenue, 48933-1609.
Telephone: 517-372-6430.
Fax: 517-372-0441.
Macomb County Office: Towne Square Development, 10 South Main Street, Suite 301, Mount Clemens, 48043-7903.
Telephone: 810-463-9770.
Fax: 810-463-8994.
Toledo, Ohio Office: 405 Madison Avenue, Suite 1500, 43604-1235.
Telephone: 419-243-4006.
Fax: 419-243-7333.
Marquette, Michigan Office: Old City Hall, 220 West Washington, Suite 500, 49855-4344.
Telephone: 906-228-0001.
Fax: 906-228-0003.

(See Next Column)

KITCH DRUTCHAS WAGNER DENARDIS & VALITUTTI A PROFESSIONAL CORPORATION—*Continued*

Ann Arbor, Michigan Office: 303 Detroit Street, Suite 400, P.O. Box 8610, 48107-8610.
Telephone: 734-994-7600.
Fax: 734-994-7626.
Grand Rapids, Michigan Office: 300 Ottawa, NW, Suite 210, 49503.
Telephone: 616-456-8384.
Fax: 616-456-8795.

FIRM PRINCIPALS

Richard A. Kitch
Ronald E. Wagner (Managing Principal)
Ralph F. Valitutti, Jr.
Richard R. DeNardis
Mona K. Majzoub
Harry J. Sherbrook
Anthony G. Arnone
Charles W. Fisher
Clyde M. Metzger, III (Principal, Ann Arbor Office)
Thomas J. Foley
Victor J. Abela
James H. Hughesian
John P. Ryan (Principal, Lansing Office)
William D. Chaklos
Steve N. Cheolas (Principal, Macomb County Office)
Richard S. Baron
Susan Healy Zitterman
John S. Wasung (Principal, Toledo, Ohio Office)
William W. Vertes
Karen Bernard Berkery
R. Michael O'Boyle
Daniel R. Shirey
John M. Sier
Richard T. Counsman
Steven M. Waclawski
Stephen R. Brzezinski
Thomas R. Shimmel
Carole S. Empey (Ann Arbor)
Carol Ann Tarnowsky
Sara Mae Gerbitz
Linda M. Garbarino
Susan Marie Beutel
Mark A. Wisniewski

FIRM ASSOCIATE PRINCIPALS

Susan M. Ramage (Grand Rapids Office)
Daniel J. Niemann (Ann Arbor Office)
Sharon A. DeWaele
Kenneth M. Essad
Kim J. Sveska
Dean A. Etsios
Barbara A. Martin
Cheryl A. Cardelli
Paula M. Burgess (Toledo, Ohio Office)
Lauri A. Read
Cullen B. McKinney
Jeffrey T. Gorcyca

FIRM SENIOR ASSOCIATES

Antonio Mauti
Joseph P. McGill
Sheley L. DeGraw
Laura L. Selzer
R. Lisa Panah
Christina A. Ginter

For Complete List of Firm Personnel, See General Section

For full biographical listings, see the Martindale-Hubbell Law Directory

MILLER, CANFIELD, PADDOCK AND STONE, P.L.C. (AV)

A Professional Limited Liability Company
Founded in 1852 by Sidney Davy Miller
150 West Jefferson, Suite 2500, 48226-4415
Telephone: 313-963-6420
Fax: 313-496-7500
Cable Address: "Stem Detroit"
URL: http://www.millercanfield.com
Ann Arbor, Michigan Office: 101 North Main Street, 7th Floor, 48104-1400.
Telephone: 734-663-2445.
Fax: 734-747-7147.
Troy, Michigan Office: 840 West Long Lake Road, Suite 200, 48098.
Telephone: 248-879-2000.
Fax: 248-879-2001.
Grand Rapids, Michigan Office: 99 Monroe, N.W., Suite 1200, 49503-2639.
Telephone: 616-454-8656.
Fax: 616-776-6322.
Howell, Michigan Office: 121 South Barnard Street, Suite 4, 48843-2305.
Telephone: 517-546-7600.
Telecopier: 517-546-6974.
Kalamazoo, Michigan Office: 444 West Michigan Avenue, 49007-3752.
Telephone: 616-381-7030.
Fax: 616-382-0244.
Lansing, Michigan Office: One Michigan Avenue, Suite 900, 48933-1609.
Telephone: 517-487-2070.
Fax: 517-374-6304.
Monroe, Michigan Office: 214 East Elm Avenue, Suite 100, 48162-2682.
Telephone: 734-243-2000.
Fax: 734-243-0901.
Washington, D.C. Office: 1900 K Street, N.W., Suite 1150. 20006.
Telephone: 202-429-5575; 785-0600.
Fax: 202-331-1118; 785-1234.
Pensacola, Florida Office: 25 West Cedar, 32501.
Telephone: 850-469-1088.
Fax: 850-432-0677.
New York, New York Office: 1450 Broadway, 41st Floor, 10018.
Telephone: 212-704-4400.
Fax: 212-704-4410.
Gdynia, Poland Office: UL. Slaska 21, 81-319.
Telephone: 011-485-831-2808.
Fax: 011-48-58-628 6411.

(See Next Column)

Warsaw, Poland Office: UL. Nowogrodzkall, 5th Floor, 00-513.
Telephone: 011-4822 529 0200.
Fax: 011-4822 529 0201.
Katowice, Poland Office: UL. Francuska 35/37, 40-027.
Telephone: 011 (48-32) 757-2414.
Fax: 011 (48-32) 757-2483.

PRINCIPALS OF FIRM

Charles E. Ritter (Kalamazoo Office)
Thomas G. Parachini
W. Mack Faison
Leland D. Barringer
Ronald E. Baylor (Kalamazoo Office)
Stephen J. Ott (Troy Office)
Pamela Chapman Enslen (Kalamazoo Office)
Brian J. Doren
Irene Bruce Hathaway

ASSOCIATE

Brian S. Westenberg (Troy Office)

Representative Firm Clients: Chrysler Corporation; Comerica, Incorporated; City of Detroit, Michigan; Detroit Tigers, Inc.; First of Michigan; Ford Motor Company; Ford Motor Credit Company; Great Lakes Bancorp; Henry Ford Hospital; INVETECH Company.

For Complete List of Firm Personnel, See General Section

For full biographical listings, see the Martindale-Hubbell Law Directory

PYTELL & VARCHETTI, P.C. (AV)

18580 Mack Avenue, 48236
Telephone: 313-343-9200; 1-888-292-4LAW
Fax: 313-343-0207
Email: PROBATE@compuserve.com *URL:* http://www.MIprobate.com

Robert H. Pytell
Henry C. Pytell (1903-1988)
Paul E. Varchetti

For full biographical listings, see the Martindale-Hubbell Law Directory

TIMMIS & INMAN L.L.P. (AV)

300 Talon Centre, 48207
Telephone: 313-396-4200
Facsimile: 313-396-4228
Email: info@timmis-inman.com *URL:* http://www.timmis-inman.com

Michael T. Timmis
Robert E. Graziani
George A. Peck
Henry J. Brennan, III
Mark W. Peyser
Bradley J. Knickerbocker
George M. Malis

Michael F. Wais
Anthony J. Long
John E.F. Gerlach

OF COUNSEL

William B. Fitzgerald

Representative Clients: Detroit Mortgage & Realty; DMR Fiancial Services, Inc.; J. Levin Sons Co.; Green Tree Financial Servicing Corp.; Hematology-Oncology Associates East, PC; Lakeshore Ear, Nose & Throat Center, PC; Micromanagement Systems, Inc.; Phoenix Crystal Corp.; Talon Surfaces LLC; Talon Automated Equipment Company.

For Complete List of Firm Personnel, See General Section

For full biographical listings, see the Martindale-Hubbell Law Directory

TROWBRIDGE LAW FIRM, P.C. (AV)

The Charles C. Trowbridge House, 1380 East Jefferson Avenue, 48207
Telephone: 313-259-6900
Fax: 313-259-3474

Stanley B. Dickson, Jr.
Stephen N. Leuchtman
Sarah W. Colegrove
Gary D. Dodds

OF COUNSEL

Robert M. Malecek

For full biographical listings, see the Martindale-Hubbell Law Directory

VALENTINE & ASSOCIATES, P.C.

(See West Bloomfield)

WILLMARTH, TANOURY, RAMAR, CORBET, GARVES & SHAW (AV)

535 Griswold, Suite 1730, 48226-3602
Telephone: 313-964-6300
Fax: 313-964-6310
Email: mdwillth@home.net

MEMBERS OF FIRM

Daniel R. Corbet
Brian R. Garves
David R. Nauts
Anthony J. Paradiso
John M. Perrin
John J. Ramar
Bruce R. Shaw
William A. Tanoury
Mark D. Willmarth

(See Next Column)

WILLMARTH, TANOURY, RAMAR, CORBET, GARVES & SHAW, *Detroit—Continued*

ASSOCIATES

Marie C. Kennedy
Wayne Walker
Elizabeth L. Sokol
Robert S. Silverman
Carmine G. Paterra
Joseph J. Ceglarek, II
Derek Steven Wilczynski
Frank Hamidi
Kristen E. Skaff
Steven J. Bonasso
Colleen P. O'Connor
Lara R. Stutz
Eric G. Tucciarone
Michael P. Robach

For full biographical listings, see the Martindale-Hubbell Law Directory

ZEFF AND ZEFF, P.C. (AV)

The Buhl Building, 535 Griswold, Suite 1630, 48226
Telephone: 313-962-3825
Fax: 313-962-6007
URL: http://www.lawyers.com/zeffzefflaw

Louis Zeff (1896-1966)
A. Robert Zeff

Sheryl L. Berenbaum
Paul W. Broschay

For full biographical listings, see the Martindale-Hubbell Law Directory

FARMINGTON HILLS, Oakland Co.

NEMIER, TOLARI, LANDRY, MAZZEO & JOHNSON, P.C. (AV)

37000 Grand River, Suite 300, 48335
Telephone: 248-476-6900
Fax: 248-476-6564
Email: firm@ntlmj.com

Craig L. Nemier
Jeffrey L. Tolari
David B. Landry
Rik Mazzeo
Mark R. Johnson

Michelle E. Mathieu
Kathy Contos Nash
Katharine R. Shishkovsky
Carol J. Surma

OF COUNSEL

William R. Still
Terry E. Pietryga

LEGAL SUPPORT PERSONNEL

Nancy Vayda Dembinski (Paralegal)

For full biographical listings, see the Martindale-Hubbell Law Directory

FLAT ROCK, Wayne Co.

TUCHOW & TRAHEY (AV)

26316 Telegraph Road, 48134
Telephone: 734-782-2900
Fax: 734-782-2123
Bloomfield Hills, Michigan Office: Americenter of Bloomfield Hills, Seven West Square Lake Road.
Telephone: 313-963-7633.
Fax: 313-782-2123.

MEMBERS OF FIRM

Gerald Tuchow
Stephen J. Trahey

Reference: Old Kent Bank.

For full biographical listings, see the Martindale-Hubbell Law Directory

*FLINT,** Genesee Co.

LAW OFFICES OF HENRY M. HANFLIK, P.C. (AV)

1380 South Linden Road, 48532-4185
Telephone: 810-720-4000
Fax: 810-720-1980
Email: hanflik@tir.com

Henry M. Hanflik

Kurtis L.V. Brown

Reference: Citizens Commercial and Savings Bank.

For full biographical listings, see the Martindale-Hubbell Law Directory

MACDONALD, FITZGERALD & MACDONALD, P.C. (AV)

200 McKinnon Building, 48502
Telephone: 810-232-3184; 234-2204
Fax: 810-232-9632

Robert J. MacDonald (1914-1987)
John J. FitzGerald (1919-1995)
R. Duncan MacDonald
Timothy J. MacDonald
Robert J MacDonald

References: Michigan National Bank; NBD Bank, N.A.; Citizen's Bank.

For full biographical listings, see the Martindale-Hubbell Law Directory

*GRAND RAPIDS,** Kent Co.

BUCHANAN, SILVER & BECKERING, P.L.C. (AV)

300 Ottawa N.W., Suite 800, 49503
Telephone: 616-458-2464
Fax: 616-458-0608
URL: http://www.bsblaw.com
Email: rbuchanan@bsblaw.com *URL:* http://www.lawyers.com/bsblaw

MEMBERS OF FIRM

John C. Buchanan
Lee T. Silver
Robert J. Buchanan
Jane M. Beckering

LEGAL SUPPORT PERSONNEL

Raymond E. Beckering, Jr., M.D. (Medical Consultant)

For full biographical listings, see the Martindale-Hubbell Law Directory

DE GROOT, KELLER, VINCENT & ALMASSIAN, P.L.C. (AV)

300 Trust Building, 40 Pearl Street, N.W., 49503
Telephone: 616-459-6251
Fax: 616-459-6352
Email: dkvkeller@aol.com

MEMBER OF FIRM

Brian D. Vincent

OF COUNSEL

Murray B. De Groot

For full biographical listings, see the Martindale-Hubbell Law Directory

DREW, COOPER & ANDING (AV)

Ledyard Building, Suite 300, 125 Ottawa Avenue, N.W., 49503-2898
Telephone: 616-454-8300
Fax: 616-454-0036
Email: DCADVOCATE@AOL.COM

Stephen R. Drew
John E. Anding
Ann M. Cooper
Christopher G. Hastings
Bridget C. Kehoe
Brian K. Lawson

For full biographical listings, see the Martindale-Hubbell Law Directory

GRUEL, MILLS, NIMS AND PYLMAN (AV)

50 Monroe Place, Suite 700 West, 49503
Telephone: 616-235-5500
Fax: 616-235-5550

MEMBERS OF FIRM

Grant J. Gruel
William F. Mills
J. Clarke Nims
Norman H. Pylman, II
Scott R. Melton
Brion J. Brooks
Thomas R. Behm
J. Paul Janes

Representative Clients: Aquinas College; Bell Helmet Co.; Blodgett Memorial Medical Center; Chem Central, Inc.; Cook Pump Co.; Grove, Inc.; NBDC; Heim Corp.

For full biographical listings, see the Martindale-Hubbell Law Directory

MILLER, CANFIELD, PADDOCK AND STONE, P.L.C. (AV)

A Professional Limited Liability Company
Founded in 1852 by Sidney Davy Miller
99 Monroe, N.W. Suite 1200, 49503-2639
Telephone: 616-454-8656
Fax: 616-776-6322
URL: http://www.millercanfield.com
Detroit, Michigan Office: 150 West Jefferson, Suite 2500, 48226-4415.
Telephone: 313-963-6420.
Fax: 313-496-7500.
Cable Address: "Stem Detroit."
Ann Arbor, Michigan Office: 101 North Main Street, 7th Floor, 48104-1400.
Telephone: 734-663-2445.
Fax: 734-747-7147.
Troy, Michigan Office: 840 West Long Lake Road, Suite 200, 48098.
Telephone: 248-879-2000.
Fax: 248-879-2001.
Howell, Michigan Office: 121 South Barnard Street, Suite 4, 48843-2305.
Telephone: 517-546-7600.
Telecopier: 517-546-6974.
Kalamazoo, Michigan Office: 444 West Michigan Avenue, 49007-3752.
Telephone: 616-381-7030.
Fax: 616-382-0244.
Lansing, Michigan Office: One Michigan Avenue, Suite 900, 48933-1609.
Telephone: 517-487-2070.
Fax: 517-374-6304.
Monroe, Michigan Office: 214 East Elm Avenue, Suite 100, 48162-2682.
Telephone: 734-243-2000.
Fax: 734-243-0901.
Washington, D.C. Office: 1900 K Street, N.W., Suite 1150. 20006.
Telephone: 202-429-5575; 785-0600.
Fax: 202-331-1118; 785-1234.

(See Next Column)

MILLER, CANFIELD, PADDOCK AND STONE P.L.C.—*Continued*

Pensacola, Florida Office: 25 West Cedar, 32501.
Telephone: 850-469-1088.
Fax: 850-432-0677.
New York, New York Office: 1450 Broadway, 41st Floor, 10018.
Telephone: 212-704-4400.
Fax: 212-704-4410.
Gdynia, Poland Office: UL. Slaska 21, 81-319.
Telephone: 011-485-831-2808.
Fax: 011-48-58-628 6411.
Warsaw, Poland Office: UL. Nowogrodzkall, 5th Floor, 00-513.
Telephone: 011-4822 529 0200.
Fax: 011-4822 529 0201.
Katowice, Poland Office: UL. Francuska 35/37, 40-027.
Telephone: 011 (48-32) 757-2414.
Fax: 011 (48-32) 757-2483.

PRINCIPALS

Robert L. DeJong
Mark E. Putney
Richard A. Gaffin
Charles S. Mishkind
Michael G. Campbell
Robert E. Lee Wright
Douglas W. Crim
Stanley J. Stek
Vernon Bennett III

OF COUNSEL/SENIOR COUNSEL

David E. Hathaway

RESIDENT SENIOR ATTORNEYS

David J. Hasper
Stephen L. Elkins

RESIDENT ASSOCIATES

John T. Stecco
Vincent E. Woltjer
Andrew T. Blum
Robert J. Nolan

Representative Firm Clients: Chrysler Corporation; Comerica, Incorporated; City of Detroit, Michigan; Detroit Tigers, Inc.; First of Michigan; Ford Motor Company; Ford Motor Credit Company; Great Lakes Bancorp; Henry Ford Hospital; INVETECH Company.

For full biographical listings, see the Martindale-Hubbell Law Directory

ROBERTS, BETZ & BLOSS, P.C. (AV)

5005 Cascade Road SE, 49546-3724
Telephone: 616-285-8899
Telecopier: 616-285-0045

Michael J. Roberts
Michael W. Betz
David J. Bloss
Gregory A. Block
Michael T. Small
Ralph M. Reisinger
Henry S. Emrich

Connie R. Thacker

For full biographical listings, see the Martindale-Hubbell Law Directory

WARDROP & WARDROP, P.C. (AV)

Suite 150 The Frey Building, 300 Ottawa Avenue, N.W., 49503
Telephone: 616-459-1225
Fax: 616-459-7273
Email: wardrop@wardroplaw.com

Robert F. Wardrop II
Thomas M. Wardrop

Mary Saur Cohn
Brian L. Groen

For full biographical listings, see the Martindale-Hubbell Law Directory

HOLLAND, Ottawa Co.

CUNNINGHAM DALMAN, P.C. (AV)

321 Settlers Road, P.O. Box 1767, 49422-1767
Telephone: 616-392-1821
Fax: 616-392-4769
Email: cunndalm@crossover.net *URL:* http://www.holland-law.com

Gordon H. Cunningham
Ronald L. Dalman
Max R. Murphy
James A. Bidol
Andrew J. Mulder
Kenneth B. Breese
Jeffrey K. Helder
Ronald J. Vander Veen
David M. Zessin
Mark H. Zietlow
Randall S. Schipper
Susan E. Vroegop
Joel G. Bouwens

Gregory J. McCoy
Jason M. Milstone
Aaron Leal
Dawn J. Ward

Representative Clients: Huntington National Bank; First of America Bank-Holland, N.A.; Ameribank; City of Holland; Auto Club Insurance Assn. (AAA); American States Insurance Co.; Holland Economic Development Corp.; Hope College; Western Theological Seminary.
Reference: Huntington National Bank.

For full biographical listings, see the Martindale-Hubbell Law Directory

*KALAMAZOO,** Kalamazoo Co.

FIELD & FIELD, P.C. (AV)

248 West Michigan Avenue, 49007
Telephone: 616-343-5581
Telecopy: 616-343-5560

Eugene Field (1916-1983)
Samuel T. Field

Reference: Keystone Community Bank.

MILLER, CANFIELD, PADDOCK AND STONE, P.L.C. (AV)

A Professional Limited Liability Company
Founded in 1852 by Sidney Davy Miller
444 West Michigan Avenue, 49007-3752
Telephone: 616-381-7030
Fax: 616-382-0244
URL: http://www.millercanfield.com
Detroit, Michigan Office: 150 West Jefferson, Suite 2500, 48226-4415.
Telephone: 313-963-6420.
Fax: 313-496-7500.
Cable Address: "Stem Detroit."
Ann Arbor, Michigan Office: 101 North Main Street, 7th Floor, 48104-1400.
Telephone: 734-663-2445.
Fax: 734-747-7147.
Troy, Michigan Office: 840 West Long Lake Road, Suite 200, 48098.
Telephone: 248-879-2000.
Fax: 248-879-2001.
Grand Rapids, Michigan Office: 99 Monroe, N.W., Suite 1200, 49503-2639.
Telephone: 616-454-8656.
Fax: 616-776-6322.
Howell, Michigan Office: 121 South Barnard Street, Suite 4, 48843-2305.
Telephone: 517-546-7600.
Telecopier: 517-546-6974.
Lansing, Michigan Office: One Michigan Avenue, Suite 900, 48933-1609.
Telephone: 517-487-2070.
Fax: 517-374-6304.
Monroe, Michigan Office: 214 East Elm Avenue, Suite 100, 48162-2682.
Telephone: 734-243-2000.
Fax: 734-243-0901.
Washington, D.C. Office: 1900 K Street, N.W., Suite 1150. 20006.
Telephone: 202-429-5575; 785-0600.
Fax: 202-331-1118; 785-1234.
Pensacola, Florida Office: 25 West Cedar, 32501.
Telephone: 850-469-1088.
Fax: 850-432-0677.
New York, New York Office: 1450 Broadway, 41st Floor, 10018.
Telephone: 212-704-4400.
Fax: 212-704-4410.
Gdynia, Poland Office: UL. Slaska 21, 81-319.
Telephone: 011-485-831-2808.
Fax: 011-48-58-628 6411.
Warsaw, Poland Office: UL. Nowogrodzkall, 5th Floor, 00-513.
Telephone: 011-4822 529 0200.
Fax: 011-4822 529 0201.
Katowice, Poland Office: UL. Francuska 35/37, 40-027.
Telephone: 011 (48-32) 757-2414.
Fax: 011 (48-32) 757-2483.

PRINCIPALS

Charles E. Ritter
Ronald E. Baylor
James E. Spurr
Pamela Chapman Enslen

RESIDENT ASSOCIATES

Kurt P. McCamman
Scott R. Sikkenga

Representative Firm Clients: Chrysler Corporation; Comerica, Incorporated; City of Detroit, Michigan; Detroit Tigers, Inc.; First of Michigan; Ford Motor Company; Ford Motor Credit Company; Great Lakes Bancorp; Henry Ford Hospital; INVETECH Company.

For Complete List of Firm Personnel, See General Section

For full biographical listings, see the Martindale-Hubbell Law Directory

LANSING, Ingham Co.

FOSTER, SWIFT, COLLINS & SMITH, P.C. (AV)

313 South Washington Square, 48933-2193
Telephone: 517-371-8100
Telecopier: 517-371-8200
URL: http://www.fosterswift.com
Farmington Hills, Michigan Office: 32300 Northwestern Highway, Suite 230.
Telephone: 248-539-9900.
Fax: 248-851-7504.

John L. Collins
William R. Schulz
David H. Aldrich
Scott A. Storey
Charles E. Barbieri
Scott L. Mandel
Michael D. Sanders
Kevin T. McGraw
Matthew W. Collins

(See Next Column)

FOSTER, SWIFT, COLLINS & SMITH P.C., *Lansing—Continued*

LEGAL SUPPORT PERSONNEL

LEGAL ASSISTANTS

Marsha M. Pullen
Carole M. Schneider
Theresa G. Solberg

For Complete List of Firm Personnel, See General Section

For full biographical listings, see the Martindale-Hubbell Law Directory

TIMMER, JAMO & O'LEARY (AV)

521 Seymour Avenue, 48933
Telephone: 517-371-3500
Fax: 517-371-4514
Email: TIMJAMOLOP@MICHBAR.ORG

MEMBERS OF FIRM

James A. Timmer
James S. O'Leary
James S. Jamo
Kathleen A. Lopilato

Representative Clients: Auto Owners Insurance Co.; Travelers/Aetna Insurance Co.; Western Surety Co.; Indiana Insurance Company/The Netherlands Insurance Companies; Michigan Municipal League; Meadowbrook Insurance; Citizens Insurance Company of America; Speedway SuperAmerica LLC; TIG/Nationwide Insurance Co.; Wolverine Mutual Insurance Co.

For full biographical listings, see the Martindale-Hubbell Law Directory

*MONROE,** Monroe Co.

BRAUNLICH, RUSSOW & BRAUNLICH, A PROFESSIONAL CORPORATION (AV)

111 South Macomb Street, 48161
Telephone: 734-241-8300
Fax: 734-241-7715

William J. Braunlich, Jr. (1924-1992)
Thomas P. Russow
William H. Braunlich

Philip A. Costello
Ann L. Nickel
Jeffrey A. Dulany, P.C.

LEGAL SUPPORT PERSONNEL

Ruth G. Flint

Representative Clients: State Farm Mutual Insurance Co.; Auto Club Insurance Assn.; Board of Road Commissioners, Monroe County; Port of Monroe; Monroe County Community College; City of Luna Pier; City of Petersburg; Auto-Owners Insurance Co.; Fremont Mutual Insurance Co.; Citizens Insurance Co. of America.

For full biographical listings, see the Martindale-Hubbell Law Directory

*MOUNT CLEMENS,** Macomb Co.

MARTIN, BACON & MARTIN, P.C. (AV)

44 First Street, 48043
Telephone: 810-979-6500
Fax: 810-468-7016
URL: http://www.lawyers.com/martin

James N. Martin
Michael R. Janes
Jonathan E. Martin
Kevin L. Moffatt
Paul R. VanTol
John W. Crimando
Victor T. Van Camp

Patrick D. Ball
Amy M. Johnston
Sean S. Cleland

Reference: Community Central Bank - Mt. Clemens.

For full biographical listings, see the Martindale-Hubbell Law Directory

*MOUNT PLEASANT,** Isabella Co.

GRAY, SOWLE & IACCO, A PROFESSIONAL CORPORATION (AV)

600 Broadway East, 48858
Telephone: 517-772-5932
Fax: 517-773-0538

Loren E. Gray
Daniel A. Iacco
Donald N. Sowle
Cheryl E. Gray

References: Isabella Bank & Trust; First of America of Mount Pleasant.

For full biographical listings, see the Martindale-Hubbell Law Directory

NORTHVILLE, Wayne & Oakland Cos.

SIMKINS & SIMKINS, P.C. (AV)

200 North Center Street, 48167-1416
Telephone: 248-349-6030
Telefax: 248-349-8982
Email: simkinsr@aol.com *URL:* http://www.lawyers.com/simkinslaw

(See Next Column)

Charles N. Simkins
Rebecca G. Simkins
Robert B. June
Kathy Ann Hosten
Anthony J. Garczynski

For full biographical listings, see the Martindale-Hubbell Law Directory

PLYMOUTH, Wayne Co.

DRAUGELIS & ASHTON, L.L.P. (AV)

843 Penniman Avenue, 48170-1690
Telephone: 734-453-4044
Fax: 734-453-2011
Clawson, Michigan Office: 380 North Main Street.
Telephone: 248-588-7704.

MEMBERS OF FIRM

Edward F. Draugelis
Lamberto DiStefano
John A. Ashton
David T. Rogers
Donald S. Scully
Joseph R. Conte
Richard T. Haynes
Steven O. Ashton

ASSOCIATES

Floyd C. Virant
Donald E. Walker
Taras P. Jarema
Heather A. Jefferson
Timothy M. McKercher
Roger D. Ajluni
Joel B. Ashton
Margaret L. Browning

For full biographical listings, see the Martindale-Hubbell Law Directory

ST. CLAIR SHORES, Macomb Co.

SAURBIER, SIEGAN & SANFIELD, P.C. (AV)

Suite 402, 400 Maple Park Boulevard, 48081
Telephone: 810-447-3700
Fax: 810-447-3755
Email: scott@saurbier.com
Detroit Office: 1028 Buhl Building.
Telephone: 313-965-2220.

SHAREHOLDERS

Scott A. Saurbier
Renée S. Siegan
Joel A. Sanfield

Marc D. Saurbier
Sara B. Keough
Lawrence T. Garcia
David C. Wiegel
John C. Valenti
Matthew J. Nagaj
Valerie Henning Mock

For full biographical listings, see the Martindale-Hubbell Law Directory

*ST. JOSEPH,** Berrien Co.

MICHAEL D. MARRS A PROFESSIONAL CORPORATION (AV)

421 Main Street, P.O. Box 124, 49085
Telephone: 616-982-4000
Fax: 616-982-0426
Email: MMarrsLaw@AOL.COM

Michael D. Marrs

For full biographical listings, see the Martindale-Hubbell Law Directory

TROFF, PETZKE & AMMESON (AV)

Law and Title Building, 811 Ship Street, P.O. Box 67, 49085
Telephone: 616-983-0161
Facsimile: 616-983-0166
Email: pnalaw@qtm.net

MEMBERS OF FIRM

Roger A. Petzke
Charles F. Ammeson

ASSOCIATE

Daniel G. Lambrecht

For full biographical listings, see the Martindale-Hubbell Law Directory

SOUTHFIELD, Oakland Co.

ROMAIN, KUCK & EGERER, P.C. (AV)

24901 Northwestern Highway, Suite 400, 48075-2255
Telephone: 248-358-4490
Facsimile: 248-358-0761

Timothy E. Egerer
David S. Robinson, Jr.
Michael Paul Daniels
David A. Kanaan
John C. Brennan
Melanie T. Frazier
Karen L. Hahn
Claude Romain (1936-1989)
Ernst W. Kuck (Retired)

Johnny A. Ioanou
Jane Kent Mills
Kenneth Guinn Harlan
Bonnie L. Bovee
Mark E. Williams
Anthony D. Shapero
Barton C. Rachwal

For full biographical listings, see the Martindale-Hubbell Law Directory

Southfield—Continued

ROSEN & LOVELL, P.C. (AV)

25505 West Twelve Mile Road Suite 1000, 48034-1811
Telephone: 248-213-2910
Fax: 248-948-6677

Paul A. Rosen

Alex J. Remick

For full biographical listings, see the Martindale-Hubbell Law Directory

SCHWARTZ & JALKANEN, P.C. (AV)

24400 Northwestern Highway, Suite 200, 48075-6821
Telephone: 248-352-2555
Facsimile: 248-352-5963

Melvin R. Schwartz
Arthur W. Jalkanen
Karl Eric Hannum

Gregory A. Light
David C. Dixon

For full biographical listings, see the Martindale-Hubbell Law Directory

SOMMERS, SCHWARTZ, SILVER & SCHWARTZ, P.C. (AV)

2000 Town Center, Suite 900, 48075
Telephone: 248-355-0300
Telecopier: 248-746-4001
Plymouth, Michigan Office: 747 South Main Street.
Telephone: 313-455-4250.

Stanley S. Schwartz
Jeffrey N. Shillman
David R. Getto
Norman D. Tucker
Robert H. Darling
Paul W. Hines
Richard D. Fox
Frank Mafrice
Richard L. Groffsky
David J. Winter
B. A. Tyler
Robert B. Sickels
Michael J. Cunningham
James D. Ledbetter
Matthew G. Curtis
Helen K. Joyner
John L. Runco
Susanne Pryce
Anne M. Schoepfle
Kenneth T. Watkins

Gerald D. Keller
Jabran G. Yasso
Randall M. Blau
Marc C. Tucker

OF COUNSEL

Howard Silver
Jeremy L. Winer
Marvin R. Stempien

General Counsel for: City of Taylor; Foodland Distributors; C.A. Muer Corporation; Vlasic & Company; Nederlander Corporation; Midwest Health Centers, P.C.
Representative Clients: Michigan National Bank; Don Lee Distributors; Rite-Aid of Michigan.

For Complete List of Firm Personnel, See General Section

For full biographical listings, see the Martindale-Hubbell Law Directory

*TRAVERSE CITY,** Grand Traverse Co.

BISHOP & HEINTZ, P.C. (AV)

440 W. Front at Oak Street, P.O. Box 707, 49685
Telephone: 616-946-4100
Fax: 616-946-8543
Email: info@bishop-heintztc.com *URL:*
http://www.lawyers.com/bishopheintzlaw

Douglas S. Bishop
Patrick E. Heintz
David A. Cvengros
Steven R. Fox

OF COUNSEL

Arthur R. Curtis

Representative Clients: Old Kent Bank-Grand Traverse; Old Kent Bank & Trust Co.; NBD Bank, N.A.; Ball Aircraft, Inc.; Power Play International Inc.; National Cherry Festival; PDM Industries, Inc.; Bolthouse Machine Corp.; Corrections Management, Inc.; Buck Wilder, Inc.

For full biographical listings, see the Martindale-Hubbell Law Directory

DINGEMAN, DANCER & CHRISTOPHERSON, P.L.C. (AV)

100 Park Street, 49684
Telephone: 231-929-0500
Fax: 231-929-0504
Email: dingeman@dingemandancer.com *URL:*
http://www.Dingemandancer.com

Mark R. Dancer

Representative Clients: Texas Instruments, Inc.; Georgia-Pacific Corporation; Martin Marietta Magesia Specialities, Inc.; Elf Atochem North America, Inc.; Busch Oil Company; Lachine Oil Company; Charmilles Technologoes Corporation; Glawe Corporations; Stomberg Carlson Products, Inc.; L'DaRu Lakeside Resort.

(See Next Column)

For full biographical listings, see the Martindale-Hubbell Law Directory

SMITH & JOHNSON, ATTORNEYS, P.C. (AV)

603 Bay Street, P.O. Box 705, 49685
Telephone: 231-946-0700
Fax: 231-946-1735
Email: sjlaw@smith-johnson.com *URL:* http://www.smith-johnson.com
Lansing, Michigan Office: Suite 402, 116 West Ottawa Street.
Telephone: 517-482-5142.

Louis A. Smith
H. Wendell Johnson
Allen G. Anderson

Thomas A. Pezzetti
Timothy Paul Smith
Matthew D. Vermetten
Gary Allen Gardner

OF COUNSEL

Barbara Ann Assendelft

Representative Clients: Empire National Bank of Traverse City; Grand Traverse Mall Limited Partnership; Green Tree Acceptance, Inc.; Lansing Automakers' Federal Credit Union; Michigan Automobile Dealers Association; Cherry Capital Oldsmobile Cadillac L.L.C.; Bill Marsh Motors, Inc.; Northern Star Broadcasting, L.L.C.; Munson Healthcare; Republic Bank.

For full biographical listings, see the Martindale-Hubbell Law Directory

SULLIVAN & CROWLEY, P.C. (AV)

735 South Garfield, Suite 202, 49686
Telephone: 616-922-1888
Fax: 616-922-2221
Email: sullcro@GTII.com *URL:*
http://www.lawyers.com/sullivancrowleylaw

James I. Sullivan
Philip J. Crowley
Jeffrey J. Noorman

For full biographical listings, see the Martindale-Hubbell Law Directory

THOMPSON, O'NEIL & VANDERVEEN (AV)

309 East Front Street, P.O. Box 429, 49685
Telephone: 231-929-9700; 1-800-678-1307
Fax: 231-929-7262
Email: tov@traverse.com *URL:* http://www.lawyers.com/tovtraverse

George R. Thompson
Daniel P. O'Neil
John R. VanderVeen

Jessica G. Rickard

For full biographical listings, see the Martindale-Hubbell Law Directory

WALTON, SMITH, PHILLIPS & DIXON, P.C. (AV)

216 Cass Street, P.O. Box 549, 49685
Telephone: 616-947-7410
Fax: 616-947-5112

Geoff G. Smith
L. Kent Walton
Thomas L. Phillips

Representative Clients: The Travelers Insurance Cos.; Farm Bureau Insurance Group; TIG Insurance.
Reference: Huntington National Bank.

For full biographical listings, see the Martindale-Hubbell Law Directory

TROY, Oakland Co.

HOLAHAN, MALLOY, MAYBAUGH, MONNICH & DELIE (AV)

Suite 100, 2690 Crooks Road, 48084-4700
Telephone: 248-362-4747
Fax: 248-362-4779
East Tawas, Michigan Office: 910 East Bay Street.
Telephone: 517-362-4747.
Fax: 517-362-7331.

MEMBERS OF FIRM

J. Michael Malloy, III
James D. Maybaugh
John R. Monnich
David L. Delie, Jr.

OF COUNSEL

Thomas H. O'Connor
Maureen Holahan (Retired; Resident, East Tawas Office)

For full biographical listings, see the Martindale-Hubbell Law Directory

POLING, MCGAW & POLING, P.C. (AV)

Suite 275, 5435 Corporate Drive, 48098
Telephone: 248-641-0500
Telecopier: 248-641-0506
URL: http://www.lawyers.com/polingmcgaw&poling

(See Next Column)

POLING, MCGAW & POLING P.C., *Troy—Continued*

Benson T. Buck (1926-1989)	Gregory C. Hamilton
Richard B. Poling	Veronica B. O'Hara
D. Douglas McGaw	James R. Parker
Richard B. Poling, Jr.	Shannon M. Acton

OF COUNSEL

Ralph S. Moore

Representative Clients: City of Troy; United States Fidelity & Guaranty Co.; Sentry Insurance Co.; Admiral Insurance; DeMaria Construction Co.; Aetna Casualty and Surety Co.; Concord Design; Pneumo-Abex.

For full biographical listings, see the Martindale-Hubbell Law Directory

SCHADEN, KATZMAN, LAMPERT & MCCLUNE (AV®)

100 West Big Beaver Road Suite 130, 48084
Telephone: 248-258-4800
Fax: 248-258-2825
Email: SCHKATZLAM@aol.com *URL:* http://www.lawyers.com/schadenlaw
Broomfield, Colorado Office: 11870 Airport Way.
Telephone: 303-465-3663.
Facsimile: 303-465-3884.

MEMBERS OF FIRM

Richard F. Schaden	Bruce A. Lampert
David I. Katzman	John D. McClune

ASSOCIATE

Kathleen M. Schaden

OF COUNSEL

Bruce O. Wilson

For full biographical listings, see the Martindale-Hubbell Law Directory

WEST BLOOMFIELD, Oakland Co.

VALENTINE & ASSOCIATES, P.C. (AV)

5767 West Maple Road, Suite 400, 48322
Telephone: 248-851-3010
Fax: 248-851-1553
Email: vallaw@umich.edu

Stephen K. Valentine, Jr.

For full biographical listings, see the Martindale-Hubbell Law Directory

PRODUCT LIABILITY LAW

ALABAMA

ALEXANDER CITY, Tallapoosa Co.

MORRIS, HAYNES & HORNSBY (AV)

131 Main Street, P.O. Box 1660, 35011-1660
Telephone: 256-329-2000
Fax: 256-329-2015
Email: morrishayn@webshoppe.net

Larry W. Morris
Randall Stark Haynes
Clay Hornsby
Nancy L. Eady

OF COUNSEL

John F. Dillon, IV (1930-1998)
Jennie Lee Kelley

Representative Clients: Aliant Bank; City of Alexander City; Town of Wadley.
Approved Attorneys for: Lawyers Title Insurance Corp.; Mississippi Valley Title Insurance Co.

For full biographical listings, see the Martindale-Hubbell Law Directory

*ANDALUSIA,** Covington Co.

ALBRITTONS, CLIFTON, ALVERSON & MOODY, P.C. (AV)

(Powell, Albritton & Albritton)
(Albrittons & Rankin)
(Albrittons, Givhan, Clifton & Alverson)
(Albrittons & Givhan)
109 Opp Avenue, P.O. Box 880, 36420
Telephone: 334-222-3177
Telecopier: 334-222-2696

Ed. T. Albritton (1857-1925)
Wm. Harold Albritton, Sr. (1881-1929)
Dempsey M. Powell (1863-1949)
Albert L. Rankin (1909-1970)
Robert Bynum Albritton (1905-1983)
William H. Albritton, Jr. (1907-1983)
James Marvin Albritton (1915-1987)
James R. Clifton
William Harold Albritton, IV
William B. Alverson, Jr.
Thomas B. Albritton
Julie S. Moody

Benjamin M. Bowden

General Counsel for: Coca-Cola Bottling Co. of Andalusia; Opp-Micolas Cotton Mills.
Attorneys for: First Alabama Bank; Alabama Power Co.; The Travelers; Liberty Mutual Ins. Co; Kemper Insurance; Crum & Forster Insurance Cos; CSX Transporation.

For full biographical listings, see the Martindale-Hubbell Law Directory

*BIRMINGHAM,** Jefferson Co.

BRADLEY ARANT ROSE & WHITE LLP (AV)

2001 Park Place, Suite 1400, P.O. Box 830709, 35283-0709
Telephone: 205-521-8000
Facsimile: 205-521-8800
Facsimile (SouthTrust Tower Office): 205-521-8500
URL: http://www.barw.com
Huntsville, Alabama Office: 200 Clinton Avenue West, Suite 900, 35801.
Telephone: 205-517-5100.
Facsimile: 205-533-5069.
Washington, D.C. Office: 801 Pennsylvania Avenue, NW, Suite 230, 20004.
Telephone: 202-347-8893.
Facsimile: 202-347-1684.

MEMBERS OF FIRM

T. Michael Brown
Philip J. Carroll III
Brittin Turner Coleman
Stewart M. Cox
Gary C. Huckaby (Resident, Huntsville Office)
David Glenn Hymer
Thad Gladden Long
Michael D. McKibben
Hobart A. McWhorter Jr.
Walter J. Sears III
Sid J. Trant
John D. Watson III

ASSOCIATES

Denise Avery Dodson
John W. Smith T

For Complete List of Firm Personnel, See General Section

For full biographical listings, see the Martindale-Hubbell Law Directory

CARR, ALLISON, PUGH, HOWARD, OLIVER & SISSON, P.C. (AV)

400 Vestavia Parkway, Suite 400, 35216
Telephone: 205-822-2006
Fax: 205-822-2057
Email: CFC@caphos.com
Florence, Alabama Office: 212 South Cedar Street, 35630.
Telephone: 256-718-6040.
Fax: 256-718-2150.
Mobile, Alabama Office: P.O. Box 781,36601-0781.
Telephone: 334-621-4340.
Fax: 334-626-8928.

Charles F. Carr (Resident, Daphne Office)
Russell Q. Allison
Bennett L. Pugh
David K. Howard (Resident, Florence Office)
Thomas L. Oliver, II
William H. Sisson (Resident, Daphne Office)
Glenn E. Ireland
Thomas C. Logan
Donald B. Kirkpatrick, II
Sarah J. Carlisle
Craig W. Goolsby (Resident, Daphne Office)

Gregg L. Smith
Joseph H. Driver
Brett A. Ross
Thomas S. Thornton, III
W. Bradford Kittrell
Jeffrey B. Carr
Joseph H. Hilley
Jeremy N. Trousdale
Ryan G. Brake
Caroline T. Pryor (Resident, Daphne Office)

For full biographical listings, see the Martindale-Hubbell Law Directory

EMOND & VINES (AV)

2200 SouthTrust Tower, 420 North 20th Street, P.O. Box 10008, 35202-0008
Telephone: 205-324-4000
Fax: 205-324-5020
Email: EmondVines@aol.com

MEMBER OF FIRM

Lanny S. Vines

ASSOCIATES

Michael Lee Allsup
Vivian D. Vines Campbell
Frank O. Hanson, Jr.

For full biographical listings, see the Martindale-Hubbell Law Directory

FRIEDMAN, LEAK & BLOOM, P.C. (AV)

3800 Colonnade Parkway, Suite 650, 35243
Telephone: 205-278-7000
Fax: 205-278-7001
Email: Info@FLB-law.com *URL:* http://www.FLB-law.com

E. Martin Bloom
Jeffrey E. Friedman
Joe L. Leak
P. Thomas Dazzio, Jr.
Christopher J. Zulanas
J. Michael Bowling
C. Mark Bain
Robert R. Bedwell III

For full biographical listings, see the Martindale-Hubbell Law Directory

HARE, WYNN, NEWELL AND NEWTON (AV)

A Partnership including Professional Corporations
Suite 800 Massey Building, 290 21st Street North, 35203
Telephone: 205-328-5330
Fax: 205-324-2165

MEMBERS OF FIRM

Francis H. Hare (1904-1983)
Carlton T. Wynn
Neal C. Newell
Alex W. Newton
C. Terrell Wynn, Jr.
James J. Thompson, Jr.
Alva C. Caine
Ray O. (Ronnie) Noojin, Jr. (1945-1996)
John W. Haley (P.C.)
D. Leon Ashford (P.C.)
Scott A. Powell
James R. Pratt, III
S. Shay Samples
Bruce J. McKee
Michael D. Ermert
Nolan Edward Awbrey
James B. Gunther, Jr.
Don McKenna
Martin E. Burke

COUNSEL

Francis H. Hare, Jr., (P.C.)
James O. Haley
James K. Baker

References: AmSouth Bank of Birmingham; First Commercial Bank of Birmingham.

For full biographical listings, see the Martindale-Hubbell Law Directory

HARRIS, CLECKLER & HOLLIS (AV)

Historic 2007 Building, 2007 Third Avenue North, 35203-2366
Telephone: 205-328-2366
Telecopier: 205-328-0013
Email: hcbr@mindspring.com *URL:* http://www.harriscleckler.com

(See Next Column)

HARRIS, CLECKLER & HOLLIS, *Birmingham—Continued*

Lyman H. Harris
Michael H. Cleckler
Jeffrey K. Hollis

ASSOCIATE

Jason A. Shamblin

For full biographical listings, see the Martindale-Hubbell Law Directory

HOGAN, SMITH & ALSPAUGH, P.C. (AV)

2323 Second Avenue, North, 35203
Telephone: 205-324-5635
Telecopier: 205-324-5637
Email: Chris@Hogan-Smith.com *URL:* http://www.hsa-pc.com

William W. Smith
Ronald R. Crook
M. Clay Alspaugh
Richard D. Stratton
R. Benjamin Hogan, III
Jack Lee Roberts, Jr.
Benjamin E. Baker, Jr.

Maxwell D. Carter

Reference: Regions Bank.

For full biographical listings, see the Martindale-Hubbell Law Directory

HUIE, FERNAMBUCQ AND STEWART, LLP (AV)

Suite 800, Regions Bank Building, 417 N. 20th Street, 35203
Telephone: 205-251-1193
Telecopy: 205-251-1256

MEMBERS OF FIRM

Thomas B. Huie (1915-1990)
Frank E. Lankford, Jr.
William B. Fernambucq (1922-1997)
M. Keith Gann
Charles H. Clark, Jr.
Charles A. Stewart, Jr. (1923-1983)
John D. Herndon
J. Allen Sydnor, Jr.
Eugene D. Martenson
D. Alan Thomas
Stanley A. Cash
William G. Gantt
James R. Shaw
T. Kelly May
Robert M. Girardeau
Christopher S. Rodgers
John S. Civils, Jr.
Walter J. Price, III
H. Lanier Brown, II

ASSOCIATES

Robert V. Rodgers
Thomas E. Bazemore, III
Gregory L. Schuck
R. Gordon Sproule, Jr.
Paul F. Malek
Martha Leach Thompson
Jennifer Devereaux Segers
Patrick O. Gray
Philip R. Collins
James W. Moss
Brandy Murphy Lee
H. Cannon Lawley
Anna Katherine Graves

Representative Clients: Deere & Co.; General Motors Corp.; Honda North America; Isuzu Motors America; Mitsubishi Motor Sales of America; Nissan Motor Corp. Ltd.; Toyota Motor Sales USA, Inc.; Mazda Motor Corp.; Navistar International; Volvo North America Corp.

For full biographical listings, see the Martindale-Hubbell Law Directory

JOHNSTON BARTON PROCTOR & POWELL LLP (AV)

2900 AmSouth/Harbert Plaza, 1901 Sixth Avenue North, 35203-2618
Telephone: 205-458-9400
Telecopier: 205-458-9500
Email: Law@JBPP.com

MEMBERS OF FIRM

Charles L. Robinson
David W. Proctor
Gilbert E. Johnston, Jr.
W. Hill Sewell
James C. Barton, Jr.
Robert S. Vance, Jr.
Thomas E. Walker
Anthony A. Joseph
Anne P. Wheeler
James P. Pewitt
William D. Jones III
Lee M. Pope

OF COUNSEL

James C. Barton

ASSOCIATES

Helen Kathryn Downs
Anna R. Minor
Gina Pearson Hunter
Keith Adrian Brown
Andrew David Block

Counsel for: Eli Lilly and Co.; General Electric Co.; General Motors Corp.; Marathon Equipment Co.; Melroe Co.; National Food Processors Assn.; Outboard Marine Corp.; Smith & Nephew, Inc.; Teva Pharmaceuticals USA, Inc.; Volvo Construction Equipment North America, Inc.

For full biographical listings, see the Martindale-Hubbell Law Directory

LIGHTFOOT, FRANKLIN & WHITE, L.L.C. (AV)

The Clark Building, 400 20th Street North, 35203
Telephone: 205-581-0700
Facsimile: 205-581-0799
Email: LFWlaw@LFWlaw.com *URL:* http://www.lfwlaw.com

(See Next Column)

Warren B. Lightfoot
Harlan I. Prater, IV
Samuel H. Franklin
Michael L. Bell
Jere F. White, Jr.
William S. Cox, III
Mac M. Moorer
William H. King, III
John M. Johnson
Madeline H. Haikala
M. Christian King
William H. Brooks
E. Glenn Waldrop, Jr.
J. Banks Sewell, III
Adam K. Peck
Lee M. Hollis
Jackson R. Sharman, III

Wynn M. Shuford
William H. Morrow
John Q. Somerville
Anne Sikes Hornsby
Suzanne Alldredge
Stephen Jackson Rowe
Stephanie Keller Womack
Ivan B. Cooper
Melody L. Hurdle
Lisa J. Wathey
Robin Hansen Graves
William Larkin Radney, IV
J. Bradley Powell
James F. Hughey, III

For full biographical listings, see the Martindale-Hubbell Law Directory

LUSK, FRALEY, MCALISTER & SIMMS, P.C. (AV)

Suite 1700 AmSouth/Harbert Plaza, 1901 Sixth Avenue North, 35203
Telephone: 205-323-7100
Fax: 205-323-7050
Email: Lusk-Fraley.com

Donald D. Lusk
David Lawrence Dean
John M. Fraley
David Thurston White, III
David L. McAlister
Susan Gilman McAlister
Keri Donald Simms
Payton Caldwell Lusk
Kenneth A. Dowdy
Leslie Ann Caldwell

For full biographical listings, see the Martindale-Hubbell Law Directory

MARSH, RICKARD & BRYAN, P.C. (AV)

800 Shades Creek Parkway, Suite 600, 35209-4532
Telephone: 205-879-1981
Facsimile: 205-879-1986
Email: attys@mrblaw.com

David H. Marsh
Nat Bryan
Jeffrey C. Rickard
Susan J. Silvernail
Dennis E. Goldasich, Jr.

Thomas M. Powell

OF COUNSEL

Irene T. Grubbs

For full biographical listings, see the Martindale-Hubbell Law Directory

PARSONS, LEE & JULIANO, P.C. (AV)

2200 AmSouth/Harbert Plaza, 1901 Sixth Avenue, North, P.O. Box 371088, 35237-1088
Telephone: 205-326-6600
Fax: 205-324-7097

Robert E. Parsons
John M. Bergquist
Jasper P. Juliano
Paul J. DeMarco
Marcus W. Lee
Deborah Ann Payne
Marda W. Sydnor
Dorothy A. Powell
David A. Lee
David Samuel Snoddy

For full biographical listings, see the Martindale-Hubbell Law Directory

PITTMAN, HOOKS, DUTTON & HOLLIS, P.C. (AV)

1100 Park Place Tower, 35203
Telephone: 205-322-8880
Telecopier: 205-328-2711
Email: PHDH@4theplaintiff.com

W. Lee Pittman
L. Andrew Hollis, Jr.
Kenneth W. Hooks
Jeffrey C. Kirby
Tom Dutton
Ralph Bohanan, Jr.

Chris T. Hellums
Michael C. Bradley
Keith T. Belt, Jr.
Page Poerschke Liddon
Leigh King Forstman
Steven William Couch
J. Chris Cochran

OF COUNSEL

James H. Davis (Not admitted in AL)
Lynn A. Crosson

For full biographical listings, see the Martindale-Hubbell Law Directory

PORTERFIELD, HARPER & MILLS, P.A. (AV)

22 Inverness Center Parkway, Suite 600, P.O. Box 530790, 35242-4821
Telephone: 205-980-5000
Fax: 205-980-5001

(See Next Column)

PORTERFIELD, HARPER & MILLS P.A.—*Continued*

Neal D. Moore, III
J. Paul Sizemore
C. Jeffery Ash

Representative Clients: CIGNA; St. Paul Insurance Co.; The Travelers; Figgie International; White Consolidated Industries; Terex Corp.; Wausau Insurance; Baptist Health Systems, Inc.; Bruno's, Inc.; Harley Davidson, Inc.

For full biographical listings, see the Martindale-Hubbell Law Directory

PORTER, PORTER & HASSINGER, P.C. (AV)

New South Federal Savings Building, 215 North 21st Street, Suite 1000, 35203
Telephone: 205-322-1744
Telecopier: 205-322-1750
Email: pphatty@earthlink.net

James W. Porter, II
David S. Hassinger
Earl C. Bloom, Jr.

General Counsel for: The Club, Inc.; Smith Coal Sales Co.

For full biographical listings, see the Martindale-Hubbell Law Directory

SMITH & ELY, LLP (AV)

2000-A Southbridge Parkway Suite 405, 35209
Telephone: 205-802-2214
Fax: 205-879-4445

MEMBERS OF FIRM

Carol Ann Smith
Brenen G. Ely

ASSOCIATES

Susan Rogers
Susan Caroline Haygood
Toby Dykes

OF COUNSEL

Lisa B. Singer

For full biographical listings, see the Martindale-Hubbell Law Directory

SMITH, SPIRES & PEDDY, P.C. (AV)

2015 Second Avenue North Suite 200, 35203
Telephone: 205-251-5885
Fax: 205-251-8642

Paul G. Smith
Thomas S. Spires
A. Joe Peddy
Todd Hamilton
Thomas Coleman, Jr.

B. Scott Tyra
James L. Sanders, II
Julie L. Jenkins
Matthew C. Williams
Clarence "Chip" Rivers, IV
Jason M. Langley
R. Timothy Estes

Representative Clients: CNA Insurance Company; St. Paul Insurance Company; Axa Global Risks, Inc.; Cincinnati Insurance Company; Great American Ins. Co.; Chubb & Son, Inc.; Federal Insurance Company; American States Ins. Co.; Bituminous Insurance Company; Auto-Owners Insurance Company; USF&G Insurance Company.

For full biographical listings, see the Martindale-Hubbell Law Directory

STARNES & ATCHISON LLP (AV)

100 Brookwood Place, 35209
Telephone: 205-868-6000
Telecopier: 205-868-6099
Mailing Address: P.O. Box 598512, 35259-8512
Email: information@starneslaw.com
Mobile, Alabama Office: Riverview Plaza, Suite 1106, 63 South Royal Street, 36602.
Telephone: 334-433-6049.

MEMBERS OF FIRM

W. Michael Atchison
John P. Scott, Jr.
J. Bentley Owens, III
Sybil Vogtle Abbot

ASSOCIATES

Rik S. Tozzi
Reed R. Bates
Bryan Oxford Balogh
Blake D. Andrews
James M. Terrell
Alfred H. Perkins, Jr.

Representative Clients: East Penn Manufacturing Company; Murray, Inc.; International Comfort Products Corporation (USA); American Honda; Kawasaki Motors Corp.; Babcock-Wilcox, Inc.; Allen-Bradley Co.; Hoffman-LaRoche, Inc.; Glaxo Wellcome, Inc.; Massey-Ferguson, Inc.

For full biographical listings, see the Martindale-Hubbell Law Directory

*CHATOM,** Washington Co.

TURNER, ONDERDONK, KIMBROUGH & HOWELL, P.A. (AV)

1021 Central Avenue, P.O. Drawer 1389, 36518
Telephone: 334-847-2237
Fax: 334-847-3115
Email: firm@tokh.com *URL:* http://www.tokh.com
Mobile, Alabama Office: 1359 Dauphin Street.
Telephone: 334-432-2855.
Fax: 334-432-2863.

Edward P. Turner, Jr.
A. Michael Onderdonk
William A. Kimbrough, Jr. (Resident, Mobile Office)
Gordon K. Howell
Marc E. Bradley (Resident, Mobile Office)
Halron W. Turner
Frank Woodson (Resident, Mobile Office)
David M. Huggins (Resident, Mobile Office)
E. Tatum Turner

LEGAL SUPPORT PERSONNEL

Thomas E. Fuller

For full biographical listings, see the Martindale-Hubbell Law Directory

*DECATUR,** Morgan Co.

EYSTER, KEY, TUBB, WEAVER & ROTH (AV)

Eyster Building, 402 East Moulton Street, S.E., P.O. Box 1607, 35602
Telephone: 256-353-6761
Fax: 256-353-6767

John C. Eyster (1863-1926)
Charles H. Eyster, Sr. (1888-1964)
Wm. B. Eyster (1921-1995)

MEMBERS OF FIRM

John S. Key
J. Glynn Tubb
Lawrence C. Weaver
Nicholas B. Roth
J. Witty Allen
William L. Middleton, III
James G. Adams, Jr.
John R. Baggette, Jr.
Jenny L. Mcleroy

General Counsel for: Alabama Farmers Cooperative.
Regional Counsel for: AmSouth Bank.
Local Counsel for: Allstate Insurance Co.; Champion International Corp; General Electric; Goodyear; Liberty Mutual Insurance Co.; Saginaw Steering Gear Division, General Motors Corp.; State Farm Mutual Automobile Insurance Co.; 3M; The Travelers.

For full biographical listings, see the Martindale-Hubbell Law Directory

HARRIS, CADDELL & SHANKS, P.C. (AV)

214 Johnston Street, S.E., P.O. Box 2688, 35602-2688
Telephone: 256-340-8000
Telecopier: 256-340-8040
Email: hcs@ala-net.com

Julian Harris (1904-1994)
Norman W. Harris (1907-1998)
Philip T. Shanks (Retired)
Charles L. Murphree (Retired)
John A. Caddell
Robert H. Harris
Jon H. Moores
Thomas A. Caddell
William E. Shinn, Jr.
Gary A. Phillips
Dow M. Perry, Jr.
Barnes F. Lovelace, Jr.
Jeffrey S. Brown
David W. Langston
Huel Harris

Attorneys for: The Industrial Development Board of the City of Decatur, Alabama; The Boeing Company; Amoco Chemical Co.; General Electric Co.; BellSouth Inc.; Auto-Owners Insurance Co.; ALFA Insurance Cos.; U.S.F. & G. Co.

For full biographical listings, see the Martindale-Hubbell Law Directory

*DOTHAN,** Houston Co.

LEE & McINISH (AV)

238 West Main Street, P.O. Box 1665, 36302
Telephone: 334-792-4156
Facsimile: 334-794-8342
Email: leemc@graceba.net

MEMBERS OF FIRM

W. L. Lee (1873-1944)
Alto V. Lee, III (1915-1987)
William L. Lee, III
Alan C. Livingston
William C. Carn, III
Peter A. McInish
Jerry M. White

ASSOCIATES

William L. Lee, IV
William W. Nichols
William C. White, II

OF COUNSEL

H. Dwight McInish

Counsel for: Seaboard Coast Line Railroad Co.; Atlanta & St. Andrews Bay Railroad Co.; ALFA; U. S. F. & G. Co.; Maryland Casualty Co.; Continental Insurance Cos.; Royal-Globe Group; Slocomb National Bank; GTE South.

(See Next Column)

LEE & MCINISH, *Dothan—Continued*

For full biographical listings, see the Martindale-Hubbell Law Directory

*EVERGREEN,** Conecuh Co.

WILLIAM D. MELTON (AV)

Melton Building, 100 Liberty Hill Drive, Drawer 800, 36401-0800
Telephone: 334-578-2423
Fax: 334-578-2427

References: Bank of Evergreen, Evergreen, Alabama; First National Bank of Brewton, Alabama.

For full biographical listings, see the Martindale-Hubbell Law Directory

*FLORENCE,** Lauderdale Co.

JONES & TROUSDALE (AV)

115 Helton Court, Suite B, P.O. Box 367, 35631-0367
Telephone: 256-767-0333
Telefax: 256-767-0331
Email: JTAttys@aol.com

MEMBERS OF FIRM

Robert E. Jones, III
Preston S. Trousdale, Jr.
A. DeLoach Stewart

For full biographical listings, see the Martindale-Hubbell Law Directory

*HUNTSVILLE,** Madison Co.

HORNSBY, WATSON & MEGINNISS (AV)

1110 Gleneagles Drive, 35801
Telephone: 256-650-5500
Fax: 256-650-5504
Email: rwhj@mindspring.com

Ralph W. Hornsby, Sr.
Ralph W. Hornsby, Jr.
S. A. "Bud" Watson, Jr.
Jeffrey G. Blackwell

OF COUNSEL

David H. Meginniss

For full biographical listings, see the Martindale-Hubbell Law Directory

MORRIS, CLOUD AND CONCHIN, P.C. (AV)

521 Madison Street, P.O. Box 248, 35804
Telephone: 256-534-0065
Fax: 256-539-0741

Harvey B. Morris (P.C.)
Joseph M. Cloud
Gary V. Conchin

Maureen "Mike" K. Cooper
Daniel B. Banks, Jr.

For full biographical listings, see the Martindale-Hubbell Law Directory

*MOBILE,** Mobile Co.

ATCHISON, CROSBY, SAAD & BEEBE, P.C. (AV)

3030 Knollwood Drive, 36693
Telephone: 334-665-7200
Fax: 334-665-7250
URL: http://www.acsblaw.com

James E. Atchison
Elias J. Saad
James H. Crosby
Donald G. Beebe

Mona Ann Vivar
Jacqueline M. McConaha
Daryl A. Atchison

Representative Clients: City of Mobile; Alabama State Docks; Mobile Area Water and Sewer Board; Owens Corning, Inc.; Pilot Catastrophe Services, Inc.; Shell Oil Co.; Premdor,Inc.; Melvin Pierce Paint Co.; Commonwealth National Bank; Fiberglass Canada,Inc.

For full biographical listings, see the Martindale-Hubbell Law Directory

BURNS, CUNNINGHAM & MACKEY, P.C. (AV)

50 St. Emanuel Street, P.O. Box 1583, 36633
Telephone: 334-432-0612
Fax: 334-432-0625
URL: http://www.bcmlawyers.com

Peter F. Burns
Peter S. Mackey
William M. Cunningham, Jr.
Gary W. Fillingim

For full biographical listings, see the Martindale-Hubbell Law Directory

CARR, ALFORD, CLAUSEN & MCDONALD, L.L.C. (AV)

One St. Louis Centre, Suite 5000, P.O. Drawer C, 36601
Telephone: 334-432-1600
Facsimile: 334-432-1700
URL: http://www.cacm.com

(See Next Column)

Davis Carr
James H. McDonald, Jr.
Helen Johnson Alford
James W. Lampkin, II
Andrew C. Clausen
Jean M. Powers

Annette McDermott Carwie
Paul V. Lagarde
M. Lauren Lemmon
Frank L. Parker, Jr.
Thomas M. Rockwell
Christina M. Adcock
Pamela Ann Moore
Kathleen Cobb Kaufman
W. Ben. Broadwater
Joseph Anthony Zarzaur, Jr.

For full biographical listings, see the Martindale-Hubbell Law Directory

CUNNINGHAM, BOUNDS, YANCE, CROWDER & BROWN, L.L.C. (AV)

1601 Dauphin Street, P.O. Box 66705, 36660
Telephone: 334-471-6191
Fax: 334-479-1031
Email: adm@cbycb.com

James A. Yance
Michael A. Worel
John T. Crowder, Jr.
David G. Wirtes, Jr.
Robert T. Cunningham, Jr.
Toby D. Brown
Joseph M. Brown, Jr.
Reggie Copeland, Jr.
Gregory B. Breedlove
Richard T. Dorman

J. Stephen Legg
George M. Dent, III

OF COUNSEL

Richard Bounds
J. Kenyon Rainer, Sr., M.D., J.D.
Robert T. Cunningham

References: Regions Bank; AmSouth Bank, N.A.

For full biographical listings, see the Martindale-Hubbell Law Directory

FINKBOHNER AND LAWLER, L.L.C. (AV)

169 Dauphin Street Suite 300, P.O. Box 3085, 36652
Telephone: 334-438-5871
Fax: 334-432-8052
Email: finkbohnerlawlerllc@zebra.net

MEMBERS OF FIRM

George W. Finkbohner, Jr.
George W. Finkbohner, III
John L. Lawler
Royce A. Ray, III

For full biographical listings, see the Martindale-Hubbell Law Directory

FRAZER, GREENE, UPCHURCH & BAKER, L.L.C. (AV)

First National Bank Building, Suite 2206 107 Saint Francis Street, 36602
Telephone: 334-431-6020
Facsimile: 334-431-6030
URL: http://www.frazergreene.com

MEMBERS OF FIRM

A. Danner Frazer, Jr.
Michael E. Upchurch
Edward C. Greene
D. Brent Baker

Bruce M. Westbrook
W. Austin Mulherin, III
Marcus Edward McDowell

For full biographical listings, see the Martindale-Hubbell Law Directory

LYONS, PIPES & COOK, P.C. (AV)

2 North Royal Street, P.O. Box 2727, 36652-2727
Telephone: 334-432-4481
Cable Address: "Lysea"
Telecopier: 334-433-1820
URL: http://www.LPCLaw.com

Joseph H. Lyons (1874-1957)
William E. Shreve, Jr.
Sam W. Pipes, III (1916-1982)
Kenneth A. Nixon
Walter M. Cook (1915-1988)
Daniel S. Cushing
Wesley Pipes
Allen E. Graham
Norton W. Brooker, Jr.
Michael C. Niemeyer
Cooper C. Thurber
M. Warren Butler
Marion A. Quina, Jr.
S. Wesley Pipes, V
Thomas F. Garth
James D. Jeffries, Jr.
Walter M. Cook, Jr.
Roger E. Cole
W. David Johnson, Jr.
S. Andrew Scharfenberg, Jr
Joseph J. Minus, Jr.
Ginger L. Pierce
Caroline C. McCarthy
Philip A. Stroud

Ryan T. Northrup

General Counsel: Inchcape Shipping Services.
Counsel: The Hertz Corp.; McKenzie Tank Lines, Inc.; SCNO Barge Lines, Inc.; Scott Paper Co.; Shell Oil Corp.
Trial Counsel: Aetna Life & Casualty Co.; Chubb Group of Insurance Companies.

For full biographical listings, see the Martindale-Hubbell Law Directory

Mobile—Continued

SINTZ, CAMPBELL, DUKE & TAYLOR (AV)

3763 Professional Parkway, 36609
Telephone: 334-344-7241
Fax: 334-344-7400

MEMBERS OF FIRM

Peter V. Sintz (1940-1997)
Robert C. Campbell, III
Frank G. Taylor
Steven L. Terry

ASSOCIATES

Wm. Kyle Morris
Kathryn W. Petersen
Barry C. Prine

OF COUNSEL

Leon G. Duke

LEGAL SUPPORT PERSONEL

James A. Koblas

Representative Clients: Aetna C & S Insurance Co.; Mobile County School Board; Auto-Owners Insurance Co.; Argonaut Insurance Co.; Mostellar Medical Clinic; Scottsdale Insurance Co.; American International Group; Alabama School of Math and Science; Mobile County Sheriff's Office.

For full biographical listings, see the Martindale-Hubbell Law Directory

*MONTGOMERY,** Montgomery Co.

BALL, BALL, MATTHEWS & NOVAK, P.A. (AV)

2000 Interstate Park Drive, Suite 204, 36109
Telephone: 334-387-7680
Fax: 334-387-3222
Email: Firm@Ball-Ball.com

Fred S. Ball (1866-1942)
Charles A. Ball (1904-1969)
Fred S. Ball, Jr. (1896-1974)
Richard A. Ball (1906-1983)
John R. Matthews, Jr.
Richard A. Ball, Jr.
Tabor R. Novak, Jr.
Clyde C. Owen, Jr.
C. Winston Sheehan, Jr.
William H. Brittain II
E. Hamilton Wilson, Jr.
Richard E. Broughton
T. Cowin Knowles
Gerald C. Swann, Jr.
Mark T. Davis
James A. Rives

Fred B. Matthews
Allison L. Alford
Michael L. White
Emily C. Marks
Brandy A. Adkins
George R. Parker

LEGAL SUPPORT PERSONNEL

Lon Worley (Office Manager)

Counsel for: Beech Aircraft Corporation; Bell Helicopter Co.; John Deere Co.; Government Employees Insurance Co.; Chubb & Son; Cigna Co.; Chrysler Corp.; Associated Aviation Underwriters.

For full biographical listings, see the Martindale-Hubbell Law Directory

BEASLEY, ALLEN, CROW, METHVIN, PORTIS & MILES, P.C. (AV)

218 Commerce Street, P.O. Box 4160, 36104
Telephone: 334-269-2343
Fax: 334-269-2371
Mailing Address: P.O. Box 4160, 36103-4160
Email: lisa@bwamc.com

Jere Locke Beasley
J. Greg Allen
J. Cole Portis
R. Graham Esdale, Jr.

LaBarron Nelson Boone
Richard D. Morrison
David B. Chancellor
Kendall C. Dunson

For full biographical listings, see the Martindale-Hubbell Law Directory

NIX, HOLTSFORD & VERCELLI, P.C. (AV)

300 A Water Street, Suite 300, P.O. Box 4128, 36103
Telephone: 334-262-2006
Fax: 334-834-3616
Email: NHV@JUNO.COM

H. E. Nix, Jr.
Alex L. Holtsford, Jr.
Charles E. Vercelli, Jr.
Floyd R. Gilliland, Jr.
T. Randall Lyons
Steven A. Higgins
Kenneth A. Hitson, Jr.

David P. Stevens
Todd E. Hughes
Rick A. Howard
Stacy Anne Linn
Jay S. Tuley

LEGAL SUPPORT PERSONNEL

Richard M. Seibert (Firm Manager)
Ashley Collins (Paralegal)
Monica E. Jayroe (Paralegal)
Suzanne H. Long (Legal Assistant)
Kelley S. Tracy (Paralegal)

For full biographical listings, see the Martindale-Hubbell Law Directory

RIGGS & NESMITH, P.A. (AV)

Lawrence Building, 472 South Lawrence Street, P.O. Box 1047, 36101
Telephone: 334-834-6990
Fax: 334-834-4796

Frank W. Riggs
Stephen M. NeSmith

LEGAL SUPPORT PERSONNEL

Patricia P. Williams (Office Manager)

For full biographical listings, see the Martindale-Hubbell Law Directory

THOMAS, MEANS, GILLIS, DEVLIN, ROBINSON & SEAY, P.C. (AV)

3121 Zelda Court, P.O. Drawer 5058, 36103-5058
Telephone: 334-270-1033
Fax: 334-260-9396
Email: tmgpc.lawfirm@tmgpc.com *URL:* http://www.tmgpc.com
Birmingham, Alabama Office: 1035 Financial Center, 505 20th Street North, 35203. Mailing Address: P.O. Box 370447, Birmingham, AL., 35237-0447.
Telephone: 205-328-7915.
Fax: 205-214-6160. E-mail: tmgpc.lawfirm@tmgpc.com. URL: http://www.tmgpc.com
Atlanta, Georgia Office: The Chandler Building, Suite 300, 127 Peachtree Street, N.E., 30303.
Telephone: 404-222-8400.
Fax: 404-222-0080. E-Mail: tmgpc.lawfirm@tmgpc.com. URL: http://www.tmgpc.com

Kenneth L. Thomas (Resident, Birmingham, Alabama Office)
Tyrone C. Means
H. Lewis Gillis
Marvin A. Devlin (Resident, Atlanta, Georgia Office)
Mark E. Robinson (Resident, Atlanta, Georgia Office)
Quinton S. Seay (Resident, Atlanta, Georgia Office)

James L. Richey (Resident, Birmingham, Alabama Office)
Wendell J. Chambliss (Resident, Birmingham Office)
Lisa F. Brown (Resident, Birmingham, Alabama Office)
Valerie L. Acoff (Resident, Birmingham, Alabama Office)
John W. Adams, Jr.
Paul C. Williams
Jennifer D. Odom (Resident, Atlanta, Georgia Office)
Darnell D. Coley
Edward J. Berry (Resident, Birmingham, Alabama Office)
Thaddeus L. Hamilton (Resident, Birmingham, Alabama Office)

LEGAL SUPPORT PERSONNEL

Joyce L. Lehmann
Tonya White
Bryan Palmer
Felicia Kolley
John Baker (Office Administrator)
Cathy Allen
Lakesha Baker
Larry Holmes
Linda Steele
Mary Duncan
Pamela Watkins
Paula Mosely
Rodney Barganier
Tamara Venice
Linda Stoudemier

For full biographical listings, see the Martindale-Hubbell Law Directory

VOLZ, PRESTWOOD & HANAN, P.C. (AV)

350 Adams Avenue, P.O. Box 1910, 36102-1910
Telephone: 334-264-6401
Fax: 334-834-4954

Charles H. Volz, Jr.
Alvin T. Prestwood
Charles H. Volz, III
Ellis D. Hanan
Richard D. Lively
Judy H. Barganier

For full biographical listings, see the Martindale-Hubbell Law Directory

WEBB & ELEY, P.C. (AV)

166 Commerce Street, Suite 300, P.O. Box 238, 36101-0238
Telephone: 334-262-1850
Fax: 334-262-1772
Email: webbeley1@mindspring.com

James W. Webb
Michael M. Eley
Kendrick E. Webb
Craig S. Dillard
Bart Harmon
William R. Chandler

Frank E. Bankston, Jr.
Pamela Robinson Higgins
Shawn Junkins Cole
Michael J. Cohan
Lisa D. Van Wagner

LEGAL SUPPORT PERSONNEL

Janice B. Miller (Business Manager)

Reference: Regions Bank.

For full biographical listings, see the Martindale-Hubbell Law Directory

Montgomery—Continued

FRANK M. WILSON (AV)

201 Monroe Street, 36101
Telephone: 334-263-2555
Fax: 334-263-2533
Email: fmw@zebra.net *URL:* http://www.lawyers.com/fmwilsonlaw

For full biographical listings, see the Martindale-Hubbell Law Directory

*TUSCUMBIA,** Colbert Co.

ASHE, TANNER, WRIGHT & KELLEY, P.C. (AV)

105 West Second Street, P.O. Box 899, 35674
Telephone: 256-383-6357
Telecopier: 256-381-4612

Braxton W. Ashe
J. Michael Tanner
Grant A. Wright
Charles J. Kelley (Resident)

Nickolas J. Steles

For full biographical listings, see the Martindale-Hubbell Law Directory

ALASKA

*ANCHORAGE,** Third Judicial District

DELANEY, WILES, HAYES, GERETY, ELLIS & YOUNG, INC. (AV)

1007 West Third Avenue, Suite 400, 99501
Telephone: 907-279-3581
Fax: 907-277-1331
Email: dwhge@alaska.net

Daniel A. Gerety
Clay A. Young
William E. Moseley
James B. Friderici
Howard A. Lazar
Donald C. Thomas

Timothy J. Lamb

Representative Clients: Crown Equipment Corporation; Ingersoll Rand Co.; J. C. Penney Co.; Gerber Products Co.; Grove Worldwide; Honda Motor Co.; Shasta Industries; Powermatic Inc.; R. D. Werner Co., Inc.; General Motors Corporation.

For Complete List of Firm Personnel, See General Section

For full biographical listings, see the Martindale-Hubbell Law Directory

LAW OFFICES OF ROBERT H. WAGSTAFF (AV)

First National Bank Building, 425 G Street, Suite 610, 99501
Telephone: 907-277-8611
Facsimile: 907-258-7329

For full biographical listings, see the Martindale-Hubbell Law Directory

ARIZONA

*PHOENIX,** Maricopa Co.

BEGAM, LEWIS, MARKS & WOLFE (AV)

A Professional Association of Lawyers
111 West Monroe Street, Suite 1400, 85003-1787
Telephone: 602-254-6071; 1-800-285-0481
Fax: 602-252-0042
Email: blmw@aol.com

Robert G. Begam
Frank Lewis
Stanley J. Marks
Elliot G. Wolfe
Kelly J. McDonald
Daniel J. Adelman
Lisa Kurtz
Dena Rosen Epstein
Steven M. Friedman
Richard P. Traulsen

Serena C. Montague

Reference: National Bank of Arizona.

For full biographical listings, see the Martindale-Hubbell Law Directory

BESS KUNZ, A PROFESSIONAL CORPORATION (AV)

7210 North 16th Street, 85020-5201
Telephone: 602-331-4600
Telecopier: 602-331-8600

Leon D. Bess
Matthew D. Kleifield

Representative Clients: Kelly Springfield Tire Co.; Goodyear Tire and Rubber Co.; Unique Equipment Co., Inc.; Big Tires.

For full biographical listings, see the Martindale-Hubbell Law Directory

RICHARD A. BLACK, P.C. (AV)

125 East Coronado Road, 85004
Telephone: 602-253-4700
Fax: 602-253-8880
Email: rickb627@aol.com

Richard A. Black

For full biographical listings, see the Martindale-Hubbell Law Directory

BONNETT, FAIRBOURN, FRIEDMAN & BALINT, P.C. (AV)

4041 North Central Avenue Suite 1100, 85012
Telephone: 602-274-1100
Fax: 602-274-1199

Jerry C. Bonnett
William G. Fairbourn
Andrew S. Friedman
Francis J. Balint, Jr.
H. Sullivan Bunch
Michael N. Widener
Robert J. Spurlock
C. Kevin Dykstra
Elaine A. Ryan
Tara L. Jackson
Wendy J. Harrison
Scott A. Erickson
Guy A. Hanson
Robert D. Ryan

Christina Bannon
Jason Ebe
Andrew Quinn Everroad
Anthony J. Fernandez
Myndi M. Eakin
Barbara A. Bagdon
David D. Weinzweig
Russell R. Yurk

OF COUNSEL

James Duke Cameron

For full biographical listings, see the Martindale-Hubbell Law Directory

CHARLES M. BREWER, LTD. (AV)

Brewer Building, 5500 North 24th Street, P.O. Box 10720, 85064
Telephone: 602-381-8787
Fax: 602-381-1152

Charles M. Brewer

Luis Pedro Guerra
John Brian Brewer

For full biographical listings, see the Martindale-Hubbell Law Directory

JAMES F. BROOK AND ASSOCIATES (AV)

11024 North 28th Drive, Suite 200, 85029
Telephone: 602-375-0414
Toll Free: 800-322-6170
Fax: 480-874-0506
Email: JFBrook@aol.com *URL:* http://www.lawyers.com/jamesbrook
Mesa, Arizona Office: 1201 South Alma School Road, Suite 14,000. 85210.
Telephone: 480-838-5591.
Fax: 480-874-0506.
Scottsdale, Arizona Office: 7150 East Camelback Road, Suite 415, 85251.
Telephone: 480-990-0104.
Fax: 480-874-0506.
Sun City, Arizona Office: 10451 Palmeras Drive, Suite 211, 85373.
Telephone: 623-972-6824.
Fax: 480-874-0506.

Adam C. E. Davis

For full biographical listings, see the Martindale-Hubbell Law Directory

BURCH & CRACCHIOLO, P.A. (AV)

702 East Osborn Road, Suite 200, 85014
Telephone: 602-274-7611
Fax: 602-234-0341
Mailing Address: P.O. Box 16882, Phoenix, AZ, 85011
Email: library@bcattorneys.com

Ian Neale

Representative Client: Bashas' Inc.

For Complete List of Firm Personnel, See General Section

For full biographical listings, see the Martindale-Hubbell Law Directory

CRONIN & STANEWICH (AV)

One Columbus Plaza, 3636 North Central Avenue, Suite 560, 85012
Telephone: 602-222-4646
Fax: 602-222-4656
Email: cslaw@msn.com

MEMBERS OF FIRM

Robert S. Cronin, Jr.
Robert B. Stanewich

For full biographical listings, see the Martindale-Hubbell Law Directory

Phoenix—Continued

FENNEMORE CRAIG, A PROFESSIONAL CORPORATION (AV)

3003 North Central Avenue, Suite 2600, 85012-2913
Telephone: 602-916-5000
Fax: 602-916-5999
Tucson, Arizona Office: One South Church Avenue, Suite 1000, 85701-1620.
Telephone: 520-879-6800.
Fax: 520-879-6899.

Kenneth J. Sherk
John D. Everroad
William L. Thorpe
Paul J. Mooney
Graeme Hancock
Christopher L. Callahan
Christopher P. Staring
Keith L. Hendricks
Douglas C. Northup

Mark H. Brain
James D. Burgess

LEGAL SUPPORT PERSONNEL

LEGAL ASSISTANTS

Beverly Cooper
Nancy E. Esser
Ann V. Kooi

For Complete List of Firm Personnel, See General Section

For full biographical listings, see the Martindale-Hubbell Law Directory

GOLDSTEIN, MCGRODER & WOODS, LTD. A PROFESSIONAL CORPORATION (AV)

2200 East Camelback Road, Suite 221, 85016-3456
Telephone: 602-957-1500
Fax: 602-956-9294
Email: pmcgroder@aol.com

Philip T. Goldstein
Patrick J. McGroder, III
Grant Woods
Suzanne P. Clarke

Jane E. Evans

LEGAL SUPPORT PERSONNEL

Kevan S. DeWitt (Paralegal)
Karen Kay Rush

For full biographical listings, see the Martindale-Hubbell Law Directory

MCALLISTER & ABROMOVITZ (AV)

2025 North Third Street Suite 100, 85004
Telephone: 602-253-8840
Telefax: 602-253-5526
Email: manda@primenet.com

Michael L. McAllister

Representative Clients: Bridgestone/Firestone, Inc.; Continental General Tire, Inc.; Cooper Tire & Rubber Company; The Dometic Corporation; Goodyear Tire and Rubber Co.; Michelin North America, Inc.; Sears, Roebuck and Co.; Sulzermedica USA, Inc.; Uniroyal Goodrich Tire Company, Inc.; White Consolidated Industries, Inc.; Yokohama Tire Corporation.

For full biographical listings, see the Martindale-Hubbell Law Directory

MUCHMORE & WALLWORK, A PROFESSIONAL CORPORATION (AV)

2700 North Central Avenue, Suite 1225, 85004-1165
Telephone: 602-240-6699
Data: 602-240-6698
Facsimile: 602-240-6697
Email: muchwork@mmww.com *URL:* http://www.mmww.com

Charles J. Muchmore
Nicholas J. Wallwork
Fredric D. Bellamy

SENIOR COUNSEL

Steve Owens

COUNSEL

Bridget S. Bade

Christopher D. Payne
Carolina L. Carver
Margaret Benny Hurst
Mindy K. Brinker

OF COUNSEL

Leslie Kyman Cooper
George H. King

LEGAL SUPPORT PERSONNEL

Gloria A. Torres (Administrator)
James R. Potts (Systems Administrator and Litigation Support Manager)
Gale James (Finance Manager)

Representative Clients: AgrEvo USA Company; BHP Copper, Inc.; Chevron U.S.A., Inc.; Cyprus Amax Minerals Company; Homes by Dave Brown, Inc.; National Indemnity Insurance Company; Standard Insurance Company; Washington Mills Electro Minerals Corporation; Cadbury Beverages, Inc.; Eisenberg Company.

(See Next Column)

For full biographical listings, see the Martindale-Hubbell Law Directory

QUARLES & BRADY LLP (AV)

One Camelback Building, One East Camelback Road, Suite 400, 85012-1649
Telephone: 602-230-5500
Fax: 602-230-5598
URL: http://www.quarles.com
Milwaukee, Wisconsin Office: 411 East Wisconsin Avenue.
Telephone: 414-277-5000.
Fax: 414-271-3552.
Madison, Wisconsin Office: First Wisconsin Plaza, One South Pinckney Street, P.O. Box 2113.
Telephone: 608-251-5000.
Fax: 608-251-9166.
West Palm Beach, Florida Office: 222 Lakeview Avenue, 4th Floor.
Telephone: 407-653-5000.
Fax: 407-653-5333.
Naples, Florida Office: Barnett Center, 4501 Tamiami Trail North, Suite 300.
Telephone: 813-262-5959.
Fax: 813-434-4999.
Chicago, Illinois Office: Quarles & Brady LLC, Citicorp Center, 500 West Madison Street, Suite 3700.
Telephone: 312-715-5000.
Fax: 312-715-5155.

MEMBER OF THE FIRM

Colleen A. Scherkenbach

ASSOCIATE

C. Christine Burns

For full biographical listings, see the Martindale-Hubbell Law Directory

SNELL & WILMER L.L.P. (AV)

One Arizona Center, 85004-2202
Telephone: 602-382-6000
Fax: 602-382-6070
Email: postmaster@snellwilmer.com *URL:* http://www.swlaw.com
Tucson, Arizona Office: One South Church Avenue, Suite 1500, 85701-1612.
Telephone: 520-882-1200.
Fax: 520-884-1294.
Orange County Office: 1920 Main Street, Suite 1200, Irvine, California 92614-7230.
Telephone: 949-253-2700.
Fax: 949-955-2507.
Salt Lake City, Utah Office: 111 East Broadway, Suite 900, 84111-1004.
Telephone: 801-237-1900.
Fax: 801-237-1950.

MEMBERS OF FIRM

Warren E. Platt
Vaughn A. Crawford
Suzanne McCann
Richard W. Shapiro
Alex B. Marconi
Steven S. Guy
Bob J. McCullough
Douglas W. Seitz
Arthur P. Greenfield
Arthur T. Anderson
Timothy G. O'Neill
Martha E. Gibbs
Patrick X. Fowler
Prithviraj S. Sivananthan
Timothy J. Casey

ASSOCIATES

Andrew S. Ashworth
Gretchen N. Smith
Barry C. Toone

Representative Clients: For list of Representative Clients, see end of biographical listings in the Martindale-Hubbell Law Directory.

For Complete List of Firm Personnel, See General Section

For full biographical listings, see the Martindale-Hubbell Law Directory

TUCKER STROHM MILLER & TUCKER, P.C. (AV)

1136 East Campbell, 85014
Telephone: 602-279-3660
Fax: 602-279-2162
Email: rlslaw@worldnet.att.net

Kenneth L. Tucker
Richard L. Strohm
Daniel P. J. Miller
Kevin J. Tucker

For full biographical listings, see the Martindale-Hubbell Law Directory

TUCSON, * Pima Co.

HEALY & STUDWELL LAW FIRM, P.C. (AV)

5210 East Williams Circle Suite 720, 85711
Telephone: 520-790-1400
Fax: 520-790-3212

William T. Healy
James R. Studwell

(See Next Column)

HEALY & STUDWELL LAW FIRM P.C., *Tucson—Continued*

Sean P. Healy

References: Bank of America; Merrill Lynch.

For full biographical listings, see the Martindale-Hubbell Law Directory

KIMBLE, NELSON, AUDILETT, MCDONOUGH & MOLLA, P.C. (AV)

335 North Wilmot Road, Suite 500, 85711
Telephone: 520-748-2440
Fax: 520-748-2469

Darwin J. Nelson
Lawrence McDonough
Daryl A. Audilett
Negatu Molla

OF COUNSEL

William Kimble

Representative Clients: State of Arizona; General Motors Corp.; Procter & Gamble Co.; St. Paul Fire and Marine Insurance Co.; City of Tucson; Tucson Electric Power Co.; United States Fidelity & Guaranty Co.; Coriegis Co.; Allstate Insurance Co.

For full biographical listings, see the Martindale-Hubbell Law Directory

KINERK, BEAL, SCHMIDT & DYER, P.C. (AV)

Suite 6000, West Tower, 5255 East Williams Circle, 85711
Telephone: 520-790-5600
Fax: 520-790-1163
Email: kbs@azstarnet.com *URL:* http://www.azinjurylaw.com

Burton J. Kinerk
Ted A. Schmidt
Robert L. Beal
James H. Dyer
Colleen L. Kinerk

Karl R. Lautz
David W. Babcock

For full biographical listings, see the Martindale-Hubbell Law Directory

RABINOVITZ & ASSOCIATES, P.C. (AV)

721 North 4th Avenue, P.O. Box 41600, 85717
Telephone: 520-624-5526
Toll Free: 1-800-365-0821
Fax: 520-622-3776

Bernard I. Rabinovitz

John D. Ellis

LEGAL SUPPORT PERSONNEL

Michael Nielson (Paralegal)
Lisa Busciglio (Paralegal)
Ruth Polizzi (Paralegal)

Representative Client: Firemans Fund Insurance Co.

For full biographical listings, see the Martindale-Hubbell Law Directory

STOMPOLY, STROUD, GLICKSMAN & ERICKSON, P.C. (AV)

1820 Norwest Tower, One South Church Avenue, 85702
Telephone: 520-628-8300
Telefax: 520-628-9948
Mailing Address: P.O. Box 190, Tucson, AZ, 85702-0190

John G. Stompoly

For Complete List of Firm Personnel, See General Section

For full biographical listings, see the Martindale-Hubbell Law Directory

*YUMA,** Yuma Co.

THE BRIAN E. SMITH LAW FIRM (AV)

The Brian Smith Building, 301 South 2nd Avenue, 85364
Telephone: 520-783-8811
Fax: 520-782-2018

Brian E. Smith
William J. Kerekes
Frank A. Fila

LEGAL SUPPORT PERSONNEL

Briget M. Marquez

Reference: Bank of America.

For full biographical listings, see the Martindale-Hubbell Law Directory

ARKANSAS

*ARKADELPHIA,** Clark Co.

WRIGHT, CHANEY, BERRY, DANIEL, SLAUGHTER & HUGHES, P.A. (AV)

303 Professional Park Drive, P.O. Drawer 947, 71923
Telephone: 501-246-6796
Telefax: 501-246-2178
Email: dchaney@arklaw.com *URL:* http://www.arklaw.com

William G. Wright
LeAnne Daniel
Donald P. Chaney, Jr.
Eric G. Hughes
Travis R. Berry
Edward M. Slaughter
Rodney Moore

Counsel for: Elk Horn Bank and Trust Co.; Farm Bureau Mutual Insurance Company of Arkansas, Inc.; Southern Farm Bureau Casualty Insurance Co.; Underwriters Adjustment Co.; Nationwide Insurance Co.; Central Production Credit Assn.; Shelter Insurance Co.; Colonial Insurance Co.
Approved Attorneys for: Farmers Home Administration; American Title Insurance Co.

For full biographical listings, see the Martindale-Hubbell Law Directory

*FAYETTEVILLE,** Washington Co.

DAVIS, COX & WRIGHT, PLC (AV)

19 East Mountain Street, P.O. Drawer 1688, 72702-1688
Telephone: 501-521-7600
Fax: 501-521-7661
Email: daviscoxwright@dcw-plc.com *URL:* http://www.dcw-plc.com

Sidney P. Davis, Jr.
Kelly P. Carithers
Walter B. Cox
Don A. Taylor
Tilden P. Wright, III
Paul H. Taylor
Constance G. Clark
John G. Trice
William Jackson Butt, II
Laura J. Andress

Mark W. Dossett
S. Lance Cox
Robin Miller

Representative Clients: Kawasaki Motors Corp.; New United Motors Manufacturing, Inc.; Tokio Marine Claims Services; Toyota Motor Sales.

For full biographical listings, see the Martindale-Hubbell Law Directory

*FORT SMITH,** Sebastian Co.

GILBREATH LAW FIRM (AV)

605 South 21st Street, 72901
Telephone: 501-782-7770
Fax: 501-782-9288
Email: attysatlaw@aol.com *URL:* http://www.lawyers.com/gilbreathlawfirm

E. C. Gilbreath
Daniel W. Gilbreath

For full biographical listings, see the Martindale-Hubbell Law Directory

LEDBETTER, COGBILL, ARNOLD & HARRISON, LLP (AV)

622 Parker Avenue, P.O. Box 185, 72902-0185
Telephone: 501-782-7294
Fax: 501-782-1493

MEMBERS OF FIRM

Charles R. Ledbetter
Ronald D. Harrison
J. Michael Cogbill
E. Diane Graham
James A. Arnold, II
R. Ray Fulmer, II

ASSOCIATES

Rebecca D. Hattabaugh
Virginia C. Trammell
Daniel A. Stewart

Representative Clients: General: First National Bank of Fort Smith; Bank of Mansfield; Commercial Bank at Alma.
Local Attorneys for: Liberty Mutual Insurance Co.; St Paul Insurance Cos.; Black & Decker Inc.; Overhead Door Corp.; Coltec Industries, Inc.; A.W. Chesterton Co..

For full biographical listings, see the Martindale-Hubbell Law Directory

WARNER, SMITH & HARRIS, PLC (AV)

214 North Sixth Street, P.O. Box 1626, 72901
Telephone: 501-782-6041
Fax: 501-782-0841

Harry Preston Warner (1885-1969)
C. Wayne Harris
Gerald L. DeLung
Cecil Randolph Warner (1890-1955)
Patrick Neill Moore
Lillard Cody Hayes
Thomas G. Graves (1939-1971)
G. Alan Wooten
Douglas O. Smith, Jr.
James Melvin Dunn

(See Next Column)

WARNER, SMITH & HARRIS PLC—*Continued*

John Alan Lewis
Joel D. Johnson
J. Randall McGinnis
Kathryn Stocks Campbell
R. Gregory Aclin

Jason Trevor Browning
Matthew C. Carter

OF COUNSEL

C. R. Warner, Jr.

District Attorneys for: Burlington Northern Railroad Co.
Counsel for: Sparks Regional Medical Center.
Local Counsel for: Planters Division, Nabisco Brands, Inc.; Gerber Products Co.; Aetna Group; Fireman's Fund-American Insurance Cos.; Hiram Walker & Sons, Inc.; Continental National American Group.

For full biographical listings, see the Martindale-Hubbell Law Directory

*LITTLE ROCK,** Pulaski Co.

ANDERSON, MURPHY & HOPKINS, L.L.P. (AV)

400 West Capitol Avenue, Suite 2640, 72201
Telephone: 501-372-1887
Fax: 501-372-7706
Email: ande@att.net

MEMBERS OF FIRM

Overton S. Anderson, II
Randy P. Murphy
Mariam T. Hopkins

ASSOCIATE

Michael P. Vanderford

For full biographical listings, see the Martindale-Hubbell Law Directory

BARBER, MCCASKILL, JONES & HALE, P.A. (AV)

2700 Regions Center, 400 West Capitol Avenue, 72201-3414
Telephone: 501-372-6175
Telecopier: 501-375-2802

Azro L. Barber (1885-1979)
Elbert A. Henry (1889-1966)
John B. Thurman (1912-1971)
Austin McCaskill, Sr.
Glenn W. Jones
Michael E. Hale
John S. Cherry, Jr.
Robert L. Henry, III
Micheal L. Alexander
William H. Edwards, Jr.
G. Spence Fricke
Gail Ponder Gaines
Michael J. Emerson
R. Kenny McCulloch
Tim A. Cheatham
Joseph F. Kolb
Scott Michael Strauss
Baucum Fulk
D. Keith Fortner
Wendy Scholtens Wood
Morris L. Williams, III
Michelle Bass Miller

Attorneys for: Associated Aviation Underwriters; CIGNA Insurance Group; CNA Insurance Company; Fireman's Fund Insurance Co.; General Motors Corp.; Hanover Insurance Co.; Royal Insurance; Tokio Marine & Fire Insurance Group; Universal Underwriters Insurance Co.

For full biographical listings, see the Martindale-Hubbell Law Directory

DUNCAN & RAINWATER TRIAL LAWYERS A PROFESSIONAL ASSOCIATION (AV)

6315 Ranch Drive, 72221-5938
Telephone: 501-228-7600
Fax: 501-228-7664
URL: http://www.lawyers.com/duncanandrainwater
Email: duncanlaw@aristotle.net *URL:* http://www.duncan-rainwater.com

Phillip J. Duncan (P.A.)
Michael R. Rainwater
Neil Ray Chamberlin
Michelle Banks Odum
J. Stephen Holt

For full biographical listings, see the Martindale-Hubbell Law Directory

HUCKABAY, MUNSON, ROWLETT & TILLEY, P.A. (AV)

Regions Center, Suite 1900, 400 West Capitol, 72201
Telephone: 501-374-6535
Fax: 501-374-5906

Mike Huckabay
Bruce E. Munson
Beverly A. Rowlett
James W. Tilley
John E. Moore
Tim Boone
Rick Runnells
Sarah Ann Presson
D. Michael Huckabay, Jr.
Carol Lockard Worley
Mark S. Breeding

Elizabeth Fletcher Rogers
Julia L. Busfield
Jane M. Yocum
Terry D. Dugger

Representative Clients: The B.F. Goodrich Co.; Federal Cartridge Co.; General Electric Co.; Hayes Wheels; Massey-Ferguson, Inc.; Varity Corp.; Morbark Industries; Sears Roebuck & Co.; Teva Pharmaceuticals USA, Inc.; U-Haul International.

For full biographical listings, see the Martindale-Hubbell Law Directory

KILPATRICK, AUD & WILLIAMS, L.L.P. (AV)

Regions Center, 400 West Capitol Avenue, Suite 1910, 72201-4849
Telephone: 501-372-0401
Facsimile: 501-372-5277

Joseph E. Kilpatrick, Jr.
Michael E. Aud
Aylmer Gene Williams

For full biographical listings, see the Martindale-Hubbell Law Directory

ROSE LAW FIRM, A PROFESSIONAL ASSOCIATION (AV)

120 East Fourth Street, 72201
Telephone: 501-375-9131
Telecopy: 501-375-1309

David L. Williams
Richard T. Donovan
Amy Lee Stewart
Michael G. Smith
Kathryn Bennett Perkins
Michael N. Shannon

COUNSEL

Phillip Carroll

Jennifer B. Hendren

Counsel for: ALLTEL Corporation; Aluminum Company of America; Bridgestone/Firestone, Inc.; The Equitable Life Assurance Society of The United States; General Motors Corp.; The Prudential Insurance Company of America; Stephens Group Inc.; Tyson Foods, Inc.

For Complete List of Firm Personnel, See General Section

For full biographical listings, see the Martindale-Hubbell Law Directory

*TEXARKANA,** Miller Co.

DUNN, NUTTER, MORGAN & SHAW (AV)

State Line Plaza, 6th Floor, P.O. Box 8030, 71854-5945
Telephone: 870-773-5651
Texas Telephone: 903-793-5651
Telecopier: 870-772-2037
Email: lawfirm@dnms.com *URL:* http://www.dnms.com

MEMBERS OF FIRM

Winford L. Dunn, Jr.
R. Gary Nutter
Nelson V. Shaw
R. David Freeze
W. David Carter

ASSOCIATES

Jeff M. Addison
Adam O. Fellows

LEGAL SUPPORT PERSONNEL

LEGAL ASSISTANTS

Myra Conaway Wells
Sonja L. Oliver

For Complete List of Firm Personnel, See General Section

For full biographical listings, see the Martindale-Hubbell Law Directory

WEST MEMPHIS, Crittenden Co.

RIEVES & MAYTON (AV)

304 East Broadway, P.O. Box 1359, 72303
Telephone: 870-735-3420
Telecopier: 870-735-4678
Email: rieves.mayton@worldnet.att.net
Little Rock, Arkansas Office: Suite 1719, First Commercial Building, 400 West Capitol.
Telephone: 501-376-0504.
Telecopier: 501-372-3482.

MEMBERS OF FIRM

Elton A. Rieves, Jr. (1909-1984)
Elton A. Rieves, III
Michael R. Mayton
Elton A. Rieves, IV

ASSOCIATES

David S. Wilson, III
Eric Newkirk

For full biographical listings, see the Martindale-Hubbell Law Directory

CALIFORNIA

ALAMO, Contra Costa Co.

LAW OFFICES OF DAVID M. BIRKA-WHITE (AV)

3240 Stone Valley Road West, Suite 102, 94507
Telephone: 925-838-2090
Facsimile: 925-362-9911
Email: d.birka-white@bending-weil.com *URL:* http://www.lawyers.com/birka-white

For full biographical listings, see the Martindale-Hubbell Law Directory

*BAKERSFIELD,** Kern Co.

BORTON, PETRINI & CONRON, LLP (AV)

The Borton, Petrini & Conron Building, 1600 Truxtun Avenue, 93301
Telephone: 661-322-3051
Voice Mail: 661-395-6700
Fax: 661-322-4628
Mailing Address: P.O. Box 2026, Bakersfield, California, 93303
Email: bpcbak@bpclaw.com *URL:* http://www.bpclaw.com
Other City Locations: Fresno, Los Angeles, Modesto, Redding, Sacramento, San Bernardino, San Diego, San Francisco, San Jose, San Luis Obispo, Santa Ana and Ventura.

MEMBERS OF FIRM

Richard E. Hitchcock
John F. Petrini
Richard E. Morton
Calvin R. Stead
Victoria R. Allard-Bernhardt

ASSOCIATES

Richard D. Brown
Dee H. Stasnopolis
Timothy B. Liebaert

For Complete List of Firm Personnel, See General Section

For full biographical listings, see the Martindale-Hubbell Law Directory

EMERYVILLE, Alameda Co.

BISHOP, BARRY, HOWE, HANEY & RYDER, A PROFESSIONAL CORPORATION (AV)

Watergate Tower III, 2000 Powell Street, Suite 1425, 94608
Telephone: 510-596-0888
Fax: 510-596-0899
Email: FirmGeneral@BBHHR.com
San Francisco Office: 44 Montgomery Street, Suite 1300, 94104.
Telephone: 415-421-8550.

Ross R. Ryder (1940-1989)
Nelson C. Barry
Drayton F. Howe, Jr.
Jeffrey N. Haney
Thomas O. Haran
Rebecca B. Aherne
Michael W. Bolechowski
Mark C. Raskoff
Patricia S. Lakner
Gregory R. de la Peña

J. Scott Wood
Mitchell J. Alward
Marco R. Sumarriva
Jane E. Carey
Carol L. Healey
Mary Margaret Ryan
Thomas Edward Foran
John F. Cooke
Jean H. Hurricane
Daniel M. O'Connell
Lisa S. Wiggins
Edward M. Lai

OF COUNSEL

Lawrence S. Molton
David P. Osako

Reference: Golden Gate Bank.

For full biographical listings, see the Martindale-Hubbell Law Directory

ENCINO, Los Angeles Co.

STEPHEN H. HELLER A PROFESSIONAL CORPORATION (AV)

16830 Ventura Boulevard, Suite B, 91436-1714
Telephone: 818-995-4646
Fax: 818-995-0668
Email: stephenheller@hellerlaw.net

Stephen H. Heller

For full biographical listings, see the Martindale-Hubbell Law Directory

*FRESNO,** Fresno Co.

MILES, SEARS & EANNI, A PROFESSIONAL CORPORATION (AV)

2844 Fresno Street, P.O. Box 1432, 93716
Telephone: 559-486-5200
Fax: 559-486-5240
Email: mse@good.attitude.com

Wm. M. Miles (1909-1991)
Robert E. Sears (1918-1992)
Carmen A. Eanni
Richard C. Watters
William J. Seiler
Douglas L. Gordon

For full biographical listings, see the Martindale-Hubbell Law Directory

GARDENA, Los Angeles Co.

McGARRY & LAUFENBERG (AV)

1125 West 190th Street, Suite 230, 90248
Telephone: 310-380-1650
Fax: 310-380-1662
Email: jjmjjlaw@aol.com

MEMBERS OF FIRM

James J. McGarry
Jeffrey J. Laufenberg
William Leamon Cummings
John E. Zegel

For full biographical listings, see the Martindale-Hubbell Law Directory

GOLD RIVER, Sacramento Co.

HACKARD, HOLT & HELLER (AV)

11335 Gold Express Drive, Suite 155, 95670
Telephone: 916-853-3000
Facsimile: 916-853-3010
Email: tholt@hackardlaw.com *URL:* http://www.hackardlaw.com

MEMBERS OF FIRM

Michael A. Hackard
Theodore J. Holt

OF COUNSEL

Steven M. Heller
Paige M. Hibbert

ASSOCIATES

David R. Zarka
Jenny M. Fickel
Eric L. Graves
Gregory W. Bayless

For full biographical listings, see the Martindale-Hubbell Law Directory

IRVINE, Orange Co.

SNELL & WILMER L.L.P. (AV)

1920 Main Street, Suite 1200, 92614-7230
Telephone: 949-253-2700
FAX: 949-955-2507
URL: http://www.swlaw.com
Phoenix, Arizona Office: One Arizona Center, 85004-2202.
Telephone: 602-382-6000.
Fax: 602-382-6070.
Tucson, Arizona Office: One South Church Avenue, Suite 1500, 85701-1630.
Telephone: 520-882-1200.
Fax: 520-884-1294.
Salt Lake City, Utah Office: 111 East Broadway, Suite 900, 84111-1004.
Telephone: 801-237-1900.
Fax: 801-237-1950.

MEMBERS OF FIRM

Robert J. Gibson
Arthur P. Greenfield
Gary A. Wolensky
Randolph T. Moore
Luke A. Torres
Ellen L. Darling
Alexander L. Conti

ASSOCIATES

John A. Chatowski
Daniel S. Rodman
Yvonne A. Yung

Representative Clients: For list of Representative Clients, see end of biographical listings in the Martindale-Hubbell Law Directory.

For Complete List of Firm Personnel, See General Section

For full biographical listings, see the Martindale-Hubbell Law Directory

LAGUNA HILLS, Orange Co.

STANTON T. MATHEWS & ASSOCIATES, A LAW CORP. (AV)

24012 Calle de la Plata, Suite 320, 92653
Telephone: 949-586-2235
Email: Triallaw@flash.net
Email: stm@injurytriallaw.com *URL:* http://www.injurytriallaw.com

Stanton T. Mathews

Paul W. Ralph
Ronald B. Funk

LEGAL SUPPORT PERSONNEL

PARALEGAL/ADMINISTRATOR

Sharing Garrett-Anderson

LEGAL ASSISTANT

Cheri C. Wickam

For full biographical listings, see the Martindale-Hubbell Law Directory

LARKSPUR, Marin Co.

WEINBERG, HOFFMAN, CASEY & ROPERS (AV)

A Partnership including a Professional Corporation
900 Larkspur Landing Circle, Suite 155, 94939
Telephone: 415-461-9666
Fax: 415-461-9681

Ivan Weinberg
Joseph Hoffman
A. Michael Casey
Mark Ropers

For full biographical listings, see the Martindale-Hubbell Law Directory

LONG BEACH, Los Angeles Co.

FORD, WALKER, HAGGERTY & BEHAR, PROFESSIONAL LAW CORPORATION (AV)

One World Trade Center, Twenty Seventh Floor, 90831
Telephone: 562-983-2500
Telecopier: 562-983-2555
Email: FWHB@FWHB.COM

(See Next Column)

FORD, WALKER, HAGGERTY & BEHAR PROFESSIONAL LAW CORPORATION—*Continued*

G. Richard Ford
Timothy L. Walker
William C. Haggerty
Jeffrey S. Behar
Mark Steven Hennings
Donna Rogers Kirby
Tina Ivankovic Mangarpan
Joseph A. Heath
Robert J. Chavez
James D. Savage
Patrick J. Gibbs
Robert Reisinger

Arthur W. Schultz
Jon T. Moseley
Maxine J. Lebowitz
Timothy P. McDonald
K. Michele Williams
Stephen Ward Moore
James O. Miller
Stanley L. Scarlett
Scott A. Ritsema
Colleen A. Deziel
Thomas L. Gourdé
Patrick J. Stark
Shayne L. Wulterin
Charles J. Schmitt
John A. Haughton
Kristen C. Vine
Joel E. D. Odou
Christopher L. Mass
Robert Montes, Jr.
Alison S. Mathews
Tatia M. Tokunaga
Mark F. Wendorff
Anneke Joan Stewart
Pamela J. Paluga

OF COUNSEL

Theodore P. Shield, P.L.C.

For full biographical listings, see the Martindale-Hubbell Law Directory

STOLPMAN • KRISSMAN • ELBER • MANDEL & KATZMAN LLP (AV)

A Limited Liability Partnership
Nineteenth Floor, 111 West Ocean Boulevard, 90802-4649
Telephone: 562-435-8300
Telecopier: 562-435-8304
Email: stolpman@ix.netcom.com
Los Angeles (Westwood), California Office: Suite 1800, 10880 Wilshire Boulevard.

MEMBERS OF FIRM

Thomas G. Stolpman
Leonard H. Mandel
Bernard Katzman (Inc.)
Joel Krissman
Mary Nielsen Abbott
Donna Silver
Dennis M. Elber

ASSOCIATES

Edwin Silver
Elaine Mandel
Michael L. Luboviski

For full biographical listings, see the Martindale-Hubbell Law Directory

WISE, WIEZOREK, TIMMONS & WISE, A PROFESSIONAL CORPORATION (AV)

3700 Santa Fe Avenue, Suite 300, P.O. Box 2190, 90801-2190
Telephone: 310-834-5028; 562-595-5318
Fax: 310-834-8018
URL: http://www.wwtw.com
Redding, California Office: 292 Hemsted Drive, Suite 101.
Telephone: 530-221-7632.
Fax: 530-221-8832.

George E. Wise
Duane H. Timmons
Anthony F. Wiezorek
Susan E. Anderson Wise
Michael J. Pearce
Mark C. Allen, III
Richard P. Dieffenbach
Steven C. Rice
Stephen M. Smith
Thomas J. Yocis
James M. Cox
Mathew J. Vande Wydeven

Susan Graham

For full biographical listings, see the Martindale-Hubbell Law Directory

WOOLLEY RUSSELL & JOHNSON (AV)

444 West Ocean Boulevard, Suite 1700, 90802
Telephone: 562-495-6000
Telecopier: 562-435-1359
Email: mail@transportlawyers.com *URL:* http://www.transportlawyers.com
Port Hueneme, California Office: 105 East Port Hueneme Road, 93041.
Telephone: 562-495-6000.
Fax: 562-435-1359.

MEMBERS OF FIRM

David E. R. Woolley
Thomas A. Russell
Philip L. Johnson

ASSOCIATE

Thomas G. Walsh

LEGAL SUPPORT PERSONNEL

PARALEGAL

Dawn C. Breaux

For full biographical listings, see the Martindale-Hubbell Law Directory

*LOS ANGELES,** Los Angeles Co.

BAUM, HEDLUND, ARISTEI, GUILFORD & DOWNEY, A PROFESSIONAL CORPORATION (AV)

Suite 950, 12100 Wilshire Boulevard, 90025
Telephone: 310-207-3233; 800-827-0087
Facsimile: 310-820-7444
Email: bhagd@bhagd.com *URL:* http://www.bhagd.com
Washington, D.C. Office: 1250 24th Street, N.W., Suite 300.
Telephone: 202-466-0513; 800-827-0097.
Facsimile: 202-466-0527.

Michael L. Baum
Paul J. Hedlund
J. Clark Aristei
Robert E. Guilford
William J. Downey III (1947-1999)

John A. Greaves
Cara J. Luther (Resident, Washington, D.C. Office)
Robert F. Foss
Karen A. Barth

OF COUNSEL

Goerge W. Murgatroyd III
Mary F. Schiavo (Not admitted in CA)

Reference: Union Bank.

For full biographical listings, see the Martindale-Hubbell Law Directory

BELCHER, HENZIE & BIEGENZAHN, A PROFESSIONAL CORPORATION (AV)

333 South Hope Street, Suite 3650, 90071-1479
Telephone: 213-624-8293
Telecopier: 213-576-9964

Frank B. Belcher (1891-1979)
Leo J. Biegenzahn (1926-1996)
David Bernard (1931-1978)
John S. Curtis
E. Lee Horton
William T. DelHagen
Julia Azrael
Jeffrey L. Horwith
Raymond E. Hane, III

Georgette Renata Herget
John Erin McOsker
Paul R. Flaherty
Ian C. Fusselman
Jeffrey D. Wolf
Debby Lynne Zajac

OF COUNSEL

George M. Henzie

Reference: Bank of America (Los Angeles Main Office).

For full biographical listings, see the Martindale-Hubbell Law Directory

BERGMAN, WEDNER & DACEY, INC. (AV)

Suite 900, 10880 Wilshire Boulevard, 90024
Telephone: 310-470-6110
Fax: 310-474-0931
Email: ofc@bergman-wedner.com *URL:* http://www.bergman-wedner.com

Gregory M. Bergman
Gregory A. Wedner
John P. Dacey
Alan Harvey Mittelman
Robert M. Mason III
Kristi Anne Sjoholm-Sierchio
John V. Tamborelli

Lisa S. Newnan
Daphne M. Humphreys
Michele M. Goldsmith
Denise G. Godfrey
William Daryl Strickland
Pamela R. Fleming
Matthew R. Hicks
Jorge J. Luna
Paul V. Rayburn
Mark W. Waterman

OF COUNSEL

Lloyd A. Bergman (1923-1994)
Jacob A. Wedner
Marvin Goldsmith
Mark K. Kitabayashi

SPECIAL COUNSEL

Richard V. Godino

For full biographical listings, see the Martindale-Hubbell Law Directory

BIREN & KATZMAN (AV)

815 Moraga Drive (Bel Air), 90049-1633
Telephone: 310-476-3031; 381-5609
Fax: 310-471-3165
Email: birenkatzman@biren.com *URL:* http://www.biren.com

Matthew B. F. Biren
Marc J. Katzman

Debra J. Tauger
Charles E. Koro

Reference: City National Bank (Beverly Hills Branch).

For full biographical listings, see the Martindale-Hubbell Law Directory

Los Angeles—Continued

CLARK & TREVITHICK, A PROFESSIONAL CORPORATION (AV)

800 Wilshire Boulevard, 12th Floor, 90017
Telephone: 213-629-5700
Telecopier: 213-624-9441
Email: postmaster@clarktrev.com
San Francisco, California Office: 456 Montgomery Street, 20th Floor.
Telephone: 415-288-6520.
Fax: 415-398-2820.

Philip W. Bartenetti
Leonard Brazil
Vincent Tricarico
Arturo Santana Jr.

For Complete List of Firm Personnel, See General Section

For full biographical listings, see the Martindale-Hubbell Law Directory

GIRARDI AND KEESE (AV)

1126 Wilshire Boulevard, 90017-1904
Telephone: 213-977-0211
FAX: 213-481-1554
San Bernardino, California Office: 155 West Hospitality Lane, Suite 260.
Telephone: 909-381-1551.
FAX: 909-381-2566.

MEMBERS OF FIRM

Thomas V. Girardi
Robert M. Keese
John A. Girardi
James B. Kropff
Robert W. Finnerty
James G. O'Callahan
V. Andre Rekte (Resident, San Bernardino Office)
John K. Courtney
Amy Fisch Solomon
Thomas C. Morgan
David N. Bigelow
Carrie J. Rognlien
David R. Lira
John Alan Roberts
Shane M. Emerson Coons
Amanda L. McClintock

ASSOCIATE

Jennifer M. Ingram

References: Wells Fargo Bank (Los Angeles Head Office); Comerica Bank.

For full biographical listings, see the Martindale-Hubbell Law Directory

GORDON, EDELSTEIN, KREPACK, GRANT, FELTON & GOLDSTEIN (AV)

Suite 1800, 3580 Wilshire Boulevard, 90010
Telephone: 213-739-7000; 213-487-1520
Fax: 213-386-1671
Email: geklaw.com

Roger L. Gordon
Mark Edelstein
Howard D. Krepack
Sherry E. Grant
Richard I. Felton
Irwin L. Goldstein
Steven J. Kleifield
David A. Goldstein

OF COUNSEL

Joshua M. Merliss

ASSOCIATES

Eugenia L. Steele
Vincent F. Bennett
Adam D. Dombchik
Jennifer S. Weisman

For full biographical listings, see the Martindale-Hubbell Law Directory

IVERSON, YOAKUM, PAPIANO & HATCH (AV)

One Wilshire Building, 27th Floor 624 South Grand Avenue, 90017
Telephone: 213-624-7444
Telecopier: 213-629-4563

Paul E. Iverson (1907-1975)
Frank B. Yoakum, Jr. (1906-1991)

MEMBERS OF FIRM

Patrick M. Mc Adam
Arnold D. Larson
John M. Garrick

ASSOCIATES

Douglas C. Pease
Andrew K. Doty
Melissa A. Immel
Mary P. Lightfoot
Mark Pearson
Adam F. Burke
Scott A. Horton

OF COUNSEL

R. Noel Hatch

Representative Clients: Lockheed Corp.; International Paper; Bridgestone/-Firestone, Inc.
Reference: Bank of America (Los Angeles Head Office).

For Complete List of Firm Personnel, See General Section

For full biographical listings, see the Martindale-Hubbell Law Directory

KERN & GONZALEZ, A PROFESSIONAL CORPORATION (AV)

601 West 5th Street, Suite 1100, 90071
Telephone: 213-629-8100
Facsimile: 213-627-8765
URL: http://www.kernlaw.net

(See Next Column)

René J. Kern, Jr.
Michael D. Gonzalez
Tina L. Gentile

Christina L. Young
Angela J. Armitage
Michele Marsh
Cynthia L. Filla
David G. Hoiles, Jr.
Michele Sherer Ancheta
Sue S. Kim
Gail S. Taningco

Representative Clients: Bridgestone/Firestone, Inc.; Dahlgren U.S.A., Inc.; Honda Motor Company, Ltd.; Makita Corporation.

For full biographical listings, see the Martindale-Hubbell Law Directory

KNOPFLER & ROBERTSON, LLP (AV)

Suite 500, 21650 Oxnard Street (Woodland Hills), 91367
Telephone: 818-227-0770; 213-624-1111
Telefax: 818-227-0777
Irvine, California Office: 19800 MacArthur Boulevard, Suite 270, 92612.
Telephone: 714-261-6191.
Pleasanton, California Office: 400 Main Street, Suite 204, 94566.
Telephone: 510-425-7250.
Las Vegas, Nevada Office: Knopfler & Robertson in Association with Broom & Vaisbort, LLP, 3753 Howard Hughes Parkway, Suite 200, 89109.
Telephone: 702-792-2413.
Camarillo, California Office: 1200 Paseo, Suite 170, 93010.
Telephone: 805-482-1903; 800-CONDOLAW.
Fax: 805-484-5917.

George Knopfler
Alexander Robertson, IV
Deborah Broom
Richard A. Capella
Jonathan S. Vick
Edward D. Vaisbort
William G. Kelsberg

OF COUNSEL

Scott C. Haith
James P. Lingl (Resident, Camarillo Office)
Christina S. Robertson

Janice M. Michaels
James M. Pazos
Mark Rohrer
Craig Smith
Robert Nation
William S. Dunlevy (Resident, Camarillo Office)
Scott A. Hunter

For full biographical listings, see the Martindale-Hubbell Law Directory

KUSSMAN & WHITEHILL (AV)

A Partnership including a Professional Corporation
Suite 1470, 10866 Wilshire Boulevard, 90024
Telephone: 310-474-4411
Fax: 310-474-6530

Russell S. Kussman (A Professional Corporation)
Michael H. Whitehill

For full biographical listings, see the Martindale-Hubbell Law Directory

LEBOVITS & DAVID, A PROFESSIONAL CORPORATION (AV)

1880 Century Park East Suite 900, 90067
Telephone: 310-277-0200
Fax: 310-552-1028
Email: mlld@msn.com *URL:* http://www.lawyers.com/lebovits&david

Moses Lebovits
Deborah A. David
Kristal M. Bowman

Reference: Imperial Bank (Main Office - Beverly Hills).

For full biographical listings, see the Martindale-Hubbell Law Directory

ROBERT L. LUTY A PROFESSIONAL CORPORATION (AV)

11999 San Vicente Boulevard, Suite 340, 90049
Telephone: 310-472-7166
Fax: 310-472-6229
Email: robert@robertlluty.com *URL:* http://www.lawyers.com/lutylaw

Robert L. Luty

Reference: Brentwood Savings Bank (Brentwood Branch).

For full biographical listings, see the Martindale-Hubbell Law Directory

MCKAY, BYRNE & GRAHAM (AV)

3250 Wilshire Boulevard, Suite 603, 90010
Telephone: 213-386-6900
Fax: 213-381-1762
Email: mbg@mbglaw.com

John P. McKay
Michael A. Byrne
Robert L. Graham
Mark G. Cunningham
Paul A. de Lorimier

(See Next Column)

McKay, Byrne & Graham—*Continued*

Jeffrey Cabot Myers
Debra Ellwood Meppen
Dawn M. Flores-Oster
April Paradise
Gabriela Escudero Goldberg
Nancy A. Ramsey

OF COUNSEL

Gail D. Solo (A Professional Corporation)

For full biographical listings, see the Martindale-Hubbell Law Directory

Law Offices of Carl A. McMahan (AV)

827 Moraga Drive (Bel Air), 90049
Telephone: 310-472-8078
Fax: 310-472-7014
Email: camcmahan@earthlink.net *URL:* http://www.lawyers.com/mcmahan

OF COUNSEL

Peter J. McNulty

Reference: City National Bank, Beverly Hills, California.

For full biographical listings, see the Martindale-Hubbell Law Directory

Robinson, Di Lando & Whitaker, A Professional Law Corporation (AV)

800 Wilshire Boulevard Suite 1100, 90017-2687
Telephone: 213-229-0100
Facsimile: 213-229-0114
Email: rdwlaw@gte.net
San Francisco, California Office: 417 Montgomery Street, Suite 910. 94104.
Telephone: 415-391-9475.
Fax: 415-391-3799.

Michael C. Robinson, Jr.
Michael A. Di Lando
Ronald S. Whitaker
Jack M. Liebhaber
Timothy L. Salazar

Steve H. Yu
Mark Kane
Cynthia A. Goodman
Bradley R. Blamires
Farzad Tabatabai
Martin J. Mendoza
David K. Stewart
Michelle B. Dykstra
Charles H. Brown, II
Michael B. Wilk

For full biographical listings, see the Martindale-Hubbell Law Directory

Schlothauer & Collins (AV)

11999 San Vicente Boulevard, Suite 340, 90049
Telephone: 310-472-1670
Fax: 310-472-5270
Affiliated San Jose California Office: Collins & Schlothauer, 60 South Market Street, Suite 1100, 95113-2204.
Telephone: 408-298-5161.
Fax: 408-297-5766.

PARTNER

Thomas L. Schlothauer

OF COUNSEL

Mark Scott Collins

For full biographical listings, see the Martindale-Hubbell Law Directory

Stone, Dolginer & Wenzel, A Law Corporation (AV)

6500 Wilshire Boulevard Suite 2060, 90048
Telephone: 323-653-2244
Fax: 323-658-1155
Email: sdwlaw@aol.com *URL:* http://www.lawyers.com/sdwfirm

Robert N. Stone
Charles I. Dolginer
Mark D. Wenzel

Henry N. Seligsohn

OF COUNSEL

A. J. Connick Doran

Reference: Union Bank (Head Office, 900 South Main Street, Los Angeles).

For full biographical listings, see the Martindale-Hubbell Law Directory

Wolf, Rifkin & Shapiro, LLP (AV)

A Partnership including a Professional Corporation
11400 West Olympic Boulevard Ninth Floor, 90064-1565
Telephone: 310-478-4100
Fax: 310-479-1422
Email: wrs@wrslawyers.com
Las Vegas, Nevada Office: Schulman & Grode, LLP, 2255-A Renaissance Drive 89119.
Telephone: 702-341-5200.
Fax: 702-341-5300.

(See Next Column)

MEMBERS OF FIRM

Michael Wolf (A Professional Corporation)
Daniel C. Shapiro
Roy G. Rifkin
Michael T. Schulman
Leslie Steven Marks
Mindy Sheps
Norman S. Wisnicki
Barry T. Mitidiere (A Professional Corporation)
Marc E. Rohatiner
Michael W. Rabkin
Andrew S. Gelb
Matthew L. Grode
Richard S. Grant
S. Michael Leventhal

ASSOCIATES

Douglas A. Lusson
Mark J. Rosenbaum
Kelly Allegra Weil
Matthew J. Hafey
Whitney B. Wilds
Keli N. Osaki
Laura S. Withrow
Lisa A. Makarem
Joseph A. Petro
Elsa M. Horowitz

OF COUNSEL

Steven A. Silver
Eric J. Feig
Jeff W. Lane
Jeffrey R. Liebster
Denise M. Parga
Simon Aron

For full biographical listings, see the Martindale-Hubbell Law Directory

MENLO PARK, San Mateo Co.

Dyer & White LLP (AV)

Suite 200, 800 Oak Grove Avenue, 94025
Telephone: 650-325-7000
Fax: 650-325-3116
Email: cdyer@dyer-white.com

MEMBERS OF FIRM

Charles A. Dyer
Rand N. White

For full biographical listings, see the Martindale-Hubbell Law Directory

O'Reilly, Collins & Danko, A Professional Corporation (AV)

2500 Sand Hill Road, Suite 201, 94025-7016
Telephone: 650-854-7700
Fax: 650-854-8350

Terry O'Reilly
James P. Collins
Michael S. Danko

Rian D. Jorgensen

For full biographical listings, see the Martindale-Hubbell Law Directory

NEWPORT BEACH, Orange Co.

Capretz & Associates (AV)

5000 Birch Street, West Tower Suite 2500, 92660-2139
Telephone: 949-724-3000
Fax: 949-757-2635
URL: http://www.lawyers.com/capretzradcliffe
Email: crlawl@ix.netcom.com *URL:* http://www.CAPRETZ.com

MEMBER OF FIRM

James T. Capretz

OF COUNSEL

William B. Lawless (Not admitted in CA)

LEGAL SUPPORT PERSONNEL

Sandra L. Koop (Law Clerk)

For full biographical listings, see the Martindale-Hubbell Law Directory

Lopez, Hodes, Restaino, Milman & Skikos, A Law Corporation (AV)

450 Newport Center Drive, 2nd Floor, 92660
Telephone: 949-640-8222
Fax: 949-640-8294
San Francisco, California Office: 625 Market Street, Fifteenth Floor, 94105.
Telephone: 415-956-5257.
Fax: 415-956-4416.

Ramon Rossi Lopez
Daniel M. Hodes
John M. Restaino, Jr.
Jeffrey A. Milman
Peter John Polos
Steven J. Skikos (Resident)

Christina A. Lopez Fountain
Steven B. Eggleston (Resident, San Francisco Office)
Gregory T. Skikos (Resident, San Francisco Office)
Thomas A. Schultz
Mark G. Crawford
Hilary Poulsen Gilles

OF COUNSEL

David L. Suggs (Not admitted in CA)
Jane E. Joseph (Not admitted in CA)

For full biographical listings, see the Martindale-Hubbell Law Directory

OAKLAND, Alameda Co.*

LAW OFFICES OF RICHARD J. BASKIN (AV)

One Kaiser Plaza, Suite 1585, 94612
Telephone: 510-444-1700
Fax: 510-444-5859
Email: rjbaskin@pacbell.net *URL:* http://www.lawyers.com/baskinlaw

For full biographical listings, see the Martindale-Hubbell Law Directory

FILICE, BROWN, EASSA & MCLEOD, LLP (AV)

1999 Harrison Street, 18th Floor, 94612
Telephone: 510-444-3131
Fax: 510-839-7940

Gennaro A. Filice III
Eugene Brown, Jr.
Robert D. Eassa
Bruce E. McLeod
Raymond J. Bergez
Nicholas D. Kayhan
John A. De Pasquale
Peter A. Strotz
Richard V. Normington III
Amee A. Mikacich
Stephen J. Valen

Jennifer Walker O'Sullivan
Jason J. Curliano
Kristin Ashurst Hughes
Lisa M. Brown
Jennifer K. Pearce
Constance J. McNeil
Michael H. Kim
Carla M. Nakata
Katrina C. Decker

OF COUNSEL

Barrie Engel
Paul R. Johnson

Representative Clients: Astra Zeneca, Inc.; ChemCentral Corp.; Chevron Corp. Dow Chemical Co.; Ethyl Corporation; ICI Americas, Inc.; Rhodia, Inc.; Tosco Refining Co.; Unocal Corp.

For full biographical listings, see the Martindale-Hubbell Law Directory

HAIMS, MACGOWAN, VALENTINO & PEEBLES, L.L.P. (AV)

490 Grand Avenue, 94610
Telephone: 510-835-0500
Facsimile: 510-835-2833

MEMBERS OF FIRM

Arnold B. Haims
Clyde L. MacGowan
Caroline N. Valentino
Dianne D. Peebles

For full biographical listings, see the Martindale-Hubbell Law Directory

LOMBARDI, LOPER & CONANT, LLP (AV)

1999 Harrison Street, Suite 1950, 94612
Telephone: 510-433-2600
Fax: 510-433-2699

Ralph A. Lombardi
Bruce P. Loper
Matthew S. Conant
Chris P. Lavdiotis
Peter O. Glaessner
Timothy J. McCaffery
GayLynn Renee Kirn

Jeffrey D Hosking
Joseph Blaise Adams
Paul S. Lecky

OF COUNSEL

George S. Peyton, Jr.
Linda C. Roodhouse
Lori A. Sebransky

For full biographical listings, see the Martindale-Hubbell Law Directory

VAN BLOIS & ASSOCIATES (AV)

Suite 2245 Ordway Building, One Kaiser Plaza, 94612
Telephone: 510-444-1906
Contra Costa County 510-947-1055
Fax: 510-444-1294
Email: rlvblaw@mindspring.com *URL:* http://www.lawyers.com/vanblois

MEMBERS OF FIRM

R. Lewis Van Blois
Thomas C. Knowles

OF COUNSEL

Charles E. Farnsworth

For full biographical listings, see the Martindale-Hubbell Law Directory

PALM DESERT, Riverside Co.

BERMAN & WEISS (AV)

73-710 Fred Waring Drive, Suite 100, 92260
Telephone: 760-773-6677
Fax: 760-346-7779
Email: weisstrial@aol.com *URL:* http://www.lawinfo.com/law/ca/berman.html

MEMBERS OF FIRM

Richard B. Weiss
Martin M. Berman

For full biographical listings, see the Martindale-Hubbell Law Directory

PASADENA, Los Angeles Co.

COLLINS, COLLINS, MUIR & TRAVER LLP (AV)

Successor to Collins & Collins
Suite 300, 265 North Euclid, 91101
Telephone: 626-793-1163
FAX: 626-793-5982
Newport Beach, California Office: 333 Bayside Drive, 92660.
Telephone: 949-723-7700.
Fax: 949-723-7701.
Affiliated Offices: Drage, Olson & Tiet, LLP, 810 S. Casino Center Boulevard, Las Vegas, Nevada, 89101.
Telephone: 702-384-1600.
Fax: 702-384-1664.

MEMBERS OF FIRM

James E. Collins (1910-1987)
Robert J. Traver (Retired)
Paul L. Rupard (Retired)
John J. Collins
Samuel J. Muir
Frank J. D'Oro
Brian K. Stewart

ASSOCIATES

Robert H. Stellwagen, Jr.
Tomas A. Guterres
Christine E. Drage
Stephen W. Olson
Peter L. Stacy
Kien C. Tiet
Martha L. Cazeneuve
Howard Franco, Jr.
Jeffrey M. Hall
Michael M. Bergfeld
Jennifer M. Gregg

For full biographical listings, see the Martindale-Hubbell Law Directory

MEENAN & LARIVIERE (AV)

790 East Colorado Boulevard Ninth Floor Penthouse, 91101-2113
Telephone: 626-398-0000
Fax: 626-585-0999
Email: meenlaw@msn.com *URL:* http://www.lawyers.com/meenlaw

Kevin Meenan
Denise L. Lariviere

For full biographical listings, see the Martindale-Hubbell Law Directory

REDDING, Shasta Co.*

DUGAN BARR & ASSOCIATES (AV)

1824 Court Street, P.O. Box 994390, 96099-1648
Telephone: 530-243-8008
Fax: 530-243-1648
URL: http://www.CA-lawyer.com

Dugan Barr

ASSOCIATES

Douglas Mudford
J. Michael Favor

Representative Clients: City of Redding; Mid Valley Bank; Scott Valley Bank; 3M; Enloe Hospital.
References: Scott Valley Bank, Redding Branch; Mid Valley Bank, Redding Branch.

For full biographical listings, see the Martindale-Hubbell Law Directory

REINER, SIMPSON & KENNEDY (AV)

2851 Park Marina Drive, Suite 200, 96001
Telephone: 530-241-1905
Fax: 530-241-0622

Russell Reiner
Robert G. Simpson
Daryl E. Kennedy

For full biographical listings, see the Martindale-Hubbell Law Directory

REDLANDS, San Bernardino Co.

WELEBIR, MCCUNE & JURE, A PROFESSIONAL LAW CORPORATION (AV)

2068 Orange Tree Lane, Suite 215, 92374
Telephone: 909-335-0444
Fax: 909-335-0452
Email: wmj@wmj-law.com *URL:* http://www.lawyers.com/wm&jlaw

Douglas F. Welebir
Richard D. McCune, Jr.
Curt W. Jure
Paul J. Burkhart
James F. Tierney, III
Melissa J. Welebir

LEGAL SUPPORT PERSONNEL

Deborah J. Marsh

For full biographical listings, see the Martindale-Hubbell Law Directory

*RIVERSIDE,** Riverside Co.

HAIGHT, BROWN & BONESTEEL, L.L.P. (AV)

A Partnership including Professional Corporations
California Tower, 3737 Main Street, Suite 800, 92501
Telephone: 909-341-8300
FAX: 909-341-8309
URL: http://www.hbblaw.com
Santa Monica, California Office: 1620 26th Street, Suite 4000 North, P.O. Box 680.
Telephone: 310-449-6000.
Telecopier: 310-829-5117.
Telex: 705837.
Santa Ana, California Office: Suite 900, 5 Hutton Centre Drive.
Telephone: 714-754-1100.
Telecopier: 714-754-0826.
San Francisco, California Office: 100 Bush Street, 27th Floor.
Telephone: 415-986-7700.
Fax: 415-986-6945.
San Diego, California Office: 101 West Broadway, Suite 1000.
Telephone: 619-595-5583.
Fax: 619-595-7873.

RESIDENT MEMBERS

Mark S. Lester
Kevin M. Osterberg

ASSOCIATES

Bonnie B. Bailey-Jones
John W. Short
Jeffrey T. Gwynn

For full biographical listings, see the Martindale-Hubbell Law Directory

*SACRAMENTO,** Sacramento Co.

CAULFIELD, DAVIES & DONAHUE (AV)

3500 American River Drive, Suite 100, 95864
Telephone: 916-487-7700
Fax: 916-487-7091
Fairfield, California Office: Fairfield West Plaza, 1455 Oliver Road, Suite 130.
Telephone: 707-426-0223.

MEMBERS OF FIRM

Richard Hyland Caulfield
Robert E. Davies
James R. Donahue
Bruce E. Leonard
Matthew Paul Donahue
Brian C. Haydon

ASSOCIATES

Chance L. Trimm
Shawn C. Moore
Catherine A.J. Woodbridge

For full biographical listings, see the Martindale-Hubbell Law Directory

HARDY ERICH BROWN & WILSON, A PROFESSIONAL CORPORATION (AV)

1000 G Street, 95814
Telephone: 916-449-3800
Fax: 916-449-3888
Mailing Address: P.O. Box 13530, Sacramento, California, 95853-4530
Email: hebw@hebw.com *URL:* http://www.hebw.com

John Quincy Brown, Jr.
Anthony D. Osmundson
Thomas C. Richards
L. Thomas Wagner
John Quincy Brown, III
David S. Worthington
Bruce E. Salenko
Brian H. Charter
Richard L. Alley
Whitney A. Davis
John C. Miller, Jr.

OF COUNSEL

Cavan Hardy
Norwood R. Erich
William A. Wilson
Richard M. Cunha

Kristine E. Balogh
Karin G. Shine
Reginald A. Dunn
Lisa L. Palombo

Representative Clients: Apria Healthcare, Inc.; Baja Marine Corporation; Charles Machine Works, Inc.; The Dexter Corporation; The Dial Corporation;The Goodyear Tire & Rubber Company; Modesto and Empire Traction Company; Sea Ray Boats; Sherwin-Williams Company; VIAD Corporation.

For full biographical listings, see the Martindale-Hubbell Law Directory

JOHNSON, SCHACHTER & COLLINS, A PROFESSIONAL CORPORATION (AV)

California Plaza, 2180 Harvard Street, #560, 95815
Telephone: 916-921-5800
Telecopier: 916-921-0247
Email: law@jscattorneys.com

Robert H. Johnson
Alesa M. Schachter
Kim H. Collins
George W. Holt
Kellie M. Murphy
Alvin Gittisriboongul

Susan E. Slager

(See Next Column)

OF COUNSEL

Ford R. Smith
Carolyn M. Wood
Susanne M. Shelley

Representative Clients: Big 5 Sporting Goods; Fireman's Fund Insurance Cos.; NAVISTAR; Rite-Aid; Sears, Roebuck and Company.
Reference: U.S. Bank, Sacramento.

For full biographical listings, see the Martindale-Hubbell Law Directory

LIVINGSTON & MATTESICH, LAW CORPORATION (AV)

1201 K Street, Suite 1100, 95814
Telephone: 916-442-1111
Fax: 916-448-1709
Email: l&m@lmlaw.net *URL:* http://www.lmlaw.net

Gene Livingston
James M. Mattesich
Carol Livingston
Rebecca M. Ceniceros
Emilio E. Varanini, III
Kenneth M. Malovos
Kathleen E. Finnerty
Joanna R. Mendoza

Steven P. Belzer
Jeffrey Leacox
Randy Pollack
Alice H. Choi
Stephen Craig Hunter
Matthew J. Goldman
Joel C. Baiocchi
Baldassaro (Bill) Di Capo
John McKinsey
Timothy E. Naccarato
Craig N. Lundgren
Mary Farrell Taylor
Brian Crone
Gay L. Carroll
Steven G. Churchwell

Representative Clients: Apollinaris & Schweppes, GMBH & Co.; Calvin Klein Cosmetics Company; Colgate-Palmolive; Combe, Inc.; Johnson & Johnson; Novartis Consumer Health, Inc.; Weider Nutrition Group.

For full biographical listings, see the Martindale-Hubbell Law Directory

MATHENY SEARS LINKERT & LONG, LLP (AV)

3638 American River Drive, P.O. Box 13711, 95853-4711
Telephone: 916-978-3434
Fax: 916-978-3430
Email: info@msll.com *URL:* http://www.msll.com

MEMBERS OF FIRM

Henry G. Matheny (1933-1984)
Douglas A. Sears
Richard S. Linkert
Ernest A. Long
Joann Georgallis
Kent M. Luckey
Matthew C. Jaime
Michael A. Bishop
Robert B. Berrigan
Ronald E. Enabnit
Eric R. Wiesel

ASSOCIATES

Andrea Croak Christensen
Michael G. Jones
Eric M. Bonzell
Mary Elizabeth Wood
Paul Richard Baleria
James F. Curran
Andreas C. Rockas
Timothy P. Chang

OF COUNSEL

James C. Damir

LEGAL SUPPORT PERSONNEL

PARALEGALS

Frances Studer
Lynell Rae Steed
Jennifer Bachman

For full biographical listings, see the Martindale-Hubbell Law Directory

PORTER, SCOTT, WEIBERG & DELEHANT, A PROFESSIONAL CORPORATION (AV)

350 University Avenue, Suite 200, 95825
Telephone: 916-929-1481
Fax: 916-927-3706
Email: pswdlaw@aol.com

Russell G. Porter
A. Irving Scott, Jr.
Edwin T. Weiberg
John W. Delehant
Anthony S. Warburg
Ned P. Telford
James K. Mirabell
Craig A. Caldwell
Terence J. Cassidy
Tom H. Bailey
Carl J. Calnero
Russ J. Wunderli
Nancy J. Sheehan
Norman V. Prior
Timothy M. Blaine
Stephen E. Horan
Carl L. Fessenden

Elisa Ungerman
Michael J. Baytosh
David A. Melton
Jennifer E. Duggan
Vanessa W. Whang
Dennis C. Huie
Michael W. Pott
Kellianne Akbar
Daniel M. Steinberg
Jack Woodside
Jonathan A. Corr
Kristina M. Hall
Alden J. Parker
Avery E. Dority
Robin Weideman
Denise A. Carnaroli

(See Next Column)

PORTER, SCOTT, WEIBERG & DELEHANT A PROFESSIONAL CORPORATION, *Sacramento—Continued*

Lara S. Hilley
Sean Allen
Ralph R. Nevis
Darrin M. Menezes
Shane Singh

For full biographical listings, see the Martindale-Hubbell Law Directory

JOE RAMSEY (AV)

1001 G Street, Suite 201, 95814
Telephone: 916-448-5353
Facsimile: 916-443-7372
Email: ojr@sna.com

For full biographical listings, see the Martindale-Hubbell Law Directory

SCHUERING ZIMMERMAN & SCULLY, LLP (AV)

400 University Avenue, 95825
Telephone: 916-567-0400
Fax: 916-568-0400
Email: szs@szs.com

MEMBERS OF FIRM

Steven T. Scully (1948-1994)
Leo H. Schuering, Jr.
Robert H. Zimmerman
Thomas J. Doyle
Lawrence S. Giardina
Anthony D. Lauria
Keith D. Chidlaw
John J. Sillis
Scott A. Linn
Donna W. Low
Raymond R. Gates

Christian Koster
Michael W. McCall
Dominique A. Pollara
Theodore D. Poppinga
John P. Rhode
Stephen L. Ramazzini
Jonathan A. Saul
Jeffrey J. Whitelaw

For full biographical listings, see the Martindale-Hubbell Law Directory

WILCOXEN, MONTGOMERY & HARBISON (AV)

A Partnership including a Professional Corporation
2114 K Street, 95816
Telephone: 916-442-2777
Email: wmh@wilcoxenlaw.com *URL:* http://www.wilcoxenlaw.com

Daniel E. Wilcoxen (Inc.)
James R. Montgomery
Joseph F. Harbison, III

Patrick L. Hinrichsen
David E. Smith
Steven H. Schultz
Michelle C. Jenni

References: SierraWest Bank; Wells Fargo Bank.

For full biographical listings, see the Martindale-Hubbell Law Directory

*SAN DIEGO,** San Diego Co.

THE LAW OFFICES OF BIRGER GREG BACINO, APC (AV)

3033 Fifth Avenue, Suite 301, 92103
Telephone: 800-801-4878
Fax: 619-299-0086
URL: http://www.bacinolaw.com
Washington, D.C. Office: 1201 Pennsylvania Avenue, Suite 300, 20004.
Telephone: 800-801-4878.
Houston, Texas Office: 510 Bering Street, Suite 300, 77057.
Telephone: 800-801-4878.

Birger Greg Bacino
Richard P. Verlasky
Philip Aman

OF COUNSEL

Patricia M. Sayre
Michael B. Sayre
Anthony J. DeLellis

For full biographical listings, see the Martindale-Hubbell Law Directory

BOUDREAU & TRENTACOSTA, A PROFESSIONAL LAW CORPORATION (AV)

401 West "A" Street, Suite 1850, 92101-9773
Telephone: 619-238-1553
Fax: 619-238-8181
Email: boutre@aol.com

Steven M. Boudreau
Robert J. Trentacosta

For full biographical listings, see the Martindale-Hubbell Law Directory

CASEY, GERRY, REED & SCHENK (AV)

110 Laurel Street, 92101
Telephone: 619-238-1811
Fax: 619-544-9232
Email: cglaw@cglaw.com *URL:* http://www.CGlaw.com

(See Next Column)

MEMBERS OF FIRM

David S. Casey
Richard F. Gerry
Scott C. Cummins
David S. Casey, Jr.
Richard D. Westbrook, Jr. (1944-1982)
T. Michael Reed
Frederick Schenk
Robert J. Francavilla
Gayle Meryl Blatt
Thomas D. Penfield
Michael P. Montgomery
Suzanne C. Etpison
Bonnie E. Kane
Thomas Luneau

Reference: San Diego National Bank.

For full biographical listings, see the Martindale-Hubbell Law Directory

CHAPIN SHEA MCNITT & CARTER, A PROFESSIONAL CORPORATION (AV)

Library, 501 West Broadway, 15th Floor, 92101
Telephone: 619-232-4261
Telefax: 619-232-4840
Email: info@chapinlaw.com *URL:* http://www.chapinlaw.com
Los Angeles, California Office: 12424 Wilshire Boulevard, 9th Floor, 90025.
Telephone: 310-826-0133.
Telefax: 310-207-4236.

Dave Carothers
Edward D. Chapin
Shirley A. Gauvin
Aaron H. Katz
Andrew G. Loeb
Earl H. Maas III
Roger L. McNitt
Steven A. Micheli
Maria C. Roberts
Lawrence W. Shea, II
Nancy L. Vaughan
Peter C. Ward

COUNSEL

Daniel P. Groszkruger
Arthur W. Jones
Thomas P. Redick

Brian A. Barnhorst
Christina A. Bernstein
Kelli Jean Brooks
Jeffery L. Caufield
Daniel W. Coffey
Amy K. Cressey-Yates
Daniel J. Curran
Glen F. Dorgan
Natasha L. Drew
Jeffrey S. Eddington
Patrick M. Howe
Bruno W. Katz
Brian Maienschein
Peter B. Maretz
Carmen M. Mosier McCormick
Jeffrey K. Miyamoto
Leticia Olivarez
Mark T. Petersen
James H. Prenton
Amanda M. Rowe
Patricia L. Sullivan
Brandy Thompson-Cody
Heather K. Van Blarcom

LOS ANGELES OFFICE

Craig H. Bell
John J. Calvagna
Richard D. Carter
Robert Ehrenreich
Leslie J. Eng
Tina Fisher
Ronald F. Gari
Neil R. Gunny
Daniel S. Imber
Shaun Dabby Jacobs
Robin James
Dana Marie Lawson
Jeffrey J. Leist
David A. Myers
Charles F. Peterson
Steven J. Renshaw
Mark Schaeffer
Mark M. Senior
Erin C. Slape
Howard J. Smith
Jeffrey C. Stodel
Stephen Z. Vegh
Irwin Waldman (A P.C.)

For full biographical listings, see the Martindale-Hubbell Law Directory

DOUGHERTY, HILDRE, DUDEK & HAKLAR (AV)

2550 Fifth Avenue, Suite 600, 92103-5624
Telephone: 619-232-9131
Telefax: 619-232-7317
Email: Douhil@aol.com

William O. Dougherty
Donald F. Hildre
Frederick M. Dudek
Thomas D. Haklar

For full biographical listings, see the Martindale-Hubbell Law Directory

DUKE GERSTEL SHEARER, LLP (AV)

A Registered Limited Liability Partnership
Sixth Floor, 101 West Broadway, P.O. Box 85470, 92186-5470
Telephone: 619-232-0816
800-405-0816
Fax: 619-232-4661
Email: lawyers@dgsllp.com *URL:* http://www.dgsllp.com
Costa Mesa, California Office: 3200 Park Center Drive, Suite 1000, 92626.
Telephone: 949-551-8664, 800-405-0816.
Los Angeles, California Office: 10866 Wilshire Boulevard, Suite 1400, 90024.
Telephone: 310-475-7118, 800-405-0816.
San Francisco, California Office: 744 Montgomery Street, Fifth Floor, 94111.
Telephone: 415-773-0101.
Palm Springs, California Office: 1111 East Tahquitz Canyon Way, Suite 110, 92262.
Telephone: 760-322-7846.

(See Next Column)

DUKE GERSTEL SHEARER LLP—*Continued*

Phoenix, Arizona Office: One Columbus Plaza, 3636 North Central Avenue, Suite 1200, 85012.
Telephone: 602-650-2060.
Fax: 602-650-2089.
Tucson, Arizona Office: 6969 East Sunrise Drive, Suite 102, 85750.
Telephone: 520-615-8858.
Fax: 520-615-1069.
Affiliate Las Vegas, Nevada Office: Parsons & Pursiano, LLP, City Center West, Suite 108, 7201 W. Lake Mead Boulevard, 89128.
Telephone: 702-384-9900.
Facsimile: 702-384-5900.

MEMBERS OF FIRM

Robert D. Shoecraft   Ronald M. Green

Reference: Bank of Commerce.

For full biographical listings, see the Martindale-Hubbell Law Directory

HAIGHT, BROWN & BONESTEEL, L.L.P. (AV)

A Partnership including Professional Corporations
101 West Broadway, Suite 1000, 92101-3544
Telephone: 619-595-5583
Telecopier: 619-595-7873
URL: http://www.hbblaw.com
Santa Monica, California Office: 1620 26th Street, Suite 4000 North, P.O. Box 680.
Telephone: 310-449-6000.
Telecopier: 310-829-5117.
Telex: 705837.
Santa Ana, California Office: Suite 900, 5 Hutton Centre Drive.
Telephone: 714-754-1100.
Telecopier: 714-754-0826.
Riverside, California Office: California Tower, 3737 Main Street, Suite 800.
Telephone: 909-341-8300.
Fax: 909-341-8309.
San Francisco, California Office: 101 Bush Street, 27th Floor.
Telephone: 415-986-7700.
Fax: 415-986-6945.

RESIDENT ASSOCIATE

Scott M. Bonesteel

For full biographical listings, see the Martindale-Hubbell Law Directory

KENNERSON SCHWARTZ SEMERDJIAN & HAILE LLP (AV)

A Limited Liability Partnership
101 West Broadway, Suite 810, 92101
Telephone: 619-236-8821
Facsimile: 619-236-8827
URL: http://www.lawyers.com/ksshlaw

OF COUNSEL

Paul R. Kennerson

MEMBERS OF FIRM

Ross J. Schwartz   Dick A. Semerdjian
Jeffrey A. Haile

James R. Ballard   John K. Grant

For full biographical listings, see the Martindale-Hubbell Law Directory

LUCE, FORWARD, HAMILTON & SCRIPPS LLP (AV)

A Partnership including Professional Corporations
600 West Broadway, Suite 2600, 92101
Telephone: 619-236-1414
Fax: 619-232-8311
URL: http://www.luce.com
La Jolla, California Office: 4275 Executive Square, Suite 800, 92037.
Telephone: 858-455-6611.
Fax: 858-232-8311.
Los Angeles, California Office: 777 South Figueroa, Suite 3600, 90017.
Telephone: 213-892-4992.
Fax: 213-892-7731.
San Francisco, California Office: 121 Spear Street, Suite 200, 94105.
Telephone: 415-356-4600.
Fax: 415-356-4610.
New York, N.Y. Office: Citicorp Center, 153 East 53rd Street, 26th Floor, 10022.
Telephone: 212-754-1414.
Fax: 212-644-9727.
Chicago, Illinois Office: 180 North La Salle Street, Suite 3110, 60601.
Telephone: 312-641-0580.
Fax: 312-641-0380.

Callie A. Bjurstrom   Lawrence J. Kouns
Edward Patrick "Pat" Swan, Jr.

(See Next Column)

ASSOCIATES

Michael L. Branch   John P. Cooley
Marjorie A. Stender

For Complete List of Firm Personnel, See General Section

For full biographical listings, see the Martindale-Hubbell Law Directory

MCCLELLAN & BROWN, A PROFESSIONAL CORPORATION (AV)

1144 State Street, 92101
Telephone: 619-231-0505
Fax: 619-544-0540
Email: mcclellan9@aol.com *URL:* http://www.lawyers.com/mcclellan&brown

Craig R. McClellan   LaMar B. Brown

For full biographical listings, see the Martindale-Hubbell Law Directory

MCCORMICK & MITCHELL, A PROFESSIONAL CORPORATION (AV)

625 Broadway, Suite 1400, 92101
Telephone: 619-235-8444
Fax: 619-235-9432
Email: mccormickandmitchell@worldnet.att.net *URL:* http://www.lawyers.com/mccormicklaw

Glenn M. Mitchell (1938-1992)   John P. McCormick
Richard N. Appleton

Konrad M. Rasmussen   Deborah K. Garvin
Geoffrey E. Bishop

Reference: San Diego Trust & Savings.

For full biographical listings, see the Martindale-Hubbell Law Directory

THORSNES, BARTOLOTTA, MCGUIRE & PADILLA (AV)

A Partnership including Professional Corporations
Fifth Avenue Financial Center, 11th Floor, 2550 Fifth Avenue, 92103
Telephone: 619-236-9363
Fax: 619-236-9653
Email: TBMPmail@TBMP.com *URL:* http://www.tbmp.com

Michael T. Thorsnes (A.P.C., P.C.)   C. Brant Noziska (P.C.)
Vincent J. Bartolotta, Jr., (P.C.)   Mitchell S. Golub (P.C.)
John F. McGuire (P.C.)   Palma Cesar Hooper (P.C.)
Kevin F. Quinn (P.C.)   Neal H. Rockwood (P.C.)
Daral B. Mazzarella (P.C.)
R. Christian Hulburt (P.C.)

ASSOCIATES

Catherine A. Richardson   James T. Atkins
Jodi L. Hautaluoma   Leo Bartolotta
Douglas J. Billings   Jill E. Cleary
Scott A. Kennedy   James B. Drimmer
Dori K. Rybacki   Timothy J. Tatro

OF COUNSEL

Robert S. Kennedy

For full biographical listings, see the Martindale-Hubbell Law Directory

*SAN FRANCISCO,** San Francisco Co.

STANLEY J. BELL A PROFESSIONAL CORPORATION (AV)

18th Floor, 505 Sansome Street, 94111
Telephone: 415-391-3700; San Jose: 408-295-1678
Fax: 415-391-3712
San Diego
San Diego, California Office: Suite 1200, 401 West A Street.
Telephone: 619-696-9445.

Stanley J. Bell

Samuel Boyd McCullagh   Craig William Morrison
Sally G. Bergman   Robert M. Dang
Steven J. Bell   Frank C. Liuzzi
J. Kevin Morrison   Hugh A. Donohoe

For full biographical listings, see the Martindale-Hubbell Law Directory

BRAZE LAW OFFICES (AV)

425 Market Street, Suite 2200, 94105
Telephone: 415-955-2612
Toll Free: 877-283-7342
Email: brazelaw@aol.com *URL:* http://www.lawyers.com/brazelaw
Petaluma, California Office: West America Bank Building. 201 Keller Street. 94952-2874.
Telephone: 707-763-2212.
Fax: 707-766-8631.
Sacramento, California Office: Chippendale Office Plaza, 4811 Chippendale Drive, Suite 704, 95814.
Telephone: 916-485-4100.

(See Next Column)

DAVID MALNICK A PROFESSIONAL CORPORATION, *San Jose—Continued*

David E. Malnick

For full biographical listings, see the Martindale-Hubbell Law Directory

REED, ELLIOTT, CREECH & ROTH (AV)
99 Almaden Boulevard, Eighth Floor, 95113
Telephone: 408-993-9911
Fax: 408-993-1335
URL: http://www.sjlegal.com

MEMBERS OF FIRM

John W. Elliott
Randall C. Creech
Thomas A. Elliott
Jeffrey S. Lawson
Peter A. Liebow
Raymond A. Brinson

ASSOCIATES

Lauren Berger
Nancy L. Mathis
Edward A. Kraus
Betty Chen
Bonnie L. Portis

OF COUNSEL

Steven J. Roth
Charles R. Reed
Thomas G. Perkins

Reference: Union Bank of California.

For full biographical listings, see the Martindale-Hubbell Law Directory

ROBINSON & WOOD, INC. (AV)
227 North First Street, 95113
Telephone: 408-298-7120
Fax: 408-298-0477
Email: rw@r-winc.com

Archie S. Robinson
Weldon S. Wood
Thomas R. Fellows
David S. Henningsen
Hugh F. Lennon
Jesse F. Ruiz
Christian B. Nielsen
Jonathan L. Lee
Jon B. Zimmerman
Mark B. Schellerup
Andrew W. Olsson
Arthur J. Casey
Joseph C. Balestrieri
John L. Winchester, III
Robert A. Nakamae

Rebecca L. Moon
Ann A. Nguyen
Kenneth I. Schumaker
Anne C. Bailey
Stephen D. Bays
Jill K. Ernst
Colin G. McCarthy
Bonnie M. Ross
Mario Alvarado
Christopher K. Karic
Alison M. Hershberger
Camille L. Acayan
Valerie M. Drogus
Jennifer L. Bautista

For full biographical listings, see the Martindale-Hubbell Law Directory

SHEA & SHEA, A PROFESSIONAL LAW CORPORATION (AV)
The James Square Building, 255 North Market Street, Suite 190, 95110
Telephone: 408-292-2434
Facsimile: 408-292-1264
Email: shea-shea@worldnet.att.net *URL:* http://www.shea-shea.com

Michael M. Shea
Michael M. Shea, Jr.

For full biographical listings, see the Martindale-Hubbell Law Directory

*SANTA ANA,** Orange Co.

BEAM, BROBECK & WEST (AV)
600 West Santa Ana Boulevard, Suite 1000, 92701
Telephone: 714-558-3944
Fax: 714-568-0129

MEMBERS OF FIRM

Byron J. Beam
David J. Brobeck, Jr.
John E. West
Kirk H. Nakamura
Daniel R. Sullivan
Charles W. Matheis, Jr.

ASSOCIATES

Gregory L. Rippetoe
Jennifer J. Miller
Donald S. Zalewski
David R. Rosenberg
Louise M. Douville
Kermit D. Marsh
Kelly A. Fortin
Barbara J. Salvini
Lil G. Delcampo
Michael J. Peffer
L. Steven Hattendorf

Representative Clients: Aetna Insurance Co.; American General Life Insurance Co.; American Hospital Supply; Carl Warren & Co.; Casualty Insurance Co.; City of Anaheim; City of Fullerton; City of Newport Beach; Empire Insurance Cos.; Physicians Interindemnity.

For full biographical listings, see the Martindale-Hubbell Law Directory

CASSIDY, WARNER, LANE & WINSTEAD, A PROFESSIONAL CORPORATION (AV)
600 West Santa Ana Boulevard, Suite 700, 92701
Telephone: 714-835-9431
Fax: 714-835-5264
Email: cdaly@cassidywarner.com

B. Kent Warner
Timothy X. Lane
Bruce A. Winstead

David C. Olson
Glen A. Stebens

OF COUNSEL

Alvin M. Cassidy

For full biographical listings, see the Martindale-Hubbell Law Directory

*SANTA CRUZ,** Santa Cruz Co.

DUNLAP & BURDICK, A PROFESSIONAL LAW CORPORATION (AV)
Britton Jackson
121 Jewell Street, 95060
Telephone: 831-426-7040
Fax: 831-426-1095
Email: DBLawSCrz@aol.com

Michael E. Dunlap
Paul P. Burdick

For full biographical listings, see the Martindale-Hubbell Law Directory

SANTA MONICA, Los Angeles Co.

BAKER, KEENER & NAHRA, LLP (AV)
2850 Ocean Park Boulevard, Suite 300, 90405-2936
Telephone: 310-399-0900
Fax: 310-399-1644
Email: general@bknlawyers.com *URL:* http://www.bknlawyers.com

MEMBERS OF FIRM

Robert C. Baker
Karl A. Keener
John P. Nahra
Michael H. Bailey
Steven T. Adams
Melissa S. Fink
Jeffrey P. Nolan
Constance A. Endelicato

Brenda K. Benson
Mitchell F. Mulbarger
James D. Hepworth
Phillip A. Baker
George P. Hawley
Thomas M. Mills
R. Jeffrey Neer
Wendy Wen Yun Chang

OF COUNSEL

Daniel P. Leonard

Reference: Wells Fargo Bank (Los Angeles Head Office).

For full biographical listings, see the Martindale-Hubbell Law Directory

HAIGHT, BROWN & BONESTEEL, L.L.P. (AV)
A Partnership including Professional Corporations
1620 26th Street, Suite 4000 North, P.O. Box 680, 90404
Telephone: 310-449-6000
Telecopier: 310-829-5117
Telex: 705837
URL: http://www.hbblaw.com
Santa Ana, California Office: Suite 900, 5 Hutton Centre Drive.
Telephone: 714-754-1100.
Telecopier: 714-754-0826.
Riverside, California Office: California Tower, 3737 Main Street, Suite 800.
Telephone: 909-341-8300.
Fax: 909-341-8309.
San Francisco, California Office: 101 Bush Street, 27th Floor.
Telephone: 415-986-7700.
Fax: 415-986-6945.
San Diego, California Office: 101 West Broadway, Suite 1000.
Telephone: 619-595-5583.
Fax: 619-595-7873.

MEMBERS OF FIRM

Peter Q. Ezzell (A Professional Corporation)
William G. Baumgaertner (A Professional Corporation)
Peter A. Dubrawski
Kevin R. Crisp
Lee Marshall
George Christensen
Kenneth G. Anderson
William O. Martin, Jr.
S. Christian Stouder

ASSOCIATES

Sean E. Judge
Shannon M. Roghair
Tyrone R. Martinez
Chandra Moore

For full biographical listings, see the Martindale-Hubbell Law Directory

Santa Monica—Continued

WATERS, McCLUSKEY & BOEHLE (AV)

3250 Ocean Park Boulevard, Suite 300, 90405-3220
Telephone: 310-396-3411
Facsimile: 310-450-0925
Email: wmb@wmboehle.com
Santa Ana, California Office: Suite 1000, 200 West Santa Ana Boulevard.
Telephone: 714-953-4407.
Facsimile: 714-953-2118.

MEMBERS OF FIRM

William W. Waters (1898-1979)
Laurence R. Corcoran (1927-1987)
Fritz B. Hax
Wayne J. Boehle
Richard A. Wall (Resident, Santa Ana Office)
Timothy R. Lee
Gregg W. Brugger
Kevin G. McCluskey
Stacey B. Spurlock (Resident, Santa Ana Office)
Michael T. Montgomery

ASSOCIATES

Quyen H. Khuong (Resident, Santa Ana)
Christine Y. Chien (Resident, Santa Ana Office)
Portasha R. Moore
Julie C. Chang-Lee (Resident, Santa Ana Office)
Joseph C. Graven
Kirk Michael Olson (Resident, Santa Ana Office)
Brett C. Drouet

References: Bank of America; Santa Monica Business Park, Santa Monica; California National Bank, Los Angeles; First Republic, Los Angeles.

For full biographical listings, see the Martindale-Hubbell Law Directory

TORRANCE, Los Angeles Co.

AGNEW & BRUSAVICH (AV)

20355 Hawthorne Boulevard, 90503
Telephone: 310-793-1400
Facsimile: 310-793-1499
Email: agnewbru@ix.netcom.com *URL:* http://www.agnew-brusavich.com

Gerald E. Agnew, Jr.
Bruce M. Brusavich

ASSOCIATES

Susan E. Hargrove
Christopher A. Kall

For full biographical listings, see the Martindale-Hubbell Law Directory

*VENTURA,** Ventura Co.

LAW OFFICES OF FREDERICK H. BYSSHE, JR. (AV)

10 South California Street, 93001
Telephone: 805-648-3224
Fax: 805-653-0267
Email: bysshe@west.net *URL:* http://www.lawyers.com/bysshelaw

Terence Geoghegan

For full biographical listings, see the Martindale-Hubbell Law Directory

WALNUT CREEK, Contra Costa Co.

ANDERSON, GALLOWAY & LUCCHESE, A PROFESSIONAL CORPORATION (AV)

1676 North California Boulevard Suite 500, 94596-4183
Telephone: 925-943-6383
Facsimile: 925-943-7542

Robert L. Anderson
George Patrick Galloway
David R. Lucchese
Martin J. Everson
Thomas J. Donnelly
Ralph J. Smith
James M. Nelson
Scott E. Murray
David A. Depolo
Karen A. Sparks
Stephen J. Brooks
Joseph S. Picchi
Erin Ruddy Sabey
Lea K. Baldacci
Michael E. Brewer
Sonja M. Dahl
Patricia A. Timm
Jeffrey S. Mitchell

Martha J. James
Shelton L. Smith
Steven M. McKinley
William L. Brelsford, Jr.

For full biographical listings, see the Martindale-Hubbell Law Directory

HINTON & ALFERT, A PROFESSIONAL CORPORATION (AV)

Suite 600, 1646 North California Boulevard, 94596-4113
Telephone: 925-932-6006
Fax: 925-932-3412
Email: ha@hintonandalfert.com *URL:* http://www.lawyers.com/hintonandalfert

Peter J. Hinton
Peter W. Alfert
Scott H. Z. Sumner

(See Next Column)

Elise Sanguinetti

For full biographical listings, see the Martindale-Hubbell Law Directory

COLORADO

*BOULDER,** Boulder Co.

COOK & LEE, P.C. (AV)

5390 Manhattan Circle, 2nd Floor, 80303
Telephone: 303-543-1000
Fax: 303-543-8582
Email: cookleepc@bewellnet.com

Stephen H. Cook
Larry D. Lee

Robert K. Reimann

For full biographical listings, see the Martindale-Hubbell Law Directory

TRINE & METCALF, P.C. (AV)

1435 Arapahoe Avenue, 80302-6390
Telephone: 303-442-0173
Fax: 303-443-7677
Email: firm@trine-metcalf.com *URL:* http://www.trine-metcalf.com

William A. Trine
J. Conard Metcalf

T. Michael Kennedy

Reference: Norwest Bank of Boulder.

For full biographical listings, see the Martindale-Hubbell Law Directory

BROOMFIELD, Boulder Co.

SCHADEN, KATZMAN, LAMPERT & McCLUNE (AV)

11870 Airport Way, 80021-2555
Telephone: 303-465-3663
Facsimile: 303-465-3884
Email: SCHKATZLAM@aol.com *URL:* http://www.lawyers.com/schadenlaw
Troy, Michigan Office; 100 West Big Beaver Road. Suite 130. 48084.
Telephone: 248-258-4800.
Fax: 248-258-2825.

MEMBERS OF FIRM

Richard F. Schaden
David I. Katzman (Not admitted in CO)
Bruce A. Lampert
John D. McClune (Not admitted in CO)

ASSOCIATE

Kathleen M. Schaden

OF COUNSEL

Bruce O. Wilson (Not admitted in CO)

For full biographical listings, see the Martindale-Hubbell Law Directory

*DENVER,** Denver Co.

BOGUE KOURY & MARYLANDER LLC (AV)

1401 17th Street, Suite 320, 80202
Telephone: 303-382-1990
Fax: 303-382-1982
URL: http://www.bkmllc.com
Email: bkmlaw@bkmllc.com *URL:* http://www.lawyers.com/bkmllc

Jeffrey A. Bogue
Victoria J. Koury
Grant Marylander

For full biographical listings, see the Martindale-Hubbell Law Directory

BYRNE, KIELY & WHITE, LLP (AV)

The Chancery, Suite 1300, 1120 Lincoln Street, 80203
Telephone: 303-861-5511
Fax: 303-861-0304

MEMBERS OF FIRM

Thomas J. Byrne
Joseph A. Kiely (1944-1992)
William White

OF COUNSEL

Michael L. Poindexter

John C. Knudsen
Laynie B. Gilida

For full biographical listings, see the Martindale-Hubbell Law Directory

Denver—Continued

CORTEZ MACAULAY BERNHARDT & SCHUETZE LLC (AV)

1600 Broadway, Suite 1600, 80202
Telephone: 303-864-1000
Facsimile: 303-864-1111
URL: http://www.cmblaw.com

Miles Cortez
Christopher T. Macaulay
Susan Bernhardt
Robert A. Schuetze
David H. Goldberg
Marian L. Carlson
Richard P. R. Cohn

For full biographical listings, see the Martindale-Hubbell Law Directory

GODFREY & ASSOCIATES, PROFESSIONAL CORPORATION (AV)

4643 S. Ulster, Suite 920, 80237
Telephone: 303-592-5980
FAX: 303-592-5985
Email: Brett_Godfrey@msn.com

Brett Marshall Godfrey
Paul B. Godfrey (1927-1998)

Michelle A. Pinkowski
James A. Johnson

For full biographical listings, see the Martindale-Hubbell Law Directory

GRUND & BRESLAU, P.C. (AV)

303 East Seventeenth Avenue, Suite 303, 80203-1263
Telephone: 303-830-7770
Facsimile: 303-830-2313
Email: g&b@grundbreslau.com

John W. Grund
Brad W. Breslau
Della S. Nelson
Richard R. Rardin
Julie J. Noonan
Graden P. Jackson

Representative Clients: Admiral Insurance Co.; Avco Corp.; Coca Cola Enterprises Inc.; Denver Coca-Cola Bottling Co.; Essex Insurance Co.; Fisher-Price, Inc.; Safway Steel Products, Inc.; Scott Aviation; Scott Technologies, Inc. (fka Figgie International, Inc.); Tyco International (U.S.), Inc.

For full biographical listings, see the Martindale-Hubbell Law Directory

MARKUSSON, GREEN & JARVIS, P.C. (AV)

Suite 2300, 1050 Seventeenth Street, 80265
Telephone: 303-572-4200
Fax: 303-595-3780

James K. Green
H. Keith Jarvis
Dennis H. Markusson
Thomas E. Napp

Kirstin G. Lindberg
Jason L. Romero
William B. Stanton
William T. Webb
Ashley E. Moller

For full biographical listings, see the Martindale-Hubbell Law Directory

MONTGOMERY LITTLE & MCGREW, P.C. (AV)

The Quadrant, 5445 DTC Parkway, Suite 800 (Englewood), 80111
Telephone: 303-773-8100
Telecopier: 303-220-0412
URL: http://www.mlmpc.com

Robert R. Montgomery
Daniel P. Murphy
Robert N. Spencer

LEGAL SUPPORT PERSONNEL

Debbie L. Kirke (Legal Assistant)

Representative Clients: BP Amoco; Bristol-Myers Squibb; Colorado Medical Society; Cyprus Minerals; Dillon Cos., Inc., d/b/a King Soopers; The St. Paul Insurance Cos.; University of Colorado Health Sciences Center; HealthOne; Teva Pharmaceuticals.

For Complete List of Firm Personnel, See General Section

For full biographical listings, see the Martindale-Hubbell Law Directory

TREECE, ALFREY, MUSAT & BOSWORTH, P.C. (AV)

999 18th Street, Suite 1600, 80202
Telephone: 303-292-2700
Facsimile: 303-295-0414
Email: tamb@tamblaw.com *URL:* http://www.tamblaw.com

Robert S. Treece
Thomas N. Alfrey
Timothy J. Judson

Nicholas Kemp

For full biographical listings, see the Martindale-Hubbell Law Directory

WELLS, ANDERSON & RACE, LLC (AV)

1700 Broadway, Suite 1850, 80290
Telephone: 303-830-1212
Fax: 303-830-0898

Mary A. Wells
Sheryl L. Anderson
Geoffrey S. Race
Suanne M. Dell

William Strohmeyer
L. Michael Brooks, Jr.
Nathalia S. A. Hardy

Representative Clients: Associated Aviation Underwriters; Baxter Healthcare Corporation; Raytheon Aircraft Company; The Cessna Aircraft Co.; State Industries Inc.; 3M; Mentor Corporation.

For full biographical listings, see the Martindale-Hubbell Law Directory

WHEELER TRIGG & KENNEDY, P.C. (AV)

Suite 3600, 1801 California Street, 80202
Telephone: 303-292-2525
Telecopier: 303-294-1879
Email: info@wtklaw.com *URL:* http://www.wtklaw.com
Roslyn, New York Office: 1800 Northern Boulevard, Suite 208, 11576.
Telephone: 516-484-9701.
Fax: 516-484-6362.

Malcolm E. Wheeler
John R. Trigg
Mark F. Kennedy
Paul F. Hultin
Michael L. O'Donnell
Robert B. Hunter
Gwen J. Young
Christopher J. Meyer
Lori L. Roberts
Habib Nasrullah
Edward C. Stewart
James E. Hooper, Jr.

OF COUNSEL

Joseph B. Valentine (Not admitted in CO)
Andrew J. Mihalick (Not admitted in CO)

Sean D. Baker
Mark T. Clouatre
Bryan D. Cross
Wendy A. Harvey
David A. Lamb
Lee A. Mickus
Amy L. Padden
Kimberly A. Stout (Not admitted in CO)

For full biographical listings, see the Martindale-Hubbell Law Directory

ENGLEWOOD, Arapahoe Co.

SALMON, LAMPERT & CLOR, PROFESSIONAL CORPORATION (AV)

Salmon Law Building, (I-25 at East Belleview) 7450 East Progress Place, 80111
Telephone: 303-771-9900
Toll Free in Colorado: 1-800-547-9055
Fax: 303-773-6843
Breckenridge, Colorado Office: Briar Rose House, 213 Briar Rose Lane.
Telephone: 1-800-547-9055

John G. Salmon
Brian J. Lampert
Penelope Clor

Francine R. Salazar
S. Jane Mitchell
Barbara Barrows Ezyk
Martha Merrill-Hall

For full biographical listings, see the Martindale-Hubbell Law Directory

CONNECTICUT

*BRIDGEPORT,** Fairfield Co.

BAI, POLLOCK AND COYNE, P.C. (AV)

Park City Plaza, 10 Middle Street, P.O. Box 1978, 06604
Telephone: 203-366-7991
Fax: 203-366-4723
Email: bpc@snet.net

Arnold J. Bai (1931-1992)
Paul E. Pollock
James E. Coyne
Jeffrey A. Blueweiss
Garie J. Mulcahey
Raymond J. Plouffe, Jr.
Philip F. von Kuhn
Madonna A. Sacco
Michael S. Lynch
David J. Robertson
Edward P. Brady III

Gaileen A. Kaufman
Kevin S. Coyne
Colleen D. Fries
Neal P. Rogan
Louis A. Annecchino
Robert J. Weber, III
Heidi Marie Priwall
Anthony D. Sutton
Kevin J. Curseaden

For full biographical listings, see the Martindale-Hubbell Law Directory

Bridgeport—Continued

KOSKOFF, KOSKOFF & BIEDER, P.C. (AV)

350 Fairfield Avenue, 06604
Telephone: 203-336-4421
Fax: 203-368-3244
Email: KKB@KOSKOFF.com
Stamford, Connecticut Office: 1172 Bedford Street.
Telephone: 203-325-3686.
Danbury, Connecticut Office: 1 Moss Avenue.
Telephone: 203-792-7100.

Michael P. Koskoff
Richard A. Bieder
Karen E. Koskoff
Carey B. Reilly
Vincent M. Musto
Michael A. Stratton
Rosalind J. Koskoff

Gertrude A. Kiaunis

For full biographical listings, see the Martindale-Hubbell Law Directory

WILLIAMS, COONEY & SHEEHY (AV)

One Lafayette Circle, 06604
Telephone: 203-331-0888
Telecopier: 203-331-0896
Email: wilcooshee@aol.com

MEMBERS OF FIRM

Ronald D. Williams
Robert J. Cooney
Edward Maum Sheehy
Dion W. Moore
Ronald D. Williams, Jr.
Francis A. Smith, Jr. (1951-1989)

Suzannah Kim Nigro
Michael Richard Brandt

Representative Clients: Zimmer Manufacturing Co.; Textron-Lycoming: The Stop & Shop Companies, Inc.; Fleet Bank; Utica Mutual Insurance Co.; Royal Insurance.

For full biographical listings, see the Martindale-Hubbell Law Directory

*HARTFORD,** Hartford Co.

KENNY, BRIMMER, MELLEY & MAHONEY (AV)

5 Grand Street, 06106
Telephone: 860-527-4226
FAX: 860-527-0214

Joseph P. Kenny (1920-1993)

MEMBERS OF FIRM

William J. Melley, III
Richard C. Mahoney
Anita M. Varunes
Dennis F. McCarthy

ASSOCIATES

Shannon K. McCarthy
Flora Pizzoferrato

OF COUNSEL

Leslie R. Brimmer

Representative Clients: Allstate Insurance Co.; Peerless Insurance Co.; Berkshire Mutual Fire Insurance Co.; Dorchester Mutual Fire Insurance Co.; Abington Mutual Fire Insurance Co.

For full biographical listings, see the Martindale-Hubbell Law Directory

*NEW HAVEN,** New Haven Co.

EARLY, LUDWICK & SWEENEY, L.L.C. (AV)

One Century Tower, 11th Floor, 265 Church Street, P.O. Box 1866, 06508-1866
Telephone: 203-777-7799
Fax: 203-785-1671
Email: INFO@ELSLAW.COM *URL:* http://www.elslaw.com

James F. Early
Lindalea P. Ludwick
Robert J. Sweeney
Michelle A. Freeman
Brian C. Fournier

Julia Cremin Wyman
John J. O'Connell

For full biographical listings, see the Martindale-Hubbell Law Directory

GALLAGHER & CALISTRO (AV)

1377 Boulevard, P.O. Box 1925, 06509
Telephone: 203-624-4165
Fax: 203-865-5598

William F. Gallagher
Roger B. Calistro
Cynthia C. Bott
Barbara L. Cox
Kurt D. Koehler
Thomas J. Airone

For full biographical listings, see the Martindale-Hubbell Law Directory

JACOBS & JACOBS (AV)

Granite Square, 700 State Street, 3rd Floor, 06511
Telephone: 203-777-2300
Fax: 203-787-5628
Email: JACOBSLAW1@AOL.com

MEMBERS OF FIRM

Israel J. Jacobs (1918-1963)
Stanley A. Jacobs
Bruce D. Jacobs
Carol Wolven
Irene Prosky Jacobs
Charles R. Douthat

Kevin Ryder

Reference: BankBoston.

For full biographical listings, see the Martindale-Hubbell Law Directory

KENNEDY, JOHNSON, D'ELIA & GILLOOLY (AV)

Long Wharf Maritime Center, 545 Long Wharf Drive, 06511
Telephone: 203-865-8430
Fax: 203-865-5345
Email: kennedyjoh@aol.com

MEMBERS OF FIRM

David H. Johnson
John J. Kennedy, Jr.
John J. D'Elia
Dennis Gillooly

ASSOCIATES

Robert L. Schwab
Stephanie Z. Roberge

Reference: Bank of Boston - Connecticut.

For full biographical listings, see the Martindale-Hubbell Law Directory

NEW LONDON, New London Co.

THE REARDON LAW FIRM, P.C. (AV)

160 Hempstead Street, Drawer 1430, 06320
Telephone: 860-442-0444
Telecopier: 860-444-6445
Email: reardonlaw@aol.com *URL:* http://www.reardonlaw.com

Robert I. Reardon, Jr.
Mark A. Dubois
Scott D. Camassar
Cynthia W. Sheppard
Gary W. Huebner

LEGAL SUPPORT PERSONNEL

Bette B. Beam (Legal Administrator)
Kimberly J. Friedel (Paralegal)
Rhonda K. Bourgeois (Paralegal)
Kyle E. Wininger (Paralegal)

For full biographical listings, see the Martindale-Hubbell Law Directory

STAMFORD, Fairfield Co.

PIAZZA & PICKEL (AV)

112 Prospect Street, P.O. Box 15390, 06901
Telephone: 203-348-2465
Fax: 203-964-9509
Email: aap@piazza-pickel.com *URL:* http://www.piazza-pickel.com

Anthony A. Piazza
Alan Scott Pickel

ASSOCIATES

Tara C.F. Ryan
Michelle M. Napoli

For full biographical listings, see the Martindale-Hubbell Law Directory

SILVER, GOLUB & TEITELL LLP (AV)

184 Atlantic Street, P.O. Box 389, 06904
Telephone: 203-325-4491
Fax: 203-325-3769
Email: silvergolubteitell.com *URL:* http://www.sgtlaw.com

MEMBERS OF FIRM

Richard A. Silver
David S. Golub
Ernest F. Teitell
Patricia M. Haugh (1942-1988)
Elaine T. Silver
John D. Josel
Mario DiNatale
Jonathan M. Levine

Marilyn J. Ramos
Richard H. Greenwood
Mary G. Curry
Kathleen L. Brandt
Paul A. Slager (Not admitted in CT)
Brad C. Gustafson

For full biographical listings, see the Martindale-Hubbell Law Directory

DELAWARE

*WILMINGTON,** New Castle Co.

CASARINO, CHRISTMAN & SHALK (AV)

Suite 1220, 222 Delaware Avenue, P.O. Box 1276, 19899
Telephone: 302-594-4500
Telecopier: 302-594-4509
URL: http://www.casarino.com

MEMBERS OF FIRM

Stephen P. Casarino
Beth H. Christman
Colin M. Shalk
Donald M. Ransom

Kenneth M. Doss
Stacey L. Cummings
Diane M. Willette
Thomas P. Leff

For full biographical listings, see the Martindale-Hubbell Law Directory

SMITH, KATZENSTEIN & FURLOW LLP (AV)

The Corporate Plaza, 800 Delaware Avenue, P.O. Box 410, 19899
Telephone: 302-652-8400
Fax: 302-652-8405
Email: info@skfdelaware.com *URL:* http://www.SKFDelaware.com

MEMBERS OF FIRM

Robert J. Katzenstein
Laurence V. Cronin

For Complete List of Firm Personnel, See General Section

For full biographical listings, see the Martindale-Hubbell Law Directory

DISTRICT OF COLUMBIA

WASHINGTON, D.C. Co.

ALLEN, JOHNSON, ALEXANDER & KARP, P.A. (AV)

1707 L Street, N.W., Suite 1050, 20036
Telephone: 202-828-4141
Fax: 202-429-8798
Email: ajakdc@aol.com
Baltimore, Maryland Office: Suite 1540, 100 East Pratt Street.
Telephone: 410-727-5000.

D'Ana E. Johnson

Representative Clients: Scottsdale Insurance Co.; Nautilus Insurance Co.; Jefferson Insurance Co.; Liberty Mutual Insurance Co.; Avis Rent-A-Car; Otis Elevator Co.; Montgomery Elevator Co.; Admiral Insurance Co.; Local Government Insurance Trust; Penn National Insurance Co.

For Complete List of Firm Personnel, See General Section

For full biographical listings, see the Martindale-Hubbell Law Directory

BAUM, HEDLUND, ARISTEI, GUILFORD & DOWNEY, A PROFESSIONAL CORPORATION (AV)

1250 24th Street, N.W., Suite 300, 20037
Telephone: 202-466-0513; 800-827-0097
Fax: 202-466-0527
Email: bhagd@bhagd.com *URL:* http://www.bhagd.com
Los Angeles, California Office: Suite 950, 12100 Wilshire Boulevard.
Telephones: 310-207-3233; 800-827-0087.
Facsimile: 310-820-7444.

Cara J. Luther

OF COUNSEL

Mary F. Schiavo

For full biographical listings, see the Martindale-Hubbell Law Directory

COALE, COOLEY, LIETZ, McINERNY & BROADUS, A PROFESSIONAL CORPORATION (AV)

818 Connecticut Avenue, N.W., Suite 857, 20006
Telephone: 202-887-4770
Facsimile: 202-887-4778

John P. Coale (A Professional Corporation)
David K. Lietz
Julia Wernett McInerny
Diane E. Cooley
Charlsa (Sandy) Broadus

Deborah St. Jean
Joseph Coale (Not admitted in DC)

For full biographical listings, see the Martindale-Hubbell Law Directory

COHEN, MILSTEIN, HAUSFELD & TOLL, P.L.L.C. (AV)

West Tower, Suite 500, 1100 New York Avenue, N.W., 20005-3964
Telephone: 202-408-4600
Facsimile: 202-408-4699
Email: lawinfo@cmht.com *URL:* http://www.CMHT.com
Seattle, Washington Office: 999 Third Avenue, Suite 3600.
Telephone: 206-521-0080.
Facsimile: 206-521-0166.

MEMBERS OF FIRM

Jerry S. Cohen (1925-1995)
Herbert E. Milstein
Michael D. Hausfeld
Steven J. Toll (Resident, Seattle, Washington Office)
Ann C. Yahner
Lisa M. Mezzetti
Andrew N. Friedman
Richard S. Lewis
Daniel S. Sommers
Daniel A. Small
Gary E. Mason
Joseph M. Sellers
Sharon A. Snyder
Mark S. Willis (Not admitted in DC)

ASSOCIATES

Lori G. Feldman (Resident, Seattle, Washington Office)
Paul T. Gallagher
Christine E. Webber
Alexander E. Barnett
Matthew James Ide (Resident, Seattle, Washington Office)
Matthew F. Pawa
Suzette M. Malveaux
Mary N. Strimel
Kristopher A. Kinkade (Resident, Seattle, Washington Office)
Agnieszka M. Fryszman
Deborah J. Vagins
Ari Karen
Charles E. Tompkins
Tamara J. Driscoll (Resident, Seattle, Washington Office)
Elizabeth Haines Cronise
Donna Solen
Lesli C. Esposito (Not admitted in DC)

OF COUNSEL

Margaret G. Farrell

For full biographical listings, see the Martindale-Hubbell Law Directory

THE FEINBERG GROUP, LLP (AV)

1120 20th Street, N.W. Suite 740 South, 20036-3437
Telephone: 202-371-1110
Fax: 202-962-9290
Email: kfeinberg@thefeinberggroup.com *URL:* http://www.krfassociates.com
New York, N.Y. Office: 780 3rd Avenue, Suite 2202.
Telephone: 212-527-9600.
Fax: 212-527-9611. Email: kfeinberg@thefeinberggroup.com.

PARTNERS

Kenneth R. Feinberg
Deborah E. Greenspan
Michael K. Rozen (Resident, New York Office)
Peter H. Woodin (Resident, New York Office)

ASSOCIATE

Fredric M. Brooks (Not admitted in DC)

SENIOR COUNSEL

Jacqueline E. Zins

For full biographical listings, see the Martindale-Hubbell Law Directory

AARON M. LEVINE & ASSOCIATES (AV)

1320 - 19th Street, N.W., 20036
Telephone: 202-833-8040
Fax: 202-833-8046
Email: lawkunst@aol.com

Brandon J. Levine
Renee L. Robinson-Meyer

For full biographical listings, see the Martindale-Hubbell Law Directory

OPPENHEIMER WOLFF DONNELLY & BAYH LLP (AV)

1350 Eye Street, N.W. Suite 200, 20005
Telephone: 202-312-8000
FAX: 202-312-8100
URL: http://www.owdlaw.com
Oppenheimer Wolff & Donnelly LLP
Minneapolis, Minnesota Office: 3300 Plaza VII, 45 South Seventh Street. 55402.
Telephone: 612-607-7000.
FAX: 612-607-7100.
Amsterdam, The Netherlands Office: Keizergracht 241.
Telephone: 31-20-423-4555.
FAX: 31-20-423-4545.
Brussels, Belgium Office: Avenue Louise 240, Box 5, 1050.
Telephone: 32-2-626-0500.
FAX: 32-2-626-0510.
Geneva, Switzerland Office: Rue Gabriel Eynard, 6, 1206.
Telephone: (41/22) 311-7410.
FAX: (41/22) 311-7407.
New York, N.Y. Office: Citicorp Center, 153 East 53rd Street, 10022.
Telephone: 212-826-5000.
FAX: 212-486-0708.

(See Next Column)

OPPENHEIMER WOLFF DONNELLY & BAYH LLP—*Continued*

Newport Beach, California Office: 500 Newport Center Drive, Suite 700, 92660.
Telephone: 949-719-6000.
FAX: 949-719-6020.
Paris, France Office: 53 Avenue Montaigne, 75008.
Telephone: (33/1) 44 95 03 50.
FAX: (33/1) 44 95 03 40.
St. Paul, Minnesota Office: 1700 First National Bank Building, 55101.
Telephone: 651-605-2000.
FAX: 651-605-2100.
Los Angeles, California Office: 2029 Century Park East, 38th Floor, 90067.
Telephone: 310-788-5000.
FAX: 310-277-1297.
Palo Alto, California Office: 3373 Hillview Avenue, Suite 200, 94304.
Telephone: 650-320-4000.
FAX: 650-320-4100.
Chicago, Illinois Office: Oppenheimer Wolff & Donnelly (Illinois), Two Prudential Plaza, 45th Floor, 180 North Stetson Avenue, 60601.
Telephone: 312-616-1800.
Fax: 312-616-5800.

RESIDENT PARTNER

John H. Korns

RESIDENT ASSOCIATE

Robin A. Williams (Not admitted in DC)

For full biographical listings, see the Martindale-Hubbell Law Directory

PANGIA & HANSEN (AV)

1717 N Street, N.W., 20036
Telephone: 202-955-6450
Fax: 202-955-9444
Email: bchansen@erols.com *URL:* http://www.lawyers.com/aviation

MEMBERS OF FIRM

Michael J. Pangia
Barry C. Hansen

ASSOCIATE

Harold E. Rambo, Jr.

For full biographical listings, see the Martindale-Hubbell Law Directory

VENABLE ATTORNEYS AT LAW VENABLE, BAETJER, HOWARD & CIVILETTI, LLP (AV)

A Partnership including Professional Corporations
Suite 1000, 1201 New York Avenue, N.W., 20005
Telephone: 202-962-4800
Fax: 202-962-8300
URL: http://www.venable.com
Baltimore, Maryland Office: Venable, Baetjer and Howard LLP, 1800 Mercantile Bank & Trust Building, 2 Hopkins Plaza.
Telephone: 410-244-7400.
Fax: 410-244-7742.
McLean, Virginia Office: Venable, Baetjer and Howard LLP, Suite 400, 2010 Corporate Ridge.
Telephone: 703-760-1600.
Fax: 703-821-8949.
Rockville, Maryland Office: Venable, Baetjer and Howard LLP, Suite 500, One Church Street, P. O. Box 1906.
Telephone: 301-217-5600.
Fax: 301-217-5617.
Towson, Maryland Office: Venable, Baetjer and Howard LLP, 210 Allegheny Avenue, P. O. Box 5517.
Telephone: 410-494-6200.
Fax: 410-821-0147.

MEMBERS OF FIRM

James K. Archibald (Also at Baltimore, Maryland Office)
Benjamin R. Civiletti (P.C.) (Also at Baltimore and Towson, Maryland Offices)
Jeffrey A. Dunn (Also at Baltimore, Maryland Office)
David W. Goewey
Gary M. Hnath
George F. Pappas (Also at Baltimore, Maryland Office)
James L. Shea (also at Baltimore, Maryland Office)

For Complete List of Firm Personnel, See General Section

For full biographical listings, see the Martindale-Hubbell Law Directory

FLORIDA

BOCA RATON, Palm Beach Co.

MICHAUD, BUSCHMANN, FOX, FERRARA & MITTELMARK, P.A. (AV)

33 Southeast 8th Street, 33432
Telephone: 561-392-0540
Fax: 561-392-0582
Email: Bocalaw@MBFFM.com *URL:* http://www.MBFFM.com

(See Next Column)

Scott H. Michaud
Paul Buschmann
Brian S. Fox
James T. Ferrara
Michael K. Mittelmark
Marc T. Millian

Marcy G. Blitz
Linda A. McCullough
Kimberly M. Hall

For full biographical listings, see the Martindale-Hubbell Law Directory

*FORT LAUDERDALE,** Broward Co.

CATRI, HOLTON, KESSLER & KESSLER, P.A. (AV)

The Litigation Building, 3rd Floor, 633 S. Andrews Avenue, 33302
Telephone: 954-463-8593
Fax: 954-462-1303

Charles T. Kessler (1930-1997)
Wesley L. Catri
Raymond O. Holton, Jr.
Paula C. Kessler
Andrea L. Kessler

Gerard A. Tuzzio
Edwina V. Kessler

For full biographical listings, see the Martindale-Hubbell Law Directory

COONEY, MATTSON, LANCE, BLACKBURN, RICHARDS & O'CONNOR, P.A. (AV)

2312 Wilton Drive, P.O. Box 14546, 33302
Telephone: Telephone: 954-568-6669
WATS: 1-800-745-3864
Telecopier: 954-568-0085
Email: cooney2312@aol.com
Orlando, Florida Office: Nations Bank Tower, 111 N. Orange Avenue, Suite 1020.
Telephone: 407-843-2100.
Fax: 407-843-2061.

David F. Cooney
Michael C. Mattson
Victor Lance (1956-1995)
Ace J. Blackburn, Jr.
John H. Richards
Dennis R. O'Connor (Resident, Orlando, Florida Office)
Bruce Michael Trybus
Walter C. Wyatt
Kieran F. O'Connor (Resident, Orlando, Florida Office)
Michele McCaul Ricca
Daniel F. Tordella

Laura Douglas
Warren Kwavnick
Rochelle Bocksch
Weslee S. Arciola
Alphonso O. Peets
Robert M. Potter, III
Elizabeth Y. Foshee (Resident, Orlando Office)

Representative Clients: The Travellers; RISCORP; CIGNA Insurance Co.; Claims Center; Fiesco; Multi-Line Claims Service, Inc.; Carpenter Contractors of America; City Furniture; CNA Insurance.

For full biographical listings, see the Martindale-Hubbell Law Directory

KRUPNICK CAMPBELL MALONE ROSELLI BUSER SLAMA HANCOCK MCNELIS LIBERMAN & MCKEE, P.A. (AV)

700 Southeast 3rd Avenue, Suite 100, 33316-1186
Telephone: 954-763-8181; 877-763-8181 (Toll Free)
Fax: 954-763-8292
Email: information@krupnicklaw.com *URL:* http://www.krupnicklaw.com

Jon E. Krupnick
Walter G. Campbell, Jr.
Kevin A. Malone
Richard J. Roselli
Thomas E. Buser
Joseph J. Slama
Kelly D. Hancock
Lisa A. McNelis
Scott S. Liberman
Robert J. McKee

Carlos Acevedo (Not admitted in FL)
Louis R. Battista
Ivan F. Cabrera
Robert D. Erben
Kelley Badger Gelb
Sean J. Greene
Holly Debra Krulik
Michael J. Ryan

OF COUNSEL

Ben J. Weaver
Dianne Jay Weaver

Reference: Mellon United National Bank.

For full biographical listings, see the Martindale-Hubbell Law Directory

WILTON L. STRICKLAND, P.A. (AV)

1401 East Broward Boulevard, Suite 303, P.O. Box 14246, 33301
Telephone: 954-760-4700; 800-760-8401
Telecopier: 954-779-7749
Email: sands@gate.net *URL:* http://www.wiltonstricklandpa.com

Wilton L. Strickland

Alexander Clark

For full biographical listings, see the Martindale-Hubbell Law Directory

*FORT MYERS,** Lee Co.

GOLDSTEIN, BUCKLEY, CECHMAN, RICE & PURTZ, P.A. (AV)

1515 Broadway, P.O. Box 2366, 33902-2366
Telephone: 941-334-1146
Fax: 941-334-3039
Email: info@gbclaw.com *URL:* http://www.GBClaw.com
Port Charlotte, Florida Office: Emerald Square, Suite 1, 2852 Tamiami Trail, 33952.
Telephone: 941-624-2393.
Fax: 941-624-2155.
Cape Coral, Florida Office: 1603 Hancock Bridge Parkway, 33990.
Telephone: 941-574-5575.
Fax: 941-574-9213.
Lehigh Acres, Florida Office: 1458 Lee Boulevard, Lee Boulevard Shopping Center, 33936.
Telephone: 941-368-6101.
Fax: 941-368-2461.
Naples, Florida Office: 4947 North Tamiami Trail, Suite 101, 34103.
Telephone: 941-262-4888.
Fax: 941-262-8716.

John B. Cechman

Approved Attorneys for: Attorneys' Title Insurance Fund.

For Complete List of Firm Personnel, See General Section

For full biographical listings, see the Martindale-Hubbell Law Directory

*JACKSONVILLE,** Duval Co.

ALFORD & KALIL, P.A. (AV)

2400 Independent Square, One Independent Drive, 32202-5064
Telephone: 904-355-3311
Fax: 904-355-5411
Email: akthefirm@aol.com

C. Wayne Alford
John S. Kalil

For full biographical listings, see the Martindale-Hubbell Law Directory

HUGH COTNEY, P.A. (AV)

905 Blackstone Building, 233 East Bay Street, 32202-3417
Telephone: 904-356-0162
FAX: 904-355-5170

Hugh Cotney

Representative Clients: First Insuramerica of Florida, Inc.; Deaf Services Center, Inc.

For full biographical listings, see the Martindale-Hubbell Law Directory

LILES, GAVIN & COSTANTINO (AV)

One Enterprise Center, Suite 1500, 225 Water Street, 32202
Telephone: 904-634-1100
Fax: 904-634-1234
Email: triallaw@bellsouth.net

Rutledge R. Liles
R. Kyle Gavin
R. Scott Costantino

ASSOCIATES

Niels P. Murphy
Robert Bruce George

For full biographical listings, see the Martindale-Hubbell Law Directory

PAJCIC & PAJCIC, P.A. (AV)

1900 Independent Square, 32202
Telephone: 904-358-8881
Fax: 904-354-1180
Email: attorneys@pajcic.com *URL:* http://www.pajcic.com

Gary Pajcic
Stephen J. Pajcic, III
William S. Burns, Jr.
Curtis Stephen Pajcic
Robert J. Link
Lee T. Griffin
Christine A. Clark
Thomas F. Slater
Curry Gary Pajcic

Reference: Barnett Bank of Jacksonville, N.A.

For full biographical listings, see the Martindale-Hubbell Law Directory

SAALFIELD, COULSON, SHAD & JAY, P.A. (AV)

225 Water Street, Suite 1000, 32202-4458
Telephone: 904-355-4401
Fax: 904-355-3503
Email: SCJ4401@BellSouth.net

John R. Saalfield
Michael I. Coulson
Charles Thomas Shad
Harvey L. Jay, III
Joseph B. Stokes, III

(See Next Column)

Gail A Stafford
Brett Q. Lucas
Carl Scott Schuler

Representative Clients: American Continental Ins. Co.; Baptist/St. Vincent's Health System; Century Products; CNA Ins. Co.; Cosco, Inc.; Crawford & Co.; Dependable Protective Mutual; Dillard Dept. Stores, Inc.; First Floridian Ins. Co.; Florida Podiatrist Trust.

For full biographical listings, see the Martindale-Hubbell Law Directory

MATTHEW W. SOWELL, P.A. (AV)

One Independent Drive, Suite 3204, 32202
Telephone: 904-358-9000
Telecopier: 904-350-9093

Matthew W. Sowell

For full biographical listings, see the Martindale-Hubbell Law Directory

MAITLAND, Orange Co.

BAILEY & MYERS, P.A. (AV)

100 East Sybelia Avenue Suite 375, 32751
Telephone: 407-628-2929
Fax: 407-628-3909
URL: http://www.baileymyers.com

Michael K. Bailey
Donald A. Myers, Jr.

For full biographical listings, see the Martindale-Hubbell Law Directory

*MIAMI,** Dade Co.

ANDREW J. ANTHONY, P.A. (AV)

999 Ponce de Leon Boulevard (Coral Gables) Suite 1035, 33134-5822
Telephone: 305-444-8927
Fax: 305-529-1072

Andrew J. Anthony

Bradley Allan Silverman

OF COUNSEL

Neal Gary Rosensweig

For full biographical listings, see the Martindale-Hubbell Law Directory

CLARKE SILVERGLATE WILLIAMS & MONTGOMERY (AV)

A Partnership of Professional Corporations
100 North Biscayne Boulevard Suite 2401, 33132
Telephone: 305-377-0700
Facsimile: 305-377-3001
Chicago, Illinois Office: Williams & Montgomery Ltd., 20 North Wacker Drive, Suite 2100.
Telephone: 312-443-3200.
Telex: 206598.
Facsimile: 312-443-1323.
Waukegan, Illinois Office: Williams & Montgomery Ltd., 20 S. Utica.
Telephone: 847-360-1220.
Wheaton, Illinois Office: Williams & Montgomery Ltd., 310 S. County Farm Road.
Telephone: 630-690-3200.
Joliet, Illinois Office: Williams & Montgomery Ltd., 81 North Chicago Avenue.
Telephone: 815-727-2653.

Mercer K. Clarke
Spencer H. Silverglate

OF COUNSEL

Henry H. Bolz, III

ASSOCIATES

Kelly Anne Luther
Richard R. Cochran
William J. Dimmig
Cynthia R. Bernard
Spencer T. Kuvin
Francisco Ramos, Jr.
Edward J. Pfister
John C. Schlesinger

For full biographical listings, see the Martindale-Hubbell Law Directory

DEUTSCH & BLUMBERG, P.A. (AV)

Suite 2802 New World Tower, 100 North Biscayne Boulevard, 33132
Telephone: 305-358-6329
Fax: 305-358-9304

Steven K. Deutsch
Edward R. Blumberg
James C. Blecke
Louis Thaler

For full biographical listings, see the Martindale-Hubbell Law Directory

Miami—Continued

FELDMAN GALE & WEBER, P.A. (AV)

201 South Biscayne Boulevard, 19th Floor, 33131-4329
Telephone: 305-358-5001
Fax: 305-358-3309
Email: fgwlaw@fgwlaw.com
Suffield, Connecticut Office: 40 Crane Hill Road, 06078.
Telephone: 860-668-0226.
Fax: 860-668-0696. Email: WCNEALON@FGWLAW.COM; WCNEALON@AOL.COM.

Jeffrey D. Feldman
James A. Gale
Michael J. Weber

Sean N. R. Wells
John C. Carey
Jennifer Johnson Watkins
Ozzie A. Farres
Nancy J. Flint
Greg Tung Nguyen

OF COUNSEL

William C. Nealon (Not admitted in FL)

For full biographical listings, see the Martindale-Hubbell Law Directory

HARDY, BISSETT & TEICHNER, P.A. (AV)

501 Northeast First Avenue, 33132
Telephone: 305-358-6200
Broward: 954-462-6377
Fax: 305-577-8230

G. Jack Hardy
G. William Bissett
Lee Philip Teichner

Lyle E. Shapiro

Representative Clients: International Paper Co.; Bridgestone/Firestone, Inc.; American International Underwriters; American International Group, Inc.; Crown Equipment Corp.; The Budd Company; Loewen Group International, Inc.; St. Paul Insurance Company; Titan International, Inc.; Sunstate Manufactured Homes of Georgia, Inc. d/b/a Peach State Homes, Inc.

For full biographical listings, see the Martindale-Hubbell Law Directory

SAMS & LISTER, P.A. (AV)

73255 West 63 Avenue, Suite 201, 33143
Telephone: 305-740-5401
Fax: 305-740-5425

Murray Sams, Jr.
David P. Lister

Arthur B. Stark

For full biographical listings, see the Martindale-Hubbell Law Directory

SEIPP, FLICK & KISSANE, P.A. (AV)

2450 Suntrust International Center, One Southeast Third Avenue, 33131
Telephone: 305-995-5600
Fax: 305-374-0494
URL: http://www.sfklaw.com

Bonnie S. Crouch
Charles P. Flick
Daniel J. Kissane
Vidian C. Mallard
James W. McCready, III
Sergio V. Medina
John C. Seipp, Jr.

For full biographical listings, see the Martindale-Hubbell Law Directory

MIAMI LAKES, Dade Co.

MARTIN, LIPSKY, KAUFMAN & WEINSTEIN, P.A. (AV)

7975 Northwest 154th Street Suite 230, 33016
Telephone: 305-362-6222
Fax: 305-362-0111
URL: http://www.lawyers.com/personalinjurypros

Timothy M. Martin
Joseph I. Lipsky
Daniel L. Kaufman
Mark S. Weinstein

For full biographical listings, see the Martindale-Hubbell Law Directory

NICEVILLE, Okaloosa Co.

STANLEY BRUCE POWELL, P.A. (AV)

107 North Partin Drive, P.O. Box 400, 32588-0400
Telephone: 850-678-2118
Fax: 850-678-8336
Email: BPOWELLPA@AOL.COM

Stanley Bruce Powell
David R. Swanick III

Representative Clients: Peoples National Bank of Niceville; Destin Bank; Big Kahuna's, Inc.
References: Peoples National Bank of Niceville; Destin Bank; Vanguard Bank and Trust Co.

For full biographical listings, see the Martindale-Hubbell Law Directory

*ORLANDO,** Orange Co.

BROWN, WARD, SALZMAN & WEISS, P.A. (AV)

111 North Orange Avenue, Suite 875, P.O. Box 2873, 32802-2873
Telephone: 407-425-9566
Fax: 407-425-9596; Email: firm@orlandolaw.net
Email: brownu@osceola.k12.fl.us *URL:* http://www.orlandolaw.net

Usher Larry Brown
John H. Ward
Gary S. Salzman
Jeffrey S. Weiss
Suzanne D'Agresta

Scott D. Danahy
James G. Vickaryous
Robert L. Butterfield, Jr.
Allison Carmine McDonald

Representative Clients: The Walt Disney Company; Walt Disney World Co.; Walt Disney World Hospitality & Recreation Corp.; General Electric Capital Modular Space; Honeywell, Inc.; Central Brevard Anesthesiologists, P.A.; Caliber; Reedy Creek Energy Services; Gallagher Bassett Services, Inc.

For full biographical listings, see the Martindale-Hubbell Law Directory

CABANISS, McDONALD, SMITH & WIGGINS, P.A. (AV)

390 N. Orange Avenue, Suite 1600, P.O. Box 2513, 32802-2513
Telephone: 407-246-1800
Facsimile: 407-246-1895
URL: http://www.cmsw.com
Atlanta, Georgia Office: 5555 Glenridge Connector, Suite 200, 30342.
Telephone: 404-531-5080.
Facsimile: 404-531-5081.

Ronald E. Cabaniss
Francis M. McDonald, Jr.
Larry D. Smith
Michael J. Wiggins
M. Gary Toole

David E. Cannella
Earnest DeLoach, Jr.
Sarah A. Long
Michelle M. Perez-Sotolongo
Douglas J. Petro
John R. Reid, Jr.
Scott A. Richman
F. Rand Wallis

For full biographical listings, see the Martindale-Hubbell Law Directory

COONEY, MATTSON, LANCE, BLACKBURN, RICHARDS & O'CONNOR, P.A. (AV)

Nations Bank Tower, 111 North Orange Avenue Suite 1020, 32801
Telephone: 407-843-2100
Fax: 407-843-2061
Fort Lauderdale, Florida Office: 2312 Wilton Drive. P.O. Box 14546. 33302.
Telephone: 954-568-6669.
Telecopier: 954-568-0085.

Dennis R. O'Connor
Kieran F. O'Connor

Elizabeth Y. Foshee (Resident)

For full biographical listings, see the Martindale-Hubbell Law Directory

DELLECKER, WILSON & KING, P.A. (AV)

719 Vassar Street, 32804
Telephone: 407-244-3000
Fax: 407-244-3033
Email: attorneys@dwklaw.com *URL:* http://www.dwklaw.com

Robert H. "Bob" Dellecker
Brian T. Wilson
Samuel P. King
Leticia J. Marques
Kenneth J. McKenna

For full biographical listings, see the Martindale-Hubbell Law Directory

HILL AND PONTON, PROFESSIONAL ASSOCIATION (AV)

Suite 500, 605 East Robinson Street, P.O. Box 2673, 32802
Telephone: 407-422-4665
URL: http://www.hillponton.com

Brian D. Hill
Carol J. Ponton

Maria D. Santana (Not admitted in FL)
Silvia R. Sanders
Jeffrey D. Starker

For full biographical listings, see the Martindale-Hubbell Law Directory

HILL, REIS, ADAMS, HALL & SCHIEFFELIN, P.A. (AV)

1417 East Concord Street, 32803
Telephone: 407-896-0425
Fax: 407-896-9236
Email: mainbox@hrahs.com

(See Next Column)

HILL, REIS, ADAMS, HALL & SCHIEFFELIN P.A., *Orlando—Continued*

G. Bruce Hill
Larry D. Hall
Gregory F. Reis
Thomas L. Schieffelin, Jr.
Janet W. Adams
William W. Large
Matthew P. Bartolomei

David O Doyle, Jr
Andrew Vlahos
Heidi Jo Haycook

Representative Clients: The Florida Hospital Trust Fund; The Florida Hospital Excess Trust Fund; Florida Hospital Workers Compensation/Self Insurance Trust Fund; Bartow Memorial Hospital; Bay Medical Center; Brooksville Regional Hospital; Cape Canaveral Hospital; Cape Coral Hospital; Desoto Memorial Hospital.

For full biographical listings, see the Martindale-Hubbell Law Directory

MAHER, GIBSON AND GUILEY A PROFESSIONAL ASSOCIATION OF LAWYERS (AV)

Suite 200, 90 East Livingston Street, 32801
Telephone: 407-839-0866
Fax: 407-425-7958

Michael Maher
Patricia M. Gibson
David D. Guiley

Steven R. Maher
Jennifer Gentry Fernandez
Robin Orosz Sharp
Melissa H. Powers

LEGAL SUPPORT PERSONNEL

INSURANCE CLAIM COORDINATOR

Charles R. Simpson

For full biographical listings, see the Martindale-Hubbell Law Directory

MCGEE & POWERS, P.A. (AV)

201 East Pine Street, Suite 700, P.O. Box 3589, 32801
Telephone: 407-422-5742
Telecopy: 407-423-1377

Patrick A. McGee
Brenda J. Newman
James K. Powers
Donna C. Valin

For full biographical listings, see the Martindale-Hubbell Law Directory

MEIER, LENGAUER, BONNER, MUSZYNSKI & DOYLE, P.A. (AV)

37 North Orange Avenue, Suite 1100, 32801
Telephone: 407-872-7774
Facsimile: 407-872-7997

George A. Meier III
Alexander Muszynski III
Steven F. Lengauer
Donna Canina Doyle
Robert E. Bonner
Donald L. O'Dell

Ernest J. Myers
Mercedes R. Wechsler
Veronica Lee Harvey
Mary Catherine Wellman
Melinda G. Baum
Melodie Brosious Jaffe

Representative Clients: AIG Aviation, Inc.; Auto Owners Insurance Company; Chubb & Son; City of Orlando; Federal Express Corp.; Gallagher-Bassett Insurance Service; Phoenix Avaition, Inc.; Westfield Companies; Zurich Insurance Co.; Crum and Forster Insurance.

For full biographical listings, see the Martindale-Hubbell Law Directory

OVERCHUCK, NEWSOME & SCHWERER, LLP (AV)

90 East Livingston Street, Suite 100, 32801
Telephone: 407-648-5977
Fax: 407-648-5282
Email: ons@onslaw.com *URL:* http://www.onslaw.com

John R. Overchuck
C. Richard Newsome
Alan M. Schwerer

For full biographical listings, see the Martindale-Hubbell Law Directory

PARRISH & FREDERICKSEN, P.A. (AV)

116 America Street, 32801
Telephone: 407-849-1776
Email: sidneyparrish@laworlando.com

Sidney H. Parrish
Kenneth S. Fredericksen

Brian F. Duckworth

For full biographical listings, see the Martindale-Hubbell Law Directory

DAVID C. SCHWARTZ, P.A. (AV)

201 East Pine Street, Suite 700, 32801
Telephone: 407-481-8500
Fax: 407-481-9010
Email: dcschwartz@prodigy.net

(See Next Column)

David C. Schwartz

For full biographical listings, see the Martindale-Hubbell Law Directory

*PENSACOLA,** Escambia Co.

BOZEMAN, JENKINS & MATTHEWS, P.A. (AV)

SunTrust Tower, 220 West Garden Street, Suite 801, P.O. Box 13105, 32501
Telephone: 850-434-6223
Fax: 850-434-5242
Email: bojema@pen.net *URL:* http://www.bojema.pen.net
Fort Walton Beach Office: 151 Mary Esther Boulevard, Suite 401.
Telephone: 850-651-2151.
Fax: 850-434-5242.
Panama City Office: 475 Harrison Avenue, Suite 203A.
Telephone: 850-872-0110.
Fax: 850-434-5242.

Frank C. Bozeman, Jr.
Larry A. Matthews
Thomas R. Jenkins
Janice K. Skievaski
Frank C. Bozeman, III

Robert T. Bleach
Raymond F. Higgins, III
John B. Fricke, Jr.
Jeremiah J. Talbott
J. Andrew Talbert
Sidney M. McCrackin

For full biographical listings, see the Martindale-Hubbell Law Directory

BRIDGERS & GILL (AV)

121 Palafox Place, Suite A, 32501
Telephone: 850-432-6484
Fax: 850-432-6383

MEMBERS OF FIRM

J. Dixon Bridgers, III (Retired)
Jeffrey P. Gill
Rachel P. Ray

ASSOCIATES

Karen L. Jordan
Brent F. Bradley

For full biographical listings, see the Martindale-Hubbell Law Directory

FULLER, JOHNSON & FARRELL, P.A. (AV)

Quayside Quarters, 700 South Palafox, Suite 170, P.O. Box 12219, 32581
Telephone: 850-434-8845
Fax: 850-432-6667
Tallahassee, Florida Office: 111 North Calhoun Street, P.O. Box 1739, 32302-1739.
Telephone: 850-224-4663.
Fax: 850-561-8839.

Michael W. Kehoe
Alan R. Horky

Jason W. Peterson (Resident)

Representative Clients: American Motors Corp.; Amoco Oil Co.; Black & Decker (U.S.), Inc.; Ford Motor Co.; Hitachi Power Tools USA, Ltd.; Hoffman-LaRoche, Inc.; Montgomery Ward and Company, Inc.; Robeson Industrial Corp.; Ryder Truck Lines, Inc.; Squibb, Inc.

For full biographical listings, see the Martindale-Hubbell Law Directory

YOUNG & ASSOCIATES, ATTORNEYS AT LAW, P.A. (AV)

Seville Tower, Seventh Floor, 226 South Palafox Place, 32501
Telephone: 850-432-2222
Fax: 850-432-1444
Tampa, Florida Office: 1517 Seventh Avenue, Suite C, 33605.
Telephone: 813-242-6262.
Fax: 813-342-6363.

B. Richard Young

Michael T. Bill
B. B. Boles, III
David A. Fugett
Ricardo J. Diaz
Peter S. Roumbos
James R. Barnes

For full biographical listings, see the Martindale-Hubbell Law Directory

ST. PETERSBURG, Pinellas Co.

CHAMBERS LAW GROUP, PROFESSIONAL ASSOCIATION (AV)

520 Fourth Street North, P.O. Box 1191, 33731-1191
Telephone: 727-896-2167
Fax: 727-822-8981
Email: CHAMLAWGRP@AOL.com

Joseph H. Chambers
Joseph W. Chambers
Jeffrey K. Chambers

John R. Mathias

Reference: NationsBank.

For full biographical listings, see the Martindale-Hubbell Law Directory

*SARASOTA,** Sarasota Co.

MARTIN & GLASER, CHARTERED (AV)

2014 Fourth Street, P.O. Box 49257, 34230-6257
Telephone: 941-365-4072
FAX: 941-365-1492
Email: martinandglaser@yahoo.com *URL:* http://www.lawyers.com/peterwmartin

Peter W. Martin — Whitney C. Glaser

For full biographical listings, see the Martindale-Hubbell Law Directory

NELSON ● HESSE (AV)

2070 Ringling Boulevard, P.O. Box 2524, 34230
Telephone: 941-366-7550
Fax: 941-955-3708

MEMBERS OF FIRM

Richard E. Nelson
Ronald Alexander Cyril (1938-1988)
Richard L. Smith
F. Steven Herb
Omer S. Causey
William A. Dooley
Michael S. Drews
Frederick J. Elbrecht
Gary W. Peal

ASSOCIATES

J. Neal Mobley
J. Corey Feist
Alison Hosmer

General Counsel for: Provident Bank; Dooley Mack Construction Co.
Representative Clients: Wellcraft Marine; American Marine Holdings; Vanliner Insurance; Time Warner Cable; SMH Radiology, Inc.; The Carlton Ranch, Inc.
References: Southtrust Bank; Provident Bank.

For full biographical listings, see the Martindale-Hubbell Law Directory

*TALLAHASSEE,** Leon Co.

FULLER, JOHNSON & FARRELL, P.A. (AV)

111 North Calhoun Street, P.O. Box 1739, 32302-1739
Telephone: 850-224-4663
Fax: 850-561-8839
Pensacola, Florida Office: Quayside Quarters, 700 South Palafox, Suite 170, P.O. Box 12219, 32581.
Telephone: 850-434-8845.
FAX: 850-432-6667.

Ben A. Andrews
Jeannette M. Andrews
Wm. Stephen Black, II
Robert C. Crabtree
Patrick J. Farrell, Jr.
S. William Fuller, Jr.
Alan R. Horky (Resident, Pensacola Office)
Fred M. Johnson
Michael W. Kehoe (Resident, Pensacola Office)
J. Craig Knox
William R. Mabile, III
P. Scott Mitchell
Steven Michael Puritz
Beverly H. Smith
Michael J. Thomas

Gregory K. Rettig
Jason W. Peterson (Resident, Pensacola Office)
Scot B. Copeland

Representative Clients: Aetna Life & Casualty; American Continental Insurance Company; American International Group; American States Insurance Company; Amoco Oil Company; Anesthesiologists' Professional Assurance Trust; Black & Decker (U.S.), Inc.; Bruno's, Inc.; CIGNA Companies; Coca-Cola Enterprises, Inc.

For full biographical listings, see the Martindale-Hubbell Law Directory

MCFARLAIN, WILEY, CASSEDY & JONES, PROFESSIONAL ASSOCIATION (AV)

215 South Monroe Street, Suite 600, P.O. Box 2174, 32316-2174
Telephone: 850-222-2107
Telecopier: 850-222-8475
Email: firm@mcfarlain.com *URL:* http://www.mcfarlain.com

Richard C. McFarlain
William B. Wiley
Douglas P. Jones
Charles A. Stampelos
H. Darrell White, Jr.
Christopher Barkas
Harold R. Mardenborough, Jr.
Terrell C. Madigan

Robert A. McNeely — P. David Brannon

LEGAL SUPPORT PERSONNEL

Diane L. Doll (Office Manager)

For full biographical listings, see the Martindale-Hubbell Law Directory

*TAMPA,** Hillsborough Co.

MICHAEL C. ADDISON (AV)

Suite 1130, 220 East Madison Street, 33602
Telephone: 813-223-2000
Facsimile: 813-228-6000
Mailing Address: P.O. Box 2175, Tampa, Florida, 33601-2175
Email: michaeladdison@compuserve.com *URL:* http://www.lawyers.com/michaeladdison-law

For full biographical listings, see the Martindale-Hubbell Law Directory

TIMOTHY G. ANDERSON, P.A. (AV)

213 South Brevard Avenue, 33606
Telephone: 813-251-0072
1-800-848-3024

Timothy G. Anderson

Leslie Longshore

For full biographical listings, see the Martindale-Hubbell Law Directory

BAVOL, BUSH & SISCO, P.L.L.C. (AV)

100 South Ashley, Suite 2100, P.O. Box 3423, 33601-3423
Telephone: 813-228-7000
Telefax: 813-273-0091

Charles D. Bavol
Ronald E. Bush
Dale R. Sisco
Jack E. Fernandez, Jr.
Dominick J. Graziano

Robert W. Bleakley
William R. Daniel
Kevin M. Gilhool
Andrew L. Rosenkranz (On Leave)
Jay P. Dinan
Jaret J. Fuente
Kerry C. McGuinn, Jr.
Pegi Money McCabe

For full biographical listings, see the Martindale-Hubbell Law Directory

CUNNINGHAM, CLARK & GREIWE, P.A. (AV)

100 Ashley Drive, South, Suite 100, 33602
Telephone: 813-228-0505
Telefax: 813-229-7982

Anthony W. Cunningham
Donald G. Greiwe
James D. Clark
D. Frank Winkles

For full biographical listings, see the Martindale-Hubbell Law Directory

LAW OFFICES OF MERKLE & MAGRI, P.A. (AV)

5510 West LaSalle Street, 33607
Telephone: 813-281-9000; Clearwater, 727-441-2699
Fax: 813-281-2223

Robert W. Merkle
Joseph D. Magri
Ward A. Meythaler
David J. Plante
Gerard J. Roble

For full biographical listings, see the Martindale-Hubbell Law Directory

RYWANT, ALVAREZ, JONES, RUSSO & GUYTON, PROFESSIONAL ASSOCIATION (AV)

Suite 500 Perry Paint & Glass Building, 109 North Brush Street, P.O. Box 3283, 33601
Telephone: 813-229-7007
Fax: 813-223-6544
Ocala, Florida Office: 3300 S.W. 34th Avenue, Suite 124C, 32674.
Telephone: 904-237-8810.
FAX: 904-237-2022.

Carmen Alpizar
Manuel J. Alvarez
Matthew R. Danahy
Matthew D. Emerson
Lisa A. Griffin
John A.C. Guyton, III
M.C. Collins Guyton
Gregory D. Jones
Burke G. Lopez
Andrew F. Russo
Michael S. Rywant

LEGAL SUPPORT PERSONNEL

Bradley Hugh Holt

Representative Clients: Peerless Insurance Co.; Gulf Insurance Group; Employers Casualty Co.; Landmark Insurance Co.

For full biographical listings, see the Martindale-Hubbell Law Directory

Tampa—Continued

CHARLES F. SANSONE (AV)

P.O. Box 18306, 33679-8306
Telephone: 813-223-9282
Fax: 813-229-0595
Email: cfsansone@aol.com

For full biographical listings, see the Martindale-Hubbell Law Directory

SANTOS, DUTTON, LYNOTT & HENRY, P.A. (AV)

One Harbour Place, Suite 950, 777 South Harbour Island Boulevard, 33602
Telephone: 813-229-1111
Fax: 813-229-3311

F. Robert Santos
Daniel J. Lynott
Scott W. Dutton
David G. Henry

Gregory Joseph Blackburn (Resident)
Harry Lee Coe, IV
Michael H. Ashy

Representative Clients: American Vehicle Insurance; Capacity Insurance Co.; Erie Insurance Co.; Fortune Insurance Group; The Hanover Insurance Co.; The Travelers Insurance Co.; The Shelby Insurance Group; State Farm Mutual Automobile Insurance Co.; Usher Insurance Co.

For full biographical listings, see the Martindale-Hubbell Law Directory

A LAW OFFICE OF JEFFERY L. SHIBLEY, P.A. (AV)

13902 North Dale Mabry Highway, Suite 102, 33618
Telephone: 813-264-7200
Fax: 813-960-2755
Email: tortsjd@aol.com *URL:* http://www.lawyers.com/jefferyshibley

Jeffery L. Shibley

For full biographical listings, see the Martindale-Hubbell Law Directory

YERRID, KNOPIK & KRIEGER, P.A. (AV)

Barnett Plaza, Suite 2160, 101 East Kennedy Boulevard, 33602
Telephone: 813-222-8222
Fax: 813-222-8224
URL: http://www.yerridknopik.com

C. Steven Yerrid
Christopher S. Knopik

Ralph L. Gonzalez

For full biographical listings, see the Martindale-Hubbell Law Directory

*VERO BEACH,** Indian River Co.

WILLIAM S. FRATES, II P.A. (AV)

830 Azalea Lane, 32963
Telephone: 561-231-5896
Fax: 561-231-5124
URL: http://www.frates.com
Email: wsflaw@gate.net *URL:* http://www.lawyers.com/wsflaw

William S. Frates, II

Brian J. Connelly

For full biographical listings, see the Martindale-Hubbell Law Directory

MOSS, HENDERSON, BLANTON & LANIER, P.A. (AV)

817 Beachland Boulevard, P.O. Box 3406, 32964-3406
Telephone: 561-231-1900
Fax: 561-231-4387

Robin A. Blanton

Representative Clients: Aetna Life & Casualty; Alcoa Florida, Inc.; Florida Power & Light Co.; Insurance Company of North America; Liberty Mutual Insurance Co.; Sears, Roebuck & Co.; Sugar Cane Growers Cooperative of Florida; Norfolk Southern Corporation/North American Van Lines, Inc.

For Complete List of Firm Personnel, See General Section

For full biographical listings, see the Martindale-Hubbell Law Directory

*WEST PALM BEACH,** Palm Beach Co.

ADAMS, COOGLER, WATSON & MERKEL, P.A. (AV)

Suite 1600, 1555 Palm Beach Lakes Boulevard, P.O. Box 2069, 33402
Telephone: 561-478-4500
Fax: 561-684-7346
Email: ACWMLAW@AOL.COM

(See Next Column)

Samuel H. Adams (1913-1981)
Catherine Lynn Kasten
Roy R. Watson
Scott S. Warburton
Robert G. Merkel
Peter A. Cooke
James C. Barry
Patricia A. Judge
Reed W. Kellner
Kathryn L. Tignor

Alexander D. Barker
James W. Flanagan
Jodi G. Barrett
Paul L. Harwood
Stephanie Brown
Thomas Hodas
Catherine M. Paris

OF COUNSEL

L. C. Shepard, Jr.

For full biographical listings, see the Martindale-Hubbell Law Directory

DAVIS, GORDON & DONER, P.A. (AV)

515 North Flagler Drive, 7th Floor, 33401
Telephone: 561-659-7337
Facsimile: 561-659-0143
Email: dgdc@flinet.com *URL:* http://www.dgdlaw.com

Zell Davis, Jr. (Retired)
Robert E. Gordon
Adam S. Doner

Eric D. Hightower
Steven G. Calamusa

OF COUNSEL

Mikel D. Jones (Not admitted in FL)

For full biographical listings, see the Martindale-Hubbell Law Directory

LYTAL, REITER, CLARK, FOUNTAIN & WILLIAMS (AV)

A Limited Liability Partnership
Tenth Floor, 515 North Flagler Drive, 33401
Telephone: 561-655-1990
Broward County: 954-426-2103
Toll Free: 1-800-654-2024
Fax: 561-832-2932
Mailing Address: P.O. Box 4056, 33402
Email: lhowden@palmbeachlaw.com *URL:* http://www.palmbeachlaw.com

Lake Lytal, Jr. (P.A.)
Mark W. Clark (P.A.)
Joseph J. Reiter (P.A.)
Donald R. Fountain, Jr. (P.A.)
William S. Williams (P.A.)

David M. Gaspari
Lake H. Lytal, III
W. Hampton Keen
Michael J. Overbeck
Nancy L. La Vista
David C. Prather
Julie H. Littky-Rubin
Kevin C. Smith
Scott Bryant Smith

Reference: United National Bank.

For full biographical listings, see the Martindale-Hubbell Law Directory

RICCI, HUBBARD, LEOPOLD, FRANKEL & FARMER, P.A. (AV)

1645 Palm Beach Lakes Boulevard, Suite 250, P.O. Box 2946, 33402
Telephone: 561-684-6500
Fax: 561-697-2383
Email: Ricci@bellsouth.net *URL:* http://www.riccihubbard.com

Edward M. Ricci
Duncan J. Farmer
James R. Hubbard
Scott C. Murray
Theodore J. Leopold
Steven G. Dell
Lois J. Frankel
Marina F. Parrish
Andrea D. McMillan

For full biographical listings, see the Martindale-Hubbell Law Directory

SEARCY DENNEY SCAROLA BARNHART & SHIPLEY, PROFESSIONAL ASSOCIATION (AV)

2139 Palm Beach Lakes Boulevard, P.O. Drawer 3626, 33402-3626
Telephone: 561-686-6300
800-780-8607
800-220-7006 (Spanish)
Fax: 561-478-0754
Email: CDS@SEARCYLAW.COM *URL:* http://www.searcylaw.com

Christian D. Searcy, Sr.
Lance J. Block, Jr.
Earl L. Denney, Jr.
C. Calvin Warriner, III
John Scarola
William A. Norton
F. Gregory Barnhart
David J. Sales
John A. Shipley
Christopher K. Speed
David K. Kelley, Jr.
William B. King
David J. White

Karen E. Terry
Patrick E. Quinlan
Sean C. Domnick
Darryl L. Lewis
Harry A. Shevin
Ellen F. Brandt

(See Next Column)

SEARCY DENNEY SCAROLA BARNHART & SHIPLEY PROFESSIONAL ASSOCIATION—*Continued*

LEGAL SUPPORT PERSONNEL

Laurie J. Briggs (Paralegal)
Deane L. Cady (Paralegal/Investigator)
Daniel J. Calloway (Paralegal/Investigator)
Emilio Diamantis (Paralegal/Investigator)
David W. Gilmore (Paralegal/Investigator)
John C. Hopkins (Paralegal/Investigator)
Thaddeus E. Kulesa (Paralegal/Investigator)
J. Peter Love (Paralegal/Investigator)
William H. Seabold (Paralegal/Investigator)
Kathleen Simon (Paralegal)
Steve M. Smith (Paralegal/Investigator)
Kevin J. Walsh (Paralegal/Investigator)
Judson Whitehorn (Paralegal/Investigator)
Samantha M. Johansen (Paralegal/Investigator)

For full biographical listings, see the Martindale-Hubbell Law Directory

GEORGIA

*ALBANY,** Dougherty Co.

CANNON, MEYER VON BREMEN & GOSS, LLP (AV)

2417 Westgate Drive, P.O. Box 70909, 31708-0909
Telephone: 912-435-1470
Telefax: 912-888-2156
Email: cmvblaw@cmvb.com

MEMBERS OF FIRM

William E. Cannon, Jr.
Michael S. Meyer von Bremen
Stephen S. Goss

ASSOCIATES

Timothy O. Davis
Toysha M. Flowers
William H. Gregory, II

For full biographical listings, see the Martindale-Hubbell Law Directory

*ATHENS,** Clarke Co.

BLASINGAME, BURCH, GARRARD, BRYANT & ASHLEY, P.C. (AV)

440 College Avenue North, P.O. Box 832, 30603
Telephone: 706-354-4000
Telecopier: 706-353-0673
Greensboro, Georgia Office: 122 N. Main Street, P.O. Box 67, 30642.
Telephone: 706-453-7139.
Fax: 706-453-7842.

J. Ralph Beaird
Gary B. Blasingame
E. Davison Burch
Henry G. Garrard, III
Everett Clay Bryant
W. Seaborn Ashley, Jr.
M. Steven Heath
Andrew J. Hill, III
Michael A. Morris
Thomas H. Rogers, Jr.
William D. Harvard
Rikard L. Bridges
Ivan A. Gustafson
David S. Thomson
Richard W. Schmidt

Matthew N. Padgett
Christopher G. Conley
Pamela Lohr Hendrix
Amy Lou Reynolds
Sean P. Dolan
Carter A. Lawson
Matthew Allen Moseley
Molly K. O'Steen
Josh B. Wages

Representative Clients: NationsBank; Georgia Power Co.; Atlanta Gas Light Company; Pittsburgh Corning Corp.; Downtown Athens Development Authority; Fowler Products Co., Inc.; Athens Newspapers, Inc.; First National Bank of Commerce; Athens First Bank & Trust Co.; Reynolds Plantation.

For full biographical listings, see the Martindale-Hubbell Law Directory

*ATLANTA,** Fulton Co.

WILLIAM Q. BIRD AND ASSOCIATES, P.C. (AV)

14 Seventeenth Street, Suite 5, P.O. Box 7009, 30357
Telephone: 404-873-4696
Fax: 404-872-3745
Email: info@williamqbird.com *URL:* http://www.williamqbird.com

William Q. Bird

John G. Mabrey
Karin Middleton Allen

For full biographical listings, see the Martindale-Hubbell Law Directory

DAVID WM. BOONE, P.C. (AV)

3166 Mathieson Drive, 30305
Telephone: 404-239-0305
Fax: 404-239-0520

(See Next Column)

David William Boone
Simone R. Siex

For full biographical listings, see the Martindale-Hubbell Law Directory

BOVIS, KYLE & BURCH, LLC (AV)

A Limited Liability Corporation including Professional Corporations
Third Floor, 53 Perimeter Center East, 30346
Telephone: 770-391-9100
Telecopier: 770-668-0878
Email: bkb@boviskyle.com *URL:* http://www.boviskyle.com

John M. Bovis (P.C.)
Steven J. Kyle (P.C.)
John V. Burch (P.C.)
C. Sam Thomas (P.C.)
James E. Singer
J. Wesley Skinner
Gregory R. Veal
Timothy J. Burson
Charles M. Medlin
John H. Peavy Jr.

J.S. Scott Busby
Christina A. Craddock
Timothy A. Hickey, Jr.
Jana B. Tabor
Carl A. Hassler
John David Etheriedge
Everett A. Kliphouse

For full biographical listings, see the Martindale-Hubbell Law Directory

BUTLER & MACDOUGALD (AV)

152 Nassau Street, 30303
Telephone: 404-688-6100
Fax: 404-688-0711
Email: dmacd@mindspring.com
Email: lbutler@mindspring.com
Jasper, Georgia Office: The Butler-Cape House, 9205 Highway 53 West, 30143.
Telephone: 706-692-6192.
Fax: 706-692-3831.

MEMBERS OF FIRM

Larry Kent Butler
Daniel MacDougald III

OF COUNSEL

Harry W. MacDougald

For full biographical listings, see the Martindale-Hubbell Law Directory

BUTLER, WOOTEN, OVERBY, FRYHOFER, DAUGHTERY & SULLIVAN (AV)

2719 Buford Highway, 30324
Telephone: 404-321-1700
WATS 1-800-242-2962
Fax: 404-321-1713
Columbus, Georgia Office: 1500 Second Avenue, P.O. Box 2766.
Telephone: 706-322-1990; National Wats: 1-800-233-4086.
Fax: 706-323-2962.

MEMBERS OF FIRM

James E. Butler, Jr.
Joel O. Wooten, Jr.
C. Frederick Overby
George W. Fryhofer III
Peter J. Daughtery
Lee Tarte Wallace
Terrance C. Sullivan

ASSOCIATES

Jason L. Crawford
Keith A. Pittman
Joshua Sacks
Teresa Thomas Abell
Cale H. Conley

Reference: Columbus Bank and Trust, Columbus, Ga.

For full biographical listings, see the Martindale-Hubbell Law Directory

DENNIS, CORRY & PORTER, L.L.P. (AV)

3300 One Atlanta Plaza, 950 East Paces Ferry Road, P.O. Box 18640, 30326
Telephone: 404-816-2800
Wats: 800-735-0838
Fax: 404-816-5656
URL: http://www.dcplaw.com

MEMBER OF FIRM

Grant B. Smith

Representative Clients: Schneider National, Inc.; Roadway Express, Inc.; Caliber System, Inc.

For Complete List of Firm Personnel, See General Section

For full biographical listings, see the Martindale-Hubbell Law Directory

DOFFERMYRE, SHIELDS, CANFIELD, KNOWLES & DEVINE (AV)

Suite 1600, 1355 Peachtree Street, 30309
Telephone: 404-881-8900
Fax: 404-881-3007

(See Next Column)

DOFFERMYRE, SHIELDS, CANFIELD, KNOWLES & DEVINE, *Atlanta—Continued*

Robert E. Shields
Georgiana Rizk
Kenneth S. Canfield
David S. Hagy
Ralph I. Knowles, Jr.
Bonnie L. Keith

For full biographical listings, see the Martindale-Hubbell Law Directory

FAIN, MAJOR, WILEY & BRENNAN, P.C. (AV)

100 Glenridge Point Parkway Suite 500, 30342-1440
Telephone: 404-688-6633
Telecopier: 404-420-1544

Gene A. Major
Thomas E. Brennan
Charles A. Wiley, Jr.
John K. Miles, Jr.
Darryl G. Haynes

Brian Alligood

Representative Clients: Allstate Insurance Co.; Budget Rent-A-Car; Arkansas Best Corp.; Chrysler Insurance Co.; Georgia Farm Bureau Mutual Insurance Co.; Hertz Corp.; Universal Underwriters Insurance Co.; Westfield Insurance Co.; Winn-Dixie Stores, Inc.

For Complete List of Firm Personnel, See General Section

For full biographical listings, see the Martindale-Hubbell Law Directory

FREEMAN, WRIGHT & HERMAN (AV)

3060 Peachtree Road, N.W. Suite 720, 30305-2240
Telephone: 404-262-2962
Fax: 404-237-1926
Email: bhi@bellsouth.net

MEMBERS OF FIRM

Joe C. Freeman, Jr.
Arnold Wright, Jr.
Robert L. Herman

For full biographical listings, see the Martindale-Hubbell Law Directory

GARLAND, SAMUEL & LOEB, P.C. (AV)

3151 Maple Drive, N.E., 30305
Telephone: 404-262-2225
Fax: 404-365-5041
Email: triallaw@atlanta.com

Edward T. M. Garland
Donald F. Samuel
Robin N. Loeb

For full biographical listings, see the Martindale-Hubbell Law Directory

GOLDNER, SOMMERS, SCRUDDER & BASS (AV)

900 Circle 75 Parkway Suite 850, 30339
Telephone: 770-612-9200
Facsimile: 770-612-9201

MEMBERS OF FIRM

Stephen L. Goldner
Henry E. Scrudder, Jr.
Glenn S. Bass

For Complete List of Firm Personnel, See General Section

For full biographical listings, see the Martindale-Hubbell Law Directory

HAWKINS & PARNELL, LLP (AV)

4000 SunTrust Plaza, 303 Peachtree Street, N.E., 30308-3243
Telephone: 404-614-7400
Fax: 404-614-7500
Email: relliott@hplegal.com *URL:* http://www.hawkinsparnell.com

MEMBERS OF FIRM

Albert H. Parnell
Warner S. Fox
A. Timothy Jones
Michael E. Hutchins
Alan F. Herman
Ollie M. Harton
Michael J. Goldman
Kimberly Houston
H. Lane Young, II
Charles R. Beans
Frank C. Bedinger, III
Kristine Berry Morain
William H. Major, III
Roger M. Goode
T. Ryan Mock, Jr.
Blanche Rose Miller
Thomas G. Tidwell

ASSOCIATES

Allen L. Broughton
Stephen Michael Bowers
Andrew A. Davenport
Michael J. Crist

Representative Clients: The Coca-Cola Co.; Atlantic Richfield; Ericsson, Inc.; Baxter Healthcare Corporation; MEDMARC; Suburban Manufacturing Company; Celanese, Ltd.

For Complete List of Firm Personnel, See General Section

For full biographical listings, see the Martindale-Hubbell Law Directory

HILL AND BLEIBERG (AV)

Suite 200, 47 Perimeter Center East, 30346
Telephone: 770-394-7800
Fax: 770-394-7802
Email: HBLAWFIRM@AOL.COM

MEMBERS OF FIRM

Robert P. Bleiberg
Gary Hill

ASSOCIATE

Bryan Hill

For full biographical listings, see the Martindale-Hubbell Law Directory

JOHNSON & WARD (AV)

2100 The Equitable Building, 100 Peachtree Street N.W., 30303-1962
Telephone: 404-524-5626
Facsimile: 404-524-1769
Email: postmaster@johnsonward.com

MEMBERS OF FIRM

William C. Lanham
John C. Dabney, Jr.
Clark H. McGehee
Bruce A. Maxwell

For Complete List of Firm Personnel, See General Section

For full biographical listings, see the Martindale-Hubbell Law Directory

MATTHEWS & STEEL (AV)

462 East Paces Ferry Road, 30305
Telephone: 404-264-1292
800-776-0098
Fax: 404-264-0161
Email: postmaster@matthewssteellaw.com

MEMBERS OF FIRM

James B. Matthews, III
John B. Briggs
John D. Steel
H. Craig Stafford

For full biographical listings, see the Martindale-Hubbell Law Directory

MILLS, MORAITAKIS, KUSHEL & PEARSON (AV)

Suite 425 3445 Peachtree Road, Northeast, 30326-1276
Telephone: 404-261-0016
Facsimile: 404-261-0024

Roger Mills
Glenn E. Kushel
Nicholas C. Moraitakis
Albert M. Pearson, III

ASSOCIATE

Martha D. Turner

For full biographical listings, see the Martindale-Hubbell Law Directory

NALL, MILLER, OWENS, HOCUTT & HOWARD, LLP (AV)

Suite 200 Peachtree & Broad Building, 66 Luckie Street, 30303
Telephone: 404-522-2200
Fax: 404-522-2208

MEMBERS OF FIRM

James S. Owens, Jr.
George Robert Neuhauser
Robert B. Hocutt
Robert L. Goldstucker
James R. Howard
Kenneth P. McDuffie
Michael D. Hostetter

COUNSEL

Samuel A. Miller

ASSOCIATES

Charles Richard Carson
Paul Jay Pontrelli
Mary Anne Palma

LEGAL SUPPORT PERSONNEL

W. Gary Bush (Registered Nurse, Legal Assistant)
Natalie D. Summers (Paralegal)
Janice F. Clark (Paralegal)
Michelle Henderson McGhee (Paralegal)

Representative Clients: Arvin Industries, Inc.; GenCorp., Inc.; Hoover Treated Wood Products; International Comfort Products Corporation (USA); Lennox International, Inc.; Whirlpool Corporation; Winnebago Industries.

For full biographical listings, see the Martindale-Hubbell Law Directory

SAMUEL P. PIERCE, JR., P.C. (AV)

5064 Roswell Road Suite C-300, 30342
Telephone: 404-843-1512
Fax: 404-843-4474
URL: http://www.lawyers.com

Samuel P. Pierce, Jr.

For full biographical listings, see the Martindale-Hubbell Law Directory

Atlanta—Continued

PIERCE & YOUNG (AV)

Building 1700, 2255 Cumberland Parkway Northwest, 30339-4575
Telephone: 770-435-0500
Telecopier: 770-435-0362

MEMBERS OF FIRM

J. Wayne Pierce
Richard M. Young

For full biographical listings, see the Martindale-Hubbell Law Directory

POPE, MCGLAMRY, KILPATRICK & MORRISON, LLP (AV)

A Partnership including Professional Corporations
The Pinnacle, 3455 Peachtree Road, N.E., 30326-3243
Telephone: 404-523-7706
Fax: 404-524-1648
Phenix City, Alabama: 334-298-7354
Mailing Address: P.O. Box 191625, Atlanta, GA, 31119-1625
Email: pmkm@pmkm.com
Columbus, Georgia Office: 318 11th Street, 2nd Floor, P.O. Box 2128, 31902-2128.
Telephone: 706-324-0050.
Fax: 706-327-1536.

MEMBERS OF FIRM

C. Neal Pope (P.C.)
Max R. McGlamry (P.C.) (Resident, Columbus, Georgia Office)
Paul V. Kilpatrick, Jr. (Resident, Columbus, Georgia Office)
R. Timothy Morrison
Michael L. McGlamry
Earle F. Lasseter
William Usher Norwood, III
Jay F. Hirsch
Wade H. Tomlinson, III
Teresa Pike Tomlinson

RESIDENT ASSOCIATE

C. Elizabeth Pope

Reference: Columbus Bank & Trust Co.

For full biographical listings, see the Martindale-Hubbell Law Directory

REYNOLDS & MCARTHUR (AV)

A Partnership including a Professional Corporation
Overlook II, Suite 270, 2839 Paces Ferry Rd., N.W., 30339
Telephone: 770-438-8997; 770-438-9062
Fax: 770-438-8536
Macon, Georgia Office: 850 Walnut Street, 31201.
Telephone: 912-741-6000.
Fax: 912-742-0750. Email: firm@rmtriallaw.com

MEMBERS OF FIRM

W. Carl Reynolds (P.C.)
Katherine L. McArthur
Charles M. Cork, III
O. Wendell Horne, III
Bradley J. Survant

For full biographical listings, see the Martindale-Hubbell Law Directory

SHIGLEY LAW FIRM, L.L.C. (AV)

3166 Mathieson Drive Suite 200, 30305
Telephone: 404-364-1999
Fax: 404-364-0880
URL: http://www.ga-law.com
Email: kshigley@mindspring.com *URL:* http://www.lawyers.com/shigleylaw

Kenneth L. Shigley

For full biographical listings, see the Martindale-Hubbell Law Directory

SMITH, HOWARD & AJAX, LLP (AV)

300 Atlanta Financial Center South, 3333 Peachtree Road, N.E., 30326
Telephone: 404-239-1900
Fax: 404-239-1930

MEMBERS OF FIRM

Fred W. Ajax, Jr.
Susan Teale Couvillon
Harvey S. Gray
Matthew G. Moffett
Michael J. Rust
Michael D. St. Amand
David K. Whatley

For full biographical listings, see the Martindale-Hubbell Law Directory

THOMAS, KENNEDY, SAMPSON & PATTERSON (AV)

3355 Main Street, 30337
Telephone: 404-688-4503
Telecopier: 404-681-2950; Litigation Dept.
Telecopier: 404-684-9515
URL: http://www.tksp.com

MEMBERS OF FIRM

R. E. Thomas, Jr. (1911-1996)
John Loren Kennedy (1942-1994)
Thomas G. Sampson
P. Andrew Patterson
Jeffrey E. Tompkins

ASSOCIATES

Thomas G. Sampson, II
Ceasar C. Mitchell, II.
Erika Nicole Jackson

(See Next Column)

LEGAL SUPPORT PERSONNEL

Gwendolyn C.H. Dixon
Elbetha (Beth) Martin (Paralegal)
Nancy Allen-Haskell
Yvonne Torrence
Shyril E. Beck
Constance Harris (Paralegal)
Lisa Russell Johnson

For full biographical listings, see the Martindale-Hubbell Law Directory

WEINBERG, WHEELER, HUDGINS, GUNN & DIAL, LLC (AV)

999 Peachtree Street, N.E. Suite 2700, 30309
Telephone: 404-876-2700
Facsimile: 404-875-9433
Email: firm@wwhgd.com

MEMBERS OF FIRM

Ben L. Weinberg, Jr.
J. Kenneth Moorman
Earl W. Gunn
Frederick N. Sager, Jr.
Carol P. Michel
Johnathan T. Krawcheck
John C. Bonnie

ASSOCIATES

Anandhi S. Rajan
Ashley P. Nichols
Beth E. Weitzman
Patrick Moore
Chloe E. Dallaire
Michael R. Boorman
Anna C. Palazzolo

Representative Clients: AIG Technical Services; American International Group; Cdse Corporation; Emory University; Merck; Proctor and Gamble Company; St. Paul Fire & Marine Insurance Co.

For Complete List of Firm Personnel, See General Section

For full biographical listings, see the Martindale-Hubbell Law Directory

WILLIAMS & HENRY, LLP (AV)

Suite 2020, 1100 Peachtree Street, N.E., 30309-4520
Telephone: 404-873-3000
Fax: 404-873-4508
URL: http://www.whlawfirm.com

MEMBERS OF FIRM

Benjamin S. Williams
Philip C. Henry
Harvey R. Spiegel

Joseph A. Fried
Edward C. Henderson, Jr.
Gary L. Wimbish

OF COUNSEL

Robert L. Callahan, III

Reference: SunTrust Bank.

For full biographical listings, see the Martindale-Hubbell Law Directory

*AUGUSTA,** Richmond Co.

WILEY S. OBENSHAIN, III, P.C. (AV)

511 Court House Lane, 30904
Telephone: 706-722-1789
Fax: 706-722-3934

Wiley S. Obenshain, III

For full biographical listings, see the Martindale-Hubbell Law Directory

*BRUNSWICK,** Glynn Co.

FENDIG, MCLEMORE, TAYLOR, WHITWORTH & DURHAM, P.C. (AV)

Suite 200 Suntrust Bank Building, P.O. Box 1996, 31521
Telephone: 912-264-4126
Telecopier: 912-264-0591

Albert Fendig, Jr.
Gilbert C. McLemore, Jr.
Philip R. Taylor
David T. Whitworth
James B. Durham
Donna L. Crossland
Beth M. Duncan

For full biographical listings, see the Martindale-Hubbell Law Directory

JORDAN & BRISTOL (AV)

1528 Ellis Street, P.O. Box 2115, 31521
Telephone: 912-262-9200
Fax: 912-262-0277
Email: jordanod@gate.net

Randall A. Jordan
Steven P. Bristol

For full biographical listings, see the Martindale-Hubbell Law Directory

*COLUMBUS,** Muscogee Co.

BUTLER, WOOTEN, OVERBY, FRYHOFER, DAUGHTERY & SULLIVAN (AV)

1500 Second Avenue, P.O. Box 2766, 31902
Telephone: 706-322-1990;
National Wats: 1-800-233-4086
Fax: 706-323-2962
Atlanta, Georgia Office: 2719 Buford Highway, 30324.
Telephone: 404-321-1700.
Fax: 404-321-1713. Wats Line: 1-800-242-2962.

MEMBERS OF FIRM

James E. Butler, Jr.
Joel O. Wooten, Jr.
C. Frederick Overby
George W. Fryhofer III
Peter J. Daughtery
Lee Tarte Wallace
Terrance C. Sullivan

ASSOCIATES

Jason L. Crawford
Keith A. Pittman
Joshua Sacks
Teresa Thomas Abell
Cale H. Conley

Reference: Columbus Bank and Trust, Columbus, Ga.

For full biographical listings, see the Martindale-Hubbell Law Directory

POPE, MCGLAMRY, KILPATRICK & MORRISON, LLP (AV)

A Partnership including Professional Corporations
318 11th Street, 2nd Floor, P.O. Box 2128, 31902-2128
Telephone: 706-324-0050
Phenix City, Alabama: 334-298-7354
Fax: 706-327-1536
Email: pmkm@pmkm.com
Atlanta, Georgia Office: The Pinnacle, 3455 Peachtree Road, N.E. (30326-3243), P.O. Box 191625 (31119-1625).
Telephone: 404-523-7706.
Fax: 404-524-1648.

MEMBERS OF FIRM

C. Neal Pope (P.C.)
Max R. McGlamry (P.C.) (Resident)
Paul V. Kilpatrick, Jr. (Resident)
R. Timothy Morrison
Michael L. McGlamry
Earle F. Lasseter
William Usher Norwood, III (Resident, Atlanta Office)
Jay F. Hirsch
Wade H. Tomlinson, III
Teresa Pike Tomlinson

RESIDENT ASSOCIATE

Matthew N. Pope

Reference: Columbus Bank & Trust Co.

For full biographical listings, see the Martindale-Hubbell Law Directory

CORNELIA, Habersham Co.

CATHEY & STRAIN (AV)

6 Irvin Street, P.O. Box 689, 30531
Telephone: 706-778-2601
Fax: 706-776-2899

MEMBERS OF FIRM

Dennis T. Cathey
Edward E. Strain, III
J. Edward Staples
David A. Sleppy

For full biographical listings, see the Martindale-Hubbell Law Directory

*HINESVILLE,** Liberty Co.

JONES, OSTEEN, JONES & ARNOLD (AV)

206 East Court Street, P.O. Box 800, 31310
Telephone: 912-876-0111
Fax: 912-368-2979
Email: JOJA1@clds.net

MEMBERS OF FIRM

Charles M. Jones
J. Noel Osteen
Billy N. Jones
Jeffery L. Arnold

ASSOCIATES

G. Brinson Williams, Jr.
Linnie L. Darden, III
Mark W. Nickerson
L. Kelly Davis

General Counsel for: The Heritage Bank; The Coastal Bank; Coastal Electric Membership Corp.; Liberty County Hospital Authority; Hinesville Area Board of Realtors; Liberty County Industrial Authority; Liberty County, Georgia; City of Hinesville.

For full biographical listings, see the Martindale-Hubbell Law Directory

*MACON,** Bibb Co.

REYNOLDS & MCARTHUR (AV)

A Partnership including a Professional Corporation
850 Walnut Street, 31201
Telephone: 912-741-6000
Fax: 912-742-0750
Email: firm@rmtriallaw.com
Atlanta, Georgia Office: Overlook II, Suite 270, 2839 Paces Ferry Road, N.W., 30339.
Telephone: 770-438-8997; 770-438-9062.
Fax: 770-438-8536.

MEMBERS OF FIRM

W. Carl Reynolds (P.C.)
Katherine L. McArthur
Charles M. Cork, III
O. Wendell Horne, III
Bradley J. Survant

For full biographical listings, see the Martindale-Hubbell Law Directory

*MARIETTA,** Cobb Co.

BROWNING & TANKSLEY, LLP (AV)

Suite 225, 166 Anderson Street, 30060
Telephone: 770-424-1500
Fax: 770-424-1740

MEMBERS OF FIRM

Charles B. Tanksley
Jerry A. Landers, Jr.
Jeffrey G. Casurella
Michael K. Jablonski

For full biographical listings, see the Martindale-Hubbell Law Directory

*ROME,** Floyd Co.

BRINSON, ASKEW, BERRY, SEIGLER, RICHARDSON & DAVIS, LLP (AV)

Omberg House, 615 West First Street, P.O. Box 5513, 30162-5513
Telephone: 706-291-8853;
Atlanta: 404-521-0908
Telecopier: 706-234-3574
Email: law@brinson-askew.com *URL:* http://www.brinson-askew.com

MEMBERS OF FIRM

Robert M. Brinson (P.C.)
C. King Askew (P.C.)
Robert L. Berry
Joseph M. Seigler, Jr.
Thomas D. Richardson
J. Anderson Davis
Hendrick L. Cromartie, III
Wright W. Smith
Mark M. J. Webb
Joseph B. Atkins
I. Stewart Duggan

ASSOCIATES

James Daniel Blitch, IV
Stephen B. Moseley

Representative Clients: Georgia Power Co.; General Electric Company; Columbia Redmond Regional Medical Center; Oglethorpe Power Corp.; Suhner Manufacturing, Inc.; ConAgra, Inc.; United States Fidelity & Guaranty Co.; The Charles Machine Works d/b/a "DitchWitch"; Shaw Industries, Inc.; Carlisle Syntec, Inc.

For full biographical listings, see the Martindale-Hubbell Law Directory

*SAVANNAH,** Chatham Co.

FORBES & BOWMAN (AV)

Park South D-14, 7505 Waters Avenue, P.O. Box 13929, 31416-0929
Telephone: 912-352-1190
FAX: 912-352-1471

Morton G. Forbes
Catherine McKenzie Bowman
John A. Foster
Scot V. Pool
D. Campbell Bowman, Jr.

Representative Clients: American International Group; AIG Claims Service; Frito-Lay, Inc.; GAB Business Services, Inc.; CNA Insurance Co.; Crawford & Co.

For full biographical listings, see the Martindale-Hubbell Law Directory

KARSMAN, BROOKS & CALLAWAY, P.C. (AV)

301 West Congress Street, P.O. Box 9149, 31412
Telephone: 912-238-2750
Cable Address: "Karbro"
Telecopier: 912-238-2767

Stanley M. Karsman
Charles C. Brooks
Timothy F. Callaway, III
Stanley E. Harris, Jr.
James L. Drake, Jr.
Dana F. Braun
R. Krannert Riddle
Edward M. Hughes
Timothy J. Haeussler

For full biographical listings, see the Martindale-Hubbell Law Directory

HAWAII

*HONOLULU,** Honolulu Co.

CRONIN, FRIED, SEKIYA, KEKINA & FAIRBANKS ATTORNEYS AT LAW, A LAW CORPORATION (AV)

1900 Davies Pacific Center, 841 Bishop Street, 96813
Telephone: 808-524-1433
Fax: 808-536-2073

Paul F. Cronin
L. Richard Fried, Jr.
Gerald Y. Sekiya
Wayne K. Kekina
David L. Fairbanks
John D. Thomas, Jr.
Stuart A. Kaneko
Bert S. Sakuda
Allen K. Williams
Keith K. H. Young

Patrick W. Border
Gregory L. Lui-Kwan
Patrick F. McTernan
Clarence S.K. Kekina
Sylvia J. Luke
Geoffrey K.S. Komeya
Frances K. Schneider

For full biographical listings, see the Martindale-Hubbell Law Directory

FUKUNAGA MATAYOSHI HERSHEY & CHING (AV)

A Partnership including a Law Corporation
841 Bishop Street, Suite 1200, 96813
Telephone: 808-533-4300
Fax: 808-531-7585

PARTNERS

Kenneth K. Fukunaga
Jerold T. Matayoshi (A Law Corporation)
James H. Hershey
Wesley H. H. Ching
Patricia Kehau Wall

ASSOCIATES

Lois H. Yamaguchi
Robert R. Sadaoka
Celia A. Urion
Sheree Kon-Herrera

OF COUNSEL

Leighton K. Chong
Kathleen M. Douglas

Representative Clients: Ford Motor Company; General Motors Corporation; Honda Motor Company, Ltd.; American Honda Motor Company; Isuzu Motors America, Inc.; Johnson Worldwide Associates, Inc.; Nissan Motor Co., Ltd.; Mitsubishi Motors Corporation; Owens-Illinois, Inc.; W.R. Grace & Co.-Conn.

For full biographical listings, see the Martindale-Hubbell Law Directory

GOODSILL ANDERSON QUINN & STIFEL (AV)

Alii Place, Suite 1800, 1099 Alakea Street, P.O. Box 3196, 96801-3196
Telephone: 808-547-5600
FAX: 808-547-5880
Email: info@goodsill.com *URL:* http://www.goodsill.com

MEMBERS OF FIRM

Martin Anderson
David J. Dezzani
John R. Lacy
William S. Miller
Jacqueline L. S. Earle
Lisa Woods Munger
Bruce L. Lamon
Mark B. Desmarais
Corlis J. Chang
Wayne H. Muraoka
LindaLee K. Farm
Margaret Jenkins Leong
Carol Ann Eblen
Roy John Tjioe
A. Richard Philpott
Lennes N. Omuro
Derek R. Kobayashi

ASSOCIATES

Thomas L. Benedict
Edmund K. Saffery
Lisa A. Bail
Normand R. Lezy

Representative Clients: American Eurocopter Corporation; E. I. du Pont de Nemours & Company; Emerson Electric Co.; Ingersol Rand; Kawasaki Motors Corporation; Lorillard Tobacco Company; MEDMARC; Minnesota Mining & Manufacturing Co.; Pfizer Inc.; Sears Roebuck & Co.

For Complete List of Firm Personnel, See General Section
For full biographical listings, see the Martindale-Hubbell Law Directory

KESSNER DUCA UMEBAYASHI BAIN & MATSUNAGA ATTORNEYS AT LAW, A LAW CORPORATION (AV)

19th Floor, Central Pacific Plaza, 220 South King Street, 96813
Telephone: 808-536-1900
Telecopier: 808-529-7177
Telex: 723 8616 OPAC IIR

Robert C. Kessner
James N. Duca
Clyde S. Umebayashi
Elton John Bain
Emma S. Matsunaga
Muriel M. Taira

Beverly S. K. Tom
Jacqueline W.S. Amai
Melanie S. Matsui
Cori Ann C. Takamiya

(See Next Column)

OF COUNSEL

Kathy K. Higham

For full biographical listings, see the Martindale-Hubbell Law Directory

JAMES KRUEGER ATTORNEY AT LAW, A LAW CORPORATION

(See Wailuku)

LAW OFFICES OF IAN L. MATTOCH (AV)

Suite 1835, 737 Bishop Street, 96813
Telephone: 808-523-2451
Fax: 808-531-2652
Email: mattoch@mattoch.com *URL:* http://www.mattoch.com
Kaneohe, Hawaii Office: 45-781 Kamehameha Highway.
Telephone: 808-247-8598.
Waimea, Hawaii Office: Spencer House, Suite 236, Waimea Center.
Telephone: 808-885-7727.
Wailuku, Hawaii Office: Suite 523, One Main Plaza, 2200 Main Street.
Telephone: 808-244-5007.
Hilo, Hawaii Office: 688 Kanoelehua Avenue, Suite 200.
Telephone: 808-969-3302.
Fax: 808-961-5599.
Kailua-Kona, Hawaii Office: Suite D211, 75-170 Hualalai Road.
Telephone: 808-326-1516.
Fax: 808-326-7416.

Ian L. Mattoch

Bruce A. Larson
Mark F. Gallagher (Also at Wailuku, Hawaii Office)
Daniel P. Kirley
Jonathan S. Kuba
Benjamin R.C. Ignacio

Reference: First Hawaiian Bank.

For full biographical listings, see the Martindale-Hubbell Law Directory

MIYAGI, NOHR & MYHRE (AV)

1001 Bishop Street, Suite 1200, 96813
Telephone: 808-524-2466
Fax: 808-524-2556

Melvyn M. Miyagi
Katharine M. Nohr
James V. Myhre
Michael H. Tsuchida
John E. Drotz

OF COUNSEL

Carleton B. Reid

Representative Clients: American International Group; State Farm Insurance; TIG Insurance; Crum & Forster; ITT Specialty Risk Services; Marriott International; The Hartford; USAA; Budget Rent A Car; Crawford & Company.

For full biographical listings, see the Martindale-Hubbell Law Directory

TOM & PETRUS (AV)

212 Merchant Street Suite 200, 96813
Telephone: 808-522-0800
Fax: 808-522-0809

MEMBERS OF FIRM

Michael D. Tom
Brad S. Petrus
Richard B. Miller

ASSOCIATES

Leslie H. Kondo
Stephen M. Teves
David R. Harada-Stone
Lauren K. Rauschenburg

COUNSEL

Lyle Minoru Ishida

Representative Clients: BHP Hawaii, Inc.; Dillingham Construction Pacific, Ltd.; Delta Construction Corporation; Kapi'olani Health (Medical Center for Women and Children and Kapi'olani Medical Center at Pali Momi); St. Francis Health System (St. Francis Medical Center and St. Francis Medical Center West); Applied Technology Corporation; Nordic/PCL (HawaiiConvention Center); Volvo Cars of North America, Inc.; Gilbarco Inc.

For full biographical listings, see the Martindale-Hubbell Law Directory

KAILUA, Honolulu Co.

WINER MEHEULA & DEVENS (AV)

970 North Kalaheo Avenue, Suite A-300, 96734
Telephone: 808-254-5855
Fax: 808-254-6872
Email: winer@pacificlaw.com *URL:* http://www.pacificlaw.com

MEMBERS OF FIRM

Andrew S. Winer
William K. Meheula
Vladimir Paul Devens

OF COUNSEL

David F. Fasi

(See Next Column)

WINER MEHEULA & DEVENS, *Kailua—Continued*

ASSOCIATE

Blue H. Kaanehe

For full biographical listings, see the Martindale-Hubbell Law Directory

*LIHUE,** Kauai Co.

JAMES KRUEGER ATTORNEY AT LAW, A LAW CORPORATION

(See Wailuku)

*WAILUKU,** Maui Co.

JAMES KRUEGER ATTORNEY AT LAW, A LAW CORPORATION (AV)

2065 Main Street, 96793
Telephone: 808-244-7444; Honolulu: 536-7474
Facsimile: 808-244-4177
Email: maulaw@maui.net *URL:* http://www.kruegerlaw-hawaii.org

James Krueger

Eve M. Green — Cynthia Kanoholani Wong

A List of Representative Clients and References will be furnished upon request.

For full biographical listings, see the Martindale-Hubbell Law Directory

IDAHO

*BOISE,** Ada Co.

LYNCH & ASSOCIATES, P.L.L.C. (AV)

Ninth and Idaho Center, 225 N. 9th Street, Suite 600, P.O. Box 739, 83701
Telephone: 208-331-5088
Fax: 208-331-0088
Email: Lynchassoc@lesbois.com *URL:* http://www.lawyers.com/lynch&associates

James B. Lynch

Katherine M. Lynch

For full biographical listings, see the Martindale-Hubbell Law Directory

MOORE, BASKIN & PARKER (AV)

Washington Federal Plaza, 1001 West Idaho Street, Suite 400, P.O. Box 6756, 83707
Telephone: 208-336-6900
Facsimile: 208-336-7031
Email: mail@MBPLAW.com *URL:* http://www.lawyers.com/moorebaskin&parker

MEMBERS OF FIRM

Michael W. Moore — Paige Alan Parker
Thomas P. Baskin, III — Richard Hansen
Wendy Cox Dvorak

ASSOCIATE

Martin C. Hendrickson

Representative Clients: Travelers Insurance Co./Aetna Casualty & Surety, Co.; Capitol Indemnity Co.; Clarendon Insurance Co.; Crawford & Co.; Empire Fire & Marine Insurance Co.; Fireman's Fund Insurance Cos.; Idaho Counties Reciprocal Management Program; Idaho State Insurance Fund; Insurance Company of the West; Protective Insurance Co.

For full biographical listings, see the Martindale-Hubbell Law Directory

ILLINOIS

*CHICAGO,** Cook Co.

BATES MECKLER BULGER & TILSON (AV)

8300 Sears Tower, 233 South Wacker, 60606
Telephone: 312-474-7900
Facsimile: 312-474-7898
URL: http://www.bmbt.com

MEMBERS OF FIRM

Robert C. Heist — Bruce R. Meckler
Mari Henry Leigh — Steven D. Pearson
Mary F. Licari — Scott M. Seaman
Brian J Williams

(See Next Column)

ASSOCIATE

Eric D. Stubenvoll

For full biographical listings, see the Martindale-Hubbell Law Directory

BLATT, HAMMESFAHR & EATON (AV)

333 W. Wacker Drive, Suite 1900, 60606
Telephone: 312-849-8000
FAX: 312-357-0198
Email: BHE@BHELAW.COM *URL:* HTTP://WWW.BHELAW.COM
New York, New York Office: 45 Broadway, 12th Floor.
Telephone: 212-363-1900.
Fax: 212-363-2600. Email: bhe@bhelaw.com.

MEMBERS OF FIRM

Richard L. Blatt — Gregory D. Hopp
Hugo Chaviano — Kathleen A. McQueeny
Matthew T. Walsh

ASSOCIATES

Mary I. Babbo — Peggy A. Glenn
Bruce M. Lichtcsien

For full biographical listings, see the Martindale-Hubbell Law Directory

CHARLES A. BOYLE & ASSOCIATES, LTD. (AV)

55 East Monroe Street, Suite 4520, 60603
Telephone: 312-346-4944
FAX: 312-368-1061

Charles A. Boyle

Reference: Northern Trust of Chicago.

For full biographical listings, see the Martindale-Hubbell Law Directory

CAHILL, CHRISTIAN & KUNKLE, LTD. (AV)

Santa Fe Building, 224 South Michigan Avenue, Suite 1300, 60604
Telephone: 312-341-1688
Fax: 312-341-1689
URL: http://www.cck.com

William J. Kunkle, Jr. — Mary Kathryn Kelly
Roseann Oliver — Suzanne M. Metzel
William T. Cahill — Matthew J. Gehringer
John M. Christian — Steven E. Nieslawski
Lorna E. Propes — Michael K. Bartosz
Scott B. Greene — Donald Lee Homyk

OF COUNSEL

Louis B. Garippo

Daniel J. Collins — Frederic T. Knape
Jeanne M. Cullen — David R. Nordwall
Elizabeth A. Kaveny — Elisha S. Rosenblum
Melisa G. Thompson

For full biographical listings, see the Martindale-Hubbell Law Directory

CLIFFORD LAW OFFICES, P.C. (AV)

120 North La Salle Street, 31st Floor, 60602
Telephone: 312-899-9090
1-800-899-0410
Fax: 312-251-1160
Email: RACA@CliffordLaw.com *URL:* http://www.cliffordlaw.com

Robert A. Clifford — Kevin P. Durkin
Keith A. Hebeisen — Thomas K. Prindable

Robert P. Walsh, Jr. — Isobel S. Thomas
Susan A. Capra — Michael S. Krzak
Jeffrey J. Kroll — Timothy S. Tomasik
Richard F. Burke, Jr. — Brian Thomas Nash
Matthew I. Baker — Donald James Storino III
Timothy P. Rhatigan — Sheri L. Tarr

OF COUNSEL

Robert P. Sheridan

For full biographical listings, see the Martindale-Hubbell Law Directory

CONNELLY & SCHROEDER (AV)

One North Franklin Street, Suite 1200, 60606-3421
Telephone: 312-251-9600
Fax: 312-251-9601
Geneva, Illinois Office: 1250 Executive Place, Suite 201.
Telephone: 630-232-6440.
FAX: 630-232-6450

MEMBERS OF FIRM

Michael P. Connelly — Daniel F. Konicek
John L. Schroeder (Resident, Geneva Office) — (Also at Geneva Office)
Thomas F. Tobin — Eugene S. Kraus
Raymond E. Stachnik — Mary Lisa Kamins
Brandt R. Madsen
Robert J. Kartholl, Jr.

(See Next Column)

CONNELLY & SCHROEDER—*Continued*

ASSOCIATES

Michelle L. Adams (Resident, Geneva Office)
Matthew Patrick Connelly
Thomas W. Dillon (Resident, Geneva Office)
John Michael Kelly
Colleen Konicek
Charina de los Reyes
Martha Swatek (Resident, Geneva Office)

For full biographical listings, see the Martindale-Hubbell Law Directory

JEFFREY M. GOLDBERG & ASSOCIATES, LTD. (AV)

20 North Clark Street, Suite 3100, 60602
Telephone: 312-236-4146
Fax: 312-236-5913
Email: firm@goldberglaw.com

Jeffrey M. Goldberg

Michael H. Berman
Suzanne M. Bonds
Anthony M. Goldner
Michael B. Gunzburg
Geoffrey G. Johnson
Michael V. Marsh

For full biographical listings, see the Martindale-Hubbell Law Directory

MICHAEL T. HANNAFAN & ASSOCIATES, LTD. (AV)

One East Wacker Drive, Suite 2710, 60601
Telephone: 312-527-0055
Fax: 312-527-0220
Email: mthannafan@aol.com

Michael T. Hannafan

Cory A. Johnson

Reference: The Northern Trust Co.

For full biographical listings, see the Martindale-Hubbell Law Directory

HASKELL & PERRIN (AV)

200 West Adams, Suite 2600, 60606
Telephone: 312-781-9393
Fax: 312-781-9178
Email: hasper@haskellperrin.com

MEMBERS OF FIRM

James Kirk Perrin
John J. Lynch
Mary Elizabeth Denefe

OF COUNSEL

Donald M. Haskell

ASSOCIATE

Nancy J. Robinson

For full biographical listings, see the Martindale-Hubbell Law Directory

KAPLAN, BEGY & VON OHLEN (AV)

One First National Plaza 51st Floor, 60603
Telephone: 312-345-3000
Fax: 312-345-3119
URL: http://www.kbvlaw.com

MEMBERS OF FIRM

Fred C. Begy, III
Larry S. Kaplan
James D. Solon
Robert C. von Ohlen, Jr.
Joseph A. Bosco
Richard A. Walker
Mitchell J. Kanaan
Patrick J. Keating

ASSOCIATES

Keith S. Yamaguchi
Thomas C. Sokol
Robert K. Villa
Nicole Halpern Murphy
Telly Andrews
Tamara S. Dykstra

For full biographical listings, see the Martindale-Hubbell Law Directory

SUSAN E. LOGGANS & ASSOCIATES, P.C. (AV)

Suite 2850, 200 West Madison Street, 60606
Telephone: 312-201-8600
Telecopier: 312-201-1180
Email: loggans@logganslaw.com *URL:* http://www.logganslaw.com

Susan E. Loggans

James G. McConnell
Gregg E. Strellis
John T. Ferjak
Patrick D. Flanagan
Norman L. Rubenstein

For full biographical listings, see the Martindale-Hubbell Law Directory

MORRIS & STELLA (AV)

Suite 1200, 200 West Adams Street, 60606
Telephone: 312-782-2345
Telecopier: 312-750-0924

(See Next Column)

MEMBERS OF FIRM

William J. Morris
Joseph N. Stella
Jeffrey W. Gunn

ASSOCIATES

Bruce J. Manos
William F. McDermott
Ronald Eric Bentsen
Austin J. Foley

For full biographical listings, see the Martindale-Hubbell Law Directory

BERNARD R. NEVORAL AND ASSOCIATES LTD. (AV)

150 North Wacker Drive, Suite 2450, 60606
Telephone: 312 263-7058
FAX: 312-263-4566

Bernard R. Nevoral

Jeremy Michael West
Daniel M. Extrom
David F Szczecin

For full biographical listings, see the Martindale-Hubbell Law Directory

NOLAN LAW GROUP (AV)

One North La Salle Street, 35th Floor, 60602
Telephone: 312-372-5400
Toll Free: 888-372-3870
Facsimile: 312-372-0558
Email: dnolan1@ix.netcom.com

Donald J. Nolan
Albert E. Durkin, Jr.
William J. Jovan
Floyd A. Wisner
James H. Lawlor, III
Thomas P. Routh
James A. Santucci
Todd R. Mcquiston

Laura L. Ruhl

For full biographical listings, see the Martindale-Hubbell Law Directory

PAVALON, GIFFORD, LAATSCH & MARINO (AV)

Two North La Salle Street, Suite 1600, 60602
Telephone: 312-419-7400
Fax: 312-419-7408
Email: pavgif@aol.com
Rockford, Illinois Office: 501 Seventh Street, Suite 501, 61104.
Telephone: 815-968-5100.

MEMBERS OF FIRM

Eugene I. Pavalon
Geoffrey L. Gifford
Gary K. Laatsch
Frank C. Marino
Henry Phillip Gruss

Christine Walsh Donnelly

For full biographical listings, see the Martindale-Hubbell Law Directory

POWER ROGERS & SMITH, P.C. (AV)

35 West Wacker Drive, Suite 3700, 60601
Telephone: 312-236-9381
Fax: 312-236-0920

Joseph A. Power, Jr.
Larry R. Rogers
Todd A. Smith

Thomas G. Siracusa
Paul L. Salzetta
Thomas M. Power
Larry R. Rogers, Jr.
Ruth M. Degnan
Devon C. Bruce

For full biographical listings, see the Martindale-Hubbell Law Directory

QUINLAN & CRISHAM, LTD. (AV)

30 North La Salle Street, Suite 2900, 60602
Telephone: 312-263-0900
Telecopier: 312-263-5013

William R. Quinlan
Thomas M. Crisham
Thomas C. Hynes
Gino L. DiVito
Mary Patricia Benz
Michael C. Bruck
James R. Carroll
Thomas C. Hofbauer
John F. Kennedy
Jeffrey T. Kubes
Eugene E. Murphy, Jr.
Michael I Rothstein
Caesar A. Tabet
Cheryl I. Niro

Frank M. Adams, Jr.
Brian J. Alesia
Michael T. Beirne
Catherine J. Casey
Jasmine De La Torre
Karina H. DeHayes
Edward Fitzsimmons Dunne
Lisa M. Hegedus
Erin Bolan Hines
John N. Hourihane, Jr.
David M. Jenkins
J. Christopher Madden
Michelle A. Michalik
James A. Niewiara
Martin J. O'Hara
John P. O'Malley

(See Next Column)

QUINLAN & CRISHAM LTD., *Chicago—Continued*

J. Jeffrey Patton
Jean M. Prendergast
Melissa M. Riahei
John H. Scheid
Daniel L. Stanner
Michael A. Steigmann

For full biographical listings, see the Martindale-Hubbell Law Directory

STONE & MOORE, CHARTERED (AV)

30 North La Salle Street, Suite 4300, 60602
Telephone: 312-332-5656
Fax: 312-332-5858
URL: http://www.stonemoore.com
Merrillville, Indiana Office: 500 E. 86th Avenue, 46410.
Telephone: 219-736-5959.
Fax: 219-736-5858.
Wheaton, Illinois Office: 600 W. Roosevelt Road, Suite 1A, 60187.
Telephone: 630-221-9292.
Fax: 630-221-9393.

William G. Stone
Robert Charles Moore (Also at Wheaton, Illinois Office)
Raymond R. Pesavento
Rosario Cibella
Richard M. Johnson, Jr.
J. Murray Pinkston, III
Julie Osswald Hooven

Christian D. Ambler
Jeffrey W. Henning
Erica Lewis Battaglia
Kevin Kemp Lyons
Kristin E. Rooney
Daniel S. Schulz
Matthew B. Stephens
A. Christine Svenson
Douglas W. Walker

For full biographical listings, see the Martindale-Hubbell Law Directory

STRIDE, CRADDOCK & STRIDE (AV)

111 West Washington Street, Suite 1837, 60602-2773
Telephone: 312-346-5800
Fax: 312-346-3870

Herbert F. Stride
J. Patrick Craddock
Herbert L. Stride

Nicholas C. Panos
Deborah A. Stride-Saran
Vickie Voukidis Blum
Michael J. Craddock
Arthur Z. Handelman

For full biographical listings, see the Martindale-Hubbell Law Directory

WILDMAN, HARROLD, ALLEN & DIXON (AV)

225 West Wacker Drive, 30th Floor, 60606-1229
Telephone: 312-201-2000
Fax: 312-201-2555
Email: hennessy@whad.com *URL:* http://www.whad.com
Aurora, Illinois Office: 1961 W. Downer Place.
Telephone: 630-892-7021.
Fax: 630-892-7158.
Waukegan, Illinois Office: 404 West Water, P. O. Box 890.
Telephone: 847-625-5550.
Fax: 847-625-5555.
Lisle, Illinois Office: 4300 Commerce Court, Suite 320.
Telephone: 630-955-0555.
Fax: 630-955-0662
Toronto, Ontario correspondent Office: Keel Cottrelle. 36 Toronto Street, Suite 920.
Telephone: 416-367-2900.
Telefax: 416-367-2791.
Telex: 062-18660.

MEMBERS OF FIRM

Richard C. Bartelt
Cal R. Burnton
Steven E. Danekas
Michael Dockterman
James P. Dorr
Robert E. Haley
Anthony G. Hopp
David A. Kanter
Elizabeth Keiley
Anne Giddings Kimball
Steven L. Larson (Waukegan Office)
Brian W. Lewis
Donald R. McGarrah
Mark P. Miller
Timothy G. Nickels
Sarah L. Olson
Richard C. Palmer
David F. Pardys (Waukegan Office)
Douglas L. Prochnow
Fred E. Schulz
Robert A. Strelecky (Lisle Office)
Peter A. Tomaras
James B. Vogts
Jeanne E. Walker
Dale G. Wills

OF COUNSEL

Thomas D. Allen

Michael J. Castellino
Paul D. Cranley
Anne-Marie Dega
Kenneth M. Gorenberg
Douglas W. Hyman
Michael A. Kaeding
Heather Huthwaite Martin
Jeffrey A. McIntyre
Ian J. McPheron
Kelly L. Murray
Martha D. Owens
Kevin B. Reid

(See Next Column)

Steven O. Schnack
Derek C. Smith (Not admitted in IL)
Susan M. Weis

For full biographical listings, see the Martindale-Hubbell Law Directory

JOHN C. WUNSCH, P.C. (AV)

77 West Washington Street, Suite 1420, 60602
Telephone: 312-977-9900
Fax: 312-236-2573

John C. Wunsch

Reference: The Northern Trust Co.

For full biographical listings, see the Martindale-Hubbell Law Directory

MATTOON, Coles Co.

CRAIG & CRAIG (AV)

1807 Broadway, P.O. Box 689, 61938-0689
Telephone: 217-234-6481
Telecopier: 217-234-6486; 258-8292
Email: craiglaw@advant.com
Mount Vernon, Illinois Office: 115 North 7th Street.
Telephone: 618-244-7511.

MEMBERS OF FIRM

Craig Van Meter (1895-1981)
Fred H. Kelly (1894-1971)
Robert M. Werden (1908-1969)
George N. Gilkerson (1911-1985)
John P. Ewart
Richard F. Record, Jr.
Stephen L. Corn
Robert G. Grierson
Gregory C. Ray
Paul R. Lynch (Resident, Mount Vernon Office)
Kenneth F. Werts (Resident, Mount Vernon Office)
John L. Barger

ASSOCIATES

Kathleen M. Stockwell
Kristine M. Tuttle
Julie A. Webb (Resident, Mount Vernon Office)
John M. O'Driscoll
Duane A. Deters
Katy C. Fain (Resident, Mount Vernon Office)
Erin E. Wisner
John F. Watson

OF COUNSEL

Jack E. Horsley

Representative Clients: Deere & Company; Chubb Group Insurance Companies; EMC Insurance Companies; Bituminous; Grinnell Mutual Reinsurance Group; Cincinnati Insurance Co.; St. Paul Insurance Co.

For full biographical listings, see the Martindale-Hubbell Law Directory

*PEORIA,** Peoria Co.

NICOARA & STEAGALL (AV)

Commerce Bank Building, 416 Main Street, Suite 815, 61602-1103
Telephone: 309-674-6085
Fax: 309-674-6032
Email: 70754.3140@compuserve.com

MEMBERS OF FIRM

John P. Nicoara
Richard L. Steagall

Representative Clients: Farmers Insurance Group; Illinois Founders Insurance Co.
Reference: Commerce Bank.

For full biographical listings, see the Martindale-Hubbell Law Directory

PERU, La Salle Co.

ANTHONY C. RACCUGLIA & ASSOCIATES (AV)

1200 Maple Drive, 61354
Telephone: 815-223-0230
Ottawa, Illinois Office: 633 La Salle Street.
Telephone: 815-434-2003.

ASSOCIATES

James A. McPhedran
Louis L. Bertrand

References: La Salle National Bank; Citizens First National Bank of Peru, Illinois.

For full biographical listings, see the Martindale-Hubbell Law Directory

*WAUKEGAN,** Lake Co.

SALVI & SCHOSTOK, P.C. (AV)

Established 1982 as Law Offices of Patrick A. Salvi, P.C.
218 North Utica Street, 60085
Telephone: 847-249-1227
Telefax: 847-249-0138
Email: salvilaw.com *URL:* http://www.salvilaw.com
Chicago, Illinois Office: 181 West Madison, Suite 3525, 60602.
Telephone: 312-372-1227.
Telefax: 312-372-3720.

(See Next Column)

SALVI & SCHOSTOK P.C.—*Continued*

Patrick A. Salvi
Michael P. Schostok
David J. Pritchard (Resident, Chicago Office)

John Andrew Kornak
J. Matthew Dudley
Peter M. Trobe
Ellen C. Smith
Scott E. Preusen

OF COUNSEL

Bernard E. Grysen

References: First Midwest Bank, Waukegan, Illinois; Northern Trust Bank, Lake Forest, Illinois; Commercial Litigation Clients; Anderson Consulting, LLP.; Baxter Healthcare; Brunswick Corporation, Lake Forest, Illinois.

For full biographical listings, see the Martindale-Hubbell Law Directory

INDIANA

*BLOOMINGTON,** Monroe Co.

KELLEY, BELCHER & BROWN, A PROFESSIONAL CORPORATION (AV)

301 West Seventh Street, P.O. Box 3250, 47402-3250
Telephone: 812-336-9963
Telecopier: 812-336-4588

William H. Kelley
Thomas J. Belcher
Darla Sue Brown

Shannon L. Robinson
Kyle M. Baker
Michael W. Phelps

For full biographical listings, see the Martindale-Hubbell Law Directory

*EVANSVILLE,** Vanderburgh Co.

BERGER AND BERGER (AV)

313 Main Street, 47708-1485
Telephone: 812-425-8101
Outside Indiana: 800-327-0182
Fax: 812-421-5909
Email: berger@bergerlaw.com *URL:* http://www.bergerlaw.com

MEMBERS OF FIRM

Charles L. Berger
Mark W. Rietman

References: Citizens National Bank of Evansville; Old National Bank in Evansville.

For full biographical listings, see the Martindale-Hubbell Law Directory

FINE & HATFIELD, A PROFESSIONAL CORPORATION (AV)

520 N.W. Second Street, P.O. Box 779, 47705-0779
Telephone: 812-425-3592
Telecopier: 812-421-4269
Email: Fine@Fine-Hatfield.com *URL:* http://www.Fine-Hatfield.com

Thomas H. Bryan
Danny E. Glass
Elaine Brown Elliott

Boyd A. Toler

A List of Representative Clients Furnished Upon Request.

For full biographical listings, see the Martindale-Hubbell Law Directory

GERLING LAW OFFICES, PROFESSIONAL CORPORATION (AV)

519 Main Street Walkway, P.O. Box 3203, 47731
Telephone: 812-423-5251
Fax: 812-423-9928
URL: http://www.gerlinglaw.com

Gary L. Gerling
Edward B. Anderson
David G. Hatfield
Christian M. Lenn
Gayle Gerling Pettinga
Stephen Hensleigh Thomas

For full biographical listings, see the Martindale-Hubbell Law Directory

*FORT WAYNE,** Allen Co.

ROBY & HOOD (AV)

Standard Federal Plaza, 200 East Main Street, Suite 520, 46802
Telephone: 219-423-3366
Fax: 219-423-3367
Anderson, Indiana Office: One Citizens Plaza, 305 Key Bank, 46016.
Telephone: 765-642-2402.
Marion, Indiana Office: 1315 West Gillespie Street, 46952.
Telephone: 765-651-0677.

(See Next Column)

MEMBERS OF FIRM

Daniel A. Roby
G. Stanley Hood
Thomas A. Manges
David Joseph Stach

References: Norwest Bank; Bank One.

For full biographical listings, see the Martindale-Hubbell Law Directory

*INDIANAPOLIS,** Marion Co.

HOVDE LAW FIRM (AV)

10585 North Meridian Street, Suite 345, P.O. Box 40849, 46240-0849
Telephone: 317-818-3100
Fax: 317-818-3111
Email: hovde@indy.net

F. Boyd Hovde
Frederick R. Hovde
Regina M. Poore
Robert T. Dassow

For full biographical listings, see the Martindale-Hubbell Law Directory

LOCKE REYNOLDS LLP (AV)

1000 Capital Center South, 201 North Illinois Street, 46204-4210
Telephone: 317-237-3800
Telecopier: 317-237-3900
Email: attys@locke.com *URL:* http://www.locke.com

Hugh E. Reynolds, Jr.
Lloyd H. Milliken, Jr.
William V. Hutchens
Michael A. Bergin
Steven J. Strawbridge
Randall R. Riggs
Richard A. Huser
Thomas J. Campbell
Thomas R. Schultz
Eric A. Riegner
Kevin C. Schiferl
Peter H. Pogue
Jeffrey J. Mortier
Nicholas C. Pappas

Stephen L. Vaughan
Nelson D. Alexander
Derek S. Burrell
T. Joseph Wendt
Michelle Davis Carmichael
Roland R. Schindler, II

OF COUNSEL

William H. Vobach

Representative Clients: American Honda Motor Co., Inc.; American Suzuki Motor Corporation; Black & Decker (U.S.) Inc.; Case Corporation; Delta International Machinery Corporation; Emerson Electric Company; Ford Motor Company; General Motors Corporation; Siemens; Toyota Motor Sales, U.S.A., Inc.

For Complete List of Firm Personnel, See General Section

For full biographical listings, see the Martindale-Hubbell Law Directory

MILLER MULLER MENDELSON & KENNEDY (AV)

8900 Keystone Crossing Suite 1250, 46240
Telephone: 317-574-4500
1-800-394-3094
Fax: 317-574-4501
Email: mmmk@iquest.net

MEMBERS OF FIRM

Michael S. Miller
John Muller
Tilden Mendelson
Timothy J. Kennedy

ASSOCIATE

Catherine A. Kling

For full biographical listings, see the Martindale-Hubbell Law Directory

MITCHELL HURST JACOBS & DICK (AV)

152 East Washington Street, 46204
Telephone: 317-636-0808
1-800-636-0808
Fax: 317-633-7680
URL: http://www.mhjd.com

MEMBERS OF FIRM

William W. Hurst
Samuel L. Jacobs
Richard J. Dick
Marshall S. Hanley
Robert W. Strohmeyer, Jr.

ASSOCIATES

Danielle A. Takla
Kimberly H. Danforth
Jennifer Levin Sinder

For full biographical listings, see the Martindale-Hubbell Law Directory

TOWNSEND & MONTROSS (AV)

230 East Ohio Street, 46204
Telephone: 317-264-4444
Fax: 317-264-2080

John F. Townsend, Jr.
W. Scott Montross

ASSOCIATE

John F. Townsend, III

(See Next Column)

TOWNSEND & MONTROSS, *Indianapolis—Continued*

OF COUNSEL

John F. Townsend

Reference: N.B.D. Bank, N.A.

For full biographical listings, see the Martindale-Hubbell Law Directory

WARD & WARD (AV)

1014 Circle Tower Building, 55 Monument Circle, 46204
Telephone: 317-639-9501
Fax: 317-637-1919
Email: cpw@wardlawfirm.com

MEMBERS OF FIRM

Donald W. Ward
Charles P. Ward

For full biographical listings, see the Martindale-Hubbell Law Directory

WILSON, KEHOE & WININGHAM (AV)

2859 North Meridian, 46208
Telephone: 317-920-6400
Fax: 317-920-6405
URL: http://www.wkw.com
Richmond, Indiana Office: 2901 East Main Street, 47374.
Telephone: 765-962-9113.
Connersville, Indiana Office: 118 West 30th Street, 47331.
Telephone: 765-827-1100.
Muncie, Indiana Office: 3310 West Fox Ridge Lane, 47304.
Telephone: 765-284-2474.
Fax: 765-288-8655.

MEMBERS OF FIRM

Harry A. Wilson, Jr.
D. Bruce Kehoe
William E. Winingham, Jr.

ASSOCIATES

Ralph E. Dowling
Gerald A. Griffin, M.D.
William E. Lukens

OF COUNSEL

Gerald L. Lawlis

Reference: The Indiana National Bank.

For full biographical listings, see the Martindale-Hubbell Law Directory

YARLING & ROBINSON (AV)

151 North Delaware, Suite 1535, P.O. Box 44128, 46204
Telephone: 317-262-8800
Fax: 317-262-3046
Email: yrhl@yarling.com *URL:* http://www.yarling.com

MEMBERS OF FIRM

Charles F. Robinson, Jr.
Douglas E. Rogers
John W. Hammel
Mark S. Gray
Linda Y. Hammel
Matthew C. Robinson

ASSOCIATE

Jeffrey R. Mitchell

OF COUNSEL

Richard W. Yarling

Representative Clients: Furnished upon request.

For full biographical listings, see the Martindale-Hubbell Law Directory

YOSHA KRAHULIK & LEVY (AV)

Pyramid II, First Floor, 3500 West DePauw Boulevard, Suite 2015, P.O. Box 68979, 46268
Telephone: 317-334-9200
Toll Free: 800-875-5759
Fax: 317-228-3355
URL: http://www.yoshalaw.com

MEMBERS OF FIRM

Louis Buddy Yosha
William Levy
Jon D. Krahulik

ASSOCIATES

David C. Krahulik
Julie C. Welp
Jeff D. Oliphant
Janice D. Heidt

Reference: National Bank of Indianapolis.

For full biographical listings, see the Martindale-Hubbell Law Directory

MERRILLVILLE, Lake Co.

HOEPPNER WAGNER & EVANS LLP (AV)

Twin Towers, Suite 606 South, 1000 East 80th Place, P.O. Box 10627, 46410-0627
Telephone: 219-769-6552; 800-263-1466 (IN, IL)
Fax: 219-738-2349
Email: hwe@hwelaw.com *URL:* http://www.hwelaw.com
Valparaiso, Indiana Office: 103 East Lincolnway, P.O. Box 2357, 46384-2357.
Telephone: 219-464-4961; 800-879-2246 (IN, IL).
Fax: 219-465-0603. Email: hwe@hwelaw.com

RESIDENT MEMBERS

John E. Hughes
F. Joseph Jaskowiak
Richard M. Davis

RESIDENT ASSOCIATE

Jack A. Kramer

For Complete List of Firm Personnel, See General Section

For full biographical listings, see the Martindale-Hubbell Law Directory

MUNSTER, Lake Co.

LAW OFFICES OF TIMOTHY F. KELLY (AV)

Suite 2A, 9250 Columbia Avenue, 46321
Telephone: 219-836-4062
Telecopier: 219-836-0167
Email: tfklaw@tfklaw.net

MEMBERS OF FIRM

Timothy F. Kelly
Karl K. Vanzo

ASSOCIATES

Steven J. Sersic
Kathleen E. Peek

LEGAL SUPPORT PERSONNEL

LEGAL ASSISTANTS

Kristen Cook Faso
Kerry E. Kelly
Lynn M. Hochstetler

For full biographical listings, see the Martindale-Hubbell Law Directory

SEYMOUR, Jackson Co.

PARDIECK, GILL, VARGO & MACTAVISH, A PROFESSIONAL CORPORATION (AV)

100 North Chestnut Street, P.O. Box 608, 47274
Telephone: 812-523-8686
Fax: 812-522-4199
Email: pgv@pgvlaw.com
Indianapolis, Indiana Office: The Old Bailey Building, 244 North College Avenue, 46202.
Telephone: 317-639-3321.

Roger L. Pardieck
John F. Vargo (Resident, Indianapolis Office)
W. Brent Gill
Bruce A. MacTavish

Thomas L. Landwerlen (Resident, Indianapolis Office)
Karen J. Mellencamp Davis
Janet O. Vargo (Resident, Indianapolis Office)

OF COUNSEL

Robert C. Rothkopf (Resident, Indianapolis Office)

References: Home Federal Savings Bank, Seymour, Indiana.

For full biographical listings, see the Martindale-Hubbell Law Directory

*SOUTH BEND,** St. Joseph Co.

DORAN • BLACKMOND LLP (AV)

1700 Valley American Bank Building, 211 W. Washington Street, 46601
Telephone: 219-288-1800
Fax: 219-236-4265

MEMBERS OF FIRM

M. Edward Doran (1895-1982)
John E. Doran
Don G. Blackmond

ASSOCIATES

Don Gregory Blackmond
Peter J. Van Dyke
Lynn M. Butcher

OF COUNSEL

A. Howard Williams

For full biographical listings, see the Martindale-Hubbell Law Directory

ROWE & ROWE (AV)

Suite 900 Keybank Building, 46601
Telephone: 219-233-8200
Fax: 219-234-5987

(See Next Column)

ROWE & ROWE—*Continued*

R. Kent Rowe R. Kent Rowe, III

ASSOCIATES

Robert D. Truitt Gregory J. Haines
Marie Anne Hendrie

For full biographical listings, see the Martindale-Hubbell Law Directory

*VALPARAISO,** Porter Co.

HOEPPNER WAGNER & EVANS LLP (AV)

103 East Lincolnway, P.O. Box 2357, 46384-2357
Telephone: 219-464-4961; 800-879-2246 (IN, IL)
Fax: 219-465-0603
Email: hwe@hwelaw.com *URL:* http://www.hwelaw.com
Merrillville, Indiana Office: Twin Towers, Suite 606 South, 1000 East 80th Place, P.O. Box 10627, 46419-0627.
Telephone: 219-769-6552; 800-263-1466 (IN, IL).
Fax: 219-738-2349. Email: hwe@hwelaw.com

MEMBERS OF FIRM

Larry G. Evans
William F. Satterlee, III
John E. Hughes (Resident, Merrillville Office)
Ronald P. Kuker
F. Joseph Jaskowiak (Resident, Merrillville Office)
Richard M. Davis (Resident, Merrillville Office)
Michael P. Blaize

ASSOCIATES

Robert L. Clark
Jeffrey W. Clymer
Jack A. Kramer (Resident, Merrillville Office)
Galen A. Bradley (Resident, Merrillville Office)
Kevin G. Kerr
Karen M. Read

Representative Clients: Bethlehem Steel Corp.; Chester, Inc.; Hunt-Wesson Foods, Inc.; Owens-Corning Fiberglas Corp.; State Farm Insurance.

For Complete List of Firm Personnel, See General Section

For full biographical listings, see the Martindale-Hubbell Law Directory

SPANGLER, JENNINGS & DOUGHERTY, P.C. (AV)

150 Lincolnway, Suite 3001, 46383
Telephone: 219-462-6151
FAX: 219-477-4935
Email: spangler@sjdlaw.com
Merrillville, Indiana Office: 8396 Mississippi Street.
Telephone: 219-769-2323.

RESIDENT PERSONNEL

Samuel J. Bernardi, Jr. Robert P. Stoner

Edward W. Hearn Christopher Grabarek

OF COUNSEL

Patrick J. Dougherty

Representative Clients: Allstate Insurance Cos.; State Farm Insurance Cos.; The Saint Paul Companies; CNA Insurance Cos.; Maryland Insurance Cos.; American Specialty Insurance Services; J&N Enterprises; Indiana Beach, Inc.; CertainTeed Corp.; Fireman's Fund.

For full biographical listings, see the Martindale-Hubbell Law Directory

*WARSAW,** Kosciusko Co.

LEMON, ARMEY, HEARN & LEININGER (AV)

210 North Buffalo Street, P.O. Box 770, 46581-0770
Telephone: 219-268-9111
Telecopier: 219-267-8647

MEMBERS OF FIRM

Robert L. Rasor (1922-1997)
Thomas R. Lemon
Michael E. Armey
R. Steven Hearn
Daniel K. Leininger
Jane L. Kauffman

ASSOCIATES

Millard P. Plumlee, III W. Douglas Lemon
Mark C. Sherer

Representative Clients: Lake City Bank; The Dalton Foundries, Inc.; Grace Schools, Inc.

For full biographical listings, see the Martindale-Hubbell Law Directory

IOWA

*DES MOINES,** Polk Co.

FINLEY, ALT, SMITH, SCHARNBERG, CRAIG, HILMES & GAFFNEY, P.C. (AV)

604 Locust Street, Fourth Floor Equitable Building, 50309
Telephone: 515-288-0145
Telecopier: 515-288-2724

(See Next Column)

Steven K. Scharnberg
John D. (Jack) Hilmes
R. Todd Gaffney
Kevin J. Driscoll

Representative Clients: ALAS; American Society of Composers, Authors and Publishers; Equitable Life Assurance Society of the U.S.; Federated Insurance Co.; Meredith Corp.
Iowa Attorneys for: Midwest Medical Insurance Co.
District Attorneys for: Norfolk & Southern Railroad; Soo Line Railroad Company.

For Complete List of Firm Personnel, See General Section

For full biographical listings, see the Martindale-Hubbell Law Directory

HUBER, BOOK, CORTESE, HAPPE & BROWN, P.L.C. (AV)

317 Sixth Avenue, Suite 200, 50309-4127
Telephone: 515-243-4148
Fax: 515-243-5481
Email: huber@desmoineslaw.com

MEMBER OF FIRM

Joseph A. Happe

Representative Clients: Atlantic Mutual Cos.; CNA Insurance Cos.; Fireman's Fund American Insurance Companies; Great West Casualty Co.; Liberty Mutual Insurance Co.; Maryland Insurance Group; Prudential Property and Casualty Insurance Co.; USF&G Company.
Reference: Bank of America.

For full biographical listings, see the Martindale-Hubbell Law Directory

PATTERSON, LORENTZEN, DUFFIELD, TIMMONS, IRISH, BECKER & ORDWAY, L.L.P. (AV)

729 Insurance Exchange Building, 50309
Telephone: 515-283-2147
Fax: 515-283-1002
Email: mail@pattersonfirm.com *URL:* http://www.pattersonfirm.com

MEMBERS OF FIRM

G. O. Patterson (1914-1982)
James A. Lorentzen (Retired)
Theodore T. Duffield
William E. Timmons (Retired)
Roy M. Irish
F. H. Becker (Retired)
Gary D. Ordway
Robin L. Hermann
Harry Perkins, III
Michael F. Lacey, Jr.
Gregory J. Wilson
Jeffrey A. Boehlert
Douglas A. Haag
Charles E. Cutler
Michael D. Huppert
Martin C. Sprock
William A. Wickett
Frederick M. Haskins
Jeffrey A. Baker
Janice M. Herfkens
Coreen K. Bezdicek
Patrick V. Waldron

ASSOCIATE

Michael S. Jones

General Counsel for: Iowa Insurance Institute.
Representative Clients: Allied Mutual Insurance Company; CNA Insurance Company; Chubb Insurance Group; Continental Western Insurance Co.; Farmers Insurance Group; Farmland Insurance Company; Grinnell Mutual Reinsurance Company; Hawkeye Security Insurance Company; Iowa Insurance Institute, St. Paul Fire & Marine Insurance Company.

For full biographical listings, see the Martindale-Hubbell Law Directory

PEDDICORD, WHARTON, THUNE AND SPENCER, A PROFESSIONAL CORPORATION (AV)

700 Des Moines Building, 405 Sixth Avenue, P.O. Box 9130, 50306-9130
Telephone: 515-243-2100
Fax: 515-243-2132
1-800-383-2100

Roland D. Peddicord

For full biographical listings, see the Martindale-Hubbell Law Directory

THE WALKER LAW FIRM (AV)

2501 Grand Avenue, Suite E, 50312
Telephone: 515-281-1488
Fax: 515-281-1489
Email: ERWJK@aol.com

E. Ralph Walker David J. Darrell
Joseph W. Fernandez

OF COUNSEL

Fred E. Rizk (Not admitted in IA)

For full biographical listings, see the Martindale-Hubbell Law Directory

KANSAS

OVERLAND PARK, Johnson Co.

FISHER, PATTERSON, SAYLER & SMITH, L.L.P. (AV)
11050 Roe Avenue, Suite 210, 66211
Telephone: 913-339-6757
FAX: 913-339-6187
Email: fpss@worldnet.att.net
Topeka, Kansas Office: 3550 S.W. 5th Street, P.O. Box 949, 66601.
Telephone: 785-232-7761.
Fax: 785-232-6604.

MEMBERS OF FIRM
Edwin Dudley Smith (Resident) Michael K. Seck (Resident)
David P. Madden (Resident)

ASSOCIATES
Kelly A. Feyh (Resident) Jennifer R. Rose (Resident)

For full biographical listings, see the Martindale-Hubbell Law Directory

RISJORD & JAMES, P.C. (AV)
Suite 100, 10680 Barkley, 66212
Telephone: 913-381-5151
Fax: 913-381-2569
Email: RJLaw@RisjordJames.com *URL:* http://www.risjordjames.com

Randy W. James Aaron N. Woods

Lisa C. Beckley

RETIRED
John C. Risjord

For full biographical listings, see the Martindale-Hubbell Law Directory

SHAMBERG, JOHNSON & BERGMAN, CHARTERED (AV)
Suite 355, 4551 West 107th Street, 66207
Telephone: 913-642-0600
Fax: 913-642-9629
Email: mail@sjblaw.com *URL:* http://www.sjblaw.com
Kansas City, Kansas Office: Suite M-4, One Security Plaza.
Telephone: 913-281-1900.
Kansas City, Missouri Office: Suite 205, Scarritt Arcade Building, 819 Walnut.
Telephone: 816-556-9431.

Lynn R. Johnson Victor A. Bergman
John M. Parisi

Steven G. Brown Steve N. Six

OF COUNSEL
John E. Shamberg

For full biographical listings, see the Martindale-Hubbell Law Directory

*TOPEKA,** Shawnee Co.

FISHER, PATTERSON, SAYLER & SMITH, L.L.P. (AV)
3550 S.W. 5th Street, P.O. Box 949, 66601
Telephone: 785-232-7761
Fax: 785-232-6604
Email: fpss@cjnetworks.com
Overland Park, Kansas Office: 11050 Roe Avenue, Suite 210, 66211.
Telephone: 913-339-6757.
Fax: 913-339-6187.

MEMBERS OF FIRM
Donald Patterson
Edwin Dudley Smith (Resident, Overland Park Office)
Larry G. Pepperdine
James P. Nordstrom
Justice B. King
J. Steven Pigg
Steve R. Fabert
Ronald J. Laskowski
Michael K. Seck (Resident, Overland Park Office)
David P. Madden (Resident, Overland Park Office)
Steven K. Johnson
Kristine A. Larscheid

ASSOCIATES
Billy E. Newman
David R. Cooper
Kelly A. Feyh (Resident, Overland Park Office)
Jennifer R. Rose (Resident, Overland Park Office)

OF COUNSEL
David H. Fisher

RETIRED
Charles Keith Sayler

Representative Clients: Gage Shopping Center, Inc.; Fireman's Fund-American Insurance Cos.; United States Fidelity and Guaranty Co.; The Procter & Gamble Company; Commercial Union Insurance Companies; National Casualty; The Hartford; Berkshire Hathaway Companies; Goodyears Tires & Rubber Co. and General Motors Corp.

(See Next Column)

For full biographical listings, see the Martindale-Hubbell Law Directory

RALSTON & POPE, LLC (AV)
2913 Southwest Maupin Lane, 66614-4139
Telephone: 913-273-8002; 888-913-2783
FAX: 913-273-0744
Email: ERalston@AOL.Com

Eugene B. Ralston Kevin L. Diehl
Ronald P. Pope

LEGAL SUPPORT PERSONNEL
PARALEGALS
Barbara Cobuluis Colleen Wright
Corri Wecker Ashanti Smith

For full biographical listings, see the Martindale-Hubbell Law Directory

*WICHITA,** Sedgwick Co.

GRACE, UNRUH & PRATT, L.C. (AV)
Suite 501, 155 North Market Street, 67202-1816
Telephone: 316-269-2006
FAX: 316-269-0437
Email: litigation@fn.net

Brian G. Grace Gilbert L. Guthrie
Terry L. Unruh Sharon A. Werner
Corlin J. Pratt Kevin A. Grace

For full biographical listings, see the Martindale-Hubbell Law Directory

HUTTON & HUTTON (AV)
8100 East 22nd Street North, Building 1200, 67226-2312
Telephone: 316-688-1166
Fax: 316-686-1077
Mailing Address: P.O. Box 638, Wichita, KS, 67201-0638
Email: huttnlaw@southwind.net *URL:* http://www.huttonlaw.com

Mark B. Hutton Andrew W. Hutton

ASSOCIATES
Derek Scott Casey Christopher P. Christian
Anne H. Pankratz Chan P. Townsley
Deborah B. McIlhenny

OF COUNSEL
M. Prudence Hutton

For full biographical listings, see the Martindale-Hubbell Law Directory

KAHRS, NELSON, FANNING, HITE & KELLOGG L.L.P. (AV)
200 W. Douglas, Suite 600, 67202
Telephone: 316-265-7761
Telecopier: 316-267-7803
URL: http://www.kahrsnelson.com

MEMBERS OF FIRM
Richard C. Hite Forrest James Robinson, Jr.
Richard L. Honeyman Don D. Gribble, II
Larry A. Withers Lisa Adrian McPherson

ASSOCIATES
Jerry D. Hawkins Scott R. Schillings

OF COUNSEL
H. W. Fanning Vince P. Wheeler

Representative Clients: American Honda Motor Company, Inc.; American Telephone & Telegraph Co.; Chrysler Corporation; Chubb Group of Companies; Conwood Company, L.P.; Epson America, Inc.; Fuji Heavy Industries; Learjet Corp.; General Motors Corp.; Gulfstream Aerospace.

For Complete List of Firm Personnel, See General Section

For full biographical listings, see the Martindale-Hubbell Law Directory

YOUNG, BOGLE, McCAUSLAND, WELLS & BLANCHARD, P.A. (AV)
106 West Douglas, Suite 923, 67202
Telephone: 316-265-7841
Facsimile: 316-265-3956
Email: ybmwblaw@aol.com

Glenn D. Young, Jr. Paul S. McCausland
Jerry D. Bogle William A. Wells
Patrick C. Blanchard

OF COUNSEL
Orlin L. Wagner

Representative Clients: Bridgestone/Firestone Inc.; Deere & Co.; Sears Roebuck & Co.; White Consolidated Industries, Inc.

For Complete List of Firm Personnel, See General Section

For full biographical listings, see the Martindale-Hubbell Law Directory

KENTUCKY

*BOWLING GREEN,** Warren Co.

COLE, MOORE & BAKER (AV)

921 College Street-Phoenix Place, P.O. Box 10240, 42102-7240
Telephone: 270-782-6666
FAX: 270-782-8666
Email: CMB@Premiernet.net

MEMBERS OF FIRM

John David Cole — Matthew J. Baker
Frank Hampton Moore, Jr. — Dov Moore

ASSOCIATES

John David Cole, Jr. — Stefan R. Hughes
Matthew P. Cook

OF COUNSEL

Frank R. Goad

Counsel for: Western Kentucky Cola-Cola Bottling Co.; Clark Distributing Co., Inc.; Scotty's Contracting & Stone Co.
Local Counsel for: General Electric Co.; Bucyrus-Erie Company; Wal-Mart Stores, Inc.; Kroger/Country Oven.
Representative Insurance Clients: Liberty Mutual Insurance Co.; Travelers Insurance Co.; Wausau Insurance Co.

For full biographical listings, see the Martindale-Hubbell Law Directory

HARLIN, PARKER, ALCOTT & CHAUDOIN, P.S.C. (AV)

519 East Tenth Street, P.O. Box 390, 42102-0390
Telephone: 502-842-5611
Telefax: 502-842-2607
Email: hpac@premiernet.net *URL:* http://www.lawyers.com/hp

William Jerry Parker — Mark D. Alcott

Insurance Clients: CIGNA/ESIS; AIG.
Railroad and Utilities Clients: District Attorneys for BellSouth Telecommunications, Inc.; CSX Transportation, Inc.
Representative Clients: Thomson Consumers Electronics Inc.
Local Counsel for: General Motors Corp.; News Publishing Co.; Holley Performance Products, Inc.

For Complete List of Firm Personnel, See General Section

For full biographical listings, see the Martindale-Hubbell Law Directory

KERRICK, GRISE & STIVERS (AV)

1025 State Street, P.O. Box 9547, 42102-9547
Telephone: 502-782-8160
Fax: 502-782-5856
Email: kgs@kgslaw.com
Elizabethtown, Kentucky Office: 2935 Dolphin Drive, Suite 102.
Telephone: 502-769-5788.
Fax: 502-737-9285.

MEMBERS OF FIRM

Thomas N. Kerrick — Gregory N. Stivers
John R. Grise — H. Brent Brennenstuhl
Laura M. Hagan

ASSOCIATES

Karl N. Crandall — Shawn Rosso Alcott
Jason B. Bell

OF COUNSEL

Jeffrey R. O'Grody

LEGAL SUPPORT PERSONNEL

Patricia Logsdon — Laura Lockhart Lico
Allison Lusk

Representative Clients: Dollar General Corp.; Columbia Greenview Regional Hospital; Hospital Corporation of America; Hardin Memorial Hospital; Fir-Star Bank; TKR Cable.

For full biographical listings, see the Martindale-Hubbell Law Directory

COVINGTON, Kenton Co.

ROBERT E. SANDERS AND ASSOCIATES, P.S.C. (AV)

The Charles H. Fisk House, 1017 Russell Street, 41011-3052
Telephone: 606-491-3000
Fax: 606-655-4642
Email: resanders@worldnet.att.net

Robert E. Sanders

Jeffrey M. Sanders — J. Pierre Tismo
Delana S. Pierce

LEGAL SUPPORT PERSONNEL

Shirley L. Sanders — Sandra A. Sturgeon
Sheila D. Rachal

For full biographical listings, see the Martindale-Hubbell Law Directory

*LEXINGTON,** Fayette Co.

PETER PERLMAN LAW OFFICES, P.S.C. (AV)

388 South Broadway, 40508
Telephone: 606-253-3919
Fax: 606-259-0493

Peter Perlman

Bryce D. Franklin, Jr.

OF COUNSEL

Thomas R. Hays

For full biographical listings, see the Martindale-Hubbell Law Directory

SAVAGE, GARMER & ELLIOTT, P.S.C. (AV)

Opera House Office Building, 141 North Broadway, 40507
Telephone: 606-254-9351
Fax: 606-233-9769

Joe C. Savage — William R. Garmer
Robert L. Elliott

For full biographical listings, see the Martindale-Hubbell Law Directory

*LONDON,** Laurel Co.

FARMER, KELLEY, BROWN AND WILLIAMS (AV)

502 West Fifth Street, Drawer 490, 40741
Telephone: 606-878-7640
Fax: 606-878-2364
Email: fpfarmer@farmerlaw.com
Lexington, Kentucky Office: 1082 Griffin Gate Drive, 40511-1384.
Telephone: 606: 263-2567.
Facsimile: 606: 878-2364.

MEMBERS OF FIRM

F. Preston Farmer — Michael P. Farmer
John F. Kelley, Jr. — Martha L. Brown
Jason E. Williams

ASSOCIATES

Suzanne S. Farmer — Jennifer S. Nicholson

Representative Clients: American Sterilizer Co.; Line Power Inc.

For full biographical listings, see the Martindale-Hubbell Law Directory

HAMM, MILBY & RIDINGS (AV)

120 North Main Street, 40741
Telephone: 606-864-4126
Fax: 606-878-8144
Email: hmrlaw@kih.net

MEMBERS OF FIRM

Robert L. Milby — Marcia Milby Ridings

James A. Ridings — Gregory A. Lay
R. Aaron Hostettler

Representative Clients: Acceleration National; Aetna Life & Casualty Ins. Co.; All Risk Claims Service, Inc.; Allstate Insurance Co.; Alexis; American Automobile Mutual Ins.; American Bankers; American Hardware Ins. Co.

For full biographical listings, see the Martindale-Hubbell Law Directory

*LOUISVILLE,** Jefferson Co.

FRANKLIN AND HANCE, P.S.C. (AV)

The Speed House, 505 West Ormsby Avenue, 40203
Telephone: 502-637-6000
Fax: 502-637-1413
Email: golfatty@aol.com *URL:* http://www.lawyers.com/fhlaw

Larry B. Franklin — Michael R. Hance

David B. Gray — Hope Fitzpatrick Brooks

Reference: First National Bank.

For full biographical listings, see the Martindale-Hubbell Law Directory

O'BRYAN, BROWN & TONER (AV)

455 South Fourth Avenue, Suite 1500, Starks Building, 40202
Telephone: 502-585-4700
Fax: 502-585-4703
Email: mail@obtlaw.com

(See Next Column)

O'BRYAN, BROWN & TONER, *Louisville—Continued*

MEMBERS OF FIRM

Donald K. Brown, Jr.
Christopher P. O'Bryan
Gerald R. Toner
John L. Dotson
Emily A. Faith
James P. Grohmann
David Scott Strite

ASSOCIATES

Andrew N. Clooney
Tracy Sullivan Prewitt
Beth H. McMasters
Cathleen Charters Palmer
Clay Edwards
Peter D. Palmer
Charles Wayne Miller

OF COUNSEL

Joseph C. O'Bryan

For full biographical listings, see the Martindale-Hubbell Law Directory

WEISS FREDERICK WILLETT & HAYNES (AV)

1425 Citizens Plaza, 40202
Telephone: 502-583-1000
FAX: 502-583-4478

Gary M. Weiss
Carl D. Frederick
Barry Willett
William T. Haynes, Jr.
Janice M. Weiss

ASSOCIATES

Karla W. Katakis
Paul J. Hershberg
Kevin M. Adams

OF COUNSEL

Henry M. Burt

For full biographical listings, see the Martindale-Hubbell Law Directory

WOODWARD, HOBSON & FULTON (AV)

2500 National City Tower, 101 South Fifth Street, 40202
Telephone: 502-581-8000
Fax: 502-581-8111
Email: WHF@IGLOU.COM
Lexington, Kentucky Office: PNC Bank Plaza, 200 West Vine Street, Suite 500.
Telephone: 606-244-7100.
Telecopier: 606-244-7111.

MEMBERS OF FIRM

William D. Grubbs
Lionel A. Hawse (Resident, Lexington, Kentucky Office)
Harry K. Herren
David R. Monohan
Will H. Fulton
Richard H. C. Clay
Elizabeth Ullmer Mendel
Jann B. Logsdon
David T. Schaefer
D. Craig York

ASSOCIATES

Christopher R. Cashen (Resident, Lexington, Kentucky Office)
Christopher L. Rhoads (Resident, Lexington Office)
Kristin M. Lomond
Stephen D. Weisskopf
W. William Cegelka (Resident, Lexington, Kentucky Office)
Katherine A. Wolfe (Not admitted in KY)

OF COUNSEL

Fielden Woodward

Representative Clients: Caterpillar Corp.; Clark Equipment Co.; General Motors Corp.; Nissan North America, Inc.; NUMMI; Snapper, Inc.; Toyota Motor Sales USA, Inc.; Volkswagen A.G.; Wyeth-Ayerst Laboratories, Inc., a division of American Home Products Corporation.

For Complete List of Firm Personnel, See General Section

For full biographical listings, see the Martindale-Hubbell Law Directory

*PADUCAH,** McCracken Co.

SALADINO LAW FIRM (AV)

700 Clark Street, P.O. Box 1246, 42002-1246
Telephone: 502-444-0406
Fax: 502-444-0454
Email: saladino@apex.net

Charles A. Saladino

ASSOCIATES

David Vance Oakes
Kristi Saladino Schaaf
Barclay Walden Banister
Gary E. Schaaf

For full biographical listings, see the Martindale-Hubbell Law Directory

LOUISIANA

*ALEXANDRIA,** Rapides Parish

BOLEN & ERWIN, LTD. A PROFESSIONAL LAW CORPORATION (AV)

709 Versailles Boulevard, P.O. Box 11590, 71315-1590
Telephone: 318-445-8236
Fax: 318-443-1770
Email: belaw@bolenlaw.com

James A. Bolen, Jr.
L. Lyle Parker
Daniel G. Brenner

Madeline J. Lee
Michael D. Hislop
Gregory Engelsman
Michael J. Gautier, Jr
Rodney Cabrera
Richard T. Conrad, III
Steven M. Rachal
Donna J. Duplechian

OF COUNSEL

Gregory S. Erwin

For full biographical listings, see the Martindale-Hubbell Law Directory

*BATON ROUGE,** East Baton Rouge Parish

LANE, FERTITTA, JANNEY & THOMAS (AV)

435 Louisiana Avenue, P.O. Box 3335, 70821
Telephone: 225-387-0241
Fax: 225-387-1238

MEMBERS OF FIRM

Horace C. Lane (1921-1989)
Frank A. Fertitta
William F. Janney
Richard S. Thomas

Representative Clients: State Farm Mutual Automobile Insurance Co.; State Farm Fire & Casualty Co.; United States Fidelity & Guaranty Co.; Aetna Casualty & Surety Co.; Employers Liability Assurance Corp., Ltd.; Allstate Insurance Co.; St. Paul Fire and Marine Insurance Co.; The Medical Protective Co.; Safeco Insurance Co. of America; Horace Mann Insurance Co.

For full biographical listings, see the Martindale-Hubbell Law Directory

POWERS & WILLARD, L.L.P. (AV)

7967 Office Park Boulevard, P.O. Box 15948, 70895
Telephone: 225-928-1951
Fax: 225-929-9834

MEMBERS OF FIRM

John Dale Powers
William E. Willard

ASSOCIATES

Neil H. Mixon
Lindsey J. Leavoy
Edwin L. Hightower
Andrew P. Sellers, Jr.
Suzanne K. Sasser
Kyle C. Marionneaux

General Counsel for: Audubon Insurance Co.
Louisiana Counsel for: Hancock Bank & Trust Co.; Hertz Corp.; Ciba-Geigy Corp.; Utica Mutual Insurance Co.

For full biographical listings, see the Martindale-Hubbell Law Directory

UNGLESBY, KOCH & REYNOLDS (AV)

246 Napoleon Street, 70802
Telephone: 225-387-0120
Fax: 225-336-4355
Email: unglkoch@premier.net

Lewis O. Unglesby
Karl J. Koch
Aidan C. Reynolds

For full biographical listings, see the Martindale-Hubbell Law Directory

WATSON, BLANCHE, WILSON & POSNER (AV)

Registered Limited Liability Partnership
505 North Boulevard, P.O. Drawer 2995, 70821-2995
Telephone: 225-387-5511
Fax: 225-387-5972

Peter T. Dazzio
Felix R. Weill
William E. Scott, III
P. Chauvin Wilkinson, Jr.
Randall L. Champagne
P. Scott Jolly

Representative Clients: Cook Pacemaker Corporation; CommunityCoffee Company, Inc.; Louisiana Hospital Association; General Health System and affiliates.

For full biographical listings, see the Martindale-Hubbell Law Directory

*COVINGTON,** St. Tammany Parish

AUBERT & PAJARES, L.L.C. (AV)

506 East Rutland Street, 70433-3219
Telephone: 504-809-2000
Fax: 504-809-2001
Email: info@aubertpajares.com *URL:* http://www.aubertpajares.com
New Orleans, Louisiana Office: 201 St. Charles Avenue, Suite 2500, 70130.

Christopher J. Aubert
Raymond J. Pajares
David J. Schexnaydre

ASSOCIATES

Tracy E. Gold
David Michael Gold
John W. Fairless
James P. Meyer
Leo R. Hemelt, II
Elizabeth Ashley Carter
William J. Perry
Richard C. Badeaux
Suzanne M. Ganucheau
John V. Lawrence
Brett M. Bollinger
Mark W. Verret
M. Paige Freeman Rosato
Cynthia A. Langston
Richard J. Garvey, Jr.

Representative Clients: Dover Elevator Company; General Star Management Company; Macrsk, Inc.; Penske Truck Leasing Company, L.P.; PHICO Services Company; Reliance National Indemnity Company; Schindler Elevator Corporation; Tenent HealthSystem; Westinghouse Electric Cotporation; Xerox Corporation.

For full biographical listings, see the Martindale-Hubbell Law Directory

*GRETNA,** Jefferson Parish

WINDHORST, GAUDRY, RANSON, HIGGINS & GREMILLION, L.L.C. (AV)

Oakwood Corporate Center, 401 Whitney Avenue Suite 500, P.O. Box 1910, 70056
Telephone: 504-362-2466; 367-9247
Telcopier: 504-362-5938
Email: wgrhg@gs.verio.net

Thomas L. Gaudry, Jr.
Daniel A. Ranson
Daryl A. Higgins
Gregory G. Gremillion
Wade A. Langlois, III
Michael D. Peytavin

OF COUNSEL

Fritz H. Windhorst (Retired)

Steven Dow Oliver
Thomas W. Darling
David J. Dowell, Jr.
John A Leslie
Walter Patrick Maestri
B. Wesley Pitts

Reference: Hibernia National Bank.

For full biographical listings, see the Martindale-Hubbell Law Directory

*HOUMA,** Terrebonne Parish

HENDERSON, HANEMANN & MORRIS, A PROFESSIONAL LAW CORPORATION (AV)

300 Lafayette Street, 70360
Telephone: 504-868-2081
New Orleans: 504-581-1434
Telecopier: 504-868-0080

Philip E. Henderson
Charles Hanemann
Robert L. Morris (1940-1986)
J. Mark Graham
Joseph A. Reilly, Jr.
Barry J. Boudreaux

Emilie Melancon Daye

Representative Clients: Alliance Insurance Company; Applied Hydraulic Systems, Inc.; Falcon Drilling Company, Inc.; Lafayette Insurance Company; Liverpool and London Steamship Protection and Indemnity Association Limited; Louisiana Medical Mutual Insurance Company; The Steamship Mutual Underwriter Association Limited; Gray & Co., Inc.; Union Oil Company of California; Minnesota Mining and Manufacturing Co.

For full biographical listings, see the Martindale-Hubbell Law Directory

*LAFAYETTE,** Lafayette Parish

BROUSSARD, DAVID & DAIGLE, A PROFESSIONAL LAW CORPORATION (AV)

557 Jefferson Street, P.O. Drawer 3308, 70502-3308
Telephone: 318-234-7000
Fax: 318-237-0344
Email: bdandd@bdandd.com *URL:* http://www.bdandd.com

Hal J. Broussard
Susan A. Daigle
Bryan D. Scofield
Ped C. Kay, III
Todd G. Crawford

(See Next Column)

James T. Rivera
Catherine E. Hensgens

Representative Clients: Certain London Underwriters per individual approval of instructions; Lloyds of London Member Syndicates; Institute of London Underwriter Member Companies; Reliance Insurance Company of Pennsylvania; Reliance Insurance Company of Illinois; Reliance National Insurance Company; The Louisiana Insurance Guaranty Association; Louisiana Oilfield Legislative Committee, Inc. (Louisiana Association of Oilfield Casing Contractors; Association of Oilwell Servicing Contractors; Louisiana Pipeline Contractors Association; Offshore Pipeline Contractors Association; Louisiana Oilfield Contractor Association).

For full biographical listings, see the Martindale-Hubbell Law Directory

DOMENGEAUX WRIGHT & ROY, A PROFESSIONAL LAW CORPORATION (AV)

556 Jefferson Street, Suite 500, P.O. Box 3668, 70502-3668
Telephone: 318-233-3033; 1-800-375-3106
Fax: 318-232-8213
Email: info@wrightroy.com *URL:* http://www.wrightroy.com

Bob F. Wright
James Parkerson Roy
Thomas R. Edwards
James H. Domengeaux
Gilbert Hennigan Dozier
Carla Marie Perron
Michael D. Goss

ASSOCIATE

Jamie D. Parker

OF COUNSEL

Jerome E. Domengeaux

Reference: Mid-South National Bank; Advocate Financial, L.L.C.

For full biographical listings, see the Martindale-Hubbell Law Directory

METAIRIE, Jefferson Parish

BERNARD, CASSISA, ELLIOTT & DAVIS, A PROFESSIONAL LAW CORPORATION (AV)

1615 Metairie Road, P.O. Box 55490, 70055-5490
Telephone: 504-834-2612
Telecopier: 504-838-9438
Email: bcande@communique.net
Oxford, Mississippi Office: 1727 East University Avenue, Suite E, 38655.
Telephone: 601-234-7236.
Fax: 601-234-7691.

Peter L. Bernard, Jr. (1920-1991)
Frank L. Micholet (1913-1972)
Paul V. Cassisa, Sr.
Stephen N. Elliott
Benjamin Franklin Davis, Jr.
Eugene M. McEachin, Jr.
Robert A. McMahon, Jr.
Carl J. Giffin, Jr.
Paul V. Cassisa, Jr.
Howard B. Kaplan
William L. Brockman
Robert A. Knight
Ann M. Sico

OF COUNSEL

Robert H. Wood, Jr.

Representative Clients: Royal Insurance Group; General Motors Corp.; Hartford Insurance Group; Nissan Motor Corp.; Honda North America, Inc.

For full biographical listings, see the Martindale-Hubbell Law Directory

*NEW ORLEANS,** Orleans Parish

BALDWIN & HASPEL, L.L.C. (AV)

Energy Centre, Suite 2200, 1100 Poydras Street, 70163-2200
Telephone: 504-585-7711
Fax: 504-585-7751
URL: http://www.baldwinhaspel.com

MEMBERS OF FIRM

Cuthbert S. Baldwin (1891-1969)
Edward Haspel (1889-1983)
Conrad Meyer, III
Jerome J. Reso, Jr.
Joel A. Mendler
Conrad Meyer, IV
Malcolm A. Meyer
Monica Tufano Surprenant
Leon H. Rittenberg, Jr.
John A. Rouchell
Jeannie Morris Randazzo
James P. Magee
Dennis M. LaBorde
Beverly Klundt Baudouin
Karl J. Zimmermann
Lance J. Arnold

OF COUNSEL

A. B. Kupperman
Frederick W. "Fritz" Veters

Leon H. Rittenberg, III
Thomas M. Long

Representative Clients: Bean Dredging Corp.; Hibernia National Bank; Alfa-Laval, Inc.

For full biographical listings, see the Martindale-Hubbell Law Directory

FRILOT, PARTRIDGE, KOHNKE & CLEMENTS, L.C. (AV)

3600 Energy Centre, 1100 Poydras Street, 70163-3600
Telephone: 504-599-8000
Telecopier: 504-599-8100
Email: postmaster@fpkc.com *URL:* http://www.fpkc.com

(See Next Column)

FRILOT, PARTRIDGE, KOHNKE & CLEMENTS L.C., *New Orleans—Continued*

Francis H. Brown, III
James H. Brown, Jr.
George E. Cain, Jr.
Michael T. Cali
Miles P. Clements
Andrew S. de Klerk
George A. Frilot, III (A Professional Law Corp.)
John J. Hainkel, III
Edward F. Kohnke, IV
Allen J. Krouse, III
J. Dwight LeBlanc, III
Douglas P. Matthews
Kenneth A. Mayeaux
Robert B. McNeal
Wayne K. McNeil
Patrick J. McShane
Joseph N. Mole
David A. Olson
Scott S. Partridge
Greg A. Pellegrini
Michael R. Phillips
James F. Shuey
James R. Silverstein
Peter E. Sperling
Patrick A. Talley (P.C.)
Patricia E. Weeks

Sidney A. Backstrom
Joel Edwin Cape (Not admitted in LA)
Nairda T. Lesa Colón
Bruce Arne Cranner
Frederick T. Greschner, Jr.
Brant David Imperatore
Stephanie Ann May
Michael B. North

For full biographical listings, see the Martindale-Hubbell Law Directory

GAINSBURGH, BENJAMIN, DAVID, MEUNIER & WARSHAUER (AV)

2800 Energy Centre, 1100 Poydras, 70163-2800
Telephone: 504-522-2304
Telecopier: 504-528-9973
Email: DPHILLIPS@GAINSBEN.COM

OF COUNSEL

Samuel C. Gainsburgh
Jack C. Benjamin

MEMBERS OF FIRM

Robert J. David
Gerald E. Meunier
Irving J. Warshauer
Stevan C. Dittman
Madeleine M. Landrieu
Darryl M. Phillips
Jeffrey A. Mitchell

ASSOCIATE

Gary B. Roth

For full biographical listings, see the Martindale-Hubbell Law Directory

MAGINNIS & HURLEY, A PROFESSIONAL LAW CORPORATION (AV)

Suite 2040 Canal Place One, 365 Canal Street, 70130
Telephone: 504-524-5353
Fax: 504-524-5403
Email: maginnis+hurley@gs.net

Michael J. Maginnis
Timothy P. Hurley
José R. Cot
Sallye Goodwin Webb
Lisa D. Kothe

For full biographical listings, see the Martindale-Hubbell Law Directory

MCGLINCHEY STAFFORD (AV)

A Professional Limited Liability Company
643 Magazine Street, 70130-3477
Telephone: 504-586-1200
Fax: 504-596-2800
TDD: (504) 596-2728
Telex: 584327
Cable Address: "MACSTAC"
Mailing Address: P.O. Box 60643, New Orleans, Louisiana, 70160-0643
Email: @mcglinchey.com *URL:* http://www.mcglinchey.com
Dallas, Texas Office: 2777 Stemmons Freeway, Suite 925, 75207-2401.
Telephone: 214-860-9700.
Fax: 214-860-9750.
Houston, Texas Office: 2727 Allen Parkway, Suite 1900, 77019.
Telephone: 713-520-1900.
Fax: 713-520-1025.
Baton Rouge, Louisiana Office: Ninth Floor, One American Place, 70825-0001.
Telephone: 504-383-9000.
Fax: 504-343-3076.
Jackson, Mississippi Office: Suite 1200, SkyTel Centre, 200 South Lamar Street, 39201.
Telephone: 601-960-8400.
Fax: 601-960-8406.
Lake Providence, Louisiana Office: 405 Morgan Street, 71254-2691.
Telephone: 318-559-1200.
Fax: 318-559-0609.
Monroe, Louisiana Office: Dean ONB Tower, 130 Desiard Street, Suite 807, 71201.
Telephone: 318-651-0807.
Fax: 318-651-0809.

(See Next Column)

MEMBERS OF FIRM

Colvin G. Norwood, Jr., (P.C.)
Henri Wolbrette, III, (P.C.)
Michael M. Noonan
Eric A. Shuman
Mark N. Bodin

ASSOCIATES

Margaret Woolverton Triebes
Elizabeth P. Blitch
Patrick J. O'Cain
Deborah A. Van Meter
Dwayne C. Jefferson
Gary G. Hebert
James E. Swinnen

OF COUNSEL

Margaret G. Diamond
Mary Lynne Friedman

MEMBERS OF FIRM

Dan E. West (Resident, Baton Rouge Office)
Deborah J. Bullion-Gascoyne (Resident, Houston Office)

ASSOCIATES

Vincent J. Bodin (Resident, Houston Office)
Craig A. Horton (Resident, Houston Office)

For full biographical listings, see the Martindale-Hubbell Law Directory

PLAUCHÉ MASELLI LANDRY & PARKERSON L.L.P. (AV)

Bank One Center, Suite 4240, 201 St. Charles Avenue, 70170-4240
Telephone: 504-582-1142
Fax: 504-582-1172
URL: http://www.pmlpnola.com

MEMBERS OF FIRM

Andrew L. Plauché, Jr.
Joseph Maselli, Jr.
Arthur W. Landry
G. Bruce Parkerson
Robert E Caraway, III

ASSOCIATES

Mark E. Young
Thomas L. Hutchinson
Cherie T. Burlett
Kenan S. Rand, Jr.
Elizabeth Salzer Schell
J. Marie Rudd
Wendy K. Lappenga
Deborah F. Malveaux
Diane S. Mitnik
Lori P. Moser

Reference: Bank One of Louisiana.

For full biographical listings, see the Martindale-Hubbell Law Directory

PULASKI, GIEGER & LABORDE, L.L.C. (AV)

Suite 4800, One Shell Square, 701 Poydras Street, 70139
Telephone: 504-561-0400
Telecopier: 504-561-1011
Covington, Louisiana Office: 434 North Columbia Street, Suite 200, 70433.
Telephone: 504-561-0400.
Telecopier: 504-809-9677.

Michael T. Pulaski
Ernest P. Gieger, Jr.
Kenneth H. Laborde
Lambert M. Laperouse
Robert W. Maxwell
Keith W. McDaniel
Sharon D. Smith
Leo R. McAloon, III
Christopher J. Wnuk
John Burke Sanders
Julianne T. Echols
Hilliard F. Kelly, III
Lorie G. DeMarcay

Marjorie Randall Brown
Gina S. Montgomery

For full biographical listings, see the Martindale-Hubbell Law Directory

SAPORITO & SLEDGE, L.L.C. (AV)

639 Loyola Avenue Suite 2100, 70113
Telephone: 504-529-5070
Fax: 504-529-5434

Jerry L. Saporito
Michael D. Sledge

Edward T. Hayes

Representative Clients: Chance Industries; Dunlop Tire Corporation; Fleetwood Enterprises; General Motors Corporation; Pacific Insurance Company; Prudential Property and Casualty Company; Royal Insurance Company; TDK Corporation; Toyota Motor Sales, USA, Inc.; TRW, Inc.

For full biographical listings, see the Martindale-Hubbell Law Directory

SLATER LAW FIRM, A PROFESSIONAL CORPORATION (AV)

650 Poydras Street Suite 2600, 70130-6101
Telephone: 504-523-7333
Fax: 504-528-1080
URL: http://www.slaterlawfirm.com

Benjamin R. Slater, Jr.
Benjamin R. Slater, III
Mark E. Van Horn
Kevin M. Wheeler
Anne Elise Brown
Donald J. Miester, Jr.

Michael O. Waguespack
Cory Rabin Cahn
Sarah Ney
S. Joseph Welborn

(See Next Column)

SLATER LAW FIRM A PROFESSIONAL CORPORATION—*Continued*

SPECIAL COUNSEL
W. Malcolm Stevenson

Representative Clients: Anheuser-Busch, Incorporated; The Quaker Oats Company; Diversified Foods and Seasonings; General Electric Company.

For full biographical listings, see the Martindale-Hubbell Law Directory

SUTTERFIELD & WEBB L.L.C. (AV)

650 Poydras Street, Suite 2715, 70130
Telephone: 504-598-2715
Fax: 504-529-7197
Email: info@swslaw.com

James R. Sutterfield — Daniel A. Webb

William J. Sommers, Jr. — Charmagne A. Padua
Gordon P. Serou, Jr.

OF COUNSEL
Robert A. Redwine

For full biographical listings, see the Martindale-Hubbell Law Directory

WAGNER & BAGOT (AV)

Suite 2660, Poydras Center, 650 Poydras Street, 70130-6105
Telephone: 504-525-2141
Telecopier: 504-523-1587
TWX: 5106017673
ELN: 62928850
"INCISIVE"

Thomas J. Wagner — Michael H. Bagot, Jr.

Thomas A. Rayer, Jr. — Thomas P. Henican
Brian P. Brancato — Dana A. Henderson

For full biographical listings, see the Martindale-Hubbell Law Directory

WARD NELSON, LLC (AV)

1539 Jackson Avenue, 6th Floor, 70130
Telephone: 504-561-5000
Fax: 504-588-1334

MEMBERS OF FIRM
Joseph R. Ward, Jr. — Craig R. Nelson
Lisa A. Condrey

ASSOCIATES
Lynn H. Frank — James Everet Brouillette

OF COUNSEL
Christina Papastavros Fay

Representative Clients: Associated Aviation Underwriters; Associated International Underwriters; Colonial Penn Insurance; Fidelity & Casualty of New York; Fireman's Insurance of Newark; Gulf Ins. Co.; Prudential Property and Cas. Ins. Co.; State Farm Fire & Casualty Co.; State Farms Mutual Automobile Insurance Co.; The Weitz Company.

For full biographical listings, see the Martindale-Hubbell Law Directory

WILSON & BOWLING (AV)

A Partnership including Professional Law Corporations
Suite 2411, Bank One Center, 201 St. Charles Avenue, 70170
Telephone: 504-586-5200
Facsimile: 504-586-5201
Email: wilsbowl@gs.net
Gulfport, Mississippi Office: 715 Markham Building, 2301 14th Street, 39501.
Telephone: 228-575-6202.
Fax: 228-864-6227.

Gordon F. Wilson, Jr., (P.L.C.) — David A. Bowling (P.L.C.)

Jeanne B. Roques — Susannah Ross Cooley
John D. Acomb

For full biographical listings, see the Martindale-Hubbell Law Directory

*RUSTON,** Lincoln Parish

GOFF AND GOFF (AV)

612 North Vienna Street, P.O. Box 2050, 71273-2050
Telephone: 318-255-1760
Fax: 318-255-7745
Email: giv@aol.com

A. Kennon Goff, III — Addison K. Goff, IV

Representative Clients: Ruston State Bank and Trust Co.; Community Trust Bank; South Central Bell Telephone Co.; Phillips Petroleum Co.; Aluminum Company of America; Society National Bank of Cleveland; Balboa Insurance Co.; Excalibur Insurance Co.; Shelter Insurance Co.; The Pyramid Life Insurance Co.;

(See Next Column)

For full biographical listings, see the Martindale-Hubbell Law Directory

*SHREVEPORT,** Caddo Parish

BARLOW AND HARDTNER L.C. (AV)

Tenth Floor, Louisiana Tower, 401 Edwards Street, 71101-3289
Telephone: 318-227-1131
Telecopier: 318-227-1141
Mailing Address: P.O. Box 8, Shreveport, Louisiana, 71161-0008

Joseph L. Shea, Jr. — Michael B. Donald

Representative Clients: Ashland Oil, Inc.; The Brinkmann Company; Kelley Oil Corporation; NorAm Energy Corp. (formerly Arkla, Inc.); Panhandle Eastern Corp.; Pennzoil Producing Co.; Southwestern Electric Power Company.

For Complete List of Firm Personnel, See General Section

For full biographical listings, see the Martindale-Hubbell Law Directory

CHARLES G. TUTT (AV)

900 Pierremont Road, Suite 206, 71106
Telephone: 318-868-6633
Fax: 318-868-5006
Email: cgtutt@softdisk.com *URL:* http://www.lawyers.com/charlestutt

ASSOCIATE
Thomas A. Bordelon

Representative Clients: Albany Insurance Co.; Bituminous Insurance Cos.; Dana Corporation; General Agents Insurance Co.; ITT Hartford; Louisiana Insurance Guaranty Assn.; Lazy Boy, Inc.; Louisiana Medical Mutual Insurance Co.; Medical Protective Insurance Company; The Millers Group.

For full biographical listings, see the Martindale-Hubbell Law Directory

MAINE

*AUGUSTA,** Kennebec Co.

JOHNSON & WEBBERT, L.L.P. (AV)

160 Capitol Street, P.O. Box 29, 04332-0029
Telephone: 207-623-5110
Fax: 207-622-4160
Email: pjohnson@johnsonwebbert.com *URL:* http://www.lawyers.com/jwl-law

Phillip E. Johnson — David G. Webbert

Representative Clients: Agway, Inc.; AVEMCO; Central Maine Power Co.; The Doctors Company; ITT/Hartford; Loss Management Services, Inc.; Shand, Morahan & Co.; Travelers Insurance Co.; Union Water Power Company.

For full biographical listings, see the Martindale-Hubbell Law Directory

PIERCE ATWOOD (AV)

77 Winthrop Street, 04330
Telephone: 207-622-6311
Fax: 207-623-9367
Email: info@PierceAtwood.com *URL:* http://www.pierceatwood.com
Portland, Maine Office: One Monument Square.
Telephone: 207-791-1100.
Fax: 207-791-1350.
Newburyport, Massachusetts Office: 6 Harris Street.
Telephone: 978-465-9599.
Fax: 978-465-9945.

MEMBERS OF FIRM
Malcolm L. Lyons — Michael D. Seitzinger
John C. Nivison

ASSOCIATE
Ann M. St. Peter-Griffith

COUNSEL
Daniel J. Stevens

For Complete List of Firm Personnel, See General Section

For full biographical listings, see the Martindale-Hubbell Law Directory

*PORTLAND,** Cumberland Co.

BURNS RAY & DELANO, PROFESSIONAL ASSOCIATION (AV)

193 Middle Street, 04101-4062
Telephone: 207-775-3581
Facsimile: 207-775-3814
Email: mailcenter@brdlaw.com

George F. Burns — Mary DeLano
David P. Ray — Elizabeth A. Burns
Arnold C. Macdonald — Carrie A. Green

(See Next Column)

BURNS RAY & DELANO PROFESSIONAL ASSOCIATION, *Portland—Continued*

OF COUNSEL

Joanne F. Cole

Representative Clients: Maine Yankee Atomic Power Company; Tractebel Power, Inc.; Hancock Lumber Co., Inc.; Jackson Laboratory; Hague International (engineering); Aetna Life & Casualty Co.; The Hartford; Great American Insurance Co.; Wausau Insurance Co.

For full biographical listings, see the Martindale-Hubbell Law Directory

FRIEDMAN BABCOCK & GAYTHWAITE (AV)

Suite 400, Six City Center, P.O. Box 4726, 04112-4726
Telephone: 207-761-0900
Telecopier: 207-761-0186
Email: info@fbg-law.com *URL:* http://www.fbg-law.com

MEMBERS OF FIRM

Harold J. Friedman
Ernest J. Babcock
Martha C. Gaythwaite
Karen Frink Wolf
Jennifer S. Riggle
Laurence H. Leavitt
Elizabeth A. Germani
Michelle Allott
Tracy D. Hill

ASSOCIATES

Susan J. Guerette
L. John Topchik
Sally A. Morris
Catherine C. Miller
Kieran N. Shields
Evan Smith

For full biographical listings, see the Martindale-Hubbell Law Directory

THOMPSON & BOWIE (AV)

Three Canal Plaza, P.O. Box 4630, 04112
Telephone: 207-774-2500
Telecopier: 207-774-3591
Email: law@thompsonbowie.com

MEMBERS OF FIRM

Roy E. Thompson, Jr.
James M. Bowie
Daniel R. Mawhinney
Rebecca H. Farnum
Glenn H. Robinson
Frank W. DeLong, III
Michael E. Saucier
Mark V. Franco
Edward R. Benjamin, Jr.
Cathy S. Roberts
Paul C. Catsos

ASSOCIATES

Elizabeth Knox Peck
Thomas G. Diebold
Michael R. Bosse
Lisa M. Fitzgibbon

For full biographical listings, see the Martindale-Hubbell Law Directory

WRIGHT & COON, P.A. (AV)

Four Canal Plaza, P.O. Box 7526, 04112
Telephone: 207-775-7722
Fax: 207-772-7045
Email: lexfori@lexfori.com

Steven F. Wright
John R. Coon
Brita J. Forssberg

For full biographical listings, see the Martindale-Hubbell Law Directory

MARYLAND

*ANNAPOLIS,** Anne Arundel Co.

BRASSEL & BALDWIN, P.A. (AV)

112 West Street, 21401
Telephone: 410-216-7900
DC Metro: 301-261-2199
Fax: 410-974-6019
URL: http://www.brasselbaldwin.com
Baltimore, Maryland Office: The B & O Building, Suite 920. 2 North Charles Street, 21201-3754.
Telephone: 410-974-6000.
Fax: 410-385-2939.

Rignal W. Baldwin, Jr.
Jon W. Brassel

Jonathan P. Kagan
Mary Coale Baldwin
Alexander John May

OF COUNSEL

Richard T. Stansbury (Resident, Baltimore, Maryland Office)

For full biographical listings, see the Martindale-Hubbell Law Directory

*BALTIMORE,** (Independent City)

ALLEN, JOHNSON, ALEXANDER & KARP, P.A. (AV)

Suite 1540, 100 East Pratt Street, 21202
Telephone: 410-727-5000
Fax: 410-727-0861
Email: ajakmd@aol.com
Washington, D.C. Office: 1707 L Street, N.W., Suite 1050.
Telephone: 202-828-4141.

Daniel Karp
D'Ana E. Johnson (Resident, Washington, D.C. Office)
Yvette M. Bryant

Representative Clients: Scottsdale Insurance Co.; Nautilus Insurance Co.; Jefferson Insurance Co.; Liberty Mutual Insurance Co.; Avis Rent-A-Car; Otis Elevator Co.; Montgomery Elevator Co.; Admiral Insurance Co.; Local Government Insurance Trust; Penn National Insurance Co.

For Complete List of Firm Personnel, See General Section

For full biographical listings, see the Martindale-Hubbell Law Directory

ANDERSON, COE & KING, L.L.P. (AV)

201 North Charles Street, Suite 2000, 21201-4135
Telephone: 410-752-1630
Cable Address: ABKO
Fax: 410-752 0085
Ocean City, Maryland Office: 12934 Kelly Bridge Lane, P.O. Box 535.
Telephone: 410-213-2681.
Fax: 410-213-2685.

COUNSEL

G. C. A. Anderson (1898-1985)
Ward B. Coe, Jr. (1913-1996)

OF COUNSEL

Frank J. Vecella
John F. King

MEMBERS OF FIRM

Robert H. Bouse, Jr.
E. Dale Adkins, III
James A. Rothschild
M. Bradley Hallwig
J. Michael Sloneker
E. Philip Franke, III
Philip C. Jacobson
Lynne B. Malone
Gregory L. VanGeison
Barbara McC. Stanley
Matthew T. Angotti
Hugh Cropper, IV (Resident, Ocean City Office)
James S. Aist

ASSOCIATES

Charles Ian Joseph
Neil R. Lebowitz
Alison J. McGriff
Stacie Free Farley
Harris Patrick Murphy
Allison Epstein Rubin
Brian P. Wyatt

Representative Clients: Hartford Accident & Indemnity Co.; The St. Paul Insurance Cos.; Chrysler Corp.; Provident Life and Accident Insurance Co.; Emerson Electric Co.; Pennsylvania Hospital Insurance Co.; Maryland Association of Boards of Education Group Insurance Pool; Pittsburg Corning Corp.; Hoover Treated Wood Products, Inc.

For full biographical listings, see the Martindale-Hubbell Law Directory

COOPER & TUERK, LLP (AV)

201 North Charles Street, Suite 2300, 21201
Telephone: 410-539-0300
Fax: 410-837-3923
Email: CANDT201@AOL.COM

MEMBERS OF FIRM

Gerald H. Cooper
Carl E. Tuerk, Jr.
Larry E. Jordan

ASSOCIATE

Marc A. Ominsky

For full biographical listings, see the Martindale-Hubbell Law Directory

CORNBLATT, BENNETT, PENHALLEGON & ROBERSON, P.A. (AV)

Suite 1800, 201 North Charles Street, 21201
Telephone: 410-752-7600
Fax: 410-752-2110
Email: mail@cbprlaw.com

Theodore B. Cornblatt
S. Woods Bennett
John R. Penhallegon
Patrick A. Roberson
Jeffrey Y. Laynor

J. Michael Harrison
Gary E. Dumer, Jr.

For full biographical listings, see the Martindale-Hubbell Law Directory

ELLIN AND BAKER (AV)

Second Floor, 1101 St. Paul Street, 21202
Telephone: 410-727-1787
Fax: 410-547-1787
1-800-237-1787
Email: Ellinlaw@aol.com

(See Next Column)

ELLIN AND BAKER—*Continued*

MEMBER OF FIRM

Marvin Ellin

For full biographical listings, see the Martindale-Hubbell Law Directory

BERTRAM M. GOLDSTEIN & ASSOCIATES, P.A. (AV)

222 Blaustein Building, One North Charles Street, 21201-3710
Telephone: 410-539-2222
Fax: 410-539-8157

Bertram M. Goldstein

Dean Kasian
Jeffrey S. Goldstein

For full biographical listings, see the Martindale-Hubbell Law Directory

GOODELL, DEVRIES, LEECH & GRAY, LLP (AV)

Suite 2000, One South Street, 21202
Telephone: 410-783-4000
Telecopy: 410-783-4040
Email: GDLG@GDLGLAW.COM

MEMBERS OF FIRM

Charles P. Goodell, Jr.
Donald L. DeVries, Jr.
Sidney G. Leech
Susan T. Preston
Richard M. Barnes
Thomas M. Goss
Bonnie J. Beavan
Linda S. Woolf
Thomas J. Cullen, Jr.

For full biographical listings, see the Martindale-Hubbell Law Directory

ISRAELSON, SALSBURY, CLEMENTS & BEKMAN, L.L.C. (AV)

300 West Pratt Street Suite 450, 21201
Telephone: 410-539-6633
FAX: 410-625-9554

MEMBERS OF FIRM

Stuart Marshall Salsbury
Paul D. Bekman
Daniel M. Clements
Matthew Zimmerman
Laurence A. Marder

Lauren R. Calia
Leslie Hayes Russo

COUNSEL TO THE FIRM

Max R. Israelson
Michael P. Smith

OF COUNSEL

Samuel Omar Jackson, Jr. (Semi-Retired)
Wendy Lozinsky Shiff

For full biographical listings, see the Martindale-Hubbell Law Directory

JANET, WILLOUGHBY & GERSHON, LLC (AV)

Executive Centre at Hooks Lane, 8 Reservoir Circle, Suite 200, 21208-1309
Telephone: 410-653-3200
Toll Free: 888-4-MED-LAW
Fax: 410-653-9030
Email: JWG@medlawlegalteam.com

Howard Alan Janet (P.C.)
Wayne M. Willoughby (P.A.)
Zev T. Gershon
Randal D. Getz

Robin R. Smith
Denise A. Greig

LEGAL SUPPORT PERSONNEL

Joan Hunter Green (Registered Nurse/Paralegal)
Sharon Marie Schmidt (Paralegal)

For full biographical listings, see the Martindale-Hubbell Law Directory

REDMOND, BURGIN & GUTIERREZ, P.A. (AV)

1301, The Fidelity Building, 210 North Charles Street, 21202
Telephone: 410-752-1555
Fax: 410-752-1064
URL: http://www.RBGLAW.com
Upper Marlboro, Maryland Office: 14746 Main Street.
Telephone: 301-952-1555.

Leonard C. Redmond, III

For Complete List of Firm Personnel, See General Section

For full biographical listings, see the Martindale-Hubbell Law Directory

ROLLINS, SMALKIN, RICHARDS & MACKIE, L.L.C. (AV)

401 North Charles Street, 21201
Telephone: 410-727-2443
Fax: 410-727-8390
URL: http://www.rsrm.com

(See Next Column)

MEMBERS OF FIRM

H. Beale Rollins (1898-1985)
Samuel S. Smalkin (1906-1982)
Edward C. Mackie
John F. Linsenmeyer
Thomas C. Gentner
Glenn W. Trimmer
Patrick G. Cullen
James P. O'Meara
Paul G. Donoghue
Ralph E. Wilson III

ASSOCIATES

Kenneth G. Macleay
Donna Lynn Kolakowski-Hollen
Meg Bantley Whiteford
J. James Roos
Jessica R. Di Cicco

OF COUNSEL

Raymond A. Richards (Retired)

LEGAL SUPPORT PERSONNEL

Guy M. Craig

For full biographical listings, see the Martindale-Hubbell Law Directory

SCANLAN, ROSEN & SHAR, LLC (AV)

26 South Street, 21202-3399
Telephone: 410-244-1155
Fax: 410-244-1157
Email: lawyers@triallaw.com *URL:* http://www.triallaw.com

Alfred L. Scanlan, Jr.
Marc Seldin Rosen
Marcus Z. Shar
Michael Stuart Warshaw

Timothy Cronin Lynch
Neil E Duke
Kristofer P. Cubello

OF COUNSEL

Colleen A. Cavanaugh
Lee H. Caplan
J. Michael McWilliams

For full biographical listings, see the Martindale-Hubbell Law Directory

SCHOCHOR, FEDERICO AND STATON, P.A. (AV)

The Paulton, 1211 St. Paul Street, 21202
Telephone: 410-234-1000
Toll Free: 888-234-0001
Facsimile: 410-234-1010
URL: http://www.sfspa.com
Washington D.C. Office: 10 G Street, N.E., Suite 650.
Telephone: 202-408-3300.

Jonathan Schochor
Philip C. Federico
Kerry D. Staton

Christopher P. Kennedy
Robert J. Farley
Bonnie Ardinger Winders

For full biographical listings, see the Martindale-Hubbell Law Directory

VENABLE ATTORNEYS AT LAW VENABLE, BAETJER AND HOWARD, LLP (AV)

A Partnership including Professional Corporations
1800 Mercantile Bank & Trust Building, 2 Hopkins Plaza, 21201
Telephone: 410-244-7400
Fax: 410-244-7742
URL: http://www.venable.com
Washington, D.C. Office: Venable, Baetjer, Howard & Civiletti LLP, Suite 1000, 1201 New York Avenue, N.W.
Telephone: 202-962-4800.
Fax: 202-962-8300.
McLean, Virginia Office: Suite 400, 2010 Corporate Ridge.
Telephone: 703-760-1600.
Fax: 703-821-8949.
Rockville, Maryland Office: Suite 500, One Church Street, P. O. Box 1906.
Telephone: 301-217-5600.
Fax: 301-217-5617.
Towson, Maryland Office: 210 Allegheny Avenue, P. O. Box 5517.
Telephone: 410-494-6200.
Fax: 410-821-0147.

MEMBERS OF FIRM

Benjamin R. Civiletti (P.C.) (Also at Washington, D.C. and Towson, Maryland Offices)
George Cochran Doub (P.C.)
Roger W. Titus (Resident, Rockville, Maryland Office)
Robert G. Smith (P.C.)
John H. Zink, III (Resident, Towson, Maryland Office)
Paul F. Strain (P.C.)
Joseph C. Wich, Jr. (Resident, Towson, Maryland Office)
Nell B. Strachan
James K. Archibald (Also at Washington, D.C. Office)
Jeffrey A. Dunn (Also at Washington, D.C. Office)
George F. Pappas (Also at Washington, D.C. Office)
James L. Shea (Also at Washington, D.C. Office)
Elizabeth C. Honeywell
C. Carey Deeley, Jr. (Also at Towson, Maryland Office)
Christopher R. Mellott
M. King Hill, III (Resident, Towson, Maryland Office)
David J. Heubeck
Gary M. Hnath (Resident, Washington, D.C. Office)
Mitchell Y. Mirviss

(See Next Column)

VENABLE ATTORNEYS AT LAW VENABLE, BAETJER AND HOWARD, LLP, *Baltimore—Continued*

MEMBERS OF FIRM (Continued)

Michael W. Robinson (Resident, McLean, Virginia Office)
David W. Goewey (Not admitted in MD; Resident, Washington, D.C. Office)
John A. McCauley
John T. Prisbe
Vicki Margolis (Also at Washington, D.C. Office)
Christine M. McAnney (Not admitted in MD; Resident, McLean, Virginia Office)
Maria F. Howell

ASSOCIATE

Paul D. Barker, Jr.

For Complete List of Firm Personnel, See General Section

For full biographical listings, see the Martindale-Hubbell Law Directory

ROBIN PAGE WEST (AV)

20 South Charles Street, Suite 703, 21201-3291
Telephone: 410-244-0400
Fax: 410-244-0402
Email: rwestn01@erols.com *URL:* http://www.lawyers.com/qui__tam

For full biographical listings, see the Martindale-Hubbell Law Directory

BETHESDA, Montgomery Co.

KARP, FROSH, LAPIDUS, WIGODSKY & NORWIND, P.A. (AV)

7475 Wisconsin Avenue, Suite 800, 20814
Telephone: 301-656-2111
Fax: 301-654-7748
Email: jackgold@erols.com
Washington, D.C. Office: 1150 Connecticut Avenue, N.W., Suite 900. 20036.
Telephone: 202-822-3777.
Fax: 202-828-4130.

Ronald A. Karp
Brian E. Frosh
Lawrence S. Lapidus
Jeffrey A. Wigodsky
Edward L. Norwind
J. Philip Kessel

Jack A. Gold
Donald C. Weinberg

OF COUNSEL

Douglas R. Smith
Stanley A. First (Not admitted in MD)
Roy I. Niedermayer
Maurice I. Burstein

For full biographical listings, see the Martindale-Hubbell Law Directory

*ROCKVILLE,** Montgomery Co.

ANDERSON & QUINN (AV)

The Adams Law Center, 25 Wood Lane, 20850
Telephone: 301-762-3303
Fax: 301-762-3776
Email: rscanlon@andersonquinn.com

MEMBERS OF FIRM

Charles C. Collins (1900-1973)
Robert E. Anderson (Retired)
Francis X. Quinn
Donald P. Maiberger
Robert P. Scanlon
John A. Rego
Alice Kelley Scanlon

ASSOCIATES

Kerry S. McGeever
Timothy J. Mulreany
Todd P. Maiberger
Jennifer D. Burke
Marc N. Steren

Representative Clients: C & P Telephone; Allstate Insurance Co.; State Farm Mutual Automobile Insurance Co.; Liberty Mutual Insurance Co.; American International Adjustment Co.; Marriott Corp.

For full biographical listings, see the Martindale-Hubbell Law Directory

BRAULT, GRAHAM, SCOTT & BRAULT, LLC (AV)

101 South Washington Street, 20850
Telephone: 301-424-1060
Fax: 301-424-7991
Email: bgsb@earthlink.net
Washington, D.C. Office: Brault, Graham, Scott & Brault, PLLC, 1140 Connecticut Avenue, N.W., Suite 250.
Telephone: 202-785-1200.
FAX: 202-785-4301.
Fairfax, Virginia Office: Suite 500, 11350 Random Hills Road, Fair Oaks Plaza, 22030-7429.
Telephone: 202-785-1200.

OF COUNSEL

Laurence T. Scott
James Robert Miller

(See Next Column)

MEMBERS OF FIRM

Denver H. Graham (1922-1987)
Albert E. Brault (Retired)
Albert D. Brault (Resident)
Leo A. Roth, Jr.
James S. Wilson (Resident)
Ronald G. Guziak
Daniel L. Shea (Resident)
M. Kathleen Parker (Resident)
David G. Mulquin (Resident)
James M. Brault (Resident)
Regina Ann Casey (Resident)

ASSOCIATES

Rhonda Ann Hurwitz (Resident)
Joan F. Brault (Resident)

Representative Clients: American Oil Co.; Crum & Forster Group; Fireman's Fund American Insurance Cos.; Kemper Group; Reliance Insurance Cos.; Safeco Group; Government Employees Insurance Co.; Medical Mutual Insurance Society of Maryland; Legal Mutual Liability Insurance Society of Maryland.

For full biographical listings, see the Martindale-Hubbell Law Directory

MICHAEL S. MORGENSTERN & ASSOCIATES, P.C. (AV)

51 Monroe Street, Suite 1604, 20850
Telephone: 301-217-9500
Fax: 301-217-9579
Toll Free: 1-888-888-0005
Mailing Address: P.O. Box 4690, Rockville, MD, 20850
Email: MSMlaw@erols.com
Washington, D.C. Office: 601 Pennsylvania Avenue, N.W. 20004.
Telephone: 202-393-2500.
Frederick, Maryland Office: 228 West Patrick Street. 21701.
Telephone: 301-620-7900.

Michael S. Morgenstern
Carl Morgenstern (Not admitted in MD)
Barbara L. Morgenstern (Not admitted in MD)

OF COUNSEL

W. David Allen

For full biographical listings, see the Martindale-Hubbell Law Directory

SILVER SPRING, Montgomery Co.

SAUNDERS & SCHMIELER (AV)

8737 Colesville Road, Suite L-200, 20910-3921
Telephone: 301-588-7717
Facsimile: 301-588-5073
Email: admin@sslawfirm.com *URL:* http://www.sslawfirm.com
Washington, D.C. Office: 1050 17th Street, N.W., #600
Telephone: 202-833-2999.
Baltimore, Maryland Office: Suite 2700, 111 South Calvert Street.
Telephone: 410-235-7558.
Arlington, Virginia Office: 2111 Wilson Boulevard, Suite 700.
Telephone: 703-243-1100.
Richmond, Virginia Office: 4900 Cutshaw Avenue.
Telephone: 804-353-9800.

MEMBER OF FIRM

Jeffrey R. Schmieler

ASSOCIATES

Nicole E. Ames
A. Benjamin Horton
Lucas F. Webster

For Complete List of Firm Personnel, See General Section

For full biographical listings, see the Martindale-Hubbell Law Directory

TIMONIUM, Baltimore Co.

DUGAN & JAKUBOWSKI, P.A. (AV)

1966 Greenspring Drive, Suite 500, 21093-4119
Telephone: 410-308-1600
Fax: 410-308-1742

Henry E. Dugan, Jr.
Ruth A. Jakubowski

Bruce J. Babij
Pamela S. Foresman
George S. Tolley, III
Yale R. Spector
Frank W. Spector

OF COUNSEL

Marian V. Fleming

For full biographical listings, see the Martindale-Hubbell Law Directory

*TOWSON,** Baltimore Co.

MUDD, HARRISON & BURCH (AV)

105 West Chesapeake Avenue, 300 Jefferson Building, 21204
Telephone: 410-828-1335
FAX: 410-828-1042
Email: mhb@mhblaw.com

MEMBERS OF FIRM

John E. Mudd
T. Rogers Harrison (1949-1995)
Richard C. Burch
Douglas W. Biser
H. Patrick Stringer, Jr.
Andrew Janquitto

(See Next Column)

MUDD, HARRISON & BURCH—*Continued*

James R. Andersen | Matthew Paul Lalumia
Nancy C. Hopkins

OF COUNSEL

Wm. T. Russell, Jr.

For full biographical listings, see the Martindale-Hubbell Law Directory

VENABLE ATTORNEYS AT LAW VENABLE, BAETJER AND HOWARD, LLP (AV)

A Partnership including Professional Corporations
210 Allegheny Avenue, P.O. Box 5517, 21204
Telephone: 410-494-6200
Fax: 410-821-0147
URL: http://www.venable.com
Baltimore, Maryland Office: 1800 Mercantile Bank & Trust Building, 2 Hopkins Plaza.
Telephone: 410-244-7400.
Fax: 410-244-7742.
Washington, D.C. Office: Venable, Baetjer, Howard & Civiletti LLP, Suite 1000, 1201 New York Avenue, N.W.
Telephone: 202-962-4800.
Fax: 202-962-8300.
McLean, Virginia Office: Suite 400, 2010 Corporate Ridge.
Telephone: 703-760-1600.
Fax: 703-821-8949.
Rockville, Maryland Office: Suite 500, One Church Street, P. O. Box 1906.
Telephone: 301-217-5600.
Fax: 301-217-5617.

PARTNERS

Benjamin R. Civiletti (P.C.) (Also at Washington, D.C. and Baltimore, Maryland Offices)
John H. Zink, III
Joseph C. Wich, Jr.
C. Carey Deeley, Jr. (Also at Baltimore, Maryland Office)
M. King Hill, III

For Complete List of Firm Personnel, See General Section

For full biographical listings, see the Martindale-Hubbell Law Directory

WHITNEY & BOGRIS, LLP (AV)

401 Washington Avenue, Twelfth Floor, 21204
Telephone: 410-583-8000
Fax: 410-583-8031
Email: HGWC@worldnet.att.net

MEMBERS OF FIRM

Daniel W. Whitney | George D. Bogris

ASSOCIATES

Kathleen D. Leslie
Henry Russell
Sandra A. Tofte
Michael A. Giacomazza
Arlene L. Sew
Gerald S. Gaetano (Not admitted in MD)
Scott A. McCabe (Not admitted in MD)
Jeffrey C. Shipley

OF COUNSEL

Joseph E. Dever
David L. Feldstein
Ronald V. Miller, Jr.

For full biographical listings, see the Martindale-Hubbell Law Directory

MASSACHUSETTS

*BOSTON,** Suffolk Co.

ANDERSON, ADLER, COHEN & HARVEY LLP (AV)

230 Congress Street, 02110
Telephone: 617-423-6674
Telefax: 617-423-7152
Email: aach@aachlaw.com *URL:* http://www.aachlaw.com

MEMBERS OF FIRM

James H. Anderson
Sidney W. Adler
Ellen Epstein Cohen
Alexandra B. Harvey
George E. Wakeman, Jr.
A. Bernard Guekguezian

ASSOCIATES

Laura Berg Susich
Charles M. Waters
Emily Haycock Fournier
Shelley A. McNamee
Windy L. Rosebush
Michael F. Conway
J. Yasmin Tayyab
Ethan I. Davis

For full biographical listings, see the Martindale-Hubbell Law Directory

BADGER, DOLAN, PARKER & COHEN (AV)

Formerly Badger, Sullivan, Kelley & Cole
2 Oliver Street, 02109
Telephone: 617-482-3030
Fax: 617-482-6919
Email: badger@badgerlaw.com *URL:* http://www.badgerlaw.com

MEMBERS OF FIRM

Walter I. Badger (1885-1926)
John J. Sullivan (1926-1979)
David W. Kelley (1935-1986)
George F. Parker, III
James B. Dolan, Jr.
Lawrence J. Cohen

ASSOCIATE

R. Christopher Green

OF COUNSEL

G. Mitchell Eckel, III | Dorothy M. Bickford

For full biographical listings, see the Martindale-Hubbell Law Directory

ELLIS & RAPACKI (AV)

85 Merrimac Street Suite 300, 02114
Telephone: 617-523-4800
Facsimile: 617-523-6901
Email: rellis4174@aol.com

Fredric L. Ellis | Edward D. Rapacki
Edward A. Broderick

For full biographical listings, see the Martindale-Hubbell Law Directory

FINNERTY & FINNERTY (AV)

Suite 230, 21 Custom House Street, 02110
Telephone: 617-737-3770
Fax: 617-737-0684
Email: AttysFandF@aol.com *URL:* http://www.finnertyfinnerty.baweb.com

MEMBERS OF FIRM

John F. Finnerty (1917-1994)
John F. Finnerty, Jr.
Brian P. Finnerty
Gail E. Finnerty

For full biographical listings, see the Martindale-Hubbell Law Directory

HINCKLEY, ALLEN & SNYDER LLP (AV)

28 State Street, 30th Floor, 02109-1775
Telephone: 617-345-9000
Email: firm@haslaw.com *URL:* http://www.haslaw.com
Providence, Rhode Island Office: 1500 Fleet Center.
Telephone: 401-274-2000.
Fax: 401-277-9600. URL: http://www.hawlaw.com.

MEMBERS OF FIRM

David D. Barricelli (Not admitted in MA)
Michael P. DeFanti
Eric F. Eisenberg
Hugh J. Gorman, III
William R. Grimm
Joel Lewin
Gerald J. Petros
Jeremy Ritzenberg
Charles E. Schaub, Jr.
Herman Snyder
Robert F. Sylvia
Howard E. Walker (Not admitted in MA)

ASSOCIATES

Mark Bianchi
Alexandra K. Callam
Kelley Jordan-Price
Catherine S. Kim
Christopher W. Morog
Elena B. Olson
Joseph D. Whelan (Not admitted in MA)

For Complete List of Firm Personnel, See General Section

For full biographical listings, see the Martindale-Hubbell Law Directory

LAW OFFICES OF MARTIN KANTROVITZ (AV)

185 Devonshire Street, Suite 510, 02110
Telephone: 617-426-3050
Fax: 617-426-3640
Hudson, Massachusetts Office: 173 Washington Street, 01749.
Telephone: 978-562-3800.
New Bedford, Massachusetts Office: 32 William Street, 02740.
Telephone: 508-994-6010.

ASSOCIATE

Lisa Baer

For full biographical listings, see the Martindale-Hubbell Law Directory

LANG & MORGERA, L.L.P. (AVⓉ)

6 Beacon Street, Suite 615, 02108
Telephone: 617-720-0176
Telecopier: 617-720-1184
URL: http://www.lawyers.com/lawdoctors
URL: http://www.lawdoctors.net
Providence, Rhode Island Office: 50 Park Row West, Suite 100.
Telephone: 401-456-0300.
Fax: 401-453-5545.

(See Next Column)

LANG & MORGERA L.L.P., *Boston—Continued*

Barry D. Lang | Vincent D. Morgera

For full biographical listings, see the Martindale-Hubbell Law Directory

MEEHAN, BOYLE & COHEN, P.C. (AV)

2 Center Plaza Suite 600, 02108
Telephone: 617-523-8300
Fax: 617-523-0525

James F. Meehan | Peter J. Black
Leo V. Boyle | John J. Carroll, Jr.
Cynthia J. Cohen | Michael B. Bogdanow
Warren F. Fitzgerald | Karen R. Ristuben

Sherry Yee Mulloy | Bradley Mead Henry
Samuel M. Furgang | Jonathan E. Tobin

For full biographical listings, see the Martindale-Hubbell Law Directory

PALMER & DODGE LLP (AV)

One Beacon Street, 02108
Telephone: 617-573-0100
Facsimile: 617-227-4420
URL: http://www.palmerdodge.com

MEMBERS OF FIRM

Michael T. Gass | Daryl J. Lapp
Jeffrey F. Jones | Francis C. Lynch
Craig E. Stewart

For Complete List of Firm Personnel, See General Section

For full biographical listings, see the Martindale-Hubbell Law Directory

SMITH & DUGGAN LLP (AV)

Two Center Plaza, 02108-1906
Telephone: 617-248-1900
Fax: 617-248-9320

MEMBERS OF FIRM

Scott A. Smith | Thomas G. Cooper
Christopher A. Duggan | H. Reed Witherby
Garrick F. Cole | Mark B. Rees

OF COUNSEL

John B. Savoca | Paul W. Johnson
Walter M. Foster | Thomas D. Herman

ASSOCIATES

Matthew J. Walko | John J. Barrett, III
Barbara E. Schultz | Kristen M. DeAngelo
Judith E. Michelman

For full biographical listings, see the Martindale-Hubbell Law Directory

SWARTZ & SWARTZ (AV)

10 Marshall Street, 02108
Telephone: 617-742-1900
Fax: 617-367-7193
Email: Attorney@Swartzlaw.com *URL:* http://www.Swartzlaw.com

Edward M. Swartz | Joan E. Swartz
Alan L. Cantor | James A. Swartz
Joseph A. Swartz | David P. Angueira
Victor A. Denaro | Jason Mark
Lisa V. Kaprielian

OF COUNSEL

Fredric A. Swartz

For full biographical listings, see the Martindale-Hubbell Law Directory

THORNTON, EARLY & NAUMES LLP (AV)

100 Summer Street, 30th Floor, 02110
Telephone: 617-720-1333; 800-431-4600
Fax: 617-720-2445
Email: tenlaw@socialaw.com *URL:* http://www.tenlaw.com

MEMBERS OF FIRM

Michael P. Thornton | Edwin L. Wallace
John T. Barrett | Robert M. Byrne, Jr.
Robert T. Naumes | David C. Strouss
Neil T. Leifer | Joseph R. Donohue
David J. McMorris | Patricia M. Flannery

OF COUNSEL

James F. Early (Not admitted in MA) | Robert P. Malone

For full biographical listings, see the Martindale-Hubbell Law Directory

BROCKTON, Plymouth Co.

VINCENT P. CAHALANE, P.C. (AV)

478 Torrey Street, Suite 12, 02301-4696
Telephone: 508-588-1222
Fax: 508-584-4748
URL: http://www.lawyers.com/cahalanelaw

Vincent P. Cahalane | Julie A. Cahalane Cahill
Robert J. Zullas | Andrew H. P. Norton
Kristopher S. Stefani

For full biographical listings, see the Martindale-Hubbell Law Directory

MICHIGAN

*ANN ARBOR,** Washtenaw Co.

GARAN, LUCOW, MILLER & SEWARD, P.C. (AV)

101 North Main Street, Suite 460, 48104-1400
Telephone: 734-930-5600
Fax: 734-930-0043
URL: http://www.garanlucow.com
Detroit, Michigan Office: 1000 Woodbridge Place.
Telephone: 313-446-1530.
Fax: 313-259-0450.
Port Huron, Michigan Office: Port Huron Office Center, 511 Fort Street, Suite 505.
Telephone: 810-985-4400.
Fax: 810-985-4107.
Grand Blanc, Michigan Office: 8332 Office Park Drive.
Telephone: 810-695-3700.
Fax: 810-695-6488.
Troy, Michigan Office: 1111 West Long Lake Road, Suite 300.
Telephone: 248-641-7600.
Fax: 248-641-0222.
Mount Clemens, Michigan Office: Towne Square Development, 10 South Main Street, Suite 307.
Telephone: 810-954-3800.
Fax: 810-954-3803.
Grand Rapids, Michigan Office: First of America Center, 171 Monroe Avenue, N.W., Suite 950.
Telephone: 616-742-5500.
Fax: 616-742-5566.
Lansing, Michigan Office: 530 Creyts Road, Suite A.
Telephone: 517-327-0300.
Fax: 517-327-0309.
Traverse City, Michigan Office: 1131 East Eighth Street, P.O. Box 3150.
Telephone: 231-941-1611.
Fax: 231-941-4420.
Marquette, Michigan Office: 228 West Washington Street, Suite 4,
Telephone: 906-228-7772.
Fax: 906-228-5999.

Judith A. Moskus (Resident) | John W. Whitman

John J. Koselka | Suzanne R. Fanning

For full biographical listings, see the Martindale-Hubbell Law Directory

BINGHAM FARMS, Oakland Co.

SMALL, TOTH, BALDRIDGE & VAN BELKUM, P.C. (AV)

30100 Telegraph Road Suite 250, 48025-4516
Telephone: 248-647-9595
Facsimile: 248-647-9599

Richard L. Small | David M. Baldridge
John M. Toth | Thomas G. Van Belkum
Keith P. Felty

Stephanie A. Griz-Kochkodan | Kristin Allen

Representative Clients: The Medical Protective Co.; Michigan Physicians Mutual Liability Insurance Co.; Physicians Insurance Company of Michigan; Shelby Insurance Group; Kemper Insurance Group; Michigan Society of Oral and Maxillofacial Surgeons; Michigan Association of Orthodontists; Michigan Association of Endodontists; AAMOS National; Mt Vernon Insurance Company.

For full biographical listings, see the Martindale-Hubbell Law Directory

BIRMINGHAM, Oakland Co.

MOFFETT & DILLON, A PROFESSIONAL CORPORATION (AV)

Brown Street Centre, Suite 340, 255 East Brown Street, 48009
Telephone: 248-646-5100
Telefax: 248-646-5332
Email: MDAAL@MSN.com
Columbus, Ohio Office: 2720 Airport Drive, Suite 100, 43219.
Telephone: 614-418-1726.

Stephen T. Moffett
Donald R. Dillon, Jr.
John M. McManus

SENIOR ASSOCIATES

Thomas L. Vitu
Robert E. Packus, Jr.
George J. David

ASSOCIATES

Jerry Lascoe
Michelle M. Holwey

LEGAL SUPPORT PERSONNEL

Debra D. Greenan
Susan M. Edwards

For full biographical listings, see the Martindale-Hubbell Law Directory

MICHAEL B. SERLING, P.C. (AV)

280 N. Old Woodward Avenue, Suite 406, 48009
Telephone: 248-647-6966
Fax: 248-647-9630

Michael B. Serling

Russell R. Beaudoen
Thomas A. Smith

OF COUNSEL

Philip J. Goodman

Reference: Comerica Bank, Birmingham, MI.

For full biographical listings, see the Martindale-Hubbell Law Directory

BLOOMFIELD HILLS, Oakland Co.

FEENEY KELLETT WIENNER & BUSH, PROFESSIONAL CORPORATION (AV)

35980 Woodward Avenue Second Floor, 48304-0394
Telephone: 248-258-1580
Fax: 248-258-0421

James P. Feeney
S. Thomas Wienner
Peter M. Kellett
Cheryl A. Bush
Thomas J. Manganello
Seth D. Gould
Patrick G. Seyferth

James J. Majernik
G. Gregory Schuetz
Erin L. Dougherty
Michael A. Tesner
Clay A. Guise
Sarah A. McLaren
Lennox Emmanuel
Kathleen M. Horchler
Helen Melia Hammond

OF COUNSEL

Jerry L. Johnson

For full biographical listings, see the Martindale-Hubbell Law Directory

DAVID D. PATTON & ASSOCIATES, P.C. (AV)

44 East Long Lake Road, Suite 100, P.O. Box 829, 48303-0829
Telephone: 248-258-6020
Fax: 248-258-6052
Email: litigation@aol.com *URL:* http://www.lawyers.com/dpattonlaw

David D. Patton

Ellen Bartman Jannette
Patricia C. White
Humma S. Siddiqi
Kelly P. Bekolay
David H. Patton (1912-1993)

OF COUNSEL

Lawrence J. Acker

For full biographical listings, see the Martindale-Hubbell Law Directory

PROVIZER & PHILLIPS, P.C. (AV)

6785 Telegraph Road, Suite 400, 48301
Telephone: 248-642-0444
Facsimile: 248-642-6661
Toll Free: 1-800-288-9080
URL: http://www.lawyers.com/provizer&phillips

Harold M. Provizer
Randall E. Phillips
Marilyn A. Madorsky
Noel F. Beck
Mark S. Baumkel

(See Next Column)

Constance S. Hall

Representative Clients: GAB; Coachman Industries; Reliance National Ins. Co.; Blackmoor Group.

For full biographical listings, see the Martindale-Hubbell Law Directory

*DETROIT,** Wayne Co.

BODMAN, LONGLEY & DAHLING LLP (AV)

34th Floor 100 Renaissance Center, 48243
Telephone: 313-259-7777
Fax: 313-393-7579
Email: info@bodmanlongley.com *URL:* http://www.bodmanlongley.com
Troy, Michigan Office: Suite 2020, 755 West Big Beaver Road.
Telephone: 248-362-2110.
Fax: 248-244-0780.
Ann Arbor, Michigan Office: 110 Miller, Suite 300.
Telephone: 734-761-3780.
Fax: 734-930-2494.
Northern Michigan Office: 229 Court Street, P.O. Box 405, Cheboygan.
Telephone: 231-627-4351.
Fax: 231-627-2802.

MEMBERS OF FIRM

James A. Smith
George G. Kemsley
Robert G. Brower
Thomas Van Dusen (Troy Office)
Lloyd C. Fell (Cheboygan Office)
Gary D. Reeves (Troy Office)
Stephen K. Postema (Ann Arbor Office)

For Representative Client List, See General Section

For Complete List of Firm Personnel, See General Section

For full biographical listings, see the Martindale-Hubbell Law Directory

GARAN, LUCOW, MILLER & SEWARD, P.C. (AV)

1000 Woodbridge Place, 48207-3192
Telephone: 313-446-1530
Fax: 313-259-0450
URL: http://www.garanlucow.com
Grand Blanc, Michigan Office: 8332 Office Park Drive.
Telephone: 810-695-3700.
Fax: 810-695-6488.
Port Huron, Michigan Office: Port Huron Office Center, 511 Fort Street, Suite 505.
Telephone: 810-985-4400.
Fax: 810-985-4107.
Ann Arbor, Michigan Office: 101 North Main Street, Suite 460.
Telephone: 734-930-5600.
Fax: 734-930-0043.
Troy, Michigan Office: 1111 West Long Lake Road, Suite 300.
Telephone: 248-641-7600.
Fax: 248-641-0222.
Mount Clemens, Michigan Office: Towne Square Development, 10 S. Main Street, Suite 307.
Telephone: 810-954-3800.
Fax: 810-954-3803.
Grand Rapids, Michigan Office: First of America Center, 171 Monroe Avenue, N.W., Suite 950.
Telephone: 616-742-5500.
Fax: 616-742-5566.
Lansing, Michigan Office: 530 Creyts Road, Suite A.
Telephone: 517-327-0300.
Fax: 517-327-0309.
Traverse City, Michigan Office: 1131 East Eighth Street, P.O. Box 3150.
Telephone: 231-941-1611.
Fax: 231-941-4420.
Marquette, Michigan Office: 228 West Washington Street, Suite 4,
Telephone: 906-228-7772.
Fax: 906-228-5999.

Daniel L. Garan (1922-1997)
Thomas F. Myers
Dennis P. Partridge
John E. McSorley
Lamont E. Buffington
Thomas L. Misuraca
Rosalind Rochkind
James J. Hayes, Jr.
Thomas W. Emery
Boyd E. Chapin, Jr.
Frederick B. Plumb
James S. Goulding
John J. Gillooly
Timothy E. O'Neill
Robert D. Goldstein
Michael J. DePolo
Thomas R. Paxton
Daniel S. Saylor
David M. Shafer
C. David Miller, II
Robert A. Obringer

Steven E. Nurenberg
Lynn E. Geist
Mark T. Rajt
Jami E. Leach
Allison L. Hoff
Charles A. Harrison, III
Erik Stamell
David M. Saperstein
Clare M. Cylkowski
Timothy James Jordan
David Allan Couch
Stacey Lynn King
Stephen Hudak

(See Next Column)

GARAN, LUCOW, MILLER & SEWARD P.C., *Detroit—Continued*

OF COUNSEL

Milton Lucow
Albert A. Miller
Matthew A. Seward
Jon P. Desenberg
Nancy J. Bourget

Counsel for: Allstate Insurance Co.; Sears, Roebuck & Co.; Liberty Mutual Insurance Co.; Continental Insurance Companies.

For full biographical listings, see the Martindale-Hubbell Law Directory

HAYDUK, ANDREWS & HYPNAR, P.C. (AV)

1700 Buhl Building, 535 Griswold, 48226
Telephone: 313-962-4500
Fax: 313-964-6577
Email: hahpc3@aol.com

Mark S. Hayduk
Robin K. Andrews
Mark A. Hypnar

Sean Angus McPhillips
Francis J. Lagrou

Representative Clients: Farmers Insurance Group; Admiral Insurance Co.; Heritage Ins. Alexis; Meijer, Inc.; Condon & Forsyth; Pinkerton's Inc.; Vik Brothers Ins.; Investors Ins. Group.

For full biographical listings, see the Martindale-Hubbell Law Directory

LUPO & KOCZKUR, P.C. (AV)

1000 First National Building, 48226
Telephone: 313-964-0110
Fax: 313-964-3711
Email: DLupo92965@aol.com *URL:* http://www.lawyers.com/l&klaw

Dane A. Lupo
Paul S. Koczkur
Ronald E. Westen

Robert P. George
Alexander B. Jarowyj
Gabriel Orzame Jr.
Dane A. Lupo, Jr.
Bradley T. Guldalian

Representative Clients: Anheuser-Busch, Inc.; United Artists; ITT; Olsten; Thermadyne Industries; National Beverage; CIGNA/Insurance Company of North America; Michigan Millers; Walt Disney World; Vic Tanny International.

For full biographical listings, see the Martindale-Hubbell Law Directory

MILLER, CANFIELD, PADDOCK AND STONE, P.L.C. (AV)

A Professional Limited Liability Company
Founded in 1852 by Sidney Davy Miller
150 West Jefferson, Suite 2500, 48226-4415
Telephone: 313-963-6420
Fax: 313-496-7500
Cable Address: "Stem Detroit"
URL: http://www.millercanfield.com
Ann Arbor, Michigan Office: 101 North Main Street, 7th Floor, 48104-1400.
Telephone: 734-663-2445.
Fax: 734-747-7147.
Troy, Michigan Office: 840 West Long Lake Road, Suite 200, 48098.
Telephone: 248-879-2000.
Fax: 248-879-2001.
Grand Rapids, Michigan Office: 99 Monroe, N.W., Suite 1200, 49503-2639.
Telephone: 616-454-8656.
Fax: 616-776-6322.
Howell, Michigan Office: 121 South Barnard Street, Suite 4, 48843-2305.
Telephone: 517-546-7600.
Telecopier: 517-546-6974.
Kalamazoo, Michigan Office: 444 West Michigan Avenue, 49007-3752.
Telephone: 616-381-7030.
Fax: 616-382-0244.
Lansing, Michigan Office: One Michigan Avenue, Suite 900, 48933-1609.
Telephone: 517-487-2070.
Fax: 517-374-6304.
Monroe, Michigan Office: 214 East Elm Avenue, Suite 100, 48162-2682.
Telephone: 734-243-2000.
Fax: 734-243-0901.
Washington, D.C. Office: 1900 K Street, N.W., Suite 1150. 20006.
Telephone: 202-429-5575; 785-0600.
Fax: 202-331-1118; 785-1234.
Pensacola, Florida Office: 25 West Cedar, 32501.
Telephone: 850-469-1088.
Fax: 850-432-0677.
New York, New York Office: 1450 Broadway, 41st Floor, 10018.
Telephone: 212-704-4400.
Fax: 212-704-4410.
Gdynia, Poland Office: UL. Slaska 21, 81-319.
Telephone: 011-485-831-2808.
Fax: 011-48-58-628 6411.

(See Next Column)

Warsaw, Poland Office: UL. Nowogrodzkall, 5th Floor, 00-513.
Telephone: 011-4822 529 0200.
Fax: 011-4822 529 0201.
Katowice, Poland Office: UL. Francuska 35/37, 40-027.
Telephone: 011 (48-32) 757-2414.
Fax: 011 (48-32) 757-2483.

PRINCIPALS OF FIRM

Charles E. Ritter (Kalamazoo Office)
Thomas G. Parachini
W. Mack Faison
Leland D. Barringer
Ronald E. Baylor (Kalamazoo Office)
Stephen J. Ott (Troy Office)
Pamela Chapman Enslen (Kalamazoo Office)
Brian J. Doren
Irene Bruce Hathaway

ASSOCIATES

Brian S. Westenberg (Troy Office)
Derek T. Montgomery
Lindsay L. Bray
Sherylle A. O. Gordon (Troy Office)

Representative Firm Clients: Chrysler Corporation; Comerica, Incorporated; City of Detroit, Michigan; Detroit Tigers, Inc.; First of Michigan; Ford Motor Company; Ford Motor Credit Company; Great Lakes Bancorp; Henry Ford Hospital; INVETECH Company.

For Complete List of Firm Personnel, See General Section

For full biographical listings, see the Martindale-Hubbell Law Directory

TIMMIS & INMAN L.L.P. (AV)

300 Talon Centre, 48207
Telephone: 313-396-4200
Facsimile: 313-396-4228
Email: info@timmis-inman.com *URL:* http://www.timmis-inman.com

Robert E. Graziani

Anthony J. Long

Representative Clients: Retail Resources, Inc.; Applied Process, Inc.; Insilco Corporation; Certain Underwriters at Lloyds of London; Various Markets, Inc.; Fel-Pro, Inc.; State Farm Fire & Casualty Company.

For Complete List of Firm Personnel, See General Section

For full biographical listings, see the Martindale-Hubbell Law Directory

VANDEVEER GARZIA, PROFESSIONAL CORPORATION (AV)

Suite 1600, 333 West Fort Street, 48226
Telephone: 313-961-4880
Fax: 313-961-3822
Email: vg@voyager.net
Oakland County Office: 220 Park Street, Suite 300, Birmingham, Michigan.
Telephone: 810-645-0100.
Fax: 810-645-2430.

Fred L. Vandeveer (1879-1972)
James E. Haggerty, Sr. (1900-1966)
Leroy G. Vandeveer (1902-1981)
Buelle A. Doelle (1902-1985)
James E. Plastow, Jr.
Michael M. Hathaway
John J. Lynch, III (Resident, Oakland County Office)
Thomas M. Peters
James K. Thome
Gary Alan Miller
William L. Kiriazis
Daniel P. Steele
Shelley K. Miller (Resident, Oakland County Office)
Terrance P. Lynch
Dennis B. Cotter
Bruce E. Pearce
Hal O. Carroll
David B. Timmis (Resident, Oakland County Office)

Nancy A. Hensley
Dawn M. Twydell
Christian E. Hildebrandt (Resident, Oakland County Office)
Donald C. Brownell

Representative Clients: Bic Corp.; CNA Insurance Group; Travelers Insurance Co.; United States Aviation Underwriters; Goodyear Tire & Rubber Co.

For full biographical listings, see the Martindale-Hubbell Law Directory

WILLMARTH, TANOURY, RAMAR, CORBET, GARVES & SHAW (AV)

535 Griswold, Suite 1730, 48226-3602
Telephone: 313-964-6300
Fax: 313-964-6310
Email: mdwillth@home.net

MEMBERS OF FIRM

Daniel R. Corbet
Brian R. Garves
David R. Nauts
Anthony J. Paradiso
John M. Perrin
John J. Ramar
Bruce R. Shaw
William A. Tanoury
Mark D. Willmarth

(See Next Column)

WILLMARTH, TANOURY, RAMAR, CORBET, GARVES & SHAW—*Continued*

ASSOCIATES

Marie C. Kennedy
Wayne Walker
Elizabeth L. Sokol
Robert S. Silverman
Carmine G. Paterra
Joseph J. Ceglarek, II
Derek Steven Wilczynski
Frank Hamidi
Kristen E. Skaff
Steven J. Bonasso
Colleen P. O'Connor
Lara R. Stutz
Eric G. Tucciarone
Michael P. Robach

For full biographical listings, see the Martindale-Hubbell Law Directory

ZEFF AND ZEFF, P.C. (AV)

The Buhl Building, 535 Griswold, Suite 1630, 48226
Telephone: 313-962-3825
Fax: 313-962-6007
URL: http://www.lawyers.com/zeffzefflaw

Louis Zeff (1896-1966)
A. Robert Zeff

Sheryl L. Berenbaum
Paul W. Broschay

For full biographical listings, see the Martindale-Hubbell Law Directory

EAST LANSING, Ingham Co.

RAYMOND JOSEPH & ASSOCIATES (AV)

713 Applegate Lane, 48823-2109
Telephone: 517-351-5540
Fax: 517-351-8343

OF COUNSEL

George R. Sidwell (1899-1983)
Michael Bowman
Bruce C. Blanton
Mary E. Low

Representative Clients: Ashland Oil, Inc.; Complete Auto Transit, Inc.; Employers Insurance of Wausau; Evans Products Co.; Grain Dealers Mutl.; Harbor Insurance Co.; Interstate Motor Freight System; Lansing Symphony Assn., Inc.; Prudential LMI Insurance Co.

For full biographical listings, see the Martindale-Hubbell Law Directory

FARMINGTON HILLS, Oakland Co.

BIRNKRANT & BIRNKRANT, P.C. (AV)

Hunters Square Office Building, 31555 West Fourteen Mile Road, Suite 201, 48334
Telephone: 248-932-7500
Facsimile: 248-932-5720

Jon J. Birnkrant
Sherwin M. Birnkrant

Dana Loewenstein

Representative Clients: Insurance Company of North America; CIGNA; City of Pontiac; ESIS; RHK Technology, Inc.; The Maccabees.

For full biographical listings, see the Martindale-Hubbell Law Directory

NEMIER, TOLARI, LANDRY, MAZZEO & JOHNSON, P.C. (AV)

37000 Grand River, Suite 300, 48335
Telephone: 248-476-6900
Fax: 248-476-6564
Email: firm@ntlmj.com

Craig L. Nemier
Jeffrey L. Tolari
David B. Landry
Rik Mazzeo
Mark R. Johnson

Michelle E. Mathieu
Kathy Contos Nash
Katharine R. Shishkovsky
Carol J. Surma

OF COUNSEL

William R. Still
Terry E. Pietryga

LEGAL SUPPORT PERSONNEL

Nancy Vayda Dembinski (Paralegal)

For full biographical listings, see the Martindale-Hubbell Law Directory

*FLINT,** Genesee Co.

MACDONALD, FITZGERALD & MACDONALD, P.C. (AV)

200 McKinnon Building, 48502
Telephone: 810-232-3184; 234-2204
Fax: 810-232-9632

Robert J. MacDonald (1914-1987)
John J. FitzGerald (1919-1995)
R. Duncan MacDonald
Timothy J. MacDonald
Robert J MacDonald

References: Michigan National Bank; NBD Bank, N.A.; Citizen's Bank.

For full biographical listings, see the Martindale-Hubbell Law Directory

*GAYLORD,** Otsego Co.

BENSINGER, COTANT, MENKES & AARDEMA, P.C. (AV)

308 West Main Street, P.O. Box 1000, 49735
Telephone: 517-732-7536
Fax: 517-732-4922
URL: http://www.bcma.net
Grand Rapids, Michigan Office: 983 Spaulding Avenue, S.E.
Telephone: 616-949-7963.
Fax: 616-949-5264.
Marquette, Michigan Office: 122 West Bluff.
Telephone: 906-225-1000.
Fax: 906-225-0818.

Dale L. Arndt (Resident, Grand Rapids)
Scott R. Eckhold

For full biographical listings, see the Martindale-Hubbell Law Directory

GRAND BLANC, Genesee Co.

GARAN, LUCOW, MILLER & SEWARD, P.C. (AV)

8332 Office Park Drive, 48439
Telephone: 810-695-3700
Fax: 810-695-6488
URL: http://www.garanlucow.com
Detroit, Michigan Office: 1000 Woodbridge Place.
Telephone: 313-446-1530.
Fax: 313-259-0450.
Port Huron, Michigan Office: Port Huron Office Center, 511 Fort Street, Suite 505.
Telephone: 810-985-4400.
Fax: 810-985-4187.
Ann Arbor, Michigan Office: 101 North Main Street, Suite 460.
Telephone: 734-930-5600.
Fax: 734-930-0043.
Troy, Michigan Office: 1111 West Long Lake Road, Suite 300.
Telephone: 248-641-7600.
Fax: 248-641-0222.
Mount Clemens, Michigan Office: Towne Square Development, 10 S. Main Street, Suite 307.
Telephone: 810-954-3800.
Fax: 810-954-3803.
Grand Rapids, Michigan Office: First of America Center, 171 Monroe Avenue, N.W., Suite 950.
Telephone: 616-742-5500.
Fax: 616-742-5566.
Lansing, Michigan Office: 530 Creyts Road, Suite A.
Telephone: 517-327-0300.
Fax: 517-327-0309.
Traverse City, Michigan Office: 1131 East Eighth Street, P.O. Box 3150.
Telephone: 231-941-1611.
Fax: 231-941-4420.
Marquette, Michigan Office: 228 West Washington Street, Suite 4,
Telephone: 906-228-7772.
Fax: 906-228-5999.

Joseph Kochis (Resident)
William J. Brickley (Resident)

Peter L. Diesel
John B. Farrell
Robert H. Shannon

For full biographical listings, see the Martindale-Hubbell Law Directory

*GRAND RAPIDS,** Kent Co.

BENSINGER, COTANT, MENKES & AARDEMA, P.C. (AV)

983 Spaulding Avenue, S.E., 49546
Telephone: 616-949-7963
Fax: 616-949-5264
URL: http://www.bcma.net
Gaylord, Michigan Office: 308 West Main, P.O. Box 1000.
Telephone: 517-732-7536.
Fax: 517-732-4922.
Marquette, Michigan Office: 122 West Bluff.
Telephone: 906-225-1000.
Fax: 906-225-0818.

Dale L. Arndt

For full biographical listings, see the Martindale-Hubbell Law Directory

BUCHANAN, SILVER & BECKERING, P.L.C. (AV)

300 Ottawa N.W., Suite 800, 49503
Telephone: 616-458-2464
Fax: 616-458-0608
URL: http://www.bsblaw.com
Email: rbuchanan@bsblaw.com *URL:* http://www.lawyers.com/bsblaw

MEMBERS OF FIRM

John C. Buchanan
Lee T. Silver
Robert J. Buchanan
Jane M. Beckering

(See Next Column)

BUCHANAN, SILVER & BECKERING P.L.C., *Grand Rapids—Continued*

LEGAL SUPPORT PERSONNEL

Raymond E. Beckering, Jr., M.D. (Medical Consultant)

Representative Clients: Melroe Ingersoll-Rand; Clark Equipment Co.; Coleman Company; Montgomery KONE; Vermont-American.

For full biographical listings, see the Martindale-Hubbell Law Directory

GARAN, LUCOW, MILLER & SEWARD, P.C. (AV)

First of America Center, 171 Monroe Avenue, N.W., Suite 950, 49503
Telephone: 616-742-5500
Fax: 616-742-5566
URL: http://www.garanlucow.com
Detroit, Michigan Office: 10000 Woodbridge Place.
Telephone: 313-446-1530.
Fax: 313-259-0450.
Grand Blanc, Michigan Office: 8332 Office Park Drive.
Telephone: 810-695-3700.
Fax: 810-695-6488.
Port Huron, Michigan Office: Port Huron Office Center, 511 Fort Street, Suite 505.
Telephone: 810-985-4400.
Fax: 810-985-4107.
Ann Arbor, Michigan Office: 101 North Main Street, Suite 460.
Telephone: 734-930-5600.
Fax: 734-930-0043.
Troy, Michigan Office: 1111 West Long Lake Road, Suite 300.
Telephone: 248-641-7600.
Fax: 248-641-0222.
Mount Clemens, Michigan Office: Towne Square Development, 10 S. Main Street, Suite 307.
Telephone: 810-954-3800.
Fax: 810-954-3803.
Lansing, Michigan Office: 530 Creyts Road, Suite A.
Telephone: 517-327-0300.
Fax: 517-327-0309.
Traverse City, Michigan Office: 1131 East Eighth Street, P.O. Box 3150.
Telephone: 231-941-1611.
Fax: 231-941-4420.
Marquette, Michigan Office: 228 West Washington Street, Suite 4,
Telephone: 906-228-7772.
Fax: 906-228-5999.

David N. Campos   Richard E. Holmes, Jr.

Thomas R. TerMaat   Michael D. Wade
Matthew P. Venema   Lori A. Ittner
Jill S Mulder

Counsel for: Allstate Insurance Co.; Sears, Roebuck & Co.; Liberty Mutual Insurance Co.; Continental Insurance Companies.

For full biographical listings, see the Martindale-Hubbell Law Directory

GROSSE POINTE PARK, Wayne Co.

ALLAN G. MEGANCK (AV)

1033 Bishop, 48230
Telephone: 313-881-0845
Fax: 313-881-0845
Email: lawtalk@aol.com

For full biographical listings, see the Martindale-Hubbell Law Directory

*KALAMAZOO,** Kalamazoo Co.

MILLER, CANFIELD, PADDOCK AND STONE, P.L.C. (AV)

A Professional Limited Liability Company
Founded in 1852 by Sidney Davy Miller
444 West Michigan Avenue, 49007-3752
Telephone: 616-381-7030
Fax: 616-382-0244
URL: http://www.millercanfield.com
Detroit, Michigan Office: 150 West Jefferson, Suite 2500, 48226-4415.
Telephone: 313-963-6420.
Fax: 313-496-7500.
Cable Address: "Stem Detroit."
Ann Arbor, Michigan Office: 101 North Main Street, 7th Floor, 48104-1400.
Telephone: 734-663-2445.
Fax: 734-747-7147.
Troy, Michigan Office: 840 West Long Lake Road, Suite 200, 48098.
Telephone: 248-879-2000.
Fax: 248-879-2001.
Grand Rapids, Michigan Office: 99 Monroe, N.W., Suite 1200, 49503-2639.
Telephone: 616-454-8656.
Fax: 616-776-6322.
Howell, Michigan Office: 121 South Barnard Street, Suite 4, 48843-2305.
Telephone: 517-546-7600.
Telecopier: 517-546-6974.

(See Next Column)

Lansing, Michigan Office: One Michigan Avenue, Suite 900, 48933-1609.
Telephone: 517-487-2070.
Fax: 517-374-6304.
Monroe, Michigan Office: 214 East Elm Avenue, Suite 100, 48162-2682.
Telephone: 734-243-2000.
Fax: 734-243-0901.
Washington, D.C. Office: 1900 K Street, N.W., Suite 1150. 20006.
Telephone: 202-429-5575; 785-0600.
Fax: 202-331-1118; 785-1234.
Pensacola, Florida Office: 25 West Cedar, 32501.
Telephone: 850-469-1088.
Fax: 850-432-0677.
New York, New York Office: 1450 Broadway, 41st Floor, 10018.
Telephone: 212-704-4400.
Fax: 212-704-4410.
Gdynia, Poland Office: UL. Slaska 21, 81-319.
Telephone: 011-485-831-2808.
Fax: 011-48-58-628 6411.
Warsaw, Poland Office: UL. Nowogrodzkall, 5th Floor, 00-513.
Telephone: 011-4822 529 0200.
Fax: 011-4822 529 0201.
Katowice, Poland Office: UL. Francuska 35/37, 40-027.
Telephone: 011 (48-32) 757-2414.
Fax: 011 (48-32) 757-2483.

PRINCIPALS

Charles E. Ritter   Ronald E. Baylor
Pamela Chapman Enslen

Representative Firm Clients: Chrysler Corporation; Comerica, Incorporated; City of Detroit, Michigan; Detroit Tigers, Inc.; First of Michigan; Ford Motor Company; Ford Motor Credit Company; Great Lakes Bancorp; Henry Ford Hospital; INVETECH Company.

For Complete List of Firm Personnel, See General Section

For full biographical listings, see the Martindale-Hubbell Law Directory

LANSING, Ingham Co.

FRASER TREBILCOCK DAVIS & FOSTER, P.C. (AV)

1000 Michigan National Tower, 48933
Telephone: 517-482-5800
Fax: 517-482-0887
URL: http://WWW.FTDF.COM
Detroit, Michigan Office: One Woodward Avenue, Suite 1550.
Telephone: 313-237-7300.
Fax: 313-961-1651.

Peter L. Dunlap   Mark R. Fox
C. Mark Hoover   Brian D. Herrington

Arthur O. Rogers II

Counsel for: Auto Club Insurance Assn. (ACIA); Auto Owners Insurance Co.; City of Mackinac Island; Federal Insurance Co.; Grand Trunk Railroad Co.; Prudential Insurance Company of America; State Farm Automobile Insurance Co.

For full biographical listings, see the Martindale-Hubbell Law Directory

GARAN, LUCOW, MILLER & SEWARD, P.C. (AV)

Office Park West, 530 Creyts Road, Suite A, 48917
Telephone: 517-327-0300
Fax: 517-327-0309
URL: http://www.garanlucow.com
Detroit, Michigan Office: 1000 Woodbridge Place.
Telephone: 313-446-1530.
Fax: 313-259-0450.
Port Huron, Michigan Office: Port Huron Office Center, 511 Fort Street, Suite 505.
Telephone: 810-985-4400.
Fax: 810-985-4187.
Ann Arbor, Michigan Office: 101 North Main Street, Suite 460.
Telephone: 734-930-5600.
Fax: 734-930-0043.
Troy, Michigan Office: 1111 West Long Lake Road, Suite 300.
Telephone: 248-641-7600.
Fax: 248-641-0222.
Mount Clemens, Michigan Office: Towne Square Development, 10 S. Main Street, Suite 307.
Telephone: 810-954-3800.
Fax: 810-954-3803.
Grand Rapids, Michigan Office: First of America Center, 171 Monroe Avenue, N.W., Suite 950.
Telephone: 616-742-5500.
Fax: 616-742-5566.
Grand Blanc, Michigan Office: 8332 Office Park Drive.
Telephone: 810-695-3700.
Fax: 810-695-6488.
Traverse City, Michigan Office: 1131 East Eighth Street, P.O. Box 3150.
Telephone: 231-941-1611.
Fax: 231-941-4420.
Marquette, Michigan Office: 228 West Washington Street, Suite 4,
Telephone: 906-228-7772.
Fax: 906-228-5999.

(See Next Column)

GARAN, LUCOW, MILLER & SEWARD P.C.—*Continued*

Kenneth V. Klaus (Resident)

Paul E. Tower (Resident)

For full biographical listings, see the Martindale-Hubbell Law Directory

*MARQUETTE,** Marquette Co.

BENSINGER, COTANT, MENKES & AARDEMA, P.C. (AV)

122 West Bluff, 49855
Telephone: 906-225-1000
Fax: 906-225-0818
URL: http://www.bcma.net
Gaylord, Michigan Office: 308 West Main, P.O. Box 1000.
Telephone: 517-732-7536.
Fax: 517-732-4922.
Grand Rapids, Michigan Office: 983 Spaulding Avenue, S.E.
Telephone: 616-949-7963.
Fax: 616-949-5264.

Glenn W. Smith

For full biographical listings, see the Martindale-Hubbell Law Directory

*MOUNT CLEMENS,** Macomb Co.

GARAN, LUCOW, MILLER & SEWARD, P.C. (AV)

Towne Square Development, 10 S. Main Street Suite 307, 48043-2370
Telephone: 810-954-3800
Fax: 810-954-3803
URL: http://www.garanlucow.com
Detroit, Michigan Office: 1000 Woodbridge Place.
Telephone: 313-446-1530.
Fax: 313-259-0450.
Grand Blanc, Michigan Office: 8332 Office Park Drive.
Telephone: 810-695-3700.
Fax: 810-695-6488.
Ann Arbor, Michigan Office: 101 North Main Street, Suite 460.
Telephone: 734-930-5600.
Fax: 734-930-0043.
Troy, Michigan Office: 1111 West Long Lake Road, Suite 300.
Telephone: 248-641-7600.
Fax: 248-641-0222.
Port Huron, Michigan Office: Port Huron Office Center, 511 Fort Street, Suite 505.
Telephone: 810-985-4400.
Fax: 810-985-4107.
Grand Rapids, Michigan Office: First of America Center, 171 Monroe Avenue, N.W., Suite 950.
Telephone: 616-742-5500.
Fax: 616-742-5566.
Lansing, Michigan Office: 530 Creyts Road, Suite A.
Telephone: 517-327-0300.
Fax: 517-327-0309.
Traverse City, Michigan Office: 1131 East Eighth Street, P.O. Box 3150.
Telephone: 231-941-1611.
Fax: 231-941-4420.
Marquette, Michigan Office: 228 West Washington Street, Suite 4,
Telephone: 906-228-7772.
Fax: 906-228-5999.

Richard E. Eaton (Resident) Robert F. MacAlpine

For full biographical listings, see the Martindale-Hubbell Law Directory

MARTIN, BACON & MARTIN, P.C. (AV)

44 First Street, 48043
Telephone: 810-979-6500
Fax: 810-468-7016
URL: http://www.lawyers.com/martin

James N. Martin
Jonathan E. Martin
Paul R. VanTol
Michael R. Janes
Kevin L. Moffatt
John W. Crimando
Victor T. Van Camp

Patrick D. Ball
Amy M. Johnston
Sean S. Cleland

Reference: Community Central Bank - Mt. Clemens.

For full biographical listings, see the Martindale-Hubbell Law Directory

*PORT HURON,** St. Clair Co.

GARAN, LUCOW, MILLER & SEWARD, P.C. (AV)

Port Huron Office Center, 511 Fort Street, Suite 505, 48060-3922
Telephone: 810-985-4400
Fax: 810-985-4107
URL: http://www.garanlucow.com
Detroit, Michigan Office: 1000 Woodbridge Place.
Telephone: 313-446-1530.
Fax: 313-259-0450.

(See Next Column)

Grand Blanc, Michigan Office: 8332 Office Park Drive.
Telephone: 810-695-3700.
Fax: 810-695-6488.
Ann Arbor, Michigan Office: 101 North Main Street, Suite 460.
Telephone: 734-930-5600.
Fax: 734-930-0043.
Troy, Michigan Office: 1111 West Long Lake Road, Suite 300.
Telephone: 248-641-7600.
Fax: 248-641-0222.
Mount Clemens, Michigan Office: Towne Square Development, 10 S. Main Street, Suite 307.
Telephone: 810-954-3800.
Fax: 810-954-3803.
Grand Rapids, Michigan Office: First of America Center, 171 Monroe Avenue, N.W., Suite 950.
Telephone: 616-742-5500.
Fax: 616-742-5566.
Lansing, Michigan Office: 530 Creyts Road, Suite A.
Telephone: 517-327-0300.
Fax: 517-327-0309.
Traverse City, Michigan Office: 1131 East Eighth Street, P.O. Box 3150.
Telephone: 231-941-1611.
Fax: 231-941-4420.
Marquette, Michigan Office: 228 West Washington Street, Suite 4,
Telephone: 906-228-7772.
Fax: 906-228-5999.

Randolph J. Martinek

Robert L. Goldenbogen Meghan A. McGlynn

For full biographical listings, see the Martindale-Hubbell Law Directory

ROYAL OAK, Oakland Co.

CARDELLI HEBERT, P.C. (AV)

322 West Lincoln, 48067
Telephone: 248-544-1100
Toll Free 1-800-411-7774
Telecopier: 248-544-1191
Email: cardelli.hebert@worldnet.att.net

Thomas G. Cardelli Deborah A. Hebert

Mary Ann J. O'Neil
Nicholas S. Andrews
John L. Weston
R. Carl Lanfear, Jr.
Robert J. Lantzy
Catherine Dritsas
Mark G. Cooper
Timothy R. Noonan

Representative Clients: Allianz Insurance Company; Dana Corporation; General Motors Corporation; Otis Elevator Company; Raymond Corporation; Robert Bosch Power Tool Corporation.

For full biographical listings, see the Martindale-Hubbell Law Directory

ST. CLAIR SHORES, Macomb Co.

SAURBIER, SIEGAN & SANFIELD, P.C. (AV)

Suite 402, 400 Maple Park Boulevard, 48081
Telephone: 810-447-3700
Fax: 810-447-3755
Email: scott@saurbier.com
Detroit Office: 1028 Buhl Building.
Telephone: 313-965-2220.

SHAREHOLDERS

Scott A. Saurbier Renée S. Siegan
Joel A. Sanfield

Marc D. Saurbier
Lawrence T. Garcia
John C. Valenti
Sara B. Keough
David C. Wiegel
Matthew J. Nagaj
Valerie Henning Mock

For full biographical listings, see the Martindale-Hubbell Law Directory

SOUTHFIELD, Oakland Co.

COLLINS, EINHORN, FARRELL & ULANOFF, A PROFESSIONAL CORPORATION (AV)

4000 Town Center, Suite 909, 48075-1473
Telephone: 248-355-4141
Facsimile: 248-355-2277

Morton H. Collins
Brian D. Einhorn
Clayton F. Farrell
Stuart A. Ulanoff
Dale J. McLellan
Kenneth C. Merritt
Noreen L. Slank
Michael J. Sullivan
Janice G. Hildenbrand
Neil W. MacCallum

(See Next Column)

COLLINS, EINHORN, FARRELL & ULANOFF A PROFESSIONAL CORPORATION, *Southfield—Continued*

Theresa M. Asoklis
Karen C. Liddle
Deborah A. Lujan
Shannon M. Kos
Kevin P. Moloughney
Susan P. Saltzman
Daniel E. Collins
J. Mark Cooney
David C. Anderson

For full biographical listings, see the Martindale-Hubbell Law Directory

ROSEN & LOVELL, P.C. (AV)

25505 West Twelve Mile Road Suite 1000, 48034-1811
Telephone: 248-213-2910
Fax: 248-948-6677

Paul A. Rosen

Alex J. Remick

For full biographical listings, see the Martindale-Hubbell Law Directory

SCHWARTZ & JALKANEN, P.C. (AV)

24400 Northwestern Highway, Suite 200, 48075-6821
Telephone: 248-352-2555
Facsimile: 248-352-5963

Melvin R. Schwartz
Arthur W. Jalkanen
Karl Eric Hannum

Gregory A. Light
David C. Dixon

For full biographical listings, see the Martindale-Hubbell Law Directory

SOMMERS, SCHWARTZ, SILVER & SCHWARTZ, P.C. (AV)

2000 Town Center, Suite 900, 48075
Telephone: 248-355-0300
Telecopier: 248-746-4001
Plymouth, Michigan Office: 747 South Main Street.
Telephone: 313-455-4250.

Leonard B. Schwartz
Robert H. Darling
James J. Vlasic
Joseph E. Grinnan
B. A. Tyler
Robert B. Sickels

General Counsel for: City of Taylor; Foodland Distributors; C.A. Muer Corporation; Vlasic & Company; Nederlander Corporation; Midwest Health Centers, P.C.
Representative Clients: Michigan National Bank; Universal Underwriters Insurance Co.; Don Lee Distributor; Rite-Aid of Michigan.

For Complete List of Firm Personnel, See General Section

For full biographical listings, see the Martindale-Hubbell Law Directory

*TRAVERSE CITY,** Grand Traverse Co.

GARAN, LUCOW, MILLER & SEWARD, P.C. (AV)

1131 East Eighth Street, P.O. Box 3150, 49685-3150
Telephone: 231-941-1611
Fax: 231-941-4420
URL: http://www.garanlucow.com
Detroit, Michigan Office: 1000 Woodbridge Place.
Telephone: 313-446-1530.
Fax: 313-259-0450.
Port Huron, Michigan Office: Port Huron Office Center, 511 Fort Street, Suite 505.
Telephone: 810-985-4400.
Fax: 810-985-4187.
Ann Arbor, Michigan Office: 101 North Main Street, Suite 460.
Telephone: 734-930-5600.
Fax: 734-930-0043.
Troy, Michigan Office: 1111 West Long Lake Road, Suite 300.
Telephone: 248-641-7600.
Fax: 248-641-0222.
Mount Clemens, Michigan Office: Towne Square Development, 10 S. Main Street, Suite 307.
Telephone: 810-954-3800.
Fax: 810-954-3803.
Grand Rapids, Michigan Office: First of America Center, 171 Monroe Avenue, N.W., Suite 950.
Telephone: 616-742-5500.
Fax: 616-742-5566.
Grand Blanc, Michigan Office: 8332 Office Park Drive.
Telephone: 810-695-3700.
Fax: 810-695-6488.
Lansing, Michigan Office: 530 Creyts Road, Suite A.
Telephone: 517-327-0300.
Fax: 517-327-0309.
Marquette, Michigan Office: 228 West Washington Street, Suite 4,
Telephone: 906-228-7772.
Fax: 906-228-5999.

(See Next Column)

Peter B. Worden, Jr.
Douglas J. Read
John W. Sharp
Michael J. Swogger

Linda Marsh-Raetz

For full biographical listings, see the Martindale-Hubbell Law Directory

THOMPSON, O'NEIL & VANDERVEEN (AV)

309 East Front Street, P.O. Box 429, 49685
Telephone: 231-929-9700; 1-800-678-1307
Fax: 231-929-7262
Email: tov@traverse.com *URL:* http://www.lawyers.com/tovtraverse

George R. Thompson
Daniel P. O'Neil
John R. VanderVeen

Jessica G. Rickard

For full biographical listings, see the Martindale-Hubbell Law Directory

TROY, Oakland Co.

BOWEN, RADABAUGH, MILTON & BROWN, P.C. (AV)

4967 Crooks Road, Suite 150, 48098
Telephone: 248-641-8000
Fax: 248-641-8219
Email: brmb@brmb.com *URL:* http://www.brmb.com

Thomas R. Bowen
James M. Radabaugh
Lisa T. Milton
Susan Leigh Brown

Geoffrey D. Marshall
Mark P. Dunn

OF COUNSEL

Meri Craver Borin

For full biographical listings, see the Martindale-Hubbell Law Directory

GARAN, LUCOW, MILLER & SEWARD, P.C. (AV)

1111 West Long Lake Road, Suite 300, 48098-6333
Telephone: 248-641-7600
Fax: 248-641-0222
URL: http://www.garanlucow.com
Detroit, Michigan Office: 10000 Woodbridge Place.
Telephone: 313-446-1530.
Fax: 313-259-0450.
Grand Blanc, Michigan Office: 8332 Office Park Drive.
Telephone: 810-695-3700.
Fax: 810-695-6488.
Port Huron, Michigan Office: Port Huron Office Center, 511 Fort Street, Suite 505.
Telephone: 810-985-4400.
Fax: 810-985-4107.
Ann Arbor, Michigan Office: 101 North Main Street, Suite 460.
Telephone: 734-930-5600.
Fax: 734-930-0043.
Mount Clemens, Michigan Office: Suite 307, Towne Square Development, 10 South Main Street.
Telephone: 810-954-3800.
Fax: 810-954-3803.
Grand Rapids, Michigan Office: First of America Center, 171 Monroe Avenue, N.W., Suite 950.
Telephone: 616-742-5500.
Fax: 616-742-5566.
Lansing, Michigan Office: 530 Creyts Road, Suite A.
Telephone: 517-327-0300.
Fax: 517-327-0309.
Traverse City, Michigan Office: 1131 East Eighth Street, P.O. Box 3150.
Telephone: 231-941-1611.
Fax: 231-941-4420.
Marquette, Michigan Office: 228 West Washington Street, Suite 4,
Telephone: 906-228-7772.
Fax: 906-228-5999.

James L. Borin
Roger A. Smith
Mark Shreve
John P. Seyfried (Resident)
Edward M. Freeland
Steven A. Matta
Ian C. Simpson
Susan M. Williams

David J. Lankford
Brian E. Etzel
Dawn M. Patterson
Kristin Stiles Smolek
Monia (Monica) C. Gregor
Beth A. Andrews
Darryl Keenan Segars
Adam K. Gordon

Counsel for: Allstate Insurance Co.; Sears, Roebuck & Co.; Liberty Mutual Insurance Co.; Continental Insurance Companies.

For full biographical listings, see the Martindale-Hubbell Law Directory

Troy—Continued

HOLAHAN, MALLOY, MAYBAUGH, MONNICH & DELIE (AV)

Suite 100, 2690 Crooks Road, 48084-4700
Telephone: 248-362-4747
Fax: 248-362-4779
East Tawas, Michigan Office: 910 East Bay Street.
Telephone: 517-362-4747.
Fax: 517-362-7331.

MEMBERS OF FIRM

J. Michael Malloy, III
John R. Monnich
James D. Maybaugh
David L. Delie, Jr.

OF COUNSEL

Thomas H. O'Connor
Maureen Holahan (Retired; Resident, East Tawas Office)

For full biographical listings, see the Martindale-Hubbell Law Directory

---

MILLER, CANFIELD, PADDOCK AND STONE, P.L.C. (AV)

A Professional Limited Liability Company
Founded in 1852 by Sidney Davy Miller
840 West Long Lake Road Suite 200, 48098
Telephone: 248-879-2000
Fax: 248-879-2001
URL: http://www.millercanfield.com
Detroit, Michigan Office: 150 West Jefferson, Suite 2500, 48226-4415.
Telephone: 313-963-6420.
Fax: 313-496-7500.
Cable Address: "Stem Detroit."
Ann Arbor, Michigan Office: 101 North Main Street, 7th Floor, 48104-1400.
Telephone: 734-663-2445.
Fax: 734-747-7147.
Grand Rapids, Michigan Office: 99 Monroe, N.W., Suite 1200, 49503-2639.
Telephone: 616-454-8656.
Fax: 616-776-6322.
Howell, Michigan Office: 121 South Barnard Street, Suite 4, 48843-2305.
Telephone: 517-546-7600.
Telecopier: 517-546-6974.
Kalamazoo, Michigan Office: 444 West Michigan Avenue, 49007-3752.
Telephone: 616-381-7030.
Fax: 616-382-0244.
Lansing, Michigan Office: One Michigan Avenue, Suite 900, 48933-1609.
Telephone: 517-487-2070.
Fax: 517-374-6304.
Monroe, Michigan Office: 214 East Elm Avenue, Suite 100, 48162-2682.
Telephone: 734-243-2000.
Fax: 734-243-0901.
Washington, D.C. Office: 1900 K Street, N.W., Suite 1150. 20006.
Telephone: 202-429-5575; 785-0600.
Fax: 202-331-1118; 785-1234.
Pensacola, Florida Office: 25 West Cedar, 32501.
Telephone: 850-469-1088.
Fax: 850-432-0677.
New York, New York Office: 1450 Broadway, 41st Floor, 10018.
Telephone: 212-704-4400.
Fax: 212-704-4410.
Gdynia, Poland Office: UL. Slaska 21, 81-319.
Telephone: 011-485-831-2808.
Fax: 011-48-58-628 6411.
Warsaw, Poland Office: UL. Nowogrodzkall, 5th Floor, 00-513.
Telephone: 011-4822 529 0200.
Fax: 011-4822 529 0201.
Katowice, Poland Office: UL. Francuska 35/37, 40-027.
Telephone: 011 (48-32) 757-2414.
Fax: 011 (48-32) 757-2483.

RESIDENT PRINCIPALS

Stephen J. Ott
Robert J. Haddad
Erich H. Hintzen

RESIDENT ASSOCIATES

Brian S. Westenberg
Sherylle A. O. Gordon
Jason S. Rose

CONTRACT ATTORNEY

Ronald P. Weitzman

Representative Firm Clients: Chrysler Corporation; Comerica, Incorporated; City of Detroit, Michigan; Detroit Tigers, Inc.; First of Michigan; Ford Motor Company; Ford Motor Credit Company; Great Lakes Bancorp; Henry Ford Hospital; INVETECH Company.

For Complete List of Firm Personnel, See General Section

For full biographical listings, see the Martindale-Hubbell Law Directory

---

POLING, MCGAW & POLING, P.C. (AV)

Suite 275, 5435 Corporate Drive, 48098
Telephone: 248-641-0500
Telecopier: 248-641-0506
URL: http://www.lawyers.com/polingmcgaw&poling

(See Next Column)

Benson T. Buck (1926-1989)
Gregory C. Hamilton
Richard B. Poling
Veronica B. O'Hara
D. Douglas McGaw
James R. Parker
Richard B. Poling, Jr.
Shannon M. Acton

OF COUNSEL

Ralph S. Moore

Representative Clients: City of Troy; United States Fidelity & Guaranty Co.; Sentry Insurance Co.; Admiral Insurance; DeMaria Construction Co.; Leo Corporation; Aetna Casualty and Surety Co.; Concord Design; Pneumo-Abex.

For full biographical listings, see the Martindale-Hubbell Law Directory

---

SCHADEN, KATZMAN, LAMPERT & MCCLUNE (AV Ⓣ)

100 West Big Beaver Road Suite 130, 48084
Telephone: 248-258-4800
Fax: 248-258-2825
Email: SCHKATZLAM@aol.com *URL:* http://www.lawyers.com/schadenlaw
Broomfield, Colorado Office: 11870 Airport Way.
Telephone: 303-465-3663.
Facsimile: 303-465-3884.

MEMBERS OF FIRM

Richard F. Schaden
Bruce A. Lampert
David I. Katzman
John D. McClune

ASSOCIATE

Kathleen M. Schaden

OF COUNSEL

Bruce O. Wilson

For full biographical listings, see the Martindale-Hubbell Law Directory

---

WEST BLOOMFIELD, Oakland Co.

CHEATHAM, ESTES & HOLLMAN, P.C. (AV)

5777 West Maple Road, Suite 130, P.O. Box 255002, 48325-5002
Telephone: 248-932-2000
Fax: 248-932-2008

Charles C. Cheatham
Lee Estes
Mary E. Hollman

Christopher P. Jelinek

COUNSEL

Lynn L. Lower

For full biographical listings, see the Martindale-Hubbell Law Directory

DOWLING, AARON & KEELER INCORPORATED—*Continued*

William J. Keeler, Jr.
Stephen M. Blumberg
Philip David Kopp
Dale Ikeda
Francine Marie Kanne
James C. Sherwood
David J. Weiland

Leigh W. Burnside

Reference: Wells Fargo Bank (Main).

For Complete List of Firm Personnel, See General Section

For full biographical listings, see the Martindale-Hubbell Law Directory

IRVINE, Orange Co.

STEVENS & KRAMER, A PROFESSIONAL CORPORATION (AV)

18022 Cowan, Suite 200D, 92614-6808
Telephone: 949-253-9553
Fax: 949-253-9643
Agoura Hills, California Office: 30401 W. Agoura Road, Suite 102.
Telephone: 818-879-1699.
Fax: 818-879-1673.

Carl R. Stevens

Lee E. Burrows

For full biographical listings, see the Martindale-Hubbell Law Directory

*LOS ANGELES,** Los Angeles Co.

BIREN & KATZMAN (AV)

815 Moraga Drive (Bel Air), 90049-1633
Telephone: 310-476-3031; 381-5609
Fax: 310-471-3165
Email: birenkatzman@biren.com *URL:* http://www.biren.com

Matthew B. F. Biren
Marc J. Katzman

Debra J. Tauger
Charles E. Koro

Reference: City National Bank (Beverly Hills Branch).

For full biographical listings, see the Martindale-Hubbell Law Directory

DAPEER, ROSENBLIT & LITVAK, LLP (AV)

11500 West Olympic Boulevard, Suite 550, 90064-1524
Telephone: 310-203-8200
Fax: 310-203-8213

William Litvak
Steven H. Rosenblit
Kenneth B. Dapeer

For full biographical listings, see the Martindale-Hubbell Law Directory

GIRARDI AND KEESE (AV)

1126 Wilshire Boulevard, 90017-1904
Telephone: 213-977-0211
FAX: 213-481-1554
San Bernardino, California Office: 155 West Hospitality Lane, Suite 260.
Telephone: 909-381-1551.
FAX: 909-381-2566.

MEMBERS OF FIRM

Thomas V. Girardi
Robert M. Keese
John A. Girardi
James B. Kropff
Robert W. Finnerty
James G. O'Callahan
V. Andre Rekte (Resident, San Bernardino Office)
John K. Courtney
Amy Fisch Solomon
Thomas C. Morgan
David N. Bigelow
Carrie J. Rognlien
David R. Lira
John Alan Roberts
Shane M. Emerson Coons
Amanda L. McClintock

ASSOCIATE

Jennifer M. Ingram

References: Wells Fargo Bank (Los Angeles Head Office); Comerica Bank.

For full biographical listings, see the Martindale-Hubbell Law Directory

PARKER MILLS & PATEL LLP (AV)

865 South Figueroa Street, Suite 850, 90017
Telephone: 213-622-4441
Fax: 213-622-1444
Email: pmp@pmplaw.com *URL:* http://www.pmplaw.com

David B. Parker
William K. Mills
Jayesh Patel
Danny T. Morin

ASSOCIATES

Rina J. Pakula
Angeli Cuesta-Aragon
Alicia J. Gonzales

For full biographical listings, see the Martindale-Hubbell Law Directory

LAW OFFICES OF ANDREA LYNN RICE A PROFESSIONAL CORPORATION (AV)

12100 Wilshire Boulevard, Suite 780, 90025
Telephone: 310-207-3717
Fax: 310-207-6785

Andrea Lynn Rice

Teresa L. Ortega

Representative Clients: Safeco Insurance Cos.; Utica Mutual Insurance Cos.; Legion Insurance Co.; Minnesota Lawyers Mutual Insurance Co.; State Farm Fire Casualty Co.; Northland Insurance Co.; Frontier Insurance Co; American Claims Management, Inc.; CNA Insurance Cos.; Carolina Casualty; Clarendon National; Attorney's Liability Protection Services; American Equity Insurance Cos.; The Bar Plan Mutual Insurance Co.; TIG Insurance Co.
Reference: Union Bank of California.

For full biographical listings, see the Martindale-Hubbell Law Directory

ROBINSON, DI LANDO & WHITAKER, A PROFESSIONAL LAW CORPORATION (AV)

800 Wilshire Boulevard Suite 1100, 90017-2687
Telephone: 213-229-0100
Facsimile: 213-229-0114
Email: rdwlaw@gte.net
San Francisco, California Office: 417 Montgomery Street, Suite 910. 94104.
Telephone: 415-391-9475.
Fax: 415-391-3799.

Michael C. Robinson, Jr.
Michael A. Di Lando
Ronald S. Whitaker
Jack M. Liebhaber
Timothy L. Salazar

Steve H. Yu
Mark Kane
Cynthia A. Goodman
Bradley R. Blamires
Farzad Tabatabai
Martin J. Mendoza
David K. Stewart
Michelle B. Dykstra
Charles H. Brown, II
Michael B. Wilk

For full biographical listings, see the Martindale-Hubbell Law Directory

NEWPORT BEACH, Orange Co.

WENTWORTH, PAOLI & PURDY, LLP (AV)

4631 Teller Avenue, Suite 100, 92660
Telephone: 949-752-7711
Fax: 949-752-8339
Email: oclawfirm@aol.com *URL:* http://www.lawyers.com/wentworthpaoli

Theodore S. Wentworth
William Delli Paoli
Nancy Morse Knight
Court Bryant Purdy
Edward L. Smilow

Reference: Wells Fargo Bank, Newport Beach, Calif.

For full biographical listings, see the Martindale-Hubbell Law Directory

*OAKLAND,** Alameda Co.

ANTHONY & CARLSON, LLP (AV)

1999 Harrison Street, Suite 2000, 94612-3517
Telephone: 510-835-8400
Fax: 510-835-5566

MEMBERS OF FIRM

Steven R. Anthony
Richard H. Carlson

Felicia C. Strankman

OF COUNSEL

Jane L. Trigero

For full biographical listings, see the Martindale-Hubbell Law Directory

LOMBARDI, LOPER & CONANT, LLP (AV)

1999 Harrison Street, Suite 1950, 94612
Telephone: 510-433-2600
Fax: 510-433-2699

Ralph A. Lombardi
Bruce P. Loper
Matthew S. Conant
Chris P. Lavdiotis
Peter O. Glaessner
Timothy J. McCaffery
GayLynn Renee Kirn

Jeffrey D Hosking
Joseph Blaise Adams
Paul S. Lecky

(See Next Column)

LOMBARDI, LOPER & CONANT LLP, *Oakland—Continued*

OF COUNSEL

George S. Peyton, Jr.
Linda C. Roodhouse
Lori A. Sebransky

For full biographical listings, see the Martindale-Hubbell Law Directory

WULFSBERG REESE & SYKES, PROFESSIONAL CORPORATION (AV)

(Formerly Lempres & Wulfsberg, Professional Corporation)
Kaiser Center, 24th Floor, 300 Lakeside Drive, 94612
Telephone: 510-835-9100
Telecopier: 510-451-2170
San Francisco, California Office: 1 Maritime Plaza, Suite 1600, 94111.

Daniel N. Lempres (May 31, 1931 - March 19, 1987)
H. James Wulfsberg
Charles W. Reese, Jr.
Jeffrey A. Sykes
Timothy A. Colvig
Eric J. Firstman
Gregory R. Aker
Matthew D. Lempres
Mark A. Stump
David A. Rosenthal
Terri Ann Kim
Stephen L. Cali
William L. Darby

Charles A. Cobb
Paulette G. Andrews
J. Kevin Moore
Gillian Small, G.M.
Edward M. Callaghan
Donald S. Simon
David J. Hyndman

OF COUNSEL

Robert L. Hughes
Dianne K. Barry (Resident, San Francisco Office)

For full biographical listings, see the Martindale-Hubbell Law Directory

*REDDING,** Shasta Co.

REINER, SIMPSON & KENNEDY (AV)

2851 Park Marina Drive, Suite 200, 96001
Telephone: 530-241-1905
Fax: 530-241-0622

Russell Reiner
Robert G. Simpson
Daryl E. Kennedy

For full biographical listings, see the Martindale-Hubbell Law Directory

*RIVERSIDE,** Riverside Co.

HAIGHT, BROWN & BONESTEEL, L.L.P. (AV)

A Partnership including Professional Corporations
California Tower, 3737 Main Street, Suite 800, 92501
Telephone: 909-341-8300
FAX: 909-341-8309
URL: http://www.hbblaw.com
Santa Monica, California Office: 1620 26th Street, Suite 4000 North, P.O. Box 680.
Telephone: 310-449-6000.
Telecopier: 310-829-5117.
Telex: 705837.
Santa Ana, California Office: Suite 900, 5 Hutton Centre Drive.
Telephone: 714-754-1100.
Telecopier: 714-754-0826.
San Francisco, California Office: 100 Bush Street, 27th Floor.
Telephone: 415-986-7700.
Fax: 415-986-6945.
San Diego, California Office: 101 West Broadway, Suite 1000.
Telephone: 619-595-5583.
Fax: 619-595-7873.

RESIDENT MEMBER

Mark S. Lester

For full biographical listings, see the Martindale-Hubbell Law Directory

*SACRAMENTO,** Sacramento Co.

JOHNSON, SCHACHTER & COLLINS, A PROFESSIONAL CORPORATION (AV)

California Plaza, 2180 Harvard Street, #560, 95815
Telephone: 916-921-5800
Telecopier: 916-921-0247
Email: law@jscattorneys.com

Robert H. Johnson
Alesa M. Schachter
Kim H. Collins
George W. Holt
Kellie M. Murphy
Alvin Gittisriboongul

Susan E. Slager

(See Next Column)

OF COUNSEL

Ford R. Smith
Carolyn M. Wood
Susanne M. Shelley

Representative Clients: Fireman's Fund Insurance Cos.; CAMICO; Insurance Company of the West; Interstate National; Shand Morahan; Westport Insurance Corporation.
Reference: U.S. Bank, Sacramento.

For full biographical listings, see the Martindale-Hubbell Law Directory

PORTER, SCOTT, WEIBERG & DELEHANT, A PROFESSIONAL CORPORATION (AV)

350 University Avenue, Suite 200, 95825
Telephone: 916-929-1481
Fax: 916-927-3706
Email: pswdlaw@aol.com

Russell G. Porter
A. Irving Scott, Jr.
Edwin T. Weiberg
John W. Delehant
Anthony S. Warburg
Ned P. Telford
James K. Mirabell
Craig A. Caldwell
Terence J. Cassidy
Tom H. Bailey
Carl L. Calnero
Russ J. Wunderli
Nancy J. Sheehan
Norman V. Prior
Timothy M. Blaine
Stephen E. Horan
Carl L. Fessenden

Elisa Ungerman
Michael J. Baytosh
David A. Melton
Jennifer E. Duggan
Vanessa W. Whang
Dennis C. Huie
Michael W. Pott
Kellianne Akbar
Daniel M. Steinberg
Jack Woodside
Jonathan A. Corr
Kristina M. Hall
Alden J. Parker
Avery E. Dority
Robin Weideman
Denise A. Carnaroli
Lara S. Hilley
Sean Allen
Ralph R. Nevis
Darrin M. Menezes
Shane Singh

For full biographical listings, see the Martindale-Hubbell Law Directory

*SAN DIEGO,** San Diego Co.

DUKE GERSTEL SHEARER, LLP (AV)

A Registered Limited Liability Partnership
Sixth Floor, 101 West Broadway, P.O. Box 85470, 92186-5470
Telephone: 619-232-0816
800-405-0816
Fax: 619-232-4661
Email: lawyers@dgsllp.com *URL:* http://www.dgsllp.com
Costa Mesa, California Office: 3200 Park Center Drive, Suite 1000, 92626.
Telephone: 949-551-8664, 800-405-0816.
Los Angeles, California Office: 10866 Wilshire Boulevard, Suite 1400, 90024.
Telephone: 310-475-7118, 800-405-0816.
San Francisco, California Office: 744 Montgomery Street, Fifth Floor, 94111.
Telephone: 415-773-0101.
Palm Springs, California Office: 1111 East Tahquitz Canyon Way, Suite 110, 92262.
Telephone: 760-322-7846.
Phoenix, Arizona Office: One Columbus Plaza, 3636 North Central Avenue, Suite 1200, 85012.
Telephone: 602-650-2060.
Fax: 602-650-2089.
Tucson, Arizona Office: 6969 East Sunrise Drive, Suite 102, 85750.
Telephone: 520-615-8858.
Fax: 520-615-1069.
Affiliate Las Vegas, Nevada Office: Parsons & Pursiano, LLP, City Center West, Suite 108, 7201 W. Lake Mead Boulevard, 89128.
Telephone: 702-384-9900.
Facsimile: 702-384-5900.

MEMBER OF FIRM

Robert D. Shoecraft

Reference: Bank of Commerce.

For full biographical listings, see the Martindale-Hubbell Law Directory

KENNERSON SCHWARTZ SEMERDJIAN & HAILE LLP (AV)

A Limited Liability Partnership
101 West Broadway, Suite 810, 92101
Telephone: 619-236-8821
Facsimile: 619-236-8827
URL: http://www.lawyers.com/ksshlaw

OF COUNSEL

Paul R. Kennerson

MEMBERS OF FIRM

Ross J. Schwartz
Dick A. Semerdjian
Jeffrey A. Haile

(See Next Column)

KENNERSON SCHWARTZ SEMERDJIAN & HAILE LLP—*Continued*

James R. Ballard
John K. Grant

For full biographical listings, see the Martindale-Hubbell Law Directory

KLINEDINST, FLIEHMAN & MCKILLOP, A PROFESSIONAL CORPORATION (AV)

The Koll Center, 501 West Broadway, Suite 600, 92101-3584
Telephone: 619-239-8131
Fax: 619-238-8707
URL: http://www.kfmlaw.com
Orange County Office: Civic Center Law Building, 611 Civic Center Drive, Suite 250, Santa Ana, California, 92701.
Telephone: 714-542-1800.
Los Angeles, California Office: Wells Fargo Center, 333 South Grand Avenue, 33rd Floor, 90071.
Telephone: 213-625-8100.

SHAREHOLDERS

John D. Klinedinst
Donald R. McKillop, Sr.
G. William (Bill) Van De Weghe, Jr.
Thomas S. Ingrassia
Douglas A. Pettit
Gregory A. Garbacz
Arthur S. Moreau, III

Kendra J. Hall
Andrew N. Kohn
M. Shawn Payment
Kurt U. Campbell
G. Dale Britton
Susan S. Kohn
Heather L. Rosing
Debora A. Cappucci
Dayna Lyn Chmelka
Jennifer N. Lehman
Dennis C. Crovella
Carey L. Cooper
Kevin J. Gramling

PARALEGALS

Mary Ann Murphy-Brown
Cam B. Picano

Reference: Bank of America.

For full biographical listings, see the Martindale-Hubbell Law Directory

LINDLEY, SCALES & CORBETT, A PROFESSIONAL CORPORATION (AV)

550 West C Street, Suite 1800, 92101
Telephone: 619-234-9181
Fax: 619-234-8475
Email: lsc@adnc.com

Luke R. Corbett

Representative Clients: Palomar Savings & Loan Assn.; McGraw-Hill Broadcasting Co.; Chicago Title Insurance Co.; San Diego Hospital Assn.; Bank United.

For full biographical listings, see the Martindale-Hubbell Law Directory

MAXIE RHEINHEIMER STEPHENS & VREVICH, LLP (AV)

600 West Broadway, Suite 900, 92101
Telephone: 619-515-1155
Fax: 619-515-1159
Los Angeles, California Office: 555 South Flower Street, Suite 4640.
Telephone: 213-236-9878.
Fax: 213-489-7559.
Newport Beach, California Office: 110 Newport Center Drive, Suite 200.
Telephone: 714-644-8136.
Fax: 714-644-7526.
Sacramento, California Office: 400 Capital Mall, Suite 235.
Telephone: 916-444-5566.
Fax: 916-444-5494.
Las Vegas, Nevada Office: Law Office of Gary P. Sinkeldam, 4270 South Decatur Blvd., Suite B6-106.
Telephone: 702-968-8037.
Fax: 702-968-8069.

Robert C. Maxie
Jane A. Rheinheimer
Sean D. Stephens
Barry M. Vrevich

Christine L. Cornick
Suzanne Lovelace Smigliani
Ann Marie Thompson
Darin L. Wessel
Theodore Dikmen
Alison J. Barry
Marie K. Peluso
Jason R. Bogni

OF COUNSEL

Gary P. Sinkeldam
Cheryl D. Davidson

For full biographical listings, see the Martindale-Hubbell Law Directory

*SAN FRANCISCO,** San Francisco Co.

BLEY AND BLEY (AV)

555 Montgomery Street, Suite 605, 94111
Telephone: 415-982-7311
Fax: 415-982-7278

(See Next Column)

Bertrand A. Bley (1903-1992)
Stephen Bruce Bley

Casimir A. Wilson
Samantha Bley DeJean
Richard S. Weil

For full biographical listings, see the Martindale-Hubbell Law Directory

HAIGHT, BROWN & BONESTEEL, L.L.P. (AV)

A Partnership including Professional Corporations
100 Bush Street, 27th Floor, 94104-3902
Telephone: 415-986-7700
Telecopier: 415-986-6945
URL: http://www.hbblaw.com
Santa Monica, California Office: 1620 26th Street, Suite 4000 North, P.O. Box 680.
Telephone: 310-449-6000.
Telecopier: 310-829-5117.
Telex: 705837.
Santa Ana, California Office: Suite 900, 5 Hutton Centre Drive.
Telephone: 714-754-1100.
Telecopier: 714-754-0826.
Riverside, California Office: California Tower, 3737 Main Street, Suite 800.
Telephone: 909-341-8300.
Fax: 909-341-8309.
San Diego, California Office: 101 West Broadway, Suite 1000.
Telephone: 619-595-5583.
Fax: 619-595-7873.

RESIDENT MEMBER

David W. Evans

ASSOCIATES

Felicia Y. Feng
Arlene Mendoza
Russell J. Smith

For full biographical listings, see the Martindale-Hubbell Law Directory

HARDIMAN & CARROLL, A LAW PARTNERSHIP (AV)

160 Pine Street, Suite 700, 94111
Telephone: 415-248-3930
Fax: 415-248-3933
Email: postmaster@hc.sflawfirm.com

Michael F. Hardiman
Gerald K. Carroll

ASSOCIATES

Dolores Bastian-Dalton
Lynn Diringer McCabe
Deirdre J. Cox
Melissa R. Meyers
Cheryl Castrogiovanni
John P. Cogger
Shaana Rahman

For full biographical listings, see the Martindale-Hubbell Law Directory

SCADDEN, HAMILTON & RYAN (AV)

220 Montgomery Street, 13th Floor, 94104-3410
Telephone: 415-362-5116
Telecopier: 415-362-4214
URL: http://www.shrlaw.com

James G. Scadden
Robert P. Hamilton
Robert J. Ryan
James P. Cunningham

Charles O. Thompson
Eileen Santana Wright
Vincent C. Milani
Timothy K. Killelea

LEGAL SUPPORT PERSONNEL

Edwin L. Lilley
Dennis Prime
Mary Sue Schroeder

For full biographical listings, see the Martindale-Hubbell Law Directory

TEHIN +PARTNERS, A PROFESSIONAL CORPORATION (AV)

Bank of America Center, 555 California Street, 33rd Floor, 94104-1609
Telephone: 415-951-8800
Fax: 415-951-8808
URL: http://www.tehin.com

Nikolai Tehin
Pamela J. Stevens
Reilly Atkinson, IV
Michael E. Brown
Bita Abdollahi

For full biographical listings, see the Martindale-Hubbell Law Directory

SANTA MONICA, Los Angeles Co.

BAKER, KEENER & NAHRA, LLP (AV)

2850 Ocean Park Boulevard, Suite 300, 90405-2936
Telephone: 310-399-0900
Fax: 310-399-1644
Email: general@bknlawyers.com *URL:* http://www.bknlawyers.com

(See Next Column)

BAKER, KEENER & NAHRA LLP, *Santa Monica—Continued*

MEMBERS OF FIRM

Robert C. Baker
Karl A. Keener
John P. Nahra
Michael H. Bailey
Steven T. Adams
Melissa S. Fink
Jeffrey P. Nolan
Constance A. Endelicato

Brenda K. Benson
Mitchell F. Mulbarger
James D. Hepworth
Phillip A. Baker
George P. Hawley
Thomas M. Mills
R. Jeffrey Neer
Wendy Wen Yun Chang

OF COUNSEL

Daniel P. Leonard

Reference: Wells Fargo Bank (Los Angeles Head Office).

For full biographical listings, see the Martindale-Hubbell Law Directory

HAIGHT, BROWN & BONESTEEL, L.L.P. (AV)

A Partnership including Professional Corporations
1620 26th Street, Suite 4000 North, P.O. Box 680, 90404
Telephone: 310-449-6000
Telecopier: 310-829-5117
Telex: 705837
URL: http://www.hbblaw.com
Santa Ana, California Office: Suite 900, 5 Hutton Centre Drive.
Telephone: 714-754-1100.
Telecopier: 714-754-0826.
Riverside, California Office: California Tower, 3737 Main Street, Suite 800.
Telephone: 909-341-8300.
Fax: 909-341-8309.
San Francisco, California Office: 101 Bush Street, 27th Floor.
Telephone: 415-986-7700.
Fax: 415-986-6945.
San Diego, California Office: 101 West Broadway, Suite 1000.
Telephone: 619-595-5583.
Fax: 619-595-7873.

MEMBERS OF FIRM

John W. Sheller (A Professional Corporation)
Morton Rosen
Lori R. Behar
Barry Z. Brodsky
Desmond J. Hinds, Jr.
Jennifer K. Saunders
Frances Mary O'Meara
Michael H. Gottschlich

ASSOCIATES

Tamra L. Bowman
Holly M. Teel
Allison Gayle Yee
Filomena E. Meyer
Jeffery E. Stockley
Patrick M. Malone
David K. Nelson
Jeannie Choi-Wolff
Mark Bradley Aldrich
Robin M. McConnell
Pamela A. Wilson
Brent M. Finch

For full biographical listings, see the Martindale-Hubbell Law Directory

COLORADO

*COLORADO SPRINGS,** El Paso Co.

WITTMAN & MCCORD (AV)

A Partnership including a Professional Corporation
Suite 320 UMB Bank Building, 5825 Delmonico Drive, 80919
Telephone: 719-590-9899
Fax: 719-590-9984
Email: wittcord-law@pcisys.net
Denver, Colorado Office: 10630 East Bethany Drive (Aurora), 80014.
Telephone: 303-337-4952.
Fax: 303-337-6165.

MEMBERS OF FIRM

Sherwin V. "Bud" Wittman, II, (P.C.)
Edward M. McCord, P.C.

ASSOCIATES

J. Bradley Hardman
Keith D. Vance

Representative Clients: Allstate Insurance Co.; Carolina Casualty Insurance Co.; E & O Professionals Insurance Co.; John Deere Transportation Insurance Co.; Motor Cargo Co.; Providian Auto & Home Insurance Co.; Safeco Insurance Co.; USAA Insurance Co.; USF & G Insurance Co.; Utica Mutual Insurance Co.

For full biographical listings, see the Martindale-Hubbell Law Directory

*DENVER,** Denver Co.

DAVIS & CERIANI, P.C. (AV)

Suite 400, Market Center, 1350 Seventeenth Street, 80202
Telephone: 303-534-9000
Telecopier: 303-534-4618
Email: davisandceriani.com

(See Next Column)

Rick G. Davis
Gary J. Ceriani
Bruce E. Rohde
Michael P. Cillo
Charles W. Bess
John W. Himmelmann

Margaret E. Peper
Patrick John Kanouff
Mark M. Osborn
Valeri Pappas

For full biographical listings, see the Martindale-Hubbell Law Directory

LAPUYADE, WASHINGTON & MOLK, LLC (AV)

4100 East Mississippi Avenue, Suite 600, 80246
Telephone: 303-759-3535
Facsimile: 303-758-2246
URL: http://www.lawyers.com/lapuyadewash&moik

Keith Dale Lapuyade
Alan G. Molk

For full biographical listings, see the Martindale-Hubbell Law Directory

MONTGOMERY LITTLE & MCGREW, P.C. (AV)

The Quadrant, 5445 DTC Parkway, Suite 800 (Englewood), 80111
Telephone: 303-773-8100
Telecopier: 303-220-0412
URL: http://www.mlmpc.com

Robert R. Montgomery
David C. Little
William H. Knapp
Christopher B. Little

Representative Clients: BP Amoco; Bristol-Myers Squibb; Colorado Medical Society; The St. Paul Insurance Cos.; University of Colorado Health Sciences Center; HealthOne; Westport Insurance Group; CNA; Design Professionals Insurance Corp.; Dentists Professional Liability Trust.

For Complete List of Firm Personnel, See General Section

For full biographical listings, see the Martindale-Hubbell Law Directory

WHEELER TRIGG & KENNEDY, P.C. (AV)

Suite 3600, 1801 California Street, 80202
Telephone: 303-292-2525
Telecopier: 303-294-1879
Email: info@wtklaw.com *URL:* http://www.wtklaw.com
Roslyn, New York Office: 1800 Northern Boulevard, Suite 208, 11576.
Telephone: 516-484-9701.
Fax: 516-484-6362.

Malcolm E. Wheeler
John R. Trigg
Mark F. Kennedy
Paul F. Hultin
Michael L. O'Donnell
Robert B. Hunter
Gwen J. Young
Christopher J. Meyer
Lori L. Roberts
Habib Nasrullah
Edward C. Stewart
James E. Hooper, Jr.

OF COUNSEL

Joseph B. Valentine (Not admitted in CO)
Andrew J. Mihalick (Not admitted in CO)

Sean D. Baker
Mark T. Clouatre
Bryan D. Cross
Wendy A. Harvey
David A. Lamb
Lee A. Mickus
Amy L. Padden
Kimberly A. Stout (Not admitted in CO)

For full biographical listings, see the Martindale-Hubbell Law Directory

WITTMAN & MCCORD (AV)

A Partnership including a Professional Corporation
10630 East Bethany Drive (Aurora), 80014
Telephone: 303-337-4952
Fax: 303-337-6165
Email: wittcord-law@pcisys.net
Colorado Springs, Colorado Office: Suite 320 UMB Bank Building, 5825 Delmonico Drive.
Telephone: 719-590-9899.
Fax: 719-590-9984.

MEMBERS OF FIRM

Sherwin V. "Bud" Wittman, II, (P.C.)
Edward M. McCord, P.C.

ASSOCIATES

J. Bradley Hardman
Keith D. Vance

Representative Clients: Allstate Insurance Co.; Carolina Casualty Insurance Co.; E & O Professionals Insurance Co.; John Deere Transportation Insurance Co.; Motor Cargo Co.; Providian Auto & Home Insurance Co.; Safeco Insurance Co.; USAA Insurance Co.; USF & G Insurance Co.; Utica Mutual Insurance Co.

For full biographical listings, see the Martindale-Hubbell Law Directory

CONNECTICUT

*NEW HAVEN,** New Haven Co.

GALLAGHER & CALISTRO (AV)

1377 Boulevard, P.O. Box 1925, 06509
Telephone: 203-624-4165
Fax: 203-865-5598

William F. Gallagher
Roger B. Calistro
Cynthia C. Bott
Barbara L. Cox
Kurt D. Koehler
Thomas J. Airone

For full biographical listings, see the Martindale-Hubbell Law Directory

KENNEDY, JOHNSON, D'ELIA & GILLOOLY (AV)

Long Wharf Maritime Center, 545 Long Wharf Drive, 06511
Telephone: 203-865-8430
Fax: 203-865-5345
Email: kennedyjoh@aol.com

MEMBERS OF FIRM

David H. Johnson
John J. Kennedy, Jr.
John J. D'Elia
Dennis Gillooly

ASSOCIATES

Robert L. Schwab
Stephanie Z. Roberge

Reference: Bank of Boston - Connecticut.

For full biographical listings, see the Martindale-Hubbell Law Directory

FLORIDA

BOCA RATON, Palm Beach Co.

MICHAUD, BUSCHMANN, FOX, FERRARA & MITTELMARK, P.A. (AV)

33 Southeast 8th Street, 33432
Telephone: 561-392-0540
Fax: 561-392-0582
Email: Bocalaw@MBFFM.com *URL:* http://www.MBFFM.com

Scott H. Michaud
Paul Buschmann
Brian S. Fox
James T. Ferrara
Michael K. Mittelmark
Marc T. Millian

Marcy G. Blitz
Linda A. McCullough
Kimberly M. Hall

For full biographical listings, see the Martindale-Hubbell Law Directory

CORAL GABLES, Dade Co.

LANE, REESE, AULICK, SUMMERS & FIELD, P.A. (AV)

Suite 304 Douglas Centre, 2600 Douglas Road, 33134
Telephone: 305-444-4418
Fax: 305-444-5504
Email: LRASF-Miami@MSN.COM

Frank A. Lane
William S. Reese
Cecilia Aulick
William L. Summers
Paul H. Field

C. Page Lane
Lorenzo Jackson, Jr.
Luis J. Perdomo

For full biographical listings, see the Martindale-Hubbell Law Directory

*FORT LAUDERDALE,** Broward Co.

COONEY, MATTSON, LANCE, BLACKBURN, RICHARDS & O'CONNOR, P.A. (AV)

2312 Wilton Drive, P.O. Box 14546, 33302
Telephone: Telephone: 954-568-6669
WATS: 1-800-745-3864
Telecopier: 954-568-0085
Email: cooney2312@aol.com
Orlando, Florida Office: Nations Bank Tower, 111 N. Orange Avenue, Suite 1020.
Telephone: 407-843-2100.
Fax: 407-843-2061.

(See Next Column)

David F. Cooney
Michael C. Mattson
Victor Lance (1956-1995)
Ace J. Blackburn, Jr.
John H. Richards
Dennis R. O'Connor (Resident, Orlando, Florida Office)
Bruce Michael Trybus
Walter C. Wyatt
Kieran F. O'Connor (Resident, Orlando, Florida Office)
Michele McCaul Ricca
Daniel F. Tordella

Laura Douglas
Warren Kwavnick
Rochelle Bocksch
Weslee S. Arciola
Alphonso O. Peets
Robert M. Potter, III
Elizabeth Y. Foshee (Resident, Orlando Office)

Representative Clients: The Travellers; RISCORP; CIGNA Insurance Co.; Claims Center; Fiesco; Multi-Line Claims Service, Inc.; Carpenter Contractors of America; City Furniture; CNA Insurance.

For full biographical listings, see the Martindale-Hubbell Law Directory

SISTARE & ASSOCIATES (AV)

600 South Andrews Avenue, Suite 600, 33301
Telephone: 954-522-2320
Fax: 954-522-2223
Email: sistare@gate.net *URL:* http://www.sistare.com

MEMBER OF FIRM

Susan P. Sistare

ASSOCIATE

Jahna Y. (Jay) Hoyte

For full biographical listings, see the Martindale-Hubbell Law Directory

*FORT MYERS,** Lee Co.

DEBOEST, KNUDSEN, STOCKMAN, WISEMAN, DECKER & DRYDEN, P.A. (AV)

1415 Hendry Street, P.O. Box 1470, 33902-1470
Telephone: 941-334-1381
Telecopier: 941-334-0266
Email: dkswlaw@gate.net
Naples, Florida Office: 600 Fifth Avenue South, Suite 301, 34102.
Telephone: 941-263-5040.
Fax: 941-263-6944.

Arthur K. Knudsen, Jr. (Retired)
Richard D. DeBoest
William E. Stockman
Tamela Eady Wiseman (Resident, Naples Office)
James G. Decker
Thomas M. Dryden

Representative Clients: Cobb Theatres, Inc.; WCI Communities, Inc.; Evelyn Jackman and Sons, Inc.

For full biographical listings, see the Martindale-Hubbell Law Directory

*JACKSONVILLE,** Duval Co.

ALFORD & KALIL, P.A. (AV)

2400 Independent Square, One Independent Drive, 32202-5064
Telephone: 904-355-3311
Fax: 904-355-5411
Email: akthefirm@aol.com

C. Wayne Alford
John S. Kalil

For full biographical listings, see the Martindale-Hubbell Law Directory

GLENN K. ALLEN A PROFESSIONAL ASSOCIATION (AV)

The Plaza Building, 353 East Forsyth Street, 32202-2822
Telephone: 904-355-7506
Facsimile: 904-353-8814
URL: http://www.glennallenpa.com
Email: GKA@glennallenpa.com *URL:* http://www.lawyers.com/glennallen

Glenn K. Allen

Jennifer Workinger Fites

For full biographical listings, see the Martindale-Hubbell Law Directory

LAKE WORTH, Palm Beach Co.

RICHARD H. WILLITS, P.A. (AV)

2290 10th Avenue North Suite 404, 33461
Telephone: 1-800-870-0573
561-582-7600
Fax: 561-588-8819
URL: http://www.lawyers.com/willitslaw

Richard H. Willits

For full biographical listings, see the Martindale-Hubbell Law Directory

*MIAMI,** Dade Co.

JOSEPHS, JACK & GAEBE, P.A. (AV)

Grove Professional Building, 2950 S.W. 27th Avenue, Suite 100, 33133-3765
Telephone: Dade County: 305-445-3800
Telecopier: 305-448-5800
Email: TheFirm@FloridaAttorneys.com *URL:* http://www.Florida-Attorneys.com

Michael R. Josephs
Lewis N. Jack, Jr.
John S. Gaebe

Elisabeth M. Allen
Helen Leen Miranda
Scott A. Cole
Stephanie E. Demos
Scott T. McCullough
Tamara D. McKeown
Christopher T. Lemos

Representative Clients: U-Haul Corporation; ITT Sheraton; Zurich-American Insurance Company; Republic Claims Service Company; Southern Fire Insurance Adjusters.

For full biographical listings, see the Martindale-Hubbell Law Directory

*ORLANDO,** Orange Co.

COONEY, MATTSON, LANCE, BLACKBURN, RICHARDS & O'CONNOR, P.A. (AV)

Nations Bank Tower, 111 North Orange Avenue Suite 1020, 32801
Telephone: 407-843-2100
Fax: 407-843-2061
Fort Lauderdale, Florida Office: 2312 Wilton Drive. P.O. Box 14546. 33302.
Telephone: 954-568-6669.
Telecopier: 954-568-0085.

Dennis R. O'Connor
Kieran F. O'Connor

Elizabeth Y. Foshee (Resident)

For full biographical listings, see the Martindale-Hubbell Law Directory

HILL, REIS, ADAMS, HALL & SCHIEFFELIN, P.A. (AV)

1417 East Concord Street, 32803
Telephone: 407-896-0425
Fax: 407-896-9236
Email: mainbox@hrahs.com

G. Bruce Hill
Gregory F. Reis
Janet W. Adams
Larry D. Hall
Thomas L. Schieffelin, Jr.
William W. Large
Matthew P. Bartolomei

Representative Clients: The Florida Hospital Trust Fund; The Florida Hospital Excess Trust Fund; Florida Hospital Workers Compensation/Self Insurance Trust Fund; Bartow Memorial Hospital; Bay Medical Center; Brooksville Regional Hospital; Cape Canaveral Hospital; Cape Coral Hospital; Desoto Memorial Hospital.

For Complete List of Firm Personnel, See General Section

For full biographical listings, see the Martindale-Hubbell Law Directory

MCEWAN, MARTINEZ, LUFF, DUKES & RUFFIER, P.A. (AV)

108 East Central Boulevard, P.O. Box 753, 32801
Telephone: 407-423-8571
Fax: 407-423-8637

Wilson Sanders (1911-1981)
O. Beverley McEwan (1913-1995)
John S. McEwan, II
Rafael E. "Ralph" Martinez
H. David Luff
Thomas E. Dukes, III
William E. Ruffier
Tyler S. McClay

Juan A. Ruiz
Ruth C. Osborne
Susan D. Kennedy

Representative Clients: Bridgestone/Firestone, Inc.; City Cab of Orlando, Inc.; CNA Insurance Company; Dependable Protective Mutual; Florida Physicians Insurance Co.; Gulf Atlantic Insurance Co.; Marine Office of America; M.C.I. Telecommunications Corporation.

For full biographical listings, see the Martindale-Hubbell Law Directory

MEYERS, MOONEY, STANLEY & HOLLINGSWORTH (AV)

(An Association of Professional Associations and Sole Proprietorships)
17 South Lake Avenue, 32801-2797
Telephone: 407-849-0940
Toll-free: 800-766-9198
Fax: 407-849-1860
Email: MeyMooMey@aol.com *URL:* http://www.lawyers.com/meyersmooney
Jacksonville Office: 2120 University Boulevard West, 32217.
Telephone: 904-367-8747; 800-951-7266.
Fax: 904-367-0650.

Irvin A. Meyers
Thomas R. Mooney
Bradley H. Hollingsworth
James A. Stanley, Jr. (Resident, Jacksonville Office)

ASSOCIATES

John V. Colvin
Thomas E. Mooney

Reference: Sun Bank & Trust of Orlando.

For full biographical listings, see the Martindale-Hubbell Law Directory

*PANAMA CITY,** Bay Co.

RICHARD SMOAK (AV)

103 West 5th Street, P.O. Box 1006, 32402-1006
Telephone: 904-747-1900
Fax: 904-747-1910

Representative Clients: Panama City - Bay County Airport & Industrial District; Florida Physicians Insurance Co.; National Casualty Co.; Church Mutual Insurance Co.; Arizona Chemical Co.; Bay Bank & Trust Co.; Mutual of Omaha Insurance Co.; Ranger Insurance Co.; St. Paul Fire & Marine Insurance Co.; Stone Container Corp.

For full biographical listings, see the Martindale-Hubbell Law Directory

*TALLAHASSEE,** Leon Co.

MCFARLAIN, WILEY, CASSEDY & JONES, PROFESSIONAL ASSOCIATION (AV)

215 South Monroe Street, Suite 600, P.O. Box 2174, 32316-2174
Telephone: 850-222-2107
Telecopier: 850-222-8475
Email: firm@mcfarlain.com *URL:* http://www.mcfarlain.com

Richard C. McFarlain
William B. Wiley
Douglas P. Jones
Charles A. Stampelos
H. Darrell White, Jr.
Christopher Barkas
Harold R. Mardenborough, Jr.
Terrell C. Madigan

Robert A. McNeely
P. David Brannon

LEGAL SUPPORT PERSONNEL

Diane L. Doll (Office Manager)

For full biographical listings, see the Martindale-Hubbell Law Directory

*TAMPA,** Hillsborough Co.

SHOFI, HENNEN, GRAMOVOT & ASSOCIATES (AV)

The Lincoln Center, Suite 560, 5401 West Kennedy Boulevard, 33609
Telephone: 813-289-7500
FAX: 813-289-5548
Mailing Address: P.O. Box 10430, Tampa, Florida, 33679-0430
Email: shglaw@gte.net

John D. Shofi
William E. Hennen
Larry I. Gramovot

Jon A. McAuliffe
Kenneth S. Takacs, Jr.
Frank Scott Williams

LEGAL SUPPORT PERSONNEL

Marianne Santucci (Legal Assistant)
Raymond Hernandez

Reference: City Bank of Tampa.

For full biographical listings, see the Martindale-Hubbell Law Directory

*WEST PALM BEACH,** Palm Beach Co.

SEARCY DENNEY SCAROLA BARNHART & SHIPLEY, PROFESSIONAL ASSOCIATION (AV)

2139 Palm Beach Lakes Boulevard, P.O. Drawer 3626, 33402-3626
Telephone: 561-686-6300
800-780-8607
800-220-7006 (Spanish)
Fax: 561-478-0754
Email: CDS@SEARCYLAW.COM *URL:* http://www.searcylaw.com

John Scarola
David J. Sales

(See Next Column)

SEARCY DENNEY SCAROLA BARNHART & SHIPLEY PROFESSIONAL ASSOCIATION—*Continued*

Sean C. Domnick

For Complete List of Firm Personnel, See General Section

For full biographical listings, see the Martindale-Hubbell Law Directory

GEORGIA

*ATLANTA,** Fulton Co.

BELTRAN & ASSOCIATES (AV)

One Atlantic Center, Suite 3095, 1201 West Peachtree Street, 30309
Telephone: 404-892-3100
Facsimile: 404-892-1222
Email: BeltranAssoc@mindspring.com

Frank J. Beltran

ASSOCIATE

Charlotte B. Perrell

Reference: NationsBank.

For full biographical listings, see the Martindale-Hubbell Law Directory

BONDURANT, MIXSON & ELMORE, LLP (AV)

1201 W. Peachtree Street Suite 3900, 30309
Telephone: 404-881-4100
Fax: 404-881-4111
URL: http://www.bondurant-mixson.com

MEMBERS OF FIRM

Emmet J. Bondurant II
H. Lamar Mixson
M. Jerome Elmore
Edward B. Krugman
Jeffrey O. Bramlett
John E. Floyd
Michael B. Terry
P. Richard Game
Jill A. Pryor
J. Scott McClain

Representative Clients: American Dairy Queen Corp.; Avon Products, Inc.; Bottlers of Coca-Cola, U.S.A.; Blue Circle of America; Delta Air Lines, Inc.; Fina Oil and Chemical Company; Four M Corporation; Penske Motorsports; Queen Carpets, Inc.; Ticketmaster Southeast.

For full biographical listings, see the Martindale-Hubbell Law Directory

BOVIS, KYLE & BURCH, LLC (AV)

A Limited Liability Corporation including Professional Corporations
Third Floor, 53 Perimeter Center East, 30346
Telephone: 770-391-9100
Telecopier: 770-668-0878
Email: bkb@boviskyle.com *URL:* http://www.boviskyle.com

John M. Bovis (P.C.)
Steven J. Kyle (P.C.)
John V. Burch (P.C.)
C. Sam Thomas (P.C.)
James E. Singer
J. Wesley Skinner
Gregory R. Veal
Timothy J. Burson
Charles M. Medlin
John H. Peavy Jr.

J.S. Scott Busby
Christina A. Craddock
Timothy A. Hickey, Jr.
Jana B. Tabor
Carl A. Hassler
John David Etheriedge
Everett A. Kliphouse

For full biographical listings, see the Martindale-Hubbell Law Directory

GOLDNER, SOMMERS, SCRUDDER & BASS (AV)

900 Circle 75 Parkway Suite 850, 30339
Telephone: 770-612-9200
Facsimile: 770-612-9201

MEMBERS OF FIRM

Stephen L. Goldner
Susan V. Sommers
Henry E. Scrudder, Jr.
Glenn S. Bass

ASSOCIATE

Tammy Spivack Skinner

For Complete List of Firm Personnel, See General Section

For full biographical listings, see the Martindale-Hubbell Law Directory

HAWKINS & PARNELL, LLP (AV)

4000 SunTrust Plaza, 303 Peachtree Street, N.E., 30308-3243
Telephone: 404-614-7400
Fax: 404-614-7500
Email: relliott@hplegal.com *URL:* http://www.hawkinsparnell.com

(See Next Column)

MEMBERS OF FIRM

J. Bruce Welch
Alan F. Herman
H. Lane Young, II
T. Ryan Mock, Jr.
Kimberly Houston
Kristine Berry Morain
Christine Lupo Mast

ASSOCIATES

Matthew F. Barr
Carl H. Anderson, Jr.
Brian M. Weiss

Representative Clients: Great American Insurance Co.; American International Group; Chicago Interstate Insurance Group; Risk Enterprise Management Company; Zurich-American Insurance Company.

For Complete List of Firm Personnel, See General Section

For full biographical listings, see the Martindale-Hubbell Law Directory

JOHNSON & WARD (AV)

2100 The Equitable Building, 100 Peachtree Street N.W., 30303-1962
Telephone: 404-524-5626
Facsimile: 404-524-1769
Email: postmaster@johnsonward.com

MEMBERS OF FIRM

William C. Lanham
Clark H. McGehee
John C. Dabney, Jr.
William D. deGolian
Bruce A. Maxwell

For Complete List of Firm Personnel, See General Section

For full biographical listings, see the Martindale-Hubbell Law Directory

WEINBERG, WHEELER, HUDGINS, GUNN & DIAL, LLC (AV)

999 Peachtree Street, N.E. Suite 2700, 30309
Telephone: 404-876-2700
Facsimile: 404-875-9433
Email: firm@wwhgd.com

MEMBERS OF FIRM

Sidney F. Wheeler
John M. Hudgins, IV, (P.C.)
Robert G. Tanner
Earl W. Gunn
David A. Dial
Carol P. Michel
John K. Train, IV
Johnathan T. Krawcheck

ASSOCIATES

Alan M. Maxwell
Molly Prichitt Lee
Ashley P. Nichols
Patrick Moore

Representative Clients: American International Group; Columbia/HCA Healthcare Corp.; Emory University; Gwinnett Hospital System; Merck; St. Paul Fire & Marine Insurance Co.; Tenant Healthcare Corporation; Zurich-American Specialities Insurance Co.

For Complete List of Firm Personnel, See General Section

For full biographical listings, see the Martindale-Hubbell Law Directory

HAWAII

*HONOLULU,** Honolulu Co.

CRONIN, FRIED, SEKIYA, KEKINA & FAIRBANKS ATTORNEYS AT LAW, A LAW CORPORATION (AV)

1900 Davies Pacific Center, 841 Bishop Street, 96813
Telephone: 808-524-1433
Fax: 808-536-2073

Paul F. Cronin
L. Richard Fried, Jr.
Gerald Y. Sekiya
Wayne K. Kekina
David L. Fairbanks
John D. Thomas, Jr.
Stuart A. Kaneko
Bert S. Sakuda
Allen K. Williams
Keith K. H. Young

Patrick W. Border
Gregory L. Lui-Kwan
Patrick F. McTernan
Clarence S.K. Kekina
Sylvia J. Luke
Geoffrey K.S. Komeya
Frances K. Schneider

For full biographical listings, see the Martindale-Hubbell Law Directory

GOODSILL ANDERSON QUINN & STIFEL (AV)

Alii Place, Suite 1800, 1099 Alakea Street, P.O. Box 3196, 96801-3196
Telephone: 808-547-5600
FAX: 808-547-5880
Email: info@goodsill.com *URL:* http://www.goodsill.com

(See Next Column)

GOODSILL ANDERSON QUINN & STIFEL, *Honolulu—Continued*

MEMBERS OF FIRM

Martin Anderson
David J. Dezzani
John R. Lacy
William S. Miller
Jacqueline L. S. Earle
Corlis J. Chang
Patricia Mathias NaPier
Wayne H. Muraoka
LindaLee K. Farm
Margaret Jenkins Leong
Carol Ann Eblen
Roy John Tjioe
A. Richard Philpott
Lennes N. Omuro
Derek R. Kobayashi

ASSOCIATES

Thomas L. Benedict
Edmund K. Saffery
Normand R. Lezy

Representative Clients: CNA Insurance Co.; Employers Reinsurance Company; Hawaii Association of Physicians/Indemnity (HAPI); CIGNA.

For Complete List of Firm Personnel, See General Section

For full biographical listings, see the Martindale-Hubbell Law Directory

KAILUA, Honolulu Co.

WINER MEHEULA & DEVENS (AV)

970 North Kalaheo Avenue, Suite A-300, 96734
Telephone: 808-254-5855
Fax: 808-254-6872
Email: winer@pacificlaw.com *URL:* http://www.pacificlaw.com

MEMBERS OF FIRM

Andrew S. Winer
William K. Meheula
Vladimir Paul Devens

OF COUNSEL

David F. Fasi

ASSOCIATE

Blue H. Kaanehe

For full biographical listings, see the Martindale-Hubbell Law Directory

ILLINOIS

*BELLEVILLE,** St. Clair Co.

NEVILLE, RICHARDS, DEFRANCO & WULLER (AV)

5 Park Place, 62226
Telephone: 618-277-0900
Facsimile: 618-277-0970
Email: nrdw@nrdw-law.com *URL:* http://www.nrdw-law.com

MEMBERS OF FIRM

James E. Neville
Timothy S. Richards
James E. DeFranco
Robert G. Wuller, Jr.

ASSOCIATES

Shari M. Brunton
Ellen M. Edmonds
Daniel L. Bradley
Matthew Charles Zittel

For full biographical listings, see the Martindale-Hubbell Law Directory

*CHICAGO,** Cook Co.

BLATT, HAMMESFAHR & EATON (AV)

333 W. Wacker Drive, Suite 1900, 60606
Telephone: 312-849-8000
FAX: 312-357-0198
Email: BHE@BHELAW.COM *URL:* HTTP://WWW.BHELAW.COM
New York, New York Office: 45 Broadway, 12th Floor.
Telephone: 212-363-1900.
Fax: 212-363-2600. Email: bhe@bhelaw.com.

MEMBERS OF FIRM

Hugo Chaviano
Larry R. Eaton

ASSOCIATES

Lesley A. Dable
Keith B. Daniels, Jr.

For full biographical listings, see the Martindale-Hubbell Law Directory

CLIFFORD LAW OFFICES, P.C. (AV)

120 North La Salle Street, 31st Floor, 60602
Telephone: 312-899-9090
1-800-899-0410
Fax: 312-251-1160
Email: RACA@CliffordLaw.com *URL:* http://www.cliffordlaw.com

Robert A. Clifford
Keith A. Hebeisen
Kevin P. Durkin
Thomas K. Prindable

(See Next Column)

Robert P. Walsh, Jr.
Susan A. Capra
Jeffrey J. Kroll
Richard F. Burke, Jr.
Matthew I. Baker
Timothy P. Rhatigan
Isobel S. Thomas
Michael S. Krzak
Timothy S. Tomasik
Brian Thomas Nash
Donald James Storino III
Sheri L. Tarr

OF COUNSEL

Robert P. Sheridan

For full biographical listings, see the Martindale-Hubbell Law Directory

ROBERT F. COLEMAN & ASSOCIATES (AV)

77 West Wacker Drive Suite 4800, 60601
Telephone: 312-444-1000
Telecopier: 312-444-1028
Email: rfca@sprynet.com

Kenneth P. Ross
Eugene J. Schiltz
Jerry S. Menge
Sean B. Crotty
Cassandra A. Crotty

For full biographical listings, see the Martindale-Hubbell Law Directory

CONNELLY & SCHROEDER (AV)

One North Franklin Street, Suite 1200, 60606-3421
Telephone: 312-251-9600
Fax: 312-251-9601
Geneva, Illinois Office: 1250 Executive Place, Suite 201.
Telephone: 630-232-6440.
FAX: 630-232-6450

MEMBERS OF FIRM

Michael P. Connelly
John L. Schroeder (Resident, Geneva Office)
Daniel F. Konicek (Also at Geneva Office)

ASSOCIATES

Michelle L. Adams (Resident, Geneva Office)
Thomas W. Dillon (Resident, Geneva Office)
John Michael Kelly
Carolyn A. Schroeder (Resident, Geneva)
Martha Swatek (Resident, Geneva Office)

For full biographical listings, see the Martindale-Hubbell Law Directory

GESSLER, HUGHES & SOCOL, LTD. (AV)

Three First National Plaza, Suite 2200, 60602
Telephone: 312-580-0100
Telecopy: 312-580-1994

Benjamin P. Beringer
Anjali Dayal
Mark S. Dym
George W. Gessler
John K. Hughes
Joshua Karsh
Peter M. Katsaros
Kimberley Marsh
Alex W. Miller
Terence J. Moran
Matthew J. Piers
Kalman D. Resnick
Frederick S. Rhine
Jonathan A. Rothstein
Michael P. Simkus
Donna Kaner Socol

Gary Chodorow
Ruth M. Dunning
S. Todd Neal
Mark A. Pellegrino
Steven C. Steinback
Dana H. Sukenik
J. Eric Vander Arend
Mark B. Weiner
Charles H. Wintersteen

OF COUNSEL

Darius S. Francescatti, M.D.
Susan R. Gzesh

For full biographical listings, see the Martindale-Hubbell Law Directory

MICHAEL T. HANNAFAN & ASSOCIATES, LTD. (AV)

One East Wacker Drive, Suite 2710, 60601
Telephone: 312-527-0055
Fax: 312-527-0220
Email: mthannafan@aol.com

Michael T. Hannafan

Cory A. Johnson

Reference: The Northern Trust Co.

For full biographical listings, see the Martindale-Hubbell Law Directory

HASKELL & PERRIN (AV)

200 West Adams, Suite 2600, 60606
Telephone: 312-781-9393
Fax: 312-781-9178
Email: hasper@haskellperrin.com

MEMBERS OF FIRM

James Kirk Perrin
John J. Lynch
Mary Elizabeth Denefe

(See Next Column)

HASKELL & PERRIN—*Continued*

OF COUNSEL

Donald M. Haskell

ASSOCIATE

Nancy J. Robinson

For full biographical listings, see the Martindale-Hubbell Law Directory

DONALD L. JOHNSON (AV)

Suite 1401, 33 North Dearborn Street, 60602
Telephone: 312-263-7000
Fax: 312-263-3051

For full biographical listings, see the Martindale-Hubbell Law Directory

POWER ROGERS & SMITH, P.C. (AV)

35 West Wacker Drive, Suite 3700, 60601
Telephone: 312-236-9381
Fax: 312-236-0920

Joseph A. Power, Jr.
Larry R. Rogers
Todd A. Smith

Thomas G. Siracusa
Paul L. Salzetta
Thomas M. Power
Larry R. Rogers, Jr.
Ruth M. Degnan
Devon C. Bruce

For full biographical listings, see the Martindale-Hubbell Law Directory

STONE & MOORE, CHARTERED (AV)

30 North La Salle Street, Suite 4300, 60602
Telephone: 312-332-5656
Fax: 312-332-5858
URL: http://www.stonemoore.com
Merrillville, Indiana Office: 500 E. 86th Avenue, 46410.
Telephone: 219-736-5959.
Fax: 219-736-5858.
Wheaton, Illinois Office: 600 W. Roosevelt Road, Suite 1A, 60187.
Telephone: 630-221-9292.
Fax: 630-221-9393.

William G. Stone
Robert Charles Moore (Also at Wheaton, Illinois Office)
Raymond R. Pesavento
Rosario Cibella
Richard M. Johnson, Jr.
J. Murray Pinkston, III
Julie Osswald Hooven

Christian D. Ambler
Jeffrey W. Henning
Erica Lewis Battaglia
Kevin Kemp Lyons
Kristin E. Rooney
Daniel S. Schulz
Matthew B. Stephens
A. Christine Svenson
Douglas W. Walker

For full biographical listings, see the Martindale-Hubbell Law Directory

LA SALLE, La Salle Co.

HERBOLSHEIMER, LANNON, HENSON, DUNCAN AND REAGAN, P.C. (AV)

State Bank Building, Suite 400, 654 First Street, P.O. Box 539, 61301
Telephone: 815-223-0111
Fax: 815-223-5829
Ottawa, Illinois Office: First Federal Savings Bank Building, 633 LaSalle Street, Suite 409.
Telephone: 815-434-1400.
Fax: 815-434-2423.

George L. Herbolsheimer (1911-1992)
R. James Lannon, Jr.
T. Donald Henson
John S. Duncan, III
Michael T. Reagan (Resident, Ottawa Office)
Douglas A. Gift
Gary R. Eiten

Karen C. Eiten
Michael C. Jansz (Resident, Ottawa Office)
Jill W. Klein
Lawrence M. Kaschak

Attorneys for: Aetna Insurance Group; St. Paul Fire and Marine Insurance Co.; State Farm Insurance Co.; La Salle State Bank; The Daily News Tribune Company, La Salle; Eureka Savings Bank; Illinois Valley Community Hospital; Community Hospital of Ottawa; Commonwealth Edison, Co.; United States Fidelity & Guaranty, Co.

For full biographical listings, see the Martindale-Hubbell Law Directory

IOWA

*DES MOINES,** Polk Co.

HUBER, BOOK, CORTESE, HAPPE & BROWN, P.L.C. (AV)

317 Sixth Avenue, Suite 200, 50309-4127
Telephone: 515-243-4148
Fax: 515-243-5481
Email: huber@desmoineslaw.com

MEMBER OF FIRM

Joseph A. Happe

Representative Clients: Atlantic Mutual Cos.; CNA Insurance Cos.; Fireman's Fund American Insurance Companies; Great West Casualty Co.; Liberty Mutual Insurance Co.; Maryland Insurance Group; Prudential Property and Casualty Insurance Co.; USF&G Company.
Reference: Bank of America.

For full biographical listings, see the Martindale-Hubbell Law Directory

PATTERSON, LORENTZEN, DUFFIELD, TIMMONS, IRISH, BECKER & ORDWAY, L.L.P. (AV)

729 Insurance Exchange Building, 50309
Telephone: 515-283-2147
Fax: 515-283-1002
Email: mail@pattersonfirm.com *URL:* http://www.pattersonfirm.com

MEMBERS OF FIRM

G. O. Patterson (1914-1982)
James A. Lorentzen (Retired)
Theodore T. Duffield
William E. Timmons (Retired)
Roy M. Irish
F. H. Becker (Retired)
Gary D. Ordway
Robin L. Hermann
Harry Perkins, III
Michael F. Lacey, Jr.
Gregory J. Wilson
Jeffrey A. Boehlert
Douglas A. Haag
Charles E. Cutler
Michael D. Huppert
Martin C. Sprock
William A. Wickett
Frederick M. Haskins
Jeffrey A. Baker
Janice M. Herfkens
Coreen K. Bezdicek
Patrick V. Waldron

ASSOCIATE

Michael S. Jones

General Counsel for: Iowa Insurance Institute.
Representative Clients: Allied Mutual Insurance Company; CNA Insurance Company; Chubb Insurance Group; Continental Western Insurance Co.; Farmers Insurance Group; Farmland Insurance Company; Grinnell Mutual Reinsurance Company; Hawkeye Security Insurance Company; Iowa Insurance Institute, St. Paul Fire & Marine Insurance Company.

For full biographical listings, see the Martindale-Hubbell Law Directory

WEST DES MOINES, Polk Co.

LAMARCA & LANDRY, P.C. (AV)

1300 50th Street, 50266
Telephone: 515-225-2600
Fax: 515-225-8581
Islamorada, Florida Office: 202 Biscayne Boulevard, 33036.
Telephone: 305-664-8527.

George A. LaMarca
Gregory W. Landry

Gary G. Mattson
Justin E. LaVan

OF COUNSEL

Martin R. Anderson
Samuel S. Duffey

For full biographical listings, see the Martindale-Hubbell Law Directory

KENTUCKY

*BOWLING GREEN,** Warren Co.

KERRICK, GRISE & STIVERS (AV)

1025 State Street, P.O. Box 9547, 42102-9547
Telephone: 502-782-8160
Fax: 502-782-5856
Email: kgs@kgslaw.com
Elizabethtown, Kentucky Office: 2935 Dolphin Drive, Suite 102.
Telephone: 502-769-5788.
Fax: 502-737-9285.

MEMBERS OF FIRM

Thomas N. Kerrick
John R. Grise
Gregory N. Stivers
H. Brent Brennenstuhl
Laura M. Hagan

ASSOCIATES

Karl N. Crandall
Shawn Rosso Alcott
Jason B. Bell

(See Next Column)

KERRICK, GRISE & STIVERS, *Bowling Green—Continued*

OF COUNSEL

Jeffrey R. O'Grody

LEGAL SUPPORT PERSONNEL

Patricia Logsdon
Laura Lockhart Lico
Allison Lusk

Representative Clients: Dollar General Corp.; Columbia Greenview Regional Hospital; Hospital Corporation of America; Hardin Memorial Hospital; Fir-Star Bank; TKR Cable.

For full biographical listings, see the Martindale-Hubbell Law Directory

LOUISIANA

*BATON ROUGE,** East Baton Rouge Parish

LONG LAW FIRM, L.L.P. (AV)

Suite 800 Two United Plaza, 8550 United Plaza Boulevard, 70809-7013
Telephone: 225-922-5110
Fax: 225-922-5105
Email: longlaw.com
Washington, D.C. Office: Market Square, Suite 750, 801 Pennsylvania Avenue, N.W., 20004-2167.
Telephone: 202-737-9212.
FAX: 202-624-0659.

MEMBERS OF FIRM

Russell B. Long
C. Kris Kirkpatrick
Michael A. Patterson
Joseph E. Juban
Albert Dale Clary
David L. Guerry
C. Stokes McConnell, Jr.

ASSOCIATES

Daniel D. Holliday, III
Jennifer J. Vosburg
Tracy Averett Morganti

OF COUNSEL

Melanie Peirron Patrick

For full biographical listings, see the Martindale-Hubbell Law Directory

METAIRIE, Jefferson Parish

CAMPBELL, MCCRANIE, SISTRUNK, ANZELMO & HARDY, P.C. (AV)

3445 North Causeway Boulevard, Suite 800, 70002
Telephone: 504-831-0946
Fax: 504-831-2492

Frederick R. Campbell
Burgess E. McCranie, Jr.
Michael R. Sistrunk
Thomas P. Anzelmo
Sidney J. Hardy
Lance S. Ostendorf
Roy C. Beard
Mishthi Grace Ratnesar
Charles E. Sutton, Jr.
Isidro René DeRojas
Mark Emerson Hanna
Geoffrey J. Orr

Angela M. Bowlin
Catherine M. Williams
Colin D. Sherman
James H. Hunter
Richard Andrew Houston, III
Paxton K. Stelly
Michele Butler Prokop
Marty D. Parlipiano
Peter J. Wanek
Ken D. Brown

Representative Clients: Wal-Mart Stores, Inc.; Delchamps, Inc.; Greyhound Lines, Inc.; The Dial Corporation; Transport Insurance Company; Burger King Corporation; CNA Insurance Companies; The Louisiana Motor Vehicle Commission; Insbrok; Patent Scaffolding.

For full biographical listings, see the Martindale-Hubbell Law Directory

HAILEY, MCNAMARA, HALL, LARMANN & PAPALE, L.L.P. (AV)

A Limited Liability Partnership including Professional Law Corporations
Suite 1400, One Galleria Boulevard, P.O. Box 8288, 70011
Telephone: 504-836-6500
Fax: 504-836-6565
URL: http://www.haileymcnamara.com

MEMBERS OF FIRM

James W. Hailey, Jr., (P.L.C.)
W. Marvin Hall (P.L.C.)
Antonio E. Papale, Jr., (P.L.C.)
Laurence E. Larmann (P.L.C.)
Michael P. Mentz
Richard T. Simmons, Jr.,(P.L.C.)
Michael J. Vondenstein
David K. Persons
Dominic J. Ovella
C. Kelly Lightfoot
John T. Culotta (P.L.C.)
John E. Unsworth, Jr.
Julie DiFulco Robles
Claude A. Greco
Valerie T. Schexnayder
W. Evan Plauche
Kurt D. Engelhardt

(See Next Column)

ASSOCIATES

William R. Seay, Jr.
W. Glenn Burns
James W. Hailey, III
Frederic Theodore Le Clercq
Barbara Bourdonnay O'Donnell
Kathryn T. Wiedorn
Joseph L. Spilman, III
Caroline D. Ibos
Robert D. Ford
Lynnette Hall-Lewis
Kevin O. Larmann
Tammy M. Stewart
Danny N. Bowz
Edward C. Vocke, IV
C. Angelle Goudeau
Alayne R. Corcoran
David K. Groome, Jr.
Kristen M. Baumer
Gabriel J. Veninata

OF COUNSEL

Henry D. McNamara, Jr., (P.L.C.)

Representative Clients: Diamond Offshore Drilling Inc.; The Flintkote Co.; Lockheed Martin Corporation; Rheem Manufacturing Co.; State Farm Fire & Casualty Co.; Textron, Inc; Travelers Companies; Coca-Cola Enterprises, Inc.

For full biographical listings, see the Martindale-Hubbell Law Directory

*NEW ORLEANS,** Orleans Parish

BEAHM AND GREEN (AV)

145 Robert E. Lee Boulevard Suite 408, 70124-2552
Telephone: 504-288-2000
Fax: 504-288-2099
Email: Frank@Beahm.com *URL:* http://www.Beahm.com

Franklin D. Beahm
Charles S. Green, Jr.

ASSOCIATES

Julie G. Hamner
Candice V. Bates

For full biographical listings, see the Martindale-Hubbell Law Directory

MCGLINCHEY STAFFORD (AV)

A Professional Limited Liability Company
643 Magazine Street, 70130-3477
Telephone: 504-586-1200
Fax: 504-596-2800
TDD: (504) 596-2728
Telex: 584327
Cable Address: "MACSTAC"
Mailing Address: P.O. Box 60643, New Orleans, Louisiana, 70160-0643
Email: @mcglinchey.com *URL:* http://www.mcglinchey.com
Dallas, Texas Office: 2777 Stemmons Freeway, Suite 925, 75207-2401.
Telephone: 214-860-9700.
Fax: 214-860-9750.
Houston, Texas Office: 2727 Allen Parkway, Suite 1900, 77019.
Telephone: 713-520-1900.
Fax: 713-520-1025.
Baton Rouge, Louisiana Office: Ninth Floor, One American Place, 70825-0001.
Telephone: 504-383-9000.
Fax: 504-343-3076.
Jackson, Mississippi Office: Suite 1200, SkyTel Centre, 200 South Lamar Street, 39201.
Telephone: 601-960-8400.
Fax: 601-960-8406.
Lake Providence, Louisiana Office: 405 Morgan Street, 71254-2691.
Telephone: 318-559-1200.
Fax: 318-559-0609.
Monroe, Louisiana Office: Dean ONB Tower, 130 Desiard Street, Suite 807, 71201.
Telephone: 318-651-0807.
Fax: 318-651-0809.

MEMBER OF FIRM

Kathleen A. Manning

ASSOCIATES

Margaret Woolverton Triebes
Mindy Brickman Patrón

For full biographical listings, see the Martindale-Hubbell Law Directory

*SHREVEPORT,** Caddo Parish

MAYER, SMITH & ROBERTS, L.L.P. (AV)

1550 Creswell, 71101
Telephone: 318-222-2135, 222-2268
Fax: 318-222-6420
Email: (Attorney's First Name)@MSRLAW.COM

MEMBERS OF FIRM

Caldwell Roberts
Walter O. Hunter, Jr.
Mark A. Goodwin
Ben Marshall, Jr.
Alexander S. Lyons
Kim Purdy Thomas
David Butterfield
Henry N. Bellamy
John C. Turnage
Paul R. Mayer, Jr.
Steven E. Soileau
Deborah Shea Baukman
Caldwell Roberts, Jr.
Frank K. Carroll
Dalton Roberts Ross

(See Next Column)

MAYER, SMITH & ROBERTS L.L.P.—*Continued*

OF COUNSEL

Paul R. Mayer

Representative Clients: CNA Insurance Companies; Liberty Mutual Insurance Company; United States Fidelity and Guaranty Company; Schumpert Medical Center; Travelers Insurance Company; Great American Insurance Company; Insurance Corporation of America; Highlands Insurance Company.

For full biographical listings, see the Martindale-Hubbell Law Directory

MAINE

*PORTLAND,** Cumberland Co.

THOMPSON & BOWIE (AV)

Three Canal Plaza, P.O. Box 4630, 04112
Telephone: 207-774-2500
Telecopier: 207-774-3591
Email: law@thompsonbowie.com

MEMBERS OF FIRM

Roy E. Thompson, Jr.
James M. Bowie
Daniel R. Mawhinney
Rebecca H. Farnum
Glenn H. Robinson
Frank W. DeLong, III
Michael E. Saucier
Mark V. Franco
Edward R. Benjamin, Jr.
Cathy S. Roberts
Paul C. Catsos

ASSOCIATES

Elizabeth Knox Peck
Thomas G. Diebold
Michael R. Bosse
Lisa M. Fitzgibbon

For full biographical listings, see the Martindale-Hubbell Law Directory

MARYLAND

*BALTIMORE,** (Independent City)

FREISHTAT & SANDLER (AV)

Suite 1500, One Calvert Plaza, 201 E. Baltimore Street, 21202
Telephone: 410-727-7740
FAX: 410-727-7356

MEMBERS OF FIRM

David Freishtat
Paul Mark Sandler
Raymond F. Altman
Raymond Daniel Burke
William Michael Mullen
Lloyd J. Snow
Stacie F. Dubnow

Roderick R. Barnes
Jeffrey S. Rosenfeld
Thomas K. Harris

OF COUNSEL

Lynn Weinberg

For full biographical listings, see the Martindale-Hubbell Law Directory

SCANLAN, ROSEN & SHAR, LLC (AV)

26 South Street, 21202-3399
Telephone: 410-244-1155
Fax: 410-244-1157
Email: lawyers@triallaw.com *URL:* http://www.triallaw.com

Alfred L. Scanlan, Jr.
Marc Seldin Rosen
Marcus Z. Shar
Michael Stuart Warshaw

Timothy Cronin Lynch
Neil E Duke
Kristofer P. Cubello

OF COUNSEL

Colleen A. Cavanaugh
Lee H. Caplan
J. Michael McWilliams

For full biographical listings, see the Martindale-Hubbell Law Directory

SILVER SPRING, Montgomery Co.

SAUNDERS & SCHMIELER (AV)

8737 Colesville Road, Suite L-200, 20910-3921
Telephone: 301-588-7717
Facsimile: 301-588-5073
Email: admin@sslawfirm.com *URL:* http://www.sslawfirm.com
Washington, D.C. Office: 1050 17th Street, N.W., #600
Telephone: 202-833-2999.
Baltimore, Maryland Office: Suite 2700, 111 South Calvert Street.
Telephone: 410-235-7558.

(See Next Column)

Arlington, Virginia Office: 2111 Wilson Boulevard, Suite 700.
Telephone: 703-243-1100.
Richmond, Virginia Office: 4900 Cutshaw Avenue.
Telephone: 804-353-9800.

MEMBER OF FIRM

Jeffrey R. Schmieler

ASSOCIATES

Nicole E. Ames
A. Benjamin Horton
Lucas F. Webster

For Complete List of Firm Personnel, See General Section

For full biographical listings, see the Martindale-Hubbell Law Directory

MASSACHUSETTS

*SPRINGFIELD,** Hampden Co.

ROBINSON DONOVAN MADDEN & BARRY, P.C. (AV)

Suite 1600, Tower Square, 1500 Main Street, 01115-5609
Telephone: 413-732-2301
Fax: 413-785-4658
Email: service@robinson-donovan.com *URL:* http://www.robinson-donovan.com

Homans Robinson (1894-1973)
Lawrence M. Sinclair (1942-1986)
Milton J. Donovan (1906-1995)

RETIRED

John H. Madden, Jr.
Edward J. Barry
Richard S. Milstein

OF COUNSEL

Victor Rosenberg

SENIOR COUNSEL

Jonathan P. Rice

Gordon H. Wentworth
James H. Tourtelotte
Ronald C. Kidd
Jeffrey W. Roberts
Jeffrey L. McCormick
James F. Martin
Robert P. Cunningham
John C. Sikorski
Nancy Frankel Pelletier
Paul S. Weinberg
Frederica H. McCarthy
Matthew J. King
Neva Kaufman Rohan
Douglas F. Boyd
James K. Bodurtha
Keith A. Minoff
Patricia M. Rapinchuk
Kimberly Davis Crear

E. Paul Amata
Lisa A. Bongiovi (Not admitted in MA)
Edward J. Carroll, III
James D. Chadwell
John E. Garber
Patrick J. Markey
Carla W. Newton
Betsy Macmillan Stevens

Representative Clients: BankBoston, N.A.; United Cooperative Bank; Fleet National Bank; CNA; Commercial Union Insurance Co.; Hanover Insurance Group.

For full biographical listings, see the Martindale-Hubbell Law Directory

MICHIGAN

BLOOMFIELD HILLS, Oakland Co.

LAWRENCE J. ACKER, P.C. (AV)

44 East Long Lake Road, 48304
Telephone: 248-594-7277
Fax: 248-594-7280

Lawrence J. Acker

For full biographical listings, see the Martindale-Hubbell Law Directory

PROVIZER & PHILLIPS, P.C. (AV)

6785 Telegraph Road, Suite 400, 48301
Telephone: 248-642-0444
Facsimile: 248-642-6661
Toll Free: 1-800-288-9080
URL: http://www.lawyers.com/provizer&phillips

Harold M. Provizer
Randall E. Phillips
Marilyn A. Madorsky
Evan A. Zagoria
Noel F. Beck
Mark S. Baumkel

(See Next Column)

PROVIZER & PHILLIPS P.C., *Bloomfield Hills—Continued*

Constance S. Hall
Ellen C. Busch
Donald J. Parthum, Jr.
Keith A. Castora
Gregory A. Nave

For full biographical listings, see the Martindale-Hubbell Law Directory

*DETROIT,** Wayne Co.

BODMAN, LONGLEY & DAHLING LLP (AV)

34th Floor 100 Renaissance Center, 48243
Telephone: 313-259-7777
Fax: 313-393-7579
Email: info@bodmanlongley.com *URL:* http://www.bodmanlongley.com
Troy, Michigan Office: Suite 2020, 755 West Big Beaver Road.
Telephone: 248-362-2110.
Fax: 248-244-0780.
Ann Arbor, Michigan Office: 110 Miller, Suite 300.
Telephone: 734-761-3780.
Fax: 734-930-2494.
Northern Michigan Office: 229 Court Street, P.O. Box 405, Cheboygan.
Telephone: 231-627-4351.
Fax: 231-627-2802.

MEMBERS OF FIRM

James A. Smith
George G. Kemsley
James J. Walsh
Thomas Van Dusen (Troy Office)
Thomas J. Tallerico
Jeffrey G. Raphelson

For Representative Clients list, See General Section

For Complete List of Firm Personnel, See General Section

For full biographical listings, see the Martindale-Hubbell Law Directory

BUTZEL LONG, A PROFESSIONAL CORPORATION (AV)

Suite 900, 150 West Jefferson, 48226
Telephone: 313-225-7000
Telecopier: 313-225-7080
Email: melnick@butzel.com *URL:* http://www.butzel.com
Birmingham, Michigan Office: Suite 200, 32270 Telegraph Road.
Telephone: 810-258-1616.
Telecopier: 810-258-1439.
Okemos, Michigan Office: Suite 300, 2127 University Park Drive.
Telephone: 517-372-6622.
Telecopier: 517-372-6672.
Ann Arbor, Michigan Office: Suite 300, 350 South Main Street.
Telephone: 313-995-3110.
Telecopier: 313-995-1777.
Grosse Pointe Farms, Michigan Office: Suite 260, 21 Kercheval.
Telephone: 313-886-5446.
Telecopier: 313-886-2114.
Boca Raton, Florida Office: Suite 411, 1200 North Federal Highway.
Telephone: 561-368-2151.
Telecopier: 561-368-4668.
Palm Beach Gardens, Florida Office: Suite 227, 11382 Prosperity Farms Road.
Telephone: 561-625-4442.
Telecopier: 561-625-6901.
Naples, Florida Office: Suite 705, 801 Laurel Oak Drive.
Telephone: 941-597-4500.
Telecopier: 941-597-5623.

Philip J. Kessler
Keefe A. Brooks
Leonard M. Niehoff (Ann Arbor)

COUNSEL

David F. DuMouchel

SENIOR ATTORNEYS

Marcia L. Proctor
Max R. Hoffman, Jr. (Okemos)
Thomas L. Sparks (Okemos)

Representative Clients: Bridgestone/Firestone, Inc.; Detroit Diesel Corp.; The Detroit News, Inc.; Kelly Services; Merrill Lynch & Co., Inc.; Stroh Companies; Takata Corp.; TRW Automotive; The University of Michigan.

For full biographical listings, see the Martindale-Hubbell Law Directory

DAVID F. DUMOUCHEL, P.C. (AV)

150 West Jefferson, Suite 900, 48226-4430
Telephone: 313-225-7004
Email: dumouchd@butzel.com

David F. DuMouchel

For full biographical listings, see the Martindale-Hubbell Law Directory

KENNETH M. MOGILL (AV)

One Kennedy Square Building, Suite 1930, 719 Griswold, 48226
Telephone: 313-962-7210
Fax: 313-961-7799
(Also Member Mogill, Posner & Cohen)

For full biographical listings, see the Martindale-Hubbell Law Directory

WILLMARTH, TANOURY, RAMAR, CORBET, GARVES & SHAW (AV)

535 Griswold, Suite 1730, 48226-3602
Telephone: 313-964-6300
Fax: 313-964-6310
Email: mdwillth@home.net

MEMBERS OF FIRM

Daniel R. Corbet
Brian R. Garves
David R. Nauts
Anthony J. Paradiso
John M. Perrin
John J. Ramar
Bruce R. Shaw
William A. Tanoury
Mark D. Willmarth

ASSOCIATES

Marie C. Kennedy
Wayne Walker
Elizabeth L. Sokol
Robert S. Silverman
Carmine G. Paterra
Joseph J. Ceglarek, II
Derek Steven Wilczynski
Frank Hamidi
Kristen E. Skaff
Steven J. Bonasso
Colleen P. O'Connor
Lara R. Stutz
Eric G. Tucciarone
Michael P. Robach

For full biographical listings, see the Martindale-Hubbell Law Directory

*GAYLORD,** Otsego Co.

BENSINGER, COTANT, MENKES & AARDEMA, P.C. (AV)

308 West Main Street, P.O. Box 1000, 49735
Telephone: 517-732-7536
Fax: 517-732-4922
URL: http://www.bcma.net
Grand Rapids, Michigan Office: 983 Spaulding Avenue, S.E.
Telephone: 616-949-7963.
Fax: 616-949-5264.
Marquette, Michigan Office: 122 West Bluff.
Telephone: 906-225-1000.
Fax: 906-225-0818.

Richard G. Bensinger
Scott R. Eckhold

For full biographical listings, see the Martindale-Hubbell Law Directory

*GRAND RAPIDS,** Kent Co.

BENSINGER, COTANT, MENKES & AARDEMA, P.C. (AV)

983 Spaulding Avenue, S.E., 49546
Telephone: 616-949-7963
Fax: 616-949-5264
URL: http://www.bcma.net
Gaylord, Michigan Office: 308 West Main, P.O. Box 1000.
Telephone: 517-732-7536.
Fax: 517-732-4922.
Marquette, Michigan Office: 122 West Bluff.
Telephone: 906-225-1000.
Fax: 906-225-0818.

Brian W. Whitelaw
Dale L. Arndt

For full biographical listings, see the Martindale-Hubbell Law Directory

*MARQUETTE,** Marquette Co.

BENSINGER, COTANT, MENKES & AARDEMA, P.C. (AV)

122 West Bluff, 49855
Telephone: 906-225-1000
Fax: 906-225-0818
URL: http://www.bcma.net
Gaylord, Michigan Office: 308 West Main, P.O. Box 1000.
Telephone: 517-732-7536.
Fax: 517-732-4922.
Grand Rapids, Michigan Office: 983 Spaulding Avenue, S.E.
Telephone: 616-949-7963.
Fax: 616-949-5264.

Gregory A. Elzinga
Michael G. Summers

For full biographical listings, see the Martindale-Hubbell Law Directory

ST. CLAIR SHORES, Macomb Co.

MERRY, FARNEN & RYAN, A PROFESSIONAL CORPORATION (AV)

27739 Jefferson Avenue, 48081-1309
Telephone: 810-776-6700
Telecopier: 810-776-1501
URL: http://www.lawyers.com/mfr

(See Next Column)

MERRY, FARNEN & RYAN A PROFESSIONAL CORPORATION—*Continued*

Cynthia E. Merry
Lynda Barbat Farnen
Michael T. Ryan

For full biographical listings, see the Martindale-Hubbell Law Directory

TROY, Oakland Co.

HOLAHAN, MALLOY, MAYBAUGH, MONNICH & DELIE (AV)

Suite 100, 2690 Crooks Road, 48084-4700
Telephone: 248-362-4747
Fax: 248-362-4779
East Tawas, Michigan Office: 910 East Bay Street.
Telephone: 517-362-4747.
Fax: 517-362-7331.

MEMBERS OF FIRM

J. Michael Malloy, III
James D. Maybaugh
John R. Monnich
David L. Delie, Jr.

OF COUNSEL

Thomas H. O'Connor
Maureen Holahan (Retired; Resident, East Tawas Office)

For full biographical listings, see the Martindale-Hubbell Law Directory

POLING, MCGAW & POLING, P.C. (AV)

Suite 275, 5435 Corporate Drive, 48098
Telephone: 248-641-0500
Telecopier: 248-641-0506
URL: http://www.lawyers.com/polingmcgaw&poling

Benson T. Buck (1926-1989)
Richard B. Poling
D. Douglas McGaw
Richard B. Poling, Jr.
Gregory C. Hamilton
Veronica B. O'Hara
James R. Parker
Shannon M. Acton

OF COUNSEL

Ralph S. Moore

Representative Clients: City of Troy; United States Fidelity & Guaranty Co.; Sentry Insurance Co.; Admiral Insurance; DeMaria Construction Co.; Leo Corporation; Aetna Casualty and Surety Co.; Concord Design; Pneumo-Abex.

For full biographical listings, see the Martindale-Hubbell Law Directory

PUBLIC UTILITIES LAW

ALABAMA

*BIRMINGHAM,** Jefferson Co.

BRADLEY ARANT ROSE & WHITE LLP (AV)

2001 Park Place, Suite 1400, P.O. Box 830709, 35283-0709
Telephone: 205-521-8000
Facsimile: 205-521-8800
Facsimile (SouthTrust Tower Office): 205-521-8500
URL: http://www.barw.com
Huntsville, Alabama Office: 200 Clinton Avenue West, Suite 900, 35801.
Telephone: 205-517-5100.
Facsimile: 205-533-5069.
Washington, D.C. Office: 801 Pennsylvania Avenue, NW, Suite 230, 20004.
Telephone: 202-347-8893.
Facsimile: 202-347-1684.

MEMBER OF FIRM

E. Cutter Hughes Jr. (Resident, Huntsville Office)

For Complete List of Firm Personnel, See General Section

For full biographical listings, see the Martindale-Hubbell Law Directory

*MONTGOMERY,** Montgomery Co.

BRANTLEY & WILKERSON, P.C. (AV)

405 South Hull Street, P.O. Box 830, 36101-0830
Telephone: 334-265-1500
Fax: 334-265-0319
Email: ashley@brantleywilkerson.com *URL:* http://www.brantleywilkerson.com

Paul A. Brantley
Mark D. Wilkerson
Leah Snell Stephens
R. Winston Lee

Representative Client: Wheeler Basin Natural Gas Company, Inc.
Reference: SouthTrust Bank, N.A.

For full biographical listings, see the Martindale-Hubbell Law Directory

ARIZONA

*PHOENIX,** Maricopa Co.

FENNEMORE CRAIG, A PROFESSIONAL CORPORATION (AV)

3003 North Central Avenue, Suite 2600, 85012-2913
Telephone: 602-916-5000
Fax: 602-916-5999
Tucson, Arizona Office: One South Church Avenue, Suite 1000, 85701-1620.
Telephone: 520-879-6800.
Fax: 520-879-6899.

C. Webb Crockett
Timothy Berg
Norman D. James
Theresa Dwyer
Jay L. Shapiro

For Complete List of Firm Personnel, See General Section

For full biographical listings, see the Martindale-Hubbell Law Directory

ROSHKA HEYMAN & DEWULF, PLC (AV)

Two Arizona Center, 400 North 5th Street, Suite 1000, 85004
Telephone: 602-256-6100
Facsimile: 602-256-6800
Email: rheyman@rhd-law.com

Paul J. Roshka, Jr.
John E. DeWulf
Raymond S. Heyman
Darlene M. Wauro
Alan S. Baskin
Randall H. Warner
Linda D. Skon

For full biographical listings, see the Martindale-Hubbell Law Directory

ARKANSAS

*LITTLE ROCK,** Pulaski Co.

CHISENHALL, NESTRUD & JULIAN, P.A. (AV)

400 West Capitol, Suite 2840, 72201
Telephone: 501-372-5800
Telecopier: 501-372-4941
Email: cnjlaw@cnjlaw.com

Lawrence E. Chisenhall, Jr.
Jim L. Julian
Charles R. Nestrud
Ann P. Faitz
Michael T. Jackson

For full biographical listings, see the Martindale-Hubbell Law Directory

ROSE LAW FIRM, A PROFESSIONAL ASSOCIATION (AV)

120 East Fourth Street, 72201
Telephone: 501-375-9131
Telecopy: 501-375-1309

Herbert C. Rule, III
Stephen N. Joiner
Brian Rosenthal

Counsel for: ALLTEL Corporation; Aluminum Company of America; Arkansas Gas Consumers; Bridgestone/Firestone, Inc.; The Equitable Life Assurance Society of The United States; General Motors Corp.; The Prudential Insurance Company of America; Stephens Group Inc.; Tyson Foods, Inc.

For Complete List of Firm Personnel, See General Section

For full biographical listings, see the Martindale-Hubbell Law Directory

CALIFORNIA

*LOS ANGELES,** Los Angeles Co.

ALLEN, MATKINS, LECK, GAMBLE & MALLORY LLP (AV)

A Limited Liability Partnership including Professional Corporations
Seventh Floor, 515 South Figueroa Street, 90071
Telephone: 213-622-5555
Telecopier: 213-620-8816
Irvine, California Office: Fourth Floor, 18400 Von Karman, 92612.
Telephone: 949-553-1313.
Telecopier: 949-553-8354.
San Diego, California Office: 501 West Broadway, Ninth Floor, 92101.
Telephone: 619-233-1155.
Facsimile: 619-233-1158.
West Los Angeles, California Office: 1999 Avenue of the Stars, Suite 1800, 90067.
Telephone: 310-788-2400.
Fax: 310-788-2410.
San Francisco, California Office: 333 Bush Street, Seventeenth Floor, 94104-2806.
Telephone: 415-837-1515.
Fax: 415-837-1516.

PARTNERS

Frederick L. Allen
John C. Gamble (Resident, Orange County and San Francisco Offices)
Brian C. Leck
Richard C. Mallory (Resident, San Francisco Office)
Michael L. Matkins
Marvin E. Garrett
Thomas C. Foster (Resident, Irvine Office)
Robert J. Cathcart
R. Michael Joyce (Resident, Irvine Office)
Gerben Hoeksma
Thomas W. Henning
Patrick E. Breen
Lawrence D. Lewis (P.C.) (Resident, Irvine Office)
George T. McDonnell
Michael F. Sfregola
Guy Rounsaville, Jr. (Resident, San Francisco Office)
David A. B. Burton (P.C.)
Monica E. Olson (Resident, Irvine Office)
Thomas E. Gibbs (Resident, Irvine Office)
Vernon C. Gauntt (Resident, San Diego Office)
Dwight L. Armstrong (Resident, Irvine Office)
Paul D. O'Connor (Resident, Irvine Office)
David L. Osias (San Diego and Los Angeles Offices)
William R. Harmsen
Debra Dison Hall
Anton N. Natsis (Resident, West Los Angeles Office)
George J. Berger (Resident, San Diego Office)
Michael C. Pruter (Resident, San Diego Office)
Michael H. Cerrina
Richard E. Stinehart (Resident, Irvine Office)
Stephen R. Thames (Resident, Irvine Office)
Dana I. Schiffman (Resident, San Diego Office)
Anne E. Klokow (Resident, Irvine Office)
Neil N. Gluck
David W. Wensley (Resident, Irvine Office)
Gary S. McKitterick (Resident, Irvine Office)
Patrick J. Grady (Resident, Irvine Office)
Thomas J. Masenga
Ray B. Gliner (Resident, San Diego Office)

(See Next Column)

ALLEN, MATKINS, LECK, GAMBLE & MALLORY LLP, *Los Angeles—Continued*

Charles N. Kenworthy (Resident, West Los Angeles Office)
Anthony J. Oliva
Mark J. Grushkin
Michael P. Durkee (Resident, San Francisco Office)
Lindbergh Porter, Jr. (Resident, San Francisco Office)
Michael D. Ryan
Edwin W. Green
Ronald K. Clausen (Resident, San Francisco Office)
Ellen B. Spellman
Robert M. Hamilton (Resident, Irvine Office)
David R. Zaro
Janet A. Winnick
H. Christian L'Orange (Resident, San Francisco Office)
Robert R. Barnes (Resident, San Diego Office)
Vincent M. Coscino (Resident, Irvine Office)
Jeffrey R. Patterson (Resident, San Diego Office)
Jerold B. Neuman (P.C.)
Mark R. Hartney
John M. Tipton (Resident, West Los Angeles Office)
Nancy Lundeen (Resident, San Francisco Office)
Joe M. Davidson (Resident, San Diego Office)
Craig D. Swanson (Resident, San Diego Office)
Gregory G. Gorman
George W. Kuney (Resident, San Diego Office)
Michael J. Kiely
Cheryl S. Prell
Bradley N. Schweitzer (Resident, Irvine Office)
Pamela L. Andes (Resident, Irvine Office)
Samuel H. Stein
Michael S. Greger (Resident, Irvine Office)
Robert A. Lurie (Resident, West Los Angeles Office)
Stephen J. Kepler (Resident, Irvine Office)
Mark J. Kelson (Resident, West Los Angeles Office)

ASSOCIATES

Henry Einar Fink
Rebecca L. Gundzik
Adela Carrasco
Catherine M. Page (Resident, Irvine Office)
Leslie Tucker Fischer (Resident, Irvine Office)
A. Kristine Floyd (Resident, Irvine Office)
Jennifer M. Casey
Cynthia Eder Bouza
Claudia Stone (Resident, West Los Angeles Office)
Michael A. Alvarado (Resident, Irvine Office)
Mary Kay Ruck (Resident, Irvine Office)
Eric J. Shelby (Resident, West Los Angeles Office)
Susan E. Graham (Resident, Irvine Office)
Martin L. Togni (Resident, San Diego Office)
Robert D. Jaffe
Stephen P. Lieske (Resident, San Francisco Office)
Loraine L. Pedowitz (Resident, San Diego Office)
Karen L. Lawlor
Drew M. Emmel (Resident, Irvine Office)
Dana R. Stone (Resident, San Francisco Office)
David H. Blackwell (Resident, San Francisco Office)
Cynthia B. Paulsen (Resident, Irvine Office)
Peter J. Roth
Thomas B. Crosbie (Resident, San Diego Office)
Rebecca Ann Thompson
Sandra J. Young (Resident, San Diego Office)
Christie M. Musser (Resident, San Francisco Office)
Bradley P. Kaplan (Resident, San Francisco Office)
Mark J. Hattam (Resident, San Diego Office)
Michael R. Farrell
Steven E. Creamer (Resident, Irvine Office)
David Y. Otsuka (Resident, San Francisco Office)
Steve Wellington (Resident, San Diego Office)
Ann Marie Maas (Resident, San Diego Office)
Todd E. Whitman
Allison L. Malin (Resident, West Los Angeles Office)
Kari Mason Desgalier (Resident, San Diego Office)
Kelly J. Brinkman (Resident, San Diego Office)
Lee A. Edlund (Resident, San Francisco Office)
John W. Kittleson (Resident, Irvine Office)
Sonia J. Ransom
Hazel Marlee Brandt (Resident, San Francisco Office)
Kimberly A. Donlon
Jeffrey N. Strug
Allen B. Walburn (Resident, San Diego Office)
Sandra A. Jacobson (Resident, Irvine Office)
Sharon Saslow (Resident, San Diego Office)
Deborah L. Babb (Resident, San Francisco Office)
Scott D. Howie (Resident, Irvine Office)
Scott Wilson Hatter
Charles D. Jarrell
Daniel R. Foster (Resident, Irvine Office)
Kathryn D. Horning (Resident, San Diego Office)
Francis N. Scollan
Darren A. Manibog
Laura B. Finkelstein (Resident, Irvine Office)
Bruce W. Hepler (Resident, Irvine Office)
A. Kenneth Hennesay, Jr. (Resident, Irvine Office)
Anne Marie LaPlace (Resident, Irvine Office)
Theodore M. Gizewski (Resident, San Francisco Office)
Jeanne M. Jorgensen (Resident, Irvine Office)
Lisa N. Machii
Kevin M. Ehrhart
Heidi K. Eick
Carrie H. Crockett (Resident, San Francisco Office)
Todd Chapman (Resident, San Francisco Office)
Gregg S. Pasternack (Resident, West Los Angeles Office)
Louis T. Antosh, Jr. (Resident, Irvine Office)
Angie Y. Yoon
Christa Stern Eilers (Resident, Irvine Office)
Hillary J. Post
Joseph S. Stuart (Resident, Irvine Office)

(See Next Column)

ASSOCIATES (Continued)

Timothy J. Hoban (Resident, Irvine Office)
William R. Ahern, III (Resident, Irvine Office)
Kushal S. Bhakta
Lisa R. Kamrath
Christine Kormanik (Resident, Irvine Office)
Patrick Austin Perry
Jennie Lau (Resident, San Francisco Office)
Cynthia Hinshaw Wertz (Resident, San Francisco Office)
Dawnmarie I. Saunders (Resident, San Diego Office)
Michael J. Holmes (Resident, San Diego Office)
Mark Edward Foster (Resident, Irvine Office)
Matthew J. Mahan
Natasha Lynn Hyman
Jennifer Erin Bromiley
Elizabeth A. Markey (Resident, Irvine Office)
Matthew J. Ertman (Resident, Irvine Office)
Brad H. Nielsen (Resident, Irvine Office)
Michael J. Betz (Resident, San Francisco Office)
Christopher B. Hansmeyer (Resident, San Diego Office)
Vanessa Alvarez (Resident, San Francisco Office)

OF COUNSEL

John G. Davies (Resident, San Diego Office)
Michael J. Murphy
S. Lee Hancock (At Irvine and San Diego Offices)
Henry Lerner (Resident, San Francisco Office)
James M. Tervo (Resident, San Francisco Office)
Madeleine E. Sloane (Resident, San Francisco Office)
Roberta V. Romberg (Resident, San Francisco Office)

Reference: Wells Fargo Bank (Los Angeles Main Office).

For full biographical listings, see the Martindale-Hubbell Law Directory

O'MELVENY & MYERS LLP (AV)

400 South Hope Street, 90071-2899
Telephone: 213-430-6000
Facsimile: 213-430-6407
Cable: MOMS
Telex: 674122
Email: omminfo@omm.com *URL:* http://www.omm.com
Century City, CA Office: 1999 Avenue of the Stars, Los Angeles, 90067-6035.
Telex: 674097. Tel: 310-553-6700.
Fax: 310-246-6779.
Newport Beach, CA Office: 610 Newport Center Drive, 92660-6429.
Telex: 4722088. Tel: 949-760-9600.
Fax: 949-823-6994.
San Francisco, CA Office: Embarcadero Center West, 275 Battery Street, 94111-3305. Tel: 415-984-8700.
Fax: 415-984-8701.
New York, NY Office: Citicorp Center, 153 East 53rd Street, 10022-4611.
Telex: 129165. Tel: 212-326-2000.
Fax: 212-326-2061.
Washington, DC Office: 555 13th Street, N.W., 20004-1109.
Cable: MOMSWSH.
Telex: 89622. Tel: 202-383-5300.
Fax: 202-383-5414.
London Office: O'Melveny & Myers, 3 Finsbury Square, London, EC2A 1LA, England. Tel: 44-171-256-8451. Fax 44-171-638-8205.
Tokyo Office: Akasaka Twin Tower, East 14F, 2-17-23, Akasaka, Minato-ku, Tokyo 107-0052, Japan. Tel: 03-5562-2800.
Fax: 03-5575-3840.
Hong Kong Office: O'Melveny & Myers, Suite 1905, Tower Two, Lippo Centre, 89 Queensway, Central, Hong Kong. Tel: 852-2523-8266.
Fax: 852-2522-1760.
Shanghai Office: Kerry Centre, 20F, 1515 Nanjing Road West, Shanghai, 200040 People's Republic of China. Tel: 86-21-5298-5600.
Fax: 86-21-5298-5500.

PARTNER

Joseph M. Malkin (San Francisco, CA Offices)

For Complete List of Firm Personnel, See General Section

For full biographical listings, see the Martindale-Hubbell Law Directory

*RIVERSIDE,** Riverside Co.

HAIGHT, BROWN & BONESTEEL, L.L.P. (AV)

A Partnership including Professional Corporations
California Tower, 3737 Main Street, Suite 800, 92501
Telephone: 909-341-8300
FAX: 909-341-8309
URL: http://www.hbblaw.com
Santa Monica, California Office: 1620 26th Street, Suite 4000 North, P.O. Box 680.
Telephone: 310-449-6000.
Telecopier: 310-829-5117.
Telex: 705837.
Santa Ana, California Office: Suite 900, 5 Hutton Centre Drive.
Telephone: 714-754-1100.
Telecopier: 714-754-0826.
San Francisco, California Office: 100 Bush Street, 27th Floor.
Telephone: 415-986-7700.
Fax: 415-986-6945.

(See Next Column)

HAIGHT, BROWN & BONESTEEL L.L.P.—*Continued*

San Diego, California Office: 101 West Broadway, Suite 1000.
Telephone: 619-595-5583.
Fax: 619-595-7873.

RESIDENT MEMBER
Kevin M. Osterberg
ASSOCIATE
Bonnie B. Bailey-Jones

For full biographical listings, see the Martindale-Hubbell Law Directory

COLORADO

*DENVER,** Denver Co.

GORSUCH KIRGIS LLP (AV)

Tower 1, Suite 1000, 1515 Arapahoe Street, 80202
Telephone: 303-376-5000
Fax: 303-376-5001

PARTNERS
Dudley P. Spiller
Peter R. Nadel
ASSOCIATES
Heather Anne Hawker
Julie Leamon Rosen

For full biographical listings, see the Martindale-Hubbell Law Directory

DISTRICT OF COLUMBIA

WASHINGTON, D.C. Co.

BRUDER, GENTILE & MARCOUX, L.L.P. (AV)

1100 New York Avenue, N.W., Suite 510 East, 20005-3934
Telephone: 202-783-1350
Telecopiers: 202-737-9117; 347-2644
Email: bgmstaff@brugen.com *URL:* http://www.brugen.com

George F. Bruder (Retired)
Carmen L. Gentile
Albert R. Simonds, Jr. (Retired)
J. Michel Marcoux
David E. Goroff
Gary E. Guy
James H. McGrew
Thomas L. Blackburn

Antonia A. Frost
David Martin Connelly
Gary D. Levenson
OF COUNSEL
Peter K. Matt

For full biographical listings, see the Martindale-Hubbell Law Directory

BRUNENKANT & HASKELL, LLP (AV)

805 15th Street, N.W., Suite 1101, 20005
Telephone: 202-408-0700
Fax: 202-408-5959
Email: brunenkant@bh-law.com

Jon L. Brunenkant
Mark R. Haskell
James W. Moeller
ASSOCIATES
Cheryl J. Walker
Melissa L. Lauderdale
Christie L. Richart (Not admitted in DC)

For full biographical listings, see the Martindale-Hubbell Law Directory

CAMERON MCKENNA LLP (AV)

2175 K Street, N.W. Fifth Floor, 20036
Telephone: 202-466-0060
Fax: 202-466-0077
Email: info@cammckenna.com *URL:* http://www.cmck.com
Associated offices in: Almaty, Brussels, Budapest, Hong Kong, London, Aberdeen, Bristol, Moscow, Prague, Toronto, Tashkent, Warsaw, Utrecht, Copenhagen, Stuttgart, Stockholm, Amsterdam, Hilversum, Arnhem, Dusseldorf, Berlin, Leipzig, Frankfurt, Chemnitz.
(Please refer to London entry for more details).

PARTNERS
Joel F. Zipp
George H. Williams, Jr.
Reinier H. J. H. Lock
Amy S. Koch
Michael S. Hindus (Resident, San Francisco, California Office)
Andrzej M. Blach (Resident, Warsaw Office)
COUNSEL
Robert C. Platt
SENIOR ASSOCIATE
Bridget Shahan

(See Next Column)

ASSOCIATES
Gunnar Birgisson
Phi H.D. Nguyen (Not admitted in DC)
Matthew E. Ross

For full biographical listings, see the Martindale-Hubbell Law Directory

TRAVIS & GOOCH (AV)

1101 15th Street, N.W. Suite 1010, 20005
Telephone: 202-721-1000
Fax: 202-721-1006
Email: T&G@travisandgooch.com *URL:* http://www.travisandgooch.com

MEMBERS OF FIRM
R. Gordon Gooch
Edmunds Travis, Jr. (Not admitted in DC)
ASSOCIATE
Judith M. Andrade
OF COUNSEL
John B. Merritt (Not admitted in DC)

For full biographical listings, see the Martindale-Hubbell Law Directory

FLORIDA

BOCA RATON, Palm Beach Co.

LAW OFFICES OF ARTHUR C. KOSKI, P.A. (AV)

568 Yamato Road, 33431
Telephone: 561-989-8800
Facsimile: 561-989-3775
Email: akoski@worldnet.att.net

Arthur C. Koski
Frank J. Badach

Thomas A. Stewart

For full biographical listings, see the Martindale-Hubbell Law Directory

*TALLAHASSEE,** Leon Co.

ROSE, SUNDSTROM & BENTLEY, LLP (AV)

2548 Blairstone Pines Drive, P.O. Box 1567, 32301-1567
Telephone: 850-877-6555
Telecopier: 850-656-4029
URL: http://www.rsbattorneys.com

MEMBERS OF FIRM
F. Marshall Deterding
Martin S. Friedman (P.A.)
John R. Jenkins (P.A.)
William E. Sundstrom (P.A.)
John L. Wharton

Representative Clients: Aloha Utilities, Inc.; AquaSource Utility, Inc.; East Central Florida Services, Inc.; North Fort Myers Utility, Inc.; Utility Board of the City of Key West; Utilities, Inc.

For full biographical listings, see the Martindale-Hubbell Law Directory

GEORGIA

*ATLANTA,** Fulton Co.

LONG ALDRIDGE & NORMAN LLP (AV)

A Limited Liability Partnership including Professional Corporations
Suite 5300, 303 Peachtree Street, 30308
Telephone: 404-527-4000
Telecopier: 404-527-4198
Email: atlanta@lanlaw.com *URL:* http://www.lanlaw.com
Washington, D.C. Office: Suite 600, 701 Pennsylvania Avenue, N.W., 20004.
Telephone: 202-624-1200.
FAX: 202-624-1298.

MEMBERS OF FIRM
Douglas L. Beresford (Resident, Washington, D.C. Office)
Michael S. Bradley
Charles E. Campbell
L. Craig Dowdy
Albert G. Norman, Jr.
Jacolyn A. Simmons (Resident, Washington, D.C. Office)
John T. Stough, Jr. (Resident, Washington, D.C. Office)
ASSOCIATES
George F. Hobday, Jr. (Resident, Washington, D.C. Office)
Thadd A. Prisco (Resident, Washington, D.C. Office)

For Complete List of Firm Personnel, See General Section

For full biographical listings, see the Martindale-Hubbell Law Directory

HAWAII

*HONOLULU,** Honolulu Co.

CARLSMITH BALL (AV)

A Partnership including Law Corporations
Suite 2200, Pacific Tower, 1001 Bishop Street, P.O. Box 656, 96809-3402
Telephone: 808-523-2500
Fax: 808-523-0842
Email: execdirector@carlsmith.com *URL:* http://www.carlsmith.com
Kapolei, Hawaii Office: Suite 318, Kapolei Building, 1001 Kamokila Boulevard, 96707.
Telephone: 808-523-2500.
Fax: 808-674-0850.
Wailuku, Maui Hawaii Office: Suite 400, One Main Plaza, 2200 Main Street, P.O. Box 1086, 96793-1086.
Telephone: 808-242-4535.
Fax: 808-244-4974.
Kailua-Kona, Hawaii Office: Suite 209, 75-1000 Henry Street, 96740.
Telephone: 808-329-6464.
Fax: 808-329-9450.
Hilo, Hawaii Office: 121 Waianuenue Avenue, P.O. Box 686, 96721-0686.
Telephone: 808-935-6644.
Fax: 808-935-7975.
Hagatna, Guam Office: Suite 401, Bank of Hawaii Building, 134 West Soledad Avenue, P.O. Box BF, 96932-5027.
Telephone: 671-472-6813.
Fax: 671-477-4375.
Telex: 721-6445 CWCMI GM.
Saipan, Commonwealth of the Northern Mariana Islands Office: Carlsmith Building, Capitol Hill, P.O. Box 5241, 96950-5241.
Telephone: 670-322-3455.
Fax: 670-322-3368.
Los Angeles, California Office: 9th Floor, 444 South Flower Street, 90071-2901.
Telephone: 213-955-1200.
Fax: 213-623-0032.
Washington, D.C. Office: Suite 300, 1201 Pennsylvania Avenue, N.W., 20004-2401.
Telephone: 202-628-2228.
Fax: 202-628-2071.
Mexico City, Mexico Office: Carlsmith Ball, Sierra Nevada 119, Lomas de Chapultepec, 11000 Mexico, D.F.
Telephone: 52-5-520-8514, 52-5-520-8757.
Fax: 52-5-540-1545.
Mexico, D.F. Office of Carlsmith Ball, S.C. (Authorized to practice as foreign legal consultants in Mexico): Sierra Nevada 119, Lomas de Chapultepec, 11000 Mexico, D.F.
Telephone: 52-5-520-8514, 52-5-520-8757.
Fax: 52-5-540-1545.

MEMBERS OF FIRM

Philip D. Isaac (Resident at Hagatna, Guam Office)
Ian L. Sandison
Robert E. Strand

ASSOCIATE

Brent K. Yamashita

For Complete List of Firm Personnel, See General Section

For full biographical listings, see the Martindale-Hubbell Law Directory

IDAHO

*POCATELLO,** Bannock Co.

MERRILL & MERRILL, CHARTERED (AV)

Key Bank Building, P.O. Box 991, 83204
Telephone: 208-232-2286
Fax: 208-232-2499
Email: mmlaw@ida.net

Stephen S. Dunn

Representative Client: Utah Power & Light Co. (PacifiCorp).

For Complete List of Firm Personnel, See General Section

For full biographical listings, see the Martindale-Hubbell Law Directory

ILLINOIS

*CHICAGO,** Cook Co.

DEFREES & FISKE (AV)

Suite 1100, 200 South Michigan Avenue, 60604
Telephone: 312-372-4000
Fax: 312-939-5617
Email: defrees@defrees.com

MEMBERS OF FIRM

Donald Defrees (1915-1968)
Kenneth M. Fiske (1928-1978)
Edward J. Griffin
Gregory E. Norwell
Timothy J. Riordan
Henry J. Underwood, Jr.
Kenneth A. von Kluck
Leslie Recht (Ms.)
Ronald W. Teeple
W. Michael Seidel
Miriam Leskovar Burkland
John L. Leonard
Charles A. Semmelhack
Michael J. Powers
Timothy S. Buckley
Phillip B. Bowman
L. Judson Todhunter

Robert J. Labate
Michael H. Erdman
Staci A. Burton

OF COUNSEL

John W. Hupp
Clement F. Springer, Jr.
William D. Carstedt
John W. Bowden
William P. Steinbrecher
J. William Cuncannan
Marvin S. Helfand

For full biographical listings, see the Martindale-Hubbell Law Directory

SAUNDERS & MONROE (AV)

1600 NBC Tower, 455 North Cityfront Plaza Drive, 60611
Telephone: 312-645-6000
Fax: 312-645-9848

MEMBERS OF FIRM

George L. Saunders, Jr.
Lee A. Monroe
Thomas F. Bush, Jr.
Matthew E. Van Tine
Thomas A. Doyle

OF COUNSEL

Victoria S. Kaplan

For full biographical listings, see the Martindale-Hubbell Law Directory

GRANITE CITY, Madison Co.

LUEDERS, ROBERTSON & KONZEN (AV)

1939 Delmar Avenue, 62040
Telephone: 618-876-8500
Telecopier: 618-876-4534
Email: lrk.il@worldnet.att.net
Danville, Illinois Office: 809 1/2 North Gilbert, 61832.
Telephone: 217-443-0304.
Fax: 217-443-0375.

MEMBERS OF FIRM

Wesley Lueders (1896-1957)
Randall Robertson
Leo H. Konzen
R. Eric Robertson
Edward C. Fitzhenry, Jr.
Brian E. Konzen
Paul G. Foran

ASSOCIATE

Anthony R. Garavalia

Representative Clients: Ameritech; Mercantile Bank (Trust Division); Granite City Steel Division of National Steel Corporation; Allied Waste Industries, Inc.; Illinois Industrial Energy Consumers (IIEC) including Olin Corporation; Archers-Daniels-Midland Company; General Motors Corporation.

For full biographical listings, see the Martindale-Hubbell Law Directory

MATTOON, Coles Co.

CRAIG & CRAIG (AV)

1807 Broadway, P.O. Box 689, 61938-0689
Telephone: 217-234-6481
Telecopier: 217-234-6486; 258-8292
Email: craiglaw@advant.com
Mount Vernon, Illinois Office: 115 North 7th Street.
Telephone: 618-244-7511.

MEMBERS OF FIRM

Craig Van Meter (1895-1981)
Fred H. Kelly (1894-1971)
Robert M. Werden (1908-1969)
George N. Gilkerson (1911-1985)
John P. Ewart
Richard F. Record, Jr.
Stephen L. Corn
Robert G. Grierson
Gregory C. Ray
Paul R. Lynch (Resident, Mount Vernon Office)
Kenneth F. Werts (Resident, Mount Vernon Office)
John L. Barger

(See Next Column)

CRAIG & CRAIG—*Continued*

ASSOCIATES

Kathleen M. Stockwell
Kristine M. Tuttle
Julie A. Webb (Resident, Mount Vernon Office)
John M. O'Driscoll
Duane A. Deters
Katy C. Fain (Resident, Mount Vernon Office)
Erin E. Wisner
John F. Watson

OF COUNSEL

Jack E. Horsley

Representative Clients: Freeman United Coal Mining Co.; Natural Gas Pipeline Company of America; Marathon Oil Company; Howell Paving, Inc.; Illinois Central R.R. Co.; Consolidated Communications Inc.; Lake Land College; Scattering Fork Drainage District of Douglas County, Illinois.

For full biographical listings, see the Martindale-Hubbell Law Directory

*PEORIA,** Peoria Co.

HOWARD & HOWARD ATTORNEYS, P.C. (AV)

The Creve Coeur Building, Suite 200, 321 Liberty Street, 61602-1403
Telephone: 309-672-1483
Telecopier: 309-672-1568
Kalamazoo, Michigan Office: The Michigan Building, Suite 200, 100 Portage Street.
Telephone: 616-382-1483.
Telecopier: 616-382-1568.
Bloomfield Hills, Michigan Office: The Pinehurst Office Center, Suite 101, 1400 North Woodward Avenue.
Telephone: 248-645-1483.
Telecopier: 248-645-1568.
Lansing, Michigan Office: Suite 500, The Phoenix Building, 222 Washington Square, North.
Telephone: 517-485-1483.
Telecopier: 517-485-1568.

Frederick G. Hoffman
Diana M. Jagiella

Representative Clients: For Representative Client list, see General Practice, Peoria, IL.

For Complete List of Firm Personnel, See General Section

For full biographical listings, see the Martindale-Hubbell Law Directory

INDIANA

*INDIANAPOLIS,** Marion Co.

BOSE MCKINNEY & EVANS LLP (AV)

2700 First Indiana Plaza, 135 North Pennsylvania Street, 46204
Telephone: 317-684-5000
Facsimile: 317-684-5173
URL: http://www.boselaw.com
Indianapolis North Office: Suite 1500, 8888 Keystone Crossing, 46240.
Telephone: 317-574-3700.
Facsimile: 317-574-3716.

MEMBERS OF FIRM

Robert K. Johnson
L. Parvin Price

ASSOCIATES

J. Christopher Janak
Jeffrey M. Reed

Representative Clients: MCI Worldcom; The Indiana Water and Wastewater Assn.; Johnson County REMC; Midwest Natural Gas Co.; Fall Creek Regional Waste District; Town of Schererville; Enron Corp.; COVAD Communications; ACI Corp.; Steel Dynamics.

For Complete List of Firm Personnel, See General Section

For full biographical listings, see the Martindale-Hubbell Law Directory

LEWIS & KAPPES, PROFESSIONAL CORPORATION (AV)

Suite 1700 One American Square, P.O. Box 82053, 46282-0003
Telephone: 317-639-1210
Telecopier: 317-639-4882
Email: Office@Lewis-Kappes.com *URL:* http://www.Lewis-Kappes.com

Ted B. Lewis (1919-1991)
Philip S. Kappes
David W. Gray
John F. Wickes, Jr.
Gary P. Price
Steven L. Tuchman
Thomas R. Ruge
M. Kent Newton
C. Duane O'Neal
Brett James Miller
Todd A. Richardson
Bette J. Dodd
Peter S. French

Brian Andrew Statz
John A. Broyles
Megan J. Kight
Christopher C. Earle
Jennifer Wheeler Terry
Stephanie Schankerman Forrest

(See Next Column)

OF COUNSEL

Samuel A. Fuller
Leslie Duvall
Lori Kyle Endris

For full biographical listings, see the Martindale-Hubbell Law Directory

IOWA

*DES MOINES,** Polk Co.

MICHAEL R. MAY (AV)

Suite 935, Two Ruan Center, 601 Locust Street, 50309
Telephone: 515-245-3757
Fax: 515-247-2210
Email: mikemay@netins.net

For full biographical listings, see the Martindale-Hubbell Law Directory

KENTUCKY

*PADUCAH,** McCracken Co.

DENTON & KEULER (AV)

Paducah Bank & Trust Company Building, 555 Jefferson Street, P.O. Box 929, 42001
Telephone: 502-443-8253
Fax: 502-442-6000
Email: dk@dklaw.com *URL:* http://www.dklaw.com

MEMBERS OF FIRM

W. David Denton
Lisa Hayden Emmons

Reference: The Paducah Bank & Trust Co.

For Complete List of Firm Personnel, See General Section

For full biographical listings, see the Martindale-Hubbell Law Directory

LOUISIANA

*BATON ROUGE,** East Baton Rouge Parish

KEAN, MILLER, HAWTHORNE, D'ARMOND, MCCOWAN & JARMAN, L.L.P. (AV)

22nd Floor, One American Place, 70825
Telephone: 225-387-0999
Fax: 225-388-9133
Mailing Address: P.O. Box 3513, Baton Rouge, Louisiana, 70821
URL: http://WWW.KMLAW.COM
New Orleans, Louisiana Office: Energy Centre, Suite 1560, 1100 Poydras Street, 70163.
Telephone: 504-585-3050.
Fax: 504-585-3051.
Plaquemine, Louisiana Office: Suite 10, 23425 Railroad Avenue, 70764.
Telephone: 225-687-9845.
Fax: 225-382-3445.
Lake Charles, Louisiana Office: One Lakeshore Drive, Suite 1220, 70629.
Telephone: 318-430-0350.
Fax: 318-436-5566.
Covington, Louisiana Office: 503 North New Hampshire Street, P.O. Box 3096, 70433.
Telephone: 504-875-0400.
Fax: 504-875-0500.

MEMBERS OF FIRM

G. William Jarman
Katherine W. King
J. Randy Young

Gordon D. Polozola

Representative Clients: Burlington Northern and Santa Fe Railroad Co., Fort Worth, TX; KMC Southeast Corp., Huntsville, AL; Louisiana Energy Users Group; MCI Worldcom, Washington, DC; Occidental Chemical Corp., Dallas, TX.

For full biographical listings, see the Martindale-Hubbell Law Directory

Baton Rouge—Continued

LONG LAW FIRM, L.L.P. (AV)

Suite 800 Two United Plaza, 8550 United Plaza Boulevard, 70809-7013
Telephone: 225-922-5110
Fax: 225-922-5105
Email: longlaw.com
Washington, D.C. Office: Market Square, Suite 750, 801 Pennsylvania Avenue, N.W., 20004-2167.
Telephone: 202-737-9212.
FAX: 202-624-0659.

MEMBERS OF FIRM

Russell B. Long
C. Kris Kirkpatrick
Michael A. Patterson
Joseph E. Juban
Albert Dale Clary
David L. Guerry
C. Stokes McConnell, Jr.

ASSOCIATES

Daniel D. Holliday, III
Jennifer J. Vosburg
Tracy Averett Morganti

OF COUNSEL

Melanie Peirron Patrick

For full biographical listings, see the Martindale-Hubbell Law Directory

*NEW ORLEANS,** Orleans Parish

MCGLINCHEY STAFFORD (AV)

A Professional Limited Liability Company
643 Magazine Street, 70130-3477
Telephone: 504-586-1200
Fax: 504-596-2800
TDD: (504) 596-2728
Telex: 584327
Cable Address: "MACSTAC"
Mailing Address: P.O. Box 60643, New Orleans, Louisiana, 70160-0643
Email: @mcglinchey.com *URL:* http://www.mcglinchey.com
Dallas, Texas Office: 2777 Stemmons Freeway, Suite 925, 75207-2401.
Telephone: 214-860-9700.
Fax: 214-860-9750.
Houston, Texas Office: 2727 Allen Parkway, Suite 1900, 77019.
Telephone: 713-520-1900.
Fax: 713-520-1025.
Baton Rouge, Louisiana Office: Ninth Floor, One American Place, 70825-0001.
Telephone: 504-383-9000.
Fax: 504-343-3076.
Jackson, Mississippi Office: Suite 1200, SkyTel Centre, 200 South Lamar Street, 39201.
Telephone: 601-960-8400.
Fax: 601-960-8406.
Lake Providence, Louisiana Office: 405 Morgan Street, 71254-2691.
Telephone: 318-559-1200.
Fax: 318-559-0609.
Monroe, Louisiana Office: Dean ONB Tower, 130 Desiard Street, Suite 807, 71201.
Telephone: 318-651-0807.
Fax: 318-651-0809.

MEMBERS OF FIRM

Constance Charles Willems
Craig Lewis Caesar

For full biographical listings, see the Martindale-Hubbell Law Directory

MILLING BENSON WOODWARD L.L.P. (AV)

A Partnership including Professional Law Corporations
Suite Twenty-Three Hundred, 909 Poydras Street, 70112-1017
Telephone: 504-569-7000
Telecopier: 504-569-7001
ABA net: 15656
MCI Mail: "Milling"
Email: milling@millinglaw.com
Lafayette, Louisiana Office: 101 La Rue France, Suite 200.
Telephone: 318-232-3929.
Telecopier: 318-233-4957.
Mandeville (North Shore), Louisiana Office: 2140 8th Street.
Telephone: 504-867-9622.
Telecopier: 504-867-8364.

MEMBER OF FIRM

David Conroy (P.C.)

MANDEVILLE (NORTH SHORE) OFFICE
RESIDENT MEMBER OF FIRM

McChord Carrico (P.C.)

See General Section for list of Representative Clients.

For Complete List of Firm Personnel, See General Section

For full biographical listings, see the Martindale-Hubbell Law Directory

*SHREVEPORT,** Caddo Parish

BARLOW AND HARDTNER L.C. (AV)

Tenth Floor, Louisiana Tower, 401 Edwards Street, 71101-3289
Telephone: 318-227-1131
Telecopier: 318-227-1141
Mailing Address: P.O. Box 8, Shreveport, Louisiana, 71161-0008

Malcolm S. Murchison
David R. Taggart
Michael B. Donald

Representative Clients: Central Louisiana Electric Co., Inc.; Central and South West Corporation; Louisiana Intrastate Gas Corp.; NorAm Energy Corp. (formerly Arkla, Inc.); Southwestern Electric Power Company; Public Service Co. of Oklahoma; Central Power and Light Co.; West Texas Utilities; Panhandle Eastern Corp.; Pennzoil Producing Co.

For Complete List of Firm Personnel, See General Section

For full biographical listings, see the Martindale-Hubbell Law Directory

WILKINSON, CARMODY & GILLIAM (AV)

1700 Beck Building, 400 Travis Street, P.O. Box 1707, 71166
Telephone: 318-221-4196
Telecopier: 318-221-3705
Email: wcg1895@aol.com

MEMBERS OF FIRM

John D. Wilkinson (1867-1929)
William Scott Wilkinson (1895-1985)
Arthur R. Carmody, Jr.
Bobby S. Gilliam
Mark E. Gilliam
William Allen Haynes

Representative Clients: Farmers Insurance Group; Home Federal Savings & Loan Association of Shreveport; The Kansas City Southern Railway Co.; KTAL-TV; Lincoln National Life Insurance Co.; Mobil Oil Co.; Schumpert Medical Center; Sears, Roebuck & Co.; Southern Pacific Transportation Co.; Southwestern Electric Power Co.

For full biographical listings, see the Martindale-Hubbell Law Directory

MAINE

*PORTLAND,** Cumberland Co.

PETRUCCELLI & MARTIN, LLP (AV)

50 Monument Square, P.O. Box 9733, 04104-5033
Telephone: 207-775-0200
Telecopier: 207-775-2360
Email: info@petruccellimartin.com *URL:* http://www.petruccellimartin.com

MEMBERS OF FIRM

Gerald F. Petruccelli
Joel C. Martin

Representative Clients: Bangor Hydro-Electric Co.; Maine Wireless, L.P.; Northeast Cellular Telephone Co., L.P.; Pine Tree Tel & Tel Co.

For full biographical listings, see the Martindale-Hubbell Law Directory

PIERCE ATWOOD (AV)

One Monument Square, 04101
Telephone: 207-791-1100
Fax: 207-791-1350
Email: info@PierceAtwood.com *URL:* http://www.pierceatwood.com
Augusta, Maine Office: 77 Winthrop Street.
Telephone: 207-622-6311.
Fax: 207-623-9367.
Newburyport, Massachusetts Office: 6 Harris Street.
Telephone: 978-465-9599.
Fax: 978-465-9945.

MEMBERS OF FIRM

Gerald M. Amero
Louise K. Thomas
John W. Gulliver
Kevin F. Gordon
David J. Champoux
Catherine R. Connors

OF COUNSEL

Vincent L. McKusick

ASSOCIATES

Deborah L. Shaw
William D. Hewitt
James H. Douglass

For Complete List of Firm Personnel, See General Section

For full biographical listings, see the Martindale-Hubbell Law Directory

Portland—Continued

PRETI, FLAHERTY, BELIVEAU, PACHIOS & HALEY, LLC (AV)

One City Center, P.O. Box 9546, 04112-9546
Telephone: 207-791-3000
Telecopier: 207-791-3111
Email: admin@preti.com *URL:* http://www.preti.com
Augusta, Maine Office: 45 Memorial Circle, P.O. Box 1058, 04332-1058.
Telephone: 207-623-5300.
Telefax: 207-623-2914.
Bath, Maine Office: Thirty Front Street, P.O. Box 665, 04530-0665.
Telephone: 207-443-5576.
Telefax: 207-443-6665.

MEMBERS OF FIRM

Severin M. Beliveau (Augusta Office)
Mark L. Haley (Bath Office)
Anthony W. Buxton (Augusta Office)
Joseph G. Donahue (Augusta Office)
Charles F. Dingman (Augusta Office)
Mark B. LeDuc (Augusta Office)

ASSOCIATE

Donald J. Sipe (Augusta Office)

Representative Clients: The Chinet Co.; Hannaford Brothers Co.; Holtra-Chem Manufacturing Co.; Industrial Energy Consumer Group (Energy Purchasers); International Paper; Fort James Corp.; Mid-Maine Telecom; National Semiconductor Corp.; Telephone Association of Maine; Tidewater Telcom, Inc.;

For Complete List of Firm Personnel, See General Section

For full biographical listings, see the Martindale-Hubbell Law Directory

MASSACHUSETTS

*BOSTON,** Suffolk Co.

HINCKLEY, ALLEN & SNYDER LLP (AV)

28 State Street, 30th Floor, 02109-1775
Telephone: 617-345-9000
Email: firm@haslaw.com *URL:* http://www.haslaw.com
Providence, Rhode Island Office: 1500 Fleet Center.
Telephone: 401-274-2000.
Fax: 401-277-9600. URL: http://www.hawlaw.com.

MEMBERS OF FIRM

Paula K. Andrews
David D. Barricelli (Not admitted in MA)
E. Jerome Batty (Not admitted in MA)
Jonathan Bell
Paul Bork
Stephen J. Carlotti (Not admitted in MA)
David Barry Connolly
Joseph P. Curran (Not admitted in MA)
Michael P. DeFanti
Eric F. Eisenberg
Malcolm Farmer, III
Margaret D. Farrell (Not admitted in MA)
Pasco Gasbarro Jr.
Hugh J. Gorman, III
Alan P. Gottlieb
William R. Grimm
Paul A. Hedstrom
Richard L. E. Jocelyn (Not admitted in MA)
Joel Lewin
Sandra Matrone Mack (Not admitted in MA)
Matthew T. Marcello, III (Not admitted in MA)
Frederick P. McClure
Elizabeth Murdock Myers
Paul F. O'Donnell, III
H. Peter Olsen (Not admitted in MA)
Julianne Palumbo
John J. Pendergast, III (Not admitted in MA)
Gerald J. Petros
James O. Reavis
Jeremy Ritzenberg
Ralph J. Rivkind
David J. Rubin
Charles E. Schaub, Jr.
Douglas F. Seaver
Herman Snyder
David R. Sullivan
Robert F. Sylvia
Howard E. Walker (Not admitted in MA)
Richard D. Wayne

ASSOCIATES

Jessica M. Bettencourt (Not admitted in MA)
Mark Bianchi
Alexandra K. Callam
Jane E. Cohen
Andrew D. Cummings
June E. Daniel (Not admitted in MA)
Kim Herman Goslant
Gloria Maria Gutierrez
Kelley Jordan-Price
Catherine S. Kim
Christopher W. Morog
Elena B. Olson
Joseph D. Whelan (Not admitted in MA)

OF COUNSEL

Willard Krasnow
Willard R. Pope
Bentley Tobin
Joachim A. Weissfeld (Not admitted in MA)

For Complete List of Firm Personnel, See General Section

For full biographical listings, see the Martindale-Hubbell Law Directory

PALMER & DODGE LLP (AV)

One Beacon Street, 02108
Telephone: 617-573-0100
Facsimile: 617-227-4420
URL: http://www.palmerdodge.com

MEMBERS OF FIRM

Jeffrey F. Jones
Stanley Keller
Kenneth W. Salinger

SENIOR COUNSEL

Jay E. Gruber

For Complete List of Firm Personnel, See General Section

For full biographical listings, see the Martindale-Hubbell Law Directory

MICHIGAN

OKEMOS, Ingham Co.

BUTZEL LONG, A PROFESSIONAL CORPORATION (AV)

Suite 300, 2127 University Park Drive, 48864-5928
Telephone: 517-372-6622
Telecopier: 517-372-6672
Email: melnick@butzel.com *URL:* http://www.butzel.com
Detroit, Michigan Office: Suite 900, 150 West Jefferson.
Telephone: 313-225-7000.
Telecopier: 313-225-7080.
Birmingham, Michigan Office: Suite 200, 32270 Telegraph Road.
Telephone: 810-258-1616.
Telecopier: 810-258-1439.
Ann Arbor, Michigan Office: Suite 300, 350 South Main Street.
Telephone: 313-995-3110.
Telecopier: 313-995-1777.
Grosse Pointe Farms, Michigan Office: Suite 260, 21 Kercheval.
Telephone: 313-886-5446.
Telecopier: 313-886-2114.
Boca Raton, Florida Office: Suite 411, 1200 North Federal Highway.
Telephone: 561-368-2151.
Telecopier: 561-368-4668.
Palm Beach Gardens, Florida Office: Suite 227, 11382 Prosperity Farms Road.
Telephone: 561-625-4442.
Telecopier: 561-625-6901.
Naples, Florida Office: Suite 705, 801 Laurel Oak Drive.
Telephone: 941-597-4500.
Telecopier: 941-597-5623.

James J. Urban

Michael F. Matheson

For full biographical listings, see the Martindale-Hubbell Law Directory

REAL ESTATE LAW

ALABAMA

*BIRMINGHAM,** Jefferson Co.

BERKOWITZ, LEFKOVITS, ISOM & KUSHNER, A PROFESSIONAL CORPORATION (AV)

SouthTrust Tower, 420 North Twentieth Street, Suite 1600, 35203-5202
Telephone: 205-328-0480
Telecopier: 205-322-8007
URL: http://www.blik.com

Arnold K. Lefkovits
Chervis Isom
Edward P. Meyerson
Denise W. Killebrew

Kirsten Hunt Kowalski
Adam Joshua Sigman

For Complete List of Firm Personnel, See General Section

For full biographical listings, see the Martindale-Hubbell Law Directory

BRADLEY ARANT ROSE & WHITE LLP (AV)

2001 Park Place, Suite 1400, P.O. Box 830709, 35283-0709
Telephone: 205-521-8000
Facsimile: 205-521-8800
Facsimile (SouthTrust Tower Office): 205-521-8500
URL: http://www.barw.com
Huntsville, Alabama Office: 200 Clinton Avenue West, Suite 900, 35801.
Telephone: 205-517-5100.
Facsimile: 205-533-5069.
Washington, D.C. Office: 801 Pennsylvania Avenue, NW, Suite 230, 20004.
Telephone: 202-347-8893.
Facsimile: 202-347-1684.

MEMBERS OF FIRM

Charles A. J. Beavers Jr.
Patrick H. Graves Jr. (Resident, Huntsville Office)
John E. Hagefstration Jr.
Stephen R. Monk
Bobby C. Underwood
Robert C. Walthall
Meade Whitaker, Jr.

OF COUNSEL

J. Robert Fleenor

Counsel for: SouthTrust Bank of Alabama, National Association; Energen Corporation; Blount, Inc.; Torchmark Corp.; Russell Corp.; Coca-Cola Bottling Company United, Inc.; Ford Motor Co.; Walter Industries, Inc.; The Birmingham Post Co. (Post-Herald); The New York Times Co.

For Complete List of Firm Personnel, See General Section

For full biographical listings, see the Martindale-Hubbell Law Directory

BURR & FORMAN LLP (AV)

3100 SouthTrust Tower, 420 North 20th Street, P.O. Box 830719, 35283-0719
Telephone: 205-251-3000
Facsimile: 205-458-5100
URL: http://www.burr.com
Huntsville, Alabama Office: Suite 204, Regency Center, 400 Meridian Street.
Telephone: 205-551-0010.
Facsimile: 205-551-0043.
Atlanta, Georgia Office: Suite 1200, One Georgia Center, 600 West Peachtree Street, 30308.
Telephone: 404-815-3000.
Facsimile: 404-817-3244.

MEMBERS OF FIRM

Jeffrey T. Baker
Eric L. Carlton
John F. DeBuys, Jr.
Deborah P. Fisher
W. Benjamin Johnson
Gail Livingston Mills
Dwight L. Mixson, Jr.
J. Fred Powell
Jack P. Stephenson, Jr.
Carol H. Stewart
Joseph G. Stewart

For Complete List of Firm Personnel, See General Section

For full biographical listings, see the Martindale-Hubbell Law Directory

CORLEY, MONCUS & WARD, P.C. (AV)

400 Shades Creek Parkway, Suite 100, P.O. Box 59807, 35259
Telephone: 205-879-5959
Telecopier: 205-871-4411

Claude McCain Moncus

For Complete List of Firm Personnel, See General Section

For full biographical listings, see the Martindale-Hubbell Law Directory

DOMINICK, FLETCHER, YEILDING, WOOD & LLOYD, P.A. (AV)

2121 Highland Avenue, 35209
Telephone: 205-939-0033
URL: http://members.aol.com/dfywandl/lawyer.htm

Frank Dominick
Walter Fletcher
Mary P. Thornton

Counsel for: Citizens Federal Savings Bank; St. Vincent's Hospital; Castle Mortgage Corporation; Thornton Construction Company, Inc.; Taylor Properties, L.L.C.

For Complete List of Firm Personnel, See General Section

For full biographical listings, see the Martindale-Hubbell Law Directory

GORDON, SILBERMAN, WIGGINS & CHILDS, P.C. (AV)

1400 SouthTrust Tower, 420 North 20th Street, 35203
Telephone: 205-328-0640
Facsimilie: 205-254-1500
Washington, D.C. Office: 1621 Connecticut Avenue, N.W., Suite 400.
Telephone: 202-238-0690.
Facsimile: 202-238-0968.

RESIDENT SHAREHOLDERS

Bruce L. Gordon
Robert F. Childs, Jr.
Ray D. Gibbons
Timothy D. Davis
Linda J. Peacock

For Complete List of Firm Personnel, See General Section

For full biographical listings, see the Martindale-Hubbell Law Directory

GORHAM & WALDREP, P.C. (AV)

2101 6th Avenue North, Suite 700, 35203
Telephone: 205-254-3216; 251-9166
Telecopier: 205-324-3802
Email: info@gorham-waldrep.com *URL:* http://www.gorham-waldrep.com
Montgomery, Alabama Office: 250 Commerce Street, P.O. Box 4837, 36103-4837.
Telephone: 334-262-0777.
Telecopier: 334-262-0742.

John T. Natter

Representative Clients: Jefferson County Personnel Board; Birmingham-Jefferson Civic Center Authority; The Water Works and Sewer Board of the City of Birmingham; City of Homewood; American Federation of Government Employees Local #1945; City of Pelham; Town of Kimberly; Alabama Tire Dealers Assn.; Southern States Body Shop Assn.

For Complete List of Firm Personnel, See General Section

For full biographical listings, see the Martindale-Hubbell Law Directory

JOHNSTON BARTON PROCTOR & POWELL LLP (AV)

2900 AmSouth/Harbert Plaza, 1901 Sixth Avenue North, 35203-2618
Telephone: 205-458-9400
Telecopier: 205-458-9500
Email: Law@JBPP.com

MEMBERS OF FIRM

Oscar M. Price III
Haskins W. Jones

COUNSEL

Richard J. Brockman

OF COUNSEL

Jerome K. Lanning

ASSOCIATES

Bradley C. Mayhew
Shannon L. Barnhill

General Counsel for: Baptist Health System, Inc..
Counsel for: The Chase Manhattan Bank; Goldome Credit Corp.; Health-Care Financial Partners REIT, Inc; Health Partners Southeast, Inc.; Jemison Investment Co.; SouthTrust Bank, National Assn.; SunBelt Golf Corp..

For full biographical listings, see the Martindale-Hubbell Law Directory

SPAIN & GILLON, L.L.C. (AV)

The Zinszer Building, 2117 2nd Avenue North, 35203
Telephone: 205-328-4100
Telecopier: 205-324-8866
Email: ddh@spain-gillon.com *URL:* http://lawlinks.com:80/atty/al/sggbn.html

MEMBERS OF FIRM

John P. McKleroy, Jr.
Samuel H. Frazier
Harold H. Goings
David S. Maxey

General Counsel for: Piggly Wiggly Alabama Distributing Co.
Counsel for: SouthTrust Mortgage Corp.; Molton, Allen & Williams Corporation; Chase Manhattan Mortgage Corp.; Compass Bank; Trans Financial Mortgage Co.; Koppers Industries; AmSouth Bank; SouthTrust Bank, N.A.; Liberty National Life Insurance Co.

(See Next Column)

SPAIN & GILLON L.L.C., *Birmingham—Continued*

For Complete List of Firm Personnel, See General Section

For full biographical listings, see the Martindale-Hubbell Law Directory

EUFAULA, Barbour Co.

WILLIAM V. NEVILLE, JR. (AV)
302 East Broad Street, P.O. Box 337, 36072-0337
Telephone: 334-687-5183
Fax: 334-687-6602
Email: anna@neville.com *URL:* http://www.lawyers.com/williamvneville

For full biographical listings, see the Martindale-Hubbell Law Directory

*HUNTSVILLE,** Madison Co.

BRADLEY ARANT ROSE & WHITE LLP (AV)
200 Clinton Avenue West, Suite 900, 35801
Telephone: 205-517-5100
Facsimile: 205-517-5200
URL: http://www.barw.com
Birmingham, Alabama Office: 2001 Park Place, Suite 1400, P.O. Box 830709.
Telephone: 205-521-8000.
Facsimile: 205-521-8800. Facsimile (SouthTrust Tower Office): 205-521-8500.
Washington, D.C. Office: 801 Pennsylvania Avenue, NW, Suite 230, 20004.
Telephone: 202-347-8893.
Facsimile: 202-347-1684.

RESIDENT PARTNERS

Patrick H Graves Jr. — Charles R. Smith Jr.

For Complete List of Firm Personnel, See General Section

For full biographical listings, see the Martindale-Hubbell Law Directory

BURR & FORMAN LLP (AV)
Suite 204, Regency Center, 400 Meridian Street, 35801
Telephone: 205-551-0010
Facsimile: 205-551-0043
Birmingham, Alabama Office: 3100 SouthTrust Tower, 420 North 20th Street.
Telephone: 205-251-3000.
Facsimile: 205-458-5100.
Atlanta, Georgia Office: Suite 1200, One Georgia Center, 600 West Peachtree Street, 30308.
Telephone: 404-815-3000.
Facsimile: 404-817-3244.

RESIDENT PARTNER

L. Tennent Lee, III

For full biographical listings, see the Martindale-Hubbell Law Directory

STEPHENS, MILLIRONS, HARRISON & GAMMONS, P.C. (AV)
333 Franklin Street, P.O. Box 307, 35801
Telephone: 256-533-7711
Telecopier: 256-536-9388

Arthur M. Stephens — James G. Harrison
Paul L. Millirons — Robert C. Gammons

Douglas A. Baymiller — Steven J. Shaw

Representative Clients: SouthTrust Bank, N.A.; Regions Mortgage, Inc.; Norwest Mortgage, Inc.; Chase Manhattan Mortgage Corp.; Commercial Federal Mortgage Corp.; SOUTHBank, A Federal Savings Bank.

For full biographical listings, see the Martindale-Hubbell Law Directory

*MOBILE,** Mobile Co.

JOHNSTONE, ADAMS, BAILEY, GORDON AND HARRIS, L.L.C. (AV)
Royal St. Francis Building, 104 St. Francis Street, 8th Floor, P.O. Box 1988, 36633
Telephone: 334-432-7682
Facsimile: 334-432-0712 or 334-432-2800
Email: attorneys@JohnstoneAdams.com *URL:* http://www.JohnstoneAdams.com
Bay Minette, Alabama Office: Dahlberg Building, 107 Hand Avenue, P.O. Box 729, 36507.
Telephone: 334-937-9473.
Facsimile: 334-937-9475.

MEMBERS OF FIRM

I. David Cherniak — Robert S. Frost

ASSOCIATE

Scott Alton Browning

For Complete List of Firm Personnel, See General Section

For full biographical listings, see the Martindale-Hubbell Law Directory

LYONS, PIPES & COOK, P.C. (AV)
2 North Royal Street, P.O. Box 2727, 36652-2727
Telephone: 334-432-4481
Cable Address: "Lysea"
Telecopier: 334-433-1820
URL: http://www.LPCLaw.com

Norton W. Brooker, Jr. — Thomas F. Garth
Marion A. Quina, Jr. — W. David Johnson, Jr.

Representative Clients: James Graham Brown Foundation; Browning-Ferris Industries of Alabama, Inc.; Champion International Corporation; Inchcape Shipping Services, Inc.; SouthTrust Bank of Mobile.

For Complete List of Firm Personnel, See General Section

For full biographical listings, see the Martindale-Hubbell Law Directory

PIERCE, LEDYARD, LATTA & WASDEN, P.C. (AV)
Colonial Bank Centre Suite 400, 41 North Beltline, 36608
Telephone: 334-344-5151
Facsimile: 334-344-9696
Mailing Address: P.O. Box 16046, Mobile, AL, 36616
URL: http://www.pllaw.com

Donald F. Pierce — H. William Wasden
Goodman G. Ledyard — W. Pemble DeLashmet

Mark Pickett Eiland

OF COUNSEL

Caroline Wells Hinds

Representative Clients: Associates Financial Services Company of Alabama, Inc.; The Prudential Home Mortgage Company, Inc.; The Mitchell Company; Colonial Bank; SouthTrust Bank of Alabama, NA; Magnolia Mortgage Company, Inc.; Regions Mortgage, Inc.; New South Federal Savings Bank; Cooper & Company, Inc.; Dauphin Realty of Mobile, Inc.

For full biographical listings, see the Martindale-Hubbell Law Directory

*MONTGOMERY,** Montgomery Co.

KAUFMAN & ROTHFEDER, P.C. (AV)
2740 Zelda Road, Drawer 4540, 36103-4540
Telephone: 334-244-1111
Fax: 334-244-1969
Email: firm@krlegal.com *URL:* http://www.krlegal.com

Samuel Kaufman — George W. Thomas
Richardson B. McKenzie III — William B. Sellers
David Bowen Hughes

Counsel For: Alfa Mutual Insurance Co.; Southern Boulevard Corporation; Aronov Realty Company, Inc.; David Kahn Co.; First American Title Insurance Co.; Lawyers Title Insurance Co.; Liz Claiborne, Inc.; Alfa Mutual Fire Insurance Company; Price Communications, Inc.

For full biographical listings, see the Martindale-Hubbell Law Directory

PARNELL & CRUM, P.A. (AV)
641 South Lawrence Street, P.O. Box 2189, 36102
Telephone: 334-832-4202
Telecopier: 334-832-4703
Fax: 334-293-3550
Email: cnparnell@aol.com

Charles N. Parnell, III — G. Barton Crum

Robert J. Russell, Jr. — Britt Batson Griggs
James McCauley Smith — Angie Hubbard Ingram

Reference: Colonial Bank of Montgomery.

For full biographical listings, see the Martindale-Hubbell Law Directory

TURNER, WILSON & SAWYER (AV)
428 South Lawrence Street, P.O. Box 98, 36104
Telephone: 334-262-2756
Fax: 334-262-2759
Email: turnerone@mindspring.com

MEMBERS OF FIRM

Wayne P. Turner — Terry P. Wilson
William P. Sawyer

LEGAL SUPPORT PERSONNEL

Dorothy Bennett (Paralegal) — Kelly Westbrook
Cara Morales (Paralegal)

For full biographical listings, see the Martindale-Hubbell Law Directory

VOLZ, PRESTWOOD & HANAN, P.C. (AV)
350 Adams Avenue, P.O. Box 1910, 36102-1910
Telephone: 334-264-6401
Fax: 334-834-4954

(See Next Column)

VOLZ, PRESTWOOD & HANAN P.C.—*Continued*

Charles H. Volz, Jr.
Alvin T. Prestwood
Charles H. Volz, III
Ellis D. Hanan
Richard D. Lively
Judy H. Barganier

For full biographical listings, see the Martindale-Hubbell Law Directory

WEBB & ELEY, P.C. (AV)

166 Commerce Street, Suite 300, P.O. Box 238, 36101-0238
Telephone: 334-262-1850
Fax: 334-262-1772
Email: webbeley1@mindspring.com

James W. Webb
Michael M. Eley
Kendrick E. Webb
Craig S. Dillard
Bart Harmon
William R. Chandler

Frank E. Bankston, Jr.
Pamela Robinson Higgins
Shawn Junkins Cole
Michael J. Cohan
Lisa D. Van Wagner

LEGAL SUPPORT PERSONNEL

Janice B. Miller (Business Manager)

Reference: Regions Bank.

For full biographical listings, see the Martindale-Hubbell Law Directory

ARIZONA

*FLAGSTAFF,** Coconino Co.

HUFFORD, HORSTMAN, MONGINI, PARNELL & McCARTHY, P.C. (AV)

323 North Leroux Street, P.O. Box B, 86002-0808
Telephone: 520-774-1453
Fax: 520-779-3621

C. Benson Hufford
Patrice M. Horstman
Michael E.J. Mongini
Eve A. Parnell
Philip (Jay) McCarthy, Jr.

E. Duane Weston

LEGAL SUPPORT PERSONNEL

R. Gehl Tucker (Legal Assistant)
Doris Utzinger (Legal Assistant)
Vickie Belman (Legal Assistant)
Jan Blackman (Paralegal)
Dawn L. Karsten (Paralegal)

Reference: Norwest Bank Arizona, N.A.

For full biographical listings, see the Martindale-Hubbell Law Directory

MANGUM, WALL, STOOPS & WARDEN, P.L.L.C. (AV)

100 North Elden, P.O. Box 10, 86002
Telephone: 520-779-6951
Fax: 520-773-1312

H. Karl Mangum (1908-1993)

OF COUNSEL

Douglas J. Wall
Robert W. Warden
Daniel J. Stoops

MEMBERS OF FIRM

A. Dean Pickett
Stephen K. Smith
Melinda L. Garrahan
Michael H. Hinson

ASSOCIATES

Annette Star Lustgarten
Rebecca Smith Currey
R. Scott Currey
Melinda K. Jacquez
Franklin Hoover

Representative Clients: Northern Arizona University; Flagstaff Unified School District; Museum of Northern Arizona; Arizona School Board Association.
Local Counsel for: Bank of America-Arizona; Arizona Public Service; U.S-.A.A.; State Farm Fire & Casualty Insurance Co.; Property Development Co.

For Complete List of Firm Personnel, See General Section

For full biographical listings, see the Martindale-Hubbell Law Directory

MESA, Maricopa Co.

JACKSON WHITE GARDNER WEECH & WALKER, P.C. (AV)

40 North Center Street, Suite 200, 85201
Telephone: 480-464-1111
Fax: 480-464-5692
Statewide: 800-243-1160
Email: firm@azmesalaw.com *URL:* http://www.azmesalaw.com
Payson, Arizona Office: 708 East Highway 260, Suite C1-E.
Telephone: 520-472-8878.

(See Next Column)

Wayne L. Gardner
Eric M. Jackson
Michael R. Pruitt
J. Grant Walker
Bradley D. Weech
Richard A. White
David L. Weed
Roger R. Foote
Otto S. Shill, III

Eric K. Macdonald
Kelly G. Black
Melody K. Seal
Patricia A. Mancabelli
Bobbie J. Rasmusson
Maureen P. Kane
James L. Tanner

For full biographical listings, see the Martindale-Hubbell Law Directory

ROBERTS & ROWLEY, LTD. (AV)

63 East Main Street, Suite 501, 85201-7423
Telephone: 480-833-1113
Fax: 480-833-1114
URL: http://www.azlegal.com

Richard Roberts
Paul S. Rowley

Brian D. Strong
Kevin J. Chapman
Jessica Carpenter
Sean M. Sabo

For full biographical listings, see the Martindale-Hubbell Law Directory

*PHOENIX,** Maricopa Co.

ANDERSON, BRODY, LEVINSON, WEISER & HORWITZ, P.A. (AV)

1112 West Camelback Road, 85013
Telephone: 602-234-0563
Fax: 602-234-2952
Email: pmw@andersonbrody.com *URL:* http://www.andersonbrody.com

Donald E. Anderson
Jeffrey H. Levinson
Paul M. Weiser
Jamie A. Brody
Ronald M. Horwitz
Bradley D. Gardner
Alan M. Levinsky
Janessa E. Shtabsky
Jan Grossman
David L. O'Daniel
Steven M. Fox
Gail I. Schwartzbard

For full biographical listings, see the Martindale-Hubbell Law Directory

ATKINSON, HAMILL & BARROWCLOUGH, P.C. (AV)

3550 North Central Avenue, Suite 1150, 85012
Telephone: 602-222-4828
Facsimile: 602-222-4820

Joseph M. Atkinson
Christopher G. Hamill
Patrick R. Barrowclough

Representative Clients: Biddulph Automotive Dealerships (Oldsmobile, Honda, Pontiac, GMC, Jeep/Eagle and RV); Del Webb Corp.; Federal Deposit Insurance Corp.; Fingerhut Cos.; First American Title Insurance Company of Arizona; John Jacobs' Golf Cos.; Motorola Inc.; PACCAR Financial Corp.; Sun Automotive Group (Scottsdale Acura, Jaguar, Range Rover, Lexus, Porsche, Audi and BMW); Sentinel Real Estate Fund.

For full biographical listings, see the Martindale-Hubbell Law Directory

BAIRD, WILLIAMS, DAVIS & SMITH (AV)

340 East Palm Lane Suite 150, 85004-4530
Telephone: 602-256-9400
Fax: 602-271-9308
Email: bwds@primenet.com *URL:* http://www.lawyers.com/bwds

MEMBERS OF FIRM

J. Ernest Baird
Daryl M. Williams

For full biographical listings, see the Martindale-Hubbell Law Directory

BEUS, GILBERT & DEVITT, P.L.L.C. (AV)

Suite 1000, Great American Tower, 3200 North Central Avenue, 85012-2417
Telephone: 602-274-8229
Fax: 602-234-5893

John V. Berry
Leo R. Beus
Laurie B. Craig
Michael R. Devitt
Nicholas J. DiCarlo
Paul E. Gilbert
Scott D. Larmore
Anthony H. Misseldine
Paul L. Mueller
Quinton F. Seamons (Not admitted in AZ)
Richard R. Thomas
Gordon M. Wasson

Jeffrey R. Adams
Diana Archer
Christopher A. Caserta
Craig D. Henley
Richard X. Herrera
J. Ridge Hicks
Christine N. Jones
Timothy G. Kasparek
Alan C. Kuffner
Malcolm Loeb
Michele L. Lorenzen
Daniel D. Maddy

(See Next Column)

BEUS, GILBERT & DEVITT P.L.L.C., *Phoenix—Continued*

Christopher E. Martin
Robert T. Mills
Jason Barclay Morris
Marc F. Pappalardo
Joseph B. Pierce
Wendy M. Rector

For full biographical listings, see the Martindale-Hubbell Law Directory

BONN, LUSCHER, PADDEN & WILKINS, CHARTERED (AV)

805 North Second Street, 85004
Telephone: 602-254-5557
Fax: 602-254-0656
Email: firm@blpw.com

Paul V. Bonn
Jeff C. Padden
Randall D. Wilkins

OF COUNSEL

Brian A. Luscher

For full biographical listings, see the Martindale-Hubbell Law Directory

BONNETT, FAIRBOURN, FRIEDMAN & BALINT, P.C. (AV)

4041 North Central Avenue Suite 1100, 85012
Telephone: 602-274-1100
Fax: 602-274-1199

Jerry C. Bonnett
Michael N. Widener
Tara L. Jackson
Scott A. Erickson
Guy A. Hanson

For full biographical listings, see the Martindale-Hubbell Law Directory

BRIER & IRISH, P.L.C. (AV)

4201 North 24th Street, Suite 300, 85016
Telephone: 602-522-3940
Fax: 602-955-6289
URL: http://www.lawyers.com/brierlaw

Robert N. Brier
Craig T. Irish

Representative Clients: The L & B Group; The RREEF Funds; Lend Lease Real Estate Investments; Jones Lang LaSalle Management Services; Prime Retail Group; Bedford Property Investors; First Industrial Realty Trust; Kitchell Development Company; Westcor Partners; Amerimar Enterprises.

For full biographical listings, see the Martindale-Hubbell Law Directory

BURCH & CRACCHIOLO, P.A. (AV)

702 East Osborn Road, Suite 200, 85014
Telephone: 602-274-7611
Fax: 602-234-0341
Mailing Address: P.O. Box 16882, Phoenix, AZ, 85011
Email: library@bcattorneys.com

Daniel Cracchiolo
Guadalupe Iniguez
Daryl Manhart
Edwin C. Bull
Andrew Abraham
Clare H. Abel
Ralph D. Harris
David M. Villadolid
Marvin Davis

Amy DeLaplace Howland
Jordan J. Rich

Representative Clients: Bashas' Inc.; Farmers Insurance Group; U-Haul International, Inc.

For Complete List of Firm Personnel, See General Section

For full biographical listings, see the Martindale-Hubbell Law Directory

CARMICHAEL & POWELL, PROFESSIONAL CORPORATION (AV)

7301 North 16th Street, Suite 103, 85020-5224
Telephone: 602-861-0777
Facsimile: 602-870-0296

Ronald W. Carmichael

Stephen Manes

Representative Clients: Home Builders Association of Central Arizona: Diamond Key Homes, Inc.; Medallion Homes.

For full biographical listings, see the Martindale-Hubbell Law Directory

COCHRAN & DAHL, P.C. (AV)

2999 North 44th Street, Suite 235, 85018
Telephone: 602-952-5300
Facsimile: 602-952-7010
Email: cochran@goodnet.com

Jerry L. Cochran
Larry J. Dahl

For full biographical listings, see the Martindale-Hubbell Law Directory

CRUSE, FIRETAG & BOCK, P.C. (AV)

5611 North 16th Street, 85016
Telephone: 602-279-9411
Facsimile: 602-241-1260
Email: cfbpc@cfbpc.com

Robert J. Cruse
Jules I. Firetag
Daniel A. Bock

John L. Stoss
Paul F. Dowdell

OF COUNSEL

Stephen T. Meadow (P.C.)

Reference: Norwest Bank, Arizona (Main Office).

For full biographical listings, see the Martindale-Hubbell Law Directory

DUSHOFF & MCCALL, A PROFESSIONAL CORPORATION (AV)

Two Renaissance Square, Suite 1000, 40 North Central, 85004
Telephone: 602-254-3800
Fax: 602-258-2551
URL: http://www.dushoff@neta.com

Jay Dushoff
Jack E. McCall (1942-1995)
Michael Riikola
Leonard M. Bell

Patrick J. McGill
Robert H. Kreutzer

LEGAL SUPPORT PERSONNEL

Thomas M. Flynn

For full biographical listings, see the Martindale-Hubbell Law Directory

FENNEMORE CRAIG, A PROFESSIONAL CORPORATION (AV)

3003 North Central Avenue, Suite 2600, 85012-2913
Telephone: 602-916-5000
Fax: 602-916-5999
Tucson, Arizona Office: One South Church Avenue, Suite 1000, 85701-1620.
Telephone: 520-879-6800.
Fax: 520-879-6899.

Robert P. Robinson
Ronald L. Ballard
Stephen M. Savage
William L. Kurtz
Mark A. Nesvig
George T. Cole
Charles M. King
Michael V. Mulchay
Don J. Miner
Margaret R. Gallogly
Jay S. Kramer
David E. Vieweg
John Randall Jefferies
M. Virginia Perry

John E. Kofron
Elizabeth M. Behnke
Jeffrey S. Pitcher
Stacey A. Kelly
Scott W. Hyder
John D. Bethea
Drew C. Flowers

LEGAL SUPPORT PERSONNEL

LEGAL ASSISTANTS

Joyce Herron
Donna M. Horwitz
Margaret Moore
Marie Morrell

For Complete List of Firm Personnel, See General Section

For full biographical listings, see the Martindale-Hubbell Law Directory

HIENTON FRY, P.C. (AV)

3636 North Central Avenue, Suite 520, 85012-1934
Telephone: 602-240-6400
Fax: 602-240-6401

Gary H. Fry
Joseph P. Hienton

Representative Clients: Arizona and California Railroad Company; Bank of Montreal; Bank of Scotland; Dillon Real Estate Co., Inc.; The Equitable Life Assurance Society of the United States; First Credit Bank; Fry's Food and Drug Stores; Imperial Bank; John Hancock Mutual Life Insurance Company; Smith's Food & Drug Centers, Inc.

For full biographical listings, see the Martindale-Hubbell Law Directory

HOLPER, WELSH & MITCHELL, LTD. (AV Ⓣ)

2415 East Camelback Road, Suite 700, 85016
Telephone: 602-508-6033
Fax: 480-483-0269
Email: rholper@aol.com *URL:* http://www.lawyers.com/holperwelsh&mitchell
Minneapolis, Minnesota Office: 4100 Multifoods Tower, 33 South Sixth Street, 55402.
Telephone: 612-317-1012.
Fax: 612-317-0947.

Richard D. Holper
Mary Ann Welsh

For full biographical listings, see the Martindale-Hubbell Law Directory

Phoenix—Continued

JENNINGS, STROUSS & SALMON, P.L.C. (AV)

A Professional Limited Liability Company
One Renaissance Square, Two North Central Avenue, 85004-2393
Telephone: 602-262-5911
Fax: 602-253-3255
Email: info@jsslaw.com *URL:* http://www.jsslaw.com
Arrowhead Office: 16150 North Arrowhead Fountains Center Drive, Suite 250, Peoria, Arizona.
Telephone: 623-878-2222.
Fax: 623-878-1333.

John R. Christian — Philip J. MacDonnell
Gary G. Keltner — Gerrit M. Steenblik
Lee E. Esch — Richard N. Morrison
Douglas G. Zimmerman — David Brnilovich
Robert J. Novak — George Esahak-Gage
R. Quinn De Angelis, Jr.

ASSOCIATES

Herbert T. Swafford — Scott Rhodes
Stephanie A. McRae — Carolyn D. Craft

For Complete List of Firm Personnel, See General Section

For full biographical listings, see the Martindale-Hubbell Law Directory

WILLIAM M. LAWSON, JR., P.A. (AV)

Suite 250 5141 North 40th Street, 85018-2100
Telephone: 602-957-8725
Facsimile: 602-957-8783
Email: blawson18@hotmail.com

William M. Lawson, Jr.

For full biographical listings, see the Martindale-Hubbell Law Directory

LEWIS AND ROCA, LLP (AV)

A Limited Liability Partnership including a Professional Corporation
40 North Central Avenue, 85004-4429
Telephone: 602-262-5311
Fax: 602-262-5747
Email: clientservice@lrlaw.com *URL:* http://www.lrlaw.com
Tucson, Arizona Office: One South Church Avenue, Suite 700, 86701-1620.
Telephone: 520-622-2090.
Fax: 520-622-3088. E-Mail: clientservice@lrlaw.com.
Las Vegas, Nevada Affiliated Office: Ashcraft and Heinz LLP, 3960 Howard Hughes Parkway, 89109.
Telephone: 702-990-3570.
Fax: 702-990-3571.

MEMBERS OF FIRM

Douglas R. Chandler — D. Randall Stokes
Kenneth Van Winkle, Jr. — Thel W. Casper
Glenn D. Forcucci — Anderson L. Carper

ASSOCIATE

Tracy M. Durchslag

OF COUNSEL

Lyman A. Manser

Representative Clients: Bank One, Arizona, NA; Gosnell Development Corp.; Phoenix Memorial Hospital; The Prudential Insurance Company of America; Scottsdale Memorial Hospitals; UDC Homes, Inc.

For Complete List of Firm Personnel, See General Section

For full biographical listings, see the Martindale-Hubbell Law Directory

LIEBERMAN, DODGE, SENDROW & GERDING, LTD. (AV)

Phoenix Corporate Center 18th Floor, 3003 North Central Avenue, 85012
Telephone: 602-277-3000
Fax: 602-277-7478
URL: http://www.azlawyers.com

Robert G. Anderson — Paul S. Gerding
David D. Dodge — Karen L. Kothe
David N. Farren — Marc R. Lieberman
Susan G. Sendrow

Paul S. Gerding, Jr.

SPECIAL COUNSEL

Michael J. Fuller — Connie J. Mableson
Lawrence J. Buckley

Representative Clients: Arizona Education Association; Public Safety Personnel Retirement System; Wells Fargo Bank and Credit Corp.; Regency Savings Bank; Baxter Healthcare Corporation; Aetna Life Insurance Company; Fairbanks Capital Corp.

For full biographical listings, see the Martindale-Hubbell Law Directory

MACLEAN & JACQUES, LTD. (AV)

Suite 202, 40 East Virginia, 85004
Telephone: 602-263-5771
FAX: 602-279-5569

John H. MacLean (1932-1992) — Raoul T. Jacques

Cary T. Inabinet — Macre S. Inabinet

LEGAL SUPPORT PERSONNEL

Sharon Petterson

For full biographical listings, see the Martindale-Hubbell Law Directory

MARISCAL, WEEKS, MCINTYRE & FRIEDLANDER, P.A. (AV)

2901 North Central Avenue Suite 200, 85012-2705
Telephone: 602-285-5000
Fax: 602-285-5100

Gary L. Birnbaum — Fred C. Fathe
Peter A. Winkler — Terry L. Tedesco

References: Northern Trust Bank of Arizona; National Bank of Arizona.

For Complete List of Firm Personnel, See General Section

For full biographical listings, see the Martindale-Hubbell Law Directory

MARTIN & ASSOCIATES, L.L.C. (AV)

Suite 2 N.W., 2715 North Third Street, 85004
Telephone: 602-230-0030
Telecopier: 602-604-0004
Email: dgmartin@primenet.com

Douglas G. Martin

OF COUNSEL

Richard H. Lee

For full biographical listings, see the Martindale-Hubbell Law Directory

MCCABE O'DONNELL, A PROFESSIONAL ASSOCIATION (AV)

3101 North Central Avenue Suite 700, P.O. Box 33457, 85012
Telephone: 602-264-0800
Facsimile: 602-274-0146
URL: http://www.lawyers.com/mccabephx.com

Joseph I. McCabe — Kathleen M. O'Donnell
Jerry W. Lawson

For full biographical listings, see the Martindale-Hubbell Law Directory

MITCHELL LAW OFFICES, A PROFESSIONAL CORPORATION (AV)

Anchor Centre One, Suite 122B, 2201 East Camelback Road, 85016
Telephone: 602-468-6450
Fax: 602-468-6451
Email: mitchell_atty@msn.com *URL:* http://www.mitchelllaw.com

Robert D. Mitchell

For full biographical listings, see the Martindale-Hubbell Law Directory

MURPHY & POSNER, L.L.P. (AV)

3200 East Camelback Road, Suite 300, 85018
Telephone: 602-224-5900
Telecopier: 602-224-5754
Email: lawfirm@murphy-posner.com *URL:* http://www.murphy-posner.com

Terry L. Rakow — K. Bellamy Brown
Don A. Davis — Earl E. Berg

ASSOCIATES

Don C. Fletcher — Samuel M. Woodruff
Brooke U. Walker

OF COUNSEL

John A. Murphy, Jr.

Representative Clients: The Westcor Companies; Westcor Partners; Amerimar Enterprises; New Mexico & Arizona Land Co.

For full biographical listings, see the Martindale-Hubbell Law Directory

MUTH, CASEBOLT, GERMAINE & DRIGGS, P.L.C. (AV)

Suite 3055, 11811 North Tatum Boulevard, 85028
Telephone: 602-953-5500
Facsimile: 602-953-5505

James R. Muth — Sanford J. Germaine
Victor S. Casebolt, II — Rebecca R. Driggs

Glenn S. McMinn

(See Next Column)

MUTH, CASEBOLT, GERMAINE & DRIGGS P.L.C., *Phoenix—Continued*

OF COUNSEL

David A. Craze

Representative Clients: The Boulders; The Westcor Cos.; The Pederson Group; Fry Investment Co.; D. Wong & Associates; The Ellman Companies; Arizona Partners; Arizona Holsum Credit Union; Chase Manhattan Bank; Loveland Industries, Inc.

For full biographical listings, see the Martindale-Hubbell Law Directory

MYERS & JENKINS, A PROFESSIONAL CORPORATION (AV)

Phoenix Corporate Center, 3003 North Central Avenue, Suite 1900, 85012
Telephone: 602-200-7900
Facsimile: 602-200-7910
Email: firm@mjlegal.com

Stephen W. Myers
William Scott Jenkins
Teresa Dawn Farrison

Gregory D. Honig

Reference: Wells Fargo Bank.

For full biographical listings, see the Martindale-Hubbell Law Directory

QUARLES & BRADY LLP (AV)

One Camelback Building, One East Camelback Road, Suite 400, 85012-1649
Telephone: 602-230-5500
Fax: 602-230-5598
URL: http://www.quarles.com
Milwaukee, Wisconsin Office: 411 East Wisconsin Avenue.
Telephone: 414-277-5000.
Fax: 414-271-3552.
Madison, Wisconsin Office: First Wisconsin Plaza, One South Pinckney Street, P.O. Box 2113.
Telephone: 608-251-5000.
Fax: 608-251-9166.
West Palm Beach, Florida Office: 222 Lakeview Avenue, 4th Floor.
Telephone: 407-653-5000.
Fax: 407-653-5333.
Naples, Florida Office: Barnett Center, 4501 Tamiami Trail North, Suite 300.
Telephone: 813-262-5959.
Fax: 813-434-4999.
Chicago, Illinois Office: Quarles & Brady LLC, Citicorp Center, 500 West Madison Street, Suite 3700.
Telephone: 312-715-5000.
Fax: 312-715-5155.

MEMBERS OF THE FIRM

Robert T. Bailes
David G. Beauchamp
Roger K. Spencer
Daniel L. Muchow
Peter A. Terry
Robert S. Bornhoft

For full biographical listings, see the Martindale-Hubbell Law Directory

ROBBINS & GREEN, A PROFESSIONAL ASSOCIATION (AV)

1800 Norwest Tower, 3300 North Central Avenue, 85012-2578
Telephone: 602-248-7600
Fax: 602-266-5369
Email: @RGLaw.com

Wayne A. Smith
Jeffrey P. Boshes
Edmund F. Richardson
Janet B. Hutchison
Jack N. Rudel
Alfred W. Ricciardi

For full biographical listings, see the Martindale-Hubbell Law Directory

SHIMMEL, HILL, BISHOP & GRUENDER, P.C. (AV)

3700 North 24th Street, 85016
Telephone: 602-224-9500
Telecopier: 602-955-6176
URL: http://www.shimmelhill.com

Joseph Wm. Kruchek
Margaret L. Steiner
S. Gregory Jones

Jennifer S. Lee

Representative Clients: Christiania Bank og Kreditkasse; Connecticut Del Mar Mortgage, Inc.; Farmers Insurance Group; First Bank and Trust fka Lacumbre Savings Bank; Harkins Amusement Enterprises, Inc.; Magellan Corporation; Mutual Trust Life Insurance Co.; Phoenix Newspapers, Inc.; Promus Hotels, Inc.; Regency Savings Bank.

For full biographical listings, see the Martindale-Hubbell Law Directory

FRANCIS J. SLAVIN, P.C. (AV)

Suite 285, 2198 East Camelback Road, 85016
Telephone: 602-381-8700
Fax: 602-381-1920
Email: fjspc@worldnet.att.net *URL:* http://www.banet.com/fjspc/law.htm

Francis J. Slavin

Joseph John Moritz, Jr.
Chad H. Kolodisner

Representative Clients: Northern Trust Bank of Arizona; The Newhall Land and Farming Company; Windsor Capital Corp.; PK Development, L.L.C.; Southwest Retirement Corp.

For full biographical listings, see the Martindale-Hubbell Law Directory

SNELL & WILMER L.L.P. (AV)

One Arizona Center, 85004-2202
Telephone: 602-382-6000
Fax: 602-382-6070
Email: postmaster@snellwilmer.com *URL:* http://www.swlaw.com
Tucson, Arizona Office: One South Church Avenue, Suite 1500, 85701-1612.
Telephone: 520-882-1200.
Fax: 520-884-1294.
Orange County Office: 1920 Main Street, Suite 1200, Irvine, California 92614-7230.
Telephone: 949-253-2700.
Fax: 949-955-2507.
Salt Lake City, Utah Office: 111 East Broadway, Suite 900, 84111-1004.
Telephone: 801-237-1900.
Fax: 801-237-1950.

MEMBERS OF FIRM

Richard K. Mallery
Robert C. Bates
Jay D. Wiley
Joyce Kline Wright
Craig K. Williams
Jody Kathleen Pokorski
Nicholas J. Wood

ASSOCIATES

David J. Carroll
Sharon L. Fabian
Elizabeth A. Fox
Todd Cannon Lockwood
Mark D. Ohre
Howard J. Powers, II
Todd J. Weiss

Representative Clients: For list of Representative Clients, see end of biographical listings in the Martindale-Hubbell Law Directory.

For Complete List of Firm Personnel, See General Section

For full biographical listings, see the Martindale-Hubbell Law Directory

STOREY & PIERONI, PLC (AV)

3030 East Camelback Road, Suite 265, 85016
Telephone: 602-468-0111
Fax: 602-468-1335
Email: kmiller@splegal.com

Rebecca Burnham Pieroni
Robert D. Anderson
Lesa J. Storey
William J. Gelm

For full biographical listings, see the Martindale-Hubbell Law Directory

WARNER ANGLE ROPER & HALLAM PLC (AV)

3550 North Central Avenue, Suite 1500, 85012
Telephone: 602-264-7101
Fax: 602-234-0419

Ted F. Warner
Stephen E. Jackson
Edward (Ted) L. Roper
Dean J. Formanek
Peter D. Ambelang
Kathryn Graham

Representative Clients: Butte Properties; Centennial Homes; Douglas Allred Company; American Bantrust Mortgage Services Corp.; Chicago Title Insurance Company, Inc.; Metropolitan Mortgage.

For full biographical listings, see the Martindale-Hubbell Law Directory

PAUL V. WENTWORTH (AV)

2901 North Central Avenue, Suite 200, 85012-2705
Telephone: 602-285-5096
Fax: 602-285-5099

For full biographical listings, see the Martindale-Hubbell Law Directory

WILENCHIK & BARTNESS, A PROFESSIONAL CORPORATION (AV)

The Wilenchik & Bartness Building, 2810 North Third Street, 85004
Telephone: 602-606-2810
Facsimile: 602-606-2811
Email: diw@wb-law.com *URL:* http://www.wb-law.com/wb-law

Dennis I. Wilenchik
George H. Foster, Jr.
Becky Ann Bartness
Adam P. Weber

(See Next Column)

WILENCHIK & BARTNESS A PROFESSIONAL CORPORATION—*Continued*

Matthew H. Sloan
Aryeh David Schwartz
Wade J. Skalsky

Representative Clients: Richmond American Homes; Saddleback Homes; C.B. Richard Ellis; Blanford Homes; Monterey Homes; Chicago Title; Chase Bank; Columbia Communities; The State of Arizona; Southwest Risk Management.

For full biographical listings, see the Martindale-Hubbell Law Directory

WITHEY & TOBIN, P.L.C. (AV)

3101 North Central Avenue, Suite 1690, 85012-2615
Telephone: 602-230-0600
Fax: 602-212-1787

Michael B. Withey
Shawn E. Tobin
Ellen Harris Hoff

For full biographical listings, see the Martindale-Hubbell Law Directory

ZEITLIN & ZEITLIN, P.C. (AV)

A Partnership including a Professional Corporation
3200 East Camelback, Suite 300, 85018-2398
Telephone: 602-648-5222
Fax: 602-648-5226
Email: zeitlin@primenet.com
Annapolis, Maryland Office: 2007 Tidewater Colony Drive, Suite 2B, 21401-8686.
Telephone: 410-266-9500.
Facsimile: 410-266-9522.
San Diego, California Office: Strauss, Asher & Zeitlin, 150 "B" Street, Suite 1950, 92101.
Telephone: 619-237-5307.
Facsimile: 619-237-5311.

Dale S. Zeitlin
Dawn Stoll Zeitlin (P.C.)

OF COUNSEL

James M. Balogh

For full biographical listings, see the Martindale-Hubbell Law Directory

*PRESCOTT,** Yavapai Co.

FAVOUR, MOORE & WILHELMSEN, A PROFESSIONAL ASSOCIATION (AV)

1580 Plaza West Drive, P.O. Box 1391, 86302
Telephone: 520-445-2444
Fax: 520-771-0450
Email: fmw@primenet.com

John M. Favour
Mark M. Moore
David K. Wilhelmsen

Representative Clients: Yavapai Title Co.; Hidden Valley Ranch; Glenn Straub Appraisers, Inc.; Lawyers Title Insurance Co.; Bullwacker Associates; The Ranch at Prescott Homeowner's Assn.; Sedona Brokers Ginny Hays Realty, Inc.; Village of Oak Creek Assn.

For Complete List of Firm Personnel, See General Section

For full biographical listings, see the Martindale-Hubbell Law Directory

SCOTTSDALE, Maricopa Co.

BENNETT, CARMICHAEL & KENNEDY, L.L.P. (AV)

6991 East Camelback Road, Suite B-111, 85251
Telephone: 602-990-1133; 602-947-8303
Fax: 602-945-2149

MEMBERS OF FIRM

William F. Bennett
David H. Carmichael
Robert T. Kennedy

For full biographical listings, see the Martindale-Hubbell Law Directory

CAMPANA, VIEH, SHORE, OWENS & LOEB (AV)

4422 North Civic Center Plaza, Suite 101, 85251
Telephone: 480-707-5000
Fax: 480-707-5005

Richard V. Campana
James E. Vieh
William F. Shore, III
Bernard C. Owens
Donald O. Loeb

LEGAL SUPPORT PERSONNEL

Lois V. Johnson (Legal Assistant)

For full biographical listings, see the Martindale-Hubbell Law Directory

PESKIND HYMSON & GOLDSTEIN, P.C. (AV)

14595 North Scottsdale Road, Suite 14, 85254
Telephone: 602-991-9077
Fax: 602-443-8854
URL: http://www.legalcounselors.com

E. J. Peskind
Irving Hymson
Marilee Miller Clarke

For full biographical listings, see the Martindale-Hubbell Law Directory

SACKS TIERNEY P.A. (AV)

4250 North Civic Center Boulevard, 85251
Telephone: 480-425-2600
Facsimile: 480-970-4610
Email: ST@sackstierney.com
Phoenix, Arizona Office: Two North Central Avenue, Suite 1960. 85004.
Telephone: 480-435-2600.
Fax: 480-970-4610.

Seymour Sacks
Marvin S. Cohen
David C. Tierney
Stephen Aron Benson
Michael R. Rooney
Robert G. Kimball
Stephen P. Linzer
Marcia J. Busching
Randall S. Yavitz
Sharon Brook Shively
James W. Armstrong
Steven M. Goldstein
Judith M. Dworkin
Robert J. Lord
Sharon S. Moyer
Candess J. Hunter
Lori R. Miller
Brian E. Ditsch

Sharyl Poulson Speaker
Steven W. Bienstock
Andrew Lane de Mars
Scott B. Cohen
Mark D. Dillon
John L. Habib
W. Kevin Bell
Isabel M. Humphrey
Julie A. Inderlied
Laura G. Meyer
Stephen A. Wolf

Reference: M&I Thunderbird Bank.

For full biographical listings, see the Martindale-Hubbell Law Directory

SPARKS, TEHAN & RYLEY, P.C. (AV)

7503 First Street, 85251-4573
Telephone: 480-949-1339
Fax: 480-949-7587

Joe P. Sparks
Kevin T. Tehan
John H. Ryley

LEGAL SUPPORT PERSONNEL

Pamela L. Sparks
Joshua Morgan Sparks
Catherine L. McComb

References: Bank One, Arizona, Trust Department; Northern Trust Bank of Arizona, N.A.; Wells Fargo Bank of Arizona.

For full biographical listings, see the Martindale-Hubbell Law Directory

TITUS, BRUECKNER & BERRY, P.C. (AV)

Scottsdale Centre Suite B-252, 7373 North Scottsdale Road, 85253-3527
Telephone: 602-483-9600
Fax: 602-483-3215
Email: TBandB@aol.com

Jon A. Titus
Kurt M. Brueckner
Charles R. Berry
Garry S. O'Rafferty
David R. Jordan

Marc D. Blonstein
Todd Michael Johnson
Matthew B. Levine
Christopher D. Lonn
Robin C. Martindale

OF COUNSEL

John R. Tellier
Timothy G. Burns

LEGAL SUPPORT PERSONNEL

Kellie E. Dicarlo
Belle Taylor

Representative Clients: Arizona Department of Insurance, Receivership Division; Beazer Homes; Cigna; Equipment Leasing Corp.; Hancock Communities; Harvard Investments; Heritage West Securities; Joseph Charles & Associates, Inc.; Peacock, Hislop, Staley Given, Inc.; Woodside Homes.

For full biographical listings, see the Martindale-Hubbell Law Directory

*TUCSON,** Pima Co.

CHANDLER, TULLAR, UDALL & REDHAIR, L.L.P. (AV)

1700 Bank of America Plaza, 33 North Stone Avenue, 85701-1415
Telephone: 520-623-4353
Telefax: 520-792-3426

MEMBERS OF FIRM

Steven Weatherspoon
Dwight M. Whitley, Jr.
E. Hardy Smith
John J. Brady

(See Next Column)

CHANDLER, TULLAR, UDALL & REDHAIR L.L.P., *Tucson—Continued*

ASSOCIATE

Elizabeth D. Bushell

Representative Clients: Arizona Electric Cooperative Power, Inc.; Atlantic Richfield Co.; Northwestern Mutual Life Insurance; Preferred Risk Life Insurance Co.; Citizen Auto Stage; Starpass Properties.

For Complete List of Firm Personnel, See General Section
For full biographical listings, see the Martindale-Hubbell Law Directory

LEONARD FELKER ALTFELD GREENBERG & BATTAILE, P.C. (AV)

250 North Meyer Avenue, P.O. Box 191, 85702-0191
Telephone: 520-622-7733
Fax: 520-622-7967

David J. Leonard
Sidney L. Felker
Jeffrey H. Greenberg
John F. Battaile III
Clifford B. Altfeld
Donna M. Aversa
R. David Sobel
Russell E. Krone
Peter B. Goldman

OF COUNSEL

Anne-Marie Brady

For full biographical listings, see the Martindale-Hubbell Law Directory

LEWIS AND ROCA, LLP (AV)

A Limited Liability Partnership including a Professional Corporation
One South Church Avenue Suite 700, 85701-1620
Telephone: 520-622-2090
Fax: 520-622-3088
Email: clientservice@lrlaw.com *URL:* http://www.lrlaw.com
Phoenix, Arizona Office: 40 North Central Avenue, 85004-4429.
Telephone: 602-262-5311.
Fax: 602-262-5747. E-Mail: clientservice@lrlaw.com.
Las Vegas, Nevada Affiliated Office: Ashcraft and Heinz LLP, 3960 Howard Hughes Parkway, 89109.
Telephone: 702-990-3570.
Fax: 702-990-3571.

RESIDENT MEMBERS

S. L. Schorr
Frank S. Bangs, Jr.
Andrew Daru Schorr
Lewis D. Schorr

Representative Clients: Advantage Health Network, Inc.; A.F. Sterling Builders; Arizona Bank; Capin Mercantile Corporation; Citibank (Arizona); Perini Land & Development Company; City of Scottsdale; Scotia Group Limited; Vistoso Partners.

For full biographical listings, see the Martindale-Hubbell Law Directory

MUNGER CHADWICK, P.L.C. (AV)

333 North Wilmot, Suite 300, 85711
Telephone: 520-721-1900
Fax: 520-747-1550
Email: m-c@mungerchadwick.com *URL:* http://www.mungerchadwick.com
Phoenix Appointment Office: 5225 N. Central, Suite 235, 85012-1452.
Telephone: 602-230-1850.

John F. Munger

Representative Clients: Tuscon Realty and Trust; Whetstone Homes; New Southwest Development Corp.; Coyote Creek Development; Jones Intercable; Tuscon Greyhound Park; Pinnacle Mortgage; The Nature Conservancy; Grapevine Canyon Ranch.

For full biographical listings, see the Martindale-Hubbell Law Directory

DANIEL H. O'CONNELL, P.C. (AV)

3573 East Sunrise Drive, Suite 120, 85718-3206
Telephone: 520-615-9802
Telefax: 520-615-9789
Email: ben@dhopc.psemail.com *URL:* http://www.lawyers.com/danieloconnell-law

Daniel H. O'Connell

Benjamin J. Burnside

OF COUNSEL

Rosanne F. Lapan

Representative Clients: Empire West Cos.; Thermal Engineering, Inc.; Alban Medical Associates; Industrial Motor & Control, Inc.; Allergy Asthma Associates, P.C.
Reference: Bank of America.

For full biographical listings, see the Martindale-Hubbell Law Directory

SNELL & WILMER L.L.P. (AV)

One South Church Avenue, Suite 1500, 85701-1612
Telephone: 520-882-1200
Fax: 520-884-1294
URL: http://www.swlaw.com
Phoenix, Arizona Office: One Arizona Center, 85004-2202.
Telephone: 602-382-6000.
Fax: 602-382-6070.
Orange County Office: 1920 Main Street, Suite 1200, Irvine, California 92614-7230.
Telephone: 949-253-2700.
Fax: 949-955-2507.
Salt Lake City, Utah Office: 111 East Broadway, Suite 900, 84111-1004.
Telephone: 801-237-1900.
Fax: 801-237-1950.

MEMBERS OF FIRM

Michael S. Milroy
Marc G. Simon
Curt D. Reimann

ASSOCIATES

Mathias G. Bildhauer
Regina L. Nassen
Jill Casson Owen
Kathryn B. Nelson
M. Roxanne Veliz

Representative Clients: For list of Representative Clients, see end of biographical listings in the Martindale-Hubbell Law Directory.

For full biographical listings, see the Martindale-Hubbell Law Directory

*YUMA,** Yuma Co.

BYRNE, BENESCH & WALSMA, P.C. (AV)

230 West Morrison Street, P.O. Box 6446, 85364
Telephone: 520-782-1805
Fax: 520-782-1808
Email: benesch1@primenet.com

Peter C. Byrne (1916-1994)
Wayne C. Benesch
Pamela Walsma
Arturo I. Villarreal
Harry W. Longbottom

For full biographical listings, see the Martindale-Hubbell Law Directory

ARKANSAS

*FORT SMITH,** Sebastian Co.

GEAN, GEAN & GEAN (AV)

511 Garrison Avenue, 72901
Telephone: 501-783-1124
Fax: 501-783-2440

Roy Gean, Sr. (1894-1969)
Roy R. Gean, Jr.
Paul B. Gean
Roy R. Gean, III

ASSOCIATES

David C. Gean
Ellen Gean Pierce

Representative Clients: Federal Savings Bank of Rogers, Arkansas; First City Finance Corp.; First National Bank, Oklahoma; Commercial Credit Plan, Inc.; Associates, Financial Services Company of Oklahoma, Inc.; K & C Properties Real Estate Developers; Cyanede Plastics.

For full biographical listings, see the Martindale-Hubbell Law Directory

*LITTLE ROCK,** Pulaski Co.

WILLIAM L. OWEN (AV)

917 West Markham Street, P.O. Box 989, 72203
Telephone: 501-372-1655
Fax: 501-372-7884
Email: wlowen@aristotle.net *URL:* http://www.lawyers.com/wlowen_law

For full biographical listings, see the Martindale-Hubbell Law Directory

ROSE LAW FIRM, A PROFESSIONAL ASSOCIATION (AV)

120 East Fourth Street, 72201
Telephone: 501-375-9131
Telecopy: 501-375-1309

George E. Campbell
Herbert C. Rule, III
Garland J. Garrett
Kevin R. Burns
John T. Hardin
Stephen N. Joiner
Brian Rosenthal

Representative Clients: ALLTEL Corporation; The Equitable Life Assurance Society of the United States; John Hancock Mutual Life Insurance Co.; Massachusetts Mutual Life Assurance Co.; Mercantile Bank of Central Arkansas; NationsBank of Arkansas, N.A.; Panhandle Eastern Corp.; Tramell Crow Companies; Tyson Foods, Inc.

(See Next Column)

ROSE LAW FIRM A PROFESSIONAL ASSOCIATION—*Continued*

For Complete List of Firm Personnel, See General Section

For full biographical listings, see the Martindale-Hubbell Law Directory

*NEWPORT,** Jackson Co.

TIMOTHY F. WATSON, SR. (AV)

209 Walnut Street, P.O. Box 988, 72112
Telephone: 870-523-8420
Fax: 870-523-4639
Email: timow1@swbell.net

For full biographical listings, see the Martindale-Hubbell Law Directory

CALIFORNIA

*BAKERSFIELD,** Kern Co.

BORTON, PETRINI & CONRON, LLP (AV)

The Borton, Petrini & Conron Building, 1600 Truxtun Avenue, 93301
Telephone: 661-322-3051
Voice Mail: 661-395-6700
Fax: 661-322-4628
Mailing Address: P.O. Box 2026, Bakersfield, California, 93303
Email: bpcbak@bpclaw.com *URL:* http://www.bpclaw.com
Other City Locations: Fresno, Los Angeles, Modesto, Redding, Sacramento, San Bernardino, San Diego, San Francisco, San Jose, San Luis Obispo, Santa Ana and Ventura.

MEMBERS OF FIRM

George F. Martin
Stephen M. Dake

ASSOCIATES

William G. Welzenbach
Raymond G. Robinson
Stephen M. Crane
Dee H. Stasnopolis
Michael S. Abril

For Complete List of Firm Personnel, See General Section

For full biographical listings, see the Martindale-Hubbell Law Directory

KLEIN, DENATALE, GOLDNER, COOPER, ROSENLIEB & KIMBALL, LLP (AV)

(Formerly Di Giorgio, Davis, Klein, Wegis, Duggan & Friedman)
ARCO Tower, 4550 California Avenue, Second Floor, 93309
Telephone: 661-395-1000
Telecopier: 661-326-0418
Mailing Address: P.O. Box 11172, Bakersfield, California, 93389-1172
Email: kleinlaw@kleinlaw.com

Anthony J. Klein (Inc.)
Barry L. Goldner
Thomas V. DeNatale, Jr.
David J. Cooper
Claude P. Kimball

Representative Clients: World Title Company; Transamerica Title Insurance Company; The Prudential America West.

For Complete List of Firm Personnel, See General Section

For full biographical listings, see the Martindale-Hubbell Law Directory

BEVERLY HILLS, Los Angeles Co.

EARLE GARY GOODMAN (AV)

415 North Camden Drive, First Floor, 90210
Telephone: 310-470-9033
Fax: 310-457-2649
Mailing Address: 23852 Pacific Coast Highway, Suite 903, Malibu, California, 90265
Email: EGGoodman@email.msn.com

Reference: Bank of America, Westwood Village Office.

For full biographical listings, see the Martindale-Hubbell Law Directory

HOCHMAN, SALKIN, RETTIG, TOSCHER & PEREZ, A PROFESSIONAL CORPORATION (AV)

9150 Wilshire Boulevard Suite 300, 90212-3414
Telephone: 310-281-3200; 273-1181
Fax: 310-859-1430
URL: http://www.taxlitigator.com

Bruce I. Hochman
Charles P. Rettig
Avram Salkin
Dennis Perez
Steven R. Toscher

OF COUNSEL

George DeRoy
Nathan Joseph Hochman

(See Next Column)

Stuart A. Simon
Steven D. Blanc
Michel R. Stein

Reference: Union Bank of California.

For full biographical listings, see the Martindale-Hubbell Law Directory

SCHWARTZ, WISOT & WILSON, LLP (AV)

315 South Beverly Drive, Suite 315, 90212
Telephone: 310-277-2323
Fax: 310-556-2308
Email: swwllp@aol.com *URL:* http://www.lawyers.com/swwllp

Bruce Edward Schwartz
Valerie Wisot
John D. Wilson

Kathleen A. Calaway-McLean

OF COUNSEL

Paula Reddish Zinnemann

Reference: City National Bank, Beverly Hills, California.

For full biographical listings, see the Martindale-Hubbell Law Directory

TURNER, AUBERT & FRIEDMAN, LLP (AV)

Formerly Turner, Gerstenfeld, Wilk & Tigerman
Suite 510, 8383 Wilshire Boulevard, 90211
Telephone: 323-653-3900
Facsimile: 323-653-3021

MEMBERS OF FIRM

Rubin M. Turner
Edward Friedman
Ronald D. Aubert
Michael J. Hanna

ASSOCIATES

Dortha Larene Pyles
Diane H. Pappas

OF COUNSEL

Yelena Yeruhim

For Complete List of Firm Personnel, See General Section

For full biographical listings, see the Martindale-Hubbell Law Directory

WILNER, KLEIN & SIEGEL, A PROFESSIONAL CORPORATION (AV)

Suite 700, 9601 Wilshire Boulevard, 90210
Telephone: 310-550-4595
Facsimile: 310-275-3509
Brea, California Office: 3230 East Imperial Highway, Suite 309.
Telephone: 714-579-2600.
Facsimile: 714-579-2549.

Walter Klein
Laura J. Snoke
Samuel Wilner
Jodi Zucker Taksar
Leonard Siegel
Edward E. Wallace
Joseph R. Serpico

Floyd W. Cranmore
Darrell J. Mariz
Edwin J. Howard
Alison M. Walz
Thomas M. Ware, II
Robert D. Moore (Resident, Brea Office)
Joshua B. Bereny
Allen Donald MacNeil (Resident, Brea Office)
Mitchell S. Brachman
Stephen Coopersmith
Steven M. Hepps (Resident, Brea Office)
Steven J. Parker (Resident, Brea Office)

OF COUNSEL

Richard B. Kott (Resident, Brea Office)

Reference: City National Bank.

For full biographical listings, see the Martindale-Hubbell Law Directory

CALABASAS, Los Angeles Co.

GARY M. GITLIN A PROFESSIONAL LAW CORPORATION (AV)

Suite 110, 23945 Calabasas Road, 91302-1552
Telephone: 818-591-3757
Telefax: 818-591-2779

Gary M. Gitlin
Jennifer L. Melton

For full biographical listings, see the Martindale-Hubbell Law Directory

CAMPBELL, Santa Clara Co.

THEODORE R. CHAVEZ (AV)

Pruneyard Towers II, 1999 South Bascom Avenue, Suite 820, 95008
Telephone: 408-371-4211
Telecopier: 408-371-3504
Email: Terraco@PacBell.net

For full biographical listings, see the Martindale-Hubbell Law Directory

COSTA MESA, Orange Co.

Albert, Weiland & Golden (AV)

Center Tower, 650 Town Center Drive, Suite 1350, 92626
Telephone: 714-966-1000
FAX: 714-966-1002
Email: awglawyers@aol.com

Theodor C. Albert
Michael J. Weiland
Jeffrey I. Golden

ASSOCIATES

Evan D. Smiley
Philip E. Strok
Lei Lei Wang Ekvall
Darlynn Campbell Morgan

OF COUNSEL

Marcus M. Kaufman
Jennifer Ann Golison
Steven J. Katzman

LEGAL SUPPORT PERSONNEL

PARALEGALS

Fran L. Russell
Patricia K. Nelson
Cynthia B. Meeker
Janet Hogan
Kim Sigismondo

For full biographical listings, see the Martindale-Hubbell Law Directory

Feldhake, August & Roquemore (AV)

Plaza Tower, Suite 1730, 600 Anton Boulevard, 92626-7124
Telephone: 714-438-3885
Fax: 714-438-3888
Email: farlaw@hqonline.com

Robert J. Feldhake
Lisa A. Roquemore
Kenneth S. August
Joshua M. Wolff

ASSOCIATES

Dimitri P. Gross
Supriya Kakkar
Katherine A. Slayton

OF COUNSEL

Arthur J. Swerdloff
Arthur M. Wilcox, Jr.

For full biographical listings, see the Martindale-Hubbell Law Directory

Rutan & Tucker, LLP (AV)

A Partnership including Professional Corporations
611 Anton Boulevard, Fourteenth Floor, P.O. Box 1950, 92626-1998
Telephone: 714-641-5100; 213-625-7586
Telecopier: 714-546-9035
Email: rutan&tucker@rutan.com *URL:* http://www.rutan.com

MEMBERS OF FIRM

James R. Moore (P.C.)
Richard A. Curnutt
John B. Hurlbut, Jr.
Michael W. Immell
Richard P. Sims
Robert C. Braun
Thomas S. Salinger (P.C.)
Clifford E. Frieden
Michael D. Rubin
Ira G. Rivin (P.C.)
Jeffrey M. Oderman (P.C.)
Marcia A. Forsyth
William J. Caplan
Randall M. Babbush
Mary M. Green
Michael F. Sitzer
Mark B. Frazier
Penelope Parmes
Lori Sarner Smith
Kim D. Thompson
Stephen A. Ellis
Adam N. Volkert
F. Kevin Brazil
Patrick D. McCalla
David H. Hochner
Paul J. Sievers
Joseph Louis Maga III
Kraig C. Kilger

SPECIAL COUNSEL

Debra Dunn Steel

ASSOCIATES

Steven John Goon
Kara S. Carlson
Marlene Pose Jurgensen
John W. Hamilton, Jr.
Philip J. Blanchard
Deja Marie Hemingway
Julie K. Whang
Charles A. Davenport, III
Daniel L. Gebert
Richard D. Arko
Nikki Nguyen

For Complete List of Firm Personnel, See General Section

For full biographical listings, see the Martindale-Hubbell Law Directory

EMERYVILLE, Alameda Co.

Bishop, Barry, Howe, Haney & Ryder, A Professional Corporation (AV)

Watergate Tower III, 2000 Powell Street, Suite 1425, 94608
Telephone: 510-596-0888
Fax: 510-596-0899
Email: FirmGeneral@BBHHR.com
San Francisco Office: 44 Montgomery Street, Suite 1300, 94104.
Telephone: 415-421-8550.

(See Next Column)

Ross R. Ryder (1940-1989)
Nelson C. Barry
Drayton F. Howe, Jr.
Jeffrey N. Haney
Thomas O. Haran
Rebecca B. Aherne
Michael W. Bolechowski
Mark C. Raskoff
Patricia S. Lakner
Gregory R. de la Peña

J. Scott Wood
Mitchell J. Alward
Marco R. Sumarriva
Jane E. Carey
Carol L. Healey
Mary Margaret Ryan
Thomas Edward Foran
John F. Cooke
Jean H. Hurricane
Daniel M. O'Connell
Lisa S. Wiggins
Edward M. Lai

OF COUNSEL

Lawrence S. Molton
David P. Osako

Representative Clients: Maxson Young & Associates; Gryphon Insurance Group.

For full biographical listings, see the Martindale-Hubbell Law Directory

ENCINO, Los Angeles Co.

Edward D. Aaronson A Law Corporation (AV)

16133 Ventura Boulevard, Suite 1080, 91436-2427
Telephone: 818-783-0444
Fax: 818-783-3873

MEMBER OF FIRM

Edward D. Aaronson

ASSOCIATE

Steven J. Berman

For full biographical listings, see the Martindale-Hubbell Law Directory

FOLSOM, Sacramento Co.

The Bleier Law Firm (AV)

110 Blue Ravine Road, Suite 201, 95630
Telephone: 916-454-2100
Fax: 916-454-2121
Email: tblf@bleier.com *URL:* http://www.bleier.com

Brenton A. Bleier

ASSOCIATE

Bradford A. Bleier

For full biographical listings, see the Martindale-Hubbell Law Directory

*FRESNO,** Fresno Co.

Bolen, Fransen & Boostrom LLP (AV)

Suite 430, East Tower Guarantee Financial Center, 1322 East Shaw Avenue, 93710
Telephone: 559-226-8177
Fax: 559-227-4971
Email: firm@bolenfransen.com *URL:* http://www.bolenfransen.com
Clovis, California Office: 414 Pollasky Avenue.
Telephone: 559-297-6250.
Fax: 559-322-6778.

PARTNERS

Hal H. Bolen II
Jeffrey A. Russell
Kenneth J. Fransen
Virginia Miller Pedreira

ASSOCIATE

Kim Marie Herold

OF COUNSEL

Donna Boostrom

For full biographical listings, see the Martindale-Hubbell Law Directory

Dietrich, Glasrud, Mallek & Aune (AV)

An Association of Attorneys including Law Corporations
5250 North Palm Avenue, Suite 402, 93704
Telephone: 559-435-5250
Facsimile: 559-435-8776
Email: info@dgmalaw.com

Richard W. Dietrich (Inc.) (1930-1999)
Donald H. Glasrud (Inc.)
Robert A. Mallek Jr. (Inc.)
Richard E. Aune (Inc.)
Bruce A. Owdom
Thomas W. Isaac

Douglas D. Schorling
Leslie G. Miessner
Daniel J. Tekunoff

OF COUNSEL

Timothy J. Buchanan

Representative Clients: Fresno Surgery and Recovery Care Center; Helm Fertilizer, Inc.; Gragnani Farms; Wathen-Castanos, Inc.; Chicago Title Company; ABC, Inc.; The McClatchy Company; Monsanto Company; Armstrong World Industries, Inc.; Stewart Title Guaranty Company.

For full biographical listings, see the Martindale-Hubbell Law Directory

Fresno—Continued

DOWLING, AARON & KEELER, INCORPORATED (AV)

6051 North Fresno Street, Suite 200, 93710
Telephone: 559-432-4500
Fax: 559-432-4590
Email: dak@daklaw.com *URL:* http://www.daklaw.com
Bakersfield, California Office: 110 South Mt. Claire, Suite 203. 93309.
Telephone: 661-396-0451. Web Site: http://www.daklaw.com.

Michael D. Dowling
Richard M. Aaron
Stephen M. Blumberg
Bruce S. Fraser
John C. Ganahl
Christopher A. Brown
James C. Sherwood
David J. Weiland

Larry B. Lindenau
Justin D. Harris

OF COUNSEL

Morris M. Sherr

Reference: Wells Fargo Bank (Main).

For Complete List of Firm Personnel, See General Section

For full biographical listings, see the Martindale-Hubbell Law Directory

LANG, RICHERT & PATCH, A PROFESSIONAL CORPORATION (AV)

Fig Garden Financial Center, 5200 North Palm Avenue, 4th Floor, P.O. Box 40012, 93755
Telephone: 559-228-6700
Fax: 559-228-6727

William T. Richert (1937-1993)
Robert L. Patch, II
Val W. Saldaña
Douglas E. Noll
Michael T. Hertz
Victoria J. Salisch
Rene Lastreto, II
Charles Trudrung Taylor
Mark L. Creede
Peter N. Zeitler
Laurie L. Quigley
Tamara L. Equals
Douglas E. Griffin
Nabil E. Zumout

Christopher B. Dorian
Matthew W. Quall
Tracy E. Sagle
Julie K. Hill
Michelle Oleksa

OF COUNSEL

Frank H. Lang

References: Wells Fargo Bank (Fresno Main Office).

For full biographical listings, see the Martindale-Hubbell Law Directory

GLENDALE, Los Angeles Co.

GREENWALD, HOFFMAN, MEYER & MONTES, L.L.P. (AV)

500 North Brand Boulevard, Suite 920, 91203-1923
Telephone: 818-507-8100; 213-381-1131
Fax: 818-507-8484

MEMBERS OF FIRM

Guy Preston Greenwald, Jr. (1914-1984)
Donald M. Hoffman
Lawrence F. Meyer
Raul M. Montes

References: Bank of America (Los Angeles and Pasadena Trust Offices); Northern Trust of California (Headquarters Office); Bank of America (Glendale Main Branch).

For full biographical listings, see the Martindale-Hubbell Law Directory

O'ROURKE, ALLAN & FONG, LLP (AV)

100 West Broadway, Suite 1250, P.O. Box 10220, 91210
Telephone: 818-247-4303
Fax: 818-247-1451
Email: OAFLAW@aol.com

MEMBERS OF FIRM

Denis M. O'Rourke
Joan H. Allan
Roderick D. Fong

ASSOCIATES

Denise Michelle O'Rourke
Marina Manoukian
Toshiko Kobayashi

References: Verdugo Banking Co. (Glendale, California); Community Bank (Glendale, California).

For full biographical listings, see the Martindale-Hubbell Law Directory

GOLD RIVER, Sacramento Co.

LAW OFFICES OF JOSEPH W. SCALIA (AV)

11335 Gold Express, Suite 105, 95670-4491
Telephone: 916-858-2286
Fax: 916-852-5777
Email: jscalia@ix.netcom.com

For full biographical listings, see the Martindale-Hubbell Law Directory

IRVINE, Orange Co.

BORCHARD & WILLOUGHBY, A PROFESSIONAL CORPORATION (AV)

18881 Von Karman Avenue, Suite 1400, 92612
Telephone: 949-263-0424
Fax: 949-263-1913

Michael D. Borchard
Michael L. Willoughby
Mark A. Rodriguez

Stephanie A. Pittaluga

For full biographical listings, see the Martindale-Hubbell Law Directory

GALFIN & PASSON, LLP (AV)

18101 Von Karman Avenue, Suite 1400, 92612-1043
Telephone: 949-752-2444
Facsimile: 949-833-8256
Email: galpas@aol.com
Santa Ana, California Office: 2122 North Broadway, Suite 100.
Telephone: 949-752-2444.

MEMBERS OF FIRM

Ted A. Galfin
Kenneth D. Passon
Lorraine Kay Smyth
Michael R. Adams
Marcelle Suzanne Strauss
Adam M. Greely

For full biographical listings, see the Martindale-Hubbell Law Directory

KASDAN, SIMONDS, MCINTYRE, EPSTEIN & MARTIN (AV)

2600 Michelson Drive, Tenth Floor, 92612-6510
Telephone: 949-851-9000
Fax: 949-833-9455
Email: info@ksmem.com *URL:* http://www.ksmem.com
San Jose, California Office: 111 West Saint John, Suite 850,
Telephone: 408-292-9220.
Fax: 408-292-9172. E Mail: INFO@KSMEM.com

MEMBERS OF FIRM

Kenneth S. Kasdan
Vance C. Simonds, Jr.
R. Donald McIntyre
David G. Epstein
Ronald B. Martin
Michael D. Turner

ASSOCIATES

Steven S. Hanagami
Randi Ellen Pinckes
Richard P. Riley
Wayne W. (Bill) Suojanen
Cathleen L. Mulligan
Heather A. Dozier
Melissa A. Pasek
James W. Markwith
Wendy Reed
Christopher J. Whelton
Daniel Peinado

Reference: Eldorado Bank.

For full biographical listings, see the Martindale-Hubbell Law Directory

OSWALD & YAP, A PROFESSIONAL CORPORATION (AV)

16148 Sand Canyon Avenue, 92618
Telephone: 949-788-8900
Telefax: 949-788-8980
URL: http://www.oswald-yap.com

Michael A. Oswald
Calvin C.S. Yap
Niall Sweetnam
Mark D. Holmes

Tzong-Bing Tsai
Joseph A. Weber
Edward W. Russey, III
Richard T. Hsueh
Carol A. Gefis

OF COUNSEL

John W. Allured
Reed M. Williams

For full biographical listings, see the Martindale-Hubbell Law Directory

PAONE CALLAHAN MCHOLM & WINTON, LLP (AV)

Eighth Floor, 19100 Von Karman Avenue, P.O. Box 19613, 92623-9613
Telephone: 949-955-2900
Facsimile: 949-955-9009
Email: info@paone.com *URL:* http://www.paone.com

MEMBERS OF FIRM

Robert E. Callahan
Richard J. Foster
Susan K. Hori
Alan Jules Kessel
Kenneth S. Kramer
Steven A. McHolm
Tim Paone
Martin J. Stein
Daniel K. Winton

OF COUNSEL

Roger A. Grable
Kathleen Carothers Paone
William P. Tanner, III

Clay Shevlin
L. Elizabeth Strahlstrom

For full biographical listings, see the Martindale-Hubbell Law Directory

KENTFIELD, Marin Co.

ALLAN M. BERLAND (AV)

6 Wolfe Canyon Road, 94904-1008
Telephone: 415-461-4711
Fax: 415-461-4704

LONG BEACH, Los Angeles Co.

CAMERON, PEARLSON & GALE (AV)

One World Trade Center, Suite 1600, 90831-1600
Telephone: 562-436-3888
Telecopier: 562-437-1967
URL: http://www.cpglawyers.com
URL: http://www.lawyers.com/cmp&glaw

MEMBERS OF FIRM

Timothy C. Cameron
Charles M. Gale
Paul R. Pearlson

ASSOCIATES

Dana K. Anderson, Jr.
Susan R. Loh

For full biographical listings, see the Martindale-Hubbell Law Directory

TAUBMAN, SIMPSON, YOUNG & SULENTOR (AV)

249 East Ocean Boulevard, Suite 700, P.O. Box 22670, 90801-5670
Telephone: 562-436-9201
FAX: 562-590-9695
Email: thefirm@tsyslaw.com

E. C. Denio (1864-1952)
Geo. A. Hart (1881-1967)
Geo. P. Taubman, Jr. (1897-1970)
Matthew C. Simpson (1900-1988)
Roger W. Young
William J. Sulentor
Peter M. Williams
Maria M. Rohaidy
Stuart C. Talley

Attorneys for: Bixby Land Co.; Renick Cadillac, Inc.; Oil Operators Inc.
Local Counsel: Crown Cork & Seal Co., Inc.

For full biographical listings, see the Martindale-Hubbell Law Directory

*LOS ANGELES,** Los Angeles Co.

ALVARADO, SMITH & SANCHEZ, A PROFESSIONAL CORPORATION (AV)

611 West Sixth Street, Suite 2650, 90017
Telephone: 213-229-2400
Facsimile: 213-229-2499
URL: http://www.alvarado-smith.com
Irvine, California Office: 4 Park Plaza, Suite 1200, 92614.
Telephone: 949-955-6800.
Fax: 949-955-6899.

Raymond G. Alvarado
Ruben A. Smith
Maurice Sanchez
John M. Sorich
Raúl F. Salinas
Frances Q. Jett
Theresa Eileen Antonucci
Diane C. Barrio
Rosario M. Tobias

OF COUNSEL

Martin N. Burton

For full biographical listings, see the Martindale-Hubbell Law Directory

ANDERSON, ABLON, LEWIS & GALE, LLP (AV)

Suite 2000 Equitable Plaza Building, 3435 Wilshire Boulevard, 90010-2006
Telephone: 213-388-3385
Fax: 213-388-8432
URL: http://www.aalg.com
San Juan Capistrano, California Office: 30240 Rancho Viejo Road, Suite F, 92675.
Telephone: 949-248-8040.
Fax: 949-248-8044.
Thousand Oaks, California Office: 220-H Briarwood Building, 299 West Hillcrest Drive, 91360.
Telephone: 805-373-5273.
Fax: 805-495-1456.

MEMBERS OF FIRM

Robert E. Lewis
Jerald E. Gale
Harris D. Bass

OF COUNSEL

Lawrence Jay Poteet
Charles R. Anderson
Herman Ablon

ASSOCIATES

Farhad Kazemzadeh
Candace Connart Bleifer
Ronald A. Gorrie
Michael D. Anderson

For full biographical listings, see the Martindale-Hubbell Law Directory

BAKER & HOSTETLER LLP (AV)

600 Wilshire Boulevard, 90017-3212
Telephone: 213-624-2400
FAX: 213-975-1740
To contact an attorney on the Internet use first initial and surname followed by @baker-hostetler.com
URL: http://www.bakerlaw.com
In Cleveland, Ohio: 3200 National City Center, 1900 East Ninth Street.
Telephone: 216-621-0200.
In Cincinnati, Ohio: 312 Walnut Street, Suite 2650.
Telephone: 513-929-3400.
In Columbus, Ohio: Capitol Square, Suite 2100, 65 East State Street.
Telephone: 614-228-1541.
In Denver, Colorado: 303 East 17th Avenue, Suite 1100.
Telephone: 303-861-0600.
In Houston, Texas: 1000 Louisiana, Suite 2000.
Telephone: 713-751-1600.
In Long Beach, California: 300 Oceangate, Suite 620.
Telephone: 562-432-2827.
In Orlando, Florida: SunBank Center, Suite 2300, 200 South Orange Avenue.
Telephone: 407-649-4000.
In Washington, D. C.: Washington Square, Suite 1100, 1050 Connecticut Avenue, N.W.
Telephone: 202-861-1500.

PARTNERS

Thomas G. Roberts
David C. Sampson

For Complete List of Firm Personnel, See General Section

For full biographical listings, see the Martindale-Hubbell Law Directory

BAKER AND JACOBSON, A PROFESSIONAL CORPORATION (AV)

Suite 500, 11377 West Olympic Boulevard, 90064-1683
Telephone: 310-914-7990
Fax: 310-914-7913
Email: do@bakjac.com

Robert P. Baker
Lawrence M. Jacobson

For full biographical listings, see the Martindale-Hubbell Law Directory

BERGMAN, WEDNER & DACEY, INC. (AV)

Suite 900, 10880 Wilshire Boulevard, 90024
Telephone: 310-470-6110
Fax: 310-474-0931
Email: ofc@bergman-wedner.com *URL:* http://www.bergman-wedner.com

Gregory M. Bergman
Gregory A. Wedner
John P. Dacey
Alan Harvey Mittelman
Robert M. Mason III
Kristi Anne Sjoholm-Sierchio
John V. Tamborelli

Lisa S. Newnan
Daphne M. Humphreys
Michele M. Goldsmith
Denise G. Godfrey
William Daryl Strickland
Pamela R. Fleming
Matthew R. Hicks
Jorge J. Luna
Paul V. Rayburn
Mark W. Waterman

OF COUNSEL

Lloyd A. Bergman (1923-1994)
Jacob A. Wedner
Marvin Goldsmith
Mark K. Kitabayashi

SPECIAL COUNSEL

Richard V. Godino

For full biographical listings, see the Martindale-Hubbell Law Directory

LAW OFFICES OF DAVID B. BLOOM A PROFESSIONAL CORPORATION (AV)

3325 Wilshire Boulevard, Ninth Floor, 90010
Telephone: 323-938-5248; 384-4088
Telecopier: 213-385-2009

David B. Bloom

Stephen S. Monroe (A Professional Corporation)
Raphael A. Rosemblat
James E. Adler
Roy A. Levun
Jonathan Udell
Susan Carole Jay
Edward Idell
Sandra Kamenir
Steven Wayne Lazarus
Andrew Edward Briseno
Shelley M. Gould
Ted L. Travis

For full biographical listings, see the Martindale-Hubbell Law Directory

Los Angeles—Continued

BRAND FARRAR & BUXBAUM LLP (AV)

515 South Flower Street, Suite 3500, 90071-2201
Telephone: 213-228-0288
Fax: 213-426-6222
Email: bfb-la@brandfarrar.com
Beijing (Peking), China Office: Suite 2518, China World Trade Centre, 1 Jian Guo Men Wai Avenue, Beijing, China.
Telephone: 86-10-6505-2288 Ext. 2523/2518.
Fax: 86-10-6505-2638. Email: bjbfbbj@public3.bta.net.cn
Chengdu, Sichuan, China Office: Suite 11A, Sichuan International Mansion, No. 1 Zhong Xi Shun Cheng Street, Chengdu, China.
Telephone: 86-28-652-1316.
Fax: 86-28-652-0547. Email: cdbfbcd@mail.sc.cninfo.net.
Chongqing, China Office: Suite 1510, Metropolitan Tower, 68 Zourong Lu, Chongqing, China.
Telephone: 86-23-6382-8381.
Fax: 86-23-6382-8373. Email: cqbfbcq@public.cta.cq.cn.
Guangzhou (Canton), China Office: Suite 1305, Main Tower, GITIC Plaza Hotel, 339 Huanshi Dong Road, Guangzhou, China.
Telephone: 86-20-8331-1888, Ext. 71305.
Fax: 86-20-8331-2671. Email: gzbfbgz@public.guangzhou.gd.cn.
Hong Kong, China Office: Brand Farrar Buxbaum LLP, 5/F., Landmark East, 12 Ice House Street, Central, Hong Kong, China.
Telephone: 852-2523-7001.
Fax: 852-2845-0947. Email: hkbfbhk@hk.super.net.
Los Angeles, California Office: Brand Farrar & Buxbaum LLP, Suite 3500, 515 South Flower Street, Los Angeles, California, 90071-2201.
Telephone: 213-228-0288.
Fax: 213-426-6222. Email: bfb-la@brandfarrar.com.
New York, New York Office: 275 Madison Avenue, 37th Floor, New York, New York, 10097.
Telephone: 212-286-0038.
Fax: 212-573-9077. Email: martineh@aol.com
Shanghai, China Office: Brand Farrar Buxbaum LLP, Suites 2611-12, Central Plaza, 227 Huangpi Bei Lu, Shanghai, China.
Telephone: 86-21-6375-8918.
Fax: 86-21-6375-8922. Email: shbfbsh@public2.sta.net.cn
Shenzhen, China Office: Suite 2103A, Shenzhen Development Center, Renmin Nan Lu, Shenzhen, China.
Telephone: 86-755-229-8009.
Fax: 86-755-229-8011. Email: szbfbsz@public.szptt.net.cn.
Ulaanbaatar, Mongolia Office: Brand Farrar Buxbaum LLP, 4/F., Time Center, No. 50 Baga Toiruu, Ulaanbaatar, Mongolia.
Telephone: 976-1-31-0711.
Fax: 976-1-32-5102. Email: mgbfbmg@magicnet.mn.
Xiamen, China Office: Suite 1182 Jian Ye Building, 28 Hubin North Road, Xiamen, China.
Telephone: 86-592-506-3059.
Fax: 86-592-511-1044. Email: xmbfbxm@public.xm.fj.cn.
Associated Office, Mumbai, Bombay, India: Shah & Sanghavi, Advocates, Solicitors & Notary, 114-A Mittal Court, Nariman Point, Mumbai 400 021 India.
Telephone: 91-22-285-5755/56 or 91-22-285-3592/93.
Fax: 91-22-284-5040.

PRINCIPALS

Michael A. Brand
David C. Buxbaum (China Offices)
Kenneth Y. Choy (Hong Kong Office)
Robert W. Dziubla
David W. Farrar
Amy E. Freilich
Margaret G. Graf
John Masao Iino
Charles K. Kolstad
Edward H. Martin (New York Office)
Gregory D. Trimarche
Li Zhuogen (China Offices)

OTHER ATTORNEYS RESIDENT IN LOS ANGELES OFFICE

Sherry L. Geyer
Joan M. Marquardt
James H. Service
Jeffrey S. Allen
Julia Sylva
Brian J. Kim
Lisa Teng

OTHER ATTORNEYS RESIDENT IN BEIJING OFFICE

Hao Xiaodong
Bin Zhao
Luo Rongping
Zhang Chunbo

OTHER ATTORNEYS RESIDENT IN CHENGDU, SICHUAN OFFICE

Zeng Xiangyu
Wu Wen

OTHER ATTORNEY RESIDENT IN CHONGQING OFFICE

Du Fei

OTHER ATTORNEYS RESIDENT IN GUANGZHOU OFFICE

Zou Wenyan (Not admitted in United States)
Feng Ruiding
Jia Guangxi

OTHER ATTORNEYS RESIDENT IN HONG KONG OFFICE

Shane F. Weir
Cheonghar Wong
N.T.S. Kularatne
Simon Woo
David William Gunson
Arthur Burton Crook
Simon K.C. Lee
Cheng Yuen Yi
Lo Wing Cheong
Nicholas C. McGrenra
Eva Y.N. Kwok

OTHER ATTORNEYS RESIDENT IN NEW YORK OFFICE

Vincent I. S. Hsieh (Of Counsel)
Jeffrey Schall
Jonathan Chun Wang

(See Next Column)

OTHER ATTORNEYS RESIDENT IN SHANGHAI OFFICE

Lin Yong
Wu Hong Liang
Tang Ying
Zhang Guoyao
Qi Zhenwen

OTHER ATTORNEYS RESIDENT IN SHENZHEN OFFICE

Zhong Wenya
Zhang He

OTHER ATTORNEYS RESIDENT IN ULAANBAATAR OFFICE

Byambaa Bayarmaa
Ajiv Enhktuya

OTHER ATTORNEY RESIDENT IN XIAMEN OFFICE

Deng Sheng

For full biographical listings, see the Martindale-Hubbell Law Directory

BROWN, WINFIELD & CANZONERI, INCORPORATED (AV)

Suite 1500 California Plaza, 300 South Grand Avenue, 90071-3125
Telephone: 213-687-2100
Fax: 213-687-2149

J. Kenneth Brown
Thomas F. Winfield III
Anthony Canzoneri
Vicki E. Land
James C. Camp
Steven Abram
Dennis S. Roy
Mark Steres
Christopher Norgaard
C. Geoffrey Mitchell
Scott H. Campbell
Joshua C. Gottheim
Donald Paul Ries
Edward J. Szczepkowski
William Balderrama
Richard J. Sestak
Robert H. Badner
John H. Holloway
Anh-Bang Bill Pham
Gregg D. Freeman
Tracy M. Noonan
Richard Charles Rey II
Jeannette R. Busek
Sylvia Diana Roth
Christopher M. Pisano

Reference: Wells Fargo Bank.

For full biographical listings, see the Martindale-Hubbell Law Directory

CLARK & TREVITHICK, A PROFESSIONAL CORPORATION (AV)

800 Wilshire Boulevard, 12th Floor, 90017
Telephone: 213-629-5700
Telecopier: 213-624-9441
Email: postmaster@clarktrev.com
San Francisco, California Office: 456 Montgomery Street, 20th Floor.
Telephone: 415-288-6520.
Fax: 415-398-2820.

Donald P. Clark
Alexander C. McGilvray, Jr.
Kevin P. Fiore
James S. Arico
Robert W. Renken

OF COUNSEL

John A. Tucker, Jr.

For Complete List of Firm Personnel, See General Section

For full biographical listings, see the Martindale-Hubbell Law Directory

DARLING, HALL & RAE, LLP (AV)

520 South Grand Avenue, 7th Floor, 90071
Telephone: 213-627-8104
Fax: 213-627-7795
Email: darlinghallrae@compuserve.com

MEMBERS OF FIRM

Hugh W. Darling (1901-1986)
Edward S. Shattuck (1901-1965)
George Gaylord Gute (1922-1981)
Donald Keith Hall (1918-1984)
Matthew S. Rae, Jr.
Richard L. Stack
Edwin Freston

OF COUNSEL

Edward F. Pearson

Reference: City National Bank (Pershing Square Office, Los Angeles, California).

For full biographical listings, see the Martindale-Hubbell Law Directory

DAVIS & FOX (AV)

1901 Avenue of the Stars, Suite 400, 90067
Telephone: 310-286-2915
Fax: 310-286-2916

Calvin E. Davis
Steven A. Fox
Elizabeth A. Kooyman
John J. Stumreiter
Amy L. Freisleben
Barbara Kekich
Gregory M. Sinderbrand

For full biographical listings, see the Martindale-Hubbell Law Directory

DEMETRIOU, DEL GUERCIO, SPRINGER & MOYER, LLP (AV)

801 South Grand Avenue, 10th Floor, 90017
Telephone: 213-624-8407
Telecopy: 213-624-0174
Email: ddsm@juno.com

(See Next Column)

DEMETRIOU, DEL GUERCIO, SPRINGER & MOYER LLP, *Los Angeles—Continued*

MEMBERS OF FIRM

Jeffrey Z. B. Springer
Michael A. Francis
Stephen A. Del Guercio
Regina Liudzius Cobb
Bradley D. Pierce

OF COUNSEL

Ronald J. Del Guercio

Reference: Bank of America, L.A. Main Office, Los Angeles, Calif.

For full biographical listings, see the Martindale-Hubbell Law Directory

EASTON & SCHIFF (AV)

A Partnership of Professional Corporations
1901 Avenue of the Stars Suite 1100, 90067
Telephone: 310-557-2436
FAX: 310-557-2432

MEMBERS OF FIRM

Harold Easton (P.C.)
Michael J. Schiff (P.C.)

References: Bank of America National Trust & Savings Assn. (Los Angeles Main Office); First Charter Bank (Beverly Hills).

For full biographical listings, see the Martindale-Hubbell Law Directory

FRIED, BIRD & CRUMPACKER, A PROFESSIONAL CORPORATION (AV)

1900 Avenue of the Stars, 25th Floor, 90067-6031
Telephone: 310-551-7400
Facsimile: 310-556-4487
Email: fbclawfirm@cs.com

Jack Fried
David W. Crumpacker, Jr.
Brian James Bird
Nikki Wolontis

David K. Johnson

For full biographical listings, see the Martindale-Hubbell Law Directory

PETER A. GELLES (AV)

1801 Century Park East Suite 1520, 90067
Telephone: 310-201-7900
Facsimile: 310-201-7925
Email: petergelles@msn.com

For full biographical listings, see the Martindale-Hubbell Law Directory

GOLDMAN & KAGON, LAW CORPORATION (AV)

1801 Century Park East, Suite 2222, 90067
Telephone: 310-552-1707
Telecopier: 310-552-7938
URL: http://www.goldmankagon.com

Mark A. Goldman
Charles D. Meyer

For Complete List of Firm Personnel, See General Section

For full biographical listings, see the Martindale-Hubbell Law Directory

LEONARD A. GOLDMAN & ASSOCIATES (AV)

(Formerly Goldman & Gordon, L.L.P.)
1900 Avenue of the Stars, Suite 1800, 90067-4409
Telephone: 310-277-7171
FAX: 310-277-1547
Email: lagoldman@earthlink.com

MEMBERS OF FIRM

A. S. Goldman (1895-1966)
Leonard A. Goldman

References: Bank of America, Fourth and Spring Branch, Los Angeles; Bank of America, Wilshire-San Vincente Branch, Beverly Hills.

For full biographical listings, see the Martindale-Hubbell Law Directory

HILL, FARRER & BURRILL LLP (AV)

A Limited Liability Partnership including Professional Corporations
37th Floor, One California Plaza, 300 South Grand Avenue, 90071-3147
Telephone: 213-620-0460
Fax: 213-624-4840
URL: http://www.hfbllp.com

MEMBERS OF FIRM

Wm. Harold Borthwick (P.C.)
Alfred M. Clark, III, (P.C.)
Michelle A. Meghrouni (P.C.)

ASSOCIATE

Stacey A. Sullivan

For Complete List of Firm Personnel, See General Section

For full biographical listings, see the Martindale-Hubbell Law Directory

SAMUEL D. INGHAM, III (AV)

1800 Avenue of the Stars, Suite 1000, 90067-4212
Telephone: 310-556-9751
Fax: 310-556-1311
Email: singham@inghamlaw.com

ASSOCIATE

John E. Rogers, Jr.

For full biographical listings, see the Martindale-Hubbell Law Directory

KESSLER & KESSLER, A LAW CORPORATION (AV)

2029 Century Park East, Suite 1520, 90067
Telephone: 310-552-9800
Fax: 310-552-0442
Email: kkalawcorp@aol.com

Warren J. Kessler
Lisa C. Alexander
Joan B. Kessler
Lisa K. Skaist

For full biographical listings, see the Martindale-Hubbell Law Directory

KNOPFLER & ROBERTSON, LLP (AV)

Suite 500, 21650 Oxnard Street (Woodland Hills), 91367
Telephone: 818-227-0770; 213-624-1111
Telefax: 818-227-0777
Irvine, California Office: 19800 MacArthur Boulevard, Suite 270, 92612.
Telephone: 714-261-6191.
Pleasanton, California Office: 400 Main Street, Suite 204, 94566.
Telephone: 510-425-7250.
Las Vegas, Nevada Office: Knopfler & Robertson in Association with Broom & Vaisbort, LLP, 3753 Howard Hughes Parkway, Suite 200, 89109.
Telephone: 702-792-2413.
Camarillo, California Office: 1200 Paseo, Suite 170, 93010.
Telephone: 805-482-1903; 800-CONDOLAW.
Fax: 805-484-5917.

George Knopfler
Richard A. Capella
Alexander Robertson, IV
Jonathan S. Vick
Deborah Broom
Edward D. Vaisbort
William G. Kelsberg

OF COUNSEL

Scott C. Haith
Christina S. Robertson
James P. Lingl (Resident, Camarillo Office)

Janice M. Michaels
Robert Nation
James M. Pazos
William S. Dunlevy (Resident, Camarillo Office)
Mark Rohrer
Scott A. Hunter
Craig Smith

For full biographical listings, see the Martindale-Hubbell Law Directory

LOEB & LOEB LLP (AV)

A Limited Liability Partnership including Professional Corporations
Suite 1800, 1000 Wilshire Boulevard, 90017-2475
Telephone: 213-688-3400
Facsimile: 213-688-3460
Email: info@loeb.com *URL:* http://www.loeb.com
Century City, California Office: Suite 2200, 10100 Santa Monica Boulevard, Los Angeles, 90067-4164.
Telephone: 310-282-2000.
Facsimile: 310-282-2192.
New York, N.Y. Office: 345 Park Avenue, 10154-0037.
Telephone: 212-407-4000.
Facsimile: 212-407-4990.
Nashville, Tennessee Office: 45 Music Square West, 37203-3205.
Telephone: 615-749-8300;
Facsimile: 615-749-8308.
Rome, Italy Office: Piazza Digione 1, 00197.
Telephone: 011-3906-808-8456.
Facsimile: 011-3906-808-8288.

MEMBERS OF FIRM

Harriet B. Alexson
Michael Bryce Kinney (New York City Office)
Michael D. Beck (A P.C.) (New York City Office)
Andrew E. Lippmann (New York City Office)
Kenneth D. Freeman (New York City Office)
Susan V. Noonoo
Joseph P. Heffernan (A P.C.)
Scott I. Schneider (New York City Office)
Karen Nielsen Higgins
Ronald Weinstein

OF COUNSEL

Frank E. Feder (A P.C.) (Century City and New York Offices)

ASSOCIATES

Nina B. Luban (New York City Office)
Samuel Mark Mizrahi (New York City Office)
Sonya Makunga
August W. Pelton

(See Next Column)

LOEB & LOEB LLP—*Continued*

For Complete List of Firm Personnel, See General Section

For full biographical listings, see the Martindale-Hubbell Law Directory

MINTON, MINTON AND RAND LLP (AV)

510 West Sixth Street, 90014
Telephone: 213-624-9394
Fax: 213-624-9323

MEMBERS OF FIRM

Carl W. Minton (1902-1974) — Carl Minton
David E. Rand

Reference: Bank of America National Trust & Savings Assn. (Seventh & Flower Office, Los Angeles, Calif.).

For full biographical listings, see the Martindale-Hubbell Law Directory

O'MELVENY & MYERS LLP (AV)

400 South Hope Street, 90071-2899
Telephone: 213-430-6000
Facsimile: 213-430-6407
Cable: MOMS
Telex: 674122
Email: omminfo@omm.com *URL:* http://www.omm.com
Century City, CA Office: 1999 Avenue of the Stars, Los Angeles, 90067-6035.
Telex: 674097. Tel: 310-553-6700.
Fax: 310-246-6779.
Newport Beach, CA Office: 610 Newport Center Drive, 92660-6429.
Telex: 4722088. Tel: 949-760-9600.
Fax: 949-823-6994.
San Francisco, CA Office: Embarcadero Center West, 275 Battery Street, 94111-3305. Tel: 415-984-8700.
Fax: 415-984-8701.
New York, NY Office: Citicorp Center, 153 East 53rd Street, 10022-4611.
Telex: 129165. Tel: 212-326-2000.
Fax: 212-326-2061.
Washington, DC Office: 555 13th Street, N.W., 20004-1109.
Cable: MOMSWSH.
Telex: 89622. Tel: 202-383-5300.
Fax: 202-383-5414.
London Office: O'Melveny & Myers, 3 Finsbury Square, London, EC2A 1LA, England. Tel: 44-171-256-8451. Fax 44-171-638-8205.
Tokyo Office: Akasaka Twin Tower, East 14F, 2-17-23, Akasaka, Minato-ku, Tokyo 107-0052, Japan. Tel: 03-5562-2800.
Fax: 03-5575-3840.
Hong Kong Office: O'Melveny & Myers, Suite 1905, Tower Two, Lippo Centre, 89 Queensway, Central, Hong Kong. Tel: 852-2523-8266.
Fax: 852-2522-1760.
Shanghai Office: Kerry Centre, 20F, 1515 Nanjing Road West, Shanghai, 200040 People's Republic of China. Tel: 86-21-5298-5600.
Fax: 86-21-5298-5500.

PARTNER

Patricia Frobes (Newport Beach and Los Angeles, CA Offices)

For Complete List of Firm Personnel, See General Section

For full biographical listings, see the Martindale-Hubbell Law Directory

PIRCHER, NICHOLS & MEEKS (AV)

1999 Avenue of the Stars, 90067
Telephone: 310-201-8900
FAX: 310-201-8922
URL: http://www.pircher.com
Chicago, Illinois Office: 900 North Michigan Avenue.
Telephone: 312-915-3112.
FAX: 312-915-3348; 312-915-3354.

MEMBERS OF FIRM

Marc A. Benjamin (Resident Partner, Chicago Office)
Michael D. Berk
Stevens A. Carey
James L. Goldman
Sheldon A. Halpern
Kathleen M. Hogaboom
John H. Irons, Jr.
Richard J. Kaplan
Gary M. Laughlin
Eugene J. M. Leone (Resident Partner, Chicago Office)
Michael McKeever (Resident Partner, Chicago Office)
Larry M. Meeks
Phillip G. Nichols
David L. Packer
Leo J. Pircher
Miryam Rosie Rees (Resident Associate, Chicago Office)
Michael E. Scheinberg
Stephanie C. Silvers
Randall C. Single
I. Bruce Speiser

ASSOCIATES

Jonathan Hague Bauman
Gregg D. Bernhard
James L. Brat
Donald M. Davis
Kathleen D. De Vaney
Philip M. J. Edison (Resident Associate, Chicago Office)
Sandra Goldstein
Christopher Hameetman
William Howard Jackson, III
Kathleen J. Kim
Suzanne M. Kopp (Resident Associate, Chicago Office)
Jonathan D. Levy (Resident Associate, Chicago Office)
Heather M. Noelte
Jane Oak
Jane E. Rudofsky
Bijal V. Vakil

(See Next Column)

OF COUNSEL

Andrea H. Bricker
John R. Cauble, Jr.
Susan A. Horn
Richard Hardison MacCracken
G. Douglas McMahon (Resident Of Counsel, Chicago Office)

For full biographical listings, see the Martindale-Hubbell Law Directory

RODI, POLLOCK, PETTKER, GALBRAITH & CAHILL, A LAW CORPORATION (AV)

444 South Flower Street, Suite 1700, 90071-2901
Telephone: 213-895-4900
Telecopiers: 213-895-4921; 895-4922; 895-4750
URL: http://www.rodipollock.com

Karl B. Rodi (1908-1982)
John D. Cahill
John D. Pettker
Daniel C. Bond (1942-1977)
William R. Christian
Henry P. Pramov, Jr.
John F. Cermak, Jr.
Allan E. Ceran
Elizabeth B. Blakely
Robert C. Norton
Tim G. Ceperley
Coralie Kupfer
Cris K. O'Neall
Scott E. Adamson
Margaret Rosenthal

Sonja A. Inglin
Michael A. Abraham
Kenneth A. Franklin
Richard Nessary
Donna Yamini
Wade E. Norwood
Deepak Nanda
David J. Elbaz

OF COUNSEL

John P. Pollock — James M. Galbraith

For full biographical listings, see the Martindale-Hubbell Law Directory

ROSENFELD, WOLFF, ARONSON, KURLAND & KLEIN, A PROFESSIONAL CORPORATION (AV)

2049 Century Park East, Suite 3090, 90067
Telephone: 310-556-1221
Fax: 310-556-0401

Morton M. Rosenfeld
Steven G. Wolff
Alan D. Aronson
Marta T. Kurland
David C. Klein

Paul R. Rosenbaum — Debra E. Best

For full biographical listings, see the Martindale-Hubbell Law Directory

SCHWARTZ, STEINSAPIR, DOHRMANN & SOMMERS, LLP (AV)

6300 Wilshire Boulevard, Suite 2000, 90048
Telephone: 323-655-4700
Fax: 323-655-4488
Pittsburgh, Pennsylvania Office: 1007 Mt. Royal Boulevard, 15223.
Telephone: 412-492-8797.
Fax: 412-492-8978.

MEMBERS OF FIRM

Laurence D. Steinsapir
Robert M. Dohrmann
Richard D. Sommers
Stuart Libicki

ASSOCIATE

Erika A. Zucker

For full biographical listings, see the Martindale-Hubbell Law Directory

SHERWOOD AND HARDGROVE (AV)

A Partnership including a Professional Corporation
Suite 240, 11990 San Vicente Boulevard, 90049-5004
Telephone: 310-826-2625
FAX: 310-826-6055

Don C. Sherwood (P.C.) — Kenneth M. Hardgrove

ASSOCIATES

Charles G. Brackins
Timothy S. Plum
Darlene R. David
Christian Stephen Molnar

For full biographical listings, see the Martindale-Hubbell Law Directory

SHIOTANI & INOUYE (AV)

1901 Avenue of the Stars Suite 1010, 90067
Telephone: 310-712-0100
Telecopier: 310-712-0110
Email: silaw@earthlink.net *URL:* http://www.lawyers.com/shiotani&inouye

MEMBERS OF FIRM

Barney B. Shiotani — Lawrence G. Inouye

ASSOCIATE

Nicole Grattan Pearson

References: First Los Angeles Bank (Airport Office); Bank of California.

For full biographical listings, see the Martindale-Hubbell Law Directory

Los Angeles—Continued

RONALD P. SLATES, P.C. (AV)

548 South Spring Street, Suite 1012, 90013-2309
Telephone: 213-624-1515; 213-654-1461
Fax: 213-624-7536; 213-654-1463
Email: rslateslaw@aol.com *URL:* http://www.lawyers.com/slateslaw

Ronald P. Slates

Donald R. Ramenian

For full biographical listings, see the Martindale-Hubbell Law Directory

LAWRENCE C. TISTAERT (AV)

11766 Wilshire Boulevard, Suite 770, 90025-6537
Telephone: 310-312-0874
Fax: 310-312-1034
Email: lctist@ix.netcom.com

Representative Clients: Bell Foundry Co.; Brendan Tours; Franklin Telecommunications Corp.; Munro Properties; United States Tour Operators Association.
Reference: Bank of America.

For full biographical listings, see the Martindale-Hubbell Law Directory

WOLF, RIFKIN & SHAPIRO, LLP (AV)

A Partnership including a Professional Corporation
11400 West Olympic Boulevard Ninth Floor, 90064-1565
Telephone: 310-478-4100
Fax: 310-479-1422
Email: wrs@wrslawyers.com
Las Vegas, Nevada Office: Schulman & Grode, LLP, 2255-A Renaissance Drive 89119.
Telephone: 702-341-5200.
Fax: 702-341-5300.

MEMBERS OF FIRM

Michael Wolf (A Professional Corporation)
Daniel C. Shapiro
Roy G. Rifkin
Michael T. Schulman
Leslie Steven Marks
Mindy Sheps
Norman S. Wisnicki
Barry T. Mitidiere (A Professional Corporation)
Marc E. Rohatiner
Michael W. Rabkin
Andrew S. Gelb
Matthew L. Grode
Richard S. Grant
S. Michael Leventhal

ASSOCIATES

Douglas A. Lusson
Mark J. Rosenbaum
Kelly Allegra Weil
Matthew J. Hafey
Whitney B. Wilds
Keli N. Osaki
Laura S. Withrow
Lisa A. Makarem
Joseph A. Petro
Elsa M. Horowitz

OF COUNSEL

Steven A. Silver
Eric J. Feig
Jeff W. Lane
Jeffrey R. Liebster
Denise M. Parga
Simon Aron

For full biographical listings, see the Martindale-Hubbell Law Directory

GERALD T. YOSHIDA (AV)

12400 Wilshire Boulevard, Suite 400, 90025-1023
Telephone: 310-571-2756
Fax: 310-207-0954

Representative Clients: Vido Artukovich & Sons Construction; McKean Construction; Spiess Construction; Gierlich-Mitchell, Inc.; Hill Crane Service, Inc.; ACI General Engineering Contractors; A.A. Portanova & Sons, Inc.; Rough Terrain, Inc.; Altfillisch Construction; Ameron.

For full biographical listings, see the Martindale-Hubbell Law Directory

STUART D. ZIMRING (AV)

12650 Riverside Drive (North Hollywood), 91607-3492
Telephone: 818-755-4848
Fax: 818-755-4853

Representative Clients: Cytec Industries Inc.; Wells Fargo Bank.

For full biographical listings, see the Martindale-Hubbell Law Directory

MANHATTAN BEACH, Los Angeles Co.

STEINBERG BARNESS FOSTER & FOLEY LLP (AV)

1334 Park View Avenue, Suite 100, 90266
Telephone: 310-546-8160
Telecopier: 310-546-8189
Email: sbgf@ix.netcom.com

MEMBERS OF FIRM

Alex Steinberg
Daniel I. Barness
Douglas B. Foster
Shannon M. Foley

(See Next Column)

ASSOCIATES

William R. (Randy) Kirkpatrick
Jeff M. Lee
Kimberly Ann White

OF COUNSEL

Jordan G. Barness
Ronald D. Hariri (Not admitted in CA)

References: California United Bank; Wells Fargo Bank; Citizens Commerical Trust & Savings Bank; Bank of America.

For full biographical listings, see the Martindale-Hubbell Law Directory

MENLO PARK, San Mateo Co.

MILLER, STARR & REGALIA, A PROFESSIONAL LAW CORPORATION (AV)

545 Middlefield Road, Suite 200, 94025
Telephone: 650-463-7800
Fax: 650-462-1010
Email: msr@msandr.com *URL:* http://www.msandr.com
Walnut Creek, California Office: 1331 North California Boulevard, Fifth Floor, P.O. Box 8177.
Telephone: 925-935-9400.
Sacramento, California Office: 455 Capitol Mall, Suite 604.
Telephone: 916-443-6700.

Gary E. Rosenberg (Resident, Walnut Creek Office)
Lance H. Anderson
Lewis J. Soffer
Basil S. Shiber
Robin B. Kennedy

William F. Devine, Jr.

Representative Clients: Bank of the West; Chicago Title Insurance Co.; First American Title Insurance Co.; Hewlett Packard; Albert D. Seeno Construction Co.; Target Stores; The Good Guys; University of California; Weyerhaeuser Co.

For full biographical listings, see the Martindale-Hubbell Law Directory

MISSION VIEJO, Orange Co.

THE BUCKLEY FIRM, P.C. (AV)

Suite 200, 26522 La Alameda, 92691
Telephone: 949-348-8300
Facsimile: 949-348-8310
Email: TBF_law@ix.netcom.com
Email: TBFlaw@ix.netcom.com *URL:* http://www.buckleyfirm.com

Lawrence J. Buckley
John W. Klein
Paula Scotland
John R. Beisner

OF COUNSEL

Timothy D. Carlyle
Jonathan C. Cavett
Sam M. Muriella
Edgar C. Smith, III

Reference: Union Bank of California

For full biographical listings, see the Martindale-Hubbell Law Directory

*MODESTO,** Stanislaus Co.

BRUNN & FLYNN, A PROFESSIONAL CORPORATION (AV)

928 12th Street, P.O. Box 3366, 95353
Telephone: 209-521-2133
Fax: 209-521-7584
Email: brunnfly@ix.netcom.com

Charles K. Brunn
Timothy T. Flynn
Gerald E. Brunn
Roger S. Matzkind

Michael G. Donovan
Andrew N. Eshoo

For full biographical listings, see the Martindale-Hubbell Law Directory

MORRO BAY, San Luis Obispo Co.

OGLE, MERZON & KIRSCHNER (AV)

A Partnership including a Professional Corporation
770 Morro Bay Boulevard, P.O. Box 720, 93443-0720
Telephone: 805-772-7353
Fax: 805-772-7713
San Luis Obispo, California Office: P.O. Box 1855, 93406.
Telephone: 805-543-0295.

Charles E. Ogle (A Professional Corporation)
James B. Merzon
Charles G. Kirschner
Charles Patrick Ogle

For full biographical listings, see the Martindale-Hubbell Law Directory

*NAPA,** Napa Co.

Gaw, Van Male, Smith, Myers & Miroglio, A Professional Law Corporation (AV)
944 Main Street, 94559-3045
Telephone: 707-252-9000
Telecopier: 707-252-0792
URL: http://www.gvmsmm.com
Fairfield, California Office: Corporate Plaza. 1261 Travis Boulevard, Suite 350, 94533-4801.
Telephone: 707-425-1250.
Fax: 707-425-1255.
Redlands, California Office: 300 E. State Street, Suite 101, 92372-5200.
Telephone: 909-798-3190.
Fax: 909-798-3092.

Wyman G. Smith, III
Bruce A. Myers
S. Scott Reynolds

Michael A. Rubin
Kathleen M. Bock

Reference: The Vintage Bank.

For full biographical listings, see the Martindale-Hubbell Law Directory

NEWPORT BEACH, Orange Co.

Davis, Punelli & Keathley LLP (AV)
610 Newport Center Drive, Suite 1000, P.O. Box 7920, 92658-7920
Telephone: 949-640-0700
Telecopier: 949-640-0714
URL: http://www.lawyers.com/dpkllp

MEMBERS OF FIRM

S. Eric Davis
Frank Punelli, Jr.
H. James Keathley
Katherine D. Keathley

OF COUNSEL

Lewis K. Uhler

For full biographical listings, see the Martindale-Hubbell Law Directory

Law Offices of Mark A. Kompa (AV)
20301 S.W. Acacia Street, Suite 200, 92660
Telephone: 949-250-9500
Facsimile: 949-250-9515

For full biographical listings, see the Martindale-Hubbell Law Directory

Millar, Hodges & Bemis (AV)
One Newport Place, Suite 900, 1301 Dove Street, 92660-2448
Telephone: 949-752-7722
Fax: 949-752-6131

MEMBERS OF FIRM

Richard W. Millar, Jr.
Kenneth R. Hodges
Larry R. Bemis

ASSOCIATE

David A. St. Clair

Reference: Manufacturers Bank, Newport Beach, California.

For full biographical listings, see the Martindale-Hubbell Law Directory

Stepp & Beauchamp LLP (AV)
A Limited Liability Partnership of Professional Corporations
1301 Dove Street, Suite 460, 92660-2422
Telephone: 949-660-9700
Fax: 949-660-9010
Email: ndh@stepp-beauchamp.com *URL:* http://www.lawyers.com/stepp&beauchampllp

Thomas E. Stepp, Jr.
Mynette D. Beauchamp
Robert B. Beauchamp
Deron Matthew Colby
Michael J. Muellerleile

For full biographical listings, see the Martindale-Hubbell Law Directory

Wolf & Richards, A Law Corporation (AV)
18 Corporate Plaza Drive, 92660-7901
Telephone: 949-720-9200
Fax: 949-720-9250
Email: Alan_Wolf@wolffirm.com *URL:* http://www.wolffirm.com

Alan S. Wolf

Donna L. La Porte
Steven K. Linkon
Mark S. Flynn
Mark R. Beckington
David B. Lally
Roland P. Reynolds
Suzanne M. Hankins
Timothy M. Ryan

(See Next Column)

OF COUNSEL

Janice L. Celotti

Representative Clients: Bank of America; Chase Manhattan Mortgage Corporation; Countrywide Home Loans, Inc.; Fannie Mae; Freddie Mac; GMAC Mortgage Corporation; Meritech Mortgage Services, Inc.; Norwest Mortgage Corporation; Ocwen Federal Savings Bank; Temple Inland Mortgage Corporation.

For full biographical listings, see the Martindale-Hubbell Law Directory

*OAKLAND,** Alameda Co.

Edward L. Blum (AV)
201 19th Street, Suite 200, 94612
Telephone: 510-452-4400
Fax: 510-452-4406
Email: edblum@blumlaw.com

For full biographical listings, see the Martindale-Hubbell Law Directory

Plageman, Lund & Miller LLP (AV)
1999 Harrison, Suite 2700, 94612
Telephone: 510-273-8553
Fax: 510-273-8559

William H. Plageman, Jr.
Richard W. Lund
Debra J. Miller

ASSOCIATES

Timothy A. DeWitt
Maureen A. Kelly
Aneke M. Plimier
Susanne Meyer Brown
Paula J. Galleano

For full biographical listings, see the Martindale-Hubbell Law Directory

ONTARIO, San Bernardino Co.

Covington & Crowe LLP (AV)
1131 West Sixth Street, P.O. Box 1515, 91762
Telephone: 909-983-9393
Fax: 909-391-6762
URL: http://www.covcrowe.com

MEMBERS OF FIRM

Maurice G. Covington (1908-1997)
Harold A. Bailin (1930-1988)
Samuel P. Crowe
George W. Porter
Robert E. Dougherty
Donald G. Haslam
Robert F. Schauer
Jette R. Anderson
Audrey A. Perri
Tracy L. Tibbals
Melanie Fisch
R. Douglas Donesky
Tammy S. Jager
Katrina West

ASSOCIATES

J. Michael Kaler
Eric S. Vail
Khymberli S. Apaloo

OF COUNSEL

Edward A. Hopson

For full biographical listings, see the Martindale-Hubbell Law Directory

OXNARD, Ventura Co.

England, Whitfield, Schröeder & Tredway, L.L.P. (AV)
300 Esplanade Drive, 6th Floor, 93030
Telephone: 805-485-9627
Ventura: 647-8237
Southern California Toll Free: 800-255-3485
Fax: 805-983-0297
URL: http://www.tsurf.com/ewst/

Theodore J. England
Anson M. Whitfield
Robert W. Schröeder
David W. Tredway
Robert A. McSorley
Stuart A. Comis
Mitchel B. Kahn
Mark A. Nelson
Eric J. Kananen
Mary E. Schröeder
Oscar C. Gonzalez
Madison M. Christian
Kurt Edward Kananen

Melissa E. Cohen
Linda Kathryn Ash
Mark T. Barney
Kevin L. Dorhout
Anthony M. Ramos
Gregory J. Ramirez

Representative Clients: Dah Chong Hong (automobile dealerships); Steve thomas BMW; Vreeland Cadillac, Inc.; Willamette Industries; The Port of Hueneme; Viola, Inc. (General Contracting); Santa Clara Chemical Co.; Nakamura Berry Growers; John Taft Electric Co.; Rodgers Mortgage Co.

For full biographical listings, see the Martindale-Hubbell Law Directory

Lowthorp, Richards, McMillan, Miller, Conway & Templeman, A Professional Corporation (AV)
300 Esplanade Drive, Suite 850, P.O. Box 5167, 93031
Telephone: 805-981-8555
Fax: 805-983-1967

(See Next Column)

LOWTHORP, RICHARDS, MCMILLAN, MILLER, CONWAY & TEMPLEMAN A PROFESSIONAL CORPORATION, *Oxnard—Continued*

Carl F. Lowthorp, Jr. (1933-1992)
Richard A. Richards
Robert C. McMillan
Paul A. Miller
Charles J. Conway, Jr.
Alan R. Templeman
Patrick T. Loughman
Glenn J. Campbell
John Q. Masteller

LEGAL SUPPORT PERSONNEL

Elizabeth T. Ladiana, CLA

Representative Clients: Pleasant Valley Mutual Water Co.; Friedrich Ranches, Inc.; Deardorff Jackson Co.; Pacific Coast Plastering; AGRX, Inc.; Terry Farms; Hurst Concrete Products; Chase Bros. Dairy; Dullam Nursery.
Reference: City National Bank.

For full biographical listings, see the Martindale-Hubbell Law Directory

PALM DESERT, Riverside Co.

CRISTE, PIPPIN & GOLDS (AV)

Suite 200, 73-550 Alessandro Drive, 92260
Telephone: 760-862-1111
Fax: 760-776-4197
Email: cpgca@aol.com

MEMBERS OF FIRM

Michael A. Criste
Robert L. Pippin
Irwin L. Golds

ASSOCIATES

Jeffrey S. Flashman
Julian S. Summers

For full biographical listings, see the Martindale-Hubbell Law Directory

PALM SPRINGS, Riverside Co.

SCHLECHT, SHEVLIN & SHOENBERGER, A LAW CORPORATION (AV)

801 East Tahquitz Canyon Way, Suite 100, P.O. Box 2744, 92263-2744
Telephone: 760-320-7161
Facsimile: 760-323-1758
Email: ssslaw@gte.net *URL:* http://www.ssslaw.com

James M. Schlecht
Daniel T. Johnson

David Darrin

Representative Clients: Outdoor Resorts of America; The Escrow Connection; Palm Hills Land Corp.; Shadowrock; Palm Springs Marquis; U.S. Home Corp.

For Complete List of Firm Personnel, See General Section

For full biographical listings, see the Martindale-Hubbell Law Directory

PALO ALTO, Santa Clara Co.

FLICKER & KERIN (AV)

Suite 460, 285 Hamilton, P.O. Box 840, 94302
Telephone: 650-321-0947
Fax: 650-326-9722

MEMBERS OF FIRM

Michael R. Flicker
Anthony J. Kerin, III
Rhesa C. Rubin

ASSOCIATES

Cheri A. Bell
Eleni Adamis

For full biographical listings, see the Martindale-Hubbell Law Directory

PASADENA, Los Angeles Co.

LAGERLOF, SENECAL, BRADLEY, GOSNEY & KRUSE, LLP (AV)

301 North Lake Avenue, 10th Floor, 91101-4108
Telephone: 626-793-9400
FAX: 626-793-5900
Email: mail@lagerlof.com

MEMBERS OF FIRM

Joseph J. Burris (1913-1980)
Stanley C. Lagerlof (1915-1998)
H. Jess Senecal
Jack T. Swafford
John F. Bradley
Timothy J. Gosney
William F. Kruse
Thomas S. Bunn, III
Andrew D. Turner
Rebecca J. Thyne
James D. Ciampa

ASSOCIATE

Shaun O. Kwon

Representative Clients: Gallo Glass Company; Orthopaedic Hospital; North American Chemical Company; Palmdale Water District; Public Water Agencies Group; Ventura Port District; Walnut Valley Water District; Metric Construction Co., Inc.

For full biographical listings, see the Martindale-Hubbell Law Directory

PIEDMONT, Alameda Co.

BICKEL & ASSOCIATES (AV)

1375 Grand Avenue, Suite 200, 94610
Telephone: 510-595-8200
Fax: 510-595-8600
Email: condolaw@slip.net *URL:* http://www.condobook.com

Branden E. Bickel

ASSOCIATE

Dawn A. Silberstein

For full biographical listings, see the Martindale-Hubbell Law Directory

PLEASANTON, Alameda Co.

GEOFFREY C. ETNIRE (AV)

4900 Hopyard Road, Suite 100, 94588
Telephone: 925-734-9950
Fax: 925-734-9170
Email: geoff@etnire.com *URL:* http://www.etnire.com
Palo Alto, California Office: 635 Emerson Street, P.O. Box 1713, 94302-1713.
Telephone: 650-327-2255.
Fax: 650-328-9327.

For full biographical listings, see the Martindale-Hubbell Law Directory

*REDWOOD CITY,** San Mateo Co.

HANNIG LAW FIRM LLP (AV)

2991 El Camino Real, Suite 100, 94061
Telephone: 650-482-3040
Facsimile: 650-482-2820
Email: tjh@hanniglaw.com *URL:* http://www.hanniglaw.com

Ted J. Hannig
H. Ann Liroff
David M. Rose

OF COUNSEL

John Antonakos
Michael D. Barry

For full biographical listings, see the Martindale-Hubbell Law Directory

*SACRAMENTO,** Sacramento Co.

BOUTIN, DENTINO, GIBSON DI GIUSTO, HODELL & WEST, A PROFESSIONAL CORPORATION (AV)

455 Capitol Mall, Suite 300, 95814-4406
Telephone: 916-321-4444
Telecopier: 916-441-7597
URL: http://www.boutindentino.com
Tucson, Arizona Office: 405 West Franklin Street, 85718.
Telephone: 520-882-2944.

Stephen F. Boutin
William Dentino
Chris Gibson
John E. Di Giusto
Douglas M. Hodell
R. Michael West
Robert D. Swanson
Ned M. Gelhaar

Kimberly L. Jackson
Mark W. Owens
James R. Moore
Michael T. Sparks
Sallie-Carol Orbas
Jeffrey B. Slaton

OF COUNSEL

Robert G. West
Thomas G. Manolakas

For full biographical listings, see the Martindale-Hubbell Law Directory

HARDY ERICH BROWN & WILSON, A PROFESSIONAL CORPORATION (AV)

1000 G Street, 95814
Telephone: 916-449-3800
Fax: 916-449-3888
Mailing Address: P.O. Box 13530, Sacramento, California, 95853-4530
Email: hebw@hebw.com *URL:* http://www.hebw.com

Thomas C. Richards
David L. Perrault
L. Kent Wyatt
Glenda N. Reager
Whitney A. Davis
Michael J. Nelson

Lisa L. Palombo

Representative Clients: American Promotional Events; Colliers Iliff Thorn & Company; Dollar Tree Stores; Donahue Schriber; E.J. Plesko & Associates, Inc.; Foamex International, Inc.; Little Caesar Enterprises, Inc.; Mather Federal Credit Union; Step Ahead Investments, Inc.; Woodmont Real Estate Services.

For full biographical listings, see the Martindale-Hubbell Law Directory

Sacramento—Continued

HUNTER RICHEY DI BENEDETTO & BREWER, LLP (AV)

A Limited Liability Partnership
Renaissance Tower, 801 K Street, 23rd Floor, 95814-3525
Telephone: 916-491-3000
Facsimile: 916-491-3080
Email: hrdb@hrdb.com *URL:* http://www.hrdb.com

MEMBERS OF FIRM

William S. Hunter
Win R. Richey
Florence L. Di Benedetto
Roy E. Brewer
Anne E. Ferguson
James F. Geary
Janet C. Eisenbeis
Stephen C. Ruehmann
Sharon K. Sandeen
Jack V. Lovell
Patricia J. Hartman

OF COUNSEL

Laurie E. Davis

LEGAL SUPPORT PERSONNEL

Lori J. Moody (Paralegal)
Deborah M. Johnson (Paralegal)
Linda Jane Hall (Executive Assistant)
Jennifer E. Mueller (Legal Assistant)
Michele L. Nickell (Legal Assistant)
Lynetta G. Goodwin

For full biographical listings, see the Martindale-Hubbell Law Directory

LIVINGSTON & MATTESICH, LAW CORPORATION (AV)

1201 K Street, Suite 1100, 95814
Telephone: 916-442-1111
Fax: 916-448-1709
Email: l&m@lmlaw.net *URL:* http://www.lmlaw.net

Gene Livingston
James M. Mattesich
Carol Livingston
Rebecca M. Ceniceros
Emilio E. Varanini, III
Kenneth M. Malovos
Kathleen E. Finnerty
Joanna R. Mendoza

Steven P. Belzer
Jeffrey Leacox
Randy Pollack
Alice H. Choi
Stephen Craig Hunter
Matthew J. Goldman
Joel C. Baiocchi
Baldassaro (Bill) Di Capo
John McKinsey
Timothy E. Naccarato
Craig N. Lundgren
Mary Farrell Taylor
Brian Crone
Gay L. Carroll
Steven G. Churchwell

Representative Clients: City of Redding; City of Rocklin; County of Del Norte; Crescent Community Services District; Guaranty Federal Bank, F.S.B.; Oak Creek Estates; Payless Cashways, Inc. (Lumberjack Stores); R. Wentz Construction, Inc.; Sacramento Regional Transit District; Tahoe Regional Planning Agency.

For full biographical listings, see the Martindale-Hubbell Law Directory

MATHENY SEARS LINKERT & LONG, LLP (AV)

3638 American River Drive, P.O. Box 13711, 95853-4711
Telephone: 916-978-3434
Fax: 916-978-3430
Email: info@msll.com *URL:* http://www.msll.com

MEMBERS OF FIRM

Henry G. Matheny (1933-1984)
Douglas A. Sears
Richard S. Linkert
Ernest A. Long
Joann Georgallis
Kent M. Luckey
Matthew C. Jaime
Michael A. Bishop
Robert B. Berrigan
Ronald E. Enabnit
Eric R. Wiesel

ASSOCIATES

Andrea Croak Christensen
Michael G. Jones
Eric M. Bonzell
Mary Elizabeth Wood
Paul Richard Baleria
James F. Curran
Andreas C. Rockas
Timothy P. Chang

OF COUNSEL

James C. Damir

LEGAL SUPPORT PERSONNEL

PARALEGALS

Frances Studer
Lynell Rae Steed
Jennifer Bachman

For full biographical listings, see the Martindale-Hubbell Law Directory

LAW OFFICES OF JOSEPH W. SCALIA

(See Gold River)

---

*SAN DIEGO,** San Diego Co.

DUKE GERSTEL SHEARER, LLP (AV)

A Registered Limited Liability Partnership
Sixth Floor, 101 West Broadway, P.O. Box 85470, 92186-5470
Telephone: 619-232-0816
800-405-0816
Fax: 619-232-4661
Email: lawyers@dgsllp.com *URL:* http://www.dgsllp.com
Costa Mesa, California Office: 3200 Park Center Drive, Suite 1000, 92626.
Telephone: 949-551-8664, 800-405-0816.
Los Angeles, California Office: 10866 Wilshire Boulevard, Suite 1400, 90024.
Telephone: 310-475-7118, 800-405-0816.
San Francisco, California Office: 744 Montgomery Street, Fifth Floor, 94111.
Telephone: 415-773-0101.
Palm Springs, California Office: 1111 East Tahquitz Canyon Way, Suite 110, 92262.
Telephone: 760-322-7846.
Phoenix, Arizona Office: One Columbus Plaza, 3636 North Central Avenue, Suite 1200, 85012.
Telephone: 602-650-2060.
Fax: 602-650-2089.
Tucson, Arizona Office: 6969 East Sunrise Drive, Suite 102, 85750.
Telephone: 520-615-8858.
Fax: 520-615-1069.
Affiliate Las Vegas, Nevada Office: Parsons & Pursiano, LLP, City Center West, Suite 108, 7201 W. Lake Mead Boulevard, 89128.
Telephone: 702-384-9900.
Facsimile: 702-384-5900.

MEMBERS OF FIRM

Stephen V. Rupp (A Professional Corporation)
Alan R. Johnston (A Professional Corporation)

ASSOCIATE

Susan K. Stewart

Reference: Bank of Commerce.

For full biographical listings, see the Martindale-Hubbell Law Directory

FERRETTE & SLATER, A LAW CORPORATION (AV)

16765 West Bernardo Drive Suite 150, 92127
Telephone: 858-487-9596; 619-233-7217
Facsimile: 858-487-9658
Email: law@ferretteslater.com

Victor J. Ferrette
Gary E. Slater
Gregory C. Alcorn
Timothy J. Truxaw

ASSOCIATE

Denise P. Blasband

For full biographical listings, see the Martindale-Hubbell Law Directory

FERRIS & BRITTON, A PROFESSIONAL CORPORATION (AV)

1600 First National Bank Center, 401 West A Street, 92101
Telephone: 619-233-3131
Fax: 619-232-9316
Email: manager@ferrisbritton.com *URL:* http://www.ferrisbritton.com

Alfred G. Ferris
Gary T. Moyer

Representative Clients: Cox Communications, Inc.; Invitrogen Corporation; Peninsula Bank; Teleport Communications Group; Southwest Airlines; ZyGam, Inc.

For Complete List of Firm Personnel, See General Section

For full biographical listings, see the Martindale-Hubbell Law Directory

FISCH, SPIEGLER, GINSBURG, LADNER & ATTARIAN, A PROFESSIONAL LAW CORPORATION (AV)

1551 Fourth Avenue, Suite 300, 92101-3184
Telephone: 619-234-1551
Telecopier: 619-234-1568
Email: FSGLA@AOL.com

Joseph J. Fisch
Mark A. Spiegler
Phillip L. Ginsburg
Karen M. Ladner
Peter J. Attarian, Jr.

For full biographical listings, see the Martindale-Hubbell Law Directory

HECHT, SOLBERG, ROBINSON & GOLDBERG, LLP (AV)

One America Plaza, 600 West Broadway, Eighth Floor, 92101
Telephone: 619-239-3444
Telecopier: 619-232-6828
Email: mail@hsrg.com

(See Next Column)

HECHT, SOLBERG, ROBINSON & GOLDBERG LLP, *San Diego—Continued*

MEMBERS OF FIRM

Alan John Hecht (A Professional Corporation)
Darryl O. Solberg (A Professional Corporation)
Jerold H. Goldberg (A Professional Corporation)
Paul E. Robinson (A Professional Corporation)
David W. Bagley, II (A Professional Corporation)
Michael J. Maher
R. Martin Bohl
Anton Dimitroff
Susan Lee Daly

SENIOR ATTORNEYS

Richard A. Schulman
Michael A. Van Horne
Peter K. Solecki
Kenneth C. Jones

ASSOCIATES

Tricia L. Greenlee
Erik Olav Valderhaug
Nataki A. Finch

For full biographical listings, see the Martindale-Hubbell Law Directory

HOVEY & KIRBY, A PROFESSIONAL CORPORATION (AV)

402 West Broadway, Suite 1500, 92101
Telephone: 619-685-4000
Fax: 619-685-4004
Email: administrator@hoveylaw.com

Gregg B. Hovey
Dean T. Kirby, Jr.
M. Leslie Hovey
Kristen S. Armstrong

For full biographical listings, see the Martindale-Hubbell Law Directory

KENNERSON SCHWARTZ SEMERDJIAN & HAILE LLP (AV)

A Limited Liability Partnership
101 West Broadway, Suite 810, 92101
Telephone: 619-236-8821
Facsimile: 619-236-8827
URL: http://www.lawyers.com/ksshlaw

OF COUNSEL

Paul R. Kennerson

MEMBERS OF FIRM

Ross J. Schwartz
Dick A. Semerdjian
Jeffrey A. Haile

James R. Ballard
John K. Grant

For full biographical listings, see the Martindale-Hubbell Law Directory

LINDLEY, SCALES & CORBETT, A PROFESSIONAL CORPORATION (AV)

550 West C Street, Suite 1800, 92101
Telephone: 619-234-9181
Fax: 619-234-8475
Email: lsc@adnc.com

Luke R. Corbett
Robert M. McLeod

Representative Clients: Chicago Title Insurance Company; Palomar Savings & Loan Association.

For full biographical listings, see the Martindale-Hubbell Law Directory

LUCE, FORWARD, HAMILTON & SCRIPPS LLP (AV)

A Partnership including Professional Corporations
600 West Broadway, Suite 2600, 92101
Telephone: 619-236-1414
Fax: 619-232-8311
URL: http://www.luce.com
La Jolla, California Office: 4275 Executive Square, Suite 800, 92037.
Telephone: 858-455-6611.
Fax: 858-232-8311.
Los Angeles, California Office: 777 South Figueroa, Suite 3600, 90017.
Telephone: 213-892-4992.
Fax: 213-892-7731.
San Francisco, California Office: 121 Spear Street, Suite 200, 94105.
Telephone: 415-356-4600.
Fax: 415-356-4610.
New York, N.Y. Office: Citicorp Center, 153 East 53rd Street, 26th Floor, 10022.
Telephone: 212-754-1414.
Fax: 212-644-9727.
Chicago, Illinois Office: 180 North La Salle Street, Suite 3110, 60601.
Telephone: 312-641-0580.
Fax: 312-641-0380.

Christopher K. Barnette
Craig K. Beam
Robert J. Bell
Robert D. Buell (Managing Partner)
Marjorie J. Burchett
Jeffrey A. Chine
Dennis J. Doucette
Roger C. Haerr
Mark Hagarty
Charles L. Hellerich
Valentine S. Hoy, VIII

(See Next Column)

(Continued)

David M. Hymer
Allan E. Low (Resident, San Francisco Office)
Thomas A. May
Thomas M. Murray
Timothy R. Pestotnik
Ronald W. Rouse
Nancy T. Scull
Stephen T. Toohill
Pamela Wagner
Steven S. Wall

ASSOCIATES

Melissa M. Allenby
Jennifer R. Barragan (Resident, San Francisco Office)
Lynn Borkenhagen
Holly Traube Cordova
Cindy Dobler Davis
Christopher H. Findley
Brian C. Fish
Lynne D. Kaelin
Stephanie E. Kish
Michael G. Ramsey
Mina S. Yang

For Complete List of Firm Personnel, See General Section

For full biographical listings, see the Martindale-Hubbell Law Directory

SOLOMON WARD SEIDENWURM & SMITH, LLP (AV)

1200 Wells Fargo Plaza, 401 B Street, 92101
Telephone: 619-231-0303
Telecopier: 619-231-4755
Email: mvafi@swsslaw.com *URL:* http://www.swsslaw.com

PARTNERS OF FIRM

Michael D. Breslauer
Cynthia L. Eldred
Lawrence J. Kaplan (P.C.)
Richard E. McCarthy
Edward J. McIntyre
Paul S. Metsch
Alison L. Pivonka
Harry J. Proctor (P.C.)
Jeffrey A. Schneider
Richard L. Seidenwurm (P.C.)
Jeffrey H. Silberman
Miguel A. Smith
Norman L. Smith
Herbert J. Solomon

ASSOCIATES

Daniel E. Gardenswartz
David T. Gluck
Amy Perkins Melden
Karl A. Sandoval
Kurt E. Scheuerman
Elizabeth A. Trevino

OF COUNSEL

Robert F. La Scala
William O. Ward, III (Retired)

For full biographical listings, see the Martindale-Hubbell Law Directory

STEPHENSON, WORLEY, GARRATT, SCHWARTZ, GARFIELD & PRAIRIE (AV)

A Limited Liability Partnership
401 "B" Street, Suite 2400, 92101-4200
Telephone: 619-696-3500
Fax: 619-696-3555
Email: SDLAW@swgsgp.com

MEMBERS OF FIRM

Gary J. Stephenson
Donald R. Worley
Gregory C. M. Garratt
William J. Schwartz, Jr.
Michael W. Prairie
Timothy K. Garfield
Laurel Lee Hyde

OF COUNSEL

Kent H. Foster
Elaine L. Chan
Ralph E. Hughes

Reference: Bank of Commerce.

For full biographical listings, see the Martindale-Hubbell Law Directory

STIPANOV & MEBANE, A PROFESSIONAL LAW CORPORATION (AV)

501 West Broadway, Suite 520, 92101
Telephone: 619-235-2686
Fax: 619-235-2692
Email: stipanov@stipmeb.com *URL:* http://www.stipmeb.com/law

Kenneth J. Stipanov
Julie S. Mebane

For full biographical listings, see the Martindale-Hubbell Law Directory

LAW OFFICES OF MAURILE C. TREMBLAY A PROFESSIONAL CORPORATION (AV)

4370 La Jolla Village Drive, Suite 675, 92122-1252
Telephone: 858-558-3030
Fax: 858-558-2502
Email: lawmct@aol.com *URL:* http://www.lawyers.com/mauriletremblay

Maurile C. Tremblay

Lana Hanisko-Greenberg

For full biographical listings, see the Martindale-Hubbell Law Directory

San Diego—Continued

ARTHUR M. WILCOX, JR. (AV)

Koll Center, 501 West Broadway, Suite 750, 92101
Telephone: 619-696-6788
Fax: 619-696-8685
Email: amwilcox@ix.netcom.com *URL:* http://www.lawyers.com/wilcoxlaw

For full biographical listings, see the Martindale-Hubbell Law Directory

*SAN FRANCISCO,** San Francisco Co.

BARTKO, ZANKEL, TARRANT & MILLER, PROFESSIONAL CORPORATION (AV)

900 Front Street, Suite 300, 94111-1427
Telephone: 415-956-1900
Fax: 415-956-1152
Email: bztm@bztm.com *URL:* http://www.bztm.com

John J. Bartko
Martin I. Zankel
Richard T. Tarrant
Charles G. Miller
Robert H. Bunzel
Michael D. Welch
Michael D. Abraham
M. Manuel Fishman
Christopher J. Hunt
John S. Lottier
Theani Christine Louskos
Howard L. Pearlman
C. Griffith Towle
Glenn P. Zwang
Christopher D. Sullivan

Thomas E. Cooper
Gail E. Kavanagh
Brenda M. Lillington
Tyler Roberts Meade
Rosanna S. Russell
Carissa Shubb
Russell G. Young

COUNSEL

Thomas A. Lee, Jr.
Darryl A. Hart

For full biographical listings, see the Martindale-Hubbell Law Directory

ELLMAN, BURKE, HOFFMAN & JOHNSON, A PROFESSIONAL CORPORATION (AV)

One Ecker, Suite 200, 94105
Telephone: 415-777-2727
Fax: 415-495-7587
Email: managingdirector@ellman-burke.com *URL:* http://www.ellman-burke.com

Howard N. Ellman
Michael J. Burke
Kenneth N. Burns
John D. Hoffman
Jeffrey W. Johnson
Thomas Paine
Jay L. Paxton
Thomas M. Sherwood
Leslie M. Browne
Jodi Billehus Fedor

JoAnne L. Dunec
Sarah Richards Gansa
Christina W. Chi

For full biographical listings, see the Martindale-Hubbell Law Directory

KAY & MERKLE (AV)

100 The Embarcadero Penthouse, 94105
Telephone: 415-357-1200
Facsimile: 415-512-9277
Email: kmlaw100@kmlaw100.com

MEMBERS OF FIRM

Steven Kay
Walter F. Merkle, Jr.
W. Bruce Bercovich
John W. Merkle
Alan J. Silver
Douglas A. Marshall
Douglas A Hutchinson

OF COUNSEL

Lionel T. Aiken

For full biographical listings, see the Martindale-Hubbell Law Directory

MORGENSTEIN & JUBELIRER, LLP (AV)

One Market, Spear Street Tower, 32nd Floor, 94105
Telephone: 415-896-0666
Fax: 415-896-5592
Email: m&j@mj-sflaw.com

Marvin D. Morgenstein (Retired)
Eliot S. Jubelirer
Lee Ann Huntington
Jean L. Bertrand
Jeffrey R. Williams
James R. Balich
Rocky N. Unruh
James L. McGinnis
Charles W. LaGrave
William J. Carroll
John S. Worden
Wendi J. Berkowitz
Stephen M. Hankins
Bruce A. Wagman

(See Next Column)

MORGENSTEIN & JUBELIRER, LLP, San Francisco—Continued

Lewis D. Barr
David H. Bromfield
Alexander P. Catalona
Michael "Cael" S. Davis
Roberta Nicol Dempster
Laura E. Gasser
Jill L. Gillen
Natasha L. Golding
Judith A. Holiber
Shawn D. Parrish
John J. Petry

For full biographical listings, see the Martindale-Hubbell Law Directory

MURPHY, PEARSON, BRADLEY & FEENEY, A PROFESSIONAL CORPORATION (AV)

88 Kearny Street, 10th Floor, 94108
Telephone: 415-788-1900
Telecopier: 415-393-8087
Email: IndividualsFirstInitialAndLastName@mpbf.com *URL:* http://www.mpbf.com
Sacramento, California Office: 701 University Avenue, Suite 150.
Telephone: 916-565-0300.
Fax: 916-565-1636.
San Jose, California Office: 80 South Market Street, 3rd Floor.
Telephone: 408-279-5792.
Facsimile: 408-279-5785.
Los Angeles, California Office: 11400 West Olympic Boulevard, Suite 249.
Telephone: 310-312-9565.
Fax: 310-312-9566.

Karen M. Goodman (Resident, Sacramento Office)
Mark S. Perelman
Jane L. O'Hara Gamp

For Complete List of Firm Personnel, See General Section

For full biographical listings, see the Martindale-Hubbell Law Directory

*SAN JOSE,** Santa Clara Co.

HOPKINS & CARLEY, A LAW CORPORATION (AV)

Sixth Floor, 2 West Santa Clara Street, 95113-1824
Telephone: 408-286-9800
Facsimile: 408-998-4790
Mailing Address: P.O. Box 1469, San Jose, CA, 95109-1469
URL: http://www.hopkinscarley.com

John F. Hopkins
Garth E. Pickett
Stephen J. Kottmeier
Ross G. Adler
Jeffrey E. Essner
Jay M. Ross
Sharon L. Wong
J. Randall Toch

For Complete List of Firm Personnel, See General Section

For full biographical listings, see the Martindale-Hubbell Law Directory

LICCARDO, ROSSI, STURGES & MCNEIL, A PROFESSIONAL LAW CORPORATION (AV)

1960 The Alameda, Suite 200, 95126-1493
Telephone: 408-244-4570
Fax: 408-244-3294
URL: http://www.LRSM.com

Salvador A. Liccardo
Ronald R. Rossi
Robert S. Sturges
R. Donald McNeil
David M. Hamerslough
Susan R. Reischl
Craig Needham
Laura Liccardo
Samuel A. Chuck
Richard B. Gullen

Robert C. Colyar
Paul Salvatore Liccardo
Thomas Eamon McNeil

For full biographical listings, see the Martindale-Hubbell Law Directory

MILLER, MORTON, CAILLAT & NEVIS (AV)

50 West San Fernando Street, Suite 1300, 95113-2413
Telephone: 408-292-1765
Telecopier: 408-292-4484
URL: http://www.mmcn-law.com

Richard W. Morton (1916-1975)
Charles V. Caillat (1920-1990)
Harvey C. Miller (1906-1993)

MEMBERS OF FIRM

David L. Nevis
Francis J. Hughes
Peter A. Kline
Stevan C. Adelman
Joseph A. Scanlan, Jr.
Carolyn Tobiason Stuart
William K. Hurley
Peter V. Dessau

OF COUNSEL

Nancy F. Symons

ASSOCIATES

Kathryn E. Barrett
Katherine S. Pak
David I. Kornbluh
Christopher J. Hersey
Julie Neale Meyer

(See Next Column)

MILLER, MORTON, CAILLAT & NEVIS, *San Jose—Continued*

Representative Clients: Trammell Crow Residential; Cornerstone Properties; Berkshire Life Insurance Co.; Artesia Mortgage Capital Corp.; Cimco, Inc.; First Community Housing; Irvine Apartment Communities; Ecumenical Association for Housing; Avalon Bay Communities; Greenbriar Homes Co.

For full biographical listings, see the Martindale-Hubbell Law Directory

TERRA LAW LLP (AV)

60 South Market Street, Suite 200, 95113
Telephone: 408-288-7325
Fax: 408-998-4895
Burlingame, California Office: 1350 Old Bayshore Highway, Suite 760, 94010.
Telephone: 650-685-7325.
Fax: 650-685-4895.

George H. Cole, Jr.
D. D. Hughmanick
R. Prescott Jaunich
Richard O. McDonald
Breck E. Milde
William L. Myers
Jane P. Relyea
Jason R. Biggs
Joan Paul
Ronald I. Rainey

Katharine L. Hardt-Mason
Thomas E. Rossmeissl

For full biographical listings, see the Martindale-Hubbell Law Directory

*SAN LUIS OBISPO,** San Luis Obispo Co.

ANDRE, MORRIS & BUTTERY, A PROFESSIONAL LAW CORPORATION (AV)

1102 Laurel Lane, P.O. Box 730, 93406-0730
Telephone: 805-543-4171
Fax: 805-543-0752
Email: amb@amblaw.com *URL:* http://www.amblaw.com

Michael J. Morris
James C. Buttery
Dennis D. Law
J. Todd Mirolla
Scott W. Wall

Mary E. McAlister
Kathryn M. Eppright
Kevin D. Morris
William V. Douglass

References: Bank of America National Trust and Savings Assn. (San Luis Obispo Main Branch); Mid-State Bank (San Luis Obispo).

For full biographical listings, see the Martindale-Hubbell Law Directory

*SAN RAFAEL,** Marin Co.

FLYNN & PHILLIPS, LLP (AV)

1099 E Street, 94901
Telephone: 415-482-9933
Fax: 415-482-9939
San Francisco, California Office: 555 Montgomery Street, Suite 720, 94111.
Telephone: 415-882-4040.
Fax: 415-882-4088.

Michael J. Flynn
Scott M. Phillips
Timothy W. Moppin
Steven A. Simontacchi

LEGAL SUPPORT PERSONNEL

Holly A.M. Lewis (Paralegal)

For full biographical listings, see the Martindale-Hubbell Law Directory

*SANTA ANA,** Orange Co.

CALLAHAN & BLAINE, A PROFESSIONAL LAW CORPORATION (AV)

3 Hutton Centre Drive, Suite 900, 92707
Telephone: 714-241-4444
Fax: 714-241-4445
Email: info@callahan-law.com *URL:* http://www.callahan-law.com

Daniel J. Callahan
Stephen E. Blaine

Jim P. Mahacek
Michael J. Sachs
Edward Susolik
Kathleen L. Dunham
Robyn Dimino
Reed N. Archambault
Nicki N. Eke
David Kam Ng
Douglas W. Schroeder

OF COUNSEL

Shelley M. Liberto
Walt D. Mahaffa

For full biographical listings, see the Martindale-Hubbell Law Directory

PIZER & MICHAELSON INC. (AV)

2122 North Broadway, Suite 100, 92706
Telephone: 714-558-0535
Telecopier: 714-550-0841
Los Angeles, California Office: 2049 Century Park East, Suite 460, 90067.
Telephone: 310-843-9729.
Fax: 310-843-9619.

Seymour S. Pizer (1930-1992)
Barry S. Michaelson
Hugh R. Coffin
Bradley J. Pizer
(Resident, Los Angeles Office)

For full biographical listings, see the Martindale-Hubbell Law Directory

ROSE POTHIER & ASSOCIATES (AV)

2122 North Broadway, 92706
Telephone: 714-953-8580
Fax: 714-558-1707
Email: ROSPO@aol.com *URL:* http://members.aol.com/Rospo/index.html

For full biographical listings, see the Martindale-Hubbell Law Directory

SWANSON AND GIESER, A PROFESSIONAL CORPORATION (AV)

4 Hutton Centre Drive, Suite 200, 92707-5770
Telephone: 714-755-3500
Fax: 714-755-3505
URL: http://www.lawyers.com/swansongieserlaw
San Diego, California Office: 600 B Street, Suite 2120, 92101.
Telephone: 619-686-6100.
Fax: 619-686-6105.

C. Brent Swanson (1941-1998)
Thomas M. Gieser

Elaine B. Alston

For full biographical listings, see the Martindale-Hubbell Law Directory

*SANTA BARBARA,** Santa Barbara Co.

ANGLE, CARLSON, GOLDRICK & ROBERTS (AV)

A Partnership including a Professional Corporation
200 East Carrillo Street, Suite 310, 93101
Telephone: 805-963-7400
Fax: 805-963-7610

Robert O. Angle
Arthur W. Carlson (A P.C.)
Miles T. Goldrick
Paul A. Roberts

For full biographical listings, see the Martindale-Hubbell Law Directory

HOLLISTER & BRACE, A PROFESSIONAL CORPORATION (AV)

1126 Santa Barbara Street, P.O. Box 630, 93101
Telephone: 805-963-6711
Fax: 805-965-0329
Email: hblaw@hbsb.com

William A. Brace (Retired)
J. James Hollister, III (Retired)
John S. Poucher
Richard C. Monk
George A. Rempe, III
Steven Evans Kirby
Bradford F. Ginder
John G. Busby
Susan H. McCollum
Robert L. Brace
Marcus Scott Bird
Charles W. Willey (P.C.)
Alexis W. Willey
Peter L. Candy

Attorneys For: Bucara Resort & Spa; Buellflat Rock Co.; Celite Corp.; Coast Rock Products; Gaviota Marine Terminal; Ian Schrager Hotels, LLC; Morehart Land Company; Santa Barbara County Rock Producers Assoc.; Santa Barbara Trust for Historic Preservation; Venoco, Inc.

For full biographical listings, see the Martindale-Hubbell Law Directory

SANTA MONICA, Los Angeles Co.

BERGER & NORTON, A LAW CORPORATION (AV)

1620 26th Street Suite 200 South, 90404
Telephone: 310-449-1000
Fax: 310-449-5000
URL: http://www.bergernorton.com

Michael M. Berger
Richard D. Norton
Ann E. Kelly
George M. Soneff
Edward G. Burg
Craig M. Collins
Pamela Schmidt

Kisu Shin
Sophie A. Castillo

OF COUNSEL

Gideon Kanner

For full biographical listings, see the Martindale-Hubbell Law Directory

Santa Monica—Continued

Gilchrist & Rutter, Professional Corporation (AV)

Wilshire Palisades Building, 1299 Ocean Avenue, Suite 900, 90401
Telephone: 310-393-4000
Facsimile: 310-394-4700
Email: POSTMASTER@GRLAWYERS.COM *URL:* http://www.grlawyers.com
Los Angeles, California Office: 355 South Grand Avenue, Suite 4100.
Telephone: 213-617-8000.
Facsimile: 213-534-8001.

MEMBERS OF THE FIRM

Jonathan S. Gross
Paul S. Rutter
James R. Andrews
Susan Fowler McNally
James M. Jimenez
Richard H. Close
Michael S. Abrams

ASSOCIATES

Steven P. Heller
Cynthia L. Masters

For full biographical listings, see the Martindale-Hubbell Law Directory

Steinberg, Nutter & Brent, Law Corporation (AV)

501 Colorado Avenue, Suite 300, 90401
Telephone: 310-451-9714
Telecopier: 310-451-0929
Woodland Hills, California Office: 21031 Ventura Boulevard, Suite 419.
Telephone: 818-703-6204.

Peter T. Steinberg
Guy B. Nutter
Paul M. Brent

ASSOCIATE

Adam E. Chaikin

Reference: Santa Monica Bank.

For full biographical listings, see the Martindale-Hubbell Law Directory

SANTA ROSA, * Sonoma Co.

Abbey, Weitzenberg, Hoffman & Emery, A Professional Corporation (AV)

1105 North Dutton Avenue, P.O. Box 1566, 95402
Telephone: 707-542-5050
Telecopier: 707-542-2589
Email: info@abbeylaw.com

Richard W. Abbey
Lewis R. Warren

Representative Clients: Exchange Bank of Santa Rosa; Westamerica Bank; Northwestern Title Security Co.; Geyser Peak Winery; Santa Rosa City School District; Sonoma National Bank; Arrowood Vineyards & Winery; Friedman Bros. Hardware, Inc.; Bank of Lake County; Lasercraft, Inc.

For full biographical listings, see the Martindale-Hubbell Law Directory

Beyers, Costin & Case, A Professional Corporation (AV)

917 College Avenue, P.O. Box 878, 95402
Telephone: 707-545-0142
Facsimile: 707-526-3672; 707-526-2746
URL: http://www.bcclaw.com

James L. Beyers
Christopher G. Costin
Nancy L. Case

Thomas Davenport, III
Peter L.D. Simon
Michelle V. Zyromski

OF COUNSEL

Mario T.R. Zepponi

For full biographical listings, see the Martindale-Hubbell Law Directory

THOUSAND OAKS, Ventura Co.

Cohen, Alexander & Clayton, A Professional Corporation (AV)

One Boardwalk, Suite 102, 91360-5799
Telephone: 805-497-0802
Fax: 805-373-6082
Email: lawcac@ix.netcom.com

Charles W. Cohen
Leonard Alexander
Raymond C. Clayton
Ruth D. Morrow
Marguerite A. Wilson

Thomas S. Cohen

Representative Clients: Comsat General Corp.; Conejo Valley Chamber of Commerce; South Coast Area Transit.

For full biographical listings, see the Martindale-Hubbell Law Directory

TORRANCE, Los Angeles Co.

Finer, Kim & Stearns (AV)

An Association of Professional Corporations
City National Bank Building, 3424 Carson Street, Suite 500, 90503
Telephone: 310-214-1477
Telecopier: 310-214-0764
Email: finerkimstearns@pobox.com *URL:* http://www.finerkimstearnslaw.com

Harry J. Kim (A Professional Corporation)
W. A. Finer (A Professional Corporation)
Robert David Ciaccio
Robert B. Parsons

OF COUNSEL

Bennett A. Rheingold
Ryan E. Stearns

LEGAL SUPPORT PERSONNEL

Marcia E. Talbert

For Complete List of Firm Personnel, See General Section

For full biographical listings, see the Martindale-Hubbell Law Directory

VALENCIA, Los Angeles Co.

Bruce A. Nahin A Professional Law Corporation (AV)

24510 Town Center Drive, 91355-1322
Telephone: 661-287-3610
Fax: 661-287-3612
Email: nu64@earthlink.net
Los Angeles, California Office: 6500 Wilshire Boulevard, Suite 17th Floor.
Telephone: 323-651-0170.
Telecopier: 323-651-0158.

Bruce A. Nahin

For full biographical listings, see the Martindale-Hubbell Law Directory

VENTURA, * Ventura Co.

Ferguson, Case, Orr, Paterson & Cunningham LLP (AV)

1050 South Kimball Road, 93004
Telephone: 805-659-6800
Telecopier: 805-659-6818
Email: info@fcopc.com *URL:* http://www.fcopc.com

Thomas R. Ferguson
Michael W. Case
John C. Orr
William E. Paterson
David L. Cunningham
Lou Carpiac
Joseph L. Strohman, Jr.
Robert L. Gallaway
Sandra M. Robertson
David L. Shain
William B. Smith
Gisele Goetz
Ramon L. Guizar
Gregory W. Herring
Douglas E. Kulper
David B. Shea

James Q. McDermott

Representative Clients: First American Title Insurance Company; Wells Fargo Bank; Area Housing Authority of the County of Ventura; Citibank; AT&T Wireless Services of California, Inc.; Catholic Health Care West, Central Coast; Autologic Information International, Inc.; GTE of California; County of Ventura; Calleguas Municipal Water District.

For full biographical listings, see the Martindale-Hubbell Law Directory

WALNUT CREEK, Contra Costa Co.

Field, Richardson & Wilhelmy (AV)

Peri Executive Centre, 2033 North Main Street, Suite 900, 94596-3729
Telephone: 925-934-7700
Telecopier: 925-934-6090
Email: frwlaw@flash.net *URL:* http://www.frwlaw.com

MEMBERS

Robert C. Field
Robert W. Richardson
Alan J. Wilhelmy

OF COUNSEL

Donald L. Edgar

Reference: Civic Bank of Commerce (Walnut Creek Regional Office).

For full biographical listings, see the Martindale-Hubbell Law Directory

WOODLAND HILLS, Los Angeles Co.

Diamond & Scharnberger (AV)

5303 Comercio Way, 91364
Telephone: 818-999-2144
Fax: 818-999-6845
Email: staff@lawcase.com *URL:* http://www.staff@lawcase.com

(See Next Column)

DIAMOND & SCHARNBERGER, *Woodland Hills—Continued*

Robert L. Diamond
Laurence M. Scharnberger
Kenneth D. Zwicker

For full biographical listings, see the Martindale-Hubbell Law Directory

COLORADO

*ASPEN,** Pitkin Co.

AUSTIN, PEIRCE & SMITH, P.C. (AV)

Suite 205, 600 East Hopkins Avenue, 81611
Telephone: 970-925-2600
FAX: 970-925-4720
Email: aps_aspen@aol.com

Ronald D. Austin
Frederick F. Peirce
Thomas Fenton Smith

John M. Lassalette

Counsel for: Chase Manhattan of Colorado, Inc.; Clark's Market; Coates, Reid & Waldron Property Management, Inc.; Crystal Palace Corp.; Snowmass Shopping Center; Coldwell Banker The Aspen Brokers, Ltd.; William Poss & Assoc., Architects; Snowmass Village Resort Association; Aspen/-Pitkin County Housing Authority.

For full biographical listings, see the Martindale-Hubbell Law Directory

J. NICHOLAS MCGRATH, P.C. (AV)

Suite 203, 600 East Hopkins Avenue, 81611
Telephone: 970-925-2612
Telecopier: 970-925-4402
Email: jnm@jnmpc.com *URL:* http://www.jnmpc.com

J. Nicholas McGrath

Representative Clients: Alpine Surveys, Inc.; Aspen Alps Condominium Assn.; Aspen Center for Physics; Gant Condominium Assn.; Old Hundred Condominum Assn; North of Nell Condominum Assn.

For full biographical listings, see the Martindale-Hubbell Law Directory

OATES, KNEZEVICH & GARDENSWARTZ, P.C. (AV)

Aspen Plaza Building, 3rd Floor, 533 East Hopkins Avenue, 81611
Telephone: 970-920-1700
Fax: 970-920-1121
Email: ohkg@rof.net

Leonard M. Oates
Ted D. Gardenswartz
Richard A. Knezevich
David B. Kelly

David B. Mueller

OF COUNSEL

John Thomas Kelly
Michael Feigenbaum

For full biographical listings, see the Martindale-Hubbell Law Directory

*BOULDER,** Boulder Co.

HOWARD BITTMAN (AV)

1406 Pearl Street, Suite 200, 80302
Telephone: 303-443-2281
Fax: 303-443-2862
Email: bittmanh@aol.com *URL:* http://www.lawyers.com/howardbittman

For full biographical listings, see the Martindale-Hubbell Law Directory

LIRTZMAN, NEHLS & HEPNER, A PROFESSIONAL CORPORATION (AV)

190 Arapahoe Avenue, 80302-5895
Telephone: 303-444-5141
Fax: 303-444-9253

Richard C. Nehls
Daniel A. Hepner

OF COUNSEL

Richard M. Lirtzman
Edward J. Roche, Jr.

For full biographical listings, see the Martindale-Hubbell Law Directory

*CASTLE ROCK,** Douglas Co.

FOLKESTAD & FAZEKAS, P.C. (AV)

316 Wilcox Street, 80104-2495
Telephone: 303-688-3045
FAX: 303-688-3189
Email: Firm@Folkestad-Fazekas.com

(See Next Column)

James B. Folkestad
Ernest F. Fazekas, II

Aaron W. Barrick
Marc C. Patoile
James M. Hunsaker

Representative Clients: Jackson Creek Ranch LLC; Crystal Vally Ranch, LLC; Ashcroft Homes of Denver LLC.
References: First National Bank of Castle Rock; First Bank of Douglas County; Castle Rock Bank.

For full biographical listings, see the Martindale-Hubbell Law Directory

*COLORADO SPRINGS,** El Paso Co.

BELTZ, EDWARDS & SABO, L.L.P. (AV)

128 South Tejon, Suite 310, 80903
Telephone: 719-634-6620
Fax: 719-634-3142
Email: BES_LLP@aol.com *URL:* http://www.lawyers.com/beslaw
Other Colorado Springs, Colorado Office: 729 South Cascade, 80903.
Telephone: 719-473-4444.
Fax: 719-444-0186.

Daniel P. Edwards
W. Thomas Beltz
John W. Sabo, III

ASSOCIATE

Daniel A. West

Representative Clients: Marth Taylor and Associates, Inc.; Martin Properties, Inc.; Phoenix Partners, LLC; Realtec Associates; WP Development Company.

For full biographical listings, see the Martindale-Hubbell Law Directory

FLYNN MCKENNA WRIGHT & KARSH (AV)

limited liability company
Plaza of the Rockies 111 South Tejon, Suite 202, 80903-3300
Telephone: 719-578-8444
Fax: 719-578-8836

OF COUNSEL

James T. Flynn

MEMBERS OF FIRM

R. Tim McKenna
Brian T. Murphy
Bruce M. Wright
Michael C. Potarf
Randolph M. Karsh
Karl A. Berg, Jr.

Representative Clients: Peregrine Joint Venture; Nor'wood Development, Inc.; Vintage Development, Inc.; The Woziwodski Group (Consulting Architects); Wal-Mart Stores; Chase Manhattan Mortgage Corp.; Hill Development; Crestone Properties; New Generation Homes; G.A. Maxwell Construction; Stewart Title of Colorado Springs.

For full biographical listings, see the Martindale-Hubbell Law Directory

*DENVER,** Denver Co.

BALLARD SPAHR ANDREWS & INGERSOLL, LLP (AV)

Seventeenth Street Plaza Building, Suite 2300, 1225 17th Street, 80202-5596
Telephone: 303-292-2400
Fax: 303-296-3956
URL: http://www.ballardspahr.com
Baltimore, Maryland Office: 300 East Lombard Street. 19th Floor.
Telephone: 410-528-5600.
Fax: 410-528-5650.
Camden, New Jersey Office: 800 Hudson Square, 5th Floor.
Telephone: 856-541-5577.
Fax: 856-541-8272.
Philadelphia, Pennsylvania Office: 1735 Market Street, 51st Floor.
Telephone: 215-665-8500.
Fax: 215-864-8999.
Salt Lake City, Utah Office: One Utah Center, Suite 1200, 201 South Main Street.
Telephone: 801-531-3000.
Fax: 801-531-3001.
Voorhees, New Jersey Office: Suite 100, 1101 Laurel Oak Drive.
Telephone: 856-627-8555.
Fax: 856-627-1153.
Washington, D.C. Office: Suite 1000 South, 601 13th Street, N.W.
Telephone: 202-661-2200.
Fax: 202-661-2299.

Beverly J. Quail

Kaye A. Jacuzzi
Christopher W. Payne

For Complete List of Firm Personnel, See General Section

For full biographical listings, see the Martindale-Hubbell Law Directory

Denver—Continued

BERENBAUM, WEINSHIENK & EASON, P.C. (AV)

Suite 2600 Republic Plaza, 370 17th Street, 80202
Telephone: 303-825-0800
Facsimile: 303-629-7610
Email: berenbaum1@aol.com *URL:* http://www.BWELaw.com

Joseph Berenbaum
Charles A. Bewley
Daniel S. Duggan
Amy L. Durfee
James L. Kurtz-Phelan
Charles P. Leder
H. Michael Miller
Ronald I. Zall

Lori L. Duwve
Heather Scheel Hagemann

Representative Clients: Home Depot; Sprint Spectrum, L.P.; Town of Vail, Colorado; First Union Corporation; City of Englewood, Colorado; Oakwood Homes; Karman, Inc.; Wells Fargo Bank, N.A.; Berkshire Life Insurance Co.; Trinity Ventures.

For full biographical listings, see the Martindale-Hubbell Law Directory

BERLINER ZISSER WALTER & GALLEGOS, A PROFESSIONAL CORPORATION (AV)

One Norwest Center, 1700 Lincoln Street, Suite 4700, 80203-4547
Telephone: 303-830-1700
Facsimile: 303-830-1705
Email: bzwg@bzwg.com

Martin M. Berliner
David A. Zisser
Robert W. Walter
Larry D. Gallegos

Stacey L. Bowers

OF COUNSEL

Phillip C. Gans

For full biographical listings, see the Martindale-Hubbell Law Directory

BRENMAN BROMBERG & TENENBAUM, P.C. (AV)

Mellon Financial Center Suite 1001, 1775 Sherman Street, 80203
Telephone: 303-894-0234
Fax: 303-839-1633
Email: bbt@bbtlaw.net

Albert Brenman
Thomas R. Bromberg
A. Thomas Tenenbaum
Steven W. McDonald

Sheryl A. Johnson
Judy A. Gooch

OF COUNSEL

Duane Woodard

For full biographical listings, see the Martindale-Hubbell Law Directory

JAMES E. BROWN & ASSOCIATES, P.C. (AV)

1350 Seventeenth Street, Suite 306, 80202
Telephone: 303-825-1818
Fax: 303-825-2828
Email: wy0j@aol.com

James E. Brown

For full biographical listings, see the Martindale-Hubbell Law Directory

BROWNSTEIN HYATT & FARBER, P.C. (AV)

Twenty-Second Floor, 410 Seventeenth Street, 80202-4437
Telephone: 303-223-1100
Telecopier: 303-223-1111
Washington, D.C. Office: 1615 L Street, N.W., Suite 450, 20036.
Telephone: 202-296-7353.
Telecopier: 202-296-7009.
Glenwood Springs, Colorado Office: Box 357, 81602.
Telephone: 970-945-5302.
Telecopier: 970-945-4921.

Norman Brownstein
Steven W. Farber
Edward N. Barad
John R. Call
Steven M. Sommers
Ronald B. Merrill
Lynda A. McNeive
Laura Jean Christman
Wayne H. Hykan
Gary M. Reiff
Bruce A. James
Robert Kaufmann
Steven C. Demby
Jay F. Kamlet
Ana Lazo Tenzer

SENIOR COUNSEL

James S. Lochhead (Resident, Glenwood Springs, Colorado Office)

OF COUNSEL

Jack N. Hyatt
Ann B. Riley

SPECIAL COUNSEL

Mark T. Shipley
David E. Tenzer
Robert P. Coyne

(See Next Column)

Howard J. Pollack
Ellen O. Kauffmann
Lea Ann T. Groesser
Joseph F. Capello
Gregory A. Vallin
Christina G. Grasso
Patricia L. Gruber
Suzanne R. Kalutkiewicz
Travis A. Willock
Michael H. Harper
Adam J. Agron
Richard A. Hardaway
Brett M. Perry

Representative Clients: Apollo Real Estate Advisors, L.P.; CDC North America, Inc.; Credit Suisse First Boston Mortgage Capital LLC; DPC Development Company; KeyBank; Prime West Real Estate Services; SunAmerica Inc.; Trammell Crow Company; U.S. Home Corporation; Vail Associates, Inc.

For Complete List of Firm Personnel, See General Section

For full biographical listings, see the Martindale-Hubbell Law Directory

CARPENTER & KLATSKIN, P.C. (AV)

1500 Denver Club Building, 518 Seventeenth Street, 80202
Telephone: 303-534-6315
Telecopier: 303-534-0514

Willis V. Carpenter
Andrew S. Klatskin

Judith C. McNerny

OF COUNSEL

Robert R. Marshall, Jr.

LEGAL SUPPORT PERSONNEL

PARALEGAL

Holly S. Hoxeng

Reference: Colorado State Bank and Trust.

For full biographical listings, see the Martindale-Hubbell Law Directory

JON B. CLARKE, P.C. (AV)

Two DTC, Suite 150, 5290 DTC Parkway (Englewood), 80111-2721
Telephone: 303-779-0600
Fax: 303-850-7115
Email: eclarkeco@cs.com

Jon B. Clarke

For full biographical listings, see the Martindale-Hubbell Law Directory

DAVIS & CERIANI, P.C. (AV)

Suite 400, Market Center, 1350 Seventeenth Street, 80202
Telephone: 303-534-9000
Telecopier: 303-534-4618
Email: davisandceriani.com

Rick G. Davis
Gary J. Ceriani
Bruce E. Rohde
Michael P. Cillo
Charles W. Bess
John W. Himmelmann

Margaret E. Peper
Patrick John Kanouff
Mark M. Osborn
Valeri Pappas

For full biographical listings, see the Martindale-Hubbell Law Directory

DUFFORD & BROWN, P.C. (AV)

1700 Broadway, Suite 1700, 80290-1701
Telephone: 303-861-8013
Facsimile: 303-832-3804
Colorado Springs, Colorado Office: 101 N. Tejon, Suite 410.
Telephone: 719-471-0559.
Facsimile: 719-471-0583.
Affiliated Office: Solomon, Pearl, Blum & Quinn, L.L.P., New York, NY and Denver, Colorado.

Thomas G. Brown
Randall J. Feuerstein
S. Kirk Ingebretsen

Representative Clients: CF&I Steel, L.P.; IDS Life Insurance Company; Hall and Hall Mortgage Corp.; Winding Brook Corporation.

For Complete List of Firm Personnel, See General Section

For full biographical listings, see the Martindale-Hubbell Law Directory

MAURICE F. FOX (AV)

4465 Kipling Street (Wheat Ridge), 80033
Telephone: 303-424-4443
Fax: 303-421-4309

References: 1st Bank of Westland; lst Bank of Wheat Ridge.

GRUND & BRESLAU, P.C. (AV)

303 East Seventeenth Avenue, Suite 303, 80203-1263
Telephone: 303-830-7770
Facsimile: 303-830-2313
Email: g&b@grundbreslau.com

(See Next Column)

GRUND & BRESLAU P.C., *Denver—Continued*

Brad W. Breslau | Julie J. Noonan
Graden P. Jackson

Representative Clients: Basic Capital Management, Inc.; Citywide Banks; Colorado Farm Bureau Mutual Insurance Co.; Gallagher, Bassett Services, Inc.

For full biographical listings, see the Martindale-Hubbell Law Directory

HOLME ROBERTS & OWEN LLP (AV)

Suite 4100, 1700 Lincoln, 80203
Telephone: 303-861-7000
Telecopier: 303-866-0200
Email: hro@hro.com *URL:* http://www.hro.com
Boulder, Colorado Office: Suite 400, 1401 Pearl Street.
Telephone: 303-444-5955.
Telecopier: 303-444-1063.
Colorado Springs, Colorado Office: Suite 1300, 90 South Cascade Avenue.
Telephone: 719-473-3800.
Telecopier: 719-633-1518.
Salt Lake City, Utah Office: Suite 1100, 111 East Broadway.
Telephone: 801-521-5800.
Telecopier: 801-521-9639.
London, England Office: Heathcoat House, 3rd Floor, 20 Savile Row.
Telephone: 011-44-171-494-5600.
Telecopier: 011-44-171-287-9344.

PARTNERS OF FIRM

Daron J. Arnold
Robert H. Bach
G. Kevin Conwick
Robert A. Holmes
David W. Isbell (Colorado Springs Office)
Bruce L. Likoff
Martha Traudt Collins Rolle (London, England Office)
Jill K. Rood (Boulder Office)
Paul V. Timmins
Richard G. Wohlgenant
John B. Wood (Boulder Office)

OF COUNSEL

Karen Campbell Jenson (Salt Lake City Office)

SPECIAL COUNSEL

Rita I. Ehrman

SENIOR COUNSEL

Louise Betcher Staab

ASSOCIATES

Brent P. Karasiuk (Colorado Springs Office)
Joli A. Messer-Liebrock

For Complete List of Firm Personnel, See General Section

For full biographical listings, see the Martindale-Hubbell Law Directory

KATZ, LOOK & MOISON, PROFESSIONAL CORPORATION (AV)

1120 Lincoln Street, Suite 1100, 80203
Telephone: 303-832-1900
Fax: 303-863-0412

Michael M. Katz
Harley K. Look, Jr.
Peter R. Moison
Kathryn A. Reeves

Brian E. Onorato
Melisa A. Vogel
Arthur T. DiMeo
Delwyn G. Haroldson
Barbara J. Stauch

SPECIAL COUNSEL

Ogborn, Summerlin & Ogborn, L.L.C., Denver, Colorado

For full biographical listings, see the Martindale-Hubbell Law Directory

LAFF STEIN CAMPBELL TUCKER & DELANEY, LLP (AV)

A Partnership including Professional Corporations
7730 East Belleview Avenue, Suite 204 (Englewood), 80111-2616
Telephone: 303-740-7200
Telecopier: 303-740-7300

Alan D. Laff (Member of Laff Campbell & Delaney, P.C.)
Alan L. Stein (Member of Alan L. Stein, P.C.)
Darrel L. Campbell (Member of Laff Campbell & Delaney, P.C.)
Ronald C. Tucker
Stacia Bank Delaney (Member of Laff Campbell & Delaney, P.C.)

JESSE N. LIPSCHUETZ, P.C. (AV)

Suite 400, 303 East 17th Avenue, 80203
Telephone: 303-860-8200
Fax: 303-860-1665
Email: jnlpc@yahoo.com

Jesse N. Lipschuetz

Reference: U.S. Bank; Norwest Bank Denver, N.A.

For full biographical listings, see the Martindale-Hubbell Law Directory

LOHF, SHAIMAN & JACOBS, P.C. (AV)

950 South Cherry Street, Suite 900, 80246-2666
Telephone: 303-753-9000
Telecopier: 303-753-9997

Charles H. Jacobs
Robert Shaiman

Reference: Vectra Bank Colorado.

For full biographical listings, see the Martindale-Hubbell Law Directory

MONTGOMERY LITTLE & MCGREW, P.C. (AV)

The Quadrant, 5445 DTC Parkway, Suite 800 (Englewood), 80111
Telephone: 303-773-8100
Telecopier: 303-220-0412
URL: http://www.mlmpc.com

James J. Soran, III
Debra Piazza
Rebecca B. Givens
Joel A. Mayo

OF COUNSEL

Thomas C. Deline
David M. Treadwell

LEGAL SUPPORT PERSONNEL

Julie M. Alvarez (Legal Assistant)
Tammy L. Jackson (Legal Assistant)
Monica L. Sharp (Legal Assistant)

Representative Clients: BP Amoco; Cyprus Minerals; Dillon Cos., Inc., d/b/a King Soopers; Butler & Co.; Kentwood Company; Monaghan Farms, Inc.; Park Investments; Perry & Butler Realty Inc.; Regency Realty Corp.; Signature Equities, Inc.

For Complete List of Firm Personnel, See General Section

For full biographical listings, see the Martindale-Hubbell Law Directory

OTTEN, JOHNSON, ROBINSON, NEFF & RAGONETTI, P.C. (AV)

950 Seventeenth Street, 16th Floor, 80202
Telephone: 303-825-8400
Telecopier: 303-825-6525
URL: http://www.ojrnr.com

Frank L. Robinson
Bruce B. Johnson
A. Bruce Campbell
William R. Neff
Thomas J. Ragonetti
Robert C. Fisher, Jr.
Neil M. Goff
J. Thomas Macdonald
John D. Sternberg
Michael Westover
Randall G. Alt
Daniel M. Minzer
Kevin A. Gliwa
David T. Brennan
Kathleen M. Bottagaro
R. Michael Shomo
Michael C. Villano
Mark F. Copertino
Victoria L. Hellmer
Christopher T. Toll
J. Bart Johnson
James C. Ellenberger
Munsey L. Ayers, Jr.
Michael C. Matheson
Nicole J. Hanak
Cheryl A. Malcolm
Lenn A. Moldenhauer
Brian P. Jumps
Berkeley I. Vogelsang

OF COUNSEL

Barbara J. Kelley

Representative Clients: The Broe Companies, Inc.; Brookfield Development Corp.; Carmel Companies, Inc.; The Genesee Co., Inc.; Land Title Guarantee Co.; OPUS Corp.; RCI West, Inc./Colorado Applebees; San Miguel Valley Corp.; Simpson Housing Limited Partnership; SunAmerica, Inc.; Union Pacific Realty Co.; U.S. Bank National Association; Vail Associates, Inc.; Western Mobile, Inc. (9 subsidiary of LaFarge Corp.).

For Complete List of Firm Personnel, See General Section

For full biographical listings, see the Martindale-Hubbell Law Directory

PREEO, SILVERMAN & GREEN, P.C. (AV)

1401 17th Street, Suite 800, 80202
Telephone: 303-296-4440
Fax: 303-296-3330

Robert L. Preeo
Eldon E. Silverman
Jersey M. Green
Martin J. Green
Gilbert R. Egle
Marilyn W. McWilliams
Timothy Kyle Jordan
Brandon S Culter

For full biographical listings, see the Martindale-Hubbell Law Directory

SENN LEWIS & VISCIANO, P.C. (AV)

1801 California Street, Suite 4300, 80202
Telephone: 303-298-1122
Facsimile: 303-296-9101

Mark A. Senn
Fredric J. Lewis
Stephen W. Arent
Ellen Kirschenbaum

Rosemarie E. Delmonte
Rufus C. "Butch" Taylor, Jr.
Margie J. Titus
Vivian Lee Perla

(See Next Column)

SENN LEWIS & VISCIANO P.C.—*Continued*

OF COUNSEL

Lawrence A. Atler
Brenda Jansen

For Complete List of Firm Personnel, See General Section

For full biographical listings, see the Martindale-Hubbell Law Directory

SLIVKA ROBINSON WATERS & O'DORISIO, A PROFESSIONAL CORPORATION (AV)

Suite 2600, 1099 18th Street, 80202-1926
Telephone: 303-297-2600
Telecopier: 303-297-2750
URL: http://www.srwo.com

SHAREHOLDERS

Richard P. Slivka
Peter A. Robinson
Stephen L. Waters
John W. O'Dorisio, Jr.
Ernest J. Panasci
Chevis F. Horne, Jr.
Margaret M. McClellan
Karen Samuels Jones

Deborah A. Hogan
Kerri M. Pertcheck
Susan R. Pierson
Elizabeth E. Pinckard
Daniel A. Sweetser
Bradley S. Taylor
Jill G. VanderPloeg

SPECIAL COUNSEL

Laura J. Vogelgesang
Christine Rothe Hoth

For full biographical listings, see the Martindale-Hubbell Law Directory

WALTERS & JOYCE, P.C. (AV)

2015 York Street, 80205
Telephone: 303-322-1404
FAX: 303-377-5668

OF COUNSEL

Julia T. Waggener

Reference: Norwest Bank of Buckingham Square; Mountain States Bank.

For Complete List of Firm Personnel, See General Section

For full biographical listings, see the Martindale-Hubbell Law Directory

*DURANGO,** La Plata Co.

FRANK J. ANESI (AV)

Suite 220, 835 East Second Avenue, P.O. Box 2185, 81302
Telephone: 970-247-9246
Fax: 970-259-2793
Email: fjanesi@frontier.net

References: First National Bank of Durango; Burns Bank, Durango.

For full biographical listings, see the Martindale-Hubbell Law Directory

ENGLEWOOD, Arapahoe Co.

BANTA, HOYT, EVERALL & FARRINGTON, L.L.C. (AV)

Suite 240E, 5690 DTC Boulevard, 80111-3232
Telephone: 303-220-8000
Fax: 303-220-0153

Richard J. Banta

Representative Clients: Cherry Creek School District No. 5; Colorado School District Self Insurance Pool; Copper Mountain Consolidated Metropolitan District; Kiewit Western Co.; Littleton Public Schools; National Union Fire Insurance Co. (local); South Arapahoe Santation District.

For Complete List of Firm Personnel, See General Section

For full biographical listings, see the Martindale-Hubbell Law Directory

THE KROVITZ LAW FIRM, P.C. (AV)

5290 DTC Parkway, Suite 150, 80111
Telephone: 303-771-4554
Fax: 303-771-4551
Email: Krovitz.Law.Firm@lawyernet.com

Rochelle G. Krovitz

For full biographical listings, see the Martindale-Hubbell Law Directory

*GOLDEN,** Jefferson Co.

HOLLEY, ALBERTSON & POLK, P.C. (AV)

Suite 100, 1667 Cole Boulevard, 80401-3295
Telephone: 303-233-7838
Fax: 303-233-2860

George Alan Holley
Scott D. Albertson
Dennis B. Polk
Eric E. Torgersen
Howard R. Stone

(See Next Column)

Heather M. Davis

Reference: First Bank of Wheat Ridge.

For full biographical listings, see the Martindale-Hubbell Law Directory

*GREELEY,** Weld Co.

BREGA & WINTERS P.C. (AV)

1100 Tenth Street, Suite 402, 80631
Telephone: 970-352-4805
Fax: 970-352-6547
Denver, Colorado Office: One Norwest Center, 1700 Lincoln Street, Suite 2222.
Telephone: 303-866-9400.
Fax: 303-861-9109.

Jerry D. Winters
Pamela A. Shaddock
William W. Hughes

Julie Scroggins Frantz
Bradley D. Laue

For full biographical listings, see the Martindale-Hubbell Law Directory

VAIL, Eagle Co.

DUNN, ABPLANALP & MAURIELLO, P.C. (AV)

Suite 300 Weststar Bank Building, 108 South Frontage Road West, 81657-5087
Telephone: 970-476-0300
Telecopier: 970-476-4765
Email: vaillaw@vail.net *URL:* http://www.lawyers.com/vaillaw

John W. Dunn
Arthur A. Abplanalp, Jr.

For Complete List of Firm Personnel, See General Section

For full biographical listings, see the Martindale-Hubbell Law Directory

OTTO, PORTERFIELD & POST, LLC (AV)

51 Eagle Road, P.O. Box 3149, 81658-3149
Telephone: 970-949-5380
Fax: 970-845-9135
Email: wbrucep@vail.net

Frederick S. Otto
Wendell B. Porterfield, Jr.
William J. Post

References: 1st Bank of Vail; WestStar Bank.

For Complete List of Firm Personnel, See General Section

For full biographical listings, see the Martindale-Hubbell Law Directory

CONNECTICUT

*BRIDGEPORT,** Fairfield Co.

ELSTEIN AND ELSTEIN, P.C. (AV)

Suite 400 1087 Broad Street, 06604-4231
Telephone: 203-367-4421
Telecopier: 203-366-8615

Henry Elstein
Bruce L. Elstein

For full biographical listings, see the Martindale-Hubbell Law Directory

GOLDSTEIN AND PECK, P.C. (AV)

1087 Broad Street, P.O. Box 1538, 06601
Telephone: 203-334-9421
Telefax: 203-334-6949
Westport, Connecticut Office: 190 Main Street, P.O. Box 5031.
Telephone: 203-226-7488.
Telefax: 203-334-6949.

David Goldstein (1898-1992)
William J. Kupinse, Jr.
Walter A. Flynn, Jr.
Eugene E. Cederbaum
John G. Dzurik
Dennis M. Laccavole
Kathleen H. Allsup
Robert L. Cavanaugh, Jr.
Jo-Ann R. Sensale

OF COUNSEL

Peter B. O'Connell

Representative Clients: Bee Publishing Co., Inc.; The Chase Manhattan Bank; Great American Insurance Companies; Physicians Health Services, Inc.; Town of Westport; Greenwich Board of Education; Newtown Savings Bank; People's Bank.

For full biographical listings, see the Martindale-Hubbell Law Directory

Bridgeport—Continued

LESSER & SOBEL, P.C. (AV)

1000 Lafayette Boulevard, 06604
Telephone: 203-336-1811
Facsimile: 203-334-8069

Robert K. Lesser
Stanton H. Lesser
Paul A. Sobel
Neil A. Lieberthal

For full biographical listings, see the Martindale-Hubbell Law Directory

DANBURY, Fairfield Co.

DRISCOLL, TALARICO, FRIZZELL, OLIVO & DRISCOLL (AV)

142 Deer Hill Avenue, 06810-7727
Telephone: 203-792-8333
Facsimile: 203-778-9570
Email: driscoll@javanet.com
Bethel, Connecticut Office: 235 Greenwood Avenue, 06801-2186.
Telephone: 203-744-5000; 743-5556.
Facsimile: 203-798-7790.
Southbury, Connecticut Office: Three Pomperaug Office Park, Suite 203, P.O. Box 252, 06488-0252.
Telephone: 203-264-9650.
Facsimile: 203-798-2175.

Julius J. Bielizna (1914-1988)
Kenneth H. Murray (1905-1984)
Herbert B. Wanderer (1902-1979)
James C. Driscoll, Jr. (Resident, Southbury Office)
Robert N. Talarico
Thomas A. Frizzell
Steven M. Olivo
James C. Driscoll, III (Resident, Bethel Office)
Jerome A. Mayer
Richard W. Hanna
D. Joseph Lane, Jr.
George S. Papazoglou

For full biographical listings, see the Martindale-Hubbell Law Directory

DARIEN, Fairfield Co.

MILLAR & AMBRETTE (AV)

23 Old King's Highway South, 06820-1267
Telephone: 203-655-7931
FAX: 203-656-2055

MEMBERS OF FIRM

Samuel D. B. Millar, Jr.
L. Conrad Ambrette

OF COUNSEL

Peter M. Ryan

ASSOCIATE

Patricia Moreland Gross

For full biographical listings, see the Martindale-Hubbell Law Directory

RUCCI, BURNHAM, CARTA & EDELBERG, LLP (AV)

800 Post Road, P.O. Box 1107, 06820
Telephone: 203-655-7695
Facsimile: 203-655-4302
URL: http://www.rbce.com
Stamford, Connecticut Office: 6 Landmark Square, Suite 470.
Telephone: 203-359-5637.

MEMBERS OF FIRM

Joseph J. Rucci, Jr.
Paul H. Burnham
Mark R. Carta
Paul B. Edelberg
William M. Carello
Robert F. Maslan, Jr.

ASSOCIATES

Colette C. Symon
Karen K. Linder
Joanna F. Bowen
David J. Rucci
Sandra J. Akoury

OF COUNSEL

Ian R. Crawford
James C. Dempsey
Lawrence H. Reilly
Alberto N. Moris (Not admitted in CT)

For full biographical listings, see the Martindale-Hubbell Law Directory

FAIRFIELD, Fairfield Co.

BRAUNSTEIN & TODISCO, LLC (AV)

One Eliot Place, 06430
Telephone: 203-254-1118
Telecopier: 203-254-2453
Email: sam@btlawfirm.com *URL:* http://www.btlawfirm.com

Samuel L. Braunstein
Amy E. Todisco

Reference: People's Bank.

For full biographical listings, see the Martindale-Hubbell Law Directory

GREENWICH, Fairfield Co.

ALBERT, WARD & JOHNSON, P.C. (AV)

125 Mason Street, P.O. Box 1668, 06836
Telephone: 203-661-8600
Telecopier: 203-661-8051

Tom S. Ward, Jr.
Scott R. Johnson
Jane D. Hogeman
Howard R. Wolfe
Christopher A. Kristoff
Vicki K. Comberiati

OF COUNSEL

David Albert
C. Robton Perelli-Minetti

For full biographical listings, see the Martindale-Hubbell Law Directory

HOLLAND KAUFMANN & BARTELS, LLC (AV)

289 Greenwich Avenue, 06830-6595
Telephone: 203-869-5600
Fax: 203-869-4648

Alexander J. Holland
Charles B. Kaufmann, III
Philip H. Bartels
Harold R. Burke
Jean Mills Aranha
Lori E. Romano
John C. Fusco

OF COUNSEL

Beth K. Hansson

For full biographical listings, see the Martindale-Hubbell Law Directory

*HARTFORD,** Hartford Co.

CRANMORE, FITZGERALD & MEANEY (AV)

49 Wethersfield Avenue, 06114-1102
Telephone: 860-522-9100
Telecopier: 860-522-3379

MEMBERS OF FIRM

J. J. Cranmore
John C. FitzGerald, Jr.
Joseph V. Meaney, Jr.
John P. McHugh
Patricia D. Anderson

ASSOCIATES

Michael P. McGoldrick
Leyla F. Kimball
Wendell G. Davis, Jr. (Not admitted in CT)

For full biographical listings, see the Martindale-Hubbell Law Directory

GORDON, MUIR AND FOLEY, LLP (AV)

Hartford Square North, Ten Columbus Boulevard, 06106-5123
Telephone: 860-525-5361
Telecopier: 860-525-4849
Email: admin@gmflaw.com *URL:* http://www.gmflaw.com

MEMBERS OF FIRM

William S. Gordon, Jr. (1946-1956)
George Muir (1939-1976)
Edward J. Foley (1955-1983)
Peter C. Schwartz
John J. Reid
John H. Goodrich, Jr.
R. Bradley Wolfe
Jon Stephen Berk
William J. Gallitto
Gerald R. Swirsky
Robert J. O'Brien
Philip J. O'Connor
Kenneth G. Williams
Mary Ann Santacroce
Mary Anne Alicia Charron
Andrew J. Hern
Reneé W. Dwyer
Patty G. Swan

ASSOCIATES

Doreen West Amata
Howard A. Steinman
Erik E. Roberts
Christopher J. Casciani

Reference: People's Bank.

For full biographical listings, see the Martindale-Hubbell Law Directory

SOROKIN, GROSS & HYDE, P.C. (AV)

One Corporate Center, 06103
Telephone: 860-525-6645
Fax: 860-522-1781
Email: sorokin@sorokinlaw.com
Simsbury, Connecticut Office: 720 Hopmeadow Street.
Telephone: 860-651-9348.
Rocky Hill, Connecticut Office: 2360 Main Street.
Telephone: 860-563-9305.
Fax: 860-529-6931.

James G. Dowling, Jr.
Barry D. Greene
John J. Kindl
Keith D. Robbins
Richard D. Tulisano (Resident, Rocky Hill Office)

Rod W. Farrell
Gwen P. Weisberg

For Complete List of Firm Personnel, See General Section

For full biographical listings, see the Martindale-Hubbell Law Directory

MILFORD, New Haven Co.

HARLOW, ADAMS & FRIEDMAN, P.C. (AV)

300 Bic Drive, 06460-3508
Telephone: 203-878-0661
Fax: 203-878-9568
Email: attorney@quidproquo.com

William D. Harlow (1921-1988)
George W. Adams, III
Dana Eric Friedman
Theodore H. Shumaker
Stephen P. Wright
Michael P. A. Williams
Eric R. Gaynor
Joseph A. Kubic
James M. Nugent
James R. Winkel

For full biographical listings, see the Martindale-Hubbell Law Directory

*NEW HAVEN,** New Haven Co.

SUSMAN, DUFFY & SEGALOFF, P.C. (AV)

55 Whitney Avenue, 06510-1300
Telephone: 203-624-9830
Fax: 203-562-8430
Mailing Address: P.O. Box 1684, New Haven, Connecticut, 06507-1684

Allen H. Duffy (1931-1986)
Michael Susman
James H. Segaloff
Joseph E. Faughnan
Susan W. Wolfson
Laura M. Sklaver
Andrew R. Lubin
James J. Perito
Matthew C. Susman
Thomas E. Katon

Jennifer L. Schancupp
Peter G. Kruzynski
Vincent J. Candelora
Karen Baldwin Kravetz

OF COUNSEL

Diana C. Ballard
David P. Hambleton

For full biographical listings, see the Martindale-Hubbell Law Directory

NEW LONDON, New London Co.

WALLER, SMITH & PALMER, P.C. (AV)

52 Eugene O'Neill Drive, P.O. Box 88, 06320
Telephone: 860-442-0367
Telecopier: 860-447-9915
Email: wspmain@snet.net *URL:* http://www.snetyp.com/wallersmithpalmer
Old Lyme Office: 103 Halls Road.
Telephone: 860-434-8063.
Telecopier: 860-434-9452. Email: wspol@snet.net

William W. Miner
Robert P. Anderson, Jr.
Robert W. Marrion
Hughes Griffis
Edward B. O'Connell
Frederick B. Gahagan
Tracy M. Collins
Philip M. Johnstone
Valerie Ann Votto

General Counsel For: Town of East Lyme.
Counsel For: Citizens Bank of Connecticut; Soneco/Northeastern, Inc.; The Nature Conservancy; Fleet Bank.
Local Counsel For: McCue Mortgage Co.; Citicorp Mortgage; U.S. Department of Housing and Urban Development.

For Complete List of Firm Personnel, See General Section

For full biographical listings, see the Martindale-Hubbell Law Directory

NORWALK, Fairfield Co.

TIERNEY, ZULLO, FLAHERTY & MURPHY, P.C. (AV)

134 East Avenue, P.O. Box 2028-Belden Station, 06852
Telephone: 203-853-7000
Fax: 203-838-4829

Thomas Tierney
Frank N. Zullo
Thomas A. Flaherty
Frank W. Murphy
Reuben S. Midler
Gary Lorusso
Andrew F. Kordas
Barbara Coughlan
Elizabeth A.B. Suchy
Creighton M. English

OF COUNSEL

Thomas A. Keating, Jr.
Vincent Gallogly

References: First Union Bank of Connecticut; Fleet Bank.

For full biographical listings, see the Martindale-Hubbell Law Directory

SOUTHPORT, Fairfield Co.

BRODY, WILKINSON AND OBER, P.C. (AV)

2507 Post Road, 06490
Telephone: 203-319-7100
Fax: 203-254-1772

(See Next Column)

Seth O. L. Brody
Peter Wilkinson
Frank Fritz Ober
S. Giles Payne
James E. Rice
William J. Britt
Barbara S. Miller
Robert L. Teicher
Ronald B. Noren
Peter T. Mott
Thomas J. Walsh, Jr.
Diane F. Martucci
Seth L. Cooper
Douglas R. Brown
Charles S. Brody (1894-1976)

OF COUNSEL

Bruce E. Dillingham
Roy W. Moore, III

For full biographical listings, see the Martindale-Hubbell Law Directory

STAMFORD, Fairfield Co.

CACACE, TUSCH & SANTAGATA (AV)

777 Summer Street, P.O. Box 15859, 06901-0859
Telephone: 203-327-2000
Telecopier: 203-353-3392
Email: lawcts@aol.com

MEMBERS OF FIRM

Michael J. Cacace
Mark P. Santagata
Paul T. Tusch
Richard S. Fisher

OF COUNSEL

Kenneth A. DellaRocco
Eric D. Grayson

ASSOCIATES

Edward F. Nemchek
Alice Ann Fitzpatrick
Ronald E. Kowalski II
Aamina Ahmad
Demaris Page Hetrick
Patrick L. Poeschl

LEGAL SUPPORT PERSONNEL

Eva L. Chan
Cynthia L. Mammone

For full biographical listings, see the Martindale-Hubbell Law Directory

CURTIS, BRINCKERHOFF & BARRETT, P.C. (AV)

666 Summer Street, 06901-1416
Telephone: 203-324-6777
Telecopier: 203-324-9621
Email: info@curtisbb.com

T. Ward Cleary (1916-1988)
Frederick M. Tobin
John Wayne Fox
Ward Frank Cleary
James D'Alton Murphy
Randolph T. Lovallo

OF COUNSEL

John D. Hertz
Jane F. Donovan
Richard L. Brinckerhoff
Patricia M. Gaug

Susan L. Stratton
Derek Gilman
Michael P. Murray
John J. Louizos

Counsel for: The F. A. Bartlett Tree Expert Co.; Town of Darien; Miller Automobile Corp.; Bolliger, Inc.; Titan Sports; People's Bank, Bridgeport; Fleet Bank; Federal Deposit Insurance Co.; William Pitt Foundation; Wood Logan Associates.

For full biographical listings, see the Martindale-Hubbell Law Directory

FOX & FOX, L.L.P. (AV)

607 Bedford Street, 06901
Telephone: 203-348-7773
Fax: 203-324-0057

Gerald M. Fox, Jr.
Gerald M. Fox, III

For full biographical listings, see the Martindale-Hubbell Law Directory

PIAZZA & PICKEL (AV)

112 Prospect Street, P.O. Box 15390, 06901
Telephone: 203-348-2465
Fax: 203-964-9509
Email: aap@piazza-pickel.com *URL:* http://www.piazza-pickel.com

Anthony A. Piazza
Alan Scott Pickel

ASSOCIATES

Tara C.F. Ryan
Michelle M. Napoli

For full biographical listings, see the Martindale-Hubbell Law Directory

WEST HARTFORD, Hartford Co.

BERMAN, BOURNS & CURRIE, LLC (AV)

970 Farmington Avenue, P.O. Box 271837, 06127-1837
Telephone: 860-232-4471
Fax: 860-523-4605

John A. Berman
Courtney B. Bourns

Mary Beth Anderson
Steven R. Dembo
Annemarie Burnham

(See Next Column)

BERMAN, BOURNS & CURRIE LLC, *West Hartford—Continued*

OF COUNSEL

John K. Currie

For full biographical listings, see the Martindale-Hubbell Law Directory

WESTPORT, Fairfield Co.

GOLDSTEIN AND PECK, P.C. (AV)

190 Main Street, P.O. Box 5031, 06881
Telephone: 203-226-7488
Telefax: 203-334-6949
Bridgeport, Connecticut Office: 1087 Broad Street, P.O. Box 1538.
Telephone: 203-334-9421.
Telefax: 203-334-6949.

David Goldstein (1898-1992)
William J. Kupinse, Jr.
Walter A. Flynn, Jr.
Eugene E. Cederbaum
John G. Dzurik
Dennis M. Laccavole
Kathleen H. Allsup
Robert L. Cavanaugh, Jr.
Jo-Ann R. Sensale

OF COUNSEL

Peter B. O'Connell

Representative Clients: Bee Publishing Co., Inc.; The Chase Manhattan Bank; Great American Insurance Companies; Physicians Health Services, Inc.; Town of Westport; Greenwich Board of Education; Newtown Savings Bank; People's Bank.

For full biographical listings, see the Martindale-Hubbell Law Directory

NEVAS, NEVAS & CAPASSE (AV)

246 Post Road East, P.O. Box 791, 06881
Telephone: 203-226-1211
Fax: 203-454-3419
Email: law@nevascapasse.com

Bernard A. Nevas (1900-1942)
Leo Nevas
Edward J. Capasse
Jamie Kay Gerard
Andrew B. Nevas

OF COUNSEL

Stephen Tate
Stephen E. Nevas

For full biographical listings, see the Martindale-Hubbell Law Directory

WILLIAM L. SCHEFFLER & ASSOCIATES (AV⓪)

P.O. Box 2773, 06880-0773
Telephone: 203-226-6600; 1-800-429-4480
Telecopier: 203-227-1873
Email: scheff@optonline.net

For full biographical listings, see the Martindale-Hubbell Law Directory

DISTRICT OF COLUMBIA

WASHINGTON, D.C. Co.

BALLARD SPAHR ANDREWS & INGERSOLL, LLP (AV)

Suite 1000 South, 601 13th Street, N.W., 20005-3807
Telephone: 202-661-2200
Fax: 202-661-2299
URL: http://www.ballardspahr.com
Baltimore, Maryland Office: 300 East Lombard Street, 19th Floor.
Telephone: 410-528-5600.
Fax: 410-528-5650.
Camden, New Jersey Office: 800 Hudson Square, 5th Floor.
Telephone: 856-541-5577.
Fax: 856-541-8772.
Denver, Colorado Office: Seventeenth Street Plaza Building, Suite 2300, 1225 17th Street.
Telephone: 303-292-2400.
Fax: 303-296-3956.
Philadelphia, Pennsylvania Office: 1735 Market Street, 51st Floor.
Telephone: 215-665-8500.
Fax: 215-834-8999.
Salt Lake City, Utah Office: 201 South Main Street, Suite 1200.
Telephone: 801-531-3000.
Fax: 801-531-3001.
Voorhees, New Jersey Office: Suite 100, 1101 Laurel Oak Drive.
Telephone: 856-627-8555.
Fax: 856-627-1153.

Paul K. Casey
Mary Jo George (Not admitted in DC)
Allan R. Winn
Kelly Mitchell Wrenn

OF COUNSEL

Katherine L. Bishop (Not admitted in DC)
James P. Cooke
B. Cheryl Terio (Not admitted in DC)

(See Next Column)

Eileen M. Greenbaum
Kurt E. Van Engen (Not admitted in DC)

For Complete List of Firm Personnel, See General Section

For full biographical listings, see the Martindale-Hubbell Law Directory

VENABLE ATTORNEYS AT LAW VENABLE, BAETJER, HOWARD & CIVILETTI, LLP (AV)

A Partnership including Professional Corporations
Suite 1000, 1201 New York Avenue, N.W., 20005
Telephone: 202-962-4800
Fax: 202-962-8300
URL: http://www.venable.com
Baltimore, Maryland Office: Venable, Baetjer and Howard LLP, 1800 Mercantile Bank & Trust Building, 2 Hopkins Plaza.
Telephone: 410-244-7400.
Fax: 410-244-7742.
McLean, Virginia Office: Venable, Baetjer and Howard LLP, Suite 400, 2010 Corporate Ridge.
Telephone: 703-760-1600.
Fax: 703-821-8949.
Rockville, Maryland Office: Venable, Baetjer and Howard LLP, Suite 500, One Church Street, P. O. Box 1906.
Telephone: 301-217-5600.
Fax: 301-217-5617.
Towson, Maryland Office: Venable, Baetjer and Howard LLP, 210 Allegheny Avenue, P. O. Box 5517.
Telephone: 410-494-6200.
Fax: 410-821-0147.

MEMBERS OF FIRM

James K. Archibald (Also at Baltimore, Maryland Office)
Benjamin R. Civiletti (P.C.) (Also at Baltimore and Towson, Maryland Offices)
Jan K. Guben (Not admitted in DC; Also at Baltimore, Maryland Office)
Thomas J. Madden
George F. Pappas (Also at Baltimore, Maryland Office)

For Complete List of Firm Personnel, See General Section

For full biographical listings, see the Martindale-Hubbell Law Directory

WATT, TIEDER, HOFFAR & FITZGERALD, L.L.P. (AV)

601 Pennsylvania Avenue, N.W., Suite 900, 20004
Telephone: 703-749-1000
Telecopier: 703-893-8029
Email: contactus@wthf.com *URL:* http://www.wthf.com
McLean Virginia Office: 7929 Westpark Drive, Suite 400,
Telephone: 703-749-1000.
Telecopier: 703-893-8029.
Irvine California Office: 3 Park Plaza, Suite 1500.
Telephone: 949-852-6700.

MEMBERS OF FIRM

John B. Tieder, Jr.
Robert K. Cox

For full biographical listings, see the Martindale-Hubbell Law Directory

WILKES, ARTIS, HEDRICK & LANE, CHARTERED (AV)

Suite 3000, 1666 K Street, N.W., 20006-2897
Telephone: 202-457-7800
URL: http://www.wilkesartis.com
Annapolis, Maryland Office: Suite 400, 47 State Circle.
Telephone: 410-263-7800.
Bethesda, Maryland Office: Suite 800, 3 Bethesda Metro Center.
Telephone: 301-654-7800.
Greenbelt, Maryland Office: Suite 500, 6305 Ivy Lane.
Telephone: 301-345-7700.
Fairfax, Virginia Office: Suite 600, 11320 Random Hills Road.
Telephone: 703-385-8000.
Waldorf, Maryland Office: Suite 101, 1 Post Office Road.
Telephone: 301-638-7500; 301-843-7610 (Metro).

James C. Wilkes (1899-1968)
James E. Artis (1907-1978)
David M. Bond
Stephen J. Braun (Resident, Waldorf, Maryland Office)
Charles A. Camalier, III
Ilene Baxt Campbell (Resident, Fairfax, Virginia Office)
Jerald S. Cohn
Christopher H. Collins
James P. Downey (Resident, Fairfax, Virginia Office)
Timothy Dugan (Resident, Bethesda, Maryland)
Maureen Ellen Dwyer
John T. Epting
Jonathan L. Farmer
Nancy G. Fax (Resident, Bethesda, Maryland Office)
Phil T. Feola
Stanley J. Fineman
David A. Fuss
Norman M. Glasgow
Norman M. Glasgow, Jr.
Larry A. Gordon (Resident, Bethesda, Maryland Office)
Robert L. Gorham
Robert M. Gurss
Patricia Ann Harris (Resident, Bethesda, Maryland Office)
Robert R. Harris (Resident, Bethesda, Maryland Office)
Allen Jones, Jr.

(See Next Column)

WILKES, ARTIS, HEDRICK & LANE CHARTERED—*Continued*

Eric S. Kassoff (Resident, Bethesda, Maryland Office)
Samuel P. Kastner
Paul J. Kiernan
Jonathan I. Kipnis (Resident, Greenbelt, Maryland Office)
William Kominers (Resident, Bethesda, Maryland Office)
John D. Lane
Lawrence G. Lerman (Resident, Bethesda, Maryland Office)
Kenneth A. Max (Resident, Bethesda, Maryland Office)
Thomas G. McGarry
Gerard P. Panaro
Allison Carney Prince
John E. Prominski, Jr.
Whayne S. Quin
Jonathan P. Rak (Resident, Fairfax, Virginia Office)
Mark S. Randall
Richard K. Reed (Resident, Greenbelt Maryland Office)
John H. Rust, Jr. (Resident, Fairfax, Virginia Office)
David H. Saffern
Kenneth L. Samuelson
Frank W. Stearns (Resident at Fairfax, Virginia Office)
Dana Brewington Stebbins
Stuart A. Turow
Lois J. Vermillion
Lorraine J. Webb (Resident, Waldorf, Maryland Office)
Joseph B. Whitebread, Jr.
David L. Winstead
Ramsey L. Woodworth

Matthew G. Ahrens (Resident, Fairfax, Virginia Office)
Antonio M. Barros, Jr.
Ronald A. Brown (Resident, Waldorf, Maryland Office)
Lisa L. Jackson (Resident, Greenbelt, Maryland Office)
Kathleen A. Marthaler (Resident, Bethesda, Maryland Office)
Marc E. Miller
Mark F. Rogers (Resident, Bethesda, Maryland Office)
Brian P. Rohde (Resident, Greenbelt, Maryland Office)
Karin M. Ryan
Sarah E. Shaw
Stacy Plotkin Silber (Resident, Greenbelt, Maryland Office)
Martin P. Sullivan
Paul A Tummonds, Jr

For full biographical listings, see the Martindale-Hubbell Law Directory

FLORIDA

BOCA RATON, Palm Beach Co.

LAW OFFICES OF CARTER & THOMAS LLP (AV)

1200 North Federal Highway, Suite 312, 33432
Telephone: 561-368-9900
Broward 954-427-0933
Fax: 561-368-0293
Email: carterboca@aol.com

John E. Carter
Donald Joseph Thomas

Colleen M. Stiger

For full biographical listings, see the Martindale-Hubbell Law Directory

DICKENSON, MURDOCH, REX AND SLOAN, CHARTERED (AV)

Suite 410 Compson Financial Center, 980 North Federal Highway, 33432
Telephone: 561-391-1900
Facsimile: 561-391-1933

David B. Dickenson
Richard A. Murdoch
Robert H. Rex
Barbara A. Sloan

For full biographical listings, see the Martindale-Hubbell Law Directory

FURR AND COHEN, P.A. (AV)

Suite 412, 1499 W. Palmetto Park Road, 33486
Telephone: 561-395-0500
Broward: 954-421-0300
Fax: 561-338-7532
Email: thefirm@furrandcohenpa.com *URL:* http://www.furrandcohenpa.com

Robert C. Furr
Charles I. Cohen

Alvin S. Goldstein
Leslie Scott Osborne
Lisa J. Chaiklin Aflalo
Bradley Scott Shraiberg

OF COUNSEL
C. William Berger

For full biographical listings, see the Martindale-Hubbell Law Directory

STEVEN I. GREENWALD, P.A. (AV)

Boca Palm Professional Plaza, 6971 North Federal Highway, Suite 105, 33487
Telephone: 561-994-5560
Facsimile: 561-994-5629

Steven I. Greenwald

(See Next Column)

OF COUNSEL
Brandon J. Douglas

For full biographical listings, see the Martindale-Hubbell Law Directory

KEELEY, HAYES, DUDLEY & GARRETT (AV)

A Partnership of Professional Associations
Suite 314 Peninsula Plaza, 2424 North Federal Highway, 33431
Telephone: 561-392-4300
Telecopier: 561-392-4409

MEMBERS OF FIRM

Rusley C. Meeker (1931-1995)
Everett H. Dudley, Jr., (P.A.)
Joseph F. Keeley (P.A.)
James B. Hayes (P.A.)
Eugene S. Garrett
Stephen Mahle (P.A.)
Stacey Leigh Burnston

Approved Attorneys for: Attorneys' Title Insurance Fund; Chicago Title Insurance Co.
Reference: NCNB National Bank of Florida; Bank America; Sun Trust Bank.

For full biographical listings, see the Martindale-Hubbell Law Directory

HARVEY G. KOPELOWITZ (AV)

7251 West Palmetto Park Road, Suite 201
Telephone: 561-392-4115
Fax: 561-392-0351

For full biographical listings, see the Martindale-Hubbell Law Directory

SCHROEDER & LARCHE, P.A. (AV)

One Boca Place, Suite 319-A, 2255 Glades Road, 33431-7383
Telephone: 561-241-0300
Broward: 954-421-0878
Telecopier: 561-241-0798
URL: http://www.lawyers.com/schroeder&larche

Michael A. Schroeder
W. Lawrence Larche

For full biographical listings, see the Martindale-Hubbell Law Directory

SHAPIRO & DECTOR, P.A. (AV)

7777 Glades Road, Suite 200, 33434
Telephone: 561-477-7800
Facsimile: 561-477-7722
Email: ShapDec@aol.com

Michael B. Shapiro
Andrew M. Dector
Vincent J. Piazza

OF COUNSEL

Michael D. Mopsick
Steven J. Asarch
Wayne Kaplan

For full biographical listings, see the Martindale-Hubbell Law Directory

WEISS & HANDLER, P.A. (AV)

Suite 218A, One Boca Place, 2255 Glades Road, 33431-7313
Telephone: 561-997-9995
Broward: 954-421-5101
Palm Beach: 561-734-8008
Telecopier: 561-997-5280
Email: weisshand@aol.com
West Palm Beach, Florida Office: 505 South Flagler Drive, Suite 1331, 33401.
Telephone: 561-655-3433.
New York, NY Office: 45 Rockefeller Plaza, Suite 1501.
Telephone: 212-332-2900.

Howard I. Weiss
Henry B. Handler

Manuel R. Comras
Donald Feldman
William M. Franz
David K. Friedman
Carol A. Kartagener
Allison L. Kay
Bruce A. Harris
Howard M. Rudolph (Resident, West Palm Beach Office)
Stacy E. Welt

OF COUNSEL

Malcolm L. Stein (Not admitted in FL)
Harry Winderman

For full biographical listings, see the Martindale-Hubbell Law Directory

*BRADENTON,** Manatee Co.

CONLEY & CLEARY (AV)

2401 Manatee Avenue West, 34205
Telephone: 941-748-8778
Telefax: 941-745-2572
Toll Free: 1-877-723-3034
Email: CONCLEAR@aol.com

Roger P. Conley
Kenneth W. Cleary

(See Next Column)

CONLEY & CLEARY, *Bradenton—Continued*

D. Robert Hoyle | Lori M. Dorman

General Counsel for: Liberty National Bank; Key Florida Bancorp., Inc.; Warner Southern College; B & J Citrus Groves, Inc.; Conley Buick-Pontiac, Inc.; Conley Subaru, Inc.
Representative Clients: Post-Browning, Inc.; Ashland, Inc.; APAC-Florida, Inc.; Metro Recycling Co.

For full biographical listings, see the Martindale-Hubbell Law Directory

GRIMES GOEBEL GRIMES HAWKINS & GLADFELTER, P.A. (AV)

The Professional Building, 1023 Manatee Avenue West, P.O. Box 1550, 34206
Telephone: 941-748-0151
Fax: 941-748-0158
Email: ggghg@gte.net
Tampa, Florida Office: Old Hyde Park Village, 1509 West Swann Avenue, Suite 275.
Telephone: 813-258-2557.
Fax: 813-258-2327.

William C. Grimes
Caleb J. Grimes
Leslie Horton Gladfelter
William S. Galvano

Counsel for: Schroeder Manatee Inc. (Agriculture and Land Development); Lombardo & Skipper & Foley, Inc. (Civil Engineers); CCI Environmental Services, Inc. (Environmental Consultants); Creekwood Investors, Ltd.; Old Hyde Park Village Center, Ltd.; First Federal Savings & Loan Association of Florida.
Approved Attorneys for: Lawyers Title Insurance Corp.; Chicago Title Insurance Co.; Attorneys Title Insurance Fund.

For full biographical listings, see the Martindale-Hubbell Law Directory

ENGLEWOOD, Sarasota & Charlotte Cos.

BATSEL, MCKINLEY, ITTERSAGEN, GUNDERSON & BERNTSSON, P.A. (AV)

Suite 204 Manor Pointe Professional Center, 1861 Placida Road, 34223
Telephone: 941-474-7713
Telefax: 941-474-8276
Email: bmi@ewol.com
Port Charlotte, Florida Office: 18401 Murdock Circle. 33948.
Telephone: 941-627-1000.
Telefax: 941-255-0684.

C. Guy Batsel (Resident, Port Charlotte and Englewood Offices)
Scott D. Ittersagen
Miko P. Gunderson
Thomas P. McLennon

For full biographical listings, see the Martindale-Hubbell Law Directory

*FORT LAUDERDALE,** Broward Co.

WILLIAM E. ASHCRAFT LAW OFFICE, P.A. (AV)

2736 Northeast 19th Street, P.O. Box 4336, 33338
Telephone: 954-561-2680
Fax: 954-561-1085
Email: ashcraftlaw@usa.net *URL:* http://www.lawyers.com/ashcraftlaw

William E. Ashcraft

For full biographical listings, see the Martindale-Hubbell Law Directory

BERGER DAVIS & SINGERMAN (AV)

350 East Las Olas Boulevard, Suite 1000, 33301
Telephone: 954-525-9900
Fax: 954-523-2872
Email: jberger@bdslaw.com *URL:* http://www.bdslaw.com
Miami, Florida Office: 200 South Biscayne Boulevard, Suite 2950.
Telephone: 305-755-9500.
Fax: 305-714-4340.
Tallahassee, Florida Office: 215 South Monroe Street, Suite 705, 32301.
Telephone: 850-561-3010.
Fax: 850-561-3013.

James L. Berger
Mitchell W. Berger
Franklin H. Caplan (Resident, Miami Office)
James B. Davis
Henry H. (Bucky) Fox
Van P. Geeker (Resident, Tallahassee Office)
Jordi Guso (Resident, Miami Office)
Nick Jovanovich
Robert B. Judd
Manuel Kushner
Daniel Lampert
Dawn M. Meyers
John D. C. Newton, II (Resident, Tallahassee Office)
Samuel E. Poole III
Leonard K. Samuels
Laz L. Schneider
Paul Steven Singerman (Resident, Miami Office)
Daniel H. Thompson (Resident, Tallahassee Office)

(See Next Column)

Robert W. Barron
Maria St. John Daugherty
James Harris Fierberg (Resident, Miami Office)
Ilyse Wrubel Homer (Resident, Miami Office)
Sherry A. Lambson
Lisa D. MacClugage
Brian G. Rich (Resident, Miami Office)
Holiday Hunt Russell
Jonathan C. Vair (Resident, Miami Office)
Jeffrey Scott Wertman

OF COUNSEL

James C. Cunningham, Jr. | Fred Goldberg

For full biographical listings, see the Martindale-Hubbell Law Directory

CAMP & CAMP, P.A. (AV)

Suite 1501 One East Broward Boulevard, 33301
Telephone: 954-524-8111
FAX: 954-524-2661
Email: JDCAMPLAW@AOL.COM

James D. Camp, Jr. | James D. Camp, III

General Counsel for: Sun Trust Bank/South Florida, N.A., Trust Division, Broward Community College; Steel Fabricators, Inc.; Steel Joists, Inc.; La-Gasse Pool Construction Co.; BRDG-Tndr Corp.
Representative Clients: Amp, Inc.; Ed Morse Chevrolet, Inc.; Gulfstream Pump and Equipment Co.; Broward Community College.

For full biographical listings, see the Martindale-Hubbell Law Directory

FERENCIK, LIBANOFF, BRANDT & BUSTAMANTE, P.A. (AV)

150 South Pine Island Road, Suite 400, 33324
Telephone: Dade County: 305-949-8003
Broward County: 954-474-8080
Fax: 954-474-7343
Email: RFerenci@Counsel.com *URL:* http://www.flbb@mindspring.com

Robert E. Ferencik, Jr.
Ira Libanoff
Alan C. (Peter) Brandt, Jr.
Nestor Bustamante III
Alexander J. Williams, Jr.

Jordana Lee Goldstein
Sandra Denise Kennedy
Gavin D. Caddy

OF COUNSEL

Carla Reece Gettlemen

For full biographical listings, see the Martindale-Hubbell Law Directory

KELLEY, HERMAN & SMITH (AV)

Suite 206, 1401 East Broward Boulevard, 33301
Telephone: 954-462-7806
Fax: 954-522-0396

MEMBERS OF FIRM

Patrick G. Kelley
Bruce K. Herman
Jeffrey B. Smith

Approved Attorneys for: Commonwealth Land Title Insurance Co.; Attorney's Title Insurance Fund.

For full biographical listings, see the Martindale-Hubbell Law Directory

LEONARD & MORRISON (AV)

Tenth Floor, 4875 North Federal Highway, P.O. Box 11025, 33339
Telephone: 954-776-3600
Fax: 954-776-3609

MEMBERS OF FIRM

William F. Leonard
Richard W. Morrison
C. Glenn Leonard

General Counsel for: Coral Ridge Golf Course, Inc.; Gill Hotels Co.; Sheraton Yankee Clipper Hotel; Royal Petroleum, Inc.
Representative Client: Plimpton Trusts.
Reference: Nations Bank; Union Bank of Florida.

For full biographical listings, see the Martindale-Hubbell Law Directory

MASTRIANA & CHRISTIANSEN, PROFESSIONAL ASSOCIATION (AV)

1500 North Federal Highway, Suite 200, 33304
Telephone: Broward: 954-566-1234
Dade: 305-949-1234
URL: http://www.lawyers.com/m&cpa

Frank A. Mastriana (1916-1991)
F. Ronald Mastriana
Michael Eric Christiansen
Stephen Vincent Hoffman
Jon M. Henning

Representative Clients: Dadeland Mall; Family Center, Inc. (A & P); Leonard L. Farber Corp.; Parkson Corp.

For full biographical listings, see the Martindale-Hubbell Law Directory

Fort Lauderdale—Continued

OPPENHEIM & PILELSKY, P.A. (AV)

1290 Weston Road, Suite 300, 33326
Telephone: 954-384-6114
Toll Free: 888-384-6114
Fax: 954-384-6115
Email: Info@oppenheimlaw.com *URL:* http://www.oppenheimlaw.com

Roy D. Oppenheim

Representative Clients: Landmark Building & Design, Inc.; Delcrest Building Corp.; Danro Homes, Inc.; Ambry Homes; Euro-Trend Realty, Inc.; Delcourt Homes, Inc.; The Hemisphere Group, Inc.; Landmark Waterfront Homes, Inc.

For full biographical listings, see the Martindale-Hubbell Law Directory

TRIPP SCOTT (AV)

110 S.E. 6th Street, P.O. Box 14245, 33301
Telephone: 954-525-7500
Telecopier: 954-761-8475
URL: http://www.trippscott.com

Norman D. Tripp
James A. Scott
Dennis Dustin Smith
Peter G. Herman
Garry W. Johnson
Kimberly A. Gilmour
Richard D. Heller
Gregory A. McLaughlin
Steven C. Elkin
Daniel E. Taylor
Matthew Zifrony
Edward J. Pozzuoli
William J. Gross

OF COUNSEL

Welcom H. Watson, Jr.

ASSOCIATES

Laura L. Hess
Scott J. Jordan
Tammy L. Knight
Paul Octavio Lopez
Milagros (Millie) G. Muñoz
Loren K. Newman
Richard J. Simeone
Heather S. Tripp
Jeffrey S. Wood
Christine T. Yates

Representative Clients: AutoNation; Colonial Bank; Commonwealth Land Title Insurance Co.; Equitable Bank; First Union National Bank of Florida; Northern Trust Bank of Florida, N.A.; Norwest Mortgage, Inc.; Re/Max Lifestyles; Union Planters Bank.

For full biographical listings, see the Martindale-Hubbell Law Directory

*FORT MYERS,** Lee Co.

DEBOEST, KNUDSEN, STOCKMAN, WISEMAN, DECKER & DRYDEN, P.A. (AV)

1415 Hendry Street, P.O. Box 1470, 33902-1470
Telephone: 941-334-1381
Telecopier: 941-334-0266
Email: dkswlaw@gate.net
Naples, Florida Office: 600 Fifth Avenue South, Suite 301, 34102.
Telephone: 941-263-5040.
Fax: 941-263-6944.

Arthur K. Knudsen, Jr. (Retired)
Richard D. DeBoest
William E. Stockman
Tamela Eady Wiseman (Resident, Naples Office)
James G. Decker
Thomas M. Dryden

Representative Clients: Cobb Theatres, Inc.; WCI Communities, Inc.; Evelyn Jackman and Sons, Inc.

For full biographical listings, see the Martindale-Hubbell Law Directory

HENDERSON, FRANKLIN, STARNES & HOLT, PROFESSIONAL ASSOCIATION (AV)

1715 Monroe Street, P.O. Box 280, 33902-0280
Telephone: 941-334-4121
Telecopier: 941-332-4494

Ronald W. Smalley
Denis H. Noah
Russell P. Schropp
Charles J. Basinait
Thomas H. Gunderson
David K. Fowler
Joseph M. Madden, Jr.

Representative Clients: CIGNA Group; CSX Transportation, Inc.; Fireman's Fund Insurance Cos.; The Hartford Insurance Group; Huntington National Bank, N.A.; NationsBank, N.A.; Travelers/Aetna Insurance Group; Sprint-Florida, Inc.

For Complete List of Firm Personnel, See General Section

For full biographical listings, see the Martindale-Hubbell Law Directory

*FORT PIERCE,** St. Lucie Co.

GONANO, HARRELL & FERGUSON (AV)

Riverside National Bank Building, 1600 South Federal Highway, Suite 200, 34950-5194
Telephone: 561-464-1032
Fax: 561-464-0282
Email: ghlaw@compuserve.com

(See Next Column)

Douglas E. Gonano
Daniel B. Harrell
Johnathan A. Ferguson

General Counsel: School Board of St. Lucie County; Reserve Community Development District; St. Lucie West Services District.
Representative Clients: East Coast Lumber & Supply Co.; Riverside National Bank of Florida; Superior Title Services, Inc.
Approved Attorneys for: Attorneys' Title Insurance Fund; Commonwealth Land Title Insurance Co.
References: Riverside National Bank of Florida; SunTrust, South Florida, N.A.

For full biographical listings, see the Martindale-Hubbell Law Directory

NEILL GRIFFIN JEFFRIES FOWLER TIERNEY & NEILL, CHARTERED (AV)

311 South Second Street, P.O. Box 1270, 34954
Telephone: 561-464-8200
Fax: 561-464-2566

Chester B. Griffin
J. Stephen Tierney, III

Local Counsel For: SunTrust Bank South Florida, N.A., (Commercial and Trust Departments); Chubb Group of Insurances Cos.
Approved Attorneys for: Attorneys' Title Insurance Fund; Commonwealth Land Title Insurance Co.
Reference: SunTrust Bank South Florida, N.A., Fort Pierce, Florida (Commercial and Trust Departments).

For full biographical listings, see the Martindale-Hubbell Law Directory

*GAINESVILLE,** Alachua Co.

WAYNE P. CASTELLO (AV)

Suite W, 2772 N.W. 43rd Street, 32606
Telephone: 352-377-4422
Telecopier: 352-373-5792
Email: wpc@prodigy.net *URL:* http://www.lawyers.com/castellolaw

LEGAL SUPPORT PERSONNEL

Griffin Stegall (Legal Assistant)
Diana Harris (Legal Assistant)

For full biographical listings, see the Martindale-Hubbell Law Directory

HOLLYWOOD, Broward Co.

STEVEN A. MASON, P.A. (AV)

3363 Sheridan Street, Suite 201, 33021
Telephone: 954-963-5900
Fax: 954-985-9811
Email: passat902@aol.com *URL:* http://www.lawyers.com/stevenmasonpa

Steven A. Mason

Representative Clients: T.S.I., Inc.; Southern Security Bank; Dental Centers of America.

For full biographical listings, see the Martindale-Hubbell Law Directory

*JACKSONVILLE,** Duval Co.

BARRY B. ANSBACHER, P.A. (AV)

1301 Riverplace Boulevard, Suite 2450 Riverplace Tower, 32207-9037
Telephone: 904-396-8050
Fax: 904-396-8076
Email: BBA@mediaone.net

Barry B. Ansbacher

Approved Attorney Agent For: Attorneys' Title Insurance Fund; Commonwealth Land Title; Old Republic.

For full biographical listings, see the Martindale-Hubbell Law Directory

DONAHOO, BALL & MCMENAMY, P.A. (AV)

(Incorporated in 1982)
50 North Laura Street, Suite 2925, 32202
Telephone: 904-354-8080
Fax: 904-791-9563
Email: office@donahooball.com

John W. Donahoo (1907-1993)
Thomas M. Donahoo
Haywood M. Ball
William B. McMenamy
Thomas M. Donahoo, Jr.

For full biographical listings, see the Martindale-Hubbell Law Directory

SAMUEL L. LEPRELL (AV)

1930 San Marco Boulevard Suite 201, St. Mark's Place, 32207-3256
Telephone: 904-390-2705
Fax: 904-390-2711
Email: juvandyleprelllaw@worldnet.att.net *URL:* http://www.lawyers.com/leprelllaw

For full biographical listings, see the Martindale-Hubbell Law Directory

Jacksonville—Continued

LOBRANO & KINCAID, P.L. (AV)

Suite 1650 Independent Life Building, 1 Independent Drive, 32202
Telephone: 904-359-2100
Facsimile: 904-353-1332

Stephen D. Lobrano
Wade McK. Hampton

OF COUNSEL

W. Douglas Smith (Not admitted in FL)

For full biographical listings, see the Martindale-Hubbell Law Directory

PAPPAS METCALF JENKS MILLER & REINSCH, P.A. (AV)

200 West Forsyth Street, Suite 1400, 32202-4327
Telephone: 904-353-1980
Telecopier: 904-353-5217
Email: pmj@papmet.com

Thomas M. Jenks
Robert A. Leapley, Jr.
John G. Metcalf
Frank Estes Miller
M. Lynn Pappas
Mark A. Reinsch

Christina P. Gillam
Gary B. Davenport
G. Todd Cottrill
Thomas Ingram

LEGAL SUPPORT PERSONNEL

Mary Beth Wimmer
Glenna Thompson (Paralegal)
Donna F. Demetree (Paralegal)

For full biographical listings, see the Martindale-Hubbell Law Directory

SMITH HULSEY & BUSEY (AV)

1800 First Union National Bank Tower, 225 Water Street, P.O. Box 53315, 32201-3315
Telephone: 904-359-7700
Facsimile: 904-359-7708; 353-9908
Email: vsharp@smithhulsey.com

Lloyd Smith (1915-1987)

MEMBERS OF FIRM

Stephen D. Busey
Earl E. Googe, Jr.
Jeanne E. Helton
Cynthia C. Jackson
G. Preston Keyes
Richard E. Klein
William E. Kuntz
Lauren P. Langham
M. Richard Lewis, Jr.
John F. MacLennan
Raymond R. Magley
E. Owen McCuller, Jr.
James H. Post
Bryan L. Putnal
E. Lanny Russell
Joel Settembrini, Jr.
Tim E. Sleeth
John R. Smith, Jr.
Harry M. Wilson, III

Brandon L. Ayscue
Brannon B. Belcastro
James A. Bolling, Jr.
Charmaine T.M. Chiu
Ryan C. Curtis
Michael R. Freed
Reynold N. Hoover
Michael J. Ivan, Jr.
Tonya L. Janney
Charles H. Keller
Bradley R. Markey
R. Leanne McKnight
Bert J. Millis
Stephen D. Moore, Jr.
Jon L. Swergold

OF COUNSEL

Mark Hulsey
John E. Thrasher

Representative Clients: ATP Tour, Inc; Baptist/St. Vincent's Health System, Inc.; Browning-Ferris Industries, Inc.; First Union National Bank of Florida; Florida Rock Industries, Inc.; PGA Tour, Inc.; KPMG Peat Marwick; The Regency Group, Inc.; The Ritz-Carlton Hotel Co.; University of Florida.

For full biographical listings, see the Martindale-Hubbell Law Directory

*KISSIMMEE,** Osceola Co.

POHL & SHORT, P.A.

(See Winter Park)

*LAKE CITY,** Columbia Co.

TERRY McDAVID (AV)

128 South Hernando Street, P.O. Box 1328, 32056-1328
Telephone: 904-752-1896
Fax: 904-752-8905

For full biographical listings, see the Martindale-Hubbell Law Directory

LAKELAND, Polk Co.

HAHN, McCLURG, WATSON, GRIFFITH & BUSH, P.A. (AV)

101 South Florida Avenue, 33801-4619
Telephone: 941-688-7747
Telecopier: 941-683-4582
Mailing Address: P.O. Box 38, 33802-0038
Email: lawfirm@hahnmcclurg.com *URL:* http://www.hmwgb@gte.net

(See Next Column)

James P. Hahn
E.V. McClurg
Stephen C. Watson
John R. Griffith
Philip H. Bush
James M. Craig, II

General Counsel: Huntington National Bank, Lakeland, Florida; Florida-First Bank, Lakeland, Florida; Publix Super Markets, Inc.
Approved Attorneys For: Attorneys' Title Insurance Fund; American Title Insurance Co.; Title & Trust Company of Florida; Federal Land Bank of Columbia, Columbia, S.C.
Reference: Huntington National Bank, Lakeland, Florida.

For full biographical listings, see the Martindale-Hubbell Law Directory

PETERSON & MYERS, P.A. (AV)

100 East Main Street, P.O. Box 24628, 33802-4628
Telephone: 941-683-6511; 676-6934
Telecopier: 941-682-8031
Lake Wales, Florida Office: 130 East Central Avenue, P.O. Box 1079.
Telephones: 941-676-7611; 683-8942.
Winter Haven, Florida Office: Lake Region Plaza, 141 5th Street, N.W., P.O. Drawer 7608.
Telephone: 941-294-3360.

M. David Alexander, III
Philip O. Allen
Jack P. Brandon
Kristen Marie Buzzanca
Debra Leigh Cline
J. Davis Connor
Dennis G. Corrick
Roy A. Craig, Jr.
Clinton A. Curtis
Jacob C. Dykxhoorn
Joseph A. Geary
Maria "Mia" Gerber
Jonn D. Hoppe
Dennis P. Johnson
Kevin C. Knowlton
Douglas A. Lockwood, III
Corneal B. Myers
E. Blake Paul
Robert E. Puterbaugh
Thomas B. Putnam, Jr.
Deborah A. Ruster
Stephen R. Senn
Andrea Teves Smith
Keith H. Wadsworth
Kerry M. Wilson

General Counsel for: SunTrust Bank Mid-Florida, N.A.; Lakeland Regional Medical Center, Inc.; Housing Finance Authority of Polk County.
Representative Clients: NationsBank, N.A.; First Union National Bank; Mutual Wholesale Co.; Ben Hill Griffin, Inc.; E. R. Jahna Industries, Inc.
Approved Attorneys for: Attorneys' Title Insurance Fund; Equitable Life Assurance Society of the United States.

For full biographical listings, see the Martindale-Hubbell Law Directory

LAKE WALES, Polk Co.

PETERSON & MYERS, P.A. (AV)

130 East Central Avenue, P.O. Box 1079, 33853
Telephone: 941-676-7611; 683-8942
Telecopier: 941-676-0643
Lakeland, Florida Office: 100 East Main Street, P.O. Box 24628.
Telephones: 941-683-6511; 676-6934.
Winter Haven, Florida Office: Lake Region Plaza, 141 5th Street, N.W., P.O. Drawer 7608.
Telephone: 941-294-3360.

M. David Alexander, III
Philip O. Allen
Jack P. Brandon
Kristen Marie Buzzanca
Debra Leigh Cline
J. Davis Connor
Dennis G. Corrick
Roy A. Craig, Jr.
Clinton A. Curtis
Jacob C. Dykxhoorn
Joseph A. Geary
Maria "Mia" Gerber
Jonn D. Hoppe
Dennis P. Johnson
Kevin C. Knowlton
Douglas A. Lockwood, III
Corneal B. Myers
E. Blake Paul
Robert E. Puterbaugh
Thomas B. Putnam, Jr.
Deborah A. Ruster
Stephen R. Senn
Andrea Teves Smith
Keith H. Wadsworth
Kerry M. Wilson

General Counsel for: SunTrust Bank Mid-Florida, N.A.; Lakeland Regional Medical Center, Inc.; Housing Finance Authority of Polk County.
Representative Clients: NationsBank, N.A.; First Union National Bank; Mutual Wholesale Co.; Ben Hill Griffin, Inc.; E. R. Jahna Industries, Inc.
Approved Attorneys for: Attorneys' Title Insurance Fund; Equitable Life Assurance Society of the United States.

For full biographical listings, see the Martindale-Hubbell Law Directory

MARCO ISLAND, Collier Co.

JOHN A. NOLD, P.A. (AV(T))

995 North Collier Boulevard, 34145
Telephone: 941-394-7811
Telefax: 941-394-9449
Email: noldatty@aol.com
Naples, Florida Office: 5100 North Tamiami Trail, Suite 103-146.
Telephone: 941-643-6868.

John A. Nold

For full biographical listings, see the Martindale-Hubbell Law Directory

*MIAMI,** Dade Co.

ADAMS, GALLINAR, IGLESIAS & MEYER, P.A. (AV)

Colonial Bank Center, 1200 Brickell Avenue, Ninth Floor, 33131
Telephone: 305-416-6800
Facsimile: 305-416-6811
Email: agimlaw@agimlaw.com *URL:* http://www.lawyers.com/agimlaw

Robert R. Adams
Michael D. Gallinar
Mario A. Iglesias
James M. Meyer

Marta M. Cil
Enrique N. Bascuas
Santiago Eljaiek, III

For full biographical listings, see the Martindale-Hubbell Law Directory

BERMAN WOLFE RENNERT VOGEL & MANDLER, P.A. (AV)

35th Floor, International Place, 100 Southeast Second Street, 33131-2130
Telephone: 305-577-4177
Fax: 305-373-6036
Email: administrator@bwr-law.com *URL:* http://www.bwr-law.com
Boca Raton, Florida Office: Boca Corporate Center, 2101 NW Corporate Boulevard, Suite 107, 33431.
Telephone: 561-995-2232.
Fax: 561-995-1668.

Neil J. Berman
Leon J. Wolfe
Charles J. Rennert
Howard J. Vogel
Jeffrey L. Mandler
Jill Nexon Berman

Jonathan L. Gaines
Miriam Cruz-Bustillo
Claire P. Menard
Shamira Klein
Julie M. Schwartz

OF COUNSEL

Anthony A. Rolle

For full biographical listings, see the Martindale-Hubbell Law Directory

CAMNER, LIPSITZ AND POLLER, PROFESSIONAL ASSOCIATION (AV)

550 Biltmore Way, Suite 700 (Coral Gables), 33134
Telephone: 305-442-4994
Fax: 305-442-2389
URL: http://www.camner-lipsitz-poller.com

Alfred R. Camner
Marc Lipsitz
Neale J. Poller
Marsha D. Bilzin

Roger A. Preziosi
Adam Mitchell Neijna
Bridget Wong
David A. Messinger
Wendy Hill El Diery

OF COUNSEL

Anne Shari Camner
Thomas R. Blake

For full biographical listings, see the Martindale-Hubbell Law Directory

J. PATRICK FITZGERALD, P.A. (AV)

110 Merrick Way (Coral Gables) Suite 3B, 33134
Telephone: 305-443-9162
Fax: 305-443-6613
Email: jpfitzgerald@ibm.net
Palm Beach, Florida Office: 189 Bradley Place, 33480.
Telephone: 561-659-6438.

J. Patrick Fitzgerald

Roberto J. Diaz
Suzanne A. Dockerty
Jorge A. Mestre

For full biographical listings, see the Martindale-Hubbell Law Directory

WARREN P. GAMMILL (AV)

Suite 1700 BIV Tower, 1101 Brickell Avenue, 33131
Telephone: 305-579-9014; 305-579-0000
Fax: 305-371-6927
Email: w.p.gammill-miami@worldnet.att.net *URL:* http://www.lawyers.com/wpglaw

For full biographical listings, see the Martindale-Hubbell Law Directory

HOLTZMAN, KRINZMAN, EQUELS & FURIA (AV)

2601 South Bayshore Drive, Suite 600, 33133
Telephone: 305-859-7700
Fax: 305-859-9996
Email: hkef@hkef.com *URL:* http://www.hkef.com
Orlando, Florida Office: 16 West Pine Street, 32801.
Telephone: 407-839-0095.
Fax: 407-839-2050.

(See Next Column)

Tallahassee, Florida Office: 542 East Park Avenue, 32301.
Telephone: 850-222-2900.
Fax: 850-222-2933.

Richard N. Krinzman
Alan E. Krinzman

OF COUNSEL

Chapman L. Smith, Jr.

For full biographical listings, see the Martindale-Hubbell Law Directory

KATZ, BARRON, SQUITERO, FAUST & BERMAN, P.A. (AV)

Seventh Floor, 2699 South Bayshore Drive, 33133-5408
Telephone: 305-856-2444; North Broward/Boca Raton: 954-781-4720; *Broward:* 954-522-3636; North Broward: 954-781-0637
Facsimile: 305-285-9227
URL: http://www.kbsfb.com
Fort Lauderdale, Florida Office: 100 Northeast 3rd Avenue, Suite 280, 33301.
Telephone: 305-860-2599.
Fax: 954-522-5119.

Michael D. Katz
Ronald M. Barron (1945-1994)
John R. Squitero
Marc L. Faust
Richard E. Berman
Anthony H. Pelle
Howard L. Friedberg
Robert C. Grady
Erica L. English
William D. Rohrer
Richard B. Ivans
Bernard Allen
W. Todd Boyd
David S. Drobner
Charles D. Robbins
Charles D. Brecker

OF COUNSEL

William A. Zeiher
Roger S. Goldman
Richard Morton

Michael I. Kean
Michele L. McNichol
Adam J. Lamb
William R. Trueba
Alex Espenkotter
Jill D. Levy
Jose R. Riguera
Monica A. Rey-Moran
Mathai Jacob

For full biographical listings, see the Martindale-Hubbell Law Directory

JAY KOENIGSBERG, P.A. (AV)

1101 Brickell Avenue, Suite 800-S, 33131
Telephone: 305-569-0600
Fax: 305-373-3233
Email: relaw@mindspring.com

Jay Koenigsberg

For full biographical listings, see the Martindale-Hubbell Law Directory

MARKOWITZ, DAVIS, RINGEL & TRUSTY, P.A. (AV)

Two Datran Center, Suite 1225, 9130 South Dadeland Boulevard, 33156-7849
Telephone: 305-670-5000
Telecopier: 305-670-5011

Thomas Ringel

For full biographical listings, see the Martindale-Hubbell Law Directory

LAW OFFICE OF WILLIAM P. MCCAUGHAN (AV)

Suite 2803 World Trade Center, 80 S.W. Eighth Street, 33130
Telephone: 305-577-0058
Fax: 305-372-0526
Email: WPMLAW@BellSouth.net

For full biographical listings, see the Martindale-Hubbell Law Directory

RITTER, RITTER & ZARETSKY (AV)

Plaza Venetia, 555 N.E. 15th Street, Suite 100, 33132
Telephone: 305-372-0933
Fax: 305-372-0836
Email: RRZLAW@AOL.COM

John H. Ritter (1913-1979)
John A. Ritter
Louis D. Zaretsky

ASSOCIATE

Mark J. Lynn

FOREIGN LEGAL CONSULTANT

John C. Cawood

For full biographical listings, see the Martindale-Hubbell Law Directory

ROSENBERG, REISMAN & STEIN, LLP (AV)

One Southeast Third Avenue Suite 3050, 33131
Telephone: 305-358-2600
Telefax: 305-375-0328
URL: http://www.rrslaw.com

(See Next Column)

ROSENBERG, REISMAN & STEIN LLP, *Miami—Continued*

MEMBERS OF FIRM

Donald S. Rosenberg
Stephen H. Reisman
Joseph B. Reisman
Gary M. Stein
Richard E. Deutch, Jr.

Representative Clients: Turner Construction Co.; The Skylake State Bank.
Approved Attorneys for: Attorneys Title Insurance Fund; Lawyers Title Insurance Corp.
Reference: The Skylake State Bank.

For full biographical listings, see the Martindale-Hubbell Law Directory

SIEGFRIED, RIVERA, LERNER, DE LA TORRE & SOBEL, P.A. (AV)

Suite 1102, 201 Alhambra Circle (Coral Gables), 33134
Telephone: 305-442-3334
Fax: 305-443-3292
URL: http://www.siegfriedlaw.com

Steven M. Siegfried
Peter H. Edwards
Oscar R. Rivera
Stuart H. Sobel
Lisa A. Lerner
Maria Victoria Arias
Helio De La Torre
James F. Harrington
Elisabeth D. Kozlow

Gary Louis Brown
Fern F. Musselwhite
David B. Israel
Grissel C. Picot
Laura Michelle Manning
Marc C. Pugliese

OF COUNSEL

H. Hugh Mc Connell

For full biographical listings, see the Martindale-Hubbell Law Directory

*NAPLES,** Collier Co.

GOODLETTE, COLEMAN & JOHNSON, P.A. (AV)

Northern Trust Bank Building, 4001 Tamiami Trail North, Suite 300, 34103
Telephone: 941-435-3535
Facsimile: 941-435-1218
Email: GCJ@sprintmail.com

Kevin G. Coleman
Linda Clare Brinkman
J. Dudley Goodlette
Harold J. Webre, III
Kenneth R. Johnson
Richard D. Yovanovich
Holly A. Harmon
Kevin R. Lottes
Scott M. Ketchum

For full biographical listings, see the Martindale-Hubbell Law Directory

QUARLES & BRADY LLP (AV)

Barnett Center, 4501 Tamiami Trail North Suite 300, 34103-3060
Telephone: 941-262-5959
Fax: 941-434-4999
URL: http://www.quarles.com
Milwaukee, Wisconsin Office: 411 East Wisconsin Avenue, 53202-4497.
Telephone: 414-277-5000.
Fax: 414-271-3552.
Madison, Wisconsin Office: Firstar Plaza, One South Pinckney Street, P.O. Box 2113, 53701-2113.
Telephone: 608-251-5000.
Fax: 608-251-9166.
West Palm Beach, Florida Office: 222 Lakeview Avenue, 4th Floor, 33401.
Telephone: 561-653-5000.
Fax: 561-653-5333.
Phoenix, Arizona Office: One Camelback Building, One East Camelback Road, Suite 400, 85012-1649.
Telephone: 602-230-5500.
Fax: 602-230-5598.
Chicago, Illinois Office: Quarles & Brady LLC, Citicorp Center, 500 West Madison Street, Suite 3700.
Telephone: 312-715-5000.
Fax: 312-715-5155.

PARTNERS

Thomas E. Maloney
Timothy G. Hains
David L. Petersen
Leo J. Salvatori
F. Joseph McMackin, III
John D. Humphreville

ASSOCIATE

C. Lane Wood

For Complete List of Firm Personnel, See General Section

For full biographical listings, see the Martindale-Hubbell Law Directory

NORTH PALM BEACH, Palm Beach Co.

COHEN, NORRIS, SCHERER, WEINBERGER & WOLMER (AV)

A Partnership of Professional Associations
712 U.S. Highway One, 33408
Telephone: 561-844-3600
Fax: 561-842-4104
URL: http://www.fcohenlaw.com

Fred C. Cohen
Gregory R. Cohen
David B. Norris
Bernard A. Conko
Kenneth J. Scherer
Peter Richard Ray
Robert M. Weinberger
Eric M. Sauerberg (P.A.)
Brent G. Wolmer
Kyle A. Silverman
Gary A. Chernay
James S. Telepman

Representative Clients: Commonwealth Land Title Insurance Company, Orlando; Attorneys Title Insurance Fund, Inc., Orlando ; American Pioneer Title Insurance Company, Casselberry; First American Title Insurance Company, Plantation; Fidelity National Title Insurance Company of New York, Maitland; Old Republic National Title Insurance Company, Deerfield Beach.

For full biographical listings, see the Martindale-Hubbell Law Directory

*ORLANDO,** Orange Co.

BAKER & HOSTETLER LLP (AV)

SunBank Center, Suite 2300, 200 South Orange Avenue, 32802-3432
Telephone: 407-649-4000
Fax: 407-841-0168
To contact an attorney on the Internet use first initial and surname followed by @baker-hostetler.com
URL: http://www.bakerlaw.com
In Cleveland, Ohio: 3200 National City Center, 1900 East Ninth Street.
Telephone: 216-621-0200.
In Cincinnati, Ohio: 312 Walnut Street, Suite 2650.
Telephone: 513-929-3400.
In Columbus, Ohio: Capitol Square, Suite 2100, 65 East State Street.
Telephone: 614-228-1541.
In Denver, Colorado: 303 East 17th Avenue, Suite 1100.
Telephone: 303-861-0600.
In Houston, Texas: 1000 Louisiana, Suite 2000.
Telephone: 713-751-1600.
In Long Beach, California: 300 Oceangate, Suite 620.
Telephone: 362-432-2827.
In Los Angeles, California: 600 Wilshire Boulevard.
Telephone: 213-624-2400.
In Washington, D. C.: Washington Square, Suite 1100, 1050 Connecticut Avenue, N.W.
Telephone: 202-861-1500.

OFFICE MANAGING PARTNER

G. Thomas Ball (Managing Partner-Orlando Office)

PARTNERS

Richard T. Fulton
Rosemary O'Shea
Kurt P. Gruber
Robert J. Webb

For Complete List of Firm Personnel, See General Section
For full biographical listings, see the Martindale-Hubbell Law Directory

BUTLER & HOSCH, P.A. (AV)

3185 South Conway Road, Suite E, 32812
Telephone: 407-381-5200
Fax: 407-381-5577
Email: bhatch@butlerandhosch.com

C. Victor Butler, Jr.
Robert H. Hosch, Jr.

Andrea L. Aylett-Hosch
Estee L. Lipenholtz
Jane E. Bond
Nancy A. Bishop
Michael W. Udowchenko
Christopher W. Conomos

Representative Clients: United Companies Financial Corp.; First Union Home Equity Corp.; Republic Bank for Savings; Capstead Mortgage Corp.; Rhode Island Hospital Trust; First National Bank of Boston; Countrywide Home Loans, Inc.; Norwest Mortgage, Inc.; Amresco; Associates Home Equity Corp.

For full biographical listings, see the Martindale-Hubbell Law Directory

DECUBELLIS & MEEKS, P.A. (AV)

Suite 801, Citrus Center, 255 South Orange Avenue, P.O. Box 4976, 32802-4976
Telephone: 407-872-2200
Telecopier: 407-423-1038

Daniel L. DeCubellis
John A. Shughart, Jr.
Mary B. Meeks
Jennifer C. Carter
Brett M. Wendt

Representative Clients: Design Professional Insurance Corp.; Florida Lawyers Mutual Insurance Corp.; International Game Technology, Inc.; Jennings Environmental Services, Inc.; Mader Southeast, Inc.; Orange County; PGA Tour, Inc.; SouthTrust Bank, N.A.

(See Next Column)

DeCubellis & Meeks P.A.—*Continued*

For full biographical listings, see the Martindale-Hubbell Law Directory

Hendry, Stoner, Sawicki & Brown, P.A. (AV)

200 East Robinson Street, Suite 500, 32801
Telephone: 407-843-5880
Fax: 407-425-7905
Email: HSSB@gdi.net

Robert R. Hendry
Richard D. Stoner
Stephen C. Sawicki
G. Steven Brown

Richard A. Barfield

OF COUNSEL

Laura A. Quigley, P.A.
Deborah J. Townsend
Carl-Christian Thier (Not admitted in FL)
Marcus R. Cigagna (Not admitted in the United States)
Jacqueline E. Danzer (Not admitted in the United States)

Counsel For: Virgin Incoming Services, Inc.; Weitnauer Trading Co. Ltd.; Dufrepex; Fairholme U.S., Inc.; Central Florida Hotel Company, L.C.; Orlando Auto Sales, Inc.; Mears Motor Leasing; Weitnauer America, Inc.; Wolf and Wolf International Inc.; New Jersey Manufacturers Insurance Co.; International Planning, Inc.

For full biographical listings, see the Martindale-Hubbell Law Directory

Moran & Shams, P.A. (AV)

111 North Orange Avenue, Suite 1200, P.O. Box 472, 32802-0472
Telephone: 407-841-4141
Fax: 407-841-4148
Email: moran-shams@moran-shams.com

Thomas P. Moran
Maurice Shams
Robert S. MacDonald
Brian J. Moran
Sidney H. Shams

Lawrence H. Haber

Representative Clients: Alliance Bank; AmSouth Bank; Cruises Only, LLC; Dayron; R.C. Dunn Oil Company; Florida Pump, Inc.; Insurance Office of America, Inc.; Photo Chemical Systems of Florida, Inc.; Southern Community Bank; Whitehill Development Group, Inc.

For full biographical listings, see the Martindale-Hubbell Law Directory

Robert W. Morrison (AV)

940 North Highland Avenue, 32803
Telephone: 407-423-3004
Cell Phone: 407-353-7726
Fax: 407-999-5273
Mailing Address: P.O. Box 1622, Orlando, FL, 32802
Email: MorrisonRW@aol.com

LEGAL SUPPORT PERSONNEL

LEGAL ASSISTANT

Eileen M. Heasley

OF COUNSEL

Bruce A. Stucker

For full biographical listings, see the Martindale-Hubbell Law Directory

Pohl & Short, P.A.

(See Winter Park)

Russell Law Offices, P.A. (AV)

537 North Magnolia Avenue, P.O. Box 886, 32802
Telephone: 407-422-1234
Telecopier: 407-423-2842
Email: RussLaw@compuserve.com *URL:* http://www.lawyers.com/russlaw

Rodney Laird Russell

For full biographical listings, see the Martindale-Hubbell Law Directory

Craig B. Ward, P.A. (AV)

Suite 501, 105 East Robinson Street, 32801-1601
Telephone: 407-843-6000
Fax: 407-839-0577
Email: CBWardlaw@aol.com

Craig B. Ward

OF COUNSEL

Charles D. Miner

Representative Clients: Gladco, Inc. (American Gladiators); Lake of the Woods Homeowners Association, Inc.; Metro One, Inc. (Real Estate); National Ambulance Builders, Inc.; Poole Construction Co., Inc.; Power Concrete Products Co.; Richard Sibley Associates, Inc. (Advertising); Scientific-Atlanta, Inc.
Approved Agent for: First American Title Insurance Co.; Attorneys' Title Insurance Fund.

For full biographical listings, see the Martindale-Hubbell Law Directory

Wilson, Leavitt & Small, P.A. (AV)

437 North Magnolia Avenue, 32801-1524
Telephone: 407-843-4321
Fax: 407-423-1505
Email: wlspa@aol.com *URL:* http://www.lawyers.com/eminentdomain

J. Christy Wilson, III
Mark R. Leavitt
Jay W. Small
Kurt H. Garber

Representative Clients: Circle K; Cumberland Farms; Hardee's Food Systems; Mobil Oil; Public Storage; Southland Corp.; U.S.F.& G.; Oerther Foods; Seventh Day Adventists; McDonald's Corporation.

For full biographical listings, see the Martindale-Hubbell Law Directory

ORMOND BEACH, Volusia Co.

Korey, Sweet, McKinnon, Simpson & Vukelja (AV)

Granada Oaks Professional Building, 595 West Granada Boulevard, Suite A, 32174-9448
Telephone: 904-677-3431
Fax: 904-673-0748

MEMBERS OF FIRM

Edward F. Simpson, Jr.
Robert Kit Korey
Noah C. McKinnon, Jr. (Also Of Counsel, Coble & Simpson, Daytona Beach)
Jeffrey C. Sweet
David A. Vukelja

OF COUNSEL

Scott E. Simpson (Also Member, Coble & Simpson, Daytona Beach)

For full biographical listings, see the Martindale-Hubbell Law Directory

PALM BEACH, Palm Beach Co.

Avis & Avis, P.A. (AV)

125 Worth Avenue, Suite 221, 33480
Telephone: 561-659-0200
Fax: 561-659-0942
Email: info@avislaw.com *URL:* http://www.avislaw.com

Warren E. Avis, Jr.
Deborah K. Avis

OF COUNSEL

Jill E. Kaufman
Richard D. Grow

Representative Clients: Florida Apple, Inc.; K-Rain Manufacturing Corp.; Sentry Paint Technology, Inc.; Palm Beach Precision Molding Co.; Arena Brands, Inc.; Wellington Industries, Inc.; Enterprise National Bank; Avis Enterprises; PAR Microsystems; Den-mat Corp.

For full biographical listings, see the Martindale-Hubbell Law Directory

Baugher, Mettler & Shelton (AV)

340 Royal Poinciana Plaza, P.O. Box 109, 33480
Telephone: 561-833-9631
Fax: 561-655-2835

MEMBERS OF FIRM

Thomas M. Mettler
John W. Shelton

ASSOCIATE

Francis X. J. Lynch

Reference: First National Bank in Palm Beach.

For full biographical listings, see the Martindale-Hubbell Law Directory

Law Offices of Harrison K. Chauncey, Jr., P.A. (AV)

241 Bradley Place, 33480
Telephone: 561-833-3001
Fax: 561-833-9060
Email: hchauncey@chaunceylaw.com

Harrison K. Chauncey Jr.
Mark R. Brown

For full biographical listings, see the Martindale-Hubbell Law Directory

Murphy, Reid, Pilotte, Ord & Austin (AV)

A Partnership of Professional Associations
Suite 100, 340 Royal Palm Way, 33480
Telephone: 561-655-4060
Facsimile: 561-832-5436
Vero Beach, Florida Office: Plantation Plaza, 6606-20th Street, 32966-7902.
Telephone: 561-567-6480.
Facsimile: 561-562-0220.

Eugene W. Murphy Jr. (P.A.)
Keith C. Austin, Jr. (P.A.)

(See Next Column)

MURPHY, REID, PILOTTE, ORD & AUSTIN, *Palm Beach—Continued*

OF COUNSEL

Philip H. Reid

For Complete List of Firm Personnel, See General Section

For full biographical listings, see the Martindale-Hubbell Law Directory

WARWICK & BANISTER, P.A. (AV)

140 Royal Palm Way, Suite 205, 33480
Telephone: 561-655-7776
Telecopier: 561-655-2271
Email: johnban140@aol.com *URL:* http://www.lawyers.com/palmbeachlaw

Charles H. Warwick, Jr. (1894-1967)
Charles H. Warwick, III
John R. Banister

For full biographical listings, see the Martindale-Hubbell Law Directory

POMPANO BEACH, Broward Co.

JOHN L. KORTHALS (AV)

1401 East Atlantic Boulevard, 33060
Telephone: 954-783-2999
Fax: 954-783-9832
Email: korthals.law@mindspring.com

For full biographical listings, see the Martindale-Hubbell Law Directory

PORT CHARLOTTE, Charlotte Co.

BATSEL, MCKINLEY, ITTERSAGEN, GUNDERSON & BERNTSSON, P.A. (AV)

18401 Murdock Circle, 33948
Telephone: 941-627-1000
Telefax: 941-255-0684
Email: BMILAW@nut-n-but.net
Englewood, Florida Office: 1861 Placida Road, Suite 204, 34223.
Telephone: 941-474-7713.
Telefax: 941-474-7713.

C. Guy Batsel (Resident, Port Charlotte and Englewood Offices)
Michael R. McKinley (Resident, Port Charlotte Office)
Scott D. Ittersagen
Miko P. Gunderson
Robert H. Berntsson (Resident, Port Charlotte Office)
Robert F. Koch (Resident, Port Charlotte Office)
Thomas P. McLennon

Jerry Paul
David L. Whigham

For full biographical listings, see the Martindale-Hubbell Law Directory

*PUNTA GORDA,** Charlotte Co.

WOTITZKY, WOTITZKY, MIZELL, ROSS & GOLDMAN, P.A. (AV)

223 Taylor Street, 33950
Telephone: 941-639-2171
Telecopier: 941-639-8617
Email: wwmr@sunline.net

Jason B. Goldman
John B. Mizell
Warren R. Ross
Ernest W. Sturges, Jr.
Edward L. Wotitzky
Hal F. Wotitzky

OF COUNSEL

Frank Wotitzky
Leo Wotitzky

Representative Clients: Punta Gorda Corp.; Developers of Southwest Florida, Inc.; Englewood Disposal Co., Inc.; Integrated Control Systems, Inc.
Approved Attorneys for: Attorneys' Title Insurance Fund, Orlando, Florida; Chicago Title Insurance Co.

For full biographical listings, see the Martindale-Hubbell Law Directory

*ST. AUGUSTINE,** St. Johns Co.

UPCHURCH, BAILEY & UPCHURCH, P.A. (AV)

780 North Ponce de Leon Boulevard, P.O. Drawer 3007, 32085-3007
Telephone: 904-829-9066
Facsimile: 904-825-4862
Email: info@ubulaw.com

John D. Bailey, Jr.
Michael A. Siragusa

OF COUNSEL

Hamilton D. Upchurch

General Counsel for: Flagler College; Flagler Hospital, Inc.; Prosperity Bank; St. Johns County School Board.
Representative Clients: Compass Bank; Bank of St. Augustine; St. Augustine-St. Johns County Board of Relators, Inc.
Approved Agents for: Commonwealth Land Title Insurance Company; Attorneys' Title Insurance Fund, Inc.

(See Next Column)

For Complete List of Firm Personnel, See General Section

For full biographical listings, see the Martindale-Hubbell Law Directory

ST. PETERSBURG, Pinellas Co.

STEIN, FORD, SCHAAF & TOWZEY, L.L.P. (AV)

501 First Avenue North, Suite 1000, 33701
Telephone: 727-894-4333
Fax: 727-894-0175

Henry A. Stein
Harvey A. Ford
Paul A. Nelson
Gary M. Schaaf
Phyllis J. Towzey
Sarah E. Williams

For full biographical listings, see the Martindale-Hubbell Law Directory

*SANFORD,** Seminole Co.

STENSTROM, MCINTOSH, COLBERT, WHIGHAM & SIMMONS, P.A. (AV)

200 West First, Suite 22, P.O. Box 4848, 32772-4848
Telephone: 407-322-2171
Fax: 407-330-2379
Orlando/Winterpark Telephone: 407-834-5119
DeLand/DeBary Telephone: 407-668-1479
URL: http://www.stenstrom.com

Thomas E. Whigham (1952-1988)
Douglas Stenstrom (Retired)
William L. Colbert
Franklin C. Whigham
Clayton D. Simmons
Robert K. McIntosh
Donna L. Surratt-McIntosh
William E. Reischmann, Jr.

Catherine D. Reischmann
James J. Partlow
Dawn M. Harrison

OF COUNSEL

Kenneth W. McIntosh
S. Kirby Moncrief

Representative Clients: City of Sanford; City of Oviedo; City of Casselberry; Seminole Community College; City of Lake Mary; Sanford Housing Authority; City of DeBary; Seminole Soccer Club, Inc.; Tuskawilla Homeowners' Association; South Seminole-North Orange Wastewater Transmission Authority.

For full biographical listings, see the Martindale-Hubbell Law Directory

*SARASOTA,** Sarasota Co.

DICKINSON & GIBBONS, P.A. (AV)

1750 Ringling Boulevard, P.O. Box 3979, 34230
Telephone: 941-366-4680
FAX: 941-953-3136
URL: http://dglawyers.com

Francis C. Dart (1902-1972)
Gary H. Larsen
Camden T. French
Ralph L. Marchbank, Jr.
A. James Rolfes
Burwell J. Jones
Richard R. Garland
Stephen G. Brannan
Deborah J. Blue
Jeffrey D. Peairs
David S. Preston

OF COUNSEL

Patrick H. Dickinson
G. Hunter Gibbons
Ward E. Dahlgren

LEGAL SUPPORT PERSONNEL

Janet E. Gadoury (Certified Legal Assistant)

Representative Clients: Ford Motor Co.; Florida Power & Light Co.; Squibb Corp.
Insurance Clients: Liberty Mutual Insurance Co.; Allstate Insurance Co.; Nationwide Insurance Group; Ohio Casualty Insurance Co.; United States Fidelity & Guaranty Co.; State Farm Insurance Company.

For Complete List of Firm Personnel, See General Section

For full biographical listings, see the Martindale-Hubbell Law Directory

WILLIAMS, PARKER, HARRISON, DIETZ & GETZEN, PROFESSIONAL ASSOCIATION (AV)

200 South Orange Avenue, 34236-6749
Telephone: 941-366-4800
Telecopier: 941-366-5109
Mailing Address: P.O. Box 3258, Sarasota, Florida, 34230-3258
Email: infodesk@williamsparker.com *URL:* http://www.williamsparker.com

William T. Harrison, Jr.
George A. Dietz
James L. Ritchey
Hugh McPheeters, Jr.
Charles D. Bailey, Jr.
J. Michael Hartenstine
Michele B. Grimes
James L. Turner
William M. Seider
Terri Salt Costa
Jeffrey A. Grebe
Morgan R. Bentley

(See Next Column)

WILLIAMS, PARKER, HARRISON, DIETZ & GETZEN PROFESSIONAL ASSOCIATION—*Continued*

LEGAL SUPPORT PERSONNEL

Mark Loveridge (Land Planner)

General Counsel for: Sarasota County Public Hospital Board; Sarasota-Manatee Airport Authority; Taylor Woodrow Homes Ltd.; FCCI Mutual Insurance Co.
Local Counsel for: Bank of America; Northern Trust Bank of Florida; SunTrust Bank, Gulfcoast.

For Complete List of Firm Personnel, See General Section

For full biographical listings, see the Martindale-Hubbell Law Directory

WILSON, JOHNSON & JAFFER, P.A. (AV)

27 South Orange Avenue, 34236-5822
Telephone: 941-955-5800
Fax: 941-955-7353
Email: wilson@lawsites.com *URL:* http://www.lawsites.com

Clyde H. Wilson (1908-1994)
Robert M. Johnson
Clyde H. Wilson, Jr.
John S. Jaffer

For full biographical listings, see the Martindale-Hubbell Law Directory

*STUART,** Martin Co.

McCARTHY, SUMMERS, BOBKO, McKEY, WOOD & SAWYER, P.A. (AV)

2081 East Ocean Boulevard, Second Floor, 34996
Telephone: 561-286-1700
Fax: 561-283-1803
URL: http://www.mcsumm.com

Terence P. McCarthy
Robert P. Summers
Noel A. Bobko
John D. McKey, Jr.
Steven J. Wood
Thomas R. Sawyer
Nicola J. Boone
Steven L. Perry

Kathryn C. Bass
Robert N. Maitland, II

Representative Clients: First National Bank and Trust Company of the Treasure Coast; Hydratech Utilities; Lost Lake at Hobe Sound; Gary Player Design Group; YMCA of Martin County; Shadow Lakes Groves, Inc.; Merrill Lynch Trust Co., (Florida); Wilmington Trust, FSB; The Huntington National Bank, N.A.; WSTU-Radio, WTCN-TV.

For full biographical listings, see the Martindale-Hubbell Law Directory

WARNER, FOX, WACKEEN, DUNGEY SEELEY, SWEET & WRIGHT, L.L.P. (AV)

1100 South Federal Highway, P.O. Drawer 6, 34995-0006
Telephone: 561-287-4444
Fax: 561-220-1489
Email: wfsds@gate.net

Thomas E. Warner
M. Lanning Fox
W. Thomas Wackeen
Richard J. Dungey
Gary L. Sweet
Tim B. Wright
Deborah Bigham Beard

Louis E. Lozeau, Jr.
William Raymond Ponsoldt, Jr.
Anthony L. Conticello
Susann Ward
Michael J. McCluskey
Shawn C. Gray

OF COUNSEL

Robert L. Seeley
Aaron A. Foosaner

Approved Attorneys for: Attorneys' Title Insurance Fund; Commonwealth Land Title Insurance Co.

For full biographical listings, see the Martindale-Hubbell Law Directory

*TALLAHASSEE,** Leon Co.

GENE D. BROWN (AV)

3848 Killearn Court, 32308
Telephone: 850-668-6103
FAX: 850-668-0441
Email: gbrown@istal.com

For full biographical listings, see the Martindale-Hubbell Law Directory

ROSE, SUNDSTROM & BENTLEY, LLP (AV)

2548 Blairstone Pines Drive, P.O. Box 1567, 32301-1567
Telephone: 850-877-6555
Telecopier: 850-656-4029
URL: http://www.rsbattorneys.com

MEMBERS OF FIRM

Chris H. Bentley (P.A.)
Martin S. Friedman (P.A.)

Representative Clients: Aloha Utilities, Inc.; Bonita Springs Utility, Inc.; First American Title Insurance Co.; North Fort Myers Utility, Inc.

(See Next Column)

Reference: Capital City Bank, Tallahassee.

For full biographical listings, see the Martindale-Hubbell Law Directory

*TAMPA,** Hillsborough Co.

BRICKLEMYER SMOLKER & BOLVES, P.A. (AV)

500 East Kennedy Boulevard, Suite 200, 33602-4708
Telephone: 813-223-3888
Fax: 813-228-6422
Email: bsb@bsbpropertylaw.com *URL:* http://www.bsbpropertylaw.com

Keith W. Bricklemyer
David Smolker
Brian A. Bolves
Jay J. Bartlett
Douglas C. Roland
David M. Corry
Richard A. Schlosser
Gregory J. Orcutt

R. Michael Brooks
Deborah M. Schmitt

OF COUNSEL

J.A. Jurgens

For full biographical listings, see the Martindale-Hubbell Law Directory

MARSHALL C. DEASON, JR. (AV)

3750 Gunn Highway, Suite 2-C, 33624
Telephone: 813-269-9448
Fax: 813-960-8902
Email: deasonlaw@rscnet.com *URL:* http://www.lawyers.com/deasonlaw

For full biographical listings, see the Martindale-Hubbell Law Directory

FUENTES AND KREISCHER (AV)

1407 West Busch Boulevard, 33612
Telephone: 813-933-6647
Fax: 813-932-8588
URL: http://www.lawyers.com/fuentesandkreischer

MEMBERS OF FIRM

Lawrence E. Fuentes
Albert C. Kreischer, Jr.

Reference: Northside Bank of Tampa.

For full biographical listings, see the Martindale-Hubbell Law Directory

GATLIN & BIRCH, P.A. (AV)

620 Twiggs Street, 33602
Telephone: 813-229-8561
FAX: 813-229-0422

C. Elmon Gatlin
Dean W. Birch

For full biographical listings, see the Martindale-Hubbell Law Directory

HARRY M. HOBBS, P.A. (AV)

3719 Swann Avenue, 33609
Telephone: 813-879-8333
Fax: 813-877-5426

Harry M. Hobbs

Robert S. Hobbs
Walter O. Hobbs

Representative Clients: Jim Walter Homes, Inc.

For full biographical listings, see the Martindale-Hubbell Law Directory

KETCHEY HORAN, P.A. (AV)

100 North Tampa Street, Suite 1900, P.O. Box 500, 33601-0500
Telephone: 813-223-9395
Fax: 813-221-1348
Email: Stephanie@KetcheyHoran.com
Sun City Center, Florida Office: 1647 Sun City Center Plaza, Suite 200.
Telephone: 813-633-1200.

SHAREHOLDERS

John B. Neukamm

ASSOCIATE

Christopher Charles Nash

For full biographical listings, see the Martindale-Hubbell Law Directory

LAW OFFICE OF JOSEPH M. PANIELLO, P.A. (AV)

Suite 2720 One Tampa City Center, 201 North Franklin Street, P.O. Box 2347, 33601
Telephone: 813-228-7004
FAX: 813-221-2418
Email: foreclosure1@paniello.com

Joseph M. Paniello
J. Mackie Paniello

Gregory T. Hall
Clay A. Holtsinger

Representative Clients: Corinthian Mortgage Corp.; GE Capital Asset Mgt. Corp.; Bank of America, FSB.

(See Next Column)

LAW OFFICE OF JOSEPH M. PANIELLO, P.A., *Tampa—Continued*

For full biographical listings, see the Martindale-Hubbell Law Directory

PARIS & ASSOCIATES, P.A. (AV)

15310 Amberly Drive, Suite 300, 33647
Telephone: 813-975-1900
Fax: 813-975-1850
Email: lawparis@ij.net

Deborah M. Paris

LEGAL SUPPORT PERSONNEL

Susan T. Wilcox
Jeffery D. Wyatt, Jr.

Representative Clients: NationsBank, N.A.; Michigan National Bank; Standard Federal Bank; Lloyds of London.

For full biographical listings, see the Martindale-Hubbell Law Directory

*VERO BEACH,** Indian River Co.

CLEM, POLACKWICH & VOCELLE (AV)

A Partnership including Professional Associations
3333 20th Street, 32960-2469
Telephone: 561-562-8111
Fax: 561-562-2870
Email: bvocelle@cpvlaw.com *URL:* http://www.cpvlaw.com

MEMBERS OF FIRM

Chester Clem (P.A.)
Alan S. Polackwich, Sr. (P.A.)
Louis B. Vocelle, Jr., (P.A.)
Paul Richard Berg

ASSOCIATE

Janet M. Carney

OF COUNSEL

Robert Golden

References: Barnett Bank of The Treasure Coast; Northern Trust Bank of Vero Beach; Indian River National Bank; Riverside National Bank of Florida.

For full biographical listings, see the Martindale-Hubbell Law Directory

COLLINS, BROWN, CALDWELL, BARKETT & GARAVAGLIA, CHARTERED (AV)

756 Beachland Boulevard, P.O. Box 3686, 32964
Telephone: 561-231-4343
FAX: 561-234-5213
Email: cbc@verolaw.com

George G. Collins, Jr.
Calvin B. Brown
William W. Caldwell
Bruce D. Barkett
Michael J. Garavaglia
Lisa N. Thompson
Susan A. Calistri

Reference: First Union Bank of Indian River County, Vero Beach, Florida.

For full biographical listings, see the Martindale-Hubbell Law Directory

MOSS, HENDERSON, BLANTON & LANIER, P.A. (AV)

817 Beachland Boulevard, P.O. Box 3406, 32964-3406
Telephone: 561-231-1900
Fax: 561-231-4387

Steve L. Henderson

Lawrence Y. Leonard

OF COUNSEL

Charles E. Garris

Representative Clients: Aetna Life & Casualty; Alcoa Florida, Inc.; Florida Power & Light Co.; Insurance Company of North America; Liberty Mutual Insurance Co.; Sears, Roebuck & Co.; Sugar Cane Growers Cooperative of Florida; Norfolk Southern Corporation/North American Van Lines, Inc.

For Complete List of Firm Personnel, See General Section

For full biographical listings, see the Martindale-Hubbell Law Directory

STEWART, EVANS & HAFNER, P.A. (AV)

3355 Ocean Drive, P.O. Box 3345, 32964-3345
Telephone: 561-231-3500
FAX: 561-231-9876
Email: firm@sneh.com

William J. Stewart
Ralph L. Evans
Cynthia L. Cambron

Representative Clients: Simons Property Group, Inc.; Beazer Homes, Inc.; Norris & Company Real Estate; Commercial Investments Partnerships.
Approved Attorneys for: Attorney's Title Insurance Fund; Commonwealth Land Title Insurance Co.

For full biographical listings, see the Martindale-Hubbell Law Directory

*WEST PALM BEACH,** Palm Beach Co.

ACKERMAN, LINK & SARTORY, P.A. (AV)

222 Lakeview Avenue, Suite 1250, Esperante, 33401
Telephone: 561-838-4100
Fax: 561-838-5305
Email: alslaw@alslaw.com *URL:* http://www.alslaw.com

David P. Ackerman
Scott J. Link
Wendy Sartory Link

Lawrence J. Diamond
John C. Kelly
Gregory J. Newcomm
Amy B. Nunziella

For full biographical listings, see the Martindale-Hubbell Law Directory

FARISH, FARISH & ROMANI (AV)

316 Banyan Boulevard, P.O. Box 4118, 33402
Telephone: 561-659-3500
1-800-401-4LAW
Fax: 561-655-3158
Email: farish@bellsouth.net

MEMBERS OF FIRM

Joseph D. Farish (1892-1977)
Joseph D. Farish, Jr.
Robert V. Romani

ASSOCIATES

S. Emory Rogers
Peter M. Bassaline

LEGAL SUPPORT PERSONNEL

Ken P. Beelner

References: 1st Union Bank.

For full biographical listings, see the Martindale-Hubbell Law Directory

KIRK GRANTHAM, P.A. (AV)

Suite 105, 1860 Forest Hill Boulevard, 33406
Telephone: 561-966-6211
Telefax: 561-966-9495

Kirk Grantham

William Carter Carroll
Edward William Hale

For full biographical listings, see the Martindale-Hubbell Law Directory

JONAS & LASORTE (AV)

Suite 1000, United National Bank Tower, 1645 Palm Beach Lakes Boulevard, 33401
Telephone: 561-684-3000
FAX: 561-684-3004
Email: alasorte@worldnet.att.net

Michael N. Jonas
Alfred A. LaSorte, Jr.

ASSOCIATE

Jane M. Gordon

For full biographical listings, see the Martindale-Hubbell Law Directory

NASON, YEAGER, GERSON, WHITE & LIOCE, P.A. (AV)

Mellon United National Bank Tower, Suite 1200, 1645 Palm Beach Lakes Boulevard, 33401
Telephone: 561-686-3307
Fax: 561-686-5442

Thomas J. Yeager
Gary N. Gerson
John White, II
Domenick R. Lioce
Alan I. Armour, II
Mark A. Pachman
Elaine Johnson James
Nathan E. Nason
Gregory L. Scott
Charles W. Edgar, III
Joseph A. Caccamo
Manuel Farach
George E. Harding
Amanda Parks Schlechter

William J. Romanos, III
Bruce E. Sands

LEGAL SUPPORT PERSONNEL

Sandra R. Gronek (Principal Administrator)
L. Ann Jaeckin (Corporate Paralegal)
Kathleen S. Loviska (Real Estate Paralegal)
Lisa M. Mroczko (Litigation/Probate Paralegal)
Elsie T. Pollak (Litigation/Probate Paralegal)
Georgina J. Popham (Corporate/Securities Paralegal)
Coral R. St. Pierre (Real Estate/Corporate Paralegal)

For full biographical listings, see the Martindale-Hubbell Law Directory

PRESSLY & PRESSLY, P.A. (AV)

Esperante, Suite 910, 222 Lakeview Avenue, 33401-6112
Telephone: 561-659-4040
FAX: 561-655-6006
URL: http://www.lawyers.com/pressly&pressly

(See Next Column)

PRESSLY & PRESSLY P.A.—*Continued*

James G. Pressly, Jr.
David S. Pressly
Trent S. Kiziah

J. Grier Pressly III

For full biographical listings, see the Martindale-Hubbell Law Directory

QUARLES & BRADY LLP (AV)

222 Lakeview Avenue, 4th Floor, 33401
Telephone: 561-653-5000
Fax: 561-653-5333
URL: http://www.quarles.com
Milwaukee, Wisconsin Office: 411 East Wisconsin Avenue, 53202-4497.
Telephone: 414-277-5000.
Fax: 414-271-3552.
Madison, Wisconsin Office: Firstar Plaza, One South Pinckney Street, P.O. Box 2113, 53701-2113.
Telephone: 608-251-5000.
Fax: 608-251-9166.
Naples, Florida Office: Barnett Center, 4501 Tamiami Trail North, Suite 300, 34103-3060.
Telephone: 941-262-5959.
Fax: 941-434-4999.
Phoenix, Arizona Office: One Camelback Building, One East Camelback Road, Suite 400, 85012-1649.
Telephone: 602-230-5500.
Fax: 602-230-5598.
Chicago, Illinois Office: Quarles & Brady LLC, Citicorp Center, 500 West Madison Street, Suite 3700.
Telephone: 312-715-5000.
Fax: 312-715-5155.

PARTNER

Ned R. Nashban

OF COUNSEL

John S. Sammond

For Complete List of Firm Personnel, See General Section

For full biographical listings, see the Martindale-Hubbell Law Directory

WARD, DAMON, BEVERLY, TITTLE & POSNER, P.A. (AV)

4420 Beacon Circle, 33407-3270
Telephone: 561-842-3000
Stuart: 561-223-5550
Fax: 561-842-3626
Email: wdbtp@wdbtp.com *URL:* http://www.wdbtp.com

James F. Cooney, Jr. (1950-1992)
Conrad Damon
Andrew Fulton, IV
Irwin R. Gilbert
Craig I. Kelley
Michael J Posner
Roger C. Stanton
James D. Tittle, Jr.
Philip H. Ward, III

OF COUNSEL

Don Beverly

For full biographical listings, see the Martindale-Hubbell Law Directory

WINTER HAVEN, Polk Co.

PETERSON & MYERS, P.A. (AV)

Lake Region Plaza, 141 5th Street N.W., P.O. Drawer 7608, 33883-7608
Telephone: 941-294-3360
Lake Wales, Florida Office: 130 East Central Avenue, P.O. Box 1079.
Telephones: 941-676-7611; 683-8942.
Lakeland, Florida Office: 100 East Main Street, P.O. Box 24628.
Telephones: 941-683-6511; 676-6934.

M. David Alexander, III
Philip O. Allen
Jack P. Brandon
Kristen Marie Buzzanca
Debra Leigh Cline
J. Davis Connor
Dennis G. Corrick
Roy A. Craig, Jr.
Clinton A. Curtis
Jacob C. Dykxhoorn
Joseph A. Geary
Maria "Mia" Gerber
Jonn D. Hoppe
Dennis P. Johnson
Kevin C. Knowlton
Douglas A. Lockwood, III
Corneal B. Myers
E. Blake Paul
Robert E. Puterbaugh
Thomas B. Putnam, Jr.
Deborah A. Ruster
Stephen R. Senn
Andrea Teves Smith
Keith H. Wadsworth
Kerry M. Wilson

General Counsel for: SunTrust Bank Mid-Florida, N.A.; Lakeland Regional Medical Center, Inc.; Housing Finance Authority of Polk County.
Representative Clients: NationsBank, N.A.; First Union National Bank; Mutual Wholesale Co.; Ben Hill Griffin, Inc.; E. R. Jahna Industries, Inc.
Approved Attorneys for: Attorneys' Title Insurance Fund; Equitable Life Assurance Society of the United States.

For full biographical listings, see the Martindale-Hubbell Law Directory

WINTER PARK, Orange Co.

GRAHAM, CLARK, JONES, BUILDER, PRATT & MARKS (AV)

Third Floor, NationsBank Building, 369 North New York Avenue, P.O. Drawer 1690, 32790
Telephone: 407-647-4455
Telefax: 407-740-7063
URL: http://www.grahamclark.com

MEMBERS OF FIRM

Jesse E. Graham
Scott D. Clark
Frederick W. Jones
J. Lindsay Builder, Jr.
James R. Pratt
Howard S. Marks

Geoffrey D. Withers
Jesse E. Graham, Jr.
Samuel M. Nelson
Jessica K. Hew
Jeffrey L. Kaplan
Douglas K. Gartenlaub
William A. Davis, Jr.

Approved Attorneys for: Chicago Title Insurance Co.
Reference: NationsBank of Florida.

For full biographical listings, see the Martindale-Hubbell Law Directory

HADDOCK PROFESSIONAL ASSOCIATION (AV)

3260 University Boulevard, Suite 210, 32792
Telephone: 407-679-6171
Fax: 407-679-8810
Email: ehaddock@fullsail.com
Mailing Address: P.O. Box 5148, Winter Park, FL, 32793-5148
Email: edhaddock@aol.com

Edward E. Haddock, Jr.

Approved Attorneys For: American Pioneer Title Insurance Co.
Reference: Colonial Bank, Orlando, Florida.

For full biographical listings, see the Martindale-Hubbell Law Directory

POHL & SHORT, P.A. (AV)

280 West Canton Avenue, Suite 410, P.O. Box 3208, 32790
Telephone: 407-647-7645; 407-647-POHL
Telefax: 407-647-2314
Email: ps@pohlshort.com

Dwight I. Cool
Alexander S. Douglas II
Gary A. Forster
E. Givens Goodspeed
Mark A. Grimes
Robert S. Hoofman
Roger A. Kelly
Adam O. Kirwan
David J. Kohs
Frank L. Pohl
James Everett Shepherd V
Houston E. Short
John R. Simpson, Jr.

Representative Clients: American Generator Co.; Copelco Capital, Inc.; Denim U.S.A., Inc.; Ford Motor Credit Co.; Lodestar Technology, Inc.; Lutheran Brotherhood; SunTrust, N.A.; Trax, Inc.

For full biographical listings, see the Martindale-Hubbell Law Directory

VOSE, BLAU & HAYES (AV)

2705 West Fairbanks Avenue, 32789
Telephone: 407-645-3735
Fax: 407-628-5670
Email: bvose@vbh-law.com *URL:* http://www.vbh-law.com

Gretchen R. H. Vose
Leslie A. Blau
Rosemary H. Hayes

ASSOCIATES

Carolyn S. Crichton
Christina M. Page
Peter J. Meadows
Aubrey Harry Ducker, Jr.

For full biographical listings, see the Martindale-Hubbell Law Directory

GEORGIA

*ALBANY,** Dougherty Co.

CANNON, MEYER VON BREMEN & GOSS, LLP (AV)

2417 Westgate Drive, P.O. Box 70909, 31708-0909
Telephone: 912-435-1470
Telefax: 912-888-2156
Email: cmvblaw@cmvb.com

MEMBERS OF FIRM

William E. Cannon, Jr.
Michael S. Meyer von Bremen
Stephen S. Goss

ASSOCIATES

Timothy O. Davis
Toysha M. Flowers
William H. Gregory, II

For full biographical listings, see the Martindale-Hubbell Law Directory

*ATLANTA,** Fulton Co.

ALTMAN, KRITZER & LEVICK, P.C. (AV)

Powers Ferry Landing, Suite 224, 6400 Powers Ferry Road, N.W., 30339
Telephone: 770-955-3555
Fax: 770-952-7821, 955-2866, 955-0038, 955-3697
Email: akl@akl.com
New York, N.Y. Office: 730 Fifth Avenue, Suite 1805, 10019.
Telephone: 212-489-3745.
Fax: 212-489-3729.
Schaumburg, Illinois Affiliate: Altman, Kritzer & Levick, Ltd., Suite 700, 1101 Perimeter Drive, 60173.
Telephone: 847-240-0340.
Fax: 847-240-0344.

Mark J. Levick
D. Charles Houk
Charles L. Wood
Ephraim Spielman
Benno G. Rothschild, Jr.
Theodore H. Sandler
Frank Slover
W. Daniel Hicks, Jr.
Robert D. Simons
Peter M. Hartman
Debra M. Thompson
John E. Taylor
John H. Lewis
Steven J. Roberts
Keith N. Wilson

OF COUNSEL

Richard P. Rubenoff
James R. Harland, Jr.
Lori E. Kilberg
Kevin M. Walsh
Gary L. Simpson

Jeremy D. Cohen
Craig P. Colburn, Jr.
Thomas D. White
Karen M. Edwards
Gil Y. Burstiner
Jack D. Pappalardo (Not admitted in GA)
Ashley C. Stanley
Ajay K. Jindia
Angela Hsu
Robert A. Chubb

Representative Clients: Home Depot, Inc.; Ingles Markets, Incorporated; Trammell Crow Co.; The Sembler Company; Uptons, Inc.; Prudential; Southtrust Bank of Ga.; First Union National Bank; Regency Retail Group; Childress-Klein Properties.

For Complete List of Firm Personnel, See General Section

For full biographical listings, see the Martindale-Hubbell Law Directory

S. MARCUS CALLOWAY, P.C. (AV)

4800 Ashford-Dunwoody Road, Suite 240, 30338
Telephone: 770-698-7960
Telecopier: 770-698-7999
Email: marcusc@titlelaw.com
Hilton Head, South Carolina Office: Calloway & Hofmann, 106 Executive Center, 29928.
Telephone: 803-686-4006.
Telecopier: 803-686-4494.

S. Marcus Calloway

Michael A. Hoover
Christine A. Hofmann (Resident, Hilton Head, South Carolina Office)
Christy B. Cheek
W. Lane Haley

References: Colonial Bank; NationsBank.

For full biographical listings, see the Martindale-Hubbell Law Directory

COHEN/DAVID & ASSOCIATES, P.C. (AV)

6000 Lake Forrest Drive, N.W. 100 Century Springs West, 30328-5902
Telephone: 404-256-7802
Fax: 404-255-0137
Email: cdstc@aol.com *URL:* http://www.lawyers.com/davidcohen&associates
Roswell, Georgia Office: Suite 400, 1172 Grimes Bridge Road, 30075.
Telephone: 770-998-8100.
Fax: 770-998-6804.

Bruce P. Cohen
John H. David, Jr. (Resident, Roswell Office)

Robert G. Bennett III

For full biographical listings, see the Martindale-Hubbell Law Directory

DAVID G. CROCKETT, P.C. (AV)

1950 Equitable Building, 100 Peachtree Street, N.W., 30303
Telephone: 404-522-4280
Telecopier: 404-589-9891
Email: CROCKLAW@BELLSOUTH.NET

David G. Crockett

Douglas L. Brooks

(See Next Column)

LEGAL SUPPORT PERSONNEL

Loraine B. Harps (Paralegal)

Approved Attorney for: Chicago Title Insurance Co.
Reference: NationsBank, N.A.

For full biographical listings, see the Martindale-Hubbell Law Directory

GRAY & GILLILAND, P.C. (AV)

400 Perimeter Center Terrace, Suite 1050, 30346-1239
Telephone: 770-392-4800
Telecopy: 770-392-4808

John C. Gray
T. Cullen Gilliland
Charles A. Ratz
Melissa A. Garrett
T. Jeffery Lehman
Robert W. Browning

P. Steven Kratsch

OF COUNSEL

E. Reid Garrett
David S. Currie
Mark B. Bullman

For full biographical listings, see the Martindale-Hubbell Law Directory

HOLT NEY ZATCOFF & WASSERMAN, LLP (AV)

A Partnership including Professional Corporations
100 Galleria Parkway, Suite 600, 30339
Telephone: 770-956-9600
Facsimile: 770-956-1490
Email: mthomas@hnzw.com

MEMBERS OF FIRM

Robert G. Holt (P.C.)
James M. Ney (P.C.)
Sanford H. Zatcoff (P.C.)
Michael G. Wasserman (P.C.)
Richard P. Vornholt
Brian P. Cain

OF COUNSEL

Penni A. Dudley

ASSOCIATES

Gregory A. Randall (Not admitted in GA)
Thomas K. Anderson

Representative Clients: Abrams Properties, Inc.; American Realty Trust, Inc.; Citicorp Real Estate, Inc.; Childress Klein Properties, Inc.; Trammell Crow Residential; First American Title Insurance Co.; Gables Residential Trust; Metric Realty; Roberts Properties, Inc.; Simmons, Vedder & Co.; Starwood Capital Group; Sterling Trust; The University Financing Foundation, Inc.

For Complete List of Firm Personnel, See General Section

For full biographical listings, see the Martindale-Hubbell Law Directory

KREVOLIN & HORST, LLC (AV)

Suite 2150, 100 Colony Square, 1175 Peachtree Street, N.E., 30361
Telephone: 404-888-9700
Fax: 404-888-9577

Douglas P. Krevolin
Jeffrey D. Horst

Michael G. Regas II
Michael D. Flint

For full biographical listings, see the Martindale-Hubbell Law Directory

LIPSHUTZ, GREENBLATT & KING (AV)

2300 Harris Tower-Peachtree Center, 233 Peachtree Street, N.E., 30303
Telephone: 404-688-2300
Fax: 404-588-0648
Email: rmllgk@aol.com

MEMBERS OF FIRM

Robert J. Lipshutz
Edward L. Greenblatt
Randall M. Lipshutz
James V. Zito

OF COUNSEL

William R. King
Tito Mazzetta

ASSOCIATE

Paula B. Smith
Mindy C. Waitsman

For full biographical listings, see the Martindale-Hubbell Law Directory

LONG ALDRIDGE & NORMAN LLP (AV)

A Limited Liability Partnership including Professional Corporations
Suite 5300, 303 Peachtree Street, 30308
Telephone: 404-527-4000
Telecopier: 404-527-4198
Email: atlanta@lanlaw.com *URL:* http://www.lanlaw.com
Washington, D.C. Office: Suite 600, 701 Pennsylvania Avenue, N.W., 20004.
Telephone: 202-624-1200.
FAX: 202-624-1298.

(See Next Column)

LONG ALDRIDGE & NORMAN LLP—*Continued*

MEMBERS OF FIRM

James L. Barkin
Clyde E. Click
Robert D. Hancock, Jr.
W. Gregory Null
Douglas D. Selph
William F. Stevens
William F. Timmons

ASSOCIATE

Michael R. Tippett

OF COUNSEL

Mindy S. Planer
Janice N. Smith
Gerald D. Walling

For Complete List of Firm Personnel, See General Section

For full biographical listings, see the Martindale-Hubbell Law Directory

MACEY, WILENSKY, COHEN, WITTNER & KESSLER, LLP (AV)

285 Peachtree Center Avenue, Suite 600, 30303-1229
Telephone: 404-584-1200
Telecopier: 404-681-4355
Email: Lawyers@MaceyWilensky.com

MEMBERS OF FIRM

Morris W. Macey
Frank B. Wilensky
M. Todd Westfall

ASSOCIATES

Pamela Gronauer Hill
Michael R. Wing

For Complete List of Firm Personnel, See General Section

For full biographical listings, see the Martindale-Hubbell Law Directory

THOMAS E. MATTIMOE LLC (AV)

Suite 3700 • Promenade II, 1230 Peachtree Street, NE, 30309
Telephone: 404-870-9797
Fax: 404-870-9787
Email: tom@mattimoe.com

Thomas E. Mattimoe

For full biographical listings, see the Martindale-Hubbell Law Directory

MCCULLOUGH SHERRILL, LLP (AV)

1409 Peachtree Street, N.E., 30309
Telephone: 404-885-1500
Telecopier: 404-892-1801
Email: info@mslegal.com *URL:* http://www.mslegal.com

MEMBERS OF FIRM

Kenneth R. McCullough
Paul M. Baisier
Mark A. Block
William D. Brunstad
Patrick J. Clarke
D. Lynn Holliday
James H. Kaminer, Jr.
Paul P. Mattingly
Chester G. Rosenberg
Bradley J. Taylor
Robert M. Trusty

ASSOCIATES

Gale G. Evans
Michael S. Rodgers
Lawrence A. Thrower
Newton Jasper Wardlaw, IV
Philip E. West

For Complete List of Firm Personnel, See General Section

For full biographical listings, see the Martindale-Hubbell Law Directory

PARKER, HUDSON, RAINER & DOBBS LLP (AV)

1500 Marquis Two Tower, 285 Peachtree Center Avenue, N.E., 30303
Telephone: 404-523-5300
Fax: 404-522-8409
Tallahassee, Florida Office: The Perkins House, 118 North Gadsden Street, 32301.
Telephone: 904-681-0191.
Fax: 904-681-9493.

MEMBERS OF FIRM

Kenneth H. Kraft
David N. Heaton

For full biographical listings, see the Martindale-Hubbell Law Directory

ROWE, FOLTZ & MARTIN, P.C. (AV)

3525 Piedmont Road, N.E. Five Piedmont Center, Suite 750, 30305-1509
Telephone: 404-231-9397
Telecopier: 404-237-1659
Email: rfm@rfmatlanta.com

Robert P. Rowe
Joseph B. Foltz
J. Marshall Martin, III
Mitchell S. Rosen
Pamela Rogers Masters
Louis Emerson Bridges, III
Kevin H. Hudson
Frederic H. Pilch, III
Paul Pei-Cheng Huang
Matthew H. Michaud

OF COUNSEL

Jeff D. Woodward

For full biographical listings, see the Martindale-Hubbell Law Directory

THOMAS, KENNEDY, SAMPSON & PATTERSON (AV)

3355 Main Street, 30337
Telephone: 404-688-4503
Telecopier: 404-681-2950; Litigation Dept.
Telecopier: 404-684-9515
URL: http://www.tksp.com

MEMBERS OF FIRM

R. E. Thomas, Jr. (1911-1996)
John Loren Kennedy (1942-1994)
Thomas G. Sampson
P. Andrew Patterson
Jeffrey E. Tompkins

ASSOCIATES

Thomas G. Sampson, II
Ceasar C. Mitchell, II.
Erika Nicole Jackson

LEGAL SUPPORT PERSONNEL

Gwendolyn C.H. Dixon
Elbetha (Beth) Martin (Paralegal)
Nancy Allen-Haskell
Yvonne Torrence
Shyril E. Beck
Constance Harris (Paralegal)
Lisa Russell Johnson

For full biographical listings, see the Martindale-Hubbell Law Directory

*AUGUSTA,** Richmond Co.

DYE, TUCKER, EVERITT, LONG & BREWTON, A PROFESSIONAL ASSOCIATION (AV)

453 Greene Street, P.O. Box 2426, 30903-2426
Telephone: 706-722-0771
Fax: 706-722-7028

A. Rowland Dye
Thomas W. Tucker
A. Zachry Everitt
John B. Long
Benjamin H. Brewton
Troy A. Lanier

OF COUNSEL

A. Montague Miller

Jon E. Ingram, Jr.

Representative Clients: State Farm Insurance Cos.; Travelers-Aetna Insurance Cos.; Georgia Power Co.; Wachovia National Bank (Augusta Division); Chubb Group; MAG Mutual Insurance Company; Augusta Board of Realtors; Canal Insurance Company; St. Paul Fire and Marine Insurance Company.

For full biographical listings, see the Martindale-Hubbell Law Directory

HALL & MULLINS, P.C. (AV)

1202 First Union Bank Building, 699 Broad Street, 30901
Telephone: 706-722-7062
Fax: 706-722-7201
URL: http://www.lawyers.com/hall&mullins

J. Randal Hall

For full biographical listings, see the Martindale-Hubbell Law Directory

HULL, TOWILL, NORMAN, BARRETT & SALLEY, A PROFESSIONAL CORPORATION (AV)

801 Broad Street, Suite 700, 30901
Telephone: 706-722-4481
Fax: 706-722-9779
Email: hullfirm@groupz.net *URL:* http://www.groupz.net/~advocate
Aiken, South Carolina Office: 111 Park Avenue, 29801.
Telephone: 803-648-4213.
Fax: 803-648-2601.

James M. Hull (1885-1975)
George B. Barrett (1894-1942)
Julian J. Willingham (1887-1963)
John Bell Towill (1907-1991)
Robert C. Norman (Retired, 1991)
W. Hale Barrett
Lawton Jordan, Jr.
Patrick J. Rice
Douglas D. Batchelor, Jr.
David E. Hudson
William H. Tucker (Not admitted in GA)
William F. Hammond
Mark S. Burgreen
George R. Hall
James B. Ellington
F. Michael Taylor
William J. Keogh, III
Edward J. Tarver
J. Noel Schweers, III
Susan D. Barrett
Ralph Emerson Hanna, III

James M. Holly (Not admitted in GA)
Timothy E. Moses
N. Shannon Gentry Lanier
Tara R. Simkins
Charles H. Weigle
Natalie A. Dopson
David C. Smith

OF COUNSEL

Julian B. Salley, Jr. (Not admitted in GA)

Counsel for: Morris Communications Corporation; Merry Land & Investment Company, Inc.; Castleberry/Snow's Brands, Inc.; Chipman-Union, Inc.; Augusta National, Inc.; Sun Trust Bank Augusta, N.A.; Georgia Power Co.; St. Joseph Hospital, Augusta, Georgia, Inc.; Norfolk Southern Corp.; Housing Authority of the City of Augusta.

(See Next Column)

HULL, TOWILL, NORMAN, BARRETT & SALLEY A PROFESSIONAL CORPORATION, *Augusta—Continued*

For full biographical listings, see the Martindale-Hubbell Law Directory

WARLICK, TRITT & STEBBINS, L.L.P. (AV)

15th Floor, First Union Bank Building, 699 Broad Street, 30901-1454
Telephone: 706-722-7543
Fax: 706-722-1822
Email: wts@wts-lawfirm.com
Columbia County Office: 119 Davis Road, Martinez, Georgia 30907.
Telephone: 706-860-7595.
Fax: 706-860-7597.

MEMBERS OF FIRM

William Byrd Warlick
Roy D. Tritt (Resident, Martinez Office)
Charles C. Stebbins, III
E. L. Clark Speese
C. Gregory Bryan

OF COUNSEL

Richard E. Miley

For full biographical listings, see the Martindale-Hubbell Law Directory

*COLUMBUS,** Muscogee Co.

HATCHER, STUBBS, LAND, HOLLIS & ROTHSCHILD (AV)

A Limited Liability Partnership
Suite 500 The Corporate Center, 233 12th Street, P.O. Box 2707, 31902-2707
Telephone: 706-324-0201
Telecopier: 706-322-7747
Email: mailman@hatcherstubbs.com

MEMBERS OF FIRM

J. Barrington Vaught
Charles T. Staples
Joseph L. Waldrep
George W. Mize, Jr.
John M. Tanzine, III
Alan F. Rothschild, Jr.
William C. Pound

General Counsel for: SunTrust Bank, West Georgia, N.A.; TOM'S Foods Inc.; Muscogee County Board of Education; The Jordan Company; Flournoy Development Company; St. Francis Hospital, Inc.; Bill Heard Enterprises, Inc.; Spectrum Stores, Inc.

For Complete List of Firm Personnel, See General Section

For full biographical listings, see the Martindale-Hubbell Law Directory

*DECATUR,** De Kalb Co.

SIMMONS, WARREN, SZCZECKO & MCFEE, PROFESSIONAL ASSOCIATION (AV)

315 West Ponce de Leon Avenue, Suite 850, 30030
Telephone: 404-378-1711
Fax: 404-377-6101

Joseph Szczecko
William C. McFee, Jr.

Representative Clients: Julian LeCraw & Company (Real Estate); Intown Suites, Inc.; Aderhold Properties, Inc.; Preferred Lodging Systems, Inc.; Royal Oldsmobile; Troncalli Motors, Inc.

For full biographical listings, see the Martindale-Hubbell Law Directory

*GAINESVILLE,** Hall Co.

SMITH, GILLIAM AND WILLIAMS (AV)

200 Old Coca-Cola Building, 301 Green Street, N.W., P.O. Box 1098, 30503
Telephone: 770-536-3381
Fax: 770-531-1481
Email: SGWFirm@Applied.net

MEMBERS OF FIRM

R. Wilson Smith, Jr. (1906-1983)
John H. Smith
Steven P. Gilliam
Jerry A. Williams
Kelly Anne Miles
Bradley J. Patten
M. Tyler Smith

ASSOCIATE

Robert A. Weber, Jr.

General Counsel for: Gainesville Industrial Electric Co.; Georgia Mutual Insurance, a Stock Company; L & R Farms; H. Wilson Manufacturing Co.; Goforth Electrical Supply; North Georgia Petroleum Co.; Gibbs Management Group, Inc.

For full biographical listings, see the Martindale-Hubbell Law Directory

*HARTWELL,** Hart Co.

THE GORDON LAW FIRM (AV)

Gordon Building, P.O. Box 870, 30643
Telephone: 706-376-5418
Fax: 706-376-5416
Email: wgordon@hartcom.net

Walter James Gordon

(See Next Column)

Kimberly A. Wilkerson

References: NationsBank of Georgia, N.A.; The Bank of Hartwell; Athens First Bank & Trust Company.

For full biographical listings, see the Martindale-Hubbell Law Directory

*LAWRENCEVILLE,** Gwinnett Co.

ANDERSEN, DAVIDSON & TATE, P.C. (AV)

1505 Lakes Parkway, Suite 100, P.O. Box 2000, 30043
Telephone: 770-822-0900
Telecopier: 770-822-9680
Email: a-dt@mindspring.com

Thomas J. Andersen
Gerald Davidson, Jr.
Thomas T. Tate
Jeffrey R. Mahaffey
Kathleen B. Guy

References: Sun Trust Bank; The Bank of Gwinnett County; Chicago Title Insurance Co.; Title Insurance Company of Minnesota.

For Complete List of Firm Personnel, See General Section

For full biographical listings, see the Martindale-Hubbell Law Directory

*MARIETTA,** Cobb Co.

MOORE INGRAM JOHNSON & STEELE, LLP (AV)

A Limited Liability Company
192 Anderson Street, P.O. Box 3305, 30060-8604
Telephone: 770-429-1499
Telecopier: 770-429-8631

MEMBERS OF FIRM

John H. Moore
G. Phillip Beggs
Eldon L. Basham
Sarah L. Bargo

ASSOCIATES

J. Kevin Moore
Susan S. Stuart

Representative Clients: Traton Corp.; Oakleigh Development Corp.
Approved Attorneys For: Chicago Title Insurance Co.; First American Title Insurance Co.; Lawyers Title Insurance Corp.
References: Charter Bank and Trust Co.; First Alliance Bank.

For full biographical listings, see the Martindale-Hubbell Law Directory

SCHAAF & HODGES (AV)

An Association of Sole Practitioners
Suite 202, 1841 Piedmont Road, 30066-4292
Telephone: 770-971-4312
Fax: 770-971-5106

Michael L. Schaaf
R.E. Hodges, Jr.

Reference: Wachovia Bank.

For full biographical listings, see the Martindale-Hubbell Law Directory

*MCDONOUGH,** Henry Co.

SMITH, WELCH & BRITTAIN (AV)

200 The Commerce Building, 235 Keys Ferry Street, P.O. Box 31, 30253
Telephone: 770-957-3937
Fax: 770-957-9165
Stockbridge, Georgia Office: 1239 Eagle's Landing Parkway.
Telephone: 770-389-4864.
Fax: 770-389-5157.

MEMBERS OF FIRM

Ernest M. Smith (1911-1992)
A. J. Welch, Jr.
J. Mark Brittain (Resident, Stockbridge Office)
E. Gilmore Maxwell

ASSOCIATES

Thomas Bruce McFarland
John P. Webb (Resident, Stockbridge Office)
Katharyne Clark Johnson
Tricia B. Smith
Bruce R. Vail

Representative Clients: Atlanta Motor Speedway, Inc.; Bellamy-Strickland Chevrolet, Inc.; Columbia/HCA Healthcare Corp.; Ceramic and Metal Coatings Corp.; Cities of Hampton, Locust Grove and Stockbridge; Georgia Farm Bureau Mutual Insurance; Killearn Properties, Inc. of Georgia; RSKCO, Inc.

For full biographical listings, see the Martindale-Hubbell Law Directory

*NEWNAN,** Coweta Co.

GLOVER & DAVIS, P.A. (AV)

10 Brown Street, P.O. Box 1038, 30264
Telephone: 770-683-6000
Fax: 770-683-6010
Peachtree City, Georgia Office: Suite 130, 200 Westpark Drive.
Telephone: 770-487-5834.
Fax: 770-487-3492.

(See Next Column)

GLOVER & DAVIS P.A.—*Continued*

Alan W. Jackson
Randy E. Connell
W. Robert Hancock, Jr. (Resident, Peachtree Office)

Mark E. Dacy (Resident, Peachtree City Office)

Representative Clients: First Citizens Corporation and Banking Subsidiaries; Putnam-Greene Financial Corporation; Farmers & Merchants Bank, Eatonton, Georgia; The Farmers Bank, Union Point, Georgia; First Bank of Coastal Georgia; Peachtree National Bank; Gas, Inc.
Local Counsel for: Inland Paperboard and Packaging, Inc.

For Complete List of Firm Personnel, See General Section

For full biographical listings, see the Martindale-Hubbell Law Directory

ROSENZWEIG, JONES & MACNABB, P.C. (AV)

32 South Court Square, P.O. Box 220, 30264
Telephone: 770-253-3282
Fax: 770-251-7262

Sidney Pope Jones, Jr.

Charles C. Witcher

Approved Attorneys for: Lawyers Title Insurance Corp.; Chicago Title Insurance Co.

For Complete List of Firm Personnel, See General Section

For full biographical listings, see the Martindale-Hubbell Law Directory

*SAVANNAH,** Chatham Co.

LEE, BLACK, SCHEER & HART, P.C. (AV)

10th Floor, 24 Drayton Street, P.O. Box 8205, 31412
Telephone: 912-233-1271
Telecopier: 912-232-7344
Other Savannah Office: 6555 Abercorn Street, Suite 121, P.O. Box 14477.
Telephone: 912-355-1131.

Edward H. Lee
W. Jerrold Black
Steven E. Scheer
R. Jonathan Hart

Christopher L. Rouse
John D. Lange

For full biographical listings, see the Martindale-Hubbell Law Directory

WEINER, SHEAROUSE, WEITZ, GREENBERG & SHAWE, L.L.P. (AV)

14 East State Street, P.O. Box 10105, 31412-0305
Telephone: 912-233-2251
Telecopier: 912-235-5464
Email: WSWGS@Sysconn.com

MEMBERS OF FIRM

Nelson Haslam (1926-1974)
Aron G. Weiner
William W. Shearouse, Jr.
N. Harvey Weitz
Stephen F. Greenberg
Mark T. Shawe
Malcolm Mackenzie, III
Edwin R. Byck

Christine Tambakis McDonnell

For full biographical listings, see the Martindale-Hubbell Law Directory

*SWAINSBORO,** Emanuel Co.

SHEPHERD, GARY & MCWHORTER (AV)

SSG Building, 109 East Moring Street, Drawer 99, 30401
Telephone: 912-237-7551
Facsimile: 912-237-7514

MEMBERS OF FIRM

Felix C. Williams (1899-1972)
George L. Smith, II (1912-1973)
Sidney B. Shepherd
Loren Gary, II
William H. McWhorter, Jr.
Millard B. Shepherd, Jr.

Representative Clients: Cities of Swainsboro, Adrian, Garfield and Nunez; The Citizens Bank of Swainsboro; Rayonier Inc.; Farm Bureau Insurance Co.
Approved Attorneys for: Lawyers Title Insurance Corp.; Ticor Title Insurance Co.; Title Insurance Company of Minnesota; Chicago Title Insurance Co.; Auto Parts & Supply.

For full biographical listings, see the Martindale-Hubbell Law Directory

HAWAII

*HONOLULU,** Honolulu Co.

AYABE, CHONG, NISHIMOTO, SIA & NAKAMURA (AV)

A Partnership including a Professional Corporation
Pauahi Tower, Suite 2500, 1001 Bishop Street, 96813
Telephone: 808-537-6119
Telecopier: 808-526-3491
Email: ACNSN@pixi.com

MEMBERS OF FIRM

Sidney K. Ayabe (P.C.)
Jeffrey H. K. Sia
Rodney S. Nishida
Gail M. Kang

Representative Clients: Travelers Insurance Co.; St. Paul Fire and Marine Insurance Co.; The Employers Group of Insurance Companies; TIG Insurance Co.; Pacific Insurance Co.; Hartford Accident and Indemnity Co.; Continental Casualty Co.; CNA Insurance Co.; DTRIC.

For full biographical listings, see the Martindale-Hubbell Law Directory

BAYS, DEAVER, HIATT, LUNG & ROSE (AV)

A Partnership including Professional Corporations
16th Floor, Alii Place, 1099 Alakea Street, P.O. Box 1760, 96806
Telephone: 808-523-9000
Telecopier: 808-533-4184
Telex: RCA 7238976
Email: bdhlr@aloha.net *URL:* http://www.bdhlr.com
Kamuela, Hawaii Office: Suite 204 Parker Square, 65-1279 Kawaihae Road.
Telephone: 808-885-3400.
Telecopier: 808-885-6765.

MEMBERS OF FIRM

A. Bernard Bays (A Law Corporation)
Phillip L. Deaver (A Law Corporation)
Jerry Michael Hiatt (A Law Corporation)
Harvey J. Lung (A Law Corporation)
Crystal K. Rose (A Law Corporation)
Jason N. Baba (A Law Corporation)
Michael W. Thomas
Karin L. Holma

ASSOCIATES

Mahilani E.K. Hiatt
Wendy J. Utsumi
Bruce Voss
Edward J. Corwin
Craig P. Wagnild
Rafael G. del Castillo
Kim A. Tomey
Liane L. Brown

Elizabeth A.C. Thompson

For full biographical listings, see the Martindale-Hubbell Law Directory

CADES SCHUTTE FLEMING & WRIGHT (AV)

Formerly Smith, Wild, Beebe & Cades
Cades Schutte Fleming & Wright Building, 1000 Bishop Street, Suite 1200, P.O. Box 939, 96808
Telephone: 808-521-9200
Telecopier: 808-521-9210
Email: cades@cades.com
Kailua-Kona, Hawaii Office: Hualalai Center, Suite B-303, 75-170 Hualalai Road.
Telephone: 808-329-5811.
Telecopier: 808-326-1175.

MEMBERS OF FIRM

Robert B. Bunn
Donald E. Scearce
Richard A. Hicks
Bernice Littman
Nicholas C. Dreher
Mark A. Hazlett
Philip J. Leas
Larry T. Takumi
Cary S. Matsushige
Gino L. Gabrio
Martin E. Hsia
Gail M. Tamashiro
Grace Nihei Kido
Donna Y. L. Leong
Jeffrey D. Watts
Michele S. Loudermilk

Laurie A. Kuribayashi

ASSOCIATES

Dean T. Yamamoto
Christopher T. Harrison

Charles K. Djou

OF COUNSEL

Harold S. Wright

Counsel for: First Hawaiian Bank; Alexander & Baldwin, Inc.; Theo. H. Davies & Co., Ltd.; C. Brewer & Company, Ltd.; Bank of America, FSB; Bank of America NT&SA; Kamehameha Schools Bernice Pauahi Bishop Estate.

For Complete List of Firm Personnel, See General Section

For full biographical listings, see the Martindale-Hubbell Law Directory

Honolulu—Continued

CARLSMITH BALL (AV)

A Partnership including Law Corporations
Suite 2200, Pacific Tower, 1001 Bishop Street, P.O. Box 656, 96809-3402
Telephone: 808-523-2500
Fax: 808-523-0842
Email: execdirector@carlsmith.com *URL:* http://www.carlsmith.com
Kapolei, Hawaii Office: Suite 318, Kapolei Building, 1001 Kamokila Boulevard, 96707.
Telephone: 808-523-2500.
Fax: 808-674-0850.
Wailuku, Maui Hawaii Office: Suite 400, One Main Plaza, 2200 Main Street, P.O. Box 1086, 96793-1086.
Telephone: 808-242-4535.
Fax: 808-244-4974.
Kailua-Kona, Hawaii Office: Suite 209, 75-1000 Henry Street, 96740.
Telephone: 808-329-6464.
Fax: 808-329-9450.
Hilo, Hawaii Office: 121 Waianuenue Avenue, P.O. Box 686, 96721-0686.
Telephone: 808-935-6644.
Fax: 808-935-7975.
Hagatna, Guam Office: Suite 401, Bank of Hawaii Building, 134 West Soledad Avenue, P.O. Box BF, 96932-5027.
Telephone: 671-472-6813.
Fax: 671-477-4375.
Telex: 721-6445 CWCMI GM.
Saipan, Commonwealth of the Northern Mariana Islands Office: Carlsmith Building, Capitol Hill, P.O. Box 5241, 96950-5241.
Telephone: 670-322-3455.
Fax: 670-322-3368.
Los Angeles, California Office: 9th Floor, 444 South Flower Street, 90071-2901.
Telephone: 213-955-1200.
Fax: 213-623-0032.
Washington, D.C. Office: Suite 300, 1201 Pennsylvania Avenue, N.W., 20004-2401.
Telephone: 202-628-2228.
Fax: 202-628-2071.
Mexico City, Mexico Office: Carlsmith Ball, Sierra Nevada 119, Lomas de Chapultepec, 11000 Mexico, D.F.
Telephone: 52-5-520-8514, 52-5-520-8757.
Fax: 52-5-540-1545.
Mexico, D.F. Office of Carlsmith Ball, S.C. (Authorized to practice as foreign legal consultants in Mexico): Sierra Nevada 119, Lomas de Chapultepec, 11000 Mexico, D.F.
Telephone: 52-5-520-8514, 52-5-520-8757.
Fax: 52-5-540-1545.

MEMBERS OF FIRM

Annie Kun Baker (Partner, Resident at Los Angeles, California Office)
Roger B. Baymiller (Resident at Los Angeles, California Office)
John F. Biehl (Resident at Saipan Office)
Edward E. Case
James H. Case (A Law Corporation)
Patricia Devlin
Randall H. Endo (Resident at Maui, Hawaii Office)
Terrence A. Everett (Resident at Los Angeles, California Office)
Philip D. Isaac (Resident at Hagatna, Guam Office)
Eric A. James
Richard Kiefer
Karl K. Kobayashi
David Patrick Ledger (Resident at Hagatna, Guam Office)
Tom C. Leuteneker (Resident at Maui, Hawaii Office)
Steven S. C. Lim (Resident at Hilo, Hawaii Office)
Tim Lui-Kwan
B. Martin Luna (Resident at Maui, Hawaii Office)
Matthew M. Matsunaga
Mark K. Murakami (Resident at Kapolei, Hawaii Office)
Craig G. Nakamura (Resident at Maui, Hawaii Office)
David R. Nevitt (Resident at Saipan Office)
Lawrence S. Okinaga (A Law Corporation)
Robert E. Strand
Lance F. Taniguchi
Robert D. Triantos (Resident at Kailua-Kona, Hawaii Office)
Paul M. Ueoka (Resident at Maui, Hawaii Office)
Charles R. Wichman
Donald C. Williams (Resident at Los Angeles, California Office)
William C. Williams, Jr. (Not admitted in HI)
Jon T. Yamamura

ASSOCIATE

Sherrill A. Atwood (Resident at Hilo, Hawaii Office)

OF COUNSEL

Donn W. Carlsmith
George G. Grubb (A Law Corporation)

For Complete List of Firm Personnel, See General Section

For full biographical listings, see the Martindale-Hubbell Law Directory

CHING, YUEN & MORIKAWA (AV)

Pacific Tower, Suite 2700, 1001 Bishop Street, 96813
Telephone: 808-524-8880
Telecopier: 808-524-7664
URL: http://www.cymlaw.com
Email: billyuen@cymlaw.com *URL:* http://www.lawyers.com/cymlaw

(See Next Column)

MEMBERS OF FIRM

Russell L. Ching
William W. L. Yuen
Randall I. Morikawa

ASSOCIATE

Chris J. Sadayasu

Representative Clients: Finance Enterprises, Ltd.; Finance Factors, Ltd.; Finance Realty, Ltd.; Goldman, Sachs & Co.; The Hertz Corporation; Kamehameha Schools Bernice Pauahi Bishop Estate; Merrill Lynch & Co.; PaineWebber Incorporated; The Sakura Bank, Ltd.; Sen Plex Corp.

For full biographical listings, see the Martindale-Hubbell Law Directory

CHUN, KERR, DODD, BEAMAN & WONG (AV)

Suite 900, 745 Fort Street Mall, 96813
Telephone: 808-528-8200
Telecopier: 808-536-5869

MEMBERS OF FIRM

Edward Y. C. Chun
William H. Dodd
Andrew V. Beaman
Danton S. Wong
Leroy E. Colombe
Trudy Burns Stone

ASSOCIATES

Andrew R. Bunn
Trevor A. Brown
Tracy D. Tanaka
John S. Nitao

References: Bank of Hawaii; First Hawaiian Bank.

For full biographical listings, see the Martindale-Hubbell Law Directory

LAW OFFICES OF MANUEL D. GARCIA (AV)

Pacific Tower of Bishop Square, 1001 Bishop Street, Suite 2800, 96813
Telephone: 808-522-0755
Facsimile: 808-522-0760

For full biographical listings, see the Martindale-Hubbell Law Directory

GERSON, GREKIN & WYNHOFF ATTORNEYS AT LAW, A LAW CORPORATION (AV)

Suite 780 Pacific Tower, 1001 Bishop Street, 96813
Telephone: 808-524-4800
Telecopier: 808-537-1420
Email: ggwlaw@aloha.net

Gaye Lynne Chun
Kristie K. Cruz
Mervyn S. Gerson
Nancy Nissen Grekin
Bruce D. Hieneman
William J. Wynhoff

For full biographical listings, see the Martindale-Hubbell Law Directory

GOODSILL ANDERSON QUINN & STIFEL (AV)

Alii Place, Suite 1800, 1099 Alakea Street, P.O. Box 3196, 96801-3196
Telephone: 808-547-5600
FAX: 808-547-5880
Email: info@goodsill.com *URL:* http://www.goodsill.com

MEMBERS OF FIRM

Conrad M. Weiser
Ronald H. W. Lum
Raymond S. Iwamoto
Lani L. Ewart
Randall K. Steverson
Peter T. Kashiwa
Russell S. Kato
Vincent A. Piekarski
Leighton J. H. S. Yuen
Carl J. Schlack, Jr.
Mark F. Ito
Audrey E. J. Ng
Alan S. Fujimoto
Gail Otsuka Ayabe
Dale Edward F.T. Zane
Kellie M. N. Sekiya

ASSOCIATES

Eric A. Elkind
Elizabeth Haemi Lee
Adrienne Y. Shimonishi

Representative Clients: AMFAC/JMB Hawaii, Inc.; Castle & Cooke, Inc.; Dole Food Company Hawaii; Graham Murata Russell; Hawaiian Trust Company; Servco Pacific Corporation; Shinwa Golf Group; Victoria Ward, Ltd.; Waikoloa Development Co.

For Complete List of Firm Personnel, See General Section

For full biographical listings, see the Martindale-Hubbell Law Directory

KOBAYASHI, SUGITA & GODA (AV)

A Partnership including Professional Corporations
999 Bishop Street, Suite 2600, 96813
Telephone: 808-539-8700
Telecopier: 808-539-8799
Telex: 6502396585 MCI
MCI Mail: 23 96585
ABA/Net: ABA2281
Email: ksg@aloha.net

OF COUNSEL

Bert T. Kobayashi, Sr.
Michael J. McGivern (Not admitted in HI)

Reference: First Hawaiian Bank.

(See Next Column)

KOBAYASHI, SUGITA & GODA—*Continued*

For Complete List of Firm Personnel, See General Section

For full biographical listings, see the Martindale-Hubbell Law Directory

McCORRISTON MIHO MILLER MUKAI (AV)

Five Waterfront Plaza, 4th Floor, 500 Ala Moana Boulevard, 96813
Telephone: 808-529-7300
Facsimile: 808-524-8293
Cable: Attorneys, Honolulu
Mailing Address: P.O. Box 2800, Honolulu, Hawaii, 96803-2800
Email: info@m4Law.com

PARTNERS

Clifford J. Miller
Franklin K. Mukai
Stanley Y. Mukai
D. Scott MacKinnon
Kenneth B. Marcus
Kenneth G. K. Hoo
Patrick K. Lau
David N. Kuriyama
Eric T. Kawatani
Sharon H. Nishi
Randall F. Sakumoto
Andrew W. Char
Alexander R. Jampel
Peter J. Hamasaki

COUNSEL

Charles E. Pear, Jr.

ASSOCIATES

Candace J. Park
Shaun M. Mukai
Stacey C. G. Hee

Representative Clients: Nauru Phosphate Royalties Trust; Victoria Ward, Limited; Kamehameha Schools Bishop Estate; Grand Wailea Resort; Mutual of New York; Long Term Credit Bank of Japan; Interval International, Inc.; Shell Group; The Walt Disney World Company.

For Complete List of Firm Personnel, See General Section

For full biographical listings, see the Martindale-Hubbell Law Directory

PETER P. J. NG (AV)

Second Floor, Bank of Hawaii Building Kaimuki Branch, 3604 Waialae Avenue, 96816
Telephone: 808-732-7788
Fax: 808-732-7780

ASSOCIATE

Jeffrey R. Niebling

For full biographical listings, see the Martindale-Hubbell Law Directory

PITLUCK KIDO SATO & STONE (AV)

701 Bishop Street, 96813
Telephone: 808-523-5030
Telecopier: 808-545-4015
Email: pitluck@pitluck.com *URL:* http://www.pitluck.com

MEMBERS OF FIRM

Wayne Marshall Pitluck
Alan Takashi Kido
Dana Kiyomi Nalani Sato
James Mauliola Keaka Stone, Jr.

OF COUNSEL

John W. Reilly

Reference: Bank of Hawaii.

For full biographical listings, see the Martindale-Hubbell Law Directory

LAW OFFICES OF PETER STARN A LAW CORPORATION (AV)

Suite 1740 Grosvenor Center Mauka Tower, 737 Bishop Street, 96813
Telephone: 808-537-6100
Fax: 808-537-5434
Email: landlaw@poi.net

Peter Starn
Duane R. Fisher
Sharon Valentine Lovejoy

Todd K. Apo

For full biographical listings, see the Martindale-Hubbell Law Directory

TAKUSHI, FUNAKI, WONG & STONE ATTORNEYS AT LAW, A LAW CORPORATION (AV)

Suite 1400 Grosvenor Center, 733 Bishop Street, 96813
Telephone: 808-543-9800
Fax: 808-543-9869
Email: tfwf@pixi.com

Roy E. Takushi
James T. Funaki
Alfred M. K. Wong
Robert M. Ehrhorn, Jr.
Dickson C. H. Lee
Peter T. Stone
James N. H. Yee
Ann L. Kurihara
Jacqueline Kong
Elizabeth A. Kane

For full biographical listings, see the Martindale-Hubbell Law Directory

TAM, O'CONNOR, HENDERSON, TAIRA & YAMAUCHI ATTORNEYS AT LAW, A LAW CORPORATION (AV)

20th Floor, Central Pacific Plaza, 220 South King Street, 96813
Telephone: 808-545-3030
Fax: 808-523-8051
Fax: 808-537-6782
Email: lawyers@50thstatelaw.com

James K. Tam
Michael F. O'Connor
Harvey E. Henderson, Jr.
Lissa H. Andrews
Robert M. Yamauchi
Darryl M. Taira
Stuart M. Kodish

Wesley H. Ikeda
Russ S. Awakuni
Kevin W. Herring
Fred I. Waki

OF COUNSEL

Paul M. Dold

For full biographical listings, see the Martindale-Hubbell Law Directory

IDAHO

*BOISE,** Ada Co.

ELAM & BURKE, A PROFESSIONAL ASSOCIATION (AV)

Key Financial Center, 702 West Idaho Street, P.O. Box 1539, 83701
Telephone: 208-343-5454
Telecopier: 208-384-5844
Email: eblaw@elamburke.com

David B. Lincoln
Ryan P. Armbruster

Representative Clients: Lincoln National Life Insurance Co.; Transamerica Financial Services; State Farm Life Insurance Co.; U.S. BanCorp Leasing, U.S. Bank.

For Complete List of Firm Personnel, See General Section

For full biographical listings, see the Martindale-Hubbell Law Directory

GREEN LAW OFFICES (AV)

P.O. Box 2597, 83701-2597
Telephone: 208-342-8915
Fax: 208-342-2718
Email: cumergreen@aol.com *URL:* http://www.greenedlaw.com

Cumer L. Green

ASSOCIATE

Debra A. Silk

LEGAL SUPPORT PERSONNEL

Gary W. Shaw (Chief, Legal Support Group)

Representative Clients: Idaho School Boards Association, Inc.; Potlatch Corporation; Bell Helmets, Inc.; R.C. Bigelow, Inc.; Fleetwood Enterprises, Inc.; United Airlines; Pacific Crown Timber; Croman Corp.; Ida-West Energy Co.; LJD Holdings, Inc.; Ram International; VFP VC Ltd.; Developers Diversified Realty Corporation; Dakota Company, Inc.

For full biographical listings, see the Martindale-Hubbell Law Directory

MEULEMAN & MILLER, L.L.P. (AV)

960 Broadway Avenue, Suite 400, P.O. Box 955, 83701
Telephone: 208-342-6066
Fax: 208-336-9712
Email: firm@lawidaho.com *URL:* http://www.lawidaho.com

MEMBERS OF FIRM

Robert L. Miller
Kimbal L. Gowland
Quentin M. Knipe
Richard W. Mollerup

Representative Clients: Albertson's, Inc.; Alliance Title and Escrow, Inc.; Alscott Real Estate LLC; Chicago Title Insurance Corporation; Greater Boise Auditorium District; Hawkins-Smith Development; Idaho State Building Authority; Kathryn Albertson Enterprises, Inc.; PACCAR Automotive, Inc.; The Terteling Company.

For full biographical listings, see the Martindale-Hubbell Law Directory

KETCHUM, Blaine Co.

JAMES L. KENNEDY, JR. (AV)

340 Second Street East, P.O. Box 2165, 83340
Telephone: 208-726-8255
Fax: 208-726-4886

Reference: First Interstate Bank of Idaho, N.A. (Ketchum-Sun Valley Branch); First Security Bank of Idaho, N.A. (Ketchum Branch)

For full biographical listings, see the Martindale-Hubbell Law Directory

Ketchum—Continued

KNEELAND, KORB, COLLIER & LEGG (AV)

Kneeland Professional Building, 128 Saddle Road, Suite 103, P.O. Box 249, 83340
Telephone: 208-726-9311
Telecopier: 208-726-4515
Email: kneeland@micron.net

MEMBERS OF FIRM

Robert Korb, III
Bruce J. Collier
Ann Legg
Michael Dorazio

OF COUNSEL

G.R. Kneeland

Reference: First Security Bank of Idaho, N. A.

For full biographical listings, see the Martindale-Hubbell Law Directory

*POCATELLO,** Bannock Co.

MERRILL & MERRILL, CHARTERED (AV)

Key Bank Building, P.O. Box 991, 83204
Telephone: 208-232-2286
Fax: 208-232-2499
Email: mmlaw@ida.net

Dave R. Gallafent
Kent L. Hawkins

Representative Client: First American Title Insurance Co.

For Complete List of Firm Personnel, See General Section

For full biographical listings, see the Martindale-Hubbell Law Directory

ILLINOIS

*BELLEVILLE,** St. Clair Co.

NEVILLE, RICHARDS, DEFRANCO & WULLER (AV)

5 Park Place, 62226
Telephone: 618-277-0900
Facsimile: 618-277-0970
Email: nrdw@nrdw-law.com *URL:* http://www.nrdw-law.com

MEMBERS OF FIRM

James E. Neville
Timothy S. Richards
James E. DeFranco
Robert G. Wuller, Jr.

ASSOCIATES

Shari M. Brunton
Ellen M. Edmonds
Daniel L. Bradley
Matthew Charles Zittel

For full biographical listings, see the Martindale-Hubbell Law Directory

BOLINGBROOK, Will Co.

MOSS AND BLOOMBERG, LTD. (AV)

305 West Briarcliff Road, Suite 201, P.O. Box 1158, 60440-0858
Telephone: 630-759-0800
Telecopier: 630-759-8504
Email: info@mb-lawyers.com

Barry L. Moss
Steven P. Bloomberg
George A. Marchetti
David J. Freeman
Daniel C. Shapiro

For full biographical listings, see the Martindale-Hubbell Law Directory

*CHICAGO,** Cook Co.

ARONBERG GOLDGEHN DAVIS & GARMISA (AV)

Suite 3000 One IBM Plaza, 60611
Telephone: 312-828-9600
Telecopier: 312-828-9635
Email: agdglaw@aol.com
Schaumberg, Illinois Office: 1901 North Roselle Road, Suite 800, 60195.
Telephone: 847-985-4060.

MEMBERS OF FIRM

William J. Garmisa
Mitchell J. Melamed
Marc W. O'Brien
Ned S. Robertson
David H. Sachs
Robert N. Sodikoff

OF COUNSEL

Ronald J. Aronberg
Steven P. Davis

ASSOCIATES

Eric M. Brown
Mary Vidal Hays

For Complete List of Firm Personnel, See General Section

For full biographical listings, see the Martindale-Hubbell Law Directory

BECKER & KAPLAN LLC (AV)

19 South La Salle Street Suite 1500, 60603
Telephone: 312-621-9500
Fax: 312-621-9011
Email: firm@beckerkaplan.com *URL:* http://www.beckerkaplan.com

Theodore M. Becker
Daniel S. Kaplan

Edward R. White
Michael J. Boxerman

For full biographical listings, see the Martindale-Hubbell Law Directory

FAGEL & HABER (AV)

140 South Dearborn Street 14th Floor, 60603
Telephone: 312-346-7500
FAX: 312-580-2201
Telex No: 754542
Cable: "NOFLAWLAW"
URL: http://www.fandh.com

MEMBERS OF FIRM

Walter D. Cupkovic
John J. Cullerton
Victor A. Des Laurier

ASSOCIATES

Christina Fazio
Patrick J. Cullerton
Thomas Bernard Golz
Ilyse D. Murman

For full biographical listings, see the Martindale-Hubbell Law Directory

FIELD & GOLAN (AV)

Three First National Plaza Suite 1500, 60602-4206
Telephone: 312-263-2300
Fax: 312-263-0939

MEMBERS OF FIRM

Robert E. Field
Stephen L. Golan
Margaret A. Christie
Donna F. Hartl

ASSOCIATES

Margaret A. Gisch
Matthew J. Cozzi
Anthony R. Taglia

OF COUNSEL

Leonard W. Golan
Stephen Edward Smith
Frank J. Dolan
John E. Vranicar

For full biographical listings, see the Martindale-Hubbell Law Directory

GOLDBERG, KOHN, BELL, BLACK, ROSENBLOOM & MORITZ, LTD. (AV)

55 East Monroe Street, Suite 3700, 60603
Telephone: 312-201-4000
Telecopier: 312-332-2196
URL: http://www.goldbergkohn.com

Stephen B. Bell
Karen Ruth Bieber
Dennis B. Black
Philip M. Blackman
Joel F. Brown
Denise B. Caplan
Andrew R. Cardonick
David J. Chizewer
Frederick H. Cohen
Natalia Delgado
David L. Dranoff
Wayne S. Gilmartin
Robert J. Goldberg (Retired)
Gerald L. Jenkins
Michael D. Karpeles
Frederic R. Klein
Randall L. Klein
Richard M. Kohn
Steven A. Levy
William R. Loesch
Michael B. Manuel
David M. Mason
William C. Meyers
Terry F. Moritz
Gerald F. Munitz
Nora A. Naughton
Kim Slotky Reich
James B. Rosenbloom
Gary N. Ruben
Daniel P. Shapiro
Alan P. Solow
Douglas P. Taber
Carole K. Towne
Kenneth S. Ulrich
Melissa Lumberg Zagon
Gary T. Zussman

Oscar L. Alcantara
Esther S. Barron
Jami L. Brodey
Nicolette L. Brown
Kelly Smith Caner
Christopher R. Clark
Jonathan M. Cooper
Everett J. Cygal
Carrie M. Garcia
Darren M. Green
Marc D. Hauser
Deborah Rzasnicki Hogan
Adam M. Laser
Michael N. Levy
Roger A. Lewis
Joseph M. Martin
Ellen C Matheeussen
Lisa D. McCoy
Christine A. Miller
David E. Morrison
Alice G. Owings
Kathryn A. Pamenter
Kelee Joy Schwenn
Sanjay Sharma
Amanda K. Williams

OF COUNSEL

Susan Atwood Jardine
Suzanne Gross Kowalski

For full biographical listings, see the Martindale-Hubbell Law Directory

Chicago—Continued

GORDON & EINSTEIN, LTD. (AV)

224 East Ontario, 60611
Telephone: 312-280-7766
Telecopier: 312-280-9599
URL: http://www.gordon-einstein.com

Raymond P. Gordon

LEGAL SUPPORT PERSONNEL

Laura A. Kozicki

For full biographical listings, see the Martindale-Hubbell Law Directory

HOLLIS AND JOHNSON (AV)

11 East Adams Street, Suite 501, 60603
Telephone: 312-427-0700
Fax: 312-427-8407
URL: http://www.digitalawyer.com/bankruptcy

Pamela S. Hollis
Donald E. Johnson

ASSOCIATE

Linda M. Kujaca

For full biographical listings, see the Martindale-Hubbell Law Directory

HOWARD GORDON KAPLAN, LTD. (AV)

180 North La Salle Street, 28th Floor, 60601
Telephone: 312-641-2555
Facsimile No.: 312-641-6265
Email: howie641@aol.com

Howard Gordon Kaplan
Leonard J. Brenner
Rhonda D. Kaplan-Katz

For full biographical listings, see the Martindale-Hubbell Law Directory

MCBRIDE BAKER & COLES (AV)

500 West Madison Street 40th Floor, 60661-2511
Telephone: 312-715-5700
Cable Address: "Chilaw"
Telex: 270258
Telecopier: 312-993-9350
Email: lastname@mbc.com *URL:* http://www.mbc.com
Oakbrook Terrace, Illinois Office: Suite 1000, One Mid America Plaza, 60181-4710.
Telephone: 630-954-2100.
Telecopier: 630-954-2112.

MEMBERS OF FIRM

John J. Cresto
Nina J. Fain
Anthony L. Frink
Francis L. Keldermans
Thomas J. Kinasz
David S. Mann
Elias N. Matsakis
Donald G. Mulack
Michael L. Weissman
Larry M. Zanger

OF COUNSEL

Robert O. Case

ASSOCIATES

Kathleen F. O'Connor
Paul R. Simons

For Complete List of Firm Personnel, See General Section

For full biographical listings, see the Martindale-Hubbell Law Directory

QUARLES & BRADY LLC (AV)

Citicorp Center, 500 West Madison Street, Suite 3700, 60661-2511
Telephone: 312-715-5000
Fax: 312-715-5155
URL: http://www.quarles.com
Milwaukee, Wisconsin Office: Quarles & Brady LLP, 411 East Wisconsin Avenue, 53202-4497.
Telephone: 414-277-5000.
Fax: 414-271-3552.
Madison, Wisconsin Office: Quarles & Brady LLP, Firstar Plaza, One South Pinckney Street, P.O. Box 2113, 53701-2113.
Telephone: 608-251-5000.
Fax: 608-251-9166.
West Palm Beach, Florida Office: Quarles & Brady LLP, 222 Lakeview Avenue, 4th Floor, 33401.
Telephone: 561-653-5000.
Fax: 561-653-5333.
Naples, Florida Office: Quarles & Brady LLP, Barnett Center, 4501 Tamiami Trail North, Suite 300, 34103-3060.
Telephone: 941-262-5959.
Fax: 941-434-4999.
Phoenix, Arizona Office: Quarles & Brady LLP, One Camelback Building, One East Camelback Road, Suite 400, 85012-1649.
Telephone: 602-230-5500.
Fax: 602-230-5598.

Peter A. Sarasek
Stephanie B. Shellenback
Richard P. Blessen
Marie K. Eitrheim

(See Next Column)

Jessamyn L. Bagley

For Complete List of Firm Personnel, See General Section

For full biographical listings, see the Martindale-Hubbell Law Directory

SCHWARTZBERG, BARNETT & COHEN (AV)

55 West Monroe Street, 2400 Xerox Centre, 60603-5040
Telephone: 312-726-3555
Fax: 312-726-6299
Cable Address: "Justice"
Email: sb&c@twty.chi.il.us

MEMBERS OF FIRM

Ralph M. Schwartzberg (1939-1975)
Mark T. Barnett (1939-1970)
Hugh J. Schwartzberg
Benjamin H. Cohen

For full biographical listings, see the Martindale-Hubbell Law Directory

SUGAR, FRIEDBERG & FELSENTHAL (AV)

30 North La Salle Street, Suite 2600, 60602
Telephone: 312-704-9400
Telecopier: 312-372-7951
Cable: "SUGARFREE"

MEMBERS OF FIRM

Richard A. Sugar
Michael R. Friedberg
Steven A. Felsenthal
Andrew B. David
Leslie J. Weiss
Ira S. Neiman
Jonathan L. Mills
Etahn M. Cohen
Howard M. Helsinger
Robert F. Simon
Martin M. Weinstein
Charles H. Braun
Kathryn A. Erickson

ASSOCIATES

Aron L. Bornstein
Annette L. Brands
Kathryn T. Cha
Norman J. Ginsparg
William F. McGuinn
Suzanne J. Massel
Deanne Elizabeth Clarke

For full biographical listings, see the Martindale-Hubbell Law Directory

WATT & SAWYIER (AV)

The Monadnock Building, 53 West Jackson Boulevard, Suite 1120, 60604-3701
Telephone: 312-663-1440
Telecopier: 312-663-1410

MEMBERS OF FIRM

Garland W. Watt
Michael T. Sawyier

OF COUNSEL

Rosalind A. Burbank

For full biographical listings, see the Martindale-Hubbell Law Directory

WILDMAN, HARROLD, ALLEN & DIXON (AV)

225 West Wacker Drive, 30th Floor, 60606-1229
Telephone: 312-201-2000
Fax: 312-201-2555
Email: hennessy@whad.com *URL:* http://www.whad.com
Aurora, Illinois Office: 1961 W. Downer Place.
Telephone: 630-892-7021.
Fax: 630-892-7158.
Waukegan, Illinois Office: 404 West Water, P. O. Box 890.
Telephone: 847-625-5550.
Fax: 847-625-5555.
Lisle, Illinois Office: 4300 Commerce Court, Suite 320.
Telephone: 630-955-0555.
Fax: 630-955-0662
Toronto, Ontario correspondent Office: Keel Cottrelle. 36 Toronto Street, Suite 920.
Telephone: 416-367-2900.
Telefax: 416-367-2791.
Telex: 062-18660.

MEMBERS OF FIRM

Benjamin P. Alschuler (Aurora Office)
Bruce L. Boruszak
Demetrius E. Carney
Bruce M. Chanen
Paul S. Chervin (Waukegan Office)
Thomas P. Duffy
David J. Fischer
Jeffrey P. Gray
Robert E. Hamilton
Ronald M. Hem (Aurora Office)
Richard C. Johnson (Lisle Office)
Dean J. Leffelman (Lisle Office)
Thomas I. Matyas
Sheldon P. Migdal
James R. Morrin
Donald J. Simantz (Resident, Aurora Office)
Sanford M. Stein
Louis P. Vitullo

OF COUNSEL

Peter H. Fritts
George W. Overton
Thomas H. Snyder
Edwin A. Wahlen

(See Next Column)

WILDMAN, HARROLD, ALLEN & DIXON, *Chicago—Continued*

Todd A. Bickel
Marcia Klenk
Mary P. Higgins
R. Lindsay Wilson II

For full biographical listings, see the Martindale-Hubbell Law Directory

DE KALB, De Kalb Co.

BOYLE, CORDES & BROWN (AV)

301 East Lincoln Highway, 60115-3307
Telephone: 815-756-6328
Fax: 815-756-8842

MEMBERS OF FIRM

John G. Boyle (1907-1996)
Gary W. Cordes
Charles G. Brown

Representative Clients: DeKalb Park District; First of America, N.A. DeKalb, Il; First National Bank in Dekalb.
References: First of America Bank-DeKalb; First National Bank in DeKalb.

For full biographical listings, see the Martindale-Hubbell Law Directory

LA SALLE, La Salle Co.

HERBOLSHEIMER, LANNON, HENSON, DUNCAN AND REAGAN, P.C. (AV)

State Bank Building, Suite 400, 654 First Street, P.O. Box 539, 61301
Telephone: 815-223-0111
Fax: 815-223-5829
Ottawa, Illinois Office: First Federal Savings Bank Building, 633 LaSalle Street, Suite 409.
Telephone: 815-434-1400.
Fax: 815-434-2423.

George L. Herbolsheimer (1911-1992)
R. James Lannon, Jr.
T. Donald Henson
John S. Duncan, III
Michael T. Reagan (Resident, Ottawa Office)
Douglas A. Gift
Gary R. Eiten

Karen C. Eiten
Michael C. Jansz (Resident, Ottawa Office)
Jill W. Klein
Lawrence M. Kaschak

Attorneys for: Aetna Insurance Group; St. Paul Fire and Marine Insurance Co.; State Farm Insurance Co.; The La Salle National Bank; La Salle State Bank; The Daily News Tribune Company, La Salle; Eureka Savings and Loan Assn.; Illinois Valley Community Hospital; Community Hospital of Ottawa; Commonwealth Edison, Co.

For full biographical listings, see the Martindale-Hubbell Law Directory

MATTOON, Coles Co.

CRAIG & CRAIG (AV)

1807 Broadway, P.O. Box 689, 61938-0689
Telephone: 217-234-6481
Telecopier: 217-234-6486; 258-8292
Email: craiglaw@advant.com
Mount Vernon, Illinois Office: 115 North 7th Street.
Telephone: 618-244-7511.

MEMBERS OF FIRM

Craig Van Meter (1895-1981)
Fred H. Kelly (1894-1971)
Robert M. Werden (1908-1969)
George N. Gilkerson (1911-1985)
John P. Ewart
Richard F. Record, Jr.
Stephen L. Corn
Robert G. Grierson
Gregory C. Ray
Paul R. Lynch (Resident, Mount Vernon Office)
Kenneth F. Werts (Resident, Mount Vernon Office)
John L. Barger

ASSOCIATES

Kathleen M. Stockwell
Kristine M. Tuttle
Julie A. Webb (Resident, Mount Vernon Office)
John M. O'Driscoll
Duane A. Deters
Katy C. Fain (Resident, Mount Vernon Office)
Erin E. Wisner
John F. Watson

OF COUNSEL

Jack E. Horsley

Representative Clients: Marathon Oil Co.; Illinois Central R.R.; Okaw Building & Loan, s.b., Mattoon, Illinois; Natural Gas Pipeline Company of America; Consolidated Communications, Inc.; Howell Paving, Inc.; D-CO, Inc.; Mattoon Enterprise Park L.L.C.; Lake Land College.

For full biographical listings, see the Martindale-Hubbell Law Directory

*MOUNT VERNON,** Jefferson Co.

MITCHELL, NEUBAUER & HANSON, P.C. (AV)

123 South 10th Street, Mercantile Bank Building, 6th Floor, P.O. Box 1088, 62864
Telephone: 618-242-0705
Telecopier: 618-242-4820
Mailing Address: P.O. Box 1088,
Email: MNHPC@Midwest.net

A. Ben Mitchell
Timothy R. Neubauer
Leslie James Hanson

T. David Purcell
David K. Overstreet
Henry P. Villani

Attorneys for: Mercantile Bank of Southern Illinois; Mt. Vernon Grade School District #80; Stewart Brothers Oil Producers; Mt. Vernon Airport Authority; J. M. Behimer Enterprises; Marion Ford-Mercury, Inc.

For full biographical listings, see the Martindale-Hubbell Law Directory

LAW OFFICE OF TERRY SHARP, P.C. (AV)

1115 Harrison Street, P.O. Box 906, 62864
Telephone: 618-242-0246
Fax: 618-242-1170
Email: TSharp.law@mvn.net
Benton, Illinois Office: 105 North Main Street.
Telephone: 618-435-5109.
FAX: 618-242-1170.

Terrell Lee Sharp

For full biographical listings, see the Martindale-Hubbell Law Directory

OAKBROOK TERRACE, DuPage Co.

MCBRIDE BAKER & COLES (AV)

Suite 1000, One Mid America Plaza, 60181-4710
Telephone: 630-954-2100
Telecopier: 630-954-2112
URL: http://www.mbc.com
Chicago, Illinois Office: 500 West Madison Street, 40th Floor, 60661-2511.
Telephone: 312-715-5700.
Telecopier: 312-993-9350.

MEMBERS OF FIRM

Steven B. Bashaw
David H. Hight
James A. Kohlstedt
Douglas C. Tibble
David E. Zajicek

OF COUNSEL

John T. Huntington

ASSOCIATES

Eric D. Filkin
Robert E. Harig
Maureen Calabrese Strauts

For Complete List of Firm Personnel, See General Section

For full biographical listings, see the Martindale-Hubbell Law Directory

*PONTIAC,** Livingston Co.

JOHNSON & TAYLOR (AV)

Formerly Ortman, Johnson & Taylor
109 North Mill Street, 61764
Telephone: 815-844-7151
Fax: 815-844-7539

MEMBERS OF FIRM

F. A. Ortman (1882-1955)
John A. Taylor
Taylor F. Johnson

OF COUNSEL

J. Kenneth Johnson

Representative Clients: Flanagan State Bank; Flanagan and Reddick and Long Point Fire; Protection Districts; Hartford Steam Boiler Insp. Co.; Metropolitan Life Ins. Co.; Good Samaritan Home of Flanagan; CAPS & Flanagan Park Districts; Evenglow Lodge; Livingston County Broadcasters; Albrecht and Oliver Trusts.

For full biographical listings, see the Martindale-Hubbell Law Directory

VERNON HILLS, Lake Co.

RICHARDS, RALPH & SCHWAB, CHARTERED (AV)

One Hawthorn Place, 175 East Hawthorn Parkway, Suite 345, 60061
Telephone: 847-367-9699
Fax: 847-367-9621
Email: dschwab@rr&s-chtd.com *URL:* http://www.lawyers.com/richardandschwab

(See Next Column)

RICHARDS, RALPH & SCHWAB CHARTERED—*Continued*

Michael L. Ralph
Alan E. Richards
David J. Schwab

For full biographical listings, see the Martindale-Hubbell Law Directory

*WAUKEGAN,** Lake Co.

DIVER, GRACH, QUADE & MASINI (AV)

Bank of Waukegan Building, 111 North County Street, 60085
Telephone: 847-662-8611
FAX: 847-662-2960

MEMBERS OF FIRM

Clarence W. Diver (1883-1962)
Thomas W. Diver
Brian S. Grach
David R. Quade
Robert J. Masini
Sarah P. Lessman
David L. Hazan

Heidi J. Aavang
Donna-Jo Rodden Vorderstrasse
Paula Vincich Randall

A list of Representative Clients will be furnished upon request.
Reference: First Midwest Bank of Waukegan.

For full biographical listings, see the Martindale-Hubbell Law Directory

INDIANA

*BLOOMINGTON,** Monroe Co.

BUNGER & ROBERTSON (AV)

226 South College Square, P.O. Box 910, 47402-0910
Telephone: 812-332-9295
Fax: 812-331-8808
Email: bunrob@iquest.net

MEMBERS OF FIRM

Don M Robertson
Thomas Bunger
Margaret M. Frisbie
William J. Beggs

ASSOCIATE

Holly M. Harvey

Representative Clients: Aetna Insurance Companies; Bloomington Hospital; Commercial Union Group; Indiana Insurance Co.; Liberty Mutual Insurance; Medical Protective Co.; Monroe County Community School Corp.; Professional Golf Car, Inc.; Prudential Insurance Company of America; State Farm Automobile Insurance Co.

For Complete List of Firm Personnel, See General Section

For full biographical listings, see the Martindale-Hubbell Law Directory

*EVANSVILLE,** Vanderburgh Co.

BOWERS, HARRISON, KENT & MILLER, LLP (AV)

25 N.W. Riverside Drive, P.O. Box 1287, 47706-1287
Telephone: 812-426-1231
Fax: 812-464-3676
Email: BOWERS,HARRISON,KENT&MILLER,LLP@BHKM.COM
URL: http://WWW.BHKM.COM

MEMBERS OF FIRM

Joseph H. Harrison
Paul E. Black
Gregory A. Kahre
Timothy J. Hubert
Sara Harrison Zeidler

ASSOCIATE

Cedric Hustace

OF COUNSEL

K. Wayne Kent

Representative Clients: Citizens Realty and Insurance, Inc.; General Growth Properties; Regency Associates, Ltd.; National Attorney's Title Assurance Fund, Inc.; Shell Mining Company; Commonwealth Land Title Insurance Company; American General Finance, Inc.

For Complete List of Firm Personnel, See General Section

For full biographical listings, see the Martindale-Hubbell Law Directory

FINE & HATFIELD, A PROFESSIONAL CORPORATION (AV)

520 N.W. Second Street, P.O. Box 779, 47705-0779
Telephone: 812-425-3592
Telecopier: 812-421-4269
Email: Fine@Fine-Hatfield.com *URL:* http://www.Fine-Hatfield.com

James E. Marchand
Leslie C. Shively

(See Next Column)

Maria T. Worthington
David D. Sanders

A List of Representative Clients Furnished Upon Request.

For full biographical listings, see the Martindale-Hubbell Law Directory

KAHN, DEES, DONOVAN & KAHN, LLP (AV)

Fifth Main Financial Plaza, Suite 305, P.O. Box 3646, 47735-3646
Telephone: 812-423-3183
Fax: 812-423-3841
Email: evvlaw@k2d2.com

MEMBERS OF FIRM

Alan N. Shovers
G. Michael Schopmeyer
Jeffrey K. Helfrich
Marjorie J. Scharpf
Kent A. Brasseale II

ASSOCIATES

Allison K. Comstock
Mark S. Samila

Representative Clients: D. Patrick, Inc.; Deaconess Hospital, Inc.; Keller-Crescent Co., Inc.; Kempf Group Inc.; Red Spot Paint & Varnish Co., Inc.; Rehabilitation Development Services, Inc.; J.H. Rudolph & Company, Inc.; J.E. Shekell, Inc.; Gray Farms, Inc.; Princeton Mining Company, Inc.

For Complete List of Firm Personnel, See General Section

For full biographical listings, see the Martindale-Hubbell Law Directory

*FORT WAYNE,** Allen Co.

BECKMAN LAWSON, LLP (AV)

800 Standard Federal Plaza, 46802
Telephone: 219-422-0800
Facsimile: 219-420-1013
Syracuse, Indiana Office: 200 West Main Street.
Telephone: 219-457-5727.
Facsimile: 219-457-2056.

MEMBERS OF FIRM

Jack W. Lawson
Frank J. Gray
Howard B. Sandler
Stephen R. Snyder
James A. Federoff
William L. Sweet, Jr.
Richard H. Blaich
John H. Brandt
Jon A. Bragalone
Brian J. T'Kindt
Douglas R. Adelsperger
Travis S. Friend
Robert L. Nicholson
David D. Cornwell
James A. Butz
Jack C. Birch
Craig R. Patterson

ASSOCIATES

John M. Ketcham
Wendy W. Davis
Jeffrey B. Harding
Martha M. Kinder
Edward J. Ormsby
Randall L. Morgan
Daniel J. Deeb
Patrick R. Hess
Georgia L. Hartman
Brian M. Simpson
James E. Rossow, Jr.
Sarah A. Hiestand
Tandra S. Johnson
Jason M. Kuchmay
Matthew J. Elliott

OF COUNSEL

Frederick A. Beckman
Neil F. Sandler
Douglas E. Miller
Loren K. Allison

Reference: National City Bank.

For full biographical listings, see the Martindale-Hubbell Law Directory

GREENWOOD, Johnson Co.

WILLIAMS HEWITT & ROBBINS, LLP (AV)

National City Bank Building, 300 South Madison Avenue Suite 400, P.O. Box 405, 46142
Telephone: 317-888-1121
Facsimile: 317-887-4069

PARTNERS

Jon E. Williams
Brian C. Hewitt
J. Lee Robbins

ASSOCIATES

John M. White
Mark E. Need
John P. Wilkowski
Stephen K. Watson

For full biographical listings, see the Martindale-Hubbell Law Directory

*INDIANAPOLIS,** Marion Co.

BACKER & BACKER, A PROFESSIONAL CORPORATION (AV)

8710 North Meridian Street, 46260
Telephone: 317-571-0500
Telecopier: 317-571-0700
Email: sabacker@ameritech.net

Herbert J. Backer (1914-1995)
Stephen A. Backer

Reference: Bank One, Indianapolis.

For full biographical listings, see the Martindale-Hubbell Law Directory

Indianapolis—Continued

BOSE MCKINNEY & EVANS LLP (AV)

2700 First Indiana Plaza, 135 North Pennsylvania Street, 46204
Telephone: 317-684-5000
Facsimile: 317-684-5173
URL: http://www.boselaw.com
Indianapolis North Office: Suite 1500, 8888 Keystone Crossing, 46240.
Telephone: 317-574-3700.
Facsimile: 317-574-3716.

MEMBERS OF FIRM

James C. Carlino
Donald K. Densborn
Kathleen G. Lucas
Daniel P. McInerny
Philip A. Nicely
Natalie J. Stucky
David L. Wills
Elizabeth Theobald Young

ASSOCIATES

Jonathan Taggart Birge
Mary E. Browne
Tammy K. Haney
Shilpa Mehta Upadhye

LEGAL SUPPORT PERSONNEL

Steven B. Granner (Zoning Consultant)

Representative Clients: Duke Realty Investments, Inc.; Citimark Development Cos.; Centex Homes; Skinner & Broadbent; Metropolitan Life Ins. Co.; New Boston Fund, Inc.; Maefield Development Corp.; Eller Media Company; Hills Communities, Inc.; The Huntington National Bank.

For Complete List of Firm Personnel, See General Section

For full biographical listings, see the Martindale-Hubbell Law Directory

CLARK, QUINN, MOSES & CLARK (AV)

One Indiana Square, Suite 2200, 46204-2011
Telephone: 317-637-1321
Fax: 317-687-2344
Email: lawyers@cqmc-law.com

MEMBERS OF FIRM

Thomas Michael Quinn
J. Murray Clark

ASSOCIATES

Michael D. Keele
Cameron F. Clark
Robert V. Clutter

Representative Clients: Justus Companies; Davis Homes; Meijer Realty, Inc.; Lowe's; Marsh; MI Shottenstein; Indianapolis Colts; Fort Harrison Reuse Authority; Indianapolis Water Company; Kroger.

For full biographical listings, see the Martindale-Hubbell Law Directory

FEIWELL & HANNOY, PROFESSIONAL CORPORATION (AV)

251 North Illinois Street, Suite 1700, P.O. Box 44141, 46244-0141
Telephone: 317-237-2727
Facsimile: 317-237-2722
Email: f&h@feiwellhannoy.com *URL:* http://www.feiwellhannoy.com

Murray J. Feiwell
Douglas J. Hannoy

Michael J. Feiwell
David J. Jurkiewicz
Susan M. Woolley
Matthew S. Love
Jerlyn S. Southwick
Phyllis A. Conditt
Jennifer D. McNair

OF COUNSEL

Lisa Kay Decker

Representative Clients: United Companies Lending Corp.; Chase Manhattan Mortgage Corp.; GMAC Mortgage Corp.; First Union Mortgage Corp.; Norwest Mortgage, Inc.; F&C Real Estate Services, Inc.; Metro Realty Ltd. Partnership; Revel & Underwood, LLC; The Money Store; Bank of America.

For full biographical listings, see the Martindale-Hubbell Law Directory

HACKMAN HULETT & CRACRAFT, LLP (AV)

2400 One Indiana Square, 46204
Telephone: 317-636-5401
Facsimile: 317-686-3288

MEMBERS OF FIRM

Marvin L. Hackman
Robert S. Hulett
Michael B. Cracraft
Timothy K. Ryan
Philip B. McKiernan
Vicki L. Anderson
John D. Cochran, Jr.
Mark S. Alderfer

Marci A. Reddick
Sherri A.B. Elder
Steven W. Krohne
Ellen J. Morrison

Representative Clients: F.C. Tucker Company, Inc.; Texas Eastern Products Pipeline Co.; Walker Information, Inc.; McGraw-Hill Broadcasting Company, Inc. (WRTV-6); Title Services, L.P.; Tucker Mortgage, LLC; Tucker Associates, Inc.

For full biographical listings, see the Martindale-Hubbell Law Directory

ICE MILLER DONADIO & RYAN (AV)

One American Square Box 82001, 46282-0002
Telephone: 317-236-2100
Fax: 317-236-2219
Email: info@imdr.com *URL:* http://www.imdr.com
South Bend, Indiana Office: 211 West Washington Street, Suite 2420.
Telephone: 219-234-7933.
Fax: 219-234-7965. Internet E-mail: info@imdr.com. Web Site Address: http://www.imdr.com.
Chicago, Illinois Office: 135 South LaSalle Street, Suite 4100.
Telephone: 312-726-1567.
Fax: 312-641-6263. Internet E-mail: info@imdr.com. Web Site Address: http://www.imdr.com.

MEMBERS OF FIRM

Charles E. Wilson
Phillip L. Bayt
Zeff A. Weiss

RETIRED PARTNER

John A. Grayson

SENIOR COUNSEL

Timothy W. Sullivan
Mark D. Grant

OF COUNSEL

James B. Burroughs
Heather K. Olinger
George H. Abel, II

ASSOCIATES

Sarah K. Funke
Timothy E. Ochs
Brian S. Short

Representative Clients: The Sexton Cos.; Citicorp Real Estate, Inc.; Mansur Group; Heitman Properties; The Buckingham Cos.; Pulte Homes; K-Mart Corp.; Super Valu, Inc.; Crossmann Communities; California Public Employees Retirement System; Whiteco Industries Inc.; Berwind Property Group, Inc.

For Complete List of Firm Personnel, See General Section

For full biographical listings, see the Martindale-Hubbell Law Directory

JOHNSON SMITH PENCE & HEATH LLP (AV)

One Indiana Square Suite 1800, 46204
Telephone: 317-634-9777
Telecopier: 317-636-9061
Email: firm@jsplaw.com *URL:* http://www.jsplaw.com
Washington, D.C. Office: 555 Twelfth Street, N.W., Suite 650.
Telephone: 202-737-5410.
Fax: 202-737-5411.

MEMBERS OF FIRM

Sean Michael Clapp
Dennis A. Johnson
Richard L. Johnson
Michael J. Kaye

ASSOCIATE

John B. Baxter

For Complete List of Firm Personnel, See General Section

For full biographical listings, see the Martindale-Hubbell Law Directory

MCNAMAR, FEARNOW & MCSHARAR, P.C. (AV)

Bank One Center Tower, 111 Monument Circle, Suite 4500, 46204-5145
Telephone: 317-630-4500
Fax: 317-630-4501
Email: mfm@indy.net

David F. McNamar
Randall R. Fearnow
Janet A. McSharar
Alastair J. Warr
John H. Sharpe
Paul (Rick) Rauch, III
Marianna P. Moran

For full biographical listings, see the Martindale-Hubbell Law Directory

MITCHELL HURST JACOBS & DICK (AV)

152 East Washington Street, 46204
Telephone: 317-636-0808
1-800-636-0808
Fax: 317-633-7680
URL: http://www.mhjd.com

MEMBERS OF FIRM

Marvin H. Mitchell
Richard J. Dick

ASSOCIATE

Michael T. McNelis

General Counsel For: Dr. Tavel's Vision Center; Calderon Bros. Vending Machines, Inc.; Grocers Supply Co., Inc.; Power Train Services, Inc.; Frank E. Irish, Inc.; Bedding Liquidators; Galyan's Trading Co.; Harcourt Management Co., Inc.; Kosene & Kosene Mgt. & Dev. Co., Inc.; Hasten Bancorp.

For full biographical listings, see the Martindale-Hubbell Law Directory

Indianapolis—Continued

SOMMER & BARNARD, ATTORNEYS AT LAW, PC (AV)

4000 Bank One Tower, 111 Monument Circle, 46204
Telephone: 317-630-4000
FAX: 317-236-9802
Email: sandb@sommerbarnard.com
North Office: 8900 Keystone Crossing, Suite 1150, Indianapolis, Indiana, 46240-2134.
Telephone: 317-630-4000.
FAX: 317-844-4780.

Dan G. Sterner
Jerald I. Ancel
Marlene Reich
Julianne S. Lis-Milam
Erick D. Ponader

Representative Clients: Comerica Bank; Federal Express; New York Life; Kimball International; Monsanto; TRW, Inc.

For Complete List of Firm Personnel, See General Section

For full biographical listings, see the Martindale-Hubbell Law Directory

STARK DONINGER & SMITH (AV)

Suite 700, 50 South Meridian Street, 46204
Telephone: 317-638-2400
Fax: 317-633-6618; 633-6619

MEMBERS OF FIRM

John C. Stark
Bruce E. Smith
John W. Van Buskirk
Richard W. Dyar
Patricia Seasor Bailey
Brian J. Tuohy
Mark A. Bailey
Lewis E. Willis, Jr.
Thomas A. Brodnik

ASSOCIATES

Richard B. Kaufman
Paul T. Belch
John J. Moore
Dennis R. Tyler

COUNSEL

Clarence H. Doninger
Gregory S. Fehribach
Robert D. Maas
William K. Byrum

Representative Clients: American Consulting Engineers, Inc.; Ost Enterprises; The C.P. Morgan Co.; Nationwide Life Insurance Co.; Trinity Homes, Inc.

For full biographical listings, see the Martindale-Hubbell Law Directory

TABBERT HAHN EARNEST & WEDDLE (AV)

Suite 2100, One Indiana Square, 46204-2101
Telephone: 317-639-5444
Fax: 317-639-5232
Email: jtyrrell@tabberthahn.com *URL:* http://www.tabberthahn.com

Don A. Tabbert
Gregory F. Hahn
Lante K. Earnest
Robert G. Weddle
Mark K. Sullivan
Judy M. Tyrrell
Lara D. Engelking
Matthew W. Conner
William W. Mathews
Heather L. Fesko
Charles R. Whybrew

OF COUNSEL

James J. Nocon
William D. Lalley
Joseph W. Hammes
Dale E. Sporleder

For full biographical listings, see the Martindale-Hubbell Law Directory

*LAFAYETTE,** Tippecanoe Co.

BALL, EGGLESTON, BUMBLEBURG, MCBRIDE, WALKEY & STAPLETON, PC (AV)

810 Bank One Building, P.O. Box 1535, 47902-1535
Telephone: 765-742-9046
Fax: 765-742-1966
Email: info@ball-law.com

Cable G. Ball (1904-1981)
Owen Crook (1908-1977)
Warren N. Eggleston (1923-1991)
Joseph T. Bumbleburg
John K. McBride
Jack L. Walkey
Michael J. Stapleton
Jeffrey J. Newell
James T. Hodson
Brian Wade Walker
Cheryl M. Knodle
Randy J. Williams
Brenda Mithoefer Clapper

General Counsel for: The Lafayette Union Railway Co.
Representative Clients: Farmers Insurance Group; General Accident Fire & Life Assurance Corp.; City of Lafayette Board of Parks and Recreation; West Lafayette Community School Corp.; Travelers Insurance Co.; Trustees, West Lafayette Public Library; Town of Dayton, Indiana.

For full biographical listings, see the Martindale-Hubbell Law Directory

STUART & BRANIGIN (AV)

The Life Building, 300 Main Street, Suite 800, P.O. Box 1010, 47902-1010
Telephone: 765-423-1561
Telecopier: 765-742-8175
Email: sb@stuartlaw.com *URL:* http://www.stuartlaw.com
Indianapolis, Indiana Office: Suite 1401, 8888 Keystone Crossing, 46240.
Telephone: 317-574-7245.
Fax: 317-574-7050.

MEMBERS OF FIRM

Allison Ellsworth Stuart (1886-1950)
Roger D. Branigin (1902-1975)
Roger D. Branigin, Jr.
Thomas L. Ryan
Thomas R. McCully
Larry R. Fisher
Nina B. Kirkpatrick
Mark Lillianfeld
Stephen R. Pennell
Anthony S. Benton
Erik D. Spykman
William E. Emerick
John C. Duffey
Bruce McSpadden
Mark E. DeYoung
Thomas B. Parent
Laura L. Bowker
Kevin D. Nicoson
Susan K. Roberts
John M. Stuckey
Deborah B. Trice
William P. Kealey
David A. Starkweather
Geoffrey L. Blazi

SENIOR COUNSEL

Russell H. Hart

COUNSEL

John F. Bodle
James V. McGlone

ASSOCIATES

Elizabeth B. Searle
Marianne Mitten Owen
David A. Locke
Karen Orr McClure
Ann Marie Waldron
Barry L. Loftus

General Counsel for: The Lafayette Life Insurance Co.; INB National Bank, N.W.; Lafayette Home Hospital, Inc.
State Counsel for: Norfolk & Western Railway Co.
Mr. Ryan is Counsel to: The Trustees of Purdue University.
Representative Clients: Aluminum Company of America; Liberty Mutual Insurance Group.

For full biographical listings, see the Martindale-Hubbell Law Directory

MERRILLVILLE, Lake Co.

HODGES & DAVIS, P.C. (AV)

8700 Broadway, 46410
Telephone: 219-641-8700
Fax: 219-641-8710
URL: http://www.hodgesdavis.com
Portage, Indiana Office: 6082 Lute Road. P.O. Box 1037.
Telephone: 219-762-9129.
Fax: 219-762-2826.

Clyde D. Compton
William B. Davis
Earle F. Hites
R. Lawrence Steele
Gregory A. Sobkowski
Bonnie C. Coleman
Jill M. Madajczyk
Laura B. Frost
David H. Kreider
Jeanne B. Blumenthal

OF COUNSEL

Edward J. Hussey

Representative Clients: Lake Mortgage Co., Inc.; McDonald's Corporation; Walgreen Co.; Century 21 Heritage Realtors.

For Complete List of Firm Personnel, See General Section

For full biographical listings, see the Martindale-Hubbell Law Directory

MISHAWAKA, St. Joseph Co.

SCHINDLER AND OLSON (AV)

122 South Mill Street, P.O. Box 100, 46544
Telephone: 219-259-5461
Fax: 219-259-5462

OF COUNSEL

John W. Schindler (1884-1971)
John W. Schindler, Jr.

MEMBER OF FIRM

James J. Olson

Representative Clients: Penn-Harris-Madison School Corp.; All Star Realty Co.; School City of Mishawaka; Edward Rose & Sons.
Reference: 1st Source Bank of Mishawaka.

For full biographical listings, see the Martindale-Hubbell Law Directory

PORTAGE, Porter Co.

HODGES & DAVIS, P.C. (AV)

6082 Lute Road, P.O. Box 1037, 46368
Telephone: 219-762-9129
Fax: 219-762-2826
URL: http://www.hodgesdavis.com
Merrillville, Indiana Office: 8700 Broadway.
Telephone: 219-641-8700.
Fax: 219-641-8710.

(See Next Column)

HODGES & DAVIS P.C., *Portage—Continued*

Clyde D. Compton | Gregory A. Sobkowski
Earle F. Hites | Bonnie C. Coleman
R. Lawrence Steele | Laura B. Frost

Representative Clients: Porter County Plan Commission; McDonald's Corporation; Walgreen Co.; Century 21 Heritage Realtors; Lake Mortgage Co., Inc.

For full biographical listings, see the Martindale-Hubbell Law Directory

*PRINCETON,** Gibson Co.

HALL, PARTENHEIMER & KINKLE (AV)

219 North Hart Street, P.O. Box 13, 47670
Telephone: 812-386-0050
FAX: 812-385-2575
Email: hpk@hpk-law.com

MEMBERS OF FIRM

Verner P. Partenheimer | J. Robert Kinkle
R. Scott Partenheimer

Representative Clients: Interlake Inc.; Civitas National Bank; East Gibson School Corporation; Union Planters National Bank; United Federal Savings Bank; Amax Minerals.
Approved Attorneys for: Lawyers Title Insurance; National Attorneys Title Fund and Stewart Title.

For full biographical listings, see the Martindale-Hubbell Law Directory

*TERRE HAUTE,** Vigo Co.

COX, ZWERNER, GAMBILL & SULLIVAN (AV)

511 Wabash Avenue, P.O. Box 1625, 47808-1625
Telephone: 812-232-6003
Fax: 812-232-6567

MEMBERS OF FIRM

Ernest J. Zwerner (1918-1980) | Robert L. Gowdy
Benjamin G. Cox (1915-1988) | Louis F. Britton
Gilbert W. Gambill, Jr. | Carroll D. Smeltzer
James E. Sullivan | Jeffry A. Lind
Benjamin G. Cox, Jr. | Ronald E. Jumps
David W. Sullivan | Scott Craig
Elizabeth A. Lewis

OF COUNSEL

Robert D. Hepburn

Counsel for: Terre Haute First National Bank; Farmers Insurance Group; Indiana-American Water Co.; Indiana State University; Merchants National Bank of Terre Haute; Rose-Hulman Institute of Technology; Tribune-Star Publishing Co., Inc.; Hendrich Title Co.
Approved Title Attorneys for: Lawyers Title Insurance Corp.; Ticor Title; Stewart Title Guaranty Company.
Title Insurance Agents for: Old Republic National Title Insurance Company.

For full biographical listings, see the Martindale-Hubbell Law Directory

*VALPARAISO,** Porter Co.

BLACHLY, TABOR, BOZIK & HARTMAN (AV)

56 South Washington Street Suite 401, 46383
Telephone: 219-464-1041
Fax: 219-464-0927
Fort Wayne, Indiana Office: 4656 West Jefferson. Suite 120. 46804.

MEMBERS OF FIRM

James S. Bozik | Thomas F. Macke
Duane W. Hartman | Randall J. Zromkoski
David L. Hollenbeck | Richard J. Rupcich
Craig R. Van Schouwen

OF COUNSEL

Glenn J. Tabor

Reference: First National Bank.

For Complete List of Firm Personnel, See General Section

For full biographical listings, see the Martindale-Hubbell Law Directory

HOEPPNER WAGNER & EVANS LLP (AV)

103 East Lincolnway, P.O. Box 2357, 46384-2357
Telephone: 219-464-4961; 800-879-2246 (IN, IL)
Fax: 219-465-0603
Email: hwe@hwelaw.com *URL:* http://www.hwelaw.com
Merrillville, Indiana Office: Twin Towers, Suite 606 South, 1000 East 80th Place, P.O. Box 10627, 46419-0627.
Telephone: 219-769-6552; 800-263-1466 (IN, IL).
Fax: 219-738-2349. Email: hwe@hwelaw.com

MEMBERS OF FIRM

William H. Wagner | Richard A. Browne
Gordon A. Etzler | Todd A. Leeth
John E. Hughes (Resident, Merrillville Office) | Michael P. Blaize
James L. Jorgensen | J. Brian Hittinger (Resident, Merrillville Office)

(See Next Column)

ASSOCIATES

Robert L. Clark | Jay S. Patheja (Resident, Merrillville Office)

Attorneys for: Aldi Inc.; Bethlehem Steel Corp.; Chester, Inc.; Hunt-Wesson Foods, Inc.; Owens-Corning Fiberglass Corp.; Valparaiso University; State Farm Insurance.

For Complete List of Firm Personnel, See General Section

For full biographical listings, see the Martindale-Hubbell Law Directory

IOWA

*CEDAR RAPIDS,** Linn Co.

SHUTTLEWORTH & INGERSOLL, P.C. (AV)

115 Third Street S.E., Suite 500, P.O. Box 2107, 52406-2107
Telephone: 319-365-9461
Fax: 319-365-8443
URL: http://www.shuttleworthlaw.com

James C. Nemmers | Dennis J. McMenimen
Michael O. McDermott | William P. Prowell
Carroll J. Reasoner | Linda M. Kirsch
Thomas P. Peffer | Brian D. Bergstrom
Dean D. Carrington

David T. Hayes | Laurie L. Dawley

OF COUNSEL

William R. Shuttleworth

COUNSEL

Joan Lipsky | Laurie Bergren

Representative Clients: Amana Society; Archer-Daniels-Midland Co.; Cargill, Inc.; Cedar River Paper Company; Firstar Bank N.A.; Lawyers Title Insurance Company; Met-Coil Systems Corporation; PMX Industries, Inc.; Ryan Construction Company; Shive-Hattery Engineers & Architects, Inc.

For Complete List of Firm Personnel, See General Section

For full biographical listings, see the Martindale-Hubbell Law Directory

*COUNCIL BLUFFS,** Pottawattamie Co.

REILLY, PETERSEN & HANNAN, P.L.C. (AV)

215 South Main Street, P.O. Box 1016, 51502-1016
Telephone: 712-328-1575
Fax: 712-328-1562

C. R. Hannan | Michael G. Reilly
Deborah L. Petersen

Craig M. Dreismeier

References: Peoples National Bank of Council Bluffs.

For full biographical listings, see the Martindale-Hubbell Law Directory

SMITH PETERSON LAW FIRM (AV)

35 Main Place, Suite 300, P.O. Box 249, 51502
Telephone: 712-328-1833
Fax: 712-328-8320
Email: email@smithpeterson.com
Omaha, Nebraska Office: 9290 West Dodge Road, Suite 205.
Telephone: 402-397-8500.
Fax: 402-397-5519.

MEMBERS OF FIRM

Raymond A. Smith (1892-1977) | Lawrence J. Beckman
John LeRoy Peterson (1895-1969) | Gregory G. Barntsen
Harold T. Beckman | W. Curtis Hewett
Robert J. Laubenthal | Steven H. Krohn
Richard A. Heininger | Randy R. Ewing
 | Joseph D. Thornton
T. J. Pattermann

ASSOCIATES

Daniel L. Fretheim | Paul M. Shotkoski

Representative Clients: Redland Insurance Group; Iowa Western Community College; Farm Credit Service of The Midlands; Demma Fruit Co.; Peoples National Bank; Council Bluffs Board of Water Works Trustee.

For full biographical listings, see the Martindale-Hubbell Law Directory

*DAVENPORT,** Scott Co.

Gosma & Gallagher, P.L.C. (AV)

Quad City Bank Building, 4500 North Brady Street, Suite 200, 52806
Telephone: 319-388-8417
Fax: 319-388-9240
Email: lawfirm@gosma-gallagher.com
Bettendorf Office: 1989 Spruce Hills Drive.
Telephone: 319-355-5304.
Fax: 319-359-7711.

MEMBERS OF FIRM

Robert D. Wells (1904-1990)
Robert H. Gallagher
John S. Gosma
James G. Noth
Marie R. Rolling-Tarbox
David A. Millage
Robert S. Gallagher
Jane E. Zimmer

OF COUNSEL

Clay LeGrand
Nicholas W. LeGrand (Not admitted in IA)

References: American Bank and Trust Company, Rock Island; Great River Bank and Trust, Princeton.

For full biographical listings, see the Martindale-Hubbell Law Directory

*DES MOINES,** Polk Co.

Connolly, O'Malley, Lillis, Hansen & Olson, L.L.P. (AV)

300 NationsBank Building, 317 Sixth Avenue, 50309-4127
Telephone: 515-243-8157
Fax: 515-243-3919
Email: clawfirm@aol.com

MEMBERS OF FIRM

William J. Lillis
Russell J. Hansen
Michael W. O'Malley
Eugene E. Olson
Streetar Cameron
Christopher R. Pose
Patrick T. Burk
David I. Hansen

A list of Representative Clients will be furnished upon request.
References will be furnished upon request.

For Complete List of Firm Personnel, See General Section

For full biographical listings, see the Martindale-Hubbell Law Directory

Finley, Alt, Smith, Scharnberg, Craig, Hilmes & Gaffney, P.C. (AV)

604 Locust Street, Fourth Floor Equitable Building, 50309
Telephone: 515-288-0145
Telecopier: 515-288-2724

Jerry P. Alt

Representative Clients: ALAS; American Society of Composers, Authors and Publishers; Equitable Life Assurance Society of the U.S.; Federated Insurance Co.; Meredith Corp.
Iowa Attorneys for: Midwest Medical Insurance Co.
District Attorneys for: Norfolk & Southern Railroad; Soo Line Railroad Company.

For Complete List of Firm Personnel, See General Section

For full biographical listings, see the Martindale-Hubbell Law Directory

Patterson, Lorentzen, Duffield, Timmons, Irish, Becker & Ordway, L.L.P. (AV)

729 Insurance Exchange Building, 50309
Telephone: 515-283-2147
Fax: 515-283-1002
Email: mail@pattersonfirm.com *URL:* http://www.pattersonfirm.com

MEMBERS OF FIRM

G. O. Patterson (1914-1982)
James A. Lorentzen (Retired)
Theodore T. Duffield
William E. Timmons (Retired)
Roy M. Irish
F. H. Becker (Retired)
Gary D. Ordway
Robin L. Hermann
Harry Perkins, III
Michael F. Lacey, Jr.
Gregory J. Wilson
Jeffrey A. Boehlert
Douglas A. Haag
Charles E. Cutler
Michael D. Huppert
Martin C. Sprock
William A. Wickett
Frederick M. Haskins
Jeffrey A. Baker
Janice M. Herfkens
Coreen K. Bezdicek
Patrick V. Waldron

ASSOCIATE

Michael S. Jones

General Counsel for: Iowa Insurance Institute.
Representative Clients: Allied Mutual Insurance Company; CNA Insurance Company; Chubb Insurance Group; Continental Western Insurance Co.; Farmers Insurance Group; Farmland Insurance Company; Grinnell Mutual Reinsurance Company; Hawkeye Security Insurance Company; Iowa Insurance Institute, St. Paul Fire & Marine Insurance Company.

For full biographical listings, see the Martindale-Hubbell Law Directory

KANSAS

*HUTCHINSON,** Reno Co.

Gilliland & Hayes, P.A. A Professional Association (AV)

20 West 2nd Avenue, 2nd Floor, P.O. Box 2977, 67504-2977
Telephone: 316-662-0537
Facsimile: 316-669-9426
URL: http://www.gillilandhayes.com
Wichita, Kansas Office: The Orpheum Centre, Suite 300, 200 North Broadway, P.O. Box 49406.
Telephone: 316-262-2266.
Facsimile: 316-263-2202.
Kansas City, Missouri Office: 12th Floor, 3100 Broadway.
Telephone: 816-753-3100.
Facsimile: 816-753-2271.

Robert J. Gilliland
John F. Hayes
James R. Gilliland
John S. Schmidt
Bruce B. Waugh (Not admitted in KS; Resident, Kansas City, Missouri Office)
Michael R. O'Neal
Bradley D. Dillon
Gerald L. Green
David N. Zimmerman (Not admitted in KS; Resident, Kansas City, Missouri Office)
Scott J. Mann
Carol Z. Smith (Resident, Kansas City, Missouri Office)
Kathleen A. Hardee (Resident, Kansas City, Missouri Office)
Kendall R. Cunningham (Resident, Wichita Office)
Mark R. Maloney (Resident, Wichita Office)

Thomas A. Dower
Tracy Applegate Cole
Laura A. Hederstedt
Terri Roberts Munsell (Resident, Kansas City, Missouri Office)
Lisa M. Ward
Kimberly Breda Bushek (Resident, Kansas City, Missouri Office)
E. Thomas Pyle, III
Tara L. Bragg

OF COUNSEL

Robert P. Reams (Not admitted in KS; Resident, Kansas City, Missouri Office)

Representative Clients: Dillon Companies; Hutchinson Clinic; Hutchinson Hospital Corp.; Leisure Hotel Corp.; Pine Development Co.; RHW Companies; Sirloin Stockade International; TSW Products; Woodwork Manufacturing; Central Bank & Trust.

For full biographical listings, see the Martindale-Hubbell Law Directory

*WICHITA,** Sedgwick Co.

Foulston & Siefkin L.L.P. (AV)

700 NationsBank Financial Center, 67202
Telephone: 316-267-6371
Facsimile: 316-267-6345
URL: http://www.foulston.com
Topeka, Kansas Office: 1515 NationsBank Tower, 534 Kansas Avenue, 66603.
Telephone: 785-233-3600.
Fax: 785-233-1610.
Dodge City, Kansas Office: 810 Frontview, P.O. Box 1147, 67801.
Telephone: 316-227-8126.
Fax: 316-227-8451.
Member: Lex Mundi, The World's Leading Association of Independent Law Firms.

MEMBERS OF FIRM

Benjamin C. Langel
Phillip S. Frick
James D. Oliver
Larry G. Rapp
Gary E. Knight

For Complete List of Firm Personnel, See General Section

For full biographical listings, see the Martindale-Hubbell Law Directory

Kahrs, Nelson, Fanning, Hite & Kellogg L.L.P. (AV)

200 W. Douglas, Suite 600, 67202
Telephone: 316-265-7761
Telecopier: 316-267-7803
URL: http://www.kahrsnelson.com

MEMBERS OF FIRM

Clark R. Nelson
Steven D. Gough
Linda S. Parks
John G. Pike

ASSOCIATE

Scott R. Schillings

Representative Clients: Garvey Center, L.C.; Maverick Development Corp.; Prairie Village Shopping Center, Inc.; The Ruffin Companies; Westway Shopping Center, Inc.

(See Next Column)

KAHRS, NELSON, FANNING, HITE & KELLOGG L.L.P., *Wichita—Continued*

For Complete List of Firm Personnel, See General Section

For full biographical listings, see the Martindale-Hubbell Law Directory

TRIPLETT, WOOLF & GARRETSON, LLC (AV)

2959 North Rock Road, Suite 300, 67226
Telephone: 316-630-8100
Fax: 316-630-8101
Email: twg@twgfirm.com

MEMBERS OF FIRM

Thomas C. Triplett | Timothy E. McKee
John P. Woolf | Ron H. Harnden

ASSOCIATES

Jeffery C. Dahlgren | Kent G. Voth

Representative Clients: Anheuser-Busch Companies, Inc.; Brite Voice Systems, Inc.; Coleman Company, Inc.; Dow Chemical Co.; Friends University; KPMG Peat Marwick; National Plastics Color, Inc.; Total Petroleum, Inc.; Travelers Insurance Co.; Willis Corroon of Kansas, Inc.

For Complete List of Firm Personnel, See General Section

For full biographical listings, see the Martindale-Hubbell Law Directory

YOUNG, BOGLE, MCCAUSLAND, WELLS & BLANCHARD, P.A. (AV)

106 West Douglas, Suite 923, 67202
Telephone: 316-265-7841
Facsimile: 316-265-3956
Email: ybmwblaw@aol.com

William A. Wells | Patrick C. Blanchard

J. Michael Peters

Representative Clients: Equitable AgriBusiness, Inc.; 1st Nationwide Bank; Transamerica Financial Corp.; Citicorp., N.A.; Security Pacific Business Credit.

For Complete List of Firm Personnel, See General Section

For full biographical listings, see the Martindale-Hubbell Law Directory

KENTUCKY

ASHLAND, Boyd Co.

HOLBROOK & PITT (AV)

200 Home Federal Building, 1500 Carter Avenue, 41101
Telephone: 606-324-5136
Fax: 606-329-8998

Charles R. Holbrook, Jr. (1909-1993) | Charles R. Holbrook III
Ernest M. Pitt, Jr.

ASSOCIATE

Anna Holmes Ruth

Reference: First American Bank.

For full biographical listings, see the Martindale-Hubbell Law Directory

*BOWLING GREEN,** Warren Co.

KERRICK, GRISE & STIVERS (AV)

1025 State Street, P.O. Box 9547, 42102-9547
Telephone: 502-782-8160
Fax: 502-782-5856
Email: kgs@kgslaw.com
Elizabethtown, Kentucky Office: 2935 Dolphin Drive, Suite 102.
Telephone: 502-769-5788.
Fax: 502-737-9285.

MEMBERS OF FIRM

Thomas N. Kerrick | Gregory N. Stivers
John R. Grise | H. Brent Brennenstuhl
Laura M. Hagan

ASSOCIATES

Karl N. Crandall | Shawn Rosso Alcott
Jason B. Bell

OF COUNSEL

Jeffrey R. O'Grody

LEGAL SUPPORT PERSONNEL

Patricia Logsdon | Laura Lockhart Lico
Allison Lusk

Representative Clients: Bowling Green Bank & Trust, N.A.; Huntington Mortgage Corp.; FirStar Bank; First American National Bank.

(See Next Column)

For full biographical listings, see the Martindale-Hubbell Law Directory

*GEORGETOWN,** Scott Co.

E. DURWARD WELDON (AV)

217 East Main Street, 40324
Telephone: 502-863-1285

Approved Attorney for: Lawyers Title Insurance Corporation of Richmond, Virginia; Louisville Title Division of Commonwealth Land Title Insurance Co. (Binder Agent); The Equitable Life Assurance Society of the United States.

For full biographical listings, see the Martindale-Hubbell Law Directory

*GLASGOW,** Barren Co.

GARMON & GOODMAN (AV)

139 North Public Square, P.O. Box 663, 42142-0663
Telephone: 270-651-8812
Telecopier: 270-651-8846

MEMBERS OF FIRM

Larry D. Garmon | Charles A. Goodman III

Approved Attorneys for: Commonwealth Land Title Insurance Co. (agent); Chicago Title Insurance Co.
References: Edmonton State Bank; South Central Bank of Barren County, Inc., Glasgow, Ky.
Representative Clients: The New Farmers National Bank of Glasgow; Green Tree Financial Services, Inc.; Commonwealth Land Title Insurance Co.; Commonwealth Relocation Services; Farm Credit Services of Mid-America, ACA; Farm Service Agency.

For full biographical listings, see the Martindale-Hubbell Law Directory

HERBERT & HERBERT (AV)

135 North Public Square, P.O. Box 1000, 42141
Telephone: 502-651-9000
Fax: 502-651-3317
Email: h&hlaw@glasgow-ky.com

MEMBERS OF FIRM

H. Jefferson Herbert, Jr. | Betty Reece Herbert

ASSOCIATES

Brian K. Pack | Wesley W. Stephens

Representative Clients: South Central Bank, South Broadway, Glasgow, Kentucky; Resort Financial Services, Inc., Park City, Kentucky; Bullek of Kentucky, Inc., Park City, Kentucky; Commonwealth Land Title Insurance Co., Louisville, Kentucky; Pan-Osten Co.

For full biographical listings, see the Martindale-Hubbell Law Directory

*HAZARD,** Perry Co.

GULLETT, COMBS, REED & BOWLING (AV)

109 Broadway, Second Floor, P.O. Box 1039, 41702-1039
Telephone: 606-439-1373; 1-800-949-8812
Fax: 606-439-4450
Email: apgullet@mis.net
Email: 1234rong@tgtel.com

MEMBERS OF FIRM

Asa P. Gullett, III | Teresa G. Combs Reed
Ronald G. Combs | Matthew Lawton Bowling

ASSOCIATE

Jameson D. Combs

LEGAL SUPPORT PERSONNEL

Jacqueline E. Goodin | Jimmie Lynn Jones

Reference: Peoples Bank and Trust Co.

For full biographical listings, see the Martindale-Hubbell Law Directory

*LEXINGTON,** Fayette Co.

GERALDS, JONES, SHERROW, SCHRADER & RICE, P.S.C. (AV)

259 West Short Street, 40507
Telephone: 606-255-7946
Fax: 606-233-4099

Oscar H. Geralds, Jr. | Billy W. Sherrow
Ernest H. Jones, II | John P. Schrader
John G. Rice

Robert L. Swisher | Patsey Ely Yewell
Cheryl D. Morgan

OF COUNSEL

Frances Geralds Rohlfing

Representative Clients: Bank of the Bluegrass & Trust Co.; Norwest Mortgage Corporation; Waterfield Financial Corporation; PHH Homequity Corporation; Commonwealth Land Title Insurance Co. (Issuing Agent).

(See Next Column)

GERALDS, JONES, SHERROW, SCHRADER & RICE P.S.C.—*Continued*

Reference: Bank of the Bluegrass & Trust Co.

For full biographical listings, see the Martindale-Hubbell Law Directory

STOLL, KEENON & PARK, LLP (AV)

201 E. Main Street, Suite 1000, 40507-1380
Telephone: 606-231-3000
Telecopier: 606-253-1093; 606-253-1027
URL: http://www.skp.com
Frankfort, Kentucky Office: 307 Washington Street, 40601.
Telephone: 502-875-6220.
Telecopier: 502-875-6235.
Henderson, Kentucky Office: 201 C North Main Street, 42420-3103.
Telephone: 270-831-1900.
Telecopier: 270-827-4060.
Louisville, Kentucky Office: 400 West Market Street, Suite 2650, 40202-3377.
Telephone: 502-568-9100.
Telecopier: 502-568-5700.

MEMBERS OF FIRM

William M. Lear, Jr.
Gary W. Barr
Frank L. Wilford
Robert W. Kellerman
Rena Gardner Wiseman
Dan M. Rose
Richard A. Nunnelley

ASSOCIATE

Steven B. Loy

OF COUNSEL

George D. Smith

Representative Clients: Ball Homes, Inc.; National Development Council; McDonalds Corp.; Kentucky River Coal Corp.; Super America, Inc.; Bank One.

For Complete List of Firm Personnel, See General Section

For full biographical listings, see the Martindale-Hubbell Law Directory

VIMONT & WILLS PLLC (AV)

Suite 300, 155 East Main Street, 40507-1317
Telephone: 606-252-2202
Telecopier: 606-259-2927
Email: vimont@lex.infi.net

Richard E. Vimont
Bernard F. Lovely, Jr.
Richard M. Wehrle
Fred E. Fugazzi, Jr.

Richard A. Whitaker
J. Thomas Rawlings
Micki Woodward McDaniel

For full biographical listings, see the Martindale-Hubbell Law Directory

*LONDON,** Laurel Co.

FARMER, KELLEY, BROWN AND WILLIAMS (AV)

502 West Fifth Street, Drawer 490, 40741
Telephone: 606-878-7640
Fax: 606-878-2364
Email: fpfarmer@farmerlaw.com
Lexington, Kentucky Office: 1082 Griffin Gate Drive, 40511-1384.
Telephone: 606: 263-2567.
Facsimile: 606: 878-2364.

MEMBERS OF FIRM

F. Preston Farmer
John F. Kelley, Jr.
Michael P. Farmer
Martha L. Brown
Jason E. Williams

ASSOCIATES

Suzanne S. Farmer
Jennifer S. Nicholson

Representative Clients: The Aetna Casualty and Surety Co.; American States Insurance Co.; Auto-Owner's Insurance Co.; Bituminous Insurance Co.; Canadian Universal Insurance Co.; Chubb Insurance Co.; Cotton States Insurance Co.; Crum & Forster Underwriters Group; Eagle Insurance Co.; Equity Mutual Insurance Co.

For full biographical listings, see the Martindale-Hubbell Law Directory

*LOUISVILLE,** Jefferson Co.

BARDENWERPER & LOBB, PLLC (AV)

8311 Shelbyville Road, 40222
Telephone: 502-426-6688
Fax: 502-425-0561

William B. Bardenwerper
James T. Lobb

ASSOCIATE

Susan T. Merrill

LEGAL SUPPORT PERSONNEL

Alice Blackburn (Paralegal)
Debra Martin (Paralegal)

For full biographical listings, see the Martindale-Hubbell Law Directory

FORE, MILLER & SCHWARTZ (AV)

First Trust Centre, Suite 700 North, 200 South Fifth Street, 40202
Telephone: 502-589-5250
Fax: 502-589-1637

MEMBERS OF FIRM

F. Larkin Fore
Dan T. Schwartz
Stephen H. Miller
Bryan J. Dillon
Donald J. LaDuke

ASSOCIATES

Louis I. Waterman
Joseph C. Spalding

OF COUNSEL

Karl M. Walz

References: American States Insurance Co.; Crawford & Company; Paragon Group, Inc.; Queens Group; Southeastern Dairies, Inc.; Ticor Title Co.; First National Bank of Louisville; Stockyards Bank; Arrow Electric Co.

For full biographical listings, see the Martindale-Hubbell Law Directory

GATHRIGHT & HARDY (AV)

Citizens Plaza, Suite 2450, 500 West Jefferson Street, 40202
Telephone: 502-569-2030
Fax: 502-569-2040
Email: ghpart@bellsouth.net

MEMBERS OF FIRM

Joseph R. Gathright, Jr.
Sharon C. Hardy

For full biographical listings, see the Martindale-Hubbell Law Directory

MAPOTHER & MAPOTHER (AV)

801 West Jefferson Street, 40202
Telephone: 502-587-5400
Fax: 502-587-5444
Email: mapother@mapother-atty.com *URL:* http://www.mapother-atty.com
Lexington, Kentucky Office: 100 East Vine Street, Suite 810.
Telephone: 606-253-0003.
Fax: 606-255-3961.
Jeffersonville, Indiana Office: 505 East Seventh Street.
Telephone: 812-288-5059.
Fax: 502-587-5444.
Cincinnati, Ohio Office: Kroger Building, Suite 2220, 1014 Vine Street.
Telephone: 513-381-4888.
Fax: 513-381-3117.
Huntington, West Virginia Office: Morris Building, Suite 701, 845 Fourth Avenue.
Telephone: 304-525-1185.
Fax: 304-529-3764.
Evansville, Indiana Office: 329 Main Street, Suite 602.
Telephone: 812-421-9108.
Fax: 812-421-9109.

MEMBERS OF FIRM

William R. Mapother
Thomas L. Canary, Jr.
Hollis L. Searcy
Charles M. Friedman

Roberta S. Dunlap (Resident, Evansville, Indiana Office)
Dean A. Langdon (Resident, Lexington, Kentucky Office)
Lee W. Grace
Brian E. Chapman (Resident, Cincinnati, Ohio Office)
T. Lawson McSwain, II
John D. Meyers (Resident, Lexington, Kentucky Office)
Lisa A. Herndon
Ronda C. Gunter (Resident, Huntington, West Virginia Office)
Steven B. Mulrooney
Dennis M. Ostrowski
Gerald O. Henderson, Jr. (Resident, Huntington, West Virginia Office)
Miles S. Apple
Joy B. Gilliam (Resident, Lexington, Kentucky Office)
Vincent A. Dimasi (Not admitted in KY; Resident, Cincinnati, Ohio Office)
Charlie W. Gordon

Representative Clients: General Electric Capital Corp; PNC Bank; Huntington Mortgage Co.; Metmor Financial Inc.; L&N Federal Credit Union; Ford Motor Credit Co.; Ford Leasing Development Co.; NationsBanc Mortgage Corp.; Chrysler Financial Corp.; Sears.

For full biographical listings, see the Martindale-Hubbell Law Directory

MORGAN & POTTINGER, P.S.C. (AV)

601 West Main Street, 40202
Telephone: 502-589-2780
Telecopier: 502-585-3498
URL: http://www.morganandpottinger.com
Lexington, Kentucky Office: 133 West Short Street.
Telephone: 606-253-1900.
Telecopier: 606-255-2038.
New Albany, Indiana Office: 120 East Market Street.
Telephone: 812-948-0008.
Telecopier: 812-944-6215.

(See Next Column)

MORGAN & POTTINGER P.S.C., *Louisville—Continued*

Patrick E. Morgan
M. Deane Stewart
James I. Murray (Resident, Lexington Office)
Mark J. Sandlin

John Allan Combs (Resident, Lexington Office)

For Complete List of Firm Personnel, See General Section

For full biographical listings, see the Martindale-Hubbell Law Directory

ROTH FOLEY BRYANT & COOPER, PLLC (AV)

First Trust Centre, Suite 300S, 200 South Fifth Street, 40202-3236
Telephone: 502-569-7550
Fax: 502-540-0123
Email: RFBC.com

Irvin D. Foley
David M. Roth
David H. Cooper
Lisa Koch Bryant
K. Gail Russell
Christian L. Juckett

OF COUNSEL

James E. Fahey
David W. Gray

Representative Clients: Bank One, Kentucky, N.A.; Huntington National Bank; Commonwealth Bank & Trust Co.; Farm Credit Services of Mid-America; Century Indemnity Co.; Travelers Casualty and Insurance Co.; Tumbleweed, LLC; John R. Gains Thoroughbreds, LLC; ARM Financial Group, Inc.; Osborn Enterprises.

For full biographical listings, see the Martindale-Hubbell Law Directory

TILFORD, DOBBINS, ALEXANDER, BUCKAWAY & BLACK (AV)

Suite 1400, One Riverfront Plaza, 40202
Telephone: 502-584-6137
Fax: 502-584-2318

MEMBERS OF FIRM

Charles W. Dobbins (1916-1992)
Henry J. Tilford (1880-1968)
George S. Wetherby (1905-1954)
Lawrence W. Wetherby (1908-1994)
John T. Metcalf (1890-1974)
Stuart E. Alexander
William A. Buckaway, Jr.
Charles W. Dobbins, Jr.
Terrell L. Black
Mark Wesley Dobbins
Stuart E. Alexander, III
John M. Nader

ASSOCIATES

John A. Wilmes
Sandra F. Keene
Patrick T. Schmidt
Thomas J.B. Hurst
H. Kevin Eddins
William J. Walsh, IV
Dana M. Taylor

OF COUNSEL

Randolph Noe
Carolyn K. Balleisen
Michael G. Karem

For full biographical listings, see the Martindale-Hubbell Law Directory

*SHELBYVILLE,** Shelby Co.

NEAL & DAVIS (AV)

931 Main Street, P.O. Box 40, 40066-0040
Telephone: 502-633-6002;
Louisville: 502-589-9888
Email: tdavis@neal-davis.com
URL: http://www.neal-davis.com

Gregg Y. Neal
Thomas Todd Davis

Reference: Republic Bank and Trust Co.

For full biographical listings, see the Martindale-Hubbell Law Directory

LOUISIANA

*BATON ROUGE,** East Baton Rouge Parish

KANTROW, SPAHT, WEAVER & BLITZER, A PROFESSIONAL LAW CORPORATION (AV)

Suite 300, City Plaza, 445 North Boulevard, P.O. Box 2997, 70821-2997
Telephone: 225-383-4703
Fax: 225-343-0630; 343-0637

Byron R. Kantrow (1909-1997)
Carlos G. Spaht
Geraldine B. Weaver
Sidney M. Blitzer, Jr.
Paul H. Spaht
Lee C. Kantrow
John C. Miller
Vincent P. Fornias
David S. Rubin
Diane L. Crochet
Richard F. Zimmerman, Jr.
Bob D. Tucker
Martin E. Golden
J. Michael Robinson, Jr.
Connell L. Archey
Randal J. Robert

(See Next Column)

C. William Belsom, Jr.
Linda Orlansky Posner

Representative Clients: CNA Insurance Cos.; Federal Deposit Insurance Corp.; Hartford Insurance Group; Air Products and Chemicals, Inc.; CF Industries, Inc.; AT&T; United Companies Financial Corp.

For full biographical listings, see the Martindale-Hubbell Law Directory

KIZER, HOOD & MORGAN, L.L.P. (AV)

A Partnership including a Professional Corporation
2111 Quail Run Drive, 70808
Telephone: 225-761-0001
Fax: 225-761-0731
URL: http://www.khmllp.com

Roland C. Kizer (1899-1988)
Roland C. Kizer, Jr., (Ltd., A Law Corporation)
Ralph E. Hood
J. Donald Morgan
Walter N. O'Roark, III
Stacy G. Butler

Blake E. Rizzo

Representative Clients: Hibernia National Bank; Bank One, Louisiana, N.A.; The Dime Savings Bank of New York, FSB; G.E. Capital Asset Management Corp.; Bankers Systems, Inc.; United Companies Lending Corporation; Rabenhorst Life Insurance Co.; General Equipment, Inc. d/b/a Scott General; Old South Builders, Inc.; P.P.R., Inc.

For full biographical listings, see the Martindale-Hubbell Law Directory

*COVINGTON,** St. Tammany Parish

LAW OFFICES OF WILLIAM J. DUTEL (AV)

325 North New Hampshire Street, 70433
Telephone: 504-892-6474
Fax: 504-892-7307
Email: bdutel@fastband.com
New Orleans, Louisiana Office: 2960 Energy Centre, 1100 Poydras Street.
Telephone: 504-582-2429.

William J. Dutel

OF COUNSEL

Kimberly Kammler Dutel

For full biographical listings, see the Martindale-Hubbell Law Directory

*LAKE CHARLES,** Calcasieu Parish

BERGSTEDT & MOUNT (AV)

Second Floor, Magnolia Life Building, P.O. Drawer 3004, 70602-3004
Telephone: 318-433-3004
Facsimile: 318-433-8080

MEMBERS OF FIRM

Thomas M. Bergstedt
Benjamin W. Mount
Van C. Seneca

ASSOCIATE

Annette N. Peltier

OF COUNSEL

Charles S. Ware

Representative Clients: ARCO Chemical Company; Ashland Oil Co.; CIGNA Property & Casualty Companies; Columbia Women's & Children's Hospital; The Hartford Steam Boiler Inspection & Insurance Company; Leach Company; Olin Corporation; Occidental Chemical Corporation; Terra Corporation; R. D. Werner Company.

For full biographical listings, see the Martindale-Hubbell Law Directory

SCOFIELD, GERARD, VERON, SINGLETARY & POHORELSKY, A PROFESSIONAL LAW CORPORATION (AV)

1114 Ryan Street, P.O. Drawer 3028, 70601
Telephone: 318-433-9436
Telefax: 318-436-0306
URL: http://www.sgvsp.com

John R. Pohorelsky

Representative Clients: Admiral Insurance Co.; Amoco Production Co.; Banc One; Browning-Ferris Industries, Inc.; Brown & Root Construction Co.; Cosmos Broadcasting Corp.; Dresser Industries, Inc.; Kansas City Southern Railway Co.; Mobil Oil Corp.; Phillips Petroleum Co.

For Complete List of Firm Personnel, See General Section

For full biographical listings, see the Martindale-Hubbell Law Directory

WRIGHT & EVERETT, L.L.C. (AV)

203 West Clarence Street, 70601
Telephone: 318-439-6930
Telecopier: 318-439-6730
URL: http://www.lawyers.com/wright&everettlaw

(See Next Column)

WRIGHT & EVERETT L.L.C.—*Continued*

Kenneth Michael Wright | John P. Everett, Jr.

For full biographical listings, see the Martindale-Hubbell Law Directory

METAIRIE, Jefferson Parish

HENICAN, JAMES & CLEVELAND (AV)

Suite 1200 Heritage Plaza, 111 Veterans Memorial Boulevard, 70005
Telephone: 504-837-8080
Facsimile: 504-833-0863
Mailing Address: P.O. Box 19300, New Orleans, Louisiana, 70179

MEMBERS OF FIRM

C. Ellis Henican (1905-1997)
Murray F. Cleveland (1913-1971)
Philip E. James, Jr.
Marshall G. Weaver
Edward N. George, III
Shawn M. Bridgewater

ASSOCIATES

Keith M. Benit
Jacob S. Capraro
David M. Packard

OF COUNSEL

Philip E. James
Louis V. Rand, II

Representative Clients: Better Business Bureau of New Orleans, Inc.; St. Paul Fire and Marine Insurance Co.; Stewart Enterprises, Inc.
Reference: Hibernia National Bank, New Orleans.

For full biographical listings, see the Martindale-Hubbell Law Directory

*NEW ORLEANS,** Orleans Parish

BALDWIN & HASPEL, L.L.C. (AV)

Energy Centre, Suite 2200, 1100 Poydras Street, 70163-2200
Telephone: 504-585-7711
Fax: 504-585-7751
URL: http://www.baldwinhaspel.com

MEMBERS OF FIRM

Cuthbert S. Baldwin (1891-1969)
Edward Haspel (1889-1983)
Conrad Meyer, III
Jerome J. Reso, Jr.
Joel A. Mendler
Conrad Meyer, IV
Malcolm A. Meyer
Monica Tufano Surprenant
Leon H. Rittenberg, Jr.
John A. Rouchell
Jeannie Morris Randazzo
James P. Magee
Dennis M. LaBorde
Beverly Klundt Baudouin
Karl J. Zimmermann
Lance J. Arnold

OF COUNSEL

A. B. Kupperman
Frederick W. "Fritz" Veters

Leon H. Rittenberg, III
Thomas M. Long

Representative Clients: Bean Dredging Corp.; Hibernia National Bank; Alfa-Laval, Inc.

For full biographical listings, see the Martindale-Hubbell Law Directory

CORRERO FISHMAN HAYGOOD PHELPS WALMSLEY & CASTEIX, L.L.P. (AV)

Bank One Center, 46th Floor, 201 St. Charles Avenue, 70170-4600
Telephone: 504-586-5252
Fax: 504-586-5250

Michael J. Casteix
Sterling Scott Willis

John D. Werner

For full biographical listings, see the Martindale-Hubbell Law Directory

GRAHAM & ARCENEAUX (AV)

Pan-American Life Center, 601 Poydras Street, Suite 1871, 70130
Telephone: 504-522-8256
Fax: 504-525-2485
Email: graarc@bellsouth.net

MEMBERS OF FIRM

George S. Graham (1894-1960)
Louis B. Graham (1916-1989)
James C. Arceneaux, III
Adriel Graham Arceneaux

ASSOCIATE

Louis Graham Arceneaux

Representative Client: Standard Mortgage Corporation, New Orleans, La.

For full biographical listings, see the Martindale-Hubbell Law Directory

MCGLINCHEY STAFFORD (AV)

A Professional Limited Liability Company
643 Magazine Street, 70130-3477
Telephone: 504-586-1200
Fax: 504-596-2800
TDD: (504) 596-2728
Telex: 584327
Cable Address: "MACSTAC"
Mailing Address: P.O. Box 60643, New Orleans, Louisiana, 70160-0643
Email: @mcglinchey.com *URL:* http://www.mcglinchey.com
Dallas, Texas Office: 2777 Stemmons Freeway, Suite 925, 75207-2401.
Telephone: 214-860-9700.
Fax: 214-860-9750.
Houston, Texas Office: 2727 Allen Parkway, Suite 1900, 77019.
Telephone: 713-520-1900.
Fax: 713-520-1025.
Baton Rouge, Louisiana Office: Ninth Floor, One American Place, 70825-0001.
Telephone: 504-383-9000.
Fax: 504-343-3076.
Jackson, Mississippi Office: Suite 1200, SkyTel Centre, 200 South Lamar Street, 39201.
Telephone: 601-960-8400.
Fax: 601-960-8406.
Lake Providence, Louisiana Office: 405 Morgan Street, 71254-2691.
Telephone: 318-559-1200.
Fax: 318-559-0609.
Monroe, Louisiana Office: Dean ONB Tower, 130 Desiard Street, Suite 807, 71201.
Telephone: 318-651-0807.
Fax: 318-651-0809.

MEMBERS OF FIRM

Frank Voelker, Jr., (P.C.)
J. Patrick Beauchamp
Susan M. Tyler
R. Keith Colvin
Joyce L. Schenewerk

ASSOCIATE

Julia Haynes Terry (Not admitted in LA)

MEMBERS OF FIRM

Michael H. Rubin (Resident, Baton Rouge Office)
Robert Marshall Grodner (Resident, Baton Rouge Office)
William S. Mendenhall (Resident, Jackson Office)
Samuel A. Bacot (Resident, Baton Rouge Office)
Richard A. Fogel (Resident, Dallas Office)
James C. Crigler, Jr. (Resident, Lake Providence Office)
S. Jess Sperry (Resident, Baton Rouge Office)

ASSOCIATES

Jolie S. Lenz (Resident, Houston Office)
Claude B. Anello (Resident, Houston Office)
Amanda K. Bishop
F. Sherman Boughton, Jr. (Resident, Lake Providence Office)

For full biographical listings, see the Martindale-Hubbell Law Directory

MIDDLEBERG, RIDDLE & GIANNA (AV)

201 St. Charles Avenue Suite 3100, 70170-3100
Telephone: 504-525-7200
Telecopier: 504-581-5983
Dallas, Texas Office: 2323 Bryan Street, Suite 1600.
Telephone: 214-220-6300;
Telecopier: 214-220-2785.
Austin, Texas Office: 1300 South Mopac Expressway, First Floor.
Telephone: 512-434-8334.
Houston, Texas Office: 7676 Woodway, Suite 325.
Telephone: 713-430-5000.
Telecopier: 713-430-5090.

MEMBERS OF FIRM

Ira Joel Middleberg
Michael Lee Riddle (Not admitted in LA)
Dominic J. Gianna

Paul J. Mirabile
John D. Person
Alan Dean Weinberger
L. Marlene Quarles
Edward T. Suffern, Jr.
Barry H. Grodsky
E. Ralph Lupin
A.J. Herbert, III
Marshall J. Simien, Jr.
Wade P. Webster
Rebecca J. King
Alvin Moon
Ernestine L. Anderson-Trahan
Steven A. Watts
R. Dean Church, Jr.
Michael M. Simpson
Michele A. Engnath

For full biographical listings, see the Martindale-Hubbell Law Directory

STEEG AND O'CONNOR, L.L.C. (AV)

Suite 3201, Bank One Center, 201 St. Charles Avenue, 70170
Telephone: 504-582-1199
Fax: 504-582-1240

(See Next Column)

STEEG AND O'CONNOR L.L.C., *New Orleans—Continued*

Moise S. Steeg, Jr.
Robert M. Steeg
Charles L. Stern, Jr.
Randy Opotowsky
Rose H. Delaney
Rose McCabe Le Breton
Jon F. Leyens, Jr.
Sally Dunlap Fleming

OF COUNSEL

Henry F. O'Connor, Jr.
Bernhardt C. Heebe
Louis M. Jones

Reference: Whitney National Bank of New Orleans.

For full biographical listings, see the Martindale-Hubbell Law Directory

*SHREVEPORT,** Caddo Parish

BARLOW AND HARDTNER L.C. (AV)

Tenth Floor, Louisiana Tower, 401 Edwards Street, 71101-3289
Telephone: 318-227-1131
Telecopier: 318-227-1141
Mailing Address: P.O. Box 8, Shreveport, Louisiana, 71161-0008

Quintin T. Hardtner, III
Malcolm S. Murchison
Stephen E. Ramey
Jay A. Greenleaf

Representative Clients: The Brinkmann Corporation; General Electric Co.; Ivan Smith Furniture Company; Transcontinental Tower, L.C.; NorAm Energy Corp. (formerly Arkla, Inc.); Central and South West Company; Panhandle Eastern Corp.; Pennzoil Producing Co.; Ashland Oil, Inc.

For Complete List of Firm Personnel, See General Section

For full biographical listings, see the Martindale-Hubbell Law Directory

BLANCHARD, WALKER, O'QUIN & ROBERTS, A PROFESSIONAL LAW CORPORATION (AV)

Fourteenth Floor, Premier Bank Tower, 400 Texas Street, P.O. Drawer 1126, 71101
Telephone: 318-221-6858
Fax: 318-227-2967
Email: BWOR@BWOR.com
Bossier City, Louisiana Office: 2285 Benton Road, Suite B-201.
Telephone: 318-742-9255.
Fax: 318-742-9210.

Wm. Timothy Allen, III
Reginald E. Cassibry
J. David Garrett
Robert W. Johnson
Julie Van Thof

For Complete List of Firm Personnel, See General Section

For full biographical listings, see the Martindale-Hubbell Law Directory

HAMILTON, PEATROSS, WRIGHT & POU (AV)

One Bellemead Centre, 6425 Youree Drive, Suite 140, 71105
Telephone: 318-797-3900
Toll Free: 800-555-4310
Fax: 318-795-3855
Email: kwright@utla.com *URL:* http://www.utla.com

George A. Hamilton
William C. Peatross
Kenneth P. Wright
John W. Pou

Terry Michael Hays
Cynthia W. Shemwell
Charlotte Guilbeaux

For full biographical listings, see the Martindale-Hubbell Law Directory

WEEMS, SCHIMPF, HAYTER, GILSOUL & CARMOUCHE, (APLC) (AV)

912 Kings Highway, 71104
Telephone: 318-222-2100
Facsimile: 318-226-5100
URL: http://www.weems-law.com

Ronald R. Weems
John O. Hayter, III

Representative Clients: First American Title Insurance Company; Lawyer's Title Insurance Company; Hibernia National Bank; Barksdale Federal Credit Union; Farm Credit Bank of Texas; Georgia-Pacific Corporation; Louisiana Title Company; Patterson Insurance; Stewart Title Guaranty Company.

For full biographical listings, see the Martindale-Hubbell Law Directory

SLIDELL, St. Tammany Parish

PATRICK J. BERRIGAN (P.L.C.) (AV)

770 Gause Boulevard, Suite B, P.O. Box 220, 70459
Telephone: 504-641-1070
Fax: 504-641-1073
Email: pjbplc@comm.net

Patrick J. Berrigan

Jenifer B. Besh
Judith Otero
Rodney J. Lacoste, Jr.
John W. Lindner, II

(See Next Column)

OF COUNSEL

Stephen A. Duczer

For full biographical listings, see the Martindale-Hubbell Law Directory

*WINNFIELD,** Winn Parish

SIMMONS AND DERR (AV)

Simmons Building, Church Street, P.O. Box 525, 71483
Telephone: 318-628-3951
Fax: 318-648-0644

MEMBERS OF FIRM

Kermit M. Simmons
Jacque D. Derr

Reference: Bank of Winnfield & Trust Co.

For full biographical listings, see the Martindale-Hubbell Law Directory

MAINE

*AUGUSTA,** Kennebec Co.

PIERCE ATWOOD (AV)

77 Winthrop Street, 04330
Telephone: 207-622-6311
Fax: 207-623-9367
Email: info@PierceAtwood.com *URL:* http://www.pierceatwood.com
Portland, Maine Office: One Monument Square.
Telephone: 207-791-1100.
Fax: 207-791-1350.
Newburyport, Massachusetts Office: 6 Harris Street.
Telephone: 978-465-9599.
Fax: 978-465-9945.

MEMBER OF FIRM

Warren E. Winslow, Jr.

ASSOCIATE

Helen L. Edmonds

For Complete List of Firm Personnel, See General Section

For full biographical listings, see the Martindale-Hubbell Law Directory

*BANGOR,** Penobscot Co.

EATON, PEABODY, BRADFORD & VEAGUE, P.A. (AV)

Fleet Center-Exchange Street, P.O. Box 1210, 04402-1210
Telephone: 207-947-0111
Telecopier: 207-942-3040
Email: eaton@eatonpeabody.com *URL:* http://www.eatonpeabody.com
Augusta, Maine Office: 77 Sewall Street, Suite 3000.
Telephone: 207-622-3747.
Telecopier: 207-622-9732.
Blue Hill, Maine Office: One East Blue Hill Road.
Telephone: 207-374-2812.
Telecopier: 207-374-2548.
Brunswick, Maine Office: 167 Park Row.
Telephone: 207-729-1144.
Telecopier: 207-729-1140.
Dover-Foxcroft, Maine Office: 30 East Main Street.
Telephone: 207-564-8378.
Telecopier: 207-564-7059.

Edward D. Leonard, III
Douglas M. Smith (Dover-Foxcroft and Augusta Offices)
John A. Cunningham (Resident, Brunswick Office)
Karen A. Huber
Jonathan B. Huntington (Resident, Dover-Foxcroft Office)
Lorena R. Rush

OF COUNSEL

Martin L. Wilk (Resident, Brunswick Office)

For Complete List of Firm Personnel, See General Section

For full biographical listings, see the Martindale-Hubbell Law Directory

GROSS, MINSKY, MOGUL & SINGAL, P.A. (AV)

Key Plaza, 23 Water Street, P.O. Box 917, 04402-0917
Telephone: 207-942-4644; 800-274-7124
Telecopier: 207-942-3699
Email: law@gmms.com

Edward I. Gross (1912-1999)
Jules L. Mogul (1930-1994)
George Z. Singal
Louis H. Kornreich
George C. Schelling
Edward W. Gould
Steven J. Mogul
James R. Wholly
Daniel A. Pileggi
Philip K. Clarke

Wayne P. Libhart (Retired)
Sandra L. Rothera
James S. Nixon

(See Next Column)

GROSS, MINSKY, MOGUL & SINGAL P.A.—*Continued*

OF COUNSEL

Norman Minsky

Approved Attorneys For: First American Title Insurance Co.; Lawyers Title Insurance Co.
Agent For: First American Title Insurance Co.; Lawyers Title Insurance Co.

For full biographical listings, see the Martindale-Hubbell Law Directory

BAR HARBOR, Hancock Co.

FENTON, CHAPMAN, FENTON, SMITH & KANE, P.A. (AV)

109 Main Street, P.O. Box B, 04609
Telephone: 207-288-3331
Fax: 207-288-9326
Email: fentonlawfirm@acadia.net *URL:* http://www.lawyers.com/fcfs&klaw

William Fenton
Douglas B. Chapman
Nathaniel R. Fenton
Chadbourn H. Smith

Margaret T. Jeffery

Reference: Bar Harbor Banking and Trust Co.

For Complete List of Firm Personnel, See General Section

For full biographical listings, see the Martindale-Hubbell Law Directory

*ELLSWORTH,** Hancock Co.

HALE & HAMLIN (AV)

10 State Street, P.O. Box 729, 04605
Telephone: 207-667-2561
Telefax: 207-667-8790
Email: barry@halehamlin.com *URL:* http://www.halehamlin.com

Eugene Hale (1836-1918)
Hannibal E. Hamlin (1858-1938)
Philip R. Lovell (1899-1961)
Charles J. Hurley (1908-1981)
Atherton Fuller (1918-1998)

MEMBERS OF FIRM

Barry K. Mills
Dale L. Worthen
Jeffrey W. Jones
Melissa Moll

LEGAL SUPPORT PERSONNEL

Donna L. Jancewicz (Paralegal)
Sylvia Joy (Paralegal)

Approved Attorneys for: Lawyers Title Insurance Corp.

For full biographical listings, see the Martindale-Hubbell Law Directory

ROSS & FERM, LLC (AV)

204 Main Street, P.O. Box 1123, 04605
Telephone: 207-667-1373
Fax: 207-667-3427
URL: http://www.lawyers.com/ross&ferm

Michael L. Ross
William N. Ferm

ASSOCIATES

William B. Entwisle
Jessica L. Shiok

For full biographical listings, see the Martindale-Hubbell Law Directory

*PORTLAND,** Cumberland Co.

BENNETT BENNETT AND TROIANO, P.A. (AV)

Suite 300, 121 Middle Street, P.O. Box 7799, 04112-7799
Telephone: 207-773-4775
Telecopier: 207-774-2366
Email: lawyers@bennettlegal.com *URL:* http://www.bennettlegal.com

Herbert H. Bennett (1928-1992)
Peter Bennett
Jeffrey Bennett
Joseph A. Troiano
Frederick B. Finberg

Julie A. Boesky

OF COUNSEL

Jonathan M. Dunitz

Counsel for: Associated Grocers of New England; General Star Indemnity Company; Coca Cola Bottling Company of Northern New England, Inc.; Northern Utilities/Bay State Gas; Pratt & Whitney (Division of United Technologies); Primerica Financial Services (Citigroup); Sprague Energy (C.H. Sprague & Son); Perrier Group of America, Inc.; Lepage Bakeries, Inc. (Country Kitchen); Texaco, Inc.

For full biographical listings, see the Martindale-Hubbell Law Directory

JENSEN BAIRD GARDNER & HENRY (AV)

Ten Free Street, P.O. Box 4510, 04112-4510
Telephone: 207-775-7271
Telecopier: 207-775-7935
Email: info@jbgh.com *URL:* http://www.jbgh.com
York County Office: 11 Main Street, Suite 4, Kennebunk, Maine, 04043.
Telephone: 207-985-4676.
Telecopier: 207-985-4932.

MEMBERS OF FIRM

Walter E. Webber
Kenneth M. Cole, III
David J. Jones (Resident, York County Office)
Ronald A. Epstein
Leslie E. Lowry, III
Richard H. Spencer, Jr.

OF COUNSEL

John D. Bradford (Resident, York County Office)

ASSOCIATE

Suzanne R. Scott

Representative Clients: General Motors Acceptance Corp.; York Insurance Co.; Maine Mall; Key Bank of Maine; Commonwealth Land Title Insurance Co.; Augusta Mall; Shaw's Supermarkets; Peoples Heritage.

For Complete List of Firm Personnel, See General Section

For full biographical listings, see the Martindale-Hubbell Law Directory

PIERCE ATWOOD (AV)

One Monument Square, 04101
Telephone: 207-791-1100
Fax: 207-791-1350
Email: info@PierceAtwood.com *URL:* http://www.pierceatwood.com
Augusta, Maine Office: 77 Winthrop Street.
Telephone: 207-622-6311.
Fax: 207-623-9367.
Newburyport, Massachusetts Office: 6 Harris Street.
Telephone: 978-465-9599.
Fax: 978-465-9945.

MEMBERS OF FIRM

Dennis C. Keeler
Elaine S. Falender
Judith A. Fletcher Woodbury

ASSOCIATES

Helen L. Edmonds (Resident, Augusta Office)
Thomas A. Loureiro

COUNSEL

Jacquelyn M. Kurz

For Complete List of Firm Personnel, See General Section

For full biographical listings, see the Martindale-Hubbell Law Directory

PRETI, FLAHERTY, BELIVEAU, PACHIOS & HALEY, LLC (AV)

One City Center, P.O. Box 9546, 04112-9546
Telephone: 207-791-3000
Telecopier: 207-791-3111
Email: admin@preti.com *URL:* http://www.preti.com
Augusta, Maine Office: 45 Memorial Circle, P.O. Box 1058, 04332-1058.
Telephone: 207-623-5300.
Telefax: 207-623-2914.
Bath, Maine Office: Thirty Front Street, P.O. Box 665, 04530-0665.
Telephone: 207-443-5576.
Telefax: 207-443-6665.

MEMBERS OF FIRM

Michael J. Gentile (Augusta Office)
Eric P. Stauffer
James C. Pitney, Jr. (Augusta Office)
Dennis C. Sbrega
Estelle A. Lavoie
Susan E. LoGiudice
Michael L. Sheehan
Jeanne T. Cohn-Connor

COUNSEL

Naomi Sakamoto

ASSOCIATE

Bonnie L. Martinolich

Representative Clients: Blethen-Maine Newspapers, Inc.; KeyBank National Assn.; Bethel Station.

For Complete List of Firm Personnel, See General Section

For full biographical listings, see the Martindale-Hubbell Law Directory

TROUBH, HEISLER & PIAMPIANO, P.C. (AV)

511 Congress Street, P.O. Box 9711, 04104-5011
Telephone: 207-780-6789
Fax: 207-774-2339
Email: info@thplaw.com

(See Next Column)

TROUBH, HEISLER & PIAMPIANO P.C., *Portland—Continued*

William B. Troubh
Edwin A. Heisler
Robert J. Piampiano
Kevin M. Gillis
Michael P. Boyd
Thomas E. Getchell
Michael Richards
William K. McKinley
Daniel F. Gilligan
Paul S. Bulger
John G. Richardson

Daniel R. Felkel
Ann Brandt
John P. Flynn, III

For full biographical listings, see the Martindale-Hubbell Law Directory

LEE D. URBAN (AV)

53 Baxter Boulevard, 04101
Telephone: 207-879-0770 Ext. 109
Fax: 207-773-4873
Email: lurban@stimson.com

VERRILL & DANA, LLP (AV)

One Portland Square, P.O. Box 586, 04112-0586
Telephone: 207-774-4000
Fax: 207-774-7499
Email: advice@verdan.com *URL:* http://www.verdan.com
Augusta, Maine Office: 45 Memorial Circle, P.O. Box 957.
Telephone: 207-623-3889.
Fax: 207-622-3117.
Kennebunk, Maine Office: 403-404 Lafayette Center, P.O. Box 147.
Telephone: 207-985-7193.
Fax: 207-985-3957.
Washington, D.C. Office: 400 North Capitol Street, Suite 585.
Telephone: 202-624-9733.
Fax: 202-393-5218.

OF COUNSEL

Louis A. Wood

MEMBERS OF FIRM

Charles R. Oestreicher
Christopher J. W. Coggeshall
Robert B. Patterson, Jr.
Christopher S. Neagle
James C. Palmer
Mark K. Googins
David C. Boyer, Jr.
Raymond A. Pelletier, Jr.
David L. Galgay, Jr.

ASSOCIATE

Anthony M. Calcagni

Counsel for: ASCAP; Bowdoin College; Fleet Bank; Hannaford Bros. Co.; Maine Blue Cross and Blue Shield; Maine Public Service Co.; Peoples Heritage Bank; Portland Water District.

For Complete List of Firm Personnel, See General Section

For full biographical listings, see the Martindale-Hubbell Law Directory

MARYLAND

*ANNAPOLIS,** Anne Arundel Co.

COUNCIL, BARADEL, KOSMERL & NOLAN, P.A. (AV)

125 West Street, Fourth Floor, P.O. Box 2289, 21404-2289
Telephone: 410-268-6600
Baltimore: 410-269-6190
Washington, D.C.: 301-261-2247
FAX: 410-269-8409
Email: cbkn@cbknlaw.com

Ronald E. Council
Ronald A. Baradel
Wayne T. Kosmerl
James P. Nolan
William F. Flood, III
Kevin M. Schaeffer
Donna McCabe Schaeffer
Frederick C. Sussman

John Naumann Strange
Susan T. Ford
Edwin H. Staples, II
Susan Stobbart Shapiro

OF COUNSEL

George N. Manis
Nicholas Goldsborough

Representative Clients: Anne Arundel County; Annapolis Bank and Trust; Bank of Maryland; State Farm Mutual Automobile Insurance Co.; Annapolis Yacht Club; Annapolis Yacht Sales, Inc.

For full biographical listings, see the Martindale-Hubbell Law Directory

HYATT, PETERS & WEBER (AV)

1919 West Street, P.O. Box 6635, 21401
Telephone: 410-266-0626
Fax: 410-841-5065
Email: info@hyatt.hpwsb.com *URL:* http://www.hpwlaw.com

(See Next Column)

Alan J. Hyatt
Paula J. Peters
Paul J. Weber

ASSOCIATES

Sara H. Arthur
Sharon M. Grosfeld
Gregg M. Weinberg
Jonathan A. Hodgson
John L. Hill
Arlette K. Bright
Bruce F. Bright
(Not admitted in MD)

OF COUNSEL

Steven G. Tyler

For full biographical listings, see the Martindale-Hubbell Law Directory

BENJAMIN MICHAELSON, JR., P.A. (AV)

275 West Street, Suite 216, 21401
Telephone: 410-267-8178
Baltimore: 410-269-6966
Washington, D.C.: 301-261-2889
Fax: 410-267-8072

Benjamin Michaelson, Jr.

Representative Clients: Annapolis Banking and Trust Co.; Crestar Bank MD.

For full biographical listings, see the Martindale-Hubbell Law Directory

P. JAMES UNDERWOOD (AV)

9A Maryland Avenue, P.O. Box 2335, 21404
Telephone: 410-268-4247

Representative Clients: R D K & W Joint Venture; Kaufmann Limited Partnership; W K D & R Real Estate Company; Elanne Corporation.

*BALTIMORE,** (Independent City)

BALLARD SPAHR ANDREWS & INGERSOLL, LLP (AV)

300 East Lombard Street, 19th Floor, 21202-3268
Telephone: 410-528-5600
Fax: 410-528-5650
URL: http://www.ballardspahr.com
Philadelphia, Pennsylvania Office: 1735 Market Street, 51st Floor.
Telephone: 215-665-8500.
Fax: 215-864-8999.
Voorhees, New Jersey Office: Suite 100, 1101 Laurel Oak Drive.
Telephone: 856-627-8555.
Fax: 856-627-1153.
Denver, Colorado Office: Seventeenth Street Plaza Building, Suite 2300, 1225 17th Street.
Telephone: 303-292-2400.
Fax: 303-296-3956.
Salt Lake City, Utah Office: One Utah Center, Suite 1200, 201 South Main Street.
Telephone: 801-531-3000.
Fax: 801-531-3001.
Washington, D.C. Office: Suite 1000 South, 601 13th Street, N.W.
Telephone: 202-661-2200.
Fax: 202-661-2299.
Camden, New Jersey Office: 800 Hudson Square, 5th Floor.
Telephone: 609-541-5577.
Fax: 609-541-8272.

Paul K. Casey
Ronald P. Fish
Morton P. Fisher, Jr.
Sophie Dagenais Goetz
Charles R. Moran
Gregory Reed
Jane Ennis Sheehan
Raymond G. Truitt
Fred Wolf, III

OF COUNSEL

Norman E. Parker, Jr.

COUNSEL

Fran S. Glushakow-Smith

Bruce L. Benshoof
Jon M. Laria
Nicole J. Papa
Jonathan M. Prince

For full biographical listings, see the Martindale-Hubbell Law Directory

GALLAGHER, EVELIUS & JONES, LLP (AV)

Park Charles Suite 400, 218 North Charles Street, 21201
Telephone: 410-727-7702
Facsimile: 410-468-2786
URL: http://www.gejlaw.com

MEMBERS OF FIRM

Francis X. Gallagher (1928-1972)
C. Edward Jones (1908-1999)
John C. Evelius (Retired)
Richard O. Berndt
Thomas N. Biddison, Jr.
Robert R. Kern, Jr.
Saul E. Gilstein
Thomas B. Lewis
Bonnie Abrams Travieso
Stephen A. Goldberg
Linda H. Jones
Jack C. Tranter
Leslie B. Speed
Christopher J. Fritz
David E. Raderman
Peter E. Keith
Nita L. Schultz
Michael W. Skojec
Kathryn Kelley Hoskins

(See Next Column)

GALLAGHER, EVELIUS & JONES LLP—*Continued*

MEMBERS OF FIRM (Continued)

Mark P. Keener
Kevin J. Davidson
Eileen M. Lunga
Lori A. Nicolle
Kenneth S. Gross
Thomas C. Dame

ASSOCIATES

Valarie K. Oulds
Margaret Stevens Jacks
Matthew W. Oakey
Rebecca A. Weaver
Michael J. Henigan
David W. Kinkopf
Paul S. Caiola
Jason W. Gaarder
M. Kirsten Andrews

LEGAL ASSISTANTS

Patricia C. Quayle
Iris T. H. Heath
Connie L. Ennis
Margaret Graff
Margo Gibson Hughes
Jonathan T. Gillis
Brenda J. Heacock
Dwayne L. Rodeheaver

Representative Clients: The Shelter Group; Enterprise Social Investment Corporation; Inner Harbor East Limited Partnerships; The Bozzuto Group; Municipal Mortgages & Equities, LLC.

For full biographical listings, see the Martindale-Hubbell Law Directory

MICHAEL H. MANNES, P.A. (AV)

1 East Franklin Street, 21202-2239
Telephone: 410-752-8090
Fax: 410-752-8099
Email: mmannes@ubmail.ubalt.edu

Michael H. Mannes

For full biographical listings, see the Martindale-Hubbell Law Directory

REDMOND, BURGIN & GUTIERREZ, P.A. (AV)

1301, The Fidelity Building, 210 North Charles Street, 21202
Telephone: 410-752-1555
Fax: 410-752-1064
URL: http://www.RBGLAW.com
Upper Marlboro, Maryland Office: 14746 Main Street.
Telephone: 301-952-1555.

Leonard C. Redmond, III

Bambi Glenn

For Complete List of Firm Personnel, See General Section

For full biographical listings, see the Martindale-Hubbell Law Directory

THOMAS & LIBOWITZ, P.A. (AV)

100 Light Street, Suite 1100, 21202-1053
Telephone: 410-752-2468
Fax: 410-752-2046; 752-2049; 752-0979
Email: thomasandlibowitz.com *URL:* http://www.thomasandlibowitz.com

Steven Anargyros Thomas
John R. Wise

C. Victoria Woodward

Representative Clients: Sinclair Broadcast Group, Inc. (Television and Radio stations); Roy Kirby & Sons, Inc. (Contractor); First Mariner Bank; Scandia Manufacturing Co. Inc. (Defense Contractor); Atlantic Automotive Corp. t/a Heritagge Automotive Group; Candy Express Franchising, Inc.; Wire Spectrum Services (Contractors-Transmission Tower Sites); Acrodyne Communications, Inc.; Alexis Logic Corporation (Software Developers); Selnic Corporation (Electronis Distributors); Liberty Mutual Insurance Company.

For full biographical listings, see the Martindale-Hubbell Law Directory

VENABLE ATTORNEYS AT LAW VENABLE, BAETJER AND HOWARD, LLP (AV)

A Partnership including Professional Corporations
1800 Mercantile Bank & Trust Building, 2 Hopkins Plaza, 21201
Telephone: 410-244-7400
Fax: 410-244-7742
URL: http://www.venable.com
Washington, D.C. Office: Venable, Baetjer, Howard & Civiletti LLP, Suite 1000, 1201 New York Avenue, N.W.
Telephone: 202-962-4800.
Fax: 202-962-8300.
McLean, Virginia Office: Suite 400, 2010 Corporate Ridge.
Telephone: 703-760-1600.
Fax: 703-821-8949.
Rockville, Maryland Office: Suite 500, One Church Street, P. O. Box 1906.
Telephone: 301-217-5600.
Fax: 301-217-5617.
Towson, Maryland Office: 210 Allegheny Avenue, P. O. Box 5517.
Telephone: 410-494-6200.
Fax: 410-821-0147.

(See Next Column)

MEMBERS OF FIRM

Russell Ronald Reno, Jr. (P.C.)
Thomas P. Perkins, III (P.C.)
James A. Cole
Benjamin R. Civiletti (P.C.) (Also at Washington, D.C. and Towson, Maryland Offices)
John B. Howard (Resident, Towson, Maryland Office)
David E. Belcher
Roger W. Titus (Resident, Rockville, Maryland Office)
Jan K. Guben (Also at Washington, D. C Office)
James D. Wright (P.C.)
John H. Zink, III (Resident, Towson, Maryland Office)
John G. Milliken (Not admitted in MD; Resident, McLean, Virginia Office)
Paul T. Glasgow (Resident, Rockville, Maryland Office)
Joseph C. Wich, Jr. (Resident, Towson, Maryland Office)
Sondra Harans Block (Resident, Rockville, Maryland Office)
David G. Lane (Resident, McLean, Virginia Office)
James K. Archibald (Also at Washington, D.C. Office)
Edward L. Wender (P.C.)
George F. Pappas (Also at Washington, D.C. Office)
Ellen F. Dyke (Not admitted in MD; Resident, McLean, Virginia Office)
James A. Dunbar (Resident, Towson, Maryland Office)
Robert A. Hoffman (Resident, Towson, Maryland Office)
J. Michael Brennan (Resident, Towson, Maryland Office)
Kevin L. Shepherd
Elizabeth Corr Smedley (Not admitted in MD; Resident, McLean, Virginia Office)
Michael W. Robinson (Resident, McLean, Virginia Office)
M. Jay Yurow (Not admitted in MD; Resident, McLean, Virginia Office)
Courtney G. Capute
John T. Prisbe
Sandra L. Howard
Vicki Margolis (Also at Washington, D.C. Office)

OF COUNSEL

Judith A. Armold (Also at Washington, D.C. Office)

ASSOCIATE

Patricia A. Malone (Resident, Towson, Maryland Office)

For Complete List of Firm Personnel, See General Section

For full biographical listings, see the Martindale-Hubbell Law Directory

*BEL AIR,** Harford Co.

BROWN, BROWN & BROWN, A PROFESSIONAL ASSOCIATION (AV)

200 South Main Street, 21014
Telephone: 410-838-5500
Baltimore: 410-879-2220
Fax: 410-893-0402

A. Freeborn Brown (1915-1998)
T. Carroll Brown
Augustus F. Brown
Albert J. A. Young

Harold Douglas Norton
Christopher R. vanRoden
David E. Carey

Attorneys for: Baltimore Gas & Electric Co.; Chesapeake & Potomac Telephone Co.; Aberdeen Proving Ground Federal Credit Union; First National Bank of Maryland; Bell Atlantic Mobile Systems; First Harbor Securities; Maryland Portable Concrete, Inc.
Approved Counsel for: The Chicago Title Insurance Co. of Maryland, Inc.

For full biographical listings, see the Martindale-Hubbell Law Directory

STARK & KEENAN, A PROFESSIONAL ASSOCIATION (AV)

30 Office Street, 21014
Telephone: 410-838-5522
Baltimore: 410-879-2222
Fax: 410-879-0688
Email: wstarkee@aol.com
Havre de Grace Office: "The Old Ordinary" 100 St. John Street, 21078.
Telephone: 410-939-0100.

Elwood V. Stark, Jr.
Charles B. Keenan, Jr.
Edwin G. Carson
Judith Cline-Silverstein
Gregory A. Szoka
Robert S. Lynch
Paul W. Ishak

Claire Prin Blomquist
Lawrence F. Kreis, Jr.
Craig H. DeRan

For full biographical listings, see the Martindale-Hubbell Law Directory

BETHESDA, Montgomery Co.

STEVEN A. LOEWY, P.A. (AV)

3 Bethesda Metro Center, Suite 700, 20814
Telephone: 301-664-8438
Fax: 301-652-6240
Email: steveloewy@aol.com *URL:* http://www.lawyers.com/steveloewy

Steven A. Loewy

For full biographical listings, see the Martindale-Hubbell Law Directory

Bethesda—Continued

POPPLETON, GARRETT & POLOTT, P.C. (AV)

6430 Rockledge Drive Suite 500, 20817
Telephone: 301-493-9800
Fax: 301-493-6585
Email: lawfirm@pgplaw.com
Fairfax, Virginia Office: 10560 Main Street, Suite 111, 22030-7182.
Telephone: 703-525-0240.

Miller John Poppleton, Jr.
Dwayne L. Garrett
Andrew R. Polott
Michael P. Chabrow (Not admitted in MD)
Richard B. Hill
Douglas A. Rubel

Richard C. Sterrn

OF COUNSEL

Stuart H. Sorkin, P.C. (Not admitted in MD)
Ellen A. Rubel

For full biographical listings, see the Martindale-Hubbell Law Directory

TENENBAUM & SAAS, P.C. (AV)

4330 East-West Highway, Suite 1150, 20814
Telephone: 301-961-5300
Fax: 301-961-5305
Email: MTENENBAUM@TSPCLAW.COM

Mark S. Tenenbaum
J. Richard Saas
Jeffrey M. Snyder
Bradshaw Rost

Caroline Hopkins Semancik
John C. Wetzel
Thomas Ward Myers, Jr
Steven G. Shapiro (Not admitted in MD)

For full biographical listings, see the Martindale-Hubbell Law Directory

*EASTON,** Talbot Co.

EWING, DIETZ, TURNER & KEHOE, PROFESSIONAL ASSOCIATION (AV)

16 South Washington Street, P.O. Box 1146, 21601
Telephone: 410-822-1988
Fax: 410-820-5053
URL: http://www.edtklaw.com

L. Clark Ewing (1919-1998)
Philip E. L. Dietz, Jr.
Christopher B. Kehoe
John F. Hall
Karen M. Kaludis
Stephen H. Kehoe

Sharon M. Shilling

OF COUNSEL

Henry P. Turner

References: The Talbot Bank of Easton, Maryland; St. Michaels Bank.

For full biographical listings, see the Martindale-Hubbell Law Directory

*FREDERICK,** Frederick Co.

OFFUTT, HORMAN, BURDETTE & FREY, P.A. (AV)

Offutt Building, 22 West Second Street, 21701
Telephone: 301-662-8248;
Hagerstown: 301-293-6032;
Montgomery Co., D.C./Va. line: 301-948-5633
Fax: 301-663-8968

W. Jerome Offutt
Amos A. Holter
John N. Burdette
George T. Horman
Charles Burton Frey

Lisa Anne Rudy
Chris M. May

Representative Clients: Donald B. Rice Tire Co., Inc.; Meadows Van and Storage Co.; Central Maryland Farm Credit, ACA; QUADS Trust Co.; Frederick Aviation, Inc.
Local Counsel: St. James Servicing Corp.; First National Bank of Maryland.
Co-Counsel for: Central Maryland Farm Credit, ACA.
Reference: Frederick Branch of First National Bank of Maryland.

For full biographical listings, see the Martindale-Hubbell Law Directory

GREENBELT, Prince Georges Co.

FOSSETT & BRUGGER, CHARTERED (AV)

6404 Ivy Lane, Suite 720, 20770
Telephone: 301-486-1900
Telecopier: 301-486-0999
La Plata, Maryland Office: 105 LaGrange Avenue, P.O. Box F.
Telephone: 301-934-4200.

(See Next Column)

George A. Brugger
Clarence L. Fossett
Nancy L. Slepicka
William M. Shipp
John C. Fredrickson
Mary A. Zambri
Eric M. Elmore
Mark S. Petrauskas
John A. Giannetti, Jr.

LEGAL SUPPORT PERSONNEL

Dean Armstrong (Consulting Land Planner)

Representative Clients: Cafritz Companies; Citicorp Real Estate, Inc.; Coscan Brookfield Homes; Crestar Bank; The Driggs Corp.; Kettler Brothers; Kiplinger Washington Editors; The Mutual Life Insurance Company of New York; Richmond-American Homes; The Simon DeBartolo Group.

For full biographical listings, see the Martindale-Hubbell Law Directory

STANLEY S. PICKETT (AV)

Suite 414 Capital Office Park, 6411 Ivy Lane, 20770
Telephone: 301-513-0613
Fax: 301-513-0618
Email: lossp@intr.net

Stanley Sinclair Pickett

ASSOCIATES

Gordon J. Brumback
Stacy S. Pickett Trimble

LEGAL SUPPORT PERSONNEL

Vivian A. Wolfe (Paralegal)

Representative Clients: B.F. Saul Co.; McDonald and Eudy Printers, Inc.; Condominium Management, Inc.; Long & Foster Realtors; Mitron Systems Corp.; Glenanden Housing Authority; Community Associations, Inc.; Hagmer Management, Inc.; Quantum Management, Inc.

For full biographical listings, see the Martindale-Hubbell Law Directory

OCEAN CITY, Worcester Co.

WILLIAMS, HAMMOND, MOORE, SHOCKLEY & HARRISON, P.A. (AV)

3509 Coastal Highway, P.O. Box 739, 21842
Telephone: 410-289-3553
Fax: 410-289-4157
Email: whmsh@shore.intercom.net
Berlin, Maryland Office: 11070 Cathell Road, Suite 19.
Telephone: 410-641-8080.
Fax: 410-641-8282.

Marcus J. Williams (1923-1995)
Edward H. Hammond, Jr.
Joseph E. Moore
Raymond C. Shockley
Joseph G. Harrison, Jr.

J. Richard Collins
Regan James Reno Smith
Jeffrey A. Pilchard
Brian D. Shockley
Olivia Harrison Phillips

For full biographical listings, see the Martindale-Hubbell Law Directory

RIVERDALE, Prince Georges Co.

MEYERS, BILLINGSLEY, RODBELL & ROSENBAUM, P.A. (AV)

Suite 400 Berkshire Building, 6801 Kenilworth Avenue, 20737-1385
Telephone: 301-699-5800
Fax: 301-779-5746
Email: mbrrlaw@martindalemail.com
Annapolis, Maryland Office: 95 Cathedral Street, Suite 100, 21401.
Telephone: 410-267-6670.
Fax: 410-267-8222.

William V. Meyers
Robert H. Rosenbaum

Reference: First National Bank of Maryland.

For Complete List of Firm Personnel, See General Section

For full biographical listings, see the Martindale-Hubbell Law Directory

*ROCKVILLE,** Montgomery Co.

CHEN, WALSH, TECLER & MCCABE, L.L.P. (AV)

Suite 300, 200-A Monroe Street, 20850
Telephone: 301-279-9500
Fax: 301-294-5195
Email: cwtm@radix.net

MEMBERS OF FIRM

William James Chen, Jr.
John Burgess Walsh, Jr.
Kenneth B. Tecler
John F. McCabe, Jr.

For Complete List of Firm Personnel, See General Section

For full biographical listings, see the Martindale-Hubbell Law Directory

Rockville—Continued

RIDGWAY AND GRIFFIN, CHARTERED (AV)

6177 Executive Boulevard, 20852
Telephone: 301-468-2545
Fax: 301-468-3538
Email: jgriffin@ltic.com
Bethesda, Maryland Office: 7250 Woodmont Avenue, Suite 300.
Telephone: 301-654-2560.
Fax: 301-654-0325.

Richard C. Ridgway
James M. Griffin
Michael C. Ridgway

Mark P. Kestner
Colleen Smyth Cogan

For full biographical listings, see the Martindale-Hubbell Law Directory

STEIN, SPERLING, BENNETT, DE JONG, DRISCOLL, GREENFEIG & METRO, P.C. (AV)

25 West Middle Lane, 20850-2204
Telephone: 301-340-2020; 800-435-5230
Telecopier: 301-340-8217
Email: lawfirm@steinsperling.com
Falls Church, Virginia Office: 6245 Leesburg Pike, Suite 140, 22044.
Telephone: 703-237-0500.
Telecopier: 703-534-2899.

Jeffrey M. Schwaber
Donald N. Sperling

William J. Scott

For Complete List of Firm Personnel, See General Section

For full biographical listings, see the Martindale-Hubbell Law Directory

*SALISBURY,** Wicomico Co.

ADKINS, POTTS & SMETHURST, L.L.P. (AV)

Suite 600, One Plaza East, P.O. Box 4247, 21803-4247
Telephone: 410-749-0161
Fax: 410-749-5021

MEMBERS OF FIRM

Raymond Stevens Smethurst, Jr.
Robert B. Taylor

Representative Clients: Campbell Soup Company; Commonwealth Land Title Co.; Delmarva Power & Light Co.; G. E. Capital Mortgage Services, Inc.; Lawyers' Title Insurance Corp.; Mellon Bank (DE); PNC Bank; Peninsula Bank; Shopco Group; WBOC-TV.

For full biographical listings, see the Martindale-Hubbell Law Directory

SILVER SPRING, Montgomery Co.

COGGINS, HARMAN & HEWITT (AV)

A Partnership of Professional Corporations
8905 Fairview Road, Suite 600, 20910
Telephone: 301-587-2880
Facsimile: 301-495-4990
Email: CHHlaw587@aol.com
Washington, D.C. Office: Suite 330, G Street Lobby, 655 15th Street, N.W.
Falls Church, Virginia Office: 254 North Washington Street.

William N. Coggins
John H. Harman
William E. Hewitt
John F. Davis

OF COUNSEL

Dale E. Duncan (Not admitted in MD)

For full biographical listings, see the Martindale-Hubbell Law Directory

GINGELL & JENKINS, P.C. (AV)

Suite 506 Wheaton Plaza South, 11160 Veirs Mill Road, 20902
Telephone: 301-949-0100
Telecopier: 301-949-0467
Email: rgingdjen@aol.com *URL:* http://www.lawyers.com/gingelljenkins

Robert A. Gingell
Donn K. Jenkins

LEGAL SUPPORT PERSONNEL

Karen Thompson
Paula Brock (Real Estate Paralegal)

Representative Clients: Air Flow Co. (Industrial Air Conditioning); Bethesda Realty Co.; Photo Science, Inc.
References: Sovran Bank; First National Bank of Maryland (Rockville, Maryland, Branch); Signet Bank Maryland.

For full biographical listings, see the Martindale-Hubbell Law Directory

LINOWES AND BLOCHER LLP (AV)

Suite 1000, 1010 Wayne Avenue, 20910-5600
Telephone: 301-588-8580
Telecopier: 301-495-9044
TTY/TDD: 301-588-3380
Email: inbox@linowes-law.com *URL:* http://www.linowes-law.com
Washington, D.C. Office: Suite 302, 1150 17th Street, N.W.
Telephone: 202-293-8510.
Telecopier: 202-293-8513.
Greenbelt, Maryland Office: Suite 202, 6411 Ivy Lane.
Telephone: 301-982-3382.
Telecopier: 301-982-0595.
Annapolis, Maryland Office: 145 Main Street.
Telephone: 410-268-0881.
Telecopier: 301-261-2603.
Frederick, Maryland Office: 228 West Patrick Street.
Telephone: 301-695-0244.
Telecopier: 301-663-6656.
Columbia, Maryland Office: Suite B215, 10015 Old Columbia Road.
Telephone: 410-312-5457.
Fax: 410-290-5285.

MEMBERS OF FIRM

David M. Cohen
Andrew M. Goldstein
Myles Hannan
William M. Hoffman, Jr.
John L. Hollingshead
Douglas M. Irvin
Andrew L. Isaacson
Midgett S. Parker, Jr. (Resident Partner, Greenbelt, Maryland office)
Raymond B. Via, Jr.
Roger D. Winston
James B. Witkin
Richard M. Zeidman

ASSOCIATES

John A. Elmendorf
Bruce C. Johnson
Lella Amiss E. Pape (Not admitted in MD)

For Complete List of Firm Personnel, See General Section

For full biographical listings, see the Martindale-Hubbell Law Directory

*TOWSON,** Baltimore Co.

VENABLE ATTORNEYS AT LAW VENABLE, BAETJER AND HOWARD, LLP (AV)

A Partnership including Professional Corporations
210 Allegheny Avenue, P.O. Box 5517, 21204
Telephone: 410-494-6200
Fax: 410-821-0147
URL: http://www.venable.com
Baltimore, Maryland Office: 1800 Mercantile Bank & Trust Building, 2 Hopkins Plaza.
Telephone: 410-244-7400.
Fax: 410-244-7742.
Washington, D.C. Office: Venable, Baetjer, Howard & Civiletti LLP, Suite 1000, 1201 New York Avenue, N.W.
Telephone: 202-962-4800.
Fax: 202-962-8300.
McLean, Virginia Office: Suite 400, 2010 Corporate Ridge.
Telephone: 703-760-1600.
Fax: 703-821-8949.
Rockville, Maryland Office: Suite 500, One Church Street, P. O. Box 1906.
Telephone: 301-217-5600.
Fax: 301-217-5617.

PARTNERS

Benjamin R. Civiletti (P.C.) (Also at Washington, D.C. and Baltimore, Maryland Offices)
John B. Howard
John H. Zink, III
Joseph C. Wich, Jr.
Robert A. Hoffman
J. Michael Brennan

ASSOCIATE

Patricia A. Malone

For Complete List of Firm Personnel, See General Section

For full biographical listings, see the Martindale-Hubbell Law Directory

*UPPER MARLBORO,** Prince Georges Co.

KNIGHT, MANZI, NUSSBAUM & LAPLACA, P.C. (AV)

14440 Old Mill Road, 20772
Telephone: 301-952-0100
Annapolis/Baltimore: 410-792-3786
Fax: 301-952-0221

William E. Knight
Robert A. Manzi
Ronald M. Miller
William C. Brennan, Jr.
Harry J. Trainor, Jr.
Andrew W. Nussbaum
Raymond G. LaPlaca
John F. Shay, Jr.
Sheldon L. Gnatt
Daniel A. LaPlaca
Gail Borjeson Viens
Roger C. Thomas
Monica M. Haley-Pierson
Daniel F. Lynch III
Norman D. Rivera

(See Next Column)

KNIGHT, MANZI, NUSSBAUM & LAPLACA P.C., *Upper Marlboro—Continued*

Robert L. Lombardo
Amy B. Glaser
Brent M. Ahalt
Terry L. Bell

Representative Clients: Washington Homes; Caruso Homes; Chesapeake Custom Homes; Miller and Smith Land, Inc.; First Washington REIT; Curtis Properties; Prince George's Plaza; Carrollton Enterprises; Albert Turner; Southland Corp.

For full biographical listings, see the Martindale-Hubbell Law Directory

*WESTMINSTER,** Carroll Co.

WALSH & FISHER, A PROFESSIONAL ASSOCIATION (AV)

179 East Main Street, 21157
Telephone: 410-848-9200; 876-2135
Telecopier: 410-848-9313
Email: wandf@qis.net

D. Eugene Walsh (1895-1980)
Charles O. Fisher
Charles O. Fisher, Jr.
David B. Weisgerber

Representative Clients: Genstar Stone Products Co., Conewago Contractors, Inc.; Westminster Bank and Trust Co.; Carroll County General Hospital, Inc.; Adams County National Bank.

For full biographical listings, see the Martindale-Hubbell Law Directory

MASSACHUSETTS

ACTON, Middlesex Co.

WILSON & ORCUTT, P.C. (AV)

201 Great Road, 01720
Telephone: 978-264-4770
Telecopier: 978-263-7142
Email: wilcutt@wilsonorcutt.com *URL:* http://www.wilsonorcutt.com

MEMBER OF FIRM

Richard M. Cotter

ASSOCIATE

Christine Connolly Morgan

For full biographical listings, see the Martindale-Hubbell Law Directory

ARLINGTON, Middlesex Co.

LAW OFFICE OF WILLIAM JOSEPH GRANNAN (AV)

Suite 408, 22 Mill Street, 02174
Telephone: 781-646-3200
Fax: 781-643-1126
Email: wjpg@ix.netcom.com *URL:* http://www.lawyers.com/williamjosephgrannan

For full biographical listings, see the Martindale-Hubbell Law Directory

*BOSTON,** Suffolk Co.

ADELSON, GOLDEN, LORIA & SIMONS, P.C. (AV)

Two Center Plaza, 02108
Telephone: 617-227-3730
Fax: 617-227-3353

Stephen M. Adelson
Neil D. Golden
Martin A. Loria
Gary P. Sanginario
Leonard M. Simons
Lisa S. Weisman

Michael H. Arwe
James A. Kelley
Amy Rothfeld Fiorino
Michael D. MacClary
Maurice Henry Sullivan, III

OF COUNSEL

Jodi M. Landau

For full biographical listings, see the Martindale-Hubbell Law Directory

BARRON & STADFELD, P.C. (AV)

50 Staniford Street, Suite 200, 02114
Telephone: 617-723-9800
Telecopier: 617-523-8359
Email: barron@barronstad.com *URL:* HTTP://WWW.BARRONSTAD.COM
Hyannis, Massachusetts Office: 258 Winter Street.
Telephone: 617-778-6622.

Thomas V. Bennett
Julie Taylor Moran
Joseph G. Butler

For Complete List of Firm Personnel, See General Section

For full biographical listings, see the Martindale-Hubbell Law Directory

BERNKOPF, GOODMAN & BASEMAN LLP (AV)

125 Summer Street, 02110-1621
Telephone: 617-790-3000
Telecopier: 617-790-3300
URL: http://www.bgblaw.com

MEMBERS OF FIRM

Abraham K. Cohen (1891-1957)
Max E. Bernkopf (1919-1967)
Sylvan A. Goodman (1935-1981)
Kenneth M. Goldberg
Alan J. Grace
Marvin N. Geller
Neil R. Markson
Gary P. Lilienthal
James B. Fox
Peter B. McGlynn
Sheryl C. Starr
Richard B. Michaud
Lydia G. Chesnick
Martin C. Pomeroy
Eric R. Allon
David L. Doyle
John B. Harkavy
James D. Friedman

OF COUNSEL

Harris I. Baseman

ASSOCIATES

Bruce D. Levin
Richard P. Bennett
Michael J. Radin
John F. Farraher, Jr.
Todd D. Goldberg
Jason A. Manekas
Elizabeth A. Long
Richard D. Vetstein

For full biographical listings, see the Martindale-Hubbell Law Directory

DIONNE & GASS (AV)

73 Tremont Street, 02108
Telephone: 617-723-3300
Fax: 617-723-4151

Richard D. Dionne
Richard D. Gass

OF COUNSEL

Maria Tilaro Higgins
Toni Ann Motta
Michael S. Sher

For full biographical listings, see the Martindale-Hubbell Law Directory

HANIFY & KING, PROFESSIONAL CORPORATION (AV)

One Federal Street, 02110-2007
Telephone: 617-423-0400
Telefax: 617-423-0498
URL: http://www.hanify.com

James Coyne King
John D. Hanify
Harold B. Murphy
David Lee Evans
Daniel J. Lyne
Donald F. Farrell, Jr.
Barbara W. Pfirrman
Gerard P. Richer
Timothy P. O'Neill
Terence P. McCourt

Jeffrey J. Upton
Michael R. Perry
Kathleen E. Cross
Robert E. Richards, Jr.
Joseph F. Cortellini
Andrew G. Lizotte
Donald Ethan Jeffery
Karen A. Whitley
Deena F. Christelis
Robyn J. Bartlett
Owen P. Kane
Sharon H. Patton
John C. McDonald
C. Alexander Hahn
Laurie J. Hurtt
Katherine T. Land
Brian P. McDonough
Lori A. Donovan
Brian R. Marinelli

For full biographical listings, see the Martindale-Hubbell Law Directory

HINCKLEY, ALLEN & SNYDER LLP (AV)

28 State Street, 30th Floor, 02109-1775
Telephone: 617-345-9000
Email: firm@haslaw.com *URL:* http://www.haslaw.com
Providence, Rhode Island Office: 1500 Fleet Center.
Telephone: 401-274-2000.
Fax: 401-277-9600. URL: http://www.hawlaw.com.

MEMBERS OF FIRM

Paula K. Andrews
David D. Barricelli (Not admitted in MA)
E. Jerome Batty (Not admitted in MA)
Jonathan Bell
Paul Bork
Stephen J. Carlotti (Not admitted in MA)
David Barry Connolly
Joseph P. Curran (Not admitted in MA)
Michael P. DeFanti
Eric F. Eisenberg
Malcolm Farmer, III
Margaret D. Farrell (Not admitted in MA)
Pasco Gasbarro Jr.
Hugh J. Gorman, III
Alan P. Gottlieb
William R. Grimm
Paul A. Hedstrom
Joel Lewin
Sandra Matrone Mack (Not admitted in MA)
Matthew T. Marcello, III (Not admitted in MA)
Elizabeth Murdock Myers
Paul F. O'Donnell, III
H. Peter Olsen (Not admitted in MA)
Gerald J. Petros
James O. Reavis
Jeremy Ritzenberg
Ralph J. Rivkind
David J. Rubin
Charles E. Schaub, Jr.
Scott E. Sheridan
Herman Snyder
David R. Sullivan

(See Next Column)

HINCKLEY, ALLEN & SNYDER LLP—*Continued*

MEMBERS OF FIRM (Continued)

Robert F. Sylvia
Christopher C. Tsouros
Howard E. Walker
(Not admitted in MA)

ASSOCIATES

Jessica M. Bettencourt
(Not admitted in MA)
Mark Bianchi
Alyssa V. Boss
Alexandra K. Callam
Jane E. Cohen
Andrew D. Cummings
June E. Daniel
(Not admitted in MA)
Kristine L. Donabedian
Kim Herman Goslant
Gloria Maria Gutierrez
Kelley Jordan-Price
Catherine S. Kim
Christopher W. Morog
Katharine Carter Noble
Elena B. Olson
Andrew F. Shure
Joseph D. Whelan
(Not admitted in MA)

OF COUNSEL

Willard R. Pope
Bentley Tobin
Joachim A. Weissfeld
(Not admitted in MA)

For Complete List of Firm Personnel, See General Section

For full biographical listings, see the Martindale-Hubbell Law Directory

NATHANSON & GOLDBERG, A PROFESSIONAL CORPORATION (AV)

Two Oliver Street, 8th Floor, 02109-4901
Telephone: 617-210-4800
Fax: 617-210-4824
Email: natgolaw@earthlink.net *URL:* http://www.natgolaw.com

Alvin S. Nathanson
Arthur Goldberg
Shannon M. Fitzpatrick
José Centeio
Stuart J. Frank

For full biographical listings, see the Martindale-Hubbell Law Directory

PALMER & DODGE LLP (AV)

One Beacon Street, 02108
Telephone: 617-573-0100
Facsimile: 617-227-4420
URL: http://www.palmerdodge.com

MEMBERS OF FIRM

Charles E. DeWitt, Jr.
Raymond M. Murphy
John E. Rattigan, Jr.
David R. Rodgers
Thomas G. Schnorr
James R. Shea, Jr.
James M. Whalen

SENIOR COUNSEL

Mary S. Tracy

COUNSEL

Susanna C. Burgett
Kathryn Cochrane Murphy
Caroline W. O'Leary
(Not admitted in MA)
Francisco X. Stork
Jane B. Thomassen

For Complete List of Firm Personnel, See General Section

For full biographical listings, see the Martindale-Hubbell Law Directory

ROCHE, CARENS & DEGIACOMO, P.C. (AV)

99 High Street, 02110
Telephone: 617-457-4000
Facsimile: 617-482-3868
Email: firm@rcdpc.com *URL:* http://www.rcdpc.com
Woburn, Massachusetts Office: 600 Unicorn Park Drive.
Telephone: 781-933-5505.

Michael T. Putziger
John W. Gahan, III
Frank M. Capezzera
John J. O'Connor, Jr.

Deirdre M. Robinson

For Complete List of Firm Personnel, See General Section

For full biographical listings, see the Martindale-Hubbell Law Directory

SHERIN AND LODGEN LLP (AV)

100 Summer Street, 02110
Telephone: 617-426-5720
Fax: 617-542-5186
Email: lawyers@sherin.com *URL:* http://www.sherin.com
Los Angeles, California Office: 11300 W. Olympic Boulevard, Suite 700.
Telephone: 310-914-7891.
Fax: 310-552-5327.

MEMBERS OF FIRM

Arthur L. Sherin (1946-1964)
George E. Lodgen (1946-1971)
Morton B. Brown
George Waldstein
John M. Reed
Robert J. Muldoon, Jr.
Alette E. Reed
Edward M. Bloom
Joshua M. Alper
Gary M. Markoff
Bryan G. Killian
David A. Guberman

(See Next Column)

MEMBERS OF FIRM (Continued)

Frank J. Bailey
Kenneth J. Mickiewicz
Craig M. Brown
Thomas A. Hippler
Ronald W. Ruth
Mark A. Nowak
Thomas P. Gorman
Steven D. Eimert
Andrew Royce
John J. Slater III
John C. La Liberte
C. Forbes Sargent III
David A. Brown
Michael S. Strauss

ASSOCIATES

Robert M. Carney
Caroline Woodward
Michael S. Bloom
Kenneth D. Small
Margaret H. Paget
Michael J. Ostroskey
James M. Wodarski
Jessica R. Yaffie
William P. Keefe
Amy D. Porter
Thomas F. Dunn
Brian G. Luneau
Michael P. Sams
Erin M. McNamara
James W. Matthews
Thomas S. Dean

OF COUNSEL

Janet E. Bostwick
Kurt A. James

For Complete List of Firm Personnel, See General Section

For full biographical listings, see the Martindale-Hubbell Law Directory

BROOKLINE, Norfolk Co.

KICKHAM LAW OFFICES (AV)

1318 Beacon Street, 02446
Telephone: 617-566-5990
FAX: 617-734-8185
Email: kickhamlaw@aol.com *URL:* http://www.lawyers.com/kickhamlaw

MEMBERS OF FIRM

Charles J. Kickham, Jr.
John W. Kickham (1923-1980)
James M. Kickham
Deborah Emello
George A. Kickham

OF COUNSEL

Constance K. Kickham
William D. Kickham

Approved Attorneys For: First American Title Insurance Co.; Stewart Title Guaranty Company.
Reference: Bank Boston, Fleet Bank; Brookline Savings Bank.

For full biographical listings, see the Martindale-Hubbell Law Directory

*CAMBRIDGE,** Middlesex Co.

WILLIAM M. O'BRIEN (AV)

185 Alewife Brook Parkway, Suite 400, 02138
Telephone: 617-661-2600
Fax: 617-868-8040

For full biographical listings, see the Martindale-Hubbell Law Directory

FRAMINGHAM, Middlesex Co.

GARRAHAN, BARBIERI & GARRAHAN, P.C. (AV)

1500 Worcester Road, P.O. Box 2482, 01701
Telephone: 508-626-9382
Facsimile: 508-626-1543

John P. Garrahan
Peter R. Barbieri
William C. Garrahan

Anna M. Corti

OF COUNSEL

Mark S. Bodner

For full biographical listings, see the Martindale-Hubbell Law Directory

HARGRAVES, KARB, WILCOX & GALVANI, LLP (AV)

The Corporate Center, 550 Cochituate Road, P.O. Box 966, 01701
Telephone: 508-620-0140
Fax: 508-875-7728
Email: Hargrave@ultranet.com *URL:* http://www.ultranet.com/~Hargrave

MEMBERS OF FIRM

Paul V. Galvani
William H. Mayer
William M. Pezzoni
Mark R. Haranas
Robert P. Jachowicz
Evans J. Carter

Charlene Denise Oliveira Cabral

OF COUNSEL

Victor H. Galvani
Brenda S. Steinberg

Counsel for: Framingham Cooperative Bank; Framingham Housing Authority; Wayland Housing Authority.
Local Counsel for: General Motors Corp. (Westwood, Mass.); Bose Corp.; Consolidated Rail Corp.; Kens Foods, Inc.; Framingham Ford.

For full biographical listings, see the Martindale-Hubbell Law Directory

FRANKLIN, Norfolk Co.

ROCHE AND MURPHY (AV)

Franklin Office Park West, 38 Pond Street, Suite 308, P.O. Box 267, 02038
Telephone: 508-528-8300
FAX: 508-528-8889
Email: jroche@ncounty.net

MEMBERS OF FIRM

Neil J. Roche
Paul G. Murphy

ASSOCIATE

John J. Roche

For full biographical listings, see the Martindale-Hubbell Law Directory

HARWICH PORT, Barnstable Co.

WILLIAM D. CROWELL (AV)

466 Main Street, P.O. Box 185, 02646
Telephone: 508-432-1643
Fax: 508-430-0631

Raymond H. Grayson (1901-1991)

For full biographical listings, see the Martindale-Hubbell Law Directory

LYNN, Essex Co.

DEMAKIS LAW OFFICES, P.C. (AV)

56 Central Avenue, 01901
Telephone: 781-595-3311
FAX: 781-592-4990

Thomas C. Demakis
Gregory C. Demakis
Sandor Rabkin

OF COUNSEL

Charles Demakis

Reference: Fleet Bank.

For full biographical listings, see the Martindale-Hubbell Law Directory

MILFORD, Worcester Co.

GREENWALD, GREENWALD, POWERS & WINSOR LLP (AV)

409 Fortune Boulevard Granite Park, 01757-1746
Telephone: 508-478-8611
Fax: 508-634-3959; 478-5937
Email: ggp@ggplaw@.com *URL:* http://www.ggplaw.com

Alan Greenwald
Steven A. Greenwald
Kathleen R. Winsor

ASSOCIATES

Anne M. Givens
Mary Jo Rett
Anna R. Vergados
Kenneth A. Northrup
Robert A. Dignan, Jr.

For full biographical listings, see the Martindale-Hubbell Law Directory

NORTH ATTLEBORO, Bristol Co.

CLAPP & McCAMBRIDGE, L.L.P. (AV)

12 Church Street, 02760
Telephone: 508-695-3554
Fax: 508-695-2523

MEMBERS OF FIRM

Stephen D. Clapp
James E. McCambridge, III

OF COUNSEL

Daniel Del Vecchio

For full biographical listings, see the Martindale-Hubbell Law Directory

*SPRINGFIELD,** Hampden Co.

ANNINO, DRAPER & MOORE, P.C. (AV)

1500 Main Street, Suite 1818, P.O. Box 15428, 01115
Telephone: 413-732-6400
Fax: 413-732-3339
Email: admatlaw@aol.com
Westfield, Massachusetts Office: 52 Court Street.
Telephone: 413-562-9829.

Calvin W. Annino, Jr.
Louis S. Moore
Mark E. Draper
Michael R. Siddall

For full biographical listings, see the Martindale-Hubbell Law Directory

ROBINSON DONOVAN MADDEN & BARRY, P.C. (AV)

Suite 1600, Tower Square, 1500 Main Street, 01115-5609
Telephone: 413-732-2301
Fax: 413-785-4658
Email: service@robinson-donovan.com *URL:* http://www.robinson-donovan.com

(See Next Column)

Homans Robinson (1894-1973)
Milton J. Donovan (1906-1995)
Lawrence M. Sinclair (1942-1986)

RETIRED

John H. Madden, Jr.
Edward J. Barry
Richard S. Milstein

OF COUNSEL

Victor Rosenberg

SENIOR COUNSEL

Jonathan P. Rice

Gordon H. Wentworth
Paul S. Weinberg
James H. Tourtelotte
Frederica H. McCarthy
Ronald C. Kidd
Matthew J. King
Jeffrey W. Roberts
Neva Kaufman Rohan
Jeffrey L. McCormick
Douglas F. Boyd
James F. Martin
James K. Bodurtha
Robert P. Cunningham
Keith A. Minoff
John C. Sikorski
Patricia M. Rapinchuk
Nancy Frankel Pelletier
Kimberly Davis Crear

E. Paul Amata
James D. Chadwell
Lisa A. Bongiovi (Not admitted in MA)
John E. Garber
Patrick J. Markey
Edward J. Carroll, III
Carla W. Newton
Betsy Macmillan Stevens

Representative Clients: BankBoston, N.A.; United Cooperative Bank; Fleet National Bank; CNA; Commercial Union Insurance Co.; Hanover Insurance Group.

For full biographical listings, see the Martindale-Hubbell Law Directory

WALTHAM, Middlesex Co.

HARNISH, JENNEY, MITCHELL AND RESH (AV)

564 Main Street, 02154
Telephone: 781-894-0000
Telecopier: 781-893-8357

MEMBERS OF FIRM

Francis E. Jenney
Joseph Melone
David L. Mitchell
Robert C. Mann
Harvey J. Resh
Margaret Manzon Skinner

ASSOCIATE

Rhonda B. Fogel

For full biographical listings, see the Martindale-Hubbell Law Directory

*WORCESTER,** Worcester Co.

MOUNTAIN, DEARBORN & WHITING LLP (AV)

370 Main Street, 01608
Telephone: 508-756-2423
Fax: 508-755-6640

MEMBERS OF FIRM

Alfred N. Whiting (1920-1989)
Francis J. Russell
Thomas R. Mountain
Dale R. Harger
Richard W. Dearborn
Mark W. Bloom
Samuel R. DeSimone
Donald J. O'Neil
Henry W. Beth
Lawrence S. Delaney
Stuart A. Hammer
Ann K. Molloy
Lisa D. Tingue

For full biographical listings, see the Martindale-Hubbell Law Directory

MICHIGAN

*ADRIAN,** Lenawee Co.

WALKER, WATTS, JACKSON & McFARLAND (AV)

160 North Winter Street, 49221
Telephone: 517-265-8138
Fax: 517-265-8286
URL: http://www.lawyers.com/wwj&m

MEMBERS OF FIRM

William H. Walker
Mark A. Jackson
Prosser M. Watts, Jr.
Michael McFarland

Attorneys for: Bank of Lenawee; Consumers Power Co.; Norfolk & Western Railway Co.; Citizens Gas Fuel Co.; Auto Owners Insurance Co.; Amerisure Co.; Citizens Mutual Liability; State Farm Mutual Insurance Co.; Tower Insurance Co.

For Complete List of Firm Personnel, See General Section

For full biographical listings, see the Martindale-Hubbell Law Directory

*ANN ARBOR,** Washtenaw Co.

BRAUN KENDRICK FINKBEINER PLC (AV)

First National Building, 210 S. Main, Suite 700, 48104
Telephone: 313-995-4100
Telecopier: 313-995-4798
Email: ALBFIE@BKF-LAW.COM *URL:* http://www.bkf-law.com
Bay City, Michigan Office: 201 Phoenix Building, P.O. Box 2039.
Telephone: 517-895-8505.
Telecopier: 517-895-8437.
Saginaw, Michigan Office: 101 N. Washington, Suite 812.
Telephone: 517-753-3461.
Telecopier: 517-753-3951.
Saginaw Township, Michigan Office: 5800 Gratiot Road, Suite 107, P.O. Box 5169.
Telephone: 517-799-8692.
Fax: 517-799-4666.
Mt. Pleasant, Michigan Office: 805 North Brown.
Telephone: 517-775-7404.
Telecopier: 517-775-3764.

Barry M. Levine

Representative Clients: The Dow Chemical Co.; General Motors Corp.; Merrill, Lynch, Inc.; Saginaw General Hospital; Saginaw News; The Wickes Foundation.

For Complete List of Firm Personnel, See General Section

For full biographical listings, see the Martindale-Hubbell Law Directory

HOOPER, HATHAWAY, PRICE, BEUCHE & WALLACE (AV)

126 South Main Street, 48104
Telephone: 313-662-4426
Fax: 313-662-9559
Email: hhpbw@voyager.net

James R. Beuche
Gregory A. Spaly

Representative Clients: Avfuel Corporation; Bank of Ann Arbor; Castrol North America; Chem-Trend Incorporated; Ervin Industries, Inc.; First Martin Corporation; Glacier Hills, Inc.; Prestolite Electric, Inc.; Southern States Cooperative; E.B. Eddy Forest Products, Ltd.

For Complete List of Firm Personnel, See General Section

For full biographical listings, see the Martindale-Hubbell Law Directory

MILLER, CANFIELD, PADDOCK AND STONE, P.L.C. (AV)

A Professional Limited Liability Company
Founded in 1852 by Sidney Davy Miller
101 North Main Street, Seventh Floor, 48104-1400
Telephone: 734-663-2445
Fax: 734-747-7147
URL: http://www.millercanfield.com
Detroit, Michigan Office: 150 West Jefferson, Suite 2500, 48226-4415.
Telephone: 313-963-6420.
Fax: 313-496-7500.
Cable Address: "Stem Detroit."
Troy, Michigan Office: 840 West Long Lake Road, Suite 200, 48098.
Telephone: 248-879-2000.
Fax: 248-879-2001.
Grand Rapids, Michigan Office: 99 Monroe, N.W., Suite 1200, 49503-2639.
Telephone: 616-454-8656.
Fax: 616-776-6322.
Howell, Michigan Office: 121 South Barnard Street, Suite 4, 48843-2305.
Telephone: 517-546-7600.
Telecopier: 517-546-6974.
Kalamazoo, Michigan Office: 444 West Michigan Avenue, 49007-3752.
Telephone: 616-381-7030.
Fax: 616-382-0244.
Lansing, Michigan Office: One Michigan Avenue, Suite 900, 48933-1609.
Telephone: 517-487-2070.
Fax: 517-374-6304.
Monroe, Michigan Office: 214 East Elm Avenue, Suite 100, 48162-2682.
Telephone: 734-243-2000.
Fax: 734-243-0901.
Washington, D.C. Office: 1900 K Street, N.W., Suite 1150. 20006.
Telephone: 202-429-5575; 785-0600.
Fax: 202-331-1118; 785-1234.
Pensacola, Florida Office: 25 West Cedar, 32501.
Telephone: 850-469-1088.
Fax: 850-432-0677.
New York, New York Office: 1450 Broadway, 41st Floor, 10018.
Telephone: 212-704-4400.
Fax: 212-704-4410.
Gdynia, Poland Office: UL. Slaska 21, 81-319.
Telephone: 011-485-831-2808.
Fax: 011-48-58-628 6411.
Warsaw, Poland Office: UL. Nowogrodzkall, 5th Floor, 00-513.
Telephone: 011-4822 529 0200.
Fax: 011-4822 529 0201.

(See Next Column)

Katowice, Poland Office: UL. Francuska 35/37, 40-027.
Telephone: 011 (48-32) 757-2414.
Fax: 011 (48-32) 757-2483.

PRINCIPALS OF FIRM

Robert E. Gilbert

Representative Firm Clients: Chrysler Corporation; Comerica, Incorporated; City of Detroit, Michigan; Detroit Tigers, Inc.; First of Michigan; Ford Motor Company; Ford Motor Credit Company; Great Lakes Bancorp; Henry Ford Hospital; INVETECH Company.

For Complete List of Firm Personnel, See General Section

For full biographical listings, see the Martindale-Hubbell Law Directory

PEAR SPERLING EGGAN & MUSKOVITZ, P.C. (AV)

Domino's Farms, 24 Frank Lloyd Wright Drive, 48105
Telephone: 734-665-4441
Fax: 734-665-8788
Email: peare@dominos.com
Ypsilanti, Michigan Offices: 5 South Washington Street.
Telephone: 734-483-3626 and 2164 Bellevue at Washtenaw.
Telephone: 734-483-7177.

Edwin L. Pear
Thomas E. Daniels
Andrew M. Eggan
Joel F. Graziani
Paul R. Fransway

Counsel For: Domino's Pizza, Inc.; Victory Lane Quick Oil Change, Inc.; Citizens Banking Corporation.

For Complete List of Firm Personnel, See General Section

For full biographical listings, see the Martindale-Hubbell Law Directory

BATTLE CREEK, Calhoun Co.

KREIS, ENDERLE, CALLANDER & HUDGINS, A PROFESSIONAL CORPORATION (AV)

One West Michigan Avenue, 49017
Telephone: 616-966-3000
Facsimile: 616-966-3022
Email: kech@kech.com *URL:* http://www.kech.com
Kalamazoo, Michigan Office: One Moorsbridge, P.O. Box 4010, 49003-4010.
Telephone: 616-324-3000.
Fax: 616-324-3010.

Alan G. Enderle (Resident, Kalamazoo Office)
C. Reid Hudgins III (Resident, Kalamazoo Office)
Stephen L. Simons
Jeffrey D. Swenarton (Resident, Kalamazoo Office)
Peter F. Davis (Resident, Kalamazoo Office)
Manuel R. Rupe (Resident, Kalamazoo Office)

OF COUNSEL

James M. Sullivan

For Complete List of Firm Personnel, See General Section

For full biographical listings, see the Martindale-Hubbell Law Directory

*BAY CITY,** Bay Co.

BRAUN KENDRICK FINKBEINER PLC (AV)

201 Phoenix Building, P.O. Box 2039, 48708
Telephone: 517-895-8505
Telecopier: 517-895-8437
Email: ALBFIE@BKF-LAW.COM *URL:* http://www.bkf-law.com
Saginaw, Michigan Office: 101 N. Washington, Suite 812. 8th Floor Second National Bank Building.
Telephone: 517-753-3461.
Telecopier: 517-753-3951.
Saginaw Township, Michigan Office: 5800 Gratiot Road, Suite 107, P.O. Box 5169.
Telephone: 517-799-8692.
Fax: 517-799-4666.
Ann Arbor, Michigan Office: First National Building. 201 S. Main, Suite 700.
Telephone: 313-995-4100.
Telecopier: 313-995-4798.
Mt. Pleasant, Michigan Office: 805 North Brown.
Telephone: 517-775-7404.
Telecopier: 517-775-3764.

Ralph J. Isackson
Daniel S. Opperman
Gregory T. Demers

Representative Clients: Bay Health Systems; Catholic Federal Credit Union; City of Saginaw; City of Vassar; City of Zilwaukee; Corporate Service; Cox Cable.

For Complete List of Firm Personnel, See General Section

For full biographical listings, see the Martindale-Hubbell Law Directory

BINGHAM FARMS, Oakland Co.

MEISNER & ASSOCIATES, P.C. (AV)

Suite 467, 30200 Telegraph Road, 48025-4506
Telephone: 248-644-4433
Fax: 248-644-2941
Email: bmeisner@mich.com *URL:* http://www.meisner-law.com

Robert M. Meisner

Robert R. Maxwell
Richard M. Delonis

For full biographical listings, see the Martindale-Hubbell Law Directory

ROBERT S. ROLLINGER, P.C. (AV)

30700 Telegraph Road, Suite 4646, 48025
Telephone: 248-646-6460
Fax: 248-642-6500

Robert S. Rollinger

LEGAL SUPPORT PERSONNEL

Kathleen Smigels (Legal Administrator)

For full biographical listings, see the Martindale-Hubbell Law Directory

BIRMINGHAM, Oakland Co.

BUTZEL LONG, A PROFESSIONAL CORPORATION (AV)

Suite 200, 32270 Telegraph Road, 48025
Telephone: 810-258-1616
Telecopier: 810-258-1439
Email: melnick@butzel.com *URL:* http://www.butzel.com
Detroit, Michigan Office: Suite 900, 150 West Jefferson.
Telephone: 313-225-7000.
Telecopier: 313-225-7080.
Okemos, Michigan Office: Suite 300, 2127 University Park Drive.
Telephone: 517-372-6622.
Telecopier: 517-372-6672.
Ann Arbor, Michigan Office: Suite 300, 350 South Main Street.
Telephone: 313-995-3110.
Telecopier: 313-995-1777.
Grosse Pointe Farms, Michigan Office: Suite 260, 21 Kercheval.
Telephone: 313-886-5446.
Telecopier: 313-886-2114.
Boca Raton, Florida Office: Suite 411, 1200 North Federal Highway.
Telephone: 561-368-2151.
Telecopier: 561-368-4668.
Palm Beach Gardens, Florida Office: Suite 227, 11382 Prosperity Farms Road.
Telephone: 561-625-4442.
Telecopier: 561-625-6901.
Naples, Florida Office: Suite 705, 801 Laurel Oak Drive.
Telephone: 941-597-4500.
Telecopier: 941-597-5623.

Stephen A. Bromberg (Resident)
Allan Nachman (Resident)
Paul L. Triemstra (Resident)
John J. Raymond, Jr.
David W. Berry (Resident)
D. Stewart Green (Resident)
Gordon W. Didier (Resident)
Alan S. Levine (Resident)
James Y. Stewart (Resident)
Anthony J. Saulino, Jr. (Resident)
Patrick A. Karbowski (Resident)
Ronald E. Reynolds (Resident)
Susan Klein Friedlaender (Resident)

For full biographical listings, see the Martindale-Hubbell Law Directory

HYMAN LIPPITT, P.C. (AV)

185 Oakland Avenue, Suite 300, 48009
Telephone: 248-646-8292
Facsimile: 248-646-8375
Email: hymalipp@tir.com

J. Leonard Hyman
Norman L. Lippitt
Douglas A. Hyman
Brian D. O'Keefe
H. Joel Newman
Nazli G. Sater
Kenneth F. Neuman
Terry S. Givens
Paul J. Fischer
John A. Sellers
Robert H. Lippitt
Roger L. Myers
Sally A. Rutledge
Joseph Pia
John P. Gonway
Leif K. Anderson
Jennifer S. Gold
Julie Lyons Kosovec
Dawn S. Spratley
Michael T. Price

For full biographical listings, see the Martindale-Hubbell Law Directory

BLOOMFIELD HILLS, Oakland Co.

JON H. BERKEY, P.C. (AV)

1700 North Woodward Avenue, Suite 101, 48304-2249
Telephone: 248-593-6460
Fax: 248-593-6470
URL: http://www.lawyers.com/jonberkeylaw

(See Next Column)

Jon H. Berkey

Anthony A. Yezbick

OF COUNSEL

Kenneth J. Wrobel, Jr.

For full biographical listings, see the Martindale-Hubbell Law Directory

DAWDA, MANN, MULCAHY & SADLER, P.L.C. (AV)

1533 North Woodward Avenue Suite 200, 48304-2815
Telephone: 248-642-3700
Fax: 248-642-7791
Email: EMail@DMMS.Com

Michael D. Mulcahy
Edward C. Dawda
Paul A. Bringer
William L. Rosin
Todd A. Schafer

Daniel M. Halprin
Daniel M. Israel
Wayne S. Segal
Nicole S. Leveque
Vincent J. Wilk
Richard S. Bailey

Representative Clients: AEGON USA Realty Advisors, Inc.; AMB Property, LP; Charter One, FSB; Ford Motor Company; Ford Motor Land Services Corp.; Home Depot U.S.A., Inc.; Northwestern Mutual Life Insurance Company; Pep Boys; Trammell Crow Company; Wal-Mart Stores, Inc.

For full biographical listings, see the Martindale-Hubbell Law Directory

DROLET, FREEMAN, COTTON & NORRIS, P.C. (AV)

33 Bloomfield Hills Parkway, Suite 100, 48304
Telephone: 248-642-2255
Fax: 248-642-6460
Email: droletfreeman@voyager.net

David G. Barnett (1915-1989)
H. William Freeman
J. Kingsley Cotton, III
Matthew C. Norris

Brian P. Henry
Suzanne S. Reynolds
Lauren D. Honet
David M. Blau

Representative Clients: Angelo Iafrate Construction Co.; ASC, Incorporated; Cadillac Asphalt Paving Co.; Carroll Packaging, Inc.; Choice Hotels International; Clawson Concrete Co.; Commerica Bank; Corrosion Control Engineering; Emcor; Farmington Public Schools.

For full biographical listings, see the Martindale-Hubbell Law Directory

HOWARD & HOWARD ATTORNEYS, P.C. (AV)

The Pinehurst Office Center, Suite 101, 1400 North Woodward Avenue, 48304-2855
Telephone: 248-645-1483
Telecopier: 248-645-1568
Kalamazoo, Michigan Office: The Michigan Building, Suite 200, 100 Portage Street.
Telephone: 616-382-1483.
Telecopier: 616-382-1568.
Lansing, Michigan Office: The Phoenix Building, Suite 500, 222 Washington Square, North.
Telephone: 517-485-1483.
Telecopier: 517-485-1568.
Peoria, Illinois Office: One Technology Plaza, Suite 600, 211 Fulton Street.
Telephone: 309-672-1483.
Telecopier: 309-672-1568.

Mark A. Davis
David B. Lipski
Timothy M. Wittebort
John E. Young

Representative Clients: For Representative Client list, see General Practice, Bloomfield Hills, MI.

For Complete List of Firm Personnel, See General Section

For full biographical listings, see the Martindale-Hubbell Law Directory

MEYER, KIRK, SNYDER & SAFFORD, PLLC (AV)

Suite 100, 100 West Long Lake Road, 48304
Telephone: 248-647-5111
Telecopier: 248-647-6079
Email: mkss@michbar.org
Detroit, Michigan Office: 1400 Ford Building, 615 Griswold, 48226.
Telephone: 313-961-1261.

George H. Meyer
John M. Kirk
Donald H. Baker, Jr.

Representative Clients: Available Upon Request.

For full biographical listings, see the Martindale-Hubbell Law Directory

Bloomfield Hills—Continued

PROVIZER & PHILLIPS, P.C. (AV)

6785 Telegraph Road, Suite 400, 48301
Telephone: 248-642-0444
Facsimile: 248-642-6661
Toll Free: 1-800-288-9080
URL: http://www.lawyers.com/provizer&phillips

Harold M. Provizer
Randall E. Phillips
Marilyn A. Madorsky
Noel F. Beck

For full biographical listings, see the Martindale-Hubbell Law Directory

CLARKSTON, Oakland Co.

BULLARD, ANDERSON & ANDERSON, PLLC (AV)

6060 Dixie Highway, Suite H, 48346-3476
Telephone: 248-623-3888
Fax: 248-623-1883
Email: firm@baalaw.com *URL:* http://www.baalaw.com

Rockwood W. Bullard III
Rae Anne Anderson
Acie G. Anderson, III

Representative Clients: ANCAR Publications, Inc.; Audio Trends, Inc.; AVC, Inc. (Advanced Visual Concepts); Clarkston Realty, Inc.; GAC Mortgage Co.; Michaelene's Granola, Inc.; Morgan Service, Inc.; Smith Disposal, Inc.; Sunview Windows, Skylights & Doors, Ltd.
Reference: NBD Bank, NA.

For full biographical listings, see the Martindale-Hubbell Law Directory

*DETROIT,** Wayne Co.

ABBOTT, NICHOLSON, QUILTER, ESSHAKI & YOUNGBLOOD, P.C. (AV)

300 River Place, Suite 3000, 48207-4225
Telephone: 313-566-2500
Telecopier: 313-566-2502
Email: anqey@anqey.com *URL:* http://www.anqey.com

C. Richard Abbott
John R. Nicholson
Thomas R. Quilter III
Gene J. Esshaki
John F. Youngblood
James B. Perry
Carl F. Jarboe
Jay A. Kennedy
Timothy A. Stoepker
Timothy J. Kramer
Norbert T. Madison, Jr.
William D. Gilbride, Jr.
Mary P. Nelson
Michael R. Blum
Anne Warren Bagno
Thomas J. Giachino

Eric J. Girdler
Jill A. Bankey
Daniel G. Kielczewski
George P. Butler III
Christopher P. Baker
Faith M. Gaudaen
Kim A. Linthorst Homan
Christopher T. Koch

OF COUNSEL

Thomas C. Shumaker
Lisa R. Gorman

For full biographical listings, see the Martindale-Hubbell Law Directory

BARRIS, SOTT, DENN & DRIKER, P.L.L.C. (AV)

211 West Fort Street, Fifteenth Floor, 48226-3281
Telephone: 313-965-9725
Telecopier: 313-965-2493
313-965-5398

Donald E. Barris
Herbert Sott
David L. Denn
Eugene Driker
William G. Barris
Sharon M. Woods
Stephen E. Glazek
Robert E. Kass
Daniel M. Share
Elaine Fieldman
Morley Witus
John A. Libby
James S. Fontichiaro
Robert E. Epstein
Daniel J. LaCombe
Dennis M. Barnes
Matthew J. Boettcher
Thomas F. Cavalier
Michael J. Reynolds
C. David Bargamian
Eric S. Rosenthal
Todd R. Mendel

COUNSEL

Leon S. Cohan

OF COUNSEL

Stanley M. Weingarden

Elizabeth A. Carrie
Monique K. Cirelli
Claudia D. Orr
Ronni Tischler
Timothy D. Batdorf
Laura Cadarette Ragold
Cynthia I. Brody
James D. VandeWyngearde

Representative Clients: Avis Rent A Car System, Inc.; Borman's, Inc.; Consumers Power Co.; County of Wayne, Michigan; Ford Motor Co.; The Great Atlantic & Pacific Tea Company, Inc.; Henry Ford Health System; Michigan Consolidated Gas Co.; NBD Bank, N.A.; Textron, Inc.

For full biographical listings, see the Martindale-Hubbell Law Directory

BIERI & AMES (AV)

1500 First National Building, 660 Woodward Avenue, 48226
Telephone: 313-962-5900
Fax: 313-962-5070
Email: sames@bieriandassoc.com *URL:* http://www.bieriandassoc.com

MEMBERS OF FIRM

James C. Bieri
Stanley L. Ames

ASSOCIATE

John M. Phelan

For full biographical listings, see the Martindale-Hubbell Law Directory

BODMAN, LONGLEY & DAHLING LLP (AV)

34th Floor 100 Renaissance Center, 48243
Telephone: 313-259-7777
Fax: 313-393-7579
Email: info@bodmanlongley.com *URL:* http://www.bodmanlongley.com
Troy, Michigan Office: Suite 2020, 755 West Big Beaver Road.
Telephone: 248-362-2110.
Fax: 248-244-0780.
Ann Arbor, Michigan Office: 110 Miller, Suite 300.
Telephone: 734-761-3780.
Fax: 734-930-2494.
Northern Michigan Office: 229 Court Street, P.O. Box 405, Cheboygan.
Telephone: 231-627-4351.
Fax: 231-627-2802.

MEMBERS OF FIRM

Michael B. Lewiston
Mark W. Griffin (Ann Arbor Office)
Joseph N. Brown
Joseph J. Kochanek
David W. Hipp
Larry R. Shulman
Michael A. Stack (Cheboygan Office)
Harvey W. Berman (Ann Arbor Office)
Stephen I. Greenhalgh
David W. Barton (Cheboygan Office)
Sandra L. Sorini (Ann Arbor Office)
Bonnie S. Sherr
Marc M. Bakst
Nicholas P. Scavone, Jr.
Sol M. Friedman

COUNSEL

Alfred C. Wortley, Jr.

ASSOCIATES

Andrew Z. Spilkin
Scott P. Gyorke
Emily M. Kellndorfer (Ann Arbor Office)
Erik S. Prater

For Representative Client List, See General Section

For Complete List of Firm Personnel, See General Section

For full biographical listings, see the Martindale-Hubbell Law Directory

BRADY, HATHAWAY, BRADY & BRETZ, PROFESSIONAL CORPORATION (AV)

1330 Buhl Building, 48226-3602
Telephone: 313-965-3700
Telecopier: 313-965-2830
Email: brady@bradyhathaway.com

Thomas P. Brady
Daniel J. Bretz

Representative Clients: The Hayman Co.; Village Green Management Co.

For Complete List of Firm Personnel, See General Section

For full biographical listings, see the Martindale-Hubbell Law Directory

BUTZEL LONG, A PROFESSIONAL CORPORATION (AV)

Suite 900, 150 West Jefferson, 48226
Telephone: 313-225-7000
Telecopier: 313-225-7080
Email: melnick@butzel.com *URL:* http://www.butzel.com
Birmingham, Michigan Office: Suite 200, 32270 Telegraph Road.
Telephone: 810-258-1616.
Telecopier: 810-258-1439.
Okemos, Michigan Office: Suite 300, 2127 University Park Drive.
Telephone: 517-372-6622.
Telecopier: 517-372-6672.
Ann Arbor, Michigan Office: Suite 300, 350 South Main Street.
Telephone: 313-995-3110.
Telecopier: 313-995-1777.
Grosse Pointe Farms, Michigan Office: Suite 260, 21 Kercheval.
Telephone: 313-886-5446.
Telecopier: 313-886-2114.
Boca Raton, Florida Office: Suite 411, 1200 North Federal Highway.
Telephone: 561-368-2151.
Telecopier: 561-368-4668.
Palm Beach Gardens, Florida Office: Suite 227, 11382 Prosperity Farms Road.
Telephone: 561-625-4442.
Telecopier: 561-625-6901.

(See Next Column)

BUTZEL LONG A PROFESSIONAL CORPORATION, *Detroit—Continued*

Naples, Florida Office: Suite 705, 801 Laurel Oak Drive.
Telephone: 941-597-4500.
Telecopier: 941-597-5623.

Stephen A. Bromberg (Birmingham)
Allan Nachman (Birmingham)
Jack D. Shumate (Birmingham)
Leonard F. Charla
David W. Berry (Birmingham)
Carl Rashid, Jr.
D. Stewart Green (Birmingham)
Gordon W. Didier (Birmingham)
Alan S. Levine (Birmingham)
Anthony J. Saulino, Jr. (Birmingham)
Clara DeMatteis Mager
Patrick A. Karbowski (Birmingham)
Ronald E. Reynolds (Birmingham)
Susan Klein Friedlaender (Birmingham)

Todd M. Fink (Birmingham)

Representative Clients: Bank of New York; Besser Co.; Blue Cross/Blue Shield of Michigan; Chrysler First; Chrysler Motor Corp.; D & N Savings Bank; The Detroit News, Inc.; Dow Chemical Co.; National City Bank; William Beaumont Hospital.

For full biographical listings, see the Martindale-Hubbell Law Directory

DYKEMA GOSSETT PLLC (AV)

400 Renaissance Center, 48243-1668
Telephone: 313-568-6800
Fax: 313-568-6545
Email: mstarrs@dykema.com *URL:* http://www.dykema.com
Ann Arbor, Michigan Office: 315 East Eisenhower Parkway, Suite 100, 48108-3306.
Telephone: 734-214-7660.
Fax: 734-214-7696.
Bloomfield Hills, Michigan Office: 1577 North Woodward Avenue, Suite 300, 48304-2820.
Telephone: 248-203-0700.
Fax: 248-203-0763.
Chicago, Illinois Office: 55 East Monroe Street, Suite 3050, 60603-5709.
Telephone: 312-551-4900.
Fax: 312-551-4919.
Grand Rapids, Michigan Office: Suite 700, 300 Ottawa Avenue, N.W., 49503-2304.
Telephone: 616-776-7500.
Fax: 616-776-7573.
Lansing, Michigan Office: 800 Michigan National Tower, 48933-1707.
Telephone: 517-374-9100.
Fax: 517-374-9191.
Washington, D.C. Office: Franklin Square, Suite 300 West, 1300 I Street, N.W., 20005-3306.
Telephone: 202-522-8600.
Fax: 202-522-8669.
Affiliated Office: Via Matconi, 3, 40122 Bologna, Italy.
Telephone: 011-39-51-228222.
Fax: 011-39-51-6593580.

MEMBERS OF FIRM

Robert A. Berlow (Resident at Bloomfield Hills Office)
David E. Doran (Resident at Grand Rapids Office)
Fred J. Fechheimer (Resident at Bloomfield Hills Office)
Alan M. Greene (Resident at Bloomfield Hills Office)
Mary Steck Kershner
Michael A. Lesha
Howard N. Luckoff (Resident at Bloomfield Hills Office)
Brian J. Page (Resident at Grand Rapids Office)
Cameron H. Piggott
Richard E. Rabbideau
Wilfred A. Steiner, Jr.

RETIRED MEMBER

James W. Draper

ASSOCIATES

David A. Antonelli (Resident at Bloomfield Hills Office)
Amy Lynn Carson (Resident at Bloomfield Hills Office)
Adam M. Fishkind
Karen R. Pifer (Resident at Bloomfield Hills Office)

For Complete List of Firm Personnel, See General Section

For full biographical listings, see the Martindale-Hubbell Law Directory

FILDEW HINKS, P.L.L.C. (AV)

3600 Penobscot Building, 645 Griswold Street, 48226-4291
Telephone: 313-961-9700
Facsimile: 313-961-0754

MEMBERS OF FIRM

Stanley L. Fildew (1896-1978)
Frank T. Hinks (1887-1974)
Richard E. Hinks (1916-1990)
John H. Fildew
Alan C. Miller
Randall S. Wangen
Mary Jane Ruffley
Robert D. Welchli
William P. Thorpe
Colleen A. Kramer
Stephen J. Pokoj
Charles S. Kennedy III

(See Next Column)

ASSOCIATE

Walter B. Fisher Jr.

References: First of America Bank-Detroit, N.A.; Comerica Bank-Detroit; National Bank of Detroit.

For full biographical listings, see the Martindale-Hubbell Law Directory

HONIGMAN MILLER SCHWARTZ AND COHN (AV)

2290 First National Building, 660 Woodward Avenue, 48226
Telephone: 313-465-7000
Telecopier: 313-465-8000
Telex: 235705
Email: mvg@honigman.com *URL:* http://law.honigman.com
Lansing, Michigan Office: Phoenix Building, 222 North Washington Square, Suite 400, 48933-1800.
Telephone: 517-484-8282.

MEMBERS OF FIRM

Jean-Vierre Adams
Joel S. Adelman
C. Leslie Banas
Thomas J. Beale
Maurice S. Binkow
Jonathan R. Borenstein
Richard J. Burstein
Gregory J. DeMars
Frederick J. Frank
Margaret E. Greene
Carl W. Herstein
Alan M. Hurvitz
Norman Hyman
Jeffrey R. Kravitz
Denise J. Lewis
Lawrence D. McLaughlin
Mitchell R. Meisner
Nancy M. Omichinski
J. Adam Rothstein
Phyllis G. Rozof
Roberta R. Russ
Laurence J. Schiff
Michael B. Shapiro
Margaret Van Meter
Randall P. Whately
Sheldon P. Winkelman
William J. Zousmer

ASSOCIATES

Jonathan David Block
John Michael Breza
Amy M. Brooks
Stephanie L. Speranza

Counsel to: Forbes/Cohen Properties; General Motors Corporation Legal Staff (General Motors Corporation, General Motors Acceptance Corporation); The Hayman Company; Hines Interests Limited Partnership; Pulte Corporation; Schostak Brothers & Company, Inc.

For Complete List of Firm Personnel, See General Section

For full biographical listings, see the Martindale-Hubbell Law Directory

JAFFE, RAITT, HEUER & WEISS, PROFESSIONAL CORPORATION (AV)

One Woodward Avenue, Suite 2400, 48226
Telephone: 313-961-8380
Telecopier: 313-961-8358
Cable Address: "Jafsni"
Southfield,Michigan Office: Travelers Tower, Suite 1520.
Telephone: 313-961-8380.

Gail A. Anderson
Robert S. Bolton
Jeffrey L. Forman
Joel S. Golden
Blair B. Hysni
Ira J. Jaffe
Robin H. Krueger
Mark P. Krysinski
Joel J. Morris
Cecil G. Raitt
Mark D. Rubenfire
Lawrence R. Shoffner
Arthur A. Weiss
Jeffrey M. Weiss
Richard A. Zussman

Ian M. Burnstein

Representative Clients: Edgemere Enterprises; Frankel Associates, Inc.; Somerset Inn & Apartments; Sosnick Development Co.; Uniprop, Inc.

For Complete List of Firm Personnel, See General Section

For full biographical listings, see the Martindale-Hubbell Law Directory

LEWIS & MUNDAY, A PROFESSIONAL CORPORATION (AV)

(Formerly Lewis, Clay & Munday, P.C.)
1300 First National Building, 660 Woodward Avenue, 48226-3531
Telephone: 313-961-2550
Fax: 313-961-1270
Email: camille.miller@lewis-pc.com *URL:* http://www.lewis-pc.com
Washington, D.C. Office: 1120 Connecticut Avenue, Suite 280. 20036.
Telephone: 202-835-0616.
Fax: 202-833-3316.
Boston, Massachusetts Office: 101 Federal Street, Suite 1900. 02110.
Telephone: 617-478-0553.
Fax: 617-478-0543.

David Baker Lewis
Reuben A. Munday
Camille Stearns Miller
Jacqueline H. Sellers
David N. Zacks
Thomas J. Guyer
Blair A. Person
Karen Kendrick Brown (Resident, Washington, D.C. Office)
Susan D. Hoffman
Hans J. Massaquoi, Jr.

(See Next Column)

LEWIS & MUNDAY A PROFESSIONAL CORPORATION—*Continued*

Althea Lynn Simpson
Donica Thomas Varner
Kris W. Krueger
Cylenthia LaToye Miller
Joseph N. Ejbeh
Yolanda R. Bates
Caroletta L. Edgar-Sprinkle
Derek G. McBride
Ayanna Weber
Deborah Jean Williamson
Darice Elizabeth Weber
Krystal M. Gardner
Syeda Taqi

COUNSEL

G. Allen Bass (Resident, Boston, Massachusetts Office)
Leamon R. Sowell, Jr.
Gail Pabarue Bennett
Roger M. Groves
Carol H. Rodriguez
Linda M. Bruton
Brian J. Kott

OF COUNSEL

Otis M. Smith (1922-1994)
Herbert O. Reid, Sr. (1915-1991)

Representative Clients: Aetna Life & Casualty Co.; Chrysler Motors Corp.; Chrysler Financial Corp.; MCI Communications Corp.; City of Detroit; City of Detroit Building Authority; City of Detroit Downtown Development Authority; Consolidated Rail Corp. (Conrail); Equitable Life Assurance Society of the United States.

For full biographical listings, see the Martindale-Hubbell Law Directory

MEYER, KIRK, SNYDER & SAFFORD, PLLC (AV)

1400 Ford Building, 615 Griswold, 48226
Telephone: 313-961-1261
Fax: 248-647-6079
Bloomfield Hills, Michigan Office: Suite 100, 100 West Long Lake Road.
Telephone: 248-647-5111.
Telecopier: 248-647-6079.

George H. Meyer
John M. Kirk
Donald H. Baker, Jr.

Representative Clients: Available Upon Request.

For full biographical listings, see the Martindale-Hubbell Law Directory

MILLER, CANFIELD, PADDOCK AND STONE, P.L.C. (AV)

A Professional Limited Liability Company
Founded in 1852 by Sidney Davy Miller
150 West Jefferson, Suite 2500, 48226-4415
Telephone: 313-963-6420
Fax: 313-496-7500
Cable Address: "Stem Detroit"
URL: http://www.millercanfield.com
Ann Arbor, Michigan Office: 101 North Main Street, 7th Floor, 48104-1400.
Telephone: 734-663-2445.
Fax: 734-747-7147.
Troy, Michigan Office: 840 West Long Lake Road, Suite 200, 48098.
Telephone: 248-879-2000.
Fax: 248-879-2001.
Grand Rapids, Michigan Office: 99 Monroe, N.W., Suite 1200, 49503-2639.
Telephone: 616-454-8656.
Fax: 616-776-6322.
Howell, Michigan Office: 121 South Barnard Street, Suite 4, 48843-2305.
Telephone: 517-546-7600.
Telecopier: 517-546-6974.
Kalamazoo, Michigan Office: 444 West Michigan Avenue, 49007-3752.
Telephone: 616-381-7030.
Fax: 616-382-0244.
Lansing, Michigan Office: One Michigan Avenue, Suite 900, 48933-1609.
Telephone: 517-487-2070.
Fax: 517-374-6304.
Monroe, Michigan Office: 214 East Elm Avenue, Suite 100, 48162-2682.
Telephone: 734-243-2000.
Fax: 734-243-0901.
Washington, D.C. Office: 1900 K Street, N.W., Suite 1150. 20006.
Telephone: 202-429-5575; 785-0600.
Fax: 202-331-1118; 785-1234.
Pensacola, Florida Office: 25 West Cedar, 32501.
Telephone: 850-469-1088.
Fax: 850-432-0677.
New York, New York Office: 1450 Broadway, 41st Floor, 10018.
Telephone: 212-704-4400.
Fax: 212-704-4410.
Gdynia, Poland Office: UL. Slaska 21, 81-319.
Telephone: 011-485-831-2808.
Fax: 011-48-58-628 6411.
Warsaw, Poland Office: UL. Nowogrodzkall, 5th Floor, 00-513.
Telephone: 011-4822 529 0200.
Fax: 011-4822 529 0201.
Katowice, Poland Office: UL. Francuska 35/37, 40-027.
Telephone: 011 (48-32) 757-2414.
Fax: 011 (48-32) 757-2483.

PRINCIPALS OF FIRM

Robert E. Gilbert (Ann Arbor Office)
Stephen G. Palms (Troy Office)
Frank L. Andrews (Troy Office)

(See Next Column)

OF COUNSEL/SENIOR COUNSEL

Allen Schwartz

SENIOR ATTORNEY

David J. Hasper (Grand Rapids Office)

Representative Firm Clients: Chrysler Corporation; Comerica, Incorporated; City of Detroit, Michigan; Detroit Tigers, Inc.; First of Michigan; Ford Motor Company; Ford Motor Credit Company; Great Lakes Bancorp; Henry Ford Hospital; INVETECH Company.

For Complete List of Firm Personnel, See General Section

For full biographical listings, see the Martindale-Hubbell Law Directory

TIMMIS & INMAN L.L.P. (AV)

300 Talon Centre, 48207
Telephone: 313-396-4200
Facsimile: 313-396-4228
Email: info@timmis-inman.com *URL:* http://www.timmis-inman.com

Michael T. Timmis
Henry J. Brennan, III
Richard M. Miettinen
Bradley J. Knickerbocker
George M. Malis

Erich J. D'Andrea
Shannon M. Nichols
Anthony J. Long
Alex N. Saleh

OF COUNSEL

David E. Costa

Representative Clients: Talon, Inc.; Talon Development Associates, Inc.; Talon Automotive Group, Inc.; Chateau Estates, CP Limited Partnership; Chateau Communities, Inc.; Windsor Corp.; N'Tandem Properties, L.P.

For Complete List of Firm Personnel, See General Section

For full biographical listings, see the Martindale-Hubbell Law Directory

FARMINGTON HILLS, Oakland Co.

COUZENS, LANSKY, FEALK, ELLIS, ROEDER & LAZAR, P.C. (AV)

39395 West 12 Mile Road, Suite 200, 48331-2913
Telephone: 248-489-8600
Facsimile: 248-489-4156
Email: info@couzens.com *URL:* http://www.couzens.com

Jack S. Couzens, II
Jerry M. Ellis
Donald M. Lansky
Bruce J. Lazar
Alan C. Roeder
Renard J. Kolasa
Kathryn Gilson Sussman
Jeffrey A. Levine
Marc L. Prey
Lisa J. Walters
Donald A. Wagner
Michael P. Witzke
Cyrus Raamin Kashef
Gregg A. Nathanson
David B. Deutsch

Alisa A. Kwang
Turkia Awada Mullin
Raoul K. Maitra

Representative Clients: Provided upon request.
Reference: Michigan National Bank.

For Complete List of Firm Personnel, See General Section

For full biographical listings, see the Martindale-Hubbell Law Directory

FLAT ROCK, Wayne Co.

TUCHOW & TRAHEY (AV)

26316 Telegraph Road, 48134
Telephone: 734-782-2900
Fax: 734-782-2123
Bloomfield Hills, Michigan Office: Americenter of Bloomfield Hills, Seven West Square Lake Road.
Telephone: 313-963-7633.
Fax: 313-782-2123.

MEMBERS OF FIRM

Gerald Tuchow
Stephen J. Trahey

Reference: Old Kent Bank.

For full biographical listings, see the Martindale-Hubbell Law Directory

*GRAND RAPIDS,** Kent Co.

BORRE, PETERSON, FOWLER & REENS, P.C. (AV)

300 Ottawa N.W., Suite 500, P.O. Box 1767, 49501-1767
Telephone: 616-459-1971
Fax: 616-459-2393
Email: 105162.1531@compuserve.com

Glen V. Borre
James B. Peterson
Ben A. Fowler
Frank H. Johnson
Mark D. Sevald
William R. Vander Sluis
John C. Arndts

(See Next Column)

BORRE, PETERSON, FOWLER & REENS P.C., *Grand Rapids—Continued*

References: Old Kent Bank; NBD Bank/First Chicago Bank; The Huntington Bank.

For Complete List of Firm Personnel, See General Section

For full biographical listings, see the Martindale-Hubbell Law Directory

MCSHANE & BOWIE, P.L.C. (AV)

1100 Campau Square Plaza, 99 Monroe Avenue, N.W., P.O. Box 360, 49501-0360
Telephone: 616-732-5000
Fax: 616-732-5099

OF COUNSEL

Jack M. Bowie (Retired)

MEMBERS OF FIRM

David L. Smith
William H. Bowie
Keith P. Walker
Dan M. Challa
Richard A. Durell
Steven E. Bratschie

ASSOCIATES

Michael D. DeVries
Laura J. Luyendyk

Representative Clients: Old Kent Bank; Hartger & Willard Mortgage Associates, Inc.; Fryling Construction Co.; Wolverine Builders, Inc.; Beta Design Group, Inc.; Ramblewood, Ltd.; M. W. VanderVeen Co.; DeVries Development; Edward Finklestein; VanKampen Group.

For Complete List of Firm Personnel, See General Section

For full biographical listings, see the Martindale-Hubbell Law Directory

MILLER, CANFIELD, PADDOCK AND STONE, P.L.C. (AV)

A Professional Limited Liability Company
Founded in 1852 by Sidney Davy Miller
99 Monroe, N.W. Suite 1200, 49503-2639
Telephone: 616-454-8656
Fax: 616-776-6322
URL: http://www.millercanfield.com
Detroit, Michigan Office: 150 West Jefferson, Suite 2500, 48226-4415.
Telephone: 313-963-6420.
Fax: 313-496-7500.
Cable Address: "Stem Detroit."
Ann Arbor, Michigan Office: 101 North Main Street, 7th Floor, 48104-1400.
Telephone: 734-663-2445.
Fax: 734-747-7147.
Troy, Michigan Office: 840 West Long Lake Road, Suite 200, 48098.
Telephone: 248-879-2000.
Fax: 248-879-2001.
Howell, Michigan Office: 121 South Barnard Street, Suite 4, 48843-2305.
Telephone: 517-546-7600.
Telecopier: 517-546-6974.
Kalamazoo, Michigan Office: 444 West Michigan Avenue, 49007-3752.
Telephone: 616-381-7030.
Fax: 616-382-0244.
Lansing, Michigan Office: One Michigan Avenue, Suite 900, 48933-1609.
Telephone: 517-487-2070.
Fax: 517-374-6304.
Monroe, Michigan Office: 214 East Elm Avenue, Suite 100, 48162-2682.
Telephone: 734-243-2000.
Fax: 734-243-0901.
Washington, D.C. Office: 1900 K Street, N.W., Suite 1150. 20006.
Telephone: 202-429-5575; 785-0600.
Fax: 202-331-1118; 785-1234.
Pensacola, Florida Office: 25 West Cedar, 32501.
Telephone: 850-469-1088.
Fax: 850-432-0677.
New York, New York Office: 1450 Broadway, 41st Floor, 10018.
Telephone: 212-704-4400.
Fax: 212-704-4410.
Gdynia, Poland Office: UL. Slaska 21, 81-319.
Telephone: 011-485-831-2808.
Fax: 011-48-58-628 6411.
Warsaw, Poland Office: UL. Nowogrodzkall, 5th Floor, 00-513.
Telephone: 011-4822 529 0200.
Fax: 011-4822 529 0201.
Katowice, Poland Office: UL. Francuska 35/37, 40-027.
Telephone: 011 (48-32) 757-2414.
Fax: 011 (48-32) 757-2483.

PRINCIPALS

Mark E. Putney

RESIDENT SENIOR ATTORNEY

David J. Hasper

Representative Firm Clients: Chrysler Corporation; Comerica, Incorporated; City of Detroit, Michigan; Detroit Tigers, Inc.; First of Michigan; Ford Motor Company; Ford Motor Credit Company; Great Lakes Bancorp; Henry Ford Hospital; INVETECH Company.

For Complete List of Firm Personnel, See General Section

For full biographical listings, see the Martindale-Hubbell Law Directory

RUSSELL & BATCHELOR (AV)

Suite 411-S Waters Building, 161 Ottawa Avenue, N.W., 49503
Telephone: 616-774-8422
Fax: 616-774-0326
Email: WJR411S@aol.com

MEMBERS OF FIRM

Walter J. Russell
James W. Batchelor

Representative Clients: First National Acceptance Company; G.E. Capital Mortgage Svcs.; Chicago Title; Dept. of Veterans Affairs; Commercial Federal Mortgage Corp.; Department of Housing & Urban Development.; First Union Home Equity; Wendover; Bank Service Center; Federal Savings Bank; AMRESCO Mortgage Svcs., Inc.

For full biographical listings, see the Martindale-Hubbell Law Directory

TOLLEY, VANDENBOSCH, WALTON, KOROLEWICZ & BRENGLE, P.C. (AV)

1700 East Beltline, N.E., Suite 200, 49525-4512
Telephone: 616-447-1800
Fax: 616-447-1881

Peter R. Tolley
Lynwood P. VandenBosch
Michael C. Walton
James B. Doezema

For full biographical listings, see the Martindale-Hubbell Law Directory

WARNER NORCROSS & JUDD LLP (AV)

900 Old Kent Building, 111 Lyon Street, N.W., 49503-2489
Telephone: 616-752-2000
Fax: 616-752-2500
URL: http://www.wnj.com
Muskegon, Michigan Office: 400 Terrace Plaza, P.O. Box 900.
Telephone: 231-727-2600.
Fax: 231-727-2699.
Holland, Michigan Office: Curtis Center, Suite 300, 170 College Avenue.
Telephone: 616-396-9800.
Fax: 616-396-3656.
Southfield, Michigan Office: 1000 Town Center, Suite 650.
Telephone: 248-223-5000.
Fax: 248-223-5005.

MEMBERS OF FIRM

John H. Logie
James H. Breay
Robert H. Skilton, III (Resident Member, Southfield Office)
Ernest M. Sharpe
Stephen R. Kretschman
W. Michael Van Haren
Thomas H. Thornhill (Resident Member, Muskegon Office)
Jeffrey O. Birkhold
Timothy Hillegonds
John G. Cameron, Jr.
Carl W. Dufendach
Rodney D. Martin
Richard E. Cassard
John D. Dunn
William W. Hall
Bruce C. Young
Paul R. Jackson (Resident Member, Muskegon Office)
John V. Byl
Sue O. Conway
Michael H. Schubert (Resident Member, Muskegon Office)
William C. Fulkerson
Mark K. Harder (Resident Member, Holland Office)
Judith Lowitz Adler (Resident Member, Southfield Office)
James J. Rabaut
Loren M. Andrulis

ASSOCIATES

Mark E. Brouwer
Karen J. Vanderwerff
Dennis J. Donohue
Andrew D. Hakken
Melissa Nestico Collar
John E. Kessler (Resident, Holland Office)
Steven D. Johnson (Resident, Muskegon Office)
Christian E. Meyer
Jaron J. Nyhof (Resident, Holland Office)

OF COUNSEL

Thomas R. Winquist

For full biographical listings, see the Martindale-Hubbell Law Directory

GROSSE POINTE FARMS, Wayne Co.

JOHNSON & MCPHERSON, P.L.C. (AV)

81 Kercheval, 48236
Telephone: 313-885-4700
Fax: 313-888-5872

Edward C. Johnson
Dale T. McPherson

RETIRED

Jarvis J. Schmidt

For full biographical listings, see the Martindale-Hubbell Law Directory

HOLLAND, Ottawa Co.

CUNNINGHAM DALMAN, P.C. (AV)

321 Settlers Road, P.O. Box 1767, 49422-1767
Telephone: 616-392-1821
Fax: 616-392-4769
Email: cunndalm@crossover.net *URL:* http://www.holland-law.com

(See Next Column)

CUNNINGHAM DALMAN P.C.—*Continued*

Gordon H. Cunningham
Ronald L. Dalman
Max R. Murphy
James A. Bidol
Andrew J. Mulder
Kenneth B. Breese
Jeffrey K. Helder
Ronald J. Vander Veen
David M. Zessin
Mark H. Zietlow
Randall S. Schipper
Susan E. Vroegop
Joel G. Bouwens

Gregory J. McCoy
Jason M. Milstone
Aaron Leal
Dawn J. Ward

Representative Clients: Huntington National Bank; First of America Bank-Holland, N.A.; Ameribank; City of Holland; Holland Economic Development Corp.

For full biographical listings, see the Martindale-Hubbell Law Directory

*KALAMAZOO,** Kalamazoo Co.

EARLY, LENNON, PETERS & CROCKER, P.C. (AV)

900 Comerica Building, 49007-4752
Telephone: 616-381-8844
Fax: 616-349-8525
Email: elpc@michbar.org

Lawrence M. Brenton
Blake D. Crocker
Robert M. Taylor
Andrew J. Vorbrich

OF COUNSEL
Vincent T. Early

Attorneys for: Aetna Insurance; Kemper Group; Medical Protective Co.; Zurich Insurance; Liberty Mutual; Home Insurance.

For Complete List of Firm Personnel, See General Section

For full biographical listings, see the Martindale-Hubbell Law Directory

HOWARD & HOWARD ATTORNEYS, P.C. (AV)

The Michigan Building, Suite 200, 100 Portage Street, 49007-4802
Telephone: 616-382-1483
Telecopier: 616-382-1568
Bloomfield Hills, Michigan Office: The Pinehurst Office Center, Suite 101, 1400 North Woodward Avenue.
Telephone: 248-645-1483.
Telecopier: 248-645-1568.
Lansing, Michigan Office: The Phoenix Building, Suite 500, 222 Washington Square North.
Telephone: 517-485-1483.
Telecopier: 517-485-1568.
Peoria, Illinois Office: One Technology Plaza, Suite 600, 211 Fulton Street.
Telephone: 309-672-1483.
Telecopier: 309-672-1568.

Jeffrey P. Chalmers

Representative Clients: For Representative Client list, see General Practice, Kalamazoo, MI.

For Complete List of Firm Personnel, See General Section

For full biographical listings, see the Martindale-Hubbell Law Directory

KREIS, ENDERLE, CALLANDER & HUDGINS, A PROFESSIONAL CORPORATION (AV)

One Moorsbridge, P.O. Box 4010, 49003-4010
Telephone: 616-324-3000
Facsimile: 616-324-3010
Email: kech@kech.com *URL:* http://www.kech.com
Battle Creek, Michigan Office: One West Michigan Avenue, 49017.
Telephone: 616-966-3000.
Fax: 616-966-3022.

Alan G. Enderle
C. Reid Hudgins III
Stephen L. Simons (Resident, Battle Creek Office)
Jeffrey D. Swenarton
Peter F. Davis
Manuel R. Rupe

OF COUNSEL
James M. Sullivan (Resident, Battle Creek Office)

For Complete List of Firm Personnel, See General Section

For full biographical listings, see the Martindale-Hubbell Law Directory

LEWIS & ALLEN, P.C. (AV)

Old Kent Bank Building, Suite 800, 136 East Michigan Avenue, 49007-3946
Telephone: 616-388-7600
Fax: 616-349-3831

(See Next Column)

Dean S. Lewis
W. Fred Allen, Jr.
Barry R. Smith
William A. Redmond
Stephen M. Denenfeld
Anne McGregor Fries
Gregory G. St. Arnauld
James M. Marquardt
Christopher T. Haenicke
Winfield J. Hollander (1906-1996)

LEGAL SUPPORT PERSONNEL
Dorothy B. Kelly

For full biographical listings, see the Martindale-Hubbell Law Directory

LANSING, Ingham Co.

FOSTER, SWIFT, COLLINS & SMITH, P.C. (AV)

313 South Washington Square, 48933-2193
Telephone: 517-371-8100
Telecopier: 517-371-8200
URL: http://www.fosterswift.com
Farmington Hills, Michigan Office: 32300 Northwestern Highway, Suite 230.
Telephone: 248-539-9900.
Fax: 248-851-7504.

Robert J. McCullen
Brent A. Titus
Brian G. Goodenough
Geoffrey D. Harrison

LEGAL SUPPORT PERSONNEL
LEGAL ASSISTANTS
Kelly A. LaGrave, CLA

For Complete List of Firm Personnel, See General Section

For full biographical listings, see the Martindale-Hubbell Law Directory

FRASER TREBILCOCK DAVIS & FOSTER, P.C. (AV)

1000 Michigan National Tower, 48933
Telephone: 517-482-5800
Fax: 517-482-0887
URL: http://WWW.FTDF.COM
Detroit, Michigan Office: One Woodward Avenue, Suite 1550.
Telephone: 313-237-7300.
Fax: 313-961-1651.

Douglas J. Austin
Michael E. Cavanaugh
Stephen L. Burlingame

Counsel for: Greater Lansing Association of Realtors.

For full biographical listings, see the Martindale-Hubbell Law Directory

HOWARD & HOWARD ATTORNEYS, P.C. (AV)

The Phoenix Building, Suite 500, 222 Washington Square, North, 48933-1817
Telephone: 517-485-1483
Telecopier: 517-485-1568
Kalamazoo, Michigan Office: The Michigan Building, Suite 200, 100 Portage Street.
Telephone: 616-382-1483.
Telecopier: 616-382-1568.
Bloomfield Hills, Michigan Office: The Pinehurst Office Center, Suite 101, 1400 North Woodward Avenue.
Telephone: 248-645-1483.
Telecopier: 248-645-1568.
Peoria, Illinois Office: One Technology Plaza, Suite 600, 211 Fulton Street.
Telephone: 309-672-1483.
Telecopier: 309-672-1568.

Todd D. Chamberlain

Representative Clients: For Representative Client list, see General Practice, Lansing, MI.

For Complete List of Firm Personnel, See General Section

For full biographical listings, see the Martindale-Hubbell Law Directory

McCLELLAND & ANDERSON, L.L.P. (AV)

1305 South Washington, 48933
Telephone: 517-482-4890
Fax: 517-482-4875
URL: http://www.mcclelland-anderson.com

Gregory L. McClelland
Gail A. Anderson
David E. Pierson
Melissa A. Hagen

Marc D. Matlock

For full biographical listings, see the Martindale-Hubbell Law Directory

*MANISTEE,** Manistee Co.

GOCKERMAN, WILSON, SAYLOR & HESSLIN, P.C. (AV)

414 Water Street, P.O. Box 537, 49660-1531
Telephone: 231-723-8333
Fax: 231-723-3888
Toll Free: 1-800-748-0534
Email: gwsh@gwsh.com *URL:* http://www.gwsh.com
Grand Rapids, Michigan Office: 124 East Fulton Street. .
Telephone: 616-458-3994.
Beulah, Michigan Office: 425 N. U.S. 31,
Telephone: 231-882-7130.

Bruce C. Gockerman
Richard M. Wilson, Jr.
George V. Saylor, III
Daniel D. Hesslin
Lisa Martinuzzi
James B. Flickinger
David J. Bedells
(Resident, Beulah Office)

For full biographical listings, see the Martindale-Hubbell Law Directory

*MIDLAND,** Midland Co.

CURRIE KENDALL POLASKY MEISEL, PLC (AV)

6024 Eastman Avenue, P.O. Box 2765, 48641-2765
Telephone: 517-839-0300
Fax: 517-832-0077
Saginaw, Michigan Office: 4800 Fashion Square Boulevard, Suite 100, 48603.
Telephone: 517-792-9300; 517-792-1111.
Fax: 517-792-7000; 517-793-6597.

Gilbert A. Currie (1882-1960)
Gilbert A. Currie (1923-1998)
Peter J. Kendall (1961-1999)
William C. Collins
Ramon F. Rolf, Jr.
Daniel J. Cline
Peter A. Poznak
Julia A. Close
Jeffrey N. Dyer
Jonathan E. Lauderbach
Amy E. Wilson
Cheryl L. Whitman
Todd M. Gambrell
Frank M. Polasky
(Resident, Saginaw Office)
Robert H. Meisel
(Resident, Saginaw Office)
Michael H. Allen
(Resident, Saginaw Office)
Larry L. Preston
(Resident, Saginaw Office)
David J. Kolat
(Resident, Saginaw Office)
M. Randall Jurrens
(Resident, Saginaw Office)
John E. Gannon
(Resident, Saginaw Office)
Carolyn Pollock Cary
(Resident, Saginaw Office)
John D. Jolley
(Resident, Saginaw Office)
W. Jay Brown
(Resident, Saginaw Office)

OF COUNSEL
James A. Kendall

Counsel for: Chemical Financial Corp.; Chemical Bank & Trust Co.; Saginaw Valley State University; Northwood University; The Midland Foundation; Elsa U. Pardee Foundation; Rollin M. Gerstacker Foundation; Charles J. Strosacker Foundation.

For full biographical listings, see the Martindale-Hubbell Law Directory

*MONROE,** Monroe Co.

BRAUNLICH, RUSSOW & BRAUNLICH, A PROFESSIONAL CORPORATION (AV)

111 South Macomb Street, 48161
Telephone: 734-241-8300
Fax: 734-241-7715

William J. Braunlich, Jr.
(1924-1992)
Thomas P. Russow
William H. Braunlich

Philip A. Costello
Ann L. Nickel
Jeffrey A. Dulany, P.C.

LEGAL SUPPORT PERSONNEL
Ruth G. Flint

Representative Clients: State Farm Mutual Insurance Co.; Auto Club Insurance Assn.; Board of Road Commissioners, Monroe County; Port of Monroe; Monroe County Community College; City of Luna Pier; City of Petersburg; Auto-Owners Insurance Co.; Fremont Mutual Insurance Co.; Citizens Insurance Co. of America.

For full biographical listings, see the Martindale-Hubbell Law Directory

*MUSKEGON,** Muskegon Co.

CULVER, SHERIDAN, KNOWLTON, EVEN & FRANKS, P.C. (AV)

250 Terrace Plaza, P.O. Box 629, 49443
Telephone: 231-724-4320
Telecopier: 231-724-4330
Email: cskef@novagate.com

Fred C. Culver, Jr.
James M. Sheridan
Michael M. Knowlton
Kevin B. Even
Eugene A. Franks

(See Next Column)

David E. Waterstradt
Foster D. Potter
Douglas Poland
Scott Knowlton
Joseph S. Bush

Representative Clients: SPX Corp.; National City Bank of Michigan/Illinois; Old Kent Bank of Grand Haven; Comerica Bank; NBD Bank; East Shore Chemical Company; Muskegon County Association of Realtors; Midland Groceries.

For full biographical listings, see the Martindale-Hubbell Law Directory

LAGUE, NEWMAN & IRISH, A PROFESSIONAL CORPORATION (AV)

600 Terrace Plaza, P.O. Box 389, 49443
Telephone: 231-725-8148
Telecopier: 231-726-3404
Email: firm@lnilaw.com

J. Scott Timmer

General Counsel: Hackley Hospital & Medical Center; Kaydon Corp.; Cole's Quality Foods; Kurdziel Industries.
Local Counsel: SPX Corp.; Booth Newspapers Inc.; National City Bank; Neway Anchorlok International.

For Complete List of Firm Personnel, See General Section

For full biographical listings, see the Martindale-Hubbell Law Directory

OKEMOS, Ingham Co.

J. RICHARD ROBINSON, P.C. (AV)

2169 Jolly Road, Suite 1, P.O. Box 1430, 48805
Telephone: 517-349-3703
Fax: 517-349-4677
Email: jrobin2680@aol.com

J. Richard Robinson

For full biographical listings, see the Martindale-Hubbell Law Directory

*SAGINAW,** Saginaw Co.

BRAUN KENDRICK FINKBEINER PLC (AV)

101 N. Washington Suite 812, 48607-1297
Telephone: 517-753-3461
Telecopier: 517-753-3951
Email: ALBFIE@BKF-LAW.COM *URL:* http://www.bkf-law.com
Saginaw Township Office, Michigan Office: 5800 Gratiot Road, Suite 107, P.O. Box 5169. Telephone 517-799-8692.
Fax: 517-799-4666.
Bay City, Michigan Office: 201 Phoenix Building, P.O. Box 2039.
Telephone: 517-895-8505.
Telecopier: 517-895-8437.
Ann Arbor, Michigan Office: First National Building. 201 S. Main, Suite 700.
Telephone: 313-995-4100.
Telecopier: 313-995-4798.
Mt. Pleasant, Michigan Office: 805 North Brown.
Telephone: 517-775-7404.
Telecopier: 517-775-3764.

James V. Finkbeiner
Hugo E. Braun, Jr.
Thomas R. Luplow
Brian F. Bauer

Representative Clients: The Dow Chemical Co.; General Motors Corp.; Merrill, Lynch, Inc.; Saginaw General Hospital; Saginaw News; The Wickes Foundation.

For Complete List of Firm Personnel, See General Section

For full biographical listings, see the Martindale-Hubbell Law Directory

CURRIE KENDALL POLASKY MEISEL, PLC (AV)

4800 Fashion Square Boulevard, Suite 100, 48603
Telephone: 517-792-1111; 517-792-9300
Fax: 517-793-6597; 517-792-7000
Midland, Michigan Office: 6024 Eastman Avenue, P.O. Box, 2765.
Telephone: 517-839-0300.
Fax: 517-832-0077.

Frank M. Polasky
Robert H. Meisel
Michael H. Allen
Larry L. Preston
David J. Kolat
M. Randall Jurrens
John E. Gannon
Carolyn Pollock Cary
John D. Jolley
W. Jay Brown
William C. Collins
(Resident, Midland Office)
Ramon F. Rolf, Jr.
(Resident, Midland Office)
Daniel J. Cline
(Resident, Midland Office)
Peter A. Poznak
(Resident, Midland Office)
Julia A. Close
(Resident, Midland Office)
Jeffrey N. Dyer
(Resident, Midland Office)
Jonathan E. Lauderbach
(Resident, Midland Office)

(See Next Column)

CURRIE KENDALL POLASKY MEISEL PLC—*Continued*

Amy E. Wilson (Resident, Midland Office)
Todd M. Gambrell (Resident, Midland Office)
Cheryl L. Whitman (Resident, Midland Office)

OF COUNSEL

James A. Kendall (Resident, Midland Office)

Counsel for: Chemical Financial Corp.; Chemical Bank & Trust Co.; Saginaw Valley State University; Northwood University; The Midland Foundation; Elsa U. Pardee Foundation; Rollin M. Gerstacker Foundation; Charles J. Strosacker Foundation.

For full biographical listings, see the Martindale-Hubbell Law Directory

*ST. JOSEPH,** Berrien Co.

TROFF, PETZKE & AMMESON (AV)

Law and Title Building, 811 Ship Street, P.O. Box 67, 49085
Telephone: 616-983-0161
Facsimile: 616-983-0166
Email: pnalaw@qtm.net

MEMBERS OF FIRM

Roger A. Petzke
Charles F. Ammeson

ASSOCIATE

Bennett S. Schwartz

For full biographical listings, see the Martindale-Hubbell Law Directory

SOUTHFIELD, Oakland Co.

MADDIN, HAUSER, WARTELL, ROTH, HELLER & PESSES, P.C. (AV)

Third Floor Essex Centre, 28400 Northwestern Highway, P.O. Box 215, 48037
Telephone: 248-354-4030, 355-5200
Telefax: 248-354-1422

Milton M. Maddin (1902-1984)
Michael W. Maddin
Mark R. Hauser
C. Robert Wartell
Richard J. Maddin
Richard F. Roth
Harvey R. Heller
Ian D. Pesses
Michael S. Leib
Robert D. Kaplow
William E. Sigler
Stewart C. W. Weiner
Charles M. Lax
Stuart M. Bordman
Steven D. Sallen
Gregory J. Gamalski
Julie Chenot Mayer
Nathaniel H. Simpson
Ronald A. Sollish
Lowell D. Salesin

Mark H. Fink
Steven M. Wolock
Lori E. Talsky
Stephen E. Handelman
Ronald M. Stern
Martin Scott Frenkel
Gary M. Remer
Jennifer S. Sternberg
George V. Cassar, Jr.
Adam J. Goldstein

OF COUNSEL

Bruce N. Goldman

Reference: Comerica Bank.

For full biographical listings, see the Martindale-Hubbell Law Directory

MASON STEINHARDT JACOBS PERLMAN & PESICK, PROFESSIONAL CORPORATION (AV)

Suite 1500, 4000 Town Center, 48075-1415
Telephone: 248-358-2090
Fax: 248-358-3599
Email: admin@msjp.com *URL:* http://www.msjp.com

John E. Jacobs
Michael B. Perlman
Neil S. Silver
L. Jeffrey Zauberman
Diane Flagg Goldstein

Representative Clients: Citibank, N.A.; City of Dearborn; DeMattia Development Co.; Forest City Enterprises; Michigan Wholesale Drug Assn.; Mortgage Bankers Association of Michigan; Nationwide Insurance Co.; City of Taylor; Union Labor Life Insurance Co.; Yellow Freight Systems, Inc.

For Complete List of Firm Personnel, See General Section

For full biographical listings, see the Martindale-Hubbell Law Directory

MORGANROTH & MORGANROTH (AV)

3000 Town Center, Suite 1500, 48075
Telephone: 248-355-3084
Fax: 248-355-3017
URL: http://www.lawyers.com/morganrothlawfirm
New York, N.Y. Office: 156 W. 56th Street, Suite 1101. 10019.
Telephone: 212-586-5905.
Fax: 212-586-7302.

(See Next Column)

MEMBERS OF FIRM

Mayer Morganroth
Jeffrey B. Morganroth
Cherie Morganroth
Jason Ross Hirsch

Representative Clients: APCOA,Inc.; ; Mayor Coleman Young (Detroit); John Z. DeLorean; Realtek Industries, Inc.; Dr. Jack Kevorkian; Carolyn Warmus; Edward J. Holland, Jr.; Lyndon LaRouche; Thomas Warmus; Walter Keating.

For full biographical listings, see the Martindale-Hubbell Law Directory

NATHAN & NATHAN, P.C. (AV)

Suite 260, Franklin Center, 29100 Northwestern Highway, 48034
Telephone: 248-351-0099
Fax: 248-351-0487
Email: rnathan@nathannathan.com

Robert B. Nathan
Kenneth A. Nathan

Robert N. Bassel

For full biographical listings, see the Martindale-Hubbell Law Directory

SOMMERS, SCHWARTZ, SILVER & SCHWARTZ, P.C. (AV)

2000 Town Center, Suite 900, 48075
Telephone: 248-355-0300
Telecopier: 248-746-4001
Plymouth, Michigan Office: 747 South Main Street.
Telephone: 313-455-4250.

Steven J. Schwartz
Gary A. Taback
David M. Black
Joseph H. Bourgon

OF COUNSEL

Norman S. Sommers
Donald R. Epstein
Marvin R. Stempien

General Counsel for: Michigan National Bank; Madison National Bank; Bank Hapoalim, B.M.; Beal Bank, S.A.; C.A. Muer Corporation; Kojaian Properties, Inc.; Vlasic & Company; Foodland Distributors; Nederlander Corporation.

For Complete List of Firm Personnel, See General Section

For full biographical listings, see the Martindale-Hubbell Law Directory

*TRAVERSE CITY,** Grand Traverse Co.

DINGEMAN, DANCER & CHRISTOPHERSON, P.L.C. (AV)

100 Park Street, 49684
Telephone: 231-929-0500
Fax: 231-929-0504
Email: dingeman@dingemandancer.com *URL:* http://www.Dingemandancer.com

Daniel J. Dingeman

Representative Clients: Black Forest Motors-Mercedes Benz; WWTV/WWUP TV 9 & 10; Heritage Broadcasting; Acme Township; Northern Physicians Organization, Inc.; Northern Physicians Company, Ltd.; The Homestead Resort; Texas Instruments, Inc.

For full biographical listings, see the Martindale-Hubbell Law Directory

OLSON, NOONAN & BZDOK, P.C. (AV)

420 East Front Street, P.O. Box 2358, 49685-2358
Telephone: 616-946-0044
Fax: 616-946-4807

James M. Olson
John D. Noonan
Christopher M. Bzdok
Karen L. Ferguson
Scott W. Howard

For full biographical listings, see the Martindale-Hubbell Law Directory

TROY, Oakland Co.

CAMPBELL, O'BRIEN & MISTELE, P.C. (AV)

850 Stephenson Highway Suite 410, 48083-1163
Telephone: 248-588-5800
Fax: 248-588-6669; 1-888-647-8353
Email: COMLAW@ADVDATA.NET *URL:* http://www.lawyers.com/comlaw

Edwin G. O'Brien (1907-1983)
Dale C. Campbell
Henry E. Mistele
Paul W. Loock
Robert J. Figa
Curtis H. Mistele

References: First Federal of Michigan; Comerica Bank.

For full biographical listings, see the Martindale-Hubbell Law Directory

HAINER & BERMAN, P.C. (AV)

888 West Big Beaver, Suite 1400, 48084
Telephone: 248-244-8424
Fax: 248-244-8455

(See Next Column)

HAINER & BERMAN P.C., *Troy—Continued*

Michael J. Hainer | Leonard K. Berman
Kay E. Malaney

Drew S. Norton | Paul S. Miller

OF COUNSEL

Michael A. Kus | Robert F. Riley
Mark S. Demorest

Representative Clients: American Empire Surplus Lines Insurance Co.; Biomass Energy Systems, Inc.; Bridgestone/Firestone, Inc.; Central Distributors of Beer, Inc.; Champion Enterprises, Inc.; City Management Corp.; Clarklift of Detroit, Inc.; Federal Reserve Bank of Chicago; Hotel Investment Services, Inc.; M&O Marketing, Inc.

For full biographical listings, see the Martindale-Hubbell Law Directory

AUSTIN HIRSCHHORN, P.C. (AV)

Suite 710 Columbia Center, 201 West Big Beaver Road, 48084-4152
Telephone: 248-680-1660
Fax: 248-680-1671
Email: austinh@ix.netcom.com

Austin Hirschhorn

For full biographical listings, see the Martindale-Hubbell Law Directory

JACOB & WEINGARTEN (AV)

2301 West Big Beaver Road, Suite 777, 48084-3300
Telephone: 248-649-1900
Facsimile: 248-649-2920
Email: law@jacobweingarten.com
North Palm Beach, Florida Office: P.O. Box 14037, 33408.
Telephone: 561-640-5600.

Harry M. Eisenberg | Carole Crosby
Steven P. Schubiner | Vicky Wood Kvicala
Peter A. Nathan (Resident, North Palm Beach, Florida Office)

Representative Clients: Dean Witter Realty, Inc.; Ethan Allen Inc.; Franklin Group, Inc.; Kimco Realty Corporation; Ruby Tuesday, Inc.

For full biographical listings, see the Martindale-Hubbell Law Directory

POLING, MCGAW & POLING, P.C. (AV)

Suite 275, 5435 Corporate Drive, 48098
Telephone: 248-641-0500
Telecopier: 248-641-0506
URL: http://www.lawyers.com/polingmcgaw&poling

Benson T. Buck (1926-1989) | Gregory C. Hamilton
Richard B. Poling | Veronica B. O'Hara
D. Douglas McGaw | James R. Parker
Richard B. Poling, Jr. | Shannon M. Acton

OF COUNSEL

Ralph S. Moore

Representative Clients: City of Troy; United States Fidelity & Guaranty Co.; Sentry Insurance Co.; Admital Insurance; DeMaria Construction Co.; Leo Corporation; Aetna Casualty and Surety Co.; Concord Design; Pneumo-Abex.

For full biographical listings, see the Martindale-Hubbell Law Directory

WEST BLOOMFIELD, Oakland Co.

VALENTINE & ASSOCIATES, P.C. (AV)

5767 West Maple Road, Suite 400, 48322
Telephone: 248-851-3010
Fax: 248-851-1553
Email: vallaw@umich.edu

Stephen K. Valentine, Jr.

For full biographical listings, see the Martindale-Hubbell Law Directory

WESTLAND, Wayne Co.

ASKER, CHAPP & CLOS, P.C. (AV)

35551 Ford Road, Suite 100, 48185
Telephone: 734-326-2101
Fax: 734-595-9771
URL: http://www.lawyers.com/michigan
Torrance, California Office: 615 Hawaii Avenue, 90503.
Telephone: 310-320-5766.

Paul P. Asker | Gary E. Perlmuter
Sandra J. Chapp | Brian J. Considine
Charles E. Clos | J. Matthew Catchick, Jr.

For full biographical listings, see the Martindale-Hubbell Law Directory

YPSILANTI, Washtenaw Co.

PEAR SPERLING EGGAN & MUSKOVITZ, P.C. (AV)

5 South Washington Street, 48197
Telephone: 734-483-3626
Fax: 734-483-1107
Email: ameggan@ameritech.net
Ann Arbor, Michigan Office: Domino's Farms, 24 Frank Lloyd Wright Drive.
Telephone: 734-665-4441
Other Ypsilanti, Michigan Office: 2164 Bellevue at Washtenaw.
Telephone: 734-483-7177.

Lawrence W. Sperling | Andrew M. Eggan
Thomas E. Daniels

Counsel for: Domino's Pizza, Inc.; Citizens Banking Corp.; Townsend and Bottum, Inc.; The Credit Bureau of Ypsilanti; City of Ypsilanti (Labor Counsel); Michigan Municipal Worker's Compensation; Self-Insurance Fund.
Approved Attorneys for: Lawyers Title Insurance Corp.

For full biographical listings, see the Martindale-Hubbell Law Directory

SECURITIES LAW

ALABAMA

*BIRMINGHAM,** Jefferson Co.

BERKOWITZ, LEFKOVITS, ISOM & KUSHNER, A PROFESSIONAL CORPORATION (AV)

SouthTrust Tower, 420 North Twentieth Street, Suite 1600, 35203-5202
Telephone: 205-328-0480
Telecopier: 205-322-8007
URL: http://www.blik.com

B. G. Minisman, Jr.
Lana K. Hawkins (Not admitted in AL)

Matthew W. Barnes
Andrew R. Chambless

For Complete List of Firm Personnel, See General Section

For full biographical listings, see the Martindale-Hubbell Law Directory

BRADLEY ARANT ROSE & WHITE LLP (AV)

2001 Park Place, Suite 1400, P.O. Box 830709, 35283-0709
Telephone: 205-521-8000
Facsimile: 205-521-8800
Facsimile (SouthTrust Tower Office): 205-521-8500
URL: http://www.barw.com
Huntsville, Alabama Office: 200 Clinton Avenue West, Suite 900, 35801.
Telephone: 205-517-5100.
Facsimile: 205-533-5069.
Washington, D.C. Office: 801 Pennsylvania Avenue, NW, Suite 230, 20004.
Telephone: 202-347-8893.
Facsimile: 202-347-1684.

MEMBERS OF FIRM

John P. Adams
Hall B. Bryant III (Resident, Huntsville Office)
J. Paul Compton Jr.
Denson Nauls Franklin III
John B. Grenier (Resident, Huntsville Office)
John G. Harrell
Michael D. McKibben
John K. Molen
Virginia Calvert Patterson
Michael R. Pennington
Paul S. Ware

OF COUNSEL

Edward M. Selfe
C. Larimore Whitaker

ASSOCIATES

Hugh Chester Boston III
Dorothy D. Pak
Joseph E. Smith

For Complete List of Firm Personnel, See General Section

For full biographical listings, see the Martindale-Hubbell Law Directory

LIGHTFOOT, FRANKLIN & WHITE, L.L.C. (AV)

The Clark Building, 400 20th Street North, 35203
Telephone: 205-581-0700
Facsimile: 205-581-0799
Email: LFWlaw@LFWlaw.com *URL:* http://www.lfwlaw.com

Warren B. Lightfoot
Samuel H. Franklin
Mac M. Moorer
Sara Anne Ford

Robin Hansen Graves

For full biographical listings, see the Martindale-Hubbell Law Directory

J. VERNON PATRICK, JR. & ASSOCIATES, P.C. (AV)

1201 Financial Center, 505 20th Street North, 35203-4607
Telephone: 205-323-5665
Telecopier: 205-324-6221

J. Vernon Patrick, Jr.

Jeffrey Venton Havercroft

For full biographical listings, see the Martindale-Hubbell Law Directory

RITCHIE & REDIKER, L.L.C. (AV)

312 North 23rd Street, 35203
Telephone: 205-251-1288
Fax: 205-324-7830

Thomas A. Ritchie
J. Michael Rediker
Carolyn L. Duncan
Thomas L. Krebs
W. Clark Goodwin
Patricia Diak
Michael C. Skotnicki
William K. Holbrook

(See Next Column)

OF COUNSEL

Peyton D. Bibb, Jr.

Representative Clients: Citation Corporation; Commerce Bank of Alabama; Heritage Bank; First Metro Bank; State Employees Retirement System of Alabama; Wall Street Deli, Inc.; Sterne, Agee & Leach, Inc.; National Office Buyers; Peoples Savings Life Insurance Co.

For full biographical listings, see the Martindale-Hubbell Law Directory

*DOTHAN,** Houston Co.

JOHNSTON, HINESLEY, FLOWERS & CLENNEY, P.C., A PROFESSIONAL CORPORATION (AV)

291 North Oates Street, 36303
Telephone: 334-793-1115
Fax: 334-793-6603

G. David Johnston
William W. Hinesley
William T. Flowers
R. Eugene Clenney, Jr.

For full biographical listings, see the Martindale-Hubbell Law Directory

*MOBILE,** Mobile Co.

ARMBRECHT, JACKSON, DEMOUY, CROWE, HOLMES & REEVES, L.L.C. (AV)

1300 Riverview Plaza, P.O. Box 290, 36601
Telephone: 334-405-1300
Facsimile: 334-432-6843; 433-3821
Email: adc@ajlaw.com

MEMBERS OF FIRM

E. B. Peebles III
James Dale Smith
Thomas P. Oldweiler

Representative Clients: Cooper/T. Smith Stevedoring Co., Inc.; Loyal American Life Insurance Co.; Mobile Gas Service Corp.; Prudential-Bache Securities, Inc.; United Bank Corporation of Alabama, Inc.; WKRG-TV-Channel 5.

For Complete List of Firm Personnel, See General Section

For full biographical listings, see the Martindale-Hubbell Law Directory

ARIZONA

*PHOENIX,** Maricopa Co.

BONNETT, FAIRBOURN, FRIEDMAN & BALINT, P.C. (AV)

4041 North Central Avenue Suite 1100, 85012
Telephone: 602-274-1100
Fax: 602-274-1199

Jerry C. Bonnett
Andrew S. Friedman
Francis J. Balint, Jr.
H. Sullivan Bunch
Elaine A. Ryan
Wendy J. Harrison

For full biographical listings, see the Martindale-Hubbell Law Directory

FENNEMORE CRAIG, A PROFESSIONAL CORPORATION (AV)

3003 North Central Avenue, Suite 2600, 85012-2913
Telephone: 602-916-5000
Fax: 602-916-5999
Tucson, Arizona Office: One South Church Avenue, Suite 1000, 85701-1620.
Telephone: 520-879-6800.
Fax: 520-879-6899.

Robert J. Hackett
Mark A. Nesvig
Karen Ciupak McConnell
Janet W. Lord
W. T. Eggleston, Jr.

Susan M. Wissink
Paul A. Krulisky
Audrey V. Dorch (Not admitted in AZ)

LEGAL SUPPORT PERSONNEL

LEGAL ASSISTANTS

Vicki Montei
Charlene Sarich

For Complete List of Firm Personnel, See General Section

For full biographical listings, see the Martindale-Hubbell Law Directory

Phoenix—Continued

JENNINGS, STROUSS & SALMON, P.L.C. (AV)

A Professional Limited Liability Company
One Renaissance Square, Two North Central Avenue, 85004-2393
Telephone: 602-262-5911
Fax: 602-253-3255
Email: info@jsslaw.com *URL:* http://www.jsslaw.com
Arrowhead Office: 16150 North Arrowhead Fountains Center Drive, Suite 250, Peoria, Arizona.
Telephone: 623-878-2222.
Fax: 623-878-1333.

I. Douglas Dunipace
George C. Spilsbury
Anne L. Kleindienst

ASSOCIATES

Stephanie A. McRae
Scott M. Berg

For Complete List of Firm Personnel, See General Section

For full biographical listings, see the Martindale-Hubbell Law Directory

LEWIS AND ROCA, LLP (AV)

A Limited Liability Partnership including a Professional Corporation
40 North Central Avenue, 85004-4429
Telephone: 602-262-5311
Fax: 602-262-5747
Email: clientservice@lrlaw.com *URL:* http://www.lrlaw.com
Tucson, Arizona Office: One South Church Avenue, Suite 700, 86701-1620.
Telephone: 520-622-2090.
Fax: 520-622-3088. E-Mail: clientservice@lrlaw.com.
Las Vegas, Nevada Affiliated Office: Ashcraft and Heinz LLP, 3960 Howard Hughes Parkway, 89109.
Telephone: 702-990-3570.
Fax: 702-990-3571.

MEMBERS OF FIRM

Thomas G. Ryan
Scott DeWald
L. Keith Beauchamp
Jesse B. Simpson
Bryant D. Barber
Richard A. Halloran
Kevin G. Hunter

OF COUNSEL

Julie M. Arvo MacKenzie

Representative Clients: MarkAir, Inc.; Rauscher Pierce Refsnes; Rockford Corp.; Samaritan Health System; Skymall, Inc.

For Complete List of Firm Personnel, See General Section

For full biographical listings, see the Martindale-Hubbell Law Directory

MEYER, HENDRICKS & BIVENS, P.A. (AV)

3003 North Central Avenue Suite 1200, 85012-2915
Telephone: 602-604-2200
Facsimile: (24 Hrs.) 602-263-5333
Mailing Address: P.O. Box 2199, 85001-2199

Tom Galbraith
Rand Haddock
Ed Hendricks
Robert K. Rogers
Scott M. Theobald

Randall Lindsey
Salmeh K. Fodor

Reference: Northern Trust Bank of Arizona.

For full biographical listings, see the Martindale-Hubbell Law Directory

MITCHELL LAW OFFICES, A PROFESSIONAL CORPORATION (AV)

Anchor Centre One, Suite 122B, 2201 East Camelback Road, 85016
Telephone: 602-468-6450
Fax: 602-468-6451
Email: mitchell_atty@msn.com *URL:* http://www.mitchelllaw.com

Robert D. Mitchell

For full biographical listings, see the Martindale-Hubbell Law Directory

QUARLES & BRADY LLP (AV)

One Camelback Building, One East Camelback Road, Suite 400, 85012-1649
Telephone: 602-230-5500
Fax: 602-230-5598
URL: http://www.quarles.com
Milwaukee, Wisconsin Office: 411 East Wisconsin Avenue.
Telephone: 414-277-5000.
Fax: 414-271-3552.
Madison, Wisconsin Office: First Wisconsin Plaza, One South Pinckney Street, P.O. Box 2113.
Telephone: 608-251-5000.
Fax: 608-251-9166.
West Palm Beach, Florida Office: 222 Lakeview Avenue, 4th Floor.
Telephone: 407-653-5000.
Fax: 407-653-5333.

(See Next Column)

Naples, Florida Office: Barnett Center, 4501 Tamiami Trail North, Suite 300.
Telephone: 813-262-5959.
Fax: 813-434-4999.
Chicago, Illinois Office: Quarles & Brady LLC, Citicorp Center, 500 West Madison Street, Suite 3700.
Telephone: 312-715-5000.
Fax: 312-715-5155.

MEMBER OF THE FIRM

P. Robert Moya

ASSOCIATES

Mary Beth Miller Orson
Mark K. Briggs
Douglas P. Martin (Not admitted in AZ)
Leezie Kim

For full biographical listings, see the Martindale-Hubbell Law Directory

ROSHKA HEYMAN & DEWULF, PLC (AV)

Two Arizona Center, 400 North 5th Street, Suite 1000, 85004
Telephone: 602-256-6100
Facsimile: 602-256-6800
Email: rheyman@rhd-law.com

Paul J. Roshka, Jr.
Raymond S. Heyman
John E. DeWulf
Darlene M. Wauro

Alan S. Baskin
Randall H. Warner
Linda D. Skon

For full biographical listings, see the Martindale-Hubbell Law Directory

SCOTTSDALE, Maricopa Co.

TITUS, BRUECKNER & BERRY, P.C. (AV)

Scottsdale Centre Suite B-252, 7373 North Scottsdale Road, 85253-3527
Telephone: 602-483-9600
Fax: 602-483-3215
Email: TBandB@aol.com

Jon A. Titus
Kurt M. Brueckner
Charles R. Berry
Garry S. O'Rafferty
David R. Jordan

Marc D. Blonstein
Todd Michael Johnson
Matthew B. Levine
Christopher D. Lonn
Robin C. Martindale

OF COUNSEL

John R. Tellier
Timothy G. Burns

LEGAL SUPPORT PERSONNEL

Kellie E. Dicarlo
Belle Taylor

Representative Clients: Arizona Department of Insurance, Receivership Division; Beazer Homes; Cigna; Equipment Leasing Corp.; Hancock Communities; Harvard Investments; Heritage West Securities; Joseph Charles & Associates, Inc.; Peacock, Hislop, Staley Given, Inc.; Woodside Homes.

For full biographical listings, see the Martindale-Hubbell Law Directory

ARKANSAS

*FAYETTEVILLE,** Washington Co.

CONNER & WINTERS, P.L.L.C. (AV)

100 West Center Street, Suite 200, 72701-6081
Telephone: 501-582-5711
Facsimile: 501-587-1426
Email: postmaster@cwlaw.com
Tulsa, Oklahoma Office: Conner & Winters, A Professional Corporation, 3700 First Place Tower, 15 East 5th Street, 74103-4344.
Telephone: 918-586-5711.
Facsimile: 918-586-8982.
Oklahoma City, Oklahoma Office: Conner & Winters, A Professional Corporation, One Leadership Square, 211 North Robinson, Suite 1700, 73102-7101.
Telephone: 405-272-5711.
Facsimile: 405-232-2695.
Washington, D.C. Office: Conner & Winters, A Professional Corporation, 1101 Seventeenth Street, N.W., Suite 606, 20036-4704.
Telephone: 202-783-5711.
Facsimile: 202-783-5720.

Greg S. Scharlau

For Complete List of Firm Personnel, See General Section

For full biographical listings, see the Martindale-Hubbell Law Directory

*LITTLE ROCK,** Pulaski Co.

ALLEN LAW FIRM, A PROFESSIONAL CORPORATION (AV)

950 Centre Place, 212 Center Street, 72201
Telephone: 501-374-7100
Telecopier: 501-374-1611
Email: hwallen@cei.net *URL:* http://www.lawyers.com/allenlawfirm

H. William Allen

Representative Clients: Empire Funding Corporation.

For full biographical listings, see the Martindale-Hubbell Law Directory

FRIDAY, ELDREDGE & CLARK (AV)

A Limited Liability Partnership of Individuals and Professional Associations
Formerly, Smith, Williams, Friday, Eldredge & Clark
2000 Regions Center, 400 West Capitol Avenue, 72201-3493
Telephone: 501-376-2011
Telecopier: 501-376-2147
Email: fecmh@fec.net

MEMBERS OF FIRM

Paul B. Benham, III (P.A.) Larry W. Burks (P.A.)

Representative Clients: Entergy Arkansas, Inc.; Dillard's, Inc.; Acxiom Corp.; Entergy Corp.; Union Pacific Railroad; Browning Arms Co.; Phillips Cos., Inc.; Liberty Mutual Ins. Co.; ALLTEL Corp.

For Complete List of Firm Personnel, See General Section

For full biographical listings, see the Martindale-Hubbell Law Directory

HILBURN, CALHOON, HARPER, PRUNISKI & CALHOUN, LTD. (AV)

P.O. Box 1256, 72203-1256
Telephone: 501-372-0110
Fax: 501-372-2029
Email: hilburn@aristotle.net
North Little Rock, Arkansas Office: Eighth Floor, Mercantile Bank Building, One Riverfront Place, P.O. Box 5551, 72119.
Telephone: 501-372-0110.
Fax: 501-372-2029.

John E. Pruniski, III Phil Campbell

Representative Clients: Mercantile Bank of Arkansas, N.A.; Merrill Lynch Pierce Fenner & Smith, Inc.; Salomon Smith Barney, Inc.

For Complete List of Firm Personnel, See General Section

For full biographical listings, see the Martindale-Hubbell Law Directory

WILLIAMS & ANDERSON (AV)

Registered Limited Liability Partnership
Twenty-Second Floor, 111 Center Street, 72201
Telephone: 501-372-0800
Fax: 501-372-6453
Email: info@williamsanderson.com *URL:* http://www.williamsanderson.com

MEMBERS OF FIRM

Peter G. Kumpe J. Leon Holmes

Representative Clients: Arkansas Democrat-Gazette, Inc.; Arkansas Development Finance Authority; Entergy Corporation; Potlatch Corporation; Texaco Inc.; Roman Catholic Diocese of Little Rock; Wal-Mart Stores, Inc.

For Complete List of Firm Personnel, See General Section

For full biographical listings, see the Martindale-Hubbell Law Directory

WRIGHT, LINDSEY & JENNINGS LLP (AV)

200 West Capitol Avenue, Suite 2200, 72201
Telephone: 501-371-0808
Fax: 501-376-9442
Email: info@wlj.com *URL:* http://www.wlj.com
Fayetteville, Arkansas Office: 101 West Mountain Street, Suite 206, 72701.
Telephone: 501-575-0808.
Fax: 501-575-0999.
Russellville, Arkansas Office: 1110 West "B" Street, Suite E, 72801.
Telephone: 501-968-7995.

C. Douglas Buford, Jr.
John William Spivey III
Charles C. Price
Walter E. May
Walter McSpadden
Kevin W. Kennedy
Fred M. Perkins III

ASSOCIATES

Michele Simmons Allgood M. Sean Hatch

Representative Clients: J.B. Hunt Transport Services, Inc.; National Home Center, Inc.; NationsBank, N.A.; StaffMark, Inc.; Stephens Inc.

For full biographical listings, see the Martindale-Hubbell Law Directory

CALIFORNIA

COSTA MESA, Orange Co.

FELDHAKE, AUGUST & ROQUEMORE (AV)

Plaza Tower, Suite 1730, 600 Anton Boulevard, 92626-7124
Telephone: 714-438-3885
Fax: 714-438-3888
Email: farlaw@hqonline.com

Robert J. Feldhake
Kenneth S. August
Lisa A. Roquemore
Joshua M. Wolff

ASSOCIATES

Dimitri P. Gross
Supriya Kakkar
Katherine A. Slayton

OF COUNSEL

Arthur J. Swerdloff Arthur M. Wilcox, Jr.

For full biographical listings, see the Martindale-Hubbell Law Directory

RUTAN & TUCKER, LLP (AV)

A Partnership including Professional Corporations
611 Anton Boulevard, Fourteenth Floor, P.O. Box 1950, 92626-1998
Telephone: 714-641-5100; 213-625-7586
Telecopier: 714-546-9035
Email: rutan&tucker@rutan.com *URL:* http://www.rutan.com

MEMBERS OF FIRM

Milford W. Dahl, Jr.
Ira G. Rivin (P.C.)
Michael T. Hornak
Thomas G. Brockington
Evridiki (Vicki) Dallas
Thomas J. Crane
Larry A. Cerutti
James S. Weisz (P.C.)

ASSOCIATES

Kent M. Clayton
Cristy Lomenzo Parker
Natalie Sibbald Dundas
Alison M. Barbarosh
W. Andrew Moore
Natasha L. Pavia

For Complete List of Firm Personnel, See General Section

For full biographical listings, see the Martindale-Hubbell Law Directory

EMERYVILLE, Alameda Co.

JAMES JAY SELTZER (AV)

Watergate Towers, Tenth Floor, 2200 Powell Street, Suite 1035, 94608
Telephone: 510-596-2500
Telecopier: 510-596-2519
URL: http://www.secureadvise.com
Email: lawoffices@jjseltzer.com *URL:* http://www.lawyers.com/jamesjayseltzer

For full biographical listings, see the Martindale-Hubbell Law Directory

*FRESNO,** Fresno Co.

DOWLING, AARON & KEELER, INCORPORATED (AV)

6051 North Fresno Street, Suite 200, 93710
Telephone: 559-432-4500
Fax: 559-432-4590
Email: dak@daklaw.com *URL:* http://www.daklaw.com
Bakersfield, California Office: 110 South Mt. Claire, Suite 203. 93309.
Telephone: 661-396-0451. Web Site: http://www.daklaw.com.

John C. Ganahl

Reference: Wells Fargo Bank (Main).

For Complete List of Firm Personnel, See General Section

For full biographical listings, see the Martindale-Hubbell Law Directory

IRVINE, Orange Co.

BORCHARD & WILLOUGHBY, A PROFESSIONAL CORPORATION (AV)

18881 Von Karman Avenue, Suite 1400, 92612
Telephone: 949-263-0424
Fax: 949-263-1913

Michael D. Borchard
Michael L. Willoughby
Mark A. Rodriguez

Stephanie A. Pittaluga

For full biographical listings, see the Martindale-Hubbell Law Directory

Irvine—Continued

GIBSON, HAGLUND & PAULSEN (AV)

2 Park Plaza, 92614
Telephone: 949-752-1100
Fax: 949-752-1144
Email: bhaglund@ghp-law.com *URL:* http://www.ghp-law.com
Draper, Utah Office: 12226 South 1000 East, Suite 11, 84020.
Telephone: 801-501-7800.
Fax: 801-501-7844.

MEMBERS OF FIRM

Robert V. Gibson
Bruce H. Haglund
Edward (Ted) B. Paulsen (Resident, Draper, Utah Office)

ASSOCIATES

Jeremy W. Rawle (Resident, Draper, Utah Office)
Arlin P. Neser

For full biographical listings, see the Martindale-Hubbell Law Directory

OSWALD & YAP, A PROFESSIONAL CORPORATION (AV)

16148 Sand Canyon Avenue, 92618
Telephone: 949-788-8900
Telefax: 949-788-8980
URL: http://www.oswald-yap.com

Michael A. Oswald
Calvin C.S. Yap
Niall Sweetnam
Mark D. Holmes

Tzong-Bing Tsai
Joseph A. Weber
Edward W. Russey, III
Richard T. Hsueh
Carol A. Gefis

OF COUNSEL

John W. Allured
Reed M. Williams

For full biographical listings, see the Martindale-Hubbell Law Directory

LA JOLLA, San Diego Co.

FISHER THURBER LLP (AV)

La Jolla Executive Tower, 4225 Executive Square Suite 1600, 92037-1483
Telephone: 619-535-9400
Fax: 619-535-1616

David A. Fisher

OF COUNSEL

Marshall Thurber
Arthur M. Wilcox, Jr.
Mark T. Mauerman

ASSOCIATES

Timothy J. Fitzpatrick
Nancy L. Mauriello

LEGAL SUPPORT PERSONNEL

Merrill R. Cannon

For full biographical listings, see the Martindale-Hubbell Law Directory

*LOS ANGELES,** Los Angeles Co.

MICHAEL A. BERTZ (AV)

Suite 2400, 1801 Century Park East, 90067
Telephone: 310-277-2811
Fax: 310-277-2914

For full biographical listings, see the Martindale-Hubbell Law Directory

BRAND FARRAR & BUXBAUM LLP (AV)

515 South Flower Street, Suite 3500, 90071-2201
Telephone: 213-228-0288
Fax: 213-426-6222
Email: bfb-la@brandfarrar.com
Beijing (Peking), China Office: Suite 2518, China World Trade Centre, 1 Jian Guo Men Wai Avenue, Beijing, China.
Telephone: 86-10-6505-2288 Ext. 2523/2518.
Fax: 86-10-6505-2638. Email: bjbfbbj@public3.bta.net.cn
Chengdu, Sichuan, China Office: Suite 11A, Sichuan International Mansion, No. 1 Zhong Xi Shun Cheng Street, Chengdu, China.
Telephone: 86-28-652-1316.
Fax: 86-28-652-0547. Email: cdbfbcd@mail.sc.cninfo.net.
Chongqing, China Office: Suite 1510, Metropolitan Tower, 68 Zourong Lu, Chongqing, China.
Telephone: 86-23-6382-8381.
Fax: 86-23-6382-8373. Email: cqbfbcq@public.cta.cq.cn.
Guangzhou (Canton), China Office: Suite 1305, Main Tower, GITIC Plaza Hotel, 339 Huanshi Dong Road, Guangzhou, China.
Telephone: 86-20-8331-1888, Ext. 71305.
Fax: 86-20-8331-2671. Email: gzbfbgz@public.guangzhou.gd.cn.
Hong Kong, China Office: Brand Farrar Buxbaum LLP, 5/F., Landmark East, 12 Ice House Street, Central, Hong Kong, China.
Telephone: 852-2523-7001.
Fax: 852-2845-0947. Email: hkbfbhk@hk.super.net.

(See Next Column)

Los Angeles, California Office: Brand Farrar & Buxbaum LLP, Suite 3500, 515 South Flower Street, Los Angeles, California, 90071-2201.
Telephone: 213-228-0288.
Fax: 213-426-6222. Email: bfb-la@brandfarrar.com.
New York, New York Office: 275 Madison Avenue, 37th Floor, New York, New York, 10097.
Telephone: 212-286-0038.
Fax: 212-573-9077. Email: martineh@aol.com
Shanghai, China Office: Brand Farrar Buxbaum LLP, Suites 2611-12, Central Plaza, 227 Huangpi Bei Lu, Shanghai, China.
Telephone: 86-21-6375-8918.
Fax: 86-21-6375-8922. Email: shbfbsh@public2.sta.net.cn
Shenzhen, China Office: Suite 2103A, Shenzhen Development Center, Renmin Nan Lu, Shenzhen, China.
Telephone: 86-755-229-8009.
Fax: 86-755-229-8011. Email: szbfbsz@public.szptt.net.cn.
Ulaanbaatar, Mongolia Office: Brand Farrar Buxbaum LLP, 4/F., Time Center, No. 50 Baga Toiruu, Ulaanbaatar, Mongolia.
Telephone: 976-1-31-0711.
Fax: 976-1-32-5102. Email: mgbfbmg@magicnet.mn.
Xiamen, China Office: Suite 1182 Jian Ye Building, 28 Hubin North Road, Xiamen, China.
Telephone: 86-592-506-3059.
Fax: 86-592-511-1044. Email: xmbfbxm@public.xm.fj.cn.
Associated Office, Mumbai, Bombay, India: Shah & Sanghavi, Advocates, Solicitors & Notary, 114-A Mittal Court, Nariman Point, Mumbai 400 021 India.
Telephone: 91-22-285-5755/56 or 91-22-285-3592/93.
Fax: 91-22-284-5040.

PRINCIPALS

Michael A. Brand
David C. Buxbaum (China Offices)
Kenneth Y. Choy (Hong Kong Office)
Robert W. Dziubla
David W. Farrar
Amy E. Freilich
Margaret G. Graf
John Masao Iino
Charles K. Kolstad
Edward H. Martin (New York Office)
Gregory D. Trimarche
Li Zhuogen (China Offices)

OTHER ATTORNEYS RESIDENT IN LOS ANGELES OFFICE

Sherry L. Geyer
Joan M. Marquardt
James H. Service
Jeffrey S. Allen
Julia Sylva
Brian J. Kim
Lisa Teng

OTHER ATTORNEYS RESIDENT IN BEIJING OFFICE

Hao Xiaodong
Bin Zhao
Luo Rongping
Zhang Chunbo

OTHER ATTORNEYS RESIDENT IN CHENGDU, SICHUAN OFFICE

Zeng Xiangyu
Wu Wen

OTHER ATTORNEY RESIDENT IN CHONGQING OFFICE

Du Fei

OTHER ATTORNEYS RESIDENT IN GUANGZHOU OFFICE

Zou Wenyan (Not admitted in United States)
Feng Ruiding
Jia Guangxi

OTHER ATTORNEYS RESIDENT IN HONG KONG OFFICE

Shane F. Weir
Cheonghar Wong
N.T.S. Kularatne
Simon Woo
David William Gunson
Arthur Burton Crook
Simon K.C. Lee
Cheng Yuen Yi
Lo Wing Cheong
Nicholas C. McGrenra
Eva Y.N. Kwok

OTHER ATTORNEYS RESIDENT IN NEW YORK OFFICE

Vincent I. S. Hsieh (Of Counsel)
Jeffrey Schall
Jonathan Chun Wang

OTHER ATTORNEYS RESIDENT IN SHANGHAI OFFICE

Lin Yong
Wu Hong Liang
Tang Ying
Zhang Guoyao
Qi Zhenwen

OTHER ATTORNEYS RESIDENT IN SHENZHEN OFFICE

Zhong Wenya
Zhang He

OTHER ATTORNEYS RESIDENT IN ULAANBAATAR OFFICE

Byambaa Bayarmaa
Ajiv Enkhtuya

OTHER ATTORNEY RESIDENT IN XIAMEN OFFICE

Deng Sheng

For full biographical listings, see the Martindale-Hubbell Law Directory

CLARK & TREVITHICK, A PROFESSIONAL CORPORATION (AV)

800 Wilshire Boulevard, 12th Floor, 90017
Telephone: 213-629-5700
Telecopier: 213-624-9441
Email: postmaster@clarktrev.com
San Francisco, California Office: 456 Montgomery Street, 20th Floor.
Telephone: 415-288-6520.
Fax: 415-398-2820.

(See Next Column)

CLARK & TREVITHICK A PROFESSIONAL CORPORATION—*Continued*

Donald P. Clark
Alexander C. McGilvray, Jr.
Kevin P. Fiore
Michael K. Wofford
Brent A. Reinke

For Complete List of Firm Personnel, See General Section

For full biographical listings, see the Martindale-Hubbell Law Directory

DONAHUE MESEREAU & LEIDS L.L.P. (AV)

A Limited Liability Partnership including Professional Corporations
1900 Avenue of the Stars Suite 2700, 90067
Telephone: 310-277-1441
Facsimile: 310-277-2888

Michael D. Donahue (A Professional Corporation)
Asher M. Leids
Dave Lenny
Kirsten L. Anderson
Jacqueline L. Shulman
Amy S. Novicoff (Not admitted in CA)
Julia A. Longjohn

OF COUNSEL

Thomas A. Mesereau, Jr. (A Professional Corporation)

For full biographical listings, see the Martindale-Hubbell Law Directory

HENNIGAN, MERCER & BENNETT (AV)

601 South Figueroa Street, Suite 3300, 90017
Telephone: 213-694-1200
Fax: 213-694-1234
Email: Silverm@hmb.com

J. Michael Hennigan
Bruce Bennett
John L. Amsden
Shawna L. Ballard
Mary H. Chu
Kirk D. Dillman
C. Dana Hobart
Jeanne E. Irving
James O. Johnston
Laura Lindgren
Bruce R. MacLeod
Peter J. Most
Robert L. Palmer
Lee W. Potts
Lauren A. Smith
Michael Swartz

ASSOCIATES

Nichole M. Auden
Gregory K. Jones
Linda A. Kontos
Joshua M. Mester
Claudia Schweikert
Thomas Bernard Watson
Jeffrey C. Henneforth

OF COUNSEL

James W. Mercer
Mark A. Albert
Kenneth A. O'Brien, Jr.

For full biographical listings, see the Martindale-Hubbell Law Directory

KONOWIECKI & RANK LLP (AV)

A Partnership including a Professional Corporation
Library Tower, 633 West 5th Street, Suite 3500, 90071-2007
Telephone: 213-229-0990
Telefax: 213-229-0992

Peter C. Rank
Joseph S. Konowiecki
Michael C. Foster
Jon N. Manzanares
Kevin B. Kroeker
Peter Roan
Peter R. Mason
Denise E. Hanna
Edna M. Chism
Scott J. Moore
Robert C. Hayden
Gail D. Schubert

ASSOCIATES

Cynthia J. Billey
Michael J. Blake
Ana Castillo
Ronan Cohen
Richard A. Cross
Rosa Kwon Easton
I-Fan C. Go
Melinda A. Hess
Sandra Lee Hitt
Lynn E. Iba
Robert M. Kessler
Harry H.W. Kim
Thomas C. Knego
Stephen J. Krause
Phillip R. Maltin
John A. Mueller
Jeffrey D. Olster
Leslie Overfelt
Gary S. Pancer
Tallien Perry
Payman Pezhman
Harold C. Pope
Robin M. Prendergast
Ira L. Robinson
Michael B. Spencer
India S. Thompson
Keith A. Weaver
John A. Zrnich

Representative Clients: PacifiCare Health Systems, Inc.; Henry Mayo Newhall Memorial Hospital; Santa Clarita Health Care Assoc.; College Health Enterprises; Granada Hills Community Hospital; Redlands Community Hospital; Health Care Partners.
Reference: Bank of America.

For full biographical listings, see the Martindale-Hubbell Law Directory

MATTHIAS & BERG LLP (AV)

1990 South Bundy Drive, Suite 790, 90025-5244
Telephone: 310-820-0083
Facsimile: 310-820-8313
Email: info@matthiasberg.com

(See Next Column)

MEMBERS OF FIRM

Michael R. Matthias
Jeffrey P. Berg

ASSOCIATES

Kenneth M. H. Hoff
Ari Lorin Markow

OF COUNSEL

Stuart R. Singer

Representative Clients: Am Tec, Inc.; Chatsworth Products, Inc.; Columbia Capital Corp.; Greater China Corp.; National Quality Care, Inc.; Network Holdings International, Inc.; Private Investors Equity Group; Residential Resources, Inc.

For full biographical listings, see the Martindale-Hubbell Law Directory

MILBANK, TWEED, HADLEY & MCCLOY LLP (AV)

601 South Figueroa Street, 90017
Telephone: 213-892-4000
Fax: 213-629-5063
Email: postmaster@milbank.com *URL:* http://www.milbank.com
New York, New York Office: 1 Chase Manhattan Plaza, 10005-1413.
Telephone: 212-530-5000.
Fax: 212- 530-5219.
Midtown Office: 375 Park Avenue, Suite 3601, 10152.
Telephone: 212-530-5800.
Fax: 212-530-0158.
Washington, D.C. Office: International Square Building, Suite 1100, 1825 Eye Street, N.W., 20006.
Telephone: 202-835-7500.
Fax: 202-835-7586.
Tokyo, Japan Office: Fukoku Seimei Building, 2-2, Uchisaiwai-cho 2-Chome, Chiyoda-ku, Tokyo 100-0011, Japan.
Telephone: 011-81-3-3504-1050.
Fax: 011-81-3-3595-2790, 011-81-3-3595-2840.
London, England Office: Dashwood House, 69 Old Broad Street, London, EC2M 1QS.
Telephone: 011-44-207-448-3000.
Fax: 011-44-207-448-3029.
Hong Kong Office: 3007 Alexandra House, 16 Charter Road.
Telephone: 011-852-2571-4888.
Fax: 011-852-2840-0792, 011-8522-845-9046.
Singapore Office: 14-00 Caltex House, 30 Raffles Place, 048622.
Telephone: 011-65-428-2400.
Fax: 011-65-428-2500.
Moscow, Russia Office: 24/27 Sadovaya-Samotyochnya, Moscow, 103051.
Telephone: 011-7-501-258-5015.
Fax: 011-7-501-258-5014.

PARTNERS

Kenneth J. Baronsky
Deborah Baumgart
Eric H. Schunk
Neil J Wertlieb

ASSOCIATES

Brett D. Goldblatt
Edward V. Kayukov
Tobin D. Lippert
Melainie K. Mansfield
Kendrick F. Royer

For Complete List of Firm Personnel, See General Section

For full biographical listings, see the Martindale-Hubbell Law Directory

O'MELVENY & MYERS LLP (AV)

400 South Hope Street, 90071-2899
Telephone: 213-430-6000
Facsimile: 213-430-6407
Cable: MOMS
Telex: 674122
Email: omminfo@omm.com *URL:* http://www.omm.com
Century City, CA Office: 1999 Avenue of the Stars, Los Angeles, 90067-6035.
Telex: 674097. Tel: 310-553-6700.
Fax: 310-246-6779.
Newport Beach, CA Office: 610 Newport Center Drive, 92660-6429.
Telex: 4722088. Tel: 949-760-9600.
Fax: 949-823-6994.
San Francisco, CA Office: Embarcadero Center West, 275 Battery Street, 94111-3305. Tel: 415-984-8700.
Fax: 415-984-8701.
New York, NY Office: Citicorp Center, 153 East 53rd Street, 10022-4611.
Telex: 129165. Tel: 212-326-2000.
Fax: 212-326-2061.
Washington, DC Office: 555 13th Street, N.W., 20004-1109.
Cable: MOMSWSH.
Telex: 89622. Tel: 202-383-5300.
Fax: 202-383-5414.
London Office: O'Melveny & Myers, 3 Finsbury Square, London, EC2A 1LA, England. Tel: 44-171-256-8451. Fax 44-171-638-8205.
Tokyo Office: Akasaka Twin Tower, East 14F, 2-17-23, Akasaka, Minato-ku, Tokyo 107-0052, Japan. Tel: 03-5562-2800.
Fax: 03-5575-3840.
Hong Kong Office: O'Melveny & Myers, Suite 1905, Tower Two, Lippo Centre, 89 Queensway, Central, Hong Kong. Tel: 852-2523-8266.
Fax: 852-2522-1760.

(See Next Column)

O'MELVENY & MYERS LLP, *Los Angeles—Continued*

Shanghai Office: Kerry Centre, 20F, 1515 Nanjing Road West, Shanghai, 200040 People's Republic of China. Tel: 86-21-5298-5600.
Fax: 86-21-5298-5500.

PARTNER

John D. Hardy, Jr.

For Complete List of Firm Personnel, See General Section

For full biographical listings, see the Martindale-Hubbell Law Directory

ROSENFELD, WOLFF, ARONSON, KURLAND & KLEIN, A PROFESSIONAL CORPORATION (AV)

2049 Century Park East, Suite 3090, 90067
Telephone: 310-556-1221
Fax: 310-556-0401

Morton M. Rosenfeld
Alan D. Aronson
Steven G. Wolff
Marta T. Kurland
David C. Klein

Paul R. Rosenbaum
Debra E. Best

For full biographical listings, see the Martindale-Hubbell Law Directory

NEWPORT BEACH, Orange Co.

KRISTIN M. CANO (AV)

One Corporate Plaza, Suite 110, 92660
Telephone: 949-759-1505
FAX: 949-640-9535
URL: http://www.lawyers.com/kcano
Email: KristinCanoLawOffice@internetMCI.com *URL:* http://www.securities-law.com

For full biographical listings, see the Martindale-Hubbell Law Directory

PALO ALTO, Santa Clara Co.

CHRISTOPHER REAM (AV)

1755 Embarcadero Road, Suite 200, 94303
Telephone: 650-424-0821
Facsimile: 650-493-7912
Email: ream@aya.yale.edu

For full biographical listings, see the Martindale-Hubbell Law Directory

*SACRAMENTO,** Sacramento Co.

BARTEL ENG LINN & SCHRODER (AV)

300 Capitol Mall, Suite 1100, 95814
Telephone: 916-442-0400
Facsimile: 916-442-3442
Email: barteleng@barteleng.com *URL:* http://www.barteleng.com

Scott E. Bartel
Roger D. Linn
Daniel B. Eng
Regina J. Schroder

Jeff D. Barlow
Eric J. Stiff

OF COUNSEL

Vincent DiCarlo

For full biographical listings, see the Martindale-Hubbell Law Directory

*SAN DIEGO,** San Diego Co.

DUCKOR SPRADLING & METZGER, A LAW CORPORATION (AV)

401 West A Street, Suite 2400, 92101-7909
Telephone: 619-231-3666
Telecopier: 619-231-6629
Email: dsm@dsm-law.com *URL:* http://www.dsm-law.com

Michael J. Duckor
Stephen A. Bond
Gary J. Spradling
R. Anthony Mahavier
Scott L. Metzger
Robin Assaf Wofford
John C. Wynne
K. Jill Osmars
John W. Cutchin
Stephen A. Colley
Robert L. Kenny
Kevin M. Bagley
Li-An C. Leonard
Robert J. Solis
John J. Freni

Jamie M. Ryan
Robert M. Shaughnessy
Pamela LaBruyere
Michael W. Vivoli
James B. Ryan
Matthew O. Osborne
Gregory P. Olson
Scott R. Omohundro
Michael A. Reed

Representative Clients: Brookstreet Securities Corp.; City of Vista, California; Invivo Research, Inc.; Leucadia National Corp.; National Dispatch Center; County of Orange, California.

For full biographical listings, see the Martindale-Hubbell Law Directory

DUKE GERSTEL SHEARER, LLP (AV)

A Registered Limited Liability Partnership
Sixth Floor, 101 West Broadway, P.O. Box 85470, 92186-5470
Telephone: 619-232-0816
800-405-0816
Fax: 619-232-4661
Email: lawyers@dgsllp.com *URL:* http://www.dgsllp.com
Costa Mesa, California Office: 3200 Park Center Drive, Suite 1000, 92626.
Telephone: 949-551-8664, 800-405-0816.
Los Angeles, California Office: 10866 Wilshire Boulevard, Suite 1400, 90024.
Telephone: 310-475-7118, 800-405-0816.
San Francisco, California Office: 744 Montgomery Street, Fifth Floor, 94111.
Telephone: 415-773-0101.
Palm Springs, California Office: 1111 East Tahquitz Canyon Way, Suite 110, 92262.
Telephone: 760-322-7846.
Phoenix, Arizona Office: One Columbus Plaza, 3636 North Central Avenue, Suite 1200, 85012.
Telephone: 602-650-2060.
Fax: 602-650-2089.
Tucson, Arizona Office: 6969 East Sunrise Drive, Suite 102, 85750.
Telephone: 520-615-8858.
Fax: 520-615-1069.
Affiliate Las Vegas, Nevada Office: Parsons & Pursiano, LLP, City Center West, Suite 108, 7201 W. Lake Mead Boulevard, 89128.
Telephone: 702-384-9900.
Facsimile: 702-384-5900.

MEMBER OF FIRM

Robert D. Shoecraft

Reference: Bank of Commerce.

For full biographical listings, see the Martindale-Hubbell Law Directory

FERRIS & BRITTON, A PROFESSIONAL CORPORATION (AV)

1600 First National Bank Center, 401 West A Street, 92101
Telephone: 619-233-3131
Fax: 619-232-9316
Email: manager@ferrisbritton.com *URL:* http://www.ferrisbritton.com

Alfred G. Ferris
Margaret Prodanov

Representative Clients: Annabooks, Inc.; Invitrogen Corporation; Global Wireless Communications; QED Biosciences, Inc.; Structural Bioinformatics, Inc.; ZyGam, Inc.

For Complete List of Firm Personnel, See General Section

For full biographical listings, see the Martindale-Hubbell Law Directory

LUCE, FORWARD, HAMILTON & SCRIPPS LLP (AV)

A Partnership including Professional Corporations
600 West Broadway, Suite 2600, 92101
Telephone: 619-236-1414
Fax: 619-232-8311
URL: http://www.luce.com
La Jolla, California Office: 4275 Executive Square, Suite 800, 92037.
Telephone: 858-455-6611.
Fax: 858-232-8311.
Los Angeles, California Office: 777 South Figueroa, Suite 3600, 90017.
Telephone: 213-892-4992.
Fax: 213-892-7731.
San Francisco, California Office: 121 Spear Street, Suite 200, 94105.
Telephone: 415-356-4600.
Fax: 415-356-4610.
New York, N.Y. Office: Citicorp Center, 153 East 53rd Street, 26th Floor, 10022.
Telephone: 212-754-1414.
Fax: 212-644-9727.
Chicago, Illinois Office: 180 North La Salle Street, Suite 3110, 60601.
Telephone: 312-641-0580.
Fax: 312-641-0380.

G. Edward Arledge
Dennis J. Doucette
Robert G. Copeland
Otto E. Sorensen

ASSOCIATES

David M. Clark
Steven J. Davis
Michael G. Fraunces

For Complete List of Firm Personnel, See General Section

For full biographical listings, see the Martindale-Hubbell Law Directory

MILLER MILOVE & KOB, P.C. (AV)

The Koll Center, 501 West Broadway, Suite 720, 92101
Telephone: 619-696-5200
Facsimile: 619-696-5393
Email: mmandkob@ix.netcom.com *URL:* http://www.lawyers.com/millermilove&kob

(See Next Column)

MILLER MILOVE & KOB P.C.—*Continued*

Brian D. Miller
Bradd L. Milove
Jeffrey S. Kob
Cynthia M. Schleindl

Beth A. Saurer

Representative Clients: Broadcort Capital Corporation; First Wall Street; Bank of Commerce; Personal Computers Products, Inc.; IDS Financial Services; Iowa Grain Company; JB Oxford & Company; Sentra Securities; Spelman & Co.; Vanguard Capital.

For full biographical listings, see the Martindale-Hubbell Law Directory

*SAN FRANCISCO,** San Francisco Co.

BERMAN, DEVALERIO, PEASE & TABACCO, LLP (AV Ⓣ)

425 California Street, 94104-2205
Telephone: 415-433-3200
Facsimile: 415-433-6382
URL: http://www.bermanesq.com
Boston, Massachusetts Office: Berman, Devalerio & Pease, One Liberty Square, 02109.
Telephone: 617-542-8300.
Facsimile: 617-542-1194.

Joseph J. Tabacco, Jr.

Christopher T. Heffelfinger, Jr.
Nicole Lavallee
Jennifer S. Abrams

OF COUNSEL

Alan Anthony Beaven

For full biographical listings, see the Martindale-Hubbell Law Directory

RAYMOND N. STELLA ERLACH (AV)

One Maritime Plaza, Fourth Floor, 94111
Telephone: 415-788-3322
Fax: 415-788-8613

OF COUNSEL

Gregory J. Erlach
Stephen Peter U. Erlach

Reference: Bank of America Private Banking, San Francisco, California.

For full biographical listings, see the Martindale-Hubbell Law Directory

GOLD BENNETT CERA & SIDENER LLP (AV)

595 Market Street, Suite 2300, 94105
Telephone: 415-777-2230
Fax: 415-777-5189
Email: info@gbcsf.com *URL:* http://www.gbcsf.com

Paul F. Bennett
Solomon B. Cera
Steven O. Sidener

George S. Trevor
Patricia A. Szumowski
Gary Garrigues
Joseph M. Barton
Steven J. Mulligan

For full biographical listings, see the Martindale-Hubbell Law Directory

LIEFF, CABRASER, HEIMANN & BERNSTEIN, LLP (AV)

Embarcadero Center West, 30th Floor, 275 Battery Street, 94111
Telephone: 415-956-1000
Telecopier: 415-956-1008
Email: mail@lchb.com *URL:* http://www.lchb.com
New York, N.Y. Office: 10 Rockefeller Plaza, 12th Floor, 10020-1903.
Telephone: 212-218-6600.
Fax: 212-218-6608.

Robert L. Lieff
Elizabeth J. Cabraser
Richard M. Heimann
William Bernstein
William B. Hirsch
James M. Finberg
Karen E. Karpen
Joseph R. Saveri
Donald C. Arbitblit
Steven E. Fineman (Resident, New York, N.Y. Office)
Robert J. Nelson
Jacqueline E. Mottek
Morris A. Ratner
Melanie M. Piech
Kelly M. Dermody
Jonathan D. Selbin
Richard M. Franco
Barry R. Himmelstein
Joshua P. Davis
Michael W. Sobol
Robert G. Eisler (Resident, New York, N.Y. Office)

Jennie L. Anderson
Lori E. Andrus
Caryn Becker
Joan T. Brown (Not admitted in CA)
Stephen H. Cassidy
Paulina do Amaral
Eric B. Fastiff
Hector D. Geribon (Resident, New York, N.Y. Office)
Pierce Gore
Rebecca M. Katz (Resident, New York, N.Y. Office)
Lisa J. Leebove
Karen J. Mandel (Resident, New York, N.Y. Office)

(See Next Column)

Scott P. Nealey
Erik L. Shawn (Resident, New York, N.Y. Office)
David S. Stellings (Resident, New York, N.Y. Office)
Steven M. Tindall
Fabrice N. Vincent
Jonathan M. Watkins
Heather A. Woodard
Yu-Yee Wu

For full biographical listings, see the Martindale-Hubbell Law Directory

MANWELL & MILTON (AV)

20 California Street, Third Floor, 94111
Telephone: 415-362-2375
Telecopier: 415-362-1010
URL: http://www.MMLAWOFFICES.COM

Edmund R. Manwell
Denise B. Milton

OF COUNSEL

Maria A. Chanco

ASSOCIATES

Ian R. Schwartz
Katayoon M. Cotto
Lissa G. Maldonado

For full biographical listings, see the Martindale-Hubbell Law Directory

MORGENSTEIN & JUBELIRER, LLP (AV)

One Market, Spear Street Tower, 32nd Floor, 94105
Telephone: 415-896-0666
Fax: 415-896-5592
Email: m&j@mj-sflaw.com

Marvin D. Morgenstein (Retired)
Eliot S. Jubelirer
Lee Ann Huntington
Jean L. Bertrand
Jeffrey R. Williams
James R. Balich
Rocky N. Unruh
James L. McGinnis
Charles W. LaGrave
William J. Carroll
John S. Worden
Wendi J. Berkowitz
Stephen M. Hankins
Bruce A. Wagman

Lewis D. Barr
David H. Bromfield
Alexander P. Catalona
Michael "Cael" S. Davis
Roberta Nicol Dempster
Laura E. Gasser
Jill L. Gillen
Natasha L. Golding
Judith A. Holiber
Shawn D. Parrish
John J. Petry

For full biographical listings, see the Martindale-Hubbell Law Directory

ROSEN, BIEN & ASARO (AV)

Eighth Floor, 155 Montgomery Street, 94104
Telephone: 415-433-6830
Fax: 415-433-7104
Email: rba@rbalaw.com

Sanford Jay Rosen
Michael W. Bien
Andrea G. Asaro

Thomas Nolan
William H. D. Fernholz
Shana J. Margolis
Ernest J. Galvan

For full biographical listings, see the Martindale-Hubbell Law Directory

*SAN JOSE,** Santa Clara Co.

BERGESON & ELIOPOULOS, LLP (AV)

55 Almaden Boulevard, Suite 400, 95113
Telephone: 408-291-6200
Fax: 408-297-6000
URL: http://www.beglaw.com
Washington, D.C. Affiliate Office: Bergeson & Campbell, P.C., 1300 Eye Street, NW, Suite 100 West, 20005.
Telephone: (202)-962-8585.
Fax: (202)-962-8599. URL: www.bclaw.com.

Daniel J. Bergeson
William T. Eliopoulos
Mary Anne Rodgers
John L. Antracoli
Donald P. Gagliardi
Ina Stangenes
Marily P. Lerner

OF COUNSEL

Anthony M. Glassman

ASSOCIATES

Marc G. Van Niekerk
Eunhae Park
Mark E. Waite
Evelyn A. Peyton
William A. Hodkowski

For full biographical listings, see the Martindale-Hubbell Law Directory

COLORADO

*COLORADO SPRINGS,** El Paso Co.

BELTZ, EDWARDS & SABO, L.L.P. (AV)

128 South Tejon, Suite 310, 80903
Telephone: 719-634-6620
Fax: 719-634-3142
Email: BES__LLP@aol.com *URL:* http://www.lawyers.com/beslaw
Other Colorado Springs, Colorado Office: 729 South Cascade, 80903.
Telephone: 719-473-4444.
Fax: 719-444-0186.

Daniel P. Edwards
W. Thomas Beltz
John W. Sabo, III

ASSOCIATE

Daniel A. West

Representative Clients: A.M.I. Industries, Inc.; Analytical Surveys, Inc.; A.C. Israel Enterprises, Inc.; Boddington Lumber Co., Inc.; Cardiovascular Surgeons of Colorado Springs, P.C.; Colorado Springs Radiologists, P.C.; Digital, Inc.; Music Semi-Conductors, Inc.; Schlage Lock Co.; Texas Instruments.

For full biographical listings, see the Martindale-Hubbell Law Directory

*DENVER,** Denver Co.

BALLARD SPAHR ANDREWS & INGERSOLL, LLP (AV)

Seventeenth Street Plaza Building, Suite 2300, 1225 17th Street, 80202-5596
Telephone: 303-292-2400
Fax: 303-296-3956
URL: http://www.ballardspahr.com
Baltimore, Maryland Office: 300 East Lombard Street. 19th Floor.
Telephone: 410-528-5600.
Fax: 410-528-5650.
Camden, New Jersey Office: 800 Hudson Square, 5th Floor.
Telephone: 856-541-5577.
Fax: 856-541-8272.
Philadelphia, Pennsylvania Office: 1735 Market Street, 51st Floor.
Telephone: 215-665-8500.
Fax: 215-864-8999.
Salt Lake City, Utah Office: One Utah Center, Suite 1200, 201 South Main Street.
Telephone: 801-531-3000.
Fax: 801-531-3001.
Voorhees, New Jersey Office: Suite 100, 1101 Laurel Oak Drive.
Telephone: 856-627-8555.
Fax: 856-627-1153.
Washington, D.C. Office: Suite 1000 South, 601 13th Street, N.W.
Telephone: 202-661-2200.
Fax: 202-661-2299.

Thomas H. Duncan

For Complete List of Firm Personnel, See General Section

For full biographical listings, see the Martindale-Hubbell Law Directory

BERENBAUM, WEINSHIENK & EASON, P.C. (AV)

Suite 2600 Republic Plaza, 370 17th Street, 80202
Telephone: 303-825-0800
Facsimile: 303-629-7610
Email: berenbaum1@aol.com *URL:* http://www.BWELaw.com

Joseph S. Borus
Daniel S. Duggan
Steven C. Hoth
James A. Jacobson
Diana L. Powell
John B. Wills

Heather Scheel Hagemann

Representative Clients: Home Depot; Sprint Spectrum, L.P.; Town of Vail, Colorado; First Union Corporation; City of Englewood, Colorado; Oakwood Homes; Karman, Inc.; Wells Fargo Bank, N.A.; Berkshire Life Insurance Co.; Trinity Ventures.

For full biographical listings, see the Martindale-Hubbell Law Directory

BERLINER ZISSER WALTER & GALLEGOS, A PROFESSIONAL CORPORATION (AV)

One Norwest Center, 1700 Lincoln Street, Suite 4700, 80203-4547
Telephone: 303-830-1700
Facsimile: 303-830-1705
Email: bzwg@bzwg.com

Martin M. Berliner
David A. Zisser
Robert W. Walter
Larry D. Gallegos

Stacey L. Bowers

(See Next Column)

OF COUNSEL

Phillip C. Gans

For full biographical listings, see the Martindale-Hubbell Law Directory

BIRGE & MAYERS, P.C. (AV)

1700 Broadway, Suite 1501, 80290
Telephone: 303-860-7100
Facsimile: 303-860-7338
URL: http://www.lawyers.com/birgemayerslaw
St. Louis, Missouri Office: 8000 Maryland Avenue, #250, 63105.
Telephone: 314-236-2203.
Telecopy: 314-236-2401.

Thomas D. Birge

Carla B. Minckley

SPECIAL COUNSEL

Terry L. Lister

Representative Clients: Morgan Stanley Dean Whitter; Walnut Street Securities; Hanifen, Imhoff Inc.; American Fronteer Financial Corporation; Cambridge Investment Research; Birchtree Financial Services; Huntleigh Securities Corporation; The Leaders Group.

For full biographical listings, see the Martindale-Hubbell Law Directory

BREGA & WINTERS P.C. (AV)

One Norwest Center, 1700 Lincoln Street, Suite 2222, 80203
Telephone: 303-866-9400
Fax: 303-861-9109
Greeley, Colorado Office: 1100 Tenth Street, Suite 402, 80631.
Telephone: 303-352-4805.
Fax: 303-352-6547.

James W. Bain
Stuart N. Bennett
Charles F. Brega
Robert R. Dormer
Wesley B. Howard, Jr.
William W. Hughes (Resident, Greeley Office)
Robert C. Kaufman
Ronald S. Loser
Brian A. Magoon
Loren L. Mall
Glenn W. Merrick
Pamela A. Shaddock (Resident, Greeley Office)
Jay John Schnell
Jerry D. Winters (Resident, Greeley Office)

Jennifer S. Fox
Julie Scroggins Frantz (Resident, Greeley Office)
Brent W. Houston
S. Scott Lasher
Bradley D. Laue (Resident, Greeley Office)
Eric B. Liebman
Kevin C. Massaro
Scott T. Rodgers

For full biographical listings, see the Martindale-Hubbell Law Directory

BRENMAN BROMBERG & TENENBAUM, P.C. (AV)

Mellon Financial Center Suite 1001, 1775 Sherman Street, 80203
Telephone: 303-894-0234
Fax: 303-839-1633
Email: bbt@bbtlaw.net

Albert Brenman
Thomas R. Bromberg
A. Thomas Tenenbaum
Steven W. McDonald

Sheryl A. Johnson
Judy A. Gooch

OF COUNSEL

Duane Woodard

For full biographical listings, see the Martindale-Hubbell Law Directory

JAMES E. BROWN & ASSOCIATES, P.C. (AV)

1350 Seventeenth Street, Suite 306, 80202
Telephone: 303-825-1818
Fax: 303-825-2828
Email: wy0j@aol.com

James E. Brown

OF COUNSEL

Michael B. Levy

For full biographical listings, see the Martindale-Hubbell Law Directory

BROWNSTEIN HYATT & FARBER, P.C. (AV)

Twenty-Second Floor, 410 Seventeenth Street, 80202-4437
Telephone: 303-223-1100
Telecopier: 303-223-1111
Washington, D.C. Office: 1615 L Street, N.W., Suite 450, 20036.
Telephone: 202-296-7353.
Telecopier: 202-296-7009.
Glenwood Springs, Colorado Office: Box 357, 81602.
Telephone: 970-945-5302.
Telecopier: 970-945-4921.

(See Next Column)

BROWNSTEIN HYATT & FARBER P.C.—*Continued*

Jeffrey M. Knetsch
Steven S. Siegel
John L. Ruppert
Gregory W. Berger
Brent T. Slosky

SENIOR COUNSEL

John R. Garrett

OF COUNSEL

Jacquelyn Kilmer

Robert M. Fogler
Christopher D. Reiss
Tad S. Rogers
J. David Hershberger
Adam J. Agron
Kurt B. Colburn

Representative Clients: Atlantic Gulf Communities Corporation; The Centennial Funds; Color Spot Nurseries; Gart Sports Company; Kohlberg & Co.; PLC Medical Systems, Inc.; Prometheus Partners, L.P.; Rocky Mountain Internet, Inc.; Samsonite Corporation; Vail Associates, Inc.

For Complete List of Firm Personnel, See General Section

For full biographical listings, see the Martindale-Hubbell Law Directory

---

FRIEDLOB SANDERSON RASKIN PAULSON & TOURTILLOTT, LLC (AV)

1400 Glenarm Place, 80202-5099
Telephone: 303-571-1400
Fax: 303-595-3159; 303-595-3970; 303-615-5472
Englewood, Colorado Office: 8400 East Prentice Avenue, 80111-2918.
Telephone: 303-571-1400.
Santa Cruz, California Office: 519 Seabright Avenue, Suite 208, 95062-3482.
Telephone: 813-460-3966.
Fax: 813-460-3968.

Raymond L. Friedlob
Gerald Raskin
John W. Kellogg

For full biographical listings, see the Martindale-Hubbell Law Directory

---

GORSUCH KIRGIS LLP (AV)

Tower 1, Suite 1000, 1515 Arapahoe Street, 80202
Telephone: 303-376-5000
Fax: 303-376-5001

PARTNERS

S. Lee Terry, Jr.
Cynthia Smith Cain

ASSOCIATES

Pantea M. Garroussi
Anastasia G. Khokhryakova

LEGAL SUPPORT PERSONNEL

Lansing Wallace
Veronica Ehrenzeller

For full biographical listings, see the Martindale-Hubbell Law Directory

---

HOLME ROBERTS & OWEN LLP (AV)

Suite 4100, 1700 Lincoln, 80203
Telephone: 303-861-7000
Telecopier: 303-866-0200
Email: hro@hro.com *URL:* http://www.hro.com
Boulder, Colorado Office: Suite 400, 1401 Pearl Street.
Telephone: 303-444-5955.
Telecopier: 303-444-1063.
Colorado Springs, Colorado Office: Suite 1300, 90 South Cascade Avenue.
Telephone: 719-473-3800.
Telecopier: 719-633-1518.
Salt Lake City, Utah Office: Suite 1100, 111 East Broadway.
Telephone: 801-521-5800.
Telecopier: 801-521-9639.
London, England Office: Heathcoat House, 3rd Floor, 20 Savile Row.
Telephone: 011-44-171-494-5600.
Telecopier: 011-44-171-287-9344.

PARTNERS OF FIRM

John P. Babb
Garth B. Jensen
Bruce R. Kohler (Resident Managing Partner, London, England Office)
David H. Little (Salt Lake City Office)
Joseph W. Morrisey, Jr.
Nick Nimmo
Susan L. (Jones) Oakes
Thomas A. Richardson
Judith L. Roberts
Martha Traudt Collins Rolle (London, England Office)
W. Dean Salter
Paul G. Thompson (London, England Office)
Francis R. Wheeler

OF COUNSEL

Harold S. Bloomenthal
Karen Campbell Jenson (Salt Lake City Office)

SPECIAL COUNSEL

Carolyn Cox (Salt Lake City Office)
Linda K. Wackwitz

(See Next Column)

ASSOCIATES

Lisa McGee Allen (London, England Office)
Troy R. Braegger
Jennifer A. D'Alessandro
William C. Holland
Hendrik F. Jordaan (Colorado Springs Office)
Brent P. Karasiuk (Colorado Springs Office)
Tammy H. Kraemer (Colorado Springs Office)
M. Mashenka Lundberg
Jill W. Rose-Tappert
Tara M. Schiller (London, England Office)
Annette M. Schüller (London, England Office)
Alec C. Sherod (Not admitted in CO)
Paul M. Wilson (Salt Lake City Office)
Maria V. Woods
Vikki Lynn Wulf (Boulder Office)

For Complete List of Firm Personnel, See General Section

For full biographical listings, see the Martindale-Hubbell Law Directory

---

KRYS BOYLE FREEDMAN & SAWYER, P.C. (AV)

Dominion Plaza, Suite 2700 South Tower 600 Seventeenth Street, 80202
Telephone: 303-893-2300
Facsimile: 303-893-2882

Thomas Boyle
Stanley F. Freedman (P.C.)
Jon D. Sawyer
James P. Beck
Andrew M. Schauer
Sharon M. Link

RETIRED COUNSEL

Joseph F. Krys

For full biographical listings, see the Martindale-Hubbell Law Directory

---

OTTEN, JOHNSON, ROBINSON, NEFF & RAGONETTI, P.C. (AV)

950 Seventeenth Street, 16th Floor, 80202
Telephone: 303-825-8400
Telecopier: 303-825-6525
URL: http://www.ojrnr.com

Blair L. Lockwood
Douglas R. Wright
Karen L. Barsch
John R. Marcil
Paul D. Zier
Jeffrey A. Sherman

Representative Clients: Coram Healthcare Corp.; Frontier Airlines; GeriMed of America, Inc.; Koala Corp.; StarTek, Inc.; TIC Holdings, Inc.

For Complete List of Firm Personnel, See General Section

For full biographical listings, see the Martindale-Hubbell Law Directory

---

REIMAN & BAYAZ, P.C. (AV)

1600 Broadway, Suite 1340, 80202
Telephone: 303-860-1500
Fax: 303-839-4380
Email: rblaw@earthlink.net

Jeff Reiman
Marcie K. Bayaz

Debra D. Asimus

For full biographical listings, see the Martindale-Hubbell Law Directory

---

SCHLUETER & ASSOCIATES, P.C. (AV)

1050 Seventeenth Street, Suite 1700, 80265
Telephone: 303-292-3883
Facsimile: 303-296-8880
Email: 76304.3546@compuserve.com

Henry F. Schlueter

Celia Velletri

For full biographical listings, see the Martindale-Hubbell Law Directory

---

ENGLEWOOD, Arapahoe Co.

NORTON • LIDSTONE, LLC (AV)

The Quadrant, 5445 DTC Parkway, Suite 850, 80111
Telephone: 303-221-5552
Fax: 303-221-5553
URL: http://www.lawyers.com/norton_lidstone_law

Michael J. Norton
Herrick K. Lidstone, Jr.

For full biographical listings, see the Martindale-Hubbell Law Directory

CONNECTICUT

*HARTFORD,** Hartford Co.

SOROKIN, GROSS & HYDE, P.C. (AV)

One Corporate Center, 06103
Telephone: 860-525-6645
Fax: 860-522-1781
Email: sorokin@sorokinlaw.com
Simsbury, Connecticut Office: 720 Hopmeadow Street.
Telephone: 860-651-9348.
Rocky Hill, Connecticut Office: 2360 Main Street.
Telephone: 860-563-9305.
Fax: 860-529-6931.

Morris W. Banks
Sharon Kowal Freilich
Andrew C. Glassman

For Complete List of Firm Personnel, See General Section

For full biographical listings, see the Martindale-Hubbell Law Directory

WESTPORT, Fairfield Co.

BLAZZARD, GRODD & HASENAUER, P.C. (AV)

943 Post Road East, P.O. Box 5108, 06881
Telephone: 203-226-7866
Telecopier: 203-454-4855
Lauderdale-By-the-Sea Office: Suite 207, W. Tradewinds Avenue, 33308.
Telephone: 954-771-6667.
Facsimile: 954-771-7689. E-Mail: BGHFL@AOL.COM

Norse N. Blazzard
Leslie E. Grodd
Judith A. Hasenauer
William E. Hasenauer
Raymond A. O'Hara, III
Lynn Korman Stone

Peter L. Cejas (Not admitted in CT)

For full biographical listings, see the Martindale-Hubbell Law Directory

DELAWARE

*WILMINGTON,** New Castle Co.

MORRIS AND MORRIS (AV)

Suite 1600, 1105 North Market Street, P.O. Box 2166, 19899-2166
Telephone: 302-426-0400
Facsimile: 302-426-0406
Email: morrisandmorris@compuserve.com

Irving Morris
Karen L. Morris
Patrick F. Morris
Seth D. Rigrodsky

ASSOCIATES

Jacqueline L. Jenkin Green (Not admitted in DE)
James A. McShane
Herbert W. Mondros

For full biographical listings, see the Martindale-Hubbell Law Directory

SMITH, KATZENSTEIN & FURLOW LLP (AV)

The Corporate Plaza, 800 Delaware Avenue, P.O. Box 410, 19899
Telephone: 302-652-8400
Fax: 302-652-8405
Email: info@skfdelaware.com *URL:* http://www.SKFDelaware.com

MEMBER OF FIRM

Craig B. Smith

For Complete List of Firm Personnel, See General Section

For full biographical listings, see the Martindale-Hubbell Law Directory

DISTRICT OF COLUMBIA

WASHINGTON, D.C. Co.

COHEN, MILSTEIN, HAUSFELD & TOLL, P.L.L.C. (AV)

West Tower, Suite 500, 1100 New York Avenue, N.W., 20005-3964
Telephone: 202-408-4600
Facsimile: 202-408-4699
Email: lawinfo@cmht.com *URL:* http://www.CMHT.com
Seattle, Washington Office: 999 Third Avenue, Suite 3600.
Telephone: 206-521-0080.
Facsimile: 206-521-0166.

(See Next Column)

MEMBERS OF FIRM

Jerry S. Cohen (1925-1995)
Herbert E. Milstein
Michael D. Hausfeld
Steven J. Toll (Resident, Seattle, Washington Office)
Ann C. Yahner
Lisa M. Mezzetti
Andrew N. Friedman
Richard S. Lewis
Daniel S. Sommers
Daniel A. Small
Gary E. Mason
Joseph M. Sellers
Sharon A. Snyder
Mark S. Willis (Not admitted in DC)

ASSOCIATES

Lori G. Feldman (Resident, Seattle, Washington Office)
Paul T. Gallagher
Christine E. Webber
Alexander E. Barnett
Matthew James Ide (Resident, Seattle, Washington Office)
Matthew F. Pawa
Suzette M. Malveaux
Mary N. Strimel
Kristopher A. Kinkade (Resident, Seattle, Washington Office)
Agnieszka M. Fryszman
Deborah J. Vagins
Ari Karen
Charles E. Tompkins
Tamara J. Driscoll (Resident, Seattle, Washington Office)
Elizabeth Haines Cronise
Donna Solen
Lesli C. Esposito (Not admitted in DC)

OF COUNSEL

Margaret G. Farrell

For full biographical listings, see the Martindale-Hubbell Law Directory

THE CUNEO LAW GROUP, P.C. (AV)

317 Massachusetts Avenue, N.E. Suite 300, 20002
Telephone: 202-789-3960
Fax: 202-789-1813
Email: contact@cuneolaw.com *URL:* http://www.cuneolaw.com

Jonathan W. Cuneo
James J. Schweitzer
David W. Stanley
Michael G. Lenett

Arthur K. Park (Not admitted in DC)
Daniel Cohen (Not admitted in DC)

COUNSEL

Charles Tiefer

For full biographical listings, see the Martindale-Hubbell Law Directory

DE MARTINO FINKELSTEIN ROSEN & VIRGA (AV)

Suite 400, 1818 N Street, N.W., 20036
Telephone: 202-659-0494
Telecopier: 202-659-1290
Email: BUSLAW@mail.dfrv.com
New York, N.Y. Office: Suite 1700, 90 Broad Street.
Telephone: 212-363-2500.
Telecopier: 212-363-2723. Email: DFRV90Brd@aol.com

MEMBERS OF FIRM

Ralph V. De Martino (Resident)
Steven R. Finkelstein (Not admitted in DC; Resident, New York, N.Y. Office)
Jeffrey S. Rosen (Resident)
Gerard A. Virga (Not admitted in DC; Resident, New York, N.Y. Office)

Keith H. Peterson (Not admitted in DC; Resident, New York, N.Y. Office)
Caroline George
Bertin Henry Pérez

OF COUNSEL

Neil R.E. Carr (Resident)
Paula A. Argento

LEGAL SUPPORT PERSONNEL

J. Keoni Robinson (Legal Assistant)

For full biographical listings, see the Martindale-Hubbell Law Directory

LEWIS & MUNDAY, A PROFESSIONAL CORPORATION (AV)

(Formerly Lewis, Clay & Munday, P.C.)
1120 Connecticut Avenue, Suite 280, 20036
Telephone: 202-835-0616
Fax: 202-833-3316
Email: karen.brown@lewis-pc.com *URL:* http://www.lewis-pc.com
Detroit, Michigan Office: 1300 First National Building, 660 Woodward Avenue. 48226-3531.
Telephone: 313-961-2550.
Fax: 313-961-1270.
Boston, Massachusetts Office: 101 Federal Street, Suite 1900. 02110.
Telephone: 617-478-0553.
Fax: 617-478-0543.

Karen Kendrick Brown (Resident)

For full biographical listings, see the Martindale-Hubbell Law Directory

Washington—Continued

MULDOON, MURPHY & FAUCETTE (AV)

5101 Wisconsin Avenue, N.W., 20016
Telephone: 202-362-0840
Telecopier: 202-966-9409; 202-363-5068

MEMBERS OF FIRM

Joseph A. Muldoon, Jr.
George W. Murphy, Jr.
Douglas P. Faucette
John R. Hall
Thomas J. Haggerty (Not admitted in DC)
Joseph P. Daly
Lori M. Beresford
Christina M. Gattuso
Lawrence M. F. Spaccasi (Not admitted in DC)
Marc Paul Levy
Paul M. Aguggia
Eric S. Kracov
Victor L. Cangelosi
Aaron M. Kaslow
Kent M. Krudys
Thomas P. Hutton

OF COUNSEL

Leslie Ann Murphy
Sean Murphy
Arthur D. Perschetz (Not admitted in DC)

For full biographical listings, see the Martindale-Hubbell Law Directory

VENABLE ATTORNEYS AT LAW VENABLE, BAETJER, HOWARD & CIVILETTI, LLP (AV)

A Partnership including Professional Corporations
Suite 1000, 1201 New York Avenue, N.W., 20005
Telephone: 202-962-4800
Fax: 202-962-8300
URL: http://www.venable.com
Baltimore, Maryland Office: Venable, Baetjer and Howard LLP, 1800 Mercantile Bank & Trust Building, 2 Hopkins Plaza.
Telephone: 410-244-7400.
Fax: 410-244-7742.
McLean, Virginia Office: Venable, Baetjer and Howard LLP, Suite 400, 2010 Corporate Ridge.
Telephone: 703-760-1600.
Fax: 703-821-8949.
Rockville, Maryland Office: Venable, Baetjer and Howard LLP, Suite 500, One Church Street, P. O. Box 1906.
Telephone: 301-217-5600.
Fax: 301-217-5617.
Towson, Maryland Office: Venable, Baetjer and Howard LLP, 210 Allegheny Avenue, P. O. Box 5517.
Telephone: 410-494-6200.
Fax: 410-821-0147.

MEMBERS OF FIRM

James K. Archibald (Also at Baltimore, Maryland Office)
Kenneth C. Bass, III (Also at McLean, Virginia Office)
Benjamin R. Civiletti (P.C.) (Also at Baltimore and Towson, Maryland Offices)
Anita J. Finkelstein
Ronald R. Glancz
Gary M. Hnath
James L. Shea (also at Baltimore, Maryland Office)
Joe A. Shull

ASSOCIATE

Donald P. Creston

For Complete List of Firm Personnel, See General Section

For full biographical listings, see the Martindale-Hubbell Law Directory

WEBSTER, CHAMBERLAIN & BEAN (AV)

Suite 1000, 1747 Pennsylvania Avenue, N.W., 20006
Telephone: 202-785-9500
Fax: 202-835-0243

MEMBERS OF FIRM

Arthur L. Herold
Alan P. Dye
Edward D. Coleman
Frank M. Northam
John W. Hazard, Jr.
Hugh K. Webster

OF COUNSEL

Charles E. Chamberlain
J. Coleman Bean
Kent Masterson Brown (Not admitted in DC)
Burkett Van Kirk
James Bopp, Jr. (Not admitted in DC)

ASSOCIATES

Charles M. Watkins
David P. Goch
Brenley Locke Elias
Raymond Cashen, II (Not admitted in DC)

For full biographical listings, see the Martindale-Hubbell Law Directory

WILMER, CUTLER & PICKERING (AV)

2445 M Street, N.W., 20037-1420
Telephone: 202-663-6000
Fax: 202-663-6363
Email: Law@Wilmer.Com *URL:* http://www.wilmer.com
Baltimore, Maryland Office: 100 Light Street, 21202.
Telephone: 410-986-2800.
Fax: 410-986-2828.

(See Next Column)

New York, New York Office: 520 Madison Avenue, 10022.
Telephone: 212-230-8800.
Fax: 212-230-8888.
European Offices:
4 Carlton Gardens, London, SW1Y 5AA, England. Telephone: +44 (20) 7 872 1000.
Fax: +44 (20) 7 839 3537.
Rue de la Loi 15# Wetstraat, B-1040 Brussels, Belgium. Telephone: +32 (2) 285 49 00.
Fax: +32 (2) 285 49 49.
Friedrichstrasse 95, D-10117 Berlin, Germany. Telephone: +49 (30) 20 22 64 00.
Fax: +49 (30) 20 22 65 00.

MEMBERS OF FIRM

Stephen H. Sachs
Louis R. Cohen
Michael R. Klein
Stephen F. Black
Richard W. Cass
John Rounsaville, Jr.
Marianne K. Smythe
Andrew B. Weissman
William R. McLucas
George P. Stamas
Harry J. Weiss
Brandon Becker
Bruce E. Coolidge
Andrew N. Vollmer
Charles E. Davidow
Philip D. Anker
Joseph K. Brenner
Matthew A. Chambers
Meredith B. Cross
Mark D. Cahn
Eric R. Markus
Jeremy N. Rubenstein
Eric J. Mogilnicki
Lewis J. Liman (Not admitted in DC; Resident, New York, New York Office)
Yoon-Young Lee
Gail C. Bernstein
Robert F. Hoyt
Thomas Mueller (Resident, European Office, Brussels, Belgium)
Soo J. Yim
James E. Anderson

COUNSEL

Robert G. Bagnall
Leon B. Greenfield
Jeffrey E. McFadden

For Complete List of Firm Personnel, See General Section

For full biographical listings, see the Martindale-Hubbell Law Directory

FLORIDA

*FORT LAUDERDALE,** Broward Co.

KIPNIS TESCHER LIPPMAN & VALINSKY (AV)

100 Northeast Third Avenue, Suite 610, 33301
Telephone: 954-467-1964
Fax: 954-467-2264

MEMBERS OF FIRM

Alan G. Kipnis
Howard A. Tescher
Steven N. Lippman
Jay L. Valinsky

ASSOCIATES

Richard B. Storfer
Patricia Fox-Butler
Michelle L. LaRue

For full biographical listings, see the Martindale-Hubbell Law Directory

*MIAMI,** Dade Co.

BERMAN WOLFE RENNERT VOGEL & MANDLER, P.A. (AV)

35th Floor, International Place, 100 Southeast Second Street, 33131-2130
Telephone: 305-577-4177
Fax: 305-373-6036
Email: administrator@bwr-law.com *URL:* http://www.bwr-law.com
Boca Raton, Florida Office: Boca Corporate Center, 2101 NW Corporate Boulevard, Suite 107, 33431.
Telephone: 561-995-2232.
Fax: 561-995-1668.

Neil J. Berman
Leon J. Wolfe
Charles J. Rennert
Howard J. Vogel
Jeffrey L. Mandler
Jill Nexon Berman

Jonathan L. Gaines
Miriam Cruz-Bustillo
Claire P. Menard
Shamira Klein
Julie M. Schwartz

OF COUNSEL

Anthony A. Rolle

For full biographical listings, see the Martindale-Hubbell Law Directory

SACHER ZELMAN PAUL BEILEY & VAN SANT, P.A. (AV)

1401 Brickell Avenue, Suite 700, 33131
Telephone: 305-371-8797
Telecopier: 305-374-2605
Email: flbuslaw@gate.net

(See Next Column)

SACHER ZELMAN PAUL BEILEY & VAN SANT P.A., *Miami—Continued*

Barton S. Sacher
Richard M. Zelman
Robert Paul
Stanley A. Beiley
Nancy J. Van Sant
Roy M. Hartman
Jeffery W. Sacher

Rhett Traband
Paul Anthony Levine
Joseph A. Sacher
Anne T. Cirasuolo

OF COUNSEL

Cyrus E. Hornsby, III

For full biographical listings, see the Martindale-Hubbell Law Directory

TEW & NOWAK (AV)

A Partnership including Professional Corporations
Miami Center, Suite 340, 201 South Biscayne Boulevard, 33131
Telephone: 305-577-3900
1-800-577-3906
Fax: 305-577-9911
Email: tewandnowak@lawyers.com *URL:* http://www.lawyers.com/tew&nowak

Jeffrey Tew
Dennis A. Nowak

ASSOCIATE

Karen Levine

For full biographical listings, see the Martindale-Hubbell Law Directory

*NAPLES,** Collier Co.

GRADY & ASSOCIATES, LEGAL PROFESSIONAL ASSOCIATION (AV)

720 Fifth Avenue South, Suite 200, 34102
Telephone: 941-261-6555
Fax: 941-261-1192
Email: gradylaw@gradylaw.com

Thomas R. Grady

For full biographical listings, see the Martindale-Hubbell Law Directory

ST. PETERSBURG, Pinellas Co.

ALLAN & SHIPP, P.A. (AV)

6675 Thirteenth Avenue North, Suite 2C, 33710
Telephone: 813-381-9800
Fax: 813-381-1155
Email: law@allan-shipp.com
Clearwater, Florida Office: 2633 McCormick Drive, Suite 101, 34619.
Telephone: 813-799-7000.
Fax: 813-381-1155.

Linda R. Allan
Wayne E. Shipp

Stephen A. Baker
Terry J. Deeb
Jeffrey L. Hinds

For full biographical listings, see the Martindale-Hubbell Law Directory

*TAMPA,** Hillsborough Co.

MICHAEL C. ADDISON (AV)

Suite 1130, 220 East Madison Street, 33602
Telephone: 813-223-2000
Facsimile: 813-228-6000
Mailing Address: P.O. Box 2175, Tampa, Florida, 33601-2175
Email: michaeladdison@compuserve.com *URL:* http://www.lawyers.com/michaeladdison-law

For full biographical listings, see the Martindale-Hubbell Law Directory

ALPERT, BARKER & RODEMS, P.A. (AV)

First Union Center, Suite 2000, 100 South Ashley Drive (33602), P.O. Box 3270, 33601-3270
Telephone: 813-223-4131
Fax: 813-228-9612
Email: Alpertfirm@Aol.com

Jonathan L. Alpert
Chris A. Barker
Ryan Christopher Rodems
David D. Ferrentino
William J. Cook

Scott J. Flint
Natalie Pedregal

For full biographical listings, see the Martindale-Hubbell Law Directory

FULLER HOLSONBACK & BIVINS, P.A. (AV)

100 North Tampa Street, Suite 2650, 33602
Telephone: 813-229-9119
Fax: Available Upon Request
Email: jfuller521@aol.com

Jeffery M. Fuller
John P. Holsonback
Robert W. Bivins
Christina C. Young
Steven F. Thompson
William D. Mercer, Jr

For full biographical listings, see the Martindale-Hubbell Law Directory

*WEST PALM BEACH,** Palm Beach Co.

ACKERMAN, LINK & SARTORY, P.A. (AV)

222 Lakeview Avenue, Suite 1250, Esperante, 33401
Telephone: 561-838-4100
Fax: 561-838-5305
Email: alslaw@alslaw.com *URL:* http://www.alslaw.com

David P. Ackerman
Scott J. Link
Wendy Sartory Link

Lawrence J. Diamond
John C. Kelly
Gregory J. Newcomm
Amy B. Nunziella

For full biographical listings, see the Martindale-Hubbell Law Directory

JOHN L. CHALIF, J.D., LL.M. (AV Ⓣ)

The Galleria International Building, 301 Clematis Street, Suite 3000, 33401
Telephone: 561-820-9488; 561-748-1954; 561-762-3397
Facsimile: 561-366-1116; 561-655-3202
URL: http://www.lawyers.com/chalif

For full biographical listings, see the Martindale-Hubbell Law Directory

SEARCY DENNEY SCAROLA BARNHART & SHIPLEY, PROFESSIONAL ASSOCIATION (AV)

2139 Palm Beach Lakes Boulevard, P.O. Drawer 3626, 33402-3626
Telephone: 561-686-6300
800-780-8607
800-220-7006 (Spanish)
Fax: 561-478-0754
Email: CDS@SEARCYLAW.COM *URL:* http://www.searcylaw.com

William A. Norton

LEGAL SUPPORT PERSONNEL

J. Peter Love (Paralegal/Investigator)

For Complete List of Firm Personnel, See General Section

For full biographical listings, see the Martindale-Hubbell Law Directory

WARD, DAMON, BEVERLY, TITTLE & POSNER, P.A. (AV)

4420 Beacon Circle, 33407-3270
Telephone: 561-842-3000
Stuart: 561-223-5550
Fax: 561-842-3626
Email: wdbtp@wdbtp.com *URL:* http://www.wdbtp.com

James F. Cooney, Jr. (1950-1992)
Conrad Damon
Andrew Fulton, IV
Irwin R. Gilbert
Craig I. Kelley
Michael J Posner
Roger C. Stanton
James D. Tittle, Jr.
Philip H. Ward, III

OF COUNSEL

Don Beverly

For full biographical listings, see the Martindale-Hubbell Law Directory

GEORGIA

*ATLANTA,** Fulton Co.

CHITWOOD & HARLEY (AV)

2900 Promenade II, 1230 Peachtree Street, N.E., 30309
Telephone: 404-873-3900
Fax: 404-876-4476
Email: mail@classlaw.com *URL:* http://www.classlaw.com

Martin D. Chitwood
Alan R. Perry, Jr.
Neal S. Berinhout
Craig G. Harley

ASSOCIATES

Nikole M. Davenport
Christi C. Mobley
John Hinton, IV
David A. Bain
Corey Daniel Holzer
Kimberly Janelle Broder

For full biographical listings, see the Martindale-Hubbell Law Directory

Atlanta—Continued

Long Aldridge & Norman LLP (AV)

A Limited Liability Partnership including Professional Corporations
Suite 5300, 303 Peachtree Street, 30308
Telephone: 404-527-4000
Telecopier: 404-527-4198
Email: atlanta@lanlaw.com *URL:* http://www.lanlaw.com
Washington, D.C. Office: Suite 600, 701 Pennsylvania Avenue, N.W., 20004.
Telephone: 202-624-1200.
FAX: 202-624-1298.

MEMBERS OF FIRM

David M. Calhoun
William L. Floyd
Margaret M. Joslin
Thomas P. Lauth, III
Maurice Ted Maloof
Leonard A. Silverstein
Edgar H. Sims, Jr. (P.C.)
Thomas R. B. Wardell
Charles E. Wilson, III

ASSOCIATES

L. Briley Brisendine, Jr.
Richard R. Willis

For Complete List of Firm Personnel, See General Section

For full biographical listings, see the Martindale-Hubbell Law Directory

Smith, Howard & Ajax, LLP (AV)

300 Atlanta Financial Center South, 3333 Peachtree Road, N.E., 30326
Telephone: 404-239-1900
Fax: 404-239-1930

MEMBERS OF FIRM

John A. Howard
Marion Smith, II

For full biographical listings, see the Martindale-Hubbell Law Directory

Thrasher, Whitley, Hampton & Morgan, A Professional Corporation (AV)

Suite 2150, Five Concourse Parkway, 30328
Telephone: 770-804-8000
Telecopier: 770-804-5555
Email: law@twhm.com
Email: main@twhm.com

H. Grady Thrasher, III

Representative Clients: First Southeastern Securities Group, Inc.; Georgia Dental Assn.; Middle Bay Oil Company, Inc.; Perry & Co.; Smallwood, Reynolds, Stewart, Stewart & Assoc., Inc.; Sunchase Holdings, Ltd.; Touch Industries, Inc.

For full biographical listings, see the Martindale-Hubbell Law Directory

*AUGUSTA,** Richmond Co.

Hull, Towill, Norman, Barrett & Salley, A Professional Corporation (AV)

801 Broad Street, Suite 700, 30901
Telephone: 706-722-4481
Fax: 706-722-9779
Email: hullfirm@groupz.net *URL:* http://www.groupz.net/~advocate
Aiken, South Carolina Office: 111 Park Avenue, 29801.
Telephone: 803-648-4213.
Fax: 803-648-2601.

James M. Hull (1885-1975)
George B. Barrett (1894-1942)
Julian J. Willingham (1887-1963)
John Bell Towill (1907-1991)
Robert C. Norman (Retired, 1991)
W. Hale Barrett
Lawton Jordan, Jr.
Patrick J. Rice
Douglas D. Batchelor, Jr.
David E. Hudson
William H. Tucker (Not admitted in GA)
William F. Hammond
Mark S. Burgreen
George R. Hall
James B. Ellington
F. Michael Taylor
William J. Keogh, III
Edward J. Tarver
J. Noel Schweers, III
Susan D. Barrett
Ralph Emerson Hanna, III

James M. Holly (Not admitted in GA)
Timothy E. Moses
N. Shannon Gentry Lanier
Tara R. Simkins
Charles H. Weigle
Natalie A. Dopson
David C. Smith

OF COUNSEL

Julian B. Salley, Jr. (Not admitted in GA)

Counsel for: Morris Communications Corporation; Merry Land & Investment Company, Inc.; Castleberry/Snow's Brands, Inc.; Chipman-Union, Inc.; Augusta National, Inc.; Sun Trust Bank Augusta, N.A.; Georgia Power Co.; St. Joseph Hospital, Augusta, Georgia, Inc.; Norfolk Southern Corp.; Housing Authority of the City of Augusta.

For full biographical listings, see the Martindale-Hubbell Law Directory

Warlick, Tritt & Stebbins, L.L.P. (AV)

15th Floor, First Union Bank Building, 699 Broad Street, 30901-1454
Telephone: 706-722-7543
Fax: 706-722-1822
Email: wts@wts-lawfirm.com
Columbia County Office: 119 Davis Road, Martinez, Georgia 30907.
Telephone: 706-860-7595.
Fax: 706-860-7597.

MEMBERS OF FIRM

William Byrd Warlick
Roy D. Tritt (Resident, Martinez Office)
Charles C. Stebbins, III
E. L. Clark Speese
C. Gregory Bryan

OF COUNSEL

Richard E. Miley

For full biographical listings, see the Martindale-Hubbell Law Directory

HAWAII

*HONOLULU,** Honolulu Co.

Carlsmith Ball (AV)

A Partnership including Law Corporations
Suite 2200, Pacific Tower, 1001 Bishop Street, P.O. Box 656, 96809-3402
Telephone: 808-523-2500
Fax: 808-523-0842
Email: execdirector@carlsmith.com *URL:* http://www.carlsmith.com
Kapolei, Hawaii Office: Suite 318, Kapolei Building, 1001 Kamokila Boulevard, 96707.
Telephone: 808-523-2500.
Fax: 808-674-0850.
Wailuku, Maui Hawaii Office: Suite 400, One Main Plaza, 2200 Main Street, P.O. Box 1086, 96793-1086.
Telephone: 808-242-4535.
Fax: 808-244-4974.
Kailua-Kona, Hawaii Office: Suite 209, 75-1000 Henry Street, 96740.
Telephone: 808-329-6464.
Fax: 808-329-9450.
Hilo, Hawaii Office: 121 Waianuenue Avenue, P.O. Box 686, 96721-0686.
Telephone: 808-935-6644.
Fax: 808-935-7975.
Hagatna, Guam Office: Suite 401, Bank of Hawaii Building, 134 West Soledad Avenue, P.O. Box BF, 96932-5027.
Telephone: 671-472-6813.
Fax: 671-477-4375.
Telex: 721-6445 CWCMI GM.
Saipan, Commonwealth of the Northern Mariana Islands Office: Carlsmith Building, Capitol Hill, P.O. Box 5241, 96950-5241.
Telephone: 670-322-3455.
Fax: 670-322-3368.
Los Angeles, California Office: 9th Floor, 444 South Flower Street, 90071-2901.
Telephone: 213-955-1200.
Fax: 213-623-0032.
Washington, D.C. Office: Suite 300, 1201 Pennsylvania Avenue, N.W., 20004-2401.
Telephone: 202-628-2228.
Fax: 202-628-2071.
Mexico City, Mexico Office: Carlsmith Ball, Sierra Nevada 119, Lomas de Chapultepec, 11000 Mexico, D.F.
Telephone: 52-5-520-8514, 52-5-520-8757.
Fax: 52-5-540-1545.
Mexico, D.F. Office of Carlsmith Ball, S.C. (Authorized to practice as foreign legal consultants in Mexico): Sierra Nevada 119, Lomas de Chapultepec, 11000 Mexico, D.F.
Telephone: 52-5-520-8514, 52-5-520-8757.
Fax: 52-5-540-1545.

MEMBERS OF FIRM

Terrence A. Everett (Resident at Los Angeles, California Office)
John E. Rogers (Resident at Mexico Office)
William C. Williams, Jr. (Not admitted in HI)

For Complete List of Firm Personnel, See General Section

For full biographical listings, see the Martindale-Hubbell Law Directory

Goodsill Anderson Quinn & Stifel (AV)

Alii Place, Suite 1800, 1099 Alakea Street, P.O. Box 3196, 96801-3196
Telephone: 808-547-5600
FAX: 808-547-5880
Email: info@goodsill.com *URL:* http://www.goodsill.com

MEMBERS OF FIRM

David J. Reber
Gregory R. Kim
Jeffrey Scott Piper

COUNSEL

E. Laurence Gay

(See Next Column)

GOODSILL ANDERSON QUINN & STIFEL, *Honolulu—Continued*

ASSOCIATES

Russell K. Kaupu
David P. Cornell

Representative Clients: C. Brewer Homes, Inc.; Castle & Cooke, Inc.; Cyanotech Corporation; Dole Food Company, Inc.; Hawaiian Electric Company, Inc.; Hawaiian Electric Industries, Inc.

For Complete List of Firm Personnel, See General Section

For full biographical listings, see the Martindale-Hubbell Law Directory

IDAHO

*BOISE,** Ada Co.

EBERLE, BERLIN, KADING, TURNBOW & MCKLVEEN, CHARTERED (AV)

Capitol Park Plaza, 300 North Sixth Street, P.O. Box 1368, 83701-1368
Telephone: 208-344-8535
Facsimile: 208-344-8542

R.M. Turnbow

Representative Clients: Piper Jaffray, Inc.; Prudential Securities Inc.; Waddell & Reed Financial Services; Edward D. Jones & Co.; Hecla Mining Corp.

For Complete List of Firm Personnel, See General Section

For full biographical listings, see the Martindale-Hubbell Law Directory

ELAM & BURKE, A PROFESSIONAL ASSOCIATION (AV)

Key Financial Center, 702 West Idaho Street, P.O. Box 1539, 83701
Telephone: 208-343-5454
Telecopier: 208-384-5844
Email: eblaw@elamburke.com

Carl P. Burke
Jeffrey A. Thomson

Representative Clients: Morrison-Knudsen, Inc.; Prudential Securities, Inc.; Sinclair Oil Co. d/b/a Sun Valley Co.; United Heritage Mutual Life Insurance Co.; United Heritage Financial Services, Inc.; Prudential Insurance Company of North America.

For Complete List of Firm Personnel, See General Section

For full biographical listings, see the Martindale-Hubbell Law Directory

ILLINOIS

*CHICAGO,** Cook Co.

FAGEL & HABER (AV)

140 South Dearborn Street 14th Floor, 60603
Telephone: 312-346-7500
FAX: 312-580-2201
Telex No: 754542
Cable: "NOFLAWLAW"
URL: http://www.fandh.com

MEMBERS OF FIRM

Joel A. Haber
Robert B. Chapman
Laura A. O'Neill

For full biographical listings, see the Martindale-Hubbell Law Directory

FREEMAN, FREEMAN & SALZMAN, P.C. (AV)

401 North Michigan Avenue, Suite 3200, 60611-4207
Telephone: 312-222-5100
Facsimile: 312-822-0870

Lee A. Freeman (1909-1995)
Lee A. Freeman, Jr.
Jerrold E. Salzman
John F. Kinney
James T. Malysiak
Glynna W. Freeman
Phillip L. Stern
Chris C. Gair

Kevin P. Kappock
Jeffrey M. Osterkamp

For full biographical listings, see the Martindale-Hubbell Law Directory

WILLIAM J. HARTE, LTD. (AV)

Suite 1100, 111 West Washington Street, 60602
Telephone: 312-726-5015
Fax: 312-641-1288

William J. Harte

(See Next Column)

Sylvia A. Sotiras
Erik D. Gruber
Stephen L. Garcia
Joan M. Mannix

OF COUNSEL

Daniel K. Schlorf
David J. Walker
P. A. Sorrentino
Robert L. Tucker

For full biographical listings, see the Martindale-Hubbell Law Directory

KAPLAN, BEGY & VON OHLEN (AV)

One First National Plaza 51st Floor, 60603
Telephone: 312-345-3000
Fax: 312-345-3119
URL: http://www.kbvlaw.com

MEMBERS OF FIRM

Fred C. Begy, III
Larry S. Kaplan
James D. Solon
Robert C. von Ohlen, Jr.
Joseph A. Bosco
Richard A. Walker
Mitchell J. Kanaan
Patrick J. Keating

ASSOCIATES

Keith S. Yamaguchi
Thomas C. Sokol
Robert K. Villa
Nicole Halpern Murphy
Telly Andrews
Tamara S. Dykstra

For full biographical listings, see the Martindale-Hubbell Law Directory

LAWRENCE, KAMIN, SAUNDERS & UHLENHOP (AV)

208 South La Salle Street, Suite 1750, 60604-1188
Telephone: 312-372-1947
Telecopier: 312-372-2389
Email: LKSU@LKSU.com

MEMBERS OF FIRM

Paul B. Uhlenhop
Kent Lawrence
Kenneth S. Perlman
Charles J. Risch
Lawrence A. Rosen
Michael Wise
David L. Reich

ASSOCIATE

Peter E. Cooper

Representative Clients: TransMarket Group, L.L.C.; Checkers, Simon & Rosner, LLP; A.G. Edwards & Sons, Inc.; Nash Weiss & Co.; Gofen & Glossberg, L.L.C.; Beacon Investment Co.

For full biographical listings, see the Martindale-Hubbell Law Directory

MCBRIDE BAKER & COLES (AV)

500 West Madison Street 40th Floor, 60661-2511
Telephone: 312-715-5700
Cable Address: "Chilaw"
Telex: 270258
Telecopier: 312-993-9350
Email: lastname@mbc.com *URL:* http://www.mbc.com
Oakbrook Terrace, Illinois Office: Suite 1000, One Mid America Plaza, 60181-4710.
Telephone: 630-954-2100.
Telecopier: 630-954-2112.

MEMBERS OF FIRM

Michael J. Boland
Lola Miranda Hale
Anne Hamblin Schiave
Robert I. Schwimmer

SENIOR COUNSEL

Lawrence A. Coles, Jr.

OF COUNSEL

Robert O. Case
William J. Cooney
G. Gale Roberson, Jr.
Thomas P. Ward

ASSOCIATES

Jerald Holisky
Mark A. Kromkowski
Michael P. Lusk
Christopher J. Rosette

For Complete List of Firm Personnel, See General Section

For full biographical listings, see the Martindale-Hubbell Law Directory

SAUNDERS & MONROE (AV)

1600 NBC Tower, 455 North Cityfront Plaza Drive, 60611
Telephone: 312-645-6000
Fax: 312-645-9848

MEMBERS OF FIRM

George L. Saunders, Jr.
Lee A. Monroe
Thomas F. Bush, Jr.
Matthew E. Van Tine
Thomas A. Doyle

OF COUNSEL

Victoria S. Kaplan

For full biographical listings, see the Martindale-Hubbell Law Directory

Chicago—Continued

PETER R. SONDERBY, P.C. (AV)

135 South La Salle Street Suite 1424, 60603
Telephone: 312-201-0999
Fax: 312-201-0749; 201-4559
Email: Psond@starnetinc.com

Peter R. Sonderby

For full biographical listings, see the Martindale-Hubbell Law Directory

SUGAR, FRIEDBERG & FELSENTHAL (AV)

30 North La Salle Street, Suite 2600, 60602
Telephone: 312-704-9400
Telecopier: 312-372-7951
Cable: "SUGARFREE"

MEMBERS OF FIRM

Richard A. Sugar
Michael R. Friedberg
Steven A. Felsenthal
Andrew B. David
Leslie J. Weiss
Ira S. Neiman
Jonathan L. Mills
Etahn M. Cohen
Howard M. Helsinger
Robert F. Simon
Martin M. Weinstein
Charles H. Braun
Kathryn A. Erickson

ASSOCIATES

Aron L. Bornstein
Annette L. Brands
Kathryn T. Cha
Norman J. Ginsparg
William F. McGuinn
Suzanne J. Massel
Deanne Elizabeth Clarke

For full biographical listings, see the Martindale-Hubbell Law Directory

WILDMAN, HARROLD, ALLEN & DIXON (AV)

225 West Wacker Drive, 30th Floor, 60606-1229
Telephone: 312-201-2000
Fax: 312-201-2555
Email: hennessy@whad.com *URL:* http://www.whad.com
Aurora, Illinois Office: 1961 W. Downer Place.
Telephone: 630-892-7021.
Fax: 630-892-7158.
Waukegan, Illinois Office: 404 West Water, P. O. Box 890.
Telephone: 847-625-5550.
Fax: 847-625-5555.
Lisle, Illinois Office: 4300 Commerce Court, Suite 320.
Telephone: 630-955-0555.
Fax: 630-955-0662
Toronto, Ontario correspondent Office: Keel Cottrelle. 36 Toronto Street, Suite 920.
Telephone: 416-367-2900.
Telefax: 416-367-2791.
Telex: 062-18660.

MEMBERS OF FIRM

John L. Eisel
Nancy J. Fuller

Samuel S. Cohen
Charles Changwon Kim

For full biographical listings, see the Martindale-Hubbell Law Directory

INDIANA

*INDIANAPOLIS,** Marion Co.

ICE MILLER DONADIO & RYAN (AV)

One American Square Box 82001, 46282-0002
Telephone: 317-236-2100
Fax: 317-236-2219
Email: info@imdr.com *URL:* http://www.imdr.com
South Bend, Indiana Office: 211 West Washington Street, Suite 2420.
Telephone: 219-234-7933.
Fax: 219-234-7965. Internet E-mail: info@imdr.com. Web Site Address: http://www.imdr.com.
Chicago, Illinois Office: 135 South LaSalle Street, Suite 4100.
Telephone: 312-726-1567.
Fax: 312-641-6263. Internet E-mail: info@imdr.com. Web Site Address: http://www.imdr.com.

MEMBERS OF FIRM

Berkley W. Duck
Harry L. Gonso
Joseph E. DeGroff
John R. Thornburgh
Stephen J. Hackman
Steven K. Humke
Elizabeth A. Smith
Dean T. Burger
Mark B. Barnes

(See Next Column)

ASSOCIATES

P. James Schumacher
Lynn Kantor
Janice C. Whiteside

For Complete List of Firm Personnel, See General Section

For full biographical listings, see the Martindale-Hubbell Law Directory

JOHNSON SMITH PENCE & HEATH LLP (AV)

One Indiana Square Suite 1800, 46204
Telephone: 317-634-9777
Telecopier: 317-636-9061
Email: firm@jsplaw.com *URL:* http://www.jsplaw.com
Washington, D.C. Office: 555 Twelfth Street, N.W., Suite 650.
Telephone: 202-737-5410.
Fax: 202-737-5411.

MEMBERS OF FIRM

James T. Crawford, Jr.
Michael W. Hile
John R. Kirkwood

ASSOCIATES

Julie Coldren Bolling
Gregory G. Taylor

For Complete List of Firm Personnel, See General Section

For full biographical listings, see the Martindale-Hubbell Law Directory

LOCKE REYNOLDS LLP (AV)

1000 Capital Center South, 201 North Illinois Street, 46204-4210
Telephone: 317-237-3800
Telecopier: 317-237-3900
Email: attys@locke.com *URL:* http://www.locke.com

Michael J. Schneider

David S. Klinestiver

Representative Clients: Baldwin & Lyons, Inc.; Conseco, Inc.; Dean Witter Reynolds, Inc.; Golden Rule Insurance Co.; Paragon Medical, Inc.; Real Silk Investments, Inc.; Thurston Springer Miller Herd & Titak, Inc.

For Complete List of Firm Personnel, See General Section

For full biographical listings, see the Martindale-Hubbell Law Directory

MCTURNAN & TURNER (AV)

2400 Market Tower, 10 West Market Street, 46204
Telephone: 317-464-8181
Telecopier: 317-464-8131

Lee B. McTurnan
Wayne C. Turner
Jackie M. Bennett, Jr.
Jacqueline Bowman Ponder
Steven M. Badger
John F. McCauley

For full biographical listings, see the Martindale-Hubbell Law Directory

SOMMER & BARNARD, ATTORNEYS AT LAW, PC (AV)

4000 Bank One Tower, 111 Monument Circle, 46204
Telephone: 317-630-4000
FAX: 317-236-9802
Email: sandb@sommerbarnard.com
North Office: 8900 Keystone Crossing, Suite 1150, Indianapolis, Indiana, 46240-2134.
Telephone: 317-630-4000.
FAX: 317-844-4780.

James K. Sommer
James A. Strain
Julianne S. Lis-Milam
Philip L. McCool

Representative Clients: Comerica Bank; Federal Express; Kimball International; Monsanto; TRW, Inc.

For Complete List of Firm Personnel, See General Section

For full biographical listings, see the Martindale-Hubbell Law Directory

IOWA

*DES MOINES,** Polk Co.

NYEMASTER, GOODE, VOIGTS, WEST, HANSELL & O'BRIEN, A PROFESSIONAL CORPORATION (AV)

700 Walnut, Suite 1600, 50309
Telephone: 515-283-3100
Telecopier: 515-283-3108
Ames, Iowa Office: 1416 Buckeye Avenue, Ames, Iowa 50010.
Telephone: 515-233-3000.
Telecopier: 515-232-3846.

(See Next Column)

NYEMASTER, GOODE, VOIGTS, WEST, HANSELL & O'BRIEN A PROFESSIONAL CORPORATION, *Des Moines—Continued*

LeRoy R. Voigts
James B. West
Edgar F. Hansell
W. Don Brittin, Jr.
Don Muyskens
R. Craig Shives
Roger L. Ferris
Lawrence E. Myers
Keith E. Luchtel
Gerald J. Newbrough
Robert A. VanOrsdel
Richard J. Sapp
G. R. Neumann
Russell E. Schrage
Carlton T. King
Gregory P. Page
Randall G. Horstmann
Jay Eaton
Bradford L. Austin
Burns Mossman
Phyllis E. Pearson
Hayward L. Draper
Sara J. Sersland
James E. Gritzner
Michael W. Thrall
Mark C. Dickinson
Gregory B. Wilcox
John F. Lorentzen
Rod Kubat
Steven J. Roy
Frank B. Harty
James C. Wine
Bruce W. Baker
Thomas W. Foley
Steven H. Lytle
Terry C. Hancock
Anthony A. Longnecker
Wade H. Schut
Mark D. Aljets
G. Thomas Sullivan
Joseph A. Quinn
Joan Fletcher
Thomas H. Walton
Willard L. Boyd III
Lisette Sell
Jeffrey William Courter
Hallie E. Still-Caris
Brian J. Humke
Deborah S. Krauth

Paula S. Dierenfeld
John B. Tuffnell
Jill M. Stevenson
Angel West
Kathryn Atkinson Overberg
Angela L. Watson
Jennifer L. Vergilii
Debra L. Dalton
Amy L. VanDuyn
Neal K. Westin
John T. Clendenin
Stephanie L. Marett

OF COUNSEL

Samuel G. O'Brien
John J. McLaughlin
Drew R. Tillotson
Frank B. Comfort
Luther L. Hill, Jr.
Barry Nadler

Representative Clients: Burlington Northern and Santa Fe Railway Company; East Des Moines National Bank; Northwestern Bell Telephone Co.; Amoco Oil Co.; Inter-State Assurance Co.; Central Life Assurance Co.; Montgomery Ward; Deere & Co.

For full biographical listings, see the Martindale-Hubbell Law Directory

KANSAS

*TOPEKA,** Shawnee Co.

GOODELL, STRATTON, EDMONDS & PALMER, L.L.P. (AV)

515 South Kansas Avenue, 66603-3999
Telephone: 785-233-0593
Fax: 785-233-8870
Email: GSEP@CJNETWORKS.COM *URL:* http://www.cjnetworks.com/~gsep
Kansas City, Missouri Office: 10401 Holmes Road, Suite 280.
Telephone: 816-943-8577.

MEMBERS OF FIRM

Gerald L. Goodell
H. Philip Elwood
Gerald J. Letourneau
John H. Stauffer, Jr.

OF COUNSEL

Robert E. Edmonds (Retired)

Counsel for: St. Paul Fire & Marine Insurance Co.
General Counsel for: American Home Life Insurance Co.; Columbian National Title Insurance Co.; The Menninger Foundation; Kansas Medical Society; Stormont-Vail Healthcare, Inc.

For Complete List of Firm Personnel, See General Section

For full biographical listings, see the Martindale-Hubbell Law Directory

*WICHITA,** Sedgwick Co.

FOULSTON & SIEFKIN L.L.P. (AV)

700 NationsBank Financial Center, 67202
Telephone: 316-267-6371
Facsimile: 316-267-6345
URL: http://www.foulston.com
Topeka, Kansas Office: 1515 NationsBank Tower, 534 Kansas Avenue, 66603.
Telephone: 785-233-3600.
Fax: 785-233-1610.
Dodge City, Kansas Office: 810 Frontview, P.O. Box 1147, 67801.
Telephone: 316-227-8126.
Fax: 316-227-8451.
Member: Lex Mundi, The World's Leading Association of Independent Law Firms.

(See Next Column)

MEMBERS OF FIRM

Benjamin C. Langel
James D. Oliver
William R. Wood, II

For Complete List of Firm Personnel, See General Section

For full biographical listings, see the Martindale-Hubbell Law Directory

KENTUCKY

*LEXINGTON,** Fayette Co.

STOLL, KEENON & PARK, LLP (AV)

201 E. Main Street, Suite 1000, 40507-1380
Telephone: 606-231-3000
Telecopier: 606-253-1093; 606-253-1027
URL: http://www.skp.com
Frankfort, Kentucky Office: 307 Washington Street, 40601.
Telephone: 502-875-6220.
Telecopier: 502-875-6235.
Henderson, Kentucky Office: 201 C North Main Street, 42420-3103.
Telephone: 270-831-1900.
Telecopier: 270-827-4060.
Louisville, Kentucky Office: 400 West Market Street, Suite 2650, 40202-3377.
Telephone: 502-568-9100.
Telecopier: 502-568-5700.

MEMBERS OF FIRM

J. David Smith, Jr.
Dan M. Rose

Representative Clients: Delta Natural Gas Co., Inc.; Farmers Capital Bank Corp.; Gamma One Laboratories, Inc.; Lexington Brewing Co.; Lexington Investment Co., Inc.; Medical Rehabilitation Centers, Inc.; MedPro, Inc.; Whitaker Bank Corporation of Kentucky.

For Complete List of Firm Personnel, See General Section

For full biographical listings, see the Martindale-Hubbell Law Directory

*LOUISVILLE,** Jefferson Co.

FORE, MILLER & SCHWARTZ (AV)

First Trust Centre, Suite 700 North, 200 South Fifth Street, 40202
Telephone: 502-589-5250
Fax: 502-589-1637

MEMBERS OF FIRM

F. Larkin Fore
Dan T. Schwartz
Stephen H. Miller
Bryan J. Dillon
Donald J. LaDuke

ASSOCIATES

Louis I. Waterman
Joseph C. Spalding

OF COUNSEL

Karl M. Walz

References: American States Insurance Co.; Crawford & Company; Paragon Group, Inc.; Queens Group; Southeastern Dairies, Inc.; Ticor Title Co.; First National Bank of Louisville; Stockyards Bank; Arrow Electric Co.

For full biographical listings, see the Martindale-Hubbell Law Directory

GOLDBERG & SIMPSON, P.S.C. (AV)

3000 National City Tower, 40202
Telephone: 502-589-4440
Telefax: 502-581-1344
Email: mail@gsatty.com *URL:* http://www.gsatty.com

Fred M. Goldberg
Jonathan D. Goldberg
Mitchell A. Charney
Steven A. Goodman
Stephen E. Smith
Mary Alice Maple
John J. McLaughlin
Charles H. Cassis
Christopher M. George
Emily L. Lawrence

Jan M. West
Sherry P. Porter
James Michael Wells
Stephanie Lynn Morgan-White
Michael F. Lawrence
Karen L. De Haan
George Hunt Rounsavall, Jr.
Stacey A. Huse

OF COUNSEL

Ronald V. Simpson
David A. Brill

Representative Clients: National City Bank; Liberty Mutual Insurance Co.; Jewish Hospital Healthcare Services, Inc.; Louisville & Jefferson County Board of Health; Providian Corp.

For full biographical listings, see the Martindale-Hubbell Law Directory

Louisville—Continued

MIDDLETON & REUTLINGER, P.S.C. (AV)

2500 Brown and Williamson Tower, 40202-3410
Telephone: 502-584-1135
Fax: 502-561-0442
URL: http://middreut.com
Jeffersonville, Indiana Office: 530 East Court Avenue, 47130.
Telephone: 812-282-1132.
Fax: 812-282-3188.

James N. Williams, Jr.
C. Kent Hatfield
D. Randall Gibson
William Jay Hunter, Jr.

Clayton R. Hume

For Complete List of Firm Personnel, See General Section

For full biographical listings, see the Martindale-Hubbell Law Directory

ROTH FOLEY BRYANT & COOPER, PLLC (AV)

First Trust Centre, Suite 300S, 200 South Fifth Street, 40202-3236
Telephone: 502-569-7550
Fax: 502-540-0123
Email: RFBC.com

Irvin D. Foley
David M. Roth
David H. Cooper
Lisa Koch Bryant
K. Gail Russell
Christian L. Juckett

OF COUNSEL

James E. Fahey
David W. Gray

Representative Clients: Blue Door Restaurants, LLC; Tumbleweed, LLC; John R. Gains Thoroughbreds, LLC; T.M. Riders, LLC; ARM Financial Group, Inc.; Apex Entertainment, LLC.

For full biographical listings, see the Martindale-Hubbell Law Directory

LOUISIANA

*NEW ORLEANS,** Orleans Parish

CORRERO FISHMAN HAYGOOD PHELPS WALMSLEY & CASTEIX, L.L.P. (AV)

Bank One Center, 46th Floor, 201 St. Charles Avenue, 70170-4600
Telephone: 504-586-5252
Fax: 504-586-5250

Anthony J. Correro, III
Louis Y. Fishman
Paul M. Haygood
Robert M. Walmsley, Jr.

Caroline B. Blitzer
Lloyd L. Drury, III

For full biographical listings, see the Martindale-Hubbell Law Directory

McGLINCHEY STAFFORD (AV)

A Professional Limited Liability Company
643 Magazine Street, 70130-3477
Telephone: 504-586-1200
Fax: 504-596-2800
TDD: (504) 596-2728
Telex: 584327
Cable Address: "MACSTAC"
Mailing Address: P.O. Box 60643, New Orleans, Louisiana, 70160-0643
Email: @mcglinchey.com *URL:* http://www.mcglinchey.com
Dallas, Texas Office: 2777 Stemmons Freeway, Suite 925, 75207-2401.
Telephone: 214-860-9700.
Fax: 214-860-9750.
Houston, Texas Office: 2727 Allen Parkway, Suite 1900, 77019.
Telephone: 713-520-1900.
Fax: 713-520-1025.
Baton Rouge, Louisiana Office: Ninth Floor, One American Place, 70825-0001.
Telephone: 504-383-9000.
Fax: 504-343-3076.
Jackson, Mississippi Office: Suite 1200, SkyTel Centre, 200 South Lamar Street, 39201.
Telephone: 601-960-8400.
Fax: 601-960-8406.
Lake Providence, Louisiana Office: 405 Morgan Street, 71254-2691.
Telephone: 318-559-1200.
Fax: 318-559-0609.
Monroe, Louisiana Office: Dean ONB Tower, 130 Desiard Street, Suite 807, 71201.
Telephone: 318-651-0807.
Fax: 318-651-0809.

MEMBERS OF FIRM

James M. Fantaci
Stephen W. Rider
Thomas A. Roberts

(See Next Column)

MEMBERS OF FIRM

Mary Terrell Joseph (Resident, Baton Rouge Office)

ASSOCIATE

D. Jeffrey Wagner

For full biographical listings, see the Martindale-Hubbell Law Directory

MAINE

*PORTLAND,** Cumberland Co.

BURNS RAY & DELANO, PROFESSIONAL ASSOCIATION (AV)

193 Middle Street, 04101-4062
Telephone: 207-775-3581
Facsimile: 207-775-3814
Email: mailcenter@brdlaw.com

George F. Burns
David P. Ray
Arnold C. Macdonald
Mary DeLano
Elizabeth A. Burns
Carrie A. Green

OF COUNSEL

Joanne F. Cole

Representative Clients: Maine Yankee Atomic Power Company; Tractebel Power, Inc.; Hancock Lumber Co., Inc.; Pharmx, Inc.; Jackson Laboratory; Hague International (engineering); Aetna Life & Casualty Co.; The Hartford; Great American Insurance Co.; Wausau Insurance Co.

For full biographical listings, see the Martindale-Hubbell Law Directory

MARYLAND

*BALTIMORE,** (Independent City)

GALLAGHER, EVELIUS & JONES, LLP (AV)

Park Charles Suite 400, 218 North Charles Street, 21201
Telephone: 410-727-7702
Facsimile: 410-468-2786
URL: http://www.gejlaw.com

MEMBERS OF FIRM

Francis X. Gallagher (1928-1972)
C. Edward Jones (1908-1999)
John C. Evelius (Retired)
Richard O. Berndt
Thomas N. Biddison, Jr.
Robert R. Kern, Jr.
Saul E. Gilstein
Thomas B. Lewis
Bonnie Abrams Travieso
Stephen A. Goldberg
Linda H. Jones
Jack C. Tranter
Leslie B. Speed
Christopher J. Fritz
David E. Raderman
Peter E. Keith
Nita L. Schultz
Michael W. Skojec
Kathryn Kelley Hoskins
Mark P. Keener
Kevin J. Davidson
Eileen M. Lunga
Lori A. Nicolle
Kenneth S. Gross
Thomas C. Dame

ASSOCIATES

Valarie K. Oulds
Margaret Stevens Jacks
Matthew W. Oakey
Rebecca A. Weaver
Michael J. Henigan
David W. Kinkopf
Paul S. Caiola
Jason W. Gaarder
M. Kirsten Andrews

LEGAL ASSISTANTS

Patricia C. Quayle
Iris T. H. Heath
Connie L. Ennis
Margaret Graff
Margo Gibson Hughes
Jonathan T. Gillis
Brenda J. Heacock
Dwayne L. Rodeheaver

Representative Clients: Roman Catholic Archdiocese of Baltimore; The Shelter Group; Mercantile-Safe Deposit and Trust Co.; The Enterprise Social Investment Corp.; Mercy Medical Center, Inc.

For full biographical listings, see the Martindale-Hubbell Law Directory

THOMAS & LIBOWITZ, P.A. (AV)

100 Light Street, Suite 1100, 21202-1053
Telephone: 410-752-2468
Fax: 410-752-2046; 752-2049; 752-0979
Email: thomasandlibowitz.com *URL:* http://www.thomasandlibowitz.com

Steven Anargyros Thomas
Clinton R. Black, IV

OF COUNSEL

Susan M. Rittenhouse

Representative Clients: Sinclair Broadcast Group, Inc. (Television and Radio stations); Roy Kirby & Sons, Inc. (Contractor); First Mariner Bank; Scandia Manufacturing Co. Inc. (Defense Contractor); Atlantic Automotive Corp. t/a Heritgage Automotive Group; Candy Express Franchising, Inc.; Wire Spectrum Services (Contractors-Transmission Tower Sites); Acrodyne Com-

(See Next Column)

THOMAS & LIBOWITZ P.A., *Baltimore—Continued*

munications, Inc.; Alexis Logic Corporation (Software Developers); Selnic Corporation (Electronis Distributors); Liberty Mutual Insurance Company.

For full biographical listings, see the Martindale-Hubbell Law Directory

VENABLE ATTORNEYS AT LAW VENABLE, BAETJER AND HOWARD, LLP (AV)

A Partnership including Professional Corporations
1800 Mercantile Bank & Trust Building, 2 Hopkins Plaza, 21201
Telephone: 410-244-7400
Fax: 410-244-7742
URL: http://www.venable.com
Washington, D.C. Office: Venable, Baetjer, Howard & Civiletti LLP, Suite 1000, 1201 New York Avenue, N.W.
Telephone: 202-962-4800.
Fax: 202-962-8300.
McLean, Virginia Office: Suite 400, 2010 Corporate Ridge.
Telephone: 703-760-1600.
Fax: 703-821-8949.
Rockville, Maryland Office: Suite 500, One Church Street, P. O. Box 1906.
Telephone: 301-217-5600.
Fax: 301-217-5617.
Towson, Maryland Office: 210 Allegheny Avenue, P. O. Box 5517.
Telephone: 410-494-6200.
Fax: 410-821-0147.

MEMBERS OF FIRM

Benjamin R. Civiletti (P.C.) (Also at Washington, D.C. and Towson, Maryland Offices)
John Henry Lewin, Jr. (P.C.)
Lee M. Miller (P.C.)
Ronald R. Glancz (Not admitted in MD; Resident, Washington, D.C. Office)
Joe A. Shull (Resident, Washington, D.C. Office)
Kenneth C. Bass, III (Not admitted in MD; Washington, D.C. and McLean, Virginia Offices)
John H. Zink, III (Resident, Towson, Maryland Office)
Joseph C. Wich, Jr. (Resident, Towson, Maryland Office)
Nell B. Strachan
G. Stewart Webb, Jr.
James K. Archibald (Also at Washington, D.C. Office)
James L. Shea (Also at Washington, D.C. Office)
Christopher R. Mellott
John L. Sullivan, III (Not admitted in MD; Resident, McLean, Virginia Office)
Elizabeth R. Hughes
Anita J. Finkelstein (Not admitted in MD; Resident, Washington, D.C. Office)
Gary M. Hnath (Resident, Washington, D.C. Office)
John T. Prisbe
Joseph C. Schmelter (Also at McLean, Virginia Office)

OF COUNSEL

Arthur W. Machen, Jr. (P.C.)
Ariel Vannier (Also at Washington, D.C. Office)

ASSOCIATES

Michael W. Conron
Donald P. Creston (Not admitted in MD; Resident, Washington, D.C. Office)
E. Anne Hamel

For Complete List of Firm Personnel, See General Section

For full biographical listings, see the Martindale-Hubbell Law Directory

*TOWSON,** Baltimore Co.

ELLYN L. BROWN CHARTERED (AV)

600 Washington Avenue, Suite 100, 21204
Telephone: 410-823-4200
Fax: 410-823-4201
Email: ellynbrown@worldnet.att.net

Ellyn L. Brown

For full biographical listings, see the Martindale-Hubbell Law Directory

MASSACHUSETTS

*BOSTON,** Suffolk Co.

GELB & GELB LLP (AV)

20 Custom House Street, 02110
Telephone: 617-345-0010
Facsimile: 617-345-0009
Email: g&g@gelbgelb.com *URL:* http://www.gelbgelb.com

MEMBERS OF FIRM

Richard M. Gelb
Gail Kleven Gelb

Aaron J. Bullwinkel
Brian G. Cafferty

For full biographical listings, see the Martindale-Hubbell Law Directory

HINCKLEY, ALLEN & SNYDER LLP (AV)

28 State Street, 30th Floor, 02109-1775
Telephone: 617-345-9000
Email: firm@haslaw.com *URL:* http://www.haslaw.com
Providence, Rhode Island Office: 1500 Fleet Center.
Telephone: 401-274-2000.
Fax: 401-277-9600. URL: http://www.hawlaw.com.

MEMBERS OF FIRM

Paula K. Andrews
David D. Barricelli (Not admitted in MA)
Jonathan Bell
Paul Bork
Stephen J. Carlotti (Not admitted in MA)
Joseph P. Curran (Not admitted in MA)
Michael P. DeFanti
Eric F. Eisenberg
Malcolm Farmer, III
Margaret D. Farrell (Not admitted in MA)
Pasco Gasbarro Jr.
Hugh J. Gorman, III
William R. Grimm
Joel Lewin
Sandra Matrone Mack (Not admitted in MA)
Matthew T. Marcello, III (Not admitted in MA)
Elizabeth Murdock Myers
Paul F. O'Donnell, III
H. Peter Olsen (Not admitted in MA)
Gerald J. Petros
James O. Reavis
Jeremy Ritzenberg
Ralph J. Rivkind
Charles E. Schaub, Jr.
Herman Snyder
David R. Sullivan
Robert F. Sylvia
Howard E. Walker (Not admitted in MA)

ASSOCIATES

Jessica M. Bettencourt (Not admitted in MA)
Mark Bianchi
Alexandra K. Callam
Jane E. Cohen
Andrew D. Cummings
June E. Daniel (Not admitted in MA)
Kelley Jordan-Price
Catherine S. Kim
Christopher W. Morog
Elena B. Olson
Joseph D. Whelan (Not admitted in MA)

OF COUNSEL

Bentley Tobin
Joachim A. Weissfeld (Not admitted in MA)

For Complete List of Firm Personnel, See General Section

For full biographical listings, see the Martindale-Hubbell Law Directory

LEWIS & MUNDAY, A PROFESSIONAL CORPORATION

(Formerly Lewis, Clay & Munday, P.C.)
101 Federal Street Suite 1900, 02110
Telephone: 617-478-0553
Fax: 617-478-0543
Email: lcmlaw@aol.com *URL:* http://www.lewis-pc.com
Washington, D.C. Office: 1120 Connecticut Avenue, Suite 280. 20036.
Telephone: 202-835-0616.
Fax: 202-833-3316.
Detroit, Michigan Office: 1300 First National Building. 660 Woodward Avenue. 48226-3531.
Telephone: 313-961-2550.
Fax: 313-961-1270.

COUNSEL

G. Allen Bass (Resident)

For full biographical listings, see the Martindale-Hubbell Law Directory

PALMER & DODGE LLP (AV)

One Beacon Street, 02108
Telephone: 617-573-0100
Facsimile: 617-227-4420
URL: http://www.palmerdodge.com

MEMBERS OF FIRM

James T. Barrett
Matthew C. Dallett
Lynnette C. Fallon
Stanley Keller

For Complete List of Firm Personnel, See General Section

For full biographical listings, see the Martindale-Hubbell Law Directory

*CAMBRIDGE,** Middlesex Co.

BARRETT & ASSOCIATES (AV)

One Kendall Square, Suite 2200, 02139
Telephone: 617-621-1579
Fax: 617-621-1556
Email: barrettd@earthlink.net

Donal B. Barrett

For full biographical listings, see the Martindale-Hubbell Law Directory

WELLESLEY, Norfolk Co.

White & McDermott, P.C. (AV)

65 William Street, 02481
Telephone: 781-431-1700
Fax: 781-237-8120
Email: mail@WhiteMcD.com

David A. White
Scott F. McDermott
Sharon Goddard White
John L. Koenig

John J. McCarthy, Jr.
Kathleen Gregg
Sarah C. Wickham

For full biographical listings, see the Martindale-Hubbell Law Directory

MICHIGAN

*ANN ARBOR,** Washtenaw Co.

Miller, Canfield, Paddock and Stone, P.L.C. (AV)

A Professional Limited Liability Company
Founded in 1852 by Sidney Davy Miller
101 North Main Street, Seventh Floor, 48104-1400
Telephone: 734-663-2445
Fax: 734-747-7147
URL: http://www.millercanfield.com
Detroit, Michigan Office: 150 West Jefferson, Suite 2500, 48226-4415.
Telephone: 313-963-6420.
Fax: 313-496-7500.
Cable Address: "Stem Detroit."
Troy, Michigan Office: 840 West Long Lake Road, Suite 200, 48098.
Telephone: 248-879-2000.
Fax: 248-879-2001.
Grand Rapids, Michigan Office: 99 Monroe, N.W., Suite 1200, 49503-2639.
Telephone: 616-454-8656.
Fax: 616-776-6322.
Howell, Michigan Office: 121 South Barnard Street, Suite 4, 48843-2305.
Telephone: 517-546-7600.
Telecopier: 517-546-6974.
Kalamazoo, Michigan Office: 444 West Michigan Avenue, 49007-3752.
Telephone: 616-381-7030.
Fax: 616-382-0244.
Lansing, Michigan Office: One Michigan Avenue, Suite 900, 48933-1609.
Telephone: 517-487-2070.
Fax: 517-374-6304.
Monroe, Michigan Office: 214 East Elm Avenue, Suite 100, 48162-2682.
Telephone: 734-243-2000.
Fax: 734-243-0901.
Washington, D.C. Office: 1900 K Street, N.W., Suite 1150. 20006.
Telephone: 202-429-5575; 785-0600.
Fax: 202-331-1118; 785-1234.
Pensacola, Florida Office: 25 West Cedar, 32501.
Telephone: 850-469-1088.
Fax: 850-432-0677.
New York, New York Office: 1450 Broadway, 41st Floor, 10018.
Telephone: 212-704-4400.
Fax: 212-704-4410.
Gdynia, Poland Office: UL. Slaska 21, 81-319.
Telephone: 011-485-831-2808.
Fax: 011-48-58-628 6411.
Warsaw, Poland Office: UL. Nowogrodzkall, 5th Floor, 00-513.
Telephone: 011-4822 529 0200.
Fax: 011-4822 529 0201.
Katowice, Poland Office: UL. Francuska 35/37, 40-027.
Telephone: 011 (48-32) 757-2414.
Fax: 011 (48-32) 757-2483.

PRINCIPALS OF FIRM

David N. Parsigian
Marta A. Manildi
John O. Renken

OF COUNSEL/SENIOR COUNSEL

Edmond F. DeVine

Representative Firm Clients: Chrysler Corporation; Comerica, Incorporated; City of Detroit, Michigan; Detroit Tigers, Inc.; First of Michigan; Ford Motor Company; Ford Motor Credit Company; Great Lakes Bancorp; Henry Ford Hospital; INVETECH Company.

For Complete List of Firm Personnel, See General Section

For full biographical listings, see the Martindale-Hubbell Law Directory

BIRMINGHAM, Oakland Co.

Hyman Lippitt, P.C. (AV)

185 Oakland Avenue, Suite 300, 48009
Telephone: 248-646-8292
Facsimile: 248-646-8375
Email: hymalipp@tir.com

J. Leonard Hyman
Norman L. Lippitt
Douglas A. Hyman
Brian D. O'Keefe
H. Joel Newman
Nazli G. Sater
Kenneth F. Neuman
Terry S. Givens
Paul J. Fischer
John A. Sellers
Robert H. Lippitt
Roger L. Myers
Sally A. Rutledge
Joseph Pia
John P. Gonway
Leif K. Anderson
Jennifer S. Gold
Julie Lyons Kosovec
Dawn S. Spratley
Michael T. Price

For full biographical listings, see the Martindale-Hubbell Law Directory

BLOOMFIELD HILLS, Oakland Co.

Hertz, Schram & Saretsky, P.C. (AV)

1760 South Telegraph Road, Suite 300, 48302
Telephone: 248-335-5000
Fax: 248-335-3346
Email: lawhss@aol.com *URL:* http://www.legalleaders.com

Bradley J. Schram
Howard Hertz
Gary M. Saretsky
Robert S. Hertzberg
Victor M. Norris
Steve J. Weiss
Robert Paul Geller
Walter J. Piszczatowski
Jeffrey A. Robbins
Mark L. Kowalsky

Dana A. Donohue
Miles D. Hart
Karen A. Gould
Paul K. Villarruel
Bradford T. Yaker
Michael F. Jacobson
Michael I. Zousmer
Brian Witus
Eva T. Cantarella
Eric Andrew Michaels

COUNSEL

Richard P. Zipser
Lisa M. Kavalhuna
(Not admitted in MI)
James W. Burdick

OF COUNSEL

David L. Steinberg
Albert L. Holtz
Elmer L. Roller
Robert A. Canner
Harvey D. Geller (1928-1989)

For full biographical listings, see the Martindale-Hubbell Law Directory

Howard & Howard Attorneys, P.C. (AV)

The Pinehurst Office Center, Suite 101, 1400 North Woodward Avenue, 48304-2855
Telephone: 248-645-1483
Telecopier: 248-645-1568
Kalamazoo, Michigan Office: The Michigan Building, Suite 200, 100 Portage Street.
Telephone: 616-382-1483.
Telecopier: 616-382-1568.
Lansing, Michigan Office: The Phoenix Building, Suite 500, 222 Washington Square, North.
Telephone: 517-485-1483.
Telecopier: 517-485-1568.
Peoria, Illinois Office: One Technology Plaza, Suite 600, 211 Fulton Street.
Telephone: 309-672-1483.
Telecopier: 309-672-1568.

Mark A. Davis
Timothy E. Kraepel
Robert L. Schwartz
John E. Young

Representative Clients: For Representative Client list, see General Practice, Bloomfield Hills, MI.

For Complete List of Firm Personnel, See General Section

For full biographical listings, see the Martindale-Hubbell Law Directory

*DETROIT,** Wayne Co.

Bodman, Longley & Dahling LLP (AV)

34th Floor 100 Renaissance Center, 48243
Telephone: 313-259-7777
Fax: 313-393-7579
Email: info@bodmanlongley.com *URL:* http://www.bodmanlongley.com
Troy, Michigan Office: Suite 2020, 755 West Big Beaver Road.
Telephone: 248-362-2110.
Fax: 248-244-0780.
Ann Arbor, Michigan Office: 110 Miller, Suite 300.
Telephone: 734-761-3780.
Fax: 734-930-2494.

(See Next Column)

Bodman, Longley & Dahling LLP, *Detroit—Continued*

Northern Michigan Office: 229 Court Street, P.O. Box 405, Cheboygan.
Telephone: 231-627-4351.
Fax: 231-627-2802.

MEMBERS OF FIRM

Richard D. Rohr
Kenneth R. Lango (Troy Office)
Herold McC. Deason
James R. Buschmann
Randolph S. Perry
Barbara A. Bowman

For Representative Client List, See General Section

For Complete List of Firm Personnel, See General Section

For full biographical listings, see the Martindale-Hubbell Law Directory

Jaffe, Raitt, Heuer & Weiss, Professional Corporation (AV)

One Woodward Avenue, Suite 2400, 48226
Telephone: 313-961-8380
Telecopier: 313-961-8358
Cable Address: "Jafsni"
Southfield,Michigan Office: Travelers Tower, Suite 1520.
Telephone: 313-961-8380.

Elliot A. Spoon
David D. Warner

Representative Clients: Edgemere Enterprises; Frankel Associates, Inc.; Somerset Inn & Apartments; Sosnick Development Co.; Uniprop, Inc.

For Complete List of Firm Personnel, See General Section

For full biographical listings, see the Martindale-Hubbell Law Directory

Lewis & Munday, A Professional Corporation (AV)

(Formerly Lewis, Clay & Munday, P.C.)
1300 First National Building, 660 Woodward Avenue, 48226-3531
Telephone: 313-961-2550
Fax: 313-961-1270
Email: camille.miller@lewis-pc.com *URL:* http://www.lewis-pc.com
Washington, D.C. Office: 1120 Connecticut Avenue, Suite 280. 20036.
Telephone: 202-835-0616.
Fax: 202-833-3316.
Boston, Massachusetts Office: 101 Federal Street, Suite 1900. 02110.
Telephone: 617-478-0553.
Fax: 617-478-0543.

David Baker Lewis
Reuben A. Munday
Camille Stearns Miller
Jacqueline H. Sellers
David N. Zacks
Thomas J. Guyer
Blair A. Person
Karen Kendrick Brown (Resident, Washington, D.C. Office)
Susan D. Hoffman
Hans J. Massaquoi, Jr.

Althea Lynn Simpson
Donica Thomas Varner
Kris W. Krueger
Cylenthia LaToye Miller
Joseph N. Ejbeh
Yolanda R. Bates
Caroletta L. Edgar-Sprinkle
Derek G. McBride
Ayanna Weber
Deborah Jean Williamson
Darice Elizabeth Weber
Krystal M. Gardner
Syeda Taqi

COUNSEL

G. Allen Bass (Resident, Boston, Massachusetts Office)
Leamon R. Sowell, Jr.
Gail Pabarue Bennett
Roger M. Groves
Carol H. Rodriguez
Linda M. Bruton
Brian J. Kott

OF COUNSEL

Otis M. Smith (1922-1994)
Herbert O. Reid, Sr. (1915-1991)

Representative Clients: Aetna Life & Casualty Co.; Chrysler Motors Corp.; Chrysler Financial Corp.; MCI Communications Corp.; City of Detroit; City of Detroit Building Authority; City of Detroit Downtown Development Authority; Consolidated Rail Corp. (Conrail); Equitable Life Assurance Society of the United States.

For full biographical listings, see the Martindale-Hubbell Law Directory

Miller, Canfield, Paddock and Stone, P.L.C. (AV)

A Professional Limited Liability Company
Founded in 1852 by Sidney Davy Miller
150 West Jefferson, Suite 2500, 48226-4415
Telephone: 313-963-6420
Fax: 313-496-7500
Cable Address: "Stem Detroit"
URL: http://www.millercanfield.com
Ann Arbor, Michigan Office: 101 North Main Street, 7th Floor, 48104-1400.
Telephone: 734-663-2445.
Fax: 734-747-7147.
Troy, Michigan Office: 840 West Long Lake Road, Suite 200, 48098.
Telephone: 248-879-2000.
Fax: 248-879-2001.

(See Next Column)

Grand Rapids, Michigan Office: 99 Monroe, N.W., Suite 1200, 49503-2639.
Telephone: 616-454-8656.
Fax: 616-776-6322.
Howell, Michigan Office: 121 South Barnard Street, Suite 4, 48843-2305.
Telephone: 517-546-7600.
Telecopier: 517-546-6974.
Kalamazoo, Michigan Office: 444 West Michigan Avenue, 49007-3752.
Telephone: 616-381-7030.
Fax: 616-382-0244.
Lansing, Michigan Office: One Michigan Avenue, Suite 900, 48933-1609.
Telephone: 517-487-2070.
Fax: 517-374-6304.
Monroe, Michigan Office: 214 East Elm Avenue, Suite 100, 48162-2682.
Telephone: 734-243-2000.
Fax: 734-243-0901.
Washington, D.C. Office: 1900 K Street, N.W., Suite 1150. 20006.
Telephone: 202-429-5575; 785-0600.
Fax: 202-331-1118; 785-1234.
Pensacola, Florida Office: 25 West Cedar, 32501.
Telephone: 850-469-1088.
Fax: 850-432-0677.
New York, New York Office: 1450 Broadway, 41st Floor, 10018.
Telephone: 212-704-4400.
Fax: 212-704-4410.
Gdynia, Poland Office: UL. Slaska 21, 81-319.
Telephone: 011-485-831-2808.
Fax: 011-48-58-628 6411.
Warsaw, Poland Office: UL. Nowogrodzkall, 5th Floor, 00-513.
Telephone: 011-4822 529 0200.
Fax: 011-4822 529 0201.
Katowice, Poland Office: UL. Francuska 35/37, 40-027.
Telephone: 011 (48-32) 757-2414.
Fax: 011 (48-32) 757-2483.

PRINCIPALS OF FIRM

Eric V. Brown, Jr. (Kalamazoo Office)
Bruce D. Birgbauer
Carl H. von Ende
David D. Joswick (P.C.)
John A. Marxer (P.C.) (Troy Office)
Clarence L. Pozza, Jr.
Jerry T. Rupley
Kent E. Shafer
John R. Cook (Kalamazoo Office)
Thomas G. Appleman (Troy Office)
Thomas H. Van Dis (Kalamazoo Office)
Brad B. Arbuckle (Bloomfield Hills Office)
Mark T. Boonstra
Karen A. McCoy
Steven M. Stankewicz (Kalamazoo Office)
David N. Parsigian (Ann Arbor Office)
Jay B. Rising (Lansing Office)
Marta A. Manildi (Ann Arbor Office)
Thomas R. Cox
John O. Renken (Washington, D.C. and Ann Arbor Offices)

Representative Firm Clients: Chrysler Corporation; Comerica, Incorporated; City of Detroit, Michigan; Detroit Tigers, Inc.; First of Michigan; Ford Motor Company; Ford Motor Credit Company; Great Lakes Bancorp; Henry Ford Hospital; INVETECH Company.

For Complete List of Firm Personnel, See General Section

For full biographical listings, see the Martindale-Hubbell Law Directory

Timmis & Inman L.L.P. (AV)

300 Talon Centre, 48207
Telephone: 313-396-4200
Facsimile: 313-396-4228
Email: info@timmis-inman.com *URL:* http://www.timmis-inman.com

Michael T. Timmis
Robert E. Graziani
George A. Peck
Henry J. Brennan, III
Mark W. Peyser
Richard M. Miettinen
Bradley J. Knickerbocker
George M. Malis

Michael F. Wais
Shannon M. Nichols
Anthony J. Long
Alex N. Saleh

OF COUNSEL

William B. Fitzgerald

Representative Clients: Retail Resources, Inc.; Applied Process, Inc.; Insilco Corporation; Talon Automotive Group, Inc.; Chateau Communities, Inc.; N'Tandem Properties, L.P.

For Complete List of Firm Personnel, See General Section

For full biographical listings, see the Martindale-Hubbell Law Directory

*GRAND RAPIDS,** Kent Co.

McShane & Bowie, P.L.C. (AV)

1100 Campau Square Plaza, 99 Monroe Avenue, N.W., P.O. Box 360, 49501-0360
Telephone: 616-732-5000
Fax: 616-732-5099

OF COUNSEL

Jack M. Bowie (Retired)

(See Next Column)

McShane & Bowie P.L.C.—*Continued*

MEMBERS OF FIRM

David L. Smith
William H. Bowie
John F. Shape

Representative Clients: M. W. VanderVeen Co.; Cambridge Development Co.

For Complete List of Firm Personnel, See General Section

For full biographical listings, see the Martindale-Hubbell Law Directory

Miller, Canfield, Paddock and Stone, P.L.C. (AV)

A Professional Limited Liability Company
Founded in 1852 by Sidney Davy Miller
99 Monroe, N.W. Suite 1200, 49503-2639
Telephone: 616-454-8656
Fax: 616-776-6322
URL: http://www.millercanfield.com
Detroit, Michigan Office: 150 West Jefferson, Suite 2500, 48226-4415.
Telephone: 313-963-6420.
Fax: 313-496-7500.
Cable Address: "Stem Detroit."
Ann Arbor, Michigan Office: 101 North Main Street, 7th Floor, 48104-1400.
Telephone: 734-663-2445.
Fax: 734-747-7147.
Troy, Michigan Office: 840 West Long Lake Road, Suite 200, 48098.
Telephone: 248-879-2000.
Fax: 248-879-2001.
Howell, Michigan Office: 121 South Barnard Street, Suite 4, 48843-2305.
Telephone: 517-546-7600.
Telecopier: 517-546-6974.
Kalamazoo, Michigan Office: 444 West Michigan Avenue, 49007-3752.
Telephone: 616-381-7030.
Fax: 616-382-0244.
Lansing, Michigan Office: One Michigan Avenue, Suite 900, 48933-1609.
Telephone: 517-487-2070.
Fax: 517-374-6304.
Monroe, Michigan Office: 214 East Elm Avenue, Suite 100, 48162-2682.
Telephone: 734-243-2000.
Fax: 734-243-0901.
Washington, D.C. Office: 1900 K Street, N.W., Suite 1150. 20006.
Telephone: 202-429-5575; 785-0600.
Fax: 202-331-1118; 785-1234.
Pensacola, Florida Office: 25 West Cedar, 32501.
Telephone: 850-469-1088.
Fax: 850-432-0677.
New York, New York Office: 1450 Broadway, 41st Floor, 10018.
Telephone: 212-704-4400.
Fax: 212-704-4410.
Gdynia, Poland Office: UL. Slaska 21, 81-319.
Telephone: 011-485-831-2808.
Fax: 011-48-58-628 6411.
Warsaw, Poland Office: UL. Nowogrodzkall, 5th Floor, 00-513.
Telephone: 011-4822 529 0200.
Fax: 011-4822 529 0201.
Katowice, Poland Office: UL. Francuska 35/37, 40-027.
Telephone: 011 (48-32) 757-2414.
Fax: 011 (48-32) 757-2483.

PRINCIPALS

Mark E. Putney

Representative Firm Clients: Chrysler Corporation; Comerica, Incorporated; City of Detroit, Michigan; Detroit Tigers, Inc.; First of Michigan; Ford Motor Company; Ford Motor Credit Company; Great Lakes Bancorp; Henry Ford Hospital; INVETECH Company.

For Complete List of Firm Personnel, See General Section

For full biographical listings, see the Martindale-Hubbell Law Directory

Patrick R. Sughroue, P.C. (AV)

3777 Sparks Drive, S.E., Suite 130, 49546
Telephone: 616-940-3399
Fax: 616-940-3592
Email: prspc@aol.com *URL:* http://www.lawyers.com/sughrouelaw

Patrick R. Sughroue

For full biographical listings, see the Martindale-Hubbell Law Directory

Warner Norcross & Judd LLP (AV)

900 Old Kent Building, 111 Lyon Street, N.W., 49503-2489
Telephone: 616-752-2000
Fax: 616-752-2500
URL: http://www.wnj.com
Muskegon, Michigan Office: 400 Terrace Plaza, P.O. Box 900.
Telephone: 231-727-2600.
Fax: 231-727-2699.
Holland, Michigan Office: Curtis Center, Suite 300, 170 College Avenue.
Telephone: 616-396-9800.
Fax: 616-396-3656.

(See Next Column)

Southfield, Michigan Office: 1000 Town Center, Suite 650.
Telephone: 248-223-5000.
Fax: 248-223-5005.

MEMBERS OF FIRM

Charles E. McCallum
William K. Holmes
John R. Marquis (Resident Member, Holland Office)
Hugh H. Makens
Gordon R. Lewis
Robert J. Chovanec
J. A. Cragwall, Jr.
Stephen R. Kretschman
Eugene E. Smary
John H. McKendry, Jr. (Resident Member, Muskegon Office)
Carl W. Dufendach
Stephen C. Waterbury
Alex J. DeYonker
William W. Hall
Bruce C. Young
Shane B. Hansen
Paul R. Jackson (Resident Member, Muskegon Office)
Tracy T. Larsen
Cameron S. DeLong
Robert J. Jonker
Michael H. Schubert (Resident Member, Muskegon Office)
Mark K. Harder (Resident Member, Holland Office)
Jeffrey S. Battershall
Jeffrey A. Ott
Melvin G. Moseley, Jr.
Timothy L. Horner
R. Paul Guerre
Loren M. Andrulis

ASSOCIATES

Mark J. Wassink
Michael P. Lunt
Michael K. Molitor
Tashia L. Rivard
Gregory E. Schmidt

For full biographical listings, see the Martindale-Hubbell Law Directory

*KALAMAZOO,** Kalamazoo Co.

Howard & Howard Attorneys, P.C. (AV)

The Michigan Building, Suite 200, 100 Portage Street, 49007-4802
Telephone: 616-382-1483
Telecopier: 616-382-1568
Bloomfield Hills, Michigan Office: The Pinehurst Office Center, Suite 101, 1400 North Woodward Avenue.
Telephone: 248-645-1483.
Telecopier: 248-645-1568.
Lansing, Michigan Office: The Phoenix Building, Suite 500, 222 Washington Square North.
Telephone: 517-485-1483.
Telecopier: 517-485-1568.
Peoria, Illinois Office: One Technology Plaza, Suite 600, 211 Fulton Street.
Telephone: 309-672-1483.
Telecopier: 309-672-1568.

Joseph B. Hemker

Representative Clients: For Representative Client list, see General Practice, Kalamazoo, MI.

For Complete List of Firm Personnel, See General Section

For full biographical listings, see the Martindale-Hubbell Law Directory

Miller, Canfield, Paddock and Stone, P.L.C. (AV)

A Professional Limited Liability Company
Founded in 1852 by Sidney Davy Miller
444 West Michigan Avenue, 49007-3752
Telephone: 616-381-7030
Fax: 616-382-0244
URL: http://www.millercanfield.com
Detroit, Michigan Office: 150 West Jefferson, Suite 2500, 48226-4415.
Telephone: 313-963-6420.
Fax: 313-496-7500.
Cable Address: "Stem Detroit."
Ann Arbor, Michigan Office: 101 North Main Street, 7th Floor, 48104-1400.
Telephone: 734-663-2445.
Fax: 734-747-7147.
Troy, Michigan Office: 840 West Long Lake Road, Suite 200, 48098.
Telephone: 248-879-2000.
Fax: 248-879-2001.
Grand Rapids, Michigan Office: 99 Monroe, N.W., Suite 1200, 49503-2639.
Telephone: 616-454-8656.
Fax: 616-776-6322.
Howell, Michigan Office: 121 South Barnard Street, Suite 4, 48843-2305.
Telephone: 517-546-7600.
Telecopier: 517-546-6974.
Lansing, Michigan Office: One Michigan Avenue, Suite 900, 48933-1609.
Telephone: 517-487-2070.
Fax: 517-374-6304.
Monroe, Michigan Office: 214 East Elm Avenue, Suite 100, 48162-2682.
Telephone: 734-243-2000.
Fax: 734-243-0901.
Washington, D.C. Office: 1900 K Street, N.W., Suite 1150. 20006.
Telephone: 202-429-5575; 785-0600.
Fax: 202-331-1118; 785-1234.
Pensacola, Florida Office: 25 West Cedar, 32501.
Telephone: 850-469-1088.
Fax: 850-432-0677.

(See Next Column)

MILLER, CANFIELD, PADDOCK AND STONE P.L.C., *Kalamazoo—Continued*

New York, New York Office: 1450 Broadway, 41st Floor, 10018.
Telephone: 212-704-4400.
Fax: 212-704-4410.
Gdynia, Poland Office: UL. Slaska 21, 81-319.
Telephone: 011-485-831-2808.
Fax: 011-48-58-628 6411.
Warsaw, Poland Office: UL. Nowogrodzkall, 5th Floor, 00-513.
Telephone: 011-4822 529 0200.
Fax: 011-4822 529 0201.
Katowice, Poland Office: UL. Francuska 35/37, 40-027.
Telephone: 011 (48-32) 757-2414.
Fax: 011 (48-32) 757-2483.

PRINCIPALS

Eric V. Brown, Jr.
James G. Vantine, Jr.
John R. Cook
Thomas H. Van Dis
Steven M. Stankewicz

Representative Firm Clients: Chrysler Corporation; Comerica, Incorporated; City of Detroit, Michigan; Detroit Tigers, Inc.; First of Michigan; Ford Motor Company; Ford Motor Credit Company; Great Lakes Bancorp; Henry Ford Hospital; INVETECH Company.

For Complete List of Firm Personnel, See General Section

For full biographical listings, see the Martindale-Hubbell Law Directory

*MONROE,** Monroe Co.

MILLER, CANFIELD, PADDOCK AND STONE, P.L.C. (AV)

A Professional Limited Liability Company
Founded in 1852 by Sidney Davy Miller
214 East Elm Avenue, Suite 100, 48162-2682
Telephone: 734-243-2000
Fax: 734-243-0901
URL: http://www.millercanfield.com
Detroit, Michigan Office: 150 West Jefferson, Suite 2500, 48226-4415.
Telephone: 313-963-6420.
Fax: 313-496-7500.
Cable Address: "Stem Detroit."
Ann Arbor, Michigan Office: 101 North Main Street, 7th Floor, 48104-1400.
Telephone: 734-663-2445.
Fax: 734-747-7147.
Troy, Michigan Office: 840 West Long Lake Road, Suite 200, 48098.
Telephone: 248-879-2000.
Fax: 248-879-2001.
Grand Rapids, Michigan Office: 99 Monroe, N.W., Suite 1200, 49503-2639.
Telephone: 616-454-8656.
Fax: 616-776-6322.
Howell, Michigan Office: 121 South Barnard Street, Suite 4, 48843-2305.
Telephone: 517-546-7600.
Telecopier: 517-546-6974.
Kalamazoo, Michigan Office: 444 West Michigan Avenue, 49007-3752.
Telephone: 616-381-7030.
Fax: 616-382-0244.
Lansing, Michigan Office: One Michigan Avenue, Suite 900, 48933-1609.
Telephone: 517-487-2070.
Fax: 517-374-6304.
Washington, D.C. Office: 1900 K Street, N.W., Suite 1150. 20006.
Telephone: 202-429-5575; 785-0600.
Fax: 202-331-1118; 785-1234.
Pensacola, Florida Office: 25 West Cedar, 32501.
Telephone: 850-469-1088.
Fax: 850-432-0677.
New York, New York Office: 1450 Broadway, 41st Floor, 10018.
Telephone: 212-704-4400.
Fax: 212-704-4410.
Gdynia, Poland Office: UL. Slaska 21, 81-319.
Telephone: 011-485-831-2808.
Fax: 011-48-58-628 6411.
Warsaw, Poland Office: UL. Nowogrodzkall, 5th Floor, 00-513.
Telephone: 011-4822 529 0200.
Fax: 011-4822 529 0201.
Katowice, Poland Office: UL. Francuska 35/37, 40-027.
Telephone: 011 (48-32) 757-2414.
Fax: 011 (48-32) 757-2483.

RESIDENT PRINCIPALS

Rocque E. Lipford (P.C.)

Representative Firm Clients: Chrysler Corporation; Comerica, Incorporated; City of Detroit, Michigan; Detroit Tigers, Inc.; First of Michigan; Ford Motor Company; Ford Motor Credit Company; Great Lakes Bancorp; Henry Ford Hospital; INVETECH Company.

For full biographical listings, see the Martindale-Hubbell Law Directory

TROY, Oakland Co.

MILLER, CANFIELD, PADDOCK AND STONE, P.L.C. (AV)

A Professional Limited Liability Company
Founded in 1852 by Sidney Davy Miller
840 West Long Lake Road Suite 200, 48098
Telephone: 248-879-2000
Fax: 248-879-2001
URL: http://www.millercanfield.com
Detroit, Michigan Office: 150 West Jefferson, Suite 2500, 48226-4415.
Telephone: 313-963-6420.
Fax: 313-496-7500.
Cable Address: "Stem Detroit."
Ann Arbor, Michigan Office: 101 North Main Street, 7th Floor, 48104-1400.
Telephone: 734-663-2445.
Fax: 734-747-7147.
Grand Rapids, Michigan Office: 99 Monroe, N.W., Suite 1200, 49503-2639.
Telephone: 616-454-8656.
Fax: 616-776-6322.
Howell, Michigan Office: 121 South Barnard Street, Suite 4, 48843-2305.
Telephone: 517-546-7600.
Telecopier: 517-546-6974.
Kalamazoo, Michigan Office: 444 West Michigan Avenue, 49007-3752.
Telephone: 616-381-7030.
Fax: 616-382-0244.
Lansing, Michigan Office: One Michigan Avenue, Suite 900, 48933-1609.
Telephone: 517-487-2070.
Fax: 517-374-6304.
Monroe, Michigan Office: 214 East Elm Avenue, Suite 100, 48162-2682.
Telephone: 734-243-2000.
Fax: 734-243-0901.
Washington, D.C. Office: 1900 K Street, N.W., Suite 1150. 20006.
Telephone: 202-429-5575; 785-0600.
Fax: 202-331-1118; 785-1234.
Pensacola, Florida Office: 25 West Cedar, 32501.
Telephone: 850-469-1088.
Fax: 850-432-0677.
New York, New York Office: 1450 Broadway, 41st Floor, 10018.
Telephone: 212-704-4400.
Fax: 212-704-4410.
Gdynia, Poland Office: UL. Slaska 21, 81-319.
Telephone: 011-485-831-2808.
Fax: 011-48-58-628 6411.
Warsaw, Poland Office: UL. Nowogrodzkall, 5th Floor, 00-513.
Telephone: 011-4822 529 0200.
Fax: 011-4822 529 0201.
Katowice, Poland Office: UL. Francuska 35/37, 40-027.
Telephone: 011 (48-32) 757-2414.
Fax: 011 (48-32) 757-2483.

RESIDENT PRINCIPALS

John A. Marxer (P.C.)
J. Kevin Trimmer
Brad B. Arbuckle

Representative Firm Clients: Chrysler Corporation; Comerica, Incorporated; City of Detroit, Michigan; Detroit Tigers, Inc.; First of Michigan; Ford Motor Company; Ford Motor Credit Company; Great Lakes Bancorp; Henry Ford Hospital; INVETECH Company.

For Complete List of Firm Personnel, See General Section

For full biographical listings, see the Martindale-Hubbell Law Directory

SPORTS AND ENTERTAINMENT LAW

ALABAMA

*BIRMINGHAM,** Jefferson Co.

JOHNSTON BARTON PROCTOR & POWELL LLP (AV)

2900 AmSouth/Harbert Plaza, 1901 Sixth Avenue North, 35203-2618
Telephone: 205-458-9400
Telecopier: 205-458-9500
Email: Law@JBPP.com

MEMBERS OF FIRM

Gilbert E. Johnston, Jr.
Hollinger F. Barnard
Anne P. Wheeler
Robert S. Vance, Jr.
Russell L. Irby, III

COUNSEL

Paul E. Toppins

ASSOCIATES

Spencer A. Kinderman
W. Jonathan Daniel
Anna R. Minor

Counsel for: Broadcast Music, Inc.; Charter Communications, Inc.; Courtroom Television Network; ESPN; Fox Inc.; National Broadcasting Company; Paramount Pictures Corporation; Public Broadcasting System; Taake-the-Field, Inc.; Wolfe-Carter Productions, Inc.

For full biographical listings, see the Martindale-Hubbell Law Directory

ARIZONA

*PHOENIX,** Maricopa Co.

FENNEMORE CRAIG, A PROFESSIONAL CORPORATION (AV)

3003 North Central Avenue, Suite 2600, 85012-2913
Telephone: 602-916-5000
Fax: 602-916-5999
Tucson, Arizona Office: One South Church Avenue, Suite 1000, 85701-1620.
Telephone: 520-879-6800.
Fax: 520-879-6899.

Jay S. Ruffner

Thomas F. O'Malley, III
Charles D. Mitchell, Jr.

For Complete List of Firm Personnel, See General Section

For full biographical listings, see the Martindale-Hubbell Law Directory

SNELL & WILMER L.L.P. (AV)

One Arizona Center, 85004-2202
Telephone: 602-382-6000
Fax: 602-382-6070
Email: postmaster@snellwilmer.com *URL:* http://www.swlaw.com
Tucson, Arizona Office: One South Church Avenue, Suite 1500, 85701-1612.
Telephone: 520-882-1200.
Fax: 520-884-1294.
Orange County Office: 1920 Main Street, Suite 1200, Irvine, California 92614-7230.
Telephone: 949-253-2700.
Fax: 949-955-2507.
Salt Lake City, Utah Office: 111 East Broadway, Suite 900, 84111-1004.
Telephone: 801-237-1900.
Fax: 801-237-1950.

MEMBERS OF FIRM

Craig K. Williams
Patrick G. Byrne

Representative Clients: For list of Representative Clients, see end of biographical listings in the Martindale-Hubbell Law Directory.

For Complete List of Firm Personnel, See General Section

For full biographical listings, see the Martindale-Hubbell Law Directory

*TUCSON,** Pima Co.

KINERK, BEAL, SCHMIDT & DYER, P.C. (AV)

Suite 6000, West Tower, 5255 East Williams Circle, 85711
Telephone: 520-790-5600
Fax: 520-790-1163
Email: kbs@azstarnet.com *URL:* http://www.azinjurylaw.com

(See Next Column)

Burton J. Kinerk
Ted A. Schmidt
Robert L. Beal
James H. Dyer
Colleen L. Kinerk

Karl R. Lautz
David W. Babcock

For full biographical listings, see the Martindale-Hubbell Law Directory

SNELL & WILMER L.L.P. (AV)

One South Church Avenue, Suite 1500, 85701-1612
Telephone: 520-882-1200
Fax: 520-884-1294
URL: http://www.swlaw.com
Phoenix, Arizona Office: One Arizona Center, 85004-2202.
Telephone: 602-382-6000.
Fax: 602-382-6070.
Orange County Office: 1920 Main Street, Suite 1200, Irvine, California 92614-7230.
Telephone: 949-253-2700.
Fax: 949-955-2507.
Salt Lake City, Utah Office: 111 East Broadway, Suite 900, 84111-1004.
Telephone: 801-237-1900.
Fax: 801-237-1950.

MEMBER OF FIRM

Curt D. Reimann

Representative Clients: For list of Representative Clients, see end of biographical listings in the Martindale-Hubbell Law Directory.

For full biographical listings, see the Martindale-Hubbell Law Directory

ARKANSAS

*LITTLE ROCK,** Pulaski Co.

ROSE LAW FIRM, A PROFESSIONAL ASSOCIATION (AV)

120 East Fourth Street, 72201
Telephone: 501-375-9131
Telecopy: 501-375-1309

William H. Kennedy, III
Ronald M. Clark
Michael N. Shannon

Counsel for: ALLTEL Corporation; Aluminum Company of America; Bridgestone/Firestone, Inc.; The Equitable Life Assurance Society of The United States; General Motors Corp.; The Prudential Insurance Company of America; Stephens Group Inc.; Tyson Foods, Inc.

For Complete List of Firm Personnel, See General Section

For full biographical listings, see the Martindale-Hubbell Law Directory

CALIFORNIA

BEVERLY HILLS, Los Angeles Co.

WEISSMANN, WOLFF, BERGMAN, COLEMAN & SILVERMAN, LLP (AV)

A Limited Liability Partnership including Professional Corporations
9665 Wilshire Boulevard, Suite 900, 90212-2316
Telephone: 310-858-7888
Facsimile: 310-550-7191
Email: wwbcs@wwbcs.com

MEMBERS OF FIRM

Michael Bergman (P.C.)
Stewart S. Brookman
David L. Burg
Stan Coleman (P.C.)
Mitchell Evall (P.C.)
Alan L. Grodin (P.C.)
Henry W. Holmes (P.C.)
Linda A. Kalm (P.C.)
Steven Katleman (P.C.)
Alan G. Kirios (Law Corporation)
Anjani Mandavia (P.C.)
Abraham M. Rudy
Andrew J. Schmerzler
Ronald J. Silverman (P.C.)
Lawrence B. Steinberg (P.C.)
Todd M. Stern
Eric Weissmann (P.C.)
Daniel H. Wolff

ASSOCIATES

Helen G. Fields
Shannon M. Hunt
Lucy Noble Inman
Wayne Kazan
David B. Miercort
Daniel R. Stutz
Julie B. Waldman

OF COUNSEL

Ira S. Epstein
John C. Kirkland

For full biographical listings, see the Martindale-Hubbell Law Directory

*FRESNO,** Fresno Co.

DOWLING, AARON & KEELER, INCORPORATED (AV)

6051 North Fresno Street, Suite 200, 93710
Telephone: 559-432-4500
Fax: 559-432-4590
Email: dak@daklaw.com *URL:* http://www.daklaw.com
Bakersfield, California Office: 110 South Mt. Claire, Suite 203. 93309.
Telephone: 661-396-0451. Web Site: http://www.daklaw.com.

Richard M. Aaron

Michael P. Dowling

Reference: Wells Fargo Bank (Main).

For Complete List of Firm Personnel, See General Section

For full biographical listings, see the Martindale-Hubbell Law Directory

GOLD RIVER, Sacramento Co.

LAW OFFICES OF JOSEPH W. SCALIA (AV)

11335 Gold Express, Suite 105, 95670-4491
Telephone: 916-858-2286
Fax: 916-852-5777
Email: jscalia@ix.netcom.com

For full biographical listings, see the Martindale-Hubbell Law Directory

*LOS ANGELES,** Los Angeles Co.

BLANC WILLIAMS JOHNSTON & KRONSTADT, LLP (AV)

A Partnership including Professional Corporations
Suite 1700, 1900 Avenue of the Stars, 90067
Telephone: 310-552-2500
Telecopier: 310-552-1191
Email: bwjk@bwjk.com

MEMBERS OF FIRM

Ronald L. Blanc (P.C.)
Harley J. Williams (P.C.)
Ronald L. Johnston (P.C.)
John A. Kronstadt
James R. Farrand
Richard T. McCoy III
Regina A. Stagg
John C. Rawls III
Daniel M. Grigsby
Suzanne V. Wilson
Dawn Weekes Glenn

James S. Blackburn
Vivian W. Yang
Allison Binder
Jennifer M. Lloyd
Mark S. Dancsecs

OF COUNSEL

Sol Rosenthal

Reference: Santa Monica Bank (Beverly Hills Office).

For full biographical listings, see the Martindale-Hubbell Law Directory

LAW OFFICES OF DAVID B. BLOOM A PROFESSIONAL CORPORATION (AV)

3325 Wilshire Boulevard, Ninth Floor, 90010
Telephone: 323-938-5248; 384-4088
Telecopier: 213-385-2009

David B. Bloom

Stephen S. Monroe (A Professional Corporation)
Raphael A. Rosemblat
James E. Adler
Roy A. Levun
Jonathan Udell
Susan Carole Jay
Edward Idell
Sandra Kamenir
Steven Wayne Lazarus
Andrew Edward Briseno
Shelley M. Gould
Ted L. Travis

For full biographical listings, see the Martindale-Hubbell Law Directory

MENES LAW CORPORATION (AV)

1801 Century Park East, Suite 1560, 90067
Telephone: 310-286-1313
Fax: 310-556-5695
Email: mlc@meneslaw.com

Barry A. Menes
Paul I. Menes

Marc M. Messineo

OF COUNSEL

John R. Climaco (Not admitted in CA)
Edward M. Bernstein (Not admitted in CA)

For full biographical listings, see the Martindale-Hubbell Law Directory

SIMKE CHODOS (AV)

A Partnership of Professional Corporations
Suite 1511, 1880 Century Park East, 90067-1615
Telephone: 310-203-3888
Fax: 310-203-3866
Email: sclawltd@aol.com

Stuart A. Simke
David M. Chodos

Richard A. Fond

OF COUNSEL

James L. Keane
Ellen Resinski Rosen

Reference: City National Bank (Wilshire-La Cienega Branch).

For full biographical listings, see the Martindale-Hubbell Law Directory

WHITE O'CONNOR CURRY GATTI & AVANZADO LLP (AV)

10100 Santa Monica Boulevard Suite 300, 90067
Telephone: 310-712-6100
Fax: 310-712-6199

Andrew M. White
Michael J. O'Connor
James E. Curry
Melvin N.A. Avanzado
John M. Gatti

OF COUNSEL

Jonathan D. Avila
Frederick F. Mumm

Jonathan H. Anschell
David E. Fink
James W. Irey
Holly J. Sadlon
Lee S. Brenner
Katherine J. Kunberger
Sydney Arfin
Edward Muir Anderson
Marci D. Friedman
Meredith C. Hightower
J Rudy Freeman, II

For full biographical listings, see the Martindale-Hubbell Law Directory

WOLF, RIFKIN & SHAPIRO, LLP (AV)

A Partnership including a Professional Corporation
11400 West Olympic Boulevard Ninth Floor, 90064-1565
Telephone: 310-478-4100
Fax: 310-479-1422
Email: wrs@wrslawyers.com
Las Vegas, Nevada Office: Schulman & Grode, LLP, 2255-A Renaissance Drive 89119.
Telephone: 702-341-5200.
Fax: 702-341-5300.

MEMBERS OF FIRM

Michael Wolf (A Professional Corporation)
Daniel C. Shapiro
Roy G. Rifkin
Michael T. Schulman
Leslie Steven Marks
Mindy Sheps
Norman S. Wisnicki
Barry T. Mitidiere (A Professional Corporation)
Marc E. Rohatiner
Michael W. Rabkin
Andrew S. Gelb
Matthew L. Grode
Richard S. Grant
S. Michael Leventhal

ASSOCIATES

Douglas A. Lusson
Mark J. Rosenbaum
Kelly Allegra Weil
Matthew J. Hafey
Whitney B. Wilds
Keli N. Osaki
Laura S. Withrow
Lisa A. Makarem
Joseph A. Petro
Elsa M. Horowitz

OF COUNSEL

Steven A. Silver
Eric J. Feig
Jeff W. Lane
Jeffrey R. Liebster
Denise M. Parga
Simon Aron

For full biographical listings, see the Martindale-Hubbell Law Directory

ZIFFREN, BRITTENHAM, BRANCA & FISCHER LLP (AV)

1801 Century Park West, 90067-6406
Telephone: 310-552-3388
Fax: 310-553-7068; 553-1648

MEMBERS OF FIRM

Kenneth Ziffren
Harry M. Brittenham
John G. Branca
Samuel N. Fischer
Paul L. Brindze
R. Dennis Luderer
David Nochimson
Gary S. Stiffelman
Clifford W. Gilbert-Lurie
Kathleen Hallberg
Jamie Young
Mitchell C. Tenzer
Steven H. Burkow
David Lande
Jamey Cohen
Matthew M. Johnson
Bryan L. Wolf

For full biographical listings, see the Martindale-Hubbell Law Directory

*SACRAMENTO,** Sacramento Co.

Law Offices of Joseph W. Scalia

(See Gold River)

*SAN DIEGO,** San Diego Co.

Wingert Grebing Brubaker & Ryan LLP (AV)

A Limited Liability Partnership including Professional Corporations
One America Plaza, Seventh Floor, 600 West Broadway, 92101
Telephone: 619-232-8151
Facsimile: 619-232-4665
URL: http://www.wgbrlaw.com
Las Vegas, Nevada Office: Ryan Marks Johnson & Todd, 1120 Town Center Drive, Suite 200, 89144.
Telephone: 702-341-7870.
Fax: 702-341-8049.

MEMBERS OF FIRM

Charles R. Grebing (A Professional Corporation)
Alan K. Brubaker (A Professional Corporation)
Norman A. Ryan
James Goodwin
Shawn D. Morris
Robert M. Juskie
Dan H. Deuprey
Robert M. Caietti
Eileen Mulligan Marks
Christopher W. Todd
Robert L. Johnson
John S. Addams
Michael Sullivan
James J. Brown, Jr.
Terie M. Theis
Craig Gross

ASSOCIATES

Stephen C. Grebing
Brian P. Worthington
Marco B. Mercaldo
Solveig Store Deuprey
Kimberly Diane Howatt
Jay A. Kenyon
T. Steven Gregor
Jana M. Beck
Brad Lovelace

OF COUNSEL

William L. Todd, Jr.
John R. Wingert (A Professional Corporation)

LEGAL SUPPORT PERSONNEL

Carol C. Berry

Representative Clients: Angelic Entertainment; Becton Dickinson; Brookfield Homes Pacific Inc.; California Casualty; Columbia/HCI; Cooper. of Amer. Physicians; Conan Davidson Homes; Discover R. Insurance; Farmers Insurance; Guaranty National.

For full biographical listings, see the Martindale-Hubbell Law Directory

*SAN FRANCISCO,** San Francisco Co.

Kay & Merkle (AV)

100 The Embarcadero Penthouse, 94105
Telephone: 415-357-1200
Facsimile: 415-512-9277
Email: kmlaw100@kmlaw100.com

MEMBERS OF FIRM

Steven Kay
Walter F. Merkle, Jr.
W. Bruce Bercovich
John W. Merkle
Alan J. Silver
Douglas A. Marshall
Douglas A Hutchinson

OF COUNSEL

Lionel T. Aiken

For full biographical listings, see the Martindale-Hubbell Law Directory

WOODLAND HILLS, Los Angeles Co.

Leon F. Bennett (AV)

6400 Canoga Avenue, Suite 354, 91367-2425
Telephone: 818-888-7731
Fax: 818-888-7674
URL: http://www.lawyers.com/leonfbennettlaw

ASSOCIATE

Debra J. Przelomiec

For full biographical listings, see the Martindale-Hubbell Law Directory

CONNECTICUT

SOUTHPORT, Fairfield Co.

Brody, Wilkinson and Ober, P.C. (AV)

2507 Post Road, 06490
Telephone: 203-319-7100
Fax: 203-254-1772

(See Next Column)

Seth O. L. Brody
Peter Wilkinson
Frank Fritz Ober
S. Giles Payne
James E. Rice
William J. Britt
Barbara S. Miller
Robert L. Teicher
Ronald B. Noren
Peter T. Mott
Thomas J. Walsh, Jr.
Diane F. Martucci
Seth L. Cooper
Douglas R. Brown
Charles S. Brody (1894-1976)

OF COUNSEL

Bruce E. Dillingham
Roy W. Moore, III

For full biographical listings, see the Martindale-Hubbell Law Directory

WESTPORT, Fairfield Co.

Alan Neigher (AV)

1804 Post Road East, 06880
Telephone: 203-259-0599
Fax: 203-255-2570
Email: aneigher@snet.net *URL:* http://www.lawyers.com/neigherlaw

OF COUNSEL

Judith M. Trutt

For full biographical listings, see the Martindale-Hubbell Law Directory

DISTRICT OF COLUMBIA

WASHINGTON, D.C. Co.

Zevnik Horton Guibord McGovern Palmer & Fognani, L.L.P. (AV)

The Warner Building, 1299 Pennsylvania Avenue, N.W. Ninth Floor, 20004
Telephone: 202-824-0950
Facsimile: 202-824-0955
Email: law@dc.zhgm.com *URL:* http://www.zevnik.com
Boston, Massachusetts Office: One International Place, Fourteenth Floor.
Telephone: 617-790-2970.
Facsimile: 617-790-2910.
San Francisco, California Office: 225 Bush Street, Seventeenth Floor.
Telephone: 415-364-6300.
Facsimile: 415-364-6333.
Los Angeles, California Office: 333 South Grande Avenue, Twenty First Floor.
Telephone: 213-437-5200.
Facsimile: 213-437-5222.
New York, New York Office: 1330 Avenue of the Americas, Eleventh Floor.
Telephone: 212-407-0600.
Facsimile: 212-407-0606.
Chicago, Illinois Office: 77 West Wacker Drive, Thirty Third Floor.
Telephone: 312-977-2500.
Facsimile: 312-977-2560.
London, England Office: 4 Kings Bench Walk, Temple, London EC4Y 7DL.
Telephone: 171-822-8822.
Facsimile: 171-822-8844.
San Diego, California Office: 101 West Broadway, Seventeenth Floor.
Telephone: 619-515-9600.
Facsimile: 619-515-9628.
Denver, Colorado Office: 555 Seventeenth Street, Twenty Sixth Floor.
Telephone: 303-382-6200.
Facsimile: 303-382-6210.
Woodcliff Lake, New Jersey Office: 50 Tice Boulevard, First Floor.
Telephone: 201-476-9600.
Facsimile: 201-476-9666.
Philadelphia, Pennsylvania Office: 620 Chestnut Street, Tenth Floor.
Telephone: 215-440-8450.
Facsimile: 215-440-8459.

Paul Anton Zevnik
Michel Yves Horton (Resident, Los Angeles, California Office)
Barbara B. Guibord (Resident, Chicago, Illinois Office)
Patrick Michael McGovern (Resident, New York, New York Office)
David G. Palmer (Resident, Denver, Colorado Office)
John D. Fognani (Resident, Denver, Colorado Office)
Joseph G. Homsy (Resident, Chicago, Illinois Office)
John K. Crossman (Resident, New York, New York Office)
Jonathan L. Osborne
John W. Roberts (Resident, Chicago, Illinois Office)
Steven E. Knott (Resident, Los Angeles, California Office)
Kenneth D. Polin (Resident, San Diego, California Office)
Steven G. Rowles (Resident, San Diego, California Office)
Charles J. Malaret (Resident, Los Angeles, California Office)
Michael John Miguel (Resident, Boston, Massachusetts Office)
Lea Leadbeater (Not admitted in DC; Resident, Chicago, Illinois Office)

(See Next Column)

ZEVNIK HORTON GUIBORD MCGOVERN PALMER & FOGNANI L.L.P.,
Washington—Continued

Michael J. Wilson
Gregory M. Cork
(Not admitted in DC)
Yolanda C. Griffin
Dolores R. Lyons
(Not admitted in DC)

For full biographical listings, see the Martindale-Hubbell Law Directory

FLORIDA

*ORLANDO,** Orange Co.

MORAN & SHAMS, P.A. (AV)
111 North Orange Avenue, Suite 1200, P.O. Box 472, 32802-0472
Telephone: 407-841-4141
Fax: 407-841-4148
Email: moran-shams@moran-shams.com

Thomas P. Moran
Robert S. MacDonald

Lawrence H. Haber

Representative Clients: One Heart Productions, Inc.; Bruno White Entertainment, Inc.; Sidekick Productions; Film Consultants International; MacStephens Productions, Inc.; J.S.S. International Group, Inc.; Mad Woodchuck Entertainment, L.L.C.; George Feder; Wright Stuff Productions, Inc.

For full biographical listings, see the Martindale-Hubbell Law Directory

*WEST PALM BEACH,** Palm Beach Co.

SEARCY DENNEY SCAROLA BARNHART & SHIPLEY, PROFESSIONAL ASSOCIATION (AV)
2139 Palm Beach Lakes Boulevard, P.O. Drawer 3626, 33402-3626
Telephone: 561-686-6300
800-780-8607
800-220-7006 (Spanish)
Fax: 561-478-0754
Email: CDS@SEARCYLAW.COM *URL:* http://www.searcylaw.com

Harry A. Shevin

For Complete List of Firm Personnel, See General Section

For full biographical listings, see the Martindale-Hubbell Law Directory

GEORGIA

*ATLANTA,** Fulton Co.

HAWKINS & PARNELL, LLP (AV)
4000 SunTrust Plaza, 303 Peachtree Street, N.E., 30308-3243
Telephone: 404-614-7400
Fax: 404-614-7500
Email: relliott@hplegal.com *URL:* http://www.hawkinsparnell.com

MEMBERS OF FIRM

Albert H. Parnell
Jack N. Sibley
Roger M. Goode
Thomas G. Tidwell

For Complete List of Firm Personnel, See General Section

For full biographical listings, see the Martindale-Hubbell Law Directory

LONG ALDRIDGE & NORMAN LLP (AV)
A Limited Liability Partnership including Professional Corporations
Suite 5300, 303 Peachtree Street, 30308
Telephone: 404-527-4000
Telecopier: 404-527-4198
Email: atlanta@lanlaw.com *URL:* http://www.lanlaw.com
Washington, D.C. Office: Suite 600, 701 Pennsylvania Avenue, N.W., 20004.
Telephone: 202-624-1200.
FAX: 202-624-1298.

MEMBERS OF FIRM

Evan Appel
Jesse J. Spikes
James J. Thomas II

For Complete List of Firm Personnel, See General Section

For full biographical listings, see the Martindale-Hubbell Law Directory

LOUISIANA

*NEW ORLEANS,** Orleans Parish

MICHAEL L. ECKSTEIN ATTORNEY AT LAW A PROFESSIONAL CORPORATION (AV)
1515 Poydras Street, Suite 2195, 70112
Telephone: 504-527-0701
Telecopier: 504-566-0040
VMX: 504-889-8876
Email: eck@eck-law.com

Michael L. Eckstein

Representative Clients: Sam Mills; Renaldo Turnbull; William Roaf.

For full biographical listings, see the Martindale-Hubbell Law Directory

*SHREVEPORT,** Caddo Parish

WILKINSON, CARMODY & GILLIAM (AV)
1700 Beck Building, 400 Travis Street, P.O. Box 1707, 71166
Telephone: 318-221-4196
Telecopier: 318-221-3705
Email: wcg1895@aol.com

MEMBERS OF FIRM

John D. Wilkinson (1867-1929)
William Scott Wilkinson
(1895-1985)
Arthur R. Carmody, Jr.
Bobby S. Gilliam
Mark E. Gilliam
William Allen Haynes

Representative Clients: Farmers Insurance Group; Home Federal Savings & Loan Association of Shreveport; The Kansas City Southern Railway Co.; KTAL-TV; Lincoln National Life Insurance Co.; Mobil Oil Co.; Schumpert Medical Center; Sears, Roebuck & Co.; Southern Pacific Transportation Co.; Southwestern Electric Power Co.

For full biographical listings, see the Martindale-Hubbell Law Directory

MASSACHUSETTS

*BOSTON,** Suffolk Co.

BLOOM & WITKIN (AV)
70 Franklin Street, 02110
Telephone: 617-443-4300
Fax: 617-443-4315

MEMBERS OF FIRM

Arnold Bloom
Mark J. Witkin

For full biographical listings, see the Martindale-Hubbell Law Directory

PALMER & DODGE LLP (AV)
One Beacon Street, 02108
Telephone: 617-573-0100
Facsimile: 617-227-4420
URL: http://www.palmerdodge.com

MEMBERS OF FIRM

Mark A. Fischer
Michael T. Gass
Laurie S. Gill
Eric F. Menoyo
Thane D. Scott
George Ticknor
John Taylor Williams

COUNSEL

Zick Rubin

For Complete List of Firm Personnel, See General Section

For full biographical listings, see the Martindale-Hubbell Law Directory

MICHIGAN

DEARBORN, Wayne Co.

RILEY, HURLEY & DOLENGA, P.C. (AV)
19853 West Outer Drive, Suite 300, 48124
Telephone: 313-565-1330
Facsimile: 313-565-1318
Email: rfrpc@pop.net

Robert F. Riley
William C. Hurley
Michael D. Dolenga

Judy L. Burgard

(See Next Column)

RILEY, HURLEY & DOLENGA P.C.—*Continued*

OF COUNSEL

Mark S. Demorest
Michael J. Hainer
Leonard K. Berman

For full biographical listings, see the Martindale-Hubbell Law Directory

SOUTHFIELD, Oakland Co.

SOMMERS, SCHWARTZ, SILVER & SCHWARTZ, P.C. (AV)

2000 Town Center, Suite 900, 48075
Telephone: 248-355-0300
Telecopier: 248-746-4001
Plymouth, Michigan Office: 747 South Main Street.
Telephone: 313-455-4250.

Patrick B. McCauley
Justin C. Ravitz
Kenneth T. Watkins

General Counsel for: City of Taylor; Foodland Distributors; C.A. Muer Corporation; Vlasic & Company; Nederlander Corporation; Midwest Health Centers, P.C.
Representative Clients: Michigan National Bank; Universal Underwriters Insurance Co.; Don Lee Distributor; Rite-Aid of Michigan.

For Complete List of Firm Personnel, See General Section

For full biographical listings, see the Martindale-Hubbell Law Directory

WESTLAND, Wayne Co.

ASKER, CHAPP & CLOS, P.C. (AV)

35551 Ford Road, Suite 100, 48185
Telephone: 734-326-2101
Fax: 734-595-9771
URL: http://www.lawyers.com/michigan
Torrance, California Office: 615 Hawaii Avenue, 90503.
Telephone: 310-320-5766.

Paul P. Asker
Sandra J. Chapp
Charles E. Clos
Gary E. Perlmuter
Brian J. Considine
J. Matthew Catchick, Jr.

For full biographical listings, see the Martindale-Hubbell Law Directory

TAX LAW

ALABAMA

*ANDALUSIA,** Covington Co.

ALBRITTONS, CLIFTON, ALVERSON & MOODY, P.C. (AV)

(Powell, Albritton & Albritton)
(Albrittons & Rankin)
(Albrittons, Givhan, Clifton & Alverson)
(Albrittons & Givhan)
109 Opp Avenue, P.O. Box 880, 36420
Telephone: 334-222-3177
Telecopier: 334-222-2696

Ed. T. Albritton (1857-1925)
Wm. Harold Albritton, Sr. (1881-1929)
Dempsey M. Powell (1863-1949)
Albert L. Rankin (1909-1970)
Robert Bynum Albritton (1905-1983)
William H. Albritton, Jr. (1907-1983)
James Marvin Albritton (1915-1987)
James R. Clifton
William Harold Albritton, IV
William B. Alverson, Jr.
Thomas B. Albritton
Julie S. Moody

Benjamin M. Bowden

General Counsel for: Coca-Cola Bottling Co. of Andalusia; Opp-Micolas Cotton Mills.
Attorneys for: First Alabama Bank; Alabama Power Co.; The Travelers; Liberty Mutual Ins. Co; Kemper Insurance; Crum & Forster Insurance Cos; CSX Transporation.

For full biographical listings, see the Martindale-Hubbell Law Directory

*BIRMINGHAM,** Jefferson Co.

BERKOWITZ, LEFKOVITS, ISOM & KUSHNER, A PROFESSIONAL CORPORATION (AV)

SouthTrust Tower, 420 North Twentieth Street, Suite 1600, 35203-5202
Telephone: 205-328-0480
Telecopier: 205-322-8007
URL: http://www.blik.com

Arnold K. Lefkovits
Harold B. Kushner
Henry I Frohsin
Barry S. Marks
Anne W. Mitchell
D. J. Simonetti
Andrew J. Potts
Thomas J. Mahoney, Jr.
Thomas O. Kolb
Nancy C. Hughes

Hewes T. Hull
Robert Buchanan Phillips, II

For Complete List of Firm Personnel, See General Section

For full biographical listings, see the Martindale-Hubbell Law Directory

BRADLEY ARANT ROSE & WHITE LLP (AV)

2001 Park Place, Suite 1400, P.O. Box 830709, 35283-0709
Telephone: 205-521-8000
Facsimile: 205-521-8800
Facsimile (SouthTrust Tower Office): 205-521-8500
URL: http://www.barw.com
Huntsville, Alabama Office: 200 Clinton Avenue West, Suite 900, 35801.
Telephone: 205-517-5100.
Facsimile: 205-533-5069.
Washington, D.C. Office: 801 Pennsylvania Avenue, NW, Suite 230, 20004.
Telephone: 202-347-8893.
Facsimile: 202-347-1684.

MEMBERS OF FIRM

Thomas Neely Carruthers Jr.
Stuart Joseph Frentz
William L. Hinds Jr.
Scott E. Ludwig (Resident, Huntsville Office)
Charles R. Smith Jr. (Resident, Huntsville Office)
Robert C. Walthall

OF COUNSEL

Edward M. Selfe
Wm. Bew White Jr. (Retired)

ASSOCIATES

K. Wood Herren
Dorothy D. Pak

For Complete List of Firm Personnel, See General Section

For full biographical listings, see the Martindale-Hubbell Law Directory

BURR & FORMAN LLP (AV)

3100 SouthTrust Tower, 420 North 20th Street, P.O. Box 830719, 35283-0719
Telephone: 205-251-3000
Facsimile: 205-458-5100
URL: http://www.burr.com
Huntsville, Alabama Office: Suite 204, Regency Center, 400 Meridian Street.
Telephone: 205-551-0010.
Facsimile: 205-551-0043.
Atlanta, Georgia Office: Suite 1200, One Georgia Center, 600 West Peachtree Street, 30308.
Telephone: 404-815-3000.
Facsimile: 404-817-3244.

MEMBERS OF FIRM

Louis H. Anders, Jr.
Henry Graham Beene
Warren C. Matthews
Marvin Glenn Perry, Jr.
Bruce A. Rawls
Jack P. Stephenson, Jr.
A. Brand Walton
Paul O. Woodall

For Complete List of Firm Personnel, See General Section

For full biographical listings, see the Martindale-Hubbell Law Directory

DOMINICK, FLETCHER, YEILDING, WOOD & LLOYD, P.A. (AV)

2121 Highland Avenue, 35209
Telephone: 205-939-0033
URL: http://members.aol.com/dfywandl/lawyer.htm

Brian T. Williams
Steven C. Pearson

Counsel for: Citizens Federal Savings Bank; St. Vincent's Hospital; Birmingham-Southern College; Castle Mortgage Corporation; Amerex.

For Complete List of Firm Personnel, See General Section

For full biographical listings, see the Martindale-Hubbell Law Directory

FELD, HYDE, LYLE, WERTHEIMER & BRYANT, P.C. (AV)

2000 Southbridge Parkway, Suite 500, 35209
Telephone: 205-802-7575
Facsimile: 205-802-7550

Louis B. Feld
Gregory D. Hyde
John F. Lyle, III
Leonard Wertheimer, III
William J. Bryant
J. Fred Kingren

Robert T. Gardner
Gwen Denoux Skinner
Allison Taylor Craft
T. Craig Williams
James J. Coomes

OF COUNSEL

Edward K. Wood, Jr.

STAFF ATTORNEY

Allison P. Smith

LEGAL SUPPORT PERSONNEL

Kelly S. Prevatte (Certified Legal Assistant)
Rebekah T. Mize (Paralegal)
Kerry Sweeney (Paralegal)

For full biographical listings, see the Martindale-Hubbell Law Directory

GORDON, SILBERMAN, WIGGINS & CHILDS, P.C. (AV)

1400 SouthTrust Tower, 420 North 20th Street, 35203
Telephone: 205-328-0640
Facsimilie: 205-254-1500
Washington, D.C. Office: 1621 Connecticut Avenue, N.W., Suite 400.
Telephone: 202-238-0690.
Facsimile: 202-238-0968.

RESIDENT SHAREHOLDERS

Wilbur G. Silberman
Bruce L. Gordon
Ray D. Gibbons
Mark P. Williams
Timothy D. Davis
Linda J. Peacock

OF COUNSEL

Robert H. Loeb

For Complete List of Firm Personnel, See General Section

For full biographical listings, see the Martindale-Hubbell Law Directory

HASKELL SLAUGHTER & YOUNG, L.L.C. (AV)

1200 AmSouth/Harbert Plaza, 1901 Sixth Avenue North, 35203
Telephone: 205-251-1000
Facsimile: 205-324-1133
Email: hsy@hsy.com
Montgomery, Alabama Office: 305 South Lawrence Street, P.O. Box 4660. 36103-4660.
Telephone: 334-265-8573.
Facsimile: 334-264-7945.

William M. Slaughter
Benjamin B. Spratling III
Robert D. Shattuck, Jr.
Ross N. Cohen

Representative Clients: HEALTHSOUTH Corporation; USX Corporation.

(See Next Column)

HASKELL SLAUGHTER & YOUNG L.L.C., *Birmingham—Continued*

For Complete List of Firm Personnel, See General Section

For full biographical listings, see the Martindale-Hubbell Law Directory

SPAIN & GILLON, L.L.C. (AV)

The Zinszer Building, 2117 2nd Avenue North, 35203
Telephone: 205-328-4100
Telecopier: 205-324-8866
Email: ddh@spain-gillon.com *URL:* http://lawlinks.com:80/atty/al/sggbn.html

MEMBERS OF FIRM

John P. McKleroy, Jr.
Glenn E. Estess, Jr.
Samuel H. Frazier
Paul S. Leonard

Representative Clients: Golden Enterprises, Inc.; City of Birmingham; First Federal of Alabama, Federal Savings Bank; Piggly Wiggly Alabama Distributing Co., Inc.; First General Lending Corporation; Alabama Health Plan; Smith Barney, Harris Upham and Co., Inc.; Auburn University Foundation; Koppers Industries; Allied Systems, Inc.

For Complete List of Firm Personnel, See General Section

For full biographical listings, see the Martindale-Hubbell Law Directory

*DECATUR,** Morgan Co.

EYSTER, KEY, TUBB, WEAVER & ROTH (AV)

Eyster Building, 402 East Moulton Street, S.E., P.O. Box 1607, 35602
Telephone: 256-353-6761
Fax: 256-353-6767

John C. Eyster (1863-1926)
Wm. B. Eyster (1921-1995)
Charles H. Eyster, Sr. (1888-1964)

MEMBERS OF FIRM

John S. Key
J. Witty Allen
J. Glynn Tubb
William L. Middleton, III
Lawrence C. Weaver
James G. Adams, Jr.
Nicholas B. Roth
John R. Baggette, Jr.
Jenny L. Mcleroy

General Counsel for: Alabama Farmers Cooperative.
Regional Counsel for: AmSouth Bank.
Local Counsel for: Allstate Insurance Co.; Champion International Corp; General Electric; Goodyear; Liberty Mutual Insurance Co.; Saginaw Steering Gear Division, General Motors Corp.; State Farm Mutual Automobile Insurance Co.; 3M; The Travelers.

For full biographical listings, see the Martindale-Hubbell Law Directory

HARRIS, CADDELL & SHANKS, P.C. (AV)

214 Johnston Street, S.E., P.O. Box 2688, 35602-2688
Telephone: 256-340-8000
Telecopier: 256-340-8040
Email: hcs@ala-net.com

Julian Harris (1904-1994)
Thomas A. Caddell
Norman W. Harris (1907-1998)
William E. Shinn, Jr.
Philip T. Shanks (Retired)
Gary A. Phillips
Charles L. Murphree (Retired)
Dow M. Perry, Jr.
John A. Caddell
Barnes F. Lovelace, Jr.
Robert H. Harris
Jeffrey S. Brown
Jon H. Moores
David W. Langston
Huel Harris

Attorneys for: First American Bank, Decatur, Alabama; SouthTrust Bank of Alabama (Morgan County); Morgan County Commission; The Industrial Development Board of the City of Decatur, Alabama; The Boeing Ccmpany; Amoco Chemical Co.; BellSouth Inc.; General Electric Co.; ConAgra, Inc.

For full biographical listings, see the Martindale-Hubbell Law Directory

*DOTHAN,** Houston Co.

JOHNSTON, HINESLEY, FLOWERS & CLENNEY, P.C., A PROFESSIONAL CORPORATION (AV)

291 North Oates Street, 36303
Telephone: 334-793-1115
Fax: 334-793-6603

G. David Johnston
William T. Flowers
William W. Hinesley
R. Eugene Clenney, Jr.

For full biographical listings, see the Martindale-Hubbell Law Directory

*FLORENCE,** Lauderdale Co.

PAINE & ASSOCIATES, P.C. (AV)

SunTrust Building, 201 South Court Street, Suite 520, P.O. Box 1609, 35631
Telephone: 256-718-3622
Fax: 256-718-4065

(See Next Column)

Peter L. Paine
Michael T. Paine

For full biographical listings, see the Martindale-Hubbell Law Directory

*HUNTSVILLE,** Madison Co.

BRADLEY ARANT ROSE & WHITE LLP (AV)

200 Clinton Avenue West, Suite 900, 35801
Telephone: 205-517-5100
Facsimile: 205-517-5200
URL: http://www.barw.com
Birmingham, Alabama Office: 2001 Park Place, Suite 1400, P.O. Box 830709.
Telephone: 205-521-8000.
Facsimile: 205-521-8800. Facsimile (SouthTrust Tower Office): 205-521-8500.
Washington, D.C. Office: 801 Pennsylvania Avenue, NW, Suite 230, 20004.
Telephone: 202-347-8893.
Facsimile: 202-347-1684.

RESIDENT PARTNERS

Scott E. Ludwig
Charles R. Smith Jr.

For Complete List of Firm Personnel, See General Section

For full biographical listings, see the Martindale-Hubbell Law Directory

*MOBILE,** Mobile Co.

ARMBRECHT, JACKSON, DEMOUY, CROWE, HOLMES & REEVES, L.L.C. (AV)

1300 Riverview Plaza, P.O. Box 290, 36601
Telephone: 334-405-1300
Facsimile: 334-432-6843; 433-3821
Email: adc@ajlaw.com

MEMBER OF FIRM

William B. Harvey

ASSOCIATE

Leah P. Ladd

Representative Clients: Cooper/T. Smith Co., Inc.; WKRG-TV-Channel 5; United States Sports Academy; Smith's Bakery, Inc.; Taca International Airlines; Scott Paper Co.; Automation Technology, Inc.; Mobile Gas Service Corporation.

For Complete List of Firm Personnel, See General Section

For full biographical listings, see the Martindale-Hubbell Law Directory

JOHNSTONE, ADAMS, BAILEY, GORDON AND HARRIS, L.L.C. (AV)

Royal St. Francis Building, 104 St. Francis Street, 8th Floor, P.O. Box 1988, 36633
Telephone: 334-432-7682
Facsimile: 334-432-0712 or 334-432-2800
Email: attorneys@JohnstoneAdams.com *URL:* http://www.JohnstoneAdams.com
Bay Minette, Alabama Office: Dahlberg Building, 107 Hand Avenue, P.O. Box 729, 36507.
Telephone: 334-937-9473.
Facsimile: 334-937-9475.

MEMBERS OF FIRM

Charles B. Bailey, Jr.
R. Gregory Watts
E. Watson Smith
Robert S. Frost

For Complete List of Firm Personnel, See General Section

For full biographical listings, see the Martindale-Hubbell Law Directory

LYONS, PIPES & COOK, P.C. (AV)

2 North Royal Street, P.O. Box 2727, 36652-2727
Telephone: 334-432-4481
Cable Address: "Lysea"
Telecopier: 334-433-1820
URL: http://www.LPCLaw.com

Wesley Pipes
Thomas F. Garth

Counsel: Florence Foundation, Inc.; McKenzie Tank Lines, Inc.; SCNO Barge Lines, Inc.; Scott Paper Co.; Shell Oil Corp.

For Complete List of Firm Personnel, See General Section

For full biographical listings, see the Martindale-Hubbell Law Directory

VICKERS, RIIS, MURRAY AND CURRAN, L.L.C. (AV)

8th Floor, Regions Bank Building, 106 Saint Francis Street, P.O. Box 2568, 36652
Telephone: 334-432-9772
Fax: 334-432-9781
Email: vickersriis.com

(See Next Column)

VICKERS, RIIS, MURRAY AND CURRAN L.L.C.—*Continued*

MEMBERS OF FIRM

J. Manson Murray
Zebulon M. P. Inge, Jr.
Ronald P. Davis

For Complete List of Firm Personnel, See General Section

For full biographical listings, see the Martindale-Hubbell Law Directory

*MONTGOMERY,** Montgomery Co.

KAUFMAN & ROTHFEDER, P.C. (AV)

2740 Zelda Road, Drawer 4540, 36103-4540
Telephone: 334-244-1111
Fax: 334-244-1969
Email: firm@krlegal.com *URL:* http://www.krlegal.com

Alan E. Rothfeder
Jo Karen Parr
Richardson B. McKenzie III
Robert E. L. Gilpin
John Ward Weiss
Robert M. Ritchey
William B. Sellers
J. Scott Pierce
Carla Cole Gilmore
Mark Monroe Gibson

Counsel For: Alfa Mutual Insurance Co.; Southern Boulevard Corp.; McInnis Corporation; The Russell Hospital Corporation; Med-South, Inc.; Russell Corporation; Sanders Lead Co., Inc.; Wiley Sanders Truck Lines, Inc.; Linden Lumber Company, Inc.; Aronov Realty Company, Inc.

For full biographical listings, see the Martindale-Hubbell Law Directory

*TUSCALOOSA,** Tuscaloosa Co.

HUBBARD, SMITH, McILWAIN, BRAKEFIELD & BROWDER, P.C. (AV)

808 Lurleen Wallace Boulevard, North, P.O. Box 2427, 35403
Telephone: 205-345-6789
Telecopier: 205-759-1195

Perry Hubbard (1921-1991)
Michael D. Smith
Christopher L. McIlwain
W. Marcus Brakefield
Herbert E. "Chip" Browder
Justice D. Smyth, III

Elizabeth Faxon Colwick
Gary E. Sullivan

Counsel for: Randall Publishing Co.; United States Fidelity & Guaranty Co.; Chubb Group of Insurance Cos.; West Alabama Health Services; City of Eutaw; Kimberly-Clark Corp.; Regions Bank; City of Tuscaloosa; West Alabama Bank & Trust; Tuscaloosa County Industrial Development Authority.

For full biographical listings, see the Martindale-Hubbell Law Directory

PHELPS, JENKINS, GIBSON & FOWLER, L.L.P. (AV)

1201 Greensboro Avenue, P.O. Box 020848, 35402-0848
Telephone: 205-345-5100
Fax: 205-758-4394
Fax: 205-391-6658
Fax: 205-391-6663

MEMBERS OF FIRM

Sam M. Phelps
James J. Jenkins
Johnson Russell Gibson, III
Randolph M. Fowler
C. Barton Adcox
Farley A. Poellnitz
A. Courtney Crowder

ASSOCIATES

Karen C. Welborn
Stephen E. Snow
W. David Ryan
Bryan Patrick Winter
John M. Compton
Charles T. Grimes
Jenny B. Compton (Not admitted in AL)
Laura C. Karns

LEGAL SUPPORT PERSONNEL

Christine Holt (Paralegal)
Lori R. Woodard (Paralegal)
Melissa D. Harvey (Paralegal)

Representative Clients: Accuchek, Inc.; Alabama Reassurance Corp.; Anderson/GEMCO News Company; Credit Bureau Systems, Inc.; Peco Foods, Inc.; Witness Wear; Vulcan Oil Company, Inc.; Cahaba Pressure Treated Forest Products, Inc.; Affiliated Paper Companies, Inc.; Ox Bodies, Inc.

For full biographical listings, see the Martindale-Hubbell Law Directory

ARIZONA

FOUNTAIN HILLS, Maricopa Co.

SCHEEHLE LAW FIRM, P.L.C. (AV)

16622 East Kingstree Boulevard, 85268-5425
Telephone: 480-837-2030/*Telecopier:* 480-827-2030
Email: info@scheehlelawfirm.com

(See Next Column)

Mark V. Scheehle
Dorothy L. Scheehle

For full biographical listings, see the Martindale-Hubbell Law Directory

MESA, Maricopa Co.

JACKSON WHITE GARDNER WEECH & WALKER, P.C. (AV)

40 North Center Street, Suite 200, 85201
Telephone: 480-464-1111
Fax: 480-464-5692
Statewide: 800-243-1160
Email: firm@azmesalaw.com *URL:* http://www.azmesalaw.com
Payson, Arizona Office: 708 East Highway 260, Suite C1-E.
Telephone: 520-472-8878.

Wayne L. Gardner
Eric M. Jackson
Michael R. Pruitt
J. Grant Walker
Bradley D. Weech
Richard A. White
David L. Weed
Roger R. Foote
Otto S. Shill, III

Eric K. Macdonald
Kelly G. Black
Melody K. Seal
Patricia A. Mancabelli
Bobbie J. Rasmusson
Maureen P. Kane
James L. Tanner

For full biographical listings, see the Martindale-Hubbell Law Directory

UDALL, SHUMWAY, BLACKHURST, ALLEN & LYONS, P.C. (AV)

30 West First Street, 85201-1446
Telephone: 480-461-5300
Facsimile: 480-461-5398
Email: usbalsea@vtc.net
Willcox, Arizona Office: 135 East Maley.
Telephone: 602-384-3389.
Fax: 602-384-2280.

David K. Udall
Dale R. Shumway
Dennis P. Blackhurst
John H. Lyons
Barry C. Dickerson
Steven H. Everts
Clark R. Richter
Roger C. Decker
Peter W. Taylor
Denise Lowell-Britt
Stephen L. West

David R. Schwartz
Robert M. Jarrett, Jr. (Resident, Willcox Office)
Brian T. Allen
Curtis M. Chipman
April A. Speelmon

Representative Clients: Mesa Public Schools; Ticor Title; University of Arizona; Wal-Mart Stores, Inc.; Church of Jesus Christ of Latter Day Saints.

For full biographical listings, see the Martindale-Hubbell Law Directory

*PHOENIX,** Maricopa Co.

BURCH & CRACCHIOLO, P.A. (AV)

702 East Osborn Road, Suite 200, 85014
Telephone: 602-274-7611
Fax: 602-234-0341
Mailing Address: P.O. Box 16882, Phoenix, AZ, 85011
Email: library@bcattorneys.com

Stephen E. Silver
Guadalupe Iniguez
Brad S. Ostroff

Martha C. Patrick

Representative Clients: Bashas' Inc.; Farmers Insurance Group; U-Haul International, Inc.; Chapman Chevrolet, Inc.

For Complete List of Firm Personnel, See General Section

For full biographical listings, see the Martindale-Hubbell Law Directory

EHMANN & HILLER, P.C. (AV)

2525 East Camelback Road, Suite 720, 85016
Telephone: 602-956-5050
Telecopier: 602-468-9775
Email: nhiller@home.com

Anthony V. Ehmann
Neil H. Hiller
John G. Pattullo
John F. Daniels, III

References: Harris Trust Bank of Arizona; Bank One, Arizona, N.A. (Trust Department); M&I Thunderbird Bank; Marshall & Ilsley Trust Company of Arizona; Wells Fargo Bank, N.A.; Colonial Trust Company; National Bank of Arizona.

For full biographical listings, see the Martindale-Hubbell Law Directory

LAW OFFICES OF JAMES J. EVERETT, P.C. (AV)

608 East Missouri Avenue, 85012
Telephone: 602-230-2212
Fax: 602-274-8761
Email: James.Everett@azbar.org

(See Next Column)

LAW OFFICES OF JAMES J. EVERETT, P.C., *Phoenix—Continued*

James J. Everett

For full biographical listings, see the Martindale-Hubbell Law Directory

FENNEMORE CRAIG, A PROFESSIONAL CORPORATION (AV)

3003 North Central Avenue, Suite 2600, 85012-2913
Telephone: 602-916-5000
Fax: 602-916-5999
Tucson, Arizona Office: One South Church Avenue, Suite 1000, 85701-1620.
Telephone: 520-879-6800.
Fax: 520-879-6899.

James Powers
Arthur D. Ehrenreich
Neal Kurn
Jay S. Ruffner
David T. Cox
Cynthia L. Shupe
Paul J. Mooney
David N. Heap
Gregg Hanks
Jim L. Wright
J. Barry Shelley
Kendis K. Muscheid
Stephen A. Good

Joel B. Shapiro
Theodore D. Setzer

For Complete List of Firm Personnel, See General Section

For full biographical listings, see the Martindale-Hubbell Law Directory

JENNINGS, STROUSS & SALMON, P.L.C. (AV)

A Professional Limited Liability Company
One Renaissance Square, Two North Central Avenue, 85004-2393
Telephone: 602-262-5911
Fax: 602-253-3255
Email: info@jsslaw.com *URL:* http://www.jsslaw.com
Arrowhead Office: 16150 North Arrowhead Fountains Center Drive, Suite 250, Peoria, Arizona.
Telephone: 623-878-2222.
Fax: 623-878-1333.

John R. Christian
Richard L. Lassen
Robert J. Werner
Scott K. Oberg
R. Quinn De Angelis, Jr.

OF COUNSEL

Ann M. Dumenil

For Complete List of Firm Personnel, See General Section

For full biographical listings, see the Martindale-Hubbell Law Directory

LANE & EHRLICH, LTD. (AV)

Fairmount Place, Suite 400, 4001 North Third Street, 85012
Telephone: 602-264-4442
Telecopier: 602-264-5006
Email: azcorplaw@aol.com

Robert L. Lane
Gerald F. Ehrlich

LEGAL SUPPORT PERSONNEL

LEGAL ASSISTANTS

Sherrie L. Lane
Janice K. Hull
Kathy S. Watkins

References: Bank One Arizona; Harris Trust & Savings Bank; The Northern Trust Bank Arizona.

For full biographical listings, see the Martindale-Hubbell Law Directory

LEWIS AND ROCA, LLP (AV)

A Limited Liability Partnership including a Professional Corporation
40 North Central Avenue, 85004-4429
Telephone: 602-262-5311
Fax: 602-262-5747
Email: clientservice@lrlaw.com *URL:* http://www.lrlaw.com
Tucson, Arizona Office: One South Church Avenue, Suite 700, 86701-1620.
Telephone: 520-622-2090.
Fax: 520-622-3088. E-Mail: clientservice@lrlaw.com.
Las Vegas, Nevada Affiliated Office: Ashcraft and Heinz LLP, 3960 Howard Hughes Parkway, 89109.
Telephone: 702-990-3570.
Fax: 702-990-3571.

MEMBERS OF FIRM

David E. Manch
Hope Leibsohn
Patrick Derdenger
Glenn D. Forcucci

Representative Clients: Blood Systems, Inc.; General Motors Corp.; MCI Telecommunications Corp.; Mervyn's Stores; Samaritan Health System; Target Stores; Unisys Corp.

For Complete List of Firm Personnel, See General Section

For full biographical listings, see the Martindale-Hubbell Law Directory

MCCABE O'DONNELL, A PROFESSIONAL ASSOCIATION (AV)

3101 North Central Avenue Suite 700, P.O. Box 33457, 85012
Telephone: 602-264-0800
Facsimile: 602-274-0146
URL: http://www.lawyers.com/mccabephx.com

Joseph I. McCabe
Kathleen M. O'Donnell

Whitney Lynn Sorrell

A List of Representative Clients will be Furnished upon Request.

For full biographical listings, see the Martindale-Hubbell Law Directory

RICHARD C. ONSAGER, P.C. (AV)

3200 North Central Avenue Suite 1112, 85012
Telephone: 602-631-6790
Fax: 602-631-6786
Email: onsager@onsager.com

Richard C. Onsager

Representative Clients: Maracay Homes; Londen Insurance Group; Catholic Healthcare West; Alpha Health Alliance; Leading Edge Technologies; Arizona Healthcare Association; The American Foundation.

For full biographical listings, see the Martindale-Hubbell Law Directory

SHIMMEL, HILL, BISHOP & GRUENDER, P.C. (AV)

3700 North 24th Street, 85016
Telephone: 602-224-9500
Telecopier: 602-955-6176
URL: http://www.shimmelhill.com

Keith F. Overholt
Margaret L. Steiner

Jennifer S. Lee

Representative Clients: Dunn Del Re Steel; The Original Apartment Movers, Inc.

For full biographical listings, see the Martindale-Hubbell Law Directory

SNELL & WILMER L.L.P. (AV)

One Arizona Center, 85004-2202
Telephone: 602-382-6000
Fax: 602-382-6070
Email: postmaster@snellwilmer.com *URL:* http://www.swlaw.com
Tucson, Arizona Office: One South Church Avenue, Suite 1500, 85701-1612.
Telephone: 520-882-1200.
Fax: 520-884-1294.
Orange County Office: 1920 Main Street, Suite 1200, Irvine, California 92614-7230.
Telephone: 949-253-2700.
Fax: 949-955-2507.
Salt Lake City, Utah Office: 111 East Broadway, Suite 900, 84111-1004.
Telephone: 801-237-1900.
Fax: 801-237-1950.

MEMBERS OF FIRM

Charles A. Pulaski, Jr.
Richard D. Blau
David E. Weiss, Jr.
L. Frederick Williams, Jr.

OF COUNSEL

Edward Jacobson

Representative Clients: For list of Representative Clients, see end of biographical listings in the Martindale-Hubbell Law Directory.

For Complete List of Firm Personnel, See General Section

For full biographical listings, see the Martindale-Hubbell Law Directory

SCOTTSDALE, Maricopa Co.

ROSEPINK & ESTES, P.L.L.C. (AV)

7373 North Scottsdale Road Suite E200, 85253
Telephone: 602-443-1280
Fax: 602-443-3664
Email: rosepink@rosepink.com *URL:* http://www.rosepink.com

MEMBERS OF FIRM

Robert J. Rosepink
David J. Estes

ASSOCIATES

Alisa J. Gray
James A. Fassold
Heather L. Illies

References: Bank of America, Arizona; Biltmore Investors Bank; Chase Trust Company of Arizona; Wells Fargo; Firstar Metropolitan Bank & Trust; M & I Marshall & Ilsley Trust Co. of Arizona; Northern Trust Bank of Arizona; Harris Trust Bank of Arizona.

For full biographical listings, see the Martindale-Hubbell Law Directory

*TUCSON,** Pima Co.

GABROY, ROLLMAN & BOSSÉ, P.C. (AV)

3507 North Campbell Avenue, Suite 111, 85719
Telephone: 520-320-1300
Telefax: 520-320-0717
Email: admin@gabroylaw.com

Steven L. Bossé | Fred A. Farsjo

For Complete List of Firm Personnel, See General Section

For full biographical listings, see the Martindale-Hubbell Law Directory

DANIEL H. O'CONNELL, P.C. (AV)

3573 East Sunrise Drive, Suite 120, 85718-3206
Telephone: 520-615-9802
Telefax: 520-615-9789
Email: ben@dhopc.psemail.com *URL:* http://www.lawyers.com/danieloconnell-law

Daniel H. O'Connell

Benjamin J. Burnside

OF COUNSEL

Rosanne F. Lapan

Representative Clients: Empire West Cos.; Thermal Engineering, Inc.; Alban Medical Associates; Industrial Motor & Control, Inc.; Allergy Asthma Associates, P.C.
Reference: Bank of America.

For full biographical listings, see the Martindale-Hubbell Law Directory

SNELL & WILMER L.L.P. (AV)

One South Church Avenue, Suite 1500, 85701-1612
Telephone: 520-882-1200
Fax: 520-884-1294
URL: http://www.swlaw.com
Phoenix, Arizona Office: One Arizona Center, 85004-2202.
Telephone: 602-382-6000.
Fax: 602-382-6070.
Orange County Office: 1920 Main Street, Suite 1200, Irvine, California 92614-7230.
Telephone: 949-253-2700.
Fax: 949-955-2507.
Salt Lake City, Utah Office: 111 East Broadway, Suite 900, 84111-1004.
Telephone: 801-237-1900.
Fax: 801-237-1950.

MEMBER OF FIRM

Charles E. Giddings

Representative Clients: For list of Representative Clients, see end of biographical listings in the Martindale-Hubbell Law Directory.

For full biographical listings, see the Martindale-Hubbell Law Directory

ARKANSAS

*FAYETTEVILLE,** Washington Co.

BALL & MOURTON, LTD., PLLC (AV)

A Professional Limited Liability Company
Suite 700, E.J. Ball Plaza, P.O. Box 1948, 72702
Telephone: 501-442-6213
Fax: 501-442-6233
Email: contact@ballandmourton.com *URL:* http://www.BallandMourton.com
Siloam Springs, Arkansas Office: 106 South Broadway. P.O. Box 1348, 72761.
Telephone: 501-524-2337.
Fax: 501-524-3693.

E. J. Ball
Kenneth R. Mourton
John T. Lee
Rayburn W. Green

David G. Bercaw
J. Michael Threet
Joseph D. Reece
Shannon L. Poore

OF COUNSEL

Neal R. Pendergraft

Representative Clients: Arkansas Western Gas Co.; Coors of Western Arkansas, Inc.; Rebel Enterprises, Inc.; Southwestern Energy Co.; Stephens Production Co.; Ohlendorf Investment Co.; Central Health Corporation; McIlroy Bank & Trust.

For full biographical listings, see the Martindale-Hubbell Law Directory

*FORT SMITH,** Sebastian Co.

WARNER, SMITH & HARRIS, PLC (AV)

214 North Sixth Street, P.O. Box 1626, 72901
Telephone: 501-782-6041
Fax: 501-782-0841

Harry Preston Warner (1885-1969)
Cecil Randolph Warner (1890-1955)
Thomas G. Graves (1939-1971)
Douglas O. Smith, Jr.
C. Wayne Harris
Gerald L. DeLung
Patrick Neill Moore
Lillard Cody Hayes
G. Alan Wooten
James Melvin Dunn
John Alan Lewis
Joel D. Johnson
J. Randall McGinnis
Kathryn Stocks Campbell
R. Gregory Aclin

Jason Trevor Browning
Matthew C. Carter

OF COUNSEL

C. R. Warner, Jr.

District Attorneys for: Burlington Northern Railroad Co.
Counsel for: Sparks Regional Medical Center.
Local Counsel for: Planters Division, Nabisco Brands, Inc.; Gerber Products Co.; Aetna Group; Fireman's Fund-American Insurance Cos.; Hiram Walker & Sons, Inc.; Continental National American Group.

For full biographical listings, see the Martindale-Hubbell Law Directory

*LITTLE ROCK,** Pulaski Co.

FRIDAY, ELDREDGE & CLARK (AV)

A Limited Liability Partnership of Individuals and Professional Associations
Formerly, Smith, Williams, Friday, Eldredge & Clark
2000 Regions Center, 400 West Capitol Avenue, 72201-3493
Telephone: 501-376-2011
Telecopier: 501-376-2147
Email: fecmh@fec.net

MEMBERS OF FIRM

Byron M. Eiseman, Jr. (P.A.)
A. Wyckliff Nisbet, Jr. (P.A.)
James E. Harris (P.A.)
James M. Saxton (P.A.)
W. Thomas Baxter (P.A.)
Joseph B. Hurst, Jr. (P.A.)
Walter M. Ebel, III (P.A.)
J. Lee Brown (P.A.)
Price C. Gardner (P.A.)
David M. Graf (P.A.)
Carla G. Spainhour (P.A.)

ASSOCIATES

James W. Smith
K. Coleman Westbrook, Jr.
Allison Cornwell
Helene Norcross Rayder

COUNSEL

H. T. Larzelere, Jr. (P.A.)

Counsel for: Union Pacific System; St. Paul Insurance Co.; Liberty Mutual Insurance Co.; Cigna Property & Casualty Co.; Entergy Arkansas, Inc.; Dillard's, Inc.; Browning Arms Co.; Phillips Petroleum Co.; Aetna Casualty & Surety Co.; ALLTEL Corp.; Acxiom Corp.

For Complete List of Firm Personnel, See General Section

For full biographical listings, see the Martindale-Hubbell Law Directory

HILBURN, CALHOON, HARPER, PRUNISKI & CALHOUN, LTD. (AV)

P.O. Box 1256, 72203-1256
Telephone: 501-372-0110
Fax: 501-372-2029
Email: hilburn@aristotle.net
North Little Rock, Arkansas Office: Eighth Floor, Mercantile Bank Building, One Riverfront Place, P.O. Box 5551, 72119.
Telephone: 501-372-0110.
Fax: 501-372-2029.

Ken F. Calhoon
Carrold E. Ray
Michael E. Hartje, Jr.

Representative Clients: Mercantile Bank of Arkansas, N.A.; Merrill Lynch Pierce Fenner & Smith, Inc.; Central Arkansas Risk Management Association; Salomon Smith Barney, Inc.

For Complete List of Firm Personnel, See General Section

For full biographical listings, see the Martindale-Hubbell Law Directory

ROSE LAW FIRM, A PROFESSIONAL ASSOCIATION (AV)

120 East Fourth Street, 72201
Telephone: 501-375-9131
Telecopy: 501-375-1309

W. Wilson Jones
C. Brantly Buck
Ronald M. Clark
Bryant K. Cranford

(See Next Column)

ROSE LAW FIRM A PROFESSIONAL ASSOCIATION, *Little Rock—Continued*

Craig S. Lair Mark Davis

Counsel for: ALLTEL Corporation; Aluminum Company of America; Donrey Media Group Inc.; Bridgestone/Firestone, Inc.; General Motors Corp.; Minnesota Mining and Manufacturing Co.; The Prudential Insurance Company of America; The Winthrop Rockefeller Foundation; Stephens Group Inc.; Tyson Foods, Inc.

For Complete List of Firm Personnel, See General Section

For full biographical listings, see the Martindale-Hubbell Law Directory

WILLIAMS & ANDERSON (AV)

Registered Limited Liability Partnership
Twenty-Second Floor, 111 Center Street, 72201
Telephone: 501-372-0800
Fax: 501-372-6453
Email: info@williamsanderson.com *URL:* http://www.williamsanderson.com

MEMBERS OF FIRM

W. Jackson Williams Patrick A. Burrow

Representative Clients: Arkansas Democrat-Gazette, Inc.; Arkansas Development Finance Authority; Entergy Corporation; Potlatch Corporation; Texaco, Inc.; Wal-Mart Stores, Inc.

For Complete List of Firm Personnel, See General Section

For full biographical listings, see the Martindale-Hubbell Law Directory

CALIFORNIA

*BAKERSFIELD,** Kern Co.

BORTON, PETRINI & CONRON, LLP (AV)

The Borton, Petrini & Conron Building, 1600 Truxtun Avenue, 93301
Telephone: 661-322-3051
Voice Mail: 661-395-6700
Fax: 661-322-4628
Mailing Address: P.O. Box 2026, Bakersfield, California, 93303
Email: bpcbak@bpclaw.com *URL:* http://www.bpclaw.com
Other City Locations: Fresno, Los Angeles, Modesto, Redding, Sacramento, San Bernardino, San Diego, San Francisco, San Jose, San Luis Obispo, Santa Ana and Ventura.

MEMBER OF FIRM

Stephen M. Dake

ASSOCIATES

Raymond G. Robinson Michael S. Abril

For Complete List of Firm Personnel, See General Section

For full biographical listings, see the Martindale-Hubbell Law Directory

KLEIN, DENATALE, GOLDNER, COOPER, ROSENLIEB & KIMBALL, LLP (AV)

(Formerly Di Giorgio, Davis, Klein, Wegis, Duggan & Friedman)
ARCO Tower, 4550 California Avenue, Second Floor, 93309
Telephone: 661-395-1000
Telecopier: 661-326-0418
Mailing Address: P.O. Box 11172, Bakersfield, California, 93389-1172
Email: kleinlaw@kleinlaw.com

Anthony J. Klein (Inc.) Claude P. Kimball
Kevin C. Findley

Representative Clients: Bank of America; Great Western Bank; Mojave Pipeline Co.; Transamerican Title Insurance Co.; Dean Whittier Reynolds, Inc.; California Republic Bank; San Joaquin Bank; Nahama & Weagant Energy Co.; Freymiller Trucking, Inc.; Westinghouse Electric Co.

For Complete List of Firm Personnel, See General Section

For full biographical listings, see the Martindale-Hubbell Law Directory

BERKELEY, Alameda Co.

LAWRENCE V. BROOKES (AV)

986 Euclid Avenue, 94708-1437
Telephone: 510-527-9865
Fax: 510-527-9812
Email: lbrookes@sirius.com

References in Tax Matters: Arkia, Shreveport, Louisiana; Automatic Data Processing, Clifton, New Jersey; Foster Enterprises, Foster City, Calif.; Willamette Industries, Portland, Oregon; U-Haul International, Phoenix, Arizona.

For full biographical listings, see the Martindale-Hubbell Law Directory

BEVERLY HILLS, Los Angeles Co.

HOCHMAN, SALKIN, RETTIG, TOSCHER & PEREZ, A PROFESSIONAL CORPORATION (AV)

9150 Wilshire Boulevard Suite 300, 90212-3414
Telephone: 310-281-3200; 273-1181
Fax: 310-859-1430
URL: http://www.taxlitigator.com

Bruce I. Hochman Charles P. Rettig
Avram Salkin Dennis Perez
Steven R. Toscher

OF COUNSEL

George DeRoy Nathan Joseph Hochman
Stuart A. Simon Steven D. Blanc
Michel R. Stein

Reference: Union Bank of California.

For full biographical listings, see the Martindale-Hubbell Law Directory

KAJAN MATHER AND BARISH, A PROFESSIONAL CORPORATION (AV)

Suite 805, 9777 Wilshire Boulevard, 90212
Telephone: 310-278-6080
Fax: 310-278-4805
URL: http://www.lawyers.com/kajanlaw
Email: KM&B@TAXDISPUTES.COM *URL:* HTTP://WWW.TAXDISPUTES.COM

Elliott H. Kajan Steven R. Mather
Kenneth M. Barish

Jason M. Silver

For full biographical listings, see the Martindale-Hubbell Law Directory

COSTA MESA, Orange Co.

RUTAN & TUCKER, LLP (AV)

A Partnership including Professional Corporations
611 Anton Boulevard, Fourteenth Floor, P.O. Box 1950, 92626-1998
Telephone: 714-641-5100; 213-625-7586
Telecopier: 714-546-9035
Email: rutan&tucker@rutan.com *URL:* http://www.rutan.com

MEMBERS OF FIRM

Paul Frederic Marx James B. O'Neal
Joseph D. Carruth Evridiki (Vicki) Dallas
James S. Weisz (P.C.)

OF COUNSEL

Edward D. Sybesma, Jr. (P.C.)

For Complete List of Firm Personnel, See General Section

For full biographical listings, see the Martindale-Hubbell Law Directory

RONALD K. VAN WERT A PROFESSIONAL CORPORATION (AV)

3200 Park Center Drive Suite 1110, 92626
Telephone: 714-546-2400
Fax: 714-546-5008

Ronald K. Van Wert

For full biographical listings, see the Martindale-Hubbell Law Directory

ESCONDIDO, San Diego Co.

GARTH O. REID, JR. A PROFESSIONAL LAW CORPORATION (AV)

319 East Second Avenue, 92025
Telephone: 760-746-6420
Fax: 760-746-2836
Email: GarthR2335@aol.com

Garth O. Reid, Jr.

For full biographical listings, see the Martindale-Hubbell Law Directory

*FRESNO,** Fresno Co.

DIETRICH, GLASRUD, MALLEK & AUNE (AV)

An Association of Attorneys including Law Corporations
5250 North Palm Avenue, Suite 402, 93704
Telephone: 559-435-5250
Facsimile: 559-435-8776
Email: info@dgmalaw.com

(See Next Column)

DIETRICH, GLASRUD, MALLEK & AUNE—*Continued*

Richard W. Dietrich (Inc.) (1930-1999)
Robert A. Mallek Jr. (Inc.)
Richard E. Aune (Inc.)
Donald H. Glasrud (Inc.)
Bruce A. Owdom
Thomas W. Isaac

Douglas D. Schorling
Leslie G. Miessner
Daniel J. Tekunoff

OF COUNSEL

Timothy J. Buchanan

Representative Clients: Fresno Surgery and Recovery Care Center; Helm Fertilizer, Inc.; Gragnani Farms; Wathen-Castanos, Inc.; Chicago Title Company; ABC, Inc.; The McClatchy Company; Monsanto Company; Armstrong World Industries, Inc.; Stewart Title Guaranty Company.

For full biographical listings, see the Martindale-Hubbell Law Directory

DOWLING, AARON & KEELER, INCORPORATED (AV)

6051 North Fresno Street, Suite 200, 93710
Telephone: 559-432-4500
Fax: 559-432-4590
Email: dak@daklaw.com *URL:* http://www.daklaw.com
Bakersfield, California Office: 110 South Mt. Claire, Suite 203. 93309.
Telephone: 661-396-0451. Web Site: http://www.daklaw.com.

Michael D. Dowling
William J. Keeler, Jr.
Richard M. Aaron
Bruce S. Fraser
John C. Ganahl

Larry B. Lindenau

OF COUNSEL

Morris M. Sherr

Reference: Wells Fargo Bank (Main).

For Complete List of Firm Personnel, See General Section

For full biographical listings, see the Martindale-Hubbell Law Directory

IRVINE, Orange Co.

GRECO, MOLLIS & O'HARA, A PROFESSIONAL CORPORATION (AV)

18400 Von Karman, Suite 500, 92612-1514
Telephone: 949-263-0600
Fax: 949-263-1513

Thomas A. Greco
Kevin O'Hara
Ronald A. Mollis
Charles A. Mollis

For full biographical listings, see the Martindale-Hubbell Law Directory

SNELL & WILMER L.L.P. (AV)

1920 Main Street, Suite 1200, 92614-7230
Telephone: 949-253-2700
FAX: 949-955-2507
URL: http://www.swlaw.com
Phoenix, Arizona Office: One Arizona Center, 85004-2202.
Telephone: 602-382-6000.
Fax: 602-382-6070.
Tucson, Arizona Office: One South Church Avenue, Suite 1500, 85701-1630.
Telephone: 520-882-1200.
Fax: 520-884-1294.
Salt Lake City, Utah Office: 111 East Broadway, Suite 900, 84111-1004.
Telephone: 801-237-1900.
Fax: 801-237-1950.

MEMBERS OF FIRM

David W. Evans
Roger A. Grad

ASSOCIATE

David S. Beard

Representative Clients: For list of Representative Clients, see end of biographical listings in the Martindale-Hubbell Law Directory.

For Complete List of Firm Personnel, See General Section

For full biographical listings, see the Martindale-Hubbell Law Directory

LONG BEACH, Los Angeles Co.

TAUBMAN, SIMPSON, YOUNG & SULENTOR (AV)

249 East Ocean Boulevard, Suite 700, P.O. Box 22670, 90801-5670
Telephone: 562-436-9201
FAX: 562-590-9695
Email: thefirm@tsyslaw.com

(See Next Column)

E. C. Denio (1864-1952)
Roger W. Young
Geo. A. Hart (1881-1967)
William J. Sulentor
Geo. P. Taubman, Jr. (1897-1970)
Peter M. Williams
Maria M. Rohaidy
Matthew C. Simpson (1900-1988)
Stuart C. Talley

Attorneys for: Bixby Land Co.; Renick Cadillac, Inc.; Oil Operators Inc.
Local Counsel: Crown Cork & Seal Co., Inc.

For full biographical listings, see the Martindale-Hubbell Law Directory

D. MICHAEL TRAINOTTI A PROFESSIONAL LAW CORPORATION (AV)

Suite 410, 200 Oceangate, 90802
Telephone: 562-590-8621
Fax: 562-590-8181
Email: mike@trainotti.com *URL:* http://www.trainotti.com

D. Michael Trainotti

Reference: Farmers & Merchants Bank; Harbor Bank.

For full biographical listings, see the Martindale-Hubbell Law Directory

*LOS ANGELES,** Los Angeles Co.

AJALAT, POLLEY & AYOOB (AV)

A Partnership including Professional Corporations
643 South Olive Street, Suite 200, 90014-1685
Telephone: 213-622-7400
Fax: 213-622-4738

MEMBERS OF FIRM

Charles R. Ajalat (A Professional Corporation)
Terry L. Polley (A Professional Corporation)
Richard J. Ayoob

Reference: Bank of America (Los Angeles Main Office).

For full biographical listings, see the Martindale-Hubbell Law Directory

MICHAEL ANTIN A LAW CORPORATION (AV)

10880 Wilshire Boulevard Suite 1010, 90024
Telephone: 310-470-0049
Fax: 310-470-0322
Email: mantin@ix.netcom.com *URL:* http://www.lawyers.com/atlaw

Michael Antin

For full biographical listings, see the Martindale-Hubbell Law Directory

PAUL L. BASILE, JR. (AV)

11400 West Olympic Boulevard, Suite 350, 90064-1558
Telephone: 310-478-2114
Toll Free: 800-511-2114
Fax: 310-478-0229
Email: pbasile@basile-law.com *URL:* http://www.basile-law.com

For full biographical listings, see the Martindale-Hubbell Law Directory

BRAND FARRAR & BUXBAUM LLP (AV)

515 South Flower Street, Suite 3500, 90071-2201
Telephone: 213-228-0288
Fax: 213-426-6222
Email: bfb-la@brandfarrar.com
Beijing (Peking), China Office: Suite 2518, China World Trade Centre, 1 Jian Guo Men Wai Avenue, Beijing, China.
Telephone: 86-10-6505-2288 Ext. 2523/2518.
Fax: 86-10-6505-2638. Email: bjbfbbj@public3.bta.net.cn
Chengdu, Sichuan, China Office: Suite 11A, Sichuan International Mansion, No. 1 Zhong Xi Shun Cheng Street, Chengdu, China.
Telephone: 86-28-652-1316.
Fax: 86-28-652-0547. Email: cdbfbcd@mail.sc.cninfo.net.
Chongqing, China Office: Suite 1510, Metropolitan Tower, 68 Zourong Lu, Chongqing, China.
Telephone: 86-23-6382-8381.
Fax: 86-23-6382-8373. Email: cqbfbcq@public.cta.cq.cn.
Guangzhou (Canton), China Office: Suite 1305, Main Tower, GITIC Plaza Hotel, 339 Huanshi Dong Road, Guangzhou, China.
Telephone: 86-20-8331-1888, Ext. 71305.
Fax: 86-20-8331-2671. Email: gzbfbgz@public.guangzhou.gd.cn.
Hong Kong, China Office: Brand Farrar Buxbaum LLP, 5/F., Landmark East, 12 Ice House Street, Central, Hong Kong, China.
Telephone: 852-2523-7001.
Fax: 852-2845-0947. Email: hkbfbhk@hk.super.net.
Los Angeles, California Office: Brand Farrar & Buxbaum LLP, Suite 3500, 515 South Flower Street, Los Angeles, California, 90071-2201.
Telephone: 213-228-0288.
Fax: 213-426-6222. Email: bfb-la@brandfarrar.com.
New York, New York Office: 275 Madison Avenue, 37th Floor, New York, New York, 10097.
Telephone: 212-286-0038.
Fax: 212-573-9077. Email: martineh@aol.com

(See Next Column)

BRAND FARRAR & BUXBAUM LLP, *Los Angeles—Continued*

Shanghai, China Office: Brand Farrar Buxbaum LLP, Suites 2611-12, Central Plaza, 227 Huangpi Bei Lu, Shanghai, China.
Telephone: 86-21-6375-8918.
Fax: 86-21-6375-8922. Email: shbfbsh@public2.sta.net.cn
Shenzhen, China Office: Suite 2103A, Shenzhen Development Center, Renmin Nan Lu, Shenzhen, China.
Telephone: 86-755-229-8009.
Fax: 86-755-229-8011. Email: szbfbsz@public.szptt.net.cn.
Ulaanbaatar, Mongolia Office: Brand Farrar Buxbaum LLP, 4/F., Time Center, No. 50 Baga Toiruu, Ulaanbaatar, Mongolia.
Telephone: 976-1-31-0711.
Fax: 976-1-32-5102. Email: mgbfbmg@magicnet.mn.
Xiamen, China Office: Suite 1182 Jian Ye Building, 28 Hubin North Road, Xiamen, China.
Telephone: 86-592-506-3059.
Fax: 86-592-511-1044. Email: xmbfbxm@public.xm.fj.cn.
Associated Office, Mumbai, Bombay, India: Shah & Sanghavi, Advocates, Solicitors & Notary, 114-A Mittal Court, Nariman Point, Mumbai 400 021 India.
Telephone: 91-22-285-5755/56 or 91-22-285-3592/93.
Fax: 91-22-284-5040.

PRINCIPALS

Michael A. Brand
David C. Buxbaum (China Offices)
Kenneth Y. Choy (Hong Kong Office)
Robert W. Dziubla
David W. Farrar
Amy E. Freilich
Margaret G. Graf
John Masao Iino
Charles K. Kolstad
Edward H. Martin (New York Office)
Gregory D. Trimarche
Li Zhuogen (China Offices)

OTHER ATTORNEYS RESIDENT IN LOS ANGELES OFFICE

Sherry L. Geyer
Joan M. Marquardt
James H. Service
Jeffrey S. Allen
Julia Sylva
Brian J. Kim
Lisa Teng

OTHER ATTORNEYS RESIDENT IN BEIJING OFFICE

Hao Xiaodong
Bin Zhao
Luo Rongping
Zhang Chunbo

OTHER ATTORNEYS RESIDENT IN CHENGDU, SICHUAN OFFICE

Zeng Xiangyu
Wu Wen

OTHER ATTORNEY RESIDENT IN CHONGQING OFFICE

Du Fei

OTHER ATTORNEYS RESIDENT IN GUANGZHOU OFFICE

Zou Wenyan (Not admitted in United States)
Feng Ruiding
Jia Guangxi

OTHER ATTORNEYS RESIDENT IN HONG KONG OFFICE

Shane F. Weir
Cheonghar Wong
N.T.S. Kularatne
Simon Woo
David William Gunson
Arthur Burton Crook
Simon K.C. Lee
Cheng Yuen Yi
Lo Wing Cheong
Nicholas C. McGrenra
Eva Y.N. Kwok

OTHER ATTORNEYS RESIDENT IN NEW YORK OFFICE

Vincent I. S. Hsieh (Of Counsel)
Jeffrey Schall
Jonathan Chun Wang

OTHER ATTORNEYS RESIDENT IN SHANGHAI OFFICE

Lin Yong
Wu Hong Liang
Tang Ying
Zhang Guoyao
Qi Zhenwen

OTHER ATTORNEYS RESIDENT IN SHENZHEN OFFICE

Zhong Wenya
Zhang He

OTHER ATTORNEYS RESIDENT IN ULAANBAATAR OFFICE

Byambaa Bayarmaa
Ajiv Enhktuya

OTHER ATTORNEY RESIDENT IN XIAMEN OFFICE

Deng Sheng

For full biographical listings, see the Martindale-Hubbell Law Directory

CLARK & TREVITHICK, A PROFESSIONAL CORPORATION (AV)

800 Wilshire Boulevard, 12th Floor, 90017
Telephone: 213-629-5700
Telecopier: 213-624-9441
Email: postmaster@clarktrev.com
San Francisco, California Office: 456 Montgomery Street, 20th Floor.
Telephone: 415-288-6520.
Fax: 415-398-2820.

Kevin P. Fiore
Dean I. Friedman
Robert F. DeMeter
Robert W. Renken

For Complete List of Firm Personnel, See General Section

For full biographical listings, see the Martindale-Hubbell Law Directory

COHEN PRIMIANI & FOSTER, A PROFESSIONAL CORPORATION (AV)

2029 Century Park East, Suite 400, 90067
Telephone: 310-277-3963
Fax: 310-277-4351
Mailing Address: 225 Santa Monica Bolevard, Suite 1002, Santa Monica, California, 90401

Marc S. Primiani
Richard Schneider
Bradford S. Cohen
Michael D. Foster
Bernard Oster
Jeffrey Forer
Michael D. Berger

Renee Wittlif
Paula Winner Barnett
Liana C. Cocanower

Reference: Western Bank (Los Angeles, Calif.).

For full biographical listings, see the Martindale-Hubbell Law Directory

DEMETRIOU, DEL GUERCIO, SPRINGER & MOYER, LLP (AV)

801 South Grand Avenue, 10th Floor, 90017
Telephone: 213-624-8407
Telecopy: 213-624-0174
Email: ddsm@juno.com

MEMBERS OF FIRM

Angela Shanahan
Stephen A. Del Guercio

OF COUNSEL

Ronald J. Del Guercio

Reference: Bank of America, L.A. Main Office, Los Angeles, Calif.

For full biographical listings, see the Martindale-Hubbell Law Directory

GREENBERG GLUSKER FIELDS CLAMAN & MACHTINGER LLP (AV)

21st Floor, 1900 Avenue of the Stars (Century City), 90067
Telephone: 310-553-3610
Fax: 310-553-0687
URL: http://www.ggfcm.com

MEMBERS OF FIRM

Sidney J. Machtinger
C. Bruce Levine
Gary L. Kaplan

Reference: Wells Fargo Bank, 1801 Ave. of the Stars, Los Angeles, CA 90067.

For Complete List of Firm Personnel, See General Section

For full biographical listings, see the Martindale-Hubbell Law Directory

HILL, FARRER & BURRILL LLP (AV)

A Limited Liability Partnership including Professional Corporations
37th Floor, One California Plaza, 300 South Grand Avenue, 90071-3147
Telephone: 213-620-0460
Fax: 213-624-4840
URL: http://www.hfbllp.com

MEMBERS OF FIRM

George Koide (P.C.)
Thomas F. Reed

OF COUNSEL

Leon S. Angvire (P.C.)

ASSOCIATE

Stacey A. Sullivan

For Complete List of Firm Personnel, See General Section

For full biographical listings, see the Martindale-Hubbell Law Directory

SAMUEL D. INGHAM, III (AV)

1800 Avenue of the Stars, Suite 1000, 90067-4212
Telephone: 310-556-9751
Fax: 310-556-1311
Email: singham@inghamlaw.com

ASSOCIATE

John E. Rogers, Jr.

For full biographical listings, see the Martindale-Hubbell Law Directory

JONES, DAY, REAVIS & POGUE (AV)

555 West Fifth Street Suite 4600, 90013-1025
Telephone: 213-489-3939
Telecopier: 213-243-2539
Email: counsel@jonesday.com *URL:* http://www.jonesday.com
In Irvine, California: 5 Park Plaza, Suite 1100.
Telephone: 949-851-3939.
Telecopier: 949-553-7539.
In Atlanta, Georgia: 3500 SunTrust Plaza, 303 Peachtree Street.
Telephone: 404-521-3939.
Telecopier: 404-581-8330.

(See Next Column)

JONES, DAY, REAVIS & POGUE—*Continued*

In Brussels, Belgium: Avenue Louise 480, 7th Floor, B-1050 Brussels.
Telephone: 32-2-645-14-11.
Telecopier: 32-2-645-14-45.
In Chicago, Illinois: 77 West Wacker.
Telephone: 312-782-3939.
Telecopier: 312-782-8585.
In Cleveland, Ohio: North Point, 901 Lakeside Avenue.
Telephone: 216-586-3939.
Telecopier: 216-579-0212.
In Columbus, Ohio: 1900 Huntington Center.
Telephone: 614-469-3939.
Telecopier: 614-461-4198.
In Dallas, Texas: 2727 North Harwood Street.
Telephone: 214-220-3939.
Telecopier: 214-969-5100.
In Frankfurt, Germany: Hochhaus am Park, Grüneburgweg 102, 60323 Frankfurt am Main.
Telephone: 49-69-9726-3939.
Telecopier: 49-69-9726-3993.
In Geneva, Switzerland: 20, rue de Candolle.
Telephone: 41-22-320-2339.
Telecopier: 41-22-320-1232.
In Hong Kong: 29th Floor, Entertainment Building, 30 Queen's Road Central.
Telephone: 852-2526-6895.
Telecopier: 852-2868-5871.
In London England: Bucklersbury House, 3 Queen Victoria Street.
Telephone: 44-20-7236-3939.
Telecopier: 44-20-7236-1113.
In New York, New York: 599 Lexington Avenue.
Telephone: 212-326-3939.
Telecopier: 212-755-7306.
In Paris, France: 120, rue du Faubourg Saint-Honoré.
Telephone: 33-1-56-59-3939.
Telecopier: 33-1-56-59-3938
In Pittsburgh, Pennsylvania: 500 Grant Street, 31st Floor.
Telephone: 412-391-3939.
Telecopier: 412-394-7959.
In Riyadh, Saudi Arabia: The International Law Firm (In Association with Jones, Day, Reavis & Pogue), Sulaymaniyah, Prince Mishari IBN, Abdulaziz Street, P.O. Box 22166.
Telephone: (966-1) 462-8866.
Telecopier: (966-1) 462-9001.
In Shanghai, China: 2805 Kerry Centre, 1515 Nanjing Road West.
Telephone: 86-21-5298-6568.
Telecopier: 86-21-5298-6569.
In Sydney, Australia: Governor Phillip Tower, Level 38, 1 Farrer Place.
Telephone: 61-2-9210-6921.
Telecopier: 61-2-9210-6926.
In Taipei, Taiwan: 8th Floor, 2 Tun Hwa South Road, Section 2.
Telephone: (886-2) 2704-6808.
Telecopier: (886-2) 2704-6791.
In Tokyo, Japan: Toranomon 45 Mori Building, 3th Floor, 1-5, Toranomon 5-Chome, Minato-ku, Tokyo 105, Japan.
Telephone: 81-3-3433-3939.
Telecopier: 81-3-5401-2725.
In Washington, D.C.: 51 Louisiana Avenue, N.W.
Telephone: 202-879-3939.
Telecopier: 202-626-1700.

MEMBERS OF FIRM IN LOS ANGELES

James F. Childs, Jr. | David S. Boyce
Elwood Lui | Sarah Heck Griffin

ASSOCIATES

Kirstin D. Poirier-Whitley | Ann-Marie Niccolai

For Complete List of Firm Personnel, See General Section

For full biographical listings, see the Martindale-Hubbell Law Directory

KESSLER & KESSLER, A LAW CORPORATION (AV)

2029 Century Park East, Suite 1520, 90067
Telephone: 310-552-9800
Fax: 310-552-0442
Email: kkalawcorp@aol.com

Warren J. Kessler | Lisa C. Alexander
Joan B. Kessler | Lisa K. Skaist

For full biographical listings, see the Martindale-Hubbell Law Directory

LOEB & LOEB LLP (AV)

A Limited Liability Partnership including Professional Corporations
Suite 1800, 1000 Wilshire Boulevard, 90017-2475
Telephone: 213-688-3400
Facsimile: 213-688-3460
Email: info@loeb.com *URL:* http://www.loeb.com
Century City, California Office: Suite 2200, 10100 Santa Monica Boulevard, Los Angeles, 90067-4164.
Telephone: 310-282-2000.
Facsimile: 310-282-2192.

(See Next Column)

New York, N.Y. Office: 345 Park Avenue, 10154-0037.
Telephone: 212-407-4000.
Facsimile: 212-407-4990.
Nashville, Tennessee Office: 45 Music Square West, 37203-3205.
Telephone: 615-749-8300;
Facsimile: 615-749-8308.
Rome, Italy Office: Piazza Digione 1, 00197.
Telephone: 011-3906-808-8456.
Facsimile: 011-3906-808-8288.

MEMBERS OF FIRM

John Arao | Paul A. Sczudlo
Terence F. Cuff | Bruce M. Stiglitz (A P.C.)
Jay Fenster (New York City Office)

OF COUNSEL

Harvey L. Silbert (Century City Office) | John S. Warren

ASSOCIATES

Paula G. Atkinson | Irving S. Gomez
Karen L. Silverman

For Complete List of Firm Personnel, See General Section

For full biographical listings, see the Martindale-Hubbell Law Directory

MATTHIAS & BERG LLP (AV)

1990 South Bundy Drive, Suite 790, 90025-5244
Telephone: 310-820-0083
Facsimile: 310-820-8313
Email: info@matthiasberg.com

MEMBERS OF FIRM

Michael R. Matthias | Jeffrey P. Berg

ASSOCIATES

Kenneth M. H. Hoff | Ari Lorin Markow

OF COUNSEL

Stuart R. Singer

Representative Clients: Chatsworth Products, Inc.; Greater China Corp.; Mexalit, S.A.; National Quality Care, Inc.; Network Holdings International, Inc.; Private Investors Equity Group; Residential Resources, Inc.

For full biographical listings, see the Martindale-Hubbell Law Directory

MITCHELL, SILBERBERG & KNUPP LLP (AV)

A Partnership including Professional Corporations
11377 West Olympic Boulevard, 90064
Telephone: 310-312-2000
Fax: 310-312-3100
Email: info@msk.com *URL:* http://www.msk.com

MEMBERS OF FIRM

Allan E. Biblin (A Professional Corporation) | David Wheeler Newman (A Professional Corporation)
Allan B. Cutrow (A Professional Corporation) | Eugene H. Veenhuis (A Professional Corporation)

ASSOCIATES

Jeffrey D. Davine | Jason H. Farber

References: Wells Fargo Bank, N.A.; Merrill, Lynch.

For Complete List of Firm Personnel, See General Section

For full biographical listings, see the Martindale-Hubbell Law Directory

OLINCY & KARPEL (AV)

10960 Wilshire Boulevard, Suite 1111, 90024-3782
Telephone: 310-478-1213
Fax: 310-478-1215
URL: http://www.lawyers.com/o&klaw

MEMBERS OF FIRM

George R. Olincy (1904-1982) | J. Dan Olincy
Philip Karpel

ASSOCIATE

Mary Kulvinskas

For full biographical listings, see the Martindale-Hubbell Law Directory

O'MELVENY & MYERS LLP (AV)

400 South Hope Street, 90071-2899
Telephone: 213-430-6000
Facsimile: 213-430-6407
Cable: MOMS
Telex: 674122
Email: omminfo@omm.com *URL:* http://www.omm.com
Century City, CA Office: 1999 Avenue of the Stars, Los Angeles, 90067-6035.
Telex: 674097. Tel: 310-553-6700.
Fax: 310-246-6779.

(See Next Column)

O'MELVENY & MYERS LLP, *Los Angeles—Continued*

Newport Beach, CA Office: 610 Newport Center Drive, 92660-6429.
Telex: 4722088. Tel: 949-760-9600.
Fax: 949-823-6994.
San Francisco, CA Office: Embarcadero Center West, 275 Battery Street, 94111-3305. Tel: 415-984-8700.
Fax: 415-984-8701.
New York, NY Office: Citicorp Center, 153 East 53rd Street, 10022-4611.
Telex: 129165. Tel: 212-326-2000.
Fax: 212-326-2061.
Washington, DC Office: 555 13th Street, N.W., 20004-1109.
Cable: MOMSWSH.
Telex: 89622. Tel: 202-383-5300.
Fax: 202-383-5414.
London Office: O'Melveny & Myers, 3 Finsbury Square, London, EC2A 1LA, England. Tel: 44-171-256-8451. Fax 44-171-638-8205.
Tokyo Office: Akasaka Twin Tower, East 14F, 2-17-23, Akasaka, Minato-ku, Tokyo 107-0052, Japan. Tel: 03-5562-2800.
Fax: 03-5575-3840.
Hong Kong Office: O'Melveny & Myers, Suite 1905, Tower Two, Lippo Centre, 89 Queensway, Central, Hong Kong. Tel: 852-2523-8266.
Fax: 852-2522-1760.
Shanghai Office: Kerry Centre, 20F, 1515 Nanjing Road West, Shanghai, 200040 People's Republic of China. Tel: 86-21-5298-5600.
Fax: 86-21-5298-5500.

PARTNER

Stuart P. Tobisman (Century City and Los Angeles, CA Offices)

For Complete List of Firm Personnel, See General Section

For full biographical listings, see the Martindale-Hubbell Law Directory

OSTROVE, KRANTZ & OSTROVE, A PROFESSIONAL CORPORATION (AV)

(Successor To: Ostrove and Lancer, A Professional Corporation; David Ostrove, A Professional Corporation)
5757 Wilshire Boulevard, Suite 535, 90036-3600
Telephone: 323-939-3400
Fax: 323-939-3500
Email: OSTROVE@AOL.COM *URL:* http://www.lawyers.com/ok&olaw

David Ostrove
David S. Krantz
Kenneth E. Ostrove

Reference: First Business Bank.

For full biographical listings, see the Martindale-Hubbell Law Directory

PASTOR & LEONARD (AV)

An Association of Professional Law Corporations
16830 Ventura Boulevard (Encino) Suite 345, 91436-1725
Telephone: 818-906-1900
Fax: 818-906-7161
Email: info@lataxlaw.com *URL:* http://www.lataxlaw.com

Mark D. Pastor
Robert T. Leonard

OF COUNSEL

Dennis A. Pastor

Representative Clients: H.F. Ahmanson & Co.; Peabody Galion Corp.; Macrodyne Industries, Inc.; General Signal Corp.

For full biographical listings, see the Martindale-Hubbell Law Directory

PILLSBURY MADISON & SUTRO LLP (AV)

Citicorp Plaza, 725 South Figueroa Street, Suite 1200, 90017-5443
Telephone: 213-488-7100
Fax: 213-629-1033
Email: pillsburylaw.com *URL:* http://pillsburylaw.com
Costa Mesa, California Office: 650 Town Center Drive, 7th Floor, 92626.
Telephone: 714-436-6800.
Fax: 714-436-2800.
Silicon Valley Office: 2550 Hanover Street, Palo Alto, 94034.
Telephone: 650-233-4500.
Fax: 650-233-4545.
Sacramento, California Office: 400 Capitol Mall, Suite 1700, 95814.
Telephone: 916-329-4700.
Fax: 916-441-3583.
San Diego, California Office: 101 West Broadway, Suite 1800, 92101.
Telephone: 619-234-5000.
Fax: 619-236-1995.
San Francisco, California Office: 50 Fremont Street, 94105.
Telephone: 415-983-1000.
Fax: 415-983-1200.
Washington, D.C. Office: 1100 New York Avenue, N.W., Ninth Floor, 20005.
Telephone: 202-861-3000.
Fax: 202-822-0944.
Vienna, Virginia Office: 8330 Boone Boulevard, Suite 400, 22182.
Telephone: 703-744-7600.
Fax: 703-744-7605.

(See Next Column)

New York, New York Office: 375 Park Avenue, Suite 3108, 10152.
Telephone: 212-826-1060.
Fax: 212-826-9255. One Liberty Plaza, 165 Broadway, 51st Floor.
Telephone: 212-374-1890.
Fax: 212-374-1852.
Tokyo, Japan Office: Pillsbury Madison & Sutro, Gaikokuho Jimu Bengoshi Jimusho, 5th Floor, Samon Eleven Building, 3-1, Samon-cho, Shinjuku-ku, Tokyo 160 Japan.
Telephone: 800-729-9830; 011-813-3354-3531.
Fax: 011-813-3354-3534.

MEMBERS OF FIRM

Anthon S. Cannon, Jr.
David L. Hayutin

For Complete List of Firm Personnel, See General Section

For full biographical listings, see the Martindale-Hubbell Law Directory

RODI, POLLOCK, PETTKER, GALBRAITH & CAHILL, A LAW CORPORATION (AV)

444 South Flower Street, Suite 1700, 90071-2901
Telephone: 213-895-4900
Telecopiers: 213-895-4921; 895-4922; 895-4750
URL: http://www.rodipollock.com

Karl B. Rodi (1908-1982)
John D. Cahill
John D. Pettker
Daniel C. Bond (1942-1977)
William R. Christian
Henry P. Pramov, Jr.
John F. Cermak, Jr.
Allan E. Ceran
Elizabeth B. Blakely
Robert C. Norton
Tim G. Ceperley
Coralie Kupfer
Cris K. O'Neall
Scott E. Adamson
Margaret Rosenthal

Sonja A. Inglin
Michael A. Abraham
Kenneth A. Franklin
Richard Nessary
Donna Yamini
Wade E. Norwood
Deepak Nanda
David J. Elbaz

OF COUNSEL

John P. Pollock
James M. Galbraith

For full biographical listings, see the Martindale-Hubbell Law Directory

RODRIGUEZ, HORII & CHOI (AV)

777 South Figueroa Street, Suite 4207, 90017
Telephone: 213-892-7700
Fax: 213-892-7777
URL: http://www.rhclaw.com

MEMBERS OF FIRM

Albert R. Rodriguez
Dwayne M. Horii
William C. Choi

ASSOCIATES

Hilary Christen Kingston
Charles E. Potter, Jr.
Amy Borlund

For full biographical listings, see the Martindale-Hubbell Law Directory

SHIOTANI & INOUYE (AV)

1901 Avenue of the Stars Suite 1010, 90067
Telephone: 310-712-0100
Telecopier: 310-712-0110
Email: silaw@earthlink.net *URL:* http://www.lawyers.com/shiotani&inouye

MEMBERS OF FIRM

Barney B. Shiotani
Lawrence G. Inouye

ASSOCIATE

Nicole Grattan Pearson

References: First Los Angeles Bank (Airport Office); Bank of California.

For full biographical listings, see the Martindale-Hubbell Law Directory

STEPHEN E. SOLOMON (AV)

2049 Century Park East Suite 3090, 90067
Telephone: 310-556-0360
Fax: 310-556-0462
Email: solomonlaw@earthlink.net

For full biographical listings, see the Martindale-Hubbell Law Directory

WEINSTEIN, BOLDT, RACINE, HALFHIDE & CAMEL, PROFESSIONAL CORPORATION (AV)

1801 Century Park East, Suite 2200, 90067-2336
Telephone: 310-203-8466
Telecopy: 310-552-7938
Email: wbrhc@compuserve.com

David A. Weinstein
Ronald M. Boldt
Scott H. Racine
Roger G. Halfhide
David J. Camel
M. Katharine Davidson

(See Next Column)

WEINSTEIN, BOLDT, RACINE, HALFHIDE & CAMEL PROFESSIONAL CORPORATION—*Continued*

Reference: City National Bank (Los Angeles, Calif.).

For full biographical listings, see the Martindale-Hubbell Law Directory

WEINSTOCK, MANION, REISMAN, SHORE & NEUMANN, A LAW CORPORATION (AV)

1875 Century Park East, 15th Floor, 90067
Telephone: 310-553-8844
Fax: 310-553-5165
URL: http://www.weinstocklaw.com

DIRECTORS

Harold Weinstock
Louis A. Reisman
Sussan H. Shore
Martin A. Neumann
Gary M. Borofsky
M. Neil Solarz
Robert E. Strauss

OF COUNSEL

Marc L. Sallus

ASSOCIATES

Susan Abraham
Blake A. Rummel
Samuel D. Shapiro
Dianna M. Burgh

References: City National Bank (Century City); Bank of America (Century City); Northern Trust Bank of California, N.A.; Sanwa Bank California.

For full biographical listings, see the Martindale-Hubbell Law Directory

WILLIAMS AND BALLAS (AV)

1800 Century Park East, Suite 510, 90067
Telephone: 310-557-8383
Fax: 310-557-8380
San Francisco, California Office: 160 Sansome Street, Suite 1200.
Telephone: 415-296-9904.
Fax: 415-981-0898.

MEMBERS OF FIRM

Lawrence D. Williams
Stephen B. Ballas

OF COUNSEL

Stanley P. Graham

ASSOCIATES

Melissa Hamilton
Laura M. Williams (Not admitted in CA)

Representative Clients: Pre-Delivery Service Corp.; Simonson Mercedes; Rockview Dairies; Sun Meat Co.; Fonda, Garrard, Hilberman & Davis; Graphic Films, Inc.; M.P. Mountains of So. Cal., Inc.; ZB Industries Inc.; Coaster Co. of America.

For full biographical listings, see the Martindale-Hubbell Law Directory

LOS OSOS, San Luis Obispo Co.

J. K. GEORGE & ASSOCIATES (AV)

P.O. Box 6129, 93412
Telephone: 805-528-3394
Telecopier: 805-528-5598
Email: info@jkgeorge.com *URL:* http://www.lawyers.com/georgelaw
San Luis Obispo, California Office: 694 Santa Rosa, P.O. Box 12710.
Telephone: 805-544-3394.
Facsimile: 805-528-5598.

J. K. George
Ray A. Gallo

Anne C. Cyr

For full biographical listings, see the Martindale-Hubbell Law Directory

*NAPA,** Napa Co.

GAW, VAN MALE, SMITH, MYERS & MIROGLIO, A PROFESSIONAL LAW CORPORATION (AV)

944 Main Street, 94559-3045
Telephone: 707-252-9000
Telecopier: 707-252-0792
URL: http://www.gvmsmm.com
Fairfield, California Office: Corporate Plaza. 1261 Travis Boulevard, Suite 350, 94533-4801.
Telephone: 707-425-1250.
Fax: 707-425-1255.
Redlands, California Office: 300 E. State Street, Suite 101, 92372-5200.
Telephone: 909-798-3190.
Fax: 909-798-3092.

Wyman G. Smith, III
Bruce A. Myers
S. Scott Reynolds

Michael A. Rubin
Kathleen M. Bock

Reference: The Vintage Bank.

For full biographical listings, see the Martindale-Hubbell Law Directory

NEWPORT BEACH, Orange Co.

STEPHEN J. SCHUMACHER (AV)

4340 Campus Drive, Suite 100, 92660
Telephone: 714-752-9425
Telecopier: 714-752-8170
Email: sjschu@aol.com

Reference: Bank of America (Irvine Industrial Branch).

For full biographical listings, see the Martindale-Hubbell Law Directory

OXNARD, Ventura Co.

ENGLAND, WHITFIELD, SCHRÖEDER & TREDWAY, L.L.P. (AV)

300 Esplanade Drive, 6th Floor, 93030
Telephone: 805-485-9627
Ventura: 647-8237
Southern California Toll Free: 800-255-3485
Fax: 805-983-0297
URL: http://www.tsurf.com/ewst/

Theodore J. England
Anson M. Whitfield
Robert W. Schröeder
David W. Tredway
Robert A. McSorley
Stuart A. Comis
Mitchel B. Kahn
Mark A. Nelson
Eric J. Kananen
Mary E. Schröeder
Oscar C. Gonzalez
Madison M. Christian
Kurt Edward Kananen

Melissa E. Cohen
Linda Kathryn Ash
Mark T. Barney
Kevin L. Dorhout
Anthony M. Ramos
Gregory J. Ramirez

Representative Clients: Dah Chong Hong (automobile dealerships); Steve thomas BMW; Vreeland Cadillac, Inc.; Willamette Industries; The Port of Hueneme; Viola, Inc. (General Contracting); Santa Clara Chemical Co.; Nakamura Berry Growers; John Taft Electric Co.; Rodgers Mortgage Co.

For full biographical listings, see the Martindale-Hubbell Law Directory

*SACRAMENTO,** Sacramento Co.

BARTEL ENG LINN & SCHRODER (AV)

300 Capitol Mall, Suite 1100, 95814
Telephone: 916-442-0400
Facsimile: 916-442-3442
Email: barteleng@barteleng.com *URL:* http://www.barteleng.com

Scott E. Bartel
Daniel B. Eng
Roger D. Linn
Regina J. Schroder

Jeff D. Barlow
Eric J. Stiff

OF COUNSEL

Vincent DiCarlo

For full biographical listings, see the Martindale-Hubbell Law Directory

DROBNY LAW OFFICES (AV)

2485 Natomas Park Drive, Suite 500, 95833
Telephone: 916-641-0526
FAX: 916-441-2352
Stockton, California Office: 7510 Shoreline Drive, Suite B-1, 95219.
Telephone: 209-464-3408.
Fax: 916-441-2352.

Mark S. Drobny

Leland J. Ellison
Todd R. Robie
Chris B. Knepshield
Leslie Ann Arnal
Lori A. Adasiewicz
Quinn Michael Jalli

For full biographical listings, see the Martindale-Hubbell Law Directory

*SAN DIEGO,** San Diego Co.

ALHADEFF CANNON ROSE SOLAR & PARKS, LLP (AV)

550 West "C" Street, Nineteenth Floor, 92101-3540
Telephone: 619-231-8700
Facsimile: 619-231-8323
Email: ksolar@acrsp.com
Temecula, California Office: The Tower Plaza, 27555 Ynez Road, Suite 203, 92591-4677.
Telephone: 909-699-9088.
Facsimile: 909-699-9878. Email: POBERHANSLEY@ACRSP.com
Los Angeles, California Office: Olympic Center, 11150 Olympic Boulevard, Suite 860, 90064.
Telephone: 310-914-4400.
Facsimile: 310-914-0030. Email: JODONNELL@ACRSP.com
Lafayette, California Office: Lafayette Terrace, 3697 Mount Diablo Boulevard, Suite 100, 94549.
Telephone: 925-283-1599.
Facsimile: 925-283-5847. Email: GMF-CA@MSN.com

(See Next Column)

ALHADEFF CANNON ROSE SOLAR & PARKS LLP, *San Diego—Continued*

PARTNERS

Samuel C. Alhadeff
Robert D. Rose
Jerry M. Cannon
Keith R. Solar
Robert J. Parks
Philip D. Oberhansley (Resident, Temecula, California Office)
Joseph L. Marshall
Leslie C. Detwiler
Glenn M. Feeley (Resident, Lafayette, California Office)
Thomas T. Lord
Madeline Clark Cahill
John L. O'Donnell, Jr. (Resident, Los Angeles, California Office)

OF COUNSEL

Craig S. Engstrand
Robert K. Edmunds
Charles F. Gorder, Sr.

ASSOCIATES

Michael J. Barry
Richard James Bayless
Craig V. Butler
Cyril J. Dantchev
Genie Harrison
S. Douglas Kerner
Frank J. Polek
Les W. Robertson
Traci M. Selby
Marjeta Duzevic Six

For full biographical listings, see the Martindale-Hubbell Law Directory

GARRISON ARMSTRONG LAW CORPORATION (AV)

First National Bank Center, 401 West A Street, Suite 1680, 92101-7922
Telephone: 619-232-1811

Garrison R. Armstrong

LEGAL SUPPORT PERSONNEL

Iris R. Daniel (Legal Assistant)

For full biographical listings, see the Martindale-Hubbell Law Directory

FERRIS & BRITTON, A PROFESSIONAL CORPORATION (AV)

1600 First National Bank Center, 401 West A Street, 92101
Telephone: 619-233-3131
Fax: 619-232-9316
Email: manager@ferrisbritton.com *URL:* http://www.ferrisbritton.com

Alfred G. Ferris
Tamara K. Fogg
Gary T. Moyer

Representative Clients: Annabooks, Inc.; Cox Communications, Inc.; Frontier Analytics, Inc.; Invitrogen Corporation; Peninsula Bank; Southwest Airlines; Structural Bioinformatics, Inc.; ZyGam, Inc.

For Complete List of Firm Personnel, See General Section

For full biographical listings, see the Martindale-Hubbell Law Directory

LAW OFFICES OF CHARLES P. LEBEAU (AV)

Historic Hayward-Patterson Building, 1887, 2148 Broadway, 92102
Telephone: 858-456-1100
Fax: 858-455-5024
Email: lebeaulaw@worldnet.att.net *URL:* http://www.lebeaulaw.com

LEGAL SUPPORT PERSONNEL

Rebecca Cisinsky (Paralegal/Secretary)
Jill Gisondo (Secretary)

For full biographical listings, see the Martindale-Hubbell Law Directory

LUCE, FORWARD, HAMILTON & SCRIPPS LLP (AV)

A Partnership including Professional Corporations
600 West Broadway, Suite 2600, 92101
Telephone: 619-236-1414
Fax: 619-232-8311
URL: http://www.luce.com
La Jolla, California Office: 4275 Executive Square, Suite 800, 92037.
Telephone: 858-455-6611.
Fax: 858-232-8311.
Los Angeles, California Office: 777 South Figueroa, Suite 3600, 90017.
Telephone: 213-892-4992.
Fax: 213-892-7731.
San Francisco, California Office: 121 Spear Street, Suite 200, 94105.
Telephone: 415-356-4600.
Fax: 415-356-4610.
New York, N.Y. Office: Citicorp Center, 153 East 53rd Street, 26th Floor, 10022.
Telephone: 212-754-1414.
Fax: 212-644-9727.
Chicago, Illinois Office: 180 North La Salle Street, Suite 3110, 60601.
Telephone: 312-641-0580.
Fax: 312-641-0380.

Phillip L. Jelsma
Mark L. Mann
Darryl Steinhause

For Complete List of Firm Personnel, See General Section

For full biographical listings, see the Martindale-Hubbell Law Directory

SELTZER CAPLAN MCMAHON & VITEK, A PROFESSIONAL CORPORATION (AV)

2100 Symphony Towers, 750 B Street, 92101
Telephone: 619-685-3003
Fax: 619-685-3100
URL: http://www.scwm.com

David J. Dorne
John H. Alspaugh
Adrienne Jeffrey

Andrew D. Brooks

Representative Clients: Chicago Title; The Goodyear Tire & Rubber Co.; W.R. Grace & Co--Conn.; McDonnell-Douglas Corp.; McMillin Communities; Western Financial Savings Bank.

For Complete List of Firm Personnel, See General Section

For full biographical listings, see the Martindale-Hubbell Law Directory

SOLOMON WARD SEIDENWURM & SMITH, LLP (AV)

1200 Wells Fargo Plaza, 401 B Street, 92101
Telephone: 619-231-0303
Telecopier: 619-231-4755
Email: mvafi@swsslaw.com *URL:* http://www.swsslaw.com

PARTNERS OF FIRM

Michael D. Breslauer
Cynthia L. Eldred
Lawrence J. Kaplan (P.C.)
Richard E. McCarthy
Edward J. McIntyre
Paul S. Metsch
Alison L. Pivonka
Harry J. Proctor (P.C.)
Jeffrey A. Schneider
Richard L. Seidenwurm (P.C.)
Jeffrey H. Silberman
Miguel A. Smith
Norman L. Smith
Herbert J. Solomon

ASSOCIATES

Daniel E. Gardenswartz
David T. Gluck
Amy Perkins Melden
Karl A. Sandoval
Kurt E. Scheuerman
Elizabeth A. Trevino

OF COUNSEL

Robert F. La Scala
William O. Ward, III (Retired)

For full biographical listings, see the Martindale-Hubbell Law Directory

LAW FIRM OF DAVID S. ZWEIG (AV)

Oceana Building, 4425 Bayard Street, Suite 200, 92109-4089
Telephone: 858-274-1818
Telefax: 858-274-8535
Email: zweiglaw@cts.com *URL:* http://www.zweiglaw.com

David S. Zweig

ASSOCIATE

Erin L. McCreary

Representative Clients: Tequila Sauza S.A. de C.V.; Dorians Tijuana S.A. de C.V.; Carlos 'N Charlies Enterprises, Inc.; Grupo Andersons S.A. de C.V.; Dupuis of California, Inc.; Comercial Mexicana S.A. de C.V.; Bufete de DeSarrollo.
References: Union Bank of California (San Diego); The RHB Trust Co., Ltd., Cayman Islands; Nevis Services Ltd.

For full biographical listings, see the Martindale-Hubbell Law Directory

*SAN FRANCISCO,** San Francisco Co.

AVERY & ASSOCIATES (AV)

49 Geary Street, Suite 202, 94108-5727
Telephone: 415-954-4800
Fax: 415-954-4810
Email: LJA@averylegal.com

Luther J. Avery

OF COUNSEL

Mark J. Avery

LEGAL SUPPORT PERSONNEL

Matthew S. Avery

For full biographical listings, see the Martindale-Hubbell Law Directory

BRAZE LAW OFFICES (AV)

425 Market Street, Suite 2200, 94105
Telephone: 415-955-2612
Toll Free: 877-283-7342
Email: brazelaw@aol.com *URL:* http://www.lawyers.com/brazelaw
Petaluma, California Office: West America Bank Building. 201 Keller Street. 94952-2874.
Telephone: 707-763-2212.
Fax: 707-766-8631.
Sacramento, California Office: Chippendale Office Plaza, 4811 Chippendale Drive, Suite 704, 95814.
Telephone: 916-485-4100.

(See Next Column)

BRAZE LAW OFFICES—*Continued*

MEMBERS OF FIRM

James J. Braze
Gail Stimmell Braze

For full biographical listings, see the Martindale-Hubbell Law Directory

RAYMOND N. STELLA ERLACH (AV)

One Maritime Plaza, Fourth Floor, 94111
Telephone: 415-788-3322
Fax: 415-788-8613

OF COUNSEL

Gregory J. Erlach
Stephen Peter U. Erlach

Reference: Bank of America Private Banking, San Francisco, California.

For full biographical listings, see the Martindale-Hubbell Law Directory

KAY & MERKLE (AV)

100 The Embarcadero Penthouse, 94105
Telephone: 415-357-1200
Facsimile: 415-512-9277
Email: kmlaw100@kmlaw100.com

MEMBERS OF FIRM

Steven Kay
Walter F. Merkle, Jr.
W. Bruce Bercovich
John W. Merkle
Alan J. Silver
Douglas A. Marshall
Douglas A Hutchinson

OF COUNSEL

Lionel T. Aiken

For full biographical listings, see the Martindale-Hubbell Law Directory

MURPHY, PEARSON, BRADLEY & FEENEY, A PROFESSIONAL CORPORATION (AV)

88 Kearny Street, 10th Floor, 94108
Telephone: 415-788-1900
Telecopier: 415-393-8087
Email: IndividualsFirstInitialAndLastName@mpbf.com *URL:* http://www.mpbf.com
Sacramento, California Office: 701 University Avenue, Suite 150.
Telephone: 916-565-0300.
Fax: 916-565-1636.
San Jose, California Office: 80 South Market Street, 3rd Floor.
Telephone: 408-279-5792.
Facsimile: 408-279-5785.
Los Angeles, California Office: 11400 West Olympic Boulevard, Suite 249.
Telephone: 310-312-9565.
Fax: 310-312-9566.

Arthur V. Pearson
Gregory A. Bastian (Resident, Sacramento Office)

For Complete List of Firm Personnel, See General Section

For full biographical listings, see the Martindale-Hubbell Law Directory

EDWARD T. PERRY (AV)

Citicorp Center, One Sansome Street, Suite 2000, 94104
Telephone: 415-951-1058
Facsimile: 415-951-4660; http://www.taxexcel.com
Email: perrylaw@taxexcel.com *URL:* http://www.lawyers.com/taxexcel

For full biographical listings, see the Martindale-Hubbell Law Directory

SILK, ADLER & COLVIN, A LAW CORPORATION (AV)

Russ Building, Suite 1120, 235 Montgomery Street, 94104
Telephone: 415-421-7555
Fax: 415-421-0712
Email: SAC@SilkLaw.com

Thomas Silk
Elizabeth Buchalter Adler
Gregory L. Colvin
Rosemary E. Fei
Robert A. Wexler
Erik D. Dryburgh

Lisa R. Appleberry
Ingrid P. Mittermaier

For full biographical listings, see the Martindale-Hubbell Law Directory

TAYLOR & FAUST, A PROFESSIONAL CORPORATION (AV)

445 Bush Street, 5th Floor, 94108-3725
Telephone: 415-421-9535
Fax: 415-956-3231

Samuel Taylor (1906-1995)
Leland H. Faust
Steven B. Kravitz

Stephen E. Clark
Justin H. Bass

For full biographical listings, see the Martindale-Hubbell Law Directory

*SAN JOSE,** Santa Clara Co.

FIORE LAW GROUP LLP (AV)

Bank of America Building, 101 Park Center Plaza, Suite 1150, 95113
Telephone: 408-293-3616
Facsimile: 408-293-0430
Email: flg@fiorelawgroup.com

Owen G. Fiore
John F. Ramsbacher

John W. Prokey

For full biographical listings, see the Martindale-Hubbell Law Directory

HOPKINS & CARLEY, A LAW CORPORATION (AV)

Sixth Floor, 2 West Santa Clara Street, 95113-1824
Telephone: 408-286-9800
Facsimile: 408-998-4790
Mailing Address: P.O. Box 1469, San Jose, CA, 95109-1469
URL: http://www.hopkinscarley.com

John F. Hopkins
Robert D. Wenzel
Dunham B. Sherer
Anthony J. McCarthy
James M. Hager
Charles H. Packer

OF COUNSEL

Theodore J. Biagini

Jennifer M. Cunneen
Tamara B. Pow

For Complete List of Firm Personnel, See General Section

For full biographical listings, see the Martindale-Hubbell Law Directory

MILLER, MORTON, CAILLAT & NEVIS (AV)

50 West San Fernando Street, Suite 1300, 95113-2413
Telephone: 408-292-1765
Telecopier: 408-292-4484
URL: http://www.mmcn-law.com

Richard W. Morton (1916-1975)
Charles V. Caillat (1920-1990)
Harvey C. Miller (1906-1993)

MEMBERS OF FIRM

David L. Nevis
Francis J. Hughes
Peter A. Kline
Stevan C. Adelman
Joseph A. Scanlan, Jr.
Carolyn Tobiason Stuart
William K. Hurley
Peter V. Dessau

OF COUNSEL

Nancy F. Symons

ASSOCIATES

Kathryn E. Barrett
Katherine S. Pak
David I. Kornbluh
Christopher J. Hersey
Julie Neale Meyer

Representative Clients: Trammell Crow Residential Services; Joe Kerley Lincoln Mercury Co.; Milligan News Co.; Joseph George Distributors; Santa Clara Dental Society; New West Foods; Bay Apartment Communities; E. A. Hathaway Co.

For full biographical listings, see the Martindale-Hubbell Law Directory

TERRA LAW LLP (AV)

60 South Market Street, Suite 200, 95113
Telephone: 408-288-7325
Fax: 408-998-4895
Burlingame, California Office: 1350 Old Bayshore Highway, Suite 760, 94010.
Telephone: 650-685-7325.
Fax: 650-685-4895.

George H. Cole, Jr.
D. D. Hughmanick
R. Prescott Jaunich
Richard O. McDonald
Breck E. Milde
William L. Myers
Jane P. Relyea
Jason R. Biggs
Joan Paul
Ronald I. Rainey

Katharine L. Hardt-Mason
Thomas E. Rossmeissl

For full biographical listings, see the Martindale-Hubbell Law Directory

*SAN LUIS OBISPO,** San Luis Obispo Co.

J. K. GEORGE & ASSOCIATES (AV)

694 Santa Rosa, P.O. Box 12710, 93406
Telephone: 805-544-3394
Facsimile: 805-528-5598
Email: info@jkgeorge.com *URL:* http://www.lawyers.com/georgelaw
Los Osos, California Office: P.O. Box 6129.
Telephone: 805-528-3394.
Telecopier: 805-528-5598.

J. K. George

(See Next Column)

J. K. GEORGE & ASSOCIATES, *San Luis Obispo—Continued*

Anne C. Cyr

For full biographical listings, see the Martindale-Hubbell Law Directory

SAN MATEO, San Mateo Co.

DANIEL G. BROWN (AV)

155 Bovet Road, Suite 405, 94402
Telephone: 650-349-7900
Facsimile: 650-349-7971
Email: dgblaw@concentric.net

For full biographical listings, see the Martindale-Hubbell Law Directory

*SANTA ROSA,** Sonoma Co.

ANDERSON, ZEIGLER, DISHAROON, GALLAGHER & GRAY, PROFESSIONAL CORPORATION (AV)

50 Old Courthouse Square, 5th Floor, P.O. Box 1498, 95404
Telephone: 707-545-4910
Fax: 707-544-0260
Other Santa Rosa, California Office: 6641 Oakmont Drive, 95409.
Telephone: 707-539-3880.
Petaluma, California Office: 17 Keller Street, 94952.
Telephone: 707-763-0937.

Edwin C. Anderson, Jr.
Kirt F. Zeigler
Robert Disharoon
Barbara Detrich Gallagher
Margaret M. Elliott
David G. Bjornstrom
Robert S. Rutherfurd
Christopher M. Mazzia
Tricia A. Shindledecker
Jeremy L. Olsan

Wendy D. Whitson
Daniel E. Post
Mary Catherine Doherty
Lisa Yoshida
Matthew E. Hannum

OF COUNSEL

John J. King, Jr.

LEGAL SUPPORT PERSONNEL

Edward J. Gibson
Daniel B. Flock (Director of Information)

For full biographical listings, see the Martindale-Hubbell Law Directory

COLORADO

*COLORADO SPRINGS,** El Paso Co.

WILTON W. COGSWELL, III (AV)

Suite 1020, Alamo Corporate Center, 102 South Tejon Street, 80903
Telephone: 719-473-1448
Facsimile: 719-473-1449
Email: wcogs3@aol.com

OF COUNSEL

Wilton W. Cogswell, IV

For full biographical listings, see the Martindale-Hubbell Law Directory

FLYNN MCKENNA WRIGHT & KARSH (AV)

limited liability company
Plaza of the Rockies 111 South Tejon, Suite 202, 80903-3300
Telephone: 719-578-8444
Fax: 719-578-8836

OF COUNSEL

James T. Flynn

MEMBERS OF FIRM

R. Tim McKenna
Bruce M. Wright
Randolph M. Karsh
Brian T. Murphy
Michael C. Potarf
Karl A. Berg, Jr.

Representative Clients: National Systems & Research, Inc.; Widefield Homes, Inc.

For full biographical listings, see the Martindale-Hubbell Law Directory

*DENVER,** Denver Co.

ATLASS PROFESSIONAL CORPORATION (AV)

3665 Cherry Creek North Drive Suite 100, 80209-3712
Telephone: 303-329-5900
Fax: 303-329-3291
Email: tatlass@atlass.com

Theodore B. Atlass

(See Next Column)

Carol Buchanan Lay

For full biographical listings, see the Martindale-Hubbell Law Directory

KATHERINE F. BECKES (AV)

1775 Sherman Street, Suite 2550, 80203
Telephone: 303-832-2732
Fax: 303-832-2733
Email: kbeckes@lawyernet.com

For full biographical listings, see the Martindale-Hubbell Law Directory

BERENBAUM, WEINSHIENK & EASON, P.C. (AV)

Suite 2600 Republic Plaza, 370 17th Street, 80202
Telephone: 303-825-0800
Facsimile: 303-629-7610
Email: berenbaum1@aol.com *URL:* http://www.BWELaw.com

Daniel S. Duggan
Steven C. Hoth
Dan A. Sciullo

Michael James Cook
Heather Scheel Hagemann

Representative Clients: Home Depot; Sprint Spectrum, L.P.; Town of Vail, Colorado; First Union Corporation; City of Englewood, Colorado; Oakwood Homes; Karman, Inc.; Wells Fargo Bank, N.A.; Berkshire Life Insurance Co.; Trinity Ventures.

For full biographical listings, see the Martindale-Hubbell Law Directory

BRENMAN BROMBERG & TENENBAUM, P.C. (AV)

Mellon Financial Center Suite 1001, 1775 Sherman Street, 80203
Telephone: 303-894-0234
Fax: 303-839-1633
Email: bbt@bbtlaw.net

Albert Brenman
Thomas R. Bromberg
A. Thomas Tenenbaum
Steven W. McDonald

Sheryl A. Johnson
Judy A. Gooch

OF COUNSEL

Duane Woodard

For full biographical listings, see the Martindale-Hubbell Law Directory

BROWNSTEIN HYATT & FARBER, P.C. (AV)

Twenty-Second Floor, 410 Seventeenth Street, 80202-4437
Telephone: 303-223-1100
Telecopier: 303-223-1111
Washington, D.C. Office: 1615 L Street, N.W., Suite 450, 20036.
Telephone: 202-296-7353.
Telecopier: 202-296-7009.
Glenwood Springs, Colorado Office: Box 357, 81602.
Telephone: 970-945-5302.
Telecopier: 970-945-4921.

Michael J. Sternick
John L. Ruppert
Gregory W. Berger

Ellen O. Kauffmann
Mark J. Maichel
Alisa B. Burns

Representative Clients: Atlantic Gulf Communities Corporation; Brothers Gourmet Coffees, Inc.; Celerity Partners; Corporate Express; Coughlin & Company, Inc.; Pacifica Holding Company; SunAmerica Inc.; U.S. Home Corporation.

For Complete List of Firm Personnel, See General Section

For full biographical listings, see the Martindale-Hubbell Law Directory

JOHN DEBRUYN LAW OFFICES (AV)

2100 East Fourteenth Avenue, 80206
Telephone: 303-377-0707
Telecopier: 303-321-2655
Email: jdebruyn@debruyn.com *URL:* http://www.debruyn.com

For full biographical listings, see the Martindale-Hubbell Law Directory

GELT, PADDISON & ASSOCIATES P.C. (AV)

1600 Broadway, Suite 2600, 80202-4926
Telephone: 303-861-1033
Fax: 303-894-0857

Theodore Z. Gelt
Jane I. Paddison
Eric Jon Zinn (Not admitted in CO)
Robert B. Keyser, II
Jack H. McQuitty, Jr.

(See Next Column)

GELT, PADDISON & ASSOCIATES P.C.—*Continued*

OF COUNSEL

Louis E. Gelt (1908-1997) Sander Jay Slatkin

Representative Clients: Aurora Dairy Corporation; Columbine Capital Services, Inc.; Community Holdings, Inc.; Customer Communications Group; Evergreen Design Group, Inc.; American State Bank; Gateway American Properties; H.C. Companies, Inc.; Hast Lumber Co.; Kaiser Steel Resources

For full biographical listings, see the Martindale-Hubbell Law Directory

GORSUCH KIRGIS LLP (AV)

Tower 1, Suite 1000, 1515 Arapahoe Street, 80202
Telephone: 303-376-5000
Fax: 303-376-5001

PARTNER

Stephen A. Weinstein

For full biographical listings, see the Martindale-Hubbell Law Directory

GUTHERY & RICKLES, P.C. (AV)

Cherry Creek Plaza II, 650 South Cherry Street Suite 1000, 80246-1812
Telephone: 303-320-5889
Fax: 303-320-5890

Peter C. Guthery Stephen P. Rickles

A list of Representative Clients that have provided written authorization will be furnished upon request.

For full biographical listings, see the Martindale-Hubbell Law Directory

HOLME ROBERTS & OWEN LLP (AV)

Suite 4100, 1700 Lincoln, 80203
Telephone: 303-861-7000
Telecopier: 303-866-0200
Email: hro@hro.com *URL:* http://www.hro.com
Boulder, Colorado Office: Suite 400, 1401 Pearl Street.
Telephone: 303-444-5955.
Telecopier: 303-444-1063.
Colorado Springs, Colorado Office: Suite 1300, 90 South Cascade Avenue.
Telephone: 719-473-3800.
Telecopier: 719-633-1518.
Salt Lake City, Utah Office: Suite 1100, 111 East Broadway.
Telephone: 801-521-5800.
Telecopier: 801-521-9639.
London, England Office: Heathcoat House, 3rd Floor, 20 Savile Row.
Telephone: 011-44-171-494-5600.
Telecopier: 011-44-171-287-9344.

PARTNERS OF FIRM

Charles B. Bruce, Jr.
Mark K. Buchi (Salt Lake City Office)
James D. Butler
James E. Bye
Carolyn E. Daniels
Judson W. Detrick
Steve L. Gaines (Colorado Springs Office)
Donald J. Hopkins
Mark M. Hrenya
William S. Huff
Lawrence L. Levin
McKay Marsden (Managing Partner, Salt Lake City Office)
David T. Mitzner
Charles A. Ramunno
Gary R. Thorup (Salt Lake City Office)
Stephanie M. Tuthill
John A. Warnick (Not admitted in CO)
Robert J. Welter
John R. Wylie (Colorado Springs Office)
Richard R. Young (Managing Partner, Colorado Springs Office)

SPECIAL COUNSEL

Karen Schauble Leaffer Norman H. Wright

ASSOCIATES

Thomas A. Geraghty, Jr.
Michelle M. Rose-Hughes
William A. Skewes, II
Lori S. Stefanoudakis
Thomas E. Yearout
Steven P. Young (Salt Lake City Office)

For Complete List of Firm Personnel, See General Section

For full biographical listings, see the Martindale-Hubbell Law Directory

KATZ, LOOK & MOISON, PROFESSIONAL CORPORATION (AV)

1120 Lincoln Street, Suite 1100, 80203
Telephone: 303-832-1900
Fax: 303-863-0412

Michael M. Katz
Harley K. Look, Jr.
Peter R. Moison
Kathryn A. Reeves

Brian E. Onorato
Melisa A. Vogel
Arthur T. DiMeo
Delwyn G. Haroldson
Barbara J. Stauch

(See Next Column)

SPECIAL COUNSEL

Ogborn, Summerlin & Ogborn, L.L.C., Denver, Colorado

For full biographical listings, see the Martindale-Hubbell Law Directory

LOHF, SHAIMAN & JACOBS, P.C. (AV)

950 South Cherry Street, Suite 900, 80246-2666
Telephone: 303-753-9000
Telecopier: 303-753-9997

Charles H. Jacobs
Moshe Luber
Robert Shaiman

Reference: Vectra Bank Colorado.

For full biographical listings, see the Martindale-Hubbell Law Directory

OTTEN, JOHNSON, ROBINSON, NEFF & RAGONETTI, P.C. (AV)

950 Seventeenth Street, 16th Floor, 80202
Telephone: 303-825-8400
Telecopier: 303-825-6525
URL: http://www.ojrnr.com

Neil M. Goff
Paul D. Zier
C. Ander Smith

For Complete List of Firm Personnel, See General Section

For full biographical listings, see the Martindale-Hubbell Law Directory

SHERMAN & HOWARD L.L.C. (AV)

Attorneys and Counselors at Law
633 Seventeenth Street, Suite 3000, 80202
Telephone: 303-297-2900
Telecopier: 303-298-0940
Colorado Springs, Colorado Office: Suite 1500, 90 South Cascade Avenue, 80903.
Telephone: 719-475-2440.
Las Vegas, Nevada Office: Swendseid & Stern, a member in Sherman & Howard L.L.C., 317 Sixth Street, 89101.
Telephone: 702-387-6073.
Reno, Nevada Office: Swendseid & Stern, a member in Sherman & Howard L.L.C., 50 West Liberty Street, Suite 660, 89501.
Telephone: 702-323-1980.

Douglas M. Cain
Duane F. Wurzer
R. Michael Sanchez
David Thomas III
Cynthia C. Benson
Carol V. Berger
Kathleen A. Odle
Michael Dubetz, Jr.

COUNSEL

Bridget K. Sullivan

Joseph M. Dencker
Ronald M. Pierce
Wendy G. Ramsey
Kirsten B. Stewart (Not admitted in CO)
Gregory T. Densen

Representative Clients: BACE Industries, LLC; Flatiron Structures Co. LLC; Hanifen, Imhoff Inc.; Hathaway Corp.; J.D. Edwards & Co.; Newmont Gold Company; Public Employees' Retirement Assn.; Tele-Communications, Inc.; United Artists Theatre Circuit, Inc.; U.S. West Communications, Inc.

For Complete List of Firm Personnel, See General Section

For full biographical listings, see the Martindale-Hubbell Law Directory

SLIVKA ROBINSON WATERS & O'DORISIO, A PROFESSIONAL CORPORATION (AV)

Suite 2600, 1099 18th Street, 80202-1926
Telephone: 303-297-2600
Telecopier: 303-297-2750
URL: http://www.srwo.com

SHAREHOLDERS

Richard P. Slivka
Peter A. Robinson
Stephen L. Waters
John W. O'Dorisio, Jr.
Ernest J. Panasci
Chevis F. Horne, Jr.
Margaret M. McClellan
Karen Samuels Jones

Deborah A. Hogan
Kerri M. Pertcheck
Susan R. Pierson
Elizabeth E. Pinckard
Daniel A. Sweetser
Bradley S. Taylor
Jill G. VanderPloeg

SPECIAL COUNSEL

Laura J. Vogelgesang Christine Rothe Hoth

For full biographical listings, see the Martindale-Hubbell Law Directory

LAW OFFICES OF JOSEPH H. THIBODEAU, P.C. (AV)

Suite 209, 155 South Madison Street, 80209
Telephone: 303-320-1250
Fax: 303-320-1577
Email: law1@ix.netcom.com

Joseph H. Thibodeau

(See Next Column)

LAW OFFICES OF JOSEPH H. THIBODEAU, P.C., *Denver—Continued*

Kandace C. Gerdes

For full biographical listings, see the Martindale-Hubbell Law Directory

ZISMAN AND INGRAHAM, P.C. (AV)
Suite 650, 3773 Cherry Creek Drive North, 80209
Telephone: 303-320-0023
Fax: 303-320-0034
Email: zisming377@aol.com

Sanford Zisman
James F. Ingraham

For full biographical listings, see the Martindale-Hubbell Law Directory

CONNECTICUT

CHESHIRE, New Haven Co.

WINTERS & FORTE (AV)
Waverly Professional Park, 315 Highland Avenue, Suite 102, P.O. Box 844, 06410
Telephone: 203-272-2927
Fax: 203-271-1222
Email: david.wayne.winters@snet.net *URL:* http://www.snetyp.com/wintersforte

MEMBERS OF FIRM

David Wayne Winters
Michael C. Forte

ASSOCIATE

Anthony R. DePaolo

A List of Representative Clients will be furnished upon request.
References: Bank of Boston, Connecticut; LaFayette American Bank & Trust Co.

For full biographical listings, see the Martindale-Hubbell Law Directory

FAIRFIELD, Fairfield Co.

BRAUNSTEIN & TODISCO, LLC (AV)
One Eliot Place, 06430
Telephone: 203-254-1118
Telecopier: 203-254-2453
Email: sam@btlawfirm.com *URL:* http://www.btlawfirm.com

Samuel L. Braunstein
Amy E. Todisco

Reference: People's Bank.

For full biographical listings, see the Martindale-Hubbell Law Directory

*HARTFORD,** Hartford Co.

COPP & BERALL, LLP (AV)
55 Farmington Avenue, Suite 703, 06105
Telephone: 860-249-5261
Fax: 860-947-6382
Email: cb@connix.com

MEMBERS OF FIRM

Frank S. Berall
Mark H. Neikrie
Suzanne Brown Walsh

Darren M. Wallace

OF COUNSEL

Belton A. Copp

References: Fleet Bank, N.A.; BankBoston.

For full biographical listings, see the Martindale-Hubbell Law Directory

SOROKIN, GROSS & HYDE, P.C. (AV)
One Corporate Center, 06103
Telephone: 860-525-6645
Fax: 860-522-1781
Email: sorokin@sorokinlaw.com
Simsbury, Connecticut Office: 720 Hopmeadow Street.
Telephone: 860-651-9348.
Rocky Hill, Connecticut Office: 2360 Main Street.
Telephone: 860-563-9305.
Fax: 860-529-6931.

Morris W. Banks
Alan S. Parker
Sharon Kowal Freilich
Barrie K. Wetstone

Margaret M. Murphy

(See Next Column)

OF COUNSEL

Charles R. Moore, Jr.

For Complete List of Firm Personnel, See General Section

For full biographical listings, see the Martindale-Hubbell Law Directory

*NEW HAVEN,** New Haven Co.

VOTRE & ASSOCIATES, P.C. (AV)
105 Court Street, Suite 302, 06511-6957
Telephone: 203-498-0065
Fax: 203-821-3595
URL: http://www.lawyers.com/votre&associates

Kenneth A. Votre

John-Henry M. Steele

OF COUNSEL

Neil K. Rutter

For full biographical listings, see the Martindale-Hubbell Law Directory

SOUTHPORT, Fairfield Co.

BRODY, WILKINSON AND OBER, P.C. (AV)
2507 Post Road, 06490
Telephone: 203-319-7100
Fax: 203-254-1772

Seth O. L. Brody
Peter Wilkinson
Frank Fritz Ober
S. Giles Payne
James E. Rice
William J. Britt
Barbara S. Miller
Robert L. Teicher
Ronald B. Noren
Peter T. Mott
Thomas J. Walsh, Jr.
Diane F. Martucci
Seth L. Cooper
Douglas R. Brown
Charles S. Brody (1894-1976)

OF COUNSEL

Bruce E. Dillingham
Roy W. Moore, III

For full biographical listings, see the Martindale-Hubbell Law Directory

STAMFORD, Fairfield Co.

CURTIS, BRINCKERHOFF & BARRETT, P.C. (AV)
666 Summer Street, 06901-1416
Telephone: 203-324-6777
Telecopier: 203-324-9621
Email: info@curtisbb.com

T. Ward Cleary (1916-1988)
Frederick M. Tobin
John Wayne Fox
Ward Frank Cleary
James D'Alton Murphy
Randolph T. Lovallo

OF COUNSEL

John D. Hertz
Jane F. Donovan
Richard L. Brinckerhoff
Patricia M. Gaug

Susan L. Stratton
Derek Gilman
Michael P. Murray
John J. Louizos

Counsel for: The F. A. Bartlett Tree Expert Co.; Town of Darien; Miller Automobile Corp.; Bolliger, Inc.; Titan Sports; People's Bank, Bridgeport; Fleet Bank; Federal Deposit Insurance Co.; William Pitt Foundation; Wood Logan Associates.

For full biographical listings, see the Martindale-Hubbell Law Directory

WOFSEY, ROSEN, KWESKIN & KURIANSKY, LLP (AV)
600 Summer Street, 06901
Telephone: 203-327-2300
Fax: 203-967-9273

MEMBERS OF FIRM

Abraham Wofsey (1915-1944)
Michael Wofsey (1927-1951)
David M. Rosen (1926-1967)
Julius B. Kuriansky (1952-1992)
Sydney C. Kweskin (1946-1998)
Monroe Silverman
Howard C. Kaplan
Edward M. Kweskin
David M. Cohen
Marshall Goldberg
Stephen A. Finn
Judith Rosenberg
Mark H. Henderson
Steven D. Grushkin
Matthew J. Forstadt
Steven M. Frederick

OF COUNSEL

Saul Kwartin
Emanuel Margolis
Anthony R. Lorenzo

SPECIAL COUNSEL

Day R. Shields

ASSOCIATES

Joseph Brachfeld
Eric M. Higgins
William A. Harrison
Daniel M. Young
Angelo A. Ziotas

(See Next Column)

WOFSEY, ROSEN, KWESKIN & KURIANSKY LLP—*Continued*

Representative Clients: Banque Paribas; Benenson Realty; Cellular Information Systems, Inc.; The Chase Manhattan Bank; First County Bank; Hartford Provision Co.; Louis Dreyfus Corp.; Norwalk Federation of Teachers; People's Bank; Ridgeway Shopping Center.

For full biographical listings, see the Martindale-Hubbell Law Directory

WESTPORT, Fairfield Co.

BLAZZARD, GRODD & HASENAUER, P.C. (AV)

943 Post Road East, P.O. Box 5108, 06881
Telephone: 203-226-7866
Telecopier: 203-454-4855
Lauderdale-By-the-Sea Office: Suite 207, W. Tradewinds Avenue, 33308.
Telephone: 954-771-6667.
Facsimile: 954-771-7689. E-Mail: BGHFL@AOL.COM

Norse N. Blazzard
Leslie E. Grodd
Judith A. Hasenauer
William E. Hasenauer
Raymond A. O'Hara, III
Lynn Korman Stone

Peter L. Cejas (Not admitted in CT)

For full biographical listings, see the Martindale-Hubbell Law Directory

LEVETT ROCKWOOD P.C. (AV)

33 Riverside Avenue, P.O. Box 5116, 06881
Telephone: 203-222-0885
Telecopier: 203-226-8025

Suzanne B. Albani
Robert O. Barberi
Edward B. Chansky
Madeleine F. Grossman
Dorit Schutzengel Heimer
Cheryl L. Johnson
Marc J. Kurzman
David R. Levett
Judy A. Rabkin
Sharon M. Schweitzer
Steven M. Siegelaub
Peter H. Struzzi
Barbara A. Young

OF COUNSEL

William O. Rockwood, Jr.

Debra R. Cardinali
Stephen M. Cowherd
Christopher M. Graham
Robin K. Higgins
Douglas R. Sansted
Rodger F. Smith, Jr.
Patricia D. Weitzman

Representative Clients: Cannondale Corp.; Caradon, Inc.; DataViz, Inc.; Dooney & Bourke, Inc.; GAF Corporation; Heyman Properties; Hospital of Saint Raphael; Marketing Corporation of America; Olin Corporation; St. Vincent's Medical Center.

For full biographical listings, see the Martindale-Hubbell Law Directory

RONALD L. SHEIMAN (AV)

1804 Post Road East, 06880
Telephone: 203-259-0599
Telecopier: 203-255-2570

For full biographical listings, see the Martindale-Hubbell Law Directory

DELAWARE

*WILMINGTON,** New Castle Co.

MORRIS, NICHOLS, ARSHT & TUNNELL (AV)

1201 North Market Street, P.O. Box 1347, 19899-1347
Telephone: 302-658-9200
Telecopier: 302-658-3989
URL: http://www.mnat.com

MEMBERS OF FIRM

Richard L. Sutton
Johannes R. Krahmer
O. Francis Biondi
Lewis S. Black, Jr.
Paul Welsh
William O. LaMotte, III
Douglas E. Whitney
William H. Sudell, Jr.
Martin P. Tully
Thomas R. Hunt, Jr.
A. Gilchrist Sparks, III
Richard D. Allen
David Ley Hamilton
John F. Johnston
Walter C. Tuthill
Donald F. Parsons, Jr.
Jack B. Blumenfeld
Donald Nelson Isken
Donald E. Reid
Denison H. Hatch, Jr.
Thomas C. Grimm
Kenneth J. Nachbar
Andrew M. Johnston
Mary B. Graham
Michael Houghton
Matthew B. Lehr
Thomas R. Pulsifer
Jon E. Abramczyk
Alan J. Stone
Louis G. Hering
Frederick H. Alexander
R. Judson Scaggs, Jr.
William M. Lafferty
Karen Jacobs Louden

(See Next Column)

MEMBERS OF FIRM (Continued)

Donna L. Culver
Julia Heaney
Jonathan I. Lessner
Robert J. Dehney
Colm F. Connolly

ASSOCIATES

Rachel A. Dwares
Jeffrey R. Wolters
Maryellen Noreika
David J. Teklits
S. Mark Hurd
Rodger D. Smith
Lisa K. W. Crossland
Eric D. Schwartz
Lucinda C. Cucuzzella
Mona A. Lee
Stanford L. Stevenson, III
J. Andrew Huffman
Derek C. Abbott
Jessica Zeldin
Bradley James Enna
David A. Harris
Elizabeth A. Brown
Patricia A. O'Neill
Gregory W. Werkheiser
Wendy L. Walter
Christopher F. Carlton
Stephanie L. Nagel
Joelle E. Polesky
Richard W. Ellis
Francis X. Gorman
John D. Pirnot
Megan E. Ward

COUNSEL

Andrew B. Kirkpatrick, Jr.
David A. Drexler
Walter L. Pepperman, II

DECEASED PARTNERS

Hugh M. Morris (1878-1966)
Alexander L. Nichols (1906-1985)
James M. Tunnell, Jr. (1910-1986)
S. Samuel Arsht (1910-1999)

Representative Clients: AstraZeneca Inc.; The Chase Manhattan Bank (USA); The Coca-Cola Company; Data General Corporation; Ford Motor Company; J.P. Morgan & Co. Incorporated; McDonald's Corporation; Merck & Co., Inc.; Texaco Inc.; U S West, Inc.

For full biographical listings, see the Martindale-Hubbell Law Directory

POTTER ANDERSON & CORROON LLP (AV)

Hercules Plaza, 1313 N. Market Street, P.O. Box 951, 19899-0951
Telephone: 302-984-6000
Fax: 302-658-1192
URL: http://www.attys.pacdelaware.com

MEMBERS OF FIRM

Leonard S. Togman
Mary E. Copper
Scott E. Waxman

ASSOCIATE

John A. Ciccarone

Representative Clients: Eastman Chemical Products, Inc.; Aramco Services Company; Republic National Bank of New York; SAFRA National Bank of New York.

For Complete List of Firm Personnel, See General Section

For full biographical listings, see the Martindale-Hubbell Law Directory

RICHARDS, LAYTON & FINGER, P.A. (AV)

One Rodney Square, P.O. Box 551, 19899
Telephone: 302-658-6541
Telecopier: 302-658-6548

Thomas P. Sweeney
Richard G. Bacon
Julian H. Baumann, Jr.
W. Donald Sparks, II

For Complete List of Firm Personnel, See General Section

For full biographical listings, see the Martindale-Hubbell Law Directory

SCHLUSSER & REIVER, P.A. (AV)

1700 West 14th Street, 19806
Telephone: 302-655-8181
Fax: 302-655-8190

Robert E. Schlusser
Joanna Reiver
George W. Kern, V

For full biographical listings, see the Martindale-Hubbell Law Directory

DISTRICT OF COLUMBIA

WASHINGTON, D.C. Co.

BAKER BOTTS L.L.P. (AV)

A Registered Limited Liability Partnership
The Warner, 1299 Pennsylvania Avenue, N.W., 20004-2400
Telephone: 202-639-7700
Fax: 202-639-7832
Email: postmaster@bakerbotts.com *URL:* http://www.bakerbotts.com
Houston, Texas Office: One Shell Plaza, 910 Louisiana.
Telephone: 713-229-1234.
Austin, Texas Office: 1600 San Jacinto Center, 98 San Jacinto Boulevard.
Telephone: 512-322-2500.

(See Next Column)

BAKER BOTTS L.L.P., *Washington—Continued*

Dallas, Texas Office: 2001 Ross Avenue.
Telephone: 214-953-6500.
New York, New York Office: 599 Lexington Avenue.
Telephone: 212-705-5000.
Moscow, Russia Office: 10 ul. Bolshaya Dimitrovka (formerly Pushkinskaya), 103031.
Telephone: 7095/921-5300 (Local); 7501/929-7070 (International).
London, England Office: 45 Ludgate Hill.
Telephone: 0171-778-1400 (Local); 011-44-171-778-1400 (International).
Baku, Azerbaijan Office: 6-10 Vagif Mustafa-zadeh Street, Third Floor, Icheri Sheher, 370004.
Telephone: 994-12-97-63-88 (Local); 011-994-12-97-63-88 (International).

MEMBERS OF FIRM

James A. Baker IV — O. Donaldson Chapoton

ASSOCIATES

Jane Boland Keough — Tamar C. Stanley

For Complete List of Firm Personnel, See General Section

For full biographical listings, see the Martindale-Hubbell Law Directory

BAKER & HOSTETLER LLP (AV)

Washington Square, Suite 1100, 1050 Connecticut Avenue, N.W., 20036-5304
Telephone: 202-861-1500
Fax: 202-861-1783
To contact an attorney on the Internet use first initial and surname followed by @baker-hostetler.com
URL: http://www.bakerlaw.com
In Cleveland, Ohio: 3200 National City Center, 1900 East Ninth Street.
Telephone: 216-621-0200.
In Cincinnati, Ohio: 312 Walnut Street, Suite 2650.
Telephone: 513-929-3400.
In Columbus, Ohio: Capitol Square, Suite 2100, 65 East State Street.
Telephone: 614-228-1541.
In Denver, Colorado: 303 East 17th Avenue, Suite 1100.
Telephone: 303-861-0600.
In Houston, Texas: 1000 Louisiana, Suite 2000.
Telephone: 713-751-1600.
In Beverly Hills, California: 9150 Wilshire Boulevard, Suite 205.
Telephone: 310-385-7500.
In Long Beach, California: 300 Oceangate, Suite 620.
Telephone: 562-432-2827.
In Los Angeles, California: 600 Wilshire Boulevard.
Telephone: 213-624-2400.
In Orlando, Florida: SunBank Center, Suite 2300, 200 South Orange Avenue.
Telephone: 407-649-4000.

PARTNER

William F. Conroy

RETIRED PARTNER

Harlan Pomeroy

For Complete List of Firm Personnel, See General Section

For full biographical listings, see the Martindale-Hubbell Law Directory

BALLARD SPAHR ANDREWS & INGERSOLL, LLP (AV)

Suite 1000 South, 601 13th Street, N.W., 20005-3807
Telephone: 202-661-2200
Fax: 202-661-2299
URL: http://www.ballardspahr.com
Baltimore, Maryland Office: 300 East Lombard Street, 19th Floor.
Telephone: 410-528-5600.
Fax: 410-528-5650.
Camden, New Jersey Office: 800 Hudson Square, 5th Floor.
Telephone: 856-541-5577.
Fax: 856-541-8772.
Denver, Colorado Office: Seventeenth Street Plaza Building, Suite 2300, 1225 17th Street.
Telephone: 303-292-2400.
Fax: 303-296-3956.
Philadelphia, Pennsylvania Office: 1735 Market Street, 51st Floor.
Telephone: 215-665-8500.
Fax: 215-834-8999.
Salt Lake City, Utah Office: 201 South Main Street, Suite 1200.
Telephone: 801-531-3000.
Fax: 801-531-3001.
Voorhees, New Jersey Office: Suite 100, 1101 Laurel Oak Drive.
Telephone: 856-627-8555.
Fax: 856-627-1153.

Frederic L. Ballard, Jr. — Charles S. Henck
Linda B. Schakel

For Complete List of Firm Personnel, See General Section

For full biographical listings, see the Martindale-Hubbell Law Directory

LAW OFFICES OF BINSTOCK, TORCHINSKY AND ASSOCIATES, P.C. (AV)

1140 Connecticut Avenue, N.W., Suite 703, 20036
Telephone: 301-657-5555
Fax: 301-657-9871
Email: shelbin@erols.com *URL:* http://www.lawyers.com/binstock_torchinsky
Chevy Chase, Maryland Office: 5454 Wisconsin Avenue, Suite 1340.
Telephone: 301-657-5555.
Fax: 301-657-9871.

Shelton M. Binstock — David B. Torchinsky

OF COUNSEL

Andrew S. Unger — George R. Adams

For full biographical listings, see the Martindale-Hubbell Law Directory

CAPLIN & DRYSDALE, CHARTERED (AV)

One Thomas Circle, N.W., 20005
Telephone: 202-862-5000
Cable Address: "Capdale"
Telex: 904001 CAPL UR WSH
Fax: 202-429-3301
URL: http://www.caplindrysdale.com
New York, N.Y. Office: 399 Park Avenue, 36th Floor.
Telephone: 212-319-7125.
Fax: 212-644-6755.

Mortimer M. Caplin
Thomas A. Troyer
David N. Webster
H. David Rosenbloom
Peter Van N. Lockwood
Richard W. Skillman
Patricia G. Lewis
Bernard S. Bailor
Albert G. Lauber, Jr.
Julie W. Davis
Trevor W. Swett III
James E. Salles
Craig A. Sharon
Catherine E. Livingston
Seth M. Green
Douglas D. Drysdale
Ralph A. Muoio
Elihu Inselbuch (Resident, New York Office)
Cono R. Namorato
Daniel B. Rosenbaum
Richard E. Timbie
Stafford Smiley
Scott D. Michel
Kent A. Mason
Robert A. Boisture
Milton Cerny
Matthew W. Frank
Jessica L. Katz
Christopher S. Rizek

Nathan D. Finch
Douglas N. Varley
Neal M. Kochman
Jason K. Bortz (Not admitted in DC)
April J. Adams (Not admitted in DC)
Elizabeth M. Sellers
Lloyd H. Mayer
Rita C. Tobin (Resident, New York Office)
H. Carter Hood (Not admitted in DC)

OF COUNSEL

Robert H. Elliott, Jr. — Myron C. Baum
Ann C. McMillan

For full biographical listings, see the Martindale-Hubbell Law Directory

CROSS, MURPHY, SMUCK & HOUSTON (AV)

1350 Connecticut Avenue, N.W., Suite 300, 20036
Telephone: 202-393-8668
Telecopier: 202-833-2351
Email: anwalt1350@aol.com *URL:* http://www.lawyers.com/cms&hlaw

MEMBERS OF FIRM

John W. Cross (1902-1971)
James Russell Murphy (1905-1986)
John C. Smuck
Stuart E. Houston

Reference: Crestar Bank, N.A.

For full biographical listings, see the Martindale-Hubbell Law Directory

DOW, LOHNES & ALBERTSON, PLLC (AV)

1200 New Hampshire Avenue, N.W. Suite 800, 20036-6802
Telephone: 202-776-2000
Facsimile: 202-776-2222
Email: info@dlalaw.com *URL:* http://www.dlalaw.com
Atlanta, Georgia Office: One Ravinia Drive, Suite 1600.
Telephone: 770-901-8800.
Telecopier: 770-901-8874.

MEMBERS OF THE FIRM

Corinne M. Antley
Richard L. Braunstein
Linda A. Fritts
Joyce Trimble Gwadz
J. Michael Hines
John C. Jost
Bernard J. Long, Jr.
Stephanie M. Loughlin
John D. Ward

Kevin P. Brandon
John E. Hinding
Anna Hong Kim (Not admitted in DC)
Stephen E. Lopez
James R. Saxenian

(See Next Column)

DOW, LOHNES & ALBERTSON PLLC—*Continued*

For Complete List of Firm Personnel, See General Section

For full biographical listings, see the Martindale-Hubbell Law Directory

FRIED, FRANK, HARRIS, SHRIVER & JACOBSON (AV)

A Partnership including Professional Corporations
Suite 800, 1001 Pennsylvania Avenue, N.W., 20004-2505
Telephone: 202-639-7000
Telecopy: 202-639-7008
Email: info@ffhsj.com
New York, New York Office: One New York Plaza.
Telephone: 212-859-8000.
Cable Address: "Steric New York." W.U. Intl.
Telex: 662119. W.U. Domestic: 128173.
Telecopier: 212-859-4000 (Dex 6200).
Los Angeles, California Office: 350 South Grand Avenue, 32nd Floor.
Telephone: 213-473-2000.
London, England Office: 4 Chiswell Street, London EC1Y 4UP.
Telephone: 011-44-171-972-9600.
Fax: 011-44-171-972-9602.
Other London, England Office: International Securities Unit, 21 Wilson Street, London EC2M 2TX.
Telephone: 011-44-171-825-3093.
Paris, France Office: 7, Rue Royale, 75008.
Telephone: (011 331) 40-17-04-04.
Fax: (011 331) 40-17-08-30.

WASHINGTON, D.C. PARTNERS

Peter V. Z. Cobb (Not admitted in DC)
Alan S. Kaden

OF COUNSEL

Martin D. Ginsburg (P.C.)

For Complete List of Firm Personnel, See General Section

For full biographical listings, see the Martindale-Hubbell Law Directory

HOPKINS & SUTTER (AV)

A Partnership including Professional Corporations
888 Sixteenth Street, N.W., 20006
Telephone: 202-835-8000
Fax: 202-835-8136
Email: postmaster@hopsut.com *URL:* http://www.hopsut.com
Chicago, Illinois Office: Three First National Plaza.
Telephone: 312-558-6600.
Telex: 206231.
Fax: 312-558-6538.
Troy, Michigan Office: 2800 Livernois, Suite 220.
Telephone: 248-740-6600.
Fax: 248-740-6613.

PARTNERS

Gordon O. Pehrson, Jr.
Richard F. Riley, Jr.

ASSOCIATE

Bobby L. Dexter

For Complete List of Firm Personnel, See General Section

For full biographical listings, see the Martindale-Hubbell Law Directory

IVINS, PHILLIPS & BARKER, CHARTERED (AV)

Suite 600, 1700 Pennsylvania Avenue, N.W., 20006
Telephone: 202-393-7600
Fax: 202-393-7601; 347-4256
Email: IPB@ipbtax.com *URL:* http://www.ipbtax.com

H. Stewart Dunn, Jr.
Carroll J. Savage
Eric R. Fox
William L. Sollee
Carol K. Nickel
Leslie Jay Schneider
Robert H. Wellen
Kevin P. O'Brien
Michael F. Solomon
Daniel B. Stone
Patrick J. Smith
Michael R. Huffstetler
Laurie E. Keenan
Jeffrey E. Moeller
Steven H. Witmer
Rosina B. Barker
Claude B. Stansbury

Jodi H. Epstein

OF COUNSEL

Jay W. Glasmann

For full biographical listings, see the Martindale-Hubbell Law Directory

JONES, DAY, REAVIS & POGUE (AV)

51 Louisiana Avenue, N.W., 20001-2113
Telephone: 202-879-3939
Telecopier: 202-626-1700
Email: counsel@jonesday.com *URL:* http://www.jonesday.com
In Atlanta, Georgia: 3500 SunTrust Plaza, 303 Peachtree Street.
Telephone: 404-521-3939.
Telecopier: 404-581-8330.

(See Next Column)

In Brussels, Belgium: Avenue Louise 480, 7th Floor, B-1050 Brussels.
Telephone: 32-2-645-14-11.
Telecopier: 32-2-645-14-45.
In Chicago, Illinois: 77 West Wacker.
Telephone: 312-782-3939.
Telecopier: 312-782-8585.
In Cleveland, Ohio: North Point, 901 Lakeside Avenue.
Telephone: 216-586-3939.
Telecopier: 216-579-0212.
In Columbus, Ohio: 1900 Huntington Center.
Telephone: 614-469-3939.
Telecopier: 614-461-4198.
In Dallas, Texas: 2727 North Harwood Street.
Telephone: 214-220-3939.
Telecopier: 214-969-5100.
In Frankfurt, Germany: Hochhaus am Park, Grüneburgweg 102, 60323, Frankfurt am Main.
Telephone: 49-69-9726-3939.
Telecopier: 49-69-9726-3993.
In Geneva, Switzerland: 20, rue de Candolle.
Telephone: 41-22-320-2339.
Telecopier: 41-22-320-1232.
In Hong Kong: 29th Floor, Entertainment Building, 30 Queen's Road Central.
Telephone: 852-2526-6895.
Telecopier: 852-2868-5871.
In Irvine, California: 5 Park Plaza, Suite 1100.
Telephone: 949-851-3939.
Telecopier: 949-553-7539.
In London, England: Bucklersbury House, 3 Queen Victoria Street.
Telephone: 44-171-236-3939.
Telecopier: 44-171-236-1113.
In Los Angeles, California: 555 West Fifth Street, Suite 4600.
Telephone: 213-489-3939.
Telecopier: 213-243-2539.
In New Delhi, India (Associate Office): Pathak & Associates (an associate firm of Jones, Day, Reavis & Pogue), 1st Floor, Dr. Gopal Das Bhaven, 28 Barakhamba Road.
Telephone: 91-11-373-8793.; 91-11-335-7345.
Telecopier: 91-11-335-3761.
In New York, New York: 599 Lexington Avenue.
Telephone: 212-326-3939.
Telecopier: 212-755-7306.
In Paris, France: 120, rue du Faubourg Saint-Honoré.
Telephone: 33-1-56-59-39-39.
Telecopier: 33-1-56-59-39-38
In Pittsburgh, Pennsylvania: 500 Grant Street, 31st Floor.
Telephone: 412-391-3939.
Telecopier: 412-394-7959.
In Riyadh, Saudi Arabia: The International Law Firm (In Association with Jones, Day, Reavis & Pogue), Sulaymaniyah, Prince Mishari IBN, Abdulaziz Street, P.O. Box 22166.
Telephone: (966-1) 462-8866.
Telecopier: (966-1) 462-9001.
In Shanghai, China: 2805 Kerry Centre, 1515 Nanjing Road West.
Telephone: 86-21-5298-6568.
Telecopier: 86-21-5298-6569.
In Sydney, Australia: Governor Phillip Tower, Level 38, 1 Farrer Place.
Telephone: 61-2-9210-6921.
Telecopier: 61-2-9210-6926.
In Taipei, Taiwan: 8th Floor, 2 Tun Hwa South Road, Section 2.
Telephone: (886-2) 2704-6808.
Telecopier: (886-2) 2704-6791.
In Tokyo, Japan: Toranomon MT Building, 4th Floor, 10-3, Toranomon 3-Chome, Minato-Ku, Tokyo 105, Japan.
Telephone: 81-3-3433-3939.
Telecopier: 81-3-5401-2725.

MEMBERS OF FIRM IN WASHINGTON, D.C.

Joseph S. Iannucci
James T. O'Hara
Lester W. Droller
Raymond J. Wiacek
Candace A. Ridgway

COUNSEL

Charles V. Stewart

ASSOCIATES

Joseph A. Goldman
Richard L. Winston

For Complete List of Firm Personnel, See General Section

For full biographical listings, see the Martindale-Hubbell Law Directory

MOORE & BRUCE, LLP (AV)

1072 Thomas Jefferson Street, N.W., 20007
Telephone: 202-965-5300
Facsimile: 202-965-7745
URL: http://www.lawyers.com/moore&brucellp

Charles M. Bruce
Jonathon R. Moore

OF COUNSEL

Mark A. Cohen
Michael C. Durney
William Morris

For full biographical listings, see the Martindale-Hubbell Law Directory

Washington—Continued

O'CONNOR & HANNAN, L.L.P. (AV)

Suite 500, 1666 K Street, N.W., 20006
Telephone: 202-887-1400
Telecopy: 202-466-2198
Vienna, Virginia Office: 8300 Boone Boulevard, Suite 554.
Telephone: 703-714-6670.
Fax: 703-848-4586.
Madrid, Spain Office: La Rinconada, 6, 3°.
Telephone: +34-1-575-0944; +34-1-357-2251.
Fax: +34-1-577-0759.

MEMBER OF FIRM

John S. Jagiela (Not admitted in DC)

OF COUNSEL

Moshe Schuldinger

For Complete List of Firm Personnel, See General Section

For full biographical listings, see the Martindale-Hubbell Law Directory

RITTER EICHNER & NORRIS, PLLC (AV)

The Jefferson Building, 1225 19th Street, N.W., 7th Floor, 20036
Telephone: 202-973-0100
Fax: 202-296-6990

MEMBERS OF FIRM

C. Willis Ritter
Richard A. Eichner
R. Wade Norris (Not admitted in DC)

ASSOCIATES

Craig S. Thomas (Not admitted in DC)
Matthew J. Bissonette
Robert A. Wrzosek

For full biographical listings, see the Martindale-Hubbell Law Directory

SILVERSTEIN AND MULLENS, P.L.L.C. (AV)

1776 K Street, N.W., 20006
Telephone: 202-452-7900
Telex: 64426
Telecopier: 202-452-7989
Email: silvmul@silvmul.com

MEMBERS OF FIRM

Leonard L. Silverstein
Gerald H. Sherman
Stuart M. Lewis
Ronald D. Abramson
John P. Warner
Donald B. Reynolds, Jr.
Patrick G. Dooher
David I. Kempler
David H. Dickieson
James J. Freedman
Aen W. Webster
Louis H. Diamond
Linda K. Shore
Gary K. Bahena
Deborah M. Beers
Carmen Irizarry-Díaz
Keith A. Mong

ASSOCIATES

Patricia R. Lesser
John S. Ross, III
Richard S. Marshall
Carmela T. Montesano
Ruth C. Shaw
Norma M. Sharara (Not admitted in DC)
Carol P. Tello
Gita Khadiri
Mary M. Baker
Jennifer M. Roof
James D. Douglas (Not admitted in DC)
Laura A. Baek (Not admitted in DC)

OF COUNSEL

Richard A. Mullens
James C. Corman
Harrison B. McCawley

For full biographical listings, see the Martindale-Hubbell Law Directory

VINYARD & ASSOCIATES (AV)

Columbia Square, 555 13th Street, N.W., 20004-1109
Telephone: 202-637-6838
Facsimile: 202-637-5910
Telex: 248370 (RCA)

Walter Darnall Vinyard

For full biographical listings, see the Martindale-Hubbell Law Directory

WEBSTER, CHAMBERLAIN & BEAN (AV)

Suite 1000, 1747 Pennsylvania Avenue, N.W., 20006
Telephone: 202-785-9500
Fax: 202-835-0243

MEMBERS OF FIRM

Arthur L. Herold
Alan P. Dye
Edward D. Coleman
Frank M. Northam
John W. Hazard, Jr.
Hugh K. Webster

OF COUNSEL

Charles E. Chamberlain
J. Coleman Bean
Kent Masterson Brown (Not admitted in DC)
Burkett Van Kirk
James Bopp, Jr. (Not admitted in DC)

(See Next Column)

ASSOCIATES

Charles M. Watkins
David P. Goch
Brenley Locke Elias
Raymond Cashen, II (Not admitted in DC)

For full biographical listings, see the Martindale-Hubbell Law Directory

WILLIAMS & CONNOLLY (AV)

725 Twelfth Street, N.W., 20005-5901
Telephone: 202-434-5000
Fax: 202-434-5029

MEMBERS OF FIRM

Lewis H. Ferguson, III
James T. Fuller, III
Mary Greer Clark
Lon E. Musslewhite

OF COUNSEL

Lyman G. Friedman

For Complete List of Firm Personnel, See General Section

For full biographical listings, see the Martindale-Hubbell Law Directory

WILMER, CUTLER & PICKERING (AV)

2445 M Street, N.W., 20037-1420
Telephone: 202-663-6000
Fax: 202-663-6363
Email: Law@Wilmer.Com *URL:* http://www.wilmer.com
Baltimore, Maryland Office: 100 Light Street, 21202.
Telephone: 410-986-2800.
Fax: 410-986-2828.
New York, New York Office: 520 Madison Avenue, 10022.
Telephone: 212-230-8800.
Fax: 212-230-8888.
European Offices:
4 Carlton Gardens, London, SW1Y 5AA, England. Telephone: +44 (20) 7 872 1000.
Fax: +44 (20) 7 839 3537.
Rue de la Loi 15# Wetstraat, B-1040 Brussels, Belgium. Telephone: +32 (2) 285 49 00.
Fax: +32 (2) 285 49 49.
Friedrichstrasse 95, D-10117 Berlin, Germany. Telephone: +49 (30) 20 22 64 00.
Fax: +49 (30) 20 22 65 00.

MEMBERS OF FIRM

F. David Lake, Jr.
Kenneth W. Gideon
William J. Wilkins
Terrill A. Hyde
Robert B. Stack
R. Scott Kilgore
Erik H. Corwin

COUNSEL

Brian J. Menkes

For Complete List of Firm Personnel, See General Section

For full biographical listings, see the Martindale-Hubbell Law Directory

FLORIDA

BOCA RATON, Palm Beach Co.

RONALD T. MARTIN P.A. (AV)

Suite 200, 7000 West Palmetto Park Road, 33433
Telephone: 561-338-4100
Fax: 561-338-9086
Email: RonTMartin@aol.com

Ronald T. Martin

For full biographical listings, see the Martindale-Hubbell Law Directory

DELRAY BEACH, Palm Beach Co.

ROBERT M. ARLEN, P.A. (AV)

110 East Atlantic Avenue, Suite 330, 33444
Telephone: 561-279-1880
Telefax: 561-278-1995

Robert M. Arlen

For full biographical listings, see the Martindale-Hubbell Law Directory

*FORT LAUDERDALE,** Broward Co.

BERGER DAVIS & SINGERMAN (AV)

350 East Las Olas Boulevard, Suite 1000, 33301
Telephone: 954-525-9900
Fax: 954-523-2872
Email: jberger@bdslaw.com *URL:* http://www.bdslaw.com
Miami, Florida Office: 200 South Biscayne Boulevard, Suite 2950.
Telephone: 305-755-9500.
Fax: 305-714-4340.

(See Next Column)

BERGER DAVIS & SINGERMAN—*Continued*

Tallahassee, Florida Office: 215 South Monroe Street, Suite 705, 32301.
Telephone: 850-561-3010.
Fax: 850-561-3013.

James L. Berger
Mitchell W. Berger
Franklin H. Caplan (Resident, Miami Office)
James B. Davis
Henry H. (Bucky) Fox
Van P. Geeker (Resident, Tallahassee Office)
Jordi Guso (Resident, Miami Office)
Nick Jovanovich
Robert B. Judd
Manuel Kushner
Daniel Lampert
Dawn M. Meyers
John D. C. Newton, II (Resident, Tallahassee Office)
Samuel E. Poole III
Leonard K. Samuels
Laz L. Schneider
Paul Steven Singerman (Resident, Miami Office)
Daniel H. Thompson (Resident, Tallahassee Office)

Robert W. Barron
Maria St. John Daugherty
James Harris Fierberg (Resident, Miami Office)
Ilyse Wrubel Homer (Resident, Miami Office)
Sherry A. Lambson
Lisa D. MacClugage
Brian G. Rich (Resident, Miami Office)
Holiday Hunt Russell
Jonathan C. Vair (Resident, Miami Office)
Jeffrey Scott Wertman

OF COUNSEL

James C. Cunningham, Jr.
Fred Goldberg

For full biographical listings, see the Martindale-Hubbell Law Directory

*FORT MYERS,** Lee Co.

HENDERSON, FRANKLIN, STARNES & HOLT, PROFESSIONAL ASSOCIATION (AV)

1715 Monroe Street, P.O. Box 280, 33902-0280
Telephone: 941-334-4121
Telecopier: 941-332-4494

William N. Horowitz
Guy E. Whitesman
Thomas P. Clark
Theresa M. Kolish
Grace Gutierrez
Neil R. Jetter

Representative Clients: CIGNA Group; CSX Transportation, Inc.; Fireman's Fund Insurance Cos.; The Hartford Insurance Group; Huntington National Bank, N.A.; NationsBank, N.A.; Travelers/Aetna Insurance Group; Sprint-Florida, Inc.

For Complete List of Firm Personnel, See General Section

For full biographical listings, see the Martindale-Hubbell Law Directory

*JACKSONVILLE,** Duval Co.

ANDERSON & STEVENS, P.A. (AV)

Suite 2640, Riverplace Tower, 1301 Riverplace Boulevard, 32207-9039
Telephone: 904-399-8000
Telecopier: 904-346-3078

Kenneth G. Anderson
James P. Stevens

Rose Marie Karadsheh Preddy

For full biographical listings, see the Martindale-Hubbell Law Directory

WILLIAM R. BLACKARD, JR. (AV)

Suite 800 121 W. Forsyth Street, 32202
Telephone: 904-354-4400
Facsimile: 904-354-5552

For full biographical listings, see the Martindale-Hubbell Law Directory

DONAHOO, BALL & MCMENAMY, P.A. (AV)

(Incorporated in 1982)
50 North Laura Street, Suite 2925, 32202
Telephone: 904-354-8080
Fax: 904-791-9563
Email: office@donahooball.com

John W. Donahoo (1907-1993)
Thomas M. Donahoo
Haywood M. Ball
William B. McMenamy
Thomas M. Donahoo, Jr.

For full biographical listings, see the Martindale-Hubbell Law Directory

FRAZIER & FRAZIER, ATTORNEYS AT LAW, P.A. (AV)

Suite A, 1515 Riverside Avenue, 32204
Telephone: 904-353-5616
Fax: 904-353-5619

William R. Frazier
W. Robinson Frazier

References: First Union National Bank of Florida; First Guaranty Bank & Trust Co.

(See Next Column)

For full biographical listings, see the Martindale-Hubbell Law Directory

SMITH HULSEY & BUSEY (AV)

1800 First Union National Bank Tower, 225 Water Street, P.O. Box 53315, 32201-3315
Telephone: 904-359-7700
Facsimile: 904-359-7708; 353-9908
Email: vsharp@smithhulsey.com

Lloyd Smith (1915-1987)

MEMBERS OF FIRM

Stephen D. Busey
Earl E. Googe, Jr.
Jeanne E. Helton
Cynthia C. Jackson
G. Preston Keyes
Richard E. Klein
William E. Kuntz
Lauren P. Langham
M. Richard Lewis, Jr.
John F. MacLennan
Raymond R. Magley
E. Owen McCuller, Jr.
James H. Post
Bryan L. Putnal
E. Lanny Russell
Joel Settembrini, Jr.
Tim E. Sleeth
John R. Smith, Jr.
Harry M. Wilson, III

Brandon L. Ayscue
Brannon B. Belcastro
James A. Bolling, Jr.
Charmaine T.M. Chiu
Ryan C. Curtis
Michael R. Freed
Reynold N. Hoover
Michael J. Ivan, Jr.
Tonya L. Janney
Charles H. Keller
Bradley R. Markey
R. Leanne McKnight
Bert J. Millis
Stephen D. Moore, Jr.
Jon L. Swergold

OF COUNSEL

Mark Hulsey
John E. Thrasher

Representative Clients: ATP Tour, Inc; Baptist/St. Vincent's Health System, Inc.; Browning-Ferris Industries, Inc.; First Union National Bank of Florida; Florida Rock Industries, Inc.; PGA Tour, Inc.; KPMG Peat Marwick; The Regency Group, Inc.; The Ritz-Carlton Hotel Co.; University of Florida.

For full biographical listings, see the Martindale-Hubbell Law Directory

JUPITER, Palm Beach Co.

JOSEPH C. KEMPE PROFESSIONAL ASSOCIATION (AV)

Attorneys and Counselors at Law
941 North Highway AIA, 33477-5111
Telephone: 561-747-7300
FAX: 561-747-7722
Email: JCKempe@msn.com *URL:* http://www.jckempe.com
Stuart, Florida Office: Royal Palm Financial Center II, Suite 200, 789 South Federal Highway.
Telephone: 561-223-0700.
Fax: 561-223-0707.
Vero Beach, Florida Office: 664 Azalea Lane, Suite B.
Telephone: 561-562-4022.
Fax: 561-234-1422.

Joseph C. Kempe

Harry S. Colburn Jr.

For full biographical listings, see the Martindale-Hubbell Law Directory

LAKELAND, Polk Co.

PETERSON & MYERS, P.A. (AV)

100 East Main Street, P.O. Box 24628, 33802-4628
Telephone: 941-683-6511; 676-6934
Telecopier: 941-682-8031
Lake Wales, Florida Office: 130 East Central Avenue, P.O. Box 1079.
Telephones: 941-676-7611; 683-8942.
Winter Haven, Florida Office: Lake Region Plaza, 141 5th Street, N.W., P.O. Drawer 7608.
Telephone: 941-294-3360.

M. David Alexander, III
Philip O. Allen
Jack P. Brandon
Kristen Marie Buzzanca
Debra Leigh Cline
J. Davis Connor
Dennis G. Corrick
Roy A. Craig, Jr.
Clinton A. Curtis
Jacob C. Dykxhoorn
Joseph A. Geary
Maria "Mia" Gerber
Jonn D. Hoppe
Dennis P. Johnson
Kevin C. Knowlton
Douglas A. Lockwood, III
Corneal B. Myers
E. Blake Paul
Robert E. Puterbaugh
Thomas B. Putnam, Jr.
Deborah A. Ruster
Stephen R. Senn
Andrea Teves Smith
Keith H. Wadsworth
Kerry M. Wilson

General Counsel for: SunTrust Bank Mid-Florida, N.A.; Lakeland Regional Medical Center, Inc.; Housing Finance Authority of Polk County.
Representative Clients: NationsBank, N.A.; First Union National Bank; Mutual Wholesale Co.; Ben Hill Griffin, Inc.; E. R. Jahna Industries, Inc.

(See Next Column)

PETERSON & MYERS P.A., *Lakeland—Continued*

Approved Attorneys for: Attorneys' Title Insurance Fund; Equitable Life Assurance Society of the United States.

For full biographical listings, see the Martindale-Hubbell Law Directory

LAKE WALES, Polk Co.

PETERSON & MYERS, P.A. (AV)

130 East Central Avenue, P.O. Box 1079, 33853
Telephone: 941-676-7611; 683-8942
Telecopier: 941-676-0643
Lakeland, Florida Office: 100 East Main Street, P.O. Box 24628.
Telephones: 941-683-6511; 676-6934.
Winter Haven, Florida Office: Lake Region Plaza, 141 5th Street, N.W., P.O. Drawer 7608.
Telephone: 941-294-3360.

M. David Alexander, III
Philip O. Allen
Jack P. Brandon
Kristen Marie Buzzanca
Debra Leigh Cline
J. Davis Connor
Dennis G. Corrick
Roy A. Craig, Jr.
Clinton A. Curtis
Jacob C. Dykxhoorn
Joseph A. Geary
Maria "Mia" Gerber
Jonn D. Hoppe
Dennis P. Johnson
Kevin C. Knowlton
Douglas A. Lockwood, III
Corneal B. Myers
E. Blake Paul
Robert E. Puterbaugh
Thomas B. Putnam, Jr.
Deborah A. Ruster
Stephen R. Senn
Andrea Teves Smith
Keith H. Wadsworth
Kerry M. Wilson

General Counsel for: SunTrust Bank Mid-Florida, N.A.; Lakeland Regional Medical Center, Inc.; Housing Finance Authority of Polk County.
Representative Clients: NationsBank, N.A.; First Union National Bank; Mutual Wholesale Co.; Ben Hill Griffin, Inc.; E. R. Jahna Industries, Inc.
Approved Attorneys for: Attorneys' Title Insurance Fund; Equitable Life Assurance Society of the United States.

For full biographical listings, see the Martindale-Hubbell Law Directory

*MIAMI,** Dade Co.

LAW OFFICES OF DAVID M. BERMAN, P.A. (AV)

13500 North Kendall Drive Suite 129, 33186
Telephone: 305-387-3351
Fax: 305-387-1929
Email: 1taxlaw@bellsouth.net

David M. Berman
Paul Franklin Berman

For full biographical listings, see the Martindale-Hubbell Law Directory

DAVID M. GARVIN, P.A. (AV)

1200 Brickell Avenue, Suite 1480, 33131
Telephone: 305-371-8101
Fax: 305-371-8848
Email: ontrial2@aol.com

David M. Garvin

For full biographical listings, see the Martindale-Hubbell Law Directory

ROBBINS, TUNKEY, ROSS, AMSEL, RABEN & WAXMAN, P.A. (AV)

2250 Southwest Third Avenue, Fourth Floor, 33129
Telephone: Dade County 305-858-9550; Broward County 954-522-6244 (All Telephones Open 24 Hours); 1-800-226-9550
Fax: 305-858-7491
Email: RTR2250@AOL.COM *URL:* http://www.crimlawfirm.com

Frederick S. Robbins
William R. Tunkey
Alan S. Ross
Robert G. Amsel
David Raben
Benjamin S. Waxman

Mark R. Eiglarsh
Marco A. Vazquez (1968-1995)

Reference: Mellon United National Bank, Miami, Florida.

For full biographical listings, see the Martindale-Hubbell Law Directory

SHUTTS & BOWEN LLP (AV)

A Partnership including Professional Associations
1500 Miami Center, 201 South Biscayne Boulevard, 33131
Telephone: 305-358-6300
Telefax: 305-381-9982
Email: MCONNORS@SHUTTS-LAW.COM *URL:* HTTP://WWW.SHUTTS-LAW.COM
Orlando, Florida Office: 20 North Orange Avenue, Suite 1000.
Telephone: 407-423-3200.
Fax: 407-425-8316.
West Palm Beach, Florida Office: One Clearlake Centre, 250 Australian Avenue, Suite 500.
Telephone: 561-835-8500.
Fax: 561-650-8530.

(See Next Column)

Tallahassee, Florida Office: 215 South Monroe Street, Suite 804.
Telephone: 850-521-0600.
Fax: 850-521-0604.
Fort Lauderdale, Florida Office: First Union Center, Suite 2000, 200 East Broward Boulevard.
Telephone: 954-524-5505.
Fax: 954-524-5506.
Amsterdam, The Netherlands Office: Shutts & Bowen, B.V., Europa Boulevard 59, 1083 AD, Amsterdam.
Telephone: (31 20) 661-0969.
Fax: (31 20) 642-1475.
London, England Office: 43 Grosvenor Street, London W1X 9PG.
Telephone: 441-71-493-4840.
Telefax: 441-71-493-4299.

MEMBERS OF FIRM

Gary J. Cohen
Robert E. Gunn (P.A.) (Resident at West Palm Beach Office)
Louis Nostro
Raul J. Salas
John B. White (P.A.)

ASSOCIATES

Michael J. Rosenbaum
Derek A. Schwartz
Miguel A. Silva

OF COUNSEL

Marshall J. Langer (P.A.) (Resident at London, England Office)
Stephen L. Perrone (P.A.)
Rosemarie N. Sanderson Schade (P.A.) (Resident at Amsterdam, The Netherlands Office)

For Complete List of Firm Personnel, See General Section

For full biographical listings, see the Martindale-Hubbell Law Directory

SPENCER AND KLEIN, PROFESSIONAL ASSOCIATION (AV)

Suite 1901, 801 Brickell Avenue, 33131
Telephone: 305-374-7700
Telecopier: 305-374-4890
Email: SandK@primenet.com

Brent D. Klein

Representative Clients: America Publishing Group; American Association of Physicians and Surgeons; Chrysler Corporation; Coldwell Banker; Editorial Televisa; Grupo Anaya, S.A.; Independent Living Care, Inc.; Managed Care of America, Inc.; New Times, Inc.; Winn-Dixie Stores.

For Complete List of Firm Personnel, See General Section

For full biographical listings, see the Martindale-Hubbell Law Directory

*ORLANDO,** Orange Co.

BAKER & HOSTETLER LLP (AV)

SunBank Center, Suite 2300, 200 South Orange Avenue, 32802-3432
Telephone: 407-649-4000
Fax: 407-841-0168
To contact an attorney on the Internet use first initial and surname followed by @baker-hostetler.com
URL: http://www.bakerlaw.com
In Cleveland, Ohio: 3200 National City Center, 1900 East Ninth Street.
Telephone: 216-621-0200.
In Cincinnati, Ohio: 312 Walnut Street, Suite 2650.
Telephone: 513-929-3400.
In Columbus, Ohio: Capitol Square, Suite 2100, 65 East State Street.
Telephone: 614-228-1541.
In Denver, Colorado: 303 East 17th Avenue, Suite 1100.
Telephone: 303-861-0600.
In Houston, Texas: 1000 Louisiana, Suite 2000.
Telephone: 713-751-1600.
In Long Beach, California: 300 Oceangate, Suite 620.
Telephone: 362-432-2827.
In Los Angeles, California: 600 Wilshire Boulevard.
Telephone: 213-624-2400.
In Washington, D. C.: Washington Square, Suite 1100, 1050 Connecticut Avenue, N.W.
Telephone: 202-861-1500.

PARTNER

Joel H. Sharp, Jr.

For Complete List of Firm Personnel, See General Section

For full biographical listings, see the Martindale-Hubbell Law Directory

HENDRY, STONER, SAWICKI & BROWN, P.A. (AV)

200 East Robinson Street, Suite 500, 32801
Telephone: 407-843-5880
Fax: 407-425-7905
Email: HSSB@gdi.net

Robert R. Hendry
Richard D. Stoner
Stephen C. Sawicki
G. Steven Brown

Richard A. Barfield

(See Next Column)

HENDRY, STONER, SAWICKI & BROWN P.A.—*Continued*

OF COUNSEL

Laura A. Quigley, P.A.
Deborah J. Townsend
Carl-Christian Thier (Not admitted in FL)
Marcus R. Cigagna (Not admitted in the United States)
Jacqueline E. Danzer (Not admitted in the United States)

Counsel For: Virgin Incoming Services, Inc.; Weitnauer Trading Co. Ltd.; Dufrepex; Fairholme U.S., Inc.; Central Florida Hotel Company, L.C.; Orlando Auto Sales, Inc.; Mears Motor Leasing; Weitnauer America, Inc.; Wolf and Wolf International Inc.; New Jersey Manufacturers Insurance Co.; International Planning, Inc.

For full biographical listings, see the Martindale-Hubbell Law Directory

MORAN & SHAMS, P.A. (AV)

111 North Orange Avenue, Suite 1200, P.O. Box 472, 32802-0472
Telephone: 407-841-4141
Fax: 407-841-4148
Email: moran-shams@moran-shams.com

Maurice Shams
Robert S. MacDonald

Representative Clients: Adventist Health System Sunbelt Healthcare Corporation; American Medical Associates, Inc.; China Group, Inc.; Cruises Only, LLC; Dayron; R.C. Dunn Oil Company; Hartman & Associates, Inc.; Insurance Office of America, Inc.; Manpower of Cedar Rapids and Central Florida; Rubio Artists, Inc.

For full biographical listings, see the Martindale-Hubbell Law Directory

PALM BEACH, Palm Beach Co.

BAUGHER, METTLER & SHELTON (AV)

340 Royal Poinciana Plaza, P.O. Box 109, 33480
Telephone: 561-833-9631
Fax: 561-655-2835

MEMBERS OF FIRM

Thomas M. Mettler
John W. Shelton

ASSOCIATE

Francis X. J. Lynch

Reference: First National Bank in Palm Beach.

For full biographical listings, see the Martindale-Hubbell Law Directory

LAW OFFICES OF HARRISON K. CHAUNCEY, JR., P.A. (AV)

241 Bradley Place, 33480
Telephone: 561-833-3001
Fax: 561-833-9060
Email: hchauncey@chaunceylaw.com

Harrison K. Chauncey Jr.
Mark R. Brown

For full biographical listings, see the Martindale-Hubbell Law Directory

PETER W. METTLER (AV)

140 Royal Palm Way Suite 202, 33480
Telephone: 561-832-7600
Fax: 561-833-0805
Email: taxman@cwix.com

For full biographical listings, see the Martindale-Hubbell Law Directory

MURPHY, REID, PILOTTE, ORD & AUSTIN (AV)

A Partnership of Professional Associations
Suite 100, 340 Royal Palm Way, 33480
Telephone: 561-655-4060
Facsimile: 561-832-5436
Vero Beach, Florida Office: Plantation Plaza, 6606-20th Street, 32966-7902.
Telephone: 561-567-6480.
Facsimile: 561-562-0220.

Frank T. Pilotte (P.A.)

For Complete List of Firm Personnel, See General Section

For full biographical listings, see the Martindale-Hubbell Law Directory

*PENSACOLA,** Escambia Co.

WILLIAM V. LINNE (AV)

127 Palafox Place, P.O. Box 12347, 32581
Telephone: 850-433-2224
Telecopier: 850-433-3301
Email: blinne@linnelaw.com

For full biographical listings, see the Martindale-Hubbell Law Directory

*SARASOTA,** Sarasota Co.

WILLIAMS, PARKER, HARRISON, DIETZ & GETZEN, PROFESSIONAL ASSOCIATION (AV)

200 South Orange Avenue, 34236-6749
Telephone: 941-366-4800
Telecopier: 941-366-5109
Mailing Address: P.O. Box 3258, Sarasota, Florida, 34230-3258
Email: infodesk@williamsparker.com *URL:* http://www.williamsparker.com

Monte K. Marshall
William G. Lambrecht
John T. Berteau
James L. Turner
Robert W. Benjamin
Ric Gregoria
Susan Barrett Hecker

General Counsel for: Sarasota County Public Hospital Board; Sarasota-Manatee Airport Authority; Taylor Woodrow Homes Ltd.; FCCI Mutual Insurance Co.
Local Counsel for: Bank of America; Northern Trust Bank of Florida; SunTrust Bank, Gulfcoast.

For Complete List of Firm Personnel, See General Section

For full biographical listings, see the Martindale-Hubbell Law Directory

*STUART,** Martin Co.

JOSEPH C. KEMPE PROFESSIONAL ASSOCIATION (AV)

Attorneys and Counselors at Law
Royal Palm Financial Center II, Suite 200, 789 South Federal Highway, 34994
Telephone: 561-223-0700
FAX: 561-223-0707
Email: JCKempe@msn.com
Jupiter, Florida Office: 941 North Highway AIA. Telephone 561-747-7300. *Fax:* 561-747-7722.
Vero Beach, Florida Office: 664 Azalea Lane, Suite B.
Telephone: 561-562-4022.
Fax: 561-234-1422.

Joseph C. Kempe

Harry S. Colburn Jr.

For full biographical listings, see the Martindale-Hubbell Law Directory

*TALLAHASSEE,** Leon Co.

JAMES R. BREWSTER (AV)

Suite 203, The Walker Building, 547 North Monroe Street, 32301
Telephone: 904-561-1037
Fax: 904-681-0560

For full biographical listings, see the Martindale-Hubbell Law Directory

ROBERT S. HIGHTOWER (AV)

241 East Virginia Street, P.O. Box 4165, 32315-4165
Telephone: 850-222-3363
Telecopier: 850-222-0992
Email: rsh@hightowerlaw.com

Representative Clients: Apalachee Center for Human Services, Inc.; Clemons, Rutherford & Associates, Inc.; Eastern Federal Corporation; Medical Center Pharmacy, Inc. of Quincy; Prescott Supply Co., Inc.; Southern Medical Group, P.A.; Tallahassee Mack Sales, Inc.; Tallahassee Plastic Surgery Clinic; GTO, Inc.

For full biographical listings, see the Martindale-Hubbell Law Directory

THE PHIPPS FIRM (AV)

P.O. Box 1351, 32302-1351
Telephone: 850-222-7000
FAX: 850-681-3998
Email: bkp@thephippsfirm.com

Benjamin K. Phipps
B. Forest Hamilton
Wayne L. Rubinas

References: Sun Trust Bank; Capital City Bank.

For full biographical listings, see the Martindale-Hubbell Law Directory

*TAMPA,** Hillsborough Co.

MANEY, DAMSKER & JONES, P.A. (AV)

606 Madison Street, P.O. Box 172009, 33672-0009
Telephone: 813-228-7371
Fax: 813-223-4846

David A. Maney
Karen Lynn Jones

For full biographical listings, see the Martindale-Hubbell Law Directory

Tampa—Continued

PREVATT & TAYLOR (AV)

A Partnership of Professional Associations
One Tampa City Center, Suite 1700, P.O. Box 2920, 33602
Telephone: 813-273-9666
Telefax: 813-273-0414

Karen J. Prevatt — Mary L. Taylor

Representative Clients: Cone Constructors Inc.; Magic Wok International, Inc.; Dallas I. Construction & Development, Inc.; Bioderm, Inc.; Mental Healthcare, Inc.; U.S.S. Forrestal Sea, Air, Space Museum, Inc.; Golden Bayou Food Service, Inc.

For full biographical listings, see the Martindale-Hubbell Law Directory

SHARP, SMITH & HARRISON, P.A. (AV)

One Urban Centre, Suite 630, 4830 West Kennedy Boulevard, 33609-2574
Telephone: 813-286-4199
Fax: 813-286-4197
Email: sharpsmith@earthlink.net

William M. Sharp, Sr. — Karen R. Smith
William T. Harrison, III

For full biographical listings, see the Martindale-Hubbell Law Directory

*VERO BEACH,** Indian River Co.

JOSEPH C. KEMPE PROFESSIONAL ASSOCIATION (AV)

Attorneys and Counselors at Law
664 Azalea Lane, Suite B, 32963
Telephone: 561-562-4022
Fax: 561-234-1442
Email: JCKempe@msn.com
Jupiter, Florida Office: 941 North Highway AIA.
Telephone: 561-747-7300.
Fax: 561-747-7722.
Stuart, Florida Office: Royal Palm Financial Center II, Suite 200, 789 S. Federal Highway.
Telephone: 561-223-0700.
Fax: 561-223-0707.

Joseph C. Kempe

Harry S. Colburn Jr.

For full biographical listings, see the Martindale-Hubbell Law Directory

MOSS, HENDERSON, BLANTON & LANIER, P.A. (AV)

817 Beachland Boulevard, P.O. Box 3406, 32964-3406
Telephone: 561-231-1900
Fax: 561-231-4387

Lawrence Y. Leonard

OF COUNSEL

Charles E. Garris

Representative Clients: Aetna Life & Casualty; Alcoa Florida, Inc.; Florida Power & Light Co.; Insurance Company of North America; Liberty Mutual Insurance Co.; Sears, Roebuck & Co.; Sugar Cane Growers Cooperative of Florida; Norfolk Southern Corporation/North American Van Lines, Inc.

For Complete List of Firm Personnel, See General Section

For full biographical listings, see the Martindale-Hubbell Law Directory

*WEST PALM BEACH,** Palm Beach Co.

AUGUST & KULUNAS, P.A. (AV)

250 Australian Avenue South Suite 1100, 33401
Telephone: 561-835-9600
Fax: 561-835-9602

Jerald David August — Joseph J. Kulunas

Adi Rappoport — Steven E. Blumenthal

OF COUNSEL

James J. Freeland

For full biographical listings, see the Martindale-Hubbell Law Directory

RICHARD B. COMITER & ASSOCIATES, P.A. (AV)

Esperante Building, 222 Lakeview Avenue, Suite 200, 33401
Telephone: 561-838-4505, 800-445-8838
Fax: 561-659-3800
Email: rcomiter@rbctax.com *URL:* http://www.lawyers.com/richardbcomiter&associate

Richard B. Comiter

Lisa Z. Hauser

(See Next Column)

OF COUNSEL

Barry A. Nelson

For full biographical listings, see the Martindale-Hubbell Law Directory

ROGERS, BOWERS, DEMPSEY AND PALADINO (AV)

Flagler Center Tower, Suite 1330, 505 South Flagler Drive, 33401
Telephone: 561-655-8980
Fax: 561-655-9480

MEMBERS OF FIRM

Robert O. Rogers — W. Glenn Dempsey
David E. Bowers — Richard Paladino

For full biographical listings, see the Martindale-Hubbell Law Directory

GEORGIA

*ATLANTA,** Fulton Co.

ALTMAN, KRITZER & LEVICK, P.C. (AV)

Powers Ferry Landing, Suite 224, 6400 Powers Ferry Road, N.W., 30339
Telephone: 770-955-3555
Fax: 770-952-7821, 955-2866, 955-0038, 955-3697
Email: akl@akl.com
New York, N.Y. Office: 730 Fifth Avenue, Suite 1805, 10019.
Telephone: 212-489-3745.
Fax: 212-489-3729.
Schaumburg, Illinois Affiliate: Altman, Kritzer & Levick, Ltd., Suite 700, 1101 Perimeter Drive, 60173.
Telephone: 847-240-0340.
Fax: 847-240-0344.

Allen D. Altman — Christian D. Shields
Duane D. Sitar — Theodore I. Blum

OF COUNSEL

Craig H. Kritzer — Mark V. Benveniste

Beth McRae Mayfield — Michael R. Deming

Representative Clients: Home Depot U.S.A., Inc.; Atlantic Southeast Airlines, Inc.; Ingles Markets, Inc.; Zartic, Inc.; Stag-Parkway, Inc.; Pacesetter Steel Service, Inc.

For Complete List of Firm Personnel, See General Section

For full biographical listings, see the Martindale-Hubbell Law Directory

HARKLEROAD & HERMANCE, A PROFESSIONAL CORPORATION (AV)

2500 International Tower-Peachtree Center, 229 Peachtree Street, N.E., 30303
Telephone: 404-588-9211
Telecopier: 404-659-0860

Donald R. Harkleroad

For full biographical listings, see the Martindale-Hubbell Law Directory

THE HISHON FIRM, LLC (AV)

999 Peachtree Street N.E. Suite 1900, 30309
Telephone: 404-817-7791
Fax: 404-817-2486

Robert H. Hishon

Nancy R. Daspit

For Complete List of Firm Personnel, See General Section

For full biographical listings, see the Martindale-Hubbell Law Directory

HOFFMAN & FOWLER, LLP (AV)

A Partnership of Professional Corporations
5040 Roswell Road, N.E. Suite 250, 30342
Telephone: 404-256-6464
Fax: 404-256-1422

MEMBER OF FIRM

Clifford G. Hoffman (P.C.)

For full biographical listings, see the Martindale-Hubbell Law Directory

HOLT NEY ZATCOFF & WASSERMAN, LLP (AV)

A Partnership including Professional Corporations
100 Galleria Parkway, Suite 600, 30339
Telephone: 770-956-9600
Facsimile: 770-956-1490
Email: mthomas@hnzw.com

(See Next Column)

HOLT NEY ZATCOFF & WASSERMAN LLP—*Continued*

MEMBER OF FIRM

Michael G. Wasserman (P.C.)

Representative Clients: Lincoln Property Company; Marathon Oil Company; Trammell Crow Residential; Primavera Financial Services; Roberts Realty Investors, Inc.; The University Financing Foundation, Inc.

For Complete List of Firm Personnel, See General Section

For full biographical listings, see the Martindale-Hubbell Law Directory

JONES, DAY, REAVIS & POGUE (AV)

3500 SunTrust Plaza, 303 Peachtree Street, 30308-3242
Telephone: 404-521-3939
Telecopier: 404-581-8330
Email: counsel@jonesday.com *URL:* http://www.jonesday.com
In Brussels, Belgium: Avenue Louise 480, 7th Floor, B-1050 Brussels.
Telephone: 32-2-645-14-11.
Telecopier: 32-2-645-14-45.
In Chicago, Illinois: 77 West Wacker.
Telephone: 312-782-3939.
Telecopier: 312-782-8585.
In Cleveland, Ohio: North Point. 901 Lakeside Avenue.
Telephone: 216-586-3939.
Telecopier: 216-579-0212.
In Columbus, Ohio: 1900 Huntington Center.
Telephone: 614-469-3939.
Telecopier: 614-461-4198.
In Dallas, Texas: 2727 North Harwood Street.
Telephone: 214-220-3939.
Telecopier: 214-969-5100.
In Frankfurt, Germany: Hochhaus am Park, Grüneburgweg 102, 60323 Frankfurt am Main.
Telephone: 49-69-9726-3939.
Telecopier: 49-69-9726-3993.
In Geneva, Switzerland: 20, rue de Candolle.
Telephone: 41-22-320-2339.
Telecopier: 41-22-320-1232.
In Hong Kong: 29th Floor, Entertainment Building, 30 Queen's Road Central.
Telephone: 852-2526-6895.
Telecopier: 852-2868-5871 or 852-2868-5699.
In Irvine, California: 5 Park Plaza, Suite 1100.
Telephone: 949-851-3939.
Telecopier: 949-553-7539.
In London, England: Bucklersbury House, 3 Queen Victoria Street.
Telephone: 44-171-236-3939.
Telecopier: 44-171-236-1113.
In Los Angeles, California: 555 West Fifth Street, Suite 4600.
Telephone: 213-489-3939.
Telecopier: 213-243-2539.
In New Delhi, India (Associate Office): Pathak & Associates (an associate firm of Jones, Day, Reavis & Pogue), 1st Floor, Dr. Gopal Das Bhaven, 28 Barakhamba Road.
Telephone: 91-11-373-8793; 91-11-335-7345.
Telecopier: 91-11-335-3761.
In New York, New York: 599 Lexington Avenue.
Telephone: 212-326-3939.
Telecopier: 212-755-7306.
In Paris, France: 120, rue du Faubourg Saint-Honoré.
Telephone: 33-1-56-59-39-39.
Telecopier: 33-1-56-59-39-38
In Pittsburgh, Pennsylvania: 500 Grant Street, 31st Floor.
Telephone: 412-391-3939.
Telecopier: 412-394-7959.
In Riyadh, Saudi Arabia: The International Law Firm (In Association with Jones, Day, Reavis & Pogue), Sulaymaniyah, Prince Mishari IBN, Abdulaziz Street, P.O. Box 22166.
Telephone: (966-1) 462-8866.
Telecopier: (966-1) 462-9001.
In Shanghai, China: 2805 Kerry Centre, 1515 Nanjing Road West.
Telephone: 86-21-5298-6568.
Telecopier: 86-21-5298-6569.
In Sydney, Australia: Governor Phillip Tower, Level 38, 1 Farrer Place.
Telephone: 61-2-9210-6921.
Telecopier: 61-2-9210-6926.
In Taipei, Taiwan: 8th Floor, 2 Tun Hwa South Road, Section 2.
Telephone: (886-2) 2704-6808.
Telecopier: (886-2) 2704-6791.
In Tokyo, Japan: Toranomon MT Building, 4th Floor, 10-3, Toranomon 3-Chome, Minato-ku, Tokyo 105, Japan.
Telephone: 81-3-3433-3939.
Telecopier: 81-3-5401-2725.
In Washington, D.C.: 51 Louisiana Avenue, N.W.
Telephone: 202-879-3939.
Telecopier: 202-626-1700.

MEMBERS OF FIRM IN ATLANTA

John R. Cornell (Not admitted in GA)
James H. Landon
Milford B. Hatcher, Jr.
Rory D. Lyons
Ralph R. Morrison

COUNSEL

Arthur G. Kent

(See Next Column)

ASSOCIATE

Charmaine L. Slack

For Complete List of Firm Personnel, See General Section

For full biographical listings, see the Martindale-Hubbell Law Directory

LONG ALDRIDGE & NORMAN LLP (AV)

A Limited Liability Partnership including Professional Corporations
Suite 5300, 303 Peachtree Street, 30308
Telephone: 404-527-4000
Telecopier: 404-527-4198
Email: atlanta@lanlaw.com *URL:* http://www.lanlaw.com
Washington, D.C. Office: Suite 600, 701 Pennsylvania Avenue, N.W., 20004.
Telephone: 202-624-1200.
FAX: 202-624-1298.

MEMBERS OF FIRM

Mark S. Lange
Patricia E. Tate
John E. Theberge (Resident, Washington, D.C. Office)
Charles T. Zink

For Complete List of Firm Personnel, See General Section

For full biographical listings, see the Martindale-Hubbell Law Directory

THE SAYLOR LAW FIRM, LLP (AV)

100 Colony Square, Suite 1224, 1175 Peachtree Street, N.E., 30361
Telephone: 404-892-4400
Telecopier: 404-892-2400
Email: SAYLOR_ATLANTA@PRODIGY.COM

C. Murray Saylor, Jr.
Jacquelyn Harmon Saylor

ASSOCIATE

Stephen C. Beeler

For full biographical listings, see the Martindale-Hubbell Law Directory

*AUGUSTA,** Richmond Co.

FLETCHER, HARLEY & FLETCHER (AV)

429 Walker Street, P.O. Box 2084, 30903-2084
Telephone: 706-724-0558
Fax: 706-724-4730
URL: http://www.lawyers.com/fletcherharley&fletcher

MEMBERS OF FIRM

Leonard O. Fletcher, Jr.
C. Thompson Harley
W. Lawrence Fletcher

For full biographical listings, see the Martindale-Hubbell Law Directory

HULL, TOWILL, NORMAN, BARRETT & SALLEY, A PROFESSIONAL CORPORATION (AV)

801 Broad Street, Suite 700, 30901
Telephone: 706-722-4481
Fax: 706-722-9779
Email: hullfirm@groupz.net *URL:* http://www.groupz.net/~advocate
Aiken, South Carolina Office: 111 Park Avenue, 29801.
Telephone: 803-648-4213.
Fax: 803-648-2601.

James M. Hull (1885-1975)
George B. Barrett (1894-1942)
Julian J. Willingham (1887-1963)
John Bell Towill (1907-1991)
Robert C. Norman (Retired, 1991)
W. Hale Barrett
Lawton Jordan, Jr.
Patrick J. Rice
Douglas D. Batchelor, Jr.
David E. Hudson
William H. Tucker (Not admitted in GA)
William F. Hammond
Mark S. Burgreen
George R. Hall
James B. Ellington
F. Michael Taylor
William J. Keogh, III
Edward J. Tarver
J. Noel Schweers, III
Susan D. Barrett
Ralph Emerson Hanna, III

James M. Holly (Not admitted in GA)
Timothy E. Moses
N. Shannon Gentry Lanier
Tara R. Simkins
Charles H. Weigle
Natalie A. Dopson
David C. Smith

OF COUNSEL

Julian B. Salley, Jr. (Not admitted in GA)

Counsel for: Morris Communications Corporation; Merry Land & Investment Company, Inc.; Castleberry/Snow's Brands, Inc.; Chipman-Union, Inc.; Augusta National, Inc.; Sun Trust Bank Augusta, N.A.; Georgia Power Co.; St. Joseph Hospital, Augusta, Georgia, Inc.; Norfolk Southern Corp.; Housing Authority of the City of Augusta.

For full biographical listings, see the Martindale-Hubbell Law Directory

*COLUMBUS,** Muscogee Co.

HATCHER, STUBBS, LAND, HOLLIS & ROTHSCHILD (AV)

A Limited Liability Partnership
Suite 500 The Corporate Center, 233 12th Street, P.O. Box 2707, 31902-2707
Telephone: 706-324-0201
Telecopier: 706-322-7747
Email: mailman@hatcherstubbs.com

MEMBERS OF FIRM

Alan F. Rothschild
Morton A. Harris
Charles T. Staples
John M. Tanzine, III
John McKay Sheftall
Alan F. Rothschild, Jr.

ASSOCIATE

Bradley R. Coppedge

General Counsel for: SunTrust Bank, West Georgia, N.A.; TOM'S Foods Inc.; Muscogee County Board of Education; The Jordan Company; Georgia Crown Distributing Co.; Flournoy Development Company; Bill Heard Enterprises, Inc.; St. Francis Hospital, Inc.

For Complete List of Firm Personnel, See General Section

For full biographical listings, see the Martindale-Hubbell Law Directory

ROTHSCHILD, MORGAN & BROWN (AV)

A Limited Liability Partnership
1025 First Avenue, P.O. Box 2788, 31902-2788
Telephone: 706-324-4167
Fax: 706-324-1969
Email: rothmor@mindspring.com

MEMBER OF FIRM

Jerome M. Rothschild

OF COUNSEL

J. Quentin Davidson, Jr.

Reference: Columbus Bank and Trust Company.

For Complete List of Firm Personnel, See General Section

For full biographical listings, see the Martindale-Hubbell Law Directory

*GAINESVILLE,** Hall Co.

SMITH, GILLIAM AND WILLIAMS (AV)

200 Old Coca-Cola Building, 301 Green Street, N.W., P.O. Box 1098, 30503
Telephone: 770-536-3381
Fax: 770-531-1481
Email: SGWFirm@Applied.net

MEMBERS OF FIRM

R. Wilson Smith, Jr. (1906-1983)
John H. Smith
Steven P. Gilliam
Jerry A. Williams
Kelly Anne Miles
Bradley J. Patten
M. Tyler Smith

ASSOCIATE

Robert A. Weber, Jr.

General Counsel for: Gainesville Industrial Electric Co.; Georgia Mutual Insurance, a Stock Company; L & R Farms; H. Wilson Manufacturing Co.; Goforth Electrical Supply; North Georgia Petroleum Co.; Gibbs Management Group, Inc.

For full biographical listings, see the Martindale-Hubbell Law Directory

*MACON,** Bibb Co.

ANDERSON, WALKER & REICHERT, LLP (AV)

Suite 404 SunTrust Bank Building, P.O. Box 6497, 31208-6497
Telephone: 912-743-8651
Telecopier: 912-743-9636

Albert P. Reichert, Jr.

Representative Clients: Riverwood International Corporation; Radiology Associates of Macon, P.C.; Thiele Kaolin Company; SunTrust Bank, Middle Georgia, N.A.
General Insurance Clients: Liberty Mutual Insurance Co.

For Complete List of Firm Personnel, See General Section

For full biographical listings, see the Martindale-Hubbell Law Directory

HALL, BLOCH, GARLAND & MEYER (AV)

1500 Charter Medical Building, P.O. Box 5088, 31208-5088
Telephone: 912-745-1625
Facsimile: 912-741-8822
Email: hbgm@hbgm.com
Midtown Macon, Georgia Office: 2452 Vineville Avenue.
Telephone: 912-745-1625.
Facsimile: 912-741-3544.

(See Next Column)

MEMBER OF FIRM

J. Patrick Meyer, Jr.

For Complete List of Firm Personnel, See General Section

For full biographical listings, see the Martindale-Hubbell Law Directory

*MARIETTA,** Cobb Co.

W. ALLEN SEPARK (AV)

250 Church Street, Second Floor, P.O. Box 3475, 30061-3475
Telephone: 770-422-3200
Fax: 770-514-1148

Representative Clients: Martin's Restaurant Systems, Inc.; Snowden Enterprises, Inc.; Sparkles Roller Rinks; Bearden & Smith, P.C.; The Halifax Group, Inc. formerly Oak Hill Farms, Inc.; Southern Polytechnic State University Foundation, Inc.; Metro North Youth Soccer Association, Inc.; Wellstar Foundation, Inc. formerly PROMINA Northwest Health Foundation, Inc.; The Georgia Ballet, Inc.

For full biographical listings, see the Martindale-Hubbell Law Directory

*MOULTRIE,** Colquitt Co.

R. LAMAR MOORE, P.C. (AV)

700 South Main Street, P.O. Box 190, 31776
Telephone: 912-985-1213
Fax: 912-890-1314

L. L. Moore (1880-1962)
R. Lamar Moore

For full biographical listings, see the Martindale-Hubbell Law Directory

*SAVANNAH,** Chatham Co.

HUNTER, MACLEAN, EXLEY & DUNN, P.C. (AV)

200 East St. Julian Street, P.O. Box 9848, 31412
Telephone: 912-236-0261
Cable Address: "Ancan"
Telecopier: 912-236-4936
Telex: 54-6483
Email: hmed.com *URL:* http://www.bobbs@hmed.com
Atlanta, Georgia Office: The Peachtree, 1355 Peachtree Street, N.E., Suite 640.
Telephone: 404-876-3611.
Fax: 404-870-2025.

Henry M. Dunn, Jr.
Craig S. Bonnell (Not admitted in GA)
David M. Hirsberg
Frank S. Macgill

OF COUNSEL

Don L. Waters

Representative Clients: Memorial Medical Center, Inc.

For Complete List of Firm Personnel, See General Section

For full biographical listings, see the Martindale-Hubbell Law Directory

HAWAII

*HONOLULU,** Honolulu Co.

CARLSMITH BALL (AV)

A Partnership including Law Corporations
Suite 2200, Pacific Tower, 1001 Bishop Street, P.O. Box 656, 96809-3402
Telephone: 808-523-2500
Fax: 808-523-0842
Email: execdirector@carlsmith.com *URL:* http://www.carlsmith.com
Kapolei, Hawaii Office: Suite 318, Kapolei Building, 1001 Kamokila Boulevard, 96707.
Telephone: 808-523-2500.
Fax: 808-674-0850.
Wailuku, Maui Hawaii Office: Suite 400, One Main Plaza, 2200 Main Street, P.O. Box 1086, 96793-1086.
Telephone: 808-242-4535.
Fax: 808-244-4974.
Kailua-Kona, Hawaii Office: Suite 209, 75-1000 Henry Street, 96740.
Telephone: 808-329-6464.
Fax: 808-329-9450.
Hilo, Hawaii Office: 121 Waianuenue Avenue, P.O. Box 686, 96721-0686.
Telephone: 808-935-6644.
Fax: 808-935-7975.
Hagatna, Guam Office: Suite 401, Bank of Hawaii Building, 134 West Soledad Avenue, P.O. Box BF, 96932-5027.
Telephone: 671-472-6813.
Fax: 671-477-4375.
Telex: 721-6445 CWCMI GM.

(See Next Column)

CARLSMITH BALL—*Continued*

Saipan, Commonwealth of the Northern Mariana Islands Office: Carlsmith Building, Capitol Hill, P.O. Box 5241, 96950-5241.
Telephone: 670-322-3455.
Fax: 670-322-3368.
Los Angeles, California Office: 9th Floor, 444 South Flower Street, 90071-2901.
Telephone: 213-955-1200.
Fax: 213-623-0032.
Washington, D.C. Office: Suite 300, 1201 Pennsylvania Avenue, N.W., 20004-2401.
Telephone: 202-628-2228.
Fax: 202-628-2071.
Mexico City, Mexico Office: Carlsmith Ball, Sierra Nevada 119, Lomas de Chapultepec, 11000 Mexico, D.F.
Telephone: 52-5-520-8514, 52-5-520-8757.
Fax: 52-5-540-1545.
Mexico, D.F. Office of Carlsmith Ball, S.C. (Authorized to practice as foreign legal consultants in Mexico): Sierra Nevada 119, Lomas de Chapultepec, 11000 Mexico, D.F.
Telephone: 52-5-520-8514, 52-5-520-8757.
Fax: 52-5-540-1545.

MEMBERS OF FIRM

Nancy M. Beckner (Resident at Washington, DC Office)
Michael I. Blaylock (Not admitted in HI; Resident at Los Angeles, California Office)
Mary Jane Connell
John C. Khil
Harry Y. Oda
James L. Starshak
David W. K. Wong

ASSOCIATE

Alton A. Murakami

OF COUNSEL

George G. Grubb (A Law Corporation)
Lorraine S. Klevansky

For Complete List of Firm Personnel, See General Section

For full biographical listings, see the Martindale-Hubbell Law Directory

CHING, YUEN & MORIKAWA (AV)

Pacific Tower, Suite 2700, 1001 Bishop Street, 96813
Telephone: 808-524-8880
Telecopier: 808-524-7664
URL: http://www.cymlaw.com
Email: billyuen@cymlaw.com *URL:* http://www.lawyers.com/cymlaw

MEMBERS OF FIRM

Russell L. Ching
William W. L. Yuen
Randall I. Morikawa

ASSOCIATE

Chris J. Sadayasu

Representative Clients: Finance Enterprises, Ltd.; Finance Factors, Ltd.; Finance Realty, Ltd.; Goldman, Sachs & Co.; The Hertz Corporation; Kamehameha Schools Bernice Pauahi Bishop Estate; Merrill Lynch & Co.; PaineWebber Incorporated; The Sakura Bank, Ltd.; Sen Plex Corp.

For full biographical listings, see the Martindale-Hubbell Law Directory

LAW OFFICES OF MANUEL D. GARCIA (AV)

Pacific Tower of Bishop Square, 1001 Bishop Street, Suite 2800, 96813
Telephone: 808-522-0755
Facsimile: 808-522-0760

For full biographical listings, see the Martindale-Hubbell Law Directory

GOODSILL ANDERSON QUINN & STIFEL (AV)

Alii Place, Suite 1800, 1099 Alakea Street, P.O. Box 3196, 96801-3196
Telephone: 808-547-5600
FAX: 808-547-5880
Email: info@goodsill.com *URL:* http://www.goodsill.com

MEMBERS OF FIRM

Lant A. Johnson
Miki Okumura
Jeffrey Scott Piper

COUNSEL

Randall W. Roth

ASSOCIATE

Kurt K. Kawafuchi

Representative Clients: Bireley's Orange (Japan), S.A.; Castle Estate; Hawaii Carpenters Trust Funds; The MacNaughton Group.

For Complete List of Firm Personnel, See General Section

For full biographical listings, see the Martindale-Hubbell Law Directory

MCCORRISTON MIHO MILLER MUKAI (AV)

Five Waterfront Plaza, 4th Floor, 500 Ala Moana Boulevard, 96813
Telephone: 808-529-7300
Facsimile: 808-524-8293
Cable: Attorneys, Honolulu
Mailing Address: P.O. Box 2800, Honolulu, Hawaii, 96803-2800
Email: info@m4Law.com

PARTNERS

Franklin K. Mukai
Stanley Y. Mukai
Donald K. O. Wong
Michael J. O'Malley
Michael Rosenthal

ASSOCIATE

Stacey C. G. Hee

Representative Clients: TSA International Limited; Eaton Vance Management; Hawaii Dental Service; Jas. Glover Holding Company; PrimeCo Investors LLC; UGI Corporation; Kids Earth Fund; Sports Shinko (Hawaii) Co., Ltd.; DIA Pacific Corporation.

For Complete List of Firm Personnel, See General Section

For full biographical listings, see the Martindale-Hubbell Law Directory

PETER P. J. NG (AV)

Second Floor, Bank of Hawaii Building Kaimuki Branch, 3604 Waialae Avenue, 96816
Telephone: 808-732-7788
Fax: 808-732-7780

ASSOCIATE

Jeffrey R. Niebling

For full biographical listings, see the Martindale-Hubbell Law Directory

REINWALD, O'CONNOR & PLAYDON (AV)

(Formerly Anthony, Hoddick, Reinwald & O'Connor)
2400 Makai Tower, Grosvenor Center, P.O. Box 3199, 96801-3199
Telephone: 808-524-8350
Telecopier: 808-531-8628
Email: info@roplaw.com *URL:* http://www.roplaw.com

MEMBER OF FIRM

Arthur B. Reinwald

OF COUNSEL

Clinton Andrew Englehart

For full biographical listings, see the Martindale-Hubbell Law Directory

TAM, O'CONNOR, HENDERSON, TAIRA & YAMAUCHI ATTORNEYS AT LAW, A LAW CORPORATION (AV)

20th Floor, Central Pacific Plaza, 220 South King Street, 96813
Telephone: 808-545-3030
Fax: 808-523-8051
Fax: 808-537-6782
Email: lawyers@50thstatelaw.com

James K. Tam
Michael F. O'Connor
Harvey E. Henderson, Jr.
Lissa H. Andrews
Robert M. Yamauchi
Darryl M. Taira
Stuart M. Kodish

Wesley H. Ikeda
Russ S. Awakuni
Kevin W. Herring
Fred I. Waki

OF COUNSEL

Paul M. Dold

For full biographical listings, see the Martindale-Hubbell Law Directory

TORKILDSON, KATZ, FONSECA, JAFFE, MOORE & HETHERINGTON ATTORNEYS AT LAW, A LAW CORPORATION (AV)

Amfac Building, 15th Floor, 700 Bishop Street, 96813-4187
Telephone: 808-523-6000
Cable Address: "Counsel"
Telex: RCA 723-8185
Telecopier: 808-523-6001
Email: info@torkildson.com
Hilo, Hawaii Office: 100 Pauahi Street, Suite 206.
Telephone: 808-961-0406.
Telecopier: 808-935-6725.

Craig K. Hirai
Ronald I. Heller

For Complete List of Firm Personnel, See General Section

For full biographical listings, see the Martindale-Hubbell Law Directory

IDAHO

*BOISE,** Ada Co.

Eberle, Berlin, Kading, Turnbow & McKlveen, Chartered (AV)

Capitol Park Plaza, 300 North Sixth Street, P.O. Box 1368, 83701-1368
Telephone: 208-344-8535
Facsimile: 208-344-8542

William J. McKlveen
Joseph H. Uberuaga, II
Steven E. Alkire

Sarah E. Scott

Representative Clients: TJ International; Hecla Mining Company; Agri Beef Co.; Key Trust Company of The West; Energy Release Products Corporation.

For Complete List of Firm Personnel, See General Section

For full biographical listings, see the Martindale-Hubbell Law Directory

ILLINOIS

*BELLEVILLE,** St. Clair Co.

Mathis, Marifian, Richter & Grandy, Ltd. (AV)

720 West Main Street, 62220
Telephone: 618-234-9800; 314-421-2325
Fax: 618-234-9786
URL: http://www.mmrg.com

Patrick B. Mathis
George E. Marifian
Kevin J. Richter
Laura Koeneman Grandy
Kevin J. Stine
Mark J. Stegman
T. Bradford Waltrip
Carl M. Markus

For full biographical listings, see the Martindale-Hubbell Law Directory

*CHICAGO,** Cook Co.

Fagel & Haber (AV)

140 South Dearborn Street 14th Floor, 60603
Telephone: 312-346-7500
FAX: 312-580-2201
Telex No: 754542
Cable: "NOFLAWLAW"
URL: http://www.fandh.com

MEMBERS OF FIRM

Sherwin M. Lesk
Norton N. Gold

ASSOCIATE

Patrick J. Cullerton

For full biographical listings, see the Martindale-Hubbell Law Directory

Hopkins & Sutter (AV)

A Partnership including Professional Corporations
Three First National Plaza, Suite 4100, 60602-4205
Telephone: 312-558-6600
Fax: 312-558-6538
Email: postmaster@hopsut.com *URL:* http://www.hopsut.com
Washington, D.C. Office: 888 Sixteenth Street, N.W.
Telephone: 202-835-8000.
Fax: 202-835-8136.
Troy, Michigan Office: 2800 Livernois, Suite 220.
Telephone: 248-740-6600.
Fax: 248-740-6613.

MEMBERS OF FIRM

Richard Bromley
R. Lee Christie
Jane Gorham Ditelberg
Lawrence M. Dubin (P.C.)
Marilyn D. Franson
George R. Goodman
Patrick A. Heffernan
James R. Hellige
John B. Palmer III
William C. Weinsheimer
Michael H. Woolever (P.C.)

SENIOR COUNSEL

Frederic W. Hickman (P.C.)

ASSOCIATES

Kathleen M. Eggers
Tracy D. Williams

For Complete List of Firm Personnel, See General Section

For full biographical listings, see the Martindale-Hubbell Law Directory

Jones, Day, Reavis & Pogue (AV)

77 West Wacker, 60601-1692
Telephone: 312-782-3939
Telecopier: 312-782-8585
Email: counsel@jonesday.com *URL:* http://www.jonesday.com
In Atlanta, Georgia: 3500 SunTrust Plaza, 303 Peachtree Street.
Telephone: 404-521-3939.
Telecopier: 404-581-8330. 34000 Brussels, Belgium: Avenue Louise 480, 7th Floor, B-1050 Brussels.
Telephone: 32-2-645-14-11.
Telecopier: 32-2-645-14-45.
In Cleveland, Ohio: North Point, 901 Lakeside Avenue.
Telephone: 216-586-3939.
Telecopier: 216-579-0212.
In Columbus, Ohio: 1900 Huntington Center.
Telephone: 614-469-3939.
Telecopier: 614-461-4198.
In Dallas, Texas: 2727 North Harwood Street.
Telephone: 214-220-3939.
Telecopier: 214-969-5100.
In Frankfurt, Germany: Hochhaus am Park, Grüneburgweg 102, 60323 Frankfurt am Main.
Telephone: 49-69-9726-3939.
Telecopier: 49-69-9726-3993.
In Geneva, Switzerland: 20, rue de Candolle.
Telephone: 41-22-320-2339.
Telecopier: 41-22-320-1232.
In Hong Kong: 29th Floor, Entertainment Building, 30 Queen's Road Central.
Telephone: 852-2526-6895.
Telecopier: 852-2868-5871 or 852-2868-5699.
In Irvine, California: 5 Park Plaza, Suite 1100.
Telephone: 949-851-3939.
Telecopier: 949-553-7539.
In London, England: Bucklersbury House, 3 Queen Victoria Street.
Telephone: 44-171-236-3939.
Telecopier: 44-171-236-1113.
In Los Angeles, California: 555 West Fifth Street, Suite 4600.
Telephone: 213-489-3939.
Telecopier: 213-243-2539.
In New Delhi, India (Associate Office): Pathak & Associates (an associate firm of Jones, Day, Reavis & Pogue), 1st Floor, Dr. Gopal Das Bhaven, 28 Barakhamba Road.
Telephone: 91-11-373-8793; 91-11-335-7345.
Telecopier: 91-11-335-3761.
In New York, New York: 599 Lexington Avenue.
Telephone: 212-326-3939.
Telecopier: 212-755-7306.
In Paris, France: 120, rue du Faubourg Saint-Honoré.
Telephone: 33-1-56-59-39-39.
Telecopier: 33-1-56-59-39-38
In Pittsburgh, Pennsylvania: 500 Grant Street, 31st Floor.
Telephone: 412-391-3939.
Telecopier: 412-394-7959.
In Riyadh, Saudi Arabia: The International Law Firm (In Association with Jones, Day, Reavis & Pogue), Sulaymaniyah, Prince Mishari IBN, Abdulaziz Street, P.O. Box 22166.
Telephone: (966-1) 462-8866.
Telecopier: (966-1) 462-9001.
In Shanghai, China: 2805 Kerry Centre, 1515 Nanjing Road West.
Telephone: 86-21-5298-6568.
Telecopier: 86-21-5298-6569.
In Sydney, Australia: Governor Phillip Tower, Level 38, 1 Farrer Place.
Telephone: 61-2-9210-6921.
Telecopier: 61-2-9210-6926.
In Taipei, Taiwan: 8th Floor, 2 Tun Hwa South Road, Section 2.
Telephone: (886-2) 2704-6808.
Telecopier: (886-2) 2704-6791.
In Tokyo, Japan: Toranomon MT Building, 4th Floor, 10-3, Toranomon 3-Chome, 34200o-ku, Tokyo 105, Japan.
Telephone: 81-3-3433-3939.
Telecopier: 81-3-5401-2725.
In Washington, D.C.: 51 Louisiana Avenue, N.W.
Telephone: 202-879-3939.
Telecopier: 202-626-1700.

MEMBERS OF FIRM IN CHICAGO

Ronald S. Rizzo
Douglas H. Walter
Stephanie Balcerzak Graves

OF COUNSEL

William S. McKay, Jr.

ASSOCIATES

John E. Hebert, IV (Not admitted in IL)
Thomas N. Molins

For Complete List of Firm Personnel, See General Section

For full biographical listings, see the Martindale-Hubbell Law Directory

Chicago—Continued

HOWARD GORDON KAPLAN, LTD. (AV)

180 North La Salle Street, 28th Floor, 60601
Telephone: 312-641-2555
Facsimile No.: 312-641-6265
Email: howie641@aol.com

Howard Gordon Kaplan
Leonard J. Brenner
Rhonda D. Kaplan-Katz

For full biographical listings, see the Martindale-Hubbell Law Directory

THE LAW OFFICES OF MARC J. LANE A PROFESSIONAL CORPORATION (AV)

Suite 2100 180 North La Salle Street, 60601-2701
Telephone: 312-372-1040
800-372-1040
Fax: 312-346-1040
Email: success@marcjlane.com *URL:* http://www.lawyers.com/marcjlane

Marc J. Lane

Gregory A. Papiernik
Scott E. Galbreath
Robert Graham Harles

For full biographical listings, see the Martindale-Hubbell Law Directory

MCBRIDE BAKER & COLES (AV)

500 West Madison Street 40th Floor, 60661-2511
Telephone: 312-715-5700
Cable Address: "Chilaw"
Telex: 270258
Telecopier: 312-993-9350
Email: lastname@mbc.com *URL:* http://www.mbc.com
Oakbrook Terrace, Illinois Office: Suite 1000, One Mid America Plaza, 60181-4710.
Telephone: 630-954-2100.
Telecopier: 630-954-2112.

MEMBERS OF FIRM

David Ackerman
Andrew R. Gelman
Thomas J. Kinasz
Steven R. Lifson
Morgan J. Ordman
Robert I. Schwimmer
David Shayne
Larry M. Zanger

OF COUNSEL

Robert O. Case

ASSOCIATES

Brian D. Hector
Mark A. Kromkowski
Michael P. Lusk
Jonathan E. Strouse

For Complete List of Firm Personnel, See General Section

For full biographical listings, see the Martindale-Hubbell Law Directory

ROBERT E. MCKENZIE (AV)

5450 North Cumberland Avenue, Suite 120, 60656
Telephone: 773-714-8040
Fax: 773-714-8055
Email: mckenziere@aol.com *URL:* http://www.mckenzielaw.com
(Partner, McKenzie & McKenzie, P.C., Chicago)

For full biographical listings, see the Martindale-Hubbell Law Directory

NISEN & ELLIOTT (AV)

200 West Adams Street, Suite 2500, 60606
Telephone: 312-346-7800
Telecopier: 312-346-9316

MEMBERS OF FIRM

Paul F. Gerbosi
Edward B. Mueller
Anthony Packard
Mark F. Zaenger
Michael J. Daley
John Foster Lesch
John K. Kneafsey
Michael H. Moirano
Robert O. Middleton
William G. Daluga, Jr.
Kenneth J. Rojc
Thomas V. McCauley
Helen M. Jensen
William A. Walker
Daniel P. Dawson
Michael J. Pavlicek

Robert Christie
Donald F. Froehlke
Thomas K. Juffernbruch
Brendan J. Kelly
Brian C. Kelly
Mary Rose C. Manczak
Bradley S. McCann
Brian D. Proctor

OF COUNSEL

Charles M. Nisen
Donald C. Shine

For full biographical listings, see the Martindale-Hubbell Law Directory

SUGAR, FRIEDBERG & FELSENTHAL (AV)

30 North La Salle Street, Suite 2600, 60602
Telephone: 312-704-9400
Telecopier: 312-372-7951
Cable: "SUGARFREE"

MEMBERS OF FIRM

Richard A. Sugar
Michael R. Friedberg
Steven A. Felsenthal
Andrew B. David
Leslie J. Weiss
Ira S. Neiman
Jonathan L. Mills
Etahn M. Cohen
Howard M. Helsinger
Robert F. Simon
Martin M. Weinstein
Charles H. Braun
Kathryn A. Erickson

ASSOCIATES

Aron L. Bornstein
Annette L. Brands
Kathryn T. Cha
Norman J. Ginsparg
William F. McGuinn
Suzanne J. Massel
Deanne Elizabeth Clarke

For full biographical listings, see the Martindale-Hubbell Law Directory

VON MANDEL & VON MANDEL (AV)

79 West Monroe Street, 60603
Telephone: 312-726-2145
Telecopier: 312-726-2261
Email: mvmtax@aol.com *URL:* http://www.lawyers.com/mvmtax

Michael J. von Mandel
Mary D. von Mandel

For full biographical listings, see the Martindale-Hubbell Law Directory

WATT & SAWYIER (AV)

The Monadnock Building, 53 West Jackson Boulevard, Suite 1120, 60604-3701
Telephone: 312-663-1440
Telecopier: 312-663-1410

MEMBER OF FIRM

Michael T. Sawyier

For full biographical listings, see the Martindale-Hubbell Law Directory

*DECATUR,** Macon Co.

R. NICHOLAS BURTON (AV)

Suite 603 Millikin Court, 132 South Water Street, 62523
Telephone: 217-423-8861

References: The First National Bank of Decatur; Union Planters Bank; Hickory Point Bank & Trust; Soy Capital Bank & Trust Co.

For full biographical listings, see the Martindale-Hubbell Law Directory

OAKBROOK TERRACE, DuPage Co.

BISHOP, ROSSI & SCARLATI, LTD. (AV)

Two TransAm Plaza, Suite 200, 60181
Telephone: 630-916-0123
Telecopier: 630-916-0567
Email: mmccawley@zootsplace.com

Raymond E. Rossi
Frank S. Scarlati Jr.
Robert A. Hall

George F. LaForte, Jr.

OF COUNSEL

Leslie R. Bishop (1928-1997)
Lucy M. Bishop (Retired)

For full biographical listings, see the Martindale-Hubbell Law Directory

*PONTIAC,** Livingston Co.

JOHNSON & TAYLOR (AV)

Formerly Ortman, Johnson & Taylor
109 North Mill Street, 61764
Telephone: 815-844-7151
Fax: 815-844-7539

MEMBERS OF FIRM

F. A. Ortman (1882-1955)
John A. Taylor
Taylor F. Johnson

OF COUNSEL

J. Kenneth Johnson

Attorneys for: Illinois Central Gulf Railroad; Flanagan State Bank; Villages of Flanagan, Long Point and Emington; Flanagan School District; Flanagan-Graymont and Reddick and Long Point Fire Districts; Hartford SteamBoiler Inspection Co.; Metro Life Insurance Co.; Good Samaritan Hone of Flanagan; Weber Metal Products, Inc.; Amtrack.

For full biographical listings, see the Martindale-Hubbell Law Directory

*ROCKFORD,** Winnebago Co.

WILLIAMS & MCCARTHY, A PROFESSIONAL CORPORATION (AV)

321 West State Street, P.O. Box 219, 61105-0219
Telephone: 815-987-8900
Fax: 815-968-0019
Email: mail@wilmac.com *URL:* http://www.wilmac.com
Oregon, Illinois Office: 607 Washington Street. P.O. Box 339.
Telephone: 815-732-2101.
Fax: 815-732-2289.

John E. Pfau

Representative Clients: Aircraft Gear Corp.; Anderson Industries, Inc.; Gallagher Bassett Insurance Co.; Liberty Mutual Insurance Co.; Atwood Industries, Inc.; The Travelers; American Mutual Insurance Co.; Rockford Health Systems; Chrysler Corp.; USF&G, West Bend.

For Complete List of Firm Personnel, See General Section

For full biographical listings, see the Martindale-Hubbell Law Directory

INDIANA

*EVANSVILLE,** Vanderburgh Co.

LAW OFFICES OF RANDALL K. CRAIG (AV)

5000 East Virginia, Suite 1, 47715
Telephone: 812-477-3337
Telefax: 812-477-3658
Email: rkcraig@dynasty.net

For full biographical listings, see the Martindale-Hubbell Law Directory

FINE & HATFIELD, A PROFESSIONAL CORPORATION (AV)

520 N.W. Second Street, P.O. Box 779, 47705-0779
Telephone: 812-425-3592
Telecopier: 812-421-4269
Email: Fine@Fine-Hatfield.com *URL:* http://www.Fine-Hatfield.com

Todd I. Glass — Thomas R. Fitzsimmons

David D. Sanders

A List of Representative Clients Furnished Upon Request.

For full biographical listings, see the Martindale-Hubbell Law Directory

KAHN, DEES, DONOVAN & KAHN, LLP (AV)

Fifth Main Financial Plaza, Suite 305, P.O. Box 3646, 47735-3646
Telephone: 812-423-3183
Fax: 812-423-3841
Email: evvlaw@k2d2.com

MEMBERS OF FIRM

Alan N. Shovers — John E. Hegeman
G. Michael Schopmeyer — Jeffrey K. Helfrich
Marjorie J. Scharpf

ASSOCIATES

Allison K. Comstock — Mark S. Samila

Representative Clients: Joe W. Morgan, Inc.; Intrametco Processing, Inc.; Crescent Plastics, Inc.; Elmer Buchta Trucking, Inc.; Schuttler Music; Deaconess Hospital, Inc.; Old National Bancorp; North Park Cinemas, Inc.; Red Spot Paint & Varnish Co.; Locust Street Company, Inc.

For Complete List of Firm Personnel, See General Section

For full biographical listings, see the Martindale-Hubbell Law Directory

LAW OFFICES OF JACK A. STONE (AV)

1400 Old National Bank Building, 47708
Telephone: 812-423-2045
Fax: 812-423-3021
Email: jastone@evansville.com

LEGAL SUPPORT PERSONNEL

Genevieve F. York (Paralegal) — Charlene M. Young (Secretary)
Alexandra Leich (Receptionist)

For full biographical listings, see the Martindale-Hubbell Law Directory

*FORT WAYNE,** Allen Co.

SHAMBAUGH, KAST, BECK & WILLIAMS, LLP (AV)

600 Standard Federal Plaza, 46802-2405
Telephone: 219-423-1430
Fax: 219-422-9038
Email: skbwlawyers@skbw.com *URL:* http://www.skbw.com

(See Next Column)

MEMBERS OF FIRM

Willard Shambaugh (1897-1976) — Daniel E. Serban
Michael H. Kast — John B. Powell
Edward E. Beck — Ronald D. Felger
Stephen J. Williams — James D. Streit
Paul R. Sturm

LEGAL SUPPORT PERSONNEL

CERTIFIED PUBLIC ACCOUNTANT

David A. Fee

Counsel for: Hagerman Construction Corp.; Rogers Markets, Inc.; K & H Realty Corp.; Olive B. Cole Foundation; M. E. Raker Foundation, Inc.; Associates Financial Services Co., of Indiana, Inc.; Professional Federal Credit Union; Fort Wayne Education Association; CBT Credit Services, Inc.; Ian & Miriam Rolland Foundation, Inc.

For full biographical listings, see the Martindale-Hubbell Law Directory

*INDIANAPOLIS,** Marion Co.

ADINAMIS & ADINAMIS, ATTORNEYS, A PROFESSIONAL CORPORATION (AV)

8710 North Meridian Street, 46260
Telephone: 317-580-9000
Fax: 317-587-0288
URL: http://www.lawyers.com/adinamislaw

George P. Adinamis — Susan L. Adinamis
Carol M. Adinamis — Jeffrey A. Saunders

For full biographical listings, see the Martindale-Hubbell Law Directory

BOSE MCKINNEY & EVANS LLP (AV)

2700 First Indiana Plaza, 135 North Pennsylvania Street, 46204
Telephone: 317-684-5000
Facsimile: 317-684-5173
URL: http://www.boselaw.com
Indianapolis North Office: Suite 1500, 8888 Keystone Crossing, 46240.
Telephone: 317-574-3700.
Facsimile: 317-574-3716.

MEMBERS OF FIRM

Gary L. Chapman — Donald M. Meyer
Robert P. Kassing — G. Pearson Smith, Jr.
R. J. McConnell — Ronald M. Soskin

ASSOCIATE

J. Gregory Shelley

Representative Clients: First Indiana Bank; Indiana League of Savings Institutions, Inc.; Indianapolis Life Insurance Co.; Duke Realty Investments, Inc.; Emmis Broadcasting Corp.; USX Corp.; Columbia Management, Inc.; Indiana Supply Company; Collins Auto Group.

For Complete List of Firm Personnel, See General Section

For full biographical listings, see the Martindale-Hubbell Law Directory

COHEN, GARELICK & GLAZIER, A PROFESSIONAL CORPORATION (AV)

Suite 800, Keystone Crossing Plaza, 8888 Keystone Crossing Boulevard, 46240
Telephone: 317-573-8888
Telecopier: 317-574-3855
Email: chuckindy@aol.com *URL:* http://www.indianapolislawyers.com

Samuel J. Mantel (1893-1978) — Steven J. Glazier
Thomas D. Mantel (Retired) — Sandra Lazarus Rothbaum
Charles A. Cohen — Steven M. Crell
Robert A. Garelick — Bradley H. Cohen
Jill Elizabeth Goldenberg

Bryan S. Redding

OF COUNSEL

Joseph J. Reiswerg — Richard L. Darst

Reference: NBD Bank.

For full biographical listings, see the Martindale-Hubbell Law Directory

ELROD & MASCHER, P.C. (AV)

4000 East Southport Road, Suite 200, 46237
Telephone: 317-786-4929
Fax: 317-786-7899
Other Indianapolis Office: 2000 First Indiana Building, 135 North Pennsylvania Street. 46204.
Telephone: 317-264-5000.
Fax: 317-264-5400.

French M. Elrod (1906-1985) — Robert G. Elrod
Gilbert E. Mascher

(See Next Column)

ELROD & MASCHER P.C.—*Continued*

Jennifer Horton Mertz

Reference: National City Bank.

For full biographical listings, see the Martindale-Hubbell Law Directory

JOSEPH D. GEESLIN, JR. (AV)

Suite 2530 One Indiana Square, 46204
Telephone: 317-632-4421
Fax: 317-637-9755

For full biographical listings, see the Martindale-Hubbell Law Directory

HALL, RENDER, KILLIAN, HEATH & LYMAN PROFESSIONAL SERVICES CORPORATION (AV)

Suite 2000, One American Square Box 82064, 46282
Telephone: 317-633-4884
Fax: 317-633-4878
Email: hrkhl@hrkhl.com *URL:* http://www.hrkhl.com
Indianapolis North Office: Suite 820, 8402 Harcourt Road, 46260.
Telephone: 317-871-6222.
Fax: 317-338-3946.
Louisville, Kentucky Office: AEGON Center, Suite 1530, 400 West Market Street, 40202.
Telephone: 502-568-1890.
Fax: 502-568-4878.

R. Terry Heath
Jeffrey Peek
Joseph R. Impicciche
Douglas P. Long
Fred J. Bachmann
Robert A. Hicks
Donald R. Russell
Jeffrey W. Short
Jon F. Spadorcia
John C. Meade
David M. Leonard

James R. Willey
William D. Roberts (Resident, Louisville, Kentucky Office)
Dave C. Bromund
David C. Lind, II
Rhett M. Stuard

For full biographical listings, see the Martindale-Hubbell Law Directory

ICE MILLER DONADIO & RYAN (AV)

One American Square Box 82001, 46282-0002
Telephone: 317-236-2100
Fax: 317-236-2219
Email: info@imdr.com *URL:* http://www.imdr.com
South Bend, Indiana Office: 211 West Washington Street, Suite 2420.
Telephone: 219-234-7933.
Fax: 219-234-7965. Internet E-mail: info@imdr.com. Web Site Address: http://www.imdr.com.
Chicago, Illinois Office: 135 South LaSalle Street, Suite 4100.
Telephone: 312-726-1567.
Fax: 312-641-6263. Internet E-mail: info@imdr.com. Web Site Address: http://www.imdr.com.

MEMBERS OF FIRM

James D. Kemper
Barton T. Sprunger
Gregory L. Pemberton
Steven K. Humke
Mark J. Richards
Joseph E. Whitsett, Jr.
Dean T. Burger

OF COUNSEL

Daniel E. Fisher

STAFF ATTORNEY

Raymond J. Schoettle

ASSOCIATES

Gareth W. Kuhl
Gina M. Giacone
Marilee J. Springer
Michael Buker

Counsel for: Cummins Engine Company, Inc.; Indianapolis Motor Speedway Corp.; Biomet, Inc.; Bristol-Myers Squibb Co.; Aluminum Company of America; Amax, Inc.; Community Hospitals of Indiana, Inc.; Pension Fund of the Christian Church; Thomson Consumer Electronics, Inc.; Reilly Industries, Inc.

For Complete List of Firm Personnel, See General Section

For full biographical listings, see the Martindale-Hubbell Law Directory

ROBERT A. LICHTENAUER (AV)

Suite 110, 8140 Knue Road, 46250
Telephone: 317-845-1988

For full biographical listings, see the Martindale-Hubbell Law Directory

LOCKE REYNOLDS LLP (AV)

1000 Capital Center South, 201 North Illinois Street, 46204-4210
Telephone: 317-237-3800
Telecopier: 317-237-3900
Email: attys@locke.com *URL:* http://www.locke.com

(See Next Column)

Michael T. Bindner
Michael J. Schneider
Jeffrey S. Dible

Counsel For: Bank One, N.A.; Caylor-Nickel Clinic, P.C.; Golden Rule Financial Corp.; Indiana Credit Union League; Indiana Motor Truck Assn.; International Business Machines Corp.; IPALCO Enterprises, Inc.; Magellan Health Services, Inc.; National Wine & Spirits, Inc.; Sisters of St. Francis Health Services, Inc.

For Complete List of Firm Personnel, See General Section

For full biographical listings, see the Martindale-Hubbell Law Directory

TABBERT HAHN EARNEST & WEDDLE (AV)

Suite 2100, One Indiana Square, 46204-2101
Telephone: 317-639-5444
Fax: 317-639-5232
Email: jtyrrell@tabberthahn.com *URL:* http://www.tabberthahn.com

Don A. Tabbert
Gregory F. Hahn
Lante K. Earnest
Robert G. Weddle
Mark K. Sullivan
Judy M. Tyrrell
Lara D. Engelking
Matthew W. Conner
William W. Mathews
Heather L. Fesko
Charles R. Whybrew

OF COUNSEL

James J. Nocon
William D. Lalley
Joseph W. Hammes
Dale E. Sporleder

For full biographical listings, see the Martindale-Hubbell Law Directory

*LAFAYETTE,** Tippecanoe Co.

STUART & BRANIGIN (AV)

The Life Building, 300 Main Street, Suite 800, P.O. Box 1010, 47902-1010
Telephone: 765-423-1561
Telecopier: 765-742-8175
Email: sb@stuartlaw.com *URL:* http://www.stuartlaw.com
Indianapolis, Indiana Office: Suite 1401, 8888 Keystone Crossing, 46240.
Telephone: 317-574-7245.
Fax: 317-574-7050.

MEMBERS OF FIRM

Allison Ellsworth Stuart (1886-1950)
Roger D. Branigin (1902-1975)
Roger D. Branigin, Jr.
Thomas L. Ryan
Thomas R. McCully
Larry R. Fisher
Nina B. Kirkpatrick
Mark Lillianfeld
Stephen R. Pennell
Anthony S. Benton
Erik D. Spykman
William E. Emerick
John C. Duffey
Bruce McSpadden
Mark E. DeYoung
Thomas B. Parent
Laura L. Bowker
Kevin D. Nicoson
Susan K. Roberts
John M. Stuckey
Deborah B. Trice
William P. Kealey
David A. Starkweather
Geoffrey L. Blazi

SENIOR COUNSEL

Russell H. Hart

COUNSEL

John F. Bodle
James V. McGlone

ASSOCIATES

Elizabeth B. Searle
Marianne Mitten Owen
David A. Locke
Karen Orr McClure
Ann Marie Waldron
Barry L. Loftus

General Counsel for: The Lafayette Life Insurance Co.; INB National Bank, N.W.; Lafayette Home Hospital, Inc.
State Counsel for: Norfolk & Western Railway Co.
Mr. Ryan is Counsel to: The Trustees of Purdue University.
Representative Clients: Aluminum Company of America; Liberty Mutual Insurance Group.

For full biographical listings, see the Martindale-Hubbell Law Directory

IOWA

*CEDAR RAPIDS,** Linn Co.

SHUTTLEWORTH & INGERSOLL, P.C. (AV)

115 Third Street S.E., Suite 500, P.O. Box 2107, 52406-2107
Telephone: 319-365-9461
Fax: 319-365-8443
URL: http://www.shuttleworthlaw.com

Michael O. McDermott
Gary J. Streit
Dean R. Einck
William S. Hochstetler
Brian D. Bergstrom
Dean D. Carrington

(See Next Column)

SHUTTLEWORTH & INGERSOLL P.C., *Cedar Rapids—Continued*

Representative Clients: Amana Society; Archer-Daniels-Midland Co.; Coe College; Firstar Bank N.A.; Hansen Lind Meyer, Inc.; McLeod USA Telecommunication Services, Inc.; Met-Coil Systems Corporation; SCI Financial Group, Inc.

For Complete List of Firm Personnel, See General Section

For full biographical listings, see the Martindale-Hubbell Law Directory

*COUNCIL BLUFFS,** Pottawattamie Co.

SMITH PETERSON LAW FIRM (AV)

35 Main Place, Suite 300, P.O. Box 249, 51502
Telephone: 712-328-1833
Fax: 712-328-8320
Email: email@smithpeterson.com
Omaha, Nebraska Office: 9290 West Dodge Road, Suite 205.
Telephone: 402-397-8500.
Fax: 402-397-5519.

MEMBERS OF FIRM

Raymond A. Smith (1892-1977)
John LeRoy Peterson (1895-1969)
Harold T. Beckman
Robert J. Laubenthal
Richard A. Heininger
Lawrence J. Beckman
Gregory G. Barntsen
W. Curtis Hewett
Steven H. Krohn
Randy R. Ewing
Joseph D. Thornton
T. J. Pattermann

ASSOCIATES

Daniel L. Fretheim
Paul M. Shotkoski

Representative Clients: Redland Insurance Group; Iowa Western Community College; Farm Credit Service of The Midlands; Demma Fruit Co.; Peoples National Bank; Council Bluffs Board of Water Works Trustee.

For full biographical listings, see the Martindale-Hubbell Law Directory

*DES MOINES,** Polk Co.

DAVIS, BROWN, KOEHN, SHORS & ROBERTS, P.C. (AV)

(Formerly Davis, Hockenberg, Wine, Brown, Koehn & Shors, P.C.)
The Financial Center, 666 Walnut Street, Suite 2500, 50309-3993
Telephone: 515-288-2500
Cable: Davis Law
Facsimile: 515-243-0654
Email: info@lawiowa.com *URL:* http://www.lawiowa.com

John D. Shors
Stephen W. Roberts
Michael G. Kulik
Frank J. Carroll
Bruce I. Campbell
Nicholas H. Roby
William A. Boatwright
Thomas J. Houser

Mark L. Stember

OF COUNSEL

William D. Thomas

For Complete List of Firm Personnel, See General Section

For full biographical listings, see the Martindale-Hubbell Law Directory

DICKINSON, MACKAMAN, TYLER & HAGEN, P.C. (AV)

Suite 1600 Hub Tower, 699 Walnut Street, 50309-3986
Telephone: 515-244-2600
Telecopier: 515-246-4550
URL: http://www.dickinsonlaw.com

F. Richard Lyford
Richard A. Malm
David M. Repp
David R. Rhein
Linda S. Weindruch

For full biographical listings, see the Martindale-Hubbell Law Directory

FINLEY, ALT, SMITH, SCHARNBERG, CRAIG, HILMES & GAFFNEY, P.C. (AV)

604 Locust Street, Fourth Floor Equitable Building, 50309
Telephone: 515-288-0145
Telecopier: 515-288-2724

David C. Craig

Representative Clients: ALAS; American Society of Composers, Authors and Publishers; Equitable Life Assurance Society of the U.S.; Federated Insurance Co.; Meredith Corp.
Iowa Attorneys for: Midwest Medical Insurance Co.
District Attorneys for: Norfolk & Southern Railroad; Soo Line Railroad Company.

For Complete List of Firm Personnel, See General Section

For full biographical listings, see the Martindale-Hubbell Law Directory

GREFE & SIDNEY, P.L.C. (AV)

2222 Grand Avenue, P.O. Box 10434, 50306
Telephone: 515-245-4300
Fax: 515-245-4452
Email: grandfirm@aol.com
Pella, Iowa Office: 725 Franklin Street, 50219.
Telephone: 515-628-9343.
Fax: 515-628-7252.

Rolland E. Grefe
Thomas W. Carpenter
Robert C. Thomson
Craig S. Shannon
Mary E. Kiener

Timothy N. Tripp

Representative Clients: Easter Enterprises, Inc.; Freeman Decorating Co.; Pella Windows.

For Complete List of Firm Personnel, See General Section

For full biographical listings, see the Martindale-Hubbell Law Directory

NYEMASTER, GOODE, VOIGTS, WEST, HANSELL & O'BRIEN, A PROFESSIONAL CORPORATION (AV)

700 Walnut, Suite 1600, 50309
Telephone: 515-283-3100
Telecopier: 515-283-3108
Ames, Iowa Office: 1416 Buckeye Avenue, Ames, Iowa 50010.
Telephone: 515-233-3000.
Telecopier: 515-232-3846.

LeRoy R. Voigts
James B. West
Edgar F. Hansell
W. Don Brittin, Jr.
Don Muyskens
R. Craig Shives
Roger L. Ferris
Lawrence E. Myers
Keith E. Luchtel
Gerald J. Newbrough
Robert A. VanOrsdel
Richard J. Sapp
G. R. Neumann
Russell E. Schrage
Carlton T. King
Gregory P. Page
Randall G. Horstmann
Jay Eaton
Bradford L. Austin
Burns Mossman
Phyllis E. Pearson
Hayward L. Draper
Sara J. Sersland
James E. Gritzner
Michael W. Thrall
Mark C. Dickinson
Gregory B. Wilcox
John F. Lorentzen
Rod Kubat
Steven J. Roy
Frank B. Harty
James C. Wine
Bruce W. Baker
Thomas W. Foley
Steven H. Lytle
Terry C. Hancock
Anthony A. Longnecker
Wade H. Schut
Mark D. Aljets
G. Thomas Sullivan
Joseph A. Quinn
Joan Fletcher
Thomas H. Walton
Willard L. Boyd III
Lisette Sell
Jeffrey William Courter
Hallie E. Still-Caris
Brian J. Humke
Deborah S. Krauth

Paula S. Dierenfeld
John B. Tuffnell
Jill M. Stevenson
Angel West
Kathryn Atkinson Overberg
Angela L. Watson
Jennifer L. Vergilii
Debra L. Dalton
Amy L. VanDuyn
Neal K. Westin
John T. Clendenin
Stephanie L. Marett

OF COUNSEL

Samuel G. O'Brien
John J. McLaughlin
Drew R. Tillotson
Frank B. Comfort
Luther L. Hill, Jr.
Barry Nadler

Representative Clients: Amoco Oil Co.; Deere & Co.; General Electric Co.; Boatmen's Bancshares of Iowa, Inc.; Musco Sports-Lighting, Inc.; Banks of Iowa; The Vernon Co.; Hubbell Realty Co.; Solo Cup Company; Heritage Communications, Inc.

For full biographical listings, see the Martindale-Hubbell Law Directory

*SIOUX CITY,** Woodbury Co.

BERENSTEIN, MOORE, BERENSTEIN, HEFFERNAN & MOELLER, L.L.P. (AV)

Firstar Bank Building, 501 Pierce Street, Suite 300, P.O. Box 3207, 51102
Telephone: 712-252-0020
Fax: 712-252-0656
Email: BMBHMLAW@aol.com

MEMBERS OF FIRM

Marvin S. Berenstein
Jeffrey A. Johnson
Mitchell A. Herigstad

Representative Clients: Aalfs Mfg., Inc.; Beef Products, Inc.; Briar Cliff College; Canal Capital Corporation - Sioux City Stockyards; Dakota Dunes Development Co.; First American Bank; Firstar Bank Iowa, N.A.; Mercy Medical Center - Sioux City; Sioux City Community School District; Wells Dairy & Blue Bunny Ice Cream.

(See Next Column)

BERENSTEIN, MOORE, BERENSTEIN, HEFFERNAN & MOELLER L.L.P.—*Continued*

For Complete List of Firm Personnel, See General Section

For full biographical listings, see the Martindale-Hubbell Law Directory

KANSAS

*DODGE CITY,** Ford Co.

FOULSTON & SIEFKIN L.L.P. (AV)

810 Frontview, P.O. Box 1147, 67801
Telephone: 316-227-8126
Fax: 316-227-8451
URL: http://www.foulston.com
Wichita, Kansas Office: 100 North Broadway, 700 NationsBank Financial Center, 67202.
Telephone: 316-267-6371.
FAX: 316-267-6345.
Topeka, Kansas Office: 1515 NationsBank Tower, 534 Kansas Avenue, 66603.
Telephone: 785-233-3600.
FAX: 785-233-1610.
Member: Lex Mundi, The World's Leading Association of Independent Law Firms.

MEMBER OF FIRM

William P. Trenkle, Jr.

For Complete List of Firm Personnel, See General Section

For full biographical listings, see the Martindale-Hubbell Law Directory

*HUTCHINSON,** Reno Co.

GILLILAND & HAYES, P.A. A PROFESSIONAL ASSOCIATION (AV)

20 West 2nd Avenue, 2nd Floor, P.O. Box 2977, 67504-2977
Telephone: 316-662-0537
Facsimile: 316-669-9426
URL: http://www.gillilandhayes.com
Wichita, Kansas Office: The Orpheum Centre, Suite 300, 200 North Broadway, P.O. Box 49406.
Telephone: 316-262-2266.
Facsimile: 316-263-2202.
Kansas City, Missouri Office: 12th Floor, 3100 Broadway.
Telephone: 816-753-3100.
Facsimile: 816-753-2271.

Robert J. Gilliland
John F. Hayes
James R. Gilliland
John S. Schmidt
Bruce B. Waugh (Not admitted in KS; Resident, Kansas City, Missouri Office)
Michael R. O'Neal
Bradley D. Dillon
Gerald L. Green
David N. Zimmerman (Not admitted in KS; Resident, Kansas City, Missouri Office)
Scott J. Mann
Carol Z. Smith (Resident, Kansas City, Missouri Office)
Kathleen A. Hardee (Resident, Kansas City, Missouri Office)
Kendall R. Cunningham (Resident, Wichita Office)
Mark R. Maloney (Resident, Wichita Office)

Thomas A. Dower
Tracy Applegate Cole
Laura A. Hederstedt
Terri Roberts Munsell (Resident, Kansas City, Missouri Office)
Lisa M. Ward
Kimberly Breda Bushek (Resident, Kansas City, Missouri Office)
E. Thomas Pyle, III
Tara L. Bragg

OF COUNSEL

Robert P. Reams (Not admitted in KS; Resident, Kansas City, Missouri Office)

Representative Clients: Dillon Companies; Hutchinson Hospital Corp.; Kansas City Southern Industries, Inc.; Leisure Hotel Corp.; Pine Development Co.; RHW Companies; Silver Dollar City, Inc.; Sirloin Stockade International; The Deramus Foundation, Inc.; The Kansas City Southern Railway.

For full biographical listings, see the Martindale-Hubbell Law Directory

*TOPEKA,** Shawnee Co.

COFFMAN, DEFRIES & NOTHERN, A PROFESSIONAL ASSOCIATION (AV)

534 S. Kansas Avenue, Suite 925, 66603-3407
Telephone: 785-234-3461
Fax: 785-234-3363
Email: cdn@cdnlaw.com

(See Next Column)

Harold R. Schroeder (1920-1986)
Barney J. Heeney, Jr. (Retired)
James Robert Groff (Retired)
H. Hurst Coffman
S. Lucky DeFries
R. Austin Nothern
Richard Harmon
Susan Krehbiel William

Jeffrey A. Wietharn
R. Mark Housley

Representative Clients: Texaco; General Dynamics; Colgate-Palmolive Co.; Simon Property Group, LP; Bertha Bean Flinsch Trusts; Hill's Pet Nutrition, Inc.; Union Carbide; U.S. West; Meade Investment Co., Inc.; Radiology & Nuclear Medicine, LLC.

For full biographical listings, see the Martindale-Hubbell Law Directory

FOULSTON & SIEFKIN L.L.P. (AV)

1515 NationsBank Tower, 534 Kansas Avenue, 66603
Telephone: 785-233-3600
Fax: 785-233-1610
URL: http://www.foulston.com
Wichita, Kansas Office: 100 North Broadway, 700 NationsBank Financial Center, 67202.
Telephone: 316-267-6371.
Fax: 316-267-6345.
Dodge City, Kansas Office: 810 Frontview, P.O. Box 1147, 67801.
Telephone: 316-227-8126.
Fax: 316-227-8451.
Member: Lex Mundi, The World's Leading Association of Independent Law Firms.

MEMBER OF FIRM

James P. Rankin

For full biographical listings, see the Martindale-Hubbell Law Directory

GOODELL, STRATTON, EDMONDS & PALMER, L.L.P. (AV)

515 South Kansas Avenue, 66603-3999
Telephone: 785-233-0593
Fax: 785-233-8870
Email: GSEP@CJNETWORKS.COM *URL:* http://www.cjnetworks.com/~gsep
Kansas City, Missouri Office: 10401 Holmes Road, Suite 280.
Telephone: 816-943-8577.

MEMBERS OF FIRM

H. Philip Elwood
Gerald J. Letourneau

OF COUNSEL

Robert A. McClure

SPECIAL COUNSEL

Joseph E. McKinney

Counsel for: St. Paul Fire & Marine Insurance Co.
General Counsel for: American Home Life Insurance Co.; Columbian National Title Insurance Co.; The Menninger Foundation; Kansas Medical Society; Kansas Hospital Association; Stormont-Vail Healthcare, Inc.

For Complete List of Firm Personnel, See General Section

For full biographical listings, see the Martindale-Hubbell Law Directory

WRIGHT, HENSON, SOMERS, SEBELIUS, CLARK & BAKER, LLP (AV)

Commerce Bank Building, 100 Southeast Ninth Street, 2nd Floor, P.O. Box 3555, 66601-3555
Telephone: 785-232-2200
FAX: 785-232-3344
Email: wrighthenson@wrighthenson.com *URL:* http://www.wrighthenson.com

OF COUNSEL

John H. Wachter
Scott S. Sumpter

For Complete List of Firm Personnel, See General Section

For full biographical listings, see the Martindale-Hubbell Law Directory

*WICHITA,** Sedgwick Co.

FOULSTON & SIEFKIN L.L.P. (AV)

700 NationsBank Financial Center, 67202
Telephone: 316-267-6371
Facsimile: 316-267-6345
URL: http://www.foulston.com
Topeka, Kansas Office: 1515 NationsBank Tower, 534 Kansas Avenue, 66603.
Telephone: 785-233-3600.
Fax: 785-233-1610.
Dodge City, Kansas Office: 810 Frontview, P.O. Box 1147, 67801.
Telephone: 316-227-8126.
Fax: 316-227-8451.
Member: Lex Mundi, The World's Leading Association of Independent Law Firms.

(See Next Column)

FOULSTON & SIEFKIN L.L.P., *Wichita—Continued*

MEMBERS OF FIRM

Stanley G. Andeel
Harvey R. Sorensen
Christopher M. Hurst
James P. Rankin
(Resident, Topeka Office)
Eric F. Melgren
William P. Trenkle, Jr.
(Resident, Dodge City Office)

For Complete List of Firm Personnel, See General Section

For full biographical listings, see the Martindale-Hubbell Law Directory

TRIPLETT, WOOLF & GARRETSON, LLC (AV)

2959 North Rock Road, Suite 300, 67226
Telephone: 316-630-8100
Fax: 316-630-8101
Email: twg@twgfirm.com

MEMBER OF FIRM

Thomas C. Triplett

ASSOCIATES

Jeffery C. Dahlgren
Christopher C. Swyers

Representative Clients: Anheuser-Busch Companies, Inc.; Brite Voice Systems, Inc.; Coleman Company, Inc.; Dow Chemical Co.; Friends University; KPMG Peat Marwick; National Plastics Color, Inc.; Total Petroleum, Inc.; Travelers Insurance Co.; Willis Corroon of Kansas, Inc.

For Complete List of Firm Personnel, See General Section

For full biographical listings, see the Martindale-Hubbell Law Directory

KENTUCKY

*GEORGETOWN,** Scott Co.

E. DURWARD WELDON (AV)

217 East Main Street, 40324
Telephone: 502-863-1285

Approved Attorney for: Lawyers Title Insurance Corporation of Richmond, Virginia; Louisville Title Division of Commonwealth Land Title Insurance Co. (Binder Agent); The Equitable Life Assurance Society of the United States.

For full biographical listings, see the Martindale-Hubbell Law Directory

*LEXINGTON,** Fayette Co.

STOLL, KEENON & PARK, LLP (AV)

201 E. Main Street, Suite 1000, 40507-1380
Telephone: 606-231-3000
Telecopier: 606-253-1093; 606-253-1027
URL: http://www.skp.com
Frankfort, Kentucky Office: 307 Washington Street, 40601.
Telephone: 502-875-6220.
Telecopier: 502-875-6235.
Henderson, Kentucky Office: 201 C North Main Street, 42420-3103.
Telephone: 270-831-1900.
Telecopier: 270-827-4060.
Louisville, Kentucky Office: 400 West Market Street, Suite 2650, 40202-3377.
Telephone: 502-568-9100.
Telecopier: 502-568-5700.

MEMBERS OF FIRM

William T. Bishop, III
C. Joseph Beavin

ASSOCIATE

Melissa Anne Stewart

OF COUNSEL

Douglas P. Romaine

Representative Clients: A.T. Massey Coal Co., Inc.; Breeders Cup Ltd.; Claiborne Farm; Delta Airlines; Keeneland Assn., Inc.; Kentucky Thoroughbred Assn., Inc.; Mill Ridge Farm, Ltd.; Pathology & Cytology Laboratories, Inc.

For Complete List of Firm Personnel, See General Section

For full biographical listings, see the Martindale-Hubbell Law Directory

*LOUISVILLE,** Jefferson Co.

MIDDLETON & REUTLINGER, P.S.C. (AV)

2500 Brown and Williamson Tower, 40202-3410
Telephone: 502-584-1135
Fax: 502-561-0442
URL: http://middreut.com
Jeffersonville, Indiana Office: 530 East Court Avenue, 47130.
Telephone: 812-282-1132.
Fax: 812-282-3188.

(See Next Column)

Brooks Alexander
D. Randall Gibson
Kipley J. McNally

Clayton R. Hume

For Complete List of Firm Personnel, See General Section

For full biographical listings, see the Martindale-Hubbell Law Directory

ROTH FOLEY BRYANT & COOPER, PLLC (AV)

First Trust Centre, Suite 300S, 200 South Fifth Street, 40202-3236
Telephone: 502-569-7550
Fax: 502-540-0123
Email: RFBC.com

Irvin D. Foley
David M. Roth
David H. Cooper
Lisa Koch Bryant
K. Gail Russell
Christian L. Juckett

OF COUNSEL

James E. Fahey
David W. Gray

Representative Clients: Bank One, Kentucky, N.A.; Huntington National Bank; Commonwealth Bank & Trust Co.; Farm Credit Services of Mid-America; Century Indemnity Co.; Travelers Casualty and Insurance Co.; Tumbleweed, LLC; John R. Gains Thoroughbreds, LLC; ARM Financial Group, Inc.; Osborn Enterprises.

For full biographical listings, see the Martindale-Hubbell Law Directory

LOUISIANA

*ALEXANDRIA,** Rapides Parish

CROWELL AND OWENS, L.L.C. (AV)

Hibernia National Bank Building Sixth Floor, P.O. Box 330, 71309-0330
Telephone: 318-445-1488
Fax: 318-445-9098

MEMBERS OF FIRM

Richard L. Crowell (1916-1994)
Richard B. Crowell
William B. Owens
W. Brent Pearson

ASSOCIATES

W. Alan Pesnell
Jeff J. Horn, Jr.

For full biographical listings, see the Martindale-Hubbell Law Directory

GOLD, WEEMS, BRUSER, SUES & RUNDELL, A PROFESSIONAL LAW CORPORATION (AV)

2001 MacArthur Drive, P.O. Box 6118, 71307-6118
Telephone: 318-445-6471
Facsimile: 318-445-6476

Charles S. Weems, III
Kenneth O. Ortego
Dorrell J. Brister

Representative Clients: Automated Prescription Systems, Inc.; Roy O. Martin Lumber Co., Inc.; Rapides Bank & Trust Company in Alexandria; Aetna Casualty Group; Allstate Insurance Co.; Texas Industries, Inc.; International Paper Company; Louisiana-Pacific Corporation.

For Complete List of Firm Personnel, See General Section

For full biographical listings, see the Martindale-Hubbell Law Directory

*BATON ROUGE,** East Baton Rouge Parish

KEAN, MILLER, HAWTHORNE, D'ARMOND, MCCOWAN & JARMAN, L.L.P. (AV)

22nd Floor, One American Place, 70825
Telephone: 225-387-0999
Fax: 225-388-9133
Mailing Address: P.O. Box 3513, Baton Rouge, Louisiana, 70821
URL: http://WWW.KMLAW.COM
New Orleans, Louisiana Office: Energy Centre, Suite 1560, 1100 Poydras Street, 70163.
Telephone: 504-585-3050.
Fax: 504-585-3051.
Plaquemine, Louisiana Office: Suite 10, 23425 Railroad Avenue, 70764.
Telephone: 225-687-9845.
Fax: 225-382-3445.
Lake Charles, Louisiana Office: One Lakeshore Drive, Suite 1220, 70629.
Telephone: 318-430-0350.
Fax: 318-436-5566.
Covington, Louisiana Office: 503 North New Hampshire Street, P.O. Box 3096, 70433.
Telephone: 504-875-0400.
Fax: 504-875-0500.

MEMBERS OF FIRM

Ben R. Miller, Jr.
Carey J. Messina
Linda Sarradet Akchin
Todd A. Rossi

(See Next Column)

KEAN, MILLER, HAWTHORNE, D'ARMOND, MCCOWAN & JARMAN L.L.P.—*Continued*

Kevin C. Curry
SPECIAL COUNSEL
Christopher J. Dicharry

Representative Clients: BASF Corporation, Geismar, LA; Uniroyal Chemical Co., Middlebury, CT.

For full biographical listings, see the Martindale-Hubbell Law Directory

GREGORY A. PLETSCH & ASSOCIATES A PROFESSIONAL LAW CORPORATION (AV)

Suite 301, Four United Plaza, 8555 United Plaza Boulevard, 70809
Telephone: 225-929-8525
Telecopier: 225-929-8520

Gregory A. Pletsch

For full biographical listings, see the Martindale-Hubbell Law Directory

SCHANEVILLE & BARINGER, L.L.C. (AV)

918 Government Street, 70802
Telephone: 225-383-9953
Fax: 225-387-3198
Email: DDSCHANE@AOL.COM

Dan D. Schaneville
Dale R. Baringer
Donald M. Meltzer
John C. Hopewell, III

Wendy E. Barberousse
OF COUNSEL
David O. Mooney

For full biographical listings, see the Martindale-Hubbell Law Directory

WATSON, BLANCHE, WILSON & POSNER (AV)

Registered Limited Liability Partnership
505 North Boulevard, P.O. Drawer 2995, 70821-2995
Telephone: 225-387-5511
Fax: 225-387-5972

Harvey H. Posner
Robert L. Roland
Richard S. Dunn

ASSOCIATE
David G. Koch

Representative Clients: CommunityCoffee Company, Inc.; Louisiana Hospital Association; General Health System and affiliates.

For full biographical listings, see the Martindale-Hubbell Law Directory

*COVINGTON,** St. Tammany Parish

L. PAUL HOOD JR. A PROFESSIONAL LAW CORPORATION (AV)

19267 Slemmer Road, Suite 101, 70433
Telephone: 504-867-8300
Facsimile: 504-867-9501
Email: paulhood@acadiacom.net *URL:* http://www.lawyers.com/paulhoodlaw

L. Paul Hood, Jr.

For full biographical listings, see the Martindale-Hubbell Law Directory

*LAKE CHARLES,** Calcasieu Parish

HUNTER, BLAZIER, O'DOWD & MORENO, A PROFESSIONAL LAW CORPORATION (AV)

1807 Lake Street, 70601
Telephone: 318-436-1600
Fax: 318-439-2505
Email: info@hunterlaw.com *URL:* http://www.hunterlaw.com

Edwin K. Hunter (P.C.)
T. Glynn Blazier
Timothy O'Dowd
Richard D. Moreno

OF COUNSEL
Robert M. Willan (Not admitted in LA)

For full biographical listings, see the Martindale-Hubbell Law Directory

KLUMPP AND BARNATT (AV)

Suite 804 901 Lakeshore Drive, 70601
Telephone: 318-436-1500
Facsimile: 318-436-1514
Email: KLUMPP@iamerica.net

Gregory J. Klumpp

For full biographical listings, see the Martindale-Hubbell Law Directory

METAIRIE, Jefferson Parish

THE DERBES LAW FIRM, L.L.C. (AV)

3027 Ridgelake Drive, 70002
Telephone: 504-837-1230
Fax: 504-837-2214
URL: http://www.DerbesLaw.com

Albert J. Derbes, III
Albert J. Derbes, IV
Eric J. Derbes

Julia C. Spear

For full biographical listings, see the Martindale-Hubbell Law Directory

HENICAN, JAMES & CLEVELAND (AV)

Suite 1200 Heritage Plaza, 111 Veterans Memorial Boulevard, 70005
Telephone: 504-837-8080
Facsimile: 504-833-0863
Mailing Address: P.O. Box 19300, New Orleans, Louisiana, 70179

MEMBERS OF FIRM
C. Ellis Henican (1905-1997)
Murray F. Cleveland (1913-1971)
Philip E. James, Jr.
Marshall G. Weaver
Edward N. George, III
Shawn M. Bridgewater

ASSOCIATES
Keith M. Benit
Jacob S. Capraro
David M. Packard

OF COUNSEL
Philip E. James
Louis V. Rand, II

Representative Clients: Better Business Bureau of New Orleans, Inc.; St. Paul Fire and Marine Insurance Co.; Stewart Enterprises, Inc.
Reference: Hibernia National Bank, New Orleans.

For full biographical listings, see the Martindale-Hubbell Law Directory

*MONROE,** Ouachita Parish

JOHN L. LUFFEY, JR. (AV)

3000 Kilpatrick Boulevard, Suite 200, Drawer 7580, 71211-7580
Telephone: 318-323-3800
Fax: 318-325-8357
Email: jluffey@iamerica.net

For full biographical listings, see the Martindale-Hubbell Law Directory

THEUS, GRISHAM, DAVIS & LEIGH, L.L.P. (AV)

1600 Lamy Lane, Drawer 4768, 71211-4768
Telephone: 318-388-0100
Fax: 318-322-8813
Email: tgdl@theuslaw.com *URL:* http://www.theuslaw.com

MEMBERS OF FIRM
John C. Theus, Sr. (1865-1938)
Orin M. Grisham (1866-1944)
Ronald L. Davis (1897-1959)
John C. Theus, Jr. (1901-1972)
E. K. Theus (1906-1974)
Thomas W. Leigh (1903-1983)
Ronald L. Davis, Jr. (1930-1999)
Robert Lee Curry, III
Charles H. Heck
Edwin K. Theus, Jr.
J. Michael Hart
Paul D. Spillers
Phillip D. Myers
David H. Nelson
Thomas G. Zentner, Jr.
James M. Edwards
Robert J. Bozeman
Sharon Ingram Marchman
C. Wendell Manning
F. Williams Sartor, Jr.
George M. Snellings, IV

ASSOCIATE
Charles H. Heck, Jr.

Representative Clients: Moore Oil Co., Inc.; CNA Insurance Company; American International Group, Inc.; Commercial Union Insurance Co.; Liberty Mutual Insurance Co.; Louisiana Medical Mutual Insurance Co.; Travelers Insurance Co.

For full biographical listings, see the Martindale-Hubbell Law Directory

THOMPSON, SPARKS, DEAN & MORRIS (AV)

A Partnership including a Professional Corporation
1401 Royal Street, P.O. Box 2867, 71207
Telephone: 318-388-1440
Fax: 318-322-0887

MEMBERS OF FIRM
M. C. Thompson (1885-1970)
James D. Sparks (1910-1987)
George B. Dean, Jr., (P.C.)
Wood T. Sparks
John C. Morris, III

(See Next Column)

THOMPSON, SPARKS, DEAN & MORRIS, *Monroe—Continued*

ASSOCIATE

Jennifer Allen Riley

Representative Clients: South Central Bell Telephone Co.; Greater Ouachita Water Company; PHH Homequity Corp.; Commonwealth Relocation Services, Inc.; Remax, Monroe; Bell South Advertising & Publishing Corp.; Premier Mortgage Corp.; Countrywide Funding Corp.
Approved Attorneys for: BankOne; Federal Land Bank.

For full biographical listings, see the Martindale-Hubbell Law Directory

*NEW ORLEANS,** Orleans Parish

BALDWIN & HASPEL, L.L.C. (AV)

Energy Centre, Suite 2200, 1100 Poydras Street, 70163-2200
Telephone: 504-585-7711
Fax: 504-585-7751
URL: http://www.baldwinhaspel.com

MEMBERS OF FIRM

Cuthbert S. Baldwin (1891-1969)
Edward Haspel (1889-1983)
Conrad Meyer, III
Jerome J. Reso, Jr.
Joel A. Mendler
Conrad Meyer, IV
Malcolm A. Meyer
Monica Tufano Surprenant
Leon H. Rittenberg, Jr.
John A. Rouchell
Jeannie Morris Randazzo
James P. Magee
Dennis M. LaBorde
Beverly Klundt Baudouin
Karl J. Zimmermann
Lance J. Arnold

OF COUNSEL

A. B. Kupperman
Frederick W. "Fritz" Veters

Leon H. Rittenberg, III
Thomas M. Long

Representative Clients: Bean Dredging Corp.; Hibernia National Bank; Alfa-Laval, Inc.

For full biographical listings, see the Martindale-Hubbell Law Directory

MICHAEL L. ECKSTEIN ATTORNEY AT LAW A PROFESSIONAL CORPORATION (AV)

1515 Poydras Street, Suite 2195, 70112
Telephone: 504-527-0701
Telecopier: 504-566-0040
VMX: 504-889-8876
Email: eck@eck-law.com

Michael L. Eckstein
David Coleman Raphael, Jr.

Representative Clients: Anserphone of New Orleans, Inc.; Dixie Web Graphic Corporation; Kencoil, Inc.; Life Point Systems, Inc.; Meeks Petroleum Company; Dan-Gulf Shipping, Inc.; Axonn Corporation; Action Ink, Inc.; TCB Industries, Inc.

For full biographical listings, see the Martindale-Hubbell Law Directory

THE GODFREY FIRM A PROFESSIONAL LAW CORPORATION (AV)

2500 Energy Centre, 1100 Poydras Street, 70163-2500
Telephone: 504-585-7538
Fax: 504-585-7535
Email: godfryfirm@aol.com

Jarrell E. Godfrey, Jr.
Cloyd F. Van Hook
Patrick M. Files
Elizabeth Earnest

For full biographical listings, see the Martindale-Hubbell Law Directory

LOWE, STEIN, HOFFMAN, ALLWEISS & HAUVER, L.L.P. (AV)

One Shell Square, 701 Poydras Street Suite 3600, 70139-7735
Telephone: 504-581-2450
Telecopier: 504-581-2461

MEMBER OF FIRM

Mark S. Stein

For Complete List of Firm Personnel, See General Section

For full biographical listings, see the Martindale-Hubbell Law Directory

MCGLINCHEY STAFFORD (AV)

A Professional Limited Liability Company
643 Magazine Street, 70130-3477
Telephone: 504-586-1200
Fax: 504-596-2800
TDD: (504) 596-2728
Telex: 584327
Cable Address: "MACSTAC"
Mailing Address: P.O. Box 60643, New Orleans, Louisiana, 70160-0643
Email: @mcglinchey.com *URL:* http://www.mcglinchey.com
Dallas, Texas Office: 2777 Stemmons Freeway, Suite 925, 75207-2401.
Telephone: 214-860-9700.
Fax: 214-860-9750.

(See Next Column)

Houston, Texas Office: 2727 Allen Parkway, Suite 1900, 77019.
Telephone: 713-520-1900.
Fax: 713-520-1025.
Baton Rouge, Louisiana Office: Ninth Floor, One American Place, 70825-0001.
Telephone: 504-383-9000.
Fax: 504-343-3076.
Jackson, Mississippi Office: Suite 1200, SkyTel Centre, 200 South Lamar Street, 39201.
Telephone: 601-960-8400.
Fax: 601-960-8406.
Lake Providence, Louisiana Office: 405 Morgan Street, 71254-2691.
Telephone: 318-559-1200.
Fax: 318-559-0609.
Monroe, Louisiana Office: Dean ONB Tower, 130 Desiard Street, Suite 807, 71201.
Telephone: 318-651-0807.
Fax: 318-651-0809.

MEMBERS OF FIRM

Kenneth A. Weiss
Katherine Conklin

ASSOCIATE

Jaye Andras Caffrey

For full biographical listings, see the Martindale-Hubbell Law Directory

MILLING BENSON WOODWARD L.L.P. (AV)

A Partnership including Professional Law Corporations
Suite Twenty-Three Hundred, 909 Poydras Street, 70112-1017
Telephone: 504-569-7000
Telecopier: 504-569-7001
ABA net: 15656
MCI Mail: "Milling"
Email: milling@millinglaw.com
Lafayette, Louisiana Office: 101 La Rue France, Suite 200.
Telephone: 318-232-3929.
Telecopier: 318-233-4957.
Mandeville (North Shore), Louisiana Office: 2140 8th Street.
Telephone: 504-867-9622.
Telecopier: 504-867-8364.

MEMBERS OF FIRM

David Conroy (P.C.)
William C. Gambel (P.C.)
Charles A. Snyder (P.C.)
Richard A. Whann (P.C.)
Hilton S. Bell (P.C.)

PARTNER EMERITUS

G. Henry Pierson, Jr., (P.C.)

ASSOCIATE

Sheila L. Moragas

SPECIAL COUNSEL

Julia M. Pearce

See General Section for list of Representative Clients.

For Complete List of Firm Personnel, See General Section

For full biographical listings, see the Martindale-Hubbell Law Directory

ORECK, BRADLEY, CRIGHTON, ADAMS & CHASE, LLC (AV)

1100 Poydras Street, Suite 1440, 70163
Telephone: 504-525-8001
Fax: 504-525-8018
Boulder, Colorado Office: 2045 Broadway, Suite 100, 80302.
Telephone: 303-444-2933.
Fax: 303-444-3441.

Frederick W. Bradley
Jesse R. Adams, III

For full biographical listings, see the Martindale-Hubbell Law Directory

PHELPS DUNBAR, L.L.P. (AV)

Texaco Center, 400 Poydras Street, 70130-3245
Telephone: 504-566-1311
Telecopier: 504-568-9130, 504-568-9007
Cable Address: "Howspencer"
Telex: 584125 WU
Telex: 6821155 WUI
Email: info@phelps.com
Baton Rouge, Louisiana Office: Suite 701, 445 North Boulevard, P.O. Box 4412.
Telephone: 225-346-0285.
Telecopier: 225-381-9197.
Jackson, Mississippi Office: Suite 500, SkyTel Centre, 200 South Lamar Street, P.O. Box 23066.
Telephone: 601-352-2300.
Telecopier: 601-360-9777.
Tupelo, Mississippi Office: Seventh Floor, One Mississippi Plaza, P.O. Box 1220.
Telephone: 662-842-7907.
Telecopier: 662-842-3873.
Houston, Texas Office: Suite 900, 3040 Post Oak Boulevard.
Telephone: 713-626-1386.
Telecopier: 713-626-1388.

(See Next Column)

PHELPS DUNBAR L.L.P.—*Continued*

London, England Office: Suite 731, Level 7, Lloyd's, 1 Lime Street, London EC3M 7DQ England.
Telephone: 011-44-207-929-4765.
Telecopier: 011-44-207-929-0046.
Telex: 987321.

RESIDENT PARTNERS

Jane E. Armstrong
F. M. Bush, III (Not admitted in LA; Resident, Tupelo, Mississippi Office)
Deborah Shelby Dees (Not admitted in LA; Resident, Jackson, Mississippi Office)
C. Delbert Hosemann, Jr. (Not admitted in LA; Resident, Jackson, Mississippi Office)
Richard E. Matheny (Resident, Baton Rouge, Louisiana Office)
Robert W. Nuzum
Gregory D. Pirkle (Not admitted in LA; Resident, Tupelo, Mississippi Office)
Glover A. Russell, Jr. (Not admitted in LA; Resident, Jackson, Mississippi Office)
David P. Webb (Not admitted in LA; Resident, Jackson, Mississippi Office)
Stephen M. Wilson (Not admitted in LA; Resident, Jackson, Mississippi Office)

COUNSEL

Linda Bounds Sherman (Not admitted in LA; Resident, Jackson, Mississippi Office)

RESIDENT ASSOCIATES

Barry L. McGraw (Not admitted in LA; Resident, Tupelo, Mississippi Office)
Elizabeth E. Thomas (Not admitted in LA; Resident, Tupelo, Mississippi Office)
Robert L. Wollfarth, Jr.

Representative Clients: Atlantic Richfield Company; Bank of Mississippi; Bank One; Citizens Utilities Company; Enron Capital & Trade Resources Corp.; Hibernia National Bank; International Business Machines Corporation; Pathology Laboratories, Inc. dba Puckett Labs; Rubicon Inc.; Vastar Resources, Inc.

For Complete List of Firm Personnel, See General Section

For full biographical listings, see the Martindale-Hubbell Law Directory

*SHREVEPORT,** Caddo Parish

BARLOW AND HARDTNER L.C. (AV)

Tenth Floor, Louisiana Tower, 401 Edwards Street, 71101-3289
Telephone: 318-227-1131
Telecopier: 318-227-1141
Mailing Address: P.O. Box 8, Shreveport, Louisiana, 71161-0008

Quintin T. Hardtner, III
Malcolm S. Murchison
David R. Taggart

OF COUNSEL

Cecil E. Ramey, Jr.
Paula Hazelrig Hickman

Representative Clients: Kelley Oil Corporation; NorAm Energy Corp. (formerly Arkla, Inc.); Central and South West Corporation; Panhandle Eastern Corp.; Pennzoil Producing Co.; Ashland Oil, Inc.; Southwestern Electric Power Company; General Electric Co.

For Complete List of Firm Personnel, See General Section

For full biographical listings, see the Martindale-Hubbell Law Directory

BLANCHARD, WALKER, O'QUIN & ROBERTS, A PROFESSIONAL LAW CORPORATION (AV)

Fourteenth Floor, Premier Bank Tower, 400 Texas Street, P.O. Drawer 1126, 71101
Telephone: 318-221-6858
Fax: 318-227-2967
Email: BWOR@BWOR.com
Bossier City, Louisiana Office: 2285 Benton Road, Suite B-201.
Telephone: 318-742-9255.
Fax: 318-742-9210.

J. Edgerton Pierson, Jr., (P.C.)

For Complete List of Firm Personnel, See General Section

For full biographical listings, see the Martindale-Hubbell Law Directory

MAINE

*PORTLAND,** Cumberland Co.

BENNETT BENNETT AND TROIANO, P.A. (AV)

Suite 300, 121 Middle Street, P.O. Box 7799, 04112-7799
Telephone: 207-773-4775
Telecopier: 207-774-2366
Email: lawyers@bennettlegal.com *URL:* http://www.bennettlegal.com

(See Next Column)

Herbert H. Bennett (1928-1992)
Peter Bennett
Jeffrey Bennett
Joseph A. Troiano
Frederick B. Finberg

Julie A. Boesky

OF COUNSEL

Jonathan M. Dunitz

Counsel for: Associated Grocers of New England; General Star Indemnity Company; Coca Cola Bottling Company of Northern New England, Inc.; Northern Utilities/Bay State Gas; Pratt & Whitney (Division of United Technologies); Primerica Financial Services (Citigroup); Sprague Energy (C.H. Sprague & Son); Perrier Group of America, Inc.; Lepage Bakeries, Inc. (Country Kitchen); Texaco, Inc.

For full biographical listings, see the Martindale-Hubbell Law Directory

LEBLANC & YOUNG (AV)

183 Middle Street, P.O. Box 7950, 04112-7950
Telephone: 207-772-2800
Facsimile: 207-772-2822
Email: firm@leblancyoung.com *URL:* http://www.leblancyoung.com

Richard P. LeBlanc
James H. Young, II
Elizabeth T. High
Abigail King Diggins

For full biographical listings, see the Martindale-Hubbell Law Directory

PIERCE ATWOOD (AV)

One Monument Square, 04101
Telephone: 207-791-1100
Fax: 207-791-1350
Email: info@PierceAtwood.com *URL:* http://www.pierceatwood.com
Augusta, Maine Office: 77 Winthrop Street.
Telephone: 207-622-6311.
Fax: 207-623-9367.
Newburyport, Massachusetts Office: 6 Harris Street.
Telephone: 978-465-9599.
Fax: 978-465-9945.

MEMBERS OF FIRM

Fred C. Scribner, Jr. (1908-1994)
Warren E. Winslow, Jr. (Resident, Augusta Office)
Everett P. Ingalls, III
James G. Good
Sarah H. Beard
Barbara K. Wheaton
Robert B. Ravenelle

OF COUNSEL

Sigrid E. Tompkins
William C. Smith

ASSOCIATES

Jonathan A. Block
Larissa S. Pratt
Mitchell R. Kops (Not admitted in ME)

COUNSEL

Michael S. Wilson

For Complete List of Firm Personnel, See General Section

For full biographical listings, see the Martindale-Hubbell Law Directory

PRETI, FLAHERTY, BELIVEAU, PACHIOS & HALEY, LLC (AV)

One City Center, P.O. Box 9546, 04112-9546
Telephone: 207-791-3000
Telecopier: 207-791-3111
Email: admin@preti.com *URL:* http://www.preti.com
Augusta, Maine Office: 45 Memorial Circle, P.O. Box 1058, 04332-1058.
Telephone: 207-623-5300.
Telefax: 207-623-2914.
Bath, Maine Office: Thirty Front Street, P.O. Box 665, 04530-0665.
Telephone: 207-443-5576.
Telefax: 207-443-6665.

MEMBERS OF FIRM

Severin M. Beliveau (Augusta Office)
James C. Pitney, Jr. (Augusta Office)
Michael L. Sheehan

ASSOCIATES

James E. Phipps
Roy T. Pierce

Representative Clients: International Business Machines Corp.; IMB Credit Corp.; Bowater Inc./Great Northern Paper Inc.; UAH Hydro-Kennebec L.P.; Stratton Energy Associates; United Timber Corp.; Mount Desert Island Hospital; Maine Coast Memorial Hospital; Maine Auto Dealers Assn.; Maine Oil Dealers Assn.

For Complete List of Firm Personnel, See General Section

For full biographical listings, see the Martindale-Hubbell Law Directory

TROUBH, HEISLER & PIAMPIANO, P.C. (AV)

511 Congress Street, P.O. Box 9711, 04104-5011
Telephone: 207-780-6789
Fax: 207-774-2339
Email: info@thplaw.com

(See Next Column)

TROUBH, HEISLER & PIAMPIANO P.C., *Portland—Continued*

William B. Troubh
Edwin A. Heisler
Robert J. Piampiano
Kevin M. Gillis
Michael P. Boyd
Thomas E. Getchell
Michael Richards
William K. McKinley
Daniel F. Gilligan
Paul S. Bulger
John G. Richardson

Daniel R. Felkel
Ann Brandt
John P. Flynn, III

For full biographical listings, see the Martindale-Hubbell Law Directory

*ROCKLAND,** Knox Co.

STROUT & PAYSON, P.A. (AV)

10 Masonic Street, P.O. Box 248, 04841-0248
Telephone: 207-594-8400
Fax: 207-594-2724
Email: splaw@midcoast.com

Arthur E. Strout
Joseph B. Pellicani (1936-1988)
Robert J. Levine
Esther R. Barnhart
Carol Ann Lundquist
Randal E. Watkinson
Elizabeth E. Biddle
James Davidson

OF COUNSEL

Curtis M. Payson
John Knight

Approved Attorneys for: First American Title Insurance Co.; Chicago Title Insurance Co.

For full biographical listings, see the Martindale-Hubbell Law Directory

SOUTH PORTLAND, Cumberland Co.

VAN MEER & BELANGER, P.A. (AV)

25 Long Creek Drive, 04106
Telephone: 207-871-7500
Fax: 207-871-7505
Email: VBLAW@GWI.NET

Thomas J. Van Meer
Norman R. Belanger
D. Kelley Young
Richard N. Bryant

Betts J. Gorsky
Mary McQuillen

For full biographical listings, see the Martindale-Hubbell Law Directory

MARYLAND

*BALTIMORE,** (Independent City)

LAW OFFICE OF EDWARD L. BLANTON, JR., P.A. (AV)

404 Allegheny Avenue, 21204
Telephone: 410-296-8160
Fax: 410-821-8113

Edward L. Blanton, Jr.

Peter T. McDowell

For full biographical listings, see the Martindale-Hubbell Law Directory

FERGUSON, SCHETELICH & HEFFERNAN, P.A. (AV)

1401 NationsBank Center, 100 South Charles Street, 21201-2725
Telephone: 410-837-2200
Fax: 410-837-1188
URL: http://www.FSHLaw.com

Robert L. Ferguson, Jr.
Thomas J. Schetelich
Christopher J. Heffernan
Craig F. Ballew
Michael N. Russo, Jr.

Peter J. Basile
Ann D. Ware
Tracey J. McLauchlin
Michele P. Zahner
Michael K. Hourigan

For full biographical listings, see the Martindale-Hubbell Law Directory

GALLAGHER, EVELIUS & JONES, LLP (AV)

Park Charles Suite 400, 218 North Charles Street, 21201
Telephone: 410-727-7702
Facsimile: 410-468-2786
URL: http://www.gejlaw.com

(See Next Column)

MEMBERS OF FIRM

Francis X. Gallagher (1928-1972)
C. Edward Jones (1908-1999)
John C. Evelius (Retired)
Richard O. Berndt
Thomas N. Biddison, Jr.
Robert R. Kern, Jr.
Saul E. Gilstein
Thomas B. Lewis
Bonnie Abrams Travieso
Stephen A. Goldberg
Linda H. Jones
Jack C. Tranter
Leslie B. Speed
Christopher J. Fritz
David E. Raderman
Peter E. Keith
Nita L. Schultz
Michael W. Skojec
Kathryn Kelley Hoskins
Mark P. Keener
Kevin J. Davidson
Eileen M. Lunga
Lori A. Nicolle
Kenneth S. Gross
Thomas C. Dame

ASSOCIATES

Valarie K. Oulds
Margaret Stevens Jacks
Matthew W. Oakey
Rebecca A. Weaver
Michael J. Henigan
David W. Kinkopf
Paul S. Caiola
Jason W. Gaarder
M. Kirsten Andrews

LEGAL ASSISTANTS

Patricia C. Quayle
Iris T. H. Heath
Connie L. Ennis
Margaret Graff
Margo Gibson Hughes
Jonathan T. Gillis
Brenda J. Heacock
Dwayne L. Rodeheaver

Representative Clients: Roman Catholic Archdiocese of Baltimore; The Shelter Group; The Enterprise Social Investment Corp.; Mercy Medical Center, Inc; The Humphries Companies.

For full biographical listings, see the Martindale-Hubbell Law Directory

MARTIN, SNYDER & BERNSTEIN, P.A. (AV)

Redwood Tower, Suite 2000, 217 East Redwood Street, 21202
Telephone: 410-547-7163
Facsimile: 410-547-1605

Gerard P. Martin
David L. Snyder
Gregg L. Bernstein

Kimberly Dunn Spelman
Caroline DeLisle Ciraolo
Steven F. Wrobel
Denis J. Charlesworth

OF COUNSEL

Steven J. Sibel

LEGAL SUPPORT PERSONNEL

Joanna L. Trela (Administrator)
D'Ann Auty (Paralegal)

For full biographical listings, see the Martindale-Hubbell Law Directory

LOUISE Y. MELEDIN (AV)

406 Bosley Avenue, 21204-0901
Telephone: 410-494-8833
Fax: 410-583-9899

OF COUNSEL

Henry L. Meledin

For full biographical listings, see the Martindale-Hubbell Law Directory

PIPER & MARBURY L.L.P. (AV)

36 South Charles Street, 21201-3018
Telephone: 410-539-2530
FAX: 410-539-0489
Email: lawfirm@pipermar.com *URL:* http://www.pipermar.com
Washington, D.C. Office: 1200 Nineteenth Street, N.W., 20036-2430.
Telephone: 202-861-3900.
FAX: 202-223-2085.
New York, N.Y. Office: 1251 Avenue of the Americas, 10020-1104.
Telephone: 212-835-6000.
FAX: 212-835-6001.
Philadelphia, Pennsylvania Office: 3400 Two Logan Square, 18th & Arch Streets, 19103-2762.
Telephone: 215-656-3300.
FAX: 215-656-3301.
Easton, Maryland Office: 117 Bay Street, 21601-2703.
Telephone: 410-820-4460.
FAX: 410-820-4463.
Princeton, N.J. Office: 116 Village Boulevard, Suite 200, Princeton Forrestal Village, 08540.
Telephone: 609-951-2252.
FAX: 609-951-2216.
Reston, Virginia Office: 1850 Centennial Park Drive, Suite 610, Commerce Executive Park III, 20191.
Telephone: 703-391-7100.
Fax: 703-309-5299.

MEMBERS OF FIRM

Lawrence M. Katz
Joseph H. Langhirt
Lee A. Sheller
Stephen M. Sharkey

(See Next Column)

PIPER & MARBURY L.L.P.—*Continued*

ASSOCIATE

Jordan I. Bailowitz

For Complete List of Firm Personnel, See General Section

For full biographical listings, see the Martindale-Hubbell Law Directory

RICHARD T. STANSBURY A PROFESSIONAL ASSOCIATION (AV)

Suite 920, The B & O Building, Two North Charles Street, 21201-3754
Telephone: 410-727-6200
Facsimile: 410-385-2939
Email: rts1law@aol.com *URL:* http://www.lawyers.com/richardstansburylaw
Annapolis, Maryland Office: 112 West Street, 21401.
Telephone: 410-974-6000.
Facsimile: 410-974-6019.

Richard T. Stansbury

For full biographical listings, see the Martindale-Hubbell Law Directory

STEWART, PLANT & BLUMENTHAL, LLC (AV)

Suite 910 7 St. Paul Street, 21202
Telephone: 410-347-0506
Fax: 410-347-0513
Email: info@spblaw.com

MEMBERS OF FIRM

C. Van Leuven Stewart
A. MacDonough Plant
Max E. Blumenthal
Hugh A. ("Jay") Mitchell, Jr.
Robert C. Young

William J. Patton
Jonathan G. Lasley
Lisa J. McGrath
Natalie B. Sherman (Not admitted in MD)

OF COUNSEL

Adena W. Testa
Charlotte A. Sherman

For full biographical listings, see the Martindale-Hubbell Law Directory

THOMSEN AND BURKE, LLP (AV)

Suite 400, One North Charles Street, 21201
Telephone: 410-539-2595
Fax: 410-783-0710
URL: http://www.T-B.com
Washington, D.C. Office: Suite 500, 1225 Eye Street, N.W.
Telephone: 202-682-4741.
Fax: 202-547-3713.

MEMBERS OF FIRM

George E. Thomsen
Paul E. Burke, Jr.
Roszel C. Thomsen, II
John B. Ward, Jr.

ASSOCIATES

Hedley A. Clark
Robin McDaniel Hough
Antoinette D. Paytas

References: NationsBank; Mercantile-Safe Deposit & Trust Co.; Carroll County Bank and Trust Co.

For full biographical listings, see the Martindale-Hubbell Law Directory

VENABLE ATTORNEYS AT LAW VENABLE, BAETJER AND HOWARD, LLP (AV)

A Partnership including Professional Corporations
1800 Mercantile Bank & Trust Building, 2 Hopkins Plaza, 21201
Telephone: 410-244-7400
Fax: 410-244-7742
URL: http://www.venable.com
Washington, D.C. Office: Venable, Baetjer, Howard & Civiletti LLP, Suite 1000, 1201 New York Avenue, N.W.
Telephone: 202-962-4800.
Fax: 202-962-8300.
McLean, Virginia Office: Suite 400, 2010 Corporate Ridge.
Telephone: 703-760-1600.
Fax: 703-821-8949.
Rockville, Maryland Office: Suite 500, One Church Street, P. O. Box 1906.
Telephone: 301-217-5600.
Fax: 301-217-5617.
Towson, Maryland Office: 210 Allegheny Avenue, P. O. Box 5517.
Telephone: 410-494-6200.
Fax: 410-821-0147.

MEMBERS OF FIRM

Jacques T. Schlenger (P.C.)
Neal D. Borden (Also at Washington, D.C. Office)
Jan K. Guben (Also at Washington, D. C Office)
Lars E. Anderson (Not admitted in MD; Resident, McLean, Virginia Office)
Alexander I. Lewis, III (P.C.) (Also at Towson, Maryland Office)
Michael Schatzow (Also at Washington, D.C. Office)
Bryson L. Cook (P.C.) (Also at Washington, D.C. Office)
Barbara E. Schlaff

(See Next Column)

MEMBERS OF FIRM (Continued)

Edward L. Wender (P.C.)
David M. Fleishman
Mitchell Kolkin
Kenneth R. Hoffman (Also at Washington, D.C. Office)
Robert Zinkham
Robert L. Waldman
John A. Roberts (Also at Rockville, Maryland Office)
Robert J. Bolger, Jr. (Also at Washington, D.C. Office)
John A. Wilhelm (Not admitted in MD; Resident, McLean, Virginia Office)
Newton B. Fowler, III
Michael J. Baader
Wallace E. Christner (Also at Washington, D.C. Office)
Jeffrey K. Gonya
Robert H. Geis, Jr.

OF COUNSEL

Robert M. Thomas (P.C.)
Robert R. Bair (P.C.)
Emried D. Cole, Jr.
Robin L. Zimelman

ASSOCIATES

Louis B. Barr
John P. Edgar
Matthew F. Kadish (Not admitted in MD; Resident, Washington, D.C. Office)
Brian J. O'Connor
Neal H. Strum

For Complete List of Firm Personnel, See General Section

For full biographical listings, see the Martindale-Hubbell Law Directory

BETHESDA, Montgomery Co.

ROBERT D. COURTLAND CHARTERED (AV(T))

Suite 203, The Seasons, 4710 Bethesda Avenue, 20814
Telephone: 301-654-0300
Fax: 301-654-5869
Email: rcourtland@aol.com

Robert D. Courtland

For full biographical listings, see the Martindale-Hubbell Law Directory

PALEY, ROTHMAN, GOLDSTEIN, ROSENBERG & COOPER, CHARTERED (AV)

Seventh Floor, One Bethesda Center, 4800 Hampden Lane, 20814
Telephone: 301-656-7603
Telecopier: 301-654-7354
Email: prg@paleyrothman.com

Victor J. Rosenberg
Mark S. Rothman
Stephen H. Paley
Ronald A. Dweck
Robert H. Maclay
Steven A. Widdes
Dennis L. Sharp
Jeffrey A. Kolender

For Complete List of Firm Personnel, See General Section

For full biographical listings, see the Martindale-Hubbell Law Directory

CHEVY CHASE, Montgomery Co.

LAW OFFICES OF BINSTOCK, TORCHINSKY AND ASSOCIATES, P.C. (AV)

Barlow Building, 5454 Wisconsin Avenue, Suite 1340, 20815
Telephone: 301-657-5555
Fax: 301-657-9871
URL: http://www.lawyers.com/binstock_torchinsky
Washington, DC Office: 1140 Connecticut Avenue, N.W., Suite 703. 20036.
Telephone: 301-657-5555.
Fax: 301-657-9871.

Shelton M. Binstock
David B. Torchinsky

OF COUNSEL

Andrew S. Unger (Not admitted in MD)
George R. Adams (Not admitted in MD)

For full biographical listings, see the Martindale-Hubbell Law Directory

*ROCKVILLE,** Montgomery Co.

STEIN, SPERLING, BENNETT, DE JONG, DRISCOLL, GREENFEIG & METRO, P.C. (AV)

25 West Middle Lane, 20850-2204
Telephone: 301-340-2020; 800-435-5230
Telecopier: 301-340-8217
Email: lawfirm@steinsperling.com
Falls Church, Virginia Office: 6245 Leesburg Pike, Suite 140, 22044.
Telephone: 703-237-0500.
Telecopier: 703-534-2899.

David S. De Jong
Ann G. Jakabcin

For Complete List of Firm Personnel, See General Section

For full biographical listings, see the Martindale-Hubbell Law Directory

MASSACHUSETTS

*BOSTON,** Suffolk Co.

Bloom & Witkin (AV)

70 Franklin Street, 02110
Telephone: 617-443-4300
Fax: 617-443-4315

MEMBERS OF FIRM

Arnold Bloom
Mark J. Witkin

For full biographical listings, see the Martindale-Hubbell Law Directory

Foley, Hoag & Eliot LLP (AV)

One Post Office Square, 02109
Telephone: 617-832-1000
Telecopier: 617-832-7000
Email: fhe@fhe.com *URL:* http://www.fhe.com
Washington, D.C. Office: 1747 Pennsylvania Avenue, N.W.
Telephone: 202-223-1200.
Telecopier: 202-785-6687.

MEMBERS OF FIRM

Robert L. Birnbaum
Leonard Schneidman
Louis P. Georgantas
Deborah A. Willard
John L. Burke, Jr. (Resident, Washington, D.C. Office)
Stefanie D. Cantor
Bruce A. Kinn
James T. Montgomery, Jr. (Resident at Washington, D.C. Office)
Richard R. Schaul-Yoder
Teresa A. Martland

ASSOCIATE

Brian A. Silikovitz

For Complete List of Firm Personnel, See General Section

For full biographical listings, see the Martindale-Hubbell Law Directory

Hinckley, Allen & Snyder LLP (AV)

28 State Street, 30th Floor, 02109-1775
Telephone: 617-345-9000
Email: firm@haslaw.com *URL:* http://www.haslaw.com
Providence, Rhode Island Office: 1500 Fleet Center.
Telephone: 401-274-2000.
Fax: 401-277-9600. URL: http://www.hawlaw.com.

MEMBERS OF FIRM

Paula K. Andrews
David D. Barricelli (Not admitted in MA)
E. Jerome Batty (Not admitted in MA)
Jonathan Bell
Leon C. Boghossian III
Paul Bork
Stephen J. Carlotti (Not admitted in MA)
David Barry Connolly
Joseph P. Curran (Not admitted in MA)
Michael P. DeFanti
Eric F. Eisenberg
Malcolm Farmer, III
Margaret D. Farrell (Not admitted in MA)
Noel M. Field, Jr. (Not admitted in MA)
Pasco Gasbarro Jr.
Hugh J. Gorman, III
Alan P. Gottlieb
William R. Grimm
Paul A. Hedstrom
Richard L. E. Jocelyn (Not admitted in MA)
Joel Lewin
Doris Jami Licht
Sandra Matrone Mack (Not admitted in MA)
Matthew T. Marcello, III (Not admitted in MA)
Frederick P. McClure
Elizabeth Murdock Myers
Paul F. O'Donnell, III
H. Peter Olsen (Not admitted in MA)
Julianne Palumbo
John J. Pendergast, III (Not admitted in MA)
Gerald J. Petros
Richard H. Pierce
James O. Reavis
Jeremy Ritzenberg
Ralph J. Rivkind
David J. Rubin
Charles E. Schaub, Jr.
Douglas F. Seaver
Paul A. Silver
Herman Snyder
David R. Sullivan
Robert F. Sylvia
Howard E. Walker (Not admitted in MA)
Richard D. Wayne

ASSOCIATES

Jessica M. Bettencourt (Not admitted in MA)
Mark Bianchi
Alyssa V. Boss
Alexandra K. Callam
Jane E. Cohen
Andrew D. Cummings
June E. Daniel (Not admitted in MA)
Josephine A. Giuffre
Kim Herman Goslant
Gloria Maria Gutierrez
Kelley Jordan-Price
Catherine S. Kim
Christopher W. Morog
Elena B. Olson
Joseph D. Whelan (Not admitted in MA)

OF COUNSEL

Willard Krasnow
Willard R. Pope
Bentley Tobin
Joachim A. Weissfeld (Not admitted in MA)

(See Next Column)

For Complete List of Firm Personnel, See General Section

For full biographical listings, see the Martindale-Hubbell Law Directory

Palmer & Dodge LLP (AV)

One Beacon Street, 02108
Telephone: 617-573-0100
Facsimile: 617-227-4420
URL: http://www.palmerdodge.com

MEMBERS OF FIRM

Neil P. Arkuss
Christopher M. Flanagan
Malcolm E. Hindin
Eric F. Menoyo
Arthur B. Page
Steven L. Paul
Thomas M. Spera
Jackson W. Wright, Jr.

For Complete List of Firm Personnel, See General Section

For full biographical listings, see the Martindale-Hubbell Law Directory

Prince, Lobel & Tye LLP (AV)

585 Commercial Street, 02109-1024
Telephone: 617-367-2202
Fax: 617-523-0977

MEMBERS OF FIRM

Martin E. Fishkin
Robert P. Maloney

ASSOCIATE

Stephen K. Fischer

For Complete List of Firm Personnel, See General Section

For full biographical listings, see the Martindale-Hubbell Law Directory

Ropes & Gray (AV)

One International Place, 02110
Telephone: 617-951-7000
Fax: 617-951-7050
Email: postmaster@ropesgray.com *URL:* http://www.ropesgray.com
Washington, D.C. Office: One Franklin Square, 1301 K Street, NW, Suite 800 East.
Telephone: 202-626-3900.
Telecopy: 202-626-3961.
Providence, Rhode Island Office: 30 Kennedy Plaza.
Telephone: 401-455-4400.
Telecopy: 401-455-4401.

MEMBERS OF FIRM

Fred R. Becker
David J. Blattner, Jr.
Ronald L. Groves
Carolyn M. Osteen
Stephen E. Shay (Not admitted in MA)
Susan A. Johnston
Eric M. Elfman
Brett A. Robbins
Adelbert L. Spitzer
Rom P. Watson
Christopher M. Leich
Loretta R. Richard

ASSOCIATES

Deborah J. Coleman
Karen A. Johnson
James R. Brown, Jr.
Debra Brown Allen

OF COUNSEL

Harry K. Mansfield

For Complete List of Firm Personnel, See General Section

For full biographical listings, see the Martindale-Hubbell Law Directory

*CAMBRIDGE,** Middlesex Co.

Mervin M. Wilf, Ltd. (AV)

2 Berkeley Place, 02138
Telephone: 617-876-5200
Email: mwilf@erols.com
Philadelphia, Pennsylvania Office: 3901 Mellon Bank Center. 1735 Market Street.
Telephone: 215-994-1430. 215-568-4842.
Facsimile: 215-994-1432.

Mervin M. Wilf

A list of Representative Clients and References will be furnished upon request.

For full biographical listings, see the Martindale-Hubbell Law Directory

FRANKLIN, Norfolk Co.

Gilmore, Rees & Carlson, P.C. (AV)

1000 Franklin Village Drive, 02038
Telephone: 508-520-2200
Fax: 508-520-2217
Wellesley, Massachusetts Office: 20 Walnut Street, 02181.
Telephone: 781-431-9788.
Fax: 781-431-1957.
Providence, Rhode Island Office: 369 South Main Street, 02903.
Telephone: 401-272-5400.
Fax: 401-453-1177.

(See Next Column)

GILMORE, REES & CARLSON P.C.—*Continued*

Daniel J. Gilmore
Christopher T. Carlson
Bruce J. Bettigole
Paul D. Bishop
Sidney A. Slobodkin
Michael P. Doherty
Craig A. Ciechanowski

OF COUNSEL

William J. Rees
Karin Blake (P.C.)

Katherine A. Botelho
Jane Fisher Carlson
Peter J. Paulousky
Brian L. Gaudet
Michael R. Fiore
Todd M. Machnik
Janis Roney Edinburgh

For full biographical listings, see the Martindale-Hubbell Law Directory

NEWTON, Middlesex Co.

VACOVEC, MAYOTTE & SINGER (AV)

Two Newton Place, Suite 340, 255 Washington Street, 02458-1633
Telephone: 617-964-0500
Fax: 617-969-2002
Email: taxgroup@vacovec.com *URL:* http://www.vacovec.com

MEMBERS OF FIRM

Kenneth J. Vacovec
Maureen C. Mayotte
Paula N. Singer
Kenneth H. Light

ASSOCIATES

Angela M. Cox
Arthur R. Kerr, II
Tonya S. James
Scott C. Cashman
Karen J. Folb
Jay R. Krasner

OF COUNSEL

Stephen P. Koster
John G. Ganick

For full biographical listings, see the Martindale-Hubbell Law Directory

*SPRINGFIELD,** Hampden Co.

ROBINSON DONOVAN MADDEN & BARRY, P.C. (AV)

Suite 1600, Tower Square, 1500 Main Street, 01115-5609
Telephone: 413-732-2301
Fax: 413-785-4658
Email: service@robinson-donovan.com *URL:* http://www.robinson-donovan.com

Homans Robinson (1894-1973)
Lawrence M. Sinclair (1942-1986)
Milton J. Donovan (1906-1995)

RETIRED

John H. Madden, Jr.
Edward J. Barry
Richard S. Milstein

OF COUNSEL

Victor Rosenberg

SENIOR COUNSEL

Jonathan P. Rice

Gordon H. Wentworth
James H. Tourtelotte
Ronald C. Kidd
Jeffrey W. Roberts
Jeffrey L. McCormick
James F. Martin
Robert P. Cunningham
John C. Sikorski
Nancy Frankel Pelletier
Paul S. Weinberg
Frederica H. McCarthy
Matthew J. King
Neva Kaufman Rohan
Douglas F. Boyd
James K. Bodurtha
Keith A. Minoff
Patricia M. Rapinchuk
Kimberly Davis Crear

E. Paul Amata
Lisa A. Bongiovi (Not admitted in MA)
Edward J. Carroll, III
James D. Chadwell
John E. Garber
Patrick J. Markey
Carla W. Newton
Betsy Macmillan Stevens

Representative Clients: BankBoston, N.A.; United Cooperative Bank; Fleet National Bank; CNA; Commercial Union Insurance Co.; Hanover Insurance Group.

For full biographical listings, see the Martindale-Hubbell Law Directory

*WORCESTER,** Worcester Co.

MOUNTAIN, DEARBORN & WHITING LLP (AV)

370 Main Street, 01608
Telephone: 508-756-2423
Fax: 508-755-6640

(See Next Column)

MEMBERS OF FIRM

Alfred N. Whiting (1920-1989)
Thomas R. Mountain
Richard W. Dearborn
Samuel R. DeSimone
Henry W. Beth
Stuart A. Hammer
Francis J. Russell
Dale R. Harger
Mark W. Bloom
Donald J. O'Neil
Lawrence S. Delaney
Ann K. Molloy
Lisa D. Tingue

For full biographical listings, see the Martindale-Hubbell Law Directory

SEDER & CHANDLER (AV)

A Partnership including a Professional Corporation
Established 1918
Burnside Building, 339 Main Street, 01608
Telephone: 508-757-7721
Telecopiers: 508-798-1863; 508-831-0955

MEMBERS OF FIRM

Samuel Seder (1918-1964)
Harold Seder (1934-1988)
Burton Chandler
J. Robert Seder
Darragh K. Kasakoff
Marvin S. Silver, P.C.
Robert S. Adler
Kevin C. McGee
Kurt L. Binder

ASSOCIATES

Paul J. O'Riordan
Jeffrey P. Greenberg
Todd Rodman

OF COUNSEL

Saul A. Seder
Gerald E. Norman
Philip C. Lombardo, Jr.

Reference: First National Bank of Boston; Safety Fund National Bank; Fleet National Bank.

For full biographical listings, see the Martindale-Hubbell Law Directory

MICHIGAN

*ANN ARBOR,** Washtenaw Co.

BRAUN KENDRICK FINKBEINER PLC (AV)

First National Building, 210 S. Main, Suite 700, 48104
Telephone: 313-995-4100
Telecopier: 313-995-4798
Email: ALBFIE@BKF-LAW.COM *URL:* http://www.bkf-law.com
Bay City, Michigan Office: 201 Phoenix Building, P.O. Box 2039.
Telephone: 517-895-8505.
Telecopier: 517-895-8437.
Saginaw, Michigan Office: 101 N. Washington, Suite 812.
Telephone: 517-753-3461.
Telecopier: 517-753-3951.
Saginaw Township, Michigan Office: 5800 Gratiot Road, Suite 107, P.O. Box 5169.
Telephone: 517-799-8692.
Fax: 517-799-4666.
Mt. Pleasant, Michigan Office: 805 North Brown.
Telephone: 517-775-7404.
Telecopier: 517-775-3764.

Barry M. Levine

Representative Clients: The Dow Chemical Co.; General Motors Corp.; Merrill, Lynch, Inc.; Saginaw General Hospital; Saginaw News; The Wickes Foundation.

For Complete List of Firm Personnel, See General Section

For full biographical listings, see the Martindale-Hubbell Law Directory

BATTLE CREEK, Calhoun Co.

KREIS, ENDERLE, CALLANDER & HUDGINS, A PROFESSIONAL CORPORATION (AV)

One West Michigan Avenue, 49017
Telephone: 616-966-3000
Facsimile: 616-966-3022
Email: kech@kech.com *URL:* http://www.kech.com
Kalamazoo, Michigan Office: One Moorsbridge, P.O. Box 4010, 49003-4010.
Telephone: 616-324-3000.
Fax: 616-324-3010.

Russell A. Kreis (Resident, Kalamazoo Office)
Janice Roark Peters (Resident, Kalamazoo Office)
Matthew S. DePerno (Resident, Kalamazoo Office)

For Complete List of Firm Personnel, See General Section

For full biographical listings, see the Martindale-Hubbell Law Directory

*BAY CITY,** Bay Co.

Braun Kendrick Finkbeiner PLC (AV)

201 Phoenix Building, P.O. Box 2039, 48708
Telephone: 517-895-8505
Telecopier: 517-895-8437
Email: ALBFIE@BKF-LAW.COM *URL:* http://www.bkf-law.com
Saginaw, Michigan Office: 101 N. Washington, Suite 812. 8th Floor Second National Bank Building.
Telephone: 517-753-3461.
Telecopier: 517-753-3951.
Saginaw Township, Michigan Office: 5800 Gratiot Road, Suite 107, P.O. Box 5169.
Telephone: 517-799-8692.
Fax: 517-799-4666.
Ann Arbor, Michigan Office: First National Building. 201 S. Main, Suite 700.
Telephone: 313-995-4100.
Telecopier: 313-995-4798.
Mt. Pleasant, Michigan Office: 805 North Brown.
Telephone: 517-775-7404.
Telecopier: 517-775-3764.

Ralph J. Isackson
Daniel S. Opperman
Gregory T. Demers

Representative Clients: Bay Health Systems; Catholic Federal Credit Union; City of Saginaw; City of Vassar; City of Zilwaukee; Corporate Service; Cox Cable.

For Complete List of Firm Personnel, See General Section

For full biographical listings, see the Martindale-Hubbell Law Directory

BIRMINGHAM, Oakland Co.

Hyman Lippitt, P.C. (AV)

185 Oakland Avenue, Suite 300, 48009
Telephone: 248-646-8292
Facsimile: 248-646-8375
Email: hymalipp@tir.com

J. Leonard Hyman
Norman L. Lippitt
Douglas A. Hyman
Brian D. O'Keefe
H. Joel Newman
Nazli G. Sater
Kenneth F. Neuman
Terry S. Givens
Paul J. Fischer
John A. Sellers
Robert H. Lippitt
Roger L. Myers
Sally A. Rutledge
Joseph Pia
John P. Gonway
Leif K. Anderson
Jennifer S. Gold
Julie Lyons Kosovec
Dawn S. Spratley
Michael T. Price

For full biographical listings, see the Martindale-Hubbell Law Directory

BLOOMFIELD HILLS, Oakland Co.

Dawda, Mann, Mulcahy & Sadler, P.L.C. (AV)

1533 North Woodward Avenue Suite 200, 48304-2815
Telephone: 248-642-3700
Fax: 248-642-7791
Email: EMail@DMMS.Com

Curtis J. Mann
Glenn G. Ross
Paul C. Apap

For full biographical listings, see the Martindale-Hubbell Law Directory

Hertz, Schram & Saretsky, P.C. (AV)

1760 South Telegraph Road, Suite 300, 48302
Telephone: 248-335-5000
Fax: 248-335-3346
Email: lawhss@aol.com *URL:* http://www.legalleaders.com

Bradley J. Schram
Howard Hertz
Gary M. Saretsky
Robert S. Hertzberg
Victor M. Norris
Steve J. Weiss
Robert Paul Geller
Walter J. Piszczatowski
Jeffrey A. Robbins
Mark L. Kowalsky

Dana A. Donohue
Miles D. Hart
Karen A. Gould
Paul K. Villarruel
Bradford T. Yaker
Michael F. Jacobson
Michael I. Zousmer
Brian Witus
Eva T. Cantarella
Eric Andrew Michaels

COUNSEL

Richard P. Zipser
Lisa M. Kavalhuna (Not admitted in MI)
James W. Burdick

(See Next Column)

OF COUNSEL

David L. Steinberg
Albert L. Holtz
Elmer L. Roller
Robert A. Canner
Harvey D. Geller (1928-1989)

For full biographical listings, see the Martindale-Hubbell Law Directory

Howard & Howard Attorneys, P.C. (AV)

The Pinehurst Office Center, Suite 101, 1400 North Woodward Avenue, 48304-2855
Telephone: 248-645-1483
Telecopier: 248-645-1568
Kalamazoo, Michigan Office: The Michigan Building, Suite 200, 100 Portage Street.
Telephone: 616-382-1483.
Telecopier: 616-382-1568.
Lansing, Michigan Office: The Phoenix Building, Suite 500, 222 Washington Square, North.
Telephone: 517-485-1483.
Telecopier: 517-485-1568.
Peoria, Illinois Office: One Technology Plaza, Suite 600, 211 Fulton Street.
Telephone: 309-672-1483.
Telecopier: 309-672-1568.

Mark A. Davis
Robert B. Johnston
Lee A. Sartori
Gina M. Torielli
James C. Wickens
John E. Young

Representative Clients: For Representative Client list, see General Practice, Bloomfield Hills, MI.

For Complete List of Firm Personnel, See General Section

For full biographical listings, see the Martindale-Hubbell Law Directory

*DETROIT,** Wayne Co.

Abbott, Nicholson, Quilter, Esshaki & Youngblood, P.C. (AV)

300 River Place, Suite 3000, 48207-4225
Telephone: 313-566-2500
Telecopier: 313-566-2502
Email: anqey@anqey.com *URL:* http://www.anqey.com

C. Richard Abbott
John R. Nicholson
Thomas R. Quilter III
Gene J. Esshaki
John F. Youngblood
James B. Perry
Carl F. Jarboe
Jay A. Kennedy
Timothy A. Stoepker
Timothy J. Kramer
Norbert T. Madison, Jr.
William D. Gilbride, Jr.
Mary P. Nelson
Michael R. Blum
Anne Warren Bagno
Thomas J. Giachino

Eric J. Girdler
Jill A. Bankey
Daniel G. Kielczewski
George P. Butler III
Christopher P. Baker
Sean A. Fraser

OF COUNSEL

Thomas C. Shumaker
Lisa R. Gorman

For full biographical listings, see the Martindale-Hubbell Law Directory

Bendure & Thomas (AV)

577 East Larned, Suite 210, 48226-4392
Telephone: 313-961-1525
Fax: 313-961-1553

MEMBERS OF FIRM

Mark R. Bendure
Marc E. Thomas

ASSOCIATES

J. Christopher Caldwell
Victor S. Valenti
Kevin P. Kavanagh

OF COUNSEL

John A. Lydick
Thomas R. Present

For full biographical listings, see the Martindale-Hubbell Law Directory

Bodman, Longley & Dahling LLP (AV)

34th Floor 100 Renaissance Center, 48243
Telephone: 313-259-7777
Fax: 313-393-7579
Email: info@bodmanlongley.com *URL:* http://www.bodmanlongley.com
Troy, Michigan Office: Suite 2020, 755 West Big Beaver Road.
Telephone: 248-362-2110.
Fax: 248-244-0780.
Ann Arbor, Michigan Office: 110 Miller, Suite 300.
Telephone: 734-761-3780.
Fax: 734-930-2494.
Northern Michigan Office: 229 Court Street, P.O. Box 405, Cheboygan.
Telephone: 231-627-4351.
Fax: 231-627-2802.

(See Next Column)

BODMAN, LONGLEY & DAHLING LLP—*Continued*

MEMBERS OF FIRM

George D. Miller, Jr.
David M. Hempstead
Randolph S. Perry
Christopher J. Dine
David P. Larsen
Barnett Jay Colvin
Carl F. Stafford

ASSOCIATES

Timothy R. Damschroder (Ann Arbor Office)
Andrew H. Curoe
Rachelle Propson Tyshka
Robert P. Tiplady
Gene P. Bowen (Troy Office)
J. Adam Behrendt

For Representative Client List, See General Section

For Complete List of Firm Personnel, See General Section

For full biographical listings, see the Martindale-Hubbell Law Directory

BUTZEL LONG, A PROFESSIONAL CORPORATION (AV)

Suite 900, 150 West Jefferson, 48226
Telephone: 313-225-7000
Telecopier: 313-225-7080
Email: melnick@butzel.com *URL:* http://www.butzel.com
Birmingham, Michigan Office: Suite 200, 32270 Telegraph Road.
Telephone: 810-258-1616.
Telecopier: 810-258-1439.
Okemos, Michigan Office: Suite 300, 2127 University Park Drive.
Telephone: 517-372-6622.
Telecopier: 517-372-6672.
Ann Arbor, Michigan Office: Suite 300, 350 South Main Street.
Telephone: 313-995-3110.
Telecopier: 313-995-1777.
Grosse Pointe Farms, Michigan Office: Suite 260, 21 Kercheval.
Telephone: 313-886-5446.
Telecopier: 313-886-2114.
Boca Raton, Florida Office: Suite 411, 1200 North Federal Highway.
Telephone: 561-368-2151.
Telecopier: 561-368-4668.
Palm Beach Gardens, Florida Office: Suite 227, 11382 Prosperity Farms Road.
Telephone: 561-625-4442.
Telecopier: 561-625-6901.
Naples, Florida Office: Suite 705, 801 Laurel Oak Drive.
Telephone: 941-597-4500.
Telecopier: 941-597-5623.

Paul L. Triemstra (Birmingham)
Philip J. Kessler
David W. Sommerfeld (Birmingham and Grosse Pointe Farms)
John J. Raymond, Jr. (Boca Raton, Naples and Palm Beach Gardens, Florida and Birmingham)
David W. Berry (Birmingham)
Carl Rashid, Jr.
Michael D. Guzick (Birmingham)
James L. Hughes
Terry O. Lang
Clara DeMatteis Mager

COUNSEL

Oscar H. Feldman (Birmingham)

OF COUNSEL

John J. Raymond, Sr. (Boca Raton, Naples and Palm Beach Gardens, Florida)

SENIOR ATTORNEY

Eric R. Wapnick

Antoinette M. Pilzner
David B. Braun

Representative Clients: Bridgestone/Firestone, Inc.; Detroit Diesel Corp.; The Detroit News, Inc.; Kelly Services; Merrill Lynch & Co., Inc.; Stroh Companies; Takata Corp.; TRW Automotive; The University of Michigan.

For full biographical listings, see the Martindale-Hubbell Law Directory

DYKEMA GOSSETT PLLC (AV)

400 Renaissance Center, 48243-1668
Telephone: 313-568-6800
Fax: 313-568-6545
Email: mstarrs@dykema.com *URL:* http://www.dykema.com
Ann Arbor, Michigan Office: 315 East Eisenhower Parkway, Suite 100, 48108-3306.
Telephone: 734-214-7660.
Fax: 734-214-7696.
Bloomfield Hills, Michigan Office: 1577 North Woodward Avenue, Suite 300, 48304-2820.
Telephone: 248-203-0700.
Fax: 248-203-0763.
Chicago, Illinois Office: 55 East Monroe Street, Suite 3050, 60603-5709.
Telephone: 312-551-4900.
Fax: 312-551-4919.
Grand Rapids, Michigan Office: Suite 700, 300 Ottawa Avenue, N.W., 49503-2304.
Telephone: 616-776-7500.
Fax: 616-776-7573.

(See Next Column)

Lansing, Michigan Office: 800 Michigan National Tower, 48933-1707.
Telephone: 517-374-9100.
Fax: 517-374-9191.
Washington, D.C. Office: Franklin Square, Suite 300 West, 1300 I Street, N.W., 20005-3306.
Telephone: 202-522-8600.
Fax: 202-522-8669.
Affiliated Office: Via Matconi, 3, 40122 Bologna, Italy.
Telephone: 011-39-51-228222.
Fax: 011-39-51-6593580.

MEMBERS OF FIRM

Michael G. Cumming (Resident at Bloomfield Hills Office)
Marie R. Deveney (Resident at Ann Arbor Office)
James M. Elsworth
William E. Fisher
Steven E. Grob
Louis W. Kasischke (Resident at Bloomfield Hills Office)
Mark C. Larson
Stewart L. Mandell
Thomas B. Spillane, Jr. (Resident at Bloomfield Hills Office)
Sherrill D. Wolford

RETIRED MEMBER

Raymond T. Huetteman, Jr. (Resident at Ann Arbor Office)

ASSOCIATES

Eric Thomas Carver
Jennifer M. Crawford (Resident at Bloomfield Hills Office)
Mary T. Malpass

For Complete List of Firm Personnel, See General Section

For full biographical listings, see the Martindale-Hubbell Law Directory

FILDEW HINKS, P.L.L.C. (AV)

3600 Penobscot Building, 645 Griswold Street, 48226-4291
Telephone: 313-961-9700
Facsimile: 313-961-0754

MEMBERS OF FIRM

Stanley L. Fildew (1896-1978)
Frank T. Hinks (1887-1974)
Richard E. Hinks (1916-1990)
John H. Fildew
Alan C. Miller
Randall S. Wangen
Mary Jane Ruffley
Robert D. Welchli
William P. Thorpe
Colleen A. Kramer
Stephen J. Pokoj
Charles S. Kennedy III

ASSOCIATE

Walter B. Fisher Jr.

References: First of America Bank-Detroit, N.A.; Comerica Bank-Detroit; National Bank of Detroit.

For full biographical listings, see the Martindale-Hubbell Law Directory

HONIGMAN MILLER SCHWARTZ AND COHN (AV)

2290 First National Building, 660 Woodward Avenue, 48226
Telephone: 313-465-7000
Telecopier: 313-465-8000
Telex: 235705
Email: mvg@honigman.com *URL:* http://law.honigman.com
Lansing, Michigan Office: Phoenix Building, 222 North Washington Square, Suite 400, 48933-1800.
Telephone: 517-484-8282.

MEMBERS OF FIRM

Roger Cook
John H. Eggertsen
Michael J. Friedman
Gerald M. Griffith
Jeffrey A. Hyman
Mary Jo Larson
Marguerite Munson Lentz
Charles Nida
James H. Novis
Sherill Siebert
Richard S. Soble
Brad M. Tomtishen
Alan M. Valade (Lansing, Michigan Office)
Patrick R. Van Tiflin (Lansing, Michigan Office)
Richard E. Zuckerman

ASSOCIATES

Kristine McKimson Renke
Scott A. Small

Representative Clients: See General Section.

For Complete List of Firm Personnel, See General Section

For full biographical listings, see the Martindale-Hubbell Law Directory

JAFFE, RAITT, HEUER & WEISS, PROFESSIONAL CORPORATION (AV)

One Woodward Avenue, Suite 2400, 48226
Telephone: 313-961-8380
Telecopier: 313-961-8358
Cable Address: "Jafsni"
Southfield, Michigan Office: Travelers Tower, Suite 1520.
Telephone: 313-961-8380.

Gary R. Glenn
Ira J. Jaffe
Robert E. Lewis
Joel J. Morris
David H. Raitt
William E. Sider
Arthur A. Weiss

(See Next Column)

JAFFE, RAITT, HEUER & WEISS PROFESSIONAL CORPORATION, *Detroit—Continued*

Milton I. Kovinsky
Jordan H. Smith

Representative Clients: Edgemere Enterprises; Frankel Associates, Inc.; Somerset Inn & Apartments; Sosnick Development Co.; Uniprop, Inc.

For Complete List of Firm Personnel, See General Section

For full biographical listings, see the Martindale-Hubbell Law Directory

JOSLYN KEYDEL & WALLACE, LLP (AV)

Albert Kahn Building, 9th Floor, 7430 Second Avenue, 48202-2717
Telephone: 313-871-4181
Fax: 313-871-6100
Email: etal@jkwlaw.com

MEMBERS OF FIRM

Lee E. Joslyn (1864-1936)
Alan W. Joslyn (1899-1990)
Lee E. Joslyn, Jr. (1895-1955)
Frederick R. Keydel (PLLC)
Harvey B. Wallace II (PLLC)

ASSOCIATE

Patrice M. Ticknor

LEGAL SUPPORT PERSONNEL

PARALEGALS

Diane C. Simpson
Alice M. Pricer
Ruth G. Spector
Sarah E. Monahan

References: NBD Bank, N.A.; Comerica Bank.

For full biographical listings, see the Martindale-Hubbell Law Directory

MILLER, CANFIELD, PADDOCK AND STONE, P.L.C. (AV)

A Professional Limited Liability Company
Founded in 1852 by Sidney Davy Miller
150 West Jefferson, Suite 2500, 48226-4415
Telephone: 313-963-6420
Fax: 313-496-7500
Cable Address: "Stem Detroit"
URL: http://www.millercanfield.com
Ann Arbor, Michigan Office: 101 North Main Street, 7th Floor, 48104-1400.
Telephone: 734-663-2445.
Fax: 734-747-7147.
Troy, Michigan Office: 840 West Long Lake Road, Suite 200, 48098.
Telephone: 248-879-2000.
Fax: 248-879-2001.
Grand Rapids, Michigan Office: 99 Monroe, N.W., Suite 1200, 49503-2639.
Telephone: 616-454-8656.
Fax: 616-776-6322.
Howell, Michigan Office: 121 South Barnard Street, Suite 4, 48843-2305.
Telephone: 517-546-7600.
Telecopier: 517-546-6974.
Kalamazoo, Michigan Office: 444 West Michigan Avenue, 49007-3752.
Telephone: 616-381-7030.
Fax: 616-382-0244.
Lansing, Michigan Office: One Michigan Avenue, Suite 900, 48933-1609.
Telephone: 517-487-2070.
Fax: 517-374-6304.
Monroe, Michigan Office: 214 East Elm Avenue, Suite 100, 48162-2682.
Telephone: 734-243-2000.
Fax: 734-243-0901.
Washington, D.C. Office: 1900 K Street, N.W., Suite 1150. 20006.
Telephone: 202-429-5575; 785-0600.
Fax: 202-331-1118; 785-1234.
Pensacola, Florida Office: 25 West Cedar, 32501.
Telephone: 850-469-1088.
Fax: 850-432-0677.
New York, New York Office: 1450 Broadway, 41st Floor, 10018.
Telephone: 212-704-4400.
Fax: 212-704-4410.
Gdynia, Poland Office: UL. Slaska 21, 81-319.
Telephone: 011-485-831-2808.
Fax: 011-48-58-628 6411.
Warsaw, Poland Office: UL. Nowogrodzkall, 5th Floor, 00-513.
Telephone: 011-4822 529 0200.
Fax: 011-4822 529 0201.
Katowice, Poland Office: UL. Francuska 35/37, 40-027.
Telephone: 011 (48-32) 757-2414.
Fax: 011 (48-32) 757-2483.

PRINCIPALS OF FIRM

Stevan Uzelac (P.C.)
Robert S. Ketchum
Samuel J. McKim, III, (P.C.)
Rocque E. Lipford (P.C.) (Monroe Office)
John A. Thurber (P.C.) (Troy Office)
Orin D. Brustad
John A. Campbell (Kalamazoo Office)
Kenneth E. Konop (Troy Office)
James W. Williams (Troy Office)
Michael R. Atkins (Lansing Office)
Jeffrey M. McHugh
Robert F. Rhoades

(See Next Column)

PRINCIPALS OF FIRM (Continued)

Gregory V. Di Censo (Troy Office)
Michael A. Indenbaum
Vernon Bennett III (Kalamazoo and Grand Rapids Offices)
Deborah W. Thompson
Dawn M. Schluter (Troy Office)
Joanne B. Faycurry
Richard I. Loebl

OF COUNSEL/SENIOR COUNSEL

Peter P. Thurber
Lawrence A. King (P.C.) (Troy Office)
Joseph F. Maycock, Jr.
George E. Parker, III
Walter A. Payne, III

ASSOCIATE

Nancy Gerarda Itnyre

Representative Firm Clients: Chrysler Corporation; Comerica, Incorporated; City of Detroit, Michigan; Detroit Tigers, Inc.; First of Michigan; Ford Motor Company; Ford Motor Credit Company; Great Lakes Bancorp; Henry Ford Hospital; INVETECH Company.

For Complete List of Firm Personnel, See General Section

For full biographical listings, see the Martindale-Hubbell Law Directory

DAVID M. THOMS & ASSOCIATES, P.C. (AV)

400 Renaissance Center, Suite 950, 48243
Telephone: 313-259-6333
Facsimile: 313-259-7037
Email: Thoms@ameritech.net *URL:* http://www.lawyers.com/thoms&associates

David M. Thoms

Audrey R. Holley
Danielle M. Spehar
Joseph A. Durocher

Representative Clients: Avion Concepts, Inc.; Gibbs World Wide Wines, Inc.; deBary Voyage, Inc.; North Management, Inc.; R.G. & G.R. Harris Funeral Home, Inc.; St. Jude Children's Research Hospital; The Salvation Army.
References: Comerica Bank-Detroit; National Bank of Detroit.

For full biographical listings, see the Martindale-Hubbell Law Directory

TIMMIS & INMAN L.L.P. (AV)

300 Talon Centre, 48207
Telephone: 313-396-4200
Facsimile: 313-396-4228
Email: info@timmis-inman.com *URL:* http://www.timmis-inman.com

Michael T. Timmis
George M. Malis

Erich J. D'Andrea
Jennifer A. Bourgoin

Representative Client: Talon Inc.; Chateau Properties, Inc.

For Complete List of Firm Personnel, See General Section

For full biographical listings, see the Martindale-Hubbell Law Directory

FARMINGTON HILLS, Oakland Co.

COUZENS, LANSKY, FEALK, ELLIS, ROEDER & LAZAR, P.C. (AV)

39395 West 12 Mile Road, Suite 200, 48331-2913
Telephone: 248-489-8600
Facsimile: 248-489-4156
Email: info@couzens.com *URL:* http://www.couzens.com

Sheldon A. Fealk
Jack S. Couzens, II
Donald M. Lansky
Alan C. Roeder
Renard J. Kolasa
Kathryn Gilson Sussman
Jeffrey A. Levine
Marc L. Prey
Lisa J. Walters
Donald A. Wagner
Michael P. Witzke
Cyrus Raamin Kashef
David B. Deutsch

Alisa A. Kwang
Turkia Awada Mullin
Raoul K. Maitra

Representative Clients: Provided upon request.
Reference: Michigan National Bank.

For Complete List of Firm Personnel, See General Section

For full biographical listings, see the Martindale-Hubbell Law Directory

*GRAND RAPIDS,** Kent Co.

BORRE, PETERSON, FOWLER & REENS, P.C. (AV)

300 Ottawa N.W., Suite 500, P.O. Box 1767, 49501-1767
Telephone: 616-459-1971
Fax: 616-459-2393
Email: 105162.1531@compuserve.com

(See Next Column)

BORRE, PETERSON, FOWLER & REENS P.C.—*Continued*

Glen V. Borre
James B. Peterson
Ben A. Fowler
William G. Krupar

Representative Clients: A.L.T.L., Inc.; Beaver Island Boat Co.; Big Rapids Products, Inc.; Herbruck Poultry Ranch, Inc.; J&H Oil Co.; Master Finish Co.; Michigan Blueberry Growers Association; NBD Bank; Pfeiffer Lincoln Mercury, Inc.

For Complete List of Firm Personnel, See General Section

For full biographical listings, see the Martindale-Hubbell Law Directory

MILLER, CANFIELD, PADDOCK AND STONE, P.L.C. (AV)

A Professional Limited Liability Company
Founded in 1852 by Sidney Davy Miller
99 Monroe, N.W. Suite 1200, 49503-2639
Telephone: 616-454-8656
Fax: 616-776-6322
URL: http://www.millercanfield.com
Detroit, Michigan Office: 150 West Jefferson, Suite 2500, 48226-4415.
Telephone: 313-963-6420.
Fax: 313-496-7500.
Cable Address: "Stem Detroit."
Ann Arbor, Michigan Office: 101 North Main Street, 7th Floor, 48104-1400.
Telephone: 734-663-2445.
Fax: 734-747-7147.
Troy, Michigan Office: 840 West Long Lake Road, Suite 200, 48098.
Telephone: 248-879-2000.
Fax: 248-879-2001.
Howell, Michigan Office: 121 South Barnard Street, Suite 4, 48843-2305.
Telephone: 517-546-7600.
Telecopier: 517-546-6974.
Kalamazoo, Michigan Office: 444 West Michigan Avenue, 49007-3752.
Telephone: 616-381-7030.
Fax: 616-382-0244.
Lansing, Michigan Office: One Michigan Avenue, Suite 900, 48933-1609.
Telephone: 517-487-2070.
Fax: 517-374-6304.
Monroe, Michigan Office: 214 East Elm Avenue, Suite 100, 48162-2682.
Telephone: 734-243-2000.
Fax: 734-243-0901.
Washington, D.C. Office: 1900 K Street, N.W., Suite 1150. 20006.
Telephone: 202-429-5575; 785-0600.
Fax: 202-331-1118; 785-1234.
Pensacola, Florida Office: 25 West Cedar, 32501.
Telephone: 850-469-1088.
Fax: 850-432-0677.
New York, New York Office: 1450 Broadway, 41st Floor, 10018.
Telephone: 212-704-4400.
Fax: 212-704-4410.
Gdynia, Poland Office: UL. Slaska 21, 81-319.
Telephone: 011-485-831-2808.
Fax: 011-48-58-628 6411.
Warsaw, Poland Office: UL. Nowogrodzkall, 5th Floor, 00-513.
Telephone: 011-4822 529 0200.
Fax: 011-4822 529 0201.
Katowice, Poland Office: UL. Francuska 35/37, 40-027.
Telephone: 011 (48-32) 757-2414.
Fax: 011 (48-32) 757-2483.

PRINCIPALS

Vernon Bennett III

Representative Firm Clients: Chrysler Corporation; Comerica, Incorporated; City of Detroit, Michigan; Detroit Tigers, Inc.; First of Michigan; Ford Motor Company; Ford Motor Credit Company; Great Lakes Bancorp; Henry Ford Hospital; INVETECH Company.

For Complete List of Firm Personnel, See General Section

For full biographical listings, see the Martindale-Hubbell Law Directory

RUSSELL & BATCHELOR (AV)

Suite 411-S Waters Building, 161 Ottawa Avenue, N.W., 49503
Telephone: 616-774-8422
Fax: 616-774-0326
Email: WJR411S@aol.com

MEMBER OF FIRM

Walter J. Russell

Representative Clients: Progressive Architects/Engineers/Planners, Inc.; Quality Brass, Inc.; Shellcast, Inc.; Victor S. Barnes and Co.; Stovall Well Drilling; F. R. Neuman Co.; Start Advertising, Inc.; Tri-River Agency; Van. R. Kipka, Inc.; Wiltzer, Gerald R., Builder.; Thomet Chevrolet and Buick, Inc.

For full biographical listings, see the Martindale-Hubbell Law Directory

WARNER NORCROSS & JUDD LLP (AV)

900 Old Kent Building, 111 Lyon Street, N.W., 49503-2489
Telephone: 616-752-2000
Fax: 616-752-2500
URL: http://www.wnj.com
Muskegon, Michigan Office: 400 Terrace Plaza, P.O. Box 900.
Telephone: 231-727-2600.
Fax: 231-727-2699.
Holland, Michigan Office: Curtis Center, Suite 300, 170 College Avenue.
Telephone: 616-396-9800.
Fax: 616-396-3656.
Southfield, Michigan Office: 1000 Town Center, Suite 650.
Telephone: 248-223-5000.
Fax: 248-223-5005.

MEMBERS OF FIRM

George L. Whitfield
Jerome M. Smith
I. John Snider, II (Resident Member, Muskegon Office)
John R. Marquis (Resident Member, Holland Office)
John H. Martin (Resident Member, Muskegon Office)
Vernon P. Saper
Stephen R. Kretschman
Carl W. Dufendach
Bruce C. Young
Paul R. Jackson (Resident Member, Muskegon Office)
Cameron S. DeLong
Jeffrey B. Power
Mark K. Harder (Resident Member, Holland Office)

ASSOCIATES

John E. Kessler (Resident, Holland Office)
Jaron J. Nyhof (Resident, Holland Office)

OF COUNSEL

Roger H. Oetting

COUNSEL

Jerry D. Hanscum (Resident Member, Southfield Office)

For full biographical listings, see the Martindale-Hubbell Law Directory

GROSSE POINTE FARMS, Wayne Co.

ALLAN NEEF (AV)

18580 Mack Avenue, 48236
Telephone: 313-343-9200
Fax: 313-343-0207

For full biographical listings, see the Martindale-Hubbell Law Directory

*JACKSON,** Jackson Co.

MARCOUX, ALLEN, ABBOTT, SCHOMER & BOWER, P.C. (AV)

145 South Jackson Street, P.O. Box 787, 49204-0787
Telephone: 517-787-4100
Fax: 517-787-9455
Email: marcoux@jacksonmi.com

William J. Marcoux (Retired)
William O. Allen
William M. Abbott
John H. Schomer
Diane Y. Bower
William B. Nichols, Jr.
Robert T. Kendall, III
Timothy R. Allen
Richard C. Lindsey, Jr.

OF COUNSEL

Walter R. Boris
Lawrence L. Bullen
Philip M. Moilanen
Terry J. Klaasen
T. Harrison Stanton

For full biographical listings, see the Martindale-Hubbell Law Directory

*KALAMAZOO,** Kalamazoo Co.

EARLY, LENNON, PETERS & CROCKER, P.C. (AV)

900 Comerica Building, 49007-4752
Telephone: 616-381-8844
Fax: 616-349-8525
Email: elpc@michbar.org

George H. Lennon, III
Robert M. Taylor

Attorneys for: Aetna Insurance; Kemper Group; Medical Protective Co.; Zurich Insurance; Liberty Mutual; Home Insurance.

For Complete List of Firm Personnel, See General Section

For full biographical listings, see the Martindale-Hubbell Law Directory

KREIS, ENDERLE, CALLANDER & HUDGINS, A PROFESSIONAL CORPORATION (AV)

One Moorsbridge, P.O. Box 4010, 49003-4010
Telephone: 616-324-3000
Facsimile: 616-324-3010
Email: kech@kech.com *URL:* http://www.kech.com
Battle Creek, Michigan Office: One West Michigan Avenue, 49017.
Telephone: 616-966-3000.
Fax: 616-966-3022.

(See Next Column)

KREIS, ENDERLE, CALLANDER & HUDGINS A PROFESSIONAL CORPORATION, *Kalamazoo—Continued*

Russell A. Kreis | Janice Roark Peters
Matthew S. DePerno

For Complete List of Firm Personnel, See General Section

For full biographical listings, see the Martindale-Hubbell Law Directory

MILLER, CANFIELD, PADDOCK AND STONE, P.L.C. (AV)

A Professional Limited Liability Company
Founded in 1852 by Sidney Davy Miller
444 West Michigan Avenue, 49007-3752
Telephone: 616-381-7030
Fax: 616-382-0244
URL: http://www.millercanfield.com
Detroit, Michigan Office: 150 West Jefferson, Suite 2500, 48226-4415.
Telephone: 313-963-6420.
Fax: 313-496-7500.
Cable Address: "Stem Detroit."
Ann Arbor, Michigan Office: 101 North Main Street, 7th Floor, 48104-1400.
Telephone: 734-663-2445.
Fax: 734-747-7147.
Troy, Michigan Office: 840 West Long Lake Road, Suite 200, 48098.
Telephone: 248-879-2000.
Fax: 248-879-2001.
Grand Rapids, Michigan Office: 99 Monroe, N.W., Suite 1200, 49503-2639.
Telephone: 616-454-8656.
Fax: 616-776-6322.
Howell, Michigan Office: 121 South Barnard Street, Suite 4, 48843-2305.
Telephone: 517-546-7600.
Telecopier: 517-546-6974.
Lansing, Michigan Office: One Michigan Avenue, Suite 900, 48933-1609.
Telephone: 517-487-2070.
Fax: 517-374-6304.
Monroe, Michigan Office: 214 East Elm Avenue, Suite 100, 48162-2682.
Telephone: 734-243-2000.
Fax: 734-243-0901.
Washington, D.C. Office: 1900 K Street, N.W., Suite 1150. 20006.
Telephone: 202-429-5575; 785-0600.
Fax: 202-331-1118; 785-1234.
Pensacola, Florida Office: 25 West Cedar, 32501.
Telephone: 850-469-1088.
Fax: 850-432-0677.
New York, New York Office: 1450 Broadway, 41st Floor, 10018.
Telephone: 212-704-4400.
Fax: 212-704-4410.
Gdynia, Poland Office: UL. Slaska 21, 81-319.
Telephone: 011-485-831-2808.
Fax: 011-48-58-628 6411.
Warsaw, Poland Office: UL. Nowogrodzkall, 5th Floor, 00-513.
Telephone: 011-4822 529 0200.
Fax: 011-4822 529 0201.
Katowice, Poland Office: UL. Francuska 35/37, 40-027.
Telephone: 011 (48-32) 757-2414.
Fax: 011 (48-32) 757-2483.

PRINCIPALS

John A. Campbell | Vernon Bennett III

Representative Firm Clients: Chrysler Corporation; Comerica, Incorporated; City of Detroit, Michigan; Detroit Tigers, Inc.; First of Michigan; Ford Motor Company; Ford Motor Credit Company; Great Lakes Bancorp; Henry Ford Hospital; INVETECH Company.

For Complete List of Firm Personnel, See General Section

For full biographical listings, see the Martindale-Hubbell Law Directory

LANSING, Ingham Co.

HONIGMAN MILLER SCHWARTZ AND COHN (AV)

A Partnership including Professional Corporations
222 North Washington Square, Suite 400, 48933-1800
Telephone: 517-484-8282
Telecopier: 517-484-8286
Email: mvg@honigman.com *URL:* http://law.honigman.com
Detroit, Michigan Office: 2290 First National Building, 660 Woodward Avenue, 48226.
Telephone: 313-465-7000.

MEMBERS

Alan M. Valade | Patrick R. Van Tiflin

For Complete List of Firm Personnel, See General Section

For full biographical listings, see the Martindale-Hubbell Law Directory

HOWARD & HOWARD ATTORNEYS, P.C. (AV)

The Phoenix Building, Suite 500, 222 Washington Square, North, 48933-1817
Telephone: 517-485-1483
Telecopier: 517-485-1568
Kalamazoo, Michigan Office: The Michigan Building, Suite 200, 100 Portage Street.
Telephone: 616-382-1483.
Telecopier: 616-382-1568.
Bloomfield Hills, Michigan Office: The Pinehurst Office Center, Suite 101, 1400 North Woodward Avenue.
Telephone: 248-645-1483.
Telecopier: 248-645-1568.
Peoria, Illinois Office: One Technology Plaza, Suite 600, 211 Fulton Street.
Telephone: 309-672-1483.
Telecopier: 309-672-1568.

Michele LaForest Halloran | Gina M. Torielli

Representative Clients: For Representative Client list, see General Practice, Lansing, MI.

For Complete List of Firm Personnel, See General Section

For full biographical listings, see the Martindale-Hubbell Law Directory

LIVONIA, Wayne Co.

FRIED & ASSOCIATES, P.C. (AV)

32900 5 Mile Road, Suite 4, 48154-3059
Telephone: 734-421-5055
Fax: 734-421-5591
URL: http://www.lawyers.com/fried&associates

William C. Fried

For full biographical listings, see the Martindale-Hubbell Law Directory

*MIDLAND,** Midland Co.

CURRIE KENDALL POLASKY MEISEL, PLC (AV)

6024 Eastman Avenue, P.O. Box 2765, 48641-2765
Telephone: 517-839-0300
Fax: 517-832-0077
Saginaw, Michigan Office: 4800 Fashion Square Boulevard, Suite 100, 48603.
Telephone: 517-792-9300; 517-792-1111.
Fax: 517-792-7000; 517-793-6597.

Gilbert A. Currie (1882-1960)
Gilbert A. Currie (1923-1998)
Peter J. Kendall (1961-1999)
William C. Collins
Ramon F. Rolf, Jr.
Daniel J. Cline
Peter A. Poznak
Julia A. Close
Jeffrey N. Dyer
Jonathan E. Lauderbach
Amy E. Wilson
Cheryl L. Whitman
Todd M. Gambrell
Frank M. Polasky (Resident, Saginaw Office)
Robert H. Meisel (Resident, Saginaw Office)
Michael H. Allen (Resident, Saginaw Office)
Larry L. Preston (Resident, Saginaw Office)
David J. Kolat (Resident, Saginaw Office)
M. Randall Jurrens (Resident, Saginaw Office)
John E. Gannon (Resident, Saginaw Office)
Carolyn Pollock Cary (Resident, Saginaw Office)
John D. Jolley (Resident, Saginaw Office)
W. Jay Brown (Resident, Saginaw Office)

OF COUNSEL

James A. Kendall

Counsel for: Chemical Financial Corp.; Chemical Bank & Trust Co.; Saginaw Valley State University; Northwood University; The Midland Foundation; Elsa U. Pardee Foundation; Rollin M. Gerstacker Foundation; Charles J. Strosacker Foundation.

For full biographical listings, see the Martindale-Hubbell Law Directory

*MONROE,** Monroe Co.

MILLER, CANFIELD, PADDOCK AND STONE, P.L.C. (AV)

A Professional Limited Liability Company
Founded in 1852 by Sidney Davy Miller
214 East Elm Avenue, Suite 100, 48162-2682
Telephone: 734-243-2000
Fax: 734-243-0901
URL: http://www.millercanfield.com
Detroit, Michigan Office: 150 West Jefferson, Suite 2500, 48226-4415.
Telephone: 313-963-6420.
Fax: 313-496-7500.
Cable Address: "Stem Detroit."
Ann Arbor, Michigan Office: 101 North Main Street, 7th Floor, 48104-1400.
Telephone: 734-663-2445.
Fax: 734-747-7147.
Troy, Michigan Office: 840 West Long Lake Road, Suite 200, 48098.
Telephone: 248-879-2000.
Fax: 248-879-2001.

(See Next Column)

MILLER, CANFIELD, PADDOCK AND STONE P.L.C.—*Continued*

Grand Rapids, Michigan Office: 99 Monroe, N.W., Suite 1200, 49503-2639.
Telephone: 616-454-8656.
Fax: 616-776-6322.
Howell, Michigan Office: 121 South Barnard Street, Suite 4, 48843-2305.
Telephone: 517-546-7600.
Telecopier: 517-546-6974.
Kalamazoo, Michigan Office: 444 West Michigan Avenue, 49007-3752.
Telephone: 616-381-7030.
Fax: 616-382-0244.
Lansing, Michigan Office: One Michigan Avenue, Suite 900, 48933-1609.
Telephone: 517-487-2070.
Fax: 517-374-6304.
Washington, D.C. Office: 1900 K Street, N.W., Suite 1150. 20006.
Telephone: 202-429-5575; 785-0600.
Fax: 202-331-1118; 785-1234.
Pensacola, Florida Office: 25 West Cedar, 32501.
Telephone: 850-469-1088.
Fax: 850-432-0677.
New York, New York Office: 1450 Broadway, 41st Floor, 10018.
Telephone: 212-704-4400.
Fax: 212-704-4410.
Gdynia, Poland Office: UL. Slaska 21, 81-319.
Telephone: 011-485-831-2808.
Fax: 011-48-58-628 6411.
Warsaw, Poland Office: UL. Nowogrodzkall, 5th Floor, 00-513.
Telephone: 011-4822 529 0200.
Fax: 011-4822 529 0201.
Katowice, Poland Office: UL. Francuska 35/37, 40-027.
Telephone: 011 (48-32) 757-2414.
Fax: 011 (48-32) 757-2483.

RESIDENT PRINCIPALS

Rocque E. Lipford (P.C.)

Representative Firm Clients: Chrysler Corporation; Comerica, Incorporated; City of Detroit, Michigan; Detroit Tigers, Inc.; Detroit Tigers, Inc.; First of Michigan; Ford Motor Company; Ford Motor Credit Company; Great Lakes Bancorp; Henry Ford Hospital; INVETECH Company.

For full biographical listings, see the Martindale-Hubbell Law Directory

*SAGINAW,** Saginaw Co.

BRAUN KENDRICK FINKBEINER PLC (AV)

101 N. Washington Suite 812, 48607-1297
Telephone: 517-753-3461
Telecopier: 517-753-3951
Email: ALBFIE@BKF-LAW.COM *URL:* http://www.bkf-law.com
Saginaw Township Office, Michigan Office: 5800 Gratiot Road, Suite 107, P.O. Box 5169. Telephone 517-799-8692.
Fax: 517-799-4666.
Bay City, Michigan Office: 201 Phoenix Building, P.O. Box 2039.
Telephone: 517-895-8505.
Telecopier: 517-895-8437.
Ann Arbor, Michigan Office: First National Building. 201 S. Main, Suite 700.
Telephone: 313-995-4100.
Telecopier: 313-995-4798.
Mt. Pleasant, Michigan Office: 805 North Brown.
Telephone: 517-775-7404.
Telecopier: 517-775-3764.

John W. Wolf
David L. Turner
Jeffrey J. Endean
Phillip J. Stahle

Representative Clients: The Dow Chemical Co.; General Motors Corp.; Merrill, Lynch, Inc.; Saginaw General Hospital; Saginaw News; The Wickes Foundation.

For Complete List of Firm Personnel, See General Section

For full biographical listings, see the Martindale-Hubbell Law Directory

CURRIE KENDALL POLASKY MEISEL, PLC (AV)

4800 Fashion Square Boulevard, Suite 100, 48603
Telephone: 517-792-1111; 517-792-9300
Fax: 517-793-6597; 517-792-7000
Midland, Michigan Office: 6024 Eastman Avenue, P.O. Box, 2765.
Telephone: 517-839-0300.
Fax: 517-832-0077.

Frank M. Polasky
Robert H. Meisel
Michael H. Allen
Larry L. Preston
David J. Kolat
M. Randall Jurrens
John E. Gannon
Carolyn Pollock Cary
John D. Jolley
W. Jay Brown
William C. Collins (Resident, Midland Office)
Ramon F. Rolf, Jr. (Resident, Midland Office)
Daniel J. Cline (Resident, Midland Office)
Peter A. Poznak (Resident, Midland Office)
Julia A. Close (Resident, Midland Office)
Jeffrey N. Dyer (Resident, Midland Office)
Jonathan E. Lauderbach (Resident, Midland Office)

(See Next Column)

Amy E. Wilson (Resident, Midland Office)
Cheryl L. Whitman (Resident, Midland Office)
Todd M. Gambrell (Resident, Midland Office)

OF COUNSEL

James A. Kendall (Resident, Midland Office)

Counsel for: Chemical Financial Corp.; Chemical Bank & Trust Co.; Saginaw Valley State University; Northwood University; The Midland Foundation; Elsa U. Pardee Foundation; Rollin M. Gerstacker Foundation; Charles J. Strosacker Foundation.

For full biographical listings, see the Martindale-Hubbell Law Directory

SOUTHFIELD, Oakland Co.

DE VINE & KOHN, PLLC (AV)

29800 Telegraph Road, 48034
Telephone: 248-353-6500
Fax: 248-353-2514

Clifford J. De Vine
Sheldon B. Kohn

For full biographical listings, see the Martindale-Hubbell Law Directory

HOFFERT & ASSOCIATES, P.C. (AV)

3000 Town Center, Suite 2990, 48075-1365
Telephone: 248-355-5600
Facsimile: 248-355-5608
Email: myles2@ix.netcom.com *URL:* http://www.lawyers.com/hoffertlaw

Myles B. Hoffert

Claris K. Cwirko
Julia Hoffert Rosen
Wayne A. Tenenbaum (Not admitted in MI)

LEGAL SUPPORT PERSONNEL

Frederick W. Morgan
Ernest E. Beren (Property Tax Consultant)
Robert A. Eckhardt
Kenneth W. Voss

Representative Clients: Toys "R" Us, Inc.; Chrysler Corp.; Tamaroff Group of Automotive Cos.; Aetna Realty; Village Green Management; IBM Corp.; Detroit Edison; Comerica Bank, Sun Life of Canada; Cargill Corporation.

For full biographical listings, see the Martindale-Hubbell Law Directory

ROBERT B. LABE, P.C. (AV)

2000 Town Center, Suite 1780, 48075
Telephone: 248-354-3100
Telecopier: 248-354-3926

Robert B. Labe

Cecile Kohl

References: Comerica Bank, N.A.; Morgan Stanley Dean Witter.

For full biographical listings, see the Martindale-Hubbell Law Directory

MADDIN, HAUSER, WARTELL, ROTH, HELLER & PESSES, P.C. (AV)

Third Floor Essex Centre, 28400 Northwestern Highway, P.O. Box 215, 48037
Telephone: 248-354-4030, 355-5200
Telefax: 248-354-1422

Milton M. Maddin (1902-1984)
Michael W. Maddin
Mark R. Hauser
C. Robert Wartell
Richard J. Maddin
Richard F. Roth
Harvey R. Heller
Ian D. Pesses
Michael S. Leib
Robert D. Kaplow
William E. Sigler
Stewart C. W. Weiner
Charles M. Lax
Stuart M. Bordman
Steven D. Sallen
Gregory J. Gamalski
Julie Chenot Mayer
Nathaniel H. Simpson
Ronald A. Sollish
Lowell D. Salesin

Mark H. Fink
Steven M. Wolock
Lori E. Talsky
Stephen E. Handelman
Ronald M. Stern
Martin Scott Frenkel
Gary M. Remer
Jennifer S. Sternberg
George V. Cassar, Jr.
Adam J. Goldstein

OF COUNSEL

Bruce N. Goldman

Reference: Comerica Bank.

For full biographical listings, see the Martindale-Hubbell Law Directory

Southfield—Continued

MASON STEINHARDT JACOBS PERLMAN & PESICK, PROFESSIONAL CORPORATION (AV)

Suite 1500, 4000 Town Center, 48075-1415
Telephone: 248-358-2090
Fax: 248-358-3599
Email: admin@msjp.com *URL:* http://www.msjp.com

OF COUNSEL

Walter B. Mason, Jr.

Representative Clients: Citibank, N.A.; City of Dearborn; DeMattia Development Co.; Forest City Enterprises; Michigan Wholesale Drug Assn.; Mortgage Bankers Association of Michigan; Nationwide Insurance Co.; City of Taylor; Union Labor Life Insurance Co.; Yellow Freight Systems, Inc.

For Complete List of Firm Personnel, See General Section

For full biographical listings, see the Martindale-Hubbell Law Directory

SIEGEL, GREENFIELD, HAYES & GROSS, P.L.C. (AV)

2000 Town Center, Suite 2700, 48075-1318
Telephone: 248-386-5900
Facsimile: 248-354-3106
URL: http://www.lawyers.com/sghandglawfirm

MEMBERS OF FIRM

Robert W. Siegel
Norman E. Greenfield
Kelly M. Hayes
Robert A. Gross

OF COUNSEL

Steven H. Schwartz

For full biographical listings, see the Martindale-Hubbell Law Directory

SOMMERS, SCHWARTZ, SILVER & SCHWARTZ, P.C. (AV)

2000 Town Center, Suite 900, 48075
Telephone: 248-355-0300
Telecopier: 248-746-4001
Plymouth, Michigan Office: 747 South Main Street.
Telephone: 313-455-4250.

Steven J. Schwartz
Leon M. Schurgin

Representative Clients: Foodland Distributors; C.A. Muer Corporation; Vlasic & Company; Nederlander Corporation; Midwest Health Centers, P.C.; Vesco Oil Corporation.

For Complete List of Firm Personnel, See General Section

For full biographical listings, see the Martindale-Hubbell Law Directory

TROY, Oakland Co.

STARK, REAGAN & FINNERTY, P.C. (AV)

Suite 202, 1111 West Long Lake Road, P.O. Box 7037, 48007-7037
Telephone: 248-641-9955
Facsimile: 248-641-9921
Email: @SRFPC.COM
Boca Raton, Florida Office: Suite 307B, 4800 North Federal Highway.
Telephone: 561-994-2266.
Traverse City, Michigan Office: 475 Eastwood Shores.
Telephone: 231-943-8230.
Facsimile: 231-943-8711.

Michael H. Whiting
Kenneth M. Boyer
Thomas H. Finnerty
R. Keith Stark
Joseph C. Bird
Joseph A. Ahern
Christopher E. LeVasseur
Daniel E. Chapman
William D. Girardot
James R. Waldvogel
Jeffrey J. Fleury
Michael D. FitzPatrick

OF COUNSEL

Harry S. Stark (Resident Of Counsel, Traverse City Office)
Willard M. Reagan
James E. Beall

For full biographical listings, see the Martindale-Hubbell Law Directory

TOXIC TORTS

ALABAMA

*MOBILE,** Mobile Co.

ATCHISON, CROSBY, SAAD & BEEBE, P.C. (AV)

3030 Knollwood Drive, 36693
Telephone: 334-665-7200
Fax: 334-665-7250
URL: http://www.acsblaw.com

James E. Atchison
James H. Crosby
Elias J. Saad
Donald G. Beebe

Mona Ann Vivar
Jacqueline M. McConaha
Daryl A. Atchison

Representative Clients: City of Mobile; Alabama State Docks; Mobile Area Water and Sewer Board; Owens Corning, Inc.; Pilot Catastrophe Services, Inc.; Shell Oil Co.; Premdor,Inc.; Melvin Pierce Paint Co.; Commonwealth National Bank; Fiberglass Canada,Inc.

For full biographical listings, see the Martindale-Hubbell Law Directory

BURNS, CUNNINGHAM & MACKEY, P.C. (AV)

50 St. Emanuel Street, P.O. Box 1583, 36633
Telephone: 334-432-0612
Fax: 334-432-0625
URL: http://www.bcmlawyers.com

Peter F. Burns
William M. Cunningham, Jr.
Peter S. Mackey
Gary W. Fillingim

For full biographical listings, see the Martindale-Hubbell Law Directory

ARKANSAS

*LITTLE ROCK,** Pulaski Co.

BARBER, MCCASKILL, JONES & HALE, P.A. (AV)

2700 Regions Center, 400 West Capitol Avenue, 72201-3414
Telephone: 501-372-6175
Telecopier: 501-375-2802

Azro L. Barber (1885-1979)
Elbert A. Henry (1889-1966)
John B. Thurman (1912-1971)
Austin McCaskill, Sr.
Glenn W. Jones
Michael E. Hale
John S. Cherry, Jr.
Robert L. Henry, III
Micheal L. Alexander
William H. Edwards, Jr.
G. Spence Fricke
Gail Ponder Gaines
Michael J. Emerson
R. Kenny McCulloch
Tim A. Cheatham
Joseph F. Kolb
Scott Michael Strauss
Baucum Fulk
D. Keith Fortner
Wendy Scholtens Wood
Morris L. Williams, III
Michelle Bass Miller

Attorneys for: AFCO Steel; AFCO Metals, Inc.; Associated Aviation Underwriters; CNA Insurance Companies; Fireman's Fund Insurance Co.; General Motors Corp.; Gennett Co., Inc.; General Motors Acceptance Corp.; Hanover Insurance Co.; Royal Insurance.

For full biographical listings, see the Martindale-Hubbell Law Directory

CALIFORNIA

LONG BEACH, Los Angeles Co.

CAMERON, PEARLSON & GALE (AV)

One World Trade Center, Suite 1600, 90831-1600
Telephone: 562-436-3888
Telecopier: 562-437-1967
URL: http://www.cpglawyers.com
URL: http://www.lawyers.com/cmp&glaw

MEMBERS OF FIRM

Timothy C. Cameron
Charles M. Gale
Paul R. Pearlson

ASSOCIATES

Dana K. Anderson, Jr.
Susan R. Loh

For full biographical listings, see the Martindale-Hubbell Law Directory

FLYNN, DELICH & WISE (AV)

One World Trade Center, Suite 1800, 90831-1800
Telephone: 562-435-2626
Fax: 562-437-7555
Email: NicholasP@FDW-LAW.COM
San Francisco, California Office: One California Street, Suite 350.
Telephone: 415-693-5566.
Fax: 415-693-0410. Email: SAMD@FDW-LAW.COM

Erich P. Wise
Nicholas S. Politis

Sook H. Lee

LEGAL SUPPORT PERSONNEL

Denise C. Orr (Legal Assistant)

Representative Clients: The Britannia Steam Ship Insurance Association; Maritime Overseas Corp.; Through Transport Mutual Insurance Association, Ltd.; Interocean Steam Ship Corp.; The United Kingdom Mutual Steam Ship Assurance Association; The Standard Steam Ship Owners Protection & Indemnity Association; The Steam Ship Mutual Underwriting Association; American Hawaii Cruises; General Steam Ship Corp. LTD.

For full biographical listings, see the Martindale-Hubbell Law Directory

*LOS ANGELES,** Los Angeles Co.

DANIELS, FINE, ISRAEL & SCHONBUCH, LLP (AV)

A Partnership including a Professional Corporation
1801 Century Park East, 9th Floor, 90067
Telephone: 310-556-7900
Telecopier: 310-556-2807

MEMBERS OF FIRM

John P. Daniels (Inc.)
Paul R. Fine
Mark R. Israel
Michael N. Schonbuch
Scott M. Leavitt
Michelle R. Press

ASSOCIATES

Scott Ashford Brooks
Spencer A. Schneider
Erin B. Hallissy
Maureen M. Michail
Shell Duncan Grimes

OF COUNSEL

Mary Hulett
Timothy J. Hughes

For full biographical listings, see the Martindale-Hubbell Law Directory

GIRARDI AND KEESE (AV)

1126 Wilshire Boulevard, 90017-1904
Telephone: 213-977-0211
FAX: 213-481-1554
San Bernardino, California Office: 155 West Hospitality Lane, Suite 260.
Telephone: 909-381-1551.
FAX: 909-381-2566.

MEMBERS OF FIRM

Thomas V. Girardi
Robert M. Keese
John A. Girardi
James B. Kropff
Robert W. Finnerty
James G. O'Callahan
V. Andre Rekte (Resident, San Bernardino Office)
John K. Courtney
Amy Fisch Solomon
Thomas C. Morgan
David N. Bigelow
Carrie J. Rognlien
David R. Lira
John Alan Roberts
Shane M. Emerson Coons
Amanda L. McClintock

ASSOCIATE

Jennifer M. Ingram

References: Wells Fargo Bank (Los Angeles Head Office); Comerica Bank.

For full biographical listings, see the Martindale-Hubbell Law Directory

GORDON, EDELSTEIN, KREPACK, GRANT, FELTON & GOLDSTEIN (AV)

Suite 1800, 3580 Wilshire Boulevard, 90010
Telephone: 213-739-7000; 213-487-1520
Fax: 213-386-1671
Email: geklaw.com

Roger L. Gordon
Mark Edelstein
Howard D. Krepack
Sherry E. Grant
Richard I. Felton
Irwin L. Goldstein
Steven J. Kleifield
David A. Goldstein

OF COUNSEL

Joshua M. Merliss

ASSOCIATES

Eugenia L. Steele
Vincent F. Bennett
Adam D. Dombchik
Jennifer S. Weisman

For full biographical listings, see the Martindale-Hubbell Law Directory

Los Angeles—Continued

KNOPFLER & ROBERTSON, LLP (AV)

Suite 500, 21650 Oxnard Street (Woodland Hills), 91367
Telephone: 818-227-0770; 213-624-1111
Telefax: 818-227-0777
Irvine, California Office: 19800 MacArthur Boulevard, Suite 270, 92612.
Telephone: 714-261-6191.
Pleasanton, California Office: 400 Main Street, Suite 204, 94566.
Telephone: 510-425-7250.
Las Vegas, Nevada Office: Knopfler & Robertson in Association with Broom & Vaisbort, LLP, 3753 Howard Hughes Parkway, Suite 200, 89109.
Telephone: 702-792-2413.
Camarillo, California Office: 1200 Paseo, Suite 170, 93010.
Telephone: 805-482-1903; 800-CONDOLAW.
Fax: 805-484-5917.

George Knopfler
Alexander Robertson, IV
Deborah Broom
Richard A. Capella
Jonathan S. Vick
Edward D. Vaisbort
William G. Kelsberg

OF COUNSEL

Scott C. Haith
James P. Lingl (Resident, Camarillo Office)
Christina S. Robertson

Janice M. Michaels
James M. Pazos
Mark Rohrer
Craig Smith
Robert Nation
William S. Dunlevy (Resident, Camarillo Office)
Scott A. Hunter

For full biographical listings, see the Martindale-Hubbell Law Directory

RODI, POLLOCK, PETTKER, GALBRAITH & CAHILL, A LAW CORPORATION (AV)

444 South Flower Street, Suite 1700, 90071-2901
Telephone: 213-895-4900
Telecopiers: 213-895-4921; 895-4922; 895-4750
URL: http://www.rodipollock.com

Karl B. Rodi (1908-1982)
John D. Cahill
John D. Pettker
Daniel C. Bond (1942-1977)
William R. Christian
Henry P. Pramov, Jr.
John F. Cermak, Jr.
Allan E. Ceran
Elizabeth B. Blakely
Robert C. Norton
Tim G. Ceperley
Coralie Kupfer
Cris K. O'Neall
Scott E. Adamson
Margaret Rosenthal

Sonja A. Inglin
Michael A. Abraham
Kenneth A. Franklin
Richard Nessary
Donna Yamini
Wade E. Norwood
Deepak Nanda
David J. Elbaz

OF COUNSEL

John P. Pollock
James M. Galbraith

For full biographical listings, see the Martindale-Hubbell Law Directory

NEWPORT BEACH, Orange Co.

CAPRETZ & ASSOCIATES (AV)

5000 Birch Street, West Tower Suite 2500, 92660-2139
Telephone: 949-724-3000
Fax: 949-757-2635
URL: http://www.lawyers.com/capretzradcliffe
Email: crlawl@ix.netcom.com *URL:* http://www.CAPRETZ.com

MEMBER OF FIRM

James T. Capretz

OF COUNSEL

William B. Lawless (Not admitted in CA)

LEGAL SUPPORT PERSONNEL

Sandra L. Koop (Law Clerk)

For full biographical listings, see the Martindale-Hubbell Law Directory

LOPEZ, HODES, RESTAINO, MILMAN & SKIKOS, A LAW CORPORATION (AV)

450 Newport Center Drive, 2nd Floor, 92660
Telephone: 949-640-8222
Fax: 949-640-8294
San Francisco, California Office: 625 Market Street, Fifteenth Floor, 94105.
Telephone: 415-956-5257.
Fax: 415-956-4416.

Ramon Rossi Lopez
Daniel M. Hodes
John M. Restaino, Jr.
Jeffrey A. Milman
Peter John Polos
Steven J. Skikos (Resident)

(See Next Column)

Christina A. Lopez Fountain
Steven B. Eggleston (Resident, San Francisco Office)
Gregory T. Skikos (Resident, San Francisco Office)
Thomas A. Schultz
Mark G. Crawford
Hilary Poulsen Gilles

OF COUNSEL

David L. Suggs (Not admitted in CA)
Jane E. Joseph (Not admitted in CA)

For full biographical listings, see the Martindale-Hubbell Law Directory

*OAKLAND,** Alameda Co.

BENNETT, SAMUELSEN, REYNOLDS AND ALLARD, A PROFESSIONAL CORPORATION (AV)

1951 Webster Street, Suite 200, 94612-2909
Telephone: 510-444-7688; 510-987-8001
Fax: 510-444-5849
Email: BSRALIT@AOL.COM

Bryant M. Bennett (Retired)
David J. Samuelsen
Richard L. Reynolds
Anthony J. Allard
John G. Cowperthwaite

Roger Blake Hohnsbeen
Thomas S. Gelini
Frederick W. Gatt
Candace Dabney-Smith
David L. Dees
Roderick D. Hill

Representative Clients: Allstate Insurance Co.; California State Automobile Assn.; The Continental Insurance Cos.; County of Alameda.

For full biographical listings, see the Martindale-Hubbell Law Directory

*SAN DIEGO,** San Diego Co.

THE LAW OFFICES OF BIRGER GREG BACINO, APC (AV)

3033 Fifth Avenue, Suite 301, 92103
Telephone: 800-801-4878
Fax: 619-299-0086
URL: http://www.bacinolaw.com
Washington, D.C. Office: 1201 Pennsylvania Avenue, Suite 300, 20004.
Telephone: 800-801-4878.
Houston, Texas Office: 510 Bering Street, Suite 300, 77057.
Telephone: 800-801-4878.

Birger Greg Bacino
Richard P. Verlasky
Philip Aman

OF COUNSEL

Patricia M. Sayre
Michael B. Sayre
Anthony J. DeLellis

For full biographical listings, see the Martindale-Hubbell Law Directory

*SAN FRANCISCO,** San Francisco Co.

FLYNN, DELICH & WISE (AV)

One California Street, Suite 350, 94111
Telephone: 415-693-5566
Fax: 415-693-0410
Email: SamD@fdw-law.com
Long Beach, California Office: 1 World Trade Center, Suite 1800.
Telephone: 562-435-2626.
Fax: 562-437-7555. Email: NicholasP@FDW-LAW.COM.

John A. Flynn (1945-1997)
Sam D. Delich
James B. Nebel

OF COUNSEL

Pecos Bill Field

Faye Lee Peterson
Conte C. Cicala
Jeanine S. Tede

Representative Clients: The Britannia Steam Ship Insurance Association; Maritime Overseas Corp.; Through Transport Mutual Insurance Association, Ltd.; Interocean Steam Ship Corp.; The United Kingdom Mutual Steam Ship Assurance Association; The Standard Steam Ship Owners Protection & Indemnity Association; The Steam Ship Mutual Underwriting Association; American Hawaii Cruises; General Steam Ship Corp. LTD.

For full biographical listings, see the Martindale-Hubbell Law Directory

HAIGHT, BROWN & BONESTEEL, L.L.P. (AV)

A Partnership including Professional Corporations
100 Bush Street, 27th Floor, 94104-3902
Telephone: 415-986-7700
Telecopier: 415-986-6945
URL: http://www.hbblaw.com
Santa Monica, California Office: 1620 26th Street, Suite 4000 North, P.O. Box 680.
Telephone: 310-449-6000.
Telecopier: 310-829-5117.
Telex: 705837.

(See Next Column)

HAIGHT, BROWN & BONESTEEL L.L.P.—*Continued*

Santa Ana, California Office: Suite 900, 5 Hutton Centre Drive.
Telephone: 714-754-1100.
Telecopier: 714-754-0826.
Riverside, California Office: California Tower, 3737 Main Street, Suite 800.
Telephone: 909-341-8300.
Fax: 909-341-8309.
San Diego, California Office: 101 West Broadway, Suite 1000.
Telephone: 619-595-5583.
Fax: 619-595-7873.

RESIDENT MEMBERS

Lisa L. Oberg
Patricia H. Perry

ASSOCIATES

Helene Emilie Swanson
Felicia Y. Feng
Arlene Mendoza
Laura Lea Allen

For full biographical listings, see the Martindale-Hubbell Law Directory

*SAN JOSE,** Santa Clara Co.

ALEXANDER, HAWES & AUDET (AV)

152 North 3rd Street, Suite 600, 95112
Telephone: 408-289-1776
Fax: 408-287-1776
URL: http://www.alexanderlaw.com
Email: access@alexanderlaw.com *URL:* http://www.lawyers.com/alexanderhawes&audet

Richard Alexander
Amanda Hawes
William M. Audet
Ann Saponara
Deborah Heller

OF COUNSEL

Michael McShane
Jana S. Stabile (Not admitted in CA)

For full biographical listings, see the Martindale-Hubbell Law Directory

SANTA MONICA, Los Angeles Co.

BAKER, KEENER & NAHRA, LLP (AV)

2850 Ocean Park Boulevard, Suite 300, 90405-2936
Telephone: 310-399-0900
Fax: 310-399-1644
Email: general@bknlawyers.com *URL:* http://www.bknlawyers.com

MEMBERS OF FIRM

Robert C. Baker
Karl A. Keener
John P. Nahra
Michael H. Bailey
Steven T. Adams
Melissa S. Fink
Jeffrey P. Nolan
Constance A. Endelicato

Brenda K. Benson
Mitchell F. Mulbarger
James D. Hepworth
Phillip A. Baker
George P. Hawley
Thomas M. Mills
R. Jeffrey Neer
Wendy Wen Yun Chang

OF COUNSEL

Daniel P. Leonard

Reference: Wells Fargo Bank (Los Angeles Head Office).

For full biographical listings, see the Martindale-Hubbell Law Directory

HAIGHT, BROWN & BONESTEEL, L.L.P. (AV)

A Partnership including Professional Corporations
1620 26th Street, Suite 4000 North, P.O. Box 680, 90404
Telephone: 310-449-6000
Telecopier: 310-829-5117
Telex: 705837
URL: http://www.hbblaw.com
Santa Ana, California Office: Suite 900, 5 Hutton Centre Drive.
Telephone: 714-754-1100.
Telecopier: 714-754-0826.
Riverside, California Office: California Tower, 3737 Main Street, Suite 800.
Telephone: 909-341-8300.
Fax: 909-341-8309.
San Francisco, California Office: 101 Bush Street, 27th Floor.
Telephone: 415-986-7700.
Fax: 415-986-6945.
San Diego, California Office: 101 West Broadway, Suite 1000.
Telephone: 619-595-5583.
Fax: 619-595-7873.

MEMBERS OF FIRM

Steven L. Hoch (A Professional Corporation)
Morton Rosen
William J. Sayers
Jeffrey B. Margulies
Farah Sohaili Nicol

ASSOCIATE

Karen B. Goldberg

For full biographical listings, see the Martindale-Hubbell Law Directory

COLORADO

*DENVER,** Denver Co.

MARKUSSON, GREEN & JARVIS, P.C. (AV)

Suite 2300, 1050 Seventeenth Street, 80265
Telephone: 303-572-4200
Fax: 303-595-3780

James K. Green
H. Keith Jarvis
Dennis H. Markusson
Thomas E. Napp

Kirstin G. Lindberg
Jason L. Romero
William B. Stanton
William T. Webb
Ashley E. Moller

For full biographical listings, see the Martindale-Hubbell Law Directory

WHEELER TRIGG & KENNEDY, P.C. (AV)

Suite 3600, 1801 California Street, 80202
Telephone: 303-292-2525
Telecopier: 303-294-1879
Email: info@wtklaw.com *URL:* http://www.wtklaw.com
Roslyn, New York Office: 1800 Northern Boulevard, Suite 208, 11576.
Telephone: 516-484-9701.
Fax: 516-484-6362.

Malcolm E. Wheeler
John R. Trigg
Mark F. Kennedy
Paul F. Hultin
Michael L. O'Donnell
Robert B. Hunter
Gwen J. Young
Christopher J. Meyer
Lori L. Roberts
Habib Nasrullah
Edward C. Stewart
James E. Hooper, Jr.

OF COUNSEL

Joseph B. Valentine (Not admitted in CO)
Andrew J. Mihalick (Not admitted in CO)

Sean D. Baker
Mark T. Clouatre
Bryan D. Cross
Wendy A. Harvey
David A. Lamb
Lee A. Mickus
Amy L. Padden
Kimberly A. Stout (Not admitted in CO)

For full biographical listings, see the Martindale-Hubbell Law Directory

CONNECTICUT

*BRIDGEPORT,** Fairfield Co.

KOSKOFF, KOSKOFF & BIEDER, P.C. (AV)

350 Fairfield Avenue, 06604
Telephone: 203-336-4421
Fax: 203-368-3244
Email: KKB@KOSKOFF.com
Stamford, Connecticut Office: 1172 Bedford Street.
Telephone: 203-325-3686.
Danbury, Connecticut Office: 1 Moss Avenue.
Telephone: 203-792-7100.

Michael P. Koskoff
Karen E. Koskoff
Michael A. Stratton
Rosalind J. Koskoff

For full biographical listings, see the Martindale-Hubbell Law Directory

*NEW HAVEN,** New Haven Co.

EARLY, LUDWICK & SWEENEY, L.L.C. (AV)

One Century Tower, 11th Floor, 265 Church Street, P.O. Box 1866, 06508-1866
Telephone: 203-777-7799
Fax: 203-785-1671
Email: INFO@ELSLAW.COM *URL:* http://www.elslaw.com

James F. Early
Lindalea P. Ludwick
Robert J. Sweeney
Michelle A. Freeman
Brian C. Fournier

Julia Cremin Wyman
John J. O'Connell

For full biographical listings, see the Martindale-Hubbell Law Directory

FLORIDA

BOCA RATON, Palm Beach Co.

MICHAUD, BUSCHMANN, FOX, FERRARA & MITTELMARK, P.A. (AV)

33 Southeast 8th Street, 33432
Telephone: 561-392-0540
Fax: 561-392-0582
Email: Bocalaw@MBFFM.com *URL:* http://www.MBFFM.com

Scott H. Michaud
Paul Buschmann
Brian S. Fox
James T. Ferrara
Michael K. Mittelmark
Marc T. Millian

Marcy G. Blitz
Linda A. McCullough
Kimberly M. Hall

For full biographical listings, see the Martindale-Hubbell Law Directory

*FORT LAUDERDALE,** Broward Co.

KRUPNICK CAMPBELL MALONE ROSELLI BUSER SLAMA HANCOCK MCNELIS LIBERMAN & MCKEE, P.A. (AV)

700 Southeast 3rd Avenue, Suite 100, 33316-1186
Telephone: 954-763-8181; 877-763-8181 (Toll Free)
Fax: 954-763-8292
Email: information@krupnicklaw.com *URL:* http://www.krupnicklaw.com

Jon E. Krupnick
Walter G. Campbell, Jr.
Kevin A. Malone
Richard J. Roselli
Thomas E. Buser
Joseph J. Slama
Kelly D. Hancock
Lisa A. McNelis
Scott S. Liberman
Robert J. McKee

Carlos Acevedo (Not admitted in FL)
Louis R. Battista
Ivan F. Cabrera
Robert D. Erben
Kelley Badger Gelb
Sean J. Greene
Holly Debra Krulik
Michael J. Ryan

OF COUNSEL

Ben J. Weaver
Dianne Jay Weaver

Reference: Mellon United National Bank.

For full biographical listings, see the Martindale-Hubbell Law Directory

*JACKSONVILLE,** Duval Co.

ALFORD & KALIL, P.A. (AV)

2400 Independent Square, One Independent Drive, 32202-5064
Telephone: 904-355-3311
Fax: 904-355-5411
Email: akthefirm@aol.com

C. Wayne Alford
John S. Kalil

For full biographical listings, see the Martindale-Hubbell Law Directory

BROWN, TERRELL, HOGAN, ELLIS, MCCLAMMA & YEGELWEL, P.A. (AV)

Suite 804 Blackstone Building, 233 East Bay Street, 32202-3417
Telephone: 904-632-2424
Fax: 904-632-2027
Email: mail@bthemy-law.com *URL:* http://www.bthemy-law.com

Thomas R. Brown
James T. Terrell
Wayne Hogan
Timothy D. Ellis
T. Edward McClamma
Evan J. Yegelwel
Thomas E. Duffy, Jr.
Christopher G. Burns
Anita Pryor
Alan M. Pickert

Carroll Cayer
Michael S. Sharrit
Theodore Samuel Pina, Jr.
Mark E. Calvin
Leslie A. Goller
Patricia M. Dodson
Jennifer Kolinski Millis

Reference: NCNB.

For full biographical listings, see the Martindale-Hubbell Law Directory

*MIAMI,** Dade Co.

RUSSO & HEFFERNAN, P.A. (AV)

7990 Red Road, 33143
Telephone: 305-665-7171
Fax: 305-665-7146
Email: lawyers@rhpa.com *URL:* http://www.lawyers.com/russo&heffernan

(See Next Column)

Don Russo
David R. Heffernan

For full biographical listings, see the Martindale-Hubbell Law Directory

*WEST PALM BEACH,** Palm Beach Co.

SEARCY DENNEY SCAROLA BARNHART & SHIPLEY, PROFESSIONAL ASSOCIATION (AV)

2139 Palm Beach Lakes Boulevard, P.O. Drawer 3626, 33402-3626
Telephone: 561-686-6300
800-780-8607
800-220-7006 (Spanish)
Fax: 561-478-0754
Email: CDS@SEARCYLAW.COM *URL:* http://www.searcylaw.com

Earl L. Denney, Jr.
John Scarola

Harry A. Shevin

LEGAL SUPPORT PERSONNEL

Deane L. Cady (Paralegal/Investigator)
Emilio Diamantis (Paralegal/Investigator)

For Complete List of Firm Personnel, See General Section

For full biographical listings, see the Martindale-Hubbell Law Directory

ILLINOIS

*CHICAGO,** Cook Co.

BLATT, HAMMESFAHR & EATON (AV)

333 W. Wacker Drive, Suite 1900, 60606
Telephone: 312-849-8000
FAX: 312-357-0198
Email: BHE@BHELAW.COM *URL:* HTTP://WWW.BHELAW.COM
New York, New York Office: 45 Broadway, 12th Floor.
Telephone: 212-363-1900.
Fax: 212-363-2600. Email: bhe@bhelaw.com.

MEMBERS OF FIRM

Richard L. Blatt
Robert W. Hammesfahr
Gregory D. Hopp
Kathleen A. McQueeny
Matthew T. Walsh

ASSOCIATES

Jennifer L. Barron
Peggy A. Glenn
Frederic C. Goodwill, II

For full biographical listings, see the Martindale-Hubbell Law Directory

STONE & MOORE, CHARTERED (AV)

30 North La Salle Street, Suite 4300, 60602
Telephone: 312-332-5656
Fax: 312-332-5858
URL: http://www.stonemoore.com
Merrillville, Indiana Office: 500 E. 86th Avenue, 46410.
Telephone: 219-736-5959.
Fax: 219-736-5858.
Wheaton, Illinois Office: 600 W. Roosevelt Road, Suite 1A, 60187.
Telephone: 630-221-9292.
Fax: 630-221-9393.

William G. Stone
Robert Charles Moore (Also at Wheaton, Illinois Office)
Raymond R. Pesavento
Rosario Cibella
Richard M. Johnson, Jr.
J. Murray Pinkston, III
Julie Osswald Hooven

Christian D. Ambler
Jeffrey W. Henning
Erica Lewis Battaglia
Kevin Kemp Lyons
Kristin E. Rooney
Daniel S. Schulz
Matthew B. Stephens
A. Christine Svenson
Douglas W. Walker

For full biographical listings, see the Martindale-Hubbell Law Directory

WILDMAN, HARROLD, ALLEN & DIXON (AV)

225 West Wacker Drive, 30th Floor, 60606-1229
Telephone: 312-201-2000
Fax: 312-201-2555
Email: hennessy@whad.com *URL:* http://www.whad.com
Aurora, Illinois Office: 1961 W. Downer Place.
Telephone: 630-892-7021.
Fax: 630-892-7158.
Waukegan, Illinois Office: 404 West Water, P. O. Box 890.
Telephone: 847-625-5550.
Fax: 847-625-5555.
Lisle, Illinois Office: 4300 Commerce Court, Suite 320.
Telephone: 630-955-0555.
Fax: 630-955-0662

(See Next Column)

WILDMAN, HARROLD, ALLEN & DIXON—*Continued*

Toronto, Ontario correspondent Office: Keel Cottrelle. 36 Toronto Street, Suite 920.
Telephone: 416-367-2900.
Telefax: 416-367-2791.
Telex: 062-18660.

MEMBERS OF FIRM

Anthony G. Hopp
Brian W. Lewis
Timothy G. Nickels
Robert L. Shuftan
Peter A. Tomaras

For full biographical listings, see the Martindale-Hubbell Law Directory

IOWA

*DES MOINES,** Polk Co.

THE WALKER LAW FIRM (AV)

2501 Grand Avenue, Suite E, 50312
Telephone: 515-281-1488
Fax: 515-281-1489
Email: ERWJK@aol.com

E. Ralph Walker
David J. Darrell
Joseph W. Fernandez

OF COUNSEL

Fred E. Rizk (Not admitted in IA)

For full biographical listings, see the Martindale-Hubbell Law Directory

LOUISIANA

*BATON ROUGE,** East Baton Rouge Parish

POWERS & WILLARD, L.L.P. (AV)

7967 Office Park Boulevard, P.O. Box 15948, 70895
Telephone: 225-928-1951
Fax: 225-929-9834

MEMBERS OF FIRM

John Dale Powers
William E. Willard

ASSOCIATES

Neil H. Mixon
Lindsey J. Leavoy
Edwin L. Hightower
Andrew P. Sellers, Jr.
Suzanne K. Sasser
Kyle C. Marionneaux

General Counsel for: Audubon Insurance Co.
Louisiana Counsel for: Hancock Bank & Trust Co.; Hertz Corp.; Ciba-Geigy Corp.; Utica Mutual Insurance Co.

For full biographical listings, see the Martindale-Hubbell Law Directory

UNGLESBY, KOCH & REYNOLDS (AV)

246 Napoleon Street, 70802
Telephone: 225-387-0120
Fax: 225-336-4355
Email: unglkoch@premier.net

Lewis O. Unglesby
Karl J. Koch
Aidan C. Reynolds

For full biographical listings, see the Martindale-Hubbell Law Directory

*LAKE CHARLES,** Calcasieu Parish

BAGGETT, MCCALL & BURGESS, A PROFESSIONAL LAW CORPORATION (AV)

3006 Country Club Road, P.O. Drawer 7820, 70606-7820
Telephone: 318-478-8888
Fax: 318-478-8946
URL: http://www.baggettmccall.com
Email: bmblf@structurex.net *URL:* http://www.occupationaldisease.com

William B. Baggett
Robert C. McCall
William B. Baggett, Jr.
Roger G. Burgess
Wells T. Watson
Erin McCall Alley
Christopher C. McCall
Rebecca F. Todd
Jeffrey Thomas Gaughan
Charles Vorndran (Not admitted in LA)

For full biographical listings, see the Martindale-Hubbell Law Directory

GUILLORY & MCCALL, L.L.C. (AV)

901 Lakeshore Drive, Suite 1030, P.O. Drawer 1607, 70602-1607
Telephone: 318-433-9996
Telefax: 318-433-9937

(See Next Column)

Robert E. Guillory, Jr.
William T. McCall
H. Clay Ward, III
Drury B. Cunningham

Representative Clients: CIGNA Property and Casualty Companies; Eagle Insurance Group (WA).

For full biographical listings, see the Martindale-Hubbell Law Directory

METAIRIE, Jefferson Parish

BERNARD, CASSISA, ELLIOTT & DAVIS, A PROFESSIONAL LAW CORPORATION (AV)

1615 Metairie Road, P.O. Box 55490, 70055-5490
Telephone: 504-834-2612
Telecopier: 504-838-9438
Email: bcande@communique.net
Oxford, Mississippi Office: 1727 East University Avenue, Suite E, 38655.
Telephone: 601-234-7236.
Fax: 601-234-7691.

Peter L. Bernard, Jr. (1920-1991)
Frank L. Micholet (1913-1972)
Paul V. Cassisa, Sr.
Stephen N. Elliott
Benjamin Franklin Davis, Jr.
Eugene M. McEachin, Jr.
Robert A. McMahon, Jr.
Carl J. Giffin, Jr.
Paul V. Cassisa, Jr.
Howard B. Kaplan
William L. Brockman
Robert A. Knight
Ann M. Sico

OF COUNSEL

Robert H. Wood, Jr.

Representative Clients: Royal Insurance Group; General Motors Corp.; Hartford Insurance Group; Nissan Motor Corp.; Honda North America, Inc.

For full biographical listings, see the Martindale-Hubbell Law Directory

*NEW ORLEANS,** Orleans Parish

BENCOMO & ASSOCIATES (AV)

Suite 2110 One Poydras Plaza, 639 Loyola Avenue, 70113
Telephone: 504-529-2929
Fax: 504-529-2018

Raul R. Bencomo

OF COUNSEL

Richard E. Anderson
Helen Hairston Babin

For full biographical listings, see the Martindale-Hubbell Law Directory

BEST KOEPPEL, A PROFESSIONAL LAW CORPORATION (AV)

LL & E Tower, 909 Poydras Street Suite 2200, 70112
Telephone: 504-593-2400
Telecopier: 504-593-2401
Email: bstkpplesq@aol.com
Houston, Texas Office: 1900 West Loop South, Suite 300, 77027.
Telephone: 713-964-4072.
Telecopier: 713-963-2503.

Laurence E. Best
Peter S. Koeppel
R. Jeffrey Bridger
James H. Daigle, Jr.
M. Davis Ready
Suzanne M. Risey

LEGAL SUPPORT PERSONNEL

PARALEGAL

Debora N. Dufrene

Representative Clients: Lexington Insurance Co.; Rowan Companies, Inc.; Rowandrill, Inc.; Rowan International, Inc.; Atlantic Maritime Services, Inc.; Rowan Drilling (U.K.), Ltd.; Hartford Insurance Co.; Trinity Marine Group; Elevating Boats, Inc.; CITGO Petroleum Corp.

For full biographical listings, see the Martindale-Hubbell Law Directory

CHRISTOVICH AND KEARNEY, L.L.P. (AV)

Suite 2300 Pan American Life Center, 601 Poydras Street, 70130-6078
Telephone: 504-561-5700
Fax: 504-561-5743
Email: c&k@christovich.com

MEMBERS OF FIRM

Alvin R. Christovich, Jr.
William K. Christovich
J. Walter Ward, Jr.
Lawrence J. Ernst
James F. Holmes
Robert E. Peyton
C. Edgar Cloutier
Charles W. Schmidt, III
Richard K. Christovich
Terry Christovich Gay
E. Phelps Gay
J. Warren Gardner, Jr.
Kevin R. Tully
Lance R. Rydberg
Elizabeth S. Cordes
Charles M. Lanier, Jr.
Philip J. Borne
James A. Holmes

ASSOCIATES

Robert D. Peyton
Craig B. Mitchell
Joseph M. Guillot
Scott J. Sonnier
John K. Nieset
Janet L. White
Mary Beth Meyer
Kory J. Ickler

(See Next Column)

CHRISTOVICH AND KEARNEY L.L.P., *New Orleans—Continued*

OF COUNSEL

John A. Stassi II

Representative Clients: Highlands Insurance Co.; Progressive Insurance Company; AIG Group; Liberty Mutual Insurance Co.; Sofamor-Danek Group, Inc.; Brown & Root, Inc.; Otis Elevator Co.; Dillard Department Stores, Inc.; A.C.& S.

For full biographical listings, see the Martindale-Hubbell Law Directory

LEE, FUTRELL & PERLES, L.L.P. (AV)

Suite 2409, 201 St. Charles Avenue, 70170-2409
Telephone: 504-569-1725
Fax: 504-569-1726
Email: mgr@leefutrell.com *URL:* http://www.lawyers.com/lf&plaw

Gary A. Lee
John Maurice Futrell
Richard M. Perles

Representative Clients: Certain Underwriters at Lloyd's, London; Institute of London Underwriters Companies.

For full biographical listings, see the Martindale-Hubbell Law Directory

MARTZELL & BICKFORD (AV)

A Partnership including a Professional Corporation
338 Lafayette Street, 70130-3244
Telephone: 504-581-9065
Fax: 504-581-7635
Email: mailbox@martzellbickford.com *URL:* http://www.martzellbickford.com

John R. Martzell (P.C.)
Scott R. Bickford

Regina O. Matthews
M. Suzanne Montero
Duggan F. Ellis
Richard A. Filce
Ray L. Rhymes

LEGAL SUPPORT PERSONNEL

LITIGATION ADMINISTRATOR

Christopher H. Sherwood

PARALEGALS

Jane B. Daigle
Connie L. Cosse
Mary Wiggenhorn

FIRM ADMINISTRATOR

Stephen C. Wolf (Certified Public Accountant)

For full biographical listings, see the Martindale-Hubbell Law Directory

MCGLINCHEY STAFFORD (AV)

A Professional Limited Liability Company
643 Magazine Street, 70130-3477
Telephone: 504-586-1200
Fax: 504-596-2800
TDD: (504) 596-2728
Telex: 584327
Cable Address: "MACSTAC"
Mailing Address: P.O. Box 60643, New Orleans, Louisiana, 70160-0643
Email: @mcglinchey.com *URL:* http://www.mcglinchey.com
Dallas, Texas Office: 2777 Stemmons Freeway, Suite 925, 75207-2401.
Telephone: 214-860-9700.
Fax: 214-860-9750.
Houston, Texas Office: 2727 Allen Parkway, Suite 1900, 77019.
Telephone: 713-520-1900.
Fax: 713-520-1025.
Baton Rouge, Louisiana Office: Ninth Floor, One American Place, 70825-0001.
Telephone: 504-383-9000.
Fax: 504-343-3076.
Jackson, Mississippi Office: Suite 1200, SkyTel Centre, 200 South Lamar Street, 39201.
Telephone: 601-960-8400.
Fax: 601-960-8406.
Lake Providence, Louisiana Office: 405 Morgan Street, 71254-2691.
Telephone: 318-559-1200.
Fax: 318-559-0609.
Monroe, Louisiana Office: Dean ONB Tower, 130 Desiard Street, Suite 807, 71201.
Telephone: 318-651-0807.
Fax: 318-651-0809.

MEMBERS OF FIRM

William V. Dalferes, Jr., (P.C.)
Eric A. Shuman

ASSOCIATES

Margaret Woolverton Triebes
Ann D. Levine
Erin Fury Parkinson
Dwayne C. Jefferson
Deirdre C. McGlinchey
Mindy Brickman Patrón

OF COUNSEL

Mary Lynne Friedman

For full biographical listings, see the Martindale-Hubbell Law Directory

PLAUCHÉ MASELLI LANDRY & PARKERSON L.L.P. (AV)

Bank One Center, Suite 4240, 201 St. Charles Avenue, 70170-4240
Telephone: 504-582-1142
Fax: 504-582-1172
URL: http://www.pmlpnola.com

MEMBERS OF FIRM

Andrew L. Plauché, Jr.
Arthur W. Landry
Joseph Maselli, Jr.
G. Bruce Parkerson
Robert E Caraway, III

ASSOCIATES

Mark E. Young
J. Marie Rudd
Thomas L. Hutchinson
Wendy K. Lappenga
Cherie T. Burlett
Deborah F. Malveaux
Kenan S. Rand, Jr.
Diane S. Mitnik
Elizabeth Salzer Schell
Lori P. Moser

Reference: Bank One of Louisiana.

For full biographical listings, see the Martindale-Hubbell Law Directory

PULASKI, GIEGER & LABORDE, L.L.C. (AV)

Suite 4800, One Shell Square, 701 Poydras Street, 70139
Telephone: 504-561-0400
Telecopier: 504-561-1011
Covington, Louisiana Office: 434 North Columbia Street, Suite 200, 70433.
Telephone: 504-561-0400.
Telecopier: 504-809-9677.

Michael T. Pulaski
Sharon D. Smith
Ernest P. Gieger, Jr.
Leo R. McAloon, III
Kenneth H. Laborde
Christopher J. Wnuk
Lambert M. Laperouse
John Burke Sanders
Robert W. Maxwell
Julianne T. Echols
Keith W. McDaniel
Hilliard F. Kelly, III
Lorie G. DeMarcay

Marjorie Randall Brown
Gina S. Montgomery

For full biographical listings, see the Martindale-Hubbell Law Directory

MAINE

*PORTLAND,** Cumberland Co.

WRIGHT & COON, P.A. (AV)

Four Canal Plaza, P.O. Box 7526, 04112
Telephone: 207-775-7722
Fax: 207-772-7045
Email: lexfori@lexfori.com

Steven F. Wright
John R. Coon
Brita J. Forssberg

For full biographical listings, see the Martindale-Hubbell Law Directory

MARYLAND

*ANNAPOLIS,** Anne Arundel Co.

BRASSEL & BALDWIN, P.A. (AV)

112 West Street, 21401
Telephone: 410-216-7900
DC Metro: 301-261-2199
Fax: 410-974-6019
URL: http://www.brasselbaldwin.com
Baltimore, Maryland Office: The B & O Building, Suite 920. 2 North Charles Street, 21201-3754.
Telephone: 410-974-6000.
Fax: 410-385-2939.

Rignal W. Baldwin, Jr.
Jon W. Brassel

Jonathan P. Kagan
Mary Coale Baldwin
Alexander John May

OF COUNSEL

Richard T. Stansbury (Resident, Baltimore, Maryland Office)

For full biographical listings, see the Martindale-Hubbell Law Directory

BETHESDA, Montgomery Co.

KARP, FROSH, LAPIDUS, WIGODSKY & NORWIND, P.A. (AV)

7475 Wisconsin Avenue, Suite 800, 20814
Telephone: 301-656-2111
Fax: 301-654-7748
Email: jackgold@erols.com
Washington, D.C. Office: 1150 Connecticut Avenue, N.W., Suite 900. 20036.
Telephone: 202-822-3777.
Fax: 202-828-4130.

Ronald A. Karp
Brian E. Frosh
Lawrence S. Lapidus
Jeffrey A. Wigodsky
Edward L. Norwind
J. Philip Kessel

Jack A. Gold
Donald C. Weinberg

OF COUNSEL

Douglas R. Smith
Stanley A. First (Not admitted in MD)
Roy I. Niedermayer
Maurice I. Burstein

For full biographical listings, see the Martindale-Hubbell Law Directory

SILVER SPRING, Montgomery Co.

SAUNDERS & SCHMIELER (AV)

8737 Colesville Road, Suite L-200, 20910-3921
Telephone: 301-588-7717
Facsimile: 301-588-5073
Email: admin@sslawfirm.com *URL:* http://www.sslawfirm.com
Washington, D.C. Office: 1050 17th Street, N.W., #600
Telephone: 202-833-2999.
Baltimore, Maryland Office: Suite 2700, 111 South Calvert Street.
Telephone: 410-235-7558.
Arlington, Virginia Office: 2111 Wilson Boulevard, Suite 700.
Telephone: 703-243-1100.
Richmond, Virginia Office: 4900 Cutshaw Avenue.
Telephone: 804-353-9800.

MEMBER OF FIRM

Jeffrey R. Schmieler

ASSOCIATES

Nicole E. Ames
A. Benjamin Horton
Lucas F. Webster

For Complete List of Firm Personnel, See General Section

For full biographical listings, see the Martindale-Hubbell Law Directory

*TOWSON,** Baltimore Co.

WHITNEY & BOGRIS, LLP (AV)

401 Washington Avenue, Twelfth Floor, 21204
Telephone: 410-583-8000
Fax: 410-583-8031
Email: HGWC@worldnet.att.net

MEMBERS OF FIRM

Daniel W. Whitney
George D. Bogris

ASSOCIATES

Kathleen D. Leslie
Henry Russell
Sandra A. Tofte
Michael A. Giacomazza
Arlene L. Sew
Gerald S. Gaetano (Not admitted in MD)
Scott A. McCabe (Not admitted in MD)
Jeffrey C. Shipley

OF COUNSEL

Joseph E. Dever
David L. Feldstein
Ronald V. Miller, Jr.

For full biographical listings, see the Martindale-Hubbell Law Directory

MASSACHUSETTS

*BOSTON,** Suffolk Co.

GOVERNO AND KAVANAGH LLP (AV)

99 High Street, 02110
Telephone: 617-423-4500
Fax: 617-423-4505
Email: dgoverno@counsel.com *URL:* http://www.governoandkavanagh.com

David M. Governo
Eileen P. Kavanagh

ASSOCIATES

Ann M. Collins
Lisa A. Hack
Michael D. Riseberg
Cynthia J. Stephens
Adam A. Larson

OF COUNSEL

Gregory J. Wenger
Timothy J. Dodd (Not admitted in MA)

For full biographical listings, see the Martindale-Hubbell Law Directory

MICHIGAN

BLOOMFIELD HILLS, Oakland Co.

PROVIZER & PHILLIPS, P.C. (AV)

6785 Telegraph Road, Suite 400, 48301
Telephone: 248-642-0444
Facsimile: 248-642-6661
Toll Free: 1-800-288-9080
URL: http://www.lawyers.com/provizer&phillips

Harold M. Provizer
Randall E. Phillips
Marilyn A. Madorsky
Evan A. Zagoria
Noel F. Beck
Mark S. Baumkel

Constance S. Hall
Ellen C. Busch
Donald J. Parthum, Jr.
Keith A. Castora
Gregory A. Nave

For full biographical listings, see the Martindale-Hubbell Law Directory

*DETROIT,** Wayne Co.

WILLMARTH, TANOURY, RAMAR, CORBET, GARVES & SHAW (AV)

535 Griswold, Suite 1730, 48226-3602
Telephone: 313-964-6300
Fax: 313-964-6310
Email: mdwillth@home.net

MEMBERS OF FIRM

Daniel R. Corbet
Brian R. Garves
David R. Nauts
Anthony J. Paradiso
John M. Perrin
John J. Ramar
Bruce R. Shaw
William A. Tanoury
Mark D. Willmarth

ASSOCIATES

Marie C. Kennedy
Wayne Walker
Elizabeth L. Sokol
Robert S. Silverman
Carmine G. Paterra
Joseph J. Ceglarek, II
Derek Steven Wilczynski
Frank Hamidi
Kristen E. Skaff
Steven J. Bonasso
Colleen P. O'Connor
Lara R. Stutz
Eric G. Tucciarone
Michael P. Robach

For full biographical listings, see the Martindale-Hubbell Law Directory

TRADEMARK, COPYRIGHT AND UNFAIR COMPETITION

(See also listings under Patent, Trademark, Copyright and Unfair Competition)

ALABAMA

*BIRMINGHAM,** Jefferson Co.

BRADLEY ARANT ROSE & WHITE LLP (AV)

2001 Park Place, Suite 1400, P.O. Box 830709, 35283-0709
Telephone: 205-521-8000
Facsimile: 205-521-8800
Facsimile (SouthTrust Tower Office): 205-521-8500
URL: http://www.barw.com
Huntsville, Alabama Office: 200 Clinton Avenue West, Suite 900, 35801.
Telephone: 205-517-5100.
Facsimile: 205-533-5069.
Washington, D.C. Office: 801 Pennsylvania Avenue, NW, Suite 230, 20004.
Telephone: 202-347-8893.
Facsimile: 202-347-1684.

MEMBERS OF FIRM

Michael S. Denniston
James W. Gewin
Linda A. Friedman
Thad Gladden Long
Michael R. Pennington

Counsel for: SouthTrust Bank of Alabama, National Association; Energen, Corporation (formerly Alagasco, Inc.); Blount, Inc.; Coca-Cola Bottling Company United, Inc.; The New York Times Col; Russell Corp.; Walter Industries, Inc.; ASCAP; Auburn University.

For Complete List of Firm Personnel, See General Section

For full biographical listings, see the Martindale-Hubbell Law Directory

ARIZONA

*PHOENIX,** Maricopa Co.

ALLEN & PRICE, P.L.C. (AV)

2850 East Camelback Road, Suite 170, 85016-4380
Telephone: 602-381-0500
Fax: 602-381-8899
Email: allen@aplaw.com
Email: price@aplaw.com
Email: schacter@aplaw.com
Email: sanders@aplaw.com

Robert E. B. Allen
Charles S. Price

Scott A. Shacter
Barry R. Sanders

For full biographical listings, see the Martindale-Hubbell Law Directory

FENNEMORE CRAIG, A PROFESSIONAL CORPORATION (AV)

3003 North Central Avenue, Suite 2600, 85012-2913
Telephone: 602-916-5000
Fax: 602-916-5999
Tucson, Arizona Office: One South Church Avenue, Suite 1000, 85701-1620.
Telephone: 520-879-6800.
Fax: 520-879-6899.

Timothy J. Burke
C. Owen Paepke
Ray K. Harris

Paul F. Wille (Not admitted in AZ)
Stacie K. Smith
Sandra L. Etherton

LEGAL SUPPORT PERSONNEL

LEGAL ASSISTANTS

Amy Thompson

For Complete List of Firm Personnel, See General Section

For full biographical listings, see the Martindale-Hubbell Law Directory

JENNINGS, STROUSS & SALMON, P.L.C. (AV)

A Professional Limited Liability Company
One Renaissance Square, Two North Central Avenue, 85004-2393
Telephone: 602-262-5911
Fax: 602-253-3255
Email: info@jsslaw.com *URL:* http://www.jsslaw.com
Arrowhead Office: 16150 North Arrowhead Fountains Center Drive, Suite 250, Peoria, Arizona.
Telephone: 623-878-2222.
Fax: 623-878-1333.

Joseph W. Mott
Anne L. Kleindienst

ASSOCIATE

Jeffrey C. Whitley

For Complete List of Firm Personnel, See General Section

For full biographical listings, see the Martindale-Hubbell Law Directory

LEWIS AND ROCA, LLP (AV)

A Limited Liability Partnership including a Professional Corporation
40 North Central Avenue, 85004-4429
Telephone: 602-262-5311
Fax: 602-262-5747
Email: clientservice@lrlaw.com *URL:* http://www.lrlaw.com
Tucson, Arizona Office: One South Church Avenue, Suite 700, 86701-1620.
Telephone: 520-622-2090.
Fax: 520-622-3088. E-Mail: clientservice@lrlaw.com.
Las Vegas, Nevada Affiliated Office: Ashcraft and Heinz LLP, 3960 Howard Hughes Parkway, 89109.
Telephone: 702-990-3570.
Fax: 702-990-3571.

MEMBERS OF FIRM

Peter D. Baird
Patricia K. Norris
Dale A. Danneman
Thomas H. Campbell
James T. Acuff, Jr.
Rosemarie Christofolo

Representative Clients: Del Webb Corp.; E & J Gallo Wineries; EMI Records Group; First Data Corp.; Jim Henson Productions; Next Base, Limited; Skymall, Inc.

For Complete List of Firm Personnel, See General Section

For full biographical listings, see the Martindale-Hubbell Law Directory

CALIFORNIA

BEVERLY HILLS, Los Angeles Co.

PAUL D. SUPNIK (AV)

9595 Wilshire Boulevard, Suite 201, 90212-2512
Telephone: 310-859-0100
Facsimile: 310-859-0177
Email: ps@supnik.com *URL:* http://www.supnik.com

For full biographical listings, see the Martindale-Hubbell Law Directory

COSTA MESA, Orange Co.

RUTAN & TUCKER, LLP (AV)

A Partnership including Professional Corporations
611 Anton Boulevard, Fourteenth Floor, P.O. Box 1950, 92626-1998
Telephone: 714-641-5100; 213-625-7586
Telecopier: 714-546-9035
Email: rutan&tucker@rutan.com *URL:* http://www.rutan.com

MEMBERS OF FIRM

Michael T. Hornak
Mark B. Frazier
James S. Weisz (P.C.)

ASSOCIATE

B. Lynn Loschin

OF COUNSEL

Edward D. Sybesma, Jr. (P.C.)

For Complete List of Firm Personnel, See General Section

For full biographical listings, see the Martindale-Hubbell Law Directory

*FRESNO,** Fresno Co.

DOWLING, AARON & KEELER, INCORPORATED (AV)

6051 North Fresno Street, Suite 200, 93710
Telephone: 559-432-4500
Fax: 559-432-4590
Email: dak@daklaw.com *URL:* http://www.daklaw.com
Bakersfield, California Office: 110 South Mt. Claire, Suite 203. 93309.
Telephone: 661-396-0451. Web Site: http://www.daklaw.com.

(See Next Column)

DOWLING, AARON & KEELER INCORPORATED, *Fresno—Continued*

Philip David Kopp
James C. Sherwood

Larry B. Lindenau
Justin D. Harris

Reference: Wells Fargo Bank (Main).

For Complete List of Firm Personnel, See General Section

For full biographical listings, see the Martindale-Hubbell Law Directory

*LOS ANGELES,** Los Angeles Co.

BAKER & HOSTETLER LLP (AV)

600 Wilshire Boulevard, 90017-3212
Telephone: 213-624-2400
FAX: 213-975-1740
To contact an attorney on the Internet use first initial and surname followed by @baker-hostetler.com
URL: http://www.bakerlaw.com
In Cleveland, Ohio: 3200 National City Center, 1900 East Ninth Street.
Telephone: 216-621-0200.
In Cincinnati, Ohio: 312 Walnut Street, Suite 2650.
Telephone: 513-929-3400.
In Columbus, Ohio: Capitol Square, Suite 2100, 65 East State Street.
Telephone: 614-228-1541.
In Denver, Colorado: 303 East 17th Avenue, Suite 1100.
Telephone: 303-861-0600.
In Houston, Texas: 1000 Louisiana, Suite 2000.
Telephone: 713-751-1600.
In Long Beach, California: 300 Oceangate, Suite 620.
Telephone: 562-432-2827.
In Orlando, Florida: SunBank Center, Suite 2300, 200 South Orange Avenue.
Telephone: 407-649-4000.
In Washington, D. C.: Washington Square, Suite 1100, 1050 Connecticut Avenue, N.W.
Telephone: 202-861-1500.

Edward J. McCutchen (1857-1933)
Harold A. Black (1895-1970)
George Harnagel (1903-1962)
G. William Shea (1911-1986)

OFFICE MANAGING PARTNER

Peter W. James (Managing Partner, Los Angeles and Long Beach, California Offices)

PARTNERS

Angela C. Agrusa
Patrick J. Cain
Penny M. Costa
Richard A. Deeb
David A. Destino
Gary L. Gilbert
Jonathan R. Hodes
Thomas G. Roberts
Jack I. Samet
David C. Sampson
Bill E. Schroeder
Glen A. Smith
Teresa R. Tracy

ASSOCIATES

Kathleen E. Bailey
Megan E. Gray
Nigel E. Jacques
Andrew Lurie
Brian A. Ross
Wendy E. Stanford
Marcos M. Tarango
Kimberly R. Wells
Cranston J. Williams

OF COUNSEL

Lisa F. Hinchliffe

RETIRED PARTNERS

G. Richard Doty
Howard J. Privett

For full biographical listings, see the Martindale-Hubbell Law Directory

BLECHER & COLLINS, A PROFESSIONAL CORPORATION (AV)

611 West Sixth Street, 20th Floor, 90017
Telephone: 213-622-4222
Telecopier: 213-622-1656

Maxwell M. Blecher
William C. Hsu
Harold R. Collins, Jr.
Gary M. Joye
John E. Andrews
James Robert Noblin
Steven J. Cannata
Donald R. Pepperman
Ralph C. Hofer
Alicia G. Rosenberg

For full biographical listings, see the Martindale-Hubbell Law Directory

JONES, DAY, REAVIS & POGUE (AV)

555 West Fifth Street Suite 4600, 90013-1025
Telephone: 213-489-3939
Telecopier: 213-243-2539
Email: counsel@jonesday.com *URL:* http://www.jonesday.com
In Irvine, California: 5 Park Plaza, Suite 1100.
Telephone: 949-851-3939.
Telecopier: 949-553-7539.

(See Next Column)

In Atlanta, Georgia: 3500 SunTrust Plaza, 303 Peachtree Street.
Telephone: 404-521-3939.
Telecopier: 404-581-8330.
In Brussels, Belgium: Avenue Louise 480, 7th Floor, B-1050 Brussels.
Telephone: 32-2-645-14-11.
Telecopier: 32-2-645-14-45.
In Chicago, Illinois: 77 West Wacker.
Telephone: 312-782-3939.
Telecopier: 312-782-8585.
In Cleveland, Ohio: North Point, 901 Lakeside Avenue.
Telephone: 216-586-3939.
Telecopier: 216-579-0212.
In Columbus, Ohio: 1900 Huntington Center.
Telephone: 614-469-3939.
Telecopier: 614-461-4198.
In Dallas, Texas: 2727 North Harwood Street.
Telephone: 214-220-3939.
Telecopier: 214-969-5100.
In Frankfurt, Germany: Hochhaus am Park, Grüneburgweg 102, 60323 Frankfurt am Main.
Telephone: 49-69-9726-3939.
Telecopier: 49-69-9726-3993.
In Geneva, Switzerland: 20, rue de Candolle.
Telephone: 41-22-320-2339.
Telecopier: 41-22-320-1232.
In Hong Kong: 29th Floor, Entertainment Building, 30 Queen's Road Central.
Telephone: 852-2526-6895.
Telecopier: 852-2868-5871.
In London England: Bucklersbury House, 3 Queen Victoria Street.
Telephone: 44-20-7236-3939.
Telecopier: 44-20-7236-1113.
In New York, New York: 599 Lexington Avenue.
Telephone: 212-326-3939.
Telecopier: 212-755-7306.
In Paris, France: 120, rue du Faubourg Saint-Honoré.
Telephone: 33-1-56-59-3939.
Telecopier: 33-1-56-59-3938
In Pittsburgh, Pennsylvania: 500 Grant Street, 31st Floor.
Telephone: 412-391-3939.
Telecopier: 412-394-7959.
In Riyadh, Saudi Arabia: The International Law Firm (In Association with Jones, Day, Reavis & Pogue), Sulaymaniyah, Prince Mishari IBN, Abdulaziz Street, P.O. Box 22166.
Telephone: (966-1) 462-8866.
Telecopier: (966-1) 462-9001.
In Shanghai, China: 2805 Kerry Centre, 1515 Nanjing Road West.
Telephone: 86-21-5298-6568.
Telecopier: 86-21-5298-6569.
In Sydney, Australia: Governor Phillip Tower, Level 38, 1 Farrer Place.
Telephone: 61-2-9210-6921.
Telecopier: 61-2-9210-6926.
In Taipei, Taiwan: 8th Floor, 2 Tun Hwa South Road, Section 2.
Telephone: (886-2) 2704-6808.
Telecopier: (886-2) 2704-6791.
In Tokyo, Japan: Toranomon 45 Mori Building, 3th Floor, 1-5, Toranomon 5-Chome, Minato-ku, Tokyo 105, Japan.
Telephone: 81-3-3433-3939.
Telecopier: 81-3-5401-2725.
In Washington, D.C.: 51 Louisiana Avenue, N.W.
Telephone: 202-879-3939.
Telecopier: 202-626-1700.

MEMBER OF FIRM IN LOS ANGELES

Victor G. Savikas

For Complete List of Firm Personnel, See General Section

For full biographical listings, see the Martindale-Hubbell Law Directory

LAW OFFICES OF STEVEN S. KARIC A PROFESSIONAL CORPORATION (AV)

800 Wilshire Boulevard, Suite 1050, 90017-2614
Telephone: 213-955-0100
Fax: 213-955-0111
Email: sskaric@kariclaw.com *URL:* http://www.kariclaw.com

Steven S. Karic

Nora Tu-Willis

For full biographical listings, see the Martindale-Hubbell Law Directory

LEOPOLD, PETRICH & SMITH, A PROFESSIONAL CORPORATION (AV)

(Formerly Youngman, Hungate & Leopold)
Suite 3110, 2049 Century Park East (Century City), 90067-3274
Telephone: 310-277-3333
Telecopier: 310-277-7444
URL: http://www.lpsla.com

(See Next Column)

LEOPOLD, PETRICH & SMITH A PROFESSIONAL CORPORATION—*Continued*

Gordon E. Youngman (1903-1983)	Vincent Cox
A. Fredric Leopold	Donald R. Gordon
Louis P. Petrich	Walter R. Sadler
Joel McCabe Smith	Daniel M. Mayeda
Edward A. Ruttenberg	David Aronoff
	Robert S. Gutierrez

Paul M. Krekorian	Lincoln D. Bandlow

OF COUNSEL

Richard Hungate

For full biographical listings, see the Martindale-Hubbell Law Directory

LOEB & LOEB LLP (AV)

A Limited Liability Partnership including Professional Corporations
Suite 1800, 1000 Wilshire Boulevard, 90017-2475
Telephone: 213-688-3400
Facsimile: 213-688-3460
Email: info@loeb.com *URL:* http://www.loeb.com
Century City, California Office: Suite 2200, 10100 Santa Monica Boulevard, Los Angeles, 90067-4164.
Telephone: 310-282-2000.
Facsimile: 310-282-2192.
New York, N.Y. Office: 345 Park Avenue, 10154-0037.
Telephone: 212-407-4000.
Facsimile: 212-407-4990.
Nashville, Tennessee Office: 45 Music Square West, 37203-3205.
Telephone: 615-749-8300;
Facsimile: 615-749-8308.
Rome, Italy Office: Piazza Digione 1, 00197.
Telephone: 011-3906-808-8456.
Facsimile: 011-3906-808-8288.

MEMBERS OF FIRM

Kenneth B. Anderson (New York City Office)	William J. Marlow (New York City Office)
David H. Carlin (New York City Office)	Stephen R. Mick (Century City Office)
Marc Chamlin (New York City Office)	Charles H. Miller (New York City Office)
David W. Grace (Century City Office)	Douglas E. Mirell
Stuart Lubitz (Century City Office)	Lee N. Steiner (New York City Office)
	James D. Taylor (New York City Office)

SENIOR COUNSEL

Dorie G. Choderker (Century City Office)

ASSOCIATES

Philip J. Graves	Wein-ing Yang (Century City Office)
David L. Lubitz (Century City Office)	

For Complete List of Firm Personnel, See General Section

For full biographical listings, see the Martindale-Hubbell Law Directory

MENES LAW CORPORATION (AV)

1801 Century Park East, Suite 1560, 90067
Telephone: 310-286-1313
Fax: 310-556-5695
Email: mlc@meneslaw.com

Barry A. Menes	Paul I. Menes

Marc M. Messineo

OF COUNSEL

John R. Climaco (Not admitted in CA)	Edward M. Bernstein (Not admitted in CA)

For full biographical listings, see the Martindale-Hubbell Law Directory

O'MELVENY & MYERS LLP (AV)

400 South Hope Street, 90071-2899
Telephone: 213-430-6000
Facsimile: 213-430-6407
Cable: MOMS
Telex: 674122
Email: omminfo@omm.com *URL:* http://www.omm.com
Century City, CA Office: 1999 Avenue of the Stars, Los Angeles, 90067-6035.
Telex: 674097. Tel: 310-553-6700.
Fax: 310-246-6779.
Newport Beach, CA Office: 610 Newport Center Drive, 92660-6429.
Telex: 4722088. Tel: 949-760-9600.
Fax: 949-823-6994.
San Francisco, CA Office: Embarcadero Center West, 275 Battery Street, 94111-3305. Tel: 415-984-8700.
Fax: 415-984-8701.

(See Next Column)

New York, NY Office: Citicorp Center, 153 East 53rd Street, 10022-4611.
Telex: 129165. Tel: 212-326-2000.
Fax: 212-326-2061.
Washington, DC Office: 555 13th Street, N.W., 20004-1109.
Cable: MOMSWSH.
Telex: 89622. Tel: 202-383-5300.
Fax: 202-383-5414.
London Office: O'Melveny & Myers, 3 Finsbury Square, London, EC2A 1LA, England. Tel: 44-171-256-8451. Fax 44-171-638-8205.
Tokyo Office: Akasaka Twin Tower, East 14F, 2-17-23, Akasaka, Minato-ku, Tokyo 107-0052, Japan. Tel: 03-5562-2800.
Fax: 03-5575-3840.
Hong Kong Office: O'Melveny & Myers, Suite 1905, Tower Two, Lippo Centre, 89 Queensway, Central, Hong Kong. Tel: 852-2523-8266.
Fax: 852-2522-1760.
Shanghai Office: Kerry Centre, 20F, 1515 Nanjing Road West, Shanghai, 200040 People's Republic of China. Tel: 86-21-5298-5600.
Fax: 86-21-5298-5500.

PARTNER

Patrick Lynch

For Complete List of Firm Personnel, See General Section

For full biographical listings, see the Martindale-Hubbell Law Directory

RICHMAN, LUNA, KICHAVEN & GLUSHON (AV)

1801 Century Park East, Suite 2400, 90067-2326
Telephone: 310-556-1444
Telecopier: 310-556-0444
URL: http://www.RLKG.com

MEMBERS OF FIRM

James D. Richman	Jeffrey G. Kichaven
Dennis R. Luna	Robert L. Glushon

OF COUNSEL

Hardy L. Thomas	Kurt E. Matthews

References: City National Bank (Beverly Hills, Calif.).

For full biographical listings, see the Martindale-Hubbell Law Directory

RINTALA, SMOOT, JAENICKE & REES (AV)

10351 Santa Monica Boulevard, Suite 400, 90025-6937
Telephone: 310-203-0935
Facsimile: 310-556-8921
Email: RSJ&R@RSJR.com

MEMBERS OF FIRM

William T. Rintala	Melodie K. Larsen
Peter C. Smoot	Frank E. Melton
J. Larson Jaenicke	Robert W. Hodges
Robert A. Rees	G. Howden Fraser

ASSOCIATES

Michael B. Garfinkel	Jeffrey H. Thaler
Emily Peters	Jaclyn A. Hoekstra

Representative Clients: William Morris Agency, Inc.; Broadcast Music, Inc.; Eaton Corp.
Reference: Santa Monica Bank.

For full biographical listings, see the Martindale-Hubbell Law Directory

RUSS, AUGUST & KABAT, A PROFESSIONAL CORPORATION (AV)

Suite 1200, 12424 Wilshire Boulevard, 90025
Telephone: 310-826-7474
Fax: 310-826-6991

Larry C. Russ	Jules L. Kabat
Richard Lee August	Laura K. Stanton

Evan M. Kent

Judith L. Meadow	Robyn K. Johnson
France D. Lemoine	Lucy Arant

OF COUNSEL

Steven M. Siemens	Jaye A. Young

For full biographical listings, see the Martindale-Hubbell Law Directory

*MODESTO,** Stanislaus Co.

RICHARD DOUGLAS BREW A PROFESSIONAL LAW CORPORATION (AV)

Suite 350 / Judge Frank C. Damrell Building, 1601 I Street, 95354-1135
Telephone: 209-572-3157
Telefax: 209-572-4641
Email: rdbplc@interleg.com

Richard Douglas Brew

For full biographical listings, see the Martindale-Hubbell Law Directory

*SACRAMENTO,** Sacramento Co.

HUNTER RICHEY DI BENEDETTO & BREWER, LLP (AV)

A Limited Liability Partnership
Renaissance Tower, 801 K Street, 23rd Floor, 95814-3525
Telephone: 916-491-3000
Facsimile: 916-491-3080
Email: hrdb@hrdb.com *URL:* http://www.hrdb.com

MEMBERS OF FIRM

William S. Hunter
Win R. Richey
Florence L. Di Benedetto
Roy E. Brewer
Anne E. Ferguson
James F. Geary
Janet C. Eisenbeis
Stephen C. Ruehmann
Sharon K. Sandeen
Jack V. Lovell
Patricia J. Hartman

OF COUNSEL

Laurie E. Davis

LEGAL SUPPORT PERSONNEL

Lori J. Moody (Paralegal)
Deborah M. Johnson (Paralegal)
Linda Jane Hall (Executive Assistant)
Jennifer E. Mueller (Legal Assistant)
Michele L. Nickell (Legal Assistant)
Lynetta G. Goodwin

For full biographical listings, see the Martindale-Hubbell Law Directory

*SAN DIEGO,** San Diego Co.

ALHADEFF CANNON ROSE SOLAR & PARKS, LLP (AV)

550 West "C" Street, Nineteenth Floor, 92101-3540
Telephone: 619-231-8700
Facsimile: 619-231-8323
Email: ksolar@acrsp.com
Temecula, California Office: The Tower Plaza, 27555 Ynez Road, Suite 203, 92591-4677.
Telephone: 909-699-9088.
Facsimile: 909-699-9878. Email: POBERHANSLEY@ACRSP.com
Los Angeles, California Office: Olympic Center, 11150 Olympic Boulevard, Suite 860, 90064.
Telephone: 310-914-4400.
Facsimile: 310-914-0030. Email: JODONNELL@ACRSP.com
Lafayette, California Office: Lafayette Terrace, 3697 Mount Diablo Boulevard, Suite 100, 94549.
Telephone: 925-283-1599.
Facsimile: 925-283-5847. Email: GMF-CA@MSN.com

PARTNER

John L. O'Donnell, Jr. (Resident, Los Angeles, California Office)

ASSOCIATES

Genie Harrison
Traci M. Selby

References: Enefco International, Ltd.; Molding International & Engineering; Health Net.

For full biographical listings, see the Martindale-Hubbell Law Directory

FERRIS & BRITTON, A PROFESSIONAL CORPORATION (AV)

1600 First National Bank Center, 401 West A Street, 92101
Telephone: 619-233-3131
Fax: 619-232-9316
Email: manager@ferrisbritton.com *URL:* http://www.ferrisbritton.com

Christopher Q. Britton
Michael R. Weinstein

Representative Clients: Cox Communications, Inc.; Enterprise Rent-A-Car; Exxon; Media One; Peninsula Bank; Teleport Communications Group; Southwest Airlines; Structural Bioinformatics, Inc.; ZyGam, Inc.

For Complete List of Firm Personnel, See General Section

For full biographical listings, see the Martindale-Hubbell Law Directory

KENNERSON SCHWARTZ SEMERDJIAN & HAILE LLP (AV)

A Limited Liability Partnership
101 West Broadway, Suite 810, 92101
Telephone: 619-236-8821
Facsimile: 619-236-8827
URL: http://www.lawyers.com/ksshlaw

OF COUNSEL

Paul R. Kennerson

MEMBERS OF FIRM

Ross J. Schwartz
Dick A. Semerdjian
Jeffrey A. Haile

James R. Ballard
John K. Grant

For full biographical listings, see the Martindale-Hubbell Law Directory

*SAN FRANCISCO,** San Francisco Co.

MURPHY, PEARSON, BRADLEY & FEENEY, A PROFESSIONAL CORPORATION (AV)

88 Kearny Street, 10th Floor, 94108
Telephone: 415-788-1900
Telecopier: 415-393-8087
Email: IndividualsFirstInitialAndLastName@mpbf.com *URL:* http://www.mpbf.com
Sacramento, California Office: 701 University Avenue, Suite 150.
Telephone: 916-565-0300.
Fax: 916-565-1636.
San Jose, California Office: 80 South Market Street, 3rd Floor.
Telephone: 408-279-5792.
Facsimile: 408-279-5785.
Los Angeles, California Office: 11400 West Olympic Boulevard, Suite 249.
Telephone: 310-312-9565.
Fax: 310-312-9566.

James A. Murphy
Arthur V. Pearson
Michael P. Bradley
John H. Feeney
Gregory A. Bastian (Resident, Sacramento Office)
Timothy J. Halloran
Karen M. Goodman (Resident, Sacramento Office)
Mark S. Perelman
Mark Ellis (Resident, Sacramento Office)
William S. Kronenberg
Gregg A. Thornton
Jane L. O'Hara Gamp
Alexander J. Berline
Margaret M. Schneck (Resident, San Jose Office)

Michele Z. Allen (Resident, San Jose Office)
Thomas N. Bell (Resident, Sacramento Office)
Alec Hunter Boyd
Shoshana Y. Chazan
Dennis W. Chiu (Resident, San Jose Office)
June D. Coleman (Resident, Sacramento Office)
Barbara A. Cotter
Peggy S. Doyle
Jan L. Gardiner (Resident, Sacramento Office)
John P. Girarde
Michael D. Haupt
Christian P. Hurley (Resident, Sacramento Office)
Anna Kapetanakos
Theresa M. La Voie (Resident, Sacramento Office)
Peter J. Linn
Joan E. Low
Anne F. Marchant
Aaron Karl McClellan
Bernard M. McGuire
Quinn Adele Moody
Van Thuc Nguyen (Resident, Sacramento Office)
Jessica B. Rudin
John A. Safyurtlu
Kelli L. Taylor (Resident, Sacramento Office)
Sylvia Wahba
Richard Sung Wang
Harlan B. Watkins

For full biographical listings, see the Martindale-Hubbell Law Directory

ROSEN, BIEN & ASARO (AV)

Eighth Floor, 155 Montgomery Street, 94104
Telephone: 415-433-6830
Fax: 415-433-7104
Email: rba@rbalaw.com

Sanford Jay Rosen
Michael W. Bien
Andrea G. Asaro

Thomas Nolan
William H. D. Fernholz
Shana J. Margolis
Ernest J. Galvan

For full biographical listings, see the Martindale-Hubbell Law Directory

LAWRENCE G. TOWNSEND (AV)

455 Market Street, 19th Floor, 94105
Telephone: 415-882-3288
FAX: 415-882-3299
(Also of Counsel to Owen, Wickersham & Erickson)

For full biographical listings, see the Martindale-Hubbell Law Directory

*SAN JOSE,** Santa Clara Co.

MCMANIS, FAULKNER & MORGAN (AV)

160 West Santa Clara Street, 10th Floor, 95113
Telephone: 408-279-8700
Fax: 408-279-3244; 408-279-0494
Email: mfm@mfmlaw.com *URL:* http://www.mfmlaw.com

James McManis
William Faulkner
Donelle Morgan
Lisa Herrick
Michael Reedy
Erica Yew

Michelle Tidalgo
Colleen Duffy Smith
Lillian Wolf
Rebecca Hughes
Kalpana Vrudhula
Ray M. Baluyot
Catherine Bechtel
Arron Nesbitt

OF COUNSEL

Mary Arand

For full biographical listings, see the Martindale-Hubbell Law Directory

COLORADO

*DENVER,** Denver Co.

Berenbaum, Weinshienk & Eason, P.C. (AV)

Suite 2600 Republic Plaza, 370 17th Street, 80202
Telephone: 303-825-0800
Facsimile: 303-629-7610
Email: berenbaum1@aol.com *URL:* http://www.BWELaw.com

M. Frances Cetrulo — Dean G. Panos

OF COUNSEL

Richard L. Eason

Representative Clients: Home Depot; Sprint Spectrum, L.P.; Town of Vail, Colorado; First Union Corporation; City of Englewood, Colorado; Oakwood Homes; Karman, Inc.; Wells Fargo Bank, N.A.; Berkshire Life Insurance Co.; Trinity Ventures.

For full biographical listings, see the Martindale-Hubbell Law Directory

Dorr, Carson, Sloan & Birney, P.C. (AV)

3010 East Sixth Avenue, 80206
Telephone: 303-333-3010
FAX: 303-333-1470
Email: bobdorr@sni.net *URL:* http://www.patnet.com/dcsb

Robert C. Dorr — Jack C. Sloan
W. Scott Carson — Thomas S. Birney

Leslie P. Kramer — John F. Thompson

OF COUNSEL

Christopher H. Munch — Steve A. Mains

Representative Clients: Winegard Co.; Intercat, Inc.; Steam Way International; Taco John's International; Dreyers Grand Ice Cream.

For full biographical listings, see the Martindale-Hubbell Law Directory

Dufford & Brown, P.C. (AV)

1700 Broadway, Suite 1700, 80290-1701
Telephone: 303-861-8013
Facsimile: 303-832-3804
Colorado Springs, Colorado Office: 101 N. Tejon, Suite 410.
Telephone: 719-471-0559.
Facsimile: 719-471-0583.
Affiliated Office: Solomon, Pearl, Blum & Quinn, L.L.P., New York, NY and Denver, Colorado.

David W. Furgason — Scott J. Mikulecky
Thomas E. J. Hazard

Representative Clients: Starbucks Coffee Company; Louis Vuitton, S.A.

For Complete List of Firm Personnel, See General Section

For full biographical listings, see the Martindale-Hubbell Law Directory

Gorsuch Kirgis LLP (AV)

Tower 1, Suite 1000, 1515 Arapahoe Street, 80202
Telephone: 303-376-5000
Fax: 303-376-5001

PARTNERS

S. Lee Terry, Jr. — Cynthia Smith Cain

ASSOCIATE

Pantea M. Garroussi

LEGAL SUPPORT PERSONNEL

Lansing Wallace — Veronica Ehrenzeller

For full biographical listings, see the Martindale-Hubbell Law Directory

Sheridan Ross, P.C. (AV)

1560 Broadway, Suite 1200, 80202
Telephone: 303-863-9700
Facsimile: 303-863-0223
Email: srlaw@sheridanross.com

David F. Zinger — Joseph E. Kovarik
Craig C. Groseth — Susan Pryor Willson
Michael L. Tompkins — Lewis D. Hansen
Todd P. Blakely — Robert R. Brunelli
Gary J. Connell — Douglas W. Swartz
Sabrina Crowley Stavish — Richard L. Hughes

Bruce A. Kugler — Benjamin Baughman Lieb
Dana Lynn Hartje — Bradley M. Knepper
Paul S. Hansra — John C. Scott
Don D. Cha — Miriam R. Drickman

(See Next Column)

OF COUNSEL

Philip H. Sheridan (P.C.) — Wannell M. Crook
Theresa A. Brown

LEGAL SUPPORT PERSONNEL

TECHNICAL SPECIALIST

Dennis J. Dupray — Angela Dallas-Pedretti

PARALEGALS

Janet E. Balent — Peggy West

Representative Clients: Ball Corporation; British Nuclear Fuels; Case Logic Inc.; COBE Laboratories; Coors Brewing Company; Heska Corporation; J.D. Edwards & Company; Maxtor Corporation; University of Colorado; Vicorp Restaurants, Inc.

For full biographical listings, see the Martindale-Hubbell Law Directory

CONNECTICUT

FAIRFIELD, Fairfield Co.

Perman & Green, LLP (AV)

425 Post Road, 06430-6232
Telephone: 203-259-1800
Facsimile: 203-255-5170
Email: pgpatent@aol.com *URL:* http://www.pgpatent.com

OF COUNSEL

Donald C. Caulfield — Paul Weinstein

For full biographical listings, see the Martindale-Hubbell Law Directory

DISTRICT OF COLUMBIA

WASHINGTON, D.C. Co.

Baker Botts L.L.P. (AV)

A Registered Limited Liability Partnership
The Warner, 1299 Pennsylvania Avenue, N.W., 20004-2400
Telephone: 202-639-7700
Fax: 202-639-7832
Email: postmaster@bakerbotts.com *URL:* http://www.bakerbotts.com
Houston, Texas Office: One Shell Plaza, 910 Louisiana.
Telephone: 713-229-1234.
Austin, Texas Office: 1600 San Jacinto Center, 98 San Jacinto Boulevard.
Telephone: 512-322-2500.
Dallas, Texas Office: 2001 Ross Avenue.
Telephone: 214-953-6500.
New York, New York Office: 599 Lexington Avenue.
Telephone: 212-705-5000.
Moscow, Russia Office: 10 ul. Bolshaya Dimitrovka (formerly Pushkinskaya), 103031.
Telephone: 7095/921-5300 (Local); 7501/929-7070 (International).
London, England Office: 45 Ludgate Hill.
Telephone: 0171-778-1400 (Local); 011-44-171-778-1400 (International).
Baku, Azerbaijan Office: 6-10 Vagif Mustafa-zadeh Street, Third Floor, Icheri Sheher, 370004.
Telephone: 994-12-97-63-88 (Local); 011-994-12-97-63-88 (International).

MEMBERS OF FIRM

Scott F. Partridge — James Remenick
Rodger L. Tate

SPECIAL COUNSEL

James B. Arpin

ASSOCIATES

Floyd B. Chapman — Laurence H. Posorske
Robert A. King (Not admitted in DC)

For Complete List of Firm Personnel, See General Section

For full biographical listings, see the Martindale-Hubbell Law Directory

Baker & Hostetler LLP (AV)

Washington Square, Suite 1100, 1050 Connecticut Avenue, N.W., 20036-5304
Telephone: 202-861-1500
Fax: 202-861-1783
To contact an attorney on the Internet use first initial and surname followed by @baker-hostetler.com
URL: http://www.bakerlaw.com
In Cleveland, Ohio: 3200 National City Center, 1900 East Ninth Street.
Telephone: 216-621-0200.
In Cincinnati, Ohio: 312 Walnut Street, Suite 2650.
Telephone: 513-929-3400.

(See Next Column)

BAKER & HOSTETLER LLP, *Washington—Continued*

In Columbus, Ohio: Capitol Square, Suite 2100, 65 East State Street.
Telephone: 614-228-1541.
In Denver, Colorado: 303 East 17th Avenue, Suite 1100.
Telephone: 303-861-0600.
In Houston, Texas: 1000 Louisiana, Suite 2000.
Telephone: 713-751-1600.
In Beverly Hills, California: 9150 Wilshire Boulevard, Suite 205.
Telephone: 310-385-7500.
In Long Beach, California: 300 Oceangate, Suite 620.
Telephone: 562-432-2827.
In Los Angeles, California: 600 Wilshire Boulevard.
Telephone: 213-624-2400.
In Orlando, Florida: SunBank Center, Suite 2300, 200 South Orange Avenue.
Telephone: 407-649-4000.

PARTNER

Belinda Jayne Scrimenti

For Complete List of Firm Personnel, See General Section

For full biographical listings, see the Martindale-Hubbell Law Directory

BANNER & WITCOFF, LTD. (AV)

Established In 1920 - Predecessor Parent
1001 G Street, N.W., 20001-4597
Telephone: 202-508-9100
Facsimile: 202-508-9299
Email: cooperman@bannerwitcoff.com *URL:* http://www.bannerwitcoff.com
Chicago, Illinois Office: Ten South Wacker Drive.
Telephone: 312-715-1000.
Facsimile: 312-715-1234.
Boston, Massachusetts Office: 28 State Street, 28th Floor.
Telephone: 617-227-7111.
Fax: 617-227-4399.
Portland, Oregon Office: 601 SW Second Avenue, Suite 1900.
Telephone: 503-279-6330.
Fax: 503-279-6328.

Robert F. Altherr, Jr.
Donald W. Banner
Pamela I. Banner
Gary D. Fedorochko
Daniel E. Fisher
William J. Fisher
Patricia E. Hong
Dale H. Hoscheit
Thomas H. Jackson
Sarah A. Kagan
Robert S. Katz
Christopher L. McKee
Edward F. McKie, Jr.
Nina L. Medlock
Frederic M. Meeker
Thomas L. Peterson
Joseph M. Potenza
Steven P. Schad
Joseph M. Skerpon
Susan A. Wolffe
Bradley C. Wright

OF COUNSEL

Brian E. Banner
William W. Beckett
Franklin D. Wolffe

ASSOCIATES

Steve S. Chang
Joseph P. Curtin
Thomas L. Evans
Holly M. Ford
Christopher R. Glembocki
Brian E. Hanlon
Lisa M. Hemmendinger
Lisa M. W. Hillman (Not admitted in DC)
Sumeet Magoon (Not admitted in DC)
Charles Miller (Not admitted in DC)
Ajay S. Pathak (Not admitted in DC)
Steven S. Payne (Not admitted in DC)
Paul M. Rivard
Christopher B. Roth (Not admitted in DC)
Kevin A. Wolff

For full biographical listings, see the Martindale-Hubbell Law Directory

BARKATS & ASSOCIATES, CHARTERED, ATTORNEYS AND COUNSELORS AT LAW (AV)

1250 Eye Street, N.W., 20005
Telephone: 202-682-1396
Telecopier: 202-789-0895
URL: http://www.lawyers.com/barkatslaw
Paris, France Office: 24, Rue de Prony, 75017 Paris, France.
Telephone: 01 44 29 32 32.
Telecopier: 44 29 31 00.
Affiliated Law Firm: Robert J. Shutak, 1424 Fourth Street, Santa Monica, California 90401.
Telephone: 310-458-3343.
Telecopier: 301-451-0043.

MEMBER OF THE FIRM IN WASHINGTON, D.C.

Pierre-Philippe Barkats

ASSOCIATES

Robert Clifton Burns
Jeffrey Thomas Gutierrez (Not admitted in DC)
Pat James Kalellis (Not admitted in DC)

(See Next Column)

OF COUNSEL

Jerome K. Tankel
Jacques R. Beghain (Not admitted in the United States)

For full biographical listings, see the Martindale-Hubbell Law Directory

FINNEGAN, HENDERSON, FARABOW, GARRETT & DUNNER, L.L.P. (AV)

Suite 700, 1300 I Street, N.W., 20005-3315
Telephone: 202-408-4000
Facsimile: 202-408-4400
URL: http://www.finnegan.com
Palo Alto, California Office: 700 Hansen Way.
Telephone: 650-849-6600.
Facsimile: 650-849-6666.
Atlanta, Georgia Office: 3200 SunTrust Plaza, 303 Peachtree Street, N.E.
Telephone: 404-653-6400.
Facsimile: 404-653-6444.
Tokyo, Japan Office: Toranomon No. 45 Mori Building, Third Floor, 1-5, Toranomon 5-chome Minato-Ku.
Telephone: 0081-3-3431-6943.
Facsimile: 0081-3-3431-6945.
Brussels, Belgium Office: Avenue Louise 326, Box 37, 1050.
Telephone: 011-322-646-0353.
Facsimile: 011-322-646-2135.

MEMBERS OF FIRM

Douglas B. Henderson
Ford F. Farabow Jr.
Arthur S. Garrett
Donald R. Dunner
Tipton D. Jennings IV
Laurence R. Hefter
Michael C. Elmer (Resident Partner, Palo Alto, California Office)
John M. Romary
Richard Lee Stroup
David W. Hill
Thomas W. Winland
E. Robert Yoches
Susan Haberman Griffen
Christopher P. Foley
John C. Paul
Griffith B. Price Jr.
John F. Hornick
Robert D. Litowitz
David M. Kelly
Mark S. Sommers
Jeffrey A. Berkowitz

COUNSEL

Arthur J. Levine

ASSOCIATES

Lisa Peller London
John R. Alison

Reference: Crestar Bank, N.A., Washington, D.C.

For full biographical listings, see the Martindale-Hubbell Law Directory

GREGORY H. GUILLOT CHARTERED (AV)

International Square, 1825 I Street, N.W., Suite 400, 20006
Telephone: 202-955-1100
Facsimile: 202-955-1101
Email: ggmark@radix.net *URL:* http://www.ggmark.com

Gregory H. Guillot

Representative Clients: OASIS Corporation; OASIS, Ireland; Riverdance-The Show; Priority E.M.S., Inc.; The Publicate Corporation; Tropical Isle, Inc.; Dynamic Systems Development Method, Ltd.; TeddysoftBV (The Netherlands); Camper Clubs of America, Inc.; Journeylink.com, Inc.

For full biographical listings, see the Martindale-Hubbell Law Directory

MIDLEN LAW CENTER (AV)

3238 Prospect Street, N.W., 20007-3214
Telephone: 202-333-1500
Facsimile: 202-333-6852
Email: john@midlen.com *URL:* http://www.midlen.com

John H. Midlen, Jr.

For full biographical listings, see the Martindale-Hubbell Law Directory

VENABLE ATTORNEYS AT LAW VENABLE, BAETJER, HOWARD & CIVILETTI, LLP (AV)

A Partnership including Professional Corporations
Suite 1000, 1201 New York Avenue, N.W., 20005
Telephone: 202-962-4800
Fax: 202-962-8300
URL: http://www.venable.com
Baltimore, Maryland Office: Venable, Baetjer and Howard LLP, 1800 Mercantile Bank & Trust Building, 2 Hopkins Plaza.
Telephone: 410-244-7400.
Fax: 410-244-7742.
McLean, Virginia Office: Venable, Baetjer and Howard LLP, Suite 400, 2010 Corporate Ridge.
Telephone: 703-760-1600.
Fax: 703-821-8949.
Rockville, Maryland Office: Venable, Baetjer and Howard LLP, Suite 500, One Church Street, P. O. Box 1906.
Telephone: 301-217-5600.
Fax: 301-217-5617.

(See Next Column)

VENABLE ATTORNEYS AT LAW VENABLE, BAETJER, HOWARD & CIVILETTI, LLP—*Continued*

Towson, Maryland Office: Venable, Baetjer and Howard LLP, 210 Allegheny Avenue, P. O. Box 5517.
Telephone: 410-494-6200.
Fax: 410-821-0147.

MEMBERS OF FIRM

Kenneth C. Bass, III (Also at McLean, Virginia Office)
Robert J. Bolger, Jr. (Also at Baltimore, Maryland Office)
William D. Coston
Jeffrey A. Dunn (Also at Baltimore, Maryland Office)
Edward F. Glynn, Jr.
David W. Goewey
Mark B. Harrison
Gary M. Hnath
Jeffrey D. Knowles
George F. Pappas (Also at Baltimore, Maryland Office)

OF COUNSEL

Barbara L. Waite

ASSOCIATE

James Nicholas Czaban

For Complete List of Firm Personnel, See General Section

For full biographical listings, see the Martindale-Hubbell Law Directory

FLORIDA

*MIAMI,** Dade Co.

ISICOFF & RAGATZ, P.A. (AV)

South Tower, 1101 Brickell Avenue, Suite 800, 33131
Telephone: 305-373-3232
Fax: 305-373-3233

Eric D. Isicoff
Teresa Ragatz

Daniel M. Stuzin
James A. Weinkle
Louise C. Perfetti

OF COUNSEL

Jay Koenigsberg

For full biographical listings, see the Martindale-Hubbell Law Directory

KENNY NACHWALTER SEYMOUR ARNOLD CRITCHLOW & SPECTOR, PROFESSIONAL ASSOCIATION (AV)

1100 Miami Center, 201 South Biscayne Boulevard, 33131-4327
Telephone: 305-373-1000
Facsimile: 305-372-1861
Email: admin@knsacs.com
Rogersville, Tennessee Office: 107 East Main Street, Suite 301.
Telephone: 423-272-5300.
Facsimile: 423-272-4961.

James J. Kenny
Michael Nachwalter
Richard Alan Arnold
Brian F. Spector
Kevin J. Murray
Harry R. Schafer
David H. Lichter
Amanda M. McGovern

Representative Clients: Cartier, Inc.; GTE Directories Corp.; Macmillan, Inc.; Mont Blanc-Simplo Gmbh.; Rolex Watch, USA, Inc.; Louis Vuitton Malletier; Livenchy, SA; NBA Properties, Inc.; Fend USA, Inc.; Business Software Alliance.

For Complete List of Firm Personnel, See General Section

For full biographical listings, see the Martindale-Hubbell Law Directory

MALLOY & MALLOY, P.A. (AV)

2800 S.W. Third Avenue, 33129
Telephone: 305-858-8000
Fort Lauderdale: 954-525-9611
In Florida: 800-337-7239
Facsimile: 305-858-0008
URL: http://www.MALLOYLAW.com
Fort Lauderdale, Florida Office: 2101 West Commercial Boulevard. Suite 4100. 33309.
Telephone: 954-525-9611.

Jennie S. Malloy
John Cyril Malloy, III
Peter A. Matos

Louis R. Gigliotti, Jr.
Andrew W. Ransom

OF COUNSEL

John Cyril Malloy
James E. Wetterling, Jr.

Representative Clients: Tasco Sales, Inc.; Turnberry Associates/Aventura Mall; Editorial Televisa; Cigarette Racing Team, Inc.; Sloppy Joe's (Bar) Int'l, Inc.; Hog's Breath (Saloon) Int'l, Inc.; Krieger Watch Corp.; Navarro Discount Pharmacies; Nailtiques Cosmetic Corp.; Cheeburger Cheeburger Restaurants.

(See Next Column)

For full biographical listings, see the Martindale-Hubbell Law Directory

*ORLANDO,** Orange Co.

ALLEN, DYER, DOPPELT, MILBRATH & GILCHRIST (AV)

255 South Orange Avenue, Suite 1401, P.O. Box 3791, 32802-3791
Telephone: 407-841-2330
Fax: 407-841-2343
Email: info@addmg.com

Herbert L. Allen
Robert Dyer
Ava K. Doppelt
Stephen D. Milbrath
Brian R. Gilchrist
Christopher F. Regan
Jeffrey S. Whittle
David L. Sigalow
Richard K. Warther
Michael W. Taylor (Not admitted in FL)
Enrique G. Estevez

LEGAL SUPPORT PERSONNEL

PATENT AGENTS

Carl M. Napolitano, Ph.D.
Jacqueline E. Hartt, Ph.D.

For full biographical listings, see the Martindale-Hubbell Law Directory

GEORGIA

*ATLANTA,** Fulton Co.

BONDURANT, MIXSON & ELMORE, LLP (AV)

1201 W. Peachtree Street Suite 3900, 30309
Telephone: 404-881-4100
Fax: 404-881-4111
URL: http://www.bondurant-mixson.com

MEMBERS OF FIRM

Emmet J. Bondurant II
H. Lamar Mixson
M. Jerome Elmore
Edward B. Krugman
Jeffrey O. Bramlett
John E. Floyd
Michael B. Terry
P. Richard Game
Jill A. Pryor
J. Scott McClain

Representative Clients: American Dairy Queen Corp.; Avon Products, Inc.; Bottlers of Coca-Cola, U.S.A.; Blue Circle of America; Delta Air Lines, Inc.; Fina Oil and Chemical Company; Four M Corporation; Penske Motorsports; Queen Carpets, Inc.; Ticketmaster Southeast.

For full biographical listings, see the Martindale-Hubbell Law Directory

HAWAII

*HONOLULU,** Honolulu Co.

EDMUNDS MAKI VERGA & THORN (AV)

Suite 2104, Davies Pacific Center, 841 Bishop Street, 96813
Telephone: 808-524-2000
Telecopier: 808-528-3585

John S. Edmunds
Paul Maki
Ronald J. Verga
Elise Owens Thorn
Joy S. Omonaka
Wesley D. Shimazu

Reference: Bank of Hawaii.

For full biographical listings, see the Martindale-Hubbell Law Directory

ILLINOIS

*CHICAGO,** Cook Co.

BANNER & WITCOFF, LTD. (AV)

Established In 1920 - Predecessor Parent
Ten South Wacker Drive, 60606-7407
Telephone: 312-715-1000
Facsimile: 312-715-1234
Email: cooperman@bannerwitcoff.com *URL:* http://www.bannerwitcoff.com
Washington, D.C. Office: 1001 G Street, N.W.
Telephone: 202-508-9100.
Facsimile: 202-508-9299.
Boston, Massachusetts Office: 28 State Street, 28th Floor.
Telephone: 617-227-7111.
Fax: 617-227-4399.
Portland, Oregon Office: 601 SW Second Avenue, 19th Floor.
Telephone: 503-279-6330.
Fax: 503-279-6328.

(See Next Column)

BANNER & WITCOFF LTD., *Chicago—Continued*

Mark T. Banner
James V. Callahan
Marc S. Cooperman
Laura J. DeMoor
Timothy C. Meece
Jon O. Nelson
Thomas K. Pratt
Christopher J. Renk
Robert H. Resis
John F. Rollins
Charles W. Shifley
J. Pieter van Es
Sheldon W. Witcoff

OF COUNSEL

Patricia A. Felch
Robert P. Hart
Joseph P. Krause
Darleen J. Stockley

ASSOCIATES

Matthew P. Becker
Joseph J. Berghammer (Not admitted in IL)
Scott A. Burow
Ronald C. Gorsché, Jr.
Gilberto Hernandez
William J. Klein
Janice V. Mitrius
Christopher P. Moreno
Binal J. Patel

For full biographical listings, see the Martindale-Hubbell Law Directory

FORAN & SCHULTZ (AV)

Suite 3000, 30 North La Salle Street, 60602
Telephone: 312-368-8330
Fax: 312-580-2600
Email: law@foran.com *URL:* http://www.Foran.com

MEMBERS OF FIRM

Thomas A. Foran
Richard G. Schultz
Stephen A. Gorman
Jeff D. Harris
Jack J. Carriglio
Steven H. Gistenson
Brooke R. Whitted
Jeffrey C. Blumenthal
Teresa F. Frisbie

For full biographical listings, see the Martindale-Hubbell Law Directory

MCDONNELL BOEHNEN HULBERT & BERGHOFF (AV)

300 South Wacker Drive 32nd Floor, 60606
Telephone: 312-913-0001
Fax: 312-913-0002
URL: http://www.mbhb.com

MEMBERS OF FIRM

John J. McDonnell
Daniel A. Boehnen
Bradley J. Hulbert
Paul H. Berghoff
Grantland G. Drutchas
Denis A. Berntsen
James C. Gumina
David M. Frischkorn
Leif R. Sigmond, Jr.
A. Blair Hughes
Lawrence H. Aaronson
Thomas A. Fairhall
Matthew J. Sampson
Curt J. Whitenack
Michael S. Greenfield
Steven J. Sarussi
Christopher M. Cavan
Kevin E. Noonan
Robert J. Irvine, III
Amir N. Penn
George I. Lee
Joshua R. Rich

ASSOCIATES

James M. McCarthy
Thomas E. Wettermann
Audrey L. Bartnicki
Enrique Perez
Stephen Lesavich (Not admitted in IL)
Sean M. Sullivan
Roger P. Zimmerman
Vernon W. Francissen (Not admitted in IL)
Emily Miao
Richard A. Machonkin
David S. Harper
Marcus Thymian
Malcolm J. Duncan
Stephen H. Docter

For full biographical listings, see the Martindale-Hubbell Law Directory

PATTISHALL, MCAULIFFE, NEWBURY, HILLIARD & GERALDSON (AV)

Suite 5000, 311 South Wacker Drive, 60606
Telephone: 312-554-8000
Facsimile: 312-554-8015
Washington, D.C. Office: 320 Watergate, Six Hundred, 20037.
Telephone: 202-338-1300.
Facsimile: 202-338-9349.

MEMBERS OF FIRM

Beverly W. Pattishall
Jeremiah D. McAuliffe
Robert M. Newbury
Benjamin S. Warren III (Resident Partner, Washington, D.C. Office)
Raymond I. Geraldson, Jr.
David Craig Hilliard
Edward G. Wierzbicki
Robert W. Sacoff
Mark V. B. Partridge
Joseph N. Welch II
Daniel D. Frohling
John Thompson Brown
Mary E. Innis
Douglas N. Masters
Brett A. August
Jonathan S. Jennings
John Michael Murphy
Kevin T. Conroy
Janet A. Marvel

OF COUNSEL

Ralph H. Lane
Diana Lee Bixler

(See Next Column)

Bradley L. Cohn
Colette A. Durst-Barkey (Resident Associate, Washington, D.C. Office)
Kathryn E. Ross
Daniel S. Goldman
Beth A. Fulkerson
Demetra Merikas
James P. Williams
Jennifer A. O'Malley
Heather F. Hines
Danielle B. Lemack
Uli Widmaier
Jennifer E. Berner
Ram Padmanabhan

For full biographical listings, see the Martindale-Hubbell Law Directory

INDIANA

*INDIANAPOLIS,** Marion Co.

ICE MILLER DONADIO & RYAN (AV)

One American Square Box 82001, 46282-0002
Telephone: 317-236-2100
Fax: 317-236-2219
Email: info@imdr.com *URL:* http://www.imdr.com
South Bend, Indiana Office: 211 West Washington Street, Suite 2420.
Telephone: 219-234-7933.
Fax: 219-234-7965. Internet E-mail: info@imdr.com. Web Site Address: http://www.imdr.com.
Chicago, Illinois Office: 135 South LaSalle Street, Suite 4100.
Telephone: 312-726-1567.
Fax: 312-641-6263. Internet E-mail: info@imdr.com. Web Site Address: http://www.imdr.com.

MEMBERS OF FIRM

Jack R. Snyder
Jay G. Taylor
David M. Mattingly
Philip A. Whistler
John F. Prescott, Jr.
Doreen J. Gridley

SENIOR COUNSEL

Bradley L. Williams
Fred H. Cate

OF COUNSEL

C. Joseph Miller

ASSOCIATES

Michael A. Swift
Russell E. Fowler, II
Brian T. Ster
James D. Wood
Christine Mayewski Orich
Angela M. Fifelski
Thomas A. Walsh
Michael E. Kondoudis (Not admitted in IN)

Counsel For: Delco Remey America, Inc.; Thomson Consumer Electronics, Inc.; Software Solutions, Inc.; Bioanalytical Systems, Inc.; Indianapolis Motor Speedway; Morgan Foods, Inc.; Guide Corporation; Dow Agro Sciences, LLC; Made2Manage Systems, Inc.; Tokheim Corp.

For Complete List of Firm Personnel, See General Section

For full biographical listings, see the Martindale-Hubbell Law Directory

*LAFAYETTE,** Tippecanoe Co.

STUART & BRANIGIN (AV)

The Life Building, 300 Main Street, Suite 800, P.O. Box 1010, 47902-1010
Telephone: 765-423-1561
Telecopier: 765-742-8175
Email: sb@stuartlaw.com *URL:* http://www.stuartlaw.com
Indianapolis, Indiana Office: Suite 1401, 8888 Keystone Crossing, 46240.
Telephone: 317-574-7245.
Fax: 317-574-7050.

MEMBERS OF FIRM

Allison Ellsworth Stuart (1886-1950)
Roger D. Branigin (1902-1975)
Roger D. Branigin, Jr.
Thomas L. Ryan
Thomas R. McCully
Larry R. Fisher
Nina B. Kirkpatrick
Mark Lillianfeld
Stephen R. Pennell
Anthony S. Benton
Erik D. Spykman
William E. Emerick
John C. Duffey
Bruce McSpadden
Mark E. DeYoung
Thomas B. Parent
Laura L. Bowker
Kevin D. Nicoson
Susan K. Roberts
John M. Stuckey
Deborah B. Trice
William P. Kealey
David A. Starkweather
Geoffrey L. Blazi

SENIOR COUNSEL

Russell H. Hart

COUNSEL

John F. Bodle
James V. McGlone

ASSOCIATES

Elizabeth B. Searle
Marianne Mitten Owen
David A. Locke
Karen Orr McClure
Ann Marie Waldron
Barry L. Loftus

General Counsel for: The Lafayette Life Insurance Co.; INB National Bank, N.W.; Lafayette Home Hospital, Inc.

(See Next Column)

STUART & BRANIGIN—*Continued*

State Counsel for: Norfolk & Western Railway Co.
Mr. Ryan is Counsel to: The Trustees of Purdue University.
Representative Clients: Aluminum Company of America; Liberty Mutual Insurance Group.

For full biographical listings, see the Martindale-Hubbell Law Directory

KANSAS

*WICHITA,** Sedgwick Co.

FOULSTON & SIEFKIN L.L.P. (AV)

700 NationsBank Financial Center, 67202
Telephone: 316-267-6371
Facsimile: 316-267-6345
URL: http://www.foulston.com
Topeka, Kansas Office: 1515 NationsBank Tower, 534 Kansas Avenue, 66603.
Telephone: 785-233-3600.
Fax: 785-233-1610.
Dodge City, Kansas Office: 810 Frontview, P.O. Box 1147, 67801.
Telephone: 316-227-8126.
Fax: 316-227-8451.
Member: Lex Mundi, The World's Leading Association of Independent Law Firms.

MEMBERS OF FIRM

James D. Oliver
R. Douglas Reagan (Resident, Dodge City Office)

For Complete List of Firm Personnel, See General Section

For full biographical listings, see the Martindale-Hubbell Law Directory

KENTUCKY

*BOWLING GREEN,** Warren Co.

KERRICK, GRISE & STIVERS (AV)

1025 State Street, P.O. Box 9547, 42102-9547
Telephone: 502-782-8160
Fax: 502-782-5856
Email: kgs@kgslaw.com
Elizabethtown, Kentucky Office: 2935 Dolphin Drive, Suite 102.
Telephone: 502-769-5788.
Fax: 502-737-9285.

MEMBERS OF FIRM

Thomas N. Kerrick
John R. Grise
Gregory N. Stivers
H. Brent Brennenstuhl
Laura M. Hagan

ASSOCIATES

Karl N. Crandall
Shawn Rosso Alcott
Jason B. Bell

OF COUNSEL

Jeffrey R. O'Grody

LEGAL SUPPORT PERSONNEL

Patricia Logsdon
Laura Lockhart Lico
Allison Lusk

Representative Clients: Dollar General Corp.; Columbia Greenview Regional Hospital; Hospital Corporation of America; Hardin Memorial Hospital; Fir-Star Bank; TKR Cable.

For full biographical listings, see the Martindale-Hubbell Law Directory

MARYLAND

*BALTIMORE,** (Independent City)

VENABLE ATTORNEYS AT LAW VENABLE, BAETJER AND HOWARD, LLP (AV)

A Partnership including Professional Corporations
1800 Mercantile Bank & Trust Building, 2 Hopkins Plaza, 21201
Telephone: 410-244-7400
Fax: 410-244-7742
URL: http://www.venable.com
Washington, D.C. Office: Venable, Baetjer, Howard & Civiletti LLP, Suite 1000, 1201 New York Avenue, N.W.
Telephone: 202-962-4800.
Fax: 202-962-8300.

(See Next Column)

McLean, Virginia Office: Suite 400, 2010 Corporate Ridge.
Telephone: 703-760-1600.
Fax: 703-821-8949.
Rockville, Maryland Office: Suite 500, One Church Street, P. O. Box 1906.
Telephone: 301-217-5600.
Fax: 301-217-5617.
Towson, Maryland Office: 210 Allegheny Avenue, P. O. Box 5517.
Telephone: 410-494-6200.
Fax: 410-821-0147.

MEMBERS OF FIRM

George Cochran Doub (P.C.)
Thomas J. Kenney, Jr. (P.C.)
Kenneth C. Bass, III (Not admitted in MD; Washington, D.C. and McLean, Virginia Offices)
Edward F. Glynn, Jr. (Resident, Washington, D.C. Office)
G. Stewart Webb, Jr.
Jeffrey D. Knowles (Not admitted in MD; Resident, Washington, D.C. Office)
Jeffrey A. Dunn (Also at Washington, D.C. Office)
George F. Pappas (Also at Washington, D.C. Office)
William D. Coston (Not admitted in MD; Resident, Washington, D.C. Office)
Mark B. Harrison (Not admitted in MD; Resident, Washington, D.C. Office)
George William Lewis (Not admitted in MD; Resident, Washington, D.C. Office)
James A. Dunbar (Resident, Towson, Maryland Office)
Robert J. Bolger, Jr. (Also at Washington, D.C. Office)
David J. Heubeck
Gary M. Hnath (Resident, Washington, D.C. Office)
Newton B. Fowler, III
David W. Goewey (Not admitted in MD; Resident, Washington, D.C. Office)
John T. Prisbe
Vicki Margolis (Also at Washington, D.C. Office)

OF COUNSEL

Barbara L. Waite (Resident, Washington, D.C. Office)

ASSOCIATES

Paul D. Barker, Jr.
James Nicholas Czaban (Not admitted in MD; Resident, Washington, D.C. Office)

For Complete List of Firm Personnel, See General Section

For full biographical listings, see the Martindale-Hubbell Law Directory

MASSACHUSETTS

*BOSTON,** Suffolk Co.

CESARI AND MCKENNA, L.L.P. (AV)

30 Rowes Wharf, 02110
Telephone: 617-951-2500
Fax: 617-951-3927

Robert A. Cesari
John F. McKenna
Martin J. O'Donnell
Thomas C. O'Konski
Joseph H. Born
Patricia A. Sheehan
Michael E. Attaya
Steven J. Frank
Charles J. Barbas
William A. Loginov

Michael R. Reinemann
Rita M. Rooney
Christopher K. Gagne (Not admitted in MA)
A. Sidney Johnston (Not admitted in MA)
John H. Emilian, Jr.
Joseph Stecewycz

LEGAL SUPPORT PERSONNEL

Dora V. Dodin (Patent Engineer)
Heather B. Shapiro (Technical Specialist)

For full biographical listings, see the Martindale-Hubbell Law Directory

DIKE, BRONSTEIN, ROBERTS & CUSHMAN, LLP (AV)

A Limited Liability Partnership including Professional Corporations
130 Water Street, 02109
Telephone: 617-523-3400
Telefax: 617-523-6440; 523-7318
Email: ipl@dbrc.com *URL:* http://www.dbrc.com
Marlborough, Massachusetts Office: 62 Cotting Avenue, P.O. Box 556, 01752-0556.
Telephone: 508-485-7772.
Fax: 508-485-0363.

David G. Conlin (P.C.)
George W. Neuner (P.C.)
Linda M. Buckley
Peter J. Manus
Peter F. Corless

Cara Zucker Lowen
William J. Daley, Jr.
Lisa Swiszcz Hazzard
Christine C. O'Day
Richard E. Gamache
David A. Tucker

(See Next Column)

DIKE, BRONSTEIN, ROBERTS & CUSHMAN LLP, *Boston—Continued*

OF COUNSEL

Sewall P. Bronstein (P.C.) (Resident, Marlborough Office)

PATENT AGENT

Robert L. Buchanan, Ph.D.

TECHNICAL SPECIALIST

Jennifer Holmes

For full biographical listings, see the Martindale-Hubbell Law Directory

HINCKLEY, ALLEN & SNYDER LLP (AV)

28 State Street, 30th Floor, 02109-1775
Telephone: 617-345-9000
Email: firm@haslaw.com *URL:* http://www.haslaw.com
Providence, Rhode Island Office: 1500 Fleet Center.
Telephone: 401-274-2000.
Fax: 401-277-9600. URL: http://www.hawlaw.com.

MEMBERS OF FIRM

Paula K. Andrews
David D. Barricelli (Not admitted in MA)
E. Jerome Batty (Not admitted in MA)
Jonathan Bell
Paul Bork
Stephen J. Carlotti (Not admitted in MA)
David Barry Connolly
Joseph P. Curran (Not admitted in MA)
Michael P. DeFanti
Eric F. Eisenberg
Malcolm Farmer, III
Margaret D. Farrell (Not admitted in MA)
Pasco Gasbarro Jr.
Hugh J. Gorman, III
Alan P. Gottlieb
William R. Grimm
Paul A. Hedstrom
Joel Lewin
Sandra Matrone Mack (Not admitted in MA)
Matthew T. Marcello, III (Not admitted in MA)
Elizabeth Murdock Myers
Paul F. O'Donnell, III
H. Peter Olsen (Not admitted in MA)
Gerald J. Petros
James O. Reavis
Jeremy Ritzenberg
Ralph J. Rivkind
David J. Rubin
Charles E. Schaub, Jr.
Herman Snyder
David R. Sullivan
Robert F. Sylvia
Howard E. Walker (Not admitted in MA)
John R. Allen (Retired)
Richard W. Billings (Retired)
Thomas J. Hogan (Retired)
Jacques V. Hopkins (Retired)
James A. Jackson (Retired)
James E. Keeley (Retired)
Robert F. Pickard (Retired)
Robert W. Shadd (Retired)
Richard F. Staples (Retired)
Edwin G. Torrance (Retired)

ASSOCIATES

Jessica M. Bettencourt (Not admitted in MA)
Mark Bianchi
Alyssa V. Boss
Alexandra K. Callam
Jane E. Cohen
Andrew D. Cummings
June E. Daniel (Not admitted in MA)
Kim Herman Goslant
Gloria Maria Gutierrez
Kelley Jordan-Price
Catherine S. Kim
Christopher W. Morog
Elena B. Olson
Joseph D. Whelan (Not admitted in MA)

OF COUNSEL

Willard R. Pope
Bentley Tobin
Joachim A. Weissfeld (Not admitted in MA)

For Complete List of Firm Personnel, See General Section

For full biographical listings, see the Martindale-Hubbell Law Directory

PALMER & DODGE LLP (AV)

One Beacon Street, 02108
Telephone: 617-573-0100
Facsimile: 617-227-4420
URL: http://www.palmerdodge.com

MEMBERS OF FIRM

F. Andrew Anderson
Mark A. Fischer
Laurie S. Gill
Francis C. Lynch
John A. Rissman (Not admitted in MA)

ASSOCIATE

Richard B. Smith

For Complete List of Firm Personnel, See General Section

For full biographical listings, see the Martindale-Hubbell Law Directory

MICHIGAN

BLOOMFIELD HILLS, Oakland Co.

ROBERT HARRISON & ASSOCIATES (AV)

Bloomfield Office Pavilion, 2550 Telegraph Road, Suite 275, 48302
Telephone: 248-253-1800
Fax: 248-253-9446
URL: http://www.lawyers.com/harrison&associates

Robert S. Harrison

ASSOCIATES

Michael J. Rex
Michael James Harrison
Rachel M. Margules

References: Comerica Bank, Southfield; Huntington Banks of Michigan, W. Bloomfield.

For full biographical listings, see the Martindale-Hubbell Law Directory

*DETROIT,** Wayne Co.

BODMAN, LONGLEY & DAHLING LLP (AV)

34th Floor 100 Renaissance Center, 48243
Telephone: 313-259-7777
Fax: 313-393-7579
Email: info@bodmanlongley.com *URL:* http://www.bodmanlongley.com
Troy, Michigan Office: Suite 2020, 755 West Big Beaver Road.
Telephone: 248-362-2110.
Fax: 248-244-0780.
Ann Arbor, Michigan Office: 110 Miller, Suite 300.
Telephone: 734-761-3780.
Fax: 734-930-2494.
Northern Michigan Office: 229 Court Street, P.O. Box 405, Cheboygan.
Telephone: 231-627-4351.
Fax: 231-627-2802.

MEMBERS OF FIRM

Randolph S. Perry
James J. Walsh
David G. Chardavoyne
Robert G. Brower
Fredrick J. Dindoffer
Susan M. Kornfield (Ann Arbor Office)
Stephen K. Postema (Ann Arbor Office)
Jeffrey G. Raphelson

For Representative Client List, See General Section

For Complete List of Firm Personnel, See General Section

For full biographical listings, see the Martindale-Hubbell Law Directory

BUTZEL LONG, A PROFESSIONAL CORPORATION (AV)

Suite 900, 150 West Jefferson, 48226
Telephone: 313-225-7000
Telecopier: 313-225-7080
Email: melnick@butzel.com *URL:* http://www.butzel.com
Birmingham, Michigan Office: Suite 200, 32270 Telegraph Road.
Telephone: 810-258-1616.
Telecopier: 810-258-1439.
Okemos, Michigan Office: Suite 300, 2127 University Park Drive.
Telephone: 517-372-6622.
Telecopier: 517-372-6672.
Ann Arbor, Michigan Office: Suite 300, 350 South Main Street.
Telephone: 313-995-3110.
Telecopier: 313-995-1777.
Grosse Pointe Farms, Michigan Office: Suite 260, 21 Kercheval.
Telephone: 313-886-5446.
Telecopier: 313-886-2114.
Boca Raton, Florida Office: Suite 411, 1200 North Federal Highway.
Telephone: 561-368-2151.
Telecopier: 561-368-4668.
Palm Beach Gardens, Florida Office: Suite 227, 11382 Prosperity Farms Road.
Telephone: 561-625-4442.
Telecopier: 561-625-6901.
Naples, Florida Office: Suite 705, 801 Laurel Oak Drive.
Telephone: 941-597-4500.
Telecopier: 941-597-5623.

Richard E. Rassel
Edward M. Kronk
Philip J. Kessler
James E. Stewart (Ann Arbor)
Lynne E. Deitch
Leonard M. Niehoff (Ann Arbor)
David H. Oermann (Birmingham)
J. Michael Huget (Ann Arbor)
Phillip C. Korovesis

James J. Giszczak
Robin K. Luce
Laurie J. Michelson
John C. Blattner (Ann Arbor)
Pamela M. Zauel

Representative Clients: Crain Communications, Inc.; Detroit Diesel Corp.; The Detroit News, Inc.; Ferndale Laboratories; General Dynamics Corp.; Kelly Services; Stroh Companies; Takata Corp.; TRW Automotive; The University of Michigan.

For full biographical listings, see the Martindale-Hubbell Law Directory

SOUTHFIELD, Oakland Co.

BROOKS & KUSHMAN, P.C. (AV)

1000 Town Center, Twenty Second Floor, 48075
Telephone: 248-358-4400

Ernie L. Brooks
James A. Kushman
David R. Syrowik
Mark A. Cantor
Ralph M. Burton
Robert C. J. Tuttle
Earl J. LaFontaine
Ronald M. Nabozny
Thomas A. Lewry
John E. Nemazi
Kevin J. Heinl
William G. Abbatt
Donald J. Harrington
Paul M. Schwartz
George R. Mosher
Frederick M. Ritchie
John M. Sheridan
Elizabeth F. Janda
Robert C. Brandenburg
A. Frank Duke
Timothy G. Newman
John M. Halan
Jeffrey M. Szuma
Maria Franek Angileri
James R. Ignatowski
Frank A. Angileri
William G. Conger
Sangeeta G. Shah
Christopher W. Quinn
Konstantine J. Diamond
David S. Bir
James N. Kallis
Hugo A. Delevie
Ralph Edwin Smith
Gigette Marie Bejin
Mark E. Stuenkel
Michael S. Brodbine
Seth E. Rodack
Pete N. Kiousis
Raymond J. Vivacqua
John J. Ignatowski
James Proscia
Ginta D. Kukainis

For full biographical listings, see the Martindale-Hubbell Law Directory

TRANSPORTATION LAW

ALABAMA

*BIRMINGHAM,** Jefferson Co.

BRADLEY ARANT ROSE & WHITE LLP (AV)

2001 Park Place, Suite 1400, P.O. Box 830709, 35283-0709
Telephone: 205-521-8000
Facsimile: 205-521-8800
Facsimile (SouthTrust Tower Office): 205-521-8500
URL: http://www.barw.com
Huntsville, Alabama Office: 200 Clinton Avenue West, Suite 900, 35801.
Telephone: 205-517-5100.
Facsimile: 205-533-5069.
Washington, D.C. Office: 801 Pennsylvania Avenue, NW, Suite 230, 20004.
Telephone: 202-347-8893.
Facsimile: 202-347-1684.

MEMBERS OF FIRM

Joseph B. Mays Jr.
Hobart A. McWhorter Jr.
John D. Watson III

For Complete List of Firm Personnel, See General Section

For full biographical listings, see the Martindale-Hubbell Law Directory

BURGE & WETTERMARK, P.C. (AV)

2300 SouthTrust Tower, 420 North 20th Street, 35203-3204
Telephone: 205-251-9729; 800-633-3733
Fax: 205-323-0512
Email: firm@bw-law.com *URL:* http://www.bw-law.com
Atlanta, Georgia Office: 3475 Lenox Road, N.E., Suite 400, 30326.
Telephone: 404-875-2500.
Jacksonville, Florida Office: 3100 Independent Drive, 32202.
Telephone: 904-353-1555; 800-498-6657.
Fax: 904-353-3905.

Frank O. Burge, Jr.
James H. Wettermark
F. Tucker Burge
Courtney Burge Brown
Monroe Dykes Barber, Jr.
Van Kirk McCombs, II
James R. Holland, II (Not admitted in AL)

References: AmSouth Bank; First Alabama Bank, Birmingham, Alabama.

For full biographical listings, see the Martindale-Hubbell Law Directory

CARR, ALLISON, PUGH, HOWARD, OLIVER & SISSON, P.C. (AV)

400 Vestavia Parkway, Suite 400, 35216
Telephone: 205-822-2006
Fax: 205-822-2057
Email: CFC@caphos.com
Florence, Alabama Office: 212 South Cedar Street, 35630.
Telephone: 256-718-6040.
Fax: 256-718-2150.
Mobile, Alabama Office: P.O. Box 781,36601-0781.
Telephone: 334-621-4340.
Fax: 334-626-8928.

Charles F. Carr (Resident, Daphne Office)
Russell Q. Allison
Bennett L. Pugh
David K. Howard (Resident, Florence Office)
Thomas L. Oliver, II
William H. Sisson (Resident, Daphne Office)
Glenn E. Ireland
Thomas C. Logan
Donald B. Kirkpatrick, II
Sarah J. Carlisle
Craig W. Goolsby (Resident, Daphne Office)

Gregg L. Smith
Joseph H. Driver
Brett A. Ross
Thomas S. Thornton, III
W. Bradford Kittrell
Jeffrey B. Carr
Joseph H. Hilley
Jeremy N. Trousdale
Ryan G. Brake
Caroline T. Pryor (Resident, Daphne Office)

For full biographical listings, see the Martindale-Hubbell Law Directory

LUSK, FRALEY, MCALISTER & SIMMS, P.C. (AV)

Suite 1700 AmSouth/Harbert Plaza, 1901 Sixth Avenue North, 35203
Telephone: 205-323-7100
Fax: 205-323-7050
Email: Lusk-Fraley.com

(See Next Column)

Donald D. Lusk
John M. Fraley
David L. McAlister
Keri Donald Simms
Kenneth A. Dowdy
David Lawrence Dean
David Thurston White, III
Susan Gilman McAlister
Payton Caldwell Lusk
Leslie Ann Caldwell

For full biographical listings, see the Martindale-Hubbell Law Directory

SMITH & ELY, LLP (AV)

2000-A Southbridge Parkway Suite 405, 35209
Telephone: 205-802-2214
Fax: 205-879-4445

MEMBERS OF FIRM

Carol Ann Smith
Brenen G. Ely

ASSOCIATES

Susan Rogers
Susan Caroline Haygood
Toby Dykes

OF COUNSEL

Lisa B. Singer

For full biographical listings, see the Martindale-Hubbell Law Directory

*MOBILE,** Mobile Co.

CUNNINGHAM, BOUNDS, YANCE, CROWDER & BROWN, L.L.C. (AV)

1601 Dauphin Street, P.O. Box 66705, 36660
Telephone: 334-471-6191
Fax: 334-479-1031
Email: adm@cbycb.com

James A. Yance
John T. Crowder, Jr.
Robert T. Cunningham, Jr.
Joseph M. Brown, Jr.
Gregory B. Breedlove
Michael A. Worel
David G. Wirtes, Jr.
Toby D. Brown
Reggie Copeland, Jr.
Richard T. Dorman

J. Stephen Legg
George M. Dent, III

OF COUNSEL

Richard Bounds
Robert T. Cunningham
J. Kenyon Rainer, Sr., M.D., J.D.

References: Regions Bank; AmSouth Bank, N.A.

For full biographical listings, see the Martindale-Hubbell Law Directory

ARIZONA

*PHOENIX,** Maricopa Co.

FENNEMORE CRAIG, A PROFESSIONAL CORPORATION (AV)

3003 North Central Avenue, Suite 2600, 85012-2913
Telephone: 602-916-5000
Fax: 602-916-5999
Tucson, Arizona Office: One South Church Avenue, Suite 1000, 85701-1620.
Telephone: 520-879-6800.
Fax: 520-879-6899.

C. Webb Crockett
Timothy Berg

Mark H. Brain

For Complete List of Firm Personnel, See General Section

For full biographical listings, see the Martindale-Hubbell Law Directory

CALIFORNIA

BEVERLY HILLS, Los Angeles Co.

MILES L. KAVALLER A PROFESSIONAL LAW CORPORATION (AV)

Suite 315, 315 South Beverly Drive, 90212
Telephone: 310-277-2323
Fax: 310-556-2308
Email: mkavaler1@earthlink.net *URL:* http://www.LA-Freight.com/kavaller

Miles L. Kavaller

Reference: City National Bank (6th & Olive Branch).

For full biographical listings, see the Martindale-Hubbell Law Directory

LONG BEACH, Los Angeles Co.

RUSSELL & MIRKOVICH (AV)
One World Trade Center, Suite 1450, 90831-1450
Telephone: 562-436-9911
FAX: 562-436-1897
Email: counsel@russell-mirkovich.com

Carlton E. Russell
Joseph N. Mirkovich

ASSOCIATE

Margaret E. Morrow
Steven Y. Otera

For full biographical listings, see the Martindale-Hubbell Law Directory

WOOLLEY RUSSELL & JOHNSON (AV)
444 West Ocean Boulevard, Suite 1700, 90802
Telephone: 562-495-6000
Telecopier: 562-435-1359
Email: mail@transportlawyers.com *URL:* http://www.transportlawyers.com
Port Hueneme, California Office: 105 East Port Hueneme Road, 93041.
Telephone: 562-495-6000.
Fax: 562-435-1359.

MEMBERS OF FIRM

David E. R. Woolley
Thomas A. Russell
Philip L. Johnson

ASSOCIATE

Thomas G. Walsh

LEGAL SUPPORT PERSONNEL

PARALEGAL

Dawn C. Breaux

For full biographical listings, see the Martindale-Hubbell Law Directory

SAN MATEO, San Mateo Co.

MICHAEL L. DWORKIN AND ASSOCIATES (AV)
155 Bovet Road, Suite 455, 94402
Telephone: 650-577-1321
Fax: 650-372-1077
Email: law@avialex.com *URL:* http://www.avialex.com

ASSOCIATE

David R. Newman

For full biographical listings, see the Martindale-Hubbell Law Directory

COLORADO

*DENVER,** Denver Co.

CUTLER & STANFIELD, L.L.P. (AV)
1675 Broadway, 80202
Telephone: 303-825-7000
Fax: 303-825-7005
Washington, D.C. Office: 700 Fourteenth Street, N.W., 10th Floor.
Telephone: 202-624-8400.
FAX: 202-624-8410.

MEMBERS OF FIRM

Eliot R. Cutler (Not admitted in CO)
Jeffrey L. Stanfield (Not admitted in CO)
Sheila D. Jones
Perry M. Rosen
Peter J. Kirsch
Barry Conaty
Stephen H. Kaplan
Sarah M. Rockwell
Thomas D. Roth (Not admitted in CO)

ASSOCIATES

Madeline S. Cohen
Polly B. Jessen
Elizabeth A. Mitchell
John E. Putnam
Daniel S. Reimer

For full biographical listings, see the Martindale-Hubbell Law Directory

FRIEDLOB SANDERSON RASKIN PAULSON & TOURTILLOTT, LLC (AV)
1400 Glenarm Place, 80202-5099
Telephone: 303-571-1400
Fax: 303-595-3159; 303-595-3970; 303-615-5472
Englewood, Colorado Office: 8400 East Prentice Avenue, 80111-2918.
Telephone: 303-571-1400.
Santa Cruz, California Office: 519 Seabright Avenue, Suite 208, 95062-3482.
Telephone: 813-460-3966.
Fax: 813-460-3968.

Raymond L. Friedlob
Christopher R. Paulson

For full biographical listings, see the Martindale-Hubbell Law Directory

GREENWOOD VILLAGE, Arapahoe Co.

ICENOGLE, NORTON & SETER, A PROFESSIONAL CORPORATION (AV)
5690 DTC Boulevard Suite 300, 80111
Telephone: 303-773-1666
Fax: 303-773-1883
Email: INS@inspc.com

T. Edward Icenogle
Barbara K. Tenney

Representative Clients: E-470 Public Highway Authority; Southeast Transportation Authority; Northwest Parkway Public Highway Authority.

For full biographical listings, see the Martindale-Hubbell Law Directory

DISTRICT OF COLUMBIA

WASHINGTON, D.C. Co.

BAKER & HOSTETLER LLP (AV)
Washington Square, Suite 1100, 1050 Connecticut Avenue, N.W., 20036-5304
Telephone: 202-861-1500
Fax: 202-861-1783
To contact an attorney on the Internet use first initial and surname followed by @baker-hostetler.com
URL: http://www.bakerlaw.com
In Cleveland, Ohio: 3200 National City Center, 1900 East Ninth Street.
Telephone: 216-621-0200.
In Cincinnati, Ohio: 312 Walnut Street, Suite 2650.
Telephone: 513-929-3400.
In Columbus, Ohio: Capitol Square, Suite 2100, 65 East State Street.
Telephone: 614-228-1541.
In Denver, Colorado: 303 East 17th Avenue, Suite 1100.
Telephone: 303-861-0600.
In Houston, Texas: 1000 Louisiana, Suite 2000.
Telephone: 713-751-1600.
In Beverly Hills, California: 9150 Wilshire Boulevard, Suite 205.
Telephone: 310-385-7500.
In Long Beach, California: 300 Oceangate, Suite 620.
Telephone: 562-432-2827.
In Los Angeles, California: 600 Wilshire Boulevard.
Telephone: 213-624-2400.
In Orlando, Florida: SunBank Center, Suite 2300, 200 South Orange Avenue.
Telephone: 407-649-4000.

PARTNER

Richard A. Hauser

For Complete List of Firm Personnel, See General Section

For full biographical listings, see the Martindale-Hubbell Law Directory

CUTLER & STANFIELD, L.L.P. (AV)
700 Fourteenth Street, N.W. 10th Floor, 20005-2014
Telephone: 202-624-8400
Fax: 202-624-8410
Denver, Colorado Office: 1675 Broadway, 80202.
Telephone: 303-825-7000.
FAX: 303-825-7005.

MEMBERS OF FIRM

Eliot R. Cutler
Jeffrey L. Stanfield
Sheila D. Jones
Perry M. Rosen
Peter J. Kirsch
Barry Conaty
Stephen H. Kaplan (Not admitted in DC)
Sarah M. Rockwell (Not admitted in DC)
Thomas D. Roth

OF COUNSEL

Byron Keith Huffman, Jr.

ASSOCIATES

Katherine Boonin Andrus
Joel D. Armstrong (Not admitted in DC)
Françoise M. Carrier
Polly B. Jessen (Not admitted in DC)
William G. Malley
Elizabeth A. Mitchell (Resident at Denver, Colorado Office)
Dana C. Nifosi
W. Eric Pilsk
Timothy A. Pohle
John E. Putnam
Daniel S. Reimer (Not admitted in DC)
Andrew T. Swers
Sara E. Wilensky

For full biographical listings, see the Martindale-Hubbell Law Directory

Washington—Continued

LaRoe, Winn, Moerman & Donovan (AV)

3900 Highwood Court, N.W., 20007
Telephone: 202-298-8100
Telecopier: 202-298-8200
Email: pmdonovan@aol.com

MEMBERS OF FIRM

Wilbur LaRoe, Jr. (1921-1957) Arthur L. Winn, Jr. (1928-1995)
Paul M. Donovan

SPECIAL COUNSEL

David A. Sutherlund

OF COUNSEL

Samuel H. Moerman

For full biographical listings, see the Martindale-Hubbell Law Directory

Carlos Rodriguez & Associates (AV)

1710 Rhode Island Avenue, N.W. Tenth Floor, 20036-3007
Telephone: 202-293-3300
Facsimile: 202-293-3307
Email: rodriguez@transportlaw.com
Email: cra@intr.net *URL:* http://www.tradecompass.com/rodriguez

Carlos G. Rodriguez

ASSOCIATES

Helen M. Cousineau (Not admitted in DC)
Henry P. Gonzalez (Not admitted in DC)
Robert R. Herrell (Not admitted in DC)
Daniel W. Lenehan, III

OF COUNSEL

Todd C. Fineberg

CUSTOMS AFFAIRS COUNSEL

Donald W. Lewis

LEGAL SUPPORT PERSONNEL

Ashley W. Craig

For full biographical listings, see the Martindale-Hubbell Law Directory

Venable Attorneys at Law Venable, Baetjer, Howard & Civiletti, LLP (AV)

A Partnership including Professional Corporations
Suite 1000, 1201 New York Avenue, N.W., 20005
Telephone: 202-962-4800
Fax: 202-962-8300
URL: http://www.venable.com
Baltimore, Maryland Office: Venable, Baetjer and Howard LLP, 1800 Mercantile Bank & Trust Building, 2 Hopkins Plaza.
Telephone: 410-244-7400.
Fax: 410-244-7742.
McLean, Virginia Office: Venable, Baetjer and Howard LLP, Suite 400, 2010 Corporate Ridge.
Telephone: 703-760-1600.
Fax: 703-821-8949.
Rockville, Maryland Office: Venable, Baetjer and Howard LLP, Suite 500, One Church Street, P. O. Box 1906.
Telephone: 301-217-5600.
Fax: 301-217-5617.
Towson, Maryland Office: Venable, Baetjer and Howard LLP, 210 Allegheny Avenue, P. O. Box 5517.
Telephone: 410-494-6200.
Fax: 410-821-0147.

MEMBERS OF FIRM

Robert G. Ames (Also at Baltimore, Maryland Office)
James K. Archibald (Also at Baltimore, Maryland Office)
Jan K. Guben (Not admitted in DC; Also at Baltimore, Maryland Office)
George F. Pappas (Also at Baltimore, Maryland Office)
Joe A. Shull
Judson W. Starr (Also at Baltimore and Towson, Maryland Offices)

For Complete List of Firm Personnel, See General Section

For full biographical listings, see the Martindale-Hubbell Law Directory

Verner, Liipfert, Bernhard, McPherson and Hand, Chartered (AV)

901 15th Street, N.W., 20005-2301
Telephone: 202-371-6000
Cable Address: "Verlip"
Fax: 202-371-6279
Email: verner.com *URL:* http://www.verner.com
Houston, Texas Office: 1111 Bagby, Suite 4700, 77002.
Telephone: 713-225-7200.
Fax: 713-752-2199.
Honolulu, Hawaii Office: 745 Fort Street, Suite 600, 96813.
Telephone: 808-566-0999.
Fax: 808-566-0995.

(See Next Column)

Austin, Texas Office: Suite 1440 San Jacinto Center, 98 San Jacinto Boulevard, 78701.
Telephone: 512-703-6000.
Fax: 512-703-6003.
Las Vegas, Nevada Affiliate Office: Gary C. Moss, Hughes Center, 3960 Howard Hughes Parkway, Suite 400, 89109.
Telephone: 702-737-3433.
Fax: 702-737-1612.
Miami, Florida Office: 3100 First Union Financial Center, 200 South Biscayne Boulevard, 33131.
Telephone: 305-371-8801.
Fax: 305-371-6545.

Berl Bernhard
Hopewell H. Darneille, III
William C. Evans
Joseph L. Manson, III
Ronald B. Natalie
Russell E. Pommer
Michael J. Roberts
Cynthia M. Surrisi (Resident, Honolulu, Hawaii Office)

OF COUNSEL

John R. Mietus, Jr.

For Complete List of Firm Personnel, See General Section

For full biographical listings, see the Martindale-Hubbell Law Directory

Weiner, Brodsky, Sidman & Kider, P.C. (AV)

1350 New York Avenue, N.W., Suite 800, 20005
Telephone: 202-628-2000
Telecopier: 202-628-2011
Email: wbsk@wbsk.com

Richard J. Andreano, Jr.
James A. Brodsky
Jo A. DeRoche
Don J. Halpern
Mitchel H. Kider
Mark H. Sidman
Rugenia Silver
Harvey E. Weiner
Joseph F. Yenouskas

OF COUNSEL

Cynthia L. Gilman
Susan L. Korytkowski

Karen Ruth Gustavson (Not admitted in DC)
Michael W. Kardash (Not admitted in DC)
Sherri L. Ledner
Todd A. Newman
Howard D. Reitz, Jr.
Leah Schmulewitz (Not admitted in DC)
John D. Socknat
Michael S. Waldron
Rose-Michele Weinryb

LEGAL SUPPORT PERSONNEL

GOVERNMENT RELATIONS SPECIALISTS

Lisa M. Noel
Ann B. Shearer

COMPLIANCE SPECIALIST

Andrew E. Zirneklis

For full biographical listings, see the Martindale-Hubbell Law Directory

Wilmer, Cutler & Pickering (AV)

2445 M Street, N.W., 20037-1420
Telephone: 202-663-6000
Fax: 202-663-6363
Email: Law@Wilmer.Com *URL:* http://www.wilmer.com
Baltimore, Maryland Office: 100 Light Street, 21202.
Telephone: 410-986-2800.
Fax: 410-986-2828.
New York, New York Office: 520 Madison Avenue, 10022.
Telephone: 212-230-8800.
Fax: 212-230-8888.
European Offices:
4 Carlton Gardens, London, SW1Y 5AA, England. Telephone: +44 (20) 7 872 1000.
Fax: +44 (20) 7 839 3537.
Rue de la Loi 15# Wetstraat, B-1040 Brussels, Belgium. Telephone: +32 (2) 285 49 00.
Fax: +32 (2) 285 49 49.
Friedrichstrasse 95, D-10117 Berlin, Germany. Telephone: +49 (30) 20 22 64 00.
Fax: +49 (30) 20 22 65 00.

MEMBERS OF FIRM

James S. Campbell
Dieter G. F. Lange (Not admitted in DC; Resident, European Office, London, England)
Stephen P. Doyle
Jeffrey N. Shane
Matthias Wissmann (Not admitted in DC; Resident, European Office, Berlin, Germany)
James S. Venit (Not admitted in DC; Resident, European Office, Brussels, Belgium)
Dr. Andreas Weitbrecht (Not admitted in DC; Resident, European Offices, Berlin, Germany and Brussels, Belgium)
Paul A. von Hehn (Not admitted in DC; Resident, European Office, Brussels, Belgium)
Dr. Natalie Lübben (Not admitted in DC; Resident, European Office, Berlin, Germany)

(See Next Column)

WILMER, CUTLER & PICKERING, *Washington—Continued*

MEMBERS OF FIRM (Continued)

Michael R. Holter (Not admitted in DC; Resident, European Office, London, England)
Christian L. Duvernoy (Resident, European Office, Brussels, Belgium)
Timothy E. Stumpff

COUNSEL

Lester Nurick
John J. Kallaugher (Not admitted in DC; European Offices, London, England and Brussels, Belgium)
Martin Seyfarth (Not admitted in DC; Resident, European Office, Berlin, Germany)

For Complete List of Firm Personnel, See General Section

For full biographical listings, see the Martindale-Hubbell Law Directory

FLORIDA

BOCA RATON, Palm Beach Co.

MICHAUD, BUSCHMANN, FOX, FERRARA & MITTELMARK, P.A. (AV)

33 Southeast 8th Street, 33432
Telephone: 561-392-0540
Fax: 561-392-0582
Email: Bocalaw@MBFFM.com *URL:* http://www.MBFFM.com

Scott H. Michaud
Paul Buschmann
Brian S. Fox
James T. Ferrara
Michael K. Mittelmark
Marc T. Millian

Marcy G. Blitz
Linda A. McCullough
Kimberly M. Hall

For full biographical listings, see the Martindale-Hubbell Law Directory

*JACKSONVILLE,** Duval Co.

MOSELEY, WARREN, PRICHARD & PARRISH, P.A. (AV)

501 West Bay Street, 32202
Telephone: 904-356-1306
Telecopier: 904-354-0194
Cable Address: "Ragland"
Email: firm@mwpplaw.com

Reuben Ragland (1882-1954)
Louis Kurz (1891-1965)
E. Dale Joyner (1943-1993)
James F. Moseley
Robert E. Warren
Joseph W. Prichard, Jr.
Robert B. Parrish
Andrew J. Knight II
Richard K. Jones
James F. Moseley, Jr.
Phillip A. Buhler

Stanley M. Weston
Kimberly Held Israel
Tracy A. Chesser
Michael A. Garfield
Eric Lee Hearn
Samuel Allen Maroon

OF COUNSEL

James E. Williams
Neil C. Taylor

Counsel for: CSX Transportation; Britannia Steam Ship Insurance Assn., Ltd.; The West of England Protection & Indemnity Assn. (Luxembourg); Crowley American Transport Services, Inc.; United Kingdom Mutual Steamship Assurance Assn., Ltd. (Bermuda); General Food Corp.; The London Steam-Ship Owners' Mutual Insurance Assn., Ltd.

For full biographical listings, see the Martindale-Hubbell Law Directory

NORTH MIAMI BEACH, Dade Co.

BECKHAM & BECKHAM, P.A. (AV)

1550 North East Miami Gardens Drive Suite 504, 33179
Telephone: 305-957-3900
Fax: 305-940-8706
Email: beckhamlaw@aol.com

Pamela Beckham
Eugene G. Beckham
Robert J. Beckham, Jr.

For full biographical listings, see the Martindale-Hubbell Law Directory

*TAMPA,** Hillsborough Co.

STEWART, JOYNER & JORDAN-HOLMES, P.A. (AV)

1112 East Kennedy Boulevard, P.O. Box 172297, 33672
Telephone: 813-229-9300
Fax: 813-229-7415
Email: cjholmes@sjjhlaw.com

(See Next Column)

Delano S. Stewart
Arthenia L. Joyner
Clark Jordan-Holmes
Eurich Z. Griffin
Karen C.D. McDonald
Steve E. Baker

For full biographical listings, see the Martindale-Hubbell Law Directory

GEORGIA

*ATLANTA,** Fulton Co.

DENNIS, CORRY & PORTER, L.L.P. (AV)

3300 One Atlanta Plaza, 950 East Paces Ferry Road, P.O. Box 18640, 30326
Telephone: 404-816-2800
Wats: 800-735-0838
Fax: 404-816-5656
URL: http://www.dcplaw.com

MEMBERS OF FIRM

Robert E. Corry, Jr.
R. Clay Porter
James S. Strawinski
Grant B. Smith
Matthew J. Jewell
Raymond J. Kurey
Ronald Ray Coleman, Jr.
Scott W. McMickle

OF COUNSEL

Douglas Dennis

ASSOCIATES

Thomas D. Trask
Christopher D. Pixley
John D. Dixon
Stephanie F. Goff
Kerry A. Quinn
George A. Koenig
Michael Goldberg
Michael F. Coogan
Todd M. Yates
Nicole L. Wolfe
Alisa W. Terry
Stephanie Collings Patel
Michael A. Prieto

Representative Clients: Schneider National, Inc.; Roadway Express, Inc.; Caliber System, Inc.

For full biographical listings, see the Martindale-Hubbell Law Directory

HAWKINS & PARNELL, LLP (AV)

4000 SunTrust Plaza, 303 Peachtree Street, N.E., 30308-3243
Telephone: 404-614-7400
Fax: 404-614-7500
Email: relliott@hplegal.com *URL:* http://www.hawkinsparnell.com

MEMBERS OF FIRM

Alan F. Herman
William H. Major, III
Warner S. Fox
Blanche Rose Miller
Thomas G. Tidwell

ASSOCIATES

Andrew A. Davenport
Robert S. Thompson

Representative Clients: J.B. Hunt; VanLiner Insurance Company; Crete Carriers Corporation; Reliance National Insurance Company; Watkins Motor Lines; Continental National Insurance Company; Global Van Lines; Saia Motor Freight; Carolina Freight; American President Lines; Corporate Express Delivery Service.

For Complete List of Firm Personnel, See General Section

For full biographical listings, see the Martindale-Hubbell Law Directory

ILLINOIS

*BELLEVILLE,** St. Clair Co.

McGLYNN & McGLYNN (AV)

65 South 65th Street, 62223
Telephone: 618-398-5112; 314-381-5112
Telecopier: 618-398-5189

MEMBERS OF FIRM

Robert E. McGlynn
James McGlynn (Retired)
Michael L. McGlynn
Stephen P. McGlynn

For full biographical listings, see the Martindale-Hubbell Law Directory

*CHICAGO,** Cook Co.

AXELROD, GOODMAN, STEINER & BAZELON (AV)

39 South LaSalle Street, Suite 920, 60603
Telephone: 312-236-9375
Fax: 312-236-2877
Email: jhs1@worldnet.att.net

(See Next Column)

AXELROD, GOODMAN, STEINER & BAZELON—*Continued*

David Axelrod (1910-1976)
Joel H. Steiner
Paul A. Gajewski

For full biographical listings, see the Martindale-Hubbell Law Directory

BELGRADE AND O'DONNELL, A PROFESSIONAL CORPORATION (AV)

311 South Wacker Drive, Suite 2770, 60606
Telephone: 312-360-9500
Facsimile: 312-360-9550
Email: bodpc@aol.com

Steven B. Belgrade
George M. Velcich
John A. O'Donnell
Kim Richard Kardas

Patrick J. Cullinan
James Kent Minnette
Lisa E. Nelson
Richard P. Girzadas

For full biographical listings, see the Martindale-Hubbell Law Directory

BLATT, HAMMESFAHR & EATON (AV)

333 W. Wacker Drive, Suite 1900, 60606
Telephone: 312-849-8000
FAX: 312-357-0198
Email: BHE@BHELAW.COM *URL:* HTTP://WWW.BHELAW.COM
New York, New York Office: 45 Broadway, 12th Floor.
Telephone: 212-363-1900.
Fax: 212-363-2600. Email: bhe@bhelaw.com.

MEMBERS OF FIRM

Hugo Chaviano
Josh M. Kantrow
Kathleen A. McQueeny

ASSOCIATE

Bruce M. Lichtcsien

For full biographical listings, see the Martindale-Hubbell Law Directory

DOWD & DOWD, LTD. (AV)

Suite 1000, 55 West Wacker Drive, 60601
Telephone: 312-704-4400
Telecopier: 312-704-4500
Lake Geneva, Wisconsin Office: P.O. Box 356.
Telephone: 414-275-0057.
Telecopier: 414-275-6786.
Des Plaines Office: 575 Lee Street.
Telephone: 847-827-5117.
Telecopier: 847-827-0076.

Joseph V. Dowd
Robert J. Golden
Michael E. Dowd (1957-1996)
Patrick J. Ruberry
Kenneth Gurber
John M. McAndrews
Patrick C. Dowd
Anthony R. Rutkowski

Daniel J. Arnett
Teri L. Meade
S. Robert Depke
Matthew J Murphy
Beth S. Dolehide
Gregory M. Norgle
David J. Farina
Michael G. Patrizio
William P. Heffernan
Michael W. Van Zalingen
Karen W. Worsek

LEGAL SUPPORT PERSONNEL

Carol Barnes

OF COUNSEL

Guenther Ahlf
Daniel C. McKay
Tobias G. Barry
Sam L. Miller
John A. Garrity, III
Joel S. Ostrow
Peter F. Higgins
Norman E. Samelson

Representative Clients: Gallagher Bassett Services, Inc.; Kemper National Insurance Companies; Schneider National Carriers; Scottsdale Insurance Company; Swift Transportation; Acceptance Insurance Companies; AI Transportation; Borg Warner Protective Services; Clarendon National Insurance Company; Landstar Inway, Inc.
Reference: American National Bank in Chicago.

For full biographical listings, see the Martindale-Hubbell Law Directory

MACCABE & MCGUIRE (AV)

Suite 3333, 77 West Wacker Drive, 60601
Telephone: 312-357-2600
Fax: 312-357-0317
Email: MacMcLaw77@aol.com

MEMBERS OF FIRM

Edward H. MacCabe
Maureen A. McGuire

ASSOCIATES

Timothy J. Murphy
Diedre S. Dunn
Margaret T. Conway

(See Next Column)

OF COUNSEL

Brian J. Mulhern

For full biographical listings, see the Martindale-Hubbell Law Directory

MCFARLAND & HERMAN (AV)

20 North Wacker Drive, Suite 1330, 60606-2902
Telephone: 312-236-0204
Fax: 312-201-9695
Email: mchermn@aol.com *URL:* http://www.lawyers.com/mcfarland&herman

MEMBERS OF FIRM

Thomas F. McFarland, Jr.
Stephen C. Herman

For full biographical listings, see the Martindale-Hubbell Law Directory

PAVALON, GIFFORD, LAATSCH & MARINO (AV)

Two North La Salle Street, Suite 1600, 60602
Telephone: 312-419-7400
Fax: 312-419-7408
Email: pavgif@aol.com
Rockford, Illinois Office: 501 Seventh Street, Suite 501, 61104.
Telephone: 815-968-5100.

MEMBERS OF FIRM

Eugene I. Pavalon
Gary K. Laatsch
Geoffrey L. Gifford
Frank C. Marino
Henry Phillip Gruss

Christine Walsh Donnelly

For full biographical listings, see the Martindale-Hubbell Law Directory

RUSIN PATTON MACIOROWSKI & FRIEDMAN, LTD. (AV)

Suite 1530 10 South Riverside Plaza, 60606
Telephone: 312-454-5110
Fax: 312-454-6166
Urbana, Illinois Office: 301 West Green Street, P.O. Box 985, 61803-0985.
Telephone: 217-328-7091.
Fax: 217-328-7093.

Michael E. Rusin
Kenneth N. Marshall
Stephen J. Friedman
Gregory G. Vacala
John W. Patton Jr.
Daniel Arkin
John A. Maciorowski
Randall R. Stark

Anuradha Y Boyapati
David M. Lewin
Todd A. Bresney
Theodore James Powers
Luke A. Casson
Gregory A. Rode
R. Mark Cosimini (Resident, Urbana Office)
Mark P. Rusin
David F. Ryan
Daniel R. Egan
Douglas Sullivan
Frederick Scott Glassman
Edward R. Tomkowiak
William J. Harrington
Cynthia M. Wallach
Daniel P. Johnston
Catherine A. Zaryczny

For full biographical listings, see the Martindale-Hubbell Law Directory

INDIANA

*BLOOMINGTON,** Monroe Co.

JONES, MCGLASSON & BENCKART, P.C. (AV)

205 South Walnut Street, P.O. Box 279, 47402
Telephone: 812-332-4431
Fax: 812-332-0554
Email: jmbattys@bloomington.in.us *URL:* http://www.Bloomington.in.us/jmbattys

Robert Delano Jones
Judith Corcoran Benckart
Thomas M. McGlasson
Gregory Scott Lauer

OF COUNSEL

David Rogers

Representative Clients: Stone Belt Freight Lines, Inc.; Best Way Express, Inc.; Don Bush Moving, Inc.; Independent Limestone Co.; Shelby Trucking, Inc.; Justin R. Blackwell Trucking & Conveying, Inc.

For full biographical listings, see the Martindale-Hubbell Law Directory

HAMMOND, Lake Co.

ABRAHAMSON, REED & ADLEY (AV)

200 Russell Street, 46320
Telephone: 219-937-1500
Fax: 219-937-3174

MEMBERS OF FIRM

Harold Abrahamson
Kenneth D. Reed
Michael C. Adley

(See Next Column)

ABRAHAMSON, REED & ADLEY, *Hammond—Continued*

ASSOCIATES

Scott R. Bilse	John P. Reed

References: Calumet National Bank, Hammond; Mercantile National Bank, Hammond.

For full biographical listings, see the Martindale-Hubbell Law Directory

*INDIANAPOLIS,** Marion Co.

SCOPELITIS, GARVIN, LIGHT & HANSON, P.C. (AV)

10 West Market Street, Suite 1500, 46204-2968
Telephone: 317-637-1777
FAX: 317-687-2414
Chicago, Illinois Office: 120 South LaSalle Street, Suite 1700.
Telephone: 312-422-1200.
Fax: 312-422-1224.

Norman R. Garvin	Gregory M. Feary
Andrew K. Light	Robert L. Browning
James H. Hanson	Steven A. Pletcher
Lynne D. Lidke	Timothy W. Wiseman
Thomas E. Farrell	Jay D. Robinson, Jr.

Michael B. Langford	Karla Cooper-Boggs
Angela D. Stemle	Jeffrey S. Toole
David C. Milne	William Todd Metzger
Carla Hounshel Stagnolia	Christopher R. Whitten

OF COUNSEL

Alki E. Scopelitis	Terry G. Fewell

LEGAL SUPPORT PERSONNEL

Susan Laetsch	Susan M. Madden
Carolyn K. Garlock	Renee L. Modrowski

CHICAGO, ILLINOIS OFFICE

Gerald F. Cooper, Jr. (Resident, Chicago, Illinois Office)	Victor P. Shane (Resident, Chicago, Illinois Office)
William D. Brejcha (Resident, Chicago, Illinois Office)	

LEGAL SUPPORT PERSONNEL

Eileen A. Neal (Legal Assistant) (Resident, Chicago, Illinois Office)

Representative Clients: American Trucking Associations, Inc.; AMTRAK; Arthur J. Gallagher & Co.; Celadon Trucking, Inc.; Chemical Leaman Corporation; Federal Express; Intrenet, Inc.; The Landstar Companies; North American Van Lines, Inc.; Penske Transportation.

For full biographical listings, see the Martindale-Hubbell Law Directory

*LAFAYETTE,** Tippecanoe Co.

STUART & BRANIGIN (AV)

The Life Building, 300 Main Street, Suite 800, P.O. Box 1010, 47902-1010
Telephone: 765-423-1561
Telecopier: 765-742-8175
Email: sb@stuartlaw.com *URL:* http://www.stuartlaw.com
Indianapolis, Indiana Office: Suite 1401, 8888 Keystone Crossing, 46240.
Telephone: 317-574-7245.
Fax: 317-574-7050.

MEMBERS OF FIRM

Allison Ellsworth Stuart (1886-1950)	William E. Emerick
	John C. Duffey
Roger D. Branigin (1902-1975)	Bruce McSpadden
Roger D. Branigin, Jr.	Mark E. DeYoung
Thomas L. Ryan	Thomas B. Parent
Thomas R. McCully	Laura L. Bowker
Larry R. Fisher	Kevin D. Nicoson
Nina B. Kirkpatrick	Susan K. Roberts
Mark Lillianfeld	John M. Stuckey
Stephen R. Pennell	Deborah B. Trice
Anthony S. Benton	William P. Kealey
Erik D. Spykman	David A. Starkweather

Geoffrey L. Blazi

SENIOR COUNSEL

Russell H. Hart

COUNSEL

John F. Bodle	James V. McGlone

ASSOCIATES

Elizabeth B. Searle	Karen Orr McClure
Marianne Mitten Owen	Ann Marie Waldron
David A. Locke	Barry L. Loftus

General Counsel for: The Lafayette Life Insurance Co.; INB National Bank, N.W.; Lafayette Home Hospital, Inc.
State Counsel for: Norfolk & Western Railway Co.
Mr. Ryan is Counsel to: The Trustees of Purdue University.
Representative Clients: Aluminum Company of America; Liberty Mutual Insurance Group.

For full biographical listings, see the Martindale-Hubbell Law Directory

IOWA

*DES MOINES,** Polk Co.

FINLEY, ALT, SMITH, SCHARNBERG, CRAIG, HILMES & GAFFNEY, P.C. (AV)

604 Locust Street, Fourth Floor Equitable Building, 50309
Telephone: 515-288-0145
Telecopier: 515-288-2724

Jerry P. Alt	R. Todd Gaffney

Kevin J. Driscoll

Representative Clients: ALAS; American Society of Composers, Authors and Publishers; Equitable Life Assurance Society of the U.S.; Federated Insurance Co.; Meredith Corp.
Iowa Attorneys for: Midwest Medical Insurance Co.
District Attorneys for: Norfolk & Southern Railroad; Soo Line Railroad Company.

For Complete List of Firm Personnel, See General Section

For full biographical listings, see the Martindale-Hubbell Law Directory

KANSAS

*TOPEKA,** Shawnee Co.

FOULSTON & SIEFKIN L.L.P. (AV)

1515 NationsBank Tower, 534 Kansas Avenue, 66603
Telephone: 785-233-3600
Fax: 785-233-1610
URL: http://www.foulston.com
Wichita, Kansas Office: 100 North Broadway, 700 NationsBank Financial Center, 67202.
Telephone: 316-267-6371.
Fax: 316-267-6345.
Dodge City, Kansas Office: 810 Frontview, P.O. Box 1147, 67801.
Telephone: 316-227-8126.
Fax: 316-227-8451.
Member: Lex Mundi, The World's Leading Association of Independent Law Firms.

SPECIAL COUNSEL

James L. Grimes, Jr.

For full biographical listings, see the Martindale-Hubbell Law Directory

LOUISIANA

*NEW ORLEANS,** Orleans Parish

PULASKI, GIEGER & LABORDE, L.L.C. (AV)

Suite 4800, One Shell Square, 701 Poydras Street, 70139
Telephone: 504-561-0400
Telecopier: 504-561-1011
Covington, Louisiana Office: 434 North Columbia Street, Suite 200, 70433.
Telephone: 504-561-0400.
Telecopier: 504-809-9677.

Michael T. Pulaski	Sharon D. Smith
Ernest P. Gieger, Jr.	Leo R. McAloon, III
Kenneth H. Laborde	Christopher J. Wnuk
Lambert M. Laperouse	Julianne T. Echols
Robert W. Maxwell	Hilliard F. Kelly, III
Keith W. McDaniel	Lorie G. DeMarcay

Marjorie Randall Brown	Gina S. Montgomery

For full biographical listings, see the Martindale-Hubbell Law Directory

SLATER LAW FIRM, A PROFESSIONAL CORPORATION (AV)

650 Poydras Street Suite 2600, 70130-6101
Telephone: 504-523-7333
Fax: 504-528-1080
URL: http://www.slaterlawfirm.com

Benjamin R. Slater, Jr.	Kevin M. Wheeler
Benjamin R. Slater, III	Anne Elise Brown
Mark E. Van Horn	Donald J. Miester, Jr.

Michael O. Waguespack	Sarah Ney
Cory Rabin Cahn	S. Joseph Welborn

(See Next Column)

SLATER LAW FIRM A PROFESSIONAL CORPORATION—*Continued*

SPECIAL COUNSEL

W. Malcolm Stevenson

Representative Clients: Norfolk Southern Corporation; The Alabama Great Southern Railroad Company; North American Van Lines; New Orleans Steamship Association; Fleet Transport Company, Inc.

For full biographical listings, see the Martindale-Hubbell Law Directory

*SHREVEPORT,** Caddo Parish

BARLOW AND HARDTNER L.C. (AV)

Tenth Floor, Louisiana Tower, 401 Edwards Street, 71101-3289
Telephone: 318-227-1131
Telecopier: 318-227-1141
Mailing Address: P.O. Box 8, Shreveport, Louisiana, 71161-0008

Malcolm S. Murchison
David R. Taggart
Michael B. Donald

Representative Clients: Kelley Oil Corporation; NorAm Energy Corp. (formerly Arkla, Inc.); NorAm Gas Transmission Company; Central and South West Corporation; Panhandle Eastern Corp.; Pennzoil Producing Co.; Ashland Oil, Inc.; Southwestern Electric Power Company; Brammer Engineering, Inc.

For Complete List of Firm Personnel, See General Section

For full biographical listings, see the Martindale-Hubbell Law Directory

WILKINSON, CARMODY & GILLIAM (AV)

1700 Beck Building, 400 Travis Street, P.O. Box 1707, 71166
Telephone: 318-221-4196
Telecopier: 318-221-3705
Email: wcg1895@aol.com

MEMBERS OF FIRM

John D. Wilkinson (1867-1929)
William Scott Wilkinson (1895-1985)
Arthur R. Carmody, Jr.
Bobby S. Gilliam
Mark E. Gilliam
William Allen Haynes

Representative Clients: Farmers Insurance Group; Home Federal Savings & Loan Association of Shreveport; The Kansas City Southern Railway Co.; KTAL-TV; Lincoln National Life Insurance Co.; Mobil Oil Co.; Schumpert Medical Center; Sears, Roebuck & Co.; Southern Pacific Transportation Co.; Southwestern Electric Power Co.

For full biographical listings, see the Martindale-Hubbell Law Directory

MARYLAND

*BALTIMORE,** (Independent City)

FERGUSON, SCHETELICH & HEFFERNAN, P.A. (AV)

1401 NationsBank Center, 100 South Charles Street, 21201-2725
Telephone: 410-837-2200
Fax: 410-837-1188
URL: http://www.FSHLaw.com

Robert L. Ferguson, Jr.
Thomas J. Schetelich
Christopher J. Heffernan
Craig F. Ballew
Michael N. Russo, Jr.

Peter J. Basile
Ann D. Ware
Tracey J. McLauchlin
Michele P. Zahner
Michael K. Hourigan

For full biographical listings, see the Martindale-Hubbell Law Directory

VENABLE ATTORNEYS AT LAW VENABLE, BAETJER AND HOWARD, LLP (AV)

A Partnership including Professional Corporations
1800 Mercantile Bank & Trust Building, 2 Hopkins Plaza, 21201
Telephone: 410-244-7400
Fax: 410-244-7742
URL: http://www.venable.com
Washington, D.C. Office: Venable, Baetjer, Howard & Civiletti LLP, Suite 1000, 1201 New York Avenue, N.W.
Telephone: 202-962-4800.
Fax: 202-962-8300.
McLean, Virginia Office: Suite 400, 2010 Corporate Ridge.
Telephone: 703-760-1600.
Fax: 703-821-8949.
Rockville, Maryland Office: Suite 500, One Church Street, P. O. Box 1906.
Telephone: 301-217-5600.
Fax: 301-217-5617.
Towson, Maryland Office: 210 Allegheny Avenue, P. O. Box 5517.
Telephone: 410-494-6200.
Fax: 410-821-0147.

(See Next Column)

MEMBERS OF FIRM

Stanley Mazaroff (P.C.)
Jan K. Guben (Also at Washington, D. C Office)
James D. Wright (P.C.)
John G. Milliken (Not admitted in MD; Resident, McLean, Virginia Office)
Joseph C. Wich, Jr. (Resident, Towson, Maryland Office)
Robert G. Ames (Also at Washington, D.C. Office)
Richard L. Wasserman (P.C.)
James K. Archibald (Also at Washington, D.C. Office)
George W. Johnston (P.C.)
Judson W. Starr (Not admitted in MD; Also at Washington, D.C. and Towson, Maryland Offices)
Jana Howard Carey (P.C.)
Mitchell Kolkin
George F. Pappas (Also at Washington, D.C. Office)
Kevin L. Shepherd
Vicki Margolis (Also at Washington, D.C. Office)

OF COUNSEL

Emried D. Cole, Jr.

For Complete List of Firm Personnel, See General Section

For full biographical listings, see the Martindale-Hubbell Law Directory

MASSACHUSETTS

*BOSTON,** Suffolk Co.

PALMER & DODGE LLP (AV)

One Beacon Street, 02108
Telephone: 617-573-0100
Facsimile: 617-227-4420
URL: http://www.palmerdodge.com

MEMBERS OF FIRM

Jean M. DeLuca
Charles E. DeWitt, Jr.
William L. Lahey
Scott P. Lewis
Thomas W. Merrill
John E. Rattigan, Jr.
David R. Rodgers
Kenneth W. Salinger
James R. Shea, Jr.
Walter J. St. Onge III
James M. Whalen

For Complete List of Firm Personnel, See General Section

For full biographical listings, see the Martindale-Hubbell Law Directory

MICHIGAN

*DETROIT,** Wayne Co.

FOSTER, MEADOWS & BALLARD, P.C. (AV)

Shelby Congress Building, 607 Shelby, Seventh Floor, 48226
Telephone: 313-961-3234
Facsimile: 313-961-6184
Email: FosterMeadows@FosterMeadows.com *URL:* http://www.lawyers.com/fm&blaw

Sparkman D. Foster (1897-1967)
Raymond A. Ballard (1921-1996)
Charles R. Hrdlicka
Paul D. Galea
Richard A. Dietz
Robert H. Fortunate
Robert G. Lahiff
Camille A. Raffa-Dietz

Michael J. Liddane

Representative Clients: Burlington Northern Railway; British Marine Mutual Insurance Association, Ltd.; Brittania Steam-Ship Insurance Association; Citizens Insurance Co.; Corrigan Air & Sea Cargo Systems; Japan Ship Owners Mutual Protection & Indemnity Association; Liverpool and London Steamship Protection & Indemnity Association, Ltd.; SurfAir Corporation.

For full biographical listings, see the Martindale-Hubbell Law Directory

LEWIS & MUNDAY, A PROFESSIONAL CORPORATION (AV)

(Formerly Lewis, Clay & Munday, P.C.)
1300 First National Building, 660 Woodward Avenue, 48226-3531
Telephone: 313-961-2550
Fax: 313-961-1270
Email: camille.miller@lewis-pc.com *URL:* http://www.lewis-pc.com
Washington, D.C. Office: 1120 Connecticut Avenue, Suite 280. 20036.
Telephone: 202-835-0616.
Fax: 202-833-3316.
Boston, Massachusetts Office: 101 Federal Street, Suite 1900. 02110.
Telephone: 617-478-0553.
Fax: 617-478-0543.

(See Next Column)

LEWIS & MUNDAY A PROFESSIONAL CORPORATION, *Detroit—Continued*

David Baker Lewis
Reuben A. Munday
Camille Stearns Miller
Jacqueline H. Sellers
David N. Zacks
Thomas J. Guyer
Blair A. Person
Karen Kendrick Brown (Resident, Washington, D.C. Office)
Susan D. Hoffman
Hans J. Massaquoi, Jr.

Althea Lynn Simpson
Donica Thomas Varner
Kris W. Krueger
Cylenthia LaToye Miller
Joseph N. Ejbeh
Yolanda R. Bates
Caroletta L. Edgar-Sprinkle
Derek G. McBride
Ayanna Weber
Deborah Jean Williamson
Darice Elizabeth Weber
Krystal M. Gardner
Syeda Taqi

COUNSEL

G. Allen Bass (Resident, Boston, Massachusetts Office)
Leamon R. Sowell, Jr.
Gail Pabarue Bennett
Roger M. Groves
Carol H. Rodriguez
Linda M. Bruton
Brian J. Kott

OF COUNSEL

Otis M. Smith (1922-1994)
Herbert O. Reid, Sr. (1915-1991)

Representative Clients: Aetna Life & Casualty Co.; Chrysler Motors Corp.; Chrysler Financial Corp.; MCI Communications Corp.; City of Detroit; City of Detroit Building Authority; City of Detroit Downtown Development Authority; Consolidated Rail Corp. (Conrail); Equitable Life Assurance Society of the United States.

For full biographical listings, see the Martindale-Hubbell Law Directory

LANSING, Ingham Co.

FOSTER, SWIFT, COLLINS & SMITH, P.C. (AV)

313 South Washington Square, 48933-2193
Telephone: 517-371-8100
Telecopier: 517-371-8200
URL: http://www.fosterswift.com
Farmington Hills, Michigan Office: 32300 Northwestern Highway, Suite 230.
Telephone: 248-539-9900.
Fax: 248-851-7504.

Robert E. McFarland
Rebecca S. Davies

OF COUNSEL

John W. Ester
Paul J. Millenbach

For Complete List of Firm Personnel, See General Section

For full biographical listings, see the Martindale-Hubbell Law Directory

HONIGMAN MILLER SCHWARTZ AND COHN (AV)

A Partnership including Professional Corporations
222 North Washington Square, Suite 400, 48933-1800
Telephone: 517-484-8282
Telecopier: 517-484-8286
Email: mvg@honigman.com *URL:* http://law.honigman.com
Detroit, Michigan Office: 2290 First National Building, 660 Woodward Avenue, 48226.
Telephone: 313-465-7000.

MEMBERS

Frederick M. Baker, Jr.
Daniel J. Demlow
Ruth E. Zimmerman

For Complete List of Firm Personnel, See General Section

For full biographical listings, see the Martindale-Hubbell Law Directory

NOVI, Oakland Co.

LAW OFFICES OF SULLIVAN & LEAVITT, P.C. (AV)

22375 Haggerty Road, 48375
Telephone: 248-349-3980
Fax: 248-349-2810
Mailing Address: P.O. Box 5490, Northville, MI, 48167
Email: mjl@sullivanleavitt.com

Robert A. Sullivan (1917-1979)
Martin J. Leavitt

Paul E. Robinson
Michael J. Leavitt
Curtis R. Willner
Joseph Richard Mariniello, Jr.

OF COUNSEL

David Loeffler

Representative Clients: Aggregate Carriers of Michigan, Inc.; D & H Mack Kenworth Sales & Service, Inc.; Gordon F. Laramie Crane Co.; Palmer Moving & Storage, Inc.; Storage and Transport; Frederick Freight, Inc.; Bill Thompson Transient, Inc.; Churchill Transportation, Inc.

For full biographical listings, see the Martindale-Hubbell Law Directory

ST. CLAIR SHORES, Macomb Co.

SAURBIER, SIEGAN & SANFIELD, P.C. (AV)

Suite 402, 400 Maple Park Boulevard, 48081
Telephone: 810-447-3700
Fax: 810-447-3755
Email: scott@saurbier.com
Detroit Office: 1028 Buhl Building.
Telephone: 313-965-2220.

SHAREHOLDERS

Scott A. Saurbier
Renée S. Siegan
Joel A. Sanfield

Marc D. Saurbier
Lawrence T. Garcia
John C. Valenti
Sara B. Keough
David C. Wiegel
Matthew J. Nagaj
Valerie Henning Mock

For full biographical listings, see the Martindale-Hubbell Law Directory

TROY, Oakland Co.

HACKETT & MAXWELL, P.C. (AV)

City Center Building, Suite 1470, 888 West Big Beaver Road, 48084
Telephone: 810-362-2600
Fax: 810-362-3610
Email: hackmax@voyager.net

Patrick E. Hackett
Phillip B. Maxwell

Representative Clients: Lake State Railway Co.; Michigan Interstate Railway Co.; CSX Transportation; Michigan Railway Assn.; Norfolk Southern Corp.; Ann Arbor Railroad; North American Van Lines.

For Complete List of Firm Personnel, See General Section

For full biographical listings, see the Martindale-Hubbell Law Directory

POLING, MCGAW & POLING, P.C. (AV)

Suite 275, 5435 Corporate Drive, 48098
Telephone: 248-641-0500
Telecopier: 248-641-0506
URL: http://www.lawyers.com/polingmcgaw&poling

Benson T. Buck (1926-1989)
Richard B. Poling
D. Douglas McGaw
Richard B. Poling, Jr.
Gregory C. Hamilton
Veronica B. O'Hara
James R. Parker
Shannon M. Acton

OF COUNSEL

Ralph S. Moore

Representative Clients: City of Troy; United States Fidelity & Guaranty Co.; Sentry Insurance Co.; Admiral Insurance; DeMaria Construction Co.; Leo Corporation; Aetna Casualty and Surety Co.; Concord Design; Pneumo-Abex.

For full biographical listings, see the Martindale-Hubbell Law Directory

TRUSTS AND ESTATES, WILLS AND PROBATE

ALABAMA

*ANDALUSIA,** Covington Co.

ALBRITTONS, CLIFTON, ALVERSON & MOODY, P.C. (AV)

(Powell, Albritton & Albritton)
(Albrittons & Rankin)
(Albrittons, Givhan, Clifton & Alverson)
(Albrittons & Givhan)
109 Opp Avenue, P.O. Box 880, 36420
Telephone: 334-222-3177
Telecopier: 334-222-2696

Ed. T. Albritton (1857-1925)
Wm. Harold Albritton, Sr. (1881-1929)
Dempsey M. Powell (1863-1949)
Albert L. Rankin (1909-1970)
Robert Bynum Albritton (1905-1983)
William H. Albritton, Jr. (1907-1983)
James Marvin Albritton (1915-1987)
James R. Clifton
William Harold Albritton, IV
William B. Alverson, Jr.
Thomas B. Albritton
Julie S. Moody

Benjamin M. Bowden

General Counsel for: Coca-Cola Bottling Co. of Andalusia; Opp-Micolas Cotton Mills.
Attorneys for: First Alabama Bank; Alabama Power Co.; The Travelers; Liberty Mutual Ins. Co; Kemper Insurance; Crum & Forster Insurance Cos; CSX Transporation.

For full biographical listings, see the Martindale-Hubbell Law Directory

*BIRMINGHAM,** Jefferson Co.

BERKOWITZ, LEFKOVITS, ISOM & KUSHNER, A PROFESSIONAL CORPORATION (AV)

SouthTrust Tower, 420 North Twentieth Street, Suite 1600, 35203-5202
Telephone: 205-328-0480
Telecopier: 205-322-8007
URL: http://www.blik.com

Arnold K. Lefkovits
Harold B. Kushner
Anne W. Mitchell
Andrew J. Potts
Thomas O. Kolb
Nancy C. Hughes

OF COUNSEL

Linda S. Lehe

For Complete List of Firm Personnel, See General Section

For full biographical listings, see the Martindale-Hubbell Law Directory

BISHOP, COLVIN, JOHNSON & KENT (AV)

317-20th Street, North, P.O. Box 370404, 35237
Telephone: 205-251-2881
Fax: 205-254-3987
Email: BCJK@BELLSOUTH.NET

MEMBERS OF FIRM

Maurice F. Bishop (1913-1982)
Gerald D. Colvin, Jr.
Carl E. Johnson, Jr.
Burgin H. Kent
Gerald DeWitt (Whit) Colvin, III

Representative Clients: Miller Transporters, Inc.; United Van Lines, Inc.; Western Steel, Inc.; Alabama Building Products, Inc.; The City of Trussville, Alabama; Utilities Board of the City of Trussville, Alabama; Jefferson County Board of Education; University of Montevallo; Milan Express, Inc.
Reference: AmSouth Bank, N.A.

For full biographical listings, see the Martindale-Hubbell Law Directory

BRADLEY ARANT ROSE & WHITE LLP (AV)

2001 Park Place, Suite 1400, P.O. Box 830709, 35283-0709
Telephone: 205-521-8000
Facsimile: 205-521-8800
Facsimile (SouthTrust Tower Office): 205-521-8500
URL: http://www.barw.com
Huntsville, Alabama Office: 200 Clinton Avenue West, Suite 900, 35801.
Telephone: 205-517-5100.
Facsimile: 205-533-5069.
Washington, D.C. Office: 801 Pennsylvania Avenue, NW, Suite 230, 20004.
Telephone: 202-347-8893.
Facsimile: 202-347-1684.

(See Next Column)

MEMBERS OF FIRM

Thomas Neely Carruthers Jr.
William L. Hinds Jr.
Scott E. Ludwig (Resident, Huntsville Office)
Ralph Howard Yeilding

OF COUNSEL

John N. Wrinkle

ASSOCIATE

Jennifer Byers McLeod (Resident, Huntsville Office)

For Complete List of Firm Personnel, See General Section

For full biographical listings, see the Martindale-Hubbell Law Directory

BURR & FORMAN LLP (AV)

3100 SouthTrust Tower, 420 North 20th Street, P.O. Box 830719, 35283-0719
Telephone: 205-251-3000
Facsimile: 205-458-5100
URL: http://www.burr.com
Huntsville, Alabama Office: Suite 204, Regency Center, 400 Meridian Street.
Telephone: 205-551-0010.
Facsimile: 205-551-0043.
Atlanta, Georgia Office: Suite 1200, One Georgia Center, 600 West Peachtree Street, 30308.
Telephone: 404-815-3000.
Facsimile: 404-817-3244.

MEMBERS OF FIRM

Warren C. Matthews
Marvin Glenn Perry, Jr.
Bruce A. Rawls
A. Brand Walton
Paul O. Woodall

For Complete List of Firm Personnel, See General Section

For full biographical listings, see the Martindale-Hubbell Law Directory

CORLEY, MONCUS & WARD, P.C. (AV)

400 Shades Creek Parkway, Suite 100, P.O. Box 59807, 35259
Telephone: 205-879-5959
Telecopier: 205-871-4411

Claude McCain Moncus

For Complete List of Firm Personnel, See General Section

For full biographical listings, see the Martindale-Hubbell Law Directory

FELD, HYDE, LYLE, WERTHEIMER & BRYANT, P.C. (AV)

2000 Southbridge Parkway, Suite 500, 35209
Telephone: 205-802-7575
Facsimile: 205-802-7550

Louis B. Feld
Gregory D. Hyde
John F. Lyle, III
Leonard Wertheimer, III
William J. Bryant
J. Fred Kingren

Robert T. Gardner
Gwen Denoux Skinner
Allison Taylor Craft
T. Craig Williams
James J. Coomes

OF COUNSEL

Edward K. Wood, Jr.

STAFF ATTORNEY

Allison P. Smith

LEGAL SUPPORT PERSONNEL

Kelly S. Prevatte (Certified Legal Assistant)
Rebekah T. Mize (Paralegal)
Kerry Sweeney (Paralegal)

For full biographical listings, see the Martindale-Hubbell Law Directory

GORDON, SILBERMAN, WIGGINS & CHILDS, P.C. (AV)

1400 SouthTrust Tower, 420 North 20th Street, 35203
Telephone: 205-328-0640
Facsimilie: 205-254-1500
Washington, D.C. Office: 1621 Connecticut Avenue, N.W., Suite 400.
Telephone: 202-238-0690.
Facsimile: 202-238-0968.

RESIDENT SHAREHOLDERS

Bruce L. Gordon
Augustus J. Beck, Jr.
Terrill W. Sanders

For Complete List of Firm Personnel, See General Section

For full biographical listings, see the Martindale-Hubbell Law Directory

Birmingham—Continued

GORHAM & WALDREP, P.C. (AV)

2101 6th Avenue North, Suite 700, 35203
Telephone: 205-254-3216; 251-9166
Telecopier: 205-324-3802
Email: info@gorham-waldrep.com *URL:* http://www.gorham-waldrep.com
Montgomery, Alabama Office: 250 Commerce Street, P.O. Box 4837, 36103-4837.
Telephone: 334-262-0777.
Telecopier: 334-262-0742.

John T. Natter — Kay L. McNabb Cason

Representative Clients: Jefferson County Personnel Board; Birmingham-Jefferson Civic Center Authority; The Water Works and Sewer Board of the City of Birmingham; City of Homewood; American Federation of Government Employees Local #1945; City of Pelham; Town of Kimberly; Alabama Tire Dealers Assn.; Southern States Body Shop Assn.

For Complete List of Firm Personnel, See General Section

For full biographical listings, see the Martindale-Hubbell Law Directory

SPAIN & GILLON, L.L.C. (AV)

The Zinszer Building, 2117 2nd Avenue North, 35203
Telephone: 205-328-4100
Telecopier: 205-324-8866
Email: ddh@spain-gillon.com *URL:* http://lawlinks.com:80/atty/al/sggbn.html

MEMBERS OF FIRM

John P. McKleroy, Jr. — Glenn E. Estess, Jr.
Samuel H. Frazier — J. Sanford Mullins, III
Paul S. Leonard

Counsel for: Liberty National Life Insurance Co.; Piggly Wiggly Alabama Distributing Co.; Alabama Insurance Guaranty Association; Alabama Life and Disability Insurance Guaranty Association; Alabama Insurance Underwriters Association; Auburn University Foundation.

For Complete List of Firm Personnel, See General Section

For full biographical listings, see the Martindale-Hubbell Law Directory

*FLORENCE,** Lauderdale Co.

PAINE & ASSOCIATES, P.C. (AV)

SunTrust Building, 201 South Court Street, Suite 520, P.O. Box 1609, 35631
Telephone: 256-718-3622
Fax: 256-718-4065

Peter L. Paine — Michael T. Paine

For full biographical listings, see the Martindale-Hubbell Law Directory

*HUNTSVILLE,** Madison Co.

BRADLEY ARANT ROSE & WHITE LLP (AV)

200 Clinton Avenue West, Suite 900, 35801
Telephone: 205-517-5100
Facsimile: 205-517-5200
URL: http://www.barw.com
Birmingham, Alabama Office: 2001 Park Place, Suite 1400, P.O. Box 830709.
Telephone: 205-521-8000.
Facsimile: 205-521-8800. Facsimile (SouthTrust Tower Office): 205-521-8500.
Washington, D.C. Office: 801 Pennsylvania Avenue, NW, Suite 230, 20004.
Telephone: 202-347-8893.
Facsimile: 202-347-1684.

RESIDENT PARTNERS

Scott E. Ludwig — Charles R. Smith Jr.

For Complete List of Firm Personnel, See General Section

For full biographical listings, see the Martindale-Hubbell Law Directory

BURR & FORMAN LLP (AV)

Suite 204, Regency Center, 400 Meridian Street, 35801
Telephone: 205-551-0010
Facsimile: 205-551-0043
Birmingham, Alabama Office: 3100 SouthTrust Tower, 420 North 20th Street.
Telephone: 205-251-3000.
Facsimile: 205-458-5100.
Atlanta, Georgia Office: Suite 1200, One Georgia Center, 600 West Peachtree Street, 30308.
Telephone: 404-815-3000.
Facsimile: 404-817-3244.

RESIDENT PARTNER

S. Dagnal Rowe

For full biographical listings, see the Martindale-Hubbell Law Directory

*MOBILE,** Mobile Co.

GALLOWAY, SMITH, WETTERMARK & EVEREST, LLP (AV)

3263 Cottage Hill Road, P.O. Box 16629, 36616-0629
Telephone: 334-476-4493
Fax: 334-479-5566
Email: GSWE@GSWELAW.COM

MEMBERS OF FIRM

Thomas M. Galloway — Lawrence M. Wettermark
Robert H. Smith — Robert M. Galloway
Thomas M. Galloway, Jr. — Mark J. Everest

ASSOCIATES

Andrew J. Rutens — Theodore L. Greenspan
Thomas O. Gaillard, III

General Counsel for: Mobile Greyhound Park.
Counsel for: Alfa Mutual Insurance Co.; American States Ins. Co.; Cigna Ins. Co.; County of Mobile.

For full biographical listings, see the Martindale-Hubbell Law Directory

HELMSING, SIMS & LEACH, P.C. (AV)

The Laclede Building, 150 Government Street, Suite 2000, P.O. Box 2767, 36652
Telephone: 334-432-5521
Telecopy: 334-432-0633

Larry U. Sims — Charles H. Dodson, Jr.
Frederick G. Helmsing — Joseph P. H. Babington
John N. Leach, Jr. — R. Alan Alexander
Warren C. Herlong, Jr. — John J. Crowley, Jr.
James B. Newman — Joseph D. Steadman
Robert H. Rouse — Todd S. Strohmeyer

William R. Lancaster — John Townsend Dukes
Robin Kilpatrick Fincher — John Casey Pipes
James Bradford Pittman, Jr.

For full biographical listings, see the Martindale-Hubbell Law Directory

JOHNSTONE, ADAMS, BAILEY, GORDON AND HARRIS, L.L.C. (AV)

Royal St. Francis Building, 104 St. Francis Street, 8th Floor, P.O. Box 1988, 36633
Telephone: 334-432-7682
Facsimile: 334-432-0712 or 334-432-2800
Email: attorneys@JohnstoneAdams.com *URL:* http://www.JohnstoneAdams.com
Bay Minette, Alabama Office: Dahlberg Building, 107 Hand Avenue, P.O. Box 729, 36507.
Telephone: 334-937-9473.
Facsimile: 334-937-9475.

MEMBERS OF FIRM

Charles B. Bailey, Jr. — R. Gregory Watts
E. Watson Smith — Robert S. Frost

For Complete List of Firm Personnel, See General Section

For full biographical listings, see the Martindale-Hubbell Law Directory

LYONS, PIPES & COOK, P.C. (AV)

2 North Royal Street, P.O. Box 2727, 36652-2727
Telephone: 334-432-4481
Cable Address: "Lysea"
Telecopier: 334-433-1820
URL: http://www.LPCLaw.com

Thomas F. Garth

General Counsel: Inchcape Shipping Services.
Counsel: The Hertz Corp.; McKenzie Tank Lines, Inc.; SCNO Barge Lines, Inc.; Scott Paper Co.; Shell Oil Corp.
Trial Counsel: Aetna Life & Casualty Co.; Chubb Group of Insurance Companies.

For Complete List of Firm Personnel, See General Section

For full biographical listings, see the Martindale-Hubbell Law Directory

PIERCE, LEDYARD, LATTA & WASDEN, P.C. (AV)

Colonial Bank Centre Suite 400, 41 North Beltline, 36608
Telephone: 334-344-5151
Facsimile: 334-344-9696
Mailing Address: P.O. Box 16046, Mobile, AL, 36616
URL: http://www.pllaw.com

Donald F. Pierce — H. William Wasden
Goodman G. Ledyard — Edward G. Isaacs Bowron
C. William Daniels, Jr.

Mark Pickett Eiland — Michael A. Montgomery

(See Next Column)

PIERCE, LEDYARD, LATTA & WASDEN P.C.—*Continued*

OF COUNSEL

Thomas E. Twitty, Jr. Caroline Wells Hinds

Representative Clients: Colonial Bank; First National Bank of Atmore; First Security Savings Bank; Regions Bank; SouthTrust Bank of Alabama, NA; South Alabama Bank of Mobile.

For full biographical listings, see the Martindale-Hubbell Law Directory

VICKERS, RIIS, MURRAY AND CURRAN, L.L.C. (AV)

8th Floor, Regions Bank Building, 106 Saint Francis Street, P.O. Box 2568, 36652
Telephone: 334-432-9772
Fax: 334-432-9781
Email: vickersriis.com

MEMBERS OF FIRM

Erling Riis, Jr.
Edwin J. Curran, Jr.
J. Manson Murray
Zebulon M. P. Inge, Jr.
Ronald P. Davis

Representative Clients: Regions Bank; AmSouth Bank; Whitney National Bank.

For Complete List of Firm Personnel, See General Section

For full biographical listings, see the Martindale-Hubbell Law Directory

*MONTGOMERY,** Montgomery Co.

KAUFMAN & ROTHFEDER, P.C. (AV)

2740 Zelda Road, Drawer 4540, 36103-4540
Telephone: 334-244-1111
Fax: 334-244-1969
Email: firm@krlegal.com *URL:* http://www.krlegal.com

Samuel Kaufman
George W. Thomas
Alan E. Rothfeder
John Ward Weiss
Jo Karen Parr
Robert M. Ritchey
Richardson B. McKenzie III
William B. Sellers
Robert E. L. Gilpin
J. Scott Pierce
Mark Monroe Gibson

Counsel for: Dale Medical Center; Evergreen Medical Center; Community Health Systems, Inc.; The Russell Hospital Corporation.

For full biographical listings, see the Martindale-Hubbell Law Directory

TURNER, WILSON & SAWYER (AV)

428 South Lawrence Street, P.O. Box 98, 36104
Telephone: 334-262-2756
Fax: 334-262-2759
Email: turnerone@mindspring.com

MEMBERS OF FIRM

Wayne P. Turner
Terry P. Wilson
William P. Sawyer

LEGAL SUPPORT PERSONNEL

Dorothy Bennett (Paralegal)
Kelly Westbrook
Cara Morales (Paralegal)

For full biographical listings, see the Martindale-Hubbell Law Directory

VOLZ, PRESTWOOD & HANAN, P.C. (AV)

350 Adams Avenue, P.O. Box 1910, 36102-1910
Telephone: 334-264-6401
Fax: 334-834-4954

Charles H. Volz, Jr.
Ellis D. Hanan
Alvin T. Prestwood
Richard D. Lively
Charles H. Volz, III
Judy H. Barganier

For full biographical listings, see the Martindale-Hubbell Law Directory

ARIZONA

*FLAGSTAFF,** Coconino Co.

HUFFORD, HORSTMAN, MONGINI, PARNELL & McCARTHY, P.C. (AV)

323 North Leroux Street, P.O. Box B, 86002-0808
Telephone: 520-774-1453
Fax: 520-779-3621

C. Benson Hufford
Michael E.J. Mongini
Patrice M. Horstman
Eve A. Parnell
Philip (Jay) McCarthy, Jr.

E. Duane Weston

(See Next Column)

LEGAL SUPPORT PERSONNEL

R. Gehl Tucker (Legal Assistant)
Vickie Belman (Legal Assistant)
Jan Blackman (Paralegal)
Doris Utzinger (Legal Assistant)
Dawn L. Karsten (Paralegal)

Reference: Norwest Bank Arizona, N.A.

For full biographical listings, see the Martindale-Hubbell Law Directory

MANGUM, WALL, STOOPS & WARDEN, P.L.L.C. (AV)

100 North Elden, P.O. Box 10, 86002
Telephone: 520-779-6951
Fax: 520-773-1312

H. Karl Mangum (1908-1993)

OF COUNSEL

Douglas J. Wall
Robert W. Warden
Daniel J. Stoops

MEMBERS OF FIRM

A. Dean Pickett
Melinda L. Garrahan
Stephen K. Smith
Michael H. Hinson

ASSOCIATES

Annette Star Lustgarten
R. Scott Currey
Rebecca Smith Currey
Melinda K. Jacquez
Franklin Hoover

Representative Clients: Bank One; First Interstate Bank of Arizona; Nordstrom & Associates, CPA's.

For Complete List of Firm Personnel, See General Section

For full biographical listings, see the Martindale-Hubbell Law Directory

LAKE HAVASU CITY, Mohave Co.

WACHTEL, BIEHN & MALM (AV)

2240 McCulloch Boulevard, 86403
Telephone: 520-855-5115
Fax: 520-855-5211
Email: wbm1@ctaz.com

MEMBERS OF FIRM

Don Biehn
Steven A. Biehn

For full biographical listings, see the Martindale-Hubbell Law Directory

MESA, Maricopa Co.

BRENT M. GUNDERSON, P.C. (AV)

123 North Centennial Way, Suite 122, 85201
Telephone: 602-655-7440
Fax: 602-655-7099
Email: Brent.Gunderson@azbar.org *URL:* http://www.lawyers.com/gundersonlaw

Brent M. Gunderson

For full biographical listings, see the Martindale-Hubbell Law Directory

JACKSON WHITE GARDNER WEECH & WALKER, P.C. (AV)

40 North Center Street, Suite 200, 85201
Telephone: 480-464-1111
Fax: 480-464-5692
Statewide: 800-243-1160
Email: firm@azmesalaw.com *URL:* http://www.azmesalaw.com
Payson, Arizona Office: 708 East Highway 260, Suite C1-E.
Telephone: 520-472-8878.

Wayne L. Gardner
Bradley D. Weech
Eric M. Jackson
Richard A. White
Michael R. Pruitt
David L. Weed
J. Grant Walker
Roger R. Foote
Otto S. Shill, III

Eric K. Macdonald
Patricia A. Mancabelli
Kelly G. Black
Bobbie J. Rasmusson
Melody K. Seal
Maureen P. Kane
James L. Tanner

For full biographical listings, see the Martindale-Hubbell Law Directory

THOMAS D. PROFFITT (AV)

1752 East Downing, P.O. Box 31222, 85275
Telephone: 602-835-5227
Fax: 602-655-7707
Email: tom@proffitt.com

For full biographical listings, see the Martindale-Hubbell Law Directory

Mesa—Continued

UDALL, SHUMWAY, BLACKHURST, ALLEN & LYONS, P.C. (AV)

30 West First Street, 85201-1446
Telephone: 480-461-5300
Facsimile: 480-461-5398
Email: usbalsea@vtc.net
Willcox, Arizona Office: 135 East Maley.
Telephone: 602-384-3389.
Fax: 602-384-2280.

David K. Udall
Dale R. Shumway
Dennis P. Blackhurst
John H. Lyons
Barry C. Dickerson
Steven H. Everts
Clark R. Richter
Roger C. Decker
Peter W. Taylor
Denise Lowell-Britt
Stephen L. West

David R. Schwartz
Robert M. Jarrett, Jr. (Resident, Willcox Office)
Brian T. Allen
Curtis M. Chipman
April A. Speelmon

Representative Clients: Mesa Public Schools; Ticor Title; University of Arizona; Wal-Mart Stores, Inc.; Church of Jesus Christ of Latter Day Saints.

For full biographical listings, see the Martindale-Hubbell Law Directory

*PHOENIX,** Maricopa Co.

DAVID W. ADLER (AV)

4141 West Bethany Home Road, Suite 1, 85019
Telephone: 602-266-6010
Fax: 602-787-9897
Mailing Address: P.O. Box 22188, Phoenix, Arizona, 85028-2188

For full biographical listings, see the Martindale-Hubbell Law Directory

BURCH & CRACCHIOLO, P.A. (AV)

702 East Osborn Road, Suite 200, 85014
Telephone: 602-274-7611
Fax: 602-234-0341
Mailing Address: P.O. Box 16882, Phoenix, AZ, 85011
Email: library@bcattorneys.com

Daniel Cracchiolo
Guadalupe Iniguez

Thomas A. Longfellow

Representative Clients: Bashas' Inc.; Farmers Insurance Group; U-Haul International, Inc.

For Complete List of Firm Personnel, See General Section

For full biographical listings, see the Martindale-Hubbell Law Directory

THOMAS W. DIETRICH (AV)

3550 North Central Avenue, Suite 1400, 85012
Telephone: 602-222-4800
Fax: 602-222-4802
URL: http://www.twdpc.com

For full biographical listings, see the Martindale-Hubbell Law Directory

EHMANN & HILLER, P.C. (AV)

2525 East Camelback Road, Suite 720, 85016
Telephone: 602-956-5050
Telecopier: 602-468-9775
Email: nhiller@home.com

Anthony V. Ehmann
Neil H. Hiller
John G. Pattullo
John F. Daniels, III

References: Harris Trust Bank of Arizona; Bank One, Arizona, N.A. (Trust Department); M&I Thunderbird Bank; Marshall & Ilsley Trust Company of Arizona; Wells Fargo Bank, N.A.; Colonial Trust Company; National Bank of Arizona.

For full biographical listings, see the Martindale-Hubbell Law Directory

LAW OFFICES OF JAMES J. EVERETT, P.C. (AV)

608 East Missouri Avenue, 85012
Telephone: 602-230-2212
Fax: 602-274-8761
Email: James.Everett@azbar.org

James J. Everett

For full biographical listings, see the Martindale-Hubbell Law Directory

FENNEMORE CRAIG, A PROFESSIONAL CORPORATION (AV)

3003 North Central Avenue, Suite 2600, 85012-2913
Telephone: 602-916-5000
Fax: 602-916-5999
Tucson, Arizona Office: One South Church Avenue, Suite 1000, 85701-1620.
Telephone: 520-879-6800.
Fax: 520-879-6899.

Neal Kurn
Louis F. Comus, Jr.
Roger T. Hargrove
Rita A. Eisenfeld
Kendis K. Muscheid

SENIOR COUNSEL

Stanley S. Weithorn (Not admitted in AZ)

Susan Marie Ciupak
Theodore D. Setzer
Jane Proctor

LEGAL SUPPORT PERSONNEL

LEGAL ASSISTANTS

Charlene Sarich
Alison Vander Ark

For Complete List of Firm Personnel, See General Section

For full biographical listings, see the Martindale-Hubbell Law Directory

GOODSON, MANLEY & DURFEE, P.L.C. (AV)

The Brookstone Building, 2025 North 3rd Street, Suite 200, 85004-1471
Telephone: 602-252-5110
Fax: 602-257-1883
URL: http://www.gmdlaw.com
Email: gmdlaw@primenet.com *URL:* http://www.lawyers.com/goodson_manley_durfee

John F. Goodson
Colleen C. Manley
Richard E. Durfee, Jr.
Benjamin D. Benedict

A list of Representative Clients will be furnished upon request.
Reference: Pacific Century Bank.

For full biographical listings, see the Martindale-Hubbell Law Directory

JABURG & WILK, P.C. (AV)

Great American Tower, 3200 North Central Avenue, Suite 2000, 85012
Telephone: 602-248-1000
Fax: 602-248-0522
Email: rcp@jaburglaw.com

Gary J. Jaburg
Lawrence E. Wilk
Roger L. Cohen
Randy Nussbaum
Mitchell Reichman
Beth S. Cohn
Loren Molever
Robert C. Houser, Jr.
Mervyn T. Braude
Michael E. Gottfried

Kathi Mann Sandweiss
Jeffry M. Edwards
Tracy A. Miller
Stephanie N. Monroe
George A. Tacker
Peter W. Ware, Jr.

OF COUNSEL

Richard M. Gerry

Representative Clients: Employee Solutions, Inc.; Sleep America, Inc.; Desert Schools Federal Credit Union; North Star Plumbing; Nations Bank of Texas; State of Arizona; FHLMC; Arizona Escrow & Financial Services.

For full biographical listings, see the Martindale-Hubbell Law Directory

JENNINGS, STROUSS & SALMON, P.L.C. (AV)

A Professional Limited Liability Company
One Renaissance Square, Two North Central Avenue, 85004-2393
Telephone: 602-262-5911
Fax: 602-253-3255
Email: info@jsslaw.com *URL:* http://www.jsslaw.com
Arrowhead Office: 16150 North Arrowhead Fountains Center Drive, Suite 250, Peoria, Arizona.
Telephone: 623-878-2222.
Fax: 623-878-1333.

John R. Christian
Richard L. Lassen
Scott K. Oberg
R. Quinn De Angelis, Jr.

For Complete List of Firm Personnel, See General Section

For full biographical listings, see the Martindale-Hubbell Law Directory

LANE & EHRLICH, LTD. (AV)

Fairmount Place, Suite 400, 4001 North Third Street, 85012
Telephone: 602-264-4442
Telecopier: 602-264-5006
Email: azcorplaw@aol.com

Robert L. Lane
Gerald F. Ehrlich

(See Next Column)

LANE & EHRLICH LTD.—*Continued*

LEGAL SUPPORT PERSONNEL

LEGAL ASSISTANTS

Sherrie L. Lane | Janice K. Hull
Kathy S. Watkins

References: Bank One Arizona; Harris Trust & Savings Bank; The Northern Trust Bank Arizona.

For full biographical listings, see the Martindale-Hubbell Law Directory

MACLEAN & JACQUES, LTD. (AV)

Suite 202, 40 East Virginia, 85004
Telephone: 602-263-5771
FAX: 602-279-5569

John H. MacLean (1932-1992) | Raoul T. Jacques

Cary T. Inabinet | Macre S. Inabinet

LEGAL SUPPORT PERSONNEL

Sharon Petterson

For full biographical listings, see the Martindale-Hubbell Law Directory

MCCABE O'DONNELL, A PROFESSIONAL ASSOCIATION (AV)

3101 North Central Avenue Suite 700, P.O. Box 33457, 85012
Telephone: 602-264-0800
Facsimile: 602-274-0146
URL: http://www.lawyers.com/mccabephx.com

Joseph I. McCabe | Kathleen M. O'Donnell

Whitney Lynn Sorrell

A List of Representative Clients will be Furnished upon Request.

For full biographical listings, see the Martindale-Hubbell Law Directory

PHILIP T. PARIS (AV)

2929 North 44th Street, Suite 120, 85018
Telephone: 602-994-5813
Telecopier: 602-667-6552
Email: bkpblaw@earthlink.net *URL:* http://www.lawyers.com/philipparislaw

For full biographical listings, see the Martindale-Hubbell Law Directory

ROBBINS & GREEN, A PROFESSIONAL ASSOCIATION (AV)

1800 Norwest Tower, 3300 North Central Avenue, 85012-2578
Telephone: 602-248-7600
Fax: 602-266-5369
Email: @RGLaw.com

Wayne A. Smith | Ronald G. Wilson

For full biographical listings, see the Martindale-Hubbell Law Directory

SHIMMEL, HILL, BISHOP & GRUENDER, P.C. (AV)

3700 North 24th Street, 85016
Telephone: 602-224-9500
Telecopier: 602-955-6176
URL: http://www.shimmelhill.com

Daniel F. Gruender | Margaret L. Steiner
Keith F. Overholt | Susan M. Swick
Scott J. Richardson | S. Gregory Jones
Joseph Wm. Kruchek | Glenn B. Hotchkiss

Jennifer S. Lee

OF COUNSEL

Charles A. Finch

For full biographical listings, see the Martindale-Hubbell Law Directory

THOMAS J. SHUMARD (AV)

4715 North 32nd Street, Suite 105, 85018
Telephone: 602-224-9706
Fax: 602-224-1376
Email: thomas.shumard@azbar.org

For full biographical listings, see the Martindale-Hubbell Law Directory

SNELL & WILMER L.L.P. (AV)

One Arizona Center, 85004-2202
Telephone: 602-382-6000
Fax: 602-382-6070
Email: postmaster@snellwilmer.com *URL:* http://www.swlaw.com
Tucson, Arizona Office: One South Church Avenue, Suite 1500, 85701-1612.
Telephone: 520-882-1200.
Fax: 520-884-1294.

(See Next Column)

Orange County Office: 1920 Main Street, Suite 1200, Irvine, California 92614-7230.
Telephone: 949-253-2700.
Fax: 949-955-2507.
Salt Lake City, Utah Office: 111 East Broadway, Suite 900, 84111-1004.
Telephone: 801-237-1900.
Fax: 801-237-1950.

MEMBERS OF FIRM

Joseph T. Melczer, III | David E. Weiss, Jr.
John C. Vryhof

ASSOCIATES

Roberta E. Berger | Elicia D. Giroux
Kevin T. Miller | Jay Douglas Wiley, II

Representative Clients: For list of Representative Clients, see end of biographical listings in the Martindale-Hubbell Law Directory.

For Complete List of Firm Personnel, See General Section

For full biographical listings, see the Martindale-Hubbell Law Directory

WARNER ANGLE ROPER & HALLAM PLC (AV)

3550 North Central Avenue, Suite 1500, 85012
Telephone: 602-264-7101
Fax: 602-234-0419

Jerry L. Angle | Larry C. Schafer
Ted F. Warner | Dean J. Formanek
Peter D. Ambelang | Jerome K. Elwell

Bryan C. Moody

Representative Clients: Fiduciary Services, Inc.; The Sun Valley Group, Inc.

For full biographical listings, see the Martindale-Hubbell Law Directory

*PRESCOTT,** Yavapai Co.

FAVOUR, MOORE & WILHELMSEN, A PROFESSIONAL ASSOCIATION (AV)

1580 Plaza West Drive, P.O. Box 1391, 86302
Telephone: 520-445-2444
Fax: 520-771-0450
Email: fmw@primenet.com

John M. Favour | Mark M. Moore
David K. Wilhelmsen

References: Bank of America; Northern Trust Bank of Arizona; Valley National Bank of Arizona; Citibank (Arizona); First Interstate Bank of Arizona; M & I Marshall & Ilsley Trust Company of Arizona.

For Complete List of Firm Personnel, See General Section

For full biographical listings, see the Martindale-Hubbell Law Directory

MURPHY, LUTEY, SCHMITT & BECK, P.L.L.C. (AV)

Elks Building, 117 East Gurley Street, 86301
Telephone: 520-445-6860
Fax: 520-445-6488
Email: MLSB@GOODNET.COM
Yuma, Arizona Office: Valley Professional Plaza, 1763 West Twenty-Fourth Street, Suite 200.
Telephone: 520-726-0314.
Fax: 520-341-1079.
Kingman, Arizona Office: 2601 Stockton Hill Road, Suite H8.
Telephone: 520-718-0888; 1-800-281-0822.

MEMBERS OF FIRM

Thelton D. Beck | Robert E. Schmitt
Michael R. Murphy | Dan A. Wilson
Selmer D. Lutey | Alex B. Vakula

Scott K. Risley

Counsel for: State Farm Mutual Automobile Insurance Co.; Allstate Insurance Co.; Farmers Insurance; Western Agricultural Insurance Co.;
Local Counsel for: Bank One Arizona, NA; The Stockmen's Bank.
Representative Clients: Prescott College; Galpin Ford, Inc.; Sedona-Oak Creek Airport Authority; Yavapai County Fair Association (Prescott Downs).

For full biographical listings, see the Martindale-Hubbell Law Directory

SCOTTSDALE, Maricopa Co.

BLUNT & ASSOCIATES, P.C. (AV)

Hayden Corporate Center, 8283 North Hayden Road, Suite 100, 85258
Telephone: 602-951-0400
Telecopier: 602-951-0463
Email: admin@bluntetal.com *URL:* http://www.bluntetal.com

A. Paul Blunt

(See Next Column)

BLUNT & ASSOCIATES P.C., *Scottsdale—Continued*

John H. Barron, III
Lawrence F. Scaringelli

For full biographical listings, see the Martindale-Hubbell Law Directory

BREGMAN & BURT, A PROFESSIONAL ASSOCIATION (AV)

7509 East First Street, 85251-4501
Telephone: 602-945-1800
Telecopier: 602-945-9594
Email: mbregman@bregmanandburt.com

Mark A. Bregman
Sandra K. Bregman
Sandra Burt

Reference: Western Security Bank.

For full biographical listings, see the Martindale-Hubbell Law Directory

PAUL J. BUSER (AV Ⓣ)

7633 East Acoma Drive, Suite 106, 85260-3486
Telephone: 480-951-1222
Fax: 480-951-2568
Email: pjbazlit@worldnet.att.net *URL:* http://www.lawyers.com/paulbusercactuslaw

For full biographical listings, see the Martindale-Hubbell Law Directory

TAMARA L. DWORSKY (AV)

8655 East Via De Ventura Suite G-226, 85258
Telephone: 480-941-8337
Fax: 480-905-8732
Email: tdworsky@earthlink.net

For full biographical listings, see the Martindale-Hubbell Law Directory

ROSEPINK & ESTES, P.L.L.C. (AV)

7373 North Scottsdale Road Suite E200, 85253
Telephone: 602-443-1280
Fax: 602-443-3664
Email: rosepink@rosepink.com *URL:* http://www.rosepink.com

MEMBERS OF FIRM

Robert J. Rosepink
David J. Estes

ASSOCIATES

Alisa J. Gray
James A. Fassold
Heather L. Illies

References: Bank of America, Arizona; Biltmore Investors Bank; Chase Trust Company of Arizona; Wells Fargo; Firstar Metropolitan Bank & Trust; M & I Marshall & Ilsley Trust Co. of Arizona; Northern Trust Bank of Arizona; Harris Trust Bank of Arizona.

For full biographical listings, see the Martindale-Hubbell Law Directory

SPARKS, TEHAN & RYLEY, P.C. (AV)

7503 First Street, 85251-4573
Telephone: 480-949-1339
Fax: 480-949-7587

Joe P. Sparks
Kevin T. Tehan
John H. Ryley

LEGAL SUPPORT PERSONNEL

Pamela L. Sparks
Joshua Morgan Sparks
Catherine L. McComb

References: Bank One, Arizona, Trust Department; Northern Trust Bank of Arizona, N.A.; Wells Fargo Bank of Arizona.

For full biographical listings, see the Martindale-Hubbell Law Directory

SUN CITY, Maricopa Co.

COOLEY & ROBBINS, L.L.C. (AV)

14805 N. Del Webb Boulevard Suite 30, 85351
Telephone: 623-977-1900
Facsimile: 623-977-2600

Susan M. Robbins
Ronald G. Cooley

For full biographical listings, see the Martindale-Hubbell Law Directory

RONALD F. LARSON, P.C. (AV)

9899 West Bell Road, Building A, 85351
Telephone: 602-933-4055
Fax: 602-972-9855
Email: rflpc@aol.com

Ronald F. Larson

Representative Clients: National Society of Tax Professionals; Moore Chrysler Plymouth, Inc.; Phoenix Foundation, Inc.; Masonic Fellowship Center, Inc.; Northwest Valley Automotive Group, L.L.C.

For full biographical listings, see the Martindale-Hubbell Law Directory

*TUCSON,** Pima Co.

FLEMING & CURTI (AV)

A Professional Limited Liability Company
330 North Granada Avenue, 85701
Telephone: 520-622-0400; 800-395-3714
FAX: 520-622-2971
Email: fleming@elder-law.com *URL:* http://www.desert.net/elder

Robert B. Fleming
Thomas A. Curti

ASSOCIATE

Julia K. Connors

For full biographical listings, see the Martindale-Hubbell Law Directory

GABROY, ROLLMAN & BOSSÉ, P.C. (AV)

3507 North Campbell Avenue, Suite 111, 85719
Telephone: 520-320-1300
Telefax: 520-320-0717
Email: admin@gabroylaw.com

Steven L. Bossé
Fred A. Farsjo

For Complete List of Firm Personnel, See General Section

For full biographical listings, see the Martindale-Hubbell Law Directory

DANIEL H. O'CONNELL, P.C. (AV)

3573 East Sunrise Drive, Suite 120, 85718-3206
Telephone: 520-615-9802
Telefax: 520-615-9789
Email: ben@dhopc.psemail.com *URL:* http://www.lawyers.com/danieloconnell-law

Daniel H. O'Connell

Benjamin J. Burnside

OF COUNSEL

Rosanne F. Lapan

Representative Clients: Empire West Cos.; Thermal Engineering, Inc.; Alban Medical Associates; Industrial Motor & Control, Inc.; Allergy Asthma Associates, P.C.
Reference: Bank of America.

For full biographical listings, see the Martindale-Hubbell Law Directory

SNELL & WILMER L.L.P. (AV)

One South Church Avenue, Suite 1500, 85701-1612
Telephone: 520-882-1200
Fax: 520-884-1294
URL: http://www.swlaw.com
Phoenix, Arizona Office: One Arizona Center, 85004-2202.
Telephone: 602-382-6000.
Fax: 602-382-6070.
Orange County Office: 1920 Main Street, Suite 1200, Irvine, California 92614-7230.
Telephone: 949-253-2700.
Fax: 949-955-2507.
Salt Lake City, Utah Office: 111 East Broadway, Suite 900, 84111-1004.
Telephone: 801-237-1900.
Fax: 801-237-1950.

MEMBER OF FIRM

Charles E. Giddings

Representative Clients: For list of Representative Clients, see end of biographical listings in the Martindale-Hubbell Law Directory.

For full biographical listings, see the Martindale-Hubbell Law Directory

TAYLOR & CAWTHORNE, LTD. (AV)

7400 North Oracle Road Suite 243, 85704-6340
Telephone: 520-742-2500
Fax: 520-742-6953
URL: http://www.lawyers.com/taylor&cawthorne
Other Tucson, Arizona (Sun City) Office: Mountain View Plaza, 1171 East Rancho Vistoso Boulevard, Suite 117, 85737.
Telephone: 520-825-0981.
Fax: 520-825-0989. Also at: 63701 East Saddlebrooke Boulevard, Suite B, 85739.

Roger W. Taylor
Hugh Cawthorne

For full biographical listings, see the Martindale-Hubbell Law Directory

ARKANSAS

*CAMDEN,** Ouachita Co.

HARRELL & LINDSEY, P.A. (AV)

201 Jackson Street, S.W., P.O. Box K, 71711
Telephone: 870-836-7725
Fax: 870-836-4643
URL: http://www.lawyers.com/harrellaw

Searcy W. Harrell, Jr. — Paul E. Lindsey

For Complete List of Firm Personnel, See General Section

For full biographical listings, see the Martindale-Hubbell Law Directory

*FAYETTEVILLE,** Washington Co.

BALL & MOURTON, LTD., PLLC (AV)

A Professional Limited Liability Company
Suite 700, E.J. Ball Plaza, P.O. Box 1948, 72702
Telephone: 501-442-6213
Fax: 501-442-6233
Email: contact@ballandmourton.com *URL:* http://www.BallandMourton.com
Siloam Springs, Arkansas Office: 106 South Broadway. P.O. Box 1348, 72761.
Telephone: 501-524-2337.
Fax: 501-524-3693.

E. J. Ball — John T. Lee
Kenneth R. Mourton — Rayburn W. Green

David G. Bercaw — Joseph D. Reece
J. Michael Threet — Shannon L. Poore

OF COUNSEL
Neal R. Pendergraft

Representative Clients: Arkansas Western Gas Co.; Coors of Western Arkansas, Inc.; Rebel Enterprises, Inc.; Southwestern Energy Co.; Stephens Production Co.; Ohlendorf Investment Co.; Central Health Corporation; McIlroy Bank & Trust.

For full biographical listings, see the Martindale-Hubbell Law Directory

*FORREST CITY,** St. Francis Co.

BUTLER, HICKY & LONG (AV)

A Partnership of Professional Corporations
2216 North Washington Street, P.O. Box 989, 72335
Telephone: 870-633-4611
FAX: 870-633-6848
Email: bhlfirm@IPA.NET

MEMBERS OF FIRM
Philip Hicky (Ltd.) — Fletcher Long, Jr. (P.A.)

ASSOCIATE
Rita Reed Harris

Representative Clients: First National Bank of Eastern Arkansas; Southern Farm Bureau Insurance Cos.; United States Aviation Underwriters Group; National Aviation Underwriters; Hartford Accident and Indemnity Co.; Peoples Implement Co.; Virginia Insurance Reciprocal.

For full biographical listings, see the Martindale-Hubbell Law Directory

*HOPE,** Hempstead Co.

PILKINTON, PILKINTON & YOCOM (AV)

116-118 East Second Street, P.O. Box 583, 71801-4401
Telephone: 870-777-8871
Fax: 870-777-2781
Email: tyocom@arkansas.net

MEMBERS OF FIRM
James H. Pilkinton (1914-1994) — James H. Pilkinton, Jr.
Tony Lynn Yocom

Representative Clients: First National Bank of Hope; Pioneer Washington Restoration Foundation; Pyramid Plastics, Inc.; John Hays Chevrolet Co.; Michigan Chrome & Chemical; Bank of Blevins, Ark.
Approved Attorneys for: Commonwealth Land Title Insurance Co.; Lawyers Title Insurance Corp.

For full biographical listings, see the Martindale-Hubbell Law Directory

*LITTLE ROCK,** Pulaski Co.

BARBER, MCCASKILL, JONES & HALE, P.A. (AV)

2700 Regions Center, 400 West Capitol Avenue, 72201-3414
Telephone: 501-372-6175
Telecopier: 501-375-2802

(See Next Column)

Azro L. Barber (1885-1979) — Gail Ponder Gaines
Elbert A. Henry (1889-1966) — Michael J. Emerson
John B. Thurman (1912-1971) — R. Kenny McCulloch
Austin McCaskill, Sr. — Tim A. Cheatham
Glenn W. Jones — Joseph F. Kolb
Michael E. Hale — Scott Michael Strauss
John S. Cherry, Jr. — Baucum Fulk
Robert L. Henry, III — D. Keith Fortner
Micheal L. Alexander — Wendy Scholtens Wood
William H. Edwards, Jr. — Morris L. Williams, III
G. Spence Fricke — Michelle Bass Miller

Attorneys for: AFCO Steel; CNA Insurance Companies; First Commercial Bank; Fireman's Fund Insurance Co.; General Motors Acceptance Corp.; Hanover Insurance Co.; Royal Insurance; Universal Underwriters Insurance Co.

For full biographical listings, see the Martindale-Hubbell Law Directory

ROSE LAW FIRM, A PROFESSIONAL ASSOCIATION (AV)

120 East Fourth Street, 72201
Telephone: 501-375-9131
Telecopy: 501-375-1309

W. Wilson Jones — Ronald M. Clark
C. Brantly Buck — Bryant K. Cranford

COUNSEL
J. Gaston Williamson — W. Dane Clay

Craig S. Lair — Mark Davis

Representative Clients: ALLTEL Corporation; Acxiom Corporation; Arkansas Association of Bank Holding Cos.; Boatmen's Trust Company of Arkansas; Winthrop Rockefeller Foundation; Mercantile Bank of Central Arkansas; Tyson Foods, Inc.

For Complete List of Firm Personnel, See General Section

For full biographical listings, see the Martindale-Hubbell Law Directory

WALKER & BLACK (AV)

1000 West Third Street, P.O. Box 3780, 72203-3780
Telephone: 501-376-2382
Fax: 501-376-3352

MEMBERS OF FIRM
W. J. Walker — Kendell R. Black

ASSOCIATE
Phillip M. Hendry

Reference: Central Bank & Trust.

For full biographical listings, see the Martindale-Hubbell Law Directory

*PINE BLUFF,** Jefferson Co.

RAMSAY, BRIDGFORTH, HARRELSON & STARLING (AV)

11th Floor, Simmons First National Building, P.O. Drawer 8509, 71611
Telephone: 870-535-9000
Fax: 870-535-8544

MEMBER OF FIRM
F. Daniel Harrelson

Representative Clients: Simmons First National Bank; Pine Bluff Sand & Gravel Co.; Stant, Inc.; McGeorge Contracting Co., Inc.; Television Station KATV.

For Complete List of Firm Personnel, See General Section

For full biographical listings, see the Martindale-Hubbell Law Directory

CALIFORNIA

ARCADIA, Los Angeles Co.

HELMS, HANRAHAN & MYERS (AV)

Suite 685 Towne Centre Building, 150 North Santa Anita Avenue, 91006
Telephone: 626-445-1177
Fax: 626-445-2085
Email: helmsj@aol.com *URL:* http://www.lawyers.com/hhmlaw

James R. Helms, Jr. — James J. Hanrahan
Sterling E. Myers

LEGAL SUPPORT PERSONNEL
PARALEGAL
Michelle L. Upp

Reference: Bank of America National Trust & Savings Assn. (Arcadia Branch).

For full biographical listings, see the Martindale-Hubbell Law Directory

*BAKERSFIELD,** Kern Co.

BORTON, PETRINI & CONRON, LLP (AV)

The Borton, Petrini & Conron Building, 1600 Truxtun Avenue, 93301
Telephone: 661-322-3051
Voice Mail: 661-395-6700
Fax: 661-322-4628
Mailing Address: P.O. Box 2026, Bakersfield, California, 93303
Email: bpcbak@bpclaw.com *URL:* http://www.bpclaw.com
Other City Locations: Fresno, Los Angeles, Modesto, Redding, Sacramento, San Bernardino, San Diego, San Francisco, San Jose, San Luis Obispo, Santa Ana and Ventura.

MEMBER OF FIRM

Stephen M. Dake

ASSOCIATE

Timothy B. Liebaert

For Complete List of Firm Personnel, See General Section

For full biographical listings, see the Martindale-Hubbell Law Directory

ELDON R. HUGIE (AV)

3403 Stockdale Highway, 93309
Telephone: 805-396-0100
Fax: 805-396-0400
Email: ERH@Lightspeed.net

Representative Clients: Swanson Family Trusts; Fanucchi Family Trusts.
References: West America Bank (Bakersfield Main Branch).

For full biographical listings, see the Martindale-Hubbell Law Directory

KLEIN, DENATALE, GOLDNER, COOPER, ROSENLIEB & KIMBALL, LLP (AV)

(Formerly Di Giorgio, Davis, Klein, Wegis, Duggan & Friedman)
ARCO Tower, 4550 California Avenue, Second Floor, 93309
Telephone: 661-395-1000
Telecopier: 661-326-0418
Mailing Address: P.O. Box 11172, Bakersfield, California, 93389-1172
Email: kleinlaw@kleinlaw.com

Anthony J. Klein (Inc.) | Claude P. Kimball
Kevin C. Findley

Representative Clients: Bank of America; Great Western Bank; Mojave Pipeline Co.; Transamerican Title Insurance Co.; Dean Whittier Reynolds, Inc.; California Republic Bank; San Joaquin Bank; Nahama & Weagant Energy Co.; Freymiller Trucking, Inc.; Westinghouse Electric Co.

For Complete List of Firm Personnel, See General Section

For full biographical listings, see the Martindale-Hubbell Law Directory

BEVERLY HILLS, Los Angeles Co.

HOCHMAN, SALKIN, RETTIG, TOSCHER & PEREZ, A PROFESSIONAL CORPORATION (AV)

9150 Wilshire Boulevard Suite 300, 90212-3414
Telephone: 310-281-3200; 273-1181
Fax: 310-859-1430
URL: http://www.taxlitigator.com

Bruce I. Hochman | Charles P. Rettig
Avram Salkin | Dennis Perez
Steven R. Toscher

OF COUNSEL

George DeRoy | Nathan Joseph Hochman
Stuart A. Simon | Steven D. Blanc
Michel R. Stein

Reference: Union Bank of California.

For full biographical listings, see the Martindale-Hubbell Law Directory

BISHOP, Inyo Co.

DOUGLAS BUCHANAN (AV)

363 Academy Avenue, 93514
Telephone: 760-873-4211
Fax: 760-873-4007
Email: dbuchanan@QNET.com

OF COUNSEL

Ronald F. Sample | Susan A. Yeck

References: Dean Witter Reynolds, Bishop; Union Bank, Bishop.

For full biographical listings, see the Martindale-Hubbell Law Directory

BREA, Orange Co.

BACON & MILLS, LLP (AV)

Three Pointe Drive, Suite 308, 92827
Telephone: 714-257-2100
Fax: 714-257-2101
Email: baconmills@earthlink.net *URL:* http://www.baconmills.com
Los Angeles, California Office: 800 Wilshire Boulevard, Suite 950.
Telephone: 213-486-6500.
Fax: 213-486-6552.

Robert L. Bacon | Theodore E. Bacon
John F. Norris

For full biographical listings, see the Martindale-Hubbell Law Directory

BURBANK, Los Angeles Co.

ALVIN N. LOSKAMP A LAW CORPORATION (AV)

290 East Verdugo Avenue, Suite 103, 91502-1331
Telephone: 818-846-9000
Fax: 818-843-1441
URL: http://www.loskamp.com
Email: aloskamp@hotmail.com *URL:* http://www.lawyers.com/loskamplaw

Alvin N. Loskamp

References: Wells Fargo Bank, Business Branch, Burbank.

For full biographical listings, see the Martindale-Hubbell Law Directory

CHULA VISTA, San Diego Co.

ATHERTON & ALLEN (AV)

210 Towne Centre Professional Building, 345 "F" Street, 91910
Telephone: 619-420-6869
Email: daveallen@estplanlaw.com

MEMBERS OF FIRM

Harvey H. Atherton (1881-1972) | Keith Atherton (1912-1998)
David R. Allen

For full biographical listings, see the Martindale-Hubbell Law Directory

COSTA MESA, Orange Co.

FELDHAKE, AUGUST & ROQUEMORE (AV)

Plaza Tower, Suite 1730, 600 Anton Boulevard, 92626-7124
Telephone: 714-438-3885
Fax: 714-438-3888
Email: farlaw@hqonline.com

Robert J. Feldhake | Lisa A. Roquemore
Kenneth S. August | Joshua M. Wolff

ASSOCIATES

Dimitri P. Gross | Supriya Kakkar
Katherine A. Slayton

OF COUNSEL

Arthur J. Swerdloff | Arthur M. Wilcox, Jr.

For full biographical listings, see the Martindale-Hubbell Law Directory

MCCORMICK, KIDMAN & BEHRENS, LLP (AV)

A Partnership of Professional Corporations
Imperial Bank Building, 695 Town Center Drive Suite 1400, 92626-7187
Telephone: 714-755-3100
Fax: 714-755-3110; 1-800-755-3125
Email: mkb1@ix.netcom.com
Sacramento, California Office: 980 Ninth Street. 16th Floor. 95814-2736.
Telephone: 916-449-9533.
Fax: 916-446-7104.
Effective April 1, 1999 the new address will be: Imperial Bank Building, 695 Town Center Drive, Suite 400.

MEMBERS OF FIRM

Homer L. (Mike) McCormick, Jr., (P.C.) | Russell G. Behrens (P.C.)
 | Suzanne M. Tague (P.C.)
Arthur G. Kidman (P.C.) | Janet R. Morningstar (P.C.)
Keith E. McCullough (P.C.)

ASSOCIATES

David D. Boyer | Gary D. Grant
Paeter E. Garcia | Edward L. Bertrand

For full biographical listings, see the Martindale-Hubbell Law Directory

RUTAN & TUCKER, LLP (AV)

A Partnership including Professional Corporations
611 Anton Boulevard, Fourteenth Floor, P.O. Box 1950, 92626-1998
Telephone: 714-641-5100; 213-625-7586
Telecopier: 714-546-9035
Email: rutan&tucker@rutan.com *URL:* http://www.rutan.com

(See Next Column)

RUTAN & TUCKER LLP—*Continued*

MEMBERS OF FIRM

Paul Frederic Marx
James B. O'Neal
James S. Weisz (P.C.)

OF COUNSEL

David J. Garibaldi III

For Complete List of Firm Personnel, See General Section

For full biographical listings, see the Martindale-Hubbell Law Directory

*EL CENTRO,** Imperial Co.

HORTON, KNOX, CARTER & FOOTE (AV)

Law Building, 895 Broadway, 92243
Telephone: 760-352-2821
Telefax: 760-352-8540
Email: hkcf@earthlink.net
Brawley Office: 195 South Second Street.
Telephone: 760-344-2360.
Fax: 760-344-9778.

MEMBER OF FIRM

Philip J. Krum, Jr.

Representative Clients: Automobile Club of Southern Calif.; Imperial Irrigation District; Union Pacific Co.; Reliance Insurance Cos.; Pioneer Memorial Hospital District; City of Imperial; San Diego Gas & Electric Co.; Chevron U.S.A.; Bixby Land Co.

For Complete List of Firm Personnel, See General Section

For full biographical listings, see the Martindale-Hubbell Law Directory

EMERYVILLE, Alameda Co.

BISHOP, BARRY, HOWE, HANEY & RYDER, A PROFESSIONAL CORPORATION (AV)

Watergate Tower III, 2000 Powell Street, Suite 1425, 94608
Telephone: 510-596-0888
Fax: 510-596-0899
Email: FirmGeneral@BBHHR.com
San Francisco Office: 44 Montgomery Street, Suite 1300, 94104.
Telephone: 415-421-8550.

Ross R. Ryder (1940-1989)
Nelson C. Barry
Drayton F. Howe, Jr.
Jeffrey N. Haney
Thomas O. Haran
Rebecca B. Aherne
Michael W. Bolechowski
Mark C. Raskoff
Patricia S. Lakner
Gregory R. de la Peña

J. Scott Wood
Mitchell J. Alward
Marco R. Sumarriva
Jane E. Carey
Carol L. Healey
Mary Margaret Ryan
Thomas Edward Foran
John F. Cooke
Jean H. Hurricane
Daniel M. O'Connell
Lisa S. Wiggins
Edward M. Lai

OF COUNSEL

Lawrence S. Molton
David P. Osako

Reference: Golden Gate Bank.

For full biographical listings, see the Martindale-Hubbell Law Directory

ESCONDIDO, San Diego Co.

DOROTHY A. COLE (AV)

Town View Professional Centre, 215 South Hickory Street, Suite 224, 92025-4361
Telephone: 760-745-6313
Fax: 760-745-6988

For full biographical listings, see the Martindale-Hubbell Law Directory

*FRESNO,** Fresno Co.

BOLEN, FRANSEN & BOOSTROM LLP (AV)

Suite 430, East Tower Guarantee Financial Center, 1322 East Shaw Avenue, 93710
Telephone: 559-226-8177
Fax: 559-227-4971
Email: firm@bolenfransen.com *URL:* http://www.bolenfransen.com
Clovis, California Office: 414 Pollasky Avenue.
Telephone: 559-297-6250.
Fax: 559-322-6778.

PARTNERS

Hal H. Bolen II
Kenneth J. Fransen
Jeffrey A. Russell
Virginia Miller Pedreira

ASSOCIATE

Kim Marie Herold

(See Next Column)

OF COUNSEL

Donna Boostrom

For full biographical listings, see the Martindale-Hubbell Law Directory

DIETRICH, GLASRUD, MALLEK & AUNE (AV)

An Association of Attorneys including Law Corporations
5250 North Palm Avenue, Suite 402, 93704
Telephone: 559-435-5250
Facsimile: 559-435-8776
Email: info@dgmalaw.com

Richard W. Dietrich (Inc.) (1930-1999)
Donald H. Glasrud (Inc.)
Robert A. Mallek Jr. (Inc.)
Richard E. Aune (Inc.)
Bruce A. Owdom
Thomas W. Isaac

Douglas D. Schorling
Leslie G. Miessner
Daniel J. Tekunoff

OF COUNSEL

Timothy J. Buchanan

Representative Clients: Fresno Surgery and Recovery Care Center; Helm Fertilizer, Inc.; Gragnani Farms; Wathen-Castanos, Inc.; Chicago Title Company; ABC, Inc.; The McClatchy Company; Monsanto Company; Armstrong World Industries, Inc.; Stewart Title Guaranty Company.

For full biographical listings, see the Martindale-Hubbell Law Directory

DOWLING, AARON & KEELER, INCORPORATED (AV)

6051 North Fresno Street, Suite 200, 93710
Telephone: 559-432-4500
Fax: 559-432-4590
Email: dak@daklaw.com *URL:* http://www.daklaw.com
Bakersfield, California Office: 110 South Mt. Claire, Suite 203. 93309.
Telephone: 661-396-0451. Web Site: http://www.daklaw.com.

Michael D. Dowling
Richard M. Aaron
William J. Keeler, Jr.
Bruce S. Fraser
John C. Ganahl

Larry B. Lindenau
Michael P. Dowling

OF COUNSEL

Morris M. Sherr

Reference: Wells Fargo Bank (Main).

For Complete List of Firm Personnel, See General Section

For full biographical listings, see the Martindale-Hubbell Law Directory

FULLERTON, Orange Co.

MARK SCOTT ROBERTS AND ASSOCIATES A PROFESSIONAL LAW CORPORATION (AV)

1440 North Harbor Boulevard, Suite 900, 92835
Telephone: 714-449-3353
Fax: 714-680-0906
URL: http://www.legacylawyer.com
Email: mroberts@legacylawyer.com *URL:* http://www.lawyers.com/msroberts

Mark Scott Roberts

For full biographical listings, see the Martindale-Hubbell Law Directory

GLENDALE, Los Angeles Co.

GILL AND BALDWIN (AV)

130 North Brand Boulevard Fourth Floor, 91203
Telephone: 818-500-7755; 323-245-3131
Fax: 818-242-4305
URL: http://www.lawyers.com/g&blaw
Email: gillandbal@aol.com *URL:* http://www.gillandbaldwin.com

MEMBERS OF FIRM

John M. Carmack
Kirk S. MacDonald

Representative Clients: Morrison-Knudsen Corp.; Bireley Foundation.
Reference: Bank of Los Angeles.

For full biographical listings, see the Martindale-Hubbell Law Directory

GREENWALD, HOFFMAN, MEYER & MONTES, L.L.P. (AV)

500 North Brand Boulevard, Suite 920, 91203-1923
Telephone: 818-507-8100; 213-381-1131
Fax: 818-507-8484

MEMBERS OF FIRM

Guy Preston Greenwald, Jr. (1914-1984)
Donald M. Hoffman
Lawrence F. Meyer
Raul M. Montes

(See Next Column)

GREENWALD, HOFFMAN, MEYER & MONTES L.L.P., *Glendale—Continued*

References: Bank of America (Los Angeles and Pasadena Trust Offices); Northern Trust of California (Headquarters Office); Bank of America (Glendale Main Branch).

For full biographical listings, see the Martindale-Hubbell Law Directory

IRVINE, Orange Co.

GRECO, MOLLIS & O'HARA, A PROFESSIONAL CORPORATION (AV)

18400 Von Karman, Suite 500, 92612-1514
Telephone: 949-263-0600
Fax: 949-263-1513

Thomas A. Greco
Kevin O'Hara
Ronald A. Mollis
Charles A. Mollis

For full biographical listings, see the Martindale-Hubbell Law Directory

JACQUELINE M. JENSEN, INC. (AV)

4010 Barranca Parkway, Suite 250, 92604
Telephone: 949-733-0050
Fax: 949-733-0051
Email: JensenInc@aol.com *URL:* http://www.lawyers.com/jmjensenlaw

Jacqueline M. Jensen

For full biographical listings, see the Martindale-Hubbell Law Directory

SNELL & WILMER L.L.P. (AV)

1920 Main Street, Suite 1200, 92614-7230
Telephone: 949-253-2700
FAX: 949-955-2507
URL: http://www.swlaw.com
Phoenix, Arizona Office: One Arizona Center, 85004-2202.
Telephone: 602-382-6000.
Fax: 602-382-6070.
Tucson, Arizona Office: One South Church Avenue, Suite 1500, 85701-1630.
Telephone: 520-882-1200.
Fax: 520-884-1294.
Salt Lake City, Utah Office: 111 East Broadway, Suite 900, 84111-1004.
Telephone: 801-237-1900.
Fax: 801-237-1950.

MEMBER OF FIRM

David W. Evans

Representative Clients: For list of Representative Clients, see end of biographical listings in the Martindale-Hubbell Law Directory.

For Complete List of Firm Personnel, See General Section

For full biographical listings, see the Martindale-Hubbell Law Directory

EDWARD H. STONE, P.C. (AV)

18201 Von Karman Avenue, Suite 1160, 92612-1005
Telephone: 949-833-7708
Fax: 949-833-7583
Email: EdHStone@aol.com

Edward H. Stone

For full biographical listings, see the Martindale-Hubbell Law Directory

LA JOLLA, San Diego Co.

FERGUSON, NEWBURN & WESTON, A PROFESSIONAL CORPORATION (AV)

7777 Fay Avenue, Suite 260, 92037
Telephone: 858-454-4233
Facsimile: 858-454-3052

Keith M. Ferguson (1903-1965)
William E. Ferguson
John L. Newburn (Retired, 1989)
David Weston

References: Union Bank (La Jolla Office); Scripps Bank (La Jolla Office).

For full biographical listings, see the Martindale-Hubbell Law Directory

LUCE, FORWARD, HAMILTON & SCRIPPS LLP (AV)

A Partnership including Professional Corporations
La Jolla Golden Triangle, 4275 Executive Square, Suite 800, 92037
Telephone: 858-455-6611
Fax: 858-232-8311
URL: http://www.luce.com
San Diego, California Office: 600 West Broadway, Suite 2600, 92101.
Telephone: 619-236-1414.
Fax: 619-232-8311.
Los Angeles, California Office: 777 South Figueroa, Suite 3600, 90017.
Telephone: 213-892-4992.
Fax: 213-892-7731.

(See Next Column)

San Francisco, California Office: 121 Spear Street, Suite 200, 94105.
Telephone: 415-356-4600.
Fax: 415-356-4610.
New York, N.Y. Office: Citicorp Center, 153 East 53rd Street, 26th Floor, 10022.
Telephone: 212-754-1414.
Fax: 212-644-9727.
Chicago, Illinois Office: 180 North La Salle Street, Suite 3110, 60601.
Telephone: 312-641-0580.
Fax: 312-641-0380.

MEMBERS OF FIRM

Jack G. Charney
Robert J. Durham, Jr.
Frederick R. Vandeveer

For full biographical listings, see the Martindale-Hubbell Law Directory

MULVANEY, KAHAN & BARRY, A PROFESSIONAL CORPORATION (AV)

Suite 315, 875 Prospect Street, P.O. Box 1168, 92038-1168
Telephone: 619-454-1780
Fax: 619-454-1792
San Diego, California Office: Seventeenth Floor, First National Bank Center, 401 West "A" Street.
Telephone: 619-238-1010.
Fax: 619-238-1981.
Los Angeles, California Office: Union Bank Plaza, 445 South Figueroa Street, Suite 2600.
Telephone: 213-612-7765.
Orange, California Office: The Koll Center, 500 North State College Boulevard, Suite 440.
Telephone: 714-634-7069.
Fax: 714-939-8000.

Thomas A. Henry, Jr.

For full biographical listings, see the Martindale-Hubbell Law Directory

LANCASTER, Los Angeles Co.

MARK E. THOMPSON A PROFESSIONAL CORPORATION (AV)

857 West Lancaster Boulevard, 93534
Telephone: 661-945-5868
Fax: 661-723-7089

Mark E. Thompson

Leonard A. Cosgrove
Kevin L. Von Tungeln

LEGAL SUPPORT PERSONNEL

Lori H. Young
Kelly Timmons

References: Antelope Valley Bank; Wells Fargo Bank; Washington Mutual Bank.

For full biographical listings, see the Martindale-Hubbell Law Directory

LONG BEACH, Los Angeles Co.

SIMON, MCKINSEY, MILLER, ZOMMICK, SANDOR & DUNDAS, A LAW CORPORATION (AV)

2750 Bellflower Boulevard, 90815
Telephone: 562-421-9354
Facsimile: 562-420-6455
Irvine, California Office: Suite 670, 4199 Campus Drive.
Telephone: 949-856-1916.
Facsimile: 949-856-3834.

Harry J. Simon (1922-1977)
David L. Sandor
Thomas W. McKinsey (1920-1990)
Geraldine G. Sandor (Resident, Irvine Office)
Arthur W. Miller (Retired)
David G. Dundas (Resident, Irvine Office)
Kenneth Zommick

Robert M. Stone
Jennifer M. Rosenblatt

For full biographical listings, see the Martindale-Hubbell Law Directory

D. MICHAEL TRAINOTTI A PROFESSIONAL LAW CORPORATION (AV)

Suite 410, 200 Oceangate, 90802
Telephone: 562-590-8621
Fax: 562-590-8181
Email: mike@trainotti.com *URL:* http://www.trainotti.com

D. Michael Trainotti

Reference: Farmers & Merchants Bank; Harbor Bank.

For full biographical listings, see the Martindale-Hubbell Law Directory

Long Beach—Continued

WISE, WIEZOREK, TIMMONS & WISE, A PROFESSIONAL CORPORATION (AV)

3700 Santa Fe Avenue, Suite 300, P.O. Box 2190, 90801-2190
Telephone: 310-834-5028; 562-595-5318
Fax: 310-834-8018
URL: http://www.wwtw.com
Redding, California Office: 292 Hemsted Drive, Suite 101.
Telephone: 530-221-7632.
Fax: 530-221-8832.

George E. Wise
Duane H. Timmons
Anthony F. Wiezorek
Susan E. Anderson Wise
Michael J. Pearce
Mark C. Allen, III
Richard P. Dieffenbach
Steven C. Rice
Stephen M. Smith
Thomas J. Yocis
James M. Cox
Mathew J. Vande Wydeven

Susan Graham

For full biographical listings, see the Martindale-Hubbell Law Directory

*LOS ANGELES,** Los Angeles Co.

MICHAEL ANTIN A LAW CORPORATION (AV)

10880 Wilshire Boulevard Suite 1010, 90024
Telephone: 310-470-0049
Fax: 310-470-0322
Email: mantin@ix.netcom.com *URL:* http://www.lawyers.com/atlaw

Michael Antin

For full biographical listings, see the Martindale-Hubbell Law Directory

PAUL L. BASILE, JR. (AV)

11400 West Olympic Boulevard, Suite 350, 90064-1558
Telephone: 310-478-2114
Toll Free: 800-511-2114
Fax: 310-478-0229
Email: pbasile@basile-law.com *URL:* http://www.basile-law.com

For full biographical listings, see the Martindale-Hubbell Law Directory

CLARK & TREVITHICK, A PROFESSIONAL CORPORATION (AV)

800 Wilshire Boulevard, 12th Floor, 90017
Telephone: 213-629-5700
Telecopier: 213-624-9441
Email: postmaster@clarktrev.com
San Francisco, California Office: 456 Montgomery Street, 20th Floor.
Telephone: 415-288-6520.
Fax: 415-398-2820.

Kevin P. Fiore
Dean I. Friedman
Robert F. DeMeter

For Complete List of Firm Personnel, See General Section

For full biographical listings, see the Martindale-Hubbell Law Directory

DARLING, HALL & RAE, LLP (AV)

520 South Grand Avenue, 7th Floor, 90071
Telephone: 213-627-8104
Fax: 213-627-7795
Email: darlinghallrae@compuserve.com

MEMBERS OF FIRM

Hugh W. Darling (1901-1986)
Edward S. Shattuck (1901-1965)
George Gaylord Gute (1922-1981)
Donald Keith Hall (1918-1984)
Matthew S. Rae, Jr.
Richard L. Stack
Edwin Freston

OF COUNSEL

Edward F. Pearson

Reference: City National Bank (Pershing Square Office, Los Angeles, California).

For full biographical listings, see the Martindale-Hubbell Law Directory

DEMETRIOU, DEL GUERCIO, SPRINGER & MOYER, LLP (AV)

801 South Grand Avenue, 10th Floor, 90017
Telephone: 213-624-8407
Telecopy: 213-624-0174
Email: ddsm@juno.com

MEMBER OF FIRM

Angela Shanahan

OF COUNSEL

Ronald J. Del Guercio

Reference: Bank of America, L.A. Main Office, Los Angeles, Calif.

For full biographical listings, see the Martindale-Hubbell Law Directory

EASTON & SCHIFF (AV)

A Partnership of Professional Corporations
1901 Avenue of the Stars Suite 1100, 90067
Telephone: 310-557-2436
FAX: 310-557-2432

MEMBERS OF FIRM

Harold Easton (P.C.)
Michael J. Schiff (P.C.)

References: Bank of America National Trust & Savings Assn. (Los Angeles Main Office); First Charter Bank (Beverly Hills).

For full biographical listings, see the Martindale-Hubbell Law Directory

GOLDSMITH & BURNS (AV)

A Partnership including a Professional Corporation
18425 Burbank Boulevard, Suite 615 (Tarzana), 91356-2800
Telephone: 818-708-2585
Telecopier: 818-996-4537
Email: info@goldsmithcalaw.com

William I. Goldsmith (A Professional Corporation)
Jack D. Hull

ASSOCIATES

Howard D. Myers
Stuart D. Meyers

Representative Clients: Wachovia Bank; Union Bank of California; American Express; First USA; Novus Services; Citibank; Chase Manhattan.
Reference: Union Bank of California, Beverly Hills.

For full biographical listings, see the Martindale-Hubbell Law Directory

GREENBERG GLUSKER FIELDS CLAMAN & MACHTINGER LLP (AV)

21st Floor, 1900 Avenue of the Stars (Century City), 90067
Telephone: 310-553-3610
Fax: 310-553-0687
URL: http://www.ggfcm.com

MEMBERS OF FIRM

Jon J. Gallo
Robert E. Bennett, Jr.
Martin H. Webster
Arnold D. Kahn

Reference: Wells Fargo Bank, 1801 Ave. of the Stars, Los Angeles, CA 90067.

For Complete List of Firm Personnel, See General Section

For full biographical listings, see the Martindale-Hubbell Law Directory

SAMUEL D. INGHAM, III (AV)

1800 Avenue of the Stars, Suite 1000, 90067-4212
Telephone: 310-556-9751
Fax: 310-556-1311
Email: singham@inghamlaw.com

ASSOCIATE

John E. Rogers, Jr.

For full biographical listings, see the Martindale-Hubbell Law Directory

KESSLER & KESSLER, A LAW CORPORATION (AV)

2029 Century Park East, Suite 1520, 90067
Telephone: 310-552-9800
Fax: 310-552-0442
Email: kkalawcorp@aol.com

Warren J. Kessler
Joan B. Kessler
Lisa C. Alexander
Lisa K. Skaist

For full biographical listings, see the Martindale-Hubbell Law Directory

LOEB & LOEB LLP (AV)

A Limited Liability Partnership including Professional Corporations
Suite 1800, 1000 Wilshire Boulevard, 90017-2475
Telephone: 213-688-3400
Facsimile: 213-688-3460
Email: info@loeb.com *URL:* http://www.loeb.com
Century City, California Office: Suite 2200, 10100 Santa Monica Boulevard, Los Angeles, 90067-4164.
Telephone: 310-282-2000.
Facsimile: 310-282-2192.
New York, N.Y. Office: 345 Park Avenue, 10154-0037.
Telephone: 212-407-4000.
Facsimile: 212-407-4990.
Nashville, Tennessee Office: 45 Music Square West, 37203-3205.
Telephone: 615-749-8300;
Facsimile: 615-749-8308.
Rome, Italy Office: Piazza Digione 1, 00197.
Telephone: 011-3906-808-8456.
Facsimile: 011-3906-808-8288.

(See Next Column)

LOEB & LOEB LLP, *Los Angeles—Continued*

MEMBERS OF FIRM

Andrew S. Garb (A P.C.)
Jerome L. Levine (New York City Office)
Jeffrey M. Loeb
David C. Nelson
Stanford K. Rubin (A P.C.) (Century City Office)
Bruce M. Stiglitz (A P.C.)
Bruce J. Wexler (New York City Office)

OF COUNSEL

James R. Birnberg
Bernard M. Silbert (Century City Office)
Harvey L. Silbert (Century City Office)
John S. Warren

SENIOR COUNSEL

Miriam J. Golbert (Century City Office)
Laurie S. Ruckel (New York City Office)

ASSOCIATE

Lynda C. Loigman (New York Office)

For Complete List of Firm Personnel, See General Section

For full biographical listings, see the Martindale-Hubbell Law Directory

---

MINTON, MINTON AND RAND LLP (AV)

510 West Sixth Street, 90014
Telephone: 213-624-9394
Fax: 213-624-9323

MEMBERS OF FIRM

Carl W. Minton (1902-1974)
Carl Minton
David E. Rand

Reference: Bank of America National Trust & Savings Assn. (Seventh & Flower Office, Los Angeles, Calif.).

For full biographical listings, see the Martindale-Hubbell Law Directory

---

MITCHELL, SILBERBERG & KNUPP LLP (AV)

A Partnership including Professional Corporations
11377 West Olympic Boulevard, 90064
Telephone: 310-312-2000
Fax: 310-312-3100
Email: info@msk.com *URL:* http://www.msk.com

MEMBERS OF FIRM

Allan B. Cutrow (A Professional Corporation)
Jeffrey K. Eisen (A Professional Corporation)

ASSOCIATES

Karl de Costa
Jeannette Hahm

References: Wells Fargo Bank, N.A.; Merrill, Lynch.

For Complete List of Firm Personnel, See General Section

For full biographical listings, see the Martindale-Hubbell Law Directory

---

OLDMAN, COOLEY & LEIGHTON, L.L.P. (AV)

Penthouse, Suite A, 16133 Ventura Boulevard (Encino), 91436-2408
Telephone: 818-986-8080
Fax: 818-789-0947
Email: info@ocllaw.com *URL:* http://www.lawyers.com/oc&lfirm

MEMBERS OF FIRM

Marshal A. Oldman
Susan J. Cooley
Walter M. Leighton
Susan R. Izenstark

OF COUNSEL

Michael L. Trope

References: City National Bank (Encino Office).

For full biographical listings, see the Martindale-Hubbell Law Directory

---

OLINCY & KARPEL (AV)

10960 Wilshire Boulevard, Suite 1111, 90024-3782
Telephone: 310-478-1213
Fax: 310-478-1215
URL: http://www.lawyers.com/o&klaw

MEMBERS OF FIRM

George R. Olincy (1904-1982)
J. Dan Olincy
Philip Karpel

ASSOCIATE

Mary Kulvinskas

For full biographical listings, see the Martindale-Hubbell Law Directory

O'MELVENY & MYERS LLP (AV)

400 South Hope Street, 90071-2899
Telephone: 213-430-6000
Facsimile: 213-430-6407
Cable: MOMS
Telex: 674122
Email: omminfo@omm.com *URL:* http://www.omm.com
Century City, CA Office: 1999 Avenue of the Stars, Los Angeles, 90067-6035.
Telex: 674097. Tel: 310-553-6700.
Fax: 310-246-6779.
Newport Beach, CA Office: 610 Newport Center Drive, 92660-6429.
Telex: 4722088. Tel: 949-760-9600.
Fax: 949-823-6994.
San Francisco, CA Office: Embarcadero Center West, 275 Battery Street, 94111-3305. Tel: 415-984-8700.
Fax: 415-984-8701.
New York, NY Office: Citicorp Center, 153 East 53rd Street, 10022-4611.
Telex: 129165. Tel: 212-326-2000.
Fax: 212-326-2061.
Washington, DC Office: 555 13th Street, N.W., 20004-1109.
Cable: MOMSWSH.
Telex: 89622. Tel: 202-383-5300.
Fax: 202-383-5414.
London Office: O'Melveny & Myers, 3 Finsbury Square, London, EC2A 1LA, England. Tel: 44-171-256-8451. Fax 44-171-638-8205.
Tokyo Office: Akasaka Twin Tower, East 14F, 2-17-23, Akasaka, Minato-ku, Tokyo 107-0052, Japan. Tel: 03-5562-2800.
Fax: 03-5575-3840.
Hong Kong Office: O'Melveny & Myers, Suite 1905, Tower Two, Lippo Centre, 89 Queensway, Central, Hong Kong. Tel: 852-2523-8266.
Fax: 852-2522-1760.
Shanghai Office: Kerry Centre, 20F, 1515 Nanjing Road West, Shanghai, 200040 People's Republic of China. Tel: 86-21-5298-5600.
Fax: 86-21-5298-5500.

PARTNER

David D. Watts

For Complete List of Firm Personnel, See General Section

For full biographical listings, see the Martindale-Hubbell Law Directory

---

OSTROVE, KRANTZ & OSTROVE, A PROFESSIONAL CORPORATION (AV)

(Successor To: Ostrove and Lancer, A Professional Corporation; David Ostrove, A Professional Corporation)
5757 Wilshire Boulevard, Suite 535, 90036-3600
Telephone: 323-939-3400
Fax: 323-939-3500
Email: OSTROVE@AOL.COM *URL:* http://www.lawyers.com/ok&olaw

David Ostrove
David S. Krantz
Kenneth E. Ostrove

Reference: First Business Bank.

For full biographical listings, see the Martindale-Hubbell Law Directory

---

POPKOFF & STERN (AV)

501 Shatto Place, Suite 100, 90020-1713
Telephone: 213-389-1358; 389-2174
Fax: 213-380-4154
Palm Springs, California Office: 225 South Civic Drive, Suite 212, 92262.
Telephone: 619-322-8041.

MEMBERS OF FIRM

Burton R. Popkoff
Gary N. Stern

RODI, POLLOCK, PETTKER, GALBRAITH & CAHILL, A LAW CORPORATION (AV)

444 South Flower Street, Suite 1700, 90071-2901
Telephone: 213-895-4900
Telecopiers: 213-895-4921; 895-4922; 895-4750
URL: http://www.rodipollock.com

Karl B. Rodi (1908-1982)
John D. Cahill
John D. Pettker
Daniel C. Bond (1942-1977)
William R. Christian
Henry P. Pramov, Jr.
John F. Cermak, Jr.
Allan E. Ceran
Elizabeth B. Blakely
Robert C. Norton
Tim G. Ceperley
Coralie Kupfer
Cris K. O'Neall
Scott E. Adamson
Margaret Rosenthal

Sonja A. Inglin
Michael A. Abraham
Kenneth A. Franklin
Richard Nessary
Donna Yamini
Wade E. Norwood
Deepak Nanda
David J. Elbaz

OF COUNSEL

John P. Pollock
James M. Galbraith

For full biographical listings, see the Martindale-Hubbell Law Directory

Los Angeles—Continued

ALICE A. SALVO (AV)

18801 Ventura Boulevard, Suite 312 (Tarzana), 91356-3372
Telephone: 818-705-1100
Fax: 818-705-0943
URL: http://www.caelderlaw.com
Email: salvolaw@pacbell.net *URL:* http://www.salvolaw.com

For full biographical listings, see the Martindale-Hubbell Law Directory

SHIOTANI & INOUYE (AV)

1901 Avenue of the Stars Suite 1010, 90067
Telephone: 310-712-0100
Telecopier: 310-712-0110
Email: silaw@earthlink.net *URL:* http://www.lawyers.com/shiotani&inouye

MEMBERS OF FIRM

Barney B. Shiotani
Lawrence G. Inouye

ASSOCIATE

Nicole Grattan Pearson

References: First Los Angeles Bank (Airport Office); Bank of California.

For full biographical listings, see the Martindale-Hubbell Law Directory

WEINSTOCK, MANION, REISMAN, SHORE & NEUMANN, A LAW CORPORATION (AV)

1875 Century Park East, 15th Floor, 90067
Telephone: 310-553-8844
Fax: 310-553-5165
URL: http://www.weinstocklaw.com

DIRECTORS

Harold Weinstock
Louis A. Reisman
Sussan H. Shore
Martin A. Neumann
Gary M. Borofsky
M. Neil Solarz
Robert E. Strauss

OF COUNSEL

Marc L. Sallus

ASSOCIATES

Susan Abraham
Blake A. Rummel
Samuel D. Shapiro
Dianna M. Burgh

References: City National Bank (Century City); Bank of America (Century City); Northern Trust Bank of California, N.A.; Sanwa Bank California.

For full biographical listings, see the Martindale-Hubbell Law Directory

WILLIAMS AND BALLAS (AV)

1800 Century Park East, Suite 510, 90067
Telephone: 310-557-8383
Fax: 310-557-8380
San Francisco, California Office: 160 Sansome Street, Suite 1200.
Telephone: 415-296-9904.
Fax: 415-981-0898.

MEMBERS OF FIRM

Lawrence D. Williams
Stephen B. Ballas

OF COUNSEL

Stanley P. Graham

ASSOCIATES

Melissa Hamilton
Laura M. Williams (Not admitted in CA)

For full biographical listings, see the Martindale-Hubbell Law Directory

STUART D. ZIMRING (AV)

12650 Riverside Drive (North Hollywood), 91607-3492
Telephone: 818-755-4848
Fax: 818-755-4853

Representative Clients: Cytec Industries Inc.; Wells Fargo Bank.

For full biographical listings, see the Martindale-Hubbell Law Directory

LOS OSOS, San Luis Obispo Co.

J. K. GEORGE & ASSOCIATES (AV)

P.O. Box 6129, 93412
Telephone: 805-528-3394
Telecopier: 805-528-5598
Email: info@jkgeorge.com *URL:* http://www.lawyers.com/georgelaw
San Luis Obispo, California Office: 694 Santa Rosa, P.O. Box 12710.
Telephone: 805-544-3394.
Facsimile: 805-528-5598.

J. K. George

(See Next Column)

Anne C. Cyr

For full biographical listings, see the Martindale-Hubbell Law Directory

MANHATTAN BEACH, Los Angeles Co.

DAVIS & CARICO LLP (AV)

1201 Morningside Drive, Suite 200, 90266
Telephone: 310-545-0010
Fax: 310-546-5477

B. Martin Davis III
Christopher D. Carico

For full biographical listings, see the Martindale-Hubbell Law Directory

STEINBERG BARNESS FOSTER & FOLEY LLP (AV)

1334 Park View Avenue, Suite 100, 90266
Telephone: 310-546-8160
Telecopier: 310-546-8189
Email: sbgf@ix.netcom.com

MEMBERS OF FIRM

Alex Steinberg
Daniel I. Barness
Douglas B. Foster
Shannon M. Foley

ASSOCIATES

William R. (Randy) Kirkpatrick
Jeff M. Lee
Kimberly Ann White

OF COUNSEL

Jordan G. Barness
Ronald D. Hariri (Not admitted in CA)

References: California United Bank; Wells Fargo Bank; Citizens Commerical Trust & Savings Bank; Bank of America.

For full biographical listings, see the Martindale-Hubbell Law Directory

*MODESTO,** Stanislaus Co.

BRUNN & FLYNN, A PROFESSIONAL CORPORATION (AV)

928 12th Street, P.O. Box 3366, 95353
Telephone: 209-521-2133
Fax: 209-521-7584
Email: brunnfly@ix.netcom.com

Charles K. Brunn
Timothy T. Flynn
Gerald E. Brunn
Roger S. Matzkind

Michael G. Donovan
Andrew N. Eshoo

For full biographical listings, see the Martindale-Hubbell Law Directory

GIANELLI & FORES, A PROFESSIONAL LAW CORPORATION (AV)

1014 16th Street, P.O. Box 3212, 95353
Telephone: 209-521-6260
Telecopier: 209-521-5971
Email: gianelli@ainet.com *URL:* http://www.gianelli-fores.com

Louis F. Gianelli
Michael L. Gianelli
Robert P. Fores
David L. Gianelli
Brett L. Dickerson
Terry L. Campbell

For full biographical listings, see the Martindale-Hubbell Law Directory

MONTEREY, Monterey Co.

JOHNSON, GAVER & LEACH, LLP (AV)

2801 Monterey-Salinas Highway, Suite B, 93940
Telephone: 831-373-2400
Fax: 831-373-2410
Email: jgl@mbay.net

Mark H. Johnson
Frances R. Gaver
Donald F. Leach

Sara B. Boyns

For full biographical listings, see the Martindale-Hubbell Law Directory

WALKER & MCPHAIL (AV)

5th Floor, Professional Building, 215 West Franklin Street, P.O. Box Law, 93942
Telephone: 831-649-1100
Fax: 831-649-6805
Email: gnpwalker@walkermcphail.com *URL:* http://www.lawyers.com/walker&mcphail
Santa Cruz, California Office: 331 Soquel Avenue, 95062.
Telephone: 831-427-2363.
Telecopier: 831-427-0511.

(See Next Column)

WALKER & MCPHAIL, *Monterey—Continued*

George R. Walker Ian D. McPhail
Kathleen Llewellyn

Representative Clients: A. F. Victor Foundation, Carmel, California; The Carmel Foundation, Carmel, California; Robert Louis Stevenson School, Pebble Beach, California; Brintons Consolidated, Inc.; C & E Farms, Inc.; The Mildred Hitchcock Huff Charitable Trust.

For full biographical listings, see the Martindale-Hubbell Law Directory

MORRO BAY, San Luis Obispo Co.

OGLE, MERZON & KIRSCHNER (AV)

A Partnership including a Professional Corporation
770 Morro Bay Boulevard, P.O. Box 720, 93443-0720
Telephone: 805-772-7353
Fax: 805-772-7713
San Luis Obispo, California Office: P.O. Box 1855, 93406.
Telephone: 805-543-0295.

Charles E. Ogle (A Professional Corporation) James B. Merzon
Charles G. Kirschner
Charles Patrick Ogle

For full biographical listings, see the Martindale-Hubbell Law Directory

*NAPA,** Napa Co.

GAW, VAN MALE, SMITH, MYERS & MIROGLIO, A PROFESSIONAL LAW CORPORATION (AV)

944 Main Street, 94559-3045
Telephone: 707-252-9000
Telecopier: 707-252-0792
URL: http://www.gvmsmm.com
Fairfield, California Office: Corporate Plaza. 1261 Travis Boulevard, Suite 350, 94533-4801.
Telephone: 707-425-1250.
Fax: 707-425-1255.
Redlands, California Office: 300 E. State Street, Suite 101, 92372-5200.
Telephone: 909-798-3190.
Fax: 909-798-3092.

David B. Gaw S. Scott Reynolds
Christine L. Craig

Kathleen M. Bock

Reference: The Vintage Bank.

For full biographical listings, see the Martindale-Hubbell Law Directory

NEWPORT BEACH, Orange Co.

CASEY & RICHARDS (AV)

610 Newport Center Drive, Suite 650, 92660-6474
Telephone: 949-640-5200
Facsimile: 949-760-9300
URL: http://www.caseyrichards.com

MEMBERS OF FIRM

Wayne J. Casey Marc H. Richards

For full biographical listings, see the Martindale-Hubbell Law Directory

THEODORE M. HANKIN (AV)

1301 Dove Street, Suite 900, 92660
Telephone: 949-752-8840
FAX: 949-752-2710
URL: http://www.lawyers.com/hankinlaw

For full biographical listings, see the Martindale-Hubbell Law Directory

THOMAS W. HENDERSON (AV)

5030 Campus Drive, 92660
Telephone: 949-252-8544
Fax: 949-252-8548

Reference: Bank of America, Westcliff Branch, Newport Beach.

For full biographical listings, see the Martindale-Hubbell Law Directory

JEFFREY R. MATSEN & ASSOCIATES (AV)

5001 Birch Street, 92660
Telephone: 949-442-9191
Fax: 949-442-9199
Email: jmatsen@urjet.net *URL:* http://www.lawyers.com/jeffreyrmatsen

For full biographical listings, see the Martindale-Hubbell Law Directory

MILLAR, HODGES & BEMIS (AV)

One Newport Place, Suite 900, 1301 Dove Street, 92660-2448
Telephone: 949-752-7722
Fax: 949-752-6131

MEMBERS OF FIRM

Richard W. Millar, Jr. Kenneth R. Hodges
Larry R. Bemis

ASSOCIATE

David A. St. Clair

Reference: Manufacturers Bank, Newport Beach, California.

For full biographical listings, see the Martindale-Hubbell Law Directory

MOZINGO & PRICE, LLP (AV)

One Newport Place, 1301 Dove Street, Suite 900, 92660
Telephone: 949-752-2255
Facsimile: 949-752-6636
Sacramento, California Office: US Bank Plaza, 980 Ninth Street, Suite 2120, 95814.
Telephone: 916-492-0525.
Facsimile: 916-492-0635.

MEMBERS OF FIRM

Glen R. Mozingo Don G. Price
Jeffrey W. Fohrman

Representative Clients: Salomon Smith Barney-Charles Schwab; Keller, Collins, Hakopian & Leisure (Investment Advisors); American River Fire District; Merchants National Bank; Good & Roberts Construction, Inc.; Essex Insurance Co.; Integrated Environmental, Inc.; International Gateway Insurance Brokers; Coastal Pacific Funding Corp.

QUINLIVAN & KANIEWSKI (AV)

1401 Dove Street, Suite 580, 92660
Telephone: 714-851-7788
Fax: 714-851-3842
URL: http://www.lawyers.com/quinlivan-kaniewski
Email: Quikanlaw@aol.com *URL:* http://qklaw.wld.com

MEMBERS OF FIRM

Patrick C. Quinlivan John A. Kaniewski

ASSOCIATES

Danniel J. Wexler Pamela Jean Richardson
Paige F. Rubinfeld

For full biographical listings, see the Martindale-Hubbell Law Directory

MICHAEL V. VOLLMER (AV)

4340 Campus Drive, Suite 100, 92660-1812
Telephone: 949-852-0833
Fax: 949-852-8731
Email: vollmer@worldnet.att.net *URL:* http://www.lawyers.com/michaelvvollmer

References: Bank of America NT&SA (Newport Beach, California); First American Trust Co. (Newport Beach, California).

For full biographical listings, see the Martindale-Hubbell Law Directory

NORTH HOLLYWOOD, Los Angeles Co.

F. BENTLEY MOONEY, JR. A LAW CORPORATION (AV)

4605 Lankershim Boulevard, Suite 718, 91602
Telephone: 818-769-4221
Fax: 818-769-5002
Email: fbmooney@pacbell.net *URL:* http://www.1bc.com/fbmoney

F. Bentley Mooney, Jr.

For full biographical listings, see the Martindale-Hubbell Law Directory

*OAKLAND,** Alameda Co.

NEAL & ASSOCIATES (AV)

Montclair Village, 6200 Antioch Street, Suite 202, 94611
Telephone: 510-339-0233
FAX: 510-339-6672
Mailing Address: P.O. Box 13314, 500, 94661-0314
Email: hdn@nealaw.com *URL:* http://www.nealaw.com

Howard D. Neal

Steven S. Miyake Barbara E. Scramstad

For full biographical listings, see the Martindale-Hubbell Law Directory

PLAGEMAN, LUND & MILLER LLP (AV)

1999 Harrison, Suite 2700, 94612
Telephone: 510-273-8553
Fax: 510-273-8559

(See Next Column)

PLAGEMAN, LUND & MILLER LLP—*Continued*

William H. Plageman, Jr. Richard W. Lund
Debra J. Miller

ASSOCIATES

Timothy A. DeWitt Aneke M. Plimier
Maureen A. Kelly Susanne Meyer Brown
Paula J. Galleano

For full biographical listings, see the Martindale-Hubbell Law Directory

ORANGE, Orange Co.

JOHN A. DUNCAN A PROFESSIONAL CORPORATION (AV)

333 City Boulevard West, Suite 1420, 92868-2924
Telephone: 714-935-9800
FAX: 714-939-1485
Email: johnduncan@OCBA.net *URL:* http://www.lawyers.com/johnduncan

John A. Duncan

For full biographical listings, see the Martindale-Hubbell Law Directory

OXNARD, Ventura Co.

LOWTHORP, RICHARDS, McMILLAN, MILLER, CONWAY & TEMPLEMAN, A PROFESSIONAL CORPORATION (AV)

300 Esplanade Drive, Suite 850, P.O. Box 5167, 93031
Telephone: 805-981-8555
Fax: 805-983-1967

Carl F. Lowthorp, Jr. (1933-1992)
Richard A. Richards
Robert C. McMillan
Paul A. Miller
Charles J. Conway, Jr.
Alan R. Templeman
Patrick T. Loughman
Glenn J. Campbell
John Q. Masteller

LEGAL SUPPORT PERSONNEL

Elizabeth T. Ladiana, CLA

Representative Clients: Pleasant Valley Mutual Water Co.; Friedrich Ranches, Inc.; Deardorff Jackson Co.; Pacific Coast Plastering; AGRX, Inc.; Terry Farms; Hurst Concrete Products; Chase Bros. Dairy; Dullam Nursery.
Reference: City National Bank.

For full biographical listings, see the Martindale-Hubbell Law Directory

PALM SPRINGS, Riverside Co.

SCHLECHT, SHEVLIN & SHOENBERGER, A LAW CORPORATION (AV)

801 East Tahquitz Canyon Way, Suite 100, P.O. Box 2744, 92263-2744
Telephone: 760-320-7161
Facsimile: 760-323-1758
Email: ssslaw@gte.net *URL:* http://www.ssslaw.com

James M. Schlecht John C. Shevlin

For Complete List of Firm Personnel, See General Section

For full biographical listings, see the Martindale-Hubbell Law Directory

PALO ALTO, Santa Clara Co.

CRIST, SCHULZ, BIORN & SHEPHERD, A PROFESSIONAL CORPORATION (AV)

550 Hamilton Avenue, Suite 300, 94301
Telephone: 650-321-5000
Fax: 650-326-2404
Email: biorn@msn.com

Robert E. Schulz Kristofer W. Biorn
Robert A. Biorn Mark R. Shepherd
Frank Lee Crist, Sr. (1898-1991)

Representative Clients: Comerica Bank; Wells Fargo Bank; Greater Bay Trust Co.

For full biographical listings, see the Martindale-Hubbell Law Directory

FINCH, MONTGOMERY & WRIGHT (AV)

350 Cambridge Avenue, Suite 175, 94306
Telephone: 650-327-0888
Fax: 650-327-5316

MEMBERS OF FIRM

Toby F. Montgomery Barbara P. Wright
Nathan C. Finch (1909-1990)

For full biographical listings, see the Martindale-Hubbell Law Directory

JOHN E. MILLER (AV)

250 Cambridge Avenue, Suite 102, 94306-1504
Telephone: 650-321-8886
Fax: 650-321-8998

(See Next Column)

ASSOCIATE

Matthew P. Pachkowski

Reference: Bank of the West.

For full biographical listings, see the Martindale-Hubbell Law Directory

PASADENA, Los Angeles Co.

LAGERLOF, SENECAL, BRADLEY, GOSNEY & KRUSE, LLP (AV)

301 North Lake Avenue, 10th Floor, 91101-4108
Telephone: 626-793-9400
FAX: 626-793-5900
Email: mail@lagerlof.com

MEMBERS OF FIRM

Joseph J. Burris (1913-1980)
Stanley C. Lagerlof (1915-1998)
H. Jess Senecal
Jack T. Swafford
John F. Bradley
Timothy J. Gosney
William F. Kruse
Thomas S. Bunn, III
Andrew D. Turner
Rebecca J. Thyne
James D. Ciampa

ASSOCIATE

Shaun O. Kwon

Representative Clients: Gallo Glass Company; Orthopaedic Hospital; North American Chemical Company; Palmdale Water District; Public Water Agencies Group; Ventura Port District; Walnut Valley Water District; Metric Construction Co., Inc.

For full biographical listings, see the Martindale-Hubbell Law Directory

RICHARD F. MILLER A PROFESSIONAL CORPORATION (AV)

Suite 511, 199 South Los Robles Avenue, 91101-2458
Telephone: 626-584-1400
Telecopier: 626-584-1447
URL: http://www.lawyers.com/rmillerlaw

Richard F. Miller

For full biographical listings, see the Martindale-Hubbell Law Directory

CAROL A. PETERS (AV)

221 East Walnut Street, Suite 136, 91101-1554
Telephone: 626-793-9383
Fax: 626-793-3552
URL: http://www.lawyers.com/elderhelp

For full biographical listings, see the Martindale-Hubbell Law Directory

PLEASANTON, Alameda Co.

JAMES J. PHILLIPS A PROFESSIONAL CORPORATION (AV)

4900 Hopyard Road, Suite 260, 94588
Telephone: 925-463-1980
Fax: 925-463-8656
Hayward, California Office: 1331 B Street, Suite 4, 94541.
Telephone: 510-886-2120.
Fax: 925-463-8656.

James J. Phillips

For full biographical listings, see the Martindale-Hubbell Law Directory

*SACRAMENTO,** Sacramento Co.

MICHAEL J. ANDERSON (AV)

425 University Avenue, Suite 210, 95825
Telephone: 916-921-2833
Fax: 916-921-2890
Email: mikeanderson@msn.com

For full biographical listings, see the Martindale-Hubbell Law Directory

DROBNY LAW OFFICES (AV)

2485 Natomas Park Drive, Suite 500, 95833
Telephone: 916-641-0526
FAX: 916-441-2352
Stockton, California Office: 7510 Shoreline Drive, Suite B-1, 95219.
Telephone: 209-464-3408.
Fax: 916-441-2352.

Mark S. Drobny

Leland J. Ellison
Todd R. Robie
Chris B. Knepshield
Leslie Ann Arnal
Lori A. Adasiewicz
Quinn Michael Jalli

For full biographical listings, see the Martindale-Hubbell Law Directory

Sacramento—Continued

WEBB, PATTERSON AND TAPELLA (AV)

906 G Street, Suite 630, 95814-1813
Telephone: 916-447-1675
Fax: 916-447-8009
Email: info@probateattorneys.com *URL:* http://www.probateattorneys.com

Borden D. Webb
Deborah K. Patterson
Carlena L. Tapella

For full biographical listings, see the Martindale-Hubbell Law Directory

TOSH G. YAMAMOTO A PROFESSIONAL CORPORATION (AV)

7201 South Land Park Drive, 95831
Telephone: 916-421-8455
Fax: 916-421-4312

Tosh G. Yamamoto
David James Richardson

For full biographical listings, see the Martindale-Hubbell Law Directory

*SAN BERNARDINO,** San Bernardino Co.

WILSON, BORROR, DUNN & DAVIS, LLP (AV)

Suite 307, The Bank of California Building, 255 North D Street, 92401
Telephone: 909-884-8855
Fax: 909-884-5161

MEMBERS OF FIRM

Fred A. Wilson (1886-1973)
Wm. H. Wilson (1915-1981)
James R. Dunn
Thomas M. Davis
Sarah L. Overton

ASSOCIATES

S. Mark Strain
C. Victor Wear

OF COUNSEL

Caywood J. Borror

Representative Clients: Travelers Insurance Co.; Rockwell International; Westinghouse Air Brake Co.; Goodyear Tire and Rubber Co.; Home Insurance Co.; Cities of: Redlands, Chino, Colton, San Bernardino, Upland, Yucapia and Corona; Lloyd's of London; Universal Health Services, Inc.-;Lawyer's Mutual Insurance; Unified School Districts of Rialto and Fontana .

For full biographical listings, see the Martindale-Hubbell Law Directory

*SAN DIEGO,** San Diego Co.

ALHADEFF CANNON ROSE SOLAR & PARKS, LLP (AV)

550 West "C" Street, Nineteenth Floor, 92101-3540
Telephone: 619-231-8700
Facsimile: 619-231-8323
Email: ksolar@acrsp.com
Temecula, California Office: The Tower Plaza, 27555 Ynez Road, Suite 203, 92591-4677.
Telephone: 909-699-9088.
Facsimile: 909-699-9878. Email: POBERHANSLEY@ACRSP.com
Los Angeles, California Office: Olympic Center, 11150 Olympic Boulevard, Suite 860, 90064.
Telephone: 310-914-4400.
Facsimile: 310-914-0030. Email: JODONNELL@ACRSP.com
Lafayette, California Office: Lafayette Terrace, 3697 Mount Diablo Boulevard, Suite 100, 94549.
Telephone: 925-283-1599.
Facsimile: 925-283-5847. Email: GMF-CA@MSN.com

PARTNERS

Samuel C. Alhadeff
Robert D. Rose
Jerry M. Cannon
Keith R. Solar
Robert J. Parks
Philip D. Oberhansley (Resident, Temecula, California Office)
Joseph L. Marshall
Leslie C. Detwiler
Glenn M. Feeley (Resident, Lafayette, California Office)
Thomas T. Lord
Madeline Clark Cahill
John L. O'Donnell, Jr. (Resident, Los Angeles, California Office)

OF COUNSEL

Craig S. Engstrand
Robert K. Edmunds
Charles F. Gorder, Sr.

ASSOCIATES

Michael J. Barry
Richard James Bayless
Craig V. Butler
Cyril J. Dantchev
Genie Harrison
S. Douglas Kerner
Frank J. Polek
Les W. Robertson
Traci M. Selby
Marjeta Duzevic Six

For full biographical listings, see the Martindale-Hubbell Law Directory

BRIERTON, JONES & JONES, LLP (AV)

2437 Second Avenue, 92101
Telephone: 619-696-7066
Fax: 619-696-6907
URL: http://www.lawyers.com/brierton&jones

(See Next Column)

MEMBERS OF FIRM

B. James Brierton
Jerilyn Satterfield Jones
Julie A. Jones

For full biographical listings, see the Martindale-Hubbell Law Directory

FERRETTE & SLATER, A LAW CORPORATION (AV)

16765 West Bernardo Drive Suite 150, 92127
Telephone: 858-487-9596; 619-233-7217
Facsimile: 858-487-9658
Email: law@ferretteslater.com

Victor J. Ferrette
Gary E. Slater
Gregory C. Alcorn
Timothy J. Truxaw

ASSOCIATE

Denise P. Blasband

For full biographical listings, see the Martindale-Hubbell Law Directory

FISCH, SPIEGLER, GINSBURG, LADNER & ATTARIAN, A PROFESSIONAL LAW CORPORATION (AV)

1551 Fourth Avenue, Suite 300, 92101-3184
Telephone: 619-234-1551
Telecopier: 619-234-1568
Email: FSGLA@AOL.com

Joseph J. Fisch
Mark A. Spiegler
Phillip L. Ginsburg
Karen M. Ladner
Peter J. Attarian, Jr.

For full biographical listings, see the Martindale-Hubbell Law Directory

DAVID L. HICKSON (AV)

8910 University Center Lane Suite 230, 92122
Telephone: 619-457-1100
Facsimile: 619-457-0109
Email: dhickson@mail.com
Email: dave@hickson.net *URL:* http://www.lawyers.com/dhickson

For full biographical listings, see the Martindale-Hubbell Law Directory

KENNERSON SCHWARTZ SEMERDJIAN & HAILE LLP (AV)

A Limited Liability Partnership
101 West Broadway, Suite 810, 92101
Telephone: 619-236-8821
Facsimile: 619-236-8827
URL: http://www.lawyers.com/ksshlaw

OF COUNSEL

Paul R. Kennerson

MEMBERS OF FIRM

Ross J. Schwartz
Dick A. Semerdjian
Jeffrey A. Haile

James R. Ballard
John K. Grant

For full biographical listings, see the Martindale-Hubbell Law Directory

MULVANEY, KAHAN & BARRY, A PROFESSIONAL CORPORATION (AV)

Seventeenth Floor, First National Bank Center, 401 West "A" Street, 92101-7994
Telephone: 619-238-1010
Fax: 619-238-1981
Email: mkb@mkblaw.com
Los Angeles, California Office: Union Bank Plaza, 445 South Figueroa Street, Suite 2600.
Telephone: 213-612-7765.
La Jolla, California Office: Suite 315, 875 Prospect Street, P.O. Box 1168.
Telephone: 619-454-1780.
Fax: 619-454-1792.
Orange, California Office: The Koll Center, 500 North State College Boulevard, Suite 440.
Telephone: 714-634-7069.
Fax: 714-939-8000.

James F. Mulvaney
Lawrence Kahan
Everett G. Barry, Jr.
Robert A. Linn
Paula Rotenberg
Melissa A. Blackburn
Mark R. Raftery
John A. Mayers
Robin L. Cahill
Kristin L. Yokomoto
Darren John Devlin

OF COUNSEL

Rex B. Beatty
Derrick W. Samuelson (Not admitted in CA)

Representative Clients: First Interstate Bank; Northern Trust Co.; San Diego Superior Court; United Negro College Fund, Inc.

For full biographical listings, see the Martindale-Hubbell Law Directory

San Diego—Continued

SOLOMON WARD SEIDENWURM & SMITH, LLP (AV)

1200 Wells Fargo Plaza, 401 B Street, 92101
Telephone: 619-231-0303
Telecopier: 619-231-4755
Email: mvafi@swsslaw.com *URL:* http://www.swsslaw.com

PARTNERS OF FIRM

Michael D. Breslauer
Cynthia L. Eldred
Lawrence J. Kaplan (P.C.)
Richard E. McCarthy
Edward J. McIntyre
Paul S. Metsch
Alison L. Pivonka
Harry J. Proctor (P.C.)
Jeffrey A. Schneider
Richard L. Seidenwurm (P.C.)
Jeffrey H. Silberman
Miguel A. Smith
Norman L. Smith
Herbert J. Solomon

ASSOCIATES

Daniel E. Gardenswartz
David T. Gluck
Amy Perkins Melden
Karl A. Sandoval
Kurt E. Scheuerman
Elizabeth A. Trevino

OF COUNSEL

Robert F. La Scala
William O. Ward, III (Retired)

For full biographical listings, see the Martindale-Hubbell Law Directory

WALTERS & WARD, A PROFESSIONAL CORPORATION (AV)

11665 Avena Place, Suite 203, 92128-2403
Telephone: 619-485-9045; 566-1480
FAX: 619-485-0398
Email: wtworkshop@aol.com *URL:* http://www.lawyers.com/walters&ward

Diane K. Ward (1939-1996)
R. Michael Walters

For full biographical listings, see the Martindale-Hubbell Law Directory

WINGERT GREBING BRUBAKER & RYAN LLP (AV)

A Limited Liability Partnership including Professional Corporations
One America Plaza, Seventh Floor, 600 West Broadway, 92101
Telephone: 619-232-8151
Facsimile: 619-232-4665
URL: http://www.wgbrlaw.com
Las Vegas, Nevada Office: Ryan Marks Johnson & Todd, 1120 Town Center Drive, Suite 200, 89144.
Telephone: 702-341-7870.
Fax: 702-341-8049.

MEMBERS OF FIRM

Charles R. Grebing (A Professional Corporation)
Alan K. Brubaker (A Professional Corporation)
Norman A. Ryan
James Goodwin
Shawn D. Morris
Robert M. Juskie
Dan H. Deuprey
Robert M. Caietti
Eileen Mulligan Marks
Christopher W. Todd
Robert L. Johnson
John S. Addams
Michael Sullivan
James J. Brown, Jr.
Terie M. Theis
Craig Gross

ASSOCIATES

Stephen C. Grebing
Brian P. Worthington
Marco B. Mercaldo
Solveig Store Deuprey
Kimberly Diane Howatt
Jay A. Kenyon
T. Steven Gregor
Jana M. Beck
Brad Lovelace

OF COUNSEL

William L. Todd, Jr.
John R. Wingert (A Professional Corporation)

LEGAL SUPPORT PERSONNEL

Carol C. Berry

Representative Clients: Angelic Entertainment; Becton Dickinson; Brookfield Homes Pacific Inc.; California Casualty; Columbia /HCI; Cooper. of Amer. Physicians; Concan Davidson Homes; Discover R. Insurance; Farmers Insurance; Guaranty National.

For full biographical listings, see the Martindale-Hubbell Law Directory

*SAN FRANCISCO,** San Francisco Co.

AVERY & ASSOCIATES (AV)

49 Geary Street, Suite 202, 94108-5727
Telephone: 415-954-4800
Fax: 415-954-4810
Email: LJA@averylegal.com

Luther J. Avery

OF COUNSEL

Mark J. Avery

LEGAL SUPPORT PERSONNEL

Matthew S. Avery

For full biographical listings, see the Martindale-Hubbell Law Directory

LAW OFFICES OF GARY D. BERGER (AV)

One Sansome Street, 19th Floor, 94104
Telephone: 415-731-2268
Fax: 415-642-7075
Email: GDBERGER@MSN.COM

For full biographical listings, see the Martindale-Hubbell Law Directory

LAW OFFICES OF ELIZABETH ANNE BIRD (AV)

One Embarcadero Center, Suite 1020, 94111-3600
Telephone: 415-956-6002
Fax: 415-981-0222
URL: http://www.lawyers.com/birdlaw
Email: eliza.bird@ebirdlaw.com *URL:* http://www.ebirdlaw.com

References: Bank of America; Union Bank of California; Mellon Trust of California.

For full biographical listings, see the Martindale-Hubbell Law Directory

G. WILLIAM FILLEY (AV)

5455 Anza Street, 94121
Telephone: 415-956-5912
Fax: 415-221-7965
Email: filleyatty@aol.com

For full biographical listings, see the Martindale-Hubbell Law Directory

FRIEDMAN, OLIVE, MCCUBBIN, SPALDING, BILTER, ROOSEVELT & MONTGOMERY, A PROFESSIONAL CORPORATION (AV)

22nd Floor, 425 California Street, 94104
Telephone: 415-434-1363
Facsimile: 415-434-1937
URL: http://www.fomlaw.com

K. Bruce Friedman
Donald J. McCubbin
Philip F. Spalding
D. Keith Bilter
Michael A. Roosevelt
George F. Montgomery II

Dale S. Adams

OF COUNSEL

William A. Seavey
Helen Olive Milowe

RETIRED

Jack H. Olive

For full biographical listings, see the Martindale-Hubbell Law Directory

MACINNIS, DONNER & KOPLOWITZ (AV)

Suite 222, 465 California Street, 94104
Telephone: 415-434-2400
FAX: 415-433-1917

MEMBERS OF FIRM

James Martin MacInnis (1914-1979)
Conrad Donner
Edward A. Koplowitz

For full biographical listings, see the Martindale-Hubbell Law Directory

STIMMEL, STIMMEL & SMITH, A PROFESSIONAL CORPORATION (AV)

100 Bush Street, Suite 850, 94104
Telephone: 415-392-2018
Fax: 415-391-2124
Email: stimmelpc@stimmel-law.com *URL:* http://www.stimmel-law.com

Norman S. Stimmel (1914-1991)
Lee D. Stimmel
Andrine K. Smith

OF COUNSEL

Jeffrey S. Rosen
Joanne M. Reming
Susan B. Jordan
Darrick T. Chase

For full biographical listings, see the Martindale-Hubbell Law Directory

*SAN JOSE,** Santa Clara Co.

FIORE LAW GROUP LLP (AV)

Bank of America Building, 101 Park Center Plaza, Suite 1150, 95113
Telephone: 408-293-3616
Facsimile: 408-293-0430
Email: flg@fiorelawgroup.com

Owen G. Fiore
John F. Ramsbacher

John W. Prokey

For full biographical listings, see the Martindale-Hubbell Law Directory

San Jose—Continued

HOPKINS & CARLEY, A LAW CORPORATION (AV)
Sixth Floor, 2 West Santa Clara Street, 95113-1824
Telephone: 408-286-9800
Facsimile: 408-998-4790
Mailing Address: P.O. Box 1469, San Jose, CA, 95109-1469
URL: http://www.hopkinscarley.com

John F. Hopkins
Robert D. Wenzel
Dunham B. Sherer
Anthony J. McCarthy
James M. Hager
Charles H. Packer

OF COUNSEL

Theodore J. Biagini

Jennifer M. Cunneen

For Complete List of Firm Personnel, See General Section

For full biographical listings, see the Martindale-Hubbell Law Directory

LICCARDO, ROSSI, STURGES & MCNEIL, A PROFESSIONAL LAW CORPORATION (AV)
1960 The Alameda, Suite 200, 95126-1493
Telephone: 408-244-4570
Fax: 408-244-3294
URL: http://www.LRSM.com

Salvador A. Liccardo
Ronald R. Rossi
Robert S. Sturges
R. Donald McNeil
David M. Hamerslough
Susan R. Reischl
Craig Needham
Laura Liccardo
Samuel A. Chuck
Richard B. Gullen

Robert C. Colyar
Paul Salvatore Liccardo
Thomas Eamon McNeil

For full biographical listings, see the Martindale-Hubbell Law Directory

MILLER, MORTON, CAILLAT & NEVIS (AV)
50 West San Fernando Street, Suite 1300, 95113-2413
Telephone: 408-292-1765
Telecopier: 408-292-4484
URL: http://www.mmcn-law.com

Richard W. Morton (1916-1975)
Charles V. Caillat (1920-1990)
Harvey C. Miller (1906-1993)

MEMBERS OF FIRM

David L. Nevis
Francis J. Hughes
Peter A. Kline
Stevan C. Adelman
Joseph A. Scanlan, Jr.
Carolyn Tobiason Stuart
William K. Hurley
Peter V. Dessau

OF COUNSEL

Nancy F. Symons

ASSOCIATES

Kathryn E. Barrett
Katherine S. Pak
David I. Kornbluh
Christopher J. Hersey
Julie Neale Meyer

Representative Clients: Trammell Crow Residential; Joe Kerley Lincoln Mercury Co.; Milligan News Co.; Joseph George Distributors; Santa Clara Dental Society; Bay Apartment Communities; Hathaway-Dinwiddie Group.

For full biographical listings, see the Martindale-Hubbell Law Directory

*SAN LUIS OBISPO,** San Luis Obispo Co.

ANDRE, MORRIS & BUTTERY, A PROFESSIONAL LAW CORPORATION (AV)
1102 Laurel Lane, P.O. Box 730, 93406-0730
Telephone: 805-543-4171
Fax: 805-543-0752
Email: amb@amblaw.com *URL:* http://www.amblaw.com

Michael J. Morris
Dennis D. Law
Scott W. Wall

References: Bank of America National Trust and Savings Assn. (San Luis Obispo Main Branch); Mid-State Bank (San Luis Obispo).

For full biographical listings, see the Martindale-Hubbell Law Directory

J. K. GEORGE & ASSOCIATES (AV)
694 Santa Rosa, P.O. Box 12710, 93406
Telephone: 805-544-3394
Facsimile: 805-528-5598
Email: info@jkgeorge.com *URL:* http://www.lawyers.com/georgelaw
Los Osos, California Office: P.O. Box 6129.
Telephone: 805-528-3394.
Telecopier: 805-528-5598.

J. K. George

(See Next Column)

Anne C. Cyr

For full biographical listings, see the Martindale-Hubbell Law Directory

SAN MATEO, San Mateo Co.

BASYE & GOLDEN (AV)
520 South El Camino Real, Suite 700, 94402
Telephone: 650-342-2500
Fax: 650-342-9560
Email: jpgolden@abanet.org

MEMBERS OF FIRM

Paul E. Basye (1901-1991)
John P. Golden

For full biographical listings, see the Martindale-Hubbell Law Directory

THIRKELL & CRETAN (AV)
181 Second Avenue, Suite 625, P.O. Box 190, 94401
Telephone: 650-348-1016
Facsimile: 650-348-2968
Email: mail@thirkell-law.com

MEMBERS OF FIRM

Edward D. Thirkell
Clifford V. Cretan
Trent E. Wright
Julia E. Lingys

For full biographical listings, see the Martindale-Hubbell Law Directory

*SANTA ANA,** Orange Co.

SWANSON AND GIESER, A PROFESSIONAL CORPORATION (AV)
4 Hutton Centre Drive, Suite 200, 92707-5770
Telephone: 714-755-3500
Fax: 714-755-3505
URL: http://www.lawyers.com/swansongieserlaw
San Diego, California Office: 600 B Street, Suite 2120, 92101.
Telephone: 619-686-6100.
Fax: 619-686-6105.

C. Brent Swanson (1941-1998)
Thomas M. Gieser

Elaine B. Alston

For full biographical listings, see the Martindale-Hubbell Law Directory

*SANTA BARBARA,** Santa Barbara Co.

ANGLE, CARLSON, GOLDRICK & ROBERTS (AV)
A Partnership including a Professional Corporation
200 East Carrillo Street, Suite 310, 93101
Telephone: 805-963-7400
Fax: 805-963-7610

Robert O. Angle
Arthur W. Carlson (A P.C.)
Miles T. Goldrick
Paul A. Roberts

For full biographical listings, see the Martindale-Hubbell Law Directory

MULLEN & HENZELL, L.L.P. (AV)
A California registered limited liability partnership
112 East Victoria Street, Post Office Drawer 789, 93102-0789
Telephone: 805-966-1501
FAX: 805-966-9204
Email: mh@mullenlaw.com

MEMBERS OF FIRM

Jay L. Beckerman
Lawrence T. Sorensen

Representative Clients: California State Auto Association (No. Calif. Auto Club); Interinsurance Exchange of the Automobile Club of Southern California; Fireman's Fund Insurance Co.; State Farm Fire & Casualty Co.; State Farm Mutual Automobile Insurance Co.

For full biographical listings, see the Martindale-Hubbell Law Directory

SANTA MONICA, Los Angeles Co.

HAIGHT, BROWN & BONESTEEL, L.L.P. (AV)
A Partnership including Professional Corporations
1620 26th Street, Suite 4000 North, P.O. Box 680, 90404
Telephone: 310-449-6000
Telecopier: 310-829-5117
Telex: 705837
URL: http://www.hbblaw.com
Santa Ana, California Office: Suite 900, 5 Hutton Centre Drive.
Telephone: 714-754-1100.
Telecopier: 714-754-0826.
Riverside, California Office: California Tower, 3737 Main Street, Suite 800.
Telephone: 909-341-8300.
Fax: 909-341-8309.
San Francisco, California Office: 101 Bush Street, 27th Floor.
Telephone: 415-986-7700.
Fax: 415-986-6945.

(See Next Column)

HAIGHT, BROWN & BONESTEEL L.L.P.—*Continued*

San Diego, California Office: 101 West Broadway, Suite 1000.
Telephone: 619-595-5583.
Fax: 619-595-7873.

MEMBER OF FIRM

Ross E. Winn

For full biographical listings, see the Martindale-Hubbell Law Directory

*SANTA ROSA,** Sonoma Co.

ANDERSON, ZEIGLER, DISHAROON, GALLAGHER & GRAY, PROFESSIONAL CORPORATION (AV)

50 Old Courthouse Square, 5th Floor, P.O. Box 1498, 95404
Telephone: 707-545-4910
Fax: 707-544-0260
Other Santa Rosa, California Office: 6641 Oakmont Drive, 95409.
Telephone: 707-539-3880.
Petaluma, California Office: 17 Keller Street, 94952.
Telephone: 707-763-0937.

Edwin C. Anderson, Jr.
Kirt F. Zeigler
Robert Disharoon
Barbara Detrich Gallagher
Margaret M. Elliott
David G. Bjornstrom
Robert S. Rutherfurd
Christopher M. Mazzia
Tricia A. Shindledecker
Jeremy L. Olsan

Wendy D. Whitson
Daniel E. Post
Mary Catherine Doherty
Lisa Yoshida
Matthew E. Hannum

OF COUNSEL

John J. King, Jr.

LEGAL SUPPORT PERSONNEL

Edward J. Gibson
Daniel B. Flock (Director of Information)

For full biographical listings, see the Martindale-Hubbell Law Directory

*STOCKTON,** San Joaquin Co.

RICHARD W. KONIG (AV)

6702 Inglewood Avenue, Suite A, 95207-3872
Telephone: 209-474-1251
Email: rwkatty@aol.com

TORRANCE, Los Angeles Co.

FINER, KIM & STEARNS (AV)

An Association of Professional Corporations
City National Bank Building, 3424 Carson Street, Suite 500, 90503
Telephone: 310-214-1477
Telecopier: 310-214-0764
Email: finerkimstearns@pobox.com *URL:* http://www.finerkimstearnslaw.com

W. A. Finer (A Professional Corporation)

LEGAL SUPPORT PERSONNEL

Marcia E. Talbert

For Complete List of Firm Personnel, See General Section

For full biographical listings, see the Martindale-Hubbell Law Directory

MCGAUGHEY & SPIRITO (AV)

2377 Crenshaw Boulevard, Suite 310, 90501
Telephone: 310-787-8783
Fax: 310-787-9937

MEMBERS OF FIRM

Terence C. McGaughey
Joseph P. Spirito Jr.

ASSOCIATE

Steven Spitzer

Reference: Bay Cities National Bank.

For full biographical listings, see the Martindale-Hubbell Law Directory

MOORE, BRYAN & SCHROFF, A LAW CORPORATION (AV)

Suite 490 California Bank & Trust Tower, 21515 Hawthorne Boulevard, 90503
Telephone: 310-540-8855
Fax: 310-316-1307
Email: mail@cmoorelaw.com

Christopher M. Moore
Sharon A. Bryan
Rebecca Lee Tomlinson Schroff

Kimberly K Davidson

For full biographical listings, see the Martindale-Hubbell Law Directory

UPLAND, San Bernardino Co.

ALTHOUSE & MCDONOUGH (AV)

Second Floor, Metro Commerce Bank Building, 188 North Euclid Avenue, P.O. Box 698, 91785
Telephone: 909-985-9828
Telecopier: 909-985-3282
Email: AltandMcD@aol.com *URL:* http://www.Alt-McD.com

Charles S. Althouse
Elizabeth A. McDonough

References: Metro Commerce Bank, Upland, California; Upland Bank, Upland, California.

For Complete List of Firm Personnel, See General Section

For full biographical listings, see the Martindale-Hubbell Law Directory

*VENTURA,** Ventura Co.

BLEUEL & MUIRHEAD (AV)

2225 Sperry Avenue, Suite 1200, 93003
Telephone: 805-650-1818
Fax: 805-650-9071
URL: http://www.bleuelmuirhead.com
Email: gavzdad@jetlink.net *URL:* http://www.lawyers.com/bleuelmuirhead

MEMBERS OF FIRM

Bartley S. Bleuel
Michael L. Muirhead

ASSOCIATE

Maria Capritto

For full biographical listings, see the Martindale-Hubbell Law Directory

FAIRFIELD & FREEMAN (AV)

290 Maple Court, Suite 200, 93003
Telephone: 805-644-7458
Fax: 805-644-4325
Email: mail@venturalaw.com *URL:* http://www.venturalaw.com

MEMBERS OF FIRM

William D. Fairfield
Wilfred J. Freeman
Kevin L. Rose

For full biographical listings, see the Martindale-Hubbell Law Directory

TAYLOR MCCORD, A LAW CORPORATION (AV)

721 East Main Street, P.O. Box 1477, 93002
Telephone: 805-648-4700
Email: vtafamlaw@aol.com

Richard L. Taylor
Robert L. McCord, Jr.
David L. Praver

Patrick Cherry
Susan D. Siple
Rebbecca F. Calderwood

LEGAL SUPPORT PERSONNEL

PARALEGALS

Stephanie Gibson
Adele Rubino (Certified Legal Assistant, California Advanced Specialist)
Diane Lovato

For full biographical listings, see the Martindale-Hubbell Law Directory

COLORADO

*ASPEN,** Pitkin Co.

OATES, KNEZEVICH & GARDENSWARTZ, P.C. (AV)

Aspen Plaza Building, 3rd Floor, 533 East Hopkins Avenue, 81611
Telephone: 970-920-1700
Fax: 970-920-1121
Email: ohkg@rof.net

Leonard M. Oates
Richard A. Knezevich
Ted D. Gardenswartz
David B. Kelly

David B. Mueller

OF COUNSEL

John Thomas Kelly
Michael Feigenbaum

For full biographical listings, see the Martindale-Hubbell Law Directory

AURORA, Arapahoe & Adams Cos.

DAVID W. KIRCH, P.C. (AV)

2260 South Xanadu Way, Suite 320, 80014
Telephone: 303-671-7726
Fax: 303-671-7679
Email: dkirch@lawyernet.com

David W. Kirch

For full biographical listings, see the Martindale-Hubbell Law Directory

*BOULDER,** Boulder Co.

DOTY & SHAPIRO, P.C. (AV)

1720 Fourteenth Street, Suite 100, 80302-6353
Telephone: 303-443-3234
Telecopier: 303-443-3438

H. McGregor Doty, II Mark R. Shapiro

For full biographical listings, see the Martindale-Hubbell Law Directory

*COLORADO SPRINGS,** El Paso Co.

BELTZ, EDWARDS & SABO, L.L.P. (AV)

128 South Tejon, Suite 310, 80903
Telephone: 719-634-6620
Fax: 719-634-3142
Email: BES__LLP@aol.com *URL:* http://www.lawyers.com/beslaw
Other Colorado Springs, Colorado Office: 729 South Cascade, 80903.
Telephone: 719-473-4444.
Fax: 719-444-0186.

Daniel P. Edwards W. Thomas Beltz
John W. Sabo, III

ASSOCIATE

Daniel A. West

For full biographical listings, see the Martindale-Hubbell Law Directory

WILTON W. COGSWELL, III (AV)

Suite 1020, Alamo Corporate Center, 102 South Tejon Street, 80903
Telephone: 719-473-1448
Facsimile: 719-473-1449
Email: wcogs3@aol.com

OF COUNSEL

Wilton W. Cogswell, IV

For full biographical listings, see the Martindale-Hubbell Law Directory

HENRY B. EASTLAND, P.C. (AV)

455 East Pikes Peak Avenue, Suite 100, 80903
Telephone: 719-578-0035
Fax: Available Upon Request

Henry B. Eastland

Representative Clients: Colorado Springs Credit Union; Pikes Peak Credit Union; Farmers State Bank of Calhan; Interstate Gas Credit Union; Cañon National Bank.
References: Norwest Bank of Colorado Springs-East, N.A.; U.S. Bank.

For full biographical listings, see the Martindale-Hubbell Law Directory

*CRAIG,** Moffat Co.

WILLIAM V. LAWRENCE (AV)

510 Breeze Street, P.O. Box 1131, 81626
Telephone: 970-824-4730
Fax: 970-824-2367

Reference: Colorado Community First National Bank.

For full biographical listings, see the Martindale-Hubbell Law Directory

*DENVER,** Denver Co.

HARRY L. ARKIN & ASSOCIATES, P.C. (AV)

Suite 2750 Lincoln Center, 1660 Lincoln Street, 80264
Telephone: 303-863-8400
Telefax: 303-832-4703
Email: harkin00@counsel.com
Email: hnikra@aol.com
London, England Office: Verulam Chambers, Peer House, 8-14 Verulam Street, WCIX 8LZ.
Telephone: 071 813-2400.
Fax: 071 405-3870.

Harry L. Arkin

Michael B. Levy

(See Next Column)

LEGAL SUPPORT PERSONNEL

Patricia A. Hanson Karen R. Loveland

For full biographical listings, see the Martindale-Hubbell Law Directory

ATLASS PROFESSIONAL CORPORATION (AV)

3665 Cherry Creek North Drive Suite 100, 80209-3712
Telephone: 303-329-5900
Fax: 303-329-3291
Email: tatlass@atlass.com

Theodore B. Atlass

Carol Buchanan Lay

For full biographical listings, see the Martindale-Hubbell Law Directory

BERENBAUM, WEINSHIENK & EASON, P.C. (AV)

Suite 2600 Republic Plaza, 370 17th Street, 80202
Telephone: 303-825-0800
Facsimile: 303-629-7610
Email: berenbaum1@aol.com *URL:* http://www.BWELaw.com

Daniel S. Duggan Dan A. Sciullo
Steven C. Hoth Ronald I. Zall

Michael James Cook

Representative Clients: Home Depot; Sprint Spectrum, L.P.; Town of Vail, Colorado; First Union Corporation; City of Englewood, Colorado; Oakwood Homes; Karman, Inc.; Wells Fargo Bank, N.A.; Berkshire Life Insurance Co.; Trinity Ventures.

For full biographical listings, see the Martindale-Hubbell Law Directory

JOHN DEBRUYN LAW OFFICES (AV)

2100 East Fourteenth Avenue, 80206
Telephone: 303-377-0707
Telecopier: 303-321-2655
Email: jdebruyn@debruyn.com *URL:* http://www.debruyn.com

For full biographical listings, see the Martindale-Hubbell Law Directory

CHARLES W. ENNIS (AV)

Suite 200 201 Fillmore Street, 80206-5015
Telephone: 303-322-2300
Fax: 303-321-3518
Email: hasklaw@gateway.net *URL:* http://www.lawyers.com/cwennislaw

Reference: Norwest Bank Colorado, N.A.

For full biographical listings, see the Martindale-Hubbell Law Directory

MICHAEL L. GILBERT (AV)

Suite 850, 50 South Steele Street, 80209-2809
Telephone: 303-320-4580
Fax: 303-320-0648
Email: mgilbert@csn.net

For full biographical listings, see the Martindale-Hubbell Law Directory

GILL PROFESSIONAL CORPORATION (AV)

Suite 610, 5000 South Quebec, 80237-2705
Telephone: 303-770-3040
Facsimile: 303-770-3041

Lawrence D. Gill

For full biographical listings, see the Martindale-Hubbell Law Directory

GLATSTEIN & O'BRIEN, LLP (AV)

2696 South Colorado Boulevard, Suite 350, 80222-5944
Telephone: 303-757-4342
Facsimile: 303-757-4570
Email: goattys@att.net *URL:* http://www.lawyers.com/g&o

MEMBERS OF FIRM

M. Carl Glatstein Marcia G. O'Brien

For full biographical listings, see the Martindale-Hubbell Law Directory

GODDARD & GODDARD, P.C. (AV)

Suite 203, 1900 Wazee Street, 80202
Telephone: 303-292-3228
Fax: 303-292-1956
Email: goddard@dimensional.com

Susan B. Goddard Jo Anna Goddard

LEGAL SUPPORT PERSONNEL

Theresa D. Cooley (Paralegal) Barbara J. Van Vliet (Paralegal)

For full biographical listings, see the Martindale-Hubbell Law Directory

Denver—Continued

GORSUCH KIRGIS LLP (AV)

Tower 1, Suite 1000, 1515 Arapahoe Street, 80202
Telephone: 303-376-5000
Fax: 303-376-5001

PARTNERS

Kenneth G. Christianssen | Stephen M. Brainerd

OF COUNSEL

William C. McGehee

LEGAL SUPPORT PERSONNEL

Martha Reed

For full biographical listings, see the Martindale-Hubbell Law Directory

GUTHERY & RICKLES, P.C. (AV)

Cherry Creek Plaza II, 650 South Cherry Street Suite 1000, 80246-1812
Telephone: 303-320-5889
Fax: 303-320-5890

Peter C. Guthery | Stephen P. Rickles

A list of Representative Clients that have provided written authorization will be furnished upon request.

For full biographical listings, see the Martindale-Hubbell Law Directory

HOLME ROBERTS & OWEN LLP (AV)

Suite 4100, 1700 Lincoln, 80203
Telephone: 303-861-7000
Telecopier: 303-866-0200
Email: hro@hro.com *URL:* http://www.hro.com
Boulder, Colorado Office: Suite 400, 1401 Pearl Street.
Telephone: 303-444-5955.
Telecopier: 303-444-1063.
Colorado Springs, Colorado Office: Suite 1300, 90 South Cascade Avenue.
Telephone: 719-473-3800.
Telecopier: 719-633-1518.
Salt Lake City, Utah Office: Suite 1100, 111 East Broadway.
Telephone: 801-521-5800.
Telecopier: 801-521-9639.
London, England Office: Heathcoat House, 3rd Floor, 20 Savile Row.
Telephone: 011-44-171-494-5600.
Telecopier: 011-44-171-287-9344.

PARTNERS OF FIRM

Charles B. Bruce, Jr.
James E. Bye
Judson W. Detrick
Steve L. Gaines (Colorado Springs Office)
Donald J. Hopkins
William S. Huff
McKay Marsden (Managing Partner, Salt Lake City Office)
Stephanie M. Tuthill
John A. Warnick (Not admitted in CO)

ASSOCIATES

Merry H. Balson
Pattie S. Christensen (Salt Lake City Office)
Michelle M. Rose-Hughes
Thomas E. Yearout

For Complete List of Firm Personnel, See General Section

For full biographical listings, see the Martindale-Hubbell Law Directory

HUTCHINS & ASSOCIATES LLC (AV)

1675 Broadway, Suite 2750, 80202
Telephone: 303-893-6500; 1-800-678-3363
Fax: 303-893-4200
Email: info@hutchinslaw.com

Steven R. Hutchins

Allen Sparkman | Michael R. Stiff
Andria Nicole Economy

For full biographical listings, see the Martindale-Hubbell Law Directory

KATZ, LOOK & MOISON, PROFESSIONAL CORPORATION (AV)

1120 Lincoln Street, Suite 1100, 80203
Telephone: 303-832-1900
Fax: 303-863-0412

Michael M. Katz
Harley K. Look, Jr.
Peter R. Moison
Kathryn A. Reeves

Brian E. Onorato
Melisa A. Vogel
Arthur T. DiMeo
Delwyn G. Haroldson
Barbara J. Stauch

SPECIAL COUNSEL

Ogborn, Summerlin & Ogborn, L.L.C., Denver, Colorado

For full biographical listings, see the Martindale-Hubbell Law Directory

MYER, SWANSON, ADAMS & WOLF, P.C. (AV)

The Colorado State Bank Building, 1600 Broadway, Suite 1480, 80202-4915
Telephone: 303-866-9800
Facsimile: 303-866-9818

Fred E. Neef (1910-1986)
Rendle Myer (1929-1999)
Allan B. Adams
Thomas J. Wolf

John M. Anderson | Karen S. Proc

OF COUNSEL

Robert Swanson

Representative Clients: The Oppenheimer Funds; Panorama Series Fund; The Centennial Trusts; Mile High Chapter of American Red Cross; Master Lease; Heartland Management Co.; Kan-Build of Colorado, Inc.
Reference: The Colorado State Bank and Trust of Denver.

For full biographical listings, see the Martindale-Hubbell Law Directory

NICHOLLS & ASSOCIATES, P.C. (AV)

1725 Gaylord Street, Suite 100, 80206-1208
Telephone: 303-329-9700, Ext. 104
Fax: 303-329-6950

Jon S. Nicholls

Stephen C. Nicholls

OF COUNSEL

Bruce R. Wyatt

Representative Clients: Little Grizzly Creek Ranch, Inc.; Clarkson Land, LLC; Lifestyle Homes, Inc.; Wheeler Realty Co., Inc; College Inn, Inc.; Dora's Mexican Restaurant, Inc.; Ramada Inn; Life Care Centers of America; First Industrial Realty.
Reference: Norwest Bank, Colorado, N.A.

For full biographical listings, see the Martindale-Hubbell Law Directory

M. KENT OLSEN (AV)

650 South Cherry Street, Suite 1250, 80246
Telephone: 303-329-4670
Facsimile: 303-329-4671

Representative Clients: Colorado Association of Homes & Services for the Aging; Allied Jewish Housing; Karis, Inc.; Colorado State Bank; Bank of Cherry Creek.

For full biographical listings, see the Martindale-Hubbell Law Directory

PREEO, SILVERMAN & GREEN, P.C. (AV)

1401 17th Street, Suite 800, 80202
Telephone: 303-296-4440
Fax: 303-296-3330

Robert L. Preeo
Eldon E. Silverman
Jersey M. Green
Martin J. Green
Gilbert R. Egle
Marilyn W. McWilliams
Timothy Kyle Jordan
Brandon S Culter

For full biographical listings, see the Martindale-Hubbell Law Directory

L. WILLIAM SCHMIDT, JR., P.C. (AV)

Suite 1700, 1050 17th Street, 80265
Telephone: 303-436-9121
Fax: 303-436-9648

L. William Schmidt, Jr.

Julia Griffith McVey

Reference: Norwest Bank Colorado, N.A.

For full biographical listings, see the Martindale-Hubbell Law Directory

SHERMAN & HOWARD L.L.C. (AV)

Attorneys and Counselors at Law
633 Seventeenth Street, Suite 3000, 80202
Telephone: 303-297-2900
Telecopier: 303-298-0940
Colorado Springs, Colorado Office: Suite 1500, 90 South Cascade Avenue, 80903.
Telephone: 719-475-2440.
Las Vegas, Nevada Office: Swendseid & Stern, a member in Sherman & Howard L.L.C., 317 Sixth Street, 89101.
Telephone: 702-387-6073.
Reno, Nevada Office: Swendseid & Stern, a member in Sherman & Howard L.L.C., 50 West Liberty Street, Suite 660, 89501.
Telephone: 702-323-1980.

Douglas M. Cain
Duane F. Wurzer
David Thomas III
Carol V. Berger

(See Next Column)

SHERMAN & HOWARD L.L.C., *Denver—Continued*

COUNSEL
Bridget K. Sullivan

Joseph M. Dencker
Wendy G. Ramsey
Gregory T. Densen

Representative Clients: BACE Industries, LLC; Flatiron Structures Co. LLC; Hanifen, Imhoff Inc.; Hathaway Corp.; J.D. Edwards & Co.; Newmont Gold Company; Public Employees' Retirement Assn.; Tele-Communications, Inc.; United Artists Theatre Circuit, Inc.; U.S. West Communications, Inc.

For Complete List of Firm Personnel, See General Section
For full biographical listings, see the Martindale-Hubbell Law Directory

ZISMAN AND INGRAHAM, P.C. (AV)

Suite 650, 3773 Cherry Creek Drive North, 80209
Telephone: 303-320-0023
Fax: 303-320-0034
Email: zisming377@aol.com

Sanford Zisman
James F. Ingraham

For full biographical listings, see the Martindale-Hubbell Law Directory

*GREELEY,** Weld Co.

BREGA & WINTERS P.C. (AV)

1100 Tenth Street, Suite 402, 80631
Telephone: 970-352-4805
Fax: 970-352-6547
Denver, Colorado Office: One Norwest Center, 1700 Lincoln Street, Suite 2222.
Telephone: 303-866-9400.
Fax: 303-861-9109.

Jerry D. Winters
Pamela A. Shaddock
William W. Hughes

Julie Scroggins Frantz
Bradley D. Laue

For full biographical listings, see the Martindale-Hubbell Law Directory

LAKEWOOD, Jefferson Co.

POLIDORI, GEROME, FRANKLIN AND JACOBSON, L.L.C. (AV)

Suite 300, 550 South Wadsworth Boulevard, 80226
Telephone: 303-936-3300
Fax: 303-936-0125

R. Jerold Gerome

For full biographical listings, see the Martindale-Hubbell Law Directory

*LAMAR,** Prowers Co.

SHINN, STEERMAN & SHINN (AV)

200 West Elm Street, P.O. Box 390, 81052
Telephone: 719-336-4313
Fax: 719-336-4315
URL: http://www.lawyers.com/shinnsteerman&shinn

MEMBERS OF FIRM
Carl M. Shinn
Wendy S. Shinn
Donald L. Steerman

Counsel for: Amity Canal; District 67 Ditch Assn.; County of Cheyenne, Colorado; County of Kiowa, Colorado; Ragsdale Farms, Inc.; Scherler Farms; Hatcher Farms, Inc.; Buffalo Canal Co.; Four States Feedyard, Inc.; Ordway Feedyard Limited, Ltd.

For full biographical listings, see the Martindale-Hubbell Law Directory

CONNECTICUT

CHESHIRE, New Haven Co.

WINTERS & FORTE (AV)

Waverly Professional Park, 315 Highland Avenue, Suite 102, P.O. Box 844, 06410
Telephone: 203-272-2927
Fax: 203-271-1222
Email: david.wayne.winters@snet.net *URL:* http://www.snetyp.com/wintersforte

MEMBERS OF FIRM
David Wayne Winters
Michael C. Forte

(See Next Column)

ASSOCIATE
Anthony R. DePaolo

A List of Representative Clients will be furnished upon request.
References: Bank of Boston, Connecticut; LaFayette American Bank & Trust Co.

For full biographical listings, see the Martindale-Hubbell Law Directory

DANBURY, Fairfield Co.

DRISCOLL, TALARICO, FRIZZELL, OLIVO & DRISCOLL (AV)

142 Deer Hill Avenue, 06810-7727
Telephone: 203-792-8333
Facsimile: 203-778-9570
Email: driscoll@javanet.com
Bethel, Connecticut Office: 235 Greenwood Avenue, 06801-2186.
Telephone: 203-744-5000; 743-5556.
Facsimile: 203-798-7790.
Southbury, Connecticut Office: Three Pomperaug Office Park, Suite 203, P.O. Box 252, 06488-0252.
Telephone: 203-264-9650.
Facsimile: 203-798-2175.

Julius J. Bielizna (1914-1988)
Kenneth H. Murray (1905-1984)
Herbert B. Wanderer (1902-1979)
James C. Driscoll, Jr. (Resident, Southbury Office)
Robert N. Talarico
Thomas A. Frizzell
Steven M. Olivo
James C. Driscoll, III (Resident, Bethel Office)
Jerome A. Mayer
Richard W. Hanna
D. Joseph Lane, Jr.
George S. Papazoglou

For full biographical listings, see the Martindale-Hubbell Law Directory

DARIEN, Fairfield Co.

MILLAR & AMBRETTE (AV)

23 Old King's Highway South, 06820-1267
Telephone: 203-655-7931
FAX: 203-656-2055

MEMBERS OF FIRM
Samuel D. B. Millar, Jr.
L. Conrad Ambrette

OF COUNSEL
Peter M. Ryan

ASSOCIATE
Patricia Moreland Gross

For full biographical listings, see the Martindale-Hubbell Law Directory

RUCCI, BURNHAM, CARTA & EDELBERG, LLP (AV)

800 Post Road, P.O. Box 1107, 06820
Telephone: 203-655-7695
Facsimile: 203-655-4302
URL: http://www.rbce.com
Stamford, Connecticut Office: 6 Landmark Square, Suite 470.
Telephone: 203-359-5637.

MEMBERS OF FIRM
Joseph J. Rucci, Jr.
Paul H. Burnham
Mark R. Carta
Paul B. Edelberg
William M. Carello
Robert F. Maslan, Jr.

ASSOCIATES
Colette C. Symon
Karen K. Linder
Joanna F. Bowen
David J. Rucci
Sandra J. Akoury

OF COUNSEL
Ian R. Crawford
James C. Dempsey
Lawrence H. Reilly
Alberto N. Moris (Not admitted in CT)

For full biographical listings, see the Martindale-Hubbell Law Directory

FAIRFIELD, Fairfield Co.

BRAUNSTEIN & TODISCO, LLC (AV)

One Eliot Place, 06430
Telephone: 203-254-1118
Telecopier: 203-254-2453
Email: sam@btlawfirm.com *URL:* http://www.btlawfirm.com

Samuel L. Braunstein
Amy E. Todisco

Reference: People's Bank.

For full biographical listings, see the Martindale-Hubbell Law Directory

GREENWICH, Fairfield Co.

ALBERT, WARD & JOHNSON, P.C. (AV)

125 Mason Street, P.O. Box 1668, 06836
Telephone: 203-661-8600
Telecopier: 203-661-8051

(See Next Column)

ALBERT, WARD & JOHNSON P.C.—*Continued*

Tom S. Ward, Jr.
Scott R. Johnson
Jane D. Hogeman
Howard R. Wolfe
Christopher A. Kristoff
Vicki K. Comberiati

OF COUNSEL

David Albert
C. Robton Perelli-Minetti

For full biographical listings, see the Martindale-Hubbell Law Directory

HOLLAND KAUFMANN & BARTELS, LLC (AV)

289 Greenwich Avenue, 06830-6595
Telephone: 203-869-5600
Fax: 203-869-4648

Alexander J. Holland
Charles B. Kaufmann, III
Philip H. Bartels
Harold R. Burke
Jean Mills Aranha
Lori E. Romano
John C. Fusco

OF COUNSEL

Beth K. Hansson

For full biographical listings, see the Martindale-Hubbell Law Directory

*HARTFORD,** Hartford Co.

COPP & BERALL, LLP (AV)

55 Farmington Avenue, Suite 703, 06105
Telephone: 860-249-5261
Fax: 860-947-6382
Email: cb@connix.com

MEMBERS OF FIRM

Frank S. Berall
Mark H. Neikrie
Suzanne Brown Walsh

Darren M. Wallace

OF COUNSEL

Belton A. Copp

References: Fleet Bank, N.A.; BankBoston.

For full biographical listings, see the Martindale-Hubbell Law Directory

GORDON, MUIR AND FOLEY, LLP (AV)

Hartford Square North, Ten Columbus Boulevard, 06106-5123
Telephone: 860-525-5361
Telecopier: 860-525-4849
Email: admin@gmflaw.com *URL:* http://www.gmflaw.com

MEMBERS OF FIRM

William S. Gordon, Jr. (1946-1956)
George Muir (1939-1976)
Edward J. Foley (1955-1983)
Peter C. Schwartz
John J. Reid
John H. Goodrich, Jr.
R. Bradley Wolfe
Jon Stephen Berk
William J. Gallitto
Gerald R. Swirsky
Robert J. O'Brien
Philip J. O'Connor
Kenneth G. Williams
Mary Ann Santacroce
Mary Anne Alicia Charron
Andrew J. Hern
Reneé W. Dwyer
Patty G. Swan

ASSOCIATES

Doreen West Amata
Howard A. Steinman
Erik E. Roberts
Christopher J. Casciani

Reference: People's Bank.

For full biographical listings, see the Martindale-Hubbell Law Directory

GOULD, KILLIAN & WYNNE (AV)

280 Trumbull Street, 25th Floor, 06103-3595
Telephone: 860-278-1270
Telecopier: 860-244-9290

MEMBERS OF FIRM

Samuel Gould (1905-1994)
Robert K. Killian
Francis J. Wynne
Martin A. Gould
Mark W. Baronas
William F. Healey
Nancy E. Gould
Robert O. Wynne

For full biographical listings, see the Martindale-Hubbell Law Directory

SHIPMAN & GOODWIN LLP (AV)

One American Row, 06103-2819
Telephone: 860-251-5000
Telecopier: 860-251-5099
Email: www@goodwin.com *URL:* http://shipman-goodwin.com
Lakeville, Connecticut Office: 12 Porter Street.
Telephone: 203-435-2539.
Stamford, Connecticut Office: One Landmark Square.
Telephone: 203-324-8100.

(See Next Column)

MEMBERS OF FIRM

Stuyvesant K. Bearns (Lakeville Office)
James T. Betts
Coleman H. Casey
Stephen K. Gellman

ASSOCIATE

Jennifer L. Veshia

OF COUNSEL

Warren S. Randall
George C. Jepsen (Stamford Office)

For Complete List of Firm Personnel, See General Section

For full biographical listings, see the Martindale-Hubbell Law Directory

SOROKIN, GROSS & HYDE, P.C. (AV)

One Corporate Center, 06103
Telephone: 860-525-6645
Fax: 860-522-1781
Email: sorokin@sorokinlaw.com
Simsbury, Connecticut Office: 720 Hopmeadow Street.
Telephone: 860-651-9348.
Rocky Hill, Connecticut Office: 2360 Main Street.
Telephone: 860-563-9305.
Fax: 860-529-6931.

Alan S. Parker
Lewis Rabinovitz
Barrie K. Wetstone

Margaret M. Murphy

OF COUNSEL

Charles R. Moore, Jr.
Ethel Silver Sorokin

For Complete List of Firm Personnel, See General Section

For full biographical listings, see the Martindale-Hubbell Law Directory

MILFORD, New Haven Co.

HARLOW, ADAMS & FRIEDMAN, P.C. (AV)

300 Bic Drive, 06460-3508
Telephone: 203-878-0661
Fax: 203-878-9568
Email: attorney@quidproquo.com

William D. Harlow (1921-1988)
George W. Adams, III
Dana Eric Friedman
Theodore H. Shumaker
Stephen P. Wright
Michael P. A. Williams
Eric R. Gaynor
Joseph A. Kubic
James M. Nugent
James R. Winkel

For full biographical listings, see the Martindale-Hubbell Law Directory

*NEW HAVEN,** New Haven Co.

COAN, LEWENDON, ROYSTON & GULLIVER, LLC (AV)

495 Orange Street, 06511
Telephone: 203-624-4756
Fax: 203-865-3673

MEMBERS OF FIRM

Richard M. Coan
Whitney M. Lewendon
Christopher M. Royston
Carl T. Gulliver
Timothy D. Miltenberger

OF COUNSEL

E. Huntington Deming

Reference: Peoples Bank.

For full biographical listings, see the Martindale-Hubbell Law Directory

NEW LONDON, New London Co.

DUPONT AND RADLAUER, L.L.P. (AV)

Captain's Walk, 165 State Street, Suite 502, P.O. Box 710, 06320-0710
Telephone: 860-447-0090
Fax: 860-437-7442
Email: radlaw@snet.net *URL:* http://www.lawyers.com/dupontandradlauer

MEMBERS OF FIRM

Ralph P. Dupont
Barbara J. Radlauer

For full biographical listings, see the Martindale-Hubbell Law Directory

WALLER, SMITH & PALMER, P.C. (AV)

52 Eugene O'Neill Drive, P.O. Box 88, 06320
Telephone: 860-442-0367
Telecopier: 860-447-9915
Email: wspmain@snet.net *URL:* http://www.snetyp.com/wallersmithpalmer
Old Lyme Office: 103 Halls Road.
Telephone: 860-434-8063.
Telecopier: 860-434-9452. Email: wspol@snet.net

(See Next Column)

WALLER, SMITH & PALMER P.C., *New London—Continued*

William W. Miner
Robert P. Anderson, Jr.
Robert W. Marrion
Philip M. Johnstone
Charles C. Anderson

General Counsel For: Town of East Lyme.
Counsel For: Citizens Bank of Connecticut; Soneco/Northeastern, Inc.; The Nature Conservancy; Fleet Bank.
Local Counsel For: McCue Mortgage Co.; Citicorp Mortgage; U.S. Department of Housing and Urban Development.

For Complete List of Firm Personnel, See General Section

For full biographical listings, see the Martindale-Hubbell Law Directory

SOUTHPORT, Fairfield Co.

BRODY, WILKINSON AND OBER, P.C. (AV)

2507 Post Road, 06490
Telephone: 203-319-7100
Fax: 203-254-1772

Seth O. L. Brody
Peter Wilkinson
Frank Fritz Ober
S. Giles Payne
James E. Rice
William J. Britt
Barbara S. Miller
Robert L. Teicher
Ronald B. Noren
Peter T. Mott
Thomas J. Walsh, Jr.
Diane F. Martucci
Seth L. Cooper
Douglas R. Brown
Charles S. Brody (1894-1976)

OF COUNSEL

Bruce E. Dillingham
Roy W. Moore, III

For full biographical listings, see the Martindale-Hubbell Law Directory

STAMFORD, Fairfield Co.

CACACE, TUSCH & SANTAGATA (AV)

777 Summer Street, P.O. Box 15859, 06901-0859
Telephone: 203-327-2000
Telecopier: 203-353-3392
Email: lawcts@aol.com

MEMBERS OF FIRM

Michael J. Cacace
Mark P. Santagata
Paul T. Tusch
Richard S. Fisher

OF COUNSEL

Kenneth A. DellaRocco
Eric D. Grayson

ASSOCIATES

Edward F. Nemchek
Alice Ann Fitzpatrick
Ronald E. Kowalski II
Aamina Ahmad
Demaris Page Hetrick
Patrick L. Poeschl

LEGAL SUPPORT PERSONNEL

Eva L. Chan
Cynthia L. Mammone

For full biographical listings, see the Martindale-Hubbell Law Directory

CURTIS, BRINCKERHOFF & BARRETT, P.C. (AV)

666 Summer Street, 06901-1416
Telephone: 203-324-6777
Telecopier: 203-324-9621
Email: info@curtisbb.com

T. Ward Cleary (1916-1988)
Frederick M. Tobin
John Wayne Fox
Ward Frank Cleary
James D'Alton Murphy
Randolph T. Lovallo

OF COUNSEL

John D. Hertz
Jane F. Donovan
Richard L. Brinckerhoff
Patricia M. Gaug

Susan L. Stratton
Derek Gilman
Michael P. Murray
John J. Louizos

Counsel for: The F. A. Bartlett Tree Expert Co.; Town of Darien; Miller Automobile Corp.; Bolliger, Inc.; Titan Sports; People's Bank, Bridgeport; Fleet Bank; Federal Deposit Insurance Co.; William Pitt Foundation; Wood Logan Associates.

For full biographical listings, see the Martindale-Hubbell Law Directory

FOX & FOX, L.L.P. (AV)

607 Bedford Street, 06901
Telephone: 203-348-7773
Fax: 203-324-0057

Gerald M. Fox, Jr.
Gerald M. Fox, III

For full biographical listings, see the Martindale-Hubbell Law Directory

WOFSEY, ROSEN, KWESKIN & KURIANSKY, LLP (AV)

600 Summer Street, 06901
Telephone: 203-327-2300
Fax: 203-967-9273

(See Next Column)

MEMBERS OF FIRM

Abraham Wofsey (1915-1944)
Michael Wofsey (1927-1951)
David M. Rosen (1926-1967)
Julius B. Kuriansky (1952-1992)
Sydney C. Kweskin (1946-1998)
Monroe Silverman
Howard C. Kaplan
Edward M. Kweskin
David M. Cohen
Marshall Goldberg
Stephen A. Finn
Judith Rosenberg
Mark H. Henderson
Steven D. Grushkin
Matthew J. Forstadt
Steven M. Frederick

OF COUNSEL

Saul Kwartin
Emanuel Margolis
Anthony R. Lorenzo

SPECIAL COUNSEL

Day R. Shields

ASSOCIATES

Joseph Brachfeld
Eric M. Higgins
William A. Harrison
Daniel M. Young
Angelo A. Ziotas

Representative Clients: Banque Paribas; Benenson Realty; Cellular Information Systems, Inc.; The Chase Manhattan Bank; First County Bank; Hartford Provision Co.; Louis Dreyfus Corp.; Norwalk Federation of Teachers; People's Bank; Ridgeway Shopping Center.

For full biographical listings, see the Martindale-Hubbell Law Directory

WEST HARTFORD, Hartford Co.

BERMAN, BOURNS & CURRIE, LLC (AV)

970 Farmington Avenue, P.O. Box 271837, 06127-1837
Telephone: 860-232-4471
Fax: 860-523-4605

John A. Berman
Courtney B. Bourns

Mary Beth Anderson
Steven R. Dembo
Annemarie Burnham

OF COUNSEL

John K. Currie

For full biographical listings, see the Martindale-Hubbell Law Directory

WESTPORT, Fairfield Co.

BLAZZARD, GRODD & HASENAUER, P.C. (AV)

943 Post Road East, P.O. Box 5108, 06881
Telephone: 203-226-7866
Telecopier: 203-454-4855
Lauderdale-By-the-Sea Office: Suite 207, W. Tradewinds Avenue, 33308.
Telephone: 954-771-6667.
Facsimile: 954-771-7689. E-Mail: BGHFL@AOL.COM

Norse N. Blazzard
Leslie E. Grodd
Judith A. Hasenauer
William E. Hasenauer
Raymond A. O'Hara, III
Lynn Korman Stone

Peter L. Cejas (Not admitted in CT)

For full biographical listings, see the Martindale-Hubbell Law Directory

EDWARD H. DIETRICH (AV)

125 Main Street, 06880
Telephone: 203-222-7600
Fax: 203-222-1830
Email: ehdlaw@webquill.com *URL:* http://www.lawyers.com/dietrichlaw
New York, N.Y. Office: 780 Third Avenue, 12th Floor, 10017.
Telephone: 212-599-5075.

Reference: The Bank of Darien at Westport.

For full biographical listings, see the Martindale-Hubbell Law Directory

HERMENZE & MARCANTONIO (AV)

62 Post Road West, P.O. Box 2747, 06880-0747
Telephone: 203-226-6552
Fax: 203-226-6035
Email: hmlaw@aol.com

David R. Hermenze
Edward Marcantonio

For full biographical listings, see the Martindale-Hubbell Law Directory

NEVAS, NEVAS & CAPASSE (AV)

246 Post Road East, P.O. Box 791, 06881
Telephone: 203-226-1211
Fax: 203-454-3419
Email: law@nevascapasse.com

Bernard A. Nevas (1900-1942)
Leo Nevas
Edward J. Capasse
Jamie Kay Gerard
Andrew B. Nevas

(See Next Column)

NEVAS, NEVAS & CAPASSE—*Continued*

OF COUNSEL

Stephen Tate — Stephen E. Nevas

For full biographical listings, see the Martindale-Hubbell Law Directory

RONALD L. SHEIMAN (AV)

1804 Post Road East, 06880
Telephone: 203-259-0599
Telecopier: 203-255-2570

For full biographical listings, see the Martindale-Hubbell Law Directory

DELAWARE

*WILMINGTON,** New Castle Co.

CONNOLLY BOVE LODGE & HUTZ LLP (AV)

1220 Market Street, P.O. Box 2207, 19899-2207
Telephone: 302-658-9141
Telecopier: 302-658-5614
Email: cblhlaw@cblhlaw.com *URL:* http://www.cblhlaw.com

James M. Mulligan, Jr. — Charles J. Durante
Richard David Levin — Anne Love Barnett

For Complete List of Firm Personnel, See General Section

For full biographical listings, see the Martindale-Hubbell Law Directory

POTTER ANDERSON & CORROON LLP (AV)

Hercules Plaza, 1313 N. Market Street, P.O. Box 951, 19899-0951
Telephone: 302-984-6000
Fax: 302-658-1192
URL: http://www.attys.pacdelaware.com

MEMBERS OF FIRM

Leonard S. Togman — Mary E. Copper
Scott E. Waxman

ASSOCIATE

John A. Ciccarone

For Complete List of Firm Personnel, See General Section

For full biographical listings, see the Martindale-Hubbell Law Directory

SCHLUSSER & REIVER, P.A. (AV)

1700 West 14th Street, 19806
Telephone: 302-655-8181
Fax: 302-655-8190

Robert E. Schlusser — Joanna Reiver
George W. Kern, V

For full biographical listings, see the Martindale-Hubbell Law Directory

DISTRICT OF COLUMBIA

WASHINGTON, D.C. Co.

LAW OFFICES OF BINSTOCK, TORCHINSKY AND ASSOCIATES, P.C. (AV)

1140 Connecticut Avenue, N.W., Suite 703, 20036
Telephone: 301-657-5555
Fax: 301-657-9871
Email: shelbin@erols.com *URL:* http://www.lawyers.com/binstock_torchinsky
Chevy Chase, Maryland Office: 5454 Wisconsin Avenue, Suite 1340.
Telephone: 301-657-5555.
Fax: 301-657-9871.

Shelton M. Binstock — David B. Torchinsky

OF COUNSEL

Andrew S. Unger — George R. Adams

For full biographical listings, see the Martindale-Hubbell Law Directory

CAPLIN & DRYSDALE, CHARTERED (AV)

One Thomas Circle, N.W., 20005
Telephone: 202-862-5000
Cable Address: "Capdale"
Telex: 904001 CAPL UR WSH
Fax: 202-429-3301
URL: http://www.caplindrysdale.com
New York, N.Y. Office: 399 Park Avenue, 36th Floor.
Telephone: 212-319-7125.
Fax: 212-644-6755.

Mortimer M. Caplin
Thomas A. Troyer
David N. Webster
H. David Rosenbloom
Peter Van N. Lockwood
Richard W. Skillman
Patricia G. Lewis
Bernard S. Bailor
Albert G. Lauber, Jr.
Julie W. Davis
Trevor W. Swett III
James E. Salles
Craig A. Sharon
Catherine E. Livingston
Seth M. Green
Douglas D. Drysdale
Ralph A. Muoio
Elihu Inselbuch (Resident, New York Office)
Cono R. Namorato
Daniel B. Rosenbaum
Richard E. Timbie
Stafford Smiley
Scott D. Michel
Kent A. Mason
Robert A. Boisture
Milton Cerny
Matthew W. Frank
Jessica L. Katz
Christopher S. Rizek

Nathan D. Finch
Douglas N. Varley
Neal M. Kochman
Jason K. Bortz (Not admitted in DC)
April J. Adams (Not admitted in DC)
Elizabeth M. Sellers
Lloyd H. Mayer
Rita C. Tobin (Resident, New York Office)
H. Carter Hood (Not admitted in DC)

OF COUNSEL

Robert H. Elliott, Jr. — Myron C. Baum
Ann C. McMillan

For full biographical listings, see the Martindale-Hubbell Law Directory

CROSS, MURPHY, SMUCK & HOUSTON (AV)

1350 Connecticut Avenue, N.W., Suite 300, 20036
Telephone: 202-393-8668
Telecopier: 202-833-2351
Email: anwalt1350@aol.com *URL:* http://www.lawyers.com/cms&hlaw

MEMBERS OF FIRM

John W. Cross (1902-1971) — John C. Smuck
James Russell Murphy (1905-1986) — Stuart E. Houston

Reference: Crestar Bank, N.A.

For full biographical listings, see the Martindale-Hubbell Law Directory

THE FALK LAW FIRM PLLC (AV)

A Professional Limited Liability Corporation
Suite 260 One Westin Center, 2445 M Street, N.W., 20037
Telephone: 202-833-8700
Telecopier: 202-872-1725
Email: FalkLaw@erols.com *URL:* http://www.falklawfirm.com

James H. Falk, Sr. — Stephen A. Best
James H. Falk, Jr. — John M. Falk

OF COUNSEL

Pierre E. Murphy — Elizabeth C. Collins

For full biographical listings, see the Martindale-Hubbell Law Directory

RENEE ISLA FOX (AV)

1725 K Street N.W. 12th Floor, Suite 1202, 20006
Telephone: 202-429-0444
Fax: 202-429-4930
Email: rif@reneefox.com *URL:* http://www.lawyers.com/reneeislafoxlaw

For full biographical listings, see the Martindale-Hubbell Law Directory

LAW OFFICES OF GARFINKLE & ASSOCIATES (AV)

1150 Connecticut Avenue, N.W., Suite 505, 20036
Telephone: 202-457-0200
Facsimile: 202-857-0550
URL: http://www.lawyers.com/washingtonartlaw

Ann M. Garfinkle

ASSOCIATE

Laura A. Possessky

OF COUNSEL

Austin P. Frum (Retired)

For full biographical listings, see the Martindale-Hubbell Law Directory

Washington—Continued

IVINS, PHILLIPS & BARKER, CHARTERED (AV)

Suite 600, 1700 Pennsylvania Avenue, N.W., 20006
Telephone: 202-393-7600
Fax: 202-393-7601; 347-4256
Email: IPB@ipbtax.com *URL:* http://www.ipbtax.com

H. Stewart Dunn, Jr.
Carroll J. Savage
Eric R. Fox
William L. Sollee
Carol K. Nickel
Leslie Jay Schneider
Robert H. Wellen
Kevin P. O'Brien
Michael F. Solomon
Daniel B. Stone
Patrick J. Smith
Michael R. Huffstetler
Laurie E. Keenan
Jeffrey E. Moeller
Steven H. Witmer
Rosina B. Barker
Claude B. Stansbury

Jodi H. Epstein

OF COUNSEL

Jay W. Glasmann

For full biographical listings, see the Martindale-Hubbell Law Directory

QUINN, RACUSIN & GAZZOLA, CHARTERED (AV)

1400 K Street, N.W. Suite 1010, 20005-2403
Telephone: 202-842-9300
Facsimile: 202-682-0148
URL: http://www.qrg-law.com
Email: qrg@qrg-law.com *URL:* http://www.lawyers.com/quinnracusin&gazzola

Aaron J. Racusin (1915-1998)
John H. Quinn, Jr.
Robert A. Gazzola
Susan Yoder Torres

Robin Duncan Culbertson

LEGAL SUPPORT PERSONNEL

Kevin Srivastava (Paralegal)
Francesca West Watson (Paralegal)

For full biographical listings, see the Martindale-Hubbell Law Directory

RAVDIN & WOFFORD, A PROFESSIONAL CORPORATION (AV)

1700 K Street, N.W., Suite 650, 20006
Telephone: 202-429-5551
Fax: 202-429-5553
URL: http://www.lawyers.com/ravdin&wofford

Linda J. Ravdin
Cindy Lynn Wofford

Kelly J. Capps
Lisa N. Seltzer (Not admitted in DC)

For full biographical listings, see the Martindale-Hubbell Law Directory

THOMPSON, O'DONNELL, MARKHAM, NORTON & HANNON (AV)

The Southern Building, 805 Fifteenth Street, N.W., Suite 705, 20005
Telephone: 202-289-1133
Facsimile: 202-289-0275
Email: Jude@mtolympus.ari.net

John Jude O'Donnell
Julian E. Markham, Jr.
Randell Hunt Norton
James W. Greene
J. Michael Hannon
Kenneth G. Stallard

ASSOCIATES

Brooke A. Pinkerton
Matthew W. Carlson
Michele L. Bulger

OF COUNSEL

James F. Bromley

Representative Clients: CNA Insurance Companies; Washington Mutual Investors Fund; FMB Trust Company, N.A.; Bernard F. Locraft, Civil Engineers, Washington, D. C.
References: Franklin National Bank; The First National Bank of Maryland; NationsBank.

For full biographical listings, see the Martindale-Hubbell Law Directory

FLORIDA

AVENTURA, Dade Co.

NELSON & ASSOCIATES, P.A. (AV)

One Turnberry Place 19495 Biscayne Boulevard, Suite 609, 33180-2320
Telephone: 305-932-2000
Telefax: 305-932-6585
URL: http://www.estaxlawyers.com

(See Next Column)

Barry A. Nelson

Rosario Ferrero Carr
Marcia E. Levine

OF COUNSEL

Richard B. Comiter

For full biographical listings, see the Martindale-Hubbell Law Directory

BOCA RATON, Palm Beach Co.

LAW OFFICES OF CARTER & THOMAS LLP (AV)

1200 North Federal Highway, Suite 312, 33432
Telephone: 561-368-9900
Broward 954-427-0933
Fax: 561-368-0293
Email: carterboca@aol.com

John E. Carter
Donald Joseph Thomas

Colleen M. Stiger

For full biographical listings, see the Martindale-Hubbell Law Directory

DICKENSON, MURDOCH, REX AND SLOAN, CHARTERED (AV)

Suite 410 Compson Financial Center, 980 North Federal Highway, 33432
Telephone: 561-391-1900
Facsimile: 561-391-1933

David B. Dickenson
Richard A. Murdoch
Robert H. Rex
Barbara A. Sloan

For full biographical listings, see the Martindale-Hubbell Law Directory

MARY SUE DONOHUE (AV)

Suite 418 Atrium Financial Center, 1515 North Federal Highway, 33432
Telephone: 561-368-5226
Fax: 561-368-9316
Email: marysue@gate.net *URL:* http://www.lawyers.com/marysuedonohue

ASSOCIATE

Christopher Gagic

OF COUNSEL

George Weinstein

For full biographical listings, see the Martindale-Hubbell Law Directory

STEVEN I. GREENWALD, P.A. (AV)

Boca Palm Professional Plaza, 6971 North Federal Highway, Suite 105, 33487
Telephone: 561-994-5560
Facsimile: 561-994-5629

Steven I. Greenwald

OF COUNSEL

Brandon J. Douglas

For full biographical listings, see the Martindale-Hubbell Law Directory

HUNT, COOK, RIGGS, MEHR & MILLER, P.A. (AV)

2200 Corporate Boulevard, N.W. Suite 401, 33431
Telephone: 561-997-9223
Telecopier: 561-997-6224
Email: admin@huntcook.com *URL:* http://www.huntcook.com

Robert J. Hunt
Joseph R. Cook
David A. Riggs
Ryna E. Mehr
Lawrence J. Miller
Andrew M. Gross
Susan E. Greenberg

David A. Greene
Sonja Trom Eayrs
Benjamin A. Jablow
Holly M. O'Neill

OF COUNSEL

Andrea G. Alpern

For full biographical listings, see the Martindale-Hubbell Law Directory

KEELEY, HAYES, DUDLEY & GARRETT (AV)

A Partnership of Professional Associations
Suite 314 Peninsula Plaza, 2424 North Federal Highway, 33431
Telephone: 561-392-4300
Telecopier: 561-392-4409

MEMBERS OF FIRM

Rusley C. Meeker (1931-1995)
Everett H. Dudley, Jr., (P.A.)
Joseph F. Keeley (P.A.)
James B. Hayes (P.A.)
Eugene S. Garrett
Stephen Mahle (P.A.)
Stacey Leigh Burnston

Approved Attorneys for: Attorneys' Title Insurance Fund; Chicago Title Insurance Co.

(See Next Column)

KEELEY, HAYES, DUDLEY & GARRETT—*Continued*

Reference: NCNB National Bank of Florida; Bank America; Sun Trust Bank.

For full biographical listings, see the Martindale-Hubbell Law Directory

RONALD T. MARTIN P.A. (AV)

Suite 200, 7000 West Palmetto Park Road, 33433
Telephone: 561-338-4100
Fax: 561-338-9086
Email: RonTMartin@aol.com

Ronald T. Martin

For full biographical listings, see the Martindale-Hubbell Law Directory

SCHROEDER & LARCHE, P.A. (AV)

One Boca Place, Suite 319-A, 2255 Glades Road, 33431-7383
Telephone: 561-241-0300
Broward: 954-421-0878
Telecopier: 561-241-0798
URL: http://www.lawyers.com/schroeder&larche

Michael A. Schroeder
W. Lawrence Larche

For full biographical listings, see the Martindale-Hubbell Law Directory

BOYNTON BEACH, Palm Beach Co.

NICHOLAS H. HAGOORT, JR., P.A. (AV)

Woolbright Corporate Center, Suite 360, 1901 South Congress Avenue, 33426
Telephone: 561-369-1010
FAX: 561-369-1254
Email: nhagoort@aol.com

Nicholas H. Hagoort, Jr.

Reference: SunTrust.

For full biographical listings, see the Martindale-Hubbell Law Directory

*BRADENTON,** Manatee Co.

GRIMES GOEBEL GRIMES HAWKINS & GLADFELTER, P.A. (AV)

The Professional Building, 1023 Manatee Avenue West, P.O. Box 1550, 34206
Telephone: 941-748-0151
Fax: 941-748-0158
Email: ggghg@gte.net
Tampa, Florida Office: Old Hyde Park Village, 1509 West Swann Avenue, Suite 275.
Telephone: 813-258-2557.
Fax: 813-258-2327.

William C. Grimes
Caleb J. Grimes

For full biographical listings, see the Martindale-Hubbell Law Directory

CORAL GABLES, Dade Co.

HENDRICKS & HENDRICKS (AV)

310 Alhambra Circle, 33134
Telephone: 305-445-3692
Fax: 305-446-8439

MEMBERS OF FIRM

R. A. Hendricks (1868-1963)
B. E. Hendricks (1904-1978)
Robert A. Hendricks

For full biographical listings, see the Martindale-Hubbell Law Directory

DAVIE, Broward Co.

WILLIAM A. SNYDER (AV)

7931 S.W. 45th Street, 33328
Telephone: Broward: 954-475-1139
Fax: 954-475-2634
Email: wasnyder@juno.com. *URL:* http://www.lawyers.com/estate-planning-lawyer

ASSOCIATE

Michele A. Maracini

For full biographical listings, see the Martindale-Hubbell Law Directory

DAYTONA BEACH, Volusia Co.

LANDIS, GRAHAM, FRENCH, HUSFELD, SHERMAN & FORD, P.A. (AV)

Formerly Hull, Landis, Graham & French
543 South Ridgewood Avenue, 32114
Telephone: 904-252-4717
Fax: 904-253-7352
Email: firm@landispa.com *URL:* http://www.landispa.com
De Land, Florida Office: 145 East Rich Avenue, P.O. Box 48.
Telephone: 904-734-3451.
Deltona, Florida Office: 204 Medical Arts Center, 1555 Saxon Boulevard.
Telephone: 407-574-1461.
Fax: 407-574-0242.

Erskine W. Landis (1900-1967)
John L. Graham (1905-1978)
Thorwald J. Husfeld (1926-1995)
Richard S. Graham
William E. Sherman
Sam N. Masters

Carol Lumb Allen (Resident)
Janet M. Strickland

OF COUNSEL

J. Compton French (Retired)

Counsel for: School Board of Volusia County; Walmart Stores, Inc.; Delco Oil, Inc.; West Volusia Hospital Authority; South Florida Natural Gas Co.; Florida Public Utilities Co.; Volusia County Industrial Development Authority; Florida United Methodist Children's Home: Volusia County Educational Facilities Authority.

For full biographical listings, see the Martindale-Hubbell Law Directory

DEERFIELD BEACH, Broward Co.

PATTERSON & HARMON, P.A. (AV)

665 S.E. 10th Street, 33441
Telephone: 954-421-7700
Fax: 954-421-7956
Email: gpbh@mindspring.com

George A. Patterson

Representative Clients: Butler Properties, Ltd.; Powerline Development, Inc.; Rivertown Apartments, Inc.; Rivertown Manor Condominium Association; Reliance Enterprises; Ransco Development, Inc.
Approved Attorneys for: Attorneys' Title Insurance Fund; Chicago Title Insurance Co.
Reference: First Union National Bank of Florida.

For Complete List of Firm Personnel, See General Section

For full biographical listings, see the Martindale-Hubbell Law Directory

C. RICHARD SHAMEL, JR. (AV)

Hauser Building, 212 North Federal Highway, 33441
Telephone: 954-428-3700
Fax: 954-428-3701
Email: Shamel@worldnet.att.net

Reference: Broward County Court Guardianship Program.

For full biographical listings, see the Martindale-Hubbell Law Directory

*DELAND,** Volusia Co.

LANDIS, GRAHAM, FRENCH, HUSFELD, SHERMAN & FORD, P.A. (AV)

Formerly Hull, Landis, Graham & French
145 East Rich Avenue, P.O. Box 48, 32721-0048
Telephone: 904-734-3451
Fax: 904-736-1350
Email: firm@landispa.com *URL:* http://www.landispa.com
Daytona Beach, Florida Office: 543 South Ridgewood Avenue, 32114.
Telephone: 904-252-4717.
Fax: 904-258-7352.
Deltona, Florida Office: 204 Medical Arts Center, 1555 Saxon Boulevard.
Telephone: 407-574-1461.
Fax: 407-574-0242.

Erskine W. Landis (1900-1967)
John L. Graham (1905-1978)
Thorwald J. Husfeld (1926-1995)
William E. Sherman
Richard S. Graham (Daytona Beach Office)
William A. Ottinger (Deltona Office)
Joe G. Dykes, Jr.
Frank A. Ford, Jr.
Sam N. Masters (Daytona Beach Office)

Edwin Channing Coolidge, Jr.
Carol Lumb Allen (Resident, Daytona Beach Office)
Janet M. Strickland
Steven N. Gosney

(See Next Column)

LANDIS, GRAHAM, FRENCH, HUSFELD, SHERMAN & FORD P.A., *DeLand—Continued*

OF COUNSEL

Frank A. Ford, Sr. J. Compton French (Daytona Beach Office; Retired)

Counsel for: School Board of Volusia County; Walmart Stores, Inc.; Delco Oil, Inc.; West Volusia Hospital Authority; South Florida Natural Gas Co.; Florida Public Utilities Co.; Volusia County Industrial Development Authority; Florida United Methodist Children's Home; Volusia County Educational Facilities Authority.

For full biographical listings, see the Martindale-Hubbell Law Directory

DELRAY BEACH, Palm Beach Co.

ROBERT M. ARLEN, P.A. (AV)

110 East Atlantic Avenue, Suite 330, 33444
Telephone: 561-279-1880
Telefax: 561-278-1995

Robert M. Arlen

For full biographical listings, see the Martindale-Hubbell Law Directory

DELTONA, Volusia Co.

LANDIS, GRAHAM, FRENCH, HUSFELD, SHERMAN & FORD, P.A. (AV)

204 Medical Arts Center, 1555 Saxon Boulevard, 32725
Telephone: 407-574-1461
Fax: 407-574-0242
Email: firm@landispa.com *URL:* http://www.landispa.com
Daytona Beach, Florida Office: 543 South Ridgewood Avenue, 32114.
Telephone: 904-252-4717.
Fax: 904-253-7352.
De Land, Florida Office: 145 East Rich Avenue, P.O. Box 48.
Telephone: 904-734-3451.

William A. Ottinger

Counsel for: School Board of Volusia County; Walmart Stores, Inc.; Delco Oil, Inc.; West Volusia Hospital Authority; South Florida Natural Gas Co.; Florida Public Utilities Co.; Volusia County Industrial Development Authority; Florida United Methodist Children's Home; Volusia County Educational Facilities Authority.

For full biographical listings, see the Martindale-Hubbell Law Directory

DESTIN, Okaloosa Co.

MILLER & ASSOCIATES (AV)

415 Mountain Drive, Suite 3, 32541
Telephone: 850-837-3860
Fax: 850-837-6158
Email: mbpa@cybertron.com

J. Jerome Miller

Toni L. Craig

For full biographical listings, see the Martindale-Hubbell Law Directory

ENGLEWOOD, Sarasota & Charlotte Cos.

BATSEL, MCKINLEY, ITTERSAGEN, GUNDERSON & BERNTSSON, P.A. (AV)

Suite 204 Manor Pointe Professional Center, 1861 Placida Road, 34223
Telephone: 941-474-7713
Telefax: 941-474-8276
Email: bmi@ewol.com
Port Charlotte, Florida Office: 18401 Murdock Circle. 33948.
Telephone: 941-627-1000.
Telefax: 941-255-0684.

C. Guy Batsel (Resident, Port Charlotte and Englewood Offices)
Scott D. Ittersagen
Miko P. Gunderson
Thomas P. McLennon

For full biographical listings, see the Martindale-Hubbell Law Directory

*FORT LAUDERDALE,** Broward Co.

CAMP & CAMP, P.A. (AV)

Suite 1501 One East Broward Boulevard, 33301
Telephone: 954-524-8111
FAX: 954-524-2661
Email: JDCAMPLAW@AOL.COM

James D. Camp, Jr. James D. Camp, III

General Counsel for: Sun Trust Bank/South Florida, N.A., Trust Division, Broward Community College; Steel Fabricators, Inc.; Steel Joists, Inc.; LaGasse Pool Construction Co.; BRDG-Tndr Corp.
Representative Clients: Amp, Inc.; Ed Morse Chevrolet, Inc.; Gulfstream Pump and Equipment Co.; Broward Community College.

(See Next Column)

For full biographical listings, see the Martindale-Hubbell Law Directory

ROBERT A. DRESSLER (AV)

1215 East Broward Boulevard, Suite 201, 33301
Telephone: 954-523-9595
Fax: 954-527-0150
Mailing Address: P.O. Box 2425, Fort Lauderdale, FL, 33301-2425
Email: dresslerra@compuserve.com *URL:* http://www.lawyers.com/dresslerlaw

For full biographical listings, see the Martindale-Hubbell Law Directory

FRIEDRICH & FRIEDRICH, P.A. (AV)

Northern Trust Bank Building, Suite 202, 2601 East Oakland Park Boulevard, 33306
Telephone: 954-564-1245
Fax: 954-563-5079

J. Peter Friedrich J. Peter Friedrich, Jr.

Approved Attorneys for: Northern Trust Bank of Florida; SunBank of S. Florida, NA.; NationsBank; Merrill Lynch Trust Company of Florida.

For full biographical listings, see the Martindale-Hubbell Law Directory

KELLEY, HERMAN & SMITH (AV)

Suite 206, 1401 East Broward Boulevard, 33301
Telephone: 954-462-7806
Fax: 954-522-0396

MEMBERS OF FIRM

Patrick G. Kelley
Bruce K. Herman
Jeffrey B. Smith

Approved Attorneys for: Commonwealth Land Title Insurance Co.; Attorney's Title Insurance Fund.

For full biographical listings, see the Martindale-Hubbell Law Directory

LEONARD & MORRISON (AV)

Tenth Floor, 4875 North Federal Highway, P.O. Box 11025, 33339
Telephone: 954-776-3600
Fax: 954-776-3609

MEMBERS OF FIRM

William F. Leonard
Richard W. Morrison
C. Glenn Leonard

General Counsel for: Coral Ridge Golf Course, Inc.; Gill Hotels Co.; Sheraton Yankee Clipper Hotel; Royal Petroleum, Inc.
Representative Client: Plimpton Trusts.
Reference: Nations Bank; Union Bank of Florida.

For full biographical listings, see the Martindale-Hubbell Law Directory

KENNETH R. MIKOS, P.A. (AV)

2780 East Oakland Park Boulevard, 33306
Telephone: 954-566-7200
Facsimile: 954-566-1568

Kenneth R. Mikos

Douglas F. Hoffman

Special Counsel to: Fort Lauderdale Civil Service Board.

For full biographical listings, see the Martindale-Hubbell Law Directory

*FORT MYERS,** Lee Co.

AVERY, WHIGHAM & WINESETT, P.A. (AV)

Corner of First and Hendry Streets, 2248 First Street, P.O. Box 610, 33902-0610
Telephone: 941-334-7040
Fax: 941-334-6258
Email: awwpa@ibm.net *URL:* http://www.lawyers.com/awwpa

Richard W. Winesett
Robert A. Winesett
Dennis L. Avery
James M. Costello
John L. Pilarski

OF COUNSEL

Dwight A. Whigham

For full biographical listings, see the Martindale-Hubbell Law Directory

DEBOEST, KNUDSEN, STOCKMAN, WISEMAN, DECKER & DRYDEN, P.A. (AV)

1415 Hendry Street, P.O. Box 1470, 33902-1470
Telephone: 941-334-1381
Telecopier: 941-334-0266
Email: dkswlaw@gate.net
Naples, Florida Office: 600 Fifth Avenue South, Suite 301, 34102.
Telephone: 941-263-5040.
Fax: 941-263-6944.

(See Next Column)

DEBOEST, KNUDSEN, STOCKMAN, WISEMAN, DECKER & DRYDEN P.A.—
Continued

Arthur K. Knudsen, Jr. (Retired)
Richard D. DeBoest
William E. Stockman
Tamela Eady Wiseman (Resident, Naples Office)
James G. Decker
Thomas M. Dryden

Representative Clients: Cobb Theatres, Inc.; WCI Communities, Inc.; Evelyn Jackman and Sons, Inc.

For full biographical listings, see the Martindale-Hubbell Law Directory

HENDERSON, FRANKLIN, STARNES & HOLT, PROFESSIONAL ASSOCIATION (AV)

1715 Monroe Street, P.O. Box 280, 33902-0280
Telephone: 941-334-4121
Telecopier: 941-332-4494

Ernest H. Hatch, Jr.
William N. Horowitz
Grace Gutierrez

Representative Clients: CIGNA Group; CSX Transportation, Inc.; Fireman's Fund Insurance Cos.; The Hartford Insurance Group; Huntington National Bank, N.A.; NationsBank, N.A.; Travelers/Aetna Insurance Group; Sprint-Florida, Inc.

For Complete List of Firm Personnel, See General Section

For full biographical listings, see the Martindale-Hubbell Law Directory

ANDRE J. PATRONE, P.A. (AV)

12685 New Brittany Boulevard, 33907
Telephone: 941-278-1800
Fax: 941-278-0608

Andre J. Patrone

For full biographical listings, see the Martindale-Hubbell Law Directory

ROBERTS & ENGVALSON, P.A. (AV)

1920 Victoria Avenue, 33901
Telephone: 941-332-7273
Fax: 941-332-3320

Charles M. Roberts
Kinley I. Engvalson
Lori W. Clifford

LEGAL SUPPORT PERSONNEL

Carolyn Glover (Legal Assistant)

For full biographical listings, see the Martindale-Hubbell Law Directory

*FORT PIERCE,** St. Lucie Co.

NEILL GRIFFIN JEFFRIES FOWLER TIERNEY & NEILL, CHARTERED (AV)

311 South Second Street, P.O. Box 1270, 34954
Telephone: 561-464-8200
Fax: 561-464-2566

Chester B. Griffin
Michael D. Fowler

Renée Marquis

Local Counsel For: SunTrust Bank South Florida, N.A., (Commercial and Trust Departments); Chubb Group of Insurances Cos.
Approved Attorneys for: Attorneys' Title Insurance Fund; Commonwealth Land Title Insurance Co.
Reference: SunTrust Bank South Florida, N.A., Fort Pierce, Florida (Commercial and Trust Departments).

For full biographical listings, see the Martindale-Hubbell Law Directory

FORT WALTON BEACH, Okaloosa Co.

JOHNNY FORTUNE, P.A. (AV)

181 Eglin Parkway N.E., P.O. Box 2376, 32549-2376
Telephone: 850-664-9199; 664-5155
Fax: 850-243-2424

Johnny A. Fortune

Representative Client: Trust Department, Vanguard Bank & Trust Co.; Synovus Trust Co.

For full biographical listings, see the Martindale-Hubbell Law Directory

*GAINESVILLE,** Alachua Co.

WAYNE P. CASTELLO (AV)

Suite W, 2772 N.W. 43rd Street, 32606
Telephone: 352-377-4422
Telecopier: 352-373-5792
Email: wpc@prodigy.net *URL:* http://www.lawyers.com/castellolaw

(See Next Column)

LEGAL SUPPORT PERSONNEL

Griffin Stegall (Legal Assistant)
Diana Harris (Legal Assistant)

For full biographical listings, see the Martindale-Hubbell Law Directory

HOLLYWOOD, Broward Co.

LAW OFFICE OF JEFFREY SOLOMON (AV)

3864 Sheridan Street, 33021
Telephone: 954-967-9800
Fax: 954-963-2227
Cooper City, Florida Office: Suite 1, 10000 Stirling Road, 33024.
Telephone: 954-967-9800.

For full biographical listings, see the Martindale-Hubbell Law Directory

*JACKSONVILLE,** Duval Co.

ANDERSON & STEVENS, P.A. (AV)

Suite 2640, Riverplace Tower, 1301 Riverplace Boulevard, 32207-9039
Telephone: 904-399-8000
Telecopier: 904-346-3078

Kenneth G. Anderson
James P. Stevens

Rose Marie Karadsheh Preddy

For full biographical listings, see the Martindale-Hubbell Law Directory

WILLIAM R. BLACKARD, JR. (AV)

Suite 800 121 W. Forsyth Street, 32202
Telephone: 904-354-4400
Facsimile: 904-354-5552

For full biographical listings, see the Martindale-Hubbell Law Directory

JEAN C. COKER, P.A. (AV)

Suite 160, 6622 Southpoint Drive South, 32216
Telephone: 904-296-1100
Fax: 904-296-1200
Email: jeccjax@bellsouth.net *URL:* http://www.lawyers.com/cokerlaw

Jean C. Coker

LEGAL SUPPORT PERSONNEL

Diana M. Len (Estate & Trust Administration Paralegal)

References: NationsBank; First Union National Bank of Florida.

For full biographical listings, see the Martindale-Hubbell Law Directory

LAW OFFICE OF C. RANDOLPH COLEMAN, P.A. (AV)

9250 Baymeadows Road, Suite 230, 32256
Telephone: 904-448-1969
Fax: 904-448-5244
Email: rcoleman@prodigy.net *URL:* http://www.estateplanning.com/coleman

C. Randolph Coleman

For full biographical listings, see the Martindale-Hubbell Law Directory

DONAHOO, BALL & MCMENAMY, P.A. (AV)

(Incorporated in 1982)
50 North Laura Street, Suite 2925, 32202
Telephone: 904-354-8080
Fax: 904-791-9563
Email: office@donahooball.com

John W. Donahoo (1907-1993)
Thomas M. Donahoo
Haywood M. Ball
William B. McMenamy
Thomas M. Donahoo, Jr.

For full biographical listings, see the Martindale-Hubbell Law Directory

FRAZIER & FRAZIER, ATTORNEYS AT LAW, P.A. (AV)

Suite A, 1515 Riverside Avenue, 32204
Telephone: 904-353-5616
Fax: 904-353-5619

William R. Frazier
W. Robinson Frazier

References: First Union National Bank of Florida; First Guaranty Bank & Trust Co.

For full biographical listings, see the Martindale-Hubbell Law Directory

LOBRANO & KINCAID, P.L. (AV)

Suite 1650 Independent Life Building, 1 Independent Drive, 32202
Telephone: 904-359-2100
Facsimile: 904-353-1332

Stephen D. Lobrano
Wade McK. Hampton

(See Next Column)

LOBRANO & KINCAID P.L., *Jacksonville—Continued*

OF COUNSEL

W. Douglas Smith (Not admitted in FL)

For full biographical listings, see the Martindale-Hubbell Law Directory

JUPITER, Palm Beach Co.

JOSEPH C. KEMPE PROFESSIONAL ASSOCIATION (AV)

Attorneys and Counselors at Law
941 North Highway AIA, 33477-5111
Telephone: 561-747-7300
FAX: 561-747-7722
Email: JCKempe@msn.com *URL:* http://www.jckempe.com
Stuart, Florida Office: Royal Palm Financial Center II, Suite 200, 789 South Federal Highway.
Telephone: 561-223-0700.
Fax: 561-223-0707.
Vero Beach, Florida Office: 664 Azalea Lane, Suite B.
Telephone: 561-562-4022.
Fax: 561-234-1422.

Joseph C. Kempe

Harry S. Colburn Jr.

For full biographical listings, see the Martindale-Hubbell Law Directory

LAKELAND, Polk Co.

HAHN, MCCLURG, WATSON, GRIFFITH & BUSH, P.A. (AV)

101 South Florida Avenue, 33801-4619
Telephone: 941-688-7747
Telecopier: 941-683-4582
Mailing Address: P.O. Box 38, 33802-0038
Email: lawfirm@hahnmcclurg.com *URL:* http://www.hmwgb@gte.net

James P. Hahn
E.V. McClurg
Stephen C. Watson
John R. Griffith
Philip H. Bush
James M. Craig, II

General Counsel: Huntington National Bank, Lakeland, Florida; Florida-First Bank, Lakeland, Florida; Publix Super Markets, Inc.
Approved Attorneys For: Attorneys' Title Insurance Fund; American Title Insurance Co.; Title & Trust Company of Florida; Federal Land Bank of Columbia, Columbia, S.C.
Reference: Huntington National Bank, Lakeland, Florida.

For full biographical listings, see the Martindale-Hubbell Law Directory

MARCO ISLAND, Collier Co.

JOHN A. NOLD, P.A. (AV⊕)

995 North Collier Boulevard, 34145
Telephone: 941-394-7811
Telefax: 941-394-9449
Email: noldatty@aol.com
Naples, Florida Office: 5100 North Tamiami Trail, Suite 103-146.
Telephone: 941-643-6868.

John A. Nold

For full biographical listings, see the Martindale-Hubbell Law Directory

MELBOURNE, Brevard Co.

LYNNE R. THOMPSON, P.A. (AV)

529 East New Haven Avenue, 32901
Telephone: 321-728-1925
Fax: 321-722-9768
Email: thompson@iu.net *URL:* http://www.lawyers.com/lynnthompson

Lynne R. Thompson

For full biographical listings, see the Martindale-Hubbell Law Directory

*MIAMI,** Dade Co.

DONLEVY-ROSEN & ROSEN, PROFESSIONAL ASSOCIATION (AV)

133 Sevilla Avenue, 33134
Telephone: 305-447-0061
Telecopier: 305-447-9888
URL: http://www.lawyers.com/weprotectyou
Email: info@protectyou.com *URL:* http://www.protectyou.com

Howard D. Rosen
Patricia Donlevy-Rosen

For full biographical listings, see the Martindale-Hubbell Law Directory

DUNWODY WHITE & LANDON, P.A. (AV)

550 Biltmore Way, Suite 810 (Coral Gables), 33134
Telephone: 305-529-1500
Fax: 305-529-8855
Email: dwl-law.com
Naples Office: 4001 Tamiami Trail North, Suite 200.
Telephone: 941-263-5885.
Fax: 941-262-1442.
Palm Beach Office: 239 South County Road, Suite 300, P.O. Box 3165.
Telephone: 561-655-2120.
Fax: 561-655-2168.

Atwood Dunwody (1912-1996)
Jonna S. Brown
Jackson M. Bruce, Jr. (Resident, Naples Office)
Neil R. Chrystal
Jack A. Falk, Jr.
John J. Grundhauser
Robert D. W. Landon, II
Thomas J. Matkov
William T. Muir
Mitchell E. Silverstein
Robert A. White

Patrick J. Lannon

For full biographical listings, see the Martindale-Hubbell Law Directory

MARSHA G. MADORSKY (AV)

2665 South Bayshore Drive Suite 603, 33133
Telephone: 305-856-0879
Fax: 305-854-6093

OF COUNSEL

W. Tucker Gibbs

ASSOCIATE

Margaret C.F. Quinlivan

For full biographical listings, see the Martindale-Hubbell Law Directory

MARKOWITZ, DAVIS, RINGEL & TRUSTY, P.A. (AV)

Two Datran Center, Suite 1225, 9130 South Dadeland Boulevard, 33156-7849
Telephone: 305-670-5000
Telecopier: 305-670-5011

Candis Trusty

For full biographical listings, see the Martindale-Hubbell Law Directory

MIAMI BEACH, Dade Co.

STEINBERG & YAFFE, P.A. (AV)

The Senator Law Center, 767 Arthur Godfrey Road, 33140-3413
Telephone: Miami-Dade: 305-538-2344; Broward 954-462-2344
Fax: 305-538-0419
Email: inbox@senatorlaw.com *URL:* http://www.senatorlaw.com

Paul B. Steinberg
Robert H. Yaffe

Richard L. Steinberg

For full biographical listings, see the Martindale-Hubbell Law Directory

*NAPLES,** Collier Co.

QUARLES & BRADY LLP (AV)

Barnett Center, 4501 Tamiami Trail North Suite 300, 34103-3060
Telephone: 941-262-5959
Fax: 941-434-4999
URL: http://www.quarles.com
Milwaukee, Wisconsin Office: 411 East Wisconsin Avenue, 53202-4497.
Telephone: 414-277-5000.
Fax: 414-271-3552.
Madison, Wisconsin Office: Firstar Plaza, One South Pinckney Street, P.O. Box 2113, 53701-2113.
Telephone: 608-251-5000.
Fax: 608-251-9166.
West Palm Beach, Florida Office: 222 Lakeview Avenue, 4th Floor, 33401.
Telephone: 561-653-5000.
Fax: 561-653-5333.
Phoenix, Arizona Office: One Camelback Building, One East Camelback Road, Suite 400, 85012-1649.
Telephone: 602-230-5500.
Fax: 602-230-5598.
Chicago, Illinois Office: Quarles & Brady LLC, Citicorp Center, 500 West Madison Street, Suite 3700.
Telephone: 312-715-5000.
Fax: 312-715-5155.

PARTNERS

Thomas E. Maloney
Kimberly Leach Johnson

ASSOCIATE

Samara S. Holland

For Complete List of Firm Personnel, See General Section

For full biographical listings, see the Martindale-Hubbell Law Directory

Naples—Continued

DENNIS R. WHITE, P.A. (AV)

Suite 300, Fifth Third Bank Building, 4099 Tamiami Trail North, 34103-3548
Telephone: 941-261-4700
Facsimile: 941-261-4721
Email: drw@whitelaw.com

Dennis R. White

For full biographical listings, see the Martindale-Hubbell Law Directory

NEW PORT RICHEY, Pasco Co.

JAMES J. ALTMAN (AV)

5628 Main Street, 34652
Telephone: 727-848-8435
Fax: 727-847-2750
Email: altman@sanctum.com *URL:* http://www.lawyers.com/altmanlaw

ASSOCIATES

Robert N. Altman
Thomas P. Altman

Approved Attorney for: Attorneys' Title Insurance Fund.
Reference: NationsBank of Florida.

For full biographical listings, see the Martindale-Hubbell Law Directory

NORTH MIAMI BEACH, Dade Co.

ROBERT D. SLEWETT, P.A. (AV)

17071 West Dixie Highway, 33160
Telephone: 305-945-1851
Fax: 305-949-7960
Email: slewlaw@msn.com

Robert D. Slewett

For full biographical listings, see the Martindale-Hubbell Law Directory

*ORLANDO,** Orange Co.

MORAN & SHAMS, P.A. (AV)

111 North Orange Avenue, Suite 1200, P.O. Box 472, 32802-0472
Telephone: 407-841-4141
Fax: 407-841-4148
Email: moran-shams@moran-shams.com

Thomas P. Moran
Maurice Shams
Robert S. MacDonald
Sidney H. Shams

References: Southern Community Bank; Sun Bank; First Union National Bank; American Express Financial Advisors.

For full biographical listings, see the Martindale-Hubbell Law Directory

POHL & SHORT, P.A.

(See Winter Park)

CRAIG B. WARD, P.A. (AV)

Suite 501, 105 East Robinson Street, 32801-1601
Telephone: 407-843-6000
Fax: 407-839-0577
Email: CBWardlaw@aol.com

Craig B. Ward

OF COUNSEL

Charles D. Miner

Representative Clients: Hospitality Management Resources, Inc.; Lake of the Woods Homeowners Association, Inc.; Metro One, Inc. (Real Estate); National Ambulance Builders, Inc.; Poole Construction Co., Inc.; Power Concrete Products Co.; Richard Sibley Associates, Inc. (Advertising); Scientific-Atlanta, Inc.
Approved Agent For: First American Title Insurance Co.; Attorneys' Title Insurance Fund.

For full biographical listings, see the Martindale-Hubbell Law Directory

PALM BEACH, Palm Beach Co.

BAUGHER, METTLER & SHELTON (AV)

340 Royal Poinciana Plaza, P.O. Box 109, 33480
Telephone: 561-833-9631
Fax: 561-655-2835

MEMBERS OF FIRM

Thomas M. Mettler
John W. Shelton

ASSOCIATE

Francis X. J. Lynch

Reference: First National Bank in Palm Beach.

For full biographical listings, see the Martindale-Hubbell Law Directory

LAW OFFICES OF HARRISON K. CHAUNCEY, JR., P.A. (AV)

241 Bradley Place, 33480
Telephone: 561-833-3001
Fax: 561-833-9060
Email: hchauncey@chaunceylaw.com

Harrison K. Chauncey Jr.
Mark R. Brown

For full biographical listings, see the Martindale-Hubbell Law Directory

MINTMIRE & ASSOCIATES (AV)

265 Sunrise Avenue, Suite 204, 33480
Telephone: 561-832-5696
Fax: 561-659-5371
Email: MintmireFL@aol.com

Donald F. Mintmire
Jeffrey A. Shaffer
Bradley F. Rothenberg

OF COUNSEL

Paul Safran, Jr.

For full biographical listings, see the Martindale-Hubbell Law Directory

MURPHY, REID, PILOTTE, ORD & AUSTIN (AV)

A Partnership of Professional Associations
Suite 100, 340 Royal Palm Way, 33480
Telephone: 561-655-4060
Facsimile: 561-832-5436
Vero Beach, Florida Office: Plantation Plaza, 6606-20th Street, 32966-7902.
Telephone: 561-567-6480.
Facsimile: 561-562-0220.

Eugene W. Murphy Jr. (P.A.)
Frank T. Pilotte (P.A.)

OF COUNSEL

Philip H. Reid

For Complete List of Firm Personnel, See General Section

For full biographical listings, see the Martindale-Hubbell Law Directory

WARWICK & BANISTER, P.A. (AV)

140 Royal Palm Way, Suite 205, 33480
Telephone: 561-655-7776
Telecopier: 561-655-2271
Email: johnban140@aol.com *URL:* http://www.lawyers.com/palmbeachlaw

Charles H. Warwick, Jr. (1894-1967)
Charles H. Warwick, III
John R. Banister

For full biographical listings, see the Martindale-Hubbell Law Directory

*PENSACOLA,** Escambia Co.

WILLIAM V. LINNE (AV)

127 Palafox Place, P.O. Box 12347, 32581
Telephone: 850-433-2224
Telecopier: 850-433-3301
Email: blinne@linnelaw.com

For full biographical listings, see the Martindale-Hubbell Law Directory

POMPANO BEACH, Broward Co.

JOHN L. KORTHALS (AV)

1401 East Atlantic Boulevard, 33060
Telephone: 954-783-2999
Fax: 954-783-9832
Email: korthals.law@mindspring.com

For full biographical listings, see the Martindale-Hubbell Law Directory

PONTE VEDRA BEACH, St. Johns Co.

GREGORY K. WEST, P.A. (AV)

13000 Sawgrass Village Circle, Suite 35, 32082
Telephone: 904-543-9800
Fax: 904-285-6098
Email: greg@gkwpa.com *URL:* http://www.gkwpa.com

Gregory K. West

For full biographical listings, see the Martindale-Hubbell Law Directory

*PUNTA GORDA,** Charlotte Co.

WOTITZKY, WOTITZKY, MIZELL, ROSS & GOLDMAN, P.A. (AV)

223 Taylor Street, 33950
Telephone: 941-639-2171
Telecopier: 941-639-8617
Email: wwmr@sunline.net

(See Next Column)

WOTITZKY, WOTITZKY, MIZELL, ROSS & GOLDMAN P.A., *Punta Gorda—Continued*

Jason B. Goldman
John B. Mizell
Warren R. Ross
Ernest W. Sturges, Jr.
Edward L. Wotitzky
Hal F. Wotitzky

OF COUNSEL

Frank Wotitzky
Leo Wotitzky

Representative Clients: Punta Gorda Corp.; Developers of Southwest Florida, Inc.; Englewood Disposal Co., Inc.; Integrated Control Systems, Inc.
Approved Attorneys for: Attorneys' Title Insurance Fund, Orlando, Florida; Chicago Title Insurance Co.

For full biographical listings, see the Martindale-Hubbell Law Directory

*ST. AUGUSTINE,** St. Johns Co.

UPCHURCH, BAILEY & UPCHURCH, P.A. (AV)

780 North Ponce de Leon Boulevard, P.O. Drawer 3007, 32085-3007
Telephone: 904-829-9066
Facsimile: 904-825-4862
Email: info@ubulaw.com

Tracy Wilson Upchurch
Michael A. Siragusa

OF COUNSEL

Hamilton D. Upchurch

Representative Clients: First Union National Bank of Florida.

For Complete List of Firm Personnel, See General Section

For full biographical listings, see the Martindale-Hubbell Law Directory

ST. PETERSBURG, Pinellas Co.

ALLAN & SHIPP, P.A. (AV)

6675 Thirteenth Avenue North, Suite 2C, 33710
Telephone: 813-381-9800
Fax: 813-381-1155
Email: law@allan-shipp.com
Clearwater, Florida Office: 2633 McCormick Drive, Suite 101, 34619.
Telephone: 813-799-7000.
Fax: 813-381-1155.

Linda R. Allan
Wayne E. Shipp

Stephen A. Baker
Terry J. Deeb
Jeffrey L. Hinds

For full biographical listings, see the Martindale-Hubbell Law Directory

STEIN, FORD, SCHAAF & TOWZEY, L.L.P. (AV)

501 First Avenue North, Suite 1000, 33701
Telephone: 727-894-4333
Fax: 727-894-0175

Henry A. Stein
Harvey A. Ford
Paul A. Nelson
Gary M. Schaaf
Phyllis J. Towzey
Sarah E. Williams

For full biographical listings, see the Martindale-Hubbell Law Directory

*SANFORD,** Seminole Co.

STENSTROM, MCINTOSH, COLBERT, WHIGHAM & SIMMONS, P.A. (AV)

200 West First, Suite 22, P.O. Box 4848, 32772-4848
Telephone: 407-322-2171
Fax: 407-330-2379
Orlando/Winterpark Telephone: 407-834-5119
DeLand/DeBary Telephone: 407-668-1479
URL: http://www.stenstrom.com

Thomas E. Whigham (1952-1988)
Douglas Stenstrom (Retired)
William L. Colbert
Franklin C. Whigham
Clayton D. Simmons
Robert K. McIntosh
Donna L. Surratt-McIntosh
William E. Reischmann, Jr.

Catherine D. Reischmann
James J. Partlow
Dawn M. Harrison

OF COUNSEL

Kenneth W. McIntosh
S. Kirby Moncrief

Representative Clients: City of Sanford; City of Oviedo; City of Casselberry; Seminole Community College; City of Lake Mary; Sanford Housing Authority; City of DeBary; Seminole Soccer Club, Inc.; Tuskawilla Homeowners' Association; South Seminole-North Orange Wastewater Transmission Authority.

For full biographical listings, see the Martindale-Hubbell Law Directory

*SARASOTA,** Sarasota Co.

BOWMAN, GEORGE, SCHEB, TOALE & ROBINSON, P.A. (AV)

22 South Tuttle Avenue, Suite 3, 34237
Telephone: 941-366-5510
FAX: 941-951-0839

I. W. Whitesell, Jr. (Retired)
David G. Bowman, Sr.
Eugene O. George
Robert P. Scheb
James E. Toale
David G. Bowman, Jr.

For Complete List of Firm Personnel, See General Section

For full biographical listings, see the Martindale-Hubbell Law Directory

DICKINSON & GIBBONS, P.A. (AV)

1750 Ringling Boulevard, P.O. Box 3979, 34230
Telephone: 941-366-4680
FAX: 941-953-3136
URL: http://dglawyers.com

Francis C. Dart (1902-1972)
Gary H. Larsen
Camden T. French
Ralph L. Marchbank, Jr.
A. James Rolfes
Burwell J. Jones
Richard R. Garland
Stephen G. Brannan
Deborah J. Blue
Jeffrey D. Peairs
David S. Preston

OF COUNSEL

Patrick H. Dickinson
G. Hunter Gibbons
Ward E. Dahlgren

LEGAL SUPPORT PERSONNEL

Janet E. Gadoury (Certified Legal Assistant)

Representative Clients: Ford Motor Co.; Florida Power & Light Co.; Squibb Corp.
Insurance Clients: Liberty Mutual Insurance Co.; Allstate Insurance Co.; Nationwide Insurance Group; Ohio Casualty Insurance Co.; United States Fidelity & Guaranty Co.; State Farm Insurance Company.

For Complete List of Firm Personnel, See General Section

For full biographical listings, see the Martindale-Hubbell Law Directory

WILLIAMS, PARKER, HARRISON, DIETZ & GETZEN, PROFESSIONAL ASSOCIATION (AV)

200 South Orange Avenue, 34236-6749
Telephone: 941-366-4800
Telecopier: 941-366-5109
Mailing Address: P.O. Box 3258, Sarasota, Florida, 34230-3258
Email: infodesk@williamsparker.com *URL:* http://www.williamsparker.com

William T. Harrison, Jr.
Monte K. Marshall
John T. Berteau
James L. Turner
Elizabeth C. Marshall
Ric Gregoria
Linda R. Getzen
Susan Barrett Hecker
R. Scott Collins

General Counsel for: Sarasota County Public Hospital Board; Sarasota-Manatee Airport Authority; Taylor Woodrow Homes Ltd.; FCCI Mutual Insurance Co.
Local Counsel for: Bank of America; Northern Trust Bank of Florida; SunTrust Bank, Gulfcoast.

For Complete List of Firm Personnel, See General Section

For full biographical listings, see the Martindale-Hubbell Law Directory

WILSON, JOHNSON & JAFFER, P.A. (AV)

27 South Orange Avenue, 34236-5822
Telephone: 941-955-5800
Fax: 941-955-7353
Email: wilson@lawsites.com *URL:* http://www.lawsites.com

Clyde H. Wilson (1908-1994)
Robert M. Johnson
Clyde H. Wilson, Jr.
John S. Jaffer

For full biographical listings, see the Martindale-Hubbell Law Directory

*STUART,** Martin Co.

BRODIE & PAWLUC (AV)

525 Camden Avenue, 34994
Telephone: 561-221-0110
Facsimile: 561-221-0113
Email: BPLAWFL@aol.com

Lawrence P. Brodie
Sonia M. Pawluc

For full biographical listings, see the Martindale-Hubbell Law Directory

Stuart—Continued

JOSEPH C. KEMPE PROFESSIONAL ASSOCIATION (AV)

Attorneys and Counselors at Law
Royal Palm Financial Center II, Suite 200, 789 South Federal Highway, 34994
Telephone: 561-223-0700
FAX: 561-223-0707
Email: JCKempe@msn.com
Jupiter, Florida Office: 941 North Highway AIA. Telephone 561-747-7300. *Fax:* 561-747-7722.
Vero Beach, Florida Office: 664 Azalea Lane, Suite B. *Telephone:* 561-562-4022. *Fax:* 561-234-1422.

Joseph C. Kempe

Harry S. Colburn Jr.

For full biographical listings, see the Martindale-Hubbell Law Directory

MCCARTHY, SUMMERS, BOBKO, MCKEY, WOOD & SAWYER, P.A. (AV)

2081 East Ocean Boulevard, Second Floor, 34996
Telephone: 561-286-1700
Fax: 561-283-1803
URL: http://www.mcsumm.com

Terence P. McCarthy
Robert P. Summers
Noel A. Bobko
John D. McKey, Jr.
Steven J. Wood
Thomas R. Sawyer
Nicola J. Boone
Steven L. Perry

Kathryn C. Bass
Robert N. Maitland, II

Representative Clients: First National Bank and Trust Company of the Treasure Coast; Hydratech Utilities; Lost Lake at Hobe Sound; Gary Player Design Group; YMCA of Martin County; Shadow Lakes Groves, Inc.; Merrill Lynch Trust Co., (Florida); Wilmington Trust, FSB; The Huntington National Bank, N.A.; WSTU-Radio, WTCN-TV.

For full biographical listings, see the Martindale-Hubbell Law Directory

*TALLAHASSEE,** Leon Co.

ROBERT S. HIGHTOWER (AV)

241 East Virginia Street, P.O. Box 4165, 32315-4165
Telephone: 850-222-3363
Telecopier: 850-222-0992
Email: rsh@hightowerlaw.com

For full biographical listings, see the Martindale-Hubbell Law Directory

*TAMPA,** Hillsborough Co.

SCOTT F. BARNETT CHARTERED (AV)

234 East Davis Boulevard, 33606-3729
Telephone: 813-251-3330
Fax: 813-251-3841
Email: SFBarnett@aol.com *URL:* http://www.lawyers.com/sfbarnett

Scott F. Barnett

For full biographical listings, see the Martindale-Hubbell Law Directory

FULLER HOLSONBACK & BIVINS, P.A. (AV)

100 North Tampa Street, Suite 2650, 33602
Telephone: 813-229-9119
Fax: Available Upon Request
Email: jfuller521@aol.com

Jeffery M. Fuller
John P. Holsonback
Robert W. Bivins
Christina C. Young
Steven F. Thompson
William D. Mercer, Jr

For full biographical listings, see the Martindale-Hubbell Law Directory

CURT GENDERS, P.A. (AV)

2304 West Cleveland Street, 33609
Telephone: 813-254-4744
FAX: 813-254-5222
Email: derekba@aol.com

Curt Genders
Derek B. Alvarez

For full biographical listings, see the Martindale-Hubbell Law Directory

KETCHEY HORAN, P.A. (AV)

100 North Tampa Street, Suite 1900, P.O. Box 500, 33601-0500
Telephone: 813-223-9395
Fax: 813-221-1348
Email: Stephanie@KetcheyHoran.com
Sun City Center, Florida Office: 1647 Sun City Center Plaza, Suite 200. *Telephone:* 813-633-1200.

SHAREHOLDERS

Phillip A. Baumann
Steven L. Hearn

ASSOCIATES

Tae Kelley Bronner
Sharon Drucker Ford

For full biographical listings, see the Martindale-Hubbell Law Directory

MANEY, DAMSKER & JONES, P.A. (AV)

606 Madison Street, P.O. Box 172009, 33672-0009
Telephone: 813-228-7371
Fax: 813-223-4846

David A. Maney
Karen Lynn Jones

For full biographical listings, see the Martindale-Hubbell Law Directory

PARIS & ASSOCIATES, P.A. (AV)

15310 Amberly Drive, Suite 300, 33647
Telephone: 813-975-1900
Fax: 813-975-1850
Email: lawparis@ij.net

Deborah M. Paris

LEGAL SUPPORT PERSONNEL

Susan T. Wilcox
Jeffery D. Wyatt, Jr.

For full biographical listings, see the Martindale-Hubbell Law Directory

PREVATT & TAYLOR (AV)

A Partnership of Professional Associations
One Tampa City Center, Suite 1700, P.O. Box 2920, 33602
Telephone: 813-273-9666
Telefax: 813-273-0414

Karen J. Prevatt
Mary L. Taylor

Representative Clients: Cone Constructors Inc.; Magic Wok International, Inc.; Dallas I. Construction & Development, Inc.; Bioderm, Inc.; Mental Healthcare, Inc.; U.S.S. Forrestal Sea, Air, Space Museum, Inc.; Golden Bayou Food Service, Inc.

For full biographical listings, see the Martindale-Hubbell Law Directory

VENICE, Sarasota Co.

MICHAEL D. HORLICK, P.A. (AV)

1314 E. Venice Avenue - Suite D, 34292
Telephone: 941-484-5656
Fax: 941-484-1650
Email: mhorlick@mdhpa.com *URL:* http://www.mdhpa.com

Michael D. Horlick

For full biographical listings, see the Martindale-Hubbell Law Directory

*VERO BEACH,** Indian River Co.

COLLINS, BROWN, CALDWELL, BARKETT & GARAVAGLIA, CHARTERED (AV)

756 Beachland Boulevard, P.O. Box 3686, 32964
Telephone: 561-231-4343
FAX: 561-234-5213
Email: cbc@verolaw.com

George G. Collins, Jr.
Calvin B. Brown
William W. Caldwell
Bruce D. Barkett
Michael J. Garavaglia
Lisa N. Thompson
Susan A. Calistri

Reference: First Union Bank of Indian River County, Vero Beach, Florida.

For full biographical listings, see the Martindale-Hubbell Law Directory

GOULD, COOKSEY, FENNELL, O'NEILL, MARINE & CARTER, PROFESSIONAL ASSOCIATION (AV)

979 Beachland Boulevard, 32963
Telephone: 561-231-1100
Fax: 561-231-2020

John R. Gould (1921-1988)
Byron T. Cooksey
Darrell Fennell
Eugene J. O'Neill
Christopher H. Marine
David M. Carter
Todd W. Fennell
Susan L. Chenault
Elsbeth T. Peshel (Not admitted in FL)

Counsel for: Indian River National Bank; Island Hopper Boats International, Inc.; Northern Trust Bank of Florida.

(See Next Column)

GOULD, COOKSEY, FENNELL, O'NEILL, MARINE & CARTER PROFESSIONAL ASSOCIATION, *Vero Beach—Continued*

Approved Attorneys for: Attorneys' Title Insurance Fund; Commonwealth Land Title Insurance Company.

For full biographical listings, see the Martindale-Hubbell Law Directory

JOSEPH C. KEMPE PROFESSIONAL ASSOCIATION (AV)

Attorneys and Counselors at Law
664 Azalea Lane, Suite B, 32963
Telephone: 561-562-4022
Fax: 561-234-1442
Email: JCKempe@msn.com
Jupiter, Florida Office: 941 North Highway AIA.
Telephone: 561-747-7300.
Fax: 561-747-7722.
Stuart, Florida Office: Royal Palm Financial Center II, Suite 200, 789 S. Federal Highway.
Telephone: 561-223-0700.
Fax: 561-223-0707.

Joseph C. Kempe

Harry S. Colburn Jr.

For full biographical listings, see the Martindale-Hubbell Law Directory

MOSS, HENDERSON, BLANTON & LANIER, P.A. (AV)

817 Beachland Boulevard, P.O. Box 3406, 32964-3406
Telephone: 561-231-1900
Fax: 561-231-4387

Lawrence Y. Leonard
OF COUNSEL
Charles E. Garris

Representative Clients: Aetna Life & Casualty; Alcoa Florida, Inc.; Florida Power & Light Co.; Insurance Company of North America; Liberty Mutual Insurance Co.; Sears, Roebuck & Co.; Sugar Cane Growers Cooperative of Florida; Norfolk Southern Corporation/North American Van Lines, Inc.

For Complete List of Firm Personnel, See General Section

For full biographical listings, see the Martindale-Hubbell Law Directory

SMITH & SMITH (AV)

Citrus Financial Center, Suite 301, 1717 Indian River Boulevard, 32960
Telephone: 561-567-4351
Fax: 561-567-4298

MEMBERS OF FIRM

Sherman N. Smith, Jr. (1914-1998)
Sherman N. Smith, III
Anthony T. Golden

References: Citrus Bank, N.A.; Northern Trust Bank of Vero Beach.

For full biographical listings, see the Martindale-Hubbell Law Directory

STEWART, EVANS & HAFNER, P.A. (AV)

3355 Ocean Drive, P.O. Box 3345, 32964-3345
Telephone: 561-231-3500
FAX: 561-231-9876
Email: firm@sneh.com

William J. Stewart
Ralph L. Evans
Troy B. Hafner

For full biographical listings, see the Martindale-Hubbell Law Directory

*WEST PALM BEACH,** Palm Beach Co.

AUGUST & KULUNAS, P.A. (AV)

250 Australian Avenue South Suite 1100, 33401
Telephone: 561-835-9600
Fax: 561-835-9602

Jerald David August
Joseph J. Kulunas

Adi Rappoport
Steven E. Blumenthal

OF COUNSEL
James J. Freeland

For full biographical listings, see the Martindale-Hubbell Law Directory

BOYES & FARINA, PROFESSIONAL ASSOCIATION (AV)

Centurion Plaza, 1601 Forum Place, Suite 900, 33401
Telephone: 561-697-9393
Fax: 561-697-8980
URL: http://www.lawyers.com/bflaw

William E. Boyes
John Farina

(See Next Column)

John Patrick Morrissey

For full biographical listings, see the Martindale-Hubbell Law Directory

RICHARD B. COMITER & ASSOCIATES, P.A. (AV)

Esperante Building, 222 Lakeview Avenue, Suite 200, 33401
Telephone: 561-838-4505, 800-445-8838
Fax: 561-659-3800
Email: rcomiter@rbctax.com *URL:* http://www.lawyers.com/richardbcomiter&associate

Richard B. Comiter

Lisa Z. Hauser
OF COUNSEL
Barry A. Nelson

For full biographical listings, see the Martindale-Hubbell Law Directory

KIRK GRANTHAM, P.A. (AV)

Suite 105, 1860 Forest Hill Boulevard, 33406
Telephone: 561-966-6211
Telefax: 561-966-9495

Kirk Grantham

William Carter Carroll
Edward William Hale

OF COUNSEL
James M. Adams

For full biographical listings, see the Martindale-Hubbell Law Directory

PRESSLY & PRESSLY, P.A. (AV)

Esperante, Suite 910, 222 Lakeview Avenue, 33401-6112
Telephone: 561-659-4040
FAX: 561-655-6006
URL: http://www.lawyers.com/pressly&pressly

James G. Pressly, Jr.
David S. Pressly
Trent S. Kiziah

J. Grier Pressly III

For full biographical listings, see the Martindale-Hubbell Law Directory

QUARLES & BRADY LLP (AV)

222 Lakeview Avenue, 4th Floor, 33401
Telephone: 561-653-5000
Fax: 561-653-5333
URL: http://www.quarles.com
Milwaukee, Wisconsin Office: 411 East Wisconsin Avenue, 53202-4497.
Telephone: 414-277-5000.
Fax: 414-271-3552.
Madison, Wisconsin Office: Firstar Plaza, One South Pinckney Street, P.O. Box 2113, 53701-2113.
Telephone: 608-251-5000.
Fax: 608-251-9166.
Naples, Florida Office: Barnett Center, 4501 Tamiami Trail North, Suite 300, 34103-3060.
Telephone: 941-262-5959.
Fax: 941-434-4999.
Phoenix, Arizona Office: One Camelback Building, One East Camelback Road, Suite 400, 85012-1649.
Telephone: 602-230-5500.
Fax: 602-230-5598.
Chicago, Illinois Office: Quarles & Brady LLC, Citicorp Center, 500 West Madison Street, Suite 3700.
Telephone: 312-715-5000.
Fax: 312-715-5155.

OF COUNSEL
John S. Sammond

For Complete List of Firm Personnel, See General Section

For full biographical listings, see the Martindale-Hubbell Law Directory

WARD, DAMON, BEVERLY, TITTLE & POSNER, P.A. (AV)

4420 Beacon Circle, 33407-3270
Telephone: 561-842-3000
Stuart: 561-223-5550
Fax: 561-842-3626
Email: wdbtp@wdbtp.com *URL:* http://www.wdbtp.com

James F. Cooney, Jr. (1950-1992)
Conrad Damon
Andrew Fulton, IV
Irwin R. Gilbert
Craig I. Kelley
Michael J Posner
Roger C. Stanton
James D. Tittle, Jr.
Philip H. Ward, III

(See Next Column)

WARD, DAMON, BEVERLY, TITTLE & POSNER P.A.—*Continued*

OF COUNSEL

Don Beverly

For full biographical listings, see the Martindale-Hubbell Law Directory

WINTER PARK, Orange Co.

POHL & SHORT, P.A. (AV)

280 West Canton Avenue, Suite 410, P.O. Box 3208, 32790
Telephone: 407-647-7645; 407-647-POHL
Telefax: 407-647-2314
Email: ps@pohlshort.com

Dwight I. Cool
Alexander S. Douglas II
Gary A. Forster
E. Givens Goodspeed
Mark A. Grimes
Robert S. Hoofman
Roger A. Kelly
Adam O. Kirwan
David J. Kohs
Frank L. Pohl
James Everett Shepherd V
Houston E. Short
John R. Simpson, Jr.

Representative Clients: American Generator Co.; Copelco Capital, Inc.; Denim U.S.A., Inc.; Ford Motor Credit Co.; Lodestar Technology, Inc.; Lutheran Brotherhood; SunTrust, N.A.; Trax, Inc.

For full biographical listings, see the Martindale-Hubbell Law Directory

GEORGIA

*ATLANTA,** Fulton Co.

ANDRE, BLAUSTEIN & GREEN, L.L.P. (AV)

The Candler Building, 127 Peachtree Street, N.E. Suite 700, 30303-1800
Telephone: 404-653-0300
Facsimile: 404-653-0338

Richard H. Andre
Jon G. Blaustein
Kevin S. Green

Cheryl A. Brown

OF COUNSEL

Edmund J. Novotny, Jr.

For full biographical listings, see the Martindale-Hubbell Law Directory

FRANCIS M. BIRD, JR. (AV)

400 Colony Square, Suite 1750, 1201 Peachtree Street, N.E., 30361
Telephone: 404-875-7990
Fax: 404-892-8560
Email: fmbirdjr@mindspring.com
Email: fmbirdjr@aol.com *URL:* http://members.aol.com/FMBIRDJR/index.html

For full biographical listings, see the Martindale-Hubbell Law Directory

BOVIS, KYLE & BURCH, LLC (AV)

A Limited Liability Corporation including Professional Corporations
Third Floor, 53 Perimeter Center East, 30346
Telephone: 770-391-9100
Telecopier: 770-668-0878
Email: bkb@boviskyle.com *URL:* http://www.boviskyle.com

John M. Bovis (P.C.)
C. Sam Thomas (P.C.)
J. Wesley Skinner

John David Etheriedge

For Complete List of Firm Personnel, See General Section

For full biographical listings, see the Martindale-Hubbell Law Directory

HOFFMAN & FOWLER, LLP (AV)

A Partnership of Professional Corporations
5040 Roswell Road, N.E. Suite 250, 30342
Telephone: 404-256-6464
Fax: 404-256-1422

MEMBERS OF FIRM

Clifford G. Hoffman (P.C.)
Michael C. Fowler (P.C.)

For full biographical listings, see the Martindale-Hubbell Law Directory

LONG ALDRIDGE & NORMAN LLP (AV)

A Limited Liability Partnership including Professional Corporations
Suite 5300, 303 Peachtree Street, 30308
Telephone: 404-527-4000
Telecopier: 404-527-4198
Email: atlanta@lanlaw.com *URL:* http://www.lanlaw.com
Washington, D.C. Office: Suite 600, 701 Pennsylvania Avenue, N.W., 20004.
Telephone: 202-624-1200.
FAX: 202-624-1298.

SENIOR COUNSEL

F. T. Davis, Jr., (P.C.)
W. Stell Huie

For Complete List of Firm Personnel, See General Section

For full biographical listings, see the Martindale-Hubbell Law Directory

RICHARD M. MORGAN, P.C. (AV)

One Midtown Plaza, Suite 1200, 1360 Peachtree Street, 30309
Telephone: 404-870-2251
Facsimile: 404-870-2213
Email: rmmpc@bellsouth.net

Richard M. Morgan

Loraine M. DiSalvo

For full biographical listings, see the Martindale-Hubbell Law Directory

THE SAYLOR LAW FIRM, LLP (AV)

100 Colony Square, Suite 1224, 1175 Peachtree Street, N.E., 30361
Telephone: 404-892-4400
Telecopier: 404-892-2400
Email: SAYLOR_ATLANTA@PRODIGY.COM

C. Murray Saylor, Jr.
Jacquelyn Harmon Saylor

ASSOCIATE

Stephen C. Beeler

For full biographical listings, see the Martindale-Hubbell Law Directory

THRASHER, WHITLEY, HAMPTON & MORGAN, A PROFESSIONAL CORPORATION (AV)

Suite 2150, Five Concourse Parkway, 30328
Telephone: 770-804-8000
Telecopier: 770-804-5555
Email: law@twhm.com
Email: main@twhm.com

Charles J. Hampton

Representative Clients: First Southeastern Securities Group, Inc.; Georgia Dental Assn.; Middle Bay Oil Company, Inc.; Perry & Co.; Smallwood, Reynolds, Stewart, Stewart & Assoc., Inc.; Sunchase Holdings, Ltd.; Touch Industries, Inc.

For full biographical listings, see the Martindale-Hubbell Law Directory

*AUGUSTA,** Richmond Co.

HULL, TOWILL, NORMAN, BARRETT & SALLEY, A PROFESSIONAL CORPORATION (AV)

801 Broad Street, Suite 700, 30901
Telephone: 706-722-4481
Fax: 706-722-9779
Email: hullfirm@groupz.net *URL:* http://www.groupz.net/~advocate
Aiken, South Carolina Office: 111 Park Avenue, 29801.
Telephone: 803-648-4213.
Fax: 803-648-2601.

James M. Hull (1885-1975)
George B. Barrett (1894-1942)
Julian J. Willingham (1887-1963)
John Bell Towill (1907-1991)
Robert C. Norman (Retired, 1991)
W. Hale Barrett
Lawton Jordan, Jr.
Patrick J. Rice
Douglas D. Batchelor, Jr.
David E. Hudson
William H. Tucker (Not admitted in GA)
William F. Hammond
Mark S. Burgreen
George R. Hall
James B. Ellington
F. Michael Taylor
William J. Keogh, III
Edward J. Tarver
J. Noel Schweers, III
Susan D. Barrett
Ralph Emerson Hanna, III

James M. Holly (Not admitted in GA)
Timothy E. Moses
N. Shannon Gentry Lanier
Tara R. Simkins
Charles H. Weigle
Natalie A. Dopson
David C. Smith

OF COUNSEL

Julian B. Salley, Jr. (Not admitted in GA)

Counsel for: Morris Communications Corporation; Merry Land & Investment Company, Inc.; Castleberry/Snow's Brands, Inc.; Sun Trust Bank Augusta, N.A.; Georgia Power Co.; St. Joseph Hospital, Augusta, Georgia,

(See Next Column)

HULL, TOWILL, NORMAN, BARRETT & SALLEY A PROFESSIONAL CORPORATION, *Augusta—Continued*

Inc.; Norfolk Southern Corp.; Housing Authority of the City of Augusta; Georgia Press Association; Columbia County, Georgia.

For full biographical listings, see the Martindale-Hubbell Law Directory

*CARROLLTON,** Carroll Co.

HEAD, HEAD & HEAD (AV)

516 Newnan Street, P.O. Box 508, 30117
Telephone: 770-832-9697
Fax: 770-834-1800

MEMBERS OF FIRM

Henry C. Head
James B. Head
David C. Head

For full biographical listings, see the Martindale-Hubbell Law Directory

*COLUMBUS,** Muscogee Co.

HATCHER, STUBBS, LAND, HOLLIS & ROTHSCHILD (AV)

A Limited Liability Partnership
Suite 500 The Corporate Center, 233 12th Street, P.O. Box 2707, 31902-2707
Telephone: 706-324-0201
Telecopier: 706-322-7747
Email: mailman@hatcherstubbs.com

MEMBERS OF FIRM

Alan F. Rothschild
Morton A. Harris
Charles T. Staples
John M. Tanzine, III
John McKay Sheftall
Alan F. Rothschild, Jr.
William C. Pound

ASSOCIATE

Bradley R. Coppedge

General Counsel for: SunTrust Bank, West Georgia, N.A.; TOM'S Foods Inc.; Kinnett Dairies, Inc.; St. Francis Hospital, Inc.; Bill Heard Enterprises, Inc.
Local Counsel for: First Union National Bank; Equitable Life Assurance Society of the United States; Prudential Insurance Company of America; Metropolitan Life Insurance Co.

For Complete List of Firm Personnel, See General Section

For full biographical listings, see the Martindale-Hubbell Law Directory

*DECATUR,** De Kalb Co.

MCCONAUGHEY & GOFF (AV)

315 W. Ponce de Leon Avenue, #1070, 30030
Telephone: 404-378-3681
Fax: 404-378-3683

H. Stephen Goff, Jr.

OF COUNSEL

Dan E. McConaughey (Retired)

For full biographical listings, see the Martindale-Hubbell Law Directory

*GRIFFIN,** Spalding Co.

JOHN M. COGBURN, JR. (AV)

115 North Sixth Street, P.O. Box 907, 30224
Telephone: 770-228-2148
Telecopier: 770-228-5018
Email: JMCOGBURN@AOL.COM *URL:* http://www.lawyers.com/cogburnlaw

Representative Clients: Griffin-Spalding County Hospital Authority; Spalding Health Care Trust (Nonprofit Community Health Care Organization); Allstar Knitwear Co., Inc. (Textiles); Dender Distributing Co. (Wholesale Beer Distributor); The Mouchet Corp. (Textile By-Products); Industrial Refrigeration Enterprises, Inc. (Refrigeration Engineers and Contractors); Cronic Chevrolet, Pontiac, Nissan (Automobile Dealership); Atlanta Tees, Inc. (Sportswear Distribution); Hi-Tech Rentals, Inc. (Computerized Audio-Visual Equipment for Trade Shows).

For full biographical listings, see the Martindale-Hubbell Law Directory

*JONESBORO,** Clayton Co.

GLAZE & GLAZE, P.C. (AV)

120 North McDonough Street, 30236
Telephone: 770-478-5555
Fax: 770-478-4555
Email: glaze@mindspring.com
Stockbridge, Georgia, 205A Corporate Center Drive, 30281. Telephone: 770-474-3347.

George E. Glaze
Kirby A. Glaze

(See Next Column)

Joe M. Harris, Jr.

For full biographical listings, see the Martindale-Hubbell Law Directory

*MACON,** Bibb Co.

ANDERSON, WALKER & REICHERT, LLP (AV)

Suite 404 SunTrust Bank Building, P.O. Box 6497, 31208-6497
Telephone: 912-743-8651
Telecopier: 912-743-9636

Thomas L. Bass
Albert P. Reichert, Jr.
Jonathan A. Alderman

OF COUNSEL

Albert P. Reichert

Representative Clients: Riverwood International Corporation; Radiology Associates of Macon, P.C.; Thiele Kaolin Company; SunTrust Bank, Middle Georgia, N.A.
General Insurance Clients: Liberty Mutual Insurance Co.

For Complete List of Firm Personnel, See General Section

For full biographical listings, see the Martindale-Hubbell Law Directory

*MARIETTA,** Cobb Co.

BROWNING & TANKSLEY, LLP (AV)

Suite 225, 166 Anderson Street, 30060
Telephone: 770-424-1500
Fax: 770-424-1740

MEMBER OF FIRM

Jerry A. Landers, Jr.

For full biographical listings, see the Martindale-Hubbell Law Directory

CUSTER & HILL, P.C. (AV)

324 Cherokee Street, P.O. Box 1224, 30061
Telephone: 770-429-8300
Fax: 770-429-8338
Email: custerhill@mindspring.com

Lawrence B. Custer
Douglas A. Hill

Vic Brown Hill

Reference: Nations Bank.

For full biographical listings, see the Martindale-Hubbell Law Directory

W. ALLEN SEPARK (AV)

250 Church Street, Second Floor, P.O. Box 3475, 30061-3475
Telephone: 770-422-3200
Fax: 770-514-1148

Representative Clients: Martin's Restaurant Systems, Inc.; Snowden Enterprises, Inc.; Sparkles Roller Rinks; Bearden & Smith, P.C.; The Halifax Group, Inc. formerly Oak Hill Farms, Inc.; Southern Polytechnic State University Foundation, Inc.; Metro North Youth Soccer Association, Inc.; Wellstar Foundation, Inc. formerly PROMINA Northwest Health Foundation, Inc.; The Georgia Ballet, Inc.

For full biographical listings, see the Martindale-Hubbell Law Directory

*NEWNAN,** Coweta Co.

GLOVER & DAVIS, P.A. (AV)

10 Brown Street, P.O. Box 1038, 30264
Telephone: 770-683-6000
Fax: 770-683-6010
Peachtree City, Georgia Office: Suite 130, 200 Westpark Drive.
Telephone: 770-487-5834.
Fax: 770-487-3492.

J. Littleton Glover
J. Littleton Glover, Jr.
Alan W. Jackson

Representative Clients: First Citizens Corporation and Banking subsidiaries; Putnam-Greene Financial Corporation; Farmers & Merchants Bank, Eatonton, Georgia; The Farmers Bank, Union Point, Georgia; First Bank of Coastal Georgia; Peachtree National Bank; Georgia Baptist Children's Homes and Family Ministries, Inc.
Local Counsel for: West Georgia Farm Credit, ACA; First Financial Bank, FSB, Stevens Point, Wisconsin.

For Complete List of Firm Personnel, See General Section

For full biographical listings, see the Martindale-Hubbell Law Directory

ROSENZWEIG, JONES & MACNABB, P.C. (AV)

32 South Court Square, P.O. Box 220, 30264
Telephone: 770-253-3282
Fax: 770-251-7262

(See Next Column)

ROSENZWEIG, JONES & MACNABB P.C.—*Continued*

George C. Rosenzweig
Sidney Pope Jones, Jr.
Joseph P. MacNabb

Charles C. Witcher
Douglas L. Dreyer
Jonathan W. Hickman

Approved Attorneys for: Lawyers Title Insurance Corp.; Chicago Title Insurance Co.

For full biographical listings, see the Martindale-Hubbell Law Directory

NORCROSS, Gwinnett Co.

THOMAS E. RAINES, P.C. (AV)

3500 Parkway Lane, Suite 130, 30092
Telephone: 770-263-0093
Facsimile: 770-840-9725
Email: TRaines166@aol.com

Thomas E. Raines

Representative Clients: Arccom Commercial Lending, Inc.; Chris Motors, Inc.; Chris Imports, Inc.; Whirlpool Financial Corp.; Citizens Bank of Gwinnett; Textron Financial Corp.

For full biographical listings, see the Martindale-Hubbell Law Directory

*SAVANNAH,** Chatham Co.

HUNTER, MACLEAN, EXLEY & DUNN, P.C. (AV)

200 East St. Julian Street, P.O. Box 9848, 31412
Telephone: 912-236-0261
Cable Address: "Ancan"
Telecopier: 912-236-4936
Telex: 54-6483
Email: hmed.com *URL:* http://www.bobbs@hmed.com
Atlanta, Georgia Office: The Peachtree, 1355 Peachtree Street, N.E., Suite 640.
Telephone: 404-876-3611.
Fax: 404-870-2025.

Malcolm R. Maclean
John B. Miller
Henry M. Dunn, Jr.
M. Lane Morrison
Craig S. Bonnell (Not admitted in GA)
J. Reid Williamson, III
William E. Dillard, III
David M. Hirsberg
Frank S. Macgill

OF COUNSEL

Don L. Waters

Representative Clients: SunTrust Bank, Savannah, N.A.; First Union National Bank of Georgia; Gulfstream Aerospace; Prudential Insurance Company of America; Historic Savannah Foundation, Inc.; John Hancock Mutual Life Insurance Co.; Norfolk Southern Corp.

For Complete List of Firm Personnel, See General Section

For full biographical listings, see the Martindale-Hubbell Law Directory

WEINER, SHEAROUSE, WEITZ, GREENBERG & SHAWE, L.L.P. (AV)

14 East State Street, P.O. Box 10105, 31412-0305
Telephone: 912-233-2251
Telecopier: 912-235-5464
Email: WSWGS@Sysconn.com

MEMBERS OF FIRM

Nelson Haslam (1926-1974)
Aron G. Weiner
William W. Shearouse, Jr.
N. Harvey Weitz
Stephen F. Greenberg
Mark T. Shawe
Malcolm Mackenzie, III
Edwin R. Byck

Christine Tambakis McDonnell

For full biographical listings, see the Martindale-Hubbell Law Directory

HAWAII

*HONOLULU,** Honolulu Co.

CADES SCHUTTE FLEMING & WRIGHT (AV)

Formerly Smith, Wild, Beebe & Cades
Cades Schutte Fleming & Wright Building, 1000 Bishop Street, Suite 1200, P.O. Box 939, 96808
Telephone: 808-521-9200
Telecopier: 808-521-9210
Email: cades@cades.com
Kailua-Kona, Hawaii Office: Hualalai Center, Suite B-303, 75-170 Hualalai Road.
Telephone: 808-329-5811.
Telecopier: 808-326-1175.

MEMBERS OF FIRM

Robert B. Bunn
David C. Larsen
Rhonda L. Griswold

ASSOCIATE

Kimberly A. Jackson (Resident, Kona Office)

For Complete List of Firm Personnel, See General Section

For full biographical listings, see the Martindale-Hubbell Law Directory

CARLSMITH BALL (AV)

A Partnership including Law Corporations
Suite 2200, Pacific Tower, 1001 Bishop Street, P.O. Box 656, 96809-3402
Telephone: 808-523-2500
Fax: 808-523-0842
Email: execdirector@carlsmith.com *URL:* http://www.carlsmith.com
Kapolei, Hawaii Office: Suite 318, Kapolei Building, 1001 Kamokila Boulevard, 96707.
Telephone: 808-523-2500.
Fax: 808-674-0850.
Wailuku, Maui Hawaii Office: Suite 400, One Main Plaza, 2200 Main Street, P.O. Box 1086, 96793-1086.
Telephone: 808-242-4535.
Fax: 808-244-4974.
Kailua-Kona, Hawaii Office: Suite 209, 75-1000 Henry Street, 96740.
Telephone: 808-329-6464.
Fax: 808-329-9450.
Hilo, Hawaii Office: 121 Waianuenue Avenue, P.O. Box 686, 96721-0686.
Telephone: 808-935-6644.
Fax: 808-935-7975.
Hagatna, Guam Office: Suite 401, Bank of Hawaii Building, 134 West Soledad Avenue, P.O. Box BF, 96932-5027.
Telephone: 671-472-6813.
Fax: 671-477-4375.
Telex: 721-6445 CWCMI GM.
Saipan, Commonwealth of the Northern Mariana Islands Office: Carlsmith Building, Capitol Hill, P.O. Box 5241, 96950-5241.
Telephone: 670-322-3455.
Fax: 670-322-3368.
Los Angeles, California Office: 9th Floor, 444 South Flower Street, 90071-2901.
Telephone: 213-955-1200.
Fax: 213-623-0032.
Washington, D.C. Office: Suite 300, 1201 Pennsylvania Avenue, N.W., 20004-2401.
Telephone: 202-628-2228.
Fax: 202-628-2071.
Mexico City, Mexico Office: Carlsmith Ball, Sierra Nevada 119, Lomas de Chapultepec, 11000 Mexico, D.F.
Telephone: 52-5-520-8514, 52-5-520-8757.
Fax: 52-5-540-1545.
Mexico, D.F. Office of Carlsmith Ball, S.C. (Authorized to practice as foreign legal consultants in Mexico): Sierra Nevada 119, Lomas de Chapultepec, 11000 Mexico, D.F.
Telephone: 52-5-520-8514, 52-5-520-8757.
Fax: 52-5-540-1545.

MEMBERS OF FIRM

Michael I. Blaylock (Not admitted in HI; Resident at Los Angeles, California Office)
Mary Jane Connell
John C. Khil
Harry Y. Oda
James L. Starshak
Sinforoso M. Tolentino (Resident at Hagatna, Guam Office)
Robert D. Triantos (Resident at Kailua-Kona, Hawaii Office)
Charles R. Wichman
David W. K. Wong

For Complete List of Firm Personnel, See General Section

For full biographical listings, see the Martindale-Hubbell Law Directory

GERSON, GREKIN & WYNHOFF ATTORNEYS AT LAW, A LAW CORPORATION (AV)

Suite 780 Pacific Tower, 1001 Bishop Street, 96813
Telephone: 808-524-4800
Telecopier: 808-537-1420
Email: ggwlaw@aloha.net

(See Next Column)

GERSON, GREKIN & WYNHOFF ATTORNEYS AT LAW, A LAW CORPORATION, *Honolulu—Continued*

Gaye Lynne Chun
Kristie K. Cruz
Mervyn S. Gerson
Nancy Nissen Grekin
Bruce D. Hieneman
William J. Wynhoff

For full biographical listings, see the Martindale-Hubbell Law Directory

GOODSILL ANDERSON QUINN & STIFEL (AV)

Alii Place, Suite 1800, 1099 Alakea Street, P.O. Box 3196, 96801-3196
Telephone: 808-547-5600
FAX: 808-547-5880
Email: info@goodsill.com *URL:* http://www.goodsill.com

MEMBERS OF FIRM

Conrad M. Weiser
Patricia Y. Lee
Raymond K. Okada
Judy Y. Lee

COUNSEL

Randall W. Roth
Eric H. Sonnenberg

ASSOCIATE

Mary A. Renfer

Representative Clients: Hawaiian Trust Company, Limited; First Hawaiian Bank.

For Complete List of Firm Personnel, See General Section

For full biographical listings, see the Martindale-Hubbell Law Directory

PETER P. J. NG (AV)

Second Floor, Bank of Hawaii Building Kaimuki Branch, 3604 Waialae Avenue, 96816
Telephone: 808-732-7788
Fax: 808-732-7780

ASSOCIATE

Jeffrey R. Niebling

For full biographical listings, see the Martindale-Hubbell Law Directory

OTA & YUEN (AV)

Pioneer Plaza, 900 Fort Street Mall, Suite 1602, 96813
Telephone: 808-532-3100
Fax: 808-532-3109

MEMBERS OF FIRM

Russell A. Ota
Curtis B. K. Yuen

For full biographical listings, see the Martindale-Hubbell Law Directory

REINWALD, O'CONNOR & PLAYDON (AV)

(Formerly Anthony, Hoddick, Reinwald & O'Connor)
2400 Makai Tower, Grosvenor Center, P.O. Box 3199, 96801-3199
Telephone: 808-524-8350
Telecopier: 808-531-8628
Email: info@roplaw.com *URL:* http://www.roplaw.com

MEMBER OF FIRM

Arthur B. Reinwald

ASSOCIATE

Jody Lynn Kellerman

OF COUNSEL

Clinton Andrew Englehart

For full biographical listings, see the Martindale-Hubbell Law Directory

STIRLING & KLEINTOP (AV)

20th Floor, 1100 Alakea Street, 96813
Telephone: 808-524-5183
FAX: 808-528-0261
Email: S&K@hifamlaw.com

MEMBER OF FIRM

Thomas L. Stirling, Jr.

For full biographical listings, see the Martindale-Hubbell Law Directory

TAKUSHI, FUNAKI, WONG & STONE ATTORNEYS AT LAW, A LAW CORPORATION (AV)

Suite 1400 Grosvenor Center, 733 Bishop Street, 96813
Telephone: 808-543-9800
Fax: 808-543-9869
Email: tfwf@pixi.com

Roy E. Takushi
James T. Funaki
Alfred M. K. Wong
Robert M. Ehrhorn, Jr.
Dickson C. H. Lee
Peter T. Stone
James N. H. Yee
Ann L. Kurihara
Jacqueline Kong
Elizabeth A. Kane

For full biographical listings, see the Martindale-Hubbell Law Directory

TAM, O'CONNOR, HENDERSON, TAIRA & YAMAUCHI ATTORNEYS AT LAW, A LAW CORPORATION (AV)

20th Floor, Central Pacific Plaza, 220 South King Street, 96813
Telephone: 808-545-3030
Fax: 808-523-8051
Fax: 808-537-6782
Email: lawyers@50thstatelaw.com

James K. Tam
Michael F. O'Connor
Harvey E. Henderson, Jr.
Lissa H. Andrews
Robert M. Yamauchi
Darryl M. Taira
Stuart M. Kodish

Wesley H. Ikeda
Russ S. Awakuni
Kevin W. Herring
Fred I. Waki

OF COUNSEL

Paul M. Dold

For full biographical listings, see the Martindale-Hubbell Law Directory

IDAHO

*BOISE,** Ada Co.

ELAM & BURKE, A PROFESSIONAL ASSOCIATION (AV)

Key Financial Center, 702 West Idaho Street, P.O. Box 1539, 83701
Telephone: 208-343-5454
Telecopier: 208-384-5844
Email: eblaw@elamburke.com

Carl P. Burke
Sandra L. Clapp

Jayne Tracy Davis

Representative Clients: U.S. BanCorp Leasing; First Security Bank of Idaho, N.A.; First Interstate Bank of Idaho, N.A.; Key Trust Company of the West.

For Complete List of Firm Personnel, See General Section

For full biographical listings, see the Martindale-Hubbell Law Directory

*POCATELLO,** Bannock Co.

MERRILL & MERRILL, CHARTERED (AV)

Key Bank Building, P.O. Box 991, 83204
Telephone: 208-232-2286
Fax: 208-232-2499
Email: mmlaw@ida.net

Dave R. Gallafent
D. Russell Wight
Gary L. Longmore

For Complete List of Firm Personnel, See General Section

For full biographical listings, see the Martindale-Hubbell Law Directory

ILLINOIS

*BELLEVILLE,** St. Clair Co.

DUNHAM, BOMAN & LESKERA (AV)

208 N. High, 62220
Telephone: 618-235-7222
Telecopier: 618-236-2800; 618-236-1899
Collinsville Office: 300 West Clay Street.
Telephone: 618-344-7734.
Telecopier: 618-344-3853.

M.F. Oehmke (1887-1963)
Wm. C. Dunham (1893-1975)
Howard Boman (1917-1985)
John W. Leskera
William L. Berry
Eric C. Young
Robert D. Francis
John L. Bitzer

For full biographical listings, see the Martindale-Hubbell Law Directory

MATHIS, MARIFIAN, RICHTER & GRANDY, LTD. (AV)

720 West Main Street, 62220
Telephone: 618-234-9800; 314-421-2325
Fax: 618-234-9786
URL: http://www.mmrg.com

Patrick B. Mathis
George E. Marifian
Kevin J. Richter
Laura Koeneman Grandy
Kevin J. Stine
Mark J. Stegman
T. Bradford Waltrip
Carl M. Markus

For full biographical listings, see the Martindale-Hubbell Law Directory

*CHICAGO,** Cook Co.

ARONBERG GOLDGEHN DAVIS & GARMISA (AV)

Suite 3000 One IBM Plaza, 60611
Telephone: 312-828-9600
Telecopier: 312-828-9635
Email: agdglaw@aol.com
Schaumberg, Illinois Office: 1901 North Roselle Road, Suite 800, 60195.
Telephone: 847-985-4060.

MEMBERS OF FIRM

James S. Jarvis — Ned S. Robertson

ASSOCIATES

Eric M. Brown — Mary Vidal Hays
Elizabeth Olen Lazzara

For Complete List of Firm Personnel, See General Section

For full biographical listings, see the Martindale-Hubbell Law Directory

HOPKINS & SUTTER (AV)

A Partnership including Professional Corporations
Three First National Plaza, Suite 4100, 60602-4205
Telephone: 312-558-6600
Fax: 312-558-6538
Email: postmaster@hopsut.com *URL:* http://www.hopsut.com
Washington, D.C. Office: 888 Sixteenth Street, N.W.
Telephone: 202-835-8000.
Fax: 202-835-8136.
Troy, Michigan Office: 2800 Livernois, Suite 220.
Telephone: 248-740-6600.
Fax: 248-740-6613.

MEMBERS OF FIRM

John T. Brooks — James R. Hellige
Jane Gorham Ditelberg — William G. McMaster, Jr.
Michael A. Ficaro — Cordell J. Overgaard (P.C.)
William C. Weinsheimer

ASSOCIATES

Kathleen M. Eggers — Samantha Weissbluth

For Complete List of Firm Personnel, See General Section

For full biographical listings, see the Martindale-Hubbell Law Directory

MCBRIDE BAKER & COLES (AV)

500 West Madison Street 40th Floor, 60661-2511
Telephone: 312-715-5700
Cable Address: "Chilaw"
Telex: 270258
Telecopier: 312-993-9350
Email: lastname@mbc.com *URL:* http://www.mbc.com
Oakbrook Terrace, Illinois Office: Suite 1000, One Mid America Plaza, 60181-4710.
Telephone: 630-954-2100.
Telecopier: 630-954-2112.

MEMBERS OF FIRM

David Ackerman — Steven R. Lifson
Andrew R. Gelman — Morgan J. Ordman
Thomas J. Kinasz — David Shayne

OF COUNSEL

Robert O. Case — G. Gale Roberson, Jr.

ASSOCIATES

Brian D. Hector — Todd J. Schneider

For Complete List of Firm Personnel, See General Section

For full biographical listings, see the Martindale-Hubbell Law Directory

NISEN & ELLIOTT (AV)

200 West Adams Street, Suite 2500, 60606
Telephone: 312-346-7800
Telecopier: 312-346-9316

MEMBERS OF FIRM

Paul F. Gerbosi — Robert O. Middleton
Edward B. Mueller — William G. Daluga, Jr.
Anthony Packard — Kenneth J. Rojc
Mark F. Zaenger — Thomas V. McCauley
Michael J. Daley — Helen M. Jensen
John Foster Lesch — William A. Walker
John K. Kneafsey — Daniel P. Dawson
Michael H. Moirano — Michael J. Pavlicek

Robert Christie — Brian C. Kelly
Donald F. Froehlke — Mary Rose C. Manczak
Thomas K. Juffernbruch — Bradley S. McCann
Brendan J. Kelly — Brian D. Proctor

(See Next Column)

OF COUNSEL

Charles M. Nisen — Donald C. Shine

For full biographical listings, see the Martindale-Hubbell Law Directory

QUARLES & BRADY LLC (AV)

Citicorp Center, 500 West Madison Street, Suite 3700, 60661-2511
Telephone: 312-715-5000
Fax: 312-715-5155
URL: http://www.quarles.com
Milwaukee, Wisconsin Office: Quarles & Brady LLP, 411 East Wisconsin Avenue, 53202-4497.
Telephone: 414-277-5000.
Fax: 414-271-3552.
Madison, Wisconsin Office: Quarles & Brady LLP, Firstar Plaza, One South Pinckney Street, P.O. Box 2113, 53701-2113.
Telephone: 608-251-5000.
Fax: 608-251-9166.
West Palm Beach, Florida Office: Quarles & Brady LLP, 222 Lakeview Avenue, 4th Floor, 33401.
Telephone: 561-653-5000.
Fax: 561-653-5333.
Naples, Florida Office: Quarles & Brady LLP, Barnett Center, 4501 Tamiami Trail North, Suite 300, 34103-3060.
Telephone: 941-262-5959.
Fax: 941-434-4999.
Phoenix, Arizona Office: Quarles & Brady LLP, One Camelback Building, One East Camelback Road, Suite 400, 85012-1649.
Telephone: 602-230-5500.
Fax: 602-230-5598.

Gary H. Kline — Thomas E. Chomicz
Thomas A. Polachek — Sarah M. Linsley
Patrick J. Bitterman

For Complete List of Firm Personnel, See General Section

For full biographical listings, see the Martindale-Hubbell Law Directory

SCHWARTZBERG, BARNETT & COHEN (AV)

55 West Monroe Street, 2400 Xerox Centre, 60603-5040
Telephone: 312-726-3555
Fax: 312-726-6299
Cable Address: "Justice"
Email: sb&c@twty.chi.il.us

MEMBERS OF FIRM

Ralph M. Schwartzberg (1939-1975) — Mark T. Barnett (1939-1970)
Hugh J. Schwartzberg
Benjamin H. Cohen

For full biographical listings, see the Martindale-Hubbell Law Directory

SUGAR, FRIEDBERG & FELSENTHAL (AV)

30 North La Salle Street, Suite 2600, 60602
Telephone: 312-704-9400
Telecopier: 312-372-7951
Cable: "SUGARFREE"

MEMBERS OF FIRM

Richard A. Sugar — Jonathan L. Mills
Michael R. Friedberg — Etahn M. Cohen
Steven A. Felsenthal — Howard M. Helsinger
Andrew B. David — Robert F. Simon
Leslie J. Weiss — Martin M. Weinstein
Ira S. Neiman — Charles H. Braun
Kathryn A. Erickson

ASSOCIATES

Aron L. Bornstein — Norman J. Ginsparg
Annette L. Brands — William F. McGuinn
Kathryn T. Cha — Suzanne J. Massel
Deanne Elizabeth Clarke

For full biographical listings, see the Martindale-Hubbell Law Directory

WATT & SAWYIER (AV)

The Monadnock Building, 53 West Jackson Boulevard, Suite 1120, 60604-3701
Telephone: 312-663-1440
Telecopier: 312-663-1410

MEMBERS OF FIRM

Garland W. Watt — Michael T. Sawyier

OF COUNSEL

Rosalind A. Burbank

For full biographical listings, see the Martindale-Hubbell Law Directory

COLLINSVILLE, Madison Co.

DUNHAM, BOMAN & LESKERA (AV)

300 West Clay Street, 62234
Telephone: 618-344-7734
Telecopier: 618-344-3853
Belleville Office: 208 N. High.
Telephone: 618-235-7222.
Telecopier: 618-236-2800; 618-236-1899.

John W. Leskera
William L. Berry
Eric C. Young
Robert D. Francis
John L. Bitzer

For full biographical listings, see the Martindale-Hubbell Law Directory

*DECATUR,** Macon Co.

R. NICHOLAS BURTON (AV)

Suite 603 Millikin Court, 132 South Water Street, 62523
Telephone: 217-423-8861

References: The First National Bank of Decatur; Union Planters Bank; Hickory Point Bank & Trust; Soy Capital Bank & Trust Co.

For full biographical listings, see the Martindale-Hubbell Law Directory

DE KALB, De Kalb Co.

BOYLE, CORDES & BROWN (AV)

301 East Lincoln Highway, 60115-3307
Telephone: 815-756-6328
Fax: 815-756-8842

MEMBERS OF FIRM

John G. Boyle (1907-1996)
Gary W. Cordes
Charles G. Brown

Representative Clients: DeKalb Park District; First of America, N.A. DeKalb, Il; First National Bank in Dekalb.
References: First of America Bank-DeKalb; First National Bank in DeKalb.

For full biographical listings, see the Martindale-Hubbell Law Directory

*GALESBURG,** Knox Co.

BARASH & STOERZBACH, P.C. (AV)

139 South Cherry Street, P.O. Box 1328, 61402-1328
Telephone: 309-341-6000
Telecopier: 309-343-7500
Email: galesburg@barashlaw.com
Galva, Illinois Office: 110 Exchange Street, P.O. Box 165, 61434.
Telephone: 309-932-2001.
Telefax: 309-932-3151. Email: galva@barashlaw.com.

Robert C. Stoerzbach
Barry M. Barash
Dwayne I. Morrison
Daniel B. Stoerzbach
Reynolds M. Everett, Jr. (Resident, Galva Office)

For Complete List of Firm Personnel, See General Section

For full biographical listings, see the Martindale-Hubbell Law Directory

HATTERY, SIMPSON & WEST (AV)

Suite 402 Hill Arcade, 61401
Telephone: 309-343-6152
Telecopier: 309-343-5103
Email: 5lawyers@galesburg.net *URL:* http://www.misslink.net/hsw/aprose.htm
Monmouth, Illinois Office: 1025 East Broadway.
Telephone: 309-734-3150.
Telefax: 309-734-7043.
Roseville, Illinois Office: 130 North Main Street.
Telephone: 309-426-2176.
Telefax: 309-426-2177.

MEMBERS OF FIRM

John J. Hattery
Roger L. Williamson
Thomas G. West
Ronald D. Stombaugh (Resident at Monmouth Office)
Carol Masden Simpson
George M. Hennenfent (Resident, Roseville Office)

For Complete List of Firm Personnel, See General Section

For full biographical listings, see the Martindale-Hubbell Law Directory

GRANITE CITY, Madison Co.

LUEDERS, ROBERTSON & KONZEN (AV)

1939 Delmar Avenue, 62040
Telephone: 618-876-8500
Telecopier: 618-876-4534
Email: lrk.il@worldnet.att.net
Danville, Illinois Office: 809 1/2 North Gilbert, 61832.
Telephone: 217-443-0304.
Fax: 217-443-0375.

(See Next Column)

MEMBERS OF FIRM

Wesley Lueders (1896-1957)
Randall Robertson
Leo H. Konzen
R. Eric Robertson
Edward C. Fitzhenry, Jr.
Brian E. Konzen
Paul G. Foran

ASSOCIATE

Anthony R. Garavalia

Representative Clients: Ameritech; Mercantile Bank (Trust Division); Granite City Steel Division of National Steel Corporation; Allied Waste Industries, Inc.; Illinois Industrial Energy Consumers (IIEC) including Olin Corporation; Archers-Daniels-Midland Company; General Motors Corporation.

For full biographical listings, see the Martindale-Hubbell Law Directory

*JOLIET,** Will Co.

MCKEOWN, FITZGERALD, ZOLLNER, BUCK, HUTCHISON & RUTTLE (AV)

2455 Glenwood Avenue, 60435
Telephone: 815-729-4800
Fax: 815-729-4711
Frankfort Office: 28 Kansas Street.
Telephone: 815-469-2176.
FAX: 815-469-0295.

MEMBERS OF FIRM

Charles J. McKeown (1908-1985)
Paul O. McKeown (1913-1982)
Richard T. Buck (1936-1992)
Douglas P. Hutchison (1939-1998)
Joseph C. Fitzgerald (Retired)
Max E. Zollner
David L. Ruttle
Theodore J. Jarz
Douglas J. McKeown
James B. Harvey
Kenneth A. Grey
Michael R. Lucas
Christopher N. Wise
Gary S. Mueller
John C. Roth
Arthur J. Wilhelmi
Thomas M. Carney

ASSOCIATE

Christopher S. Ward (Resident)

OF COUNSEL

George E. Sangmeister
Stewart C. Hutchison

Representative Clients: First Midwest Bank, N.A.; Silver Cross Hospital; Villages of: Plainfield and Mokena; Southwest Agency for Risk Management; Joliet Junior College Foundation; Cornerstone Services, Inc.; Nicor Inc.; Express Riverboat Casino, Joliet, Inc.; Joliet Valves, Inc.

For full biographical listings, see the Martindale-Hubbell Law Directory

MATTOON, Coles Co.

CRAIG & CRAIG (AV)

1807 Broadway, P.O. Box 689, 61938-0689
Telephone: 217-234-6481
Telecopier: 217-234-6486; 258-8292
Email: craiglaw@advant.com
Mount Vernon, Illinois Office: 115 North 7th Street.
Telephone: 618-244-7511.

MEMBERS OF FIRM

Craig Van Meter (1895-1981)
Fred H. Kelly (1894-1971)
Robert M. Werden (1908-1969)
George N. Gilkerson (1911-1985)
John P. Ewart
Richard F. Record, Jr.
Stephen L. Corn
Robert G. Grierson
Gregory C. Ray
Paul R. Lynch (Resident, Mount Vernon Office)
Kenneth F. Werts (Resident, Mount Vernon Office)
John L. Barger

ASSOCIATES

Kathleen M. Stockwell
Kristine M. Tuttle
Julie A. Webb (Resident, Mount Vernon Office)
John M. O'Driscoll
Duane A. Deters
Katy C. Fain (Resident, Mount Vernon Office)
Erin E. Wisner
John F. Watson

OF COUNSEL

Jack E. Horsley

Representative Clients: First Mid-Illinois Bank & Trust, Mattoon, Illinois; BANKCENTRAL TRUST, a Division of BankChampaign, N.A.; Lake Land College.

For full biographical listings, see the Martindale-Hubbell Law Directory

OAKBROOK TERRACE, DuPage Co.

MCBRIDE BAKER & COLES (AV)

Suite 1000, One Mid America Plaza, 60181-4710
Telephone: 630-954-2100
Telecopier: 630-954-2112
URL: http://www.mbc.com
Chicago, Illinois Office: 500 West Madison Street, 40th Floor, 60661-2511.
Telephone: 312-715-5700.
Telecopier: 312-993-9350.

(See Next Column)

McBRIDE BAKER & COLES—*Continued*

MEMBERS OF FIRM

Robert C. Aument
James A. Kohlstedt
Carl A. Neumann

ASSOCIATE

Maureen Calabrese Strauts

For Complete List of Firm Personnel, See General Section

For full biographical listings, see the Martindale-Hubbell Law Directory

OAK PARK, Cook Co.

GOEDERT, HUNTINGTON & DEBOER (AV)

1011 Lake Street Suite 303, 60301-1138
Telephone: 708-848-6066
Fax: 708-848-6067
Email: mdeboer@csi.com *URL:* http://www.lawyers.com/gh&dlaw

MEMBERS OF FIRM

John P. Goedert
Robert A. Huntington
Michael J. DeBoer

For full biographical listings, see the Martindale-Hubbell Law Directory

*PEKIN,** Tazewell Co.

ELLIFF, KEYSER, OBERLE & DANCEY, P.C. (AV)

109 South Fourth Street, P.O. Box 873, 61554
Telephone: 309-346-4148
Fax: 309-346-0633

John T. Elliff (1872-1960)
Nathan T. Elliff (1905-1993)
Patrick E. Oberle
Burt L. Dancey
William P. Streeter

OF COUNSEL

Ronald L. Keyser

Representative Clients: City of Pekin Central Illinois Dock.
Local Counsel for: The Prudential Insurance Company of America.

For full biographical listings, see the Martindale-Hubbell Law Directory

*PEORIA,** Peoria Co.

JEROLD I. HORN (AV)

124 S.W. Adams Street, Suite 515, 61602-1355
Telephone: 309-676-2778
Fax: 309-676-2779
Email: JIHORN@AOL.COM
References: National City Bank

For full biographical listings, see the Martindale-Hubbell Law Directory

*PONTIAC,** Livingston Co.

JOHNSON & TAYLOR (AV)

Formerly Ortman, Johnson & Taylor
109 North Mill Street, 61764
Telephone: 815-844-7151
Fax: 815-844-7539

MEMBERS OF FIRM

F. A. Ortman (1882-1955)
John A. Taylor
Taylor F. Johnson

OF COUNSEL

J. Kenneth Johnson

Representative Clients: Flanagan State Bank; Flanagan-Graymont and Reddick and Long Point Fire Districts; Hartford Steam Boiler Inspection Co.; Metro Life Insurance Co.; Good Samaritan Home of Flanagan; CAPS and Flanagan Park Districts; Evenglow Lodge; Livingston County Broadcasters; Albrecht and Oliver Trusts.

For full biographical listings, see the Martindale-Hubbell Law Directory

*SULLIVAN,** Moultrie Co.

MCLAUGHLIN AND FLORINI, LTD. (AV)

16 South Washington Street, P.O. Box 228, 61951
Telephone: 217-728-7325
Fax: 217-728-8122
Email: twtignor@one-eleven.net

Joseph L. McLaughlin (1884-1963)
James M. McLaughlin
Joseph V. Florini

Representative Clients: Scott State Bank, Bethany, Ill.; Shank Road Oil & Culvert Co., Mattoon, Ill.; State Bank of Arthur, Ill.; First Mid-Illinois Bank & Trust.

For full biographical listings, see the Martindale-Hubbell Law Directory

*WAUKEGAN,** Lake Co.

DIVER, GRACH, QUADE & MASINI (AV)

Bank of Waukegan Building, 111 North County Street, 60085
Telephone: 847-662-8611
FAX: 847-662-2960

MEMBERS OF FIRM

Clarence W. Diver (1883-1962)
Thomas W. Diver
Brian S. Grach
David R. Quade
Robert J. Masini
Sarah P. Lessman
David L. Hazan

Heidi J. Aavang
Donna-Jo Rodden Vorderstrasse
Paula Vincich Randall

A list of Representative Clients will be furnished upon request.
Reference: First Midwest Bank of Waukegan.

For full biographical listings, see the Martindale-Hubbell Law Directory

*WHEATON,** DuPage Co.

ROLEWICK & GUTZKE, P.C. (AV)

Danada West Professional Center, 1776 South Naperville Road, Suite 104A, 60187-8133
Telephone: 630-653-1577
Fax: 630-653-1579
Email: rgpclaw@aol.com *URL:* http://www.lawyers.com/rolewickandgutzke

David F. Rolewick
John D. Gutzke
Karen Johnson Guilde
Christopher L. Cook

For full biographical listings, see the Martindale-Hubbell Law Directory

INDIANA

*BLOOMINGTON,** Monroe Co.

BUNGER & ROBERTSON (AV)

226 South College Square, P.O. Box 910, 47402-0910
Telephone: 812-332-9295
Fax: 812-331-8808
Email: bunrob@iquest.net

MEMBERS OF FIRM

Don M Robertson
Thomas Bunger
Margaret M. Frisbie

ASSOCIATE

Holly M. Harvey

Representative Clients: Aetna Insurance Companies; Bloomington Hospital; Commercial Union Group; Indiana Insurance Co.; Liberty Mutual Insurance; Medical Protective Co.; Monroe County Community School Corp.; Professional Golf Car, Inc.; Prudential Insurance Company of America; State Farm Automobile Insurance Co.

For Complete List of Firm Personnel, See General Section

For full biographical listings, see the Martindale-Hubbell Law Directory

JONES, MCGLASSON & BENCKART, P.C. (AV)

205 South Walnut Street, P.O. Box 279, 47402
Telephone: 812-332-4431
Fax: 812-332-0554
Email: jmbattys@bloomington.in.us *URL:* http://www.Bloomington.in.us/jmbattys

Robert Delano Jones
Thomas M. McGlasson
Judith Corcoran Benckart
Gregory Scott Lauer

OF COUNSEL

David Rogers

Representative Clients: Monroe County Bank; Indiana University Foundation; Blackwell Construction Inc.; Rogers Group Investments.
Reference: Monroe County Bank.

For full biographical listings, see the Martindale-Hubbell Law Directory

CARMEL, Hamilton Co.

KNOWLES & ASSOCIATES, LLC (AV)

811 South Range Line Road, 46032
Telephone: 317-848-4360
Telecopier: 317-848-4363
Email: knowlesassociates@worldnet.att.net *URL:* http://www.lawyers.com/knowles

William W. Knowles

(See Next Column)

KNOWLES & ASSOCIATES LLC, *Carmel—Continued*

D. Brandon Johnston

For full biographical listings, see the Martindale-Hubbell Law Directory

*COLUMBIA CITY,** Whitley Co.

GATES LAW OFFICE (AV)

407 Pinecrest Drive, P.O. Box 251, 46725-0251
Telephone: 219-244-5175
Fax: 219-244-5177

MEMBER OF FIRM

Benton E. Gates, Jr.

Attorneys for: Furnished upon request.

For full biographical listings, see the Martindale-Hubbell Law Directory

*COLUMBUS,** Bartholomew Co.

SHARPNACK, BIGLEY, DAVID & RUMPLE (AV)

321 Washington Street, P.O. Box 310, 47202-0310
Telephone: 812-372-1553
Fax: 812-372-1567
Email: sbdr@hsonline.net

MEMBERS OF FIRM

Thomas C. Bigley, Jr.
John R. Rumple
Jeffrey S. Washburn

For Complete List of Firm Personnel, See General Section

For full biographical listings, see the Martindale-Hubbell Law Directory

*EVANSVILLE,** Vanderburgh Co.

LAW OFFICES OF RANDALL K. CRAIG (AV)

5000 East Virginia, Suite 1, 47715
Telephone: 812-477-3337
Telefax: 812-477-3658
Email: rkcraig@dynasty.net

For full biographical listings, see the Martindale-Hubbell Law Directory

FINE & HATFIELD, A PROFESSIONAL CORPORATION (AV)

520 N.W. Second Street, P.O. Box 779, 47705-0779
Telephone: 812-425-3592
Telecopier: 812-421-4269
Email: Fine@Fine-Hatfield.com *URL:* http://www.Fine-Hatfield.com

James E. Marchand
Todd I. Glass
Thomas R. Fitzsimmons

Maria T. Worthington
David D. Sanders

A List of Representative Clients Furnished Upon Request.

For full biographical listings, see the Martindale-Hubbell Law Directory

RUDOLPH, FINE, PORTER & JOHNSON LLP (AV)

221 N.W. Fifth Street, Second Floor, P.O. Box 1507, 47706
Telephone: 812-422-9444
Fax: 812-421-7459
URL: http://www.rfpj@rfpj.com

MEMBERS OF FIRM

Marc D. Fine
Krista B. Lockyear

ASSOCIATE

Jeffrey D. Thompson

Reference: National City Bank of Evansville.

For full biographical listings, see the Martindale-Hubbell Law Directory

LAW OFFICES OF JACK A. STONE (AV)

1400 Old National Bank Building, 47708
Telephone: 812-423-2045
Fax: 812-423-3021
Email: jastone@evansville.com

LEGAL SUPPORT PERSONNEL

Genevieve F. York (Paralegal)
Charlene M. Young (Secretary)
Alexandra Leich (Receptionist)

For full biographical listings, see the Martindale-Hubbell Law Directory

*FORT WAYNE,** Allen Co.

HELMKE, BEAMS, BOYER & WAGNER (AV)

300 Metro Building, Berry & Harrison Streets, 46802-2242
Telephone: 219-422-7422
Telecopier: 219-422-6764
Email: hbbwdjb@aol.com
Email: rdboyer1@fortwayne.infi.net

(See Next Column)

MEMBERS OF FIRM

Walter E. Helmke (1901-1976)
Robert A. Wagner
Walter P. Helmke
J. Timothy McCaulay
R. David Boyer
Daniel J. Borgmann
Trina Glusenkamp Gould

ASSOCIATES

Payne D. Brown
R. David Boyer, II

OF COUNSEL

Glen J. Beams
William A. Berning

Representative Clients: Aalco Distributing Co., Inc.; Brotherhood Mutual Insurance Co.; Fremont Community Schools; Air-O-Mat, Inc.; Leo Distributors, Inc.; The City of Fort Wayne, Indiana; Foellinger Foundation, Inc.

For full biographical listings, see the Martindale-Hubbell Law Directory

SHAMBAUGH, KAST, BECK & WILLIAMS, LLP (AV)

600 Standard Federal Plaza, 46802-2405
Telephone: 219-423-1430
Fax: 219-422-9038
Email: skbwlawyers@skbw.com *URL:* http://www.skbw.com

MEMBERS OF FIRM

Willard Shambaugh (1897-1976)
Daniel E. Serban
Michael H. Kast
John B. Powell
Edward E. Beck
Ronald D. Felger
Stephen J. Williams
James D. Streit
Paul R. Sturm

LEGAL SUPPORT PERSONNEL

CERTIFIED PUBLIC ACCOUNTANT

David A. Fee

Counsel for: Hagerman Construction Corp.; Rogers Markets, Inc.; K & H Realty Corp.; Olive B. Cole Foundation; M. E. Raker Foundation, Inc.; Associates Financial Services Co., of Indiana, Inc.; Professional Federal Credit Union; Fort Wayne Education Association; CBT Credit Services, Inc.; Ian & Miriam Rolland Foundation, Inc.

For full biographical listings, see the Martindale-Hubbell Law Directory

GREENWOOD, Johnson Co.

WILLIAMS HEWITT & ROBBINS, LLP (AV)

National City Bank Building, 300 South Madison Avenue Suite 400, P.O. Box 405, 46142
Telephone: 317-888-1121
Facsimile: 317-887-4069

PARTNERS

Jon E. Williams
Brian C. Hewitt
J. Lee Robbins

ASSOCIATES

John M. White
John P. Wilkowski
Mark E. Need
Stephen K. Watson

For full biographical listings, see the Martindale-Hubbell Law Directory

*INDIANAPOLIS,** Marion Co.

ADINAMIS & ADINAMIS, ATTORNEYS, A PROFESSIONAL CORPORATION (AV)

8710 North Meridian Street, 46260
Telephone: 317-580-9000
Fax: 317-587-0288
URL: http://www.lawyers.com/adinamislaw

George P. Adinamis
Susan L. Adinamis
Carol M. Adinamis
Jeffrey A. Saunders

For full biographical listings, see the Martindale-Hubbell Law Directory

CONOUR • DOEHRMAN • STARKEY (AV)

III Meridian Plaza, Suite 100, 10333 N. Meridian Street, 46290
Telephone: 317-705-4444
Fax: 317-705-4455
Toll Free: 800-269-3443
URL: http://www.indianalaw.com

MEMBER OF FIRM

Martha T. Starkey

For full biographical listings, see the Martindale-Hubbell Law Directory

ELROD & MASCHER, P.C. (AV)

4000 East Southport Road, Suite 200, 46237
Telephone: 317-786-4929
Fax: 317-786-7899
Other Indianapolis Office: 2000 First Indiana Building, 135 North Pennsylvania Street. 46204.
Telephone: 317-264-5000.
Fax: 317-264-5400.

(See Next Column)

ELROD & MASCHER P.C.—*Continued*

French M. Elrod (1906-1985)
Robert G. Elrod
Gilbert E. Mascher

Jennifer Horton Mertz

Reference: National City Bank.

For full biographical listings, see the Martindale-Hubbell Law Directory

HALL & BROGDEN, P.C. (AV)

9200 Keystone Crossing, Suite 230, 46240-2167
Telephone: 317-580-4959
Fax: 317-580-4960
Email: hallbrog@indy.net

Richard M. Hall
Annette T. Brogden

Douglas S. Byrum
Pamela K. Koehler

For full biographical listings, see the Martindale-Hubbell Law Directory

HALL, RENDER, KILLIAN, HEATH & LYMAN PROFESSIONAL SERVICES CORPORATION (AV)

Suite 2000, One American Square Box 82064, 46282
Telephone: 317-633-4884
Fax: 317-633-4878
Email: hrkhl@hrkhl.com *URL:* http://www.hrkhl.com
Indianapolis North Office: Suite 820, 8402 Harcourt Road, 46260.
Telephone: 317-871-6222.
Fax: 317-338-3946.
Louisville, Kentucky Office: AEGON Center, Suite 1530, 400 West Market Street, 40202.
Telephone: 502-568-1890.
Fax: 502-568-4878.

William S. Hall
R. Terry Heath
Jeffrey Peek
Douglas P. Long
Fred J. Bachmann
Jon F. Spadorcia

James R. Willey
Edward L. Schoenbaechler (Not admitted in IN; Resident, Louisville, Kentucky Office)

For full biographical listings, see the Martindale-Hubbell Law Directory

ICE MILLER DONADIO & RYAN (AV)

One American Square Box 82001, 46282-0002
Telephone: 317-236-2100
Fax: 317-236-2219
Email: info@imdr.com *URL:* http://www.imdr.com
South Bend, Indiana Office: 211 West Washington Street, Suite 2420.
Telephone: 219-234-7933.
Fax: 219-234-7965. Internet E-mail: info@imdr.com. Web Site Address: http://www.imdr.com.
Chicago, Illinois Office: 135 South LaSalle Street, Suite 4100.
Telephone: 312-726-1567.
Fax: 312-641-6263. Internet E-mail: info@imdr.com. Web Site Address: http://www.imdr.com.

MEMBERS OF FIRM

Gordon D. Wishard
Lisa A. Stone

SENIOR COUNSEL

Gene E. Wilkins

STAFF ATTORNEY

Raymond J. Schoettle

ASSOCIATES

Gina M. Giacone
Veronica L. Jarnagin
Kristine J. Bouaichi

For Complete List of Firm Personnel, See General Section

For full biographical listings, see the Martindale-Hubbell Law Directory

ROBERT A. LICHTENAUER (AV)

Suite 110, 8140 Knue Road, 46250
Telephone: 317-845-1988

For full biographical listings, see the Martindale-Hubbell Law Directory

TABBERT HAHN EARNEST & WEDDLE (AV)

Suite 2100, One Indiana Square, 46204-2101
Telephone: 317-639-5444
Fax: 317-639-5232
Email: jtyrrell@tabberthahn.com *URL:* http://www.tabberthahn.com

(See Next Column)

Don A. Tabbert
Gregory F. Hahn
Lante K. Earnest
Robert G. Weddle
Mark K. Sullivan
Judy M. Tyrrell
Lara D. Engelking
Matthew W. Conner
William W. Mathews
Heather L. Fesko
Charles R. Whybrew

OF COUNSEL

James J. Nocon
William D. Lalley
Joseph W. Hammes
Dale E. Sporleder

For full biographical listings, see the Martindale-Hubbell Law Directory

YARLING & ROBINSON (AV)

151 North Delaware, Suite 1535, P.O. Box 44128, 46204
Telephone: 317-262-8800
Fax: 317-262-3046
Email: yrhl@yarling.com *URL:* http://www.yarling.com

MEMBERS OF FIRM

Charles F. Robinson, Jr.
John W. Hammel
Linda Y. Hammel
Douglas E. Rogers
Mark S. Gray
Matthew C. Robinson

ASSOCIATE

Jeffrey R. Mitchell

OF COUNSEL

Richard W. Yarling

Representative Clients: Furnished upon request.

For full biographical listings, see the Martindale-Hubbell Law Directory

*LAFAYETTE,** Tippecanoe Co.

BALL, EGGLESTON, BUMBLEBURG, MCBRIDE, WALKEY & STAPLETON, PC (AV)

810 Bank One Building, P.O. Box 1535, 47902-1535
Telephone: 765-742-9046
Fax: 765-742-1966
Email: info@ball-law.com

Cable G. Ball (1904-1981)
Owen Crook (1908-1977)
Warren N. Eggleston (1923-1991)
Joseph T. Bumbleburg
John K. McBride
Jack L. Walkey
Michael J. Stapleton
Jeffrey J. Newell
James T. Hodson
Brian Wade Walker
Cheryl M. Knodle
Randy J. Williams
Brenda Mithoefer Clapper

General Counsel for: The Lafayette Union Railway Co.
Representative Clients: Farmers Insurance Group; General Accident Fire & Life Assurance Corp.; City of Lafayette Board of Parks and Recreation; West Lafayette Community School Corp.; Travelers Insurance Co.; Trustees, West Lafayette Public Library; Town of Dayton, Indiana.

For full biographical listings, see the Martindale-Hubbell Law Directory

STUART & BRANIGIN (AV)

The Life Building, 300 Main Street, Suite 800, P.O. Box 1010, 47902-1010
Telephone: 765-423-1561
Telecopier: 765-742-8175
Email: sb@stuartlaw.com *URL:* http://www.stuartlaw.com
Indianapolis, Indiana Office: Suite 1401, 8888 Keystone Crossing, 46240.
Telephone: 317-574-7245.
Fax: 317-574-7050.

MEMBERS OF FIRM

Allison Ellsworth Stuart (1886-1950)
Roger D. Branigin (1902-1975)
Roger D. Branigin, Jr.
Thomas L. Ryan
Thomas R. McCully
Larry R. Fisher
Nina B. Kirkpatrick
Mark Lillianfeld
Stephen R. Pennell
Anthony S. Benton
Erik D. Spykman
William E. Emerick
John C. Duffey
Bruce McSpadden
Mark E. DeYoung
Thomas B. Parent
Laura L. Bowker
Kevin D. Nicoson
Susan K. Roberts
John M. Stuckey
Deborah B. Trice
William P. Kealey
David A. Starkweather
Geoffrey L. Blazi

SENIOR COUNSEL

Russell H. Hart

COUNSEL

John F. Bodle
James V. McGlone

ASSOCIATES

Elizabeth B. Searle
Marianne Mitten Owen
David A. Locke
Karen Orr McClure
Ann Marie Waldron
Barry L. Loftus

General Counsel for: The Lafayette Life Insurance Co.; INB National Bank, N.W.; Lafayette Home Hospital, Inc.

(See Next Column)

STUART & BRANIGIN, *Lafayette—Continued*

State Counsel for: Norfolk & Western Railway Co.
Mr. Ryan is Counsel to: The Trustees of Purdue University.
Representative Clients: Aluminum Company of America; Liberty Mutual Insurance Group.

For full biographical listings, see the Martindale-Hubbell Law Directory

MISHAWAKA, St. Joseph Co.

SCHINDLER AND OLSON (AV)

122 South Mill Street, P.O. Box 100, 46544
Telephone: 219-259-5461
Fax: 219-259-5462

OF COUNSEL

John W. Schindler (1884-1971)
John W. Schindler, Jr.

MEMBER OF FIRM

James J. Olson

A List of Representative Clients Will Be Furnished Upon Request.
Reference: 1st Source Bank of Mishawaka.

For full biographical listings, see the Martindale-Hubbell Law Directory

*TERRE HAUTE,** Vigo Co.

COX, ZWERNER, GAMBILL & SULLIVAN (AV)

511 Wabash Avenue, P.O. Box 1625, 47808-1625
Telephone: 812-232-6003
Fax: 812-232-6567

MEMBERS OF FIRM

Ernest J. Zwerner (1918-1980)
Benjamin G. Cox (1915-1988)
Gilbert W. Gambill, Jr.
James E. Sullivan
Benjamin G. Cox, Jr.
David W. Sullivan
Robert L. Gowdy
Louis F. Britton
Carroll D. Smeltzer
Jeffry A. Lind
Ronald E. Jumps
Scott Craig
Elizabeth A. Lewis

OF COUNSEL

Robert D. Hepburn

Counsel for: Terre Haute First National Bank; Farmers Insurance Group; Indiana-American Water Co.; Indiana State University; Merchants National Bank of Terre Haute; Rose-Hulman Institute of Technology; Tribune-Star Publishing Co., Inc.

For full biographical listings, see the Martindale-Hubbell Law Directory

*VALPARAISO,** Porter Co.

BLACHLY, TABOR, BOZIK & HARTMAN (AV)

56 South Washington Street Suite 401, 46383
Telephone: 219-464-1041
Fax: 219-464-0927
Fort Wayne, Indiana Office: 4656 West Jefferson. Suite 120. 46804.

MEMBERS OF FIRM

James S. Bozik
Duane W. Hartman
David L. Hollenbeck
Thomas F. Macke
Randall J. Zromkoski
Richard J. Rupcich
Craig R. Van Schouwen

OF COUNSEL

Glenn J. Tabor

Reference: First National Bank.

For Complete List of Firm Personnel, See General Section

For full biographical listings, see the Martindale-Hubbell Law Directory

*WARSAW,** Kosciusko Co.

LEMON, ARMEY, HEARN & LEININGER (AV)

210 North Buffalo Street, P.O. Box 770, 46581-0770
Telephone: 219-268-9111
Telecopier: 219-267-8647

MEMBERS OF FIRM

Robert L. Rasor (1922-1997)
Thomas R. Lemon
Michael E. Armey
R. Steven Hearn
Daniel K. Leininger
Jane L. Kauffman

Representative Clients: Lake City Bank; The Dalton Foundries, Inc.; Grace Schools, Inc.

For full biographical listings, see the Martindale-Hubbell Law Directory

IOWA

*CEDAR RAPIDS,** Linn Co.

SHUTTLEWORTH & INGERSOLL, P.C. (AV)

115 Third Street S.E., Suite 500, P.O. Box 2107, 52406-2107
Telephone: 319-365-9461
Fax: 319-365-8443
URL: http://www.shuttleworthlaw.com

Michael O. McDermott
Gary J. Streit
Carroll J. Reasoner
William P. Prowell
Dean R. Einck
William S. Hochstetler
Gilda L. Boyer
Dean D. Carrington

David T. Hayes

OF COUNSEL

William R. Shuttleworth

Representative Clients: Firstar Bank N.A.; First National Bank of Cedar Rapids; Norwest Bank Iowa, N.A.

For Complete List of Firm Personnel, See General Section

For full biographical listings, see the Martindale-Hubbell Law Directory

*COUNCIL BLUFFS,** Pottawattamie Co.

SMITH PETERSON LAW FIRM (AV)

35 Main Place, Suite 300, P.O. Box 249, 51502
Telephone: 712-328-1833
Fax: 712-328-8320
Email: email@smithpeterson.com
Omaha, Nebraska Office: 9290 West Dodge Road, Suite 205.
Telephone: 402-397-8500.
Fax: 402-397-5519.

MEMBERS OF FIRM

Raymond A. Smith (1892-1977)
John LeRoy Peterson (1895-1969)
Harold T. Beckman
Robert J. Laubenthal
Richard A. Heininger
Lawrence J. Beckman
Gregory G. Barntsen
W. Curtis Hewett
Steven H. Krohn
Randy R. Ewing
Joseph D. Thornton
T. J. Pattermann

ASSOCIATES

Daniel L. Fretheim
Paul M. Shotkoski

Representative Clients: Redland Insurance Group; Iowa Western Community College; Farm Credit Service of The Midlands; Demma Fruit Co.; Peoples National Bank; Council Bluffs Board of Water Works Trustee.

For full biographical listings, see the Martindale-Hubbell Law Directory

*DAVENPORT,** Scott Co.

GOSMA & GALLAGHER, P.L.C. (AV)

Quad City Bank Building, 4500 North Brady Street, Suite 200, 52806
Telephone: 319-388-8417
Fax: 319-388-9240
Email: lawfirm@gosma-gallagher.com
Bettendorf Office: 1989 Spruce Hills Drive.
Telephone: 319-355-5304.
Fax: 319-359-7711.

MEMBERS OF FIRM

Robert D. Wells (1904-1990)
Robert H. Gallagher
John S. Gosma
James G. Noth
Marie R. Rolling-Tarbox
David A. Millage
Robert S. Gallagher
Jane E. Zimmer

OF COUNSEL

Clay LeGrand
Nicholas W. LeGrand (Not admitted in IA)

References: American Bank and Trust Company, Rock Island; Great River Bank and Trust, Princeton.

For full biographical listings, see the Martindale-Hubbell Law Directory

*DES MOINES,** Polk Co.

CONNOLLY, O'MALLEY, LILLIS, HANSEN & OLSON, L.L.P. (AV)

300 NationsBank Building, 317 Sixth Avenue, 50309-4127
Telephone: 515-243-8157
Fax: 515-243-3919
Email: clawfirm@aol.com

MEMBERS OF FIRM

William J. Lillis
Russell J. Hansen
Michael W. O'Malley
Eugene E. Olson
Streetar Cameron
Douglas A. Fulton
Daniel L. Manning
Christopher R. Pose

(See Next Column)

CONNOLLY, O'MALLEY, LILLIS, HANSEN & OLSON L.L.P.—*Continued*

A list of Representative Clients will be furnished upon request.
References will be furnished upon request.

For Complete List of Firm Personnel, See General Section

For full biographical listings, see the Martindale-Hubbell Law Directory

DICKINSON, MACKAMAN, TYLER & HAGEN, P.C. (AV)

Suite 1600 Hub Tower, 699 Walnut Street, 50309-3986
Telephone: 515-244-2600
Telecopier: 515-246-4550
URL: http://www.dickinsonlaw.com

Barbara G. Barrett
David M. Repp
David R. Rhein
Paul R. Tyler

For full biographical listings, see the Martindale-Hubbell Law Directory

FINLEY, ALT, SMITH, SCHARNBERG, CRAIG, HILMES & GAFFNEY, P.C. (AV)

604 Locust Street, Fourth Floor Equitable Building, 50309
Telephone: 515-288-0145
Telecopier: 515-288-2724

David C. Craig

Representative Clients: ALAS; American Society of Composers, Authors and Publishers; Equitable Life Assurance Society of the U.S.; Federated Insurance Co.; Meredith Corp.
Iowa Attorneys for: Midwest Medical Insurance Co.
District Attorneys for: Norfolk & Southern Railroad; Soo Line Railroad Company.

For Complete List of Firm Personnel, See General Section

For full biographical listings, see the Martindale-Hubbell Law Directory

GREFE & SIDNEY, P.L.C. (AV)

2222 Grand Avenue, P.O. Box 10434, 50306
Telephone: 515-245-4300
Fax: 515-245-4452
Email: grandfirm@aol.com
Pella, Iowa Office: 725 Franklin Street, 50219.
Telephone: 515-628-9343.
Fax: 515-628-7252.

Rolland E. Grefe
Thomas W. Carpenter
Robert C. Thomson
Craig S. Shannon
Mary E. Kiener

Timothy N. Tripp

Representative Clients: Boatmen's National Bank of Des Moines; Easter Enterprises, Inc.; Freeman Decorating Co.; Pella Corp.

For Complete List of Firm Personnel, See General Section

For full biographical listings, see the Martindale-Hubbell Law Directory

PATTERSON, LORENTZEN, DUFFIELD, TIMMONS, IRISH, BECKER & ORDWAY, L.L.P. (AV)

729 Insurance Exchange Building, 50309
Telephone: 515-283-2147
Fax: 515-283-1002
Email: mail@pattersonfirm.com *URL:* http://www.pattersonfirm.com

MEMBERS OF FIRM

G. O. Patterson (1914-1982)
James A. Lorentzen (Retired)
Theodore T. Duffield
William E. Timmons (Retired)
Roy M. Irish
F. H. Becker (Retired)
Gary D. Ordway
Robin L. Hermann
Harry Perkins, III
Michael F. Lacey, Jr.
Gregory J. Wilson
Jeffrey A. Boehlert
Douglas A. Haag
Charles E. Cutler
Michael D. Huppert
Martin C. Sprock
William A. Wickett
Frederick M. Haskins
Jeffrey A. Baker
Janice M. Herfkens
Coreen K. Bezdicek
Patrick V. Waldron

ASSOCIATE

Michael S. Jones

General Counsel for: Iowa Insurance Institute.
Representative Clients: Allied Mutual Insurance Company; CNA Insurance Company; Chubb Insurance Group; Continental Western Insurance Co.; Farmers Insurance Group; Farmland Insurance Company; Grinnell Mutual Reinsurance Company; Hawkeye Security Insurance Company; Iowa Insurance Institute, St. Paul Fire & Marine Insurance Company.

For full biographical listings, see the Martindale-Hubbell Law Directory

*IOWA CITY,** Johnson Co.

JOHNSTON, POTTERFIELD & NATHANSON, P.C. (AV)

1902 Broadway, P.O. Box 3400, 52244
Telephone: 319-354-1712
Fax: 319-354-7265
URL: http://www.lawyers.com/johnstonlaw
Cedar Rapids Office: 129 First Avenue, S.W., P.O. Box 74210.
Telephone: 319-366-1000.
Fax: 319-366-6973.
Waterloo Office: 1506 LaPorte Road, P.O. Box 2787.
Telephone: 319-235-3000.
Fax: 319-235-2108.

Joseph C. Johnston
Amanda Potterfield
Henry E. Nathanson
Cathy L. Fitzmaurice
David Burbidge

OF COUNSEL

Carl J. Goetz, Jr.

For full biographical listings, see the Martindale-Hubbell Law Directory

*MARSHALLTOWN,** Marshall Co.

HARRISON, BRENNECKE, MOORE, SMAHA & MCKIBBEN (AV)

302 Masonic Temple Building, P.O. Box 618, 50158
Telephone: 515-752-4271
Fax: 515-752-5266
Email: MWW@MTNIA.COM

MEMBERS OF FIRM

G. A. Mote (1874-1965)
Arley J. Wilson (1913-1982)
William L. Welp (1920-1997)
Allen E. Brennecke
James R. Moore
Leslie E. Smaha
Larry E. McKibben
James L. Goodman

OF COUNSEL

Roger E. Harrison

A List of Representatve Clients will be furnished upon request.

For Complete List of Firm Personnel, See General Section

For full biographical listings, see the Martindale-Hubbell Law Directory

*MASON CITY,** Cerro Gordo Co.

WINSTON & BYRNE, LAWYERS, A PROFESSIONAL CORPORATION (AV)

119 Second Street, N.W., 50401
Telephone: 515-423-1913
Fax: 515-423-8998
Email: winston.byrne@mach3ww.com

Harold R. Winston
Michael G. Byrne
Patrick B. Byrne

Representative Clients: Woodharbor Molding & Millworks, Inc.; Winkleman Farms, Inc.; Sparboe Iowa Corporation; Schmidt Family Farms, Inc.; First Citizen's National Bank of Mason City; Norwest Bank Iowa, N.A.

For full biographical listings, see the Martindale-Hubbell Law Directory

*NEVADA,** Story Co.

CAHILL LAW OFFICES (AV)

1015 Fifth Street, 50201
Telephone: 515-382-6571
Fax: 515-382-4338

MEMBERS OF FIRM

Donald L. Nelson (1922-1984)
Thomas J. Cahill
Joseph R. Cahill

General Counsel for: Community Bank.
Representative Clients: Colo Telephone Co.; Allied Group; Iowa Mutual Insurance Co.

For full biographical listings, see the Martindale-Hubbell Law Directory

*SIOUX CITY,** Woodbury Co.

BERENSTEIN, MOORE, BERENSTEIN, HEFFERNAN & MOELLER, L.L.P. (AV)

Firstar Bank Building, 501 Pierce Street, Suite 300, P.O. Box 3207, 51102
Telephone: 712-252-0020
Fax: 712-252-0656
Email: BMBHMLAW@aol.com

MEMBERS OF FIRM

Marvin S. Berenstein
Jeffrey A. Johnson
Mitchell A. Herigstad

ASSOCIATE

Kimberly K. Wolff

Representative Clients: Aalfs Mfg., Inc.; Beef Products, Inc.; Briar Cliff College; Canal Capital Corporation - Sioux City Stockyards; Dakota Dunes Development Co.; First American Bank; Firstar Bank Iowa, N.A.; Mercy Medi-

(See Next Column)

BERENSTEIN, MOORE, BERENSTEIN, HEFFERNAN & MOELLER L.L.P., *Sioux City—Continued*

cal Center - Sioux City; Sioux City Community School District; Wells Dairy & Blue Bunny Ice Cream.

For Complete List of Firm Personnel, See General Section

For full biographical listings, see the Martindale-Hubbell Law Directory

KANSAS

*DODGE CITY,** Ford Co.

FOULSTON & SIEFKIN L.L.P. (AV)

810 Frontview, P.O. Box 1147, 67801
Telephone: 316-227-8126
Fax: 316-227-8451
URL: http://www.foulston.com
Wichita, Kansas Office: 100 North Broadway, 700 NationsBank Financial Center, 67202.
Telephone: 316-267-6371.
FAX: 316-267-6345.
Topeka, Kansas Office: 1515 NationsBank Tower, 534 Kansas Avenue, 66603.
Telephone: 785-233-3600.
FAX: 785-233-1610.
Member: Lex Mundi, The World's Leading Association of Independent Law Firms.

MEMBERS OF FIRM

William P. Trenkle, Jr.
Thomas W. Young

For Complete List of Firm Personnel, See General Section

For full biographical listings, see the Martindale-Hubbell Law Directory

*HUTCHINSON,** Reno Co.

GILLILAND & HAYES, P.A. A PROFESSIONAL ASSOCIATION (AV)

20 West 2nd Avenue, 2nd Floor, P.O. Box 2977, 67504-2977
Telephone: 316-662-0537
Facsimile: 316-669-9426
URL: http://www.gillilandhayes.com
Wichita, Kansas Office: The Orpheum Centre, Suite 300, 200 North Broadway, P.O. Box 49406.
Telephone: 316-262-2266.
Facsimile: 316-263-2202.
Kansas City, Missouri Office: 12th Floor, 3100 Broadway.
Telephone: 816-753-3100.
Facsimile: 816-753-2271.

Robert J. Gilliland
John F. Hayes
James R. Gilliland
John S. Schmidt
Bruce B. Waugh (Not admitted in KS; Resident, Kansas City, Missouri Office)
Michael R. O'Neal
Bradley D. Dillon
Gerald L. Green
David N. Zimmerman (Not admitted in KS; Resident, Kansas City, Missouri Office)
Scott J. Mann
Carol Z. Smith (Resident, Kansas City, Missouri Office)
Kathleen A. Hardee (Resident, Kansas City, Missouri Office)
Kendall R. Cunningham (Resident, Wichita Office)
Mark R. Maloney (Resident, Wichita Office)

Thomas A. Dower
Tracy Applegate Cole
Laura A. Hederstedt
Terri Roberts Munsell (Resident, Kansas City, Missouri Office)
Lisa M. Ward
Kimberly Breda Bushek (Resident, Kansas City, Missouri Office)
E. Thomas Pyle, III
Tara L. Bragg

OF COUNSEL

Robert P. Reams (Not admitted in KS; Resident, Kansas City, Missouri Office)

Representative Clients: Allied Group; CNA Insurance; Dillon Companies; Farm Bureau Mutual Insurance Co.; Fidelity Deposit Co. of Maryland; Kansas Medical Mutual Insurance Co.; Hutchinson Clinic; Hutchinson Hospital Corp.; Central Bank & Trust; U.S. Fidelity Corp.

For full biographical listings, see the Martindale-Hubbell Law Directory

*TOPEKA,** Shawnee Co.

GOODELL, STRATTON, EDMONDS & PALMER, L.L.P. (AV)

515 South Kansas Avenue, 66603-3999
Telephone: 785-233-0593
Fax: 785-233-8870
Email: GSEP@CJNETWORKS.COM *URL:* http://www.cjnetworks.com/~gsep
Kansas City, Missouri Office: 10401 Holmes Road, Suite 280.
Telephone: 816-943-8577.

MEMBERS OF FIRM

Gerald L. Goodell
H. Philip Elwood
Gerald J. Letourneau

OF COUNSEL

Robert A. McClure
John A. Bausch

ASSOCIATE

Scott C. Palecki

SPECIAL COUNSEL

Joseph E. McKinney

Counsel for: American Home Life Insurance Co.

For Complete List of Firm Personnel, See General Section

For full biographical listings, see the Martindale-Hubbell Law Directory

*WICHITA,** Sedgwick Co.

DEPEW AND GILLEN, L.L.C. (AV)

151 North Main, Suite 800, 67202-1409
Telephone: 316-262-4000
Facsimile: 316-265-3819
Email: DG@DEPEWGILLEN.COM *URL:* HTTP://WWW.DEPEWGILLEN.COM

Spencer L. Depew

For Complete List of Firm Personnel, See General Section

For full biographical listings, see the Martindale-Hubbell Law Directory

FOULSTON & SIEFKIN L.L.P. (AV)

700 NationsBank Financial Center, 67202
Telephone: 316-267-6371
Facsimile: 316-267-6345
URL: http://www.foulston.com
Topeka, Kansas Office: 1515 NationsBank Tower, 534 Kansas Avenue, 66603.
Telephone: 785-233-3600.
Fax: 785-233-1610.
Dodge City, Kansas Office: 810 Frontview, P.O. Box 1147, 67801.
Telephone: 316-227-8126.
Fax: 316-227-8451.
Member: Lex Mundi, The World's Leading Association of Independent Law Firms.

MEMBERS OF FIRM

Stanley G. Andeel
Harvey R. Sorensen
Jim H. Goering
Kevin J. Arnel
William P. Trenkle, Jr. (Resident, Dodge City Office)
Stewart T. Weaver

For Complete List of Firm Personnel, See General Section

For full biographical listings, see the Martindale-Hubbell Law Directory

TRIPLETT, WOOLF & GARRETSON, LLC (AV)

2959 North Rock Road, Suite 300, 67226
Telephone: 316-630-8100
Fax: 316-630-8101
Email: twg@twgfirm.com

MEMBERS OF FIRM

Thomas C. Triplett
Rachael K. Pirner

ASSOCIATES

Jeffery C. Dahlgren
Christopher C. Swyers

Representative Clients: Anheuser-Busch Companies, Inc.; Brite Voice Systems, Inc.; Coleman Company, Inc.; Dow Chemical Co.; Friends University; KPMG Peat Marwick; National Plastics Color, Inc.; Total Petroleum, Inc.; Travelers Insurance Co.; Willis Corroon of Kansas, Inc.

For Complete List of Firm Personnel, See General Section

For full biographical listings, see the Martindale-Hubbell Law Directory

YOUNG, BOGLE, MCCAUSLAND, WELLS & BLANCHARD, P.A. (AV)

106 West Douglas, Suite 923, 67202
Telephone: 316-265-7841
Facsimile: 316-265-3956
Email: ybmwblaw@aol.com

(See Next Column)

YOUNG, BOGLE, MCCAUSLAND, WELLS & BLANCHARD P.A.—*Continued*

Jerry D. Bogle
William A. Wells
Patrick C. Blanchard

References provided upon request.

For Complete List of Firm Personnel, See General Section

For full biographical listings, see the Martindale-Hubbell Law Directory

KENTUCKY

*GEORGETOWN,** Scott Co.

E. DURWARD WELDON (AV)

217 East Main Street, 40324
Telephone: 502-863-1285

Approved Attorney for: Lawyers Title Insurance Corporation of Richmond, Virginia; Louisville Title Division of Commonwealth Land Title Insurance Co. (Binder Agent); The Equitable Life Assurance Society of the United States.

For full biographical listings, see the Martindale-Hubbell Law Directory

*GLASGOW,** Barren Co.

GARMON & GOODMAN (AV)

139 North Public Square, P.O. Box 663, 42142-0663
Telephone: 270-651-8812
Telecopier: 270-651-8846

MEMBER OF FIRM

Larry D. Garmon

Representative Clients: James N. Gray Company (construction); Pedigo-Lessenberry Insurance Agency, Inc.; Manning Motor Express, Inc.; Glasgow Pediatric Associates, P.S.C.; Glasgow Radiology, P.S.C.; Cardiology Associates of Southern Kentucky, P.S.C.
Approved Attorneys For: Chicago Title Insurance Co.; Commonwealth Land Title Insurance Co. (Agent).
Reference: The New Farmers National Bank of Glasgow, Glasgow, KY.

For Complete List of Firm Personnel, See General Section

For full biographical listings, see the Martindale-Hubbell Law Directory

*LEXINGTON,** Fayette Co.

STOLL, KEENON & PARK, LLP (AV)

201 E. Main Street, Suite 1000, 40507-1380
Telephone: 606-231-3000
Telecopier: 606-253-1093; 606-253-1027
URL: http://www.skp.com
Frankfort, Kentucky Office: 307 Washington Street, 40601.
Telephone: 502-875-6220.
Telecopier: 502-875-6235.
Henderson, Kentucky Office: 201 C North Main Street, 42420-3103.
Telephone: 270-831-1900.
Telecopier: 270-827-4060.
Louisville, Kentucky Office: 400 West Market Street, Suite 2650, 40202-3377.
Telephone: 502-568-9100.
Telecopier: 502-568-5700.

MEMBER OF FIRM

William T. Bishop, III

ASSOCIATE

Melissa Anne Stewart

OF COUNSEL

Douglas P. Romaine

For Complete List of Firm Personnel, See General Section

For full biographical listings, see the Martindale-Hubbell Law Directory

VIMONT & WILLS PLLC (AV)

Suite 300, 155 East Main Street, 40507-1317
Telephone: 606-252-2202
Telecopier: 606-259-2927
Email: vimont@lex.infi.net

Richard E. Vimont
Bernard F. Lovely, Jr.
Richard M. Wehrle
Fred E. Fugazzi, Jr.

Micki Woodward McDaniel

For full biographical listings, see the Martindale-Hubbell Law Directory

*LOUISVILLE,** Jefferson Co.

LAWRENCE AND LAWRENCE (AV)

Suite 300, 200 South Seventh Street, 40202
Telephone: 502-583-4484
Fax: 502-583-4486

William W. Lawrence

Reference: PNC Bank & Trust Co.

For full biographical listings, see the Martindale-Hubbell Law Directory

MIDDLETON & REUTLINGER, P.S.C. (AV)

2500 Brown and Williamson Tower, 40202-3410
Telephone: 502-584-1135
Fax: 502-561-0442
URL: http://middreut.com
Jeffersonville, Indiana Office: 530 East Court Avenue, 47130.
Telephone: 812-282-1132.
Fax: 812-282-3188.

Ian Y. Henderson
Charles G. Middleton, III
Brooks Alexander
Kipley J. McNally

Clayton R. Hume

For Complete List of Firm Personnel, See General Section

For full biographical listings, see the Martindale-Hubbell Law Directory

MORGAN & POTTINGER, P.S.C. (AV)

601 West Main Street, 40202
Telephone: 502-589-2780
Telecopier: 502-585-3498
URL: http://www.morganandpottinger.com
Lexington, Kentucky Office: 133 West Short Street.
Telephone: 606-253-1900.
Telecopier: 606-255-2038.
New Albany, Indiana Office: 120 East Market Street.
Telephone: 812-948-0008.
Telecopier: 812-944-6215.

Patrick E. Morgan
C. Edward Hastie (Resident, Lexington Office)

For Complete List of Firm Personnel, See General Section

For full biographical listings, see the Martindale-Hubbell Law Directory

ROTH FOLEY BRYANT & COOPER, PLLC (AV)

First Trust Centre, Suite 300S, 200 South Fifth Street, 40202-3236
Telephone: 502-569-7550
Fax: 502-540-0123
Email: RFBC.com

Irvin D. Foley
David M. Roth
David H. Cooper
Lisa Koch Bryant
K. Gail Russell
Christian L. Juckett

OF COUNSEL

James E. Fahey
David W. Gray

Representative Clients: Bank One, Kentucky, N.A.; Huntington National Bank; Commonwealth Bank & Trust Co.; Farm Credit Services of Mid-America; Century Indemnity Co.; Travelers Casualty and Insurance Co.; Tumbleweed, LLC; John R. Gains Thoroughbreds, LLC; ARM Financial Group, Inc.; Osborn Enterprises.

For full biographical listings, see the Martindale-Hubbell Law Directory

TILFORD, DOBBINS, ALEXANDER, BUCKAWAY & BLACK (AV)

Suite 1400, One Riverfront Plaza, 40202
Telephone: 502-584-6137
Fax: 502-584-2318

MEMBERS OF FIRM

Charles W. Dobbins (1916-1992)
Henry J. Tilford (1880-1968)
George S. Wetherby (1905-1954)
Lawrence W. Wetherby (1908-1994)
John T. Metcalf (1890-1974)
Stuart E. Alexander
William A. Buckaway, Jr.
Charles W. Dobbins, Jr.
Terrell L. Black
Mark Wesley Dobbins
Stuart E. Alexander, III

John M. Nader

ASSOCIATES

John A. Wilmes
Sandra F. Keene
Patrick T. Schmidt
Thomas J.B. Hurst
H. Kevin Eddins
William J. Walsh, IV

Dana M. Taylor

OF COUNSEL

Randolph Noe
Carolyn K. Balleisen

Michael G. Karem

For full biographical listings, see the Martindale-Hubbell Law Directory

LOUISIANA

*ALEXANDRIA,** Rapides Parish

CROWELL AND OWENS, L.L.C. (AV)

Hibernia National Bank Building Sixth Floor, P.O. Box 330, 71309-0330
Telephone: 318-445-1488
Fax: 318-445-9098

MEMBERS OF FIRM

Richard L. Crowell (1916-1994)
William B. Owens
Richard B. Crowell
W. Brent Pearson

ASSOCIATES

W. Alan Pesnell
Jeff J. Horn, Jr.

For full biographical listings, see the Martindale-Hubbell Law Directory

*BATON ROUGE,** East Baton Rouge Parish

KANTROW, SPAHT, WEAVER & BLITZER, A PROFESSIONAL LAW CORPORATION (AV)

Suite 300, City Plaza, 445 North Boulevard, P.O. Box 2997, 70821-2997
Telephone: 225-383-4703
Fax: 225-343-0630; 343-0637

Byron R. Kantrow (1909-1997)
Carlos G. Spaht
Geraldine B. Weaver
Sidney M. Blitzer, Jr.
Paul H. Spaht
Lee C. Kantrow
John C. Miller
Vincent P. Fornias
David S. Rubin
Diane L. Crochet
Richard F. Zimmerman, Jr.
Bob D. Tucker
Martin E. Golden
J. Michael Robinson, Jr.
Connell L. Archey
Randal J. Robert

C. William Belsom, Jr.
Linda Orlansky Posner

Representative Clients: CNA Insurance Cos.; Federal Deposit Insurance Corp.; Hartford Insurance Group; Air Products and Chemicals, Inc.; CF Industries, Inc.; AT&T; United Companies Financial Corp.

For full biographical listings, see the Martindale-Hubbell Law Directory

GREGORY A. PLETSCH & ASSOCIATES A PROFESSIONAL LAW CORPORATION (AV)

Suite 301, Four United Plaza, 8555 United Plaza Boulevard, 70809
Telephone: 225-929-8525
Telecopier: 225-929-8520

Gregory A. Pletsch

For full biographical listings, see the Martindale-Hubbell Law Directory

*COVINGTON,** St. Tammany Parish

LAW OFFICES OF WILLIAM J. DUTEL (AV)

325 North New Hampshire Street, 70433
Telephone: 504-892-6474
Fax: 504-892-7307
Email: bdutel@fastband.com
New Orleans, Louisiana Office: 2960 Energy Centre, 1100 Poydras Street.
Telephone: 504-582-2429.

William J. Dutel

OF COUNSEL

Kimberly Kammler Dutel

For full biographical listings, see the Martindale-Hubbell Law Directory

L. PAUL HOOD JR. A PROFESSIONAL LAW CORPORATION (AV)

19267 Slemmer Road, Suite 101, 70433
Telephone: 504-867-8300
Facsimile: 504-867-9501
Email: paulhood@acadiacom.net *URL:* http://www.lawyers.com/paulhoodlaw

L. Paul Hood, Jr.

For full biographical listings, see the Martindale-Hubbell Law Directory

*LAKE CHARLES,** Calcasieu Parish

THE GRAY LAW FIRM A PROFESSIONAL LAW CORPORATION (AV)

Hibernia Tower, One Lakeshore Drive, Suite 900, P.O. Box 1467, 70602-1467
Telephone: 318-494-0694
Facsimile: 318-494-0697
Email: graylaw@graylawfirm.com

(See Next Column)

Andrew J. Gray, III
Anna R. Gray
David L. Sigler
Leslie Qvale Knox

Wade Thomas Visconte

For full biographical listings, see the Martindale-Hubbell Law Directory

HUNTER, BLAZIER, O'DOWD & MORENO, A PROFESSIONAL LAW CORPORATION (AV)

1807 Lake Street, 70601
Telephone: 318-436-1600
Fax: 318-439-2505
Email: info@hunterlaw.com *URL:* http://www.hunterlaw.com

Edwin K. Hunter (P.C.)
Timothy O'Dowd
T. Glynn Blazier
Richard D. Moreno

OF COUNSEL

Robert M. Willan (Not admitted in LA)

For full biographical listings, see the Martindale-Hubbell Law Directory

KLUMPP AND BARNATT (AV)

Suite 804 901 Lakeshore Drive, 70601
Telephone: 318-436-1500
Facsimile: 318-436-1514
Email: KLUMPP@iamerica.net

Gregory J. Klumpp
Theresa Ann Barnatt

For full biographical listings, see the Martindale-Hubbell Law Directory

METAIRIE, Jefferson Parish

HENICAN, JAMES & CLEVELAND (AV)

Suite 1200 Heritage Plaza, 111 Veterans Memorial Boulevard, 70005
Telephone: 504-837-8080
Facsimile: 504-833-0863
Mailing Address: P.O. Box 19300, New Orleans, Louisiana, 70179

MEMBERS OF FIRM

C. Ellis Henican (1905-1997)
Murray F. Cleveland (1913-1971)
Philip E. James, Jr.
Marshall G. Weaver
Edward N. George, III
Shawn M. Bridgewater

ASSOCIATES

Keith M. Benit
Jacob S. Capraro
David M. Packard

OF COUNSEL

Philip E. James
Louis V. Rand, II

Representative Clients: Better Business Bureau of New Orleans, Inc.; St. Paul Fire and Marine Insurance Co.; Stewart Enterprises, Inc.
Reference: Hibernia National Bank, New Orleans.

For full biographical listings, see the Martindale-Hubbell Law Directory

WEIR AND WALLEY (AV)

2721 Division Street, 70002-7084
Telephone: 504-455-7264
Fax: 504-455-7266
Email: weirwall@iamerica.net *URL:* http://www.weirandwalley.com

Andrew M. Weir
James M. Walley

ASSOCIATES

Mark Needham
Lisa A. Colby
Kenneth S. Moran

References: The Whitney National Bank; Omni Bank.

For full biographical listings, see the Martindale-Hubbell Law Directory

*MONROE,** Ouachita Parish

THEUS, GRISHAM, DAVIS & LEIGH, L.L.P. (AV)

1600 Lamy Lane, Drawer 4768, 71211-4768
Telephone: 318-388-0100
Fax: 318-322-8813
Email: tgdl@theuslaw.com *URL:* http://www.theuslaw.com

MEMBERS OF FIRM

John C. Theus, Sr. (1865-1938)
Orin M. Grisham (1866-1944)
Ronald L. Davis (1897-1959)
John C. Theus, Jr. (1901-1972)
E. K. Theus (1906-1974)
Thomas W. Leigh (1903-1983)
Ronald L. Davis, Jr. (1930-1999)
Robert Lee Curry, III
Charles H. Heck
Edwin K. Theus, Jr.
J. Michael Hart
Paul D. Spillers
Phillip D. Myers
David H. Nelson
Thomas G. Zentner, Jr.
James M. Edwards
Robert J. Bozeman
Sharon Ingram Marchman
C. Wendell Manning
F. Williams Sartor, Jr.
George M. Snellings, IV

(See Next Column)

THEUS, GRISHAM, DAVIS & LEIGH L.L.P.—*Continued*

ASSOCIATE

Charles H. Heck, Jr.

Representative Clients: Moore Oil Co., Inc.; CNA Insurance Company; American International Group, Inc.; Commercial Union Insurance Co.; Liberty Mutual Insurance Co.; Louisiana Medical Mutual Insurance Co.; Travelers Insurance Co.

For full biographical listings, see the Martindale-Hubbell Law Directory

THOMPSON, SPARKS, DEAN & MORRIS (AV)

A Partnership including a Professional Corporation
1401 Royal Street, P.O. Box 2867, 71207
Telephone: 318-388-1440
Fax: 318-322-0887

MEMBERS OF FIRM

M. C. Thompson (1885-1970)
George B. Dean, Jr., (P.C.)
James D. Sparks (1910-1987)
Wood T. Sparks
John C. Morris, III

ASSOCIATE

Jennifer Allen Riley

Representative Clients: South Central Bell Telephone Co.; Greater Ouachita Water Company; PHH Homequity Corp.; Commonwealth Relocation Services, Inc.; Remax, Monroe; Bell South Advertising & Publishing Corp.; Premier Mortgage Corp.; Countrywide Funding Corp.
Approved Attorneys for: BankOne; Federal Land Bank.

For full biographical listings, see the Martindale-Hubbell Law Directory

*NEW ORLEANS,** Orleans Parish

CORRERO FISHMAN HAYGOOD PHELPS WALMSLEY & CASTEIX, L.L.P. (AV)

Bank One Center, 46th Floor, 201 St. Charles Avenue, 70170-4600
Telephone: 504-586-5252
Fax: 504-586-5250

Paul M. Haygood

For full biographical listings, see the Martindale-Hubbell Law Directory

MICHAEL L. ECKSTEIN ATTORNEY AT LAW A PROFESSIONAL CORPORATION (AV)

1515 Poydras Street, Suite 2195, 70112
Telephone: 504-527-0701
Telecopier: 504-566-0040
VMX: 504-889-8876
Email: eck@eck-law.com

Michael L. Eckstein
David Coleman Raphael, Jr.

Representative Clients: Anserphone of New Orleans, Inc.; Dixie Web Graphic Corporations; Kencoil, Inc.; Life Point Systems, Inc.; Meeks Petroleum Company; Dan-Gulf Shipping, Inc.; Action, Inc.; TCB Industries, Inc.

For full biographical listings, see the Martindale-Hubbell Law Directory

LANDWEHR & HOF (AV)

225 Baronne Street Suite 2116, 70112
Telephone: 504-561-8086

MEMBERS OF FIRM

Merrill T. Landwehr
Ronald J. Hof
Darryl T. Landwehr

Reference: Bank of Louisiana, New Orleans, La.

For full biographical listings, see the Martindale-Hubbell Law Directory

LOWE, STEIN, HOFFMAN, ALLWEISS & HAUVER, L.L.P. (AV)

One Shell Square, 701 Poydras Street Suite 3600, 70139-7735
Telephone: 504-581-2450
Telecopier: 504-581-2461

MEMBER OF FIRM

Mark S. Stein

Charlton D. Hunley

For Complete List of Firm Personnel, See General Section

For full biographical listings, see the Martindale-Hubbell Law Directory

MCGLINCHEY STAFFORD (AV)

A Professional Limited Liability Company
643 Magazine Street, 70130-3477
Telephone: 504-586-1200
Fax: 504-596-2800
TDD: (504) 596-2728
Telex: 584327
Cable Address: "MACSTAC"
Mailing Address: P.O. Box 60643, New Orleans, Louisiana, 70160-0643
Email: @mcglinchey.com *URL:* http://www.mcglinchey.com
Dallas, Texas Office: 2777 Stemmons Freeway, Suite 925, 75207-2401.
Telephone: 214-860-9700.
Fax: 214-860-9750.
Houston, Texas Office: 2727 Allen Parkway, Suite 1900, 77019.
Telephone: 713-520-1900.
Fax: 713-520-1025.
Baton Rouge, Louisiana Office: Ninth Floor, One American Place, 70825-0001.
Telephone: 504-383-9000.
Fax: 504-343-3076.
Jackson, Mississippi Office: Suite 1200, SkyTel Centre, 200 South Lamar Street, 39201.
Telephone: 601-960-8400.
Fax: 601-960-8406.
Lake Providence, Louisiana Office: 405 Morgan Street, 71254-2691.
Telephone: 318-559-1200.
Fax: 318-559-0609.
Monroe, Louisiana Office: Dean ONB Tower, 130 Desiard Street, Suite 807, 71201.
Telephone: 318-651-0807.
Fax: 318-651-0809.

MEMBERS OF FIRM

Frank Voelker, Jr., (P.C.)
Kenneth A. Weiss
Katherine Conklin

ASSOCIATES

David Ball
Jaye Andras Caffrey

MEMBER OF FIRM

Richard A. Fogel (Resident, Dallas Office)

ASSOCIATES

Jon Ann H. Giblin (Resident, Baton Rouge Office)
F. Sherman Boughton, Jr. (Resident, Lake Providence Office)
Amanda K. Bishop

For full biographical listings, see the Martindale-Hubbell Law Directory

WALTER J. SUTHON III (AV)

1010 Whitney Building, 228 St. Charles Avenue, 70130
Telephone: 504-524-0681
Fax: 504-524-0685

For full biographical listings, see the Martindale-Hubbell Law Directory

TARCZA & GELDERMAN, L.L.C. (AV)

Thirteen Ten Whitney Building, Two Twenty Eight St. Charles Avenue, 70130
Telephone: 504-525-6696
Fax: 504-525-6701

Robert E. Tarcza
G. Anthony Gelderman, III

ASSOCIATE

Juliet Puissegur Bland

For full biographical listings, see the Martindale-Hubbell Law Directory

*SHREVEPORT,** Caddo Parish

BARLOW AND HARDTNER L.C. (AV)

Tenth Floor, Louisiana Tower, 401 Edwards Street, 71101-3289
Telephone: 318-227-1131
Telecopier: 318-227-1141
Mailing Address: P.O. Box 8, Shreveport, Louisiana, 71161-0008

Quintin T. Hardtner, III
Stephen E. Ramey

OF COUNSEL

Cecil E. Ramey, Jr.
Paula Hazelrig Hickman

For Complete List of Firm Personnel, See General Section

For full biographical listings, see the Martindale-Hubbell Law Directory

BLANCHARD, WALKER, O'QUIN & ROBERTS, A PROFESSIONAL LAW CORPORATION (AV)

Fourteenth Floor, Premier Bank Tower, 400 Texas Street, P.O. Drawer 1126, 71101
Telephone: 318-221-6858
Fax: 318-227-2967
Email: BWOR@BWOR.com
Bossier City, Louisiana Office: 2285 Benton Road, Suite B-201.
Telephone: 318-742-9255.
Fax: 318-742-9210.

(See Next Column)

BLANCHARD, WALKER, O'QUIN & ROBERTS A PROFESSIONAL LAW CORPORATION, *Shreveport—Continued*

J. Edgerton Pierson, Jr., (P.C.) Gary H. Love

For Complete List of Firm Personnel, See General Section

For full biographical listings, see the Martindale-Hubbell Law Directory

SOCKRIDER, BOLIN, ANGLIN & BATTE, A PROFESSIONAL LAW CORPORATION (AV)

327 Crockett Street, 71101
Telephone: 318-221-5503
Fax: 318-221-3849

John R. Pleasant (1905-1983)
H. F. Sockrider, Jr.
James E. Bolin, Jr.
D. Rex Anglin
Gregory H. Batte

For full biographical listings, see the Martindale-Hubbell Law Directory

*WINNFIELD,** Winn Parish

SIMMONS AND DERR (AV)

Simmons Building, Church Street, P.O. Box 525, 71483
Telephone: 318-628-3951
Fax: 318-648-0644

MEMBERS OF FIRM

Kermit M. Simmons
Jacque D. Derr

Reference: Bank of Winnfield & Trust Co.

For full biographical listings, see the Martindale-Hubbell Law Directory

MAINE

*BANGOR,** Penobscot Co.

EATON, PEABODY, BRADFORD & VEAGUE, P.A. (AV)

Fleet Center-Exchange Street, P.O. Box 1210, 04402-1210
Telephone: 207-947-0111
Telecopier: 207-942-3040
Email: eaton@eatonpeabody.com *URL:* http://www.eatonpeabody.com
Augusta, Maine Office: 77 Sewall Street, Suite 3000.
Telephone: 207-622-3747.
Telecopier: 207-622-9732.
Blue Hill, Maine Office: One East Blue Hill Road.
Telephone: 207-374-2812.
Telecopier: 207-374-2548.
Brunswick, Maine Office: 167 Park Row.
Telephone: 207-729-1144.
Telecopier: 207-729-1140.
Dover-Foxcroft, Maine Office: 30 East Main Street.
Telephone: 207-564-8378.
Telecopier: 207-564-7059.

Calvin E. True
Clarissa B. Edelston
Douglas M. Smith (Dover-Foxcroft and Augusta Offices)
John A. Cunningham (Resident, Brunswick Office)

Nathaniel S. Putnam

For Complete List of Firm Personnel, See General Section

For full biographical listings, see the Martindale-Hubbell Law Directory

GROSS, MINSKY, MOGUL & SINGAL, P.A. (AV)

Key Plaza, 23 Water Street, P.O. Box 917, 04402-0917
Telephone: 207-942-4644; 800-274-7124
Telecopier: 207-942-3699
Email: law@gmms.com

Edward I. Gross (1912-1999)
Jules L. Mogul (1930-1994)
George Z. Singal
Louis H. Kornreich
George C. Schelling
Edward W. Gould
Steven J. Mogul
James R. Wholly
Daniel A. Pileggi
Philip K. Clarke

Wayne P. Libhart (Retired)
Sandra L. Rothera
James S. Nixon

OF COUNSEL

Norman Minsky

Representative Client: Dahl Chase Pathology Associates.
Local Counsel for: The St. Paul Insurance Cos.; Aetna Life & Casualty Co.; Imperial Casualty & Indemnity Co.

For full biographical listings, see the Martindale-Hubbell Law Directory

RUDMAN & WINCHELL, LLC (AV)

84 Harlow Street, P.O. Box 1401, 04402-1401
Telephone: 207-947-4501
Telecopy: 207-941-9715
URL: http://www.rudman-winchell.com

MEMBERS OF FIRM

Abraham M. Rudman (1896-1970)
Albert H. Winchell, Jr. (1924-1992)
Gerald E. Rudman
Phillip D. Buckley
Michael P. Friedman
Winfred A. Stevens
Robert E. Sutcliffe
Paul W. Chaiken
David C. King
John W. McCarthy
Frank T. McGuire
Bruce C. Mallonee
Paul H. Sighinolfi
William H. Hanson
George F. Eaton, II
Edith A. Richardson
Michael M. McAleer
Brett D. Baber
Barbara A. Cardone
Robert E. Murray, Jr.
Edmond J. Bearor
Curtis E. Kimball
Brent A. Singer

ASSOCIATES

Jane E. Skelton
Leigh Stephens McCarthy
Virginia Kozak Putnam
Ajaz S. Fiazzuddin
Anne-Marie Storey Hamer
Hans S. Peterson
Christopher J. Austin

Counsel for: Penobscot Shoe Co.; Sherman Lumber Co.; Webber Oil Co.; Fleet Bank of Maine; Key Bank of Maine; McCain Foods, Inc.
Local Counsel for: Commercial Union York Insurance Cos.; Hanover Insurance Company; Liberty Mutual Insurance Co.

For full biographical listings, see the Martindale-Hubbell Law Directory

BAR HARBOR, Hancock Co.

FENTON, CHAPMAN, FENTON, SMITH & KANE, P.A. (AV)

109 Main Street, P.O. Box B, 04609
Telephone: 207-288-3331
Fax: 207-288-9326
Email: fentonlawfirm@acadia.net *URL:* http://www.lawyers.com/fcfs&klaw

William Fenton
Douglas B. Chapman
Nathaniel R. Fenton
Chadbourn H. Smith
Daniel H. Kane (1940-1995)
Hancock Griffin, Jr. (1912-1980)

Margaret T. Jeffery

Reference: Bar Harbor Banking and Trust Co.

For full biographical listings, see the Martindale-Hubbell Law Directory

*ELLSWORTH,** Hancock Co.

HALE & HAMLIN (AV)

10 State Street, P.O. Box 729, 04605
Telephone: 207-667-2561
Telefax: 207-667-8790
Email: barry@halehamlin.com *URL:* http://www.halehamlin.com

Eugene Hale (1836-1918)
Hannibal E. Hamlin (1858-1938)
Philip R. Lovell (1899-1961)
Charles J. Hurley (1908-1981)
Atherton Fuller (1918-1998)

MEMBERS OF FIRM

Barry K. Mills
Dale L. Worthen
Jeffrey W. Jones
Melissa Moll

LEGAL SUPPORT PERSONNEL

Donna L. Jancewicz (Paralegal)
Sylvia Joy (Paralegal)

Approved Attorneys for: Lawyers Title Insurance Corp.

For full biographical listings, see the Martindale-Hubbell Law Directory

*PORTLAND,** Cumberland Co.

BENNETT BENNETT AND TROIANO, P.A. (AV)

Suite 300, 121 Middle Street, P.O. Box 7799, 04112-7799
Telephone: 207-773-4775
Telecopier: 207-774-2366
Email: lawyers@bennettlegal.com *URL:* http://www.bennettlegal.com

Herbert H. Bennett (1928-1992)
Peter Bennett
Jeffrey Bennett
Joseph A. Troiano
Frederick B. Finberg

Julie A. Boesky

OF COUNSEL

Jonathan M. Dunitz

Counsel for: Associated Grocers of New England; General Star Indemnity Company; Coca Cola Bottling Company of Northern New England, Inc.; Northern Utilities/Bay State Gas; Pratt & Whitney (Division of United Technologies); Primerica Financial Services (Citigroup); Sprague Energy (C.H. Sprague & Son); Perrier Group of America, Inc.; Lepage Bakeries, Inc. (Country Kitchen); Texaco, Inc.

(See Next Column)

BENNETT BENNETT AND TROIANO P.A.—*Continued*

For full biographical listings, see the Martindale-Hubbell Law Directory

DAVID E. HUNT (AV)

75 Market Street, 04101
Telephone: 207-773-5100
Fax: 207-773-8200
Email: info@mainewills.com *URL:* http://www.mainewills.com

OF COUNSEL

Elizabeth P. Hunt

For full biographical listings, see the Martindale-Hubbell Law Directory

JENSEN BAIRD GARDNER & HENRY (AV)

Ten Free Street, P.O. Box 4510, 04112-4510
Telephone: 207-775-7271
Telecopier: 207-775-7935
Email: info@jbgh.com *URL:* http://www.jbgh.com
York County Office: 11 Main Street, Suite 4, Kennebunk, Maine, 04043.
Telephone: 207-985-4676.
Telecopier: 207-985-4932.

MEMBERS OF FIRM

Frank H. Frye
R. Lee Ivy

OF COUNSEL

Merton G. Henry
John D. Bradford (Resident, York County Office)

Representative Clients: Margaret Chase Smith Foundation; Peoples Heritage Bank.

For Complete List of Firm Personnel, See General Section

For full biographical listings, see the Martindale-Hubbell Law Directory

LEBLANC & YOUNG (AV)

183 Middle Street, P.O. Box 7950, 04112-7950
Telephone: 207-772-2800
Facsimile: 207-772-2822
Email: firm@leblancyoung.com *URL:* http://www.leblancyoung.com

Richard P. LeBlanc
James H. Young, II
Elizabeth T. High
Abigail King Diggins

For full biographical listings, see the Martindale-Hubbell Law Directory

PETRUCCELLI & MARTIN, LLP (AV)

50 Monument Square, P.O. Box 9733, 04104-5033
Telephone: 207-775-0200
Telecopier: 207-775-2360
Email: info@petruccellimartin.com *URL:* http://www.petruccellimartin.com

MEMBER OF FIRM

Linda C. Russell

Bruce A. McGlauflin

For full biographical listings, see the Martindale-Hubbell Law Directory

PIERCE ATWOOD (AV)

One Monument Square, 04101
Telephone: 207-791-1100
Fax: 207-791-1350
Email: info@PierceAtwood.com *URL:* http://www.pierceatwood.com
Augusta, Maine Office: 77 Winthrop Street.
Telephone: 207-622-6311.
Fax: 207-623-9367.
Newburyport, Massachusetts Office: 6 Harris Street.
Telephone: 978-465-9599.
Fax: 978-465-9945.

MEMBERS OF FIRM

Fred C. Scribner, Jr. (1908-1994)
Warren E. Winslow, Jr. (Resident, Augusta Office)
Everett P. Ingalls, III
Barbara K. Wheaton

OF COUNSEL

Sigrid E. Tompkins
William C. Smith
Jeremiah D. Newbury

ASSOCIATE

Larissa S. Pratt

For Complete List of Firm Personnel, See General Section

For full biographical listings, see the Martindale-Hubbell Law Directory

PRETI, FLAHERTY, BELIVEAU, PACHIOS & HALEY, LLC (AV)

One City Center, P.O. Box 9546, 04112-9546
Telephone: 207-791-3000
Telecopier: 207-791-3111
Email: admin@preti.com *URL:* http://www.preti.com
Augusta, Maine Office: 45 Memorial Circle, P.O. Box 1058, 04332-1058.
Telephone: 207-623-5300.
Telefax: 207-623-2914.
Bath, Maine Office: Thirty Front Street, P.O. Box 665, 04530-0665.
Telephone: 207-443-5576.
Telefax: 207-443-6665.

MEMBERS OF FIRM

Michael J. Gentile (Augusta Office)
Estelle A. Lavoie
Michael L. Sheehan

COUNSEL

Robert F. Preti
Albert J. Beliveau, Jr.
Robert W. Smith

For Complete List of Firm Personnel, See General Section

For full biographical listings, see the Martindale-Hubbell Law Directory

TROUBH, HEISLER & PIAMPIANO, P.C. (AV)

511 Congress Street, P.O. Box 9711, 04104-5011
Telephone: 207-780-6789
Fax: 207-774-2339
Email: info@thplaw.com

William B. Troubh
Edwin A. Heisler
Robert J. Piampiano
Kevin M. Gillis
Michael P. Boyd
Thomas E. Getchell
Michael Richards
William K. McKinley
Daniel F. Gilligan
Paul S. Bulger
John G. Richardson

Daniel R. Felkel
Ann Brandt
John P. Flynn, III

For full biographical listings, see the Martindale-Hubbell Law Directory

VERRILL & DANA, LLP (AV)

One Portland Square, P.O. Box 586, 04112-0586
Telephone: 207-774-4000
Fax: 207-774-7499
Email: advice@verdan.com *URL:* http://www.verdan.com
Augusta, Maine Office: 45 Memorial Circle, P.O. Box 957.
Telephone: 207-623-3889.
Fax: 207-622-3117.
Kennebunk, Maine Office: 403-404 Lafayette Center, P.O. Box 147.
Telephone: 207-985-7193.
Fax: 207-985-3957.
Washington, D.C. Office: 400 North Capitol Street, Suite 585.
Telephone: 202-624-9733.
Fax: 202-393-5218.

OF COUNSEL

Robert B. Williamson, Jr.
Carolyn S. Wollen

MEMBERS OF FIRM

Judith M. Coburn
John D. Duncan
Gregory L. Foster

ASSOCIATES

Kenneth F. Ginder
Kurt E. Klebe

Counsel for: ASCAP; Bowdoin College; Fleet Bank; Hannaford Bros. Co.; Maine Blue Cross and Blue Shield; Maine Public Service Co.; Peoples Heritage Bank; Portland Water District.

For Complete List of Firm Personnel, See General Section

For full biographical listings, see the Martindale-Hubbell Law Directory

SOUTH PORTLAND, Cumberland Co.

VAN MEER & BELANGER, P.A. (AV)

25 Long Creek Drive, 04106
Telephone: 207-871-7500
Fax: 207-871-7505
Email: VBLAW@GWI.NET

Thomas J. Van Meer
Norman R. Belanger
D. Kelley Young
Richard N. Bryant

Betts J. Gorsky
Mary McQuillen

For full biographical listings, see the Martindale-Hubbell Law Directory

MARYLAND

*ANNAPOLIS,** Anne Arundel Co.

COUNCIL, BARADEL, KOSMERL & NOLAN, P.A. (AV)

125 West Street, Fourth Floor, P.O. Box 2289, 21404-2289
Telephone: 410-268-6600
Baltimore: 410-269-6190
Washington, D.C.: 301-261-2247
FAX: 410-269-8409
Email: cbkn@cbknlaw.com

Ronald E. Council
Ronald A. Baradel
Wayne T. Kosmerl
James P. Nolan
William F. Flood, III
Kevin M. Schaeffer
Donna McCabe Schaeffer
Frederick C. Sussman

John Naumann Strange
Susan T. Ford
Edwin H. Staples, II
Susan Stobbart Shapiro

OF COUNSEL

George N. Manis
Nicholas Goldsborough

Representative Clients: Anne Arundel County; Annapolis Bank and Trust; Bank of Maryland; State Farm Mutual Automobile Insurance Co.; Annapolis Yacht Club; Annapolis Yacht Sales, Inc.

For full biographical listings, see the Martindale-Hubbell Law Directory

ABEL J. MERRILL, P.A. (AV)

Clock Tower Place, 1410 Forest Drive, Suite 32, 21403
Telephone: 410-268-0006
Baltimore: 410-269-0155
Fax: 410-269-5126
http: //www.estateplanning.com/merrillaw
Email: abelj@merrillaw.com *URL:* http://www.estateplanning.com/merrillaw

Danielle M. Cruttenden

Reference: Annapolis Banking & Trust Company.

For full biographical listings, see the Martindale-Hubbell Law Directory

*BALTIMORE,** (Independent City)

FERGUSON, SCHETELICH & HEFFERNAN, P.A. (AV)

1401 NationsBank Center, 100 South Charles Street, 21201-2725
Telephone: 410-837-2200
Fax: 410-837-1188
URL: http://www.FSHLaw.com

Robert L. Ferguson, Jr.
Thomas J. Schetelich
Christopher J. Heffernan
Craig F. Ballew
Michael N. Russo, Jr.

Peter J. Basile
Ann D. Ware
Tracey J. McLauchlin
Michele P. Zahner
Michael K. Hourigan

For full biographical listings, see the Martindale-Hubbell Law Directory

GALLAGHER, EVELIUS & JONES, LLP (AV)

Park Charles Suite 400, 218 North Charles Street, 21201
Telephone: 410-727-7702
Facsimile: 410-468-2786
URL: http://www.gejlaw.com

MEMBERS OF FIRM

Francis X. Gallagher (1928-1972)
C. Edward Jones (1908-1999)
John C. Evelius (Retired)
Richard O. Berndt
Thomas N. Biddison, Jr.
Robert R. Kern, Jr.
Saul E. Gilstein
Thomas B. Lewis
Bonnie Abrams Travieso
Stephen A. Goldberg
Linda H. Jones
Jack C. Tranter
Leslie B. Speed
Christopher J. Fritz
David E. Raderman
Peter E. Keith
Nita L. Schultz
Michael W. Skojec
Kathryn Kelley Hoskins
Mark P. Keener
Kevin J. Davidson
Eileen M. Lunga
Lori A. Nicolle
Kenneth S. Gross
Thomas C. Dame

ASSOCIATES

Valarie K. Oulds
Margaret Stevens Jacks
Matthew W. Oakey
Rebecca A. Weaver
Michael J. Henigan
David W. Kinkopf
Paul S. Caiola
Jason W. Gaarder
M. Kirsten Andrews

(See Next Column)

LEGAL ASSISTANTS

Patricia C. Quayle
Iris T. H. Heath
Connie L. Ennis
Margaret Graff
Margo Gibson Hughes
Jonathan T. Gillis
Brenda J. Heacock
Dwayne L. Rodeheaver

Representative Clients: Roman Catholic Archdiocese of Baltimore; Associated Catholic Charities; Mercantile-Safe Deposit and Trust Co.; The Enterprise Social Investment Corp.; Mercy Medical Center, Inc.

For full biographical listings, see the Martindale-Hubbell Law Directory

RICHARD T. STANSBURY A PROFESSIONAL ASSOCIATION (AV)

Suite 920, The B & O Building, Two North Charles Street, 21201-3754
Telephone: 410-727-6200
Facsimile: 410-385-2939
Email: rts1law@aol.com *URL:* http://www.lawyers.com/richardstansburylaw
Annapolis, Maryland Office: 112 West Street, 21401.
Telephone: 410-974-6000.
Facsimile: 410-974-6019.

Richard T. Stansbury

For full biographical listings, see the Martindale-Hubbell Law Directory

STEWART, PLANT & BLUMENTHAL, LLC (AV)

Suite 910 7 St. Paul Street, 21202
Telephone: 410-347-0506
Fax: 410-347-0513
Email: info@spblaw.com

MEMBERS OF FIRM

C. Van Leuven Stewart
A. MacDonough Plant
Max E. Blumenthal
Hugh A. ("Jay") Mitchell, Jr.
Robert C. Young

William J. Patton
Jonathan G. Lasley
Lisa J. McGrath
Natalie B. Sherman (Not admitted in MD)

OF COUNSEL

Adena W. Testa
Charlotte A. Sherman

For full biographical listings, see the Martindale-Hubbell Law Directory

THOMAS & LIBOWITZ, P.A. (AV)

100 Light Street, Suite 1100, 21202-1053
Telephone: 410-752-2468
Fax: 410-752-2046; 752-2049; 752-0979
Email: thomasandlibowitz.com *URL:* http://www.thomasandlibowitz.com

Steven Anargyros Thomas
Charles B. Jones

OF COUNSEL

Basil A. Thomas
Susan M. Rittenhouse

LEGAL SUPPORT PERSONNEL

PARALEGALS

Melissa A. Johnson
Kelley Atkins
Kimberly Beard

Representative Clients: Sinclair Broadcast Group, Inc. (Television and Radio stations); Roy Kirby & Sons, Inc. (Contractor); First Mariner Bank; Scandia Manufacturing Co. Inc. (Defense Contractor); Atlantic Automotive Corp. t/a Heritgage Automotive Group; Candy Express Franchising, Inc.; Wire Spectrum Services (Contractors-Transmission Tower Sites); Acrodyne Communications, Inc.; Alexis Logic Corporation (Software Developers); Selnic Corporation (Electronis Distributors); Liberty Mutual Insurance Company.

For full biographical listings, see the Martindale-Hubbell Law Directory

THOMSEN AND BURKE, LLP (AV)

Suite 400, One North Charles Street, 21201
Telephone: 410-539-2595
Fax: 410-783-0710
URL: http://www.T-B.com
Washington, D.C. Office: Suite 500, 1225 Eye Street, N.W.
Telephone: 202-682-4741.
Fax: 202-547-3713.

MEMBERS OF FIRM

George E. Thomsen
Paul E. Burke, Jr.
Roszel C. Thomsen, II
John B. Ward, Jr.

ASSOCIATES

Hedley A. Clark
Robin McDaniel Hough
Antoinette D. Paytas

References: NationsBank; Mercantile-Safe Deposit & Trust Co.; Carroll County Bank and Trust Co.

For full biographical listings, see the Martindale-Hubbell Law Directory

Baltimore—Continued

VENABLE ATTORNEYS AT LAW VENABLE, BAETJER AND HOWARD, LLP (AV)

A Partnership including Professional Corporations
1800 Mercantile Bank & Trust Building, 2 Hopkins Plaza, 21201
Telephone: 410-244-7400
Fax: 410-244-7742
URL: http://www.venable.com
Washington, D.C. Office: Venable, Baetjer, Howard & Civiletti LLP, Suite 1000, 1201 New York Avenue, N.W.
Telephone: 202-962-4800.
Fax: 202-962-8300.
McLean, Virginia Office: Suite 400, 2010 Corporate Ridge.
Telephone: 703-760-1600.
Fax: 703-821-8949.
Rockville, Maryland Office: Suite 500, One Church Street, P. O. Box 1906.
Telephone: 301-217-5600.
Fax: 301-217-5617.
Towson, Maryland Office: 210 Allegheny Avenue, P. O. Box 5517.
Telephone: 410-494-6200.
Fax: 410-821-0147.

MEMBERS OF FIRM

Jacques T. Schlenger (P.C.)
John Henry Lewin, Jr. (P.C.)
Roger W. Titus (Resident, Rockville, Maryland Office)
Alexander I. Lewis, III (P.C.) (Also at Towson, Maryland Office)
Paul T. Glasgow (Resident, Rockville, Maryland Office)
Joseph C. Wich, Jr. (Resident, Towson, Maryland Office)
Jeffrey J. Radowich
Nell B. Strachan
James K. Archibald (Also at Washington, D.C. Office)
Christopher R. Mellott
M. King Hill, III (Resident, Towson, Maryland Office)
James A. Dunbar (Resident, Towson, Maryland Office)
Robert L. Waldman
David J. Heubeck
Jeffrey K. Gonya

OF COUNSEL

Robert M. Thomas (P.C.)
Robert R. Bair (P.C.)
Emried D. Cole, Jr.

ASSOCIATES

John P. Edgar
Matthew F. Kadish (Not admitted in MD; Resident, Washington, D.C. Office)
William A. McComas

For Complete List of Firm Personnel, See General Section

For full biographical listings, see the Martindale-Hubbell Law Directory

WRIGHT, CONSTABLE & SKEEN, LLP (AV)

One Charles Center, 16th Floor, 100 N. Charles Street, 21201
Telephone: 410-659-1300
Telex: 710 234-2383 CALDAS
Fax: 410-659-1350

MEMBERS OF FIRM

Wm. Pepper Constable (1882-1976)
John D. Wright (1903-1976)
George W. Constable (Retired)
Read A. McCaffrey (1913-1995)
William A. Skeen (Retired)
John Brentnall Powell, Jr.
Michael J. Abromaitis
Monte Fried
James W. Constable
David W. Skeen
James D. Skeen
Douglas G. Worrall
Kenneth F. Davies
Stephen F. White
Brian S. Goodman
Frederick L. Kobb
Paul F. Evelius
Lois A. Fenner McBride
Charles J. Morton, Jr.

ASSOCIATES

Mary Alice Smolarek
Catherine H. Bellinger
Carol J. Glover
Tracey D. King
David J. Shuster
Howard S. Stevens

COUNSEL

Francis N. Iglehart, Jr.
P. McEvoy Cromwell
C. Gordon Haines

Representative Clients: Conowingo Power Co.; Weyerhaeuser Co.; Commercial Credit Corp.; Noxell Corp.; Consolidated Rail Corp.; Murray Corp.; Atlantic Mutual Insurance Co.; Sea Containers, Ltd.; Great Atlantic & Pacific Tea Co.; Tyson Foods, Inc.

For full biographical listings, see the Martindale-Hubbell Law Directory

*BEL AIR,** Harford Co.

BROWN, BROWN & BROWN, A PROFESSIONAL ASSOCIATION (AV)

200 South Main Street, 21014
Telephone: 410-838-5500
Baltimore: 410-879-2220
Fax: 410-893-0402

A. Freeborn Brown (1915-1998)
T. Carroll Brown
Augustus F. Brown
Albert J. A. Young

(See Next Column)

Harold Douglas Norton
Christopher R. vanRoden
David E. Carey

Attorneys for: Baltimore Gas & Electric Co.; Chesapeake & Potomac Telephone Co.; Aberdeen Proving Ground Federal Credit Union; First National Bank of Maryland; Bell Atlantic Mobile Systems; First Harbor Securities; Maryland Portable Concrete, Inc.
Approved Counsel for: The Chicago Title Insurance Co. of Maryland, Inc.

For full biographical listings, see the Martindale-Hubbell Law Directory

STARK & KEENAN, A PROFESSIONAL ASSOCIATION (AV)

30 Office Street, 21014
Telephone: 410-838-5522
Baltimore: 410-879-2222
Fax: 410-879-0688
Email: wstarkee@aol.com
Havre de Grace Office: "The Old Ordinary" 100 St. John Street, 21078.
Telephone: 410-939-0100.

Elwood V. Stark, Jr.
Charles B. Keenan, Jr.
Edwin G. Carson
Judith Cline-Silverstein
Gregory A. Szoka
Robert S. Lynch
Paul W. Ishak

Claire Prin Blomquist
Lawrence F. Kreis, Jr.
Craig H. DeRan

For full biographical listings, see the Martindale-Hubbell Law Directory

BETHESDA, Montgomery Co.

EIG AND SCHWARTZ, CHARTERED (AV)

7475 Wisconsin Avenue, Suite 500, 20814
Telephone: 301-654-4884
Telecopier: 301-654-0165

Linda D. Schwartz
Wayne D. Eig
Katherine Palumbo
Paul G. Marcotte, Jr.
Arnold B. Sherman

For full biographical listings, see the Martindale-Hubbell Law Directory

LEE F. HOLDMANN CHARTERED (AV)

9207 Old Georgetown Road, 20814
Telephone: 301-530-0900
Fax: 301-530-2852
La Plata Office: 200 Centennial Street.
Telephone: 301-934-1152.
Fax: 301-530-2852.
Annapolis Office: Glenco Building, 410 Rowe Boulevard.
Telephone: 410-268-0200.
Fax: 301-530-2852.
Leonardtown Office: Camalier Building, 22635 Washington Street.
Telephone: 301-457-2645.
Fax: 301-530-2852.

Lee F. Holdmann

Shelley R. Culhane
Larry W. Brown
Charles W. Bills
Tina B. Fernandes

LEGAL SUPPORT PERSONNEL

Sharon Lightner (Senior Paralegal)

Reference: Marriott Corporation Senior Living Services, Washington, D.C.

For full biographical listings, see the Martindale-Hubbell Law Directory

RON M. LANDSMAN, P.A. (AV)

4550 Montgomery Avenue, Suite 901N, 20814
Telephone: 301-652-5050
Fax: 301-961-8615
Email: RLANDS7369@AOL.COM

Ron M. Landsman

Erin Adele Mahony

OF COUNSEL

May-Lis A. Manley

For full biographical listings, see the Martindale-Hubbell Law Directory

NELSON & NELSON LLP (AV)

3 Bethesda Metro Center Suite 750, 20814
Telephone: 301-961-1958
Fax: 301-656-5122
Email: sswen@aol.com *URL:* http://www.lawyers.com/nelson&nelson

(See Next Column)

NELSON & NELSON LLP, *Bethesda—Continued*

MEMBERS OF FIRM

William E. Nelson
Sherlee Stanford Nelson (Not admitted in MD)

For full biographical listings, see the Martindale-Hubbell Law Directory

POPPLETON, GARRETT & POLOTT, P.C. (AV)

6430 Rockledge Drive Suite 500, 20817
Telephone: 301-493-9800
Fax: 301-493-6585
Email: lawfirm@pgplaw.com
Fairfax, Virginia Office: 10560 Main Street, Suite 111, 22030-7182.
Telephone: 703-525-0240.

Miller John Poppleton, Jr.
Dwayne L. Garrett
Andrew R. Polott
Michael P. Chabrow (Not admitted in MD)
Richard B. Hill
Douglas A. Rubel

Richard C. Sterrn

OF COUNSEL

Stuart H. Sorkin, P.C. (Not admitted in MD)
Ellen A. Rubel

For full biographical listings, see the Martindale-Hubbell Law Directory

BOWIE, Prince Georges Co.

THE SINCLAIR LAW FIRM (AV)

OMNI Building, Suite A210, 4000 Mitchellville Road, 20716
Telephone: 301-352-2300; 800-366-4615
Fax: 301-352-2306
URL: http://www.sinclairlawfirm.com
Annapolis, Maryland Office: 170 Jennifer Road, Suite, 110.
Telephone: 800-366-4615.
Fax: 301-352-2306.
Millersville, Maryland Office: 1120 C. Benfield Boulevard.
Telephone: 800-366-4615.
Fax: 301-352-2306.

R. Ronald Sinclair
Colleen Sinclair Prosser

For full biographical listings, see the Martindale-Hubbell Law Directory

CABIN JOHN, Montgomery Co.

SUSAN E. PFEIFER (AV)

Suite 200C - MacArthur Plaza I, 7945 MacArthur Boulevard, 20818
Telephone: 301-229-7500
Fax: 301-229-0862
Email: SiroccoMD@aol.com *URL:* http://www.lawyers.com/pfeiferlaw

For full biographical listings, see the Martindale-Hubbell Law Directory

CHEVY CHASE, Montgomery Co.

LAW OFFICES OF BINSTOCK, TORCHINSKY AND ASSOCIATES, P.C. (AV)

Barlow Building, 5454 Wisconsin Avenue, Suite 1340, 20815
Telephone: 301-657-5555
Fax: 301-657-9871
URL: http://www.lawyers.com/binstock_torchinsky
Washington, DC Office: 1140 Connecticut Avenue, N.W., Suite 703. 20036.
Telephone: 301-657-5555.
Fax: 301-657-9871.

Shelton M. Binstock
David B. Torchinsky

OF COUNSEL

Andrew S. Unger (Not admitted in MD)
George R. Adams (Not admitted in MD)

For full biographical listings, see the Martindale-Hubbell Law Directory

PYNE & DERRY, P.C. (AV)

Chevy Chase Metro Building Suite 640, Two Wisconsin Circle, 20815
Telephone: 301-961-0240
Fax: 301-907-3920
Email: pyne-derry@juno.com

John J. Pyne
Peter E. Derry

For full biographical listings, see the Martindale-Hubbell Law Directory

*EASTON,** Talbot Co.

EWING, DIETZ, TURNER & KEHOE, PROFESSIONAL ASSOCIATION (AV)

16 South Washington Street, P.O. Box 1146, 21601
Telephone: 410-822-1988
Fax: 410-820-5053
URL: http://www.edtklaw.com

(See Next Column)

L. Clark Ewing (1919-1998)
Philip E. L. Dietz, Jr.
Christopher B. Kehoe
John F. Hall
Karen M. Kaludis
Stephen H. Kehoe

Sharon M. Shilling

OF COUNSEL

Henry P. Turner

References: The Talbot Bank of Easton, Maryland; St. Michaels Bank.

For full biographical listings, see the Martindale-Hubbell Law Directory

WHEELER, THOMPSON, PARKER & COUNTS, LLP (AV)

129 North Washington Street, P.O. Box 1209, 21601
Telephone: 410-822-1122
Fax: 410-822-3635
Email: wtpc@dmv.com

MEMBERS OF FIRM

Edward T. Miller (1895-1968)
Ernest M. Thompson (1921-1989)
Charles E. Wheeler
Dorothy H. Thompson
Willard C. Parker, II
Richard L. Counts, III
Douglas A. Collison

OF COUNSEL

Donald H. Olson

Representative Clients: Chicago Title Insurance Company of Maryland; State Farm Mutual Insurance Co.; Chesapeake College; Habitat for Humanity of Talbot County; Talbot County Board of Education; Fuller Motor Sales, Inc.; St. Michaels Housing Authority.
References: Nationsbank, Easton Branch; Talbot Bank, Easton, Maryland; St. Michaels Bank, Eston, Maryland.

For full biographical listings, see the Martindale-Hubbell Law Directory

*FREDERICK,** Frederick Co.

OFFUTT, HORMAN, BURDETTE & FREY, P.A. (AV)

Offutt Building, 22 West Second Street, 21701
Telephone: 301-662-8248;
Hagerstown: 301-293-6032;
Montgomery Co., D.C./Va. line: 301-948-5633
Fax: 301-663-8968

W. Jerome Offutt
Amos A. Holter
John N. Burdette
George T. Horman
Charles Burton Frey

Lisa Anne Rudy
Chris M. May

Representative Clients: Donald B. Rice Tire Co., Inc.; Meadows Van and Storage Co.; Central Maryland Farm Credit, ACA; QUADS Trust Co.; Frederick Aviation, Inc.
Local Counsel: St. James Servicing Corp.; First National Bank of Maryland.
Co-Counsel for: Central Maryland Farm Credit, ACA.
Reference: Frederick Branch of First National Bank of Maryland.

For full biographical listings, see the Martindale-Hubbell Law Directory

GREENBELT, Prince Georges Co.

STANLEY S. PICKETT (AV)

Suite 414 Capital Office Park, 6411 Ivy Lane, 20770
Telephone: 301-513-0613
Fax: 301-513-0618
Email: lossp@intr.net

Stanley Sinclair Pickett

ASSOCIATES

Gordon J. Brumback
Stacy S. Pickett Trimble

LEGAL SUPPORT PERSONNEL

Vivian A. Wolfe (Paralegal)

Representative Clients: B.F. Saul Co.; McDonald and Eudy Printers, Inc.; Condominium Management, Inc.; Long & Foster Realtors; Mitron Systems Corp.; Glenanden Housing Authority; Community Associations, Inc.; Hagmer Management, Inc.; Quantum Management, Inc.

For full biographical listings, see the Martindale-Hubbell Law Directory

*ROCKVILLE,** Montgomery Co.

ANDREW D. BALL, P.C. (AV)

Adams Law Center, 33 Wood Lane, 20850
Telephone: 301-251-9100
Fax: 301-251-3755
Email: adball@worldnet.att.net

Andrew D. Ball

Reference: NationsBank.

For full biographical listings, see the Martindale-Hubbell Law Directory

Rockville—Continued

STEVEN M. KATZ, P.A. (AV)

Suite 208 401 East Jefferson Street, 20850
Telephone: 301-738-8441
Fax: 301-294-9484
Email: smkatz@intr.net *URL:* http://www.lawyers.com/stevenkatz

Steven M. Katz

Jeffrey D. Katz

For full biographical listings, see the Martindale-Hubbell Law Directory

WILLIAM H. ROBERGE, JR. (AV)

9210 Corporate Boulevard Suite 390, 20850-4608
Telephone: 301-990-8875
Fax: 301-990-8720
Email: wroblaw@erols.com

For full biographical listings, see the Martindale-Hubbell Law Directory

STEIN, SPERLING, BENNETT, DE JONG, DRISCOLL, GREENFEIG & METRO, P.C. (AV)

25 West Middle Lane, 20850-2204
Telephone: 301-340-2020; 800-435-5230
Telecopier: 301-340-8217
Email: lawfirm@steinsperling.com
Falls Church, Virginia Office: 6245 Leesburg Pike, Suite 140, 22044.
Telephone: 703-237-0500.
Telecopier: 703-534-2899.

David S. De Jong — Ann G. Jakabcin

Edward D. McGuire, Jr.

For Complete List of Firm Personnel, See General Section

For full biographical listings, see the Martindale-Hubbell Law Directory

SILVER SPRING, Montgomery Co.

GINGELL & JENKINS, P.C. (AV)

Suite 506 Wheaton Plaza South, 11160 Veirs Mill Road, 20902
Telephone: 301-949-0100
Telecopier: 301-949-0467
Email: rgingdjen@aol.com *URL:* http://www.lawyers.com/gingelljenkins

Robert A. Gingell — Donn K. Jenkins

LEGAL SUPPORT PERSONNEL

Karen Thompson — Paula Brock (Real Estate Paralegal)

Representative Clients: Air Flow Co. (Industrial Air Conditioning); Bethesda Realty Co.; Photo Science, Inc.
References: Sovran Bank; First National Bank of Maryland (Rockville, Maryland, Branch); Signet Bank Maryland.

For full biographical listings, see the Martindale-Hubbell Law Directory

*TOWSON,** Baltimore Co.

BLUE & EDWARDS P.A. (AV)

409 Washington Avenue, Suite 625, 21204-4903
Telephone: 410-296-9292
Fax: 410-296-2004
Email: wilmalaw@connext.net

William F. Blue — Mary Baker Edwards

Robert G. Blue

For full biographical listings, see the Martindale-Hubbell Law Directory

LAW OFFICES OF RICHARD W. MOORE (AV)

40 West Chesapeake Avenue Suite 518, 21204
Telephone: 410-938-2222
Fax: 410-938-2225

Richard W. Moore

LEGAL SUPPORT PERSONNEL

Renee C. Guckert (Legal Assistant)

For full biographical listings, see the Martindale-Hubbell Law Directory

NOLAN, PLUMHOFF & WILLIAMS, CHARTERED (AV)

Suite 700, Nottingham Centre, 502 Washington Avenue, 21204-4528
Telephone: 410-823-7800
Fax: 410-296-2765
Email: npw@nolanplumhoff.com

Thomas J. Renner — E. Bruce Jones

For Complete List of Firm Personnel, See General Section

For full biographical listings, see the Martindale-Hubbell Law Directory

VENABLE ATTORNEYS AT LAW VENABLE, BAETJER AND HOWARD, LLP (AV)

A Partnership including Professional Corporations
210 Allegheny Avenue, P.O. Box 5517, 21204
Telephone: 410-494-6200
Fax: 410-821-0147
URL: http://www.venable.com
Baltimore, Maryland Office: 1800 Mercantile Bank & Trust Building, 2 Hopkins Plaza.
Telephone: 410-244-7400.
Fax: 410-244-7742.
Washington, D.C. Office: Venable, Baetjer, Howard & Civiletti LLP, Suite 1000, 1201 New York Avenue, N.W.
Telephone: 202-962-4800.
Fax: 202-962-8300.
McLean, Virginia Office: Suite 400, 2010 Corporate Ridge.
Telephone: 703-760-1600.
Fax: 703-821-8949.
Rockville, Maryland Office: Suite 500, One Church Street, P. O. Box 1906.
Telephone: 301-217-5600.
Fax: 301-217-5617.

PARTNERS

Alexander I. Lewis, III (P.C.) (Also at Baltimore, Maryland Office) — Joseph C. Wich, Jr. — M. King Hill, III

For Complete List of Firm Personnel, See General Section

For full biographical listings, see the Martindale-Hubbell Law Directory

*WESTMINSTER,** Carroll Co.

DULANY & LEAHY, LLP (AV)

127 East Main Street, 21157-5012
Telephone: 410-848-3333; Baltimore Line: 410-876-2117
FAX: 410-876-0747
Email: dulany@dulany.com

MEMBERS OF FIRM

William B. Dulany — Amber Dahlgreen Curtis
J. Brooks Leahy — Kenneth Michael Williams

Representative Clients: Lehigh Portland Cement Co.; Pizza Hut of Maryland, Inc.; McGregor Printing Corporation; Mutual Fire Insurance Company of Carroll County; Carroll Lutheran Village, Inc.; Western Maryland College.
Reference: Carroll County Bank and Trust Co.

For full biographical listings, see the Martindale-Hubbell Law Directory

MASSACHUSETTS

AMESBURY, Essex Co.

THE HAMEL LAW FIRM (AV)

Five Market Square, P.O. Box 198, 01913-0398
Telephone: 978-388-3558
Telecopier: 978-388-0441
Email: hamellaw@excelr8.net
Email: hamellaw@lawyers.com *URL:* http://www.lawyers.com/hamellaw

MEMBER OF FIRM

Richard P. Hamel

ASSOCIATE

Peter R. Ayer, Jr.

Representative Clients: First and Ocean National Bank, Newburyport, MA.
Approved Attorneys for: Chicago Title Insurance; Old Republic Title Insurance Co.

For Complete List of Firm Personnel, See General Section

For full biographical listings, see the Martindale-Hubbell Law Directory

ARLINGTON, Middlesex Co.

LAW OFFICE OF WILLIAM JOSEPH GRANNAN (AV)

Suite 408, 22 Mill Street, 02174
Telephone: 781-646-3200
Fax: 781-643-1126
Email: wjpg@ix.netcom.com *URL:* http://www.lawyers.com/williamjosephgrannan

For full biographical listings, see the Martindale-Hubbell Law Directory

*BARNSTABLE,** Barnstable Co.

THOMAS J. MCNULTY, JR. (AV)

1441 Route 132, P.O. Box 1059, 02630
Telephone: 508-771-8000
Fax: 508-778-1441
Email: mcnulty@capeonramp.com *URL:* http://www.lawyers.com/mcnutly_capecod

Reference: Cape Cod Bank & Trust Co.

For full biographical listings, see the Martindale-Hubbell Law Directory

*BOSTON,** Suffolk Co.

HEMENWAY & BARNES (AV)

60 State Street, 02109
Telephone: 617-227-7940
Fax: 617-227-0781

MEMBERS OF FIRM

Roy A. Hammer
Lawrence T. Perera
George T. Shaw
Timothy F. Fidgeon
Michael J. Puzo
Deborah J. Hall
Kurt F. Somerville
Brian C. Broderick
Charles Fayerweather

ASSOCIATE

Dennis R. Delaney

OF COUNSEL

George H. Kidder

For Complete List of Firm Personnel, See General Section

For full biographical listings, see the Martindale-Hubbell Law Directory

HINCKLEY, ALLEN & SNYDER LLP (AV)

28 State Street, 30th Floor, 02109-1775
Telephone: 617-345-9000
Email: firm@haslaw.com *URL:* http://www.haslaw.com
Providence, Rhode Island Office: 1500 Fleet Center.
Telephone: 401-274-2000.
Fax: 401-277-9600. URL: http://www.hawlaw.com.

MEMBERS OF FIRM

Leon C. Boghossian III
Noel M. Field, Jr. (Not admitted in MA)
Doris Jami Licht
Richard H. Pierce
James O. Reavis
Paul A. Silver

ASSOCIATE

Lynn E. Riley

For Complete List of Firm Personnel, See General Section

For full biographical listings, see the Martindale-Hubbell Law Directory

MENARD, MURPHY & WALSH LLP (AV)

One Financial Center, 02111
Telephone: 617-832-2500
Telecopier: 617-832-2550
Email: mmw@mmwlaw.com
Washington, D.C. Office: Farragut Park, 910 17th Street, NW, Suite 800, 20006.
Telephone: 202-293-3500.
Telecopier: 202-293-3596.

Arthur P. Menard
Paul J. Murphy
Joseph H. Walsh
John E. Coyne
John S. Leonard

COUNSEL

Theodore E. Daiber

ASSOCIATES

Kevin G. Mahoney
Kevin P. Sweeney
Robert S. Steinberg

For full biographical listings, see the Martindale-Hubbell Law Directory

PACKENHAM, SCHMIDT & FEDERICO, P.C. (AV)

Four Longfellow Place, 35th Floor, 02114-2832
Telephone: 617-742-6565
Fax: 617-742-0292

Richard D. Packenham
Mary H. Schmidt
Phyllis E. Federico

Jennifer Rivera-Ulwick
Nicole R. Manny

OF COUNSEL

W. Sanford Durland III

For full biographical listings, see the Martindale-Hubbell Law Directory

PALMER & DODGE LLP (AV)

One Beacon Street, 02108
Telephone: 617-573-0100
Facsimile: 617-227-4420
URL: http://www.palmerdodge.com

MEMBERS OF FIRM

Lawrence B. Cohen
Laurie J. Hall
Eric F. Menoyo
Arthur B. Page
R. Robert Woodburn, Jr.
Jackson W. Wright, Jr.

SENIOR COUNSEL

Joan Garrity Flynn
Rhonda G. Hollander
Pamela M. Veasy

For Complete List of Firm Personnel, See General Section

For full biographical listings, see the Martindale-Hubbell Law Directory

PRINCE, LOBEL & TYE LLP (AV)

585 Commercial Street, 02109-1024
Telephone: 617-367-2202
Fax: 617-523-0977

MEMBERS OF FIRM

Robert P. Maloney
Samuel C. Sichko
Patricia M. Annino

ASSOCIATE

Stephen K. Fischer

OF COUNSEL

Richard E. Kaplan
Susan M. Miller
Neil R. Schauer

For Complete List of Firm Personnel, See General Section

For full biographical listings, see the Martindale-Hubbell Law Directory

ROCHE, CARENS & DEGIACOMO, P.C. (AV)

99 High Street, 02110
Telephone: 617-457-4000
Facsimile: 617-482-3868
Email: firm@rcdpc.com *URL:* http://www.rcdpc.com
Woburn, Massachusetts Office: 600 Unicorn Park Drive.
Telephone: 781-933-5505.

James R. DeGiacomo
Judith K. Wyman
Anne Hanford

OF COUNSEL

Lynne Callahan DeGiacomo

For Complete List of Firm Personnel, See General Section

For full biographical listings, see the Martindale-Hubbell Law Directory

ARNOLD L. SLAVET (AV)

Sixty State Street, Suite 700, 02109
Telephone: 617-371-2977; 781-894-1022
Telecopier: 781-647-1436
Email: ArnoldSlavet@worldnet.att.net

For full biographical listings, see the Martindale-Hubbell Law Directory

TAYLOR, GANSON & PERRIN, L.L.P. (AV)

20th Floor 160 Federal Street, 02110
Telephone: 617-951-2777
Fax: 617-951-0989
Beverly, Massachusetts Office: P.O. Box 5315, 398 Essex Street.
Telephone: 508-921-7330.
Fax: 508-921-7332.

MEMBERS OF FIRM

Varnum Taylor (1909-1979)
Charles M. Ganson (1908-1982)
Wm. Gardner Perrin (Retired)
Bradley R. Cook
Charles F. O'Connell
John A. Leith
Raymond W. Rawlings
John C. Prescott, Jr.
Paul F. Donovan
John Paul Fulginiti

ASSOCIATES

Joanne Craig
Joseph G. Imbriani
Edward R. Martin
Patricia M. Darrigo
Maria C. Lampasona
Susan M. Kealy
Nina J. Pelletier
Maureen B. Carney
Michael J. Starr
Gianpiero Spino

OF COUNSEL

James D. Colt
William F. Kehoe

For full biographical listings, see the Martindale-Hubbell Law Directory

BROOKLINE, Norfolk Co.

KICKHAM LAW OFFICES (AV)

1318 Beacon Street, 02446
Telephone: 617-566-5990
FAX: 617-734-8185
Email: kickhamlaw@aol.com *URL:* http://www.lawyers.com/kickhamlaw

(See Next Column)

KICKHAM LAW OFFICES—*Continued*

MEMBERS OF FIRM

Charles J. Kickham, Jr.
John W. Kickham (1923-1980)
James M. Kickham
Deborah Emello
George A. Kickham

OF COUNSEL

Constance K. Kickham
William D. Kickham

Approved Attorneys For: First American Title Insurance Co.; Stewart Title Guaranty Company.
Reference: Bank Boston, Fleet Bank; Brookline Savings Bank.

For full biographical listings, see the Martindale-Hubbell Law Directory

*CAMBRIDGE,** Middlesex Co.

JOHN J. ROCHE & ASSOCIATES (AV)

One Cambridge Center, Suite 405, 02142
Telephone: 617-621-3100
Telecopier: 617-621-3140

For full biographical listings, see the Martindale-Hubbell Law Directory

MERVIN M. WILF, LTD. (AV)

2 Berkeley Place, 02138
Telephone: 617-876-5200
Email: mwilf@erols.com
Philadelphia, Pennsylvania Office: 3901 Mellon Bank Center. 1735 Market Street.
Telephone: 215-994-1430. 215-568-4842.
Facsimile: 215-994-1432.

Mervin M. Wilf

A list of Representative Clients and References will be furnished upon request.

For full biographical listings, see the Martindale-Hubbell Law Directory

CENTERVILLE, Barnstable Co.

BOYD & BOYD, P.C. (AV)

1185 Falmouth Road, Suite 101, 02632
Telephone: 508-775-7800
Fax: 508-775-5666

F. Keats Boyd, Jr.
F. Keats Boyd, III

For full biographical listings, see the Martindale-Hubbell Law Directory

FITCHBURG, Worcester Co.

O'CONNOR AND RYAN, P.C. (AV)

61 Academy Street, 01420
Telephone: 978-345-4166
Fax: 978-343-8416

John M. O'Connor
Edward P. Ryan, Jr.

Eugene P. O'Donnell, Jr.

For full biographical listings, see the Martindale-Hubbell Law Directory

FRAMINGHAM, Middlesex Co.

HARGRAVES, KARB, WILCOX & GALVANI, LLP (AV)

The Corporate Center, 550 Cochituate Road, P.O. Box 966, 01701
Telephone: 508-620-0140
Fax: 508-875-7728
Email: Hargrave@ultranet.com *URL:* http://www.ultranet.com/~Hargrave

MEMBERS OF FIRM

Paul V. Galvani
William H. Mayer
William M. Pezzoni
Mark R. Haranas
Robert P. Jachowicz
Evans J. Carter

Charlene Denise Oliveira Cabral

OF COUNSEL

Victor H. Galvani
Brenda S. Steinberg

Counsel for: Framingham Cooperative Bank; Framingham Housing Authority; Wayland Housing Authority.
Local Counsel for: General Motors Corp. (Westwood, Mass.); Bose Corp.; Consolidated Rail Corp.; Kens Foods, Inc.; Framingham Ford.

For full biographical listings, see the Martindale-Hubbell Law Directory

FRANKLIN, Norfolk Co.

GILMORE, REES & CARLSON, P.C. (AV)

1000 Franklin Village Drive, 02038
Telephone: 508-520-2200
Fax: 508-520-2217
Wellesley, Massachusetts Office: 20 Walnut Street, 02181.
Telephone: 781-431-9788.
Fax: 781-431-1957.
Providence, Rhode Island Office: 369 South Main Street, 02903.
Telephone: 401-272-5400.
Fax: 401-453-1177.

Daniel J. Gilmore
Christopher T. Carlson
Bruce J. Bettigole
Paul D. Bishop
Sidney A. Slobodkin
Michael P. Doherty
Craig A. Ciechanowski

OF COUNSEL

William J. Rees
Karin Blake (P.C.)

Katherine A. Botelho
Jane Fisher Carlson
Peter J. Paulousky
Brian L. Gaudet
Michael R. Fiore
Todd M. Machnik
Janis Roney Edinburgh

For full biographical listings, see the Martindale-Hubbell Law Directory

HOLYOKE, Hampden Co.

LYON, FERRITER & FITZPATRICK, LLP (AV)

Whitney Place, 14 Bobala Road, 01040
Telephone: 413-536-4000
Fax: 413-536-3773
Email: lyonferr@aol.com

MEMBERS OF FIRM

Maurice J. Ferriter
Clarke S. Lyon
William D. Fitzpatrick
James F. Donnelly
Peter C. Connor
John J. Ferriter
Priscilla Fifield Chesky
Robert C. Sacco

ASSOCIATE

Robyn Andrea Porter

OF COUNSEL

William E. Begley

Representative Clients: Mount Holyoke College; Newspapers of New England, Inc.; Loomis House Retirement Community; Atlas Copco Compressors Inc.; Hazen Paper Company.

For full biographical listings, see the Martindale-Hubbell Law Directory

HYANNIS, Barnstable Co.

HADDLETON & COLLINS, P.C. (AV)

251 South Street, P.O. Box 1298, 02601
Telephone: 508-771-3132
Fax: 508-790-3760

Russell E. Haddleton
Joyce M. Collins

Michael Toivo Lahti

For full biographical listings, see the Martindale-Hubbell Law Directory

SYKES AND COLE (AV)

420 South Street, P.O. Box 1358, 02601
Telephone: 508-775-9147, 775-2334
Fax: 508-775-5682

MEMBERS OF FIRM

Peter M. Sykes (1914-1997)
David Bruce Cole

ASSOCIATE

Joseph V. Maruca

For full biographical listings, see the Martindale-Hubbell Law Directory

LOWELL, Middlesex Co.

DONAHUE & DONAHUE, ATTORNEYS, P.C. (AV)

21 George Street, 01852
Telephone: 978-458-6887
Fax: 978-458-3424

Daniel J. Donahue (1860-1939)
Joseph P. Donahue (1889-1973)
Charles A. Donahue (1891-1964)
Richard K. Donahue
Joseph P. Donahue, Jr.
Joseph D. Regan
Michael W. Gallagher
Richard K. Donahue, Jr.
Andrea S. Barisano
Matthew C. Donahue
Richard E. Cavanaugh
Kelly R. Spencer
Alicia A. Donahue

(See Next Column)

DONAHUE & DONAHUE ATTORNEYS, P.C., *Lowell—Continued*

Kelly M. Quigley

Representative Clients: The Travelers Insurance Co.; Ciro's Restaurants; Black & Decker; Burger King Corp.; White Consolidated, Inc.

For full biographical listings, see the Martindale-Hubbell Law Directory

MILFORD, Worcester Co.

GREENWALD, GREENWALD, POWERS & WINSOR LLP (AV)

409 Fortune Boulevard Granite Park, 01757-1746
Telephone: 508-478-8611
Fax: 508-634-3959; 478-5937
Email: ggp@ggplaw@.com *URL:* http://www.ggplaw.com

ASSOCIATE

Anna R. Vergados

For full biographical listings, see the Martindale-Hubbell Law Directory

ORLEANS, Barnstable Co.

D'ELIA & CAVANAUGH (AV)

161 Cranberry Highway, P.O. Box 707, 02653
Telephone: 508-255-2255
Telecopier: 508-255-2563
URL: http://www.lawyers.com/delia&cavanaugh

Joseph H. D'Elia
George B. Cavanaugh

For full biographical listings, see the Martindale-Hubbell Law Directory

FREDERICK K. PLUMB (AV)

19A Cove Road, P.O. Box 247, 02653
Telephone: 508-255-5566
FAX: Furnished Upon Request
Email: plumb@capecod.net

References: First National Bank of Boston; Cape Cod Bank & Trust Co.; Cape Cod Five Cents Savings Bank.

For full biographical listings, see the Martindale-Hubbell Law Directory

*SPRINGFIELD,** Hampden Co.

ROBINSON DONOVAN MADDEN & BARRY, P.C. (AV)

Suite 1600, Tower Square, 1500 Main Street, 01115-5609
Telephone: 413-732-2301
Fax: 413-785-4658
Email: service@robinson-donovan.com *URL:* http://www.robinson-donovan.com

Homans Robinson (1894-1973)
Lawrence M. Sinclair (1942-1986)
Milton J. Donovan (1906-1995)

RETIRED

John H. Madden, Jr.
Edward J. Barry
Richard S. Milstein

OF COUNSEL

Victor Rosenberg

SENIOR COUNSEL

Jonathan P. Rice

Gordon H. Wentworth
James H. Tourtelotte
Ronald C. Kidd
Jeffrey W. Roberts
Jeffrey L. McCormick
James F. Martin
Robert P. Cunningham
John C. Sikorski
Nancy Frankel Pelletier
Paul S. Weinberg
Frederica H. McCarthy
Matthew J. King
Neva Kaufman Rohan
Douglas F. Boyd
James K. Bodurtha
Keith A. Minoff
Patricia M. Rapinchuk
Kimberly Davis Crear

E. Paul Amata
Lisa A. Bongiovi (Not admitted in MA)
Edward J. Carroll, III
James D. Chadwell
John E. Garber
Patrick J. Markey
Carla W. Newton
Betsy Macmillan Stevens

Representative Clients: BankBoston, N.A.; United Cooperative Bank; Fleet National Bank; CNA; Commercial Union Insurance Co.; Hanover Insurance Group.

For full biographical listings, see the Martindale-Hubbell Law Directory

WALTHAM, Middlesex Co.

HARNISH, JENNEY, MITCHELL AND RESH (AV)

564 Main Street, 02154
Telephone: 781-894-0000
Telecopier: 781-893-8357

(See Next Column)

MEMBERS OF FIRM

Francis E. Jenney
David L. Mitchell
Harvey J. Resh
Joseph Melone
Robert C. Mann
Margaret Manzon Skinner

ASSOCIATE

Rhonda B. Fogel

For full biographical listings, see the Martindale-Hubbell Law Directory

*WORCESTER,** Worcester Co.

ERSKINE & ERSKINE (AV)

30 Highland Street, 01609-2704
Telephone: 508-753-7100
Fax: 508-753-8088

William T. Forbes (1876-1931)
Linwood M. Erskine, Sr. (1909-1956)
Linwood M. Erskine, Jr.
Matthew F. Erskine

Donna Toman Salvidio

For full biographical listings, see the Martindale-Hubbell Law Directory

MOUNTAIN, DEARBORN & WHITING LLP (AV)

370 Main Street, 01608
Telephone: 508-756-2423
Fax: 508-755-6640

MEMBERS OF FIRM

Alfred N. Whiting (1920-1989)
Thomas R. Mountain
Richard W. Dearborn
Samuel R. DeSimone
Henry W. Beth
Stuart A. Hammer
Francis J. Russell
Dale R. Harger
Mark W. Bloom
Donald J. O'Neil
Lawrence S. Delaney
Ann K. Molloy
Lisa D. Tingue

For full biographical listings, see the Martindale-Hubbell Law Directory

SEDER & CHANDLER (AV)

A Partnership including a Professional Corporation
Established 1918
Burnside Building, 339 Main Street, 01608
Telephone: 508-757-7721
Telecopiers: 508-798-1863; 508-831-0955

MEMBERS OF FIRM

Samuel Seder (1918-1964)
Harold Seder (1934-1988)
Burton Chandler
J. Robert Seder
Darragh K. Kasakoff
Marvin S. Silver, P.C.
Robert S. Adler
Kevin C. McGee
Kurt L. Binder

ASSOCIATES

Paul J. O'Riordan
Jeffrey P. Greenberg
Todd Rodman

OF COUNSEL

Saul A. Seder
Gerald E. Norman
Philip C. Lombardo, Jr.

Reference: First National Bank of Boston; Safety Fund National Bank; Fleet National Bank.

For full biographical listings, see the Martindale-Hubbell Law Directory

MICHIGAN

*ADRIAN,** Lenawee Co.

WALKER, WATTS, JACKSON & MCFARLAND (AV)

160 North Winter Street, 49221
Telephone: 517-265-8138
Fax: 517-265-8286
URL: http://www.lawyers.com/wwj&m

MEMBERS OF FIRM

William H. Walker
Prosser M. Watts, Jr.
Mark A. Jackson
Michael McFarland

ASSOCIATE

David Christopher McFarland

Attorneys for: Bank of Lenawee; Consumers Power Co.; Norfolk & Western Railway Co.; Citizens Gas Fuel Co.; Auto Owners Insurance Co.; Amerisure Co.; Blissfield Manufacturing Co.; Adrian College.

For full biographical listings, see the Martindale-Hubbell Law Directory

*ANN ARBOR,** Washtenaw Co.

BRAUN KENDRICK FINKBEINER PLC (AV)

First National Building, 210 S. Main, Suite 700, 48104
Telephone: 313-995-4100
Telecopier: 313-995-4798
Email: ALBFIE@BKF-LAW.COM *URL:* http://www.bkf-law.com
Bay City, Michigan Office: 201 Phoenix Building, P.O. Box 2039.
Telephone: 517-895-8505.
Telecopier: 517-895-8437.
Saginaw, Michigan Office: 101 N. Washington, Suite 812.
Telephone: 517-753-3461.
Telecopier: 517-753-3951.
Saginaw Township, Michigan Office: 5800 Gratiot Road, Suite 107, P.O. Box 5169.
Telephone: 517-799-8692.
Fax: 517-799-4666.
Mt. Pleasant, Michigan Office: 805 North Brown.
Telephone: 517-775-7404.
Telecopier: 517-775-3764.

Barry M. Levine

Representative Clients: The Dow Chemical Co.; General Motors Corp.; Merrill, Lynch, Inc.; Saginaw General Hospital; Saginaw News; The Wickes Foundation.

For Complete List of Firm Personnel, See General Section

For full biographical listings, see the Martindale-Hubbell Law Directory

HOOPER, HATHAWAY, PRICE, BEUCHE & WALLACE (AV)

126 South Main Street, 48104
Telephone: 313-662-4426
Fax: 313-662-9559
Email: hhpbw@voyager.net

Alan E. Price

Representative Clients: Avfuel Corporation; Bank of Ann Arbor; Castrol North America; Chem-Trend Incorporated; Ervin Industries, Inc.; First Martin Corporation; Glacier Hills, Inc.; Prestolite Electric, Inc.; Southern States Cooperative; E.B. Eddy Forest Products, Ltd.

For Complete List of Firm Personnel, See General Section

For full biographical listings, see the Martindale-Hubbell Law Directory

PEAR SPERLING EGGAN & MUSKOVITZ, P.C. (AV)

Domino's Farms, 24 Frank Lloyd Wright Drive, 48105
Telephone: 734-665-4441
Fax: 734-665-8788
Email: peare@dominos.com
Ypsilanti, Michigan Offices: 5 South Washington Street.
Telephone: 734-483-3626 and 2164 Bellevue at Washtenaw.
Telephone: 734-483-7177.

Edwin L. Pear — Andrew M. Eggan

For Complete List of Firm Personnel, See General Section

For full biographical listings, see the Martindale-Hubbell Law Directory

BATTLE CREEK, Calhoun Co.

KREIS, ENDERLE, CALLANDER & HUDGINS, A PROFESSIONAL CORPORATION (AV)

One West Michigan Avenue, 49017
Telephone: 616-966-3000
Facsimile: 616-966-3022
Email: kech@kech.com *URL:* http://www.kech.com
Kalamazoo, Michigan Office: One Moorsbridge, P.O. Box 4010, 49003-4010.
Telephone: 616-324-3000.
Fax: 616-324-3010.

C. Reid Hudgins III (Resident, Kalamazoo Office)
Robert B. Borsos (Resident, Kalamazoo Office)
Stephen L. Simons
Daniel P. McGlinn (Resident, Kalamazoo Office)
Janice Roark Peters (Resident, Kalamazoo Office)
Matthew S. DePerno (Resident, Kalamazoo Office)

OF COUNSEL

James M. Sullivan

For Complete List of Firm Personnel, See General Section
For full biographical listings, see the Martindale-Hubbell Law Directory

*BAY CITY,** Bay Co.

BRAUN KENDRICK FINKBEINER PLC (AV)

201 Phoenix Building, P.O. Box 2039, 48708
Telephone: 517-895-8505
Telecopier: 517-895-8437
Email: ALBFIE@BKF-LAW.COM *URL:* http://www.bkf-law.com
Saginaw, Michigan Office: 101 N. Washington, Suite 812. 8th Floor Second National Bank Building.
Telephone: 517-753-3461.
Telecopier: 517-753-3951.
Saginaw Township, Michigan Office: 5800 Gratiot Road, Suite 107, P.O. Box 5169.
Telephone: 517-799-8692.
Fax: 517-799-4666.
Ann Arbor, Michigan Office: First National Building. 201 S. Main, Suite 700.
Telephone: 313-995-4100.
Telecopier: 313-995-4798.
Mt. Pleasant, Michigan Office: 805 North Brown.
Telephone: 517-775-7404.
Telecopier: 517-775-3764.

Ralph J. Isackson
Gregory E. Meter
Gregory T. Demers

Representative Clients: Bay Health Systems; Catholic Federal Credit Union; City of Saginaw; City of Vassar; City of Zilwaukee; Corporate Service; Cox Cable.

For Complete List of Firm Personnel, See General Section

For full biographical listings, see the Martindale-Hubbell Law Directory

BIRMINGHAM, Oakland Co.

BUTZEL LONG, A PROFESSIONAL CORPORATION (AV)

Suite 200, 32270 Telegraph Road, 48025
Telephone: 810-258-1616
Telecopier: 810-258-1439
Email: melnick@butzel.com *URL:* http://www.butzel.com
Detroit, Michigan Office: Suite 900, 150 West Jefferson.
Telephone: 313-225-7000.
Telecopier: 313-225-7080.
Okemos, Michigan Office: Suite 300, 2127 University Park Drive.
Telephone: 517-372-6622.
Telecopier: 517-372-6672.
Ann Arbor, Michigan Office: Suite 300, 350 South Main Street.
Telephone: 313-995-3110.
Telecopier: 313-995-1777.
Grosse Pointe Farms, Michigan Office: Suite 260, 21 Kercheval.
Telephone: 313-886-5446.
Telecopier: 313-886-2114.
Boca Raton, Florida Office: Suite 411, 1200 North Federal Highway.
Telephone: 561-368-2151.
Telecopier: 561-368-4668.
Palm Beach Gardens, Florida Office: Suite 227, 11382 Prosperity Farms Road.
Telephone: 561-625-4442.
Telecopier: 561-625-6901.
Naples, Florida Office: Suite 705, 801 Laurel Oak Drive.
Telephone: 941-597-4500.
Telecopier: 941-597-5623.

Paul L. Triemstra (Resident)
T. Gordon Scupholm II (Resident)
David W. Sommerfeld
John J. Raymond, Jr.
Robert P. Perry

SENIOR ATTORNEYS

Katherine B. Albrecht (Resident)
Amy L. Glenn (Resident)

Monica Demko Moons (Resident)

For full biographical listings, see the Martindale-Hubbell Law Directory

HYMAN LIPPITT, P.C. (AV)

185 Oakland Avenue, Suite 300, 48009
Telephone: 248-646-8292
Facsimile: 248-646-8375
Email: hymalipp@tir.com

J. Leonard Hyman
Norman L. Lippitt
Douglas A. Hyman
Brian D. O'Keefe
H. Joel Newman
Nazli G. Sater
Kenneth F. Neuman
Terry S. Givens
Paul J. Fischer
John A. Sellers
Robert H. Lippitt
Roger L. Myers
Sally A. Rutledge
Joseph Pia
John P. Gonway
Leif K. Anderson

(See Next Column)

HYMAN LIPPITT P.C., *Birmingham—Continued*

Jennifer S. Gold	Dawn S. Spratley
Julie Lyons Kosovec	Michael T. Price

For full biographical listings, see the Martindale-Hubbell Law Directory

BLOOMFIELD HILLS, Oakland Co.

BEIER HOWLETT, PROFESSIONAL CORPORATION (AV)

200 East Long Lake Road, Suite 110, 48304-2361
Telephone: 248-645-9400
Fax: 248-645-9344
URL: http://www.beierhowlett.com

James L. Howlett	Mark W. Hafeli
Daniel C. Devine	Timothy J. Currier
Lawrence R. Ternan	Mary T. Schmitt Smith
Stephen W. Jones	Joseph F. Yamin
Frank S. Galgan	John D. Staran
Kenneth J. Sorensen	Phyllis Aiuto Zimmerman
Thomas J. Trenta	P. Daniel Christ

Lauren M. Underwood

Elizabeth A. Barrett Bonner	Jon M. Midtgard
Mary M. Kucharek	Paul L. Nystrom
Richard A. Joslin, Jr.	Genevieve Dwaihy Hopkins
Michael C. Gibbons	Jeffrey S. Kragt

OF COUNSEL

Dean G. Beier	Catherine J. Hulbert
Robert G. Waddell	Thomas V. Trainer

For full biographical listings, see the Martindale-Hubbell Law Directory

DAWDA, MANN, MULCAHY & SADLER, P.L.C. (AV)

1533 North Woodward Avenue Suite 200, 48304-2815
Telephone: 248-642-3700
Fax: 248-642-7791
Email: EMail@DMMS.Com

Edward C. Dawda	Curtis J. Mann

Glenn G. Ross

Paul C. Apap

For full biographical listings, see the Martindale-Hubbell Law Directory

DROLET, FREEMAN, COTTON & NORRIS, P.C. (AV)

33 Bloomfield Hills Parkway, Suite 100, 48304
Telephone: 248-642-2255
Fax: 248-642-6460
Email: droletfreeman@voyager.net

David G. Barnett (1915-1989)	J. Kingsley Cotton, III
H. William Freeman	Matthew C. Norris

Brian P. Henry	Lauren D. Honet
Suzanne S. Reynolds	David M. Blau

Representative Clients: Angelo Iafrate Construction Co.; ASC, Incorporated; Cadillac Asphalt Paving Co.; Carroll Packaging, Inc.; Choice Hotels International; Clawson Concrete Co.; Commerica Bank; Corrosion Control Engineering; Emcor; Farmington Public Schools.

For full biographical listings, see the Martindale-Hubbell Law Directory

JOYCE Q. LOWER (AV)

800 West Long Lake Road, Suite 210, 48302
Telephone: 248-642-1056
Fax: 248-642-1156
Email: jlower@voyager.net

ASSOCIATE

Laura Ann Schreiner

For full biographical listings, see the Martindale-Hubbell Law Directory

MEYER, KIRK, SNYDER & SAFFORD, PLLC (AV)

Suite 100, 100 West Long Lake Road, 48304
Telephone: 248-647-5111
Telecopier: 248-647-6079
Email: mkss@michbar.org
Detroit, Michigan Office: 1400 Ford Building, 615 Griswold, 48226.
Telephone: 313-961-1261.

George H. Meyer	John M. Kirk

Donald H. Baker, Jr.

Michelle R. Puricelli

Representative Clients: Available Upon Request.

For full biographical listings, see the Martindale-Hubbell Law Directory

*DETROIT,** Wayne Co.

ABBOTT, NICHOLSON, QUILTER, ESSHAKI & YOUNGBLOOD, P.C. (AV)

300 River Place, Suite 3000, 48207-4225
Telephone: 313-566-2500
Telecopier: 313-566-2502
Email: anqey@anqey.com *URL:* http://www.anqey.com

C. Richard Abbott	Timothy A. Stoepker
John R. Nicholson	Timothy J. Kramer
Thomas R. Quilter III	Norbert T. Madison, Jr.
Gene J. Esshaki	William D. Gilbride, Jr.
John F. Youngblood	Mary P. Nelson
James B. Perry	Michael R. Blum
Carl F. Jarboe	Anne Warren Bagno
Jay A. Kennedy	Thomas J. Giachino

Eric J. Girdler	George P. Butler III
Jill A. Bankey	Christopher P. Baker
Daniel G. Kielczewski	Sean A. Fraser

OF COUNSEL

Thomas C. Shumaker	Lisa R. Gorman

For full biographical listings, see the Martindale-Hubbell Law Directory

BODMAN, LONGLEY & DAHLING LLP (AV)

34th Floor 100 Renaissance Center, 48243
Telephone: 313-259-7777
Fax: 313-393-7579
Email: info@bodmanlongley.com *URL:* http://www.bodmanlongley.com
Troy, Michigan Office: Suite 2020, 755 West Big Beaver Road.
Telephone: 248-362-2110.
Fax: 248-244-0780.
Ann Arbor, Michigan Office: 110 Miller, Suite 300.
Telephone: 734-761-3780.
Fax: 734-930-2494.
Northern Michigan Office: 229 Court Street, P.O. Box 405, Cheboygan.
Telephone: 231-627-4351.
Fax: 231-627-2802.

MEMBERS OF FIRM

George D. Miller, Jr.	David M. Hempstead
Mark W. Griffin (Ann Arbor Office)	David P. Larsen
	Barnett Jay Colvin

COUNSEL

John S. Dobson (Ann Arbor Office)

ASSOCIATES

Andrew H. Curoe	Emily M. Kellndorfer (Ann Arbor Office)
Robert P. Tiplady	

For Representative Client List, See General Section

For Complete List of Firm Personnel, See General Section

For full biographical listings, see the Martindale-Hubbell Law Directory

BOOTHMAN, HEBERT & ELLER, P.C. (AV)

Marquette Building, 243 West Congress, Suite 950, 48226
Telephone: 313-964-0150
Fax: 313-964-2226
Email: boothman@mail.mich.com

Dale L. Hebert	Richard C. Boothman

Gary S. Eller

Edward C. Reynolds, Jr.	Marta J. Hoffman

Representative Clients: University of Michigan; Mutual Insurance Corporation of America; Emergency Physicians Medical Group; Pronational; HCR Manor Care, Inc.
Reference: Comerica Bank-Detroit.

For full biographical listings, see the Martindale-Hubbell Law Directory

FILDEW HINKS, P.L.L.C. (AV)

3600 Penobscot Building, 645 Griswold Street, 48226-4291
Telephone: 313-961-9700
Facsimile: 313-961-0754

MEMBERS OF FIRM

Stanley L. Fildew (1896-1978)	Mary Jane Ruffley
Frank T. Hinks (1887-1974)	Robert D. Welchli
Richard E. Hinks (1916-1990)	William P. Thorpe
John H. Fildew	Colleen A. Kramer
Alan C. Miller	Stephen J. Pokoj
Randall S. Wangen	Charles S. Kennedy III

ASSOCIATE

Walter B. Fisher Jr.

References: First of America Bank-Detroit, N.A.; Comerica Bank-Detroit; National Bank of Detroit.

(See Next Column)

FILDEW HINKS P.L.L.C.—*Continued*

For full biographical listings, see the Martindale-Hubbell Law Directory

HAYDUK, ANDREWS & HYPNAR, P.C. (AV)

1700 Buhl Building, 535 Griswold, 48226
Telephone: 313-962-4500
Fax: 313-964-6577
Email: hahpc3@aol.com

Mark S. Hayduk
Robin K. Andrews
Mark A. Hypnar

Sean Angus McPhillips
Francis J. Lagrou

Representative Clients: Farmers Insurance Group; Admiral Insurance Co.; Heritage Insurance; Meijer, Inc.; Alexis Condon & Forsyth; Pinkerton's Inc.; Vik Brothers Ins.; American Modern Home Ins.

For full biographical listings, see the Martindale-Hubbell Law Directory

JAFFE, RAITT, HEUER & WEISS, PROFESSIONAL CORPORATION (AV)

One Woodward Avenue, Suite 2400, 48226
Telephone: 313-961-8380
Telecopier: 313-961-8358
Cable Address: "Jafsni"
Southfield,Michigan Office: Travelers Tower, Suite 1520.
Telephone: 313-961-8380.

Derek S. Adolf
Joel S. Golden
Shirley A. Powers Kaigler

For Complete List of Firm Personnel, See General Section

For full biographical listings, see the Martindale-Hubbell Law Directory

JOSLYN KEYDEL & WALLACE, LLP (AV)

Albert Kahn Building, 9th Floor, 7430 Second Avenue, 48202-2717
Telephone: 313-871-4181
Fax: 313-871-6100
Email: etal@jkwlaw.com

MEMBERS OF FIRM

Lee E. Joslyn (1864-1936)
Alan W. Joslyn (1899-1990)
Lee E. Joslyn, Jr. (1895-1955)
Frederick R. Keydel (PLLC)
Harvey B. Wallace II (PLLC)

ASSOCIATE

Patrice M. Ticknor

LEGAL SUPPORT PERSONNEL

PARALEGALS

Diane C. Simpson
Alice M. Pricer
Ruth G. Spector
Sarah E. Monahan

References: NBD Bank, N.A.; Comerica Bank.

For full biographical listings, see the Martindale-Hubbell Law Directory

KELLER, THOMA, SCHWARZE, SCHWARZE, DUBAY & KATZ, P.C. (AV)

440 East Congress, 5th Floor, 48226
Telephone: 313-965-7610
Fax: 313-965-4480
Bingham Farms, Michigan Office: 30150 Telegraph Road, Suite 444, 48025.
Telephone: 248-642-5218.

James R. Miller
Anthony J. Heckemeyer

Counsel for: Livonia Public Schools; Ludington News Co., Inc.
Representative Clients: Borg-Warner Corp.; E & L Transport Co.; The Kroger Co.; Holnam, Inc.
Public Employer Clients: City of Farmington Hills; City of Flint; City of Grosse Pointe Woods; Saginaw Public Schools.

For Complete List of Firm Personnel, See General Section

For full biographical listings, see the Martindale-Hubbell Law Directory

MAY AND MAY, PROFESSIONAL CORPORATION

(See Southfield)

MEYER, KIRK, SNYDER & SAFFORD, PLLC (AV)

1400 Ford Building, 615 Griswold, 48226
Telephone: 313-961-1261
Fax: 248-647-6079
Bloomfield Hills, Michigan Office: Suite 100, 100 West Long Lake Road.
Telephone: 248-647-5111.
Telecopier: 248-647-6079.

George H. Meyer
John M. Kirk
Donald H. Baker, Jr.

(See Next Column)

Michelle R. Puricelli

Representative Clients: Available Upon Request.

For full biographical listings, see the Martindale-Hubbell Law Directory

MILLER, CANFIELD, PADDOCK AND STONE, P.L.C. (AV)

A Professional Limited Liability Company
Founded in 1852 by Sidney Davy Miller
150 West Jefferson, Suite 2500, 48226-4415
Telephone: 313-963-6420
Fax: 313-496-7500
Cable Address: "Stem Detroit"
URL: http://www.millercanfield.com
Ann Arbor, Michigan Office: 101 North Main Street, 7th Floor, 48104-1400.
Telephone: 734-663-2445.
Fax: 734-747-7147.
Troy, Michigan Office: 840 West Long Lake Road, Suite 200, 48098.
Telephone: 248-879-2000.
Fax: 248-879-2001.
Grand Rapids, Michigan Office: 99 Monroe, N.W., Suite 1200, 49503-2639.
Telephone: 616-454-8656.
Fax: 616-776-6322.
Howell, Michigan Office: 121 South Barnard Street, Suite 4, 48843-2305.
Telephone: 517-546-7600.
Telecopier: 517-546-6974.
Kalamazoo, Michigan Office: 444 West Michigan Avenue, 49007-3752.
Telephone: 616-381-7030.
Fax: 616-382-0244.
Lansing, Michigan Office: One Michigan Avenue, Suite 900, 48933-1609.
Telephone: 517-487-2070.
Fax: 517-374-6304.
Monroe, Michigan Office: 214 East Elm Avenue, Suite 100, 48162-2682.
Telephone: 734-243-2000.
Fax: 734-243-0901.
Washington, D.C. Office: 1900 K Street, N.W., Suite 1150. 20006.
Telephone: 202-429-5575; 785-0600.
Fax: 202-331-1118; 785-1234.
Pensacola, Florida Office: 25 West Cedar, 32501.
Telephone: 850-469-1088.
Fax: 850-432-0677.
New York, New York Office: 1450 Broadway, 41st Floor, 10018.
Telephone: 212-704-4400.
Fax: 212-704-4410.
Gdynia, Poland Office: UL. Slaska 21, 81-319.
Telephone: 011-485-831-2808.
Fax: 011-48-58-628 6411.
Warsaw, Poland Office: UL. Nowogrodzkall, 5th Floor, 00-513.
Telephone: 011-4822 529 0200.
Fax: 011-4822 529 0201.
Katowice, Poland Office: UL. Francuska 35/37, 40-027.
Telephone: 011 (48-32) 757-2414.
Fax: 011 (48-32) 757-2483.

PRINCIPALS OF FIRM

Kenneth E. Konop (Troy Office)
Dawn M. Schluter (Troy Office)
James W. Williams (Troy Office)
John G. VanSlambrouck (Kalamazoo Office)
Gregory V. Di Censo (Troy Office)

OF COUNSEL/SENIOR COUNSEL

Peter P. Thurber
George E. Parker, III
Lawrence A. King (P.C.) (Troy Office)

SENIOR ATTORNEY

Stephen L. Elkins (Grand Rapids Office)

Representative Firm Clients: Chrysler Corporation; Comerica, Incorporated; City of Detroit, Michigan; Detroit Tigers, Inc.; First of Michigan; Ford Motor Company; Ford Motor Credit Company; Great Lakes Bancorp; Henry Ford Hospital; INVETECH Company.

For Complete List of Firm Personnel, See General Section

For full biographical listings, see the Martindale-Hubbell Law Directory

PYTELL & VARCHETTI, P.C. (AV)

18580 Mack Avenue, 48236
Telephone: 313-343-9200; 1-888-292-4LAW
Fax: 313-343-0207
Email: PROBATE@compuserve.com *URL:* http://www.MIprobate.com

Robert H. Pytell
Henry C. Pytell (1903-1988)
Paul E. Varchetti

For full biographical listings, see the Martindale-Hubbell Law Directory

Detroit—Continued

DAVID M. THOMS & ASSOCIATES, P.C. (AV)

400 Renaissance Center, Suite 950, 48243
Telephone: 313-259-6333
Facsimile: 313-259-7037
Email: Thoms@ameritech.net *URL:* http://www.lawyers.com/thoms&associates

David M. Thoms

Audrey R. Holley
Danielle M. Spehar
Joseph A. Durocher

Representative Clients: deBary Voyage, Inc.; R.G. & G.R. Harris Funeral Home, Inc.; St. Jude Children's Research Hospital; The Salvation Army; American Red Cross; Comerica Bank-Detroit; National Bank of Detroit; Sterling Bank; Margaret Varney Charitable Remainder Trust; Cremation Society of Michigan, Inc.

For full biographical listings, see the Martindale-Hubbell Law Directory

TIMMIS & INMAN L.L.P. (AV)

300 Talon Centre, 48207
Telephone: 313-396-4200
Facsimile: 313-396-4228
Email: info@timmis-inman.com *URL:* http://www.timmis-inman.com

Michael T. Timmis
George A. Peck
George M. Malis

Erich J. D'Andrea

Representative Clients: Retail Resources, Inc.; Applied Process, Inc.; Certain Underwriters at Lloyds of London; Eastpointe Radiologists, P.C.; Talon Automotive Group, Inc.; G&L Industries, Inc.; Hawthorne Metal Products Co.; Foam Rubber Products Co.; Diamond Automations, Inc.; Veltri Metal Products Co.; J&R Manufacturing, Inc.; Spiralock Corporation.

For Complete List of Firm Personnel, See General Section

For full biographical listings, see the Martindale-Hubbell Law Directory

FARMINGTON HILLS, Oakland Co.

COUZENS, LANSKY, FEALK, ELLIS, ROEDER & LAZAR, P.C. (AV)

39395 West 12 Mile Road, Suite 200, 48331-2913
Telephone: 248-489-8600
Facsimile: 248-489-4156
Email: info@couzens.com *URL:* http://www.couzens.com

Jack S. Couzens, II
Donald M. Lansky
Bruce J. Lazar
Alan C. Roeder
Renard J. Kolasa
Kathryn Gilson Sussman
Jeffrey A. Levine
Marc L. Prey
Lisa J. Walters
Michael P. Witzke

Alisa A. Kwang
Turkia Awada Mullin
Raoul K. Maitra

Representative Clients: Provided upon request.
Reference: Michigan National Bank.

For Complete List of Firm Personnel, See General Section

For full biographical listings, see the Martindale-Hubbell Law Directory

FLAT ROCK, Wayne Co.

TUCHOW & TRAHEY (AV)

26316 Telegraph Road, 48134
Telephone: 734-782-2900
Fax: 734-782-2123
Bloomfield Hills, Michigan Office: Americenter of Bloomfield Hills, Seven West Square Lake Road.
Telephone: 313-963-7633.
Fax: 313-782-2123.

MEMBERS OF FIRM

Gerald Tuchow
Stephen J. Trahey

Reference: Old Kent Bank.

For full biographical listings, see the Martindale-Hubbell Law Directory

*FLINT,** Genesee Co.

GAULT DAVISON A PROFESSIONAL SERVICE CORPORATION (AV)

Tenth Floor, Northbank Center, 432 North Saginaw Street, 48502-2032
Telephone: 810-234-3633
Fax: 810-233-3387
Email: gltdav@tir.com *URL:* http://www.gaultdavison.com

Russell E. Bowers
Bernard L. McAra

(See Next Column)

Christine A. Waun

Representative Clients: BankOne; Citizens Banking Corporation.

For full biographical listings, see the Martindale-Hubbell Law Directory

*GRAND RAPIDS,** Kent Co.

BORRE, PETERSON, FOWLER & REENS, P.C. (AV)

300 Ottawa N.W., Suite 500, P.O. Box 1767, 49501-1767
Telephone: 616-459-1971
Fax: 616-459-2393
Email: 105162.1531@compuserve.com

Glen V. Borre
James B. Peterson
Ben A. Fowler
William G. Krupar

Michelle H. Anthes

References: Old Kent Bank; NBD Bank/First Chicago Bank; The Huntington Bank.

For Complete List of Firm Personnel, See General Section

For full biographical listings, see the Martindale-Hubbell Law Directory

MCSHANE & BOWIE, P.L.C. (AV)

1100 Campau Square Plaza, 99 Monroe Avenue, N.W., P.O. Box 360, 49501-0360
Telephone: 616-732-5000
Fax: 616-732-5099

MEMBERS OF FIRM

William H. Bowie
Keith P. Walker
John F. Shape
Wayne P. Bryan

Representative Clients: Old Kent Bank; Amway Hotel Corp.; Randers Engineering, Inc.; BETA Design Group, Inc.; Wolverine Gas & Oil Co., Inc.; M. W. VanderVeen Co.

For Complete List of Firm Personnel, See General Section

For full biographical listings, see the Martindale-Hubbell Law Directory

MILLER, CANFIELD, PADDOCK AND STONE, P.L.C. (AV)

A Professional Limited Liability Company
Founded in 1852 by Sidney Davy Miller
99 Monroe, N.W. Suite 1200, 49503-2639
Telephone: 616-454-8656
Fax: 616-776-6322
URL: http://www.millercanfield.com
Detroit, Michigan Office: 150 West Jefferson, Suite 2500, 48226-4415.
Telephone: 313-963-6420.
Fax: 313-496-7500.
Cable Address: "Stem Detroit."
Ann Arbor, Michigan Office: 101 North Main Street, 7th Floor, 48104-1400.
Telephone: 734-663-2445.
Fax: 734-747-7147.
Troy, Michigan Office: 840 West Long Lake Road, Suite 200, 48098.
Telephone: 248-879-2000.
Fax: 248-879-2001.
Howell, Michigan Office: 121 South Barnard Street, Suite 4, 48843-2305.
Telephone: 517-546-7600.
Telecopier: 517-546-6974.
Kalamazoo, Michigan Office: 444 West Michigan Avenue, 49007-3752.
Telephone: 616-381-7030.
Fax: 616-382-0244.
Lansing, Michigan Office: One Michigan Avenue, Suite 900, 48933-1609.
Telephone: 517-487-2070.
Fax: 517-374-6304.
Monroe, Michigan Office: 214 East Elm Avenue, Suite 100, 48162-2682.
Telephone: 734-243-2000.
Fax: 734-243-0901.
Washington, D.C. Office: 1900 K Street, N.W., Suite 1150. 20006.
Telephone: 202-429-5575; 785-0600.
Fax: 202-331-1118; 785-1234.
Pensacola, Florida Office: 25 West Cedar, 32501.
Telephone: 850-469-1088.
Fax: 850-432-0677.
New York, New York Office: 1450 Broadway, 41st Floor, 10018.
Telephone: 212-704-4400.
Fax: 212-704-4410.
Gdynia, Poland Office: UL. Slaska 21, 81-319.
Telephone: 011-485-831-2808.
Fax: 011-48-58-628 6411.
Warsaw, Poland Office: UL. Nowogrodzkall, 5th Floor, 00-513.
Telephone: 011-4822 529 0200.
Fax: 011-4822 529 0201.
Katowice, Poland Office: UL. Francuska 35/37, 40-027.
Telephone: 011 (48-32) 757-2414.
Fax: 011 (48-32) 757-2483.

(See Next Column)

MILLER, CANFIELD, PADDOCK AND STONE P.L.C.—*Continued*

RESIDENT SENIOR ATTORNEY

Stephen L. Elkins

Representative Firm Clients: Chrysler Corporation; Comerica, Incorporated; City of Detroit, Michigan; Detroit Tigers, Inc.; First of Michigan; Ford Motor Company; Ford Motor Credit Company; Great Lakes Bancorp; Henry Ford Hospital; INVETECH Company.

For Complete List of Firm Personnel, See General Section

For full biographical listings, see the Martindale-Hubbell Law Directory

---

RHOADES, MCKEE, BOER, GOODRICH & TITTA (AV)

600 Waters Building, 161 Ottawa Avenue NW, 49503-2793
Telephone: 616-235-3500
Fax: 616-235-1639
Email: webmaster@grlaw.com *URL:* http://www.grlaw.com

Roger W. Boer
Edward B. Goodrich
Peter A. Titta
Richard G. Leonard
Arthur C. Spalding
Bruce W. Neckers
Robert J. Dugan
Terrence L. Groesser
Thomas P. Hogan
James M. Flaggert
Mary Ann Cartwright
Daniel L. Elve
Thomas L. Saxe
James L. Schipper
Laurie M. Strong
Stephen A. Hilger
Gregory G. Timmer
Mary Lynette Williams
Scott J. Steiner
Douglas P. Vanden Berge
Robert C. Shaver
John M. Lichtenberg
Dan E. Bylenga, Jr.
Mark E. Fatum

Paul A. McCarthy
Todd Allen Hendricks
Kenneth M. Horjus
Randy J. Kolar
Molly M. McNamara
Peter J. Lozicki
David E. Bevins
Mark S. Pendery
Terry L. Zabel
Mary L. Cranmer
Patrick Drueke
Anthony Allan Pearson

OF COUNSEL

Dale W. Rhoades
F. William McKee
Jean McKee
Charles T. Zimmerman
Robert F. Williams

Reference: First Michigan Bank.

For full biographical listings, see the Martindale-Hubbell Law Directory

WARNER NORCROSS & JUDD LLP (AV)

900 Old Kent Building, 111 Lyon Street, N.W., 49503-2489
Telephone: 616-752-2000
Fax: 616-752-2500
URL: http://www.wnj.com
Muskegon, Michigan Office: 400 Terrace Plaza, P.O. Box 900.
Telephone: 231-727-2600.
Fax: 231-727-2699.
Holland, Michigan Office: Curtis Center, Suite 300, 170 College Avenue.
Telephone: 616-396-9800.
Fax: 616-396-3656.
Southfield, Michigan Office: 1000 Town Center, Suite 650.
Telephone: 248-223-5000.
Fax: 248-223-5005.

MEMBERS OF FIRM

Jerome M. Smith
I. John Snider, II (Resident Member, Muskegon Office)
John R. Marquis (Resident Member, Holland Office)
John H. Martin (Resident Member, Muskegon Office)
W. Michael Van Haren
Carl W. Dufendach
Bruce C. Young
Jeffrey B. Power
Mark K. Harder (Resident Member, Holland Office)
Susan Gell Meyers

ASSOCIATES

Karen J. Vanderwerff
John E. Kessler (Resident, Holland Office)
Christian E. Meyer
Jonathan J. Siebers
Jaron J. Nyhof (Resident, Holland Office)

For full biographical listings, see the Martindale-Hubbell Law Directory

---

GROSSE POINTE FARMS, Wayne Co.

JOHNSON & MCPHERSON, P.L.C. (AV)

81 Kercheval, 48236
Telephone: 313-885-4700
Fax: 313-888-5872

Edward C. Johnson
Dale T. McPherson

RETIRED

Jarvis J. Schmidt

For full biographical listings, see the Martindale-Hubbell Law Directory

ALLAN NEEF (AV)

18580 Mack Avenue, 48236
Telephone: 313-343-9200
Fax: 313-343-0207

For full biographical listings, see the Martindale-Hubbell Law Directory

---

GROSSE POINTE WOODS, Wayne Co.

PATRICIA L. PATTERSON (AV)

19678 Harper, 48236-1966
Telephone: 313-884-8300
Fax: 313-881-9050

ASSOCIATE

Michele P Fuller

For full biographical listings, see the Martindale-Hubbell Law Directory

---

HARBOR SPRINGS, Emmet Co.

RAMER, MOORE & GLASS (AV)

First Community Bank Building, One Hundred Spring Street Post Office Box 5, 49740
Telephone: 616-526-6214
Fax: 616-526-9343
http: //www.ramerandmoore.com
Email: jramer@ramerandmoore.com *URL:* http://www.lawyers.com/ramerandmoore

MEMBERS OF FIRM

James T. Ramer
Joel B. Moore
Charles F. Glass

Representative Clients: City of Harbor Springs; Roaring Brook Assn.; Forest Beach Assn.; Birchwood Farms Property Owners Assn.; Pride Hunters & Jumpers, Inc.; Black Forest Farm.

For full biographical listings, see the Martindale-Hubbell Law Directory

---

*HILLSDALE,** Hillsdale Co.

PARKER, HAYES & LOVINGER, P.C. (AV)

14-16 South Howell Street, P.O. Box 358, 49242
Telephone: 517-437-7210
Fax: 517-437-0260

James B. Parker
Lawrence L. Hayes, Jr.
John P. Lovinger

Representative Clients: Hillsdale County National Bank; Villages of Jonesville and Camden; Hillsdale County (Labor Counsel); Hillsdale College; Powell Petroleum Co.; Foulke Construction Co.; Somerset Township; Hillsdale Tool

For full biographical listings, see the Martindale-Hubbell Law Directory

---

HOLLAND, Ottawa Co.

CUNNINGHAM DALMAN, P.C. (AV)

321 Settlers Road, P.O. Box 1767, 49422-1767
Telephone: 616-392-1821
Fax: 616-392-4769
Email: cunndalm@crossover.net *URL:* http://www.holland-law.com

Gordon H. Cunningham
Ronald L. Dalman
Max R. Murphy
James A. Bidol
Andrew J. Mulder
Kenneth B. Breese
Jeffrey K. Helder
Ronald J. Vander Veen
David M. Zessin
Mark H. Zietlow
Randall S. Schipper
Susan E. Vroegop
Joel G. Bouwens

Gregory J. McCoy
Jason M. Milstone
Aaron Leal
Dawn J. Ward

Representative Clients: Huntington National Bank; First of America Bank-Holland, N.A.; Ameribank; City of Holland; Auto Club Insurance Assn. (AAA); American States Insurance Co.; Holland Economic Development Corp.; Hope College; Western Theological Seminary.
Reference: Huntington National Bank.

For full biographical listings, see the Martindale-Hubbell Law Directory

---

*KALAMAZOO,** Kalamazoo Co.

DEMENT AND MARQUARDT, P.L.C. (AV)

407 West Michigan Avenue, 49007
Telephone: 616-343-2106
Fax: 616-343-2107
Email: daNdmplc@net-link.net

Daniel L. DeMent
Michele C. Marquardt

For full biographical listings, see the Martindale-Hubbell Law Directory

Kalamazoo—Continued

EARLY, LENNON, PETERS & CROCKER, P.C. (AV)

900 Comerica Building, 49007-4752
Telephone: 616-381-8844
Fax: 616-349-8525
Email: elpc@michbar.org

George H. Lennon, III
Gordon C. Miller
Robert M. Taylor

Attorneys for: Aetna Insurance; Kemper Group; Medical Protective Co.; Zurich Insurance; Liberty Mutual; Home Insurance.

For Complete List of Firm Personnel, See General Section

For full biographical listings, see the Martindale-Hubbell Law Directory

KREIS, ENDERLE, CALLANDER & HUDGINS, A PROFESSIONAL CORPORATION (AV)

One Moorsbridge, P.O. Box 4010, 49003-4010
Telephone: 616-324-3000
Facsimile: 616-324-3010
Email: kech@kech.com *URL:* http://www.kech.com
Battle Creek, Michigan Office: One West Michigan Avenue, 49017.
Telephone: 616-966-3000.
Fax: 616-966-3022.

C. Reid Hudgins III
Robert B. Borsos
Stephen L. Simons (Resident, Battle Creek Office)
Daniel P. McGlinn
Janice Roark Peters
Matthew S. DePerno

OF COUNSEL

James M. Sullivan (Resident, Battle Creek Office)

For Complete List of Firm Personnel, See General Section

For full biographical listings, see the Martindale-Hubbell Law Directory

LEWIS & ALLEN, P.C. (AV)

Old Kent Bank Building, Suite 800, 136 East Michigan Avenue, 49007-3946
Telephone: 616-388-7600
Fax: 616-349-3831

Dean S. Lewis
W. Fred Allen, Jr.
Barry R. Smith
William A. Redmond
Stephen M. Denenfeld
Anne McGregor Fries
Gregory G. St. Arnauld
James M. Marquardt
Christopher T. Haenicke
Winfield J. Hollander (1906-1996)

Dorothy B. Kelly

For full biographical listings, see the Martindale-Hubbell Law Directory

MILLER, CANFIELD, PADDOCK AND STONE, P.L.C. (AV)

A Professional Limited Liability Company
Founded in 1852 by Sidney Davy Miller
444 West Michigan Avenue, 49007-3752
Telephone: 616-381-7030
Fax: 616-382-0244
URL: http://www.millercanfield.com
Detroit, Michigan Office: 150 West Jefferson, Suite 2500, 48226-4415.
Telephone: 313-963-6420.
Fax: 313-496-7500.
Cable Address: "Stem Detroit."
Ann Arbor, Michigan Office: 101 North Main Street, 7th Floor, 48104-1400.
Telephone: 734-663-2445.
Fax: 734-747-7147.
Troy, Michigan Office: 840 West Long Lake Road, Suite 200, 48098.
Telephone: 248-879-2000.
Fax: 248-879-2001.
Grand Rapids, Michigan Office: 99 Monroe, N.W., Suite 1200, 49503-2639.
Telephone: 616-454-8656.
Fax: 616-776-6322.
Howell, Michigan Office: 121 South Barnard Street, Suite 4, 48843-2305.
Telephone: 517-546-7600.
Telecopier: 517-546-6974.
Lansing, Michigan Office: One Michigan Avenue, Suite 900, 48933-1609.
Telephone: 517-487-2070.
Fax: 517-374-6304.
Monroe, Michigan Office: 214 East Elm Avenue, Suite 100, 48162-2682.
Telephone: 734-243-2000.
Fax: 734-243-0901.
Washington, D.C. Office: 1900 K Street, N.W., Suite 1150. 20006.
Telephone: 202-429-5575; 785-0600.
Fax: 202-331-1118; 785-1234.
Pensacola, Florida Office: 25 West Cedar, 32501.
Telephone: 850-469-1088.
Fax: 850-432-0677.

(See Next Column)

New York, New York Office: 1450 Broadway, 41st Floor, 10018.
Telephone: 212-704-4400.
Fax: 212-704-4410.
Gdynia, Poland Office: UL. Slaska 21, 81-319.
Telephone: 011-485-831-2808.
Fax: 011-48-58-628 6411.
Warsaw, Poland Office: UL. Nowogrodzkall, 5th Floor, 00-513.
Telephone: 011-4822 529 0200.
Fax: 011-4822 529 0201.
Katowice, Poland Office: UL. Francuska 35/37, 40-027.
Telephone: 011 (48-32) 757-2414.
Fax: 011 (48-32) 757-2483.

PRINCIPALS

Eric V. Brown, Jr.
John A. Campbell
John G. VanSlambrouck

OF COUNSEL/SENIOR COUNSEL

Gerard Thomas

Representative Firm Clients: Chrysler Corporation; Comerica, Incorporated; City of Detroit, Michigan; Detroit Tigers, Inc.; First of Michigan; Ford Motor Company; Ford Motor Credit Company; Great Lakes Bancorp; Henry Ford Hospital; INVETECH Company.

For Complete List of Firm Personnel, See General Section

For full biographical listings, see the Martindale-Hubbell Law Directory

LANSING, Ingham Co.

FOSTER, SWIFT, COLLINS & SMITH, P.C. (AV)

313 South Washington Square, 48933-2193
Telephone: 517-371-8100
Telecopier: 517-371-8200
URL: http://www.fosterswift.com
Farmington Hills, Michigan Office: 32300 Northwestern Highway, Suite 230.
Telephone: 248-539-9900.
Fax: 248-851-7504.

Allan J. Claypool
Charles A. Janssen
Louis K. Nigg
Patricia A. Calore
Douglas A. Mielock

LEGAL SUPPORT PERSONNEL

LEGAL ASSISTANTS

Sandra L. De Santis
Kelly A. LaGrave, CLA

For Complete List of Firm Personnel, See General Section

For full biographical listings, see the Martindale-Hubbell Law Directory

FRASER TREBILCOCK DAVIS & FOSTER, P.C. (AV)

1000 Michigan National Tower, 48933
Telephone: 517-482-5800
Fax: 517-482-0887
URL: http://WWW.FTDF.COM
Detroit, Michigan Office: One Woodward Avenue, Suite 1550.
Telephone: 313-237-7300.
Fax: 313-961-1651.

Joe C. Foster, Jr.
Everett R. Zack
Richard C. Lowe
Nancy L. Little
Sharon A. Bruner
Michelyn E. Pasteur

Counsel for: Bank One, East Lansing; Comerica Bank; First of America Bank-Central; Michigan National Bank; Old Kent Bank; Citizens Bank.

For full biographical listings, see the Martindale-Hubbell Law Directory

MILLER, CANFIELD, PADDOCK AND STONE, P.L.C. (AV)

A Professional Limited Liability Company
Founded in 1852 by Sidney Davy Miller
Suite 900, One Michigan Avenue, 48933-1609
Telephone: 517-487-2070
Fax: 517-374-6304
URL: http://www.millercanfield.com
Detroit, Michigan Office: 150 West Jefferson, Suite 2500, 48226-4415.
Telephone: 313-963-6420.
Fax: 313-496-7500.
Cable Address: "Stem Detroit."
Ann Arbor, Michigan Office: 101 North Main Street, 7th Floor, 48104-1400.
Telephone: 734-663-2445.
Fax: 734-747-7147.
Troy, Michigan Office: 840 West Long Lake Road, Suite 200, 48098.
Telephone: 248-879-2000.
Fax: 248-879-2001.
Grand Rapids, Michigan Office: 99 Monroe, N.W., Suite 1200, 49503-2639.
Telephone: 616-454-8656.
Fax: 616-776-6322.
Howell, Michigan Office: 121 South Barnard Street, Suite 4, 48843-2305.
Telephone: 517-546-7600.
Telecopier: 517-546-6974.

(See Next Column)

MILLER, CANFIELD, PADDOCK AND STONE P.L.C.—*Continued*

Kalamazoo, Michigan Office: 444 West Michigan Avenue, 49007-3752.
Telephone: 616-381-7030.
Fax: 616-382-0244.
Monroe, Michigan Office: 214 East Elm Avenue, Suite 100, 48162-2682.
Telephone: 734-243-2000.
Fax: 734-243-0901.
Washington, D.C. Office: 1900 K Street, N.W., Suite 1150. 20006.
Telephone: 202-429-5575; 785-0600.
Fax: 202-331-1118; 785-1234.
Pensacola, Florida Office: 25 West Cedar, 32501.
Telephone: 850-469-1088.
Fax: 850-432-0677.
New York, New York Office: 1450 Broadway, 41st Floor, 10018.
Telephone: 212-704-4400.
Fax: 212-704-4410.
Gdynia, Poland Office: UL. Slaska 21, 81-319.
Telephone: 011-485-831-2808.
Fax: 011-48-58-628 6411.
Warsaw, Poland Office: UL. Nowogrodzkall, 5th Floor, 00-513.
Telephone: 011-4822 529 0200.
Fax: 011-4822 529 0201.
Katowice, Poland Office: UL. Francuska 35/37, 40-027.
Telephone: 011 (48-32) 757-2414.
Fax: 011 (48-32) 757-2483.

RESIDENT PRINCIPALS

Michael R. Atkins

Representative Firm Clients: Chrysler Corporation; Comerica, Incorporated; City of Detroit, Michigan; Detroit Tigers, Inc.; First of Michigan; Ford Motor Company; Ford Motor Credit Company; Great Lakes Bancorp; Henry Ford Hospital; INVETECH Company.

For Complete List of Firm Personnel, See General Section

For full biographical listings, see the Martindale-Hubbell Law Directory

LIVONIA, Wayne Co.

FRIED & ASSOCIATES, P.C. (AV)

32900 5 Mile Road, Suite 4, 48154-3059
Telephone: 734-421-5055
Fax: 734-421-5591
URL: http://www.lawyers.com/fried&associates

William C. Fried

For full biographical listings, see the Martindale-Hubbell Law Directory

*MONROE,** Monroe Co.

BRAUNLICH, RUSSOW & BRAUNLICH, A PROFESSIONAL CORPORATION (AV)

111 South Macomb Street, 48161
Telephone: 734-241-8300
Fax: 734-241-7715

William J. Braunlich, Jr. (1924-1992)
Thomas P. Russow
William H. Braunlich

Philip A. Costello
Ann L. Nickel
Jeffrey A. Dulany, P.C.

LEGAL SUPPORT PERSONNEL

Ruth G. Flint

Representative Clients: State Farm Mutual Insurance Co.; Auto Club Insurance Assn.; Board of Road Commissioners, Monroe County; Port of Monroe; Monroe County Community College; City of Luna Pier; City of Petersburg; Auto-Owners Insurance Co.; Fremont Mutual Insurance Co.; Citizens Insurance Co. of America.

For full biographical listings, see the Martindale-Hubbell Law Directory

PLYMOUTH, Wayne Co.

DRAUGELIS & ASHTON, L.L.P. (AV)

843 Penniman Avenue, 48170-1690
Telephone: 734-453-4044
Fax: 734-453-2011
Clawson, Michigan Office: 380 North Main Street.
Telephone: 248-588-7704.

MEMBERS OF FIRM

Edward F. Draugelis
John A. Ashton
Donald S. Scully
Richard T. Haynes
Lamberto DiStefano
David T. Rogers
Joseph R. Conte
Steven O. Ashton

ASSOCIATES

Floyd C. Virant
Taras P. Jarema
Timothy M. McKercher
Joel B. Ashton
Donald E. Walker
Heather A. Jefferson
Roger D. Ajluni
Margaret L. Browning

(See Next Column)

Representative Client: State Farm Mutual Automobile Insurance Co.
Reference: National Bank of Detroit, Plymouth Branch.

For full biographical listings, see the Martindale-Hubbell Law Directory

*SAGINAW,** Saginaw Co.

BRAUN KENDRICK FINKBEINER PLC (AV)

101 N. Washington Suite 812, 48607-1297
Telephone: 517-753-3461
Telecopier: 517-753-3951
Email: ALBFIE@BKF-LAW.COM *URL:* http://www.bkf-law.com
Saginaw Township Office, Michigan Office: 5800 Gratiot Road, Suite 107, P.O. Box 5169. Telephone 517-799-8692.
Fax: 517-799-4666.
Bay City, Michigan Office: 201 Phoenix Building, P.O. Box 2039.
Telephone: 517-895-8505.
Telecopier: 517-895-8437.
Ann Arbor, Michigan Office: First National Building. 201 S. Main, Suite 700.
Telephone: 313-995-4100.
Telecopier: 313-995-4798.
Mt. Pleasant, Michigan Office: 805 North Brown.
Telephone: 517-775-7404.
Telecopier: 517-775-3764.

James V. Finkbeiner
Hugo E. Braun, Jr.
John W. Wolf
David L. Turner
Jeffrey J. Endean
Thomas R. Luplow
Phillip J. Stahle

Representative Clients: The Dow Chemical Co.; General Motors Corp.; Merrill, Lynch, Inc.; Saginaw General Hospital; Saginaw News; The Wickes Foundation.

For Complete List of Firm Personnel, See General Section

For full biographical listings, see the Martindale-Hubbell Law Directory

*ST. JOSEPH,** Berrien Co.

FISHER LAW OFFICE (AV)

Law & Title Building, 811 Ship Street, P.O. Box 83, 49085-0083
Telephone: 616-983-5511
Telecopier: 616-893-5571
Email: fisherv@fisherlaw.com *URL:* http://www.fisherlaw.com

Vance A. Fisher

For full biographical listings, see the Martindale-Hubbell Law Directory

TROFF, PETZKE & AMMESON (AV)

Law and Title Building, 811 Ship Street, P.O. Box 67, 49085
Telephone: 616-983-0161
Facsimile: 616-983-0166
Email: pnalaw@qtm.net

MEMBERS OF FIRM

Roger A. Petzke
Charles F. Ammeson

For full biographical listings, see the Martindale-Hubbell Law Directory

SOUTHFIELD, Oakland Co.

DE VINE & KOHN, PLLC (AV)

29800 Telegraph Road, 48034
Telephone: 248-353-6500
Fax: 248-353-2514

Clifford J. De Vine
Sheldon B. Kohn

For full biographical listings, see the Martindale-Hubbell Law Directory

ROBERT B. LABE, P.C. (AV)

2000 Town Center, Suite 1780, 48075
Telephone: 248-354-3100
Telecopier: 248-354-3926

Robert B. Labe

Cecile Kohl

References: Comerica Bank, N.A.; Morgan Stanley Dean Witter.

For full biographical listings, see the Martindale-Hubbell Law Directory

MADDIN, HAUSER, WARTELL, ROTH, HELLER & PESSES, P.C. (AV)

Third Floor Essex Centre, 28400 Northwestern Highway, P.O. Box 215, 48037
Telephone: 248-354-4030, 355-5200
Telefax: 248-354-1422

(See Next Column)

MADDIN, HAUSER, WARTELL, ROTH, HELLER & PESSES P.C., *Southfield—Continued*

Milton M. Maddin (1902-1984)
Michael W. Maddin
Mark R. Hauser
C. Robert Wartell
Richard J. Maddin
Richard F. Roth
Harvey R. Heller
Ian D. Pesses
Michael S. Leib
Robert D. Kaplow
William E. Sigler
Stewart C. W. Weiner
Charles M. Lax
Stuart M. Bordman
Steven D. Sallen
Gregory J. Gamalski
Julie Chenot Mayer
Nathaniel H. Simpson
Ronald A. Sollish
Lowell D. Salesin

Mark H. Fink
Steven M. Wolock
Lori E. Talsky
Stephen E. Handelman
Ronald M. Stern
Martin Scott Frenkel
Gary M. Remer
Jennifer S. Sternberg
George V. Cassar, Jr.
Adam J. Goldstein

OF COUNSEL

Bruce N. Goldman

Reference: Comerica Bank.

For full biographical listings, see the Martindale-Hubbell Law Directory

MASON STEINHARDT JACOBS PERLMAN & PESICK, PROFESSIONAL CORPORATION (AV)

Suite 1500, 4000 Town Center, 48075-1415
Telephone: 248-358-2090
Fax: 248-358-3599
Email: admin@msjp.com *URL:* http://www.msjp.com

Gordon I. Ginsberg
Irving I. Boigon
Jack Schon
Frederick D. Steinhardt
John E. Jacobs
Michael B. Perlman
Jerome P. Pesick
Richard A. Polk
Neil S. Silver
L. Jeffrey Zauberman
Howard A. Lax
H. Adam Cohen
Diane Flagg Goldstein

Jeffrey B. Linden
David E. Nykanen
Jacquelyn L. Lane

OF COUNSEL

Walter B. Mason, Jr.
Erwin B. Ellmann
Walter J. Goldsmith
Randolph J. Friedman
Marvin C. Daitch

Representative Clients: Citibank, N.A.; City of Dearborn; DeMattia Development Co.; Forest City Enterprises; Michigan Wholesale Drug Assn.; Mortgage Bankers Association of Michigan; Nationwide Insurance Co.; City of Taylor; Union Labor Life Insurance Co.; Yellow Freight Systems, Inc.

For full biographical listings, see the Martindale-Hubbell Law Directory

MAY AND MAY, PROFESSIONAL CORPORATION (AV)

3000 Town Center, Suite 2600, 48075
Telephone: 248-358-3800
Fax: 248-358-1627
Email: MAYMAYPC@AOL.COM

Alan A. May

Lawrence G. Snyder
Laura M. Kystad
Barbara P. Andruccioli

For full biographical listings, see the Martindale-Hubbell Law Directory

SIEGEL, GREENFIELD, HAYES & GROSS, P.L.C. (AV)

2000 Town Center, Suite 2700, 48075-1318
Telephone: 248-386-5900
Facsimile: 248-354-3106
URL: http://www.lawyers.com/sghandglawfirm

MEMBERS OF FIRM

Robert W. Siegel
Norman E. Greenfield
Kelly M. Hayes
Robert A. Gross

OF COUNSEL

Steven H. Schwartz

For full biographical listings, see the Martindale-Hubbell Law Directory

SOMMERS, SCHWARTZ, SILVER & SCHWARTZ, P.C. (AV)

2000 Town Center, Suite 900, 48075
Telephone: 248-355-0300
Telecopier: 248-746-4001
Plymouth, Michigan Office: 747 South Main Street.
Telephone: 313-455-4250.

Victor A. Coen
Tracy L. Allen

(See Next Column)

OF COUNSEL

Paul Groffsky
H. Rollin Allen

General Counsel for: City of Taylor; Foodland Distributors; C.A. Muer Corporation; Vlasic & Company; Nederlander Corporation; Midwest Health Centers, P.C.

Representative Clients: Michigan National Bank; Universal Underwriters Insurance Co.; Don Lee Distributor; Rite-Aid of Michigan.

For Complete List of Firm Personnel, See General Section

For full biographical listings, see the Martindale-Hubbell Law Directory

*TAWAS CITY,** Iosco Co.

LAW OFFICES OF MYLES AND MARTIN (AV)

502 Lake Street, P.O. Box 518, 48764-0518
Telephone: 517-362-4405
Telefax: 517-362-7840

Kenneth J. Myles
Christopher P. Martin

For full biographical listings, see the Martindale-Hubbell Law Directory

*TRAVERSE CITY,** Grand Traverse Co.

DINGEMAN, DANCER & CHRISTOPHERSON, P.L.C. (AV)

100 Park Street, 49684
Telephone: 231-929-0500
Fax: 231-929-0504
Email: dingeman@dingemandancer.com *URL:* http://www.Dingemandancer.com

Daniel J. Dingeman

ASSOCIATE

Brian L. Johnson

Representative Clients: Black Forest Motors-Mercedes Benz; WWTV/WWUP TV 9 & 10; Heritage Broadcasting; Acme Township; Northern Physicians Organization, Inc.; Northern Physicians Company, Ltd.; The Homestead Resort; Texas Instruments, Inc.; Empire National Bank Trust Department; Old Kent Bank Trust Department.

For full biographical listings, see the Martindale-Hubbell Law Directory

TROY, Oakland Co.

BOOKHOLDER & BASSETT, P.C. (AV)

Long Lake Crossings, 1301 West Long Lake Road, Suite 355, 48098-6349
Telephone: 248-641-0100
Fax: 248-641-0109
Email: info@bookholderbassett.com *URL:* http://www.lawyers.com/bookholder&bassett

Ronald M. Bookholder
Scott Bassett

Patricia S. Leary

For full biographical listings, see the Martindale-Hubbell Law Directory

CAMPBELL, O'BRIEN & MISTELE, P.C. (AV)

850 Stephenson Highway Suite 410, 48083-1163
Telephone: 248-588-5800
Fax: 248-588-6669; 1-888-647-8353
Email: COMLAW@ADVDATA.NET *URL:* http://www.lawyers.com/comlaw

Edwin G. O'Brien (1907-1983)
Dale C. Campbell
Henry E. Mistele
Paul W. Loock
Robert J. Figa
Curtis H. Mistele

References: First Federal of Michigan; Comerica Bank.

For full biographical listings, see the Martindale-Hubbell Law Directory

HAINER & BERMAN, P.C. (AV)

888 West Big Beaver, Suite 1400, 48084
Telephone: 248-244-8424
Fax: 248-244-8455

Michael J. Hainer
Leonard K. Berman
Kay E. Malaney

Drew S. Norton
Paul S. Miller

OF COUNSEL

Michael A. Kus
Robert F. Riley
Mark S. Demorest

Representative Clients: American Empire Surplus Lines Insurance Co.; Biomass Energy Systems, Inc.; Bridgestone/Firestone, Inc.; Central Distributors of Beer, Inc.; Champion Enterprises, Inc.; City Management Corp.; Clarklift of Detroit, Inc.; Federal Reserve Bank of Chicago; Hotel Investment Services, Inc.; M&O Marketing, Inc.

For full biographical listings, see the Martindale-Hubbell Law Directory

Troy—Continued

HOLAHAN, MALLOY, MAYBAUGH, MONNICH & DELIE (AV)

Suite 100, 2690 Crooks Road, 48084-4700
Telephone: 248-362-4747
Fax: 248-362-4779
East Tawas, Michigan Office: 910 East Bay Street.
Telephone: 517-362-4747.
Fax: 517-362-7331.

MEMBERS OF FIRM

J. Michael Malloy, III
James D. Maybaugh
John R. Monnich
David L. Delie, Jr.

OF COUNSEL

Thomas H. O'Connor
Maureen Holahan (Retired; Resident, East Tawas Office)

Representative Clients: Johnson & Higgens; Employers Reinsurance; Chubb Companies; American States Insurance Co.; Travelers Insurance; Pontiac Osteopathic Hospital; Michigan Health Care Corporation.

For full biographical listings, see the Martindale-Hubbell Law Directory

POLING, MCGAW & POLING, P.C. (AV)

Suite 275, 5435 Corporate Drive, 48098
Telephone: 248-641-0500
Telecopier: 248-641-0506
URL: http://www.lawyers.com/polingmcgaw&poling

Benson T. Buck (1926-1989)
Richard B. Poling
D. Douglas McGaw
Richard B. Poling, Jr.
Gregory C. Hamilton
Veronica B. O'Hara
James R. Parker
Shannon M. Acton

OF COUNSEL

Ralph S. Moore

Representative Clients: City of Troy; United States Fidelity & Guaranty Co.; Sentry Insurance Co.; Admiral Insurance; DeMaria Construction Co.; Leo Corporation; Aetna Casualty and Surety Co.; Concord Design; Pneumo-Abex.

For full biographical listings, see the Martindale-Hubbell Law Directory

POWERS, CHAPMAN, DEAGOSTINO, MEYERS & MILIA, PROFESSIONAL CORPORATION (AV)

Suite 704, 3001 West Big Beaver Road, 48084
Telephone: 248-643-6500
Telecopier: 248-643-0280

Conrad D. Chapman
L. Gene DeAgostino
Allen M. Meyers
Richard A. Novak, Jr.
Robert P. Milia
Joseph M. McGlynn
Nelson B. Stieper
Richard T. Chapman
Randy J. Ordway

Michael S. Holmes
Ronald T. Charlebois
Connie Skinner McNealy
Craig Tarpinian
David A. Perez, II
Kevin A Casey
Robert M. Yonkers

OF COUNSEL

Ward D. Powers
John R. Brown

General Counsel for: Davis Industries, Inc.; Fuller Tool Co.; Charles Dalgleish Cadillac, Inc.
Reference: Huntington National Bank.

For full biographical listings, see the Martindale-Hubbell Law Directory

STARK, REAGAN & FINNERTY, P.C. (AV)

Suite 202, 1111 West Long Lake Road, P.O. Box 7037, 48007-7037
Telephone: 248-641-9955
Facsimile: 248-641-9921
Email: @SRFPC.COM
Boca Raton, Florida Office: Suite 307B, 4800 North Federal Highway.
Telephone: 561-994-2266.
Traverse City, Michigan Office: 475 Eastwood Shores.
Telephone: 231-943-8230.
Facsimile: 231-943-8711.

Michael H. Whiting
Kenneth M. Boyer
Thomas H. Finnerty
R. Keith Stark
Joseph C. Bird
Joseph A. Ahern
Christopher E. LeVasseur
Daniel E. Chapman
William D. Girardot
James R. Waldvogel
Jeffrey J. Fleury
Michael D. FitzPatrick

OF COUNSEL

Harry S. Stark (Resident Of Counsel, Traverse City Office)
Willard M. Reagan
James E. Beall

For full biographical listings, see the Martindale-Hubbell Law Directory

WEST BLOOMFIELD, Oakland Co.

CHEATHAM, ESTES & HOLLMAN, P.C. (AV)

5777 West Maple Road, Suite 130, P.O. Box 255002, 48325-5002
Telephone: 248-932-2000
Fax: 248-932-2008

Charles C. Cheatham
Lee Estes
Mary E. Hollman

Christopher P. Jelinek

COUNSEL

Lynn L. Lower

For full biographical listings, see the Martindale-Hubbell Law Directory

WESTLAND, Wayne Co.

ASKER, CHAPP & CLOS, P.C. (AV)

35551 Ford Road, Suite 100, 48185
Telephone: 734-326-2101
Fax: 734-595-9771
URL: http://www.lawyers.com/michigan
Torrance, California Office: 615 Hawaii Avenue, 90503.
Telephone: 310-320-5766.

Paul P. Asker
Sandra J. Chapp
Charles E. Clos
Gary E. Perlmuter
Brian J. Considine
J. Matthew Catchick, Jr.

For full biographical listings, see the Martindale-Hubbell Law Directory

YPSILANTI, Washtenaw Co.

PEAR SPERLING EGGAN & MUSKOVITZ, P.C. (AV)

5 South Washington Street, 48197
Telephone: 734-483-3626
Fax: 734-483-1107
Email: ameggan@ameritech.net
Ann Arbor, Michigan Office: Domino's Farms, 24 Frank Lloyd Wright Drive.
Telephone: 734-665-4441
Other Ypsilanti, Michigan Office: 2164 Bellevue at Washtenaw.
Telephone: 734-483-7177.

Andrew M. Eggan

Counsel for: Domino's Pizza, Inc.; Citizens Banking Corp.; Townsend and Bottum, Inc.; The Credit Bureau of Ypsilanti; City of Ypsilanti (Labor Counsel); Michigan Municipal Worker's Compensation; Self-Insurance Fund.
Approved Attorneys for: Lawyers Title Insurance Corp.

For Complete List of Firm Personnel, See General Section

For full biographical listings, see the Martindale-Hubbell Law Directory

WORKERS COMPENSATION

ALABAMA

*ANDALUSIA,** Covington Co.

ALBRITTONS, CLIFTON, ALVERSON & MOODY, P.C. (AV)

(Powell, Albritton & Albritton)
(Albrittons & Rankin)
(Albrittons, Givhan, Clifton & Alverson)
(Albrittons & Givhan)
109 Opp Avenue, P.O. Box 880, 36420
Telephone: 334-222-3177
Telecopier: 334-222-2696

Ed. T. Albritton (1857-1925)
Wm. Harold Albritton, Sr. (1881-1929)
Dempsey M. Powell (1863-1949)
Albert L. Rankin (1909-1970)
Robert Bynum Albritton (1905-1983)
William H. Albritton, Jr. (1907-1983)
James Marvin Albritton (1915-1987)
James R. Clifton
William Harold Albritton, IV
William B. Alverson, Jr.
Thomas B. Albritton
Julie S. Moody

Benjamin M. Bowden

General Counsel for: Coca-Cola Bottling Co. of Andalusia; Opp-Micolas Cotton Mills.
Attorneys for: First Alabama Bank; Alabama Power Co.; The Travelers; Liberty Mutual Ins. Co; Kemper Insurance; Crum & Forster Insurance Cos; CSX Transporation.

For full biographical listings, see the Martindale-Hubbell Law Directory

POWELL, PEEK & WEAVER (AV)

201 East Troy Street, Drawer 969, 36420
Telephone: 334-222-4103
Facsimile: 334-222-4105
Email: ppw@alaweb.com

MEMBERS OF FIRM

Abner R. Powell, III
Gary L. Weaver

Representative Clients: State Farm Insurance Group; ALFA Insurance Companies; U.S.F.& G. Co.; CNA Insurance; Auto Owners Insurance Co.; Southern Guaranty Co.; Covington County Bank; Colonial Bank of Opp, Alabama.

For Complete List of Firm Personnel, See General Section

For full biographical listings, see the Martindale-Hubbell Law Directory

*BIRMINGHAM,** Jefferson Co.

BRADLEY ARANT ROSE & WHITE LLP (AV)

2001 Park Place, Suite 1400, P.O. Box 830709, 35283-0709
Telephone: 205-521-8000
Facsimile: 205-521-8800
Facsimile (SouthTrust Tower Office): 205-521-8500
URL: http://www.barw.com
Huntsville, Alabama Office: 200 Clinton Avenue West, Suite 900, 35801.
Telephone: 205-517-5100.
Facsimile: 205-533-5069.
Washington, D.C. Office: 801 Pennsylvania Avenue, NW, Suite 230, 20004.
Telephone: 202-347-8893.
Facsimile: 202-347-1684.

MEMBERS OF FIRM

John William Hargrove
Jay D. St. Clair

COUNSEL

Amy K. Myers

ASSOCIATES

David M. Lawson
T. Matthew Miller
John W. Smith T

For Complete List of Firm Personnel, See General Section
For full biographical listings, see the Martindale-Hubbell Law Directory

CARR, ALLISON, PUGH, HOWARD, OLIVER & SISSON, P.C. (AV)

400 Vestavia Parkway, Suite 400, 35216
Telephone: 205-822-2006
Fax: 205-822-2057
Email: CFC@caphos.com
Florence, Alabama Office: 212 South Cedar Street, 35630.
Telephone: 256-718-6040.
Fax: 256-718-2150.

(See Next Column)

Mobile, Alabama Office: P.O. Box 781,36601-0781.
Telephone: 334-621-4340.
Fax: 334-626-8928.

Charles F. Carr (Resident, Daphne Office)
Russell Q. Allison
Bennett L. Pugh
David K. Howard (Resident, Florence Office)
Thomas L. Oliver, II
William H. Sisson (Resident, Daphne Office)
Glenn E. Ireland
Thomas C. Logan
Donald B. Kirkpatrick, II
Sarah J. Carlisle
Craig W. Goolsby (Resident, Daphne Office)

Gregg L. Smith
Joseph H. Driver
Brett A. Ross
Thomas S. Thornton, III
W. Bradford Kittrell
Jeffrey B. Carr
Joseph H. Hilley
Jeremy N. Trousdale
Ryan G. Brake
Caroline T. Pryor (Resident, Daphne Office)

For full biographical listings, see the Martindale-Hubbell Law Directory

CLARK & SCOTT, P.C. (AV)

3500 Blue Lake Drive, Suite 350, P.O. Box 380548, 35238-0548
Telephone: 205-967-9675
Telecopier: 205-967-7563
WATS: 800-955-8678
Mobile, Alabama Office: Clark, Scott & Sullivan, P.C., 10th Floor, Regions Bank Building, 56 St. Joseph Street, P.O. Box 1034.
Telephone: 205-433-1346.
Telecopier: 205-433-1086. WATS: 800-239-6733.
Jackson, Mississippi Office: Clark, Scott & Streetman, P.A., 447 Northpark Drive, Ridgeland, 39157.
Telephone: 601-977-0102.
Telecopier: 601-957-0690.

William A. Scott, Jr.
John W. Clark, Jr.
G. Steven Henry
Anthony N. Fox
Judith E. Dolan
Wayne Morse
James C. Ayers, Jr.
Kelly W. Otto
David Whittington McDowell
Joseph E. Stott
Shane M. Oncale

Cynthia A. Martin
Tommy C. Ritter, Jr.
J. Craig Lewis
Rosemary Sizemore Moore
Freddie N. Harrington, Jr.

Representative Clients: American International Group; ITT Hartford; Fireman's Fund Insurance Company; American Medical Systems, Inc.; Crum & Forster Companies; MEDMARC Insurance Company; Parke Davis/Warner Lambert Co.; Pfizer, Inc.; GAINSCO; Southern Heritage Insurance Company.

For full biographical listings, see the Martindale-Hubbell Law Directory

LUSK, FRALEY, MCALISTER & SIMMS, P.C. (AV)

Suite 1700 AmSouth/Harbert Plaza, 1901 Sixth Avenue North, 35203
Telephone: 205-323-7100
Fax: 205-323-7050
Email: Lusk-Fraley.com

Donald D. Lusk
John M. Fraley
David L. McAlister
Keri Donald Simms
Kenneth A. Dowdy
David Lawrence Dean
David Thurston White, III
Susan Gilman McAlister
Payton Caldwell Lusk
Leslie Ann Caldwell

For full biographical listings, see the Martindale-Hubbell Law Directory

PORTER, PORTER & HASSINGER, P.C. (AV)

New South Federal Savings Building, 215 North 21st Street, Suite 1000, 35203
Telephone: 205-322-1744
Telecopier: 205-322-1750
Email: pphatty@earthlink.net

James W. Porter, II
David S. Hassinger
Earl C. Bloom, Jr.

General Counsel for: The Club, Inc.; Smith Coal Sales Co.

For full biographical listings, see the Martindale-Hubbell Law Directory

SMITH & ELY, LLP (AV)

2000-A Southbridge Parkway Suite 405, 35209
Telephone: 205-802-2214
Fax: 205-879-4445

MEMBERS OF FIRM

Carol Ann Smith
Brenen G. Ely

ASSOCIATES

Susan Rogers
Susan Caroline Haygood
Toby Dykes

(See Next Column)

SMITH & ELY LLP, *Birmingham—Continued*

OF COUNSEL

Lisa B. Singer

For full biographical listings, see the Martindale-Hubbell Law Directory

SMITH, SPIRES & PEDDY, P.C. (AV)

2015 Second Avenue North Suite 200, 35203
Telephone: 205-251-5885
Fax: 205-251-8642

Paul G. Smith
Thomas S. Spires
A. Joe Peddy
Todd Hamilton
Thomas Coleman, Jr.

B. Scott Tyra
James L. Sanders, II
Julie L. Jenkins
Matthew C. Williams
Clarence "Chip" Rivers, IV
Jason M. Langley
R. Timothy Estes

Representative Clients: Birmingham Steel Erectors; Winn Dixie Inc.; Southern Risk Services.

For full biographical listings, see the Martindale-Hubbell Law Directory

*CHATOM,** Washington Co.

TURNER, ONDERDONK, KIMBROUGH & HOWELL, P.A. (AV)

1021 Central Avenue, P.O. Drawer 1389, 36518
Telephone: 334-847-2237
Fax: 334-847-3115
Email: firm@tokh.com *URL:* http://www.tokh.com
Mobile, Alabama Office: 1359 Dauphin Street.
Telephone: 334-432-2855.
Fax: 334-432-2863.

Edward P. Turner, Jr.
A. Michael Onderdonk
William A. Kimbrough, Jr. (Resident, Mobile Office)
Gordon K. Howell
Marc E. Bradley (Resident, Mobile Office)
Halron W. Turner
Frank Woodson (Resident, Mobile Office)
David M. Huggins (Resident, Mobile Office)
E. Tatum Turner

LEGAL SUPPORT PERSONNEL

Thomas E. Fuller

For full biographical listings, see the Martindale-Hubbell Law Directory

*CULLMAN,** Cullman Co.

DRAKE & DRAKE (AV)

Suite A, 419 Second Avenue, S.W., P.O. Box 1165, 35055-4106
Telephone: 256-734-7602
Fax: 256-734-7696

MEMBERS OF FIRM

Tom Drake
Christine McKoy Drake

ASSOCIATE

Thomas E. Drake, II

OF COUNSEL

G. Whit Drake

Representative Clients: Cullman Electric Corp.; Shaver Poultry Breeding Farm, a Division of Cargill.
References: First National Bank of Birmingham; Peoples Bank of Cullman County.

For full biographical listings, see the Martindale-Hubbell Law Directory

ST. JOHN & ST. JOHN, L.L.C. (AV)

108 Third Street South East, P.O. Drawer K, 35056-3542
Telephone: 256-734-3542
Fax: 256-734-3544

MEMBERS OF FIRM

F. E. St. John (1874-1943)
Finis E. St. John (1909-1984)
Finis E. St. John, III (1933-1984)
Finis E. St. John, IV
Gaynor L. St. John

ASSOCIATE

Rita P. Farris

OF COUNSEL

Juliet G. St. John

Attorneys for: U.S. Fidelity & Guaranty Co.; Travelers Insurance Co.; Liberty Mutual Insurance Co.; ALFA Mutual Insurance Co.; First Federal Savings & Loan; The Atlanta Casualty Companies; Auto-Owners Insurance Co.; Golden-Rod Broilers, Inc.; Cullman Products, Inc.; McGriff Industries, Inc.

For full biographical listings, see the Martindale-Hubbell Law Directory

*ELBA,** Coffee Co.

L. MERRILL SHIRLEY (AV)

431 North Court Street, P.O. Box 408, 36323
Telephone: 334-897-5775
Fax: 334-897-2304

Representative Clients: National Security Insurance Co.; Peoples Bank of Elba; ALFA Mutual Insurance Co.; Fireman's Fund Insurance Group; Southern Guaranty Insurance Co.; Elba General Hospital and Nursing Home.
References: Peoples Bank; National Security Insurance Co.

For full biographical listings, see the Martindale-Hubbell Law Directory

*HUNTSVILLE,** Madison Co.

HORNSBY, WATSON & MEGINNISS (AV)

1110 Gleneagles Drive, 35801
Telephone: 256-650-5500
Fax: 256-650-5504
Email: rwhj@mindspring.com

Ralph W. Hornsby, Sr.
S. A. "Bud" Watson, Jr.
Ralph W. Hornsby, Jr.
Jeffrey G. Blackwell

OF COUNSEL

David H. Meginniss

For full biographical listings, see the Martindale-Hubbell Law Directory

MORRIS, CLOUD AND CONCHIN, P.C. (AV)

521 Madison Street, P.O. Box 248, 35804
Telephone: 256-534-0065
Fax: 256-539-0741

Harvey B. Morris (P.C.)
Joseph M. Cloud
Gary V. Conchin

Maureen "Mike" K. Cooper
Daniel B. Banks, Jr.

For full biographical listings, see the Martindale-Hubbell Law Directory

THE LAW FIRM OF SINIARD, MCKINNEY & BRASWELL, P.C. (AV)

125 Holmes Avenue, P.O. Box 2767, 35804
Telephone: 256-536-0770
Facsimile: 256-539-0540
URL: http://www.lawyers.com/smblawfirm
URL: http://www.law-injury.com/scripts/template.cgi?index

Tommy H. Siniard
Jeffery W. McKinney
M. Roy Braswell

Michael Kenan Timberlake
James William League

For full biographical listings, see the Martindale-Hubbell Law Directory

WOLFE, JONES & BOSWELL (AV)

905 Bob Wallace Avenue Suite 100, 35801
Telephone: 205-534-2205
Fax: 205-534-0854
Email: wjb@traveller.com

MEMBERS OF FIRM

R. Wayne Wolfe
Keith S. Jones
Daniel C. Boswell

ASSOCIATES

Gary P. Wolfe
Joel R. Hamner
James Rayburn Kennamer

Representative Clients: First Union Home Equity Corp.; Norwest Financial Services; ALTUS Bank.
Approved Agents for: Stewart Title Guaranty Co.

For full biographical listings, see the Martindale-Hubbell Law Directory

*MOBILE,** Mobile Co.

GARDNER, MIDDLEBROOKS, FLEMING, GIBBONS & KITTRELL, P.C. (AV)

64 North Royal Street, Drawer 3103, 36652
Telephone: 334-433-8100
Telecopier: 334-433-8181
Email: GMFH@WORLDNET.ATT.NET
Birmingham, Alabama Office: Suite 450, 2013 1st Avenue, North.
Telephone: 205-250-7776.
Telecopier: 205-250-7675.
Washington, D.C. Office: 1919 S Street NW, Washington, D.C.
Telephone: 202-667-8278.
Telecopier: 202-234-1003.

(See Next Column)

GARDNER, MIDDLEBROOKS, FLEMING, GIBBONS & KITTRELL P.C.—*Continued*

J. Cecil Gardner
Charles J. Fleming
Sherwood C. Middlebrooks, III
John D. Gibbons
Braxton L. Kittrell, Jr.

Mary Elizabeth Olsen
Kimberly J. Calametti
Walter G. (Stoney) Chavers

Representative Clients: CNA Insurance Cos.; Canal Insurance Co.; Safeway Insurance Company of Alabama; Honda Motor Co.; Toyota Motor Co., U.S.A.; Bay Equipment Co.; Lyon Properties, Inc.; Southside Storage, Inc.

For full biographical listings, see the Martindale-Hubbell Law Directory

SINTZ, CAMPBELL, DUKE & TAYLOR (AV)

3763 Professional Parkway, 36609
Telephone: 334-344-7241
Fax: 334-344-7400

MEMBERS OF FIRM

Peter V. Sintz (1940-1997)
Frank G. Taylor
Robert C. Campbell, III
Steven L. Terry

ASSOCIATES

Wm. Kyle Morris
Kathryn W. Petersen
Barry C. Prine

OF COUNSEL

Leon G. Duke

LEGAL SUPPORT PERSONEL

James A. Koblas

Representative Clients: Aetna C & S Insurance Co.; Mobile County School Board; Auto-Owners Insurance Co.; Argonaut Insurance Co.; Mostellar Medical Clinic; Scottsdale Insurance Co.; American International Group; Alabama School of Math and Science; Mobile County Sheriff's Office.

For full biographical listings, see the Martindale-Hubbell Law Directory

*MONTGOMERY,** Montgomery Co.

BRANTLEY & WILKERSON, P.C. (AV)

405 South Hull Street, P.O. Box 830, 36101-0830
Telephone: 334-265-1500
Fax: 334-265-0319
Email: ashley@brantleywilkerson.com *URL:* http://www.brantleywilkerson.com

Paul A. Brantley

Representative Clients: MidCoast, Inc.; ALLTEL; Southeastern Cellular; TDS; Construction Claims Management, Inc.
Reference: SouthTrust Bank, N.A.

For full biographical listings, see the Martindale-Hubbell Law Directory

NIX, HOLTSFORD & VERCELLI, P.C. (AV)

300 A Water Street, Suite 300, P.O. Box 4128, 36103
Telephone: 334-262-2006
Fax: 334-834-3616
Email: NHV@JUNO.COM

H. E. Nix, Jr.
Floyd R. Gilliland, Jr.
Alex L. Holtsford, Jr.
T. Randall Lyons
Charles E. Vercelli, Jr.
Steven A. Higgins
Kenneth A. Hitson, Jr.

David P. Stevens
Rick A. Howard
Todd E. Hughes
Stacy Anne Linn
Jay S. Tuley

LEGAL SUPPORT PERSONNEL

Richard M. Seibert (Firm Manager)
Monica E. Jayroe (Paralegal)
Ashley Collins (Paralegal)
Suzanne H. Long (Legal Assistant)
Kelley S. Tracy (Paralegal)

Representative Clients: Kemper Group; Waffle House, Inc.; Sabel Industries, Inc.; Alfa Mutual Insurance Company; United States Fidelity & Guaranty Insurance Company.

For full biographical listings, see the Martindale-Hubbell Law Directory

WEBB & ELEY, P.C. (AV)

166 Commerce Street, Suite 300, P.O. Box 238, 36101-0238
Telephone: 334-262-1850
Fax: 334-262-1772
Email: webbeley1@mindspring.com

James W. Webb
Craig S. Dillard
Michael M. Eley
Bart Harmon
Kendrick E. Webb
William R. Chandler

(See Next Column)

Frank E. Bankston, Jr.
Shawn Junkins Cole
Pamela Robinson Higgins
Michael J. Cohan
Lisa D. Van Wagner

LEGAL SUPPORT PERSONNEL

Janice B. Miller (Business Manager)

Reference: Regions Bank.

For full biographical listings, see the Martindale-Hubbell Law Directory

*TUSCALOOSA,** Tuscaloosa Co.

ZEANAH, HUST, SUMMERFORD, DAVIS, JONES & WILLIAMSON, L.L.C. (AV)

Seventh Floor, AmSouth Bank Building, P.O. Box 1310, 35403
Telephone: 205-349-1383
Fax: 205-391-1319
Email: ZHSDJ@mail.dbtech.net

MEMBERS OF FIRM

Olin W. Zeanah (1922-1987)
Kenneth D. Davis
Wilbor J. Hust, Jr.
Christopher H. Jones
E. Clark Summerford
Beverly Smith Williamson

OF COUNSEL

Marvin T. Ormond

Representative Clients: Alfa Insurance Cos.; Hartford Insurance Group; Home Insurance Co.; Nationwide Insurance Co.; Alabama Power Co.; Liberty Mutual Insurance Co.; The Uniroyal Goodrich Tire Co.

For full biographical listings, see the Martindale-Hubbell Law Directory

*TUSCUMBIA,** Colbert Co.

ASHE, TANNER, WRIGHT & KELLEY, P.C. (AV)

105 West Second Street, P.O. Box 899, 35674
Telephone: 256-383-6357
Telecopier: 256-381-4612

Braxton W. Ashe
Grant A. Wright
J. Michael Tanner
Charles J. Kelley (Resident)

Nickolas J. Steles

For full biographical listings, see the Martindale-Hubbell Law Directory

ARIZONA

*PHOENIX,** Maricopa Co.

DOHERTY & VENEZIA, A PROFESSIONAL CORPORATION (AV)

100 West Clarendon, Suite 1720, 85013
Telephone: 602-277-1585
Fax: 602-277-1182

Julie A. Doherty
Stephen M. Venezia

Representative Clients: Cigna Property and Casualty Insurance; Insurance Company of the West; Intel; ITT Hartford; Kemper Risk Management; Liberty Mutual Insurance Group; Marriott International; Matrix Self Insurance Resources, Inc.; Motel 6; Alexis Risk Management.

For full biographical listings, see the Martindale-Hubbell Law Directory

DON A. FENDON, P.C. (AV)

320 East McDowell, Suite 230, 85004
Telephone: 602-256-2000
Toll Free: 800-228-2300
Fax: 602-256-6383
Mailing Address: P.O. Box 36365, Phoenix, AZ, 85067-6365

Don A. Fendon

LEGAL SUPPORT PERSONNEL

PARALEGALS

Lynne Carmody
Carole St. Pierre

For full biographical listings, see the Martindale-Hubbell Law Directory

FENNEMORE CRAIG, A PROFESSIONAL CORPORATION (AV)

3003 North Central Avenue, Suite 2600, 85012-2913
Telephone: 602-916-5000
Fax: 602-916-5999
Tucson, Arizona Office: One South Church Avenue, Suite 1000, 85701-1620.
Telephone: 520-879-6800.
Fax: 520-879-6899.

Scott M. Finical
Jean Marie Sullivan

Vera E. Munoz

(See Next Column)

FENNEMORE CRAIG A PROFESSIONAL CORPORATION, *Phoenix—Continued*

LEGAL SUPPORT PERSONNEL

LEGAL ASSISTANTS

Ann V. Kooi
Claudia L. Parks

For Complete List of Firm Personnel, See General Section

For full biographical listings, see the Martindale-Hubbell Law Directory

HERZOG AND O'CONNOR, P.C. (AV)

5353 North 16th Street, Suite 175, 85016
Telephone: 602-277-5710
Fax: 602-277-6124

Michael W. Herzog
Mark S. O'Connor

Kirk A. Barberich

For full biographical listings, see the Martindale-Hubbell Law Directory

JOHN W. MAIN, P.C. (AV)

4020 North 20th Street Suite 218, 85016-6028
Telephone: 602-266-7704
Fax: 602-266-7705

John W. Main

Representative Clients: AlliedSignal Aerospace Company; ASARCO Incorporated; Bashas' Markets Inc.; Pennzoil Company; State Farm Fire and Casualty Company; U S West Communications.

For full biographical listings, see the Martindale-Hubbell Law Directory

*TUCSON,** Pima Co.

RABINOVITZ & ASSOCIATES, P.C. (AV)

721 North 4th Avenue, P.O. Box 41600, 85717
Telephone: 520-624-5526
Toll Free: 1-800-365-0821
Fax: 520-622-3776

Bernard I. Rabinovitz

John D. Ellis

LEGAL SUPPORT PERSONNEL

Michael Nielson (Paralegal)
Lisa Busciglio (Paralegal)
Ruth Polizzi (Paralegal)

Representative Client: Firemans Fund Insurance Co.

For full biographical listings, see the Martindale-Hubbell Law Directory

DEE-DEE SAMET, P.C. (AV)

717 North Sixth Avenue, 85705
Telephone: 520-624-8595
Fax: 520-623-4560
Email: Dee-Dee.Same@azbar.org

Dee-Dee Samet

References: Bank of America; Norwest Bank.

For full biographical listings, see the Martindale-Hubbell Law Directory

LAW OFFICES OF DAVID M. WATERMAN (AV)

900 East River Road, Suite 204, 85718
Telephone: 520-882-9001
Fax: 520-882-9010
Email: dw7ivt@azstarnet.com

Lynda J. Russell

For full biographical listings, see the Martindale-Hubbell Law Directory

ARKANSAS

*FORT SMITH,** Sebastian Co.

LEDBETTER, COGBILL, ARNOLD & HARRISON, LLP (AV)

622 Parker Avenue, P.O. Box 185, 72902-0185
Telephone: 501-782-7294
Fax: 501-782-1493

MEMBERS OF FIRM

Charles R. Ledbetter
J. Michael Cogbill
James A. Arnold, II
Ronald D. Harrison
E. Diane Graham
R. Ray Fulmer, II

(See Next Column)

ASSOCIATES

Rebecca D. Hattabaugh
Virginia C. Trammell
Daniel A. Stewart

Representative Clients: Liberty Mutual Insurance Company; St. Paul Insurance Company; CIGNA; Houston General; Fireman's Fund; Alexsis, Inc.; Arkansas Nursing Home Self-Insured Trust; Gerber Products'; Franklin Electric; Consolidated Freightways.

For full biographical listings, see the Martindale-Hubbell Law Directory

WALKER, SHOCK, HARP & HILL, P.L.L.C. (AV)

400 North Sixth Street, P.O. Box 998, 72902-0998
Telephone: 501-783-7600
Fax: 501-783-0420
Email: walsharp@ipa.net

MEMBERS OF FIRM

Eddie H. Walker, Jr.
J. Randolph Shock
David K. Harp
William A. Hill, Jr.

References: Deposit Guarranty National Bank; First National Bank.

For full biographical listings, see the Martindale-Hubbell Law Directory

*LITTLE ROCK,** Pulaski Co.

ANDERSON, MURPHY & HOPKINS, L.L.P. (AV)

400 West Capitol Avenue, Suite 2640, 72201
Telephone: 501-372-1887
Fax: 501-372-7706
Email: ande@att.net

MEMBERS OF FIRM

Randy P. Murphy
Mariam T. Hopkins

ASSOCIATES

Michael P. Vanderford
Penny Brown Wilbourn
David A. Littleton
Scott D. Provencher

For full biographical listings, see the Martindale-Hubbell Law Directory

BARBER, MCCASKILL, JONES & HALE, P.A. (AV)

2700 Regions Center, 400 West Capitol Avenue, 72201-3414
Telephone: 501-372-6175
Telecopier: 501-375-2802

Azro L. Barber (1885-1979)
Elbert A. Henry (1889-1966)
John B. Thurman (1912-1971)
Austin McCaskill, Sr.
Glenn W. Jones
Michael E. Hale
John S. Cherry, Jr.
Robert L. Henry, III
Micheal L. Alexander
William H. Edwards, Jr.
G. Spence Fricke
Gail Ponder Gaines
Michael J. Emerson
R. Kenny McCulloch
Tim A. Cheatham
Joseph F. Kolb
Scott Michael Strauss
Baucum Fulk
D. Keith Fortner
Wendy Scholtens Wood
Morris L. Williams, III
Michelle Bass Miller

Attorneys for: Associated Aviation Underwriters; Baptist Health; CNA Insurance Company; Fireman's Fund Insurance Co.; GAB Robins; Hanover Insurance Co.; Minnesota Mining & Manufacturing; Royal Insurance; United States Fidelity & Guaranty Co.; Universal Underwriters Insurance Co.

For full biographical listings, see the Martindale-Hubbell Law Directory

HUCKABAY, MUNSON, ROWLETT & TILLEY, P.A. (AV)

Regions Center, Suite 1900, 400 West Capitol, 72201
Telephone: 501-374-6535
Fax: 501-374-5906

Mike Huckabay
Bruce E. Munson
Beverly A. Rowlett
James W. Tilley
John E. Moore
Tim Boone
Rick Runnells
Sarah Ann Presson
D. Michael Huckabay, Jr.
Carol Lockard Worley
Mark S. Breeding

Elizabeth Fletcher Rogers
Julia L. Busfield
Jane M. Yocum
Terry D. Dugger

Representative Clients: AIG Claims Services, Inc.; Crawford & Company; Employers Mutual Insurance Company; Farmers Insurance Group; General Adjustment Bureau; Hanover Insurance Company; Houston General Insurance Company; Lumber Mutual Insurance Co.; Lindsey Morden; Reliance Insurance Co.

For full biographical listings, see the Martindale-Hubbell Law Directory

KILPATRICK, AUD & WILLIAMS, L.L.P. (AV)

Regions Center, 400 West Capitol Avenue, Suite 1910, 72201-4849
Telephone: 501-372-0401
Facsimile: 501-372-5277

(See Next Column)

KILPATRICK, AUD & WILLIAMS L.L.P.—*Continued*

Joseph E. Kilpatrick, Jr. Michael E. Aud
Aylmer Gene Williams

For full biographical listings, see the Martindale-Hubbell Law Directory

LASER, WILSON, BUFFORD & WATTS, P.A. (AV)

101 South Spring Street, Suite 300, 72201-2488
Telephone: 501-376-2981
Telecopier: 501-376-2417
Email: laser@laserlaw.com

Frank B. Newell

Thomas J. Diaz Keith Martin McPherson
Andy L. Turner

OF COUNSEL

Ralph R. Wilson

Representative Clients: AIG Claim Services; Arkansas Insurance Adjusting, Inc.; Continental Loss Adjusting, Little Rock, AR, Metairie, LA, Dallas, TX, Fort Lauderdale, FL and Chicago, IL; Crawford & Co.; Gallagher Bassett Services, Inc.; The Silvey Cos.; State Farm Insurance Co.; Columbia Insurance Group; Farm Bureau Insurance; Great West Casualty Co.

For Complete List of Firm Personnel, See General Section

For full biographical listings, see the Martindale-Hubbell Law Directory

ROSE LAW FIRM, A PROFESSIONAL ASSOCIATION (AV)

120 East Fourth Street, 72201
Telephone: 501-375-9131
Telecopy: 501-375-1309

Tim Boe Kathryn Bennett Perkins
David P. Martin Michael N. Shannon

COUNSEL

Phillip Carroll

Counsel for: Aluminum Company of America; Bridgestone/Firestone, Inc.; The Equitable Life Assurance Society of The United States; General Motors Corp.; Georgia-Pacific Corp.; The Prudential Insurance Company of America; Stephens Group Inc.; Tyson Foods, Inc.

For Complete List of Firm Personnel, See General Section

For full biographical listings, see the Martindale-Hubbell Law Directory

WEST MEMPHIS, Crittenden Co.

RIEVES & MAYTON (AV)

304 East Broadway, P.O. Box 1359, 72303
Telephone: 870-735-3420
Telecopier: 870-735-4678
Email: rieves.mayton@worldnet.att.net
Little Rock, Arkansas Office: Suite 1719, First Commercial Building, 400 West Capitol.
Telephone: 501-376-0504.
Telecopier: 501-372-3482.

MEMBERS OF FIRM

Elton A. Rieves, Jr. (1909-1984) Michael R. Mayton
Elton A. Rieves, III Elton A. Rieves, IV

ASSOCIATES

David S. Wilson, III Eric Newkirk

For full biographical listings, see the Martindale-Hubbell Law Directory

CALIFORNIA

CHINO, San Bernardino Co.

LAW OFFICES OF ELLEN VAN WAGNER (AV)

12490 Central Avenue, Suite 104, 91710
Telephone: 909-902-1210
Fax: 909-902-1215

For full biographical listings, see the Martindale-Hubbell Law Directory

ENCINO, Los Angeles Co.

SOBELSOHN & JOHNSON, LLP (AV)

17323 Ventura Boulevard, Suite 310, 91316
Telephone: 818-986-6700
Fax: 818-986-6880

(See Next Column)

MEMBERS OF FIRM

Bernard Sobelsohn Michael E. Johnson

Reference: Western Financial Bank, Encino.

For full biographical listings, see the Martindale-Hubbell Law Directory

*LOS ANGELES,** Los Angeles Co.

GORDON, EDELSTEIN, KREPACK, GRANT, FELTON & GOLDSTEIN (AV)

Suite 1800, 3580 Wilshire Boulevard, 90010
Telephone: 213-739-7000; 213-487-1520
Fax: 213-386-1671
Email: geklaw.com

Roger L. Gordon Richard I. Felton
Mark Edelstein Irwin L. Goldstein
Howard D. Krepack Steven J. Kleifield
Sherry E. Grant David A. Goldstein

OF COUNSEL

Joshua M. Merliss

ASSOCIATES

Eugenia L. Steele Adam D. Dombchik
Vincent F. Bennett Jennifer S. Weisman

For full biographical listings, see the Martindale-Hubbell Law Directory

*OAKLAND,** Alameda Co.

KAZAN, MCCLAIN, EDISES, SIMON & ABRAMS, A PROFESSIONAL LAW CORPORATION (AV)

171 Twelfth Street, Suite 300, 94607
Telephone: 510-465-7728; 893-7211
TDD: (510) 763-8808
Fax: 510-835-4913
Email: postmaster@kmesa.com *URL:* http://www.KMESA.COM

Victoria Edises

Michelle Diane Perry

For full biographical listings, see the Martindale-Hubbell Law Directory

*SACRAMENTO,** Sacramento Co.

MASTAGNI, HOLSTEDT & CHIURAZZI, A PROFESSIONAL CORPORATION (AV)

1912 I Street, Suite 102, 95814
Telephone: 916-446-4692
Fax: 916-447-4614
Email: mhcmailbox@mastagni.com

David P. Mastagni John R. Holstedt
Richard J. Chiurazzi

Stephen Curtis Winter Brian A. Dixon
Dennis W. Hargrave Elaine M. Cawley
Michael D. Amick Michael R. Kelly
Barbara M. Jacobson Mark Regalbuti
Kasey Christopher Clark Christopher W. Miller

Representative Clients: Alameda County Probation Assn.; Cannery Workers, El Dorado County Deputy Sheriffs Assn.; Folsom Police Officers Assn.; Jackson Police Officers Assn.; United Food & Commercial Workers 588, Northern California; P.O.R.A.C. Insurance Board.

For full biographical listings, see the Martindale-Hubbell Law Directory

TWEEDY, PENNEY & CRAWFORD, A LAW PARTNERSHIP (AV)

2151 River Plaza Drive, Suite 225, 95833
Telephone: 916-921-2500
Fax: 916-921-2800
Email: dougpenney@tpcworkcomplaw.com
Email: scottcrawford@tpcworkcomplaw.com *URL:* http://www.lawyers.com/tp&claw

MEMBERS OF FIRM

Douglass F. Penney Scott E. Crawford
John W. Jackson

OF COUNSEL

Thomas A. Tweedy

Representative Clients: Rice Growers Association of California; Fremont Compensation Company; Claims Management, Inc.; L.W.P. Services, Inc.; City of Sacramento; Sacramento Regional Transit; Cypress Insurance.

For full biographical listings, see the Martindale-Hubbell Law Directory

*SAN BERNARDINO,** San Bernardino Co.

BOLSON KUNTZ & SEREMBE (AV)

600 North Arrowhead Avenue, Suite 215, 92401
Telephone: 909-889-0421
Fax: 909-889-6236

MEMBERS OF FIRM

John H. Bolson (Retired)
Janet Rice Kuntz
John A. Kuntz
C. Robert Bakke
Stephen J. Serembe
Louis David Seaman

ASSOCIATES

Myrle Rountree Petty
Donald R. Franklin
Robert J. Parsons (P.A.)
Ameneh K. Ernst
Linda L. Adams

OF COUNSEL

S. Henslee Smith

For full biographical listings, see the Martindale-Hubbell Law Directory

*SAN DIEGO,** San Diego Co.

EGGER & TALMADGE (AV)

600 B Street, Suite 2200, 92101-4507
Telephone: 619-236-9377
Fax: 619-236-1329
Email: eggertalsd@aol.com *URL:* http://www.lawyers.com/egger&talmadge
Pleasant Hill, California Office: 3478 Buskirk Avenue, Suite 110, 94523.
Telephone: 925-937-2477.
Fax: 925-937-1611. E-Mail: eggertalph@aol.com.
Salinas, California Office: 975 West Alisal, Unit I, 93901.
Telephone: 831-771-1414.
Fax: 831-771-1408. E-Mail: eggertalsa@aol.com.
Fresno, California Office: 516 West Shaw Avenue, Suite 200, 93704.
Telephone: 559-445-9089.
Fax: 559-445-9091. E-Mail: eggertalfs@aol.com.

Patrick R. Egger (Managing Partner, Salinas and Fresno Offices)
Michael G. McDonald (Managing Partner, Pleasant Hill Office)
Keith R. Talmadge (Managing Partner, San Diego Office)
Kenneth J. Stein (Resident, Pleasant Hill Office)
Stephen A. Jacobs (Resident)

LEGAL SUPPORT PERSONNEL

Leo A. Akulian (Paralegal)

Representative Clients: Paula Insurance Co.; Kemper Insurance Co.; American International Group; Republic Indemnity of America; Legion Insurance Co.; City of Riverside; The St. Paul/U.S.F.&G.; Clarendon Insurance Company; Pinnacle Risk Mgmt.; Swift Trucking.

For full biographical listings, see the Martindale-Hubbell Law Directory

*SAN FRANCISCO,** San Francisco Co.

HARBINSON, TUNE, MANGOLD & KASSELIK, A PROFESSIONAL CORPORATION (AV)

100 Bush Street, Suite 1200, 94104
Telephone: 415-986-3992
Fax: 415-986-3995
Email: hctmail@worldnet.att.net

Thomas J. Harbinson
Martha M. Mangold
Mark H. Tune
Lisa Erickson Kasselik

Kame O. Yoo
Donald R. Shearer

For full biographical listings, see the Martindale-Hubbell Law Directory

LEACH, MCGREEVY & BAUTISTA, LLP (AV)

2833 Laguna Street, 94123
Telephone: 415-775-4455
Telefax: 415-775-7435
Email: LMLawSF@aol,com
Southern California Office: 24752 Via San Fernando, Mission Viejo, CA 92692.
Telephone: 949-859-7464.

Theodore Tamba (1900-1973)
A. Marquez Bautista
John T. Harmon (1928-1993)
Robert W. Shinnick
David G. Leach
Philip T. Kilduff
Richard E. McGreevy
Peter C. Labrador

ASSOCIATES

John C. Connolly
Annadel A. Almendras
Larry B. Carr
David Emerson Beeby

OF COUNSEL

Lloyd F. Postel

For full biographical listings, see the Martindale-Hubbell Law Directory

SAN JUAN CAPISTRANO, Orange Co.

JOHN H.F. UFKES (AV)

31411 Camino Capistrano, Suite 100, 92675
Telephone: 949-240-3334
Email: ufkes@pacbell.net *URL:* http://www.lawyers.com/jufkeslaw

For full biographical listings, see the Martindale-Hubbell Law Directory

*VENTURA,** Ventura Co.

LOUIS J. VIGORITA (AV)

5450 Ralston Avenue, Suite 202, 93003
Telephone: 805-656-8111; 800-341-1335
Fax: 805-642-1579
Email: lvigorita@vigorita.com *URL:* http://www.vigorita.com

Andrew T. Koenig

For full biographical listings, see the Martindale-Hubbell Law Directory

COLORADO

*COLORADO SPRINGS,** El Paso Co.

BELTZ, EDWARDS & SABO, L.L.P. (AV)

128 South Tejon, Suite 310, 80903
Telephone: 719-634-6620
Fax: 719-634-3142
Email: BES__LLP@aol.com *URL:* http://www.lawyers.com/beslaw
Other Colorado Springs, Colorado Office: 729 South Cascade, 80903.
Telephone: 719-473-4444.
Fax: 719-444-0186.

Daniel P. Edwards
W. Thomas Beltz
John W. Sabo, III

ASSOCIATE

Daniel A. West

Representative Clients: A.M.I. Industries, Inc.; Analytical Surveys, Inc.; A.C. Israel Enterprises, Inc.; Boddington Lumber Co., Inc.; Cardiovascular Surgeons of Colorado Springs, P.C.; Colorado Springs Radiologists, P.C.; Digital, Inc.; Music Semi-Conductors, Inc.; Schlage Lock Co.; Texas Instruments.

For full biographical listings, see the Martindale-Hubbell Law Directory

*DENVER,** Denver Co.

DOUGLAS R. PHILLIPS, P.C. (AV)

Suite 330, 155 South Madison Street, 80209
Telephone: 303-399-8033
Fax: 303-399-8037

Douglas R. Phillips

Reference: Bank of Denver.

For full biographical listings, see the Martindale-Hubbell Law Directory

TREECE, ALFREY, MUSAT & BOSWORTH, P.C. (AV)

999 18th Street, Suite 1600, 80202
Telephone: 303-292-2700
Facsimile: 303-295-0414
Email: tamb@tamblaw.com *URL:* http://www.tamblaw.com

Karen Gail Treece
James B. Fairbanks
Kathleen M. North

Nicolle H. Martin
Suzanne M. Gall

For full biographical listings, see the Martindale-Hubbell Law Directory

CONNECTICUT

*BRIDGEPORT,** Fairfield Co.

COTTER, COTTER AND SOHON, P.C. (AV)

P.O. Box 5660 Bayview Station, 06610
Telephone: 203-335-3131
Fax: 203-874-1983
Email: tcotter@cottercottersohon.com
Milford, Connecticut Office: 500 Boston Post Road, 06460.
Telephone: 203-882-7143.
Fax: 203-874-1983.

(See Next Column)

COTTER, COTTER AND SOHON P.C.—*Continued*

D. Harold Cotter (1893-1961)
Thomas H. Cotter
John J. Cotter
Thomas Galvin Cotter
Catherine N. Anderson
Kevin M. Blake
James F. Mullen
Catherine A. Stewart
Michael V. Vocalina
Bryan L. LeClerc
Brian W. Smith

Gina M. Hall

Representative Clients: Royal Globe Indemnity Co.; Covenant Group; United States Fidelity & Guaranty Co.; Commercial Union Insurance Co.; Transport Insurance Co.; Metropolitan Insurance Co.; CNA; Nationwide Insurance Co.; Employers of Wassau Insurance Co.; Peerless Insurance Co.

For full biographical listings, see the Martindale-Hubbell Law Directory

GLASTONBURY, Hartford Co.

POMERANZ, DRAYTON & STABNICK (AV)

95 Glastonbury Boulevard, 06033-4412
Telephone: 860-657-8000; 800-246-5541
Fax: 860-657-9838
Email: pdsesq@aol.com

Douglas L. Drayton
James L. Pomeranz
Richard T. Stabnick
Lucas D. Strunk
Jason M. Dodge
Anne Kelly Zovas
Richard L. Aiken, Jr.
Margaret E. Corrigan
Michael J. McAuliffe

For full biographical listings, see the Martindale-Hubbell Law Directory

*NEW HAVEN,** New Haven Co.

KENNEDY, JOHNSON, D'ELIA & GILLOOLY (AV)

Long Wharf Maritime Center, 545 Long Wharf Drive, 06511
Telephone: 203-865-8430
Fax: 203-865-5345
Email: kennedyjoh@aol.com

MEMBERS OF FIRM

David H. Johnson
John J. Kennedy, Jr.
John J. D'Elia
Dennis Gillooly

ASSOCIATES

Robert L. Schwab
Stephanie Z. Roberge

Reference: Bank of Boston - Connecticut.

For full biographical listings, see the Martindale-Hubbell Law Directory

DELAWARE

*WILMINGTON,** New Castle Co.

CASARINO, CHRISTMAN & SHALK (AV)

Suite 1220, 222 Delaware Avenue, P.O. Box 1276, 19899
Telephone: 302-594-4500
Telecopier: 302-594-4509
URL: http://www.casarino.com

MEMBERS OF FIRM

Stephen P. Casarino
Colin M. Shalk
Beth H. Christman
Donald M. Ransom

Kenneth M. Doss
Diane M. Willette
Stacey L. Cummings
Thomas P. Leff

For full biographical listings, see the Martindale-Hubbell Law Directory

ROBERT W. RALSTON (AV)

10 East 13th Street, P.O. Box 1396, 19899
Telephone: 302-429-0758
Fax: 302-429-0193

For full biographical listings, see the Martindale-Hubbell Law Directory

DISTRICT OF COLUMBIA

WASHINGTON, D.C. Co.

MACLEAY, LYNCH, GREGG & LYNCH, P.C. (AV)

Suite 1150, 1629 K Street, N.W., 20006
Telephone: 202-785-0123
FAX: 202-393-3390
Email: maclmac@aol.com

(See Next Column)

Donald Macleay (1908-1994)
Hugh Lynch, Jr. (1913-1994)
John C. Lynch
Michael Maloney
Robert P. Lynch
Robert G. McGinley
James C. Gregg

Jack David Lapidus
David C. Numrych

For full biographical listings, see the Martindale-Hubbell Law Directory

FLORIDA

BOCA RATON, Palm Beach Co.

STILES, TAYLOR & GRACE, P.A. (AV)

The Compson Financial Center, 980 North Federal Highway, Suite 305, 33432
Telephone: 561-393-7600
Fax: 561-393-7038
Tampa, Florida Office: 315 Plant Avenue.
Telephone: 813-251-2880.
Fax: 813-254-9073.
Miami, Florida Office: 1101 Brickell Avenue, North Tower, Suite 403, 33131.
Telephone: 305-358-3556.
Fax: 305-358-7210.
Orlando, Florida Office: The AmSouth Tower, 111 North Orange Avenue, Suite 850, 32801.
Telephone: 407-843-9900.
Fax: 407-843-9808.
Tallahassee, Florida Office: 317 North Calhoun Street, 32301.
Telephone: 904-222-2229.
FAX: 904-561-3642.

Diane M. Antell
David W. Evoy

For full biographical listings, see the Martindale-Hubbell Law Directory

CORAL GABLES, Dade Co.

MILLER, KAGAN, RODRIGUEZ AND SILVER, PROFESSIONAL ASSOCIATION (AV)

75 Valencia Avenue, 33134
Telephone: 305-446-5228
Fax: 305-446-7110
Email: georgek@mkrs.com
Fort Lauderdale, Florida Office: 5900 N. Andrews Avenue, Suite 920, 33309.
Telephone: 954-776-9966.
West Palm Beach, Florida Office: 250 Australian Avenue South, Suite 1600, 33401.
Telephone: 561-833-1860.

DADE OFFICE

Paul A. Herman
Robert J. Rodriguez
Salvatore J. Sicuso

OF COUNSEL

H. Jack Miller

Joel A. Brown
Vivian Taranco Carsello
Robert Andrew Friedman
Elena Maria Gomez
Nicole E. Jacomo
Ivette E. Linares-Moreno
Kristina M. Llerena
Olga L. Martin
Rafael DeJesus Pozo
Camille D. Riviere
Javier I. Rodriguez
Mitchell S. Shea

Walter H. Djokic
Mark A. Faris
Wendy Ellen Knecht
Trent Dale Miller
Ann Marie O'Brien
Maura B. Sorenson
Elaine L. Thompson

Representative Client: Chubb Indemnity Group.

For full biographical listings, see the Martindale-Hubbell Law Directory

*FORT LAUDERDALE,** Broward Co.

COONEY, MATTSON, LANCE, BLACKBURN, RICHARDS & O'CONNOR, P.A. (AV)

2312 Wilton Drive, P.O. Box 14546, 33302
Telephone: Telephone: 954-568-6669
WATS: 1-800-745-3864
Telecopier: 954-568-0085
Email: cooney2312@aol.com
Orlando, Florida Office: Nations Bank Tower, 111 N. Orange Avenue, Suite 1020.
Telephone: 407-843-2100.
Fax: 407-843-2061.

(See Next Column)

COONEY, MATTSON, LANCE, BLACKBURN, RICHARDS & O'CONNOR P.A., *Fort Lauderdale—Continued*

David F. Cooney
Michael C. Mattson
Victor Lance (1956-1995)
Ace J. Blackburn, Jr.
John H. Richards
Dennis R. O'Connor (Resident, Orlando, Florida Office)
Bruce Michael Trybus
Walter C. Wyatt
Kieran F. O'Connor (Resident, Orlando, Florida Office)
Michele McCaul Ricca
Daniel F. Tordella

Laura Douglas
Warren Kwavnick
Rochelle Bocksch
Weslee S. Arciola
Alphonso O. Peets
Robert M. Potter, III
Elizabeth Y. Foshee (Resident, Orlando Office)

Representative Clients: The Travellers; RISCORP; CIGNA Insurance Co.; Claims Center; Fiesco; Multi-Line Claims Service, Inc.; Carpenter Contractors of America; City Furniture; CNA Insurance.

For full biographical listings, see the Martindale-Hubbell Law Directory

HALICZER, PETTIS & WHITE, P.A. (AV)

101 Northeast Third Avenue, Sixth Floor, 33301
Telephone: 954-523-9922
Fax: 954-522-2512
Orlando, Florida Office: NationsBank Building, Suite 1275, 111 North Orange Avenue. 32801.
Telephone: 407-841-9866.
Fax: 407-841-9915.

James S. Haliczer
Eugene K. Pettis
Kenneth E. White

Amy B. Talisman
Anthony K. Goodman
Anthony V. Scalese
Debra B. Potter
William Bassett, Jr.
Frank J. Taddeo

For full biographical listings, see the Martindale-Hubbell Law Directory

KELLEY, KRONENBERG, KELLEY, GILMARTIN, FICHTEL & WANDER, P.A. (AV)

Suite 4000 8201 Peters Road, 33324
Telephone: 954-370-9970
Dade Line: 305-940-2701
West Palm Beach Line: 561-687-4224
Fax: 954-382-1988
Miami Lakes, Florida Office: Suite 204, 15600 NW 67th Avenue, 33014.
Telephone: 305-826-7260. Broward Line: 954-522-5991.
Fax: 305-826-0936.
West Palm Beach, Florida Office: 1400 Centrepark Boulevard. Suite 200. 33401.
Telephone: 561-684-5956. Broward Line: 954-761-8554.
Fax: 561-684-5753.
Orlando, Florida Office: 20 North Orange Avenue, Suite 807, First Union Tower, 32801.
Telephone: 407-648-9450.
Fax: 407-648-4167.

W. L. Adams (1924-1984)
Steven P. Kronenberg (Miami Office)
John M. Kelley (Fort Lauderdale Office)
Karen Baust Gilmartin (Miami Office)
Michael J. Fichtel (Fort Lauderdale Office)
Howard L. Wander (West Palm Beach Office)
Vivianne A. Wicker (Liability Dept., Ft. Lauderdale Office)
Robert L. Bamdas (Longshore Dept., West Palm Beach Office)

OF COUNSEL
Charles E. Kelley

For full biographical listings, see the Martindale-Hubbell Law Directory

*FORT MYERS,** Lee Co.

DIAMOND AND DIAMOND, P.A. (AV)

2036 McGregor Boulevard, P.O. Drawer 2590, 33902
Telephone: 941-334-4401
Facsimile: 941-334-8699

Anthony J. Diamond
Stella Diamond

For full biographical listings, see the Martindale-Hubbell Law Directory

GOLDSTEIN, BUCKLEY, CECHMAN, RICE & PURTZ, P.A. (AV)

1515 Broadway, P.O. Box 2366, 33902-2366
Telephone: 941-334-1146
Fax: 941-334-3039
Email: info@gbclaw.com *URL:* http://www.GBClaw.com
Port Charlotte, Florida Office: Emerald Square, Suite 1, 2852 Tamiami Trail, 33952.
Telephone: 941-624-2393.
Fax: 941-624-2155.

(See Next Column)

Cape Coral, Florida Office: 1603 Hancock Bridge Parkway, 33990.
Telephone: 941-574-5575.
Fax: 941-574-9213.
Lehigh Acres, Florida Office: 1458 Lee Boulevard, Lee Boulevard Shopping Center, 33936.
Telephone: 941-368-6101.
Fax: 941-368-2461.
Naples, Florida Office: 4947 North Tamiami Trail, Suite 101, 34103.
Telephone: 941-262-4888.
Fax: 941-262-8716.

Jerome A. Sico

Approved Attorneys for: Attorneys' Title Insurance Fund.

For Complete List of Firm Personnel, See General Section

For full biographical listings, see the Martindale-Hubbell Law Directory

*JACKSONVILLE,** Duval Co.

THE CRAMER LAW FIRM (AV)

1 Independent Drive, Suite 3300, 32202
Telephone: 904-632-2211
Fax: 904-632-2324
Email: cramerjax@worldnet.att.net

Jeffrey A. Cramer

Leonard S. Magid
Richard L. Ruth

Reference: Suntrust Bank.

For full biographical listings, see the Martindale-Hubbell Law Directory

MARTIN L. LEIBOWITZ, P.A. (AV)

2254 Riverside Avenue, P.O. Box 47530, 32247-7530
Telephone: 904-384-8878
Fax: 904-384-8588
URL: http://www.lawyers.com/mleibowitzlaw

Martin L. Leibowitz

For full biographical listings, see the Martindale-Hubbell Law Directory

*MIAMI,** Dade Co.

ABRAMSON & MAGIDSON, P.A. (AV)

Suite 904, 800 Brickell Avenue, 33131
Telephone: 305-358-4400
Fax: 305-539-0477
Email: abramson@icanect.net

John M. Abramson
David L. Magidson

For full biographical listings, see the Martindale-Hubbell Law Directory

DANIELS, KASHTAN & FORNARIS, P.A. (AV)

241 Sevilla Avenue, Penthouse 2, 33134
Telephone: 305-448-7988
Telecopier: 305-448-7978
URL: http://www.dkflaw.com

Richard G. Daniels
Michael F. Kashtan
Martha D. Fornaris
John E. Oramas
Ana Latour Grande
Albert Blair

Elizabeth M. Touma
Tracey A. Wright
Mercy Blasa Piña
John M. Haney
Omar Perez, Jr.
Chad J. Schatzle
Joseph W. Carey
Christopher G. Berga
Liane T. Alvarez
Ricardo Morales-Gomez

OF COUNSEL
Joseph W. Downs, III

Reference: Barnett Bank.

For full biographical listings, see the Martindale-Hubbell Law Directory

LEVINE, BUSCH, SCHNEPPER & STEIN, P.A. (AV)

Suite 1010 One Datran Center, 9100 South Dadeland Boulevard, 33156
Telephone: 305-670-2333
Fax: 305-670-0716
Email: LEVBUSSCHS@aol.com *URL:* http://www.lawofficesoflbss.com
Broward Office: 100 South Pine Island Road, Suite 202, Plantation, Florida, 33324.
Telephone: 954-922-0800.

David H. Levine
Edward P. Busch
R. Cory Schnepper
Barry A. Stein

Sanford M. Reinstein

For full biographical listings, see the Martindale-Hubbell Law Directory

Miami—Continued

STILES, TAYLOR & GRACE, P.A. (AV)

1101 Brickell Avenue, North Tower Suite 403, 33131
Telephone: 305-358-3556
Fax: 305-358-7210
Tampa, Florida Office: Old Hyde Park, 315 Plant Avenue, 33606.
Telephone: 813-251-2880.
Fax: 813-254-9073.
Orlando, Florida Office: The AmSouth Tower, 111 North Orange Avenue, Suite 850, 32801.
Telephone: 407-843-9900.
Fax: 407-843-9808.
Tallahassee, Florida Office: 317 North Calhoun Street, 32301.
Telephone: 904-222-2229.
FAX: 904-561-3642.
Boca Raton, Florida Office: The Compson Financial Center, 980 North Federal Highway, Suite 305, 33432.
Telephone: 561-393-7600.
Fax: 561-393-7038.

Robert J. Grace, Jr.

Felicia B. Kaufman
Jeffrey C. Perlman
John D. Adorno

For full biographical listings, see the Martindale-Hubbell Law Directory

*ORLANDO,** Orange Co.

COONEY, MATTSON, LANCE, BLACKBURN, RICHARDS & O'CONNOR, P.A. (AV)

Nations Bank Tower, 111 North Orange Avenue Suite 1020, 32801
Telephone: 407-843-2100
Fax: 407-843-2061
Fort Lauderdale, Florida Office: 2312 Wilton Drive. P.O. Box 14546. 33302.
Telephone: 954-568-6669.
Telecopier: 954-568-0085.

Dennis R. O'Connor
Kieran F. O'Connor

Elizabeth Y. Foshee (Resident)

For full biographical listings, see the Martindale-Hubbell Law Directory

EUBANKS, HILYARD & BOGAN, P.A. (AV)

Suite 600 First Union Building, 20 North Orange Avenue, P.O. Box 4973, 32802-4973
Telephone: 407-425-4251
Telecopier: 407-841-8431

Ernest H. Eubanks
Rodney G. Ross (1934-1982)
Sutton G. Hilyard, Jr.
Bruce R. Bogan

Bobby G. Palmer, Jr.
W. Gregory Lockeby

Representative Clients: AIG Aviation, Inc.; AVEMCO Insurance Co.; Phoenix Aviation Managers, Inc.; Ranger Insurance Co.; Old Republic Insurance Co.; Signal Aviation Underwriters; Underwriters at Lloyds; Orange County Sheriff's Office; United Technologies Corp.; Reliance Insurance Co.

For full biographical listings, see the Martindale-Hubbell Law Directory

GROWER, KETCHAM, MORÉ, RUTHERFORD, NOECKER, BRONSON, SIBONI & EIDE, P.A. (AV)

390 North Orange Avenue, Suite 1900, P.O. Box 538065, 32853-8065
Telephone: 407-423-9545
Telefacsimile: 407-425-7104
Ocala, Florida Office: 307 N.W. 3rd Street.
Telephone: 352-629-7441.
Telefacsimile: 352-629-7745.

Mason H. Grower, III
Walter A. Ketcham, Jr.
Hector A. Moré
Launa K. Rutherford
A. Scott Noecker
Michael C. Siboni (Resident Partner, Ocala Office)
Jeanelle G. Bronson
Eric R. Eide
David W. Henry
Kelly Gardner Hamer (Resident Partner, Ocala Office)
David B. Blessing
Patrick H. Telan

Benjamin W. Newman
Jack Erskine Holt, III
William H. Olney
Robert B. Buchanan
John M. Crotty
Christopher R. Fay
Scot D. Warner
M. Suzanne Chistolini
Stephen P. Matzuk
Diego "Woody" Rodriguez
Michael Richard Jackson
Jeremy K. Markman
Sharon T. De Shazo

For full biographical listings, see the Martindale-Hubbell Law Directory

MEYERS, MOONEY, STANLEY & HOLLINGSWORTH (AV)

(An Association of Professional Associations and Sole Proprietorships)
17 South Lake Avenue, 32801-2797
Telephone: 407-849-0940
Toll-free: 800-766-9198
Fax: 407-849-1860
Email: MeyMooMey@aol.com *URL:* http://www.lawyers.com/meyersmooney
Jacksonville Office: 2120 University Boulevard West, 32217.
Telephone: 904-367-8747; 800-951-7266.
Fax: 904-367-0650.

Irvin A. Meyers
Thomas R. Mooney
Bradley H. Hollingsworth
James A. Stanley, Jr. (Resident, Jacksonville Office)

ASSOCIATES

John V. Colvin
Thomas E. Mooney

Reference: Sun Bank & Trust of Orlando.

For full biographical listings, see the Martindale-Hubbell Law Directory

MORAN & SHAMS, P.A. (AV)

111 North Orange Avenue, Suite 1200, P.O. Box 472, 32802-0472
Telephone: 407-841-4141
Fax: 407-841-4148
Email: moran-shams@moran-shams.com

James F. Kidd

Clinton C. Lyons, Jr.
David E. Ackley
Yuvora Nong

Representative Clients: CNA Insurance Company; RSKCo.; Professional Business Owners Association, Inc.; United Self Insured Services Claims Center; Superior National Insurance; Managed Care USA; Kemper Insurance Companies Claims Center; Frito Lay; Public Storage.

For full biographical listings, see the Martindale-Hubbell Law Directory

MORGAN COLLING & GILBERT, A PROFESSIONAL ASSOCIATION (AV)

20 North Orange Avenue, 16th Floor, Suite 1607, P.O. Box 4979, 32802-4979
Telephone: 407-420-1414
Fax: 407-425-8171
URL: http://www.morgancollinggilbert.com
Tampa, Florida Office: 101 East Kennedy Boulevard, Suite 1790, 33602.
Telephone: 813-223-5505.
Fax: 813-223-5402.

Stewart L. Colling
James W. Keeter
Michael A. Mandeville
Richard Jay Manno
David I. Rickey
David A. Spain
Tony A. Turner (Resident, Tampa Office)
Basil Andres Valdivia

Reference: Sun Bank.

For full biographical listings, see the Martindale-Hubbell Law Directory

STILES, TAYLOR & GRACE, P.A. (AV)

The AmSouth Tower, 111 North Orange Avenue, Suite 850, 32801
Telephone: 407-843-9900
Fax: 407-843-9808
Miami, Florida Office: 1101 Brickell Avenue, North Tower, Suite 403, 33131.
Telephone: 305-358-3556.
Fax: 305-358-7210.
Tampa, Florida Office: 315 Plant Avenue.
Telephone: 813-251-2880.
Fax: 813-254-9073.
Tallahassee, Florida Office: 317 North Calhoun Street, 32301.
Telephone: 904-222-2229.
Fax: 904-561-3642.
Boca Raton, Florida Office: Compson Financial Center, 980 North Federal Highway, Suite 305, 33432.
Telephone: 561-393-7600.
Fax: 561-393-7038.

Stephen B. Wilson
Mark Glaser

For full biographical listings, see the Martindale-Hubbell Law Directory

PALM BEACH GARDENS, Palm Beach Co.

KEITH R. PALLO & ASSOCIATES, P.A. (AV)

4800 Riverside Drive, Suite 101, 33410
Telephone: 561-624-1051
Fax: 561-624-7441
Email: KRP2@AOL.com *URL:* http://www.pallolaw.com

Keith R. Pallo

(See Next Column)

KEITH R. PALLO & ASSOCIATES, P.A., *Palm Beach Gardens—Continued*

Carlos J. Hernandez
Jeffrey L. Marks
Christopher Charles Riggio
Judith S. Hernandez
Jonathan D. Wald

Representative Clients: Auto Owners Insurance; FCCI Mutual Insurance Company; Stirling Cooke; Boca Raton Resort & Club; Gallagher Bassett Services; Sheriff of Palm Beach County; Unisource Administrators; F.A. Richard; E.B.I.; Florida Restaurant Fund.

For full biographical listings, see the Martindale-Hubbell Law Directory

*PENSACOLA,** Escambia Co.

BOZEMAN, JENKINS & MATTHEWS, P.A. (AV)

SunTrust Tower, 220 West Garden Street, Suite 801, P.O. Box 13105, 32501
Telephone: 850-434-6223
Fax: 850-434-5242
Email: bojema@pen.net *URL:* http://www.bojema.pen.net
Fort Walton Beach Office: 151 Mary Esther Boulevard, Suite 401.
Telephone: 850-651-2151.
Fax: 850-434-5242.
Panama City Office: 475 Harrison Avenue, Suite 203A.
Telephone: 850-872-0110.
Fax: 850-434-5242.

Frank C. Bozeman, Jr.
Thomas R. Jenkins
Larry A. Matthews
Janice K. Skievaski
Frank C. Bozeman, III

Robert T. Bleach
John B. Fricke, Jr.
J. Andrew Talbert
Raymond F. Higgins, III
Jeremiah J. Talbott
Sidney M. McCrackin

For full biographical listings, see the Martindale-Hubbell Law Directory

ST. PETERSBURG, Pinellas Co.

NANCY L. CAVEY (AV)

821 Sixteenth Street North, P.O. Box 7508, 33705
Telephone: 813-894-3188
Fax: 813-821-2751

For full biographical listings, see the Martindale-Hubbell Law Directory

*SARASOTA,** Sarasota Co.

BROWN CLARK, A PROFESSIONAL ASSOCIATION (AV)

Suite 500, Sarasota City Center, 1819 Main Street, 34236
Telephone: 941-957-3800
Telefax: 941-957-3888
Email: brownclark@mindspring.com *URL:* http://www.brownclark.com

Daniel J. DeMay

Manatee County: RSKCo; Liberty Mutual.

For full biographical listings, see the Martindale-Hubbell Law Directory

*TALLAHASSEE,** Leon Co.

McCONNAUGHHAY, DUFFY, COONROD, POPE & WEAVER, P.A. (AV)

Suite 900, 101 North Monroe Street, P.O. Drawer 229, 32302-0229
Telephone: 850-222-8121
Telecopier: 850-222-4359
Pensacola, Florida Office: 316 South Baylen Street, Suite 500.
Telephone: 850-434-7122.
Telecopier: 850-435-0924.
Panama City, Florida Office: 306 E. 19th Street.
Telephone: 850-784-2599.
Telecopier: 850-769-5461.
Jacksonville, Florida Office: 8381 Dix Ellis Trail, Suite 100.
Telephone: 904-363-1950.
Telecopier: 904-363-1510.
Sarasota, Florida Office: 1800 Second Street, Suite 954.
Telephone: 941-955-6141.
Telecopier: 941-955-6244.
Ocala, Florida Office: Building 600, Laurel Run Professional Center, 2100 S.E. 17th Street.
Telephone: 352-840-0330.
Fax: 352-401-9518.
Gainesville, Florida Office: 5024 N.W. 27th Court.
Telephone: 352-378-4422.
Fax: 352-378-7826.

James N. McConnaughhay
Brian S. Duffy
R. Stephen Coonrod
Robert D. Pope
(Resident at Jacksonville)
Patrick E. Weaver
(Resident at Panama City)
E. Louis Stern
(Resident at Sarasota)

(See Next Column)

Michael J. Rudicell
(Resident at Pensacola)
Mary Lalley Wakeman
Michael C. Crumpler
(Resident at Jacksonville)
M. Kemmerly Thomas
Elizabeth F. Campo
(Resident at Gainesville)
Betty D. Marion
(Resident at Ocala)
Holly A. Davis
(Resident at Ocala)
Robert A. Keeter
(Resident at Gainesville)

Mary Ellen Ingley
Jana E. McConnaughhay
Sarah M. Stokes
Tracey J. Hyde
(Resident at Panama City)
Jacqueline L. Blanton
(Resident at Sarasota)
Susan L. Fara
(Resident at Sarasota)
Susan N. Marks
(Resident at Pensacola)
Kyle Lee Redfearn
William Jemison Mims, Jr.
(Resident at Pensacola)
Renee M. Armbruster
(Resident at Sarasota)
Wallace W. Hardy
Kathryn L. Johnson
Jeffrey R. Richardson
Eric D. Schurger
(Resident at Pensacola)
Monett B. Kent
(Resident at Jacksonville)
Timothy R. Whitney
(Resident at Panama City)
Dale J. Stone
(Resident at Jacksonville)
Teri A. Bussey
Joe G. Durrett
W. Scott Van Ness
(Resident at Sarasota)
H. Lee Futch
Nicole D. Lindsey
(Resident at Ocala)
Mark A. Massey
(Resident at Ocala)
Sharon Neil Ruth
(Resident at Gainesville)
Gary S. Weisman
Gregory Carter Harrell
Sean S. O'Connor
(Resident at Ocala)
Iris M. DuBois
(Resident at Sarasota)

For full biographical listings, see the Martindale-Hubbell Law Directory

STILES, TAYLOR & GRACE, P.A. (AV)

317 North Calhoun Street, 32301
Telephone: 904-222-2229
Fax: 904-561-3642
Miami, Florida Office: 1101 Brickell Avenue, North Tower, Suite 403, 33131.
Telephone: 305-358-3556.
Fax: 305-358-7210.
Tampa, Florida Office: 315 Plant Avenue.
Telephone: 813-251-2880.
Fax: 813-254-9073.
Boca Raton, Florida Office: Compson Financial Center, 980 North Federal Highway, Suite 305, 33432.
Telephone: 561-393-7600.
Fax: 561-393-7038.
Orlando, Florida Office: The AmSouth Tower, 111 North Orange Avenue, Suite 850, 32801.
Telephone: 407-843-9900.
Fax: 407-843-9808.

Mary Ann Stiles
Rayford H. Taylor
Tamela W. Ivey
Ferman M. Fernandez

OF COUNSEL

Daniel J. Wiser
Cynthia L. Jakeman
Gene H. Williams

For full biographical listings, see the Martindale-Hubbell Law Directory

*TAMPA,** Hillsborough Co.

BARBAS WEED KOENIG NUÑEZ & WHEELEY (AV)

1802 West Cleveland Street, 33606
Telephone: 813-254-6575
Fax: 813-254-4690
Lakeland, Florida Office: 500 South Florida Avenue, Suite 600, 38801.
Telephone: 941-680-2712.
Palm Harbor, Florida Office: 2708 Alternate 19 North Suite 701, 34683.
Telephone: 813-443-5323.
New Port Richey, Florida Office: 6014 U.S. 19, Suite 101-4.
Telephone: 813-849-0592.

Martha-Irene Weed
Stephen M. Barbas
Matthew B. Wheeley
David F. Koenig
Kelly Barcia Nuñez
L. Gray Sanders
Nilo J. Sanchez, Jr.

ASSOCIATES

Jimmie Butler
Steven Edward Hovsepian

For full biographical listings, see the Martindale-Hubbell Law Directory

BARR, MURMAN, TONELLI, HERZFELD & RUBIN (AV)

Suite 1750, 201 East Kennedy Boulevard, P.O. Box 172669, 33672-0669
Telephone: 813-223-3951
Fax: 813-229-2254
URL: http://www.hrfirm.com
New Port Richey, Florida Office: 7613 Little Road, 34654.
Telephone: 727-846-8646;
Fax: 727-846-8913.

(See Next Column)

BARR, MURMAN, TONELLI, HERZFELD & RUBIN—*Continued*

James A. Murman
Michael A. Tonelli
Daniel H. Sleet
T. Gregory Slother
John W. Boult
Gregory G. Frazier
Joseph S. Silver

ASSOCIATES

John J. Kozak
Morris D. Purcell, Jr.
Robert J. Scanlan
Pamela A. Walton

OF COUNSEL

Billy R. Barr

Representative Clients: School Board of Hillsborough County, Florida; Royal Insurance Co.; CIGNA Insurance Co.; Wastequip; USIS.

For full biographical listings, see the Martindale-Hubbell Law Directory

WILLIAM P. LEVENS (AV)

1907 West Kennedy Boulevard, 33606
Telephone: 813-251-5775
Toll Free: 1-800-395-0463
Fax: 813-251-3240
Email: watty1@tampabay.rr.com *URL:* http://www.lawyers.com/flworkcomp

For full biographical listings, see the Martindale-Hubbell Law Directory

ROSEN & OSBORNE, P.A. (AV)

3444 South Westshore Boulevard, 33629
Telephone: 813-902-1200
Telefax: 813-832-4627
Email: mrwc44u@aol.com

Stephen L. Rosen
Richard W. Osborne
Cynthia L. Maynard

For full biographical listings, see the Martindale-Hubbell Law Directory

SMITH, ANDREWS, ROGERS & BRADY (AV)

Biglow Mansion Office Building, 4807 Bayshore Boulevard, Suite 200, P.O. Box 13500, 33681-3500
Telephone: 813-831-7978
Fax: 813-832-2961
Email: JSmith@TFCTPA.com

James H. Smith
Dana G. Andrews
Dawn M. Rogers
John G. Brady

ASSOCIATE

Benjamin Andrew Winter

For full biographical listings, see the Martindale-Hubbell Law Directory

STILES, TAYLOR & GRACE, P.A. (AV)

Old Hyde Park, 315 Plant Avenue, 33606
Telephone: 813-251-2880
Fax: 813-254-9073
Miami, Florida Office: 1101 Brickell Avenue, North Tower, Suite 403, 33131.
Telephone: 305-358-3556.
Fax: 305-358-7210.
Orlando, Florida Office: The AmSouth Tower, 111 North Orange Avenue, Suite 850, 32801.
Telephone: 407-843-9900.
Fax: 407-843-9808.
Tallahassee, Florida Office: 317 North Calhoun Street, 32301.
Telephone: 904-222-2229.
FAX: 904-561-3642.
Boca Raton, Florida Office: The Compson Financial Center, 980 North Federal Highway, Suite 305, 33432.
Telephone: 561-393-7600.
Fax: 561-393-7038.

Mary Ann Stiles
Robert J. Grace, Jr.
John S. Smith

Felice D. Rivers
Gary G. Carpenter
Courtney Rivers

For full biographical listings, see the Martindale-Hubbell Law Directory

*VERO BEACH,** Indian River Co.

MOSS, HENDERSON, BLANTON & LANIER, P.A. (AV)

817 Beachland Boulevard, P.O. Box 3406, 32964-3406
Telephone: 561-231-1900
Fax: 561-231-4387

(See Next Column)

Anthony M. Amelio
David C. Chafin

Representative Clients: Aetna Life & Casualty; Alcoa Florida, Inc.; Florida Power & Light Co.; Insurance Company of North America; Liberty Mutual Insurance Co.; Sears, Roebuck & Co.; Sugar Cane Growers Cooperative of Florida; Norfolk Southern Corporation/North American Van Lines, Inc.

For Complete List of Firm Personnel, See General Section

For full biographical listings, see the Martindale-Hubbell Law Directory

*WEST PALM BEACH,** Palm Beach Co.

ADAMS, COOGLER, WATSON & MERKEL, P.A. (AV)

Suite 1600, 1555 Palm Beach Lakes Boulevard, P.O. Box 2069, 33402
Telephone: 561-478-4500
Fax: 561-684-7346
Email: ACWMLAW@AOL.COM

Samuel H. Adams (1913-1981)
Roy R. Watson
Robert G. Merkel
James C. Barry
Reed W. Kellner
Catherine Lynn Kasten
Scott S. Warburton
Peter A. Cooke
Patricia A. Judge
Kathryn L. Tignor

Alexander D. Barker
Jodi G. Barrett
Stephanie Brown
James W. Flanagan
Paul L. Harwood
Thomas Hodas
Catherine M. Paris

OF COUNSEL

L. C. Shepard, Jr.

For full biographical listings, see the Martindale-Hubbell Law Directory

GEORGIA

*ATHENS,** Clarke Co.

FOY S. HORNE, JR., P.C. (AV)

2425 West Broad Street, Suite 200, P.O. Box 706, 30603
Telephone: 706-549-6376
Fax: 706-613-2508

Foy S. Horne, Jr.

Bank Reference: NationsBank of Georgia, N.A.

For full biographical listings, see the Martindale-Hubbell Law Directory

*ATLANTA,** Fulton Co.

BOVIS, KYLE & BURCH, LLC (AV)

A Limited Liability Corporation including Professional Corporations
Third Floor, 53 Perimeter Center East, 30346
Telephone: 770-391-9100
Telecopier: 770-668-0878
Email: bkb@boviskyle.com *URL:* http://www.boviskyle.com

Steven J. Kyle (P.C.)
Charles M. Medlin

Carl A. Hassler

For Complete List of Firm Personnel, See General Section

For full biographical listings, see the Martindale-Hubbell Law Directory

FAIN, MAJOR, WILEY & BRENNAN, P.C. (AV)

100 Glenridge Point Parkway Suite 500, 30342-1440
Telephone: 404-688-6633
Telecopier: 404-420-1544

Gene A. Major
Charles A. Wiley, Jr.
John K. Miles, Jr.
Darryl G. Haynes

Brian Alligood
Kim Monroe Jackson

Representative Clients: Allstate Insurance Co.; Budget Rent-A-Car; Arkansas Best Corp.; Chrysler Insurance Co.; Georgia Farm Bureau Mutual Insurance Co.; Hertz Corp.; Universal Underwriters Insurance Co.; Westfield Insurance Co.; Winn-Dixie Stores, Inc.

For Complete List of Firm Personnel, See General Section

For full biographical listings, see the Martindale-Hubbell Law Directory

GOLDNER, SOMMERS, SCRUDDER & BASS (AV)

900 Circle 75 Parkway Suite 850, 30339
Telephone: 770-612-9200
Facsimile: 770-612-9201

(See Next Column)

GOLDNER, SOMMERS, SCRUDDER & BASS, *Atlanta—Continued*

MEMBERS OF FIRM

Susan V. Sommers
Alfred A. Quillian, Jr.
Sandra G. Chase
Linda Jacobsen Pollock

ASSOCIATE

Jane Carol Taylor

For Complete List of Firm Personnel, See General Section

For full biographical listings, see the Martindale-Hubbell Law Directory

GOODMAN, MCGUFFEY, AUST & LINDSEY, LLP (AV)

2100 Tower Place, 3340 Peachtree Road, N.E., 30326-1084
Telephone: 404-264-1500
Fax: 404-264-1737
Email: gmal@atlanta.com

MEMBERS OF FIRM

William S. Goodman
C. Wade McGuffey, Jr.
Judy Farrington Aust
Edward H. Lindsey, Jr.
Joe David Jackson
Kathryn A. Cater
Debra L. Dalton
Lisa A. Wade

Michael A. Dalton
Danielle F. Forte

For full biographical listings, see the Martindale-Hubbell Law Directory

PIERCE & YOUNG (AV)

Building 1700, 2255 Cumberland Parkway Northwest, 30339-4575
Telephone: 770-435-0500
Telecopier: 770-435-0362

MEMBER OF FIRM

J. Wayne Pierce

For full biographical listings, see the Martindale-Hubbell Law Directory

THEODORE SALTER, JR. & ASSOCIATES, P.C. (AV)

Suite 510, 2970 Peachtree Road, N.W., P.O. Box 53138, 30355
Telephone: 404-239-0106
Fax: 404-365-0811
Email: tsalter@mindspring.com

Theodore Salter, Jr.

Thomas A. Soderberg
Carolyn A. Wilson

For full biographical listings, see the Martindale-Hubbell Law Directory

SWIFT, CURRIE, MCGHEE & HIERS (AV)

1355 Peachtree Street, N.E., 30309-3238
Telephone: 404-874-8800
Telecopier: 404-888-6199
Email: scmhlaw.com

MEMBERS OF FIRM

James T. McDonald, Jr.
John F. Sacha
Michael H. Schroder
Stephen L. Cotter
Robert R. Potter
Douglas A. Bennett
Mark T. Dietrichs
Lynn M. Roberson
Mark J. Goodman
Joseph A. Munger
R. Briggs Peery
Thomas D. Martin
Bradley S. Wolff
Frederick Owen Ferrand
John W. Campbell
Stephen M. Schatz
Richard H. Sapp, III
Charles M. McDaniel, Jr.
Michael Ryder
Susan A. Dewberry

OF COUNSEL

Frank M. Swift
Warner S. Currie
Glover McGhee
James B. Hiers, Jr.

ASSOCIATES

Michael H. Friedman
Debra Dawn Chambers
Micheal D. Watson
Thomas E. Best
Richard A. Watts
Peggy R. Goodnight
Kenneth B. Still
Michael C. Kendall
Timothy C. Lemke
Bright Kinnett Wright
Douglas W. Brown, Jr.
Christopher D. Balch
Joan Perkins Shaker
David Charles King
Willie C. Adams
W. Wright Mitchell
H. Lee Pruett
Thomas J. Mazziotti
Robert E. Jones
Kristine J. Moschella
Megan W. Grout
Kenneth A. David
J. Michael Parsons
Lloyd N. Bell
Erik S. Rodriguez
James D. Johnson
Cabell D. Townsend
Scott M. Williamson
Sharon Leah Neal
John F. Blount
Casey W. Stevens
Amy Greenstein

Representative Clients: Chubb Insurance Group; Cagle's Inc.; Gold Kist, Inc.; Kemper Insurance Group; Maryland Casualty Cos.; PHH Homequity; Sedgwick James; State Farm Fire & Casualty Co.; The Travelers Cos.; Super Valu.

For full biographical listings, see the Martindale-Hubbell Law Directory

WEBB, CARLOCK, COPELAND, SEMLER & STAIR, LLP (AV)

A Partnership including Professional Corporations
2600 Marquis Two Tower, 285 Peachtree Center Avenue, P.O. Box 56887, 30343-0887
Telephone: 404-522-8220
Fax: 404-523-2345; 404-222-9482

MEMBERS OF FIRM

Robert C. Semler (P.C.)
Christopher A. Whitlock

ASSOCIATES

Lynn B. Olmert
Jerry W. Cain, Jr.

For full biographical listings, see the Martindale-Hubbell Law Directory

ZIRKLE AND HOFFMAN (AV)

Five Concourse Parkway, Suite 2900, 30328
Telephone: 770-551-8700
Fax: 770-512-0329
Email: zh@zirklaw.com *URL:* http://www.zirklaw.com

MEMBERS OF FIRM

Charles B. Zirkle, Jr.
G. Scott Hoffman
Eric S. Jones
Ben E. Pellegrini
Deborah G. Krotenberg

ASSOCIATES

Donnell J. Collins
Nancy C. Collins
Brian J. Mongelluzzo
Deborah S. Urbach

LEGAL SUPPORT PERSONNEL

PARALEGALS

Karen H. Jones (Paralegal)
Susan J. Millican (Paralegal)

For full biographical listings, see the Martindale-Hubbell Law Directory

*DALTON,** Whitfield Co.

KINNEY, KEMP, SPONCLER, JOINER & THARPE (AV)

A Partnership including a Professional Corporation
225 West King Street, P.O. Box 398, 30722-0398
Telephone: 706-278-5211
Fax: 706-275-6566
Email: attorney@kinneyandkemp.com

MEMBERS OF FIRM

R. Carter Pittman (1898-1972)
Hinton Eugene Kinney (1913-1996)
L. Hugh Kemp (P.C.)
Maurice M. Sponcler, Jr.
Horace Greely Joiner, Jr.
Henry C. Tharpe, Jr.
F. Gregory Melton
Richard W. Andrews
Timothy H. Allred
Mark D. Newberry
Robert Adam Cowan

ASSOCIATE

Chad D. Plumley

OF COUNSEL

Susan W. Bisson
William J. Kimsey
J. Tracy Ward

General Counsel for: North Georgia Electric Membership Corporation; Queen Carpet Corp.; Hardwick Bank & Trust Company.
Representative Clients: Allstate Insurance Co.; Liberty Mutual Insurance Co.; State Farm Mutual Automobile Insurance Co.; Norfolk Southern Railway Company; General Motors Corporation; Dalton Board of Education.

For full biographical listings, see the Martindale-Hubbell Law Directory

*DECATUR,** De Kalb Co.

HYATT & HYATT, P.C. (AV)

Suite 201, Trust Building, 545 North McDonough Street, 30030
Telephone: 404-378-3635
Fax: 404-377-8304
Email: jhyatt@mindspring.com *URL:* http://www.lawyers.com/hyattlaw

Charles H. Hyatt (1924-1995)
John M. Hyatt

For full biographical listings, see the Martindale-Hubbell Law Directory

*MACON,** Bibb Co.

SELL & MELTON, L.L.P. (AV)

A Limited Liability Partnership including a Professional Corporation
14th Floor, 577 Mulberry Street, P.O. Box 229, 31202-0229
Telephone: 912-746-8521
Telecopier: 912-745-6426

Doye E. Green
Russell M. Boston (P.C.)

General Counsel for: Macon Telegraph Publishing Co. (The Macon Telegraph); Macon-Bibb County Hospital Authority; County of Bibb; Smith & Sons Foods, Inc. (S & S Cafeterias); Macon Bibb County Industrial Authority; Burgess Pigment Co.
Local Counsel For: United States Aircraft Insurance Group (USAIG); United States Aviation Underwriters, Inc. (USAU).

(See Next Column)

SELL & MELTON L.L.P.—*Continued*

For Complete List of Firm Personnel, See General Section

For full biographical listings, see the Martindale-Hubbell Law Directory

NORCROSS, Gwinnett Co.

DEMING, PARKER, HOFFMAN, GREEN & CAMPBELL, P.C. (AV)

4851 Jimmy Carter Boulevard, 30093
Telephone: 770-564-2600
Fax: 770-564-2267
Covington, Georgia Office: Suite 11, 3236 Highway 278.
Telephone: 770-787-2600.
Fax: 770-564-2267.
Cumming, Georgia Office: 425 Tribble Gap Road, Suite 398, 30130.
Telephone: 770-889-2600.
Fax: 770-564-2267.

Michael D. Deming
Franklin E. Parker
Paul M. Hoffman
Jim R. Green, Jr.
Richard A. Campbell
Stephen R. Williams

OF COUNSEL

Robert E. Born

Mark L. Wells
Christopher W. T. Daly
E. Nicole Harrison
Suzanne M. Boykin

For full biographical listings, see the Martindale-Hubbell Law Directory

*SAVANNAH,** Chatham Co.

BOUHAN, WILLIAMS & LEVY LLP (AV)

The Armstrong House, 447 Bull Street, P.O. Box 2139, 31402-2139
Telephone: 912-236-2491
Fax: 912-233-0811
Email: bouhan@bellsouth.net

MEMBER OF FIRM

B. H. Levy, Jr.

General Counsel for: Savannah Electric and Power Co.; Wachovia Bank of Georgia, N.A.; Southeastern Maritime Co.; Solomons Co.; Fiduciary Services Corp.; Peeples Industry, Inc.; Board of Education of the City of Savannah and County of Chatham; The Branigar Organization, Inc.

For Complete List of Firm Personnel, See General Section

For full biographical listings, see the Martindale-Hubbell Law Directory

KARSMAN, BROOKS & CALLAWAY, P.C. (AV)

301 West Congress Street, P.O. Box 9149, 31412
Telephone: 912-238-2750
Cable Address: "Karbro"
Telecopier: 912-238-2767

Stanley M. Karsman
Charles C. Brooks
Timothy F. Callaway, III
Stanley E. Harris, Jr.
James L. Drake, Jr.
Dana F. Braun
R. Krannert Riddle
Edward M. Hughes
Timothy J. Haeussler

For full biographical listings, see the Martindale-Hubbell Law Directory

*VALDOSTA,** Lowndes Co.

CLYATT, CLYATT & DEVAUGHN, P.C. (AV)

410 North Valdosta Road, P.O. Box 5799, 31603
Telephone: 912-241-9091
Fax: 912-245-1635
Email: ccd1@surfsouth.com

Robert M. Clyatt
Melissa M. Clyatt
C. Elizabeth DeVaughn
Carl G. Fulp, III
N. Daniel Lovein
Sandra Guest Sanders

For full biographical listings, see the Martindale-Hubbell Law Directory

HAWAII

*HONOLULU,** Honolulu Co.

CARLSMITH BALL (AV)

A Partnership including Law Corporations
Suite 2200, Pacific Tower, 1001 Bishop Street, P.O. Box 656, 96809-3402
Telephone: 808-523-2500
Fax: 808-523-0842
Email: execdirector@carlsmith.com *URL:* http://www.carlsmith.com
Kapolei, Hawaii Office: Suite 318, Kapolei Building, 1001 Kamokila Boulevard, 96707.
Telephone: 808-523-2500.
Fax: 808-674-0850.

(See Next Column)

Wailuku, Maui Hawaii Office: Suite 400, One Main Plaza, 2200 Main Street, P.O. Box 1086, 96793-1086.
Telephone: 808-242-4535.
Fax: 808-244-4974.
Kailua-Kona, Hawaii Office: Suite 209, 75-1000 Henry Street, 96740.
Telephone: 808-329-6464.
Fax: 808-329-9450.
Hilo, Hawaii Office: 121 Waianuenue Avenue, P.O. Box 686, 96721-0686.
Telephone: 808-935-6644.
Fax: 808-935-7975.
Hagatna, Guam Office: Suite 401, Bank of Hawaii Building, 134 West Soledad Avenue, P.O. Box BF, 96932-5027.
Telephone: 671-472-6813.
Fax: 671-477-4375.
Telex: 721-6445 CWCMI GM.
Saipan, Commonwealth of the Northern Mariana Islands Office: Carlsmith Building, Capitol Hill, P.O. Box 5241, 96950-5241.
Telephone: 670-322-3455.
Fax: 670-322-3368.
Los Angeles, California Office: 9th Floor, 444 South Flower Street, 90071-2901.
Telephone: 213-955-1200.
Fax: 213-623-0032.
Washington, D.C. Office: Suite 300, 1201 Pennsylvania Avenue, N.W., 20004-2401.
Telephone: 202-628-2228.
Fax: 202-628-2071.
Mexico City, Mexico Office: Carlsmith Ball, Sierra Nevada 119, Lomas de Chapultepec, 11000 Mexico, D.F.
Telephone: 52-5-520-8514, 52-5-520-8757.
Fax: 52-5-540-1545.
Mexico, D.F. Office of Carlsmith Ball, S.C. (Authorized to practice as foreign legal consultants in Mexico): Sierra Nevada 119, Lomas de Chapultepec, 11000 Mexico, D.F.
Telephone: 52-5-520-8514, 52-5-520-8757.
Fax: 52-5-540-1545.

MEMBERS OF FIRM

Anna M. Elento-Sneed
Terry E. Thomason

For Complete List of Firm Personnel, See General Section

For full biographical listings, see the Martindale-Hubbell Law Directory

KESSNER DUCA UMEBAYASHI BAIN & MATSUNAGA ATTORNEYS AT LAW, A LAW CORPORATION (AV)

19th Floor, Central Pacific Plaza, 220 South King Street, 96813
Telephone: 808-536-1900
Telecopier: 808-529-7177
Telex: 723 8616 OPAC IIR

Robert C. Kessner
James N. Duca
Clyde S. Umebayashi
Elton John Bain
Emma S. Matsunaga
Muriel M. Taira

Beverly S. K. Tom
Jacqueline W.S. Amai
Melanie S. Matsui
Cori Ann C. Takamiya

OF COUNSEL

Kathy K. Higham

For full biographical listings, see the Martindale-Hubbell Law Directory

IDAHO

*BOISE,** Ada Co.

ELAM & BURKE, A PROFESSIONAL ASSOCIATION (AV)

Key Financial Center, 702 West Idaho Street, P.O. Box 1539, 83701
Telephone: 208-343-5454
Telecopier: 208-384-5844
Email: eblaw@elamburke.com

Ryan P. Armbruster
James A. Ford

Rebecca A. Broadbent

Representative Client: Idaho State Insurance Fund.

For Complete List of Firm Personnel, See General Section

For full biographical listings, see the Martindale-Hubbell Law Directory

GARDNER & CHARNEY, P.L.L.P. (AV)

350 North 9th Street - Suite B-60, 83702
Telephone: 208-387-0881
Fax: 208-387-3501
Email: agboi@aol.com

(See Next Column)

GARDNER & CHARNEY P.L.L.P., *Boise—Continued*

Alan R. Gardner
Dennis M. Charney

Representative Clients: Safeco Insurance Cos.; Wausau Insurance Cos.; Farmers Insurance Group; St. Paul Insurance Company; Traveler's Insurance Cos.; Fremont Insurance Co.; Intermountain Health Care; Chubb Insurance Company; Reliance Insurance Co.; Albertson's, Inc.

For full biographical listings, see the Martindale-Hubbell Law Directory

ILLINOIS

*CHICAGO,** Cook Co.

ANESI, OZMON, RODIN, NOVAK & KOHEN, LTD. (AV)

161 North Clark Street, 21st Floor, 60601
Telephone: 312-372-3822
Fax: 312-372-3833

Nat P. Ozmon
Curt N. Rodin
Mark Novak
Bruce M. Kohen
Douglas A. Colby
Joseph J. Miroballi
Marc A. Taxman
Daniel V. O'Connor

David J. Comeau
Alain Leval
Scott H. Rudin
John A. Salzeider
Telly C. Nakos
Martin J. Lucas
John M. Popelka
Edward D. D'Arcy, Jr.
Paul W. Pasche
Mark Murnane
Samantha Kavathas
Bruce D. Ogron
James G. McCarthy
Steven A. Berman
Peter J. Stavropoulos
George G. Argionis
Steven W. Burrows
Andrew M. DeLuca
Bradley Michael Arnold
Michael P. Hellman

OF COUNSEL

Noel C. Lindenmuth
Irving D. Fasman
Charles E. Anesi (1912-1995)
Richard A. Lewin (1925-1985)

For full biographical listings, see the Martindale-Hubbell Law Directory

BERNARD R. NEVORAL AND ASSOCIATES LTD. (AV)

150 North Wacker Drive, Suite 2450, 60606
Telephone: 312 263-7058
FAX: 312-263-4566

Bernard R. Nevoral

Daniel M. Extrom
David F Szczecin

For full biographical listings, see the Martindale-Hubbell Law Directory

ROOKS, PITTS AND POUST (AV)

10 South Wacker Drive, Suite 2300, 60606
Telephone: 312-876-1700
Fax: 312-876-1155
Lisle, Illinois Office: 4200 Commerce Court, Suite 300.
Telephone: 630-245-0400.
Facsimile: 630-245-0140.
Joliet, Illinois Office: 111 North Ottawa Street.
Telephone: 815-727-4511.
Facsimile: 815-727-1586.
Winnetka, Illinois Office: 560 Green Bay Road.
Telephone: 847-441-5615.
Fax: 847-441-9367.

MEMBERS OF FIRM

Frank C. Rowland
Ian M. Sherman
Geoffrey A. Bryce
Michael Gahan
J. Barrett Long

Ellen D. Holzman
David L. Miller

For Complete List of Firm Personnel, See General Section

For full biographical listings, see the Martindale-Hubbell Law Directory

RUSIN PATTON MACIOROWSKI & FRIEDMAN, LTD. (AV)

Suite 1530 10 South Riverside Plaza, 60606
Telephone: 312-454-5110
Fax: 312-454-6166
Urbana, Illinois Office: 301 West Green Street, P.O. Box 985, 61803-0985.
Telephone: 217-328-7091.
Fax: 217-328-7093.

Michael E. Rusin
Stephen J. Friedman
John W. Patton Jr.
John A. Maciorowski
Kenneth N. Marshall
Gregory G. Vacala
Daniel Arkin
Randall R. Stark

(See Next Column)

Anuradha Y Boyapati
Todd A. Bresney
Luke A. Casson
R. Mark Cosimini (Resident, Urbana Office)
Daniel R. Egan
Frederick Scott Glassman
William J. Harrington
Daniel P. Johnston
David M. Lewin
Theodore James Powers
Gregory A. Rode
Mark P. Rusin
David F. Ryan
Douglas Sullivan
Edward R. Tomkowiak
Cynthia M. Wallach
Catherine A. Zaryczny

For full biographical listings, see the Martindale-Hubbell Law Directory

SCHIFF & HULBERT (AV)

311 South Wacker Drive, Suite 2625, 60606
Telephone: 312-427-7570
Fax: 312-427-7560
Email: SchiffHulb@aol.com

MEMBERS OF FIRM

Matthew B. Schiff
James W. Hulbert

ASSOCIATES

Bridget A. Neuson
Linda Cecchin Kramer
Lynn M. Kreutzberg

For full biographical listings, see the Martindale-Hubbell Law Directory

STONE & MOORE, CHARTERED (AV)

30 North La Salle Street, Suite 4300, 60602
Telephone: 312-332-5656
Fax: 312-332-5858
URL: http://www.stonemoore.com
Merrillville, Indiana Office: 500 E. 86th Avenue, 46410.
Telephone: 219-736-5959.
Fax: 219-736-5858.
Wheaton, Illinois Office: 600 W. Roosevelt Road, Suite 1A, 60187.
Telephone: 630-221-9292.
Fax: 630-221-9393.

William G. Stone
Robert Charles Moore (Also at Wheaton, Illinois Office)
Raymond R. Pesavento
Rosario Cibella
Richard M. Johnson, Jr.
J. Murray Pinkston, III
Julie Osswald Hooven

Christian D. Ambler
Jeffrey W. Henning
Erica Lewis Battaglia
Kevin Kemp Lyons
Kristin E. Rooney
Daniel S. Schulz
Matthew B. Stephens
A. Christine Svenson
Douglas W. Walker

For full biographical listings, see the Martindale-Hubbell Law Directory

YELTON & KEHL, LTD. (AV)

One East Wacker Drive Suite 3720, 60601
Telephone: 312-832-9255
Fax: 312-832-9277
URL: http://www.yeltonkehl.com

Karen M. Talty

For full biographical listings, see the Martindale-Hubbell Law Directory

*HARRISBURG,** Saline Co.

JELLIFFE, FERRELL, MORRIS, DOERGE & FOSTER (AV)

108 East Walnut Street, P.O. Box 406, 62946
Telephone: 618-253-7153; 253-7647
Telecopier: 618-252-1843

OF COUNSEL

Charles R. Jelliffe

MEMBERS OF FIRM

DeWitt Twente (1904-1976)
Donald V. Ferrell
Walden E. Morris
Michal Doerge
Thomas J. Foster

Representative Clients: Auto-Owners Insurance; Country Cos; Metropolitan Life Insurance; Ohio Casualty Group; Standard Mutual Insurance Co.; State Farm Cos.; Aetna Casualty & Surety Co.; Sahara Coal Co.

For full biographical listings, see the Martindale-Hubbell Law Directory

LA SALLE, La Salle Co.

HERBOLSHEIMER, LANNON, HENSON, DUNCAN AND REAGAN, P.C. (AV)

State Bank Building, Suite 400, 654 First Street, P.O. Box 539, 61301
Telephone: 815-223-0111
Fax: 815-223-5829
Ottawa, Illinois Office: First Federal Savings Bank Building, 633 LaSalle Street, Suite 409.
Telephone: 815-434-1400.
Fax: 815-434-2423.

(See Next Column)

HERBOLSHEIMER, LANNON, HENSON, DUNCAN AND REAGAN P.C.—*Continued*

George L. Herbolsheimer (1911-1992)
R. James Lannon, Jr.
T. Donald Henson
John S. Duncan, III
Michael T. Reagan (Resident, Ottawa Office)
Douglas A. Gift
Gary R. Eiten

Karen C. Eiten
Michael C. Jansz (Resident, Ottawa Office)
Jill W. Klein
Lawrence M. Kaschak

Attorneys for: Aetna Insurance Group; St. Paul Fire and Marine Insurance Co.; State Farm Insurance Co.; La Salle State Bank; The Daily News Tribune Company, La Salle; Eureka Savings Bank; Illinois Valley Community Hospital; Community Hospital of Ottawa; Commonwealth Edison, Co.; United States Fidelity & Guaranty, Co.

For full biographical listings, see the Martindale-Hubbell Law Directory

*MARION,** Williamson Co.

HARRIS, LAMBERT, HOWERTON & DORRIS (AV)

300 West Main Street, 62959
Telephone: 618-993-2616
Fax: 618-997-1845
Email: robi8@midamer.net *URL:* http://www.lawyers.com/hlh&d

MEMBERS OF FIRM

Ralph W. Harris (1904-1982)
Richard Gordon Lambert (Retired)
Robert H. Howerton
Douglas N. Dorris

ASSOCIATES

Stephen W. Stone
Kelley Ray Phelps

For full biographical listings, see the Martindale-Hubbell Law Directory

MATTOON, Coles Co.

CRAIG & CRAIG (AV)

1807 Broadway, P.O. Box 689, 61938-0689
Telephone: 217-234-6481
Telecopier: 217-234-6486; 258-8292
Email: craiglaw@advant.com
Mount Vernon, Illinois Office: 115 North 7th Street.
Telephone: 618-244-7511.

MEMBERS OF FIRM

Craig Van Meter (1895-1981)
Fred H. Kelly (1894-1971)
Robert M. Werden (1908-1969)
George N. Gilkerson (1911-1985)
John P. Ewart
Richard F. Record, Jr.
Stephen L. Corn
Robert G. Grierson
Gregory C. Ray
Paul R. Lynch (Resident, Mount Vernon Office)
Kenneth F. Werts (Resident, Mount Vernon Office)
John L. Barger

ASSOCIATES

Kathleen M. Stockwell
Kristine M. Tuttle
Julie A. Webb (Resident, Mount Vernon Office)
John M. O'Driscoll
Duane A. Deters
Katy C. Fain (Resident, Mount Vernon Office)
Erin E. Wisner
John F. Watson

OF COUNSEL

Jack E. Horsley

Representative Clients: Marathon Oil Company; Freeman United Coal Mining Co.; Continental General Tire, Inc.; R. R. Donnelley & Sons Co.; Kal Kan Foods, Inc.; Illinois Municipal League Risk Management Association; ESIS, Inc.; Kemper Insurance Group.

For full biographical listings, see the Martindale-Hubbell Law Directory

*SPRINGFIELD,** Sangamon Co.

METNICK, CHERRY & FRAZIER (AV)

Second Floor, Myers Building, 1 West Old State Capitol Plaza, P.O. Box 12140, 62791
Telephone: 217-753-4242
Telefax: 217-753-4642
Email: SPRINGLAW@AOL.COM

MEMBERS OF FIRM

Michael B. Metnick
Richard D. Frazier

ASSOCIATE

Scott A. Sabin

For full biographical listings, see the Martindale-Hubbell Law Directory

WEST FRANKFORT, Franklin Co.

SAM C. MITCHELL & ASSOCIATES (AV)

115 1/2 East Main Street, P.O. Box 280, 62896
Telephone: 618-932-2772; 937-2662
Telecopier: 618-932-3456

(See Next Column)

Sam C. Mitchell

ASSOCIATE

Bruce D. Irish

For full biographical listings, see the Martindale-Hubbell Law Directory

INDIANA

*EVANSVILLE,** Vanderburgh Co.

RUDOLPH, FINE, PORTER & JOHNSON LLP (AV)

221 N.W. Fifth Street, Second Floor, P.O. Box 1507, 47706
Telephone: 812-422-9444
Fax: 812-421-7459
URL: http://www.rfpj@rfpj.com

MEMBER OF FIRM

Ross E. Rudolph

ASSOCIATE

Keith A. Sermersheim

Reference: National City Bank of Evansville.

For full biographical listings, see the Martindale-Hubbell Law Directory

*INDIANAPOLIS,** Marion Co.

BUSCHMANN, CARR & SHANKS, PROFESSIONAL CORPORATION (AV)

1020 Market Tower, 10 West Market Street, 46204-2963
Telephone: 317-636-5511
Fax: 317-636-3661
Email: bcs@indy.net *URL:* http://www.buschmanncarr.com

Stephen R. Buschmann
John N. Shanks II

Representative Clients: Archer-Daniels Midland Co.; Ball Corp.; Industrial Valley Title Insurance; Creative Risk Management, Inc.; Deflecto Corporation; Glenfed Mortgage Corp.; Gates McDonald; Merchants National Bank & Trust Company of Muncie; Monumental Life Insurance Co.; National Council on Compensation Insurance.

For full biographical listings, see the Martindale-Hubbell Law Directory

IOWA

*COUNCIL BLUFFS,** Pottawattamie Co.

SHELDON GALLNER, P.C. (AV)

300 West Broadway, Suite 145, P.O. Box 1588, 51503
Telephone: 712-323-0999
Fax: 712-323-0814
URL: http://www.lawyers.com/gallnerlaw

Sheldon M. Gallner
Laura Laubenthal Pattermann
Eric C. Hanson

For full biographical listings, see the Martindale-Hubbell Law Directory

*DES MOINES,** Polk Co.

FINLEY, ALT, SMITH, SCHARNBERG, CRAIG, HILMES & GAFFNEY, P.C. (AV)

604 Locust Street, Fourth Floor Equitable Building, 50309
Telephone: 515-288-0145
Telecopier: 515-288-2724

V. Glenn Goodwin, Jr.

Representative Clients: ALAS; American Society of Composers, Authors and Publishers; Equitable Life Assurance Society of the U.S.; Federated Insurance Co.; Meredith Corp.
Iowa Attorneys for: Midwest Medical Insurance Co.
District Attorneys for: Norfolk & Southern Railroad; Soo Line Railroad Company.

For Complete List of Firm Personnel, See General Section

For full biographical listings, see the Martindale-Hubbell Law Directory

HANSEN, MCCLINTOCK & RILEY (AV)

Eighth Floor - Fleming Building, 218 Sixth Avenue, 50309
Telephone: 515-244-2141
Fax: 515-244-2931
Email: hmrlaw@aol.com

(See Next Column)

HANSEN, MCCLINTOCK & RILEY, *Des Moines—Continued*

MEMBERS OF FIRM

Haemer Wheatcraft (1904-1983) Chester C. Woodburn, III
J. Rudolph Hansen (1904-1995) William D. Scherle
John A. McClintock David L. Brown
Ronald A. Riley John E. Swanson

ASSOCIATES

James M. Ballard Aaron T. Oliver

Representative Clients: The St. Paul Companies; Bituminous Insurance Companies; Northwestern National Insurance Co.; The Travelers Insurance Companies; United States Aviation Insurance Group; American International Companies; Iowa Credit Union League; The McAninch Corp.; R. J. Reynolds Tobacco Co.; Brown Bros., Inc. Electrical Contractors.

For full biographical listings, see the Martindale-Hubbell Law Directory

LAW OFFICES OF HOFFMANN & MCCONKEY, P.L.C. (AV)

3708 75th Street, 50322
Telephone: 515-270-8899
Fax: 515-270-0115
Email: h&m@hoffman-mcconkey.com *URL:* http://www.iowaworkcomp.com

Michael R. Hoffmann Nathan R. McConkey

For full biographical listings, see the Martindale-Hubbell Law Directory

HUBER, BOOK, CORTESE, HAPPE & BROWN, P.L.C. (AV)

317 Sixth Avenue, Suite 200, 50309-4127
Telephone: 515-243-4148
Fax: 515-243-5481
Email: huber@desmoineslaw.com

MEMBERS OF FIRM

James C. Huber Joseph A. Happe
Richard G. Book Terrence D. Brown
Joseph S. Cortese II Patrick D. Smith

ASSOCIATES

Deborah M. Stein Jeffrey W. Lanz

Representative Clients: Atlantic Mutual Cos.; CNA Insurance Cos.; Fireman's Fund American Insurance Companies; Great West Casualty Co.; Liberty Mutual Insurance Co.; Maryland Insurance Group; Prudential Property and Casualty Insurance Co.; USF&G Company.
Reference: Bank of America.

For full biographical listings, see the Martindale-Hubbell Law Directory

PATTERSON, LORENTZEN, DUFFIELD, TIMMONS, IRISH, BECKER & ORDWAY, L.L.P. (AV)

729 Insurance Exchange Building, 50309
Telephone: 515-283-2147
Fax: 515-283-1002
Email: mail@pattersonfirm.com *URL:* http://www.pattersonfirm.com

MEMBERS OF FIRM

G. O. Patterson (1914-1982) Jeffrey A. Boehlert
James A. Lorentzen (Retired) Douglas A. Haag
Theodore T. Duffield Charles E. Cutler
William E. Timmons (Retired) Michael D. Huppert
Roy M. Irish Martin C. Sprock
F. H. Becker (Retired) William A. Wickett
Gary D. Ordway Frederick M. Haskins
Robin L. Hermann Jeffrey A. Baker
Harry Perkins, III Janice M. Herfkens
Michael F. Lacey, Jr. Coreen K. Bezdicek
Gregory J. Wilson Patrick V. Waldron

ASSOCIATE

Michael S. Jones

General Counsel for: Iowa Insurance Institute.
Representative Clients: Allied Mutual Insurance Company; CNA Insurance Company; Chubb Insurance Group; Continental Western Insurance Co.; Farmers Insurance Group; Farmland Insurance Company; Grinnell Mutual Reinsurance Company; Hawkeye Security Insurance Company; Iowa Insurance Institute, St. Paul Fire & Marine Insurance Company.

For full biographical listings, see the Martindale-Hubbell Law Directory

PEDDICORD, WHARTON, THUNE AND SPENCER, A PROFESSIONAL CORPORATION (AV)

700 Des Moines Building, 405 Sixth Avenue, P.O. Box 9130, 50306-9130
Telephone: 515-243-2100
Fax: 515-243-2132
1-800-383-2100

Paul C. Thune Lee P. Hook
Stephen W. Spencer Joseph M. Barron
Timothy W. Wegman

(See Next Column)

Michael S. Roling Steven T. Durick

For full biographical listings, see the Martindale-Hubbell Law Directory

KEOKUK, Lee Co.

LAW OFFICES OF JAMES P. HOFFMAN (AV)

Middle Road, P.O. Box 1087, 52632-1087
Telephone: 319-524-4441
Fax: 319-524-1638

For full biographical listings, see the Martindale-Hubbell Law Directory

*SIOUX CITY,** Woodbury Co.

HEIDMAN, REDMOND, FREDREGILL, PATTERSON, PLAZA & DYKSTRA, L.L.P. (AV)

A Registered Limited Liability Partnership including Professional Corporations
701 Pierce Street, Suite 200, P.O. Box 3086, 51102
Telephone: 712-255-8838
Fax: 712-258-6714
Email: lawyers@pionet.net

MEMBERS OF FIRM

Marvin F. Heidman Gregg E. Williams
James W. Redmond Cynthia C. Moser
Alan E. Fredregill (P.C.) Judith A. Higgs
Charles T. Patterson John C. Gray
Thomas M. Plaza Daniel B. Shuck
Daniel D. Dykstra Rita C. Grimm
Lance D. Ehmcke Edward C."Ted" Poulsen
Margaret M. Prahl Patrick L. Sealey

ASSOCIATES

Jeff W. Wright Kathleen M. Deegan
Sarah J. Kuehl (Not admitted in IA)

OF COUNSEL

John W. Gleysteen (Retired) Jacob C. Gleysteen (1883-1943)
Robert R. Eidsmoe (Retired) H. Clifford Harper (1891-1959)

Representative Clients: Mercy Medical Center; Allied Insurance Group; Irving F. Jensen, Co.; Terra International, Inc.; P.I.C. International Group, P.L.C.; Grinnell Mutual Reinsurance Co.; Travelers Insurance Co.; United Fire & Casualty; Kemper Insurance Group; American Family Insurance.

For full biographical listings, see the Martindale-Hubbell Law Directory

MAYNE & MAYNE (AV)

400 Pioneer Bank Building, 701 Pierce Street, P.O. Box 5049, 51102-5049
Telephone: 712-252-3220
Fax: 712-252-1535
Email: maynelaw@aol.com

MEMBER OF FIRM

Robert J. Pierson

Representative Clients: American Telephone & Telegraph Co.; Amoco Oil Company; Central United Life Insurance Company; Century 21-Marketplace; Credit Bureau of Sioux City; Ford Motor Credit Company; Intensive Medical Services of Siouxland, P.C.; Metz Baking Company; Shell Chemical Company; U.S. West Communications Company.

For full biographical listings, see the Martindale-Hubbell Law Directory

SMITH & MCELWAIN (AV)

505 Fifth, Suite 530, P.O. Box 1194, 51102
Telephone: 712-255-8094
Fax: 712-255-3825
Email: smitmcel@aol.com

MEMBERS OF FIRM

MacDonald Smith Dennis M. McElwain
Harry H. Smith (1916-1999)

Representative Clients: Iowa Federation of Labor; Iowa State Building & Construction Trades Council; Bakers' Pension Fund.
Reference: Norwest Bank, N.A.

For full biographical listings, see the Martindale-Hubbell Law Directory

WEST DES MOINES, Polk Co.

LAMARCA & LANDRY, P.C. (AV)

1300 50th Street, 50266
Telephone: 515-225-2600
Fax: 515-225-8581
Islamorada, Florida Office: 202 Biscayne Boulevard, 33036.
Telephone: 305-664-8527.

George A. LaMarca Gregory W. Landry

Gary G. Mattson Justin E. LaVan

(See Next Column)

LAMARCA & LANDRY P.C.—*Continued*

OF COUNSEL

Martin R. Anderson
Samuel S. Duffey

For full biographical listings, see the Martindale-Hubbell Law Directory

KANSAS

*HUTCHINSON,** Reno Co.

GILLILAND & HAYES, P.A. A PROFESSIONAL ASSOCIATION (AV)

20 West 2nd Avenue, 2nd Floor, P.O. Box 2977, 67504-2977
Telephone: 316-662-0537
Facsimile: 316-669-9426
URL: http://www.gillilandhayes.com
Wichita, Kansas Office: The Orpheum Centre, Suite 300, 200 North Broadway, P.O. Box 49406.
Telephone: 316-262-2266.
Facsimile: 316-263-2202.
Kansas City, Missouri Office: 12th Floor, 3100 Broadway.
Telephone: 816-753-3100.
Facsimile: 816-753-2271.

Robert J. Gilliland
John F. Hayes
James R. Gilliland
John S. Schmidt
Bruce B. Waugh (Not admitted in KS; Resident, Kansas City, Missouri Office)
Michael R. O'Neal
Bradley D. Dillon
Gerald L. Green
David N. Zimmerman (Not admitted in KS; Resident, Kansas City, Missouri Office)
Scott J. Mann
Carol Z. Smith (Resident, Kansas City, Missouri Office)
Kathleen A. Hardee (Resident, Kansas City, Missouri Office)
Kendall R. Cunningham (Resident, Wichita Office)
Mark R. Maloney (Resident, Wichita Office)

Thomas A. Dower
Tracy Applegate Cole
Laura A. Hederstedt
Terri Roberts Munsell (Resident, Kansas City, Missouri Office)
Lisa M. Ward
Kimberly Breda Bushek (Resident, Kansas City, Missouri Office)
E. Thomas Pyle, III
Tara L. Bragg

OF COUNSEL

Robert P. Reams (Not admitted in KS; Resident, Kansas City, Missouri Office)

Representative Clients: City of Hutchinson; CGU Hawkeye Securities; Collins Industries; Columbia Insurance Company; Dillon Companies; Firemen's Fund Insurance; Jackson Ice Cream; Phico; Riverside Hospital; Hutchinson Hospital Corp.

For full biographical listings, see the Martindale-Hubbell Law Directory

MISSION, Johnson Co.

MARK & BURKHEAD (AV)

6700 Squibb, Suite 103, 66202
Telephone: 913-677-1010
Fax: 913-677-3780

MEMBERS OF FIRM

Keith L. Mark
Leah Brown Burkhead

For full biographical listings, see the Martindale-Hubbell Law Directory

*TOPEKA,** Shawnee Co.

FISHER, PATTERSON, SAYLER & SMITH, L.L.P. (AV)

3550 S.W. 5th Street, P.O. Box 949, 66601
Telephone: 785-232-7761
Fax: 785-232-6604
Email: fpss@cjnetworks.com
Overland Park, Kansas Office: 11050 Roe Avenue, Suite 210, 66211.
Telephone: 913-339-6757.
Fax: 913-339-6187.

MEMBERS OF FIRM

Donald Patterson
Edwin Dudley Smith (Resident, Overland Park Office)
Larry G. Pepperdine
James P. Nordstrom
Justice B. King
J. Steven Pigg
Steve R. Fabert
Ronald J. Laskowski
Michael K. Seck (Resident, Overland Park Office)
David P. Madden (Resident, Overland Park Office)
Steven K. Johnson
Kristine A. Larscheid

(See Next Column)

ASSOCIATES

Billy E. Newman
David R. Cooper
Kelly A. Feyh (Resident, Overland Park Office)
Jennifer R. Rose (Resident, Overland Park Office)

OF COUNSEL

David H. Fisher

RETIRED

Charles Keith Sayler (Retired)

Representative Clients: Gage Shopping Center, Inc.; Fireman's Fund-American Insurance Cos.; United States Fidelity and Guaranty Co.; The Procter & Gamble Company; Commercial Union Insurance Companies; National Casualty; The Hartford; Berkshire Hathaway Companies.

For full biographical listings, see the Martindale-Hubbell Law Directory

KENTUCKY

*BOWLING GREEN,** Warren Co.

HARNED, BACHERT & DENTON (AV)

324 East 10th Avenue, P.O. Box 1270, 42102-1270
Telephone: 502-782-3938
Telecopier: 502-781-4737

MEMBER OF FIRM

Norman E. Harned

ASSOCIATE

Jefferson V. Layson, III

For full biographical listings, see the Martindale-Hubbell Law Directory

KERRICK, GRISE & STIVERS (AV)

1025 State Street, P.O. Box 9547, 42102-9547
Telephone: 502-782-8160
Fax: 502-782-5856
Email: kgs@kgslaw.com
Elizabethtown, Kentucky Office: 2935 Dolphin Drive, Suite 102.
Telephone: 502-769-5788.
Fax: 502-737-9285.

MEMBERS OF FIRM

Thomas N. Kerrick
John R. Grise
Gregory N. Stivers
H. Brent Brennenstuhl
Laura M. Hagan

ASSOCIATES

Karl N. Crandall
Shawn Rosso Alcott
Jason B. Bell

OF COUNSEL

Jeffrey R. O'Grody

LEGAL SUPPORT PERSONNEL

Patricia Logsdon
Laura Lockhart Lico
Allison Lusk

Representative Clients: Dollar General Corp.; Columbia Greenview Regional Hospital; Hospital Corporation of America; Hardin Memorial Hospital; FirStar Bank; TKR Cable.

For full biographical listings, see the Martindale-Hubbell Law Directory

COVINGTON, Kenton Co.

WARE, BRYSON, WEST & KUMMER (AV)

157 Barnwood Drive, 41017
Telephone: 606-341-0255
Fax: 606-341-1876

MEMBERS OF FIRM

Rodney S. Bryson
Larry C. West
John R. Kummer
Mark W. Howard
Greg D. Voss
Robert B. Cetrulo
Susanne M. Cetrulo
David W. Martin

ASSOCIATE

James M. West
Orie S. Ware (1882-1974)
William O. Ware (1908-1961)
James C. Ware (1913-1991)

Attorneys For: First National Bank of Northern Ky.; State Farm Insurance Co.; Reliance Insurance Group; Maryland Casualty Insurance Co.; Kemper Insurance Co.; Shelby Mutual Insurance Co.; Cincinnati Insurance Co.; Travelers/Aetna Group; Kentucky Employers Mutual Insurance; Gallagher Bassett Services.

For full biographical listings, see the Martindale-Hubbell Law Directory

*LEXINGTON,** Fayette Co.

BOEHL STOPHER & GRAVES (AV)

444 West Second Street, 40508
Telephone: 606-252-6721
FAX: 606-253-1445
Louisville, Kentucky Office: Suite 2300, Aegon Center, 400 West Market Street.
Telephone: 502-589-5980.
Fax: 502-561-9400.
Paducah, Kentucky Office: Suite 340 Executive Inn Riverfront, One Executive Boulevard.
Telephone: 270-442-4369.
Fax: 270-442-4689.
Prestonsburg, Kentucky Office: 105 West Court Street.
Telephone: 606-886-8004.
Fax: 606-886-9579.
New Albany, Indiana Office: Elsby East, Suite 204, 400 Pearl Street.
Telephone: 812-948-5053.
Fax: 812-948-9233.

RESIDENT PARTNERS

W. T. Adkins
Nolan Carter, Jr.
Ronald L. Green
Kim Martin Wilkie
Guillermo A. Carlos
James B. Cooper
Steven R. Armstrong

RESIDENT ASSOCIATES

Brennen C. Ragone
William E. Brown, II
Ronald E. Thornsberry

Counsel For: Amerisure Companies; Baptist Healthcare System; CIGNA Companies; CNA Insurance Companies; Ford Motor Co.; Kemper National Insurance Group; Levi Strauss & Co.; Monroe County Insurance Company; Old Republic Insurance; Peabody Coal Company.

For full biographical listings, see the Martindale-Hubbell Law Directory

FERRERI, FOGLE & PICKLESIMER (AV)

500 Quality Place, 300 East Main Street, 40507
Telephone: 606-253-4700
Telefax: 606-253-4702
Email: fflex@pop.net
Louisville, Kentucky Office: 203 Speed Building, 333 Guthrie Green.
Telephone: 502-582-1381.
Telefax: 502-581-9887.

MEMBERS OF FIRM

Thomas L. Ferreri
Max D. Picklesimer
Joel W. Aubrey
Sherri P. Brown

ASSOCIATES

Hugh Brett Stonecipher
Stephanie Dawn Ross
Gary A. Stephens

Representative Clients: American International Group; Chubb Group of Insurance Companies; Commercial General Union Insurance Companies; GAB Robins, Inc.; Gallagher Bassett Services; Indiana Insurance Company; Kentucky Employers' Mutual Insurance; Liberty Mutual Group; Louisville Gas & Electric Company; United Parcel Service.

For full biographical listings, see the Martindale-Hubbell Law Directory

LYNN, FULKERSON, NICHOLS AND KINKEL, PLLC (AV)

267 West Short Street, 40507
Telephone: 606-253-0523
Telefax: 606-254-2098
Email: mail@LFNK.com

MEMBER OF FIRM

Calvin R. Fulkerson

ASSOCIATE

Jo Alice Van Nagell

OF COUNSEL

Gordon W. Moss

Representative Clients: Argonaut Insurance Co.; The Northern Group/-Laurier Indemnity Co.; Kemper National Insurance Group.

For full biographical listings, see the Martindale-Hubbell Law Directory

VIMONT & WILLS PLLC (AV)

Suite 300, 155 East Main Street, 40507-1317
Telephone: 606-252-2202
Telecopier: 606-259-2927
Email: vimont@lex.infi.net

Timothy C. Wills

Dawn S. Logsdon

For full biographical listings, see the Martindale-Hubbell Law Directory

*LONDON,** Laurel Co.

HAMM, MILBY & RIDINGS (AV)

120 North Main Street, 40741
Telephone: 606-864-4126
Fax: 606-878-8144
Email: hmrlaw@kih.net

MEMBERS OF FIRM

Robert L. Milby
Marcia Milby Ridings

James A. Ridings
Gregory A. Lay
R. Aaron Hostettler

Representative Clients: Acceleration National; Aetna Life & Casualty Ins. Co.; All Risk Claims Service, Inc.; Allstate Insurance Co.; Alexis; American Automobile Mutual Ins.; American Bankers; American Hardware Ins. Co.

For full biographical listings, see the Martindale-Hubbell Law Directory

*LOUISVILLE,** Jefferson Co.

BOEHL STOPHER & GRAVES (AV)

Suite 2300 Aegon Center, 400 West Market Street, 40202-3354
Telephone: 502-589-5980
FAX: 502-561-9400
Lexington, Kentucky Office: 444 West Second Street.
Telephone: 606-252-6721.
Fax: 606-253-1445.
Paducah, Kentucky Office: Suite 340 Executive Inn Riverfront, One Executive Boulevard.
Telephone: 270-442-4369.
Fax: 270-442-4689.
Prestonsburg, Kentucky Office: 105 West Court Street.
Telephone: 606-886-8004.
Fax: 606-886-9579.
New Albany, Indiana Office: Elsby East, Suite 204, 400 Pearl Street.
Telephone: 812-948-5053.
Fax: 812-948-9233.

MEMBERS OF FIRM

Larry L. Johnson
Wesley G. Gatlin
Philip J. Reverman, Jr.
Peter J. Glauber
Walter E. Harding
Douglas A. U'Sellis

ASSOCIATES

Mary Ann Kiwala
William J. Crowe
Denise Basford Askin
George T. T. Kitchen III

Counsel For: Amerisure Companies; Baptist Healthcare System; CIGNA Companies; CNA Insurance Companies; Ford Motor Co.; Kemper National Insurance Group; Levi Strauss & Co.; Monroe County Insurance Company; Old Republic Insurance; Peabody Coal Company.

For Complete List of Firm Personnel, See General Section

For full biographical listings, see the Martindale-Hubbell Law Directory

FERRERI, FOGLE & PICKLESIMER (AV)

203 Speed Building, 333 Guthrie Green, 40202
Telephone: 502-582-1381
Telefax: 502-581-9887
Email: fflou@aye.net
Lexington, Kentucky Office: 500 Quality Place, 300 East Main Street.
Telephone: 606-253-4700.
Telefax: 606-253-4702.

MEMBERS OF FIRM

Thomas L. Ferreri
James G. Fogle
Max D. Picklesimer
Phillipe W. Rich
Walter C. Jobson
Brian Timothy Gannon

ASSOCIATES

J. D. Raine, Jr.
Allan Weiss

OF COUNSEL

William A. Miller
Glenn L. Schilling

Representative Clients: American International Group; Chubb Group of Insurance Companies; Commercial General Union Insurance Companies; GAB Robins, Inc.; Gallagher Bassett Services; Indiana Insurance Company; Kentucky Employers' Mutual Insurance; Liberty Mutual Group; Louisville Gas & Electric Company; United Parcel Service.

For full biographical listings, see the Martindale-Hubbell Law Directory

O'BRYAN, BROWN & TONER (AV)

455 South Fourth Avenue, Suite 1500, Starks Building, 40202
Telephone: 502-585-4700
Fax: 502-585-4703
Email: mail@obtlaw.com

MEMBERS OF FIRM

Donald K. Brown, Jr.
Christopher P. O'Bryan
Gerald R. Toner
John L. Dotson
Emily A. Faith
James P. Grohmann
David Scott Strite

(See Next Column)

O'BRYAN, BROWN & TONER—*Continued*

ASSOCIATES

Andrew N. Clooney
Tracy Sullivan Prewitt
Beth H. McMasters
Cathleen Charters Palmer
Clay Edwards
Peter D. Palmer
Charles Wayne Miller

OF COUNSEL

Joseph C. O'Bryan

For full biographical listings, see the Martindale-Hubbell Law Directory

*PAINTSVILLE,** Johnson Co.

WELLS, PORTER, SCHMITT & JONES (AV)

327 Main Street, 41240
Telephone: 606-789-3747; 789-3749; 789-3775
Fax: 606-789-3790
URL: http://www.wpsj.com

MEMBER OF FIRM

John V. Porter, Jr.

ASSOCIATE

Johnny L. Griffith

Representative Clients: Wausau; Travelers; Fireman's Fund; Ladegast & Heffner; CNA.

For Complete List of Firm Personnel, See General Section

For full biographical listings, see the Martindale-Hubbell Law Directory

LOUISIANA

*BATON ROUGE,** East Baton Rouge Parish

SHOCKEY & ZIOBER, A PROFESSIONAL LAW CORPORATION (AV)

5551 Corporate Boulevard, Suite 3-A, P.O. Box 80286, 70898-0286
Telephone: 225-929-8929
Telecopier: 225-928-7694

William C. Shockey

Douglas J. Cochran

For full biographical listings, see the Martindale-Hubbell Law Directory

*HOUMA,** Terrebonne Parish

HENDERSON, HANEMANN & MORRIS, A PROFESSIONAL LAW CORPORATION (AV)

300 Lafayette Street, 70360
Telephone: 504-868-2081
New Orleans: 504-581-1434
Telecopier: 504-868-0080

Philip E. Henderson
Charles Hanemann
Robert L. Morris (1940-1986)
J. Mark Graham
Joseph A. Reilly, Jr.
Barry J. Boudreaux

Emilie Melancon Daye

Representative Clients: Alliance Insurance Company; Applied Hydraulic Systems, Inc.; Falcon Drilling Company, Inc.; Lafayette Insurance Company; Liverpool and London Steamship Protection and Indemnity Association Limited; Louisiana Medical Mutual Insurance Company; The Steamship Mutual Underwriter Association Limited; Gray & Co., Inc.; Union Oil Company of California; Minnesota Mining and Manufacturing Co.

For full biographical listings, see the Martindale-Hubbell Law Directory

*NEW ORLEANS,** Orleans Parish

BEST KOEPPEL, A PROFESSIONAL LAW CORPORATION (AV)

LL & E Tower, 909 Poydras Street Suite 2200, 70112
Telephone: 504-593-2400
Telecopier: 504-593-2401
Email: bstkpplesq@aol.com
Houston, Texas Office: 1900 West Loop South, Suite 300, 77027.
Telephone: 713-964-4072.
Telecopier: 713-963-2503.

Laurence E. Best
Peter S. Koeppel
R. Jeffrey Bridger
James H. Daigle, Jr.
M. Davis Ready
Suzanne M. Risey

(See Next Column)

LEGAL SUPPORT PERSONNEL

PARALEGAL

Debora N. Dufrene

Representative Clients: Lexington Insurance Co.; Rowan Companies, Inc.; Rowandrill, Inc.; Rowan International, Inc.; Atlantic Maritime Services, Inc.; Rowan Drilling (U.K.), Ltd.; Hartford Insurance Co.; Trinity Marine Group; Elevating Boats, Inc.; CITGO Petroleum Corp.

For full biographical listings, see the Martindale-Hubbell Law Directory

BUCKLEY & HAYES, L.L.P. (AV)

A Partnership including a Professional Corporation
1555 Poydras Street Suite 1700, 70112
Telephone: 504-523-5100
Fax: 504-523-5698
Covington, Louisiana Office: 2301 North HIghway 190, Suite 3, 70433.
Telephone: 504-871-7005.
Fax: 504-871-7051.

MEMBERS OF FIRM

Lloyd W. Hayes
E. Ross Buckley, Jr., (A Professional Law Corp.)
Marianne S. Pensa
William H. Voigt

ASSOCIATES

Michele D. Ahlers
Ernest Philip Legier, Jr.
Elton A. Foster

OF COUNSEL

Harold A. Thomas

For full biographical listings, see the Martindale-Hubbell Law Directory

JOHNSON, JOHNSON, BARRIOS & YACOUBIAN, A PROFESSIONAL LAW CORPORATION (AV)

One Shell Square, 701 Poydras Street, Suite 4900, 70139-7701
Telephone: 504-528-3001
Facsimile: 504-528-3030
Email: jjbylaw@bellsouth.net

Ronald A. Johnson
Edward S. Johnson
Bettye A. Barrios
Alan J. Yacoubian
Salvador J. Pusateri
Rene S. Paysse, Jr.

Cindy T. Matherne
Lance E. Harwell
Salvatore A. Faso, II
Michael W. Mallory
Kevin G. Barreca
Wesley S. Alost
Thomas A. French
T. Gavin Hoppe

Representative Clients: Liberty Mutual Insurance Company; Louisiana Nursing Home Association; Louisiana Restaurant Association; Tulane University.

For full biographical listings, see the Martindale-Hubbell Law Directory

McGLINCHEY STAFFORD (AV)

A Professional Limited Liability Company
643 Magazine Street, 70130-3477
Telephone: 504-586-1200
Fax: 504-596-2800
TDD: (504) 596-2728
Telex: 584327
Cable Address: "MACSTAC"
Mailing Address: P.O. Box 60643, New Orleans, Louisiana, 70160-0643
Email: @mcglinchey.com *URL:* http://www.mcglinchey.com
Dallas, Texas Office: 2777 Stemmons Freeway, Suite 925, 75207-2401.
Telephone: 214-860-9700.
Fax: 214-860-9750.
Houston, Texas Office: 2727 Allen Parkway, Suite 1900, 77019.
Telephone: 713-520-1900.
Fax: 713-520-1025.
Baton Rouge, Louisiana Office: Ninth Floor, One American Place, 70825-0001.
Telephone: 504-383-9000.
Fax: 504-343-3076.
Jackson, Mississippi Office: Suite 1200, SkyTel Centre, 200 South Lamar Street, 39201.
Telephone: 601-960-8400.
Fax: 601-960-8406.
Lake Providence, Louisiana Office: 405 Morgan Street, 71254-2691.
Telephone: 318-559-1200.
Fax: 318-559-0609.
Monroe, Louisiana Office: Dean ONB Tower, 130 Desiard Street, Suite 807, 71201.
Telephone: 318-651-0807.
Fax: 318-651-0809.

MEMBER OF FIRM

Joseph F. Clark, Jr.

For full biographical listings, see the Martindale-Hubbell Law Directory

New Orleans—Continued

MOULEDOUX, BLAND, LEGRAND & BRACKETT, LLC (AV)

Poydras Center, 650 Poydras Street, Suite 2150, 70130
Telephone: 504-595-3000
Fax: 504-522-2121
Email: admin@mblb.com *URL:* http://www.mblb.com

André J. Mouledoux
Alan Guy Brackett
Wilton E. Bland, III
Daniel J. Hoerner
Gerard Joseph Dragna

For full biographical listings, see the Martindale-Hubbell Law Directory

WILSON & BOWLING (AV)

A Partnership including Professional Law Corporations
Suite 2411, Bank One Center, 201 St. Charles Avenue, 70170
Telephone: 504-586-5200
Facsimile: 504-586-5201
Email: wilsbowl@gs.net
Gulfport, Mississippi Office: 715 Markham Building, 2301 14th Street, 39501.
Telephone: 228-575-6202.
Fax: 228-864-6227.

Gordon F. Wilson, Jr., (P.L.C.)
David A. Bowling (P.L.C.)

Jeanne B. Roques
Susannah Ross Cooley
John D. Acomb

For full biographical listings, see the Martindale-Hubbell Law Directory

*SHREVEPORT,** Caddo Parish

MAYER, SMITH & ROBERTS, L.L.P. (AV)

1550 Creswell, 71101
Telephone: 318-222-2135, 222-2268
Fax: 318-222-6420
Email: (Attorney's First Name)@MSRLAW.COM

MEMBERS OF FIRM

Caldwell Roberts
Henry N. Bellamy
Walter O. Hunter, Jr.
John C. Turnage
Mark A. Goodwin
Paul R. Mayer, Jr.
Ben Marshall, Jr.
Steven E. Soileau
Alexander S. Lyons
Deborah Shea Baukman
Kim Purdy Thomas
Caldwell Roberts, Jr.
David Butterfield
Frank K. Carroll
Dalton Roberts Ross

OF COUNSEL

Paul R. Mayer

Representative Clients: CNA Insurance Companies; Liberty Mutual Insurance Company; United States Fidelity and Guaranty Company; Schumpert Medical Center; Travelers Insurance Company; Great American Insurance Company; Insurance Corporation of America; Highlands Insurance Company.

For full biographical listings, see the Martindale-Hubbell Law Directory

SLIDELL, St. Tammany Parish

JAMES R. STRAIN, JR. (AV)

103 Galeria Boulevard, 70458
Telephone: 504-649-3662
Fax: 504-649-2462
Mailing Address: P.O. Box 2590, Slidell, LA, 70459

Representative Clients: Louisiana Medical Mutual Insurance Co.; Louisiana Patients' Compensation Fund; Medical Fitness Centers of America, Inc.; Thirstrup Medical Enterprises, Inc.; Wellness Aerobic & Sports Medicine Clinic; Jefferson Insurance Group; State of Louisiana-Dept. of Transportation and Development; State of Louisiana-Office of Risk Management.

For full biographical listings, see the Martindale-Hubbell Law Directory

MAINE

*BANGOR,** Penobscot Co.

WEATHERBEE, WOODCOCK, BURLOCK & WOODCOCK (AV)

136 Broadway, P.O. Box 1127, 04402-1127
Telephone: 207-942-9900
Telefax: 207-942-6999
Email: info@weathwood.com

MEMBERS OF FIRM

Peter M. Weatherbee
Stephen J. Burlock
John A. Woodcock, Jr.
Timothy C. Woodcock

For full biographical listings, see the Martindale-Hubbell Law Directory

*PORTLAND,** Cumberland Co.

THOMPSON & BOWIE (AV)

Three Canal Plaza, P.O. Box 4630, 04112
Telephone: 207-774-2500
Telecopier: 207-774-3591
Email: law@thompsonbowie.com

MEMBERS OF FIRM

Roy E. Thompson, Jr.
Frank W. DeLong, III
James M. Bowie
Michael E. Saucier
Daniel R. Mawhinney
Mark V. Franco
Rebecca H. Farnum
Edward R. Benjamin, Jr.
Glenn H. Robinson
Cathy S. Roberts
Paul C. Catsos

ASSOCIATES

Elizabeth Knox Peck
Michael R. Bosse
Thomas G. Diebold
Lisa M. Fitzgibbon

For full biographical listings, see the Martindale-Hubbell Law Directory

TROUBH, HEISLER & PIAMPIANO, P.C. (AV)

511 Congress Street, P.O. Box 9711, 04104-5011
Telephone: 207-780-6789
Fax: 207-774-2339
Email: info@thplaw.com

William B. Troubh
Thomas E. Getchell
Edwin A. Heisler
Michael Richards
Robert J. Piampiano
William K. McKinley
Kevin M. Gillis
Daniel F. Gilligan
Michael P. Boyd
Paul S. Bulger
John G. Richardson

Daniel R. Felkel
Ann Brandt
John P. Flynn, III

For full biographical listings, see the Martindale-Hubbell Law Directory

MARYLAND

*BALTIMORE,** (Independent City)

CORNBLATT, BENNETT, PENHALLEGON & ROBERSON, P.A. (AV)

Suite 1800, 201 North Charles Street, 21201
Telephone: 410-752-7600
Fax: 410-752-2110
Email: mail@cbprlaw.com

Theodore B. Cornblatt
John R. Penhallegon
S. Woods Bennett
Patrick A. Roberson
Jeffrey Y. Laynor

J. Michael Harrison
Gary E. Dumer, Jr.

For full biographical listings, see the Martindale-Hubbell Law Directory

GALLAGHER, EVELIUS & JONES, LLP (AV)

Park Charles Suite 400, 218 North Charles Street, 21201
Telephone: 410-727-7702
Facsimile: 410-468-2786
URL: http://www.gejlaw.com

MEMBERS OF FIRM

Francis X. Gallagher (1928-1972)
Leslie B. Speed
C. Edward Jones (1908-1999)
Christopher J. Fritz
John C. Evelius (Retired)
David E. Raderman
Richard O. Berndt
Peter E. Keith
Thomas N. Biddison, Jr.
Nita L. Schultz
Robert R. Kern, Jr.
Michael W. Skojec
Saul E. Gilstein
Kathryn Kelley Hoskins
Thomas B. Lewis
Mark P. Keener
Bonnie Abrams Travieso
Kevin J. Davidson
Stephen A. Goldberg
Eileen M. Lunga
Linda H. Jones
Lori A. Nicolle
Jack C. Tranter
Kenneth S. Gross
Thomas C. Dame

ASSOCIATES

Valarie K. Oulds
Michael J. Henigan
Margaret Stevens Jacks
David W. Kinkopf
Matthew W. Oakey
Paul S. Caiola
Rebecca A. Weaver
Jason W. Gaarder
M. Kirsten Andrews

LEGAL ASSISTANTS

Patricia C. Quayle
Margo Gibson Hughes
Iris T. H. Heath
Jonathan T. Gillis
Connie L. Ennis
Brenda J. Heacock
Margaret Graff
Dwayne L. Rodeheaver

(See Next Column)

GALLAGHER, EVELIUS & JONES LLP—*Continued*

Representative Clients: Roman Catholic Archdiocese of Baltimore; The Shelter Group; Mercy Medical Center, Inc.; Caronia Corporation; Sisco, Inc.

For full biographical listings, see the Martindale-Hubbell Law Directory

LORD & WHIP, A PROFESSIONAL ASSOCIATION (AV)

800 One Center Plaza, 120 West Fayette Street, 21201-3700
Telephone: 410-539-5881
Fax: 410-685-6726
URL: http://www.lordwhip.com

George W. P. Whip (1884-1961)
Robert E. Coughlan, Jr. (1899-1971)
Frederick J. Green, Jr. (1919-1988)
George L. Huber, Jr.
Edward M. Ranier
J. Paul Mullen
Robert C. Erlandson
John J. Boyd
Frank F. Daily
W. John Vernon
Pamela Thomas Broache

OF COUNSEL

Robert P. Schlenger

Michael S. DeBaugh
Michelle J. Abrams
Christopher M. Erwin
Kathleen M. Bustraan
Michael H. Daney
Cynthia M. Dietz
J. Daniel Vorsteg

Representative Clients: Associated Aviation Underwriters; CIGNA; CNA; General Star Management; Government Employees Insurance Companies; Great American Insurance Companies; Harbison-Walker Refactories; Lockheed Martin Corp.; Reliance Insurance Company; Unilever, Inc.

For full biographical listings, see the Martindale-Hubbell Law Directory

ROLLINS, SMALKIN, RICHARDS & MACKIE, L.L.C. (AV)

401 North Charles Street, 21201
Telephone: 410-727-2443
Fax: 410-727-8390
URL: http://www.rsrm.com

MEMBERS OF FIRM

H. Beale Rollins (1898-1985)
Samuel S. Smalkin (1906-1982)
Edward C. Mackie
John F. Linsenmeyer
Thomas C. Gentner
Glenn W. Trimmer
Patrick G. Cullen
James P. O'Meara
Paul G. Donoghue
Ralph E. Wilson III

ASSOCIATES

Kenneth G. Macleay
Donna Lynn Kolakowski-Hollen
Meg Bantley Whiteford
J. James Roos
Jessica R. Di Cicco

OF COUNSEL

Raymond A. Richards (Retired)

LEGAL SUPPORT PERSONNEL

Guy M. Craig

For full biographical listings, see the Martindale-Hubbell Law Directory

*BEL AIR,** Harford Co.

BROWN, BROWN & BROWN, A PROFESSIONAL ASSOCIATION (AV)

200 South Main Street, 21014
Telephone: 410-838-5500
Baltimore: 410-879-2220
Fax: 410-893-0402

A. Freeborn Brown (1915-1998)
T. Carroll Brown
Augustus F. Brown
Albert J. A. Young

Harold Douglas Norton
Christopher R. vanRoden
David E. Carey

Attorneys for: Baltimore Gas & Electric Co.; Chesapeake & Potomac Telephone Co.; Aberdeen Proving Ground Federal Credit Union; First National Bank of Maryland; Bell Atlantic Mobile Systems; First Harbor Securities; Maryland Portable Concrete, Inc.
Approved Counsel for: The Chicago Title Insurance Co. of Maryland, Inc.

For full biographical listings, see the Martindale-Hubbell Law Directory

*ROCKVILLE,** Montgomery Co.

ANDERSON & QUINN (AV)

The Adams Law Center, 25 Wood Lane, 20850
Telephone: 301-762-3303
Fax: 301-762-3776
Email: rscanlon@andersonquinn.com

MEMBERS OF FIRM

Charles C. Collins (1900-1973)
Robert E. Anderson (Retired)
Francis X. Quinn
Donald P. Maiberger
Robert P. Scanlon
John A. Rego
Alice Kelley Scanlon

(See Next Column)

ASSOCIATES

Kerry S. McGeever
Timothy J. Mulreany
Todd P. Maiberger
Jennifer D. Burke
Marc N. Steren

Representative Clients: C & P Telephone; Allstate Insurance Co.; State Farm Mutual Automobile Insurance Co.; Liberty Mutual Insurance Co.; American International Adjustment Co.; Marriott Corp.

For full biographical listings, see the Martindale-Hubbell Law Directory

MASSACHUSETTS

*BOSTON,** Suffolk Co.

HINCKLEY, ALLEN & SNYDER LLP (AV)

28 State Street, 30th Floor, 02109-1775
Telephone: 617-345-9000
Email: firm@haslaw.com *URL:* http://www.haslaw.com
Providence, Rhode Island Office: 1500 Fleet Center.
Telephone: 401-274-2000.
Fax: 401-277-9600. URL: http://www.hawlaw.com.

MEMBERS OF FIRM

Paula K. Andrews
David D. Barricelli (Not admitted in MA)
Jonathan Bell
Paul Bork
Stephen J. Carlotti (Not admitted in MA)
Joseph P. Curran (Not admitted in MA)
Michael P. DeFanti
Eric F. Eisenberg
Malcolm Farmer, III
Margaret D. Farrell (Not admitted in MA)
Pasco Gasbarro Jr.
Hugh J. Gorman, III
William R. Grimm
Richard L. E. Jocelyn (Not admitted in MA)
Joel Lewin
Sandra Matrone Mack (Not admitted in MA)
Matthew T. Marcello, III (Not admitted in MA)
Frederick P. McClure
Elizabeth Murdock Myers
Paul F. O'Donnell, III
H. Peter Olsen (Not admitted in MA)
Julianne Palumbo
John J. Pendergast, III (Not admitted in MA)
Gerald J. Petros
James O. Reavis
Jeremy Ritzenberg
Ralph J. Rivkind
Charles E. Schaub, Jr.
Douglas F. Seaver
Herman Snyder
David R. Sullivan
Robert F. Sylvia
Howard E. Walker (Not admitted in MA)
Richard D. Wayne

ASSOCIATES

Jessica M. Bettencourt (Not admitted in MA)
Mark Bianchi
Alexandra K. Callam
Jane E. Cohen
Andrew D. Cummings
June E. Daniel (Not admitted in MA)
Kelley Jordan-Price
Catherine S. Kim
Christopher W. Morog
Elena B. Olson
Joseph D. Whelan (Not admitted in MA)

OF COUNSEL

Willard Krasnow
Bentley Tobin
Joachim A. Weissfeld (Not admitted in MA)

For Complete List of Firm Personnel, See General Section

For full biographical listings, see the Martindale-Hubbell Law Directory

FRAMINGHAM, Middlesex Co.

MORTON J. SHUMAN (AV)

The Trolley Square Building, 855 Worcester Road (Route 9 West), 01701-5248
Telephone: 508-879-4040
Fax: 508-879-4080
Boston Telephone: 617-422-0012
Email: msh7832495@aol.com *URL:* http://www.lawyers.com/mortonjshuman

For full biographical listings, see the Martindale-Hubbell Law Directory

SOMERSET, Bristol Co.

SABRA & ASPDEN, PROFESSIONAL ASSOCIATION (AV)

1026 County Street, 02726
Telephone: 508-674-0890
Fax: 508-679-5998
Email: sabra@efortress.com

Steven P. Sabra
Matthew Mark Aspden

For full biographical listings, see the Martindale-Hubbell Law Directory

*SPRINGFIELD,** Hampden Co.

Robinson Donovan Madden & Barry, P.C. (AV)
Suite 1600, Tower Square, 1500 Main Street, 01115-5609
Telephone: 413-732-2301
Fax 413-785-4658
Email: service@robinson-donovan.com *URL:* http://www.robinson-donovan.com

Homans Robinson (1894-1973) Milton J. Donovan (1906-1995)
Lawrence M. Sinclair (1942-1986)

RETIRED

John H. Madden, Jr. Edward J. Barry
Richard S. Milstein

OF COUNSEL

Victor Rosenberg

SENIOR COUNSEL

Jonathan P. Rice

Gordon H. Wentworth
James H. Tourtelotte
Ronald C. Kidd
Jeffrey W. Roberts
Jeffrey L. McCormick
James F. Martin
Robert P. Cunningham
John C. Sikorski
Nancy Frankel Pelletier
Paul S. Weinberg
Frederica H. McCarthy
Matthew J. King
Neva Kaufman Rohan
Douglas F. Boyd
James K. Bodurtha
Keith A. Minoff
Patricia M. Rapinchuk
Kimberly Davis Crear

E. Paul Amata
Lisa A. Bongiovi (Not admitted in MA)
Edward J. Carroll, III
James D. Chadwell
John E. Garber
Patrick J. Markey
Carla W. Newton
Betsy Macmillan Stevens

Representative Clients: BankBoston, N.A.; United Cooperative Bank; Fleet National Bank; CNA; Commercial Union Insurance Co.; Hanover Insurance Group.

For full biographical listings, see the Martindale-Hubbell Law Directory

*WORCESTER,** Worcester Co.

Milton, Laurence & Dixon (AV)
100 Front Street, Suite 1020, 01608-1402
Telephone: 508-791-6386
Fax: 508-799-4879
Email: mld@chamber.worcester.ma.us

MEMBERS OF FIRM

Stanley B. Milton (1924-1992)
Robert C. Milton (1932-1977)
Gerard R. Laurence
Charles W. Dixon
Paul P. O'Connor
Karen A. Loughlin
Daniel M. Wrenn
Karyn E. Polito

OF COUNSEL

John G. Preston Judy Eldredge

Reference: Shawmut, Worcester County Bank, N.A.

For full biographical listings, see the Martindale-Hubbell Law Directory

MICHIGAN

*ANN ARBOR,** Washtenaw Co.

Braun Kendrick Finkbeiner PLC (AV)
First National Building, 210 S. Main, Suite 700, 48104
Telephone: 313-995-4100
Telecopier: 313-995-4798
Email: ALBFIE@BKF-LAW.COM *URL:* http://www.bkf-law.com
Bay City, Michigan Office: 201 Phoenix Building, P.O. Box 2039.
Telephone: 517-895-8505.
Telecopier: 517-895-8437.
Saginaw, Michigan Office: 101 N. Washington, Suite 812.
Telephone: 517-753-3461.
Telecopier: 517-753-3951.
Saginaw Township, Michigan Office: 5800 Gratiot Road, Suite 107, P.O. Box 5169.
Telephone: 517-799-8692.
Fax: 517-799-4666.
Mt. Pleasant, Michigan Office: 805 North Brown.
Telephone: 517-775-7404.
Telecopier: 517-775-3764.

Barry M. Levine

Representative Client: General Motors Corporation.

(See Next Column)

For Complete List of Firm Personnel, See General Section

For full biographical listings, see the Martindale-Hubbell Law Directory

*BAY CITY,** Bay Co.

Braun Kendrick Finkbeiner PLC (AV)
201 Phoenix Building, P.O. Box 2039, 48708
Telephone: 517-895-8505
Telecopier: 517-895-8437
Email: ALBFIE@BKF-LAW.COM *URL:* http://www.bkf-law.com
Saginaw, Michigan Office: 101 N. Washington, Suite 812. 8th Floor Second National Bank Building.
Telephone: 517-753-3461.
Telecopier: 517-753-3951.
Saginaw Township, Michigan Office: 5800 Gratiot Road, Suite 107, P.O. Box 5169.
Telephone: 517-799-8692.
Fax: 517-799-4666.
Ann Arbor, Michigan Office: First National Building. 201 S. Main, Suite 700.
Telephone: 313-995-4100.
Telecopier: 313-995-4798.
Mt. Pleasant, Michigan Office: 805 North Brown.
Telephone: 517-775-7404.
Telecopier: 517-775-3764.

Frank M. Quinn Gregory E. Meter
Jeffrey C. Wilson

Michael E. Wooley

Representative Clients: Bay Health Systems; Catholic Federal Credit Union; City of Saginaw; City of Vassar; City of Zilwaukee; Corporate Service; Cox Cable.

For Complete List of Firm Personnel, See General Section

For full biographical listings, see the Martindale-Hubbell Law Directory

BIRMINGHAM, Oakland Co.

Lacey & Jones, LLP (AV)
600 South Adams Road, Suite 300, 48009-6827
Telephone: 248-433-1414
Fax: 248-433-1241
URL: http://www.laceyjones.com
Ann Arbor, Michigan Office: Suite 525, 220 East Huron, 48104.
Telephone: 734-761-8358.
Fax: 734-761-3134.
Detroit, Michigan Office: Suite 3250, Penobscot Building, 645 Griswold, 48226.
Telephone: 313-961-6474.
Fax: 313-961-5688.
Grand Rapids, Michigan Office: Suite 430, Ledyard Building, 125 Ottawa Avenue, N.W., 49503.
Telephone: 616-776-3641.
Fax: 616-776-3516.
Jackson, Michigan Office: 740 West Michigan Avenue, 49201.
Telephone: 517-782-2000.
Fax: 517-782-3917.

Ralph B. Lacey (1885-1966)
William J. Jones (1908-1991)
Robert B. Lacey (1912-1976)
John A. Hilgendorf (Retired)
Theodore A. Lughezzani (Retired)
Steve N. Yardley (Retired)

MEMBERS OF FIRM

Brian S. Ahearn (Resident, Detroit)
Kathleen McNichol Behn
Larry P. Beidelman
Mary F. Clinton (Resident, Ann Arbor)
William A. Day
David J. Duthie (Resident, Grand Rapids)
T. F. Felker, Jr.
John Hayes
Charles J. Hurbis (Resident, Ann Arbor)
Lawrence G. Kozaruk
Richard N. Lovernick (Resident, Ann Arbor)
Charles E. Mann
Gerald M. Marcinkoski
J. Patrick O'Neill
Sean J. Powers
Michael T. Reinholm
Bruce C. Roberts
Peter M. Roggenbaum
Thomas J. Sullivan (Resident, Jackson)
Dennis E. Zacharski

Carrie G. Barrett
John C. Dickinson
Dawn M. Drobnich
Timothy D. Finegan
Timothy M. McAree (Resident, Grand Rapids)
D. Michael McCann
Dallas G. Moon
Robert H. Orlowski, Jr.
Johnnie B. Rambus
Kenneth S. Wilson

OF COUNSEL

Robert L. Beardslee
Georgette E. David (Resident, Ann Arbor)
Robert G. Lewandowski
William G. Sinn

(See Next Column)

LACEY & JONES LLP—*Continued*

Representative Clients: Alexsis, Inc.; Ameritech; Chrysler Corporation; CIGNA; Liberty Mutual Insurance Company; Meijer, Inc.; Metropolitan Prop. & Casualty; Michigan Hospital Association; Travelers Insurance Company; University of Michigan.

For full biographical listings, see the Martindale-Hubbell Law Directory

BLOOMFIELD HILLS, Oakland Co.

PROVIZER & PHILLIPS, P.C. (AV)

6785 Telegraph Road, Suite 400, 48301
Telephone: 248-642-0444
Facsimile: 248-642-6661
Toll Free: 1-800-288-9080
URL: http://www.lawyers.com/provizer&phillips

Harold M. Provizer
Randall E. Phillips

Keith A. Castora

For full biographical listings, see the Martindale-Hubbell Law Directory

*DETROIT,** Wayne Co.

BRADY, HATHAWAY, BRADY & BRETZ, PROFESSIONAL CORPORATION (AV)

1330 Buhl Building, 48226-3602
Telephone: 313-965-3700
Telecopier: 313-965-2830
Email: brady@bradyhathaway.com

John F. Brady
Thomas P. Brady
Tracy A. Leahy

Representative Clients: Beam Stream, Inc.; Bundy Corporation; Energy Conversion Devices, Inc.; Schering Corporation; Warner-Lambert; Wolverine Technologies; ABB Environmental Services.

For Complete List of Firm Personnel, See General Section

For full biographical listings, see the Martindale-Hubbell Law Directory

CHARFOOS, REITER, PETERSON, HOLMQUIST & PILCHAK, P.C. (AV)

476 State of Michigan Plaza Building, 1200 Sixth Street, 48226
Telephone: 313-961-7011
Email: CRPHP@crphp.com
Farmington Hills, Michigan Office: 30500 Northwestern Highway, Suite 400.
Telephone: 248-626-7300.
Fax: 248-626-7305.

Myron B. Charfoos
James A. Reiter
Daniel Peterson
C. John Holmquist, Jr.
William E. Pilchak
Daniel G. Cohen

Kenneth E. Jones
Deborah S. Dorland
Danial J. Hébert
Robert C. Tice
Nedra D. Campbell

Representative Clients: The Accident Fund Co.; CNA Insurance Co.; Detroit Board of Education; Frankenmuth Insurance Co.; Hyatt Regency; Meadowbrook Insurance Group; MAXCIS, Inc.; Michigan Auto Dealers' Self-Insured Fund; Michigan Health & Hospital Assn.; Sedgewick James of Mich.

For full biographical listings, see the Martindale-Hubbell Law Directory

CONKLIN, BENHAM, DUCEY, LISTMAN & CHUHRAN, P.C. (AV)

1740 First National Building, 48226
Telephone: 313-961-8690
Fax: 313-961-4786
Traverse City, Michigan Office: 415 East Front Street.
Telephone: 616-947-4300.
Fax: 616-947-3924.

S. Gerard Conklin (1903-1975)
Donald G. Ducey
William R. Listman
Thomas P. Chuhran
Thomas J. McNally
David J. Watts
Martin L. Critchell
Thomas A. Plagens
John S. Chapman
David J. Berge
Dwight D. Labadie

Martin M. Summer

Representative Clients: General Motors Corp.; Great Lakes Division, National Steel Corp.; The Accident Fund Co.; Frankenmuth Mutual Insurance Co.; The Budd Co.; CIGNA/INA-Aetna; Michigan Health & Hospital Association; Oakwood Health Services Corp.; Chrysler Corp.; Sedgewick James of Michigan.

For full biographical listings, see the Martindale-Hubbell Law Directory

KELLER, THOMA, SCHWARZE, SCHWARZE, DUBAY & KATZ, P.C. (AV)

440 East Congress, 5th Floor, 48226
Telephone: 313-965-7610
Fax: 313-965-4480
Bingham Farms, Michigan Office: 30150 Telegraph Road, Suite 444, 48025.
Telephone: 248-642-5218.

Thomas L. Fleury
John J. Rabaut

Counsel for: Livonia Public Schools; Ludington News Co., Inc.
Representative Clients: Borg-Warner Corp.; E & L Transport Co.; The Kroger Co.; Holnam, Inc.
Public Employer Clients: City of Farmington Hills; City of Flint; City of Grosse Pointe Woods; Saginaw Public Schools.

For Complete List of Firm Personnel, See General Section

For full biographical listings, see the Martindale-Hubbell Law Directory

FARMINGTON HILLS, Oakland Co.

CHARFOOS, REITER, PETERSON, HOLMQUIST & PILCHAK, P.C. (AV)

30500 Northwestern Highway, Suite 400, 48334-3179
Telephone: 248-626-7300
Facsimile: 248-626-7305
Email: CRPHP@crphp.com
Detroit, Michigan Office: 1200 Sixth Street.
Telephone: 313-961-7011.

Myron B. Charfoos
James A. Reiter
Daniel Peterson
C. John Holmquist, Jr.
William E. Pilchak
Daniel G. Cohen

Kenneth E. Jones
Deborah S. Dorland
Danial J. Hébert
Robert C. Tice
Nedra D. Campbell

Representative Clients: The Accident Fund Co.; CNA Insurance Co.; Detroit Board of Education; Frankenmuth Insurance Co.; Hyatt Regency; Meadowbrook Insurance Group; MAXCIS, Inc.; Michigan Auto Dealers' Self-Insured Fund; Michigan Health & Hospital Assn.; Sedgewick James of Mich.

For full biographical listings, see the Martindale-Hubbell Law Directory

*FLINT,** Genesee Co.

MACDONALD, FITZGERALD & MACDONALD, P.C. (AV)

200 McKinnon Building, 48502
Telephone: 810-232-3184; 234-2204
Fax: 810-232-9632

Robert J. MacDonald (1914-1987)
John J. FitzGerald (1919-1995)
R. Duncan MacDonald
Timothy J. MacDonald
Robert J MacDonald

References: Michigan National Bank; NBD Bank, N.A.; Citizen's Bank.

For full biographical listings, see the Martindale-Hubbell Law Directory

*KALAMAZOO,** Kalamazoo Co.

EARLY, LENNON, PETERS & CROCKER, P.C. (AV)

900 Comerica Building, 49007-4752
Telephone: 616-381-8844
Fax: 616-349-8525
Email: elpc@michbar.org

John T. Peters, Jr.

Attorneys for: Aetna Insurance; Kemper Group; Medical Protective Co.; Zurich Insurance; Liberty Mutual; Home Insurance.

For Complete List of Firm Personnel, See General Section

For full biographical listings, see the Martindale-Hubbell Law Directory

*MOUNT PLEASANT,** Isabella Co.

GRAY, SOWLE & IACCO, A PROFESSIONAL CORPORATION (AV)

600 Broadway East, 48858
Telephone: 517-772-5932
Fax: 517-773-0538

Loren E. Gray
Donald N. Sowle
Daniel A. Iacco
Cheryl E. Gray

References: Isabella Bank & Trust; First of America of Mount Pleasant.

For full biographical listings, see the Martindale-Hubbell Law Directory

*SAGINAW,** Saginaw Co.

BRAUN KENDRICK FINKBEINER PLC (AV)

101 N. Washington Suite 812, 48607-1297
Telephone: 517-753-3461
Telecopier: 517-753-3951
Email: ALBFIE@BKF-LAW.COM *URL:* http://www.bkf-law.com
Saginaw Township Office, Michigan Office: 5800 Gratiot Road, Suite 107, P.O. Box 5169. Telephone 517-799-8692.
Fax: 517-799-4666.
Bay City, Michigan Office: 201 Phoenix Building, P.O. Box 2039.
Telephone: 517-895-8505.
Telecopier: 517-895-8437.
Ann Arbor, Michigan Office: First National Building. 201 S. Main, Suite 700.
Telephone: 313-995-4100.
Telecopier: 313-995-4798.
Mt. Pleasant, Michigan Office: 805 North Brown.
Telephone: 517-775-7404.
Telecopier: 517-775-3764.

Harold J. Blanchet, Jr.
Bruce L. Dalrymple
E. Louis Ognisanti
Charles A. Gilfeather

Representative Client: General Motors Corporation; Dow Chemical Co.

For Complete List of Firm Personnel, See General Section

For full biographical listings, see the Martindale-Hubbell Law Directory

SOUTHFIELD, Oakland Co.

SOMMERS, SCHWARTZ, SILVER & SCHWARTZ, P.C. (AV)

2000 Town Center, Suite 900, 48075
Telephone: 248-355-0300
Telecopier: 248-746-4001
Plymouth, Michigan Office: 747 South Main Street.
Telephone: 313-455-4250.

John F. Vos, III
Allen J. Wall

Gerald D. Keller

General Counsel for: City of Taylor; Foodland Distributors; C.A. Muer Corporation; Vlasic & Company; Nederlander Corporation; Midwest Health Centers, P.C.
Representative Clients: Michigan National Bank; Universal Underwriters Insurance Co.; Don Lee Distributor; Rite-Aid of Michigan.

For Complete List of Firm Personnel, See General Section

For full biographical listings, see the Martindale-Hubbell Law Directory

*TRAVERSE CITY,** Grand Traverse Co.

CONKLIN, BENHAM, DUCEY, LISTMAN & CHUHRAN, P.C. (AV)

415 East Front Street, 49684
Telephone: 616-947-4300
Fax: 616-947-3924
Detroit, Michigan Office: 1740 First National Building.
Telephone: 313-961-8690.
Fax: 313-961-4786.

Michael J. Gillman

C. Bruce Taylor

Representative Clients: The Accident Fund Co.; Alexsis Risk Management Service; Amerisure Companies; American International Adjusting; Citizens Management, Inc.; Lake State Insurance Co.; Michigan Association of Counties; Michigan Construction Industry Self-Insurers' Fund; Michigan Health & Hospital Assn.; State of Michigan.

For full biographical listings, see the Martindale-Hubbell Law Directory

WALTON, SMITH, PHILLIPS & DIXON, P.C. (AV)

216 Cass Street, P.O. Box 549, 49685
Telephone: 616-947-7410
Fax: 616-947-5112

Geoff G. Smith
L. Kent Walton
Thomas L. Phillips

Representative Clients: The Travelers Insurance Cos.; Farm Bureau Insurance Group; TIG Insurance.
Reference: Huntington National Bank.

For full biographical listings, see the Martindale-Hubbell Law Directory

MARTINDALE-HUBBELL®

BAR REGISTER OF PREEMINENT LAWYERS™ 2000

VOLUME II

MINNESOTA–WYOMING
CANADA
INTERNATIONAL

EIGHTY-FOURTH EDITION

MARTINDALE-HUBBELL
A Member of LEXIS Publishing™

LEXIS Publishing™
LEXIS-NEXIS • MARTINDALE-HUBBELL
MATTHEW BENDER • MICHIE • SHEPARD'S

121 Chanlon Road, New Providence, NJ 07974 • 1-800-526-4902
Email: info@martindale.com • www.martindale.com

Published by Martindale-Hubbell®, A Member of LEXIS® Publishing™

Louis J. Andreozzi, President and Chief Executive Officer
Carol D. Cooper, Publisher, Senior Vice President, Marketing and Product Development
Larry D. Thompson, Senior Vice President, U.S. Sales and Customer Relations
Andrew W. Meyer, Vice President, Administration
Vera Lang, Vice President and Chief Financial Officer
Dean Hollister, Vice President, Database Production
John Roney, Vice President, Chief Information Officer

International Standard Book Number: 1-56160-424-0 (set)

Printed and bound in the United States of America
by Quebecor World Book Services
Taunton, Massachusetts

ISBN 1 - 56160 - 424 - 0

9 781561 604241

TABLE OF CONTENTS

TABLE OF CONTENTS — *Continued*

PRACTICE AREAS SECTION, VOLUME II (Minnesota–Wyoming, Canada, International)

FOREWORD

We are pleased to present the 84th edition of the **Martindale-Hubbell® Bar Register of Preeminent Lawyers™**, the definitive guide to America's leading lawyers and law firms.

The **Martindale-Hubbell Bar Register** lists only the most distinguished law practices – those that have achieved the highest "AV®" rating in the **Martindale-Hubbell Law Directory**. The "A" signifies the highest levels of legal ability, while the "V" denotes "very high" adherence to professional standards of conduct, ethics, reliability and diligence. This rating is the result of a peer review system based upon the confidential opinions of practicing attorneys and members of the judiciary.

The 2000 **Bar Register** contains concise listings and full contact data for more than 9,000 sole practitioners and law firms in the United States and Canada. It lists lawyers and firms excelling in 61 practice areas, from Administrative Law to Workers Compensation. Five new Practice Areas are included this year – Education Law, Elder Law, Franchise Law, Legal Malpractice, and Nonprofit & Tax Exemption Organizations. Also with this edition, Probate, Trusts and Estate Planning is now Trusts and Estates, Wills and Probate.

We believe you will find the **Bar Register** invaluable whenever you need to identify today's most highly regarded law firms in a particular geographic location or area of expertise. In addition, your **Bar Register** status is noted in your professional listing emphasizing your firm's prestige and standing. Your listing on *martindale.com* will feature an icon to instantly alert potential clients to your **Bar Register** status.

As always, we invite you to contact us with any suggestions for new practice areas or ideas to further improve the next edition.

Thank you for your support.

Louis J. Andreozzi
President and Chief Executive Officer

MARTINDALE-HUBBELL®/LEXIS®-NEXIS® LEGAL ADVISORY BOARD

The Martindale-Hubbell/LEXIS-NEXIS Legal Advisory Board was formed to ensure that Martindale-Hubbell and LEXIS-NEXIS are responsive to the constantly changing needs of the legal profession. The following lawyers selected from the private, corporate and international sectors of the profession comprise the 1999-2000 Board.

MARTHA W. BARNETT of Holland & Knight, Tallahassee, Florida. Ms. Barnett is a former Chair of the House of Delegates of the American Bar Association, the first woman lawyer to be so honored, and has served on the ABA's Board of Governors. Currently, she is the President-Elect of the American Bar Association, to serve as such from August 1999 to July 2000, and to serve as President from July 2000 to August 2001.

ALLEN E. BRENNECKE of Harrison, Brennecke, Moore, Smaha & McKibben, Marshaltown, Iowa. Mr. Brennecke has served as a Member of the Board of Directors of the National Judicial College, President of the Iowa State Bar Association, a Member of the ABA House of Delegates since 1975 and its Chair, 1984-1986. His prior service to the ABA also includes four years on the Board of Governors and three years as Chair of the IOLTA Commission. He previously served on the Board of Editors of the American Bar Association Journal and served as Chair from 1989 to 1995.

BENJAMIN R. CIVILETTI of Venable, Baetjer, Howard & Civiletti, Washington, D.C. and Baltimore, Maryland. Mr. Civiletti is a former Attorney General of the United States under President Carter, 1979-1981. He is the former Chairman of the ABA Litigation Section and has been a member of the ABA House of Delegates since 1991. He also serves as the ABA Representative to the United Nations. He is the Chairman of Venable. Mr. Civiletti is a Fellow of the American College of Trial Lawyers and the American Law Institute.

DOUGLAS B. HENDERSON is the Founding and Senior Partner of Finnegan, Henderson, Farabow, Garrett & Dunner, Washington, D.C. Mr. Henderson is a Member of the Advisory Council of the United States Court of Federal Claims, and a Member of the Board of the Federal Circuit Bar Association. He was formerly Chairman of the Patent Division and Member of Council of the Section of Intellectual Property Law of the American Bar Association. He was the Founder of the Federal Circuit Bar Association, a co-founder of the U.S. Court of Federal Claims Bar Association, and a co-founder of the ITC Trial Lawyers Association.

THOMAS G. HEINTZMAN, O.C., Q.C., of McCarthy Tétrault, Toronto, Ontario, is a past President of the Canadian Bar Association (1994-1995). He is a member of the International Bar Association and the past Canadian member of the Council. Mr. Heintzman is a Fellow of the International Academy of Trial Lawyers, and the American College of Trial Lawyers and the past Chair of its Canadian Judiciary Committee. He is an Officer of the Order of Canada.

THOMAS J. KLITGAARD, formerly Senior Vice President and General Counsel of Sega of America, Inc., is now a partner with Dillingham & Murphy, San Francisco. He is a former Chairman of the California State Bar's Committee on the Maintenance of Professional Competence. He is a member of the panel of technology arbitrators of the American Arbitration Association in New York and a member of the Advisory Board of the Southwestern Legal Foundation in Dallas. He is currently the chairman of a graduate business management program in Shanghai, China.

RALPH I. LANCASTER, JR. of Pierce Atwood, Portland, Maine is currently serving as Independent Counsel, In Re Herman, by appointment of the Special Division of the D.C. Court of Appeals. He previously served as Counsel for the United States before the International Court of Justice in a case concerning delimitation of the Maritime Boundary in the Gulf of Maine and as Special Master by appointment of the Untied States Supreme Court in State of New Jersey vs. State of Nebraska. Mr. Lancaster began his legal career as a law clerk to the Honorable Edward T. Gignoux. He is a Past-President of the Maine State Bar Association and a former member of the House of Delegates of the American Bar Association. He served as Chair of the Standing Committee on Federal Judiciary of the ABA. He is a Fellow of the American College of Trial Lawyers and served as its President, 1989-1990.

JERALYN E. MERRITT, a sole practitioner from Denver, Colorado, is an author and frequent lecturer on criminal defense. She was selected by Chairman Bill McCollum, House Judiciary Committee, Subcommittee on Crime, to present oral and written congressional testimony on federal marijuana sentencing laws on behalf of the National Association of Criminal Defense Lawyers (NACDL) on March 6, 1996, in Washington, D.C. She served as Chair from 1995-1996 while a judicially appointed member of the Standing Committee on the Criminal Justice Act for the United States District Court for the District of Colorado from 1994-1996. Ms. Merritt is currently a member of the Board of Directors and Chair of the Advisory Board for the National Association of Criminal Defense Lawyers, the Director of the Cyberspace Bar Association and a member of the Board of Governors for the American Board of Criminal Lawyers.

HARRIET E. MIERS, Co-Managing Partner of Locke Liddell & Sapp LLP, has previously served as President and director of the State Bar of Texas as well as President and Chairman of the Board of Directors for the Dallas Bar Association. She is currently a member of the House of Delegates for the American Bar Association and State Delegate for the State of Texas. Ms. Miers also serves as a Trustee of the Southwestern Legal Foundation, a member of the Executive Board for the Southern Methodist University School of Law and Chair of the Texas Lottery Commission.

WILLIAM G. PAUL of Crowe & Dunlevy, Oklahoma City, Oklahoma. Mr. Paul is the former Senior Vice President & General Counsel, Phillips Petroleum Company, Bartlesville, Oklahoma. In February 1998, he was nominated to be President-Elect of the American Bar Association, to serve as such from August 1998 to August 1999, and is now the President to serve as such from August 1999 to July 2000. He has served as President of the Oklahoma State Bar Association, President of the National Conference of Bar Presidents, a Member of the American Bar Association, House of Delegates 1975-1999 and is a Fellow in the American College of Trial Lawyers.

FERNANDO POMBO, Founder and Senior Partner of Gomez-Acebo & Pombo, Madrid, Spain, has contributed to and authored several publications in the field of international business law. Currently, he is the International Bar Association Chairman of SLP. Mr. Pombo has been a visiting professor at the Institute on International Legal Studies in Salzburg, Austria since 1985. He is also a former President of LES International and a member of the Spanish Arbitration Court. He is fluent in Spanish, English, French and German.

WM. REECE SMITH, JR. of Tampa, Florida, is the senior member of Carlton, Fields, Ward, Emmanuel, Smith & Cutler, P.A. A Rhodes Scholar at Oxford University, England, he was later President of The Florida Bar (1972-73), the American Bar Association (1980-81), and the International Bar Association (1988-90). He is a Fellow of the American College of Trial Lawyers and the International Academy of Trial Lawyers and serves on the Council of the American Law Institute. He received the American Bar Association's Gold Medal for "exceptionally distinguished service to the cause of American Jurisprudence."

WALTER H. WHITE, JR. is a Partner of Bryan Cave L.L.P. in London, England. Mr. White previously has served as a Partner of Steptoe & Johnson L.L.P. in Washington, D.C. and as the Managing Director of its Moscow office. Mr. White is a former Commissioner of Securities for the State of Wisconsin 1988-1991. He has served as a member of the ABA House of Delegates, as the Chair of the Section of Individual Rights and Responsibilities and as chair of the Young Lawyers Division. Mr. White has also been a member of the State Bar of Wisconsin Board of Governors, on the Board of the Milwaukee Foundation and is currently a Board member of the Central-Asian-American Enterprise Fund by appointment of President Clinton.

USER'S GUIDE

The **Martindale-Hubbell Bar Register of Preeminent Lawyers** is a two-volume registry of firms and attorneys of significant stature. The 2000 edition presents sixty-one alphabetically sequenced practice area sections and an index to the firms listed in each practice area.

This **Subscriber Locator**, arranged alphabetically by subscriber name, will assist the user in identifying those practice areas and geographic location(s) where the subscriber lists.

A typical entry appears as follows:

Firm Name → **LEWANDOWSKI & BERRY, P.C.**

Roseland, NJ . . . . . .Banking Law; Bankruptcy Law; Civil Trial Practice; General Practice; Tax Law ← *Practice Areas*

Geographic Location → New York, NY . . . . .Banking Law; Bankruptcy Law; Tax Law

The **Practice Areas Section** clearly lists the practice area at the top of the page, along with the geographic location. Listings for the United States and Canada are arranged in alphabetic sequence by state (or Canadian province) and within state (or Canadian province) by city name and finally by listee name. For countries other than the United States and Canada, alphabetic country name is the major sequence, followed by city and then listee name.

A typical section entry appears as follows:

Practice Area → **GENERAL PRACTICE** — **NEW YORK—AMSTERDAM** ← *Geographic Location*

County Seat Indicator → AMSTERDAM,* Montgomery Co.

Firm Name → **LETTERMAN AND KOLACKOVSKY, P.C.** (AV) ← *Firm Rating*

Contact Information →
46 Rose Street, P.O. Box 2429, 12010
Telephone: 515-214-9291
Fax: 515-214-6153
Email: postmaster@lettkol.com *URL:* http://www.lettkol.com

Mitchell J. Letterman — John Kolackovsky

——— ← *Associate Indicator*

Megan Brett — Ann Kolackovsky

Doris Vayda

Clients →
Representative Clients: New York Home Security, Inc.; American Flight School, Inc.; East Coast Recycling Center, New York Casualty, Inc.; American Fire Insurance Corp.
Reference: Atlantic National Bank.

Martindale-Hubbell Professional Biographies Reference → *For full biographical listings, see the Martindale-Hubbell Law Directory.*

For additional help or explanation, please call Martindale-Hubbell Customer Relations, at (800) 526-4902.

INDEX SECTION

AAFEDT, FORDE, GRAY & MONSON, P.A.
Minneapolis, MN....................Insurance Defense

AARON, WILLIAM
Miami, FL....................Criminal Trial Practice

AARONS LAW FIRM, P.C.
Santa Fe, NM....................Criminal Trial Practice

AARONSON, EDWARD D., A LAW CORPORATION
Encino, CA....................Real Estate Law

ABBATE, LAWRENCE & WORDEN, P.C.
Melville, NY....................Medical Malpractice; Product Liability Law

ABBEY, WEITZENBERG, HOFFMAN & EMERY, A PROFESSIONAL CORPORATION
Santa Rosa, CA....................Banking Law; Bankruptcy Law; Business Law; Civil Trial Practice; Construction Law; Labor and Employment Law; Medical Malpractice; Personal Injury; Real Estate Law

ABBOT, MURPHY AND HARVEY, P.C.
Louisville, GA....................Business Law; General Practice

ABBOTT, C. MICHAEL, P.C.
Atlanta, GA....................Appellate Practice; Criminal Trial Practice

ABBOTT, NICHOLSON, QUILTER, ESSHAKI & YOUNGBLOOD, P.C.
Detroit, MI....................Business Law; Civil Trial Practice; Employment Benefits Law; Family Law; Labor and Employment Law; Municipal and Zoning Law; Real Estate Law; Tax Law; Trust and Estates, Wills and Probate

ABBOTT & NOLEN
Sacramento, CA....................Civil Trial Practice; Insurance Defense

ABDO AND ABDO, P.A.
Minneapolis, MN....................Appellate Practice; Business Law; Civil Trial Practice; Environmental Law; General Practice; Real Estate Law; Securities Law; Sports and Entertainment Law; Trust and Estates, Wills and Probate

ABELE & SANDERSON, L.L.C.
St. Louis, MO....................Personal Injury; Product Liability Law; Workers Compensation

ABEL, MUSSER, SOKOLOSKY, MARES & KOURI
Oklahoma City, OK....................Personal Injury

ABELSON LAW FIRM, THE
Washington, DC....................Medical Malpractice

ABEYTA-NELSON P.C.
Yakima, WA....................Personal Injury; Product Liability Law

ABLONDI, FOSTER, SOBIN & DAVIDOW, P.C.
Washington, DC....................International Trade Law

ABOWITZ, RHODES & DAHNKE, P.C.
Oklahoma City, OK....................Civil Trial Practice; Insurance Defense; Personal Injury; Securities Law

ABRAHAMS KASLOW & CASSMAN
Omaha, NE....................General Practice

ABRAHAMSON, REED & ADLEY
Hammond, IN....................Civil Trial Practice; Commercial Litigation; Insurance Defense; Transportation Law

ABRAMOWITZ & POMERANTZ, P.A.
Fort Lauderdale, FL....................Medical Malpractice; Personal Injury

ABRAMS, GORELICK, FRIEDMAN & JACOBSON, P.C.
New York, NY....................Civil Trial Practice; Insurance Defense

ABRAMS & SMITH, A PROFESSIONAL ASSOCIATION
Minneapolis, MN....................Civil Trial Practice; Insurance Defense; Personal Injury; Product Liability Law

ABRAMSON & FOX
Chicago, IL....................Civil Trial Practice

ABRAMSON & FREEDMAN, L.L.C.
Philadelphia, PA....................Administrative Law; Civil Trial Practice; Commercial Litigation

ABRAMSON & MAGIDSON, P.A.
Miami, FL....................Admiralty/Maritime Law; Personal Injury; Workers Compensation

ABRAMSON, REIS, BROWN & DUGAN
Manchester, NH....................Medical Malpractice; Personal Injury

ACKER, LAWRENCE J., P.C.
Bloomfield Hills, MI....................Medical Malpractice; Professional Liability

ACKERMAN, JAMES H. LAW OFFICES OF
Long Beach, CA....................Admiralty/Maritime Law; General Practice

ACKERMAN & ACKERMAN, P.C.
Troy, MI....................Eminent Domain

ACKERMAN, ALLAN A., P.C.
Chicago, IL....................Appellate Practice; Criminal Trial Practice

ACKERMAN, LEE B., P.C., LAW OFFICES OF
Los Angeles, CA....................Legal Malpractice

ACKERMAN, LINK & SARTORY, P.A.
West Palm Beach, FL....................Business Law; Real Estate Law; Securities Law

ACKERMAN & TERRY, LLC
Westbury, NY....................Bankruptcy Law; Commercial Litigation

ACKMAN, MAREK & BOYD, LTD.
Kankakee, IL....................Civil Trial Practice; Insurance Defense; Medical Malpractice
Watseka, IL....................General Practice

ADAMI, GOLDMAN & SHUFFIELD, INCORPORATED
San Antonio, TX....................Insurance Defense

ADAMO AND NEWMAN
Westerly, RI....................Criminal Trial Practice; Family Law; Personal Injury

ADAMS & ADAMS
Miami, FL....................Civil Trial Practice; General Practice

ADAMS & ASSOCIATES
Oklahoma City, OK....................Civil Trial Practice; Criminal Trial Practice; Personal Injury

ADAMS, BARFIELD, DUNAWAY & HANKINSON, LLP
Thomaston, GA....................General Practice

ADAMS, COOGLER, WATSON & MERKEL, P.A.
West Palm Beach, FL....................Civil Trial Practice; Commercial Litigation; Insurance Defense; Medical Malpractice; Personal Injury; Product Liability Law; Workers Compensation

ADAMS, GALLINAR, IGLESIAS & MEYER, P.A.
Miami, FL....................Aviation Law; Banking Law; International Business Law; Real Estate Law

ADAMS & GRAHAM, L.L.P.
Harlingen, TX....................Appellate Practice; Civil Trial Practice; Insurance Defense; Medical Malpractice; Product Liability Law; Professional Liability; Workers Compensation

ADAMS AND JOHNSTON, A PROFESSIONAL LAW CORPORATION
New Orleans, LA....................Civil Trial Practice

ADAMS, LYNCH & LOFTIN, P.C.
Bedford, TX....................Banking Law; Business Law; Labor and Employment Law; Real Estate Law

ADAMS AND REESE LLP
New Orleans, LA....................General Practice

ADAMS, WESTON, LAW FIRM
Columbia, SC....................General Practice

ADDISON, MICHAEL C.
Tampa, FL....................Antitrust Law; Civil Trial Practice; Construction Law; Product Liability Law; Securities Law

ADDUCI, MASTRIANI & SCHAUMBERG, L.L.P.
Washington, DC....................Administrative Law; International Trade Law; Patent, Trademark, Copyright and Unfair Competition

ADELMAN LAVINE GOLD AND LEVIN, A PROFESSIONAL CORPORATION
Philadelphia, PA....................Bankruptcy Law; Corporate Law; Real Estate Law

ADELMAN, ROBERT A., A LAW CORPORATION
Beverly Hills, CA....................Family Law

ADELSON, GOLDEN, LORIA & SIMONS, P.C.
Boston, MA....................Real Estate Law

ADINAMIS & ADINAMIS, ATTORNEYS, A PROFESSIONAL CORPORATION
Indianapolis, IN....................Tax Law; Trust and Estates, Wills and Probate

ADKINS & KELSTON, P.C.
Boston, MA....................Commercial Litigation; Criminal Trial Practice

ADKINS, POTTS & SMETHURST, L.L.P.
Salisbury, MD....................Civil Trial Practice; Environmental Law; Municipal and Zoning Law; Real Estate Law

ADKISON, CYNTHIA, P.C.
Bloomfield Hills, MI....................Insurance Defense; Labor and Employment Law

ADKISON, NEED, GREEN & ALLEN
Bloomfield Hills, MI....................Banking Law; Business Law; Commercial Litigation; Communications Law; Computer Law; Corporate Law; Family Law; General Practice; Land Use Law; Municipal and Zoning Law

ADKISSON & JACKSON, L.L.P.
San Antonio, TX........Medical Malpractice; Personal Injury; Product Liability Law

ADLER, ALAN R.
Morristown, NJ........Tax Law

ADLER, DAVID W.
Phoenix, AZ........Family Law; Trust and Estates, Wills and Probate

ADLER, JOHN S., A PROF. CORP., LAW OFFICES OF
San Diego, CA........Labor and Employment Law

ADOLPH & BINTINGER, P.S.
Seattle, WA........Civil Trial Practice

AGAPAY, LEVYN & HALLING, A PROFESSIONAL CORPORATION
Los Angeles, CA........Civil Trial Practice

AGINS HAAZ & SEIDEL, L.L.P.
Philadelphia, PA........Personal Injury

AGNEW & BRUSAVICH
Torrance, CA........Civil Trial Practice; Medical Malpractice; Personal Injury; Product Liability Law

AHLERS, COONEY, DORWEILER, HAYNIE, SMITH & ALLBEE, P.C.
Des Moines, IA........General Practice

AHMUTY, DEMERS & MCMANUS
New York, NY........Civil Trial Practice; Insurance Defense

AIKIN, WENDY L., P.A.
Winter Park, FL........Commercial Litigation; Family Law; Personal Injury

AIKINS, MACAULAY & THORVALDSON
Winnipeg, MB, Canada........Business Law; Civil Trial Practice; General Practice; Insurance Defense; Personal Injury; Tax Law; Trust and Estates, Wills and Probate

AINSA PARTNERS, LLP
El Paso, TX........Banking Law; Business Law; Commercial Litigation; Construction Law; Corporate Law; Eminent Domain; Government Contracts; Land Use Law; Municipal and Zoning Law; Real Estate Law

AINSWORTH, SULLIVAN, TRACY, KNAUF, WARNER & RUSLANDER, P.C.
Albany, NY........Appellate Practice; General Practice; Insurance Defense; Product Liability Law

AIRD & BERLIS
Toronto, ON, Canada........General Practice

AITKEN, SCHAUBLE, PATRICK, NEILL & RUFF
Pullman, WA........Trust and Estates, Wills and Probate

AJALAT, POLLEY & AYOOB
Los Angeles, CA........Tax Law

AKIN, GUMP, STRAUSS, HAUER & FELD
Brussels, Belgium........General Practice
Washington, DC........General Practice
Austin, TX........General Practice
Dallas, TX........General Practice
Houston, TX........General Practice
San Antonio, TX........General Practice

AKINS, JEFFREY R.
San Antonio, TX........Civil Trial Practice

ALBERT, WARD & JOHNSON, P.C.
Greenwich, CT........Business Law; Civil Trial Practice; Construction Law; Corporate Law; General Practice; Municipal and Zoning Law; Real Estate Law; Trust and Estates, Wills and Probate

ALBERT, WEILAND & GOLDEN
Costa Mesa, CA........Appellate Practice; Bankruptcy Law; Civil Trial Practice; Commercial Litigation; Creditors Rights; Real Estate Law

ALBERT, WHITEHEAD & MCGAUGH, P.C.
Chicago, IL........Business Law; Civil Trial Practice; Labor and Employment Law

ALBRIGHT BROWN & GOERTEMILLER, LLC
Baltimore, MD........Civil Trial Practice; Criminal Trial Practice

ALBRIGHT, STODDARD, WARNICK & ALBRIGHT, A PROFESSIONAL CORPORATION
Las Vegas, NV........Appellate Practice; Banking Law; Bankruptcy Law; Civil Trial Practice; Commercial Law; Construction Law; Family Law; General Practice; Insurance Defense; Real Estate Law; Trust and Estates, Wills and Probate

ALBRITTONS, CLIFTON, ALVERSON & MOODY, P.C.
Andalusia, AL........Civil Trial Practice; General Practice; Insurance Defense; Product Liability Law; Professional Liability; Tax Law; Trust and Estates, Wills and Probate; Workers Compensation

ALCORN, JOHN R. LAW OFFICES OF
Irvine, CA........Immigration and Naturalization

ALDEN ARONOVSKY & SAX LLP
San Francisco, CA........Civil Trial Practice; Commercial Litigation; Environmental Law

ALDERMAN AND ALDERMAN
Syracuse, NY........Family Law; Real Estate Law; Trust and Estates, Wills and Probate

ALDRICH & BONNEFIN, P.L.C.
Irvine, CA........Banking Law

ALEXANDER & CLEAVER, P.A.
Annapolis, MD........Business Law; Commercial Law; Personal Injury

ALEXANDER, HAWES & AUDET
San Jose, CA........Antitrust Law; Civil Trial Practice; Personal Injury; Product Liability Law; Toxic Torts

ALEXANDER, HOLBURN, BEAUDIN & LANG
Vancouver, BC, Canada........General Practice; Insurance Defense; Labor and Employment Law

ALEXANDER RALSTON, SPECKHARD & SPECKHARD, L.L.P.
Greensboro, NC........Civil Trial Practice; Commercial Law; Corporate Law; Medical Malpractice; Personal Injury; Real Estate Law; Trust and Estates, Wills and Probate; Workers Compensation

ALEXANDER, TOM, & ASSOCIATES
Houston, TX........Civil Trial Practice; Family Law

ALEXANDER & VANN, LLP
Thomasville, GA........General Practice

ALFERS & CARVER, LLC
Denver, CO........International Business Law; Natural Resources Law; Oil and Gas Law

ALFORD, E. GREGORY
San Diego, CA........Family Law

ALFORD & KALIL, P.A.
Jacksonville, FL........Product Liability Law; Professional Liability; Toxic Torts

ALHADEFF CANNON ROSE SOLAR & PARKS, LLP
San Diego, CA........Bankruptcy Law; Business Law; Civil Trial Practice; Labor and Employment Law; Tax Law; Trademark, Copyright and Unfair Competition; Trust and Estates, Wills and Probate

ALI, PAPPAS & COX, P.C.
Syracuse, NY........Civil Trial Practice; Commercial Litigation; Creditors Rights; General Practice; Real Estate Law

ALKON, RHEA & HART
Christiansted, St. Croix, VI........Civil Trial Practice; Personal Injury

ALLAN & SHIPP, P.A.
St. Petersburg, FL........General Practice; Securities Law; Trust and Estates, Wills and Probate

ALLE, JAMES
Grosse Pointe, MI........Family Law

ALLEN, RICHARD E.
Augusta, GA........Civil Trial Practice; Criminal Trial Practice; Family Law; General Practice

ALLEN, ALLEN, ALLEN & ALLEN, A PROFESSIONAL CORPORATION
Richmond, VA........Personal Injury; Product Liability Law

ALLEN, ALLEN, BOERNER & BREELAND
Brookhaven, MS........Banking Law; Civil Trial Practice; Commercial Law; Family Law; General Practice; Insurance Defense; Labor and Employment Law; Personal Injury; Real Estate Law; Trust and Estates, Wills and Probate

ALLEN, BRINTON, SIMMONS & MCCARTHY, P.A.
Jacksonville, FL........Business Law; Civil Trial Practice; Commercial Litigation; Construction Law

ALLEN, COOLEY & ALLEN
Lawrence, KS........General Practice

ALLEN, DELL, FRANK & TRINKLE, P.A.
Tampa, FL........Civil Trial Practice; Family Law; General Practice

ALLEN, DYER, DOPPELT, MILBRATH & GILCHRIST
Orlando, FL........Commercial Litigation; Intellectual Property Law; Patent, Trademark, Copyright and Unfair Competition; Trademark, Copyright and Unfair Competition

ALLEN & FLATT INCORPORATED
Newport Beach, CA........Personal Injury

ALLEN, GLENN K., A PROFESSIONAL ASSOCIATION
Jacksonville, FL ....Civil Trial Practice; Family Law; Medical Malpractice; Personal Injury; Professional Liability

ALLEN GUTHRIE & MCHUGH
Charleston, WV....................Administrative Law; Appellate Practice; Civil Trial Practice; Criminal Trial Practice; Health Care Law; Tax Law

ALLEN, JOHNSON, ALEXANDER & KARP, P.A.
Washington, DC....................Civil Trial Practice; General Practice; Insurance Defense; Product Liability Law
Baltimore, MD ....Civil Rights; Civil Trial Practice; General Practice; Insurance Defense; Product Liability Law

ALLEN AND KIMBELL, LLP
Santa Barbara, CA..................General Practice

ALLEN LAW FIRM, A PROFESSIONAL CORPORATION
Little Rock, AR ....Banking Law; Commercial Litigation; Insurance Defense; Securities Law

ALLEN, MATKINS, LECK, GAMBLE & MALLORY LLP
Irvine, CA...............................General Practice
Los Angeles, CA ....General Practice; Public Utilities Law
San Diego, CA ....General Practice
San Francisco, CA ....General Practice

ALLEN & MOORE, L.L.P.
Raleigh, NC.............................Administrative Law; Business Law; Civil Trial Practice

ALLEN AND PINNIX, P.A.
Raleigh, NC.............................Administrative Law; Antitrust Law; Immigration and Naturalization; International Business Law

ALLEN, POLGAR, PROIETTI & FAGALDE
Merced, CA.............................Civil Trial Practice; General Practice

ALLEN & PRICE, P.L.C.
Phoenix, AZ ....Antitrust Law; Civil Trial Practice; Health Care Law; Patent, Trademark, Copyright and Unfair Competition; Trademark, Copyright and Unfair Competition

ALLEN, SCRUGGS, SOSSAMAN & THOMPSON, P.C.
Memphis, TN..........................Business Law; Labor and Employment Law; Workers Compensation

ALLEN, VAHRENWALD & JOHNSON, LLC
Fort Collins, CO ....General Practice

ALLEN, VAUGHN, COBB & HOOD, P.A.
Gulfport, MS...........................Banking Law; Business Law; Civil Trial Practice; Corporate Law; General Practice; Insurance Defense; Personal Injury; Product Liability Law; Real Estate Law; Workers Compensation

ALLEN, W. RILEY, P.A.
Orlando, FL.............................Civil Trial Practice

ALLEN, YURASEK & MERKLIN
Marysville, OH........................General Practice

ALLEY, RAYMOND A., JR., P.A.
Tampa, FL ....Family Law

ALLISON & BASSETT, L.L.P.
Austin, TX ....Criminal Trial Practice

ALLISON, MACKENZIE, HARTMAN, SOUMBENIOTIS & RUSSELL, LTD.
Carson City, NV ....General Practice

ALLMAN SPRY LEGGETT & CRUMPLER, P.A.
Winston-Salem, NC ....General Practice

ALLOTT, ANN, A PROFESSIONAL CORPORATION
Denver, CO ....Immigration and Naturalization

ALLRED, BACON, HALFHILL, LANDAU & YOUNG, PC
Fairfax, VA ....General Practice

ALLRED, JOEL M., P.C.
Salt Lake City, UT..................Appellate Practice; Aviation Law; Civil Trial Practice; Medical Malpractice; Personal Injury; Product Liability Law

ALLRED LAW FIRM, THE
Jackson, MS ....Insurance Defense

ALPER & MCCULLOCH
San Francisco, CA ....Civil Trial Practice; Commercial Litigation

ALPERT, BARKER & RODEMS, P.A.
Tampa, FL ....Civil Trial Practice; Commercial Litigation; General Practice; Insurance Defense; Securities Law

ALPERT, BUTLER & SANDERS, P.C.
West Orange, NJ......................Antitrust Law; Banking Law; Commercial Litigation; Communications Law; Trademark, Copyright and Unfair Competition

ALSCHULER GROSSMAN STEIN & KAHAN LLP
Los Angeles, CA.....................General Practice

AL-SHUBAIKI, TORKI A., LEGAL ADVISORS
Riyadh, Saudi Arabia..............General Practice

ALSTON & JONES
Jackson, MS ....Antitrust Law; Civil Trial Practice; Communications Law; General Practice; Natural Resources Law; Tax Law

ALTHEIMER & GRAY
Chicago, IL..............................General Practice

ALTHOUSE & MCDONOUGH
Upland, CA ....Business Law; Civil Trial Practice; General Practice; Trust and Estates, Wills and Probate

ALTICK & CORWIN CO., L.P.A.
Dayton, OH.............................General Practice

ALTMAN, JAMES J.
New Port Richey, FL ....Trust and Estates, Wills and Probate

ALTMAN, LAWRENCE J.
Chesterfield, MO ....Labor and Employment Law

ALTMAN, D. DAVID CO., A LEGAL PROFESSIONAL ASSOCIATION
Cincinnati, OH ....Environmental Law

ALTMAN, KRITZER & LEVICK, P.C.
Atlanta, GA ....General Practice; Real Estate Law; Tax Law

ALTON, WALTER G., JR., & ASSOCIATES, P.C.
New York, NY.........................Medical Malpractice; Personal Injury

ALVARADO, SMITH & SANCHEZ, A PROFESSIONAL CORPORATION
Los Angeles, CA......................Business Law; Civil Trial Practice; Commercial Litigation; Corporate Law; Environmental Law; International Business Law; Real Estate Law

ALVERSON, TAYLOR, MORTENSEN, NELSON & SANDERS
Las Vegas, NV ....Administrative Law; Banking Law; Bankruptcy Law; Business Law; Civil Trial Practice; Commercial Law; Commercial Litigation; Construction Law; Immigration and Naturalization; Insurance Defense; International Business Law; Medical Malpractice; Municipal Bond/Public Authority Financing; Real Estate Law; Trust and Estates, Wills and Probate

AMADO, HONEY KESSLER
Beverly Hills, CA....................Appellate Practice

AMBROSE, WILSON, GRIMM & DURAND
Knoxville, TN ....Civil Trial Practice; General Practice; Insurance Defense

AMELUNG, WULFF & WILLENBROCK, P.C.
St. Louis, MO..........................Insurance Defense

AMES & AMES
Onancock, VA..........................General Practice

AMLONG & AMLONG, P.A.
Fort Lauderdale, FL ....Family Law; Labor and Employment Law

AMSTER, ROTHSTEIN & EBENSTEIN
New York, NY.........................Patent, Trademark, Copyright and Unfair Competition

AMUNDSEN, MOORE & TORPY
Tallahassee, FL ....Environmental Law; Health Care Law

ANAPOL, SCHWARTZ, WEISS, COHAN, FELDMAN AND SMALLEY, P.C.
Philadelphia, PA ....Civil Trial Practice; Commercial Litigation; Environmental Law; Medical Malpractice; Personal Injury; Professional Liability; Toxic Torts

ANCEL & DUNLAP, LLP
Indianapolis, IN ....Bankruptcy Law

ANDERLINI, FINKELSTEIN & EMERICK, A PROFESSIONAL CORPORATION
San Mateo, CA.........................Commercial Litigation; Personal Injury

ANDERSEN, BERKSHIRE, LAURITSEN & BROWER
Omaha, NE ....General Practice; Labor and Employment Law

ANDERSEN, DAVIDSON & TATE, P.C.
Lawrenceville, GA ....Banking Law; Business Law; Civil Trial Practice; Family Law; General Practice; Real Estate Law

ANDERSON, JEFFREY C. LAW OFFICES OF
San Antonio, TX......................Medical Malpractice

ANDERSON, MICHAEL J.
Sacramento, CA ....Trust and Estates, Wills and Probate

ANDERSON, ABLON, LEWIS & GALE, LLP
Los Angeles, CA......................Commercial Litigation; Insurance Defense; Real Estate Law

ANDERSON, ADLER, COHEN & HARVEY LLP
Boston, MA....Civil Trial Practice; Labor and Employment Law; Medical Malpractice; Product Liability Law

ANDERSON & ASSOCIATES, P.A.
Columbia, SC....Bankruptcy Law

ANDERSON, BRODY, LEVINSON, WEISER & HORWITZ, P.A.
Phoenix, AZ....General Practice; Real Estate Law

ANDERSON, COE & KING, L.L.P.
Baltimore, MD....Civil Trial Practice; Product Liability Law

ANDERSON, DANIEL & COXE
Wrightsville Beach, NC....Insurance Defense

ANDERSON, GALLOWAY & LUCCHESE, A PROFESSIONAL CORPORATION
Walnut Creek, CA....Civil Trial Practice; Insurance Defense; Medical Malpractice; Product Liability Law

ANDERSON & GILBERT
St. Louis, MO....Civil Trial Practice; General Practice

ANDERSON, JOHNSON, LAWRENCE, BUTLER & BOCK
Fayetteville, NC....Insurance Defense

ANDERSON KILL & OLICK, L.L.P.
Washington, DC....Civil Trial Practice; General Practice

ANDERSON KILL & OLICK, P.C.
New York, NY....Antitrust Law; Civil Trial Practice

ANDERSON, MURPHY & HOPKINS, L.L.P.
Little Rock, AR....Insurance Defense; Medical Malpractice; Product Liability Law; Workers Compensation

ANDERSON & QUINN
Rockville, MD....Civil Trial Practice; Commercial Litigation; General Practice; Insurance Defense; Medical Malpractice; Personal Injury; Product Liability Law; Workers Compensation

ANDERSON, SHANNON, O'BRIEN, RICE & BERTZ
Stevens Point, WI....General Practice

ANDERSON & STEVENS, P.A.
Jacksonville, FL....Tax Law; Trust and Estates, Wills and Probate

ANDERSON, THOMAS T., P.C.
Indio, CA....General Practice

ANDERSON, TIMOTHY G., P.A.
Tampa, FL....Civil Trial Practice; Personal Injury; Product Liability Law

ANDERSON, WALKER & REICHERT, LLP
Macon, GA....General Practice; Insurance Defense; Tax Law; Trust and Estates, Wills and Probate

ANDERSON, ZEIGLER, DISHAROON, GALLAGHER & GRAY, PROFESSIONAL CORPORATION
Santa Rosa, CA....Business Law; Corporate Law; General Practice; Tax Law; Trust and Estates, Wills and Probate

ANDRADE & ASSOCIATES
Irvine, CA....Construction Law; Insurance Defense; Labor and Employment Law

ANDRE, BLAUSTEIN & GREEN, L.L.P.
Atlanta, GA....Trust and Estates, Wills and Probate

ANDRE, MORRIS & BUTTERY, A PROFESSIONAL LAW CORPORATION
San Luis Obispo, CA....Business Law; Civil Trial Practice; Corporate Law; Environmental Law; Labor and Employment Law; Land Use Law; Mergers and Acquisitions; Real Estate Law; Trust and Estates, Wills and Probate

ANDRES & BERGER, A PROFESSIONAL CORPORATION
Haddonfield, NJ....Medical Malpractice

ANDREWS, SALLY S.
Houston, TX....Trust and Estates, Wills and Probate

ANDREWS DAVIS LEGG BIXLER MILSTEN & PRICE, A PROFESSIONAL CORPORATION
Oklahoma City, OK....Antitrust Law; Banking Law; Bankruptcy Law; Civil Trial Practice; General Practice; Health Care Law; Labor and Employment Law; Real Estate Law; Securities Law; Tax Law; Trust and Estates, Wills and Probate

ANDREWS & KURTH L.L.P.
Los Angeles, CA....General Practice
Washington, DC....General Practice
New York, NY....General Practice
Dallas, TX....General Practice
Houston, TX....General Practice

ANDREWS LAW OFFICES
Syracuse, NY....Civil Trial Practice; Insurance Defense; Product Liability Law

ANDRUS, SCEALES, STARKE & SAWALL, LLP
Milwaukee, WI....Patent, Trademark, Copyright and Unfair Competition

ANESI, FRANK J.
Durango, CO....Commercial Law; General Practice; Real Estate Law

ANESI, OZMON, RODIN, NOVAK & KOHEN, LTD.
Chicago, IL....Civil Trial Practice; Personal Injury; Workers Compensation

ANGELO, KILDAY & KILDUFF
Sacramento, CA....Civil Rights; Labor and Employment Law

ANGINO & ROVNER, P.C.
Harrisburg, PA....Appellate Practice; Civil Trial Practice; Medical Malpractice; Personal Injury; Product Liability Law; Professional Liability

ANGLE, CARLSON, GOLDRICK & ROBERTS
Santa Barbara, CA....Appellate Practice; Bankruptcy Law; Commercial Litigation; Family Law; Personal Injury; Real Estate Law; Trust and Estates, Wills and Probate

ANGLE, MURPHY, VALENTINO & CAMPBELL, P.C.
York, NE....General Practice

ANGONES, HUNTER, MCCLURE, LYNCH & WILLIAMS, P.A.
Miami, FL....Civil Trial Practice; General Practice; Insurance Defense; Medical Malpractice

ANNINO, DRAPER & MOORE, P.C.
Springfield, MA....Construction Law; Elder Law; Environmental Law; Health Care Law; Real Estate Law

ANSBACHER, BARRY B., P.A.
Jacksonville, FL....Real Estate Law

ANSPACH & ASSOCIATES
Chicago, IL....Environmental Law

ANSPACH & SERRAINO
Toledo, OH....General Practice

ANSTANDIG, MCDYER, BURDETTE & YURCON, P.C.
Pittsburgh, PA....Civil Trial Practice; General Practice; Insurance Defense

ANTHENELLI & OTWAY
Salisbury, MD....Civil Trial Practice; Criminal Trial Practice; Personal Injury

ANTHONY, ANDREW J., P.A.
Miami, FL....Civil Rights; Insurance Defense; Personal Injury; Product Liability Law

ANTHONY & CARLSON, LLP
Oakland, CA....Civil Trial Practice; Insurance Defense; Labor and Employment Law; Medical Malpractice; Personal Injury; Professional Liability

ANTIN, MICHAEL, A LAW CORPORATION
Los Angeles, CA....Employment Benefits Law; Tax Law; Trust and Estates, Wills and Probate

ANTON, BRUCE
Dallas, TX....Criminal Trial Practice

ANTONELLI, TERRY, STOUT & KRAUS, LLP
Arlington, VA....Intellectual Property Law; Patent, Trademark, Copyright and Unfair Competition

ANWYL, SCOFFIELD, STEPP & UNIVERSAL
Sacramento, CA....Insurance Defense

ANZALONE LAW OFFICES
Wilkes-Barre, PA....Personal Injury

APFELBAUM, APFELBAUM & APFELBAUM
Sunbury, PA....Business Law; Trust and Estates, Wills and Probate

APICELLA AND TRAPP
Cleveland, OH....Medical Malpractice; Personal Injury

APPLE AND APPLE, A PROFESSIONAL CORPORATION
Pittsburgh, PA....Bankruptcy Law; Commercial Law; Creditors Rights

APRUZZESE, MCDERMOTT, MASTRO & MURPHY, A PROFESSIONAL CORPORATION
Liberty Corner, NJ....Commercial Law; Labor and Employment Law
Newark, NJ....Commercial Law; Labor and Employment Law
Springfield, NJ....Commercial Law; Labor and Employment Law

ARAGON, RAYMOND GEORGE
Chula Vista, CA....Criminal Trial Practice

ARAGON, BURLINGTON, WEIL & CROCKETT, P.A.
Miami, FL....Commercial Litigation; Criminal Trial Practice

ARBES, JAKE
Atlanta, GA ....Appellate Practice; Criminal Trial Practice

ARCHER, DAVID G., P.C.
Cartersville, GA ....Civil Trial Practice; Labor and Employment Law; Municipal and Zoning Law

ARENT FOX KINTNER PLOTKIN & KAHN, PLLC
Washington, DC......................Intellectual Property Law

ARESTY INTERNATIONAL LAW OFFICES, P.C.
Boston, MA...............................International Business Law

ARIANO, ANDERSON, HARDY & CASTILLO, P.C. A PROFESSIONAL CORPORATION
Elgin, IL ....General Practice

ARKIN, HARRY L., & ASSOCIATES, P.C.
Denver, CO ....Arbitration; Business Law; International Business Law; Trust and Estates, Wills and Probate

ARKIN SCHAFFER & KAPLAN LLP
New York, NY...........................Appellate Practice; Arbitration; Civil Trial Practice; Criminal Trial Practice; Labor and Employment Law; Securities Law

ARLEN, ROBERT M., P.A.
Delray Beach, FL.....................Tax Law; Trust and Estates, Wills and Probate

ARMBRECHT, JACKSON, DEMOUY, CROWE, HOLMES & REEVES, L.L.C.
Mobile, AL...............................Administrative Law; Admiralty/Maritime Law; Antitrust Law; Banking Law; Bankruptcy Law; Business Law; Civil Trial Practice; Commercial Litigation; Employment Benefits Law; General Practice; Insurance Defense; Labor and Employment Law; Medical Malpractice; Natural Resources Law; Securities Law; Tax Law

ARMOR, G. W.
Laverne, OK............................Trust and Estates, Wills and Probate

ARMSTRONG, E. ALAN
Atlanta, GA ....Aviation Law

ARMSTRONG ALLEN PREWITT GENTRY JOHNSTON & HOLMES, PLLC
Memphis, TN...........................Antitrust Law; Banking Law; Bankruptcy Law; Business Law; Civil Trial Practice; Commercial Law; Commercial Litigation; Communications Law; Computer Law; Employment Benefits Law; Environmental Law; Family Law; General Practice; Health Care Law; Insurance Defense; Labor and Employment Law; Medical Malpractice; Municipal Bond/Public Authority Financing; Personal Injury; Product Liability Law; Real Estate Law; Securities Law; Tax Law; Trademark, Copyright and Unfair Competition; Trust and Estates, Wills and Probate; Workers Compensation

ARMSTRONG & ARMSTRONG, P.A.
Smithfield, NC ....Family Law; Medical Malpractice; Personal Injury

ARMSTRONG, DONOHUE, CEPPOS & VAUGHAN, CHARTERED
Rockville, MD..........................Civil Trial Practice; Criminal Trial Practice; Insurance Defense; Medical Malpractice; Personal Injury

ARMSTRONG, GARRISON, LAW CORPORATION
San Diego, CA ....Pension and Profit Sharing; Tax Law

ARMSTRONG & MEJER, P.A.
Miami, FL................................Admiralty/Maritime Law; Business Law; Civil Trial Practice; Insurance Defense

ARMSTRONG TEASDALE LLP
Kansas City, MO......................General Practice
St. Louis, MO..........................Antitrust Law; Civil Trial Practice; Environmental Law; General Practice; Labor and Employment Law; Tax Law

ARNETT, DRAPER & HAGOOD
Knoxville, TN ....Civil Trial Practice; General Practice; Labor and Employment Law

ARNOLD, RICHARD P.
Greenbelt, MD.........................Criminal Trial Practice

ARNOLD & ANDERSON
Atlanta, GA ....Labor and Employment Law

ARNOLD, ANDERSON & DOVE, P.L.L.P.
Minneapolis, MN.....................Business Law; Civil Trial Practice; Family Law; General Practice; Personal Injury; Real Estate Law

ARNOLD GALLAGHER SAYDACK PERCELL & ROBERTS, P.C.
Eugene, OR ....General Practice

ARNOLD & PORTER
Washington, DC.......................General Practice

ARNOLD WHITE & DURKEE, A PROFESSIONAL CORPORATION
Menlo Park, CA.......................Patent, Trademark, Copyright and Unfair Competition
Washington, DC.......................Patent, Trademark, Copyright and Unfair Competition
Chicago, IL.............................Patent, Trademark, Copyright and Unfair Competition
Minneapolis, MN ....Patent, Trademark, Copyright and Unfair Competition
Austin, TX ....Patent, Trademark, Copyright and Unfair Competition
Houston, TX ....Patent, Trademark, Copyright and Unfair Competition

ARONBERG GOLDGEHN DAVIS & GARMISA
Chicago, IL..............................Appellate Practice; Banking Law; Civil Trial Practice; Commercial Litigation; Corporate Law; Family Law; General Practice; Health Care Law; Insurance Defense; Labor and Employment Law; Real Estate Law; Trust and Estates, Wills and Probate

ARONSOHN WEINER, A PROFESSIONAL CORPORATION
Hackensack, NJ.......................Commercial Litigation; Family Law

ARONSON, ROBERT H.
Chicago, IL..............................Criminal Trial Practice

ARSENEAULT & FASSETT
Chatham, NJ ....Appellate Practice; Civil Trial Practice; Criminal Trial Practice

ARTER & HADDEN LLP
Los Angeles, CA ....General Practice
Washington, DC.......................General Practice
Cleveland, OH.........................General Practice; Labor and Employment Law; Tax Law
Columbus, OH ....General Practice

ARTHUR AND PERLMUTTER
Denver, CO ....Creditors Rights

ARTZ, WILLIAM E., A PROFESSIONAL CORPORATION
Arlington, VA ....Medical Malpractice; Personal Injury

ASBILL, JUNKIN & MOFFITT, CHTD.
Washington, DC.......................Civil Trial Practice; Criminal Trial Practice

ASHBY & GEDDES
Wilmington, DE.......................Civil Trial Practice; General Practice

ASHCRAFT, WILLIAM E., LAW OFFICE, P.A.
Fort Lauderdale, FL ....Real Estate Law

ASHCROFT WILES, LLP
Salem, OR ....Insurance Defense; Trust and Estates, Wills and Probate

ASHE, TANNER, WRIGHT & KELLEY, P.C.
Tuscumbia, AL.........................Civil Trial Practice; Insurance Defense; Medical Malpractice; Personal Injury; Product Liability Law; Workers Compensation

ASHLEY, ASHLEY & ARNOLD
Dyersburg, TN ....Construction Law; Government Contracts

ASHMORE, JOSEPH E., JR., P.C.
Dallas, TX................................Banking Law; General Practice; Health Care Law; Trust and Estates, Wills and Probate

ASKER, CHAPP & CLOS, P.C.
Westland, MI ....Business Law; Commercial Litigation; Real Estate Law; Sports and Entertainment Law; Trust and Estates, Wills and Probate

ASKEW & ARCHBOLD, A PROFESSIONAL CORPORATION
Stockton, CA............................Business Law

ASPEY, WATKINS & DIESEL, P.L.L.C.
Flagstaff, AZ ....Criminal Trial Practice; Personal Injury

ASTOR WEISS KAPLAN & ROSENBLUM, LLP
Philadelphia, PA ....Business Law; Commercial Litigation; Family Law; General Practice; Personal Injury; Real Estate Law; Trust and Estates, Wills and Probate

ASTUNO, JOHN JR.
Denver, CO ....Medical Malpractice; Personal Injury

ASWAD & INGRAHAM
Binghamton, NY ....Civil Trial Practice; Criminal Trial Practice; Labor and Employment Law; Medical Malpractice; Real Estate Law

ATCHISON, CROSBY, SAAD & BEEBE, P.C.
Mobile, AL...............................Business Law; Civil Trial Practice; Construction Law; Corporate Law; Environmental Law; Personal Injury; Product Liability Law; Toxic Torts

ATCHLEY, RUSSELL, WALDROP & HLAVINKA, L.L.P.
Texarkana, TX ....Civil Trial Practice; General Practice

ATER WYNNE LLP
Portland, OR..........General Practice

ATES & ASSOCIATES, A PROFESSIONAL LAW CORPORATION
New Orleans, LA..........General Practice

ATHERTON & ALLEN
Chula Vista, CA..........General Practice; Trust and Estates, Wills and Probate

ATHERTON & HUTH
Emporia, KS..........General Practice

ATKINS & COHEN
Philadelphia, PA..........Civil Trial Practice

ATKINSON, HAMILL & BARROWCLOUGH, P.C.
Phoenix, AZ..........Bankruptcy Law; Commercial Litigation; Real Estate Law

ATKINSON, HASKINS, NELLIS, BOUDREAUX, HOLEMAN, PHIPPS & BRITTINGHAM, A PROFESSIONAL CORPORATION
Tulsa, OK..........Antitrust Law; Appellate Practice; Aviation Law; Bankruptcy Law; Business Law; Civil Rights; Civil Trial Practice; Commercial Litigation; Environmental Law; Insurance Defense; Medical Malpractice; Personal Injury; Product Liability Law

ATKINSON & KELSEY, P.A.
Albuquerque, NM..........Family Law

ATKINSON, PERRY, ATKINSON & BALHOFF, L.L.C.
Baton Rouge, LA..........Environmental Law; Insurance Defense; Personal Injury

ATLAS & HALL, L.L.P.
McAllen, TX..........General Practice

ATLASS PROFESSIONAL CORPORATION
Denver, CO..........Tax Law; Trust and Estates, Wills and Probate

ATLEE, HALL & BROOKHART, L.L.P.
Lancaster, PA..........Medical Malpractice; Personal Injury; Product Liability Law

ATTERBURY & RILEY, S.C.
Madison, WI..........Medical Malpractice; Personal Injury; Product Liability Law

ATWOOD & CHERNY
Boston, MA..........Civil Trial Practice; Family Law

ATWOOD, MALONE, TURNER & SABIN, A PROFESSIONAL ASSOCIATION
Roswell, NM..........Insurance Defense; Medical Malpractice

ATWOOD, RONALD W., P.C.
Portland, OR..........Workers Compensation

AUBERT & PAJARES, L.L.C.
Covington, LA..........Insurance Defense; Product Liability Law

AUERBACH, MARSHALL J., & ASSOCIATES, LTD.
Chicago, IL..........Family Law

AUERBACH, PHILIP G., A PROFESSIONAL CORPORATION
Red Bank, NJ..........Appellate Practice; Civil Trial Practice; Criminal Trial Practice; General Practice; Medical Malpractice; Personal Injury; Product Liability Law

AUGUST & KULUNAS, P.A.
West Palm Beach, FL..........Tax Law; Trust and Estates, Wills and Probate

AULTMAN, TYNER, RUFFIN & YARBOROUGH, LTD., A PROFESSIONAL LAW CORPORATION
Columbia, MS..........Admiralty/Maritime Law; Banking Law; Civil Trial Practice; Commercial Law; Environmental Law; General Practice; Insurance Defense
Gulfport, MS..........Admiralty/Maritime Law; Banking Law; Civil Trial Practice; Commercial Law; Environmental Law; General Practice; Insurance Defense
Hattiesburg, MS..........Admiralty/Maritime Law; Banking Law; Civil Trial Practice; Commercial Law; Environmental Law; General Practice; Insurance Defense

AUSLEY & ALGERT, L.L.P.
Austin, TX..........Family Law

AUSLEY & MCMULLEN, P.A.
Tallahassee, FL..........General Practice

AUSTIN, PEIRCE & SMITH, P.C.
Aspen, CO..........Appellate Practice; Civil Trial Practice; General Practice; Municipal and Zoning Law; Real Estate Law

AUSTIN & PEPPERMAN
Leesburg, FL..........Appellate Practice; Civil Trial Practice; General Practice

AUTREY, D. ROBERT, JR., P.C.
Marietta, GA..........Civil Trial Practice

AVERY & ASSOCIATES
San Francisco, CA..........Tax Law; Trust and Estates, Wills and Probate

AVERY, WHIGHAM & WINESETT, P.A.
Fort Myers, FL..........Trust and Estates, Wills and Probate

AVIS & AVIS, P.A.
Palm Beach, FL..........Commercial Litigation; Corporate Law; Real Estate Law

AWSUMB, R. A., & ASSOCIATES, PLC
St. Paul, MN..........Personal Injury; Product Liability Law

AXE, JOHN R. AND ASSOCIATES
Grosse Pointe Farms, MI..........Municipal Bond/Public Authority Financing

AXELROD, GOODMAN, STEINER & BAZELON
Chicago, IL..........Transportation Law

AXLEY BRYNELSON, LLP
Madison, WI..........Civil Trial Practice; Commercial Law; Environmental Law; General Practice; Insurance Defense; Medical Malpractice; Personal Injury; Trust and Estates, Wills and Probate

AYABE, CHONG, NISHIMOTO, SIA & NAKAMURA
Honolulu, HI..........Construction Law; Insurance Defense; Legal Malpractice; Medical Malpractice; Personal Injury; Real Estate Law

AYCOCK, HORNE & COLEMAN
Franklin, LA..........General Practice

AYE LAW FIRM, P.A.
Tampa, FL..........Labor and Employment Law

AYRES, JENKINS, GORDY & ALMAND, P.A.
Ocean City, MD..........Civil Trial Practice; Criminal Trial Practice

AZAR & AZAR, L.L.C.
Montgomery, AL..........General Practice

BABIN, SEEGER, CROW & MANWELL, LLP
Santa Rosa, CA..........Business Law; Insurance Defense

BABST, CALLAND, CLEMENTS AND ZOMNIR, A PROFESSIONAL CORPORATION
Pittsburgh, PA..........Commercial Law; Construction Law; Environmental Law; Labor and Employment Law; Municipal and Zoning Law

BACALSKI, BYRNE & KOSKA
San Diego, CA..........Civil Trial Practice; General Practice

BACHMAN & LAPOINTE, P.C.
New Haven, CT..........Patent, Trademark, Copyright and Unfair Competition

BACHMANN, HESS, BACHMANN & GARDEN, P.L.L.C.
Wheeling, WV..........General Practice; Insurance Defense; Personal Injury

BACINO, BIRGER GREG, APC, THE LAW OFFICES OF
San Diego, CA..........Aviation Law; Elder Law; Personal Injury; Product Liability Law; Toxic Torts

BACKER & BACKER, A PROFESSIONAL CORPORATION
Indianapolis, IN..........Business Law; Commercial Law; Construction Law; Real Estate Law

BACKES & HILL
Trenton, NJ..........Civil Trial Practice; General Practice

BACKMAN & BLUMEL, P.S.
Spokane, WA..........Medical Malpractice; Personal Injury

BACKUS, LELAND EUGENE, & ASSOCIATES LTD.
Las Vegas, NV..........Construction Law; Insurance Defense; International Business Law

BACON & DEAR, PLC
Phoenix, AZ..........Employment Benefits Law; Immigration and Naturalization

BACON & MILLS, LLP
Brea, CA..........Corporate Law; Trust and Estates, Wills and Probate
Los Angeles, CA..........Business Law; Insurance Defense

BADDOUR, PARKER & HINE, PROFESSIONAL CORPORATION
Goldsboro, NC..........General Practice

BADGER, DAVID R., P.A.
Charlotte, NC..........Bankruptcy Law

BADGER, DOLAN, PARKER & COHEN
Boston, MA..........Commercial Law; Insurance Defense; Product Liability Law

BADGLEY - MULLINS
Seattle, WA .... Commercial Litigation

BADIAK WILL & RUDDY
New York, NY .... Admiralty/Maritime Law; Aviation Law; Civil Trial Practice; General Practice; Insurance Defense; Transportation Law

BAER MARKS & UPHAM LLP
New York, NY .... Civil Trial Practice; General Practice

BAGGETT, MCCALL & BURGESS, A PROFESSIONAL LAW CORPORATION
Lake Charles, LA .... Personal Injury; Toxic Torts

BAI, POLLOCK AND COYNE, P.C.
Bridgeport, CT .... Civil Trial Practice; Insurance Defense; Medical Malpractice; Personal Injury; Product Liability Law

BAILEY & BROWN
Sacramento, CA .... Insurance Defense

BAILEY & DIXON, L.L.P.
Raleigh, NC .... Appellate Practice; Civil Trial Practice; Insurance Defense; Personal Injury; Product Liability Law; Public Utilities Law

BAILEY LAW FIRM
Mountain Home, AR .... Medical Malpractice

BAILEY & MYERS, P.A.
Maitland, FL .... Medical Malpractice; Personal Injury; Product Liability Law

BAILEY, PATTERSON, CADDELL, HART, MILLIKEN & BAILEY, P.A.
Charlotte, NC .... Civil Trial Practice; Criminal Trial Practice; Personal Injury; Tax Law

BAILEY & PETERSON, P.C.
Denver, CO .... General Practice

BAILEY, RALPH, P.A.
Greenville, SC .... Patent, Trademark, Copyright and Unfair Competition

BAILEY & STOCK
Cheyenne, WY .... Civil Trial Practice

BAIN, TROY E.
Shreveport, LA .... Civil Trial Practice; Medical Malpractice; Personal Injury

BAIN & MCRAE
Lillington, NC .... General Practice

BAINTON MCCARTHY & SIEGEL, LLC
New York, NY .... Civil Trial Practice

BAIRD, BAIRD, BAIRD AND JONES, P.S.C.
Pikeville, KY .... General Practice

BAIRD, WILLIAMS, DAVIS & SMITH
Phoenix, AZ .... Commercial Litigation; Real Estate Law

BAISE, MILLER & FREER, P.C.
Washington, DC .... Environmental Law

BAKAS, JOHN W. JR.
Tampa, FL .... Commercial Litigation; Construction Law; Government Contracts

BAKER, J. NORMAN
Mountain View, CA .... Family Law

BAKER, BAKER & TWOMEY, P.A.
Baltimore, MD .... Civil Trial Practice

BAKER BOTTS, L.L.P.
Washington, DC .... Administrative Law; Business Law; Civil Trial Practice; Commercial Law; Environmental Law; General Practice; Natural Resources Law; Patent, Trademark, Copyright and Unfair Competition; Tax Law; Trademark, Copyright and Unfair Competition
New York, NY .... Business Law; Civil Trial Practice; Commercial Law; General Practice; Patent, Trademark, Copyright and Unfair Competition; Tax Law; Trademark, Copyright and Unfair Competition
Austin, TX .... Administrative Law; Banking Law; Bankruptcy Law; Business Law; Civil Trial Practice; Commercial Law; Environmental Law; General Practice; Patent, Trademark, Copyright and Unfair Competition; Real Estate Law; Trademark, Copyright and Unfair Competition
Dallas, TX .... Administrative Law; Antitrust Law; Banking Law; Bankruptcy Law; Business Law; Civil Trial Practice; Commercial Law; General Practice; Labor and Employment Law; Patent, Trademark, Copyright and Unfair Competition; Personal Injury; Real Estate Law; Trademark, Copyright and Unfair Competition
Houston, TX .... Administrative Law; Admiralty/Maritime Law; Antitrust Law; Banking Law; Bankruptcy Law; Business Law; Civil Trial Practice; Commercial Law; Environmental Law; General Practice; Labor and Employment Law; Patent, Trademark, Copyright and Unfair Competition; Personal Injury; Real Estate Law; Tax Law; Trust and Estates, Wills and Probate

BAKER & BOYAN, P.L.L.C.
High Point, NC .... General Practice

BAKER, CAMPBELL & PARSONS
Nashville, TN .... General Practice

BAKER & DANIELS
Washington, DC .... General Practice
Elkhart, IN .... General Practice
Fort Wayne, IN .... General Practice
Indianapolis, IN .... General Practice
South Bend, IN .... General Practice
Qingdao, China .... General Practice

BAKER, DONELSON, BEARMAN & CALDWELL
Jackson, MS .... Civil Trial Practice; Commercial Litigation; Environmental Law; General Practice; Health Care Law; Insurance Defense; Labor and Employment Law; Tax Law; Trust and Estates, Wills and Probate
Chattanooga, TN .... Commercial Litigation; General Practice; Health Care Law; Immigration and Naturalization; Intellectual Property Law; Labor and Employment Law; Real Estate Law; Securities Law; Tax Law; Trust and Estates, Wills and Probate
Huntsville, TN .... Civil Trial Practice; General Practice
Johnson City, TN .... Civil Trial Practice; Commercial Litigation; General Practice; Labor and Employment Law; Securities Law
Knoxville, TN .... Civil Trial Practice; Environmental Law; General Practice; Securities Law; Tax Law
Memphis, TN .... Banking Law; Bankruptcy Law; Business Law; Civil Trial Practice; Environmental Law; General Practice; Health Care Law; Immigration and Naturalization; Insurance Defense; Labor and Employment Law; Municipal Bond/Public Authority Financing; Securities Law; Tax Law
Nashville, TN .... Antitrust Law; Bankruptcy Law; Civil Trial Practice; Corporate Law; Environmental Law; General Practice; Health Care Law; Labor and Employment Law; Mergers and Acquisitions; Real Estate Law; Securities Law; Tax Law

BAKER, DUBLIKAR, BECK, WILEY & MATHEWS
Canton, OH .... Civil Trial Practice; Insurance Defense

BAKER, ELIZABETH S., P.A., LAW OFFICES OF
Miami, FL .... Family Law

BAKER & HOSTETLER LLP
Long Beach, CA .... Admiralty/Maritime Law; General Practice
Los Angeles, CA .... Admiralty/Maritime Law; Bankruptcy Law; Civil Trial Practice; Environmental Law; General Practice; Labor and Employment Law; Real Estate Law; Trademark, Copyright and Unfair Competition
Denver, CO .... Civil Trial Practice; Environmental Law; General Practice
Washington, DC .... Administrative Law; Antitrust Law; Banking Law; Civil Trial Practice; Communications Law; Environmental Law; General Practice; Labor and Employment Law; Tax Law; Trademark, Copyright and Unfair Competition; Transportation Law
Orlando, FL .... Civil Trial Practice; Construction Law; General Practice; Municipal Bond/Public Authority Financing; Real Estate Law; Tax Law
Cleveland, OH .... Antitrust Law; Banking Law; Bankruptcy Law; Civil Trial Practice; Communications Law; Construction Law; Employment Benefits Law; Environmental Law; General Practice; Immigration and Naturalization; Labor and Employment Law; Municipal Bond/Public Authority Financing; Real Estate Law; Tax Law; Trademark, Copyright and Unfair Competition; Trust and Estates, Wills and Probate
Columbus, OH .... Bankruptcy Law; Civil Trial Practice; Employment Benefits Law; General Practice; Labor and Employment Law; Tax Law; Transportation Law
Houston, TX .... Civil Trial Practice; General Practice

BAKER AND JACOBSON, A PROFESSIONAL CORPORATION
Los Angeles, CA .... Bankruptcy Law; Civil Trial Practice; Construction Law; Real Estate Law

BAKER, JENKINS, JONES & DALY, P.A.
Ahoskie, NC .... Insurance Defense

BAKER, KEENER & NAHRA, LLP
Santa Monica, CA .... Commercial Litigation; Construction Law; Labor and Employment Law; Legal Malpractice; Medical Malpractice; Personal Injury; Product Liability Law; Professional Liability; Toxic Torts

BAKER, LANCIANESE, CAMPBELL & CONATY
Huntington, WV .... Bankruptcy Law; Creditors Rights; Health Care Law; Insurance Defense; Labor and Employment Law; Medical Malpractice; Product Liability Law; Professional Liability; Real Estate Law; Toxic Torts

BAKER LAW FIRM, THE
Little Rock, AR .... Civil Trial Practice; Personal Injury

BAKER, MANOCK & JENSEN, A PROFESSIONAL CORPORATION
Fresno, CA .... General Practice

BAKER & MAXHAM, A PROFESSIONAL CORPORATION
San Diego, CA .... Patent, Trademark, Copyright and Unfair Competition

BAKER & MCKENZIE
Palo Alto, CA .... General Practice
San Diego, CA .... General Practice
San Francisco, CA .... General Practice
Washington, DC .... General Practice
Miami, FL .... General Practice
Chicago, IL .... General Practice
New York, NY .... General Practice
Dallas, TX .... General Practice
Houston, TX .... General Practice
Toronto, ON, Canada .... General Practice
Buenos Aires, Argentina .... General Practice
Melbourne, Victoria, Australia .... General Practice
Sydney, New South Wales, Australia .... General Practice
Baku, Azerbaijan .... General Practice
Manama, Bahrain .... General Practice
Brussels, Belgium .... General Practice
Santiago, Chile .... General Practice
Beijing, China .... General Practice
Hong Kong, China .... General Practice
Prague, Czech Republic .... General Practice
Cairo, Egypt .... General Practice
Paris, France .... General Practice
Milan, Italy .... General Practice
Rome, Italy .... General Practice
Almaty, Kazakhstan .... General Practice
Ciudad Juarez, Chihuahua, Mexico .... General Practice
Mexico, D.F., Mexico .... General Practice
Monterrey, Nuevo León, Mexico .... General Practice
Tijuana, Baja California, Mexico .... General Practice
Moscow, Russia .... General Practice
St. Petersburg, Russia .... General Practice
Singapore, Singapore .... General Practice
Barcelona, Spain .... General Practice
Madrid, Spain .... General Practice
Zürich, Switzerland .... General Practice
Hsinchu, Taiwan .... General Practice
Taipei, Taiwan .... General Practice
Bangkok, Thailand .... General Practice
Kyiv (Kiev), Ukraine .... General Practice
Caracas, Venezuela .... General Practice
Valencia, Venezuela .... General Practice
Hanoi, Vietnam .... General Practice
Ho Chi Minh City, Vietnam .... General Practice
Geneva, Switzerland .... General Practice
Stockholm, Sweden .... General Practice
Warsaw, Poland .... General Practice
Berlin, Germany .... General Practice
Düsseldorf, Germany .... General Practice
Frankfurt/Main, Germany .... General Practice
Munich, Germany .... General Practice

BALCH & BINGHAM LLP
Birmingham, AL .... General Practice

BALCOMB & GREEN, P.C.
Glenwood Springs, CO .... General Practice

BALDWIN & HASPEL, L.L.C.
New Orleans, LA .... Business Law; Product Liability Law; Real Estate Law; Tax Law

BALFOUR MOSS
Regina, SK, Canada .... Civil Trial Practice; Commercial Law; General Practice

BALISLE & ROBERSON, S.C.
Madison, WI .... Appellate Practice; Family Law; Trust and Estates, Wills and Probate

BALK, OXFELD, MANDELL & COHEN, A PROFESSIONAL CORPORATION
Newark, NJ .... General Practice; Labor and Employment Law

BALL, ANDREW D., P.C.
Rockville, MD .... Trust and Estates, Wills and Probate

BALLARD, ROSENBERG & GOLPER
Universal City, CA .... Arbitration; Labor and Employment Law

BALLARD SPAHR ANDREWS & INGERSOLL, LLP
Denver, CO .... Civil Trial Practice; Commercial Law; Environmental Law; General Practice; Municipal Bond/Public Authority Financing; Natural Resources Law; Real Estate Law; Securities Law
Washington, DC .... General Practice; Municipal Bond/Public Authority Financing; Real Estate Law; Tax Law
Baltimore, MD .... Banking Law; Bankruptcy Law; Civil Trial Practice; Commercial Law; Real Estate Law
Philadelphia, PA .... Antitrust Law; Banking Law; Bankruptcy Law; Civil Trial Practice; Commercial Law; Employment Benefits Law; Environmental Law; General Practice; Health Care Law; Labor and Employment Law; Municipal Bond/Public Authority Financing; Real Estate Law; Tax Law; Trust and Estates, Wills and Probate
Salt Lake City, UT .... Municipal Bond/Public Authority Financing; Real Estate Law

BALL, BALL, MATTHEWS & NOVAK, P.A.
Montgomery, AL .... Civil Trial Practice; Corporate Law; General Practice; Insurance Defense; Product Liability Law

BALL, BARDEN & BELL, P.A.
Asheville, NC .... Insurance Defense

BALL, BARTON & HOFFMAN, A PROFESSIONAL ASSOCIATION
Monticello, AR .... General Practice

BALL, EGGLESTON, BUMBLEBURG, MCBRIDE, WALKEY & STAPLETON, PC
Lafayette, IN .... Appellate Practice; Civil Trial Practice; General Practice; Insurance Defense; Municipal and Zoning Law; Personal Injury; Real Estate Law; Trust and Estates, Wills and Probate

BALL JANIK LLP
Portland, OR .... General Practice

BALL & KOONS
Bay Minette, AL .... Criminal Trial Practice

BALL, MCDONOUGH & ARTZ, P.C.
Binghamton, NY .... Personal Injury; Real Estate Law

BALL & MOURTON, LTD., PLLC
Fayetteville, AR .... Business Law; General Practice; Tax Law; Trust and Estates, Wills and Probate

BALLON STOLL BADER & NADLER, P.C.
New York, NY .... General Practice

BAMBERGER & FEIBLEMAN
Indianapolis, IN .... Bankruptcy Law; Civil Rights; Commercial Law; International Business Law

BANDER, FOX-ISICOFF & ASSOCIATES, P.A.
Miami, FL .... Immigration and Naturalization

BANGEL, BANGEL & BANGEL, L.L.P.
Portsmouth, VA .... Personal Injury

BANGS, MCCULLEN, BUTLER, FOYE & SIMMONS, L.L.P.
Rapid City, SD .... Civil Trial Practice; Corporate Law; General Practice; Health Care Law; Labor and Employment Law; Personal Injury; Trust and Estates, Wills and Probate

BANKS & UNDERHILL, P.C.
Portland, OR .... Business Law; Civil Rights; Professional Liability; Securities Law

BANKSTON & RICHARDSON, L.L.P.
Austin, TX .... Appellate Practice; Civil Trial Practice

BANNER & WITCOFF, LTD.
Washington, DC .... Patent, Trademark, Copyright and Unfair Competition; Trademark, Copyright and Unfair Competition
Chicago, IL .... Patent, Trademark, Copyright and Unfair Competition; Trademark, Copyright and Unfair Competition
Boston, MA .... Patent, Trademark, Copyright and Unfair Competition
Portland, OR .... Patent, Trademark, Copyright and Unfair Competition

BANNIGAN & KELLY, P.A.
St. Paul, MN .... Civil Trial Practice; Labor and Employment Law; Municipal and Zoning Law

BANTA, HOYT, EVERALL & FARRINGTON, L.L.C.
Englewood, CO .... Civil Trial Practice; General Practice; Real Estate Law

BANTZ, GOSCH, CREMER, PETERSON & SOMMERS
Aberdeen, SD .... Banking Law; Business Law; Insurance Defense

BANZET, BANZET & THOMPSON
Warrenton, NC .... General Practice

BARASH & STOERZBACH, P.C.
Galesburg, IL .... General Practice; Trust and Estates, Wills and Probate

BARBAS WEED KOENIG NUÑEZ & WHEELEY
Tampa, FL .... Personal Injury; Workers Compensation

BARBER, JAMES C. LAW OFFICES OF
Dallas, TX .... Medical Malpractice; Personal Injury

BARBER, EMERSON, SPRINGER, ZINN & MURRAY, L.C.
Lawrence, KS .... General Practice

BARBER, HAMILTON & SHOULDERS
Evansville, IN .... General Practice

BARBER, MCCASKILL, JONES & HALE, P.A.
Little Rock, AR .... Commercial Law; General Practice; Health Care Law; Insurance Defense; Legal Malpractice; Medical Malpractice; Personal Injury; Product Liability Law; Toxic Torts; Trust and Estates, Wills and Probate; Workers Compensation

BARBERA, CLAPPER, BEENER, RULLO & MELVIN
Somerset, PA .... General Practice

BARBIERI, CHRISTINA J. & ASSOCIATES
Philadelphia, PA .... Workers Compensation

BARBOSA GARCIA LLP
Los Angeles, CA .... Business Law; Commercial Litigation; Construction Law; Eminent Domain; Labor and Employment Law; Mergers and Acquisitions; Municipal and Zoning Law

BARCLAY & GOERING, P.C.
Phoenix, AZ .... Health Care Law

BARDENWERPER & LOBB, PLLC
Louisville, KY .... Land Use Law; Municipal and Zoning Law; Real Estate Law

BARFORD, BURNS F. JR.
Valatie, NY .... General Practice; Municipal and Zoning Law; Real Estate Law; Trust and Estates, Wills and Probate

BARGER, HERMANSEN, MCKIBBEN & VILLARREAL, L.L.P.
Corpus Christi, TX .... Appellate Practice; Civil Trial Practice; Insurance Defense

BARHAM & ARCENEAUX, A PROFESSIONAL LAW CORPORATION
New Orleans, LA .... Appellate Practice; Civil Trial Practice

BARISH, MARVIN I., LAW OFFICES, A PROF. CORP.
Philadelphia, PA .... Admiralty/Maritime Law; Civil Trial Practice; Medical Malpractice; Personal Injury; Transportation Law

BARKATS & ASSOCIATES, CHARTERED, ATTORNEYS AND COUNSELORS AT LAW
Washington, DC .... Aviation Law; Computer Law; Intellectual Property Law; International Business Law; Trademark, Copyright and Unfair Competition

BARKER, BROWN, BUSBY, CHRISMAN & THOMAS, A PROFESSIONAL CORPORATION
Las Vegas, NV .... Civil Trial Practice; Commercial Litigation; Insurance Defense; Labor and Employment Law

BARKER THOMAS & WALTERS, A PROFESSIONAL LAW CORPORATION
San Diego, CA .... Commercial Litigation; Construction Law; Labor and Employment Law

BARKLEY, ALICE SUET YEE
San Francisco, CA .... Environmental Law; Land Use Law

BARKLEY & KENNEDY, CHARTERED
Rockville, MD .... Bankruptcy Law; Commercial Litigation; Creditors Rights

BARLEY, SNYDER, SENFT & COHEN, LLC
Chambersburg, PA .... Business Law; General Practice; Health Care Law
Hanover, PA .... Commercial Litigation; General Practice; Labor and Employment Law
Harrisburg, PA .... Commercial Litigation; General Practice; Tax Law
Lancaster, PA .... Commercial Litigation; General Practice; Health Care Law
Reading, PA .... General Practice; Intellectual Property Law; Labor and Employment Law
York, PA .... Commercial Litigation; General Practice; Health Care Law

BARLOW & DERBY
Troy, MI .... Business Law; Health Care Law; Labor and Employment Law

BARLOW AND HARDTNER L.C.
Shreveport, LA .... Administrative Law; Appellate Practice; Business Law; Civil Trial Practice; Commercial Law; Communications Law; Construction Law; Environmental Law; General Practice; Insurance Defense; Land Use Law; Natural Resources Law; Product Liability Law; Public Utilities Law; Real Estate Law; Tax Law; Transportation Law; Trust and Estates, Wills and Probate

BARMANN, KRAMER & BOHLEN, P.C.
Kankakee, IL .... Commercial Law; Commercial Litigation; General Practice; Health Care Law; Personal Injury

BARNES, ALFORD, STORK & JOHNSON, L.L.P.
Columbia, SC .... Appellate Practice; Arbitration; Banking Law; Construction Law; General Practice; Insurance Defense; Legal Malpractice; Medical Malpractice; Product Liability Law; Real Estate Law; Tax Law; Workers Compensation

BARNES, CROSBY, FITZGERALD & ZEMAN LLP
Irvine, CA .... Civil Trial Practice

BARNES, F. SMITH, P.C.
Oklahoma City, OK .... Business Law; Trust and Estates, Wills and Probate

BARNES & THORNBURG
Washington, DC .... General Practice
Chicago, IL .... Bankruptcy Law; Creditors Rights; General Practice
Elkhart, IN .... Bankruptcy Law; Creditors Rights; General Practice
Fort Wayne, IN .... Bankruptcy Law; Creditors Rights; General Practice
Indianapolis, IN .... Bankruptcy Law; Creditors Rights; General Practice
South Bend, IN .... Bankruptcy Law; Creditors Rights; General Practice

BARNETT, LYNN D.
St. Louis, MO .... Workers Compensation

BARNETT, BARCLAY & SPRINGMANN, P.A.
Orlando, FL .... Criminal Trial Practice; Family Law

BARNETT • MATTICE
Fairfield, CA .... Personal Injury

BARNETT, SCOTT F., CHARTERED
Tampa, FL .... Trust and Estates, Wills and Probate

BARNEY, GROSSMAN, DUBOW & MARCUS
Ithaca, NY .... General Practice

BARNHART, STEVEN D., & ASSOCIATES, P.C.
Atlanta, GA .... Civil Trial Practice; Labor and Employment Law

BARNWELL WHALEY PATTERSON & HELMS, LLC
Charleston, SC .... Civil Trial Practice; Construction Law; Health Care Law; Insurance Defense; Labor and Employment Law; Product Liability Law

BAROKAS, MARTIN, AHLERS & TOMLINSON
Seattle, WA .... Business Law; Construction Law

BARON, SAR, GOODWIN, GILL & LOHR
Sioux City, IA .... General Practice

BAROUSSE & CRATON
Crowley, LA .... Civil Trial Practice; General Practice

BARR, BURT, & ASSOCIATES, L.L.P.
Dallas, TX .... Insurance Defense; International Business Law

BARR, DUGAN, & ASSOCIATES
Redding, CA .... Aviation Law; Civil Trial Practice; Personal Injury; Product Liability Law

BARR, JOSEPH J., JR., A PROFESSIONAL CORPORATION
San Diego, CA .... Civil Trial Practice; Insurance Defense

BARR, MURMAN, TONELLI, HERZFELD & RUBIN
Tampa, FL .... Civil Trial Practice; Commercial Litigation; Insurance Defense; Medical Malpractice; Personal Injury; Workers Compensation

BARR, UNGER AND MCINTOSH, L.L.C.
Charleston, SC .... Civil Trial Practice; Criminal Trial Practice

BARRACK, RODOS & BACINE
Philadelphia, PA .... Antitrust Law; Securities Law

BARRAN LIEBMAN LLP
Portland, OR .... Labor and Employment Law

BARRET, HAYNES, MAY, CARTER AND ROARK, P.S.C.
Hazard, KY .... General Practice

BARRETT, DANIEL R. LAW OFFICES OF
Fort Worth, TX .... Medical Malpractice

BARRETT & ASSOCIATES
Cambridge, MA .... Business Law; Mergers and Acquisitions; Securities Law

BARRETT BURKE WILSON CASTLE DAFFIN & FRAPPIER, L.L.P.
Addison, TX .... Banking Law; Bankruptcy Law; Civil Trial Practice; Corporate Law; Real Estate Law

BARRETT & DEACON, A PROFESSIONAL ASSOCIATION
Jonesboro, AR .... Civil Trial Practice; General Practice; Insurance Defense

BARRETT GILMAN & ZIKER
Seattle, WA .... Commercial Litigation; Environmental Law

BARRETT GRAVANTE CARPINELLO & STERN LLP
New York, NY .... Appellate Practice; Civil Trial Practice; Criminal Trial Practice

BARRETT & WEBER, A LEGAL PROFESSIONAL ASSOCIATION
Cincinnati, OH .... Administrative Law; Municipal and Zoning Law; Real Estate Law; Trust and Estates, Wills and Probate

BARRIS, SOTT, DENN & DRIKER, P.L.L.C.
Detroit, MI .... Civil Trial Practice; Real Estate Law

BARRON & BERRY, L.L.P.
Greensboro, NC .... Civil Trial Practice; Medical Malpractice; Personal Injury

BARRON & STADFELD, P.C.
Boston, MA .... Banking Law; Business Law; Civil Trial Practice; Environmental Law; General Practice; Personal Injury; Real Estate Law

BARROW GADDIS GRIFFITH & GRIMM, A PROFESSIONAL CORPORATION
Tulsa, OK .... Bankruptcy Law; Business Law; Civil Trial Practice; Tax Law

BARROW, SIMS & LEE, A PROFESSIONAL CORPORATION
Savannah, GA .... Insurance Defense

BARRY, MCTIERNAN & MOORE
New York, NY .... Civil Trial Practice; Insurance Defense

BARRY, RICHARD, AND SHARON MAH
San Rafael, CA .... Family Law

BARTEL ENG LINN & SCHRODER
Sacramento, CA .... Securities Law; Tax Law

BARTELS & FEUREISEN, LLP
White Plains, NY .... General Practice

BARTHOLOMEW, WASZNICKY & MOLINARO LLP
Sacramento, CA .... Family Law

BARTIMUS, FRICKLETON & PRESLEY, A PROFESSIONAL CORPORATION
Kansas City, MO .... Aviation Law; Health Care Law; Medical Malpractice; Personal Injury; Product Liability Law

BARTKO, ZANKEL, TARRANT & MILLER, PROFESSIONAL CORPORATION
San Francisco, CA .... Civil Trial Practice; Commercial Litigation; Real Estate Law

BARTLETT, BARBARA ANN
Tulsa, OK .... Family Law

BARTLETT, MCDONOUGH, BASTONE & MONAGHAN, LLP
Mineola, NY .... Medical Malpractice; Personal Injury

BARTON, KLUGMAN & OETTING LLP
Los Angeles, CA .... Civil Trial Practice

BARTON, RICHARDSON, CANSECO & WHITNEY, L.L.P.
New Orleans, LA .... Commercial Litigation

BARTON & SCHNEIDER, L.L.P.
San Antonio, TX .... Real Estate Law

BARTON AND STREVER, P.C.
Newport, OR .... Personal Injury

BASILE, PAUL L. JR.
Los Angeles, CA .... Business Law; Tax Law; Trust and Estates, Wills and Probate

BASILE & TESTA, A PROFESSIONAL CORPORATION
Vineland, NJ .... Civil Trial Practice; General Practice

BASKIN, RICHARD J. LAW OFFICES OF
Oakland, CA .... Personal Injury; Product Liability Law

BASKIN, BENNETT & KOMKOV, L.L.P.
Austin, TX .... Commercial Litigation; Construction Law

BASS, SUZANNE
Jacksonville, FL .... Criminal Trial Practice

BASS, BERRY & SIMS PLC
Nashville, TN .... Antitrust Law; Bankruptcy Law; Environmental Law; Health Care Law; Labor and Employment Law; Municipal Bond/Public Authority Financing; Securities Law; Tax Law

BASS & CARLSON, P.A.
Minneapolis, MN .... Personal Injury

BASS, JAMES R., INC., LAW OFFICES OF
San Antonio, TX .... Civil Trial Practice; Family Law; Trust and Estates, Wills and Probate

BASSETT LAW FIRM
Fayetteville, AR .... Civil Trial Practice; General Practice

BASSFORD, LOCKHART, TRUESDELL & BRIGGS, P.A.
Minneapolis, MN .... Civil Trial Practice; Environmental Law; General Practice; Insurance Defense; Personal Injury

BASTEDO STEWART SMITH
Toronto, ON, Canada .... Family Law

BASTIANELLI, BROWN & KELLEY, CHARTERED
Washington, DC .... Admiralty/Maritime Law; Government Contracts

BASTONE ASSOCIATES
Boston, MA .... Immigration and Naturalization

BASYE & GOLDEN
San Mateo, CA .... Trust and Estates, Wills and Probate

BATES, PHILIP A.
Pensacola, FL .... Business Law; Commercial Litigation; Creditors Rights

BATES & CASEY
Fort Worth, TX .... Criminal Trial Practice

BATES MECKLER BULGER & TILSON
Chicago, IL .... Civil Trial Practice; Commercial Law; Insurance Defense; Labor and Employment Law; Product Liability Law

BATHGATE, WEGENER & WOLF, P.C.
Lakewood, NJ .... Civil Trial Practice; Environmental Law; General Practice; Municipal Bond/Public Authority Financing

BATJER & WAGSTAFF, P.C.
Abilene, TX .... General Practice; Insurance Defense

BATSEL, MCKINLEY, ITTERSAGEN, GUNDERSON & BERNTSSON, P.A.
Englewood, FL .... Real Estate Law; Trust and Estates, Wills and Probate
Port Charlotte, FL .... Real Estate Law

BATSON, NOLAN, BRICE, HARVEY & WILLIAMSON, PLLC
Clarksville, TN .... Commercial Litigation; General Practice; Insurance Defense

BATTLE FOWLER LLP
New York, NY .... General Practice

BATZAR & WEINBERG, A PROFESSIONAL CORPORATION
Rockville Centre, NY .... Bankruptcy Law; Commercial Law; Commercial Litigation

BAUDLER, BAUDLER, MAUS & BLAHNIK
Austin, MN .... General Practice
Spring Valley, MN .... General Practice

BAUER, BERNARD K., CO., L.P.A.
Findlay, OH .... Personal Injury

BAUER, CRIDER & PELLEGRINO
Clearwater, FL .... Criminal Trial Practice
Tampa, FL .... Criminal Trial Practice

BAUGHER, METTLER & SHELTON
Palm Beach, FL .... Real Estate Law; Tax Law; Trust and Estates, Wills and Probate

BAUM & ASSOCIATES
Bloomfield Hills, MI .... Criminal Trial Practice

BAUMEISTER & SAMUELS, P.C.
Morristown, NJ .... Aviation Law; Civil Trial Practice; Environmental Law; Medical Malpractice; Personal Injury; Product Liability Law; Toxic Torts
New York, NY .... Aviation Law; Civil Trial Practice; Environmental Law; Medical Malpractice; Personal Injury; Product Liability Law; Toxic Torts

BAUM, HEDLUND, ARISTEI, GUILFORD & DOWNEY, A PROFESSIONAL CORPORATION
Los Angeles, CA .... Aviation Law; Personal Injury; Product Liability Law

Washington, DC....................Aviation Law; Personal Injury; Product Liability Law

BAUS, HAMMOND & DALY, L.L.P.
New Orleans, LA....................Insurance Defense

BAVOL, BUSH & SISCO, P.L.L.C.
Tampa, FL....................Commercial Litigation; Medical Malpractice; Product Liability Law

BAXLEY, DILLARD, DAUPHIN & MCKNIGHT
Birmingham, AL....................Administrative Law; Criminal Trial Practice; Personal Injury

BAXTER, JENSEN, PAYNE, YOUNG & SMITH
Benton, AR....................Civil Trial Practice; Insurance Defense

BAYARD, FORREST S.
Chicago, IL....................Family Law

BAYER, THEODORE R.
Miami, FL....................Arbitration

BAYER, KARL
Austin, TX....................Appellate Practice; Civil Trial Practice; Computer Law; Medical Malpractice; Patent, Trademark, Copyright and Unfair Competition; Personal Injury; Product Liability Law

BAYKO GIBSON CARNEGIE HAGAN SCHOONMAKER & MEYER LLP
Houston, TX....................Appellate Practice; Civil Trial Practice; General Practice; Labor and Employment Law

BAYLESS & STOKES
Houston, TX....................Civil Trial Practice; Commercial Litigation; Creditors Rights; Trust and Estates, Wills and Probate

BAYLOR, EVNEN, CURTISS, GRIMIT & WITT
Lincoln, NE....................General Practice

BAYS, DEAVER, HIATT, LUNG & ROSE
Honolulu, HI....................Commercial Law; Construction Law; Real Estate Law

BEACH, BURCKE, HELFERS, MITTLEMAN AND STEWART, L.L.C.
St. Louis, MO....................Civil Trial Practice

BEACH LAW FIRM, P.A.
Columbia, SC....................Commercial Law; Public Utilities Law; Securities Law

BEAHM AND GREEN
New Orleans, LA....................Health Care Law; Medical Malpractice; Professional Liability

BEAM, BROBECK & WEST
Santa Ana, CA....................Employment Benefits Law; General Practice; Insurance Defense; Medical Malpractice; Product Liability Law

BEAN, KINNEY & KORMAN, A PROFESSIONAL CORPORATION
Arlington, VA....................Banking Law; Family Law; Personal Injury

BEARD, RUSSELL C. (RUSTY)
Abilene, TX....................Commercial Litigation; Insurance Defense

BEARDEN, BRECKENRIDGE & GIDLOW
St. Louis, MO....................Labor and Employment Law

BEARD, STEVEN L., P.C.
Marietta, GA....................Medical Malpractice; Personal Injury

BEASLEY, ALLEN, CROW, METHVIN, PORTIS & MILES, P.C.
Montgomery, AL....................Commercial Litigation; Personal Injury; Product Liability Law

BEASLEY, CASEY & ERBSTEIN
Philadelphia, PA....................General Practice

BEASLEY, LEACOCK & HAUSER, P.A.
West Palm Beach, FL....................Appellate Practice; Business Law; Commercial Litigation

BEATIE AND OSBORN LLP
New York, NY....................Civil Trial Practice; Commercial Law; Commercial Litigation; Environmental Law; Insurance Defense; Product Liability Law; Securities Law

BEATTIE PADOVANO, LLC
Montvale, NJ....................Civil Trial Practice; Commercial Law; General Practice

BEATTY, THOMAS D.
Las Vegas, NV....................Appellate Practice; Civil Trial Practice; Criminal Trial Practice

BEATTY, CRAMP, KAUFFMAN & LINCKE
Media, PA....................Corporate Law; General Practice; Insurance Defense; Medical Malpractice; Municipal and Zoning Law; Trust and Estates, Wills and Probate

BECK, PAUL A. & ASSOCIATES
Pittsburgh, PA....................Intellectual Property Law; Patent, Trademark, Copyright and Unfair Competition

BECK, CHAET, MOLONY & BAMBERGER, S.C.
Milwaukee, WI....................Corporate Law; Health Care Law; Labor and Employment Law

BECK, DE CORSO, DALY, BARRERA & KREINDLER, A PROFESSIONAL LAW CORPORATION
Los Angeles, CA....................Administrative Law; Business Law; Civil Trial Practice; Criminal Trial Practice

BECKER, GLYNN, MELAMED & MUFFLY LLP
New York, NY....................General Practice

BECKER, HICKS, IRVING & HADEED, P.C.
Springfield, VA....................Business Law; Civil Trial Practice; Criminal Trial Practice; Family Law; Immigration and Naturalization

BECKER & KAPLAN LLC
Chicago, IL....................Business Law; Civil Trial Practice; Commercial Litigation; Construction Law; Franchise Law; Labor and Employment Law; Real Estate Law

BECKER LAW OFFICE
San Francisco, CA....................Bankruptcy Law

BECKER, STEVEN A., A PROFESSIONAL LAW CORPORATION
San Bernardino, CA....................Family Law

BECKERMAN & BECKERMAN, LLP
Rochester, NY....................Family Law; General Practice

BECKES, KATHERINE F.
Denver, CO....................Tax Law

BECKHAM & BECKHAM, P.A.
North Miami Beach, FL....................Appellate Practice; Transportation Law

BECKLEY, JAMES F., P.A.
Albuquerque, NM....................Trust and Estates, Wills and Probate

BECKLEY & MADDEN
Harrisburg, PA....................Construction Law; General Practice; Labor and Employment Law

BECKMAN LAWSON, LLP
Fort Wayne, IN....................Bankruptcy Law; General Practice; Labor and Employment Law; Land Use Law; Real Estate Law

BECKMAN, MILLMAN & SANDERS, LLP
New York, NY....................Business Law

BECK, REDDEN & SECREST
Houston, TX....................Appellate Practice; Civil Trial Practice; Commercial Litigation

BEDZOW, KORN, BROWN, MILLER & ZEMEL, P.A.
Aventura, FL....................Commercial Litigation

BEELER, JOSEPH, P.A.
Miami, FL....................Criminal Trial Practice

BEEMER & BEEMER
Clarks Summit, PA....................Civil Trial Practice

BEEM & MANN, PROFESSIONAL CORPORATION
Denver, CO....................Civil Trial Practice; Commercial Litigation; Personal Injury

BEER & TOONE, P.C.
Phoenix, AZ....................Aviation Law; Insurance Defense

BEERY & SPURLOCK CO., L.P.A.
Columbus, OH....................Transportation Law

BEGAM, LEWIS, MARKS & WOLFE
Phoenix, AZ....................Civil Trial Practice; Medical Malpractice; Personal Injury; Product Liability Law; Professional Liability

BEGGS & LANE
Pensacola, FL....................General Practice

BEGLEY, CARLIN & MANDIO
Bristol, PA....................Civil Trial Practice; General Practice
Langhorne, PA....................Civil Trial Practice; General Practice

BEHR, MANTOVANI, MCCARTER & POTTER, P.C.
St. Louis, MO....................Insurance Defense

BEIER HOWLETT, PROFESSIONAL CORPORATION
Bloomfield Hills, MI....................Commercial Litigation; Corporate Law; Family Law; Insurance Defense; Municipal and Zoning Law; Trust and Estates, Wills and Probate

BEIL, JACOB
Columbus, GA....................Commercial Law

BEIRNE, MAYNARD & PARSONS, L.L.P.
Houston, TX .... Civil Trial Practice; General Practice

BELAIR & EVANS LLP
New York, NY .... Civil Trial Practice; Legal Malpractice; Medical Malpractice

BELANGER & PLIMPTON
Lovelock, NV .... Civil Trial Practice; General Practice; Personal Injury

BELCHER, HENZIE & BIEGENZAHN, A PROFESSIONAL CORPORATION
Los Angeles, CA .... Aviation Law; General Practice; Insurance Defense; Product Liability Law

BELDEN, BELDEN, PERSIN & JOHNSTON
Greensburg, PA .... Criminal Trial Practice; General Practice; Workers Compensation

BELDOCK LEVINE & HOFFMAN LLP
New York, NY .... Civil Trial Practice; Criminal Trial Practice; Family Law

BELES, ROBERT J.
Oakland, CA .... Criminal Trial Practice

BELETIC, ANNE TURNER
Dallas, TX .... Family Law

BELGRADE AND O'DONNELL, A PROFESSIONAL CORPORATION
Chicago, IL .... Admiralty/Maritime Law; Insurance Defense; Transportation Law

BELIN LAMSON MCCORMICK ZUMBACH FLYNN, A PROFESSIONAL CORPORATION
Des Moines, IA .... Civil Trial Practice; General Practice

BELIN RAWLINGS & BADAL LLP
Los Angeles, CA .... Antitrust Law; Business Law; Commercial Litigation

BELLAMY, RUTENBERG, COPELAND, EPPS, GRAVELY & BOWERS, P.A.
Myrtle Beach, SC .... Appellate Practice; Business Law; Civil Trial Practice; Commercial Law; General Practice; Insurance Defense; Labor and Employment Law; Personal Injury; Product Liability Law; Real Estate Law; Trust and Estates, Wills and Probate

BELLAND, STANTON P., P.C.
Los Angeles, CA .... International Trade Law

BELL & ASSOCIATES, P.A.
Madison, MS .... Business Law; Family Law; Medical Malpractice; Personal Injury; Toxic Torts

BELLATTI, FAY, BELLATTI & BEARD
Jacksonville, IL .... General Practice

BELL, CHARLES M., A PROFESSIONAL ASSOCIATION
Ellicott City, MD .... Aviation Law

BELL, DAVIS & PITT, P.A.
Winston-Salem, NC .... General Practice

BELL, LEEPER & ROPER, P.A.
Orlando, FL .... Insurance Defense

BELL, ORROCK & WATASE, LLP
Riverside, CA .... Insurance Defense; Personal Injury

BELL, RYNIKER & LETOURNEAU, P.C.
Houston, TX .... Admiralty/Maritime Law; Government Contracts; Insurance Defense; International Business Law

BELL, STANLEY J., A PROFESSIONAL CORPORATION
San Francisco, CA .... Construction Law; Personal Injury; Product Liability Law

BELSKY & ASSOCIATES
San Diego, CA .... Insurance Defense; Medical Malpractice

BELTRAN & ASSOCIATES
Atlanta, GA .... Professional Liability

BELTZ, EDWARDS & SABO, L.L.P.
Colorado Springs, CO .... Business Law; Civil Trial Practice; Construction Law; Family Law; General Practice; Personal Injury; Real Estate Law; Securities Law; Trust and Estates, Wills and Probate; Workers Compensation

BELZ & JONES, P.C.
St. Louis, MO .... Corporate Law

BENCKENSTEIN, NORVELL & NATHAN, L.L.P.
Beaumont, TX .... Civil Trial Practice; Insurance Defense; Personal Injury

BENCKENSTEIN & OXFORD, L.L.P.
Beaumont, TX .... Admiralty/Maritime Law; Civil Trial Practice; Environmental Law; General Practice; Natural Resources Law

BENCOMO & ASSOCIATES
New Orleans, LA .... Admiralty/Maritime Law; Personal Injury; Toxic Torts

BENDER, HAROLD J.
Charlotte, NC .... Criminal Trial Practice

BENDURE & THOMAS
Detroit, MI .... Appellate Practice; Civil Trial Practice; Tax Law

BENEDICT AND ALTMAN
New Brunswick, NJ .... Appellate Practice; Criminal Trial Practice

BENETAR BERNSTEIN SCHAIR & STEIN
New York, NY .... Labor and Employment Law

BENJAMIN & BENSON
Cambridge, MA .... Family Law

BENJAMIN, MICHAEL D., P.C.
Philadelphia, PA .... Medical Malpractice

BENNARDO, JACK A.
Merrick, NY .... Real Estate Law; Tax Law; Trust and Estates, Wills and Probate

BENNETT, EDMUND C.
Providence, RI .... Tax Law; Trust and Estates, Wills and Probate

BENNETT, LEON F.
Woodland Hills, CA .... Family Law; Sports and Entertainment Law

BENNETT & BENNETT
Eaton, OH .... Civil Trial Practice; Criminal Trial Practice; General Practice; Trust and Estates, Wills and Probate

BENNETT BENNETT AND TROIANO, P.A.
Portland, ME .... Business Law; Civil Trial Practice; Employment Benefits Law; General Practice; Labor and Employment Law; Mergers and Acquisitions; Real Estate Law; Tax Law; Trust and Estates, Wills and Probate

BENNETT BIGELOW & LEEDOM, P.S.
Seattle, WA .... Health Care Law

BENNETT, BOEHNING & CLARY
Lafayette, IN .... General Practice

BENNETT, CARMICHAEL & KENNEDY, L.L.P.
Scottsdale, AZ .... Business Law; Civil Trial Practice; Personal Injury; Real Estate Law

BENNETT & GUTHRIE, P.L.L.C.
Winston-Salem, NC .... Commercial Litigation; Construction Law; Environmental Law; Insurance Defense; Medical Malpractice; Workers Compensation

BENNETT & HALL, L.L.P.
Fort Worth, TX .... Insurance Defense

BENNETT JONES
Calgary, AB, Canada .... Appellate Practice; Banking Law; Business Law; Civil Trial Practice; Commercial Law; Employment Benefits Law; Environmental Law; General Practice; Health Care Law; International Business Law; Medical Malpractice; Natural Resources Law; Public Utilities Law; Real Estate Law; Securities Law; Trust and Estates, Wills and Probate
Edmonton, AB, Canada .... General Practice
Toronto, ON, Canada .... General Practice

BENNETT LOTTERHOS SULSER & WILSON, P.A.
Jackson, MS .... Bankruptcy Law; Commercial Litigation; Environmental Law; Insurance Defense

BENNETT, SAMUELSEN, REYNOLDS AND ALLARD, A PROFESSIONAL CORPORATION
Oakland, CA .... Civil Trial Practice; Insurance Defense; Personal Injury; Toxic Torts

BENOIT, ALEXANDER, SINCLAIR, HARWOOD & HIGH, L.L.P.
Twin Falls, ID .... Insurance Defense

BENSINGER, COTANT, MENKES & AARDEMA, P.C.
Gaylord, MI .... Civil Trial Practice; Insurance Defense; Legal Malpractice; Medical Malpractice; Product Liability Law; Professional Liability
Grand Rapids, MI .... Insurance Defense; Legal Malpractice; Medical Malpractice; Product Liability Law; Professional Liability
Marquette, MI .... Insurance Defense; Legal Malpractice; Medical Malpractice; Patent, Trademark, Copyright and Unfair Competition; Product Liability Law; Professional Liability

BENSON, JAMES R. JR.
Denver, CO .... Commercial Litigation

BENTON & CENTENO, L.L.P.
Birmingham, AL .... Bankruptcy Law; Commercial Litigation

BENTON CLARK & TAYLOR, P.C.
San Antonio, TX .... Banking Law; Corporate Law; Real Estate Law; Tax Law; Trust and Estates, Wills and Probate

BERCHEM, MOSES & DEVLIN, A PROFESSIONAL CORPORATION
Milford, CT .... Commercial Law; General Practice; Labor and Employment Law

BERENBAUM, WEINSHIENK & EASON, P.C.
Denver, CO .... Appellate Practice; Banking Law; Bankruptcy Law; Business Law; Civil Trial Practice; Environmental Law; Health Care Law; Labor and Employment Law; Real Estate Law; Securities Law; Tax Law; Trademark, Copyright and Unfair Competition; Trust and Estates, Wills and Probate

BERENS & TATE, P.C.
Omaha, NE .... Employment Benefits Law; General Practice; Labor and Employment Law

BERENSTEIN, MOORE, BERENSTEIN, HEFFERNAN & MOELLER, L.L.P.
Sioux City, IA .... General Practice; Tax Law; Trust and Estates, Wills and Probate

BERESFORD, BOOTH, DEMARAY & TROMPETER, INC., P.S.
Seattle, WA .... Commercial Litigation

BERESKIN & PARR
Toronto, ON, Canada .... Business Law; Patent, Trademark, Copyright and Unfair Competition

BERESTON, MICHAEL H., P.A.
Annapolis, MD .... Medical Malpractice

BERG & ANDROPHY
Houston, TX .... Civil Trial Practice; Commercial Litigation; Criminal Trial Practice; Medical Malpractice; Personal Injury; Product Liability Law

BERGER, FRANCES C. LAW OFFICES OF
New York, NY .... Immigration and Naturalization

BERGER, GARY D. LAW OFFICES OF
San Francisco, CA .... Trust and Estates, Wills and Probate

BERGER AND BERGER
Evansville, IN .... Civil Trial Practice; Labor and Employment Law; Personal Injury; Product Liability Law

BERGER DAVIS & SINGERMAN
Fort Lauderdale, FL .... Bankruptcy Law; Business Law; Civil Trial Practice; Creditors Rights; Real Estate Law; Tax Law

BERGER & MONTAGUE, P.C.
Philadelphia, PA .... Antitrust Law; Securities Law

BERGER & NORTON, A LAW CORPORATION
Santa Monica, CA .... Eminent Domain; Land Use Law; Real Estate Law

BERGER STERN & WEBB, LLP
New York, NY .... Intellectual Property Law

BERGER & ZAVESKY CO., L.P.A.
Cleveland, OH .... Personal Injury

BERGERON, PARADIS & FITZPATRICK, LLP
Burlington, VT .... Personal Injury

BERGERT & BERGERT
Arlington, VA .... Intellectual Property Law; Patent, Trademark, Copyright and Unfair Competition

BERGESON & ELIOPOULOS, LLP
San Jose, CA .... Civil Trial Practice; Commercial Litigation; Intellectual Property Law; Securities Law

BERGHOLTZ, RICHARD S., P.A.
Mount Dora, FL .... Construction Law

BERGMAN & BARRETT
Princeton, NJ .... Arbitration; Civil Trial Practice; Commercial Law; Commercial Litigation; Family Law; Labor and Employment Law; Personal Injury; Trust and Estates, Wills and Probate; Workers Compensation

BERGMAN, WEDNER & DACEY, INC.
Los Angeles, CA .... Business Law; Civil Trial Practice; Construction Law; Labor and Employment Law; Product Liability Law; Real Estate Law

BERGSTEDT & MOUNT
Lake Charles, LA .... Admiralty/Maritime Law; Banking Law; Civil Trial Practice; General Practice; Insurance Defense; Real Estate Law

BERGSTRESSER AND ASSOCIATES, P.C., LAW OFFICES
Boston, MA .... Medical Malpractice; Personal Injury

BERICK, PEARLMAN & MILLS, A LEGAL PROFESSIONAL ASSOCIATION
Cleveland, OH .... General Practice

BERKE, ROBERT LAW OFFICES OF
Santa Monica, CA .... Criminal Trial Practice

BERKEY, JON H., P.C.
Bloomfield Hills, MI .... Commercial Law; Environmental Law; Real Estate Law

BERKOWITZ, LEFKOVITS, ISOM & KUSHNER, A PROFESSIONAL CORPORATION
Birmingham, AL .... Antitrust Law; Business Law; Civil Trial Practice; General Practice; Health Care Law; Intellectual Property Law; Labor and Employment Law; Real Estate Law; Securities Law; Tax Law; Trust and Estates, Wills and Probate

BERKOWITZ, TRAGER & TRAGER, LLC
Westport, CT .... Corporate Law

BERLACK, ISRAELS & LIBERMAN LLP
New York, NY .... Administrative Law; Bankruptcy Law; Business Law; Civil Trial Practice; Employment Benefits Law; Energy Law; Public Utilities Law; Securities Law; Tax Law; Trust and Estates, Wills and Probate

BERLAND, ALLAN M.
Kentfield, CA .... Real Estate Law

BERLINER, CANDON & JIMISON
Washington, DC .... Administrative Law

BERLINER ZISSER WALTER & GALLEGOS, A PROFESSIONAL CORPORATION
Denver, CO .... Arbitration; Corporate Law; Mergers and Acquisitions; Real Estate Law; Securities Law

BERMAN, DAVID
Medford, MA .... Civil Trial Practice

BERMAN, BOURNS & CURRIE, LLC
West Hartford, CT .... Civil Trial Practice; Family Law; General Practice; Real Estate Law; Trust and Estates, Wills and Probate

BERMAN, DAVID C., A PROFESSIONAL CORPORATION
Morristown, NJ .... Commercial Litigation

BERMAN, DAVID M., P.A., LAW OFFICES OF
Miami, FL .... Tax Law

BERMAN, DEVALERIO, PEASE & TABACCO, LLP
San Francisco, CA .... Antitrust Law; Securities Law

BERMAN, ELIHU H., P.A.
Clearwater, FL .... Business Law; Civil Trial Practice; Personal Injury

BERMAN, GAUFIN, TOMSIC, SAVAGE & CAMPBELL, A PROFESSIONAL CORPORATION
Salt Lake City, UT .... Civil Trial Practice

BERMAN, PALEY, GOLDSTEIN & KANNRY, LLP
New York, NY .... Construction Law; Environmental Law

BERMAN & WEISS
Palm Desert, CA .... Medical Malpractice; Personal Injury; Product Liability Law

BERMAN WOLFE RENNERT VOGEL & MANDLER, P.A.
Miami, FL .... Commercial Litigation; Real Estate Law; Securities Law

BERNARD, CASSISA, ELLIOTT & DAVIS, A PROFESSIONAL LAW CORPORATION
Metairie, LA .... General Practice; Product Liability Law; Toxic Torts

BERNARD, HAFFEY & BOHNERT CO., L.P.A.
Cleveland, OH .... Business Law; Civil Trial Practice; Commercial Litigation; Criminal Trial Practice; General Practice

BERNAUER, THOMAS A., A PROFESSIONAL CORPORATION
Newport Beach, CA .... Family Law

BERNKOPF, GOODMAN & BASEMAN LLP
Boston, MA .... Business Law; General Practice; Real Estate Law

BERNSTEIN, BRENDA JOY, P.C.
Atlanta, GA .... Criminal Trial Practice

BERNSTEIN LITOWITZ BERGER & GROSSMANN LLP
New York, NY .... Antitrust Law; Civil Rights; Securities Law

BERNSTEIN, SHUR, SAWYER & NELSON, A PROFESSIONAL CORPORATION
Portland, ME .... General Practice

BERNSTEIN, STAIR & MCADAMS LLP
Knoxville, TN .... Business Law; Civil Trial Practice; Commercial Litigation; Construction Law; Creditors Rights; Family Law; General Practice; Product Liability Law

BERRIGAN, PATRICK J., (P.L.C.)
Slidell, LA .... Commercial Litigation; Real Estate Law

BERRY, THOMAS A. & ASSOCIATES
Bloomington, IN .... Civil Trial Practice

BERRY & BERRY, A PROFESSIONAL CORPORATION
Oakland, CA .... Civil Trial Practice

BERRY, KELLEY & HANSEN
Lincoln, NE .... Appellate Practice; Criminal Trial Practice

BERTHOLD, TIANO & O'DELL
Charleston, WV .... Aviation Law; Medical Malpractice; Product Liability Law

BERTINE, HUFNAGEL, HEADLEY, ZELTNER, DRUMMOND & DOHN, LLP
Scarsdale, NY .... Corporate Law

BERTZ, MICHAEL A.
Los Angeles, CA .... Securities Law

BESHARA, EDWARD C., P.A.
Winter Park, FL .... Immigration and Naturalization

BESS KUNZ, A PROFESSIONAL CORPORATION
Phoenix, AZ .... Civil Trial Practice; Insurance Defense; Personal Injury; Product Liability Law

BEST & ANDERSON, P.A.
Crystal River, FL .... Civil Trial Practice; Medical Malpractice; Personal Injury
Melbourne, FL .... Civil Trial Practice; Medical Malpractice; Personal Injury
Orlando, FL .... Civil Trial Practice; Environmental Law; Medical Malpractice; Personal Injury

BEST KOEPPEL, A PROFESSIONAL LAW CORPORATION
New Orleans, LA .... Admiralty/Maritime Law; General Practice; Insurance Defense; Toxic Torts; Workers Compensation

BEST & SHARP, A PROFESSIONAL CORPORATION
Tulsa, OK .... Civil Trial Practice; Insurance Defense; Medical Malpractice; Personal Injury; Professional Liability; Workers Compensation

BESUNDER, HARVEY B. LAW OFFICES OF
Hauppauge, NY .... Commercial Litigation; Real Estate Law

BETTERMAN & DIXON
Omaha, NE .... Commercial Litigation

BETTS & HOLT
Washington, DC .... Energy Law

BETTS, PATTERSON & MINES, P.S.
Seattle, WA .... General Practice

BEUS, GILBERT & DEVITT, P.L.L.C.
Phoenix, AZ .... Commercial Litigation; Municipal and Zoning Law; Professional Liability; Real Estate Law

BEVERIDGE & DIAMOND, P.C.
Washington, DC .... General Practice
New York, NY .... General Practice

BEVERIDGE & DIAMOND LLP
San Francisco, CA .... General Practice

BEYERS, COSTIN & CASE, A PROFESSIONAL CORPORATION
Santa Rosa, CA .... Real Estate Law

BIALAC, JAMES T.
Phoenix, AZ .... General Practice

BIANCO & MURPHY
San Francisco, CA .... Civil Trial Practice; Labor and Employment Law; Personal Injury

BIBLE, HOY & TRACHOK, A PROFESSIONAL CORPORATION
Reno, NV .... Appellate Practice; Business Law; Commercial Litigation; Construction Law

BICKEL & ASSOCIATES
Piedmont, CA .... Real Estate Law

BICKEL & BREWER
Dallas, TX .... Civil Trial Practice; General Practice

BICKFORD, HARRY L. LAW OFFICE
Ardmore, OK .... Civil Trial Practice; General Practice; Workers Compensation

BIDNA & KEYS, A PROFESSIONAL LAW CORPORATION
Newport Beach, CA .... Business Law

BIEBEL & FRENCH, A LEGAL PROFESSIONAL ASSOCIATION
Dayton, OH .... Patent, Trademark, Copyright and Unfair Competition

BIEN & SUMMERS LLP
Novato, CA .... Appellate Practice

BIENSTOCK & CLARK
Santa Monica, CA .... Civil Trial Practice

BIERI & AMES
Detroit, MI .... Real Estate Law

BIERMAN & BIERMAN, P.C.
Grinnell, IA .... General Practice

BIERMAN, SHOHAT, LOEWY & KLEIN, PROFESSIONAL ASSOCIATION
Miami, FL .... Appellate Practice; Criminal Trial Practice; General Practice; International Business Law

BIESER, GREER & LANDIS
Dayton, OH .... Civil Trial Practice; General Practice

BIGGS AND BATTAGLIA
Wilmington, DE .... Civil Trial Practice; Criminal Trial Practice; General Practice

BIGHAM ENGLAR JONES & HOUSTON
New York, NY .... Insurance Defense

BILLET & CONNOR
Philadelphia, PA .... Civil Trial Practice

BILLING, COCHRAN, HEATH, LYLES & MAURO, P.A.
Fort Lauderdale, FL .... Insurance Defense; Medical Malpractice

BILLINGS, CUNNINGHAM, MORGAN & BOATWRIGHT, PROFESSIONAL ASSOCIATION
Orlando, FL .... Medical Malpractice; Personal Injury

BILLINGS & SOLOMON, P.C.
Houston, TX .... Admiralty/Maritime Law

BILZIN SUMBERG DUNN PRICE & AXELROD LLP
Miami, FL .... General Practice

BINDERMAN, WILLIAM N.
New York, NY .... General Practice
Philadelphia, PA .... General Practice

BINGAMAN, HESS, COBLENTZ & BELL, A PROFESSIONAL CORPORATION
Reading, PA .... Banking Law; Bankruptcy Law; Civil Trial Practice; Creditors Rights; General Practice

BINGHAM DANA LLP
Hartford, CT .... General Practice
Washington, DC .... General Practice
Boston, MA .... General Practice
London, England .... General Practice

BINKLEY & ASSOCIATES
Birmingham, MI .... Civil Trial Practice

BINKLEY, MICHAEL W., P.C.
Nashville, TN .... Family Law; Personal Injury; Workers Compensation

BINNING, J. BOYD
Columbus, OH .... Personal Injury

BINSTOCK, TORCHINSKY AND ASSOCIATES, P.C., LAW OFFICES OF
Washington, DC .... Tax Law; Trust and Estates, Wills and Probate
Chevy Chase, MD .... Tax Law; Trust and Estates, Wills and Probate

BIOFF SINGER AND FINUCANE, LLP
Kansas City, MO .... Civil Trial Practice; Labor and Employment Law

BIRCH, STEWART, KOLASCH & BIRCH, LLP
Falls Church, VA .... Patent, Trademark, Copyright and Unfair Competition

BIRD, ELIZABETH ANNE LAW OFFICES OF
San Francisco, CA .... Trust and Estates, Wills and Probate

BIRD, FRANCIS M. JR.
Atlanta, GA .... General Practice; Trust and Estates, Wills and Probate

BIRD & BIRD, A LAW CORPORATION
Torrance, CA .... Criminal Trial Practice

BIRD, SVENDSEN, BROTHERS, SCHESKE & PATTISON, P.C.
Sturgis, MI .... General Practice

BIRDWELL, JANKE & DURANDO, LLP
Portland, OR .... Patent, Trademark, Copyright and Unfair Competition

BIRD, WILLIAM Q., AND ASSOCIATES, P.C.
Atlanta, GA .... Civil Trial Practice; Medical Malpractice; Personal Injury; Product Liability Law

BIREN & KATZMAN
Los Angeles, CA .... Personal Injury; Product Liability Law; Professional Liability

BIRGE & MAYERS, P.C.
Denver, CO .... Arbitration; Commercial Law; Criminal Trial Practice; Securities Law

BIRKA-WHITE, DAVID M. LAW OFFICES OF
Alamo, CA .... Construction Law; Product Liability Law

BIRNKRANT & BIRNKRANT, P.C.
Farmington Hills, MI .... Commercial Litigation; Insurance Defense; Product Liability Law

BISCEGLIE & FRIEDMAN, LLC
Newark, NJ .... Labor and Employment Law

BISGYER, BERT NEIL LAW OFFICES OF
Washington, DC .... Labor and Employment Law

BISHOP, JAMES A. LAW OFFICES OF
Brunswick, GA .... General Practice

BISHOP, BARRY, HOWE, HANEY & RYDER, A PROFESSIONAL CORPORATION
Emeryville, CA .... Arbitration; Aviation Law; Civil Trial Practice; Construction Law; Environmental Law; Insurance Defense; Product Liability Law; Real Estate Law; Trust and Estates, Wills and Probate

BISHOP & BISHOP
Ashdown, AR .... General Practice

BISHOP, COLVIN, JOHNSON & KENT
Birmingham, AL .... General Practice; Personal Injury; Trust and Estates, Wills and Probate

BISHOP & HEINTZ, P.C.
Traverse City, MI .... Business Law; Corporate Law; Patent, Trademark, Copyright and Unfair Competition; Personal Injury

BISHOP, PAYNE, HARVARD & KAITCER, L.L.P.
Fort Worth, TX .... Civil Trial Practice; Real Estate Law

BISHOP, ROSSI & SCARLATI, LTD.
Oakbrook Terrace, IL .... Business Law; Tax Law

BITTMAN, HOWARD
Boulder, CO .... Civil Trial Practice; Criminal Trial Practice; Family Law; Real Estate Law

BLACHLY, TABOR, BOZIK & HARTMAN
Valparaiso, IN .... Civil Trial Practice; General Practice; Personal Injury; Real Estate Law; Trust and Estates, Wills and Probate

BLACK, A. CLIFTON
Kissimmee, FL .... Civil Trial Practice

BLACK, MICHAEL V.
Phoenix, AZ .... Criminal Trial Practice

BLACKARD, WILLIAM R. JR.
Jacksonville, FL .... Tax Law; Trust and Estates, Wills and Probate

BLACK & BLACK
Port Arthur, TX .... General Practice

BLACK COMPEAN & HALL, A LIMITED LIABILITY PARTNERSHIP
Los Angeles, CA .... Appellate Practice; Civil Trial Practice; Insurance Defense

BLACK HELTERLINE, LLP
Portland, OR .... Banking Law; Bankruptcy Law; Civil Trial Practice; Commercial Law; Environmental Law; General Practice; Immigration and Naturalization; Natural Resources Law; Real Estate Law; Tax Law

BLACK, MCCUSKEY, SOUERS & ARBAUGH, A LEGAL PROFESSIONAL ASSOCIATION
Canton, OH .... Civil Trial Practice; General Practice; Labor and Employment Law

BLACK & MCLAREN, A PROFESSIONAL CORPORATION
Memphis, TN .... Civil Trial Practice

BLACKMON & SNELLINGS, LLP
Sacramento, CA .... Criminal Trial Practice

BLACKMORE & BLACKMORE
Fort Lauderdale, FL .... Criminal Trial Practice; Insurance Defense; Personal Injury

BLACK, NOLAND & READ, P.L.C.
Staunton, VA .... General Practice

BLACK, RICHARD A., P.C.
Phoenix, AZ .... Medical Malpractice; Product Liability Law

BLACKWELL & WHITE
Gulfport, MS .... Corporate Law; Eminent Domain; General Practice; Municipal Bond/Public Authority Financing

BLAIR CONAWAY BOGRAD & MARTIN, P.A.
Charlotte, NC .... Commercial Litigation; Construction Law

BLAIR AND PARSONS
Pell City, AL .... Civil Trial Practice; General Practice; Insurance Defense

BLAIR, SCHAEFER, HUTCHISON & WOLFE, LLP
Vancouver, WA .... General Practice

BLAIR, STROUD & DAVIDSON
Batesville, AR .... General Practice

BLAKE, CASSELS & GRAYDON LLP
Calgary, AB, Canada .... General Practice
Vancouver, BC, Canada .... General Practice
Ottawa, ON, Canada .... General Practice
Toronto, ON, Canada .... General Practice
Beijing, China .... General Practice
London, England .... General Practice

BLAKE, KIRCHNER, SYMONDS, MACFARLANE, LARSON & SMITH, P.C.
Detroit, MI .... Insurance Defense

BLAKESLEE, WESLEY D.
Westminster, MD .... General Practice

BLANC WILLIAMS JOHNSTON & KRONSTADT, LLP
Los Angeles, CA .... Business Law; Commercial Litigation; Computer Law; Intellectual Property Law; Labor and Employment Law; Sports and Entertainment Law

BLANCHARD, ROBERTSON, MITCHELL & CARTER, P.C.
Joplin, MO .... General Practice; Insurance Defense

BLANCHARD, WALKER, O'QUIN & ROBERTS, A PROFESSIONAL LAW CORPORATION
Shreveport, LA .... Appellate Practice; Bankruptcy Law; Civil Trial Practice; Commercial Law; Commercial Litigation; Criminal Trial Practice; Energy Law; Environmental Law; General Practice; Insurance Defense; Labor and Employment Law; Natural Resources Law; Real Estate Law; Tax Law; Trust and Estates, Wills and Probate

BLANCO TACKABERY COMBS & MATAMOROS, P.A.
Winston-Salem, NC .... Bankruptcy Law; Commercial Law

BLANEY MCMURTRY LLP
Toronto, ON, Canada .... General Practice

BLANK, CHRISTOPHER L.
Newport Beach, CA .... Bankruptcy Law; Business Law

BLANKINGSHIP & KOOMEY, P.C.
Alexandria, VA .... Commercial Litigation

BLANK ROME COMISKY & MCCAULEY LLP
Philadelphia, PA .... General Practice

BLANTON, EDWARD L., JR., P.A., LAW OFFICE OF
Baltimore, MD .... Bankruptcy Law; Civil Trial Practice; Corporate Law; Tax Law

BLASINGAME, BURCH, GARRARD, BRYANT & ASHLEY, P.C.
Athens, GA .... Civil Trial Practice; General Practice; Insurance Defense; Product Liability Law

BLATT, FRANKLIN R. LAW OFFICES OF
Harrisonburg, VA .... Family Law

BLATT, HAMMESFAHR & EATON
Chicago, IL .... Admiralty/Maritime Law; Civil Trial Practice; Construction Law; Corporate Law; Environmental Law; Government Contracts; Health Care Law; Insurance Defense; Labor and Employment Law; Medical Malpractice; Product Liability Law; Professional Liability; Toxic Torts; Transportation Law
New York, NY .... Banking Law; Civil Trial Practice; International Business Law

BLAUGRUND, HERBERT & MARTIN, INCORPORATED
Dublin, OH .... Administrative Law; Appellate Practice; Banking Law; Bankruptcy Law; Business Law; Civil Rights; Civil Trial Practice; Environmental Law; Family Law; Labor and Employment Law; Land Use Law; Municipal and Zoning Law; Nonprofit and Tax Exempt Organizations; Personal Injury; Real Estate Law; Tax Law; Trust and Estates, Wills and Probate; Workers Compensation

BLAU, KRAMER, WACTLAR & LIEBERMAN, P.C.
Jericho, NY .... Corporate Law; Real Estate Law; Securities Law

BLAZZARD, GRODD & HASENAUER, P.C.
Westport, CT .... General Practice; Securities Law; Tax Law; Trust and Estates, Wills and Probate

BLECHER & COLLINS, A PROFESSIONAL CORPORATION
Los Angeles, CA .... Antitrust Law; Appellate Practice; Business Law; Civil Trial Practice; Trademark, Copyright and Unfair Competition

BLEDSOE & BLEDSOE, P.L.L.C.
Charlotte, NC .... General Practice; Real Estate Law

BLEDSOE, SCHMIDT, LIPPES, MOONLY & ROBERSON, P.A.
Jacksonville, FL .... Civil Trial Practice

BLEIER LAW FIRM, THE
Folsom, CA .... Civil Trial Practice; Commercial Litigation; Communications Law; Eminent Domain; Environmental Law; Real Estate Law

BLEUEL & MUIRHEAD
Ventura, CA .... Trust and Estates, Wills and Probate

BLEY AND BLEY
San Francisco, CA .... Family Law; Personal Injury; Professional Liability

BLISH & CAVANAGH
Providence, RI .... Antitrust Law; Civil Trial Practice; Commercial Law; Commercial Litigation; Construction Law; Environmental Law; General Practice; Labor and Employment Law; Medical Malpractice; Municipal Bond/Public Authority Financing; Personal Injury

BLISS & WILKENS, LLC
Anchorage, AK .... Aviation Law; Civil Trial Practice; Health Care Law

BLOCK & COLUCCI, P.C.
Buffalo, NY .... Banking Law; Corporate Law; Real Estate Law

BLOND & ALLISON, P.C., LAW OFFICES OF
Kansas City, MO .... Family Law

BLOOM & BUELL
Boston, MA .... Civil Trial Practice; General Practice; Health Care Law; Insurance Defense

BLOOM, DAVID B., A PROF. CORP., LAW OFFICES OF
Los Angeles, CA .... Banking Law; Bankruptcy Law; Business Law; Civil Trial Practice; Commercial Law; Construction Law; General Practice; International Business Law; Personal Injury; Real Estate Law; Sports and Entertainment Law

BLOOM, LEONARD, & ASSOCIATES, LLC
Towson, MD .... Patent, Trademark, Copyright and Unfair Competition

BLOOM & WITKIN
Boston, MA .... Sports and Entertainment Law; Tax Law

BLOOSTON, MORDKOFSKY, JACKSON & DICKENS
Washington, DC .... Communications Law

BLUE & EDWARDS, P.A.
Towson, MD .... Trust and Estates, Wills and Probate

BLUM, EDWARD L.
Oakland, CA .... Commercial Law; Real Estate Law

BLUM, LORIN B. LAW OFFICES OF
Oakland, CA .... Family Law

BLUM, BAMBI G., P.A.
Miami, FL .... Appellate Practice

BLUMENFELD, NORMAN L. LAW OFFICES OF
Washington, DC .... Personal Injury

BLUMENFELD & COHEN
Washington, DC .... Antitrust Law; Communications Law; Computer Law

BLUNT & ASSOCIATES, P.C.
Scottsdale, AZ .... Trust and Estates, Wills and Probate

BLUT, JEROME L., CHARTERED
Las Vegas, NV .... Tax Law; Trust and Estates, Wills and Probate

BOBO, SPICER, CIOTOLI, FULFORD, BOCCHINO & DEBEVOISE, P.A.
North Palm Beach, FL .... Health Care Law; Insurance Defense; Medical Malpractice
Orlando, FL .... Health Care Law; Insurance Defense; Medical Malpractice

BOBROFF, HESSE, LINDMARK & MARTONE, P.C.
St. Louis, MO .... Labor and Employment Law

BOCK, JOHN GORDON
Houston, TX .... Civil Trial Practice; Family Law

BODDINGTON & BROWN, CHARTERED
Kansas City, KS .... General Practice

BODELL, GERALD E.
Bridgeport, CT .... Appellate Practice; Civil Rights; Civil Trial Practice; Criminal Trial Practice

BODMAN, LONGLEY & DAHLING LLP
Ann Arbor, MI .... Intellectual Property Law
Cheboygan, MI .... Banking Law
Detroit, MI .... Administrative Law; Antitrust Law; Appellate Practice; Banking Law; Bankruptcy Law; Business Law; Civil Trial Practice; Commercial Law; Communications Law; Construction Law; Creditors Rights; Environmental Law; General Practice; Health Care Law; Intellectual Property Law; Labor and Employment Law; Mergers and Acquisitions; Municipal and Zoning Law; Municipal Bond/Public Authority Financing; Natural Resources Law; Pension and Profit Sharing; Product Liability Law; Professional Liability; Real Estate Law; Securities Law; Tax Law; Trademark, Copyright and Unfair Competition; Trust and Estates, Wills and Probate

BODYFELT, MOUNT, STROUP & CHAMBERLAIN
Portland, OR .... Civil Trial Practice; Insurance Defense

BOEGGEMAN, GEORGE, HODGES & CORDE, P.C.
White Plains, NY .... Appellate Practice; Arbitration; Civil Trial Practice; Commercial Litigation; Construction Law; Corporate Law; Insurance Defense; Medical Malpractice; Product Liability Law; Transportation Law

BOEHL STOPHER & GRAVES
Lexington, KY .... Civil Trial Practice; General Practice; Workers Compensation
Louisville, KY .... Civil Trial Practice; General Practice; Workers Compensation
Paducah, KY .... Civil Trial Practice; General Practice

BOELTER & ASSOCIATES
Seattle, WA .... Tax Law

BOESCHE, MCDERMOTT & ESKRIDGE
Tulsa, OK .... Banking Law; Bankruptcy Law; Civil Trial Practice; Commercial Litigation; Employment Benefits Law; Energy Law; General Practice; Health Care Law; International Business Law; International Trade Law; Mergers and Acquisitions; Natural Resources Law; Oil and Gas Law; Pension and Profit Sharing

BOGENSCHUTZ & DUTKO, P.A.
Fort Lauderdale, FL .... Criminal Trial Practice

BOGGS, LOEHN & RODRIGUE
New Orleans, LA .... Environmental Law; Health Care Law; Insurance Defense; Medical Malpractice

BOGIN, PATTERSON & BOHMAN LLP
Dayton, OH .... Bankruptcy Law; Business Law

BOGUE KOURY & MARYLANDER LLC
Denver, CO .... Medical Malpractice; Personal Injury; Product Liability Law

BOKELMAN & BENJAMIN, A PROFESSIONAL LAW CORPORATION
San Francisco, CA .... Medical Malpractice; Personal Injury

BOLEN & ERWIN, LTD., A PROF. LAW CORP.
Alexandria, LA .... Insurance Defense; Product Liability Law

BOLEN, FRANSEN & BOOSTROM LLP
Fresno, CA .... Business Law; Real Estate Law; Trust and Estates, Wills and Probate

BOLSON KUNTZ & SEREMBE
San Bernardino, CA .... Workers Compensation

BONAPARTE & MIYAMOTO, A PROFESSIONAL LAW CORPORATION
Los Angeles, CA .... Immigration and Naturalization

BONDURANT, MIXSON & ELMORE, LLP
Atlanta, GA .... Antitrust Law; Appellate Practice; Civil Trial Practice; Commercial Litigation; Constitutional Law; Criminal Trial Practice; Environmental Law; Professional Liability; Trademark, Copyright and Unfair Competition

BONE, BILL, P.A., THE LAW OFFICE OF
West Palm Beach, FL .... Personal Injury

BONEZZI SWITZER MURPHY & POLITO, CO. L.P.A.
Cleveland, OH .... Medical Malpractice; Toxic Torts

BONINA & BONINA, P.C.
Brooklyn, NY .... Civil Trial Practice; Medical Malpractice; Personal Injury; Product Liability Law

BONN, LUSCHER, PADDEN & WILKINS, CHARTERED
Phoenix, AZ .... Appellate Practice; Business Law; Civil Trial Practice; Commercial Litigation; Health Care Law; Real Estate Law

BONNE, BRIDGES, MUELLER, O'KEEFE & NICHOLS, PROFESSIONAL CORPORATION
Los Angeles, CA .... Medical Malpractice

BONNETT, FAIRBOURN, FRIEDMAN & BALINT, P.C.
Phoenix, AZ .... Bankruptcy Law; Civil Trial Practice; Commercial Litigation; Insurance Defense; Municipal and Zoning Law; Personal Injury; Product Liability Law; Real Estate Law; Securities Law

BONYA GAZZA & DEGORY, LLP
Indiana, PA .... General Practice

BOOKHOLDER & BASSETT, P.C.
Troy, MI .... Appellate Practice; Family Law; Trust and Estates, Wills and Probate

BOONE, CELIA TRIMBLE
Abilene, TX .... Family Law

BOONE, BEALE, COSBY & LONG
Richmond, VA .... Criminal Trial Practice; Personal Injury

BOONE, DAVID WM., P.C.
Atlanta, GA .... Aviation Law; Civil Trial Practice; Medical Malpractice; Personal Injury; Product Liability Law

BOONE, KARLBERG AND HADDON P.C.
Missoula, MT .... General Practice

BOONE, SMITH, DAVIS, HURST & DICKMAN, A PROFESSIONAL CORPORATION
Tulsa, OK .... General Practice; Health Care Law; Labor and Employment Law; Municipal and Zoning Law; Real Estate Law; Workers Compensation

BOOTH, MITCHELL B.
New York, NY .... Trust and Estates, Wills and Probate

BOOTH, BATE, GRIECO AND BRIODY
Montclair, NJ .... Trust and Estates, Wills and Probate

BOOTH, MITCHEL & STRANGE
Los Angeles, CA .... Insurance Defense

BOOTHMAN, HEBERT & ELLER, P.C.
Detroit, MI .... Civil Trial Practice; Corporate Law; General Practice; Insurance Defense; Medical Malpractice; Mergers and Acquisitions; Trust and Estates, Wills and Probate

BORCHARD & WILLOUGHBY, A PROFESSIONAL CORPORATION
Irvine, CA .... Appellate Practice; General Practice; Real Estate Law; Securities Law

BORDEN & ELLIOT
Toronto, ON, Canada .... Admiralty/Maritime Law; Antitrust Law; Banking Law; Bankruptcy Law; Business Law; Civil Trial Practice; Commercial Law; Communications Law; Construction Law; Employment Benefits Law; Environmental Law; Family Law; General Practice; Health Care Law; Insurance Defense; International Business Law; Labor and Employment Law; Medical Malpractice; Municipal and Zoning Law; Natural Resources Law; Patent, Trademark, Copyright and Unfair Competition; Personal Injury; Real Estate Law; Securities Law; Tax Law; Trust and Estates, Wills and Probate

BORDEN ELLIOT SCOTT & AYLEN
Ottawa, ON, Canada .... Business Law; Civil Trial Practice; Commercial Litigation; Patent, Trademark, Copyright and Unfair Competition; Real Estate Law; Securities Law; Tax Law

BOREN, JAMES E.
Baton Rouge, LA .... Criminal Trial Practice

BORENE LAW FIRM, P.A.
Minneapolis, MN .... Immigration and Naturalization

BORING & PILGER, P.C.
Vienna, VA .... Appellate Practice; Civil Trial Practice; Commercial Law; Commercial Litigation; Employment Benefits Law

BORINS, SETEL, SNITZER & BROWNSTEIN
Buffalo, NY .... Family Law; General Practice; Trust and Estates, Wills and Probate

BORKON, RAMSTEAD, MARIANI & LETOURNEAU, LTD.
Minneapolis, MN .... Medical Malpractice; Personal Injury; Product Liability Law; Workers Compensation

BOROD & KRAMER, P.C.
Memphis, TN .... Bankruptcy Law; Civil Trial Practice; General Practice; Securities Law

BOROWSKY, PHILIP, A PROF. CORP., LAW OFFICES OF
San Francisco, CA .... Commercial Litigation; Labor and Employment Law; Personal Injury

BORRE, PETERSON, FOWLER & REENS, P.C.
Grand Rapids, MI .... Banking Law; Bankruptcy Law; Business Law; Civil Trial Practice; Commercial Law; Commercial Litigation; Corporate Law; Environmental Law; General Practice; Real Estate Law; Tax Law; Trust and Estates, Wills and Probate

BORRON & DELAHAYE, A PROFESSIONAL LAW CORPORATION
Plaquemine, LA .... General Practice

BORRUS, GOLDIN & FOLEY, A PROFESSIONAL CORPORATION
New Brunswick, NJ .... General Practice

BORRUS, GOLDIN, FOLEY, VIGNUOLO, HYMAN, STAHL & CLARKIN, A PROFESSIONAL CORPORATION
North Brunswick, NJ .... Administrative Law; Business Law; Civil Trial Practice; Commercial Law; Criminal Trial Practice; Family Law; General Practice; Municipal and Zoning Law; Personal Injury; Product Liability Law; Real Estate Law; Tax Law; Trust and Estates, Wills and Probate

BORSODY, ROBERT P., P.C.
New York, NY .... Health Care Law

BORSTEIN & SHEINBAUM
New York, NY .... Civil Trial Practice

BORTON, PETRINI & CONRON, LLP
Bakersfield, CA .... Administrative Law; Appellate Practice; Banking Law; Business Law; Commercial Litigation; Constitutional Law; Construction Law; Energy Law; Environmental Law; General Practice; Health Care Law; Insurance Defense; Labor and Employment Law; Medical Malpractice; Municipal and Zoning Law; Municipal Bond/Public Authority Financing; Natural Resources Law; Product Liability Law; Real Estate Law; Tax Law; Trust and Estates, Wills and Probate

BOSE MCKINNEY & EVANS LLP
Indianapolis, IN .... Antitrust Law; Banking Law; Bankruptcy Law; Civil Trial Practice; Communications Law; Environmental Law; General Practice; Labor and Employment Law; Municipal Bond/Public Authority Financing; Public Utilities Law; Real Estate Law; Tax Law

BOS & GLAZIER, P.L.C.
Grand Rapids, MI .... Civil Trial Practice; Environmental Law; Insurance Defense

BOSSIN, PHYLLIS G., CO., L.P.A.
Cincinnati, OH .... Family Law

BOSSO, WILLIAMS, SACHS, BOOK, ATACK & GALLAGHER, A PROFESSIONAL CORPORATION
Santa Cruz, CA .... General Practice

BOSTON, HOLT & SOCKWELL, PLLC
Lawrenceburg, TN .... General Practice

BOSTON, JAMES R., & ASSOCIATES, P.C.
Houston, TX .... Medical Malpractice

BOSTON, WILLIAM C., P.L.L.C.
Oklahoma City, OK .... Aviation Law; Commercial Law; Transportation Law

BOSWELL & SIMS
Paducah, KY .... Civil Trial Practice

BOTTS, R. DAVID
Atlanta, GA .... Criminal Trial Practice

BOUDREAU & TRENTACOSTA, A PROFESSIONAL LAW CORPORATION
San Diego, CA .... Medical Malpractice; Personal Injury; Product Liability Law

BOUHAN, WILLIAMS & LEVY LLP
Savannah, GA .... Admiralty/Maritime Law; Business Law; Environmental Law; General Practice; Workers Compensation

BOULAND & BRUSH, L.L.C.
Baltimore, MD .... Civil Trial Practice

BOULT, CUMMINGS, CONNERS & BERRY, PLC
Nashville, TN .... General Practice

BOURNE, NOLL & KENYON, A PROFESSIONAL CORPORATION
Summit, NJ .... Banking Law; Commercial Law; General Practice; Real Estate Law; Tax Law; Trust and Estates, Wills and Probate

BOUTIN, DENTINO, GIBSON DI GIUSTO, HODELL & WEST, A PROFESSIONAL CORPORATION
Sacramento, CA .... Business Law; Civil Trial Practice; Patent, Trademark, Copyright and Unfair Competition; Real Estate Law

BOVIS, KYLE & BURCH, LLC
Atlanta, GA ....Business Law; Commercial Litigation; Construction Law; Environmental Law; General Practice; Insurance Defense; Personal Injury; Product Liability Law; Professional Liability; Trust and Estates, Wills and Probate; Workers Compensation

BOWEN, RADABAUGH, MILTON & BROWN, P.C.
Troy, MI............Commercial Law; Corporate Law; Insurance Defense; Labor and Employment Law; Product Liability Law

BOWEN, WILLIAM M., P.A.
Hilton Head Island, SC............General Practice

BOWERS, HARRISON, KENT & MILLER, LLP
Evansville, IN............Appellate Practice; Banking Law; Bankruptcy Law; Business Law; Civil Trial Practice; Commercial Law; Corporate Law; General Practice; Labor and Employment Law; Land Use Law; Real Estate Law

BOWLES AND BOWLES
Richmond, VA............Civil Trial Practice

BOWLES RICE MCDAVID GRAFF & LOVE, PLLC
Charleston, WV............Civil Trial Practice; General Practice
Fairmont, WV............Civil Trial Practice; General Practice
Martinsburg, WV............Civil Trial Practice; General Practice
Morgantown, WV............Civil Trial Practice; General Practice
Parkersburg, WV............Civil Trial Practice; General Practice

BOWMAN, ANDREW B.
Westport, CT............Appellate Practice; Civil Trial Practice; Constitutional Law; Criminal Trial Practice

BOWMAN, ALAN DEXTER, P.A.
Newark, NJ............Civil Trial Practice; Criminal Trial Practice

BOWMAN AND BROOKE
Minneapolis, MN............Civil Trial Practice; Product Liability Law

BOWMAN, GEORGE, SCHEB, TOALE & ROBINSON, P.A.
Sarasota, FL............General Practice; Trust and Estates, Wills and Probate

BOWMAN & SMITH, P.C.
Yuma, AZ............Personal Injury

BOYCE & BOYCE, A PROFESSIONAL ASSOCIATION
Newport, AR............General Practice

BOYCE, MURPHY, MCDOWELL & GREENFIELD, L.L.P.
Sioux Falls, SD............General Practice

BOYD AGNEW DRYER & STORAASLI, LTD.
Duluth, MN............General Practice

BOYD & BOYD, P.C.
Centerville, MA............Trust and Estates, Wills and Probate

BOYER, REYNOLDS & DEMARCO, LTD.
Providence, RI............Insurance Defense

BOYER AND SCHILTZ, P.A.
Clearwater, FL............Family Law

BOYES & FARINA, PROFESSIONAL ASSOCIATION
West Palm Beach, FL............Trust and Estates, Wills and Probate

BOYLAN & RICHARDS, P.C.
Springfield, VT............General Practice

BOYLE, CHARLES A., & ASSOCIATES, LTD.
Chicago, IL............Personal Injury; Product Liability Law

BOYLE, CORDES & BROWN
De Kalb, IL............General Practice; Real Estate Law; Trust and Estates, Wills and Probate

BOZEMAN, JENKINS & MATTHEWS, P.A.
Pensacola, FL............Civil Trial Practice; Commercial Litigation; Health Care Law; Insurance Defense; Medical Malpractice; Product Liability Law; Workers Compensation

BOZICEVIC, FIELD & FRANCIS, LLP
Palo Alto, CA............Intellectual Property Law

BRACEWELL & PATTERSON, L.L.P.
Houston, TX............General Practice

BRACH, EICHLER, ROSENBERG, SILVER, BERNSTEIN, HAMMER & GLADSTONE, A PROFESSIONAL CORPORATION
Roseland, NJ............Banking Law; Business Law; Civil Trial Practice; Commercial Litigation; Construction Law; Environmental Law; Family Law; General Practice; Health Care Law; Insurance Defense; Land Use Law; Personal Injury; Real Estate Law; Tax Law

BRACKEN & MARGOLIN, LLP
Islandia, NY............Business Law; Civil Trial Practice; General Practice

BRADEN & OLSON
Lake Geneva, WI............Civil Trial Practice; Personal Injury; Real Estate Law; Trust and Estates, Wills and Probate

BRADFORD, MICHAEL E. LAW OFFICES OF
Phoenix, AZ............Insurance Defense; Medical Malpractice; Personal Injury

BRADFORD, COENEN & WELSH
Omaha, NE............Civil Trial Practice; General Practice

BRADLEY ARANT ROSE & WHITE LLP
Birmingham, AL............Antitrust Law; Appellate Practice; Banking Law; Bankruptcy Law; Business Law; Civil Rights; Civil Trial Practice; Commercial Law; Communications Law; Computer Law; Construction Law; Employment Benefits Law; Environmental Law; Family Law; General Practice; Health Care Law; Immigration and Naturalization; Insurance Defense; International Business Law; Labor and Employment Law; Land Use Law; Municipal and Zoning Law; Municipal Bond/Public Authority Financing; Natural Resources Law; Patent, Trademark, Copyright and Unfair Competition; Personal Injury; Product Liability Law; Public Utilities Law; Real Estate Law; Securities Law; Tax Law; Trademark, Copyright and Unfair Competition; Transportation Law; Trust and Estates, Wills and Probate; Workers Compensation
Huntsville, AL............Civil Trial Practice; Communications Law; Environmental Law; General Practice; Insurance Defense; Labor and Employment Law; Personal Injury; Real Estate Law; Tax Law; Trust and Estates, Wills and Probate

BRADLEY, DRENDEL & JEANNEY
Reno, NV............Aviation Law; Medical Malpractice; Personal Injury; Product Liability Law

BRADSHAW, STEELE, COCHRANE & BERENS, L.C.
Cape Girardeau, MO............General Practice

BRADY, BROOKS & O'CONNELL, LLP
Salamanca, NY............Arbitration; Commercial Litigation; Corporate Law; Personal Injury; Trust and Estates, Wills and Probate

BRADY, HATHAWAY, BRADY & BRETZ, PROFESSIONAL CORPORATION
Detroit, MI............Administrative Law; Admiralty/Maritime Law; Arbitration; Civil Trial Practice; General Practice; Labor and Employment Law; Real Estate Law; Workers Compensation

BRADY, VORWERCK & RYDER
Orange, CA............Insurance Defense

BRAFF, HARRIS & SUKONECK
Livingston, NJ............Civil Trial Practice

BRAFMAN & ROSS, P.C.
New York, NY............Criminal Trial Practice

BRAINARD LAW OFFICES, THE
Charleston, IL............General Practice; Insurance Defense

BRAMNICK, JON M.
Scotch Plains, NJ............Personal Injury

BRANCH LAW FIRM
Albuquerque, NM............Civil Trial Practice; Medical Malpractice; Personal Injury; Product Liability Law; Toxic Torts

BRANCH, THOMPSON, PHILHOURS & WARMATH, A PROFESSIONAL ASSOCIATION
Paragould, AR............General Practice

BRAND FARRAR & BUXBAUM LLP
Los Angeles, CA............Corporate Law; International Business Law; International Trade Law; Land Use Law; Mergers and Acquisitions; Real Estate Law; Securities Law; Tax Law

BRANDON, SCHMIDT, GOFFINET & SOLVERSON
Carbondale, IL............Insurance Defense; Medical Malpractice

BRANDON & YARC, LLP
Long Beach, CA............Family Law

BRANDT AND BEESON, P.C.
Johnson City, TN............Business Law; Real Estate Law; Trust and Estates, Wills and Probate

BRANDT, JENNINGS, ROBERTS, DAVIS & SNEE, PLLC
Falls Church, VA............General Practice

BRANDT, LARRY C., P.A.
Walhalla, SC............Appellate Practice; Civil Trial Practice; General Practice; Medical Malpractice; Personal Injury; Product Liability Law

BRANNON, BROWN, HALEY, ROBINSON & BULLOCK, P.A.
Lake City, FL............General Practice

BRANSDORFER & BRANSDORFER, P.C.
Grand Rapids, MI .... Civil Trial Practice

BRANSON BRINKOP GRIFFITH & STRONG LLP
Redwood City, CA .... Insurance Defense

BRANSON, FRANK L., P.C., LAW OFFICES OF
Dallas, TX .... Business Law; Civil Trial Practice; Medical Malpractice; Personal Injury

BRANSTETTER, KILGORE, STRANCH & JENNINGS
Nashville, TN .... Labor and Employment Law

BRANTLEY & WILKERSON, P.C.
Montgomery, AL .... Administrative Law; Business Law; Commercial Litigation; Communications Law; Corporate Law; Health Care Law; Insurance Defense; Public Utilities Law; Workers Compensation

BRASHER LAW FIRM, L.C.
St. Louis, MO .... Personal Injury

BRASSEL & BALDWIN, P.A.
Annapolis, MD .... Aviation Law; Family Law; Medical Malpractice; Product Liability Law; Toxic Torts

BRASSEY, WETHERELL, CRAWFORD & MCCURDY, L.L.P.
Boise, ID .... Insurance Defense

BRATTAIN & MINNIX
Indianapolis, IN .... Civil Trial Practice; General Practice

BRATTON, WILLIAM A. III
Dallas, TX .... Criminal Trial Practice

BRAUDE & MARGULIES, P.C.
Washington, DC .... Administrative Law; Civil Trial Practice; Construction Law

BRAULT, GRAHAM, SCOTT & BRAULT, LLC
Rockville, MD .... Business Law; Civil Trial Practice; Commercial Law; General Practice; Insurance Defense; Medical Malpractice; Personal Injury; Product Liability Law

BRAULT, PALMER, GROVE, ZIMMERMAN, WHITE & STEINHILBER
Fairfax, VA .... Civil Trial Practice; General Practice; Insurance Defense; Product Liability Law; Workers Compensation

BRAUN, HARLAND W., PROFESSIONAL CORPORATION
Los Angeles, CA .... Criminal Trial Practice

BRAUN KENDRICK FINKBEINER PLC
Ann Arbor, MI .... Banking Law; Commercial Law; Environmental Law; General Practice; Insurance Defense; Labor and Employment Law; Natural Resources Law; Real Estate Law; Tax Law; Trust and Estates, Wills and Probate; Workers Compensation
Bay City, MI .... Banking Law; Bankruptcy Law; Commercial Law; Environmental Law; General Practice; Insurance Defense; Labor and Employment Law; Natural Resources Law; Personal Injury; Real Estate Law; Tax Law; Trust and Estates, Wills and Probate; Workers Compensation
Saginaw, MI .... Banking Law; Bankruptcy Law; Commercial Law; Environmental Law; General Practice; Insurance Defense; Labor and Employment Law; Natural Resources Law; Real Estate Law; Tax Law; Trust and Estates, Wills and Probate; Workers Compensation

BRAUNER BARON ROSENZWEIG & KLEIN, L.L.P.
New York, NY .... Bankruptcy Law; Trust and Estates, Wills and Probate

BRAUNLICH, RUSSOW & BRAUNLICH, A PROFESSIONAL CORPORATION
Monroe, MI .... Business Law; Construction Law; Environmental Law; Insurance Defense; Labor and Employment Law; Municipal and Zoning Law; Personal Injury; Real Estate Law; Trust and Estates, Wills and Probate

BRAUNSTEIN & TODISCO, LLC
Fairfield, CT .... Real Estate Law; Tax Law; Trust and Estates, Wills and Probate

BRAUWERMAN & ASSOCIATES, P.A.
Miami, FL .... Immigration and Naturalization

BRAVERMAN AND ROSSI, P.A., LAW OFFICES OF
Fort Lauderdale, FL .... Criminal Trial Practice; Family Law

BRAY, GEIGER, RUDQUIST & NUSS
Stockton, CA .... General Practice

BRAZE LAW OFFICES
San Francisco, CA .... Insurance Defense; Product Liability Law; Tax Law

BREAZEALE, SACHSE & WILSON, L.L.P.
Baton Rouge, LA .... Antitrust Law; Civil Trial Practice; General Practice; Labor and Employment Law; Municipal Bond/Public Authority Financing; Natural Resources Law
New Orleans, LA .... General Practice

BRECKENRIDGE, HUGH LAW OFFICES OF
Irvine, CA .... Business Law

BREEDEN, MACMILLAN & GREEN, P.L.C.
Norfolk, VA .... Civil Trial Practice; General Practice

BREGA & WINTERS P.C.
Denver, CO .... Civil Trial Practice; Criminal Trial Practice; General Practice; Securities Law
Greeley, CO .... Business Law; Civil Trial Practice; Real Estate Law; Trust and Estates, Wills and Probate

BREGMAN & BURT, A PROFESSIONAL ASSOCIATION
Scottsdale, AZ .... Bankruptcy Law; Trust and Estates, Wills and Probate

BREIT, DRESCHER & BREIT, P.C.
Norfolk, VA .... Admiralty/Maritime Law; Medical Malpractice; Personal Injury; Product Liability Law

BREMYER & WISE, P.A.
McPherson, KS .... General Practice

BRENMAN BROMBERG & TENENBAUM, P.C.
Denver, CO .... Administrative Law; Appellate Practice; Business Law; Civil Trial Practice; Commercial Litigation; Construction Law; Corporate Law; Mergers and Acquisitions; Real Estate Law; Securities Law; Tax Law

BRENNAN & BARNARD
Quincy, IL .... Insurance Defense

BRENNAN & COLLINS
Milwaukee, WI .... Insurance Defense

BRENNAN, HAYSKAR, JEFFERSON, WALKER & SCHWERER, PROFESSIONAL ASSOCIATION
Fort Pierce, FL .... Appellate Practice; Civil Trial Practice; General Practice

BRENNAN, REHFUSS AND LIGUORI, P.C.
Albany, NY .... Civil Trial Practice; General Practice

BRENNAN, STEIL, BASTING & MACDOUGALL, S.C.
Janesville, WI .... General Practice

BRENNAN & WASDEN LLP
Savannah, GA .... Insurance Defense; Medical Malpractice

BRENNEMAN, DIANE M.
Washington, DC .... Family Law

BRENNER, BROWN, GOLIAN & MCCAFFREY CO., L.P.A.
Columbus, OH .... Employment Benefits Law; Insurance Defense

BRENNER, DOHNAL, EVANS & YOFFY, P.C.
Richmond, VA .... Criminal Trial Practice; Family Law; Insurance Defense; Medical Malpractice; Personal Injury; Product Liability Law

BRESLOW & WALKER, LLP
New York, NY .... Business Law; Securities Law

BREW, RICHARD DOUGLAS, A PROFESSIONAL LAW CORPORATION
Modesto, CA .... Business Law; International Business Law; Trademark, Copyright and Unfair Competition

BREWER, BREWER, ANTHONY & MIDDLEBROOK
Irving, TX .... Civil Trial Practice; Nonprofit and Tax Exempt Organizations

BREWER, CHARLES M., LTD.
Phoenix, AZ .... Appellate Practice; Aviation Law; Civil Trial Practice; Medical Malpractice; Personal Injury; Product Liability Law

BREWER & PRITCHARD, A PROFESSIONAL CORPORATION
Houston, TX .... Construction Law; Insurance Defense; Securities Law

BREWSTER, JAMES R.
Tallahassee, FL .... Tax Law

BREWSTER, SHALLCROSS AND DEANGELIS
Tulsa, OK .... Medical Malpractice

BRICKER & ECKLER LLP
Columbus, OH .... Civil Trial Practice; Commercial Litigation; Computer Law; Construction Law; Environmental Law; General Practice; Health Care Law; Labor and Employment Law; Mergers and Acquisitions; Municipal Bond/Public Authority Financing; Nonprofit and Tax Exempt Organizations; Public Utilities Law; Real Estate Law; Securities Law; Tax Law; Workers Compensation

BRICKFIELD, BURCHETTE & RITTS, P.C.
Washington, DC .... Natural Resources Law

BRICKLEMYER SMOLKER & BOLVES, P.A.
Tampa, FL ....Eminent Domain; Land Use Law; Municipal and Zoning Law; Real Estate Law

BRIDGERS & GILL
Pensacola, FL....Insurance Defense; Product Liability Law

BRIDGES, TERRY LAW OFFICES OF
Riverside, CA....Civil Trial Practice

BRIDGES, YOUNG, MATTHEWS & DRAKE PLC
Pine Bluff, AR....General Practice

BRIDGFORTH & BUNTIN
Southaven, MS....Civil Trial Practice; Real Estate Law

BRIER & IRISH, P.L.C.
Phoenix, AZ....Real Estate Law

BRIERLY LAW OFFICE, L.L.P.
Newton, IA....General Practice

BRIERTON, JONES & JONES, LLP
San Diego, CA....Trust and Estates, Wills and Probate

BRIGDEN & PETAJAN, S.C.
Milwaukee, WI....Labor and Employment Law

BRIGHAM AND TREVOR, P.C.
Philadelphia, PA....Product Liability Law

BRIGHT AND BROWN
Glendale, CA....Business Law; Environmental Law; Oil and Gas Law

BRINIG, JOSEPH K.
Phoenix, AZ....Bankruptcy Law

BRINKER & DOYEN, L.L.P.
St. Louis, MO....Insurance Defense

BRINKLEY, MCNERNEY, MORGAN, SOLOMON & TATUM, LLP
Fort Lauderdale, FL....Business Law; Corporate Law

BRINKS HOFER GILSON & LIONE, A PROFESSIONAL CORPORATION
Chicago, IL....General Practice

BRINK, SOBOLIK, SEVERSON, MALM & ALBRECHT, P.A.
Hallock, MN....Civil Trial Practice; General Practice; Insurance Defense; Personal Injury

BRINSON, ASKEW, BERRY, SEIGLER, RICHARDSON & DAVIS, LLP
Rome, GA....Business Law; Civil Rights; Civil Trial Practice; General Practice; Insurance Defense; Product Liability Law

BRIOL & ASSOCIATES
Minneapolis, MN....Commercial Litigation; Securities Law

BRIONES LAW FIRM, A PROFESSIONAL ASSOCIATION
Farmington, NM....Civil Trial Practice

BRISKMAN & BINION, P.C.
Mobile, AL....Civil Trial Practice; Criminal Trial Practice; Family Law; General Practice; Insurance Defense; Personal Injury

BRISTOL, DOUGLAS
Chicago, IL....Immigration and Naturalization

BRITT, HANKINS, SCHAIBLE & MOUGHAN
Philadelphia, PA....Insurance Defense

BRITTON, GRAY AND HILL, P.C.
Oklahoma City, OK....Banking Law; Business Law; Civil Trial Practice

BROAD, ALAN H., P.C., LAW OFFICES
Grosse Pointe Woods, MI....Civil Trial Practice

BROAD AND CASSEL
Boca Raton, FL....General Practice
Fort Lauderdale, FL....General Practice
Miami, FL....General Practice
Orlando, FL....General Practice
Tallahassee, FL....General Practice
Tampa, FL....General Practice
West Palm Beach, FL....General Practice

BROBECK, PHLEGER & HARRISON LLP
Irvine, CA....General Practice
Los Angeles, CA....General Practice
Palo Alto, CA....General Practice
San Diego, CA....General Practice
San Francisco, CA....General Practice
New York, NY....General Practice

BROCK, CARPENTER & MCGUIRE, P.S.
Davenport, WA....Land Use Law

BROCKINTON, BROCKINTON & KERR, P.A.
Charleston, SC....General Practice

BROCK & PERSON, A PROFESSIONAL CORPORATION
San Antonio, TX....Insurance Defense; Personal Injury; Product Liability Law; Workers Compensation

BRODERICK & THORNTON
Bowling Green, KY....Commercial Litigation; General Practice; Insurance Defense

BRODER, SHERRY P., A LAW CORPORATION, LAW OFFICE OF
Honolulu, HI....Civil Trial Practice

BRODIE & PAWLUC
Stuart, FL....Trust and Estates, Wills and Probate

BRODSKY, GREENBLATT & RENEHAN, CHARTERED
Gaithersburg, MD....Family Law

BRODSKY, RICHARD E., P.A.
Miami, FL....Appellate Practice

BRODY FABIANI & COHEN
New York, NY....Insurance Defense

BRODY, WILKINSON AND OBER, P.C.
Southport, CT....Business Law; Civil Trial Practice; Employment Benefits Law; Real Estate Law; Sports and Entertainment Law; Tax Law; Trust and Estates, Wills and Probate

BROMBERG, ROSENTHAL, SIEGEL & GOODMAN
Rockville, MD....General Practice

BROMBERG & SUNSTEIN LLP
Boston, MA....Business Law; Civil Trial Practice; Patent, Trademark, Copyright and Unfair Competition

BRONSTEIN, VAN VEEN & BRONSTEIN, P.C.
New York, NY....Family Law

BRONSTON, EDYTHE L. LAW OFFICES OF
Los Angeles, CA....Bankruptcy Law

BROOK, JAMES F. AND ASSOCIATES
Phoenix, AZ....Medical Malpractice; Personal Injury; Product Liability Law

BROOKES, LAWRENCE V.
Berkeley, CA....Tax Law

BROOKS, GARY L. AND ASSOCIATES
Oklahoma City, OK....Civil Trial Practice; Medical Malpractice; Personal Injury; Product Liability Law

BROOKS & KUSHMAN, P.C.
Southfield, MI....Intellectual Property Law; Trademark, Copyright and Unfair Competition

BROOKS, LEBOEUF, BENNETT & FOSTER, P.A.
Tallahassee, FL....Criminal Trial Practice; Personal Injury

BROOKS, PIERCE, MCLENDON, HUMPHREY & LEONARD, L.L.P.
Greensboro, NC....Civil Trial Practice; General Practice

BROOKS, STEVENS & POPE, P.A.
Cary, NC....Civil Trial Practice; Workers Compensation

BROOME, DAVID P.
Mobile, AL....Civil Trial Practice; Commercial Litigation; Family Law

BROPHY, MILLS, SCHMOR, GERKING & BROPHY, LLP
Medford, OR....General Practice

BROUDE, SMITH & JENNINGS, P.C.
Fort Worth, TX....Bankruptcy Law; Real Estate Law; Tax Law; Trust and Estates, Wills and Probate

BROUSSARD, DAVID & DAIGLE, A PROFESSIONAL LAW CORPORATION
Lafayette, LA....Admiralty/Maritime Law; Civil Trial Practice; Insurance Defense; Personal Injury; Product Liability Law

BROWDY AND NEIMARK
Washington, DC....Patent, Trademark, Copyright and Unfair Competition

BROWN, DANIEL G.
San Mateo, CA....Tax Law

BROWN, DOUGLAS C.
San Diego, CA....Criminal Trial Practice

BROWN, GENE D.
Tallahassee, FL....Business Law; Real Estate Law

BROWN, HAROLD & ASSOCIATES, LAW OFFICES OF
Boston, MA............................Antitrust Law; Franchise Law

BROWN, KENT MASTERSON LAW OFFICES OF
Danville, KY............................Appellate Practice; Civil Trial Practice

BROWN AND AMODIO, A LEGAL PROFESSIONAL ASSOCIATION
Medina, OH............................General Practice

BROWN, BEMILLER, MURRAY & MCINTYRE
Mansfield, OH............................General Practice; Insurance Defense

BROWN & BOLAND
San Francisco, CA............................Insurance Defense

BROWN AND BROWN
St. Ignace, MI............................General Practice

BROWN, BROWN & BROWN, A PROFESSIONAL ASSOCIATION
Bel Air, MD............................Civil Trial Practice; Criminal Trial Practice; Family Law; Personal Injury; Real Estate Law; Trust and Estates, Wills and Probate; Workers Compensation

BROWN CLARK, A PROFESSIONAL ASSOCIATION
Sarasota, FL............................Commercial Litigation; Construction Law; Workers Compensation

BROWN & CONNERY, LLP
Camden, NJ............................Admiralty/Maritime Law; Civil Trial Practice; General Practice; Insurance Defense
Westmont, NJ............................Admiralty/Maritime Law; Civil Trial Practice; General Practice; Insurance Defense

BROWN, CUMMINS & BROWN CO., L.P.A.
Cincinnati, OH............................Business Law; Civil Trial Practice; Health Care Law; Labor and Employment Law; Securities Law

BROWN, DREW & MASSEY, LLP
Casper, WY............................Administrative Law; Appellate Practice; Banking Law; Bankruptcy Law; Business Law; Civil Trial Practice; Commercial Law; Construction Law; Creditors Rights; Environmental Law; Family Law; General Practice; Insurance Defense; Labor and Employment Law; Natural Resources Law; Public Utilities Law; Real Estate Law; Trust and Estates, Wills and Probate

BROWN, ELLYN L., CHARTERED
Towson, MD............................Franchise Law; Securities Law

BROWN ENVIRONMENTAL LAW GROUP, P.C., THE
Chicago, IL............................Environmental Law

BROWN, ERNEST, & COMPANY, A PROFESSIONAL CORPORATION
San Francisco, CA............................Construction Law; International Business Law

BROWN & GREEN, P.A.
Orlando, FL............................Labor and Employment Law

BROWN, HAY & STEPHENS
Springfield, IL............................Business Law; General Practice

BROWN, JAMES E., & ASSOCIATES, P.C.
Denver, CO............................Business Law; Civil Trial Practice; Real Estate Law; Securities Law

BROWN, JEFFERIES AND BOULWARE
Barnwell, SC............................General Practice

BROWN & KELLY, L.L.P.
Buffalo, NY............................Business Law; Commercial Litigation; Criminal Trial Practice; Insurance Defense; Labor and Employment Law; Personal Injury; Real Estate Law; Trust and Estates, Wills and Probate

BROWN, KINSEY & FUNKHOUSER, P.L.C.
Mason City, IA............................General Practice

BROWN LAW FIRM, P.C.
Billings, MT............................General Practice; Insurance Defense; Medical Malpractice; Tax Law; Trust and Estates, Wills and Probate

BROWN, MALCOLM H., P.C.
Bismarck, ND............................Commercial Law

BROWN RAYSMAN MILLSTEIN FELDER & STEINER LLP
New York, NY............................Civil Trial Practice; General Practice

BROWN, ROSETA, LONG, MCCONVILLE, KILCULLEN & CARLSON
Eugene, OR............................Insurance Defense

BROWN SCHWARTZ PATTERSON & ANKERS, P.C.
Troy, MI............................Civil Rights; Labor and Employment Law

BROWN, SIMS, WISE & WHITE, A PROFESSIONAL CORPORATION
Houston, TX............................Admiralty/Maritime Law; Insurance Defense

BROWN, TERRELL, HOGAN, ELLIS, MCCLAMMA & YEGELWEL, P.A.
Jacksonville, FL............................Civil Rights; Environmental Law; Labor and Employment Law; Medical Malpractice; Personal Injury; Toxic Torts

BROWN, WARD & HAYNES, P.A.
Waynesville, NC............................Business Law

BROWN, WARD, SALZMAN & WEISS, P.A.
Orlando, FL............................Administrative Law; Business Law; Civil Trial Practice; Commercial Litigation; Government Contracts; Labor and Employment Law; Product Liability Law

BROWN, WATT & BUCHANAN, P.A.
Biloxi, MS............................Corporate Law; Environmental Law; Insurance Defense; Product Liability Law; Transportation Law; Workers Compensation
Pascagoula, MS............................Corporate Law; Environmental Law; Insurance Defense; Product Liability Law; Transportation Law; Workers Compensation

BROWN & WICHMER, P.C.
St. Louis, MO............................Immigration and Naturalization

BROWN, WINFIELD & CANZONERI, INCORPORATED
Los Angeles, CA............................Municipal and Zoning Law; Real Estate Law

BROWN, WINICK, GRAVES, GROSS, BASKERVILLE AND SCHOENEBAUM, P.L.C.
Des Moines, IA............................General Practice

BROWN & WOOD LLP
Washington, DC............................General Practice
New York, NY............................General Practice

BROWNING BUSHMAN, A PROFESSIONAL CORPORATION
Houston, TX............................Patent, Trademark, Copyright and Unfair Competition

BROWNING, KALECZYC, BERRY & HOVEN, P.C.
Helena, MT............................Administrative Law; Commercial Law; Environmental Law; Health Care Law; Immigration and Naturalization; Insurance Defense; Natural Resources Law

BROWNING & LIPTON
Dallas, TX............................Insurance Defense

BROWNING & TANKSLEY, LLP
Marietta, GA............................Banking Law; Civil Trial Practice; Family Law; Medical Malpractice; Personal Injury; Product Liability Law; Trust and Estates, Wills and Probate

BROWNSTEIN HYATT & FARBER, P.C.
Denver, CO............................Administrative Law; Business Law; Civil Trial Practice; Commercial Litigation; Corporate Law; Environmental Law; General Practice; Labor and Employment Law; Land Use Law; Municipal Bond/Public Authority Financing; Real Estate Law; Securities Law; Tax Law

BROYLES & PRATT, A PROFESSIONAL CORPORATION
Austin, TX............................Civil Trial Practice; Insurance Defense; Public Utilities Law
Corpus Christi, TX............................Civil Trial Practice; Insurance Defense; Legal Malpractice; Public Utilities Law

BRUCKER MORRA & HILTUNEN, A PROFESSIONAL CORPORATION
Los Angeles, CA............................Employment Benefits Law

BRUCKNER & SYKES, L.L.P.
Houston, TX............................Labor and Employment Law

BRUDER, GENTILE & MARCOUX, L.L.P.
Washington, DC............................Administrative Law; Energy Law; Public Utilities Law

BRUINOOGE & ASSOCIATES
Rutherford, NJ............................Land Use Law; Real Estate Law

BRUNENKANT & HASKELL, LLP
Washington, DC............................Administrative Law; Energy Law; Natural Resources Law; Public Utilities Law

BRUNN & FLYNN, A PROFESSIONAL CORPORATION
Modesto, CA............................Civil Trial Practice; Insurance Defense; Real Estate Law; Trust and Estates, Wills and Probate

BRUNO, FREDERIC & ASSOCIATES
Minneapolis, MN............................Criminal Trial Practice

BRYAN CAVE LLP
St. Louis, MO............................General Practice

BRYAN, NELSON, SCHROEDER, CASTIGLIOLA & BANAHAN
Pascagoula, MS............................Business Law; Civil Trial Practice; Corporate Law; Insurance Defense

BRYANT AND HIGBY, CHARTERED
Panama City, FL............................General Practice

BRYANT LAW OFFICES
Wilmington, OH............................General Practice

BRYANT, LOVLIEN & JARVIS, P.C.
Bend, OR....General Practice

BRYCE, WILLIAM D.
Georgetown, TX....Business Law

BRYDGER, GORDON C., P.A.
Fort Lauderdale, FL....Family Law

BRYDGES, MAHAN, O'BRIEN & FRUCCI, P.C.
Virginia Beach, VA....Civil Trial Practice; Criminal Trial Practice; Family Law; Medical Malpractice; Personal Injury; Product Liability Law

BRYDON, SWEARENGEN & ENGLAND, PROFESSIONAL CORPORATION
Jefferson City, MO....General Practice

BUCCI, BAILEY & JAVINS, L.C.
Charleston, WV....Medical Malpractice; Personal Injury; Product Liability Law

BUCHANAN, DOUGLAS
Bishop, CA....Criminal Trial Practice; General Practice; Trust and Estates, Wills and Probate

BUCHANAN, ROBERT L. JR.
Aiken, SC....Civil Trial Practice

BUCHANAN, JURDEM & ZULAUF, P.C.
Denver, CO....Personal Injury

BUCHANAN, SILVER & BECKERING, P.L.C.
Grand Rapids, MI....Civil Trial Practice; Commercial Litigation; Medical Malpractice; Personal Injury; Product Liability Law

BUCK & BUCK
Smithville, TN....General Practice

BUCK & GORDON LLP
Seattle, WA....Environmental Law; Municipal and Zoning Law; Real Estate Law

BUCKINGHAM, HOLZAPFEL, ZEIHER, WALDOCK & SCHELL CO., L.P.A.
Sandusky, OH....Commercial Law; General Practice

BUCKLEY FIRM, THE, P.C.
Mission Viejo, CA....Bankruptcy Law; Civil Trial Practice; General Practice; Real Estate Law

BUCKLEY & HAYES, L.L.P.
New Orleans, LA....Civil Trial Practice; Health Care Law; Insurance Defense; Medical Malpractice; Personal Injury; Workers Compensation

BUCKLEY KING & BLUSO, A LEGAL PROFESSIONAL ASSOCIATION
Cleveland, OH....Civil Trial Practice

BUCKLEY, MENDLESON & CRISCIONE, P.C.
Albany, NY....Workers Compensation

BUCKLEY, NAGLE, GENTRY, BRION, MCGUIRE & MORRIS
West Chester, PA....General Practice; Municipal and Zoning Law; Trust and Estates, Wills and Probate

BUCKNELL STEHLIK
Seattle, WA....Commercial Law

BUDNER, BRUCE A. & ASSOCIATES
Dallas, TX....Legal Malpractice; Personal Injury

BUESSER, BUESSER, BLACK, LYNCH, FRYHOFF & GRAHAM, P.C.
Bloomfield Hills, MI....Family Law; General Practice

BUFALINI, DAVID A., P.S., INC.
Tacoma, WA....Personal Injury

BUHLER LAW FIRM, THE
Memphis, TN....Corporate Law; Securities Law

BUIST, MOORE, SMYTHE & MCGEE, P.A.
Charleston, SC....Admiralty/Maritime Law; Bankruptcy Law; Civil Trial Practice; Commercial Law; Construction Law; Environmental Law; General Practice; Health Care Law; Insurance Defense; Labor and Employment Law; Product Liability Law; Real Estate Law

BULLARD, ANDERSON & ANDERSON, PLLC
Clarkston, MI....Arbitration; Aviation Law; Business Law; Civil Trial Practice; International Business Law; Real Estate Law

BULLARD, KORSHOJ, SMITH & JERNSTEDT, A PROFESSIONAL CORPORATION
Portland, OR....Labor and Employment Law

BULL, HOUSSER & TUPPER
Vancouver, BC, Canada....General Practice

BULLOCK, CHILDS, PENDLEY, REED, HERZFELD & RUBIN
Jacksonville, FL....Civil Trial Practice; Insurance Defense

BULUA, STANLEY E., ATTORNEY AT LAW, LLC
Scarsdale, NY....Tax Law

BUMP AND BUMP
Chadron, NE....General Practice

BUNCH & BROCK
Lexington, KY....Bankruptcy Law

BUNGER & ROBERTSON
Bloomington, IN....Banking Law; Business Law; Civil Trial Practice; General Practice; Health Care Law; Insurance Defense; Personal Injury; Real Estate Law; Trust and Estates, Wills and Probate

BUONAURO, ROBERT J., P.A.
Orlando, FL....Criminal Trial Practice

BURAK ANDERSON & MELLONI, PLC
Burlington, VT....General Practice

BURBIDGE AND MITCHELL
Salt Lake City, UT....Commercial Litigation; Personal Injury

BURCH & CRACCHIOLO, P.A.
Phoenix, AZ....Appellate Practice; Bankruptcy Law; Civil Trial Practice; Commercial Law; Criminal Trial Practice; Environmental Law; Family Law; General Practice; Insurance Defense; Medical Malpractice; Personal Injury; Product Liability Law; Real Estate Law; Tax Law; Trust and Estates, Wills and Probate

BURCH, PORTER & JOHNSON
Memphis, TN....General Practice

BURD MAGATHAN LOZANO & ZACHERL, L.L.P.
Miami, FL....Aviation Law; Civil Trial Practice

BURD & NAYLOR
Santa Ana, CA....Bankruptcy Law

BURESH, FREDRIC C., P.A.
Fort Lauderdale, FL....Bankruptcy Law; Business Law

BURESH, KAPLAN, JANG & FELLER
Berkeley, CA....Insurance Defense

BURG SIMPSON ELDREDGE & HERSH, P.C.
Englewood, CO....Civil Trial Practice; Commercial Law; Insurance Defense

BURGE, DAVID A., CO., L.P.A.
Cleveland, OH....Patent, Trademark, Copyright and Unfair Competition

BURGER, WILLIAM KENNERLY
Murfreesboro, TN....Civil Trial Practice

BURGER & BENNETT, P.C.
McCook, NE....Civil Trial Practice; Real Estate Law

BURGETT & ROBBINS
Jamestown, NY....Civil Trial Practice; Family Law; General Practice; Personal Injury; Product Liability Law

BURGE & WETTERMARK, P.C.
Birmingham, AL....Personal Injury; Transportation Law

BURGOYNE, MICHAEL H., P.A., LAW OFFICE OF
Towson, MD....General Practice

BURKE, DANIEL V.
Carlsbad, CA....Family Law

BURKE COSTANZA & CUPPY LLP
Merrillville, IN....General Practice

BURKE, MARLIN W., P.C.
Denver, CO....Health Care Law

BURKE & MAYER, A PROFESSIONAL LAW CORPORATION
New Orleans, LA....Admiralty/Maritime Law; Environmental Law

BURKE, THOMAS M., P.C., LAW OFFICES
St. Louis, MO....Personal Injury; Workers Compensation

BURKERT & HART
Fort Myers, FL....Personal Injury

BURK LAW FIRM, THE, A PROFESSIONAL CORPORATION
Austin, TX....Civil Trial Practice; Commercial Litigation

BURK & SEATON, P.A.
Minneapolis, MN....Labor and Employment Law

BURLEIGH, LAWRENCE K., LTD., A PROF. LAW CORP.
Lafayette, LA....Admiralty/Maritime Law; Aviation Law; Personal Injury

BURNHAM & BROWN, A PROFESSIONAL CORPORATION
Oakland, CA .... General Practice

BURNS ANDERSON JURY & BRENNER, L.L.P.
Austin, TX .... Insurance Defense; Transportation Law; Workers Compensation

BURNS, BRYANT, HINCHEY, COX & ROCKEFELLER, P.A.
Dover, NH .... Insurance Defense; Medical Malpractice; Personal Injury

BURNS, CUNNINGHAM & MACKEY, P.C.
Mobile, AL .... Commercial Law; Medical Malpractice; Personal Injury; Product Liability Law; Toxic Torts

BURNS, DOANE, SWECKER & MATHIS, L.L.P.
Alexandria, VA .... Patent, Trademark, Copyright and Unfair Competition; Trademark, Copyright and Unfair Competition

BURNS & FARREY
Worcester, MA .... Insurance Defense

BURNS & LEVINSON LLP
Boston, MA .... Business Law; Corporate Law; Creditors Rights; General Practice

BURNS, MCDONALD, BRADFORD, PATRICK & TINSLEY, L.L.P.
Greenwood, SC .... Civil Trial Practice; General Practice

BURNS RAY & DELANO, PROFESSIONAL ASSOCIATION
Portland, ME .... Business Law; Commercial Litigation; Construction Law; General Practice; Insurance Defense; Labor and Employment Law; Product Liability Law; Securities Law

BURNSIDE, WALL, DANIEL, ELLISON & REVELL
Augusta, GA .... Civil Trial Practice; Commercial Litigation; General Practice; Municipal and Zoning Law; Personal Injury

BURR & FORMAN LLP
Birmingham, AL .... Antitrust Law; Banking Law; Business Law; Civil Trial Practice; Communications Law; Environmental Law; General Practice; Labor and Employment Law; Municipal Bond/Public Authority Financing; Real Estate Law; Tax Law; Trust and Estates, Wills and Probate
Huntsville, AL .... Banking Law; Business Law; Real Estate Law; Trust and Estates, Wills and Probate

BURR, JEFFREY L., & ASSOCIATES
Las Vegas, NV .... Trust and Estates, Wills and Probate

BURRIS, MACMILLAN, PEARCE & MAYER, L.L.P.
Charlotte, NC .... Real Estate Law

BURROUGHS, HEPLER, BROOM, MACDONALD & HEBRANK
Edwardsville, IL .... Civil Trial Practice

BURROW & PARROTT, L.L.P.
Houston, TX .... Civil Trial Practice; Personal Injury; Toxic Torts

BURSTEIN, HERTOGS & MCFARLAND, P.A.
Minneapolis, MN .... General Practice

BURT, ROBERT G., P.C.
Portland, OR .... Business Law; General Practice; Mergers and Acquisitions; Tax Law; Trust and Estates, Wills and Probate

BURTON, JOHN C.
Pasadena, CA .... Appellate Practice; Civil Rights; Civil Trial Practice; Medical Malpractice; Personal Injury

BURTON, R. NICHOLAS
Decatur, IL .... Tax Law; Trust and Estates, Wills and Probate

BURTON & MURPHY
Tampa, FL .... Commercial Litigation; Computer Law

BURTON & SUE, L.L.P.
Greensboro, NC .... Civil Trial Practice; Insurance Defense; Personal Injury; Workers Compensation

BURTON, VOLKMANN & SCHMAL, LLP
Santa Cruz, CA .... Insurance Defense

BUSCH AND BUSCH, LLP
North Brunswick, NJ .... Business Law; Civil Trial Practice; Family Law; General Practice; Insurance Defense; Municipal and Zoning Law; Personal Injury; Real Estate Law; Trust and Estates, Wills and Probate

BUSCH PROFESSIONAL CORPORATION
Golden, CO .... General Practice

BUSCHMANN, CARR & SHANKS, PROFESSIONAL CORPORATION
Indianapolis, IN .... Bankruptcy Law; Civil Trial Practice; Commercial Law; Creditors Rights; Labor and Employment Law; Workers Compensation

BUSER, PAUL J.
Scottsdale, AZ .... Business Law; Elder Law; Family Law; Trust and Estates, Wills and Probate

BUSH CRADDOCK & RENEKER, L.L.P.
Dallas, TX .... Civil Trial Practice; Personal Injury

BUSH, HAUDER & ADKERSON
Dallas, TX .... Insurance Defense; Workers Compensation

BUSH, JAMES, P.C., LAW OFFICES OF
Phoenix, AZ .... Commercial Litigation

BUSSART, WEST, ROSSETTI, PIAIA & TYLER, P.C.
Rock Springs, WY .... Civil Trial Practice; General Practice

BUSTO & JENNINGS, PROFESSIONAL ASSOCIATION
Miami, FL .... Commercial Litigation

BUTKUS & REIMER, P.C.
Albuquerque, NM .... Insurance Defense; Medical Malpractice

BUTLER, JACK A. LAW OFFICES OF
Nashville, TN .... Personal Injury

BUTLER BURNETTE PAPPAS
Miami, FL .... Insurance Defense
Tallahassee, FL .... Insurance Defense
Tampa, FL .... Insurance Defense

BUTLER, HICKY & LONG
Forrest City, AR .... Aviation Law; Civil Trial Practice; General Practice; Insurance Defense; Medical Malpractice; Trust and Estates, Wills and Probate

BUTLER & HOSCH, P.A.
Orlando, FL .... Banking Law; Bankruptcy Law; Real Estate Law

BUTLER, JAMES T., & ASSOCIATES, P.A.
Tampa, FL .... Personal Injury

BUTLER & MACDOUGALD
Atlanta, GA .... Personal Injury; Product Liability Law

BUTLER, SNOW, O'MARA, STEVENS & CANNADA, PLLC
Jackson, MS .... General Practice

BUTLER, WOOTEN, OVERBY, FRYHOFER, DAUGHTERY & SULLIVAN
Atlanta, GA .... Civil Trial Practice; Medical Malpractice; Personal Injury; Product Liability Law
Columbus, GA .... Civil Trial Practice; Medical Malpractice; Personal Injury; Product Liability Law

BUTT, THORNTON & BAEHR, P.C.
Albuquerque, NM .... Civil Trial Practice; Insurance Defense; Labor and Employment Law; Product Liability Law

BUTTERMAN KAHN & GARDNER, LLP
New York, NY .... Family Law

BUTZ DUNN DESANTIS & BINGHAM, A PROFESSIONAL CORPORATION
San Diego, CA .... Civil Trial Practice

BUTZEL LONG, A PROFESSIONAL CORPORATION
Ann Arbor, MI .... Antitrust Law; Appellate Practice; Banking Law; Commercial Litigation; Constitutional Law; Intellectual Property Law
Birmingham, MI .... Commercial Litigation; Family Law; Municipal and Zoning Law; Real Estate Law; Trust and Estates, Wills and Probate
Detroit, MI .... Administrative Law; Antitrust Law; Appellate Practice; Business Law; Civil Trial Practice; Commercial Litigation; Constitutional Law; Construction Law; Employment Benefits Law; Environmental Law; Health Care Law; Immigration and Naturalization; Intellectual Property Law; International Business Law; Labor and Employment Law; Mergers and Acquisitions; Professional Liability; Real Estate Law; Tax Law; Trademark, Copyright and Unfair Competition
Okemos, MI .... Administrative Law; Construction Law; Public Utilities Law

BYE, GOFF & ROHDE, LTD.
River Falls, WI .... Personal Injury

BYERS, FRITZ
Toledo, OH .... Appellate Practice; Civil Trial Practice; Communications Law; Labor and Employment Law

BYERS CASGRAIN
Montreal, QU, Canada .... General Practice

BYNUM, ARLEN DEAN SPIDER, P.C., LAW OFFICES OF
Dallas, TX .... Insurance Defense

BYRD, BYRD, ERVIN, WHISNANT, MCMAHON & ERVIN, P.A.
Morganton, NC .... Criminal Trial Practice; General Practice; Personal Injury; Trust and Estates, Wills and Probate

BYRD, DAVIS AND EISENBERG, L.L.P.
Austin, TX ....Aviation Law; Medical Malpractice; Personal Injury; Product Liability Law

BYRD, MISCHE, BEVIS, BOWEN, JOSEPH & O'CONNOR, P.C.
Fairfax, VA ....Family Law

BYRNE, BENESCH & WALSMA, P.C.
Yuma, AZ....Real Estate Law

BYRNE, EDWARD O., & ASSOCIATES P.C.
Denver, CO ....International Business Law

BYRNE, JAMES B., JR., P.A.
Longwood, FL....Civil Trial Practice

BYRNE, KIELY & WHITE, LLP
Denver, CO ....Aviation Law; Insurance Defense; Product Liability Law

BYSSHE, FREDERICK H. JR., LAW OFFICES OF
Ventura, CA....Medical Malpractice; Personal Injury; Product Liability Law

CABANISS, JOHNSTON, GARDNER, DUMAS & O'NEAL
Birmingham, AL....Civil Trial Practice; General Practice
Mobile, AL....Civil Trial Practice; General Practice

CABANISS, MCDONALD, SMITH & WIGGINS, P.A.
Orlando, FL ....Civil Trial Practice; Product Liability Law

CABELL, ROBERT & ASSOCIATES
Richmond, VA....Criminal Trial Practice

CACACE, TUSCH & SANTAGATA
Stamford, CT....Business Law; Civil Trial Practice; Commercial Litigation; Corporate Law; Municipal and Zoning Law; Personal Injury; Real Estate Law; Trust and Estates, Wills and Probate

CACCIATORE, RONALD K., P.A.
Tampa, FL ....Criminal Trial Practice

CACHERIS, PLATO, LAW OFFICES OF
Washington, DC....Criminal Trial Practice
Alexandria, VA ....Criminal Trial Practice

CADES SCHUTTE FLEMING & WRIGHT
Honolulu, HI....Banking Law; Civil Trial Practice; General Practice; Patent, Trademark, Copyright and Unfair Competition; Real Estate Law; Trust and Estates, Wills and Probate
Kailua-Kona, HI....Civil Trial Practice; General Practice

CADWALADER, WICKERSHAM & TAFT
New York, NY....General Practice

CAESAR, RIVISE, BERNSTEIN, COHEN & POKOTILOW, LTD.
Philadelphia, PA ....Computer Law; Intellectual Property Law; Patent, Trademark, Copyright and Unfair Competition

CAHALANE, VINCENT P., P.C.
Brockton, MA ....Arbitration; Civil Trial Practice; Construction Law; Insurance Defense; Personal Injury; Product Liability Law

CAHILL, CHRISTIAN & KUNKLE, LTD.
Chicago, IL....Commercial Litigation; Construction Law; Environmental Law; Intellectual Property Law; Product Liability Law

CAHILL GORDON & REINDEL
Washington, DC....General Practice
New York, NY....General Practice; Municipal Bond/Public Authority Financing
Paris, France....General Practice

CAHILL, KATHLEEN, LLC, THE LAW OFFICES OF
Baltimore, MD ....Labor and Employment Law; Medical Malpractice; Personal Injury

CAHILL LAW OFFICES
Nevada, IA....General Practice; Trust and Estates, Wills and Probate

CAHILL & MARQUART, P.A.
Moorhead, MN ....General Practice
Fargo, ND....General Practice

CAHN WISHOD & KNAUER, LLP
Melville, NY....Banking Law; Business Law; Commercial Litigation; Corporate Law; Environmental Law; Municipal and Zoning Law

CALAFELL, RAY, JR., P.A.
Tampa, FL ....Civil Trial Practice

CALAWAY, STEPHEN G.
Winston-Salem, NC ....Real Estate Law

CALBOM & SCHWAB, P.S.C.
Moses Lake, WA....Personal Injury; Workers Compensation

CALCUTT CUNNINGHAM DAVISON ROGERS BOYNTON & PETTERSON, P.L.L.C.
Traverse City, MI....Corporate Law

CALDWELL, BERNER & CALDWELL
Woodstock, IL ....Civil Trial Practice; General Practice

CALDWELL & PACETTI
Palm Beach, FL....General Practice; Municipal Bond/Public Authority Financing

CALFEE, HALTER & GRISWOLD LLP
Cleveland, OH....General Practice; Trademark, Copyright and Unfair Competition
Columbus, OH ....General Practice

CALHOUN, FAULK, WATKINS & FAIRCLOTH, L.L.C.
Troy, AL ....Civil Trial Practice; General Practice; Insurance Defense

CALHOUN, KADEMENOS & HEICHEL CO., L.P.A.
Mansfield, OH....General Practice

CALHOUN & STACY
Dallas, TX....Appellate Practice; Banking Law; Bankruptcy Law; Business Law; Civil Trial Practice; Commercial Law; Commercial Litigation; Communications Law; Construction Law; Corporate Law; Environmental Law; General Practice; Health Care Law; Insurance Defense; Labor and Employment Law; Medical Malpractice; Municipal and Zoning Law; Patent, Trademark, Copyright and Unfair Competition; Personal Injury; Product Liability Law; Real Estate Law; Securities Law; Tax Law; Transportation Law; Trust and Estates, Wills and Probate

CALKINS & CALKINS
Eugene, OR ....General Practice; Insurance Defense

CALLAHAN & BLAINE, A PROFESSIONAL LAW CORPORATION
Santa Ana, CA....Business Law; Commercial Litigation; Construction Law; Environmental Law; General Practice; Patent, Trademark, Copyright and Unfair Competition; Real Estate Law

CALLAHAN & DEACON
Sacramento, CA ....Civil Trial Practice; Personal Injury

CALLAHAN LAW FIRM
Tallahassee, FL ....Insurance Defense; Medical Malpractice; Personal Injury

CALLAHAN, REBECCA, A PROFESSIONAL LAW CORPORATION
Newport Beach, CA....Appellate Practice; Bankruptcy Law; Civil Trial Practice; Commercial Litigation

CALLAN, REGENSTREICH, KOSTER & BRADY
New York, NY....Civil Trial Practice; Criminal Trial Practice; Insurance Defense; Medical Malpractice; Personal Injury; Product Liability Law

CALLENDER, JOHN F.
Jacksonville, FL ....Commercial Litigation; Personal Injury

CALLISTER NEBEKER & MCCULLOUGH, A PROFESSIONAL CORPORATION
Salt Lake City, UT....Antitrust Law; Banking Law; Bankruptcy Law; Business Law; Civil Trial Practice; Commercial Law; Corporate Law; Employment Benefits Law; Environmental Law; General Practice; Labor and Employment Law; Municipal Bond/Public Authority Financing; Natural Resources Law; Nonprofit and Tax Exempt Organizations; Pension and Profit Sharing; Personal Injury; Real Estate Law; Securities Law; Tax Law; Trust and Estates, Wills and Probate

CALLOWAY, NORRIS & BURDETTE
Dallas, TX....Trust and Estates, Wills and Probate

CALLOWAY, S. MARCUS, P.C.
Atlanta, GA ....Real Estate Law

CALVERT, MELANIE A.
Pasadena, CA ....Labor and Employment Law

CAMERON, MARRIOTT, WALSH, HODGES & COLEMAN, P.A.
Orlando, FL....Civil Trial Practice; Insurance Defense

CAMERON MCKENNA LLP
Washington, DC....Energy Law; Public Utilities Law

CAMERON & MITTLEMAN LLP
Providence, RI....Business Law; Health Care Law

CAMERON, PEARLSON & GALE
Long Beach, CA....Banking Law; Civil Trial Practice; Environmental Law; Labor and Employment Law; Land Use Law; Real Estate Law; Toxic Torts

CAMNER, LIPSITZ AND POLLER, PROFESSIONAL ASSOCIATION
Miami, FL..............................Corporate Law; General Practice; Real Estate Law

CAMP & CAMP, P.A.
Fort Lauderdale, FL...............Real Estate Law; Trust and Estates, Wills and Probate

CAMP CHURCH & ASSOCIATES
Vancouver, BC, Canada...........Administrative Law; Aviation Law; Commercial Litigation

CAMPANA, VIEH, SHORE, OWENS & LOEB
Scottsdale, AZ.........................Commercial Litigation; Family Law; Medical Malpractice; Personal Injury; Real Estate Law

CAMPBELL, JAMES M.
Orlando, FL.............................Criminal Trial Practice; Family Law

CAMPBELL, ARELLANO & RICH
Charlotte Amalie, St. Thomas, VI..............................Appellate Practice; Bankruptcy Law; Commercial Litigation; Environmental Law

CAMPBELL, BLACK, CARNINE, HEDIN, BALLARD & MCDONALD, P.C.
Mount Vernon, IL...................Civil Trial Practice; General Practice; Insurance Defense

CAMPBELL, DILLE AND BARNETT P.L.L.C.
Puyallup, WA..........................Civil Trial Practice

CAMPBELL, LEA, MICHAEL, MCCONNELL & PIGOT
Charlottetown, PE, Canada.....Administrative Law; Business Law; Civil Trial Practice; General Practice; Insurance Defense; Personal Injury

CAMPBELL & LEVINE, LLC
Pittsburgh, PA........................Bankruptcy Law; Commercial Law

CAMPBELL, MCCRANIE, SISTRUNK, ANZELMO & HARDY, P.C.
Metairie, LA............................Appellate Practice; Civil Trial Practice; Commercial Law; Medical Malpractice; Professional Liability

CAMPBELL, O'BRIEN & MISTELE, P.C.
Troy, MI..................................Business Law; General Practice; Real Estate Law; Trust and Estates, Wills and Probate

CAMPBELL, WALLER & MCCALLUM, L.L.C.
Birmingham, AL......................Commercial Litigation; Personal Injury

CAMPBELL, WOODS, BAGLEY, EMERSON, MCNEER & HERNDON, P.L.L.C.
Charleston, WV.......................General Practice
Huntington, WV.......................General Practice

CAMPEAU & THOMAS, A LAW CORPORATION
San Jose, CA...........................Bankruptcy Law; Civil Trial Practice; Commercial Law

CAMPNEY & MURPHY
Vancouver, BC, Canada...........General Practice

CAMRUD, MADDOCK, OLSON & LARSON, LTD.
Grand Forks, ND.....................General Practice

CANALES & SIMONSON, P.C.
Corpus Christi, TX.................Appellate Practice; Civil Trial Practice; Commercial Litigation; Criminal Trial Practice

CANGES, IWASHKO & BETHKE, A PROFESSIONAL CORPORATION
Denver, CO.............................Civil Trial Practice; Commercial Litigation; Criminal Trial Practice; Family Law

CANNON & DUNPHY, S.C.
Brookfield, WI........................Personal Injury; Professional Liability

CANNON, MEYER VON BREMEN & GOSS, LLP
Albany, GA.............................Civil Trial Practice; Personal Injury; Product Liability Law; Real Estate Law

CANO, KRISTIN M.
Newport Beach, CA................Corporate Law; Securities Law

CANSLER, LOCKHART, CAMPBELL, EVANS, BRYANT & GARLITZ, P.A.
Charlotte, NC..........................Business Law; Commercial Litigation; Insurance Defense

CANTEY & HANGER
Dallas, TX...............................General Practice; Insurance Defense; Personal Injury
Fort Worth, TX.......................General Practice; Insurance Defense; Labor and Employment Law; Personal Injury; Tax Law
Austin, TX...............................Administrative Law; Insurance Defense; International Business Law; Tax Law

CANTOR, DAVID MICHAEL, P.C., LAW OFFICES OF
Mesa, AZ.................................Criminal Trial Practice

CANTRILL, SKINNER, SULLIVAN & KING
Boise, ID.................................General Practice; Insurance Defense

CAPITELLI & WICKER
New Orleans, LA.....................Admiralty/Maritime Law; Civil Trial Practice; Criminal Trial Practice; Medical Malpractice; Personal Injury

CAPLAN, BUCKNER, ROHRBAUGH & KOSTECKA, CHTD.
Bethesda, MD..........................General Practice

CAPLIN & DRYSDALE, CHARTERED
Washington, DC.......................Business Law; Civil Trial Practice; Criminal Trial Practice; Tax Law; Trust and Estates, Wills and Probate
New York, NY.........................Business Law; Civil Trial Practice; Criminal Trial Practice; Trust and Estates, Wills and Probate

CAPRETZ & ASSOCIATES
Newport Beach, CA.................Business Law; Civil Trial Practice; Commercial Law; Commercial Litigation; Construction Law; General Practice; Product Liability Law; Toxic Torts

CAPUTO, ANTHONY J., P.C.
White Plains, NY.....................Civil Trial Practice; Insurance Defense

CAPUTO, JOHN A., & ASSOCIATES
Pittsburgh, PA........................Medical Malpractice; Personal Injury; Product Liability Law

CARB, LURIA, COOK & KUFELD, LLP
New York, NY.........................Commercial Litigation; Real Estate Law; Trust and Estates, Wills and Probate

CARDELLI HEBERT, P.C.
Royal Oak, MI.........................Commercial Law; Insurance Defense; Product Liability Law

CARDILLO & CORBETT
New York, NY.........................Admiralty/Maritime Law; Corporate Law

CARELLA, BYRNE, BAIN, GILFILLAN, CECCHI, STEWART & OLSTEIN, A PROFESSIONAL CORPORATION
Roseland, NJ............................General Practice; Municipal Bond/Public Authority Financing; Patent, Trademark, Copyright and Unfair Competition

CAREY, AUSTIN, JR., P.C.
Hartford, CT............................Environmental Law

CAREY & HILBERT
Clearwater, FL.........................Personal Injury

CAREY, O'MALLEY, WHITAKER & MANSON, P.A.
Tampa, FL...............................Commercial Litigation; Construction Law; Environmental Law

CARIDDI, MEE, RUÉ, AVOCATS ASSOCIÉS À LA COUR DE PARIS
Paris, France...........................General Practice

CARLBERG, GWENDOLYN JO M.
Alexandria, VA........................Family Law

CARLIN, HELLSTROM & BITTNER
Davenport, IA..........................General Practice

CARLIN, MADDOCK, FAY & CERBONE, P.C.
Florham Park, NJ.....................Civil Trial Practice; Commercial Litigation; Environmental Law; General Practice; Labor and Employment Law; Product Liability Law

CARLIN & VASVARI, LLC
Youngstown, OH......................Civil Trial Practice

CARLINER, REMES AND MIRBAGHERI-SMITH, P.C.
Washington, DC.......................Immigration and Naturalization

CARLOCK, DAVID, P.C.
Dallas, TX...............................Family Law

CARLSMITH BALL
Los Angeles, CA.....................General Practice
Washington, DC.......................General Practice
Hilo, HI...................................General Practice
Honolulu, HI...........................Administrative Law; Admiralty/Maritime Law; Antitrust Law; Appellate Practice; Arbitration; Banking Law; Bankruptcy Law; Business Law; Civil Trial Practice; Commercial Law; Commercial Litigation; Construction Law; Corporate Law; Creditors Rights; Employment Benefits Law; Energy Law; Environmental Law; General Practice; Government Contracts; Health Care Law; Immigration and Naturalization; Intellectual Property Law; International Business Law; Labor and Employment Law; Land Use Law; Mergers and Acquisitions; Nonprofit and Tax Exempt Organizations; Patent, Trademark, Copyright and Unfair Competition; Pension and Profit Sharing; Public Utilities Law; Real Estate Law; Securities Law; Tax Law; Trust and Estates, Wills and Probate; Workers Compensation
Kailua-Kona, HI.....................General Practice
Wailuku, HI............................General Practice
Hagåtña, GU...........................General Practice
Saipan, TT..............................General Practice
Mexico, D.F., Mexico.............General Practice

CARLSON, HAMMOND & PADDOCK, L.L.C.
Denver, CO .... Environmental Law

CARLSON WENDLER & ASSOCIATES, P.C.
Edwardsville, IL .... Personal Injury

CARLTON, FIELDS, WARD, EMMANUEL, SMITH & CUTLER, P.A.
Miami, FL .... General Practice
Orlando, FL .... General Practice
Pensacola, FL .... General Practice
St. Petersburg, FL .... General Practice
Tallahassee, FL .... General Practice
Tampa, FL .... General Practice
West Palm Beach, FL .... General Practice

CARMAN, BEAUCHAMP, SANG & TOPKIN, P.A.
Deerfield Beach, FL .... Insurance Defense

CARMAN, CALLAHAN & INGHAM
Farmingdale, NY .... Banking Law; Commercial Law; Insurance Defense; Trust and Estates, Wills and Probate

CARMICHAEL & POWELL, PROFESSIONAL CORPORATION
Phoenix, AZ .... Administrative Law; Bankruptcy Law; Construction Law; Personal Injury; Real Estate Law

CARMODY LAW OFFICES
Albuquerque, NM .... Family Law

CARMODY & TORRANCE LLP
New Haven, CT .... General Practice
Waterbury, CT .... General Practice

CARNEY BADLEY SMITH & SPELLMAN, P.S.
Seattle, WA .... General Practice

CARON & STEVENS/BAKER & MCKENZIE
Amsterdam, Netherlands .... General Practice

CAROSELLI, BEACHLER, MCTIERNAN & CONBOY, LLC
Pittsburgh, PA .... Personal Injury; Workers Compensation

CARPENTER & ASSOCIATES
Houston, TX .... Civil Trial Practice; Criminal Trial Practice; Legal Malpractice

CARPENTER, BENNETT & MORRISSEY
Newark, NJ .... Admiralty/Maritime Law; Antitrust Law; Appellate Practice; Banking Law; Civil Trial Practice; Commercial Law; Employment Benefits Law; Environmental Law; General Practice; Health Care Law; Labor and Employment Law; Personal Injury; Real Estate Law; Tax Law; Trust and Estates, Wills and Probate; Workers Compensation

CARPENTER & CHÁVEZ, LTD.
Albuquerque, NM .... Aviation Law; Civil Trial Practice; Medical Malpractice; Personal Injury; Product Liability Law

CARPENTER & KLATSKIN, P.C.
Denver, CO .... Commercial Law; Real Estate Law

CARPENTER & NIXON, LLP
Santa Fe, NM .... Natural Resources Law; Public Utilities Law

CARPENTER & O'CONNOR
Knoxville, TN .... General Practice; Insurance Defense

CARPONELLI & KRUG
Chicago, IL .... Civil Trial Practice

CARR, ALFORD, CLAUSEN & MCDONALD, L.L.C.
Mobile, AL .... Appellate Practice; Civil Trial Practice; Health Care Law; Insurance Defense; Product Liability Law; Professional Liability

CARR, ALLISON, PUGH, HOWARD, OLIVER & SISSON, P.C.
Birmingham, AL .... Civil Trial Practice; Insurance Defense; Labor and Employment Law; Product Liability Law; Transportation Law; Workers Compensation

CARR GOODSON WARNER, A PROFESSIONAL CORPORATION
Washington, DC .... Environmental Law; General Practice; Insurance Defense; Labor and Employment Law

CARR, HUNT & JOY L.L.P.
Lubbock, TX .... Appellate Practice; Commercial Law; Family Law; General Practice; Insurance Defense

CARR, KENNEDY, PETERSON & FROST, A LAW CORPORATION
Redding, CA .... Civil Trial Practice; General Practice

CARR & LISTON
Boston, MA .... Civil Trial Practice; Labor and Employment Law

CARR, MCCLELLAN, INGERSOLL, THOMPSON & HORN, PROFESSIONAL CORPORATION
Burlingame, CA .... General Practice

CARR, TABB & POPE
Atlanta, GA .... Civil Trial Practice

CARRINGTON, COLEMAN, SLOMAN & BLUMENTHAL, L.L.P.
Dallas, TX .... Antitrust Law; General Practice; Tax Law

CARROLL, MICHAEL BROOKS
San Francisco, CA .... Antitrust Law

CARROLL, CARROLL, DAVIDSON & YOUNG, P.C.
Syracuse, NY .... Civil Trial Practice; General Practice; Personal Injury; Trust and Estates, Wills and Probate

CARROLL, KELLY & MURPHY
Providence, RI .... Civil Trial Practice; General Practice

CARROW, ROBERT D.
San Francisco, CA .... Civil Trial Practice; Construction Law; Criminal Trial Practice; Personal Injury

CARRUTHERS & ROTH, P.A.
Greensboro, NC .... Civil Trial Practice; General Practice

CARSON, CHARLES T.
Phoenix, AZ .... Insurance Defense

CARSON, LESLIE J. JR.
Philadelphia, PA .... Trust and Estates, Wills and Probate

CARSON & COIL, P.C.
Jefferson City, MO .... Appellate Practice; Bankruptcy Law; Civil Trial Practice; Family Law; Insurance Defense; Medical Malpractice; Personal Injury; Real Estate Law; Trust and Estates, Wills and Probate; Workers Compensation

CARTER & COLEMAN
Alexandria, VA .... Civil Trial Practice; Employment Benefits Law; Health Care Law; Insurance Defense; Labor and Employment Law; Sports and Entertainment Law

CARTER, NOLAN, P.A.
Orlando, FL .... Medical Malpractice; Personal Injury

CARTER & THOMAS LLP, LAW OFFICES OF
Boca Raton, FL .... Civil Trial Practice; Elder Law; Personal Injury; Real Estate Law; Trust and Estates, Wills and Probate

CARTON, WITT, ARVANITIS & BARISCILLO, L.L.C.
Asbury Park, NJ .... Banking Law; Civil Trial Practice; Corporate Law; General Practice; Insurance Defense
Manasquan, NJ .... Banking Law; Civil Trial Practice; Corporate Law; General Practice; Insurance Defense

CARTWRIGHT, DRUKER & RYDEN
Marshalltown, IA .... General Practice

CARUANA AND LORENZEN, P.A.
Miami, FL .... Commercial Litigation; Family Law

CARUSO, BURLINGTON, BOHN & COMPIANI, P.A.
West Palm Beach, FL .... Appellate Practice

CARUSO & GEORGETTI
Toledo, OH .... Personal Injury

CARVER, DARDEN, KORETZKY, TESSIER, FINN, BLOSSMAN & AREAUX, L.L.C.
New Orleans, LA .... Banking Law; Oil and Gas Law

CARY, WELCH & HICKMAN, L.L.P.
Hannibal, MO .... General Practice

CASARINO, CHRISTMAN & SHALK
Wilmington, DE .... Civil Trial Practice; Insurance Defense; Personal Injury; Product Liability Law; Workers Compensation

CASASSA AND RYAN
Hampton, NH .... Corporate Law; General Practice; Real Estate Law; Trust and Estates, Wills and Probate

CASE & DUSTERHOFF, LLP
Beaverton, OR .... Insurance Defense; Product Liability Law

CASEY, DONALD C.
Alexandria, VA .... Patent, Trademark, Copyright and Unfair Competition

CASEY, JOHN F.
Columbus, OH .... Business Law

CASEY & BARNETT, LLC
New York, NY .... Admiralty/Maritime Law

CASEY, GENTZ & SIFUENTES, L.L.P.
Austin, TX .... Communications Law

CASEY, GERRY, REED & SCHENK
San Diego, CA .... Business Law; Civil Trial Practice; Personal Injury; Product Liability Law

CASEY & RICHARDS
Newport Beach, CA .... Trust and Estates, Wills and Probate

CASH JONES, L.L.P.
Houston, TX .... Civil Trial Practice; Real Estate Law

CASKIE & FROST, A PROFESSIONAL CORPORATION
Lynchburg, VA .... General Practice

CASNER & EDWARDS, LLP
Boston, MA .... Business Law; Civil Trial Practice; General Practice

CASPER AND CASPER
Middletown, OH .... Personal Injury; Workers Compensation

CASPER & DE TOLEDO LLC
Stamford, CT .... Civil Trial Practice; Labor and Employment Law; Personal Injury

CASPER, MEADOWS & SCHWARTZ, A PROFESSIONAL CORPORATION
Walnut Creek, CA .... Personal Injury

CASSADY, FULLER & MARSH, LLP
Enterprise, AL .... Civil Trial Practice; General Practice; Insurance Defense

CASSELS BROCK & BLACKWELL LLP
Toronto, ON, Canada .... General Practice

CASSIDAY, SCHADE & GLOOR
Chicago, IL .... General Practice

CASSIDY, SEAN
Greensburg, PA .... Oil and Gas Law

CASSIDY, BRUCE G., & ASSOCIATES, P.A.
Philadelphia, PA .... Civil Trial Practice; Criminal Trial Practice; International Business Law; Personal Injury

CASSIDY & MUELLER
Peoria, IL .... Civil Trial Practice; General Practice; Insurance Defense

CASSIDY, MYERS, COGAN, VOEGELIN & TENNANT, L.C.
Wheeling, WV .... Civil Trial Practice; Labor and Employment Law; Personal Injury

CASSIDY, WARNER, LANE & WINSTEAD, A PROFESSIONAL CORPORATION
Santa Ana, CA .... Civil Trial Practice; Environmental Law; Insurance Defense; Product Liability Law

CASSTEVENS, HANNER, GUNTER & CONRAD, P.A.
Charlotte, NC .... General Practice

CASTELLO, WAYNE P.
Gainesville, FL .... Real Estate Law; Trust and Estates, Wills and Probate

CATALDO LAW OFFICES, LLP
Franklin, MA .... Criminal Trial Practice; Family Law

CATAPANO-FRIEDMAN, ROBERT S., P.C.
Albany, NY .... Employment Benefits Law; Labor and Employment Law; Tax Law

CATES & HOLLOWAY
Scottsdale, AZ .... Patent, Trademark, Copyright and Unfair Competition

CATHEY & STRAIN
Cornelia, GA .... Civil Trial Practice; Personal Injury; Product Liability Law

CATRI, HOLTON, KESSLER & KESSLER, P.A.
Fort Lauderdale, FL .... Appellate Practice; Civil Trial Practice; Insurance Defense; Personal Injury; Product Liability Law

CATRON, CATRON & SAWTELL, A PROFESSIONAL ASSOCIATION
Santa Fe, NM .... Appellate Practice; Banking Law; Civil Trial Practice; Commercial Law; General Practice; Real Estate Law; Tax Law; Trust and Estates, Wills and Probate

CATTERTON, KEMP & GREENBERG, P.A.
Rockville, MD .... Civil Trial Practice; Criminal Trial Practice

CATTS, AUSTIN E.
Brunswick, GA .... Civil Trial Practice; Personal Injury

CAUDLE & SPEARS, P.A.
Charlotte, NC .... Civil Trial Practice; Commercial Litigation; Environmental Law; General Practice; Insurance Defense; Personal Injury; Tax Law

CAULFIELD, DAVIES & DONAHUE
Sacramento, CA .... Construction Law; Insurance Defense; Personal Injury; Product Liability Law

CAUSEY, CAYWOOD, TAYLOR, MCMANUS & BAILEY
Memphis, TN .... Criminal Trial Practice; Family Law; General Practice; Trust and Estates, Wills and Probate

CAVAZOS, HENDRICKS, POIROT & DEWEY, P.C.
Dallas, TX .... Bankruptcy Law; Creditors Rights

CAVEY, NANCY L.
St. Petersburg, FL .... Workers Compensation

CAYER, KILSTOFTE & CRATON, A PROFESSIONAL LAW CORPORATION
Long Beach, CA .... Banking Law; Civil Trial Practice; General Practice

CEARLEY LAW FIRM, P.A.
Little Rock, AR .... Civil Trial Practice; General Practice

CEBALLOS, M. ALAN, P.A.
Jacksonville, FL .... Criminal Trial Practice

CELLA, MCKEON & WILLIAMS, P.C.
North Haven, CT .... Insurance Defense

CELLI, SCHLOSSBERG & DIAMOND, L.L.C.
Morristown, NJ .... Civil Trial Practice; Family Law

CENATIEMPO & DITTA, LLP
Houston, TX .... Trust and Estates, Wills and Probate

CERRATO, DAWES, COLLINS, SAKER & BROWN, A PROFESSIONAL CORPORATION
Freehold, NJ .... Civil Trial Practice; General Practice; Personal Injury

CERTILMAN BALIN ADLER & HYMAN, LLP
East Meadow, NY .... Bankruptcy Law; Civil Trial Practice; General Practice; Municipal and Zoning Law; Real Estate Law; Securities Law; Tax Law; Trust and Estates, Wills and Probate

CERUSSI & SPRING, A PROFESSIONAL CORPORATION
White Plains, NY .... Civil Trial Practice; Insurance Defense

CERVANTES & ASSOCIATES
St. Louis, MO .... Personal Injury

CESARANO, MARILYN J. W., P.A.
Miami, FL .... Family Law

CESARI AND MCKENNA, L.L.P.
Boston, MA .... Antitrust Law; Patent, Trademark, Copyright and Unfair Competition; Trademark, Copyright and Unfair Competition

CETRULO, ROBERT C., P.S.C.
Covington, KY .... Civil Trial Practice

CHADBOURNE & PARKE
London, England .... General Practice
Los Angeles, CA .... General Practice
Washington, DC .... General Practice
New York, NY .... General Practice
Hong Kong, China .... General Practice
Moscow, Russia .... General Practice

CHADWELL, STEELE R.
Princeton, NJ .... Health Care Law; Trust and Estates, Wills and Probate

CHAFFE, MCCALL, PHILLIPS, TOLER & SARPY, L.L.P.
New Orleans, LA .... Admiralty/Maritime Law; Commercial Litigation; General Practice; Labor and Employment Law; Natural Resources Law

CHAIKIN & SHERMAN, P.C.
Washington, DC .... Medical Malpractice; Personal Injury

CHAIREZ & ASSOCIATES
Irvine, CA .... Civil Trial Practice

CHALAT LAW OFFICES, P.C.
Denver, CO .... Medical Malpractice; Personal Injury

CHALIF, JOHN L. J.D., LL.M.
West Palm Beach, FL .... Securities Law

CHAMBERS, JOY S.
Alexandria, VA .... Trust and Estates, Wills and Probate

CHAMBERS LAW GROUP, PROFESSIONAL ASSOCIATION
St. Petersburg, FL .... Medical Malpractice; Personal Injury; Product Liability Law

CHAMPION, JAN
San Jose, CA .... Civil Trial Practice; Medical Malpractice; Personal Injury; Product Liability Law

CHANCE & MADDOX
Calhoun, GA........General Practice

CHANDLER & BRITT, LLC
Buford, GA........Criminal Trial Practice; General Practice

CHANDLER LAW OFFICES
Lufkin, TX........Personal Injury

CHANDLER, TULLAR, UDALL & REDHAIR, L.L.P.
Tucson, AZ........Civil Trial Practice; Commercial Law; Environmental Law; General Practice; Insurance Defense; Natural Resources Law; Personal Injury; Real Estate Law

CHANFRAU, CHANFRAU & BOUCK
Daytona Beach, FL........Medical Malpractice; Personal Injury

CHANG, CHRISTOPHER E. LAW OFFICES OF
New York, NY........Criminal Trial Practice

CHAPIN SHEA MCNITT & CARTER, A PROFESSIONAL CORPORATION
San Diego, CA........Business Law; Civil Trial Practice; Commercial Law; Insurance Defense; Product Liability Law

CHAPMAN, MICHAEL L.
Atlanta, GA........Commercial Law; Construction Law

CHAPMAN, BYRHOLDT & YON
Anderson, SC........Criminal Trial Practice; Personal Injury; Workers Compensation

CHAPMAN AND CUTLER
Chicago, IL........General Practice; Municipal Bond/Public Authority Financing
Salt Lake City, UT........General Practice

CHAPMAN, GLUCKSMAN & DEAN, A PROFESSIONAL CORPORATION
Los Angeles, CA........Construction Law; Insurance Defense

CHAPMAN, LEWIS & SWAN
Clarksdale, MS........General Practice; Personal Injury

CHAPPANO WOOD PLL
Columbus, OH........International Business Law

CHAPPELL, E. HUGH, JR., P.A.
Fort Lauderdale, FL........Personal Injury

CHAPPELL, PARMELEE, JOHNSON & HILL, P.C.
Fort Worth, TX........Civil Trial Practice; Education Law; General Practice

CHAR SAKAMOTO ISHII LUM & CHING
Honolulu, HI........Civil Trial Practice

CHARAPP, DEESE & WEISS, LLP
Washington, DC........Commercial Litigation; Corporate Law; Government Contracts; Labor and Employment Law

CHARFOOS, REITER, PETERSON, HOLMQUIST & PILCHAK, P.C.
Detroit, MI........Civil Rights; Employment Benefits Law; Labor and Employment Law; Workers Compensation
Farmington Hills, MI........Civil Rights; Employment Benefits Law; Labor and Employment Law; Workers Compensation

CHARITON & SCHWAGER
Wilkes-Barre, PA........Business Law; Civil Trial Practice

CHARLSON BREDEHOFT, P.C.
Reston, VA........Labor and Employment Law

CHARLSON, MARBEN & JORGENSON, P.A.
Thief River Falls, MN........General Practice

CHARTERS, HECK, O'DONNELL, PETRULIS & ZORZA, P.C.
Troy, MI........General Practice

CHARWAT, MARK S., P.C.
Garden City, NY........Trust and Estates, Wills and Probate

CHASON & CHASON, P.C.
Bay Minette, AL........General Practice

CHATHAM LAW FIRM
Hernando, MS........General Practice; Medical Malpractice

CHATTERTON, ROBERT D.
Orange, CA........Criminal Trial Practice

CHATTMAN, GAINES & STERN
Cleveland, OH........Commercial Litigation; Corporate Law; Labor and Employment Law; Trust and Estates, Wills and Probate

CHAUNCEY, HARRISON K., JR., P.A., LAW OFFICES OF
Palm Beach, FL........Business Law; Real Estate Law; Tax Law; Trust and Estates, Wills and Probate

CHAVEZ, THEODORE R.
Campbell, CA........Real Estate Law

CHEADLE & CHEADLE
Nashville, TN........Commercial Litigation; Creditors Rights

CHEATHAM, ESTES & HOLLMAN, P.C.
West Bloomfield, MI........Civil Trial Practice; Environmental Law; Insurance Defense; Medical Malpractice; Product Liability Law; Trust and Estates, Wills and Probate

CHEEK & ZEEHANDELAR, LLP
Columbus, OH........Creditors Rights

CHEHARDY, SHERMAN, ELLIS, BRESLIN & MURRAY, L.L.P.
Metairie, LA........General Practice

CHEN, WALSH, TECLER & MCCABE, L.L.P.
Rockville, MD........General Practice; Real Estate Law

CHENEY & CHENEY, P.C.
Reidsville, GA........General Practice; Personal Injury

CHERNAU, CHAFFIN & BURNSED, PLLC
Nashville, TN........Banking Law; Civil Trial Practice; Labor and Employment Law; Real Estate Law; Trademark, Copyright and Unfair Competition

CHERNIN & GOLD, LLP
Binghamton, NY........General Practice

CHERNOFF, VILHAUER, MCCLUNG & STENZEL, LLP
Portland, OR........Patent, Trademark, Copyright and Unfair Competition

CHERNOV, STERN & KRINGS, S.C.
Milwaukee, WI........Appellate Practice; Commercial Law; Commercial Litigation; Corporate Law; Creditors Rights; Product Liability Law; Real Estate Law; Trust and Estates, Wills and Probate

CHERWIN, GLICKMAN & THEISE, LLP
Boston, MA........Business Law; Commercial Law; General Practice

CHESNUT, LIVINGSTON & PYE, P.C.
Doraville, GA........General Practice

CHESNUTT, CHARLES R.
Dallas, TX........Bankruptcy Law

CHESTER, WILLCOX AND SAXBE LLP
Columbus, OH........Bankruptcy Law; Business Law; Civil Trial Practice; International Business Law; Public Utilities Law; Real Estate Law; Securities Law; Trust and Estates, Wills and Probate

CHICOINE & HALLETT, P.S.
Seattle, WA........Tax Law

CHIERICI, CHIERICI & SMITH, A PROFESSIONAL CORPORATION
Moorestown, NJ........Appellate Practice; Civil Trial Practice; Commercial Litigation; General Practice; Insurance Defense; Medical Malpractice; Personal Injury; Product Liability Law; Toxic Torts

CHILVERS & TAYLOR, PC
Emeryville, CA........Commercial Litigation; Health Care Law

CHIMEL DORADO
New York, NY........Corporate Law; International Business Law; Real Estate Law

CHIMICLES & TIKELLIS LLP
Haverford, PA........Civil Trial Practice

CHING, YUEN & MORIKAWA
Honolulu, HI........Banking Law; Real Estate Law; Tax Law

CHINN & ASSOCIATES, PLLC
Jackson, MS........Family Law

CHINNERY, CARL, & ASSOCIATES, P.C.
Lee's Summit, MO........Business Law; Real Estate Law; Trust and Estates, Wills and Probate

CHISENHALL, NESTRUD & JULIAN, P.A.
Little Rock, AR........Civil Trial Practice; Corporate Law; Environmental Law; Public Utilities Law

CHITWOOD & HARLEY
Atlanta, GA........Antitrust Law; Securities Law

CHOATE, HALL & STEWART
Boston, MA........General Practice

CHOPIN, WAGAR, COLE, RICHARD, REBOUL & KUTCHER, LLP
Metairie, LA........General Practice

CHORCHES & NOVAK, P.C.
Wethersfield, CT........Bankruptcy Law

CHOREY, TAYLOR & FEIL, A PROFESSIONAL CORPORATION
Atlanta, GA .... Administrative Law; Civil Trial Practice; Communications Law; General Practice

CHORNENKY, O. JOSEPH, P.C.
Phoenix, AZ .... Criminal Trial Practice

CHRISS, WILLIAM J., P.C., LAW OFFICES OF
Corpus Christi, TX .... Civil Trial Practice; Commercial Litigation; Personal Injury

CHRISTENSEN & AUER
Pasadena, CA .... Health Care Law

CHRISTENSEN & FREDERICKSON LAW OFFICES
Deadwood, SD .... General Practice

CHRISTENSEN, O'CONNOR, JOHNSON & KINDNESS, PLLC
Seattle, WA .... Patent, Trademark, Copyright and Unfair Competition

CHRISTIAN, SPARTZ, KEOGH & CHRISTIAN
Le Center, MN .... General Practice

CHRISTIE, PABARUE, MORTENSEN AND YOUNG, A PROFESSIONAL CORPORATION
Philadelphia, PA .... Employment Benefits Law; Insurance Defense; Medical Malpractice; Professional Liability

CHRISTOPHER & TAYLOR
Indianapolis, IN .... Civil Trial Practice

CHRISTOVICH AND KEARNEY, L.L.P.
New Orleans, LA .... Admiralty/Maritime Law; General Practice; Insurance Defense; Toxic Torts

CHUBBUCK SMITH & RHODES, A PROFESSIONAL CORPORATION
Oklahoma City, OK .... Insurance Defense

CHUN, KERR, DODD, BEAMAN & WONG
Honolulu, HI .... Commercial Litigation; General Practice; Real Estate Law

CHURCH, CHURCH, HITTLE & ANTRIM
Noblesville, IN .... Family Law; General Practice; Municipal Bond/Public Authority Financing; Personal Injury

CHURCH & HOUFF, P.A.
Baltimore, MD .... Insurance Defense

CIANCIO & JONSEN, P.C.
Westminster, CO .... Civil Trial Practice; Family Law; Intellectual Property Law; Personal Injury

CIARDI, MASCHMEYER & KARALIS, P.C.
Philadelphia, PA .... Bankruptcy Law; Creditors Rights

CITY, HAYES, MEAGHER & DISSETTE, P.C.
Boston, MA .... Construction Law

CIVEROLO, GRALOW & HILL, A PROFESSIONAL ASSOCIATION
Albuquerque, NM .... Civil Trial Practice; General Practice; Insurance Defense

CLAPP & MCCAMBRIDGE, L.L.P.
North Attleboro, MA .... Real Estate Law

CLAREY, ROBERT L.
Mineola, NY .... Criminal Trial Practice; Trust and Estates, Wills and Probate

CLARK, BRUCE G. & ASSOCIATES
New York, NY .... Civil Trial Practice; Medical Malpractice

CLARK AND ASSOCIATES
Yuma, AZ .... Commercial Litigation; Insurance Defense; Labor and Employment Law; Personal Injury

CLARK, BEVERLY, P.C.
Detroit, MI .... Family Law

CLARK BLOSS & MCIVER, PLLC
Greensboro, NC .... Civil Trial Practice; General Practice; Medical Malpractice; Personal Injury; Securities Law

CLARK, CHARLTON, MARTINO & BORDERS, P.A.
Tampa, FL .... Civil Trial Practice; Medical Malpractice; Personal Injury

CLARK, DEEN & COPELAND, P.C.
Mobile, AL .... Appellate Practice; Criminal Trial Practice

CLARK & DEGRAND
Chicago, IL .... Civil Trial Practice; Commercial Litigation; General Practice

CLARK DRUMMIE
Saint John, NB, Canada .... Administrative Law; Admiralty/Maritime Law; Banking Law; Bankruptcy Law; Civil Trial Practice; Commercial Law; Environmental Law; General Practice; Insurance Defense; Labor and Employment Law; Municipal and Zoning Law; Personal Injury; Real Estate Law; Transportation Law; Trust and Estates, Wills and Probate

CLARKE, LAURENCE R.
Los Angeles, CA .... Arbitration

CLARKE, JOHNSON, PETERSON & MCLEAN, A PROFESSIONAL ASSOCIATION
Florence, SC .... Insurance Defense

CLARKE, JON B., P.C.
Denver, CO .... Bankruptcy Law; Real Estate Law

CLARKE SILVERGLATE WILLIAMS & MONTGOMERY
Miami, FL .... Admiralty/Maritime Law; Commercial Law; Employment Benefits Law; Personal Injury; Product Liability Law

CLARK HILL PLC
Detroit, MI .... Administrative Law; General Practice

CLARK, JEFF B., P.A.
Orlando, FL .... Family Law

CLARK, LINDAUER, MCCLINTON, FETHERSTON, EDMONDS & LIPPOLD
Salem, OR .... General Practice

CLARK, MIZE & LINVILLE, CHARTERED
Salina, KS .... General Practice

CLARK, QUINN, MOSES & CLARK
Indianapolis, IN .... Commercial Litigation; Land Use Law; Municipal and Zoning Law; Real Estate Law

CLARK & SCOTT, P.C.
Birmingham, AL .... Civil Trial Practice; Insurance Defense; Workers Compensation

CLARK, SCOTT & SULLIVAN, P.C.
Mobile, AL .... Civil Trial Practice

CLARKSON, FORTSON, WALSH & RHENEY, P.A.
Greenville, SC .... Commercial Litigation; Construction Law; Insurance Defense; Labor and Employment Law; Workers Compensation

CLARK & TREVITHICK, A PROFESSIONAL CORPORATION
Los Angeles, CA .... Banking Law; Bankruptcy Law; Business Law; Civil Trial Practice; Commercial Law; Commercial Litigation; Environmental Law; General Practice; Insurance Defense; Labor and Employment Law; Product Liability Law; Real Estate Law; Securities Law; Tax Law; Trust and Estates, Wills and Probate

CLARK, WEST, KELLER, BUTLER & ELLIS, L.L.P.
Dallas, TX .... Civil Trial Practice; Corporate Law; Family Law; General Practice; Labor and Employment Law; Product Liability Law; Real Estate Law

CLARK & WILLIAMS
Tulsa, OK .... Family Law; General Practice

CLAWSON & STAUBES, L.L.C.
Charlotte, NC .... Bankruptcy Law; Civil Trial Practice
Charleston, SC .... Bankruptcy Law; Civil Trial Practice

CLAY, BILL, P.A., II
Miami, FL .... Criminal Trial Practice

CLAYSON, MANN, YAEGER & HANSEN, A PROFESSIONAL LAW CORPORATION
Corona, CA .... Business Law; General Practice

CLAYTON, HOWARTH & CANNON, P.C.
Salt Lake City, UT .... Intellectual Property Law
Sandy, UT .... Computer Law; Intellectual Property Law; Patent, Trademark, Copyright and Unfair Competition

CLEAR, MICHAEL GENE LAW OFFICES OF
Stamford, CT .... Civil Trial Practice; Insurance Defense; Personal Injury

CLEARY, GOTTLIEB, STEEN & HAMILTON
Washington, DC .... General Practice
New York, NY .... General Practice
Brussels, Belgium .... General Practice
Hong Kong, China .... General Practice
London, England .... General Practice
Paris, France .... General Practice
Frankfurt/Main, Germany .... General Practice
Rome, Italy .... General Practice
Tokyo, Japan .... General Practice

CLEARY SHAHI ASSOCIATES, A PROFESSIONAL CORPORATION
Rutland, VT .... General Practice; Product Liability Law

CLEMENT & ASSOCIATES
Sacramento, CA .... Medical Malpractice

CLEMENT & WHEATLEY, A PROFESSIONAL CORPORATION
Danville, VA .... General Practice

CLEMENTS, MAHIN & COHEN
Cincinnati, OH .... Personal Injury; Workers Compensation

CLEMENTS, O'NEILL, PIERCE NICKENS & WILSON, L.L.P.
Houston, TX .... Civil Trial Practice

CLEM, POLACKWICH & VOCELLE
Vero Beach, FL .... Civil Trial Practice; Personal Injury; Real Estate Law

CLENDENEN, WILLIAM H., JR., A PROFESSIONAL CORPORATION
New Haven, CT .... Civil Trial Practice; General Practice

CLIFFORD CHANCE ROGERS & WELLS LLP
Washington, DC .... General Practice
New York, NY .... Civil Trial Practice; General Practice

CLIFFORD CLENDENIN O'HALE & JONES, L.L.P.
Greensboro, NC .... Criminal Trial Practice; Personal Injury; Workers Compensation

CLIFFORD LAW OFFICES, P.C.
Chicago, IL .... Aviation Law; Civil Trial Practice; Commercial Litigation; Medical Malpractice; Personal Injury; Product Liability Law; Professional Liability

CLIFTON, SANDERS & SMITH, P.C.
Toccoa, GA .... General Practice

CLINE, CLINE & GRIFFIN
Flint, MI .... Civil Trial Practice

CLINE, WILLIAMS, WRIGHT, JOHNSON & OLDFATHER
Lincoln, NE .... Administrative Law; Antitrust Law; Arbitration; Bankruptcy Law; Civil Trial Practice; Commercial Law; Commercial Litigation; Criminal Trial Practice; Employment Benefits Law; Environmental Law; General Practice; Health Care Law; Insurance Defense; Intellectual Property Law; Labor and Employment Law; Mergers and Acquisitions; Municipal Bond/Public Authority Financing; Pension and Profit Sharing; Personal Injury; Product Liability Law; Professional Liability; Real Estate Law; Securities Law; Tax Law; Trust and Estates, Wills and Probate
Omaha, NE .... Arbitration; Civil Trial Practice; Commercial Litigation; Employment Benefits Law; General Practice; Health Care Law; Labor and Employment Law; Product Liability Law; Securities Law

CLONTZ & COX
Mount Vernon, KY .... Criminal Trial Practice; General Practice

CLYATT, CLYATT & DEVAUGHN, P.C.
Valdosta, GA .... Insurance Defense; Workers Compensation

COALE, COOLEY, LIETZ, MCINERNY & BROADUS, A PROFESSIONAL CORPORATION
Washington, DC .... Aviation Law; Civil Trial Practice; Personal Injury; Product Liability Law

COAN, LEWENDON, ROYSTON & GULLIVER, LLC
New Haven, CT .... Bankruptcy Law; Trust and Estates, Wills and Probate

COBB & SHEALY, P.A.
Dothan, AL .... Civil Trial Practice; General Practice; Insurance Defense

COBB, STANTON L., P.A., LAW FIRM OF
Orlando, FL .... Family Law

COBRIN & GITTES
New York, NY .... Civil Trial Practice; Computer Law; Environmental Law; Intellectual Property Law; Patent, Trademark, Copyright and Unfair Competition; Real Estate Law; Trademark, Copyright and Unfair Competition

COCHRAN & DAHL, P.C.
Phoenix, AZ .... Real Estate Law

CODDINGTON, HICKS & DANFORTH, A PROFESSIONAL CORPORATION
Redwood City, CA .... Civil Trial Practice

COFER, WILLIAM L., P.A.
Winston-Salem, NC .... Criminal Trial Practice

COFFEY & GRIESBACH
St. Louis, MO .... Medical Malpractice; Personal Injury; Product Liability Law; Toxic Torts

COFFMAN, COLEMAN, ANDREWS & GROGAN, PROFESSIONAL ASSOCIATION
Jacksonville, FL .... Labor and Employment Law

COFFMAN, DEFRIES & NOTHERN, A PROFESSIONAL ASSOCIATION
Topeka, KS .... Tax Law

COGAVIN AND WAYSTACK
Boston, MA .... Civil Trial Practice; Insurance Defense

COGBURN, JOHN M. JR.
Griffin, GA .... Business Law; Trust and Estates, Wills and Probate

COGGINS, HARMAN & HEWITT
Silver Spring, MD .... Bankruptcy Law; Civil Trial Practice; Commercial Litigation; Creditors Rights; Real Estate Law

COGSWELL, WILTON W. III
Colorado Springs, CO .... Tax Law; Trust and Estates, Wills and Probate

COGSWELL NAKAZAWA & CHANG
Long Beach, CA .... Admiralty/Maritime Law

COHAN, DARVY MACK
La Jolla, CA .... Civil Trial Practice

COHAN, SIMPSON, COWLISHAW & WULFF, L.L.P.
Dallas, TX .... Commercial Litigation; Labor and Employment Law

COHEN, ERNEST ALLEN
Tucson, AZ .... Business Law; Labor and Employment Law

COHEN, GARY I.
Greenwich, CT .... Family Law

COHEN, JEROME S.
Long Beach, CA .... Bankruptcy Law

COHEN, PAUL F.
Los Angeles, CA .... Commercial Litigation

COHEN, ALEXANDER & CLAYTON, A PROFESSIONAL CORPORATION
Thousand Oaks, CA .... Business Law; Family Law; General Practice; Land Use Law; Real Estate Law

COHEN, CONWAY, COPELAND & PAIVA, P.A.
Stuart, FL .... Civil Trial Practice

COHEN DARNELL & COHEN
Dallas, TX .... Civil Trial Practice; Immigration and Naturalization

COHEN & FEELEY, P.C.
Easton, PA .... Commercial Litigation; Medical Malpractice; Personal Injury; Product Liability Law

COHEN AND FROMM, P.C.
Phoenix, AZ .... Family Law

COHEN, GARELICK & GLAZIER, A PROFESSIONAL CORPORATION
Indianapolis, IN .... Business Law; Family Law; Tax Law

COHEN, GETTINGS & DUNHAM, P.C.
Arlington, VA .... Civil Trial Practice; Commercial Litigation; Criminal Trial Practice

COHEN, HENNESSEY & BIENSTOCK, P.C.
New York, NY .... Family Law

COHEN, JAYSON & FOSTER, P.A., THE LAW FIRM OF
Tampa, FL .... Civil Trial Practice; Criminal Trial Practice

COHEN KENNEDY DOWD & QUIGLEY, P.C.
Phoenix, AZ .... Civil Trial Practice; Commercial Litigation

COHEN & LOMBARDO, P.C.
Buffalo, NY .... Business Law; Civil Trial Practice; General Practice; Insurance Defense

COHEN & MALAD, P.C.
Indianapolis, IN .... Civil Trial Practice; Personal Injury

COHEN, MILSTEIN, HAUSFELD & TOLL, P.L.L.C.
Washington, DC .... Antitrust Law; Civil Rights; Commercial Litigation; Employment Benefits Law; Environmental Law; Labor and Employment Law; Natural Resources Law; Product Liability Law; Securities Law

COHEN MOHR LLP
Washington, DC .... Government Contracts

COHEN, NORRIS, SCHERER, WEINBERGER & WOLMER
North Palm Beach, FL .... Real Estate Law

COHEN PRIMIANI & FOSTER, A PROFESSIONAL CORPORATION
Los Angeles, CA .... Tax Law

COHEN & SMALL
Houston, TX .... Business Law; Commercial Litigation

COHEN AND WOLF, P.C.
Bridgeport, CT .... General Practice

COHEN/DAVID & ASSOCIATES, P.C.
Atlanta, GA .... Real Estate Law

COHN, FREDERICK H.
New York, NY .... Civil Trial Practice; Criminal Trial Practice

COHN, GOLDBERG & DEUTSCH, LLC
Towson, MD .... Creditors Rights

COHN & KELAKOS LLP
Boston, MA .... Bankruptcy Law

COHN LIFLAND PEARLMAN HERRMANN & KNOPF LLP
Saddle Brook, NJ .... Appellate Practice; Bankruptcy Law; Civil Trial Practice; Commercial Law; Corporate Law; Family Law; Franchise Law; Medical Malpractice; Personal Injury; Product Liability Law; Securities Law

COHN AND MARKS
Washington, DC .... Administrative Law; Communications Law

COHN, POWELL AND HIND, P.C.
St. Louis, MO .... Patent, Trademark, Copyright and Unfair Competition

COKER, JEAN C., P.A.
Jacksonville, FL .... Trust and Estates, Wills and Probate

COKER, MYERS, SCHICKEL, SORENSON, HIGGINBOTHAM & GREEN, P.A.
Jacksonville, FL .... Family Law; Insurance Defense; Medical Malpractice; Personal Injury

COK, WHEAT, BROWN & MCGARRY, PLLP
Bozeman, MT .... Civil Trial Practice

COLBERT, FREEMAN & STRIBLING
Austin, TX .... Medical Malpractice; Personal Injury

COLBY, MONET, DEMERS, DELAGE & CREVIER
Montreal, QU, Canada .... General Practice

COLE, DOROTHY A.
Escondido, CA .... Trust and Estates, Wills and Probate

COLE LAW OFFICES, P.C.
Bath, NY .... Banking Law; Commercial Litigation; General Practice; Real Estate Law; Trust and Estates, Wills and Probate

COLELLA & KOLCZUN, P.L.L.
Lorain, OH .... Business Law

COLEMAN, JOSEPH C.
Columbia, SC .... Civil Trial Practice

COLEMAN, LARRY K.
Bradenton, FL .... Family Law

COLEMAN, ROBERT F. & ASSOCIATES
Chicago, IL .... Commercial Litigation; Professional Liability

COLEMAN, C. RANDOLPH, P.A., LAW OFFICE OF
Jacksonville, FL .... Trust and Estates, Wills and Probate

COLEMAN, EASTON, LOCHMILLER & HALL
Elizabethtown, KY .... General Practice; Insurance Defense; Medical Malpractice

COLEMAN, HULL & VAN VLIET, P.L.L.P.
Minneapolis, MN .... Commercial Litigation; Construction Law

COLEMAN, TALLEY, NEWBERN, KURRIE, PRESTON & HOLLAND, LLP
Valdosta, GA .... Civil Trial Practice; General Practice; Insurance Defense

COLE, MOORE & BAKER
Bowling Green, KY .... Civil Trial Practice; General Practice; Insurance Defense; Medical Malpractice; Product Liability Law

COLE, RAYWID & BRAVERMAN, L.L.P.
Washington, DC .... Business Law; Commercial Litigation; Communications Law

COLFER, WOOD, LYONS & WOOD
McCook, NE .... General Practice

COLINGO, WILLIAMS, HEIDELBERG, STEINBERGER & MCELHANEY, P.A.
Pascagoula, MS .... Business Law; Civil Trial Practice; Commercial Litigation; Employment Benefits Law; Environmental Law; Government Contracts; Insurance Defense; Medical Malpractice; Personal Injury; Product Liability Law; Real Estate Law; Workers Compensation

COLLERAN, JAMES E. LAW OFFICES OF
Philadelphia, PA .... Civil Trial Practice; Medical Malpractice; Personal Injury; Product Liability Law

COLLERAN, O'HARA & MILLS
Garden City, NY .... General Practice; Labor and Employment Law; Real Estate Law

COLLINS, DAVID W.
Monticello, FL .... Criminal Trial Practice

COLLINS, MARK L.
Tucson, AZ .... Commercial Litigation

COLLINS, BROWN, CALDWELL, BARKETT & GARAVAGLIA, CHARTERED
Vero Beach, FL .... Civil Trial Practice; General Practice; Real Estate Law; Trust and Estates, Wills and Probate

COLLINS, BUCKLEY, SAUNTRY AND HAUGH, P.L.L.P.
St. Paul, MN .... Family Law; General Practice; Insurance Defense; Personal Injury

COLLINS, COLLINS, MUIR & TRAVER LLP
Pasadena, CA .... Civil Trial Practice; Construction Law; Insurance Defense; Personal Injury; Product Liability Law

COLLINS, DAN A., & ASSOCIATES, P.A.
Greenville, SC .... Trust and Estates, Wills and Probate

COLLINS, EINHORN, FARRELL & ULANOFF, A PROFESSIONAL CORPORATION
Southfield, MI .... Appellate Practice; Civil Trial Practice; Commercial Law; Communications Law; Construction Law; Environmental Law; Insurance Defense; Product Liability Law

COLLINS & LACY, P.C.
Columbia, SC .... Civil Trial Practice; General Practice

COLLINS & SCHLOTHAUER
San Jose, CA .... Civil Trial Practice

COLMAN-SCHWIMMER & WARREN, A PROFESSIONAL LAW CORPORATION
Beverly Hills, CA .... Family Law

COLOMBO AND COLOMBO, P.C.
Bloomfield Hills, MI .... Business Law; Commercial Litigation

COLQUHOUN & COLQUHOUN, A PROFESSIONAL CORPORATION
Morristown, NJ .... Banking Law; Insurance Defense

COLSON, HICKS, EIDSON, COLSON, MATTHEWS, MARTINEZ & MENDOZA
Miami, FL .... Commercial Law; General Practice; Personal Injury

COLUCCI & UMANS
New York, NY .... Commercial Litigation; Patent, Trademark, Copyright and Unfair Competition; Trademark, Copyright and Unfair Competition
Scarsdale, NY .... Patent, Trademark, Copyright and Unfair Competition

COLWELL, WILLIAM S.
Springfield, VA .... Arbitration; Labor and Employment Law

COMEAU, MALDEGEN, TEMPLEMAN & INDALL, L.L.P.
Santa Fe, NM .... Civil Trial Practice; Commercial Law; General Practice; Insurance Defense; Natural Resources Law

COMERFORD & BRITT, L.L.P.
Winston-Salem, NC .... Aviation Law; Medical Malpractice; Personal Injury

COMITER, RICHARD B., & ASSOCIATES, P.A.
West Palm Beach, FL .... Tax Law; Trust and Estates, Wills and Probate

COMPTON, PREWETT, THOMAS & HICKEY, P.A.
El Dorado, AR .... General Practice

CONANT FRENCH & CHANEY, LLP
Dallas, TX .... Antitrust Law; Appellate Practice; Bankruptcy Law; Business Law; Civil Trial Practice; Commercial Litigation; Professional Liability; Securities Law

CONBOY, MCKAY, BACHMAN & KENDALL, LLP
Carthage, NY .... General Practice
Watertown, NY .... General Practice; Insurance Defense

CONDO & MASTERMAN, P.C.
Vienna, VA .... Family Law

CONKLIN, BENHAM, DUCEY, LISTMAN & CHUHRAN, P.C.
Detroit, MI .... Workers Compensation
Traverse City, MI .... Workers Compensation

CONLEY & CLEARY
Bradenton, FL .... Real Estate Law

CONLIN, ROXANNE B., AND ASSOCIATES, P.C.
Des Moines, IA .... Civil Rights; Medical Malpractice; Personal Injury

CONMY, FESTE, HUBBARD, CORWIN & BRUST, LTD.
Fargo, ND .... Banking Law; Civil Trial Practice; General Practice; Personal Injury; Real Estate Law; Trust and Estates, Wills and Probate

CONNELL, FOLEY & GEISER LLP
Roseland, NJ .... Civil Trial Practice; General Practice; Insurance Defense

CONNELLY & SCHROEDER
Chicago, IL....Appellate Practice; Aviation Law; Civil Trial Practice; Commercial Litigation; Insurance Defense; Medical Malpractice; Personal Injury; Product Liability Law; Professional Liability

CONNER & RILEY
Erie, PA....Personal Injury

CONNER & WINTERS, A PROFESSIONAL CORPORATION
Washington, DC....Employment Benefits Law
Oklahoma City, OK....Antitrust Law; Bankruptcy Law; Civil Trial Practice; General Practice; Labor and Employment Law; Natural Resources Law; Real Estate Law; Securities Law; Tax Law
Tulsa, OK....Bankruptcy Law; Civil Trial Practice; Employment Benefits Law; General Practice; Labor and Employment Law; Natural Resources Law; Real Estate Law; Securities Law; Tax Law

CONNER & WINTERS, P.L.L.C.
Fayetteville, AR....Civil Trial Practice; General Practice; Securities Law

CONNOLLY BOVE LODGE & HUTZ LLP
Wilmington, DE....Business Law; Commercial Law; General Practice; Intellectual Property Law; Patent, Trademark, Copyright and Unfair Competition; Trust and Estates, Wills and Probate

CONNOLLY, O'MALLEY, LILLIS, HANSEN & OLSON, L.L.P.
Des Moines, IA....General Practice; Real Estate Law; Trust and Estates, Wills and Probate

CONNOR, BUNN, ROGERSON & WOODARD, P.L.L.C.
Wilson, NC....General Practice

CONNORS & CORCORAN, L.L.P.
Rochester, NY....Civil Trial Practice; General Practice; Insurance Defense; Product Liability Law

CONNORS & VILARDO, LLP
Buffalo, NY....Appellate Practice; Civil Trial Practice; Criminal Trial Practice

CONOLY, DAVID Z., P.C.
Corpus Christi, TX....Real Estate Law

CONOUR • DOEHRMAN • STARKEY
Indianapolis, IN....Civil Trial Practice; Medical Malpractice; Personal Injury; Trust and Estates, Wills and Probate

CONRAD O'BRIEN GELLMAN & ROHN, P.C.
Philadelphia, PA....Civil Trial Practice; Commercial Litigation; Criminal Trial Practice

CONRAD & SCHERER
Fort Lauderdale, FL....Admiralty/Maritime Law; Civil Trial Practice; Commercial Litigation; General Practice; Health Care Law; Insurance Defense; Legal Malpractice; Medical Malpractice; Personal Injury

CONROY, BALLMAN & DAMERON, CHARTERED
Gaithersburg, MD....Civil Trial Practice

CONSTANTINE & PARTNERS
New York, NY....Antitrust Law

CONTANT, SCHERBY & ATKINS
Hackensack, NJ....Banking Law; Civil Trial Practice; Commercial Law; General Practice; Municipal and Zoning Law; Real Estate Law; Trust and Estates, Wills and Probate

CONTE, MELTON & D'ANTONIO
Conway, PA....Medical Malpractice; Personal Injury

CONTIGUGLIA & GIACONA
Auburn, NY....General Practice; Real Estate Law; Trust and Estates, Wills and Probate

CONTRADA & ASSOCIATES
Toledo, OH....Personal Injury

CONWAY, JACK K.
San Marino, CA....Personal Injury

CONWAY, JOSEPH WM.
Pittsburgh, PA....Civil Trial Practice

CONWAY, FARRELL, CURTIN & KELLY, P.C.
New York, NY....Insurance Defense; Professional Liability; Real Estate Law

CONWAY & HALL, A LEGAL PROFESSIONAL ASSOCIATION
Dayton, OH....Banking Law; General Practice

CONWAY, MARKEN, WYNER, KURANT & KERN CO., L.P.A.
Cleveland, OH....Business Law; Commercial Litigation; Mergers and Acquisitions; Real Estate Law

COOK, CATHY R.
Cincinnati, OH....Criminal Trial Practice; Family Law

COOK, H. CLAYTON JR.
Washington, DC....Admiralty/Maritime Law

COOK, ROBERT M.
Yuma, AZ....Arbitration; Bankruptcy Law; Civil Trial Practice; Commercial Law

COOK, ALEX, MCFARRON, MANZO, CUMMINGS & MEHLER
Chicago, IL....Intellectual Property Law

COOK, BROWN & PRAGER, LLP
Sacramento, CA....Labor and Employment Law
Salinas, CA....Labor and Employment Law
Santa Ana, CA....Labor and Employment Law

COOK & CONNELLY
Summerville, GA....Civil Trial Practice; Criminal Trial Practice

COOKE & COOKE
Greensboro, NC....General Practice

COOK & FRANKE S.C.
Milwaukee, WI....Admiralty/Maritime Law; General Practice; Tax Law

COOK & LEE, P.C.
Boulder, CO....Civil Trial Practice; Medical Malpractice; Personal Injury; Product Liability Law

COOK, NOELL, TOLLEY, BATES & MICHAEL, LLP
Athens, GA....Criminal Trial Practice; Medical Malpractice

COOK, ROACH & LAWLESS, L.L.P.
Houston, TX....Appellate Practice; Civil Trial Practice

COOK, TUCKER, NETTER & CLOONAN, P.C.
Kingston, NY....General Practice; Insurance Defense

COOLEY GODWARD LLP
Menlo Park, CA....General Practice
Palo Alto, CA....General Practice
San Diego, CA....General Practice
San Francisco, CA....General Practice
Boulder, CO....General Practice
Denver, CO....General Practice
Kirkland, WA....General Practice

COOLEY & ROBBINS, L.L.C.
Sun City, AZ....Trust and Estates, Wills and Probate

COOLING & HERBERS, P.C.
Kansas City, MO....Aviation Law

COONEY, MATTSON, LANCE, BLACKBURN, RICHARDS & O'CONNOR, P.A.
Fort Lauderdale, FL....Medical Malpractice; Personal Injury; Product Liability Law; Professional Liability; Workers Compensation
Orlando, FL....Medical Malpractice; Personal Injury; Product Liability Law; Professional Liability; Workers Compensation

COOPER, C. JAMES
Denver, CO....Immigration and Naturalization

COOPER, LAWRENCE A.
Atlanta, GA....Family Law; Medical Malpractice

COOPER CARVIN & ROSENTHAL, PLLC
Washington, DC....Administrative Law; Constitutional Law

COOPER & CLOUGH, P.C.
Denver, CO....Insurance Defense; Medical Malpractice

COOPER, COPPINS & MONROE, P.A.
Tallahassee, FL....Civil Trial Practice; Labor and Employment Law

COOPER & DUNHAM LLP
New York, NY....General Practice; Patent, Trademark, Copyright and Unfair Competition; Trademark, Copyright and Unfair Competition

COOPER, HALL, WHITTUM AND SHILLABER, P.C.
Rochester, NH....General Practice

COOPER, KENNETH D., P.A.
Fort Lauderdale, FL....Commercial Litigation; Personal Injury

COOPER & LARSEN
Pocatello, ID....Insurance Defense

COOPER, MARVIN A., P.C.
White Plains, NY....Personal Injury; Product Liability Law

COOPER & PRESTON
Parsons, WV....Civil Trial Practice

COOPER, SPONG & DAVIS, P.C.
Portsmouth, VA — Environmental Law; General Practice; Health Care Law

COOPER & STIELER
New Providence, NJ — Intellectual Property Law; Patent, Trademark, Copyright and Unfair Competition

COOPER & TUERK, LLP
Baltimore, MD — Personal Injury; Product Liability Law

COOPER & WOLFE, P.A.
Miami, FL — Appellate Practice

COOPER & WOODRUFF, A LAW CORPORATION
Abbeville, LA — General Practice

COOPERMAN LEVITT WINIKOFF LESTER & NEWMAN, P.C.
New York, NY — Civil Trial Practice; Corporate Law; General Practice

COOVER & COOVER
Corpus Christi, TX — Family Law

COPE, JOSEPH ADAMS
Boulder, CO — Civil Trial Practice; Natural Resources Law

COPELAND COOK TAYLOR & BUSH, A PROFESSIONAL ASSOCIATION
Jackson, MS — Banking Law; Civil Trial Practice; Commercial Law; Insurance Defense; Natural Resources Law; Tax Law

COPELAND, LANDYE, BENNETT AND WOLF, LLP
Portland, OR — Bankruptcy Law; Business Law; Environmental Law; Real Estate Law; Securities Law

COPP & BERALL, LLP
Hartford, CT — Tax Law; Trust and Estates, Wills and Probate

COPPLE, CHAMBERLIN, BOEHM & MURPHY, P.C.
Phoenix, AZ — Appellate Practice; Insurance Defense; Medical Malpractice; Personal Injury

CORBAN & GUNN
Biloxi, MS — Business Law; General Practice; Insurance Defense

CORBETT CROCKETT & LECKRONE
Nashville, TN — Commercial Law; Commercial Litigation; Real Estate Law; Tax Law

CORBETT GORDON & ASSOCIATES, P.C.
Portland, OR — Labor and Employment Law

CORBIN SILVERMAN & SANSEVERINO LLP
New York, NY — Banking Law; Corporate Law; Securities Law

CORBITT & JOHNSON, P.C.
Tulsa, OK — Family Law

CORBOY & DEMETRIO, P.C.
Chicago, IL — Civil Trial Practice; Medical Malpractice; Personal Injury

CORCORAN, WILLIAM E.
McAllen, TX — Family Law; Personal Injury

CORCORAN, ROBERT T., P.C.
Hackensack, NJ — Appellate Practice; Family Law

CORDA, WILLIAM J.
Lakeland, FL — Personal Injury

CORDRAY & GOODRICH, PROFESSIONAL CORPORATION
Houston, TX — Business Law; Mergers and Acquisitions; Real Estate Law; Tax Law; Trust and Estates, Wills and Probate

CORETTE POHLMAN & KEBE, A PROFESSIONAL CORPORATION
Butte, MT — General Practice

CORKERN & CREWS, L.L.C.
Natchitoches, LA — Insurance Defense

CORLEY, MONCUS & WARD, P.C.
Birmingham, AL — Bankruptcy Law; General Practice; Insurance Defense; Real Estate Law; Trust and Estates, Wills and Probate

CORNBLATT, BENNETT, PENHALLEGON & ROBERSON, P.A.
Baltimore, MD — Insurance Defense; Medical Malpractice; Product Liability Law; Workers Compensation

CORNELIUS & COLLINS, LLP
Nashville, TN — Civil Trial Practice; General Practice

CORNELL & GOLLUB
Boston, MA — Civil Trial Practice; General Practice; Insurance Defense; Medical Malpractice

CORRERO FISHMAN HAYGOOD PHELPS WALMSLEY & CASTEIX, L.L.P.
New Orleans, LA — Banking Law; Business Law; Commercial Litigation; Corporate Law; Mergers and Acquisitions; Real Estate Law; Securities Law; Trust and Estates, Wills and Probate

CORSI, MARIO D.
Dover, OH — Real Estate Law; Trust and Estates, Wills and Probate

CORTEZ MACAULAY BERNHARDT & SCHUETZE LLC
Denver, CO — Arbitration; Business Law; Civil Trial Practice; Commercial Litigation; Labor and Employment Law; Personal Injury; Product Liability Law

CORWIN, BRENT E., P.C.
Scottsdale, AZ — Commercial Litigation; Personal Injury

CORY, TIMOTHY S. & ASSOCIATES, LAW OFFICES OF
Las Vegas, NV — Bankruptcy Law

CORY, KENNETH C., A PROFESSIONAL CORPORATION
Las Vegas, NV — Civil Trial Practice; Criminal Trial Practice; Personal Injury

CORY, MEREDITH, WITTER, ROUSH & CHENEY, A LEGAL PROFESSIONAL ASSOCIATION
Lima, OH — General Practice

COSGRAVE, VERGEER & KESTER, L.L.P.
Portland, OR — General Practice

COSTELLO COONEY & FEARON, LLP
Syracuse, NY — Bankruptcy Law; Civil Trial Practice; Corporate Law; General Practice; Health Care Law; Labor and Employment Law; Real Estate Law; Tax Law; Trademark, Copyright and Unfair Competition

COSTILLA, FRANK, JR., P.L.L.C.
Brownsville, TX — Personal Injury

COTHRAN, JAMES C. JR.
Spartanburg, SC — Civil Trial Practice

COTKIN, COLLINS & GINSBURG, A PROFESSIONAL CORPORATION
Los Angeles, CA — General Practice
Santa Ana, CA — General Practice

COTNEY, HUGH, P.A.
Jacksonville, FL — Criminal Trial Practice; Personal Injury; Product Liability Law

COTSIRILOS, JOHN G.
San Diego, CA — Criminal Trial Practice

COTTER, COTTER AND SOHON, P.C.
Bridgeport, CT — Insurance Defense; Workers Compensation

COTTINGHAM & PORTER, P.C.
Douglas, GA — General Practice

COTTON, JOHN H., & ASSOCIATES, LTD.
Scottsdale, AZ — Civil Trial Practice; Commercial Litigation; Medical Malpractice

COUCH WHITE, LLP
Albany, NY — Administrative Law; Construction Law; Energy Law; General Practice; Health Care Law; Public Utilities Law

COUGHLIN & GERHART, L.L.P.
Binghamton, NY — Civil Trial Practice; General Practice

COULOMBE LAW FIRM, THE, A PROFESSIONAL CORPORATION
Costa Mesa, CA — Civil Trial Practice

COUNCIL, BARADEL, KOSMERL & NOLAN, P.A.
Annapolis, MD — Business Law; Civil Trial Practice; Environmental Law; Family Law; Insurance Defense; Labor and Employment Law; Municipal and Zoning Law; Personal Injury; Real Estate Law; Trust and Estates, Wills and Probate

COURBOIS, FRANCIS
Oklahoma City, OK — Criminal Trial Practice

COURTLAND, ROBERT D., CHARTERED
Bethesda, MD — Tax Law

COUSINEAU, MCGUIRE & ANDERSON, CHARTERED
Minneapolis, MN — Insurance Defense

COUZENS, LANSKY, FEALK, ELLIS, ROEDER & LAZAR, P.C.
Farmington Hills, MI — Bankruptcy Law; Business Law; Civil Trial Practice; Commercial Law; Corporate Law; Employment Benefits Law; General Practice; Labor and Employment Law; Pension and Profit Sharing; Real Estate Law; Tax Law; Trust and Estates, Wills and Probate

COVINGTON & BURLING
Washington, DC......General Practice

COVINGTON & CROWE LLP
Ontario, CA......Civil Trial Practice; Employment Benefits Law; Family Law; General Practice; Real Estate Law

COVINGTON, PATRICK, HAGINS, STERN & LEWIS, P.A.
Greenville, SC......Civil Trial Practice; Product Liability Law

COWAN, DENNIS K.
Redding, CA......Bankruptcy Law

COWARD, HICKS & SILER, P.A.
Sylva, NC......Civil Trial Practice; Real Estate Law; Trust and Estates, Wills and Probate

COWART, ROY N., P.C.
Warner Robins, GA......Corporate Law; General Practice

COWLES & THOMPSON, A PROFESSIONAL CORPORATION
Dallas, TX......Civil Trial Practice; Commercial Law; General Practice; Insurance Defense; Municipal and Zoning Law
McKinney, TX......General Practice
Tyler, TX......General Practice

COX, GOUDY, MCNULTY & WALLACE, P.L.L.P.
Minneapolis, MN......Civil Trial Practice; Commercial Law; Personal Injury

COX HANSON O'REILLY MATHESON
Fredericton, NB, Canada......Administrative Law; Appellate Practice; Banking Law; Bankruptcy Law; Civil Trial Practice; Commercial Law; Construction Law; Environmental Law; Family Law; General Practice; Insurance Defense; Labor and Employment Law; Real Estate Law; Tax Law
Saint John, NB, Canada......Tax Law
St. John's, NF, Canada......General Practice; Insurance Defense
Halifax, NS, Canada......General Practice

COX, LEVAN, SPRADER & PATTON, P.L.L.C.
Nashville, TN......Insurance Defense; Transportation Law

COX & MOYER, A PROFESSIONAL CORPORATION
San Francisco, CA......Antitrust Law; Aviation Law; Civil Trial Practice; Medical Malpractice; Personal Injury; Product Liability Law

COX PADMORE SKOLNIK & SHAKARCHY
Denver, CO......Commercial Litigation; International Business Law
New York, NY......General Practice

COX & SMITH INCORPORATED
San Antonio, TX......Antitrust Law; Banking Law; Bankruptcy Law; Business Law; Civil Trial Practice; Computer Law; General Practice; Health Care Law; Labor and Employment Law; Natural Resources Law; Patent, Trademark, Copyright and Unfair Competition; Real Estate Law; Securities Law; Tax Law; Trust and Estates, Wills and Probate

COX, ZWERNER, GAMBILL & SULLIVAN
Terre Haute, IN......Banking Law; Civil Trial Practice; General Practice; Insurance Defense; Real Estate Law; Trust and Estates, Wills and Probate

COY, GILBERT & GILBERT
Richmond, KY......General Practice

COYNE, NIESS, SCHULTZ, BECKER & BAUER, S.C.
Madison, WI......Civil Trial Practice

COZEN AND O'CONNOR, A PROFESSIONAL CORPORATION
Philadelphia, PA......Civil Trial Practice; Commercial Law; General Practice; Insurance Defense; Personal Injury

CRABBE, BROWN, JONES, POTTS & SCHMIDT
Columbus, OH......Civil Trial Practice; General Practice; Insurance Defense

CRABTREE, SCHMIDT, ZEFF, JACOBS & FARRAR
Modesto, CA......General Practice

CRACKEN, HARKEY & PAYNE, LLP
Dallas, TX......Civil Trial Practice; Medical Malpractice; Personal Injury; Product Liability Law

CRADDICK, CANDLAND & CONTI, PROFESSIONAL CORPORATION
Danville, CA......Business Law; Civil Trial Practice; Insurance Defense; Medical Malpractice

CRAFT, PATRICIA J., P.C.
Decatur, GA......Labor and Employment Law

CRAIG, RANDALL K. LAW OFFICES OF
Evansville, IN......Business Law; Tax Law; Trust and Estates, Wills and Probate

CRAIG & CRAIG
Mattoon, IL......Banking Law; Business Law; Civil Trial Practice; Commercial Law; Environmental Law; General Practice; Labor and Employment Law; Land Use Law; Medical Malpractice; Natural Resources Law; Product Liability Law; Public Utilities Law; Real Estate Law; Trust and Estates, Wills and Probate; Workers Compensation

CRAIG AND MACAULEY, PROFESSIONAL CORPORATION
Boston, MA......Banking Law; Bankruptcy Law; Business Law; Commercial Litigation; General Practice; Insurance Defense

CRAIGE, BRAWLEY, LIIPFERT & WALKER, L.L.P.
Winston-Salem, NC......General Practice; Insurance Defense; Trust and Estates, Wills and Probate

CRAMER & ANDERSON LLP
Litchfield, CT......General Practice

CRAMER LAW FIRM, THE
Jacksonville, FL......Insurance Defense; Labor and Employment Law; Personal Injury; Workers Compensation

CRAMER, MULTHAUF & HAMMES, LLP
Waukesha, WI......Business Law

CRANFILL, SUMNER & HARTZOG, L.L.P.
Raleigh, NC......Insurance Defense; Personal Injury

CRANMORE, FITZGERALD & MEANEY
Hartford, CT......Banking Law; Civil Trial Practice; Real Estate Law

CRARY, HUFF, INKSTER, HECHT & SHEEHAN, P.C.
Sioux City, IA......General Practice

CRAVATH, SWAINE & MOORE
New York, NY......General Practice
Hong Kong, China......General Practice
London, England......General Practice

CRAWFORD, B. HAYDEN
Tulsa, OK......Civil Trial Practice

CRAWFORD, JOHN A. JR.
San Diego, CA......Criminal Trial Practice

CRAWFORD, RUSSELL E.
Orlando, FL......Criminal Trial Practice

CRAWFORD & MCKINNEY
Houston, TX......Personal Injury; Professional Liability

CREEDON & FELICIANI, P.C.
Norristown, PA......Civil Trial Practice; Medical Malpractice; Personal Injury; Product Liability Law

CREMEN, FRANK J.
Las Vegas, NV......Criminal Trial Practice

CREMINS & ASSOCIATES, P.C.
Fairfax, VA......Appellate Practice; Civil Trial Practice; Health Care Law; Medical Malpractice

CRENSHAW, DUPREE & MILAM, L.L.P.
Lubbock, TX......Insurance Defense; Medical Malpractice; Trust and Estates, Wills and Probate

CREWS & HANCOCK, P.L.C.
Richmond, VA......Business Law; Commercial Law; Health Care Law; Medical Malpractice

CREWS & KLEIN, P.C.
Charlotte, NC......Insurance Defense

CRIBBS & MCFARLAND, A PROFESSIONAL CORPORATION
Arlington, TX......General Practice

CRIMMINS, ROBERT C.
Riverhead, NY......Civil Trial Practice; Commercial Litigation

CRISLIP, PHILIP & ASSOCIATES
Memphis, TN......General Practice

CRISP PAGE & CURRIN, L.L.P.
Raleigh, NC......Communications Law

CRIST, SCHULZ, BIORN & SHEPHERD, A PROFESSIONAL CORPORATION
Palo Alto, CA......Trust and Estates, Wills and Probate

CRISTE, VIRGINIA S. LAW OFFICES OF
Indian Wells, CA......Family Law

CRISTE, PIPPIN & GOLDS
Palm Desert, CA......Bankruptcy Law; Business Law; Civil Trial Practice; Real Estate Law

CRITTENDEN • MARTIN
Birmingham, AL......Family Law

CRITTENDEN & CRITTENDEN, P.A.
Winter Haven, FL....................General Practice

CROCKETT, DAVID G., P.C.
Atlanta, GA ....Bankruptcy Law; Civil Trial Practice; Commercial Law; Creditors Rights; Real Estate Law

CROCKETT & MYERS, LTD., A PROFESSIONAL CORPORATION
Las Vegas, NV.........................Medical Malpractice; Personal Injury; Workers Compensation

CROFTS, CALLAWAY & JEFFERSON, A PROFESSIONAL CORPORATION
San Antonio, TX......................Appellate Practice

CROLEY, DAVIDSON & HUIE
Knoxville, TN ....Real Estate Law

CROMWELL, MARGRIT E. LAW OFFICE OF
Tucson, AZ ....Family Law

CRONIN, FRIED, SEKIYA, KEKINA & FAIRBANKS, ATTORNEYS AT LAW, A LAW CORPORATION
Honolulu, HI...........................Admiralty/Maritime Law; Aviation Law; Medical Malpractice; Personal Injury; Product Liability Law; Professional Liability

CRONIN & STANEWICH
Phoenix, AZ ....Insurance Defense; Medical Malpractice; Personal Injury; Product Liability Law

CROSS, MURPHY, SMUCK & HOUSTON
Washington, DC.......................Tax Law; Trust and Estates, Wills and Probate

CROSSETT, EDGAR L., III, P.C.
Atlanta, GA ....Personal Injury

CROW AND CROW
Pomeroy, OH ....General Practice

CROWE & DUNLEVY
Norman, OK ....Banking Law; Bankruptcy Law; Civil Trial Practice; Commercial Law; Corporate Law; General Practice; Health Care Law; Labor and Employment Law; Municipal Bond/Public Authority Financing; Real Estate Law
Oklahoma City, OK.................Antitrust Law; Appellate Practice; Banking Law; Bankruptcy Law; Civil Trial Practice; Commercial Law; Commercial Litigation; Corporate Law; General Practice; Health Care Law; Intellectual Property Law; Labor and Employment Law; Municipal Bond/Public Authority Financing; Oil and Gas Law; Patent, Trademark, Copyright and Unfair Competition; Real Estate Law; Securities Law; Tax Law; Workers Compensation
Tulsa, OK................................Banking Law; Bankruptcy Law; Civil Trial Practice; Commercial Law; Commercial Litigation; Corporate Law; General Practice; Health Care Law; Intellectual Property Law; Labor and Employment Law; Municipal Bond/Public Authority Financing; Oil and Gas Law; Real Estate Law; Securities Law; Workers Compensation

CROWE & SCOTT, P.A.
Phoenix, AZ ....Civil Trial Practice; Criminal Trial Practice

CROWELL, WILLIAM D.
Harwich Port, MA...................Real Estate Law

CROWELL & MORING
London, England ....General Practice
Irvine, CA................................General Practice
Washington, DC.......................General Practice

CROWELL AND OWENS, L.L.C.
Alexandria, LA ....Business Law; Tax Law; Trust and Estates, Wills and Probate

CROWELL, SUSICH, OWEN & TACKES, LTD., A PROF. LAW CORP.
Carson City, NV ....Administrative Law; Business Law

CROWLEY BARRETT & KARABA, LTD.
Chicago, IL..............................Commercial Litigation

CROWLEY, HAUGHEY, HANSON, TOOLE & DIETRICH, P.L.L.P.
Billings, MT ....Administrative Law; Banking Law; Bankruptcy Law; Business Law; Civil Trial Practice; Commercial Law; Criminal Trial Practice; Employment Benefits Law; Environmental Law; Family Law; General Practice; Health Care Law; Immigration and Naturalization; Insurance Defense; Labor and Employment Law; Medical Malpractice; Municipal Bond/Public Authority Financing; Natural Resources Law; Personal Injury; Product Liability Law; Public Utilities Law; Real Estate Law; Securities Law; Tax Law; Trademark, Copyright and Unfair Competition; Transportation Law; Trust and Estates, Wills and Probate; Workers Compensation

CROWSON & INGRAM
El Paso, TX.............................Banking Law; Bankruptcy Law; Business Law; Civil Trial Practice; Commercial Law; Commercial Litigation; Creditors Rights; General Practice; Real Estate Law

CRUMP, TOLSON & PAGE LLP
Tulsa, OK................................Commercial Litigation; Environmental Law; General Practice

CRUMPLER O'CONNOR & WYNNE
El Dorado, AR ....General Practice

CRUSE, FIRETAG & BOCK, P.C.
Phoenix, AZ ....Banking Law; Commercial Law; Real Estate Law

CRUSE, SCOTT, HENDERSON & ALLEN, L.L.P.
Houston, TX ....Civil Trial Practice; Medical Malpractice; Professional Liability

CRUTSINGER & BOOTH
Dallas, TX...............................Patent, Trademark, Copyright and Unfair Competition

CRYSTAL, HEYTOW & WARNICK, P.C.
Chicago, IL..............................Insurance Defense

CUCCIO AND CUCCIO
Hackensack, NJ.......................General Practice

CULBERTSON, THOMAS A.
Santa Ana, CA ....Civil Trial Practice

CULBRETH, STEPHEN E.
Wilmington, NC.......................Appellate Practice; Criminal Trial Practice; Personal Injury; Workers Compensation

CULLEN LAW FIRM, LTD.
Minneapolis, MN ....Civil Trial Practice

CULP ELLIOTT & CARPENTER, P.L.L.C.
Charlotte, NC..........................Tax Law

CULVER, SHERIDAN, KNOWLTON, EVEN & FRANKS, P.C.
Muskegon, MI.........................Business Law; Commercial Litigation; General Practice; Real Estate Law

CUMMINGS & SNYDER, P.A.
Fort Lauderdale, FL ....Administrative Law; Construction Law; Government Contracts
Tallahassee, FL ....Administrative Law; Construction Law; Government Contracts

CUMMINS, BERNARD F.
Martinez, CA...........................General Practice

CUNEO LAW GROUP, THE, P.C.
Washington, DC.......................Administrative Law; Antitrust Law; Commercial Litigation; Corporate Law; Securities Law

CUNNINGHAM, BLACKBURN, FRANCIS, BROCK & CUNNINGHAM
Grand Island, NE ....General Practice

CUNNINGHAM, BOUNDS, YANCE, CROWDER & BROWN, L.L.C.
Mobile, AL..............................Admiralty/Maritime Law; Aviation Law; Civil Trial Practice; General Practice; Medical Malpractice; Personal Injury; Product Liability Law; Professional Liability; Transportation Law

CUNNINGHAM, CLARK & GREIWE, P.A.
Tampa, FL ....Civil Trial Practice; General Practice; Medical Malpractice; Personal Injury; Product Liability Law

CUNNINGHAM DALMAN, P.C.
Holland, MI ....Banking Law; Business Law; Civil Trial Practice; Environmental Law; Family Law; General Practice; Insurance Defense; Personal Injury; Real Estate Law; Trust and Estates, Wills and Probate

CUNNINGHAM, DARLOW, ZOOK & CHAPOTON, LLP
Houston, TX ....Antitrust Law; Commercial Litigation; Intellectual Property Law; Securities Law

CUNNINGHAM LAW FIRM
Phoenix, AZ ....Personal Injury

CURAN, MICHAEL E., P.C., THE LAW OFFICES OF
New York, NY.........................Administrative Law; Civil Trial Practice; Insurance Defense; Personal Injury

CURET & BARRON
Hammond, LA.........................General Practice

CURIALE DELLAVERSON HIRSCHFELD KELLY & KRAEMER, LLP
Los Angeles, CA ....Labor and Employment Law
San Francisco, CA ....Labor and Employment Law

CURLEY & CURLEY, P.C.
Boston, MA.............................Civil Trial Practice; General Practice; Insurance Defense

CURRAN, DENNIS J.
Boston, MA.............................Civil Trial Practice; Personal Injury

CURRAN & CURRAN
Fort Lauderdale, FL ....Corporate Law

CURRAN, JAMES, P.A.
Fort Lauderdale, FL..............Administrative Law

CURRAN & PARRY
Las Vegas, NV..............Construction Law; Municipal and Zoning Law; Real Estate Law

CURRAN AND WATSON
Fullerton, CA..............Criminal Trial Practice

CURRIE JOHNSON GRIFFIN GAINES & MYERS, PLLC
Jackson, MS..............Civil Trial Practice; General Practice; Insurance Defense; Medical Malpractice

CURRIE KENDALL POLASKY MEISEL, PLC
Midland, MI..............Banking Law; Civil Trial Practice; Family Law; General Practice; Real Estate Law; Tax Law
Saginaw, MI..............Banking Law; Civil Trial Practice; Family Law; General Practice; Real Estate Law; Tax Law

CURRY, MORIN AND GOUDARZI, P.C.
Marshall, TX..............Aviation Law; Civil Trial Practice; Personal Injury

CURTIN & HEEFNER, LLP
Morrisville, PA..............General Practice

CURTIN, MURPHY & O'REILLY, P.C.
Boston, MA..............Civil Trial Practice; Insurance Defense

CURTIS, BRINCKERHOFF & BARRETT, P.C.
Stamford, CT..............Administrative Law; Business Law; Civil Trial Practice; Commercial Law; Commercial Litigation; Corporate Law; Elder Law; Eminent Domain; Family Law; General Practice; Land Use Law; Personal Injury; Real Estate Law; Tax Law; Trust and Estates, Wills and Probate

CURTIS & LAMBERT, A PROFESSIONAL LAW CORPORATION
Lafayette, LA..............Admiralty/Maritime Law; Personal Injury

CURTIS LAW OFFICE
Oshkosh, WI..............Civil Trial Practice; Personal Injury; Trust and Estates, Wills and Probate; Workers Compensation

CURTIS, MALLET-PREVOST, COLT & MOSLE
Mexico, D.F., Mexico..............General Practice
Washington, DC..............General Practice
Newark, NJ..............General Practice
New York, NY..............Admiralty/Maritime Law; Bankruptcy Law; Civil Trial Practice; Criminal Trial Practice; International Business Law; Real Estate Law; Tax Law; Trust and Estates, Wills and Probate
London, England..............General Practice
Paris, France..............General Practice
Frankfurt/Main, Germany..............General Practice

CUSHING, PETER
Orlando, FL..............Family Law

CUSHING, MORRIS, ARMBRUSTER & JONES, LLP
Atlanta, GA..............Business Law

CUSTER & HILL, P.C.
Marietta, GA..............Family Law; General Practice; Trust and Estates, Wills and Probate

CUTHBERT LAW OFFICES, A PROFESSIONAL CORPORATION
Petersburg, VA..............Personal Injury

CUTLER, LAURENCE J.
Morristown, NJ..............Family Law

CUTLER & STANFIELD, L.L.P.
Denver, CO..............Transportation Law
Washington, DC..............Aviation Law; Energy Law; Environmental Law; Municipal and Zoning Law; Natural Resources Law; Transportation Law

CUTRIGHT & CUTRIGHT
Chillicothe, OH..............General Practice; Real Estate Law; Trust and Estates, Wills and Probate

CUYLER BURK
Parsippany, NJ..............Appellate Practice; Arbitration; Banking Law; Business Law; Civil Trial Practice; Commercial Litigation; Corporate Law; Environmental Law; General Practice; Insurance Defense; Personal Injury; Real Estate Law; Toxic Torts

CYPERT, CROUCH, CLARK & HARWELL
Springdale, AR..............Commercial Litigation; General Practice; Insurance Defense

CYRIL & CROWLEY LLP
San Francisco, CA..............Civil Trial Practice; Insurance Defense; Product Liability Law

CZYGIER, JOHN M. JR.
Riverhead, NY..............Trust and Estates, Wills and Probate

DAAR & NEWMAN, PROFESSIONAL CORPORATION
Los Angeles, CA..............General Practice; Insurance Defense; International Business Law

D'AGOSTINO, KRACKELER, BAYNES & MAGUIRE, P.C.
Albany, NY..............General Practice

DAHL, JAMES E. & ASSOCIATES
Chicago, IL..............Civil Trial Practice

DAHLGREN AND CLOSE
Washington, DC..............International Business Law

DAILEY, GARRETT C.
Oakland, CA..............Family Law

DAILY & WOODS, P.L.L.C.
Fort Smith, AR..............Civil Trial Practice; General Practice; Insurance Defense; Oil and Gas Law

DALEIDEN & TREMAINE, LTD.
Arlington Heights, IL..............General Practice

DALE & KLEIN, L.L.P.
McAllen, TX..............Civil Trial Practice; Family Law; Insurance Defense

D'ALESSANDRO, JACOVINO & GERSON
Florham Park, NJ..............Civil Trial Practice; General Practice; Insurance Defense; Medical Malpractice

DALEY, BLACK & MOREIRA
Halifax, NS, Canada..............General Practice

DALLER GREENBERG & DIETRICH, LLP
Fort Washington, PA..............Commercial Litigation; Construction Law; Environmental Law; Labor and Employment Law; Product Liability Law; Toxic Torts

DALNEKOFF & MASON, P.A.
Annapolis, MD..............Civil Trial Practice; Criminal Trial Practice; Family Law

DALTON, TREASURE & MOWRER
Kennett, MO..............General Practice

DALY LAVERY & HALL
Ossining, NY..............General Practice

D'AMATO & LYNCH
New York, NY..............Civil Trial Practice; Insurance Defense

DAMON KEY LEONG KUPCHAK HASTERT, ATTORNEYS AT LAW, A LAW CORPORATION
Honolulu, HI..............General Practice

DAMON & MOREY LLP
Buffalo, NY..............Civil Trial Practice; Commercial Litigation; Health Care Law; Insurance Defense; Intellectual Property Law; Labor and Employment Law

DAMON, OOSTERHOUSE & WITTE, L.L.P.
Grand Rapids, MI..............Business Law

DAMRELL, NELSON, SCHRIMP, PALLIOS & LADINE, A PROFESSIONAL CORPORATION
Modesto, CA..............Civil Trial Practice; General Practice

DANAHER, TEDFORD, LAGNESE & NEAL, P.C.
Hartford, CT..............Insurance Defense

DANIEL, CLAMPETT, POWELL & CUNNINGHAM, L.L.C.
Springfield, MO..............Civil Trial Practice

DANIEL & DANIEL
Pawleys Island, SC..............General Practice; Personal Injury

DANIEL, LAWSON, TUGGLE & JERLES, L.L.P.
Perry, GA..............General Practice

DANIEL & OBERMAN
Knoxville, TN..............Civil Trial Practice; Criminal Trial Practice

DANIELS, FINE, ISRAEL & SCHONBUCH, LLP
Los Angeles, CA..............Construction Law; Insurance Defense; Toxic Torts

DANIELS, KASHTAN & FORNARIS, P.A.
Miami, FL..............Construction Law; Workers Compensation

DANIELS LAW OFFICES, P.C.
Boston, MA..............Bankruptcy Law; Commercial Litigation; Creditors Rights

DANIELS, SANDERS, PIANOWSKI, TODD & THOMAS
Elkhart, IN..............Civil Trial Practice; Corporate Law; Labor and Employment Law

DANIELSON HARRIGAN & TOLLEFSON, LLP
Seattle, WA..............Admiralty/Maritime Law; Civil Trial Practice; Commercial Litigation; Construction Law

DANKENBRING GREIMAN OSTERHOLT & HOFFMANN, P.C.
St. Louis, MO .... Real Estate Law; Tax Law; Trademark, Copyright and Unfair Competition

DANKNER & MILSTEIN, P.C.
New York, NY .... Civil Trial Practice

DANN, DORFMAN, HERRELL AND SKILLMAN, A PROFESSIONAL CORPORATION
Philadelphia, PA .... Computer Law; Intellectual Property Law; Patent, Trademark, Copyright and Unfair Competition

DANNING, GILL, DIAMOND & KOLLITZ, LLP
Los Angeles, CA .... Bankruptcy Law

DANZIGER & MARKHOFF LLP
White Plains, NY .... Pension and Profit Sharing

DAPEER, ROSENBLIT & LITVAK, LLP
Los Angeles, CA .... Civil Trial Practice; Municipal and Zoning Law; Professional Liability

DARBY, PEELE, BOWDOIN, PAYNE & KENNON
Lake City, FL .... General Practice

DARCHE, GARY M.
Kew Gardens, NY .... Civil Trial Practice

DARK, CLAYTON E. JR.
Lufkin, TX .... General Practice; Insurance Defense

DARLING, HALL & RAE, LLP
Los Angeles, CA .... Business Law; Civil Trial Practice; Corporate Law; Real Estate Law; Trust and Estates, Wills and Probate

DART ADAMSON DONOVAN & HANSON
Salt Lake City, UT .... Commercial Litigation; Construction Law; Family Law; Municipal and Zoning Law; Personal Injury; Real Estate Law

DASCHBACH, COOPER, HOTCHKISS & CSATARI, PROFESSIONAL ASSOCIATION
Lebanon, NH .... General Practice

DASILVA, HILOWITZ & MCEVILY LLP
Garden City, NY .... Family Law; Trust and Estates, Wills and Probate

DATSOPOULOS, MACDONALD & LIND, P.C.
Missoula, MT .... Business Law; Commercial Litigation

DAUER & THOMPSON
Sacramento, CA .... Administrative Law; Appellate Practice; Construction Law; Government Contracts

DAUGHERTY, DAVID H.
Huntington, WV .... Trust and Estates, Wills and Probate

DAVENPORT, EVANS, HURWITZ & SMITH, L.L.P.
Sioux Falls, SD .... Banking Law; Bankruptcy Law; Business Law; Civil Trial Practice; General Practice; Insurance Defense; Personal Injury; Real Estate Law; Tax Law

DAVENPORT, FILES & KELLY, L.L.P.
Monroe, LA .... Criminal Trial Practice; General Practice; Insurance Defense

DAVEY & BROGAN, P.C.
Norfolk, VA .... Admiralty/Maritime Law; Insurance Defense; Transportation Law

DAVID, ANTHONY P., A PROFESSIONAL CORPORATION
San Francisco, CA .... Commercial Litigation; Personal Injury

DAVIDOFF, PAUL F., A PROFESSIONAL CORPORATION
Kalamazoo, MI .... Bankruptcy Law; Commercial Litigation

DAVIDSON, THOMAS M.
McLean, VA .... Business Law; Corporate Law; Mergers and Acquisitions

DAVIDSON, DAVIDSON & KAPPEL, LLC
New York, NY .... Patent, Trademark, Copyright and Unfair Competition

DAVIDSON, MEAUX, SONNIER, MCELLIGOTT & SWIFT
Lafayette, LA .... Aviation Law; Business Law; Civil Trial Practice; Commercial Litigation; General Practice; Insurance Defense

DAVIDSON, NIX & JONES, A PROFESSIONAL LAW CORPORATION
Shreveport, LA .... Business Law; Labor and Employment Law; Oil and Gas Law

DAVIDSON, WIGGINS, JONES & COLEMAN, P.C.
Tuscaloosa, AL .... Civil Trial Practice; General Practice; Insurance Defense

DAVIES & HUMPHREYS
Nashville, TN .... Insurance Defense; Medical Malpractice; Product Liability Law; Workers Compensation

DAVIES MCFARLAND & CARROLL, P.C.
Pittsburgh, PA .... Civil Trial Practice; General Practice; Insurance Defense; Medical Malpractice; Product Liability Law; Workers Compensation

DAVIES, WARD & BECK
Toronto, ON, Canada .... Antitrust Law; Banking Law; Business Law; Civil Trial Practice; Commercial Law; Computer Law; Environmental Law; General Practice; Real Estate Law; Securities Law; Tax Law

DAVIS, JAMES MARTIN
Omaha, NE .... Criminal Trial Practice; Personal Injury

DAVIS, STEPHEN J.
Minneapolis, MN .... Real Estate Law

DAVIS, BROWN, KOEHN, SHORS & ROBERTS, P.C.
Des Moines, IA .... General Practice; Patent, Trademark, Copyright and Unfair Competition; Tax Law

DAVIS AND BUJOLD
Manchester, NH .... Patent, Trademark, Copyright and Unfair Competition

DAVIS & CANNON
Sheridan, WY .... Civil Trial Practice

DAVIS & CARICO LLP
Manhattan Beach, CA .... Trust and Estates, Wills and Probate

DAVIS, CEDILLO & MENDOZA, INCORPORATED
San Antonio, TX .... Commercial Litigation

DAVIS & CERIANI, P.C.
Denver, CO .... Arbitration; Bankruptcy Law; Civil Trial Practice; Commercial Litigation; Legal Malpractice; Professional Liability; Real Estate Law

DAVIS & COMPANY
Vancouver, BC, Canada .... General Practice

DAVIS, COX & WRIGHT, PLC
Fayetteville, AR .... Civil Trial Practice; Commercial Law; Commercial Litigation; General Practice; Insurance Defense; Product Liability Law

DAVIS & DAVIS, P.C.
Austin, TX .... Administrative Law; Civil Trial Practice; General Practice; Health Care Law; Insurance Defense

DAVIS, DAVIS & KAAR
Milton, PA .... General Practice

DAVIS FIRM, THE
Seattle, WA .... Admiralty/Maritime Law; Medical Malpractice; Personal Injury; Product Liability Law

DAVIS & FOX
Los Angeles, CA .... Business Law; Civil Trial Practice; General Practice; Insurance Defense; Real Estate Law

DAVIS, GORDON & DONER, P.A.
West Palm Beach, FL .... Medical Malpractice; Personal Injury; Product Liability Law

DAVIS, GRAHAM & STUBBS LLP
Denver, CO .... General Practice

DAVIS & HAMRICK, L.L.P.
Winston-Salem, NC .... General Practice

DAVIS, HOWARD M., P.C.
West Orange, NJ .... Civil Trial Practice; Commercial Law; General Practice

DAVIS & KUELTHAU, S.C.
Milwaukee, WI .... Admiralty/Maritime Law; Business Law; Environmental Law; Labor and Employment Law; Municipal Bond/Public Authority Financing; Real Estate Law; Tax Law; Trust and Estates, Wills and Probate

DAVIS & LOWE, P.C.
Phoenix, AZ .... Bankruptcy Law; Creditors Rights

DAVIS, MURRELLE & LUMSDEN, P.A.
Beaufort, NC .... Admiralty/Maritime Law; Civil Trial Practice; Personal Injury

DAVIS, ORETSKY & GUILFOYLE, P.C.
Houston, TX .... Commercial Litigation; Insurance Defense; Labor and Employment Law; Personal Injury; Professional Liability; Toxic Torts

DAVIS POLK & WARDWELL
Washington, DC .... General Practice
New York, NY .... General Practice
London, England .... General Practice
Paris, France .... General Practice

DAVIS, PUNELLI & KEATHLEY LLP
Newport Beach, CA................Business Law; Civil Trial Practice; Real Estate Law

DAVIS, STURGES & TOMLINSON
Louisburg, NC........................General Practice; Insurance Defense

DAVIS, TUPPER & GRIMSLEY, L.L.P.
Beaufort, SC..........................Arbitration; Corporate Law; Family Law; Insurance Defense; Medical Malpractice; Product Liability Law; Real Estate Law; Trust and Estates, Wills and Probate

DAVIS, WALTER LEE, JR., A PROFESSIONAL CORPORATION
Johnson City, TN....................Trust and Estates, Wills and Probate

DAVIS & WEISMAN, P.C.
St. Louis, MO.........................Creditors Rights

DAVIS & WILKERSON, P.C.
Austin, TX..............................Civil Trial Practice; Commercial Litigation; Health Care Law; Insurance Defense; Labor and Employment Law; Medical Malpractice

DAVIS & YOUNG
Cleveland, OH.........................General Practice; Insurance Defense; Medical Malpractice; Product Liability Law

DAWDA, MANN, MULCAHY & SADLER, P.L.C.
Bloomfield Hills, MI...............Business Law; Civil Trial Practice; Commercial Litigation; Corporate Law; Environmental Law; Labor and Employment Law; Mergers and Acquisitions; Real Estate Law; Tax Law; Trust and Estates, Wills and Probate

DAWSON, JOHN B., JR., P.C.
Mineola, NY...........................Trust and Estates, Wills and Probate

DAWSON, SODD & BEARD, P.C.
Corsicana, TX.........................Civil Trial Practice

DAY, BERRY & HOWARD LLP
Hartford, CT...........................General Practice
Stamford, CT..........................General Practice
Boston, MA.............................General Practice

DAY, EDWARDS, FEDERMAN, PROPESTER & CHRISTENSEN, P.C.
Oklahoma City, OK..................Appellate Practice; Arbitration; Banking Law; Bankruptcy Law; Business Law; Civil Trial Practice; Commercial Law; Commercial Litigation; Construction Law; Corporate Law; Creditors Rights; Energy Law; Environmental Law; General Practice; Health Care Law; Insurance Defense; Intellectual Property Law; International Business Law; Labor and Employment Law; Natural Resources Law; Oil and Gas Law; Product Liability Law; Real Estate Law; Securities Law; Toxic Torts; Workers Compensation

DAY & SAWDEY, A PROFESSIONAL CORPORATION
Grand Rapids, MI....................Corporate Law

DEAN, KRISTI WEILER LAW OFFICES OF
Encino, CA..............................Insurance Defense

DEAN & GIBSON, L.L.P.
Charlotte, NC..........................Aviation Law; Civil Trial Practice; Commercial Litigation; Insurance Defense

DEANER, DEANER, SCANN, MALAN & LARSEN
Las Vegas, NV........................Civil Trial Practice; Commercial Litigation; General Practice; Real Estate Law

DEARTH, MARKHAM & JACK, CHARTERED
Parsons, KS............................General Practice

DEASEY, MAHONEY & BENDER, LTD.
Philadelphia, PA.....................Civil Trial Practice; Insurance Defense

DEASON, CHARLES A. JR.
El Paso, TX.............................Personal Injury; Product Liability Law

DEASON, EDWARD J.
Torrance, CA...........................Personal Injury

DEASON, MARSHALL C. JR.
Tampa, FL...............................Real Estate Law

DEATON, DAVISON & KESSINGER, A PROFESSIONAL CORPORATION
Ada, OK..................................General Practice; Insurance Defense

DEBEVOISE & PLIMPTON
Washington, DC......................General Practice
New York, NY..........................General Practice
Hong Kong, China....................General Practice
London, England.....................General Practice
Paris, France...........................General Practice
Moscow, Russia......................General Practice

DE BLASIO, FIGMAN, EPSTEIN & LA ROCCA, P.C.
New York, NY..........................Civil Trial Practice; Legal Malpractice; Medical Malpractice; Personal Injury; Product Liability Law

DEBOEST, KNUDSEN, STOCKMAN, WISEMAN, DECKER & DRYDEN, P.A.
Fort Myers, FL.......................Appellate Practice; Business Law; Civil Trial Practice; Professional Liability; Real Estate Law; Trust and Estates, Wills and Probate

DEBRUYN, JOHN LAW OFFICES
Denver, CO.............................Tax Law; Trust and Estates, Wills and Probate

DEBUS KAZAN & WESTERHAUSEN, LTD.
Phoenix, AZ............................Criminal Trial Practice; Personal Injury

DECARLO, CONNOR & SELVO, A PROFESSIONAL CORPORATION
Los Angeles, CA.....................Employment Benefits Law; Labor and Employment Law

DECAROLIS, SAENZ & TROPE, LLP
Los Angeles, CA.....................Civil Trial Practice; Family Law

DECHERT PRICE & RHOADS
Washington, DC......................General Practice
Boston, MA.............................General Practice
Princeton, NJ..........................General Practice
New York, NY..........................General Practice
Harrisburg, PA........................General Practice
Philadelphia, PA.....................General Practice
Brussels, Belgium...................General Practice
London, England.....................General Practice
Paris, France...........................General Practice

DECKER, JONES, MCMACKIN, MCCLANE, HALL & BATES, A PROFESSIONAL CORPORATION
Fort Worth, TX........................Business Law; Civil Trial Practice; Commercial Litigation; Corporate Law; General Practice; Insurance Defense; Intellectual Property Law; Medical Malpractice; Mergers and Acquisitions; Oil and Gas Law; Real Estate Law; Tax Law; Toxic Torts; Trademark, Copyright and Unfair Competition; Trust and Estates, Wills and Probate; Workers Compensation

DECUBELLIS & MEEKS, P.A.
Orlando, FL............................Business Law; Civil Trial Practice; General Practice; Real Estate Law

DEEGAN & DEEGAN, L.L.P.
Hempstead, NY........................Civil Trial Practice; General Practice; Insurance Defense; Professional Liability

DEEHL, DAVID L., P.A.
Miami, FL...............................Personal Injury

DEENER, FEINGOLD & STERN, A PROFESSIONAL CORPORATION
Hackensack, NJ......................Administrative Law; Business Law; Civil Trial Practice; Commercial Law; General Practice; Tax Law; Trust and Estates, Wills and Probate

DEEP & WOMACK
Henderson, KY........................Civil Trial Practice; General Practice; Insurance Defense

DEES, J. GORDON, A PROFESSIONAL CORPORATION
Houston, TX............................Criminal Trial Practice

DEETH WILLIAMS WALL, LLP
Toronto, ON, Canada...............Computer Law; Intellectual Property Law; Patent, Trademark, Copyright and Unfair Competition

DEFINO, MICHAEL G.
Media, PA...............................Criminal Trial Practice; Personal Injury

DEFOREST & KOSCELNIK
Pittsburgh, PA........................Civil Trial Practice; Commercial Law; Labor and Employment Law

DEFREES & FISKE
Chicago, IL.............................Public Utilities Law

DE GRANDPRÉ CHAIT
Montreal, QU, Canada.............Civil Trial Practice; Construction Law; General Practice; Real Estate Law

DEGRAVELLES, PALMINTIER & HOLTHAUS
Baton Rouge, LA.....................Criminal Trial Practice; Personal Injury

DE GROOT, KELLER, VINCENT & ALMASSIAN, P.L.C.
Grand Rapids, MI....................Bankruptcy Law; Civil Trial Practice; Commercial Law; Commercial Litigation; Personal Injury

DEGUERIN & DICKSON
Houston, TX............................Criminal Trial Practice

DEHAY & ELLISTON, L.L.P.
Dallas, TX...............................Civil Trial Practice; Insurance Defense; Personal Injury; Product Liability Law

DEKLE, PATRICK H., P.A.
Tampa, FL .... Civil Trial Practice; Medical Malpractice; Personal Injury

DE LA GARZA, BILL, & ASSOCIATES, P.C.
Houston, TX .... Family Law; Real Estate Law

DELANEY AND O'CONNOR LLP
Syracuse, NY .... Elder Law; Health Care Law; Trust and Estates, Wills and Probate

DELANEY & SUMNER
Rapid City, SD .... Civil Trial Practice; Family Law; Insurance Defense; Oil and Gas Law; Personal Injury

DELANEY, WILES, HAYES, GERETY, ELLIS & YOUNG, INC.
Anchorage, AK .... Environmental Law; General Practice; Insurance Defense; Labor and Employment Law; Medical Malpractice; Natural Resources Law; Product Liability Law

DELANOY, ENGLISH, SCHUETZE & MCGAHA, A PROFESSIONAL CORPORATION
Las Vegas, NV .... Commercial Litigation; Insurance Defense

DELAP, HERBERT A., & ASSOCIATES, P.C.
Denver, CO .... General Practice

DE LA PARTE, GILBERT & BALES, PROFESSIONAL ASSOCIATION
Tampa, FL .... Commercial Litigation; Environmental Law

DELBELLO DONNELLAN WEINGARTEN & TARTAGLIA, LLP
White Plains, NY .... Banking Law; Commercial Litigation; Environmental Law; Insurance Defense; Land Use Law; Real Estate Law

DELEON, BOGGINS & ICENOGLE, A PROFESSIONAL CORPORATION
Austin, TX .... Administrative Law; Civil Trial Practice; Insurance Defense

DELGADO, ACOSTA, BRADEN & JONES, P.C.
El Paso, TX .... General Practice

D'ELIA & CAVANAUGH
Orleans, MA .... Trust and Estates, Wills and Probate

DELISIO MORAN GERAGHTY & ZOBEL, P.C.
Anchorage, AK .... Business Law; Civil Trial Practice; Insurance Defense

DELLECKER, WILSON & KING, P.A.
Orlando, FL .... Medical Malpractice; Personal Injury; Product Liability Law

DEL SOLE & DEL SOLE, L.L.P.
New Haven, CT .... Civil Trial Practice

DELSTON, ROSS S.
Washington, DC .... Banking Law

DEL TORO & SANTANA
San Juan, PR .... Civil Trial Practice

DEMA, JOHN K., P.C., LAW OFFICES OF
Christiansted, St. Croix, VI ..... Environmental Law

DEMAKIS LAW OFFICES, P.C.
Lynn, MA .... Civil Trial Practice; Commercial Law; Personal Injury; Real Estate Law

DEMARIA ELLIS & BAUCH L.L.C.
Newark, NJ .... Labor and Employment Law

DEMARTINI, D'AQUILA & VOLK, A PROFESSIONAL LAW CORPORATION
Kenner, LA .... Commercial Litigation

DE MARTINO FINKELSTEIN ROSEN & VIRGA
Washington, DC .... Business Law; Securities Law

DEMENT AND MARQUARDT, P.L.C.
Kalamazoo, MI .... Trust and Estates, Wills and Probate

DEMENT, VANDIVORT AND DEMENT
Sikeston, MO .... Civil Trial Practice

DEMERSSEMAN JENSEN, L.L.P.
Rapid City, SD .... General Practice

DEMET & DEMET, S.C.
Milwaukee, WI .... Corporate Law

DEMETRIOU, DEL GUERCIO, SPRINGER & MOYER, LLP
Los Angeles, CA .... Administrative Law; Business Law; Civil Trial Practice; Commercial Law; Eminent Domain; Environmental Law; Health Care Law; Natural Resources Law; Real Estate Law; Tax Law; Trust and Estates, Wills and Probate

DEMING, PARKER, HOFFMAN, GREEN & CAMPBELL, P.C.
Norcross, GA .... Civil Trial Practice; Corporate Law; Criminal Trial Practice; Personal Injury; Workers Compensation

DEMPSEY & SASSO
Orlando, FL .... Antitrust Law; Civil Trial Practice; Construction Law; Criminal Trial Practice; Labor and Employment Law

DENHAM & KING, PLLC
Ocean Springs, MS .... Personal Injury

DENIUS, FRANKLIN W.
Austin, TX .... Civil Trial Practice

DENLINGER, ROSENTHAL & GREENBERG, A LEGAL PROFESSIONAL ASSOCIATION
Cincinnati, OH .... Labor and Employment Law

DENMEAD & MALONEY
Columbus, OH .... Civil Trial Practice; General Practice; Personal Injury

DENNIN, TIMOTHY J., P.C.
New York, NY .... Securities Law

DENNIS, HARRY D. JR.
Pompano Beach, FL .... Civil Trial Practice; Family Law

DENNIS, CORRY & PORTER, L.L.P.
Atlanta, GA .... Aviation Law; Civil Trial Practice; General Practice; Insurance Defense; Personal Injury; Product Liability Law; Transportation Law

DENTON & CARY
Bolivar, TN .... General Practice

DENTON & KEULER
Paducah, KY .... Admiralty/Maritime Law; Banking Law; Commercial Litigation; General Practice; Public Utilities Law

DENTON & LOPEZ
Las Vegas, NV .... Civil Trial Practice; General Practice; Trust and Estates, Wills and Probate

DE ORCHIS, WALKER & CORSA, LLP
New York, NY .... Admiralty/Maritime Law; Civil Trial Practice; Commercial Law; Insurance Defense; Product Liability Law; Transportation Law

DEPEW AND GILLEN, L.L.C.
Wichita, KS .... Aviation Law; Business Law; Civil Trial Practice; Corporate Law; Environmental Law; General Practice; Insurance Defense; Natural Resources Law; Personal Injury; Trust and Estates, Wills and Probate

DERBES LAW FIRM, THE, L.L.C.
Metairie, LA .... Commercial Litigation; Tax Law

DERICKSON, DAVID G., P.C.
Phoenix, AZ .... Criminal Trial Practice; Health Care Law

DERR, ALLEN
Boise, ID .... Personal Injury

DERR, DAILEY J., P.A.
Durham, NC .... Construction Law

DESANTO, JAMES J., A PROFESSIONAL CORPORATION
Libertyville, IL .... Commercial Litigation; Labor and Employment Law; Personal Injury

DESHAZO, GARY F. & ASSOCIATES
Austin, TX .... Civil Trial Practice; Legal Malpractice

DESJARDINS DUCHARME STEIN MONAST
Montreal, QU, Canada .... General Practice
Quebec, QU, Canada .... General Practice

DESSEN, MOSES & SHEINOFF
Philadelphia, PA .... Civil Trial Practice

DETISCH & CHRISTENSEN
San Diego, CA .... Civil Trial Practice; General Practice

DEUSCHLE, BRIAN C., CHARTERED
Fort Lauderdale, FL .... Commercial Law; Commercial Litigation

DEUTCH & FALK, A PROFESSIONAL CORPORATION
Woodbridge, NJ .... Construction Law; Health Care Law; Securities Law

DEUTSCH & BLUMBERG, P.A.
Miami, FL .... Civil Trial Practice; Medical Malpractice; Personal Injury; Product Liability Law

DEUTSCH, DAVID M., CO., L.P.A.
Dayton, OH .... Medical Malpractice; Personal Injury; Product Liability Law

DEUTSCH WILLIAMS BROOKS DERENSIS HOLLAND & DRACHMAN, P.C.
Boston, MA .... Civil Trial Practice
Nantucket, MA .... Civil Trial Practice

DEVEAU, COLTON & MARQUIS
Atlanta, GA .... Patent, Trademark, Copyright and Unfair Competition

DEVEREUX, MURPHY, STRILER, BRICKEY & SHER, L.L.C.
St. Louis, MO .... Commercial Litigation; Real Estate Law

DE VINE & KOHN, PLLC
Southfield, MI .... Business Law; Construction Law; Tax Law; Trust and Estates, Wills and Probate

DEVINE, MILLIMET & BRANCH, PROFESSIONAL ASSOCIATION
Manchester, NH .... General Practice

DEVLIN, JOHN GERARD, & ASSOCIATES, P.C.
Philadelphia, PA .... Civil Trial Practice; Environmental Law; Insurance Defense; Product Liability Law; Transportation Law

DEVORSETZ STINZIANO GILBERTI HEINTZ & SMITH, P.C.
Syracuse, NY .... Environmental Law; Land Use Law

DE VRIES, PRICE & DAVENPORT, A PROFESSIONAL CORPORATION
Mason City, IA .... Insurance Defense

DEWEY BALLANTINE LLP
Washington, DC .... General Practice
New York, NY .... General Practice; Municipal Bond/Public Authority Financing

DEWITT ROSS & STEVENS S.C.
Madison, WI .... General Practice; Patent, Trademark, Copyright and Unfair Competition

DEWOSKIN, ALAN E., P.C.
St. Louis, MO .... Commercial Litigation; Family Law

DEYOE HEISSENBUTTEL, L.L.C.
Wayne, NJ .... Appellate Practice; Civil Trial Practice; Environmental Law; Family Law; General Practice; Insurance Defense; Legal Malpractice; Personal Injury; Product Liability Law; Professional Liability

DIAMOND AND DIAMOND, P.A.
Fort Myers, FL .... Workers Compensation

DIAMOND RASH GORDON & JACKSON, P.C.
El Paso, TX .... Civil Trial Practice; Municipal Bond/Public Authority Financing

DIAMOND & SCHARNBERGER
Woodland Hills, CA .... Business Law; Personal Injury; Real Estate Law

DICERBO & PALUMBO
Olean, NY .... General Practice

DICKENSON, MURDOCH, REX AND SLOAN, CHARTERED
Boca Raton, FL .... Real Estate Law; Trust and Estates, Wills and Probate

DICKERSON, DICKERSON, CONSUL & POCKER
Las Vegas, NV .... Civil Trial Practice; Commercial Litigation; Family Law; Personal Injury

DICK AND HARRIS
Chicago, IL .... Intellectual Property Law; Patent, Trademark, Copyright and Unfair Competition

DICKIE, MCCAMEY & CHILCOTE, A PROFESSIONAL CORPORATION
Pittsburgh, PA .... General Practice

DICKINSON & GIBBONS, P.A.
Sarasota, FL .... Civil Trial Practice; General Practice; Insurance Defense; Medical Malpractice; Real Estate Law; Trust and Estates, Wills and Probate

DICKINSON, MACKAMAN, TYLER & HAGEN, P.C.
Des Moines, IA .... Banking Law; Labor and Employment Law; Tax Law; Trust and Estates, Wills and Probate

DICKINSON WRIGHT PLLC
Washington, DC .... General Practice; Patent, Trademark, Copyright and Unfair Competition
Bloomfield Hills, MI .... General Practice
Detroit, MI .... Civil Trial Practice; Environmental Law; General Practice; Labor and Employment Law; Municipal Bond/Public Authority Financing
Grand Rapids, MI .... General Practice
Lansing, MI .... General Practice

DICKSTEIN SHAPIRO MORIN & OSHINSKY LLP
Washington, DC .... General Practice

DIDONATO & WINTERHALTER, P.C.
Philadelphia, PA .... Bankruptcy Law; Commercial Law; Commercial Litigation; Creditors Rights; Municipal and Zoning Law

DIEPENBROCK & COSTA
Sacramento, CA .... Environmental Law; Insurance Defense

DIETRICH, EDWARD H.
Westport, CT .... Trust and Estates, Wills and Probate

DIETRICH, THOMAS W.
Phoenix, AZ .... Trust and Estates, Wills and Probate

DIETRICH, GLASRUD, MALLEK & AUNE
Fresno, CA .... Commercial Litigation; Corporate Law; Pension and Profit Sharing; Real Estate Law; Tax Law; Trust and Estates, Wills and Probate

DIKE, BRONSTEIN, ROBERTS & CUSHMAN, LLP
Boston, MA .... Patent, Trademark, Copyright and Unfair Competition; Trademark, Copyright and Unfair Competition

DIKMAN AND DIKMAN
Lake Success, NY .... Criminal Trial Practice; Family Law; Personal Injury; Real Estate Law; Trust and Estates, Wills and Probate

DILL, MATTHEW T.
Wilmington, NC .... Trust and Estates, Wills and Probate

DILLARD & GALLOWAY, LLC
Atlanta, GA .... Family Law; Municipal and Zoning Law

DILLARD AND KATONA
Tappahannock, VA .... General Practice

DILLINGHAM & MURPHY, LLP
San Francisco, CA .... Insurance Defense; Intellectual Property Law

DILLON MCCANDLESS KING COULTER & GRAHAM L.L.P.
Butler, PA .... General Practice

DILL & SHOWLER
Redlands, CA .... General Practice

DILWORTH & BARRESE
Uniondale, NY .... Patent, Trademark, Copyright and Unfair Competition

DILWORTH PAXSON LLP
Philadelphia, PA .... General Practice

DIMASCIO, JOHN P. THE LAW OFFICES OF
Garden City, NY .... Family Law

DIMITRIOU, EMMANUEL H., P.C.
Pottsville, PA .... Criminal Trial Practice
Reading, PA .... Criminal Trial Practice

DIMMICH, GULDIN, DINKELACKER & BRIENZA, P.C.
Orefield, PA .... Civil Trial Practice

DIMOCK STRATTON CLARIZIO
Toronto, ON, Canada .... Computer Law; Patent, Trademark, Copyright and Unfair Competition; Trademark, Copyright and Unfair Competition

DIMURO, GINSBERG & MOOK, P.C.
Alexandria, VA .... Commercial Litigation; General Practice

DINES, GROSS & ESQUIVEL, P.C.
Albuquerque, NM .... Communications Law; Health Care Law; Insurance Defense; Labor and Employment Law; Professional Liability

DINGEMAN, DANCER & CHRISTOPHERSON, P.L.C.
Traverse City, MI .... Business Law; Civil Trial Practice; Commercial Litigation; Corporate Law; Environmental Law; Health Care Law; Personal Injury; Real Estate Law; Trust and Estates, Wills and Probate

DINN, HOCHMAN AND POTTER, LLC
Cleveland, OH .... Labor and Employment Law

DINSE, KNAPP & MCANDREW, P.C.
Burlington, VT .... Civil Trial Practice; General Practice; Health Care Law; Insurance Defense; Labor and Employment Law

DIONNE & GASS
Boston, MA .... Business Law; Real Estate Law

DIORIO & SERENI, LLP
Media, PA .... Civil Trial Practice; Family Law; General Practice; Personal Injury

DI RENZO AND BOMIER, LLC
Neenah, WI .... Business Law; General Practice; Insurance Defense

DIRMANN, JAMES R., P.A.
Sarasota, FL .... Criminal Trial Practice

DIVER, GRACH, QUADE & MASINI
Waukegan, IL .... Banking Law; Civil Trial Practice; Family Law; Municipal and Zoning Law; Real Estate Law; Trust and Estates, Wills and Probate

DJORDJEVIC, MICHAEL M., CO. LPA
Akron, OH ....Medical Malpractice; Professional Liability

DOBBERTEEN & LUNA
Los Angeles, CA ....Bankruptcy Law

DOBSON & BROWN, P.A.
St. Augustine, FL....................Commercial Litigation; Environmental Law

DODD AND DENNIS, P.C.
Valdosta, GA ....Civil Trial Practice; Criminal Trial Practice; Family Law; Personal Injury

DODDS, KIDD, RYAN & MOORE
Little Rock, AR ....Personal Injury

DODGE, DAVID A., P.C.
Grand Rapids, MI ....Criminal Trial Practice

DODSON AND ASSOCIATES, P.C.
Denver, CO ....Commercial Litigation

DOERING, STEVEN B.
Garnett, KS..............................General Practice

DOERNER, SAUNDERS, DANIEL & ANDERSON, L.L.P.
Tulsa, OK.................................General Practice; Labor and Employment Law; Natural Resources Law; Securities Law

DOFFERMYRE, SHIELDS, CANFIELD, KNOWLES & DEVINE
Atlanta, GA ....Civil Trial Practice; Medical Malpractice; Personal Injury; Product Liability Law

DOHERTY & SHERIDAN, L.L.P.
Fairfax, VA ....Insurance Defense; Trust and Estates, Wills and Probate

DOHERTY & VENEZIA, A PROFESSIONAL CORPORATION
Phoenix, AZ ....Insurance Defense; Workers Compensation

DOHERTY, WALLACE, PILLSBURY AND MURPHY, P.C.
Springfield, MA........................General Practice; Patent, Trademark, Copyright and Unfair Competition

DOK, LEVY & PERRIN
San Jose, CA ....Family Law

DOLAN AND DOLAN, P.A. A PROFESSIONAL CORPORATION
Newton, NJ ....General Practice

DOLE, COALWELL, CLARK, MOUNTAINSPRING & MORNARICH, P.C.
Roseburg, OR ....Civil Trial Practice; General Practice

DOLIN, NORMAN M. LAW OFFICES OF
Beverly Hills, CA.....................Family Law

DOLIN & ASSOCIATES, P.C.
Rochester, NY...........................Civil Trial Practice; Labor and Employment Law

DOLLINGER, GONSKI & GROSSMAN
Carle Place, NY ....Civil Trial Practice; Commercial Law; General Practice; Real Estate Law

DOMENGEAUX WRIGHT & ROY, A PROFESSIONAL LAW CORPORATION
Lafayette, LA ....Admiralty/Maritime Law; Civil Trial Practice; Personal Injury; Product Liability Law

DOMESTICO & BARRY
Framingham, MA ....Civil Trial Practice; Commercial Litigation; Labor and Employment Law

DOMINA LAW PC
Omaha, NE ....Civil Trial Practice; Criminal Trial Practice; Personal Injury

DOMINICK, FLETCHER, YEILDING, WOOD & LLOYD, P.A.
Birmingham, AL ....Civil Trial Practice; General Practice; Real Estate Law; Tax Law

DONAHOE, PECARO & VOLLENDER, P.A.
Fort Lauderdale, FL.................Civil Trial Practice; Insurance Defense; Personal Injury

DONAHOO, BALL & MCMENAMY, P.A.
Jacksonville, FL ....Real Estate Law; Tax Law; Trust and Estates, Wills and Probate

DONAHUE & DONAHUE, ATTORNEYS, P.C.
Lowell, MA ....Business Law; General Practice; Insurance Defense; Trust and Estates, Wills and Probate

DONAHUE MESEREAU & LEIDS L.L.P.
Los Angeles, CA.......................Business Law; Corporate Law; Securities Law

DONAHUE, WOOD, LOVING & VOGEL
Sacramento, CA ....Civil Trial Practice; Insurance Defense

DONALD, RANDALL, DONALD & TIPTON
Tuscaloosa, AL ....General Practice; Insurance Defense

DONALDSON, BELL & PICKETT, P.C.
Albany, GA...............................Criminal Trial Practice; General Practice

DONAU & BOLT
Tucson, AZ ....Criminal Trial Practice; Family Law

DONENFELD, JACK A., A LEGAL PROF. ASSN., LAW OFFICES OF
Cincinnati, OH ....Securities Law

DONLEVY-ROSEN & ROSEN, PROFESSIONAL ASSOCIATION
Miami, FL ....Trust and Estates, Wills and Probate

DONNELLY, DANIEL
Garrison, NY ....Civil Trial Practice

DONOHUE, JAMES F.
White Plains, NY ....Administrative Law; Criminal Trial Practice; Personal Injury

DONOHUE, MARY SUE
Boca Raton, FL ....Trust and Estates, Wills and Probate

DONOHUE AND DONOHUE
Philadelphia, PA ....Administrative Law; Corporate Law; Criminal Trial Practice; International Trade Law

DONOHUE, SABO, VARLEY & ARMSTRONG, P.C.
Albany, NY...............................Civil Trial Practice; Insurance Defense

DONOVAN, MARTIN K.
Providence, RI..........................Civil Trial Practice; General Practice; Insurance Defense; Personal Injury

DONOVAN PARRY CARBIN MCDERMOTT & RADZIK
New York, NY...........................Insurance Defense

DONOVAN, PAUL F., PROFESSIONAL CORPORATION
Lancaster, NH...........................General Practice

DONOVAN AND ROBERTS, P.C.
Wheaton, IL ....Civil Trial Practice; Commercial Litigation; General Practice; Personal Injury

DORAMUS, TRAUGER & NEY
Nashville, TN ....Business Law; Civil Trial Practice

DORAN • BLACKMOND LLP
South Bend, IN ....Bankruptcy Law; Civil Trial Practice; Commercial Law; Environmental Law; Insurance Defense; Personal Injury; Product Liability Law

DORAN & NOWALIS
Wilkes-Barre, PA ....Bankruptcy Law

DORF & DORF, A PROFESSIONAL CORPORATION
Rahway, NJ...............................Labor and Employment Law

DORITY & MANNING, P.A.
Greenville, SC...........................Patent, Trademark, Copyright and Unfair Competition

DORNAN, DONALD C. JR.
Biloxi, MS.................................Civil Trial Practice

DORR, CARSON, SLOAN & BIRNEY, P.C.
Denver, CO ....Patent, Trademark, Copyright and Unfair Competition; Trademark, Copyright and Unfair Competition

DORSEY & WHITNEY LLP
Minneapolis, MN.....................General Practice

DORWART, FREDERIC
Tulsa, OK..................................Banking Law; Natural Resources Law; Oil and Gas Law

DOSTART CLAPP & COVENEY, LLP
San Diego, CA ....Business Law

DOTY & SHAPIRO, P.C.
Boulder, CO ....Business Law; Trust and Estates, Wills and Probate

DOUGHERTY, HILDRE, DUDEK & HAKLAR
San Diego, CA ....Admiralty/Maritime Law; Personal Injury; Product Liability Law

DOUGLAS, ALEXA, KOEPPEN & HURLEY
Valparaiso, IN..........................General Practice

DOUGLAS, DENHAM, ROGERS & HOOD
Portland, ME ....General Practice

DOUGLAS, ROBINSON, LEONARD & GARVEY, P.C.
Concord, NH ....Civil Trial Practice; Family Law; Labor and Employment Law; Personal Injury; Trust and Estates, Wills and Probate

DOVER & DIXON, P.A.
Little Rock, AR ....General Practice

DOW, COGBURN & FRIEDMAN, P.C.
Houston, TX ....Real Estate Law

DOW, EINHAUS & MATTISON, P.A.
Owatonna, MN ....General Practice

DOW, LOHNES & ALBERTSON, PLLC
Washington, DC ....Antitrust Law; Communications Law; General Practice; Tax Law

DOWD & DOWD, LTD.
Chicago, IL ....Appellate Practice; Insurance Defense; Transportation Law

DOWLER, ROBERT W.
Fairfax, VA ....Civil Trial Practice

DOWLING, AARON & KEELER, INCORPORATED
Fresno, CA ....Bankruptcy Law; Business Law; Civil Trial Practice; Commercial Law; Environmental Law; General Practice; Health Care Law; Insurance Defense; Municipal Bond/Public Authority Financing; Professional Liability; Real Estate Law; Securities Law; Sports and Entertainment Law; Tax Law; Trademark, Copyright and Unfair Competition; Trust and Estates, Wills and Probate

DOWNEY, BRAND, SEYMOUR & ROHWER LLP
Sacramento, CA ....Environmental Law; General Practice; Natural Resources Law

DOWNEY & CLEVELAND, LLP
Marietta, GA ....Civil Trial Practice; General Practice; Insurance Defense; Medical Malpractice; Personal Injury

DOWNEY, WILLIAM J., P.C.
Phoenix, AZ ....Civil Trial Practice; Insurance Defense; Personal Injury

DOYLE & HARRIS, A PROFESSIONAL CORPORATION
Tulsa, OK ....Antitrust Law; Civil Trial Practice; Securities Law

DOYLE, LEWIS & WARNER
Toledo, OH ....Appellate Practice; Business Law; Civil Trial Practice; Corporate Law; General Practice; Insurance Defense; Real Estate Law; Tax Law; Transportation Law; Trust and Estates, Wills and Probate

DOYLE & NELSON
Augusta, ME ....Administrative Law

DOYLE & WINTHROP, P.C.
Phoenix, AZ ....Construction Law; Health Care Law; Insurance Defense; Medical Malpractice; Personal Injury

DOZIER, MILLER, POLLARD & MURPHY
Charlotte, NC ....Bankruptcy Law; Business Law; Civil Trial Practice; Criminal Trial Practice; Family Law; Immigration and Naturalization; Personal Injury; Trust and Estates, Wills and Probate

DRAGE, DE BEAUBIEN, KNIGHT, SIMMONS, MANTZARIS & NEAL
Orlando, FL ....Civil Trial Practice

DRAKE & DRAKE
Cullman, AL ....Personal Injury; Workers Compensation

DRAKE, SOMMERS, LOEB, TARSHIS & CATANIA, PLLC
Newburgh, NY ....General Practice

DRANOFF & GOLDSCHMIDT, L.L.P.
Pearl River, NY ....Family Law

DRATH, CLIFFORD, MURPHY, WENNERHOLM & HAGEN, A PROFESSIONAL CORPORATION
San Francisco, CA ....Civil Trial Practice; Insurance Defense

DRAUGELIS & ASHTON, L.L.P.
Plymouth, MI ....Business Law; Civil Trial Practice; General Practice; Insurance Defense; Personal Injury; Trust and Estates, Wills and Probate

DREHER LANGER & TOMKIES L.L.P.
Mandeville, LA ....Banking Law
Columbus, OH ....Banking Law

DREILING, BIEKER & HOFFMAN, LLP
Hays, KS ....General Practice

DRENDEL TATNALL, A PROFESSIONAL CORPORATION
Batavia, IL ....General Practice

DRENNER & STUART, L.L.P.
Austin, TX ....Real Estate Law

DRESNICK & ELLSWORTH, P.A.
Miami, FL ....Health Care Law

DRESSER, DRESSER, GILBERT & HAAS, P.C.
Sturgis, MI ....General Practice

DRESSLER, ROBERT A.
Fort Lauderdale, FL ....Trust and Estates, Wills and Probate

DREW, COOPER & ANDING
Grand Rapids, MI ....Civil Rights; Civil Trial Practice; Personal Injury

DREYER, BABICH, BUCCOLA & CALLAHAM, LLP
Sacramento, CA ....Personal Injury

DRIGGERS, SCHULTZ & HERBST, A PROFESSIONAL CORPORATION
Troy, MI ....Business Law

DRINKA, LEVINE & MASSON, S.C.
Milwaukee, WI ....Corporate Law; Family Law; Real Estate Law; Tax Law; Trust and Estates, Wills and Probate

DRINKER BIDDLE & REATH LLP
Washington, DC ....General Practice
Philadelphia, PA ....General Practice

DRINKER BIDDLE & SHANLEY LLP
Florham Park, NJ ....Banking Law; Bankruptcy Law; Civil Trial Practice; Corporate Law; Environmental Law; General Practice; Health Care Law; Labor and Employment Law; Real Estate Law; Tax Law

DRISCOLL, TALARICO, FRIZZELL, OLIVO & DRISCOLL
Danbury, CT ....Civil Trial Practice; Commercial Law; Corporate Law; Real Estate Law; Trust and Estates, Wills and Probate

DROBNY LAW OFFICES
Sacramento, CA ....Business Law; Tax Law; Trust and Estates, Wills and Probate

DROLET, FREEMAN, COTTON & NORRIS, P.C.
Bloomfield Hills, MI ....Business Law; Construction Law; Real Estate Law; Trust and Estates, Wills and Probate

DRUBNER, HARTLEY, O'CONNOR & MENGACCI
Waterbury, CT ....Commercial Litigation; Health Care Law

DRUMMOND & DRUMMOND, LLP
Portland, ME ....General Practice

DRUMMOND & DUCKWORTH
Newport Beach, CA ....Intellectual Property Law; Patent, Trademark, Copyright and Unfair Competition

DRUMM & THORNTON
Sikeston, MO ....Civil Trial Practice; General Practice; Trust and Estates, Wills and Probate

DUANE, W. FORD
Orlando, FL ....Criminal Trial Practice

DUANE, MORRIS & HECKSCHER LLP
San Francisco, CA ....General Practice
Wilmington, DE ....General Practice
Washington, DC ....General Practice
Miami, FL ....General Practice
Palm Beach, FL ....General Practice
Boston, MA ....General Practice
Cherry Hill, NJ ....General Practice
Newark, NJ ....General Practice
New York, NY ....General Practice
Allentown, PA ....General Practice
Harrisburg, PA ....General Practice
Philadelphia, PA ....General Practice
Wayne, PA ....General Practice

DUBÉ & GOODGAL, P.C.
Baltimore, MD ....Labor and Employment Law

DUBE, PATRICIA KAY, P.C.
Houston, TX ....Civil Trial Practice; Construction Law; Health Care Law; Insurance Defense; Product Liability Law

DUBOIS BILLIG LOUGHLIN CONATY & WEISMAN
Mineola, NY ....Medical Malpractice

DUCKOR SPRADLING & METZGER, A LAW CORPORATION
San Diego, CA ....Civil Trial Practice; Commercial Law; Securities Law

DUDLEY, DUDLEY & WINDLE
El Paso, TX ....Insurance Defense; Personal Injury

DUDLEY, GALUMBECK & NECESSARY
Tazewell, VA ....Civil Trial Practice; Criminal Trial Practice; Personal Injury

DUÉ, CABALLERO, PRICE & GUIDRY, (A PROFESSIONAL ASSOCIATION)
Baton Rouge, LA ....Admiralty/Maritime Law; Personal Injury

DUFF, DUBBERLY, TURNER, WHITE & BOYKIN, L.L.C.
Columbia, SC .... Labor and Employment Law

DUFFORD & BROWN, P.C.
Denver, CO .... Antitrust Law; Bankruptcy Law; Business Law; Commercial Law; Energy Law; Environmental Law; General Practice; Labor and Employment Law; Natural Resources Law; Real Estate Law; Trademark, Copyright and Unfair Competition

DUFFY, VIRGINIA M.
Jenkintown, PA .... Real Estate Law

DUFFY & GREEN
West Chester, PA .... Criminal Trial Practice; General Practice; Personal Injury

DUGAN & JAKUBOWSKI, P.A.
Timonium, MD .... Medical Malpractice; Product Liability Law

DUKE GERSTEL SHEARER, LLP
San Diego, CA .... Appellate Practice; Business Law; Construction Law; Elder Law; Personal Injury; Product Liability Law; Professional Liability; Real Estate Law; Securities Law

DUKES, DUKES, KEATING AND FANECA, P.A.
Gulfport, MS .... Administrative Law; Admiralty/Maritime Law; Bankruptcy Law; Business Law; Civil Trial Practice; Commercial Law; Commercial Litigation; Construction Law; Corporate Law; Environmental Law; General Practice; Insurance Defense; Labor and Employment Law; Land Use Law; Municipal and Zoning Law; Personal Injury; Product Liability Law; Real Estate Law; Transportation Law; Workers Compensation

DULANY & LEAHY, LLP
Westminster, MD .... General Practice; Trust and Estates, Wills and Probate

DUMOUCHEL, DAVID F., P.C.
Detroit, MI .... Appellate Practice; Criminal Trial Practice; Professional Liability

DUNAWAY & CROSS, A PROFESSIONAL CORPORATION
Washington, DC .... Administrative Law; Antitrust Law

DUNCAN, GREEN, BROWN, LANGENESS & ECKLEY, A PROFESSIONAL CORPORATION
Des Moines, IA .... General Practice

DUNCAN, JOHN A., A PROFESSIONAL CORPORATION
Orange, CA .... Trust and Estates, Wills and Probate

DUNCAN & RAINWATER, TRIAL LAWYERS, A PROF. ASSN.
Little Rock, AR .... Civil Trial Practice; Medical Malpractice; Personal Injury; Product Liability Law

DUNCAN, THOMASSON, LEONARD & SHATTUCK
La Grange, GA .... General Practice

DUNHAM, BOMAN & LESKERA
Belleville, IL .... Civil Trial Practice; General Practice; Insurance Defense; Trust and Estates, Wills and Probate
Collinsville, IL .... Civil Trial Practice; Criminal Trial Practice; General Practice; Insurance Defense; Trust and Estates, Wills and Probate

DUNLAP & BURDICK, A PROFESSIONAL LAW CORPORATION
Santa Cruz, CA .... Personal Injury; Product Liability Law

DUNLAP, CODDING & ROGERS, P.C.
Oklahoma City, OK .... Patent, Trademark, Copyright and Unfair Competition

DUNLAP & SEEGER, P.A.
Rochester, MN .... General Practice

DUNN, ABPLANALP & MAURIELLO, P.C.
Vail, CO .... Civil Trial Practice; General Practice; Real Estate Law

DUNN, FRANKLIN & MURPHY
Lexington, KY .... Land Use Law; Municipal and Zoning Law

DUNN, JAMES F., & ASSOCIATES, P.A.
St. Paul, MN .... Civil Trial Practice

DUNN, KACAL, ADAMS, PAPPAS & LAW, A PROFESSIONAL CORPORATION
Houston, TX .... Civil Trial Practice; Medical Malpractice

DUNN, MACDONALD & COLEMAN, P.C.
Knoxville, TN .... General Practice; Insurance Defense

DUNN, NUTTER, MORGAN & SHAW
Texarkana, AR .... Civil Trial Practice; Commercial Litigation; General Practice; Medical Malpractice; Natural Resources Law; Product Liability Law

DUNN, ROGASKI, PREOVOLOS & WEBER
Vallejo, CA .... General Practice; Insurance Defense

DUNN, STANCZAK & WILLARD
Bloomington, IL .... Commercial Litigation; Education Law; General Practice

DUNN & WEATHERED, P.C.
Corpus Christi, TX .... Appellate Practice; Civil Trial Practice; Insurance Defense

DUNNAM & DUNNAM, L.L.P.
Waco, TX .... Civil Trial Practice; Criminal Trial Practice; Family Law; General Practice; Real Estate Law

DUNTON, SIMMONS & DUNTON, L.L.P
White Stone, VA .... Civil Trial Practice; General Practice

DUNWODY WHITE & LANDON, P.A.
Miami, FL .... Commercial Litigation; Trust and Estates, Wills and Probate

DUPLASS, ZWAIN & BOURGEOIS, A PROFESSIONAL LAW CORPORATION
Metairie, LA .... Civil Trial Practice

DUPONT AND RADLAUER, L.L.P.
New London, CT .... Business Law; Civil Trial Practice; Trust and Estates, Wills and Probate

DURANDO, BIRDWELL & JANKE, LLP
Tucson, AZ .... Intellectual Property Law

DURBIN, LARIMORE & BIALICK, P.C.
Oklahoma City, OK .... Commercial Law; Insurance Defense; Real Estate Law

DURHAM, EDWARD D.
Montrose, CO .... Civil Trial Practice; Family Law; General Practice

DURHAM JONES & PINEGAR, A PROFESSIONAL CORPORATION
Salt Lake City, UT .... Business Law; Civil Trial Practice; Real Estate Law; Securities Law; Tax Law

DURKIN & BOGGIA
Ridgefield Park, NJ .... Civil Trial Practice

DURKIN, THOMAS ANTHONY, P.C.
Chicago, IL .... Criminal Trial Practice

DUSHOFF & MCCALL, A PROFESSIONAL CORPORATION
Phoenix, AZ .... Civil Trial Practice; Commercial Litigation; Eminent Domain; Land Use Law; Municipal and Zoning Law; Real Estate Law

DUTEL, WILLIAM J., LAW OFFICES OF
Covington, LA .... Commercial Law; Commercial Litigation; Corporate Law; Real Estate Law; Trust and Estates, Wills and Probate

DUTTON, BRAUN, STAACK & HELLMAN, P.L.C.
Waterloo, IA .... General Practice

DUVALL & DUVALL, L.L.P.
Salisbury, MD .... Civil Trial Practice; Criminal Trial Practice; General Practice; Health Care Law

DUVIN, CAHN & HUTTON, A LEGAL PROFESSIONAL ASSOCIATION
Cleveland, OH .... Appellate Practice; Civil Trial Practice; Employment Benefits Law; Labor and Employment Law; Workers Compensation

DWORKEN & BERNSTEIN CO., L.P.A., A PROFESSIONAL CORPORATION
Painesville, OH .... Corporate Law; Real Estate Law

DWORKIN, MICHAEL L. AND ASSOCIATES
San Mateo, CA .... Aviation Law; Transportation Law

DWORSKY, TAMARA L.
Scottsdale, AZ .... Trust and Estates, Wills and Probate

DWYER & BLACK, P.C.
Olean, NY .... Personal Injury

DWYER, DALY, BROTZEN & BRUNO, LLP
Los Angeles, CA .... Appellate Practice; Aviation Law; Civil Trial Practice

DWYER, HUDDLESON & RAY, P.C.
Fort Collins, CO .... General Practice

DWYER, SMITH, GARDNER, LAZER, POHREN, ROGERS & FORREST
Omaha, NE .... Bankruptcy Law; Business Law; Civil Trial Practice; Commercial Law; Computer Law; Corporate Law; General Practice; Health Care Law; Labor and Employment Law; Personal Injury; Tax Law; Trust and Estates, Wills and Probate

DWYER & WHITE
Atlanta, GA .... Medical Malpractice; Personal Injury

DYE, TUCKER, EVERITT, LONG & BREWTON, A PROFESSIONAL ASSOCIATION
Augusta, GA .... Bankruptcy Law; Business Law; Civil Trial Practice; General Practice; Insurance Defense; Medical Malpractice; Real Estate Law

DYER, GAROFALO, MANN & SCHULTZ, A LEGAL PROFESSIONAL ASSOCIATION
Dayton, OH .... Personal Injury

DYER & WHITE LLP
Menlo Park, CA .... Civil Trial Practice; Labor and Employment Law; Personal Injury; Product Liability Law

DYKAS, FRANK J., P.A.
Boise, ID .... Patent, Trademark, Copyright and Unfair Competition

DYKEMA GOSSETT PLLC
Washington, DC .... General Practice
Chicago, IL .... General Practice
Ann Arbor, MI .... General Practice
Bloomfield Hills, MI .... General Practice
Detroit, MI .... Antitrust Law; Civil Trial Practice; Environmental Law; General Practice; Health Care Law; International Business Law; Labor and Employment Law; Municipal Bond/Public Authority Financing; Patent, Trademark, Copyright and Unfair Competition; Personal Injury; Real Estate Law; Tax Law
Grand Rapids, MI .... General Practice
Lansing, MI .... General Practice

DYTRYCH, TERRENCE F., P.A., THE LAW OFFICE OF
West Palm Beach, FL .... Commercial Litigation; Personal Injury

EAGAN, MICHAEL Q.
San Francisco, CA .... Commercial Litigation

EAGLETON, EAGLETON AND HARRISON, INC.
Tulsa, OK .... Business Law; Employment Benefits Law; Family Law; Pension and Profit Sharing; Tax Law; Trust and Estates, Wills and Probate

EARDLEY LAW OFFICES, P.C.
Cannonsburg, MI .... Personal Injury

EARL, BLANK, KAVANAUGH & STOTTS, PROFESSIONAL ASSOCIATION
Miami, FL .... Environmental Law; Natural Resources Law
Sarasota, FL .... Environmental Law; Natural Resources Law

EARL, CURLEY & LAGARDE, P.C.
Phoenix, AZ .... Land Use Law; Municipal and Zoning Law

EARLE & PATCHEN, PROFESSIONAL ASSOCIATION
Miami, FL .... Eminent Domain

EARLEY, JACK M. LAW OFFICE OF, THE
Costa Mesa, CA .... Criminal Trial Practice

EARLY, LENNON, PETERS & CROCKER, P.C.
Kalamazoo, MI .... Business Law; Corporate Law; General Practice; Insurance Defense; Real Estate Law; Tax Law; Trust and Estates, Wills and Probate; Workers Compensation

EARLY, LUDWICK & SWEENEY, L.L.C.
New Haven, CT .... Product Liability Law; Toxic Torts

EARLY, S. ALLEN, & ASSOCIATES
Detroit, MI .... Criminal Trial Practice; Labor and Employment Law

EARP COHN P.C.
Westmont, NJ .... Business Law; Civil Trial Practice; Real Estate Law

EASTLAND, HENRY B., P.C.
Colorado Springs, CO .... Trust and Estates, Wills and Probate

EASTMAN & SMITH LTD.
Toledo, OH .... Banking Law; Business Law; Civil Trial Practice; Environmental Law; General Practice; Health Care Law; Insurance Defense; Labor and Employment Law; Real Estate Law; Tax Law; Trust and Estates, Wills and Probate; Workers Compensation

EASTON, W. DOUGLAS LAW OFFICES OF
Costa Mesa, CA .... Medical Malpractice; Personal Injury

EASTON & SCHIFF
Los Angeles, CA .... Corporate Law; Real Estate Law; Trust and Estates, Wills and Probate

EATON, MARTINEZ & HART, P.C.
Albuquerque, NM .... Civil Trial Practice; Medical Malpractice; Personal Injury; Product Liability Law

EATON, PEABODY, BRADFORD & VEAGUE, P.A.
Bangor, ME .... Administrative Law; Antitrust Law; Banking Law; Business Law; Civil Trial Practice; Environmental Law; General Practice; Health Care Law; Insurance Defense; Labor and Employment Law; Municipal and Zoning Law; Municipal Bond/Public Authority Financing; Personal Injury; Real Estate Law; Trust and Estates, Wills and Probate

EAVES, BARDACKE, BAUGH KIERST & KIERNAN, P.A.
Albuquerque, NM .... Antitrust Law; Banking Law; Civil Trial Practice; Commercial Law; Commercial Litigation; Employment Benefits Law; Environmental Law; Insurance Defense; Oil and Gas Law

EBERLE, BERLIN, KADING, TURNBOW & MCKLVEEN, CHARTERED
Boise, ID .... Antitrust Law; Civil Trial Practice; General Practice; Natural Resources Law; Securities Law; Tax Law

ECKER, LOEHR, ECKER & ECKER, L.L.P.
Yonkers, NY .... Civil Trial Practice; Corporate Law; Family Law; Personal Injury; Real Estate Law

ECKER & STANDISH, CHARTERED
Las Vegas, NV .... Family Law

ECKERT KOST & VOCKE
Rhinelander, WI .... Appellate Practice; Civil Trial Practice; General Practice; Insurance Defense

ECKERT SEAMANS CHERIN & MELLOTT, LLC
Washington, DC .... General Practice
Harrisburg, PA .... General Practice
Pittsburgh, PA .... General Practice; Patent, Trademark, Copyright and Unfair Competition

ECKHOFF & HOPPE
San Francisco, CA .... Patent, Trademark, Copyright and Unfair Competition

ECKSTEIN, MICHAEL L., ATTORNEY AT LAW, A PROF. CORP.
New Orleans, LA .... Business Law; Mergers and Acquisitions; Sports and Entertainment Law; Tax Law; Trust and Estates, Wills and Probate

EDERER & PRICE, L.L.C.
San Antonio, TX .... Criminal Trial Practice; General Practice

EDGARTON, ST. PETER, PETAK, MASSEY & BULLON
Fond du Lac, WI .... General Practice

EDMONSON, BIGGS & MOZINGO, P.A.
Jackson, MS .... Banking Law; Commercial Law; Insurance Defense

EDMUNDS MAKI VERGA & THORN
Honolulu, HI .... Commercial Law; Criminal Trial Practice; Personal Injury; Trademark, Copyright and Unfair Competition

EDMUNDS & WILLIAMS, P.C.
Lynchburg, VA .... General Practice

EDSON, LAPLANTE & SPINELLI
Sacramento, CA .... Insurance Defense

EDWARDS & ANGELL, LLP
Providence, RI .... Antitrust Law; Civil Trial Practice; Communications Law; Environmental Law; General Practice; Labor and Employment Law; Municipal Bond/Public Authority Financing; Natural Resources Law; Tax Law; Trademark, Copyright and Unfair Competition

EDWARDS & ANTHOLIS, P.C.
Morristown, NJ .... Commercial Law; Tax Law

EDWARDS, BALLARD, BISHOP, STURM, CLARK & KEIM, P.A.
Spartanburg, SC .... Employment Benefits Law; Environmental Law; Immigration and Naturalization; Labor and Employment Law; Workers Compensation

EDWARDS, SOOY & BYRON, A PROFESSIONAL CORPORATION
San Diego, CA .... Civil Trial Practice; Insurance Defense
Las Vegas, NV .... Civil Trial Practice; Commercial Litigation; Construction Law; Insurance Defense; Product Liability Law

EDWARDS, TOLSTEDT & FRICKLE
Billings, MT .... Personal Injury

EDWARDS & WINTERTON, CHTD.
Las Vegas, NV .... Bankruptcy Law; Commercial Litigation; Corporate Law; Real Estate Law; Tax Law; Trust and Estates, Wills and Probate

EFFRON, WAYNE D., P.C.
Greenwich, CT .... Family Law; Personal Injury

EFMAN & OBEDIN
Central Islip, NY .... Criminal Trial Practice

EGAN, FLANAGAN AND COHEN, P.C.
Springfield, MA .... General Practice

EGAN & MAZZARA, PLLC
Troy, MI .... Commercial Litigation

EGAN, THOMAS F., P.A.
Orlando, FL .... Commercial Litigation; Criminal Trial Practice

EGERTON, MCAFEE, ARMISTEAD & DAVIS, P.C.
Knoxville, TN ....Banking Law; Civil Trial Practice; Health Care Law; Tax Law; Trust and Estates, Wills and Probate; Workers Compensation

EGGER & TALMADGE
San Diego, CA ....Insurance Defense; Workers Compensation

EHLINGER & KRILL, S.C.
Milwaukee, WI ....Business Law; Civil Trial Practice; Health Care Law

EHMANN & HILLER, P.C.
Phoenix, AZ ....Employment Benefits Law; Tax Law; Trust and Estates, Wills and Probate

EHRENBERG & FROST, P.C.
Chicago, IL ....Bankruptcy Law; Commercial Litigation

EHRENPREIS, RALPH, A PROFESSIONAL LAW CORPORATION
Los Angeles, CA ....Immigration and Naturalization

EHRLICH, FRAZER & FELDMAN
Garden City, NY ....Labor and Employment Law

EIDSON & ASSOCIATES, P.C.
Atlanta, GA ....Civil Trial Practice

EIG AND SCHWARTZ, CHARTERED
Bethesda, MD ....Business Law; Trust and Estates, Wills and Probate

EIKENBURG & STILES, P.C.
Houston, TX ....General Practice

EISEN & JOHNSTON
Sacramento, CA ....Appellate Practice

EISENBERG, ANDERSON, MICHALIK & LYNCH, L.L.P.
New Britain, CT ....Labor and Employment Law

EISENBERG & FINK, LLP
Irvine, CA ....Commercial Litigation; Construction Law; Personal Injury

EISENBERG & KIRSCH
Liberty, NY ....Insurance Defense

EISENBERG, SUE ELLEN, P.C.
Bloomfield Hills, MI ....Arbitration; Labor and Employment Law

EISENBUD, FREDERICK
Hauppauge, NY ....Environmental Law

EISENHART & EISENHART
Cambridge, NE ....General Practice

EISENSTAT, GABAGE, BERMAN & FURMAN, A PROFESSIONAL CORPORATION
Vineland, NJ ....Civil Trial Practice; General Practice; Insurance Defense

EISENSTEIN, GWEN M.
Dallas, TX ....Real Estate Law

EISFELDER, ROBERT W., P.C., LAW OFFICES OF
Los Angeles, CA ....Civil Trial Practice; Family Law

EISNER & HUBBARD, P.C.
New York, NY ....Labor and Employment Law

ELAM & BURKE, A PROFESSIONAL ASSOCIATION
Boise, ID ....Antitrust Law; Banking Law; Bankruptcy Law; Business Law; Civil Trial Practice; Commercial Law; Environmental Law; General Practice; Insurance Defense; Labor and Employment Law; Municipal Bond/Public Authority Financing; Natural Resources Law; Real Estate Law; Securities Law; Trust and Estates, Wills and Probate; Workers Compensation

ELAM & GLASGOW
Union City, TN ....General Practice; Insurance Defense

ELARBEE, THOMPSON & TRAPNELL, LLP
Atlanta, GA ....Employment Benefits Law; Immigration and Naturalization; Labor and Employment Law

ELDEN LAW FIRM, THE
Chicago, IL ....Health Care Law

ELDER, KURZMAN & VACCARELLA, P.A.
Miami, FL ....Construction Law

ELLENBOGEN & GOLDSTEIN, P.C.
New York, NY ....Family Law

ELLIFF, KEYSER, OBERLE & DANCEY, P.C.
Pekin, IL ....Business Law; Municipal and Zoning Law; Trust and Estates, Wills and Probate

ELLIN AND BAKER
Baltimore, MD ....Civil Trial Practice; Medical Malpractice; Personal Injury; Product Liability Law

ELLIOTT & BLACKBURN
Valdosta, GA ....Civil Trial Practice; General Practice

ELLIOTT REIHNER SIEDZIKOWSKI & EGAN, P.C.
Blue Bell, PA ....Civil Trial Practice; Commercial Law

ELLIS, RONALD D.
Torrance, CA ....Commercial Law

ELLIS, HOOPER, WARLICK & MORGAN, LLP
Jacksonville, NC ....General Practice

ELLIS LAW FIRM
Benton, AR ....Civil Trial Practice; Insurance Defense

ELLIS, LI & MCKINSTRY PLLC
Seattle, WA ....Commercial Litigation

ELLIS & MORGAN
Stillwater, OK ....Commercial Law; Trust and Estates, Wills and Probate

ELLIS & RAPACKI
Boston, MA ....Civil Trial Practice; Personal Injury; Product Liability Law

ELLISON & HINKLE, A PROFESSIONAL LAW CORPORATION
Ventura, CA ....Personal Injury

ELLISTON & ORMESHER, L.L.P.
Dallas, TX ....Civil Trial Practice; Criminal Trial Practice

ELLMAN, BURKE, HOFFMAN & JOHNSON, A PROFESSIONAL CORPORATION
San Francisco, CA ....Civil Trial Practice; Land Use Law; Municipal and Zoning Law; Real Estate Law

ELMAN & ASSOCIATES, A PROFESSIONAL CORPORATION
Media, PA ....Patent, Trademark, Copyright and Unfair Competition

ELMAN & EHARDT, LTD.
Harvard, IL ....General Practice

ELMORE, ELMORE & WILLIAMS, P.A.
Asheville, NC ....Criminal Trial Practice; Medical Malpractice; Personal Injury; Workers Compensation

ELROD & MASCHER, P.C.
Indianapolis, IN ....Municipal and Zoning Law; Tax Law; Trust and Estates, Wills and Probate

ELSENER & CADENHEAD, P.C.
Seminole, OK ....Civil Trial Practice; General Practice

ELSTEIN AND ELSTEIN, P.C.
Bridgeport, CT ....Business Law; Personal Injury; Real Estate Law

ELWOOD, O'DONOHOE, O'CONNOR & STOCHL
Charles City, IA ....General Practice
Cresco, IA ....General Practice
New Hampton, IA ....General Practice

ELY AND TRUE
Batavia, OH ....Insurance Defense

EMANUEL AND DUNN
Raleigh, NC ....Business Law

EMCH, SCHAFFER, SCHAUB & PORCELLO CO., L.P.A.
Toledo, OH ....Intellectual Property Law; Patent, Trademark, Copyright and Unfair Competition

EMERY CUTI BRINCKERHOFF & ABADY PC
New York, NY ....Appellate Practice; Civil Rights; Civil Trial Practice; Commercial Litigation; Constitutional Law; Criminal Trial Practice

EMERY JAMIESON
Edmonton, AB, Canada ....Civil Trial Practice; General Practice; Patent, Trademark, Copyright and Unfair Competition

EMISON, DOOLITTLE, KOLB & ROELLGEN
Vincennes, IN ....General Practice; Insurance Defense

EMMANUEL, SHEPPARD & CONDON
Pensacola, FL ....Civil Trial Practice

EMMETT, COBB, WAITS, KESSENICH & O'NEIL, A PROFESSIONAL LAW CORPORATION
New Orleans, LA ....Admiralty/Maritime Law; Medical Malpractice

EMMOTT, JACK H. III, & ASSOCIATES, P.C.
Houston, TX ....Civil Trial Practice; Family Law

EMOND & VINES
Birmingham, AL .... Antitrust Law; Commercial Litigation; Medical Malpractice; Personal Injury; Product Liability Law

ENGINEER, RUMI LAW OFFICES OF
Denver, CO .... Immigration and Naturalization

ENGLAND & COHEN, LLP
Oxnard, CA .... General Practice

ENGLAND, WHITFIELD, SCHRÖEDER & TREDWAY, L.L.P.
Oxnard, CA .... Business Law; Construction Law; Education Law; Land Use Law; Real Estate Law; Tax Law

ENGLISH & VAN HORNE, P.C.
Detroit, MI .... Immigration and Naturalization

ENGLISH & WOOD, P.C.
Tulsa, OK .... Bankruptcy Law

ENNIS, CHARLES W.
Denver, CO .... Trust and Estates, Wills and Probate

ENTERPRISE COUNSEL GROUP THE
Irvine, CA .... Civil Trial Practice; Computer Law; Labor and Employment Law

ENTWISTLE & CAPPUCCI LLP
New York, NY .... Securities Law

ENWALL & GRANT, L.L.C.
Boulder, CO .... Civil Trial Practice; Criminal Trial Practice

EPPERSON & RENCHER, A PROFESSIONAL CORPORATION
Salt Lake City, UT .... Medical Malpractice

EPPS AND EPPS, LAW OFFICE OF
Johnson City, TN .... Construction Law; General Practice; Land Use Law; Municipal and Zoning Law

EPSTEIN BECKER & GREEN, P.C.
New York, NY .... General Practice

EPSTEIN, SHAPIRO & EPSTEIN
Philadelphia, PA .... Tax Law

EPTING & HACKNEY
Chapel Hill, NC .... Civil Trial Practice; Family Law; General Practice; Personal Injury; Real Estate Law

ERHARD, RUEBEL & JENNINGS, A PROFESSIONAL CORPORATION
Dallas, TX .... Civil Trial Practice; Corporate Law; Labor and Employment Law

ERICKSON, DAVIS, MURPHY, JOHNSON, GRIFFITH & WALSH, LTD.
Decatur, IL .... Commercial Litigation; Insurance Defense

ERICKSON & SEDERSTROM, P.C.
Lincoln, NE .... Civil Trial Practice; General Practice; Health Care Law; Insurance Defense; Labor and Employment Law; Municipal and Zoning Law; Personal Injury; Real Estate Law; Trust and Estates, Wills and Probate
Omaha, NE .... Bankruptcy Law; Civil Trial Practice; Environmental Law; General Practice; Insurance Defense; Labor and Employment Law; Personal Injury; Securities Law; Tax Law; Trust and Estates, Wills and Probate

ERICKSON, THORPE & SWAINSTON, LTD.
Reno, NV .... Civil Trial Practice; Construction Law; General Practice; Insurance Defense; Labor and Employment Law; Medical Malpractice; Product Liability Law

ERICKSON, WEBB & SCOLTON
Jamestown, NY .... Corporate Law; General Practice; Personal Injury; Real Estate Law; Trust and Estates, Wills and Probate

ERLACH, RAYMOND N. STELLA
San Francisco, CA .... Business Law; Civil Trial Practice; Securities Law; Tax Law

ERMAN, TEICHER, MILLER, ZUCKER, FREEDMAN & GORDON, A PROFESSIONAL CORPORATION
Southfield, MI .... Bankruptcy Law

ERNSTROM & DRESTE, LLP
Rochester, NY .... Commercial Litigation; Construction Law

ERSKINE & ERSKINE
Worcester, MA .... Trust and Estates, Wills and Probate

ERSKINE & MCMAHON, L.L.P.
Longview, TX .... Personal Injury; Product Liability Law; Toxic Torts

ERWIN THOMPSON & HASCHEFF
Reno, NV .... Business Law; Civil Trial Practice; Corporate Law; Labor and Employment Law; Natural Resources Law; Real Estate Law

ESDAILE, BARRETT & ESDAILE
Boston, MA .... Civil Trial Practice; General Practice; Personal Injury

ESLER & LINDIE, P.A.
Fort Lauderdale, FL .... Business Law; Civil Trial Practice; Commercial Litigation; General Practice; Insurance Defense; Personal Injury

ESPY, ALAN C., P.A.
West Palm Beach, FL .... Insurance Defense; Personal Injury

ESSEN, ESSEN, SUSANECK, CANET & LIPSON, P.A.
Miami, FL .... Criminal Trial Practice

ESTES, HOYT & HANSEN, A PROFESSIONAL CORPORATION
San Diego, CA .... Bankruptcy Law; Civil Trial Practice

ETHERIDGE, MOSER, GARNER AND BRUNER, P.A.
Laurinburg, NC .... General Practice

ETNIRE, GEOFFREY C.
Pleasanton, CA .... Real Estate Law

EUBANKS, HILYARD & BOGAN, P.A.
Orlando, FL .... Aviation Law; Civil Trial Practice; General Practice; Insurance Defense; Medical Malpractice; Personal Injury; Workers Compensation

EVANS, CARTER, KUNES & BENNETT, P.A.
Charleston, SC .... Tax Law; Trust and Estates, Wills and Probate

EVANS AND CLESI, A PROFESSIONAL LAW CORPORATION
New Orleans, LA .... Insurance Defense

EVANS & DIXON, L.L.C.
St. Louis, MO .... Civil Trial Practice; Insurance Defense; Workers Compensation

EVANS, GANDY, DANIEL & MOORE
Fort Worth, TX .... Criminal Trial Practice

EVANS, JOHN F., & ASSOCIATES
Hamilton, ON, Canada .... Civil Trial Practice

EVANS, JONES & REYNOLDS, A PROFESSIONAL CORPORATION
Nashville, TN .... General Practice

EVANS, KAREN, LITIGATION RESOLUTION, INC.
Miami, FL .... Commercial Law; Labor and Employment Law

EVANS, KEANE LLP
Boise, ID .... General Practice
Kellogg, ID .... General Practice

EVANS, OSBORNE & KREIZMAN
Ocean Township, NJ .... Admiralty/Maritime Law; Civil Trial Practice; Corporate Law; General Practice; Insurance Defense

EVANS & PETREE
Memphis, TN .... Banking Law; Civil Trial Practice; Commercial Law; Criminal Trial Practice; General Practice; Insurance Defense; Tax Law

EVANS, PORTNOY & QUINN
Pittsburgh, PA .... Legal Malpractice; Medical Malpractice; Personal Injury; Product Liability Law

EVERETT, JAMES J., P.C., LAW OFFICES OF
Phoenix, AZ .... Tax Law; Trust and Estates, Wills and Probate

EVERSON, WHITNEY, EVERSON & BREHM, S.C.
Green Bay, WI .... General Practice; Insurance Defense; Medical Malpractice; Product Liability Law

EWING, DIETZ, TURNER & KEHOE, PROFESSIONAL ASSOCIATION
Easton, MD .... Civil Trial Practice; Commercial Litigation; Family Law; General Practice; Municipal and Zoning Law; Real Estate Law; Trust and Estates, Wills and Probate

EWING & EWING, P.C.
Denver, CO .... Personal Injury

EWING & HOBEROCK
Nevada, MO .... General Practice

EWING, JOHNSON, GRAVES & DRISKILL, PROFESSIONAL LAW CORPORATION
El Centro, CA .... General Practice

EYSTER, KEY, TUBB, WEAVER & ROTH
Decatur, AL .... General Practice; Insurance Defense; Medical Malpractice; Product Liability Law; Tax Law

FABRICANT & YESKOO, LLP
New York, NY .... Commercial Litigation; Patent, Trademark, Copyright and Unfair Competition

FAEGRE BENSON HOBSON AUDLEY
London, England .... General Practice

FAEGRE & BENSON LLP
Denver, CO .... General Practice
Minneapolis, MN .... General Practice

FAGELBAUM & HELLER, LLP
Los Angeles, CA .... Civil Trial Practice; Commercial Litigation

FAGEL & HABER
Chicago, IL .... Banking Law; Bankruptcy Law; Real Estate Law; Securities Law; Tax Law

FAIN, MAJOR, WILEY & BRENNAN, P.C.
Atlanta, GA .... Civil Trial Practice; General Practice; Insurance Defense; Labor and Employment Law; Medical Malpractice; Personal Injury; Product Liability Law; Workers Compensation

FAIRCHILD, HANEY & BUCK, P.A.
Topeka, KS .... General Practice

FAIRCHILD, PRICE, THOMAS, HALEY & WILLINGHAM, L.L.P.
Center, TX .... General Practice; Insurance Defense; Medical Malpractice; Product Liability Law; Professional Liability; Real Estate Law; Toxic Torts
Houston, TX .... General Practice; Insurance Defense; Medical Malpractice; Product Liability Law; Professional Liability; Real Estate Law; Toxic Torts
Nacogdoches, TX .... General Practice; Insurance Defense; Medical Malpractice; Product Liability Law; Professional Liability; Real Estate Law; Toxic Torts

FAIRFIELD, FARROW, FLOWERS, PIERSON & STROTZ, P.C.
Albuquerque, NM .... Commercial Litigation; Government Contracts; Real Estate Law

FAIRFIELD & FREEMAN
Ventura, CA .... Trust and Estates, Wills and Probate

FAIRFIELD, JEFFREY J., P.C.
Herndon, VA .... Commercial Law

FAKES, ARTHUR, P.C.
Chicago, IL .... Computer Law; International Business Law
Lombard, IL .... Computer Law; Intellectual Property Law; International Business Law

FALK LAW FIRM, THE, PLLC
Washington, DC .... Government Contracts; Health Care Law; Insurance Defense; Labor and Employment Law; Trust and Estates, Wills and Probate

FALK & SIEMER, LLP
Buffalo, NY .... General Practice

FANCHER, C. LARRY
La Habra, CA .... Family Law

FANT, PHILIP A.
San Francisco, CA .... Admiralty/Maritime Law

FARACI & LANGE, LLP
Rochester, NY .... Medical Malpractice; Personal Injury; Product Liability Law; Real Estate Law

FARAGE, MCBRIDE & RUGGIERI
Philadelphia, PA .... Civil Trial Practice; Medical Malpractice; Product Liability Law

FARBER, STEVEN G.
Santa Fe, NM .... Criminal Trial Practice; Personal Injury

FARBER, SEGALL & PAPPALARDO
White Plains, NY .... Commercial Litigation

FARISH, FARISH & ROMANI
West Palm Beach, FL .... Civil Trial Practice; Family Law; Personal Injury; Real Estate Law

FARMER, KELLEY, BROWN AND WILLIAMS
London, KY .... Banking Law; Civil Trial Practice; General Practice; Insurance Defense; Medical Malpractice; Product Liability Law; Real Estate Law

FARMER, PRICE, HORNSBY & WEATHERFORD, L.L.P.
Dothan, AL .... Commercial Litigation; Personal Injury

FARMER & WATLINGTON, L.L.P.
Yanceyville, NC .... General Practice

FARNSWORTH & VONBERG
Houston, TX .... Business Law; Commercial Law; Natural Resources Law

FARR, DAVIS & FITZE
Tunkhannock, PA .... Civil Trial Practice; General Practice; Real Estate Law; Trust and Estates, Wills and Probate

FARR, FARR, EMERICH, SIFRIT, HACKETT AND CARR, P.A.
Punta Gorda, FL .... General Practice

FARRELL, J. MICHAEL
Philadelphia, PA .... Civil Trial Practice

FARRELL, FARRELL & FARRELL, L.C.
Huntington, WV .... Commercial Litigation

FARRIS, MATHEWS, BRANAN & HELLEN, P.L.C.
Memphis, TN .... Administrative Law; Admiralty/Maritime Law; Banking Law; Civil Trial Practice; Communications Law; General Practice; Insurance Defense; Municipal and Zoning Law; Real Estate Law

FARRIS, VAUGHAN, WILLS & MURPHY
Vancouver, BC, Canada .... General Practice

FARRIS, WARFIELD & KANADAY, PLC
Nashville, TN .... General Practice

FARRISH, JOHNSON & MASCHKA, P.L.L.P.
Mankato, MN .... Civil Trial Practice; General Practice; Insurance Defense

FARRUGIA, VICTOR R., A PROFESSIONAL LAW CORPORATION
New Orleans, LA .... Labor and Employment Law

FARUKI GILLIAM & IRELAND P.L.L.
Dayton, OH .... Commercial Litigation

FASKEN MARTINEAU DUMOULIN
Vancouver, BC, Canada .... General Practice
Toronto, ON, Canada .... General Practice; Trademark, Copyright and Unfair Competition
Montreal, QU, Canada .... General Practice
Quebec, QU, Canada .... General Practice
London, England .... General Practice

FAUST, HARRELSON, FULKER, MCCARTHY & SCHLEMMER
Troy, OH .... General Practice

FAVOUR, MOORE & WILHELMSEN, A PROFESSIONAL ASSOCIATION
Prescott, AZ .... Appellate Practice; Business Law; Civil Trial Practice; Commercial Law; Family Law; General Practice; Real Estate Law; Trust and Estates, Wills and Probate

FAVRET, DEMAREST, RUSSO & LUTKEWITTE, A PROFESSIONAL LAW CORPORATION
New Orleans, LA .... Civil Trial Practice; General Practice

FAW, FOLGER, JOHNSON & CAMPBELL, L.L.P.
Mount Airy, NC .... General Practice

FAY, SHARPE, FAGAN, MINNICH & MCKEE, LLP
Cleveland, OH .... Intellectual Property Law; Patent, Trademark, Copyright and Unfair Competition; Trademark, Copyright and Unfair Competition

FEARER, NYE, AHLBERG & CHADWICK
Rochelle, IL .... General Practice

FEATHERSTONE DESISTO LLP
Denver, CO .... Commercial Litigation

FEATHERSTONHAUGH, CONWAY, WILEY & CLYNE, L.L.P.
Albany, NY .... Administrative Law; Business Law; Commercial Litigation; Corporate Law; Labor and Employment Law; Medical Malpractice; Personal Injury; Product Liability Law

FECHTER & DICKSON, P.A.
Tampa, FL .... Civil Rights; Labor and Employment Law

FECZKO AND SEYMOUR
Pittsburgh, PA .... Civil Trial Practice; Personal Injury; Trust and Estates, Wills and Probate

FEDER LAW OFFICE, P.A.
Phoenix, AZ .... Criminal Trial Practice; Medical Malpractice; Personal Injury

FEDERLEIN & KERANEN, P.C.
Bloomfield Hills, MI .... Civil Trial Practice; Commercial Litigation; Construction Law; Insurance Defense; Land Use Law

FEENEY KELLETT WIENNER & BUSH, PROFESSIONAL CORPORATION
Bloomfield Hills, MI .... Civil Trial Practice; Commercial Law; Product Liability Law

FEINBERG GROUP, THE, LLP
Washington, DC .... Business Law; Civil Trial Practice; Commercial Law; Construction Law; Employment Benefits Law; General Practice; Insurance Defense; Labor and Employment Law; Medical Malpractice; Patent, Trademark, Copyright and Unfair Competition; Product Liability Law

FEINGERTS & ASSOCIATES, A PROFESSIONAL LAW CORPORATION
New Orleans, LA .... General Practice; Government Contracts

FEINGOLD, EUGENE M. LAW OFFICES OF
Munster, IN .... Civil Trial Practice; General Practice; Municipal and Zoning Law

FEINGOLD & ALPERT, L.L.P.
New York, NY .... Tax Law

FEIRICH/MAGER/GREEN/RYAN
Carbondale, IL .... General Practice

FEIWELL & HANNOY, PROFESSIONAL CORPORATION
Indianapolis, IN .... Bankruptcy Law; Commercial Law; Real Estate Law

FELDERSTEIN WILLOUGHBY & PASCUZZI LLP
Sacramento, CA .... Bankruptcy Law

FELDESMAN, TUCKER, LEIFER, FIDELL & BANK LLP
Washington, DC .... Business Law; Family Law; Health Care Law

FELDHAKE, AUGUST & ROQUEMORE
Costa Mesa, CA .... Appellate Practice; Banking Law; Bankruptcy Law; Business Law; Civil Trial Practice; Commercial Law; Commercial Litigation; Environmental Law; General Practice; International Business Law; International Trade Law; Mergers and Acquisitions; Real Estate Law; Securities Law; Trust and Estates, Wills and Probate

FELD, HYDE, LYLE, WERTHEIMER & BRYANT, P.C.
Birmingham, AL .... Tax Law; Trust and Estates, Wills and Probate

FELDMAN & FIORELLO
Wayne, NJ .... Family Law

FELDMAN, FRANDEN, WOODARD & FARRIS
Tulsa, OK .... Civil Trial Practice; Medical Malpractice

FELDMAN GALE & WEBER, P.A.
Miami, FL .... Commercial Litigation; Medical Malpractice; Patent, Trademark, Copyright and Unfair Competition; Product Liability Law

FELDMAN, JOEL H., P.A.
Boca Raton, FL .... Family Law

FELDMAN, KIEFFER & HERMAN, LLP
Buffalo, NY .... Civil Trial Practice; Environmental Law; Health Care Law; Insurance Defense; Medical Malpractice; Product Liability Law

FELDMAN, KLEIDMAN & COFFEY, L.L.P.
Fishkill, NY .... Personal Injury

FELDMAN & ORLANSKY
Anchorage, AK .... Appellate Practice; Civil Trial Practice; Criminal Trial Practice

FELDSTEIN GRINBERG STEIN & MCKEE, A PROFESSIONAL CORPORATION
Pittsburgh, PA .... Business Law; Civil Trial Practice; Employment Benefits Law; Family Law; Health Care Law; Insurance Defense; Personal Injury

FELHABER, LARSON, FENLON & VOGT, PROFESSIONAL ASSOCIATION
Minneapolis, MN .... General Practice; Labor and Employment Law
St. Paul, MN .... General Practice

FELLERS, SNIDER, BLANKENSHIP, BAILEY & TIPPENS, A PROFESSIONAL CORPORATION
Oklahoma City, OK .... General Practice
Tulsa, OK .... General Practice

FELLOWS, PIPER & SCHMIDT
Milwaukee, WI .... Insurance Defense

FELSMAN, BRADLEY, GUNTER & DILLON, LLP
Fort Worth, TX .... Patent, Trademark, Copyright and Unfair Competition

FENDIG, MCLEMORE, TAYLOR, WHITWORTH & DURHAM, P.C.
Brunswick, GA .... Civil Trial Practice; General Practice; Insurance Defense; Legal Malpractice; Medical Malpractice; Personal Injury; Product Liability Law

FENDLER, OSCAR
Blytheville, AR .... General Practice

FENDON, DON A., P.C.
Phoenix, AZ .... Workers Compensation

FENNEMORE CRAIG, A PROFESSIONAL CORPORATION
Phoenix, AZ .... Administrative Law; Antitrust Law; Appellate Practice; Banking Law; Bankruptcy Law; Business Law; Civil Trial Practice; Commercial Law; Commercial Litigation; Communications Law; Computer Law; Constitutional Law; Construction Law; Criminal Trial Practice; Employment Benefits Law; Environmental Law; General Practice; Health Care Law; Immigration and Naturalization; Insurance Defense; Intellectual Property Law; International Business Law; Labor and Employment Law; Land Use Law; Medical Malpractice; Mergers and Acquisitions; Municipal and Zoning Law; Natural Resources Law; Patent, Trademark, Copyright and Unfair Competition; Pension and Profit Sharing; Personal Injury; Product Liability Law; Professional Liability; Public Utilities Law; Real Estate Law; Securities Law; Sports and Entertainment Law; Tax Law; Trademark, Copyright and Unfair Competition; Transportation Law; Trust and Estates, Wills and Probate; Workers Compensation
Tucson, AZ .... General Practice; Labor and Employment Law

FENTON, CHAPMAN, FENTON, SMITH & KANE, P.A.
Bar Harbor, ME .... Civil Trial Practice; Corporate Law; Environmental Law; General Practice; International Business Law; Personal Injury; Real Estate Law; Trust and Estates, Wills and Probate

FERENCIK, LIBANOFF, BRANDT & BUSTAMANTE, P.A.
Fort Lauderdale, FL .... Construction Law; Real Estate Law

FERGUSON, CASE, ORR, PATERSON & CUNNINGHAM LLP
Ventura, CA .... Civil Trial Practice; Real Estate Law

FERGUSON, NEWBURN & WESTON, A PROFESSIONAL CORPORATION
La Jolla, CA .... Trust and Estates, Wills and Probate

FERGUSON, SCHETELICH & HEFFERNAN, P.A.
Baltimore, MD .... Admiralty/Maritime Law; Aviation Law; Civil Trial Practice; Construction Law; Environmental Law; Insurance Defense; Labor and Employment Law; Tax Law; Transportation Law; Trust and Estates, Wills and Probate

FERGUSON, STEIN, WALLAS, ADKINS, GRESHAM & SUMTER, P.A.
Charlotte, NC .... Appellate Practice; Civil Rights; Civil Trial Practice; Criminal Trial Practice; Education Law; Labor and Employment Law; Medical Malpractice; Personal Injury

FERNANDEZ, JOHN D., P.A.
Clearwater, FL .... Criminal Trial Practice; Personal Injury

FERNANDEZ & KNEBEL, A PROFESSIONAL CORPORATION
Dallas, TX .... Civil Trial Practice; Commercial Litigation; Corporate Law; Health Care Law; Real Estate Law

FERRARA, FIORENZA, LARRISON, BARRETT & REITZ, P.C.
Syracuse, NY .... Education Law; Labor and Employment Law

FERRARO & ASSOCIATES, P.A.
Miami, FL .... Civil Trial Practice; Personal Injury

FERRARO, RUSSELL J., JR. AND ASSOCIATES, P.A.
Stuart, FL .... Family Law

FERRELL, WAYNE E. JR.
Jackson, MS .... Aviation Law

FERRELLE, JOHN R., P.C.
Brunswick, GA .... Medical Malpractice

FERRELL SCHULTZ CARTER & FERTEL, P.A.
Miami, FL .... Civil Trial Practice; Criminal Trial Practice

FERRERI, FOGLE & PICKLESIMER
Lexington, KY .... Insurance Defense; Workers Compensation
Louisville, KY .... Insurance Defense; Workers Compensation

FERRETTE & SLATER, A LAW CORPORATION
San Diego, CA .... Real Estate Law; Trust and Estates, Wills and Probate

FERRIS & BRITTON, A PROFESSIONAL CORPORATION
San Diego, CA .... Antitrust Law; Banking Law; Business Law; Civil Trial Practice; Commercial Law; Communications Law; General Practice; Insurance Defense; Labor and Employment Law; Real Estate Law; Securities Law; Tax Law; Trademark, Copyright and Unfair Competition

FERRIS & SALTER, P.C.
Ann Arbor, MI .... Criminal Trial Practice; Medical Malpractice; Personal Injury

FERRO LABELLA LOGERFO & ZUCKER, A PROFESSIONAL CORPORATION
Hackensack, NJ .... Banking Law; Commercial Law; Real Estate Law; Trust and Estates, Wills and Probate

FERRUZZO & FERRUZZO
Santa Ana, CA .... Business Law

FERRY, WARREN D., P.C.
Butler, PA .... Civil Trial Practice

FETTERLY & GORDON, P.A.
Minneapolis, MN .... Civil Trial Practice; Insurance Defense; Personal Injury

FIDDLER GONZÁLEZ & RODRÍGUEZ, LLP
San Juan, PR .... Antitrust Law; Banking Law; Bankruptcy Law; Civil Trial Practice; Commercial Law; Environmental Law; General Practice; Immigration and Naturalization; Insurance Defense; Labor and Employment Law; Municipal Bond/Public Authority Financing; Real Estate Law; Tax Law; Trademark, Copyright and Unfair Competition

FIEDELMAN & MCGAW
Jericho, NY .... Insurance Defense

FIELD & FIELD, P.C.
Kalamazoo, MI ....Personal Injury

FIELD & GOLAN
Chicago, IL..............................Banking Law; Business Law; Commercial Litigation; Mergers and Acquisitions; Real Estate Law

FIELD, RICHARDSON & WILHELMY
Walnut Creek, CA ....Construction Law; Real Estate Law

FIELDS, JOHN W., P.A.
Seneca, SC ....Real Estate Law

FIGARI DAVENPORT & GRAVES, L.L.P.
Dallas, TX................................Business Law; Civil Trial Practice; General Practice; Insurance Defense; Labor and Employment Law

FIGLIULO & SILVERMAN, P.C.
Chicago, IL..............................Civil Trial Practice; Commercial Litigation; Eminent Domain; Land Use Law; Legal Malpractice

FILDEW HINKS, P.L.L.C.
Detroit, MI..............................Civil Trial Practice; General Practice; Real Estate Law; Tax Law; Trust and Estates, Wills and Probate

FILE, PAYNE, SCHERER & FILE
Beckley, WV ....Banking Law; General Practice; Insurance Defense; Real Estate Law

FILICE, BROWN, EASSA & MCLEOD, LLP
Oakland, CA ....Civil Trial Practice; Environmental Law; General Practice; Product Liability Law

FILION, WAKELY & THORUP
Toronto, ON, Canada.............Labor and Employment Law

FILLEY, G. WILLIAM
San Francisco, CA ....Family Law; Trust and Estates, Wills and Probate

FINCH, MONTGOMERY & WRIGHT
Palo Alto, CA ....Trust and Estates, Wills and Probate

FINCK, KEVIN W. LAW OFFICES OF
San Francisco, CA ....Business Law; Commercial Law; International Business Law

FINE & FAURE
Albuquerque, NM...................Personal Injury

FINE & HATFIELD, A PROFESSIONAL CORPORATION
Evansville, IN..........................Appellate Practice; Bankruptcy Law; Business Law; Civil Trial Practice; Environmental Law; Health Care Law; Insurance Defense; Labor and Employment Law; Product Liability Law; Real Estate Law; Tax Law; Trust and Estates, Wills and Probate

FINER, KIM & STEARNS
Torrance, CA...........................Bankruptcy Law; Business Law; Civil Trial Practice; Environmental Law; General Practice; Real Estate Law; Trust and Estates, Wills and Probate

FINESTONE & MORRIS
Atlanta, GA ....Commercial Litigation; Criminal Trial Practice

FINK, DAVID E.
Baltimore, MD ....Civil Trial Practice

FINKBOHNER AND LAWLER, L.L.C.
Mobile, AL...............................Bankruptcy Law; Civil Trial Practice; Commercial Law; General Practice; Municipal and Zoning Law; Personal Injury; Product Liability Law

FINKEL & ALTMAN, L.L.C.
Columbia, SC ....Bankruptcy Law; Civil Trial Practice; Commercial Law; Construction Law; Criminal Trial Practice; Insurance Defense; Personal Injury; Real Estate Law; Tax Law

FINKEL GOLDSTEIN BERZOW ROSENBLOOM & NASH, LLP
New York, NY.........................Bankruptcy Law; Commercial Litigation; Creditors Rights

FINKELMEIER & FARRELL
Cincinnati, OH........................Workers Compensation

FINLAYSON, MAC D., P.C.
Tulsa, OK................................Bankruptcy Law; Creditors Rights

FINLEY, WARREN
Laguna Beach, CA..................General Practice

FINLEY, ALT, SMITH, SCHARNBERG, CRAIG, HILMES & GAFFNEY, P.C.
Des Moines, IA ....Appellate Practice; Banking Law; Business Law; Civil Trial Practice; Construction Law; Employment Benefits Law; General Practice; Health Care Law; Insurance Defense; Labor and Employment Law; Medical Malpractice; Personal Injury; Product Liability Law; Real Estate Law; Tax Law; Transportation Law; Trust and Estates, Wills and Probate; Workers Compensation

FINMAN, SHELDON E., P.A.
Fort Myers, FL ....Family Law

FINNEGAN, HENDERSON, FARABOW, GARRETT & DUNNER, L.L.P.
Washington, DC......................Patent, Trademark, Copyright and Unfair Competition; Trademark, Copyright and Unfair Competition

FINNERTY & FINNERTY
Boston, MA.............................Insurance Defense; Product Liability Law

FINNERTY & LAROCCA, P.C.
Paramus, NJ ....Appellate Practice; Civil Trial Practice; Family Law

FINNEY, DANIEL P. JR.
St. Louis, MO..........................Personal Injury

FIORE LAW GROUP, LLP
San Jose, CA ....Tax Law; Trust and Estates, Wills and Probate

FIORETTI, MICHAEL D.
Philadelphia, PA ....Family Law

FISCH, SPIEGLER, GINSBURG, LADNER & ATTARIAN, A PROFESSIONAL LAW CORPORATION
San Diego, CA ....Business Law; Civil Trial Practice; Labor and Employment Law; Real Estate Law; Trust and Estates, Wills and Probate

FISCHER, BESSETTE & MULDOWNEY, L.L.P.
Malone, NY.............................Civil Trial Practice; Insurance Defense; Personal Injury

FISCHER, BROWN & GUNN, P.C.
Fort Collins, CO ....General Practice

FISCHETTE, OWEN, HELD & MCBURNEY
Jacksonville, FL ....Bankruptcy Law; Commercial Litigation

FISH, EMANUEL S. LAW OFFICES OF
Maplewood, NJ.......................Civil Trial Practice; Personal Injury; Product Liability Law

FISH & NEAVE
Palo Alto, CA ....Patent, Trademark, Copyright and Unfair Competition
New York, NY.........................Patent, Trademark, Copyright and Unfair Competition

FISHBACH, HERTAN & IVES
New York, NY.........................Commercial Law; Commercial Litigation

FISHEL, GRACE J.
St. Louis, MO..........................Patent, Trademark, Copyright and Unfair Competition

FISHER, ARTHUR W., III, P.A.
Tampa, FL ....Intellectual Property Law; Patent, Trademark, Copyright and Unfair Competition

FISHER, BOYD, BROWN, BOUDREAUX & HUGUENARD, L.L.P.
Houston, TX ....Aviation Law; Commercial Litigation; Personal Injury; Product Liability Law

FISHER CLINARD & CRAIG, PLLC
High Point, NC........................General Practice

FISHER, FISHER & BERGER
New York, NY.........................Civil Trial Practice; Commercial Litigation; Construction Law; Corporate Law; General Practice

FISHER LAW OFFICE
St. Joseph, MI ....Trust and Estates, Wills and Probate

FISHER & NEWSOM, P.C,
Austin, TX ....Municipal Bond/Public Authority Financing

FISHER, OLSON, DALEY & BATA, LTD.
Grand Forks, ND ....General Practice

FISHER, PATTERSON, SAYLER & SMITH, L.L.P.
Overland Park, KS..................Civil Rights; Civil Trial Practice; Commercial Law; Insurance Defense; Labor and Employment Law; Medical Malpractice; Product Liability Law
Topeka, KS..............................Appellate Practice; Bankruptcy Law; Civil Rights; Civil Trial Practice; Commercial Law; General Practice; Insurance Defense; Labor and Employment Law; Legal Malpractice; Personal Injury; Product Liability Law; Workers Compensation

FISHER & PHILLIPS LLP
Newport Beach, CA................Labor and Employment Law
Redwood City, CA ....Labor and Employment Law
Fort Lauderdale, FL...............Labor and Employment Law
Atlanta, GA ....Employment Benefits Law; Labor and Employment Law
New Orleans, LA ....Labor and Employment Law
Houston, TX ....Labor and Employment Law

FISHER THURBER LLP
La Jolla, CA....Securities Law

FISHER WAYLAND COOPER LEADER & ZARAGOZA L.L.P.
Washington, DC....Communications Law; General Practice; Intellectual Property Law

FISHMAN & JAKLITSCH
Upper Marlboro, MD....Personal Injury

FISHMAN & MORGENTHAL
Carlisle, PA....Commercial Law; Land Use Law; Municipal and Zoning Law; Trust and Estates, Wills and Probate

FITCH, EVEN, TABIN & FLANNERY
San Diego, CA....Patent, Trademark, Copyright and Unfair Competition
Washington, DC....Patent, Trademark, Copyright and Unfair Competition
Chicago, IL....Patent, Trademark, Copyright and Unfair Competition

FITE & O'BRIEN, LTD.
McLean, VA....Family Law

FITZGERALD, HENRY ST. JOHN
Arlington, VA....Appellate Practice; Commercial Litigation

FITZGERALD, ABBOTT & BEARDSLEY LLP
Oakland, CA....General Practice

FITZGERALD & ASSOCIATES
Palm Springs, CA....Labor and Employment Law

FITZGERALD, J. PATRICK, P.A.
Miami, FL....Real Estate Law

FITZGERALD LAW FIRM, THE
Cheyenne, WY....Civil Trial Practice; Medical Malpractice; Personal Injury; Product Liability Law

FITZGERALD MORRIS BAKER FIRTH
Glens Falls, NY....Business Law; Civil Trial Practice; Trust and Estates, Wills and Probate

FITZGIBBONS, JOHN M.
Sarasota, FL....Criminal Trial Practice
Tampa, FL....Criminal Trial Practice

FITZGIBBONS & ANDERSON
Las Vegas, NV....Civil Trial Practice

FITZGIBBONS BROTHERS
Estherville, IA....General Practice

FITZPATRICK, BLACKEY & DEVANIE
La Crosse, WI....General Practice; Product Liability Law

FITZPATRICK, CELLA, HARPER & SCINTO
Washington, DC....Patent, Trademark, Copyright and Unfair Competition
New York, NY....Patent, Trademark, Copyright and Unfair Competition

FITZPATRICK, F. EMMETT, P.C.
Philadelphia, PA....Appellate Practice; Civil Trial Practice; Commercial Law; Commercial Litigation; Computer Law; Criminal Trial Practice; General Practice; International Business Law; International Trade Law; Real Estate Law

FITZPATRICK & WATERMAN
Bayonne, NJ....General Practice; Municipal Bond/Public Authority Financing; Tax Law
Secaucus, NJ....General Practice; Municipal Bond/Public Authority Financing; Tax Law

FITZSIMMONS, LAURA WIGHTMAN
Las Vegas, NV....Eminent Domain

FITZSIMMONS RINGLE & JACOBS, P.C.
Newark, NJ....Civil Trial Practice; Criminal Trial Practice; Personal Injury; Product Liability Law

FIXEL & MAGUIRE
Orlando, FL....Eminent Domain
Tallahassee, FL....Eminent Domain

FJELDAL & ASSOCIATES, A PROFESSIONAL CORPORATION
Houston, TX....Civil Trial Practice; Insurance Defense

FLAHERTY, MEISLER & COURTNEY
Vernon, CT....Civil Trial Practice; Criminal Trial Practice; General Practice; Personal Injury

FLAHERTY, SENSABAUGH & BONASSO, P.L.L.C.
Charleston, WV....Civil Trial Practice; Product Liability Law; Professional Liability

FLAHIVE, OGDEN & LATSON, A PROFESSIONAL CORPORATION
Austin, TX....Workers Compensation

FLANAGAN, BOOTH, UNGER & MOSES
Glendale, CA....Criminal Trial Practice; Personal Injury

FLANAGAN, MANIOTIS & BERGER, P.A.
West Palm Beach, FL....Insurance Defense

FLASTER/GREENBERG, P.C.
Cherry Hill, NJ....Business Law; Commercial Law; Commercial Litigation; Health Care Law; Labor and Employment Law; Land Use Law; Pension and Profit Sharing; Real Estate Law; Tax Law; Trust and Estates, Wills and Probate

FLAXMAN, NEIL, PROFESSIONAL ASSOCIATION
Miami, FL....Administrative Law; Labor and Employment Law

FLEISCHMANN, ROGER JUSTICE LAW OFFICES OF
San Francisco, CA....Business Law

FLEISSNER, PHILLIP A., PLLC
Chattanooga, TN....Civil Trial Practice; Environmental Law; Labor and Employment Law; Product Liability Law

FLEMING & ASSOCIATES, L.L.P.
Houston, TX....Aviation Law; Environmental Law; Personal Injury; Product Liability Law

FLEMING & CURTI
Tucson, AZ....Trust and Estates, Wills and Probate

FLEMING, JOSEPH Z., P.A.
Miami, FL....Communications Law; Environmental Law; Labor and Employment Law; Natural Resources Law

FLEMING, PATTRIDGE & RUNNERSTROM, P.C.
Golden, CO....General Practice

FLETCHER, HARLEY & FLETCHER
Augusta, GA....Corporate Law; General Practice; Government Contracts; Tax Law

FLETCHER, HEALD & HILDRETH, P.L.C.
Washington, DC....Communications Law

FLETCHER, SIBELL & MIGATZ, P.C.
Manhasset, NY....General Practice

FLETCHER, TILTON & WHIPPLE, P.C.
Worcester, MA....General Practice

FLEURIET SCHELL LAW FIRM, THE, LLP
Harlingen, TX....Civil Trial Practice

FLICKER & KERIN
Palo Alto, CA....Business Law; Family Law; Real Estate Law

FLIGELTAUB, WILLIAM H.
Seattle, WA....Criminal Trial Practice; Personal Injury

FLORES, CASSO & PETTITT, L.L.P.
McAllen, TX....General Practice; Personal Injury; Product Liability Law

FLORIN, ROEBIG, WALKER, HUDDLESTUN & ROGERS, P.A.
Palm Harbor, FL....Labor and Employment Law; Medical Malpractice; Personal Injury

FLOYD LAW FIRM, P.C.
Norman, OK....Municipal Bond/Public Authority Financing
St. Louis, MO....Personal Injury; Product Liability Law

FLOYD LAW FIRM, THE, PC
Surfside Beach, SC....General Practice

FLYNN, DELICH & WISE
Long Beach, CA....Admiralty/Maritime Law; Civil Trial Practice; Insurance Defense; International Business Law; Patent, Trademark, Copyright and Unfair Competition; Toxic Torts
San Francisco, CA....Admiralty/Maritime Law; Civil Trial Practice; Insurance Defense; International Business Law; Patent, Trademark, Copyright and Unfair Competition; Toxic Torts

FLYNN & GASKINS, L.L.P.
Minneapolis, MN....Civil Trial Practice; Insurance Defense; Labor and Employment Law; Product Liability Law

FLYNN MCKENNA WRIGHT & KARSH
Colorado Springs, CO....Banking Law; Commercial Law; Commercial Litigation; International Business Law; Real Estate Law; Tax Law

FLYNN, PALMER & TAGUE
Champaign, IL....General Practice

FLYNN & PHILLIPS, LLP
San Rafael, CA........................Real Estate Law

FLYNN, PY & KRUSE, A LEGAL PROFESSIONAL ASSOCIATION
Sandusky, OH........................General Practice

FOGARTY COHEN SELBY & NEMIROFF LLC
Greenwich, CT........................Business Law; Civil Trial Practice; Corporate Law; General Practice

FOGEL, FELDMAN, OSTROV, RINGLER & KLEVENS, A LAW CORPORATION
Santa Monica, CA........................Civil Trial Practice; Labor and Employment Law; Personal Injury

FOGEL, JO BENSON, P.A.
Rockville, MD........................Family Law

FOGEL, LAMBER & BRONNENKANT, PROFESSIONAL ASSOCIATION
Phoenix, AZ........................Appellate Practice; Arbitration; Business Law; Civil Trial Practice; Commercial Litigation; Personal Injury

FOGG, FOGG & HANDLEY
El Reno, OK........................Civil Trial Practice

FOLEY, COGNETTI, COMERFORD & CIMINI
Scranton, PA........................Insurance Defense

FOLEY & FOLEY
Palmyra, NY........................Medical Malpractice; Personal Injury; Product Liability Law; Workers Compensation

FOLEY, HOAG & ELIOT LLP
Washington, DC........................General Practice
Boston, MA........................General Practice; Labor and Employment Law; Tax Law

FOLEY & JONES
Las Vegas, NV........................Civil Trial Practice; Construction Law; Personal Injury

FOLEY & JUDELL, L.L.P.
New Orleans, LA........................Municipal Bond/Public Authority Financing

FOLEY & LARDNER
Los Angeles, CA........................Health Care Law
San Diego, CA........................General Practice
San Francisco, CA........................General Practice
Denver, CO........................General Practice
Washington, DC........................General Practice
Jacksonville, FL........................General Practice
Orlando, FL........................General Practice; Labor and Employment Law
Tallahassee, FL........................General Practice
Tampa, FL........................General Practice
West Palm Beach, FL........................General Practice
Chicago, IL........................General Practice
Annapolis, MD........................General Practice
Madison, WI........................General Practice
Milwaukee, WI........................Antitrust Law; General Practice; Tax Law

FOLEY, MCLANE, FOLEY, MCDONALD & MACGREGOR
Scranton, PA........................Medical Malpractice; Personal Injury; Product Liability Law

FOLGER LEVIN & KAHN LLP
San Francisco, CA........................General Practice

FOLKESTAD & FAZEKAS, P.C.
Castle Rock, CO........................General Practice; Municipal and Zoning Law; Real Estate Law

FOLLICK & BESSICH, P.C.
Huntington Station, NY........................International Trade Law

FOLLIN & OVERFIELD, L.L.P.
Greensboro, NC........................Bankruptcy Law

FONDA, HILBERMAN & FRASER LLP
Los Angeles, CA........................Insurance Defense

FONZONE & ASHLEY
Allentown, PA........................General Practice; Insurance Defense; Municipal and Zoning Law

FORAN & SCHULTZ
Chicago, IL........................Civil Trial Practice; Construction Law; Criminal Trial Practice; Eminent Domain; Health Care Law; Municipal and Zoning Law; Trademark, Copyright and Unfair Competition

FORBES & BOWMAN
Savannah, GA........................Insurance Defense; Labor and Employment Law; Product Liability Law

FORCHELLI, CURTO, SCHWARTZ, MINEO, CARLINO & COHN, LLP
Mineola, NY........................Civil Trial Practice; Real Estate Law

FORD, JON R.
Enid, OK........................Family Law

FORD, FRANCIS A., P.C.
Worcester, MA........................Personal Injury

FORD & HARRISON LLP
Los Angeles, CA........................Labor and Employment Law
Miami, FL........................Labor and Employment Law
Tampa, FL........................Civil Trial Practice; Labor and Employment Law
Atlanta, GA........................Labor and Employment Law
Memphis, TN........................Labor and Employment Law

FORD AND HOWARD, P.C.
Gadsden, AL........................Civil Trial Practice; General Practice; Insurance Defense

FORD LAW FIRM, THE
Los Angeles, CA........................Appellate Practice; Civil Trial Practice

FORD MARRIN ESPOSITO WITMEYER & GLESER, L.L.P.
New York, NY........................Business Law; Civil Trial Practice; Corporate Law; General Practice

FORD & RICHARDSON
Lewisburg, WV........................General Practice

FORD & SINCLAIR, P.A.
Miami, FL........................Medical Malpractice

FORD, WALKER, HAGGERTY & BEHAR, PROFESSIONAL LAW CORPORATION
Long Beach, CA........................Civil Trial Practice; Commercial Litigation; Construction Law; General Practice; Insurance Defense; Product Liability Law

FOREMAN, BOUDREAUX, SMITH & JOHNSON
Dallas, TX........................Personal Injury; Product Liability Law

FORE, MILLER & SCHWARTZ
Louisville, KY........................Business Law; Commercial Law; General Practice; Real Estate Law; Securities Law

FORMAN HOLT & ELIADES LLC
Rochelle Park, NJ........................Banking Law; Bankruptcy Law; Commercial Litigation; Real Estate Law

FORSYTH, HOWE, O'DWYER, KALB & MURPHY, P.C.
Rochester, NY........................Banking Law; Bankruptcy Law; Commercial Law; Creditors Rights; Eminent Domain; Real Estate Law

FORTINO, PLAXTON, MOSKAL & COSTANZO, P.C.
Alma, MI........................General Practice; Insurance Defense

FORTNEY & KLINGSHIRN
Akron, OH........................Construction Law; Labor and Employment Law

FORTUNE, JOHNNY, P.A.
Fort Walton Beach, FL........................Trust and Estates, Wills and Probate

FOSSETT & BRUGGER, CHARTERED
Greenbelt, MD........................Civil Trial Practice; Land Use Law; Real Estate Law

FOSTER, FOSTER, ALLEN & DURRENCE, P.C.
Chattanooga, TN........................Civil Trial Practice; Construction Law; Environmental Law; General Practice; Insurance Defense; Medical Malpractice; Personal Injury; Real Estate Law; Securities Law

FOSTER, MEADOWS & BALLARD, P.C.
Detroit, MI........................Admiralty/Maritime Law; Transportation Law

FOSTER PEPPER & SHEFELMAN PLLC
Seattle, WA........................General Practice

FOSTER, PURDY, ALLAN, PETERSON & DAHLIN, LLP
Medford, OR........................General Practice

FOSTER, SWIFT, COLLINS & SMITH, P.C.
Lansing, MI........................Banking Law; Civil Trial Practice; Employment Benefits Law; Environmental Law; General Practice; Health Care Law; Immigration and Naturalization; Insurance Defense; International Business Law; Labor and Employment Law; Patent, Trademark, Copyright and Unfair Competition; Personal Injury; Real Estate Law; Transportation Law; Trust and Estates, Wills and Probate

FOULKROD, S. WALTER III & ASSOCIATES
Harrisburg, PA........................Administrative Law; Civil Trial Practice

FOULSTON & SIEFKIN L.L.P.
Dodge City, KS........................Business Law; Civil Trial Practice; General Practice; Tax Law; Trust and Estates, Wills and Probate
Topeka, KS........................Administrative Law; Business Law; Employment Benefits Law; Tax Law; Transportation Law
Wichita, KS........................Administrative Law; Antitrust Law; Banking Law; Bankruptcy Law; Business Law; Civil Trial Practice; Commercial Law; Construction Law; Employment Benefits Law; Environmental Law; General Practice; Health Care Law; Insurance Defense; International Business Law; Labor and Employment Law; Medical Malpractice; Natural Resources Law; Personal Injury; Real Estate Law; Securities Law; Tax Law; Trademark, Copyright and Unfair Competition; Trust and Estates, Wills and Probate

FOURNARIS & SANET, P.A.
Miami, FL ..... Medical Malpractice; Personal Injury

FOURNET, M. MICHELE
Baton Rouge, LA ..... Criminal Trial Practice

FOWLER, MEASLE & BELL, L.L.P.
Lexington, KY ..... Bankruptcy Law; Insurance Defense

FOX, MAURICE F.
Denver, CO ..... Real Estate Law

FOX, RENEE ISLA
Washington, DC ..... Trust and Estates, Wills and Probate

FOX & FOX, L.L.P.
Stamford, CT ..... Real Estate Law; Trust and Estates, Wills and Probate

FOX, GROVE, ABBEY, ADAMS, BYELICK & KIERNAN
St. Petersburg, FL ..... Insurance Defense

FOX HORAN & CAMERINI LLP
New York, NY ..... Civil Trial Practice; International Business Law; Securities Law

FOX, OLDT & BROWN
Easton, PA ..... Elder Law; Personal Injury; Trust and Estates, Wills and Probate

FOX, ROTHSCHILD, O'BRIEN & FRANKEL, LLP
Trenton, NJ ..... General Practice
Philadelphia, PA ..... General Practice; Real Estate Law; Tax Law

FRALEY & FRALEY, L.L.P.
Dallas, TX ..... Civil Trial Practice; Commercial Litigation; Health Care Law; Insurance Defense; Medical Malpractice; Personal Injury; Professional Liability

FRAMME LAW FIRM, PLC
Richmond, VA ..... Civil Trial Practice

FRAMPTON, WILLIAMS & LITTLE, A PROFESSIONAL ASSOCIATION
Fresno, CA ..... Labor and Employment Law

FRANCHISE LAW TEAM
Rancho Santa Margarita, CA ..... Franchise Law

FRANCZEK SULLIVAN P.C.
Chicago, IL ..... Arbitration; Civil Trial Practice; Education Law; Employment Benefits Law; Labor and Employment Law

FRANKE, RAINEY & SALLOUM, PLLC
Gulfport, MS ..... Admiralty/Maritime Law; Civil Trial Practice; Commercial Law; Environmental Law; General Practice; Insurance Defense; Real Estate Law; Trust and Estates, Wills and Probate; Workers Compensation

FRANKE & SCHULTZ, A PROFESSIONAL CORPORATION
Kansas City, MO ..... Civil Trial Practice; Insurance Defense; Personal Injury; Product Liability Law

FRANK LAW FIRM, THE, L.L.P.
St. Louis, MO ..... Personal Injury

FRANKLIN, CARDWELL & JONES
Houston, TX ..... Civil Trial Practice; Commercial Litigation; Medical Malpractice; Personal Injury

FRANKLIN, COOPER & MARCUS, PLLC
Chattanooga, TN ..... Civil Trial Practice; Insurance Defense; Labor and Employment Law; Personal Injury; Product Liability Law

FRANKLIN, GORDON & HOBGOOD
Madisonville, KY ..... Insurance Defense; Medical Malpractice

FRANKLIN AND HANCE, P.S.C.
Louisville, KY ..... Civil Trial Practice; Medical Malpractice; Personal Injury; Product Liability Law

FRANKOVITCH, ANETAKIS, COLANTONIO & SIMON
Weirton, WV ..... General Practice; Personal Injury

FRANKS, E. BEN LAW OFFICES OF
Texarkana, TX ..... Civil Trial Practice

FRANSEN & HARDIN, A P.L.C.
New Orleans, LA ..... Admiralty/Maritime Law

FRANTZ, MCCONNELL & SEYMOUR, LLP
Knoxville, TN ..... Civil Trial Practice; Commercial Litigation; General Practice; Insurance Defense; Labor and Employment Law

FRASER MILNER
Vancouver, BC, Canada ..... General Practice
Ottawa, ON, Canada ..... General Practice
Toronto, ON, Canada ..... General Practice

FRASER, STRYKER, VAUGHN, MEUSEY, OLSON, BOYER & BLOCH, P.C.
Omaha, NE ..... Banking Law; Commercial Law; Environmental Law; General Practice; Insurance Defense; Labor and Employment Law; Real Estate Law; Tax Law

FRASER TREBILCOCK DAVIS & FOSTER, P.C.
Lansing, MI ..... Civil Trial Practice; Employment Benefits Law; Environmental Law; Health Care Law; Insurance Defense; Labor and Employment Law; Medical Malpractice; Product Liability Law; Real Estate Law; Trust and Estates, Wills and Probate

FRASIER, FRASIER & HICKMAN
Tulsa, OK ..... Personal Injury; Product Liability Law; Workers Compensation

FRATES, WILLIAM S., II P.A.
Vero Beach, FL ..... Product Liability Law

FRAZER, S. STEWART
Dallas, TX ..... General Practice

FRAZER, GREENE, UPCHURCH & BAKER, L.L.C.
Mobile, AL ..... Civil Trial Practice; Commercial Litigation; Insurance Defense; Medical Malpractice; Product Liability Law; Professional Liability

FRAZER SCHAPIRO & RICH, S.C.
Milwaukee, WI ..... Environmental Law; Tax Law

FRAZIER & FRAZIER, ATTORNEYS AT LAW, P.A.
Jacksonville, FL ..... Tax Law; Trust and Estates, Wills and Probate

FREDERICKS, BARRY I.
Englewood Cliffs, NJ ..... Civil Trial Practice; Intellectual Property Law

FREEARK, HARVEY, MENDILLO, DENNIS, WULLER & CAIN, P.C.
Belleville, IL ..... Commercial Litigation; Insurance Defense

FREEBURG, JUDY & NETTELS
Pasadena, CA ..... Civil Trial Practice; Environmental Law; Insurance Defense; Medical Malpractice

FREEDMAN BOYD DANIELS HOLLANDER GOLDBERG & CLINE P.A.
Albuquerque, NM ..... Antitrust Law; Appellate Practice; Civil Rights; Civil Trial Practice; Commercial Litigation; Criminal Trial Practice; Securities Law

FREEDMAN AND FISH
New York, NY ..... Elder Law; Trust and Estates, Wills and Probate

FREEDMAN, LEVY, KROLL & SIMONDS
Washington, DC ..... General Practice

FREELAND & FREELAND
Oxford, MS ..... Banking Law; Bankruptcy Law; Civil Trial Practice; Commercial Law; Commercial Litigation; Constitutional Law; Insurance Defense; Product Liability Law; Real Estate Law

FREEMAN, FREEMAN & SALZMAN, P.C.
Chicago, IL ..... Antitrust Law; Commercial Litigation; Securities Law

FREEMAN, LOFTUS & MANLEY
New City, NY ..... Banking Law; Real Estate Law; Trust and Estates, Wills and Probate

FREEMAN MATHIS & GARY, LLP
Atlanta, GA ..... Civil Rights; Construction Law; Insurance Defense; Labor and Employment Law

FREEMAN & SUPRAN, P.A.
West Palm Beach, FL ..... Medical Malpractice; Personal Injury

FREEMAN, WOLFE & GREENBAUM, P.A.
Towson, MD ..... Civil Trial Practice; Criminal Trial Practice

FREEMAN, WRIGHT & HERMAN
Atlanta, GA ..... Civil Trial Practice; Environmental Law; Labor and Employment Law; Personal Injury; Product Liability Law

FREISHTAT & SANDLER
Baltimore, MD ..... Civil Trial Practice; Commercial Litigation; Construction Law; Professional Liability

FREITAS, MCCARTHY, MACMAHON & KEATING, LLP
San Rafael, CA ..... Insurance Defense

FRENCH & STONE, P.C.
Boulder, CO ..... Civil Trial Practice; Commercial Law; Personal Injury

FREUND, FREEZE & ARNOLD, A LEGAL PROFESSIONAL ASSOCIATION
Dayton, OH ..... Civil Trial Practice; Commercial Law; Construction Law; Insurance Defense; Medical Malpractice; Product Liability Law

FRIDAY, ELDREDGE & CLARK
Little Rock, AR .... Antitrust Law; Banking Law; Civil Trial Practice; General Practice; Insurance Defense; Labor and Employment Law; Municipal Bond/Public Authority Financing; Personal Injury; Securities Law; Tax Law

FRIED & ASSOCIATES, P.C.
Livonia, MI .... Tax Law; Trust and Estates, Wills and Probate

FRIEDBERG, JOSEPH S., CHARTERED
Minneapolis, MN .... Criminal Trial Practice

FRIED, BIRD & CRUMPACKER, A PROFESSIONAL CORPORATION
Los Angeles, CA .... Banking Law; Commercial Litigation; Labor and Employment Law; Real Estate Law

FRIED, FRANK, HARRIS, SHRIVER & JACOBSON
Washington, DC .... General Practice; Tax Law
New York, NY .... General Practice
London, England .... General Practice
Paris, France .... General Practice

FRIEDLOB SANDERSON RASKIN PAULSON & TOURTILLOTT, LLC
Denver, CO .... Civil Trial Practice; Corporate Law; Environmental Law; Natural Resources Law; Securities Law; Transportation Law

FRIEDMAN, AVERY S.
Cleveland, OH .... Civil Rights

FRIEDMAN, BARRY A. & ASSOCIATES
Mobile, AL .... Creditors Rights

FRIEDMAN & ATHERTON
Boston, MA .... Civil Trial Practice; Family Law; General Practice

FRIEDMAN & BABBITT CO., L.P.A.
Columbus, OH .... Family Law

FRIEDMAN BABCOCK & GAYTHWAITE
Portland, ME .... Civil Trial Practice; Environmental Law; Health Care Law; Insurance Defense; Personal Injury; Product Liability Law

FRIEDMAN, C. MARSHALL, A PROFESSIONAL CORPORATION
St. Louis, MO .... Civil Trial Practice

FRIEDMAN, COLLARD, CUTTER & PANNETON, PROFESSIONAL CORPORATION
Sacramento, CA .... General Practice; Personal Injury

FRIEDMAN, DOMIANO & SMITH CO., L.P.A.
Cleveland, OH .... Medical Malpractice; Personal Injury; Product Liability Law

FRIEDMAN AND FRIEDMAN, P.A.
Miami, FL .... Medical Malpractice; Personal Injury

FRIEDMAN KAPLAN & SEILER LLP
New York, NY .... Business Law; Civil Trial Practice; Commercial Litigation; Labor and Employment Law; Securities Law

FRIEDMAN, LEAK & BLOOM, P.C.
Birmingham, AL .... Insurance Defense; Product Liability Law

FRIEDMAN, LEVY & GOLDFARB, P.C.
New York, NY .... Medical Malpractice; Personal Injury

FRIEDMAN, OLIVE, MCCUBBIN, SPALDING, BILTER, ROOSEVELT & MONTGOMERY, A PROFESSIONAL CORPORATION
San Francisco, CA .... Trust and Estates, Wills and Probate

FRIEDMAN, WITTENSTEIN & HOCHMAN, A PROFESSIONAL CORPORATION
New York, NY .... Civil Trial Practice; Corporate Law; General Practice

FRIEDRICH & FRIEDRICH, P.A.
Fort Lauderdale, FL .... Trust and Estates, Wills and Probate

FRIELING, LEONARD I., P.C.
Boulder, CO .... Criminal Trial Practice

FRIEND, KARL E.
Allentown, PA .... Bankruptcy Law
Reading, PA .... Bankruptcy Law

FRIEND & ASSOCIATES, L.L.P.
Houston, TX .... Medical Malpractice

FRIERSON & WATSON
Stuart, FL .... Criminal Trial Practice; Personal Injury

FRIJOUF, RUST & PYLE, P.A.
Tampa, FL .... Patent, Trademark, Copyright and Unfair Competition

FRILOT, PARTRIDGE, KOHNKE & CLEMENTS, L.C.
New Orleans, LA .... Admiralty/Maritime Law; Environmental Law; General Practice; Insurance Defense; Product Liability Law

FRINK, FOY & YOUNT, P.A.
Shallotte, NC .... General Practice
Southport, NC .... General Practice

FRISK, FRANK W., JR., P.C.
Washington, DC .... Natural Resources Law

FRISTOE, TAYLOR & SCHULTZ, LTD., P.S.
Olympia, WA .... General Practice

FROELICH & WEPRIN CO. LPA
Dayton, OH .... Business Law; Real Estate Law

FROHNMAYER, DEATHERAGE, PRATT, JAMIESON, CLARKE & MOORE, P.C.
Medford, OR .... Commercial Litigation; General Practice; Insurance Defense

FROIMSON, JEROME L.
Phoenix, AZ .... Labor and Employment Law

FROMME SCHWARTZ NEWMAN & CORNICELLO, LLP
New York, NY .... Commercial Litigation; Corporate Law; Real Estate Law

FROMMER LAWRENCE & HAUG LLP
New York, NY .... Patent, Trademark, Copyright and Unfair Competition

FROSS ZELNICK LEHRMAN & ZISSU, P.C.
New York, NY .... Trademark, Copyright and Unfair Competition

FROST & JACOBS LLP
Cincinnati, OH .... Antitrust Law; Banking Law; Bankruptcy Law; Civil Trial Practice; Commercial Law; Communications Law; Environmental Law; General Practice; Health Care Law; Intellectual Property Law; Labor and Employment Law; Patent, Trademark, Copyright and Unfair Competition; Real Estate Law; Tax Law
Middletown, OH .... General Practice

FROST & SAUNDERS, P.A.
Bartow, FL .... Civil Trial Practice; Commercial Litigation; General Practice; Medical Malpractice; Personal Injury

FRUE LAW FIRM, THE, L.L.P.
Asheville, NC .... Real Estate Law

FRYER & ROSS
New York, NY .... Civil Trial Practice

FTHENAKIS, BASIL P.
Palo Alto, CA .... Antitrust Law; Civil Trial Practice; Patent, Trademark, Copyright and Unfair Competition

FUCHSBERG & FUCHSBERG
New York, NY .... Civil Trial Practice; Medical Malpractice; Personal Injury; Product Liability Law

FUCHSBERG, JACOB D., THE, LAW FIRM
New York, NY .... Medical Malpractice; Personal Injury

FUENTES AND KREISCHER
Tampa, FL .... Real Estate Law

FUJIYAMA, DUFFY & FUJIYAMA, ATTORNEYS AT LAW, A LAW CORPORATION
Honolulu, HI .... Civil Trial Practice; General Practice

FUKUNAGA MATAYOSHI HERSHEY & CHING
Honolulu, HI .... Civil Trial Practice; Insurance Defense; Intellectual Property Law; Product Liability Law

FULBRIGHT & JAWORSKI L.L.P.
Houston, TX .... General Practice

FULCHER, HAGLER, REED, HANKS & HARPER, LLP
Augusta, GA .... General Practice

FULLENWEIDER & ASSOCIATES
Houston, TX .... Family Law

FULLER, BECTON, SLIFKIN & BELL, P.A.
Raleigh, NC .... Medical Malpractice; Personal Injury

FULLER HOLSONBACK & BIVINS, P.A.
Tampa, FL .... Commercial Litigation; Mergers and Acquisitions; Securities Law; Trust and Estates, Wills and Probate

FULLER, JOHNSON & FARRELL, P.A.
Pensacola, FL .... Civil Trial Practice; Product Liability Law
Tallahassee, FL .... Civil Trial Practice; Product Liability Law

FULLER, TELLINGHUISEN, GORDON & PERCY, P.C.
Lead, SD....................Administrative Law; Business Law; Civil Trial Practice; Corporate Law; Criminal Trial Practice; Family Law; General Practice; Personal Injury; Trust and Estates, Wills and Probate; Workers Compensation

FULLER, VAUGHN AND GOTT
Kingsport, TN....................Insurance Defense

FULLER-JACOBS, NANCY & ASSOCIATES
San Diego, CA....................Immigration and Naturalization; International Business Law; International Trade Law

FULTON, PHILIP J. & ASSOCIATES
Columbus, OH....................Workers Compensation

FULWIDER PATTON LEE & UTECHT, LLP
Los Angeles, CA....................Patent, Trademark, Copyright and Unfair Competition

FUNDERBURK & ANDREWS
Baton Rouge, LA....................Insurance Defense

FUNK & BOLTON, A PROFESSIONAL ASSOCIATION
Baltimore, MD....................Administrative Law; Appellate Practice; Business Law; Insurance Defense; Municipal Bond/Public Authority Financing

FURBEE, AMOS, WEBB & CRITCHFIELD
Fairmont, WV....................Civil Trial Practice; Commercial Litigation; General Practice; Insurance Defense; Real Estate Law
Morgantown, WV....................General Practice

FUREY & FUREY, P.C.
Hempstead, NY....................Civil Trial Practice

FUREY, KERLEY, WALSH, MATERA & CINQUEMANI, A PROFESSIONAL CORPORATION
Mineola, NY....................Appellate Practice; Insurance Defense

FURGANG & ADWAR, LLP
New York, NY....................Intellectual Property Law

FURIA AND TURNER
Philadelphia, PA....................Civil Trial Practice; Medical Malpractice; Personal Injury; Product Liability Law; Real Estate Law; Trust and Estates, Wills and Probate; Workers Compensation

FURR AND COHEN, P.A.
Boca Raton, FL....................Bankruptcy Law; Creditors Rights; Family Law; Real Estate Law

FURR AND HENSHAW
Myrtle Beach, SC....................Civil Trial Practice; Medical Malpractice; Personal Injury

FUSCO LEGAL GROUP, THE, L.C.
Morgantown, WV....................Antitrust Law; Civil Trial Practice; Commercial Litigation; General Practice; Health Care Law; Mergers and Acquisitions

FUTERFAS, ALAN S. LAW OFFICES OF
New York, NY....................Criminal Trial Practice

GABEL INTERNATIONAL LAW FIRM
Burlington, VT....................International Business Law

GABLER & ASSOCIATES, P.C.
Pittsburgh, PA....................Employment Benefits Law

GABROY, ROLLMAN & BOSSÉ, P.C.
Tucson, AZ....................Civil Trial Practice; General Practice; Personal Injury; Tax Law; Trust and Estates, Wills and Probate

GACA MATIS BAUM & RIZZA, A PROFESSIONAL CORPORATION
Pittsburgh, PA....................Civil Trial Practice

GADSBY & HANNAH LLP
Boston, MA....................Civil Trial Practice; General Practice

GAGER & PETERSON, LLP
Waterbury, CT....................General Practice

GAGE & WILLIAMS LAW FIRM
Muskogee, OK....................Civil Trial Practice; General Practice

GAILOR & ASSOCIATES, P.L.L.C.
Raleigh, NC....................Family Law

GAINES & HELINGER
Clearwater, FL....................Eminent Domain

GAINSBURGH, BENJAMIN, DAVID, MEUNIER & WARSHAUER
New Orleans, LA....................Admiralty/Maritime Law; Criminal Trial Practice; Environmental Law; General Practice; Medical Malpractice; Personal Injury; Product Liability Law

GAIR, GAIR, CONASON, STEIGMAN & MACKAUF
New York, NY....................Civil Trial Practice; General Practice; Personal Injury

GALATZ, EARL, & ASSOCIATES
Las Vegas, NV....................Civil Trial Practice; Medical Malpractice; Personal Injury; Product Liability Law

GALFAND BERGER, LLP
Philadelphia, PA....................Labor and Employment Law; Medical Malpractice; Personal Injury; Product Liability Law; Toxic Torts; Trust and Estates, Wills and Probate; Workers Compensation

GALFIN & PASSON, LLP
Irvine, CA....................Business Law; Commercial Litigation; Real Estate Law

GALLAGHER & CALISTRO
New Haven, CT....................Appellate Practice; Civil Trial Practice; General Practice; Medical Malpractice; Personal Injury; Product Liability Law; Professional Liability

GALLAGHER, EVELIUS & JONES, LLP
Baltimore, MD....................Banking Law; Business Law; Civil Trial Practice; Commercial Law; Commercial Litigation; Corporate Law; Education Law; Health Care Law; Nonprofit and Tax Exempt Organizations; Real Estate Law; Securities Law; Tax Law; Trust and Estates, Wills and Probate; Workers Compensation

GALLAGHER GOSSEEN FALLER KAPLAN & CROWLEY
Garden City, NY....................Civil Trial Practice; Employment Benefits Law; General Practice; Insurance Defense; Labor and Employment Law; Personal Injury; Product Liability Law

GALLAGHER, JAMES J., LAW OFFICES OF
Fort Lauderdale, FL....................Insurance Defense

GALLAGHER, JOHN J., P.C., LAW OFFICES OF
Philadelphia, PA....................Business Law; Civil Trial Practice; Commercial Litigation; Personal Injury; Public Utilities Law

GALLAGHER & LATHROP, A PROFESSIONAL CORPORATION
San Francisco, CA....................Patent, Trademark, Copyright and Unfair Competition

GALLAGHER, REILLY, LACHAT & EGBERT, P.C.
Philadelphia, PA....................Insurance Defense

GALLAGHER, SHARP, FULTON & NORMAN
Cleveland, OH....................Civil Trial Practice; Environmental Law; General Practice; Insurance Defense; Medical Malpractice; Product Liability Law; Professional Liability

GALLAGHER, WALKER, BIANCO & PLASTARAS
Mineola, NY....................Business Law; Insurance Defense; Medical Malpractice; Product Liability Law

GALLAGHER, YOUNG, LEWIS, HAMPTON & DOWNEY, L.L.P.
Houston, TX....................Aviation Law; Civil Trial Practice; Commercial Law; Environmental Law; Medical Malpractice; Personal Injury; Product Liability Law

GALLAS & SCHULTZ
Kansas City, MO....................Bankruptcy Law

GALLAWA • BROWN • KROESCH, A PROFESSIONAL CORPORATION
Sacramento, CA....................Insurance Defense; Personal Injury

GALLET DREYER & BERKEY, LLP
New York, NY....................Civil Trial Practice; Real Estate Law; Trust and Estates, Wills and Probate

GALLIGAN & NEWMAN
McMinnville, TN....................General Practice

GALLIGAN, TULLY, DOYLE & REID, P.C.
Des Moines, IA....................Medical Malpractice

GALLIHER, KEITH E., JR., CHARTERED
Las Vegas, NV....................Personal Injury

GALLION, BAKER & BRAY, P.S.C.
Lexington, KY....................Civil Trial Practice; Medical Malpractice

GALLNER, SHELDON, P.C.
Council Bluffs, IA....................Family Law; Personal Injury; Workers Compensation

GALLON, E. S., & ASSOCIATES
Dayton, OH....................Administrative Law; Personal Injury; Product Liability Law; Workers Compensation

GALLOP, JOHNSON & NEUMAN, L.C.
St. Louis, MO....................General Practice

GALLOWAY, SMITH, WETTERMARK & EVEREST, LLP
Mobile, AL....................Insurance Defense; Trust and Estates, Wills and Probate

GALTON & HELM LLP
Los Angeles, CA .... Civil Trial Practice; Health Care Law; Insurance Defense

GAMBERG, JAY M., P.A.
Hollywood, FL .... Bankruptcy Law

GAMBRELL & STOLZ, L.L.P.
Atlanta, GA .... Civil Trial Practice; General Practice

GAMMILL, WARREN P.
Miami, FL .... Business Law; Real Estate Law

GANDIN, SCHOTSKY, RAPPAPORT, GLASS & GREENE, LLP
Melville, NY .... Civil Trial Practice; Medical Malpractice; Personal Injury; Product Liability Law

GANDY, FRANCIS I. JR.
Corpus Christi, TX .... Civil Trial Practice

GANNON, COTTRELL & WARD, P.C.
Alexandria, VA .... Civil Trial Practice; Family Law
Fairfax, VA .... Family Law

GAONA MOORE, P.C.
Phoenix, AZ .... Construction Law; Labor and Employment Law

GARAN, LUCOW, MILLER & SEWARD, P.C.
Ann Arbor, MI .... Civil Trial Practice; General Practice; Insurance Defense; Product Liability Law
Detroit, MI .... Civil Trial Practice; General Practice; Insurance Defense; Product Liability Law
Grand Blanc, MI .... Civil Trial Practice; General Practice; Insurance Defense; Product Liability Law
Grand Rapids, MI .... Civil Trial Practice; General Practice; Insurance Defense; Product Liability Law
Lansing, MI .... Civil Trial Practice; General Practice; Insurance Defense; Product Liability Law
Mount Clemens, MI .... Civil Trial Practice; General Practice; Insurance Defense; Product Liability Law
Port Huron, MI .... Civil Trial Practice; General Practice; Insurance Defense; Product Liability Law
Traverse City, MI .... Civil Trial Practice; General Practice; Insurance Defense; Product Liability Law
Troy, MI .... Civil Trial Practice; General Practice; Insurance Defense; Product Liability Law

GARBARINI & SCHER, P.C.
New York, NY .... Medical Malpractice; Product Liability Law

GARCIA, MANUEL D. LAW OFFICES OF
Honolulu, HI .... International Business Law; Real Estate Law; Tax Law

GARDERE & WYNNE, L.L.P.
Dallas, TX .... General Practice

GARDNER, BARROW & SHARPE, A PROFESSIONAL CORPORATION
Danville, VA .... General Practice; Personal Injury

GARDNER BOND TRABOLSI ST. LOUIS & CLEMENT, PLLC
Seattle, WA .... Insurance Defense

GARDNER, CARTON & DOUGLAS
Chicago, IL .... General Practice

GARDNER & CHARNEY, P.L.L.P.
Boise, ID .... Insurance Defense; Workers Compensation

GARDNER, GARDNER, BARROW & SHARPE, A PROFESSIONAL CORPORATION
Martinsville, VA .... General Practice; Personal Injury

GARDNER, MIDDLEBROOKS, FLEMING, GIBBONS & KITTRELL, P.C.
Mobile, AL .... Insurance Defense; Labor and Employment Law; Workers Compensation

GARFINKLE & ASSOCIATES, LAW OFFICES OF
Washington, DC .... Family Law; Intellectual Property Law; Trust and Estates, Wills and Probate

GARFINKLE, MCLEMORE & WALKER, PLLC
Nashville, TN .... Bankruptcy Law; Personal Injury

GARFUNKEL, WILD & TRAVIS, P.C.
Great Neck, NY .... Health Care Law

GARGARO, WILLIAM J., JR., A PROFESSIONAL CORPORATION
Los Angeles, CA .... Medical Malpractice

GARIPPA AND DAVENPORT, A PROFESSIONAL CORPORATION
Montclair, NJ .... Civil Trial Practice; Real Estate Law; Tax Law

GARLAND, SAMUEL & LOEB, P.C.
Atlanta, GA .... Appellate Practice; Civil Trial Practice; Criminal Trial Practice; Labor and Employment Law; Medical Malpractice; Personal Injury; Product Liability Law

GARLINGTON, LOHN & ROBINSON, PLLP
Missoula, MT .... General Practice

GARMON & GOODMAN
Glasgow, KY .... Bankruptcy Law; General Practice; Real Estate Law; Trust and Estates, Wills and Probate

GARNER & STEIN, LLP
Amarillo, TX .... Civil Trial Practice; Commercial Law; Personal Injury

GARNIER & GARNIER, P.C.
Falls Church, VA .... Insurance Defense

GARRAHAN, BARBIERI & GARRAHAN, P.C.
Framingham, MA .... Real Estate Law

GARRETT & GARRETT, A PROF. CORP., LAW OFFICES
Bedford, VA .... General Practice

GARRETT & GILLIARD
Augusta, GA .... Appellate Practice; Criminal Trial Practice

GARRETT & JENSEN
Santa Ana, CA .... Insurance Defense; Personal Injury

GARRIGLE, PALM AND THOMASSON
Cherry Hill, NJ .... General Practice

GARSON GERSPACH DECORATO & COHEN, LLP
New York, NY .... Civil Trial Practice; Insurance Defense; Medical Malpractice

GARTNER, BENNETT & SCHUPP, P.C.
Minneapolis, MN .... Civil Trial Practice; Personal Injury; Product Liability Law

GARTNER & YOUNG, A PROFESSIONAL CORPORATION
Los Angeles, CA .... Labor and Employment Law

GARVER LAW OFFICES, P.C.
Reston, VA .... Civil Trial Practice; Criminal Trial Practice; Medical Malpractice; Personal Injury

GARVEY, ANDERSON, JOHNSON, GABLER & GERACI, S.C.
Eau Claire, WI .... General Practice; Insurance Defense

GARVEY, SCHUBERT & BARER
Portland, OR .... General Practice
Seattle, WA .... Admiralty/Maritime Law; General Practice

GARVIN, DAVID M., P.A.
Miami, FL .... Criminal Trial Practice; Tax Law

GARVIN & TRIPP, A PROFESSIONAL ASSOCIATION
Fort Myers, FL .... Appellate Practice; Commercial Litigation; Personal Injury

GARWOOD, MCKENNA, MCKENNA & WOLF, P.A.
Orlando, FL .... Labor and Employment Law

GARY & GOODMAN LIMITED
Vienna, VA .... Business Law; Commercial Law; Corporate Law; Mergers and Acquisitions; Real Estate Law; Tax Law

GARZA & GARZA, L.L.P.
Brownsville, TX .... Civil Trial Practice

GARZA, REGAN & ROSENBLATT, P.C.
Rockville, MD .... Bankruptcy Law; Commercial Litigation

GASSMAN, STEPHEN, LAW OFFICES OF
Garden City, NY .... Civil Trial Practice; Family Law

GATES LAW OFFICE
Columbia City, IN .... Trust and Estates, Wills and Probate

GATHRIGHT & HARDY
Louisville, KY .... Real Estate Law

GATLIN & BIRCH, P.A.
Tampa, FL .... Business Law; Commercial Litigation; Real Estate Law

GATZKE, DILLON & BALLANCE
Carlsbad, CA .... Aviation Law; Civil Trial Practice; Environmental Law

GAULEY & CO.
Saskatoon, SK, Canada .... Civil Trial Practice; Commercial Law; General Practice; Labor and Employment Law

GAULT DAVISON, A PROFESSIONAL SERVICE CORPORATION
Flint, MI .... Business Law; Civil Trial Practice; Commercial Law; Corporate Law; Environmental Law; Insurance Defense; Labor and Employment Law; Trust and Estates, Wills and Probate

GAUNTLETT & ASSOCIATES
Irvine, CA....Appellate Practice; Intellectual Property Law

GAVIN LAW FIRM
Belleville, IL....Admiralty/Maritime Law; Commercial Litigation; Environmental Law

GAW, VAN MALE, SMITH, MYERS & MIROGLIO, A PROFESSIONAL LAW CORPORATION
Napa, CA....Business Law; Civil Trial Practice; Family Law; Land Use Law; Real Estate Law; Tax Law; Trust and Estates, Wills and Probate

GAWTHROP, GREENWOOD & HALSTED, A PROFESSIONAL CORPORATION
West Chester, PA....Business Law; General Practice; Health Care Law; Municipal and Zoning Law; Trust and Estates, Wills and Probate

GAY & CHACKER, A PROFESSIONAL CORPORATION
Philadelphia, PA....Personal Injury

GAYLORD, MCNALLY, STRICKLAND & SNYDER, L.L.P.
Greenville, NC....Business Law; Commercial Litigation; General Practice; Insurance Defense; Personal Injury; Real Estate Law

GEAN, GEAN & GEAN
Fort Smith, AR....Bankruptcy Law; Corporate Law; Real Estate Law

GEARHISER, PETERS, LOCKABY & TALLANT, PLLC
Chattanooga, TN....Business Law; Civil Trial Practice; General Practice; Tax Law; Trust and Estates, Wills and Probate

GEARY, WILLIAM L.
Columbus, OH....Family Law

GEARY, PORTER & DONOVAN, P.C.
Dallas, TX....Civil Trial Practice; Eminent Domain; Family Law; Real Estate Law; Trust and Estates, Wills and Probate

GEBHARDT, JOSEPH D., P.C.
Washington, DC....Civil Rights; Labor and Employment Law

GEBHARDT & KIEFER, P.C.
Clinton, NJ....General Practice

GEDNEY, SEAMAN & HILGENDORFF
Florham Park, NJ....General Practice; Tax Law; Trust and Estates, Wills and Probate

GEESLIN, JOSEPH D. JR.
Indianapolis, IN....Tax Law

GEHLHAUSEN, JOHN, P.C.
Lamar, CO....Civil Trial Practice; Personal Injury

GEHRING, ROBERT J., CO., L.P.A.
Cincinnati, OH....Civil Trial Practice; Insurance Defense; Personal Injury; Product Liability Law; Professional Liability

GEIMER LAW FIRM, S.C.
Green Bay, WI....Trust and Estates, Wills and Probate

GELB & GELB LLP
Boston, MA....Civil Trial Practice; Family Law; Intellectual Property Law; Securities Law

GELERMAN, CASHMAN & DONAHUE
Dedham, MA....Civil Trial Practice; General Practice

GELLES, PETER A.
Los Angeles, CA....International Business Law; Real Estate Law

GELT, PADDISON & ASSOCIATES P.C.
Denver, CO....Tax Law

GEMRICH, MOSER, BOWSER, MURPHY & GRAHAM, LLP
Kalamazoo, MI....Corporate Law

GENDERS, CURT, P.A.
Tampa, FL....Personal Injury; Trust and Estates, Wills and Probate

GENDRY & SPRAGUE, P.C.
San Antonio, TX....Aviation Law; Insurance Defense

GENN, JONATHAN M.
Silver Spring, MD....Corporate Law

GENNET, KALLMANN, ANTIN & ROBINSON, A PROFESSIONAL CORPORATION
Parsippany, NJ....Appellate Practice; Civil Trial Practice; Insurance Defense; Personal Injury

GENOVA, BURNS & VERNOIA
Livingston, NJ....Administrative Law; Appellate Practice; Civil Trial Practice; Environmental Law; Health Care Law; Insurance Defense; Labor and Employment Law

GENTRY & HASKINS LLP
Colorado Springs, CO....Criminal Trial Practice

GENTRY, NICHOLAS R., L.L.C., LAW OFFICES OF
Albuquerque, NM....Civil Trial Practice

GENTRY, PHILLIPS AND HODAK, P.A.
Jacksonville, FL....Civil Trial Practice; Medical Malpractice; Personal Injury

GEORGE & DONALDSON, L.L.P.
Austin, TX....Appellate Practice; Civil Trial Practice

GEORGE, EDWARD P., JR., INC., A PROF. CORP.
Long Beach, CA....Appellate Practice; Civil Trial Practice; Criminal Trial Practice; Personal Injury

GEORGE AND GEORGE, LTD., A PROFESSIONAL LAW CORPORATION
Baton Rouge, LA....Admiralty/Maritime Law; Personal Injury

GEORGE, HARTZ, LUNDEEN, FLAGG & FULMER
Miami, FL....Insurance Defense; Medical Malpractice

GEORGE, J. K., & ASSOCIATES
Los Osos, CA....Tax Law; Trust and Estates, Wills and Probate

GEORGE, J.K., & ASSOCIATES
San Luis Obispo, CA....Tax Law; Trust and Estates, Wills and Probate

GEORGE & SHIELDS, LLP
Irvine, CA....Business Law; Civil Trial Practice; Labor and Employment Law

GEORGESON, THOMPSON & ANGARAN, CHARTERED
Reno, NV....Insurance Defense

GEORGE, THOMAS, P.C.
Austin, TX....Civil Trial Practice; Health Care Law

GERAGHTY, O'LOUGHLIN & KENNEY, PROFESSIONAL ASSOCIATION
St. Paul, MN....Civil Trial Practice; Construction Law; Insurance Defense; Labor and Employment Law; Medical Malpractice

GERAGHTY, PATRICK E., A PROFESSIONAL ASSOCIATION
Fort Myers, FL....Civil Rights; Civil Trial Practice; Commercial Law; Personal Injury

GERAGOS & GERAGOS
Los Angeles, CA....Criminal Trial Practice

GERALDS, JONES, SHERROW, SCHRADER & RICE, P.S.C.
Lexington, KY....General Practice; Insurance Defense; Real Estate Law

GERARD SINGER & LEVICK, P.C.
Addison, TX....Bankruptcy Law; Business Law; Civil Trial Practice; Commercial Litigation; Insurance Defense

GERBER & BATEMAN, A PROFESSIONAL ASSOCIATION
Santa Fe, NM....Family Law; Trust and Estates, Wills and Probate

GERBER & GERBER
Blue Bell, PA....Business Law; Civil Trial Practice; Criminal Trial Practice; Eminent Domain; General Practice; Personal Injury; Real Estate Law

GERBER & SAMSON, L.L.C.
Wayne, NJ....Civil Trial Practice; Labor and Employment Law; Municipal and Zoning Law

GERDING & O'LOUGHLIN, P.C.
Farmington, NM....Civil Trial Practice

GERLING LAW OFFICES, PROFESSIONAL CORPORATION
Evansville, IN....Medical Malpractice; Personal Injury; Product Liability Law

GERRITY AND BURRIER
Columbus, OH....Family Law; Personal Injury

GERSON, GREKIN & WYNHOFF, ATTORNEYS AT LAW, A LAW CORPORATION
Honolulu, HI....Real Estate Law; Trust and Estates, Wills and Probate

GERSTEIN GRAYSON, LLP
Haddonfield, NJ....General Practice

GERSTEIN, JOE W., P.C.
Doraville, GA....General Practice

GERTNER & GERTNER
Columbus, OH....Civil Trial Practice; Criminal Trial Practice; Personal Injury

GESSLER, HUGHES & SOCOL, LTD.
Chicago, IL....Civil Rights; Civil Trial Practice; Commercial Litigation; Health Care Law; Immigration and Naturalization; Insurance Defense; Labor and Employment Law; Medical Malpractice; Personal Injury; Professional Liability

GETMAN LAW FIRM
Oneonta, NY ....General Practice; Real Estate Law; Trust and Estates, Wills and Probate

GETNICK & GETNICK
New York, NY ....Business Law; Civil Trial Practice; Commercial Litigation; Criminal Trial Practice

GHOLSON, HICKS & NICHOLS, A PROFESSIONAL ASSOCIATION
Columbus, MS ....General Practice

GIACOMINI, J. ANTHONY, PC
Klamath Falls, OR ....General Practice

GIANELLI & FORES, A PROFESSIONAL LAW CORPORATION
Modesto, CA ....Business Law; Commercial Litigation; Trust and Estates, Wills and Probate

GIAUQUE, CROCKETT, BENDINGER & PETERSON, A PROFESSIONAL CORPORATION
Salt Lake City, UT ....Antitrust Law; Commercial Law

GIBBES GRAVES MULLINS HORTMAN HARLOW MARTINDALE & JONES, PLLC
Laurel, MS ....Environmental Law; General Practice; Insurance Defense; Real Estate Law

GIBBONS, JOHN B.
Cleveland, OH ....Criminal Trial Practice

GIBBONS, WILLIAM P.
Cleveland, OH ....Business Law

GIBBONS, SMITH, COHN & ARNETT, A PROFESSIONAL ASSOCIATION
Tampa, FL ....General Practice

GIBBS & BRUNS, L.L.P.
Houston, TX ....Civil Trial Practice; Commercial Law

GIBBS & HOLMES
Charleston, SC ....Labor and Employment Law

GIBBS AND SCHWARTZMAN
San Antonio, TX ....Tax Law; Trust and Estates, Wills and Probate

GIBNEY, ANTHONY & FLAHERTY, LLP
New York, NY ....General Practice; Tax Law

GIBSON, DUNN & CRUTCHER LLP
Los Angeles, CA ....General Practice

GIBSON, HAGLUND & PAULSEN
Irvine, CA ....Securities Law

GIBSON, HOTCHKISS, ROACH & DAVENPORT
Wichita Falls, TX ....Banking Law; Business Law; Civil Trial Practice; Construction Law; General Practice; Trust and Estates, Wills and Probate

GIBSON, LEFLER & ASSOCIATES
Princeton, WV ....Banking Law; Civil Trial Practice; Criminal Trial Practice; Medical Malpractice; Personal Injury; Product Liability Law; Workers Compensation

GIBSON, MCCLURE & WALLACE, L.L.P.
Dallas, TX ....Civil Trial Practice; Commercial Litigation; Insurance Defense; Labor and Employment Law

GIBSON, OCHSNER & ADKINS, LLP
Amarillo, TX ....General Practice

GIBSON, RICHARD H., A PROF. CORP., LAW OFFICES OF
Los Angeles, CA ....Bankruptcy Law; Civil Trial Practice

GIFFEN LEE
Kitchener, ON, Canada ....Civil Trial Practice; Family Law; Insurance Defense; Personal Injury; Trust and Estates, Wills and Probate

GIFFIN, WINNING, COHEN & BODEWES, P.C.
Springfield, IL ....Bankruptcy Law; Civil Trial Practice; General Practice; Insurance Defense

GIGNILLIAT, SAVITZ & BETTIS
Columbia, SC ....Employment Benefits Law; Labor and Employment Law

GILBERT, MICHAEL L.
Denver, CO ....Elder Law; Trust and Estates, Wills and Probate

GILBERT, HARRELL, GILBERT, SUMERFORD & MARTIN, P.C.
Brunswick, GA ....Civil Trial Practice; General Practice; Insurance Defense

GILBERT, MCGLOAN, GILLIS
Saint John, NB, Canada ....Business Law; Civil Trial Practice; General Practice; Insurance Defense

GILBREATH LAW FIRM
Fort Smith, AR ....Medical Malpractice; Product Liability Law

GILCHRIST & RUTTER, PROFESSIONAL CORPORATION
Los Angeles, CA ....Labor and Employment Law
Santa Monica, CA ....Bankruptcy Law; Business Law; Creditors Rights; Real Estate Law

GILCREASE, GLYNN W. JR., LAW OFFICES OF
Tempe, AZ ....Personal Injury

GILDEMEISTER, WILLIA, KEANE, STAHLE & ANDREASEN, L.L.P.
Sioux City, IA ....General Practice

GILKEY, STEPHENSON & WEESE, P.A.
Albuquerque, NM ....Labor and Employment Law

GILLARY, RANDALL J., P.C.
Troy, MI ....Commercial Litigation

GILL AND BALDWIN
Glendale, CA ....Business Law; Civil Trial Practice; Construction Law; Trust and Estates, Wills and Probate

GILLESPIE, GOLDMAN & KRONENGOLD
Fort Lauderdale, FL ....Civil Trial Practice; Commercial Litigation; Personal Injury

GILLESPIE, HART, ALTIZER & WHITESELL, P.C.
Tazewell, VA ....General Practice

GILLESPIE, JAMES R., P.A.
Boise, ID ....General Practice

GILLESPIE, ROZEN & WATSKY, P.C.
Dallas, TX ....Labor and Employment Law

GILLILAND & ASSOCIATES
Covington, KY ....Health Care Law; Labor and Employment Law

GILLILAND & HAYES, P.A. A PROFESSIONAL ASSOCIATION
Hutchinson, KS ....Civil Trial Practice; Commercial Litigation; Construction Law; Employment Benefits Law; General Practice; Health Care Law; Insurance Defense; Labor and Employment Law; Medical Malpractice; Real Estate Law; Tax Law; Trust and Estates, Wills and Probate; Workers Compensation

GILLIN, JACOBSON, ELLIS & LARSEN
Orinda, CA ....Civil Trial Practice; Commercial Litigation; Labor and Employment Law; Personal Injury

GILLIS, NORMAN B. JR.
Mc Comb, MS ....General Practice

GILLIS & ANGLEY
Hingham, MA ....Corporate Law; General Practice

GILLIS & SLOGAR
Houston, TX ....Bankruptcy Law; Business Law; Civil Trial Practice; Commercial Law; Real Estate Law; Tax Law

GILLOCK, MARKLEY & KILLEBREW
Las Vegas, NV ....Medical Malpractice; Personal Injury

GILLOTTI, CAPRISTO & BECK, P.C.
Pittsburgh, PA ....Family Law

GILL PROFESSIONAL CORPORATION
Denver, CO ....Trust and Estates, Wills and Probate

GILMAN, MCLAUGHLIN & HANRAHAN, LLP
Boston, MA ....General Practice

GILMER, SADLER, INGRAM, SUTHERLAND & HUTTON
Blacksburg, VA ....General Practice; Insurance Defense; Personal Injury
Pulaski, VA ....General Practice; Insurance Defense; Personal Injury

GILMORE, R. PATRICK
Chandler, OK ....Civil Trial Practice

GILMORE & BELL, A PROFESSIONAL CORPORATION
Kansas City, MO ....Municipal Bond/Public Authority Financing

GILMORE, REES & CARLSON, P.C.
Franklin, MA ....Tax Law; Trust and Estates, Wills and Probate

GILPIN, PAXSON & BERSCH
Houston, TX ....Appellate Practice; Banking Law; Bankruptcy Law; Civil Trial Practice; Construction Law; Environmental Law; Insurance Defense; Personal Injury; Product Liability Law; Real Estate Law

GILREATH & ASSOCIATES
Knoxville, TN ....Aviation Law; Environmental Law; Medical Malpractice; Personal Injury; Product Liability Law

GILSTRAP, WILLIAM G.
Albuquerque, NM ....Personal Injury

GINGELL & JENKINS, P.C.
Silver Spring, MD ....General Practice; Real Estate Law; Trust and Estates, Wills and Probate

GINSBERG, EUGENE S.
Garden City, NY .... Arbitration; Labor and Employment Law; Real Estate Law

GINSBERG & BROOME
New York, NY .... Civil Trial Practice; Medical Malpractice; Personal Injury; Product Liability Law

GIOFFRE & GIOFFRE, PROFESSIONAL CORPORATION
Purchase, NY .... General Practice; Real Estate Law; Trust and Estates, Wills and Probate

GIORDANO, HALLERAN & CIESLA, A PROFESSIONAL CORPORATION
Middletown, NJ .... General Practice

GIRARDI AND KEESE
Los Angeles, CA .... Civil Trial Practice; Commercial Litigation; Medical Malpractice; Personal Injury; Product Liability Law; Professional Liability; Toxic Torts

GISLASON & HUNTER, LLP
Mankato, MN .... Civil Trial Practice
Minneapolis, MN .... Civil Trial Practice
New Ulm, MN .... Civil Trial Practice; General Practice

GITLIN, GARY M., A PROFESSIONAL LAW CORPORATION
Calabasas, CA .... Real Estate Law

GITTLER, AMY J., PLC
Phoenix, AZ .... Civil Trial Practice; Commercial Litigation; Labor and Employment Law

GLASER, HAROLD I.
Baltimore, MD .... Civil Trial Practice; Criminal Trial Practice

GLASGOW AND VEAZEY
Nashville, TN .... Insurance Defense

GLASS, JOSEPH G.
Louisville, KY .... General Practice

GLASSMAN, JETER, EDWARDS & WADE, P.C.
Memphis, TN .... Civil Trial Practice; Construction Law; Insurance Defense; Labor and Employment Law; Personal Injury; Product Liability Law

GLATSTEIN & O'BRIEN, LLP
Denver, CO .... Trust and Estates, Wills and Probate

GLAZE & GLAZE, P.C.
Jonesboro, GA .... Banking Law; Commercial Litigation; Corporate Law; Trust and Estates, Wills and Probate

GLEASON, FLYNN & EMIG, CHARTERED
Rockville, MD .... Insurance Defense

GLEAVES SWEARINGEN LARSEN POTTER SCOTT & SMITH, LLP
Eugene, OR .... General Practice

GLEICHER & PATEK, P.C.
Detroit, MI .... Health Care Law; Medical Malpractice; Personal Injury

GLENN, MILLS & FISHER, P.A.
Durham, NC .... Civil Rights; Civil Trial Practice; Personal Injury

GLENN MURPHY GRAY & STEPP, L.L.P.
Columbia, SC .... Civil Trial Practice; Commercial Litigation; Criminal Trial Practice; General Practice; Personal Injury; Product Liability Law

GLENNON, GOODMAN, LUBELEY, VAUGHN & WALKER, L.L.P.
Reston, VA .... General Practice

GLICKMAN, SUGARMAN, KNEELAND & GRIBOUSKI
Worcester, MA .... Criminal Trial Practice; General Practice

GLICK & RETAMAR
Boca Raton, FL .... Medical Malpractice; Personal Injury

GLOSSER & SHREVE
Pittsburgh, PA .... Bankruptcy Law; Commercial Law; Creditors Rights; Real Estate Law

GLOVER, ANDERSON, LEWIS & PREBEG P.C., PROFESSIONAL CORPORATION
Houston, TX .... Appellate Practice; Civil Trial Practice; Personal Injury; Product Liability Law

GLOVER & DAVIS, P.A.
Newnan, GA .... Bankruptcy Law; Business Law; Civil Trial Practice; Construction Law; General Practice; Municipal and Zoning Law; Personal Injury; Real Estate Law; Trust and Estates, Wills and Probate

GLOVER & VAN COTT, A PROFESSIONAL ASSOCIATION
Phoenix, AZ .... Commercial Litigation

GLOVER, YOUNG, WALTON, PHILLIPS & TUCKER, PLLC
Meridian, MS .... Civil Trial Practice; General Practice; Insurance Defense; Labor and Employment Law; Real Estate Law; Trust and Estates, Wills and Probate

GOBER, GARY R. THE LAW OFFICE OF
Nashville, TN .... Personal Injury

GOCKERMAN, WILSON, SAYLOR & HESSLIN, P.C.
Manistee, MI .... Civil Trial Practice; Municipal and Zoning Law; Real Estate Law

GODARD, WEST & ADELMAN, P.C.
Fairfax, VA .... Insurance Defense

GODDARD & GODDARD, P.C.
Denver, CO .... Trust and Estates, Wills and Probate

GODFREY & ASSOCIATES, PROFESSIONAL CORPORATION
Denver, CO .... Civil Trial Practice; Product Liability Law

GODFREY FIRM, THE, A PROFESSIONAL LAW CORPORATION
New Orleans, LA .... Civil Trial Practice; General Practice; Municipal Bond/Public Authority Financing; Tax Law

GODFREY & KAHN, S.C.
Green Bay, WI .... General Practice
Madison, WI .... General Practice
Milwaukee, WI .... General Practice
Oshkosh, WI .... General Practice

GODFREY, VANDOVER & BURNS, INC., A PROFESSIONAL CORPORATION
St. Louis, MO .... Insurance Defense

GODLOVE, MAYHALL, DZIALO, DUTCHER & ERWIN, A PROFESSIONAL CORPORATION
Lawton, OK .... General Practice

GODWIN WHITE & GRUBER, A PROFESSIONAL CORPORATION
Dallas, TX .... Banking Law; Bankruptcy Law; Civil Trial Practice; Commercial Law; General Practice; Insurance Defense; Labor and Employment Law; Tax Law; Trust and Estates, Wills and Probate

GOEDERT, HUNTINGTON & DEBOER
Oak Park, IL .... Business Law; Trust and Estates, Wills and Probate

GOERING, ROBERTS, BERKMAN, RUBIN & BROGNA, P.C.
Tucson, AZ .... Civil Trial Practice; General Practice; Insurance Defense; Medical Malpractice; Personal Injury

GOFF AND GOFF
Ruston, LA .... Product Liability Law

GOFFSTEIN, RASKAS, POMERANTZ, KRAUS, SHERMAN, RUTHMEYER & SUSMAN, L.L.C.
St. Louis, MO .... Insurance Defense

GOICOECHEA & DI GRAZIA, LTD., A PROF. CORP., LAW OFFICES
Elko, NV .... Business Law; Civil Trial Practice; General Practice

GOINS, UNDERKOFLER, CRAWFORD & LANGDON, L.L.P.
Dallas, TX .... Business Law; Construction Law

GOLD, ESTELLA S.
Moorestown, NJ .... Civil Trial Practice; Computer Law; Intellectual Property Law; Trademark, Copyright and Unfair Competition

GOLD, SALLY B. LAW OFFICES OF
Baltimore, MD .... Family Law

GOLD & ASSOCIATES
New York, NY .... International Business Law; International Trade Law

GOLD BENNETT CERA & SIDENER LLP
San Francisco, CA .... Securities Law

GOLDBERG & CONNOLLY
Rockville Centre, NY .... Construction Law

GOLDBERG, GRUENER, GENTILE, HOROHO & AVALLI, P.C.
Pittsburgh, PA .... Family Law

GOLDBERG, JAY, P.C.
New York, NY .... Civil Trial Practice; Criminal Trial Practice; Real Estate Law

GOLDBERG, JEFFREY M., & ASSOCIATES, LTD.
Chicago, IL .... Aviation Law; Medical Malpractice; Personal Injury; Product Liability Law

GOLDBERG, KATZMAN & SHIPMAN, P.C.
Harrisburg, PA .... Antitrust Law; Business Law; Civil Trial Practice; Commercial Law; Criminal Trial Practice; Family Law; General Practice; Insurance Defense; Medical Malpractice; Municipal and Zoning Law; Municipal Bond/Public Authority Financing; Personal Injury; Product Liability Law; Real Estate Law; Tax Law; Trust and Estates, Wills and Probate

GOLDBERG, KOHN, BELL, BLACK, ROSENBLOOM & MORITZ, LTD.
Chicago, IL .... Real Estate Law

GOLDBERG, MUFSON & SPAR, A PROFESSIONAL CORPORATION
West Orange, NJ ....Business Law; Civil Trial Practice; Tax Law; Trust and Estates, Wills and Probate

GOLDBERG & SIMPSON, P.S.C.
Louisville, KY ....Bankruptcy Law; Civil Trial Practice; Corporate Law; Insurance Defense; Securities Law

GOLDBERG, STINNETT, MEYERS & DAVIS, A PROFESSIONAL CORPORATION
San Francisco, CA ....Bankruptcy Law

GOLDBERGER AND DUBIN, P.C.
New York, NY ....Appellate Practice; Criminal Trial Practice; Insurance Defense

GOLDBLATT, LIPKIN & COHEN, P.C.
Norfolk, VA ....Bankruptcy Law; Commercial Law; Family Law; Personal Injury; Trust and Estates, Wills and Probate; Workers Compensation

GOLDEN, TAYLOR & POTTERFIELD
Columbia, SC ....Civil Trial Practice; Family Law

GOLDEN, WEXLER & SARNESE, P.C.
Garden City, NY ....General Practice

GOLDFARB, BERNARD S.
Cleveland, OH ....Business Law; Commercial Litigation; Labor and Employment Law

GOLDFEIN & JOSEPH, A PROFESSIONAL CORPORATION
Philadelphia, PA ....Civil Trial Practice; Commercial Litigation; Insurance Defense; Medical Malpractice; Product Liability Law; Professional Liability; Workers Compensation

GOLD & GOLD
Plano, TX ....Civil Trial Practice; Creditors Rights

GOLDING HOLDEN COSPER POPE & BAKER, L.L.P.
Charlotte, NC ....Civil Trial Practice; Insurance Defense

GOLD LANGE & MAJOROS, P.C.
Southfield, MI ....Bankruptcy Law; Creditors Rights

GOLD, LAWRENCE M., P.C.
Atlanta, GA ....Mergers and Acquisitions

GOLDMAN, LAURENCE R.
Woodland Hills, CA ....Family Law

GOLDMAN ANTONETTI & CÓRDOVA
San Juan, PR ....Banking Law; Civil Trial Practice; Commercial Law; Environmental Law; General Practice; Labor and Employment Law; Municipal Bond/Public Authority Financing; Natural Resources Law; Real Estate Law; Tax Law

GOLDMAN & CURTIS, P.C.
Lowell, MA ....Business Law; General Practice

GOLDMAN & HAFETZ
New York, NY ....Civil Trial Practice; Criminal Trial Practice

GOLDMAN & KAGON, LAW CORPORATION
Los Angeles, CA ....Family Law; General Practice; Real Estate Law

GOLDMAN, LEONARD A., & ASSOCIATES
Los Angeles, CA ....Bankruptcy Law; Civil Trial Practice; Commercial Law; Real Estate Law

GOLDMAN & ROSEN, LTD.
Akron, OH ....Bankruptcy Law; Family Law; Tax Law; Trust and Estates, Wills and Probate

GOLD MORRISON & LAUGHLIN PC
Alexandria, VA ....Bankruptcy Law

GOLDNER, SOMMERS, SCRUDDER & BASS
Atlanta, GA ....Civil Trial Practice; Commercial Law; General Practice; Health Care Law; Insurance Defense; Labor and Employment Law; Legal Malpractice; Medical Malpractice; Personal Injury; Product Liability Law; Professional Liability; Workers Compensation

GOLDSHORE & WOLF, P.C.
Plainsboro, NJ ....Environmental Law

GOLDSMITH & BURNS
Los Angeles, CA ....Insurance Defense; Trust and Estates, Wills and Probate

GOLDSTEIN, BERTRAM M., & ASSOCIATES, P.A.
Baltimore, MD ....Medical Malpractice; Product Liability Law

GOLDSTEIN, BUCKLEY, CECHMAN, RICE & PURTZ, P.A.
Fort Myers, FL ....Commercial Law; Construction Law; General Practice; Personal Injury; Product Liability Law; Workers Compensation

GOLDSTEIN, FLANZ & FISHMAN
Montreal, QU, Canada ....Banking Law; Bankruptcy Law; Civil Trial Practice; Commercial Law; Real Estate Law

GOLDSTEIN, GOLDSTEIN AND HILLEY
San Antonio, TX ....Criminal Trial Practice

GOLDSTEIN, KENNEDY & PETITO
Los Angeles, CA ....Labor and Employment Law

GOLDSTEIN, MCGRODER & WOODS, LTD. A PROFESSIONAL CORPORATION
Phoenix, AZ ....Appellate Practice; Civil Trial Practice; Medical Malpractice; Personal Injury; Product Liability Law

GOLDSTEIN & MORRIS, LLP
New York, NY ....Civil Trial Practice; Commercial Litigation; Labor and Employment Law; Sports and Entertainment Law

GOLDSTEIN & MUSTO, A PROFESSIONAL CORPORATION
San Francisco, CA ....Civil Trial Practice

GOLDSTEIN AND PECK, P.C.
Bridgeport, CT ....General Practice; Real Estate Law
Westport, CT ....General Practice; Real Estate Law

GOLDSTEIN AND PRICE, L.C.
St. Louis, MO ....Admiralty/Maritime Law

GOLDSTEIN, RICHARD S., P.C., LAW OFFICES OF
New York, NY ....Immigration and Naturalization

GOLDSTEIN, STUART
Phoenix, AZ ....Medical Malpractice; Personal Injury

GOLD & VANARIA, P.C.
Springfield, MA ....Commercial Litigation; Creditors Rights

GOLD, WEEMS, BRUSER, SUES & RUNDELL, A PROFESSIONAL LAW CORPORATION
Alexandria, LA ....General Practice; Tax Law

GOLENBOCK, EISEMAN, ASSOR & BELL
New York, NY ....Civil Trial Practice; Commercial Law; Corporate Law; General Practice; Securities Law

GOLOB, MICHAEL H.
Farmington Hills, MI ....Civil Trial Practice; Commercial Law; Family Law

GOLOMB, DAVID B. LAW OFFICES OF
New York, NY ....Medical Malpractice; Personal Injury; Product Liability Law; Professional Liability

GOLOMB, GEORGE E.
Baltimore, MD ....Civil Rights; Labor and Employment Law

GOMEZ, ROLAND H.
Miami, FL ....Insurance Defense; Personal Injury

GOMEZ, DAVID F., A PROFESSIONAL CORPORATION
Phoenix, AZ ....Civil Trial Practice; Labor and Employment Law

GONANO, HARRELL & FERGUSON
Fort Pierce, FL ....Land Use Law; Real Estate Law

GONZALEZ, MARCE JR.
Merrillville, IN ....Appellate Practice; Criminal Trial Practice; Personal Injury

GONZALEZ-MIRANDA, NOEL S.
San Juan, PR ....Commercial Law

GOODELL, DEVRIES, LEECH & GRAY, LLP
Baltimore, MD ....Insurance Defense; Medical Malpractice; Product Liability Law

GOODELL, STRATTON, EDMONDS & PALMER, L.L.P.
Topeka, KS ....Arbitration; Bankruptcy Law; Civil Trial Practice; Communications Law; Corporate Law; Elder Law; Environmental Law; General Practice; Health Care Law; Insurance Defense; Labor and Employment Law; Legal Malpractice; Nonprofit and Tax Exempt Organizations; Securities Law; Tax Law; Trust and Estates, Wills and Probate

GOODING & DODSON, P.C.
Texarkana, TX ....Civil Trial Practice; Insurance Defense

GOODING, HUFFMAN, KELLEY & BECKER
Lima, OH ....Civil Trial Practice; Insurance Defense

GOODLETTE, COLEMAN & JOHNSON, P.A.
Naples, FL ....Real Estate Law

GOODMAN, EARLE GARY
Beverly Hills, CA ....Real Estate Law

GOODMAN CHESNOFF & KEACH, A PROFESSIONAL CORPORATION
Las Vegas, NV ....Constitutional Law; Criminal Trial Practice; Personal Injury

GOODMAN & CLARK
Arlington, TX .... Family Law

GOODMAN & GOODMAN, A LEGAL PROFESSIONAL ASSOCIATION
Cincinnati, OH .... Family Law; Health Care Law; Labor and Employment Law; Personal Injury; Real Estate Law; Trust and Estates, Wills and Probate

GOODMAN, MCGUFFEY, AUST & LINDSEY, LLP
Atlanta, GA .... Civil Trial Practice; Insurance Defense; Workers Compensation

GOODMAN PHILLIPS & VINEBERG
Montreal, QU, Canada .... General Practice
Hong Kong, China .... General Practice

GOODMAN, ROBERT U., P.L.C.
Shreveport, LA .... Business Law; Civil Trial Practice; Commercial Law

GOODMAN WEISS MILLER LLP
Cleveland, OH .... Business Law; Civil Trial Practice; Securities Law

GOODSILL ANDERSON QUINN & STIFEL
Honolulu, HI .... Admiralty/Maritime Law; Banking Law; Civil Trial Practice; Commercial Litigation; Communications Law; Construction Law; Environmental Law; General Practice; Health Care Law; Immigration and Naturalization; Insurance Defense; Intellectual Property Law; International Business Law; Labor and Employment Law; Mergers and Acquisitions; Product Liability Law; Professional Liability; Real Estate Law; Securities Law; Tax Law; Trust and Estates, Wills and Probate

GOODSON, MANLEY & DURFEE, P.L.C.
Phoenix, AZ .... Business Law; General Practice; Trust and Estates, Wills and Probate

GOODWIN & GOODWIN
Charleston, WV .... Civil Trial Practice; Corporate Law; General Practice; Government Contracts; Labor and Employment Law; Municipal Bond/Public Authority Financing; Personal Injury
Parkersburg, WV .... General Practice
Ripley, WV .... General Practice

GOODWIN, PROCTER & HOAR LLP
Boston, MA .... General Practice

GOODY, W. KEITH
Jackson, WY .... Criminal Trial Practice; Family Law; Personal Injury

GOOLD PATTERSON DEVORE ALES & ROADHOUSE
Las Vegas, NV .... Commercial Law; Commercial Litigation; General Practice; International Business Law; Real Estate Law

GORANSON, BAIN & LARSEN, L.C.
Dallas, TX .... Family Law

GORDON, ARATA, MCCOLLAM, DUPLANTIS & EAGAN, L.L.P.
Lafayette, LA .... Oil and Gas Law
New Orleans, LA .... Environmental Law; General Practice; Oil and Gas Law

GORDON, EDELSTEIN, KREPACK, GRANT, FELTON & GOLDSTEIN
Los Angeles, CA .... Construction Law; Environmental Law; Medical Malpractice; Personal Injury; Product Liability Law; Toxic Torts; Workers Compensation

GORDON & EINSTEIN, LTD.
Chicago, IL .... Business Law; Real Estate Law

GORDON & HENESON, P.A.
Baltimore, MD .... Civil Trial Practice

GORDON LAW FIRM, THE
Hartwell, GA .... Civil Trial Practice; General Practice; Real Estate Law

GORDON, MUIR AND FOLEY, LLP
Hartford, CT .... Banking Law; Civil Trial Practice; Commercial Law; Construction Law; General Practice; Insurance Defense; Medical Malpractice; Real Estate Law; Trust and Estates, Wills and Probate

GORDON, SIEGEL, MASTRO, MULLANEY, GORDON & GALVIN, P.C.
Latham, NY .... Corporate Law

GORDON, SILBERMAN, WIGGINS & CHILDS, P.C.
Birmingham, AL .... Banking Law; Bankruptcy Law; Business Law; Civil Rights; Civil Trial Practice; Commercial Law; Employment Benefits Law; General Practice; Labor and Employment Law; Personal Injury; Real Estate Law; Tax Law; Trust and Estates, Wills and Probate

GORHAM & WALDREP, P.C.
Birmingham, AL .... Business Law; Civil Rights; Civil Trial Practice; Criminal Trial Practice; Family Law; General Practice; Labor and Employment Law; Municipal and Zoning Law; Municipal Bond/Public Authority Financing; Natural Resources Law; Personal Injury; Real Estate Law; Trust and Estates, Wills and Probate

GORMAN, WASZKIEWICZ, GORMAN & SCHMITT
Utica, NY .... Civil Trial Practice; General Practice

GORNBEIN, HENRY S.
Bloomfield Hills, MI .... Family Law

GORSUCH KIRGIS LLP
Denver, CO .... Business Law; Commercial Litigation; Communications Law; Computer Law; Construction Law; Corporate Law; Environmental Law; Government Contracts; Health Care Law; Insurance Defense; Intellectual Property Law; Labor and Employment Law; Land Use Law; Mergers and Acquisitions; Municipal and Zoning Law; Natural Resources Law; Public Utilities Law; Securities Law; Tax Law; Trademark, Copyright and Unfair Competition; Trust and Estates, Wills and Probate

GOSMA & GALLAGHER, P.L.C.
Davenport, IA .... Banking Law; Business Law; Commercial Litigation; General Practice; Real Estate Law; Trust and Estates, Wills and Probate

GOSNEY, CLIFF B. JR.
Port Orange, FL .... Civil Trial Practice

GOTT, YOUNG & BOGLE, P.A.
Wichita, KS .... General Practice

GOTTLIEB & PEARSON
Montreal, QU, Canada .... International Trade Law

GOUBEAUX & GOUBEAUX
Greenville, OH .... General Practice

GOUGH, SHANAHAN, JOHNSON & WATERMAN
Helena, MT .... General Practice

GOULD, COOKSEY, FENNELL, O'NEILL, MARINE & CARTER, PROFESSIONAL ASSOCIATION
Vero Beach, FL .... Civil Trial Practice; General Practice; Trust and Estates, Wills and Probate

GOULD, KILLIAN & WYNNE
Hartford, CT .... Business Law; General Practice; Insurance Defense; Trust and Estates, Wills and Probate

GOURVITZ, ELLIOT H., P.A.
Springfield, NJ .... Family Law

GOUVEIA & MILLER
Merrillville, IN .... Bankruptcy Law; Personal Injury

GOVERNALI, JOSEPH P.
White Plains, NY .... Commercial Litigation; Family Law; General Practice

GOVERNO AND KAVANAGH LLP
Boston, MA .... Civil Trial Practice; Insurance Defense; Toxic Torts

GOZIGIAN, WASHBURN & CLINTON
Cooperstown, NY .... General Practice; Personal Injury; Real Estate Law; Trust and Estates, Wills and Probate

GRACE, JOHN PHILIP, P.C.
Phoenix, AZ .... Personal Injury

GRACE, UNRUH & PRATT, L.C.
Wichita, KS .... Civil Trial Practice; Commercial Litigation; Insurance Defense; Labor and Employment Law; Product Liability Law

GRADY & ASSOCIATES, LEGAL PROFESSIONAL ASSOCIATION
Naples, FL .... Securities Law

GRAHAM & ARCENEAUX
New Orleans, LA .... Real Estate Law

GRAHAM, CAMPAIGN, P.C.
New York, NY .... Computer Law; Intellectual Property Law; Nonprofit and Tax Exempt Organizations; Trademark, Copyright and Unfair Competition

GRAHAM, CLARK, JONES, BUILDER, PRATT & MARKS
Winter Park, FL .... Civil Trial Practice; Real Estate Law

GRAHAM, CURTIN & SHERIDAN, A PROFESSIONAL ASSOCIATION
Morristown, NJ .... General Practice

GRAHAM & DUNN PC
Seattle, WA .... General Practice

GRAHAM AND GRAHAM, LTD.
Springfield, IL .... General Practice

GRAHAM & JAMES LLP
Los Angeles, CA .... General Practice
Palo Alto, CA .... General Practice
San Francisco, CA .... Admiralty/Maritime Law; General Practice
Washington, DC .... General Practice

Milan, Italy....General Practice

GRAHAM LAW FIRM, THE
St. Louis, MO....Civil Trial Practice

GRAHAM, MARJORIE GADARIAN, P.A.
Palm Beach Gardens, FL....Appellate Practice

GRAMPP, GLENN A.
Evansville, IN....Criminal Trial Practice

GRANAHAN, THOMAS F., P.A.
Tampa, FL....Criminal Trial Practice; Insurance Defense; Personal Injury

GRANNAN, WILLIAM JOSEPH LAW OFFICE OF
Arlington, MA....Real Estate Law; Trust and Estates, Wills and Probate

GRANT, RUSSELL P. JR.
Jackson, MS....Natural Resources Law

GRANT, FRIDKIN, PEARSON, ATHAN & CROWN, P.A.
Naples, FL....General Practice

GRANT & GRANT, LLP
Longmont, CO....General Practice

GRANT, LEATHERWOOD & PITTS, P.A.
Greenville, SC....Civil Trial Practice; Commercial Litigation; Environmental Law; Insurance Defense; Product Liability Law

GRANTHAM, KIRK, P.A.
West Palm Beach, FL....Real Estate Law; Trust and Estates, Wills and Probate

GRATCH JACOBS & BROZMAN, P.C.
New York, NY....Bankruptcy Law; Commercial Litigation; Corporate Law

GRATTAN & GALATI
Sacramento, CA....Administrative Law; Energy Law; Environmental Law; Land Use Law; Natural Resources Law

GRAVEL AND SHEA, A PROFESSIONAL CORPORATION
Burlington, VT....Antitrust Law; Appellate Practice; Banking Law; Business Law; Civil Trial Practice; Commercial Law; Criminal Trial Practice; Environmental Law; General Practice; Immigration and Naturalization; Municipal and Zoning Law; Real Estate Law; Tax Law; Trust and Estates, Wills and Probate

GRAVES, DOUGHERTY, HEARON & MOODY, A PROFESSIONAL CORPORATION
Austin, TX....General Practice

GRAY CARY WARE & FREIDENRICH LLP
El Centro, CA....General Practice
La Jolla, CA....General Practice
Palo Alto, CA....General Practice
San Diego, CA....General Practice
San Francisco, CA....General Practice

GRAY & GILLILAND, P.C.
Atlanta, GA....Aviation Law; Bankruptcy Law; Civil Trial Practice; Family Law; Insurance Defense; Land Use Law; Real Estate Law

GRAY LAW FIRM, THE, A PROFESSIONAL LAW CORPORATION
Lake Charles, LA....Commercial Litigation; Eminent Domain; Oil and Gas Law; Trust and Estates, Wills and Probate

GRAY, SOWLE & IACCO, A PROFESSIONAL CORPORATION
Mount Pleasant, MI....Medical Malpractice; Personal Injury; Workers Compensation

GRAY, YORK & DUFFY LLP
Los Angeles, CA....Business Law; Civil Trial Practice; Construction Law; Insurance Defense

GREBEN & ASSOCIATES
Sacramento, CA....Commercial Litigation; Environmental Law

GRECO, MOLLIS & O'HARA, A PROFESSIONAL CORPORATION
Irvine, CA....Business Law; Tax Law; Trust and Estates, Wills and Probate

GREEN, JOHN R.
Duncan, OK....General Practice

GREEN, BRUCE DAVID, P.A.
Fort Lauderdale, FL....Aviation Law

GREEN CORDONNIER & HOUSE, LLP
St. Louis, MO....Family Law

GREEN LAW OFFICES
Boise, ID....Civil Trial Practice; General Practice; Real Estate Law

GREEN, LUNDGREN & RYAN, A PROFESSIONAL CORPORATION
Cherry Hill, NJ....General Practice; Insurance Defense

GREEN, SCHAAF & JACOBSON, P.C.
St. Louis, MO....Business Law; Commercial Litigation; Securities Law

GREENBAUM, ROWE, SMITH, RAVIN, DAVIS AND HIMMEL LLP
Woodbridge, NJ....Bankruptcy Law; Civil Trial Practice; General Practice; Real Estate Law; Tax Law

GREENBERG, GARY J.
New York, NY....Commercial Litigation

GREENBERG DAUBER EPSTEIN & TUCKER, A PROFESSIONAL CORPORATION
Newark, NJ....Banking Law; Civil Trial Practice; Commercial Law; Criminal Trial Practice; General Practice; Tax Law

GREENBERG GLUSKER FIELDS CLAMAN & MACHTINGER LLP
Los Angeles, CA....General Practice; Tax Law; Trust and Estates, Wills and Probate

GREENBERG & PLEBAN
St. Louis, MO....Criminal Trial Practice; Medical Malpractice; Personal Injury; Product Liability Law

GREENBERG & SCHULMAN
Woodbridge, NJ....Tax Law; Trust and Estates, Wills and Probate

GREENBERG, STEWART G., P.A.
Miami, FL....Personal Injury

GREENBLATT, JAY H., & ASSOCIATES, A PROF. CORP.
Vineland, NJ....Civil Trial Practice; General Practice; Insurance Defense; Personal Injury; Product Liability Law; Professional Liability

GREENE, BROILLET, TAYLOR, WHEELER & PANISH, LLP
Santa Monica, CA....Personal Injury

GREENE & CURTIS, L.L.P.
Springfield, MO....Business Law

GREENE, CYNTHIA L., P.A.
Miami, FL....Family Law

GREENE AND LETTS
Chicago, IL....Insurance Defense; Labor and Employment Law

GREENE, RALEIGH "LEE", III
St. Petersburg, FL....Commercial Litigation; Family Law

GREENE AND REID
Syracuse, NY....Insurance Defense; Personal Injury

GREENE & ZINNER, P.C.
White Plains, NY....Civil Trial Practice; Commercial Litigation; Corporate Law; General Practice

GREENEBAUM DOLL & MCDONALD PLLC
Louisville, KY....General Practice; Labor and Employment Law

GREENFELDER, MANDER, HANSON, MURPHY & DWYER
Dade City, FL....Criminal Trial Practice; Personal Injury

GREENFIELD, BREWER, BAILOR & KAY
Pittsburgh, PA....Civil Trial Practice; Criminal Trial Practice

GREENHAW & GREENHAW
Fayetteville, AR....Insurance Defense

GREENLEE, WINNER AND SULLIVAN, P.C.
Boulder, CO....Patent, Trademark, Copyright and Unfair Competition

GREENMAN, GOLDBERG, RABY & MARTINEZ, PROFESSIONAL CORPORATION
Las Vegas, NV....Personal Injury; Workers Compensation

GREENSPAN & GREENSPAN
White Plains, NY....Civil Trial Practice; Criminal Trial Practice; Securities Law; Tax Law

GREENSPUN, PETER D., & ASSOCIATES, P.C.
Fairfax, VA....Civil Trial Practice; Criminal Trial Practice; Personal Injury

GREENWALD, GREENWALD, POWERS & WINSOR LLP
Milford, MA....Civil Trial Practice; Municipal and Zoning Law; Personal Injury; Real Estate Law; Trust and Estates, Wills and Probate

GREENWALD, HOFFMAN, MEYER & MONTES, L.L.P.
Glendale, CA....Business Law; Real Estate Law; Trust and Estates, Wills and Probate

GREENWALD, STEVEN I., P.A.
Boca Raton, FL....Real Estate Law; Trust and Estates, Wills and Probate

GREER, HERZ & ADAMS, L.L.P.
Galveston, TX........................Commercial Litigation; General Practice

GREESON & ASSOCIATES
Greensboro, NC........................Medical Malpractice; Personal Injury

GREFE & SIDNEY, P.L.C.
Des Moines, IA........................Civil Trial Practice; General Practice; Insurance Defense; Tax Law; Trust and Estates, Wills and Probate

GREGG & FARRIS
Batesville, AR........................Banking Law; Commercial Litigation; Insurance Defense

GREGG & GREGG, P.C.
Houston, TX........................Civil Trial Practice; General Practice; Municipal and Zoning Law; Real Estate Law

GREGORIO, SAM N., A PROFESSIONAL LAW CORPORATION
Shreveport, LA........................Personal Injury

GREGORY, CHRISTY & MANIKLAL
Cordele, GA........................Civil Trial Practice

GREGORY, EASLEY AND COURTNEY
Murray, KY........................General Practice; Personal Injury

GREINES, MARTIN, STEIN & RICHLAND LLP
Beverly Hills, CA........................Appellate Practice

GRELL, CHRISTOPHER E. LAW OFFICES OF
San Francisco, CA........................Personal Injury

GRENADIER, SIMPSON & DUFFETT, P.C.
Alexandria, VA........................Family Law

GRESENS & GILLEN LLP
Buffalo, NY........................Commercial Litigation; Construction Law

GRESHAM, DAVIS, GREGORY, WORTHY & MOORE, A PROFESSIONAL CORPORATION
San Antonio, TX........................Corporate Law; General Practice

GREVE, CLIFFORD, WENGEL & PARAS, LLP
Sacramento, CA........................Civil Trial Practice; Insurance Defense

GRIEM, DAVID
Detroit, MI........................Civil Trial Practice; Criminal Trial Practice
Mount Clemens, MI........................Civil Trial Practice; Criminal Trial Practice

GRIFFIN COCHRANE & MARSHALL, A PROFESSIONAL CORPORATION
Atlanta, GA........................Construction Law

GRIFFIN, COOGAN & VENERUSO, P.C.
Bronxville, NY........................Banking Law; Business Law; Civil Trial Practice; Corporate Law; Real Estate Law; Tax Law

GRIFFIN & FLETCHER
Cincinnati, OH........................Real Estate Law

GRIFFIN & GOULKA
Boston, MA........................Insurance Defense; Personal Injury

GRIFFIN & LINDER, P.A.
Orlando, FL........................Personal Injury

GRIFFITH & GRIFFITH
Cleveland, MS........................Civil Rights; Civil Trial Practice; Insurance Defense; Natural Resources Law

GRIFFITH LAW OFFICES
Rome, NY........................General Practice; Real Estate Law; Trust and Estates, Wills and Probate

GRIFFITH & NIXON, P.C.
Dallas, TX........................Business Law; Construction Law; Real Estate Law

GRIFFITHS & CASTLE, INC.
Palo Alto, CA........................Construction Law

GRIMES GOEBEL GRIMES HAWKINS & GLADFELTER, P.A.
Bradenton, FL........................Civil Trial Practice; Eminent Domain; Land Use Law; Personal Injury; Real Estate Law; Trust and Estates, Wills and Probate

GRIMES & WARWICK
San Diego, CA........................Criminal Trial Practice

GRIMMER, EDWARD P.
Crown Point, IN........................Civil Trial Practice; Commercial Litigation

GRISI & RIEGLER
Akron, OH........................Personal Injury

GRISSIM & HODGES
Nashville, TN........................Real Estate Law

GRISWOLD, LASALLE, COBB, DOWD & GIN, L.L.P.
Hanford, CA........................General Practice

GRODSKY, IRVIN, P.C.
Mobile, AL........................Bankruptcy Law; Commercial Litigation

GROGAN, GRAFFAM, MCGINLEY & LUCCHINO, P.C.
Pittsburgh, PA........................General Practice

GROSMAN & GROSMAN
Millburn, NJ........................Appellate Practice; Family Law

GROSS, MCGINLEY, LABARRE & EATON, LLP
Allentown, PA........................Civil Trial Practice; Communications Law

GROSS, MINSKY, MOGUL & SINGAL, P.A.
Bangor, ME........................Banking Law; Bankruptcy Law; Civil Trial Practice; Corporate Law; Criminal Trial Practice; General Practice; Health Care Law; Medical Malpractice; Real Estate Law; Trust and Estates, Wills and Probate

GROSS, NEMETH & SILVERMAN, P.L.C.
Detroit, MI........................Appellate Practice

GROSS SHUMAN BRIZDLE & GILFILLAN, P.C.
Buffalo, NY........................General Practice

GROSSBART, ROBERT N., P.A.
Baltimore, MD........................Bankruptcy Law

GROSSMAN, KRUTTSCHNITT, HEAVEY & JACOB, A PROFESSIONAL CORPORATION
Brick, NJ........................Insurance Defense; Medical Malpractice

GROSSMAN LAW OFFICES
Columbus, OH........................Family Law

GROSSMAN & WALDMAN, L.L.P.
Houston, TX........................Personal Injury

GROWE & BUCHHOLZ
St. Louis, MO........................Personal Injury

GROWER, KETCHAM, MORÉ, RUTHERFORD, NOECKER, BRONSON, SIBONI & EIDE, P.A.
Orlando, FL........................Aviation Law; Insurance Defense; Workers Compensation

GRUCCIO, PEPPER, GIOVINAZZI, DESANTO & FARNOLY, P.A.
Vineland, NJ........................Banking Law; Bankruptcy Law; Civil Trial Practice; General Practice; Insurance Defense; Labor and Employment Law; Municipal and Zoning Law; Personal Injury; Trust and Estates, Wills and Probate

GRUEL, MILLS, NIMS AND PYLMAN
Grand Rapids, MI........................Civil Trial Practice; Commercial Law; Commercial Litigation; Environmental Law; General Practice; Health Care Law; Medical Malpractice; Personal Injury

GRUND & BRESLAU, P.C.
Denver, CO........................Aviation Law; Commercial Law; Insurance Defense; Product Liability Law; Real Estate Law

GRUNERT STOUT & BRUCH
Charlotte Amalie, St. Thomas, VI........................Aviation Law; Banking Law; Business Law; Civil Rights; Civil Trial Practice; Commercial Law; General Practice; Insurance Defense; International Business Law; Personal Injury; Real Estate Law; Tax Law; Trust and Estates, Wills and Probate

GRUNSKY, EBEY, FARRAR & HOWELL, A PROFESSIONAL CORPORATION
Watsonville, CA........................General Practice

GRZECA, JEROME G., S.C.
Milwaukee, WI........................Immigration and Naturalization

GUDMUNDSON, SIGGINS, STONE & SKINNER, LLP
San Francisco, CA........................Insurance Defense

GUEBERT & YEOMANS, P.C.
Albuquerque, NM........................Civil Trial Practice; Commercial Litigation; Insurance Defense; Personal Injury; Product Liability Law

GUICE, JUDY M., A PROFESSIONAL ASSOCIATION
Biloxi, MS........................Admiralty/Maritime Law; Civil Trial Practice; Medical Malpractice; Personal Injury; Product Liability Law

GUIDA & EAGAN, P.A.
Columbia, MD........................Civil Trial Practice; Personal Injury

GUILD, RUSSELL, GALLAGHER & FULLER, LTD.
Reno, NV........................Administrative Law; Business Law; Civil Trial Practice; Corporate Law; General Practice; Trust and Estates, Wills and Probate

GUILLORY & MCCALL, L.L.C.
Lake Charles, LA.....Insurance Defense; Toxic Torts

GUILLOT, GREGORY H., CHARTERED
Washington, DC.....Communications Law; Trademark, Copyright and Unfair Competition

GULICK, JOHN N. JR.
San Francisco, CA.....Civil Trial Practice

GULLAHORN & HARE, P.C.
Albertville, AL.....Banking Law; Civil Trial Practice; General Practice; Municipal Bond/Public Authority Financing

GULLETT, COMBS, REED & BOWLING
Hazard, KY.....Civil Trial Practice; General Practice; Natural Resources Law; Personal Injury; Real Estate Law

GUMBINER & ESKRIDGE LLP
Walnut Creek, CA.....Commercial Litigation

GUM & HILLIER, P.A.
Asheville, NC.....Bankruptcy Law; Family Law

GUMP, RICHARD A., JR., P.C., LAW OFFICES OF
Dallas, TX.....Immigration and Naturalization

GUNDERSON, MICHAEL A.
Detroit, MI.....Insurance Defense

GUNDERSON, BRENT M., P.C.
Mesa, AZ.....Immigration and Naturalization; Trust and Estates, Wills and Probate

GUNDLACH, LEE, EGGMANN, BOYLE & ROESSLER
Belleville, IL.....General Practice

GUNHUS, GRINNELL, KLINGER, SWENSON & GUY, LTD.
Moorhead, MN.....Civil Trial Practice; General Practice
Fargo, ND.....General Practice

GUNSBERG & BRESKIN, P.C.
Bloomfield Hills, MI.....Arbitration; Civil Rights; Civil Trial Practice; Labor and Employment Law

GUNSTER, YOAKLEY, VALDES-FAULI & STEWART, P.A.
West Palm Beach, FL.....General Practice

GUNTA & REAK, S.C.
Milwaukee, WI.....Admiralty/Maritime Law; Constitutional Law; Construction Law

GURNEY & HANDLEY, P.A.
Orlando, FL.....Civil Trial Practice; General Practice

GUSRAE, KAPLAN & BRUNO
New York, NY.....Securities Law

GUTGLASS ERICKSON & BONVILLE, S.C.
Milwaukee, WI.....Insurance Defense

GUTHERY & RICKLES, P.C.
Denver, CO.....Nonprofit and Tax Exempt Organizations; Pension and Profit Sharing; Tax Law; Trust and Estates, Wills and Probate

GUTMAN & GUTMAN LLP
Mineola, NY.....Commercial Law; Commercial Litigation; Creditors Rights; Real Estate Law

GUTTERMAN, CARLTON & HECKENBACH, L.L.P.
Lone Tree, CO.....Family Law

GWIN, LEWIS & PUNCHES, LLP
Natchez, MS.....General Practice; Insurance Defense
Woodville, MS.....General Practice

HAASIS & GOODIN
San Diego, CA.....Civil Trial Practice; Insurance Defense

HABBESHAW, KALMANS & SCHWARTZ, P.C.
San Antonio, TX.....Bankruptcy Law; Commercial Litigation

HABEDANK, CUMMING, BEST & SAVAGE
Sidney, MT.....General Practice

HABUSH, HABUSH, DAVIS & ROTTIER, S.C.
Appleton, WI.....Medical Malpractice; Personal Injury; Product Liability Law
Green Bay, WI.....Medical Malpractice; Personal Injury; Product Liability Law
Lake Geneva, WI.....Medical Malpractice; Personal Injury; Product Liability Law
Madison, WI.....Medical Malpractice; Personal Injury; Product Liability Law
Milwaukee, WI.....Medical Malpractice; Personal Injury; Product Liability Law
Racine, WI.....Medical Malpractice; Personal Injury; Product Liability Law
Rhinelander, WI.....Medical Malpractice; Personal Injury; Product Liability Law
Waukesha, WI.....Medical Malpractice; Personal Injury; Product Liability Law
Wausau, WI.....Medical Malpractice; Personal Injury; Product Liability Law

HACKARD, HOLT & HELLER
Gold River, CA.....Commercial Litigation; Environmental Law; Product Liability Law

HACKETT & MAXWELL, P.C.
Troy, MI.....Antitrust Law; Business Law; Civil Trial Practice; Commercial Litigation; Corporate Law; General Practice; Transportation Law

HACKMAN HULETT & CRACRAFT, LLP
Indianapolis, IN.....Administrative Law; General Practice; Real Estate Law

HACK, PIRO, O'DAY, MERKLINGER, WALLACE & MCKENNA, P.A.
Florham Park, NJ.....Bankruptcy Law; Civil Trial Practice; Environmental Law; General Practice; Insurance Defense; Personal Injury; Product Liability Law; Professional Liability; Real Estate Law; Trust and Estates, Wills and Probate; Workers Compensation

HADDAD, SUSAN CHRISTINE
Chicago, IL.....Family Law

HADDLETON & COLLINS, P.C.
Hyannis, MA.....Trust and Estates, Wills and Probate

HADDOCK PROFESSIONAL ASSOCIATION
Winter Park, FL.....Business Law; Education Law; Real Estate Law

HADIPUTRANTO, HADINOTO & PARTNERS
Jakarta, Indonesia.....General Practice

HAGEN, DYE, HIRSCHY & DILORENZO, P.C.
Portland, OR.....Business Law; Commercial Law; Real Estate Law; Tax Law; Trust and Estates, Wills and Probate

HAGERTY, JOHNSON, ALBRIGHTSON & BEITZ, P.A.
Minneapolis, MN.....Civil Trial Practice; Real Estate Law; Trust and Estates, Wills and Probate

HAGGARD, PARKS & STONE, P.A.
Miami, FL.....Aviation Law; Civil Trial Practice; Personal Injury

HAGOORT, NICHOLAS H., JR., P.A.
Boynton Beach, FL.....Trust and Estates, Wills and Probate

HAHN, MCCLURG, WATSON, GRIFFITH & BUSH, P.A.
Lakeland, FL.....Commercial Litigation; General Practice; Real Estate Law; Trust and Estates, Wills and Probate

HAIGHT, BROWN & BONESTEEL, L.L.P.
Riverside, CA.....Bankruptcy Law; Civil Trial Practice; Commercial Law; Constitutional Law; Labor and Employment Law; Municipal and Zoning Law; Personal Injury; Product Liability Law; Professional Liability; Public Utilities Law
San Diego, CA.....Civil Trial Practice; Commercial Litigation; Corporate Law; Environmental Law; Health Care Law; Insurance Defense; International Business Law; Labor and Employment Law; Personal Injury; Product Liability Law
San Francisco, CA.....Civil Trial Practice; Commercial Litigation; Computer Law; Creditors Rights; Environmental Law; Health Care Law; Insurance Defense; Labor and Employment Law; Product Liability Law; Professional Liability; Toxic Torts
Santa Ana, CA.....Civil Trial Practice; Commercial Litigation; Insurance Defense; Personal Injury
Santa Monica, CA.....Appellate Practice; Bankruptcy Law; Civil Trial Practice; Commercial Litigation; Environmental Law; Health Care Law; Insurance Defense; Intellectual Property Law; Labor and Employment Law; Personal Injury; Product Liability Law; Professional Liability; Toxic Torts; Trust and Estates, Wills and Probate

HAIGHT GARDNER HOLLAND & KNIGHT
New York, NY.....General Practice

HAILEY, MCNAMARA, HALL, LARMANN & PAPALE, L.L.P.
Metairie, LA.....Admiralty/Maritime Law; General Practice; Insurance Defense; Professional Liability

HAIMS, MACGOWAN, VALENTINO & PEEBLES, L.L.P.
Oakland, CA.....Civil Trial Practice; Construction Law; Environmental Law; General Practice; Health Care Law; Insurance Defense; Personal Injury; Product Liability Law

HAINER & BERMAN, P.C.
Troy, MI.....Business Law; Civil Trial Practice; Environmental Law; Labor and Employment Law; Real Estate Law; Trust and Estates, Wills and Probate

HAINES, MARTIN L., III, CHARTERED
Lake Park, FL....................Family Law

HALABY CROSS & SCHLUTER
Denver, CO....................Civil Trial Practice; General Practice; Insurance Defense

HALE AND DORR LLP
Washington, DC....................General Practice
Boston, MA....................General Practice

HALE, FOGLEMAN & ROGERS
West Memphis, AR....................Civil Trial Practice; Personal Injury

HALE & HAMLIN
Ellsworth, ME....................Civil Trial Practice; Real Estate Law; Trust and Estates, Wills and Probate

HALE HEADRICK DEWEY & WOLF, PLLC
Memphis, TN....................Antitrust Law; Bankruptcy Law; Business Law; Commercial Litigation; Communications Law; Construction Law; Corporate Law; Creditors Rights; Criminal Trial Practice; Eminent Domain; Health Care Law; Medical Malpractice; Mergers and Acquisitions; Personal Injury; Product Liability Law; Tax Law

HALE, KINCAID & SKINNER, P.C.
Liberty, MO....................General Practice

HALE LANE PEEK DENNISON HOWARD AND ANDERSON
Carson City, NV....................Business Law; Corporate Law; General Practice; Real Estate Law
Las Vegas, NV....................Administrative Law; Bankruptcy Law; Commercial Litigation; Corporate Law; General Practice; Health Care Law; Real Estate Law; Tax Law; Trust and Estates, Wills and Probate
Reno, NV....................Bankruptcy Law; Business Law; Commercial Litigation; Corporate Law; General Practice; Health Care Law; Natural Resources Law; Real Estate Law; Securities Law; Tax Law; Trust and Estates, Wills and Probate

HALE LAW FIRM
St. Louis, MO....................Insurance Defense

HALE & WAGNER, S.C.
Milwaukee, WI....................Commercial Litigation

HALEY BADER & POTTS P.L.C.
Arlington, VA....................Communications Law; Trademark, Copyright and Unfair Competition

HALEY, PURCHIO, SAKAI & SMITH
Hayward, CA....................General Practice; Land Use Law

HALICZER, PETTIS & WHITE, P.A.
Fort Lauderdale, FL....................Appellate Practice; Civil Trial Practice; Insurance Defense; Medical Malpractice; Workers Compensation

HALIO & HALIO
Charleston, SC....................Civil Trial Practice

HALIW SICILIANO AND MYCHALOWYCH
Farmington Hills, MI....................Business Law; Commercial Litigation; Insurance Defense

HALKIDES & MORGAN, A PROFESSIONAL CORPORATION
Redding, CA....................Insurance Defense

HALL, H. GLENN JR.
Austin, TX....................Banking Law; Real Estate Law

HALL, THOMAS J.
Reno, NV....................Real Estate Law

HALL, ANSLEY, RODGERS & CONDRY, A PROFESSIONAL CORPORATION
Springfield, MO....................Insurance Defense

HALL, BLOCH, GARLAND & MEYER
Macon, GA....................Banking Law; Business Law; Civil Trial Practice; General Practice; Insurance Defense; Personal Injury; Tax Law

HALL, BOOTH, SMITH & SLOVER, A PROFESSIONAL CORPORATION
Atlanta, GA....................Civil Trial Practice; Insurance Defense; Medical Malpractice

HALL & BROGDEN, P.C.
Indianapolis, IN....................Business Law; Trust and Estates, Wills and Probate

HALL, CASHWELL & SULLIVAN, L.L.P.
Wilmington, NC....................Criminal Trial Practice; Personal Injury

HALL, CONERLY, MUDD & BOLVIG, P.C.
Birmingham, AL....................General Practice; Insurance Defense

HALL, DAVID AND JOSEPH, P.A.
Miami, FL....................Civil Trial Practice; Commercial Law; Family Law; Personal Injury

HALL, DAVID W., ATTORNEY AT LAW, A LAW CORPORATION
Honolulu, HI....................Civil Trial Practice; Criminal Trial Practice

HALLENBECK, LASCELL, NORRIS & HELLER
Rochester, NY....................Civil Trial Practice; Commercial Litigation; Medical Malpractice; Personal Injury; Product Liability Law

HALL, ESTILL, HARDWICK, GABLE, GOLDEN & NELSON, A PROFESSIONAL CORPORATION
Tulsa, OK....................General Practice

HALL & EVANS, L.L.C.
Colorado Springs, CO....................General Practice
Denver, CO....................General Practice

HALL & HALL
Staten Island, NY....................Banking Law

HALL, JOHN WESLEY, JR., A PROFESSIONAL CORPORATION
Little Rock, AR....................Appellate Practice; Constitutional Law; Criminal Trial Practice

HALL AND LEWIS, P.C.
Mount Pleasant, MI....................General Practice

HALL & MULLINS, P.C.
Augusta, GA....................Business Law; Real Estate Law

HALLORAN & SAGE LLP
Hartford, CT....................General Practice
Middletown, CT....................General Practice

HALL, PARTENHEIMER & KINKLE
Princeton, IN....................General Practice; Natural Resources Law; Real Estate Law

HALL, RENDER, KILLIAN, HEATH & LYMAN, PROFESSIONAL SERVICES CORPORATION
Indianapolis, IN....................Health Care Law; Medical Malpractice; Tax Law; Trust and Estates, Wills and Probate
Louisville, KY....................Construction Law; Health Care Law; Insurance Defense; Labor and Employment Law

HALL AND SICKELS, P.C.
Reston, VA....................General Practice; Personal Injury

HALVERSON & APPLEGATE, P.S.
Yakima, WA....................General Practice

HALVERSON, WATTERS, DOWNS, REYELTS & BATEMAN, LTD.
Duluth, MN....................General Practice; Insurance Defense

HAMEL LAW FIRM, THE
Amesbury, MA....................Business Law; Commercial Law; General Practice; Personal Injury; Trust and Estates, Wills and Probate
Charlotte, NC....................General Practice

HAMILTON, BROOK, SMITH & REYNOLDS, P.C.
Lexington, MA....................Patent, Trademark, Copyright and Unfair Competition

HAMILTON AND FAATZ, A PROFESSIONAL CORPORATION
Denver, CO....................Business Law; Civil Trial Practice; Corporate Law; General Practice

HAMILTON, GIBSON, NICKELSEN, RUSH & MOORE
Honolulu, HI....................General Practice

HAMILTON & LINDER
Meridian, MS....................General Practice; Personal Injury; Workers Compensation

HAMILTON, PEATROSS, WRIGHT & POU
Shreveport, LA....................Real Estate Law

HAMMAN & BENN
Chicago, IL....................Commercial Law; Computer Law; Intellectual Property Law

HAMMER, BILL C., & ASSOCIATES
Las Vegas, NV....................Administrative Law; Corporate Law; Real Estate Law

HAMMER & JACOBS
San Jose, CA....................Family Law

HAMM, MILBY & RIDINGS
London, KY....................General Practice; Insurance Defense; Product Liability Law; Workers Compensation

HAMMOND AND CLARK
Loveland, CO....................General Practice

HAMMOND & SEWARDS
Columbus, OH....................Commercial Litigation; Insurance Defense; Medical Malpractice

HAMPTON & ROYCE, L.C.
Salina, KS ....General Practice

HANCOCK & ESTABROOK, LLP
Syracuse, NY ....General Practice; Municipal Bond/Public Authority Financing; Tax Law

HANCOCK ROTHERT & BUNSHOFT LLP
San Francisco, CA ....General Practice

HANDLIN & ASSOCIATES
Houston, TX ....Insurance Defense

HANDY & ROBINSON, P.C.
Fort Worth, TX ....Personal Injury

HANEN, ALEXANDER, JOHNSON & SPALDING, L.L.P.
Houston, TX ....Civil Trial Practice; Commercial Litigation; Insurance Defense; Medical Malpractice; Product Liability Law

HANEY, PHILIP S., ASSOCIATES
Tulsa, OK ....Nonprofit and Tax Exempt Organizations

HANFLIK, HENRY M., P.C., LAW OFFICES OF
Flint, MI ....Personal Injury

HANFT, FRIDE, O'BRIEN, HARRIES, SWELBAR & BURNS, P.A.
Duluth, MN ....Civil Trial Practice; General Practice; Insurance Defense; Trust and Estates, Wills and Probate

HANIFY & KING, PROFESSIONAL CORPORATION
Boston, MA ....Antitrust Law; Bankruptcy Law; Civil Trial Practice; Commercial Law; Real Estate Law

HANKIN, THEODORE M.
Newport Beach, CA ....Business Law; Trust and Estates, Wills and Probate

HANKIN, HANIG, STALL, CAPLICKI, REDL & CURTIN, LLP
Poughkeepsie, NY ....General Practice; Labor and Employment Law; Personal Injury; Real Estate Law; Trust and Estates, Wills and Probate

HANLEY, CHRISTINE D., & ASSOCIATES, P.A.
West Palm Beach, FL ....Labor and Employment Law

HANLEY & DEJORAS, P.A.
Minneapolis, MN ....Criminal Trial Practice

HANLON & LAVIGNE, A PROFESSIONAL CORPORATION
Edison, NJ ....Civil Trial Practice; Labor and Employment Law; Product Liability Law

HANNA, KERNS & STRADER, A PROFESSIONAL CORPORATION
Portland, OR ....Real Estate Law; Tax Law; Trust and Estates, Wills and Probate

HANNA & PLAUT, L.L.P.
Austin, TX ....Insurance Defense

HANNAFAN, MICHAEL T., & ASSOCIATES, LTD.
Chicago, IL ....Antitrust Law; Civil Trial Practice; Commercial Litigation; Intellectual Property Law; Product Liability Law; Professional Liability

HANNIG LAW FIRM LLP
Redwood City, CA ....Civil Trial Practice; Corporate Law; Real Estate Law

HANOVER & SCHNITZER
San Bernardino, CA ....Bankruptcy Law

HANOVER, WALSH, JALENAK & BLAIR, PLLC
Memphis, TN ....General Practice

HANSEN, JOEL F. & ASSOCIATES
Las Vegas, NV ....Civil Trial Practice; Insurance Defense

HANSEN, HUBBARD & SWANSON
Sturgis, SD ....General Practice

HANSEN, MCCLINTOCK & RILEY
Des Moines, IA ....Civil Trial Practice; General Practice; Insurance Defense; Legal Malpractice; Workers Compensation

HANSEN, MEAGHER, SHAMBEAU & MARONEY, S.C.
Waupaca, WI ....General Practice

HANSON, BRIDGETT, MARCUS, VLAHOS & RUDY, LLP
San Francisco, CA ....General Practice

HANSON, CURRAN, PARKS & WHITMAN
Providence, RI ....Admiralty/Maritime Law; Appellate Practice; Civil Trial Practice; Environmental Law; General Practice; Insurance Defense; Labor and Employment Law

HANSON & HANSON
McCook, NE ....General Practice

HANSON, LULIC & KRALL
Minneapolis, MN ....Insurance Defense

HANSON MAREK BOLKCOM & GREENE, LTD.
Minneapolis, MN ....Civil Trial Practice; Product Liability Law

HARAD, GITTLEMAN, GREENBERG, BRUNNER & LOVE
Philadelphia, PA ....Insurance Defense

HARALSON, MILLER, PITT & MCANALLY, P.L.C.
Tucson, AZ ....Aviation Law; Civil Trial Practice; General Practice; Medical Malpractice; Personal Injury

HARBINSON, TUNE, MANGOLD & KASSELIK, A PROFESSIONAL CORPORATION
San Francisco, CA ....Workers Compensation

HARBISON, KESSINGER, LISLE & BUSH
Lexington, KY ....General Practice

HARBOLD, R. CHRIS AND ASSOCIATES
Columbus, OH ....Family Law

HARDIG, LEE AND GROVES, PROFESSIONAL ASSOCIATION
South Bend, IN ....Medical Malpractice; Personal Injury

HARDIG PARSONS PEDERSEN & STOUT, PLLC
Bloomfield Hills, MI ....Business Law; Civil Trial Practice; Corporate Law; Family Law; Insurance Defense

HARDIMAN & CARROLL, A LAW PARTNERSHIP
San Francisco, CA ....Civil Trial Practice; Insurance Defense; Professional Liability

HARDIN, HAL D.
Nashville, TN ....General Practice

HARDIN, KUNDLA, MCKEON, POLETTO & POLIFRONI, P.A., A PROFESSIONAL CORPORATION
Springfield, NJ ....Civil Trial Practice; Commercial Litigation; Construction Law; Environmental Law; Health Care Law; Insurance Defense; Medical Malpractice; Product Liability Law; Transportation Law

HARDING, BASS, FARGASON, BOOTH & ST. CLAIR, L.L.P.
Lubbock, TX ....General Practice

HARDT, FREDERICK W.
Moorestown, NJ ....Government Contracts; Land Use Law; Municipal and Zoning Law; Real Estate Law; Trust and Estates, Wills and Probate

HARDWICK & HARRIS
Baltimore, MD ....Insurance Defense

HARDWICK, HAUSE & SEGREST
Dothan, AL ....Civil Trial Practice; Education Law; General Practice; Insurance Defense

HARDWICK LAW FIRM
Renton, WA ....Personal Injury

HARDY, BISSETT & TEICHNER, P.A.
Miami, FL ....Civil Trial Practice; General Practice; Insurance Defense; Product Liability Law

HARDY ERICH BROWN & WILSON, A PROFESSIONAL CORPORATION
Sacramento, CA ....Bankruptcy Law; Civil Trial Practice; Construction Law; Environmental Law; Insurance Defense; Labor and Employment Law; Medical Malpractice; Personal Injury; Product Liability Law; Real Estate Law

HARDY, G.P., III, P.C.
Houston, TX ....Civil Trial Practice; Commercial Law; Personal Injury

HARE, WYNN, NEWELL AND NEWTON
Birmingham, AL ....Civil Trial Practice; Medical Malpractice; Personal Injury; Product Liability Law

HARGAN, MARK C.
Newport Beach, CA ....Construction Law

HARGRAVES, KARB, WILCOX & GALVANI, LLP
Framingham, MA ....Family Law; Land Use Law; Real Estate Law; Trust and Estates, Wills and Probate

HARGROVE, PESNELL & WYATT, A P.L.C.
Shreveport, LA ....Civil Trial Practice; Natural Resources Law

HARHAI, STEPHEN J.
Denver, CO ....Family Law

HARKAVY, SHAINBERG, KOSTEN, KAPLAN & DUNSTAN, PC
Memphis, TN ....Business Law; Environmental Law; General Practice; Labor and Employment Law; Municipal and Zoning Law; Real Estate Law; Trust and Estates, Wills and Probate

HARKLEROAD & HERMANCE, A PROFESSIONAL CORPORATION
Atlanta, GA ....Administrative Law; Banking Law; Business Law; International Business Law; Tax Law

HARLAN & FLORA, P.C.
Norfolk, VA ....Aviation Law; Medical Malpractice; Personal Injury; Product Liability Law

HARLEY & BROWNE
New York, NY............................Civil Trial Practice; Medical Malpractice

HARLIN, PARKER, ALCOTT & CHAUDOIN, P.S.C.
Bowling Green, KY ....Civil Trial Practice; General Practice; Insurance Defense; Product Liability Law

HARLOW, ADAMS & FRIEDMAN, P.C.
Milford, CT ....Bankruptcy Law; General Practice; Real Estate Law; Trust and Estates, Wills and Probate

HARMAN, CLAYTOR, CORRIGAN & WELLMAN, A PROFESSIONAL CORPORATION
Richmond, VA ....Insurance Defense

HARMAN, OWEN, SAUNDERS & SWEENEY, A PROFESSIONAL CORPORATION
Atlanta, GA ....Business Law; Insurance Defense

HARMATA LAW OFFICES
Sacramento, CA ....Administrative Law; Construction Law; General Practice; Government Contracts

HARMON, STEVEN L.
Riverside, CA............................Criminal Trial Practice

HARMON, SUSAN M.
Bala Cynwyd, PA............................Trust and Estates, Wills and Probate

HARNED, BACHERT & DENTON
Bowling Green, KY ....Business Law; Civil Trial Practice; Workers Compensation

HARNESS, DICKEY & PIERCE, P.L.C.
Washington, DC............................Intellectual Property Law; Patent, Trademark, Copyright and Unfair Competition
Ann Arbor, MI ....Intellectual Property Law; Patent, Trademark, Copyright and Unfair Competition
Troy, MI............................Computer Law; Intellectual Property Law; Patent, Trademark, Copyright and Unfair Competition

HARNISH, JENNEY, MITCHELL AND RESH
Waltham, MA ....Civil Trial Practice; General Practice; Real Estate Law; Trust and Estates, Wills and Probate

HARPER, DAVID W.
Louisville, KY............................Mergers and Acquisitions

HARPER, EDWARD J. II
Greenville, NC ....Bankruptcy Law; Commercial Litigation

HARPER, FERGUSON & DAVIS
Louisville, KY............................Municipal Bond/Public Authority Financing

HARPER, HORNBAKER, ALTENHOFEN & OPAT, CHARTERED
Junction City, KS............................Civil Trial Practice

HARPER LAW FIRM, THE, P.A.
Greenville, SC............................Commercial Litigation; Construction Law

HARRANG LONG GARY RUDNICK P.C.
Eugene, OR ....General Practice

HARRAY & LINKER
Monterey, CA ....Appellate Practice; Civil Trial Practice; Insurance Defense; Medical Malpractice

HARRELL AND HARRELL
Trenton, TN............................Criminal Trial Practice; Personal Injury

HARRELL & LINDSEY, P.A.
Camden, AR ....General Practice; Trust and Estates, Wills and Probate

HARRINGTON, THOMAS S.
Eden, NC............................General Practice
Wentworth, NC............................General Practice

HARRINGTON, HOPPE & MITCHELL, LTD.
Warren, OH............................General Practice
Youngstown, OH ....Bankruptcy Law; General Practice

HARRINGTON, THOMPSON, ACKER & HARRINGTON, LTD.
Chicago, IL............................Civil Trial Practice; Personal Injury

HARRIS, DAVID J.
Wilkes-Barre, PA ....Bankruptcy Law

HARRIS, CADDELL & SHANKS, P.C.
Decatur, AL ....Civil Trial Practice; Corporate Law; General Practice; Insurance Defense; Product Liability Law; Tax Law

HARRIS, CLECKLER & HOLLIS
Birmingham, AL ....Civil Trial Practice; Insurance Defense; Medical Malpractice; Personal Injury; Product Liability Law

HARRIS, DOWELL, FISHER & HARRIS, L.C.
St. Louis, MO............................Labor and Employment Law

HARRIS, FEARS, DAVIS, LYNCH & MCDANIEL
Norfolk, VA ....Insurance Defense

HARRIS • GINSBERG LLP
Los Angeles, CA ....Family Law

HARRIS & HARRIS
Austin, TX ....Administrative Law; Civil Trial Practice; Workers Compensation

HARRIS AND HARRIS, A PROFESSIONAL CORPORATION
Warrington, PA............................Civil Trial Practice; Municipal and Zoning Law

HARRIS, JOHN D., P.C.
Phoenix, AZ ....Business Law; Commercial Litigation

HARRIS, LAMBERT, HOWERTON & DORRIS
Marion, IL............................Personal Injury; Workers Compensation

HARRIS, LAVERN D., ATTORNEY AT LAW, P.C.
Kerrville, TX ....Civil Trial Practice

HARRIS, MIDYETTE & DARBY, P.A.
Lakeland, FL............................General Practice

HARRIS, NANCY HUTCHESON, P.A.
Tampa, FL ....Family Law

HARRIS, PALUMBO, POWERS & CUNNINGHAM, P.L.L.C.
Phoenix, AZ ....Insurance Defense; Medical Malpractice; Personal Injury

HARRIS, SHELTON, DUNLAP AND COBB, P.L.L.C.
Memphis, TN ....Criminal Trial Practice; Environmental Law; General Practice; Health Care Law; Insurance Defense; Mergers and Acquisitions

HARRIS, TIM L., AND ASSOCIATES
Charlotte, NC............................Medical Malpractice; Personal Injury; Workers Compensation
Gastonia, NC ....Medical Malpractice; Personal Injury
Monroe, NC ....Personal Injury

HARRIS, TRIMMER & THOMPSON
Reno, NV ....Environmental Law; Natural Resources Law

HARRIS, WELSH & LUKMANN
Chesterton, IN ....General Practice

HARRISON, JOSEPH
Boca Raton, FL ....Administrative Law; Health Care Law

HARRISON, BRENNECKE, MOORE, SMAHA & MCKIBBEN
Marshalltown, IA............................General Practice; Trust and Estates, Wills and Probate

HARRISON & HUGHES, P.C.
Alexandria, VA ....Civil Trial Practice

HARRISON & RIAL, L.L.P.
Austin, TX ....Commercial Litigation; Natural Resources Law; Product Liability Law

HARRISON, ROBERT, & ASSOCIATES
Bloomfield Hills, MI............................Civil Trial Practice; Commercial Litigation; Criminal Trial Practice; Labor and Employment Law; Trademark, Copyright and Unfair Competition

HARRISON, TUCKER & HYDE, LLP
Springfield, MO............................Medical Malpractice; Personal Injury; Product Liability Law; Workers Compensation

HARRISON & WALL
Eastman, GA............................General Practice

HARRISON, WHITE, SMITH, HAYES & COGGINS, P.A.
Spartanburg, SC............................Civil Trial Practice; Personal Injury; Workers Compensation

HART, RICHARD H. JR., LAW OFFICES
Milwaukee, WI............................Corporate Law

HART, BROOK, ATTORNEY AT LAW, A LAW CORPORATION
Honolulu, HI............................Criminal Trial Practice

HART & CALLEY, P.C.
Alexandria, VA ....Municipal and Zoning Law

HART, GEORGE W., P.C.
Atlanta, GA ....Medical Malpractice; Personal Injury

HART AND HART
Benton, IL ....Civil Trial Practice; General Practice

HART & HORAN, P.C.
Fairfax, VA ....Construction Law

HARTE, WILLIAM J., LTD.
Chicago, IL............Civil Trial Practice; Commercial Law; Securities Law

HARTLEY, DENNIS W., P.C., PROFESSIONAL CORPORATION
Colorado Springs, CO............Criminal Trial Practice

HARTLEY, WALL & NORMAN
Orlando, FL ....Civil Trial Practice; Commercial Litigation

HARTNETT LAW FIRM, THE
Dallas, TX............Trust and Estates, Wills and Probate

HARTSELL, HARTSELL & WHITE, PA
Concord, NC............Insurance Defense

HARTZELL, GLIDDEN, TUCKER AND HARTZELL
Carthage, IL............General Practice

HARTZOG CONGER & CASON, A PROFESSIONAL CORPORATION
Oklahoma City, OK............Banking Law; Civil Trial Practice; Commercial Law; General Practice; Health Care Law; Labor and Employment Law; Real Estate Law; Securities Law; Tax Law; Trust and Estates, Wills and Probate

HARTZOG, SILVA & DAVIES
Franklin, TN............General Practice

HARVEY & BATTEY, P.A.
Beaufort, SC............Commercial Litigation; Elder Law; Environmental Law; Family Law; General Practice; Municipal and Zoning Law; Personal Injury; Real Estate Law; Tax Law; Trust and Estates, Wills and Probate

HARVEY AND MUMFORD
Albany, NY............Appellate Practice; Arbitration; Civil Trial Practice; Commercial Litigation; General Practice; Medical Malpractice; Personal Injury; Product Liability Law; Professional Liability

HARVEY, PENNINGTON, CABOT, GRIFFITH & RENNEISEN, LTD.
Philadelphia, PA ....General Practice

HARVIN, WESLEY R., P.A.
Stuart, FL............Commercial Litigation

HARWELL & PLANT
Lawrenceburg, TN............Insurance Defense; Real Estate Law

HARWICK, MAURICE
North Hollywood, CA............Civil Trial Practice

HASH & O'BRIEN, PLLP
Kalispell, MT............General Practice; Insurance Defense; Real Estate Law; Tax Law

HASKELL & PERRIN
Chicago, IL............Civil Trial Practice; Insurance Defense; Medical Malpractice; Product Liability Law; Professional Liability

HASKELL SLAUGHTER & YOUNG, L.L.C.
Birmingham, AL............Antitrust Law; Banking Law; Business Law; Civil Trial Practice; Commercial Law; General Practice; Health Care Law; Labor and Employment Law; Municipal Bond/Public Authority Financing; Tax Law

HASKELL SLAUGHTER YOUNG & GALLION, L.L.C.
Montgomery, AL............Civil Trial Practice; General Practice; Labor and Employment Law

HASLAM FIRM, THE
Fort Worth, TX............Civil Trial Practice; Personal Injury

HASPEL & MEISELMAN, CHARTERED
Rockville, MD............Family Law

HASS, D. WINTHROP, S.C.
Milwaukee, WI............Corporate Law; Mergers and Acquisitions

HASSENFELD & LEDERMAN
Boston, MA............Commercial Law

HASSETT & DONNELLY
Worcester, MA............Insurance Defense

HATCH AND PARENT
Santa Barbara, CA............Land Use Law

HATCHER, B. PAUL
Chattanooga, TN............Real Estate Law

HATCHER, STUBBS, LAND, HOLLIS & ROTHSCHILD
Columbus, GA............Banking Law; Bankruptcy Law; Commercial Law; Employment Benefits Law; General Practice; Insurance Defense; Municipal Bond/Public Authority Financing; Real Estate Law; Tax Law; Trust and Estates, Wills and Probate

HATTER, DONOVAN & MCFAUL, LLP
Mineola, NY............Civil Trial Practice; Insurance Defense; Personal Injury; Trust and Estates, Wills and Probate

HATTERY, SIMPSON & WEST
Galesburg, IL............General Practice; Personal Injury; Trust and Estates, Wills and Probate

HAUER, HARVEY I., P.C.
Bingham Farms, MI............Family Law

HAUGEN LAW FIRM, PLLP
Minneapolis, MN............International Business Law; Patent, Trademark, Copyright and Unfair Competition

HAUGH & HAUGH, P.C.
Charlottesville, VA............Civil Trial Practice; Criminal Trial Practice

HAUPTMAN & RICHMOND, P.A.
West Orange, NJ............Tax Law; Trust and Estates, Wills and Probate

HAURY, WILLIAM W. JR.
Fort Lauderdale, FL............Civil Trial Practice; Commercial Litigation

HAUSHALTER, HARRY
Hamilton Square, NJ............Civil Trial Practice; Tax Law

HAVERSTOCK, GARRETT AND ROBERTS
St. Louis, MO............Patent, Trademark, Copyright and Unfair Competition

HAWKINS • BLICK
San Jose, CA............Civil Trial Practice; Legal Malpractice; Medical Malpractice; Personal Injury

HAWKINS, MOODY, BINGHAM, MILLER & ASSOCIATES, P.C.
Kingsport, TN............Medical Malpractice; Personal Injury; Product Liability Law; Workers Compensation

HAWKINS & NORRIS
Des Moines, IA............Antitrust Law; Business Law; Civil Trial Practice; Personal Injury

HAWKINS & PARNELL, LLP
Atlanta, GA............Civil Rights; Civil Trial Practice; Commercial Law; Environmental Law; General Practice; Municipal and Zoning Law; Product Liability Law; Professional Liability; Sports and Entertainment Law; Transportation Law

HAWKINS, SCHNABEL, LINDAHL & BECK, LLP
Los Angeles, CA............Civil Trial Practice; Insurance Defense

HAWLEY, HUDSON & HAWLEY
Mt. Vernon, IN............Natural Resources Law

HAWORTH RIGGS
High Point, NC............General Practice

HAYDEN AND MILLIKEN, P.A.
Miami, FL............Admiralty/Maritime Law; Business Law; Corporate Law; Insurance Defense
Tampa, FL............Admiralty/Maritime Law; Business Law; Corporate Law; Insurance Defense

HAYDEN, THOMAS C., JR., P.A.
La Plata, MD............General Practice

HAYDUK, ANDREWS & HYPNAR, P.C.
Detroit, MI............Civil Trial Practice; Environmental Law; Insurance Defense; Labor and Employment Law; Product Liability Law; Trust and Estates, Wills and Probate

HAYES, J. MICHAEL
Buffalo, NY............Civil Trial Practice; Personal Injury

HAYES, HARKEY, SMITH & CASCIO, L.L.P.
Monroe, LA............Civil Trial Practice; General Practice; Insurance Defense; Medical Malpractice

HAYES LORENZEN, PLC
Iowa City, IA............Medical Malpractice

HAYES, PHILLIPS & MALONEY, P.C.
Denver, CO............Municipal and Zoning Law

HAYGOOD, LYNCH, HARRIS & MELTON
Forsyth, GA............General Practice
Monticello, GA............General Practice

HAYNES AND BOONE, LLP
Dallas, TX............General Practice

HAYNES, HULL, RIEDER & EWELL, P.A.
Tullahoma, TN....General Practice

HAYNSWORTH BALDWIN JOHNSON & GREAVES LLC
Jacksonville, FL....Labor and Employment Law
Tampa, FL....Labor and Employment Law
Charlotte, NC....Labor and Employment Law
Greensboro, NC....Labor and Employment Law
Raleigh, NC....Labor and Employment Law
Columbia, SC....Labor and Employment Law
Greenville, SC....Labor and Employment Law

HAYNSWORTH, MARION, MCKAY & GUÉRARD, L.L.P.
Charleston, SC....Administrative Law; Business Law; Civil Trial Practice; Employment Benefits Law; General Practice; Health Care Law; Insurance Defense; Medical Malpractice; Municipal Bond/Public Authority Financing; Product Liability Law; Real Estate Law; Securities Law; Tax Law; Trust and Estates, Wills and Probate
Columbia, SC....Administrative Law; Banking Law; Bankruptcy Law; Business Law; Civil Trial Practice; Employment Benefits Law; Environmental Law; General Practice; Insurance Defense; Medical Malpractice; Municipal Bond/Public Authority Financing; Product Liability Law; Public Utilities Law; Real Estate Law; Securities Law
Greenville, SC....Administrative Law; Banking Law; Bankruptcy Law; Business Law; Civil Trial Practice; Construction Law; Employment Benefits Law; Environmental Law; General Practice; Health Care Law; Insurance Defense; Medical Malpractice; Municipal Bond/Public Authority Financing; Patent, Trademark, Copyright and Unfair Competition; Product Liability Law; Real Estate Law; Tax Law; Trust and Estates, Wills and Probate; Workers Compensation

HAYNSWORTH, PERRY, BRYANT, MARION & JOHNSTONE
Greenville, SC....General Practice

HAYS, MCCONN, RICE & PICKERING
Houston, TX....Banking Law; Civil Trial Practice; Insurance Defense; Personal Injury

HAZLETT & WILKES
Tucson, AZ....General Practice; Insurance Defense; Medical Malpractice

HEAD, HEAD & HEAD
Carrollton, GA....Family Law; Personal Injury; Trust and Estates, Wills and Probate

HEAD, SEIFERT & VANDER WEIDE, A PROFESSIONAL ASSOCIATION
Minneapolis, MN....Commercial Litigation; General Practice; Securities Law

HEAD, THOMAS & WEBB, LLC
Atlanta, GA....Criminal Trial Practice

HEALTH LAW FIRM, THE
Little Rock, AR....Health Care Law

HEALY, GEORGE W. IV
New Orleans, LA....Admiralty/Maritime Law; Personal Injury

HEALY & BAILLIE, LLP
Stamford, CT....Admiralty/Maritime Law; General Practice
New York, NY....Admiralty/Maritime Law; General Practice

HEALY & STUDWELL LAW FIRM, P.C.
Tucson, AZ....Medical Malpractice; Personal Injury; Product Liability Law

HEARD LINEBARGER GRAHAM GOGGAN BLAIR PEÑA & SAMPSON, LLP
San Antonio, TX....Criminal Trial Practice; Family Law; General Practice; International Business Law

HEARN, BRITTAIN & MARTIN, P.A.
Conway, SC....Criminal Trial Practice; Family Law; Personal Injury

HEARNE, EPPRIGHT & GEST, A PROFESSIONAL CORPORATION
Austin, TX....Civil Trial Practice; General Practice

HECHT, SOLBERG, ROBINSON & GOLDBERG, LLP
San Diego, CA....Business Law; Land Use Law; Real Estate Law

HECKER & HARRIMAN
Los Angeles, CA....Patent, Trademark, Copyright and Unfair Competition

HECTOR & HARKE LLP
Miami, FL....Commercial Litigation

HEDEEN, HUGHES, WETERING & KNESS
Worthington, MN....General Practice

HEDLAND, BRENNAN, HEIDEMAN & COOKE, A PROFESSIONAL CORPORATION
Anchorage, AK....Civil Trial Practice

HEDRICK, DEWBERRY & REGAN, P.A.
Jacksonville, FL....Civil Trial Practice; Commercial Litigation; Construction Law; Labor and Employment Law

HEENAN BLAIKIE
Montreal, QU, Canada....General Practice

HEENEY, ARMSTRONG & HEENEY
Rockville, MD....Criminal Trial Practice

HEIDELL, PITTONI, MURPHY & BACH, LLP
Stamford, CT....Medical Malpractice
New York, NY....Insurance Defense; Medical Malpractice

HEIDMAN, REDMOND, FREDREGILL, PATTERSON, PLAZA & DYKSTRA, L.L.P.
Sioux City, IA....Civil Trial Practice; General Practice; Insurance Defense; Workers Compensation

HEILIG, MCKENRY, FRAIM & LOLLAR, A PROFESSIONAL CORPORATION
Norfolk, VA....Insurance Defense

HEILIGENSTEIN & BADGLEY, PROFESSIONAL CORPORATION
Belleville, IL....Personal Injury

HEIN, SMITH, BEREZIN, MALOOF & JACOBS, L.L.C.
Hackensack, NJ....Business Law; Civil Trial Practice; Commercial Law; Employment Benefits Law; General Practice; Insurance Defense; Medical Malpractice; Personal Injury; Product Liability Law; Real Estate Law; Workers Compensation

HEINRICH GORDON HARGROVE WEIHE & JAMES, P.A.
Fort Lauderdale, FL....Civil Trial Practice; General Practice; Personal Injury

HEINTZMAN, WARREN, WISE & FORNELLA, P.C.
Pittsburgh, PA....Admiralty/Maritime Law; Civil Trial Practice; Insurance Defense; Medical Malpractice; Product Liability Law

HEISE MARKARIAN P.A.
Miami, FL....Civil Trial Practice

HEISERMAN, ROBERT G., P.C.
Denver, CO....Immigration and Naturalization

HELEIN & ASSOCIATES, P.C.
McLean, VA....Communications Law

HELFREY, SIMON & JONES, P.C.
St. Louis, MO....Criminal Trial Practice; Intellectual Property Law; International Business Law; Mergers and Acquisitions; Real Estate Law

HELLER, DRAPER, HAYDEN & HORN, L.L.C.
New Orleans, LA....Bankruptcy Law

HELLER, STEPHEN H., A PROFESSIONAL CORPORATION
Encino, CA....Medical Malpractice; Personal Injury; Product Liability Law

HELLRING LINDEMAN GOLDSTEIN & SIEGAL LLP
Newark, NJ....Antitrust Law; Appellate Practice; Bankruptcy Law; Civil Trial Practice; Commercial Litigation; Criminal Trial Practice; Environmental Law; Family Law; General Practice; Intellectual Property Law; Labor and Employment Law; Natural Resources Law; Real Estate Law; Securities Law; Tax Law; Trust and Estates, Wills and Probate

HELM & ASSOCIATES
Anchorage, AK....Medical Malpractice

HELMKE, BEAMS, BOYER & WAGNER
Fort Wayne, IN....Bankruptcy Law; Civil Trial Practice; Creditors Rights; General Practice; Municipal and Zoning Law; Trust and Estates, Wills and Probate

HELMS, HANRAHAN & MYERS
Arcadia, CA....Family Law; General Practice; Trust and Estates, Wills and Probate

HELMSING, SIMS & LEACH, P.C.
Mobile, AL....Aviation Law; Civil Trial Practice; Commercial Law; Commercial Litigation; Criminal Trial Practice; General Practice; Insurance Defense; Personal Injury; Trust and Estates, Wills and Probate

HELSELL FETTERMAN LLP
Seattle, WA....General Practice

HEMENWAY & BARNES
Boston, MA....Business Law; General Practice; Trust and Estates, Wills and Probate

HENDERSON, THOMAS W.
Newport Beach, CA................Trust and Estates, Wills and Probate

HENDERSON & BRENNAN
White Plains, NY....................Civil Trial Practice

HENDERSON & BUTLER
Huntsville, AL.........................Insurance Defense

HENDERSON, FRANKLIN, STARNES & HOLT, PROFESSIONAL ASSOCIATION
Fort Myers, FL........................Business Law; Civil Trial Practice; Corporate Law; General Practice; Insurance Defense; Personal Injury; Real Estate Law; Tax Law; Trust and Estates, Wills and Probate

HENDERSON, HANEMANN & MORRIS, A PROFESSIONAL LAW CORPORATION
Houma, LA.............................Admiralty/Maritime Law; Insurance Defense; Product Liability Law; Workers Compensation

HENDREN AND ANDRAE
Jefferson City, MO..................General Practice; Insurance Defense

HENDRICK, PHILLIPS, SCHEMM & SALZMAN, A PROFESSIONAL CORPORATION
Atlanta, GA............................Construction Law

HENDRICKS, NATHAN V. III
Atlanta, GA............................Municipal and Zoning Law

HENDRICKS & HENDRICKS
Coral Gables, FL....................Trust and Estates, Wills and Probate

HENDRICKSON, RAY
Irvine, CA...............................Family Law

HENDRY, STONER, SAWICKI & BROWN, P.A.
Orlando, FL............................International Trade Law; Real Estate Law; Tax Law

HENICAN, JAMES & CLEVELAND
Metairie, LA...........................Corporate Law; Mergers and Acquisitions; Real Estate Law; Tax Law; Trust and Estates, Wills and Probate

HENINGER, BURGE, VARGO AND DAVIS, LLP
Birmingham, AL......................Medical Malpractice; Personal Injury

HENINGER AND HENINGER, PROFESSIONAL CORPORATION
Davenport, IA.........................General Practice; Medical Malpractice

HENKE-BUFKIN, A PROFESSIONAL ASSOCIATION
Clarksdale, MS.......................Insurance Defense; Product Liability Law

HENNENBERG & ASSOCIATES
Cleveland, OH........................Civil Rights; Criminal Trial Practice; Real Estate Law; Trust and Estates, Wills and Probate

HENNENHOEFER, JAMES A., A PROFESSIONAL CORPORATION
Vista, CA................................Family Law

HENNIGAN, MERCER & BENNETT
Los Angeles, CA.....................Antitrust Law; Bankruptcy Law; Civil Trial Practice; Commercial Litigation; Securities Law

HENRICKSEN & HENRICKSEN, INC.
El Reno, OK............................General Practice

HENRY & BEAVER LLP
Lebanon, PA...........................Civil Trial Practice; General Practice

HENRY, BUCHANAN, HUDSON, SUBER & CARTER, P.A.
Tallahassee, FL......................Civil Trial Practice; General Practice; Insurance Defense

HENRY, MCCORD, BEAN & MILLER, P.L.L.C.
Tullahoma, TN........................General Practice

HENSHAW, TODD MAXWELL
Tulsa, OK...............................Bankruptcy Law

HENSLEE, FOWLER, HEPWORTH & SCHWARTZ, L.L.P.
Austin, TX..............................Insurance Defense

HENSLEY & HENSLEY
Raymore, MO..........................Criminal Trial Practice; Family Law; Personal Injury; Workers Compensation

HENSON & EFRON, P.A.
Minneapolis, MN.....................Commercial Litigation; Environmental Law; Family Law; General Practice; Product Liability Law; Securities Law

HENSON AND FUERST, P.A.
Rocky Mount, NC....................Medical Malpractice; Personal Injury

HENSON & HENSON, L.L.P.
Greensboro, NC.......................Civil Trial Practice; Insurance Defense; Personal Injury

HENSON, HENSON, HENSON, MARSHALL & MILBURN, LLP
Shawnee, OK..........................General Practice

HEPFER, CHERYL LYNN
Rockville, MD.........................Family Law

HERBERT & HERBERT
Glasgow, KY...........................Civil Trial Practice; Family Law; General Practice; Personal Injury; Real Estate Law

HERBOLSHEIMER, LANNON, HENSON, DUNCAN AND REAGAN, P.C.
La Salle, IL............................Appellate Practice; Civil Trial Practice; General Practice; Insurance Defense; Medical Malpractice; Professional Liability; Real Estate Law; Workers Compensation

HERLOCKER, ROBERTS & ST. PETER, L.L.C.
Winfield, KS...........................General Practice

HERMAN, GOLDSTEIN & FORSYTH, P.C.
Scottsdale, AZ........................Civil Trial Practice; Insurance Defense; Personal Injury

HERMAN, HERMAN, KATZ & COTLAR, L.L.P.
New Orleans, LA.....................Civil Trial Practice; General Practice

HERMAN & HOWRY, L.L.P.
Austin, TX..............................Civil Trial Practice; Commercial Litigation

HERMANN, CAHN & SCHNEIDER
Cleveland, OH........................Business Law; Civil Trial Practice; Family Law; Insurance Defense; Personal Injury; Product Liability Law

HERMENZE & MARCANTONIO
Westport, CT..........................Trust and Estates, Wills and Probate

HERNER, DONALD A. LAW OFFICES OF
Stamford, CT..........................Business Law; Corporate Law

HEROLD AND HAINES, PROFESSIONAL ASSOCIATION
Warren, NJ.............................General Practice

HERRERA, LONG & POUND, P.A.
Santa Fe, NM.........................Civil Trial Practice; Health Care Law; Insurance Defense; Land Use Law; Municipal and Zoning Law; Product Liability Law; Real Estate Law

HERRICK LAW OFFICE, S.C.
Fond du Lac, WI.....................Insurance Defense

HERRING, D. JEFFERSON
Nashville, TN.........................Tax Law; Trust and Estates, Wills and Probate

HERRMANN, LAWRENCE M.
Jackson Heights, NY...............Criminal Trial Practice

HERSH, NEAL RAYMOND LAW OFFICES OF
Beverly Hills, CA....................Family Law

HERSH FAMILYLAW PRACTICE, A PROFESSIONAL CORPORATION
San Francisco, CA..................Family Law

HERSHEWE & GULICK, P.C.
Joplin, MO.............................Medical Malpractice; Personal Injury

HERSHNER, HUNTER, ANDREWS, NEILL & SMITH, LLP
Eugene, OR............................General Practice

HERTEN, BURSTEIN, SHERIDAN, CEVASCO, BOTTINELLI & LITT, L.L.C.
Hackensack, NJ......................Appellate Practice; Civil Trial Practice; Land Use Law; Product Liability Law

HERTZ, SCHRAM & SARETSKY, P.C.
Bloomfield Hills, MI................Banking Law; Bankruptcy Law; Business Law; Commercial Law; Commercial Litigation; Family Law; Securities Law; Tax Law

HERTZBERG, RICHARD J.
Phoenix, AZ...........................Civil Trial Practice; Criminal Trial Practice

HERZFELD & RUBIN, P.C.
New York, NY.........................General Practice

HERZOG, CREBS & MCGHEE, LLP
St. Louis, MO.........................Civil Trial Practice

HERZOG, FISHER, GRAYSON & WOLFE, A LAW CORPORATION
Beverly Hills, CA....................Business Law; Commercial Litigation; Health Care Law; Insurance Defense

HERZOG AND O'CONNOR, P.C.
Phoenix, AZ...........................Insurance Defense; Personal Injury; Workers Compensation

HESLIN & ROTHENBERG, P.C.
Albany, NY.............................Intellectual Property Law; Patent, Trademark, Copyright and Unfair Competition

HESSIAN & MCKASY, P.A.
Minneapolis, MN....................Bankruptcy Law; Labor and Employment Law; Municipal and Zoning Law; Real Estate Law

HESSION & BEKOFF
Mineola, NY............................Criminal Trial Practice; Personal Injury

HESTER, GRADY, HESTER, GREENE & PAYNE
Elizabethtown, NC................General Practice

HESTER, JON L., P.C., A PROFESSIONAL CORPORATION
Oklahoma City, OK................Family Law

HEWITT, JAMES W.
Lincoln, NE.............................General Practice

HEWLETT, COLLINS AND ALLARD
Wilmington, NC.......................Criminal Trial Practice

HEYL, ROYSTER, VOELKER & ALLEN, PROFESSIONAL CORPORATION
Edwardsville, IL.......................Insurance Defense
Peoria, IL................................Insurance Defense
Rockford, IL ....Insurance Defense
Springfield, IL ....Insurance Defense
Urbana, IL...............................Insurance Defense

HICKEY, MACKEY, EVANS & WALKER
Cheyenne, WY.........................Banking Law; Civil Trial Practice; Commercial Law; Criminal Trial Practice; General Practice; Personal Injury; Public Utilities Law

HICKS, H. MELVILLE JR.
New York, NY..........................Commercial Law

HICKS & ANDERSON, P.A.
Miami, FL................................Appellate Practice; General Practice

HICKS, BRAMS & SCHER
West Palm Beach, FL.............Civil Trial Practice

HICKS & LUCKY, A PROFESSIONAL CORPORATION
El Paso, TX.............................Civil Trial Practice; Insurance Defense; Medical Malpractice; Personal Injury

HICKSON, DAVID L.
San Diego, CA ....Trust and Estates, Wills and Probate

HIENTON FRY, P.C.
Phoenix, AZ ....Real Estate Law

HIERING, DUPIGNAC & STANZIONE, A PROFESSIONAL CORPORATION
Toms River, NJ........................General Practice

HIGBEE, JENSEN & MACFARLANE, P.C.
Cedar City, UT ....General Practice; Personal Injury

HIGGINS, CAVANAGH & COONEY
Providence, RI.........................Civil Trial Practice; General Practice; Insurance Defense

HIGGS, FLETCHER & MACK LLP
San Diego, CA ....Banking Law; Civil Trial Practice; General Practice

HIGH, STACK, LAZENBY, PALAHACH & FEILER
Miami, FL................................Civil Trial Practice; Personal Injury

HIGH, SWARTZ, ROBERTS & SEIDEL, LLP
Norristown, PA........................General Practice

HIGHSAW, MAHONEY & CLARKE, P.C.
Washington, DC.......................Labor and Employment Law

HIGHTOWER, ROBERT S.
Tallahassee, FL ....Corporate Law; Mergers and Acquisitions; Tax Law; Trust and Estates, Wills and Probate

HILBRECHT & ASSOCIATES, CHARTERED
Las Vegas, NV ....Administrative Law; General Practice; Personal Injury

HILBURN, CALHOON, HARPER, PRUNISKI & CALHOUN, LTD.
Little Rock, AR ....Civil Trial Practice; General Practice; Labor and Employment Law; Securities Law; Tax Law

HILDER, PHILIP H., & ASSOCIATES, P.C.
Houston, TX............................Criminal Trial Practice

HILL, JOHN E. LAW OFFICES OF
San Francisco, CA..................Civil Trial Practice

HILL & BARLOW, A PROFESSIONAL CORPORATION
Boston, MA..............................General Practice

HILL AND BLEIBERG
Atlanta, GA ....Medical Malpractice; Personal Injury; Product Liability Law

HILLENCAMP & ALVAREZ, P.A.
Miami, FL................................Medical Malpractice; Personal Injury

HILL, EVANS, DUNCAN, JORDAN & DAVIS
Greensboro, NC......................Civil Trial Practice; General Practice

HILL, FARRER & BURRILL LLP
Los Angeles, CA ....Appellate Practice; Civil Trial Practice; Eminent Domain; General Practice; Labor and Employment Law; Real Estate Law; Tax Law

HILL & HILL
Houston, TX ....General Practice

HILL, HILL, CARTER, FRANCO, COLE & BLACK, P.C.
Montgomery, AL ....Civil Trial Practice; General Practice

HILLIARD, FRANK P.
Louisville, KY ....Civil Trial Practice; General Practice; Insurance Defense

HILLIS CLARK MARTIN & PETERSON, A PROFESSIONAL SERVICE CORPORATION
Seattle, WA ....General Practice

HILLMAN, FORMAN, NELSEN CHILDERS, LINGO & MCCORMACK
Omaha, NE ....General Practice

HILL & PARKER, A PROFESSIONAL CORPORATION
Houston, TX ....Civil Trial Practice; Personal Injury

HILL AND PONTON, PROFESSIONAL ASSOCIATION
Orlando, FL ....Aviation Law; Civil Trial Practice; Medical Malpractice; Personal Injury; Product Liability Law

HILL, REIS, ADAMS, HALL & SCHIEFFELIN, P.A.
Orlando, FL ....Antitrust Law; Appellate Practice; Civil Trial Practice; General Practice; Health Care Law; Insurance Defense; Medical Malpractice; Personal Injury; Product Liability Law; Professional Liability

HINCKLEY, ALLEN & SNYDER LLP
Boston, MA.............................Banking Law; Bankruptcy Law; Business Law; Commercial Law; Commercial Litigation; Computer Law; Construction Law; Creditors Rights; Employment Benefits Law; Energy Law; General Practice; Health Care Law; Intellectual Property Law; International Business Law; International Trade Law; Labor and Employment Law; Mergers and Acquisitions; Municipal and Zoning Law; Municipal Bond/Public Authority Financing; Patent, Trademark, Copyright and Unfair Competition; Pension and Profit Sharing; Product Liability Law; Public Utiiities Law; Real Estate Law; Securities Law; Tax Law; Trademark, Copyright and Unfair Competition; Trust and Estates, Wills and Probate; Workers Compensation
Providence, RI........................Banking Law; Bankruptcy Law; Business Law; Commercial Law; Commercial Litigation; Computer Law; Construction Law; Creditors Rights; Employment Benefits Law; Energy Law; General Practice; Health Care Law; Intellectual Property Law; International Business Law; International Trade Law; Labor and Employment Law; Mergers and Acquisitions; Municipal and Zoning Law; Municipal Bond/Public Authority Financing; Patent, Trademark, Copyright and Unfair Competition; Pension and Profit Sharing; Product Liability Law; Public Utilities Law; Real Estate Law; Securities Law; Tax Law; Trademark, Copyright and Unfair Competition; Trust and Estates, Wills and Probate; Workers Compensation

HINDMAN, GOLDSTEIN & HARDER, P.C.
Columbia, MO ....Civil Trial Practice

HINDS, ROBERT T., JR. AND ASSOCIATES, P.C.
Greenwood Village, CO..........Family Law

HINES & THOMAS
San Francisco, CA ....Insurance Defense

HINKLEY & GIUNTA
Midland, TX ....Personal Injury

HINMAN, HOWARD & KATTELL, LLP
Binghamton, NY......................Civil Trial Practice; Corporate Law; General Practice; Labor and Employment Law; Municipal Bond/Public Authority Financing; Natural Resources Law; Oil and Gas Law; Tax Law

HINMAN, STRAUB, PIGORS & MANNING, P.C.
Albany, NY..............................Health Care Law; Labor and Employment Law

HINSHAW & CULBERTSON
Chicago, IL.............................General Practice

HINTON & ALFERT, A PROFESSIONAL CORPORATION
Walnut Creek, CA ....Aviation Law; Civil Trial Practice; Commercial Litigation; Personal Injury; Product Liability Law

HIRSCH LAW OFFICE, P.C.
Phoenix, AZ ....Bankruptcy Law; Family Law

HIRSCHHORN, AUSTIN, P.C.
Troy, MI....Bankruptcy Law; Business Law; Civil Trial Practice; Commercial Law; General Practice; Real Estate Law

HIRSCHHORN, JOEL, P.A.
Coral Gables, FL....Appellate Practice; Criminal Trial Practice

HIRSH, BJORGAARD & ROGERS, P.L.C.
Tucson, AZ....Criminal Trial Practice

HIRSON WEXLER PERL & STARK, A PROFESSIONAL CORPORATION
Newport Beach, CA....Immigration and Naturalization

HIRST & APPLEGATE, A PROFESSIONAL CORPORATION
Cheyenne, WY....Civil Trial Practice; Real Estate Law; Trust and Estates, Wills and Probate

HISCOCK & BARCLAY, LLP
Syracuse, NY....Banking Law; Business Law; Commercial Litigation; General Practice

HISHON FIRM, THE, LLC
Atlanta, GA....Business Law; Civil Trial Practice; General Practice; Tax Law

HOAGLAND, LONGO, MORAN, DUNST & DOUKAS
New Brunswick, NJ....Business Law; Civil Trial Practice; Construction Law; Environmental Law; Insurance Defense

HOBBS & HAIN, P.C.
Selma, AL....General Practice

HOBBS, HARRY M., P.A.
Tampa, FL....Real Estate Law

HOBBS, LARRY F., P.C.
Denver, CO....Labor and Employment Law

HOBSON, CADY & CADY
Hampton, IA....Civil Trial Practice; General Practice

HOCHMAN, SALKIN, RETTIG, TOSCHER & PEREZ, A PROFESSIONAL CORPORATION
Beverly Hills, CA....Business Law; Corporate Law; Criminal Trial Practice; Real Estate Law; Tax Law; Trust and Estates, Wills and Probate

HOCKEMA, TIPPIT & ESCOBEDO, L.L.P.
Edinburg, TX....Commercial Litigation; Personal Injury

HODGDEN, HALLREN, SMITHTON & HODGDEN, P.L.L.C.
Woodward, OK....General Practice

HODGES, CHARLES R., P.C.
Dallas, TX....Family Law

HODGES & DAVIS, P.C.
Merrillville, IN....Civil Trial Practice; Commercial Law; General Practice; Health Care Law; Real Estate Law
Portage, IN....Civil Trial Practice; Commercial Law; General Practice; Health Care Law; Real Estate Law

HODGES & LEVERETT, L.L.C.
Elberton, GA....General Practice

HODGSON, RUSS, ANDREWS, WOODS & GOODYEAR, LLP
Albany, NY....General Practice
Buffalo, NY....Civil Trial Practice; General Practice; Immigration and Naturalization; Labor and Employment Law; Patent, Trademark, Copyright and Unfair Competition; Tax Law

HODOSH, SPINELLA & ANGELONE
Providence, RI....Civil Trial Practice

HOEFFNER, JAMES V.
Austin, TX....Bankruptcy Law

HOEPPNER WAGNER & EVANS LLP
Merrillville, IN....General Practice; Insurance Defense; Labor and Employment Law; Product Liability Law
Valparaiso, IN....Employment Benefits Law; General Practice; Insurance Defense; Labor and Employment Law; Product Liability Law; Real Estate Law

HOFELICH & KING
Cleveland, OH....Civil Trial Practice

HOFF, CURTIS, PACHT, CASSIDY & FRAME, P.C.
Burlington, VT....General Practice

HOFFERT & ASSOCIATES, P.C.
Southfield, MI....Tax Law

HOFFINGER FRIEDLAND DOBRISH & STERN, P.C.
New York, NY....Appellate Practice; Civil Trial Practice; Commercial Litigation; Corporate Law; Criminal Trial Practice; Family Law; Real Estate Law; Securities Law; Tax Law

HOFFMAN, JAMES P. LAW OFFICES OF
Keokuk, IA....Personal Injury; Workers Compensation

HOFFMAN DREWRY HANCOCK & SIMMONS
Indianapolis, IN....Commercial Law; Commercial Litigation; Construction Law; Government Contracts

HOFFMAN & FOWLER, LLP
Atlanta, GA....Business Law; Civil Trial Practice; Family Law; Personal Injury; Tax Law; Trust and Estates, Wills and Probate

HOFFMAN & HERTZIG, P.A.
Miami, FL....Aviation Law; Business Law; Civil Trial Practice

HOFFMAN & LYONS, P.C.
Rockville, MD....Commercial Litigation

HOFFMAN POLLOK & PICKHOLZ LLP
New York, NY....Criminal Trial Practice; Securities Law

HOFFMAN, WACHTELL, KOSTER & MAIER
White Plains, NY....Civil Trial Practice; General Practice; Municipal and Zoning Law; Real Estate Law; Workers Compensation

HOFFMANN & BARON, LLP
Parsippany, NJ....Intellectual Property Law; Patent, Trademark, Copyright and Unfair Competition
Syosset, NY....Intellectual Property Law; Patent, Trademark, Copyright and Unfair Competition

HOFFMANN & MCCONKEY, P.L.C., LAW OFFICES OF
Des Moines, IA....Workers Compensation

HOFLER, HAYES, & ASSOCIATES, P.A.
Durham, NC....Civil Trial Practice; Construction Law; Personal Injury

HOGAN, THOMAS R. LAW OFFICES OF
San Jose, CA....Business Law; Civil Trial Practice; Construction Law; General Practice

HOGAN DUBOSE & TOWNSEND, L.L.P.
Houston, TX....Appellate Practice; Civil Trial Practice

HOGAN & HARTSON
Prague, Czech Republic....General Practice
Colorado Springs, CO....General Practice
Denver, CO....General Practice
Washington, DC....General Practice
Baltimore, MD....General Practice
Rockville, MD....General Practice
McLean, VA....General Practice
Brussels, Belgium....General Practice
London, England....General Practice
Paris, France....General Practice
Moscow, Russia....General Practice
Warsaw, Poland....General Practice

HOGAN & HOGAN
East Providence, RI....General Practice

HOGAN, PALACE & SCULLY
Hackensack, NJ....Civil Trial Practice; Commercial Litigation; Real Estate Law; Trust and Estates, Wills and Probate

HOGAN & SARZYNSKI, L.L.P.
Binghamton, NY....Arbitration; Education Law; Labor and Employment Law; Municipal and Zoning Law

HOGAN, SMITH & ALSPAUGH, P.C.
Birmingham, AL....Civil Trial Practice; Environmental Law; Medical Malpractice; Personal Injury; Product Liability Law

HOGG, RYCE & HUDSON
West Palm Beach, FL....Labor and Employment Law

HOGUE, HILL, JONES, NASH AND LYNCH, L.L.P.
Wilmington, NC....Civil Trial Practice; General Practice; Insurance Defense

HOGUE & LANNIS
Pittsburgh, PA....Business Law; Commercial Litigation

HOHMANN & TAUBE, L.L.P.
Austin, TX....Banking Law; Bankruptcy Law; Civil Trial Practice; Insurance Defense

HOHN & SCHEÜERLE
Philadelphia, PA....Civil Trial Practice

HOIDAL & HANNAH, P.L.C.
Phoenix, AZ....Criminal Trial Practice

HOLAHAN, GUMPPER & DOWLING
Fairfield, CT....Civil Trial Practice

HOLAHAN, MALLOY, MAYBAUGH, MONNICH & DELIE
Troy, MI....................Civil Trial Practice; Environmental Law; Insurance Defense; Medical Malpractice; Personal Injury; Product Liability Law; Professional Liability; Trust and Estates, Wills and Probate

HOLBROOK, HEAVEN & OSBORN, P.A.
Kansas City, KS....................Civil Trial Practice; General Practice; Insurance Defense

HOLBROOK & PITT
Ashland, KY....................Real Estate Law

HOLCOMB DUNBAR, A PROFESSIONAL ASSOCIATION
Clarksdale, MS....................Civil Trial Practice; Commercial Law; General Practice; Insurance Defense; Trust and Estates, Wills and Probate; Workers Compensation
Oxford, MS....................Bankruptcy Law; Civil Trial Practice; Commercial Law; General Practice; Insurance Defense; Labor and Employment Law
Southaven, MS....................Civil Trial Practice; Commercial Law; General Practice; Insurance Defense

HOLCOMBE, BOMAR, GUNN AND BRADFORD, P.A.
Spartanburg, SC....................Civil Trial Practice; General Practice; Medical Malpractice; Product Liability Law

HOLDER, HOLLY I., P.C.
Denver, CO....................Environmental Law; Natural Resources Law

HOLDMANN, LEE F., CHARTERED
Bethesda, MD....................Arbitration; Trust and Estates, Wills and Probate

HOLLAND & BONZAGNI, P.C.
Springfield, MA....................Patent, Trademark, Copyright and Unfair Competition

HOLLAND & HART LLP
Denver, CO....................General Practice

HOLLAND KAUFMANN & BARTELS, LLC
Greenwich, CT....................Business Law; Civil Trial Practice; Commercial Litigation; Family Law; General Practice; Land Use Law; Real Estate Law; Trust and Estates, Wills and Probate

HOLLAND & KNIGHT LLP
San Francisco, CA....................General Practice
Washington, DC....................General Practice
Fort Lauderdale, FL....................General Practice
Jacksonville, FL....................General Practice
Lakeland, FL....................General Practice
Melbourne, FL....................General Practice
Miami, FL....................General Practice
Orlando, FL....................General Practice
St. Petersburg, FL....................General Practice
Tallahassee, FL....................General Practice
Tampa, FL....................General Practice
West Palm Beach, FL....................General Practice
Atlanta, GA....................General Practice
Falls Church, VA....................General Practice

HOLLEMAN, BOYCE, A PROFESSIONAL CORPORATION
Gulfport, MS....................Business Law; Civil Trial Practice; Corporate Law; Criminal Trial Practice; Family Law; General Practice; Government Contracts; Medical Malpractice; Personal Injury; Product Liability Law; Workers Compensation

HOLLEY, ALBERTSON & POLK, P.C.
Golden, CO....................Civil Trial Practice; Construction Law; Land Use Law; Real Estate Law

HOLLIMAN LANGHOLZ RUNNELS FORSMAN & SELLERS, A PROFESSIONAL CORPORATION
Tulsa, OK....................General Practice; Natural Resources Law

HOLLINS, SCHECHTER, FEINSTEIN & CONDAS, A PROFESSIONAL CORPORATION
Orange, CA....................Insurance Defense

HOLLINS, WAGSTER & YARBROUGH, P.C.
Nashville, TN....................Civil Trial Practice; Criminal Trial Practice; Insurance Defense

HOLLIS AND JOHNSON
Chicago, IL....................Banking Law; Bankruptcy Law; Business Law; Commercial Law; Commercial Litigation; Real Estate Law

HOLLISTER & BRACE, A PROFESSIONAL CORPORATION
Santa Barbara, CA....................Business Law; Civil Trial Practice; Energy Law; Environmental Law; Land Use Law; Natural Resources Law; Real Estate Law

HOLLOMAN, CHARLES R., P.A.
Ocala, FL....................Criminal Trial Practice

HOLLORAN LAW FIRM, THE, P.C.
St. Louis, MO....................Medical Malpractice; Personal Injury; Product Liability Law

HOLLOWAY, DOBSON, BACHMAN & JENNINGS, A PROFESSIONAL CORPORATION
Oklahoma City, OK....................Civil Trial Practice

HOLLOWAY ODEGARD & SWEENEY, P.C.
Phoenix, AZ....................Insurance Defense

HOLLOWAY & ROWLEY, P.C.
Houston, TX....................Civil Trial Practice

HOLLOWELL, PEACOCK & MEYER, P.A.
Raleigh, NC....................Health Care Law

HOLLSTEIN KEATING CATTELL JOHNSON & GOLDSTEIN, P.C.
Philadelphia, PA....................Admiralty/Maritime Law; Commercial Litigation; Product Liability Law; Toxic Torts

HOLME ROBERTS & OWEN LLP
Boulder, CO....................General Practice; Intellectual Property Law
Colorado Springs, CO....................General Practice; Intellectual Property Law; Nonprofit and Tax Exempt Organizations
Denver, CO....................Banking Law; Civil Trial Practice; Environmental Law; General Practice; Health Care Law; Intellectual Property Law; International Business Law; Labor and Employment Law; Municipal Bond/Public Authority Financing; Natural Resources Law; Nonprofit and Tax Exempt Organizations; Patent, Trademark, Copyright and Unfair Competition; Real Estate Law; Securities Law; Tax Law; Trust and Estates, Wills and Probate
Salt Lake City, UT....................General Practice; Nonprofit and Tax Exempt Organizations
London, England....................General Practice

HOLMES FIRM, THE, A PROFESSIONAL CORPORATION
Dallas, TX....................Real Estate Law

HOLMES WEDDLE & BARCOTT, A PROFESSIONAL CORPORATION
Anchorage, AK....................General Practice
Seattle, WA....................General Practice

HOLMES, WOODS & GARZA
Dallas, TX....................Family Law; Trust and Estates, Wills and Probate

HOLMSTROM & KENNEDY, P.C.
Rockford, IL....................General Practice

HOLPER, WELSH & MITCHELL, LTD.
Phoenix, AZ....................Bankruptcy Law; Business Law; Commercial Litigation; Real Estate Law
Minneapolis, MN....................Bankruptcy Law; Business Law; Commercial Litigation; Real Estate Law

HOLT, LONGEST, WALL & BLAETZ, P.L.L.C.
Burlington, NC....................General Practice

HOLT NEY ZATCOFF & WASSERMAN, LLP
Atlanta, GA....................Business Law; Civil Trial Practice; Commercial Law; Communications Law; Environmental Law; General Practice; Municipal and Zoning Law; Real Estate Law; Tax Law

HOLT & WATT
Reidsville, NC....................Real Estate Law

HOLT YORK MCDARRIS, LLP
Raleigh, NC....................Municipal and Zoning Law

HOLTON HOWARD & GOODMAN, P.C.
Nashville, TN....................Tax Law; Trust and Estates, Wills and Probate

HOLTORF, KOVARIK, ELLISON & MATHIS, P.C.
Gering, NE....................General Practice; Insurance Defense

HOLTZMAN, ERIC H.
Hauppauge, NY....................Civil Trial Practice; Commercial Law; Commercial Litigation; Environmental Law; General Practice; Product Liability Law

HOLTZMAN, KRINZMAN, EQUELS & FURIA
Miami, FL....................Administrative Law; Bankruptcy Law; Civil Trial Practice; Commercial Litigation; Corporate Law; Real Estate Law

HONEYCHURCH AND FINKAS
Fairfield, CA....................Criminal Trial Practice

HONIGMAN MILLER SCHWARTZ AND COHN
Detroit, MI....................Antitrust Law; Bankruptcy Law; Civil Trial Practice; Communications Law; Criminal Trial Practice; Environmental Law; General Practice; Health Care Law; Labor and Employment Law; Municipal Bond/Public Authority Financing; Natural Resources Law; Real Estate Law; Tax Law
Lansing, MI....................Civil Trial Practice; Environmental Law; General Practice; Insurance Defense; Natural Resources Law; Tax Law; Transportation Law

HOOD LAW FIRM
Charleston, SC ....Civil Trial Practice; General Practice; Insurance Defense; Medical Malpractice; Personal Injury; Product Liability Law; Professional Liability

HOOD, L. PAUL, JR., A PROFESSIONAL LAW CORPORATION
Covington, LA ....Tax Law; Trust and Estates, Wills and Probate

HOOD & RAYNOLDS, P.C.
Tulsa, OK ....Family Law

HOOKER & RODRIGUEZ
Tucson, AZ ....Criminal Trial Practice

HOOPER, HATHAWAY, PRICE, BEUCHE & WALLACE
Ann Arbor, MI ....Business Law; Civil Trial Practice; Commercial Litigation; Corporate Law; Criminal Trial Practice; Employment Benefits Law; Environmental Law; Family Law; General Practice; Labor and Employment Law; Medical Malpractice; Personal Injury; Real Estate Law; Trust and Estates, Wills and Probate

HOOPER, LUNDY & BOOKMAN, INC.
Los Angeles, CA ....Health Care Law

HOOVER, ROBERT D., P.L.C., LAW OFFICES OF
Baton Rouge, LA ....Insurance Defense; Personal Injury

HOPGOOD, CALIMAFDE, KALIL & JUDLOWE LLP
New York, NY ....Intellectual Property Law; Patent, Trademark, Copyright and Unfair Competition

HOPKINS & CARLEY, A LAW CORPORATION
San Jose, CA ....Commercial Law; Corporate Law; Environmental Law; General Practice; Patent, Trademark, Copyright and Unfair Competition; Real Estate Law; Tax Law; Trust and Estates, Wills and Probate

HOPKINS, CRAWLEY, BAGWELL & UPSHAW, P.L.L.C.
Gulfport, MS ....Civil Trial Practice; Environmental Law; Insurance Defense; Personal Injury; Product Liability Law; Workers Compensation

HOPKINS LAW FIRM, A PROFESSIONAL ASSOCIATION
Little Rock, AR ....Commercial Law

HOPKINS RODEN CROCKETT HANSEN & HOOPES, PLLC
Boise, ID ....General Practice
Idaho Falls, ID ....General Practice

HOPKINS & SUTTER
Washington, DC ....General Practice; Tax Law
Chicago, IL ....Commercial Litigation; General Practice; Tax Law; Trust and Estates, Wills and Probate

HOPPE & STOKES, P.A.
Miami, FL ....Admiralty/Maritime Law; Medical Malpractice; Personal Injury

HOPPEL, MAYER & COLEMAN
Washington, DC ....Admiralty/Maritime Law

HOPPER, GALLIHER & TUCKER, P.C.
Indianapolis, IN ....Bankruptcy Law; Commercial Litigation; Creditors Rights

HOPSON AND HABENICHT, LTD.
Chester, VA ....Civil Trial Practice

HORGER, BARNWELL & REID, L.L.P.
Orangeburg, SC ....General Practice

HÖRGER, HÖRGER, LANIER & KNIGHT, L.L.P.
Orangeburg, SC ....Civil Trial Practice

HORLICK, MICHAEL D., P.A.
Venice, FL ....Corporate Law; Trust and Estates, Wills and Probate

HORN, JEROLD I.
Peoria, IL ....Trust and Estates, Wills and Probate

HORN, ARTHUR S., P.A.
Nutley, NJ ....Real Estate Law; Trust and Estates, Wills and Probate

HORNBERGER, GHAZARIANS & BREWER
Los Angeles, CA ....Civil Trial Practice

HORNE, BISTROW & DULBERG, P.C.
Phoenix, AZ ....Civil Trial Practice; Commercial Litigation; Construction Law; Intellectual Property Law; Personal Injury

HORNE, FOY S., JR., P.C.
Athens, GA ....Personal Injury; Workers Compensation

HORNE, HOLLINGSWORTH & PARKER, A PROFESSIONAL ASSOCIATION
Little Rock, AR ....General Practice

HORNECKER, COWLING, HASSEN & HEYSELL, L.L.P.
Medford, OR ....General Practice

HORNSBY, WATSON & MEGINNISS
Huntsville, AL ....Civil Trial Practice; Personal Injury; Product Liability Law; Workers Compensation

HORNTHAL, RILEY, ELLIS & MALAND, L.L.P.
Elizabeth City, NC ....Civil Trial Practice; General Practice

HOROWITZ, EDWARD J., A PROFESSIONAL CORPORATION
Los Angeles, CA ....Appellate Practice

HOROWITZ, FORAN & SONNTAG, P.A.
Greenbelt, MD ....Medical Malpractice; Personal Injury

HORRIGAN & GOEHRS, L.L.P.
Houston, TX ....Trust and Estates, Wills and Probate

HORTON, KNOX, CARTER & FOOTE
El Centro, CA ....General Practice; Insurance Defense; Trust and Estates, Wills and Probate

HORTY, SPRINGER & MATTERN, P.C.
Pittsburgh, PA ....Health Care Law

HORVITZ & LEVY, LLP
Los Angeles, CA ....Appellate Practice; Commercial Litigation; Health Care Law; Insurance Defense; Intellectual Property Law

HORWATT, MICHAEL, & ASSOCIATES P.C.
McLean, VA ....Business Law; Commercial Law; Real Estate Law

HORWITZ & FUSSELL, A PROF. ASSN., LAW OFFICES OF
Orlando, FL ....Criminal Trial Practice

HOSKIN, FARINA, ALDRICH & KAMPF, PROFESSIONAL CORPORATION
Grand Junction, CO ....General Practice

HOSTAK, HENZL & BICHLER, S.C.
Racine, WI ....General Practice

HOSTETLER & KOWALIK, P.C.
Indianapolis, IN ....Bankruptcy Law; Commercial Law; Creditors Rights

HOTTELL, DENNIS M. & ASSOCIATES
Fairfax, VA ....Family Law

HOTZ & ASSOCIATES, P.C.
Tucker, GA ....Banking Law; Civil Trial Practice

HOURIGAN, KLUGER & QUINN, A PROFESSIONAL CORPORATION
Wilkes-Barre, PA ....General Practice; Labor and Employment Law; Medical Malpractice; Personal Injury; Real Estate Law; Trust and Estates, Wills and Probate

HOUSE, KINGSMILL & RIESS, L.L.C.
New Orleans, LA ....Civil Trial Practice

HOUSSIERE, DURANT & HOUSSIERE, LLP
Houston, TX ....Medical Malpractice; Product Liability Law; Securities Law

HOUSTON, PHILLIP C., P.A.
West Palm Beach, FL ....Personal Injury

HOVDE LAW FIRM
Indianapolis, IN ....Construction Law; Medical Malpractice; Personal Injury; Product Liability Law

HOVEY & KIRBY, A PROFESSIONAL CORPORATION
San Diego, CA ....Bankruptcy Law; Business Law; Civil Trial Practice; Commercial Law; Construction Law; Environmental Law; Municipal and Zoning Law; Real Estate Law

HOWARD, JOHN H.
Ventura, CA ....Civil Trial Practice

HOWARD, BRENNER & NASS, P.C.
Philadelphia, PA ....Civil Trial Practice; Toxic Torts

HOWARD, CARSWELL & BENNETT, P.C.
Jesup, GA ....General Practice; Insurance Defense

HOWARD, DAVIS & BUNT, P.C.
Tyler, TX ....Medical Malpractice

HOWARD, GREEN & MCDARRIS, L.L.P.
Raleigh, NC ....Family Law; General Practice

HOWARD & HOWARD ATTORNEYS, P.C.
Peoria, IL ....Banking Law; Business Law; Commercial Litigation; Communications Law; Environmental Law; General Practice; Labor and Employment Law; Municipal Bond/Public Authority Financing; Public Utilities Law

HOWARD & HOWARD ATTORNEYS, P.C. — *Continued*
Bloomfield Hills, MI..........Antitrust Law; Banking Law; Bankruptcy Law; Business Law; Commercial Litigation; Environmental Law; General Practice; Immigration and Naturalization; Labor and Employment Law; Municipal Bond/Public Authority Financing; Patent, Trademark, Copyright and Unfair Competition; Real Estate Law; Securities Law; Tax Law
Kalamazoo, MI..........Banking Law; Bankruptcy Law; Business Law; Commercial Litigation; General Practice; Real Estate Law; Securities Law
Lansing, MI..........Administrative Law; Banking Law; Business Law; Commercial Litigation; General Practice; Labor and Employment Law; Municipal Bond/Public Authority Financing; Real Estate Law; Tax Law

HOWARD, LEGGANS, PIERCY & HOWARD
Mount Vernon, IL..........General Practice

HOWARD, MACKIE
Calgary, AB, Canada..........General Practice

HOWARD ROME MARTIN & RIDLEY LLP
Redwood City, CA..........Civil Trial Practice; Insurance Defense

HOWD & LUDORF
Hartford, CT..........General Practice; Insurance Defense

HOWE, EDWIN A., P.C., THE LAW FIRM OF
Denver, CO..........Civil Trial Practice; Medical Malpractice; Personal Injury

HOWE, GEDNEY M., III, P.A.
Charleston, SC..........Civil Trial Practice; Criminal Trial Practice; Personal Injury; Product Liability Law

HOWE, WATERS & CARPENTER, P.A.
Hendersonville, NC..........General Practice; Real Estate Law

HOWELL, JOEL W. III
Jackson, MS..........Civil Trial Practice

HOWELL & HAFERKAMP, L.C.
St. Louis, MO..........Patent, Trademark, Copyright and Unfair Competition

HOWELL, LEMBHARD G., P.S., LAW OFFICES OF
Seattle, WA..........Personal Injury

HOWES, JOHN R., A PROFESSIONAL ASSOCIATION
Fort Lauderdale, FL..........Criminal Trial Practice

HOWETT, KISSINGER & MILES, P.C.
Harrisburg, PA..........Family Law

HOWIE & SWEENEY, L.L.P.
Dallas, TX..........Aviation Law; Medical Malpractice; Personal Injury; Product Liability Law

HOWLAND, DAVID R. LAW OFFICES OF
Miami, FL..........Insurance Defense

HOWREY & SIMON
Washington, DC..........General Practice

HOWSER, NEWMAN & BESLEY, L.L.C.
Columbia, SC..........Insurance Defense; Product Liability Law; Professional Liability; Workers Compensation

HOWSON & HOWSON
Spring House, PA..........Patent, Trademark, Copyright and Unfair Competition

HOYLE, MORRIS & KERR LLP
Philadelphia, PA..........Civil Trial Practice; General Practice

HOYLE, WILLIAM V., JR., P.C.
Newport News, VA..........Civil Trial Practice

HRONES AND GARRITY
Boston, MA..........Criminal Trial Practice

HUANG & MITCHELL, A PROFESSIONAL LAW CORPORATION
Los Angeles, CA..........Commercial Litigation

HUBBARD, CATES & LONG
Roxboro, NC..........General Practice

HUBBARD, SMITH, MCILWAIN, BRAKEFIELD & BROWDER, P.C.
Tuscaloosa, AL..........Banking Law; Bankruptcy Law; Business Law; Civil Trial Practice; General Practice; Tax Law

HUBER, BOOK, CORTESE, HAPPE & BROWN, P.L.C.
Des Moines, IA..........Civil Trial Practice; Creditors Rights; Insurance Defense; Legal Malpractice; Personal Injury; Product Liability Law; Professional Liability; Workers Compensation

HUBER AND WALDRON
Allentown, PA..........Criminal Trial Practice; Personal Injury

HUCKABAY, MUNSON, ROWLETT & TILLEY, P.A.
Little Rock, AR..........Civil Trial Practice; Insurance Defense; Medical Malpractice; Personal Injury; Product Liability Law; Workers Compensation

HUCKABY, FLEMING, FRAILEY, CHAFFIN, CORDELL, GREENWOOD & PERRYMAN, L.L.P.
Oklahoma City, OK..........Civil Trial Practice; Insurance Defense

HUDDLESTON, BOLEN, BEATTY, PORTER & COPEN
Charleston, WV..........General Practice
Huntington, WV..........General Practice

HUDGINS LAW FIRM
Alexandria, VA..........Civil Trial Practice; Insurance Defense

HUERTA, MARCELINO J., III, P.A.
Tampa, FL..........Criminal Trial Practice

HUFF LAW OFFICES
Harlan, KY..........General Practice; Insurance Defense; Labor and Employment Law

HUFF, MORAN & ORRON
Cranbury, NJ..........Elder Law

HUFFAKER & CONWAY, A PROFESSIONAL CORPORATION
Albuquerque, NM..........Antitrust Law; Commercial Litigation; Insurance Defense
Santa Fe, NM..........Administrative Law; Antitrust Law; Appellate Practice; Commercial Litigation; Environmental Law; Insurance Defense; Natural Resources Law

HUFFAKER, GREEN & HUFFAKER
Tahoka, TX..........General Practice

HUFFINE, DAVID E., P.A.
Wilmington, NC..........Real Estate Law

HUFFORD, HORSTMAN, MONGINI, PARNELL & MCCARTHY, P.C.
Flagstaff, AZ..........Arbitration; Commercial Law; Family Law; Labor and Employment Law; Municipal and Zoning Law; Real Estate Law; Trust and Estates, Wills and Probate

HUGHES, AMYS
Toronto, ON, Canada..........Insurance Defense

HUGHES LAW OFFICES
Sioux Falls, SD..........Business Law; Civil Trial Practice; Health Care Law; Municipal and Zoning Law; Personal Injury; Real Estate Law

HUGHES & LUCE, L.L.P.
Dallas, TX..........Arbitration; Banking Law; Bankruptcy Law; Business Law; Civil Trial Practice; Commercial Law; Criminal Trial Practice; Employment Benefits Law; Energy Law; General Practice; Intellectual Property Law; Labor and Employment Law; Real Estate Law; Securities Law; Sports and Entertainment Law; Tax Law; Trust and Estates, Wills and Probate

HUGHES, MATHEWS & DIDIER, P.A.
St. Cloud, MN..........Business Law; Civil Trial Practice; Commercial Law; Health Care Law; Labor and Employment Law

HUGHES & NUNN
San Diego, CA..........Insurance Defense

HUGHES & SCHACHT, P.S.
Bellingham, WA..........Patent, Trademark, Copyright and Unfair Competition

HUGHES & STRUMOR, LTD. CO.
Albuquerque, NM..........Municipal Bond/Public Authority Financing; Securities Law

HUGHEY, FLICK & CATANIA
Media, PA..........Criminal Trial Practice; Personal Injury

HUGIE, ELDON R.
Bakersfield, CA..........Business Law; Trust and Estates, Wills and Probate

HUIE, FERNAMBUCQ AND STEWART, LLP
Birmingham, AL..........Civil Trial Practice; Medical Malpractice; Product Liability Law

HULL, NORMAN LINDER, P.A.
Orlando, FL..........Bankruptcy Law; Business Law; Civil Trial Practice; Commercial Litigation; Construction Law

HULL, TOWILL, NORMAN, BARRETT & SALLEY, A PROFESSIONAL CORPORATION
Augusta, GA..........Arbitration; Business Law; Civil Trial Practice; Construction Law; Corporate Law; Environmental Law; General Practice; Insurance Defense; Real Estate Law; Securities Law; Tax Law; Trust and Estates, Wills and Probate

HULLVERSON & HULLVERSON, L.L.C.
St. Louis, MO..........Medical Malpractice; Personal Injury

HULLVERSON LAW FIRM, THE
St. Louis, MO..........Admiralty/Maritime Law; Medical Malpractice; Personal Injury; Product Liability Law

HULL, WEBBER & REIS, LLP
Rutland, VT..........General Practice

HULTSTRAND, CHARLES, P.C.
Mesa, AZ..........Commercial Litigation

HUMMEL & COAN
Louisville, KY..........Insurance Defense; Personal Injury

HUMPHREYS DUNLAP WELLFORD ACUFF & STANTON, A PROFESSIONAL CORPORATION
Memphis, TN..........General Practice

HUNEGS, STONE, KOENIG, LENEAVE & KVAS, P.A.
Minneapolis, MN..........Admiralty/Maritime Law; Aviation Law; Civil Trial Practice; Medical Malpractice; Personal Injury; Product Liability Law

HUNT, DAVID E.
Portland, ME..........Trust and Estates, Wills and Probate

HUNT, RUSSELL DAVID
Waco, TX..........Criminal Trial Practice

HUNT, COOK, RIGGS, MEHR & MILLER, P.A.
Boca Raton, FL..........Family Law; General Practice; Trust and Estates, Wills and Probate

HUNT & ROSS, A PROFESSIONAL ASSOCIATION
Clarksdale, MS..........Administrative Law; General Practice; Municipal and Zoning Law; Natural Resources Law; Public Utilities Law; Real Estate Law

HUNTER, RICHARD S. JR.
Raleigh, NC..........Personal Injury

HUNTER, BLAZIER, O'DOWD & MORENO, A PROFESSIONAL LAW CORPORATION
Lake Charles, LA..........Tax Law; Trust and Estates, Wills and Probate

HUNTER, JOHNSTON, ELAM & BENJAMIN, PLLC
Greensboro, NC..........General Practice

HUNTER, MACLEAN, EXLEY & DUNN, P.C.
Savannah, GA..........Business Law; Civil Trial Practice; Environmental Law; General Practice; Labor and Employment Law; Tax Law; Trust and Estates, Wills and Probate

HUNTER RICHEY DI BENEDETTO & BREWER, LLP
Sacramento, CA..........Business Law; Civil Trial Practice; Construction Law; Environmental Law; Health Care Law; Land Use Law; Mergers and Acquisitions; Patent, Trademark, Copyright and Unfair Competition; Real Estate Law; Trademark, Copyright and Unfair Competition

HUNTER, SMITH & DAVIS, LLP
Johnson City, TN..........General Practice
Kingsport, TN..........Banking Law; Civil Trial Practice; Environmental Law; General Practice; Labor and Employment Law; Municipal Bond/Public Authority Financing; Tax Law

HUNTON & WILLIAMS
Richmond, VA..........General Practice

HUPPERT & SWINDLEHURST, P.C.
Livingston, MT..........General Practice

HUPY, MICHAEL F., & ASSOCIATES, S.C.
Milwaukee, WI..........Personal Injury

HURLEY, FOX, SELIG & KELLEHER
Stony Point, NY..........Civil Trial Practice; Commercial Law; General Practice; Land Use Law; Municipal and Zoning Law; Personal Injury; Product Liability Law; Real Estate Law

HURLEY, JOSEPH A., P.A.
Wilmington, DE..........Criminal Trial Practice

HURLEY, LYNCH & RE, P.C.
Bend, OR..........Civil Trial Practice; General Practice

HURTUK & DAROFF CO., L.P.A.
Cleveland, OH..........Real Estate Law

HUSKEY, DOW T.
Dothan, AL..........Business Law

HUSTEAD LAW FIRM, THE, A PROFESSIONAL CORPORATION
Denver, CO..........Commercial Litigation; Insurance Defense; Labor and Employment Law

HUTCHINS & ASSOCIATES, LLC
Denver, CO..........Trust and Estates, Wills and Probate

HUTCHINS, WHEELER & DITTMAR, A PROFESSIONAL CORPORATION
Boston, MA..........General Practice

HUTCHISON, MAMELE & COOVER, P.A.
Sanford, FL..........Family Law

HUTCHISON & MASON PLLC
Raleigh, NC..........Business Law

HUTTON & HUTTON
Wichita, KS..........Medical Malpractice; Personal Injury; Product Liability Law

HUTTON, LAURY, YOUNG & LIETZ
Danville, IL..........Civil Trial Practice; General Practice; Insurance Defense

HWANG & ASSOCIATES, P.C.
Philadelphia, PA..........Civil Trial Practice

HYATT & HYATT, P.C.
Decatur, GA..........General Practice; Personal Injury; Workers Compensation

HYATT, PETERS & WEBER
Annapolis, MD..........Banking Law; Civil Trial Practice; Commercial Law; Family Law; Insurance Defense; Medical Malpractice; Real Estate Law

HYDE, MILLER, OWEN & TROST, A PROFESSIONAL CORPORATION
Sacramento, CA..........Government Contracts; Municipal and Zoning Law

HYMAN LIPPITT, P.C.
Birmingham, MI..........Bankruptcy Law; Business Law; Civil Trial Practice; Commercial Law; Commercial Litigation; Corporate Law; Family Law; General Practice; International Business Law; Labor and Employment Law; Land Use Law; Mergers and Acquisitions; Municipal and Zoning Law; Real Estate Law; Securities Law; Tax Law; Trust and Estates, Wills and Probate

HYMAN, STUART I., P.A.
Orlando, FL..........Criminal Trial Practice

ICE MILLER DONADIO & RYAN
Indianapolis, IN..........Antitrust Law; Banking Law; Bankruptcy Law; Civil Trial Practice; Commercial Law; Communications Law; Construction Law; Creditors Rights; Employment Benefits Law; Environmental Law; General Practice; Health Care Law; Immigration and Naturalization; International Trade Law; Labor and Employment Law; Medical Malpractice; Municipal Bond/Public Authority Financing; Natural Resources Law; Personal Injury; Real Estate Law; Securities Law; Tax Law; Trademark, Copyright and Unfair Competition; Trust and Estates, Wills and Probate

ICENOGLE, NORTON & SETER, A PROFESSIONAL CORPORATION
Greenwood Village, CO..........Civil Trial Practice; Municipal and Zoning Law; Transportation Law

IFSHIN & FRIEDMAN, P.L.L.C.
Washington, DC..........Civil Trial Practice

IMAI, TADLOCK & KEENEY, LLP
San Francisco, CA..........Insurance Defense

INDIANO, WILLIAMS & WEINSTEIN-BACAL
San Juan, PR..........Bankruptcy Law; Civil Trial Practice; Commercial Law; Construction Law; Personal Injury

INGBER & ARONSON, P.A.
Minneapolis, MN..........Immigration and Naturalization

INGERMAN & HORWITZ, L.L.P.
Baltimore, MD..........Personal Injury

INGE, TWITTY & DUFFY
Mobile, AL..........Civil Trial Practice; General Practice; Insurance Defense; Professional Liability

INGHAM, SAMUEL D. III
Los Angeles, CA..........Natural Resources Law; Real Estate Law; Tax Law; Trust and Estates, Wills and Probate

INGLESBY, FALLIGANT, HORNE, COURINGTON & NASH, A PROFESSIONAL CORPORATION
Savannah, GA..........Bankruptcy Law

INGLIS, LEDBETTER & GOWER
Los Angeles, CA..........Corporate Law

INGLISH & MONACO, P.C.
Jefferson City, MO..........Civil Trial Practice; General Practice; Insurance Defense

INGRAM YUZEK GAINEN CARROLL & BERTOLOTTI, LLP
New York, NY....Appellate Practice; Banking Law; Business Law; Civil Trial Practice; Commercial Law; Construction Law; General Practice; Insurance Defense; Real Estate Law; Tax Law

INTERNATIONAL LAW FIRM, THE
Riyadh, Saudi Arabia....General Practice

INZER, HANEY, JOHNSON & MCWHORTER, P.A.
Gadsden, AL....Civil Trial Practice; Corporate Law; General Practice

IRELAND, CARROLL & KELLEY, P.C.
Tyler, TX....Appellate Practice; Bankruptcy Law; Civil Trial Practice; Insurance Defense

IRELL & MANELLA LLP
Los Angeles, CA....General Practice

IRESON & WEIZEL, P.C.
Houston, TX....Personal Injury; Product Liability Law

IRVIN, STANFORD & KESSLER, LLP
Atlanta, GA....Labor and Employment Law

ISAACSON & ISAACSON
Greensboro, NC....Business Law; Commercial Law; General Practice; Municipal and Zoning Law; Real Estate Law

ISEMAN, CUNNINGHAM, RIESTER & HYDE, LLP
Albany, NY....Civil Trial Practice; Commercial Litigation; Construction Law; Corporate Law; Health Care Law; Nonprofit and Tax Exempt Organizations; Personal Injury; Real Estate Law; Tax Law; Toxic Torts

ISICOFF & RAGATZ, P.A.
Miami, FL....Trademark, Copyright and Unfair Competition

ISOM, DAVID K. LAW OFFICES
Salt Lake City, UT....Commercial Litigation

ISRAELSON, SALSBURY, CLEMENTS & BEKMAN, L.L.C.
Baltimore, MD....Admiralty/Maritime Law; Civil Trial Practice; Medical Malpractice; Personal Injury; Product Liability Law

IVENER & HOLT LLP
Los Angeles, CA....Immigration and Naturalization

IVERSON, YOAKUM, PAPIANO & HATCH
Los Angeles, CA....Appellate Practice; Business Law; Civil Trial Practice; Environmental Law; General Practice; Labor and Employment Law; Product Liability Law

IVEY, BARNUM & O'MARA, LLC
Greenwich, CT....General Practice

IVEY, MCCLELLAN, GATTON & TALCOTT, L.L.P.
Greensboro, NC....Bankruptcy Law; General Practice

IVINS, PHILLIPS & BARKER, CHARTERED
Washington, DC....Tax Law; Trust and Estates, Wills and Probate

IVONE, DEVINE & JENSEN, LLP
Lake Success, NY....Civil Trial Practice; Insurance Defense; Medical Malpractice

JABURG & WILK, P.C.
Phoenix, AZ....Bankruptcy Law; Business Law; Commercial Litigation; Trust and Estates, Wills and Probate

JACKS, ADAMS & WESTERFIELD, P.A.
Cleveland, MS....General Practice; Insurance Defense; Product Liability Law

JACKSON & CAMPBELL, P.C.
Washington, DC....General Practice

JACKSON HARRIS BURLINGAME & HUBERT, LLC
Danielson, CT....General Practice

JACKSON & JESSUP, P.C.
Arlington, VA....Transportation Law

JACKSON & KELLY
Washington, DC....General Practice
Lexington, KY....General Practice
Charleston, WV....Administrative Law; Admiralty/Maritime Law; Antitrust Law; Banking Law; Bankruptcy Law; Civil Trial Practice; Commercial Law; Construction Law; Criminal Trial Practice; Employment Benefits Law; Environmental Law; General Practice; Health Care Law; Insurance Defense; Labor and Employment Law; Municipal Bond/Public Authority Financing; Natural Resources Law; Public Utilities Law; Real Estate Law; Securities Law; Tax Law; Transportation Law; Trust and Estates, Wills and Probate; Workers Compensation
Martinsburg, WV....General Practice
Morgantown, WV....General Practice
New Martinsville, WV....General Practice

JACKSON, LEWIS, SCHNITZLER & KRUPMAN
White Plains, NY....Labor and Employment Law

JACKSON, O'KEEFE AND PHELAN
Hartford, CT....Appellate Practice; Civil Trial Practice; Family Law; General Practice; Insurance Defense; Medical Malpractice; Personal Injury

JACKSON WALKER L.L.P.
Austin, TX....Administrative Law; Business Law; Communications Law; Environmental Law; General Practice; Health Care Law; Labor and Employment Law
Dallas, TX....Appellate Practice; Business Law; Civil Trial Practice; Communications Law; Computer Law; General Practice; Health Care Law; Insurance Defense; International Business Law; Labor and Employment Law; Patent, Trademark, Copyright and Unfair Competition; Personal Injury; Product Liability Law; Real Estate Law; Tax Law
Fort Worth, TX....Civil Trial Practice; General Practice; Insurance Defense; Labor and Employment Law; Real Estate Law
Houston, TX....Business Law; Civil Trial Practice; Communications Law; Energy Law; Environmental Law; General Practice; Insurance Defense; International Business Law; Personal Injury
San Angelo, TX....Civil Trial Practice; General Practice
San Antonio, TX....Civil Trial Practice; General Practice; Health Care Law; Insurance Defense; Labor and Employment Law; Patent, Trademark, Copyright and Unfair Competition; Personal Injury

JACKSON WHITE GARDNER WEECH & WALKER, P.C.
Mesa, AZ....Business Law; Commercial Litigation; Construction Law; Elder Law; Labor and Employment Law; Municipal and Zoning Law; Personal Injury; Real Estate Law; Tax Law; Trust and Estates, Wills and Probate

JACOB, ARTHUR LAW OFFICES OF
Hackensack, NJ....Patent, Trademark, Copyright and Unfair Competition

JACOB & WEINGARTEN
Troy, MI....Commercial Litigation; Creditors Rights; Real Estate Law

JACOBOWITZ, GARFINKEL & LESMAN
New York, NY....Insurance Defense

JACOBOWITZ, GRABELLE, DEFINO, MCGOUGHRAN & LATIMER
Oakhurst, NJ....Family Law

JACOBS, REX W.
Long Beach, CA....Personal Injury

JACOBS, DARLEEN M., A PROFESSIONAL LAW CORPORATION
New Orleans, LA....Admiralty/Maritime Law; Personal Injury

JACOBS, GRUDBERG, BELT & DOW, P.C.
New Haven, CT....Civil Trial Practice; General Practice

JACOBS & JACOBS
New Haven, CT....Civil Trial Practice; Medical Malpractice; Personal Injury; Product Liability Law

JACOBS AND SLAWSKY, P.A.
Atlanta, GA....Labor and Employment Law

JACOBSON AND GOLDBERG, LLP
Garden City, NY....Administrative Law; Health Care Law

JACOBSON, PRICE, HOLMAN & STERN, PLLC
Washington, DC....Patent, Trademark, Copyright and Unfair Competition

JACOBSON & SCHWARTZ
Rockville Centre, NY....Appellate Practice; Insurance Defense; Product Liability Law

JAECKLE FLEISCHMANN & MUGEL, LLP
Buffalo, NY....General Practice

JAFFE AND CLEMENS
Beverly Hills, CA....Family Law

JAFFE, RAITT, HEUER & WEISS, PROFESSIONAL CORPORATION
Detroit, MI....Bankruptcy Law; Business Law; Civil Trial Practice; Commercial Litigation; Employment Benefits Law; Environmental Law; Family Law; General Practice; Health Care Law; Municipal and Zoning Law; Municipal Bond/Public Authority Financing; Real Estate Law; Securities Law; Tax Law; Trust and Estates, Wills and Probate
Southfield, MI....General Practice

JAMES, GARY J.
Oklahoma City, OK.................Criminal Trial Practice

JAMES, DENECKE, URRUTIA, MARMADUKE & LAWSON, P.C.
Portland, OR..........................Business Law; Civil Trial Practice; Mergers and Acquisitions; Real Estate Law

JAMES, GOLDMAN & HAUGLAND, P.C. A PROFESSIONAL CORPORATION
El Paso, TX............................Banking Law; Bankruptcy Law; General Practice; Insurance Defense

JAMES, GRAY, BRONSON & SWANBERG, P.C.
Great Falls, MT......................Civil Trial Practice

JAMES, POTTS AND WULFERS, INC.
Tulsa, OK...............................Business Law; Commercial Law; Real Estate Law; Tax Law; Trust and Estates, Wills and Probate

JAMIESON, MOORE, PESKIN & SPICER, A PROFESSIONAL CORPORATION
Princeton, NJ..........................General Practice

JAMIN, EBELL, SCHMITT & MASON, A PROFESSIONAL CORPORATION
Kodiak, AK.............................General Practice

JANET, WILLOUGHBY & GERSHON, LLC
Baltimore, MD........................Medical Malpractice; Personal Injury; Product Liability Law

JANIK & FORBES
Cleveland, OH.........................Appellate Practice; Civil Trial Practice; Construction Law; Environmental Law; General Practice; Insurance Defense; Labor and Employment Law; Personal Injury; Product Liability Law; Securities Law; Trademark, Copyright and Unfair Competition

JANUSZEWSKI, MCQUILLAN AND DENIGRIS
New Britain, CT......................General Practice

JARDINE & PAGANO, A PROFESSIONAL CORPORATION
Springfield, NJ........................Labor and Employment Law; Trust and Estates, Wills and Probate

JAVERBAUM WURGAFT HICKS & ZARIN, A PROFESSIONAL CORPORATION
Springfield, NJ........................Civil Trial Practice; Commercial Litigation; Medical Malpractice; Personal Injury; Product Liability Law; Professional Liability

JEANSONNE & REMONDET, L.L.C.
Lafayette, LA.........................Civil Trial Practice; Insurance Defense

JEFFCOAT, PIKE & NAPPIER, LLC
Myrtle Beach, SC...................Trust and Estates, Wills and Probate

JEFFER, HOPKINSON & VOGEL
Hawthorne, NJ........................Business Law; Civil Trial Practice; General Practice; Municipal and Zoning Law; Municipal Bond/Public Authority Financing; Real Estate Law

JEFFERS & BANACK, INCORPORATED
San Antonio, TX.....................Appellate Practice

JEFFERS, DANIELSON, SONN & AYLWARD, P.S.
Wenatchee, WA.......................General Practice

JEFFRIES, OLSON, FLOM & BULLIS, P.A.
Moorhead, MN.......................Civil Trial Practice; General Practice
Fargo, ND..............................Civil Trial Practice; General Practice

JELLIFFE, FERRELL, MORRIS, DOERGE & FOSTER
Harrisburg, IL.........................Civil Trial Practice; General Practice; Insurance Defense; Workers Compensation

JENKENS & GILCHRIST, A PROFESSIONAL CORPORATION
Dallas, TX..............................General Practice

JENKINS, GOODMAN & NEUMAN
San Francisco, CA..................Commercial Law

JENKINS & KLING, P.C.
St. Louis, MO.........................Criminal Trial Practice; Real Estate Law

JENKINS MARZBAN LOGAN
Vancouver, BC, Canada...........Arbitration; Civil Trial Practice; Commercial Litigation; Construction Law; Family Law; Real Estate Law

JENKINS & NELSON, P.C.
Cartersville, GA......................General Practice

JENKINS & WILSON, P.A.
Durham, NC............................Intellectual Property Law; Patent, Trademark, Copyright and Unfair Competition

JENNE, SCOTT & JENNE
Cleveland, TN.........................Civil Trial Practice; Construction Law; Medical Malpractice; Personal Injury; Product Liability Law; Workers Compensation

JENNER & BLOCK
Chicago, IL.............................General Practice

JENNINGS, HAUG & CUNNINGHAM, L.L.P.
Phoenix, AZ............................Business Law; Civil Trial Practice; Construction Law; Personal Injury

JENNINGS, STROUSS & SALMON, P.L.C.
Phoenix, AZ............................Banking Law; Bankruptcy Law; Civil Trial Practice; Environmental Law; General Practice; Health Care Law; Insurance Defense; Labor and Employment Law; Medical Malpractice; Municipal Bond/Public Authority Financing; Natural Resources Law; Personal Injury; Real Estate Law; Securities Law; Tax Law; Trademark, Copyright and Unfair Competition; Trust and Estates, Wills and Probate

JENSEN BAIRD GARDNER & HENRY
Kennebunk, ME.......................General Practice
Portland, ME..........................Banking Law; Civil Trial Practice; Environmental Law; General Practice; Real Estate Law; Trust and Estates, Wills and Probate

JENSEN, JACQUELINE M., INC.
Irvine, CA...............................Trust and Estates, Wills and Probate

JENSEN & KELLEY, P.A.
Phoenix, AZ............................Family Law

JEPPSON, H. ROY, A PROFESSIONAL CORPORATION
Los Angeles, CA.....................Business Law; Commercial Litigation; Labor and Employment Law
Oxnard, CA............................Business Law; Commercial Litigation; Labor and Employment Law

JESSOP & COMPANY, P.C.
Denver, CO............................Bankruptcy Law

JESTER, MICHAEL H.
San Diego, CA........................Patent, Trademark, Copyright and Unfair Competition

JETER & WILLIAMS, P.A.
Columbia, SC..........................Business Law

JEWELL, COLLINS & DELAY
Norfolk, NE............................General Practice

JG, P.C. BUSINESS & CORPORATE LAW
Pleasanton, CA.......................Business Law; Corporate Law

JIMÉNEZ, GRAFFAM & LAUSELL
San Juan, PR..........................Admiralty/Maritime Law; Civil Trial Practice; Construction Law; Environmental Law; General Practice; Insurance Defense; Labor and Employment Law; Medical Malpractice; Personal Injury; Product Liability Law; Transportation Law

JIMENEZ, JORGE R., LAW OFFICES
San Juan, PR..........................Antitrust Law; Banking Law; Civil Trial Practice; Commercial Law; General Practice; Real Estate Law

JINKERSON, GUYTON N.
San Jose, CA..........................Criminal Trial Practice

JOANIS LAW GROUP, THE
Minneapolis, MN....................Bankruptcy Law

JOANNES, JOHN A., A PROFESSIONAL CORPORATION
Los Angeles, CA.....................Immigration and Naturalization

JOENS, TIMOTHY L., & ASSOC., A PROF. CORP.
Irvine, CA...............................Appellate Practice; Business Law; Civil Trial Practice

JOHNS & CHRISTENSEN, A PROFESSIONAL CORPORATION
San Rafael, CA........................Appellate Practice; Civil Trial Practice; Commercial Litigation; Insurance Defense; Legal Malpractice

JOHNS, FLAHERTY & RICE, S.C.
La Crosse, WI.........................General Practice

JOHNSON, DONALD L.
Chicago, IL.............................Professional Liability

JOHNSON, JAMES M.
Minden, LA.............................Business Law; Civil Trial Practice; Criminal Trial Practice; Family Law; Personal Injury

JOHNSON, JAY M.
Ventura, CA............................Criminal Trial Practice; Family Law

JOHNSON AND ANGELO
Cleveland, OH.........................Environmental Law; Insurance Defense; Labor and Employment Law

JOHNSON, AYERS & MATTHEWS
Roanoke, VA...........................Insurance Defense

JOHNSON, BARRY L., P.A.
Hilton Head Island, SC..........Bankruptcy Law; Business Law; Commercial Litigation; Personal Injury; Real Estate Law

JOHNSON & BELL, LTD.
Chicago, IL..........Civil Trial Practice; Environmental Law; Insurance Defense; Medical Malpractice

JOHNSON, BLAKELY, POPE, BOKOR, RUPPEL & BURNS, P.A.
Clearwater, FL..........General Practice
Tampa, FL..........General Practice

JOHNSON & BOWEN
El Paso, TX..........General Practice

JOHNSON, BUNCE & NOBLE, P.C.
Peoria, IL..........General Practice

JOHNSON, CLIFTON, LARSON & CORSON, P.C.
Eugene, OR..........Personal Injury; Product Liability Law

JOHNSON & EDWARDS LLP
San Diego, CA..........Civil Trial Practice

JOHNSON EIESLAND HUFFMAN & CLAYBORNE LAW FIRM, LLP
Rapid City, SD..........Commercial Law; Insurance Defense; Medical Malpractice

JOHNSON, FERGUSON & PIPKIN
Houston, TX..........Personal Injury; Toxic Torts

JOHNSON, FLODMAN, GUENZEL, ESKE & WIDGER
Lincoln, NE..........Civil Trial Practice; Family Law; Health Care Law; Insurance Defense; Trust and Estates, Wills and Probate

JOHNSON, GARY C., P.S.C.
Pikeville, KY..........Commercial Law; Personal Injury

JOHNSON, GAVER & LEACH, LLP
Monterey, CA..........Trust and Estates, Wills and Probate

JOHNSON, GREEN, MILLER & GIBSON, P.A.
Milton, FL..........General Practice

JOHNSON, GRUSIN, KEE & SURPRISE, P.C.
Memphis, TN..........General Practice; Real Estate Law

JOHNSON, HESTER, WALTER & BRECKENRIDGE, L.L.P.
Ottumwa, IA..........General Practice

JOHNSON & HOULIHAN, S.C.
Rhinelander, WI..........General Practice

JOHNSON, JEAN E., JR., P.C.
Marietta, GA..........Medical Malpractice; Personal Injury

JOHNSON & JOHNSON, LAW OFFICES
Las Vegas, NV..........Trust and Estates, Wills and Probate

JOHNSON & JOHNSON, P.L.C.
Newport, KY..........Personal Injury

JOHNSON, JOHNSON, BARRIOS & YACOUBIAN, A PROFESSIONAL LAW CORPORATION
New Orleans, LA..........Admiralty/Maritime Law; Insurance Defense; Workers Compensation

JOHNSON, KENNEDY, DAHL & WILLIS
Wichita, KS..........General Practice; Insurance Defense

JOHNSON & LAMBETH
Wilmington, NC..........Criminal Trial Practice; Insurance Defense

JOHNSON LAW GROUP, THE
Seattle, WA..........Business Law; Commercial Law

JOHNSON & MCPHERSON, P.L.C.
Grosse Pointe Farms, MI..........Business Law; Real Estate Law; Trust and Estates, Wills and Probate

JOHNSON & OLIVER, A LEGAL PROFESSIONAL ASSOCIATION
Portsmouth, OH..........General Practice; Trust and Estates, Wills and Probate

JOHNSON & ROCHE
McLean, VA..........Personal Injury

JOHNSON, RODNEY G., LTD.
Phoenix, AZ..........Labor and Employment Law

JOHNSON, SCHACHTER & COLLINS, A PROFESSIONAL CORPORATION
Sacramento, CA..........Civil Trial Practice; Insurance Defense; Personal Injury; Product Liability Law; Professional Liability

JOHNSON, SIMMERMAN & BROUGHTON, L.C.
Clarksburg, WV..........Civil Trial Practice; Construction Law; Environmental Law; Medical Malpractice; Personal Injury; Tax Law; Trust and Estates, Wills and Probate

JOHNSON SMITH PENCE & HEATH LLP
Indianapolis, IN..........Administrative Law; Banking Law; Bankruptcy Law; Civil Trial Practice; Commercial Law; Environmental Law; General Practice; Health Care Law; Insurance Defense; Intellectual Property Law; Real Estate Law; Securities Law

JOHNSON & SYLVAN, P.C.
Dallas, TX..........Insurance Defense; Medical Malpractice

JOHNSON & TAYLOR
Pontiac, IL..........Real Estate Law; Tax Law; Trust and Estates, Wills and Probate

JOHNSON & WARD
Atlanta, GA..........Aviation Law; Business Law; Civil Trial Practice; General Practice; Personal Injury; Product Liability Law; Professional Liability

JOHNSON & WEBBERT, L.L.P.
Augusta, ME..........Aviation Law; Insurance Defense; Labor and Employment Law; Product Liability Law

JOHNSON & YANG, P.C.
Wheaton, MD..........Immigration and Naturalization

JOHNSTON, ALLISON & HORD, P.A.
Charlotte, NC..........Construction Law; General Practice

JOHNSTON, ARONSON & DIAMOND, A PROFESSIONAL CORPORATION
Harrisburg, PA..........Employment Benefits Law; Labor and Employment Law; Pension and Profit Sharing

JOHNSTON BARTON PROCTOR & POWELL LLP
Birmingham, AL..........Banking Law; Commercial Litigation; Communications Law; Construction Law; Health Care Law; Labor and Employment Law; Product Liability Law; Real Estate Law; Sports and Entertainment Law

JOHNSTON & DODD, P.L.C.
Phoenix, AZ..........Administrative Law; Civil Trial Practice; Health Care Law

JOHNSTON, HINESLEY, FLOWERS & CLENNEY, P.C., A PROFESSIONAL CORPORATION
Dothan, AL..........Mergers and Acquisitions; Securities Law; Tax Law

JOHNSTON, HOLROYD & ASSOCIATES
Princeton, WV..........General Practice; Personal Injury

JOHNSTON, POTTERFIELD & NATHANSON, P.C.
Iowa City, IA..........Bankruptcy Law; Civil Trial Practice; Commercial Law; Criminal Trial Practice; Family Law; Personal Injury; Trust and Estates, Wills and Probate

JOHNSTON • TOBEY, P.C.
Dallas, TX..........Legal Malpractice; Professional Liability

JOHNSTONE, ADAMS, BAILEY, GORDON AND HARRIS, L.L.C.
Mobile, AL..........Admiralty/Maritime Law; Antitrust Law; Banking Law; Bankruptcy Law; Business Law; Civil Trial Practice; Construction Law; Employment Benefits Law; Environmental Law; General Practice; Health Care Law; Insurance Defense; Labor and Employment Law; Natural Resources Law; Real Estate Law; Tax Law; Trust and Estates, Wills and Probate

JOHNSTONE, ADAMS, BAILEY, GORDON AND HARRIS, L.L.C.
Bay Minette, AL..........Business Law; Civil Trial Practice; General Practice

JOLLEY, URGA, WIRTH & WOODBURY
Las Vegas, NV..........Administrative Law; Appellate Practice; Banking Law; Bankruptcy Law; Business Law; Civil Trial Practice; Commercial Law; Commercial Litigation; Construction Law; Environmental Law; Family Law; General Practice; Labor and Employment Law; Municipal and Zoning Law; Natural Resources Law; Personal Injury; Real Estate Law; Transportation Law; Trust and Estates, Wills and Probate

JONAS & LASORTE
West Palm Beach, FL..........Commercial Litigation; Real Estate Law

JONASSEN, WILLIAM S., P.A.
Largo, FL..........Medical Malpractice; Personal Injury

JONES, JIM
Sallisaw, OK..........General Practice

JONES, O. F. III, LAW OFFICE OF
Victoria, TX..........Civil Trial Practice

JONES, RANDOLPH B.
Nashville, TN..........Arbitration; Commercial Law; Corporate Law; General Practice

JONES & BAHRET, CO., L.P.A.
Holland, OH..........Civil Trial Practice; Insurance Defense

JONES, BLECHMAN, WOLTZ & KELLY, P.C.
Newport News, VA ....General Practice

JONES, CHARTERED
Pocatello, ID ....General Practice

JONES, CORK & MILLER, LLP
Macon, GA ....General Practice

JONES, DAY, REAVIS & POGUE
Irvine, CA................................Civil Trial Practice; General Practice
Los Angeles, CA ....Antitrust Law; Bankruptcy Law; Civil Trial Practice; General Practice; Insurance Defense; Labor and Employment Law; Patent, Trademark, Copyright and Unfair Competition; Tax Law; Trademark, Copyright and Unfair Competition
Washington, DC......................Antitrust Law; Civil Trial Practice; Criminal Trial Practice; General Practice; Labor and Employment Law; Municipal Bond/Public Authority Financing; Tax Law
Atlanta, GA ....Antitrust Law; Civil Trial Practice; General Practice; Labor and Employment Law; Municipal Bond/Public Authority Financing; Tax Law
Chicago, IL..............................Antitrust Law; Civil Trial Practice; Criminal Trial Practice; General Practice; Labor and Employment Law; Municipal Bond/Public Authority Financing; Tax Law
New York, NY..........................Civil Trial Practice; Criminal Trial Practice; General Practice; Insurance Defense; Municipal Bond/Public Authority Financing; Patent, Trademark, Copyright and Unfair Competition; Trademark, Copyright and Unfair Competition
Cleveland, OH..........................Antitrust Law; Civil Trial Practice; Criminal Trial Practice; General Practice; Insurance Defense; Labor and Employment Law; Municipal Bond/Public Authority Financing; Patent, Trademark, Copyright and Unfair Competition; Real Estate Law; Tax Law; Trademark, Copyright and Unfair Competition
Columbus, OH ....Civil Trial Practice; General Practice; Labor and Employment Law; Municipal Bond/Public Authority Financing
Pittsburgh, PA ....Civil Trial Practice; General Practice; Insurance Defense; Labor and Employment Law
Dallas, TX................................Antitrust Law; Civil Trial Practice; General Practice; Labor and Employment Law; Municipal Bond/Public Authority Financing; Tax Law
Sydney, New South Wales, Australia ....General Practice
Brussels, Belgium ....General Practice
Hong Kong, China.....................General Practice
London, England ....General Practice; Tax Law
Paris, France.............................General Practice
Frankfurt/Main, Germany ......General Practice
Tokyo, Japan.............................General Practice
Geneva, Switzerland.................General Practice
Taipei, Taiwan...........................General Practice

JONES, E. STEWART
Troy, NY...................................Civil Trial Practice; Criminal Trial Practice; General Practice; Medical Malpractice; Personal Injury; Product Liability Law

JONES, GALLIGAN, KEY & LOZANO, L.L.P.
Weslaco, TX.............................Civil Trial Practice; General Practice

JONES, GARY L., CO., L.P.A.
Columbus, OH ....Administrative Law

JONES, GIVENS, GOTCHER & BOGAN, A PROFESSIONAL CORPORATION
Tulsa, OK..................................Business Law; General Practice

JONES, HEWSON & WOOLARD
Charlotte, NC............................General Practice

JONES, JACKSON & MOLL, PLC
Fort Smith, AR ....Civil Trial Practice; Insurance Defense

JONES AND JONES
Hackensack, NJ.........................Banking Law; Commercial Law; Trust and Estates, Wills and Probate

JONES & JONES
Garden City, NY ....Civil Trial Practice; General Practice; Trust and Estates, Wills and Probate
Marshall, TX.............................Civil Trial Practice; Personal Injury

JONES, JONES & LUSHBAUGH, PLC
Fayetteville, AR ....Insurance Defense

JONES, JONES, VINES & HUNKINS
Wheatland, WY.........................General Practice

JONES, KEY, MELVIN & PATTON, P.A.
Franklin, NC.............................General Practice

JONES, MCGLASSON & BENCKART, P.C.
Bloomington, IN ....Business Law; Personal Injury; Transportation Law; Trust and Estates, Wills and Probate

JONES OBENCHAIN, LLP
South Bend, IN ....General Practice

JONES, OSTEEN, JONES & ARNOLD
Hinesville, GA.........................General Practice; Personal Injury; Product Liability Law

JONES, ROGERS & NAVARRO
San Antonio, TX......................Insurance Defense

JONES, SNEAD, WERTHEIM, WENTWORTH & JARAMILLO, P.A.
Santa Fe, NM...........................Commercial Litigation

JONES & TROUSDALE
Florence, AL ....Insurance Defense; Medical Malpractice; Personal Injury; Product Liability Law

JONES, WALKER, WAECHTER, POITEVENT, CARRÈRE & DENÈGRE, L.L.P.
New Orleans, LA ....General Practice

JONES & WYATT
Enid, OK ....Civil Trial Practice; Criminal Trial Practice

JORDAN & BRISTOL
Brunswick, GA.........................Insurance Defense; Product Liability Law

JORDAN AND HAMBURG
New York, NY.........................Patent, Trademark, Copyright and Unfair Competition

JORDAN, HYDEN, WOMBLE & CULBRETH, P.C.
Corpus Christi, TX ....Bankruptcy Law; Commercial Litigation

JORDAN PRICE WALL GRAY JONES & CARLTON
Raleigh, NC..............................Construction Law; General Practice

JORDON, WAYNE A.
Alamogordo, NM ....General Practice

JORGENSON, SIEGEL, MCCLURE & FLEGEL, LLP
Menlo Park, CA.......................General Practice

JORY, PETERSON, WATKINS & SMITH
Fresno, CA...............................Civil Trial Practice; Labor and Employment Law

JOSCELYN, MCNAIR AND JEFFREY, P.C.
Ann Arbor, MI ....General Practice

JOSE, HENRY, BRANTLEY & KELTNER, L.L.P.
Fort Worth, TX ....Appellate Practice; Civil Trial Practice; Medical Malpractice; Personal Injury; Product Liability Law

JOSEPH, RAYMOND & ASSOCIATES
East Lansing, MI ....Civil Trial Practice; Insurance Defense; Product Liability Law

JOSEPH, GREENWALD AND LAAKE, P.A.
Greenbelt, MD ....Commercial Litigation

JOSEPH & JOSEPH
Columbus, OH ....Family Law; Real Estate Law

JOSEPHS, BONNIE P.
New York, NY..........................Civil Trial Practice

JOSEPHS, JACK & GAEBE, P.A.
Miami, FL ....Civil Trial Practice; Commercial Litigation; Insurance Defense; Personal Injury; Professional Liability

JOSEPHSON, LOVELL & DRINGMAN
Big Timber, MT ....Real Estate Law; Trust and Estates, Wills and Probate

JOSLYN KEYDEL & WALLACE, LLP
Detroit, MI...............................Tax Law; Trust and Estates, Wills and Probate

JUDICE & ADLEY, A PROFESSIONAL LAW CORPORATION
Lafayette, LA ....Insurance Defense

JULIAN & PERTZ, P.C.
Utica, NY ....Civil Trial Practice; Medical Malpractice; Personal Injury; Product Liability Law

JULIEN & SCHLESINGER, P.C.
New York, NY..........................Civil Trial Practice; Medical Malpractice; Personal Injury; Product Liability Law

JUNEAU FIRM, THE, A PROFESSIONAL LAW CORPORATION
Lafayette, LA ....Admiralty/Maritime Law; Insurance Defense

KABALA & GEESEMAN, A PROFESSIONAL CORPORATION
Pittsburgh, PA ....General Practice

KAHN, DEES, DONOVAN & KAHN, LLP
Evansville, IN..........................Admiralty/Maritime Law; Banking Law; Civil Trial Practice; Corporate Law; Environmental Law; General Practice; Health Care Law; Insurance Defense; Labor and Employment Law; Real Estate Law; Tax Law

KAHN, KLEINMAN, YANOWITZ & ARNSON CO., L.P.A.
Cleveland, OH..........General Practice

KAHN, SMITH & COLLINS, P.A.
Baltimore, MD..........Administrative Law; Labor and Employment Law; Medical Malpractice; Personal Injury

KAHRS, NELSON, FANNING, HITE & KELLOGG L.L.P.
Wichita, KS..........Business Law; Civil Trial Practice; Commercial Litigation; Corporate Law; General Practice; Insurance Defense; Natural Resources Law; Product Liability Law; Real Estate Law

KAISER, JACK I. LAW OFFICES
San Francisco, CA..........Immigration and Naturalization

KAJAN MATHER AND BARISH, A PROFESSIONAL CORPORATION
Beverly Hills, CA..........Tax Law

KALCHEIM, SCHATZ & BERGER
Chicago, IL..........Family Law

KALEEL & KALEEL, P.A.
St. Petersburg, FL..........Civil Trial Practice

KALISON, MCBRIDE & JACKSON, P.A.
Liberty Corner, NJ..........Health Care Law; Mergers and Acquisitions; Tax Law; Trust and Estates, Wills and Probate

KALOW, SPRINGUT & BRESSLER LLP
New York, NY..........Intellectual Property Law

KAMBERG, BERMAN, P.C.
Springfield, MA..........Bankruptcy Law; Commercial Law; Commercial Litigation

KAMER & ZUCKER
Las Vegas, NV..........Labor and Employment Law

KANE, DONLEY & JOHNSON, P.C.
Colorado Springs, CO..........Civil Trial Practice; Family Law; General Practice; Insurance Defense

KANE, RUSSELL, COLEMAN & LOGAN, A PROFESSIONAL CORPORATION
Dallas, TX..........Bankruptcy Law; Civil Trial Practice; General Practice; Real Estate Law; Tax Law

KANE & SILVERMAN, PROFESSIONAL CORPORATION
Philadelphia, PA..........Civil Trial Practice; Medical Malpractice; Personal Injury; Product Liability Law

KANIA, LINDNER, LASAK AND FEENEY
Bala Cynwyd, PA..........Business Law; Civil Trial Practice; Commercial Law; Commercial Litigation; Corporate Law; Mergers and Acquisitions; Real Estate Law

KANTROVITZ, MARTIN LAW OFFICES OF
Boston, MA..........Personal Injury; Product Liability Law

KANTROW, SPAHT, WEAVER & BLITZER, A PROFESSIONAL LAW CORPORATION
Baton Rouge, LA..........Civil Trial Practice; Commercial Law; General Practice; Real Estate Law; Trust and Estates, Wills and Probate

KAPETAN MEYERS ROSEN & LOUIK, P.C.
Pittsburgh, PA..........Medical Malpractice; Personal Injury; Product Liability Law

KAPLAN, JOEL S.
Garden City, NY..........Civil Trial Practice; General Practice

KAPLAN, BEGY & VON OHLEN
Chicago, IL..........Commercial Litigation; Construction Law; Insurance Defense; Labor and Employment Law; Product Liability Law; Securities Law

KAPLAN, HOWARD GORDON, LTD.
Chicago, IL..........Business Law; Employment Benefits Law; Real Estate Law; Tax Law

KAPLAN, STRANGIS AND KAPLAN, P.A.
Minneapolis, MN..........General Practice

KAPLIN STEWART MELOFF REITER & STEIN, PROFESSIONAL CORPORATION
Blue Bell, PA..........Bankruptcy Law; Civil Trial Practice; Commercial Law; Health Care Law; Real Estate Law; Tax Law

KAPNER, LEWIS, P.A.
West Palm Beach, FL..........Civil Trial Practice; Family Law

KARASZKIEWICZ, KIRK T., & ASSOCIATES, P.C.
Philadelphia, PA..........Criminal Trial Practice

KARGIANIS WATKINS WERNER, L.L.P., P.S.
Seattle, WA..........Personal Injury; Product Liability Law

KARIC, STEVEN S., A PROF.CORP., LAW OFFICES OF
Los Angeles, CA..........Civil Trial Practice; Commercial Litigation; Trademark, Copyright and Unfair Competition

KARNS & KARABIAN
Los Angeles, CA..........Administrative Law

KARP, DAVID I.
Van Nuys, CA..........Civil Trial Practice

KARP, FROSH, LAPIDUS, WIGODSKY & NORWIND, P.A.
Bethesda, MD..........Commercial Litigation; Medical Malpractice; Personal Injury; Product Liability Law; Toxic Torts

KARR, CHARLES, P.A., LAW OFFICES OF
Fort Smith, AR..........Medical Malpractice

KARSMAN, BROOKS & CALLAWAY, P.C.
Savannah, GA..........Bankruptcy Law; Business Law; Civil Trial Practice; Commercial Law; Insurance Defense; Labor and Employment Law; Product Liability Law; Workers Compensation

KASDAN, SIMONDS, MCINTYRE, EPSTEIN & MARTIN
Irvine, CA..........Construction Law; Real Estate Law

KASDIN, PETER D., LTD.
Chicago, IL..........Medical Malpractice; Personal Injury

KASDORF, LEWIS & SWIETLIK, S.C.
Milwaukee, WI..........Aviation Law; Insurance Defense; Labor and Employment Law; Product Liability Law; Professional Liability; Workers Compensation

KASS LAW FIRM
Portsmouth, VA..........Personal Injury

KATARINCIC & SALMON
Pittsburgh, PA..........Civil Trial Practice; Securities Law

KATSKEE, HENATSCH & SUING
Omaha, NE..........Civil Trial Practice; General Practice; Insurance Defense; Professional Liability

KATTEN MUCHIN & ZAVIS
Chicago, IL..........General Practice

KATZ, BARRON, SQUITERO, FAUST & BERMAN, P.A.
Miami, FL..........Commercial Litigation; Insurance Defense; Real Estate Law

KATZ, GREENBERGER & NORTON
Cincinnati, OH..........General Practice

KATZ, KANTOR & PERKINS
Bluefield, WV..........General Practice

KATZ & KLEIN
White Plains, NY..........General Practice

KATZ, KUTTER, HAIGLER, ALDERMAN, BRYANT & YON, PROFESSIONAL ASSOCIATION
Tallahassee, FL..........Administrative Law

KATZ, LOOK & MOISON, PROFESSIONAL CORPORATION
Denver, CO..........Business Law; Civil Trial Practice; Commercial Litigation; Real Estate Law; Tax Law; Trust and Estates, Wills and Probate

KATZ & MANKA, LTD.
Minneapolis, MN..........Family Law

KATZ, STEVEN M., P.A.
Rockville, MD..........Business Law; Trust and Estates, Wills and Probate

KATZ, TELLER, BRANT & HILD, A LEGAL PROFESSIONAL ASSOCIATION
Cincinnati, OH..........Banking Law; Bankruptcy Law; Business Law; Civil Trial Practice; Employment Benefits Law; Environmental Law; Family Law; General Practice; Health Care Law; Labor and Employment Law; Municipal and Zoning Law; Real Estate Law; Securities Law; Tax Law; Trust and Estates, Wills and Probate

KAUFFMAN, EARL G.
Philadelphia, PA..........Criminal Trial Practice

KAUFMAN & CANOLES, A PROFESSIONAL CORPORATION
Chesapeake, VA..........General Practice
Newport News, VA..........General Practice
Norfolk, VA..........General Practice
Virginia Beach, VA..........General Practice
Williamsburg, VA..........General Practice

KAUFMAN, COREN, RESS & WEIDMAN, P.C.
Philadelphia, PA..........Civil Trial Practice; Commercial Litigation

KAUFMAN & CUMBERLAND CO., L.P.A.
Cleveland, OH..........Antitrust Law; Business Law; Civil Trial Practice; Commercial Litigation; Municipal Bond/Public Authority Financing; Product Liability Law; Real Estate Law

KAUFMAN & FLORENCE
Lebanon, OH..........General Practice

KAUFMAN & GREEN, L.L.P.
Wilmington, NC.....................Banking Law; Creditors Rights; Health Care Law; Real Estate Law

KAUFMAN & LOGAN LLP
San Francisco, CA ....Appellate Practice; Bankruptcy Law; Civil Trial Practice; Commercial Litigation; Environmental Law

KAUFMAN AND PAYTON
Farmington Hills, MI ....Insurance Defense

KAUFMAN & ROTHFEDER, P.C.
Montgomery, AL.....................Bankruptcy Law; Business Law; Commercial Law; Commercial Litigation; Environmental Law; Health Care Law; Real Estate Law; Tax Law; Trust and Estates, Wills and Probate

KAUFMAN, SCHNEIDER & BIANCO, LLP
Jericho, NY ....Employment Benefits Law; Labor and Employment Law

KAUFMAN & YOUNG, A PROFESSIONAL CORPORATION
Beverly Hills, CA....................Family Law

KAVALLER, MILES L., A PROFESSIONAL LAW CORPORATION
Beverly Hills, CA....................Transportation Law

KAVANAGH, SCULLY, SUDOW, WHITE & FREDERICK, P.C.
Galesburg, IL..........................General Practice
Peoria, IL................................Civil Trial Practice; General Practice; Labor and Employment Law

KAWACHIKA & OSAKI
Honolulu, HI...........................Civil Trial Practice

KAY, J. BENJAMIN III
Augusta, GA............................Bankruptcy Law; Corporate Law; Creditors Rights

KAY & ANDERSEN, S.C.
Madison, WI ....Civil Trial Practice; Construction Law; Environmental Law; Insurance Defense

KAY CASTO & CHANEY PLLC
Charleston, WV.......................Civil Trial Practice; General Practice

KAY & MERKLE
San Francisco, CA ....Business Law; Real Estate Law; Sports and Entertainment Law; Tax Law

KAYE, ALLEN E., P.C.
New York, NY.........................Immigration and Naturalization

KAYE, ROSE & PARTNERS, LLP
Los Angeles, CA......................Admiralty/Maritime Law
San Diego, CA ....Admiralty/Maritime Law
San Francisco, CA ....Admiralty/Maritime Law
Miami, FL...............................Admiralty/Maritime Law

KAYE, SCHOLER, FIERMAN, HAYS & HANDLER, LLP
Los Angeles, CA......................General Practice
Washington, DC.......................General Practice
New York, NY.........................General Practice
Hong Kong, China...................General Practice

KAYLOR, ROBERT W., P.A.
Raleigh, NC.............................Public Utilities Law

KAZAN, MCCLAIN, EDISES, SIMON & ABRAMS, A PROFESSIONAL LAW CORPORATION
Oakland, CA ....Civil Trial Practice; Personal Injury; Workers Compensation

KAZEE, KINNER & CHAFIN
Prestonsburg, KY ....General Practice; Insurance Defense; Natural Resources Law

KEAN, MILLER, HAWTHORNE, D'ARMOND, MCCOWAN & JARMAN, L.L.P.
Baton Rouge, LA.....................Admiralty/Maritime Law; Civil Trial Practice; Commercial Law; Environmental Law; Health Care Law; Intellectual Property Law; Labor and Employment Law; Public Utilities Law; Tax Law

KEANE & BEANE, P.C.
White Plains, NY ....Commercial Law; Environmental Law; General Practice; Labor and Employment Law; Municipal and Zoning Law; Personal Injury; Real Estate Law

KEANE, REESE & VESELY, P.A.
St. Petersburg, FL..................Civil Trial Practice

KEANE, WILLIAM T., P.C.
Phoenix, AZ ....Personal Injury

KEARNEY, GARY W.
Pasadena, CA ....Family Law

KEARNEY & WESTFALL
Fort Worth, TX ....Criminal Trial Practice

KEATING JONES BILDSTEIN & HUGHES, P.C.
Portland, OR...........................Insurance Defense

KEATING, MUETHING & KLEKAMP, P.L.L.
Cincinnati, OH ....Banking Law; Bankruptcy Law; Civil Trial Practice; Environmental Law; General Practice; Insurance Defense; Medical Malpractice; Real Estate Law; Securities Law; Tax Law; Trademark, Copyright and Unfair Competition

KEATS, JOHN A.
Fairfax, VA ....General Practice

KEEFER, O'REILLY & FERRARIO
Las Vegas, NV ....Business Law; Civil Trial Practice

KEEFER WOOD ALLEN & RAHAL, LLP
Harrisburg, PA.........................Civil Trial Practice; General Practice; Health Care Law; Tax Law

KEEGAN, RAYMOND J., & ASSOC., LLP
White Plains, NY ....Personal Injury

KEELEY, HAYES, DUDLEY & GARRETT
Boca Raton, FL ....Real Estate Law; Trust and Estates, Wills and Probate

KEENER DOUCHER CURLEY & PATTERSON, A LEGAL PROFESSIONAL ASSOCIATION
Columbus, OH ....Civil Trial Practice; Insurance Defense; Personal Injury; Product Liability Law

KEENER & KEENER
Centre, AL ....General Practice

KEGLER, BROWN, HILL & RITTER
Columbus, OH ....Administrative Law; Banking Law; Bankruptcy Law; Business Law; Civil Trial Practice; Construction Law; Employment Benefits Law; Environmental Law; General Practice; Health Care Law; Immigration and Naturalization; Labor and Employment Law; Municipal and Zoning Law; Natural Resources Law; Public Utilities Law; Real Estate Law; Tax Law; Trademark, Copyright and Unfair Competition; Trust and Estates, Wills and Probate

KEHART, SHAFTER & WEBBER, P.C.
Decatur, IL..............................General Practice; Insurance Defense

KEHOE, DENNIS J., A LAW CORPORATION
Aptos, CA ....Environmental Law

KEILP, JOE, P.C.
Phoenix, AZ ....Criminal Trial Practice

KEIL & WEINKAUF
Washington, DC.......................Patent, Trademark, Copyright and Unfair Competition

KEISER, LARRY S.
Wilkes-Barre, PA ....Civil Trial Practice; Personal Injury

KEITGES & BANGLE, A PROFESSIONAL LAW CORPORATION
Sacramento, CA ....Insurance Defense

KEITH, DARRELL, P.C., LAW FIRM OF
Fort Worth, TX ....Legal Malpractice; Medical Malpractice

KEKER & VAN NEST, L.L.P.
San Francisco, CA ....Civil Trial Practice

KELAHER, CONNELL & CONNOR, P.C.
Surfside Beach, SC ....Civil Trial Practice; Personal Injury

KELAHER LAW OFFICES, P.A.
Orlando, FL ....Medical Malpractice; Personal Injury

KELEHER & MCLEOD, P.A.
Albuquerque, NM....................Insurance Defense; Trust and Estates, Wills and Probate

KELL, ALTERMAN & RUNSTEIN, LLP
Portland, OR...........................Admiralty/Maritime Law; Bankruptcy Law; Business Law; Civil Trial Practice; Corporate Law; Creditors Rights; Family Law; Labor and Employment Law; Mergers and Acquisitions; Personal Injury; Real Estate Law; Tax Law; Trust and Estates, Wills and Probate

KELLER, JENNIFER L. LAW OFFICES OF
Newport Beach, CA.................Criminal Trial Practice

KELLER AND CURTIN CO., L.P.A.
Cleveland, OH.........................Business Law; Civil Trial Practice; Corporate Law; Environmental Law; Insurance Defense; Product Liability Law

KELLER & HOUCK, A PROFESSIONAL ASSOCIATION
Miami, FL ....Admiralty/Maritime Law

KELLER, REYNOLDS, DRAKE, JOHNSON & GILLESPIE, P.C.
Helena, MT .... Civil Trial Practice; Insurance Defense

KELLER, THOMA, SCHWARZE, SCHWARZE, DUBAY & KATZ, P.C.
Detroit, MI .... Arbitration; Civil Trial Practice; Employment Benefits Law; General Practice; Insurance Defense; Labor and Employment Law; Trust and Estates, Wills and Probate; Workers Compensation

KELLER, WAHLBERG & MORRATO, P.C.
Denver, CO .... Personal Injury

KELLEY, BELCHER & BROWN, A PROFESSIONAL CORPORATION
Bloomington, IN .... Civil Trial Practice; Insurance Defense; Personal Injury; Product Liability Law

KELLEY DRYE & WARREN LLP
New York, NY .... General Practice

KELLEY, HERMAN & SMITH
Fort Lauderdale, FL .... Real Estate Law; Trust and Estates, Wills and Probate

KELLEY, JAMES C., P.A.
Miami, FL .... Insurance Defense

KELLEY, JASONS, MCGUIRE & SPINELLI, L.L.P.
Philadelphia, PA .... Civil Trial Practice; Commercial Law; Insurance Defense; Personal Injury; Product Liability Law; Toxic Torts

KELLEY, KRONENBERG, KELLEY, GILMARTIN, FICHTEL & WANDER, P.A.
Fort Lauderdale, FL .... Insurance Defense; Workers Compensation

KELLEY, MCCANN & LIVINGSTONE, LLP
Cleveland, OH .... Appellate Practice; Bankruptcy Law; Business Law; Civil Trial Practice; Environmental Law; Family Law; General Practice; Labor and Employment Law; Municipal and Zoning Law; Real Estate Law

KELLEY & MURPHY
Blue Bell, PA .... Administrative Law; Business Law; Civil Trial Practice; Commercial Law; Commercial Litigation; Corporate Law; General Practice; Insurance Defense; Labor and Employment Law; Personal Injury; Real Estate Law; Workers Compensation

KELLEY, WEBER, PIETZ & SLATER, S.C.
Wausau, WI .... Civil Trial Practice

KELL & FLACH
St. Charles, MO .... Personal Injury

KELLUM & JONES, P.A.
New Bern, NC .... Civil Trial Practice; Personal Injury; Workers Compensation

KELLY AFFLECK GREENE
Toronto, ON, Canada .... Administrative Law; Antitrust Law; Banking Law; Civil Trial Practice; Commercial Litigation; Construction Law; Environmental Law; Insurance Defense; Intellectual Property Law; Medical Malpractice; Municipal and Zoning Law; Patent, Trademark, Copyright and Unfair Competition; Personal Injury; Product Liability Law; Professional Liability

KELLY, BAUERSFELD, LOWRY & KELLEY, LLP
Woodland Hills, CA .... Patent, Trademark, Copyright and Unfair Competition

KELLY & HAMMERS, A PROFESSIONAL CORPORATION
Santa Monica, CA .... Family Law

KELLY, HART & HALLMAN, A PROFESSIONAL CORPORATION
Fort Worth, TX .... General Practice

KELLY, RODE & KELLY, LLP
Mineola, NY .... Insurance Defense

KELLY, TIMOTHY F., LAW OFFICES OF
Munster, IN .... Civil Trial Practice; General Practice; Insurance Defense; Labor and Employment Law; Medical Malpractice; Personal Injury; Product Liability Law

KELSCH KELSCH RUFF & KRANDA
Mandan, ND .... Environmental Law; General Practice

KEMP, DUCKETT, SPRADLEY, CURRY & ARNOLD
Little Rock, AR .... General Practice

KEMP, SMITH, DUNCAN & HAMMOND, A PROFESSIONAL CORPORATION
El Paso, TX .... Antitrust Law; General Practice; Labor and Employment Law; Tax Law

KEMPE, JOSEPH C., PROFESSIONAL ASSOCIATION
Jupiter, FL .... Tax Law; Trust and Estates, Wills and Probate
Stuart, FL .... Tax Law; Trust and Estates, Wills and Probate
Vero Beach, FL .... Tax Law; Trust and Estates, Wills and Probate

KEMPER & BARLOW
Madison, IN .... General Practice

KENDALL, HUGH F., ATTORNEY, P.C.
Chattanooga, TN .... Real Estate Law; Tax Law; Trust and Estates, Wills and Probate

KENDRICKS BORDEAU, P.C.
Marquette, MI .... General Practice

KENNEDY, JAMES L. JR.
Ketchum, ID .... Environmental Law; Natural Resources Law; Real Estate Law

KENNEDY & CHRISTOPHER, P.C.
Denver, CO .... Civil Trial Practice; Medical Malpractice

KENNEDY, CICCONETTI & KNOWLTON, L.P.A.
Wooster, OH .... Civil Trial Practice; Trust and Estates, Wills and Probate

KENNEDY COVINGTON LOBDELL & HICKMAN, L.L.P.
Charlotte, NC .... General Practice
Raleigh, NC .... General Practice
Rock Hill, SC .... General Practice

KENNEDY, FULTON, KOONTZ & FARINASH
Chattanooga, TN .... Bankruptcy Law

KENNEDY, JOHNSON, D'ELIA & GILLOOLY
New Haven, CT .... Civil Trial Practice; Medical Malpractice; Personal Injury; Product Liability Law; Professional Liability; Workers Compensation

KENNEDY, NERVIG & CARLISLE, LLP
Wadena, MN .... General Practice

KENNEDY, RICHARD R., A PROFESSIONAL LAW CORPORATION
Lafayette, LA .... Admiralty/Maritime Law; Appellate Practice; Civil Trial Practice; Personal Injury

KENNELLY, DENNIS LAWRENCE LAW OFFICE OF
Menlo Park, CA .... Labor and Employment Law

KENNERSON SCHWARTZ SEMERDJIAN & HAILE LLP
San Diego, CA .... Business Law; Civil Trial Practice; Commercial Law; Construction Law; Corporate Law; Insurance Defense; Intellectual Property Law; Labor and Employment Law; Personal Injury; Product Liability Law; Professional Liability; Real Estate Law; Trademark, Copyright and Unfair Competition; Trust and Estates, Wills and Probate

KENNEY & KEARNEY LLP
Cherry Hill, NJ .... Civil Trial Practice; Commercial Litigation; Environmental Law; Labor and Employment Law

KENNY, BRIMMER, MELLEY & MAHONEY
Hartford, CT .... General Practice; Insurance Defense; Medical Malpractice; Personal Injury; Product Liability Law

KENNY NACHWALTER SEYMOUR ARNOLD CRITCHLOW & SPECTOR, PROFESSIONAL ASSOCIATION
Miami, FL .... Antitrust Law; Civil Trial Practice; General Practice; Trademark, Copyright and Unfair Competition

KENNY & STEARNS
Newark, NJ .... Admiralty/Maritime Law; Civil Trial Practice
New York, NY .... Admiralty/Maritime Law; Civil Trial Practice; Insurance Defense

KENT, HAZZARD, JAEGER, GREER, WILSON & FAY
White Plains, NY .... Corporate Law; General Practice; Real Estate Law; Trust and Estates, Wills and Probate

KENT & MCBRIDE, P.C.
Philadelphia, PA .... Civil Trial Practice

KENT, WORSHAM & SMART
Savannah, GA .... Civil Trial Practice; Insurance Defense

KENYON & KENYON
Washington, DC .... Patent, Trademark, Copyright and Unfair Competition
New York, NY .... Patent, Trademark, Copyright and Unfair Competition

KEPLEY, GILLIGAN & EYRICH, A LEGAL PROFESSIONAL ASSOCIATION
Cincinnati, OH .... Business Law; Civil Trial Practice; Personal Injury; Real Estate Law; Workers Compensation

KERKAM, STOWELL, KONDRACKI & CLARKE, P.C.
Falls Church, VA .... Patent, Trademark, Copyright and Unfair Competition

KERN & GONZALEZ, A PROFESSIONAL CORPORATION
Los Angeles, CA .... Civil Trial Practice; Insurance Defense; Labor and Employment Law; Medical Malpractice; Product Liability Law

KERR, ANN LOUGHRIDGE
Clearwater, FL .... Family Law
Tampa, FL .... Family Law

KERR, IRVINE, RHODES & ABLES, A PROFESSIONAL CORPORATION
Oklahoma City, OK .... Administrative Law; Civil Trial Practice; Corporate Law; Environmental Law; General Practice; Insurance Defense; Labor and Employment Law

KERR MCDONALD, LLP
Baltimore, MD .... Civil Trial Practice

KERR & WARD, L.L.P.
Midland, TX .... Business Law; Civil Trial Practice; General Practice; Health Care Law; Natural Resources Law

KERRICK, GRISE & STIVERS
Bowling Green, KY .... Banking Law; Business Law; Civil Trial Practice; Commercial Law; General Practice; Health Care Law; Insurance Defense; Labor and Employment Law; Medical Malpractice; Personal Injury; Product Liability Law; Professional Liability; Real Estate Law; Trademark, Copyright and Unfair Competition; Workers Compensation

KERRIGAN, ESTESS, RANKIN & MCLEOD
Pensacola, FL .... Civil Trial Practice; Medical Malpractice; Personal Injury

KERSTEN & MCKINNON, S.C.
Milwaukee, WI .... Antitrust Law; Business Law; Civil Trial Practice; Personal Injury

KESSLER, COHEN & ROTH, A PROFESSIONAL CORPORATION
Philadelphia, PA .... Civil Trial Practice; Medical Malpractice; Personal Injury; Product Liability Law

KESSLER, DOUGLAS W., P.C.
Atlanta, GA .... Business Law

KESSLER & KESSLER, A LAW CORPORATION
Los Angeles, CA .... Commercial Litigation; Corporate Law; Real Estate Law; Tax Law; Trust and Estates, Wills and Probate

KESSLER & SCHWARZ, P.C.
Atlanta, GA .... Family Law

KESSNER DUCA UMEBAYASHI BAIN & MATSUNAGA, ATTORNEYS AT LAW, A LAW CORPORATION
Honolulu, HI .... Banking Law; Bankruptcy Law; Insurance Defense; Product Liability Law; Workers Compensation

KESTENBAUM, HAROLD L., P.C.
Garden City, NY .... Franchise Law

KETCHAM & KETCHAM
Columbus, OH .... Criminal Trial Practice; Trust and Estates, Wills and Probate

KETCHEY HORAN, P.A.
Tampa, FL .... Bankruptcy Law; Business Law; Commercial Litigation; Corporate Law; Creditors Rights; Real Estate Law; Trust and Estates, Wills and Probate

KEULING-STOUT, P.C.
Big Stone Gap, VA .... Civil Trial Practice; General Practice

KEYSER MASON BALL
Mississauga, ON, Canada .... Banking Law

KEZIAH, GATES & SAMET, L.L.P.
High Point, NC .... General Practice

KICKHAM LAW OFFICES
Brookline, MA .... Real Estate Law; Trust and Estates, Wills and Probate

KIENBAUM, KAREN SMITH & ASSOCIATES
Detroit, MI .... Arbitration; Labor and Employment Law

KIENBAUM OPPERWALL HARDY & PELTON, P.L.C.
Birmingham, MI .... Labor and Employment Law
Detroit, MI .... Labor and Employment Law

KIERNAN, PLUNKETT & REDIHAN
Providence, RI .... Civil Trial Practice

KIESEWETTER WISE KAPLAN SCHWIMMER & PRATHER, PLC
Memphis, TN .... Labor and Employment Law

KIESLER & BERMAN
Chicago, IL .... Civil Trial Practice; Insurance Defense

KIGER & ALPERN
Pittsburgh, PA .... Civil Trial Practice; Insurance Defense; Medical Malpractice; Personal Injury; Product Liability Law

KILBORNE, ROBERT S. IV, LAW OFFICES OF
Rancho Santa Fe, CA .... Business Law; Civil Trial Practice; Medical Malpractice; Personal Injury

KILBURN, JONES, GILL & CAMPBELL, L.L.P.
Houston, TX .... Civil Trial Practice; Oil and Gas Law

KILCULLEN, WILSON AND KILCULLEN, CHARTERED
Washington, DC .... Construction Law; Government Contracts

KILE MCINTYRE HARBIN & LEE
Washington, DC .... Intellectual Property Law

KILGORE, DONALD C.
Portsmouth, VA .... Commercial Law; General Practice

KILGORE & KILGORE, A PROFESSIONAL CORPORATION
Dallas, TX .... Civil Trial Practice; General Practice; Labor and Employment Law; Natural Resources Law

KILLEEN & FIERRO
Houston, TX .... Admiralty/Maritime Law; Civil Trial Practice; Energy Law; Insurance Defense

KILLIAN, DONOHUE & SHIPMAN, LLC
Hartford, CT .... Administrative Law; Energy Law; Land Use Law; Municipal and Zoning Law

KILLIAN & GEPHART, LLP
Harrisburg, PA .... Administrative Law; Civil Trial Practice; Criminal Trial Practice; Environmental Law; Labor and Employment Law

KILLWORTH, GOTTMAN, HAGAN & SCHAEFF, L.L.P.
Dayton, OH .... Patent, Trademark, Copyright and Unfair Competition

KILPATRICK, AUD & WILLIAMS, L.L.P.
Little Rock, AR .... Insurance Defense; Legal Malpractice; Medical Malpractice; Product Liability Law; Professional Liability; Workers Compensation

KIMBLE, NELSON, AUDILETT, MCDONOUGH & MOLLA, P.C.
Tucson, AZ .... Insurance Defense; Product Liability Law

KIMERER & LAVELLE, P.L.C.
Phoenix, AZ .... Antitrust Law; Civil Trial Practice; Commercial Litigation; Criminal Trial Practice; Environmental Law; Personal Injury

KINCAID, TAYLOR & GEYER
Zanesville, OH .... General Practice

KINERK, BEAL, SCHMIDT & DYER, P.C.
Tucson, AZ .... Medical Malpractice; Personal Injury; Product Liability Law; Professional Liability; Sports and Entertainment Law

KING, JEAN LEDWITH
Ann Arbor, MI .... Family Law

KING & ATTRIDGE
Rockville, MD .... Commercial Litigation; Construction Law

KING & BALLOW
San Diego, CA .... General Practice
Nashville, TN .... Antitrust Law; Civil Trial Practice; Communications Law; General Practice; Labor and Employment Law; Tax Law; Trademark, Copyright and Unfair Competition

KING, BLACKWELL & DOWNS, P.A.
Orlando, FL .... Civil Trial Practice; Commercial Litigation; Personal Injury

KING & KING
Greeneville, TN .... Family Law

KING AND KING, L.L.C.
Jackson, WY .... Civil Trial Practice; Personal Injury

KING LAW FIRM
Oklahoma City, OK .... Civil Trial Practice; Insurance Defense; Product Liability Law

KING, PAGANO & HARRISON
Washington, DC .... Antitrust Law; Civil Trial Practice; Criminal Trial Practice; Health Care Law; Intellectual Property Law; Labor and Employment Law
New York, NY .... Civil Trial Practice; Health Care Law; Intellectual Property Law; Labor and Employment Law

KING • PETERSON • DYMOND LLP
Englewood, CO .... Civil Trial Practice; Commercial Law

KING AND SCHICKLI
Lexington, KY .... Intellectual Property Law; Patent, Trademark, Copyright and Unfair Competition

KING & VERNON, P.A.
Columbia, SC .... Civil Trial Practice; Criminal Trial Practice; Family Law; General Practice

KINGCADE, THOMAS E., PROFESSIONAL ASSOCIATION
West Palm Beach, FL............Civil Trial Practice; Commercial Litigation; Personal Injury

KINGERY DURREE WAKEMAN & RYAN, ASSOC.
Peoria, IL............Civil Trial Practice; General Practice; Medical Malpractice

KINGSLEY, JOHN P., P.C.
Catskill, NY............Insurance Defense

KINNARD, CLAYTON & BEVERIDGE
Nashville, TN............Medical Malpractice

KINNEY, KEMP, SPONCLER, JOINER & THARPE
Dalton, GA............Insurance Defense; Workers Compensation

KINSEY VINCENT PYLE, P.A.
Daytona Beach, FL............Construction Law

KIPLE, KIPLE, DENEFE, BEAVER & GARDNER, L.L.P.
Ottumwa, IA............General Practice

KIPNIS TESCHER LIPPMAN & VALINSKY
Fort Lauderdale, FL............Commercial Litigation; Creditors Rights; Securities Law

KIPP AND CHRISTIAN, P.C.
Salt Lake City, UT............Civil Trial Practice; General Practice; Insurance Defense; Personal Injury

KIRBY, PATRICK M.
Flint, MI............General Practice

KIRBY & HOLT, L.L.P.
Raleigh, NC............Medical Malpractice; Personal Injury

KIRCH, DAVID W., P.C.
Aurora, CO............Trust and Estates, Wills and Probate

KIRCHER, C. WILLIAM, JR., A PROF. CORP., LAW OFFICES OF
Irvine, CA............Business Law

KIRKENDALL & ISGUR
Houston, TX............Bankruptcy Law

KIRKLAND & ELLIS
Los Angeles, CA............Criminal Trial Practice; General Practice
Washington, DC............General Practice
Chicago, IL............General Practice
New York, NY............General Practice
London, England............General Practice

KIRKPATRICK & LOCKHART LLP
Pittsburgh, PA............General Practice

KIRLIN, CAMPBELL & KEATING
New York, NY............Admiralty/Maritime Law

KIRSCHNER AND VENKER, P.C.
Atlanta, GA............Medical Malpractice; Personal Injury

KIRSCHNIK, JAMES L., S.C.
Milwaukee, WI............Construction Law

KIRSHENBAUM LAW ASSOCIATES
Warwick, RI............Civil Trial Practice; Family Law; Personal Injury

KIRSHMAN, HARRIS & BRANTON, A PROFESSIONAL CORPORATION
Beverly Hills, CA............Business Law
Las Vegas, NV............Civil Trial Practice; Labor and Employment Law

KIRTON & MCCONKIE, A PROFESSIONAL CORPORATION
Salt Lake City, UT............Civil Trial Practice; Commercial Law; General Practice; Insurance Defense; Personal Injury; Real Estate Law; Trust and Estates, Wills and Probate

KIRVEN & KIRVEN, P.C.
Buffalo, WY............General Practice; Real Estate Law; Trust and Estates, Wills and Probate

KIRWAN & BARRETT, P.C.
Bozeman, MT............Appellate Practice; Banking Law; Business Law; Civil Trial Practice; Commercial Law; Construction Law; Labor and Employment Law; Municipal and Zoning Law; Personal Injury; Real Estate Law; Trust and Estates, Wills and Probate

KISSOON, CLUGG, LINDER & DITTBERNER, LTD.
Edina, MN............Family Law

KITCH DRUTCHAS WAGNER DENARDIS & VALITUTTI, A PROFESSIONAL CORPORATION
Ann Arbor, MI............General Practice
Detroit, MI............Civil Trial Practice; Environmental Law; General Practice; Health Care Law; Insurance Defense; Labor and Employment Law; Medical Malpractice; Personal Injury
Grand Rapids, MI............General Practice
Lansing, MI............General Practice
Mount Clemens, MI............General Practice

KITCHEN, JUDKINS, SIMPSON & HIGH
Tallahassee, FL............Civil Trial Practice; Commercial Litigation; Criminal Trial Practice; Personal Injury

KITCHENS, BENTON, KITCHENS & WARREN, A PROFESSIONAL LAW CORPORATION
Minden, LA............General Practice

KITCHIN, NEAL, WEBB, WEBB & FUTRELL, P.A.
Rockingham, NC............General Practice

KITRICK, MARK, CO., L.P.A.
Columbus, OH............Civil Trial Practice; Personal Injury

KITTAY, GOLD & GERSHFELD, P.C.
New York, NY............Bankruptcy Law; Commercial Litigation

KITTREDGE, DONLEY, ELSON, FULLEM & EMBICK, LLP
Philadelphia, PA............Commercial Litigation; Environmental Law; Insurance Defense; Labor and Employment Law

KIVITZ & LIPTZ, LLC
Chevy Chase, MD............Civil Trial Practice

KIZER AND BLACK
Maryville, TN............Civil Trial Practice

KIZER, HOOD & MORGAN, L.L.P.
Baton Rouge, LA............Bankruptcy Law; Real Estate Law

KIZER & NEU
Bremen, IN............General Practice
Plymouth, IN............General Practice

K.K.M., P.A.
Bethesda, MD............Business Law

KLAMANN & HUBBARD, P.A.
Overland Park, KS............Civil Trial Practice

KLAUBER & JACKSON
Hackensack, NJ............Patent, Trademark, Copyright and Unfair Competition; Trademark, Copyright and Unfair Competition

KLEHR, HARRISON, HARVEY, BRANZBURG & ELLERS LLP
Philadelphia, PA............General Practice

KLEIN, HOWARD BRUCE LAW OFFICES OF
Philadelphia, PA............Criminal Trial Practice

KLEIN, DENATALE, GOLDNER, COOPER, ROSENLIEB & KIMBALL, LLP
Bakersfield, CA............Bankruptcy Law; Business Law; Civil Trial Practice; Commercial Law; Construction Law; Corporate Law; Environmental Law; General Practice; Labor and Employment Law; Personal Injury; Real Estate Law; Tax Law; Trust and Estates, Wills and Probate

KLEIN, JOEL, & ASSOCIATES
San Antonio, TX............Commercial Law; Creditors Rights

KLEINBARD, BELL & BRECKER LLP
Philadelphia, PA............Business Law; Commercial Litigation; Corporate Law; Creditors Rights; Environmental Law; General Practice; Labor and Employment Law; Mergers and Acquisitions; Municipal and Zoning Law; Pension and Profit Sharing; Securities Law; Toxic Torts

KLEINFELD, KAPLAN AND BECKER
Washington, DC............Administrative Law

KLEINPETER & KLEINPETER
Baton Rouge, LA............Civil Trial Practice; Commercial Litigation; Insurance Defense

KLENDA, MITCHELL, AUSTERMAN & ZUERCHER, L.L.C.
Wichita, KS............General Practice

KLIEWER, BREEN, GARATONI, PATTERSON & MALONE, INCORPORATED
San Antonio, TX............Tax Law

KLINE, JOHN R., P.C.
Helena, MT............Tax Law; Trust and Estates, Wills and Probate

KLINE & SPECTER, P.C.
Philadelphia, PA............Civil Trial Practice

KLINEDINST, FLIEHMAN & MCKILLOP, A PROFESSIONAL CORPORATION
San Diego, CA............Civil Trial Practice; Commercial Litigation; Construction Law; Labor and Employment Law; Professional Liability

KLUGER, PERETZ, KAPLAN & BERLIN, P.A.
Fort Lauderdale, FL............Civil Trial Practice
Miami, FL............Civil Trial Practice

KLUMPP AND BARNATT
Lake Charles, LA....................Tax Law; Trust and Estates, Wills and Probate

KLUNDER, CARL J.
Irvine, CA....................Insurance Defense

KLUTTZ, REAMER, BLANKENSHIP, HAYES & RANDOLPH, L.L.P.
Salisbury, NC....................General Practice; Insurance Defense

KNAPP, MARSH, JONES & DORAN, L.L.P.
Los Angeles, CA....................General Practice

KNECHT, MICHAEL C., & ASSOCIATES, P.A.
Palm Beach Gardens, FL.........Civil Trial Practice; Personal Injury

KNEE & ROSS, LLP
Los Angeles, CA....................Labor and Employment Law

KNEELAND, KORB, COLLIER & LEGG
Ketchum, ID....................Family Law; Real Estate Law

KNIGHT, JOHN DAVID
Cullman, AL....................General Practice

KNIGHT & FISHER
Macon, GA....................Medical Malpractice

KNIGHT, FORD, ATWILL, PARSHALL & BAKER
Columbia, MO....................General Practice; Insurance Defense

KNIGHT, MANZI, NUSSBAUM & LAPLACA, P.C.
Upper Marlboro, MD..............Administrative Law; Banking Law; Business Law; Civil Trial Practice; Commercial Law; Criminal Trial Practice; Family Law; General Practice; Municipal Bond/Public Authority Financing; Real Estate Law

KNOLL, JAMES L.
Portland, OR....................Arbitration; Construction Law

KNOPFLER & ROBERTSON, LLP
Los Angeles, CA....................Business Law; Construction Law; Corporate Law; Environmental Law; Labor and Employment Law; Oil and Gas Law; Product Liability Law; Real Estate Law; Toxic Torts

KNOTT, JOHN K. JR.
Cheshire, CT....................Municipal and Zoning Law

KNOWLES, JOHN L.
Geneva, AL....................General Practice

KNOWLES & ASSOCIATES, LLC
Carmel, IN....................Business Law; Civil Trial Practice; Criminal Trial Practice; Trust and Estates, Wills and Probate

KNOX MCLAUGHLIN GORNALL & SENNETT, P.C.
Erie, PA....................General Practice

KNOX AND SWAN
Thomson, GA....................General Practice

KNUDSEN, BERKHEIMER, RICHARDSON & ENDACOTT
Lincoln, NE....................General Practice

KOBAYASHI, SUGITA & GODA
Honolulu, HI....................Business Law; Commercial Law; General Practice; Real Estate Law

KOBLENTZ & KOBLENTZ
Cleveland, OH....................Civil Trial Practice; Criminal Trial Practice; Family Law

KOCH & HARRINGTON, P.A.
Clearwater, FL....................Family Law

KOCH, RON, P.A.
Albuquerque, NM....................Criminal Trial Practice

KODNER, WATKINS, MUCHNICK & DUNNE, L.C.
St. Louis, MO....................Securities Law

KOENIGSBERG, JAY, P.A.
Miami, FL....................Real Estate Law

KOEPKE, KARL O.
Orlando, FL....................Medical Malpractice; Personal Injury

KOEPPEL MARTONE LEISTMAN & HERMAN, L.L.P.
Mineola, NY....................Municipal and Zoning Law; Real Estate Law

KOFF, HOWARD M., P.C.
Albany, NY....................Tax Law

KOFF, WENDOLOWSKI, FERGUSON & MANGAN, P.C.
Wilkes-Barre, PA....................Labor and Employment Law

KOHLER & HART
Milwaukee, WI....................Criminal Trial Practice

KOHN, MICHAEL G.
Cincinnati, OH....................Civil Trial Practice

KOHN, KOHN & COLAPINTO, P.C.
Washington, DC....................Labor and Employment Law

KOHN PARTNERSHIP, THE, L.P.
St. Louis, MO....................Mergers and Acquisitions; Tax Law

KOHN, SHANDS, ELBERT, GIANOULAKIS & GILJUM, LLP
St. Louis, MO....................Antitrust Law; Labor and Employment Law; Tax Law

KOHNER, MANN & KAILAS, S.C.
Milwaukee, WI....................Banking Law; Bankruptcy Law; Business Law; Civil Trial Practice; Commercial Law; Commercial Litigation; Construction Law; Creditors Rights

KOHRS & FISKE
Santa Monica, CA....................Insurance Defense

KOLCZYNSKI, PHILLIP J., LAW CORPORATION
Santa Ana, CA....................Aviation Law

KOLESAR & LEATHAM, CHARTERED
Las Vegas, NV....................Banking Law; Bankruptcy Law; Business Law; Commercial Litigation; Real Estate Law; Trust and Estates, Wills and Probate

KOLEY, JESSEN, DAUBMAN & RUPIPER, PROFESSIONAL CORPORATION
Omaha, NE....................General Practice

KOLLIN, GARY, P.A.
Fort Lauderdale, FL..............Criminal Trial Practice

KOLLMAN & SHEEHAN, P.A.
Baltimore, MD....................Business Law; Commercial Law; Construction Law; Labor and Employment Law

KOLODINSKY, SEITZ & TRESHER
Daytona Beach, FL..............Medical Malpractice; Personal Injury
New Smyrna Beach, FL..........Medical Malpractice; Personal Injury

KOLODNY & ANTEAU
Beverly Hills, CA....................Family Law

KOLVOORD, OVERTON AND WILSON
Essex Junction, VT....................General Practice

KOMPA, MARK A. LAW OFFICES OF
Newport Beach, CA..............Bankruptcy Law; Real Estate Law

KONCILJA & ASSOCIATES, P.C.
Denver, CO....................Civil Trial Practice; Commercial Litigation

KONIG, RICHARD W.
Stockton, CA....................Trust and Estates, Wills and Probate

KONOWIECKI & RANK LLP
Los Angeles, CA....................Corporate Law; Health Care Law; Mergers and Acquisitions; Securities Law

KOO, LARRABEE & LAU-KEE, LLP
Ardsley, NY....................Corporate Law

KOONS, FULLER, VANDEN EYKEL & ROBERTSON, A PROFESSIONAL CORPORATION
Dallas, TX....................Family Law
Plano, TX....................Family Law

KOONS, STEPHEN R., P.A.
West Palm Beach, FL..............Personal Injury

KOONZ, MCKENNEY, JOHNSON, DEPAOLIS & LIGHTFOOT
Washington, DC....................Personal Injury

KOOPERSMITH & BROWN, LLP
Lake Success, NY....................Family Law

KOPELMAN AND PAIGE, P.C.
Boston, MA....................Civil Trial Practice; Environmental Law; General Practice; Insurance Defense; International Business Law; Municipal and Zoning Law

KOPELOWITZ, HARVEY G.
Boca Raton, FL....................Business Law; Commercial Litigation; Real Estate Law

KOREY, SWEET, MCKINNON, SIMPSON & VUKELJA
Ormond Beach, FL....................General Practice; Real Estate Law

KORMEIER & WALTERS
Houston, TX....................Trust and Estates, Wills and Probate

KORN, ANDREW R., P.C.
Dallas, TX....................Commercial Litigation

KORN & COHN, PROFESSIONAL CORPORATION
Plymouth Meeting, PA............Construction Law

KORNBERG, HOWARD CRAIG
Los Angeles, CA....................Personal Injury

KORNIEVSKY, GEORGE M., A PROF. CORP., LAW OFFICES OF
Irvine, CA....................Family Law

KORTHALS, JOHN L.
Pompano Beach, FL....................Real Estate Law; Trust and Estates, Wills and Probate

KOSKI, ARTHUR C., P.A., LAW OFFICES OF
Boca Raton, FL....................Construction Law; Public Utilities Law

KOSKOFF, KOSKOFF & BIEDER, P.C.
Bridgeport, CT....................Aviation Law; Civil Rights; Commercial Litigation; Health Care Law; Medical Malpractice; Personal Injury; Product Liability Law; Toxic Torts

KOSTELANETZ & FINK, LLP
New York, NY....................Appellate Practice; Civil Trial Practice; Commercial Litigation; Criminal Trial Practice; Intellectual Property Law; Securities Law; Tax Law; Trust and Estates, Wills and Probate

KOZYAK TROPIN & THROCKMORTON, P.A.
Miami, FL....................Bankruptcy Law

KRAEMER, BURNS, MYTELKA, LOVELL & KULKA, P.A.
Springfield, NJ....................Business Law; Civil Trial Practice; Commercial Litigation

KRAGE & JANVEY, L.L.P.
Dallas, TX....................Appellate Practice; Civil Trial Practice; Commercial Litigation; Corporate Law; Creditors Rights; Real Estate Law; Securities Law; Tax Law

KRAMER, GILDA L.
Philadelphia, PA....................Civil Trial Practice

KRAMER, DILLOF, TESSEL, DUFFY & MOORE
New York, NY....................Civil Trial Practice; Medical Malpractice; Personal Injury

KRAMER, FEINGOLD & CASTROVINCI, PLLC
Commack, NY....................Civil Trial Practice; Family Law

KRAMER & FRANK, P.C.
St. Louis, MO....................Commercial Litigation; Creditors Rights

KRAMER LEVIN NAFTALIS & FRANKEL LLP
New York, NY....................Civil Trial Practice; General Practice

KRAMER, RAYSON, LEAKE, RODGERS & MORGAN, LLP
Knoxville, TN....................General Practice

KRAMON & GRAHAM, P.A.
Baltimore, MD....................General Practice

KRAMSKY, ELLIOTT N. LAW OFFICES OF
Woodland Hills, CA....................Patent, Trademark, Copyright and Unfair Competition

KRATHEN, DAVID, A PROF. ASSOC., THE LAW OFFICES OF
Fort Lauderdale, FL....................Medical Malpractice

KRATZIG, PAUL G. LAW OFFICES OF
Corpus Christi, TX....................Commercial Litigation; Criminal Trial Practice

KRAUS, SHERRY S.
Rochester, NY....................Tax Law

KRAVIT, GASS, HOVEL & LEITNER S.C.
Milwaukee, WI....................Insurance Defense

KRAVITZ, SCHNITZER & SLOANE, CHARTERED, A PROFESSIONAL CORPORATION
Las Vegas, NV....................Banking Law; Bankruptcy Law; Civil Trial Practice; Commercial Litigation; Insurance Defense; Real Estate Law

KREDER, BROOKS, HAILSTONE & LUDWIG
Scranton, PA....................Banking Law; Business Law; Civil Trial Practice; General Practice; Insurance Defense; Personal Injury; Product Liability Law

KREHBIEL, BANNERMAN & HORN, P.A.
Albuquerque, NM....................Commercial Law; Commercial Litigation; Health Care Law; Natural Resources Law

KREINDLER & KREINDLER
New York, NY....................Aviation Law; Medical Malpractice; Personal Injury; Product Liability Law

KREIS, ENDERLE, CALLANDER & HUDGINS, A PROFESSIONAL CORPORATION
Battle Creek, MI....................Banking Law; Bankruptcy Law; Business Law; Civil Trial Practice; Commercial Law; Construction Law; Corporate Law; Employment Benefits Law; Environmental Law; Family Law; General Practice; Health Care Law; Immigration and Naturalization; Labor and Employment Law; Mergers and Acquisitions; Municipal and Zoning Law; Real Estate Law; Tax Law; Trust and Estates, Wills and Probate
Kalamazoo, MI....................Banking Law; Bankruptcy Law; Business Law; Civil Trial Practice; Commercial Law; Construction Law; Corporate Law; Employment Benefits Law; Environmental Law; Family Law; General Practice; Health Care Law; Immigration and Naturalization; Labor and Employment Law; Mergers and Acquisitions; Municipal and Zoning Law; Real Estate Law; Tax Law; Trust and Estates, Wills and Probate

KREITZMAN, MORTENSEN, SIMON & IRGANG
New York, NY....................Labor and Employment Law

KREMBS & ALKIRE LLP
Cleveland, OH....................Commercial Litigation; Medical Malpractice; Personal Injury; Product Liability Law

KRETSCHMAN, KAREN L.
Austin, TX....................Family Law

KREUSLER-WALSH, JANE, P.A.
West Palm Beach, FL....................Appellate Practice

KREVOLIN & HORST, LLC
Atlanta, GA....................Business Law; Civil Trial Practice; Commercial Litigation; Corporate Law; Personal Injury; Real Estate Law

KRIEGER, ALBERT J., P.A.
Miami, FL....................Criminal Trial Practice

KRIEGER & KRIEGER
Omaha, NE....................Immigration and Naturalization

KRIGER, MARK J.
Detroit, MI....................Criminal Trial Practice

KRIST LAW FIRM, THE, P.C.
Houston, TX....................Civil Trial Practice; Personal Injury

KRISZTAL, RUBEN J.
Overland Park, KS....................Medical Malpractice

KRIVCHER MAGIDS PLC
Memphis, TN....................Bankruptcy Law; Commercial Law; Family Law; General Practice; Insurance Defense; Real Estate Law; Trust and Estates, Wills and Probate

KROLL, RUBIN & FIORELLA LLP
New York, NY....................General Practice

KROLOFF, BELCHER, SMART, PERRY & CHRISTOPHERSON
Stockton, CA....................General Practice

KRONEY • MINCEY, INC.
Dallas, TX....................Business Law; Trust and Estates, Wills and Probate

KRONTZ, KENNETH W., P.C.
Douglasville, GA....................Criminal Trial Practice; Family Law; Personal Injury

KROVITZ LAW FIRM, THE, P.C.
Englewood, CO....................Real Estate Law

KRUCHKO & FRIES
Baltimore, MD....................Labor and Employment Law
McLean, VA....................Labor and Employment Law

KRUEGER, JAMES, ATTORNEY AT LAW, A LAW CORPORATION
Honolulu, HI....................Civil Trial Practice; Medical Malpractice; Personal Injury; Product Liability Law
Lihue, HI....................Civil Trial Practice; Medical Malpractice; Personal Injury; Product Liability Law
Wailuku, HI....................Civil Trial Practice; Medical Malpractice; Personal Injury; Product Liability Law

KRUGER, ALLEN J., P.A.
Laurel, MD....................Family Law

KRUGLIAK, WILKINS, GRIFFITHS & DOUGHERTY CO., L.P.A.
Canton, OH....................General Practice

KRUGMAN & KAILES LLP
Saddle Brook, NJ....................Civil Trial Practice; Commercial Law; Commercial Litigation; Corporate Law; Environmental Law; General Practice; International Business Law; Securities Law; Tax Law; Trust and Estates, Wills and Probate

KRUKOWSKI & COSTELLO, S.C.
Milwaukee, WI....................Labor and Employment Law

KRUM, MARK JAY
Philadelphia, PA....................Civil Trial Practice; Criminal Trial Practice

KRUPIN GREENBAUM & O'BRIEN, LLC
Washington, DC....................Immigration and Naturalization; Labor and Employment Law

KRUPNICK CAMPBELL MALONE ROSELLI BUSER SLAMA HANCOCK MCNELIS LIBERMAN & MCKEE, P.A.
Fort Lauderdale, FL................Admiralty/Maritime Law; Aviation Law; Civil Trial Practice; Environmental Law; General Practice; Medical Malpractice; Personal Injury; Product Liability Law; Toxic Torts

KRYS BOYLE FREEDMAN & SAWYER, P.C.
Denver, CO ....Securities Law

KUBASIAK, CREMIEUX, FYLSTRA, REIZEN & ROTUNNO, PROFESSIONAL CORPORATION
Chicago, IL...............................Commercial Litigation

KUBICKI DRAPER
Fort Lauderdale, FL................Insurance Defense
Miami, FL.................................Insurance Defense
West Palm Beach, FL.............Insurance Defense

KUBOVCIK & KUBOVCIK
Washington, DC.......................Intellectual Property Law

KUHN & BELZ
Laguna Niguel, CA..................Personal Injury

KUMMER KAEMPFER BONNER & RENSHAW
Las Vegas, NV.........................Civil Trial Practice; Commercial Law; Insurance Defense; Securities Law

KUNIHOLM, ELIZABETH F.
Raleigh, NC.............................Medical Malpractice

KUNKEL MILLER & HAMENT
Fort Myers, FL........................Labor and Employment Law
Sarasota, FL............................Labor and Employment Law
Tampa, FL................................Labor and Employment Law

KUPFER, RICHARD A., P.A.
West Palm Beach, FL.............Appellate Practice

KURLBAUM STOLL SEAMAN & MUSTOE, P.C.
Kansas City, MO.....................Commercial Law; Corporate Law

KURRUS, THOMAS W.
Gainesville, FL........................Criminal Trial Practice

KURZMAN & EISENBERG, LLP
White Plains, NY.....................Trust and Estates, Wills and Probate

KUSSMAN & WHITEHILL
Los Angeles, CA......................Medical Malpractice; Personal Injury; Product Liability Law

KUTAK ROCK
Denver, CO..............................General Practice
Washington, DC.......................General Practice
Atlanta, GA.............................General Practice
Omaha, NE...............................General Practice

KUTNER, RUBINOFF, BUSH & LERNER
Miami, FL.................................Civil Trial Practice; General Practice

KUVIN & STETTIN, P.A.
Fort Lauderdale, FL................Medical Malpractice; Personal Injury

KWALL, SHOWERS & COLEMAN, P.A.
Clearwater, FL........................Administrative Law; Business Law; Civil Rights; Commercial Litigation; Criminal Trial Practice; General Practice; Labor and Employment Law; Personal Injury

KYNES, MARKMAN & FELMAN, P.A.
Tampa, FL................................Appellate Practice; Criminal Trial Practice

LABARRE, JEROME, A PROFESSIONAL CORPORATION
Portland, OR............................Civil Trial Practice; Securities Law

L'ABBATE, BALKAN, COLAVITA & CONTINI, L.L.P.
Garden City, NY.....................Civil Trial Practice; General Practice; Insurance Defense; Product Liability Law; Toxic Torts

LABE, ROBERT B., P.C.
Southfield, MI.........................Business Law; Tax Law; Trust and Estates, Wills and Probate

LABER, EDWARD HARRIS, LTD.
Tucson, AZ..............................Civil Trial Practice; Criminal Trial Practice

LACEY & JONES, LLP
Birmingham, MI.......................Civil Trial Practice; Insurance Defense; Labor and Employment Law; Workers Compensation

LACKEY, NUSBAUM, HARRIS, RENY & TORZEWSKI, A LEGAL PROFESSIONAL ASSOCIATION
Toledo, OH..............................Admiralty/Maritime Law; Family Law; Labor and Employment Law; Personal Injury; Product Liability Law

LACKEY, RODGERS, PRICE AND SNEDEKER
Nashville, TN...........................Civil Trial Practice

LACY, KATZEN, RYEN & MITTLEMAN, LLP
Rochester, NY..........................Bankruptcy Law; Family Law; General Practice; Personal Injury; Trust and Estates, Wills and Probate

LADAR & LADAR
San Francisco, CA..................Criminal Trial Practice

LADENDORF, MARK C. & ASSOCIATES
Indianapolis, IN.......................Medical Malpractice; Personal Injury

LADNER DOWNS
Vancouver, BC, Canada...........General Practice; Real Estate Law

LAFF STEIN CAMPBELL TUCKER & DELANEY, LLP
Denver, CO..............................Business Law; Real Estate Law

LAFF, WHITESEL & SARET, LTD., A PROFESSIONAL CORPORATION
Chicago, IL..............................Patent, Trademark, Copyright and Unfair Competition

LAFLEUR BROWN
Montreal, QU, Canada...........General Practice

LAGARENNÉ, LAWRENCE E.
Monticello, NY........................Civil Trial Practice

LAGERLOF, SENECAL, BRADLEY, GOSNEY & KRUSE, LLP
Los Angeles, CA.....................Civil Trial Practice; General Practice
Pasadena, CA..........................Administrative Law; Bankruptcy Law; Civil Trial Practice; Environmental Law; Municipal and Zoning Law; Natural Resources Law; Real Estate Law; Trust and Estates, Wills and Probate

LAGUE, NEWMAN & IRISH, A PROFESSIONAL CORPORATION
Muskegon, MI.........................Business Law; Civil Trial Practice; Corporate Law; Environmental Law; General Practice; Health Care Law; Medical Malpractice; Real Estate Law

LAHIVE & COCKFIELD, LLP
Boston, MA..............................Patent, Trademark, Copyright and Unfair Competition

LAIRD, DALLAS J.
Casper, WY..............................Civil Trial Practice

LAKE TINDALL, LLP
Greenville, MS........................Admiralty/Maritime Law; General Practice

LAKE, TOBACK & YAVITZ
Chicago, IL..............................Family Law

LALOS & KEEGAN
Washington, DC.......................Patent, Trademark, Copyright and Unfair Competition

LAMAR, BURGESS, HALE, MILLER, NORRIS & FELDMAN, P.C.
Birmingham, AL......................Civil Trial Practice

LAMARCA & LANDRY, P.C.
West Des Moines, IA..............Civil Trial Practice; Commercial Law; Commercial Litigation; Medical Malpractice; Personal Injury; Professional Liability; Workers Compensation

LAMB & BARNOSKY, LLP
Melville, NY............................Administrative Law; Appellate Practice; Banking Law; Business Law; Civil Trial Practice; Commercial Law; Computer Law; Corporate Law; Environmental Law; Health Care Law; International Business Law; Labor and Employment Law; Land Use Law; Mergers and Acquisitions; Municipal and Zoning Law; Real Estate Law; Securities Law; Tax Law; Trust and Estates, Wills and Probate

LAMBDIN, JOHNSON, HERLOCKER, SODERBERG & LAMBDIN, CHARTERED
Wichita, KS.............................Family Law

LAMBERT, JAY
Louisville, KY.........................Criminal Trial Practice

LAMBERT, PAUL WATSON
Tallahassee, FL.......................Health Care Law

LAMBERT & ROFFMAN, L.L.C.
Madison, GA............................General Practice

LAMBERTH, BONAPFEL, CIFELLI & STOKES, P.A.
Atlanta, GA.............................Bankruptcy Law; Business Law; Creditors Rights

LAMBOS & JUNGE
New York, NY.........................Admiralty/Maritime Law; Civil Trial Practice; Labor and Employment Law

LAMKIN, VAN EMAN, TRIMBLE, BEALS & ROURKE
Columbus, OH.........................Civil Trial Practice; Medical Malpractice; Personal Injury; Product Liability Law

LAMMERS, LAMMERS & KLEIBACKER, L.L.P.
Madison, SD............................General Practice

LAMPF, LIPKIND, PRUPIS, PETIGROW & LABUE, A PROFESSIONAL CORPORATION
West Orange, NJ....................Tax Law; Trust and Estates, Wills and Probate

LANDAU, JULIE ELLEN LAW OFFICE OF
Baltimore, MD........................Family Law

LAND, CLARK, CARROLL, MENDELSON & BLAIR, P.C.
Alexandria, VA........................General Practice

LANDELS RIPLEY & DIAMOND, LLP
San Francisco, CA.................General Practice

LANDERS & PARSONS
Tallahassee, FL......................Energy Law; Environmental Law

LANDIS, GRAHAM, FRENCH, HUSFELD, SHERMAN & FORD, P.A.
Daytona Beach, FL..................Criminal Trial Practice; General Practice; Personal Injury; Trust and Estates, Wills and Probate
DeLand, FL..............................General Practice; Personal Injury; Trust and Estates, Wills and Probate
Deltona, FL..............................General Practice; Trust and Estates, Wills and Probate

LANDOE, BROWN, PLANALP, BRAAKSMA & REIDA, P.C.
Bozeman, MT...........................General Practice

LANDRUM & LANDRUM
Jasper, GA...............................General Practice

LANDRUM & SHOUSE
Lexington, KY..........................Appellate Practice; General Practice; Insurance Defense
Louisville, KY..........................Civil Rights; Civil Trial Practice

LANDRY & WATKINS
New Iberia, LA........................General Practice; Insurance Defense

LANDSMAN, RON M., P.A.
Bethesda, MD..........................Trust and Estates, Wills and Probate

LANDWEHR & HOF
New Orleans, LA.....................Bankruptcy Law; Trust and Estates, Wills and Probate

LANE, AITKEN & MCCANN, L.L.P.
Washington, DC......................Patent, Trademark, Copyright and Unfair Competition

LANE & EHRLICH, LTD.
Phoenix, AZ............................Business Law; Tax Law; Trust and Estates, Wills and Probate

LANE, FERTITTA, JANNEY & THOMAS
Baton Rouge, LA.....................Insurance Defense; Medical Malpractice; Personal Injury; Product Liability Law

LANE, GANNON & TALIAFERRO, L.L.P.
San Antonio, TX......................Aviation Law; Commercial Litigation; Insurance Defense; Product Liability Law

LANE & LANE
Chicago, IL..............................Medical Malpractice; Personal Injury

LANE, LANE AND KELLY
Braintree, MA.........................General Practice

LANE, MARC J., A PROF. CORP., THE LAW OFFICES OF
Chicago, IL..............................Business Law; Tax Law

LANE POWELL SPEARS LUBERSKY LLP
Portland, OR...........................Antitrust Law; General Practice; Labor and Employment Law
Seattle, WA.............................Antitrust Law; Bankruptcy Law; Civil Trial Practice; Environmental Law; General Practice; Labor and Employment Law; Land Use Law; Real Estate Law; Tax Law

LANE, REESE, AULICK, SUMMERS & FIELD, P.A.
Coral Gables, FL.....................Admiralty/Maritime Law; Appellate Practice; Civil Trial Practice; Insurance Defense; Professional Liability

LANE, TROHN, BERTRAND & VREELAND, P.A.
Lakeland, FL...........................Civil Trial Practice; General Practice

LANE & WATERMAN
Rock Island, IL.......................General Practice
Davenport, IA.........................General Practice

LANER, MUCHIN, DOMBROW, BECKER, LEVIN AND TOMINBERG, LTD.
Chicago, IL..............................Employment Benefits Law; Labor and Employment Law

LANG MICHENER
Ottawa, ON, Canada...............General Practice
Toronto, ON, Canada..............General Practice

LANG & MORGERA, L.L.P.
Boston, MA.............................Medical Malpractice; Personal Injury; Product Liability Law

LANG, RICHERT & PATCH, A PROFESSIONAL CORPORATION
Fresno, CA..............................Bankruptcy Law; Civil Trial Practice; Construction Law; Environmental Law; General Practice; Labor and Employment Law; Medical Malpractice; Personal Injury; Real Estate Law

LANGAN, DEMPSEY AND BRODIGAN
Boston, MA.............................Civil Trial Practice; Construction Law

LANGLAIS & SCHUMACHER, P.A.
Hastings, MN..........................Real Estate Law; Tax Law

LANIER, PARKER & SULLIVAN, P.C.
Houston, TX............................Appellate Practice; Commercial Litigation; Medical Malpractice; Personal Injury; Product Liability Law

LANKLER SIFFERT & WOHL LLP
New York, NY.........................Appellate Practice; Civil Trial Practice; Commercial Litigation; Criminal Trial Practice

LANO, NELSON, O'TOOLE & BENGTSON, LTD.
Grand Rapids, MN..................Civil Trial Practice; Insurance Defense

LANSDEN, MITCHELL BAYLOR
Houston, TX............................Criminal Trial Practice

LAPPAS, SPERO T. THE LAW OFFICES OF
Harrisburg, PA........................Criminal Trial Practice; Personal Injury

LAPPIN & KUSMER LLP
Boston, MA.............................Patent, Trademark, Copyright and Unfair Competition

LAPUYADE, WASHINGTON & MOLK, LLC
Denver, CO.............................Commercial Litigation; Professional Liability

LARA, ART B. JR.
Amarillo, TX...........................Civil Trial Practice; General Practice

LARKY, SHELDON G.
Bingham Farms, MI................Family Law

LAROE, WINN, MOERMAN & DONOVAN
Washington, DC......................Transportation Law

LA ROSSA & ROSS
New York, NY.........................Criminal Trial Practice; General Practice

LARSON, RONALD F., P.C.
Sun City, AZ...........................Trust and Estates, Wills and Probate

LARSON & TAYLOR
Alexandria, VA.......................Patent, Trademark, Copyright and Unfair Competition

LASCHER & LASCHER, A PROFESSIONAL CORPORATION
Ventura, CA............................Appellate Practice; International Business Law

LASER, WILSON, BUFFORD & WATTS, P.A.
Little Rock, AR.......................Civil Trial Practice; Education Law; General Practice, Insurance Defense; Medical Malpractice; Workers Compensation

LASH & GOLDBERG LLP
Miami, FL...............................Commercial Litigation

LASKY, HAAS & COHLER, PROFESSIONAL CORPORATION
San Francisco, CA..................Civil Trial Practice

LASPADA, ANTHONY J., P.A.
Tampa, FL...............................Criminal Trial Practice; Personal Injury

LASSER, MYRON G., P.C.
Staten Island, NY...................Personal Injury

LASTER, G. A.
San Mateo, CA........................Business Law; Municipal Bond/Public Authority Financing

LATHAM & WATKINS
Los Angeles, CA.....................General Practice

LATHROP & CLARK, LLP
Madison, WI...........................General Practice; Patent, Trademark, Copyright and Unfair Competition; Trademark, Copyright and Unfair Competition

LATHROP & RUTLEDGE, A PROFESSIONAL CORPORATION
Cheyenne, WY........................Civil Trial Practice; General Practice; Insurance Defense

LAUB & FRANCHINO, L.L.C., LAW OFFICES OF
Raritan, NJ.............................Insurance Defense; Product Liability Law

LAUCHENGCO, JOSÉ Y. JR.
Los Angeles, CA .... Civil Trial Practice; Criminal Trial Practice; Personal Injury

LAUER, PHILIP D., P.C.
Easton, PA .... Civil Trial Practice; Criminal Trial Practice

LAUFMAN, ALAN K., J.D., M.D., A PROF. CORP., LAW OFFICES OF
Dallas, TX .... Medical Malpractice; Personal Injury; Product Liability Law

LAUGHLIN AND BOWEN
Hilton Head Island, SC .... Admiralty/Maritime Law; Civil Trial Practice; Construction Law

LAUGHLIN, PETERSON & LANG
Omaha, NE .... Civil Trial Practice; General Practice; Real Estate Law; Tax Law; Trust and Estates, Wills and Probate

LAURO, JOHN F., P.A.
Tampa, FL .... Commercial Litigation; Criminal Trial Practice

LAUTSCH LAW CORPORATION
Newport Beach, CA .... Business Law

LAVELLE, WILLIAM A.
Athens, OH .... Trust and Estates, Wills and Probate

LAVERY, DE BILLY
Montreal, QU, Canada .... General Practice
Quebec, QU, Canada .... General Practice

LAVIN, COLEMAN, O'NEIL, RICCI, FINARELLI & GRAY
New York, NY .... Civil Trial Practice; Insurance Defense; Product Liability Law
Philadelphia, PA .... Civil Trial Practice; Insurance Defense; Product Liability Law

LAW, SNAKARD & GAMBILL, A PROFESSIONAL CORPORATION
Fort Worth, TX .... Business Law; Commercial Litigation; General Practice

LAWING SHARPLESS & STAVOLA, P.A.
Greensboro, NC .... Civil Trial Practice; General Practice; Medical Malpractice

LAWLER, ANDREW M., P.C.
New York, NY .... Criminal Trial Practice

LAWRENCE, WILLIAM V.
Craig, CO .... Trust and Estates, Wills and Probate

LAWRENCE, BACA & DONOHUE PLLC
Houston, TX .... Bankruptcy Law

LAWRENCE FIRM, THE, L.P.A.
Cincinnati, OH .... Medical Malpractice; Personal Injury; Product Liability Law

LAWRENCE, KAMIN, SAUNDERS & UHLENHOP
Chicago, IL .... Civil Trial Practice; Construction Law; Corporate Law; Labor and Employment Law; Securities Law

LAWRENCE AND LAWRENCE
Louisville, KY .... Trust and Estates, Wills and Probate

LAWRENCE AND WALSH, P.C.
Hempstead, NY .... Business Law

LAWRENCE, WERNER, KESSELRING, SWARTOUT & BROWN, LLP
Rochester, NY .... Banking Law; Bankruptcy Law; Commercial Law; Commercial Litigation; Creditors Rights; Municipal and Zoning Law; Trust and Estates, Wills and Probate

LAWS & MURDOCH, P.A.
Russellville, AR .... General Practice

LAWSON, KIPP, FORBES & AYRES
Fairfax, VA .... Civil Trial Practice

LAWSON LUNDELL LAWSON & MCINTOSH
Vancouver, BC, Canada .... General Practice

LAWSON, WILLIAM M., JR., P.A.
Phoenix, AZ .... Real Estate Law

LAWTON & CATES, S.C.
Madison, WI .... Civil Trial Practice; Construction Law; Criminal Trial Practice; Labor and Employment Law; Personal Injury

LAXALT & NOMURA, LTD.
Reno, NV .... Civil Trial Practice

LAYDEN & LAYDEN
Lafayette, IN .... Civil Trial Practice; General Practice

LAZARUS, PAUL D.
Miami, FL .... Criminal Trial Practice

LAZARUS & ASSOCIATES, A PROFESSIONAL CORPORATION
Phoenix, AZ .... Land Use Law; Municipal and Zoning Law

LAZZARO AND KRAUS
Cleveland, OH .... Family Law

LEA, ARDEN J. LAW OFFICES OF
Fort Walton Beach, FL .... Admiralty/Maritime Law; Insurance Defense

LEACH, RAY
San Antonio, TX .... Civil Trial Practice; Personal Injury

LEACH, KENNETH C., P.C.
Albuquerque, NM .... Business Law; Corporate Law; Oil and Gas Law; Real Estate Law; Trust and Estates, Wills and Probate

LEACH, MCGREEVY & BAUTISTA, LLP
San Francisco, CA .... Construction Law; Environmental Law; Insurance Defense; Medical Malpractice; Product Liability Law; Workers Compensation

LEACH, SULLIVAN, SULLIVAN & WATKINS
Duncan, OK .... General Practice; Trust and Estates, Wills and Probate

LEAHEY & JOHNSON, P.C.
New York, NY .... Civil Trial Practice; Construction Law; Insurance Defense; Medical Malpractice; Product Liability Law

LEAHY & DENAULT, LLP
Claremont, NH .... General Practice

LEAKE, ANDERSSON & MANN, L.L.P.
New Orleans, LA .... Civil Trial Practice; Commercial Law; Construction Law; General Practice; Insurance Defense

LEARY, BRIDE, TINKER & MORAN, A PROFESSIONAL CORPORATION
Cedar Knolls, NJ .... Civil Trial Practice; Construction Law; Environmental Law; Insurance Defense; Product Liability Law

LEATH, BOUCH & CRAWFORD, L.L.P.
Charleston, SC .... Construction Law; Creditors Rights; Environmental Law; Toxic Torts

LEATHERMAN, WITZLER, DOMBEY & HART
Perrysburg, OH .... General Practice; Trust and Estates, Wills and Probate

LEATHERWOOD WALKER TODD & MANN, P.C.
Greenville, SC .... Antitrust Law; Bankruptcy Law; Civil Trial Practice; Construction Law; Environmental Law; General Practice; Health Care Law; Insurance Defense; Patent, Trademark, Copyright and Unfair Competition; Real Estate Law; Tax Law; Transportation Law
Spartanburg, SC .... Civil Trial Practice; General Practice; Insurance Defense

LEAVELL, JEFFREY, S.C.
Racine, WI .... Civil Trial Practice; Environmental Law; Insurance Defense

LEAVY, SCHULTZ, DAVIS & FEARING, P.S.
Kennewick, WA .... General Practice

LEBEAU, CHARLES P. LAW OFFICES OF
San Diego, CA .... Business Law; International Business Law; Tax Law

LEBLANC & YOUNG
Portland, ME .... Tax Law; Trust and Estates, Wills and Probate

LEBOVITS & DAVID, A PROFESSIONAL CORPORATION
Los Angeles, CA .... Aviation Law; Civil Trial Practice; Personal Injury; Product Liability Law

LECLAIR RYAN, A PROFESSIONAL CORPORATION
Richmond, VA .... Administrative Law; Appellate Practice; Bankruptcy Law; Business Law; Civil Trial Practice; Health Care Law; Immigration and Naturalization; Labor and Employment Law; Patent, Trademark, Copyright and Unfair Competition; Product Liability Law; Real Estate Law; Securities Law; Tax Law

LEDBETTER, COGBILL, ARNOLD & HARRISON, LLP
Fort Smith, AR .... General Practice; Insurance Defense; Medical Malpractice; Product Liability Law; Workers Compensation

LEDGEWOOD LAW FIRM, A PROFESSIONAL CORPORATION
Philadelphia, PA .... Trust and Estates, Wills and Probate

LEDY-GURREN & BLUMENSTOCK, L.L.P.
New York, NY .... Insurance Defense; Product Liability Law; Toxic Torts

LEE, DAVID L. LAW OFFICES OF
Chicago, IL..............................Labor and Employment Law

LEE, ROTAN E.
Philadelphia, PA.....................Corporate Law; Municipal Bond/Public Authority Financing

LEE, BLACK, SCHEER & HART, P.C.
Savannah, GA..........................Business Law; Civil Trial Practice; General Practice; Real Estate Law

LEE, DUROCHER, KISNER, WALKER & REID
Oklahoma City, OK................Civil Trial Practice; Insurance Defense; Medical Malpractice; Personal Injury; Product Liability Law; Professional Liability

LEE, EADON, ISGETT AND POPWELL, P.A.
Columbia, SC..........................Medical Malpractice; Personal Injury; Product Liability Law; Workers Compensation

LEE, ERTER, WILSON, HOLLER & SMITH, L.L.C.
Sumter, SC..............................Civil Trial Practice; Criminal Trial Practice; Family Law; Insurance Defense

LEE, FUTRELL & PERLES, L.L.P.
New Orleans, LA....................Admiralty/Maritime Law; Civil Trial Practice; Energy Law; General Practice; Insurance Defense; Toxic Torts

LEE, GODDARD & DUFFY LLP
Irvine, CA...............................Business Law; Civil Trial Practice

LEE, JOHN PETER, LTD.
Las Vegas, NV........................Bankruptcy Law; Business Law; Civil Trial Practice; Commercial Litigation; General Practice; Real Estate Law; Trust and Estates, Wills and Probate

LEE, LEE & GARNER
Whiteville, NC........................General Practice

LEE, MARTIN, GREEN & REITER, INC.
Bellefonte, PA........................General Practice
State College, PA...................General Practice

LEE & MCINISH
Dothan, AL..............................Civil Trial Practice; General Practice; Insurance Defense; Product Liability Law

LEE, ROBERT W., & ASSOCIATES, P.C.
Birmingham, AL.....................Personal Injury

LEE, SMART, COOK, MARTIN & PATTERSON, P.S., INC.
Seattle, WA............................Insurance Defense

LEESFIELD, LEIGHTON, RUBIO & MAHFOOD, P.A.
Miami, FL...............................Civil Trial Practice; General Practice

LEFEBVRE, BARRON & VIVONE, CHTD.
Las Vegas, NV.......................Civil Trial Practice; Construction Law; Insurance Defense; Personal Injury; Product Liability Law; Toxic Torts

LEFEBVRE, FRANCIS, BUREAU
New York, NY........................Business Law; Tax Law

LEFFLER, HYLAND & THOMPSON, A PROFESSIONAL CORPORATION
Fairfax, VA............................Civil Trial Practice; Criminal Trial Practice; Labor and Employment Law; Real Estate Law

LEFTWICH & DOUGLAS, P.L.L.C.
Washington, DC.....................General Practice

LEGAL STRATEGIES GROUP
Emeryville, CA.......................Civil Trial Practice; General Practice; Intellectual Property Law

LEGER & MESTAYER
New Orleans, LA....................Admiralty/Maritime Law

LEGROS LAW PARTNERS, P.C.
Berwyn, PA.............................Environmental Law

LEHMAN & EILEN, LLP
Uniondale, NY........................Business Law; Civil Trial Practice; Securities Law; Trademark, Copyright and Unfair Competition

LEHNER, MITCHELL, RODRIGUES AND SEARS
Portland, OR..........................Insurance Defense

LEHR MIDDLEBROOKS PRICE & PROCTOR, P.C.
Birmingham, AL.....................Labor and Employment Law

LEIB & KATT, S.C.
Milwaukee, WI........................Civil Trial Practice

LEIBOWITZ & COHEN
Knoxville, TN..........................Business Law; Civil Trial Practice; Construction Law; Criminal Trial Practice; Labor and Employment Law; Land Use Law; Medical Malpractice; Personal Injury; Trust and Estates, Wills and Probate

LEIBOWITZ, MARTIN L., P.A.
Jacksonville, FL.....................Workers Compensation

LEIBY CONSTRUCTION LAW FIRM, PROFESSIONAL ASSOCIATION
Fort Lauderdale, FL...............Construction Law; Government Contracts

LEICK, HAMMONS AND BRITTAIN
Corbin, KY..............................General Practice

LEINOFF, ANDREW M., & ASSOCIATES, P.A.
Miami, FL...............................Family Law

LEISAWITZ HELLER ABRAMOWITCH PHILLIPS, P.C.
Wyomissing, PA.....................Bankruptcy Law; Commercial Litigation; Mergers and Acquisitions; Personal Injury; Real Estate Law

LEITER, WILLIAM
Tulsa, OK...............................Trust and Estates, Wills and Probate

LEITNER, WILLIAMS, DOOLEY & NAPOLITAN, PLLC
Chattanooga, TN....................General Practice
Knoxville, TN..........................General Practice
Memphis, TN..........................General Practice
Nashville, TN.........................General Practice

LELAND, PARACHINI, STEINBERG, MATZGER & MELNICK, L.L.P.
San Francisco, CA.................General Practice

LEMON, ARMEY, HEARN & LEININGER
Warsaw, IN............................Civil Trial Practice; Corporate Law; Product Liability Law; Trust and Estates, Wills and Probate

LEMON, SHEARER, EHRLICH, PHILLIPS & GOOD, A PROFESSIONAL CORPORATION
Perryton, TX..........................Civil Trial Practice; General Practice; Natural Resources Law

LENAHAN & DEMPSEY, A PROFESSIONAL CORPORATION
Scranton, PA.........................Civil Trial Practice; General Practice; Insurance Defense; Personal Injury; Securities Law; Workers Compensation

LEON, AMBERSON & CARROLL, L.L.P.
San Antonio, TX....................Civil Trial Practice; Criminal Trial Practice

LEONARD FELKER ALTFELD GREENBERG & BATTAILE, P.C.
Tucson, AZ............................Bankruptcy Law; Civil Trial Practice; Commercial Litigation; Real Estate Law

LEONARD & MORRISON
Fort Lauderdale, FL...............Real Estate Law; Trust and Estates, Wills and Probate

LEONARD, STREET AND DEINARD, PROFESSIONAL ASSOCIATION
Minneapolis, MN...................General Practice

LEONE, LAWRENCE E.
Los Angeles, CA...................Family Law

LEOPOLD, PETRICH & SMITH, A PROFESSIONAL CORPORATION
Los Angeles, CA...................Civil Trial Practice; Trademark, Copyright and Unfair Competition

LEPLEY, PATRICK H.
Bellevue, WA.........................Personal Injury

LEPRELL, SAMUEL L.
Jacksonville, FL.....................Business Law; Real Estate Law

LERNER, DAVID, LITTENBERG, KRUMHOLZ & MENTLIK
Westfield, NJ.........................Patent, Trademark, Copyright and Unfair Competition

LERUM, NORMAN J.
Chicago, IL............................Appellate Practice; Civil Trial Practice; Commercial Litigation

LESLIE & SMITH, P.C.
El Paso, TX...........................Bankruptcy Law

LESS, GETZ & LIPMAN
Memphis, TN.........................Construction Law

LESSER & SOBEL, P.C.
Bridgeport, CT.......................Civil Trial Practice; Personal Injury; Real Estate Law

LEUPP, WACHOB & WOODALL
Auburn, CA............................Criminal Trial Practice; Insurance Defense

LEVENE, NEALE, BENDER & RANKIN L.L.P.
Los Angeles, CA...................Bankruptcy Law

LEVENS, WILLIAM P.
Tampa, FL.............................Personal Injury; Workers Compensation

LEVENTHAL LAW FIRM, THE, P.C.
Denver, CO...........................Civil Trial Practice; Medical Malpractice; Personal Injury

LEVENTHAL & SLAUGHTER, P.A.
Orlando, FL ....Criminal Trial Practice

LEVERTY & ASSOCIATES LAW, CHARTERED
Reno, NV ....Administrative Law; Civil Trial Practice

LEVETT ROCKWOOD P.C.
Westport, CT............................Business Law; General Practice; Health Care Law; Labor and Employment Law; Patent, Trademark, Copyright and Unfair Competition; Tax Law

LEVIN, MARK
Roseland, NJ............................Tax Law; Trust and Estates, Wills and Probate

LEVIN, FISHBEIN, SEDRAN & BERMAN
Philadelphia, PA ....Admiralty/Maritime Law; Antitrust Law; Civil Trial Practice; Commercial Litigation; Environmental Law; General Practice; Medical Malpractice; Product Liability Law; Securities Law

LEVIN & GILLEY
Beaufort, SC ....General Practice; Real Estate Law; Trust and Estates, Wills and Probate

LEVIN, MARMAROS & CHARMS CO., L.P.A.
Cleveland, OH............................Commercial Litigation; Medical Malpractice; Personal Injury; Product Liability Law

LEVIN, MICHAEL I., AND ASSOCIATES, P.C.
Huntingdon Valley, PA ....Labor and Employment Law

LEVINE, AARON M. & ASSOCIATES
Washington, DC............................Medical Malpractice; Personal Injury; Product Liability Law

LEVINE & ASSOCIATES
Los Angeles, CA ....Business Law

LEVINE, BLASZAK, BLOCK & BOOTHBY, LLP
Washington, DC............................Communications Law

LEVINE, BUSCH, SCHNEPPER & STEIN, P.A.
Miami, FL ....Medical Malpractice; Personal Injury; Workers Compensation

LEVINE, CARL S., & ASSOCIATES, P.C.
Roslyn, NY ....Commercial Litigation

LEVINE, HIRSCH, SEGALL & BRENNAN, P.A.
Tampa, FL ....Civil Trial Practice; Criminal Trial Practice; Family Law; Personal Injury

LEVINE & PARTNERS, P.A.
Miami, FL ....Commercial Litigation; General Practice; Insurance Defense

LEVINE, STEINBERG & MILLER
San Diego, CA ....Civil Trial Practice; Personal Injury

LEVINE SULLIVAN & KOCH, L.L.P.
Washington, DC............................Communications Law; Intellectual Property Law

LEVINE AND YATES, P.C.
Arlington, VA ....Immigration and Naturalization

LEVINGSTON & LEVINGSTON
Cleveland, MS............................Bankruptcy Law; Corporate Law

LEVIT, MANN & HALLIGAN, P.C.
Richmond, VA............................Labor and Employment Law

LEVY, HERBERT MONTE
New York, NY............................Appellate Practice

LEVY, ANGSTREICH, FINNEY, BALDANTE, RUBENSTEIN & COREN, P.C.
Philadelphia, PA ....Civil Trial Practice; Commercial Litigation

LEVY, EHRLICH & PETRIELLO, A PROFESSIONAL CORPORATION
Newark, NJ ....General Practice; Tax Law; Trust and Estates, Wills and Probate

LEVY, JAMES L., P.C.
St. Albans, VT ....Personal Injury

LEVY & LAMBDIN, P.C.
Denver, CO ....Civil Trial Practice; Commercial Litigation; Environmental Law; Insurance Defense

LEVY, STEVEN B., LTD.
Naperville, IL............................Civil Trial Practice; Medical Malpractice; Personal Injury
Wheaton, IL ....Civil Trial Practice; Medical Malpractice; Personal Injury

LEWALLEN, JO BETSY LAW OFFICES OF
Austin, TX ....Family Law

LEWANDOWSKI LAW FIRM, THE, A PROFESSIONAL CORPORATION
Kansas City, MO ....Transportation Law

LEWIS, JOHN B.
Sacramento, CA ....Civil Trial Practice

LEWIS & ALLEN, P.C.
Kalamazoo, MI ....Business Law; Commercial Law; Commercial Litigation; Corporate Law; Family Law; General Practice; Labor and Employment Law; Real Estate Law; Trust and Estates, Wills and Probate

LEWIS & ASSOCIATES
Beaumont, TX............................Civil Trial Practice; Insurance Defense

LEWIS, BABCOCK & HAWKINS, L.L.P.
Columbia, SC ....Civil Trial Practice

LEWIS, D'AMATO, BRISBOIS & BISGAARD LLP
Los Angeles, CA ....General Practice

LEWIS, FISHER, HENDERSON & CLAXTON, LLP
Memphis, TN ....Labor and Employment Law

LEWIS & GREER, P.C.
Poughkeepsie, NY ....Construction Law; Municipal and Zoning Law; Public Utilities Law; Real Estate Law

LEWIS & KAPPES, PROFESSIONAL CORPORATION
Indianapolis, IN ....General Practice; Immigration and Naturalization; Public Utilities Law

LEWIS, KULLMAN & STERBCOW
New Orleans, LA ....Admiralty/Maritime Law; Medical Malpractice; Personal Injury

LEWIS LAW FIRM, THE, A PROFESSIONAL CORPORATION
Washington, DC............................Family Law

LEWIS & MUNDAY, A PROFESSIONAL CORPORATION
Washington, DC............................Environmental Law; Municipal Bond/Public Authority Financing; Securities Law
Boston, MA............................Municipal Bond/Public Authority Financing; Securities Law
Detroit, MI............................Banking Law; Business Law; Civil Trial Practice; Environmental Law; Health Care Law; Municipal Bond/Public Authority Financing; Real Estate Law; Securities Law; Transportation Law

LEWIS & PRESTON
Elizabethtown, KY ....General Practice

LEWIS, RICE & FINGERSH
St. Louis, MO............................Admiralty/Maritime Law; Antitrust Law; Civil Trial Practice; General Practice; Labor and Employment Law; Municipal Bond/Public Authority Financing; Tax Law

LEWIS & ROBERTS, P.L.L.C.
Raleigh, NC............................Construction Law; Insurance Defense; Workers Compensation

LEWIS AND ROCA, LLP
Phoenix, AZ ....Antitrust Law; Banking Law; Bankruptcy Law; Business Law; Civil Trial Practice; Commercial Law; Criminal Trial Practice; Environmental Law; General Practice; Health Care Law; Labor and Employment Law; Real Estate Law; Securities Law; Tax Law; Trademark, Copyright and Unfair Competition
Tucson, AZ ....Real Estate Law

LEWIS, ROGERS & KUDRLE, P.C.
Plattsburgh, NY............................Banking Law; Corporate Law; General Practice; Municipal and Zoning Law; Trust and Estates, Wills and Probate

LEWIS, TAYLOR, TODD & DIXON, P.C.
La Grange, GA ....General Practice

LEYDIG, VOIT & MAYER, LTD.
Washington, DC............................Patent, Trademark, Copyright and Unfair Competition
Chicago, IL............................Patent, Trademark, Copyright and Unfair Competition
Rockford, IL ....Patent, Trademark, Copyright and Unfair Competition

LIBERT, JACK L. LAW OFFICES OF
Garden City, NY ....Municipal and Zoning Law

LIBERT, VICTOR E., LAW OFFICE OF
Simsbury, CT............................Patent, Trademark, Copyright and Unfair Competition

LICATA, ARTHUR F., P.C.
Boston, MA............................Civil Trial Practice

LICCARDO, ROSSI, STURGES & MCNEIL, A PROFESSIONAL LAW CORPORATION
San Jose, CA ....Personal Injury; Product Liability Law; Real Estate Law; Trust and Estates, Wills and Probate

LICHTENAUER, ROBERT A.
Indianapolis, IN ....Tax Law; Trust and Estates, Wills and Probate

LIDDLE & ROBINSON, L.L.P.
New York, NY........................Civil Trial Practice; Family Law; Labor and Employment Law

LIEBER & LIEBER
New York, NY........................Insurance Defense; Product Liability Law

LIEBERMAN, MAX L. & ASSOCIATES
Fort Washington, PA..............Real Estate Law

LIEBERMAN, DODGE, SENDROW & GERDING, LTD.
Phoenix, AZ ....Commercial Litigation; Real Estate Law

LIEBERMAN, MARTIN, P.C.
Phoenix, AZ ....Criminal Trial Practice

LIEBERMAN & NOWAK, LLP
New York, NY........................Patent, Trademark, Copyright and Unfair Competition

LIEBERTHAL, DAVID H.
Tucson, AZ ....Family Law

LIEFF, CABRASER, HEIMANN & BERNSTEIN, LLP
San Francisco, CA ....Antitrust Law; Civil Trial Practice; Environmental Law; Labor and Employment Law; Product Liability Law; Securities Law

LIGGIO, BENRUBI & WILLIAMS, P.A.
West Palm Beach, FL ....Civil Trial Practice; Health Care Law; Personal Injury

LIGHTCAP, ROBERT P.
Latrobe, PA.............................Construction Law

LIGHTFOOT, FRANKLIN & WHITE, L.L.C.
Birmingham, AL ....Antitrust Law; Appellate Practice; Civil Trial Practice; Commercial Litigation; Construction Law; Environmental Law; Labor and Employment Law; Personal Injury; Product Liability Law; Securities Law

LIGHTMAN, MANOCHI & KORNILOWICZ
Philadelphia, PA ....Civil Trial Practice

LIGMAN, MARTIN & EVANS, P.L.
Miami, FL ....Commercial Law; Insurance Defense

LILES, GAVIN & COSTANTINO
Jacksonville, FL.....................Civil Trial Practice; Commercial Litigation; Medical Malpractice; Personal Injury; Product Liability Law

LILLY, ANDERSON, MORGAN
Toronto, ON, Canada.............Insurance Defense

LIMANDRI, CHARLES S.
Rancho Santa Fe, CA.............Civil Trial Practice

LIMBACH & LIMBACH, L.L.P.
San Francisco, CA ....Patent, Trademark, Copyright and Unfair Competition

LIM, RUGER & KIM, LLP
Los Angeles, CA.....................Civil Trial Practice

LINDABURY, MCCORMICK & ESTABROOK, P.A.
Westfield, NJ ....Banking Law; Civil Trial Practice; Commercial Law; Construction Law; General Practice; Health Care Law; Labor and Employment Law; Municipal Bond/Public Authority Financing; Public Utilities Law; Real Estate Law; Tax Law

LINDER & HOLLOWELL, A PROFESSIONAL CORPORATION
Indianapolis, IN ....Insurance Defense

LINDHORST & DREIDAME CO., L.P.A.
Cincinnati, OH ....Civil Trial Practice; General Practice; Insurance Defense; Medical Malpractice

LINDLEY, SCALES & CORBETT, A PROFESSIONAL CORPORATION
San Diego, CA ....Banking Law; Business Law; Civil Trial Practice; Commercial Law; Commercial Litigation; Creditors Rights; Health Care Law; Professional Liability; Real Estate Law

LINDNER & MARSACK, S.C.
Milwaukee, WI ....Labor and Employment Law

LINDOW & TREAT, L.L.P.
San Antonio, TX.....................Insurance Defense

LINDSAY, HART, NEIL & WEIGLER, LLP
Portland, OR...........................Admiralty/Maritime Law; Antitrust Law; Labor and Employment Law

LINES, HINSON AND LINES
Quincy, FL..............................General Practice

LINIAK, BERENATO, LONGACRE & WHITE, LLC
Bethesda, MD ....Patent, Trademark, Copyright and Unfair Competition

LINNE, WILLIAM V.
Pensacola, FL..........................Tax Law; Trust and Estates, Wills and Probate

LINOWES AND BLOCHER LLP
Silver Spring, MD ....Bankruptcy Law; Business Law; Commercial Litigation; Environmental Law; General Practice; Land Use Law; Municipal and Zoning Law; Real Estate Law

LIONEL SAWYER & COLLINS
Las Vegas, NV ....Bankruptcy Law; Civil Trial Practice; General Practice; Labor and Employment Law; Land Use Law; Real Estate Law
Reno, NV ....General Practice

LIPKIN, STANLEY G.
Denver, CO ....Family Law

LIPKIN, MARSHALL, BOHORAD & THORNBURG, A PROFESSIONAL CORPORATION
Pottsville, PA ....General Practice

LIPMAN, ANTONELLI, BATT, DUNLAP, WODLINGER & GILSON, A PROFESSIONAL CORPORATION
Vineland, NJ...........................Civil Trial Practice; General Practice

LIPMAN & KATZ, P.A.
Augusta, ME ....Civil Trial Practice; Commercial Litigation; Labor and Employment Law; Personal Injury

LIPPE & ASSOCIATES, LAW OFFICES OF
Dallas, TX...............................Appellate Practice; Civil Trial Practice

LIPPMAN, MAHFOUZ & MARTIN
Morgan City, LA ....General Practice; Personal Injury

LIPSCHUETZ, JESSE N., P.C.
Denver, CO ....Real Estate Law

LIPSCOMB, J. RANDOLPH
Columbus, MS.........................Civil Trial Practice

LIPSHUTZ, GREENBLATT & KING
Atlanta, GA ....Civil Trial Practice; General Practice; Real Estate Law

LIPSIG, SHAPEY, MANUS & MOVERMAN, P.C.
New York, NY.........................Personal Injury; Product Liability Law

LIPSTET & HIRSCH, L.L.P.
Houston, TX ....Commercial Law; Family Law; International Business Law

LIRTZMAN, NEHLS & HEPNER, A PROFESSIONAL CORPORATION
Boulder, CO ....Bankruptcy Law; Real Estate Law

LISS AND ASSOCIATES, P.C.
Bloomfield Hills, MI...............Civil Trial Practice; Commercial Law; Personal Injury

LISTON/LANCASTER
Grenada, MS...........................Civil Trial Practice; General Practice
Jackson, MS ....Civil Trial Practice; General Practice
Winona, MS ....Civil Trial Practice; General Practice

LITCHFORD & CHRISTOPHER, PROFESSIONAL ASSOCIATION
Orlando, FL ....Antitrust Law; Appellate Practice; Civil Trial Practice; Commercial Litigation; General Practice

LITE, DE PALMA, GREENBERG & RIVAS, LLC
Newark, NJ.............................Admiralty/Maritime Law; Appellate Practice; Civil Trial Practice; Criminal Trial Practice; Environmental Law

LITMAN, ASCHE & GIOIELLA, LLP
New York, NY.........................Civil Trial Practice; Criminal Trial Practice; Personal Injury

LITMAN, KRAAI AND BROWN, L.L.C.
Kansas City, MO ....Patent, Trademark, Copyright and Unfair Competition

LITMAN LAW OFFICES, LTD.
Arlington, VA ....Patent, Trademark, Copyright and Unfair Competition

LITMAN LITMAN HARRIS & BROWN, P.C.
Pittsburgh, PA ....Civil Trial Practice

LITTEN & SIPE, L.L.P.
Harrisonburg, VA...................General Practice

LITTLE, GILMAN & VELASQUEZ, P.A.
Albuquerque, NM...................Family Law

LITTLE, LITTLE, LITTLE, WINDEL & COPPEDGE
Madill, OK..........General Practice

LITTLE, PARSLEY & CLUVERIUS, P.C.
Richmond, VA..........Environmental Law; Real Estate Law; Trust and Estates, Wills and Probate

LITTLER MENDELSON, A PROFESSIONAL CORPORATION
San Francisco, CA..........General Practice

LITTNER, DESCHLER & LITTNER
Allentown, PA..........General Practice; Real Estate Law; Trust and Estates, Wills and Probate
Bethlehem, PA..........General Practice; Real Estate Law; Trust and Estates, Wills and Probate
Easton, PA..........General Practice; Real Estate Law; Trust and Estates, Wills and Probate

LITVAK, LITVAK, MEHRTENS & EPSTEIN, PROFESSIONAL CORPORATION
Denver, CO..........Family Law

LIVINGSTON & MATTESICH, LAW CORPORATION
Sacramento, CA..........Administrative Law; Appellate Practice; Business Law; Civil Trial Practice; Commercial Litigation; Construction Law; Eminent Domain; Energy Law; Environmental Law; General Practice; Health Care Law; Intellectual Property Law; Labor and Employment Law; Natural Resources Law; Patent, Trademark, Copyright and Unfair Competition; Product Liability Law; Real Estate Law

LLOYD, DINNING, BOGGS & DINNING
Demopolis, AL..........General Practice

LLOYD, GOSSELINK, BLEVINS, ROCHELLE, BALDWIN & TOWNSEND, P.C.
Austin, TX..........Environmental Law

LLOYD, SCHREIBER & GRAY, P.C.
Birmingham, AL..........Civil Trial Practice; Insurance Defense

LOBEL & OPERA LLP
Irvine, CA..........Bankruptcy Law; Commercial Law; Commercial Litigation

LOBRANO & KINCAID, P.L.
Jacksonville, FL..........Business Law; Commercial Litigation; Construction Law; Real Estate Law; Trust and Estates, Wills and Probate

LOCKE & HERBERT
New York, NY..........Civil Trial Practice; Insurance Defense

LOCKE LIDDELL & SAPP LLP
Dallas, TX..........General Practice

LOCKE REYNOLDS LLP
Indianapolis, IN..........Banking Law; Civil Trial Practice; Construction Law; General Practice; Health Care Law; Insurance Defense; Labor and Employment Law; Medical Malpractice; Patent, Trademark, Copyright and Unfair Competition; Personal Injury; Product Liability Law; Securities Law; Tax Law

LOE, WARREN, ROSENFIELD, KAITCER & HIBBS, A PROFESSIONAL CORPORATION
Fort Worth, TX..........Business Law; Family Law

LOEB & LOEB LLP
Los Angeles, CA..........Antitrust Law; Appellate Practice; Banking Law; Bankruptcy Law; Civil Trial Practice; Environmental Law; General Practice; Intellectual Property Law; Labor and Employment Law; Real Estate Law; Tax Law; Trademark, Copyright and Unfair Competition; Trust and Estates, Wills and Probate
New York, NY..........Antitrust Law; Appellate Practice; Banking Law; Bankruptcy Law; Civil Trial Practice; General Practice; Real Estate Law; Tax Law; Trademark, Copyright and Unfair Competition; Trust and Estates, Wills and Probate
Rome, Italy..........General Practice

LOEWY, STEVEN A., P.A.
Bethesda, MD..........Real Estate Law

LOFTON, LIONEL S.
Charleston, SC..........Criminal Trial Practice

LOGAN, CHARLES E.
San Jose, CA..........Bankruptcy Law

LOGAN, GARY
Las Vegas, NV..........Aviation Law; Medical Malpractice; Personal Injury

LOGGANS, SUSAN E., & ASSOCIATES, P.C.
Chicago, IL..........Civil Trial Practice; Medical Malpractice; Personal Injury; Product Liability Law

LOHF, SHAIMAN & JACOBS, P.C.
Denver, CO..........Business Law; Natural Resources Law; Real Estate Law; Tax Law

LOMBARDI, LOPER & CONANT, LLP
Oakland, CA..........Civil Trial Practice; Education Law; Insurance Defense; Medical Malpractice; Product Liability Law; Professional Liability

LOMELL, MUCCIFORI, ADLER, RAVASCHIERE, AMABILE & PEHLIVANIAN, A PROFESSIONAL CORPORATION
Toms River, NJ..........Civil Trial Practice; Environmental Law; General Practice; Insurance Defense; Municipal and Zoning Law; Personal Injury; Product Liability Law; Toxic Torts; Workers Compensation

LOMMEN, NELSON, COLE & STAGEBERG, P.A.
Minneapolis, MN..........Business Law; Civil Trial Practice; Insurance Defense; Real Estate Law

LONDON FISCHER LLP
New York, NY..........Admiralty/Maritime Law; Appellate Practice; Civil Trial Practice; Construction Law; Insurance Defense; Product Liability Law

LONG ALDRIDGE & NORMAN LLP
Atlanta, GA..........Administrative Law; Antitrust Law; Appellate Practice; Bankruptcy Law; Business Law; Civil Trial Practice; Communications Law; Computer Law; Creditors Rights; Employment Benefits Law; Environmental Law; Family Law; General Practice; Health Care Law; Immigration and Naturalization; Labor and Employment Law; Municipal Bond/Public Authority Financing; Public Utilities Law; Real Estate Law; Securities Law; Sports and Entertainment Law; Tax Law; Trust and Estates, Wills and Probate

LONG, BURNER, PARKS & SEALY, A PROFESSIONAL CORPORATION
Austin, TX..........Administrative Law; Insurance Defense

LONG & JAUDON, P.C.
Denver, CO..........Civil Trial Practice; General Practice; Insurance Defense; Labor and Employment Law; Legal Malpractice; Medical Malpractice

LONG LAW FIRM, L.L.P.
Baton Rouge, LA..........Commercial Litigation; Insurance Defense; Professional Liability; Public Utilities Law

LONG & LEVIT LLP
San Francisco, CA..........General Practice

LONG & LONG
Chapel Hill, NC..........Civil Trial Practice; Family Law

LONG, PARKER, WARREN & JONES, P.A.
Asheville, NC..........Civil Trial Practice; Criminal Trial Practice

LONG, TUMINELLO, BESSO, SELIGMAN, QUINLAN & WERNER
Bay Shore, NY..........Civil Trial Practice; Criminal Trial Practice; Personal Injury

LONG & WILLIAMSON, A PROFESSIONAL CORPORATION
Santa Ana, CA..........Insurance Defense

LOOMIS, EWERT, PARSLEY, DAVIS & GOTTING, P.C.
Lansing, MI..........Commercial Litigation; Corporate Law

LOONEY & GROSSMAN LLP
Boston, MA..........Bankruptcy Law; Business Law; Civil Trial Practice; General Practice

LOONEY, NICHOLS & JOHNSON, PLLC
Oklahoma City, OK..........Civil Trial Practice; General Practice

LOPEZ, DAVID T. & ASSOCIATES
Houston, TX..........Arbitration; Labor and Employment Law

LOPEZ, SCOTT P. LAW OFFICE OF
Boston, MA..........Civil Trial Practice; Criminal Trial Practice

LOPEZ, HODES, RESTAINO, MILMAN & SKIKOS, A LAW CORPORATION
Newport Beach, CA..........Civil Trial Practice; Labor and Employment Law; Medical Malpractice; Personal Injury; Product Liability Law; Toxic Torts

LORD, BISSELL & BROOK
Los Angeles, CA..........General Practice
Atlanta, GA..........General Practice
Chicago, IL..........General Practice
Rockford, IL..........General Practice

LORD & WHIP, A PROFESSIONAL ASSOCIATION
Baltimore, MD..........General Practice; Workers Compensation

LORENZO & GIANVITO, P.C.
Punxsutawney, PA..........Civil Trial Practice; Commercial Litigation; Personal Injury

LORUSSO & LOUD
Boston, MA..........Patent, Trademark, Copyright and Unfair Competition

LOSKAMP, ALVIN N., A LAW CORPORATION
Burbank, CA..........Business Law; Trust and Estates, Wills and Probate

LOTT, FRANKLIN, FONDA & FLANAGAN
Greenwood, MS..........General Practice

LOVE, THORNTON, ARNOLD & THOMASON, P.A.
Greenville, SC..........Civil Trial Practice; Corporate Law; Criminal Trial Practice; Environmental Law; General Practice; Insurance Defense; Medical Malpractice; Product Liability Law; Real Estate Law

LOVELESS, CURTIS M.
Denton, TX..........Family Law

LOVELL & STEWART, LLP
New York, NY..........Antitrust Law; Civil Trial Practice; Commercial Law; Corporate Law; Criminal Trial Practice; Securities Law

LOVETT, THOMAS G. JR.
Minneapolis, MN..........Bankruptcy Law; General Practice; Trust and Estates, Wills and Probate

LOVICH & PENN
Los Angeles, CA..........Insurance Defense

LOVITZ AND GOLD, P.C.
Philadelphia, PA..........Civil Trial Practice; Labor and Employment Law

LOW & CHILDERS, P.C.
Phoenix, AZ..........Administrative Law

LOWE, BRYAN A, & ASSOCIATES, A PROF. LAW CORP.
Las Vegas, NV..........Elder Law; Real Estate Law; Trust and Estates, Wills and Probate

LOWE • EKLUND • WAKEFIELD CO., L.P.A.
Cleveland, OH..........Business Law; Commercial Litigation; Medical Malpractice; Personal Injury; Product Liability Law

LOWE, MOBLEY & LOWE
Haleyville, AL..........Insurance Defense

LOWE, STEIN, HOFFMAN, ALLWEISS & HAUVER, L.L.P.
New Orleans, LA..........Administrative Law; Business Law; Civil Trial Practice; Commercial Law; Corporate Law; Family Law; General Practice; Insurance Defense; Labor and Employment Law; Personal Injury; Tax Law; Trust and Estates, Wills and Probate

LOWENBAUM PARTNERSHIP, THE, L.L.C.
St. Louis, MO..........Commercial Litigation; Corporate Law; Health Care Law; Labor and Employment Law; Securities Law

LOWENHAUPT & CHASNOFF, L.L.C.
St. Louis, MO..........General Practice; Tax Law

LOWENTHAL, BETTY L.
Sylvan Lake, MI..........Family Law

LOWER, JOYCE Q.
Bloomfield Hills, MI..........Trust and Estates, Wills and Probate

LOWTHORP, RICHARDS, MCMILLAN, MILLER, CONWAY & TEMPLEMAN, A PROFESSIONAL CORPORATION
Oxnard, CA..........Corporate Law; Real Estate Law; Trust and Estates, Wills and Probate

LOWY, RONALD S. THE LAW OFFICES OF
Miami, FL..........Commercial Litigation; Criminal Trial Practice; Personal Injury

LUBIN & ENOCH, P.C.
Phoenix, AZ..........Labor and Employment Law

LUBIN, RICHARD G., P.A.
West Palm Beach, FL..........Criminal Trial Practice

LUCAS, HENRY C. III
Philadelphia, PA..........Admiralty/Maritime Law; Commercial Litigation

LUCAS BOWKER & WHITE
Edmonton, AB, Canada..........Civil Trial Practice; Commercial Law; Environmental Law; General Practice

LUCAS, HOLCOMB & MEDREA
Merrillville, IN..........General Practice

LUCAS LAW FIRM, THE
San Francisco, CA..........Civil Trial Practice; Labor and Employment Law

LUCAS & TONN, P.C.
Miles City, MT..........General Practice

LUCCO BROWN & MUDGE
Edwardsville, IL..........Civil Trial Practice; Criminal Trial Practice

LUCE, FORWARD, HAMILTON & SCRIPPS LLP
La Jolla, CA..........Trust and Estates, Wills and Probate
San Diego, CA..........Banking Law; Bankruptcy Law; Business Law; Environmental Law; Family Law; General Practice; Insurance Defense; Intellectual Property Law; International Business Law; Labor and Employment Law; Municipal Bond/Public Authority Financing; Personal Injury; Product Liability Law; Real Estate Law; Securities Law; Tax Law

LUCKETT LAW FIRM, A PROFESSIONAL ASSOCIATION
Clarksdale, MS..........General Practice; Insurance Defense

LUDENS, POTTER & BURCH
Morrison, IL..........General Practice

LUDWIG GOLDBERG & KRENZEL, A PROFESSIONAL CORPORATION
San Francisco, CA..........Employment Benefits Law

LUEDEKA, NEELY & GRAHAM, P.C.
Knoxville, TN..........Computer Law; Intellectual Property Law; Patent, Trademark, Copyright and Unfair Competition

LUEDERS, ROBERTSON & KONZEN
Granite City, IL..........Commercial Litigation; Energy Law; General Practice; Public Utilities Law; Trust and Estates, Wills and Probate

LUFFEY, JOHN L. JR.
Monroe, LA..........Tax Law

LUGENBUHL, BURKE, WHEATON, PECK, RANKIN & HUBBARD, A LAW CORPORATION
New Orleans, LA..........Admiralty/Maritime Law; Commercial Litigation; Environmental Law

LUNDEEN, DAVID F.
Fergus Falls, MN..........Elder Law; Employment Benefits Law; General Practice; Pension and Profit Sharing; Real Estate Law; Tax Law; Trust and Estates, Wills and Probate

LUNDIN, JOHN W., P.S.
Seattle, WA..........Criminal Trial Practice; Environmental Law

LUNDY & ASSOCIATES, P.C.
Fort Wayne, IN..........Patent, Trademark, Copyright and Unfair Competition
Indianapolis, IN..........Patent, Trademark, Copyright and Unfair Competition

LUNDY & DAVIS, L.L.P.
Lake Charles, LA..........Admiralty/Maritime Law; Personal Injury

LUPO, DAVID G., P.C.
St. Louis, MO..........Elder Law

LUPO & KOCZKUR, P.C.
Detroit, MI..........Insurance Defense; Product Liability Law

LUSK, FRALEY, MCALISTER & SIMMS, P.C.
Birmingham, AL..........Civil Trial Practice; Commercial Litigation; Employment Benefits Law; Insurance Defense; Medical Malpractice; Personal Injury; Product Liability Law; Professional Liability; Transportation Law; Workers Compensation

LUSK & LUSK
Guntersville, AL..........General Practice; Insurance Defense

LUSTBADER, PHILIP M., & DAVID LUSTBADER, A PROFESSIONAL CORPORATION
Livingston, NJ..........Appellate Practice; Civil Trial Practice; Insurance Defense; Medical Malpractice; Personal Injury; Product Liability Law; Workers Compensation

LUTHER, ANDERSON, PLLP
Chattanooga, TN..........Insurance Defense

LUTY, ROBERT L., A PROFESSIONAL CORPORATION
Los Angeles, CA..........Medical Malpractice; Personal Injury; Product Liability Law

LUXAN & MURFITT
Helena, MT..........General Practice

LUXENBERG, GARBETT, KELLY & SAPIENZA, P.C.
New Castle, PA..........Insurance Defense; Personal Injury

LYKKEBAK, DONALD A.
Orlando, FL..........Criminal Trial Practice

LYLES, DARR & CLARK
Spartanburg, SC..........General Practice

LYNBERG & WATKINS, A PROFESSIONAL CORPORATION
Los Angeles, CA..........Civil Trial Practice

LYNCH & ASSOCIATES, P.L.L.C.
Boise, ID..........General Practice; Insurance Defense; Product Liability Law

LYNCH, CHAPPELL & ALSUP, A PROFESSIONAL CORPORATION
Midland, TX .... General Practice; Natural Resources Law; Tax Law

LYNCH, DALLAS, SMITH & HARMAN, P.C.
Cedar Rapids, IA .... Civil Trial Practice; General Practice

LYNCH, GALLAGHER, LYNCH & MARTINEAU, P.L.L.C.
Mount Pleasant, MI .... Environmental Law; General Practice; Natural Resources Law; Oil and Gas Law

LYNCH, MARTIN, KANE, KUPER, KEEFE & BARTELS, LLC
North Brunswick, NJ .... Civil Trial Practice; General Practice; Insurance Defense; Personal Injury; Product Liability Law

LYNN, FULKERSON, NICHOLS AND KINKEL, PLLC
Lexington, KY .... Insurance Defense; Medical Malpractice; Workers Compensation

LYNN, JACKSON, SHULTZ & LEBRUN, P.C.
Rapid City, SD .... Civil Trial Practice; General Practice; Personal Injury

LYNN LAW OFFICE
Syracuse, NY .... Civil Trial Practice; Criminal Trial Practice; Personal Injury; Trust and Estates, Wills and Probate

LYNN STODGHILL MELSHEIMER & TILLOTSON, L.L.P.
Dallas, TX .... Commercial Law

LYON & ARTZ PLC
Bloomfield Hills, MI .... Intellectual Property Law; Patent, Trademark, Copyright and Unfair Competition
Southfield, MI .... Intellectual Property Law; Patent, Trademark, Copyright and Unfair Competition

LYON, FERRITER & FITZPATRICK, LLP
Holyoke, MA .... Business Law; Corporate Law; General Practice; Trust and Estates, Wills and Probate

LYON KIRWIN, P.A.
Winter Park, FL .... Commercial Law; Commercial Litigation; Construction Law; Government Contracts

LYON & LYON LLP
Los Angeles, CA .... Antitrust Law; Patent, Trademark, Copyright and Unfair Competition

LYON, WEIGAND & GUSTAFSON, P.S.
Yakima, WA .... General Practice

LYONS, BRANDT, COOK & HIRAMATSU
Honolulu, HI .... Civil Trial Practice; Insurance Defense

LYONS LAW FIRM, THE
Wilmington, DE .... Criminal Trial Practice; Personal Injury

LYONS, PIPES & COOK, P.C.
Mobile, AL .... Admiralty/Maritime Law; Appellate Practice; Banking Law; Bankruptcy Law; Civil Trial Practice; Commercial Law; Environmental Law; General Practice; Labor and Employment Law; Municipal Bond/Public Authority Financing; Natural Resources Law; Pension and Profit Sharing; Product Liability Law; Professional Liability; Real Estate Law; Tax Law; Trust and Estates, Wills and Probate

LYONS & RHODES, P.C.
San Antonio, TX .... Medical Malpractice; Personal Injury

LYTAL, REITER, CLARK, FOUNTAIN & WILLIAMS
West Palm Beach, FL .... Medical Malpractice; Personal Injury; Product Liability Law

LYTLE, THOMAS F.
Sacramento, CA .... Civil Trial Practice; Personal Injury

MACCABE & MCGUIRE
Chicago, IL .... Civil Trial Practice; Insurance Defense; Transportation Law

MACCARTHY, POJANI & HURLEY, LLP
Worcester, MA .... Banking Law; Civil Trial Practice; General Practice; Insurance Defense

MACCARTNEY, MACCARTNEY, KERRIGAN & MACCARTNEY
Nyack, NY .... General Practice; Insurance Defense

MACCORKLE LAVENDER & CASEY PLLC
Charleston, WV .... Product Liability Law

MACDONALD & ASSOCIATES
San Francisco, CA .... Bankruptcy Law

MACDONALD, FITZGERALD & MACDONALD, P.C.
Flint, MI .... General Practice; Personal Injury; Product Liability Law; Workers Compensation

MACDONALD, ILLIG, JONES & BRITTON LLP
Erie, PA .... General Practice

MACELREE, HARVEY, GALLAGHER, FEATHERMAN & SEBASTIAN, LTD.
Exton, PA .... General Practice
Kennett Square, PA .... General Practice
West Chester, PA .... Banking Law; Civil Trial Practice; General Practice; Personal Injury

MACEY, WILENSKY, COHEN, WITTNER & KESSLER, LLP
Atlanta, GA .... Bankruptcy Law; Civil Trial Practice; Creditors Rights; General Practice; Real Estate Law

MACIE, JAMES J.
Jonesboro, GA .... Family Law

MACINNIS, DONNER & KOPLOWITZ
San Francisco, CA .... Business Law; Family Law; Trust and Estates, Wills and Probate

MACKALL, CROUNSE & MOORE, PLC
Minneapolis, MN .... General Practice; Patent, Trademark, Copyright and Unfair Competition

MACKALL, MACKALL & GIBB, A PROFESSIONAL CORPORATION
Fairfax, VA .... Real Estate Law; Trust and Estates, Wills and Probate

MACKENZIE FUJISAWA BREWER STEVENSON
Vancouver, BC, Canada .... General Practice

MACKOFF KELLOGG LAW FIRM
Dickinson, ND .... General Practice

MACLEAN & JACQUES, LTD.
Phoenix, AZ .... Appellate Practice; Commercial Law; Family Law; Real Estate Law; Trust and Estates, Wills and Probate

MACLEAY, LYNCH, GREGG & LYNCH, P.C.
Washington, DC .... Civil Trial Practice; Insurance Defense; Workers Compensation

MACPHERSON LESLIE & TYERMAN
Regina, SK, Canada .... Administrative Law; Appellate Practice; Banking Law; Bankruptcy Law; Business Law; Civil Trial Practice; Commercial Law; Commercial Litigation; Construction Law; Criminal Trial Practice; Employment Benefits Law; Environmental Law; Family Law; General Practice; Health Care Law; Insurance Defense; Labor and Employment Law; Medical Malpractice; Natural Resources Law; Professional Liability; Real Estate Law; Securities Law; Tax Law; Trust and Estates, Wills and Probate; Workers Compensation

MACRAE, GERALD C.
Los Angeles, CA .... Civil Trial Practice

MACVEAN, LEWIS, SHERWIN & MCDERMOTT, P.C.
Middletown, NY .... Banking Law; General Practice; Insurance Defense; Personal Injury; Real Estate Law; Trust and Estates, Wills and Probate

MADDEN, FRANK, & ASSOCIATES
Plymouth, MN .... Employment Benefits Law

MADDEN, MADDEN AND DEL DUCA, P.A.
Haddonfield, NJ .... General Practice

MADDEN, POLIAK, MACDOUGALL & WILLIAMSON
Seattle, WA .... Admiralty/Maritime Law; Insurance Defense

MADDIN, HAUSER, WARTELL, ROTH, HELLER & PESSES, P.C.
Southfield, MI .... Banking Law; Business Law; Civil Trial Practice; Employment Benefits Law; Pension and Profit Sharing; Real Estate Law; Tax Law; Trust and Estates, Wills and Probate

MADDOX, THOMAS E., JR., P.C.
Atlanta, GA .... Civil Rights; Criminal Trial Practice; Medical Malpractice

MADEWELL, JARED & HALFACRE
Cookeville, TN .... Civil Trial Practice; General Practice; Insurance Defense

MADIGAN & SCOTT, INC.
Springfield, VA .... Business Law; Civil Trial Practice; Real Estate Law

MADISON, HARBOUR, MROZ & BRENNAN, P.A.
Albuquerque, NM .... Commercial Litigation; Insurance Defense; Medical Malpractice; Product Liability Law

MADORSKY, MARSHA G.
Miami, FL .... Trust and Estates, Wills and Probate

MADORY, ZELL AND PLEISS, A PROFESSIONAL CORPORATION
Tustin, CA .... Medical Malpractice

MADSON & METCALF, A PROFESSIONAL CORPORATION
Salt Lake City, UT .... Intellectual Property Law; Patent, Trademark, Copyright and Unfair Competition

MAEDER, JEROME A., LAW OFFICES, S.C.
Wausau, WI....Medical Malpractice; Personal Injury

MAGAÑA, CATHCART & MCCARTHY
Los Angeles, CA....Personal Injury

MAGEE AND ISHERWOOD, L.L.P.
Wall Township, NJ....Civil Trial Practice; General Practice; Insurance Defense; Municipal and Zoning Law; Personal Injury

MAGER LAW FIRM, THE, P.C.
Philadelphia, PA....Labor and Employment Law

MAGGIO & KATTAR, P.C.
Washington, DC....Immigration and Naturalization

MAGIE, ANDRESEN, HAAG, PACIOTTI, BUTTERWORTH & MCCARTHY, P.A.
Duluth, MN....Civil Trial Practice; General Practice; Insurance Defense; Real Estate Law

MAGINNIS & HURLEY, A PROFESSIONAL LAW CORPORATION
New Orleans, LA....Admiralty/Maritime Law; Insurance Defense; Product Liability Law

MAGRUDER & SUMNER
Rome, GA....Civil Trial Practice

MAGUIRE & KRESS, P.C.
Pocatello, ID....Insurance Defense

MAHASSNI, HASSAN, LAW OFFICE OF
Jeddah, Saudi Arabia....General Practice

MAHER, GIBSON AND GUILEY, A PROF. ASSN. OF LAWYERS
Orlando, FL....Medical Malpractice; Personal Injury; Product Liability Law

MAHER & MAHER, LLP
Irvine, CA....Environmental Law; General Practice

MAHL REHON WALWORTH & ROBERTS, A PROFESSIONAL CORPORATION
San Jose, CA....Banking Law; Commercial Litigation; Construction Law

MAHON & FARLEY, P.A.
Jacksonville, FL....Family Law; Personal Injury

MAHONEY, DOUGHERTY AND MAHONEY, P.A. PROFESSIONAL ASSOCIATION
Minneapolis, MN....Civil Trial Practice; Insurance Defense

MAIN, JOHN W., P.C.
Phoenix, AZ....Workers Compensation

MAIN, RONALD, P.C.
Tulsa, OK....Business Law; Civil Trial Practice; Family Law; General Practice; Real Estate Law

MAINERO, MARIO W., JR., INC.
Newport Beach, CA....Civil Trial Practice

MAINES & LOEB, PLLC
Washington, DC....Appellate Practice

MAINOR & HARRIS
Las Vegas, NV....Construction Law; Medical Malpractice; Personal Injury; Product Liability Law

MAIRE, MANSELL & BEASLEY, A LAW CORPORATION
Redding, CA....Insurance Defense; Personal Injury

MAJESTIC, PARSONS, SIEBERT & HSUE, A PROFESSIONAL CORPORATION
San Francisco, CA....Intellectual Property Law; Patent, Trademark, Copyright and Unfair Competition

MALFITANO CAMPBELL & DICKINSON
Jacksonville, FL....Labor and Employment Law
Tampa, FL....Labor and Employment Law

MALIN, HALEY & DIMAGGIO, P.A.
Fort Lauderdale, FL....Patent, Trademark, Copyright and Unfair Competition
Miami, FL....Patent, Trademark, Copyright and Unfair Competition
West Palm Beach, FL....Patent, Trademark, Copyright and Unfair Competition

MALLINCKRODT & MALLINCKRODT
Salt Lake City, UT....Patent, Trademark, Copyright and Unfair Competition

MALLOY & MALLOY, P.A.
Miami, FL....Intellectual Property Law; Patent, Trademark, Copyright and Unfair Competition; Trademark, Copyright and Unfair Competition

MALLOY & SULLIVAN, LAWYERS PROFESSIONAL CORPORATION
Hingham, MA....Communications Law

MALNICK, DAVID, A PROFESSIONAL CORPORATION
San Jose, CA....Civil Trial Practice; Personal Injury; Product Liability Law

MALONE, THOMAS WILLIAM
Atlanta, GA....Medical Malpractice; Personal Injury

MALONE, THOMAS P., & ASSOCIATES, P.C.
Denver, CO....Family Law

MALONEY, HUENNEKENS, PARKS, GECKER & PARSONS, A PROFESSIONAL CORPORATION
Richmond, VA....Bankruptcy Law; Business Law; Commercial Law; Commercial Litigation; Construction Law; General Practice; Labor and Employment Law; Personal Injury; Securities Law; Workers Compensation

MALONEY & MALONEY
Aberdeen, SD....Construction Law; Employment Benefits Law; Labor and Employment Law; Personal Injury

MALONEY & YURACHEK, P.C.
Falls Church, VA....Trust and Estates, Wills and Probate

MALOON, JERRY L., CO., L.P.A.
Columbus, OH....Medical Malpractice

MANAHAN, PIETRYKOWSKI, BAMMAN & DELANEY
Toledo, OH....Commercial Litigation; Insurance Defense

MANATT, PHELPS & PHILLIPS, LLP
Los Angeles, CA....General Practice

MANCHESTER, BENNETT, POWERS & ULLMAN, A LEGAL PROFESSIONAL ASSOCIATION
Youngstown, OH....General Practice

MANCHESTER LAW OFFICES, PROFESSIONAL CORPORATION
Burlington, VT....Civil Trial Practice; Commercial Law; Environmental Law; Medical Malpractice; Personal Injury

MANCHESTER & PIGNATO, P.C.
Oklahoma City, OK....Civil Rights; Insurance Defense

MANCHESTER & WILLIAMS
San Jose, CA....Criminal Trial Practice

MANCKE, WAGNER, HERSHEY AND TULLY
Harrisburg, PA....Civil Trial Practice; Criminal Trial Practice; General Practice; Personal Injury; Transportation Law

MANDELBAUM, SALSBURG, GOLD, LAZRIS, DISCENZA & STEINBERG, P.A.
West Orange, NJ....General Practice

MANDEL, LIPTON AND STEVENSON LIMITED
Chicago, IL....Civil Trial Practice; Family Law; General Practice; Immigration and Naturalization

MANDELL LAW FIRM, THE, A PROFESSIONAL CORPORATION
Vienna, VA....Business Law

MANDELSTAMM, JEROME R.
St. Louis, MO....Business Law; Real Estate Law; Trust and Estates, Wills and Probate

MANEY, DAMSKER & JONES, P.A.
Tampa, FL....Appellate Practice; Civil Trial Practice; Commercial Litigation; Criminal Trial Practice; Family Law; Tax Law; Trust and Estates, Wills and Probate

MANEY & GORDON, P.A.
Tampa, FL....Immigration and Naturalization

MANGUM, WALL, STOOPS & WARDEN, P.L.L.C.
Flagstaff, AZ....Business Law; Civil Trial Practice; Commercial Law; Construction Law; Corporate Law; Family Law; General Practice; Insurance Defense; Labor and Employment Law; Personal Injury; Real Estate Law; Trust and Estates, Wills and Probate

MANLEY, BURKE, LIPTON & COOK, A LEGAL PROFESSIONAL ASSOCIATION
Cincinnati, OH....Land Use Law; Municipal and Zoning Law

MANLEY, TRAEGER, PERRY & STAPP
Demopolis, AL....General Practice

MANN, FREDERICK R., JR., P.A.
Winter Park, FL....Criminal Trial Practice

MANN, KENNETH L., P.A.
Orlando, FL....Appellate Practice; Arbitration; Civil Trial Practice; Commercial Litigation; Legal Malpractice

MANN LAW FIRM
Terre Haute, IN....Civil Trial Practice; Personal Injury

MANN & MITCHELL
Providence, RI..........Civil Rights; Criminal Trial Practice

MANN & WOOLDRIDGE, P.C.
Newnan, GA..........General Practice

MANNES, MICHAEL H., P.A.
Baltimore, MD..........Real Estate Law

MANNING & CROUCH
Raleigh, NC..........Civil Trial Practice; Criminal Trial Practice

MANNING CURTIS BRADSHAW & BEDNAR, LLC
Salt Lake City, UT..........General Practice

MANNING, FULTON & SKINNER, P.A.
Raleigh, NC..........General Practice

MANOS, MARTIN, PERGRAM & DIETZ, L.P.A.
Delaware, OH..........General Practice

MANSFIELD TANICK & COHEN, P.A.
Minneapolis, MN..........Bankruptcy Law; Civil Trial Practice; Labor and Employment Law; Trust and Estates, Wills and Probate

MANSOUR, GAVIN, GERLACK & MANOS CO., L.P.A.
Cleveland, OH..........Civil Trial Practice

MANTA AND WELGE, A PROFESSIONAL CORPORATION
Philadelphia, PA..........Commercial Law; Commercial Litigation; Environmental Law; Insurance Defense; Labor and Employment Law; Product Liability Law

MANWELL & MILTON
San Francisco, CA..........Business Law; Securities Law

MAPOTHER & MAPOTHER
Louisville, KY..........Banking Law; Bankruptcy Law; Creditors Rights; Real Estate Law

MARAN & MARAN
Newark, NJ..........Legal Malpractice; Medical Malpractice; Product Liability Law; Professional Liability

MARCH & LILEY, P.C.
Fort Collins, CO..........General Practice

MARCOUX, ALLEN, ABBOTT, SCHOMER & BOWER, P.C.
Jackson, MI..........Banking Law; Civil Trial Practice; Corporate Law; General Practice; Insurance Defense; Labor and Employment Law; Tax Law

MARCUS, GOULD & SUSSMAN, LLP
White Plains, NY..........Commercial Litigation; Real Estate Law; Trust and Estates, Wills and Probate

MARCUS, GRYGIEL & CLEGG, P.A.
Portland, ME..........Banking Law; Bankruptcy Law; Business Law; Commercial Law; Commercial Litigation; General Practice; Health Care Law

MARCUS & SHAPIRA LLP
Pittsburgh, PA..........Antitrust Law; Bankruptcy Law; Civil Trial Practice; Commercial Law; Corporate Law; General Practice; Insurance Defense; Labor and Employment Law; Personal Injury; Real Estate Law; Securities Law; Tax Law; Trust and Estates, Wills and Probate; Workers Compensation

MARDEROSIAN, OREN & PABOOJIAN, A PROFESSIONAL CORPORATION
Fresno, CA..........Business Law; Insurance Defense; Labor and Employment Law

MAREADY, WILLIAM F. THE LAW OFFICES OF
Winston-Salem, NC..........Aviation Law; Product Liability Law

MARGER, JOHNSON & MCCOLLOM, P.C.
Portland, OR..........Intellectual Property Law; Patent, Trademark, Copyright and Unfair Competition; Trademark, Copyright and Unfair Competition

MARGOLIS & CASSIDY
Milwaukee, WI..........Family Law

MARGULIS GRANT & MARGULIS, P.C.
St. Louis, MO..........Criminal Trial Practice

MARISCAL, WEEKS, MCINTYRE & FRIEDLANDER, P.A.
Phoenix, AZ..........Bankruptcy Law; Commercial Litigation; Family Law; General Practice; Real Estate Law

MARK & BURKHEAD
Mission, KS..........Workers Compensation
Kansas City, MO..........Workers Compensation

MARKLE, RAMOS & ZITO, A PROFESSIONAL CORPORATION
Houston, TX..........Insurance Defense; Medical Malpractice; Personal Injury

MARKOW, WALKER & REEVES, P.A.
Jackson, MS..........Environmental Law; Insurance Defense; Medical Malpractice

MARKOWITZ, DAVIS, RINGEL & TRUSTY, P.A.
Miami, FL..........Bankruptcy Law; Commercial Litigation; Creditors Rights; Real Estate Law; Trust and Estates, Wills and Probate

MARK & PEARLSTEIN, P.A.
Phoenix, AZ..........Family Law; Insurance Defense; Medical Malpractice; Personal Injury

MARKS GRAY
Jacksonville, FL..........General Practice

MARKS, MADSEN & HIRSCHBACH
Sioux City, IA..........General Practice

MARKS, O'NEILL, REILLY, O'BRIEN & COURTNEY, P.C.
Philadelphia, PA..........Civil Trial Practice; Environmental Law; Insurance Defense; Medical Malpractice; Personal Injury; Product Liability Law; Toxic Torts; Workers Compensation

MARKUSON, GLORIA CROWLEY
Scarsdale, NY..........General Practice; Trust and Estates, Wills and Probate

MARKUSSON, GREEN & JARVIS, P.C.
Denver, CO..........Civil Trial Practice; Environmental Law; Insurance Defense; Product Liability Law; Toxic Torts

MARLIN & SALTZMAN, A PROFESSIONAL LAW CORPORATION
Santa Ana, CA..........Business Law; Insurance Defense

MARR HIPP JONES & PEPPER
Honolulu, HI..........Labor and Employment Law

MARRINER, JONES & FITCH
Washington, PA..........General Practice

MARRONE ROBINSON FREDERICK & FOSTER, PROFESSIONAL CORPORATION
Burbank, CA..........Insurance Defense

MARRS, MICHAEL D., A PROFESSIONAL CORPORATION
St. Joseph, MI..........Personal Injury

MARS, RICHARD D., P.A.
Bartow, FL..........Criminal Trial Practice

MARSH, RICKARD & BRYAN, P.C.
Birmingham, AL..........Personal Injury; Product Liability Law

MARSH, SPAEDER, BAUR, SPAEDER & SCHAAF, LLP
Erie, PA..........General Practice; Insurance Defense; Tax Law

MARSHACK SHULMAN & HODGES LLP
Irvine, CA..........Bankruptcy Law; Commercial Litigation

MARSHALL, MARILYN J.
Tallahassee, FL..........General Practice

MARSHALL CONWAY & WRIGHT, P.C.
New York, NY..........Insurance Defense

MARSHALL HILL CASSAS & DE LIPKAU
Reno, NV..........Civil Trial Practice; Corporate Law; Natural Resources Law

MARSHALL LAW FIRM
New York, NY..........Intellectual Property Law; Trademark, Copyright and Unfair Competition

MARSHALL, O'TOOLE, GERSTEIN, MURRAY & BORUN
Chicago, IL..........Intellectual Property Law; Patent, Trademark, Copyright and Unfair Competition

MARSHALL, WILLIAMS & GORHAM, L.L.P.
Wilmington, NC..........Admiralty/Maritime Law; Civil Trial Practice; General Practice

MARSTILLER, PHILIP S., P.C.
Richmond, VA..........Labor and Employment Law; Product Liability Law

MARTEN & BROWN LLP
Seattle, WA..........Environmental Law

MARTENS DUNAJ MARLOWE DAVIS & MARLOWE
Miami, FL..........Commercial Litigation; Computer Law

MARTIN, ADE, BIRCHFIELD & MICKLER, P.A.
Jacksonville, FL..........General Practice

MARTIN & ASSOCIATES, L.L.C.
Phoenix, AZ..........Real Estate Law

MARTIN & ASSOCIATES, P.A.
Minneapolis, MN..........Business Law; Nonprofit and Tax Exempt Organizations; Real Estate Law; Tax Law; Trust and Estates, Wills and Probate

MARTIN, BACON & MARTIN, P.C.
Mount Clemens, MI................Civil Trial Practice; Insurance Defense; Medical Malpractice; Personal Injury; Product Liability Law

MARTIN, BROWNE, HULL & HARPER, P.L.L.
Springfield, OH........................General Practice

MARTIN, CHARLES L., LAW OFFICES OF
Decatur, GA...........................Administrative Law

MARTIN, CHURCHILL, BLAIR, HILL, COLE & HOLLANDER, CHARTERED
Wichita, KS.............................Labor and Employment Law

MARTIN & GLASER, CHARTERED
Sarasota, FL...........................Personal Injury; Product Liability Law

MARTIN, GUNN & MARTIN, A PROFESSIONAL CORPORATION
Westmont, NJ........................Civil Trial Practice

MARTIN, JOHN O., P.C.
Denver, CO.............................Medical Malpractice

MARTIN, JUSTICE & VINCENT
Ashland, KY............................Civil Trial Practice; General Practice; Insurance Defense; Personal Injury

MARTIN LAW FIRM, THE
Chicago, IL.............................Environmental Law

MARTIN LAW OFFICE
Oklahoma City, OK.................Criminal Trial Practice

MARTIN, LIPSKY, KAUFMAN & WEINSTEIN, P.A.
Miami Lakes, FL....................Medical Malpractice; Personal Injury; Product Liability Law

MARTIN, MAGNUSON, MCCARTHY & KENNEY
Boston, MA.............................General Practice; Insurance Defense

MARTIN & MARTIN, P.A.
Lakeland, FL...........................General Practice

MARTIN, MARTIN & WOODARD, LLP
Syracuse, NY..........................Bankruptcy Law; Civil Trial Practice; Commercial Law; Personal Injury; Trust and Estates, Wills and Probate

MARTIN & MEHAFFY, LLC
Boulder, CO............................Insurance Defense

MARTIN, RONALD T., P.A.
Boca Raton, FL.......................Pension and Profit Sharing; Tax Law; Trust and Estates, Wills and Probate

MARTIN, SHOWERS, SMITH & MCDONALD, L.L.P.
Hillsboro, TX..........................General Practice

MARTIN, SHUDT, WALLACE, DILORENZO & JOHNSON
Troy, NY.................................Commercial Law; Corporate Law; Real Estate Law; Trust and Estates, Wills and Probate

MARTIN, SNYDER & BERNSTEIN, P.A.
Baltimore, MD........................Civil Trial Practice; Criminal Trial Practice; Tax Law

MARTIN, TATE, MORROW & MARSTON, P.C.
Memphis, TN..........................General Practice

MARTIN, VAN DE WALLE, DONOHUE, MCGAHAN, CATALANO & FAIRGRIEVE
Jericho, NY.............................Banking Law; Civil Trial Practice; Commercial Litigation; Insurance Defense; Personal Injury; Real Estate Law; Trust and Estates, Wills and Probate

MARTIN, WILSON & MACDOWELL, A PROFESSIONAL CORPORATION
Santa Ana, CA.........................Civil Trial Practice

MARTÍNEZ ODELL & CALABRIA
San Juan, PR...........................Banking Law; Bankruptcy Law; Civil Trial Practice; Commercial Law; Environmental Law; General Practice; Labor and Employment Law; Municipal Bond/Public Authority Financing; Real Estate Law; Tax Law

MARTONYI ÉS KAJTÁR BAKER & MCKENZIE
Budapest, Hungary..................General Practice

MARTSON DEARDORFF WILLIAMS & OTTO, A PROFESSIONAL CORPORATION
Carlisle, PA............................General Practice

MARTZELL & BICKFORD
New Orleans, LA.....................Commercial Litigation; Criminal Trial Practice; Environmental Law; Medical Malpractice; Oil and Gas Law; Personal Injury; Toxic Torts

MARVIN, DOUGLAS R., P.C.
Fairfax, VA............................International Business Law

MARX & MARX
Atlanta, GA............................Civil Trial Practice; Labor and Employment Law
New York, NY.........................Civil Trial Practice; Labor and Employment Law

MARZIK, ROBERT K., P.C., LAW OFFICES OF
Stratford, CT..........................Admiralty/Maritime Law

MASERITZ, GUY B.
Columbia, MD.........................Business Law

MASKALERIS & ASSOCIATES
Morristown, NJ.......................Civil Trial Practice

MASON, GRIFFIN & PIERSON, A PROFESSIONAL CORPORATION
Princeton, NJ..........................Civil Trial Practice; Real Estate Law; Trust and Estates, Wills and Probate

MASON, J. CHENEY, P.A.
Orlando, FL............................Criminal Trial Practice; Family Law

MASON, JOHN, PARTNERS, LTD.
Stateline, NV..........................Sports and Entertainment Law

MASON, SLOVIN & SCHILLING CO., L.P.A.
Cincinnati, OH.......................Banking Law; Commercial Law; Creditors Rights

MASON STEINHARDT JACOBS PERLMAN & PESICK, PROFESSIONAL CORPORATION
Southfield, MI........................Commercial Law; Corporate Law; Environmental Law; General Practice; Land Use Law; Municipal and Zoning Law; Real Estate Law; Tax Law; Trust and Estates, Wills and Probate

MASON, STEVEN A., P.A.
Hollywood, FL........................Civil Trial Practice; Commercial Litigation; Family Law; Real Estate Law

MASON & THOMAS
Sacramento, CA......................Civil Trial Practice; Insurance Defense; Personal Injury

MASSA, PATRICK C., P.A., LAW OFFICES OF
North Palm Beach, FL............Civil Trial Practice; Personal Injury

MASTAGNI, HOLSTEDT & CHIURAZZI, A PROFESSIONAL CORPORATION
Sacramento, CA......................Labor and Employment Law; Personal Injury; Workers Compensation

MASTERS & TAYLOR, L.C.
Charleston, WV......................Personal Injury

MASTERSON, THOMAS A., & ASSOCIATES, P.C.
Norristown, PA.......................Arbitration

MASTRIANA & CHRISTIANSEN, PROFESSIONAL ASSOCIATION
Fort Lauderdale, FL................Business Law; Real Estate Law

MASUD, GILBERT & PATTERSON, P.C.
Saginaw, MI...........................Labor and Employment Law

MATHENY SEARS LINKERT & LONG, LLP
Sacramento, CA......................Appellate Practice; Business Law; Civil Trial Practice; Employment Benefits Law; Insurance Defense; Personal Injury; Product Liability Law; Real Estate Law

MATHEW & MATHEW, P.C.
Phoenix, AZ...........................Criminal Trial Practice

MATHEWS, COLLINS, SHEPHERD & GOULD, A PROFESSIONAL CORPORATION
Princeton, NJ..........................Intellectual Property Law; Trademark, Copyright and Unfair Competition

MATHEWS, STANTON T., & ASSOCIATES, A LAW CORP.
Laguna Hills, CA....................Elder Law; Labor and Employment Law; Medical Malpractice; Personal Injury; Product Liability Law

MATHIS, MARIFIAN, RICHTER & GRANDY, LTD.
Belleville, IL..........................Tax Law; Trust and Estates, Wills and Probate

MATISON, CHARLES A., P.C., THE LAW OFFICES OF
Northfield, NJ........................Family Law

MATKOV, SALZMAN, MADOFF & GUNN
Chicago, IL............................Labor and Employment Law

MATSEN, JEFFREY R. & ASSOCIATES
Newport Beach, CA................Business Law; International Business Law; Trust and Estates, Wills and Probate

MATTHEWS, EDWIN R., P.C.
Short Hills, NJ.......................Commercial Law; Environmental Law; Insurance Defense; Municipal and Zoning Law; Product Liability Law

MATTHEWS & STEEL
Atlanta, GA...........................Civil Trial Practice; Commercial Litigation; Medical Malpractice; Personal Injury; Product Liability Law

MATTHIAS & BERG LLP
Los Angeles, CA....................Business Law; Commercial Litigation; International Business Law; Mergers and Acquisitions; Securities Law; Tax Law

MATTHIESEN, CHASE & ERWIN, L.L.P.
Houston, TX....................Civil Trial Practice; Insurance Defense

MATTIMOE, THOMAS E., LLC
Atlanta, GA....................Corporate Law; Real Estate Law

MATTIONI, LTD.
Philadelphia, PA....................Admiralty/Maritime Law; Civil Trial Practice; Environmental Law; General Practice

MATTOCH, IAN L., LAW OFFICES OF
Honolulu, HI....................Personal Injury; Product Liability Law

MATTOX & MATTOX
New Albany, IN....................General Practice; Medical Malpractice; Personal Injury

MATTSON, RICKETTS, DAVIES, STEWART & CALKINS
Lincoln, NE....................General Practice

MATZ, JEFFREY A. LAW OFFICES OF
Los Angeles, CA....................Civil Trial Practice

MAUPIN TAYLOR & ELLIS, P.A.
Raleigh, NC....................General Practice; Labor and Employment Law

MAURER, EUGENE J., JR., P.A.
Wilmington, DE....................Criminal Trial Practice

MAURER LAW FIRM
La Jolla, CA....................Civil Trial Practice

MAURO, GOLDBERG & LILLING
Great Neck, NY....................Appellate Practice

MAUTZ BAUM & O'HANLON, LLP
Pendleton, OR....................General Practice

MAUZY LAW FIRM
Minneapolis, MN....................Criminal Trial Practice

MAXIE RHEINHEIMER STEPHENS & VREVICH, LLP
San Diego, CA....................Construction Law; Labor and Employment Law; Professional Liability

MAY, MICHAEL P.
Baltimore, MD....................General Practice

MAY, MICHAEL R.
Des Moines, IA....................Public Utilities Law

MAY, ADAM, GERDES & THOMPSON, L.L.P.
Pierre, SD....................General Practice

MAY AND MAY, PROFESSIONAL CORPORATION
Detroit, MI....................Trust and Estates, Wills and Probate
Southfield, MI....................Trust and Estates, Wills and Probate

MAYALL, HURLEY, KNUTSEN, SMITH & GREEN, A PROFESSIONAL CORPORATION
Stockton, CA....................Insurance Defense

MAYER, BROWN & PLATT
Los Angeles, CA....................General Practice
Washington, DC....................General Practice
Chicago, IL....................General Practice
New York, NY....................General Practice
Charlotte, NC....................General Practice
Houston, TX....................General Practice
London, England....................General Practice
Berlin, Germany....................General Practice
Cologne, Germany....................General Practice
Bishkek, Kyrgyzstan....................General Practice
Ashgabat, Turkmenistan....................General Practice
Tashkent, Uzbekistan....................General Practice

MAYER, FRIEDLICH, SPIESS, TIERNEY, BROWN & PLATT
Chicago, IL....................General Practice

MAYER & RISER, PLLC
Highlands, NC....................General Practice

MAYER, SMITH & ROBERTS, L.L.P.
Shreveport, LA....................Civil Trial Practice; General Practice; Insurance Defense; Medical Malpractice; Professional Liability; Workers Compensation

MAYFIELD & PERRENOT, P.C.
El Paso, TX....................Banking Law; General Practice; Immigration and Naturalization; Insurance Defense; International Trade Law; Trust and Estates, Wills and Probate

MAYNARD, O'CONNOR, SMITH & CATALINOTTO, LLP
Albany, NY....................Appellate Practice; Insurance Defense; Medical Malpractice; Personal Injury

MAYNE & MAYNE
Sioux City, IA....................Civil Trial Practice; Insurance Defense; Labor and Employment Law; Workers Compensation

MAYNES, BRADFORD, SHIPPS & SHEFTEL LLP
Durango, CO....................General Practice

MAYOCK, W. MICHAEL
Pasadena, CA....................Appellate Practice; Criminal Trial Practice

MAYOR, DAY, CALDWELL & KEETON, L.L.P.
Austin, TX....................General Practice
Houston, TX....................General Practice

MAYS, KARBERG & WACHTER
Cleveland, OH....................Real Estate Law

MAZUR, CARP & RUBIN, P.C.
New York, NY....................Civil Trial Practice; Construction Law; Trust and Estates, Wills and Probate

MCAFEE & TAFT, A PROFESSIONAL CORPORATION
Oklahoma City, OK....................Employment Benefits Law; General Practice; Labor and Employment Law; Natural Resources Law; Patent, Trademark, Copyright and Unfair Competition; Tax Law

MCALLISTER & ABROMOVITZ
Phoenix, AZ....................Insurance Defense; Product Liability Law

MCALLISTER, HYBERG & WHITE
Northfield, NJ....................Civil Trial Practice; Insurance Defense; Personal Injury; Product Liability Law

MCALOON & FRIEDMAN, P.C.
New York, NY....................Civil Trial Practice; Health Care Law; Medical Malpractice; Personal Injury; Real Estate Law

MCANDREW, THOMAS J., ESQ., LTD.
Providence, RI....................Labor and Employment Law

MCANGUS, GOUDELOCK & COURIE, L.L.C.
Columbia, SC....................Civil Trial Practice; Workers Compensation

MCBRIDE BAKER & COLES
Chicago, IL....................Antitrust Law; Banking Law; Business Law; Commercial Litigation; Computer Law; Employment Benefits Law; Environmental Law; General Practice; Intellectual Property Law; Labor and Employment Law; Real Estate Law; Securities Law; Tax Law; Trust and Estates, Wills and Probate
Oakbrook Terrace, IL....................Banking Law; Business Law; Commercial Litigation; General Practice; Real Estate Law; Trust and Estates, Wills and Probate

MCBRIDE AND MCBRIDE, P.C.
Grove City, PA....................General Practice

MCCABE, COLLINS, MCGEOUGH & FOWLER, LLP
Mineola, NY....................Insurance Defense

MCCABE & MACK LLP
Poughkeepsie, NY....................General Practice

MCCABE O'DONNELL, A PROFESSIONAL ASSOCIATION
Phoenix, AZ....................Commercial Litigation; Real Estate Law; Tax Law; Trust and Estates, Wills and Probate

MCCAFFREY & TAWWATER
Oklahoma City, OK....................Civil Trial Practice; Labor and Employment Law; Medical Malpractice; Personal Injury; Workers Compensation

MCCAHILL, JOHN A.
Washington, DC....................Criminal Trial Practice

MCCALLAR AND ASSOCIATES
Savannah, GA....................Bankruptcy Law; Civil Trial Practice; Commercial Litigation

MCCALLA, THOMPSON, PYBURN, HYMOWITZ & SHAPIRO
New Orleans, LA....................General Practice; Labor and Employment Law

MCCALL, DOUGHTON & BLANCATO, P.L.L.C.
Winston-Salem, NC....................Corporate Law

MCCALL & RITCHIE, LLP
Austin, TX....................Oil and Gas Law

MCCAMPBELL & YOUNG, A PROFESSIONAL CORPORATION
Knoxville, TN....................General Practice

MCCANDLISH & LILLARD, A PROFESSIONAL CORPORATION
Fairfax, VA....................Banking Law; Business Law; Civil Trial Practice; Commercial Litigation; Computer Law; General Practice; Health Care Law; Intellectual Property Law; Medical Malpractice; Real Estate Law; Trust and Estates, Wills and Probate

MCCANNA, KONZ, DUDAS, KEWLEY & PAPENDORF, S.C.
Appleton, WI ....Civil Trial Practice; Insurance Defense

MCCARROLL, NUNLEY & HARTZ
Owensboro, KY ....General Practice; Insurance Defense

MCCARTER & ENGLISH, LLP
Wilmington, DE ....General Practice
Cherry Hill, NJ ....Civil Trial Practice; General Practice
Newark, NJ ....Admiralty/Maritime Law; Antitrust Law; Banking Law; Bankruptcy Law; Civil Trial Practice; Commercial Law; Communications Law; Computer Law; Employment Benefits Law; Family Law; General Practice; Health Care Law; Insurance Defense; International Business Law; Labor and Employment Law; Municipal Bond/Public Authority Financing; Natural Resources Law; Personal Injury; Real Estate Law; Securities Law; Tax Law; Trademark, Copyright and Unfair Competition; Transportation Law; Trust and Estates, Wills and Probate
Philadelphia, PA ....General Practice

MCCARTHY, JOHN C.
Claremont, CA ....Civil Trial Practice; Labor and Employment Law

MCCARTHY & COSTELLO, L.L.P.
Lanham, MD ....General Practice; Personal Injury

MCCARTHY, LEBIT, CRYSTAL & HAIMAN CO., L.P.A.
Cleveland, OH ....Tax Law

MCCARTHY, LEONARD, KAEMMERER, OWEN, LAMKIN & MCGOVERN, L.C.
St. Louis, MO ....Business Law; Labor and Employment Law

MCCARTHY & MASSEY, P.C.
Manassas, VA ....Commercial Litigation; Labor and Employment Law; Medical Malpractice; Workers Compensation

MCCARTHY, PALMER, VOLKEMA & THOMAS, A LEGAL PROFESSIONAL ASSOCIATION
Columbus, OH ....Appellate Practice; Civil Trial Practice; Medical Malpractice; Personal Injury; Product Liability Law

MCCARTHY AND SCHATZMAN, P.A.
Princeton, NJ ....Appellate Practice; Banking Law; Business Law; Civil Trial Practice; Commercial Law; Creditors Rights; Family Law; General Practice; Municipal and Zoning Law; Real Estate Law; Trust and Estates, Wills and Probate

MCCARTHY, SUMMERS, BOBKO, MCKEY, WOOD & SAWYER, P.A.
Stuart, FL ....Banking Law; Civil Trial Practice; Commercial Law; Commercial Litigation; Construction Law; Corporate Law; Family Law; General Practice; Land Use Law; Real Estate Law; Trust and Estates, Wills and Probate

MCCARTHY TÉTRAULT
Calgary, AB, Canada ....General Practice
Vancouver, BC, Canada ....General Practice
London, ON, Canada ....General Practice
Ottawa, ON, Canada ....General Practice
Toronto, ON, Canada ....General Practice
Montreal, QU, Canada ....General Practice
Quebec, QU, Canada ....General Practice
London, England ....General Practice

MCCAUGHAN, WILLIAM P. LAW OFFICE OF
Miami, FL ....General Practice; Real Estate Law

MCCAUGHEY & METOS
Salt Lake City, UT ....Criminal Trial Practice

MCCAULEY & ASSOCIATES ALC
Newport Beach, CA ....Business Law; Civil Trial Practice

MCCLAIN, RAY P., ATTORNEY, P.A.
Charleston, SC ....Labor and Employment Law; Personal Injury

MCCLELLAN & BROWN, A PROFESSIONAL CORPORATION
San Diego, CA ....Civil Trial Practice; Personal Injury; Product Liability Law

MCCLELLAN, POWERS, EHMLING & DIX, P.C.
Gallatin, TN ....Civil Trial Practice; Insurance Defense

MCCLELLAND & ANDERSON, L.L.P.
Lansing, MI ....Commercial Law; Commercial Litigation; Construction Law; Land Use Law; Real Estate Law

MCCLUNG, PETERS AND SIMON
Albany, NY ....Banking Law; Commercial Litigation; General Practice

MCCOLLOUGH & ASSOCIATES, P.C.
Austin, TX ....Communications Law; Public Utilities Law

MCCOLLOUGH, TERRY L., P.A.
Orlando, FL ....Civil Trial Practice; Commercial Litigation; Personal Injury

MCCOLLUM, CROWLEY, VEHANEN, MOSCHET & MILLER, LTD.
Minneapolis, MN ....Insurance Defense

MCCONAUGHEY & GOFF
Decatur, GA ....Trust and Estates, Wills and Probate

MCCONNAUGHHAY, DUFFY, COONROD, POPE & WEAVER, P.A.
Tallahassee, FL ....Civil Trial Practice; Workers Compensation

MCCONNELL AND FINNERTY
North Vernon, IN ....General Practice

MCCONNELL VALDÉS
San Juan, PR ....General Practice

MCCORKLE, PEDIGO & JOHNSON, LLP
Savannah, GA ....General Practice

MCCORMACK & EPSTEIN
Boston, MA ....Civil Trial Practice; Insurance Defense; Personal Injury

MCCORMICK AND CHRISTOPH, P.C.
Boulder, CO ....Criminal Trial Practice; Personal Injury

MCCORMICK, HOFFMAN, REES, FAUBION, VAN BUSKIRK, JOHNSON & SCHUMOCK, P.S.
Lakewood, WA ....General Practice

MCCORMICK, KIDMAN & BEHRENS, LLP
Costa Mesa, CA ....Civil Trial Practice; Eminent Domain; Environmental Law; General Practice; Natural Resources Law; Trust and Estates, Wills and Probate

MCCORMICK & MITCHELL, A PROFESSIONAL CORPORATION
San Diego, CA ....Arbitration; Construction Law; Insurance Defense; Product Liability Law

MCCORMICK, PAULDING & HUBER, LLP
Hartford, CT ....Intellectual Property Law
Springfield, MA ....Intellectual Property Law

MCCORMICK & PRIORE, P.C.
Philadelphia, PA ....Civil Trial Practice; Environmental Law; Insurance Defense; Medical Malpractice; Product Liability Law; Toxic Torts

MCCORRISTON MIHO MILLER MUKAI
Honolulu, HI ....Business Law; Civil Trial Practice; General Practice; Insurance Defense; International Business Law; Real Estate Law; Tax Law

MCCOY & ASSOCIATES, P.C.
Philadelphia, PA ....Civil Rights; Labor and Employment Law

MCCOY ROBERTS BEGNAUD & FRIEDMAN, A LAW CORPORATION
Natchitoches, LA ....General Practice

MCCOY, WEAVER, WIGGINS, CLEVELAND & RAPER, PLLC
Fayetteville, NC ....General Practice

MCCOY & WEST
Lexington, KY ....Civil Trial Practice; Criminal Trial Practice

MCCOY, WILKINS, STEPHENS & TIPTON, P.A.
Jackson, MS ....Insurance Defense

MCCULLOUGH SHERRILL, LLP
Atlanta, GA ....Business Law; Civil Trial Practice; General Practice; Immigration and Naturalization; International Business Law; Labor and Employment Law; Real Estate Law

MCCULLOUGH, SMITH, WRIGHT & KEMPE, P.A.
St. Paul, MN ....Family Law; Personal Injury

MCCURDY & CANDLER, L.L.C.
Decatur, GA ....General Practice

MCCURLEY, KINSER, MCCURLEY & NELSON, L.L.P.
Dallas, TX ....Family Law

MCCUTCHEN, BLANTON, RHODES & JOHNSON, L.L.P.
Columbia, SC ....Appellate Practice; Civil Trial Practice; General Practice; Insurance Defense

MCCUTCHEN, DOYLE, BROWN & ENERSEN, LLP
Los Angeles, CA ....General Practice
San Francisco, CA ....General Practice
Walnut Creek, CA ....General Practice
Taipei, Taiwan ....General Practice

MCCUTCHEON, MCCUTCHEON & BAXTER, P.A.
Conway, SC ....Civil Trial Practice; General Practice; Insurance Defense; Medical Malpractice

MCDADE, FOGLER, MAINES & LOHSE, L.L.P.
Houston, TX .... Civil Trial Practice

MCDANIEL, DUKE A.
Petersburg, WV .... General Practice

MCDANIEL & MARSH
Baltimore, MD .... Appellate Practice; Civil Trial Practice; Commercial Litigation; Criminal Trial Practice

MCDANIEL & WELLS, P.A.
Jonesboro, AR .... Personal Injury

MCDAVID, TERRY
Lake City, FL .... Real Estate Law

MCDERMOTT & MCGEE
Millburn, NJ .... Appellate Practice; Civil Trial Practice; General Practice; Insurance Defense; Medical Malpractice; Personal Injury; Professional Liability

MCDONALD, E. DANDRIDGE
Charleston, WV .... Public Utilities Law

MCDONALD, BROWN & FAGEN
Dallas Center, IA .... General Practice

MCDONALD CARANO WILSON MCCUNE BERGIN FRANKOVICH & HICKS LLP
Las Vegas, NV .... Civil Trial Practice; Commercial Law; Construction Law; General Practice; Municipal and Zoning Law; Real Estate Law; Tax Law; Trust and Estates, Wills and Probate
Reno, NV .... Administrative Law; Civil Trial Practice; Commercial Law; Construction Law; Employment Benefits Law; Environmental Law; General Practice; Intellectual Property Law; Labor and Employment Law; Municipal and Zoning Law; Real Estate Law; Tax Law; Trust and Estates, Wills and Probate; Workers Compensation

MCDONALD, FRANCES B., P.C.
Denver, CO .... Labor and Employment Law; Nonprofit and Tax Exempt Organizations

MCDONALD GROUP, THE, L.L.P.
Erie, PA .... General Practice

MCDONALD & HAYDEN
Toronto, ON, Canada .... Business Law; Family Law; Personal Injury; Real Estate Law; Securities Law; Tax Law; Trademark, Copyright and Unfair Competition

MCDONALD, HOPKINS, BURKE & HABER CO., L.P.A.
Cleveland, OH .... Appellate Practice; Business Law; Civil Trial Practice; Commercial Litigation; Employment Benefits Law; General Practice; Pension and Profit Sharing; Real Estate Law; Tax Law; Trust and Estates, Wills and Probate

MCDONALD & KANYUK, P.L.L.C.
Concord, NH .... Trust and Estates, Wills and Probate

MCDONALD KUHN
Memphis, TN .... General Practice; Insurance Defense; Product Liability Law; Workers Compensation

MCDONALD, MARYBETH, P.A.
Orlando, FL .... Insurance Defense

MCDONALD & MCDONALD
Miami, FL .... Aviation Law

MCDONALD, SAELTZER, MORRIS, CREEGGAN & WADDOCK
Sacramento, CA .... Civil Trial Practice; Insurance Defense

MCDONALD, WILLIAM H., & ASSOCIATES, P.C.
Springfield, MO .... Antitrust Law; Civil Trial Practice; Commercial Law; General Practice; Patent, Trademark, Copyright and Unfair Competition; Product Liability Law

MCDONNELL BOEHNEN HULBERT & BERGHOFF
Chicago, IL .... Intellectual Property Law; Patent, Trademark, Copyright and Unfair Competition; Trademark, Copyright and Unfair Competition

MCDONNELL TRIAL LAWYERS
Naples, FL .... Civil Trial Practice; Criminal Trial Practice; Personal Injury

MCDONOUGH, HOLLAND & ALLEN, A PROFESSIONAL CORPORATION
Sacramento, CA .... General Practice

MCDONOUGH, KORN & EICHHORN, A PROFESSIONAL CORPORATION
Springfield, NJ .... Admiralty/Maritime Law; Aviation Law; Civil Trial Practice; Criminal Trial Practice; General Practice; Insurance Defense; Medical Malpractice; Personal Injury; Product Liability Law; Professional Liability

MCDOUGALL & SELF, L.L.P.
Sumter, SC .... Family Law

MCDOWALL, COTTER, DUNN, VALE & BRACCO, A PROFESSIONAL CORPORATION
San Mateo, CA .... Civil Trial Practice; Insurance Defense

MCDOWELL & BEASON
Russellville, AL .... Corporate Law; General Practice; Insurance Defense

MCDOWELL, JOSEPH F., III, P.A.
Manchester, NH .... General Practice

MCDOWELL, WICK, DALY, GALLUP, HAUSER AND HARTLE
Bradford, PA .... General Practice

MCDUFFEE, PAUL G. II
Tampa, FL .... Personal Injury

MCELDREW & FULLAM, P.C.
Philadelphia, PA .... Civil Trial Practice; Labor and Employment Law; Medical Malpractice; Personal Injury; Product Liability Law; Professional Liability; Transportation Law

MCELROY, DEUTSCH AND MULVANEY
Morristown, NJ .... Civil Trial Practice; Commercial Law; Construction Law; Environmental Law; General Practice; Insurance Defense

MCEWAN, MARTINEZ, LUFF, DUKES & RUFFIER, P.A.
Orlando, FL .... Civil Trial Practice; Commercial Litigation; Insurance Defense; Medical Malpractice; Professional Liability

MCEWEN, SCHMITT & CO.
Vancouver, BC, Canada .... Admiralty/Maritime Law

MCFADDEN & DILLON, A PROFESSIONAL CORPORATION
Chicago, IL .... Banking Law; Civil Trial Practice; Commercial Litigation; General Practice; Labor and Employment Law

MCFARLAIN, WILEY, CASSEDY & JONES, PROFESSIONAL ASSOCIATION
Tallahassee, FL .... Administrative Law; Appellate Practice; Business Law; Civil Trial Practice; Commercial Law; Commercial Litigation; Family Law; Health Care Law; Insurance Defense; Medical Malpractice; Personal Injury; Product Liability Law; Professional Liability

MCFARLAND & HERMAN
Chicago, IL .... Transportation Law

MCGAHN, FRISS, FRANKS & TRIPICIAN
Atlantic City, NJ .... General Practice

MCGARITY & ASSOCIATES
Lawrenceville, GA .... Personal Injury

MCGARRY & LAUFENBERG
Gardena, CA .... Insurance Defense; Personal Injury; Product Liability Law

MCGAUGHEY & SPIRITO
Torrance, CA .... Family Law; Trust and Estates, Wills and Probate

MCGEE & GELMAN
Buffalo, NY .... Civil Trial Practice; General Practice; Patent, Trademark, Copyright and Unfair Competition

MCGEE & MASON, P.A.
Brooksville, FL .... General Practice

MCGEE & POWERS, P.A.
Orlando, FL .... Commercial Litigation; Insurance Defense; Product Liability Law

MCGILL, GOTSDINER, WORKMAN & LEPP, P.C.
Omaha, NE .... Banking Law; Civil Trial Practice; Commercial Litigation; Creditors Rights; General Practice; Health Care Law; International Business Law; Labor and Employment Law; Mergers and Acquisitions; Tax Law; Workers Compensation

MCGILLICUDDY, TERRENCE J., P.C.
Phoenix, AZ .... Aviation Law; Personal Injury

MCGIMPSEY & CAFFERTY
Somerset, NJ .... Communications Law; General Practice

MCGINLEY, O'DONNELL, REYNOLDS & EDWARDS, P.C.
Ogallala, NE .... General Practice

MCGINNIS, LOCHRIDGE & KILGORE, L.L.P.
Austin, TX .... General Practice
Houston, TX .... General Practice

MCGLINCHEY STAFFORD
New Orleans, LA .... Admiralty/Maritime Law; Antitrust Law; Appellate Practice; Arbitration; Aviation Law; Banking Law; Bankruptcy Law; Business Law; Civil Trial Practice; Commercial Litigation; Construction Law; Corporate Law; Employment Benefits Law; Environmental Law; Health Care Law; Immigration and Naturalization; Insurance Defense; Intellectual Property Law; International Trade Law; Labor and Employment Law; Medical Malpractice; Municipal and Zoning Law; Municipal Bond/Public Authority Financing; Pension and Profit Sharing; Product Liability Law; Professional Liability; Public Utilities Law; Real Estate Law; Securities Law; Tax Law; Toxic Torts; Trust and Estates, Wills and Probate; Workers Compensation

MCGLINN, MICHAEL D.
San Diego, CA ....Criminal Trial Practice

MCGLOTHREN, MICHAEL S., P.C.
Fairhope, AL..........................Personal Injury

MCGLYNN & MCGLYNN
Belleville, IL ....Commercial Law; Personal Injury; Transportation Law
St. Louis, MO..........................Personal Injury

MCGOUGAN, WRIGHT, WORLEY AND HARPER, L.L.P.
Tabor City, NC.........................General Practice

MCGOVERN, CONNELLY & DAVIDSON
New Rochelle, NY ....Tax Law

MCGOVERN AND DAWSON
White Plains, NY.....................Civil Trial Practice; Trust and Estates, Wills and Probate

MCGOWN, MICHAEL R.
Beaumont, TX..........................Civil Trial Practice; Personal Injury; Product Liability Law

MCGRANE & NOSICH, P.A.
Miami, FL ....Insurance Defense

MCGRATH, J. NICHOLAS, P.C.
Aspen, CO ....Civil Trial Practice; General Practice; Real Estate Law

MCGRATH, NORTH, MULLIN & KRATZ, P.C.
Omaha, NE ....Antitrust Law; Civil Trial Practice; General Practice; Insurance Defense; Intellectual Property Law; Labor and Employment Law; Tax Law

MCGREGOR & ASSOCIATES, P.C.
Boston, MA..............................Environmental Law

MCGUANE AND HOGAN LLP
Denver, CO ....Family Law

MCGUINESS, ROBERT D.
Oakland, CA ....Family Law

MCGUINESS NORRIS & WILLIAMS, LLP
Washington, DC........................Labor and Employment Law

MCGUINN, HILLSMAN & PALEFSKY, A PROFESSIONAL CORPORATION
San Francisco, CA ....Admiralty/Maritime Law; Labor and Employment Law; Personal Injury

MCGUIRE, KEHL & NEALON, LLP
New York, NY..........................Civil Trial Practice; Education Law; Intellectual Property Law; Sports and Entertainment Law

MCGUIRE, WOOD & BISSETTE, P.A.
Asheville, NC ....Civil Trial Practice; General Practice

MCGUIRE, WOODS, BATTLE & BOOTHE LLP
Washington, DC........................General Practice
Jacksonville, FL......................General Practice
Charlottesville, VA...................General Practice
McLean, VA.............................General Practice
Norfolk, VA ....General Practice
Richmond, VA ....Antitrust Law; General Practice; Labor and Employment Law; Municipal Bond/Public Authority Financing; Tax Law

MCHENRY LAW FIRM
Little Rock, AR ....Medical Malpractice

MCHIE, MYERS, MCHIE & ENSLEN
Hammond, IN..........................Civil Trial Practice; General Practice

MCINNES COOPER
Fredericton, NB, Canada..........Appellate Practice; Banking Law; Bankruptcy Law; Business Law; Civil Trial Practice; Commercial Law; Commercial Litigation; Construction Law; Corporate Law; Creditors Rights; Employment Benefits Law; Energy Law; General Practice; Government Contracts; Labor and Employment Law; Medical Malpractice; Mergers and Acquisitions; Personal Injury; Product Liability Law; Professional Liability; Real Estate Law; Securities Law; Tax Law; Trust and Estates, Wills and Probate
Moncton, NB, Canada.............Administrative Law; Appellate Practice; Banking Law; Bankruptcy Law; Business Law; Civil Rights; Civil Trial Practice; Commercial Law; Commercial Litigation; Construction Law; Corporate Law; Creditors Rights; Employment Benefits Law; Environmental Law; General Practice; Insurance Defense; Medical Malpractice; Municipal and Zoning Law; Natural Resources Law; Oil and Gas Law; Personal Injury; Product Liability Law; Professional Liability; Real Estate Law; Securities Law
St. John's, NF, Canada............Admiralty/Maritime Law; Appellate Practice; Arbitration; Aviation Law; Banking Law; Bankruptcy Law; Business Law; Civil Rights; Civil Trial Practice; Commercial Law; Commercial Litigation; Computer Law; Construction Law; Corporate Law; Creditors Rights; Criminal Trial Practice; Employment Benefits Law; Energy Law; Environmental Law; General Practice; Health Care Law; Insurance Defense; Intellectual Property Law; Labor and Employment Law; Medical Malpractice; Mergers and Acquisitions; Natural Resources Law; Oil and Gas Law; Patent, Trademark, Copyright and Unfair Competition; Personal Injury; Product Liability Law; Professional Liability; Public Utilities Law; Real Estate Law; Securities Law; Sports and Entertainment Law; Tax Law; Trademark, Copyright and Unfair Competition; Workers Compensation
Halifax, NS, Canada ....Administrative Law; Admiralty/Maritime Law; Appellate Practice; Arbitration; Aviation Law; Banking Law; Bankruptcy Law; Business Law; Civil Rights; Civil Trial Practice; Commercial Law; Commercial Litigation; Computer Law; Constitutional Law; Construction Law; Corporate Law; Creditors Rights; Employment Benefits Law; Energy Law; Environmental Law; General Practice; Government Contracts; Insurance Defense; Intellectual Property Law; International Business Law; International Trade Law; Labor and Employment Law; Land Use Law; Medical Malpractice; Mergers and Acquisitions; Municipal and Zoning Law; Municipal Bond/Public Authority Financing; Natural Resources Law; Oil and Gas Law; Pension and Profit Sharing; Personal Injury; Product Liability Law; Professional Liability; Public Utilities Law; Real Estate Law; Securities Law; Sports and Entertainment Law; Tax Law; Toxic Torts; Trademark, Copyright and Unfair Competition; Transportation Law; Trust and Estates, Wills and Probate; Workers Compensation
Charlottetown, PE, Canada.....Administrative Law; Appellate Practice; Banking Law; Bankruptcy Law; Business Law; Civil Trial Practice; Commercial Law; Commercial Litigation; Construction Law; Corporate Law; Creditors Rights; Energy Law; General Practice; Health Care Law; Immigration and Naturalization; Insurance Defense; Labor and Employment Law; Land Use Law; Medical Malpractice; Mergers and Acquisitions; Oil and Gas Law; Personal Injury; Professional Liability; Public Utilities Law; Real Estate Law; Trust and Estates, Wills and Probate

MCINTOSH & LEE
Florence, SC ....Insurance Defense

MCINTOSH, SHERARD & SULLIVAN
Anderson, SC..........................General Practice

MCKAY, BYRNE & GRAHAM
Los Angeles, CA ....Civil Trial Practice; Insurance Defense; Product Liability Law

MCKAY & GUÉRARD, P.A.
Charleston, SC ....General Practice
Columbia, SC ....General Practice

MCKAY, JOHN J., JR., P.A.
Hilton Head Island, SC...........Civil Trial Practice

MCKAY & MCKAY, P.A.
Columbia, SC ....Civil Trial Practice; General Practice; Medical Malpractice; Product Liability Law

MCKENDREE, JOHN W. LAW OFFICES OF
Denver, CO ....Arbitration; Civil Rights; Civil Trial Practice; Constitutional Law; Criminal Trial Practice; Family Law; Labor and Employment Law

MCKENNA, JAMES L., P.C.
Cherry Hill, NJ ....Environmental Law; Insurance Defense

MCKENZIE, ROBERT E.
Chicago, IL.............................Tax Law

MCKENZIE, MCRAE, VASSER & BARBER, PLLC
Prescott, AR............................General Practice

MCKENZIE & TAYLOR, P.A.
Pensacola, FL..........................Personal Injury

MCKEOWN, FITZGERALD, ZOLLNER, BUCK, HUTCHISON & RUTTLE
Joliet, IL ....Civil Trial Practice; General Practice; Personal Injury; Trust and Estates, Wills and Probate

MCKINNEY, ANNE M., P.C.
Knoxville, TN ....Trust and Estates, Wills and Probate

MCKIRDY AND RISKIN, A PROFESSIONAL CORPORATION
Morristown, NJ.......................Civil Trial Practice; Eminent Domain; Real Estate Law

MCKISSOCK & HOFFMAN, P.C.
Philadelphia, PA ....Aviation Law; Civil Trial Practice; Commercial Law; Commercial Litigation; Health Care Law; Insurance Defense; Medical Malpractice; Product Liability Law

MCKOOL SMITH, A PROFESSIONAL CORPORATION
Dallas, TX...............................Civil Trial Practice

MCLAUGHLIN, LESLIE G.
Midland, TX ....Civil Trial Practice; General Practice; Insurance Defense; Personal Injury

MCLAUGHLIN AND FLORINI, LTD.
Sullivan, IL.............................Trust and Estates, Wills and Probate

MCLENNAN ROSS
Calgary, AB, Canada...............Civil Trial Practice; Labor and Employment Law
Edmonton, AB, Canada ....Civil Trial Practice; General Practice; Labor and Employment Law

MCLEOD, ALEXANDER, POWEL & APFFEL, A PROFESSIONAL CORPORATION
Galveston, TX .... General Practice

MCLEOD & MOYNE, P.C.
Okemos, MI .... Intellectual Property Law; Patent, Trademark, Copyright and Unfair Competition

MCLEOD VERLANDER
Monroe, LA .... Civil Trial Practice; Family Law; Health Care Law; Medical Malpractice; Personal Injury

MCLEOD, WATKINSON & MILLER
Washington, DC .... Administrative Law

MCMAHAN, CARL A. LAW OFFICES OF
Los Angeles, CA .... Civil Trial Practice; Medical Malpractice; Personal Injury; Product Liability Law

MCMAHON, BERGER, HANNA, LINIHAN, CODY & MCCARTHY, A PROFESSIONAL CORPORATION
St. Louis, MO .... Labor and Employment Law

MCMAHON, PATRICK R., A PROF. CORP., LAW OFFICES OF
San Jose, CA .... Personal Injury

MCMAHON & SPIEGEL
Los Angeles, CA .... Oil and Gas Law

MCMAHON, TIDWELL, HANSEN, ATKINS & PEACOCK, P.C.
Odessa, TX .... General Practice

MCMANIMON & SCOTLAND, L.L.C.
Newark, NJ .... Banking Law; Commercial Law; Corporate Law; Environmental Law; General Practice; Municipal Bond/Public Authority Financing; Real Estate Law; Securities Law; Tax Law

MCMANIS, FAULKNER & MORGAN
San Jose, CA .... Antitrust Law; Appellate Practice; Civil Rights; Civil Trial Practice; Commercial Litigation; Construction Law; Criminal Trial Practice; Environmental Law; Family Law; Intellectual Property Law; Labor and Employment Law; Land Use Law; Personal Injury; Trademark, Copyright and Unfair Competition

MCMASTER, CLIFFORD F.
Fort Worth, TX .... Bankruptcy Law

MCMASTER GERVAIS
Montreal, QU, Canada .... Administrative Law; Admiralty/Maritime Law; Arbitration; Banking Law; Bankruptcy Law; Business Law; Civil Trial Practice; Commercial Law; Commercial Litigation; Computer Law; Construction Law; Corporate Law; Environmental Law; General Practice; Health Care Law; Immigration and Naturalization; Insurance Defense; Intellectual Property Law; International Business Law; Labor and Employment Law; Medical Malpractice; Municipal and Zoning Law; Municipal Bond/Public Authority Financing; Personal Injury; Product Liability Law; Professional Liability; Public Utilities Law; Real Estate Law; Securities Law; Tax Law; Trademark, Copyright and Unfair Competition; Transportation Law; Trust and Estates, Wills and Probate; Workers Compensation

MCMATH, VEHIK, DRUMMOND, HARRISON & LEDBETTER, P.A.
Little Rock, AR .... Civil Trial Practice; Medical Malpractice

MCMILLAN BINCH
Toronto, ON, Canada .... General Practice

MCMILLAN CONSTABILE, LLP
Larchmont, NY .... General Practice

MCMILLEN, REINHART & VOGHT, P.A.
Orlando, FL .... Medical Malpractice

MCMORAN & ASSOCIATES, P.C.
Iselin, NJ .... Labor and Employment Law

MCMULLEN LAW FIRM
Fort Worth, TX .... Civil Trial Practice; Commercial Litigation; Construction Law; Insurance Defense; Personal Injury

MCMURRY & LIVINGSTON
Paducah, KY .... General Practice

MCMURRY & TALBOTT
Louisville, KY .... Legal Malpractice; Medical Malpractice

MCNABB, DOUGLAS C.
Houston, TX .... Appellate Practice; Criminal Trial Practice

MCNAIR LAW FIRM, P.A.
Columbia, SC .... General Practice

MCNAMAR, FEARNOW & MCSHARAR, P.C.
Indianapolis, IN .... Administrative Law; Health Care Law; Real Estate Law

MCNAMARA, F. TIMOTHY, P.C.
Hartford, CT .... Criminal Trial Practice

MCNAMARA AND MCNAMARA
Columbus, OH .... Construction Law; Insurance Defense

MCNAMARA, TODD J., P.C.
Denver, CO .... Labor and Employment Law

MCNAUL EBEL NAWROT HELGREN & VANCE P.L.L.C.
Seattle, WA .... Civil Trial Practice; General Practice

MCNEER, HIGHLAND, MCMUNN AND VARNER, L.C.
Clarksburg, WV .... Appellate Practice; Banking Law; Bankruptcy Law; Business Law; Civil Trial Practice; Commercial Law; Commercial Litigation; Construction Law; Environmental Law; General Practice; Insurance Defense; Labor and Employment Law; Medical Malpractice; Mergers and Acquisitions; Natural Resources Law; Personal Injury; Product Liability Law; Real Estate Law; Tax Law; Trust and Estates, Wills and Probate; Workers Compensation

MCNEES, WALLACE & NURICK
Columbus, OH .... Energy Law
Harrisburg, PA .... Commercial Litigation; Construction Law; Energy Law; General Practice; Intellectual Property Law; Labor and Employment Law; Real Estate Law; Transportation Law

MCNEIL, SILVEIRA & RICE
San Rafael, CA .... Business Law

MCNEIL, SUSSON, PARRETT & TROPP, A PROFESSIONAL CORPORATION
Santa Ana, CA .... Health Care Law; Medical Malpractice

MCNICHOLAS & MCNICHOLAS, LLP
Los Angeles, CA .... Civil Trial Practice; Labor and Employment Law; Personal Injury

MCNULTY, THOMAS J. JR.
Barnstable, MA .... Trust and Estates, Wills and Probate

MCPHERSON & ROCAMORA, PLLC
Durham, NC .... Trust and Estates, Wills and Probate

MCQUADES, THE, CO., L.P.A.
Swanton, OH .... General Practice; Personal Injury; Trust and Estates, Wills and Probate

MCREYNOLDS, GREGG C., P.C.
Denver, CO .... Civil Trial Practice

MCREYNOLDS, MARY A., P.C.
Washington, DC .... Civil Trial Practice; Commercial Law

MCSHANE & BOWIE, P.L.C.
Grand Rapids, MI .... Business Law; Commercial Litigation; Corporate Law; General Practice; Real Estate Law; Securities Law; Trust and Estates, Wills and Probate

MCSHANE, DAVIS & HANCE, L.L.P.
Dallas, TX .... Family Law

MCSHEA TECCE, P.C.
Philadelphia, PA .... Civil Trial Practice

MCTAGUE LAW FIRM
Windsor, ON, Canada .... Civil Trial Practice; Commercial Law; General Practice; Insurance Defense; Labor and Employment Law; Real Estate Law

MCTIGHE, WEISS, O'ROURKE & MILNER, P.C.
Norristown, PA .... General Practice; Insurance Defense

MCTURNAN & TURNER
Indianapolis, IN .... Antitrust Law; Appellate Practice; Civil Trial Practice; Commercial Litigation; Labor and Employment Law; Securities Law

MCVAY, WILLIAM W.
Pittsburgh, PA .... Personal Injury

MCWHORTER, COBB & JOHNSON, L.L.P.
Lubbock, TX .... Civil Trial Practice; General Practice

MEAD & ASSOCIATES
Glendale, AZ .... General Practice

MEADE, BRODOVSKY, AIKEN, JACOBSEN & HINE, A LIMITED LIABILITY PARTNERSHIP
Sacramento, CA .... Personal Injury

MEAD, HECHT, CONKLIN & GALLAGHER
White Plains, NY .... General Practice

MEADOWS, ICHTER & TRIGG, P.C. A PROFESSIONAL CORPORATION
Atlanta, GA .... Civil Trial Practice

MEADOWS, OWENS, COLLIER, REED, COUSINS & BLAU, L.L.P.
Dallas, TX .... Corporate Law; General Practice; Mergers and Acquisitions; Real Estate Law; Securities Law; Tax Law; Trust and Estates, Wills and Probate

MEADOWS RILEY LAW FIRM
Gulfport, MS .... Bankruptcy Law; Business Law; Civil Trial Practice; Corporate Law; Environmental Law; Family Law; Real Estate Law; Trust and Estates, Wills and Probate

MEAHER, AUGUSTINE, III, P.C.
Mobile, AL .... Civil Trial Practice; General Practice

MEARDON, SUEPPEL, DOWNER & HAYES P.L.C.
Iowa City, IA .... Civil Trial Practice; General Practice; Municipal and Zoning Law

MEARS, CHRISTOPHER B., A P.C.
Irvine, CA .... Personal Injury

MEDEIROS + SANFORD INC.
Providence, RI .... Antitrust Law; Business Law; Civil Trial Practice; Commercial Litigation; Labor and Employment Law; Securities Law

MEDLEN & CARROLL, LLP
San Francisco, CA .... Patent, Trademark, Copyright and Unfair Competition

MEEHAN & ASSOCIATES, LAW OFFICES OF
Tucson, AZ .... Commercial Litigation

MEEHAN, BOYLE & COHEN, P.C.
Boston, MA .... Appellate Practice; Aviation Law; Civil Trial Practice; Medical Malpractice; Personal Injury; Product Liability Law

MEEKS, W. EDWARD JR.
Albany, GA .... General Practice; Medical Malpractice; Personal Injury

MEENAN & LARIVIERE
Pasadena, CA .... Civil Trial Practice; Medical Malpractice; Personal Injury; Product Liability Law

MEGANCK, ALLAN G.
Grosse Pointe Park, MI .... Insurance Defense; Medical Malpractice; Product Liability Law

MEHAFFY & WEBER, A PROFESSIONAL CORPORATION
Beaumont, TX .... Admiralty/Maritime Law; Civil Trial Practice; Employment Benefits Law; Environmental Law; General Practice; Insurance Defense; Medical Malpractice; Personal Injury; Product Liability Law
Houston, TX .... Civil Trial Practice; Environmental Law; Insurance Defense; Personal Injury; Product Liability Law
Orange, TX .... Civil Trial Practice; Environmental Law; Insurance Defense; Personal Injury

MEHLMAN & GREENBLATT, LLC
Baltimore, MD .... Bankruptcy Law; Civil Trial Practice; Criminal Trial Practice; Medical Malpractice

MEHR & LAFRANCE
Freehold, NJ .... General Practice

MEHRENS AND WILEMON, P.A.
Phoenix, AZ .... Criminal Trial Practice

MEIER, LENGAUER, BONNER, MUSZYNSKI & DOYLE, P.A.
Orlando, FL .... Civil Trial Practice; Insurance Defense; Product Liability Law

MEIGHEN DEMERS
Toronto, ON, Canada .... General Practice

MEIROSE & FRISCIA, P.A.
Tampa, FL .... Commercial Litigation; Construction Law; Insurance Defense

MEISLIK & LEVAVY
Montclair, NJ .... Business Law; Real Estate Law

MEISNER & ASSOCIATES, P.C.
Bingham Farms, MI .... Business Law; Civil Trial Practice; Real Estate Law

MEISSNER TIERNEY FISHER & NICHOLS S.C.
Milwaukee, WI .... Antitrust Law; Business Law; Commercial Litigation; Elder Law; Employment Benefits Law; Environmental Law; Health Care Law; Nonprofit and Tax Exempt Organizations; Real Estate Law; Securities Law; Tax Law; Trust and Estates, Wills and Probate

MELAT, PRESSMAN, EZELL & HIGBIE, LLP
Colorado Springs, CO .... Civil Trial Practice; Commercial Litigation; Personal Injury

MELEDIN, LOUISE Y.
Baltimore, MD .... Tax Law

MELLEY, STEVEN M.
Rhinebeck, NY .... Personal Injury

MELLI, WALKER, PEASE & RUHLY, S.C.
Madison, WI .... General Practice; Labor and Employment Law

MELLON LAW FIRM, THE
Denver, CO .... Civil Trial Practice; Construction Law

MELLON, WEBSTER & MELLON, A PROF. CORP., THE LAW OFFICES OF
Doylestown, PA .... Personal Injury

MELTON, FLOYD M. JR.
Greenwood, MS .... Trust and Estates, Wills and Probate

MELTON, WILLIAM D.
Evergreen, AL .... Civil Trial Practice; Personal Injury; Product Liability Law

MELTZER, SANFORD
Syracuse, NY .... Criminal Trial Practice; Family Law

MELTZER, PETER E., & ASSOCIATES, P.C., LAW OFFICES OF
Philadelphia, PA .... Creditors Rights

MELVIN & MELVIN
Laurel, MS .... Medical Malpractice; Personal Injury; Product Liability Law
Syracuse, NY .... General Practice

MENARD, MURPHY & WALSH LLP
Boston, MA .... Business Law; Civil Trial Practice; Commercial Litigation; Family Law; Labor and Employment Law; Trust and Estates, Wills and Probate

MENDELSOHN ROSENTZVEIG SHACTER
Montreal, QU, Canada .... Banking Law; Bankruptcy Law; Commercial Law; Commercial Litigation; Labor and Employment Law; Patent, Trademark, Copyright and Unfair Competition; Real Estate Law; Securities Law; Tax Law

MENDES & MOUNT, LLP
New York, NY .... Insurance Defense

MENES LAW CORPORATION
Los Angeles, CA .... Intellectual Property Law; Sports and Entertainment Law; Trademark, Copyright and Unfair Competition

MENTZER, VUILLEMIN AND MYGRANT LTD.
Akron, OH .... Bankruptcy Law; Commercial Law; Commercial Litigation; Criminal Trial Practice

MERCALDO, RONALD D., LTD.
Tucson, AZ .... Medical Malpractice; Personal Injury

MERCER & MERCER
Pittsburgh, PA .... Personal Injury

MERKIN, STEWART A. LAW OFFICE OF
Miami, FL .... Business Law

MERKLE & MAGRI, P.A., LAW OFFICES OF
Tampa, FL .... Civil Trial Practice; Commercial Litigation; Criminal Trial Practice; Personal Injury; Product Liability Law

MERLIN & HERTZ, P.A.
Coral Gables, FL .... Family Law

MERLINE & THOMAS, P.A.
Greenville, SC .... Mergers and Acquisitions; Pension and Profit Sharing; Tax Law; Trust and Estates, Wills and Probate

MERLO, KANOFSKY & BRINKMEIER, LTD.
Chicago, IL .... Aviation Law; Insurance Defense

MERLY, LAWRENCE J.
Bridgeport, CT .... Civil Trial Practice; Personal Injury

MERRILL, ABEL J., P.A.
Annapolis, MD .... Trust and Estates, Wills and Probate

MERRILL & MERRILL, CHARTERED
Pocatello, ID .... Appellate Practice; Business Law; Civil Trial Practice; General Practice; Health Care Law; Insurance Defense; Public Utilities Law; Real Estate Law; Trust and Estates, Wills and Probate

MERRILL, MULLINS & SPEARS, A PROFESSIONAL ASSOCIATION
Memphis, TN .... Commercial Law

MERRILL, SCHULTZ & WOLDS, LIMITED
San Diego, CA .... Employment Benefits Law; Labor and Employment Law

MERRILL, STONE & HAMILTON, LLC
Swainsboro, GA......................Civil Trial Practice

MERRIMAN, PATTERSON & ALLISON, L.L.P.
Longview, TX..........................Insurance Defense

MERRITT & ASSOCIATES, P.C.
Oklahoma City, OK....................Medical Malpractice; Personal Injury; Product Liability Law

MERRITT, WOOTEN & JANVIER, P.A.
Raleigh, NC............................Business Law

MERRY, FARNEN & RYAN, A PROFESSIONAL CORPORATION
St. Clair Shores, MI.................Medical Malpractice; Professional Liability

MERVIS, CLARK D.
Miami, FL...............................Criminal Trial Practice

MESH, GENE & ASSOCIATES
Cincinnati, OH.........................Civil Trial Practice; Commercial Litigation; Securities Law

MESHBESHER & SPENCE
Minneapolis, MN.......................Civil Trial Practice; Criminal Trial Practice; Medical Malpractice; Personal Injury

MESSER, HOWARD F., P.C.
Pittsburgh, PA.........................Civil Trial Practice; Medical Malpractice; Personal Injury; Product Liability Law; Transportation Law

MESSINA BULZOMI
Tacoma, WA.............................Personal Injury

METNICK, CHERRY & FRAZIER
Springfield, IL..........................Civil Trial Practice; Criminal Trial Practice; Family Law; Personal Injury; Workers Compensation

METTE, EVANS & WOODSIDE, A PROFESSIONAL CORPORATION
Harrisburg, PA.........................Administrative Law; Banking Law; Civil Trial Practice; Commercial Law; Construction Law; Environmental Law; General Practice; Municipal Bond/Public Authority Financing; Real Estate Law; Tax Law

METTLER, PETER W.
Palm Beach, FL.........................Tax Law

METZGER & ASSOCIATES, LTD.
Chicago, IL..............................Appellate Practice

METZGER, DIRK T., A PROFESSIONAL CORPORATION
San Diego, CA..........................Commercial Litigation

METZGER, WICKERSHAM, KNAUSS & ERB, P.C.
Harrisburg, PA.........................Civil Trial Practice; General Practice; Insurance Defense; Medical Malpractice; Personal Injury; Product Liability Law; Trust and Estates, Wills and Probate

MEULEMAN & MILLER, L.L.P.
Boise, ID.................................Construction Law; Real Estate Law

MEYER, CAPEL, HIRSCHFELD, MUNCY, JAHN & ALDEEN, P.C.
Champaign, IL..........................Business Law; Commercial Litigation; General Practice

MEYER, FLUEGGE AND TENNEY, P.S.
Yakima, WA.............................General Practice

MEYER, HENDRICKS & BIVENS, P.A.
Phoenix, AZ.............................Business Law; Commercial Litigation; International Business Law; Mergers and Acquisitions; Professional Liability; Securities Law

MEYER, JIM, & ASSOCIATES, P.C.
Waco, TX.................................Civil Trial Practice; Family Law; Personal Injury

MEYER, KIRK, SNYDER & SAFFORD, PLLC
Bloomfield Hills, MI..................Business Law; Civil Trial Practice; Family Law; Real Estate Law; Trust and Estates, Wills and Probate
Detroit, MI...............................Business Law; Civil Trial Practice; Family Law; Real Estate Law; Trust and Estates, Wills and Probate

MEYER, UNKOVIC & SCOTT LLP
Pittsburgh, PA.........................General Practice

MEYERS, BILLINGSLEY, RODBELL & ROSENBAUM, P.A.
Riverdale, MD..........................Bankruptcy Law; Commercial Litigation; General Practice; Municipal Bond/Public Authority Financing; Real Estate Law

MEYERS, HENTEMANN & REA CO., L.P.A.
Cleveland, OH..........................Civil Trial Practice; General Practice; Insurance Defense; Product Liability Law

MEYERS, MOONEY, STANLEY & HOLLINGSWORTH
Orlando, FL.............................Aviation Law; Medical Malpractice; Personal Injury; Professional Liability; Workers Compensation

MEYNER AND LANDIS
Newark, NJ..............................Administrative Law; Banking Law; Bankruptcy Law; Civil Trial Practice; Commercial Law; Communications Law; Corporate Law; Creditors Rights; General Practice; Immigration and Naturalization; Land Use Law; Nonprofit and Tax Exempt Organizations; Public Utilities Law; Real Estate Law; Trust and Estates, Wills and Probate

MEZVINSKY, EDWARD M.
Narberth, PA...........................General Practice; International Business Law; International Trade Law

MICHAEL, ROBERT J.
Rochester, NY..........................Civil Trial Practice; Personal Injury; Product Liability Law

MICHAEL BEST & FRIEDRICH LLP
Madison, WI............................General Practice
Milwaukee, WI.........................Antitrust Law; General Practice; Labor and Employment Law; Municipal Bond/Public Authority Financing; Natural Resources Law; Patent, Trademark, Copyright and Unfair Competition; Tax Law

MICHAELIS, MONTANARI & JOHNSON, A PROFESSIONAL LAW CORPORATION
Westlake Village, CA.................Insurance Defense

MICHAELS & BONNER, P.C.
Washington, DC........................Health Care Law

MICHAELS, JONES, MARTIN, PARRIS & TESSENER LAW OFFICES, PLLC
Raleigh, NC.............................Medical Malpractice; Personal Injury; Product Liability Law; Workers Compensation

MICHAELS & SMOLAK, P.C.
Auburn, NY..............................Civil Trial Practice

MICHAELSON, BENJAMIN, JR., P.A.
Annapolis, MD..........................Real Estate Law

MICHAUD, BUSCHMANN, FOX, FERRARA & MITTELMARK, P.A.
Boca Raton, FL.........................Civil Trial Practice; Construction Law; Insurance Defense; Medical Malpractice; Product Liability Law; Professional Liability; Toxic Torts; Transportation Law

MICHELI, BALDWIN, BOPELEY & NORTHRUP CO., L.P.A.
Zanesville, OH..........................Civil Trial Practice; Insurance Defense; Medical Malpractice

MICHENER, LARIMORE, SWINDLE, WHITAKER, FLOWERS, SAWYER, REYNOLDS & CHALK, L.L.P.
Fort Worth, TX..........................Business Law; Tax Law

MICKEY, WILSON, WEILER & RENZI, P.C.
Aurora, IL...............................General Practice

MIDDENDORF, HENRY S. JR.
New York, NY...........................General Practice

MIDDLEBERG, RIDDLE & GIANNA
New Orleans, LA.......................Commercial Law; Insurance Defense; Real Estate Law
Dallas, TX...............................Civil Trial Practice; Commercial Law; Insurance Defense; Real Estate Law

MIDDLEBROOK, KAISER & POPKA, A PROFESSIONAL CORPORATION
San Bernardino, CA...................Civil Trial Practice; Insurance Defense

MIDDLEBROOKS & SHAPIRO, P.C.
Parsippany, NJ..........................Bankruptcy Law; Commercial Litigation

MIDDLETON, MATHIS, ADAMS & TATE, P.C.
Atlanta, GA.............................General Practice
Milledgeville, GA.....................General Practice
Savannah, GA...........................General Practice

MIDDLETON & REUTLINGER, P.S.C.
Louisville, KY..........................Antitrust Law; Banking Law; Bankruptcy Law; Civil Trial Practice; Environmental Law; General Practice; Insurance Defense; Patent, Trademark, Copyright and Unfair Competition; Personal Injury; Securities Law; Tax Law; Trust and Estates, Wills and Probate

MIDLEN LAW CENTER
Washington, DC........................Business Law; Communications Law; Trademark, Copyright and Unfair Competition

MIKKELBORG, BROZ, WELLS & FRYER, PLLC
Seattle, WA.............................Admiralty/Maritime Law; General Practice

MIKOS, KENNETH R., P.A.
Fort Lauderdale, FL..................Civil Trial Practice; Elder Law; Trust and Estates, Wills and Probate

MIKUS LAW ASSOCIATES
Lancaster, PA..........................Personal Injury; Product Liability Law

MILANO, JAY LAW OFFICES OF
Rocky River, OH....................Civil Trial Practice; Criminal Trial Practice

MILBANK, TWEED, HADLEY & MCCLOY LLP
Los Angeles, CA....................General Practice; Securities Law
Washington, DC....................General Practice
New York, NY....................Aviation Law; Banking Law; Commercial Litigation; General Practice; Securities Law; Transportation Law
Hong Kong, China....................General Practice; Securities Law
London, England....................General Practice; Securities Law
Tokyo, Japan....................Aviation Law; General Practice; Transportation Law
Moscow, Russia....................General Practice
Singapore, Singapore....................General Practice

MILBERG WEISS BERSHAD HYNES & LERACH LLP
New York, NY....................Antitrust Law; Civil Trial Practice

MILDE, HOFFBERG & MACKLIN, LLP
White Plains, NY....................Patent, Trademark, Copyright and Unfair Competition

MILES AND MILES, A PROFESSIONAL ASSOCIATION
Plymouth, MA....................Family Law

MILES, SEARS & EANNI, A PROFESSIONAL CORPORATION
Fresno, CA....................Civil Trial Practice; Medical Malpractice; Personal Injury; Product Liability Law

MILIDES, GUS
Easton, PA....................Family Law; General Practice; Medical Malpractice; Personal Injury; Product Liability Law

MILITELLO, ZANCK & COEN, P.C.
Crystal Lake, IL....................Commercial Law; General Practice; Municipal and Zoning Law

MILLAR & AMBRETTE
Darien, CT....................Family Law; General Practice; Real Estate Law; Trust and Estates, Wills and Probate

MILLAR, HODGES & BEMIS
Newport Beach, CA....................Civil Trial Practice; Real Estate Law; Trust and Estates, Wills and Probate

MILLEDGE, JOHN M., P.A.
Fort Lauderdale, FL....................Municipal and Zoning Law

MILLEN, WHITE, ZELANO & BRANIGAN, P.C.
Arlington, VA....................Patent, Trademark, Copyright and Unfair Competition
Richmond, VA....................Patent, Trademark, Copyright and Unfair Competition

MILLER, JOHN E.
Palo Alto, CA....................Family Law; Trust and Estates, Wills and Probate

MILLER, ROBERT A.
Oklahoma City, OK....................Oil and Gas Law

MILLER & ASSOCIATES
Destin, FL....................Trust and Estates, Wills and Probate

MILLER, CANFIELD, PADDOCK AND STONE, P.L.C.
Washington, DC....................Communications Law; Labor and Employment Law; Municipal Bond/Public Authority Financing
Ann Arbor, MI....................Antitrust Law; Civil Rights; Civil Trial Practice; Commercial Litigation; General Practice; Health Care Law; Insurance Defense; International Business Law; Labor and Employment Law; Municipal Bond/Public Authority Financing; Real Estate Law; Securities Law
Detroit, MI....................Antitrust Law; Banking Law; Bankruptcy Law; Business Law; Civil Rights; Civil Trial Practice; Commercial Litigation; Communications Law; Computer Law; Construction Law; Creditors Rights; Employment Benefits Law; Environmental Law; General Practice; Health Care Law; Intellectual Property Law; International Business Law; Labor and Employment Law; Medical Malpractice; Mergers and Acquisitions; Municipal and Zoning Law; Municipal Bond/Public Authority Financing; Patent, Trademark, Copyright and Unfair Competition; Personal Injury; Product Liability Law; Real Estate Law; Securities Law; Tax Law; Trust and Estates, Wills and Probate
Grand Rapids, MI....................Antitrust Law; Business Law; Computer Law; Creditors Rights; Environmental Law; General Practice; Intellectual Property Law; International Business Law; Personal Injury; Real Estate Law; Securities Law; Tax Law; Trust and Estates, Wills and Probate
Kalamazoo, MI....................Antitrust Law; Bankruptcy Law; Business Law; Civil Trial Practice; Commercial Law; Computer Law; Construction Law; Creditors Rights; Employment Benefits Law; Environmental Law; General Practice; Insurance Defense; Labor and Employment Law; Medical Malpractice; Mergers and Acquisitions; Municipal and Zoning Law; Personal Injury; Product Liability Law; Securities Law; Tax Law; Trust and Estates, Wills and Probate
Lansing, MI....................Antitrust Law; Banking Law; Bankruptcy Law; Environmental Law; General Practice; Municipal Bond/Public Authority Financing; Trust and Estates, Wills and Probate
Monroe, MI....................Antitrust Law; General Practice; International Business Law; Securities Law; Tax Law
Troy, MI....................General Practice; Mergers and Acquisitions; Product Liability Law; Securities Law
New York, NY....................Civil Trial Practice; General Practice; International Business Law

MILLER CARSON BOXBERGER & MURPHY, LLP
Bloomington, IN....................Insurance Defense
Fort Wayne, IN....................Banking Law; Business Law; Insurance Defense

MILLER & COHEN, P.C.
Longmont, CO....................Civil Trial Practice; Creditors Rights

MILLER & COMPANY P.C.
Washington, DC....................International Trade Law
Kansas City, MO....................International Trade Law

MILLER, EGGLESTON & CRAMER, LTD.
Burlington, VT....................Antitrust Law; Civil Trial Practice; General Practice; Health Care Law; Immigration and Naturalization; Labor and Employment Law; Public Utilities Law; Securities Law; Tax Law; Trademark, Copyright and Unfair Competition

MILLER FAIGNANT & BEHRENS, P.C.
Rutland, VT....................Appellate Practice; Civil Trial Practice; General Practice; Insurance Defense; Medical Malpractice; Personal Injury; Product Liability Law; Professional Liability; Workers Compensation

MILLER, G. SPENCER, L.L.C., LAW OFFICES OF
Gladstone, MO....................Medical Malpractice; Personal Injury; Professional Liability

MILLER AND HARRISON, LLC
Boulder, CO....................Criminal Trial Practice; Personal Injury

MILLER, J. BRUCE, LAW GROUP
Louisville, KY....................Business Law; Civil Trial Practice; General Practice

MILLER, KAGAN, RODRIGUEZ AND SILVER, PROFESSIONAL ASSOCIATION
Coral Gables, FL....................Workers Compensation

MILLER, KATHLEEN ORTMAN, S.C.
Milwaukee, WI....................Family Law

MILLER, KISTLER, CAMPBELL, MILLER, WILLIAMS & BENSON, INC.
Bellefonte, PA....................Civil Trial Practice
State College, PA....................Civil Trial Practice

MILLER LAW FIRM, A PROFESSIONAL CORPORATION
Kansas City, MO....................Commercial Litigation; Construction Law

MILLER LAW GROUP
Larkspur, CA....................Labor and Employment Law

MILLER LAW OFFICES, THE
Studio City, CA....................Immigration and Naturalization

MILLER & MARKLE, L.L.P.
Atlanta, GA....................Civil Trial Practice

MILLER & MARTIN LLP
Chattanooga, TN....................General Practice

MILLER, MELVIN B., LTD.
Bala Cynwyd, PA....................Business Law; Real Estate Law

MILLER, MILLER & CANBY, CHARTERED
Rockville, MD....................Business Law; General Practice; Municipal and Zoning Law

MILLER MILOVE & KOB, P.C.
San Diego, CA....................Business Law; Securities Law

MILLER, MORTON, CAILLAT & NEVIS
San Jose, CA....................Bankruptcy Law; Business Law; Civil Trial Practice; Construction Law; General Practice; Real Estate Law; Tax Law; Trust and Estates, Wills and Probate

MILLER MULLER MENDELSON & KENNEDY
Indianapolis, IN....................Business Law; Civil Trial Practice; Medical Malpractice; Personal Injury; Product Liability Law

MILLER NASH LLP
Portland, OR....................Admiralty/Maritime Law; Antitrust Law; General Practice; Labor and Employment Law; Patent, Trademark, Copyright and Unfair Competition

MILLER, PEARSON, GLOE, BURNS, BEATTY & COWIE, P.C.
Decorah, IA....................General Practice; Insurance Defense; Personal Injury

MILLER, PORTER & MULLER, P.C.
Princeton, NJ ....General Practice

MILLER, RICHARD F., A PROFESSIONAL CORPORATION
Pasadena, CA ....Trust and Estates, Wills and Probate

MILLER, SCHWARTZ AND MILLER, P.A.
Hollywood, FL ....General Practice

MILLER, SHINE & BRYAN, P.A.
St. Augustine, FL ....Civil Trial Practice; Family Law

MILLER, STARR & REGALIA, A PROFESSIONAL LAW CORPORATION
Menlo Park, CA ....Real Estate Law

MILLER, STRATVERT & TORGERSON, P.A.
Albuquerque, NM ....Banking Law; Civil Trial Practice; Commercial Law; General Practice; Insurance Defense; Natural Resources Law; Real Estate Law; Tax Law; Trust and Estates, Wills and Probate

MILLER THOMSON
Calgary, AB, Canada ....General Practice
Edmonton, AB, Canada ....General Practice
Markham, ON, Canada ....General Practice
Toronto, ON, Canada ....General Practice

MILLER & VAN EATON, P.L.L.C.
Washington, DC ....Communications Law

MILLER & WELCH, L.L.C.
Denver, CO ....Civil Trial Practice; Commercial Litigation; Labor and Employment Law

MILLER & WRUBEL P.C.
New York, NY ....Civil Trial Practice; Commercial Law

MILLIKEN LAW FIRM
Bowling Green, KY ....Criminal Trial Practice; Insurance Defense; Medical Malpractice

MILLING BENSON WOODWARD L.L.P.
New Orleans, LA ....Admiralty/Maritime Law; Antitrust Law; Banking Law; Commercial Litigation; Energy Law; General Practice; Health Care Law; Labor and Employment Law; Natural Resources Law; Public Utilities Law; Tax Law

MILLS, WILLIAM S.
McPherson, KS ....General Practice

MILLS LAW FIRM, THE, P.C.
Oklahoma City, OK ....Civil Rights; Civil Trial Practice; Insurance Defense; Medical Malpractice; Personal Injury; Product Liability Law

MILLS, MORAITAKIS, KUSHEL & PEARSON
Atlanta, GA ....Civil Trial Practice; Medical Malpractice; Product Liability Law

MILLS PRESBY AND ASSOCIATES, L.L.P.
Dallas, TX ....Civil Trial Practice; Criminal Trial Practice

MILLS, SHIRLEY, ECKEL & BASSETT, L.L.P.
Galveston, TX ....Insurance Defense
Houston, TX ....Insurance Defense

MILLSAP, MIKE
Lubbock, TX ....Civil Trial Practice; Medical Malpractice; Personal Injury; Product Liability Law

MILLSAP & SINGER, P.C.
St. Louis, MO ....Real Estate Law

MILLSTEIN & KNUPP
Youngwood, PA ....Appellate Practice; Business Law; Civil Trial Practice; General Practice; Real Estate Law

MILNER, LOBEL, GORANSON, SORRELS, UDASHEN & WELLS
Dallas, TX ....Criminal Trial Practice

MILODRAGOVICH, DALE, STEINBRENNER & BINNEY, P.C.
Missoula, MT ....General Practice

MILTON, LAURENCE & DIXON
Worcester, MA ....Insurance Defense; Personal Injury; Workers Compensation

MINEO & WHITTAKER
Charlotte, NC ....Patent, Trademark, Copyright and Unfair Competition
Raleigh, NC ....Aviation Law; Patent, Trademark, Copyright and Unfair Competition

MINIER, STANLEY, INC., LAW OFFICES OF
Santa Ana, CA ....Bankruptcy Law

MINK & BLAIR
Nashville, TN ....Civil Trial Practice; Insurance Defense

MINOR AND ASSOCIATES
Biloxi, MS ....Admiralty/Maritime Law; Civil Trial Practice; General Practice; Medical Malpractice; Personal Injury; Product Liability Law

MINSKY, MCCORMICK & HALLAGAN, P.C.
Chicago, IL ....Immigration and Naturalization

MINTMIRE & ASSOCIATES
Palm Beach, FL ....Business Law; Civil Trial Practice; Insurance Defense; Trust and Estates, Wills and Probate

MINTON, HARVEY S. & ASSOCIATES
Columbus, OH ....Business Law; Real Estate Law; Trust and Estates, Wills and Probate

MINTON, BURTON, FOSTER & COLLINS, A PROFESSIONAL CORPORATION
Austin, TX ....Civil Trial Practice; Criminal Trial Practice

MINTON FIRM, THE
Chicago, IL ....Family Law

MINTON, MINTON AND RAND LLP
Los Angeles, CA ....Business Law; Real Estate Law; Trust and Estates, Wills and Probate

MINTZ, LEVIN, COHN, FERRIS, GLOVSKY AND POPEO, P.C.
Washington, DC ....Antitrust Law; Communications Law; General Practice
Boston, MA ....Antitrust Law; Civil Trial Practice; Communications Law; Criminal Trial Practice; General Practice; Municipal Bond/Public Authority Financing

MINYARD AND MORRIS, LLP
Orange, CA ....Family Law

MIRES, DOUGLAS W.
Rochester Hills, MI ....Banking Law

MIRICK, O'CONNELL, DEMALLIE & LOUGEE, LLP
Worcester, MA ....General Practice

MIROFF, CROSS & KLINEMAN
Indianapolis, IN ....Family Law

MISHAN, SLOTO, GREENBERG, HELLINGER & UDOLF, P.A.
Miami, FL ....Bankruptcy Law; Commercial Litigation; Creditors Rights

MITCHELL, LINCOLN A.
Palo Alto, CA ....Family Law

MITCHELL, SHELLEY M.
Fort Lauderdale, FL ....Family Law

MITCHELL, BRISSO, DELANEY & VRIEZE
Eureka, CA ....General Practice; Insurance Defense

MITCHELL & DECLERCK, P.L.L.C.
Enid, OK ....General Practice

MITCHELL, EDDIE C., P.A.
Winston-Salem, NC ....Criminal Trial Practice

MITCHELL HURST JACOBS & DICK
Indianapolis, IN ....Business Law; Civil Trial Practice; Medical Malpractice; Personal Injury; Product Liability Law; Real Estate Law

MITCHELL, JOINER, & HARDESTY, PSC
Madisonville, KY ....Civil Trial Practice; Personal Injury

MITCHELL LAW OFFICES, A PROFESSIONAL CORPORATION
Phoenix, AZ ....Real Estate Law; Securities Law

MITCHELL, MCNUTT, THREADGILL, SMITH & SAMS, P.A.
Columbus, MS ....General Practice
Tupelo, MS ....General Practice

MITCHELL & MITCHELL, P.C.
Dalton, GA ....Civil Trial Practice; General Practice

MITCHELL, MITCHELL & BRADLEY
Marion, IL ....Commercial Litigation; General Practice; Insurance Defense

MITCHELL, MITCHELL, GRAY & GALLAGHER, A PROFESSIONAL CORPORATION
Williamsport, PA ....Aviation Law; Civil Trial Practice; Insurance Defense; Medical Malpractice; Personal Injury; Product Liability Law; Workers Compensation

MITCHELL, NEUBAUER & HANSON, P.C.
Mount Vernon, IL ....Banking Law; General Practice; Real Estate Law

MITCHELL, RALLINGS, SINGER, MCGIRT & TISSUE, PLLC
Charlotte, NC ....Bankruptcy Law; Civil Trial Practice; Commercial Law

MITCHELL, SAM C., & ASSOCIATES
West Frankfort, IL....Personal Injury; Workers Compensation

MITCHELL, SHELDON, LTD.
Phoenix, AZ....Family Law

MITCHELL, SILBERBERG & KNUPP LLP
Los Angeles, CA....Antitrust Law; Commercial Law; Environmental Law; General Practice; Intellectual Property Law; Labor and Employment Law; Patent, Trademark, Copyright and Unfair Competition; Tax Law; Trust and Estates, Wills and Probate

MITCHELL, VOGE, CORBAN AND MORRIS
Tupelo, MS....General Practice

MITHOFF & JACKS, L.L.P.
Austin, TX....Civil Trial Practice; Personal Injury

MIYAGI, NOHR & MYHRE
Honolulu, HI....Arbitration; Civil Trial Practice; Construction Law; Insurance Defense; Product Liability Law

MIZE, JAMES M.
Sacramento, CA....Family Law

MOBBS, DENNY E.
Cleveland, TN....Civil Trial Practice; General Practice; Insurance Defense

MOCKBEE HALL & DRAKE, A PROFESSIONAL ASSOCIATION
Jackson, MS....Construction Law

MODRALL, SPERLING, ROEHL, HARRIS & SISK, P.A.
Albuquerque, NM....General Practice
Las Cruces, NM....General Practice
Santa Fe, NM....General Practice

MOEN, BRUCE R.
Seattle, WA....Trust and Estates, Wills and Probate

MOEN, CAIN & O'BRIEN
Houston, TX....Appellate Practice; Criminal Trial Practice

MOEN, SHEEHAN, MEYER, LTD.
La Crosse, WI....General Practice

MOERER & BURTON, L.L.P.
Houston, TX....Corporate Law

MOFFETT & DILLON, A PROFESSIONAL CORPORATION
Birmingham, MI....Product Liability Law

MOGEL, SPEIDEL, BOBB & KERSHNER, A PROFESSIONAL CORPORATION
Reading, PA....Banking Law; Bankruptcy Law; Business Law; Commercial Law; Family Law; General Practice; Real Estate Law; Tax Law; Trust and Estates, Wills and Probate

MOGILL, KENNETH M.
Detroit, MI....Appellate Practice; Criminal Trial Practice; Professional Liability

MOHR, HACKETT, PEDERSON, BLAKLEY & RANDOLPH, P.C.
Phoenix, AZ....General Practice

MOIR & HARDMAN
Washington, DC....Communications Law

MOLDAWER & MARSHALL, P.C.
Rockville, MD....Business Law

MOLDOF, HILLIARD E., P.A.
Fort Lauderdale, FL....Criminal Trial Practice

MOLLER, ARTHUR C., P.A.
Miami, FL....Insurance Defense

MOLLICA & MURRAY
Pittsburgh, PA....Business Law; Construction Law; Insurance Defense; Municipal and Zoning Law; Real Estate Law

MOMBACH, BOYLE & HARDIN, P.A.
Fort Lauderdale, FL....Commercial Law

MONACO, MONACO & BIRDER
Gainesville, FL....Insurance Defense

MONAGHAN & GOLD, P.C.
Elkins Park, PA....Appellate Practice; Civil Trial Practice; Commercial Law; Insurance Defense; Labor and Employment Law; Medical Malpractice; Product Liability Law

MONAGHAN, LEAHY, HOCHADEL & LIBBY, LLP
Portland, ME....Banking Law; Civil Rights; Insurance Defense; Municipal and Zoning Law

MONDSCHEIN ASSOCIATES
Allentown, PA....Family Law

MONE, D'AMBROSE & HANYEN, P.C.
Brockton, MA....Civil Trial Practice

MONNET, HAYES, BULLIS, THOMPSON & EDWARDS
Oklahoma City, OK....Civil Trial Practice; General Practice; Natural Resources Law

MONTAVON, MICHAEL C., P.C.
Fairfax, VA....Commercial Litigation

MONTELEONE & MCCRORY, LLP
Los Angeles, CA....Commercial Litigation; Construction Law; General Practice

MONTERO FINIZIO VELASQUEZ WEISSING AND REYES, P.A.
Fort Lauderdale, FL....Aviation Law; International Business Law; Personal Injury

MONTFORT, HEALY, MCGUIRE & SALLEY
Garden City, NY....Appellate Practice; Civil Rights; Civil Trial Practice; Environmental Law; General Practice; Health Care Law; Insurance Defense; Medical Malpractice; Product Liability Law; Professional Liability

MONTGOMERY & ANDREWS, PROFESSIONAL ASSOCIATION
Santa Fe, NM....Administrative Law; Appellate Practice; Civil Rights; Civil Trial Practice; Environmental Law; General Practice; Insurance Defense; Labor and Employment Law; Natural Resources Law

MONTGOMERY LITTLE & MCGREW, P.C.
Denver, CO....Civil Trial Practice; Commercial Law; Commercial Litigation; Construction Law; General Practice; Health Care Law; Insurance Defense; Medical Malpractice; Product Liability Law; Professional Liability; Real Estate Law

MONTGOMERY, MCCRACKEN, WALKER & RHOADS, LLP
Philadelphia, PA....General Practice

MOODIE, MOODIE & WORTMAN
West Point, NE....General Practice

MOODY & HAYS, L.L.P.
Lubbock, TX....General Practice

MOODY, STROPLE & KLOEPPEL, INC.
Portsmouth, VA....Civil Trial Practice; Personal Injury

MOONEY, F. BENTLEY, JR., A LAW CORPORATION
North Hollywood, CA....Business Law; Trust and Estates, Wills and Probate

MOONEY LAW FIRM
Jonesboro, AR....General Practice

MOORE, JOHN R.
Selinsgrove, PA....General Practice; Trust and Estates, Wills and Probate

MOORE, R. ERIC
Christiansted, St. Croix, VI....Civil Trial Practice; Insurance Defense; Product Liability Law

MOORE, BASKIN & PARKER
Boise, ID....General Practice; Insurance Defense; Product Liability Law

MOORE & BERKOWITZ
Southampton, PA....Civil Trial Practice

MOORE & BROWN
Winston-Salem, NC....Antitrust Law
San Francisco, CA....Civil Rights; Labor and Employment Law; Personal Injury; Product Liability Law

MOORE & BRUCE, LLP
Washington, DC....Business Law; Tax Law

MOORE, BRYAN & SCHROFF, A LAW CORPORATION
Torrance, CA....Family Law; Trust and Estates, Wills and Probate

MOORE, GEORGE E., A PROFESSIONAL LAW CORPORATION
Pasadena, CA....Medical Malpractice; Personal Injury

MOORE & HANSEN
Minneapolis, MN....Patent, Trademark, Copyright and Unfair Competition

MOORE INGRAM JOHNSON & STEELE, LLP
Marietta, GA....Civil Trial Practice; Insurance Defense; Real Estate Law

MOORE, O'BRIEN, JACQUES & YELENAK
Cheshire, CT....Aviation Law; Civil Trial Practice; Medical Malpractice

MOORE, R. LAMAR, P.C.
Moultrie, GA....General Practice; Tax Law

MOORE, RADER, CLIFT AND FITZPATRICK, P.C.
Cookeville, TN .... Civil Trial Practice; General Practice; Insurance Defense

MOORE, RICHARD W., LAW OFFICES OF
Towson, MD .... Trust and Estates, Wills and Probate

MOORE, RUTTER & EVANS
Long Beach, CA .... Admiralty/Maritime Law; Civil Trial Practice; Criminal Trial Practice; Insurance Defense

MOORE & VAN ALLEN, PLLC
Charlotte, NC .... General Practice
Durham, NC .... Intellectual Property Law; Patent, Trademark, Copyright and Unfair Competition; Trademark, Copyright and Unfair Competition

MOORE, VIRGADAMO & LYNCH, LTD.
Newport, RI .... General Practice

MOORMAN, TATE, MOORMAN, URQUHART & HALEY, L.L.P.
Brenham, TX .... General Practice

MOOTY & ASSOCIATES, P.C.
Montgomery, AL .... Insurance Defense

MORAN & MORAN
Toledo, OH .... Bankruptcy Law; Civil Trial Practice; Family Law; General Practice; Personal Injury; Real Estate Law; Trust and Estates, Wills and Probate

MORAN & SHAMS, P.A.
Orlando, FL .... Civil Trial Practice; Commercial Law; Commercial Litigation; Intellectual Property Law; Labor and Employment Law; Real Estate Law; Sports and Entertainment Law; Tax Law; Trust and Estates, Wills and Probate; Workers Compensation

MORCHOWER, LUXTON AND WHALEY
Richmond, VA .... Criminal Trial Practice; Personal Injury

MORELLI, BENEDICT P., & ASSOCIATES, P.C.
New York, NY .... Civil Trial Practice

MOREY, CARTER, P.C.
Tucson, AZ .... Civil Trial Practice; Medical Malpractice; Personal Injury

MORGAN, BROWN & JOY, LLP
Boston, MA .... Labor and Employment Law

MORGAN COLLING & GILBERT, A PROFESSIONAL ASSOCIATION
Orlando, FL .... Business Law; Medical Malpractice; Personal Injury; Workers Compensation

MORGAN, DAVID JAY, A PROFESSIONAL CORPORATION
San Mateo, CA .... Civil Trial Practice

MORGAN & FINNEGAN, L.L.P.
Washington, DC .... Patent, Trademark, Copyright and Unfair Competition
New York, NY .... Patent, Trademark, Copyright and Unfair Competition

MORGAN AND GOTCHER
Greenville, TX .... Family Law; General Practice; Trust and Estates, Wills and Probate

MORGAN, LEWIS & BOCKIUS LLP
Philadelphia, PA .... General Practice

MORGAN, MEYER & RICE, L.C.
Salt Lake City, UT .... Civil Trial Practice; Construction Law; General Practice; Insurance Defense; Personal Injury; Product Liability Law

MORGAN & POTTINGER, P.S.C.
Louisville, KY .... Appellate Practice; Banking Law; Bankruptcy Law; Commercial Litigation; Creditors Rights; General Practice; Real Estate Law; Trust and Estates, Wills and Probate

MORGAN, RICHARD M., P.C.
Atlanta, GA .... Trust and Estates, Wills and Probate

MORGAN & WEISBROD, L.L.P.
Dallas, TX .... Medical Malpractice; Personal Injury; Product Liability Law; Professional Liability

MORGANROTH & MORGANROTH
Southfield, MI .... Business Law; Civil Trial Practice; Commercial Law; Criminal Trial Practice; Real Estate Law
New York, NY .... Business Law; Civil Trial Practice; Commercial Law; Criminal Trial Practice; Real Estate Law

MORGANROTH, MORGANROTH, JACKMAN & NYE, P.C.
Birmingham, MI .... Family Law

MORGANSTERN, MACADAMS & DEVITO CO., L.P.A.
Cleveland, OH .... Business Law; Commercial Litigation; Family Law

MORGENSTEIN & JUBELIRER, LLP
San Francisco, CA .... Antitrust Law; Civil Trial Practice; Commercial Litigation; Construction Law; Environmental Law; General Practice; Labor and Employment Law; Product Liability Law; Real Estate Law; Securities Law

MORGENSTERN, MICHAEL S., & ASSOCIATES, P.C.
Rockville, MD .... Civil Trial Practice; Medical Malpractice; Personal Injury; Product Liability Law

MORITT, HOCK & HAMROFF, LLP
Garden City, NY .... Bankruptcy Law; Civil Trial Practice; Commercial Law; Commercial Litigation; Real Estate Law

MORLEDGE, W. FRANK, P.A.
Forrest City, AR .... Civil Trial Practice; General Practice

MORRILL THOMAS NOONEY & BRAUN, LLP
Rapid City, SD .... General Practice

MORRIS, EDITH H.
New Orleans, LA .... Family Law

MORRIS, JOHN P.
Bridgeton, NJ .... Appellate Practice; Civil Trial Practice; Criminal Trial Practice; Personal Injury; Professional Liability

MORRIS, CLOUD AND CONCHIN, P.C.
Huntsville, AL .... Civil Trial Practice; Criminal Trial Practice; Personal Injury; Product Liability Law; Workers Compensation

MORRIS, DUFFY, ALONSO & FALEY, LLP
New York, NY .... Civil Trial Practice

MORRIS & FLOREY, L.L.P.
Austin, TX .... Criminal Trial Practice

MORRIS, HAYNES & HORNSBY
Alexander City, AL .... Civil Trial Practice; Personal Injury; Product Liability Law

MORRIS, JAMES, HITCHENS & WILLIAMS, LLP
Dover, DE .... General Practice
Newark, DE .... General Practice
Wilmington, DE .... Civil Trial Practice; General Practice

MORRIS, LAING, EVANS, BROCK & KENNEDY, CHARTERED
Wichita, KS .... Bankruptcy Law; Civil Trial Practice; General Practice; Labor and Employment Law; Natural Resources Law

MORRIS AND MORRIS
Wilmington, DE .... Securities Law

MORRIS, NEIL A., ASSOCIATES, P.C.
Philadelphia, PA .... Civil Rights; General Practice; Labor and Employment Law

MORRIS, NICHOLS, ARSHT & TUNNELL
Wilmington, DE .... General Practice; Intellectual Property Law; Tax Law

MORRIS, PAUL, PROFESSIONAL ASSOCIATION
Miami, FL .... Appellate Practice

MORRIS & STELLA
Chicago, IL .... Product Liability Law

MORRIS, WILLIAM, LAW OFFICES
Hamilton, ON, Canada .... Personal Injury

MORRIS YORK WILLIAMS SURLES & BARRINGER, L.L.P.
Charlotte, NC .... Insurance Defense

MORRISON, ROBERT W.
Orlando, FL .... Real Estate Law

MORRISON COHEN SINGER & WEINSTEIN, LLP
New York, NY .... General Practice

MORRISON & FOERSTER LLP
San Francisco, CA .... General Practice

MORRISON & MILLS, P.A.
Tampa, FL .... Banking Law; Business Law; Civil Trial Practice; Health Care Law; Municipal and Zoning Law; Municipal Bond/Public Authority Financing

MORRISON & SHELTON, A PROFESSIONAL CORPORATION
Wichita Falls, TX .... Civil Trial Practice; General Practice; Personal Injury

MORRISONS, MCCARTHY & BARABAN
Whitefish, MT .... Civil Trial Practice

MORRISSEY & MORRISSEY, LLP
New York, NY .... Trust and Estates, Wills and Probate

MORROW & OTOROWSKI
Bainbridge Island, WA..........Admiralty/Maritime Law; Medical Malpractice; Personal Injury

MORROW, ROMINE & PEARSON, P.C.
Montgomery, AL..........Insurance Defense

MORROW & WHITE
Costa Mesa, CA..........Insurance Defense

MORSE & ALTMAN
Boston, MA..........Patent, Trademark, Copyright and Unfair Competition

MORSE & BRATT
Vancouver, WA..........General Practice

MORSE, KENNETH D., A PROFESSIONAL ASSOCIATION
Orlando, FL..........Commercial Litigation; Family Law

MORSE & MOWBRAY, A PROFESSIONAL CORPORATION
Las Vegas, NV..........Civil Trial Practice; Construction Law; Medical Malpractice; Real Estate Law; Trust and Estates, Wills and Probate

MORTIMER SOURWINE & SLOANE, LTD.
Reno, NV..........Civil Trial Practice; General Practice

MORTON & MORTON, PLLC
Knoxville, TN..........Civil Trial Practice

MORVILLO, ABRAMOWITZ, GRAND, IASON & SILBERBERG, P.C.
New York, NY..........Criminal Trial Practice; General Practice

MOSCATO & HALLOCK
Portland, OR..........Insurance Defense

MOSCOWITZ STARKMAN & MAGOLNICK
Miami, FL..........Commercial Litigation; Criminal Trial Practice

MOSELEY & ASSOCIATES, A PROFESSIONAL LAW CORPORATION
New Orleans, LA..........Civil Trial Practice; Family Law

MOSELEY, WARREN, PRICHARD & PARRISH, P.A.
Jacksonville, FL..........Admiralty/Maritime Law; General Practice; Insurance Defense; Transportation Law

MOSER AND MARSALEK, P.C.
St. Louis, MO..........Civil Trial Practice; Insurance Defense

MOSKOWITZ & MOSKOWITZ
Cincinnati, OH..........Family Law

MOSS, BENTON & WALLIS, PLLC
Jackson, TN..........Civil Trial Practice; General Practice; Insurance Defense

MOSS AND BLOOMBERG, LTD.
Bolingbrook, IL..........Banking Law; Insurance Defense; Municipal and Zoning Law; Real Estate Law

MOSS & ENOCHIAN, A LAW CORPORATION
Redding, CA..........Civil Trial Practice

MOSS, HENDERSON, BLANTON & LANIER, P.A.
Vero Beach, FL..........Admiralty/Maritime Law; Business Law; Civil Trial Practice; Commercial Litigation; Construction Law; General Practice; Insurance Defense; Land Use Law; Medical Malpractice; Personal Injury; Product Liability Law; Real Estate Law; Tax Law; Trust and Estates, Wills and Probate; Workers Compensation

MOSS, STRICKLER & SACHITANO, P.A.
Bethesda, MD..........Civil Trial Practice; Family Law

MOSTEN & TUFFIAS
Los Angeles, CA..........Civil Trial Practice; Family Law

MOTLEY & MOTLEY
Branson, MO..........Trust and Estates, Wills and Probate

MOULDER, WILLIAM C. A., P.A.
Jacksonville, FL..........Criminal Trial Practice; Family Law

MOULEDOUX, BLAND, LEGRAND & BRACKETT, LLC
New Orleans, LA..........Admiralty/Maritime Law; Commercial Litigation; Corporate Law; Workers Compensation

MOULTON, BELLINGHAM, LONGO & MATHER, P.C.
Billings, MT..........General Practice

MOUNCE, GREEN, MYERS, SAFI & GALATZAN, A PROFESSIONAL CORPORATION
El Paso, TX..........Antitrust Law; Appellate Practice; General Practice; Insurance Defense; Labor and Employment Law; Medical Malpractice; Product Liability Law

MOUND, COTTON & WOLLAN
New York, NY..........Civil Trial Practice; Commercial Litigation; General Practice; Insurance Defense; International Business Law

MOUNTAIN, DEARBORN & WHITING LLP
Worcester, MA..........Commercial Litigation; General Practice; Labor and Employment Law; Municipal and Zoning Law; Real Estate Law; Tax Law; Trust and Estates, Wills and Probate

MOWER, KOELLER, NEBEKER, CARLSON & HALUCK, LLP
Irvine, CA..........Civil Trial Practice; Insurance Defense
San Diego, CA..........Civil Trial Practice

MOYER & BERGMAN, P.L.C.
Cedar Rapids, IA..........Bankruptcy Law; Creditors Rights

MOYERS, MARTIN, SANTEE, IMEL & TETRICK
Tulsa, OK..........General Practice

MOYES STOREY
Phoenix, AZ..........Natural Resources Law

MOYLE & DRAPER, P.C.
Salt Lake City, UT..........General Practice

MOYLER, MOYLER, RAINEY & COBB, P.L.C.
Franklin, VA..........General Practice

MOZINGO & PRICE, LLP
Newport Beach, CA..........Civil Trial Practice; Corporate Law; Trust and Estates, Wills and Probate

MUCHMORE & WALLWORK, A PROFESSIONAL CORPORATION
Phoenix, AZ..........Civil Trial Practice; Commercial Litigation; Environmental Law; Insurance Defense; Personal Injury; Product Liability Law

MUDD, HARRISON & BURCH
Towson, MD..........Construction Law; Family Law; Insurance Defense; Product Liability Law

MUDD, MUDD & FITZGERALD, P.A.
La Plata, MD..........Criminal Trial Practice; Family Law; Land Use Law; Personal Injury

MUDIE, F. PATRICIA, A PROFESSIONAL CORPORATION
Los Angeles, CA..........Family Law

MUELLER & GALLIOS, P.C.
Phoenix, AZ..........Family Law

MUELLER, GOSS & POSSI, S.C.
Milwaukee, WI..........Insurance Defense

MUELLER AND SMITH, A LEGAL PROFESSIONAL ASSOCIATION
Columbus, OH..........Computer Law; Patent, Trademark, Copyright and Unfair Competition

MUELLER, THOMAS F., A PROFESSIONAL CORPORATION
San Jose, CA..........Criminal Trial Practice

MUETH, JOSEPH E., A LAW CORPORATION
Pasadena, CA..........Patent, Trademark, Copyright and Unfair Competition

MUHLHEIM PALMER & WADE, A PROFESSIONAL CORPORATION
Eugene, OR..........Bankruptcy Law; Commercial Law; Commercial Litigation; Creditors Rights

MULDOON, MURPHY & FAUCETTE
Washington, DC..........Banking Law; Securities Law

MULHEARN & MULHEARN
Natchez, MS..........Civil Trial Practice; General Practice; Personal Injury; Real Estate Law; Trust and Estates, Wills and Probate

MULLEN & HENZELL, L.L.P.
Santa Barbara, CA..........Civil Trial Practice; Insurance Defense; Labor and Employment Law; Trust and Estates, Wills and Probate

MULLER, CHANDLER R., P.A., LAW OFFICES OF
Winter Park, FL..........Criminal Trial Practice

MULLER, MINTZ, KORNREICH, CALDWELL, CASEY, CROSLAND & BRAMNICK, P.A.
Miami, FL..........Labor and Employment Law
Orlando, FL..........Labor and Employment Law

MULLIKEN, GLEASON, WEINER & WHITNEY, P.C.
Colorado Springs, CO..........General Practice

MULLIN HOARD & BROWN, L.L.P.
Amarillo, TX..........General Practice

MULLIN, JOHN C., JR., P.A.
Miami, FL..........Insurance Defense

MULLINS, HARRIS & JESSEE, A PROFESSIONAL CORPORATION
Norton, VA..........General Practice; Insurance Defense

MULVANEY, KAHAN & BARRY, A PROFESSIONAL CORPORATION
La Jolla, CA............................Antitrust Law; Banking Law; General Practice; Municipal and Zoning Law; Trust and Estates, Wills and Probate

MULVANEY, KAHAN & BARRY, A PROFESSIONAL CORPORATION
San Diego, CA..........................Antitrust Law; Banking Law; General Practice; Municipal and Zoning Law; Trust and Estates, Wills and Probate

MULVANIA, WALTER L.
Rock Port, MO........................Trust and Estates, Wills and Probate

MULVEY & FLANAGAN, P.C.
Philadelphia, PA......................Civil Trial Practice; Personal Injury; Workers Compensation

MUNDAY & NATHAN, THE LAW OFFICES OF
Chicago, IL..............................Civil Trial Practice; Medical Malpractice; Personal Injury

MUNDY & GAMMAGE, P.C.
Cedartown, GA........................Civil Trial Practice; General Practice; Personal Injury

MUNDY, ROGERS & FRITH, LLP
Roanoke, VA...........................Family Law; Medical Malpractice; Personal Injury

MUNGER CHADWICK, P.L.C.
Tucson, AZ..............................Commercial Law; Real Estate Law

MUNGER, TOLLES & OLSON LLP
Los Angeles, CA......................General Practice

MUNLEY, MUNLEY & CARTWRIGHT, P.C.
Scranton, PA...........................Appellate Practice; Civil Trial Practice; Commercial Litigation; Criminal Trial Practice; Medical Malpractice; Personal Injury; Product Liability Law; Workers Compensation

MUNSILL, JOHN W.
Sacramento, CA.......................Family Law

MURAI, WALD, BIONDO & MORENO, P.A.
Miami, FL................................Civil Trial Practice; General Practice; International Business Law

MURCHISON, TAYLOR & GIBSON, L.L.P.
Wilmington, NC........................Civil Trial Practice; Commercial Law; Real Estate Law; Tax Law

MURNAGHAN & FERGUSON, P.A.
Tampa, FL...............................Commercial Litigation; Personal Injury

MURNANE, CONLIN, WHITE & BRANDT, PROFESSIONAL ASSOCIATION
St. Paul, MN...........................General Practice

MUROV & WARD, L.L.C.
New Orleans, LA......................Immigration and Naturalization

MURPHY, MICHAEL C.
Lawrenceville, GA....................Civil Trial Practice; Family Law; Labor and Employment Law

MURPHY, BARTOL & O'BRIEN, LLP
Mineola, NY.............................Civil Trial Practice

MURPHY & DESMOND, S.C.
Madison, WI............................General Practice

MURPHY, GILLICK, WICHT & PRACHTHAUSER
Milwaukee, WI.........................Civil Trial Practice; Personal Injury

MURPHY, HESSE, TOOMEY AND LEHANE
Quincy, MA..............................Labor and Employment Law

MURPHY, HUPP, FOOTE, MIELKE AND KINNALLY
Aurora, IL................................Civil Trial Practice; Environmental Law; General Practice; Immigration and Naturalization; Insurance Defense; Personal Injury

MURPHY, KIRKPATRICK & FAIN, P.L.L.P.
Billings, MT............................Business Law; Commercial Litigation; Real Estate Law

MURPHY, LUTEY, SCHMITT & BECK, P.L.L.C.
Kingman, AZ...........................Personal Injury
Prescott, AZ............................Civil Trial Practice; Commercial Litigation; General Practice; Personal Injury; Trust and Estates, Wills and Probate
Yuma, AZ................................Personal Injury

MURPHY AND MURPHY
Hyannis, MA............................General Practice

MURPHY AND O'CONNOR
Philadelphia, PA......................Civil Trial Practice

MURPHY, OLIVER, CAIOLA & GOWEN, A PROFESSIONAL LAW CORPORATION
Norristown, PA........................Business Law; Civil Trial Practice; Commercial Litigation; Elder Law; Family Law; Insurance Defense; Legal Malpractice; Medical Malpractice; Personal Injury; Product Liability Law; Toxic Torts; Trust and Estates, Wills and Probate

MURPHY, PEARSON, BRADLEY & FEENEY, A PROFESSIONAL CORPORATION
San Francisco, CA..................Appellate Practice; Banking Law; Civil Rights; Civil Trial Practice; Construction Law; Employment Benefits Law; General Practice; Insurance Defense; Medical Malpractice; Product Liability Law; Real Estate Law; Tax Law; Trademark, Copyright and Unfair Competition

MURPHY, PIAZZA & GENELLO, P.C.
Scranton, PA...........................Civil Trial Practice

MURPHY & POSNER, L.L.P.
Phoenix, AZ............................Commercial Litigation; Creditors Rights; Real Estate Law

MURPHY, POST, THOMPSON, ARNOLD & SKINNER
Batesville, AR.........................Civil Trial Practice

MURPHY, REID, PILOTTE, ORD & AUSTIN
Palm Beach, FL.......................General Practice; Real Estate Law; Tax Law; Trust and Estates, Wills and Probate

MURPHY, ROGERS & SLOSS, A PROFESSIONAL LAW CORPORATION
New Orleans, LA......................Admiralty/Maritime Law

MURPHY, THOMAS D., P.C.
Rockville, MD..........................General Practice

MURPHY, WILLIAM T., LAW OFFICES, INC.
Providence, RI.........................Banking Law; Bankruptcy Law; Civil Trial Practice; Commercial Law; Criminal Trial Practice; Insurance Defense; Labor and Employment Law

MURRAY, DUNHAM & MURRAY
Seattle, WA............................Insurance Defense

MURRAY, JOHN A., & ASSOCIATES, LTD.
St. Paul, MN...........................Commercial Litigation; Real Estate Law; Tax Law

MURRAY LAW FIRM
New Orleans, LA......................Personal Injury

MURRAY, PLUMB & MURRAY
Portland, ME...........................General Practice

MUSSELMAN, ROBERT M. & ASSOCIATES
Charlottesville, VA...................Bankruptcy Law; Pension and Profit Sharing; Tax Law; Trust and Estates, Wills and Probate

MUSTO & SAUNDERS, P.C.
Plymouth, PA...........................Health Care Law; Insurance Defense

MUTH, CASEBOLT, GERMAINE & DRIGGS, P.L.C.
Phoenix, AZ............................Real Estate Law

MYER, SWANSON, ADAMS & WOLF, P.C.
Denver, CO.............................Business Law; Civil Trial Practice; Commercial Law; Commercial Litigation; General Practice; Trust and Estates, Wills and Probate

MYERS, DAUGHERITY, BERRY, O'CONOR & KUZMA, LTD.
Ottawa, IL...............................Banking Law; General Practice; Insurance Defense
Streator, IL..............................General Practice

MYERS & FLEMING, LLP
Newport Beach, CA..................Construction Law; International Business Law; Natural Resources Law

MYERS & JENKINS, A PROFESSIONAL CORPORATION
Phoenix, AZ............................Bankruptcy Law; Commercial Litigation; Health Care Law; Real Estate Law

MYERS, OLIVER & PRICE, P.C.
Albuquerque, NM.....................Land Use Law; Real Estate Law

MYERS, ROBERT J., & ASSOCIATES
San Antonio, TX.......................Civil Trial Practice; Tax Law

MYLES AND MARTIN, LAW OFFICES OF
Tawas City, MI.........................Municipal and Zoning Law; Trust and Estates, Wills and Probate

MYLOTTE, DAVID & FITZPATRICK
Philadelphia, PA......................Civil Trial Practice; Toxic Torts

NACHSHIN & WESTON, LLP
Los Angeles, CA......................Family Law

NAGELEY, MEREDITH & MILLER, INC.
Sacramento, CA.......................Business Law; Civil Trial Practice; Construction Law; Insurance Defense; Labor and Employment Law

NAGIN GALLOP FIGUEREDO, P.A.
Miami, FL .... Antitrust Law; Environmental Law; Land Use Law; Patent, Trademark, Copyright and Unfair Competition

NAGLE, THOMAS C., A PROF. CORP., LAW OFFICES OF
Walnut Creek, CA .... Eminent Domain

NAGY & PINTÉR HOGAN & HARTSON LAW OFFICE
Budapest, Hungary .... General Practice

NAHIN, BRUCE A., A PROFESSIONAL LAW CORPORATION
Valencia, CA .... Business Law; Real Estate Law

NAKAMURA, QUINN & WALLS, LLP
Birmingham, AL .... Labor and Employment Law

NALL, MILLER, OWENS, HOCUTT & HOWARD, LLP
Atlanta, GA .... Civil Trial Practice; Commercial Litigation; Insurance Defense; Medical Malpractice; Product Liability Law

NAMAN, HOWELL, SMITH & LEE, A PROFESSIONAL CORPORATION
Austin, TX .... General Practice
Fort Worth, TX .... General Practice
Temple, TX .... General Practice
Waco, TX .... General Practice

NANCE, CACCIATORE AND HAMILTON
Melbourne, FL .... Civil Trial Practice; General Practice; Medical Malpractice; Personal Injury

NARDONI, SILVIO
Glendale, CA .... Civil Trial Practice

NARRON, O'HALE & WHITTINGTON, P.A.
Smithfield, NC .... General Practice

NASATIR, HIRSCH & PODBERESKY
Santa Monica, CA .... Criminal Trial Practice

NASH, COHENOUR, KELLEY & HUNT, P.C.
Oklahoma City, OK .... Bankruptcy Law; Commercial Law; Trust and Estates, Wills and Probate

NASH & COMPANY, A PROFESSIONAL CORPORATION
Pittsburgh, PA .... General Practice; Health Care Law

NASH & EDGERTON
Hermosa Beach, CA .... Mergers and Acquisitions

NASH, WALTER B., III, P.C.
Tucson, AZ .... Criminal Trial Practice

NASON, YEAGER, GERSON, WHITE & LIOCE, P.A.
West Palm Beach, FL .... Business Law; Civil Trial Practice; Real Estate Law

NASTASI, NICHOLAS J., A PROFESSIONAL CORPORATION
Philadelphia, PA .... Criminal Trial Practice

NATH & ASSOCIATES
Washington, DC .... Patent, Trademark, Copyright and Unfair Competition

NATHAN & NATHAN, P.C.
Southfield, MI .... Bankruptcy Law; Real Estate Law

NATHANSON & GOLDBERG, A PROFESSIONAL CORPORATION
Boston, MA .... Civil Trial Practice; Construction Law; Personal Injury; Real Estate Law

NATISS, NATISS & GORDON, P.C.
Roslyn Heights, NY .... Commercial Litigation; Corporate Law; Family Law; General Practice; Personal Injury; Real Estate Law; Trust and Estates, Wills and Probate

NAUFUL, ERNEST J., JR., P.C.
Columbia, SC .... Civil Trial Practice; General Practice; Medical Malpractice; Product Liability Law

NAVRATIL, HARDY & BOURGEOIS L.L.P.
Baton Rouge, LA .... Business Law; Insurance Defense

NAWROCKI, ROONEY & SIVERTSON, P.A.
Minneapolis, MN .... Intellectual Property Law

NEAL & ASSOCIATES
Oakland, CA .... Business Law; Trust and Estates, Wills and Probate

NEAL & DAVIS
Shelbyville, KY .... Civil Trial Practice; Personal Injury; Real Estate Law

NEARY, BRIAN J.
Hackensack, NJ .... Appellate Practice; Criminal Trial Practice

NEBEL, TOM, A PROF. CORP., LAW OFFICES OF
Nashville, TN .... Personal Injury

NEBLETT, BEARD & ARSENAULT
Alexandria, LA .... Civil Trial Practice

NEEDELL, SIEKERKA & CASTELLANI, A PROFESSIONAL CORPORATION
Trenton, NJ .... Appellate Practice; Civil Rights; Civil Trial Practice; Commercial Law; Construction Law; Employment Benefits Law; Family Law; Insurance Defense; Labor and Employment Law; Product Liability Law

NEEDHAM JOHNSON, A PROFESSIONAL CORPORATION
Dallas, TX .... Medical Malpractice

NEEF, ALLAN
Grosse Pointe Farms, MI .... Corporate Law; Tax Law; Trust and Estates, Wills and Probate

NEEL, HOOPER & KALMANS, P.C.
Houston, TX .... Labor and Employment Law

NEFF LAW FIRM, THE, LTD.
Bucyrus, OH .... Civil Trial Practice; General Practice

NEIDER & BOUCHER, S.C.
Madison, WI .... Business Law; Intellectual Property Law; Patent, Trademark, Copyright and Unfair Competition; Real Estate Law; Securities Law; Tax Law; Trademark, Copyright and Unfair Competition; Trust and Estates, Wills and Probate

NEIGHER, ALAN
Westport, CT .... Sports and Entertainment Law

NEILL GRIFFIN JEFFRIES FOWLER TIERNEY & NEILL, CHARTERED
Fort Pierce, FL .... Appellate Practice; Civil Trial Practice; Personal Injury; Real Estate Law; Trust and Estates, Wills and Probate

NEIMAN GINSBURG & MAIRANZ P.C.
New York, NY .... Administrative Law; Bankruptcy Law; Commercial Litigation; Health Care Law

NEJAME, MARK E., P.A., LAW OFFICES OF
Orlando, FL .... Criminal Trial Practice

NELSON & ASSOCIATES, P.A.
Aventura, FL .... Trust and Estates, Wills and Probate

NELSON, DRIES, CONNELL & KRAMER, S.C.
Brookfield, WI .... Civil Trial Practice; Insurance Defense; Workers Compensation

NELSON • HESSE
Sarasota, FL .... Civil Trial Practice; Commercial Law; General Practice; Product Liability Law

NELSON AND KREUGER, PROFESSIONAL CORPORATION
Grand Rapids, MI .... Commercial Litigation; Insurance Defense

NELSON, MCMAHAN & NOBLETT
Chattanooga, TN .... Environmental Law; Insurance Defense; Municipal and Zoning Law; Personal Injury

NELSON MULLINS RILEY & SCARBOROUGH, L.L.P.
Columbia, SC .... General Practice

NELSON & NELSON LLP
Bethesda, MD .... Trust and Estates, Wills and Probate

NELSON OYEN TORVIK
Montevideo, MN .... General Practice

NEMETH BURWELL, P.C.
Detroit, MI .... Labor and Employment Law

NEMETH, CABORN & BUTAUSKI
Columbus, OH .... Civil Trial Practice; Insurance Defense; Legal Malpractice; Personal Injury

NEMIER, TOLARI, LANDRY, MAZZEO & JOHNSON, P.C.
Farmington Hills, MI .... Appellate Practice; Insurance Defense; Personal Injury; Product Liability Law

NEMLAHA, BEATRICE H., P.C.
Los Angeles, CA .... Family Law

NEUBERGER, QUINN, GIELEN, RUBIN & GIBBER, P.A.
Baltimore, MD .... General Practice

NEUFELD & O'LEARY
New York, NY .... Environmental Law; Trust and Estates, Wills and Probate

NEUMEYER & BOYD, LLP
Los Angeles, CA .... Appellate Practice; Insurance Defense

NEUMILLER & BEARDSLEE, A PROFESSIONAL CORPORATION
Stockton, CA .... General Practice

NEVAS, NEVAS & CAPASSE
Westport, CT .... Business Law; Real Estate Law; Trust and Estates, Wills and Probate

NEVILLE, WILLIAM V. JR.
Eufaula, AL .... General Practice; Real Estate Law

NEVILLE & KELLEY
Cambridge, MA .... Insurance Defense

NEVILLE, RICHARDS, DEFRANCO & WULLER
Belleville, IL .... Civil Trial Practice; Commercial Litigation; General Practice; Insurance Defense; Medical Malpractice; Professional Liability; Real Estate Law

NEVILLE SHAVER HUBBARD & MCLEAN
Stamford, CT .... General Practice

NEVIN, EDWARD J.
San Francisco, CA .... Civil Trial Practice

NEVIN GRUEN, LLP
Oakland, CA .... Civil Trial Practice

NEVORAL, BERNARD R., AND ASSOCIATES LTD.
Chicago, IL .... Civil Trial Practice; Medical Malpractice; Personal Injury; Product Liability Law; Workers Compensation

NEWBY, LEWIS, KAMINSKI & JONES
La Porte, IN .... General Practice

NEWCOMB, BRIAN W.
Menlo Park, CA .... Civil Trial Practice

NEWELL & MARTENS
Denver, CO .... Criminal Trial Practice

NEWLAN, DOUGLAS H.
Redding, CA .... Insurance Defense

NEWMAN, CRAIG
Casper, WY .... Natural Resources Law

NEWMAN, DAVID, CHARTERED
La Plata, MD .... Patent, Trademark, Copyright and Unfair Competition

NEWMAN FITCH ALTHEIM MYERS, P.C.
New York, NY .... Civil Trial Practice; Insurance Defense

NEWMAN, FREYMAN, KLEIN & GAMACHE, P.C.
St. Louis, MO .... Commercial Litigation; Family Law; Trust and Estates, Wills and Probate

NEWMAN, MATHIS, BRADY, WAKEFIELD & SPEDALE, A PROFESSIONAL LAW CORPORATION
Metairie, LA .... Banking Law; Commercial Litigation

NEWMAN SCHWARTZ & GREENBERG
New York, NY .... Appellate Practice; Criminal Trial Practice

NEWSOM, GRAHAM, HEDRICK & KENNON, P.A.
Durham, NC .... General Practice

NEWTON AND HOFF, L.L.P.
Gulfport, MS .... Business Law; Civil Trial Practice; Corporate Law; Real Estate Law; Trust and Estates, Wills and Probate

NEXSEN PRUET JACOBS & POLLARD, LLP
Columbia, SC .... Commercial Litigation; Construction Law; Creditors Rights; Environmental Law; General Practice; Health Care Law; Intellectual Property Law; Labor and Employment Law; Land Use Law; Municipal Bond/Public Authority Financing; Tax Law

NG, PETER P. J.
Honolulu, HI .... Real Estate Law; Tax Law; Trust and Estates, Wills and Probate

NICHOLLS & ASSOCIATES, P.C.
Denver, CO .... Bankruptcy Law; Trust and Estates, Wills and Probate

NICHOLS, RICHARD L.
Jacksonville, FL .... Family Law; Medical Malpractice

NICHOLS, DAVID E., P.C.
Charlotte Amalie, St. Thomas, VI .... Business Law

NICHOLS, JACKSON, DILLARD, HAGER & SMITH, L.L.P.
Dallas, TX .... Insurance Defense; Municipal and Zoning Law

NICHOLS, SACKS, SLANK & SWEET, A PROFESSIONAL CORPORATION
Ann Arbor, MI .... Family Law

NICHOLSON, GARNER & DUGGAN
Maryville, TN .... Civil Trial Practice; Commercial Litigation; Elder Law; General Practice; Personal Injury; Product Liability Law; Real Estate Law

NICKLAUS & WICKS, P.A.
Miami, FL .... Insurance Defense

NICOARA & STEAGALL
Peoria, IL .... Insurance Defense; Medical Malpractice; Personal Injury; Product Liability Law

NICOLETTE & PERKINS, P.A.
Hackensack, NJ .... Administrative Law; Bankruptcy Law; Civil Trial Practice; Commercial Law; Corporate Law; General Practice; Trust and Estates, Wills and Probate

NICOLINI & PARADISE
Mineola, NY .... Civil Trial Practice; Insurance Defense

NIKAIDO, MARMELSTEIN, MURRAY & ORAM, LLP
Washington, DC .... Patent, Trademark, Copyright and Unfair Competition

NIKOLAI, MERSEREAU & DIETZ, P.A.
Minneapolis, MN .... International Business Law; Patent, Trademark, Copyright and Unfair Competition

NILES, BARTON & WILMER
Baltimore, MD .... Admiralty/Maritime Law; Civil Trial Practice; General Practice

NILLES, HANSEN & DAVIES, LTD.
Fargo, ND .... Banking Law; Civil Trial Practice; Commercial Law; General Practice; Insurance Defense; Labor and Employment Law; Personal Injury; Real Estate Law; Tax Law; Trust and Estates, Wills and Probate

NIMS, HOWES, COLLISON, HANSEN & LACKERT
New York, NY .... Intellectual Property Law; Trademark, Copyright and Unfair Competition

NIRO, SCAVONE, HALLER & NIRO
Chicago, IL .... Intellectual Property Law; Patent, Trademark, Copyright and Unfair Competition

NISCHWITZ, PEMBRIDGE & CHRISZT CO., L.P.A.
Cleveland, OH .... Business Law; Commercial Litigation; Family Law

NISEN & ELLIOTT
Chicago, IL .... Business Law; Commercial Law; Commercial Litigation; Corporate Law; Employment Benefits Law; Mergers and Acquisitions; Tax Law; Trust and Estates, Wills and Probate

NIX, HOLTSFORD & VERCELLI, P.C.
Montgomery, AL .... Business Law; Civil Trial Practice; Environmental Law; Government Contracts; Insurance Defense; Product Liability Law; Professional Liability; Workers Compensation

NIX & WINEGEART, P.C.
Sherman, TX .... Bankruptcy Law; Creditors Rights

NIXON PEABODY LLP
New York, NY .... General Practice
Rochester, NY .... General Practice

NIXON & VANDERHYE P.C.
Arlington, VA .... Patent, Trademark, Copyright and Unfair Competition

NOCE & BUCKLEY, L.L.C.
St. Louis, MO .... Insurance Defense

NOEDING & MOODY, P.C.
Albuquerque, NM .... Labor and Employment Law

NOKES, DAVIS & QUINN, A PROFESSIONAL CORPORATION
Laguna Beach, CA .... Civil Trial Practice; Commercial Litigation; Construction Law; Family Law

NOLAN, ARMSTRONG & BARTON, LLP
Palo Alto, CA .... Criminal Trial Practice

NOLAN LAW GROUP
Chicago, IL .... Appellate Practice; Aviation Law; Civil Trial Practice; Medical Malpractice; Personal Injury; Product Liability Law

NOLAN, PLUMHOFF & WILLIAMS, CHARTERED
Towson, MD .... Civil Trial Practice; Criminal Trial Practice; General Practice; Personal Injury; Trust and Estates, Wills and Probate

NOLAND, HAMERLY, ETIENNE & HOSS, A PROFESSIONAL CORPORATION
Salinas, CA .... General Practice

NOLD, JOHN A., P.A.
Marco Island, FL .... Real Estate Law; Trust and Estates, Wills and Probate

NOONAN & PROKUP
Allentown, PA .... Trust and Estates, Wills and Probate

NOONAN, THOMAS J., P.C., THE LAW OFFICES OF
St. Louis, MO..........Insurance Defense

NORDMAN, CORMANY, HAIR & COMPTON
Oxnard, CA..........General Practice

NORMAN, DOWLER, SAWYER, ISRAEL, WALKER & BARTON
Ventura, CA..........General Practice

NORMAN, HANSON & DETROY, LLC
Portland, ME..........General Practice

NORMANDIN, CHENEY & O'NEIL
Laconia, NH..........Banking Law; Civil Trial Practice; Commercial Law; Corporate Law; Environmental Law; General Practice; Personal Injury; Product Liability Law; Real Estate Law; Trust and Estates, Wills and Probate

NORMINTON & WIITA
Beverly Hills, CA..........Civil Trial Practice

NORRIS, RAYMOND M. LAW OFFICES OF
Phoenix, AZ..........Personal Injury

NORRIS & NORRIS
Richmond, CA..........Civil Trial Practice

NORRIS & ROSSI LLP
San Mateo, CA..........Family Law

NORTH, STEVEN E., P.C.
New York, NY..........Medical Malpractice; Personal Injury

NORTHCUTT, CLARK, GARDNER, HRON & TATE
Ponca City, OK..........General Practice

NORTHEN BLUE, L.L.P.
Chapel Hill, NC..........Bankruptcy Law; Business Law

NORTON & CHRISTENSEN
Goshen, NY..........Construction Law; Environmental Law; General Practice

NORTON • LIDSTONE, LLC
Englewood, CO..........Civil Trial Practice; Corporate Law; Securities Law

NORTON & LUHN, P.C.
Knoxville, TN..........Civil Trial Practice

NORTON, MANCINI, ARGENTATI, WEILER & DEANO
Wheaton, IL..........Civil Trial Practice; Insurance Defense

NOTTAGE AND WARD
Chicago, IL..........Family Law

NOUMAIR, GEORGE J., P.C.
New York, NY..........Tax Law

NOVACK AND MACEY
Chicago, IL..........Civil Trial Practice

NOVINS, YORK & PENTONY, A PROFESSIONAL CORPORATION
Toms River, NJ..........Civil Trial Practice; Criminal Trial Practice; General Practice; Insurance Defense; Medical Malpractice; Personal Injury; Real Estate Law

NOVIT, SCARMINACH & WILLIAMS, P.A.
Hilton Head Island, SC..........Real Estate Law

NOVOSELSKY, DAVID A., & ASSOCIATES
Chicago, IL..........Appellate Practice

NOWELL, GEORGE W. LAW OFFICES OF
San Francisco, CA..........Admiralty/Maritime Law

NOWELL AMOROSO KLEIN BIERMAN, P.A.
Hackensack, NJ..........Civil Trial Practice; Environmental Law; Product Liability Law

NURENBERG, PLEVIN, HELLER & MCCARTHY CO., L.P.A.
Cleveland, OH..........Aviation Law; Civil Trial Practice; Commercial Litigation; Medical Malpractice; Personal Injury; Product Liability Law; Workers Compensation

NUSBAUM & PARRINO, P.C.
Westport, CT..........Family Law

NUTTALL BERMAN ATTORNEYS
Fresno, CA..........Criminal Trial Practice

NUTTER, MCCLENNEN & FISH, LLP
Boston, MA..........General Practice

NUZZO & ROBERTS, L.L.C.
Cheshire, CT..........Civil Trial Practice

NYEMASTER, GOODE, VOIGTS, WEST, HANSELL & O'BRIEN, A PROFESSIONAL CORPORATION
Des Moines, IA..........Civil Trial Practice; General Practice; Securities Law; Tax Law

OATES, KNEZEVICH & GARDENSWARTZ, P.C.
Aspen, CO..........Business Law; Civil Trial Practice; Family Law; General Practice; Land Use Law; Real Estate Law; Trust and Estates, Wills and Probate

O'BANION & RITCHEY LLP
Sacramento, CA..........Patent, Trademark, Copyright and Unfair Competition

OBENSHAIN, WILEY S., III, P.C.
Augusta, GA..........Civil Trial Practice; Insurance Defense; Medical Malpractice; Product Liability Law

OBERMAN & OBERMAN
Charleston, SC..........Civil Trial Practice; Family Law; General Practice; Real Estate Law

OBERMAYER, REBMANN, MAXWELL & HIPPEL LLP
Philadelphia, PA..........General Practice

OBLON, SPIVAK, MCCLELLAND, MAIER & NEUSTADT, P.C.
Arlington, VA..........Patent, Trademark, Copyright and Unfair Competition

O'BRIEN, WILLIAM M.
Cambridge, MA..........Banking Law; Commercial Law; General Practice; Real Estate Law

O'BRIEN, ANDERSON, BURGY, GARBOWICZ & BROWN, LLP
Eagle River, WI..........General Practice

O'BRIEN, EHRICK, WOLF, DEANER & MAUS, L.L.P.
Rochester, MN..........Civil Trial Practice; General Practice; Real Estate Law

O'BRIEN, TANSKI & YOUNG
Hartford, CT..........Health Care Law; Insurance Defense; Medical Malpractice

O'BRIEN WATTERS & DAVIS, LLP
Santa Rosa, CA..........General Practice

O'BRYAN, BROWN & TONER
Louisville, KY..........Insurance Defense; Medical Malpractice; Product Liability Law; Workers Compensation

OBUCHOWSKI LAW OFFICE
Bethel, VT..........Bankruptcy Law

OCHOA & SILLAS
Los Angeles, CA..........Administrative Law; Civil Trial Practice; Construction Law; Insurance Defense; Labor and Employment Law; Municipal Bond/Public Authority Financing

O'CONNELL AND ARONOWITZ, P.C.
Albany, NY..........Appellate Practice; Civil Trial Practice; Criminal Trial Practice; Health Care Law; Labor and Employment Law

O'CONNELL, BENJAMIN & COGHLAN, L.L.P.
San Antonio, TX..........Civil Trial Practice; Commercial Litigation; Construction Law; Insurance Defense; Labor and Employment Law; Medical Malpractice; Product Liability Law; Professional Liability; Toxic Torts

O'CONNELL, DANIEL H., P.C.
Tucson, AZ..........Corporate Law; Pension and Profit Sharing; Real Estate Law; Tax Law; Trust and Estates, Wills and Probate

O'CONNOR, DEGRAZIA & TAMM, P.C.
Bloomfield Hills, MI..........Civil Rights; Medical Malpractice; Municipal and Zoning Law

O'CONNOR & DEMAS, P.C.
Chatham, NJ..........Civil Trial Practice; Personal Injury

O'CONNOR, GACIOCH, POPE & TAIT, L.L.P.
Binghamton, NY..........Construction Law; Environmental Law; Insurance Defense; Labor and Employment Law; Medical Malpractice; Personal Injury

O'CONNOR & HANNAN, L.L.P.
Washington, DC..........General Practice; Tax Law

O'CONNOR, MCGUINNESS, CONTE, DOYLE & OLESON
White Plains, NY..........Product Liability Law; Professional Liability; Trust and Estates, Wills and Probate

O'CONNOR & MEYERS, P.A.
Miami, FL..........Insurance Defense

O'CONNOR, O'CONNOR, MAYBERGER & FIRST, P.C.
Albany, NY..........Commercial Litigation; Insurance Defense; Medical Malpractice; Product Liability Law; Toxic Torts

O'CONNOR AND RYAN, P.C.
Fitchburg, MA..........Civil Trial Practice; Criminal Trial Practice; Family Law; Labor and Employment Law; Personal Injury; Trust and Estates, Wills and Probate

O'CONNOR & THOMAS, P.C.
Dubuque, IA .... General Practice; Personal Injury

ODELL, JAMES R., P.S.C.
Lexington, KY .... General Practice

ODIN, FELDMAN & PITTLEMAN, P.C.
Fairfax, VA .... Banking Law; Civil Trial Practice; Commercial Law; Family Law; General Practice; Intellectual Property Law; International Business Law; Labor and Employment Law; Real Estate Law; Tax Law; Trademark, Copyright and Unfair Competition

ODOM & DES ROCHES, LLP
Hahira, GA .... Civil Trial Practice
New Orleans, LA .... Civil Trial Practice; Commercial Litigation

ODOM & ELLIOTT
Fayetteville, AR .... Civil Trial Practice; Medical Malpractice; Personal Injury

O'DONNELL, ROBERT G.
White Plains, NY .... Civil Trial Practice; Commercial Litigation

O'DONNELL, SCHWARTZ, GLANSTEIN, ROSEN, DI PRETA & GOLDSTEIN, L.L.P.
New York, NY .... Admiralty/Maritime Law; Employment Benefits Law; Labor and Employment Law

O'DONOHUE & O'DONOHUE
Toronto, ON, Canada .... General Practice

OFFUTT, FISHER & NORD
Huntington, WV .... Commercial Litigation; Insurance Defense; Medical Malpractice

OFFUTT, HORMAN, BURDETTE & FREY, P.A.
Frederick, MD .... General Practice; Real Estate Law; Trust and Estates, Wills and Probate

OGBORN, SUMMERLIN & OGBORN, L.L.C.
Denver, CO .... Civil Trial Practice

OGDEN, LEN W. JR.
Paducah, KY .... Criminal Trial Practice; Personal Injury

OGGEL, STEPHEN P., A P.C., THE LAW OFFICES OF
San Diego, CA .... Antitrust Law; Business Law

OGILVIE, DAVID A., P.C.
Denver, CO .... Criminal Trial Practice

OGILVY RENAULT
Vancouver, BC, Canada .... General Practice
Ottawa, ON, Canada .... General Practice
Toronto, ON, Canada .... General Practice
Montreal, QU, Canada .... General Practice
Quebec, QU, Canada .... General Practice
London, England .... General Practice

OGLE, MERZON & KIRSCHNER
Morro Bay, CA .... General Practice; Real Estate Law; Trust and Estates, Wills and Probate

OGLETREE, DEAKINS, NASH, SMOAK & STEWART, P.C.
Washington, DC .... Labor and Employment Law
Atlanta, GA .... Labor and Employment Law
Raleigh, NC .... Labor and Employment Law
Winston-Salem, NC .... Labor and Employment Law
Charleston, SC .... Labor and Employment Law
Columbia, SC .... Labor and Employment Law
Greenville, SC .... Environmental Law; Labor and Employment Law
Houston, TX .... Labor and Employment Law

O'HARA & HANLON, LLP
Cazenovia, NY .... General Practice

O'HARA, PATRICK M., P.A.
West Palm Beach, FL .... Commercial Litigation; Personal Injury

O'HARE & HEITCZMAN
Bethlehem, PA .... Civil Trial Practice; Criminal Trial Practice; Family Law; General Practice

OHNEGIAN, DONALD C.
Ramsey, NJ .... General Practice

OHNSTAD TWICHELL, P.C.
Fargo, ND .... Criminal Trial Practice; General Practice; Municipal Bond/Public Authority Financing; Trust and Estates, Wills and Probate

OHRENSTEIN & BROWN, L.L.P.
New York, NY .... Insurance Defense; Toxic Torts

O'KEEFFE & LINDGREN, LLP
White Plains, NY .... Civil Trial Practice; Personal Injury

OLDFIELD, E. LAWRENCE, & ASSOCIATES
Oak Brook, IL .... General Practice

OLDHAM & DOWLING
Akron, OH .... Civil Trial Practice; Insurance Defense; Trust and Estates, Wills and Probate

OLDMAN, COOLEY & LEIGHTON, L.L.P.
Los Angeles, CA .... Trust and Estates, Wills and Probate

OLENDER, JACK H., AND ASSOCIATES, P.C.
Washington, DC .... Medical Malpractice; Personal Injury

OLES, MORRISON, RINKER & BAKER L.L.P.
Seattle, WA .... Construction Law; General Practice; Insurance Defense

OLIFF & BERRIDGE, PLC
Alexandria, VA .... Patent, Trademark, Copyright and Unfair Competition

OLINCY & KARPEL
Los Angeles, CA .... Tax Law; Trust and Estates, Wills and Probate

OLINGER, LOVALD, ROBBENNOLT, MCCAHREN AND REIMERS, P.C.
Pierre, SD .... General Practice

OLINS, FOERSTER & HAYES
San Diego, CA .... Civil Trial Practice; Family Law; Labor and Employment Law; Personal Injury

OLIVE AND OLIVE, P.A.
Durham, NC .... Intellectual Property Law; Patent, Trademark, Copyright and Unfair Competition

OLIVER, DUCKWORTH, SPARGER & WINKLE, P.C.
Jonesboro, GA .... Civil Trial Practice; General Practice

OLIVER, OLIVER & WALTZ, P.C.
Cape Girardeau, MO .... Civil Trial Practice; General Practice; Insurance Defense

OLIVER, VOSE, SANDIFER, MURPHY & LEE, A PROFESSIONAL CORPORATION
Los Angeles, CA .... Eminent Domain; Environmental Law; Municipal and Zoning Law

OLIVER, WALKER, WILSON & EHRHARDT, LLC
Columbia, MO .... Civil Trial Practice; Insurance Defense; Workers Compensation

OLSEN, M. KENT
Denver, CO .... Elder Law; Trust and Estates, Wills and Probate

OLSON, JANTSCH, BAKKER & BLAKEY, P.A.
Phoenix, AZ .... Medical Malpractice

OLSON, NOONAN & BZDOK, P.C.
Traverse City, MI .... Civil Trial Practice; Corporate Law; Environmental Law; Municipal and Zoning Law; Real Estate Law

OLTMAN, FLYNN AND KUBLER
Fort Lauderdale, FL .... Patent, Trademark, Copyright and Unfair Competition

OLUP & ASSOCIATES
Minneapolis, MN .... Family Law

O'MALLEY & HARRIS, P.C.
Scranton, PA .... Appellate Practice; Bankruptcy Law; Business Law; Civil Trial Practice; Commercial Litigation; Environmental Law; Family Law; General Practice; Insurance Defense; Medical Malpractice; Personal Injury; Product Liability Law; Real Estate Law; Workers Compensation

O'MALLEY & LANGAN, A PROFESSIONAL CORPORATION
Scranton, PA .... Workers Compensation

O'MALLEY LAW FIRM, THE, P.C.
St. Louis, MO .... Criminal Trial Practice; Insurance Defense

OMAN, GENTRY & YNTEMA, P.A.
Albuquerque, NM .... Business Law; Real Estate Law

O'MELVENY & MYERS LLP
Los Angeles, CA .... Antitrust Law; Appellate Practice; Banking Law; Bankruptcy Law; Business Law; Civil Trial Practice; Commercial Law; Communications Law; Construction Law; Criminal Trial Practice; Employment Benefits Law; Environmental Law; General Practice; Immigration and Naturalization; Insurance Defense; International Business Law; Labor and Employment Law; Municipal and Zoning Law; Natural Resources Law; Patent, Trademark, Copyright and Unfair Competition; Public Utilities Law; Real Estate Law; Securities Law; Tax Law; Trademark, Copyright and Unfair Competition; Trust and Estates, Wills and Probate

OMER, JAMES R., & ASSOCIATES
Nashville, TN....................Personal Injury

O'NEAL, BROWN & SIZEMORE, A PROFESSIONAL CORPORATION
Macon, GA....................General Practice; Personal Injury

O'NEAL, WALKER & BOEHM
Chattanooga, TN....................Personal Injury

ONEBANE, BERNARD, TORIAN, DIAZ, MCNAMARA & ABELL
Lafayette, LA....................Admiralty/Maritime Law; Business Law; Civil Trial Practice; Energy Law; Environmental Law; General Practice; Insurance Defense; Labor and Employment Law

O'NEILL, CHAPIN, LIEBMAN & COOPER
Orlando, FL....................Civil Trial Practice; Commercial Law; Commercial Litigation; Insurance Defense

O'NEILL CRAWFORD & GREEN, P.C.
Burlington, VT....................Commercial Litigation; Criminal Trial Practice; Personal Injury

O'NEILL, JOSEPH D., A PROFESSIONAL CORPORATION
Vineland, NJ....................Criminal Trial Practice; Medical Malpractice; Personal Injury

O'NEILL, LYSAGHT & SUN LLP
Santa Monica, CA....................Appellate Practice; Civil Trial Practice; Commercial Law; Criminal Trial Practice

O'NEILL, PATRICK H., LAW OFFICES OF
Fort Worth, TX....................Civil Trial Practice; Commercial Litigation; Health Care Law; Medical Malpractice; Personal Injury; Product Liability Law

O'NEILL, WALLACE & DOYLE, P.C.
Saginaw, MI....................General Practice; Insurance Defense

ONSAGER, RICHARD C., P.C.
Phoenix, AZ....................Tax Law

ONSTAD LAW FIRM, THE
Austin, TX....................Aviation Law; Medical Malpractice; Personal Injury

OPIE, GLENN E.
Great Bend, KS....................General Practice

OPPENHEIMER, BLEND, HARRISON & TATE, INC.
San Antonio, TX....................General Practice

OPPENHEIMER WOLFF & DONNELLY (ILLINOIS)
Chicago, IL....................Commercial Litigation

OPPENHEIMER WOLFF DONNELLY & BAYH LLP
Washington, DC....................Commercial Litigation; Environmental Law; Intellectual Property Law; Patent, Trademark, Copyright and Unfair Competition; Product Liability Law

OPPENHEIMER WOLFF & DONNELLY LLP
Los Angeles, CA....................Banking Law; Bankruptcy Law; Commercial Litigation; Environmental Law; Intellectual Property Law; Patent, Trademark, Copyright and Unfair Competition
Newport Beach, CA....................Commercial Litigation; Intellectual Property Law; Patent, Trademark, Copyright and Unfair Competition
Palo Alto, CA....................Commercial Litigation; Environmental Law; Intellectual Property Law; Patent, Trademark, Copyright and Unfair Competition
Minneapolis, MN....................Banking Law; Bankruptcy Law; Commercial Litigation; Environmental Law; General Practice; Intellectual Property Law; Patent, Trademark, Copyright and Unfair Competition; Product Liability Law
St. Paul, MN....................Commercial Litigation
New York, NY....................Banking Law; Bankruptcy Law; Commercial Litigation; Environmental Law; Intellectual Property Law; Patent, Trademark, Copyright and Unfair Competition
Brussels, Belgium....................Environmental Law

OPPENHEIM & PILELSKY, P.A.
Fort Lauderdale, FL....................Commercial Litigation; Personal Injury; Real Estate Law

ORANS, ELSEN & LUPERT LLP
New York, NY....................General Practice

ORECK, BRADLEY, CRIGHTON, ADAMS & CHASE, LLC
New Orleans, LA....................Tax Law

O'REILLY, COLLINS & DANKO, A PROFESSIONAL CORPORATION
Menlo Park, CA....................Aviation Law; Civil Trial Practice; Personal Injury; Product Liability Law

O'REILLY LAW OFFICES
Wheaton, IL....................Commercial Litigation; Medical Malpractice; Personal Injury

O'REILLY, MARSH & CORTESELLI, P.C.
Garden City, NY....................Banking Law

ORGAIN, BELL & TUCKER, L.L.P.
Beaumont, TX....................General Practice

ORLOW AND ORLOW, P.C.
Philadelphia, PA....................Immigration and Naturalization

O'ROURKE, ALLAN & FONG, LLP
Glendale, CA....................Business Law; Civil Trial Practice; Construction Law; Personal Injury; Real Estate Law

ORRICK, HERRINGTON & SUTCLIFFE LLP
San Francisco, CA....................General Practice

ORSINGER & NARDONE
Westerly, RI....................Real Estate Law; Trust and Estates, Wills and Probate

ORTALE, KELLEY, HERBERT & CRAWFORD
Nashville, TN....................Insurance Defense

ORTON, TOOMAN, HALE, MCKOWN AND KIEL, P.C.
Allegan, MI....................General Practice

OSBORN, J. KIRK
Chapel Hill, NC....................Criminal Trial Practice; Family Law; Personal Injury

OSBORN SMITH, P.L.L.C.
Seattle, WA....................Personal Injury

OSBORNE, LOWE, HELMAN & SMITH, L.L.P.
Austin, TX....................Tax Law; Trust and Estates, Wills and Probate

OSBORNE, WILLIAM G., P.A.
Orlando, FL....................Civil Trial Practice; Commercial Litigation; Personal Injury

O'SHAUGHNESSY, PHILLIPS P., P.A.
Fort Lauderdale, FL....................Civil Trial Practice; Legal Malpractice
Baltimore, MD....................Civil Trial Practice; General Practice; Legal Malpractice; Medical Malpractice

O'SHEA, REYNOLDS & CUMMINGS
Buffalo, NY....................Insurance Defense; Legal Malpractice; Medical Malpractice; Product Liability Law

OSHINS & ASSOCIATES, P.C.
Las Vegas, NV....................Business Law; General Practice; Tax Law; Trust and Estates, Wills and Probate

OSLER, HOSKIN & HARCOURT LLP
Calgary, AB, Canada....................General Practice
Ottawa, ON, Canada....................General Practice
Toronto, ON, Canada....................General Practice

OSSICK, JOHN J., JR., P.C.
Kingsland, GA....................Civil Trial Practice; Criminal Trial Practice

OSTERHOUDT, FERGUSON, NATT, AHERON & AGEE, A PROFESSIONAL CORPORATION
Roanoke, VA....................Bankruptcy Law; Business Law; General Practice

OSTER & WEGENER, A P.L.C.
Slidell, LA....................Family Law

OSTGARD, JAMES E. II
Minneapolis, MN....................Criminal Trial Practice

OSTROLENK, FABER, GERB & SOFFEN, LLP
New York, NY....................Patent, Trademark, Copyright and Unfair Competition

OSTROVE, NONA L.
Voorhees, NJ....................Bankruptcy Law

OSTROVE, KRANTZ & OSTROVE, A PROFESSIONAL CORPORATION
Los Angeles, CA....................Admiralty/Maritime Law; Commercial Law; Insurance Defense; Mergers and Acquisitions; Tax Law; Trust and Estates, Wills and Probate

OSTROW AND TAUB, LLP
Garden City, NY....................Family Law

OSWALD, COTTEY & TEMPLETON, A PROFESSIONAL CORPORATION
Kirksville, MO....................Civil Trial Practice; Family Law; General Practice; Insurance Defense

OSWALD AND REED
Pascagoula, MS....................Civil Trial Practice; Personal Injury

OSWALD & YAP, A PROFESSIONAL CORPORATION
Irvine, CA....................Immigration and Naturalization; Labor and Employment Law; Real Estate Law; Securities Law

OTA & YUEN
Honolulu, HI....................Trust and Estates, Wills and Probate

OTERI, WEINBERG & LAWSON, P.A.
Boston, MA....Criminal Trial Practice

OTJEN, VAN ERT, LIEB & WEIR, S.C.
Milwaukee, WI....Insurance Defense

O'TOOLE LAW FIRM, THE
Los Angeles, CA....Environmental Law

OTT & HOFFMAN, A PROFESSIONAL CORPORATION
Glendale, CA....Appellate Practice; Civil Trial Practice; Labor and Employment Law

OTTEN, JOHNSON, ROBINSON, NEFF & RAGONETTI, P.C.
Denver, CO....Banking Law; Bankruptcy Law; Business Law; Commercial Litigation; Construction Law; Corporate Law; Eminent Domain; Environmental Law; General Practice; Health Care Law; Labor and Employment Law; Land Use Law; Municipal and Zoning Law; Real Estate Law; Securities Law; Tax Law

OTTERBOURG, STEINDLER, HOUSTON & ROSEN, P.C.
New York, NY....Antitrust Law; Appellate Practice; Banking Law; Bankruptcy Law; Business Law; Civil Trial Practice; Commercial Law; Construction Law; Employment Benefits Law; General Practice; International Business Law; Real Estate Law; Securities Law; Trademark, Copyright and Unfair Competition; Trust and Estates, Wills and Probate

OTTERMAN & ALLEN, P.C.
Barre, VT....Trust and Estates, Wills and Probate

OTTO, PORTERFIELD & POST, LLC
Vail, CO....Banking Law; General Practice; Real Estate Law

OTTS, MOORE & JORDAN
Brewton, AL....General Practice; Insurance Defense

OTTSEN, MAUZÉ, LEGGAT & BELZ, L.C.
St. Louis, MO....Business Law; Constitutional Law; Trust and Estates, Wills and Probate

OUTTEN, BARRETT, BURR & SHARRETT, P.C.
Emporia, VA....General Practice
Lawrenceville, VA....General Practice

OVERBEY, HAWKINS & SELZ
Rustburg, VA....Civil Trial Practice; Personal Injury

OVERCHUCK, NEWSOME & SCHWERER, LLP
Orlando, FL....Personal Injury; Product Liability Law

OWEN, WILLIAM L.
Little Rock, AR....Civil Trial Practice; Real Estate Law

OWEN, BIRD
Vancouver, BC, Canada....General Practice

OWEN & DAVIS PC
New York, NY....Appellate Practice; Civil Trial Practice

OWEN & GALLOWAY
Gulfport, MS....Personal Injury

OWENS & ALMOND, LLP
Tuscaloosa, AL....Civil Trial Practice; General Practice

OWENS, CLARY & AIKEN, L.L.P.
Dallas, TX....Civil Trial Practice; Real Estate Law

OWENS DAVIES MACKIE, P.S., A PROFESSIONAL SERVICES CORPORATION
Olympia, WA....General Practice

OWENS & TURNER, A PROFESSIONAL CORPORATION
Anchorage, AK....Commercial Law; Labor and Employment Law

OWNBEY, LLOYD C. JR.
Pasadena, CA....Labor and Employment Law

OWSEN, JOHN D., P.C.
Irving, TX....Tax Law

OXLEY, MALONE, FITZGERALD & HOLLISTER
Findlay, OH....General Practice; Insurance Defense

OZZARD, WILLIAM E.
Bridgewater, NJ....Trust and Estates, Wills and Probate

PACIFICO, PAUL J. LAW OFFICES OF
Westport, CT....Civil Trial Practice; Medical Malpractice; Personal Injury

PACKENHAM, SCHMIDT & FEDERICO, P.C.
Boston, MA....Appellate Practice; Family Law; Trust and Estates, Wills and Probate

PAGE FIRM, THE, A P.C.
San Diego, CA....Civil Trial Practice; General Practice; International Business Law

PAGE, MANNINO, PERESICH & MCDERMOTT
Biloxi, MS....General Practice; Insurance Defense; Medical Malpractice; Personal Injury; Product Liability Law

PAHL & GOSSELIN, A PROFESSIONAL CORPORATION
San Francisco, CA....Employment Benefits Law

PAIN AND GARLAND
Anadarko, OK....General Practice

PAINE & ASSOCIATES, P.C.
Florence, AL....Tax Law; Trust and Estates, Wills and Probate

PAINE EDMONDS
Vancouver, BC, Canada....General Practice; Insurance Defense

PAJCIC & PAJCIC, P.A.
Jacksonville, FL....Medical Malpractice; Personal Injury; Product Liability Law

PALEY, ROTHMAN, GOLDSTEIN, ROSENBERG & COOPER, CHARTERED
Bethesda, MD....General Practice; Labor and Employment Law; Tax Law

PALKOVITZ, HERBERT
Cleveland, OH....Family Law

PALLO, KEITH R., & ASSOCIATES, P.A.
Palm Beach Gardens, FL....Workers Compensation

PALMER & DODGE LLP
Boston, MA....Antitrust Law; Appellate Practice; Banking Law; Bankruptcy Law; Business Law; Civil Trial Practice; Communications Law; Computer Law; Construction Law; Education Law; Employment Benefits Law; Environmental Law; General Practice; Immigration and Naturalization; Insurance Defense; International Business Law; Labor and Employment Law; Land Use Law; Municipal Bond/Public Authority Financing; Product Liability Law; Public Utilities Law; Real Estate Law; Securities Law; Sports and Entertainment Law; Tax Law; Trademark, Copyright and Unfair Competition; Transportation Law; Trust and Estates, Wills and Probate

PALMER LAW FIRM
Dyersburg, TN....Commercial Law; Personal Injury

PALMER, ROBERT M. N., P.C., LAW OFFICES OF
Springfield, MO....Product Liability Law

PALMERI, CHARLES J., CO., L.P.A.
Cleveland, OH....Creditors Rights

PALMIERI, TYLER, WIENER, WILHELM & WALDRON, LLP
Irvine, CA....General Practice

PALMISANO, JAMES ANTHONY, LTD.
Palos Heights, IL....Family Law

PANGIA & HANSEN
Washington, DC....Aviation Law; Medical Malpractice; Personal Injury; Product Liability Law

PANIELLO, JOSEPH M., P.A., LAW OFFICE OF
Tampa, FL....Real Estate Law

PANKOFF, PHILIP E., P.C.
Denver, CO....Commercial Litigation

PANSLER & MOODY, P.A.
Bartow, FL....Civil Trial Practice

PAONE CALLAHAN MCHOLM & WINTON, LLP
Irvine, CA....Civil Trial Practice; Real Estate Law

PAPA, HERMAN D.
San Francisco, CA....Civil Trial Practice

PAPARELLI & PARTNERS LLP
Irvine, CA....Immigration and Naturalization

PAPERNICK & GEFSKY, A PROFESSIONAL CORPORATION
Pittsburgh, PA....Real Estate Law

PAPPAS METCALF JENKS MILLER & REINSCH, P.A.
Jacksonville, FL....Environmental Law; General Practice; Land Use Law; Municipal and Zoning Law; Real Estate Law

PARADISO, DACK, TAUB & OLER, P.C.
Bethesda, MD....Family Law

PARDIECK, GILL, VARGO & MACTAVISH, A PROFESSIONAL CORPORATION
Seymour, IN....Medical Malpractice; Personal Injury; Product Liability Law

PARENTI, FALK, WAAS, HERNANDEZ & CORTINA, P.A.
Coral Gables, FL....................Insurance Defense; Medical Malpractice

PARHAM, HELMS, HARRIS, BLYTHE & MORTON
Charlotte, NC....................Banking Law; Bankruptcy Law; Real Estate Law

PARHAM & SMITH, L.L.C.
Greenville, SC....................Civil Trial Practice; Medical Malpractice; Personal Injury; Product Liability Law

PARIS, PHILIP T.
Phoenix, AZ....................Mergers and Acquisitions; Trust and Estates, Wills and Probate

PARIS & ASSOCIATES, P.A.
Tampa, FL....................Real Estate Law; Trust and Estates, Wills and Probate

PARIS AND PARIS, LLP
Santa Monica, CA....................Bankruptcy Law; Creditors Rights

PARISH, WILLIAM W. LAW OFFICES OF
Dallas, TX....................Personal Injury

PARISH & NELSON, A PROFESSIONAL CORPORATION
Stockton, CA....................Civil Trial Practice

PARKER CHAPIN LLP
New York, NY....................Antitrust Law; Banking Law; Bankruptcy Law; Civil Trial Practice; Commercial Law; General Practice; Insurance Defense; Intellectual Property Law; Labor and Employment Law; Mergers and Acquisitions; Product Liability Law; Real Estate Law; Securities Law; Tax Law; Trust and Estates, Wills and Probate

PARKER, DAVID YOUNG, P.C.
Nashville, TN....................General Practice

PARKER, HAYES & LOVINGER, P.C.
Hillsdale, MI....................Commercial Litigation; General Practice; Trust and Estates, Wills and Probate

PARKER, HUDSON, RAINER & DOBBS LLP
Atlanta, GA....................Antitrust Law; Banking Law; Bankruptcy Law; Business Law; Commercial Litigation; Health Care Law; Real Estate Law

PARKER, LANDERMAN & PARKER, P.A.
Orlando, FL....................Civil Rights; Civil Trial Practice; Medical Malpractice; Personal Injury

PARKER, LAWRENCE, CANTRELL & DEAN
Nashville, TN....................Civil Trial Practice; Insurance Defense

PARKER, MCCAY & CRISCUOLO, P.A.
Cherry Hill, NJ....................Civil Trial Practice; General Practice
Marlton, NJ....................Civil Trial Practice; General Practice

PARKER MILLS & PATEL LLP
Los Angeles, CA....................Commercial Litigation; Professional Liability

PARKER, POE, ADAMS & BERNSTEIN GMBH-IG
Frankfurt/Main, Germany......General Practice

PARKER, POE, ADAMS & BERNSTEIN L.L.P.
Charlotte, NC....................General Practice
Raleigh, NC....................General Practice
Columbia, SC....................General Practice
Spartanburg, SC....................General Practice

PARKER & WAICHMAN
New York, NY....................Civil Trial Practice; Medical Malpractice

PARKHURST & WENDEL, L.L.P.
Alexandria, VA....................Civil Trial Practice; Patent, Trademark, Copyright and Unfair Competition

PARKINSON, JAMES W. THE LAW OFFICES OF
Palm Desert, CA....................Personal Injury

PARK, KEITH H., P.A.
West Palm Beach, FL....................Civil Trial Practice; Family Law

PARLEE MCLAWS
Calgary, AB, Canada....................Administrative Law; Banking Law; Bankruptcy Law; Civil Trial Practice; Commercial Law; Corporate Law; Environmental Law; General Practice; Insurance Defense; Intellectual Property Law; Labor and Employment Law; Natural Resources Law; Personal Injury; Real Estate Law; Securities Law; Tax Law; Trust and Estates, Wills and Probate
Edmonton, AB, Canada....................Administrative Law; Appellate Practice; Banking Law; Bankruptcy Law; Business Law; Civil Trial Practice; Commercial Law; Constitutional Law; Construction Law; Corporate Law; Environmental Law; General Practice; Immigration and Naturalization; Insurance Defense; Intellectual Property Law; International Business Law; Labor and Employment Law; Municipal and Zoning Law; Personal Injury; Public Utilities Law; Real Estate Law; Securities Law; Tax Law; Trust and Estates, Wills and Probate

PARNELL & CRUM, P.A.
Montgomery, AL....................Banking Law; Bankruptcy Law; Commercial Law; Commercial Litigation; Construction Law; Creditors Rights; Family Law; Real Estate Law

PARR WADDOUPS BROWN GEE & LOVELESS, A PROFESSIONAL CORPORATION
Salt Lake City, UT....................Bankruptcy Law; Civil Trial Practice; Construction Law; Employment Benefits Law; Environmental Law; General Practice; Insurance Defense; Intellectual Property Law; International Business Law; Labor and Employment Law; Municipal and Zoning Law; Natural Resources Law; Product Liability Law; Public Utilities Law; Real Estate Law; Securities Law; Tax Law; Trust and Estates, Wills and Probate

PARRA, DEL VALLE, FRAU & LIMERES
Ponce, PR....................General Practice

PARRETT, PORTO, PARESE & COLWELL, P.C.
New Haven, CT....................Civil Trial Practice

PARRILLO, ROBERT D.
Providence, RI....................Civil Trial Practice

PARRISH & FREDERICKSEN, P.A.
Orlando, FL....................Medical Malpractice; Personal Injury; Product Liability Law

PARRY, WILLIAM D.
Philadelphia, PA....................Civil Trial Practice; Personal Injury

PARSINEN KAPLAN LEVY ROSBERG & GOTLIEB P.A.
Minneapolis, MN....................Corporate Law; Labor and Employment Law; Real Estate Law; Trust and Estates, Wills and Probate

PARSONS BEHLE & LATIMER, A PROFESSIONAL CORPORATION
Salt Lake City, UT....................Civil Trial Practice; Environmental Law; General Practice; Natural Resources Law

PARSONS, DAVIES, KINGHORN & PETERS, P.C.
Salt Lake City, UT....................Bankruptcy Law; Business Law; Commercial Law; Commercial Litigation; Creditors Rights; Energy Law; Environmental Law; General Practice; Health Care Law; Land Use Law; Municipal and Zoning Law; Natural Resources Law; Pension and Profit Sharing; Real Estate Law; Tax Law; Trademark, Copyright and Unfair Competition; Trust and Estates, Wills and Probate

PARSONS, LEE & JULIANO, P.C.
Birmingham, AL....................General Practice; Health Care Law; Insurance Defense; Municipal and Zoning Law; Product Liability Law

PASCOE & RAFTON
San Rafael, CA....................Bankruptcy Law; Business Law

PASHMAN STEIN, A PROFESSIONAL CORPORATION
Hackensack, NJ....................Appellate Practice; Bankruptcy Law; Commercial Law; Family Law; General Practice; Labor and Employment Law; Trust and Estates, Wills and Probate

PASSEN, STEPHEN M., LTD.
Chicago, IL....................Civil Trial Practice; Personal Injury

PASTOR & LEONARD
Los Angeles, CA....................Tax Law

PASULKA, DAVID P., & ASSOCIATES, P.C.
Chicago, IL....................Family Law

PATE & DODSON
Beaumont, TX....................Commercial Litigation; Insurance Defense; Product Liability Law

PATHAK & ASSOCIATES
New Delhi, India....................General Practice

PATLA, STRAUS, ROBINSON & MOORE, P.A.
Asheville, NC....................General Practice

PATRICK, HARPER & DIXON L.L.P.
Hickory, NC....................General Practice

PATRICK, J. VERNON, JR., & ASSOCIATES, P.C.
Birmingham, AL....................Antitrust Law; Appellate Practice; Civil Trial Practice; Securities Law

PATRICK & STOWELL, P.C.
Aspen, CO....................Environmental Law; Natural Resources Law

PATRONE, ANDRE J., P.A.
Fort Myers, FL....................Trust and Estates, Wills and Probate

PATTERSON, PATRICIA L.
Grosse Pointe Woods, MI.......Trust and Estates, Wills and Probate

PATTERSON & ASSOCIATES
Corpus Christi, TX ....Personal Injury; Product Liability Law

PATTERSON, BELKNAP, WEBB & TYLER LLP
New York, NY.........................Civil Trial Practice; General Practice

PATTERSON, DILTHEY, CLAY & BRYSON, L.L.P.
Raleigh, NC.............................Insurance Defense; Medical Malpractice; Personal Injury

PATTERSON & HARMON, P.A.
Deerfield Beach, FL................General Practice; Trust and Estates, Wills and Probate

PATTERSON, LORENTZEN, DUFFIELD, TIMMONS, IRISH, BECKER & ORDWAY, L.L.P.
Des Moines, IA........................Civil Trial Practice; General Practice; Insurance Defense; Personal Injury; Product Liability Law; Professional Liability; Real Estate Law; Trust and Estates, Wills and Probate; Workers Compensation

PATTERSON & PATTERSON
Aberdeen, MS..........................Bankruptcy Law; Civil Trial Practice; General Practice; Labor and Employment Law; Natural Resources Law

PATTERSON, PHIFER & PHILLIPS, P.C.
Detroit, MI..............................Civil Trial Practice; Insurance Defense

PATTERSON, ROBERT B., LTD., LAW OFFICES OF
Chicago, IL..............................Personal Injury

PATTISHALL, MCAULIFFE, NEWBURY, HILLIARD & GERALDSON
Chicago, IL..............................International Business Law; Patent, Trademark, Copyright and Unfair Competition; Trademark, Copyright and Unfair Competition

PATTON BOGGS LLP
Washington, DC......................General Practice

PATTON, DAVID D., & ASSOCIATES, P.C.
Bloomfield Hills, MI...............Administrative Law; Business Law; Civil Trial Practice; Health Care Law; Insurance Defense; Labor and Employment Law; Medical Malpractice; Personal Injury; Product Liability Law

PATTON, HALTOM, ROBERTS, MCWILLIAMS & GREER, L.L.P.
Texarkana, TX ....Bankruptcy Law; Civil Trial Practice; General Practice; Insurance Defense; Personal Injury; Real Estate Law; Tax Law; Trust and Estates, Wills and Probate

PATTON, LATHAM, LEGGE & COLE
Athens, AL...............................General Practice; Insurance Defense

PATTON, TIDWELL & SANDEFUR, L.L.P.
Texarkana, TX ....Civil Trial Practice; Employment Benefits Law; General Practice; Medical Malpractice; Personal Injury; Product Liability Law

PATULA & ASSOCIATES
Chicago, IL..............................Patent, Trademark, Copyright and Unfair Competition

PATURIS, E. MICHAEL
Alexandria, VA ....Business Law; Tax Law; Trust and Estates, Wills and Probate

PAULE, CAMAZINE & BLUMENTHAL, A PROFESSIONAL CORPORATION
St. Louis, MO..........................Corporate Law; Family Law; Trust and Estates, Wills and Probate

PAULEY PETERSEN KINNE & FEJER
Chicago, IL..............................Intellectual Property Law; Patent, Trademark, Copyright and Unfair Competition
Hoffman Estates, IL ....Intellectual Property Law; Patent, Trademark, Copyright and Unfair Competition

PAUL, HASTINGS, JANOFSKY & WALKER LLP
Costa Mesa, CA......................General Practice
Los Angeles, CA.....................General Practice
San Francisco, CA ....General Practice
Stamford, CT..........................General Practice
Washington, DC......................General Practice
Atlanta, GA ....General Practice
New York, NY.........................General Practice
London, England ....General Practice
Tokyo, Japan ....General Practice

PAULIG AND SINGER
Urbana, OH.............................General Practice

PAUL & JANOFSKY
Santa Monica, CA...................Civil Trial Practice

PAUL, JOHNSON, PARK & NILES, ATTORNEYS AT LAW, A LAW CORPORATION
Honolulu, HI...........................General Practice
Wailuku, HI ....General Practice

PAUL & PAUL
Philadelphia, PA ....Intellectual Property Law; Patent, Trademark, Copyright and Unfair Competition; Trademark, Copyright and Unfair Competition

PAULSON & NACE
Washington, DC......................Civil Trial Practice; Medical Malpractice; Personal Injury

PAUL, WEISS, RIFKIND, WHARTON & GARRISON
Washington, DC......................General Practice
New York, NY.........................General Practice
Beijing, China.........................General Practice
Hong Kong, China...................General Practice
Paris, France...........................General Practice
Tokyo, Japan ....General Practice

PAVALON, GIFFORD, LAATSCH & MARINO
Chicago, IL..............................Aviation Law; Civil Trial Practice; Commercial Litigation; Medical Malpractice; Personal Injury; Product Liability Law; Transportation Law

PAXTON, CROW, BRAGG, SMITH & NELSON, P.A.
West Palm Beach, FL.............Civil Trial Practice

PAYNE & BLANCHARD, L.L.P.
Dallas, TX ....Civil Trial Practice; General Practice

PAYNE, GATES, FARTHING & RADD, P.C.
Norfolk, VA ....Banking Law; Business Law; Civil Trial Practice; Commercial Law; Commercial Litigation; Construction Law; Insurance Defense; Intellectual Property Law; International Business Law; Labor and Employment Law; Mergers and Acquisitions; Patent, Trademark, Copyright and Unfair Competition; Personal Injury; Securities Law; Tax Law; Trust and Estates, Wills and Probate

PAYNE, LUNDEEN, D'AMBROSIO & ARISMENDI, L.L.P.
Houston, TX ....Patent, Trademark, Copyright and Unfair Competition

PAYNE, WATSON, KLING, MILLER & MALECHEK, P.C.
Bryan, TX................................Insurance Defense

PAYNE, WOOD & LITTLEJOHN
Bridgehampton, NY.................Banking Law; General Practice; Real Estate Law
Melville, NY............................Banking Law; General Practice; Real Estate Law

PAYTON & CARLSON, P.A.
Miami, FL................................Civil Trial Practice; Commercial Litigation

PEABODY & ARNOLD LLP
Portland, ME ....General Practice
Boston, MA.............................General Practice
Providence, RI.........................General Practice

PEACOCK KELLER ECKER & CROTHERS, LLP
Washington, PA ....Business Law; Civil Trial Practice; General Practice; Trust and Estates, Wills and Probate

PEAR SPERLING EGGAN & MUSKOVITZ, P.C.
Ann Arbor, MI ....Banking Law; Business Law; Civil Trial Practice; Corporate Law; Family Law; Franchise Law; General Practice; Insurance Defense; Labor and Employment Law; Real Estate Law; Trust and Estates, Wills and Probate
Ypsilanti, MI ....Banking Law; Civil Trial Practice; Corporate Law; Family Law; Franchise Law; General Practice; Real Estate Law; Trust and Estates, Wills and Probate

PEARCE AND DURICK, PLLP
Bismarck, ND ....Appellate Practice; Civil Trial Practice; Commercial Law; Commercial Litigation; Communications Law; General Practice; Insurance Defense; Labor and Employment Law; Natural Resources Law; Product Liability Law; Real Estate Law; Tax Law

PEARL & SMITH, LAW OFFICES OF
Rochester, NY.........................Product Liability Law

PEARSON, PATTON, SHEA, FOLEY & KURTZ, P.C.
Las Vegas, NV ....Insurance Defense

PEARSON & PRICE, PLLC
Corpus Christi, TX ....General Practice; Tax Law; Trust and Estates, Wills and Probate

PECKAR & ABRAMSON, A PROFESSIONAL CORPORATION
River Edge, NJ........................Construction Law; Labor and Employment Law

PEDDICORD, WHARTON, THUNE AND SPENCER, A PROFESSIONAL CORPORATION
Des Moines, IA........................Arbitration; Aviation Law; Insurance Defense; Medical Malpractice; Product Liability Law; Workers Compensation

PEDLEY ZIELKE GORDINIER OLT & PENCE, PLLC
Louisville, KY..........Civil Trial Practice; Corporate Law; Insurance Defense; Municipal Bond/Public Authority Financing

PEIFER, K. LEE LAW OFFICES OF
Albuquerque, NM..........Labor and Employment Law

PEIRSON & PATTERSON, L.L.P.
Dallas, TX..........Real Estate Law

PELEROSE, DEBBIE CROSBY, P.C., LAW OFFICES OF
Marietta, GA..........Family Law

PELINO & LENTZ, A PROFESSIONAL CORPORATION
Philadelphia, PA..........General Practice

PELTZ & WALKER
New York, NY..........Insurance Defense; Medical Malpractice; Personal Injury

PENDLETON, FRIEDBERG, WILSON & HENNESSEY, P.C.
Denver, CO..........Civil Trial Practice; General Practice

PENNIE & EDMONDS LLP
Washington, DC..........Patent, Trademark, Copyright and Unfair Competition
New York, NY..........Patent, Trademark, Copyright and Unfair Competition; Trademark, Copyright and Unfair Competition

PENNINGTON, MOORE, WILKINSON, BELL & DUNBAR, P.A.
Tallahassee, FL..........General Practice

PEPPER & CORAZZINI, L.L.P.
Washington, DC..........Communications Law

PEPPER HAMILTON LLP
Wilmington, DE..........General Practice
Washington, DC..........General Practice
Detroit, MI..........General Practice
Cherry Hill, NJ..........General Practice
Berwyn, PA..........General Practice
Harrisburg, PA..........General Practice
Philadelphia, PA..........General Practice
Pittsburgh, PA..........General Practice

PERANTINIDES & NOLAN CO., L.P.A.
Akron, OH..........General Practice; Insurance Defense; Medical Malpractice; Personal Injury; Product Liability Law

PERDUE LAW FIRM, THE, L.L.P.
Houston, TX..........Medical Malpractice; Personal Injury

PEREY, RON LAW OFFICE OF
Seattle, WA..........Medical Malpractice; Personal Injury; Product Liability Law

PEREZ & MCNABB, A PROFESSIONAL CORPORATION
Orinda, CA..........Business Law

PERKIN & HOSODA
Honolulu, HI..........Civil Trial Practice; Personal Injury

PERKINS, ROGER A.
Annapolis, MD..........Family Law

PERKINS COIE LLP
Washington, DC..........General Practice
Bellevue, WA..........General Practice
Seattle, WA..........Antitrust Law; General Practice; Labor and Employment Law; Municipal Bond/Public Authority Financing; Tax Law

PERKINS, OLSON & PRATT, P.A.
Portland, ME..........Bankruptcy Law; Commercial Litigation

PERKINS, THOMPSON, HINCKLEY & KEDDY, P.A.
Portland, ME..........Civil Trial Practice; General Practice; International Trade Law

PERLA, RANDALL M.
Cleveland, OH..........Family Law

PERLMAN, PETER, LAW OFFICES, P.S.C.
Lexington, KY..........Civil Trial Practice; Personal Injury; Product Liability Law

PERMAN & GREEN, LLP
Fairfield, CT..........Intellectual Property Law; Patent, Trademark, Copyright and Unfair Competition; Trademark, Copyright and Unfair Competition

PERONA, LANGER, BECK & LALLANDE, A PROFESSIONAL CORPORATION
Long Beach, CA..........Civil Trial Practice; Personal Injury

PERRIN, PERRIN, MANN & PATTERSON, L.L.P.
Spartanburg, SC..........Commercial Law; General Practice

PERRONI AND JAMES
Little Rock, AR..........Business Law; Criminal Trial Practice; Personal Injury

PERRY, EDWARD T.
San Francisco, CA..........Tax Law

PERRY, GREGORY M.
Commerce, GA..........General Practice

PERRY, FIALKOWSKI & PERRY
Philadelphia, PA..........Civil Trial Practice; Health Care Law; Medical Malpractice; Personal Injury; Product Liability Law

PERRY, KITTRELL, BLACKBURN & BLACKBURN
Henderson, NC..........General Practice

PERRY & MURR
Gulfport, MS..........Personal Injury

PERRY, PATRICK, FARMER & MICHAUX, P.A.
Charlotte, NC..........General Practice; Real Estate Law
Raleigh, NC..........General Practice; Real Estate Law

PERRY & SPANN, A PROFESSIONAL CORPORATION
Las Vegas, NV..........Insurance Defense
Reno, NV..........Insurance Defense

PERRY & WOMACK
Longview, TX..........Personal Injury

PERSHES & SCHWARTZ, P.A.
Coral Springs, FL..........Construction Law; Patent, Trademark, Copyright and Unfair Competition

PERSKIE NEHMAD & PERILLO, A PROFESSIONAL CORPORATION
Atlantic City, NJ..........Civil Trial Practice; Land Use Law

PERSON, WHITWORTH, RAMOS, BORCHERS & MORALES, L.L.P.
Laredo, TX..........General Practice; Natural Resources Law

PERTNOY, SOLOWSKY, ALLEN & HABER, P.A.
Miami, FL..........General Practice

PESIN, EDWARD, A PROFESSIONAL CORPORATION
North Bergen, NJ..........Tax Law; Trust and Estates, Wills and Probate

PESKIND HYMSON & GOLDSTEIN, P.C.
Scottsdale, AZ..........Bankruptcy Law; Business Law; Civil Trial Practice; Commercial Law; Construction Law; Family Law; Real Estate Law

PETERS, CAROL A.
Pasadena, CA..........Trust and Estates, Wills and Probate

PETERS, JOHN C., P.C.
West Hartford, CT..........General Practice

PETERS LAW FIRM, P.C.
Council Bluffs, IA..........General Practice

PETERS ROBERTSON DEMAHY PARSONS MOWERS PASSARO & DRAKE P.A.
Fort Lauderdale, FL..........General Practice
Fort Myers, FL..........General Practice
Miami, FL..........General Practice
West Palm Beach, FL..........General Practice

PETERS, RUSH, HABIB & MCKENNA
Chico, CA..........Insurance Defense

PETERS & WASILEFSKI
Harrisburg, PA..........Business Law; Civil Trial Practice; Insurance Defense; Medical Malpractice; Product Liability Law

PETERSEN, G. RUSSELL, P.A.
Vero Beach, FL..........Family Law

PETERSON, NILS GEORGE
Arlington, VA..........Labor and Employment Law

PETERSON & MYERS, P.A.
Lakeland, FL..........Banking Law; Civil Trial Practice; Environmental Law; General Practice; Real Estate Law; Tax Law
Lake Wales, FL..........Banking Law; Civil Trial Practice; Environmental Law; General Practice; Real Estate Law; Tax Law
Winter Haven, FL..........Banking Law; Civil Trial Practice; Environmental Law; Family Law; General Practice; Real Estate Law

PETERSON & ROSS
Chicago, IL..........General Practice

PETERSON RUSSELL COFANO PLLC
Bellevue, WA..........Business Law; Mergers and Acquisitions

PETOCK, MICHAEL F.
Valley Forge, PA....................Patent, Trademark, Copyright and Unfair Competition; Trademark, Copyright and Unfair Competition

PETRIE & STOCKING S.C.
Milwaukee, WI....................Commercial Litigation

PETRIKIN, WELLMAN, DAMICO, BROWN & PETROSA, A PROFESSIONAL CORPORATION
Media, PA....................General Practice

PETRONE & PETRONE, P.C.
Utica, NY....................Environmental Law; Insurance Defense

PETRUCCELLI & MARTIN, LLP
Portland, ME....................Appellate Practice; Civil Trial Practice; Commercial Litigation; Construction Law; Environmental Law; Insurance Defense; Public Utilities Law; Trust and Estates, Wills and Probate

PETTIS & VAN ROYEN, P.A.
Tampa, FL....................Patent, Trademark, Copyright and Unfair Competition

PETTY, DAVID K., A PROFESSIONAL CORPORATION
Guymon, OK....................Civil Trial Practice

PEYTON, GORDON P., P.C.
Alexandria, VA....................Bankruptcy Law; Trust and Estates, Wills and Probate

PFEIFER, MAXWELL S.
Bronx, NY....................Civil Trial Practice; General Practice; Medical Malpractice; Personal Injury; Product Liability Law

PFEIFER, SUSAN E.
Cabin John, MD....................Trust and Estates, Wills and Probate

PFUNDER, CURTIS C.
Boston, MA....................Civil Trial Practice

PHEARS & MOLDOVAN
Norcross, GA....................Health Care Law; Land Use Law

PHELAN & MITRI
Stamford, CT....................Business Law; Corporate Law

PHELPS, J. MICHAEL
San Francisco, CA....................Civil Trial Practice

PHELPS DUNBAR, L.L.P.
Baton Rouge, LA....................Civil Trial Practice; General Practice
New Orleans, LA....................Admiralty/Maritime Law; Banking Law; Civil Trial Practice; Environmental Law; General Practice; Labor and Employment Law; Natural Resources Law; Tax Law
Jackson, MS....................Civil Trial Practice; General Practice; Labor and Employment Law
Tupelo, MS....................Civil Trial Practice; General Practice
Houston, TX....................Admiralty/Maritime Law; Civil Trial Practice

PHELPS & FARA
Indianapolis, IN....................Family Law

PHELPS, JENKINS, GIBSON & FOWLER, L.L.P.
Tuscaloosa, AL....................Business Law; Civil Trial Practice; Commercial Litigation; Insurance Defense; Tax Law

PHELPS, KASTEN, RUYLE, BURNS, CARMODY & SIMS
Carlinville, IL....................Civil Trial Practice; General Practice

PHILIPS, HOPKINS, EAMES & COBB, P.C.
Denton, TX....................Civil Trial Practice; Criminal Trial Practice; Family Law; Personal Injury; Real Estate Law, Trust and Estates, Wills and Probate

PHILLIPS, DOROTHY K.
Philadelphia, PA....................Family Law

PHILLIPS, BECKWITH & HALL
Fairfax, VA....................Criminal Trial Practice

PHILLIPS & BOHYER, P.C.
Missoula, MT....................Commercial Litigation; Insurance Defense; Product Liability Law

PHILLIPS, DOUGLAS R., P.C.
Denver, CO....................Workers Compensation

PHILLIPS, GARDILL, KAISER & ALTMEYER
Wheeling, WV....................General Practice

PHILLIPS, JAMES J., A PROFESSIONAL CORPORATION
Pleasanton, CA....................Trust and Estates, Wills and Probate

PHILLIPS, LYTLE, HITCHCOCK, BLAINE & HUBER LLP
Buffalo, NY....................General Practice; Labor and Employment Law; Tax Law
Fredonia, NY....................General Practice
Jamestown, NY....................General Practice
New York, NY....................General Practice
Rochester, NY....................General Practice

PHILLIPS MCFALL MCCAFFREY MCVAY & MURRAH, P.C.
Oklahoma City, OK....................General Practice

PHILLIPS & POTACH, P.A.
Minneapolis, MN....................General Practice

PHIPPS FIRM, THE
Tallahassee, FL....................Tax Law

PIAZZA & PICKEL
Stamford, CT....................Civil Trial Practice; Family Law; Medical Malpractice; Personal Injury; Product Liability Law; Real Estate Law

PICADIO MCCALL MILLER & NORTON
Pittsburgh, PA....................Civil Trial Practice

PICCARRETA & DAVIS, P.C.
Tucson, AZ....................Criminal Trial Practice

PICCIONE, KEELEY & ASSOCIATES, LTD.
Wheaton, IL....................General Practice

PICKENS, BARNES & ABERNATHY
Cedar Rapids, IA....................Civil Trial Practice; Insurance Defense

PICKER, ROBERT K. JR.
Atlanta, GA....................Commercial Litigation

PICKERING LAW FIRM, THE, P.C.
Fort Collins, CO....................Personal Injury

PICKETT, STANLEY S.
Greenbelt, MD....................Civil Trial Practice; Criminal Trial Practice; Family Law; General Practice; Real Estate Law; Trust and Estates, Wills and Probate

PICKREL, SCHAEFFER & EBELING
Dayton, OH....................Health Care Law; Insurance Defense; Labor and Employment Law; Mergers and Acquisitions

PICO & MITCHELL
Las Vegas, NV....................Business Law; Civil Trial Practice; Commercial Law; Construction Law; Family Law; General Practice; Health Care Law; Insurance Defense; Labor and Employment Law; Medical Malpractice; Personal Injury; Product Liability Law; Real Estate Law; Trust and Estates, Wills and Probate

PIERCE ATWOOD
Augusta, ME....................Administrative Law; Bankruptcy Law; Civil Trial Practice; Criminal Trial Practice; General Practice; Medical Malpractice; Personal Injury; Product Liability Law; Real Estate Law
Portland, ME....................Administrative Law; Antitrust Law; Banking Law; Bankruptcy Law; Business Law; Civil Trial Practice; Commercial Law; Construction Law; Criminal Trial Practice; Environmental Law; General Practice; Immigration and Naturalization; Insurance Defense; Intellectual Property Law; International Business Law; Labor and Employment Law; Municipal and Zoning Law; Municipal Bond/Public Authority Financing; Natural Resources Law; Personal Injury; Public Utilities Law; Real Estate Law; Tax Law; Trust and Estates, Wills and Probate

PIERCE COUCH HENDRICKSON BAYSINGER & GREEN, L.L.P.
Oklahoma City, OK....................General Practice; Insurance Defense; Medical Malpractice; Product Liability Law

PIERCE AND HAHN
Ann Arbor, MI....................Immigration and Naturalization

PIERCE, LEDYARD, LATTA & WASDEN, P.C.
Mobile, AL....................Admiralty/Maritime Law; Appellate Practice; Banking Law; Business Law; Civil Trial Practice; Insurance Defense; Real Estate Law; Trust and Estates, Wills and Probate

PIERCE, SAMUEL P., JR., P.C.
Atlanta, GA....................Medical Malpractice; Product Liability Law

PIERCE & YOUNG
Atlanta, GA....................Civil Trial Practice; Commercial Law; Family Law; Health Care Law; Insurance Defense; International Business Law; Legal Malpractice; Medical Malpractice; Personal Injury; Product Liability Law; Workers Compensation

PIERSON & BURNETT, L.L.P.
Washington, DC....................Commercial Litigation; Communications Law

PIERSON, PIERSON & NOLAN
Baltimore, MD....................Appellate Practice; Civil Trial Practice; General Practice

PIGG, GAIL P.
Nashville, TN........Civil Trial Practice; Commercial Law; Real Estate Law

PILECKAS, PAUL L.
Rome, NY........Civil Trial Practice; Family Law; General Practice; Personal Injury; Trust and Estates, Wills and Probate

PILIERO GOLDSTEIN JENKINS & SULLIVAN, LLP
New York, NY........Antitrust Law; Appellate Practice; Arbitration; Banking Law; Business Law; Civil Trial Practice; Commercial Law; Commercial Litigation; Computer Law; Creditors Rights; Franchise Law; General Practice; Intellectual Property Law; International Business Law; International Trade Law; Labor and Employment Law; Mergers and Acquisitions; Product Liability Law; Real Estate Law; Securities Law; Trademark, Copyright and Unfair Competition

PILKA & ASSOCIATES, P.A.
Brandon, FL........Insurance Defense; Personal Injury

PILKINTON, PILKINTON & YOCOM
Hope, AR........Trust and Estates, Wills and Probate

PILLAR • MULROY & FERBER, PROFESSIONAL CORPORATION
Pittsburgh, PA........Family Law; Transportation Law

PILLSBURY MADISON & SUTRO LLP
Los Angeles, CA........Admiralty/Maritime Law; Antitrust Law; Civil Trial Practice; General Practice; Tax Law
San Diego, CA........Admiralty/Maritime Law; General Practice
San Francisco, CA........General Practice
Washington, DC........General Practice

PINGEL & TEMPLER, P.C.
Des Moines, IA........Commercial Law; Construction Law; General Practice; Labor and Employment Law

PINNEY, PAYNE, VAN LENTEN, BURRELL, WOLFE & DILLMAN, P.C.
Danbury, CT........Civil Trial Practice; Commercial Litigation; Criminal Trial Practice

PINSKY & SKANDALIS
Syracuse, NY........Insurance Defense

PINTO COATES KYRE & BROWN, PLLC
Greensboro, NC........Civil Trial Practice; Insurance Defense; Personal Injury

PIPER & MARBURY L.L.P.
Baltimore, MD........Antitrust Law; General Practice; Labor and Employment Law; Municipal Bond/Public Authority Financing; Tax Law

PIPER MARBURY RUDNICK & WOLFE LLP
Washington, DC........General Practice

PIPER, WELLMAN & BOWERS
Lexington, KY........Civil Trial Practice; Health Care Law; Insurance Defense; Personal Injury

PIPKIN, KNOTT, CLARK & BERGER, L.L.P.
Raleigh, NC........General Practice; Personal Injury

PIPPINGER, RICHARD G., P.A.
Tampa, FL........Family Law; Personal Injury

PIRCHER, NICHOLS & MEEKS
Los Angeles, CA........Real Estate Law

PITLUCK KIDO SATO & STONE
Honolulu, HI........Antitrust Law; Business Law; Real Estate Law

PITNEY, HARDIN, KIPP & SZUCH LLP
Morristown, NJ........Antitrust Law; Banking Law; Bankruptcy Law; Business Law; Civil Trial Practice; Criminal Trial Practice; Employment Benefits Law; Environmental Law; General Practice; Labor and Employment Law; Real Estate Law; Trust and Estates, Wills and Probate

PITTMAN, THOMAS H.
Tifton, GA........Family Law

PITTMAN, HOOKS, DUTTON & HOLLIS, P.C.
Birmingham, AL........Admiralty/Maritime Law; Medical Malpractice; Personal Injury; Product Liability Law

PITTON LAW OFFICES, P.A.
Iowa City, IA........Civil Trial Practice; Personal Injury

PITTS, PITTS & THOMPSON
Selma, AL........General Practice

PIZER & MICHAELSON INC.
Los Angeles, CA........Bankruptcy Law; Civil Trial Practice
Santa Ana, CA........Bankruptcy Law; Business Law; Civil Trial Practice; Real Estate Law

PLAGEMAN, LUND & MILLER LLP
Oakland, CA........Construction Law; Real Estate Law; Trust and Estates, Wills and Probate

PLANT, WALLACE, CHRISTENSEN & KANELL, A PROFESSIONAL CORPORATION
Salt Lake City, UT........General Practice; Insurance Defense; Medical Malpractice; Workers Compensation

PLASSMAN, RUPP, HENSAL & SHORT
Archbold, OH........General Practice

PLASTIRAS & TERRIZZI
San Rafael, CA........Insurance Defense

PLAUCHÉ MASELLI LANDRY & PARKERSON L.L.P.
New Orleans, LA........Environmental Law; General Practice; Insurance Defense; Product Liability Law; Toxic Torts

PLAUCHÉ SMITH & NIESET, A PROFESSIONAL LAW CORPORATION
Lake Charles, LA........Admiralty/Maritime Law; Civil Trial Practice; General Practice; Insurance Defense; Personal Injury

PLEDGER & FEORD P.L.C.
McLean, VA........Civil Trial Practice; General Practice; Insurance Defense; Medical Malpractice

PLETSCH, GREGORY A., & ASSOCIATES, A PROF. LAW CORP.
Baton Rouge, LA........Tax Law; Trust and Estates, Wills and Probate

PLEWS SHADLEY RACHER & BRAUN
Indianapolis, IN........Environmental Law

PLOPPER, STEPHEN E. & ASSOCIATES
Indianapolis, IN........International Business Law

PLOURDE & LEONARD, LTD.
Providence, RI........Tax Law

PLOWMAN, SPIEGEL & LEWIS, P.C.
Pittsburgh, PA........Banking Law; Bankruptcy Law; Civil Trial Practice; Commercial Law; Construction Law; Environmental Law; General Practice; Insurance Defense; Municipal and Zoning Law; Real Estate Law; Securities Law; Trust and Estates, Wills and Probate

PLUMB, FREDERICK K.
Orleans, MA........Trust and Estates, Wills and Probate

PLUMMER & FARMER
Houston, TX........Civil Trial Practice; Family Law

PLUNKETT & GIBSON, INC.
San Antonio, TX........Civil Trial Practice; General Practice; Insurance Defense

PLUNKETT & JAFFE, P.C.
New York, NY........Administrative Law; Commercial Litigation; Construction Law; General Practice; Trust and Estates, Wills and Probate

POCHE, STEPHEN S., P.A.
Shalimar, FL........Family Law

PODELL & PODELL
Milwaukee, WI........Family Law

PODHURST, ORSECK, JOSEFSBERG, EATON, MEADOW, OLIN & PERWIN, P.A.
Miami, FL........Appellate Practice; Aviation Law; Civil Trial Practice; Commercial Litigation; Criminal Trial Practice; General Practice; Personal Injury

POEHLMANN, THEODORE A.E., P.C., LAW OFFICE OF
Woodstock, IL........Civil Trial Practice

POHL & SHORT, P.A.
Kissimmee, FL........Civil Trial Practice; International Business Law; Real Estate Law
Orlando, FL........Banking Law; Business Law; Civil Trial Practice; Commercial Law; Construction Law; International Business Law; Real Estate Law; Trust and Estates, Wills and Probate
Winter Park, FL........Banking Law; Business Law; Civil Trial Practice; Commercial Law; Construction Law; International Business Law; Real Estate Law; Trust and Estates, Wills and Probate

POIDMORE, ANTHONY J. LAW OFFICES OF
Sacramento, CA........Labor and Employment Law

POLATSEK, HARRY D., P.A.
Fort Lauderdale, FL........Immigration and Naturalization

POLIDORI, GEROME, FRANKLIN AND JACOBSON, L.L.C.
Lakewood, CO........Criminal Trial Practice; Family Law; Personal Injury; Trust and Estates, Wills and Probate

POLING, MCGAW & POLING, P.C.
Troy, MI........Business Law; Civil Rights; Civil Trial Practice; Commercial Law; Commercial Litigation; Construction Law; Corporate Law; Employment Benefits Law; Environmental Law; Family Law; General Practice; Health Care Law; Insurance Defense; Labor and Employment Law; Mergers and Acquisitions; Personal Injury; Product Liability Law; Professional Liability; Real Estate Law; Transportation Law; Trust and Estates, Wills and Probate

POLLACK, DAVID S.
Port Washington, NY ....Medical Malpractice

POLLI, ROBERT P., P.A.
Tampa, FL ....Appellate Practice; Criminal Trial Practice

POLLOCK, MEYERS, EICKSTEADT & WEECH, LTD.
Marengo, IL ....General Practice

POLLOCK, VANDE SANDE & AMERNICK, R.L.L.P.
Washington, DC............Patent, Trademark, Copyright and Unfair Competition

POLSTER, LIEDER, WOODRUFF & LUCCHESI, L.C.
St. Louis, MO............Patent, Trademark, Copyright and Unfair Competition

POLSTON, DEAN & HEALY, P.A.
Tallahassee, FL ....Commercial Litigation; Computer Law; Constitutional Law; Insurance Defense; Labor and Employment Law

POMERANZ, DRAYTON & STABNICK
Glastonbury, CT ....Workers Compensation

POPE & BERGER
San Diego, CA ....Construction Law; Insurance Defense; Labor and Employment Law

POPE, MCGLAMRY, KILPATRICK & MORRISON, LLP
Atlanta, GA ....Civil Trial Practice; General Practice; Medical Malpractice; Personal Injury; Product Liability Law
Columbus, GA ....Civil Trial Practice; General Practice; Medical Malpractice; Personal Injury; Product Liability Law

POPE, MCMILLAN, KUTTEH, SIMON & BAKER, P.A.
Statesville, NC............General Practice

POPE & RODGERS
Columbia, SC ....Business Law; Civil Trial Practice

POPKOFF & STERN
Los Angeles, CA............Trust and Estates, Wills and Probate

POPPLETON, GARRETT & POLOTT, P.C.
Bethesda, MD ....Real Estate Law; Trust and Estates, Wills and Probate

PORES, JOEL MICHAEL THE LAW OFFICE OF
Laguna Hills, CA............Legal Malpractice

PORTERFIELD, HARPER & MILLS, P.A.
Birmingham, AL ....Civil Trial Practice; Insurance Defense; Medical Malpractice; Product Liability Law

PORTER, J. CHESTER, & ASSOCIATES
Shepherdsville, KY............Banking Law

PORTER & PORTER
Cincinnati, OH ....Tax Law; Trust and Estates, Wills and Probate

PORTER, PORTER & HASSINGER, P.C.
Birmingham, AL ....Product Liability Law; Workers Compensation

PORTER, SCOTT, WEIBERG & DELEHANT, A PROFESSIONAL CORPORATION
Sacramento, CA............Civil Trial Practice; Construction Law; Insurance Defense; Labor and Employment Law; Medical Malpractice; Product Liability Law; Professional Liability

PORTER WRIGHT MORRIS & ARTHUR LLP
Washington, DC............General Practice
Naples, FL............General Practice
Cincinnati, OH............General Practice
Cleveland, OH............General Practice
Columbus, OH ....Antitrust Law; Banking Law; Bankruptcy Law; Civil Trial Practice; Environmental Law; General Practice; Labor and Employment Law; Municipal Bond/Public Authority Financing; Patent, Trademark, Copyright and Unfair Competition; Tax Law
Dayton, OH............General Practice

PORTNOY, PIDGEON & ROTH, P.C.
Bloomfield Hills, MI............Civil Trial Practice; Health Care Law; Insurance Defense; Medical Malpractice; Personal Injury

PORZIO, BROMBERG & NEWMAN, A PROFESSIONAL CORPORATION
Morristown, NJ............Environmental Law; General Practice

POSNER, POSNER & ASSOCIATES, PC
White Plains, NY............Bankruptcy Law; Commercial Law; Environmental Law; Real Estate Law; Trust and Estates, Wills and Probate

POST KIRBY NOONAN & SWEAT LLP
San Diego, CA ....Antitrust Law; Business Law; Civil Trial Practice

POST, POLAK, GOODSELL & MACNEILL, P.A.
Roseland, NJ............Business Law; Civil Trial Practice; Commercial Law; Commercial Litigation; Family Law; General Practice; Labor and Employment Law; Medical Malpractice; Real Estate Law

POST & POST
High Point, NC............General Practice

POST & SCHELL, P.C.
Philadelphia, PA ....Civil Trial Practice

POSTLEWAITE & JORDAN
Columbus, OH ....Business Law; Commercial Litigation; Construction Law

POSTNER & RUBIN
New York, NY............Civil Trial Practice; Construction Law; Environmental Law; Government Contracts; Insurance Defense; Professional Liability

POTHIER, ROSE & ASSOCIATES
Santa Ana, CA............Real Estate Law

POTTER ANDERSON & CORROON LLP
Wilmington, DE............Banking Law; Bankruptcy Law; Civil Trial Practice; Employment Benefits Law; Environmental Law; General Practice; Municipal Bond/Public Authority Financing; Patent, Trademark, Copyright and Unfair Competition; Personal Injury; Tax Law; Trust and Estates, Wills and Probate

POULIOT, MERCURE
Montreal, QU, Canada ....Administrative Law; Banking Law; Bankruptcy Law; Business Law; Civil Trial Practice; Commercial Litigation; Environmental Law; General Practice; Intellectual Property Law; Labor and Employment Law; Mergers and Acquisitions; Municipal Bond/Public Authority Financing; Real Estate Law; Trademark, Copyright and Unfair Competition

POULSON, JON C.
Accomac, VA ....Criminal Trial Practice; Personal Injury; Real Estate Law

POULSON, ODELL & PETERSON, LLC
Denver, CO ....Arbitration; Natural Resources Law; Oil and Gas Law

POWELL, DAVID A.
Gainesville, GA............Civil Trial Practice; Criminal Trial Practice; Family Law

POWELL, RICHARD L.
Marietta, GA............Medical Malpractice; Personal Injury

POWELL, GOLDSTEIN, FRAZER & MURPHY LLP
Washington, DC............General Practice
Atlanta, GA ....General Practice; Immigration and Naturalization; Municipal Bond/Public Authority Financing

POWELL, PEEK & WEAVER
Andalusia, AL............Civil Trial Practice; General Practice; Insurance Defense; Personal Injury; Workers Compensation

POWELL, STANLEY BRUCE, P.A.
Niceville, FL............Commercial Litigation; Medical Malpractice; Personal Injury; Product Liability Law

POWER ROGERS & SMITH, P.C.
Chicago, IL............Aviation Law; Civil Trial Practice; Medical Malpractice; Personal Injury; Product Liability Law; Professional Liability

POWERS, CHAPMAN, DEAGOSTINO, MEYERS & MILIA, PROFESSIONAL CORPORATION
Troy, MI............Business Law; Trust and Estates, Wills and Probate

POWERS, PYLES, SUTTER & VERVILLE, P.C.
Washington, DC............Administrative Law; Health Care Law

POWERS & SANTOLA
Albany, NY ....Civil Trial Practice; Medical Malpractice; Personal Injury; Product Liability Law

POWERS & WILLARD, L.L.P.
Baton Rouge, LA............Banking Law; Business Law; Civil Trial Practice; Commercial Litigation; Corporate Law; General Practice; Legal Malpractice; Medical Malpractice; Product Liability Law; Toxic Torts

POZNER, LARRY, P.C.
Denver, CO ....Criminal Trial Practice

PRATHER & ASSOCIATES, P.C.
Detroit, MI............Family Law

PRATHER, JOHN G., THE FIRM OF
Somerset, KY ....General Practice; Medical Malpractice

PRAY, WALKER, JACKMAN, WILLIAMSON & MARLAR, A PROFESSIONAL CORPORATION
Tulsa, OK .... Civil Trial Practice; General Practice

PREEO, SILVERMAN & GREEN, P.C.
Denver, CO .... Commercial Litigation; Construction Law; Corporate Law; Legal Malpractice; Real Estate Law; Trust and Estates, Wills and Probate

PREG O'DONNELL & GILLETT PLLC
Seattle, WA .... Insurance Defense

PREIS, BERGERON & ATCHISON
Baton Rouge, LA .... Business Law; Commercial Litigation; Mergers and Acquisitions

PREIS KRAFT & ROY, A PROFESSIONAL LAW CORPORATION
Lafayette, LA .... Admiralty/Maritime Law; General Practice; Insurance Defense

PREMINGER, DANIEL M., P.C.
Philadelphia, PA .... Appellate Practice; Criminal Trial Practice; Personal Injury

PRENDERGAST, RICHARD J., LTD.
Chicago, IL .... Civil Trial Practice; Commercial Litigation

PRESBERG, ANDREW D., P.C., LAW OFFICES OF
Islandia, NY .... Business Law; Commercial Litigation; Real Estate Law

PRESSLY & PRESSLY, P.A.
West Palm Beach, FL .... Real Estate Law; Trust and Estates, Wills and Probate

PRESTHOLT, KLEEGER, FIDONE & VILLASENOR
Los Angeles, CA .... Civil Trial Practice; Insurance Defense; Personal Injury

PRESTON & PRESTON, P.C.
Douglas, GA .... General Practice

PRETI, FLAHERTY, BELIVEAU, PACHIOS & HALEY, LLC
Augusta, ME .... General Practice
Bath, ME .... General Practice
Portland, ME .... Administrative Law; Bankruptcy Law; Business Law; Civil Trial Practice; Commercial Law; Communications Law; Environmental Law; General Practice; Health Care Law; Insurance Defense; Intellectual Property Law; International Business Law; Labor and Employment Law; Medical Malpractice; Municipal Bond/Public Authority Financing; Public Utilities Law; Real Estate Law; Tax Law; Trust and Estates, Wills and Probate

PRETTY, SCHROEDER & POPLAWSKI, A PROFESSIONAL CORPORATION
Los Angeles, CA .... Patent, Trademark, Copyright and Unfair Competition

PREUSS WALKER & SHANAGHER LLP
San Francisco, CA .... Civil Trial Practice; Commercial Litigation; Product Liability Law

PREVATT & TAYLOR
Tampa, FL .... Tax Law; Trust and Estates, Wills and Probate

PREVIANT, GOLDBERG, UELMEN, GRATZ, MILLER & BRUEGGEMAN, S.C.
Milwaukee, WI .... Labor and Employment Law

PREZANT & MOLLATH
Reno, NV .... Land Use Law

PRICE, SMITH, HARGETT, PETHO & ANDERSON
Charlotte, NC .... Personal Injury

PRICKETT, JONES & ELLIOTT, P.A.
Dover, DE .... General Practice
Wilmington, DE .... General Practice
Kennett Square, PA .... General Practice

PRINCE, GLICK & MCFARLANE, P.A., LAW OFFICES
Fort Lauderdale, FL .... Personal Injury

PRINCE & HELLINGER, P.C.
Nashville, TN .... Civil Trial Practice; Insurance Defense

PRINCE, LOBEL & TYE LLP
Boston, MA .... Civil Trial Practice; Criminal Trial Practice; Family Law; General Practice; Labor and Employment Law; Tax Law; Trust and Estates, Wills and Probate

PRINCE, POOLE & CROSS, P.C.
Tuscaloosa, AL .... Personal Injury

PRINCE, YEATES & GELDZAHLER
Park City, UT .... General Practice
Salt Lake City, UT .... General Practice; Labor and Employment Law; Real Estate Law; Tax Law

PRINCE, YOUNGBLOOD & MASSAGEE
Hendersonville, NC .... General Practice

PRINDLE, MALAND, SELLNER, STENNES AND KNUTSEN, CHARTERED
Montevideo, MN .... General Practice

PRINGLE & PRINGLE, A PROFESSIONAL CORPORATION
Oklahoma City, OK .... Banking Law; Bankruptcy Law; Commercial Litigation; General Practice; Mergers and Acquisitions

PRITCHARD, ROBERT A.
Pascagoula, MS .... Personal Injury; Product Liability Law

PRITCHARD, MCCALL & JONES, L.L.C.
Birmingham, AL .... Bankruptcy Law

PROFFITT, THOMAS D.
Mesa, AZ .... Trust and Estates, Wills and Probate

PROLY & LAPORTE, P.A.
Port Richey, FL .... Personal Injury

PROSKAUER ROSE
Paris, France .... General Practice
Los Angeles, CA .... General Practice
Washington, DC .... General Practice
Boca Raton, FL .... General Practice
New York, NY .... General Practice; Labor and Employment Law

PROSPERE & RUSSELL
Dallas, TX .... Criminal Trial Practice

PROTAS, MARTIN S., P.C.
Bethesda, MD .... Civil Trial Practice

PROVIZER & PHILLIPS, P.C.
Bloomfield Hills, MI .... Banking Law; Business Law; Civil Rights; Civil Trial Practice; Commercial Law; Commercial Litigation; Computer Law; Construction Law; Elder Law; Employment Benefits Law; Environmental Law; Health Care Law; Insurance Defense; Medical Malpractice; Personal Injury; Product Liability Law; Professional Liability; Real Estate Law; Toxic Torts; Workers Compensation

PRUITT, GUSHEE & BACHTELL
Salt Lake City, UT .... Natural Resources Law

PRYOR, BARRY, SMITH, KARBER AND ALFORD P.L.C.
Fort Smith, AR .... Insurance Defense

PRYOR, FLYNN, PRIEST & HARBER
Knoxville, TN .... Civil Trial Practice; Criminal Trial Practice; General Practice; Medical Malpractice; Personal Injury; Product Liability Law

PRYOR & MANDELUP, L.L.P.
Westbury, NY .... Bankruptcy Law; Civil Trial Practice; Commercial Litigation

PUCCINELLI & PUCCINELLI
Elko, NV .... Civil Trial Practice; General Practice

PUGH AND VAN BUREN
Orlando, FL .... Civil Trial Practice; Commercial Litigation; Environmental Law; Personal Injury

PULASKI, GIEGER & LABORDE, L.L.C.
New Orleans, LA .... Aviation Law; Environmental Law; Insurance Defense; Natural Resources Law; Oil and Gas Law; Product Liability Law; Toxic Torts; Transportation Law

PURCELL, KRUG & HALLER
Harrisburg, PA .... Bankruptcy Law

PURCELL, RIES, SHANNON, MULCAHY & O'NEILL
Bedminster, NJ .... Business Law; Civil Trial Practice; Corporate Law; Environmental Law; General Practice; Insurance Defense; Labor and Employment Law; Product Liability Law; Real Estate Law

PURDY AND FLYNN, P.A.
Fort Lauderdale, FL .... Commercial Litigation; Personal Injury

PURVIS, GRAY & GORDON, LLP
Boulder, CO .... Civil Trial Practice; Legal Malpractice; Personal Injury
Denver, CO .... Civil Trial Practice; Legal Malpractice; Personal Injury

PYNE & DERRY, P.C.
Chevy Chase, MD .... Insurance Defense; Personal Injury; Trust and Estates, Wills and Probate

PYSZKA, BLACKMON, LEVY & SAVOLA, P.A.
Miami Lakes, FL .... Civil Trial Practice; Insurance Defense

PYTELL & VARCHETTI, P.C.
Detroit, MI ..... Commercial Law; Commercial Litigation; Creditors Rights; Medical Malpractice; Personal Injury; Trust and Estates, Wills and Probate

QUACKENBUSH & QUACKENBUSH
San Mateo, CA ..... Labor and Employment Law

QUALE, FELDBRUEGGE, CALVELLI, THOM & CROKE, S.C.
Milwaukee, WI ..... Insurance Defense; Product Liability Law

QUANDT, GIFFELS & BUCK CO., L.P.A.
Cleveland, OH ..... Civil Trial Practice; General Practice; Insurance Defense

QUARLES & BRADY LLC
Chicago, IL ..... Business Law; Civil Trial Practice; General Practice; Real Estate Law; Trust and Estates, Wills and Probate

QUARLES & BRADY LLP
Phoenix, AZ ..... Administrative Law; Business Law; Civil Trial Practice; Commercial Law; Commercial Litigation; Environmental Law; Health Care Law; International Business Law; Labor and Employment Law; Municipal Bond/Public Authority Financing; Natural Resources Law; Patent, Trademark, Copyright and Unfair Competition; Personal Injury; Product Liability Law; Real Estate Law; Securities Law
Naples, FL ..... Banking Law; Business Law; Civil Trial Practice; Construction Law; General Practice; Land Use Law; Real Estate Law; Trust and Estates, Wills and Probate
West Palm Beach, FL ..... Bankruptcy Law; Business Law; Commercial Law; Construction Law; General Practice; Labor and Employment Law; Land Use Law; Patent, Trademark, Copyright and Unfair Competition; Real Estate Law; Trust and Estates, Wills and Probate
Madison, WI ..... Admiralty/Maritime Law; Antitrust Law; Business Law; Civil Trial Practice; Construction Law; Environmental Law; General Practice; Health Care Law; Municipal Bond/Public Authority Financing; Patent, Trademark, Copyright and Unfair Competition; Product Liability Law; Securities Law
Milwaukee, WI ..... Administrative Law; Antitrust Law; Banking Law; Bankruptcy Law; Business Law; Civil Trial Practice; Commercial Law; Construction Law; Employment Benefits Law; Environmental Law; Family Law; General Practice; Health Care Law; Immigration and Naturalization; International Business Law; Labor and Employment Law; Land Use Law; Municipal and Zoning Law; Municipal Bond/Public Authority Financing; Patent, Trademark, Copyright and Unfair Competition; Product Liability Law; Public Utilities Law; Real Estate Law; Securities Law; Tax Law; Trust and Estates, Wills and Probate

QUIGLEY, DILL & QUIGLEY
Valentine, NE ..... General Practice

QUINLAN & CRISHAM, LTD.
Chicago, IL ..... Civil Trial Practice; Commercial Litigation; Insurance Defense; Product Liability Law

QUINLIVAN & KANIEWSKI
Newport Beach, CA ..... Business Law; Civil Trial Practice; Trust and Estates, Wills and Probate

QUINN, PAUL G.
Denver, CO ..... Bankruptcy Law

QUINN, DAY & BARKER, P.L.L.C.
Belle Fourche, SD ..... Civil Trial Practice; Medical Malpractice; Personal Injury
Rapid City, SD ..... Civil Trial Practice

QUINN, JOHNSTON, HENDERSON & PRETORIUS, CHARTERED
Peoria, IL ..... Civil Trial Practice; General Practice

QUINN, MCGARRY & CAFFERY, P.C.
Buffalo, NY ..... Insurance Defense; Personal Injury

QUINN, PATTERSON & WILLARD
Columbia, SC ..... Business Law; Civil Trial Practice; General Practice; Real Estate Law

QUINN, RACUSIN & GAZZOLA, CHARTERED
Washington, DC ..... Business Law; Trust and Estates, Wills and Probate

QUIRK AND BAKALOR, P.C.
New York, NY ..... Appellate Practice; Civil Trial Practice; Insurance Defense

QUISUMBING TORRES
Metro Manila, Philippines ..... General Practice

RAAB & RAAB
Fort Lauderdale, FL ..... Family Law

RABBITT, PITZER & SNODGRASS, P.C.
St. Louis, MO ..... Civil Trial Practice; Insurance Defense

RABE, GEORGE F.
Lexington, KY ..... General Practice

RABIN & PECKEL LLP
New York, NY ..... Antitrust Law; Securities Law

RABINOVITZ & ASSOCIATES, P.C.
Tucson, AZ ..... Civil Trial Practice; Insurance Defense; Medical Malpractice; Personal Injury; Product Liability Law; Workers Compensation

RABINOWITZ, TRENK, LUBETKIN & TULLY, P.C.
West Orange, NJ ..... Bankruptcy Law; Commercial Litigation; Creditors Rights; Land Use Law; Municipal and Zoning Law

RABON, WOLF & RABON
Hugo, OK ..... General Practice

RACCUGLIA, ANTHONY C. & ASSOCIATES
Peru, IL ..... Civil Trial Practice; Medical Malpractice; Personal Injury; Product Liability Law

RACINE, OLSON, NYE, BUDGE & BAILEY, CHARTERED
Pocatello, ID ..... Insurance Defense

RADER, FISHMAN, GRAUER & MCGARRY PLLC
Grand Rapids, MI ..... Intellectual Property Law; Patent, Trademark, Copyright and Unfair Competition

RADER, FISHMAN & GRAUER PLLC
Washington, DC ..... Intellectual Property Law; Patent, Trademark, Copyright and Unfair Competition
Bloomfield Hills, MI ..... Intellectual Property Law; Patent, Trademark, Copyright and Unfair Competition

RAGGIO, CAPPEL, CHOZEN & BERNIARD
Lake Charles, LA ..... Civil Trial Practice; General Practice

RAGGIO AND RAGGIO, P.L.L.C.
Dallas, TX ..... Family Law

RAGSDALE LIGGETT, PLLC
Raleigh, NC ..... Business Law; Civil Trial Practice; Real Estate Law

RAICHLE, BANNING, WEISS & STEPHENS
Buffalo, NY ..... Business Law; Commercial Law; Corporate Law; Environmental Law; General Practice; Labor and Employment Law

RAINES, THOMAS E., P.C.
Norcross, GA ..... Trust and Estates, Wills and Probate

RAINS & POGREBIN, P.C.
Mineola, NY ..... Labor and Employment Law

RAISBECK, LARA, RODRIGUEZ & RUEDA
Bogotá, Colombia ..... General Practice

RAIZMAN & FRISCHMAN, P.C.
Pittsburgh, PA ..... Medical Malpractice

RAJALA, ERIC C.
Overland Park, KS ..... Bankruptcy Law

RAJKOWSKI HANSMEIER LTD.
St. Cloud, MN ..... Insurance Defense

RAKESTRAW & RAKESTRAW
Findlay, OH ..... General Practice

RALSTON, ROBERT W.
Wilmington, DE ..... Insurance Defense; Workers Compensation

RALSTON & POPE, LLC
Topeka, KS ..... Civil Trial Practice; Medical Malpractice; Personal Injury; Product Liability Law

RAMBO, ANDREW C., P.C.
Shelbyville, TN ..... Insurance Defense

RAMER, MOORE & GLASS
Harbor Springs, MI ..... Commercial Litigation; Trust and Estates, Wills and Probate

RAMEY & FLOCK, A PROFESSIONAL CORPORATION
Tyler, TX ..... Appellate Practice; Civil Rights; Civil Trial Practice; Commercial Law; Health Care Law; Labor and Employment Law; Medical Malpractice; Product Liability Law; Workers Compensation

RAMMELKAMP, BRADNEY, KUSTER, KEATON, FRITSCHE & LINDSAY, P.C.
Jacksonville, IL ..... General Practice; Insurance Defense

RAMSAY, BRIDGFORTH, HARRELSON & STARLING
Pine Bluff, AR ..... Civil Trial Practice; General Practice; Labor and Employment Law; Trust and Estates, Wills and Probate

RAMSEY, JOE
Sacramento, CA ....Arbitration; Civil Trial Practice; Product Liability Law

RAMSEY & MURRAY, A PROFESSIONAL CORPORATION
Houston, TX ....Appellate Practice; Arbitration; Civil Trial Practice; Environmental Law; Insurance Defense; Labor and Employment Law; Personal Injury; Product Liability Law; Toxic Torts; Workers Compensation

RAND, ALGEIER, TOSTI & WOODRUFF, A PROFESSIONAL CORPORATION
Morristown, NJ........................Civil Rights; Civil Trial Practice; Commercial Law; Construction Law; Education Law; General Practice; Labor and Employment Law; Personal Injury

RANKIN, HILL, PORTER & CLARK LLP
Cleveland, OH........................Intellectual Property Law; Patent, Trademark, Copyright and Unfair Competition

RANKIN & SULTAN
Boston, MA........................Criminal Trial Practice

RANSOME AND RAY, P.C.
Brownsville, TX ....Bankruptcy Law; Construction Law

RANSON, ARTHUR J. III
Orlando, FL ....Civil Trial Practice

RAPPORT, MEYERS, WHITBECK, SHAW & RODENHAUSEN, LLP
Hudson, NY........................General Practice

RASMUSSEN & MITCHELL
Omaha, NE ....Bankruptcy Law; Commercial Litigation; Corporate Law; Creditors Rights; Personal Injury; Real Estate Law; Trust and Estates, Wills and Probate

RASOR, C. LEWIS JR.
Greenville, SC........................Trust and Estates, Wills and Probate

RATH, YOUNG AND PIGNATELLI, PROFESSIONAL ASSOCIATION
Concord, NH ....Civil Trial Practice; Environmental Law; General Practice; Insurance Defense; Medical Malpractice; Personal Injury; Public Utilities Law; Tax Law
Nashua, NH ....General Practice; Insurance Defense; Medical Malpractice

RATHJE, WOODWARD, DYER & BURT
Wheaton, IL........................General Practice

RATTET & PASTERNAK, LLP
Harrison, NY ....Bankruptcy Law

RAUSCHER, DAVID J., P.C.
St. Louis, MO........................Personal Injury

RAVDIN & WOFFORD, A PROFESSIONAL CORPORATION
Washington, DC........................Family Law; Trust and Estates, Wills and Probate

RAVIN, GREENBERG & MARKS, A PROFESSIONAL CORPORATION
Roseland, NJ........................Bankruptcy Law

RAWLE & HENDERSON LLP
Philadelphia, PA ....Admiralty/Maritime Law; Product Liability Law

RAWLES, O'BYRNE, STANKO & KEPLEY, P.C.
Champaign, IL ....Business Law; General Practice

RAWLINGS, NIELAND, PROBASCO, KILLINGER, ELLWANGER, JACOBS & MOHRHAUSER
Sioux City, IA ....General Practice

RAWLINGS, OLSON, CANNON, GORMLEY & DESRUISSEAUX, A PROFESSIONAL CORPORATION
Las Vegas, NV ....Insurance Defense

RAWLS & DICKINSON, P.A.
Charlotte, NC........................Criminal Trial Practice; Personal Injury

RAY, CHARLES R.
Nashville, TN........................Criminal Trial Practice

RAY, MCCHRISTIAN & JEANS, A PROFESSIONAL CORPORATION
El Paso, TX........................Civil Trial Practice; Commercial Litigation; Insurance Defense; Labor and Employment Law; Medical Malpractice; Product Liability Law; Professional Liability

RAY, QUINNEY & NEBEKER, A PROFESSIONAL CORPORATION
Provo, UT........................General Practice
Salt Lake City, UT........................Antitrust Law; Banking Law; Bankruptcy Law; Civil Trial Practice; Commercial Law; General Practice; Insurance Defense; Labor and Employment Law; Natural Resources Law; Real Estate Law; Tax Law; Trust and Estates, Wills and Probate

RAY, ROBINSON, CARLE & DAVIES P.L.L.
Cleveland, OH........................Admiralty/Maritime Law; Civil Trial Practice; General Practice

RAYBURN, MOON & SMITH, P.A.
Charlotte, NC........................Business Law; Civil Trial Practice; General Practice; Securities Law

RAYBURN & PIERCE
Oxford, MS........................Civil Trial Practice

RAYMOND, GREER & SASSAMAN, P.C.
Phoenix, AZ ....Insurance Defense; Personal Injury

RAYNES, MCCARTY, BINDER, ROSS & MUNDY
Philadelphia, PA ....Personal Injury

READY, SULLIVAN & READY, L.L.P.
Monroe, MI........................General Practice

REAGER & ADLER, P.C.
Camp Hill, PA ....Civil Trial Practice; Construction Law; Municipal and Zoning Law; Real Estate Law

REAM, CHRISTOPHER
Palo Alto, CA ....Business Law; Securities Law

REARDON LAW FIRM, THE, P.C.
New London, CT........................Medical Malpractice; Personal Injury; Product Liability Law

REAUD, MORGAN & QUINN
Beaumont, TX........................Commercial Law; Personal Injury; Product Liability Law

REBMAN WAGENER & LINHARES, P.C.
St. Louis, MO........................Transportation Law

RECKLESS, WALTER W.
Columbus, OH ....Civil Trial Practice; Personal Injury; Product Liability Law

REDDEN, MILLS & CLARK
Birmingham, AL ....Appellate Practice; Criminal Trial Practice; Family Law; Labor and Employment Law

REDFEARN & BROWN, A PROFESSIONAL CORPORATION
Kansas City, MO ....Medical Malpractice; Personal Injury; Product Liability Law

REDMAN, JAMES E.
Milwaukie, OR........................General Practice

REDMON, BOYKIN & BRASWELL, L.L.P.
Alexandria, VA ....General Practice

REDMOND, MARGARET ANN
San Jose, CA ....Immigration and Naturalization

REDMOND, BURGIN & GUTIERREZ, P.A.
Baltimore, MD ....Administrative Law; Aviation Law; Civil Rights; Criminal Trial Practice; Employment Benefits Law; Family Law; General Practice; Insurance Defense; Personal Injury; Product Liability Law; Real Estate Law

REED, ARMSTRONG, GORMAN, COFFEY, GILBERT & MUDGE, PROFESSIONAL CORPORATION
Edwardsville, IL........................Civil Trial Practice; Insurance Defense

REED, CARRERA & MCLAIN, L.L.P.
Edinburg, TX ....Appellate Practice; Civil Trial Practice

REED, ELLIOTT, CREECH & ROTH
San Jose, CA ....Business Law; Commercial Litigation; Construction Law; Energy Law; Environmental Law; Product Liability Law

REED, LUCE, TOSH, WOLFORD & DOUGLASS, A PROFESSIONAL CORPORATION
Beaver, PA........................General Practice

REED MCCLURE
Seattle, WA ....General Practice

REED, RONALD S., P.A.
Tampa, FL ....Family Law

REED SMITH HAZEL & THOMAS LLP
Falls Church, VA........................General Practice
Leesburg, VA ....General Practice
McLean, VA........................Employment Benefits Law; Labor and Employment Law
Richmond, VA ....General Practice

REED SMITH SHAW & MCCLAY LLP
Washington, DC........................Labor and Employment Law; Municipal Bond/Public Authority Financing
Newark, NJ ....Labor and Employment Law
Princeton, NJ ....Labor and Employment Law; Municipal Bond/Public Authority Financing
New York, NY........................Employment Benefits Law; Labor and Employment Law

Harrisburg, PA....Labor and Employment Law
Philadelphia, PA....Employment Benefits Law; Labor and Employment Law; Municipal Bond/Public Authority Financing
Pittsburgh, PA....Employment Benefits Law; Labor and Employment Law; Municipal Bond/Public Authority Financing

REES, BROOME & DIAZ, P.C.
Vienna, VA....Business Law; Tax Law; Trust and Estates, Wills and Probate

REEVES, CHAVEZ, GREENFIELD & WALKER, P.A.
Las Cruces, NM....Banking Law; Civil Trial Practice; Commercial Litigation; Health Care Law; Insurance Defense; Real Estate Law; Trust and Estates, Wills and Probate

REEVES & STEWART, P.C.
Selma, AL....General Practice; Insurance Defense

REGAN & CANTWELL
Charleston, SC....Municipal and Zoning Law

REGAN, MICHAEL P., P.C., LAW OFFICES OF
Danville, VA....Civil Trial Practice; General Practice

REHM LAW FIRM, A PROFESSIONAL CORPORATION
Lincoln, NE....Personal Injury; Workers Compensation

REICH, MEEKS & TREADAWAY, L.L.C.
Metairie, LA....Admiralty/Maritime Law; Insurance Defense

REID, BURGE, PREVALLET & COLEMAN
Blytheville, AR....Civil Trial Practice; Insurance Defense

REID, GARTH O., JR., A PROFESSIONAL LAW CORPORATION
Escondido, CA....Tax Law

REID AND RIEGE, P.C.
Hartford, CT....General Practice

REID, STRICKLAND & GILLETTE, L.L.P.
Baytown, TX....General Practice

REILLY LAW ASSOCIATES, INC.
Providence, RI....Tax Law

REILLY, PETERSEN & HANNAN, P.L.C.
Council Bluffs, IA....Bankruptcy Law; General Practice; Personal Injury; Real Estate Law

REILLY, STUART J., P.C.
Phoenix, AZ....Medical Malpractice; Personal Injury

REIMAN & BAYAZ, P.C.
Denver, CO....Antitrust Law; Appellate Practice; Civil Trial Practice; Commercial Litigation; Construction Law; Securities Law

REINER, SIMPSON & KENNEDY
Redding, CA....Personal Injury; Product Liability Law; Professional Liability

REINERT & ROURKE, P.C.
St. Louis, MO....Commercial Litigation

REINGLASS, MICHELLE A.
Laguna Hills, CA....Labor and Employment Law

REINHART, BOERNER, VAN DEUREN, NORRIS & RIESELBACH, S.C.
Milwaukee, WI....General Practice

REINIS & REINIS
Los Angeles, CA....Business Law

REINWALD, O'CONNOR & PLAYDON
Honolulu, HI....Civil Trial Practice; Commercial Litigation; Tax Law; Trust and Estates, Wills and Probate

REISEMAN SHARP KELSEY & BROWN LLP
Parsippany, NJ....Civil Trial Practice; Insurance Defense; Medical Malpractice; Personal Injury; Product Liability Law

REISER, MICHAEL J. LAW OFFICES OF
Walnut Creek, CA....Labor and Employment Law; Legal Malpractice

REISH & LUFTMAN, A PROFESSIONAL CORPORATION
Los Angeles, CA....Pension and Profit Sharing

REISING, ETHINGTON, BARNES, KISSELLE, LEARMAN & MCCULLOCH, P.C.
Saginaw, MI....Intellectual Property Law; Patent, Trademark, Copyright and Unfair Competition
Troy, MI....Intellectual Property Law; Patent, Trademark, Copyright and Unfair Competition

REISMAN, GLENN M.
Shelton, CT....Bankruptcy Law; Creditors Rights

RELIN, GOLDSTEIN AND CRANE, LLP
Rochester, NY....Creditors Rights

RELPH, ROBERT B.
Grand Rapids, MI....Family Law

REMCHO, JOHANSEN AND PURCELL
San Francisco, CA....Appellate Practice; Civil Trial Practice; Constitutional Law

REMICK MARTONE, A PROFESSIONAL CORPORATION
Philadelphia, PA....Insurance Defense; Sports and Entertainment Law

REMY, THOMAS AND MOOSE, LLP
Sacramento, CA....Environmental Law; Land Use Law

RENALDO, MYERS & PALUMBO, P.C.
Buffalo, NY....Personal Injury

RENDLEN LAW FIRM, THE, P.C.
Hannibal, MO....General Practice

RENICK, SINGER AND KAMBER
Lake Worth, FL....Family Law

RENNER CLARK BUCKWALTER & VOLTZ, P.C.
Wayne, PA....Business Law; Mergers and Acquisitions; Real Estate Law; Securities Law

RENNER, KENNER, GREIVE, BOBAK, TAYLOR & WEBER, A LEGAL PROFESSIONAL ASSOCIATION
Akron, OH....Intellectual Property Law; Patent, Trademark, Copyright and Unfair Competition
Canton, OH....Intellectual Property Law; Patent, Trademark, Copyright and Unfair Competition

RENNER, OTTO, BOISSELLE & SKLAR, P.L.L.
Cleveland, OH....Intellectual Property Law; Trademark, Copyright and Unfair Competition

RESTOVICH, GEORGE F. & ASSOCIATES
Rochester, MN....Criminal Trial Practice; Family Law; Personal Injury

RETHERFORD, MULLEN, JOHNSON & BRUCE, L.L.C.
Colorado Springs, CO....Civil Trial Practice; General Practice; Insurance Defense

RETTIG, OSBORNE, FORGETTE, O'DONNELL, ILLER & ADAMSON, LLP
Kennewick, WA....Civil Trial Practice

REVELLE, BURLESON, LEE & REVELLE, L.L.P.
Murfreesboro, NC....General Practice

REXON, FREEDMAN, KLEPETAR & HAMBLETON, A PROFESSIONAL CORPORATION
Los Angeles, CA....Labor and Employment Law

REYNOLDS & CONWAY, P.C.
Springfield, MO....General Practice

REYNOLDS & MCARTHUR
Atlanta, GA....Civil Trial Practice; Medical Malpractice; Personal Injury; Product Liability Law
Macon, GA....Civil Trial Practice; Medical Malpractice; Personal Injury; Product Liability Law

REYNOLDS, SMITH & WINTERS, P.C.
Norfolk, VA....Insurance Defense

RHEES, HOPKINS & KREAMER
Phoenix, AZ....Commercial Litigation; Construction Law; Insurance Defense

RHEINGOLD, VALET, RHEINGOLD & SHKOLNIK, P.C.
New York, NY....Medical Malpractice; Personal Injury; Product Liability Law

RHOADES, MCKEE, BOER, GOODRICH & TITTA
Grand Rapids, MI....Business Law; Civil Trial Practice; Labor and Employment Law; Trust and Estates, Wills and Probate

RHOADS & SINON LLP
Harrisburg, PA....Banking Law; Civil Trial Practice; Environmental Law; General Practice; Municipal Bond/Public Authority Financing; Tax Law

RHODA, STOUDT & BRADLEY
Reading, PA....General Practice

RHODEN, LACY, DOWNEY & COLBERT
Jackson, MS....Business Law; Insurance Defense; Real Estate Law

RHODES, HIERONYMUS, JONES, TUCKER & GABLE, P.L.L.C.
Tulsa, OK....Appellate Practice; Arbitration; Aviation Law; Bankruptcy Law; Civil Rights; Civil Trial Practice; Eminent Domain; Environmental Law; Health Care Law; Insurance Defense; Labor and Employment Law; Medical Malpractice; Personal Injury; Product Liability Law; Professional Liability; Toxic Torts; Transportation Law; Workers Compensation

RHODES & MASON, P.L.L.C.
Greensboro, NC .... Patent, Trademark, Copyright and Unfair Competition
Wilmington, NC .... Patent, Trademark, Copyright and Unfair Competition

RIBET, CLAUDIA
Los Angeles, CA .... Appellate Practice; Civil Trial Practice

RICCI, HUBBARD, LEOPOLD, FRANKEL & FARMER, P.A.
West Palm Beach, FL .... Civil Trial Practice; Personal Injury; Product Liability Law

RICCIARDI & PAUSTIAN
Las Vegas, NV .... Labor and Employment Law

RICCOLO & BAKER, P.C.
Cedar Rapids, IA .... Medical Malpractice; Personal Injury

RICE, ANDREA LYNN, LAW OFFICES OF A PROF. CORP.
Los Angeles, CA .... Professional Liability

RICE & HENDRICKSON
Harlan, KY .... Administrative Law; General Practice; Insurance Defense; Labor and Employment Law

RICHARDS, CHARLES L.
Warren, OH .... Insurance Defense; Medical Malpractice

RICHARDS & CONNOR
Tulsa, OK .... Civil Trial Practice; Insurance Defense; Medical Malpractice

RICHARDS, LAYTON & FINGER, P.A.
Wilmington, DE .... General Practice; Tax Law

RICHARDS, RALPH & SCHWAB, CHARTERED
Vernon Hills, IL .... Banking Law; Bankruptcy Law; Business Law; Commercial Litigation; Land Use Law; Real Estate Law

RICHARDS SPEARS KIBBE & ORBE
New York, NY .... Corporate Law; Securities Law

RICHARDSON, PLOWDEN, CARPENTER & ROBINSON, P.A.
Columbia, SC .... Appellate Practice; Banking Law; Business Law; Civil Trial Practice; Commercial Law; Construction Law; Environmental Law; General Practice; Health Care Law; Insurance Defense; Medical Malpractice; Personal Injury; Product Liability Law; Real Estate Law; Trust and Estates, Wills and Probate

RICHARDSON, WHITMAN, LARGE & BADGER, A PROFESSIONAL CORPORATION
Portland, ME .... Insurance Defense; Personal Injury

RICHESON, J. DAVID, & ASSOCIATES, P.A.
Fort Pierce, FL .... Labor and Employment Law
West Palm Beach, FL .... Labor and Employment Law

RICHEY, WILLIAM L., P.A.
Miami, FL .... Appellate Practice; Banking Law; Civil Trial Practice; Creditors Rights; Criminal Trial Practice

RICHILANO & RIDLEY, P.C.
Denver, CO .... Civil Trial Practice; Criminal Trial Practice

RICHMAN, GERALD M.
Ellicott City, MD .... Civil Trial Practice; Criminal Trial Practice

RICHMAN GREER WEIL BRUMBAUGH MIRABITO & CHRISTENSEN, P.A.
Miami, FL .... Civil Trial Practice

RICHMAN & JONES, P.C.
Denver, CO .... Medical Malpractice; Personal Injury

RICHMAN, LUNA, KICHAVEN & GLUSHON
Los Angeles, CA .... Natural Resources Law; Trademark, Copyright and Unfair Competition

RICKS & ANDERSON, A LAW CORPORATION
Costa Mesa, CA .... Civil Trial Practice; Labor and Employment Law

RICK, STEINER, P.C.
New York, NY .... Corporate Law; Real Estate Law

RIDBERG, PRESS & SHERBILL
Bethesda, MD .... Arbitration; Business Law; Commercial Litigation

RIDDLE & BAUMGARTNER
Houston, TX .... Personal Injury

RIDENOUR, RIDENOUR & FOX
Clinton, TN .... Personal Injury

RIDER, WEINER, FRANKEL & CALHELHA, P.C.
Newburgh, NY .... Business Law; Civil Trial Practice; Real Estate Law; Trust and Estates, Wills and Probate

RIDGWAY AND GRIFFIN, CHARTERED
Rockville, MD .... Real Estate Law

RIDOUT & MAYBEE
Ottawa, ON, Canada .... Patent, Trademark, Copyright and Unfair Competition
Toronto, ON, Canada .... Patent, Trademark, Copyright and Unfair Competition

RIEGELS CAMPOS & KENYON LLP
Sacramento, CA .... Business Law; Insurance Defense

RIEKE & SAVAGE, P.C.
Portland, OR .... Personal Injury; Professional Liability

RIESEN LAW FIRM, L.L.P.
North Charleston, SC .... Admiralty/Maritime Law; Personal Injury

RIESENBURGER & KIZNER, P.C.
Vineland, NJ .... Appellate Practice; Civil Trial Practice; Environmental Law; Real Estate Law

RIEVES & MAYTON
West Memphis, AR .... Business Law; Civil Trial Practice; General Practice; Insurance Defense; Product Liability Law; Workers Compensation

RIFKIN AND ASSOCIATES, P.A.
Miami, FL .... Immigration and Naturalization

RIGBY, THATCHER, ANDRUS, RIGBY, KAM & MOELLER, CHARTERED
Rexburg, ID .... General Practice

RIGGS & NESMITH, P.A.
Montgomery, AL .... Personal Injury; Product Liability Law

RIGHTHAND, SCOTT, P.C., LAW OFFICE OF
San Francisco, CA .... Civil Trial Practice

RIKER, DANZIG, SCHERER, HYLAND & PERRETTI LLP
Morristown, NJ .... General Practice
Trenton, NJ .... General Practice

RILEY, JOSEPH H. JR.
Tucson, AZ .... Family Law

RILEY & HARRIS, L.L.P.
Brownsville, TX .... Civil Trial Practice; Medical Malpractice; Personal Injury
Houston, TX .... Civil Trial Practice; Medical Malpractice; Personal Injury

RILEY, HURLEY & DOLENGA, P.C.
Dearborn, MI .... Civil Trial Practice; Labor and Employment Law; Sports and Entertainment Law

RILEY, MCNULTY, HEWITT & SWEITZER, A PROFESSIONAL CORPORATION
Pittsburgh, PA .... Civil Trial Practice; Commercial Law; General Practice

RILEY AND ROUMELL, P.C.
Detroit, MI .... General Practice; Labor and Employment Law

RILEY, TOM, LAW FIRM, P.L.C.
Cedar Rapids, IA .... Personal Injury

RINELLA AND RINELLA, LTD.
Chicago, IL .... Family Law

RINGO, STUBER, ENSOR & HADLOCK, P.C.
Corvallis, OR .... Personal Injury

RINGUET DANIELS & COLLIER, A PROFESSIONAL LAW CORPORATION
Lafayette, LA .... Civil Trial Practice; Commercial Law; Natural Resources Law

RINTALA, SMOOT, JAENICKE & REES
Los Angeles, CA .... Commercial Litigation; Labor and Employment Law; Trademark, Copyright and Unfair Competition

RION, RION & RION, L.P.A. INC.
Dayton, OH .... Criminal Trial Practice

RISJORD & JAMES, P.C.
Overland Park, KS .... Aviation Law; Civil Trial Practice; Personal Injury; Product Liability Law

RITCHIE & REDIKER, L.L.C.
Birmingham, AL .... Securities Law

RITER, MAYER, HOFER, WATTIER & BROWN, L.L.P.
Pierre, SD .... General Practice

RITTER EICHNER & NORRIS, PLLC
Washington, DC .... Municipal Bond/Public Authority Financing; Tax Law

RITTER AND JESPERSON
Bridgeton, NJ ..... Civil Trial Practice; General Practice

RITTER, RITTER & ZARETSKY
Miami, FL ..... Real Estate Law

RITTER, ROBINSON, MCCREADY & JAMES
Toledo, OH ..... Civil Trial Practice; Corporate Law; General Practice; Insurance Defense; Municipal and Zoning Law; Personal Injury; Real Estate Law

RIVKIN, RADLER & KREMER LLP
Uniondale, NY ..... Civil Trial Practice; General Practice

RIVKIND & PEDRAZA, P.A.
Miami, FL ..... Admiralty/Maritime Law

RIVLIN, LEWIS A., P.C., LAW OFFICES OF
Washington, DC ..... General Practice

ROACH, JAMES T.
Albuquerque, NM ..... Personal Injury; Product Liability Law

ROACH, BROWN, MCCARTHY & GRUBER, P.C.
Buffalo, NY ..... Civil Trial Practice; General Practice; Insurance Defense; Legal Malpractice; Medical Malpractice; Product Liability Law

ROACH & CARPENTER, P.C.
Boston, MA ..... Bankruptcy Law; Civil Trial Practice; Commercial Litigation

ROACH LAW FIRM, THE, P.C.
Tulsa, OK ..... Insurance Defense; Personal Injury; Product Liability Law

ROBBINS, STEPHEN
Sacramento, CA ..... Land Use Law

ROBBINS & GREEN, A PROFESSIONAL ASSOCIATION
Phoenix, AZ ..... Bankruptcy Law; Commercial Law; Commercial Litigation; Insurance Defense; Personal Injury; Real Estate Law; Trust and Estates, Wills and Probate

ROBBINS & KEEHN, A PROFESSIONAL CORPORATION
San Diego, CA ..... Bankruptcy Law; Civil Trial Practice

ROBBINS & RHODES, ATTORNEYS AT LAW, A LAW CORPORATION
Honolulu, HI ..... Appellate Practice; Civil Trial Practice; Health Care Law; Insurance Defense; Medical Malpractice

ROBBINS, TUNKEY, ROSS, AMSEL, RABEN & WAXMAN, P.A.
Miami, FL ..... Administrative Law; Appellate Practice; Civil Rights; Constitutional Law; Criminal Trial Practice; Tax Law

ROBEIN, URANN & LURYE, A PROFESSIONAL LAW CORPORATION
Metairie, LA ..... Labor and Employment Law

ROBENALT & ROBENALT
Lima, OH ..... General Practice; Health Care Law

ROBERGE, WILLIAM H. JR.
Rockville, MD ..... Trust and Estates, Wills and Probate

ROBERTS, FRANK H.
Reno, NV ..... Insurance Defense

ROBERTS, ALLEN P., P.A.
Camden, AR ..... Civil Trial Practice; General Practice; Labor and Employment Law

ROBERTS, BETZ & BLOSS, P.C.
Grand Rapids, MI ..... Civil Trial Practice; Commercial Litigation; Construction Law; Environmental Law; Insurance Defense; Personal Injury

ROBERTS & ENGVALSON, P.A.
Fort Myers, FL ..... Family Law; Trust and Estates, Wills and Probate

ROBERTS, LARRY K., INC.
Newport Beach, CA ..... Intellectual Property Law; Patent, Trademark, Copyright and Unfair Competition

ROBERTS, MARKEL & FOLGER, L.L.P.
Houston, TX ..... Admiralty/Maritime Law; Insurance Defense; Real Estate Law

ROBERTS, MARK SCOTT, AND ASSOCIATES, A PROF. LAW CORP.
Fullerton, CA ..... Trust and Estates, Wills and Probate

ROBERTS, PERRYMAN, BOMKAMP & MEIVES, P.C.
St. Louis, MO ..... Civil Trial Practice; Environmental Law; Insurance Defense; Product Liability Law; Workers Compensation

ROBERTS & ROWLEY, LTD.
Mesa, AZ ..... Business Law; Corporate Law; Real Estate Law

ROBERTS & SALAZAR, L.L.P.
Key Biscayne, FL ..... General Practice

ROBERTS & SMITH
Lexington, KY ..... Criminal Trial Practice; General Practice; Insurance Defense; Personal Injury

ROBERTSON, WILLIAM DIXON III
Columbia, SC ..... Construction Law

ROBERTSON & ASSOCIATES
Charleston, SC ..... Construction Law

ROBERTSON, BEASLEY, COWAN & KETCHAM, PLLC
Fort Smith, AR ..... Civil Trial Practice; General Practice

ROBERTSON, JAYNE JARNIGAN, P.C.
Oklahoma City, OK ..... Commercial Litigation; Environmental Law

ROBERTSON, MONAGLE & EASTAUGH, A PROFESSIONAL CORPORATION
Anchorage, AK ..... General Practice
Juneau, AK ..... General Practice

ROBERTSON & WILLIAMS, INC.
Oklahoma City, OK ..... General Practice

ROBERTSON, WILLIAMS & MCDONALD, P.A.
Orlando, FL ..... Civil Trial Practice

ROBINETTE, GILBERT H.
Baltimore, MD ..... Legal Malpractice; Medical Malpractice; Personal Injury

ROBINS, KAPLAN, MILLER & CIRESI L.L.P.
Minneapolis, MN ..... General Practice

ROBINSON, BERT K. LAW OFFICES OF
Baton Rouge, LA ..... Construction Law

ROBINSON, BRADSHAW & HINSON, P.A.
Charlotte, NC ..... General Practice
Rock Hill, SC ..... General Practice

ROBINSON, CALCAGNIE & ROBINSON, A PROFESSIONAL CORPORATION
Newport Beach, CA ..... Civil Trial Practice; Personal Injury

ROBINSON, DIAMANT & BRILL, A PROFESSIONAL CORPORATION
Los Angeles, CA ..... Bankruptcy Law

ROBINSON, DI LANDO & WHITAKER, A PROFESSIONAL LAW CORPORATION
Los Angeles, CA ..... Insurance Defense; Labor and Employment Law; Product Liability Law; Professional Liability

ROBINSON DONOVAN MADDEN & BARRY, P.C.
Springfield, MA ..... Banking Law; Commercial Litigation; Construction Law; Insurance Defense; Labor and Employment Law; Professional Liability; Real Estate Law; Tax Law; Trust and Estates, Wills and Probate; Workers Compensation

ROBINSON, J. RICHARD, P.C.
Okemos, MI ..... Municipal and Zoning Law; Real Estate Law

ROBINSON LAW FIRM, THE
Washington, DC ..... Civil Trial Practice; Commercial Litigation; Criminal Trial Practice; Medical Malpractice
Tulsa, OK ..... Insurance Defense

ROBINSON, PALMER & LOGAN
Bakersfield, CA ..... Civil Trial Practice; General Practice; Insurance Defense

ROBINSON SHEPPARD SHAPIRO, G.P.
Montreal, QU, Canada ..... General Practice

ROBINSON & WOOD, INC.
San Jose, CA ..... Civil Trial Practice; Commercial Litigation; Insurance Defense; Product Liability Law

ROBINSON WOOLSON O'CONNELL, LLP
Baltimore, MD ..... Civil Trial Practice

ROBISON, BELAUSTEGUI, ROBB AND SHARP, A PROFESSIONAL CORPORATION
Reno, NV ..... General Practice

ROBISON & BELSER, P.A.
Montgomery, AL ..... Business Law; Civil Trial Practice; Criminal Trial Practice; Family Law; Insurance Defense; Labor and Employment Law

ROBISON & ROBISON
Denton, TX ..... Labor and Employment Law; Personal Injury; Trust and Estates, Wills and Probate

ROBY & HOOD
Fort Wayne, IN ..... Civil Trial Practice; Personal Injury; Product Liability Law

ROCA & SHARPE, P.A.
West Palm Beach, FL............Civil Trial Practice; Personal Injury

ROCAP, WITCHGER & THRELKELD
Indianapolis, IN............Commercial Litigation; General Practice; Insurance Defense

ROCHE, JOHN J. & ASSOCIATES
Cambridge, MA............Trust and Estates, Wills and Probate

ROCHE, CARENS & DEGIACOMO, P.C.
Boston, MA............Banking Law; Bankruptcy Law; Construction Law; Family Law; General Practice; Labor and Employment Law; Real Estate Law; Trust and Estates, Wills and Probate

ROCHE CORRIGAN MCCOY & BUSH
Albany, NY............Civil Trial Practice; Construction Law; General Practice; Insurance Defense; Legal Malpractice; Personal Injury; Professional Liability

ROCHE AND MURPHY
Franklin, MA............Civil Trial Practice; Land Use Law; Municipal and Zoning Law; Real Estate Law

ROCHELLE, MCCULLOCH & AULDS
Lebanon, TN............General Practice

ROCKEY, MILNAMOW & KATZ, LTD.
Chicago, IL............Intellectual Property Law; Patent, Trademark, Copyright and Unfair Competition

ROCKHILL, PINNICK, PEQUIGNOT, HELM, LANDIS & RIGDON
Warsaw, IN............Business Law; Civil Trial Practice; Corporate Law; Insurance Defense; Municipal and Zoning Law

RODEHEFFER, STEPHEN C.
Portsmouth, OH............General Practice

RODEY, DICKASON, SLOAN, AKIN & ROBB, P.A.
Albuquerque, NM............Administrative Law; Antitrust Law; Banking Law; Bankruptcy Law; Business Law; Commercial Law; Construction Law; Criminal Trial Practice; General Practice; Health Care Law; Insurance Defense; International Business Law; Labor and Employment Law; Land Use Law; Medical Malpractice; Natural Resources Law; Personal Injury; Product Liability Law; Public Utilities Law; Real Estate Law; Securities Law; Tax Law; Trust and Estates, Wills and Probate
Santa Fe, NM............General Practice

RODGERS, JAMES R.
Blackwell, OK............General Practice; Trust and Estates, Wills and Probate

RODGERS AND CO., L.P.A.
Cleveland, OH............Civil Trial Practice; Commercial Litigation; Construction Law; Insurance Defense; Product Liability Law; Real Estate Law

RODGERS, MENARD & COPPOLA, LLP
Buffalo, NY............Civil Trial Practice

RODI, POLLOCK, PETTKER, GALBRAITH & CAHILL, A LAW CORPORATION
Los Angeles, CA............Business Law; Civil Trial Practice; Commercial Litigation; Corporate Law; Employment Benefits Law; Environmental Law; Labor and Employment Law; Real Estate Law; Tax Law; Toxic Torts; Trust and Estates, Wills and Probate

RODRIGUEZ, CARLOS, & ASSOCIATES
Washington, DC............Admiralty/Maritime Law; International Trade Law; Transportation Law

RODRIGUEZ, COLVIN & CHANEY, L.L.P.
Brownsville, TX............Appellate Practice; Civil Trial Practice; Environmental Law; General Practice; Insurance Defense; Personal Injury; Product Liability Law
McAllen, TX............Appellate Practice; Civil Trial Practice; Environmental Law; General Practice; Insurance Defense; Personal Injury; Product Liability Law

RODRIGUEZ, HORII & CHOI
Los Angeles, CA............Tax Law

ROEDER AND ASSOCIATES, P.C.
McLean, VA............Corporate Law; Real Estate Law

ROETZEL & ANDRESS, A LEGAL PROFESSIONAL ASSOCIATION
Akron, OH............General Practice

ROGAN GUIDA & ORENSTEIN
White Plains, NY............Appellate Practice; Business Law; Commercial Litigation; Corporate Law; Family Law; Insurance Defense; Personal Injury; Product Liability Law; Real Estate Law; Trust and Estates, Wills and Probate

ROGERS, BOWERS, DEMPSEY AND PALADINO
West Palm Beach, FL............Tax Law

ROGERS & GREENBERG
Dayton, OH............Business Law; Family Law; General Practice

ROGERS & KILLEEN
Alexandria, VA............Intellectual Property Law; Patent, Trademark, Copyright and Unfair Competition; Trademark, Copyright and Unfair Competition

ROGERS LAW OFFICE
Toronto, ON, Canada............Patent, Trademark, Copyright and Unfair Competition

ROGERS & SHEFFIELD, LLP
Santa Barbara, CA............Business Law; Civil Trial Practice

ROGERS TOWNSEND & THOMAS, PC
Columbia, SC............Aviation Law; Bankruptcy Law; Construction Law; Family Law; General Practice; Real Estate Law; Trust and Estates, Wills and Probate; Workers Compensation

ROGERS & WHALEN, P.A.
Phoenix, AZ............Administrative Law; Labor and Employment Law

ROGIN, NASSAU, CAPLAN, LASSMAN & HIRTLE, LLC
Hartford, CT............Business Law; Civil Trial Practice; General Practice

ROHRBACHERS, LIGHT, CRON, ZMUDA & TRIMBLE CO., L.P.A.
Toledo, OH............Business Law; Environmental Law; Insurance Defense; Labor and Employment Law; Product Liability Law; Tax Law

ROLEWICK & GUTZKE, P.C.
Wheaton, IL............Business Law; Commercial Litigation; Corporate Law; Trust and Estates, Wills and Probate

ROLLINGER, ROBERT S., P.C.
Bingham Farms, MI............Real Estate Law

ROLLINS, SMALKIN, RICHARDS & MACKIE, L.L.C.
Baltimore, MD............Civil Trial Practice; Insurance Defense; Personal Injury; Product Liability Law; Workers Compensation

ROLLS KOHN & ASSOCIATES, LLP
Buffalo, NY............Business Law; Communications Law; Corporate Law; General Practice; Real Estate Law

ROMAIN, KUCK & EGERER, P.C.
Southfield, MI............Insurance Defense; Personal Injury

ROOKER & GIBSON
Henderson, NV............Antitrust Law; Business Law; Civil Trial Practice; Commercial Law; Construction Law; Corporate Law; Environmental Law; Health Care Law; Labor and Employment Law; Mergers and Acquisitions; Municipal and Zoning Law; Real Estate Law; Securities Law

ROOKS, PITTS AND POUST
Chicago, IL............General Practice; Workers Compensation

ROOT & SCHINDLER, P.C.
Denver, CO............Environmental Law; Natural Resources Law

ROPER & QUIGG
Chicago, IL............Intellectual Property Law; Patent, Trademark, Copyright and Unfair Competition
Arlington, VA............Intellectual Property Law; Patent, Trademark, Copyright and Unfair Competition

ROPERS, MAJESKI, KOHN & BENTLEY, A PROFESSIONAL CORPORATION
Los Angeles, CA............General Practice
Redwood City, CA............General Practice
San Francisco, CA............General Practice
San Jose, CA............General Practice

ROPES & GRAY
Washington, DC............General Practice
Boston, MA............Civil Trial Practice; General Practice; Tax Law

ROSE, MICHAEL T.
Summerville, SC............Business Law; Civil Trial Practice

ROSE LAW FIRM, A PROFESSIONAL ASSOCIATION
Little Rock, AR............Appellate Practice; Banking Law; Bankruptcy Law; Civil Trial Practice; Commercial Law; Communications Law; Corporate Law; Creditors Rights; Employment Benefits Law; Environmental Law; General Practice; Insurance Defense; International Business Law; Labor and Employment Law; Municipal Bond/Public Authority Financing; Patent, Trademark, Copyright and Unfair Competition; Pension and Profit Sharing; Personal Injury; Product Liability Law; Professional Liability; Public Utilities Law; Real Estate Law; Sports and Entertainment Law; Tax Law; Trust and Estates, Wills and Probate; Workers Compensation

ROSE, RAND, ORCUTT, CAULEY, BLAKE & ELLIS, P.A.
Wilson, NC....General Practice

ROSE & ROSE
Kenosha, WI....Criminal Trial Practice; General Practice

ROSE, SCHMIDT, HASLEY & DISALLE, P.C.
Pittsburgh, PA....Antitrust Law; Civil Trial Practice; General Practice; Labor and Employment Law

ROSE, SUNDSTROM & BENTLEY, LLP
Tallahassee, FL....Administrative Law; Environmental Law; Health Care Law; Public Utilities Law; Real Estate Law

ROSEN, AVRUM J. LAW OFFICES OF
Huntington, NY....Bankruptcy Law

ROSEN, CHARLES A.
Roseland, NJ....Commercial Law; General Practice

ROSEN, BIEN & ASARO
San Francisco, CA....Antitrust Law; Appellate Practice; Civil Trial Practice; Commercial Law; Commercial Litigation; Labor and Employment Law; Securities Law; Trademark, Copyright and Unfair Competition

ROSEN, COOK, SLEDGE, DAVIS, CADE & SHATTUCK, P.A.
Tuscaloosa, AL....General Practice

ROSEN & DOLAN, P.C.
New Haven, CT....Appellate Practice; Civil Rights; Civil Trial Practice; Family Law; General Practice; Labor and Employment Law; Personal Injury

ROSEN, EINBINDER & DUNN, P.C.
New York, NY....Civil Trial Practice; Real Estate Law

ROSEN & LOVELL, P.C.
Southfield, MI....Construction Law; Personal Injury; Product Liability Law

ROSEN, MICHAEL J., P.A.
Miami, FL....Commercial Litigation; Criminal Trial Practice

ROSEN & OSBORNE, P.A.
Tampa, FL....Workers Compensation

ROSENBAUM, RICHARD L.
Fort Lauderdale, FL....Appellate Practice; Criminal Trial Practice

ROSENBERG LAW FIRM, THE
Des Moines, IA....Appellate Practice; Business Law; Criminal Trial Practice; General Practice; Personal Injury

ROSENBERG, REISMAN & STEIN, LLP
Miami, FL....Construction Law; Real Estate Law

ROSENBERG, ROBERT MERRILL, P.A.
Minneapolis, MN....General Practice; Real Estate Law

ROSENBLATT, STANLEY M., PROFESSIONAL ASSOCIATION
Miami, FL....Civil Trial Practice

ROSENBLUM & FILAN, L.L.C.
Stamford, CT....Civil Trial Practice; General Practice; Health Care Law; Medical Malpractice
New York, NY....Medical Malpractice
White Plains, NY....Medical Malpractice

ROSENBLUM, GOLDENHERSH, SILVERSTEIN & ZAFFT, P.C.
St. Louis, MO....Commercial Litigation; Corporate Law; Real Estate Law; Tax Law

ROSENBLUM & ROSENBLUM, L.L.C.
Alexandria, VA....Bankruptcy Law; Personal Injury

ROSENBLUM, SCHWARTZ & ROGERS, L.L.C.
St. Louis, MO....Criminal Trial Practice

ROSENBLUM, WOLF & LLOYD, A PROFESSIONAL CORPORATION
Teaneck, NJ....Real Estate Law; Tax Law

ROSENFELD, WOLFF, ARONSON, KURLAND & KLEIN, A PROFESSIONAL CORPORATION
Los Angeles, CA....Business Law; Real Estate Law; Securities Law

ROSENN, JENKINS & GREENWALD, L.L.P.
Wilkes-Barre, PA....Bankruptcy Law; General Practice; Labor and Employment Law; Real Estate Law; Tax Law; Trust and Estates, Wills and Probate

ROSENTHAL, MARTIN R.
Boston, MA....Civil Trial Practice; Criminal Trial Practice

ROSENTHAL & CURRY
East Meadow, NY....General Practice

ROSENTHAL & OSHA, L.L.P.
Houston, TX....Intellectual Property Law; Patent, Trademark, Copyright and Unfair Competition

ROSENTHAL AND SCHANFIELD, PROFESSIONAL CORPORATION
Chicago, IL....Civil Trial Practice; General Practice

ROSENTHAL, SIEGEL, MUENKEL & MALONEY, LLP
Amherst, NY....Personal Injury
Buffalo, NY....Medical Malpractice; Personal Injury

ROSENTHAL AND WEISBERG, P.C.
Philadelphia, PA....Criminal Trial Practice; Health Care Law; Medical Malpractice; Personal Injury; Product Liability Law

ROSENZWEIG, JEFF
Little Rock, AR....Criminal Trial Practice

ROSENZWEIG, JONES & MACNABB, P.C.
Newnan, GA....Bankruptcy Law; Civil Trial Practice; Commercial Law; Family Law; General Practice; Personal Injury; Real Estate Law; Trust and Estates, Wills and Probate

ROSEPINK & ESTES, P.L.L.C.
Scottsdale, AZ....Tax Law; Trust and Estates, Wills and Probate

ROSHKA HEYMAN & DEWULF, PLC
Phoenix, AZ....Commercial Litigation; Communications Law; Public Utilities Law; Securities Law

ROSS, HARRIET
San Francisco, CA....Criminal Trial Practice

ROSS, RICHARD M.
Sacramento, CA....Administrative Law; Environmental Law

ROSS & ASSOCIATES
Miami, FL....Insurance Defense

ROSS, BRITTAIN & SCHONBERG CO., L.P.A.
Cleveland, OH....Labor and Employment Law

ROSS & COHEN, LLP
New York, NY....Construction Law; Real Estate Law

ROSS, DIXON & BELL, L.L.P.
Irvine, CA....Civil Trial Practice
San Diego, CA....Civil Trial Practice
Washington, DC....Civil Trial Practice

ROSS & FERM, LLC
Ellsworth, ME....Personal Injury; Real Estate Law

ROSS & HARDIES
Chicago, IL....General Practice
New York, NY....General Practice

ROSS, JAMES A., JR. LAW OFFICE
Monticello, AR....General Practice

ROSSBACHER & ASSOCIATES
Los Angeles, CA....Commercial Litigation; Constitutional Law

ROSSI, MURNANE & HUGHES
Utica, NY....General Practice; Insurance Defense

ROSSIE, LUCKETT, PARKER & RIDDER, P.C.
Memphis, TN....General Practice; Insurance Defense; Real Estate Law; Trust and Estates, Wills and Probate

ROSSMAN, BAUMBERGER & REBOSO, A PROFESSIONAL ASSOCIATION
Miami, FL....Civil Trial Practice

ROST & GEIGER
Wailuku, HI....Personal Injury

ROTH, STEPHEN H.
Hackensack, NJ....Administrative Law; Appellate Practice; Civil Trial Practice; Commercial Law; Family Law; Real Estate Law

ROTH AND DUNCAN, P.A.
West Palm Beach, FL....Criminal Trial Practice

ROTH FOLEY BRYANT & COOPER, PLLC
Louisville, KY....Banking Law; Bankruptcy Law; Civil Trial Practice; Creditors Rights; Family Law; General Practice; Personal Injury; Real Estate Law; Securities Law; Tax Law; Trust and Estates, Wills and Probate

ROTHBERG & LOGAN
Fort Wayne, IN....Banking Law; Commercial Litigation; Family Law; General Practice

ROTHENBERG, ALLEN L., LAW FIRM OF
Philadelphia, PA....Personal Injury

ROTHENBERG SILVERMAN & FURMAN, P.C.
Elkins Park, PA....Labor and Employment Law

ROTHFELDER LAW OFFICES, THE
Westfield, NJ....Communications Law; Energy Law; Public Utilities Law

ROTHSCHILD, BARRY & MYERS
Chicago, IL....................Antitrust Law; Aviation Law; General Practice

ROTHSCHILD, MORGAN & BROWN
Columbus, GA....................General Practice; Health Care Law; Insurance Defense; Tax Law

ROTHSCHILD, WISHEK & SANDS
Sacramento, CA....................Administrative Law; Criminal Trial Practice

ROTHSTEIN, DONATELLI, HUGHES, DAHLSTROM & SCHOENBURG, LLP
Santa Fe, NM....................Civil Trial Practice; Criminal Trial Practice

ROTHWELL, FIGG, ERNST & KURZ, A PROFESSIONAL CORPORATION
Washington, DC....................Intellectual Property Law

ROUDA, FEDER & TIETJEN
San Francisco, CA....................Personal Injury

ROUNTREE & SEAGLE, L.L.P.
Wilmington, NC....................Admiralty/Maritime Law; Civil Trial Practice

ROUTMAN, MOORE, GOLDSTONE & VALENTINO
New Castle, PA....................General Practice
Sharon, PA....................General Practice

ROVNER, GERALD C.
Boston, MA....................Immigration and Naturalization

ROWE, GORDON H. JR.
South Fork, CO....................General Practice

ROWE, FOLTZ & MARTIN, P.C.
Atlanta, GA....................Real Estate Law

ROWE LAW FIRM, THE, P.C.
Albuquerque, NM....................General Practice

ROWE & ROWE
South Bend, IN....................Civil Trial Practice; General Practice; Insurance Defense; Medical Malpractice; Personal Injury; Product Liability Law

ROWLEY LAW FIRM, P.C.
Clovis, NM....................Banking Law; General Practice

ROY, FORREST & LOPRESTO, LTD.
New Iberia, LA....................Insurance Defense

ROY SHECTER & VOCHT
Bloomfield Hills, MI....................Antitrust Law; Business Law

ROYALS, THOMAS E.
Jackson, MS....................Civil Trial Practice; Criminal Trial Practice; General Practice

ROYCE, THOMAS L. JR.
Houston, TX....................Criminal Trial Practice

ROYLANCE, ABRAMS, BERDO & GOODMAN, L.L.P.
Washington, DC....................Antitrust Law; Patent, Trademark, Copyright and Unfair Competition

ROYSTON, MUELLER, MCLEAN & REID, LLP
Towson, MD....................General Practice

ROYSTON, RAYZOR, VICKERY & WILLIAMS, L.L.P.
Brownsville, TX....................General Practice
Corpus Christi, TX....................General Practice
Galveston, TX....................General Practice
Houston, TX....................Admiralty/Maritime Law; General Practice

ROZELLE AND CALL
West Palm Beach, FL....................Civil Trial Practice; Insurance Defense

RUBENSTEIN, SUSAN LAW OFFICES OF
San Francisco, CA....................Labor and Employment Law

RUBERTI, GIRVIN & FERLAZZO, P.C.
Albany, NY....................Education Law; General Practice; Labor and Employment Law; Personal Injury

RUBIN, MILES J. LAW OFFICES OF
Los Angeles, CA....................Family Law

RUBIN & DORNBAUM
Newark, NJ....................Immigration and Naturalization

RUBIN & HAYS
Louisville, KY....................Municipal Bond/Public Authority Financing

RUBINBAUM LLP
New York, NY....................General Practice

RUBNER & KUTNER, P.C.
Denver, CO....................Bankruptcy Law

RUCCI, BURNHAM, CARTA & EDELBERG, LLP
Darien, CT....................Banking Law; Bankruptcy Law; Business Law; Civil Trial Practice; Real Estate Law; Trust and Estates, Wills and Probate

RUDDY, BRADLEY, KOLKHORST & REGES, A PROFESSIONAL CORPORATION
Juneau, AK....................Civil Trial Practice; Environmental Law; Natural Resources Law

RUDEN, MCCLOSKY, SMITH, SCHUSTER & RUSSELL, P.A.
Fort Lauderdale, FL....................General Practice

RUDLOFF & RUDLOFF
Bowling Green, KY....................Civil Trial Practice; Insurance Defense; Personal Injury

RUDMAN & WINCHELL, LLC
Bangor, ME....................Business Law; Insurance Defense; Labor and Employment Law; Trust and Estates, Wills and Probate

RUDOLF & MAHER, P.A.
Chapel Hill, NC....................Civil Trial Practice; Criminal Trial Practice

RUDOLPH, DORIAN, GOLDSTEIN, ROCHESTIE, WISNIEWSKI & TAYLOR, P.C.
Bensalem, PA....................Commercial Litigation; Medical Malpractice; Personal Injury; Product Liability Law; Real Estate Law; Toxic Torts

RUDOLPH, FINE, PORTER & JOHNSON LLP
Evansville, IN....................Business Law; Commercial Law; Health Care Law; Insurance Defense; Labor and Employment Law; Trust and Estates, Wills and Probate; Workers Compensation

RUFFIN, JOSEPH LUIS, P.C.
Oklahoma City, OK....................Criminal Trial Practice

RUMRELL, WAGNER & COSTABEL, LLP
Jacksonville, FL....................Civil Trial Practice

RUNFOLA, JOHN M.
San Francisco, CA....................Criminal Trial Practice

RUNNING, WISE, FORD AND PHILLIPS, P.L.C.
Traverse City, MI....................Corporate Law; Insurance Defense

RUNYON AND RUNYON, PLLC
Clarksville, TN....................Family Law; Personal Injury; Trust and Estates, Wills and Probate

RUS, MILIBAND & SMITH
Irvine, CA....................Bankruptcy Law; Civil Trial Practice; Commercial Litigation

RUSH MOORE CRAVEN SUTTON MORRY & BEH
Honolulu, HI....................General Practice

RUSHFORD & BONOTTO, LLP
Sacramento, CA....................Civil Trial Practice; Insurance Defense

RUSHING & GUICE
Biloxi, MS....................Admiralty/Maritime Law; Banking Law; Business Law; Civil Trial Practice; Commercial Litigation; Product Liability Law

RUSIN PATTON MACIOROWSKI & FRIEDMAN, LTD.
Chicago, IL....................Civil Trial Practice; Insurance Defense; Transportation Law; Workers Compensation

RUSS, AUGUST & KABAT, A PROFESSIONAL CORPORATION
Los Angeles, CA....................Trademark, Copyright and Unfair Competition

RUSSELL & BATCHELOR
Grand Rapids, MI....................Real Estate Law; Tax Law

RUSSELL, BROWN, BICKEL & BRECKENRIDGE
Nevada, MO....................General Practice

RUSSELL LAW OFFICES, P.A.
Orlando, FL....................Business Law; Civil Trial Practice; Commercial Litigation; Construction Law; Real Estate Law

RUSSELL, MCINTYRE, HILLIGOSS & WELKE
Kokomo, IN....................Medical Malpractice; Personal Injury

RUSSELL & MIRKOVICH
Long Beach, CA....................Admiralty/Maritime Law; Civil Trial Practice; Commercial Law; International Business Law; Personal Injury; Transportation Law

RUSSELL, RICHARD A., A PROFESSIONAL CORPORATION
Ocean City, NJ....................Family Law

RUSSELL, TURNER, LAIRD & JONES, L.L.P.
Fort Worth, TX....................Civil Trial Practice; Commercial Law; Medical Malpractice; Personal Injury; Product Liability Law

RUSSO APPELLATE FIRM, P.A.
Miami, FL ....Appellate Practice

RUSSO & HEFFERNAN, P.A.
Miami, FL ....Civil Trial Practice; Medical Malpractice; Toxic Torts

RUST, ARMENIS, SCHWARTZ, LAMB & BILLS, A PROFESSIONAL CORPORATION
Sacramento, CA ....Insurance Defense; Medical Malpractice
San Francisco, CA ....Insurance Defense

RUTAN & TUCKER, LLP
Costa Mesa, CA ....Antitrust Law; Appellate Practice; Bankruptcy Law; Business Law; Civil Rights; Civil Trial Practice; Commercial Law; Communications Law; Computer Law; Construction Law; Employment Benefits Law; Environmental Law; General Practice; Labor and Employment Law; Land Use Law; Municipal and Zoning Law; Municipal Bond/Public Authority Financing; Real Estate Law; Securities Law; Tax Law; Trademark, Copyright and Unfair Competition; Trust and Estates, Wills and Probate

RUTH & MACNEILLE, PROFESSIONAL ASSOCIATION
Hilton Head Island, SC ....Civil Trial Practice; Corporate Law; Elder Law; Tax Law; Trust and Estates, Wills and Probate

RUTHRAUFF & ARMBRUST, P.C.
Philadelphia, PA ....Personal Injury; Product Liability Law; Professional Liability

RUTKIN AND OLDHAM, L.L.C
Westport, CT ....Family Law; Personal Injury

RUTLEDGE, MANION, RABAUT, TERRY & THOMAS, P.C.
Detroit, MI ....Insurance Defense

RUTTER, ROBERT P.
Cleveland, OH ....Personal Injury

RYAN, BROWN, MCDONNELL, BERGER GIBBONS & LAROCCA, LLP
Philadelphia, PA ....Civil Trial Practice; Insurance Defense; Personal Injury

RYAN AND GANNON
Florham Park, NJ ....Appellate Practice; Civil Trial Practice; Insurance Defense

RYAN, JAMIESON, MORRIS & RYAN
Kalamazoo, MI ....Insurance Defense

RYAN KROMHOLZ & MANION, S.C.
Brookfield, WI ....Intellectual Property Law; Patent, Trademark, Copyright and Unfair Competition

RYAN MARKS JOHNSON TODD & BRODER
Las Vegas, NV ....Civil Trial Practice; Construction Law; Insurance Defense

RYAN & RYAN
Aitkin, MN ....General Practice

RYAN, RYAN, JOHNSON & DELUCA, LLP
Stamford, CT ....Civil Trial Practice; General Practice

RYAN SMITH & CARBINE, LTD.
Rutland, VT ....General Practice

RYMER, WM. W.
Providence, RI ....Intellectual Property Law; Patent, Trademark, Copyright and Unfair Competition

RYWANT, ALVAREZ, JONES, RUSSO & GUYTON, PROFESSIONAL ASSOCIATION
Tampa, FL ....Civil Trial Practice; Insurance Defense; Medical Malpractice; Product Liability Law

SAALFIELD, COULSON, SHAD & JAY, P.A.
Jacksonville, FL ....Civil Trial Practice; Insurance Defense; Medical Malpractice; Product Liability Law

SABRA & ASPDEN, PROFESSIONAL ASSOCIATION
Somerset, MA ....Criminal Trial Practice; Personal Injury; Workers Compensation

SACCA AND SACCA
Lockport, NY ....Corporate Law; General Practice; Trust and Estates, Wills and Probate

SACHER ZELMAN PAUL BEILEY & VAN SANT, P.A.
Miami, FL ....Securities Law

SACHNOFF & WEAVER, LTD.
Chicago, IL ....General Practice

SACHS, LESTER G. LAW OFFICES
San Jose, CA ....Construction Law

SACHS, MAITLIN, FLEMING, GREENE, WILSON & MAROTTE
West Orange, NJ ....Appellate Practice; Environmental Law; Insurance Defense; Medical Malpractice; Product Liability Law

SACHS & WERDINE, P.A.
Tampa, FL ....Eminent Domain

SACKS MONTGOMERY, P.C.
New York, NY ....Civil Trial Practice; Commercial Litigation; Construction Law; General Practice; Government Contracts

SACKS & SACKS, A PROFESSIONAL CORPORATION
Norfolk, VA ....Appellate Practice; Civil Trial Practice; Criminal Trial Practice; General Practice; Personal Injury; Product Liability Law

SACKS TIERNEY P.A.
Scottsdale, AZ ....Commercial Law; Commercial Litigation; General Practice; Health Care Law; Real Estate Law

SACOPULOS, JOHNSON, CARTER & SACOPULOS
Terre Haute, IN ....Insurance Defense

SADOW, STEVEN H., P.C.
Atlanta, GA ....Criminal Trial Practice

SAEGERT, ANGENEND & AUGUSTINE, P.C.
Austin, TX ....Business Law; Civil Trial Practice; Real Estate Law

SAGASER, FRANSON & JONES, A PROFESSIONAL CORPORATION
Fresno, CA ....Civil Trial Practice; Commercial Litigation; Environmental Law; Labor and Employment Law

SAIKLEY, GARRISON & COLOMBO, LTD.
Danville, IL ....Commercial Law

ST. JOHN, HOWARD C. AND ASSOCIATES
Kingston, NY ....General Practice; Real Estate Law; Trust and Estates, Wills and Probate

ST. JOHN & ST. JOHN, L.L.C.
Cullman, AL ....Civil Trial Practice; Insurance Defense; Labor and Employment Law; Workers Compensation

ST. JOHN & WAYNE, L.L.C.
Newark, NJ ....Banking Law; Bankruptcy Law; Civil Trial Practice; Commercial Law; Environmental Law; General Practice; Insurance Defense; Labor and Employment Law; Municipal Bond/Public Authority Financing; Tax Law

ST. MARTIN & WILLIAMS, A PROFESSIONAL LAW CORPORATION
Houma, LA ....Personal Injury

ST. ONGE STEWARD JOHNSTON & REENS, LLC
Stamford, CT ....Patent, Trademark, Copyright and Unfair Competition

SALADINO LAW FIRM
Paducah, KY ....Admiralty/Maritime Law; Personal Injury; Product Liability Law

SALEH, JOHN
Lamesa, TX ....Civil Trial Practice

SALESE & MCCARTHY, P.C.
Tucson, AZ ....Family Law

SALES, RONALD, P.A.
West Palm Beach, FL ....Family Law

SALITERMAN & SIEFFERMAN, P.C.
Minneapolis, MN ....General Practice; Securities Law

SALLEY & ASSOCIATES
Metairie, LA ....Admiralty/Maritime Law

SALLY & FITCH
Boston, MA ....Civil Trial Practice

SALMON, LAMPERT & CLOR, PROFESSIONAL CORPORATION
Englewood, CO ....Medical Malpractice; Personal Injury; Product Liability Law

SALSBERY & DRUCKMAN
Charleston, WV ....Civil Trial Practice; Commercial Litigation; Criminal Trial Practice; Medical Malpractice; Personal Injury; Product Liability Law

SALTER, JAMES W., III, P.A.
Rockville, MD ....Civil Trial Practice

SALTER, THEODORE, JR., & ASSOCIATES, P.C.
Atlanta, GA ....Workers Compensation

SALTMAN & STEVENS, P.C.
Washington, DC ....Business Law; Commercial Law

SALTMARSH, SARA E. LAW OFFICES OF
Austin, TX....................Family Law

SALVI & SCHOSTOK, P.C.
Waukegan, IL....................Aviation Law; Commercial Litigation; Medical Malpractice; Personal Injury; Product Liability Law

SALVO, ALICE A.
Los Angeles, CA....................Trust and Estates, Wills and Probate

SAMEL, JEFFREY, & PARTNERS
New York, NY....................Civil Trial Practice; General Practice; Insurance Defense; Personal Injury; Product Liability Law

SAMET, DEE-DEE, P.C.
Tucson, AZ....................Personal Injury; Workers Compensation

SAMMONS & PARKER, A PROFESSIONAL CORPORATION
Tyler, TX....................Civil Trial Practice; Insurance Defense; Real Estate Law

SAMPSON, WILLIAM A. II & ASSOCIATES
Pacific Palisades, CA....................Civil Trial Practice; Personal Injury

SAMS & LISTER, P.A.
Miami, FL....................Appellate Practice; Civil Trial Practice; General Practice; Medical Malpractice; Personal Injury; Product Liability Law

SAMUEL, RALPH D. & CO., A PROFESSIONAL CORPORATION
Philadelphia, PA....................Arbitration; Civil Trial Practice; Commercial Litigation; Constitutional Law; Medical Malpractice; Personal Injury; Product Liability Law; Workers Compensation

SAMUELS, HARVEY M.
Columbus, OH....................Family Law

SAMUELSON RIEGER & YOVINO, LLP
Garden City, NY....................Family Law

SANDALS, LANGER & TAYLOR, LLP
Philadelphia, PA....................Antitrust Law; Commercial Litigation; Employment Benefits Law

SANDENAW, CARRILLO & PIAZZA, P.C.
Las Cruces, NM....................Civil Trial Practice; Insurance Defense; Medical Malpractice

SANDERS, AUSTIN, SWOPE & FLANIGAN
Princeton, WV....................Civil Trial Practice; Personal Injury; Product Liability Law; Workers Compensation

SANDERS, HAUGEN & SEARS, P.C.
Newnan, GA....................General Practice

SANDERS, ROBERT E., AND ASSOCIATES, P.S.C.
Covington, KY....................Appellate Practice; Business Law; Civil Trial Practice; Criminal Trial Practice; Environmental Law; Medical Malpractice; Personal Injury; Product Liability Law

SANDLER, TRAVIS & ROSENBERG, P.A.
Miami, FL....................International Trade Law

SANDS, KENTON V. LAW OFFICE OF
Orlando, FL....................Appellate Practice; Criminal Trial Practice

SANDS & MOSKOWITZ, P.A.
Miami, FL....................Criminal Trial Practice

SANFORD HOLSHOUSER LAW FIRM PLLC, THE
Raleigh, NC....................Banking Law

SANGER & SWYSEN
Santa Barbara, CA....................Criminal Trial Practice

SANGERMAN, JAY J. & ASSOCIATES
New York, NY....................Elder Law; Trust and Estates, Wills and Probate

SANSONE, CHARLES F.
Tampa, FL....................Civil Trial Practice; Personal Injury; Product Liability Law

SANTOS, DUTTON, LYNOTT & HENRY, P.A.
Tampa, FL....................Insurance Defense; Product Liability Law

SANTWIER, RICKARD
Pasadena, CA....................Criminal Trial Practice

SAPORITO & SLEDGE, L.L.C.
New Orleans, LA....................Insurance Defense; Product Liability Law

SAPP, SAPP & WHITE, P.C.
Austin, TX....................Administrative Law; Commercial Litigation

SARNOFF & BAYER
Miami, FL....................Admiralty/Maritime Law

SARRAIL, LYNCH & HALL
San Francisco, CA....................Insurance Defense; Product Liability Law

SARROUF, TARRICONE & FLEMMING
Boston, MA....................Aviation Law; Civil Trial Practice; Personal Injury

SASSER, CESTERO & SASSER, P.A.
West Palm Beach, FL....................Family Law; General Practice

SATHER, BYERLY & HOLLOWAY, LLP
Portland, OR....................Administrative Law; Civil Trial Practice; Insurance Defense; Labor and Employment Law; Professional Liability; Workers Compensation

SATTERFIELD, BONNIE S., P.A.
Coral Springs, FL....................Appellate Practice; Civil Trial Practice
Fort Lauderdale, FL....................Appellate Practice; Civil Trial Practice

SATZ & KIRSHON, P.C.
Poughkeepsie, NY....................Appellate Practice; Civil Trial Practice; Family Law

SAUCEDO & CORSIGLIA, A LAW CORPORATION
San Jose, CA....................Civil Trial Practice; Medical Malpractice; Personal Injury

SAUER & WAGNER LLP
Los Angeles, CA....................Civil Trial Practice

SAUL, EWING, REMICK & SAUL LLP
New York, NY....................General Practice
Berwyn, PA....................General Practice
Philadelphia, PA....................General Practice

SAUNDERS & MONROE
Chicago, IL....................Antitrust Law; Civil Trial Practice; Communications Law; Public Utilities Law; Securities Law

SAUNDERS & SCHMIELER
Silver Spring, MD....................Construction Law; Environmental Law; General Practice; Insurance Defense; Intellectual Property Law; Product Liability Law; Professional Liability; Toxic Torts

SAURBIER, SIEGAN & SANFIELD, P.C.
St. Clair Shores, MI....................Civil Trial Practice; Health Care Law; Insurance Defense; Medical Malpractice; Personal Injury; Product Liability Law; Transportation Law

SAVAGE, GARMER & ELLIOTT, P.S.C.
Lexington, KY....................Civil Trial Practice; Medical Malpractice; Personal Injury; Product Liability Law

SAVAGE, HERNDON & TURNER, P.C.
Savannah, GA....................Civil Trial Practice

SAVAGE, ROYALL AND SHEHEEN, L.L.P.
Camden, SC....................Civil Trial Practice; General Practice

SAVAGE & SAVAGE, P.A.
Charleston, SC....................Criminal Trial Practice; Personal Injury

SAVETT FRUTKIN PODELL & RYAN, P.C.
Philadelphia, PA....................Antitrust Law; Civil Trial Practice; Commercial Litigation; Securities Law

SAWAYA, ROSE, ROBERTS & SAWAYA, P.C.
Denver, CO....................Personal Injury

SAWYER, J. E. JR.
Enterprise, AL....................Civil Trial Practice; General Practice

SAWYER, DAVIS, HALPERN & DEMETRI
Garden City, NY....................Civil Trial Practice; Medical Malpractice; Personal Injury

SAXON, JOHN D., P.C.
Birmingham, AL....................Civil Trial Practice; Labor and Employment Law

SAYAD & BIREN, A PROFESSIONAL CORPORATION
San Francisco, CA....................Labor and Employment Law

SAYLES & EVANS
Elmira, NY....................Civil Trial Practice; Corporate Law

SAYLES & LIDJI, A PROFESSIONAL CORPORATION
Dallas, TX....................Corporate Law

SAYLOR LAW FIRM, THE, LLP
Atlanta, GA....................Business Law; Tax Law; Trust and Estates, Wills and Probate

SAYRE LAW OFFICES
Seattle, WA....................General Practice

SAYRE & SAYRE, P.S.
Spokane, WA....................Elder Law

SCADDEN, HAMILTON & RYAN
San Francisco, CA....................Appellate Practice; Civil Trial Practice; Environmental Law; Insurance Defense; Product Liability Law; Professional Liability

SCALIA, JOSEPH W. LAW OFFICES OF
Gold River, CA........................Business Law; Real Estate Law; Sports and Entertainment Law

SCALIA, JOSEPH W., LAW OFFICES OF
Sacramento, CA........................Business Law; Real Estate Law; Sports and Entertainment Law

SCALLEY & READING, A PROFESSIONAL CORPORATION
Salt Lake City, UT....................Environmental Law; Insurance Defense; Real Estate Law

SCANLAN, EDMUND J., LTD., LAW OFFICES OF
Chicago, IL............................Civil Trial Practice; Medical Malpractice; Personal Injury

SCANLAN, ROSEN & SHAR, LLC
Baltimore, MD.........................Aviation Law; Civil Trial Practice; Commercial Litigation; Medical Malpractice; Personal Injury; Product Liability Law; Professional Liability

SCANLON & GEARINGER CO., L.P.A.
Akron, OH..............................Medical Malpractice; Personal Injury; Product Liability Law

SCANLON, HOWLEY, SCANLON & DOHERTY
Scranton, PA...........................Civil Trial Practice; General Practice; Insurance Defense; Medical Malpractice; Personal Injury; Product Liability Law; Workers Compensation

SCARIANO, ELLCH, HIMES, SRAGA AND PETRARCA, CHARTERED
Chicago, IL............................Civil Trial Practice; Employment Benefits Law; Insurance Defense; Labor and Employment Law; Municipal and Zoning Law; Municipal Bond/Public Authority Financing

SCARPELLO & ALLING, LTD. A PROFESSIONAL CORPORATION
Carson City, NV.......................General Practice
Stateline, NV..........................General Practice

SCARZAFAVA LAW OFFICE, THE
Oneonta, NY............................Personal Injury; Product Liability Law

SCATES, J. C. TIM
Denver, CO.............................Business Law

SCHAAF & HODGES
Marietta, GA...........................Real Estate Law

SCHACHTER, KRISTOFF, ORENSTEIN & BERKOWITZ, L.L.P.
Menlo Park, CA........................Labor and Employment Law
Sacramento, CA........................Labor and Employment Law
San Francisco, CA.....................Labor and Employment Law

SCHACHTER, TROMBADORE, OFFEN, STANTON & PAVICS, A PROFESSIONAL CORPORATION
Somerville, NJ.........................Appellate Practice; Bankruptcy Law; Business Law; Civil Trial Practice; Commercial Law; Commercial Litigation; Corporate Law; Criminal Trial Practice; Family Law; Land Use Law; Municipal and Zoning Law; Personal Injury; Real Estate Law; Trust and Estates, Wills and Probate

SCHADEN, KATZMAN, LAMPERT & MCCLUNE
Broomfield, CO........................Aviation Law; Civil Trial Practice; Personal Injury; Product Liability Law
Troy, MI.................................Aviation Law; Civil Trial Practice; Personal Injury; Product Liability Law

SCHAFER, GERALD S.
Greensboro, NC........................Bankruptcy Law

SCHAFFNER & VAN DER SNICK, P.C.
Geneva, IL..............................Criminal Trial Practice; Family Law

SCHANEVILLE & BARINGER, L.L.C.
Baton Rouge, LA.......................Bankruptcy Law; Tax Law

SCHANTZ, STEWART T.
Poughkeepsie, NY......................Family Law

SCHAPER, CARLOS E. LAW OFFICE
Broken Bow, NE........................General Practice; Real Estate Law; Trust and Estates, Wills and Probate

SCHECHNER, STEPHEN H. LAW OFFICES OF
Millburn, NJ............................Insurance Defense; Medical Malpractice; Professional Liability

SCHECHTER LAW FIRM, THE, P.C.
St. Louis, MO..........................Family Law

SCHEEHLE LAW FIRM, P.L.C.
Fountain Hills, AZ.....................Tax Law

SCHEFFLER, WILLIAM L. & ASSOCIATES
Westport, CT...........................Business Law; Municipal and Zoning Law; Real Estate Law

SCHELL BRAY AYCOCK ABEL & LIVINGSTON P.L.L.C.
Greensboro, NC........................Business Law; Mergers and Acquisitions; Real Estate Law; Securities Law; Trust and Estates, Wills and Probate

SCHELLINGER & DOYLE, S.C.
Milwaukee, WI.........................Insurance Defense

SCHENCK, PRICE, SMITH & KING, LLP
Morristown, NJ........................Civil Trial Practice; General Practice

SCHENK, BONCHER AND PRASHER, P.C.
Grand Rapids, MI......................Commercial Litigation; Environmental Law

SCHERNER, HANSON & CORNWELL, LLC
Columbus, OH..........................Civil Trial Practice; Medical Malpractice; Personal Injury; Product Liability Law

SCHEUER, YOST & PATTERSON, A PROFESSIONAL CORPORATION
Santa Fe, NM...........................Banking Law; Civil Trial Practice; Environmental Law; General Practice; Labor and Employment Law; Real Estate Law; Trust and Estates, Wills and Probate

SCHIER, DENEWETH & PARFITT, P.C.
Troy, MI.................................Commercial Litigation; Construction Law

SCHIFF HARDIN & WAITE
Washington, DC........................General Practice
Chicago, IL.............................General Practice

SCHIFF & HULBERT
Chicago, IL.............................Labor and Employment Law; Workers Compensation

SCHIFFRIN OLSON SCHLEMLEIN & HOPKINS, P.L.L.C.
Seattle, WA.............................Commercial Law; Construction Law

SCHILD, PETER
Boulder, CO............................Criminal Trial Practice

SCHILLER, MARVIN
Raleigh, NC............................Appellate Practice; Environmental Law; Labor and Employment Law; Securities Law

SCHILLER & ASSOCIATES, P.C.
New York, NY..........................Computer Law; Real Estate Law

SCHILLER, DU CANTO AND FLECK
Chicago, IL.............................Family Law
Lake Forest, IL........................Family Law

SCHINDLER AND OLSON
Mishawaka, IN.........................Personal Injury; Real Estate Law; Trust and Estates, Wills and Probate

SCHLANGER, MILLS, MAYER & SILVER, L.L.P.
Houston, TX............................Real Estate Law

SCHLAPPRIZZI, DONALD L., P.C.
St. Louis, MO..........................Personal Injury

SCHLECHT, SHEVLIN & SHOENBERGER, A LAW CORPORATION
Palm Springs, CA......................Business Law; Civil Trial Practice; Family Law; General Practice; Real Estate Law; Trust and Estates, Wills and Probate

SCHLICHTER, BOGARD & DENTON
St. Louis, MO..........................Personal Injury

SCHLOTHAUER & COLLINS
Los Angeles, CA.......................Aviation Law; Medical Malpractice; Product Liability Law

SCHLUETER & ASSOCIATES, P.C.
Denver, CO.............................Business Law; International Business Law; Mergers and Acquisitions; Securities Law

SCHLUSSER & REIVER, P.A.
Wilmington, DE........................Tax Law; Trust and Estates, Wills and Probate

SCHMELTZER, APTAKER & SHEPARD, P.C.
Washington, DC........................Admiralty/Maritime Law; Business Law; Civil Trial Practice; Employment Benefits Law; Health Care Law; Labor and Employment Law

SCHMIDT FIRM, THE
Dallas, TX..............................Civil Trial Practice; Medical Malpractice; Personal Injury

SCHMIDT, L. WILLIAM, JR., P.C.
Denver, CO.............................Trust and Estates, Wills and Probate

SCHMIDT, RONCA AND KRAMER, P.C.
Harrisburg, PA.........................Personal Injury

SCHMIDT, SCHROYER & MORENO, P.C.
Pierre, SD...............................General Practice

SCHMITTINGER & RODRIGUEZ, PROFESSIONAL ASSOCIATION
Dover, DE..............................General Practice

SCHMUKLER, MARTIN L., P.C.
New York, NY..........................Criminal Trial Practice

SCHNADER HARRISON SEGAL & LEWIS LLP
Philadelphia, PA.....................General Practice

SCHNAPP, ROGER H., A PROFESSIONAL CORPORATION
Newport Beach, CA................Labor and Employment Law

SCHNEIDER, IRWIN, & ASSOCIATES, P.C.
Scranton, PA...........................General Practice

SCHNEIDER, KLEINICK, WEITZ, DAMASHEK & SHOOT
New York, NY..........................Civil Trial Practice; Insurance Defense; Medical Malpractice; Personal Injury; Product Liability Law

SCHNEIDER LAW FIRM
Willmar, MN.............................Civil Trial Practice; Personal Injury; Product Liability Law

SCHNEIDER & MCWILLIAMS, P.C.
George West, TX....................General Practice; Natural Resources Law

SCHNEIDER, REILLY, ZABIN & COSTELLO, P.C.
Boston, MA.............................Civil Trial Practice

SCHNEIDLER, JON G.
Seattle, WA............................Business Law; Real Estate Law

SCHNORF & SCHNORF CO., L.P.A., A PROFESSIONAL CORPORATION
Toledo, OH.............................Civil Trial Practice; Corporate Law; General Practice; Insurance Defense; Labor and Employment Law; Personal Injury; Trust and Estates, Wills and Probate

SCHOCH & WOODRUFF, L.L.P.
Greensboro, NC......................Family Law; Tax Law
High Point, NC.......................Family Law; Personal Injury; Tax Law

SCHOCHOR, FEDERICO AND STATON, P.A.
Baltimore, MD........................Civil Trial Practice; Medical Malpractice; Personal Injury; Product Liability Law

SCHOELLERMAN, JACK L.
Irvine, CA...............................Business Law

SCHOEL, OGLE, LILES AND UPSHAW, LLP
Birmingham, AL.....................Antitrust Law; Bankruptcy Law; Civil Trial Practice; Construction Law; General Practice

SCHOENBAUM, CURPHY & SCANLAN, P.C.
San Antonio, TX....................Business Law; Employment Benefits Law; Real Estate Law; Tax Law; Trust and Estates, Wills and Probate

SCHOFIELD & ASSOCIATES
Las Vegas, NV........................Construction Law; Eminent Domain

SCHOLZ, LOOS, PALMER, SIEBERS & DUESTERHAUS
Quincy, IL..............................General Practice

SCHOONMAKER, GEORGE & COLIN, P.C.
Greenwich, CT........................Family Law

SCHOTTENSTEIN, ZOX & DUNN, A LEGAL PROFESSIONAL ASSOCIATION
Columbus, OH........................Banking Law; Bankruptcy Law; Business Law; Construction Law; Employment Benefits Law; Environmental Law; General Practice; Health Care Law; Intellectual Property Law; Labor and Employment Law; Real Estate Law; Tax Law; Trust and Estates, Wills and Probate

SCHRADER BYRD & COMPANION, PLLC
Wheeling, WV.........................Banking Law; Bankruptcy Law; Civil Trial Practice; Commercial Litigation; Criminal Trial Practice; Employment Benefits Law; Family Law; General Practice; Insurance Defense; Labor and Employment Law; Medical Malpractice; Personal Injury; Real Estate Law; Tax Law

SCHRAGGER, LAVINE & NAGY
Trenton, NJ............................Business Law; Civil Trial Practice; Criminal Trial Practice; General Practice; Health Care Law; Insurance Defense; Land Use Law; Municipal and Zoning Law; Real Estate Law; Trust and Estates, Wills and Probate

SCHRAMM & PINES, L.L.C.
St. Louis, MO.........................Business Law; Civil Trial Practice; Commercial Litigation; Family Law; International Business Law; Trust and Estates, Wills and Probate

SCHRECK MORRIS
Las Vegas, NV........................Appellate Practice; Bankruptcy Law; Civil Trial Practice; Commercial Law; Labor and Employment Law; Product Liability Law; Real Estate Law

SCHROEDER & LARCHE, P.A.
Boca Raton, FL.......................Real Estate Law; Trust and Estates, Wills and Probate

SCHROETER, GOLDMARK & BENDER, P.S.
Seattle, WA............................Criminal Trial Practice; Employment Benefits Law; Medical Malpractice; Personal Injury; Product Liability Law

SCHROPP, BUELL & ELLIGETT, PROFESSIONAL ASSOCIATION
Tampa, FL...............................Appellate Practice; Civil Trial Practice

SCHUBERT, BELLWOAR, CAHILL & QUINN, A PROFESSIONAL CORPORATION
Philadelphia, PA.....................Corporate Law; Employment Benefits Law; Health Care Law; Public Utilities Law; Trust and Estates, Wills and Probate

SCHUERING ZIMMERMAN & SCULLY, LLP
Sacramento, CA......................Civil Trial Practice; Insurance Defense; Medical Malpractice; Product Liability Law

SCHULER & HALVORSON, P.A.
West Palm Beach, FL.............Medical Malpractice; Personal Injury

SCHULMAN, LEROY AND BENNETT, P.C.
Nashville, TN..........................General Practice

SCHULMAN & MCMILLAN, INCORPORATED
Costa Mesa, CA......................Criminal Trial Practice

SCHULTE ROTH & ZABEL LLP
New York, NY..........................Civil Trial Practice; Criminal Trial Practice; General Practice

SCHUMACHER, STEPHEN J.
Newport Beach, CA................Tax Law

SCHWARTZ, AMITAI
San Francisco, CA..................Appellate Practice; Civil Rights

SCHWARTZ, THEODORE F.
Clayton, MO...........................Commercial Litigation

SCHWARTZ, ARTHUR M., P.C.
Denver, CO.............................Civil Rights; Criminal Trial Practice

SCHWARTZ & BLACKMAN
Philadelphia, PA.....................Commercial Litigation; Personal Injury

SCHWARTZ, BON, WALKER & STUDER, LLC
Casper, WY............................Business Law; Commercial Litigation

SCHWARTZ, BRENDA KEEN, P.C.
Houston, TX...........................Family Law

SCHWARTZ & CERA LLP
San Francisco, CA..................Civil Trial Practice

SCHWARTZ, DAVID C., P.A.
Orlando, FL............................Civil Trial Practice; Insurance Defense; Product Liability Law

SCHWARTZ & EICHELBAUM, P.C.
Austin, TX...............................Civil Rights; Insurance Defense; Labor and Employment Law

SCHWARTZ AND ELLIS, LTD.
Arlington, VA..........................Civil Trial Practice; Family Law; International Business Law; Medical Malpractice; Personal Injury

SCHWARTZ & JALKANEN, P.C.
Southfield, MI.........................Civil Trial Practice; Family Law; Insurance Defense; Medical Malpractice; Personal Injury; Product Liability Law

SCHWARTZ, JOHN B., & ASSOCIATES
Chicago, IL.............................Civil Trial Practice; Medical Malpractice; Personal Injury

SCHWARTZ JUNELL CAMPBELL & OATHOUT, L.L.P.
Houston, TX...........................Admiralty/Maritime Law; Appellate Practice; Business Law; Civil Trial Practice; Commercial Law; Construction Law; Energy Law; Insurance Defense; Labor and Employment Law

SCHWARTZ KUCK & ASSOCIATES LLP
Atlanta, GA............................Immigration and Naturalization

SCHWARTZ & SCHWARTZ
Hallettsville, TX.....................Personal Injury

SCHWARTZ SIMON EDELSTEIN CELSO & KESSLER
Florham Park, NJ....................Civil Trial Practice; Commercial Law; Environmental Law; Family Law; Health Care Law; Labor and Employment Law

SCHWARTZ, STEINSAPIR, DOHRMANN & SOMMERS, LLP
Los Angeles, CA.....................Arbitration; Civil Trial Practice; Employment Benefits Law; Labor and Employment Law; Real Estate Law

SCHWARTZ, WISOT & WILSON, LLP
Beverly Hills, CA....................Business Law; Civil Trial Practice; Real Estate Law

SCHWARTZBERG, BARNETT & COHEN
Chicago, IL..............................Appellate Practice; Business Law; Civil Rights; Commercial Law; Construction Law; Family Law; General Practice; Health Care Law; Real Estate Law; Trust and Estates, Wills and Probate

SCHWARTZMAN, JAMES C., & ASSOCIATES, P.C.
Philadelphia, PA ....Civil Trial Practice; Commercial Litigation; Criminal Trial Practice

SCHWERIN CAMPBELL BARNARD LLP
Seattle, WA ....Labor and Employment Law

SCOBLIONKO, SCOBLIONKO, MUIR, BARTHOLOMEW & MELMAN, A PROFESSIONAL CORPORATION
Allentown, PA ....General Practice

SCOFIELD, GERARD, VERON, SINGLETARY & POHORELSKY, A PROFESSIONAL LAW CORPORATION
Lake Charles, LA.....................Civil Trial Practice; General Practice; Real Estate Law

SCOPELITIS, GARVIN, LIGHT & HANSON, P.C.
Indianapolis, IN ....Transportation Law

SCOTT, HULSE, MARSHALL, FEUILLE, FINGER & THURMOND, P.C.
El Paso, TX.............................General Practice

SCRUDATO, PAUL A.
New York, NY..........................Civil Trial Practice; Commercial Litigation; Personal Injury; Product Liability Law; Toxic Torts

SCRUGGS, JORDAN, DODD & DODD
Fort Payne, AL........................Civil Trial Practice; Corporate Law; General Practice; Insurance Defense; Personal Injury

SCUDDER LAW FIRM, P.C.
Lincoln, NE.............................Mergers and Acquisitions; Real Estate Law; Securities Law

SCULLY, SCOTT, MURPHY & PRESSER, A PROFESSIONAL CORPORATION
Garden City, NY ....Intellectual Property Law; Patent, Trademark, Copyright and Unfair Competition

SEALE, SMITH, ZUBER & BARNETTE
Baton Rouge, LA.....................Civil Trial Practice; Commercial Litigation; Insurance Defense; Personal Injury

SEARCY DENNEY SCAROLA BARNHART & SHIPLEY, PROFESSIONAL ASSOCIATION
West Palm Beach, FL ....Aviation Law; Civil Trial Practice; Commercial Law; Commercial Litigation; General Practice; Health Care Law; Labor and Employment Law; Medical Malpractice; Personal Injury; Product Liability Law; Professional Liability; Securities Law; Sports and Entertainment Law; Toxic Torts

SEARS, M.H., THE, LAW FIRM
Washington, DC.......................Patent, Trademark, Copyright and Unfair Competition

SEBALY, SHILLITO & DYER, A LEGAL PROFESSIONAL ASSOCIATION
Dayton, OH.............................Bankruptcy Law; Business Law; Civil Trial Practice; Environmental Law; Health Care Law; Labor and Employment Law; Mergers and Acquisitions; Securities Law; Trust and Estates, Wills and Probate

SEBASTIAN, DAVID A.
Birmingham, MI.......................General Practice

SECOR, CASSIDY & MCPARTLAND, P.C.
Southbury, CT..........................General Practice
Waterbury, CT ....General Practice

SECREST, HILL & FOLLUO
Tulsa, OK................................Insurance Defense; Medical Malpractice; Product Liability Law

SECREST, WARDLE, LYNCH, HAMPTON, TRUEX AND MORLEY
Farmington Hills, MI ....Insurance Defense

SEDER & CHANDLER
Worcester, MA.........................Bankruptcy Law; Business Law; Civil Trial Practice; Commercial Law; Tax Law; Trust and Estates, Wills and Probate

SEDGWICK, DETERT, MORAN & ARNOLD
San Francisco, CA ....General Practice

SEDIVY, WHITE AND WHITE, P.C. PROFESSIONAL CORPORATION
Bozeman, MT...........................General Practice

SEDWICK, EDWIN S. LAW OFFICE OF
Jeffersonville, IN ....Personal Injury

SEED AND BERRY LLP
Seattle, WA ....Intellectual Property Law; Patent, Trademark, Copyright and Unfair Competition

SEELEY, SAVIDGE AND EBERT, A LEGAL PROFESSIONAL ASSOCIATION
Cleveland, OH.........................Civil Trial Practice; General Practice; Insurance Defense; Labor and Employment Law; Municipal and Zoning Law; Securities Law; Trust and Estates, Wills and Probate

SEELIE, JOHN F.
Cleveland, OH.........................Family Law

SEGAL AND SHANKS
Louisville, KY ....Insurance Defense

SEGEL, GOLDMAN & MAZZOTTA, P.C.
Albany, NY.............................Business Law; Real Estate Law

SEHAM SEHAM MELTZ & PETERSEN, LLP
New York, NY.........................Labor and Employment Law; Public Utilities Law

SEIB LAW FIRM, THE, A PROFESSIONAL CORPORATION
Dallas, TX...............................Commercial Litigation; Creditors Rights

SEID, GERALD P.
Skillman, NJ............................Business Law; Corporate Law; General Practice

SEIDMAN, SILVERMAN & SEIDMAN, P.C.
New York, NY.........................Appellate Practice; Business Law; Civil Trial Practice; Criminal Trial Practice; Tax Law; Trademark, Copyright and Unfair Competition

SEIGEL & WOLFF, P.C.
St. Louis, MO..........................Commercial Litigation

SEIPP, FLICK & KISSANE, P.A.
Miami, FL ....Product Liability Law

SEITELMAN, MARK E. LAW OFFICES
New York, NY.........................Civil Trial Practice; Personal Injury

SELDEN LAW FIRM
San Diego, CA ....Civil Trial Practice; Construction Law; Personal Injury

SELF, GIDDENS & LEES, INC.
Oklahoma City, OK................Banking Law; Bankruptcy Law; Civil Trial Practice; Commercial Law; Natural Resources Law; Real Estate Law

SELF & SELF
Florence, AL ....Civil Trial Practice; Commercial Law; Personal Injury
Tuscumbia, AL........................Civil Trial Practice; Commercial Law

SELLAR RICHARDSON, P.C.
Roseland, NJ ....Appellate Practice; Civil Trial Practice; Insurance Defense; Product Liability Law

SELL & MELTON, L.L.P.
Macon, GA ....Banking Law; Bankruptcy Law; Business Law; Civil Trial Practice; General Practice; Health Care Law; Municipal Bond/Public Authority Financing; Personal Injury; Workers Compensation

SELMAN • BREITMAN
Los Angeles, CA ....Civil Trial Practice; Construction Law; Insurance Defense; Personal Injury

SELTZER, JAMES JAY
Emeryville, CA.........................Administrative Law; Civil Rights; Criminal Trial Practice; Health Care Law; Securities Law

SELTZER CAPLAN MCMAHON & VITEK, A PROFESSIONAL CORPORATION
San Diego, CA ....Antitrust Law; Civil Trial Practice; Criminal Trial Practice; General Practice; Tax Law

SELTZER LAW GROUP
San Francisco, CA ....Construction Law

SEMANOFF, ORMSBY & GREENBERG, LLP
Jenkintown, PA........................Business Law; Labor and Employment Law; Real Estate Law

SEMMES, JOHN GIBSON
Potomac, MD..........................Intellectual Property Law

SEMMES, BOWEN & SEMMES, A PROFESSIONAL CORPORATION
Baltimore, MD ....General Practice

SEMPLE, MILLER & MOONEY, P.C.
Denver, CO ....Education Law; Labor and Employment Law

SENECZKO LAW OFFICES, S.C.
Milwaukee, WI ....Labor and Employment Law; Workers Compensation

SENN LEWIS & VISCIANO, P.C.
Denver, CO ....Appellate Practice; Business Law; Commercial Law; Commercial Litigation; Corporate Law; General Practice; Real Estate Law

SENNIGER, POWERS, LEAVITT & ROEDEL
St. Louis, MO....Patent, Trademark, Copyright and Unfair Competition

SENTER GOLDFARB & RICE, L.L.C.
Denver, CO....Insurance Defense

SEPARK, W. ALLEN
Marietta, GA....Business Law; Commercial Law; Tax Law; Trust and Estates, Wills and Probate

SERCHUK & ZELERMYER, LLP
White Plains, NY....Banking Law; Corporate Law

SERKO & SIMON LLP
New York, NY....International Business Law; International Trade Law; Transportation Law

SERLING, MICHAEL B., P.C.
Birmingham, MI....Personal Injury; Product Liability Law

SEROTTE, ROCKMAN & WESCOTT, P.A.
Baltimore, MD....Labor and Employment Law

SESSIONS & FISHMAN, L.L.P.
New Orleans, LA....General Practice

SESSUMS, MASON & BLACK, P.A.
Tampa, FL....Family Law

SESTRIC LAW FIRM, THE
St. Louis, MO....Appellate Practice; Civil Trial Practice

SEVIER LAW FIRM, P.C.
Memphis, TN....Family Law; General Practice; Insurance Defense

SEVILA, SAUNDERS, HUDDLESTON & WHITE, A PROFESSIONAL CORPORATION
Leesburg, VA....Civil Trial Practice; Family Law; General Practice; Land Use Law; Personal Injury

SEWARD & KISSEL LLP
Washington, DC....General Practice
New York, NY....General Practice

SEYFARTH, SHAW, FAIRWEATHER & GERALDSON
Chicago, IL....General Practice

SHACKELFORD, HONENBERGER, THOMAS, WILLIS & GREGG, P.L.C.
Orange, VA....Civil Trial Practice; Criminal Trial Practice; General Practice; Personal Injury; Real Estate Law; Trust and Estates, Wills and Probate

SHACKLEFORD, PHILLIPS, WINELAND & RATCLIFF, P.A.
El Dorado, AR....Civil Trial Practice; General Practice

SHACKLETON, HAZELTINE AND BISHOP
Ship Bottom, NJ....Admiralty/Maritime Law; Civil Trial Practice; General Practice; Insurance Defense; Medical Malpractice; Personal Injury; Product Liability Law; Real Estate Law

SHAFER, DAVIS, ASHLEY, O'LEARY & STOKER, A PROFESSIONAL CORPORATION
Odessa, TX....General Practice

SHAFER, SWICK, BAILEY, IRWIN, STACK & MILLIN
Meadville, PA....General Practice

SHAFFER, RICHARD W.
Allentown, PA....Environmental Law; Land Use Law; Trust and Estates, Wills and Probate

SHAIN, SCHAFFER & RAFANELLO, A PROFESSIONAL CORPORATION
Bernardsville, NJ....Banking Law; Business Law; Corporate Law; General Practice; Real Estate Law

SHALHOUB, ROBERT M.W., P.A., LAW OFFICES OF
West Palm Beach, FL....Family Law

SHAMBAUGH, KAST, BECK & WILLIAMS, LLP
Fort Wayne, IN....Civil Trial Practice; General Practice; Tax Law; Trust and Estates, Wills and Probate

SHAMBERG, JOHNSON & BERGMAN, CHARTERED
Overland Park, KS....Civil Trial Practice; Environmental Law; Medical Malpractice; Personal Injury; Product Liability Law

SHAMBERG MARWELL HOCHERMAN DAVIS & HOLLIS, P.C.
Mount Kisco, NY....Environmental Law; Municipal and Zoning Law

SHAMBERG, WOLF, MCDERMOTT & DEPUÉ
Grand Island, NE....General Practice

SHAMEL, C. RICHARD JR.
Deerfield Beach, FL....Trust and Estates, Wills and Probate

SHANDELL, BLITZ, BLITZ, GLASS, BOOKSON & KERN, LLP
New York, NY....Medical Malpractice; Personal Injury; Product Liability Law; Toxic Torts

SHANKLIN & MCDANIEL, L.L.P.
Wilmington, NC....Commercial Law; Real Estate Law

SHANLEY, THOMAS M.
Greenwich, CT....Family Law

SHANLEY, SWEENEY, REILLY & ALLEN, P.C.
Albany, NY....Commercial Litigation; Corporate Law; Environmental Law; General Practice; Municipal and Zoning Law; Municipal Bond/Public Authority Financing; Real Estate Law

SHANNON & FLEMING, P.C.
Phoenix, AZ....Creditors Rights

SHANNONHOUSE, JOSEPH G. IV
Oklahoma City, OK....Tax Law

SHAPIRO, LEONARD H.
Owings Mills, MD....Criminal Trial Practice

SHAPIRO, WILLIAM D. LAW OFFICES OF
San Bernardino, CA....Personal Injury

SHAPIRO & ASSOCIATES
Boston, MA....Insurance Defense; Personal Injury

SHAPIRO, COHEN
Ottawa, ON, Canada....Patent, Trademark, Copyright and Unfair Competition

SHAPIRO & CROLAND
Hackensack, NJ....Bankruptcy Law; Business Law; Civil Trial Practice; Commercial Litigation; Corporate Law; Family Law; General Practice; Real Estate Law; Tax Law

SHAPIRO & DECTOR, P.A.
Boca Raton, FL....Commercial Litigation; Real Estate Law

SHAPIRO, LIFSCHITZ AND SCHRAM, P.C.
Washington, DC....Construction Law

SHARP, CHRISTOPHER G., P.C.
Dallas, TX....Administrative Law; Health Care Law; Real Estate Law

SHARP, SMITH & HARRISON, P.A.
Tampa, FL....International Business Law; Tax Law

SHARP, TERRY, P.C., LAW OFFICE OF
Mount Vernon, IL....Bankruptcy Law; Commercial Law; Real Estate Law

SHARPE & KRUEGER
Kingsville, TX....General Practice

SHARPNACK, BIGLEY, DAVID & RUMPLE
Columbus, IN....Civil Trial Practice; Family Law; General Practice; Insurance Defense; Trust and Estates, Wills and Probate

SHARTSIS, FRIESE & GINSBURG LLP
San Francisco, CA....General Practice

SHAW LAW FIRM
Fort Smith, AR....General Practice

SHAW, LICITRA, BOHNER, ESERNIO & SCHWARTZ, P.C.
Garden City, NY....Appellate Practice; Bankruptcy Law; General Practice

SHAW, MADDOX, GRAHAM, MONK & BOLING, LLP
Rome, GA....Civil Trial Practice; General Practice

SHAWE & ROSENTHAL
Baltimore, MD....Labor and Employment Law

SHAYNE, DACHS, STANISCI, CORKER & SAUER
Mineola, NY....Insurance Defense; Medical Malpractice; Personal Injury; Professional Liability

SHEA & ASSOCIATES
Cincinnati, OH....Civil Trial Practice; Medical Malpractice; Personal Injury; Product Liability Law

SHEA & SHEA, A PROFESSIONAL LAW CORPORATION
San Jose, CA....Civil Trial Practice; Personal Injury; Product Liability Law

SHEAFFER, WILLIAM J., P.A.
Orlando, FL....Criminal Trial Practice

SHEARMAN & STERLING
San Francisco, CA....General Practice
Washington, DC....General Practice
New York, NY....General Practice
Beijing, China....General Practice
Hong Kong, China....General Practice
London, England....General Practice

Paris, France....................General Practice
Düsseldorf, Germany..........General Practice
Frankfurt/Main, Germany......General Practice
Tokyo, Japan......................General Practice
Singapore, Singapore............General Practice
Abu Dhabi, United Arab Emirates.....................General Practice

SHEEHAN PHINNEY BASS + GREEN, PROFESSIONAL ASSOCIATION
Manchester, NH....................Commercial Law; Environmental Law; General Practice; Insurance Defense; Labor and Employment Law; Personal Injury; Product Liability Law; Securities Law; Tax Law
Portsmouth, NH....................Labor and Employment Law; Tax Law

SHEEHY, LOVELACE & MAYFIELD, P.C. A PROFESSIONAL CORPORATION
Waco, TX....................Civil Trial Practice; General Practice

SHEFFER • HUTCHINSON • KINNEY
Henderson, KY....................General Practice
Louisville, KY....................General Practice
Owensboro, KY....................General Practice
Paducah, KY....................General Practice

SHEIMAN, RONALD L.
Westport, CT....................Business Law; Tax Law; Trust and Estates, Wills and Probate

SHEKETOFF & HOMAN
Boston, MA....................Criminal Trial Practice

SHELL, BUFORD, BUFKIN, CALLICUTT & PERRY
Jackson, MS....................Civil Trial Practice; Insurance Defense

SHELL, FLEMING, DAVIS & MENGE, P.A.
Pensacola, FL....................General Practice

SHELLOW, SHELLOW & GLYNN, S.C.
Milwaukee, WI....................Criminal Trial Practice

SHELTON & VALADEZ, P.C.
San Antonio, TX....................Civil Trial Practice; Insurance Defense

SHENKER, ARDEN E.
Portland, OR....................Civil Trial Practice

SHEPARD, FILBURN & GOODBLATT, P.A.
Orlando, FL....................Civil Trial Practice; Insurance Defense

SHEPHERD & CRABTREE
Chico, CA....................Insurance Defense; Labor and Employment Law

SHEPHERD, GARY & MCWHORTER
Swainsboro, GA....................Insurance Defense; Real Estate Law

SHEPPARD, MULLIN, RICHTER & HAMPTON LLP
Los Angeles, CA....................General Practice

SHEPPARD, WHITE & THOMAS, P.A.
Jacksonville, FL....................Appellate Practice; Civil Rights; Criminal Trial Practice

SHER GARNER CAHILL RICHTER KLEIN MCALISTER & HILBERT, L.L.C.
New Orleans, LA....................General Practice

SHERESKY ARONSON & MAYEFSKY, LLP
New York, NY....................Family Law

SHERIDAN ROSS, P.C.
Denver, CO....................Intellectual Property Law; Patent, Trademark, Copyright and Unfair Competition; Trademark, Copyright and Unfair Competition

SHERIN AND LODGEN LLP
Boston, MA....................Business Law; Civil Trial Practice; General Practice; Real Estate Law

SHERMAN, WILLIAM F.
Little Rock, AR....................General Practice

SHERMAN & HOWARD L.L.C.
Colorado Springs, CO....................General Practice
Denver, CO....................Antitrust Law; Banking Law; Civil Trial Practice; General Practice; Labor and Employment Law; Municipal Bond/Public Authority Financing; Natural Resources Law; Tax Law; Trust and Estates, Wills and Probate

SHERMAN & SHALLOWAY
Alexandria, VA....................Patent, Trademark, Copyright and Unfair Competition

SHERMAN, SILVERSTEIN, KOHL, ROSE & PODOLSKY, A PROFESSIONAL CORPORATION
Pennsauken, NJ....................General Practice; Pension and Profit Sharing

SHERMAN, STEPHEN A., & ASSOCIATES
Oklahoma City, OK....................Commercial Law; Real Estate Law

SHERMETA, CHIMKO & KILPATRICK, P.C.
Rochester Hills, MI....................Bankruptcy Law; Commercial Law; Commercial Litigation

SHERRILL, CROSNOE & GOFF, A PROFESSIONAL CORPORATION
Wichita Falls, TX....................General Practice

SHERRILL & ROOF, L.L.P.
Columbia, SC....................Banking Law; Business Law; Elder Law; Public Utilities Law

SHERWOOD AND HARDGROVE
Los Angeles, CA....................Real Estate Law

SHERWOOD, KLEIN, DUDLEY & ABRAM, P.A.
Phoenix, AZ....................Commercial Litigation; Personal Injury

SHIBLEY, JEFFERY L., P.A., A LAW OFFICE OF
Tampa, FL....................Civil Trial Practice; Personal Injury; Product Liability Law

SHIBLEY RIGHTON
Toronto, ON, Canada....................General Practice

SHIELDS LAW OFFICE, P.A.
St. John, KS....................General Practice

SHIGLEY LAW FIRM, L.L.C.
Atlanta, GA....................Personal Injury; Product Liability Law

SHIMKO, TIMOTHY A., & ASSOCIATES, A LEGAL PROF. ASSN.
Cleveland, OH....................Antitrust Law; Civil Trial Practice; Labor and Employment Law; Medical Malpractice; Personal Injury; Product Liability Law

SHIMMEL, HILL, BISHOP & GRUENDER, P.C.
Phoenix, AZ....................Bankruptcy Law; Civil Trial Practice; Commercial Litigation; Construction Law; Creditors Rights; Employment Benefits Law; Family Law; Insurance Defense; Labor and Employment Law; Real Estate Law; Tax Law; Trust and Estates, Wills and Probate

SHINE & MASON LAW OFFICE
Kingsport, TN....................General Practice; Labor and Employment Law; Workers Compensation

SHINGLES & CAPPELLI
Blue Bell, PA....................Appellate Practice; Civil Trial Practice; Criminal Trial Practice; Personal Injury

SHINN, STEERMAN & SHINN
Lamar, CO....................General Practice; Trust and Estates, Wills and Probate

SHIOTANI & INOUYE
Los Angeles, CA....................Business Law; Real Estate Law; Tax Law; Trust and Estates, Wills and Probate

SHIPLEY & ASSOCIATES
Fort Wayne, IN....................Bankruptcy Law; Commercial Law; Commercial Litigation

SHIPLEY, JENNINGS & CHAMPLIN, P.C.
Tulsa, OK....................Civil Trial Practice; Environmental Law

SHIPMAN & ASSOCIATES, L.L.P.
Wilmington, NC....................Construction Law; Medical Malpractice; Personal Injury

SHIPMAN & GOODWIN LLP
Hartford, CT....................Environmental Law; General Practice; Labor and Employment Law; Trust and Estates, Wills and Probate
Lakeville, CT....................General Practice
Stamford, CT....................General Practice

SHIRINIAN & ROITMAN
Las Vegas, NV....................Commercial Litigation; Construction Law; Corporate Law; Trust and Estates, Wills and Probate

SHIRK, WORK & ROBINSON, P.C.
Oklahoma City, OK....................General Practice

SHIRLEY, L. MERRILL
Elba, AL....................Insurance Defense; Personal Injury; Workers Compensation

SHLIMBAUM, SHLIMBAUM AND JABLONSKI
Islip, NY....................Family Law; Municipal and Zoning Law; Personal Injury

SHOCKEY & ZIOBER, A PROFESSIONAL LAW CORPORATION
Baton Rouge, LA....................Bankruptcy Law; Civil Trial Practice; Environmental Law; Insurance Defense; Workers Compensation

SHOECRAFT, JAMES W., P.C., ATTORNEYS' OFFICES OF
Dallas, TX....................Personal Injury

SHOFI, HENNEN, GRAMOVOT & ASSOCIATES
Tampa, FL .... Insurance Defense; Professional Liability

SHOOK, HARDY & BACON L.L.P.
Kansas City, MO .... General Practice

SHOR, FRANK LAW OFFICES OF
Carrollton, TX .... Civil Trial Practice; Criminal Trial Practice

SHORALL & STEVENS, P.C.
Phoenix, AZ .... Insurance Defense

SHORT, KEVIN J.
Minneapolis, MN .... Criminal Trial Practice

SHORT & JENKINS, A PROFESSIONAL LEGAL CORPORATION
Houston, TX .... Civil Trial Practice

SHOUN & BACH, P.C.
Fairfax, VA .... Family Law

SHRAGER, MCDAID, LOFTUS, FLUM & SPIVEY
Philadelphia, PA .... Medical Malpractice; Personal Injury

SHREVE, DAVID WILLIAM
Altavista, VA .... Civil Trial Practice

SHUFORD, CADDELL & FRALEY
Salisbury, NC .... General Practice

SHUGHART THOMSON & KILROY, A PROFESSIONAL CORPORATION
Overland Park, KS .... General Practice
Kansas City, MO .... Antitrust Law; Civil Trial Practice; General Practice; Labor and Employment Law

SHULLAW, WAYNE A.
Lafayette, LA .... Banking Law; Commercial Litigation

SHULMAN, CURTIN, GRUNDNER, REGAN & SNYDER, P.C.
Syracuse, NY .... Municipal and Zoning Law; Real Estate Law

SHULTZ & ROLLINS, LTD.
Tucson, AZ .... Civil Trial Practice; Medical Malpractice; Personal Injury

SHUMAKER, LOOP & KENDRICK, LLP
Columbus, OH .... Environmental Law
Toledo, OH .... Commercial Litigation; Construction Law; Environmental Law

SHUMAN, MORTON J.
Framingham, MA .... Personal Injury; Workers Compensation

SHUMAN ANNAND BAILEY WYANT & EARLES
Charleston, WV .... Appellate Practice; Business Law; Construction Law; General Practice; Insurance Defense; Medical Malpractice; Product Liability Law

SHUMARD, THOMAS J.
Phoenix, AZ .... Trust and Estates, Wills and Probate

SHUPE, REAGAN & WYNE
Santa Ana, CA .... Insurance Defense

SHUSTERMAN, CARL LAW OFFICES OF
Los Angeles, CA .... Immigration and Naturalization

SHUTTLEWORTH & INGERSOLL, P.C.
Cedar Rapids, IA .... Administrative Law; Banking Law; Civil Trial Practice; General Practice; Insurance Defense; Labor and Employment Law; Patent, Trademark, Copyright and Unfair Competition; Real Estate Law; Tax Law; Trust and Estates, Wills and Probate

SHUTTLEWORTH RULOFF & GIORDANO, P.C.
Virginia Beach, VA .... Criminal Trial Practice; Medical Malpractice; Personal Injury; Product Liability Law

SHUTTS & BOWEN LLP
Miami, FL .... Admiralty/Maritime Law; Antitrust Law; General Practice; Tax Law
Orlando, FL .... General Practice
West Palm Beach, FL .... General Practice

SIBBISON, WENDY
Greenfield, MA .... Appellate Practice

SIBLEY, THOMAS J., P.C.
Beaumont, TX .... Commercial Law

SIDKOFF, PINCUS & GREEN, P.C.
Philadelphia, PA .... Civil Trial Practice

SIDLEY & AUSTIN
Washington, DC .... General Practice
Chicago, IL .... General Practice

SIDLEY & BELL LLP
Los Angeles, CA .... Civil Trial Practice; Criminal Trial Practice

SIEBEN, GROSE, VON HOLTUM & CAREY, LTD.
Minneapolis, MN .... Medical Malpractice; Personal Injury; Workers Compensation

SIEBEN, POLK, LAVERDIERE, JONES & HAWN, A PROFESSIONAL ASSOCIATION
Hastings, MN .... Civil Trial Practice; Personal Injury

SIEGEL, BRILL, GREUPNER, DUFFY & FOSTER, P.A.
Minneapolis, MN .... Antitrust Law; Civil Trial Practice; General Practice; Land Use Law

SIEGEL, GREENFIELD, HAYES & GROSS, P.L.C.
Southfield, MI .... Corporate Law; Tax Law; Trust and Estates, Wills and Probate

SIEGFRIED, RIVERA, LERNER, DE LA TORRE & SOBEL, P.A.
Miami, FL .... Civil Trial Practice; Commercial Law; Commercial Litigation; Construction Law; Corporate Law; Real Estate Law

SIEMION, HUCKABAY, BODARY, PADILLA, MORGANTI & BOWERMAN, P.C.
Southfield, MI .... Civil Trial Practice; Insurance Defense

SIFFORD & ANDERSON, L.L.P.
Dallas, TX .... Aviation Law; Insurance Defense; Personal Injury; Product Liability Law

SIGERMAN, JON B. THE LAW OFFICES OF
San Francisco, CA .... Labor and Employment Law

SIGMON, CLARK, MACKIE, HUTTON & HANVEY, P.A.
Hickory, NC .... Civil Trial Practice; General Practice; Real Estate Law

SIKES, GRIFFIN JR.
Montgomery, AL .... Civil Trial Practice

SIKORA, FREDERICK J., P.A.
Warren, NJ .... Family Law

SILBER & VALENTE, P.A.
West Palm Beach, FL .... Aviation Law; Personal Injury

SILK, ADLER & COLVIN, A LAW CORPORATION
San Francisco, CA .... Tax Law

SILLS, NANCY M.
Albany, NY .... Tax Law; Trust and Estates, Wills and Probate

SILLS CUMMIS RADIN TISCHMAN EPSTEIN & GROSS, A PROFESSIONAL CORPORATION
Atlantic City, NJ .... General Practice
Newark, NJ .... Administrative Law; Antitrust Law; Appellate Practice; Banking Law; Bankruptcy Law; Business Law; Civil Rights; Civil Trial Practice; Commercial Law; Commercial Litigation; Communications Law; Computer Law; Construction Law; Criminal Trial Practice; Employment Benefits Law; Energy Law; Environmental Law; Family Law; General Practice; Health Care Law; Insurance Defense; International Business Law; International Trade Law; Labor and Employment Law; Land Use Law; Medical Malpractice; Municipal and Zoning Law; Municipal Bond/Public Authority Financing; Natural Resources Law; Patent, Trademark, Copyright and Unfair Competition; Personal Injury; Product Liability Law; Public Utilities Law; Real Estate Law; Securities Law; Sports and Entertainment Law; Tax Law; Transportation Law; Trust and Estates, Wills and Probate
New York, NY .... General Practice

SÍLVA, RIEDER & MAESTAS, P.C.
Albuquerque, NM .... Civil Trial Practice; Commercial Litigation; Criminal Trial Practice; Labor and Employment Law

SILVER & BROWN, A PROFESSIONAL CORPORATION
Fairfax, VA .... Commercial Litigation

SILVER, FREEDMAN & TAFF, L.L.P.
Washington, DC .... Banking Law; Mergers and Acquisitions

SILVER, GOLUB & TEITELL LLP
Stamford, CT .... Civil Trial Practice; Commercial Litigation; Criminal Trial Practice; Family Law; General Practice; Medical Malpractice; Personal Injury; Product Liability Law

SILVERMAN & DECARIA, CHARTERED
Reno, NV .... Family Law

SILVERMAN FRIMMER BERNHEIM & MCDONNELL, A PROFESSIONAL CORPORATION
Philadelphia, PA .... Banking Law; Insurance Defense

SILVERSTEIN AND MULLENS, P.L.L.C.
Washington, DC....................Tax Law

SIM, HUGHES, ASHTON & MCKAY
Toronto, ON, Canada..............Computer Law; Intellectual Property Law; Patent, Trademark, Copyright and Unfair Competition

SIMKE CHODOS
Los Angeles, CA....................Civil Trial Practice; Commercial Litigation; Sports and Entertainment Law

SIMKINS & SIMKINS, P.C.
Northville, MI........................Personal Injury

SIMMONS AND DERR
Winnfield, LA..........................Banking Law; Civil Trial Practice; General Practice; Real Estate Law; Trust and Estates, Wills and Probate

SIMMONS, GRIFFIN & LYDON, L.L.P.
Columbia, SC..........................Environmental Law

SIMMONS, OLSEN, EDIGER, SELZER, FERGUSON & CARNEY, P.C.
Scottsbluff, NE.......................General Practice

SIMMONS, WARREN, SZCZECKO & MCFEE, PROFESSIONAL ASSOCIATION
Decatur, GA............................Business Law; Civil Trial Practice; Family Law; Real Estate Law

SIMON, FITZGERALD, COOKE, REED & WELCH
Shreveport, LA........................Bankruptcy Law; General Practice

SIMON, MCKINSEY, MILLER, ZOMMICK, SANDOR & DUNDAS, A LAW CORPORATION
Long Beach, CA.......................Trust and Estates, Wills and Probate

SIMON & SCHMIDT
Delray Beach, FL....................General Practice

SIMON AND SIMON
Kansas City, MO.....................Criminal Trial Practice

SIMON, TURNBULL & MARTIN, CHARTERED
Washington, DC.......................Business Law

SIMONCINI & ASSOCIATES
San Jose, CA..........................Construction Law; Insurance Defense

SIMONE, ROBERTS & WEISS, P.A.
Albuquerque, NM....................Civil Trial Practice; Insurance Defense; Medical Malpractice; Personal Injury; Product Liability Law

SIMONS, CUDDY & FRIEDMAN, LLP
Santa Fe, NM..........................Insurance Defense; Labor and Employment Law

SIMPSON, GARY HOWARD
Bethesda, MD..........................Arbitration; Civil Rights; Civil Trial Practice; Constitutional Law; Labor and Employment Law

SIMPSON AYCOCK, P.A.
Morganton, NC........................General Practice

SIMPSON & BOYD, P.L.L.C.
Decatur, TX............................Civil Trial Practice; Commercial Litigation; Product Liability Law

SIMPSON, KABLACK & BELL
Indiana, PA............................General Practice

SIMPSON, KEPLER & EDWARDS, LC
Cody, WY................................General Practice; Trust and Estates, Wills and Probate

SIMPSON, STEVEN D., P.A., LAW OFFICES OF
Raleigh, NC............................Nonprofit and Tax Exempt Organizations

SIMPSON THACHER & BARTLETT
New York, NY.........................General Practice
Columbus, OH.........................General Practice
Hong Kong, China....................General Practice
London, England......................General Practice
Tokyo, Japan..........................General Practice
Singapore, Singapore................General Practice

SIMS, FLEMING & SPURLIN, P.C.
Tifton, GA..............................General Practice

SINCLAIR, I.B. LAW OFFICES
State College, PA....................Family Law

SINCLAIR LAW FIRM, THE
Bowie, MD.............................Trust and Estates, Wills and Probate

SINDEL & SINDEL, P.C.
St. Louis, MO.........................Criminal Trial Practice; Personal Injury

SINGER, ROBERT S.
Miami, FL...............................Personal Injury

SINGER FRUMENTO LLP
New York, NY.........................Securities Law

SINGLETARY LAW FIRM, P.A.
Tampa, FL..............................Personal Injury

SINGLETON & SINGLETON
Mount Kisco, NY.....................General Practice; Municipal and Zoning Law; Real Estate Law

SINGLETON URQUHART
Vancouver, BC, Canada...........Construction Law; Environmental Law; General Practice; Insurance Defense; Product Liability Law; Toxic Torts

SINIARD, MCKINNEY & BRASWELL, P.C., THE LAW FIRM OF
Huntsville, AL.........................Medical Malpractice; Personal Injury; Workers Compensation

SINKELDAM, GARY P. LAW OFFICE OF
Las Vegas, NV........................Construction Law

SINKLER & BOYD, P.A.
Charleston, SC........................Admiralty/Maritime Law; Civil Trial Practice; General Practice; Municipal Bond/Public Authority Financing
Columbia, SC..........................Admiralty/Maritime Law; Civil Trial Practice; General Practice; Municipal Bond/Public Authority Financing
Greenville, SC.........................Municipal Bond/Public Authority Financing

SINK, POWERS, SINK & POTTER, L.L.P.
Raleigh, NC............................General Practice

SINNOTT, DITO, MOURA & PUEBLA
Los Angeles, CA.....................Commercial Litigation

SINOFF, BARRY S., P.A., LAW OFFICE OF
Jacksonville, FL......................Family Law

SINSHEIMER, SCHIEBELHUT & BAGGETT, A PROFESSIONAL CORPORATION
San Luis Obispo, CA...............General Practice

SINTZ, CAMPBELL, DUKE & TAYLOR
Mobile, AL.............................Civil Rights; Civil Trial Practice; Constitutional Law; Corporate Law; Education Law; Insurance Defense; Labor and Employment Law; Product Liability Law; Workers Compensation

SIRKIN PINALES MEZIBOV & SCHWARTZ
Cincinnati, OH........................Civil Trial Practice; Constitutional Law; Criminal Trial Practice; Labor and Employment Law

SIROTA & SIROTA, LLP
New York, NY.........................Securities Law

SISTARE & ASSOCIATES
Fort Lauderdale, FL................Civil Trial Practice; Insurance Defense; Medical Malpractice; Personal Injury; Professional Liability

SITLINGER, MCGLINCY, STEINER, THEILER & KAREM
Louisville, KY.........................Civil Trial Practice; Insurance Defense; Medical Malpractice

SIXBEY, FRIEDMAN, LEEDOM & FERGUSON, P.C.
McLean, VA............................Patent, Trademark, Copyright and Unfair Competition

SJOBERG & VOTTA LAW OFFICES
Warwick, RI............................Trust and Estates, Wills and Probate

SKADDEN, ARPS, SLATE, MEAGHER & FLOM LLP
New York, NY.........................Bankruptcy Law; Criminal Trial Practice; General Practice; Labor and Employment Law

SKARECKY & HOLDER, A PROFESSIONAL ASSOCIATION
Phoenix, AZ............................Creditors Rights

SKELDING, LABASKY & DAWS, A PROFESSIONAL ASSOCIATION
Tallahassee, FL......................Administrative Law

SKELLEY ROTTNER P.C.
Hartford, CT...........................Insurance Defense

SKELTON, TAINTOR & ABBOTT, A PROFESSIONAL CORPORATION
Auburn, ME.............................General Practice

SKJERVEN, MORRILL, MACPHERSON, FRANKLIN & FRIEL LLP
Newport Beach, CA.................Patent, Trademark, Copyright and Unfair Competition
San Francisco, CA..................General Practice; Patent, Trademark, Copyright and Unfair Competition
San Jose, CA..........................General Practice; Patent, Trademark, Copyright and Unfair Competition

SKOKOS, BEQUETTE & BILLINGSLEY, P.A.
Little Rock, AR.......................Business Law; Civil Trial Practice; Commercial Litigation

SKOLER, ABBOTT & PRESSER, P.C.
Springfield, MA........................Employment Benefits Law; Labor and Employment Law
Worcester, MA........................Employment Benefits Law; Labor and Employment Law

SKOLOFF & WOLFE, P.C.
Livingston, NJ........................Family Law; General Practice; Municipal and Zoning Law; Real Estate Law; Tax Law

SKOUSEN, SKOUSEN, GULBRANDSEN & PATIENCE, P.C.
Mesa, AZ........................Personal Injury

SKULINA, THOMAS R.
Westlake, OH........................Civil Trial Practice

SLACK & DAVIS, L.L.P.
Austin, TX........................Aviation Law; Commercial Litigation; Personal Injury; Product Liability Law

SLADE & ASSOCIATES, P.C.
New York, NY........................Commercial Litigation; Criminal Trial Practice; Labor and Employment Law; Trademark, Copyright and Unfair Competition

SLATER, MILDRED FLETCHER
Upperville, VA........................Real Estate Law

SLATER LAW FIRM, A PROFESSIONAL CORPORATION
New Orleans, LA........................Antitrust Law; Business Law; Commercial Litigation; Environmental Law; Product Liability Law; Transportation Law

SLATES, RONALD P., P.C.
Los Angeles, CA........................Bankruptcy Law; Commercial Litigation; Creditors Rights; Real Estate Law

SLAVET, ARNOLD L.
Boston, MA........................Trust and Estates, Wills and Probate

SLAVIN, FRANCIS J., P.C.
Phoenix, AZ........................Real Estate Law

SLAWSON CUNNINGHAM WHALEN & STEWART, P.L.
Palm Beach Gardens, FL........Civil Trial Practice; Personal Injury

SLAYDON, KATHLEEN AMELIA, P.C.
Houston, TX........................Commercial Litigation

SLEVIN & HART, P.C.
Washington, DC........................Employment Benefits Law

SLEWETT, ROBERT D., P.A.
North Miami Beach, FL........Trust and Estates, Wills and Probate

SLICKER, FREDERICK K.
Tulsa, OK........................Business Law

SLIVKA ROBINSON WATERS & O'DORISIO, A PROFESSIONAL CORPORATION
Denver, CO........................Banking Law; Labor and Employment Law; Mergers and Acquisitions; Real Estate Law; Tax Law

SLOAN, TODD M. LAW OFFICES OF
Malibu, CA........................Civil Trial Practice

SLOAN, RUBENS & PEEPLES
West Memphis, AR........................Banking Law; Civil Trial Practice; General Practice

SLOMSKI, RAYMOND J., P.C., LAW OFFICES OF
Phoenix, AZ........................Medical Malpractice; Personal Injury

SLOTCHIVER & SLOTCHIVER, L.L.P.
Charleston, SC........................Civil Trial Practice; Tax Law

SMALL, DANIEL W.
Nashville, TN........................Banking Law; Commercial Litigation

SMALLEY, ROBERT H., JR., P.C.
Griffin, GA........................Banking Law; Civil Trial Practice; General Practice

SMALL LARKIN, LLP
Los Angeles, CA........................Intellectual Property Law; Patent, Trademark, Copyright and Unfair Competition

SMALL, TOTH, BALDRIDGE & VAN BELKUM, P.C.
Bingham Farms, MI........................Business Law; Civil Trial Practice; Construction Law; Health Care Law; Insurance Defense; Medical Malpractice; Product Liability Law

SMALLWOOD-COOK & SCHMIEDER
Warsaw, NY........................Family Law; General Practice; Real Estate Law; Trust and Estates, Wills and Probate

SMART & BIGGAR
Vancouver, BC, Canada........Intellectual Property Law; Patent, Trademark, Copyright and Unfair Competition; Trademark, Copyright and Unfair Competition
Ottawa, ON, Canada........................Intellectual Property Law; Patent, Trademark, Copyright and Unfair Competition; Trademark, Copyright and Unfair Competition
Toronto, ON, Canada........................Intellectual Property Law; Patent, Trademark, Copyright and Unfair Competition; Trademark, Copyright and Unfair Competition

SMITH, DANIEL T.
Denver, CO........................Criminal Trial Practice

SMITH, DAVID RANDOLPH & ASSOCIATES
Nashville, TN........................Civil Trial Practice; Medical Malpractice; Personal Injury; Product Liability Law

SMITH, E. ALFRED & ASSOCIATES
Philadelphia, PA........................Civil Trial Practice

SMITH, ROBERT B.
Jesup, GA........................Civil Trial Practice; Personal Injury

SMITH, WALTER LANDRY
Baton Rouge, LA........................Personal Injury

SMITH, A. RUSSELL
Akron, OH........................Civil Trial Practice; Medical Malpractice; Personal Injury

SMITH, ANDREWS, ROGERS & BRADY
Tampa, FL........................Workers Compensation

SMITH, BARTLETT, HEEKE, CARPENTER, LEWIS & THOMPSON
Jeffersonville, IN........................General Practice

SMITH & BEMENDERFER
Indianapolis, IN........................Insurance Defense

SMITH, BRIAN E., THE LAW FIRM
Yuma, AZ........................Civil Trial Practice; Personal Injury; Product Liability Law

SMITH & BROOKER, P.C.
Bay City, MI........................Insurance Defense

SMITH & CASHION, PLC
Nashville, TN........................Commercial Litigation; Construction Law

SMITH, CURRIE & HANCOCK LLP
Atlanta, GA........................Construction Law; Environmental Law; Government Contracts; Labor and Employment Law

SMITH DEBNAM NARRON WYCHE STORY & MYERS, L.L.P.
Raleigh, NC........................Administrative Law; Appellate Practice; Bankruptcy Law; Civil Trial Practice; Commercial Law

SMITH & DUGGAN LLP
Boston, MA........................Commercial Litigation; Product Liability Law

SMITH ELLIOTT SMITH & GARMEY, P.A.
Saco, ME........................Civil Trial Practice; General Practice; Medical Malpractice; Personal Injury

SMITH & ELY, LLP
Birmingham, AL........................Appellate Practice; Civil Trial Practice; Commercial Litigation; Insurance Defense; Personal Injury; Product Liability Law; Professional Liability; Transportation Law; Workers Compensation

SMITH, FINKELSTEIN, LUNDBERG, ISLER AND YAKABOSKI, LLP
Riverhead, NY........................Civil Trial Practice; General Practice

SMITH, GAMBRELL & RUSSELL, LLP
Washington, DC........................Intellectual Property Law; Patent, Trademark, Copyright and Unfair Competition

SMITH, GENDLER, SHIELL, SHEFF & FORD, P.A.
Minneapolis, MN........................Real Estate Law

SMITH, GILLIAM AND WILLIAMS
Gainesville, GA........................Corporate Law; General Practice; Insurance Defense; Real Estate Law; Tax Law

SMITH, GOLDSTEIN, MAGRAM & BERENATO, A PROFESSIONAL CORPORATION
Burlington, NJ........................Civil Trial Practice; General Practice; Medical Malpractice; Personal Injury; Product Liability Law

SMITH, GRIMSLEY, BAUMAN, PINKERTON, PETERMANN & WELLS
Fort Walton Beach, FL........General Practice

SMITH & HALE
Columbus, OH........................Municipal Bond/Public Authority Financing; Real Estate Law

SMITH AND HAMM, P.A.
Lake Alfred, FL........................Family Law

SMITH & HARRINGTON
Eastman, GA........................Civil Trial Practice

SMITH HAUGHEY RICE & ROEGGE, P.C.
East Lansing, MI........................Civil Trial Practice; General Practice; Insurance Defense; Medical Malpractice
Grand Rapids, MI........................Civil Trial Practice; General Practice; Insurance Defense; Medical Malpractice

Lansing, MI....Civil Trial Practice; General Practice; Insurance Defense; Medical Malpractice
Traverse City, MI....Civil Trial Practice; General Practice; Insurance Defense; Medical Malpractice

SMITH HELMS MULLISS & MOORE, L.L.P.
Charlotte, NC....General Practice
Greensboro, NC....General Practice
Raleigh, NC....General Practice

SMITH, HOWARD & AJAX, LLP
Atlanta, GA....Aviation Law; Civil Trial Practice; Construction Law; Insurance Defense; Medical Malpractice; Patent, Trademark, Copyright and Unfair Competition; Product Liability Law; Securities Law

SMITH HULSEY & BUSEY
Jacksonville, FL....Business Law; Commercial Litigation; Environmental Law; Health Care Law; Real Estate Law; Tax Law

SMITH & JAKUBOWSKI
Abington, PA....Trust and Estates, Wills and Probate

SMITH & JENSEN, P.C. A PROFESSIONAL CORPORATION
Richmond, VA....Insurance Defense; Product Liability Law

SMITH & JOHNSON, ATTORNEYS, P.C.
Traverse City, MI....Commercial Litigation; Corporate Law; Family Law; Personal Injury

SMITH, KATZENSTEIN & FURLOW LLP
Wilmington, DE....Bankruptcy Law; Business Law; Civil Trial Practice; Commercial Law; General Practice; Insurance Defense; Labor and Employment Law; Medical Malpractice; Personal Injury; Product Liability Law; Securities Law

SMITH LARSEN & WIXOM, CHARTERED
Las Vegas, NV....Banking Law; Commercial Litigation; Construction Law; Insurance Defense; Real Estate Law

SMITH LAW FIRM, THE, L.L.P.
Leesville, LA....Personal Injury

SMITH, LEWIS, BECKETT, POWELL, ROARK & DURLEY, L.L.P.
Columbia, MO....General Practice

SMITH LYONS
Toronto, ON, Canada....General Practice

SMITH, MARSHALL, WEAVER AND VERGON
Cleveland, OH....Civil Trial Practice; Insurance Defense; Product Liability Law

SMITH, MAURRAS, COHEN, REDD & HORAN, PLC
Fort Smith, AR....Business Law; Commercial Litigation

SMITH MAZURE DIRECTOR WILKINS YOUNG YAGERMAN & TARALLO, P.C.
New York, NY....Civil Trial Practice; General Practice; Insurance Defense; Toxic Torts

SMITH MCCULLOUGH, P.C.
Denver, CO....Franchise Law

SMITH & MCELWAIN
Sioux City, IA....Labor and Employment Law; Workers Compensation

SMITH & MOORE
Dallas, TX....Aviation Law; Insurance Defense

SMITH, NEVILLE, LAW FIRM OF
Manchester, KY....General Practice

SMITH AND NOWLIN
Ventura, CA....Family Law

SMITH PETERSON LAW FIRM
Council Bluffs, IA....Business Law; Commercial Law; Insurance Defense; Labor and Employment Law; Real Estate Law; Tax Law; Trust and Estates, Wills and Probate

SMITH, PHILLIP R., P.C.
Martinsville, IN....General Practice

SMITH, PHILLIPS, MITCHELL, SCOTT & RUTHERFORD
Batesville, MS....Personal Injury

SMITH, RANSCHT, CONNORS, MUTINO, NORDELL & SIRIGNANO, P.C.
White Plains, NY....Commercial Litigation; Corporate Law; General Practice; Real Estate Law; Tax Law; Trust and Estates, Wills and Probate

SMITH, SABBATINI & MCLEARY, PLLC
Memphis, TN....Civil Trial Practice; Commercial Litigation; General Practice; Health Care Law; Insurance Defense; Labor and Employment Law; Medical Malpractice; Personal Injury; Product Liability Law; Professional Liability; Toxic Torts; Workers Compensation

SMITH, SAUER & DEMARIA
Pensacola, FL....General Practice

SMITH & SMITH
Vero Beach, FL....Civil Trial Practice; General Practice; Trust and Estates, Wills and Probate

SMITH AND SMITH
Louisville, KY....Labor and Employment Law

SMITH, SOVIK, KENDRICK & SUGNET, P.C.
Syracuse, NY....General Practice; Medical Malpractice; Workers Compensation

SMITH, SPIRES & PEDDY, P.C.
Birmingham, AL....Civil Trial Practice; Health Care Law; Insurance Defense; Product Liability Law; Workers Compensation

SMITH, STRATTON, WISE, HEHER & BRENNAN
Princeton, NJ....General Practice

SMITH, UNDERWOOD & PERKINS, A PROFESSIONAL CORPORATION
Dallas, TX....Banking Law; Business Law; Civil Trial Practice; Commercial Law; Commercial Litigation; Construction Law; Employment Benefits Law; General Practice; Insurance Defense; Intellectual Property Law; International Business Law; Labor and Employment Law; Land Use Law; Medical Malpractice; Mergers and Acquisitions; Pension and Profit Sharing; Professional Liability; Real Estate Law; Securities Law; Tax Law; Trust and Estates, Wills and Probate

SMITH & URE
Santa Ana, CA....Personal Injury

SMITH, WELCH & BRITTAIN
McDonough, GA....Civil Trial Practice; Family Law; General Practice; Municipal and Zoning Law; Personal Injury; Real Estate Law

SMITH & WILLIAMS
Las Vegas, NV....Medical Malpractice; Personal Injury

SMOAK, RICHARD
Panama City, FL....General Practice; Professional Liability

SMOCK AND WEINBERGER
Phoenix, AZ....Antitrust Law; Commercial Litigation; Insurance Defense

SMOLEN & PLEVY P.C.
Vienna, VA....Business Law; Family Law; Trust and Estates, Wills and Probate

SMYTH, JEFFREY A., P.S.
Seattle, WA....Civil Trial Practice

SMYTH & LACK
Huntington, NY....Banking Law; Corporate Law; General Practice; Real Estate Law; Trust and Estates, Wills and Probate

SNAPKA, KATHRYN
Corpus Christi, TX....Personal Injury

SNEAD, WILLIAM O. P. III
Fairfax, VA....Personal Injury

SNEED LANG, P.C.
Tulsa, OK....Antitrust Law; Banking Law; Bankruptcy Law; Civil Trial Practice; Commercial Law; Commercial Litigation; Criminal Trial Practice; Energy Law; Insurance Defense; Natural Resources Law; Personal Injury; Real Estate Law; Securities Law; Trust and Estates, Wills and Probate

SNEERINGER, EUGENE M. JR.
Albany, NY....Real Estate Law

SNELBAKER, BRENNEMAN & SPARE, P.C.
Mechanicsburg, PA....General Practice; Municipal and Zoning Law

SNELLGROVE, LANGLEY, LOVETT & CULPEPPER
Jonesboro, AR....General Practice; Insurance Defense

SNELLINGS, BREARD, SARTOR, INABNETT & TRASCHER, LLP
Monroe, LA....Civil Trial Practice; General Practice

SNELL & WILMER L.L.P.
Phoenix, AZ....Antitrust Law; Banking Law; Bankruptcy Law; Civil Trial Practice; Commercial Law; Commercial Litigation; Construction Law; Employment Benefits Law; Environmental Law; General Practice; Health Care Law; Intellectual Property Law; Labor and Employment Law; Municipal Bond/Public Authority Financing; Natural Resources Law; Product Liability Law; Real Estate Law; Sports and Entertainment Law; Tax Law; Trust and Estates, Wills and Probate

SNELL & WILMER L.L.P. — *Continued*

Tucson, AZ ....Antitrust Law; Banking Law; Bankruptcy Law; Environmental Law; Intellectual Property Law; Labor and Employment Law; Municipal Bond/Public Authority Financing; Real Estate Law; Sports and Entertainment Law; Tax Law; Trust and Estates, Wills and Probate

Irvine, CA.............................Corporate Law; General Practice; Intellectual Property Law; Labor and Employment Law; Product Liability Law; Tax Law; Trust and Estates, Wills and Probate

Salt Lake City, UT.............................Environmental Law; General Practice; Intellectual Property Law; Labor and Employment Law; Municipal Bond/Public Authority Financing; Natural Resources Law; Product Liability Law; Tax Law

SNOW, CHRISTENSEN & MARTINEAU, P.C.

Salt Lake City, UT.............................General Practice

SNYDER, WILLIAM A.

Davie, FL.............................Trust and Estates, Wills and Probate

SNYDER, MALLON A., CHARTERED

Rockville, MD.............................Arbitration

SOBEL, EDWARD B.

Bradenton, FL.............................Family Law

SOBEL, EDWARD B.

Sarasota, FL.............................Family Law

SOBELSOHN & JOHNSON, LLP

Encino, CA.............................Workers Compensation

SOBIESKI, MESSER & ASSOCIATES

Knoxville, TN.............................Appellate Practice; Civil Rights; Construction Law; Family Law

SOCKRIDER, BOLIN, ANGLIN & BATTE, A PROFESSIONAL LAW CORPORATION

Shreveport, LA.............................Civil Trial Practice; Family Law; Personal Injury; Trust and Estates, Wills and Probate

SOKOL, BEHOT AND FIORENZO

Hackensack, NJ.............................Business Law; Civil Trial Practice; Commercial Law; Environmental Law; General Practice; Real Estate Law

SOKOLOFF, CHARLES S., INCORPORATED

Smithfield, RI.............................Business Law; Commercial Litigation; Corporate Law; Franchise Law; Land Use Law; Nonprofit and Tax Exempt Organizations; Real Estate Law; Trust and Estates, Wills and Probate

SOLOMON, JEFFREY LAW OFFICE OF

Hollywood, FL.............................Bankruptcy Law; Trust and Estates, Wills and Probate

SOLOMON, STEPHEN E.

Los Angeles, CA.............................Tax Law

SOLOMON & BENEDICT, P.A.

Tampa, FL.............................Commercial Litigation

SOLOMON, BUDMAN, STRICKER & SCHWARTZ, L.L.P.

Charleston, SC.............................Civil Trial Practice; Family Law; Personal Injury; Real Estate Law; Tax Law

SOLOMON WARD SEIDENWURM & SMITH, LLP

San Diego, CA.............................Civil Trial Practice; Commercial Law; Real Estate Law; Tax Law; Trust and Estates, Wills and Probate

SOLOVAY, EDLIN & EISEMAN

New York, NY.............................Civil Trial Practice; Commercial Litigation; Corporate Law; General Practice; Real Estate Law; Securities Law

SOMMER & BARNARD, ATTORNEYS AT LAW, PC

Indianapolis, IN.............................Administrative Law; Antitrust Law; Bankruptcy Law; Business Law; Civil Trial Practice; Commercial Law; Computer Law; Environmental Law; General Practice; Labor and Employment Law; Real Estate Law; Securities Law

SOMMERS, SCHWARTZ, SILVER & SCHWARTZ, P.C.

Southfield, MI.............................Appellate Practice; Banking Law; Bankruptcy Law; Business Law; Civil Trial Practice; Commercial Law; Criminal Trial Practice; Employment Benefits Law; Environmental Law; Family Law; General Practice; Health Care Law; Insurance Defense; Labor and Employment Law; Medical Malpractice; Personal Injury; Product Liability Law; Real Estate Law; Sports and Entertainment Law; Tax Law; Trust and Estates, Wills and Probate; Workers Compensation

SONDERBY, PETER R., P.C.

Chicago, IL.............................Civil Trial Practice; Commercial Litigation; Securities Law

SONNENSCHEIN NATH & ROSENTHAL

Los Angeles, CA.............................General Practice
San Francisco, CA.............................General Practice
Washington, DC.............................General Practice
Chicago, IL.............................General Practice
Kansas City, MO.............................General Practice
St. Louis, MO.............................General Practice
New York, NY.............................General Practice

SOPUCH NOUHAN HIGGINS & ARNETT, L.L.P.

Dallas, TX.............................Commercial Litigation; Construction Law

SORLING, NORTHRUP, HANNA, CULLEN AND COCHRAN, LTD.

Springfield, IL.............................General Practice

SOROKIN, GROSS & HYDE, P.C.

Hartford, CT.............................Administrative Law; Antitrust Law; Appellate Practice; Business Law; Civil Trial Practice; Commercial Law; Construction Law; Employment Benefits Law; Family Law; General Practice; Insurance Defense; Labor and Employment Law; Real Estate Law; Securities Law; Tax Law; Trust and Estates, Wills and Probate

SOULE, JOEL V.

Grand Rapids, MI.............................Business Law

SOUTHWELL & O'ROURKE, P.S.

Spokane, WA.............................Bankruptcy Law

SOWDERS, A. GLENN JR.

Kansas City, MO.............................Tax Law

SOWELL, MATTHEW W., P.A.

Jacksonville, FL.............................Medical Malpractice; Product Liability Law

SPAETH & MCGRATH

San Francisco, CA.............................Administrative Law

SPAIN & GILLON, L.L.C.

Birmingham, AL.............................Antitrust Law; Banking Law; Bankruptcy Law; Civil Trial Practice; Commercial Law; Environmental Law; General Practice; Insurance Defense; Labor and Employment Law; Medical Malpractice; Municipal Bond/Public Authority Financing; Personal Injury; Real Estate Law; Tax Law; Trust and Estates, Wills and Probate

SPANGENBERG, SHIBLEY & LIBER LLP

Cleveland, OH.............................General Practice; Medical Malpractice; Personal Injury; Product Liability Law

SPANGLER, JENNINGS & DOUGHERTY, P.C.

Merrillville, IN.............................Civil Trial Practice; General Practice; Insurance Defense; Personal Injury
Valparaiso, IN.............................General Practice; Insurance Defense; Personal Injury; Product Liability Law

SPARBER, FERGUSON, PONDER & RYAN, A PROFESSIONAL LAW CORPORATION

San Diego, CA.............................General Practice

SPARKMAN, ROBB & MASON

Miami, FL.............................Civil Trial Practice; Insurance Defense

SPARKS, TEHAN & RYLEY, P.C.

Scottsdale, AZ.............................Commercial Litigation; Environmental Law; Natural Resources Law; Real Estate Law; Trust and Estates, Wills and Probate

SPARLING, DENSFORD AND REYNOLDS, P.A.

Lexington Park, MD.............................General Practice

SPEARS, MICHAEL E., P.A.

Spartanburg, SC.............................Medical Malpractice

SPECTOR GADON & ROSEN, P.C.

Philadelphia, PA.............................Business Law; Civil Trial Practice; Commercial Litigation

SPECTOR & ROSEMAN, A PROFESSIONAL CORPORATION

Philadelphia, PA.............................Antitrust Law; Civil Trial Practice; Commercial Litigation; Securities Law

SPEISER KRAUSE, A PROFESSIONAL CORPORATION

Irvine, CA.............................Aviation Law
Dallas, TX.............................Aviation Law
Arlington, VA.............................Aviation Law
New York, NY.............................Aviation Law

SPEISER, LAURENCE A., LTD.

Las Vegas, NV.............................Business Law

SPENCE, KOHLER, CHRISTIE & PULVER, P.A.

Baltimore, MD.............................Medical Malpractice; Personal Injury

SPENCE, MORIARITY & SCHUSTER, LLC

Jackson, WY.............................Civil Trial Practice; Criminal Trial Practice; General Practice; Medical Malpractice; Personal Injury; Product Liability Law

SPENCE, RICKE & THURMER, P.A.
St. Paul, MN ....Insurance Defense; Labor and Employment Law; Transportation Law

SPENCER FANE BRITT & BROWNE LLP
Kansas City, MO ....Civil Trial Practice; Environmental Law; Labor and Employment Law

SPENCER AND KLEIN, PROFESSIONAL ASSOCIATION
Miami, FL ....Civil Trial Practice; General Practice; International Business Law; Tax Law

SPENCER & SPENCER, PROFESSIONAL ASSOCIATION
Rock Hill, SC ....General Practice

SPERLING, DEAN P.
Santa Ana, CA ....Commercial Law

SPESIA, AYERS & ARDAUGH
Joliet, IL ....General Practice; Personal Injury

SPIEGEL LIAO & KAGAY
San Francisco, CA ....Antitrust Law; Appellate Practice; Commercial Litigation

SPIETH, BELL, MCCURDY & NEWELL CO., L.P.A.
Cleveland, OH ....Civil Trial Practice; General Practice; Labor and Employment Law; Real Estate Law; Tax Law; Trust and Estates, Wills and Probate

SPILMAN THOMAS & BATTLE, PLLC
Charleston, WV ....General Practice

SPITLER, VOGTSBERGER & HUFFMAN, LLP
Bowling Green, OH ....Personal Injury

SPITZ & CARR
Edmonton, AB, Canada ....Civil Trial Practice

SPITZER & FELDMAN, P.C.
New York, NY ....Civil Trial Practice; Corporate Law

SPOHRER, WILNER, MAXWELL & MATTHEWS, P.A.
Jacksonville, FL ....Aviation Law

SPRECHMAN & ASSOCIATES, P.A.
Miami, FL ....Commercial Litigation; Creditors Rights

SPRENGER & LANG, P.L.L.C.
Washington, DC ....Civil Rights; Labor and Employment Law
Minneapolis, MN ....Labor and Employment Law

SPRINGER, CASEY & DIENSTAG, P.C.
Chicago, IL ....General Practice

SPRINGER, LYLE & WATT L.L.P.
Denton, TX ....Personal Injury

SPRINGER & STEINBERG, A PROFESSIONAL CORPORATION
Denver, CO ....Criminal Trial Practice; Personal Injury

SPURRIER, RICE, WOOD & HALL
Huntsville, AL ....Civil Trial Practice; Insurance Defense

SQUIRE, SANDERS & DEMPSEY
London, England ....General Practice
Almaty, Kazakhstan ....General Practice
Moscow, Russia ....General Practice
Madrid, Spain ....General Practice
Taipei, Taiwan ....General Practice
Phoenix, AZ ....General Practice
Washington, DC ....General Practice
Jacksonville, FL ....General Practice
Miami, FL ....General Practice
New York, NY ....General Practice
Cleveland, OH ....General Practice
Columbus, OH ....General Practice
Houston, TX ....General Practice
Brussels, Belgium ....General Practice
Hong Kong, China ....General Practice
Budapest, Hungary ....General Practice
Bratislava, Slovakia ....General Practice
Kyiv (Kiev), Ukraine ....General Practice
Prague, Czech Republic ....General Practice

SREENAN, GREGORY P., P.A., LAW OFFICES OF
Miami, FL ....Aviation Law; Insurance Defense

STACEY & WALEN
Billings, MT ....General Practice; Insurance Defense

STACKHOUSE, SMITH & NEXSEN
Norfolk, VA ....Banking Law; Bankruptcy Law; Business Law; Civil Trial Practice; General Practice; Insurance Defense

STADTMAUER BAILKIN, LLP
New York, NY ....Real Estate Law

STAHANCYK, GEARING & RACKNER, P.C.
Portland, OR ....Family Law; Trust and Estates, Wills and Probate

STAITMAN SNYDER TANNENBAUM & DORENFELD, LLP
Encino, CA ....Civil Trial Practice; Insurance Defense

STALMACK, JOSEPH, & ASSOCIATES, P.C.
Hammond, IN ....Civil Trial Practice

STAMBLER, ERROL H.
Los Angeles, CA ....Criminal Trial Practice

STAMOS & TRUCCO
Chicago, IL ....Health Care Law

STAMPER, HADLEY & REASOR
Antlers, OK ....Civil Trial Practice; General Practice; Insurance Defense; Labor and Employment Law

STANISLAW ASHBAUGH, LLP
Seattle, WA ....Construction Law

STANSBURY, RICHARD T., A PROFESSIONAL ASSOCIATION
Baltimore, MD ....Business Law; Mergers and Acquisitions; Tax Law; Trust and Estates, Wills and Probate

STANTON, WILLIAM E.
Millbrook, NY ....Civil Trial Practice; Criminal Trial Practice; Medical Malpractice

STANTON & ASSOCIATES, A PROFESSIONAL CORPORATION
Washington, DC ....Bankruptcy Law

STANTON, HUGHES, DIANA, SALSBERG, CERRA & MARIANI, P.C.
Morristown, NJ ....Labor and Employment Law

STANYAR, CAROLE M.
Detroit, MI ....Appellate Practice; Criminal Trial Practice

STAPLETON & STAPLETON, A PROFESSIONAL ASSOCIATION
Tustin, CA ....Criminal Trial Practice; Family Law

STARBIRD, RUSSELL B., P.C.
Houston, TX ....Commercial Litigation

STARK DONINGER & SMITH
Indianapolis, IN ....Business Law; Environmental Law; General Practice; Real Estate Law

STARKEY, KELLY, BLANEY & WHITE
Toms River, NJ ....Civil Trial Practice; General Practice; Insurance Defense; Personal Injury; Real Estate Law; Workers Compensation

STARK & KEENAN, A PROFESSIONAL ASSOCIATION
Bel Air, MD ....Appellate Practice; Business Law; Civil Trial Practice; General Practice; Municipal and Zoning Law; Personal Injury; Real Estate Law; Trust and Estates, Wills and Probate

STARK & KNOLL CO., L.P.A.
Akron, OH ....Corporate Law; Trust and Estates, Wills and Probate

STARK, REAGAN & FINNERTY, P.C.
Troy, MI ....Business Law; Civil Trial Practice; Construction Law; Employment Benefits Law; Labor and Employment Law; Tax Law; Trust and Estates, Wills and Probate

STARK & STARK, A PROFESSIONAL CORPORATION
Princeton, NJ ....Business Law; Commercial Litigation; Family Law; Personal Injury; Product Liability Law; Real Estate Law; Securities Law; Trust and Estates, Wills and Probate; Workers Compensation

STARN, PETER, A LAW CORPORATION, LAW OFFICES OF
Honolulu, HI ....Commercial Law; Real Estate Law

STARNES & ATCHISON LLP
Birmingham, AL ....Civil Trial Practice; Construction Law; Environmental Law; Insurance Defense; Medical Malpractice; Personal Injury; Product Liability Law

STATON, PERKINSON, DOSTER, POST, SILVERMAN & ADCOCK, P.A.
Sanford, NC ....General Practice

STEAKLEY & WETSEL
Sweetwater, TX ....Oil and Gas Law

STEEFEL, LEVITT & WEISS, A PROFESSIONAL CORPORATION
San Francisco, CA ....Civil Trial Practice; General Practice

STEEG AND O'CONNOR, L.L.C.
New Orleans, LA ....Real Estate Law

STEEL, JOHN H. LAW OFFICES OF
Telluride, CO............................Business Law; Civil Trial Practice

STEELE, JERRY
Phoenix, AZ............................Civil Trial Practice

STEELE, STEELE, MCSOLEY & MCSOLEY
Bedford, IN............................Banking Law; Civil Trial Practice; General Practice

STEEL HECTOR & DAVIS LLP
Miami, FL............................General Practice

STEELMAN, BARRY L., P.A.
Baltimore, MD............................Civil Trial Practice

STEEL, RUDNICK & RUBEN
Philadelphia, PA............................Immigration and Naturalization

STEEN REYNOLDS & DALEHITE, LLP
Jackson, MS............................Civil Trial Practice; Insurance Defense

STEIN, RICK M. LAW OFFICES OF
Palm Springs, CA............................Civil Trial Practice

STEIN, FORD, SCHAAF & TOWZEY, L.L.P.
St. Petersburg, FL............................Civil Trial Practice; Commercial Litigation; Labor and Employment Law; Real Estate Law; Trust and Estates, Wills and Probate

STEIN, HARVEY W., A PROFESSIONAL CORPORATION
Oakland, CA............................Commercial Law

STEIN, MOORE & FAY, P.A.
St. Paul, MN............................Bankruptcy Law; Real Estate Law

STEIN RISO MANTEL HASPEL & JACOBS LLP
New York, NY............................Criminal Trial Practice; Family Law; Tax Law

STEIN, SCHIFINO & VAN DER WALL
Tampa, FL............................Intellectual Property Law

STEIN, SPERLING, BENNETT, DE JONG, DRISCOLL, GREENFEIG & METRO, P.C.
Rockville, MD............................Bankruptcy Law; Business Law; Civil Trial Practice; Commercial Law; Commercial Litigation; Corporate Law; Criminal Trial Practice; Family Law; General Practice; Labor and Employment Law; Medical Malpractice; Personal Injury; Real Estate Law; Tax Law; Trust and Estates, Wills and Probate

STEIN, STEPHEN, CHARTERED
Las Vegas, NV............................Criminal Trial Practice

STEINBERG BARNESS FOSTER & FOLEY LLP
Manhattan Beach, CA............................Bankruptcy Law; Business Law; Civil Trial Practice; General Practice; Real Estate Law; Trust and Estates, Wills and Probate

STEINBERG, NUTTER & BRENT, LAW CORPORATION
Santa Monica, CA............................Bankruptcy Law; Civil Trial Practice; Real Estate Law

STEINBERG & RASKIN, P.C.
New York, NY............................Patent, Trademark, Copyright and Unfair Competition

STEINBERG & YAFFE, P.A.
Miami Beach, FL............................Trust and Estates, Wills and Probate

STEINBURG, CARWILE, HERZIK & PRIETO
Houston, TX............................Personal Injury

STEINER AND STEINER
Kittanning, PA............................General Practice

STEINHEIMER, RIGGIO, HAYDEL & MORDAUNT, A PROFESSIONAL LAW CORPORATION
Stockton, CA............................Civil Trial Practice; General Practice

STENGER & FINNERTY
Buffalo, NY............................Civil Trial Practice; Commercial Litigation; Constitutional Law; Environmental Law

STENSTROM, MCINTOSH, COLBERT, WHIGHAM & SIMMONS, P.A.
Sanford, FL............................Civil Trial Practice; Family Law; General Practice; Real Estate Law; Trust and Estates, Wills and Probate

STEPHENS, BARONI, REILLY & LEWIS LLP
White Plains, NY............................Civil Trial Practice; Corporate Law; Criminal Trial Practice; General Practice; Municipal and Zoning Law

STEPHENS LAW FIRM, PLLC
McLean, VA............................General Practice

STEPHENS, MILLIRONS, HARRISON & GAMMONS, P.C.
Huntsville, AL............................Banking Law; Bankruptcy Law; Civil Trial Practice; Corporate Law; Family Law; General Practice; Personal Injury; Real Estate Law

STEPHENSON, WORLEY, GARRATT, SCHWARTZ, GARFIELD & PRAIRIE
San Diego, CA............................Employment Benefits Law; Land Use Law; Real Estate Law

STEPONOVICH & ASSOCIATES, A PROFESSIONAL LAW CORPORATION
Irvine, CA............................Civil Trial Practice

STEPP & BEAUCHAMP LLP
Newport Beach, CA............................Business Law; Civil Trial Practice; Corporate Law; Real Estate Law

STEPP & SULLIVAN, P.C.
Houston, TX............................Admiralty/Maritime Law; Civil Trial Practice

STEPTOE & JOHNSON LLP
Phoenix, AZ............................General Practice
Los Angeles, CA............................General Practice
Washington, DC............................General Practice

STERN & EDLIN, P.C.
Atlanta, GA............................Family Law

STERN & KLEPFER, L.L.P.
Greensboro, NC............................Business Law; Commercial Law; Labor and Employment Law; Real Estate Law

STERNS & WEINROTH, A PROFESSIONAL CORPORATION
Atlantic City, NJ............................General Practice
Trenton, NJ............................General Practice

STETINA BRUNDA GARRED & BRUCKER, A PROFESSIONAL CORPORATION
Laguna Hills, CA............................Antitrust Law; Commercial Litigation; Computer Law; Patent, Trademark, Copyright and Unfair Competition

STETTNER, MILLER AND COHN, P.C.
Denver, CO............................Labor and Employment Law

STEVENS, RICHARD W.
Jenkintown, PA............................Trust and Estates, Wills and Probate

STEVENS, BAGLEY & STEVENS
Fayetteville, TN............................General Practice

STEVENS & JOHNSON
Allentown, PA............................Insurance Defense

STEVENS & KRAMER, A PROFESSIONAL CORPORATION
Irvine, CA............................Arbitration; Civil Trial Practice; Elder Law; Insurance Defense; Personal Injury; Professional Liability

STEVENS LAW FIRM, P.C.
Loris, SC............................Civil Trial Practice; Eminent Domain; Labor and Employment Law; Personal Injury; Product Liability Law; Real Estate Law; Workers Compensation

STEVENS, MCGHEE, MORGAN, LENNON, O'QUINN & TOLL
Wilmington, NC............................Commercial Litigation; Trust and Estates, Wills and Probate

STEVENS & MINTER
Secaucus, NJ............................Insurance Defense

STEVENS & O'CONNELL LLP
Sacramento, CA............................Civil Trial Practice; Commercial Litigation; Criminal Trial Practice; Environmental Law

STEWART, TIMOTHY A.
Hagåtña, GU............................General Practice

STEWART, COOK, CONSTANCE, STEWART & MINTON, L.L.C.
Independence, MO............................General Practice

STEWART AND DE CHANT CO., L.P.A.
Cleveland, OH............................Medical Malpractice; Personal Injury; Product Liability Law; Workers Compensation

STEWART, ESTES & DONNELL
Nashville, TN............................Insurance Defense; Sports and Entertainment Law

STEWART, EVANS & HAFNER, P.A.
Vero Beach, FL............................Health Care Law; Real Estate Law; Trust and Estates, Wills and Probate

STEWART, JAMES D., AND ASSOCIATES, INC.
San Antonio, TX............................Family Law

STEWART, JOYNER & JORDAN-HOLMES, P.A.
Tampa, FL............................Insurance Defense; Personal Injury; Transportation Law

STEWART MCKELVEY STIRLING SCALES
Fredericton, NB, Canada............................General Practice
Moncton, NB, Canada............................General Practice
Saint John, NB, Canada............................General Practice
St. John's, NF, Canada............................General Practice

Halifax, NS, Canada ....General Practice
Sydney, NS, Canada ....General Practice
Charlottetown, PE, Canada.....General Practice

STEWART, MELVIN & FROST, LLP
Gainesville, GA....................General Practice

STEWART, PLANT & BLUMENTHAL, LLC
Baltimore, MD........................Tax Law; Trust and Estates, Wills and Probate

STEWART AND STEWART
Washington, DC......................General Practice; International Business Law

STEWART TILGHMAN FOX & BIANCHI, P.A.
Miami, FL...............................Civil Trial Practice

STICHTER, RIEDEL, BLAIN & PROSSER, P.A.
Tampa, FL...............................Bankruptcy Law

STIKEMAN ELLIOTT
Vancouver, BC, Canada..........General Practice
Ottawa, ON, Canada..............General Practice
Toronto, ON, Canada.............General Practice
Montreal, QU, Canada...........General Practice
Hong Kong, China..................General Practice
London, England....................General Practice

STILES BYRUM & HORNE, L.L.P.
Charlotte, NC..........................Insurance Defense

STILES, TAYLOR & GRACE, P.A.
Boca Raton, FL.......................Workers Compensation
Miami, FL...............................Workers Compensation
Orlando, FL............................Workers Compensation
Tallahassee, FL.......................Workers Compensation
Tampa, FL...............................Workers Compensation

STILLMAN & FRIEDMAN, P.C.
New York, NY........................Civil Trial Practice; Criminal Trial Practice

STIMMEL, STIMMEL & SMITH, A PROFESSIONAL CORPORATION
San Francisco, CA..................Business Law; Construction Law; Corporate Law; International Business Law; Trust and Estates, Wills and Probate

STINSON, JOSEPH M.
Tylertown, MS........................General Practice

STINSON, LOUIS, JR., P.A.
Miami, FL...............................Admiralty/Maritime Law

STIPANOV & MEBANE, A PROFESSIONAL LAW CORPORATION
San Diego, CA........................Real Estate Law

STIRLING & KLEINTOP
Honolulu, HI..........................Family Law; Trust and Estates, Wills and Probate

STITES & HARBISON
Frankfort, KY.........................General Practice
Lexington, KY........................General Practice; Natural Resources Law
Louisville, KY........................General Practice; Municipal Bond/Public Authority Financing

STITES, HOPKINS & FAIR
Kansas City, MO....................Medical Malpractice; Personal Injury; Product Liability Law

STITES, MCELWAIN & FOWLER
Louisville, KY........................General Practice

STOCKS AND FENTIN, LLP
San Diego, CA........................Family Law

STOCKTON & SADLER
Modesto, CA..........................Civil Trial Practice

STOCKWELL, SIEVERT, VICCELLIO, CLEMENTS & SHADDOCK, L.L.P.
Lake Charles, LA....................General Practice

STOCKWOOD SPIES
Toronto, ON, Canada.............Civil Trial Practice

STOEL RIVES LLP
Portland, OR..........................General Practice

STOKES, FRED
Albemarle, NC........................Criminal Trial Practice

STOKES & BARTHOLOMEW, P.A.
Nashville, TN.........................General Practice

STOKES & MURPHY, P.C.
San Diego, CA........................Labor and Employment Law
Atlanta, GA............................Labor and Employment Law

STOLAR PARTNERSHIP, THE
St. Louis, MO.........................Creditors Rights; Environmental Law; Health Care Law; Mergers and Acquisitions

STOLDT, HORAN AND KOWAL, A PROFESSIONAL CORPORATION
Hackensack, NJ......................Civil Trial Practice; Employment Benefits Law; Environmental Law; Land Use Law; Municipal and Zoning Law; Real Estate Law

STOLL, KEENON & PARK, LLP
Frankfort, KY.........................General Practice
Lexington, KY........................Administrative Law; Antitrust Law; Banking Law; Bankruptcy Law; Business Law; Civil Trial Practice; Commercial Law; Communications Law; Employment Benefits Law; Environmental Law; Family Law; General Practice; Health Care Law; Insurance Defense; Labor and Employment Law; Municipal and Zoning Law; Municipal Bond/Public Authority Financing; Natural Resources Law; Patent, Trademark, Copyright and Unfair Competition; Real Estate Law; Securities Law; Tax Law; Trust and Estates, Wills and Probate
Louisville, KY........................Commercial Law; General Practice

STOLPMAN • KRISSMAN • ELBER • MANDEL & KATZMAN LLP
Long Beach, CA......................Civil Trial Practice; Personal Injury; Product Liability Law

STOLTZ, MELVIN I.
Milford, CT............................Patent, Trademark, Copyright and Unfair Competition

STOMPOLY, STROUD, GLICKSMAN & ERICKSON, P.C.
Tucson, AZ............................Civil Trial Practice; Family Law; General Practice; Medical Malpractice; Personal Injury; Product Liability Law

STONE, JACK A. LAW OFFICES OF
Evansville, IN.........................Tax Law; Trust and Estates, Wills and Probate

STONE, NANCY J.
Amarillo, TX..........................Civil Trial Practice; Commercial Litigation; Personal Injury

STONE, DOLGINER & WENZEL, A LAW CORPORATION
Los Angeles, CA.....................Civil Trial Practice; Medical Malpractice; Personal Injury; Product Liability Law

STONE, EDWARD H., P.C.
Irvine, CA..............................Trust and Estates, Wills and Probate

STONE, JED, LTD., THE LAW OFFICES OF
Chicago, IL............................Criminal Trial Practice

STONE JESSUP, P.C.
Tulsa, OK..............................Municipal Bond/Public Authority Financing

STONE, KAPLAN & CHAPMAN, P.C.
Macon, GA.............................Family Law

STONE, LEYTON & GERSHMAN, A PROFESSIONAL CORPORATION
St. Louis, MO.........................Bankruptcy Law; Commercial Litigation; Real Estate Law

STONE & MOORE, CHARTERED
Chicago, IL............................Civil Trial Practice; Commercial Litigation; Construction Law; Insurance Defense; Legal Malpractice; Product Liability Law; Professional Liability; Toxic Torts; Workers Compensation

STONE, PIGMAN, WALTHER, WITTMANN & HUTCHINSON, L.L.P.
New Orleans, LA....................General Practice

STONE & ROSENBLATT, A LAW CORPORATION
Encino, CA.............................Insurance Defense

STONEMAN, CHANDLER & MILLER LLP
Boston, MA............................Education Law; Labor and Employment Law

STOREY & PIERONI, PLC
Phoenix, AZ...........................Real Estate Law

STORM, HAWK MESA
Angel Fire, NM......................Arbitration

STOUP, ARTHUR H., & ASSOCIATES, P.C.
Kansas City, MO....................Civil Trial Practice; Medical Malpractice; Personal Injury; Workers Compensation

STOUT, MICHAEL L. LAW OFFICES OF
Roswell, NM..........................Criminal Trial Practice; Personal Injury

STRADLEY & WRIGHT
Dallas, TX.............................Insurance Defense

STRADLING YOCCA CARLSON & RAUTH, A PROFESSIONAL CORPORATION
Newport Beach, CA................General Practice

STRAIN, JAMES R. JR.
Slidell, LA.............................Medical Malpractice; Personal Injury; Workers Compensation

STRAIN, DENNIS, MAYHALL & BATES, L.L.P.
Baton Rouge, LA....................Oil and Gas Law

STRAMONDO, SALVATORE F.
Lexington, MA....................Aviation Law; Civil Trial Practice

STRANG, FLETCHER, CARRIGER, WALKER, HODGE & SMITH, PLLC
Chattanooga, TN....................General Practice

STRASBURGER & PRICE, L.L.P.
Austin, TX....................General Practice
Dallas, TX....................General Practice
Houston, TX....................General Practice
Mexico, D.F., Mexico....................General Practice

STRASSER & ASSOCIATES, A PROFESSIONAL CORPORATION
Paramus, NJ....................Civil Trial Practice; Commercial Law; General Practice; Health Care Law; Real Estate Law

STRAUSS & TROY, A LEGAL PROFESSIONAL ASSOCIATION
Covington, KY....................General Practice
Cincinnati, OH....................Business Law; Civil Trial Practice; Employment Benefits Law; General Practice; Insurance Defense; Medical Malpractice; Real Estate Law; Securities Law; Tax Law

STRAUSS • URITZ, A PROFESSIONAL CORPORATION
Ventura, CA....................Business Law; Civil Trial Practice; Environmental Law; Labor and Employment Law

STREATER & MURPHY, P.A.
Winona, MN....................General Practice; Personal Injury; Product Liability Law

STRECKER & ASSOCIATES, P.C.
Tulsa, OK....................Civil Trial Practice; Labor and Employment Law

STREET, STREET, STREET, SCOTT & BOWMAN
Grundy, VA....................General Practice

STREETER, PATRICIA A.
Chicago, IL....................Civil Trial Practice
Detroit, MI....................Civil Trial Practice

STRICKLAND & STRICKLAND, P.C.
Tucson, AZ....................Environmental Law; Medical Malpractice; Natural Resources Law; Personal Injury

STRICKLAND, WILTON L., P.A.
Fort Lauderdale, FL....................Medical Malpractice; Personal Injury; Product Liability Law

STRIDE, CRADDOCK & STRIDE
Chicago, IL....................Aviation Law; Civil Trial Practice; Medical Malpractice; Personal Injury; Product Liability Law

STRIFLING, JAN S., P.A.
Columbia, SC....................Criminal Trial Practice

STRIPLING, MCMICHAEL & STRIPLING, P.A.
Gainesville, FL....................Medical Malpractice; Personal Injury

STRODEL, ROBERT C., LTD.
Peoria, IL....................Civil Trial Practice; General Practice; Medical Malpractice; Personal Injury

STROEBEL, EDWARD
Wapakoneta, OH....................Trust and Estates, Wills and Probate

STRONG & HANNI, A PROFESSIONAL CORPORATION
Salt Lake City, UT....................Business Law; General Practice; Insurance Defense; Labor and Employment Law; Medical Malpractice; Product Liability Law; Trust and Estates, Wills and Probate

STRONG LAW FIRM, THE, A PROFESSIONAL CORPORATION
Springfield, MO....................Personal Injury

STRONG, PIPKIN, NELSON, BISSELL & LEDYARD, L.L.P.
Beaumont, TX....................General Practice

STRONG & STRONG, A PROFESSIONAL CORPORATION
Maryville, MO....................Civil Trial Practice

STROOCK & STROOCK & LAVAN LLP
Los Angeles, CA....................General Practice
Washington, DC....................General Practice
Miami, FL....................General Practice
Boston, MA....................General Practice
New York, NY....................Bankruptcy Law; General Practice; Tax Law

STROUD, WILLINK & HOWARD, LLC
Madison, WI....................General Practice; Real Estate Law; Trademark, Copyright and Unfair Competition; Trust and Estates, Wills and Probate

STROUP & JONES, L.L.P.
Longview, TX....................Product Liability Law

STROUT & PAYSON, P.A.
Rockland, ME....................Civil Trial Practice; General Practice; Tax Law

STRUCKMEYER AND WILSON
Phoenix, AZ....................Insurance Defense

STRYKER, DUENSING, CASNER & DOLLISON
Charlotte Amalie, St. Thomas, VI....................General Practice

STRYKER, TAMS & DILL LLP
Newark, NJ....................General Practice

STUART, CHARLES M. JR.
Greenville, SC....................Trust and Estates, Wills and Probate

STUART & BRANIGIN
Lafayette, IN....................Appellate Practice; Banking Law; Bankruptcy Law; Business Law; Civil Trial Practice; Commercial Law; Employment Benefits Law; Environmental Law; General Practice; Health Care Law; Insurance Defense; Labor and Employment Law; Land Use Law; Medical Malpractice; Municipal Bond/Public Authority Financing; Real Estate Law; Tax Law; Trademark, Copyright and Unfair Competition; Transportation Law; Trust and Estates, Wills and Probate

STUBBS & PERDUE, P.A.
New Bern, NC....................Bankruptcy Law

STUCKERT AND YATES
Newtown, PA....................General Practice

STUDDARD & MELBY, A PROFESSIONAL CORPORATION
El Paso, TX....................General Practice

STUMP, T. DOUGLAS
Oklahoma City, OK....................Immigration and Naturalization

STUMPF CRADDOCK MASSEY & PULMAN, A PROFESSIONAL CORPORATION
Houston, TX....................Commercial Litigation; Real Estate Law

STUTMAN, TREISTER & GLATT, PROFESSIONAL CORPORATION
Los Angeles, CA....................Bankruptcy Law; Commercial Law

STUTZ, GALLAGHER, ARTIANO, SHINOFF & HOLTZ, A PROFESSIONAL CORPORATION
San Diego, CA....................Civil Trial Practice

SUAREZ & WARDELL, P.A.
Tampa, FL....................Criminal Trial Practice

SUDEKUM, ROSENBERG & CASSIDY, CHARTERED
Chicago, IL....................Insurance Defense

SUGAR, FRIEDBERG & FELSENTHAL
Chicago, IL....................Business Law; Civil Trial Practice; Commercial Litigation; Mergers and Acquisitions; Real Estate Law; Securities Law; Tax Law; Trust and Estates, Wills and Probate

SUGARMAN AND SUGARMAN, P.C.
Boston, MA....................Personal Injury

SUGARMAN, WALLACE, MANHEIM & SCHOENWALD
Buffalo, NY....................Insurance Defense
Syracuse, NY....................Appellate Practice; Civil Trial Practice; Construction Law; Insurance Defense; Legal Malpractice; Personal Injury; Professional Liability

SUGHROUE, PATRICK R., P.C.
Grand Rapids, MI....................Securities Law

SUITER & ASSOCIATES P.C.
Omaha, NE....................Intellectual Property Law; Patent, Trademark, Copyright and Unfair Competition

SUKKAR, MAZEN M., P.A.
Hollywood, FL....................Immigration and Naturalization

SULLIVAN, MIKKI ROSEMARY
San Diego, CA....................Creditors Rights

SULLIVAN & CROMWELL
Los Angeles, CA....................General Practice
Washington, DC....................General Practice
New York, NY....................Civil Trial Practice; General Practice
Melbourne, Victoria, Australia....................General Practice
Hong Kong, China....................General Practice
London, England....................General Practice
Paris, France....................General Practice
Frankfurt/Main, Germany....................General Practice
Tokyo, Japan....................General Practice
Beijing, China....................General Practice

SULLIVAN & CROWLEY, P.C.
Traverse City, MI....................Civil Trial Practice; Commercial Litigation; Environmental Law; Personal Injury

SULLIVAN, CUNNINGHAM, KEENAN, MRAZ & LEMIRE
Albany, NY....................Real Estate Law; Workers Compensation

SULLIVAN HILL LEWIN REZ & ENGEL, A PROFESSIONAL LAW CORPORATION
San Diego, CA....................Civil Trial Practice

SULLIVAN & LARGEY
Quincy, MA....................Civil Trial Practice

SULLIVAN LAW CORPORATION
Los Angeles, CA....................Aviation Law; Business Law; Civil Trial Practice; Government Contracts

SULLIVAN & LEAVITT, P.C., LAW OFFICES OF
Novi, MI....................Commercial Litigation; Corporate Law; Transportation Law

SULLIVAN, MAHONEY
Niagara Falls, ON, Canada.....General Practice
St. Catharines, ON, Canada....Business Law; General Practice

SULLIVAN & OLIVERIO
Buffalo, NY....................Appellate Practice; Civil Trial Practice; Commercial Law; Commercial Litigation; Family Law; General Practice; Real Estate Law

SULLIVAN AND SULLIVAN
Jackson, MS....................Civil Trial Practice; Commercial Litigation; Construction Law; General Practice; Medical Malpractice; Personal Injury; Product Liability Law

SULLIVAN & WARD, P.C.
Des Moines, IA....................General Practice

SULLIVAN, WARD, BONE, TYLER & ASHER, P.C.
Southfield, MI....................Insurance Defense

SULLOWAY & HOLLIS, P.L.L.C.
Concord, NH....................General Practice

SULMEYER, KUPETZ, BAUMANN & ROTHMAN, A PROFESSIONAL CORPORATION
Los Angeles, CA....................Bankruptcy Law; Commercial Law

SUMMA & RYAN, P.C.
Waterbury, CT....................Labor and Employment Law

SUMMERS, COMPTON, WELLS AND HAMBURG, PROFESSIONAL CORPORATION
St. Louis, MO....................Intellectual Property Law

SUMMERS & WYATT, P.C.
Chattanooga, TN....................Civil Trial Practice; Criminal Trial Practice; General Practice; Labor and Employment Law; Medical Malpractice; Personal Injury; Workers Compensation

SUMMIT LAW GROUP, PLLC
Seattle, WA....................Business Law; Commercial Litigation; Corporate Law; Environmental Law; Labor and Employment Law; Securities Law

SUMNER, DAVID W.
Blue Bell, PA....................Medical Malpractice

SUNDAHL, POWERS, KAPP & MARTIN, L.L.C.
Cheyenne, WY....................Administrative Law; Civil Trial Practice; Insurance Defense

SUNDERLAND, MURPHY, SPENN, JOHNSON AND LUEBCHOW
Watseka, IL....................General Practice

SUPNIK, PAUL D.
Beverly Hills, CA....................Trademark, Copyright and Unfair Competition

SUROVELL, JACKSON, COLTEN & DUGAN, P.C.
Fairfax, VA....................Family Law

SURRATT, JOHN R., P.A.
Winston-Salem, NC....................Civil Trial Practice; Commercial Law; Commercial Litigation; Real Estate Law

SURRETT & COLEMAN, P.A.
Augusta, GA....................Bankruptcy Law; Civil Trial Practice; Family Law; General Practice; Insurance Defense

SUSMAN, DUFFY & SEGALOFF, P.C.
New Haven, CT....................Business Law; Civil Trial Practice; Family Law; Real Estate Law

SUSMAN GODFREY L.L.P.
Los Angeles, CA....................Civil Trial Practice
Dallas, TX....................Civil Trial Practice
Houston, TX....................Civil Trial Practice
Seattle, WA....................Civil Trial Practice

SUTHERLAND, RICHARD T.
Wichita Falls, TX....................Family Law

SUTHERLAND ASBILL & BRENNAN LLP
Atlanta, GA....................General Practice

SUTHON, WALTER J. III
New Orleans, LA....................Trust and Estates, Wills and Probate

SUTKOWSKI & WASHKUHN LTD.
Peoria, IL....................General Practice

SUTTERFIELD & WEBB L.L.C.
New Orleans, LA....................Insurance Defense; Personal Injury; Product Liability Law

SUTTS, STROSBERG LLP
Windsor, ON, Canada....................Civil Trial Practice; Commercial Law; Criminal Trial Practice; Family Law; General Practice; Insurance Defense; Labor and Employment Law; Medical Malpractice; Personal Injury; Product Liability Law

SWADEN LAW OFFICES
Edina, MN....................Family Law

SWAIM & SCHRANDT, P.C.
Albuquerque, NM....................Tax Law; Trust and Estates, Wills and Probate

SWAINE, HARRIS, SHEEHAN & MCCLURE, P.A.
Lake Placid, FL....................General Practice
Sebring, FL....................General Practice

SWANN, HADLEY & ALVAREZ, P.A.
Winter Park, FL....................Insurance Defense

SWANSEN, SAMUEL T., P.C.
Blue Bell, PA....................Trust and Estates, Wills and Probate

SWANSON & DETTMANN
Marquette, MI....................Civil Trial Practice; Insurance Defense

SWANSON AND GIESER, A PROFESSIONAL CORPORATION
Santa Ana, CA....................Civil Trial Practice; Real Estate Law; Trust and Estates, Wills and Probate

SWANSON MIDGLEY, LLC
Kansas City, MO....................Banking Law; Business Law; Civil Trial Practice; Education Law; Franchise Law; General Practice; Intellectual Property Law; Labor and Employment Law; Real Estate Law; Tax Law; Trust and Estates, Wills and Probate

SWANSON, THOMAS & COON
Portland, OR....................Medical Malpractice; Personal Injury; Product Liability Law; Toxic Torts; Workers Compensation

SWARTZ, GERALD NEAL LAW OFFICES, THE
New York, NY....................Personal Injury; Product Liability Law

SWARTZ & REED
Washington, DC....................Medical Malpractice

SWARTZ & SWARTZ
Boston, MA....................Admiralty/Maritime Law; Civil Trial Practice; Commercial Litigation; Environmental Law; Medical Malpractice; Personal Injury; Product Liability Law

SWEDLOW, BUTLER, LEVINE, LEWIS & DYE CO., L.P.A.
Columbus, OH....................Business Law; Commercial Litigation; Mergers and Acquisitions; Real Estate Law

SWEENEY, DABAGIA, THORNE, JANES & PAGOS, L.L.P.
Michigan City, IN....................General Practice

SWENDSEID & STERN
Las Vegas, NV....................Municipal Bond/Public Authority Financing
Reno, NV....................Municipal Bond/Public Authority Financing

SWENSEN PERER & KONTOS
Pittsburgh, PA....................Civil Trial Practice; Criminal Trial Practice; Medical Malpractice; Personal Injury; Product Liability Law

SWERDLOW FLORENCE SANCHEZ & RATHBUN, A LAW CORPORATION
Beverly Hills, CA....................Labor and Employment Law

SWERGOLD, NATHANIEL M.
Cedarhurst, NY....................Civil Trial Practice

SWERLING, JACK B.
Columbia, SC....................Appellate Practice; Criminal Trial Practice

SWIFT, CURRIE, MCGHEE & HIERS
Atlanta, GA....................Commercial Litigation; Insurance Defense; Workers Compensation

SWOPE, CARDILLO, P.A.
Tampa, FL....................Personal Injury

SYKES AND COLE
Hyannis, MA....................Trust and Estates, Wills and Probate

SYLVESTER & MALEY, INC.
Burlington, VT .... Civil Trial Practice; Medical Malpractice; Personal Injury

SYNNESTVEDT & LECHNER LLP
Philadelphia, PA .... Antitrust Law; Computer Law; Intellectual Property Law; Patent, Trademark, Copyright and Unfair Competition

SZAFERMAN, LAKIND, BLUMSTEIN, WATTER & BLADER, P.C.
Lawrenceville, NJ .... Appellate Practice; Banking Law; Business Law; Civil Trial Practice; Commercial Litigation; Environmental Law; Family Law; Labor and Employment Law; Land Use Law; Personal Injury; Professional Liability; Securities Law

TABBERT HAHN EARNEST & WEDDLE
Indianapolis, IN .... Administrative Law; Banking Law; Business Law; Civil Trial Practice; Commercial Litigation; Criminal Trial Practice; Environmental Law; Health Care Law; Insurance Defense; International Business Law; Medical Malpractice; Natural Resources Law; Real Estate Law; Tax Law; Trust and Estates, Wills and Probate

TABNER, RYAN AND KENIRY
Albany, NY .... Business Law; Civil Trial Practice; General Practice; Medical Malpractice; Municipal and Zoning Law; Personal Injury; Real Estate Law; Trust and Estates, Wills and Probate

TAFARO & FLYNN, P.A.
New Providence, NJ .... Civil Trial Practice; Medical Malpractice; Personal Injury

TAFT & MCSALLY
Cranston, RI .... General Practice; Trust and Estates, Wills and Probate

TAFT, STETTINIUS & HOLLISTER LLP
Covington, KY .... General Practice
Cincinnati, OH .... General Practice
Cleveland, OH .... General Practice
Columbus, OH .... General Practice

TAGLIA, FETTE, DUMKE, PASSARO & KAHNE, P.C.
St. Joseph, MI .... General Practice

TAIT, DONALD H. Q.C.
Windsor, ON, Canada .... Criminal Trial Practice

TAKUSHI, FUNAKI, WONG & STONE, ATTORNEYS AT LAW, A LAW CORPORATION
Honolulu, HI .... Bankruptcy Law; Business Law; Creditors Rights; Family Law; Real Estate Law; Trust and Estates, Wills and Probate

TALBOTT AND GALLAGHER, A PROFESSIONAL CORPORATION
McLean, VA .... Business Law; Corporate Law; Real Estate Law; Securities Law

TALCOTT, LIGHTFOOT, VANDEVELDE SADOWSKY, MEDVENE & LEVINE
Los Angeles, CA .... Civil Trial Practice; Criminal Trial Practice

TALIAFERRO, MEHLING, SHIROONI & CARRAN
Covington, KY .... Civil Trial Practice; Criminal Trial Practice; Family Law; Labor and Employment Law; Personal Injury

TALLACKSON, JEFFREY S.
New York, NY .... Banking Law; Commercial Law

TALLEY & SHARP, P.C.
Conyers, GA .... General Practice

TALLMAN, HUDDERS & SORRENTINO, P.C.
Allentown, PA .... Civil Trial Practice; General Practice; Trust and Estates, Wills and Probate

TAM, O'CONNOR, HENDERSON, TAIRA & YAMAUCHI, ATTORNEYS AT LAW, A LAW CORPORATION
Honolulu, HI .... Business Law; Commercial Litigation; Corporate Law; Employment Benefits Law; Insurance Defense; Labor and Employment Law; Personal Injury; Real Estate Law; Tax Law; Trust and Estates, Wills and Probate

TANENBAUM, MARK C., P.A.
Charleston, SC .... Personal Injury; Product Liability Law

TANKARD AND GORDON
Eastville, VA .... Criminal Trial Practice; General Practice; Trust and Estates, Wills and Probate

TANNER, ROD, & ASSOCIATES, P.C.
Fort Worth, TX .... Labor and Employment Law

TANSEY, JAMES J.
Washington, DC .... Commercial Litigation

TARASI LAW FIRM, THE, P.C.
Pittsburgh, PA .... Civil Trial Practice; General Practice; Medical Malpractice; Personal Injury

TARCZA & GELDERMAN, L.L.C.
New Orleans, LA .... Civil Trial Practice; Corporate Law; Trust and Estates, Wills and Probate

TARGAN, DONALD G., & ASSOCIATES, A PROF. CORP.
Atlantic City, NJ .... Civil Trial Practice

TARLOW, BARRY, A PROF. CORP., LAW OFFICES OF
Los Angeles, CA .... Appellate Practice; Criminal Trial Practice

TARNOW, HERMAN H.
New York, NY .... Family Law

TARUTIS & BARRON, P.S.
Seattle, WA .... Health Care Law

TASCHNER, DANA B., P.C.
Los Angeles, CA .... Civil Trial Practice

TATE LAW FIRM, THE
Abingdon, VA .... Commercial Litigation; General Practice; Labor and Employment Law; Medical Malpractice; Personal Injury; Product Liability Law

TATUM & MCDOWELL
Clovis, NM .... General Practice; Tax Law; Trust and Estates, Wills and Probate

TAUBMAN, SIMPSON, YOUNG & SULENTOR
Long Beach, CA .... Civil Trial Practice; Environmental Law; Oil and Gas Law; Real Estate Law; Tax Law

TAUNT, CHARLES J., & ASSOCIATES, P.L.L.C.
Birmingham, MI .... Bankruptcy Law

TAVSS, FLETCHER, MAIDEN & KING, P.C.
Norfolk, VA .... Banking Law; Civil Trial Practice; General Practice; Personal Injury; Real Estate Law

TAX, ESTATE & BUSINESS LAW N.A. LLC
Albuquerque, NM .... Business Law; Tax Law; Trust and Estates, Wills and Probate

TAYLOR, LAWRENCE THE LAW OFFICES OF
Irvine, CA .... Criminal Trial Practice

TAYLOR & CAWTHORNE, LTD.
Tucson, AZ .... Trust and Estates, Wills and Probate

TAYLOR & CIRE
Houston, TX .... Civil Trial Practice

TAYLOR, DUANE, BARTON & GILMAN, LLP
Boston, MA .... Civil Trial Practice; General Practice; Insurance Defense

TAYLOR & FAUST, A PROFESSIONAL CORPORATION
San Francisco, CA .... Tax Law

TAYLOR, GANSON & PERRIN, L.L.P.
Boston, MA .... Trust and Estates, Wills and Probate

TAYLOR, HARP & CALLIER
Columbus, GA .... Civil Trial Practice; Personal Injury

TAYLOR, LAWRENCE, THE LAW OFFICES OF
Beverly Hills, CA .... Criminal Trial Practice
Los Angeles, CA .... Criminal Trial Practice

TAYLOR MCCORD, A LAW CORPORATION
Ventura, CA .... Appellate Practice; Civil Trial Practice; Environmental Law; Family Law; Labor and Employment Law; Personal Injury; Trust and Estates, Wills and Probate

TAYLOR, MILLER, SPROWL, HOFFNAGLE & MERLETTI
Chicago, IL .... General Practice; Insurance Defense

TAYLOR, OLSON, ADKINS, SRALLA & ELAM, L.L.P.
Fort Worth, TX .... Municipal and Zoning Law

TAYLOR, PORTER, BROOKS & PHILLIPS, L.L.P.
Baton Rouge, LA .... General Practice

TAYLOR, STAFFORD, WOODY, CLITHERO & FITZGERALD, LLP
Springfield, MO .... Personal Injury

TAYLOR & TAYLOR
Morehead City, NC .... General Practice

TAYLOR & WALKER, P.C.
Norfolk, VA .... Business Law; Commercial Law; Insurance Defense

TAYLOR, ZUNKA, MILNOR & CARTER, LTD.
Charlottesville, VA .... General Practice; Insurance Defense

TEAFORD, RICH, CRITES & WESP
Columbus, OH .... Personal Injury; Real Estate Law

TEAGUE, CAMPBELL, DENNIS & GORHAM, L.L.P.
Raleigh, NC....Insurance Defense; Workers Compensation

TEAHAN & CONSTANTINO
Poughkeepsie, NY....Tax Law; Trust and Estates, Wills and Probate

TECHMEIER & VAN GRUNSVEN, S.C.
Milwaukee, WI....Personal Injury

TEGTMEIER LAW FIRM, P.C.
Colorado Springs, CO....Civil Trial Practice; Criminal Trial Practice; Personal Injury

TEHIN +PARTNERS, A PROFESSIONAL CORPORATION
San Francisco, CA....Admiralty/Maritime Law; Civil Trial Practice; Commercial Litigation; Labor and Employment Law; Medical Malpractice; Personal Injury; Product Liability Law; Professional Liability

TEICH, GROH AND FROST
Trenton, NJ....Bankruptcy Law; Commercial Law; Family Law; General Practice

TEITLER, STANLEY A., P.C.
New York, NY....Appellate Practice; Civil Trial Practice; Criminal Trial Practice

TEKELL, BOOK, MATTHEWS & LIMMER, L.L.P.
Houston, TX....Civil Trial Practice; Insurance Defense; Personal Injury

TELLER, CHANEY, HASSELL & HOPSON, LLP
Vicksburg, MS....General Practice

TELPNER, PETERSON, SMITH & RUESCH
Council Bluffs, IA....General Practice

TEMPLE & TEMPLE
Austin, TX....Administrative Law; Banking Law

TENENBAUM & SAAS, P.C.
Bethesda, MD....Real Estate Law

TERAOKA & ASSOCIATES, A LAW CORPORATION
San Francisco, CA....Business Law

TERRA LAW LLP
San Jose, CA....Commercial Litigation; Construction Law; Creditors Rights; Land Use Law; Real Estate Law; Tax Law

TERRIBERRY, CARROLL & YANCEY, L.L.P.
New Orleans, LA....Admiralty/Maritime Law; Corporate Law; General Practice

TERRY, EDWIN J. (TED) JR., LAW OFFICES OF
Austin, TX....Family Law

TERRY, WILLIAM B., CHARTERED
Las Vegas, NV....Criminal Trial Practice

TERWILLIGER, WAKEEN, PIEHLER & CONWAY, S.C.
Wausau, WI....Insurance Defense

TESTA, HURWITZ & THIBEAULT, LLP
Boston, MA....General Practice

TEW & ATCHISON, P.A.
Clayton, NC....General Practice

TEW & NOWAK
Miami, FL....Business Law; Securities Law

THAYER, BERNSTEIN & BASS, P.C.
Kansas City, MO....Family Law

THAYER, STEVEN W., P.S.
Vancouver, WA....Criminal Trial Practice

THE LOUDERBACK LAW FIRM
San Francisco, CA....Civil Trial Practice; Labor and Employment Law

THELEN REID & PRIEST LLP
Los Angeles, CA....General Practice
San Francisco, CA....General Practice
San Jose, CA....General Practice
Washington, DC....General Practice
New York, NY....General Practice

THERIAULT & JOSLIN, P.C.
Montpelier, VT....General Practice; Insurance Defense; Medical Malpractice; Product Liability Law; Professional Liability

THEUS, GRISHAM, DAVIS & LEIGH, L.L.P.
Monroe, LA....Insurance Defense; Tax Law; Trust and Estates, Wills and Probate

THÉVER, SHAN K., & ASSOCIATES, A PROF. CORP.
Los Angeles, CA....Medical Malpractice

THIBODEAU, JOSEPH H., P.C., LAW OFFICES OF
Denver, CO....Tax Law

THINNES, THOMAS A., P.A.
Phoenix, AZ....Criminal Trial Practice

THIRKELL & CRETAN
San Mateo, CA....Trust and Estates, Wills and Probate

THOMAN SOULE GAGE
Hamilton, ON, Canada....Civil Trial Practice; Insurance Defense; Product Liability Law

THOMAS, ARCHIBALD J. III, LAW OFFICES OF
Jacksonville, FL....Labor and Employment Law

THOMAS, CLAYTON H. JR.
Philadelphia, PA....Environmental Law; Insurance Defense; Product Liability Law; Toxic Torts; Workers Compensation

THOMAS, RICHARD C.
Columbia, MO....Civil Trial Practice; Personal Injury; Product Liability Law

THOMAS, BIRDSONG & BECKER, P.C.
Rolla, MO....General Practice

THOMAS & CULP, L.L.P.
Dallas, TX....Appellate Practice; Civil Trial Practice

THOMAS & ELARDO, P.C.
Phoenix, AZ....Insurance Defense

THOMAS, FELDMAN & WILSHUSEN, L.L.P.
Dallas, TX....Civil Trial Practice; Commercial Litigation; Construction Law

THOMAS, KAYDEN, HORSTEMEYER & RISLEY, L.L.P.
Atlanta, GA....Patent, Trademark, Copyright and Unfair Competition

THOMAS, KENNEDY, SAMPSON & PATTERSON
Atlanta, GA....Civil Trial Practice; Commercial Law; Insurance Defense; Medical Malpractice; Municipal Bond/Public Authority Financing; Personal Injury; Product Liability Law; Real Estate Law

THOMAS & LIBOWITZ, P.A.
Baltimore, MD....Banking Law; Business Law; Communications Law; Corporate Law; Family Law; Franchise Law; Insurance Defense; Mergers and Acquisitions; Real Estate Law; Securities Law; Trust and Estates, Wills and Probate

THOMAS, MAMER & HAUGHEY
Champaign, IL....General Practice

THOMAS, MEANS, GILLIS, DEVLIN, ROBINSON & SEAY, P.C.
Birmingham, AL....Civil Rights; Civil Trial Practice; Constitutional Law; Labor and Employment Law
Montgomery, AL....Civil Rights; Civil Trial Practice; Constitutional Law; Government Contracts; Labor and Employment Law; Personal Injury; Product Liability Law

THOMAS, SCOTT G., LAW OFFICES OF
Milwaukee, WI....Insurance Defense

THOMAS & SELF, A PROFESSIONAL CORPORATION
Dallas, TX....Civil Trial Practice

THOMAS, THOMAS & HAFER, LLP
Harrisburg, PA....Civil Trial Practice; Health Care Law; Insurance Defense; Labor and Employment Law; Medical Malpractice; Workers Compensation

THOMASSON, GILBERT, COOK & MAGUIRE, L.C.
Cape Girardeau, MO....Civil Trial Practice

THOMPSON, BETTY A., LTD.
Arlington, VA....Family Law

THOMPSON & BOWIE
Portland, ME....Civil Trial Practice; Construction Law; Insurance Defense; Legal Malpractice; Medical Malpractice; Personal Injury; Product Liability Law; Professional Liability; Workers Compensation

THOMPSON COBURN LLP
Washington, DC....General Practice
Belleville, IL....General Practice
St. Louis, MO....Civil Trial Practice; Commercial Law; General Practice

THOMPSON, COE, COUSINS & IRONS, L.L.P.
Dallas, TX....Administrative Law; Bankruptcy Law; Business Law; Civil Trial Practice; General Practice; Insurance Defense; Labor and Employment Law

THOMPSON, E.C., III, P.C.
Warsaw, NC....General Practice

THOMPSON, GARRETT & HINES
Brewton, AL....General Practice

THOMPSON KNIGHT BROWN PARKER & LEAHY L.L.P.
Houston, TX....Appellate Practice; Arbitration; Aviation Law; Business Law; Civil Trial Practice; Construction Law; Corporate Law; Energy Law; General Practice; Health Care Law; Insurance Defense; Intellectual Property Law; Labor and Employment Law; Legal Malpractice; Medical Malpractice; Natural Resources Law; Product Liability Law; Real Estate Law; Securities Law; Tax Law; Toxic Torts

THOMPSON & KNIGHT L.L.P.
Austin, TX....Administrative Law; Appellate Practice; Business Law; Civil Trial Practice; Corporate Law; Energy Law; Environmental Law; General Practice; Health Care Law; Insurance Defense; International Business Law; Labor and Employment Law; Medical Malpractice; Municipal and Zoning Law; Natural Resources Law; Product Liability Law; Securities Law; Tax Law; Toxic Torts; Trademark, Copyright and Unfair Competition
Dallas, TX....Administrative Law; Antitrust Law; Appellate Practice; Arbitration; Aviation Law; Banking Law; Bankruptcy Law; Business Law; Civil Trial Practice; Commercial Law; Computer Law; Construction Law; Corporate Law; Employment Benefits Law; Energy Law; Environmental Law; Franchise Law; General Practice; Health Care Law; Immigration and Naturalization; Insurance Defense; Intellectual Property Law; International Business Law; Labor and Employment Law; Legal Malpractice; Medical Malpractice; Mergers and Acquisitions; Municipal and Zoning Law; Natural Resources Law; Patent, Trademark, Copyright and Unfair Competition; Product Liability Law; Real Estate Law; Securities Law; Tax Law; Toxic Torts; Trademark, Copyright and Unfair Competition; Trust and Estates, Wills and Probate
Fort Worth, TX....Aviation Law; Banking Law; Business Law; Civil Trial Practice; Construction Law; General Practice; Health Care Law; Insurance Defense; International Business Law; Medical Malpractice; Product Liability Law; Real Estate Law; Securities Law; Tax Law; Trust and Estates, Wills and Probate
Garza Garcia, Nuevo Leon, Mexico....Business Law; General Practice; International Business Law; Securities Law

THOMPSON LAW FIRM, THE, P.A.
Conway, SC....Civil Trial Practice; Construction Law; General Practice; Insurance Defense
Myrtle Beach, SC....Civil Trial Practice; Construction Law; General Practice; Insurance Defense

THOMPSON LAW OFFICE, THE
Monterey, CA....Business Law; Civil Trial Practice; Personal Injury

THOMPSON AND LLEWELLYN, P.A.
Fort Smith, AR....Aviation Law; Commercial Litigation

THOMPSON, LYNNE R., P.A.
Melbourne, FL....Trust and Estates, Wills and Probate

THOMPSON, MARK E., A PROFESSIONAL CORPORATION
Lancaster, CA....Trust and Estates, Wills and Probate

THOMPSON, O'BRIEN, KEMP & NASUTI, P.C.
Norcross, GA....Banking Law; Commercial Litigation; Creditors Rights

THOMPSON, O'DONNELL, MARKHAM, NORTON & HANNON
Washington, DC....Civil Trial Practice; Trust and Estates, Wills and Probate

THOMPSON, O'NEIL & VANDERVEEN, P.C.
Traverse City, MI....Civil Trial Practice; Medical Malpractice; Personal Injury; Product Liability Law

THOMPSON & SMITH, P.C.
Augusta, GA....General Practice; Insurance Defense

THOMPSON, SPARKS, DEAN & MORRIS
Monroe, LA....Banking Law; Bankruptcy Law; Business Law; Commercial Law; Land Use Law; Tax Law; Trust and Estates, Wills and Probate

THOMPSON & SWEENY, P.C.
Lawrenceville, GA....General Practice

THOMPSON & THOMAS, A PROFESSIONAL CORPORATION
Lubbock, TX....Commercial Litigation; Insurance Defense

THOMPSON & WALDRON
Alexandria, VA....Construction Law

THOMS, DAVID M., & ASSOCIATES, P.C.
Detroit, MI....Business Law; Tax Law; Trust and Estates, Wills and Probate

THOMSEN AND BURKE, LLP
Washington, DC....Business Law; International Trade Law
Baltimore, MD....Business Law; International Trade Law; Tax Law; Trust and Estates, Wills and Probate

THOMSON LAW OFFICE
Edwardsville, IL....Civil Trial Practice; Insurance Defense

THOMSON & NELSON, A PROFESSIONAL LAW CORPORATION
Whittier, CA....General Practice

THOMSON, RHODES & COWIE, P.C.
Pittsburgh, PA....General Practice

THOMSON, ROGERS
Toronto, ON, Canada....General Practice

THON, BECK, VANNI, PHILLIPI & NUTT, A PROFESSIONAL CORPORATION
Pasadena, CA....Personal Injury

THORBURN, SAKOL & THRONE
Boulder, CO....Family Law

THORN AND GERSHON, LLP
Albany, NY....Medical Malpractice; Product Liability Law; Toxic Torts

THORNDAL, ARMSTRONG, DELK, BALKENBUSH & EISINGER, A PROFESSIONAL CORPORATION
Las Vegas, NV....Civil Trial Practice; Insurance Defense; Workers Compensation

THORNE, GRODNIK, RANSEL, DUNCAN, BYRON, HOSTETLER & TRIPPEL, LLP
Elkhart, IN....Bankruptcy Law; Corporate Law; Creditors Rights; Education Law; Personal Injury

THORNTON, EARLY & NAUMES LLP
Boston, MA....Civil Trial Practice; Product Liability Law

THORNTON, HEGG, REIF, DOLAN & BOWEN, P.A.
Alexandria, MN....General Practice

THORNTON, MASTRUCCI & MINKIN
Miami, FL....Medical Malpractice; Personal Injury

THORNTON & ROTHMAN, P.A.
Miami, FL....Criminal Trial Practice

THORNTON, TAYLOR, DOWNS, BECKER, TOLSON & DOHERTY
San Francisco, CA....Insurance Defense

THORP AND CLARKE
Fayetteville, NC....General Practice

THORPE, NORTH & WESTERN, L.L.P.
Sandy, UT....Computer Law; Intellectual Property Law; Patent, Trademark, Copyright and Unfair Competition

THORSNES, BARTOLOTTA, MCGUIRE & PADILLA
San Diego, CA....Business Law; Civil Trial Practice; Construction Law; Eminent Domain; Medical Malpractice; Personal Injury; Product Liability Law

THORSTEINSSONS
Vancouver, BC, Canada....Tax Law
Toronto, ON, Canada....Tax Law

THRAILKILL, HARRIS & WOOD, PLC
Brentwood, TN....Business Law; Tax Law; Trust and Estates, Wills and Probate

THRASHER, WHITLEY, HAMPTON & MORGAN, A PROFESSIONAL CORPORATION
Atlanta, GA....Business Law; International Business Law; Securities Law; Trust and Estates, Wills and Probate

THREET, MARTIN E., & ASSOCIATES
Albuquerque, NM....Appellate Practice; Civil Trial Practice; Creditors Rights; General Practice

THURBER CAPPELL, L.L.C.
Hackensack, NJ....Civil Trial Practice; Construction Law; Family Law; Labor and Employment Law; Trust and Estates, Wills and Probate

THURMAN, HOWALD, WEBER, SENKEL & NORRICK, L.L.C.
Hillsboro, MO....Civil Trial Practice; General Practice

TIERNEY & HAUGHWOUT
West Palm Beach, FL....Criminal Trial Practice

TIERNEY, ZULLO, FLAHERTY & MURPHY, P.C.
Norwalk, CT....General Practice; Real Estate Law

TIGHE, PATTON & BABBIN, P.L.L.C.
Washington, DC....Business Law

TILFORD, DOBBINS, ALEXANDER, BUCKAWAY & BLACK
Louisville, KY....Business Law; Civil Rights; Commercial Litigation; General Practice; Insurance Defense; Real Estate Law; Trust and Estates, Wills and Probate

TILL, PETER W.
Short Hills, NJ....Civil Rights; Civil Trial Practice; Criminal Trial Practice

TILLINGHAST LICHT & SEMONOFF LTD.
Providence, RI....General Practice

TIMBERLAKE, SMITH, THOMAS & MOSES, P.C.
Staunton, VA....General Practice

TIMMER, JAMO & O'LEARY
Lansing, MI....Civil Trial Practice; General Practice; Insurance Defense; Medical Malpractice; Personal Injury

TIMMIS & INMAN L.L.P.
Detroit, MI....Antitrust Law; Appellate Practice; Business Law; Civil Trial Practice; Commercial Law; Commercial Litigation; Corporate Law; Employment Benefits Law; Environmental Law; General Practice; Health Care Law; Insurance Defense; Intellectual Property Law; Labor and Employment Law; Mergers and Acquisitions; Pension and Profit Sharing; Personal Injury; Product Liability Law; Real Estate Law; Securities Law; Tax Law; Trust and Estates, Wills and Probate

TIMMONS & KELLY
Dallas, TX....Intellectual Property Law; Patent, Trademark, Copyright and Unfair Competition

TINDALL & FOSTER, P.C.
Houston, TX....Family Law; Immigration and Naturalization

TINLEY, NASTRI, RENEHAN & DOST, LLP
Waterbury, CT....General Practice

TINSMAN & HOUSER, INC.
San Antonio, TX....Civil Trial Practice; Commercial Law; Medical Malpractice; Personal Injury; Product Liability Law

TIROLA & HERRING
Westport, CT....General Practice

TISHLER, NICHOLAS E.
Niskayuna, NY....Appellate Practice

TISTAERT, LAWRENCE C.
Los Angeles, CA....Business Law; Real Estate Law

TITUS, BRUECKNER & BERRY, P.C.
Scottsdale, AZ....Business Law; Commercial Litigation; Real Estate Law; Securities Law

TOBIN, CRAIG D., & ASSOCIATES
Chicago, IL....Civil Trial Practice; Criminal Trial Practice

TODD, HOLLOWAY & WARD, P.C.
Columbia, SC....Commercial Litigation

TODD, VANDERBLOEMEN AND BRADY, P.A.
Lenoir, NC....General Practice

TODD & WAKEFIELD
Seattle, WA....Insurance Defense

TODD & WELD
Boston, MA....Civil Trial Practice

TODT LAW FIRM, THE, P.C.
St. Louis, MO....Family Law

TODTMAN, NACHAMIE, SPIZZ & JOHNS, P.C.
New York, NY....Bankruptcy Law; Tax Law

TOGUT, SEGAL & SEGAL
New York, NY....Bankruptcy Law

TOKYO AOYAMA LAW OFFICE
Tokyo, Japan....General Practice

TOLLEY, VANDENBOSCH, WALTON, KOROLEWICZ & BRENGLE, P.C.
Grand Rapids, MI....Civil Trial Practice; Construction Law; Insurance Defense; Real Estate Law

TOLLISON LAW FIRM, P.A.
Oxford, MS....Civil Trial Practice; Personal Injury

TOMAR, SIMONOFF, ADOURIAN, O'BRIEN, KAPLAN, JACOBY & GRAZIANO, A PROFESSIONAL CORPORATION
Cherry Hill, NJ....Labor and Employment Law; Natural Resources Law; Personal Injury
Northfield, NJ....Environmental Law; Labor and Employment Law

TOMASETTI, DOROTHY H.
Littleton, CO....Family Law

TOMAZIN, THOMAS J., P.C.
Englewood, CO....Civil Trial Practice; Medical Malpractice; Personal Injury

TOMITA & SIMPSON, P.C.
Albuquerque, NM....Trust and Estates, Wills and Probate

TOM & PETRUS
Honolulu, HI....Civil Trial Practice; Construction Law; Insurance Defense; Product Liability Law

TOMPKINS, CLOUGH, HIRSHON & LANGER, P.A.
Portland, ME....Admiralty/Maritime Law; Banking Law; Commercial Law

TOMPKINS, MCGUIRE, WACHENFELD & BARRY
Newark, NJ....Banking Law; Civil Trial Practice; Criminal Trial Practice; General Practice; Insurance Defense

TOMPKINS AND MCMASTER
Columbia, SC....Business Law; Civil Trial Practice; Criminal Trial Practice; General Practice

TONKIN & MONDL, L.C.
St. Louis, MO....Admiralty/Maritime Law

TOOLEY & VOSS
Dallas, TX....Appellate Practice; Civil Rights; Civil Trial Practice; Constitutional Law; Insurance Defense; Labor and Employment Law; Municipal and Zoning Law; Personal Injury; Product Liability Law

TOOMS & HOUSE
London, KY....Civil Trial Practice; Commercial Litigation; Corporate Law; Insurance Defense

TORBERT & TORBERT, P.A.
Gadsden, AL....Insurance Defense

TORKILDSON, KATZ, FONSECA, JAFFE, MOORE & HETHERINGTON, ATTORNEYS AT LAW, A LAW CORPORATION
Honolulu, HI....General Practice; Health Care Law; Labor and Employment Law; Pension and Profit Sharing; Tax Law

TORSHEN, SPREYER, GARMISA & SLOBIG, LTD.
Chicago, IL....Appellate Practice; Commercial Litigation

TORYS
New York, NY....Business Law
Toronto, ON, Canada....General Practice

TOWNSEND, LAWRENCE G.
San Francisco, CA....Trademark, Copyright and Unfair Competition

TOWNSEND & BRANNON
Tampa, FL....Bankruptcy Law; Commercial Litigation

TOWNSEND, COURTLAND K., JR., CHARTERED
Ocean City, MD....Civil Trial Practice; Criminal Trial Practice

TOWNSEND & MONTROSS
Indianapolis, IN....Aviation Law; Medical Malpractice; Personal Injury; Product Liability Law

TOWNSEND AND TOWNSEND AND CREW LLP
Palo Alto, CA....Patent, Trademark, Copyright and Unfair Competition
San Francisco, CA....Patent, Trademark, Copyright and Unfair Competition

TRACI & MARX CO., L.P.A.
Cleveland, OH....Commercial Litigation; Medical Malpractice; Personal Injury; Product Liability Law

TRAGER, SUSAN M., A PROF. CORP., LAW OFFICES OF
Irvine, CA....Environmental Law; Natural Resources Law

TRAGOS, GEORGE E.
Clearwater, FL....Criminal Trial Practice

TRAINOTTI, D. MICHAEL, A PROFESSIONAL LAW CORPORATION
Long Beach, CA....Corporate Law; Tax Law; Trust and Estates, Wills and Probate

TRALINS AND ASSOCIATES, P.A.
Miami, FL....Commercial Litigation; General Practice

TRAPASSO, DOLAN & HOLLANDER
Newton, NJ....Real Estate Law; Trust and Estates, Wills and Probate

TRASK, BRITT & ROSSA, A PROFESSIONAL CORPORATION
Salt Lake City, UT....Patent, Trademark, Copyright and Unfair Competition

TRAUB, BONACQUIST & FOX LLP
New York, NY....Bankruptcy Law; Business Law

TRAVERS & GARGAS, P.C.
Boston, MA........Family Law

TRAVIS, WILLIAM R. LAW OFFICE OF
Austin, TX........Family Law

TRAVIS & GOOCH
Washington, DC........Public Utilities Law

TRAYNOR, RUTTEN & TRAYNOR
Devils Lake, ND........General Practice

TREDENNICK, STEVEN B.
Round Rock, TX........Business Law

TREECE, ALFREY, MUSAT & BOSWORTH, P.C.
Denver, CO........Aviation Law; Civil Trial Practice; Commercial Litigation; Environmental Law; Medical Malpractice; Product Liability Law; Workers Compensation

TREMAYNE, PAMELA L. LAW OFFICES OF
Atlanta, GA........Creditors Rights; Family Law

TREMBLAY & HOLSENBACK
La Jolla, CA........Civil Trial Practice

TREMBLAY, MAURILE C., A PROF. CORP., LAW OFFICES OF
San Diego, CA........Civil Trial Practice; Insurance Defense; Real Estate Law

TREMBLAY & SMITH, LLP
Charlottesville, VA........Civil Trial Practice; General Practice

TRENAM, KEMKER, SCHARF, BARKIN, FRYE, O'NEILL & MULLIS, PROFESSIONAL ASSOCIATION
Tampa, FL........General Practice

TRENCH, ROSSI E WATANABE
Brasília, Brazil........General Practice
Rio de Janeiro, Brazil........General Practice
São Paulo, Brazil........General Practice

TRENTI LAW FIRM
Virginia, MN........General Practice

TREON, STRICK, LUCIA & AGUIRRE, A PROF. ASSN. OF LAWYERS
Phoenix, AZ........Medical Malpractice; Personal Injury

TREVETT, LENWEAVER & SALZER, P.C.
Rochester, NY........Civil Trial Practice; Criminal Trial Practice; Insurance Defense; Labor and Employment Law; Personal Injury

TREXLER, BUSHNELL, GIANGIORGI & BLACKSTONE, LTD.
Chicago, IL........Patent, Trademark, Copyright and Unfair Competition

TRIBLER ORPETT & CRONE, A PROFESSIONAL CORPORATION
Chicago, IL........Civil Trial Practice; Insurance Defense

TRICHILO, BANCROFT, MCGAVIN, HORVATH & JUDKINS, P.C.
Fairfax, VA........Civil Trial Practice; Insurance Defense

TRIMBLE, SHERINIAN, & VARANINI
Sacramento, CA........Insurance Defense

TRINE & METCALF, P.C.
Boulder, CO........Civil Trial Practice; Environmental Law; Medical Malpractice; Personal Injury; Product Liability Law

TRINKLE, REDMAN, SWANSON, BYRD & COTON, P.A.
Plant City, FL........General Practice

TRIPLETT, WOOLF & GARRETSON, LLC
Wichita, KS........Business Law; Civil Trial Practice; Commercial Law; Commercial Litigation; Construction Law; General Practice; Insurance Defense; Labor and Employment Law; Mergers and Acquisitions; Real Estate Law; Tax Law; Trust and Estates, Wills and Probate

TRIPP SCOTT
Fort Lauderdale, FL........Environmental Law; Labor and Employment Law; Real Estate Law

TROFF, PETZKE & AMMESON
St. Joseph, MI........Business Law; Labor and Employment Law; Personal Injury; Real Estate Law; Trust and Estates, Wills and Probate

TROMBADORE, RAYMOND R., & DAVID W., P.C.
Somerville, NJ........Business Law; Civil Trial Practice; Commercial Law; Corporate Law; Criminal Trial Practice; General Practice; Real Estate Law

TROPE AND TROPE
Los Angeles, CA........Family Law

TROUBH, HEISLER & PIAMPIANO, P.C.
Portland, ME........Banking Law; Bankruptcy Law; Business Law; Civil Trial Practice; Commercial Law; General Practice; Labor and Employment Law; Personal Injury; Real Estate Law; Tax Law; Trust and Estates, Wills and Probate; Workers Compensation

TROUT & RICHARDS, P.L.L.C.
Washington, DC........Civil Trial Practice; Criminal Trial Practice

TROUTMAN, RICHARD B., P.A.
Orlando, FL........Medical Malpractice; Personal Injury
Winter Park, FL........Medical Malpractice; Personal Injury

TROUTMAN, WILLIAMS, IRVIN, GREEN & HELMS, PROFESSIONAL ASSOCIATION
Winter Park, FL........Civil Trial Practice; General Practice

TROWBRIDGE & BASINE, P.C.
Glastonbury, CT........Construction Law; Environmental Law; Insurance Defense

TROWBRIDGE LAW FIRM, P.C.
Detroit, MI........Corporate Law; Personal Injury

TRULY, SMITH & LATHAM
Natchez, MS........Banking Law; Civil Trial Practice; Energy Law; Real Estate Law; Trust and Estates, Wills and Probate

TRUMAN, CRAIG L., P.C.
Denver, CO........Criminal Trial Practice

TRYON & ASSOCIATES, P.C.
Garden City, NY........Commercial Litigation; Construction Law

TSCHIDER & SMITH
Bismarck, ND........Civil Trial Practice; Tax Law; Trust and Estates, Wills and Probate

TUCHOW & TRAHEY
Flat Rock, MI........Family Law; Personal Injury; Real Estate Law; Trust and Estates, Wills and Probate

TUCKER, STEVEN L.
Santa Fe, NM........Appellate Practice

TUCKER, HENDRYX, TAUNTON, SNYDER & SLADE, P.C.
Houston, TX........Insurance Defense

TUCKER STROHM MILLER & TUCKER, P.C.
Phoenix, AZ........Appellate Practice; Criminal Trial Practice; Medical Malpractice; Personal Injury; Product Liability Law; Professional Liability

TUCKER AND TUCKER, P.C.
Paoli, IN........General Practice

TUKE YOPP & SWEENEY, PLC
Nashville, TN........Commercial Litigation; Mergers and Acquisitions; Trademark, Copyright and Unfair Competition

TULAC, JOHN W.
Claremont, CA........International Business Law; International Trade Law

TURBIN, RICHARD, A LAW CORPORATION, LAW OFFICES OF
Honolulu, HI........Medical Malpractice; Personal Injury

TURK, PAUL A., JR., P.A.
Palm Beach, FL........Civil Trial Practice; Eminent Domain

TURLEY & STUTZ, P.C.
Dallas, TX........Medical Malpractice; Personal Injury; Product Liability Law

TURLEY, WINDLE, P.C., LAW OFFICES OF
Dallas, TX........Aviation Law; Civil Trial Practice; Personal Injury

TURNER, BRUCE E.
Addison, TX........Real Estate Law

TURNER, CHARLES B. LAW OFFICE OF
South Orange, NJ........Commercial Law; General Practice

TURNER, AUBERT & FRIEDMAN, LLP
Beverly Hills, CA........Business Law; Civil Trial Practice; General Practice; Real Estate Law

TURNER & DAVIS, A PROFESSIONAL CORPORATION
Midland, TX........Commercial Litigation; Natural Resources Law

TURNER, JONES & BITTING
Clarinda, IA........General Practice

TURNER, ONDERDONK, KIMBROUGH & HOWELL, P.A.
Chatom, AL........Civil Trial Practice; Criminal Trial Practice; General Practice; Personal Injury; Product Liability Law; Workers Compensation
Mobile, AL........General Practice

TURNER, PADGET, GRAHAM & LANEY, P.A.
Columbia, SC........Administrative Law; Antitrust Law; Banking Law; Bankruptcy Law; Business Law; Civil Trial Practice; Commercial Law; Construction Law; Creditors Rights; Criminal Trial Practice; Environmental Law; General Practice; Government Contracts; Health Care Law; Insurance Defense; Medical Malpractice; Municipal and Zoning Law; Personal Injury; Product Liability Law; Real Estate Law; Securities Law; Trust and Estates, Wills and Probate; Workers Compensation

TURNER, REID, DUNCAN, LOOMER & PATTON, P.C.
Springfield, MO....................Civil Trial Practice

TURNER, SEABERRY & WARFORD
Eastland, TX....................General Practice

TURNER & TURNER, P.C.
Tuscaloosa, AL....................General Practice

TURNER, TURNER & TURNER, PROFESSIONAL CORPORATION
Atlanta, GA....................Family Law

TURNER, WILSON & SAWYER
Montgomery, AL....................Family Law; Real Estate Law; Trust and Estates, Wills and Probate

TUSA, MICHAEL T. JR.
Metairie, LA....................Labor and Employment Law

TUTT, CHARLES G.
Shreveport, LA....................Civil Trial Practice; Product Liability Law

TUTTLE & TAYLOR, A LAW CORPORATION
Los Angeles, CA....................General Practice

TUTTLE, TAYLOR & HERON
Washington, DC....................General Practice

TWEEDY, PENNEY & CRAWFORD, A LAW PARTNERSHIP
Sacramento, CA....................Workers Compensation

TWIGGS, ABRAMS, STRICKLAND & TREHY, P.A.
Raleigh, NC....................Civil Trial Practice; Communications Law; Medical Malpractice; Personal Injury; Product Liability Law

TWITCHELL AND RICE
Santa Maria, CA....................General Practice

TWOHIG, RAY, P.C.
Albuquerque, NM....................Civil Rights; Criminal Trial Practice

TYAN & ASSOCIES
Beirut, Lebanon....................General Practice

TYE AND TYE
Dayton, OH....................General Practice; Trust and Estates, Wills and Probate

TYLER, BARTL, BURKE AND ALBERT, P.L.C.
Alexandria, VA....................Bankruptcy Law

TYLER, CASSELL, JACKSON, PEACE & SILVER, L.L.P.
Columbia, SC....................Commercial Law; Construction Law; Real Estate Law

TYLER COOPER & ALCORN, LLP
Hartford, CT....................General Practice
New Haven, CT....................General Practice
Stamford, CT....................General Practice

TYSON, GEORGE H. JR.
Houston, TX....................Criminal Trial Practice

UDALL, SHUMWAY, BLACKHURST, ALLEN & LYONS, P.C.
Mesa, AZ....................Commercial Litigation; Education Law; Family Law; Insurance Defense; Legal Malpractice; Personal Injury; Tax Law; Trust and Estates, Wills and Probate

UFKES, JOHN H.F.
San Juan Capistrano, CA........Workers Compensation

ULMER & BERNE LLP
Cleveland, OH....................Business Law; Civil Trial Practice; General Practice; Labor and Employment Law; Tax Law

ULRICH, KESSLER & ANGER, P.C.
Phoenix, AZ....................Antitrust Law; Appellate Practice; Commercial Litigation; Health Care Law; Medical Malpractice; Municipal and Zoning Law; Natural Resources Law

UNDERBERG & KESSLER LLP
Rochester, NY....................Banking Law; Business Law; Civil Trial Practice; Environmental Law; General Practice; Health Care Law; Insurance Defense; Labor and Employment Law; Tax Law

UNDERWOOD, P. JAMES
Annapolis, MD....................Real Estate Law

UNDERWOOD KINSEY WARREN & TUCKER, P.A.
Charlotte, NC....................General Practice

UNDERWOOD LAW FIRM
Jackson, MS....................Bankruptcy Law; Real Estate Law

UNDERWOOD, WILSON, BERRY, STEIN & JOHNSON, P.C.
Amarillo, TX....................General Practice

UNGERMAN, MAYNARD I., LAW OFFICES OF
Tulsa, OK....................Family Law; Labor and Employment Law; Personal Injury

UNGLESBY, KOCH & REYNOLDS
Baton Rouge, LA....................Criminal Trial Practice; Product Liability Law; Toxic Torts

UPCHURCH, BAILEY & UPCHURCH, P.A.
St. Augustine, FL....................Civil Trial Practice; Environmental Law; General Practice; Land Use Law; Municipal and Zoning Law; Real Estate Law; Trust and Estates, Wills and Probate

UPSHAW, WILLIAMS, BIGGERS, BECKHAM & RIDDICK, LLP
Greenwood, MS....................Civil Trial Practice; Environmental Law; General Practice; Insurance Defense; Workers Compensation
Jackson, MS....................Civil Trial Practice; General Practice; Insurance Defense; Workers Compensation

URBAN, LEE D.
Portland, ME....................Real Estate Law

URBELIS, FIELDSTEEL & BAILIN, LLP
Boston, MA....................Civil Trial Practice

URICCHIO, HOWE, KRELL, JACOBSON, TOPOREK & THEOS, P.A.
Charleston, SC....................Civil Trial Practice; Criminal Trial Practice; Family Law; Workers Compensation

USSERY & PARRISH, P.A.
Albuquerque, NM....................Real Estate Law

UTZ, LITVAK, SUMMERS, POWERS & MANRING
St. Joseph, MO....................General Practice

VAAGE, ROBERT F.
San Diego, CA....................Civil Trial Practice

VAALER, ZIMNEY, FOSTER & JOHNSON, CHARTERED
Grand Forks, ND....................General Practice

VACOVEC, MAYOTTE & SINGER
Newton, MA....................International Business Law; Tax Law

VAGLICA & MEINHOLD, L.L.C.
Colorado Springs, CO....................Civil Trial Practice

VAIRO, MECHLIN, TOMASI, JOHNSON & MANCHESTER
Houghton, MI....................General Practice; Insurance Defense

VAKA, LARSON & JOHNSON, P.L.
Tampa, FL....................Appellate Practice; Personal Injury

VALENTINE, ADAMS & LAMAR, L.L.P.
Nashville, NC....................General Practice

VALENTINE & ASSOCIATES, P.C.
Detroit, MI....................Civil Trial Practice; Labor and Employment Law; Personal Injury
West Bloomfield, MI....................Business Law; Civil Trial Practice; Labor and Employment Law; Personal Injury; Real Estate Law

VALENZUELA, HENRY E., P.A.
Tampa, FL....................Medical Malpractice; Personal Injury

VALLE & CRAIG, P.A.
Miami, FL....................Admiralty/Maritime Law; Civil Trial Practice; Commercial Law; Insurance Defense

VAN BLOIS & ASSOCIATES
Oakland, CA....................Aviation Law; Medical Malpractice; Personal Injury; Product Liability Law

VAN CAMP, HAYES & MEACHAM, A PROFESSIONAL ASSOCIATION
Pinehurst, NC....................General Practice

VAN COTT, BAGLEY, CORNWALL & MCCARTHY, A PROFESSIONAL CORPORATION
Ogden, UT....................General Practice
Park City, UT....................General Practice
Salt Lake City, UT....................Administrative Law; Antitrust Law; Appellate Practice; Arbitration; Banking Law; Bankruptcy Law; Business Law; Civil Trial Practice; Commercial Law; Commercial Litigation; Communications Law; Constitutional Law; Construction Law; Corporate Law; Creditors Rights; Eminent Domain; Employment Benefits Law; Energy Law; Environmental Law; Family Law; General Practice; Government Contracts; Health Care Law; Immigration and Naturalization; Insurance Defense; Intellectual Property Law; International Trade Law; Labor and Employment Law; Land Use Law; Medical Malpractice; Mergers and Acquisitions; Municipal and Zoning Law; Natural Resources Law; Oil and Gas Law; Pension and Profit Sharing; Personal Injury; Product Liability Law; Professional Liability; Public Utilities Law; Real Estate Law; Securities Law; Tax Law; Toxic Torts; Trademark, Copyright and Unfair Competition; Trust and Estates, Wills and Probate

VANDEBERG JOHNSON & GANDARA
Tacoma, WA............General Practice

VANDEMARK, RUTH E. LAW OFFICES OF
Chicago, IL............Appellate Practice

VANDEN BOS & CHAPMAN
Portland, OR............Bankruptcy Law

VANDER MALE, BELLAMY, GILCHRIST, VANDE VUSSE & CAFFERTY
Detroit, MI............Civil Trial Practice; Criminal Trial Practice; Health Care Law

VANDEVEER GARZIA, PROFESSIONAL CORPORATION
Birmingham, MI............Insurance Defense
Detroit, MI............Aviation Law; Civil Trial Practice; Commercial Litigation; Construction Law; Insurance Defense; Medical Malpractice; Municipal and Zoning Law; Product Liability Law

VANDEVENTER BLACK LLP
Norfolk, VA............Admiralty/Maritime Law; Bankruptcy Law; Civil Trial Practice; Environmental Law; General Practice; Immigration and Naturalization; Labor and Employment Law; Real Estate Law; Tax Law

VAN DEWATER & VAN DEWATER
Poughkeepsie, NY............Banking Law; Bankruptcy Law; Communications Law; Family Law; General Practice; Real Estate Law; Tax Law

VAN HOY, REUTLINGER & TAYLOR
Charlotte, NC............Health Care Law; Labor and Employment Law

VAN MEER & BELANGER, P.A.
South Portland, ME............Business Law; Employment Benefits Law; Health Care Law; Tax Law; Trust and Estates, Wills and Probate

VANN LAW FIRM
Camilla, GA............General Practice

VANNAH COSTELLO CANEPA RIEDY & RUBINO
Las Vegas, NV............Construction Law; Insurance Defense; Medical Malpractice; Personal Injury; Product Liability Law

VANNOY, COLVARD, TRIPLETT & VANNOY, P.L.L.C.
North Wilkesboro, NC............General Practice

VAN STEENBERG, CHALOUPKA, MULLIN, HOLYOKE, PAHLKE, SMITH, SNYDER & HOFMEISTER, P.C.
Scottsbluff, NE............Commercial Litigation

VAN SUILICHEM & ASSOCIATES, P.C.
Troy, MI............Civil Rights; Labor and Employment Law

VAN WAGNER, ELLEN LAW OFFICES OF
Chino, CA............Workers Compensation

VAN WERT, RONALD K., A PROFESSIONAL CORPORATION
Costa Mesa, CA............Civil Trial Practice; Tax Law

VAN WINKLE, BUCK, WALL, STARNES AND DAVIS, P.A.
Asheville, NC............Business Law; General Practice; Insurance Defense; Medical Malpractice

VARNADORE, M. DEWAYNE, P.C., LAW OFFICES OF
Tyler, TX............Oil and Gas Law

VASSALLO, EDDIE, P.C., LAW OFFICES OF
Dallas, TX............Civil Trial Practice; Eminent Domain; Personal Injury

VAUGHAN & HULL, LTD., A PROF. CORP., LAW OFFICES
Elko, NV............General Practice

VEAL & ASSOCIATES
Birmingham, AL............Intellectual Property Law; Patent, Trademark, Copyright and Unfair Competition

VEDDER, PRICE, KAUFMAN & KAMMHOLZ
Chicago, IL............General Practice

VEEN, WILLIAM L., A PROFESSIONAL CORPORATION
San Francisco, CA............Personal Injury

VELTMANN & LETO
San Diego, CA............Family Law

VENABLE, ATTORNEYS AT LAW, VENABLE, BAETJER, HOWARD & CIVILETTI, LLP
Washington, DC............Administrative Law; Admiralty/Maritime Law; Antitrust Law; Appellate Practice; Banking Law; Bankruptcy Law; Business Law; Civil Trial Practice; Commercial Law; Communications Law; Construction Law; Criminal Trial Practice; Employment Benefits Law; Environmental Law; General Practice; Health Care Law; Insurance Defense; Intellectual Property Law; Labor and Employment Law; Natural Resources Law; Patent, Trademark, Copyright and Unfair Competition; Product Liability Law; Real Estate Law; Securities Law; Trademark, Copyright and Unfair Competition; Transportation Law
Baltimore, MD............Administrative Law; Admiralty/Maritime Law; Antitrust Law; Appellate Practice; Banking Law; Bankruptcy Law; Business Law; Civil Trial Practice; Commercial Law; Communications Law; Construction Law; Criminal Trial Practice; Employment Benefits Law; Environmental Law; Family Law; General Practice; Health Care Law; Immigration and Naturalization; Insurance Defense; Intellectual Property Law; Labor and Employment Law; Municipal and Zoning Law; Municipal Bond/Public Authority Financing; Natural Resources Law; Patent, Trademark, Copyright and Unfair Competition; Personal Injury; Product Liability Law; Real Estate Law; Securities Law; Tax Law; Trademark, Copyright and Unfair Competition; Transportation Law; Trust and Estates, Wills and Probate
Rockville, MD............Administrative Law; Appellate Practice; Banking Law; Business Law; Civil Trial Practice; General Practice; Labor and Employment Law
Towson, MD............Appellate Practice; Banking Law; Business Law; Civil Trial Practice; Commercial Law; Construction Law; General Practice; Insurance Defense; Labor and Employment Law; Municipal Bond/Public Authority Financing; Personal Injury; Product Liability Law; Real Estate Law; Trust and Estates, Wills and Probate
McLean, VA............Appellate Practice; Banking Law; Civil Trial Practice; Commercial Law; Construction Law; General Practice; Real Estate Law

VENZIE, PHILLIPS & WARSHAWER, A PROFESSIONAL CORPORATION
Philadelphia, PA............Arbitration; Construction Law

VEON, LESLIE L. LAW OFFICES OF
Chicago, IL............Family Law

VERCRUYSSE METZ & MURRAY, A PROFESSIONAL CORPORATION
Bingham Farms, MI............Labor and Employment Law

VERNER & BRUMLEY, A PROFESSIONAL CORPORATION
Dallas, TX............Family Law

VERNER, LIIPFERT, BERNHARD, MCPHERSON AND HAND, CHARTERED
Washington, DC............Bankruptcy Law; Commercial Law; Communications Law; Energy Law; Environmental Law; General Practice; International Business Law; Labor and Employment Law; Transportation Law

VERNER SIMON LLP
New York, NY............Insurance Defense

VERRILL & DANA, LLP
Portland, ME............Administrative Law; Bankruptcy Law; Business Law; Civil Trial Practice; Commercial Litigation; Construction Law; Employment Benefits Law; Environmental Law; General Practice; Health Care Law; Labor and Employment Law; Land Use Law; Real Estate Law; Trust and Estates, Wills and Probate

VERTERANO & MANOLIS
New Castle, PA............General Practice

VETTER & WHITE, INCORPORATED
Providence, RI............Appellate Practice; Business Law; Civil Trial Practice; Employment Benefits Law; Insurance Defense; Intellectual Property Law; Product Liability Law; Trademark, Copyright and Unfair Competition

VIAL, HAMILTON, KOCH & KNOX, L.L.P.
Dallas, TX............General Practice

VICKERS, RIIS, MURRAY AND CURRAN, L.L.C.
Mobile, AL............Admiralty/Maritime Law; Business Law; Commercial Law; Environmental Law; General Practice; Tax Law; Trust and Estates, Wills and Probate

VICTOR, RAYMOND M., P.C.
Norristown, PA............Legal Malpractice; Medical Malpractice; Personal Injury; Product Liability Law

VIGORITA, LOUIS J.
Ventura, CA............Workers Compensation

VIMONT & WILLS PLLC
Lexington, KY............Construction Law; Family Law; Insurance Defense; Labor and Employment Law; Real Estate Law; Trust and Estates, Wills and Probate; Workers Compensation

VINAR, BENJAMIN
Garden City, NY............Appellate Practice; Civil Trial Practice

VINSON & ELKINS
London, England............General Practice
Washington, DC............Civil Trial Practice; General Practice
Austin, TX............Civil Trial Practice; General Practice
Dallas, TX............Civil Trial Practice; General Practice

Houston, TX .... Admiralty/Maritime Law; Antitrust Law; Civil Trial Practice; Energy Law; General Practice; Labor and Employment Law; Municipal Bond/Public Authority Financing; Natural Resources Law; Patent, Trademark, Copyright and Unfair Competition; Tax Law

VINYARD & ASSOCIATES
Washington, DC .... Tax Law

VIRTUE NAJJAR BARTELL MATTHEWS & BROWN P.C.
Santa Fe, NM .... General Practice

VITTAL AND STERNBERG
Los Angeles, CA .... Civil Trial Practice

VLADECK, WALDMAN, ELIAS & ENGELHARD, P.C.
New York, NY .... Labor and Employment Law

VLASSIS & VLASSIS
Phoenix, AZ .... Business Law; Immigration and Naturalization; Natural Resources Law

VOGEL, WEIR, BYE, HUNKE & MCCORMICK, LTD.
Fargo, ND .... Banking Law; Bankruptcy Law; Civil Trial Practice; Commercial Law; Criminal Trial Practice; General Practice; Insurance Defense; Labor and Employment Law; Personal Injury; Real Estate Law; Tax Law; Trust and Estates, Wills and Probate

VOGL & MEREDITH
San Francisco, CA .... Civil Trial Practice; Commercial Litigation; Environmental Law; Insurance Defense

VOLK LAW FIRM, THE, P.C.
Sewickley, PA .... Labor and Employment Law

VOLLMER, MICHAEL V.
Newport Beach, CA .... Trust and Estates, Wills and Probate

VOLLMER RULONG & KEATING, P.C.
Pittsburgh, PA .... Bankruptcy Law; Civil Trial Practice; Commercial Litigation; Creditors Rights; Personal Injury

VOLPE, EDWARD L., P.C.
Denver, CO .... Commercial Litigation

VOLZ, PRESTWOOD & HANAN, P.C.
Montgomery, AL .... Administrative Law; Appellate Practice; Business Law; Civil Rights; Civil Trial Practice; Commercial Law; Constitutional Law; Employment Benefits Law; General Practice; Labor and Employment Law; Product Liability Law; Real Estate Law; Trust and Estates, Wills and Probate

VON MANDEL & VON MANDEL
Chicago, IL .... Tax Law

VOORHEES & OUDA
Morris Plains, NJ .... Civil Trial Practice; Legal Malpractice; Medical Malpractice; Professional Liability

VOORHIES & LABBÉ, A PROFESSIONAL LAW CORPORATION
Lafayette, LA .... Insurance Defense; Personal Injury

VORT, ROBERT A.
Tenafly, NJ .... Appellate Practice; Family Law

VORYS, SATER, SEYMOUR AND PEASE LLP
Washington, DC .... General Practice
Cincinnati, OH .... General Practice
Cleveland, OH .... General Practice; Labor and Employment Law
Columbus, OH .... Antitrust Law; Banking Law; Bankruptcy Law; General Practice; Labor and Employment Law; Municipal Bond/Public Authority Financing; Natural Resources Law; Real Estate Law; Tax Law

VOSE, BLAU & HAYES
Winter Park, FL .... Commercial Litigation; Construction Law; Environmental Law; Land Use Law; Real Estate Law

VOTRE & ASSOCIATES, P.C.
New Haven, CT .... Commercial Law; Health Care Law; International Business Law; Tax Law

VOUTÉ, LOHRFINK, MAGRO & COLLINS, LLP
White Plains, NY .... Civil Trial Practice; General Practice; Insurance Defense; Medical Malpractice; Personal Injury; Product Liability Law

VRANESH AND RAISCH, L.L.P.
Boulder, CO .... Environmental Law; Natural Resources Law
Denver, CO .... Environmental Law; Natural Resources Law

WACHTEL, BIEHN & MALM
Lake Havasu City, AZ .... Arbitration; Family Law; Personal Injury; Trust and Estates, Wills and Probate

WACHTEL & MASYR, LLP
New York, NY .... Civil Trial Practice; Corporate Law; Tax Law

WADDICK LAW FIRM, THE, P.C.
Indianapolis, IN .... Personal Injury

WADE CLARK MULCAHY
New York, NY .... Civil Trial Practice; Insurance Defense; Product Liability Law

WADLEIGH, STARR & PETERS, P.L.L.C.
Manchester, NH .... General Practice

WAGNER, CRAIG E.
Englewood, CO .... Commercial Litigation

WAGNER & BAGOT
New Orleans, LA .... Admiralty/Maritime Law; Commercial Litigation; Environmental Law; Insurance Defense; International Business Law; Labor and Employment Law; Product Liability Law

WAGNER, DAVIS & GOLD, P.C.
New York, NY .... Commercial Litigation; Construction Law; General Practice; Real Estate Law; Trust and Estates, Wills and Probate

WAGNER AND GRUNDY
Tulsa, OK .... Family Law

WAGNER, JOHNSON, MCAFEE & BODIK, P.A.
West Palm Beach, FL .... Civil Trial Practice; Personal Injury

WAGNER LAW FIRM, THE
Fort Worth, TX .... Personal Injury

WAGNER, MYERS & SANGER, A PROFESSIONAL CORPORATION
Knoxville, TN .... Civil Trial Practice; General Practice; Health Care Law; Natural Resources Law; Public Utilities Law; Tax Law

WAGSTAFF, ROBERT H. LAW OFFICES OF
Anchorage, AK .... Appellate Practice; Aviation Law; Insurance Defense; Medical Malpractice; Product Liability Law

WAGSTAFF, ALVIS, STUBBEMAN, SEAMSTER & LONGACRE, L.L.P.
Abilene, TX .... General Practice; Insurance Defense

WAGSTAFF & CARTMELL, LLP
Kansas City, MO .... Civil Trial Practice; Commercial Litigation; Medical Malpractice; Product Liability Law; Professional Liability

WAITE, SCHNEIDER, BAYLESS & CHESLEY CO., L.P.A.
Cincinnati, OH .... Antitrust Law; Appellate Practice; Aviation Law; Civil Trial Practice; International Business Law; Labor and Employment Law; Personal Injury; Product Liability Law; Real Estate Law; Securities Law

WALDBAUM, CORN, KOFF AND BERGER, P.C.
Denver, CO .... General Practice

WALDECK & LIND, P.A.
Minneapolis, MN .... Appellate Practice; Civil Trial Practice; Insurance Defense

WALDER, SONDAK & BROGAN, A PROFESSIONAL CORPORATION
Roseland, NJ .... Appellate Practice; Business Law; Civil Trial Practice; Commercial Law; Criminal Trial Practice; Environmental Law; General Practice; Insurance Defense; Tax Law

WALDRON AND FANN
Murfreesboro, TN .... Personal Injury

WALKER, WOODROW W.
Arlington, VA .... Creditors Rights

WALKER & BLACK
Little Rock, AR .... Commercial Law; Trust and Estates, Wills and Probate

WALKER, GEORGE G., INC.
San Francisco, CA .... Criminal Trial Practice

WALKER, HULBERT, GRAY & BYRD, L.L.P.
Perry, GA .... General Practice

WALKER, KEELING & CARROLL, L.L.P.
Victoria, TX .... Environmental Law; Insurance Defense; Labor and Employment Law

WALKER LAW FIRM, THE
Des Moines, IA .... Civil Trial Practice; Personal Injury; Product Liability Law; Toxic Torts
Newport Beach, CA .... Civil Trial Practice

WALKER & MCPHAIL
Monterey, CA .... Trust and Estates, Wills and Probate

WALKER, SHOCK, HARP & HILL, P.L.L.C.
Fort Smith, AR........................Workers Compensation

WALKER & WALKER, P.C.
Knoxville, TN..........................Banking Law; Bankruptcy Law; Creditors Rights; General Practice

WALKER, WATTS, JACKSON & MCFARLAND
Adrian, MI..............................Banking Law; General Practice; Real Estate Law; Trust and Estates, Wills and Probate

WALKER, WILLIAM G., P.C.
Tucson, AZ..............................Civil Trial Practice; Commercial Litigation; Criminal Trial Practice

WALKUP, MELODIA, KELLY & ECHEVERRIA, A PROFESSIONAL CORPORATION
San Francisco, CA....................Employment Benefits Law; Labor and Employment Law; Medical Malpractice; Personal Injury; Product Liability Law

WALLACE & DE MAYO, P.C.
Norcross, GA...........................Bankruptcy Law; Commercial Law; Creditors Rights

WALLACE, KLOR & MANN, P.C.
Portland, OR...........................Workers Compensation

WALLACE, MORRIS & BARWICK, P.A.
Kinston, NC............................General Practice

WALLACE, SAUNDERS, AUSTIN, BROWN & ENOCHS, CHARTERED
Overland Park, KS..................General Practice

WALLENSTEIN & WAGNER, LTD.
Chicago, IL.............................Intellectual Property Law; Patent, Trademark, Copyright and Unfair Competition

WALLER LANSDEN DORTCH & DAVIS
Columbia, TN..........................General Practice
Nashville, TN..........................General Practice

WALLER, SMITH & PALMER, P.C.
New London, CT....................Banking Law; Business Law; Civil Trial Practice; Commercial Law; Corporate Law; General Practice; Municipal and Zoning Law; Real Estate Law; Trust and Estates, Wills and Probate
Old Lyme, CT.........................General Practice

WALLMAN, GREENBERG, GASMAN & MCKNIGHT, LLP
New York, NY.........................Corporate Law; Family Law; Real Estate Law; Trust and Estates, Wills and Probate

WALSH, MICHAEL R.
Orlando, FL............................Family Law

WALSH, TIMOTHY J.
Mishawaka, IN.......................Civil Trial Practice

WALSH, ANDERSON, BROWN, SCHULZE & ALDRIDGE, P.C.
Austin, TX..............................Civil Trial Practice; Insurance Defense

WALSH, COLUCCI, STACKHOUSE, EMRICH & LUBELEY, P.C.
Arlington, VA.........................Business Law; Civil Trial Practice; Land Use Law; Municipal and Zoning Law; Real Estate Law
Leesburg, VA..........................Real Estate Law
Woodbridge, VA......................Real Estate Law

WALSH, DANIEL R., THE LAW OFFICE OF
Carson City, NV......................Energy Law; Environmental Law; Land Use Law

WALSH & DECLUES, LLP
Encino, CA..............................Labor and Employment Law
Santa Ana, CA........................Insurance Defense; Labor and Employment Law

WALSH & FISHER, A PROFESSIONAL ASSOCIATION
Westminster, MD....................General Practice; Real Estate Law

WALSH & KEATING, S.C.
Milwaukee, WI........................Commercial Law; Corporate Law; Real Estate Law; Tax Law; Trust and Estates, Wills and Probate

WALSH, MICHAEL P., P.A.
West Palm Beach, FL.............Family Law

WALSH, O'NEAL, & ASSOCIATES
Baton Rouge, LA.....................Insurance Defense

WALSTON, WELLS, ANDERSON & BAINS, LLP
Birmingham, AL......................Civil Trial Practice; General Practice

WALSWORTH, FRANKLIN, BEVINS & MCCALL
Orange, CA.............................Environmental Law

WALTER & HAVERFIELD, P.L.L.
Cleveland, OH........................Civil Trial Practice; Communications Law; Employment Benefits Law; Environmental Law; General Practice; Health Care Law; International Business Law; Labor and Employment Law; Mergers and Acquisitions; Municipal and Zoning Law; Pension and Profit Sharing; Real Estate Law; Tax Law; Trust and Estates, Wills and Probate

WALTERS, DAVIS & PUJADAS, P.C.
Ocilla, GA...............................Civil Trial Practice; Criminal Trial Practice; General Practice

WALTERS FRAZIER CAIETTI RUTAN & LOPEZ, LLP
San Diego, CA........................Civil Trial Practice

WALTERS & JOYCE, P.C.
Denver, CO.............................Antitrust Law; Civil Trial Practice; General Practice; Real Estate Law

WALTERS & WARD, A PROFESSIONAL CORPORATION
San Diego, CA........................Trust and Estates, Wills and Probate

WALTHER ASSOCIATES
Albuquerque, NM...................Family Law
Santa Fe, NM..........................Family Law

WALTHER, KEY, MAUPIN, OATS, COX & LEGOY, A PROFESSIONAL CORPORATION
Reno, NV................................Arbitration; Business Law; Civil Trial Practice; Commercial Litigation; Construction Law; Corporate Law; Employment Benefits Law; Environmental Law; Health Care Law; Pension and Profit Sharing; Personal Injury; Real Estate Law; Tax Law; Trust and Estates, Wills and Probate

WALTHER LAW OFFICES, S.C.
Milwaukee, WI........................Transportation Law

WALTON LANTAFF SCHROEDER & CARSON
Fort Lauderdale, FL...............General Practice
Miami, FL...............................General Practice
West Palm Beach, FL.............General Practice

WALTON, SMITH, PHILLIPS & DIXON, P.C.
Traverse City, MI...................Civil Trial Practice; Commercial Litigation; Personal Injury; Workers Compensation

WANSKER, HENRY B.
Rockingham, NC....................Personal Injury

WARBURTON, ADAMI, MCNEILL, PAISLEY & APPELL, P.C.
Alice, TX...............................Banking Law; Family Law; General Practice; Trust and Estates, Wills and Probate

WARD, CRAIG B., P.A.
Orlando, FL............................General Practice; Real Estate Law; Trust and Estates, Wills and Probate

WARD, DAMON, BEVERLY, TITTLE & POSNER, P.A.
West Palm Beach, FL.............Antitrust Law; Banking Law; Bankruptcy Law; Commercial Litigation; Real Estate Law; Securities Law; Trust and Estates, Wills and Probate

WARD, KERSHAW & MINTON, A PROFESSIONAL ASSOCIATION
Baltimore, MD........................Admiralty/Maritime Law; Antitrust Law; Civil Trial Practice; Insurance Defense

WARD NELSON, LLC
New Orleans, LA....................Commercial Litigation; Health Care Law; Insurance Defense; Medical Malpractice; Product Liability Law

WARDROP & WARDROP, P.C.
Grand Rapids, MI...................Bankruptcy Law; Commercial Law; Immigration and Naturalization; Personal Injury

WARD & WARD
Indianapolis, IN.....................Civil Trial Practice; Personal Injury; Product Liability Law

WARE, DAVID A. M. & ASSOCIATES
Metairie, LA...........................Immigration and Naturalization

WARE, MICHAEL L.
Fort Worth, TX.......................Criminal Trial Practice

WARE, BRYSON, WEST & KUMMER
Covington, KY.......................Civil Trial Practice; General Practice; Insurance Defense; Workers Compensation

WARING COX, PLC
Memphis, TN..........................Civil Trial Practice; General Practice; Insurance Defense; Intellectual Property Law; Labor and Employment Law; Municipal Bond/Public Authority Financing; Real Estate Law; Securities Law; Tax Law

WARLICK MILSTED DOTSON & CARTER
Jacksonville, NC....................General Practice

WARLICK, TRITT & STEBBINS, L.L.P.
Augusta, GA..........................Banking Law; Bankruptcy Law; Civil Trial Practice; General Practice; Real Estate Law; Securities Law

WARNER, CHARLES G. LAW OFFICES OF
Monterey, CA.........................Civil Trial Practice

WARNER ANGLE ROPER & HALLAM PLC
Phoenix, AZ ....Appellate Practice; Business Law; Commercial Litigation; Construction Law; Personal Injury; Real Estate Law; Trust and Estates, Wills and Probate

WARNER, FOX, WACKEEN, DUNGEY SEELEY, SWEET & WRIGHT, L.L.P.
Stuart, FL................................Civil Trial Practice; Commercial Litigation; Real Estate Law

WARNER, MAYOUE & BATES, P.C.
Atlanta, GA ....Family Law

WARNER NORCROSS & JUDD LLP
Grand Rapids, MI ....Antitrust Law; Banking Law; Bankruptcy Law; Business Law; Civil Trial Practice; Computer Law; Corporate Law; Employment Benefits Law; Environmental Law; Health Care Law; Immigration and Naturalization; International Business Law; Labor and Employment Law; Patent, Trademark, Copyright and Unfair Competition; Real Estate Law; Securities Law; Tax Law; Trust and Estates, Wills and Probate

WARNER, SMITH & HARRIS, PLC
Fort Smith, AR.......................Civil Trial Practice; Corporate Law; Insurance Defense; Product Liability Law; Tax Law

WARNICKE & LITTLER, P.L.C.
Phoenix, AZ ....Bankruptcy Law; Commercial Litigation; Construction Law

WARREN & SINKLER, L.L.P.
Charleston, SC ....Business Law; General Practice; Real Estate Law; Securities Law; Tax Law

WARREN AND YOUNG PLL
Ashtabula, OH ....Business Law; General Practice; Insurance Defense; Labor and Employment Law

WARRICK, BENJAMIN R.
Clinton, NC.............................Family Law

WARTNICK, CHABER, HAROWITZ, SMITH & TIGERMAN, A PROFESSIONAL CORPORATION
San Francisco, CA ....Business Law; Commercial Litigation; Personal Injury; Product Liability Law

WARWICK & BANISTER, P.A.
Palm Beach, FL.......................Commercial Litigation; Real Estate Law; Trust and Estates, Wills and Probate

WASKA, RONALD J., A PROFESSIONAL CORPORATION
Houston, TX ....Commercial Litigation; Criminal Trial Practice

WASSER, ROSENSON & CARTER
Los Angeles, CA ....Family Law

WASSERMAN, MANCINI & CHANG
Washington, DC......................Immigration and Naturalization

WATANABE, ING & KAWASHIMA
Honolulu, HI...........................Civil Trial Practice; Commercial Law; General Practice; Insurance Defense

WATERMAN, DAVID M. LAW OFFICES OF
Tucson, AZ ....Workers Compensation

WATERS, HOLT & FIELDS
Pampa, TX ....General Practice

WATERS, MCCLUSKEY & BOEHLE
Santa Monica, CA...................Civil Trial Practice; Construction Law; Insurance Defense; Personal Injury; Product Liability Law

WATERS, MCPHERSON, MCNEILL, P.C.
Secaucus, NJ...........................Civil Trial Practice; General Practice

WATERS & MORSE, P.C.
Grand Rapids, MI ....Patent, Trademark, Copyright and Unfair Competition

WATERS, WARNER & HARRIS, PLLC
Clarksburg, WV ....Business Law; Civil Trial Practice; Commercial Litigation; General Practice; Insurance Defense; Mergers and Acquisitions; Natural Resources Law; Real Estate Law

WATKINS, JOHN E. JR.
White Plains, NY ....Corporate Law; Municipal and Zoning Law; Real Estate Law; Tax Law

WATKINS, BOULWARE, LUCAS, MINER, MURPHY & TAYLOR
St. Joseph, MO.......................General Practice

WATKINS & EAGER
Jackson, MS ....Banking Law; Bankruptcy Law; Civil Trial Practice; Commercial Law; Commercial Litigation; Environmental Law; General Practice; Insurance Defense; Labor and Employment Law; Natural Resources Law; Personal Injury; Real Estate Law; Tax Law; Trust and Estates, Wills and Probate

WATKINSON LAIRD RUBENSTEIN LASHWAY & BALDWIN, P.C.
Eugene, OR ....General Practice; Health Care Law; Real Estate Law

WATLEY, KEVIN D.
Norman, OK ....Tax Law

WATROUS & REARDON
Albuquerque, NM....................Bankruptcy Law; Commercial Litigation; Labor and Employment Law; Real Estate Law

WATSON, TIMOTHY F. SR.
Newport, AR ....Business Law; Real Estate Law

WATSON, WILLIAM E. & ASSOCIATES
Wellsburg, WV........................General Practice

WATSON, BISHOP, LONDON, GALOW, P.C.
Austin, TX ....Civil Trial Practice; Commercial Litigation; Personal Injury

WATSON, BLANCHE, WILSON & POSNER
Baton Rouge, LA....................Commercial Litigation; Health Care Law; Medical Malpractice; Product Liability Law; Tax Law

WATSON, FARLEY & WILLIAMS
New York, NY........................Admiralty/Maritime Law; Banking Law; General Practice; Transportation Law

WATSON, HOLLOW & REEVES, P.L.C.
Knoxville, TN ....Civil Trial Practice; Communications Law; General Practice; Insurance Defense; Labor and Employment Law; Medical Malpractice; Product Liability Law

WATSON, STEVENS, FIORILLA & RUTTER, LLP
New Brunswick, NJ ....Transportation Law

WATT & SAWYIER
Chicago, IL..............................Mergers and Acquisitions; Municipal Bond/Public Authority Financing; Real Estate Law; Tax Law; Trust and Estates, Wills and Probate

WATT, TIEDER, HOFFAR & FITZGERALD, L.L.P.
Washington, DC......................Commercial Law; Construction Law; Environmental Law; International Business Law; Real Estate Law
McLean, VA............................Construction Law; International Business Law; Real Estate Law

WAYCASTER, MORRIS, JOHNSON & DEAN
Dalton, GA ....Personal Injury

WAYMAN, IRVIN & MCAULEY
Pittsburgh, PA ....Insurance Defense

WEADON & ASSOCIATES
Washington, DC......................International Business Law

WEARN, JAMES MCCARTNEY, P.A.
West Palm Beach, FL ....Commercial Litigation; General Practice; Municipal and Zoning Law

WEARY, DAVIS, HENRY, STRUEBING, TROUP, KAUS & RYAN, L.C.
Junction City, KS....................General Practice

WEATHERBEE, WOODCOCK, BURLOCK & WOODCOCK
Bangor, ME.............................Insurance Defense; Workers Compensation

WEBB, BURNETT, JACKSON, CORNBROOKS, WILBER, VORHIS & DOUSE, LLP
Salisbury, MD ....Business Law; Civil Trial Practice; Criminal Trial Practice

WEBB, CARLOCK, COPELAND, SEMLER & STAIR, LLP
Atlanta, GA ....Civil Trial Practice; Insurance Defense; Workers Compensation

WEBB & ELEY, P.C.
Montgomery, AL ....Commercial Litigation; Insurance Defense; Labor and Employment Law; Product Liability Law; Real Estate Law; Workers Compensation

WEBB, PATTERSON AND TAPELLA
Sacramento, CA ....Trust and Estates, Wills and Probate

WEBB, SANDERS, BALDUCCI & SMITH, P.L.L.C.
Tupelo, MS..............................Civil Trial Practice; Insurance Defense

WEBB, STOKES & SPARKS
San Angelo, TX ....Personal Injury

WEBB & TIHOLIZ, LLP
Dallas, TX...............................Family Law

WEBB ZIESENHEIM LOGSDON ORKIN & HANSON, P.C.
Pittsburgh, PA ....Patent, Trademark, Copyright and Unfair Competition

WEBBER, CHRISTOPHER A. JR.
Wallingford, VT ....Trust and Estates, Wills and Probate

WEBBER, JOSEPH P. LAW OFFICES OF
Austin, TX ......Civil Trial Practice; Commercial Litigation

WEBER & WEBER
Weston, WV ......Civil Trial Practice; Real Estate Law

WEBSTER, GEOFFREY E.
Columbus, OH ......Health Care Law

WEBSTER, BRANNON & BISORDI, P.A.
Shalimar, FL ......Family Law

WEBSTER, CHAMBERLAIN & BEAN
Washington, DC......Administrative Law; Business Law; Securities Law; Tax Law

WEBSTER, FREDRICKSON & BRACKSHAW
Washington, DC......Bankruptcy Law; Labor and Employment Law

WEEMS, SCHIMPF, HAYTER, GILSOUL & CARMOUCHE, (APLC)
Shreveport, LA......Civil Trial Practice; Construction Law; Real Estate Law

WEGMAN, HESSLER, VANDERBURG & O'TOOLE, A LEGAL PROFESSIONAL ASSOCIATION
Cleveland, OH......Business Law; Trust and Estates, Wills and Probate

WEGMANN, GASAWAY, STEWART, SCHNEIDER, DIEFFENBACH, TESREAU & SHERMAN, P.C.
Hillsboro, MO......General Practice

WEHNER AND PERLMAN LLP
Los Angeles, CA ......Business Law

WEHNER & YORK
Washington, DC......Civil Trial Practice; Criminal Trial Practice

WEICHSEL, JOHN L.
Hackensack, NJ......Civil Trial Practice; Criminal Trial Practice

WEILER & BORST, LLP
San Ramon, CA ......Family Law

WEIL, GOTSHAL & MANGES LLP
New York, NY......General Practice

WEIL & PETROCCHI, A PROFESSIONAL CORPORATION
Dallas, TX......Civil Trial Practice; Commercial Litigation

WEINBERG, HOFFMAN, CASEY & ROPERS
Larkspur, CA ......Business Law; Insurance Defense; Medical Malpractice; Personal Injury; Product Liability Law

WEINBERG, MCCORMICK, CHATZINOFF AND PAUL, A PROFESSIONAL ASSOCIATION
Haddonfield, NJ......Bankruptcy Law; Family Law

WEINBERG, WHEELER, HUDGINS, GUNN & DIAL, LLC
Atlanta, GA ......Construction Law; General Practice; Medical Malpractice; Product Liability Law; Professional Liability

WEINER & ARGO, P.A.
Ocala, FL......Insurance Defense

WEINER, BRODSKY, SIDMAN & KIDER, P.C.
Washington, DC......Banking Law; Transportation Law

WEINER, JEFFREY S., P.A.
Miami, FL ......Appellate Practice; Criminal Trial Practice; Environmental Law; Health Care Law

WEINER, SAMUEL B., CO., L.P.A.
Columbus, OH ......Criminal Trial Practice

WEINER, SHEAROUSE, WEITZ, GREENBERG & SHAWE, L.L.P.
Savannah, GA ......Civil Trial Practice; Real Estate Law; Trust and Estates, Wills and Probate

WEINHAUS AND DOBSON
St. Louis, MO......Employment Benefits Law; Health Care Law

WEINSTEIN & BERGMAN LAWYERS, A PROFESSIONAL SERVICES CORP.
Seattle, WA ......Product Liability Law

WEINSTEIN, BOLDT, RACINE, HALFHIDE & CAMEL, PROFESSIONAL CORPORATION
Los Angeles, CA ......Tax Law

WEINSTEIN SNYDER, A PROFESSIONAL CORPORATION
Roseland, NJ......Family Law

WEINSTEIN, STEPHEN S., A PROFESSIONAL CORPORATION
Morristown, NJ......Civil Trial Practice; Commercial Litigation; Criminal Trial Practice; Insurance Defense; Medical Malpractice; Personal Injury; Product Liability Law; Professional Liability

WEINSTOCK, MANION, REISMAN, SHORE & NEUMANN, A LAW CORPORATION
Los Angeles, CA ......Tax Law; Trust and Estates, Wills and Probate

WEINTRAUB, STOCK, BENNETT, GRISHAM & UNDERWOOD, P.C.
Memphis, TN......General Practice; Labor and Employment Law

WEIR & ALVARADO, P.C.
San Antonio, TX......Civil Trial Practice; Criminal Trial Practice; Labor and Employment Law

WEIR & PARTNERS LLP
Philadelphia, PA ......Banking Law; Bankruptcy Law; Business Law; Civil Trial Practice; Commercial Law; Commercial Litigation; Creditors Rights; Real Estate Law

WEIR AND WALLEY
Metairie, LA......Commercial Law; Trust and Estates, Wills and Probate

WEISFUSE & WEISFUSE
New York, NY......Personal Injury

WEISMAN GOLDMAN BOWEN & GROSS LLP
Pittsburgh, PA ......Bankruptcy Law; Civil Trial Practice; Commercial Law; Real Estate Law

WEISS, DAVID J. LAW OFFICES OF
Santa Monica, CA......Legal Malpractice; Medical Malpractice

WEISS & ASSOCIATES
Cleveland, OH......Appellate Practice; Civil Trial Practice

WEISS BERRETT PETTY, L.C.
Salt Lake City, UT......Civil Trial Practice; Criminal Trial Practice; Insurance Defense

WEISS FREDERICK WILLETT & HAYNES
Louisville, KY......Medical Malpractice; Personal Injury; Product Liability Law

WEISS & HANDLER, P.A.
Boca Raton, FL ......Civil Trial Practice; Commercial Law; Commercial Litigation; Family Law; Personal Injury; Real Estate Law

WEISSMAN, DERVISHI, BORGO & NORDLUND, P.A.
Miami, FL......Commercial Litigation

WEISSMAN, JOEL M., P.A.
West Palm Beach, FL......Family Law

WEISSMANN, WOLFF, BERGMAN, COLEMAN & SILVERMAN, LLP
Beverly Hills, CA......Sports and Entertainment Law

WEISZ & ASSOCIATES
Atlanta, GA ......Business Law; Civil Trial Practice; Commercial Law; Construction Law

WELBAUM, GUERNSEY, HINGSTON, GREENLEAF & GREGORY, L.L.P.
Miami, FL ......Civil Trial Practice; Construction Law; General Practice

WELBORN SULLIVAN MECK & TOOLEY, P.C.
Denver, CO ......Civil Trial Practice; Environmental Law; General Practice; International Business Law; Oil and Gas Law

WELCH, MICHAEL
Atlanta, GA ......Construction Law

WELCH, JONES & SMITH, P.C.
Oklahoma City, OK......Insurance Defense

WELDON, CHARLES R.
Norwalk, CA......Personal Injury

WELDON, E. DURWARD
Georgetown, KY......General Practice; Real Estate Law; Tax Law; Trust and Estates, Wills and Probate

WELDON, HUSTON & KEYSER
Mansfield, OH......Bankruptcy Law; General Practice

WELEBIR, MCCUNE & JURE, A PROFESSIONAL LAW CORPORATION
Redlands, CA......Personal Injury; Product Liability Law

WELKER, PAUL
Clarksville, TN......Personal Injury

WELLBORN, HOUSTON, ADKISON, MANN, SADLER & HILL, L.L.P.
Henderson, TX......Commercial Law; Personal Injury; Product Liability Law

WELLER, GREEN, TOUPS & TERRELL, L.L.P.
Beaumont, TX......Insurance Defense; Personal Injury

WELLES & MCGRATH
Scranton, PA......Business Law; Commercial Law; General Practice; Real Estate Law; Trust and Estates, Wills and Probate

WELLS, ANDERSON & RACE, LLC
Denver, CO .... Aviation Law; Civil Trial Practice; Insurance Defense; Product Liability Law

WELLS, GREGORY K., & ASSOCIATES, P.A.
Largo, MD .... Civil Trial Practice; Medical Malpractice; Personal Injury

WELLS, PEYTON, GREENBERG & HUNT, L.L.P.
Beaumont, TX .... Admiralty/Maritime Law; General Practice

WELLS, PORTER, SCHMITT & JONES
Paintsville, KY .... General Practice; Insurance Defense; Workers Compensation

WELLS, PURCELL & KRAATZ
Fort Worth, TX .... Personal Injury

WELTY, JEAN L.
New Haven, CT .... Family Law

WENDEROTH, LIND & PONACK, L.L.P.
Washington, DC .... Patent, Trademark, Copyright and Unfair Competition

WENTWORTH, PAUL V.
Phoenix, AZ .... Real Estate Law

WENTWORTH, PAOLI & PURDY, LLP
Newport Beach, CA .... Personal Injury; Professional Liability

WESIERSKI & ZUREK, LLP
Irvine, CA .... Civil Trial Practice; Insurance Defense

WESNER, KEMPTON, RUSSELL AND DOMINIQUE
Jefferson City, MO .... General Practice
Sedalia, MO .... General Practice

WESSELS & PAUTSCH, P.C.
St. Charles, IL .... Labor and Employment Law

WESSELS, STOJAN & STEPHENS P.C.
Rock Island, IL .... General Practice

WEST, ROBIN PAGE
Baltimore, MD .... Civil Trial Practice; Personal Injury; Product Liability Law

WEST, GREGORY K., P.A.
Ponte Vedra Beach, FL .... Trust and Estates, Wills and Probate

WEST & ROSE
Kingsport, TN .... Aviation Law; Civil Rights; Civil Trial Practice; Insurance Defense; Medical Malpractice

WESTERMANN HAMILTON & SHEEHY
Garden City, NY .... Construction Law

WESTERVELT, JOHNSON, NICOLL & KELLER
Peoria, IL .... General Practice

WESTLING, RICHARD W., L.L.C., LAW OFFICES OF
New Orleans, LA .... Criminal Trial Practice

WESTMORELAND, VESPER & SCHWARTZ, A PROFESSIONAL CORPORATION
Atlantic City, NJ .... Banking Law; Commercial Litigation; Personal Injury; Real Estate Law

WESTON HURD FALLON PAISLEY & HOWLEY L.L.P.
Cleveland, OH .... Civil Trial Practice; Environmental Law; General Practice; Insurance Defense; Tax Law; Trademark, Copyright and Unfair Competition

WHALEN, RALPH S. JR.
New Orleans, LA .... Criminal Trial Practice; Personal Injury

WHALEN & COMPTON, A LEGAL PROFESSIONAL ASSOCIATION
Akron, OH .... Labor and Employment Law

WHAM & WHAM
Centralia, IL .... General Practice; Insurance Defense

WHARTON LEVIN EHRMANTRAUT KLEIN & NASH, A PROFESSIONAL ASSOCIATION
Annapolis, MD .... Civil Trial Practice
Baltimore, MD .... Civil Trial Practice

WHEAT, JOE F.
Houston, TX .... Real Estate Law

WHEELER, THOMPSON, PARKER & COUNTS, LLP
Easton, MD .... General Practice; Trust and Estates, Wills and Probate

WHEELER TRIGG & KENNEDY, P.C.
Denver, CO .... Civil Trial Practice; Franchise Law; Product Liability Law; Professional Liability; Toxic Torts

WHELCHEL, BROWN, READDICK & BUMGARTNER
Brunswick, GA .... Civil Trial Practice; Commercial Litigation; General Practice; Insurance Defense; Labor and Employment Law

WHELCHEL & DUNLAP, LLP
Gainesville, GA .... General Practice

WHELCHEL, WHELCHEL & CARLTON
Moultrie, GA .... General Practice

WHETSTONE LAW FIRM
Little Rock, AR .... Personal Injury

WHIPPLE AND VIELE, A PROFESSIONAL LAW CORPORATION
Ventura, CA .... Criminal Trial Practice; Family Law; Personal Injury

WHITAKER, RIDLEY M.
New York, NY .... Civil Trial Practice; Communications Law; Employment Benefits Law

WHITE, WILLIAM A. THE LAW OFFICE OF
Austin, TX .... Criminal Trial Practice

WHITE, ALLINDER & GRAHAM, L.L.C.
Independence, MO .... Business Law; Commercial Litigation; Labor and Employment Law; Medical Malpractice; Personal Injury

WHITE & CASE
Washington, DC .... General Practice
New York, NY .... Civil Trial Practice; Criminal Trial Practice; General Practice
London, England .... General Practice
Paris, France .... General Practice
Tokyo, Japan .... General Practice
Singapore, Singapore .... General Practice
Ankara, Turkey .... General Practice
Istanbul, Turkey .... General Practice
Stockholm, Sweden .... General Practice
Hong Kong, China .... General Practice

WHITE, COFFEY, GALT & FITE, P.C.
Oklahoma City, OK .... General Practice

WHITE AND CRUMPLER
Winston-Salem, NC .... Criminal Trial Practice; Family Law; Personal Injury

WHITE, CUMMINGS & LONGINO, P.C.
Phoenix, AZ .... Commercial Litigation

WHITE, DENNIS R., P.A.
Naples, FL .... Trust and Estates, Wills and Probate

WHITE & FISH, L.P.A., INC.
Columbus, OH .... Bankruptcy Law; Civil Trial Practice; Family Law; Personal Injury

WHITE, FLEISCHNER & FINO
Red Bank, NJ .... Appellate Practice; Civil Trial Practice; Insurance Defense; Intellectual Property Law; Legal Malpractice; Medical Malpractice; Product Liability Law; Professional Liability
New York, NY .... Appellate Practice; Civil Trial Practice; Commercial Litigation; Construction Law; Environmental Law; General Practice; Insurance Defense; Intellectual Property Law; Labor and Employment Law; Legal Malpractice; Medical Malpractice; Personal Injury; Product Liability Law; Professional Liability; Sports and Entertainment Law; Toxic Torts

WHITEFORD, TAYLOR & PRESTON L.L.P.
Washington, DC .... General Practice
Baltimore, MD .... General Practice; Labor and Employment Law; Municipal Bond/Public Authority Financing
Towson, MD .... General Practice

WHITEHURST, HARKNESS, OZMUN & ARCHULETA, A PROFESSIONAL CORPORATION
Austin, TX .... Aviation Law; Medical Malpractice; Personal Injury; Product Liability Law

WHITE, KOCH, KELLY & MCCARTHY, A PROFESSIONAL ASSOCIATION
Santa Fe, NM .... Commercial Law; Commercial Litigation; Criminal Trial Practice; Family Law; General Practice; Insurance Defense; Labor and Employment Law; Natural Resources Law; Oil and Gas Law; Public Utilities Law; Real Estate Law; Trust and Estates, Wills and Probate

WHITE LAW FIRM
Oklahoma City, OK .... Civil Trial Practice; Criminal Trial Practice; Personal Injury

WHITE & MCDERMOTT, P.C.
Wellesley, MA .... Corporate Law; Immigration and Naturalization; Mergers and Acquisitions; Securities Law

WHITENER & WHARTON, P.A.
Columbia, SC .... Banking Law; Corporate Law; Real Estate Law

WHITE O'CONNOR CURRY GATTI & AVANZADO LLP
Los Angeles, CA .... Civil Trial Practice; Commercial Litigation; Intellectual Property Law; Sports and Entertainment Law

WHITE & REED LLP
Los Angeles, CA .... Civil Trial Practice

WHITE, REGEN & GARTON, PLC
Dickson, TN .... General Practice

WHITE, WHITE, ASKEW & CRENSHAW
Hopkinsville, KY .... Business Law; Corporate Law

WHITFIELD & EDDY, P.L.C.
Des Moines, IA .... Banking Law; Civil Trial Practice; General Practice; Insurance Defense

WHITHAM, CURTIS & WHITHAM, PLC
Reston, VA .... Intellectual Property Law

WHITING, HAGG & HAGG
Rapid City, SD .... Banking Law; Insurance Defense; Personal Injury

WHITMAN BREED ABBOTT & MORGAN LLP
Greenwich, CT .... General Practice
New York, NY .... General Practice
London, England .... General Practice

WHITNEY & BOGRIS, LLP
Towson, MD .... Appellate Practice; Civil Trial Practice; Environmental Law; General Practice; Insurance Defense; Medical Malpractice; Personal Injury; Product Liability Law; Toxic Torts

WHITTEN, JAMES M.
Corpus Christi, TX .... Civil Trial Practice; Personal Injury

WHITTENBURG WHITTENBURG & SCHACHTER, P.C.
Amarillo, TX .... Bankruptcy Law; Civil Trial Practice; General Practice; Professional Liability
Dallas, TX .... Civil Trial Practice; General Practice; Professional Liability; Securities Law

WHITTEN, MCGUIRE, WOOD, TERRY, ROSELIUS & DITTRICH, A PROF. LTD. LIABILITY CO.
Oklahoma City, OK .... Civil Rights; Civil Trial Practice; Insurance Defense; Medical Malpractice; Personal Injury; Product Liability Law

WHITTEN & YOUNG, P.C.
Abilene, TX .... Commercial Law; Family Law; General Practice

WICKENS, HERZER & PANZA, A LEGAL PROFESSIONAL ASSOCIATION
Lorain, OH .... General Practice

WIED, C. W., PROFESSIONAL CORPORATION
San Diego, CA .... Bankruptcy Law

WIEDERHOLD, MOSES, BULFIN & RUBIN, P.A.
West Palm Beach, FL .... Civil Trial Practice; Health Care Law; Insurance Defense; Personal Injury

WIENER AND WIENER LLP
Allentown, PA .... Bankruptcy Law; Business Law; Family Law

WIEST, SAYLOR, MUOLO, NOON & SWINEHART
Sunbury, PA .... General Practice

WIGGIN & DANA
Hartford, CT .... General Practice
New Haven, CT .... Antitrust Law; Civil Trial Practice; General Practice; Health Care Law; Labor and Employment Law; Patent, Trademark, Copyright and Unfair Competition
Stamford, CT .... General Practice

WIGGIN & NOURIE, P.A.
Manchester, NH .... General Practice; Insurance Defense

WIGGINS AND MASSON, LLP
Ithaca, NY .... Civil Trial Practice; Criminal Trial Practice; Elder Law; Family Law; General Practice; Medical Malpractice; Personal Injury; Trust and Estates, Wills and Probate

WIGHT, RICHARD W.
Manasquan, NJ .... Real Estate Law

WIGODA, WILLIAM S., LTD.
Chicago, IL .... Commercial Litigation; Family Law

WILBRAHAM, LAWLER & BUBA, A PROFESSIONAL CORPORATION
Haddonfield, NJ .... Appellate Practice; Civil Trial Practice; Criminal Trial Practice; Environmental Law; Insurance Defense; Land Use Law; Product Liability Law; Toxic Torts
Philadelphia, PA .... Appellate Practice; Civil Trial Practice; Criminal Trial Practice; Environmental Law; Insurance Defense; Land Use Law; Product Liability Law; Toxic Torts

WILBURN, MASTERSON & SMILING
Tulsa, OK .... Insurance Defense; Medical Malpractice

WILCOX, ARTHUR M. JR.
San Diego, CA .... Business Law; Real Estate Law

WILCOX, GORDON W., INC. P.S.
Seattle, WA .... Family Law

WILCOX, WILCOX, ENRIGHT, HALLSTEIN, MCMAHON & ADLER, LLC
Eau Claire, WI .... Civil Trial Practice; General Practice; Insurance Defense; Real Estate Law

WILCOXEN, MONTGOMERY & HARBISON
Sacramento, CA .... Civil Trial Practice; Medical Malpractice; Personal Injury; Product Liability Law

WILDMAN, HARROLD, ALLEN & DIXON
Chicago, IL .... Antitrust Law; Appellate Practice; Aviation Law; Civil Trial Practice; Commercial Law; Commercial Litigation; Corporate Law; Creditors Rights; Criminal Trial Practice; Environmental Law; Government Contracts; Health Care Law; Insurance Defense; Intellectual Property Law; Labor and Employment Law; Medical Malpractice; Mergers and Acquisitions; Patent, Trademark, Copyright and Unfair Competition; Product Liability Law; Real Estate Law; Securities Law; Toxic Torts

WILENCHIK & BARTNESS, A PROFESSIONAL CORPORATION
Phoenix, AZ .... Civil Trial Practice; Real Estate Law

WILENTZ, GOLDMAN & SPITZER, A PROFESSIONAL CORPORATION
Eatontown, NJ .... General Practice
Perth Amboy, NJ .... General Practice
Woodbridge, NJ .... Banking Law; Civil Trial Practice; Commercial Law; Criminal Trial Practice; Environmental Law; Family Law; General Practice; Health Care Law; Labor and Employment Law; Municipal Bond/Public Authority Financing; Real Estate Law; Sports and Entertainment Law; Tax Law; Trust and Estates, Wills and Probate

WILES, BOYLE, BURKHOLDER & BRINGARDNER CO., L.P.A.
Columbus, OH .... Insurance Defense

WILES AND WILES
Marietta, GA .... Commercial Law

WILEY PRICE & RADULOVICH, LLP
Alameda, CA .... Labor and Employment Law

WILEY, REIN & FIELDING
Washington, DC .... General Practice

WILF, MERVIN M., LTD.
Cambridge, MA .... Pension and Profit Sharing; Tax Law; Trust and Estates, Wills and Probate
Philadelphia, PA .... Pension and Profit Sharing; Tax Law; Trust and Estates, Wills and Probate

WILKES, ARTIS, HEDRICK & LANE, CHARTERED
Washington, DC .... General Practice; Real Estate Law

WILKINS, TOM LAW OFFICES OF
McAllen, TX .... General Practice

WILKINS, FROHLICH, JONES, HEVIA, RUSSELL & SUTTER, P.A.
Port Charlotte, FL .... General Practice; Personal Injury

WILKINS & MADDEN, P.A.
Greenville, SC .... Civil Trial Practice; Family Law

WILKINSON, CARMODY & GILLIAM
Shreveport, LA .... Appellate Practice; Civil Trial Practice; Environmental Law; General Practice; Insurance Defense; Labor and Employment Law; Public Utilities Law; Sports and Entertainment Law; Transportation Law

WILLARD, ROBERT H.
Columbus, OH .... Insurance Defense

WILLARDSON & LIPSCOMB, LLP
Wilkesboro, NC .... General Practice; Insurance Defense

WILLCOX, PIROZZOLO AND MCCARTHY, PROFESSIONAL CORPORATION
Boston, MA .... Civil Trial Practice; General Practice; Patent, Trademark, Copyright and Unfair Competition

WILLETTE & GUERRA, L.L.P.
Brownsville, TX .... Civil Trial Practice; Insurance Defense

WILLEY & CHAMBERLAIN, L.L.P.
Grand Rapids, MI .... Criminal Trial Practice

WILLIAMS, J. SCOTT
Irvine, CA................................Bankruptcy Law

WILLIAMS, PETER C.
Alexandria, VA........................Banking Law; Creditors Rights

WILLIAMS & ANDERSON
Little Rock, AR........................Antitrust Law; Civil Trial Practice; Commercial Law; General Practice; Municipal Bond/Public Authority Financing; Securities Law; Tax Law

WILLIAMS & ASSOCIATES, P.C.
Nashville, TN..........................Medical Malpractice; Personal Injury

WILLIAMS AND BALLAS
Los Angeles, CA.......................Tax Law; Trust and Estates, Wills and Probate

WILLIAMS, BOX, FORSHEE & BULLARD, P.C.
Oklahoma City, OK...................Commercial Law; General Practice; Land Use Law; Municipal and Zoning Law; Municipal Bond/Public Authority Financing; Public Utilities Law; Real Estate Law

WILLIAMS & CONNOLLY
Washington, DC.......................Civil Trial Practice; Criminal Trial Practice; General Practice; Tax Law

WILLIAMS, COONEY & SHEEHY
Bridgeport, CT.........................Civil Trial Practice; General Practice; Insurance Defense; Medical Malpractice; Personal Injury; Product Liability Law

WILLIAMS & EOANNOU, P.C.
Bethesda, MD..........................Civil Trial Practice

WILLIAMS, H. DOHN, JR., P.A.
Fort Lauderdale, FL..................Criminal Trial Practice

WILLIAMS, HAMMOND, MOORE, SHOCKLEY & HARRISON, P.A.
Ocean City, MD........................Civil Trial Practice; Real Estate Law

WILLIAMS & HENRY, LLP
Atlanta, GA.............................Medical Malpractice; Personal Injury; Product Liability Law

WILLIAMS & HENRY, PROFESSIONAL ASSOCIATION
Greenville, SC..........................Business Law; Commercial Law; Commercial Litigation; General Practice; Real Estate Law

WILLIAMS HEWITT & ROBBINS, LLP
Greenwood, IN.........................Banking Law; Real Estate Law; Trust and Estates, Wills and Probate

WILLIAMS & JENSEN, A PROFESSIONAL CORPORATION
Washington, DC.......................Administrative Law

WILLIAMS, KATHRYN, P.A.
Greenville, SC..........................Workers Compensation

WILLIAMS & MCCARTHY, A PROFESSIONAL CORPORATION
Oregon, IL...............................Civil Trial Practice; General Practice
Rockford, IL............................Civil Trial Practice; General Practice; Tax Law

WILLIAMS & MONTGOMERY LTD.
Chicago, IL..............................Civil Trial Practice; General Practice

WILLIAMS, MORGAN & AMERSON, P.C.
Houston, TX............................Patent, Trademark, Copyright and Unfair Competition

WILLIAMS, MULLEN, CLARK & DOBBINS, A PROFESSIONAL CORPORATION
Richmond, VA..........................Administrative Law; Antitrust Law; Banking Law; Bankruptcy Law; Business Law; Civil Trial Practice; Commercial Law; Communications Law; Construction Law; Employment Benefits Law; Environmental Law; General Practice; Health Care Law; Immigration and Naturalization; Insurance Defense; Intellectual Property Law; International Business Law; Labor and Employment Law; Municipal and Zoning Law; Municipal Bond/Public Authority Financing; Real Estate Law; Securities Law; Tax Law; Trademark, Copyright and Unfair Competition; Trust and Estates, Wills and Probate

WILLIAMS, PARKER, HARRISON, DIETZ & GETZEN, PROFESSIONAL ASSOCIATION
Sarasota, FL............................Aviation Law; Banking Law; Civil Trial Practice; General Practice; Health Care Law; International Business Law; Labor and Employment Law; Municipal Bond/Public Authority Financing; Real Estate Law; Tax Law; Trust and Estates, Wills and Probate

WILLIAMS, PATTILLO, SQUIRES & WREN, L.L.P.
Waco, TX................................Civil Trial Practice

WILLIAMS, POLAN & PATTIS, LLC
New Haven, CT........................Appellate Practice; Civil Rights; Civil Trial Practice; Criminal Trial Practice

WILLIAMS, PORTER, DAY & NEVILLE, P.C.
Casper, WY.............................Civil Trial Practice; Environmental Law; General Practice; Insurance Defense

WILLIAMS, SENNETT & SCULLY CO., L.P.A.
Twinsburg, OH........................Civil Trial Practice; Insurance Defense

WILLIAMS, STROBEL, MALONE, MASON & RALPH, P.A.
Dodge City, KS........................General Practice

WILLIAMS & WILLIAMS
Buffalo, NY.............................Civil Trial Practice; Insurance Defense; Workers Compensation

WILLIAMS, WILLIAMS AND MONTGOMERY, P.A.
Poplarville, MS........................General Practice; Personal Injury

WILLIAMS, ZOGRAFOS & PECK, A PROFESSIONAL CORPORATION
Lake Oswego, OR.....................Labor and Employment Law

WILLIAMSON, DEAN, WILLIAMSON, PURCELL & SOJKA, L.L.P.
Laurinburg, NC........................General Practice

WILLIAMSON, STEPHEN T.
Louisville, CO..........................Natural Resources Law

WILLIS, JOHN M.
Philadelphia, PA......................Personal Injury

WILLIS & SACKETT
Perry, IA.................................General Practice

WILLITS, RICHARD H., P.A.
Lake Worth, FL........................Civil Trial Practice; Personal Injury; Professional Liability

WILLKIE FARR & GALLAGHER
Washington, DC.......................General Practice
New York, NY..........................Civil Trial Practice; General Practice; Municipal Bond/Public Authority Financing
London, England......................General Practice
Paris, France............................General Practice

WILLMAN & ARNOLD, LLP
Pittsburgh, PA.........................Environmental Law; Insurance Defense

WILLMARTH, TANOURY, RAMAR, CORBET, GARVES & SHAW
Detroit, MI..............................Civil Trial Practice; Commercial Litigation; Health Care Law; Insurance Defense; Labor and Employment Law; Legal Malpractice; Medical Malpractice; Personal Injury; Product Liability Law; Professional Liability; Toxic Torts

WILLONER, CALABRESE & ROSEN, P.A.
College Park, MD.....................General Practice

WILLOUGHBY & HOEFER, P.A.
Columbia, SC...........................Communications Law; Public Utilities Law; Securities Law; Transportation Law

WILL, ROBERT P., & ASSOCIATES
Waukegan, IL...........................Criminal Trial Practice

WILMER, CUTLER & PICKERING
Washington, DC.......................Antitrust Law; Banking Law; Bankruptcy Law; Business Law; Civil Trial Practice; Communications Law; Criminal Trial Practice; Environmental Law; General Practice; Insurance Defense; International Business Law; Securities Law; Tax Law; Transportation Law
New York, NY..........................General Practice
Brussels, Belgium.....................General Practice
London, England......................General Practice
Berlin, Germany.......................General Practice

WILNER, KLEIN & SIEGEL, A PROFESSIONAL CORPORATION
Beverly Hills, CA......................Insurance Defense; Real Estate Law

WILSHIRE SCOTT & DYER, A PROFESSIONAL CORPORATION
Houston, TX............................Civil Trial Practice

WILSMAN & SCHOONOVER
Cleveland, OH.........................Family Law

WILSON, BRUCE H.
Akron, OH...............................Civil Trial Practice

WILSON, FRANK M.
Montgomery, AL......................Appellate Practice; Commercial Litigation; Product Liability Law

WILSON AND BARROWS, LTD.
Elko, NV.................................General Practice; Real Estate Law; Trust and Estates, Wills and Probate

WILSON, BAVE, CONBOY, COZZA & COUZENS, P.C.
White Plains, NY.....................General Practice; Insurance Defense; Medical Malpractice; Personal Injury

WILSON, BORROR, DUNN & DAVIS, LLP
San Bernardino, CA .... Appellate Practice; Civil Trial Practice; General Practice; Insurance Defense; Trust and Estates, Wills and Probate

WILSON & BOWLING
New Orleans, LA .... Admiralty/Maritime Law; Civil Trial Practice; Commercial Litigation; Environmental Law; Health Care Law; Medical Malpractice; Personal Injury; Product Liability Law; Workers Compensation

WILSON & CRAIG, PROFESSIONAL CORPORATION
Eldora, IA .... General Practice

WILSON, CRAIG R., P.A.
North Palm Beach, FL .... Criminal Trial Practice

WILSON, DECAMP & TALBOTT, P.S.C.
Lexington, KY .... General Practice

WILSON, ELSER, MOSKOWITZ, EDELMAN & DICKER LLP
New York, NY .... Civil Trial Practice; Insurance Defense

WILSON, ENGSTROM, CORUM & COULTER
Little Rock, AR .... Civil Trial Practice; Criminal Trial Practice

WILSON GROSENHEIDER MOORE & JACOBS, L.L.P.
Austin, TX .... Insurance Defense

WILSON, HALBROOK & BAYARD, PROFESSIONAL ASSOCIATION
Georgetown, DE .... General Practice

WILSON, JANE P., & ASSOCIATES CO., L.P.A.
Eastlake, OH .... Workers Compensation

WILSON, JOHNSON & JAFFER, P.A.
Sarasota, FL .... Business Law; Computer Law; Real Estate Law; Trust and Estates, Wills and Probate

WILSON, KEHOE & WININGHAM
Indianapolis, IN .... Aviation Law; Medical Malpractice; Personal Injury; Product Liability Law

WILSON, LEAVITT & SMALL, P.A.
Orlando, FL .... Commercial Litigation; Eminent Domain; Environmental Law; Real Estate Law

WILSON, MCRAE, IVY, MCTYIER AND STRAIN
Memphis, TN .... General Practice; Insurance Defense

WILSON & ORCUTT, P.C.
Acton, MA .... Business Law; Commercial Litigation; Real Estate Law

WILSON, PETTY, KOSMO & TURNER LLP
San Diego, CA .... Civil Trial Practice

WILSON SONSINI GOODRICH & ROSATI, PROFESSIONAL CORPORATION
Palo Alto, CA .... General Practice

WILSON, WORLEY & GAMBLE, P.C.
Kingsport, TN .... General Practice

WIMBERLY LAWSON & SEALE, PLLC
Knoxville, TN .... Labor and Employment Law; Workers Compensation

WIMPFHEIMER, STEVEN
Great Neck, NY .... Commercial Law; Real Estate Law

WINCKLER & HARVEY, L.L.P.
Austin, TX .... Legal Malpractice; Medical Malpractice; Personal Injury

WINDELS, MARX, DAVIES & IVES
New York, NY .... General Practice

WINDER & HASLAM, P.C.
Salt Lake City, UT .... Business Law; Civil Trial Practice; General Practice

WINDHORST, GAUDRY, RANSON, HIGGINS & GREMILLION, L.L.C.
Gretna, LA .... Business Law; Commercial Litigation; Health Care Law; Insurance Defense; Medical Malpractice; Product Liability Law

WINER MEHEULA & DEVENS
Kailua, HI .... Arbitration; Civil Trial Practice; Commercial Litigation; Medical Malpractice; Personal Injury; Product Liability Law; Professional Liability

WINETSKY AND WINETSKY
Linden, NJ .... General Practice; Real Estate Law

WINGERT GREBING BRUBAKER & RYAN LLP
San Diego, CA .... Civil Trial Practice; Construction Law; Insurance Defense; Sports and Entertainment Law; Trust and Estates, Wills and Probate

WINGET & KANE
Peoria, IL .... Civil Trial Practice; Family Law

WINIKATES & WINIKATES
Frisco, TX .... Banking Law; Civil Trial Practice; Corporate Law; Insurance Defense; Trust and Estates, Wills and Probate

WINN, BEAUDRY & WINN, LLP
Dallas, TX .... Trust and Estates, Wills and Probate

WINNINGHAM & STEIN
Oklahoma City, OK .... Immigration and Naturalization

WINSHIP & BYRNE
Miami, FL .... Intellectual Property Law

WINSTEAD SECHREST & MINICK P.C.
Austin, TX .... General Practice
Dallas, TX .... General Practice
Houston, TX .... General Practice

WINSTEIN, KAVENSKY & WALLACE
Rock Island, IL .... Civil Trial Practice; Criminal Trial Practice; Personal Injury

WINSTON, BARRY T.
Chapel Hill, NC .... Civil Trial Practice; Criminal Trial Practice

WINSTON & BYRNE, LAWYERS, A PROFESSIONAL CORPORATION
Mason City, IA .... Civil Trial Practice; General Practice; Trust and Estates, Wills and Probate

WINSTON & STRAWN
Washington, DC .... General Practice
Chicago, IL .... Antitrust Law; General Practice
New York, NY .... General Practice

WINTERBAUER & DIAMOND, P.L.L.C.
Seattle, WA .... Labor and Employment Law

WINTER & RHODEN
Gaffney, SC .... General Practice

WINTERS, BREWSTER, CROSBY & PATCHETT
Marion, IL .... General Practice

WINTERS, FEATHERSTUN, GAUMER, KENNEY, POSTLEWAIT & STOCKS
Decatur, IL .... Insurance Defense

WINTERS & FORTE
Cheshire, CT .... Business Law; Commercial Law; Tax Law; Trust and Estates, Wills and Probate

WINTERS, KRUG, DELBON & NASTARI
Burlingame, CA .... Insurance Defense

WINTERS & MERKLE
Columbus, OH .... Criminal Trial Practice

WINTHROP COUCHOT, PROFESSIONAL CORPORATION
Newport Beach, CA .... Bankruptcy Law; Commercial Litigation

WINTHROP, STIMSON, PUTNAM & ROBERTS
Stamford, CT .... General Practice
Washington, DC .... General Practice
Palm Beach, FL .... General Practice
New York, NY .... Antitrust Law; Banking Law; Bankruptcy Law; Civil Trial Practice; General Practice; Tax Law
Hong Kong, China .... General Practice
London, England .... General Practice
Tokyo, Japan .... General Practice

WINTHROP & WEINSTINE, A PROFESSIONAL ASSOCIATION
St. Paul, MN .... General Practice

WIRE, R. THOMAS, A PROFESSIONAL CORPORATION
Westlake Village, CA .... Personal Injury

WIRKEN GROUP, THE, A PROFESSIONAL CORPORATION
Kansas City, MO .... Civil Trial Practice

WISE & MARSAC, PROFESSIONAL CORPORATION
Detroit, MI .... Business Law; Civil Trial Practice

WISE, WIEZOREK, TIMMONS & WISE, A PROFESSIONAL CORPORATION
Long Beach, CA .... Civil Trial Practice; Insurance Defense; Product Liability Law; Trust and Estates, Wills and Probate

WITCHER, JACK F.
Bremen, GA .... Personal Injury

WITHERED CORRIGAN & SERVICE
Lafayette, IN .... Civil Trial Practice; Personal Injury

WITHERS, BRANT, IGOE & MULLENNIX, P.C.
Liberty, MO .... Civil Trial Practice; General Practice

WITHERSPOON, KELLEY, DAVENPORT & TOOLE, P.S.
Spokane, WA .... Communications Law; General Practice

WITHEY & TOBIN, P.L.C.
Phoenix, AZ .... Land Use Law; Municipal and Zoning Law; Real Estate Law

WITMER, KARP, WARNER & THUOTTE LLP
Boston, MA .... Civil Trial Practice; Family Law

WITT, GAITHER & WHITAKER, P.C.
Chattanooga, TN .... Civil Trial Practice; Employment Benefits Law; Environmental Law; General Practice; Labor and Employment Law; Securities Law; Trust and Estates, Wills and Probate

WITTMAN & MCCORD
Colorado Springs, CO .... Insurance Defense; Oil and Gas Law; Personal Injury; Professional Liability
Denver, CO .... Insurance Defense; Personal Injury; Professional Liability

WITWER, OLDENBURG, BARRY & BEDINGFIELD, LLP
Greeley, CO .... General Practice

WITWER, POLTROCK & GIAMPIETRO
Chicago, IL .... Labor and Employment Law

WOBENSMITH, ZACHARY T. III
Valley Forge, PA .... Patent, Trademark, Copyright and Unfair Competition; Trademark, Copyright and Unfair Competition

WOFSEY, ROSEN, KWESKIN & KURIANSKY, LLP
Stamford, CT .... Banking Law; Bankruptcy Law; Business Law; Civil Trial Practice; Commercial Law; Corporate Law; Family Law; General Practice; Personal Injury; Tax Law; Trust and Estates, Wills and Probate

WOHLFORD, PAUL R.
Bristol, TN .... Family Law

WOLCOTT, RIVERS, WHEARY, BASNIGHT & KELLY, P.C.
Virginia Beach, VA .... Banking Law; Bankruptcy Law; Family Law; General Practice; Personal Injury; Real Estate Law

WOLF, WAYNE C.
Albuquerque, NM .... Civil Trial Practice

WOLF AND AKERS, A LEGAL PROFESSIONAL ASSOCIATION
Cleveland, OH .... Family Law

WOLF, ARNOLD & CARDOSO, P.C.
Washington, DC .... International Business Law; International Trade Law

WOLF, JUDITH M., P.C.
Phoenix, AZ .... Arbitration; Family Law

WOLF & RICHARDS, A LAW CORPORATION
Newport Beach, CA .... Banking Law; Bankruptcy Law; Real Estate Law

WOLF, RIFKIN & SHAPIRO, LLP
Los Angeles, CA .... Civil Trial Practice; Product Liability Law; Real Estate Law; Sports and Entertainment Law

WOLF & TIEDEKEN
Cheyenne, WY .... Criminal Trial Practice; Medical Malpractice; Personal Injury

WOLFE, JONES & BOSWELL
Huntsville, AL .... Personal Injury; Workers Compensation

WOLFE, SNOWDEN, HURD, LUERS & AHL
Lincoln, NE .... Corporate Law; Insurance Defense; Trust and Estates, Wills and Probate

WOLFF AND D'AGROSA, LAW OFFICES OF
Clayton, MO .... Criminal Trial Practice

WOLFF & SAMSON, A PROFESSIONAL CORPORATION
Roseland, NJ .... General Practice

WOLFF, WHORLEY, DE HOOGH & THOMPSON
Sheldon, IA .... General Practice

WOLFSDORF, BERNARD P., A PROFESSIONAL CORPORATION
Los Angeles, CA .... Immigration and Naturalization

WOLK & GENTER
Philadelphia, PA .... Aviation Law

WOLSKE & BLUE, A LEGAL PROFESSIONAL ASSOCIATION
Columbus, OH .... Appellate Practice; Medical Malpractice; Personal Injury

WOMACK, LANDIS, PHELPS, MCNEILL & MCDANIEL, A PROFESSIONAL ASSOCIATION
Jonesboro, AR .... General Practice; Insurance Defense

WOMACK LAW FIRM, THE
La Fayette, GA .... General Practice

WOMACK, MCCLISH & WALL, P.C.
Austin, TX .... Eminent Domain

WOMBLE CARLYLE SANDRIDGE & RICE
Charlotte, NC .... Appellate Practice; Banking Law; Business Law; Civil Trial Practice; Commercial Law; Construction Law; Employment Benefits Law; Environmental Law; General Practice; Insurance Defense; International Business Law; Labor and Employment Law; Municipal Bond/Public Authority Financing; Natural Resources Law; Real Estate Law; Securities Law; Tax Law
Raleigh, NC .... Administrative Law; Antitrust Law; Appellate Practice; Banking Law; Business Law; Civil Trial Practice; Commercial Law; Computer Law; Construction Law; Employment Benefits Law; Environmental Law; General Practice; Health Care Law; Insurance Defense; International Business Law; Labor and Employment Law; Municipal Bond/Public Authority Financing; Natural Resources Law; Patent, Trademark, Copyright and Unfair Competition; Product Liability Law; Real Estate Law; Securities Law; Tax Law
Winston-Salem, NC .... Administrative Law; Antitrust Law; Appellate Practice; Banking Law; Bankruptcy Law; Business Law; Civil Rights; Civil Trial Practice; Commercial Law; Communications Law; Computer Law; Construction Law; Employment Benefits Law; Environmental Law; Family Law; General Practice; Health Care Law; Insurance Defense; International Business Law; Labor and Employment Law; Medical Malpractice; Municipal and Zoning Law; Municipal Bond/Public Authority Financing; Natural Resources Law; Product Liability Law; Real Estate Law; Securities Law; Tax Law; Trust and Estates, Wills and Probate

WONER, GLENN, REEDER & GIRARD, P.A.
Kansas City, KS .... Bankruptcy Law; Commercial Law; Commercial Litigation
Lawrence, KS .... Bankruptcy Law; Commercial Law; Commercial Litigation
Overland Park, KS .... Bankruptcy Law; Commercial Law; Commercial Litigation
Topeka, KS .... Bankruptcy Law; Commercial Law; Commercial Litigation

WONG, MARGARET W. & ASSOCIATES
Cleveland, OH .... Immigration and Naturalization

WONG, MICHAEL J. Y.
Honolulu, HI .... Civil Trial Practice; Family Law; General Practice; Personal Injury

WONG FLEMING, P.C.
Edison, NJ .... Bankruptcy Law; Civil Rights; Commercial Litigation; General Practice; Immigration and Naturalization; Labor and Employment Law

WONG & LEOW
Singapore, Singapore .... General Practice

WOODARD, JOHN L. III
Orlando, FL .... Criminal Trial Practice

WOODARD, EMHARDT, NAUGHTON, MORIARTY & MCNETT
Indianapolis, IN .... Intellectual Property Law; Patent, Trademark, Copyright and Unfair Competition

WOOD & ASSOCIATES, P.A.
St. Petersburg, FL .... Insurance Defense; Medical Malpractice

WOODBURN AND WEDGE
Reno, NV .... Bankruptcy Law; Business Law; Civil Trial Practice; Commercial Law; Natural Resources Law; Real Estate Law; Trust and Estates, Wills and Probate

WOODBURY, DAVID P.
Prairie Village, KS .... Family Law

WOODBURY, J. WAYNE
Silver City, NM .... General Practice

WOODCOCK WASHBURN KURTZ MACKIEWICZ & NORRIS LLP
Philadelphia, PA .... Intellectual Property Law; Patent, Trademark, Copyright and Unfair Competition

WOOD CRAPO LLC
Salt Lake City, UT .... Commercial Litigation; Labor and Employment Law; Tax Law

WOODEN & MCLAUGHLIN LLP
Indianapolis, IN .... General Practice

WOOD GORDON, P.C.
Pittsburgh, PA .... Business Law

WOOD & GRANT
Atlanta, GA .... Civil Trial Practice; Medical Malpractice; Personal Injury

WOODLEY, WILLIAMS, BOUDREAU, NORMAN, BROWN & DOYLE
Lake Charles, LA....................Admiralty/Maritime Law; Commercial Law; Insurance Defense

WOOD, ODOM AND EDGE, P.A.
Newnan, GA....................General Practice

WOOD, RIS & HAMES, PROFESSIONAL CORPORATION
Denver, CO....................Insurance Defense

WOODRUFF, GORDON C.
Smithfield, NC....................Bankruptcy Law; Civil Trial Practice

WOODRUFF & ASSOCIATES
Dallas, TX....................Insurance Defense

WOODRUFF, O'HAIR & POSNER, INC. A LAW CORPORATION
Sacramento, CA....................Family Law

WOODS, BARRY A.
San Juan, PR....................Corporate Law; General Practice; Tax Law

WOODS, RONALD G.
Houston, TX....................Criminal Trial Practice

WOODS & BATES
Lincoln, IL....................General Practice

WOODS & PARTNERS
Montreal, QU, Canada....................Arbitration; Civil Trial Practice; Commercial Litigation; Construction Law; General Practice; Labor and Employment Law; Product Liability Law; Professional Liability; Sports and Entertainment Law

WOODSON, DANNY LAW OFFICES OF
Mount Pleasant, TX....................Family Law; Personal Injury

WOOD, THACKER & WEATHERLY, P.C.
Denton, TX....................Business Law; Civil Trial Practice; Family Law; Labor and Employment Law; Personal Injury

WOODWARD COTHRAN & HERNDON
Columbia, SC....................Banking Law; Business Law; Civil Trial Practice; Construction Law; Personal Injury; Real Estate Law

WOODWARD, HOBSON & FULTON
Louisville, KY....................Antitrust Law; Civil Trial Practice; Environmental Law; General Practice; Health Care Law; Insurance Defense; Labor and Employment Law; Product Liability Law

WOOLFOLK, KEOUGH, DUBOSE & DEBARI, P.A.
Orlando, FL....................Medical Malpractice; Personal Injury

WOOLLEY RUSSELL & JOHNSON
Long Beach, CA....................Admiralty/Maritime Law; Aviation Law; Civil Trial Practice; Commercial Law; Environmental Law; General Practice; International Business Law; Product Liability Law; Transportation Law

WOOTEN & HART, A PROFESSIONAL CORPORATION
Roanoke, VA....................Banking Law; Business Law; Civil Trial Practice; Commercial Litigation; Constitutional Law; Corporate Law; Creditors Rights; Environmental Law; Family Law; Health Care Law; Insurance Defense; Medical Malpractice; Product Liability Law; Professional Liability; Trust and Estates, Wills and Probate; Workers Compensation

WOOTON, JAMES R., P.A.
Baltimore, MD....................Bankruptcy Law

WOOTTON, RICHARD H., P.A.
Hot Springs National Park, AR....................General Practice

WORDEN, THANE & HAINES, P.C.
Missoula, MT....................General Practice

WORKER & POWER
Chicago, IL....................Civil Trial Practice; Insurance Defense

WORKMAN, NYDEGGER & SEELEY, A PROFESSIONAL CORPORATION
Salt Lake City, UT....................Intellectual Property Law

WORREL & WORREL
Fresno, CA....................Patent, Trademark, Copyright and Unfair Competition

WOTITZKY, WOTITZKY, MIZELL, ROSS & GOLDMAN, P.A.
Punta Gorda, FL....................Personal Injury; Real Estate Law; Trust and Estates, Wills and Probate

WREN, RONALD D.
Bedford, TX....................Appellate Practice; Civil Trial Practice

WRIGHT, CHANEY, BERRY, DANIEL, SLAUGHTER & HUGHES, P.A.
Arkadelphia, AR....................General Practice; Product Liability Law

WRIGHT, CONSTABLE & SKEEN, LLP
Baltimore, MD....................Admiralty/Maritime Law; Bankruptcy Law; Commercial Litigation; General Practice; Insurance Defense; Trust and Estates, Wills and Probate

WRIGHT & COON, P.A.
Portland, ME....................Civil Trial Practice; Environmental Law; Insurance Defense; Product Liability Law; Toxic Torts

WRIGHT, DALE, JETT & CARTER
Guymon, OK....................General Practice

WRIGHT & EVERETT, L.L.C.
Lake Charles, LA....................Real Estate Law

WRIGHT, HENSON, SOMERS, SEBELIUS, CLARK & BAKER, LLP
Topeka, KS....................Administrative Law; Banking Law; Bankruptcy Law; Civil Trial Practice; Commercial Law; Family Law; General Practice; Insurance Defense; Labor and Employment Law; Medical Malpractice; Patent, Trademark, Copyright and Unfair Competition; Personal Injury; Tax Law

WRIGHT, JUDD & WINCKLER
Las Vegas, NV....................Appellate Practice; Civil Trial Practice; Commercial Litigation; Criminal Trial Practice; Health Care Law

WRIGHT, LINDSEY & JENNINGS LLP
Little Rock, AR....................Bankruptcy Law; Commercial Litigation; Intellectual Property Law; Labor and Employment Law; Municipal Bond/Public Authority Financing; Securities Law

WRIGHT, MAX E., A PROFESSIONAL CORPORATION
Midland, TX....................Medical Malpractice

WRIGHT & MILLS, P.A.
Skowhegan, ME....................Civil Trial Practice; Criminal Trial Practice

WRIGHT, STOUT, FITE & WILBURN
Muskogee, OK....................General Practice

WRIGHT, TOLLIVER AND GUTHALS, A PROFESSIONAL SERVICE CORPORATION
Billings, MT....................Bankruptcy Law; Commercial Law; Family Law; Insurance Defense; Labor and Employment Law

WUERFEL & CHOLAKIAN, A PROFESSIONAL CORPORATION
San Francisco, CA....................Civil Trial Practice; Commercial Litigation; Construction Law; Insurance Defense; Labor and Employment Law

WUESTLING & JAMES, L.C.
St. Louis, MO....................Insurance Defense; Professional Liability

WULFMEIER & OTTENWESS, PLC
Detroit, MI....................Family Law; Insurance Defense; Labor and Employment Law; Medical Malpractice

WULFSBERG REESE & SYKES, PROFESSIONAL CORPORATION
Oakland, CA....................Construction Law; Professional Liability

WULIGER, FADEL & BEYER
Cleveland, OH....................General Practice

WUNSCH, JOHN C., P.C.
Chicago, IL....................Aviation Law; Medical Malpractice; Personal Injury; Product Liability Law

WUSINICH AND BROGAN
Downingtown, PA....................Medical Malpractice; Personal Injury; Workers Compensation

WYATT, JAMES F. III, LAW OFFICES OF
Charlotte, NC....................Civil Trial Practice; Criminal Trial Practice

WYATT, EARLY, HARRIS & WHEELER, L.L.P.
High Point, NC....................Civil Trial Practice; General Practice

WYATT, TARRANT & COMBS
New Albany, IN....................General Practice
Frankfort, KY....................General Practice
Lexington, KY....................General Practice
Louisville, KY....................Banking Law; Civil Trial Practice; Communications Law; General Practice
Nashville, TN....................Communications Law; General Practice; Trademark, Copyright and Unfair Competition

WYLIE, PAUL R., A PROFESSIONAL CORPORATION
Bozeman, MT....................Patent, Trademark, Copyright and Unfair Competition

WYNNE SPIEGEL ITKIN, A LAW CORPORATION
Los Angeles, CA....................Bankruptcy Law

WYRSCH HOBBS MIRAKIAN & LEE, P.C.
Kansas City, MO....................Appellate Practice; Civil Trial Practice; Criminal Trial Practice; General Practice

YAMAMOTO, TOSH G., A PROFESSIONAL CORPORATION
Sacramento, CA .... Trust and Estates, Wills and Probate

YANNI, PALMA R.
Washington, DC .... Immigration and Naturalization

YARLING & ROBINSON
Indianapolis, IN .... Bankruptcy Law; Civil Trial Practice; Commercial Law; Insurance Defense; Personal Injury; Product Liability Law; Trust and Estates, Wills and Probate

YATES, MCLAMB & WEYHER, L.L.P.
Raleigh, NC .... Civil Trial Practice; Insurance Defense; Medical Malpractice; Product Liability Law; Workers Compensation

YELTON & KEHL, LTD.
Chicago, IL .... Appellate Practice; Civil Trial Practice; Insurance Defense; Workers Compensation

YENGICH, RICH & XAIZ
Salt Lake City, UT .... Criminal Trial Practice

YERRID, KNOPIK & KRIEGER, P.A.
Tampa, FL .... Commercial Litigation; Medical Malpractice; Personal Injury; Product Liability Law

YERUSHALMI & ASSOCIATES, L.L.P.
New York, NY .... International Business Law; International Trade Law

YODER, AINLAY, ULMER & BUCKINGHAM
Goshen, IN .... General Practice

YORK & YORK, P.C.
Cedartown, GA .... General Practice

YOSHA KRAHULIK & LEVY
Indianapolis, IN .... Civil Trial Practice; Medical Malpractice; Personal Injury; Product Liability Law

YOSHIDA, GERALD T.
Los Angeles, CA .... Business Law; Construction Law; Real Estate Law

YOST & TRETTA
Philadelphia, PA .... Insurance Defense

YOUNG, FRANCIS X.
White Plains, NY .... Civil Trial Practice; Personal Injury

YOUNG & ALEXANDER CO., L.P.A.
Dayton, OH .... Insurance Defense

YOUNG & ASSOCIATES, ATTORNEYS AT LAW, P.A.
Pensacola, FL .... Civil Trial Practice; Construction Law; Insurance Defense; Product Liability Law

YOUNG & ASSOCIATES, P.C.
Southfield, MI .... Antitrust Law; Civil Trial Practice; Commercial Litigation

YOUNG, BOGLE, MCCAUSLAND, WELLS & BLANCHARD, P.A.
Wichita, KS .... Civil Trial Practice; Commercial Law; Criminal Trial Practice; Environmental Law; General Practice; Insurance Defense; Natural Resources Law; Personal Injury; Product Liability Law; Real Estate Law; Trust and Estates, Wills and Probate

YOUNG CONAWAY STARGATT & TAYLOR, LLP
Georgetown, DE .... General Practice
Wilmington, DE .... General Practice

YOUNG, GOLDMAN & VAN BEEK, A PROFESSIONAL CORPORATION
Alexandria, VA .... Business Law; Creditors Rights; Real Estate Law

YOUNG & PICKETT
Texarkana, TX .... Civil Trial Practice; Commercial Litigation; Criminal Trial Practice; General Practice

YOUNG, RICHARD W., A PROF. CORP., LAW OFFICES OF
Reno, NV .... Criminal Trial Practice; Family Law

YOUNG & THOMPSON
Arlington, VA .... Patent, Trademark, Copyright and Unfair Competition

YOUNG & VALKENET, L.L.C.
Baltimore, MD .... Business Law; Commercial Law; Construction Law; Insurance Defense

YOUNG WOOLDRIDGE, LAW OFFICES OF
Bakersfield, CA .... Civil Trial Practice; Corporate Law; General Practice; Personal Injury

YOUNKIN, JACK C.
Danville, PA .... General Practice
Shamokin, PA .... Civil Trial Practice; General Practice

YU STROMBERG CLEVELAND, P.C.
Denver, CO .... Health Care Law

YUDES, JAMES P., A PROFESSIONAL CORPORATION
Springfield, NJ .... Family Law

YUEN, RENEE M. L., ATTORNEY AT LAW, A LAW CORPORATION
Honolulu, HI .... Civil Trial Practice; Criminal Trial Practice; General Practice

YUKEVICH, MARCHETTI, LIEKAR & ZANGRILLI, P.C.
Pittsburgh, PA .... Banking Law; Business Law; Civil Trial Practice; Corporate Law; Oil and Gas Law

YURASKO, FRANK N.
Somerville, NJ .... General Practice

YURKO & OWENS, P.A.
Charlotte, NC .... Criminal Trial Practice

ZABEL, JUDITH L., P.A.
Albuquerque, NM .... Tax Law; Trust and Estates, Wills and Probate

ZAGRANS LAW FIRM, A LEGAL PROFESSIONAL ASSOCIATION
Elyria, OH .... Antitrust Law; Appellate Practice; Civil Trial Practice; Medical Malpractice; Product Liability Law; Securities Law

ZALKIND, RODRIGUEZ, LUNT & DUNCAN
Boston, MA .... Criminal Trial Practice

ZALK & WOOD, P.A.
Minneapolis, MN .... Family Law

ZAMANSKY PROFESSIONAL ASSOCIATION
Minneapolis, MN .... Business Law; Real Estate Law

ZANE AND RUDOFSKY
New York, NY .... Commercial Litigation; General Practice

ZAPPITELL & KAPRAL, P.A.
Boca Raton, FL .... Personal Injury

ZARLEY, MCKEE, THOMTE, VOORHEES & SEASE, P.L.C.
Des Moines, IA .... Patent, Trademark, Copyright and Unfair Competition

ZARWIN, BAUM, DEVITO, KAPLAN & O'DONNELL, P.C.
Philadelphia, PA .... Civil Trial Practice; Insurance Defense

ZAVARELLO, A. WILLIAM, CO., L.P.A.
Akron, OH .... Civil Trial Practice; Medical Malpractice

ZAZZALI, ZAZZALI, FAGELLA & NOWAK, A PROFESSIONAL CORPORATION
Newark, NJ .... Administrative Law; Appellate Practice; Civil Trial Practice; Labor and Employment Law

ZDARSKY, SAWICKI & AGOSTINELLI
Buffalo, NY .... Appellate Practice; Civil Trial Practice; Commercial Litigation; Construction Law

ZEANAH, HUST, SUMMERFORD, DAVIS, JONES & WILLIAMSON, L.L.C.
Tuscaloosa, AL .... Civil Trial Practice; General Practice; Insurance Defense; Workers Compensation

ZEFF AND ZEFF, P.C.
Detroit, MI .... Civil Trial Practice; Personal Injury; Product Liability Law

ZEGAS, ALAN L.
Chatham, NJ .... Appellate Practice; Civil Trial Practice; Commercial Litigation; Criminal Trial Practice; General Practice

ZEIGER & CARPENTER
Columbus, OH .... Commercial Litigation; Communications Law; Franchise Law; Product Liability Law

ZEIGLER COHEN & KOCH
Indianapolis, IN .... Health Care Law; Insurance Defense; Medical Malpractice

ZEISLER & ZEISLER, P.C.
Bridgeport, CT .... Bankruptcy Law; Creditors Rights

ZEITLIN & ZEITLIN, P.C.
Phoenix, AZ .... Land Use Law; Real Estate Law

ZELDES, NEEDLE & COOPER, A PROFESSIONAL CORPORATION
Bridgeport, CT .... General Practice

ZELLE, HOFMANN, VOELBEL & GETTE, LLP
Minneapolis, MN .... Civil Trial Practice; General Practice

ZELLNER, KATHLEEN T. & ASSOCIATES
Naperville, IL .... Medical Malpractice; Personal Injury

ZEMAN, WILLIAM S.
Hartford, CT .... Labor and Employment Law

ZERMAN & MOGERMAN, L.L.C.
St. Louis, MO .... Family Law

ZERRENNER & ROANE
Grand Rapids, MI ....Family Law

ZEVNIK HORTON GUIBORD MCGOVERN PALMER & FOGNANI, L.L.P.
Washington, DC......................Civil Trial Practice; Environmental Law; Sports and Entertainment Law

ZICKERT, LLOYD L.
Chicago, IL.............................Intellectual Property Law

ZIDE & O'BIECUNAS
Los Angeles, CA.....................Commercial Law; Commercial Litigation

ZIEMAN, SPEEGLE, JACKSON & HOFFMAN, L.L.C.
Mobile, AL...............................Business Law; Commercial Litigation; Mergers and Acquisitions

ZIEMER, STAYMAN, WEITZEL & SHOULDERS, LLP
Evansville, IN..........................Banking Law; Bankruptcy Law; Business Law; Commercial Law; Construction Law; Health Care Law; Labor and Employment Law

ZIFFREN, BRITTENHAM, BRANCA & FISCHER LLP
Los Angeles, CA.....................Sports and Entertainment Law

ZIMMER KUNZ, PROFESSIONAL CORPORATION
Pittsburgh, PA ....Civil Trial Practice; General Practice; Insurance Defense

ZIMMER AND ZIMMER, L.L.P.
Wilmington, NC......................Criminal Trial Practice; Personal Injury

ZIMMERMAN, ROBERT H.
Philadelphia, PA ....Environmental Law; Real Estate Law

ZIMMERMAN, LIEBERMAN & DERENZO
Pottsville, PA ....General Practice

ZIMMERMAN, PFANNEBECKER, NUFFORT & ALBERT, LLP
Lancaster, PA..........................Civil Trial Practice; General Practice

ZIMRING, STUART D.
Los Angeles, CA.....................Real Estate Law; Trust and Estates, Wills and Probate

ZINOBER & MCCREA, P.A.
Tampa, FL ....General Practice; Labor and Employment Law

ZINSER AND PATTERSON, P.L.L.C.
Nashville, TN.........................Labor and Employment Law

ZIRKLE AND HOFFMAN
Atlanta, GA ....Insurance Defense; Workers Compensation

ZISMAN AND INGRAHAM, P.C.
Denver, CO ....Tax Law; Trust and Estates, Wills and Probate

ZIZIK, LASALLE & POWERS, A PROFESSIONAL CORPORATION
Wellesley, MA.........................Civil Trial Practice; Insurance Defense

ZOLLA AND MEYER
Los Angeles, CA.....................Family Law

ZUCKER, HOWARD B.
Denver, CO ....Family Law

ZUCKERMAN, SPAEDER, GOLDSTEIN, TAYLOR & KOLKER, L.L.P.
Washington, DC......................Criminal Trial Practice

ZUETEL & TOMLINSON
Pasadena, CA.........................Civil Trial Practice; Medical Malpractice

ZUGER KIRMIS & SMITH
Bismarck, ND ....Civil Trial Practice; General Practice

ZUKOWSKI, ROGERS, FLOOD & MCARDLE
Crystal Lake, IL......................Family Law; General Practice; Municipal and Zoning Law

ZVARA, WILLIAM L., P.A.
Jacksonville, FL ....Municipal Bond/Public Authority Financing

ZWEIG, DAVID S., LAW FIRM OF
San Diego, CA ....Tax Law

PRACTICE AREAS SECTION

Volume II

Minnesota–Wyoming
Canada
International

ADMINISTRATIVE LAW

MISSISSIPPI

*CLARKSDALE,** Coahoma Co.

HUNT & ROSS, A PROFESSIONAL ASSOCIATION (AV)

123 Court Street, P.O. Box 1196, 38614
Telephone: 601-627-5251
Telecopier No.: 601-627-5254
Email: huntross@clarksdale.com *URL:* http://www.lawyers.com/h&rlaw

Tom T. Ross (1903-1993) David R. Hunt
Tom T. Ross, Jr.

Thomas W. Allen Katherine Blackwell Parker

Representative Client: Mississippi Delta Council for Farmworkers Opportunities, Inc., Clarksdale, Mississippi.

For full biographical listings, see the Martindale-Hubbell Law Directory

*GULFPORT,** Harrison Co.

DUKES, DUKES, KEATING AND FANECA, P.A. (AV)

2909 13th Street, 6th Floor, P.O. Drawer W, 39501
Telephone: 228-868-1111
Fax: 228-863-2886
Email: ddkf@ddkf.com

Hugh D. Keating Cy Faneca

For Complete List of Firm Personnel, See General Section

For full biographical listings, see the Martindale-Hubbell Law Directory

MONTANA

*BILLINGS,** Yellowstone Co.

CROWLEY, HAUGHEY, HANSON, TOOLE & DIETRICH, P.L.L.P. (AV)

500 Transwestern II, 490 North 31st Street, P.O. Box 2529, 59103
Telephone: 406-252-3441
Fax: 406-259-4159
Email: crowley@crowleylaw.com
Helena, Montana Office: IBM Building, 100 North Park Avenue, Suite 300, 59601.
Telephone: 406-449-4165.
Fax: 406-449-5149.
Kalispell, Montana Office: 431 1st Avenue West, 59901.
Telephone: 406-752-6644.
Fax: 406-752-5108.
Williston, North Dakota Office: 113 East Broadway, 58801.
Telephone: 701-572-2200.
Fax: 701-572-7072.

MEMBERS OF FIRM

Terry B. Cosgrove (Resident, Helena, Montana Office)
Janice L. Rehberg
Michael S. Lahr (Resident, Helena, Montana Office)

Representative Clients: Montana Power Co.; First Interstate Bank of Commerce; MDU Resources Group, Inc.; Chevron U.S.A., Inc.; Noranda Minerals Corp.; United Parcel Service.
Insurance Clients: Farmers Insurance Group; New York Life Insurance Co.

For Complete List of Firm Personnel, See General Section

For full biographical listings, see the Martindale-Hubbell Law Directory

*HELENA,** Lewis and Clark Co.

BROWNING, KALECZYC, BERRY & HOVEN, P.C. (AV)

139 North Last Chance Gulch, P.O. Box 1697, 59624
Telephone: 406-443-6820
Telefax: 406-443-6882
Email: BKBH@BKBH.COM *URL:* http://www.BKBH.com

Stanley T. Kaleczyc J. Daniel Hoven
Leo Berry Catherine A. Laughner
Mark D. Etchart

(See Next Column)

Mary K. Giddings Steven T. Wade
Mark R. Taylor

Representative Clients: The Burlington Northern Santa Fe Railway Co.; Columbia Falls Aluminum Company; Burlington Resources Oil & Gas Company; Crane Company; R-Y Timber Company; Pacific Steel and Recycling; Rhone-Poulene.

For full biographical listings, see the Martindale-Hubbell Law Directory

NEBRASKA

*LINCOLN,** Lancaster Co.

CLINE, WILLIAMS, WRIGHT, JOHNSON & OLDFATHER (AV)

1900 U.S. Bank Building, 233 South 13th Street, 68508
Telephone: 402-474-6900
Fax: 402-474-5393
Email: postmaster@cline-law.com *URL:* http://www.cline-law.com
Omaha, Nebraska Office: Suite 720, One Pacific Place, 1125 South 103rd Street, 68124.
Telephone: 402-397-1700.
Fax: 402-397-1806.

ATTORNEYS

Allen L. Graves
Charles M. Pallesen, Jr.
Fredric H. Kauffman
Donald F. Burt
Alan E. Peterson
Stephen E. Gehring
Robert J. Routh
Kevin Colleran
L. Bruce Wright
James M. Bausch
Larry A. Holle
David R. Buntain
Stephen H. Nelsen
Michael C. Mueller
Lauren W. Wismer
Daniel R. Stogsdill
Scott D. Kelly
Terry R. Wittler
Pamela Hastings Carrier
Mark A. Christensen
Richard P. Garden, Jr.
Shawn D. Renner
John C. Miles
Mary Kay Frank
Thomas C. Huston
Sonya S. Ekart
Don R. Janssen
Susan Kubert Sapp
Kevin J. Schneider
Andrew D. Strotman
Jill Gossin Jensen
Rochelle A. Mullen
John L. Horan
Bryan S. Hatch
Steven C. Likes
Tracy A. Oldemeyer
Jolene M. Papa
Timothy G. Aschoff
Eric N. Bergquist
Janis J. Winterhof
Andrea Dylan Snowden

OF COUNSEL

Charles E. Wright Richard P. Jeffries
Mary M. Campbell

RETIRED PARTNERS

Flavel A. Wright (Retired) Warren C. Johnson (Retired)
Charles E. Oldfather (1927-1998)

Representative Clients: U.S. Bank National Association; University of Nebraska; Nebraska Medical Assn.; Saint Elizabeth Regional Medical Center; Media of Nebraska; Cargill Inc.; State Farm Insurance Cos.; Wal-Mart Stores, Inc.; Textron/Cushman; Isco, Inc.

For full biographical listings, see the Martindale-Hubbell Law Directory

NEVADA

*CARSON CITY,** (Independent City)

CROWELL, SUSICH, OWEN & TACKES, LTD. A PROFESSIONAL LAW CORPORATION (AV)

510 West Fourth Street, P.O. Box 1000, 89702
Telephone: 775-882-1311; 775-588-5448
Fax: 775-882-0257
Email: thefirm@advocacy.net

William J. Crowell, Jr. J. Thomas Susich
Robert L. Crowell Steven E. Tackes
Sandra-Mae Pickens

For full biographical listings, see the Martindale-Hubbell Law Directory

*LAS VEGAS,** Clark Co.

ALVERSON, TAYLOR, MORTENSEN, NELSON & SANDERS (AV)

7401 West Charleston Boulevard, 89117
Telephone: 702-384-7000
FAX: 702-385-7000
Email: alverson@intermind.net
Reno, Nevada Office: 245 East Liberty, Suite 520, 89505.
Telephone: 775-329-0473.
Fax: 775-329-3303.

MEMBERS OF FIRM

J. Bruce Alverson
Eric K. Taylor
David J. Mortensen
Erven T. Nelson
LeAnn Sanders

OF COUNSEL

Jack C. Cherry
Kurt D. Anderson
Philip C. Van Alstyne

ASSOCIATES

Rebecca Hopkins Miller
Sandra Smagac
Victoria L. Nelson
Aaron D. Lovaas
Diane Obritsch
Michael A. Olsen
Randal D. Shimon
Catherine A. Olendorff
Monica L. Pierce
Gabriel D. Lither
Kurt R. Bonds
Darius F. Rafie
Mark J. King, IV
Shell L. Mercer
Carrie S. Bourdeau
Jason Lane Earnest
Nathan R. Reinmiller
Donn C. Alexander
Afshin Tadayon
Eric O. Freeman
Lindsay L. Stadtlander
Julie M. Sueoka

Representative Clients: Checker Cab Company; Nevada Fleet Management, Inc.; Star Cab Co.; Yellow Cab Company; National Moving & Storage, Inc.; Southwest Pools & Landscaping; White Gove Delivery, Inc.; Fleet Deliver Service Northwest.

For full biographical listings, see the Martindale-Hubbell Law Directory

HALE LANE PEEK DENNISON HOWARD AND ANDERSON (AV)

Nevada Financial Center, 2300 West Sahara Avenue, Eighth Floor, Box 8, 89102
Telephone: 702-222-2500
Fax: 702-365-6940
Email: info@halelane.com
Reno, Nevada Office: 100 West Liberty Street, Tenth Floor, P.O. Box 3237.
Telephone: 775-327-3000.
Telefax: 775-786-6179.
Carson City, Nevada Office: 777 East William Street, Suite 200, P.O. Box 2620.
Telephone: 775-684-6000.
Telefax: 775-684-6001.

MEMBERS OF FIRM

J. Stephen Peek
Kristin B. McMillan

Representative Clients: Sprint; ITT Sheraton Corporation.

For Complete List of Firm Personnel, See General Section
For full biographical listings, see the Martindale-Hubbell Law Directory

BILL C. HAMMER & ASSOCIATES (AV)

BankWest Building, 4270 South Decatur Boulevard, Suite B-10, 89103
Telephone: 702-387-0530
Fax: 702-387-0928
Email: bchlawoff@aol.com *URL:* http://www.lawyers.com/billchammer

Bill C. Hammer

For full biographical listings, see the Martindale-Hubbell Law Directory

HILBRECHT & ASSOCIATES, CHARTERED (AV)

723 South Casino Center Boulevard, 89101-6716
Telephone: 702-384-1036
Facsimile: 702-384-2LAW
URL: http://www.lawyers.com/hilbrecht&associates
Email: hilbrcht@skylink.net *URL:* http://1stpage.sharednet.com/1/hilbrecht

Norman Ty Hilbrecht

Representative Clients: Bristol-Myers Squibb; Calzona Tankways; City Wide Enterprises; Coldwell Banker; Desert Chrysler-Plymouth; Enstrom Helicopter Co.; Las Vegas Congeneration; New England Life; Paul Revere Insurance;
Reference: First Security Bank of Nevada.

For full biographical listings, see the Martindale-Hubbell Law Directory

JOLLEY, URGA, WIRTH & WOODBURY (AV)

3800 Howard Hughes Parkway Suite 1600, 89109
Telephone: 702-699-7500
Facsimile: 702-699-7555
URL: http://www.juww.com
Boulder City, Nevada Office: Suite 105, 1000 Nevada Highway, 89005.
Telephone: 702-293-3674.

MEMBERS OF FIRM

William R. Urga
Brian E. Holthus

Representative Clients: Wells Fargo Bank and its predecessor, First Interstate Bank of Nevada; Nevada State Bank; Chicago Title Insurance Co.; Melvin Simon & Associates, Inc.; General Motors Acceptance Corp.; Toyota Motor Credit Corporation; Champion Home Builders Co.; Circus Circus Casinos, Inc.

For Complete List of Firm Personnel, See General Section
For full biographical listings, see the Martindale-Hubbell Law Directory

*RENO,** Washoe Co.

GUILD, RUSSELL, GALLAGHER & FULLER, LTD. (AV)

100 West Liberty, Suite 800, P.O. Box 2838, 89505
Telephone: 775-786-2366
Telecopier: 775-322-9105
Email: attorneys@grgflaw.com

Clark J. Guild (1887-1971)
Clark J. Guild, Jr.
C. David Russell
John K. Gallagher
Gary M. Fuller

Jason J. Freelin

Representative Clients: Caithness Resources, Inc.; Chevron USA, Inc.; Dickson Realty; DRGM Advertising Agency; Federal Deposit Insurance Corp.; Intermountain Power Project; Land Rover North America; Porsche Cars North America; Jones-West Ford; City of Los Angeles, Department of Water & Power; Metropolitan Water District of Southern California; Microsoft Corporation; 100 W. Liberty Ltd. Partnership.

For full biographical listings, see the Martindale-Hubbell Law Directory

LEVERTY & ASSOCIATES LAW, CHARTERED (AV)

Reno Gould House, 832 Willow Street, 89502
Telephone: 775-322-6636
Fax: 775-322-3953
Email: levertyassoc@law.reno.nv.us *URL:* http://www.lawyers.com/levertylaw
San Diego, California Office: 110 West "C" Street. Suite 1300. 92101.
Telephone: 619-234-6636.
Fax: 619-234-6634. Email: levlaw@pacbell.net
Las Vegas, Nevada Office: 2110 East Flamingo Road, Suite 106, 89119.
Telephone: 702-733-0556.
Fax: 702-733-0563.

Vernon E. Leverty
Matthew L. Sharp

Betty C. Baker
Rebecca D. Lack (Not admitted in NV; Resident, San Diego, California Office)

For full biographical listings, see the Martindale-Hubbell Law Directory

MCDONALD CARANO WILSON MCCUNE BERGIN FRANKOVICH & HICKS LLP (AV)

241 Ridge Street, 89501
Telephone: 775-788-2000
Telecopier: 775-788-2020
URL: http://www.mcdonaldcarano.com
Las Vegas, Nevada Office: Suite 1000, 2300 West Sahara Avenue.
Telephone: 702-873-4100.
Telecopier: 702-873-9966.

MEMBERS OF FIRM

Robert L. McDonald
Thomas R. C. Wilson
John J. Frankovich
Alvin J. (Bud) Hicks
Robert E. Armstrong
James C. Giudici

ASSOCIATES

David F. Grove
Bonnie Fleischer Drinkwater
Andrew S. Gabriel
Jane M. Long (Not admitted in NV)

OF COUNSEL

Donald L. Carano
William S. Boyd
Charles E. Huff

Representative Clients: Boyd Gaming Corporation; Eldorado Hotel & Casino; AT&T Communications of Nevada; John Acuaga's Nugget; Coast Resorts, LLC; Jackpot Enterprises, Inc.; Universal Distributing of Nevada, Inc.

For Complete List of Firm Personnel, See General Section
For full biographical listings, see the Martindale-Hubbell Law Directory

NEW JERSEY

*HACKENSACK,** Bergen Co.

DEENER, FEINGOLD & STERN, A PROFESSIONAL CORPORATION (AV)

2 University Plaza, Suite 503, 07601
Telephone: 201-343-8788
Fax: 201-343-4640
Email: JeromeDeener@DeenerFeingold.com *URL:* http://www.lawyers.com/deenerfeingold&stern

Jerome A. Deener
Cal R. Feingold
Robert A. Stern
David M. Edelblum
Anthony M. Vizzoni

Debra T. Hirsch
Andrew M. Grumet
Ronen Gabbay

References: Hudson United Bank; Commerce Bank.

For full biographical listings, see the Martindale-Hubbell Law Directory

NICOLETTE & PERKINS, P.A. (AV)

3 University Plaza, Fifth Floor, 07601
Telephone: 201-488-9080
Telecopier: 201-488-5580
Email: nicoletteperkins@juno.com *URL:* http://www.lawyers.com/nicolette&perkins

David A. Nicolette, Jr.
Eric R. Perkins

Jeanette A. Odynski
Laura N. Keenan
Toni Marie McPhillips

For full biographical listings, see the Martindale-Hubbell Law Directory

STEPHEN H. ROTH (AV)

62 Summit Avenue, 07601
Telephone: 201-489-3737
Fax: 201-489-0557

ASSOCIATE

Michele M. De Santis

For full biographical listings, see the Martindale-Hubbell Law Directory

LIVINGSTON, Essex Co.

GENOVA, BURNS & VERNOIA (AV)

Eisenhower Plaza II, 354 Eisenhower Parkway, 07039
Telephone: 973-533-0777
Facsimile: 973-533-1112
URL: http://www.gbvlaw.com
Trenton, New Jersey Office: The Princeton House, 160 West State Street.
Telephone: 609-393-1131.

MEMBERS OF FIRM

Angelo J. Genova
James M. Burns
Francis J. Vernoia
John C. Petrella
James J. McGovern, III
Carmel Joy Decker

ASSOCIATES

Sandro Polledri
Celia S. Bosco
Lynn S. Degen
Elizabeth A. Daly
Brian O. Lipman
J. Frank Vespa-Papaleo
Susan B. Burns
Bruno Genova
Robert C. Gifford, Jr.
Courtney Gaccione

For full biographical listings, see the Martindale-Hubbell Law Directory

*NEWARK,** Essex Co.

MEYNER AND LANDIS (AV)

One Gateway Center, Suite 2500, 07102-5311
Telephone: 973-624-2800
Fax: 973-624-0356
Email: attys@meyner.com *URL:* http://www.meyner.com

Robert B. Meyner (1908-1990)
Edwin C. Landis, Jr.
John N. Malyska
William J. Fiore
Anthony F. Siliato
Francis R. Perkins
Howard O. Thompson
Scott T. McCleary
Linda Townley Snyder
William H. Schmidt, Jr.
David B. Grantz

For full biographical listings, see the Martindale-Hubbell Law Directory

SILLS CUMMIS RADIN TISCHMAN EPSTEIN & GROSS, A PROFESSIONAL CORPORATION (AV)

One Riverfront Plaza, 07102-5400
Telephone: 973-643-7000
Fax: 973-643-6500
Telex: 820630 Sillsbeck Nwk
Email: sillsmail@sillscummis.com *URL:* http://www.sillscummis.com
Atlantic City, New Jersey Office: 17 Gordon's Alley.
Telephone: 609-344-2800.
New York, N.Y. Office: 712 Fifth Avenue.
Telephone: 212-643-7000.
Washington, D.C. Office: 1800 K Street, N.W.
Telephone: 202-296-4750.

MEMBERS OF FIRM

Clive S. Cummis
Stephen J. Moses
William J. Martini
Noah Bronkesh
Lester Aron
Kenneth F. Oettle
Philip R. Sellinger
James M. Hirschhorn

OF COUNSEL

Mitchel E. Ostrer
Cherie L. Maxwell

Paul P. Josephson
Robert I. Siegel

Representative Clients: GAF Corporation; Public Service Enterprise Group; Bally Manufacturing Corp.; GTE Sprint; GAF Corporation; U.S. Generating Co.; Bertex Laboratories, Inc.; Jersey City Medical Center.; Englewood Hospital Compost America.

For Complete List of Firm Personnel, See General Section

For full biographical listings, see the Martindale-Hubbell Law Directory

ZAZZALI, ZAZZALI, FAGELLA & NOWAK, A PROFESSIONAL CORPORATION (AV)

One Riverfront Plaza, 07102-5410
Telephone: 973-623-1822
Telecopier: 973-623-2209
URL: http://www.lawyers.com/zazzali
Trenton, New Jersey Office: 150 West State Street.
Telephone: 609-392-8172.
Facsimile: 609-392-8933.
New York, New York Office: 15 West 72nd Street.
Telephone: 212-529-3927.
Facsimile: 212-875-8275.

Andrew F. Zazzali (1925-1969)
Andrew F. Zazzali, Jr.
James R. Zazzali
Robert A. Fagella
Kenneth I. Nowak
Paul L. Kleinbaum
Richard A. Friedman

Kathleen Anne Naprstek
Aileen M. O'Driscoll
Edward H. O'Hare
Jason Solowkowski

For full biographical listings, see the Martindale-Hubbell Law Directory

NORTH BRUNSWICK, Middlesex Co.

BORRUS, GOLDIN, FOLEY, VIGNUOLO, HYMAN, STAHL & CLARKIN, A PROFESSIONAL CORPORATION (AV)

2875 U.S. Highway 1, Route 1 & Finnigans Lane, P.O. Box 7463, 08902
Telephone: 732-422-1000
Fax: 732-422-1016
Email: attys@borrus.com *URL:* http://www.borrus.com

Jack Borrus
Martin S. Goldin
David M. Foley
Anthony B. Vignuolo
Jeffrey M. Hyman
James E. Stahl
James F. Clarkin III
Eileen Mary Foley

Robert C. Nisenson
Rosalind Westlake
Lisa M. Vignuolo
Steven L. Fox
Peter A. Vignuolo
Gerald T. Foley (1903-1976)

Representative Clients: Summit Bank; R. J. Reynolds Tobacco Co.; K. Hovnanian Enterprises, Inc.; Johnson and Johnson; Foster Wheeler, Inc.; Hartz Mountain Industries; Middlesex County Vocational Services Commission; Borough of South Plainfield Board of Adjustment; U-Haul of Northern NJ.

For full biographical listings, see the Martindale-Hubbell Law Directory

NEW MEXICO

*ALBUQUERQUE,** Bernalillo Co.

RODEY, DICKASON, SLOAN, AKIN & ROBB, P.A. (AV)

Albuquerque Plaza, Suite 2200, 201 Third Street, N.W., P.O. Box 1888, 87103-1888
Telephone: 505-765-5900
Fax: 505-768-7395
Email: info@rodey.com *URL:* http://www.rodey.com
Santa Fe, New Mexico Office: Suite 101 Marcy Plaza, 123 East Marcy Street, P.O. Box 1357, 87504-1357.
Telephone: 505-984-0100.
Fax: 505-989-9542.

Mark K. Adams
Joseph B. Rochelle
John P. Salazar
David W. Bunting
W. Mark Mowery (Resident, Santa Fe Office)
Susan K. Barger

COUNSEL

Richard C. Minzner

For Complete List of Firm Personnel, See General Section

For full biographical listings, see the Martindale-Hubbell Law Directory

*SANTA FE,** Santa Fe Co.

HUFFAKER & CONWAY, A PROFESSIONAL CORPORATION (AV)

155 Grant Avenue, P.O. Box 1868, 87504-1868
Telephone: 505-988-8921
Fax: 505-983-3927
Email: sfstaff@sisna.com
Albuquerque, New Mexico Office: 201 Third Street, N.W., Suite 1910.
Telephone: 505-244-0021.
Facsimile: 505-244-1372.

Gregory D. Huffaker, Jr.
Lisa A. Joynes
Ann Maloney Conway
Seth L. Sparks
Edward C. Bagley

Representative Clients: Chevron Products Company; The State Farm Insurance Companies.

For full biographical listings, see the Martindale-Hubbell Law Directory

MONTGOMERY & ANDREWS, PROFESSIONAL ASSOCIATION (AV)

325 Paseo de Peralta, P.O. Box 2307, 87504-2307
Telephone: 505-982-3873
Fax: 505-982-4289
Email: montand@montand.com

Gary Kilpatric
Galen M. Buller
Thomas W. Olson
Edmund H. Kendrick
John B. Draper
Louis W. Rose
Nancy M. Anderson King
Carolyn Wolf

Representative Clients: Allstate Insurance Co.; Conoco, Inc.; El Paso Corp.; Giant Industries Arizona, Inc.; INTEL Corporation; LAC Minerals (USA), Inc.; McKinley Paper Co.; Mobil Exploration and Producing U.S. Inc.; New Mexico-American Water Company; New Mexico Utilities, Inc.; U S WEST Communications, Inc.

For Complete List of Firm Personnel, See General Section

For full biographical listings, see the Martindale-Hubbell Law Directory

NEW YORK

*ALBANY,** Albany Co.

COUCH WHITE, LLP (AV)

540 Broadway, P.O. Box 22222, 12201
Telephone: 518-426-4600
Telecopier: 518-426-0376
Email: CouchWhiteBrenn@Global2000.net *URL:* http://www.couchwhite.com
Washington, D.C. Office: 700 Thirteenth Street, N.W., Suite 950.
Telephone: 202-434-4503.
Fax: 202-434-4562.

MEMBERS OF FIRM

Leslie F. Couch
Leonard H. Singer
Algird F. White, Jr.
Keith B. Rose
Barbara S. Brenner
Christopher A. Cernik
Joel M. Howard, III
Michael B. Mager
Paul A. Feigenbaum
Mark F. Glaser
Robert M. Loughney
Pamela A. Madeiros
Harold N. Iselin
James J. Barriere
Doreen Unis Saia

(See Next Column)

SENIOR COUNSEL

Lawrence H. Cooke

ASSOCIATES

David G. Anderson
James S. King
Tricia A. Asaro
Marc A. Madia

For full biographical listings, see the Martindale-Hubbell Law Directory

FEATHERSTONHAUGH, CONWAY, WILEY & CLYNE, L.L.P. (AV)

99 Pine Street, Suite 207, 12207
Telephone: 518-436-0786
Fax: 518-427-0452
URL: http://www.fcwc-law.com

MEMBERS OF FIRM

James D. Featherstonhaugh
Stephen J. Wiley
Thomas A. Conway
Elizabeth K. Clyne

ASSOCIATES

Nadine Feiden Shadlock
William F. Conway, IV
Denis R. Hurley, Jr.
Gerard L. Conway, Jr.
Andrew W. Kirby
Steven M. Connolly

OF COUNSEL

William F. Conway
David Weinraub
Jeffrey J. Conklin
Randall J. Ezick

LEGAL SUPPORT PERSONNEL

GOVERNMENTAL RELATIONS

John L. Hardy
John P. Griffin
Daniel G. Plummer
David F. Fleming

For full biographical listings, see the Martindale-Hubbell Law Directory

GARDEN CITY, Nassau Co.

JACOBSON AND GOLDBERG, LLP (AV)

585 Stewart Avenue, 11530
Telephone: 516-222-2330
Telex: 80-4294 BARRISTER
Fax: 516-222-2339
Email: JacobsonandGoldberg@worldnet.att.net

MEMBERS OF FIRM

Arthur I. Goldberg
Amy T. Kulb
Miles R. Jacobson
Daniel M. Goldberg
Jeffrey A. Granat

For full biographical listings, see the Martindale-Hubbell Law Directory

MELVILLE, Suffolk Co.

LAMB & BARNOSKY, LLP (AV)

534 Broadhollow Road-CS 9034, 11747-9034
Telephone: 631-694-2300
Telecopier: 631-694-2309
Email: thefirm@lambbarnosky.com *URL:* http://www.lambbarnosky.com

PARTNERS

Eugene R. Barnosky
Scott M. Karson
Robert H. Cohen
P. L. Lamb
Marcia Lyn Finkelstein
Arthur A. Lane
Michael J. Heller
Joel M. Markowitz
Gary Holman
Gerald P. Rosenberg
Patrice Dowd Shenn

OF COUNSEL

Louis E. Black
Howard W. Newman
James F. Gesualdi
Joseph J. Salvatore
Joseph H. Wishod

COUNSEL

Lloyd K. Chanin
Scott P. McBride

ASSOCIATES

Cathleen D. Allen
Rita Fishman Sheena
Catherine Healy Kanzler
Shari Lee Sugarman

For full biographical listings, see the Martindale-Hubbell Law Directory

*NEW YORK,** New York Co.

BERLACK, ISRAELS & LIBERMAN LLP (AV)

120 West 45th Street, 10036
Telephone: 212-704-0100
Cable Address: "Berilib"
Telecopier: 212-704-0196
Email: info@berlack.com
Morristown, New Jersey Office: 65 Madison Avenue.
Telephone: 201-644-3400.
Telecopier: 201-644-3159.

MEMBERS OF FIRM

Harris Berlack (1946-1968)
Wade M. Boswell
Carlos L. Israels (1946-1969)
Douglas E. Davidson
Kenneth R. Asher
Alan N. Forman
Claude A. Baum
Steven E. Greenbaum
Scott M. Berman
Harvey M. Katz

(See Next Column)

BERLACK, ISRAELS & LIBERMAN LLP—*Continued*

MEMBERS OF FIRM (Continued)

James B. Liberman
Stuart Neuhauser
Robert D. Schmicker
Martin S. Siegel
Steven F. Wasserman
Edward S. Weisfelner

SENIOR ATTORNEYS

Andrew S. Dash
Erica M. Ryland

ASSOCIATES

John P. Biedermann
Anne M. Cunningham
Pauline Foley (Resident, Morristown, New Jersey Office)
Julie L. Friedberg (Resident, Morristown, New Jersey Office)
Emilio A. Galván
Linda B. Goebel
Louis Lombardo
Rachel F. Mayerson (Not admitted in NY)
Amy P. K. Motzenbecker (Resident, Morristown, New Jersey Office)
Antonio Peguero, Jr.
Elizabeth Quirk (Resident, Morristown, New Jersey Office)
Marcela M. Sanchez
Melissa Sarubbi

OF COUNSEL

Gerald W. Conway (Not admitted in NY; Resident, Morristown, New Jersey Office)
Marc B. Lasky (Resident, Morristown, New Jersey Office)

For full biographical listings, see the Martindale-Hubbell Law Directory

THE LAW OFFICES OF MICHAEL E. CURAN, P.C. (AV)

59 John Street, Third Floor, 10038
Telephone: 212-513-1578
Fax: 212-513-1592

Michael E. Curan

Anthony Van Zwaren
Robert J. Callahan
Steven R. Mitlitzky

OF COUNSEL

William H. Maloney, Jr.

For full biographical listings, see the Martindale-Hubbell Law Directory

NEIMAN GINSBURG & MAIRANZ P.C. (AV)

39 Broadway, 25th Floor, 10006-3003
Telephone: 212-269-1000
Telecopier: 212-635-9302
Email: ngmpc@concentric.net *URL:* http://www.ngmpc.com

Marvin Neiman
Theodore T. Mairanz
Gary Ginsburg

Betsy R. Malik
Susie Chovev

For full biographical listings, see the Martindale-Hubbell Law Directory

PLUNKETT & JAFFE, P.C. (AV)

230 Park Avenue, Suite 1847, 10169
Telephone: 212-922-1800
Facsimile: 212-922-1819
Email: plunkettjaffe.com
White Plains, New York Office: 1 North Broadway.
Telephone: 914-948-7722.
Facsimile: 914-948-7603.
Albany, New York Office: 111 Washington Avenue.
Telephone: 518-462-1800.
Facsimile: 518-462-4875.

William F. Plunkett, Jr.
Kevin J. Plunkett
Patrick E. Brown
John S. Harris
Kathleen P. O'Connor

For Complete List of Firm Personnel, See General Section

For full biographical listings, see the Martindale-Hubbell Law Directory

*WHITE PLAINS,** Westchester Co.

JAMES F. DONOHUE (AV)

81 Main Street, Suite 505, 10601
Telephone: 914-949-7766
Fax: 914-949-0324

ASSOCIATE

Thomas M. Roach, Jr.

Representative Clients: Nova Casualty Co.
Reference: Chase Bank/NBW Division, White Plains Branch.

For full biographical listings, see the Martindale-Hubbell Law Directory

NORTH CAROLINA

*RALEIGH,** Wake Co.

ALLEN & MOORE, L.L.P. (AV)

3700 Computer Drive, Suite 320, 27609-8627
Telephone: 919-783-8023
Fax: 919-783-8282
Email: ALLNMOORE@AOL.COM

Arch T. Allen, III
Joseph C. Moore, III
Ann Strader Hanley

For full biographical listings, see the Martindale-Hubbell Law Directory

ALLEN AND PINNIX, P.A. (AV)

333 Fayetteville Street, Mall, Suite 1200, 27601
Telephone: 919-755-0505
Facsimile: 919-829-8098

Noel L. Allen
John L. Pinnix
C. Lynn Calder
M. Jackson Nichols
D. James Jones, Jr.
Michael L. Weisel
Alice S. Glover

General Counsel For: North Carolina State Board of CPA Examiners; North Carolina Board of Architecture; NCAE.

For full biographical listings, see the Martindale-Hubbell Law Directory

SMITH DEBNAM NARRON WYCHE STORY & MYERS, L.L.P. (AV)

Hedingham Oaks, 4700 New Bern Avenue, P.O. Box 26268, 27611-6268
Telephone: 919-250-2000
Facsimile: 919-250-2100
Email: smithdebnamlaw.com

MEMBERS OF FIRM

W. Thurston Debnam, Jr.
John W. Narron
Jerry T. Myers
Terri L. Gardner
Byron L. Saintsing
Franklin Drake
Gerald H. Groon, Jr.
Terry M. Kilbride
Elizabeth B. Godfrey
N. Hunter Wyche, Jr.
Ashley H. Story
Bettie Kelley Sousa
Laura K. Howell
Rose H. Stout
Susan Yelton Ellinger
Caren Davis Enloe
Connie E. Carrigan
Jeff D. Rogers
Kevin L. Sink

ASSOCIATES

Melanie J. Hogg
Staci Flaxman Katz
Tabatha L. Cruden
Tracy T. Hyde
Nina L. Gunther
Matthew E. Roehm
Sharon B. Christopher
J. Michael Mackay
Cynthia V. Mcalister

OF COUNSEL

Fred J. Smith, Jr.
Jane Flowers Finch

For full biographical listings, see the Martindale-Hubbell Law Directory

WOMBLE CARLYLE SANDRIDGE & RICE (AV)

A Professional Limited Liability Company
2100 First Union Capitol Center, 150 Fayetteville Street Mall, P.O. Box 831, 27602
Telephone: 919-755-2100
Fax: 919-755-2150
Email: lawyers@wcsr.com *URL:* http://www.wcsr.com
Charlotte, North Carolina Office: 3300 One First Union Center, 301 South College Street.
Telephone: 704-331-4900.
Fax: 704-331-4955.
Winston-Salem, North Carolina Office: 200 West Second Street, P.O. Drawer 84.
Telephone: 336-721-3600.
Fax: 336-721-3660.
Research Triangle Park, North Carolina Office: 2505 Meridian Parkway, Suite 300 (Durham), 27713.
Telephone: 919-484-2300.
Fax: 919-484-2340.
Atlanta, Georgia Office: One Atlantic Center, 1201 West Peachtree Street, Suite 3500.
Telephone: 404-872-7000.
Fax: 404-888-7490.
Other Atlanta, Georgia Office: Suite 404, 2296 Henderson Mill Road, N.E.
Telephone: 770-492-9030.
Fax: 770-492-9609.
Washington, D.C. Office: 1120 Nineteenth Street, N.W., Eighth Floor.
Telephone: 202-857-4400.
Fax: 202-467-6910.
Greenville, South Carolina Office: 15 South Main Street, Suite 601, P.O. Box 10208.
Telephone: 864-255-5400.
Fax: 864-255-5440.

(See Next Column)

WOMBLE CARLYLE SANDRIDGE & RICE, *Raleigh—Continued*

RESIDENT MEMBERS

Johnny M. Loper
Alexander P. Sands, III

RESIDENT ASSOCIATE

Samuel M. Taylor

RESIDENT OF COUNSEL

E. Lawrence Davis, III

Representative Clients: Aetna Casualty and Surety Co., Inc.; ALSCO/AmeriMark Building Products, Inc.; Aoki Corporation America, Inc.; Hackney Brothers, Inc.; Lawyers Mutual Liability Insurance Company of North Carolina; Meredith College; Regency Park Corp.; Wachovia Bank, N.A.

For Complete List of Firm Personnel, See General Section

For full biographical listings, see the Martindale-Hubbell Law Directory

*WINSTON-SALEM,** Forsyth Co.

WOMBLE CARLYLE SANDRIDGE & RICE (AV)

A Professional Limited Liability Company
200 West Second Street, P.O. Drawer 84, 27102
Telephone: 336-721-3600
Fax: 336-721-3660
Email: lawyers@wcsr.com *URL:* http://www.wcsr.com
Charlotte, North Carolina Office: 3300 One First Union Center, 301 South College Street.
Telephone: 704-331-4900.
Fax: 704-331-4955.
Raleigh, North Carolina Office: 2100 First Union Capitol Center, 150 Fayetteville Street Mall, P.O. Box 831.
Telephone: 919-755-2100.
Fax: 919-755-2150.
Research Triangle Park, North Carolina Office: 2505 Meridian Parkway, Suite 300 (Durham), 27713.
Telephone: 919-484-2300.
Fax: 919-484-2340.
Atlanta, Georgia Office: One Atlantic Center, 1201 West Peachtree Street, Suite 3500.
Telephone: 404-872-7000.
Fax: 404-888-7490.
Other Atlanta, Georgia Office: Suite 404, 2296 Henderson Mill Road, N.E.
Telephone: 770-492-9030.
Fax: 770-492-9609.
Washington, D.C. Office: 1120 Nineteenth Street, N.W., Eighth Floor.
Telephone: 202-857-4400.
Fax: 202-467-6910.
Greenville, South Carolina Office: 15 South Main Street, Suite 601, P.O. Box 10208.
Telephone: 864-255-5400.
Fax: 864-255-5440.

RESIDENT MEMBER

Ashley O. Thrift

Representative Clients: Brad Ragan, Inc.; Brenner Companies, Inc.; Food Lion, Inc.; Hanes Companies, Inc.; North Carolina Baptist Hospitals, Inc.; R.J. Reynolds Tobacco Company; Thomasville Furniture Industries, Inc.; Wachovia Corp.; Wake Forest University.

For Complete List of Firm Personnel, See General Section

For full biographical listings, see the Martindale-Hubbell Law Directory

OHIO

*CINCINNATI,** Hamilton Co.

BARRETT & WEBER A LEGAL PROFESSIONAL ASSOCIATION (AV)

500 Fourth & Walnut Centre, 105 East Fourth Street, 45202
Telephone: 513-721-2120
Facsimile: 513-721-2139

C. Francis Barrett

For full biographical listings, see the Martindale-Hubbell Law Directory

*COLUMBUS,** Franklin Co.

GARY L. JONES CO., L.P.A. (AV)

42 East Gay Street, Suite 1500, 43215
Telephone: 614-221-2300
URL: http://www.lawyers.com/garyjones

Gary L. Jones
James J. Andrioff

OF COUNSEL

Roland Thomas Gilbert

For full biographical listings, see the Martindale-Hubbell Law Directory

KEGLER, BROWN, HILL & RITTER (AV)

Capitol Square Suite 1800, 65 East State Street, 43215-4294
Telephone: 614-462-5400
Telecopier: 614-464-2634
Cable Address: "Law KBHR"
Telex: 246671
Email: info@kbhr.com *URL:* http://www.kbhr.com
Marion, Ohio Office: 250 Executive Drive, Suite B, P.O. Box 919.
Telephone: 614-387-3501.
Facsimile: 614-387-3630.

Donald A. Antrim
William J. Brown
Lawrence F. Feheley
Daniel G. Hilson
Gene W. Holliker
R. Kevin Kerns
Ronald L. Mason
Richard W. Schuermann, Jr.
Roger P. Sugarman
R. Douglas Wrightsel
Michael E. Zatezalo

COUNSEL

Leigh Anne Reardon

Thomas M. L. Metzger

Representative Clients: Medco Containment Services, Inc.; Ohio Manufactured Housing Association.

For Complete List of Firm Personnel, See General Section

For full biographical listings, see the Martindale-Hubbell Law Directory

*DAYTON,** Montgomery Co.

E. S. GALLON & ASSOCIATES (AV)

40 West Fourth Street Centre Suite 2200, 45402
Telephone: 937-586-3100; 800-998-4374
Fax: 937-586-3200
URL: http://www.esgallon.com

MEMBERS OF FIRM

Jack A. Cervay
David A. Saphire
Joseph R. Ebenger
Joan B. Brenner
James D. Dennis
James R. Piercy
Richard M. Malone
Kyle D. Martin
Natalie J. Tackett

ASSOCIATE

David R. Salyer

For full biographical listings, see the Martindale-Hubbell Law Directory

DUBLIN, Franklin Co.

BLAUGRUND, HERBERT & MARTIN, INCORPORATED (AV)

5455 Rings Road, Suite 500, 43017-7517
Telephone: 614-764-0681
Fax: 614-764-0774
Email: bhm@bhmlaw.net

David S. Blaugrund
John W. Herbert
John S. Jones
David S. Kessler
Emily J. Lewis
Marc E. Myers
Stephen P. Postalakis

For full biographical listings, see the Martindale-Hubbell Law Directory

OKLAHOMA

*OKLAHOMA CITY,** Oklahoma Co.

KERR, IRVINE, RHODES & ABLES, A PROFESSIONAL CORPORATION (AV)

201 Robert S. Kerr Avenue, Suite 600, 73102-4267
Telephone: 405-272-9221
Fax: 405-236-3121
Email: kira201@aol.com

Horace G. Rhodes
J. Angela Ables
James W. Rhodes
James R. Barnett
R. Thomas Lay

Kevin R. Wisner

OF COUNSEL

Henry B. Taliaferro, Jr.

Representative Clients: Allstate Insurance Co.; Clarendon Insurance Group; Community Care HMO; Causeco Co.; Pre-Paid Legal Services, Inc.; Delta Dental Plan of Oklahoma; Harbor Insurance Co.; Insurance Data Resources (IDR); Life Assurance Co.. Inc.; 66 Federal Credit Union.

For Complete List of Firm Personnel, See General Section

For full biographical listings, see the Martindale-Hubbell Law Directory

OREGON

*PORTLAND,** Multnomah Co.

Sather, Byerly & Holloway, LLP (AV)

621 Southwest Morrison Street, Suite 650, 97205
Telephone: 503-225-5858
Fax: 503-721-9272
Email: sbh@teleport.com *URL:* http://www.teleport.com/~sbh/sbh.htm

Deborah L. Sather
Bruce L. Byerly
Ronald C. Holloway
Krishna Balasubramani
Tracy J. White
Constance Lynn Wold

For full biographical listings, see the Martindale-Hubbell Law Directory

PENNSYLVANIA

BLUE BELL, Montgomery Co.

Kelley & Murphy (AV)

Union Meeting Corporate Center V, Suite 160 925 Harvest Drive, 19422
Telephone: 215-643-6500
Fax: 215-643-8356
Cable Address: "BIGTIME"
Email: kmlaw@counsel.com

Joseph T. Kelley, Jr.
Patrick G. Murphy
Joseph T. Kelley, III

LEGAL SUPPORT PERSONNEL

Marianne Rowen
Tanja M.Z. Barron

For full biographical listings, see the Martindale-Hubbell Law Directory

*HARRISBURG,** Dauphin Co.

S. Walter Foulkrod, III & Associates (AV)

2215 Forest Hills Drive, Suite 35, P.O. Box 6600, 17112-0600
Telephone: 717-541-0400
Fax: 717-541-1727
Email: law@foulkrod.com *URL:* http://www.foulkrod.com

ASSOCIATES

S. Walter Foulkrod, IV
Andrew H. Foulkrod

Representative Clients: Aegis Security Insurance Company; Allianz Life Insurance Company of North America; Allstate Insurance Co.; ATI Title Co.; Physicians Insurance Company of Ohio; Physicians Mutual Insurance Co.; Pennsylvania Medical Society Liability Insurance Co.; Pennsylvania National Mutual Casualty Insurance Co.; Tighe Industries, Inc.; United Investors Life Insurance Co.

For full biographical listings, see the Martindale-Hubbell Law Directory

Killian & Gephart, LLP (AV)

218 Pine Street, P.O. Box 886, 17108
Telephone: 717-232-1851
Telecopier: 717-238-0592
Email: kg@killiangephart.com *URL:* http://www.killiangephart.com

MEMBERS OF FIRM

John D. Killian
Smith B. Gephart
Thomas W. Scott
Jane Gowen Penny
Terrence J. McGowan
Paula J. McDermott
J. Paul Helvy

ASSOCIATE

Bradley A. Schutjer

Reference: Fulton Bank.

For full biographical listings, see the Martindale-Hubbell Law Directory

Mette, Evans & Woodside, A Professional Corporation (AV)

3401 North Front Street, P.O. Box 5950, 17110-0950
Telephone: 717-232-5000
Fax: 717-236-1816
Email: MEW@Mette.com *URL:* HTTP://WWW.METTE.COM

Howell C. Mette
James W. Evans
Charles B. Zwally
Lloyd R. Persun
Christopher C. Conner
P. Daniel Altland
Michael D. Reed
David A. Fitzsimons
Guy P. Beneventano

(See Next Column)

Robyn Katzman Bowman
Kathleen Doyle Yaninek
Elizabeth J. Goldstein
Bryan Scott Megary
John M. Hartzell

For Complete List of Firm Personnel, See General Section

For full biographical listings, see the Martindale-Hubbell Law Directory

*PHILADELPHIA,** Philadelphia Co.

Abramson & Freedman, L.L.C. (AV)

2128 Locust Street, 19103
Telephone: 215-545-2400
Telecopier: 215-545-8537
Haddonfield, New Jersey Office: 20 Kings Highway West.
Telephone: 609-795-5363.
Fax: 609-354-0020.

Gilbert B. Abramson
Jeffrey M. Freedman

Michael B. Tolcott
Stanley B. Cheiken (Resident, Haddonfield, New Jersey Office)
Glen L. Abramson

For full biographical listings, see the Martindale-Hubbell Law Directory

Donohue and Donohue (AV)

232 South Fourth Street, 19106
Telephone: 215-574-1080
Fax: 215-574-1255
URL: http://www.lawyers.com/donohuelaw
New York, N.Y. Office: 26 Broadway.
Telephone: 212-269-2330.
Telecopier: 212-269-5016.

John P. Donohue (Resident)

Patrick J. Egan
Melissa G. Pinheiro

For full biographical listings, see the Martindale-Hubbell Law Directory

SOUTH CAROLINA

*CHARLESTON,** Charleston Co.

Haynsworth, Marion, McKay & Guérard, L.L.P. (AV)

134 Meeting Street, P.O. Box 1119, 29402
Telephone: 843-722-7606
Facsimile: 843-724-8016
Columbia, South Carolina Office: Suite 2400 Affinity Building, 1201 Main Street, P.O. Drawer 7157, 29202.
Telephone: 803-765-1818. Facsimile 803-765-2399.
Greenville, South Carolina Office: 75 Beattie Place, Eleventh Floor, P.O. Box 2048, 29602.
Telephone: 864-240-3200.
Facsimile: 864-240-3300.

MEMBERS OF FIRM

William C. Cleveland
James J. Hinchey, Jr.
James E. Lady

Counsel for: Baker Hospital; Healthsource of South Carolina; Allstate Insurance Co.; CSX Corp.; Lloyd's Underwriters; Coward-Hund Construction Co.; City of Hanahan; Duke Power Co.; Anheuser Busch Co.

For Complete List of Firm Personnel, See General Section

For full biographical listings, see the Martindale-Hubbell Law Directory

*COLUMBIA,** Richland Co.

Haynsworth, Marion, McKay & Guérard, L.L.P. (AV)

Suite 2400 Affinity Building, 1201 Main Street, P.O. Drawer 7157, 29202
Telephone: 803-765-1818
Facsimile: 803-765-2399
Greenville, South Carolina Office: 75 Beattie Place, Eleventh Floor, P.O. Box 2048, 29602.
Telephone: 864-240-3200.
Facsimile: 864-240-3300.
Charleston, South Carolina Office: 134 Meeting Street, P.O. Box 1119, 29402.
Telephone: 843-722-7606.
Facsimile: 843-724-8016.

MEMBERS OF FIRM

William P. Simpson
Steven Todd Moon
Stephen F. McKinney
Michael R. Daniel
Russell B. Shetterly

(See Next Column)

HAYNSWORTH, MARION, MCKAY & GUÉRARD L.L.P., *Columbia—Continued*

ASSOCIATES

Gina L. Campano
Theodore D. Riley

OF COUNSEL

Julius W. McKay

Counsel for: St. Paul Insurance Group; Allstate Insurance Co.; Fluor-Daniel Corp.; South Carolina Jobs - Economic Development Authority; Anheuser Busch Company; CSX Transportation; Ernst & Young, LLP; Willis Corroon of South Carolina, Inc.; Westinghouse Savannah River Co.; Wachovia Bank of South Carolina, N.A.

For Complete List of Firm Personnel, See General Section

For full biographical listings, see the Martindale-Hubbell Law Directory

TURNER, PADGET, GRAHAM & LANEY, P.A. (AV)

Seventeenth Floor, 1901 Main Street, P.O. Box 1473, 29202
Telephone: 803-254-2200
Telecopy: 803-799-3957
Florence, South Carolina Office: Fourth Floor, 1831 West Evans Street, P.O. Box 5478, 29502.
Telephone: 843-662-9008.
Fax: 843-667-0828.
Charleston, South Carolina Office: 21 Broad Street, 1st Floor, P.O. Box 836, 29402.
Telephone: 843-723-1622.
Fax: 843-577-3369.

Thomas C. Salane
Danny C. Crowe
Arthur E. Justice, Jr. (Resident, Florence, SC, Office)

For Complete List of Firm Personnel, See General Section

For full biographical listings, see the Martindale-Hubbell Law Directory

*GREENVILLE,** Greenville Co.

HAYNSWORTH, MARION, MCKAY & GUÉRARD, L.L.P. (AV)

75 Beattie Place, Eleventh Floor, P.O. Box 2048, 29602
Telephone: 864-240-3200
Facsimile: 864-240-3300
Columbia, South Carolina Office: Suite 2400 Affinity Building, 1201 Main Street, P.O. Drawer 7157, 29202
Telephone: 803-765-1818.
Facsimile: 803-765-2399.
Charleston, South Carolina Office: 134 Meeting Street, P.O. Box 1119, 29402.
Telephone: 843-722-7606.
Facsimile: 843-724-8016.

MEMBERS OF FIRM

Thomas H. Coker, Jr.
H. Sam Mabry, III

ASSOCIATE

Boyd B. Nicholson, Jr.

OF COUNSEL

Julius W. McKay

Counsel for: Duke Power Co.; ASCI, Inc.; Fluor-Daniel Corp.; Synalloy Corp.; Greenville Hospital System.

For Complete List of Firm Personnel, See General Section

For full biographical listings, see the Martindale-Hubbell Law Directory

SOUTH DAKOTA

LEAD, Lawrence Co.

FULLER, TELLINGHUISEN, GORDON & PERCY, P.C. (AV)

203 West Main Street, P.O. Box 898, 57754
Telephone: 605-584-2440
Fax: 605-584-1979
Email: leadlaw@mato.com
Spearfish, South Dakota Office: 132 East Illinois, 57783.
Telephone: 605-642-8080.
Fax: 605-642-1756. E-mail: spflaw@mato.com

A. P. Fuller
Roger A. Tellinghuisen
Bradley P. Gordon
Michelle Palmer Percy

Representative Clients: Homestake Mining Co.; Hotel Franklin & Gaming; Black Hills Novelty/Automatic Vending, Inc.; Northern Hills General Hospital; Lantis Enterprises, Inc.; Norwest Bank South Dakota N.A.; Lead-Deadwood Independent School District # 40-1; City of Lead.

For full biographical listings, see the Martindale-Hubbell Law Directory

TENNESSEE

*MEMPHIS,** Shelby Co.

FARRIS, MATHEWS, BRANAN & HELLEN, P.L.C. (AV)

One Commerce Square, Suite 2000, 38103
Telephone: 901-259-7100
Fax: 901-259-7150
Email: firm@farris-law.com
East Memphis, Tennessee Office: Suite 400. First Commercial Bank Building. 5384 Poplar Avenue.
Telephone: 901-763-4000.
Fax: 901-763-4095.
Nashville, Tennessee Office: Nashville City Center, 511 Union Street, Suite 2400.
Telephone: 615-726-1200.
Fax: 615-726-1776.

MEMBERS OF FIRM

Harlan Mathews
Homer B. Branan, III
Edwin Dean White, III
Charles B. Welch, Jr. (Resident, Nashville Office)
John M. Farris
Dedrick Brittenum, Jr.

ASSOCIATES

Steven Caines Brammer
Harold W. Fonville, II
Fred D. Thompson, Jr. (Resident, Nashville Office)

For Complete List of Firm Personnel, See General Section

For full biographical listings, see the Martindale-Hubbell Law Directory

TEXAS

*AUSTIN,** Travis Co.

BAKER BOTTS L.L.P. (AV)

1600 San Jacinto Center, 98 San Jacinto Boulevard, 78701
Telephone: 512-322-2500
Fax: 512-322-2501
Email: postmaster@bakerbotts.com *URL:* http://www.bakerbotts.com
Houston, Texas Office: One Shell Plaza, 910 Louisiana.
Telephone: 713-229-1234.
Dallas, Texas Office: 2001 Ross Avenue.
Telephone: 214-953-6500.
Washington, D.C. Office: The Warner, 1299 Pennsylvania Avenue, N.W.
Telephone: 202-639-7700.
New York, New York Office: 599 Lexington Avenue.
Telephone: 212-705-5000.
Moscow, Russia Office: 10 ul. Bolshaya Dimitrovka (formerly Pushkinskaya), 103031.
Telephone: 7095/921-5300 (Local); 7501/929-7070 (International).
London, England Office: 45 Ludgate Hill.
Telephone: 0171-778-1400 (Local); 011-44-171-778-1400 (International).
Baku, Azerbaijan Office: 6-10 Vagif Mustafa-zadeh Street, Third Floor, Icheri Sheher, 370004.
Telephone: 994-12-97-63-88 (Local); 011-994-12-97-63-88 (International).
Fax: 994-12-97-63-61 (Local); 011-994-12-97-63-91 (International).

MEMBERS OF FIRM

Pamela M. Giblin
Mark R. Robeck
Robert T. Stewart
Larry F. York

OF COUNSEL

Joe R. Greenhill
Bob E. Shannon

ASSOCIATE

Derek R. McDonald

For Complete List of Firm Personnel, See General Section

For full biographical listings, see the Martindale-Hubbell Law Directory

CANTEY & HANGER ROAN & AUTREY L.L.P. (AV)

200 First State Bank Tower, 400 West Fifteenth Street, 78701-4200
Telephone: 512-474-4200
FAX: 512-469-0470; 512-469-0474
Email: FIRM@ROAN-AUTREY.COM *URL:* http://www.Roan-Autrey.com
Fort Worth, Texas Office: Cantey & Hanger, 2100 Burnett Plaza, 801 Cherry Street.
Telephone: 817-877-2800, Metro Line: 429-3815.
Telex: 758631.
FAX: 877-2807. Email: cantey@onramp.net
Dallas, Texas Office: Cantey & Hanger, 3330 Harwood Center, 1999 Bryan Street.
Telephone: 214-978-4100.
FAX: 214-978-4150. Email: chdallas@onramp.net

(See Next Column)

CANTEY & HANGER ROAN & AUTREY L.L.P.—*Continued*

Forrest C. Roan
Stephen L. Phillips
Jeff W. Autrey
Brian C. Newby
Julie K. Lane

OF COUNSEL

Tieman H. Dippel, Jr.

LEGAL SUPPORT PERSONNEL

Mary B. Jordan
Mary Perroni Blevins

Representative Clients: American Insurance Assn.; American Bankers Insurance Group; Manufacturers Life Insurance Co.; Prudential Insurance Co.; Zenith Insurance Co.; Zurich Commercial Insurance Co.; Metropolitan Life Insurance Company; Zurich American Life Insurance Company; Commercial General Union Insurance Co.; Tokio Marine & Fire Insurance Co.; Raytheon; National Semiconductor; Motorola; Texas Instruments; Chase Bank, Brenham National Bank.

For full biographical listings, see the Martindale-Hubbell Law Directory

DAVIS & DAVIS, P.C. (AV)

Arboretum Plaza One, 9th Floor, 9442 Capital of Texas Highway, P.O. Box 1588, 78759
Telephone: 512-343-6248
Fax: 512-343-0121
Mailing Address: P.O. Box 1588, Austin, Texas, 78767

C. Dean Davis
Ruth Russell-Schafer
Fred E. Davis
Michael L. Neely
Alexis J. Fuller, Jr.
Brian Gregory Jackson
Monte F. James

Bill Cline, Jr.
Kenda B. Dalrymple
Mark Alan Keene
Marian J. Wu
Mark S. La Spina

For Complete List of Firm Personnel, See General Section

For full biographical listings, see the Martindale-Hubbell Law Directory

DELEON, BOGGINS & ICENOGLE, A PROFESSIONAL CORPORATION (AV)

Bank One Tower, 221 West 6th Street, Suite 1050, 78701
Telephone: 512-478-5308
Fax: 512-482-8628
Email: deleon@dandb.com

Hector DeLeon
Anthony Icenogle
Thomas P. Washburn

OF COUNSEL

Joseph C. Boggins
Waggoner Carr
L. Dean Coff

Reference: Bank One, Austin.

For full biographical listings, see the Martindale-Hubbell Law Directory

HARRIS & HARRIS (AV)

Building III, 5300 Bee Cave Road, Suite 200, 78746
Telephone: 512-346-5533
Fax: 512-346-2539
Email: info@harriswc.com *URL:* http://www.harriswc.com

MEMBERS OF FIRM

H. S. Harris, Jr. (1916-1991)
Charles E. Morse, Jr.
H. S. Harris, III
Frances A. Lout
Christopher J. Ameel
William J. Grove, Jr.

ASSOCIATES

Camille L. Espey
LeeAnna Gainer
Janice G. Menzies
Paul Kelley
Stuart Colburn
Jessica Mendes Warren
Ricky D. Green
Robert F. Josey
Mark H. Sickles

For full biographical listings, see the Martindale-Hubbell Law Directory

JACKSON WALKER L.L.P. (AV)

100 Congress Avenue, Suite 1100, 78701-4099
Telephone: 512-236-2000
Fax: 512-236-2002
Email: hloftin@jw.com *URL:* http://www.jw.com
Dallas, Texas Office: 901 Main Street, Suite 6000.
Telephone: 214-953-6000.
Fax: 214-953-5822.
Fort Worth, Texas Office: 301 Commerce Street, Suite 2400.
Telephone: 817-334-7200.
Fax: 817-334-7290.
Houston, Texas Office: 1100 Louisiana, Suite 4200.
Telephone: 713-752-4200.
Fax: 713-752-4221.
Richardson, Texas Office: 2435 North Central Expressway, Suite 600.
Telephone: 972-671-2560.
Fax: 972-671-2566.

(See Next Column)

San Angelo, Texas Office: 225 West Beauregard Avenue.
Telephone: 915-481-2550.
Fax: 915-481-2552.
San Antonio, Texas Office: 112 E. Pecan Street, Suite 2100.
Telephone: 210-978-7700.
Fax: 210-978-7790.

MEMBERS OF FIRM

Carla J. Cox
Louis K. Obdyke, IV
J. Stephen Dillawn
Thomas T. Rogers
J. Matthew Dow
Thomas F. Sedberry
James M. Nias
Edward C. Small
Fred B. Werkenthin

For Complete List of Firm Personnel, See General Section

For full biographical listings, see the Martindale-Hubbell Law Directory

LONG, BURNER, PARKS & SEALY, A PROFESSIONAL CORPORATION (AV)

515 Congress Avenue, Suite 1500, P.O. Box 2212, 78768-2212
Telephone: 512-474-1587
Fax: 512-322-0301

Burnie Burner
Elisabeth DeLargy
Christopher A. McClellan

For full biographical listings, see the Martindale-Hubbell Law Directory

SAPP, SAPP & WHITE, P.C. (AV)

710 West Avenue, 78701
Telephone: 512-474-1801
Facsimile: 512-474-8230
URL: http://sapplaw.wld.com
URL: http://www.lawyers.com/sapplaw
Affiliated Office: Gay N. Sapp, 703 West 10th Street, Austin, Texas, 78701.
Telephone: 512-481-9401.
Facsimile: 512-478-9882.

David R. Sapp
Gay N. Sapp
Susan G. White

James "Beau" Eccles

OF COUNSEL

Russell Harding

For full biographical listings, see the Martindale-Hubbell Law Directory

TEMPLE & TEMPLE (AV)

400 West 15th Street, Suite 1510, 78701
Telephone: 512-477-4467
Fax: 512-477-4478

Larry E. Temple
J. Lawrence Temple

For full biographical listings, see the Martindale-Hubbell Law Directory

THOMPSON & KNIGHT L.L.P. (AV)

(Attorneys and Counselors)
1200 San Jacinto Center, 98 San Jacinto Boulevard, 78701
Telephone: 512-469-6100
Telecopy: 512-469-6180
URL: http://www.tklaw.com
Dallas, Texas Office: 1700 Pacific Avenue, Suite 3300, 75201.
Telephone: 214-969-1700.
Telecopy: 512-969-1751.
Telex: 732298.
Fort Worth, Texas Office: 801 Cherry Street, Suite 1600, 76102.
Telephone: 817-347-1700.
Telecopy: 817-347-1799.
Houston, Texas Office: Thompson Knight Brown Parker & Leahy L.L.P., 1200 Smith Street, Suite 3600, 77002-4595.
Telephone: 713-654-8111.
Telecopier: 713-654-1871.
San Pedro Garza Garcia, Nuevo León, Mexico Office: Edificio Losoles PD-4, Av. Lázaro Cárdenas No. 2400 Pte., C.P. 66220.
Telephone: (52-8) 363-0096.
Telecopy: (52-8) 363-3067.

PARTNERS

James E. Cousar
Regina C. Williams

For Complete List of Firm Personnel, See General Section

For full biographical listings, see the Martindale-Hubbell Law Directory

*DALLAS,** Dallas Co.

BAKER BOTTS L.L.P. (AV)

2001 Ross Avenue, 75201
Telephone: 214-953-6500
Fax: 214-953-6503
Email: postmaster@bakerbotts.com *URL:* http://www.bakerbotts.com
Houston, Texas Office: One Shell Plaza, 910 Louisiana.
Telephone: 713-229-1234.
Washington, D.C. Office: The Warner, 1299 Pennsylvania Avenue, N.W.
Telephone: 202-639-7700.
Austin, Texas Office: 1600 San Jacinto Center, 98 San Jacinto Boulevard.
Telephone: 512-322-2500.
New York, New York Office: 599 Lexington Avenue.
Telephone: 212-705-5000.
Moscow, Russia Office: 10 ul. Bolshaya Dimitrovka (formerly Pushkinskaya), 103031.
Telephone: 7095/921-5300 (Local); 7095/929-7070.
London, England Office: 45 Ludgate Hill.
Telephone: 0171-778-1400 (Local); 011-44-171-778-1400 (International).
Baku, Azerbaijan Office: 6-10 Vagif Mustafa-zadeh Street, Third Floor, Icheri Sheher, 370004.
Telephone: 994-12-97-63-88 (Local); 011-994-12-97-63-88 (International).

MEMBER OF FIRM

Edwin J. Tomko

ASSOCIATE

Ardita L. Vick

For Complete List of Firm Personnel, See General Section

For full biographical listings, see the Martindale-Hubbell Law Directory

CHRISTOPHER G. SHARP, P.C. (AV)

6116 North Central Expressway, Suite 520, 75206
Telephone: 214-368-3600
Fax: 214-368-3632
Email: CGSPC@Prodigy.com *URL:* http://www.lawyers.com/christophergsharplaw

Christopher G. Sharp

For full biographical listings, see the Martindale-Hubbell Law Directory

THOMPSON, COE, COUSINS & IRONS, L.L.P. (AV)

200 Crescent Court, Eleventh Floor, 75201-1853
Telephone: 214-871-8200
Fax: 214-871-8209
Austin, Texas Office: Suite 1500, Austin Centre, 701 Brazos, 78701.
Telephone: 512-708-8200.
Fax: 512-708-8777.

PARTNERS

Emory L. White, Jr.
Richard S. Geiger
Jack M. Cleaveland, Jr.
Rodney D. Bucker
Michael W. Jones
Rider Scott

ASSOCIATE

Loyd Ross Earley

Representative Clients: Association of Fire and Casualty Companies in Texas; Great American Insurance Companies; Universal Surety of America; Texas Insurance Organization; Texas Automobile Insurance Plan Association; TIG Insurance Company; Maclean Oddy & Associates, Inc.

For Complete List of Firm Personnel, See General Section

For full biographical listings, see the Martindale-Hubbell Law Directory

THOMPSON & KNIGHT L.L.P. (AV)

(Attorneys and Counselors)
1700 Pacific Avenue Suite 3300, 75201
Telephone: 214-969-1700
Telecopy: 214-969-1751
Telex: 732 298
URL: http://www.tklaw.com
Austin, Texas Office: 1200 San Jacinto Center, 98 San Jacinto Boulevard, 78701.
Telephone: 512-469-6100.
Telecopy: 512-469-6180.
Fort Worth, Texas Office: 801 Cherry Street, Suite 1600, 76102.
Telephone: 817-347-1700.
Telecopy: 817-347-1799.
Houston, Texas Office: Thompson Knight Brown Parker & Leahy L.L.P., 1200 Smith Street, Suite 3600, 77002-4595.
Telephone: 713-654-8111.
Telecopier: 713-654-1871.
San Pedro Garza Garcia, Nuevo León, Mexico Office: Edificio Losoles PD-4, Av. Lázaro Cárdenas No. 2400 Pte., C.P. 66220.
Telephone: (52-8) 363-0096.
Telecopy: (52-8) 363-3067.

(See Next Column)

PARTNER

Bennett W. Cervin

For Complete List of Firm Personnel, See General Section

For full biographical listings, see the Martindale-Hubbell Law Directory

*HOUSTON,** Harris Co.

BAKER BOTTS L.L.P. (AV)

One Shell Plaza, 910 Louisiana, 77002
Telephone: 713-229-1234
Cable Address: "Boterlove"
Fax: 713-229-1522
Email: postmaster@bakerbotts.com *URL:* http://www.bakerbotts.com
Washington, D.C. Office: The Warner, 1299 Pennsylvania Avenue, N.W.
Telephone: 202-639-7700.
New York, New York Office: 599 Lexington Avenue.
Telephone: 212-705-5000.
Austin, Texas Office: 1600 San Jacinto Center, 98 San Jacinto Boulevard.
Telephone: 512-322-2500.
Dallas, Texas Office: 2001 Ross Avenue.
Telephone: 214-953-6500.
Moscow, Russia Office: 10 ul. Bolshaya Dimitrovka (formerly Pushkinskaya), 103031.
Telephone: 7095/921-5300 (Local); 7095/929-7070 (International).
London, England Office: 45 Ludgate Hill.
Telephone: 0171-778-1400 (Local); 011-44-171-778-1400 (International).
Baku, Azerbaijan Office: 6-10 Vagif Mustafa-zadeh Street, Third Floor, Icheri Sheher, 370004.
Telephone: 994-12-97-63-88 (Local); 011-994-12-97-63-88 (International).
Fax: 994-12-97-63-91 (Local); 011-994-12-97-63-91 (International)

MEMBERS OF FIRM

I. Jay Golub
George F. Goolsby
Scott E. Rozzell

ASSOCIATES

Gretchen Gibbons Allen
James H. Barkley
Sarah Sharlot Dietrich

For Complete List of Firm Personnel, See General Section

For full biographical listings, see the Martindale-Hubbell Law Directory

UTAH

*SALT LAKE CITY,** Salt Lake Co.

VAN COTT, BAGLEY, CORNWALL & MCCARTHY, A PROFESSIONAL CORPORATION (AV)

50 South Main Street, Suite 1600, P.O. Box 45340, 84145-0340
Telephone: 801-532-3333
Telecopier: 801-534-0058
Email: info@vancott.com *URL:* http://www.vancott.com
Ogden, Utah Office: 2404 Washington Boulevard, Suite 900.
Telephone: 801-394-5783.
Park City, Utah Office: 2200 Park Avenue, Suite C200-A.
Telephone: 435-649-3889.

Thomas T. Billings
Thomas W. Clawson
H. Michael Keller
Matthew F. McNulty, III
Gregory P. Williams

Mara A. Brown
Kim S Colton

OF COUNSEL

M. Scott Woodland

For Complete List of Firm Personnel, See General Section

For full biographical listings, see the Martindale-Hubbell Law Directory

VIRGINIA

RICHMOND, (Independent City)

LECLAIR RYAN, A PROFESSIONAL CORPORATION (AV)

707 East Main Street, 11th Floor, 23219
Telephone: 804-783-2003
Facsmile: 804-783-2294
Email: email@leclairryan.com
Glen Allen, Virginia Office: 4201 Dominion Boulevard, Suite 200, 23060.
Telephone: 804-270-0070.
Facsimile: 804-270-4715.
Blacksburg, Virginia Office: 1872 Pratt Drive, Suite 1865, 24060.
Telephone: 540-961-2762.
Fax: 540-961-2781.

(See Next Column)

LeClair Ryan A Professional Corporation—*Continued*

Norfolk, Virginia Office: 999 Waterside Drive, Suite 2025.
Telephone: 757-624-1454.
Facsimile: 757-624-3773.
Alexandria, Virginia Office: 225 Reinekers Lane, Suite 290, 22314.
Telephone: 703-684-8007.
Facsimile: 703-684-8075.
Charlottesville, Virginia Office: 108 S.E. Second Street, P.O. Box 2017, 22902.
Telephone: 804-971-7771.
Facsimile: 804-296-0905.

Rodney K. Adams
Robert J. Grey, Jr.
James Patrick Guy, II
Micheal L. Hern
Thomas A. Lisk
Lawrence E. Marshall, II
Eric Michael Page
John A. Pirko
Kirk T. Schroder
David G. Shuford
George B. Wickham

Ellen Duffy McKay (Not admitted in VA)
Robert A. Omberg

For full biographical listings, see the Martindale-Hubbell Law Directory

Williams, Mullen, Clark & Dobbins, A Professional Corporation (AV)

Two James Center, 1021 East Cary Street, P.O. Box 1320, 23218-1320
Telephone: 804-643-1991
Fax: 804-783-6507
URL: http://www.wmcd.com
Newport News Office: Harbor Bank Center, Suite 210, One Old Oyster Point Road, 23602-7119.
Telephone: 757-249-5100.
Fax: 757-249-5109.
Virginia Beach Office: One Columbus Center, 23462-6763.
Telephone: 757-499-8800.
Fax: 757-473-0395.
Vienna Office: 1593 Spring Hill Road, Suite 510, 22182.
Telephone: 703-760-5200.
Fax: 703-748-0244.
Washington, D.C. Office: The Farragut Building, 900 17th Street, N.W., Suite 700, 20006.
Telephone: 202-293-0213.
Fax: 804-783-6507. Fax Within D.C.: 202-293-5939.
London, England Office: Blake Lodge, Bridge Lane, SW11 3AD.
Telephone: (011-44-71) 223-2756.
Fax: (011-44-71) 350-0156.
Riyadh, Saudi Arabia Affiliate Office: Saudi-American Legal Consultants Commercial Building #2, Diplomatic Quarter, P.O. Box 57270, 11574.
Telephone: (011-966-1) 488-1563.
Fax: (011-966-1) 488-0542.

R. Brian Ball
Sarah Hopkins Finley
Reginald N. Jones
Thomas B. McVey (Resident, Washington, D.C. Office)
Walter H. Ryland
C. William Waechter, Jr.
Charles E. Wall
Clayton L. Walton

For Complete List of Firm Personnel, See General Section

For full biographical listings, see the Martindale-Hubbell Law Directory

WEST VIRGINIA

*CHARLESTON,** Kanawha Co.

Allen Guthrie & McHugh (AV)

1300 Bank One Center, P.O. Box 3394, 25333
Telephone: 304-345-7250
Telecopier: 304-345-9941
Email: kagwv@kagwv.com

George G. Guthrie
Robert B. Allen
Thomas E. McHugh
R. Terrance Rodgers
S. Benjamin Bryant
Wm. Scott Wickline
Pamela Lynn Kandzari
James P. McHugh

Michelle M. Price
John K. McHugh
Teresa K. Thompson

For full biographical listings, see the Martindale-Hubbell Law Directory

Jackson & Kelly (AV)

1600 Laidley Tower, P.O. Box 553, 25322
Telephone: 304-340-1000
Fax: 304-340-1130
Email: info@jacksonkelly.com *URL:* http://www.jacksonkelly.com
Martinsburg, West Virginia Office: 300 Foxcroft Avenue, P.O. Box 1068.
Telephone: 304-263-8800.
Fax: 304-263-7110.
Morgantown, West Virginia Office: 6000 Hampton Center, P.O. Box 619.
Telephone: 304-599-3000.
Fax: 304-285-2040.
New Martinsville, West Virginia Office: 256 Russell Avenue, P.O. Box 68.
Telephone: 304-455-1751.
Fax: 304-455-6314.
Parkersburg, West Virginia Office: 412 Market Street, Suite 202, P.O. Box 1144.
Telephone: 304-424-3490.
Fax: 304-424-3499.
Fairmont, West Virginia Office: 1000 Technology Drive, Suite 1310.
Telephone: 304-368-2000.
Fax: 304-368-2020.
Lexington, Kentucky Office: 175 East Main Street, Suite 500, P.O. Box 2150.
Telephone: 606-255-9500.
Fax: 606-281-6478.
Washington, D. C. Office: 2401 Pennsylvania Avenue, N.W., Suite 400.
Telephone: 202-973-0200.
Fax: 202-973-0232.
Denver, Colorado Office: Suite 2710, 1660 Lincoln Street.
Telephone: 303-390-0003.
Fax: 303-390-0040.
Wheeling, West Virginia Office: 1144 Market Street.
Telephone: 304-233-4000.
Fax: 304-233-4077.

MEMBERS OF FIRM

John L. McClaugherty
Thomas E. Potter
W. Warren Upton
Michael A. Albert
Allen R. Prunty
James W. Thomas
Samme L. Gee
John Philip Melick
William E. Doll, Jr. (Resident, Lexington, Kentucky Office)
Thad S. Huffman (Administrative Manager, Washington, D.C. Office)

ASSOCIATE

Brooks K. Barkwill (Resident, New Martinsville, West Virginia Office)

Representative Clients: Central West Virginia Regional Airport Authority; Kanawha Valley Regional Transportation Authority; Kanawha County Parks and Recreation Commission; CONSOL Inc.; Pittston Coal Management Co.; Union Carbide Corp.; Rhone-Poulenc Ag Co.

For Complete List of Firm Personnel, See General Section

For full biographical listings, see the Martindale-Hubbell Law Directory

WISCONSIN

*MILWAUKEE,** Milwaukee Co.

Quarles & Brady LLP (AV)

411 East Wisconsin Avenue, 53202-4497
Telephone: 414-277-5000
Fax: 414-271-3552
URL: http://www.quarles.com
Madison, Wisconsin Office: Firstar Plaza, One South Pinckney Street, P.O. Box 2113, 53701-2113.
Telephone: 608-251-5000.
Fax: 608-251-9166.
West Palm Beach, Florida Office: 222 Lakeview Avenue, 4th Floor, 33401.
Telephone: 561-653-5000.
Fax: 561-653-5333.
Naples, Florida Office: Barnett Center, 4501 Tamiami Trail North, Suite 300, 34103-3060.
Telephone: 941-262-5959.
Fax: 941-434-4999.
Phoenix, Arizona Office: One Camelback Building, One East Camelback Road, Suite 400, 85012-1649.
Telephone: 602-230-5500.
Fax: 602-230-5598.
Chicago, Illinois Office: Quarles & Brady LLC, Citicorp Center, 500 West Madison Street, Suite 3700.
Telephone: 312-715-5000.
Fax: 312-715-5155.

MEMBERS OF FIRM
(ALPHABETICALLY BY YEAR OF ADMISSION TO BAR)

Charles Q. Kamps
Michael S. Weiden (Resident, Madison Office)
Anthony H. Driessen
Michael S. McCauley
Thomas P. McElligott
Nancy K. Peterson

(See Next Column)

QUARLES & BRADY LLP, *Milwaukee—Continued*

ASSOCIATES

Lauri D. Morris (Resident, Madison Office)

For Complete List of Firm Personnel, See General Section

For full biographical listings, see the Martindale-Hubbell Law Directory

WYOMING

*CASPER,** Natrona Co.

BROWN, DREW & MASSEY, LLP (AV)

Casper Business Center, Suite 800, 123 West First Street, 82601-2486
Telephone: 307-234-1000
800-877-6755
Telefax: 307-265-8025
Email: brwndrew@coffey.com

MEMBERS OF FIRM

Morris R. Massey
Harry B. Durham, III
Donn J. McCall
Thomas F. Reese
Rex O. Arney
P. Jaye Rippley
Courtney Robert Kepler

ASSOCIATES

Scott P. Klosterman
Timothy M. Stubson

Attorneys for: Norwest Bank Wyoming, N.A.; The CIT Group/Equipment Financing; Bituminous Insurance Companies; The Doctor's Co.; MED-MARC; Westech, Inc.; Chevron USA; Enron Group of Energy Companies; North American Resources Co.

For Complete List of Firm Personnel, See General Section

For full biographical listings, see the Martindale-Hubbell Law Directory

*CHEYENNE,** Laramie Co.

SUNDAHL, POWERS, KAPP & MARTIN, L.L.C. (AV)

1725 Carey Avenue, P.O. Box 328, 82001
Telephone: 307-632-6421
Fax: 307-632-7216
Email: atty@spkm.org

MEMBERS OF FIRM

John Alan Sundahl
George E. Powers, Jr.
Paul Kapp
Raymond W. Martin

ASSOCIATES

John A. Coppede
Kay Lynn Bestol
Deborah G. M. Kellam
Brian J. Hanify

A list of Representative Clients will be furnished upon request.

For full biographical listings, see the Martindale-Hubbell Law Directory

CANADA ALBERTA

*CALGARY,** Calgary Jud. Dist.

PARLEE MCLAWS (AV)

3400 Petro-Canada Centre, 150 - 6th Avenue, SW, T2P 3Y7
Telephone: 403-294-7000
Telecopier: 403-265-8263
Email: lawyers@parlee.com *URL:* http://www.parlee.com
Edmonton, Alberta Office: 15th Floor Manulife Place, 10180 101st Street.
Telephone: 403-423-8500.
Telecopier: 403-423-2870.

MEMBERS OF FIRM

Patrick J. McGovern
Terry R. Davis

For Complete List of Firm Personnel, See General Section

For full biographical listings, see the Martindale-Hubbell Law Directory

*EDMONTON,** Edmonton Jud. Dist.

PARLEE MCLAWS (AV)

15th Floor Manulife Place, 10180 101st Street, T5J 4K1
Telephone: 403-423-8500
Telecopier: 403-423-2870
Email: lawyers@parlee.com *URL:* http://www.parlee.com
Calgary, Alberta Office: 3400 Petro-Canada Centre, 150 - 6th Avenue, SW.
Telephone: 403-294-7000.
Telecopier: 403-265-8263.

(See Next Column)

MEMBERS OF FIRM

Michael D. MacDonald
Walter J. Pavlic
Richard W. Wilson
Brian J. Curial

For Complete List of Firm Personnel, See General Section

For full biographical listings, see the Martindale-Hubbell Law Directory

CANADA BRITISH COLUMBIA

*VANCOUVER,** Vancouver Co.

CAMP CHURCH & ASSOCIATES (AV)

4th Floor, The Randall Building, 555 West Georgia Street, V6B 1Z5
Telephone: 604-689-7555
Fax: 604-689-7554
URL: http://www.campchurch.com

MEMBERS OF FIRM

J.J. Camp, Q.C.
David P. Church

Giuseppe (Joe) Fiorante
Andrew J. Pearson
Sharon D. Matthews
Ian G. Schildt

For full biographical listings, see the Martindale-Hubbell Law Directory

CANADA NEW BRUNSWICK

*FREDERICTON,** York Co.

COX HANSON O'REILLY MATHESON (AV)

(Formerly Hanson Hashey)
Suite 400, Phoenix Square, P.O. Box 310, E3B 4Y9
Telephone: 506-453-7771
Fax: 506-453-9600
Email: fredericton@coxhanson.ca *URL:* http://www.coxhanson.ca
Halifax, Nova Scotia Office: Suite 1100, Purdy's Wharf Tower 1, P.O. Box 2380 Station Central RPO, B3J 3E5.
Telephone: 902-421-6262.
Fax: 902-421-3130. E-Mail: halifax@coxhanson.ca
Saint John, New Brunswick Office: 1212-One Brunswick Square, 1 Germain St. E2L 4V1.
Telephone: 506-652-7771.
Fax: 506-632-9600.
St. John's, Newfoundland Office: Scotia Centre, 401-235 Water Street, A1C 1B6.
Telephone: 709-726-3321.
Fax: 709-726-2992. E-Mail: stjohns@coxhanson.ca
Charlottetown, Prince Edward Island Office: Queen Square, Suite 202, 119 Queen Street, P.O. Box 875, Station Central, C1A 7L9.
Telephone: 902-894-7051.
Fax: 902-368-3762. E-Mail: charlottetown@coxhanson.ca

MEMBERS OF FIRM

H. A. Hanson, Q.C. (1909-1985)
David T. Hashey, Q.C.
David M. Norman, Q.C.
J. Ian M. Whitcomb, Q.C.
John M. Hanson, Q.C.
Walter D. Vail, Q.C.
Michael E. Bowlin
John D. Larlee, Q.C.
Bruce D. Hatfield, Q.C.
Julian A. G. Dickson, Q.C.
Anne D. Wooder
Terrence J. Morrison
Lucie Richard
Catherine M. Bowlen
J. Marc Richard

ASSOCIATES

Amanda J. Frenette
Monika M. L. Zauhar
Jade A. Spalding
William E. Gould
Christopher R. DeLong
Deborah M. Power
Corinne A. Godbout
Marc-Antoine Chiasson

For full biographical listings, see the Martindale-Hubbell Law Directory

*MONCTON,** Westmorland Co.

MCINNES COOPER (AV)

Barristers, Solicitors & Trade Mark Agents
Place Moncton Place, 655 Main Street, P.O. Box 1368, E1C 8T6
Telephone: 506-857-8970
Fax: 506-857-4095
Email: mcrmctn@mcrlaw.com *URL:* http://www.mcrlaw.com
Halifax, Nova Scotia Office: Summit Place, 1601 Lower Water Street, P.O. Box 730, B3J 2V1.
Telephone: 902-425-6500.
Fax: 902-425-6350. Email: mcrhfx@mcrlaw.com.

(See Next Column)

McInnes Cooper—*Continued*

St. John's, Newfoundland Office: Baine Johnston Centre, 5th Floor, 10 Fort William Place, P.O. Box 5939, A1C 5X4.
Telephone: 709-722-8735.
Telecopier: 709-722-1763. Email: mcrsj@mcrlaw.com.
Charlottetown, Prince Edward Island Office: BDC Place, Suite 620, 119 Kent Street, C1A 1N3.
Telephone: 902-368-8473.
Fax: 902-368-8346. Email: mcrpei@mcrlaw.com.
Fredericton, New Brunswick Office: Suite 600, 570 Queen Street, P.O. Box 610.
Telephone: 506-458-8572.
Fax: 506-458-9903. Email: mcrfton@mcrlaw.com.

ASSOCIATES

John C. Friel, Q.C. — Christa A. Bourque

For Complete List of Firm Personnel, See General Section

For full biographical listings, see the Martindale-Hubbell Law Directory

*SAINT JOHN,** Saint John Co.

Clark Drummie (AV)

40 Wellington Row, P.O. Box 6850, E2L 4S3
Telephone: 506-633-3800
Telecopier (Automatic): 506-633-3811
Email: cd@nbnet.nb.ca

MEMBERS OF FIRM

Deno P. Pappas, Q.C. — M. Robert Jette

Reference: Royal Bank of Canada.

For Complete List of Firm Personnel, See General Section

For full biographical listings, see the Martindale-Hubbell Law Directory

CANADA NOVA SCOTIA

*HALIFAX,** Regional Munic. of Halifax

McInnes Cooper (AV)

Barristers, Solicitors & Trade Mark Agents
Summit Place, 1601 Lower Water Street, P.O. Box 730, B3J 2V1
Telephone: 902-425-6500
Fax: 902-425-6350
Email: mcrhfx@mcrlaw.com *URL:* http://www.mcrlaw.com
St. John's, Newfoundland Office: Baine Johnston Centre, 5th Floor, 10 Fort William Place, P.O. Box 5939, A1C 5X4.
Telephone: 709-722-8735.
Telecopier: 709-722-1763. Email: mcrsj@mcrlaw.com.
Moncton, New Brunswick Office: Place Moncton Place, 655 Main Street, P.O. Box 1368, E1C 8T6.
Telephone: 506-857-8970.
Fax: 506-857-4095. Email: mcrmctn@mcrlaw.com.
Charlottetown, Prince Edward Island Office: BDC Place, Suite 620, 119 Kent Street, C1A 1N3.
Telephone: 902-368-8473.
Fax: 902-368-8346. Email: mcrpei@mcrlaw.com.
Fredericton, New Brunswick Office: Suite 600, 570 Queen Street, P.O. Box 610.
Telephone: 506-458-8572.
Fax: 506-458-9903. Email: mcrfton@mcrlaw.com.

PARTNERS

Reginald A. Cluney, Q.C.
Alan J. Stern, Q.C.
Eric Durnford, Q.C.
Malcolm D. Boyle
Stewart McInnes, P.C., Q.C.
George T. H. Cooper, Q.C.
Peter McLellan, Q.C.
John H. (Jack) Graham

ASSOCIATES

Paul McLean
Rebecca Saturley
Tara A. Erskine
Janet Clark

For Complete List of Firm Personnel, See General Section

For full biographical listings, see the Martindale-Hubbell Law Directory

CANADA ONTARIO

*TORONTO,** Regional Munic. of Toronto

Kelly Affleck Greene (AV)

One First Canadian Place, Suite 840, P.O. Box 489, M5X 1E5
Telephone: 416-360-2800
Fax: 416-360-5960
Email: info@kag.net *URL:* http://www.kag.net

MEMBERS OF FIRM

W. Anthony Kelly, Q.C.
Donald S. Affleck, Q.C.
Peter R. Greene
Donald B. Houston
James C. Orr
Peter C. Wardle
Helen A. Daley
Melissa J. Kennedy

ASSOCIATES

Kenneth A. Dekker
W. Michael G. Osborne
Jason C. Markwell
Patrice F. Band

For full biographical listings, see the Martindale-Hubbell Law Directory

CANADA PRINCE EDWARD ISLAND

*CHARLOTTETOWN,** Queen's Co.

Campbell, Lea, Michael, McConnell & Pigot (AV)

15 Queen Street, P.O. Box 429, C1A 7K7
Telephone: 902-566-3400
Telecopier: 902-566-9266
Email: www.office@campbelllea.com

MEMBERS OF FIRM

William G. Lea, Q.C. — Paul D. Michael, Q.C.
Kenneth L. Godfrey

General Counsel in Prince Edward Island for: Canadian Imperial Bank of Commerce; Maritime Electric Co., Ltd.; Michelin Tires (Canada) Ltd.; Newsco Investments Ltd. (Dundas Farms); Imperial Oil Limited; General Motors of Canada; Co-op Atlantic; Liberty Mutual; Employers Reinsurance Group.

For Complete List of Firm Personnel, See General Section

For full biographical listings, see the Martindale-Hubbell Law Directory

McInnes Cooper (AV Ⓣ)

Barristers, Solicitors & Trade Mark Agents
BDC Place, Suite 620, 119 Kent Street, C1A 1N3
Telephone: 902-368-8473
Fax: 902-368-8346
Email: mcrpei@mcrlaw.com *URL:* http://www.mcrlaw.com
Halifax, Nova Scotia Office: Summit Place, 1601 Lower Water Street, P.O. Box 730, B3J 2V1.
Telephone: 902-425-6500.
Fax: 902-425-6350. Email: mcrhfx@mcrlaw.com.
St. John's, Newfoundland Office: Baine Johnston Centre, 5th Floor, 10 Fort William Place, P.O. Box 5939, A1C 5X4.
Telephone: 709-722-8735.
Telecopier: 709-722-1763. Email: mcrsj@mcrlaw.com.
Moncton, New Brunswick Office: Place Moncton Place, 655 Main Street, P.O. Box 1368, E1C 8T6.
Telephone: 506-857-8970.
Fax: 506-857-4095. Email: mcrmctn@mcrlaw.com.
Fredericton, New Brunswick Office: Suite 600, 570 Queen Street, P.O. Box 610.
Telephone: 506-458-8572.
Fax: 506-458-9903. Email: mcrfton@mcrlaw.com.

PARTNERS

Horace B. Carver, Q.C. — Mark Ledwell
Michele M. Murphy

ASSOCIATES

L. Charles Keizer
Murray L. Murphy
Kevin J. Kiley
Kim Petrie

For Complete List of Firm Personnel, See General Section

For full biographical listings, see the Martindale-Hubbell Law Directory

CANADA
QUEBEC

*MONTREAL,** Montreal Dist.

McMaster Gervais (AV)

A General Partnership
1000 de La Gauchetière Street West, Suite 900, H3B 5H4
Telephone: 514-879-1212
Fax: 514-954-1905
Email: info@mcmastergervais.com *URL:* http://www.mcmastergervais.com

MEMBERS OF FIRM

Pierre Flageole
Thomas M. Davis
Philippe C. Vachon
Jacques Gauthier
Catherine Guertin

COUNSEL

Richard J. Riendeau, Q.C.

For Complete List of Firm Personnel, See General Section

For full biographical listings, see the Martindale-Hubbell Law Directory

Pouliot, Mercure (AV)

CIBC Tower, 31st Floor, 1155 René-Lévesque Boulevard, West, H3B 3S6
Telephone: 514-875-5210
Telecopier: 514-875-4308
Email: POUMER@CEDEP.COM
Genève, Suisse Office: 8, Rue de la Rôtisserie, 1204 Geneva, Switzerland.
Telephone: +41 22-28 79 40.
Telecopier: +41 22-21 23 67.

MEMBERS OF FIRM

Georges A. Pouliot, Q.C.
Gilles Brunelle
Luc Gratton
Brian Riordan
Pierre Paquet
Anne-Marie Gauthier
Yvon Brizard
Robert Tessier
Daniel Gagné
Lilia Pouliot
Marco Veilleux
Alain Nadon
Jean H. Gagnon
Richard Fontaine
Normand Royal
Gilles Bertrand
Jean Larivière
Louis-Michel Tremblay
David I. Johnston
Stéphane Hébert
Jacques LeBel, Q.C.
Joel A. Silcoff
Ronald M. Auclair
Philippe Roy
Maxime B. Rhéaume
Serge Desrochers
C. Keenan LaPierre
Alain Bond
Louis Coallier
Nicole Chouinard
Stéphane Teasdale

ASSOCIATES

Micheline Perrault
Caroline Lemoine
Béatrice Arronis
Yvan Nantel
Sylvie Boulanger
Vincent Frenette
Robert Cardin
Alexandre Henri
Brent J. Muir
Louise Tremblay
Chantal Joubert
Normand D'Amour
Pascale Cloutier
Eric Couture
Frédéric Chatel
Mary-Lynn Breton
Alexandre Ajami

For full biographical listings, see the Martindale-Hubbell Law Directory

CANADA
SASKATCHEWAN

*REGINA,** Regina Jud. Centre

MacPherson Leslie & Tyerman (AV)

1500-1874 Scarth Street, S4P 4E9
Telephone: 306-347-8000
Telecopier: 306-352-5250
Email: mltreg@mlt.com
Saskatoon, Saskatchewan Office: 1500-410 22nd Street East, S7K 5T6.
Telephone: 306-975-7100.
Telecopier: 306-975-7145.

MEMBERS OF FIRM

Dennis P. Ball, Q.C.
Larry B. LeBlanc, Q.C.
Robert G. Richards, Q.C.
Brian J. Kenny
A. Robson Garden, Q.C. (Resident, Saskatoon Office)
Melissa A. Brunsdon (Resident, Saskatoon Office)
Eileen V. Libby

ASSOCIATES

Vanessa Monar Enweani (Resident, Saskatoon Office)
M. Jean Torrens (Resident, Saskatoon Office)
Heather D. Heavin

(See Next Column)

COUNSEL

W. Thomas Molloy, O.C., Q.C. (Resident, Saskatoon Office)

For Complete List of Firm Personnel, See General Section

For full biographical listings, see the Martindale-Hubbell Law Directory

ADMIRALTY/MARITIME LAW

MINNESOTA

*MINNEAPOLIS,** Hennepin Co.

HUNEGS, STONE, KOENIG, LENEAVE & KVAS, P.A. (AV)

1650 International Center Building, 900 Second Avenue South, 55402
Telephone: 612-339-4511; 800-328-4340
Fax: 612-339-5150
URL: http://hunegslaw.com

William H. DeParcq (1905-1988)
Richard Gene Hunegs
Robert N. Stone
Ralph E. Koenig
Randal W. LeNeave
Cortney S. LeNeave
William Kvas
Richard L. Carlson
Steven M. Hunegs
Kermit N. Fruechte

Reference: National City Bank of Minneapolis.

For full biographical listings, see the Martindale-Hubbell Law Directory

MISSISSIPPI

BILOXI, Harrison Co.

JUDY M. GUICE A PROFESSIONAL ASSOCIATION (AV)

750 Dr. Martin Luther King Jr. Boulevard, P.O. Box 1919, 39533
Telephone: 228-374-9787
Fax: 228-374-9436
Email: judy@judyguice.com *URL:* http://www.judyguice.com

Judy Guice

For full biographical listings, see the Martindale-Hubbell Law Directory

MINOR AND ASSOCIATES (AV)

A Partnership including a Professional Association
160 Main Street, Drawer 1388, 39533-1388
Telephone: 228-374-5151
Fax: 228-374-6630
Email: pminoratty@aol.com

Paul S. Minor (P.A.)

Mark D. Lumpkin
James R. Reeves, Jr.
Christopher C. VanCleave

For full biographical listings, see the Martindale-Hubbell Law Directory

RUSHING & GUICE (AV)

683 Water Street, P.O. Box 1925, 39533-1925
Telephone: 228-374-2313
Telecopier: 228-374-8155
Email: rushguice@rushing-guice.com *URL:* http://www.rushing-guice.com

MEMBERS OF FIRM

Charles L. Rushing (1881-1923)
William L. Guice (1887-1971)
William Lee Guice III

OF COUNSEL

Jacob D. Guice

ASSOCIATES

R. Scott Wells
Maria M. Cobb

LEGAL SUPPORT PERSONNEL

Antonia Strong

Representative Clients: Caterpillar Financial Services Corp.; Zions; Weems Brothers Seafood; R.A. Lesso Seafood; Business Loan Center, Inc.

For full biographical listings, see the Martindale-Hubbell Law Directory

*COLUMBIA,** Marion Co.

AULTMAN, TYNER, RUFFIN & YARBOROUGH, LTD., A PROFESSIONAL LAW CORPORATION (AV)

329 Church Street, P.O. Drawer 707, 39429
Telephone: 601-736-2222
FAX: 601-736-9884
Email: rfyjr@cblink.com
Hattiesburg, Mississippi Office: 315 Hemphill Street, P.O. Drawer 750.
Telephone: 601-583-2671.
FAX: 601-583-2677.
Gulfport, Mississippi Office: 1201 25th Avenue, Suite 300, P.O. Box 607.
Telephone: 228-863-6913.
FAX: 228-868-8505. Email: atmr@digiscape.com.

(See Next Column)

New Orleans, Louisiana Office: The Texaco Center, 400 Poydras Street, Suite 2250.
Telephone: 504-528-9616.
FAX: 504-528-9640.

Richard F. Yarborough, Jr.

OF COUNSEL

Ernest Ray Duff

Representative Clients: Hercules, Inc.; United States Steel Corp.; Ford Motor Co.; International Paper Co.; Phillips Petroleum Co.; Aetna Casualty & Surety Co.; CNA Group; Liberty Mutual Insurance Co.; St. Paul Fire & Marine Insurance Co.; Fireman's Fund.

For full biographical listings, see the Martindale-Hubbell Law Directory

*GREENVILLE,** Washington Co.

LAKE TINDALL, LLP (AV)

127 South Poplar Street, P.O. Box 918, 38701
Telephone: 601-378-2121
Facsimile: 601-378-2183
Jackson, Mississippi Office: One Jackson Place, 188 East Capitol Street, Suite 450, P.O. Box 1789.
Telephone: 601-948-2121.
Facsimile: 601-948-0603.

Franklin S. Thackston, Jr. (Resident, Greenville)
Clinton W. Walker, III (Resident, Greenville)

General Counsel for: Bunge Towing, Inc.; Greenville Port Commission; Delta and Pine Land Co.
Local Counsel for: Insurance: Aetna Casualty & Surety Co.; Cigna-Aetna Insurance Co.; Neare Gibbs & Company; Mutual Marine Office, Inc.; Institute of London Underwriters.

For Complete List of Firm Personnel, See General Section

For full biographical listings, see the Martindale-Hubbell Law Directory

*GULFPORT,** Harrison Co.

AULTMAN, TYNER, RUFFIN & YARBOROUGH, LTD., A PROFESSIONAL LAW CORPORATION (AV)

1201 25th Avenue, Suite 300, P.O. Box 607, 39502
Telephone: 228-863-6913
FAX: 228-868-8505
Email: atmr@digiscape.com
Hattiesburg, Mississippi Office: 315 Hemphill Street, P.O. Drawer 750.
Telephone: 601-583-2671.
FAX: 601-583-2677.
Columbia, Mississippi Office: 329 Church Street, P.O. Drawer 707.
Telephone: 601-736-2222.
FAX: 601-736-9884. Email: rfyjr@cblink.com.
New Orleans, Louisiana Office: The Texaco Center, 400 Poydras Street, Suite 2250.
Telephone: 504-528-9616.
FAX: 504-528-9640.

Ben E. Sheely
Dorrance (Dee) Aultman, Jr.

For Complete List of Firm Personnel, See General Section

For full biographical listings, see the Martindale-Hubbell Law Directory

DUKES, DUKES, KEATING AND FANECA, P.A. (AV)

2909 13th Street, 6th Floor, P.O. Drawer W, 39501
Telephone: 228-868-1111
Fax: 228-863-2886
Email: ddkf@ddkf.com

Walter W. Dukes
Hugh D. Keating
Cy Faneca

For Complete List of Firm Personnel, See General Section

For full biographical listings, see the Martindale-Hubbell Law Directory

FRANKE, RAINEY & SALLOUM, PLLC (AV)

2605 14th Street, P.O. Drawer 460, 39502
Telephone: 228-868-7070
Telecopier: 228-868-7090
Email: frs@diversicomm.com

Paul M. Franke, Jr.
William M. Rainey
Richard P. Salloum
Paul B. Howell
Fredrick B. Feeney, II
Traci M. Castille
Donald P. Moore

Kaleel G. Salloum, Jr.
Brandi C. Schwartz
James C. Simpson, Jr.

For full biographical listings, see the Martindale-Hubbell Law Directory

*HATTIESBURG,** Forrest Co.

AULTMAN, TYNER, RUFFIN & YARBOROUGH, LTD., A PROFESSIONAL LAW CORPORATION (AV)

315 Hemphill Street, P.O. Drawer 750, 39403-0750
Telephone: 601-583-2671
FAX: 601-583-2677
Email: aultyn@c-gate.net
Columbia, Mississippi Office: 329 Church Street, P.O. Drawer 707.
Telephone: 601-736-2222.
FAX: 601-736-9884. Email: rfyjr@cblink.com.
Gulfport, Mississippi Office: 1201 25th Avenue, Suite 300, P.O. Box 607.
Telephone: 228-863-6913.
FAX: 228-868-8505. Email: atmr@digiscape.com.
New Orleans, Louisiana Office: The Texaco Center, 400 Poydras Street, Suite 2250.
Telephone: 504-528-9616.
FAX: 504-528-9640.

Dorrance Aultman
Thomas W. Tyner
Louie F. Ruffin
Richard F. Yarborough, Jr. (Resident, Columbia Office)
Ben E. Sheely (Resident, Gulfport Office)
R. Curtis Smith, II
Dorrance (Dee) Aultman, Jr. (Resident, Gulfport Office)
William Nelson Graham

Victor A. DuBose

OF COUNSEL

Ernest Ray Duff (Resident, Columbia Office)

Representative Clients: Hercules, Inc.; U.S. Steel Corp.; Ford Motor Co.; Phillips Petroleum Co.; Aetna Casualty & Surety Co.; CNA Group; Liberty Mutual Insurance Co.; St. Paul Fire & Marine Insurance Co.; Fireman's Fund; L & A Contracting Co.

For Complete List of Firm Personnel, See General Section

For full biographical listings, see the Martindale-Hubbell Law Directory

MISSOURI

ST. LOUIS, (Independent City)

GOLDSTEIN AND PRICE, L.C. (AV)

Suite 1000, 100 North Broadway, 63102
Telephone: 314-421-0710
Telecopier: 314-421-2832
Email: gplaw@gandplc.com

Hubert I. Binowitz (1933-1990)
Milton I. Goldstein (Retired)
Elmer Price (Retired)
Gary T. Sacks
Daryl F. Sohn
Robert Dale Nienhuis
John R. Halpern
Alan K. Goldstein
Douglas E. Gossow
Teresa A. McNail

OF COUNSEL

Jeanne Knowles Townsend

David A. Perney
Daniel E. Tranen
Derrick Shane Kirby

Representative Clients: American River Transportation Co.; Apex Oil Co.; Commercial Union Insurance Cos.; Marine Office of America Corp.; Midland Enterprises Inc.; Peavey Barge Line, division of ConAgra, Inc.; Riverway Harbor Services, St. Louis, Inc.; Southern Towing Co.; GRE America.

For full biographical listings, see the Martindale-Hubbell Law Directory

THE HULLVERSON LAW FIRM (AV)

Suite 1550, 1010 Market Street, 63101-2091
Telephone: 314-421-2313
Fax: 314-421-2341
URL: http://www.hullverson.com

Everett Hullverson (1897-1975)
Thomas C. Hullverson
Stephen H. Ringkamp
Philip C. Denton
Spencer E. Farris
Mark J. Becker
John E. Hullverson
Theresa A. Appelbaum

For full biographical listings, see the Martindale-Hubbell Law Directory

LEWIS, RICE & FINGERSH (AV)

A Limited Liability Company
500 North Broadway, Suite 2000, 63102-2147
Telephone: 314-444-7600
Telecopier: 314-241-6056
URL: http://www.lrf.com
Belleville, Illinois Office: 325 South High Street.
Telephone: 618-234-8636.

(See Next Column)

Leawood, Kansas Office: Suite 375, 8900 State Line Road.
Telephone: 913-381-8898.
Creve Coeur, Missouri Office: 700 Office Parkway, Suite 15.
Telephone: 314-569-2262.
Kansas City, Missouri Office: 1010 Walnut, Suite 500.
Telephone: 816-421-2500.
Washington, Missouri Office: 216 West Main, P.O. Box 1040.
Telephone: 636-239-7747.

RESIDENT MEMBERS

James W. Herron
Andrew Rothschild
James V. O'Brien

For Complete List of Firm Personnel, See General Section

For full biographical listings, see the Martindale-Hubbell Law Directory

TONKIN & MONDL, L.C. (AV)

701 Market Street, Suite 260, 63101
Telephone: 314-231-2794
Telecopier: 314-231-1481
Email: tonkmond@aol.com *URL:* http://www.lawyers.com/tonkinmondl

Simon Tonkin
James K. Mondl

For full biographical listings, see the Martindale-Hubbell Law Directory

NEW JERSEY

*CAMDEN,** Camden Co.

BROWN & CONNERY, LLP (AV)

518 Market Street, P.O. Box 1449, 08101
Telephone: 609-365-5100
Facsimile: 609-858-4967
Westmont, New Jersey Office: 360 Haddon Avenue, P.O. Box 539.
Telephone: 609-854-8900.

MEMBERS OF FIRM

Thomas F. Connery, Jr.
Warren W. Faulk
Dennis P. Blake
William M. Tambussi

Representative Clients: Camden County Health Services Center; Delaware River Port Authority; Federal Deposit Insurance Corp.; Mercedes-Benz Credit Corp.; Philadelphia Newspaper, Inc.; Philip Morris Inc.; Pollution Control Financing Authority of Camden County; Underwood-Memorial Hospital.

For Complete List of Firm Personnel, See General Section

For full biographical listings, see the Martindale-Hubbell Law Directory

*NEWARK,** Essex Co.

CARPENTER, BENNETT & MORRISSEY (AV)

Three Gateway Center, 17th Floor, 100 Mulberry Street, 07102-4079
Telephone: 973-622-7711
New York City: 212-943-6530
Telex: 139405
Telecopier: 973-622-5314
Email: cbm@carpben.com

MEMBER OF FIRM

John P. Dwyer

Reference: Summit Bank.

For Complete List of Firm Personnel, See General Section

For full biographical listings, see the Martindale-Hubbell Law Directory

KENNY & STEARNS (AV)

56 Park Place, 07102
Telephone: 201-624-7779
New York, N.Y. Office: 26 Broadway.
Telephone: 212-422-6111.
Fax: 212-422-6544.

PARTNERS IN CHARGE

James M. Kenny
Joseph T. Stearns
Gino A. Zonghetti

ASSOCIATES

Michael C. Mulé
Christina M. Kenny
John D. Blomquist

For full biographical listings, see the Martindale-Hubbell Law Directory

LITE, DE PALMA, GREENBERG & RIVAS, LLC (AV)

Two Gateway Center, 12th Floor, 07102-5003
Telephone: 973-623-3000
Fax: 973-623-0858

(See Next Column)

LITE, DE PALMA, GREENBERG & RIVAS LLC—*Continued*

MEMBER OF FIRM

Joseph J. De Palma

For full biographical listings, see the Martindale-Hubbell Law Directory

McCARTER & ENGLISH, LLP (AV)

Four Gateway Center, 100 Mulberry Street, P.O. Box 652, 07101-0652
Telephone: 973-622-4444
Telecopier: 973-624-7070
URL: http://www.mccarter.com
Cherry Hill, New Jersey Office: 1820 Chapel Avenue West, Suite 380.
Telephone: 609-662-8444.
Telecopier: 609-662-6203.
New York, New York Office: Suite 2247, One World Trade Center.
Telephone: 212-466-9018.
Telecopier: 212-432-6568.
Boca Raton, Florida Office: 2255 Glades Road, Suite 319-A.
Telephone: 561-994-6262.
Telecopier: 561-241-0798.
Wilmington, Delaware Office: Mellon Bank Center, 919 Market Street.
Telephone: 302-654-8010.
Telecopier: 302-654-0795.
Philadelphia, Pennsylvania Office: One Commerce Square, 2005 Market Street, Suite 3600.
Telephone: 215-557-7700.
Telecopier: 215-557-6544.

MEMBER OF FIRM

James F. Hammill (Resident Partner, Cherry Hill, New Jersey Office)

OF COUNSEL

Thomas F. Daly

For Complete List of Firm Personnel, See General Section

For full biographical listings, see the Martindale-Hubbell Law Directory

OCEAN TOWNSHIP, Monmouth Co.

EVANS, OSBORNE & KREIZMAN (AV)

CN 7808 1500 Lawrence Avenue, 07712-7808
Telephone: 732-643-0300
Fax: 732-643-0340
New York, New York Office: Suite 7967, One World Trade Center.
Telephone: 212-466-1207.

MEMBERS OF FIRM

Harry S. Evans
Harry V. Osborne, II
Joel N. Kreizman
Mary O'Keefe Massey
Kevin E. Hoffman

ASSOCIATES

Marie A. Accardi
James F. McDonough
Kenneth P. Skibinski

Representative Clients: United Kingdom P&I Club (Thomas R. Miller Insurance Services); American Marine Underwriters, Inc.; Continental Insurance Cos.; Hartford Insurance Cos.; CIGNA Cos.; Jersey Central Power & Light Co.; First Union Bank; CNA Insurance Cos.; Princess Cruises, Inc.; APL Limited.

For full biographical listings, see the Martindale-Hubbell Law Directory

SHIP BOTTOM, Ocean Co.

SHACKLETON, HAZELTINE AND BISHOP (AV)

22nd Street and Long Beach Boulevard, P.O. Box 410, 08008
Telephone: 609-494-2136
Telefax: 609-494-0870
Fairfield, New Jersey Office: One Passaic Avenue.
Telephone: 201-882-4646.
Telefax: 201-882-4620.

MEMBERS OF FIRM

Richard J. Shackleton
Colin R. Hazeltine
James E. Bishop

ASSOCIATES

Laura M. O'Regan
Marc Baden Powell
Robert Emmet Rue

OF COUNSEL

Kenneth L. Leiby, Jr. (Resident, Fairfield Office)

References: Commerce Bank/Shore N/A; Summit Bank Corp.

For full biographical listings, see the Martindale-Hubbell Law Directory

SPRINGFIELD, Union Co.

McDONOUGH, KORN & EICHHORN, A PROFESSIONAL CORPORATION (AV)

Park Place Legal Center, 959 South Springfield Avenue, P.O. Box 712, 07081-0712
Telephone: 973-912-9099
Fax: 973-912-8604

(See Next Column)

Matthew S. Schorr

Representative Clients: Yosuda Fire & Marine Insurance Co.; Lurich American Insurance Co.; Chubb Insurance Co.; AIG Insurance Co.; St. Paul Fire & Marine Insurance Co.

For Complete List of Firm Personnel, See General Section

For full biographical listings, see the Martindale-Hubbell Law Directory

WESTMONT, Camden Co.

BROWN & CONNERY, LLP (AV)

360 Haddon Avenue, P.O. Box 539, 08108
Telephone: 609-854-8900
Facsimile: 609-858-4967
Camden, New Jersey Office: 518 Market Street, P.O. Box 1449.
Telephone: 609-365-5100.
Telecopier: 609-858-4967.

MEMBERS OF FIRM

Warren W. Faulk
Dennis P. Blake
William M. Tambussi

Representative Clients: Camden County Health Services Center; Delaware River Port Authority; Federal Deposit Insurance Corp.; Mercedes-Benz Credit Corp.; Philadelphia Newspaper, Inc.; Philip Morris Inc.; Pollution Control Financing Authority of Camden County; Underwood-Memorial Hospital.

For Complete List of Firm Personnel, See General Section

For full biographical listings, see the Martindale-Hubbell Law Directory

NEW YORK

*NEW YORK,** New York Co.

BADIAK WILL & RUDDY (AV)

Suite 1040, 120 Broadway, 10271
Telephone: 212-376-6767
Telecopier: 212-376-6777
Telex: 6716686 BANDW
Email: admiralaw@aol.com
North Miami Beach, Florida Office: Badiak, Will & Kallen, 17071 West Dixie Highway, P.O. Box 600550.
Telephone: 305-945-1851.

MEMBERS OF FIRM

Roman Badiak
Alfred J. Will
James J. Ruddy
John D. Kallen (Resident, North Miami, Florida Office)
David L. Maloof (1924-1992)

ASSOCIATES

Stephen A. Frank
Nicholas Kalfa
James P. Krauzlis
Martin L. Lindahl
Lisa A. Scognamillo
Deborah R. Reid

OF COUNSEL

Charles C. Goodenough

For full biographical listings, see the Martindale-Hubbell Law Directory

CARDILLO & CORBETT (AV)

29 Broadway, 10006
Telephone: 212-344-0464
Telex: 421757
Cable Address: "Avocard, N.Y."
Telecopier: 212-797-1212

MEMBERS OF FIRM

Joseph Cardillo, Jr. (1913-1980)
Robert V. Corbett
Christophil B. Costas
Tulio R. Prieto
James P. Rau
Peter G. Drakos

OF COUNSEL

Francis H. McNamara
Donald Burke

For full biographical listings, see the Martindale-Hubbell Law Directory

CASEY & BARNETT, LLC (AV)

521 Fifth Avenue, Suite 3800, 10175
Telephone: 212-370-9322
Fax: 212-682-7447
Email: mfclaw@msn.com

Martin F. Casey
Gregory G. Barnett

For full biographical listings, see the Martindale-Hubbell Law Directory

New York—Continued

CURTIS, MALLET-PREVOST, COLT & MOSLE LLP (AV)

101 Park Avenue, 10178-0061
Telephone: 212-696-6000
Telecopier: 212-697-1559
Email: info@cm-p.com *URL:* http://www.cm-p.com
Washington, D.C. Office: Suite 1205L, 1801 K Street, N.W.
Telephone: 202-452-7373.
Telecopier: 202-452-7333.
Newark, New Jersey Office: One Gateway Center, Suite 403.
Telephone: 973-622-0605.
Telecopier: 973-622-5646.
Houston, Texas Office: 2 Houston Center, 909 Fannin Street, Suite 3725.
Telephone: 713-759-9555.
Telecopier: 713-759-0712.
Stamford, Connecticut Office: One Canterbury Green.
Telephone: 203-359-6200.
Telecopier: 203-328-2617.
Mexico City, D.F., Mexico Office: Curtis, Mallet-Prevost, Colt & Mosle, Ruben Dario 281, Piso 9, Col. Bosque de Chapultepec, 11530 Mexico, D.F.
Telephone: 525-282-0444.
Telecopier: 525-282-0637.
Paris, France Office: 15 rue d'Astorg, 75008.
Telephone: +33-1 42-66-39-10.
Telecopier: +33-1 42-66-39-62.
London, England Office: Two Throgmorton Avenue, EC2N 2DL.
Telephone: 0207-638-7957.
Telecopier: 0207-638-5512.
Frankfurt am Main 1, Germany Office: Staufenstrasse 42.
Telephone: +49-69-971-4420.
Telecopier: +49-69-17 33 99.
Muscat, Sultanate of Oman Office: Jewel Beach-134.
Telephone: 968-607-725.
Telecopier: 968-607-724.
Milan, Italy Office: Curtis, Mallet-Prevost & Gilioli, Piazzale Principessa Clotilde 8, 20121.
Telephone: +(39) 02 29 00 29 32.
Telefax: +(39) 02 65 75 969.

MEMBERS OF FIRM

Robert J. Gruendel
Herbert M. Lord

For full biographical listings, see the Martindale-Hubbell Law Directory

DE ORCHIS, WALKER & CORSA, LLP (AV)

One Battery Park Plaza, Second Floor, 10004-1480
Telephone: 212-344-4700
MCI Telex: 673-4608
Telefax: 212-509-7886
Email: DW&C@MCIMAIL.COM *URL:* http://www.marinelex.com
Union, New Jersey Office: 1495 Morris Avenue, P.O. Box 1718.
Telephone: 973-467-4740.
Telefax: 908-687-0255.
Stamford, Connecticut Office: 999 Summer Street.
Telephone: 203-323-9120.
Telefax: 203-323-9015.
Boston, Massachusetts Office: One Boston Place, 5th Floor, 02180.
Telephone: 617-619-3610.
Telefax: 617-619-3924.
Miami, Florida Office: De Orchis, Corsa & Hillerbrand, LLP, 2650 Biscayne Boulevard, 33137.
Telephone: 305-571-9200.
Telefax: 305-571-9250.

PARTNERS

LeRoy S. Corsa
Vincent M. De Orchis
Christopher H. Mansuy
Alexander V. Sansone
John A. Orzel
Michael E. Unger
Cary R. Wiener

ASSOCIATES

R. Brett Kelly
William E. Lakis
Marc I. Kunkin
Francesco A. Di Pietro

RESIDENT COUNSEL

M. E. De Orchis

OF COUNSEL

Ara A. Shimshidian
Bruce H. Neuman

For full biographical listings, see the Martindale-Hubbell Law Directory

HEALY & BAILLIE, LLP (AV)

29 Broadway, 10006-3293
Telephone: 212-943-3980
Telecopier: 212-425-0131
Cable Address: "Mainbrace New York"
Telex: 422089
Email: reception@healy.com *URL:* http://www.healy.com
Hong Kong Office: Healy & Baillie, Suite 1303, Dina House, Ruttonjee Centre, 11 Duddell Street, Central.
Telephone: 852-2537-8628.
Telecopier: 852-2521-9072. Email: gryu@healy.com.hk.

(See Next Column)

Stamford, Connecticut Office: Stamford Harbor Park, 333 Ludlow Street, 06902-6987.
Telephone: 203-961-7250.
Telecopier: 203-357-7909. Email: reception@healy.com.

MEMBERS OF FIRM

Allan A. Baillie (1911-1983)
W. Cameron Beard
Nigel J. Binnersley (Resident Partner, Hong Kong Office)
Andrew V. Buchsbaum
Sharon S.H. Chen (Resident Partner, Hong Kong Office)
William N. France, II
Jack A. Greenbaum
Karen I. Hansen
Simon Harter
Jeremy J. Harwood
Nicholas J. Healy
John G. Ingram
John D. Kimball
John C. Koster
Andrew N. Krinsky
LeRoy Lambert
Philip S. LaPenta
Matthew A. Marion
Howard M. McCormack
Michael J. Murphy
Glen T. Oxton
Robert G. Shaw
Richard V. Singleton, II
John W. Wall (Resident Partner, Stamford, Connecticut Office)
Robert E. Wilder
Genrong Yu (Resident Partner, Hong Kong Office)

OF COUNSEL

Gordon W. Paulsen

For Complete List of Firm Personnel, See General Section

For full biographical listings, see the Martindale-Hubbell Law Directory

KENNY & STEARNS (AV)

26 Broadway, 10004-1882
Telephone: 212-422-6111
Fax: 212-422-6544
Email: kenny-stearns@erols.com
Newark, New Jersey Office: 56 Park Place.
Telephone: 201-624-7779.

MEMBERS OF FIRM

James M. Kenny
Joseph T. Stearns
Gino A. Zonghetti

ASSOCIATES

Michael C. Mulé
Christina M. Kenny (Not admitted in NY)
John D. Blomquist

For full biographical listings, see the Martindale-Hubbell Law Directory

KIRLIN, CAMPBELL & KEATING (AV)

5 Hanover Square, 14th Floor, 10004
Telephone: 212-425-7800
Cable Address: "Vasefield NewYork"
Telex: ITT 422219; TRT 177117
Facsimile: 212-425-7856
Email: kirlin@kck.com
Other Offices Located in: Long Beach, California, Washington, D.C., Stamford, Connecticut and Hoboken, New Jersey.

MEMBERS OF FIRM

Richard H. Brown, Jr.
John R. Geraghty
Albert Charles Goudvis
Marshall P. Keating
Ernesto V. Luzzatto
Todd L. Platek
J. Scot Provan
Michael D. Wilson

OF COUNSEL

John E. Grimmer
Selwyn Nimaroff
Mary L. O'Connor
Richard H. Sommer

ASSOCIATES

Keith A. Brady
Vivienne M. Clerissi (Not admitted in NY)
Mark D. Cole (Not admitted in NY)
James M. Maloney
Daniel F. Paige
Robert A. Suarez

For full biographical listings, see the Martindale-Hubbell Law Directory

LAMBOS & JUNGE (AV)

29 Broadway, 9th Floor, 10006-3101
Telephone: 212-943-2470; 212-269-0061
Telecopiers: 212-797-9213; 212-269-0172
Email: nyoffice@lambosjunge.com *URL:* http://lambosjunge.wld.com
San Francisco, California Office (A California Partnership): Three Embarcadero Center, 28th Floor, 94111.
Telephone: 415-986-7450.
Fax: 415-986-7499.
Tampa, Florida Office: 13992 W. Hillsborough Avenue, 33635.
Telephone: 813-855-5400.
Fax: 813-855-9735.
Bayonne, New Jersey Office: 473 Broadway, Bayonne Plaza, Suite 209, 07002.
Telephone: 201-823-1000.
Fax: 201-823-3097.
Boston, Massachusetts Office: The Vermont Marble Building, 10 Thacher Street, Suite 114, 02113.
Telephone: 617-227-5500.
Fax: 617-227-5500.

(See Next Column)

LAMBOS & JUNGE—*Continued*

MEMBERS OF FIRM

Constantine P. Lambos
Peter A. Junge
Richard P. Lerner
Robert J. Attaway
Donato Caruso
William M. Spelman
Nicholas G. Maglaras
Peter C. Lambos (1945-1991)

SPECIAL COUNSEL

Steven L. Barkan
George W. Sullivan

ASSOCIATES

Ann Marie Flynn
Richard J. Ciampi, Jr.
Armand P. Mele
Carol Notias Lambos
James R. Campbell, Jr.
Robert F. Sloan (Resident Associate, New Jersey Office; Also Practicing Individually in Bayonne, New Jersey)
Daniel Amo Gronda

OF COUNSEL

Edward M. Kovach (Resident California Partner)
Edward J. Heine, Jr.
Vincent De Vito
E. Gordon Cleland

For full biographical listings, see the Martindale-Hubbell Law Directory

LONDON FISCHER LLP (AV)

59 Maiden Lane, 10038
Telephone: 212-972-1000
Facsimile: 212-972-1030
Email: Law@LondonFischer.com

MEMBERS OF FIRM

Bernard London
James L. Fischer
Daniel Zemann, Jr.
John E. Sparling
Richard S. Endres
Leah Campbell
Marvin B. Segal
James Walsh
Anthony F. Tagliagambe

For full biographical listings, see the Martindale-Hubbell Law Directory

O'DONNELL, SCHWARTZ, GLANSTEIN, ROSEN, DI PRETA & GOLDSTEIN, L.L.P. (AV)

Suite 1022, 60 East 42nd Street, 10165
Telephone: 212-370-5100
Fax: 212-697-6299
Email: odsgr@worldnet.att.net
Washington, D.C. Offices: O'Donnell, Schwartz & Anderson, Suite 1200, 1300 L Street, N.W.
Telephone: 202-898-1707.
Telex: 202-429-8928 and Suite 707, 1900 L Street, N.W.
Telephone: 202-898-1824.

RESIDENT MEMBERS

John F. O'Donnell (1907-1993)
Asher W. Schwartz
Joel C. Glanstein
David B. Rosen
Malcolm A. Goldstein
Manlio Di Preta

RESIDENT ASSOCIATES

Edmond V. Pendleton
David M. Glanstein

OF COUNSEL

Suzanne McCarthy

For full biographical listings, see the Martindale-Hubbell Law Directory

WATSON, FARLEY & WILLIAMS (AV)

380 Madison Avenue, 10017
Telephone: 212-922-2200
Telex: 6790626 WFWNY
Fax: 212-922-1512
Email: josborne@wfw.com *URL:* http://www.wfw.com
London, England Office: 15 Appold Street, London EC2A 2HB.
Telephone: (44 171) 814 8000.
Telex: 8955707 WFWLON G.
Fax: (44 171) 814 8141.
Paris, France Office: 47, rue de Monceau, 75008 Paris.
Telephone: (33 1) 53 83 12 12.
Telex: WFWPAR 651096 F.
Fax: (33 1) 45 61 09 01.
Athens, Greece Office: 5th Floor, Alassia Building, Defteras Merarchias 13, 185-35 Piraeus.
Telephone: (30 1) 422 3660.
Telex: 24 1311 WFWGR.
Fax: (30 1) 422 3664.
Singapore Office: 16 Collyer Quay, #12-02 Hitachi Tower, Singapore 049318.
Telephone: (65) 532-5335.
Fax: (65) 532-5454.
Moscow, Russia Office: 16/2 Tverskaya Ulitsa, Business Centre Bldg. 3, The Actor Gallery, Moscow 103009.
Telephone: 7502 237 7770 (international only); 7095 935 7770.
Fax: 7502 237 7771 (international only); 7095 935 7771.
Copenhagen, Denmark Office: Lille Kongensgade 20 DK-1074 Copenhagen K.
Telephone: (45 33) 91 33 03.
Fax: (45 33) 91 49 12.

(See Next Column)

Associated Office: Abbas F. Ghazzawi Law Firm, Saudi Arabia.

MEMBERS OF FIRM

Leo Chang
John S. Osborne, Jr.
Alfred E. Yudes, Jr.
Richard L. Jarashow
William S. Haft
Christopher P. Belisle

For Complete List of Firm Personnel, See General Section

For full biographical listings, see the Martindale-Hubbell Law Directory

NORTH CAROLINA

*BEAUFORT,** Carteret Co.

DAVIS, MURRELLE & LUMSDEN, P.A. (AV)

412 Front Street, P.O. Box 819, 28516
Telephone: 252-728-4080
Fax: 252-728-3235
URL: http://www.lawyers.com/dmtlaw

Edward L. Murrelle
Treve B. Lumsden

Janet M. Lyles

OF COUNSEL

Warren J. Davis

Representative Clients: Cooperative Bank for Savings; Roman Catholic Diocese of Raleigh for Carteret County; International Longshoreman's Association Local 1807; Town of Cedar Point; John Yancey Corp.; Morehead City Export Terminal, Inc.; Crow Hill Farms, Inc.; Phoenix Foods, Inc.; Core Sound Waterfowl Museum, Inc.; Northland Ins. Co.

For full biographical listings, see the Martindale-Hubbell Law Directory

*WILMINGTON,** New Hanover Co.

MARSHALL, WILLIAMS & GORHAM, L.L.P. (AV)

14 South Fifth Street, P.O. Drawer 2088, 28402-2088
Telephone: 910-763-9891
Telecopier: 910-343-8604
URL: http://www.mwglaw.com

MEMBERS OF FIRM

Lonnie B. Williams
John Dearman Martin
John L. Coble

Representative Clients: Almont Shipping Company; Skuld; Danish Shipowner's Defense Assoc.; McAllister Towing; Akzo Salt and Basic Chemical.

For Complete List of Firm Personnel, See General Section

For full biographical listings, see the Martindale-Hubbell Law Directory

ROUNTREE & SEAGLE, L.L.P. (AV)

2419 Market Street, P.O. Box 1409, 28403
Telephone: 910-763-3404
Telecopier: 910-763-0320
URL: http://www.ltinet.com/rountree&seagle

MEMBERS OF FIRM

George Rountree, III
J. Harold Seagle
Geoffrey A. Losee
Brian N. Bishop

Representative Clients: American International Marine Agency; Fireman's Fund Insurance Cos.; The Japan Shipowners' Mutual Protection & Indemnity Assn., Ltd.; Time Warner Cable - Advance/Newhouse Partnership.
Approved Attorneys for: Chicago Title Insurance Co.; Commonwealth Land Insurance Co.; Investors Title Insurance Co.; Lawyers Title Insurance Corp.
References: Centura Bank; First Union National Bank of North Carolina.

For full biographical listings, see the Martindale-Hubbell Law Directory

OHIO

*CLEVELAND,** Cuyahoga Co.

RAY, ROBINSON, CARLE & DAVIES P.L.L. (AV)

1650 The East Ohio Building, 1717 East 9th Street, 44114-2898
Telephone: 216-861-4533
Facsimile: 216-861-4568
Email: rayrob@rayrobcle.com

MEMBERS OF FIRM

David G. Davies
Douglas R. Denny
Gene B. George
Julia R. Brouhard
Robert T. Coniam
Sandra Maurer Kelly

ASSOCIATE

Thomas More Wynne

(See Next Column)

RAY, ROBINSON, CARLE & DAVIES P.L.L., *Cleveland—Continued*

OF COUNSEL

Lucian Y. Ray (1903-1987)
Theodore C. Robinson (Retired)
William D. Carle, III (Senior Counsel)

Representative Clients: Bethlehem Steel Corp., Great Lakes Steamship Division; Canada Steamship Lines; The M.A. Hanna Co.; Ispat Inland, Inc. Assuranceforeningen Gard; West of England Shipowners P & I Assn., Ltd.; The London Steam-Ship Owners Insurance Assn.; Inland Lakes Management; BP Amoco Corp.; American Steamship Owners P & I Assn.

For full biographical listings, see the Martindale-Hubbell Law Directory

*TOLEDO,** Lucas Co.

LACKEY, NUSBAUM, HARRIS, RENY & TORZEWSKI A LEGAL PROFESSIONAL ASSOCIATION (AV)

Two Maritime Plaza Third Floor, 43604
Telephone: 419-243-1105
Fax: 419-243-8953

D. Michael Reny

References: Fifth Third Bank; Society Bank.

For full biographical listings, see the Martindale-Hubbell Law Directory

OREGON

*PORTLAND,** Multnomah Co.

KELL, ALTERMAN & RUNSTEIN, LLP (AV)

1001 S.W. Fifth Avenue, Suite 1800, 97204
Telephone: 503-222-3531
Telecopier: 503-227-2980
Email: kell@teleport.com

MEMBERS OF FIRM

Raymond M. Kell (1911-1991)
Clifford B. Alterman (1925-1995)
Ted E. Runstein
Lee Davis Kell
Wayne D. Palmer
Lloyd R. Summers
William D. Dickas
Gary P. Compa
Charles R. Williamson
Mary Ellen Page Farr
Eric Sogge
Thomas J. Matsuda
Thomas R. Rask, III
Nicholas S. Fish

Dana L. Barnes
Cory Larvik
Robert E. Kabacy
Robin M. Runstein

References: Union Bank of California, N.A. (Portland Branch); The Bank of Tokyo-Mitsubishi, Ltd. (Portland Branch); Bank of America (5th S. Main Branch).

For full biographical listings, see the Martindale-Hubbell Law Directory

LINDSAY, HART, NEIL & WEIGLER, LLP (AV)

3400 Wells Fargo Center, 1300 S.W. Fifth Avenue, 97201-5696
Telephone: 503-226-7677
Telecopier: 503-226-7697
Email: LHNW@Europa.com
Washington, D.C. Office: 1201 Pennsylvania Avenue, N.W., Suite 821, 20004.
Telephone: 202-467-8383.
Fax: 202-467-8581.

MEMBERS OF FIRM

Dennis J. Lindsay
Carl R. Neil
Jerard S. Weigler
Thomas E. McDermott

ASSOCIATE

John D. Kimmerlein

Representative Clients: Master Contracting Stevedore Association of the Pacific Coast, Inc.; Pacific Northwest Grain Elevator Operators.

For full biographical listings, see the Martindale-Hubbell Law Directory

MILLER NASH LLP (AV)

A Limited Liability Partnership including Professional Corporations
111 S.W. Fifth Avenue, 97204-3699
Telephone: 503-224-5858
Telex: 364462, Kingmar PTL
Facsimile: 503-224-0155, 503-224-2450
Email: e-mail@millernash.com *URL:* http://www.millernash.com
Seattle, Washington Office: 4400 Two Union Square, 601 Union Street, 98101-2322.
Telephone: 206-622-8484.
Facsimile: 206-622-7485.

(See Next Column)

PORTLAND, OREGON PARTNERS

Dean D. DeChaine, P.C.
James F. Dulcich, P.C.
M. Christie Helmer, P.C.

Representative Clients: The London Steam-Ship Owners' Mutual Insurance Assn., Ltd.; Mitsui Marine & Fire Insurance Co., Ltd.; The Charterers P & I Club; International Marine Underwriters; Ocean Marine Mutual Protection & Indemnity Assn.; Transmarine Mutual Assurance Assn.

For Complete List of Firm Personnel, See General Section

For full biographical listings, see the Martindale-Hubbell Law Directory

PENNSYLVANIA

*PHILADELPHIA,** Philadelphia Co.

MARVIN I. BARISH LAW OFFICES A PROFESSIONAL CORPORATION (AV)

6th and Walnut Streets, Suite 801E, 19106-3308
Telephone: 215-923-8900; 800-233-7101
Email: mbarish@aol.com *URL:* http://www.lawyers.com/barishlawoffices
Cherry Hill, New Jersey Office: 1930 East Marlton Pike, Suite Q-38.
Telephone: 609-338-0550.

Marvin I. Barish

Gregory L. Nester

For full biographical listings, see the Martindale-Hubbell Law Directory

HOLLSTEIN KEATING CATTELL JOHNSON & GOLDSTEIN, P.C. (AV)

Suite 1602 1608 Walnut Street, 19103
Telephone: 215-893-9488
Fax: 215-893-9480
Email: JFJ@HKCJG.com
Voorhees, New Jersey Office: 1016 Laurel Oak Road, Suite 2, 08043.
Telephone: 609-309-9000.
Fax: 609-309-0337.
Wilmington, Delaware Office: One Commerce Center, Suite 730, 12th and Orange Streets, 19801.
Telephone: 302-884-6700.
Fax: 302-573-2507.

Richard W. Hollstein
E. Michael Keating, III
Edward V. Cattell, Jr.
James W. Johnson
Stuart M. Goldstein (Resident, Voorhees, New Jersey Office)
Mark G. Lionetti
John E. Tyrrell
Lynne M. Parker (at Voorhees, New Jersey and Wilmington, Delaware Offices)
Paul F. Weisbein
James D. Lloyd
Nancy D. Wagman
Margaret M. Grasso

LEGAL SUPPORT PERSONNEL

Nancy Hevener (Paralegal)
Libby Carrol (Paralegal)

For full biographical listings, see the Martindale-Hubbell Law Directory

LEVIN, FISHBEIN, SEDRAN & BERMAN (AV)

Suite 500, 510 Walnut Street, 19106-3697
Telephone: 215-592-1500
Fax: 215-592-4663
Email: lfsb@psinet.com

MEMBERS OF FIRM

Arnold Levin
Michael D. Fishbein
Howard J. Sedran
Laurence S. Berman
Frederick S. Longer

Craig D. Ginsburg
Cheryl R. Brown Hill
Donald E. Haviland, Jr.
Daniel C. Levin
Terrianne Benedetto
Charles E. Schaffer
Austin B. Cohen

LEGAL SUPPORT PERSONNEL

Lee Ann Fitzpatrick
Cheryl Hesson

For full biographical listings, see the Martindale-Hubbell Law Directory

HENRY C. LUCAS, III (AV)

2000 Market Street, 6th Floor, 19103
Telephone: 215-851-6620
Fax: 215-851-6644
Email: 6762434@mcimail.com *URL:* http://www.lawyers.com/henryclucas111

For full biographical listings, see the Martindale-Hubbell Law Directory

Philadelphia—Continued

Mattioni, Ltd. (AV)

399 Market Street, 2nd Floor, 19106
Telephone: 215-629-1600
Cable Address: "Mattioni"
Fax: 215-923-2227
Email: firmmail@mattioni.com *URL:* http://www.mattioni.com
Westmont, New Jersey Office: Mattioni, LLP, Suite 100, Sentry Office Plaza, 216 Haddon Avenue, 08108.
Telephone: 856-854-6200.
Fax: 856-854-3338.
Montgomery County Office: Suite 200, 1101 Fayette Street, Conshohocken, Pennsylvania, 19428.
Telephone: 610-941-9530.
Fax: 610-940-4489.

Dante Mattioni
Faustino Mattioni
John Mattioni
Blasco Mattioni *
Eugene Mattioni
Francis X. Kelly
George R. Zacharkow
Andrew H. Quinn
Eva Helena Bleich
Robert W. Weidner, Jr.
Scott J. Schwarz
Anthony Granato
Stephen M. Martin
Stephen J. Galati
Joseph F. Bouvier
Michael Mattioni
Bruce A. O'Neill
Alan Mattioni
Itzchak E. Kornfeld
Sarah Wilson Weingast (Not admitted in PA)
Mary Alice Cleve
Paul A. Kettunen
Donald S. Sabatini
Mark David Hasenauer
Bridget C. Sciamanna
Mette Deleuran
Dante C. Rohr

Frank Carano *
Ronald R. Donatucci *
John A. DiPietro **
Kristi L. Treadway **

*Counsel to the Firm
**Of Counsel

For full biographical listings, see the Martindale-Hubbell Law Directory

Rawle & Henderson LLP (AV)

(Rawle Law Offices Founded 1783)
The Widener Building, One South Penn Square, 19107
Telephone: 215-575-4200
Telecopier: 215-563-2583
Email: info@rawle.com *URL:* http://www.rawle.com
Marlton, New Jersey Office: Suite 204, Ten Lake Center Executive Park, 401 Route 73 North.
Telephone: 609-596-4800.
Telecopier: 609-596-6164.
New York, N.Y. Office: 140 Broadway, Forty-Sixth Floor.
Telephone: 212-858-7570. Fax 212-858-7750.

Carl D. Buchholz, III
David P. Thompson
Michael P. Zipfel

Jon Michael Dumont
Angela M. Heim
Ann-Michele G. Higgins
Michael A. Meehan
James A. Wescoe

For full biographical listings, see the Martindale-Hubbell Law Directory

*PITTSBURGH,** Allegheny Co.

Heintzman, Warren, Wise & Fornella, P.C. (AV)

The 35th Floor, Gulf Tower, 707 Grant Street, 15219
Telephone: 412-394-7810
Fax: 412-263-5222
Email: hww@hwwlaw.com *URL:* http://www.hwwlaw.com

Leonard Fornella
Kenneth F. Klanica

Max T. Busatto

For full biographical listings, see the Martindale-Hubbell Law Directory

RHODE ISLAND

*PROVIDENCE,** Providence Co.

Hanson, Curran, Parks & Whitman (AV)

146 Westminster Street, 02903-2218
Telephone: 401-421-2154
Telecopier: 401-521-7040
URL: http://www.hcpw.com

Kirk Hanson (1948-1991)

(See Next Column)

MEMBERS OF FIRM

A. Lauriston Parks
David P. Whitman
Michael T. F. Wallor
Dennis J. McCarten
James T. Murphy
Seth E. Bowerman
Thomas R. Bender
Mark W. Dana

ASSOCIATES

Richard H. Burrows
Christopher J. Zangari (Resident)
Wendy J. Taylor

OF COUNSEL

William A. Curran

General Counsel for: Medical Malpractice Joint Underwriting Association of Rhode Island.
Rhode Island Counsel for: Amica Mutual Insurance Co.; CIGNA; St. Paul Insurance Cos.; Occidental Life Insurance Co.; Exchange Mutual Insurance Co.; Aetna Casualty & Surety Co.

For full biographical listings, see the Martindale-Hubbell Law Directory

SOUTH CAROLINA

*CHARLESTON,** Charleston Co.

Buist, Moore, Smythe & McGee, P.A. (AV)

Successors to Buist, Buist, Smythe and Smythe and Moore, Mouzon and McGee.
Five Exchange Street, P.O. Box 999, 29402
Telephone: 843-722-3400
Cable Address: "Conferees"
Telex: 57-6488
Telecopier: 843-723-7398
Email: bmsm@lawyer-sc.com *URL:* http://www.lawyer-sc.com

Benjamin Allston Moore, Jr.
Gordon D. Schreck
Douglas M. Muller

Julius H. Hines

OF COUNSEL

David M. Collins

Representative Clients: Thomas Miller (Americas), Inc.; Lamorte, Burns & Co., Inc.; Shipowners Claims Bureau, Inc.; Scandinavian Marine Claims Office, Inc.; MOAC; Zurich-American Insurance Group (Ocean Marine); Sea-Land Services, Inc; Trimar Defense Services, Inc.; Anchor Marine Services, Inc.; St. Paul Fire and Marine Insurance Co.; Brunswick Corp.; Viking Yachts; Bombardier, Inc.

For Complete List of Firm Personnel, See General Section

For full biographical listings, see the Martindale-Hubbell Law Directory

Sinkler & Boyd, P.A. (AV)

160 East Bay Street, P.O. Box 340, 29402-0340
Telephone: 843-722-3366
FAX: 843-722-2266
Email: firm@sinklerboyd.com *URL:* http://www.sinklerboyd.com
Columbia, South Carolina Office: Suite 1200 The Palmetto Center, 1426 Main Street, P.O. Box 11889.
Telephone: 803-779-3080.
FAX: 803-765-1243.
Greenville, South Carolina Office: 15 South Main Street, Insignia Financial Center on Main, Suite 500, P.O. Box 275.
Telephone: 864-467-1100.
FAX: 864-467-1521.

Stephen E. Darling
Marvin D. Infinger

Joseph D. Thompson, III

For Complete List of Firm Personnel, See General Section

For full biographical listings, see the Martindale-Hubbell Law Directory

*COLUMBIA,** Richland Co.

Sinkler & Boyd, P.A. (AV)

Suite 1200 The Palmetto Center, 1426 Main Street, P.O. Box 11889, 29211-1889
Telephone: 803-779-3080
FAX: 803-765-1243
Email: firm@sinklerboyd.com *URL:* http://www.sinklerboyd.com
Charleston, South Carolina Office: 160 East Bay Street, P.O. Box 340.
Telephone: 843-722-3366.
FAX: 843-722-2266.
Greenville, South Carolina Office: 15 South Main Street, Insignia Financial Center on Main, Suite 500, P.O. Box 275.
Telephone: 864-467-1100.
FAX: 864-467-1521.

(See Next Column)

SINKLER & BOYD P.A., *Columbia—Continued*

Stephen E. Darling (Resident, Charleston Office)
Marvin D. Infinger (Resident, Charleston Office)

Joseph D. Thompson, III (Resident, Charleston Office)

For Complete List of Firm Personnel, See General Section

For full biographical listings, see the Martindale-Hubbell Law Directory

HILTON HEAD ISLAND, Beaufort Co.

LAUGHLIN AND BOWEN (AV)

20 Palmetto Parkway, Suites A & B, Drawer 21119, 29925-1119
Telephone: 843-689-5700
Fax: 843-689-9300
Email: Jazzlaw@Hargray.com

MEMBERS OF FIRM

Drew A. Laughlin
John R. C. Bowen

For full biographical listings, see the Martindale-Hubbell Law Directory

NORTH CHARLESTON, Charleston Co.

RIESEN LAW FIRM, L.L.P. (AV)

3660 West Montague Avenue, P.O. Box 40997, 29423-0997
Telephone: 843-760-2450
FAX: 843-767-3282

MEMBERS OF FIRM

John D. Bradley, III (1946-1998)
Fred W. Riesen, Jr.
Gary Alan Ling
E. Paul Gibson
Timothy Clay Kulp
Philip A. Berlinsky
Allison A. Stover
Jody V. McKnight

Ellen Howard

For full biographical listings, see the Martindale-Hubbell Law Directory

TENNESSEE

*MEMPHIS,** Shelby Co.

FARRIS, MATHEWS, BRANAN & HELLEN, P.L.C. (AV)

One Commerce Square, Suite 2000, 38103
Telephone: 901-259-7100
Fax: 901-259-7150
Email: firm@farris-law.com
East Memphis, Tennessee Office: Suite 400. First Commercial Bank Building. 5384 Poplar Avenue.
Telephone: 901-763-4000.
Fax: 901-763-4095.
Nashville, Tennessee Office: Nashville City Center, 511 Union Street, Suite 2400.
Telephone: 615-726-1200.
Fax: 615-726-1776.

MEMBERS OF FIRM

G. Ray Bratton
Eugene Stone Forrester, Jr.

ASSOCIATE

Gregory W. O'Neal

For Complete List of Firm Personnel, See General Section

For full biographical listings, see the Martindale-Hubbell Law Directory

TEXAS

*BEAUMONT,** Jefferson Co.

BENCKENSTEIN & OXFORD, L.L.P. (AV)

Community Bank Building, P.O. Box 150, 77704
Telephone: 409-833-9182
Cable Address: "Bmor"
Telex: 779485
Telefax: 409-833-8819
Email: lawfirm@benoxford.com
Houston, Texas Office: Two Post Oak Central, 1980 Post Oak Boulevard, Suite 1600, 77056.
Telephone: 713-629-0345.
Fax: 713-629-0614.

(See Next Column)

MEMBERS OF FIRM

L. J. Benckenstein (1894-1966)
F. L. Benckenstein (1918-1987)
Hubert Oxford, III
Alan G. Sampson
Frank D. Calvert
Dana Timaeus
Frances Blair Bethea
Robert J. Rose, Sr.

ASSOCIATES

F. Blair Clarke
Michael K. Eaves
Alex J. Stelly, Jr.
Robert W. Craft
Lauren Miller Robbins (Resident, Houston Office)

Representative Clients: Marine Office of American Corp. (MOAC); Moran Towing and Transportation Co., Inc.

For full biographical listings, see the Martindale-Hubbell Law Directory

MEHAFFY & WEBER, A PROFESSIONAL CORPORATION (AV)

2615 Calder Avenue, Suite 800, P.O. Box 16, 77704
Telephone: 409-835-5011
Fax: 409-835-5729; 835-5177
Email: MehaffyWeber.com
Orange, Texas Office: 1006 Green Avenue, P.O. Drawer 189.
Telephone: 409-886-7766.
Houston, Texas Office: One Allen Center, 500 Dallas, Suite 1200.
Telephone: 713-655-1200.

Louis M. Scofield
David B. Gaultney
M. C. Carrington
John E. Haught

OF COUNSEL

Otto J. Weber, Jr.
Dewey J. Gonsoulin
John J. Durkay

Representative Clients: E.I. du Pont de Nemours and Co.; Eli Lilly & Co.; Merrell Dow; Jefferson County Tax Appraisal District; W.R. Grace & Co.-Conn.; Burlington Northern Santa Fe Railway; Christus St. Elizabeth; Christus Health.
Approved Attorneys for: Stewart Title Guaranty Co.

For Complete List of Firm Personnel, See General Section

For full biographical listings, see the Martindale-Hubbell Law Directory

WELLS, PEYTON, GREENBERG & HUNT, L.L.P. (AV)

6th Floor, Petroleum Building, P.O. Box 3708, 77704-3708
Telephone: 409-838-2644
Fax: 409-838-4713
Email: wellspeyton@ih2000.net

MEMBERS OF FIRM

Peter Boyd Wells, III
Bruce M. Partain

OF COUNSEL

Louis H. Beard

For Complete List of Firm Personnel, See General Section

For full biographical listings, see the Martindale-Hubbell Law Directory

*HOUSTON,** Harris Co.

BAKER BOTTS L.L.P. (AV)

One Shell Plaza, 910 Louisiana, 77002
Telephone: 713-229-1234
Cable Address: "Boterlove"
Fax: 713-229-1522
Email: postmaster@bakerbotts.com *URL:* http://www.bakerbotts.com
Washington, D.C. Office: The Warner, 1299 Pennsylvania Avenue, N.W.
Telephone: 202-639-7700.
New York, New York Office: 599 Lexington Avenue.
Telephone: 212-705-5000.
Austin, Texas Office: 1600 San Jacinto Center, 98 San Jacinto Boulevard.
Telephone: 512-322-2500.
Dallas, Texas Office: 2001 Ross Avenue.
Telephone: 214-953-6500.
Moscow, Russia Office: 10 ul. Bolshaya Dimitrovka (formerly Pushkinskaya), 103031.
Telephone: 7095/921-5300 (Local); 7095/929-7070 (International).
London, England Office: 45 Ludgate Hill.
Telephone: 0171-778-1400 (Local); 011-44-171-778-1400 (International).
Baku, Azerbaijan Office: 6-10 Vagif Mustafa-zadeh Street, Third Floor, Icheri Sheher, 370004.
Telephone: 994-12-97-63-88 (Local); 011-994-12-97-63-88 (International).
Fax: 994-12-97-63-91 (Local); 011-994-12-97-63-91 (International)

MEMBER OF FIRM

Joseph D. Cheavens

For Complete List of Firm Personnel, See General Section

For full biographical listings, see the Martindale-Hubbell Law Directory

BELL, RYNIKER & LETOURNEAU, P.C. (AV)

Five Post Oak Park, Suite 1300, 77027
Telephone: 713-871-8822
Fax: 713-871-8844
URL: http://www.brlpc.com
Email: mkbell@brlpc.com *URL:* http://www.lawyers.com/brlpc

(See Next Column)

BELL, RYNIKER & LETOURNEAU P.C.—*Continued*

Michael K. Bell
Keith B. Letourneau
Robert J. Ryniker
Thomas R. Nork

Douglas J. Shoemaker
Deborah T. Busby
Wesley T. Welmaker

For full biographical listings, see the Martindale-Hubbell Law Directory

BILLINGS & SOLOMON, P.C. (AV)

460 Riviana Building, 2777 Allen Parkway, 77019-2174
Telephone: 713-528-2111
Fax: 713-528-0980; 528-3138
Email: bsolomonpc@aol.com

Frank E. Billings
Cecil L. Solomon
Richard P. Martini

Ford C. Thanheiser
James C. Bollom

For full biographical listings, see the Martindale-Hubbell Law Directory

BROWN, SIMS, WISE & WHITE, A PROFESSIONAL CORPORATION (AV)

One Post Oak Central, 21st Floor, 2000 Post Oak Boulevard, 77056-4496
Telephone: 713-629-1580
Fax: 713-629-5027
Telex: 775557
Email: bsww@neosoft.com *URL:* http://www.neosoft.com/~bsww/bsww.htm

G. Byron Sims
James D. Wise, Jr.
Ronald L. White
Kenneth G. Engerrand
Innes Alexander Henderson Mackillop
James N. Isbell
Thomas O. Deen
Michael D. Williams
Thomas W. Burch, III
Ronnie W. Baham, Jr.
Polly A. Kinnibrugh
Deanna H. Brewer
Mark C. Clemer
James R. Koecher
John R. Walker
William A. Galerston
Cynthia A. Galvan
Michael A. Varner
Walter Joseph Gallant
Philip Robert Brinson
Monica A. Fekete
Gregory L. Deans
Nelson D. Skyler
James A. Tatem, III
Sheri E. Moore
Lisa L. Gambrell
Jeromy D. Hughes
Robbie A. Moehlmann
Hal Davis Hale, Jr.
Thomas A. Brown (1932-1997)

For full biographical listings, see the Martindale-Hubbell Law Directory

KILLEEN & FIERRO (AV)

1717 St. James Place, Suite 620, 77056
Telephone: 713-626-5100
Facsimile: 713-626-4545

Robert Joseph Killeen, Jr.
John M. Longoria
L. Byron Wilson

Candace A. Ourso

OF COUNSEL

Gerald M. Johnson, III

For full biographical listings, see the Martindale-Hubbell Law Directory

PHELPS DUNBAR, L.L.P. (AV)

Suite 900, 3040 Post Oak Boulevard, 77056
Telephone: 713-626-1386
Telecopier: 713-626-1388
Email: info@phelps.com
New Orleans, Louisiana Office: Texaco Center, 400 Poydras Street.
Telephone: 504-566-1311.
Telecopier: 504-568-9130, 504-568-9007.
Cable Address: "Howspencer."
Telex: 584125 WU.
Telex: 6821155 WUI.
Baton Rouge, Louisiana Office: Suite 701, 445 North Boulevard, P.O. Box 4412.
Telephone: 225-346-0285.
Telecopier: 225-381-9197.
Jackson, Mississippi Office: Suite 500, SkyTel Centre, 200 South Lamar Street, P.O. Box 23066.
Telephone: 601-352-2300.
Telecopier: 601-360-9777.
Tupelo, Mississippi Office: Seventh Floor, One Mississippi Plaza, P.O. Box 1220.
Telephone: 662-842-7907.
Telecopier: 662-842-3873.

(See Next Column)

London, England Office: Suite 731, Level 7, Lloyd's, 1 Lime Street, London EC3M 7DQ England.
Telephone: 011-44-207-929-4765.
Telecopier: 011-44-207-929-0046.
Telex: 987321.

RESIDENT PARTNERS

Julia Marie Adams
Matthew R. Muth
Claude LeRoy Stuart, III
Kent E. Westmoreland (Also at London, England Office)

RESIDENT ASSOCIATES

Jennifer M. Benson
Karen Klaas Milhollin
Stanley T. Proctor
John L. Schouest

Representative Clients: Atlantic Mutual Insurance Co.; Bludworth Bond Shipyard; Commercial Union Assurance, PLC; Edison Chouest Offshore, L.L.C.; Entex; GATX Terminals Corp.; Global Industries; Highlands Insurance Company; McDonough Marine Service, A Division of MARMAC Corp.; Underwriters at Lloyd's, London.

For full biographical listings, see the Martindale-Hubbell Law Directory

ROBERTS, MARKEL & FOLGER, L.L.P. (AV)

A Limited Liability Partnership of Professional Corporations
Weslayan Tower, Suite 2000, 24 Greenway Plaza, 77046
Telephone: 713-840-1666
Telecopier: 713-840-9404

MEMBERS OF FIRM

Jeffrey D. Roberts
Alan B. Folger
Theodore L. Guerry, Jr.

ASSOCIATE

John Bradley Mitchell

For full biographical listings, see the Martindale-Hubbell Law Directory

ROYSTON, RAYZOR, VICKERY & WILLIAMS, L.L.P. (AV)

600 Travis Street, Suite 2200, 77002-2913
Telephone: 713-224-8380
Cable Address: "Houport"
Telex: 6869017
Telecopier: 713-225-9945
Email: royston@roystonlaw.com *URL:* http://www.roystonlaw.com
Brownsville, Texas Office: 55 Cove Circle, P.O. Box 3509.
Telephone: 956-542-4377.
Cable Address: "Padre"
Telex: 767-817.
Telecopier: 956-542-4370.
Corpus Christi, Texas Office: 1700 Wilson Plaza West, 606 North Carancahua.
Telephone: 361-884-8808.
Cable Address: "CC PORT"
Telex: 6866625.
Telecopier: 361-884-7261.
Galveston, Texas Office: 205 Cotton Exchange Building, 2102 Mechanic Street.
Telephone: 409-763-1623.
Cable Address: "Houport"
Telex: 6869017.
Telecopier: 409-763-3853.
Lubbock, Texas Office: 1401 Avenue G.
Telephone: 806-763-9252.
Telex: 6869017.
Telecopier: 806-763-9254.
San Antonio, Texas Office: 2000 Riverview Towers, 111 Soledad Street.
Telephone: 210-228-0655.
Telecopier: 210-228-0839.

PARTNERS

Kenneth D. Kuykendall
Ted C. Litton
William M. Jensen
W. Robins Brice
James Patrick Cooney
Bradley A. Jackson
Robert H. Etnyre, Jr.
James G. Blain, II
John M. Elsley
David R. Walker
John F. Unger
Mark Cohen
William R. Towns
Marilyn Tanner Hebinck
C. Scott Kinzel
Marcus R. Tucker
Jennifer S. Sickler

OF COUNSEL

Edward D. Vickery
Gus A. Schill, Jr.
Ben L. Reynolds
Decatur J. Holcombe
Richard L. Lionberger

ASSOCIATES

Scott R. Breitenwischer
Stephen K. Hubchen
I. Ray Kerlick

Representative Clients: West of England Steam Ship Owners' Protection & Indemnity Assn., Ltd.; The United Kingdom Mutual Steam Ship Assurance Assn. Ltd.

For Complete List of Firm Personnel, See General Section

For full biographical listings, see the Martindale-Hubbell Law Directory

Houston—Continued

SCHWARTZ JUNELL CAMPBELL & OATHOUT, L.L.P. (AV)

Two Houston Center, 909 Fannin, Suite 2000, 77010
Telephone: 713-752-0017
Telecopier: 713-752-0327
Email: dschwartz@schwartz-junell.com

Richard A. Schwartz
William Edward Junell, Jr.
Marshall S. Campbell
Monica F. Oathout
Steven R. Rech

Phillip W. Bechter
J. Parker Fauntleroy, Jr.

OF COUNSEL

Joe H. Reynolds
A. R. Schwartz

LEGAL SUPPORT PERSONNEL

PARALEGALS

Nannette Koger
Maria Woods
Shelly A. Savage, CLA

For full biographical listings, see the Martindale-Hubbell Law Directory

STEPP & SULLIVAN, P.C. (AV)

Three Allen Center, 333 Clay Street, Suite 4750, 77002
Telephone: 713-336-7200
Fax: 713-336-7250
URL: http://www.ss-pc.com

Jad J. Stepp
Dennis J. Sullivan

Mark H. Barber
Richard C. Brister
Kimberly Y. Delaney
Kevin Troy Dossett

For full biographical listings, see the Martindale-Hubbell Law Directory

VINSON & ELKINS L.L.P. (AV)

2300 First City Tower, 1001 Fannin, 77002-6760
Telephone: 713-758-2222
Fax: 713-758-2346
Email: info@velaw.com *URL:* http://www.velaw.com
Austin, Texas Office: One American Center Suite 2700, 600 Congress Avenue, Austin, Texas, 78701-3200.
Telephone: 512-495-8400.
Fax: 512-495-8612.
Beijing, China Office: 20/F, Beijing Silver Tower, No. 2, Dong San Huan Bei Lu, Chaoyang District, 100027.
Telephone: +86-10-6410-6300.
Fax: +86-10-6410-6360.
Dallas, Texas Office: 3700 Trammell Crow Center, 2001 Ross Avenue, Dallas, Texas, 75201-2975.
Telephone: 214-220-7700.
Fax: 214-220-7716.
London, England Office: Regis House, 8th Floor, 45 King William Street, London, EC4R 9AN, England.
Telephone: (44-171) 618-6000.
Fax: (44-171) 618-6001.
Moscow, Russia Office: 16 Ulitsa Spiridonovka, Second Floor, 103001 Moscow, Russia.
Telephone: (7-095) 956-1995. Local
Fax: (7-095) 956-1996. U.S. Satellite
Fax: (212) 803-0142.
New York, N.Y. Office: 1325 Avenue of the Americas, 17th Floor, New York, N.Y., 10019.
Telephone: 917-206-8000.
Fax: 917-206-8100.
Singapore Office: 6 Battery Road, #39-01, Singapore, 049909.
Telephone: (65) 536-8300.
Fax: (65) 536-8311.
Washington, D.C. Office: The Willard Office Building, 1455 Pennsylvania Avenue, N.W., Washington, D.C., 20004-1008.
Telephone: 202-639-6500.
Fax: 202-639-6604.

MEMBERS OF FIRM

David H. Brown
Phillip B. Dye, Jr.
Louis E. McCarter
Robert M. Schick
Eugene J. Silva

ASSOCIATES

Matthew D. Eisele
Kevin Michael O'Gorman
Daniel B. Shilliday

For Complete List of Firm Personnel, See General Section

For full biographical listings, see the Martindale-Hubbell Law Directory

VIRGINIA

NORFOLK, (Independent City)

BREIT, DRESCHER & BREIT, P.C. (AV)

1000 Dominion Tower, 999 Waterside Drive, 23510
Telephone: 757-670-3888
Fax: 757-670-3895
Email: jbreit@livenet.net

John W. Drescher
Jeffrey A. Breit
George T. Albiston
Michael F. Imprevento
Latane' Ware Brown
John L. Watts

For full biographical listings, see the Martindale-Hubbell Law Directory

DAVEY & BROGAN, P.C. (AV)

101 Granby Street, Suite 300, 23510
Telephone: 757-622-0100
Telecopier: 757-622-4924
Email: daveylaw@pilot.infi.net *URL:* http://www.lawyers.com/davey&associates

Philip N. Davey
Patrick M. Brogan
R. Arthur Jett, Jr.

Representative Clients: GRE Insurance Group; Marine Office of America Corp.; Spliethoff's Bevrachtingskantoor B.V.; W.F. Magann Corp.; The North of England Protecting and Indemnity Association Limited; Evergreen America Corporation; Sveriges Angfartygs Assurans Forening "The Swedish Club"; Mediterranean Shipping Co., S.A.
Reference: Crestar Bank.

For full biographical listings, see the Martindale-Hubbell Law Directory

VANDEVENTER BLACK LLP (AV)

500 World Trade Center, 23510-1699
Telephone: 757-446-8600
Cable Address: "Hughsvan"
Telecopier: 757-446-8670
URL: http://www.vanblk.com
Kitty Hawk, North Carolina Office: 6 Juniper Trail.
Telephone: 252-261-5055.
Fax: 252-261-8444. E-Mail: nshearin@pinn.net.
London, England Office: Mitre House, 4th Floor, 12-14 Mitre Street.
Telephone: (0171) 623-2081.
Facsimile: (0171) 929-0043.

PARTNERS OF FIRM

Walter B. Martin, Jr.
Morton H. Clark
John M. Ryan
G. William Birkhead
Geoffrey F. Birkhead
Carter T. Gunn
Mark T. Coberly
F. Nash Bilisoly
Henry P. Bouffard
Edward J. Powers
Lawrence G. Cohen

For Complete List of Firm Personnel, See General Section

For full biographical listings, see the Martindale-Hubbell Law Directory

WASHINGTON

BAINBRIDGE ISLAND, Kitsap Co.

MORROW & OTOROWSKI (AV)

298 Winslow Way West, 98110
Telephone: 206-842-1000
Facsimile: 206-842-0797
URL: http://www.medilaw.com
Email: m-o@medilaw.com *URL:* http://www.lawyers.com/medilaw

MEMBERS OF FIRM

Albert Morrow
Christopher L. Otorowski

ASSOCIATE

Carol N. Johnston

For full biographical listings, see the Martindale-Hubbell Law Directory

*SEATTLE,** King Co.

DANIELSON HARRIGAN & TOLLEFSON, LLP (AV)

A Limited Liability Partnership including a Professional Service Corporation
999 Third Avenue, 44th Floor, 98104
Telephone: 206-623-1700
Facsimile: 206-623-8717
Email: lawfirm@dh-t.com

(See Next Column)

DANIELSON HARRIGAN & TOLLEFSON LLP—*Continued*

David Danielson (P.S.)
Arthur W. Harrigan, Jr.
G. Val Tollefson
Timothy G. Leyh
Michelle Buhler
Karl F. Oles
Charles Jordan

COUNSEL

Richard H. Holmquist
Katherine See Kennedy
Matthew R. Kenney
Terence K. McGee

ASSOCIATES

Randall Thomsen
Michael M.K. Hemphill

For full biographical listings, see the Martindale-Hubbell Law Directory

THE DAVIS FIRM (AV)

5301 Ballard Avenue N.W., 98107
Telephone: 206-789-1056
Fax: 206-789-9690
Email: thedavisfirm@seanet.com *URL:* http://www.lawyers.com/thedavisfirm

MEMBERS OF FIRM

Susan R. Davis
Donald K. Davis

For full biographical listings, see the Martindale-Hubbell Law Directory

GARVEY, SCHUBERT & BARER (AV)

1191 Second Avenue, 18th Floor, 98101
Telephone: 206-464-3939
Cable Address: "Lex, Seattle"
Telecopier: 206-464- 0125
Washington, D.C. Office: 5th Floor, 1000 Potomac Street, N.W., 20007.
Telephone: 202-965-7880.
Telecopier: 202-965-1729.
Portland, Oregon Office: Eleventh Floor, 121 S.W. Morrison Street, 97204.
Telephone: 503-228-3939.
Telecopier: 503-226-0259.

MEMBERS OF FIRM

Barbara L. Holland
Stephen B. Johnson
James G. Kibble
E. Charles Routh
Alan P. Sherbrooke
Gary J. Strauss
David R. West
Susan Richardson Willert

RESIDENT ASSOCIATES

Elizabeth Lynn Hubbard
Pegeen Mulhern
Donald B. Scaramastra

OF COUNSEL

Stanley H. Barer
Steven M. Dickinson
Kenneth L. Karlberg
Bruce A. King

Representative Clients: B.P. America, Inc.; China Ocean Shipping (Group) Company; Foss Maritime Co.; Totem Ocean Trailer Express, Inc.; United Kingdom Mutual Steamship Assurance Assn.

For Complete List of Firm Personnel, See General Section

For full biographical listings, see the Martindale-Hubbell Law Directory

MADDEN, POLIAK, MACDOUGALL & WILLIAMSON (AV)

1001 Fourth Avenue Plaza, Suite 2800, 98154
Telephone: 206-621-1011
Telecopier: 206-622-6805
Email: maddenpoliak@msn.com

William J. Madden (1908-1987)
Paul M. Poliak
Allan L. MacDougall
Michael H. Williamson
Rodney Q. Fonda
Craig L. Watson
Bradley P. Scarp
Tom Montgomery

Representative Clients: American International Marine Agency; Chubb Pacific Indemnity; CIGNA; Colony Insurance Company; Commercial Fisherman's Inter-Insurance Exchange; Commercial Union; Fireman's Fund Insurance Company; GRE (Albany); Great American Insurance Company; Highlands Insurance Company.

For full biographical listings, see the Martindale-Hubbell Law Directory

MIKKELBORG, BROZ, WELLS & FRYER, PLLC (AV)

Suite 3600, 1001 Fourth Avenue, 98154
Telephone: 206-623-5890
Facsimile: 206-623-0965
Email: mail@mbwf.com

MEMBERS OF FIRM

Robert O. Wells, Jr.
Douglas M. Fryer
Richard L. Phillips
Jeffrey L. Jernegan
Margaret Doyle Fitzpatrick
Jess G. Webster
Newell D. Smith
Mitchell A. Broz

ASSOCIATES

Victor V. Hoff
Rebecca T. White

OF COUNSEL

G. Lawrence Salkield
John E. Lenker

(See Next Column)

COUNSEL

Jacob A. Mikkelborg
Richard F. Broz

LEGAL SUPPORT PERSONNEL

M. Brigid Browne

Representative Clients: Alaska Ocean Seafoods; All Alaskan Seafoods, Inc.; Alyeska Ocean, Inc.; Alyeska Seafoods, Inc.; Arctic Alaska, Inc. Arctic Fjord, Inc.; Arctic Storm, Inc.; Premier Pacific Seafoods, Inc.; TAMS Consultants, Inc.; Wards Cove Packing Co., Inc.

For full biographical listings, see the Martindale-Hubbell Law Directory

WEST VIRGINIA

*CHARLESTON,** Kanawha Co.

JACKSON & KELLY (AV)

1600 Laidley Tower, P.O. Box 553, 25322
Telephone: 304-340-1000
Fax: 304-340-1130
Email: info@jacksonkelly.com *URL:* http://www.jacksonkelly.com
Martinsburg, West Virginia Office: 300 Foxcroft Avenue, P.O. Box 1068.
Telephone: 304-263-8800.
Fax: 304-263-7110.
Morgantown, West Virginia Office: 6000 Hampton Center, P.O. Box 619.
Telephone: 304-599-3000.
Fax: 304-285-2040.
New Martinsville, West Virginia Office: 256 Russell Avenue, P.O. Box 68.
Telephone: 304-455-1751.
Fax: 304-455-6314.
Parkersburg, West Virginia Office: 412 Market Street, Suite 202, P.O. Box 1144.
Telephone: 304-424-3490.
Fax: 304-424-3499.
Fairmont, West Virginia Office: 1000 Technology Drive, Suite 1310.
Telephone: 304-368-2000.
Fax: 304-368-2020.
Lexington, Kentucky Office: 175 East Main Street, Suite 500, P.O. Box 2150.
Telephone: 606-255-9500.
Fax: 606-281-6478.
Washington, D. C. Office: 2401 Pennsylvania Avenue, N.W., Suite 400.
Telephone: 202-973-0200.
Fax: 202-973-0232.
Denver, Colorado Office: Suite 2710, 1660 Lincoln Street.
Telephone: 303-390-0003.
Fax: 303-390-0040.
Wheeling, West Virginia Office: 1144 Market Street.
Telephone: 304-233-4000.
Fax: 304-233-4077.

MEMBERS OF FIRM

A. L. Emch
Larry W. Blalock (Administrative Manager, New Martinsville and Wheeling, West Virginia Offices)
Thomas J. Hurney, Jr.
William J. Powell

Representative Clients: Madison Coal & Supply Company; Crounse Corporation.

For Complete List of Firm Personnel, See General Section

For full biographical listings, see the Martindale-Hubbell Law Directory

WISCONSIN

*MADISON,** Dane Co.

QUARLES & BRADY LLP (AV)

Firstar Plaza, One South Pinckney Street, P.O. Box 2113, 53701-2113
Telephone: 608-251-5000
Fax: 608-251-9166
URL: http://www.quarles.com
Milwaukee, Wisconsin Office: 411 East Wisconsin Avenue, 53202-4497.
Telephone: 414-277-5000.
Fax: 414-271-3552.
West Palm Beach, Florida Office: 222 Lakeview Avenue, 4th Floor, 33401.
Telephone: 561-653-5000.
Fax: 561-653-5333.
Naples, Florida Office: Barnett Center, 4501 Tamiami Trail North, Suite 300, 34103-3060.
Telephone: 941-262-5959.
Fax: 941-434-4999.

(See Next Column)

QUARLES & BRADY LLP, *Madison—Continued*

Phoenix, Arizona Office: One Camelback Building, One East Camelback Road, Suite 400, 85012-1649.
Telephone: 602-230-5500.
Fax: 602-230-5598.
Chicago, Illinois Office: Quarles & Brady LLC, Citicorp Center, 500 West Madison Street, Suite 3700.
Telephone: 312-715-5000.
Fax: 312-715-5155.

PARTNER

Anthony H. Driessen

For Complete List of Firm Personnel, See General Section

For full biographical listings, see the Martindale-Hubbell Law Directory

*MILWAUKEE,** Milwaukee Co.

COOK & FRANKE S.C. (AV)

660 East Mason Street, 53202
Telephone: 414-271-5900
Facsimile: 414-271-2002

William A. Jennaro

Representative Clients: The United Kingdom Mutual Steam Ship Assurance Association; The Liverpool and London Steamship P&I Association, Ltd.; The Standard Steamship Owners' P&I Association, Ltd.; Assuranceforeningen Gard; Newcastle P&I Association; The Steamship Mutual Underwriting Association, Ltd.; The North of England P&I Association, Ltd.; The Britannia Steamship Insurance Association, Ltd.; The London Steamship Owners' Mutual Insurance Association, Ltd.; West of England Ship Owners Mutual Insurance Association.

For Complete List of Firm Personnel, See General Section

For full biographical listings, see the Martindale-Hubbell Law Directory

DAVIS & KUELTHAU, S.C. (AV)

111 East Kilbourn Avenue, Suite 1400, 53202-6613
Telephone: 414-276-0200
Facsimile: 414-276-9369
Cable Address: "Shiplaw"
Email: info@daviskuelthau.com *URL:* http://www.daviskuelthau.com
Madison, Wisconsin Office: Ten East Doty Street, Suite 600, P.O. Box 1068, 53703.
Telephone: 608-280-8235.
Fax: 608-280-8231.
Sheboygan, Wisconsin Office: 605 North Eighth, Suite 610, P.O. Box 1287.
Telephone: 920-451-1461.
Fax: 920-451-1465.
Green Bay, Wisconsin Office: 414 East Walnut Street, Suite 240.
Telephone: 920-435-9378.
Fax: 920-435-9391.

James E. Braza
David W. Neeb
James E. Culhane
Kathy L. Nusslock
Louis F. Raymond

Admiralty Counsel For: The American Club; Great Lakes Towing Co.; Through Transport Insurance; Marine Office of America Corp.; Mutual Marine Office, Inc.; The Mutual Assurance Association SKULD; Scandinavian Marine Claims Office, Inc.; Shipowners Claims Bureau, Inc.; Swedish Shipowners Insurance Assn.; West of England Ship Owners Mutual Insurance Association.

For full biographical listings, see the Martindale-Hubbell Law Directory

GUNTA & REAK, S.C. (AV)

219 North Milwaukee Street, 53202
Telephone: 414-291-7979
Facsimile: 414-291-7960
Email: gntareak@execpc.com *URL:* http://www.lawyers.com/gntareak

Gregg J. Gunta
Kevin P. Reak
Joseph A. McCarthy

Ann C. Wirth

OF COUNSEL

Gary A. Gerlach

For full biographical listings, see the Martindale-Hubbell Law Directory

PUERTO RICO

SAN JUAN, San Juan Dist.

JIMÉNEZ, GRAFFAM & LAUSELL

Suite 505, Midtown Building, 421 Muñoz Rivera Avenue, Hato Rey, P.O. Box 366104, 00936-6104
Telephone: 787-767-1030; 767-1000; 767-1061; 767-1064
Telefax: 787-751-4068;
Cable: "Nezte"
RCA Telex: 325-2730
Email: manager@jgl.com *URL:* http://www.jgl.com

MEMBERS OF FIRM

William A. Graffam
J. Ramón Rivera-Morales
Manolo T. Rodríguez-Bird

ASSOCIATES

Patricia A. Garrity
Edgardo A. Vega-López
Isabel J. Vélez-Serrano
Jorge F. Blasini

Representative Clients: Crowley Maritime Corp.; Sea-Land Service, Inc.; The United Kingdom Steamship P & I Association; The Japan Ship Owners' Mutual Protection & Indemnity Association; The West of England Ship Owners Mutual Protection and Indemnity Association (Luxembourg); The Britannia Steamship Insurance Association, Ltd.; Assuranceforeningen Skuld, Norway; The Standard Steamship Owners' Protection & Indemnity Association (Bermuda); Liverpool & London Steamship Protection & Indemnity Association, Ltd.

For Complete List of Firm Personnel, See General Section

For full biographical listings, see the Martindale-Hubbell Law Directory

CANADA
BRITISH COLUMBIA

*VANCOUVER,** Vancouver Co.

MCEWEN, SCHMITT & CO. (AV)

1615 - 1055 West Georgia Street, P.O. Box 11174 - Royal Centre, V6E 3R5
Telephone: 604-683-1223
Telecopier: 604-683-2359
Telex: 04-51388
Email: mail@marinelawcanada.com *URL:* http://www.marinelawcanada.com

MEMBERS OF FIRM

David F. McEwen
Douglas G. Schmitt
John M. McEwen (1911-1988)

ASSOCIATES

Gregory G. Blue
Susan A. Stonier
Roger S. Watts

For full biographical listings, see the Martindale-Hubbell Law Directory

CANADA
NEW BRUNSWICK

*SAINT JOHN,** Saint John Co.

CLARK DRUMMIE (AV)

40 Wellington Row, P.O. Box 6850, E2L 4S3
Telephone: 506-633-3800
Telecopier (Automatic): 506-633-3811
Email: cd@nbnet.nb.ca

MEMBER OF FIRM

M. Robert Jette

Reference: Royal Bank of Canada.

For Complete List of Firm Personnel, See General Section

For full biographical listings, see the Martindale-Hubbell Law Directory

CANADA NEWFOUNDLAND

*ST. JOHN'S,**

McInnes Cooper (AV)

Barristers, Solicitors & Trade Mark Agents
Baine Johnston Centre, 5th Floor, 10 Fort William Place, P.O. Box 5939, A1C 5X4
Telephone: 709-722-8735
Telecopier: 709-722-1763
Email: mcrsj@mcrlaw.com *URL:* http://www.mcrlaw.com
Halifax, Nova Scotia Office: Summit Place, 1601 Lower Water Street, P.O. Box 730, B3J 2V1.
Telephone: 902-425-6500.
Fax: 902-425-6350. Email: mcrhfx@mcrlaw.com.
Moncton, New Brunswick Office: Place Moncton Place, 655 Main Street, P.O. Box 1368, E1C 8T6.
Telephone: 506-857-8970.
Fax: 506-857-4095. Email: mcrmctn@mcrlaw.com.
Charlottetown, Prince Edward Island Office: BDC Place, Suite 620, 119 Kent Street, C1A 1N3.
Telephone: 902-368-8473.
Fax: 902-368-8346. Email: mcrpei@mcrlaw.com.
Fredericton, New Brunswick Office: Suite 600, 570 Queen Street, P.O. Box 610.
Telephone: 506-458-8572.
Fax: 506-458-9903. Email: mcrfton@mcrlaw.com.

PARTNERS

W. Gary Rowe, Q.C.
Deborah L. J. Hutchings

ASSOCIATE

Dennis N. Clarke

For Complete List of Firm Personnel, See General Section

For full biographical listings, see the Martindale-Hubbell Law Directory

CANADA NOVA SCOTIA

*HALIFAX,** Regional Munic. of Halifax

McInnes Cooper (AV)

Barristers, Solicitors & Trade Mark Agents
Summit Place, 1601 Lower Water Street, P.O. Box 730, B3J 2V1
Telephone: 902-425-6500
Fax: 902-425-6350
Email: mcrhfx@mcrlaw.com *URL:* http://www.mcrlaw.com
St. John's, Newfoundland Office: Baine Johnston Centre, 5th Floor, 10 Fort William Place, P.O. Box 5939, A1C 5X4.
Telephone: 709-722-8735.
Telecopier: 709-722-1763. Email: mcrsj@mcrlaw.com.
Moncton, New Brunswick Office: Place Moncton Place, 655 Main Street, P.O. Box 1368, E1C 8T6.
Telephone: 506-857-8970.
Fax: 506-857-4095. Email: mcrmctn@mcrlaw.com.
Charlottetown, Prince Edward Island Office: BDC Place, Suite 620, 119 Kent Street, C1A 1N3.
Telephone: 902-368-8473.
Fax: 902-368-8346. Email: mcrpei@mcrlaw.com.
Fredericton, New Brunswick Office: Suite 600, 570 Queen Street, P.O. Box 610.
Telephone: 506-458-8572.
Fax: 506-458-9903. Email: mcrfton@mcrlaw.com.

PARTNERS

James E. Gould, Q.C.
Wylie Spicer, Q.C.
Thomas E. Hart

ASSOCIATE

Hugh Wright

For Complete List of Firm Personnel, See General Section

For full biographical listings, see the Martindale-Hubbell Law Directory

CANADA ONTARIO

*TORONTO,** Regional Munic. of Toronto

Borden & Elliot (AV)

Barristers & Solicitors
Scotia Plaza, 40 King Street West, M5H 3Y4
Telephone: 416-367-6000
Telecopier: 416-367-6749
Email: info@borden.com *URL:* http://www.borden.com
Ottawa, Ontario Office: Borden Elliot Scott & Aylen, 1000-60 Rue Queen Street.
Telephone: 613-237-5160; 800-661-4237. General
Facsimile: 613-230-8842. IP Dept.
Facsimile: 613-787-3558. Email: ottinfo@scottaylen.com. URL: http://www.borden.com.

Norman Letalik

For Complete List of Firm Personnel, See General Section

For full biographical listings, see the Martindale-Hubbell Law Directory

CANADA QUEBEC

*MONTREAL,** Montreal Dist.

McMaster Gervais (AV)

A General Partnership
1000 de La Gauchetière Street West, Suite 900, H3B 5H4
Telephone: 514-879-1212
Fax: 514-954-1905
Email: info@mcmastergervais.com *URL:* http://www.mcmastergervais.com

MEMBERS OF FIRM

Sean J. Harrington
Robert E. Charbonneau
D. James Papadimitriou
Yvan Houle
Caroline Matte
Georges R. Thibaudeau
P. Jeremy Bolger
Peter G. Pamel
Darren E.G. McGuire
Manon Gauthier
Stéphane Pitre

COUNSEL

A. Stuart Hyndman, Q.C.

For Complete List of Firm Personnel, See General Section

For full biographical listings, see the Martindale-Hubbell Law Directory

ANTITRUST LAW

MINNESOTA

*MINNEAPOLIS,** Hennepin Co.

SIEGEL, BRILL, GREUPNER, DUFFY & FOSTER, P.A. (AV)

1300 Washington Square, 100 Washington Avenue South, 55401
Telephone: 612-339-7131
Telecopier: 612-339-6591

Gerald S. Duffy
Wood R. Foster, Jr.
Wm. Christopher Penwell
Sherri L. Rohlf
Jordan M. Lewis

Representative Clients: Champion Auto Stores, Inc.; Ron-Vik, Inc.; Aveda Corporation; Applied Spectrum Technology, Inc.; Richard Manufacturing Co.; Mann Theaters; Homecraft Builders, Inc.; The McNeilus Companies; AVR, Inc.

For Complete List of Firm Personnel, See General Section

For full biographical listings, see the Martindale-Hubbell Law Directory

MISSISSIPPI

*JACKSON,** Hinds Co.

ALSTON & JONES (AV)

A Professional Limited Liability Company
121 North State Street, P.O. Drawer 1532, 39215-1532
Telephone: 601-948-6882
Fax: 601-948-6902
Email: ARVS@Teclink.net

MEMBER OF FIRM

Alex A. Alston, Jr.

Counsel for: Ford Motor Co.; E.I. du Pont de Nemours Co.; Gannett Co., Inc.; Conoco, Inc.; Jostens, Inc.; General Electric Company; Georgia-Pacific Corp.; Dean Witter Reynolds, Inc.; Prudential Securities, Inc.; Transcontinental Gas Pipeline Inc.

For Complete List of Firm Personnel, See General Section

For full biographical listings, see the Martindale-Hubbell Law Directory

MISSOURI

KANSAS CITY, Jackson, Clay, Platte & Cass Cos.

SHUGHART THOMSON & KILROY, A PROFESSIONAL CORPORATION (AV)

Twelve Wyandotte Plaza, 120 West 12th Street, 64105
Telephone: 816-421-3355
Email: Solutions@KC.STKLAW.COM *URL:* http://www.STKLAW.COM
Overland Park, Kansas Office: Suite 1100, 32 Corporate Woods, 9225 Indian Creek Parkway 66210.
Telephone: 913-451-3355.
Springfield, Missouri Office: Suite 1200, Hammons Tower, 901 St. Louis, 65806.
Telephone: 417-869-3353.
Denver, Colorado Office: 1050 17th Street, Suite 2350. 80265.
Telephone: 303-572-9300.
Fax: 303-572-7883.

R. Lawrence Ward
George E. Leonard
John M. Kilroy, Jr.
Dennis D. Palmer
William E. Quirk
Jennifer Gille Bacon
Philip W. Bledsoe

OF COUNSEL

Robert R. Raymond

For Complete List of Firm Personnel, See General Section

For full biographical listings, see the Martindale-Hubbell Law Directory

ST. LOUIS, (Independent City)

ARMSTRONG TEASDALE LLP (AV)

A Partnership including Professional Corporations
One Metropolitan Square, 63102-2740
Telephone: 314-621-5070
Facsimile: 314-621-5065
Twx: 910 761-2246
Cable: ATKV LAW
Email: armstrongteasdale@armstrongteasdale.com *URL:* http://www.armstrongteasdale.com
Kansas City, Missouri Office: 2345 Grand Boulevard, Suite 2000, 64108.
Telephone: 816-221-3420.
Facsimile: 816-221-0786.
Jefferson City, Missouri Office: 3405 W. Truman Blvd., Suite 210, 65109.
Telephone: 573-636-8394.
Washington, D.C. Office: 1747 Pennsylvania Avenue, N.W., Suite 300, 20006.
Telephone: 202-347-0259.
Belleville, Illinois Office: 23 South First Street, 62220.
Telephone: 618-397-4411.
Olathe, Kansas Office: 100 East Park, 66061.
Telephone: 913-345-0706.
Shanghai, China Office: A-T International Consultants, LLC, Suite 310, No. 12 Zhongshan Road (E1), Shanghai 200002 P.R.C.
Telephone: 86-21-6326-7001.
Facsimile: 86-21-6326-0626.

MEMBERS OF FIRM

Thomas Cummings (P.C.)
Glenn E. Davis (Assistant Chair, Litigation Department. Chair, Antitrust Trade Regulation and Distribution Law Practice Group)
Byron E. Francis (P.C.)
Jay A. Summerville
Therese Rolufs Trelz

ASSOCIATE

Daniel C. Nelson

Representative Clients: Advanced Elastomer Systems, L.P.; AmerenUE; Clark Oil & Refining Corporation; Enterprise Capital Companies; Jefferson Smurfit Corporation; Manna Pro Corporation; M.D. Consult, L.L.C.; Southwestern Bell Corporation.

For Complete List of Firm Personnel, See General Section

For full biographical listings, see the Martindale-Hubbell Law Directory

KOHN, SHANDS, ELBERT, GIANOULAKIS & GILJUM, LLP (AV)

24th Floor, One Mercantile Center, 63101
Telephone: 314-241-3963
Telecopier: 314-241-2509
Email: attys@ksegg.com

Alan C. Kohn
John Gianoulakis
Mark J. Bremer

For full biographical listings, see the Martindale-Hubbell Law Directory

LEWIS, RICE & FINGERSH (AV)

A Limited Liability Company
500 North Broadway, Suite 2000, 63102-2147
Telephone: 314-444-7600
Telecopier: 314-241-6056
URL: http://www.lrf.com
Belleville, Illinois Office: 325 South High Street.
Telephone: 618-234-8636.
Leawood, Kansas Office: Suite 375, 8900 State Line Road.
Telephone: 913-381-8898.
Creve Coeur, Missouri Office: 700 Office Parkway, Suite 15.
Telephone: 314-569-2262.
Kansas City, Missouri Office: 1010 Walnut, Suite 500.
Telephone: 816-421-2500.
Washington, Missouri Office: 216 West Main, P.O. Box 1040.
Telephone: 636-239-7747.

RESIDENT MEMBERS

Allen S. Boston
Barry A. Short
Richard B. Walsh, Jr.

OF COUNSEL

Robert Smith Allen

For Complete List of Firm Personnel, See General Section

For full biographical listings, see the Martindale-Hubbell Law Directory

*SPRINGFIELD,** Greene Co.

WILLIAM H. McDONALD & ASSOCIATES, P.C. (AV)

300 South Jefferson, Suite 600, P.O. Box 1245, 65801
Telephone: 417-869-0581
Facsimile: 417-831-7852
Email: mcdassoc@dialnet.net *URL:* http://www.mcdonaldassoc.com

William H. McDonald

(See Next Column)

WILLIAM H. MCDONALD & ASSOCIATES, P.C., *Springfield—Continued*

Stuart H. King
James A. Endicott
Dana A. Chamblee

For Complete List of Firm Personnel, See General Section

For full biographical listings, see the Martindale-Hubbell Law Directory

NEBRASKA

*LINCOLN,** Lancaster Co.

CLINE, WILLIAMS, WRIGHT, JOHNSON & OLDFATHER (AV)

1900 U.S. Bank Building, 233 South 13th Street, 68508
Telephone: 402-474-6900
Fax: 402-474-5393
Email: postmaster@cline-law.com *URL:* http://www.cline-law.com
Omaha, Nebraska Office: Suite 720, One Pacific Place, 1125 South 103rd Street, 68124.
Telephone: 402-397-1700.
Fax: 402-397-1806.

ATTORNEYS

Allen L. Graves
Charles M. Pallesen, Jr.
Fredric H. Kauffman
Donald F. Burt
Alan E. Peterson
Stephen E. Gehring
Robert J. Routh
Kevin Colleran
L. Bruce Wright
James M. Bausch
Larry A. Holle
David R. Buntain
Stephen H. Nelsen
Michael C. Mueller
Lauren W. Wismer
Daniel R. Stogsdill
Scott D. Kelly
Terry R. Wittler
Pamela Hastings Carrier
Mark A. Christensen
Richard P. Garden, Jr.
Shawn D. Renner
John C. Miles
Mary Kay Frank
Thomas C. Huston
Sonya S. Ekart
Don R. Janssen
Susan Kubert Sapp
Kevin J. Schneider
Andrew D. Strotman
Jill Gossin Jensen
Rochelle A. Mullen
John L. Horan
Bryan S. Hatch
Steven C. Likes
Tracy A. Oldemeyer
Jolene M. Papa
Timothy G. Aschoff
Eric N. Bergquist
Janis J. Winterhof
Andrea Dylan Snowden

OF COUNSEL

Charles E. Wright
Richard P. Jeffries
Mary M. Campbell

RETIRED PARTNERS

Flavel A. Wright (Retired)
Warren C. Johnson (Retired)
Charles E. Oldfather (1927-1998)

Representative Clients: U.S. Bank National Association; University of Nebraska; Nebraska Medical Assn.; Saint Elizabeth Regional Medical Center; Media of Nebraska; Cargill Inc.; State Farm Insurance Cos.; Wal-Mart Stores, Inc.; Textron/Cushman; Isco, Inc.

For full biographical listings, see the Martindale-Hubbell Law Directory

*OMAHA,** Douglas Co.

MCGRATH, NORTH, MULLIN & KRATZ, P.C. (AV)

Suite 1400, One Central Park Plaza, 68102
Telephone: 402-341-3070
Fax: 402-341-0216

John P. Passarelli
Mark F. Enenbach
Edward G. Warin
David H. Roe
Sandra D. Morar

General Counsel for: ConAgra, Inc.; InaCom Corp.; Omaha Airport Authority; Physicians Mutual Insurance Co.; Supertel Hospitality, Inc.; Valmont Industries, Inc.
Representative Clients: Clarkson Hospital; Omaha Chamber of Commerce.
Insurance Clients: American Family Insurance Group; Blue Cross-Blue Shield of Nebraska.

For Complete List of Firm Personnel, See General Section

For full biographical listings, see the Martindale-Hubbell Law Directory

NEVADA

HENDERSON, Clark Co.

ROOKER & GIBSON (AV)

Suite 105, 701 North Green Valley Parkway, 89014
Telephone: 702-990-8100
Telecopier: 702-932-5266

C. Keith Rooker
James B. Gibson

Reference: BankWest of Nevada.

For full biographical listings, see the Martindale-Hubbell Law Directory

NEW JERSEY

*MORRISTOWN,** Morris Co.

PITNEY, HARDIN, KIPP & SZUCH LLP (AV)

P.O. Box 1945, 07962-1945
Telephone: 973-966-6300
New York City: 212-687-6000
Telex: 642014
Telecopier: 973-966-1550
URL: http://www.phks.com
New York, New York Office: 711 Third Avenue, 10017-4014.
Telephone: 212-687-6000.
Fax: 212-682-3485.

MEMBERS OF FIRM

Clyde A. Szuch
Murray J. Laulicht
Frederick L. Whitmer

Representative Clients: AGFA Division-Bayer Corporation; Sony Electronics.

For Complete List of Firm Personnel, See General Section

For full biographical listings, see the Martindale-Hubbell Law Directory

*NEWARK,** Essex Co.

CARPENTER, BENNETT & MORRISSEY (AV)

Three Gateway Center, 17th Floor, 100 Mulberry Street, 07102-4079
Telephone: 973-622-7711
New York City: 212-943-6530
Telex: 139405
Telecopier: 973-622-5314
Email: cbm@carpben.com

MEMBERS OF FIRM

Michael S. Waters
John F. Lynch, Jr.
Robert J. Stickles
Lois H. Goodman

ASSOCIATES

Daniel J. O'Hern, Jr.
Steven J. Santarsiero
Marc E. Wolin
Melissa B. Popkin
Kerry A. O'Shea

Representative Clients: General Motors Corp.; E. I. du Pont de Nemours and Co.; Texaco Inc.; AT&T; Litton Industries; ITT Industries, Inc.; International Flavors & Fragrances Inc.; Prudential Insurance Company of America; Rutgers, The State University of New Jersey; Johnson & Johnson.

For Complete List of Firm Personnel, See General Section

For full biographical listings, see the Martindale-Hubbell Law Directory

HELLRING LINDEMAN GOLDSTEIN & SIEGAL LLP (AV)

One Gateway Center, 07102-5386
Telephone: 973-621-9020
Fax: 973-621-7406
Englewood, New Jersey Office: 32-40 North Dean Street.
Telephone: 201-871-3060.

Jonathan L. Goldstein
Richard D. Shapiro
Robert S. Raymar
Stephen L. Dreyfuss
Matthew E. Moloshok

For Complete List of Firm Personnel, See General Section

For full biographical listings, see the Martindale-Hubbell Law Directory

MCCARTER & ENGLISH, LLP (AV)

Four Gateway Center, 100 Mulberry Street, P.O. Box 652, 07101-0652
Telephone: 973-622-4444
Telecopier: 973-624-7070
URL: http://www.mccarter.com
Cherry Hill, New Jersey Office: 1820 Chapel Avenue West, Suite 380.
Telephone: 609-662-8444.
Telecopier: 609-662-6203.

(See Next Column)

McCarter & English LLP—*Continued*

New York, New York Office: Suite 2247, One World Trade Center.
Telephone: 212-466-9018.
Telecopier: 212-432-6568.
Boca Raton, Florida Office: 2255 Glades Road, Suite 319-A.
Telephone: 561-994-6262.
Telecopier: 561-241-0798.
Wilmington, Delaware Office: Mellon Bank Center, 919 Market Street.
Telephone: 302-654-8010.
Telecopier: 302-654-0795.
Philadelphia, Pennsylvania Office: One Commerce Square, 2005 Market Street, Suite 3600.
Telephone: 215-557-7700.
Telecopier: 215-557-6544.

MEMBERS OF FIRM

William J. O'Shaughnessy
Richard M. Eittreim
Seth T. Taube
Harvey C. Kaish

For Complete List of Firm Personnel, See General Section

For full biographical listings, see the Martindale-Hubbell Law Directory

Sills Cummis Radin Tischman Epstein & Gross, A Professional Corporation (AV)

One Riverfront Plaza, 07102-5400
Telephone: 973-643-7000
Fax: 973-643-6500
Telex: 820630 Sillsbeck Nwk
Email: sillsmail@sillscummis.com *URL:* http://www.sillscummis.com
Atlantic City, New Jersey Office: 17 Gordon's Alley.
Telephone: 609-344-2800.
New York, N.Y. Office: 712 Fifth Avenue.
Telephone: 212-643-7000.
Washington, D.C. Office: 1800 K Street, N.W.
Telephone: 202-296-4750.

MEMBERS OF FIRM

Lawrence S. Horn
Jeffrey J. Greenbaum

Jennifer L. Borofsky

For Complete List of Firm Personnel, See General Section

For full biographical listings, see the Martindale-Hubbell Law Directory

WEST ORANGE, Essex Co.

Alpert, Butler & Sanders, P.C. (AV)

The Alpert Professional Building, 449 Mount Pleasant Avenue, 07052
Telephone: 973-325-1188
Fax: 973-325-3399
Email: mailbox@abslaw.com *URL:* http://www.abslaw.com
New York, New York Office: 509 Madison Avenue.
Telephone: 212-758-6958.
Fax: 212-758-2817.

Clark E. Alpert
David N. Butler
William D. Sanders

OF COUNSEL

Martin L. Bearg
Ted M. Rosen (Not admitted in NJ)

Elliot L. Lewis
Matthew J. Rice

LEGAL SUPPORT PERSONNEL

PARALEGAL

Robin S. Karpel

For full biographical listings, see the Martindale-Hubbell Law Directory

NEW MEXICO

*ALBUQUERQUE,** Bernalillo Co.

Eaves, Bardacke, Baugh Kierst & Kiernan, P.A. (AV)

6400 Uptown Boulevard, N.E., Suite 110-W, P.O. Box 35670, 87176
Telephone: 505-888-4300
Facsimile: 505-883-4406
Email: LGLEAVES@EB-B.com

John M. Eaves
Paul Bardacke
John G. Baugh
Peter S. Kierst
Kerry Kiernan

Derek V. Larson
Karen S. Mendenhall
C. Shannon Bacon

(See Next Column)

OF COUNSEL

Jennifer J. Pruett

For full biographical listings, see the Martindale-Hubbell Law Directory

Freedman Boyd Daniels Hollander Goldberg & Cline P.A. (AV)

20 First Plaza, Suite 700, 87102
Telephone: 505-842-9960
Fax: 505-842-0761

Joseph Goldberg

Scott M. Davidson

For full biographical listings, see the Martindale-Hubbell Law Directory

Huffaker & Conway, A Professional Corporation (AV)

201 Third Street, N.W., Suite 1910, 87103-1190
Telephone: 505-244-0021
Facsimile: 505-244-1372
Email: albstaff@sisna.com
Santa Fe, New Mexico Office: 155 Grant Avenue, P.O. Box 1868.
Telephone: 505-988-8921.
Fax: 505-983-3927.

Gregory D. Huffaker, Jr.
Ann Maloney Conway
Lisa A. Joynes
Seth L. Sparks
Edward C. Bagley

For full biographical listings, see the Martindale-Hubbell Law Directory

Rodey, Dickason, Sloan, Akin & Robb, P.A. (AV)

Albuquerque Plaza, Suite 2200, 201 Third Street, N.W., P.O. Box 1888, 87103-1888
Telephone: 505-765-5900
Fax: 505-768-7395
Email: info@rodey.com *URL:* http://www.rodey.com
Santa Fe, New Mexico Office: Suite 101 Marcy Plaza, 123 East Marcy Street, P.O. Box 1357, 87504-1357.
Telephone: 505-984-0100.
Fax: 505-989-9542.

William S. Dixon
John P. Burton (Resident, Santa Fe Office)
Edward Ricco

For Complete List of Firm Personnel, See General Section

For full biographical listings, see the Martindale-Hubbell Law Directory

*SANTA FE,** Santa Fe Co.

Huffaker & Conway, A Professional Corporation (AV)

155 Grant Avenue, P.O. Box 1868, 87504-1868
Telephone: 505-988-8921
Fax: 505-983-3927
Email: sfstaff@sisna.com
Albuquerque, New Mexico Office: 201 Third Street, N.W., Suite 1910.
Telephone: 505-244-0021.
Facsimile: 505-244-1372.

Gregory D. Huffaker, Jr.
Ann Maloney Conway
Lisa A. Joynes
Seth L. Sparks
Edward C. Bagley

For full biographical listings, see the Martindale-Hubbell Law Directory

NEW YORK

*NEW YORK,** New York Co.

Anderson Kill & Olick, P.C. (AV)

1251 Avenue of the Americas, 10020-1182
Telephone: 212-278-1000
Fax: 212-278-1733
Email: AKO@andersonkill.com *URL:* http://www.andersonkill.com
Washington, D.C. Office: Anderson Kill & Olick, L.L.P., 2000 Pennsylvania Avenue, N.W., Suite 7500.
Telephone: 202-728-3100.
Fax: 202-728-3199.
Philadelphia, Pennsylvania Office: 1600 Market Street.
Telephone: 215-568-4202.
Fax: 215-568-4573.
Newark, New Jersey Office: One Gateway Center, Suite 0901.
Telephone: 973-642-5858.
Fax: 973-621-6361.
Chicago, Illinois Office: Anderson Kill & Olick, 227 West Monroe Street, Mezzanine Level.
Telephone: 312-857-2500.
Fax: 312-857-0122.

(See Next Column)

ANDERSON KILL & OLICK P.C., *New York—Continued*

Eugene R. Anderson
Michael A. Berkowitz (Not admitted in NY)
John B. Berringer
Malcolm T. Brown
Jeannine W. Chanes
Steven Cooper
John H. Doyle, III
David A. Einhorn
Kirsten M. Eriksson
Jean M. Farrell
Jeremy J. Flanagan
Gloria J. Frank
Mark Garbowski
John P. Gasior
Linda Gerstel
Ann S. Ginsberg
Jeffrey L. Glatzer
Joshua Gold
Finley T. R. Harckham
Robert M. Horkovich
Edward M. Joyce
R. Mark Keenan
Thomas L. Kent
Lawrence Kill
Whitman G.S. Knapp
Ann V. Kramer
Richard P. Lewis
Sandra L. Mallenbaum
John G. Nevius
William G. Passannante
Bennett Pine
Anthony Princi
J. Andrew Rahl, Jr.
Maria-Christina Ricarte
David M. Schlecker
David J. Schwartz
Edan Dawn Segal
Jordan W. Siev
Mark D. Silverschotz
Edward J. Stein (Not admitted in NY)
C. Alexander Teu
Irene C. Warshauer
Mark L. Weyman
Judith A. Yavitz
Nicholas J. Zoogman

OF COUNSEL

Roy Babitt
Dona Seeman Kahn
Arthur S. Olick
Melvin Salberg

For full biographical listings, see the Martindale-Hubbell Law Directory

BERNSTEIN LITOWITZ BERGER & GROSSMANN LLP (AV)

1285 Avenue of the Americas, 10019
Telephone: 212-554-1400
Telecopier: 212-554-1444
Email: blbg@blbglaw.com *URL:* http://www.blbglaw.com

MEMBERS OF FIRM

Paul M. Bernstein (1929-1990)
Max W. Berger
Edward A. Grossmann
Jeffrey A. Klafter
Daniel L. Berger
Douglas M. McKeige
Seth R. Lesser
John P. Coffey
Robert S. Gans
Darnley Dickinson Stewart

ASSOCIATES

Lisa K. Buckser
Thomas E. Chase
Patricia S. Gillane
Leah Beth Guggenheimer
Rochelle Feder Hansen
Jeffrey N. Leibell
Nancy Bea Lipin
Louis C. Paul
Ryan D. Poliakoff
Robert W. Rodriguez (Not admitted in NY)
Gerald H. Silk
Steven B. Singer

OF COUNSEL

Ronald Litowitz

For full biographical listings, see the Martindale-Hubbell Law Directory

CONSTANTINE & PARTNERS (AV)

477 Madison Avenue, 11th Floor, 10022
Telephone: 212-350-2700
Facsimile: 212-350-2701
Email: info@cpny.com *URL:* http://www.cpny.com

Lloyd Constantine
Mitchell C. Shapiro
Robert L. Begleiter
Yang Chen
Jeffrey Shinder
Abby S. Milstein
Stacey A. Mahoney
Philip G. Barber
Allen Dolberg
Douglas J. Goglia
Gary J. Malone
Gordon Schnell
Matthew L. Cantor
Alysia A. Dashef
Amy N. Roth

For full biographical listings, see the Martindale-Hubbell Law Directory

LOEB & LOEB LLP (AV)

A Limited Liability Partnership including Professional Corporations
345 Park Avenue, 10154-0037
Telephone: 212-407-4000
Facsimile: 212-407-4990
Email: info@loeb.com *URL:* http://www.loeb.com
Los Angeles, California Office: Suite 1800, 1000 Wilshire Boulevard, 90017-2475.
Telephone: 213-688-3400.
Facsimile: 213-688-3460.
Century City (Los Angeles), California Office: Suite 2200, 10100 Santa Monica Boulevard, Los Angeles, 90067-4164.
Telephone: 310-282-2000.
Facsimile: 310-282-2192.
Nashville, Tennessee Office: 45 Music Square West, 37203-3205.
Telephone: 615-749-8300.
Facsimile: 615-749-8308.

(See Next Column)

Rome, Italy Office: Piazza Digione 1, 00197.
Telephone: 011-3906-808-8456.
Facsimile: 011-3906-808-8288.

MEMBER OF FIRM

Charles H. Miller

For Complete List of Firm Personnel, See General Section

For full biographical listings, see the Martindale-Hubbell Law Directory

LOVELL & STEWART, LLP (AV)

A Limited Liability Partnership including a Professional Corporation
500 Fifth Avenue, 10110
Telephone: 212-608-1900
Telefax: 212-719-4677
Email: sklovell@aol.com

Christopher Lovell, P.C.
Victor E. Stewart
Gary S. Jacobson

Peggy J. Wedgworth
Geoffrey M. Horn
William W. Foshay, III
Ian T. Stoll

For full biographical listings, see the Martindale-Hubbell Law Directory

MILBERG WEISS BERSHAD HYNES & LERACH LLP (AV)

One Pennsylvania Plaza, 10119
Telephone: 212-594-5300
San Diego, California Office: 600 West Broadway, 1800 One America Plaza.
Telephone: 619-231-1058.
San Francisco, California Office: 100 Pine Street, 26th Floor.
Telephone: 415-288-4545.
Fax: 415-288-4534.
Los Angeles, California Office: 355 South Grand Avenue, Suite 4170, 90071.
Telephone: 213-617-9007.
Fax: 213-617-9185.
Boca Raton, Florida Office: The Plaza, 5355 Town Center Road, Suite 900.
Telephone: 561-361-5000.
Telecopier: 561-367-8400.

MEMBERS OF FIRM

Melvyn I. Weiss (Resident at Boca Raton Office)
Lawrence Milberg (1913-1989)
David J. Bershad
Patricia M. Hynes
Steven G. Schulman
Michael C. Spencer
Keith M. Fleischman
Sol Schreiber
Jerome M. Congress
Arnold N. Bressler
Robert A. Wallner
Sanford P. Dumain
George A. Bauer III
Barry A. Weprin
Richard H. Weiss
Deborah Clark-Weintraub
Joshua H. Vinik
Edith M. Kallas
Janine L. Pollack
Salvatore J. Graziano

ASSOCIATES

Elaine Simek Kusel
U. Seth Ottensoser

OF COUNSEL

Richard M. Meyer
Jared Specthrie

For full biographical listings, see the Martindale-Hubbell Law Directory

OTTERBOURG, STEINDLER, HOUSTON & ROSEN, P.C. (AV)

230 Park Avenue, 29th Floor, 10169
Telephone: 212-661-9100
Telecopier: 212-682-6104

Peter L. Feldman

COUNSEL

Bernard Beitel

Lloyd M. Green

For Complete List of Firm Personnel, See General Section

For full biographical listings, see the Martindale-Hubbell Law Directory

PARKER CHAPIN LLP (AV)

Chrysler Building, 405 Lexington Avenue, 10017
Telephone: 212-704-6000
Telecopier: 212-704-6288
URL: http://www.parkerchapin.com
Great Neck, New York Office: 175 Great Neck Road.
Telephone: 516-482-4422.
Telecopier: 516-482-4469.
Hackensack, New Jersey: 190 Morre Street, Suite 307.
Telephone: 210-883-6400.
Telecopier: 210-883-6404.
Beverly Hills, California: 9454 Wilshire Boulevard.
Telephone: 310-288-8367.
Telecopier: 310-288-8365.

(See Next Column)

PARKER CHAPIN LLP—*Continued*

MEMBERS OF FIRM

Barry J. Brett
Aurora Cassirer
Michael D. Friedman
Charles P. Greenman
Stephen G. Rinehart
Alvin M. Stein

OF COUNSEL

Mark I. Schlesinger

For Complete List of Firm Personnel, See General Section

For full biographical listings, see the Martindale-Hubbell Law Directory

PILIERO GOLDSTEIN JENKINS & SULLIVAN, LLP (AV)

292 Madison Avenue, 10017
Telephone: 212-213-8200
Fax: 212-685-2028
Email: lawyers@pgjhlaw.com *URL:* http://www.pgjhlaw.com
Carlstadt, New Jersey Office: One Palmer Terrace.
Telephone: 201-507-5157.
FAX: 201-507-5221.
Washington, D.C. Office: 888 17th Street, N.W., Suite 1100.
Telephone: 202-467-6991.
FAX: 202-467-6703.
San Francisco, California Office: 507 Howard Street, Suite 200.
Telephone: 415-281-3631.
Fax: 415-281-3630.

MEMBERS OF FIRM

Kimberlee S. Bogen
Edward J. Goldstein
Jon Mark Jenkins
Marc A. Lebowitz
Robert D. Piliero
George O. Richardson, III
Michael T. Sullivan

ASSOCIATES

Craig Avedisian
Rosemary G. Feit
Eric M. Kogan
Mariano Schwed

OF COUNSEL

Kenneth D. Arbeeny
Christopher P. Hall

For full biographical listings, see the Martindale-Hubbell Law Directory

RABIN & PECKEL LLP (AV)

275 Madison Avenue, 10016
Telephone: 212-682-1818
Telecopier: 212-682-1892
Email: email@rabinlaw.com *URL:* http://www.rabinlaw.com

I. Stephen Rabin
Allan K. Peckel
Brian P. Murray
Marvin L. Frank

Jacqueline Sailer
Joseph V. McBride
Donald J. Wallace
Shaye J. Fuchs (Not admitted in NY)

For full biographical listings, see the Martindale-Hubbell Law Directory

WINTHROP, STIMSON, PUTNAM & ROBERTS (AV)

One Battery Park Plaza, 10004-1490
Telephone: 212-858-1000
Telex: 62854 WINSTIM
Telefax: 212-858-1500
URL: http://www.winstim.com
Stamford, Connecticut Office: Financial Centre, 695 East Main Street, P.O. Box 6760, 06904-6760.
Telephone: 203-348-2300.
Fax: 203-965-8226.
Washington, D.C. Office: 1133 Connecticut Avenue, N.W., 20036.
Telephone: 202-775-9800.
Fax: 202-833-8491.
Palm Beach, Florida Office: 125 Worth Avenue, Suite 310, 33480.
Telephone: 561-655-7297.
Fax: 561-833-6726.
London Office: 54 Lombard Street, London EC3V 9DH, England.
Telephone: 011-44207-648-9200.
Fax: 011-44207-283-1656.
Tokyo, Japan Office: 608 Atagoyama Bengoshi Building 6-7, Atago 1-chome, Minato-ku, Tokyo 105 Japan.
Telephone: 011-813-3437-9740.
Fax: 011-813-3437-9261.
Hong Kong, China Office: 2505 Asia Pacific Finance Tower, Citibank Plaza, 3 Garden Road, Central.
Telephone: 011-852-2530-3400.
Fax: 011-852-2530-3355.
Singapore Office: 6 Battery Road #38-01/B, Singapore 049909.
Telephone: 65-227-4700.
Fax: 65-227-4711.

NEW YORK OFFICE
MEMBERS OF FIRM

Leo T. Crowley
Sutton Keany
David G. Keyko
David M. Lindley
Edwin J. Wesely

(See Next Column)

SENIOR COUNSEL

Merrell E. Clark, Jr.

STAMFORD OFFICE
MEMBER OF FIRM

Thomas F. Clauss, Jr.

WASHINGTON, D.C. OFFICE
MEMBER OF FIRM

Donald A. Carr

WASHINGTON, D.C.
COUNSEL

Aileen Meyer

For Complete List of Firm Personnel, See General Section

For full biographical listings, see the Martindale-Hubbell Law Directory

NORTH CAROLINA

*RALEIGH,** Wake Co.

ALLEN AND PINNIX, P.A. (AV)

333 Fayetteville Street, Mall, Suite 1200, 27601
Telephone: 919-755-0505
Facsimile: 919-829-8098

Noel L. Allen

For full biographical listings, see the Martindale-Hubbell Law Directory

WOMBLE CARLYLE SANDRIDGE & RICE (AV)

A Professional Limited Liability Company
2100 First Union Capitol Center, 150 Fayetteville Street Mall, P.O. Box 831, 27602
Telephone: 919-755-2100
Fax: 919-755-2150
Email: lawyers@wcsr.com *URL:* http://www.wcsr.com
Charlotte, North Carolina Office: 3300 One First Union Center, 301 South College Street.
Telephone: 704-331-4900.
Fax: 704-331-4955.
Winston-Salem, North Carolina Office: 200 West Second Street, P.O. Drawer 84.
Telephone: 336-721-3600.
Fax: 336-721-3660.
Research Triangle Park, North Carolina Office: 2505 Meridian Parkway, Suite 300 (Durham), 27713.
Telephone: 919-484-2300.
Fax: 919-484-2340.
Atlanta, Georgia Office: One Atlantic Center, 1201 West Peachtree Street, Suite 3500.
Telephone: 404-872-7000.
Fax: 404-888-7490.
Other Atlanta, Georgia Office: Suite 404, 2296 Henderson Mill Road, N.E.
Telephone: 770-492-9030.
Fax: 770-492-9609.
Washington, D.C. Office: 1120 Nineteenth Street, N.W., Eighth Floor.
Telephone: 202-857-4400.
Fax: 202-467-6910.
Greenville, South Carolina Office: 15 South Main Street, Suite 601, P.O. Box 10208.
Telephone: 864-255-5400.
Fax: 864-255-5440.

RESIDENT MEMBER

Pressly M. Millen

RESIDENT ASSOCIATE

Samuel M. Taylor

RESIDENT OF COUNSEL

E. Lawrence Davis, III

Representative Clients: Aetna Casualty and Surety Co., Inc.; ALSCO/AmeriMark Building Products, Inc.; Aoki Corporation America, Inc.; Hackney Brothers, Inc.; Lawyers Mutual Liability Insurance Company of North Carolina; Meredith College; Regency Park Corp.; Wachovia Bank, N.A.

For Complete List of Firm Personnel, See General Section

For full biographical listings, see the Martindale-Hubbell Law Directory

*WINSTON-SALEM,** Forsyth Co.

MOORE & BROWN (AV)

A Partnership including Professional Corporations
1014 West Fifth Street, 27101-2522
Telephone: 336-723-7966
Fax: 336-723-1035
Washington, D.C. Office: 4900 Massachusetts Avenue, N.W., Suite 230.
Telephone: 202-364-1032.
Fax: 202-363-6912.

MEMBERS OF FIRM

Beverly C. Moore, Jr., P.C. (Resident, Washington, D.C. Office)
B. Ervin Brown, II

OF COUNSEL

Stuart J. Logan (Resident, Washington, D.C. Office)

ASSOCIATES

James S. Gibbs, Jr.
John Pillette (Not admitted in NC; Resident, Washington D.C. Office)

For full biographical listings, see the Martindale-Hubbell Law Directory

WOMBLE CARLYLE SANDRIDGE & RICE (AV)

A Professional Limited Liability Company
200 West Second Street, P.O. Drawer 84, 27102
Telephone: 336-721-3600
Fax: 336-721-3660
Email: lawyers@wcsr.com *URL:* http://www.wcsr.com
Charlotte, North Carolina Office: 3300 One First Union Center, 301 South College Street.
Telephone: 704-331-4900.
Fax: 704-331-4955.
Raleigh, North Carolina Office: 2100 First Union Capitol Center, 150 Fayetteville Street Mall, P.O. Box 831.
Telephone: 919-755-2100.
Fax: 919-755-2150.
Research Triangle Park, North Carolina Office: 2505 Meridian Parkway, Suite 300 (Durham), 27713.
Telephone: 919-484-2300.
Fax: 919-484-2340.
Atlanta, Georgia Office: One Atlantic Center, 1201 West Peachtree Street, Suite 3500.
Telephone: 404-872-7000.
Fax: 404-888-7490.
Other Atlanta, Georgia Office: Suite 404, 2296 Henderson Mill Road, N.E.
Telephone: 770-492-9030.
Fax: 770-492-9609.
Washington, D.C. Office: 1120 Nineteenth Street, N.W., Eighth Floor.
Telephone: 202-857-4400.
Fax: 202-467-6910.
Greenville, South Carolina Office: 15 South Main Street, Suite 601, P.O. Box 10208.
Telephone: 864-255-5400.
Fax: 864-255-5440.

RESIDENT MEMBERS

W. Andrew Copenhaver
James K. Phillips
Mark N. Poovey
David A. Shirlen
Ashley O. Thrift

RESIDENT ASSOCIATES

Andrew J. Logan
David J. Mazza (Not admitted in NC)

MEMBER OF COUNSEL

Susan P. Strommer

Representative Clients: Brad Ragan, Inc.; Brenner Companies; Food Lion, Inc.; Hanes Companies, Inc.; North Carolina Baptist Hospitals, Inc.; R.J. Reynolds Tobacco Co.; Thomasville Furniture Industries, Inc.; Wachovia Corp.; Wake Forest University.

For Complete List of Firm Personnel, See General Section

For full biographical listings, see the Martindale-Hubbell Law Directory

OHIO

*CINCINNATI,** Hamilton Co.

FROST & JACOBS LLP (AV)

2500 PNC Center, 201 East Fifth Street, 45202
Telephone: 513-651-6800
Telecopier: 513-651-6981
URL: http://www.frojac.com
Columbus, Ohio Office: One Columbus, 10 West Broad Street, 43215.
Telephone: 614-464-1211.
Telecopier: 614-464-1737.
Lexington, Kentucky Office: 1100 Vine Center Tower, 333 West Vine Street, 40507.
Telephone: 606-254-1100.
Telecopier: 606-253-2990.
Middletown, Ohio Office: 400 First National Bank Building, 2 North Main Street, 45042.
Telephone: 513-422-2001.
Telecopier: 513-422-3010.
Frankfort, Kentucky Office: 201 W. Main Street, 40601.
Telephone: 502-223-1400.
Telecopier: 502-223-1410.

MEMBERS OF FIRM

James R. Adams
Myron L. Dale

SENIOR ATTORNEY

Daniel W. Scharff

ASSOCIATE

Jeffrey R. Teeters

OF COUNSEL

John K. Rose
Clayton R. Sanders Jr. (Not admitted in OH)

PATENT, TRADEMARK AND COPYRIGHT ATTORNEY
MEMBERS OF FIRM

Steven J. Goldstein

OF COUNSEL

Stephen E. Gillen

LEXINGTON, KENTUCKY OFFICE
ASSOCIATE

Andrew W. Green

Representative Clients: Armco Inc.; Arthur Andersen & Co.; Cincinnati Bell Inc.; Cincinnati Machine; Federated Department Stores Inc.; Mercy Health Systems; PNC Bank, National Association; Sencorp.; totes Isotoner Corporation.

For Complete List of Firm Personnel, See General Section

For full biographical listings, see the Martindale-Hubbell Law Directory

WAITE, SCHNEIDER, BAYLESS & CHESLEY CO., L.P.A. (AV)

1513 Central Trust Tower, Fourth and Vine Streets, 45202
Telephone: 513-621-0267
Fax: 513-381-2375; 621-0262

Stanley M. Chesley

Thomas F. Rehme
Robert A. Steinberg
Fay E. Stilz
Louise M. Roselle
D. Arthur Rabourn
Jerome L. Skinner
Janet G. Abaray
Paul M. De Marco
Terrence L. Goodman
Colleen M. Hegge
Jane H. Walker
Renée Infante
James F. Keller
Jean M. Geoppinger
Robert Heuck II

For full biographical listings, see the Martindale-Hubbell Law Directory

*CLEVELAND,** Cuyahoga Co.

BAKER & HOSTETLER LLP (AV)

3200 National City Center, 1900 East Ninth Street, 44114-3485
Telephone: 216-621-0200
Telecopier: 216-696-0740
TWX: 810 421 8375
RCA Telex: 215032
To contact an attorney on the Internet use first initial and surname followed by @baker-hostetler.com
URL: http://www.bakerlaw.com
In Cincinnati, Ohio: 312 Walnut Street, Suite 2650.
Telephone: 513-929-3400.
In Columbus, Ohio: Capitol Square, Suite 2100, 65 East State Street.
Telephone: 614-228-1541.
In Denver, Colorado: 303 East 17th Avenue, Suite 1100.
Telephone: 303-861-0600.
In Houston, Texas: 1000 Louisiana, Suite 2000.
Telephone: 713-751-1600.
In Beverly Hills, California: 9150 Wilshire Boulevard, Suite 205.
Telephone: 310-385-7500.

(See Next Column)

BAKER & HOSTETLER LLP—*Continued*

In Long Beach, California: 300 Oceangate, Suite 620.
Telephone: 562-432-2827.
In Los Angeles, California: 600 Wilshire Boulevard.
Telephone: 213-624-2400.
In Orlando, Florida: SunBank Center, Suite 2300, 200 South Orange Avenue.
Telephone: 407-649-4000.
In Washington, D.C.: Washington Square, Suite 1100, 1050 Connecticut Avenue, N.W.
Telephone: 202-861-1500.

PARTNERS

Paul P. Eyre (Head of Litigation Practice)
John D. Parker
Ernest E. Vargo, Jr.

For Complete List of Firm Personnel, See General Section

For full biographical listings, see the Martindale-Hubbell Law Directory

JONES, DAY, REAVIS & POGUE (AV)

North Point, 901 Lakeside Avenue, 44114
Telephone: 216-586-3939
Telecopier: 216-579-0212
Email: counsel@jonesday.com *URL:* http://www.jonesday.com
In Columbus, Ohio: 1900 Huntington Center.
Telephone: 614-469-3939.
Telecopier: 614-461-4198.
In Atlanta, Georgia: 3500 SunTrust Plaza, 303 Peachtree Street.
Telephone: 404-521-3939.
Telecopier: 404-581-8330.
In Brussels, Belgium: Avenue Louise 480, 7th Floor. B-1050 Brussels.
Telephone: 32-2-645-14-11.
Telecopier: 32-2-645-14-45.
In Chicago, Illinois: 77 West Wacker.
Telephone: 312-782-3939.
Telecopier: 312-782-8585.
In Dallas, Texas: 2727 North Harwood Street.
Telephone: 214-220-3939.
Telecopier: 214-969-5100.
In Frankfurt, Germany: Hochhaus am Park, Grüneburgweg 102, 60323 Frankfurt am Main.
Telephone: 49-69-9726-3939.
Telecopier: 49-69-9726-3993.
In Geneva, Switzerland: 20, rue de Candolle.
Telephone: 41-22-320-2339.
Telecopier: 41-22-320-1232.
In Hong Kong, China: 29th Floor, Entertainment Building, 30 Queen's Road Central.
Telephone: 852-2526-6895.
Telecopier: 852-2868-5871 or 852-2868-5699.
In Irvine, California: 5 Park Plaza, Suite 1100.
Telephone: 949-851-3939.
Telecopier: 949-553-7539.
In London, England: Bucklersbury House, 3 Queen Victoria Street.
Telephone: 44-171-236-3939.
Telecopier: 44-171-236-1113.
In Los Angeles, California: 555 West Fifth Street, Suite 4600.
Telephone: 213-489-3939.
Telecopier: 213-243-2539.
In New Delhi, India (Associate Office): Pathak & Associates (an associate firm of Jones, Day, Reavis & Pogue), 1st Floor, Dr. Gopal Das Bhaven, 28 Barakhamba Road.
Telephone: 91-11-373-8793; 91-11-335-7345.
Telecopier: 91-11-335-3761.
In New York, N.Y.: 599 Lexington Avenue.
Telephone: 212-326-3939.
Telecopier: 212-755-7306.
In Paris, France: 120, rue du Faubourg Saint-Honoré.
Telephone: 33-1-56-59-39-39.
Telecopier: 33-1-56-59-39-38
In Pittsburgh, Pennsylvania: 500 Grant Street, 31st Floor.
Telephone: 412-391-3939.
Telecopier: 412-394-7959.
In Riyadh, Saudi Arabia: The International Law Firm (In Association with Jones, Day, Reavis & Pogue), Sulaymaniyah, Prince Mishari IBN, Abdulaziz Street, P.O. Box 22166.
Telephone: (966-1) 462-8866.
Telecopier: (966-1) 462-9001.
In Shanghai, China: 2805 Kerry Centre, 1515 Nanjing Road West.
Telephone: 86-21-5298-6568.
Telecopier: 86-21-5298-6569.
In Sydney, Australia: Governor Phillip Tower, Level 38, 1 Farrer Place.
Telephone: 61-2-9210-6921.
Telecopier: 61-2-9210-6926.
In Taipei, Taiwan: 8th Floor, Tun Hwa South Road, Section 2.
Telephone: (886-2) 2704-6808.
Telecopier: (886-2) 2704-6791.
In Tokyo, Japan: Toranomon MT Building, 4th Floor, 10-3, Toranomon 3-Chome, Minato-ku, Tokyo 105, Japan.
Telephone: 81-3-3433-3939.
Telecopier: 81-3-5401-2725.

(See Next Column)

In Washington, D.C.: 51 Louisiana Avenue, N.W.
Telephone: 202-879-3939.
Telecopier: 202-626-1700.

MEMBERS OF FIRM IN CLEVELAND

William Thomas Plesec
Robert H. Rawson, Jr.
Thomas Demitrack
Stephen J. Squeri
Michelle K. Fischer
Deborah Platt Herman

ASSOCIATE

Susanne H. Deegan

For Complete List of Firm Personnel, See General Section

For full biographical listings, see the Martindale-Hubbell Law Directory

KAUFMAN & CUMBERLAND CO., L.P.A. (AV)

1500 Republic Building, 25 Prospect Avenue, West, 44115-1000
Telephone: 216-861-0707
Telefax: 216-694-6883
TDD: 216-694-6891

Steven S. Kaufman
Frank J. Cumberland, Jr. (Retired)
Frank R. DeSantis
William W. Jacobs

Representative Client: CertainTeed Corp.

For full biographical listings, see the Martindale-Hubbell Law Directory

TIMOTHY A. SHIMKO & ASSOCIATES A LEGAL PROFESSIONAL ASSOCIATION (AV)

2010 Huntington Building, 925 Euclid Avenue, 44115
Telephone: 216-241-8300
Fax: 216-241-2702
Email: taslaw@ix.netcom.com *URL:* http://www.netcom.com/~taslaw

Timothy A. Shimko

Frank E. Piscitelli, Jr.

Reference: National City Bank, Cleveland.

For full biographical listings, see the Martindale-Hubbell Law Directory

*COLUMBUS,** Franklin Co.

PORTER WRIGHT MORRIS & ARTHUR LLP (AV)

41 South High Street, 43215-6194
Telephone: 614-227-2000; (800-533-2794)
Fax: 614-227-2100
Email: cmh@porterwright.com *URL:* http://www.porterwright.com
Cincinnati, Ohio Office: 250 E. Fifth Street, Suite 2200, 45202-4199.
Telephones: 513-381-4700; (800-582-5813).
Fax: 513-421-0991. Internet: cvg@porterwright.com.
Cleveland, Ohio Office: 925 Euclid Avenue, Suite 1700, 44115-1483.
Telephones: 216-443-9000; (800-824-1980).
Fax: 216-443-9011. Internet: cle@porterwright.com.
Dayton, Ohio Office: One Dayton Centre, One South Main Street, Suite 1600, 45402-2028.
Telephones: 937-449-6810; (800-533-4434).
Fax: 937-449-6820. Internet: day@porterwright.com.
Naples, Florida Office: 5801 Pelican Bay Boulevard, Suite 300, 34108-2709.
Telephones: 941-593-2900; (800-876-7962).
Fax: 941-593-2990. Internet: apf@porterwright.com.
Washington, D.C. Office: 1667 K Street, N.W., Suite 1100, 20006-1605.
Telephones: 202-778-3000; (800-456-7962).
Fax: 202-778-3063. Internet: dca@porterwright.com.

MEMBERS OF FIRM
COLUMBUS, OHIO OFFICE

Edwin M. Baranowski
Dixon F. Miller
Robert J. Nordstrom
Jean Yingling Teteris
Kathleen McManus Trafford

CINCINNATI, OHIO OFFICE
RESIDENT MEMBER

Jerome J. Metz, Jr.

WASHINGTON, D.C. OFFICE
MEMBER

Thomas O. Gorman

For Complete List of Firm Personnel, See General Section

For full biographical listings, see the Martindale-Hubbell Law Directory

VORYS, SATER, SEYMOUR AND PEASE LLP (AV)

52 East Gay Street, P.O. Box 1008, 43216-1008
Telephone: 614-464-6400
Telecopier: 614-464-6350
URL: http://www.vssp.com
Washington, D.C. Office: 1828 L Street, N.W., 20036-5109.
Telephone: 202-467-8800.
Telex: 440693.
Telecopier: 202-467-8900.

(See Next Column)

VORYS, SATER, SEYMOUR AND PEASE LLP, *Columbus—Continued*

Cleveland, Ohio Office: 2100 One Cleveland Center, 1375 East Ninth Street, 44114-1724.
Telephone: 216-479-6100.
Telecopier: 216-479-6060.
Cincinnati, Ohio Office: Suite 2100, 221 East Fourth Street, P.O. Box 0236, 45201-0236.
Telephone: 513-723-4000.
Telecopier: 513-723-4056.
Alexandria, Virginia Office: 277 South Washington St., Suite 310, 22314.
Telephone: 703-549-4282.
Telecopier: 703-549-4492.

MEMBERS OF FIRM

James P. Kennedy — Ivery D. Foreman
David S. Cupps — Laura G. Kuykendall
Michael J. Canter — Carl D. Smallwood
James A. Wilson

OF COUNSEL

John C. Elam — Russell P. Herrold, Jr.
Jacob E. Davis, II

Local Counsel: Abbott Laboratories; Anheuser-Busch, Inc.; Connecticut General Life Insurance Co.; General Motors Corp.; The Kroger Co.; Navistar International Corporation; Ohio Manufacturers Assn.; Wendy's International, Inc.

For Complete List of Firm Personnel, See General Section

For full biographical listings, see the Martindale-Hubbell Law Directory

*ELYRIA,** Lorain Co.

ZAGRANS LAW FIRM A LEGAL PROFESSIONAL ASSOCIATION (AV)

5338 Meadow Lane Court, 44035-1469
Telephone: 440-934-7000
Facsimile: 440-934-7001
Email: eric@zagrans.com *URL:* http://www.zagrans.com

Eric H. Zagrans

Joshua M. Marks

LEGAL SUPPORT PERSONNEL

Jeannette M. Wolff (Legal Assistant)

For full biographical listings, see the Martindale-Hubbell Law Directory

OKLAHOMA

*OKLAHOMA CITY,** Oklahoma Co.

ANDREWS DAVIS LEGG BIXLER MILSTEN & PRICE, A PROFESSIONAL CORPORATION (AV)

500 West Main, Suite 500, 73102
Telephone: 405-272-9241
FAX: 405-235-8786
Email: andrewsdavis@andrewsdavis.com *URL:* http://www.andrewsdavis.com

John F. Fischer, II — Don G. Holladay
R. Brown Wallace

For Complete List of Firm Personnel, See General Section

For full biographical listings, see the Martindale-Hubbell Law Directory

CONNER & WINTERS, A PROFESSIONAL CORPORATION (AV)

One Leadership Square, 211 North Robinson, Suite 1700, 73102-7101
Telephone: 405-272-5711
Facsimile: 405-232-2695
Email: postmaster@cwlaw.com
Tulsa, Oklahoma Office: 3700 First Place Tower, 15 East 5th Street, 74103-4344.
Telephone: 918-586-5711.
Facsimile: 918-586-8982.
Fayetteville, Arkansas Office: Conner & Winters, P.L.L.C., 100 West Center Street, Suite 200, 72701-6081.
Telephone: 501-582-5711.
Facsimile: 501-587-1426.
Washington, D.C. Office: 1050 Seventeenth Street, N.W., Suite 810, 20036-5503.
Telephone: 202-783-5711.
Facsimile: 202-783-5720.

Peter B. Bradford — Raymond E. Tompkins
Timothy J. Bomhoff

For Complete List of Firm Personnel, See General Section

For full biographical listings, see the Martindale-Hubbell Law Directory

CROWE & DUNLEVY, A PROFESSIONAL CORPORATION (AV)

1800 Mid-America Tower, 20 North Broadway, 73102-8273
Telephone: 405-235-7700
Fax: 405-239-6651
Email: marketing@crowedunlevy.com *URL:* http://www.crowedunlevy.com
Tulsa, Oklahoma Office: 500 Kennedy Building, 321 South Boston Avenue, 74103-3313.
Telephone: 918-592-9800.
Fax: 918-592-9801.
Norman, Oklahoma Office: Crowe & Dunlevy, 2500 South McGee, Suite 140, 73072-6705.
Telephone: 405-321-7317.
Fax: 405-360-4002.

D. Kent Meyers — Mack J. Morgan III
Joseph J. Ferretti

Mary Hirth Tolbert — Eric S. Fisher
Paige S. Bass

For Complete List of Firm Personnel, See General Section

For full biographical listings, see the Martindale-Hubbell Law Directory

*TULSA,** Tulsa Co.

ATKINSON, HASKINS, NELLIS, BOUDREAUX, HOLEMAN, PHIPPS & BRITTINGHAM, A PROFESSIONAL CORPORATION (AV)

1500 ParkCentre, 525 South Main Street, 74103
Telephone: 918-582-8877
Fax: 918-585-8096
Email: ahnmail@ahn-law.com

John J. Carwile

Representative Clients: Allstate Insurance Co.; Bayer Corp.; Crum & Forster Insurance Co.; Hartford Insurance Company; National American Insurance Co.; Federated Insurance Co.; Liberty Mutual Insurance Co.; Physicians Liability Insurance Co.; State Farm Mutual Automobile Insurance Co.; United States Aviation Underwriters.

For full biographical listings, see the Martindale-Hubbell Law Directory

DOYLE & HARRIS, A PROFESSIONAL CORPORATION (AV)

1350 Boulder, P.O. Box 1679, 74119
Telephone: 918-592-1276
Fax: 918-592-4389
Email: D&H@CommerciaLaw.com *URL:* http://www.CommerciaLaw.com

Stan P. Doyle — Steven M. Harris

Michael D. Davis — Douglas R. Haughey
Bruce A. Spence

Reference: Peoples State Bank.

For full biographical listings, see the Martindale-Hubbell Law Directory

SNEED LANG, P.C. (AV)

2300 Williams Center Tower II, Two West Second Street, 74103
Telephone: 918-583-3145
Telecopier: 918-582-0410

James C. Lang — Robbie Emery Burke
D. Faith Orlowski — Patrick O. Waddel
Brian S. Gaskill — Randolph P. Stainer
G. Steven Stidham — Steven K. Balman
Stephen R. McNamara — Brian T. Inbody
Thomas E. Black, Jr. — D. Michael McBride III

OF COUNSEL

James L. Sneed

Representative Clients: Amoco Production Co.; Bank One, Texas; Enron Corp.; Halliburton Energy Services; Helmerich & Payne, Inc.; Shell Oil Co.; State Farm Mutual Automobile Insurance Co.; The Williams Companies.

For full biographical listings, see the Martindale-Hubbell Law Directory

OREGON

*PORTLAND,** Multnomah Co.

LANE POWELL SPEARS LUBERSKY LLP (AV)

Limited Liability Partnership composed of Individuals and Professional Service Corporations
601 S.W. Second Avenue, Suite 2100, 97204
Telephone: 503-778-2100
Facsimile: 503-778-2200
Email: information@lanepowell.com *URL:* http://www.lanepowell.com
Other Offices at: Seattle, Washington; Anchorage, Alaska; Olympia and Mount Vernon, Washington; London, England.

MEMBERS OF FIRM

Craig D. Bachman
Milo Petranovich
Donald H. Pyle

For Complete List of Firm Personnel, See General Section

For full biographical listings, see the Martindale-Hubbell Law Directory

LINDSAY, HART, NEIL & WEIGLER, LLP (AV)

3400 Wells Fargo Center, 1300 S.W. Fifth Avenue, 97201-5696
Telephone: 503-226-7677
Telecopier: 503-226-7697
Email: LHNW@Europa.com
Washington, D.C. Office: 1201 Pennsylvania Avenue, N.W., Suite 821, 20004.
Telephone: 202-467-8383.
Fax: 202-467-8581.

MEMBER OF FIRM

Dennis J. Lindsay

Representative Clients: Merchants Exchange of Portland; Grain Exchange of Portland; United Grain Corporation.

For full biographical listings, see the Martindale-Hubbell Law Directory

MILLER NASH LLP (AV)

A Limited Liability Partnership including Professional Corporations
111 S.W. Fifth Avenue, 97204-3699
Telephone: 503-224-5858
Telex: 364462, Kingmar PTL
Facsimile: 503-224-0155, 503-224-2450
Email: e-mail@millernash.com *URL:* http://www.millernash.com
Seattle, Washington Office: 4400 Two Union Square, 601 Union Street, 98101-2322.
Telephone: 206-622-8484.
Facsimile: 206-622-7485.

PORTLAND, OREGON PARTNERS

Jeffrey D. Austin, P.C.
John D. Burns
William B. Crow, P.C.
Thomas C. Sand, P.C.
R. Alan Wight

Representative Clients: U.S. Bancorp; Louisiana-Pacific Corp.; Willamette Industries, Inc.; Portland Public Schools; St. Vincent Hospital and Medical Center; Merrill Lynch, Pierce, Fenner & Smith, Inc.

For Complete List of Firm Personnel, See General Section

For full biographical listings, see the Martindale-Hubbell Law Directory

PENNSYLVANIA

*HARRISBURG,** Dauphin Co.

GOLDBERG, KATZMAN & SHIPMAN, P.C. (AV)

320 Market Street - Strawberry Square, P.O. Box 1268, 17108-1268
Telephone: 717-234-4161
Telecopier: 717-234-6808; 717-234-6810
Email: gks@gkslaw.com

Ronald M. Katzman

Steven E. Grubb

Representative Clients: Ameralum, Inc.; Cincinnati Insurance Co.; The Atlantic Mutual Cos.; Erie Insurance Group; Maryland Commercial Insurance Group; State Auto Insurance Co.; Dauphin County General Authority; Flight Systems, Inc.; Tressler Lutheran Services; Merchants & Businessman's Mutual Insurance Co.
Reference: Fulton Bank.

For Complete List of Firm Personnel, See General Section

For full biographical listings, see the Martindale-Hubbell Law Directory

*PHILADELPHIA,** Philadelphia Co.

BALLARD SPAHR ANDREWS & INGERSOLL, LLP (AV)

1735 Market Street, 51st Floor, 19103-7599
Telephone: 215-665-8500
Fax: 215-864-8999
URL: http://www.ballardspahr.com
Baltimore, Maryland Office: 300 East Lombard Street. 19th Floor.
Telephone: 410-528-5600.
Fax: 410-528-5650.
Camden, New Jersey Office: 800 Hudson Square, 5th Floor.
Telephone: 856-541-5577.
Fax: 856-541-8272.
Denver, Colorado Office: Seventeenth Street Plaza Building, Suite 2300, 1225 17th Street.
Telephone: 303-292-2400.
Fax: 303-296-3956.
Salt Lake City, Utah Office: One Utah Center, Suite 1200, 201 South Main Street.
Telephone: 801-531-3000.
Fax: 801-531-3001.
Voorhees, New Jersey Office: Suite 100, 1101 Laurel Oak Drive.
Telephone: 856-627-8555.
Fax: 856-627-1153.
Washington, D.C. Office: Suite 1000 South, 601 13th Street, N.W.
Telephone: 202-661-2200.
Fax: 202-661-2299.

Geoffrey A. Kahn
Matthew M. Strickler

For Complete List of Firm Personnel, See General Section

For full biographical listings, see the Martindale-Hubbell Law Directory

BARRACK, RODOS & BACINE (AV)

A Partnership including Professional Corporations
3300 Two Commerce Square, 2001 Market Street, 19103
Telephone: 215-963-0600
Telecopier: 215-963-0838
URL: http://www.barrack.com
San Diego, California Office: 600 West Broadway, Suite 1700. 92101.
Telephone: 619-230-0800.
Telecopier: 619-230-1874.
New York, New York Courtesy Office: 18 East 50th Street, 7th Floor. 10022.
Telephone: 212-688-0782.
Telecopier: 212-688-0783.
Haddonfield, New Jersey Office: 14 Kings Highway West. 08033.
Telephone: 856-354-0707.
Telecopier: 856-354-9404.
Boston, Massachusetts Office: 90 Canal Street, 5th Floor. 02114.
Telephone: 617-367-1040.
Telecopier: 617-742-8280.

Leonard Barrack (P.C.)
Gerald J. Rodos (P.C.)
Daniel E. Bacine (P.C.)
Sheldon L. Albert
Steven A. Asher
Jeffrey Alan Barrack
Stephen R. Basser (Resident, San Diego, California Office)
Sara Jones Biden
Edward M. Gergosian (Resident, San Diego, California Office)
Jeffrey B. Gittleman
Jeffrey W. Golan
Robert A. Hoffman (Resident, Haddonfield, New Jersey Office)
David L. Kelston (Resident, Boston, Massachusetts Office)
M. Richard Komins
Leslie Bornstein Molder
Matthew P. Montgomery (Resident, San Diego, California Office)
Blair A. Nicholas (Resident, San Diego, California Office)
Mark R. Rosen
Samuel R. Simon

For full biographical listings, see the Martindale-Hubbell Law Directory

BERGER & MONTAGUE, P.C. (AV)

1622 Locust Street, 19103
Telephone: 215-875-3000
Telecopier: 215-875-4604; 875-4608
URL: http://home.bm.net

David Berger
Harold Berger
H. Laddie Montague, Jr.
Merrill G. Davidoff
Sherrie Raiken Savett
Daniel Berger
Todd S. Collins
Jay Robert Stiefel
Gary E. Cantor
Stephen A. Whinston
Martin I. Twersky
Carole A. Broderick
Peter R. Kahana
Ruthanne Gordon
Stephen D. Ramos
Karen S. Orman
Jeanne A. Markey
Russell D. Henkin
Peter B. Nordberg
Lawrence Deutsch
Lawrence J. Lederer
Jerome M. Marcus
David F. Sorensen
Arthur Stock

OF COUNSEL

Stanley R. Wolfe
Sandra Diane Stein

(See Next Column)

BERGER & MONTAGUE P.C., *Philadelphia—Continued*

Jonathan D. Berger
Susan Schneider Thomas
Sheryl S. Levy
Bart D. Cohen
Michael T. Fantini
Stuart J. Guber
Michael L. Block
Jonathan Auerbach
Edward W. Millstein
Bret P. Flaherty
Genna Driscoll Kidd
Charles Pearsall Goodwin
Kendall S. Zylstra
Neil F. Mara
Jacob A. Goldberg
Eric L. Cramer
Daniel M. Cohen
Laura Sabrina Stein
Phyllis Maza Parker
Jill E. Sterbakov
Lane L. Vines
Douglas M. Risen

For full biographical listings, see the Martindale-Hubbell Law Directory

LEVIN, FISHBEIN, SEDRAN & BERMAN (AV)

Suite 500, 510 Walnut Street, 19106-3697
Telephone: 215-592-1500
Fax: 215-592-4663
Email: lfsb@psinet.com

MEMBERS OF FIRM

Arnold Levin
Michael D. Fishbein
Howard J. Sedran
Laurence S. Berman
Frederick S. Longer

Craig D. Ginsburg
Cheryl R. Brown Hill
Donald E. Haviland, Jr.
Daniel C. Levin
Terrianne Benedetto
Charles E. Schaffer
Austin B. Cohen

LEGAL SUPPORT PERSONNEL

Lee Ann Fitzpatrick
Cheryl Hesson

For full biographical listings, see the Martindale-Hubbell Law Directory

SANDALS, LANGER & TAYLOR, LLP (AV)

One Liberty Place 50th Floor, 1650 Market Street, 19103-7301
Telephone: 215-419-6500
Fax: 215-419-6501
Email: Main@SLT-LAW.COM *URL:* http://www.slt-law.com

Howard I. Langer
Alan M. Sandals
John R. Taylor

Scott M. Lempert
Kay E. Sickles

For full biographical listings, see the Martindale-Hubbell Law Directory

SAVETT FRUTKIN PODELL & RYAN, P.C. (AV)

Suite 700, 325 Chestnut Street, 19106
Telephone: 215-923-5400
FAX: 923-9353
Email: SFPRPC@OP.NET

Stuart H. Savett
Robert P. Frutkin
Barbara A. Podell
Katharine M. Ryan

For full biographical listings, see the Martindale-Hubbell Law Directory

SPECTOR & ROSEMAN, A PROFESSIONAL CORPORATION (AV)

1818 Market Street, Suite 2500, 19103
Telephone: 215-496-0300
Telecopier: 215-496-6611
Email: espector@spectorandroseman.com *URL:* http://www.spectorandroseman.com
San Diego, California Office: 600 West Broadway, 1600 One American Plaza, 92101.
Telephone: 619-338-4514.
Telecopier: 619-231-7423.

Eugene A. Spector
Robert M. Roseman
Jeffrey L. Kodroff
Ellen Gusikoff Stewart (Not admitted in PA)

Ronnie D. Seidel
Diane Doherty (Not admitted in PA)
Anthony Chu
Andrew D. Abramowitz (Not admitted in PA)
Joshua H. Grabar
Howard C. Gottlieb
Michael P. Nachman
Beth Mandel Rosenthal

OF COUNSEL

Anthony J. Bolognese

LEGAL SUPPORT PERSONNEL

PARALEGALS

Joseph Morrison
Michelle Adams
Carole Staiger

For full biographical listings, see the Martindale-Hubbell Law Directory

SYNNESTVEDT & LECHNER LLP (AV)

2600 Aramark Tower, 1101 Market Street, 19107-2950
Telephone: 215-923-4466
Facsimile: 215-923-2189
Email: synnlech@synnlech.com *URL:* http://www.synnlech.com

Paul Synnestvedt (1870-1950)
Harvey L. Lechner (1885-1954)
Raymond H. Synnestvedt (1902-1986)
Andrew R. Klein (1928-1987)
Albert L. Free (1922-1996)
William H. Elliott, Jr. (1918-1997)

MEMBERS OF FIRM

John T. Synnestvedt
Charles H. Lindrooth
Alexis Barron
Joseph F. Posillico
Bryna S. Silver
Gary A. Hecht
Theodore Naccarella

SENIOR COUNSEL

Irving Newman (Not admitted in PA)

ASSOCIATES

Lisa B. Lane
Stephen J. Driscoll
Joshua R. Slavitt
Mark D. Simpson
Patrick John Kelly
John A. Chionchio
Gregory S. Bernabeo
Stephen James Weed (Not admitted in PA)
Peter J. Butch III (Not admitted in PA)

OF COUNSEL

Richard D. Weber

LEGAL SUPPORT PERSONNEL

SCIENTIFIC ADVISORS

Brett T. Freeman
Gene J. Yao

For full biographical listings, see the Martindale-Hubbell Law Directory

*PITTSBURGH,** Allegheny Co.

MARCUS & SHAPIRA LLP (AV)

35th Floor, One Oxford Centre, 301 Grant Street, 15219-6401
Telephone: 412-471-3490
Telecopier: 412-391-8758
Email: info@marcus-shapira.com *URL:* http://www.marcus-shapira.com

MEMBERS OF FIRM

Robert L. Allman, II
Robert M. Barnes
Scott D. Livingston
Bernard D. Marcus
Daniel H. Shapira

For Complete List of Firm Personnel, See General Section

For full biographical listings, see the Martindale-Hubbell Law Directory

ROSE, SCHMIDT, HASLEY & DISALLE, P.C. (AV)

900 Oliver Building, 15222-2310
Telephone: 412-434-8600
Fax: 412-263-2829
Email: rshd@rshdlaw.com
Washington, Pennsylvania Office: 7th Floor, Millcraft Center.
Telephone: 724-228-8883.

Steven M. Petrikis

For Complete List of Firm Personnel, See General Section

For full biographical listings, see the Martindale-Hubbell Law Directory

RHODE ISLAND

*PROVIDENCE,** Providence Co.

BLISH & CAVANAGH (AV)

Commerce Center, 30 Exchange Terrace, 02903
Telephone: 401-831-8900
Telecopier: 401-751-7542
Email: BLISHCAV@AOL.COM

MEMBERS OF FIRM

Joseph V. Cavanagh, Jr.
William R. Landry
Edmund L. Alves, Jr.
Stephen J. Reid, Jr.
Karen A. Pelczarski
Scott T. Spear
Raymond A. Marcaccio

Michael W. Carroll
Staci L. Sawyer
Kristin Rodgers Sullivan

OF COUNSEL

John H. Blish

Representative Clients: Providence Journal Co.; Rhode Island Hospital Trust National Bank; Fleet Bank; Metropolitan Insurance Co.; Allstate Insurance Co.; Delta Dental of Rhode Island; Colony Communications; Providence Housing Authority; Textron; A.T. Cross.

For full biographical listings, see the Martindale-Hubbell Law Directory

Providence—Continued

EDWARDS & ANGELL, LLP (AV)

A Partnership including Professional Corporations
2800 BankBoston Plaza, 02903
Telephone: 401-274-9200
Telecopier: 401-276-6611
Cable Address: "Edwangle Providence"
Telex: 952001 "E A PVD"
Email: postmaster@ealaw.com *URL:* http://www.ealaw.com
Boston, Massachusetts Office: 101 Federal Street, 02110-1800.
Telephone: 617-439-4444.
Telecopier: 617-439-4170.
New York, New York Office: 750 Lexington Avenue, 10022-1200.
Telephone: 212-308-4411.
Telecopier: 212-308-4844.
Palm Beach, Florida Office: 250 Royal Palm Way, Suite 300, 33480-4356.
Telephone: 561-833-7700.
Telecopier: 561-655-8719.
Short Hills, New Jersey Office: 51 John F. Kennedy Parkway, 07078.
Telephone: 973-376-7700.
Telecopier: 973-376-3380.
Hartford, Connecticut Office: 90 State House Square, 06103-2715.
Telephone: 860-525-5065.
Telecopier: 860-527-4198.
Newport, Rhode Island Office: 130 Bellevue Avenue, 02840.
Telephone: 401-849-7800.
Telecopier: 401-849-7887.

MEMBER OF FIRM

Patricia A. Sullivan

ASSOCIATE

Jon M. Anderson

For Complete List of Firm Personnel, See General Section

For full biographical listings, see the Martindale-Hubbell Law Directory

MEDEIROS + SANFORD INC. (AV)

One Turks Head Place, Suite 700, 02903-2215
Telephone: 401-831-0700
Fax: 401-274-2752 or 401-861-7249

Matthew F. Medeiros
Paul M. Sanford
Stacey P. Nakasian

Jane E. Brockmann

For full biographical listings, see the Martindale-Hubbell Law Directory

SOUTH CAROLINA

*COLUMBIA,** Richland Co.

TURNER, PADGET, GRAHAM & LANEY, P.A. (AV)

Seventeenth Floor, 1901 Main Street, P.O. Box 1473, 29202
Telephone: 803-254-2200
Telecopy: 803-799-3957
Florence, South Carolina Office: Fourth Floor, 1831 West Evans Street, P.O. Box 5478, 29502.
Telephone: 843-662-9008.
Fax: 843-667-0828.
Charleston, South Carolina Office: 21 Broad Street, 1st Floor, P.O. Box 836, 29402.
Telephone: 843-723-1622.
Fax: 843-577-3369.

W. Duvall Spruill
R. Wayne Byrd (Resident, Florence, SC, Office)

OF COUNSEL

Michael S. Church

For Complete List of Firm Personnel, See General Section

For full biographical listings, see the Martindale-Hubbell Law Directory

*GREENVILLE,** Greenville Co.

LEATHERWOOD WALKER TODD & MANN, P.C. (AV)

100 East Coffee Street, P.O. Box 87, 29602
Telephone: 864-242-6440
FAX: 864-240-2477
Email: leatherwood@lwtm.com *URL:* http://www.lwtm.com
Spartanburg, South Carolina Office: 1451 East Main Street, P.O. Box 3188.
Telephone: 864-582-4365.
Telefax: 864-583-8961.

(See Next Column)

Harvey G. Sanders, Jr.
Steven E. Farrar
Natalma M. McKnew
James T. Hewitt

COUNSEL

J. D. Todd, Jr.
James H. Watson
Fletcher C. Mann
J. Brantley Phillips, Jr.

Counsel for: John D. Hollingsworth on Wheels, Inc.; Bi-Lo, Inc.; Suitt Construction, Co., Inc.; Platt Saco Lowell Corp.; The Litchfield Company of South Carolina.
Representative Clients: NationsBank; Springs Industries, Inc.; American Federal Bank, F.S.B.; General Motor Acceptance Corp.

For Complete List of Firm Personnel, See General Section

For full biographical listings, see the Martindale-Hubbell Law Directory

TENNESSEE

*MEMPHIS,** Shelby Co.

ARMSTRONG ALLEN PREWITT GENTRY JOHNSTON & HOLMES, PLLC (AV)

Brinkley Plaza, Suite 700, 80 Monroe Avenue, 38103-2467
Telephone: 901-523-8211
Facsimile: 901-524-4936
Little Rock, Arkansas Office: Suite 100, 100 Morgan Keegan Drive, 72202.
Telephone: 501-280-0100.
Facsimile: 501-280-0166.
Jackson, Mississippi Office: 2525 Lakeward Drive, Suite 200, 39216.
Telephone: 601-713-1192.
Facsimile: 601-713-2049.
Jackson, Tennessee Office: 464 North Parkway, Suite A, 38305.
Telephone: 901-660-2332.
Facsimile: 901-664-1109.

MEMBERS OF FIRM

Thomas F. Johnston
Mark S. Norris

For Complete List of Firm Personnel, See General Section

For full biographical listings, see the Martindale-Hubbell Law Directory

HALE HEADRICK DEWEY & WOLF, PLLC (AV)

One Memphis Place, 200 Jefferson Avenue Suite 1450, 38103
Telephone: 901-523-1123
Fax: 901-523-7472
Nashville, Tennessee Office: Suntrust Bank Building, 201 Fourth Avenue North, Suite 1450, 37219.
Telephone: 615-843-5160.
Fax: 615-843-5165

Stephen P. Hale
H. Tucker Dewey
S. Russell Headrick
Herbert B. Wolf, Jr.
John S. Golwen

OF COUNSEL

Steven L. Gill

Jennifer Ziegenhorn
Holly N. Knight
Wendy A. Geurin
Charles S. Blatteis
John W. Campbell
Jennifer S. Kiesewetter
Joseph M. Koury
J. William Williams

For full biographical listings, see the Martindale-Hubbell Law Directory

*NASHVILLE,** Davidson Co.

BAKER, DONELSON, BEARMAN & CALDWELL (AV)

1700 Nashville City Center, 511 Union Street, 37219
Telephone: 615-726-5600
Telecopier: 615-726-0464
Email: info@bdbc.com *URL:* http://www.bakerdonelson.com
Memphis, Tennessee Office: 20th Floor, First Tennessee Building, 165 Madison, 38103.
Telephone: 901-526-2000.
Telecopier: 901-577-2303.
Chattanooga, Tennessee Office: 1800 Republic Centre, 633 Chestnut Street, 37450-1800.
Telephone: 423-756-2010.
Telecopier: 423-756-3447.
Knoxville, Tennessee Office: 2200 Riverview Tower, 900 South Gay Street, 37901.
Telephone: 423-549-7000.
Telecopier: 423-525-8569.
Johnson City, Tennessee Office: SunTrust Bank Building, 207 Mockingbird Lane, P.O. Box 3038, 37602.
Telephone: 423-928-0181.
Telecopier: 423-928-5694; 423-928-3654; Kingsport: 423-246-6191.
Huntsville, Tennessee Office: 3 Courthouse Square, 37756.
Telephone: 423-663-2321.
Telecopier: 423-663-2111.

(See Next Column)

BAKER, DONELSON, BEARMAN & CALDWELL, *Nashville—Continued*

Washington, D.C. Office: Market Square, 801 Pennsylvania Avenue, N.W., 20004.
Telephone: 202-508-3400.
Telecopier: 202-508-3402.
Jackson, Mississippi Office: Suite 500, 700 North State Street, 39202.
Telephone: 601-351-2400.
Telecopier: 601-351-2424.

OF COUNSEL

Peter C. Ward (Not admitted in TN)

For Complete List of Firm Personnel, See General Section

For full biographical listings, see the Martindale-Hubbell Law Directory

---

BASS, BERRY & SIMS PLC (AV)

2700 First American Center, 37238-2700
Telephone: 615-742-6200
Telecopy: 615-742-6293
URL: http://www.bassberry.com
Knoxville, Tennessee Office: 1700 Riverview Tower, 900 S. Gay Street, 37902 and P.O. Box 1509, 37901-1509.
Telephone: 423-521-6200.
Telecopy: 423-521-6234.
Memphis, Tennessee Office: 119 S. Main Street, Suite 500, 38103.
Telephone: 901-312-9100.
Fax: 901-312-9101.

MEMBERS OF FIRM

James O. Bass, Jr.
Robert J. Walker
R. Dale Grimes

Representative Clients: BellSouth Telecommunications, Inc.; The Vanderbilt University; Ingram Industries, Inc.; Amana Refrigeration, Inc.; Blue Cross and Blue Shield of Tennessee, Inc.; Service Merchandise Company, Inc.; Voluntary Hospitals of America, Inc.; Levi Strauss & Co., Inc.; Bristol-Myers Squibb Co.; Kimberly Clark Corp.

For full biographical listings, see the Martindale-Hubbell Law Directory

---

KING & BALLOW (AV)

Union Street Plaza, 315 Union Street, Suite 1100, 37201
Telephone: 615-259-3456
Fax: 615-254-7907
Email: lawfirm@king-ballow.com *URL:* http://www.king-ballow.com
San Diego, California Office: 2700 Symphony Towers, 750 B Street, 92101.
Telephone: 619-236-9401.
Fax: 619-236-9437.

MEMBERS OF FIRM

Frank S. King, Jr.
Robert L. Ballow
Alan L. Marx
Paul H. Duvall (Resident, San Diego, California Office)
Steven C. Douse
Mark E. Hunt

ASSOCIATES

Patrick M. Thomas
Elizabeth S. Washko (Not admitted in TN)

Representative Clients: Denver Post, Denver, Colorado; Dollar General Corporation, Nashville, Tennessee; Ingram Industries, Inc., Nashville, Tennessee; MediaNews Group, Denver, Colorado; Oakland Tribune, Oakland, California; Schneider National Carriers Incorporated, Greenbay, Wisconsin; Tulsa World, Tulsa, Oaklahoma; Union Tribune, San Diego, California; York Newspaper Co., York, Pennsylvania; National Newspaper Association, Washington, D.C.

For Complete List of Firm Personnel, See General Section

For full biographical listings, see the Martindale-Hubbell Law Directory

---

TEXAS

*DALLAS,** Dallas Co.

BAKER BOTTS L.L.P. (AV)

2001 Ross Avenue, 75201
Telephone: 214-953-6500
Fax: 214-953-6503
Email: postmaster@bakerbotts.com *URL:* http://www.bakerbotts.com
Houston, Texas Office: One Shell Plaza, 910 Louisiana.
Telephone: 713-229-1234.
Washington, D.C. Office: The Warner, 1299 Pennsylvania Avenue, N.W.
Telephone: 202-639-7700.
Austin, Texas Office: 1600 San Jacinto Center, 98 San Jacinto Boulevard.
Telephone: 512-322-2500.
New York, New York Office: 599 Lexington Avenue.
Telephone: 212-705-5000.
Moscow, Russia Office: 10 ul. Bolshaya Dimitrovka (formerly Pushkinskaya), 103031.
Telephone: 7095/921-5300 (Local); 7095/929-7070.

(See Next Column)

London, England Office: 45 Ludgate Hill.
Telephone: 0171-778-1400 (Local); 011-44-171-778-1400 (International).
Baku, Azerbaijan Office: 6-10 Vagif Mustafa-zadeh Street, Third Floor, Icheri Sheher, 370004.
Telephone: 994-12-97-63-88 (Local); 011-994-12-97-63-88 (International).

MEMBERS OF FIRM

Robert W. Jordan
Robert W. Kantner
Ronald L. Palmer

ASSOCIATE

Samara Lackman Kline

For Complete List of Firm Personnel, See General Section

For full biographical listings, see the Martindale-Hubbell Law Directory

---

CARRINGTON, COLEMAN, SLOMAN & BLUMENTHAL, L.L.P. (AV)

200 Crescent Court, Suite 1500, 75201
Telephone: 214-855-3000
Telecopy: 214-855-1333
Email: ccsb@ccsb.com *URL:* http://www.carringtoncoleman.com

MEMBERS OF FIRM

James E. Coleman, Jr.
Fletcher L. Yarbrough
Lyman G. Hughes
Tyler A. Baker, III
Tim Gavin
Diane M. Sumoski

SENIOR COUNSEL

Marvin S. Sloman

For Complete List of Firm Personnel, See General Section

For full biographical listings, see the Martindale-Hubbell Law Directory

---

CONANT FRENCH & CHANEY, LLP (AV)

3880 Bank One Center, 1717 Main Street, 75201
Telephone: 214-915-0620
Fasimile: 214-915-0634
Email: cfc@cfc-law.com *URL:* http://www.cfc-law.com

A. B. Conant, Jr.
William J. French
William B. Chaney
Linda A. Hale
Glen E. Lavy
Shawn W. Phelan
James D. MacIntyre

For full biographical listings, see the Martindale-Hubbell Law Directory

---

JONES, DAY, REAVIS & POGUE (AV)

2727 North Harwood Street, 75201-1515
Telephone: 214-220-3939
Telecopier: 214-969-5100
Email: counsel@jonesday.com *URL:* http://www.jonesday.com
In Atlanta, Georgia: 3500 SunTrust Plaza, 303 Peachtree Street.
Telephone: 404-521-3939.
Telecopier: 404-581-8330.
In Brussels, Belgium: Avenue Louise 480, 7th Floor, B-1050 Brussels.
Telephone: 32-2-645-14-11.
Telecopier: 32-2-645-14-45.
In Chicago, Illinois: 77 West Wacker.
Telephone: 312-782-3939.
Telecopier: 312-782-8585.
In Cleveland, Ohio: North Point, 901 Lakeside Avenue.
Telephone: 216-586-3939.
Telecopier: 216-579-0212.
In Columbus, Ohio: 1900 Huntington Center.
Telephone: 614-469-3939.
Telecopier: 614-461-4198.
In Frankfurt, Germany: Hochhaus am Park, Grüneburgweg 102, 60323 Frankfurt am Main.
Telephone: 49-69-9726-3939.
Telecopier: 49-69-9726-3993.
In Geneva, Switzerland: 20, rue de Candolle.
Telephone: 41-22-320-2339.
Telecopier: 41-22-320-1232.
In Hong Kong: 29th Floor, Entertainment Building, 30 Queen's Road Central.
Telephone: 852-2526-6895.
Telecopier: 852-2868-5871.
In Irvine, California: 5 Park Plaza, Suite 1100.
Telephone: 949-851-3939.
Telecopier: 949-553-7539.
In London, England: Bucklersbury House, 3 Queen Victoria Street.
Telephone: 44-20-7236-3939.
Telecopier: 44-20-7236-1113.
In Los Angeles, California: 555 West Fifth Street, Suite 4600.
Telephone: 213-489-3939.
Telecopier: 213-243-2539.
In New York, New York: 599 Lexington Avenue.
Telephone: 212-326-3939.
Telecopier: 212-755-7306.
In Paris, France: 120, rue du Faubourg Saint-Honoré.
Telephone: 33-1-56-59-39-39.
Telecopier: 33-1-56-59-39-38

(See Next Column)

JONES, DAY, REAVIS & POGUE—*Continued*

In Pittsburgh, Pennsylvania: 500 Grant Street, 31st Floor.
Telephone: 412-391-3939.
Telecopier: 412-394-7959.
Riyadh, Saudi Arabia: The International Law Firm (In Association with Jones, Day, Reavis & Pogue), Sulaymaniyah, Prince Mishari IBN, Addulaziz Street, P.O. Box 22166.
Telephone: (966-1) 462-8866.
Telecopier: (966-1) 462-9001.
In Shanghai, China: 2805 Kerry Centre, 1515 Nanjing Road West.
Telephone: 86-21-5298-6568.
Telecopier: 86-21-5298-6569.
In Sydney, Australia: Governor Phillip Tower, Level 38, 1 Farrer Place.
Telephone: 61-2-9210-6921.
Telecopier: 61-2-9210-6926.
In Taipei, Taiwan: 8th Floor, 2 Tun Hwa South Road, Section 2.
Telephone: (886-2) 2704-6808.
Telecopier: (886-2) 2704-6791.
In Tokyo, Japan: Toranomon 45 Mori Building, 3rd Floor, 1-5, Toranomon, 5-Chome, Minato-ku, Tokyo 105, Japan.
Telephone: 81-3-3433-3939.
Telecopier: 81-3-5401-2725.
In Washington, D.C.: 51 Louisiana Avenue, N.W.
Telephone: 202-879-3939.
Telecopier: 202-626-1700.

MEMBERS OF FIRM IN DALLAS

Joseph L. McEntee — Thomas R. Jackson

For Complete List of Firm Personnel, See General Section

For full biographical listings, see the Martindale-Hubbell Law Directory

THOMPSON & KNIGHT L.L.P. (AV)

(Attorneys and Counselors)
1700 Pacific Avenue Suite 3300, 75201
Telephone: 214-969-1700
Telecopy: 214-969-1751
Telex: 732 298
URL: http://www.tklaw.com
Austin, Texas Office: 1200 San Jacinto Center, 98 San Jacinto Boulevard, 78701.
Telephone: 512-469-6100.
Telecopy: 512-469-6180.
Fort Worth, Texas Office: 801 Cherry Street, Suite 1600, 76102.
Telephone: 817-347-1700.
Telecopy: 817-347-1799.
Houston, Texas Office: Thompson Knight Brown Parker & Leahy L.L.P., 1200 Smith Street, Suite 3600, 77002-4595.
Telephone: 713-654-8111.
Telecopier: 713-654-1871.
San Pedro Garza Garcia, Nuevo León, Mexico Office: Edificio Losoles PD-4, Av. Lázaro Cárdenas No. 2400 Pte., C.P. 66220.
Telephone: (52-8) 363-0096.
Telecopy: (52-8) 363-3067.

PARTNERS

L. James Berglund, II — Veronica Smith Lewis
Gregory S. C. Huffman — Timothy R. McCormick
Peter J. Thoma

SENIOR ATTORNEY

David S. White

ASSOCIATE

William M. Katz, Jr.

OF COUNSEL

David C. Cain (Not admitted in TX) — Laura Peterson Elkind

For Complete List of Firm Personnel, See General Section

For full biographical listings, see the Martindale-Hubbell Law Directory

*EL PASO,** El Paso Co.

KEMP, SMITH, DUNCAN & HAMMOND, A PROFESSIONAL CORPORATION (AV)

221 North Kansas, Suite 1700, 79901, P.O. Drawer 2800, 79999
Telephone: 915-533-4424
Fax: 915-546-5360
Email: ksdh@kempsmith.com *URL:* http://www.kempsmith.com
Austin, Texas Office: 816 Congress, Suite 1650.
Telephone: 512-320-5466.
Fax: 512-320-5431.

Mark N. Osborn

Attorneys for: Magnolia Coca Cola; Asarco.

For Complete List of Firm Personnel, See General Section

For full biographical listings, see the Martindale-Hubbell Law Directory

MOUNCE, GREEN, MYERS, SAFI & GALATZAN, A PROFESSIONAL CORPORATION (AV)

100 N. Stanton, Suite 1700, P.O. Box 1977, 79950-1977
Telephone: 915-532-2000
Fax: 915-541-1597
Email: mouncegreenmyers@worldnet.att.net

S. Anthony Safi

Attorneys for: El Paso Natural Gas Co.; El Paso Independent School District; Commercial Union Assurance Cos.; State Farm Mutual Automobile Insurance Co.; Greater El Paso Association of Realtors.

For Complete List of Firm Personnel, See General Section

For full biographical listings, see the Martindale-Hubbell Law Directory

*HOUSTON,** Harris Co.

BAKER BOTTS L.L.P. (AV)

One Shell Plaza, 910 Louisiana, 77002
Telephone: 713-229-1234
Cable Address: "Boterlove"
Fax: 713-229-1522
Email: postmaster@bakerbotts.com *URL:* http://www.bakerbotts.com
Washington, D.C. Office: The Warner, 1299 Pennsylvania Avenue, N.W.
Telephone: 202-639-7700.
New York, New York Office: 599 Lexington Avenue.
Telephone: 212-705-5000.
Austin, Texas Office: 1600 San Jacinto Center, 98 San Jacinto Boulevard.
Telephone: 512-322-2500.
Dallas, Texas Office: 2001 Ross Avenue.
Telephone: 214-953-6500.
Moscow, Russia Office: 10 ul. Bolshaya Dimitrovka (formerly Pushkinskaya), 103031.
Telephone: 7095/921-5300 (Local); 7095/929-7070 (International).
London, England Office: 45 Ludgate Hill.
Telephone: 0171-778-1400 (Local); 011-44-171-778-1400 (International).
Baku, Azerbaijan Office: 6-10 Vagif Mustafa-zadeh Street, Third Floor, Icheri Sheher, 370004.
Telephone: 994-12-97-63-88 (Local); 011-994-12-97-63-88 (International).
Fax: 994-12-97-63-91 (Local); 011-994-12-97-63-91 (International)

MEMBERS OF FIRM

J. Michael Baldwin — J. Bruce McDonald
Rufus W. Oliver, III

SENIOR COUNSEL

E. William Barnett

ASSOCIATES

Samuel W. Cooper — Paul J. Stancil
Keith D. Jaasma — Jennifer L. Walker Elrod
M. Shane Kimzey — Mark L. Walters

For Complete List of Firm Personnel, See General Section

For full biographical listings, see the Martindale-Hubbell Law Directory

CUNNINGHAM, DARLOW, ZOOK & CHAPOTON, LLP (AV)

1000 Louisiana, Suite 6900, 77002
Telephone: 713-659-5522
Fax: 713-659-4466
Email: sgosslee@cdzc.com

Tom Alan Cunningham — Richard J. Zook
Debbie Crupain Darlow — John E. Chapoton, Jr.

ASSOCIATES

Kelley M. Keller — Jon T. Powell

For full biographical listings, see the Martindale-Hubbell Law Directory

VINSON & ELKINS L.L.P. (AV)

2300 First City Tower, 1001 Fannin, 77002-6760
Telephone: 713-758-2222
Fax: 713-758-2346
Email: info@velaw.com *URL:* http://www.velaw.com
Austin, Texas Office: One American Center Suite 2700, 600 Congress Avenue, Austin, Texas, 78701-3200.
Telephone: 512-495-8400.
Fax: 512-495-8612.
Beijing, China Office: 20/F, Beijing Silver Tower, No. 2, Dong San Huan Bei Lu, Chaoyang District, 100027.
Telephone: +86-10-6410-6300.
Fax: +86-10-6410-6360.
Dallas, Texas Office: 3700 Trammell Crow Center, 2001 Ross Avenue, Dallas, Texas, 75201-2975.
Telephone: 214-220-7700.
Fax: 214-220-7716.
London, England Office: Regis House, 8th Floor, 45 King William Street, London, EC4R 9AN, England.
Telephone: (44-171) 618-6000.
Fax: (44-171) 618-6001.

(See Next Column)

VINSON & ELKINS L.L.P., *Houston—Continued*

Moscow, Russia Office: 16 Ulitsa Spiridonovka, Second Floor, 103001 Moscow, Russia.
Telephone: (7-095) 956-1995. Local
Fax: (7-095) 956-1996. U.S. Satellite
Fax: (212) 803-0142.
New York, N.Y. Office: 1325 Avenue of the Americas, 17th Floor, New York, N.Y., 10019.
Telephone: 917-206-8000.
Fax: 917-206-8100.
Singapore Office: 6 Battery Road, #39-01, Singapore, 049909.
Telephone: (65) 536-8300.
Fax: (65) 536-8311.
Washington, D.C. Office: The Willard Office Building, 1455 Pennsylvania Avenue, N.W., Washington, D.C., 20004-1008.
Telephone: 202-639-6500.
Fax: 202-639-6604.

MEMBER OF FIRM

Harry M. Reasoner (Managing Partner)

MEMBERS OF FIRM

Alden L. Atkins (Resident, Washington, D.C. Office)
Scott J. Atlas
David M. Bond
C. Michael Buxton (Resident, Washington, D.C. Office)
Christopher W. Byrd
Edward A. Carr
John L. Carter
Ky P. Ewing, Jr. (Resident, Washington, D.C. Office)
Celso M. Gonzalez-Falla
Orrin L. Harrison, III (Resident, Dallas, Texas Office)
David T. Harvin
David T. Hedges, Jr.
Max Hendrick, III
Michael J. Henke (Resident, Washington, D.C. Office)
Neil W. Imus (Resident, Washington, D.C. Office)
Karen Jewell
Erica L. Krennerich
Thomas S. Leatherbury (Resident, Dallas, Texas Office)
Cathy A. Lewis (Resident, Washington, D.C. Office)
Michael L. Malone (Resident, Dallas, Texas Office)
Richard D. Milvenan (Resident, Austin, Texas Office)
John L. Murchison, Jr.
Charles T. Newton, Jr.
Betty R. Owens
James Arthur Reeder, Jr.
Charles W. Schwartz
James I. Serota (Resident. New York, N.Y. Office)
William D. Sims, Jr. (Resident, Dallas, Texas Office)
Alison L. Smith
Karl S. Stern
Walter B. Stuart IV
John D. Taurman (Resident, Washington, D. C. Office)
Charles D. Tetrault (Resident, Washington, D.C. Office)
Mark H. Tuohey, III (Resident, Washington, D.C. Office)
Allan Van Fleet
Robert C. Walters (Resident, Dallas, Texas Office)
Russell Yager (Resident, Dallas, Texas Office)
Paul L. Yde (Resident, Washington, D.C. Office)

WASHINGTON, D.C. OF COUNSEL

Tegan M. Flynn
William E. Lawler, III

NEW YORK OF COUNSEL

Michael M. Zaitz

ASSOCIATES

Bruce A. Blefeld
Vanessa Y. Chandler (Resident, Washington, D.C. Office)
William J. Cobb III (Resident, Austin, Texas Office)
Stephanie Crain
John P. DeGeeter
John M. Faust (Resident, Washington, D.C. Office)
Wallis M. Hampton
Dean W. Harvey (Resident, Austin, Texas Office)
Lisa R. Helgoe
Karl K. Hennessee
Michael C. Holmes
Joseph E. Hunsader (Resident, Washington, D.C. Office)
Jeffrey S. Johnston
Bruce C. McCulloch (Resident, Washington, D.C. Office)
Christopher H. Meakin
D. John Neese, Jr.
Jason M. Powers
Michael L. Raiff (Resident, Dallas, Texas Office)
Tomasz J. Sikora
Kathleen Bone Spangler
Jerome A. Swindell (Resident, Washington, D.C. Office)
Fred I. Williams
Richard C. Williams

For Complete List of Firm Personnel, See General Section

For full biographical listings, see the Martindale-Hubbell Law Directory

*SAN ANTONIO,** Bexar Co.

COX & SMITH INCORPORATED (AV)

112 East Pecan Street, Suite 1800, 78205-1521
Telephone: 210-554-5500
Fax: 210-226-8395
Email: info@coxsmith.com *URL:* http://www.coxsmith.com

J. Burleson Smith
Keith E. Kaiser
James B. Smith, Jr.
A. Michael Ferrill
James K. Spivey
Leslie S. Hyman
John M. Black

Representative Clients: Agency Rent-A-Car; Blue Cross Blue Shield of Texas; Boral Industries, Inc.; Eastman Kodak Co.; Miller Brewing Co.; Nashua Corp.; National Skeet Shooting Association; Owens-Corning Fiberglass Corp.; Santa Rosa Health Care; Southwest Oncology Group.

(See Next Column)

For Complete List of Firm Personnel, See General Section

For full biographical listings, see the Martindale-Hubbell Law Directory

UTAH

*SALT LAKE CITY,** Salt Lake Co.

CALLISTER NEBEKER & MCCULLOUGH, A PROFESSIONAL CORPORATION (AV)

Gateway Tower East, Suite 900, 10 East South Temple, 84133
Telephone: 801-530-7300
Telecopier: 801-364-9127
Email: mjeaston@cnmlaw.com *URL:* http://www.cnmlaw.com

James R. Holbrook
Mark L. Callister

Representative Clients: GTE Directories Corp.; University of Utah; Zions First National Bank.

For Complete List of Firm Personnel, See General Section

For full biographical listings, see the Martindale-Hubbell Law Directory

GIAUQUE, CROCKETT, BENDINGER & PETERSON, A PROFESSIONAL CORPORATION (AV)

Wells Fargo Plaza, 170 South Main, Suite 400, 84101-1664
Telephone: 801-533-8383
Fax: 801-531-1486
Email: gcbp@xmission.com

PARTNERS

Stephen G. Crockett
Gary F. Bendinger
Robert A. Peterson
Richard W. Casey
Stephen T. Hard
Milo Steven Marsden
Jeffery S. Williams

OF COUNSEL

Richard W. Giauque
Roger D. Sandack
Kevin M. McDonough
Robert J. Moore
Patricia A. O'Rorke

Sean N. Egan
Wesley D. Felix
Rebecca S. Parr
John H. Bogart
Lisa R. Petersen
J. Robert Sonne
Karen L. Martinez
Andrew G. Deiss (On Leave)

For full biographical listings, see the Martindale-Hubbell Law Directory

RAY, QUINNEY & NEBEKER, A PROFESSIONAL CORPORATION (AV)

79 South Main Street, Suite 400, P.O. Box 45385, 84145-0385
Telephone: 801-532-1500
Fax: 801-532-7543
Email: rqn@rqn.com *URL:* http://www.rqn.com
Provo, Utah Office: 92 North University Avenue, Suite 210, 84601-4420.
Telephone: 801-342-2400.
Fax: 801-375-8379.
Albuquerque, New Mexico Office: Suite 620, 40 First Plaza, N.W.
Telephone: 505-243-6665.
Fax: 505-764-9890.

Jonathan A. Dibble
James S. Jardine
Allan T. Brinkerhoff
Keith A. Kelly

Representative Clients: First Security Bank, N.A.; Borden, Inc.; Salt Lake Organizing Committee for the Winter Olympic Games of 2002; Southern Pacific Transportation; Utah Power & Light Co.; Travelers Insurance Co.; U.S. West.

For Complete List of Firm Personnel, See General Section

For full biographical listings, see the Martindale-Hubbell Law Directory

VAN COTT, BAGLEY, CORNWALL & MCCARTHY, A PROFESSIONAL CORPORATION (AV)

50 South Main Street, Suite 1600, P.O. Box 45340, 84145-0340
Telephone: 801-532-3333
Telecopier: 801-534-0058
Email: info@vancott.com *URL:* http://www.vancott.com
Ogden, Utah Office: 2404 Washington Boulevard, Suite 900.
Telephone: 801-394-5783.
Park City, Utah Office: 2200 Park Avenue, Suite C200-A.
Telephone: 435-649-3889.

David A. Greenwood
Kenneth W. Yeates

For Complete List of Firm Personnel, See General Section

For full biographical listings, see the Martindale-Hubbell Law Directory

VERMONT

*BURLINGTON,** Chittenden Co.

GRAVEL AND SHEA, A PROFESSIONAL CORPORATION (AV)

Corporate Plaza, 76 St. Paul Street, P.O. Box 369, 05402-0369
Telephone: 802-658-0220
Fax: 802-658-1456

Robert B. Hemley Dennis R. Pearson

SPECIAL COUNSEL

Norman Williams

For Complete List of Firm Personnel, See General Section

For full biographical listings, see the Martindale-Hubbell Law Directory

MILLER, EGGLESTON & CRAMER, LTD. (AV)

150 South Champlain Street, P.O. Box 1489, 05402-1489
Telephone: 802-864-0880
Telecopier: 802-864-0328

Martin K. Miller Anne E. Cramer
Peter F. Young

For Complete List of Firm Personnel, See General Section

For full biographical listings, see the Martindale-Hubbell Law Directory

VIRGINIA

RICHMOND, (Independent City)

MCGUIRE, WOODS, BATTLE & BOOTHE LLP (AV)

One James Center, 901 East Cary Street, 23219-4030
Telephone: 804-775-1000
Fax: 804-775-1061
Email: info@mwbb.com *URL:* http://www.mwbb.com
Atlanta, Georgia Office: 285 Peachtree Center Avenue, N.E., Suite 2200, Marquis Tower Two, 30303-1234.
Telephone: 404-443-5500.
Fax: 404-443-5599.
Baltimore, Maryland Office: 7 Saint Paul Street, Suite 1000, 21202-1671.
Telephone: 410-659-4400.
Fax: 410-659-4599.
Charlotte, North Carolina Offices: 3700 Bank of America Plaza, 101 South Tryon Street, 28280.
Telephone: 704-373-8999.
Fax: 704-373-8990 and Bank of America Corporate Center, Suite 2900, 100 North Tryon Street, 28202.
Telephone: 704-373-8999.
Fax: 704-373-8935.
Charlottesville, Virginia Office: Court Square Building, 310 Fourth Street, N.E., Suite 300, P.O. Box 1288, 22902-1288.
Telephone: 804-977-2500.
Fax: 804-980-2222.
Chicago, Illinois Office: R.R. Donnelly Building, 77 West Wacker Drive, Suite 4500, 60601-1635.
Telephone: 312-849-3699.
Fax: 312-849-3690.
Jacksonville, Florida Office: 50 North Laura Street, 32202-3635.
Telephone: 904-798-3200.
Fax: 904-798-3207.
McLean, (Tysons Corner) Virginia Office: 1750 Tysons Boulevard, Suite 1800, 22102-3892.
Telephone: 703-712-5000.
Fax: 703-712-5050.
Norfolk, Virginia Office: World Trade Center, 101 West Main Street, Suite 9000, 23510-1655.
Telephone: 757-640-3700.
Fax: 757-640-3701. 23219-4030.
Washington, D.C. Office: Washington Square, 1050 Connecticut Avenue, N.W., Suite 1200, 20036-5317.
Telephone: 202-857-1700.
Fax: 202-857-1737.
Almaty, Republic of Kazakhstan Office: Park Palace, 41 Kazibek Bi Street, 2nd Floor, 480100.
Telephone: 7-3272-608-300.
Fax: 7-3272-608-305.
Brussels, Belgium Office: 250 Avenue Louise, Bte. 64, 1050.
Telephone: 32-2-629-42-11.
Fax: 32-2-629-42-22.
Moscow, Russia Office: Paveltskaya Square, 1 Valovaya Street, 7th Floor, 13054.
Telephone: 7-502-937-0774.
Fax: 7-502-937-0776.

(See Next Column)

MEMBERS OF FIRM

Howard Feller James H. Walsh
Anne Marie Whittemore

For Complete List of Firm Personnel, See General Section

For full biographical listings, see the Martindale-Hubbell Law Directory

WILLIAMS, MULLEN, CLARK & DOBBINS, A PROFESSIONAL CORPORATION (AV)

Two James Center, 1021 East Cary Street, P.O. Box 1320, 23218-1320
Telephone: 804-643-1991
Fax: 804-783-6507
URL: http://www.wmcd.com
Newport News Office: Harbor Bank Center, Suite 210, One Old Oyster Point Road, 23602-7119.
Telephone: 757-249-5100.
Fax: 757-249-5109.
Virginia Beach Office: One Columbus Center, 23462-6763.
Telephone: 757-499-8800.
Fax: 757-473-0395.
Vienna Office: 1593 Spring Hill Road, Suite 510, 22182.
Telephone: 703-760-5200.
Fax: 703-748-0244.
Washington, D.C. Office: The Farragut Building, 900 17th Street, N.W., Suite 700, 20006.
Telephone: 202-293-0213.
Fax: 804-783-6507. Fax Within D.C.: 202-293-5939.
London, England Office: Blake Lodge, Bridge Lane, SW11 3AD.
Telephone: (011-44-71) 223-2756.
Fax: (011-44-71) 350-0156.
Riyadh, Saudi Arabia Affiliate Office: Saudi-American Legal Consultants Commercial Building #2, Diplomatic Quarter, P.O. Box 57270, 11574.
Telephone: (011-966-1) 488-1563.
Fax: (011-966-1) 488-0542.

Stephen E. Baril David R. Johnson

For Complete List of Firm Personnel, See General Section

For full biographical listings, see the Martindale-Hubbell Law Directory

WASHINGTON

*SEATTLE,** King Co.

LANE POWELL SPEARS LUBERSKY LLP (AV)

Limited Liability Partnership composed of Individuals and Professional Service Corporations
1420 Fifth Avenue, Suite 4100, 98101-2338
Telephone: 206-223-7000
Facsimile: 206-223-7107
Email: information@lanepowell.com *URL:* http://www.lanepowell.com
Other Offices at: Portland, Oregon; Anchorage, Alaska; Olympia and Mount Vernon, Washington; London, England.

MANAGING PARTNER

James L. Robart

MEMBERS OF FIRM

Larry S. Gangnes Richard C. Siefert
D. Wayne Gittinger Douglas E. Smith
Christian N. Oldham David C. Spellman

COUNSEL

Minaksi Bhatt (Not admitted in WA)

Representative Clients: Coca-Cola Bottling Co. of Yakima & Tri-Cities; Fred Hutchinson Cancer Research Center; Mitsui & Co., Ltd.; Nordstrom, Inc.; Simpson Investment Co. and Affiliates; Texaco Inc.

For Complete List of Firm Personnel, See General Section

For full biographical listings, see the Martindale-Hubbell Law Directory

PERKINS COIE LLP (AV)

Strategic Alliance with Russell & DuMoulin
1201 Third Avenue, Suite 4800, 98101-3099
Telephone: 206-583-8888
Facsimile: 206-583-8500
Email: perkins@perkinscoic.com *URL:* http://www.perkinscoie.com
Anchorage, Alaska: 1029 West Third Avenue, Suite 300, 99501-1970.
Telephone: 907-279-8561.
Facsimile: 907-276-3108.
Los Angeles, California: 1620 26th Street, 6th Floor, 90404.
Telephone: 310-788-9900.
Facsimile: 310-788-3399.
Menlo Park, California: 135 Commonwealth Drive, Suite 250, 94025-1105.
Telephone: 650-752-6000.
Facsimile: 650-752-6050.

(See Next Column)

PERKINS COIE LLP, *Seattle—Continued*

San Francisco, California: 180 Townsend Street, 94107-1909.
Telephone: 415-781-3200.
Facsimile: 415-781-2525.
Denver, Colorado: World Trade Center, 1675 Broadway, Suite 2800, 80202-062.
Telephone: 303-571-6100.
Facsimile: 303-571-6111.
Washington, D.C.: 607 Fourteenth Street, N.W., 20005-2011.
Telephone: 202-628-6600.
Telex: 44-0277 PCSO.
Facsimile: 202-434-1690.
Boise, Idaho: 714 West State Street, 83702.
Telephone: 208-343-3434.
Facsimile: 208-343-3232.
Portland, Oregon: Suite 1500, 1211 Southwest Fifth Avenue.
Telephone: 503-727-2000.
Facsimile: 503-727-2222.
Bellevue, Washington: Suite 1800, One Bellevue Center, 411 - 108th Avenue N.E., 98004-5584.
Telephone: 425-453-6980.
Facsimile: 425-453-7350.
Spokane, Washington: North 221 Wall Street, Suite 600, 99201-0826.
Telephone: 509-624-2212.
Facsimile: 509-458-3399.
Hong Kong: 17/F, Standard Charter Bank Building, 4 Des Voeux Road.
Telephone: 852-2878-1177.
Facsimile: 852-2524-9988.
Taipei, Taiwan, R.O.C.: 8/F Cathay United Bank Tower, 85 Jen Ai Rd., Section 5.
Telephone: 886-2-2778-1177.
Facsimile: 886-2-2777-9898.
Canada: Strategic Alliance with Russell & DuMoulin, 1700-1075 West Georgia Street. Vancouver, British Columbia, V6E 3G2.
Telephone: 604-631-3131.

PARTNERS

Richard L. Baum (Resident, Portland Oregon Office)
Thomas L. Boeder
David J. Burman
Ronald M. Gould
Ramer B. Holtan, Jr.
Bobbee J. Musgrave (Resident, Denver, Colorado Office)
Michael H. Simon (Resident, Portland, Oregon Office)

Counsel for: The Boeing Company; Puget Sound Power Energy; US West; Amazon.com; Louisiana-Pacific; Lloyd's of London (Aviation); Weyerhauser.

For Complete List of Firm Personnel, See General Section

For full biographical listings, see the Martindale-Hubbell Law Directory

WEST VIRGINIA

*CHARLESTON,** Kanawha Co.

JACKSON & KELLY (AV)

1600 Laidley Tower, P.O. Box 553, 25322
Telephone: 304-340-1000
Fax: 304-340-1130
Email: info@jacksonkelly.com *URL:* http://www.jacksonkelly.com
Martinsburg, West Virginia Office: 300 Foxcroft Avenue, P.O. Box 1068.
Telephone: 304-263-8800.
Fax: 304-263-7110.
Morgantown, West Virginia Office: 6000 Hampton Center, P.O. Box 619.
Telephone: 304-599-3000.
Fax: 304-285-2040.
New Martinsville, West Virginia Office: 256 Russell Avenue, P.O. Box 68.
Telephone: 304-455-1751.
Fax: 304-455-6314.
Parkersburg, West Virginia Office: 412 Market Street, Suite 202, P.O. Box 1144.
Telephone: 304-424-3490.
Fax: 304-424-3499.
Fairmont, West Virginia Office: 1000 Technology Drive, Suite 1310.
Telephone: 304-368-2000.
Fax: 304-368-2020.
Lexington, Kentucky Office: 175 East Main Street, Suite 500, P.O. Box 2150.
Telephone: 606-255-9500.
Fax: 606-281-6478.
Washington, D. C. Office: 2401 Pennsylvania Avenue, N.W., Suite 400.
Telephone: 202-973-0200.
Fax: 202-973-0232.
Denver, Colorado Office: Suite 2710, 1660 Lincoln Street.
Telephone: 303-390-0003.
Fax: 303-390-0040.
Wheeling, West Virginia Office: 1144 Market Street.
Telephone: 304-233-4000.
Fax: 304-233-4077.

(See Next Column)

MEMBERS OF FIRM

James Knight Brown
W. Henry Jernigan, Jr.
James R. Snyder
David Allen Barnette
Elizabeth Osenton Lord

For Complete List of Firm Personnel, See General Section

For full biographical listings, see the Martindale-Hubbell Law Directory

*MORGANTOWN,** Monongalia Co.

THE FUSCO LEGAL GROUP, L.C. (AV)

2400 Cranberry Square, 26505-9209
Telephone: 304-594-1000
Telecopier: 304-594-1181
URL: http://www.fuscolegalgroup.com
Email: fnlaw@wvlaw.com *URL:* http://www.wvlaw.com

Andrew G. Fusco

Jeffrey A. Ray

For Complete List of Firm Personnel, See General Section

For full biographical listings, see the Martindale-Hubbell Law Directory

WISCONSIN

*MADISON,** Dane Co.

QUARLES & BRADY LLP (AV)

Firstar Plaza, One South Pinckney Street, P.O. Box 2113, 53701-2113
Telephone: 608-251-5000
Fax: 608-251-9166
URL: http://www.quarles.com
Milwaukee, Wisconsin Office: 411 East Wisconsin Avenue, 53202-4497.
Telephone: 414-277-5000.
Fax: 414-271-3552.
West Palm Beach, Florida Office: 222 Lakeview Avenue, 4th Floor, 33401.
Telephone: 561-653-5000.
Fax: 561-653-5333.
Naples, Florida Office: Barnett Center, 4501 Tamiami Trail North, Suite 300, 34103-3060.
Telephone: 941-262-5959.
Fax: 941-434-4999.
Phoenix, Arizona Office: One Camelback Building, One East Camelback Road, Suite 400, 85012-1649.
Telephone: 602-230-5500.
Fax: 602-230-5598.
Chicago, Illinois Office: Quarles & Brady LLC, Citicorp Center, 500 West Madison Street, Suite 3700.
Telephone: 312-715-5000.
Fax: 312-715-5155.

PARTNER

Michael L. Zaleski

For Complete List of Firm Personnel, See General Section

For full biographical listings, see the Martindale-Hubbell Law Directory

*MILWAUKEE,** Milwaukee Co.

FOLEY & LARDNER (AV)

Firstar Center, 777 East Wisconsin Avenue, 53202-5367
Telephone: 414-271-2400
Telex: 26-819 (Foley Lard Mil)
Facsimile: 414-297-4900
Email: foleylardner@worldnet.att.net *URL:* http://www.foleylardner.com
Los Angeles, California Office: 2029 Century Park East, 35th Floor.
Telephone: 310-277-2223.
Fax: 310-557-8475.
Sacramento, California Office: 300 Capitol Mall, Suite 1125.
Telephone: 916-443-8005.
Fax: 916-443-2240.
San Diego, California Office: 402 West Broadway, 23rd Floor.
Telephone: 619-234-6655.
Fax: 619-234-3510.
San Francisco, California Office: One Maritime Plaza, Sixth Floor.
Telephone: 415-434-4484.
Fax: 415-434-4507.
Denver, Colorado Office: 1999 Broadway, Suite 2560.
Telephone: 303-297-0260.
Fax: 303-297-0266.
Washington, D.C. Office: Washington Harbour, Suite 500, 3000 K Street, N.W.
Telephone: 202-672-5300.
Telex: 904136 (Foley Lard Wash).
Facsimile: 202-672-5399.

(See Next Column)

FOLEY & LARDNER—*Continued*

Jacksonville, Florida Office: The Greenleaf Building, 200 Laura Street. P.O. Box 240.
Telephone: 904-359-2000.
Facsimile: 904-359-8700.
Orlando, Florida Office: Suite 1800, 111 North Orange Avenue, P.O. Box 2193.
Telephone: 407-423-7656.
Facsimile: 407-648-1743.
Tallahassee, Florida Office: 300 East Park Avenue, P.O. Box 1454.
Telephone: 850-222-6100.
Facsimile: 850-561-6475.
Tampa, Florida Offices: Suite 2700, One Hundred N. Tampa Street, P.O. Box 3391.
Telephones: 813-229-2300; Pinellas County: 813-442-3296.
Facsimile: 813-221-4210.
West Palm Beach, Florida Office: Suite 200, Phillips Point East Tower, 777 South Flagler Drive.
Telephone: 561-655-5050.
Facsimile: 561-655-6925.
Chicago, Illinois Office: Suite 3300, One IBM Plaza, 330 N. Wabash Avenue.
Telephone: 312-755-1900.
Facsimile: 312-755-1925.
Annapolis, Maryland Office: Suite 102, 175 Admiral Cochrane Drive.
Telephone: 410-266-8077.
Telex: 899149 (Oldtownpat).
Facsimile: 410-266-8664.
Madison, Wisconsin Office: Verex Plaza, 150 East Gilman Street, P.O. Box 1497.
Telephone: 608-257-5035.
Facsimile: 608-258-4258.
Brussels, Belgium Office: Avenue Louise, 283.
Telephone: 32-2-646-2777.
Facsimile: 32-2-646-7574.

PARTNERS

Russell J. Barron
Ralf-Reinhard Böer
Richard H. Casper
Robert A. DuPuy
Richard S. Florsheim
Maurice J. (Marc) McSweeney
Christian G. Steinmetz
Ronald M. Wawrzyn
Edwin P. Wiley

RETIRED PARTNERS

David E. Beckwith
James P. Brody

For Complete List of Firm Personnel, See General Section

For full biographical listings, see the Martindale-Hubbell Law Directory

KERSTEN & MCKINNON, S.C. (AV)

231 West Wisconsin Avenue, Suite 1200, 53203
Telephone: 414-271-0054
Fax: 414-271-7131
Email: Kersten3@ExecPc.com

Charles J. Kersten (1929-1972)
Arlo McKinnon (1929-1999)
J. P. McKinnon (1943-1973)
E. Campion Kersten
George P. Kersten
Kenan J. Kersten
Leslie Van Buskirk
Matthew T. Fricker

For full biographical listings, see the Martindale-Hubbell Law Directory

MEISSNER TIERNEY FISHER & NICHOLS S.C. (AV)

The Milwaukee Center, 111 East Kilbourn Avenue, 19th Floor, 53202-6622
Telephone: 414-273-1300
Facsimile: 414-273-5840
URL: http://www.mtfn.com

Joseph E. Tierney III
Dennis L. Fisher
Thomas J. Nichols
Michael J. Cohen

Justin B. Nelsen

OF COUNSEL

Paul F. Meissner

For full biographical listings, see the Martindale-Hubbell Law Directory

MICHAEL BEST & FRIEDRICH LLP (AV)

100 East Wisconsin Avenue, 53202-4108
Telephone: 414-271-6560
Telecopier: 414-277-0656
Cable Address: "Mibef"
Email: info@mbf-law.com *URL:* http://www.mbf-law.com
Madison, Wisconsin Office: One South Pinckney Street, Firstar Plaza, P.O. Box 1806, 53701-1806.
Telephone: 608-257-3501.
Telecopier: 283-2275.
Manitowoc, Wisconsin Office: 1000 Maritime Drive, 54220.
Telephone: 920-686-2800.
Fax: 920-686-2810.

(See Next Column)

Chicago, Illinois Office: Michael Best & Friedrich LLC, 77 West Wacker Drive, Suite 4300, 60601-1635.
Telephone: 312-845-5800.
Telecopier: 312-845-5828.

PARTNERS

John K. MacIver
David V. Meany

For Complete List of Firm Personnel, See General Section

For full biographical listings, see the Martindale-Hubbell Law Directory

QUARLES & BRADY LLP (AV)

411 East Wisconsin Avenue, 53202-4497
Telephone: 414-277-5000
Fax: 414-271-3552
URL: http://www.quarles.com
Madison, Wisconsin Office: Firstar Plaza, One South Pinckney Street, P.O. Box 2113, 53701-2113.
Telephone: 608-251-5000.
Fax: 608-251-9166.
West Palm Beach, Florida Office: 222 Lakeview Avenue, 4th Floor, 33401.
Telephone: 561-653-5000.
Fax: 561-653-5333.
Naples, Florida Office: Barnett Center, 4501 Tamiami Trail North, Suite 300, 34103-3060.
Telephone: 941-262-5959.
Fax: 941-434-4999.
Phoenix, Arizona Office: One Camelback Building, One East Camelback Road, Suite 400, 85012-1649.
Telephone: 602-230-5500.
Fax: 602-230-5598.
Chicago, Illinois Office: Quarles & Brady LLC, Citicorp Center, 500 West Madison Street, Suite 3700.
Telephone: 312-715-5000.
Fax: 312-715-5155.

MEMBERS OF FIRM

(ALPHABETICALLY BY YEAR OF ADMISSION TO BAR)

Harry G. Holz
Thomas W. Ehrmann
Samuel J. Recht
Wayne E. Babler, Jr.
W. Stuart Parsons
John A. Casey
Peter C. Karegeannes
Quinn W. Martin
Darryl S. Bell
Matthew J. Flynn
Michael H. Schaalman
Carl R. Schwartz
David R. Cross

OF COUNSEL

Elwin J. Zarwell

ASSOCIATE

Brian D. Winters

For Complete List of Firm Personnel, See General Section

For full biographical listings, see the Martindale-Hubbell Law Directory

PUERTO RICO

SAN JUAN, San Juan Dist.

FIDDLER GONZÁLEZ & RODRÍGUEZ, LLP

254 Muñoz Rivera Avenue (Hato Rey), P.O. Box 363507, 00936-3507
Telephone: 787-753-3113
Telecopier: 787-759-3123
Email: fiddler@fgrlaw.com *URL:* http://www.fgrlaw.com

MEMBERS OF FIRM

Salvador Antonetti-Zequeira
Ricardo F. Casellas

Representative Clients: The Chase Manhattan Bank, N.A.; Kodak Caribbean Ltd.; Pfizer, Inc.; Merck & Co., Inc.; Bacardi Corp.

For Complete List of Firm Personnel, See General Section

For full biographical listings, see the Martindale-Hubbell Law Directory

JORGE R. JIMENEZ LAW OFFICES

Suite 807 IBM Building, 654 Muñoz Rivera Avenue (Hato Rey), 00918
Telephone: 787-763-0106
Fax: 787-763-0574

MEMBERS OF FIRM

Jorge R. Jimenez
Juan F. Doval

For full biographical listings, see the Martindale-Hubbell Law Directory

CANADA
ONTARIO

*TORONTO,** Regional Munic. of Toronto

BORDEN & ELLIOT (AV)

Barristers & Solicitors
Scotia Plaza, 40 King Street West, M5H 3Y4
Telephone: 416-367-6000
Telecopier: 416-367-6749
Email: info@borden.com *URL:* http://www.borden.com
Ottawa, Ontario Office: Borden Elliot Scott & Aylen, 1000-60 Rue Queen Street.
Telephone: 613-237-5160; 800-661-4237. General
Facsimile: 613-230-8842. IP Dept.
Facsimile: 613-787-3558. Email: ottinfo@scottaylen.com. URL: http://www.borden.com.

Simon B. Scott, Q.C.

For Complete List of Firm Personnel, See General Section

For full biographical listings, see the Martindale-Hubbell Law Directory

DAVIES, WARD & BECK (AV)

1 First Canadian Place, M5X 1B1
Telephone: 416-863-0900
Fax: 416-863-0871
Email: info@dwb.com *URL:* http://www.dwb.com

PARTNERS AND ASSOCIATES

Calvin S. Goldman, Q.C.
Joel T. Kissack
Paul S. Crampton
Richard F. D. Corley
Christine J. Prudham
Brian A. Facey
Neil Finkelstein
John D. Bodrug
Mark C. Katz
Milos Barutciski
Lori A. Cornwall
Dany H. Assaf

For Complete List of Firm Personnel, See General Section

For full biographical listings, see the Martindale-Hubbell Law Directory

KELLY AFFLECK GREENE (AV)

One First Canadian Place, Suite 840, P.O. Box 489, M5X 1E5
Telephone: 416-360-2800
Fax: 416-360-5960
Email: info@kag.net *URL:* http://www.kag.net

MEMBERS OF FIRM

W. Anthony Kelly, Q.C.
Donald S. Affleck, Q.C.
Peter R. Greene
Donald B. Houston
James C. Orr
Peter C. Wardle
Helen A. Daley
Melissa J. Kennedy

ASSOCIATES

Kenneth A. Dekker
W. Michael G. Osborne
Jason C. Markwell
Patrice F. Band

For full biographical listings, see the Martindale-Hubbell Law Directory

APPELLATE PRACTICE

MINNESOTA

*MINNEAPOLIS,** Hennepin Co.

ABDO AND ABDO, P.A. (AV)
710 Northstar West 625 Marquette Avenue, 55402
Telephone: 612-333-1526
Fax: 612-342-2608
Email: abdoabdo@aol.com *URL:* http://www.abdo.com.br

E. John Abdo (1912-1993)
Robert P. Abdo
Steven R. Hedges
Keith J. Broady
Kenneth J. Abdo
Timothy C. Matson

Representative Client: ADT Security Services, Inc.

For Complete List of Firm Personnel, See General Section

For full biographical listings, see the Martindale-Hubbell Law Directory

WALDECK & LIND, P.A. (AV)
Suite 730, TCF Tower, 121 South Eighth Street, 55402
Telephone: 612-375-1550
Facsimilie: 612-375-0647

Timothy W. Waldeck
Peter E. Lind

Steven D. Pattee

For full biographical listings, see the Martindale-Hubbell Law Directory

MISSOURI

*JEFFERSON CITY,** Cole Co.

CARSON & COIL, P.C. (AV)
515 East High, P.O. Box 28, 65102
Telephone: 573-636-2177
Telecopier: 573-636-7119
Email: general@carsoncoil.com

Forrest P. Carson (1910-1981)
Cullen Coil (1907-1989)
Michael P. Riley
Ronald R. McMillin
Eugene G. Bushmann
James W. Gallaher
Lori J. Levine
Rudolph L. Veit
Michael Madsen
R. Max Humphreys
Mark A. Ludwig
Dana L. Frese
Edward C. Clausen
Carla G. Holste
Kent L. Brown
Douglas W. Hennon
Charles J. McPheeters
Paul T. Graham

Jack C. Hauser, Jr.
Charles A. "Chip" Gentry
James W. "Jamie" Gallaher, Jr.

General Counsel for: Capital Reserve Life Insurance Co.; Missouri Farm Bureau; Healthcare Services Group.
Reference: Central Trust Bank.

For full biographical listings, see the Martindale-Hubbell Law Directory

KANSAS CITY, Jackson, Clay, Platte & Cass Cos.

WYRSCH HOBBS MIRAKIAN & LEE, P.C. (AV)
1300 Mercantile Tower 1101 Walnut, 64106-2122
Telephone: 816-221-0080
Fax: 816-221-3280
Email: whml@sprintmail.com

James R. Wyrsch
Stephen G. Mirakian
Ronald D. Lee
James R. Hobbs
Keith E. Drill
Jacqueline A. Cook
Charles M. Rogers
Marilyn B. Keller
Cheryl A. Pilate
W. Brian Gaddy

OF COUNSEL
James W. Fletcher

David Andrew Kelly

LEGAL SUPPORT PERSONNEL
Darlene Wyrsch (Paralegal)
Dru A. Colhour (Paralegal)
Katherine Vetsch (Paralegal)
Leslie R. Elkins (Paralegal)
William J. Baltrusaitis, II (Investigator)

For full biographical listings, see the Martindale-Hubbell Law Directory

ST. LOUIS, (Independent City)

THE SESTRIC LAW FIRM (AV)
801 North Second Street, Suite 401, 63102-2560
Telephone: 314-241-8600
Fax: 314-241-8603
Email: AJSESTRIC@JUNO.COM *URL:* http://www.lawyers.com/thesestriclawfirm

MEMBER OF FIRM
Anthony J. Sestric
ASSOCIATE
Nancy K. Troutman
LEGAL SUPPORT PERSONNEL
Laura A. Schulte

Reference: Mercantile Bank and Trust Co.

For full biographical listings, see the Martindale-Hubbell Law Directory

MONTANA

*BOZEMAN,** Gallatin Co.

KIRWAN & BARRETT, P.C. (AV)
215 West Mendenhall, P.O. Box 1348, 59771-1348
Telephone: 406-586-1553
Fax: 406-586-8971

Peter M. Kirwan
Stephen M. Barrett

For full biographical listings, see the Martindale-Hubbell Law Directory

NEBRASKA

*LINCOLN,** Lancaster Co.

BERRY, KELLEY & HANSEN (AV)
2650 North 48th Street, P.O. Box 4554, 68504
Telephone: 402-466-8444
Fax: 402-466-1793
URL: http://www.JSBerrylaw.com

MEMBERS OF FIRM
John Stevens Berry
James M. Kelley
Michael J. Hansen

For full biographical listings, see the Martindale-Hubbell Law Directory

NEVADA

*LAS VEGAS,** Clark Co.

ALBRIGHT, STODDARD, WARNICK & ALBRIGHT, A PROFESSIONAL CORPORATION (AV)
Quail Park I, Building D-4, 801 South Rancho Drive, 89106
Telephone: 702-384-7111
Fax: 702-384-0605
URL: http://www.aswalaw.com

G. Vern Albright
William H. Stoddard
Whitney B. Warnick
G. Mark Albright

D. Chris Albright
Tami C. Budo
Corey D. Randall (Not admitted in NV)

Representative Clients: Tokio Marine and Fire Insurance Co.; INAPRO, a CIGNA Co.; Nevada Ready Mix; North American Health Care, Inc. (Nursing Home); Royal Insurance; First Security Bank of Utah; Nevada Community Bank; Nationwide Insurance Co.; Liberty Mutual Insurance; CB Commercial.

For full biographical listings, see the Martindale-Hubbell Law Directory

THOMAS D. BEATTY (AV)
601 East Bridger Avenue, 89101
Telephone: 702-382-5111
Facsimile: 702-382-2892

(See Next Column)

THOMAS D. BEATTY, *Las Vegas—Continued*

ASSOCIATE

Rena G. Hughes

Representative Clients: Liberty Mutual Insurance Co.; Aetna Casualty & Surety Co.; Bayliner Marine Corporation; Clark County Association of School Administrators.
Reference: Wells Fargo Bank.

For full biographical listings, see the Martindale-Hubbell Law Directory

JOLLEY, URGA, WIRTH & WOODBURY (AV)

3800 Howard Hughes Parkway Suite 1600, 89109
Telephone: 702-699-7500
Facsimile: 702-699-7555
URL: http://www.juww.com
Boulder City, Nevada Office: Suite 105, 1000 Nevada Highway, 89005.
Telephone: 702-293-3674.

MEMBERS OF FIRM

Roger A. Wirth
Brian E. Holthus

Representative Clients: Wells Fargo Bank and its predecessor, First Interstate Bank of Nevada; Nevada State Bank; Chicago Title Insurance Co.; Melvin Simon & Associates, Inc.; General Motors Acceptance Corp.; Toyota Motor Credit Corporation; Champion Home Builders Co.; Circus Circus Casinos, Inc.

For Complete List of Firm Personnel, See General Section

For full biographical listings, see the Martindale-Hubbell Law Directory

SCHRECK MORRIS (AV)

1200 Bank of America Plaza, 300 South Fourth Street, 89101
Telephone: 702-382-2101
Fax: 702-382-8135; 702-474-9422
URL: http://www.schreckmorris.com
Reno, Nevada Office: 100 West Liberty, Suite 940, 89501.
Telephone: 775-322-7777.
Facsimile: 775-322-7791.

MEMBERS OF FIRM

Frank A. Schreck
Steve Morris
Andrew S. Brignone
Leslie Terry Jones
Mary Kristina Pickering
John A. Godfrey
Ann Morgan
Sean T. McGowan
Ellen Schulhofer
James J. Pisanelli
Clark V. Vellis
Todd L. Bice

ASSOCIATES

James R. Chamberlain
Dennis V. Gallagher
Margaret L. Sanner
F. Edward Mulholland, II
Elizabeth M. Fielder
Elayna Youchah
Sonia C. Vermeys
Denise Michaelides
Mary J. Drury
John P. Desmond
Adam P. Segal
Matthew McCaughey
Amelia R. De Los Santos
Wendy Medura
Robert J. Grasso
Shawn G. Pearson
David Dornak
Matthew L. Heinhold
Paul D. Colton

For full biographical listings, see the Martindale-Hubbell Law Directory

WRIGHT, JUDD & WINCKLER (AV)

302 East Carson Avenue, 3rd Floor, 89101
Telephone: 702-382-4004
FAX: 702-382-4800
Email: wjw@netxs.net

MEMBERS OF FIRM

Richard A. Wright
Bruce M. Judd
Karen C. Winckler

For full biographical listings, see the Martindale-Hubbell Law Directory

*RENO,** Washoe Co.

BIBLE, HOY & TRACHOK, A PROFESSIONAL CORPORATION (AV)

201 West Liberty Street, Third Floor, 89501
Telephone: 775-786-8000
Fax: 775-786-7426
Email: firm@nevadalaw.com *URL:* http://www.nevadalaw.com

Paul A. Bible
David R. Hoy
Richard M. Trachok, II
Michael D. Hoy
Mark S. Sertic
Jon M. Ludwig

Mark F. Bruce
Mark J. Lenz
Andrew Alan List
Ralph A. Fellows (Not admitted in NV)

For full biographical listings, see the Martindale-Hubbell Law Directory

NEW JERSEY

*BRIDGETON,** Cumberland Co.

JOHN P. MORRIS (AV)

200 West Commerce Street, P.O. Box 299, 08302
Telephone: 609-453-1000
Fax: 609-453-0200
URL: http://www.lawyers.com/johnpmorris

LEGAL SUPPORT PERSONNEL

Tara Dickson (Paralegal)

For full biographical listings, see the Martindale-Hubbell Law Directory

CHATHAM, Morris Co.

ARSENEAULT & FASSETT (AV)

560 Main Street, 07928-2119
Telephone: 973-635-3366
Fax: 973-635-0855
Email: www.aklaw.com *URL:* http://www.lawyers.com/arsenaultkrovatinattys

MEMBERS OF FIRM

Jack Arseneault
David W. Fassett

ASSOCIATE

Steven G. Sanders (Not admitted in NJ)

For full biographical listings, see the Martindale-Hubbell Law Directory

ALAN L. ZEGAS (AV)

552 Main Street, 07928
Telephone: 973-701-7080
Fax: 973-701-7081
Email: alanatLaw@aol.com *URL:* http://www.lawyers.com/zegas

Gina L. Mendola
Sharon B. Kean
Patricia A. Lee
Aimee Blakeslee

For full biographical listings, see the Martindale-Hubbell Law Directory

FLORHAM PARK, Morris Co.

RYAN AND GANNON (AV)

Suite 201, 147 Columbia Turnpike, 07932
Telephone: 201-966-1000
Fax: 201-966-6215
URL: http://www.lawyers.com/ryanandgannon

MEMBERS OF FIRM

William J. Gannon
Gerald J. Helfrich

ASSOCIATE

Edward George Fattell, III

OF COUNSEL

George P. Helfrich
Edward V. Ryan
Thomas A. Shepard, Jr.

For full biographical listings, see the Martindale-Hubbell Law Directory

*HACKENSACK,** Bergen Co.

ROBERT T. CORCORAN, P.C. (AV)

401 Hackensack Avenue, 07601
Telephone: 201-342-5151
Facsimile: 201-342-7190
URL: http://www.lawyers.com/robertcorcoran
Email: law@robertcorcoran.com *URL:* http://www.robertcorcoran.com

Robert T. Corcoran
Jason J. Miller
Karen M. Venice
Christopher R. Cavalli

OF COUNSEL

Michael J. Powers

For full biographical listings, see the Martindale-Hubbell Law Directory

HERTEN, BURSTEIN, SHERIDAN, CEVASCO, BOTTINELLI & LITT, L.L.C. (AV)

Court Plaza North, 25 Main Street, 07601
Telephone: 201-342-6000
Telecopier: 201-342-6611

Thomas J. Herten
Albert Burstein
Philip F. Sheridan, Jr.
Andrew J. Cevasco
Terry Paul Bottinelli
Arnold D. Litt
Brian T. Campion
Menelaos W. Toskos
Mark P. Marotta
Susan M. Marra
John L. Molinelli
Kevin P. Kelly

(See Next Column)

HERTEN, BURSTEIN, SHERIDAN, CEVASCO, BOTTINELLI & LITT L.L.C.—*Continued*

ASSOCIATES

Patrick Papalia
Anthony Ronald Suarez
Thomas S. McGuire
Donna T. Tamayne

For full biographical listings, see the Martindale-Hubbell Law Directory

BRIAN J. NEARY (AV)

190 Moore Street, 07601
Telephone: 201-488-0544
Fax: 201-488-0240
Email: brianneary@erols.com *URL:* http://www.lawyers.com/brianneary criminaldefense
New York, N.Y. Office: 475 Park Avenue, South, Suite 3300.
Telephone: 212-683-8000.

Judith A. Eisenberg

For full biographical listings, see the Martindale-Hubbell Law Directory

PASHMAN STEIN, A PROFESSIONAL CORPORATION (AV)

45 Essex Street, 07601-5415
Telephone: 201-488-8200
Fax: 201-488-5556
Email: info@pashmanstein.com *URL:* http://www.lawyers.com/pashmanstein

Louis Pashman
Samuel J. Samaro
Dennis T. Smith
Michael S. Stein

Amy E. Whitteaker
John T. Whipple

SPECIAL COUNSEL

Morris Pashman

For full biographical listings, see the Martindale-Hubbell Law Directory

STEPHEN H. ROTH (AV)

62 Summit Avenue, 07601
Telephone: 201-489-3737
Fax: 201-489-0557

ASSOCIATE

Michele M. De Santis

For full biographical listings, see the Martindale-Hubbell Law Directory

HADDONFIELD, Camden Co.

WILBRAHAM, LAWLER & BUBA, A PROFESSIONAL CORPORATION (AV Ⓣ)

24 Kings Highway West, 08033-2122
Telephone: 856-795-4422
Fax: 856-795-4699
Philadelphia, Pennsylvania Office: 1818 Market Street, Suite 3100.
Telephone: 215-564-4141.
Fax: 215-564-4385.
Wilmington, Delaware Office: Stoney Batter Office Building, 5301 Limestone Road, Suite 221.
Telephone: 302-234-8217.
Fax: 302-234-8218.

Edward J. Wilbraham
Michael J. Block
Mary S. Cook

For full biographical listings, see the Martindale-Hubbell Law Directory

LAWRENCEVILLE, Mercer Co.

SZAFERMAN, LAKIND, BLUMSTEIN, WATTER & BLADER, P.C. (AV)

Suite 104 Quakerbridge Executive Center, 101 Grovers Mill Road, 08648
Telephone: 609-275-0400
Telefax: 609-275-4511

Arnold C. Lakind
Barry D. Szaferman
Jeffrey P. Blumstein
Paul N. Watter
Steven Blader
Sidney H. Lehmann
Gerald B. Schenkman
David B. Beckett
Scott P. Borsack
Mary Lou Delahanty

Jennifer Weisberg Millner
Cathyanne A. Pisciotta
Jason N. Fruhschein
Demery J. Roberts
Stuart A. Tucker
Brian G. Paul
Victoria Rivera-Cruz
Thomas J. Burns III

LEGAL SUPPORT PERSONNEL

Paula M. Rossi (Office Administrator)
Patricia Hallstrum (Controller)

Representative Clients: Sun National Bank; First Washington Bank; Gilmore Securities & Co.; Communication Workers of America; The Eagle Group; Water's Edge Convalescent Center; Ronson Aviation, Inc.; Holmdel Township Board of Adjustment; Public Service Managers Association; Chemical Leaman Tank Lines.

For full biographical listings, see the Martindale-Hubbell Law Directory

LIVINGSTON, Essex Co.

GENOVA, BURNS & VERNOIA (AV)

Eisenhower Plaza II, 354 Eisenhower Parkway, 07039
Telephone: 973-533-0777
Facsimile: 973-533-1112
URL: http://www.gbvlaw.com
Trenton, New Jersey Office: The Princeton House, 160 West State Street.
Telephone: 609-393-1131.

MEMBERS OF FIRM

Angelo J. Genova
James M. Burns
Francis J. Vernoia
John C. Petrella
James J. McGovern, III
Carmel Joy Decker

ASSOCIATES

Sandro Polledri
Celia S. Bosco
Lynn S. Degen
Elizabeth A. Daly
Brian O. Lipman
J. Frank Vespa-Papaleo
Susan B. Burns
Bruno Genova
Robert C. Gifford, Jr.
Courtney Gaccione

For full biographical listings, see the Martindale-Hubbell Law Directory

PHILIP M. LUSTBADER & DAVID LUSTBADER A PROFESSIONAL CORPORATION (AV)

615 West Mount Pleasant Avenue, 07039
Telephone: 973-740-1000
Fax: 973-740-1520
URL: http://www.lawyers.com/lustbader,law

Philip M. Lustbader
David Lustbader

John L. Riordan, Jr.
James S. Colavito

For full biographical listings, see the Martindale-Hubbell Law Directory

MILLBURN, Essex Co.

GROSMAN & GROSMAN (AV)

75 Main Street Suite 205, 07041
Telephone: 973-467-9520
FAX: 973-467-0322
Email: agrosman@bellatlantic.net

Charles M. Grosman (1921-1970)
Alan M. Grosman

References: The Bank of New York; National Community Bank Division.

For full biographical listings, see the Martindale-Hubbell Law Directory

McDERMOTT & McGEE (AV)

75 Main Street, P.O. Box 192, 07041-0192
Telephone: 973-467-8080
Fax: 973-376-8669

MEMBERS OF FIRM

John L. McDermott
John P. McGee
Richard P. Maggi
Thomas A. Wester
Richard M. Tango
Frank P. Leanza
John L. McDermott, Jr.
David J. Dickinson
A. Charles Lorenzo
Robert A. McDermott
Kevin John McGee

ASSOCIATES

Anthony John Verardi
Lindsay K. O'Shaughnessy
Andre L. McGuire

OF COUNSEL

Daniel K. Van Dorn

Representative Clients: Affiliated Building Service, Inc.; Allstate Insurance Co.; General Agents Insurance Company of America; Greater New York Mutual; General Accident Group; ISS International Service System, Inc.; Zurich-American Insurance Co.; Penn National Insurance Co.; Tokio Marine & Fire Insurance Co.; Medical Inter-Insurance Exchange of New Jersey.

For full biographical listings, see the Martindale-Hubbell Law Directory

MOORESTOWN, Burlington Co.

CHIERICI, CHIERICI & SMITH, A PROFESSIONAL CORPORATION (AV)

Blason Campus - III, 509 South Lenola Road Building Six, 08057-1561
Telephone: 856-234-6300
Fax: 856-234-9490

Donald R. Chierici, Jr.
Elizabeth Coleman Chierici
Julie C. Smith

(See Next Column)

CHIERICI, CHIERICI & SMITH A PROFESSIONAL CORPORATION, *Moorestown—Continued*

Carolyn J. Kornas
Mark G. Esposito
Richard D. DiTomaso
Melvin McDowell
David J. Karbasian
Peter P. Sanchez
Donald R. Chierici, III

For full biographical listings, see the Martindale-Hubbell Law Directory

*NEWARK,** Essex Co.

CARPENTER, BENNETT & MORRISSEY (AV)

Three Gateway Center, 17th Floor, 100 Mulberry Street, 07102-4079
Telephone: 973-622-7711
New York City: 212-943-6530
Telex: 139405
Telecopier: 973-622-5314
Email: cbm@carpben.com

MEMBERS OF FIRM

Laurence Reich
John P. Dwyer
Rosemary J. Bruno
Patrick G. Brady
Robert J. Stickles
Stephen F. Payerle
Kevin C. Donovan
Lois H. Goodman
David J. Reilly

Representative Clients: General Motors Corp.; E.I. du Pont de Nemours and Co.; ITT Industries, Inc.; Texaco Inc.; Prudential Insurance Company of America; Litton Industries; AT&T; Chubb & Son, Inc.; Rutgers, The State University of New Jersey; Johnson & Johnson.

For Complete List of Firm Personnel, See General Section

For full biographical listings, see the Martindale-Hubbell Law Directory

HELLRING LINDEMAN GOLDSTEIN & SIEGAL LLP (AV)

One Gateway Center, 07102-5386
Telephone: 973-621-9020
Fax: 973-621-7406
Englewood, New Jersey Office: 32-40 North Dean Street.
Telephone: 201-871-3060.

Robert S. Raymar
Ronny Jo Greenwald Siegal
Stephen L. Dreyfuss
Sheryl E. Koomer

For Complete List of Firm Personnel, See General Section

For full biographical listings, see the Martindale-Hubbell Law Directory

LITE, DE PALMA, GREENBERG & RIVAS, LLC (AV)

Two Gateway Center, 12th Floor, 07102-5003
Telephone: 973-623-3000
Fax: 973-623-0858

MEMBERS OF FIRM

Allyn Z. Lite
Joseph J. De Palma
Bruce D. Greenberg
Alberto Rivas

ASSOCIATES

Michele Soto
Mary Jean Pizza
Stephanie Kay Austin

For full biographical listings, see the Martindale-Hubbell Law Directory

SILLS CUMMIS RADIN TISCHMAN EPSTEIN & GROSS, A PROFESSIONAL CORPORATION (AV)

One Riverfront Plaza, 07102-5400
Telephone: 973-643-7000
Fax: 973-643-6500
Telex: 820630 Sillsbeck Nwk
Email: sillsmail@sillscummis.com *URL:* http://www.sillscummis.com
Atlantic City, New Jersey Office: 17 Gordon's Alley.
Telephone: 609-344-2800.
New York, N.Y. Office: 712 Fifth Avenue.
Telephone: 212-643-7000.
Washington, D.C. Office: 1800 K Street, N.W.
Telephone: 202-296-4750.

MEMBERS OF FIRM

Clive S. Cummis
James M. Hirschhorn

OF COUNSEL

Steven R. Rowland

Steven S. Katz

Representative Clients: International Fidelity Insurance Co.; Midlantic National Bank.

For Complete List of Firm Personnel, See General Section

For full biographical listings, see the Martindale-Hubbell Law Directory

ZAZZALI, ZAZZALI, FAGELLA & NOWAK, A PROFESSIONAL CORPORATION (AV)

One Riverfront Plaza, 07102-5410
Telephone: 973-623-1822
Telecopier: 973-623-2209
URL: http://www.lawyers.com/zazzali
Trenton, New Jersey Office: 150 West State Street.
Telephone: 609-392-8172.
Facsimile: 609-392-8933.
New York, New York Office: 15 West 72nd Street.
Telephone: 212-529-3927.
Facsimile: 212-875-8275.

Andrew F. Zazzali (1925-1969)
Andrew F. Zazzali, Jr.
James R. Zazzali
Robert A. Fagella
Kenneth I. Nowak
Paul L. Kleinbaum
Richard A. Friedman

Kathleen Anne Naprstek
Aileen M. O'Driscoll
Edward H. O'Hare
Jason Solowkowski

For full biographical listings, see the Martindale-Hubbell Law Directory

*NEW BRUNSWICK,** Middlesex Co.

BENEDICT AND ALTMAN (AV)

247 Livingston Avenue, 08901
Telephone: 732-745-9000
Fax: 732-214-1897

MEMBERS OF FIRM

Joseph J. Benedict
Steven D. Altman

ASSOCIATE

Doris E. McNeil

For full biographical listings, see the Martindale-Hubbell Law Directory

PARAMUS, Bergen Co.

FINNERTY & LAROCCA, P.C. (AV)

Country Club Plaza, W 115 Century Road, 07652
Telephone: 201-845-4000
Facsimile: 201-845-6799
URL: http://finnertylarocca
URL: http://www.familylaw-nj.com

John E. Finnerty
Frank J. LaRocca

Erin K. Burke
Gina R. Pacinella

OF COUNSEL

Eugenie F. Temmler

For full biographical listings, see the Martindale-Hubbell Law Directory

PARSIPPANY, Morris Co.

CUYLER BURK (AV)

Parsippany Corporate Center, Four Century Drive, 07054-4663
Telephone: 973-734-3200
Telex: 429071
Telecopier: 973-734-3201
Email: Main@Cuyler.com *URL:* http://www.cuyler.com
New York, New York Office: 350 Fifth Avenue, Suite 3304. 10018.
Telephone: 212-645-4039.

MEMBERS OF FIRM

Stephen D. Cuyler
Jo Ann Burk
Stefano Calogero
David L. Menzel
Peter Petrou
Richard A. Crooker
Michael J. Jones

COUNSEL

Anne M. Mohan
Frank J. Miele

ASSOCIATES

Jan C. Walker
Kathleen Jane Olear
Claudia L. Marchese
Mark G. Eliades
Kimberly A. Joel
Christy A. Ramunno
Catherine E. Youngman
Andrew K. Craig
Mark S. Winter
Thomas J. Castano
Hugo A. Hilgendorff, IV

LEGAL SUPPORT PERSONNEL

Frederick M. H. Currie, Jr.

For full biographical listings, see the Martindale-Hubbell Law Directory

GENNET, KALLMANN, ANTIN & ROBINSON, A PROFESSIONAL CORPORATION (AV)

6 Campus Drive, 07054-4406
Telephone: 973-285-1919
Fax: 973-285-1177
Email: gkar@nac.net
New York, New York Office: Litman Suite, 45 Broadway Atrium, 10006.
Telephone: 212-406-1919.

(See Next Column)

GENNET, KALLMANN, ANTIN & ROBINSON A PROFESSIONAL CORPORATION— *Continued*

Stanley W. Kallmann
Mark L. Antin
Harry Robinson, III
Richard S. Nichols

William Gary Hanft
Thomas J. Olsen, IV
Francie E. Joseph
Paul A. Tumbleson

LEGAL SUPPORT PERSONNEL

Eleanor Dawalt (Administrator)

Representative Clients: Aetna Insurance Co.; Hartford Fire; Lloyds of London; New England Mutuals.
Reference: United Jersey Bank.

For full biographical listings, see the Martindale-Hubbell Law Directory

PRINCETON, Mercer Co.

MCCARTHY AND SCHATZMAN, P.A. (AV)

228 Alexander Street, P.O. Box 2329, 08543-2329
Telephone: 609-924-1199
Fax: 609-683-5251

John F. McCarthy, Jr.
Richard Schatzman
G. Christopher Baker
John F. McCarthy, III
Michael A. Spero
Barbara Strapp Nelson
W. Scott Stoner
James J. Britt, Jr.

Charly Gayden

Representative Clients: Trustees of Princeton University; Carnegie Center Associates; Merrill Lynch Pierce Fenner & Smith, Inc.; Calton Homes, Inc.

For full biographical listings, see the Martindale-Hubbell Law Directory

RED BANK, Monmouth Co.

PHILIP G. AUERBACH A PROFESSIONAL CORPORATION (AV)

231 Maple Avenue, P.O. Box Y, 07701
Telephone: 732-842-6660
Fax: 732-530-7925

Philip G. Auerbach

Edward A. Genz
John J. Ryan
John F. McLaughlin

For full biographical listings, see the Martindale-Hubbell Law Directory

WHITE, FLEISCHNER & FINO (AV)

272 Broad Street, 07701
Telephone: 732-530-7787
Telecopier: 732-530-8552
New York, New York Office: 140 Broadway.
Telephone: 212-487-9700.
Telecopier: 212-487-9777.

Benjamin A. Fleischner

ASSOCIATE

Nancy D. Lyness

Representative Clients: Chicago Insurance Group; London Market; Interstate Insurance Group; Wausau Insurance Companies.

For full biographical listings, see the Martindale-Hubbell Law Directory

ROSELAND, Essex Co.

SELLAR RICHARDSON, P.C. (AV)

Six Becker Farm Road, 07068-1735
Telephone: 973-535-1400
Fax: 973-535-6522
Email: info@sellarrichardson.com

James P. Richardson
Wendy H. Smith
John M. Kearney
Denise M. Luckenbach
Shawn R. Stowell

Patricia R. Carley
Julia C. Talarick
Deborah M. Taub
Albert N. Montano
Jennifer R. Sentivan
Victoria F. Pratt

OF COUNSEL

Alastair J. Sellar
E. Scott Garrett
Anthony C. Stuart

For full biographical listings, see the Martindale-Hubbell Law Directory

WALDER, SONDAK & BROGAN, A PROFESSIONAL CORPORATION (AV)

5 Becker Farm Road, P.O. Box 901, 07068
Telephone: 973-992-5300
Telecopier: 973-992-1505; 992-1006
Email: general@wsbesqs.com *URL:* http://www.wsbesqs.com

Justin P. Walder
John A. Brogan
Barry A. Kozyra
James A. Plaisted

Shalom D. Stone
Judith A. Hartz
Christopher M. Farella

For Complete List of Firm Personnel, See General Section

For full biographical listings, see the Martindale-Hubbell Law Directory

SADDLE BROOK, Bergen Co.

COHN LIFLAND PEARLMAN HERRMANN & KNOPF LLP (AV)

Park 80 Plaza West-One, 07663
Telephone: 201-845-9600
Telecopier: 201-845-9423
Email: info@njlawfirm.com *URL:* http://www.njlawfirm.com

MEMBERS OF FIRM

Albert L. Cohn
Peter S. Pearlman
Barry A. Knopf
Daniel Crystal (Retired)
Jeffrey W. Herrmann
Robert D. Zatorski
Allen Susser
Mary Ann T. Stokes
Brian D. Zinn
Joshua P. Cohn

ASSOCIATES

Virginia A. Harper
Leonard Z. Kaufmann
Audra DePaolo
Robert Ricci, Jr.
Maurice W. McLaughlin
Andrew C. Abrams
Jessica V. Henry

OF COUNSEL

Sylvia J. Cohn
Jodi B. Scherl

For full biographical listings, see the Martindale-Hubbell Law Directory

*SOMERVILLE,** Somerset Co.

SCHACHTER, TROMBADORE, OFFEN, STANTON & PAVICS, A PROFESSIONAL CORPORATION (AV)

45 East High Street, P.O. Box 520, 08876-0520
Telephone: 908-722-5700
Fax: 908-722-8853

Richard J. Schachter
Stephen M. Offen

For full biographical listings, see the Martindale-Hubbell Law Directory

TENAFLY, Bergen Co.

ROBERT A. VORT (AV)

45 Central Avenue, P.O. Box 142, 07670-0142
Telephone: 201-816-9444
Fax: 201-894-1718
Email: r.vort@vortlaw.com *URL:* http://www.vortlaw.com

ASSOCIATE

Avrin Slatkin

OF COUNSEL

Anne M. Ronan

For full biographical listings, see the Martindale-Hubbell Law Directory

*TRENTON,** Mercer Co.

NEEDELL, SIEKERKA & CASTELLANI, A PROFESSIONAL CORPORATION (AV)

Quakerbridge Commons, 2681 Quakerbridge Road, 08619-1625
Telephone: 609-584-7700
Fax: 609-584-0123
Email: nsclaw@aol.com

Stanley H. Needell
Michele N. Siekerka
Anthony P. Castellani

John M. Cinti
Dean C. Gresek

LEGAL SUPPORT PERSONNEL

PARALEGALS

Marlene Griesbach
Carolyn D. Shaw
Veronica A. Mitchell

For full biographical listings, see the Martindale-Hubbell Law Directory

VINELAND, Cumberland Co.

RIESENBURGER & KIZNER, P.C. (AV)
190 South Main Road, P.O. Box 640, 08362-0640
Telephone: 856-691-6200
Telecopier: 856-696-8150
Email: rieskizn@eticomm.net *URL:* http://www.rklawyers.com
Cherry Hill Office: 413 Route 70 East.
Telephone: 609-354-7500.

Franklin J. Riesenburger
Mitchell H. Kizner

Vivian R. Salmon
Robert P. Merenich

For full biographical listings, see the Martindale-Hubbell Law Directory

WAYNE, Passaic Co.

DEYOE HEISSENBUTTEL, L.L.C. (AV)
401 Hamburg Turnpike, P.O. Box 2449, 07474-2449
Telephone: 973-595-6300
Fax: 973-595-0146
Email: deyoelaw@ix.netcom.com *URL:* http://www.deyoe.com

MEMBERS OF FIRM

Charles P. DeYoe (1923-1973)
Wood M. DeYoe
Frederick C. Heissenbuttel
Scott B. Piekarsky

ASSOCIATES

Raymond F. Shenekji
Anne Hutton
Albert C. Buglione
Laureen A. Moloney

LEGAL SUPPORT PERSONNEL

Marilyn Moore (Office Manager)

Representative Clients: Hanover Insurance Inc.; Maryland Casualty Co.; Ohio Casualty Insurance Co.; Motor Club of America; Selective Insurance Co.; Prudential Property & Casualty; Reliance Ins. Co.

For full biographical listings, see the Martindale-Hubbell Law Directory

WEST ORANGE, Essex Co.

SACHS, MAITLIN, FLEMING, GREENE, WILSON & MAROTTE (AV)
80 Main Street, 3rd Floor, 07052
Telephone: 973-731-3400
Fax: 973-731-2896

Harold D. Feuerstein (1933-1967)
Marvin A. Sachs
Allan Maitlin
Raymond J. Fleming
Peter A. Greene
Bradley M. Wilson
Michael Marotte

ASSOCIATES

Steven L. Albertson
Philip B. Harrison
David Eric Maitlin
Theresa Mullen
Rosa Marques
Laura L. Milcsik

Reference: Fidelity Union Trust Co.

For full biographical listings, see the Martindale-Hubbell Law Directory

NEW MEXICO

*ALBUQUERQUE,** Bernalillo Co.

FREEDMAN BOYD DANIELS HOLLANDER GOLDBERG & CLINE P.A. (AV)
20 First Plaza, Suite 700, 87102
Telephone: 505-842-9960
Fax: 505-842-0761

David A. Freedman
John W. Boyd
Charles W. Daniels
Nancy Hollander
John D. Cline

Scott M. Davidson
Eric J. Knapp
K.C. Maxwell

For full biographical listings, see the Martindale-Hubbell Law Directory

MARTIN E. THREET & ASSOCIATES (AV)
6400 Uptown Boulevard N.E. Suite 500 West Tower, 87110
Telephone: 505-881-5155
Fax: 505-881-5356
Email: threetlaw@aol.com

MEMBER OF FIRM

Martin E. Threet

(See Next Column)

ASSOCIATES

Joseph L. Romero
Joey B. Wright

For Complete List of Firm Personnel, See General Section

For full biographical listings, see the Martindale-Hubbell Law Directory

*SANTA FE,** Santa Fe Co.

CATRON, CATRON & SAWTELL, A PROFESSIONAL ASSOCIATION (AV)
2006 Botulph Road, P.O. Box 788, 87504-0788
Telephone: 505-982-1947
Telecopier: 505-986-1013
Email: catronlaw@aol.com

John S. Catron
Fletcher R. Catron
W. Anthony Sawtell
Michael T. Pottow
Bryan P. Biedscheid

For Complete List of Firm Personnel, See General Section

For full biographical listings, see the Martindale-Hubbell Law Directory

HUFFAKER & CONWAY, A PROFESSIONAL CORPORATION (AV)
155 Grant Avenue, P.O. Box 1868, 87504-1868
Telephone: 505-988-8921
Fax: 505-983-3927
Email: sfstaff@sisna.com
Albuquerque, New Mexico Office: 201 Third Street, N.W., Suite 1910.
Telephone: 505-244-0021.
Facsimile: 505-244-1372.

Gregory D. Huffaker, Jr.
Ann Maloney Conway
Lisa A. Joynes
Seth L. Sparks
Edward C. Bagley

For full biographical listings, see the Martindale-Hubbell Law Directory

MONTGOMERY & ANDREWS, PROFESSIONAL ASSOCIATION (AV)
325 Paseo de Peralta, P.O. Box 2307, 87504-2307
Telephone: 505-982-3873
Fax: 505-982-4289
Email: montand@montand.com

Bruce Herr
Sarah Michael Singleton
Carolyn Wolf
Andrew S. Montgomery
Grace Philips
Jennifer Lynn Weed

OF COUNSEL

William R. Federici

Representative Clients: Chrysler Corporation; El Paso Corporation; Johnson Controls Northern New Mexico, L.L.C.; State of New Mexico; U S WEST Communications, Inc.

For Complete List of Firm Personnel, See General Section

For full biographical listings, see the Martindale-Hubbell Law Directory

STEVEN L. TUCKER (AV)
125 Lincoln Avenue, Suite 400, 87501-2005
Telephone: 505-982-3467
Fax: 505-982-3270
URL: http://www.lawyers.com/stevenltucker

For full biographical listings, see the Martindale-Hubbell Law Directory

NEW YORK

*ALBANY,** Albany Co.

AINSWORTH, SULLIVAN, TRACY, KNAUF, WARNER & RUSLANDER, P.C. (AV)
Brandon Place, 403 New Karner Road, P.O. Box 12849, 12212-2849
Telephone: 518-464-0600
Fax: 518-464-0679
Email: foc@brokerlaw.com *URL:* http://www.brokerlaw.com

Danforth E. Ainsworth (1908-1927)
Charles B. Sullivan (1881-1975)
Thomas F. Tracy (1914-1994)
John E. Knauf (1914-1996)
Frank J. Warner, Jr.
Robert K. Ruslander
James E. McHenry
John W. Bailey
Frank M. Pell
Elizabeth M. Dumas
Margaret Comard Lynch
Michael J. Murphy
Timothy J. O'Connor
Dennis W. Habel
Maria C. Tebano

Colleen M. O'Connell
Anthony V. Cardona, Jr.
Rebecca A. Slezak
Scott R. Almas

(See Next Column)

AINSWORTH, SULLIVAN, TRACY, KNAUF, WARNER & RUSLANDER P.C.—*Continued*

OF COUNSEL

Bruce R. Sullivan

Local Counsel for: Liberty Insurance Co.; United Service Auto Assn.; Continental Insurance Cos.; American International Insurance Co.; Aetna Insurance Co.; Kemper Insurance Co.; Sears Roebuck & Co.; Yamaha Motor Corp.; Chubb & Sons, Inc.; Grand Union Co.

For full biographical listings, see the Martindale-Hubbell Law Directory

HARVEY AND MUMFORD (AV)

20 Corporate Woods Boulevard, 12211-2396
Telephone: 518-463-4491
Telecopier: 518-463-5665
Email: thefirm@harveyandmumford.com

Arthur J. Harvey (1903-1986)

MEMBERS OF FIRM

Jonathan P. Harvey
Brian F. Mumford

ASSOCIATES

Eva Lynn M. Hayko
Karen Hendricks
Peter Baird Joslin, Jr.
Trudy L. Boulia
Keith J. Starlin

OF COUNSEL

Jack D. Harvey

For full biographical listings, see the Martindale-Hubbell Law Directory

MAYNARD, O'CONNOR, SMITH & CATALINOTTO, LLP (AV)

Seventh Floor, 80 State Street, 12207
Telephone: 518-465-3553
Fax: 518-465-5845
Saugerties, New York Office: Route 9W, P.O. Box 180.
Telephone: 914-246-3666.
Fax: 914-246-0390.

MEMBERS OF FIRM

William C. Maynard (1883-1972)
Gerald W. O'Connor (1896-1965)
J. Vincent Smith (1916-1991)
Michael E. Catalinotto
Stephen C. Prudente
Christopher K.H. Dressler
Thomas G. Daley
James R. Schultz
Bruce A. Bell
Concetta R. Lomanto
Edwin J. Tobin, Jr.

ASSOCIATES

Michael E. Catalinotto, Jr.
Robert A. Rausch
Teresa M. Morrisey
Aaron M. Baldwin
Laurel L. Bohl

OF COUNSEL

Earl S. Jones, Jr.

Local Counsel for: Utica Mutual Insurance Co.; General Motors; Medical Liability Mutual Insurance; Metropolitan Insurance Co.

For full biographical listings, see the Martindale-Hubbell Law Directory

O'CONNELL AND ARONOWITZ, P.C. (AV)

100 State Street, 12207-1885
Telephone: 518-462-5601
Telecopier: 518-462-2670
Email: info@oalaw.com
Plattsburgh, New York Office: 206 West Bay Plaza.
Telephone: 518-562-0600.
Fax: 518-562-0657.
Saratoga Springs, New York Office: Suite 204, 358 Broadway.
Telephone: 518-587-0425.

Cornelius D. Murray

Representative Clients: The New York State Health Facilities Association, Inc.; Time Warner Entertainment; First Albany Corporation (Retirement Plan Counsel).

For full biographical listings, see the Martindale-Hubbell Law Directory

*BUFFALO,** Erie Co.

CONNORS & VILARDO, LLP (AV)

1020 Liberty Building, 420 Main Street, 14202
Telephone: 716-852-5533
Fax: 716-852-5649
Email: c-v@connors-vilardo.com

MEMBERS OF FIRM

Joseph J. Ricotta (1921-1993)
Terrence M. Connors
Lawrence J. Vilardo
Kevin A. Ricotta
Randall D. White
John T. Loss
Vincent E. Doyle III

(See Next Column)

ASSOCIATES

Michael J. Roach
Mark R. Uba
Margaret L. Phillips
Henry J. Nowak
Lawlor F. Quinlan III
James W. Grable, Jr.

For full biographical listings, see the Martindale-Hubbell Law Directory

SULLIVAN & OLIVERIO (AV)

600 Main Place Tower, 14202-3706
Telephone: 716-854-5300
Telecopier: 716-854-5299
Email: sulliolaw@aol.com

MEMBERS OF FIRM

Richard T. Sullivan
B. P. Oliverio
Bruce W. Hoover

Thomas M. Moll
Michael E. Appelbaum
Kevin M. Carter

OF COUNSEL

Paul D. Pearson

For full biographical listings, see the Martindale-Hubbell Law Directory

ZDARSKY, SAWICKI & AGOSTINELLI (AV)

404 Cathedral Place, 298 Main Street, 14202
Telephone: 716-855-3200
Telecopier: 716-855-3101
Email: zsagtw@buffnet.net

MEMBERS OF FIRM

Joseph E. Zdarsky
K. Michael Sawicki
Guy J. Agostinelli
Gerald T. Walsh
Mark J. Schlant

ASSOCIATES

Patrick A. Dudley
John A. Moscati, Jr.

Reference: Marine Midland Bank, N.A.

For full biographical listings, see the Martindale-Hubbell Law Directory

GARDEN CITY, Nassau Co.

MONTFORT, HEALY, MCGUIRE & SALLEY (AV)

1140 Franklin Avenue, 11530
Telephone: 516-747-4082
Telecopier: 516-746-0748

MEMBERS OF FIRM

E. Richard Rimmels, Jr. (1930-1999)
Frank J. Cafaro
Philip J. Catapano
Fredric C. Montfort
Donald S. Neumann, Jr.
James J. Keefe, Jr.
Michael A. Baranowicz
James Michael Murphy

OF COUNSEL

Fredric H. Montfort
Edward M. Salley, Jr.
David J. Fleming
Robert J. Mettalia

ASSOCIATES

Claudia C. Glacken
Marcie K. Glasser
Bruce A. Cook
Jeffrey D. Present
Joan E. Resnik
Susan H. Dempsey
Camille L. Hansen
Christopher T. Cafaro
Kathleen Dumont
Jeffrey B. Siler
Michael G. Kruzynski
Karen J. Cooper

For full biographical listings, see the Martindale-Hubbell Law Directory

SHAW, LICITRA, BOHNER, ESERNIO & SCHWARTZ, P.C. (AV)

1010 Franklin Avenue, 11530
Telephone: 516-742-0610
Telecopier: 516-742-2670
Email: shaw0610@aol.com

Joseph Licitra (1930-1987)
J. Stanley Shaw
Robert J. Bohner
George P. Esernio
Jeffrey L. Schwartz
Anton J. Borovina
Edward M. Flint
Stuart I. Gordon
John H. Hall, Jr.
Sarah M. Keenan
Frank J. Livoti
Alan E. Marder
Peter Marullo
Roberta L. McManus

David P. Gesser
Steven H. Blatt
Michael Clark

COUNSEL

Victor G. Beaudet (1919-1993)
Alan M. Parente

For full biographical listings, see the Martindale-Hubbell Law Directory

Garden City—Continued

BENJAMIN VINAR (AV)
1050 Franklin Avenue, 11530
Telephone: 516-746-0241
Telecopier: 516-747-9759
Email: BVinar@compuserve.com *URL:* http://www.vinarlaw.com

For full biographical listings, see the Martindale-Hubbell Law Directory

GREAT NECK, Nassau Co.

MAURO, GOLDBERG & LILLING (AV)
60 Cutter Mill Road, Suite 415, 11021
Telephone: 516-487-5800
Fax: 516-487-5811
URL: http://www.mglappeals.com

Kenneth Mauro
Barbara DeCrow Goldberg
Caryn L. Lilling

ASSOCIATES

Timothy Robert Capowski
Christopher F. Simone
Katherine E. Herr

Representative Clients: Amici Curiae and Appellate Counsel for: American Insurance Association; American Urological Association; American International Group; City of New York; State of New York; Defense Association of New York; Frontier Insurance Co.; General Star; Group Council Mutual Insurance Co.; Liberty Mutual Insurance Co.

For full biographical listings, see the Martindale-Hubbell Law Directory

MELVILLE, Suffolk Co.

LAMB & BARNOSKY, LLP (AV)
534 Broadhollow Road-CS 9034, 11747-9034
Telephone: 631-694-2300
Telecopier: 631-694-2309
Email: thefirm@lambbarnosky.com *URL:* http://www.lambbarnosky.com

PARTNERS

Eugene R. Barnosky
Robert H. Cohen
Marcia Lyn Finkelstein
Michael J. Heller
Gary Holman
Scott M. Karson
P. L. Lamb
Arthur A. Lane
Joel M. Markowitz
Gerald P. Rosenberg
Patrice Dowd Shenn

OF COUNSEL

Louis E. Black
James F. Gesualdi
Howard W. Newman
Joseph J. Salvatore
Joseph H. Wishod

COUNSEL

Lloyd K. Chanin
Scott P. McBride

ASSOCIATES

Cathleen D. Allen
Catherine Healy Kanzler
Rita Fishman Sheena
Shari Lee Sugarman

For full biographical listings, see the Martindale-Hubbell Law Directory

*MINEOLA,** Nassau Co.

FUREY, KERLEY, WALSH, MATERA & CINQUEMANI, A PROFESSIONAL CORPORATION (AV)
200 Old Country Road, Suite 660, 11501
Telephone: 516-248-8880
Fax: 516-873-8786

Raymond J. Furey
Brian P. Kerley
Jeffrey G. Walsh
Rosemary A. Cinquemani
Glenn J. Matera

Lauren B. Bristol
Jeffrey M. Di Luccio
Peter X. Dodge
Kathleen Lindsay
MaryAnne Powers Richardson
Bryan L Salamone
William Scott Matlin
Alejandro Monroy

LEGAL SUPPORT PERSONNEL

Arthetta Baldock

For full biographical listings, see the Martindale-Hubbell Law Directory

*NEW YORK,** New York Co.

ARKIN SCHAFFER & KAPLAN LLP (AV)
590 Madison Avenue, 10022
Telephone: 212-333-0200
Fax: 212-333-2350
Email: info@ARKIN-LAW.com

Stanley S. Arkin
Hyman L. Schaffer
Jeffrey M. Kaplan
Mark S. Cohen
Howard J. Kaplan

(See Next Column)

ASSOCIATES

Harry B. Feder
Sean R. O'Brien
Robert Pfeffer

OF COUNSEL

Michelle A. Rice

For full biographical listings, see the Martindale-Hubbell Law Directory

BARRETT GRAVANTE CARPINELLO & STERN LLP (AV)
570 Lexington Avenue, 10022
Telephone: 212-446-2300
Telecopier: 212-446-2350
Albany, New York Office: 100 State Street, 12207.
Telephone: 518-434-0600.
Telecopier: 518-434-0665.
Fort Lauderdale, Florida Office: Barnett Bank Plaza, One East Broward Boulevard, 33301.
Telephone: 954-356-0011.
Telecopier: 954-356-0022.

David A. Barrett
Nicholas A. Gravante, Jr.
George F. Carpinello
Jack G. Stern
Michael I. Endler
Harlan A. Levy
Kathleen M. Franklin
Roland G. Riopelle
Steven I. Froot
Andrew B. Peretz, P.A.
Carla E. Hogan

OF COUNSEL

Michael Straus
Howard A. Wintner
Norman P. Fivel
Karen Martino Valle
Philippa Bainbridge

Jeffrey S. Shelly
Kenneth G. Walsh
Philip J. Iovieno
Evan Glassman
Bradley J. Gross (Resident, Fort Lauderdale, Florida Office)
Jessica M. Tourk
Magda M. Jimenez
Kahlia E. Fisher
Elizabeth Ann Butler
Ryan K. Higgins

For full biographical listings, see the Martindale-Hubbell Law Directory

EMERY CUTI BRINCKERHOFF & ABADY PC (AV)
545 Madison Avenue, 3rd Floor, 10022-4219
Telephone: 212-763-5000
Facsimile: 212-763-5001
Email: mail@ecbalaw.com *URL:* http://www.ecbalaw.com

Richard D. Emery
Matthew D. Brinckerhoff
Jonathan S. Abady
John R. Cuti

Ilann M. Maazel
David H. Gans
Alexandra D. Lahav (Not admitted in NY)

For full biographical listings, see the Martindale-Hubbell Law Directory

GOLDBERGER AND DUBIN, P.C. (AV)
401 Broadway, 10013
Telephone: 212-431-9380
Fax: 212-966-0588
Email: GND401@aol.com *URL:* http://www.ny-attorney.com

Paul A. Goldberger
Lawrence Dubin

Robert A. Horne

For full biographical listings, see the Martindale-Hubbell Law Directory

HOFFINGER FRIEDLAND DOBRISH & STERN, P.C. (AV)
A Professional Corporation including Professional Corporations
110 East 59th Street, 10022-1392
Telephone: 212-421-4000
Telecopier: 212-223-3857

Jack S. Hoffinger
Lawrence N. Friedland
Robert Z. Dobrish (P.C.)
Stephen R. Stern (P.C.)
Samuel P. Ross
Warren R. Gleicher
Philip S. Ross

Michael J. Sherman
Fran Hoffinger
John H. Friedland
Lydia A. Milone
Devorah S. Weinschneider
Eric I. Wrubel
Nina S. Gross
Scott Lawrence D'Aloise

For full biographical listings, see the Martindale-Hubbell Law Directory

INGRAM YUZEK GAINEN CARROLL & BERTOLOTTI, LLP (AV)
250 Park Avenue, 10177
Telephone: 212-907-9600
Facsimile: 212-907-9681

(See Next Column)

INGRAM YUZEK GAINEN CARROLL & BERTOLOTTI LLP—*Continued*

MEMBERS OF FIRM

Ernest J. Bertolotti (1942-1999)
Daniel L. Carroll
Roger Cukras
David G. Ebert
Larry F. Gainen
Samuel W. Ingram, Jr.
Paulette Kendler
Steven Mastbaum
Shane O'Neill
Dean G. Yuzek

ASSOCIATES

Warren E. Barrows
Amy Bertolotti
Patricia Hewitt
Theodore M. Kakoyiannis
Jeanne F. Pucci
Leigh A. Roveda
Jennifer E. Schwartz
Paul H. Slaney

OF COUNSEL

Karin J. Barkhorn
Beverly L. Deickler
Mark E. Klein
Paulette Lemay Peters
Cory L. Weiss

For full biographical listings, see the Martindale-Hubbell Law Directory

---

KOSTELANETZ & FINK, LLP (AV)

530 Fifth Avenue, 22nd Floor, 10036
Telephone: 212-808-8100
Fax: 212-808-8108
Email: mail@kostelanetzfink.com

SENIOR COUNSEL

Boris Kostelanetz

MEMBERS OF FIRM

Robert S. Fink
Kevin M. Flynn
Bryan C. Skarlatos

COUNSEL

Norman Sinrich
Theodore F. Dickson
Caroline Rule
Brian C. Wille
William F. Cuozzi, III
Dawn Ngo

For full biographical listings, see the Martindale-Hubbell Law Directory

---

LANKLER SIFFERT & WOHL LLP (AV)

33rd Floor, 500 Fifth Avenue, 10110-3398
Telephone: 212-921-8399
Telefax: 212-764-3701
Telex: 4939413 LSWU1
URL: http://www.LSWLAW.com

MEMBERS OF FIRM

Jess Fardella
Helen Gredd
Roderick C. Lankler
John Sand Siffert
Charles T. Spada
Frank H. Wohl

OF COUNSEL

Susan L. Sommer
Peter Herbert

Lisa A. Baroni
Brett S. Deutsch
Brian Fleischer (Not admitted in NY)
Rebecca E. Hollander-Blumoff
Sara Lesch
Ghillaine A Reid
Daniel E. Reynolds
Laura H. Stasior

For full biographical listings, see the Martindale-Hubbell Law Directory

---

HERBERT MONTE LEVY (AV)

60 East 42nd Street, 10165
Telephone: 212-370-4950

For full biographical listings, see the Martindale-Hubbell Law Directory

---

LOEB & LOEB LLP (AV)

A Limited Liability Partnership including Professional Corporations
345 Park Avenue, 10154-0037
Telephone: 212-407-4000
Facsimile: 212-407-4990
Email: info@loeb.com *URL:* http://www.loeb.com
Los Angeles, California Office: Suite 1800, 1000 Wilshire Boulevard, 90017-2475.
Telephone: 213-688-3400.
Facsimile: 213-688-3460.
Century City (Los Angeles), California Office: Suite 2200, 10100 Santa Monica Boulevard, Los Angeles, 90067-4164.
Telephone: 310-282-2000.
Facsimile: 310-282-2192.
Nashville, Tennessee Office: 45 Music Square West, 37203-3205.
Telephone: 615-749-8300.
Facsimile: 615-749-8308.
Rome, Italy Office: Piazza Digione 1, 00197.
Telephone: 011-3906-808-8456.
Facsimile: 011-3906-808-8288.

(See Next Column)

MEMBERS OF FIRM

David B. Eizenman
Helen Gavaris
John F. Lang
Charles H. Miller
Martin R. Pollner
David M. Satnick
P. Gregory Schwed
Brian R. Socolow
Michael P. Zweig

ASSOCIATES

Christian D. Carbone
Paula K. Colbath
Philippa J. Smith
Maria L. Zanfini

For Complete List of Firm Personnel, See General Section

For full biographical listings, see the Martindale-Hubbell Law Directory

---

LONDON FISCHER LLP (AV)

59 Maiden Lane, 10038
Telephone: 212-972-1000
Facsimile: 212-972-1030
Email: Law@LondonFischer.com

MEMBERS OF FIRM

Bernard London
James L. Fischer
Daniel Zemann, Jr.
John E. Sparling
Richard S. Endres
Leah Campbell
Marvin B. Segal
James Walsh
Anthony F. Tagliagambe

For full biographical listings, see the Martindale-Hubbell Law Directory

---

NEWMAN SCHWARTZ & GREENBERG (AV)

950 Third Avenue, 10022
Telephone: 212-308-7900
Telecopier: 212-826-3273

MEMBERS OF FIRM

Gustave H. Newman
Robert Hill Schwartz
Richard A. Greenberg

ASSOCIATES

Karl E. Pflanz
Annemarie Hassett
Steven Y. Yurowitz

For full biographical listings, see the Martindale-Hubbell Law Directory

---

OTTERBOURG, STEINDLER, HOUSTON & ROSEN, P.C. (AV)

230 Park Avenue, 29th Floor, 10169
Telephone: 212-661-9100
Telecopier: 212-682-6104

William M. Silverman
Peter H. Stolzar
Daniel Wallen
Anthony M. Piccione
Stanley L. Lane, Jr.
Peter L. Feldman
Richard G. Haddad

GENERAL COUNSEL

Kurt J. Wolff

COUNSEL

Bernard Beitel
Morton L. Gitter

Lloyd M. Green
Enid Nagler Stuart

For Complete List of Firm Personnel, See General Section

For full biographical listings, see the Martindale-Hubbell Law Directory

---

OWEN & DAVIS PC (AV)

805 Third Avenue, 10022-7513
Telephone: 212-754-1700
Fax: 212-754-1727
Email: odny@owendavis.com

James M. Davis
Robert D. Owen
James H. Neale
Anita Tucker Smith (Not admitted in NY)
Allen Craig Wasserman
India De Carmine
Henry G. Burnett
James L. Fuchs

Lori J. Hoffman

For full biographical listings, see the Martindale-Hubbell Law Directory

---

PILIERO GOLDSTEIN JENKINS & SULLIVAN, LLP (AV)

292 Madison Avenue, 10017
Telephone: 212-213-8200
Fax: 212-685-2028
Email: lawyers@pgjhlaw.com *URL:* http://www.pgjhlaw.com
Carlstadt, New Jersey Office: One Palmer Terrace.
Telephone: 201-507-5157.
FAX: 201-507-5221.
Washington, D.C. Office: 888 17th Street, N.W., Suite 1100.
Telephone: 202-467-6991.
FAX: 202-467-6703.

(See Next Column)

PILIERO GOLDSTEIN JENKINS & SULLIVAN LLP, *New York—Continued*

San Francisco, California Office: 507 Howard Street, Suite 200.
Telephone: 415-281-3631.
Fax: 415-281-3630.

MEMBERS OF FIRM

Kimberlee S. Bogen
Edward J. Goldstein
Jon Mark Jenkins
Marc A. Lebowitz
Robert D. Piliero
George O. Richardson, III
Michael T. Sullivan

ASSOCIATES

Craig Avedisian
Rosemary G. Feit
Eric M. Kogan
Mariano Schwed

OF COUNSEL

Kenneth D. Arbeeny
Christopher P. Hall

For full biographical listings, see the Martindale-Hubbell Law Directory

QUIRK AND BAKALOR, P.C. (AV)

845 Third Avenue, 10022
Telephone: 212-319-1000

Robert E. Quirk
Richard H. Bakalor
Stephen K. Blunda
Jeffrey J. Ellis
Richard M. Freiman
Scott P. Taylor
Henry Nicholas Goodman
Timothy J. Keane

Alice J. Jaffe
Loretta A. Redmond
Michael W. Hecht
Debra E. Seidman
Dominic S. Curcio
A. Lorenzo Bryan
Steven A. Lee
Anoushka Sharifi-Bayley
Brian P. Sexton
Donna Hope Bakalor
Alyssa M. Cohen
James M. Andriola
Liza R. Berliner
Pablo A. Sosa
Christopher J. Gray
Anne E. Pettit
Todd A. Paradeis
Andrew M. Premisler

For full biographical listings, see the Martindale-Hubbell Law Directory

SEIDMAN, SILVERMAN & SEIDMAN, P.C. (AV)

600 Third Avenue 33rd Floor, 10016-2001
Telephone: 212-922-1900

Irving P. Seidman
Lawrence H. Silverman
Brian William Seidman

Joseph M. Fein

For full biographical listings, see the Martindale-Hubbell Law Directory

STANLEY A. TEITLER, P.C. (AV)

299 Broadway, Suite 1500, 10007
Telephone: 212-233-8031
Fax: 212-233-8864

Stanley A. Teitler

For full biographical listings, see the Martindale-Hubbell Law Directory

WHITE, FLEISCHNER & FINO (AV)

140 Broadway, 10005
Telephone: 212-487-9700
Telecopier: 212-487-9777
Email: infor@wff-law.com
Red Bank, New Jersey Office: 272 Broad Street.
Telephone: 732-530-7787.
Telecopier: 732-530-8552.

MEMBER OF FIRM

Benjamin A. Fleischner

ASSOCIATE

Nancy D. Lyness

Representative Clients: Chicago Insurance Co.; London Syndicates; Utica Mutual Ins. Co.; New York Central Ins. Co.; Interstate Insurance Group; State Insurance Fund; Marriott International; Wausau Insurance Companies; London Market Companies.

For Complete List of Firm Personnel, See General Section

For full biographical listings, see the Martindale-Hubbell Law Directory

NISKAYUNA, Schenectady Co.

NICHOLAS E. TISHLER (AV)

1917 Mayfair Road, 12309-5429
Telephone: 518-372-1357
Fax: 518-382-8934
Email: appealsNY@aol.com *URL:* http://www.lawyers.com/nicholasetishlerlaw

For full biographical listings, see the Martindale-Hubbell Law Directory

*POUGHKEEPSIE,** Dutchess Co.

SATZ & KIRSHON, P.C. (AV)

309 Mill Street, 12601
Telephone: 914-454-4040
Fax: 914-454-2938
URL: http://www.lawyers.com/satz&kirshon

Perry Satz

Juliana Muyot Lobiondo

Reference: Premier National Bank.

For full biographical listings, see the Martindale-Hubbell Law Directory

ROCKVILLE CENTRE, Nassau Co.

JACOBSON & SCHWARTZ (AV)

510 Merrick Road, P.O. Box 46, 11571
Telephone: 516-536-0900
Telecopier: 516-536-2371

Jacob N. Schwartz
Ronald A. Jacobson (1935-1993)
Gary R. Schwartz
Robert M. Bridges

Paul Goodovitch
Eric P. Tosca
Jeffrey D. Kadushin
Walter P. Wagner
Rhonda Hammer Barry
Susan B. Mandiberg
Anthony Eugene Graziani
Marc G. Schultz

OF COUNSEL

Bernard Adler

For full biographical listings, see the Martindale-Hubbell Law Directory

*SYRACUSE,** Onondaga Co.

SUGARMAN, WALLACE, MANHEIM & SCHOENWALD (AV)

HSBC Center, Fifth Floor, 360 South Warren Street, 13202-2680
Telephone: 315-474-2943
Fax: 315-474-0235
URL: http://www.sugarmanlaw.com
Buffalo Office: 1720 Rand Building, 14 Lafayette Square, 14203.
Telephone: 716-847-2523.
Fax: 716-847-2589.

MEMBERS OF FIRM

Timothy J. Perry
Sherry R. Bruce

Representative Clients: Allstate Insurance Co.; CNA Insurance Companies; Chubb & Son; Liberty Mutual Insurance Co.; Carpenter Manufacturing Co., Inc.; General Accident Group; Hartford Accident & Indemnity Co.; Firemans Fund; New York Central Mutual; Progressive Insurance Co.
Reference: HSBC.

For full biographical listings, see the Martindale-Hubbell Law Directory

*WHITE PLAINS,** Westchester Co.

BOEGGEMAN, GEORGE, HODGES & CORDE, P.C. (AV)

11 Martine Avenue, 10606
Telephone: 914-761-2252
Telecopier: 914-761-5211
Email: boeggeman@bghc-law.com *URL:* http://www.bghc-law.com
Albany, New York Office: 46 Columbia Street, 12207-2716.
Telephone: 518-465-1100.
Fax: 518-465-1800.

George S. Hodges
Richard G. Corde
John J. Walsh, II
Harold L. Moroknek
Robert S. Ondrovic
Thomas A. Sica (Resident Managing Attorney, Albany Office)

Karen A.D. Jockimo
William M. Wingertzahn
Elizabeth C. Mirisola
Cynthia Dolan
Marcella M. Green
Paul A. Hurley
Leslie K. Arfine
John T. Holden
James J. Lofrese
Jeanne M. Hurley
Ira H. Lapp
Matt Randolph Belkin
Cynthia K. Messemer

OF COUNSEL

Joseph H. George
John E. Boeggeman (1919-1993)

Representative Clients: American Telephone & Telegraph; Anheuser-Busch Companies, Inc.; Lowe's Home Centers; Great Atlantic & Pacific Tea Company; Reliance National Insurance Company; Metropolitan Property & Casualty Insurance Company; Fisher Price, Inc.; CGU Insurance Company; United Services Automobile Association; New York Central Mutual Fire Insurance Company.

For full biographical listings, see the Martindale-Hubbell Law Directory

White Plains—Continued

Rogan Guida & Orenstein (AV)

235 Mamaroneck Avenue, 10605
Telephone: 1-888-WIN-WITH-US; 914-328-4480
Fax: 914-328-4479
URL: http://www.NYlawyers.com
Email: RoganGO@aol.com *URL:* http://www.lawyers.com/personalinjury

Jeffrey P. Rogan	Toni M. Guida

David L. Orenstein

Representative Clients: Recore One Mortgage Corp.; LEASCO; Pappas Enterprises Inc.; Steelcase, Inc.; Printing Center of Westchester Inc.; Corporate Imaging, Inc.; King Jolo's Flowers, Inc.; Systems Exchange, Inc.; Domus Realty.
Reference: Fleet Bank.

For full biographical listings, see the Martindale-Hubbell Law Directory

NORTH CAROLINA

*CHARLOTTE,** Mecklenburg Co.

Ferguson, Stein, Wallas, Adkins, Gresham & Sumter, P.A. (AV)

741 Kenilworth Avenue, Suite 300, 28204-2828
Telephone: 704-375-8461
Fax: 704-334-5654
Mailing Address: P.O. Box 36486, 28236-6486
Email: FSWAGS@aol.com
Chapel Hill, North Carolina Office: Suite 2, 312 West Franklin Street.
Telephone: 919-933-5300.
Fax: 919-967-4953.

James E. Ferguson, II	Geraldine Sumter
Adam Stein (Resident, Chapel Hill Office)	Henderson Hill
Jonathan Wallas	Thomas M. Stern (Resident, Chapel Hill Office)
Karl Adkins	C. Margaret Errington
John W. Gresham	Stephen Luke Largess

Rebecca Ann Thorne	Corie Diane Pauling
James E. Ferguson, III	Ann C. Todd

For full biographical listings, see the Martindale-Hubbell Law Directory

Womble Carlyle Sandridge & Rice (AV)

A Professional Limited Liability Company
3300 One First Union Center, 301 South College Street, 28202-6025
Telephone: 704-331-4900
Fax: 704-331-4955
Email: lawyers@wcsr.com *URL:* http://www.wcsr.com
Winston-Salem, North Carolina Office: 200 West Second Street, P.O. Drawer 84.
Telephone: 336-721-3600.
Fax: 336-721-3660.
Raleigh, North Carolina Office: 2100 First Union Capitol Center, 150 Fayetteville Street Mall, P.O. Box 831.
Telephone: 919-755-2100.
Fax: 919-755-2150.
Research Triangle Park, North Carolina Office: 2505 Meridian Parkway, Suite 300 (Durham), 27713.
Telephone: 919-484-2300.
Fax: 919-484-2340.
Atlanta, Georgia Office: One Atlantic Center, 1201 West Peachtree Street, Suite 3500.
Telephone: 404-872-7000.
Fax: 404-888-7490.
Other Atlanta, Georgia Office: Suite 404, 2296 Henderson Mill Road, N.E.
Telephone: 770-492-9030.
Fax: 770-492-9609.
Washington, D.C. Office: 1120 Nineteenth Street, N.W., Eighth Floor.
Telephone: 202-857-4400.
Fax: 202-467-6910.
Greenville, South Carolina Office: 15 South Main Street, Suite 601, P.O. Box 10208.
Telephone: 864-255-5400.
Fax: 864-255-5440.

RESIDENT MEMBERS

Timothy G. Barber	Debbie Weston Harden
G. Michael Barnhill	Mark P. Henriques
Jim D. Cooley	William C. Raper
Bradford A. DeVore	F. Lane Williamson

(See Next Column)

RESIDENT ASSOCIATES

Patricia E. Dowds	W. Clark Goodman
Steven D. Gardner	Brian E. Heim

Representative Clients: Childress Klein Properties, Inc.; Food Lion, Inc.; J.A. Jones Construction Co.; Parkdale Mills, Inc.; Pillowtex; Duke Power Co.; Bowles Hollowell Conner & Co.; ALLTEL Carolina, Inc.; Belk Store Services, Inc.; Philip Holzmann A.G.

For Complete List of Firm Personnel, See General Section

For full biographical listings, see the Martindale-Hubbell Law Directory

*RALEIGH,** Wake Co.

Bailey & Dixon, L.L.P. (AV)

2500 Two Hannover Square, 434 Fayetteville Street Mall, P.O. Box 1351, 27602
Telephone: 919-828-0731
Facsimile: 919-828-6592
Email: info@bdixon.com *URL:* http://www.bdixon.com

MEMBERS OF FIRM

Ralph McDonald	Patricia P. Kerner
Gary S. Parsons	Cathleen M. Plaut
Carson Carmichael, III	David S. Coats
Alan J. Miles	M. Denise Stanford

Kenyann Brown Stanford

OF COUNSEL

J. Ruffin Bailey	James H. Walker (1920-1994)
Wright T. Dixon, Jr. (Retired)	David M. Britt

ASSOCIATES

David Scott Wisz	Dayatra T. King
Warren Tobin Savage, IV	Philip Todd Gray
Rita Lane Hanshumaker	Ali John Hoomani

Representative Clients: Nationwide Insurance Co.; Lawyers Mutual Liability Insurance Company of North Carolina; Aetna Life and Casualty Insurance Company; GAB Business Services, Inc.; Hartford Insurance Group; Interlocal Risk Financing Fund of North Carolina; Jefferson Pilot Life Insurance Co.; North Carolina League of Municipalities Risk Management Services; Southern Pilot Insurance Co.

For full biographical listings, see the Martindale-Hubbell Law Directory

Marvin Schiller (AV)

Two Hannover Square, Suite 1250, 434 Fayetteville Street Mall, 27601
Telephone: 919-836-8800
Fax: 919-836-8838
URL: http://www.lawyers.com/marvinschiller

For full biographical listings, see the Martindale-Hubbell Law Directory

Smith Debnam Narron Wyche Story & Myers, L.L.P. (AV)

Hedingham Oaks, 4700 New Bern Avenue, P.O. Box 26268, 27611-6268
Telephone: 919-250-2000
Facsimile: 919-250-2100
Email: smithdebnamlaw.com

MEMBERS OF FIRM

W. Thurston Debnam, Jr.	N. Hunter Wyche, Jr.
John W. Narron	Ashley H. Story
Jerry T. Myers	Bettie Kelley Sousa
Terri L. Gardner	Laura K. Howell
Byron L. Saintsing	Rose H. Stout
Franklin Drake	Susan Yelton Ellinger
Gerald H. Groon, Jr.	Caren Davis Enloe
Terry M. Kilbride	Connie E. Carrigan
Elizabeth B. Godfrey	Jeff D. Rogers

Kevin L. Sink

ASSOCIATES

Melanie J. Hogg	Nina L. Gunther
Staci Flaxman Katz	Matthew E. Roehm
Tabatha L. Cruden	Sharon B. Christopher
Tracy T. Hyde	J. Michael Mackay

Cynthia V. Mcalister

OF COUNSEL

Fred J. Smith, Jr.	Jane Flowers Finch

For full biographical listings, see the Martindale-Hubbell Law Directory

Womble Carlyle Sandridge & Rice (AV)

A Professional Limited Liability Company
2100 First Union Capitol Center, 150 Fayetteville Street Mall, P.O. Box 831, 27602
Telephone: 919-755-2100
Fax: 919-755-2150
Email: lawyers@wcsr.com *URL:* http://www.wcsr.com
Charlotte, North Carolina Office: 3300 One First Union Center, 301 South College Street.
Telephone: 704-331-4900.
Fax: 704-331-4955.

(See Next Column)

WOMBLE CARLYLE SANDRIDGE & RICE, *Raleigh—Continued*

Winston-Salem, North Carolina Office: 200 West Second Street, P.O. Drawer 84.
Telephone: 336-721-3600.
Fax: 336-721-3660.
Research Triangle Park, North Carolina Office: 2505 Meridian Parkway, Suite 300 (Durham), 27713.
Telephone: 919-484-2300.
Fax: 919-484-2340.
Atlanta, Georgia Office: One Atlantic Center, 1201 West Peachtree Street, Suite 3500.
Telephone: 404-872-7000.
Fax: 404-888-7490.
Other Atlanta, Georgia Office: Suite 404, 2296 Henderson Mill Road, N.E.
Telephone: 770-492-9030.
Fax: 770-492-9609.
Washington, D.C. Office: 1120 Nineteenth Street, N.W., Eighth Floor.
Telephone: 202-857-4400.
Fax: 202-467-6910.
Greenville, South Carolina Office: 15 South Main Street, Suite 601, P.O. Box 10208.
Telephone: 864-255-5400.
Fax: 864-255-5440.

RESIDENT MEMBERS

Jerry S. Alvis
Susan Davis Crooks
Charles A. Edwards
Robert E. Fields III
Marilyn R. Forbes
Christopher T. Graebe
Johnny M. Loper
Pressly M. Millen
Burley B. Mitchell, Jr.
Robert H. Sasser, III

RESIDENT ASSOCIATES

Coleman M. Cowan
Mark A. Davis
Jeffrey M. Hahn
G. Christopher Olson
M. Todd Sullivan

RESIDENT OF COUNSEL

Elizabeth LeVan Riley

Representative Clients: Aetna Casualty and Surety Co., Inc.; ALSCO/AmeriMark Building Products, Inc.; Aoki Corporation America, Inc.; Hackney Brothers, Inc.; Lawyers Mutual Liability Insurance Company of North Carolina; Meredith College; Regency Park Corp.; Wachovia Bank, N.A.

For Complete List of Firm Personnel, See General Section

For full biographical listings, see the Martindale-Hubbell Law Directory

*WILMINGTON,** New Hanover Co.

STEPHEN E. CULBRETH (AV)

514 Chestnut Street, P.O. Box 446, 28402
Telephone: 910-763-3416
Facsimile: 910-763-9975
Email: culbreth@wilmington.net *URL:* http://www.lawyers.com/culbrethlaw

For full biographical listings, see the Martindale-Hubbell Law Directory

*WINSTON-SALEM,** Forsyth Co.

WOMBLE CARLYLE SANDRIDGE & RICE (AV)

A Professional Limited Liability Company
200 West Second Street, P.O. Drawer 84, 27102
Telephone: 336-721-3600
Fax: 336-721-3660
Email: lawyers@wcsr.com *URL:* http://www.wcsr.com
Charlotte, North Carolina Office: 3300 One First Union Center, 301 South College Street.
Telephone: 704-331-4900.
Fax: 704-331-4955.
Raleigh, North Carolina Office: 2100 First Union Capitol Center, 150 Fayetteville Street Mall, P.O. Box 831.
Telephone: 919-755-2100.
Fax: 919-755-2150.
Research Triangle Park, North Carolina Office: 2505 Meridian Parkway, Suite 300 (Durham), 27713.
Telephone: 919-484-2300.
Fax: 919-484-2340.
Atlanta, Georgia Office: One Atlantic Center, 1201 West Peachtree Street, Suite 3500.
Telephone: 404-872-7000.
Fax: 404-888-7490.
Other Atlanta, Georgia Office: Suite 404, 2296 Henderson Mill Road, N.E.
Telephone: 770-492-9030.
Fax: 770-492-9609.
Washington, D.C. Office: 1120 Nineteenth Street, N.W., Eighth Floor.
Telephone: 202-857-4400.
Fax: 202-467-6910.
Greenville, South Carolina Office: 15 South Main Street, Suite 601, P.O. Box 10208.
Telephone: 864-255-5400.
Fax: 864-255-5440.

(See Next Column)

RESIDENT MEMBERS

Reid C. Adams, Jr.
Conrad C. Baldwin, Jr.
H. Grady Barnhill, Jr.
Jimmy H. Barnhill
S. Fraley Bost
Charles A. Burke
Karen Estelle Carey
Keith A. Clinard
Clayton M. Custer
Tyrus V. Dahl, Jr.
Jeffrey L. Furr
Allan R. Gitter
Ellen M. Gregg
R. Howard Grubbs
Hada V. Haulsee
Lori Privette Hinnant
Martin L. Holton, III
R. Michael Leonard
James R. Morgan, Jr.
Alexander S. Nicholas
Robert S. Pierce
Michael E. Ray
Richard T. Rice
Thomas D. Schroeder
J. Keith Tart
Keith W. Vaughan
G. Criston Windham
Erna A. P. Womble
William F. Womble, Jr.

RESIDENT ASSOCIATES

Kenneth R. Ashford
Amy L. Bircher
John J. Bowers
Ursula M. Henninger
Kenneth R. Michael
John F. Morrow, Jr.

MEMBER OF COUNSEL

W. David Edwards
Kurt C. Stakeman
Dewey W. Wells

Representative Clients: Brad Ragan, Inc.; Brenner Companies; Food Lion, Inc.; Hanes Companies, Inc.; North Carolina Baptist Hospitals, Inc.; R.J. Reynolds Tobacco Co.; Thomasville Furniture Industries, Inc.; Wachovia Corp.; Wake Forest University.

For Complete List of Firm Personnel, See General Section

For full biographical listings, see the Martindale-Hubbell Law Directory

NORTH DAKOTA

*BISMARCK,** Burleigh Co.

PEARCE AND DURICK, PLLP (AV)

314 East Thayer Avenue, P.O. Box 400, 58502
Telephone: 701-223-2890
Fax: 701-223-7865
Email: law.office@pearce-durick.com *URL:* http://www.pearce-durick.com

MEMBERS OF FIRM

William P. Pearce
Gary R. Thune
Larry L. Boschee

Representative Clients: Amoco Oil Co.; Deere & Co.; First Bank; MDU Resources Group; Minnesota Mining and Manufacturing Co.; Monsanto Agricultural Products Co.; North Dakota Insurance Reserve Fund; Northwest Airlines, Inc.; Texaco Inc; Travelers Insurance Co.

For Complete List of Firm Personnel, See General Section

For full biographical listings, see the Martindale-Hubbell Law Directory

OHIO

*CINCINNATI,** Hamilton Co.

WAITE, SCHNEIDER, BAYLESS & CHESLEY CO., L.P.A. (AV)

1513 Central Trust Tower, Fourth and Vine Streets, 45202
Telephone: 513-621-0267
Fax: 513-381-2375; 621-0262

Stanley M. Chesley

Thomas F. Rehme
Robert A. Steinberg
Fay E. Stilz
Louise M. Roselle
D. Arthur Rabourn
Jerome L. Skinner
Janet G. Abaray
Paul M. De Marco
Terrence L. Goodman
Colleen M. Hegge
Jane H. Walker
Renée Infante
James F. Keller
Jean M. Geoppinger
Robert Heuck II

For full biographical listings, see the Martindale-Hubbell Law Directory

*CLEVELAND,** Cuyahoga Co.

DUVIN, CAHN & HUTTON A LEGAL PROFESSIONAL ASSOCIATION (AV)

Erieview Tower, 20th Floor, 1301 East Ninth Street, 44114
Telephone: 216-696-7600
Facsimile: 216-696-2038
Email: attorneys@duvin.com *URL:* http://www.duvinlaw.com
Southfield, Michigan Office: 26211 Central Park Boulevard, Suite 500, 48076.
Telephone: 248-945-1977.
Fax: 248-945-1162.

Robert P. Duvin
Stephen J. Cahn
Lee J. Hutton
Marc J. Bloch
Andrew C. Meyer
Martin S. List
Craig M. Brown
Frank W. Buck
Neal B. Wainblat
Kenneth B. Stark
Martin T. Wymer
Robert M. Wolff
Steven W. Albert
Stephen J. Sferra
Christine C. Covey
Richard C. Hubbard, III
Jon M. Dileno
Suellen Oswald
David A. Posner
Janette McCarthy Louard

Lisa Froimson Mann
David W. Neel
Kathleen M. Kordeleski
Michael T. Pearson
Kenneth D. Schwartz
Brett S. Krantz
Barry Y. Freeman
Bradley A. Sherman
Jonathan S. Forman
Mark F. Humenik
Robert C. Pivonka
Fredrick W Englehart
Jonathan T. Hyman
Latha M. Srinivasan
Shannon K. Patton

OF COUNSEL

Mark V. Webber

Representative Clients: Ameritech; Lincoln Electric; Cleveland-Akron-Canton Supermarket Industry; Cleveland Clinic Foundation; The Scott Fetzer Co.; LTV Steel Company; Electronic Data Systems Corporation; Steris.

For full biographical listings, see the Martindale-Hubbell Law Directory

JANIK & FORBES (AV)

Building Two, 8223 Brecksville Road, 44141-1371
Telephone: 440-838-7600
Fax: 440-838-7601

MEMBER OF FIRM

Steven G. Janik

For Complete List of Firm Personnel, See General Section

For full biographical listings, see the Martindale-Hubbell Law Directory

KELLEY, MCCANN & LIVINGSTONE, LLP (AV)

3500 BP Tower, 200 Public Square, 44114-2302
Telephone: 216-241-3141
Fax: 216-241-3707
Email: Attorneys@kmlegal.com

MEMBERS OF FIRM

Stephen M. O'Bryan
John D. Brown
Mark J. Valponi
Thomas J. Lee
Mary Grace Balazs
Carl A. Murway
David H. Wallace
Robert A. Brindza II
Peter M. Poulos

ASSOCIATES

Timothy J. Duff
Colleen G. Treml
Gregory J. O'Brien

For Complete List of Firm Personnel, See General Section

For full biographical listings, see the Martindale-Hubbell Law Directory

MCDONALD, HOPKINS, BURKE & HABER CO., L.P.A. (AV)

2100 Bank One Center, 600 Superior Avenue, E., 44114-2653
Telephone: 216-348-5400
Telecopier: 216-348-5474
Email: attorney@mhbh.com *URL:* http://www.mhbh.com

Patrick J. Berry
Jeffrey P. Consolo
Jerome W. Cook
Richard S. Cooper
Anthony J. DiVenere
Paul N. Edwards
Theodore J. Esborn
Steven L. Gardner
Carl J. Grassi
James A. Griffith
Jeffrey R. Huntsberger
Brian J. Jereb
Bernard L. Karr
Thomas W. Keen
Roger L. Kleinman
Joseph J. LoPresti, Jr.
Dan L. Makee
George L. McGaughey, Jr.
John T. Mulligan
Brian M. O'Neill
William J. O'Neill
Stephen T. Parisi
R. Jeffrey Pollock
Michael G. Riley

(See Next Column)

Shawn M. Riley
Albert N. Salvatore
Thomas C. Schrader
Roger L. Shumaker
Barbara J. Smith
James M. Stone
Dale R. Vlasek
Kenneth J. Walsh
John M. Wirtshafter
Jane Marie Pine Wood
Charles B. Zellmer

OF COUNSEL

John J. Monroe

Julie A. Callsen
Anne T. Corrigan
Steven A. Eisenberg
G. Andrew Gardner
Anuj Goswami
Donald E. Kacmar
David M. Kall
Jeffrey B. Keiper
Kevin J. Kessinger
Mark D. Klimek
Alan M. Koschik
Deviani M. Kuhar
Paul W. Linehan
Tyler L. Mathews
Jennifer A. Mills
Antoinette K. Palmer
Ketan K. Patel
Sharon Szolosi Regas
Douglas B. Schnee
Michele Smolin
Glenn D. Southworth
Michael R. Spreng

For full biographical listings, see the Martindale-Hubbell Law Directory

WEISS & ASSOCIATES (AV)

1600 Midland Building Landmark Office Towers, 101 Prospect Avenue West, 44115
Telephone: 216-589-9993
Fax: 216-589-9723
Email: jweiss@jweisslaw.com

MEMBERS OF FIRM

Jerome F. Weiss
Robert H. Hanna (Deceased)

For full biographical listings, see the Martindale-Hubbell Law Directory

*COLUMBUS,** Franklin Co.

MCCARTHY, PALMER, VOLKEMA & THOMAS A LEGAL PROFESSIONAL ASSOCIATION (AV)

140 East Town Street, Suite 1100, 43215
Telephone: Telephone: 614-221-4400
Telecopier: 614-221-6010
URL: http://www.mccarthypalmer.com
Email: attorneys@mccarthypalmer.com *URL:* http://www.lawyers.com/attorneysmccarthy

Dennis M. McCarthy
Robert Gray Palmer
Daniel R. Volkema
Warner M. Thomas, Jr.
Michael S. Miller
Elizabeth Schorpp Burkett
Craig P. Scott
Tony C. Merry

Jennifer K. Thivener

Reference: Huntington National Bank.

For full biographical listings, see the Martindale-Hubbell Law Directory

WOLSKE & BLUE A LEGAL PROFESSIONAL ASSOCIATION (AV)

580 South High Street, 43215-5672
Telephone: 614-228-6969
Fax: 614-228-4367
URL: http://www.lawyers.com/wolske&blue
Cincinnati, Ohio Office: The Grand Baldwin Building, 655 Eden Park Drive, Suite 770, 45202.
Telephone: 513-579-1181.
Fax: 513-579-0320.

Jason A. Blue
Walter J. Wolske, Jr.

Reference: Bank One of Columbus, N.A.

For full biographical listings, see the Martindale-Hubbell Law Directory

DUBLIN, Franklin Co.

BLAUGRUND, HERBERT & MARTIN, INCORPORATED (AV)

5455 Rings Road, Suite 500, 43017-7517
Telephone: 614-764-0681
Fax: 614-764-0774
Email: bhm@bhmlaw.net

David S. Blaugrund
John W. Herbert
John S. Jones
David S. Kessler
Emily J. Lewis
Steven A. Martin
Marc E. Myers
Stephen P. Postalakis
Teri G. Rasmussen

For full biographical listings, see the Martindale-Hubbell Law Directory

*ELYRIA,** Lorain Co.

ZAGRANS LAW FIRM A LEGAL PROFESSIONAL ASSOCIATION (AV)
5338 Meadow Lane Court, 44035-1469
Telephone: 440-934-7000
Facsimile: 440-934-7001
Email: eric@zagrans.com *URL:* http://www.zagrans.com

Eric H. Zagrans

Joshua M. Marks
LEGAL SUPPORT PERSONNEL
Jeannette M. Wolff (Legal Assistant)

For full biographical listings, see the Martindale-Hubbell Law Directory

*TOLEDO,** Lucas Co.

FRITZ BYERS (AV)
Suite 824 The Spitzer Building, 43604
Telephone: 419-241-8013
Telecopier: 419-241-4215
Email: fbyers@accesstoledo.com

General Counsel for: Blade Communications, Inc.; Toledo Blade Co.; Buckeye Cablevision, Inc.; Pittsburgh Post Gazette.
Reference: Capital Bank N.A.

For full biographical listings, see the Martindale-Hubbell Law Directory

DOYLE, LEWIS & WARNER (AV)
202 North Erie Street, P.O. Box 2168, 43603
Telephone: 419-248-1500
Fax: 419-248-2002
Email: dlw1@primenet.com

MEMBERS OF FIRM

Steven Timonere
Richard F. Ellenberger
Michael E. Hyrne
Michael A. Bruno
David W. Doerner

ASSOCIATES

Kevin A. Pituch
Maureen O. Atkins

Counsel for: Consolidated Rail Corp.; The Lakefront Dock & Railroad Terminal Co.; Prudential Insurance Co. of America; Equitable Life Assurance Society of the U.S.; Metropolitan Life Insurance Co.; Greyhound Lines; Fireman's Fund Insurance Cos.

For Complete List of Firm Personnel, See General Section

For full biographical listings, see the Martindale-Hubbell Law Directory

OKLAHOMA

*OKLAHOMA CITY,** Oklahoma Co.

CROWE & DUNLEVY, A PROFESSIONAL CORPORATION (AV)
1800 Mid-America Tower, 20 North Broadway, 73102-8273
Telephone: 405-235-7700
Fax: 405-239-6651
Email: marketing@crowedunlevy.com *URL:* http://www.crowedunlevy.com
Tulsa, Oklahoma Office: 500 Kennedy Building, 321 South Boston Avenue, 74103-3313.
Telephone: 918-592-9800.
Fax: 918-592-9801.
Norman, Oklahoma Office: Crowe & Dunlevy, 2500 South McGee, Suite 140, 73072-6705.
Telephone: 405-321-7317.
Fax: 405-360-4002.

L. E. Stringer
Clyde A. Muchmore
Richard C. Ford
Kelley C. Callahan
Harvey D. Ellis, Jr.

For Complete List of Firm Personnel, See General Section

For full biographical listings, see the Martindale-Hubbell Law Directory

DAY, EDWARDS, FEDERMAN, PROPESTER & CHRISTENSEN, P.C. (AV)
Suite 2900 Oklahoma Tower, 210 Park Avenue, 73102-5605
Telephone: 405-239-2121
Telecopier: 405-236-1012
URL: http://lawlinks.com/attys/ok/defpc.html

Bruce W. Day
Joe E. Edwards
Rodney J. Heggy

(See Next Column)

Ricki Valerie Sonders
Thomas Pitchlynn Howell, IV

Representative Clients: Bank of America Corporation; Federal Deposit Insurance Corporation; LSB Industries, Inc.; Merrill Lynch, Pierce, Fenner & Smith, Inc.

For Complete List of Firm Personnel, See General Section

For full biographical listings, see the Martindale-Hubbell Law Directory

*TULSA,** Tulsa Co.

ATKINSON, HASKINS, NELLIS, BOUDREAUX, HOLEMAN, PHIPPS & BRITTINGHAM, A PROFESSIONAL CORPORATION (AV)
1500 ParkCentre, 525 South Main Street, 74103
Telephone: 918-582-8877
Fax: 918-585-8096
Email: ahnmail@ahn-law.com

Galen Lee Brittingham, P.C.
Marthanda J. Beckworth
James N. Edmonds

Kirsten E. Pace
Jeffrey L. Wilson
Margaret A. Nunnery
Roni S. Rierson
Christine M. Benson

OF COUNSEL

Joseph F. Glass

Representative Clients: Allstate Insurance Co.; Bayer Corp.; Crum & Forster Insurance Co.; Hartford Insurance Company; National American Insurance Co.; Federated Insurance Co.; Liberty Mutual Insurance Co.; Physicians Liability Insurance Co.; State Farm Mutual Automobile Insurance Co.; United States Aviation Underwriters.

For full biographical listings, see the Martindale-Hubbell Law Directory

RHODES, HIERONYMUS, JONES, TUCKER & GABLE, P.L.L.C. (AV)
Oneok Plaza, 100 West 5th Street, Suite 400, P.O. Box 21100, 74121-1100
Telephone: 918-582-1173
Fax: 918-592-3390
URL: http://www.rhodesokla.com

MEMBERS OF FIRM

Kevin D. Berry
Jo Anne Deaton
Richard M. Eldridge
E. D. Hieronymus (1908 -1994)
Bert M. Jones
William S. Leach
Michael W. McGivern
William D. Perrine
Mary Quinn-Cooper
Robert P. Redemann
David P. Reid
Chris L. Rhodes, III
Thomas E. Steichen
Catherine C. Taylor
John H. Tucker
Wilson T. White
Harold C. Zuckerman

Ann E. Allison
Steven K. Bunting
Robert P. Coffey, Jr.
J. Christopher Davis
Andrew D. Downing
Dana L. Gish
Kerry R. Lewis
Andrew L. Richardson
Michael F. Smith
Leslie J. Southerland
Kimberly E. West
Keith A. Wilkes

OF COUNSEL

George W. Gable (Retired Partner)
Larry J. Fulton
Kelly M. Greenough

Representative Clients: American International Companies; Bechtel; Chubb Group of Insurance Companies; General Motors Corporation; Merrill, Lynch; Nissan Motor Corporation in U.S.A.; Pfizer, Inc.; Volkswagen of America, Volkswagen, A.G.; Zurich U.S.

For full biographical listings, see the Martindale-Hubbell Law Directory

PENNSYLVANIA

BLUE BELL, Montgomery Co.

SHINGLES & CAPPELLI (AV)
794 Pennllyn Blue Bell Pike, Suite 101, 19422
Telephone: 610-941-4444
Fax: 610-941-9880
800-974-9444
URL: http://www.lawyers.com/shingles&cappelli

MEMBERS OF FIRM

Stanley M. Shingles
Joseph J. Cappelli

ASSOCIATES

Elizabeth L. Schmidt
Shawn M. Sassaman

OF COUNSEL

Robert J. F. Brobyn

(See Next Column)

SHINGLES & CAPPELLI—*Continued*

SPECIAL COUNSEL

Joseph S. Ziccardi

For full biographical listings, see the Martindale-Hubbell Law Directory

ELKINS PARK, Montgomery Co.

MONAGHAN & GOLD, P.C. (AV)

Manor Professional Building, 7837 Old York Road, 19027
Telephone: 215-782-1800
Fax: 215-782-1010
URL: http://www.MNG-LAW.com

Alan S. Gold — John F. X. Monaghan, Jr.

Murray R. Glickman — Robert F. Fortin
Tanya M. Sweet — Sean Robins
Mitchell K. Brudno — Kenneth W. Taylor
Francis D. Hennessy, Jr.

OF COUNSEL

Alan L. Butkovitz — Steven M. Zelitch
Barbara Malett Weitz

LEGAL SUPPORT PERSONNEL

Andrew Logan (Paralegal) — Janet McCrossen (Registered Nurse)
Carol Veach (Paralegal)

For full biographical listings, see the Martindale-Hubbell Law Directory

*HARRISBURG,** Dauphin Co.

ANGINO & ROVNER, P.C. (AV)

4503 North Front Street, 17110
Telephone: 717-238-6791
Fax: 717-238-5610
Email: lawfirm@angino-rovner.com *URL:* http://www.angino-rovner.com
Carlisle, Pennsylvania Office: 28 South Pitt Street, 17013.
Telephone: 717-241-2661.

Richard C. Angino — Neil J. Rovner

References: Credit Bureau of Greater Harrisburg; CoreStates.

For full biographical listings, see the Martindale-Hubbell Law Directory

*PHILADELPHIA,** Philadelphia Co.

F. EMMETT FITZPATRICK, P.C. (AV)

926 Public Ledger Building, 19106
Telephone: 215-925-5200
Fax: 215-925-5991
Email: info@toplaw.com *URL:* http://www.toplaw.com

F. Emmett Fitzpatrick — F. Emmett Fitzpatrick, III

NiaLena Caravasos

LEGAL SUPPORT PERSONNEL

Doreen Howley (Paralegal)

For full biographical listings, see the Martindale-Hubbell Law Directory

DANIEL M. PREMINGER, P.C. (AV)

Suite 1050, Robinson Building, 42 South 15th Street, 19102
Telephone: 215-564-1227
Fax: 215-564-0396
Cape May, New Jersey Office: 811 Columbia Avenue, P.O. Box 908, 08204.
Telephone: 609-463-9091.
Fax: 609-465-4061.

Daniel M. Preminger

For full biographical listings, see the Martindale-Hubbell Law Directory

WILBRAHAM, LAWLER & BUBA, A PROFESSIONAL CORPORATION (AV)

1818 Market Street, Suite 3100, 19103-3631
Telephone: 215-564-4141
Fax: 215-564-4385
Email: @wlbdeflaw.com
Haddonfield, New Jersey Office: 24 Kings Highway West.
Telephone: 856-795-4422.
Fax: 856-795-4699.
Wilmington, Delaware Office: Stoney Batter Office Building, 5301 Limestone Road, Suite 221.
Telephone: 302-234-8217.
Fax: 302-234-8218.

Edward J. Wilbraham — Barbara J. Buba
Robert B. Lawler — Michael J. Block

(See Next Column)

R. Erick Chizmar — John S. Howarth
Kevin J. Maginnis — David M. Maselli
InSook Kim — Renee E. Berger
Sandra D. Terry-Crawford — Edward T. Finch
Sean P. Buggy

OF COUNSEL

Walter J. Timby, Jr. — Daniel J. Allan

Representative Clients: GAF Corporation; Armstrong World Industries, Inc.; U.S. Gypsum Company; Georgia-Pacific Corporation; ARCO; Shell; Royal; AIG; Chubb; Keystone.

For full biographical listings, see the Martindale-Hubbell Law Directory

*SCRANTON,** Lackawanna Co.

MUNLEY, MUNLEY & CARTWRIGHT, P.C. (AV)

205 Madison Avenue, 18503
Telephone: 570-346-7401
Fax: 570-346-3452
URL: http://www.lawyers.com/mmclaw
Email: lawyers@munley.com *URL:* http://www.munley.com

Robert W. Munley — James Christopher Munley
Marion Munley — Daniel W. Munley
Matthew A. Cartwright — Robert W. Munley, III

Reference: First National Bank of Jermyn.

For full biographical listings, see the Martindale-Hubbell Law Directory

O'MALLEY & HARRIS, P.C. (AV)

345 Wyoming Avenue, 18503
Telephone: 570-348-3711
Fax: 570-348-4092
Email: ohpc@epix.net *URL:* http://www.ohpclaw.com
Stroudsburg, Pennsylvania Office: 111 North Seventh Street.
Telephone: 570-421-2252; 570-422-1280.
FAX: 570-422-1281. Email: cerato@ptdprolog.net.
Wilkes-Barre, Pennsylvania Office: 61 North Washington Street.
Telephone: 570-829-3232.
FAX: 570-829-4418. Email: ohpcwb@epix.net.
Williamsport, Pennsylvania Office: 321 Pine Street, Suite 308.
Telephone: 570-323-4380.

Eugene Nogi (1905-1975) — Bruce L. Coyer
Henry Nogi (1900-1976) — John Q. Durkin
Russell J. O'Malley, Sr. (1904-1993) — Gerald J. Hanchulak
Norman Harris (1907-1998) — Richard K. Hodges
William H. Amesbury (Resident, Wilkes-Barre Office) — Timothy J. Holland (Resident, Wilkes-Barre Office)
Paul A. Barrett — John F. Kennedy (Resident, Wilkes-Barre Office)
Matthew P. Barrett — Daniel Morgan
J. Scott Brady (Resident, Wilkes-Barre Office) — Michael Perry
Lori J. Cerato (Resident, Stroudsburg Office) — James M. Tressler
Joseph Timothy Healey
A. Ruth Whalen (Resident, Wilkes-Barre Office)

Representative Clients: Pennsylvania Hospital Insurance Co.; MMI Systems Agency, Inc.; State Farm Insurance Company; ITT Specialty Risk Services; St. Paul Fire & Marine Insurance Co.; Chubb Group of Insurance Companies; Geisingen System Services; Princeton Insurance Company; Northeastern Pennsylvania Physicians Organization; Catholic Healthcare Partners.

For full biographical listings, see the Martindale-Hubbell Law Directory

YOUNGWOOD, Westmoreland Co.

MILLSTEIN & KNUPP (AV)

Cherry Creek Commons Armbrust Road, P.O. Box 467, 15697-0467
Telephone: 724-837-3333
Fax: 724-837-8344

David J. Millstein

For Complete List of Firm Personnel, See General Section

For full biographical listings, see the Martindale-Hubbell Law Directory

RHODE ISLAND

*PROVIDENCE,** Providence Co.

HANSON, CURRAN, PARKS & WHITMAN (AV)

146 Westminster Street, 02903-2218
Telephone: 401-421-2154
Telecopier: 401-521-7040
URL: http://www.hcpw.com

Kirk Hanson (1948-1991)

(See Next Column)

HANSON, CURRAN, PARKS & WHITMAN, *Providence—Continued*

MEMBERS OF FIRM

A. Lauriston Parks
David P. Whitman
Michael T. F. Wallor
Dennis J. McCarten
James T. Murphy
Seth E. Bowerman
Thomas R. Bender
Mark W. Dana

ASSOCIATES

Richard H. Burrows
Christopher J. Zangari (Resident)
Wendy J. Taylor

OF COUNSEL

William A. Curran

General Counsel for: Medical Malpractice Joint Underwriting Association of Rhode Island.
Rhode Island Counsel for: Amica Mutual Insurance Co.; CIGNA; St. Paul Insurance Cos.; Occidental Life Insurance Co.; Exchange Mutual Insurance Co.; Aetna Casualty & Surety Co.

For full biographical listings, see the Martindale-Hubbell Law Directory

VETTER & WHITE, INCORPORATED (AV)

20 Washington Place, 02903
Telephone: 401-421-3060
Telecopier: 401-272-6803
Email: vetlit@aol.com

Benjamin V. White, III
Gordon P. Cleary
Howard A. Merten, Jr.
Brooks R. Magratten

OF COUNSEL

George Vetter

Kimberly A. Simpson
Michael W. Long

For full biographical listings, see the Martindale-Hubbell Law Directory

SOUTH CAROLINA

*COLUMBIA,** Richland Co.

BARNES, ALFORD, STORK & JOHNSON, L.L.P. (AV)

1613 Main Street, P.O. Box 8448, 29202
Telephone: 803-799-1111
Telefax: 803-254-1335
Email: basj@basjlaw.com

Weldon R. Johnson

Andrea C. Pope

For Complete List of Firm Personnel, See General Section

For full biographical listings, see the Martindale-Hubbell Law Directory

McCUTCHEN, BLANTON, RHODES & JOHNSON, L.L.P. (AV)

1414 Lady Street, P.O. Drawer 11209, 29211
Telephone: 803-799-9791
Telecopier: 803-253-6084
Email: Firm1414@aol.com
Winnsboro, South Carolina Office: 120 West Washington Street, 29180.
Telephone: 803-635-6884.

MEMBERS OF FIRM

Thomas E. McCutchen
Jeter E. Rhodes, Jr.
T. English McCutchen, III
Pope D. Johnson, III
William R. Taylor
Evans Taylor Barnette
G. D. Morgan, Jr.
John C. Bradley, Jr.
Creighton B. Coleman
Ruskin C. Foster
William E. Hopkins, Jr.

ASSOCIATE

Anthony W. Livoti

OF COUNSEL

Hoover C. Blanton

Representative Clients: Allstate Insurance Co.; Sears, Roebuck and Co.; J.B. White Co.; Anchor Continental Inc.; Western Fire Insurance Co.; Liberty Mutual Insurance Co.; Southeastern Freight Lines; Continental Life Insurance Co.; State Farm Fire & Casualty Co.

For full biographical listings, see the Martindale-Hubbell Law Directory

RICHARDSON, PLOWDEN, CARPENTER & ROBINSON, P.A. (AV)

1600 Marion Street, P.O. Drawer 7788, 29202
Telephone: 803-771-4400
Telecopy: 803-779-0016
Email: atty@rpcrlaw.com *URL:* http://www.rpcrlaw.com
Myrtle Beach, South Carolina Office: 2103 B Farlow Street, P.O. Box 3646, 29578.
Telephone: 843-448-1008.
FAX: 843-448-1533.

Charles E. Carpenter, Jr.
Steven W. Hamm

S. Elizabeth Brosnan

Representative Clients: Insurance: CNA Insurance Co.; Commercial Union Insurance Co.; The Hartford; Kemper Insurance Co.; Pennsylvania National Mutual Casualty Insurance Co.; Wausau Insurance Cos. Real Estate, Corporate and Banking: Richland Memorial Hospital; First Union Bank. Construction: S.C. Department of Transportation.

For Complete List of Firm Personnel, See General Section

For full biographical listings, see the Martindale-Hubbell Law Directory

JACK B. SWERLING (AV)

1720 Main Street, Suite 301, 29201
Telephone: 803-765-2626
Fax: 803-799-4059
Email: jacklaw@aol.com

For full biographical listings, see the Martindale-Hubbell Law Directory

MYRTLE BEACH, Horry Co.

BELLAMY, RUTENBERG, COPELAND, EPPS, GRAVELY & BOWERS, P.A. (AV)

1000 29th Avenue North, P.O. Box 357, 29578
Telephone: 843-448-2400
Telecopier: 843-448-3022

Howell V. Bellamy, Jr.
John K. Rutenberg
John E. Copeland
Claude M. Epps, Jr.
David R. Gravely
Edward B. Bowers, Jr.
Bradley D. King
Henrietta U. Golding
M. Edwin Hinds, Jr.
Jill F. Griffith
Kathryn M. Cook
David B. Miller
C. Winfield Johnson, III
Sarah A. Johnson
Douglas M. Zayicek
Jeffrey W. King
Mary Anna Malpass
Martin Charles Dawsey

Representative Clients: Dargan Construction Co.; Coastal Federal Savings Bank; Sands Investments; Wachovia Bank of South Carolina; AVX Corp.; Bank of America; Parthenon Insurance Co.; Burroughs & Chapin Co.; International Paper Co.; Hospital Corporation of America.

For full biographical listings, see the Martindale-Hubbell Law Directory

*WALHALLA,** Oconee Co.

LARRY C. BRANDT, P.A. (AV)

205 West Main Street, P.O. Drawer 738, 29691
Telephone: 864-638-5406
864-638-7873
Email: lbrandt@innova.net

Larry C. Brandt

LEGAL SUPPORT PERSONNEL

Debra C. Miller

For full biographical listings, see the Martindale-Hubbell Law Directory

TENNESSEE

*KNOXVILLE,** Knox Co.

SOBIESKI, MESSER & ASSOCIATES (AV)

900 South Gay Street, Suite 1801, 37902
Telephone: 423-546-7770
Fax: 423-546-7969
Email: sobilaw@aol.com

Wanda G. Sobieski
Diane M. Messer

ASSOCIATE

R. Richard Carl, II

For full biographical listings, see the Martindale-Hubbell Law Directory

TEXAS

*AUSTIN,** Travis Co.

BANKSTON & RICHARDSON, L.L.P. (AV)

400 West 15th Street, Suite 710, 78701
Telephone: 512-499-8855
Fax: 512-499-8886
Email: brmlaw@brmlaw.com

Milton L. Bankston — James M. Richardson

For full biographical listings, see the Martindale-Hubbell Law Directory

KARL BAYER (AV)

900 Norwood Tower, 114 West Seventh Street, 78701
Telephone: 512-476-1226
Fax: 512-476-1280
Email: karl@karlbayer.com

Karl Bayer

For full biographical listings, see the Martindale-Hubbell Law Directory

GEORGE & DONALDSON, L.L.P. (AV)

1100 Norwood Tower, 114 West 7th Street, 78701
Telephone: 512-495-1400
Facsimile: 512-499-0094
Email: gdf@gdf.com *URL:* http://www.gdf.com

MEMBERS OF FIRM

R. James George, Jr.
David H. Donaldson, Jr.
Ben J. Cunningham
Renea Hicks
Peter D. Kennedy
J. Roger Williams, Jr.
Gary L. Lewis
James A. Hemphill

ASSOCIATES

Todd S. George — Paul Vigushin

For full biographical listings, see the Martindale-Hubbell Law Directory

THOMPSON & KNIGHT L.L.P. (AV)

(Attorneys and Counselors)
1200 San Jacinto Center, 98 San Jacinto Boulevard, 78701
Telephone: 512-469-6100
Telecopy: 512-469-6180
URL: http://www.tklaw.com
Dallas, Texas Office: 1700 Pacific Avenue, Suite 3300, 75201.
Telephone: 214-969-1700.
Telecopy: 512-969-1751.
Telex: 732298.
Fort Worth, Texas Office: 801 Cherry Street, Suite 1600, 76102.
Telephone: 817-347-1700.
Telecopy: 817-347-1799.
Houston, Texas Office: Thompson Knight Brown Parker & Leahy L.L.P., 1200 Smith Street, Suite 3600, 77002-4595.
Telephone: 713-654-8111.
Telecopier: 713-654-1871.
San Pedro Garza Garcia, Nuevo León, Mexico Office: Edificio Losoles PD-4, Av. Lázaro Cárdenas No. 2400 Pte., C.P. 66220.
Telephone: (52-8) 363-0096.
Telecopy: (52-8) 363-3067.

PARTNERS

Debora Beck Alsup — Jeffrey S. Boyd

For Complete List of Firm Personnel, See General Section

For full biographical listings, see the Martindale-Hubbell Law Directory

BEDFORD, Tarrant Co.

RONALD D. WREN (AV)

1244 Harwood Road, Suite 220, 76021
Telephone: 817-540-6522 (Metro)
Fax: 817-540-0650 (Metro)
Email: ronaldwren@airmail.net

For full biographical listings, see the Martindale-Hubbell Law Directory

*BROWNSVILLE,** Cameron Co.

RODRIGUEZ, COLVIN & CHANEY, L.L.P. (AV)

1201 East Van Buren, P.O. Box 2155, 78520
Telephone: 956-542-7441
Fax: 956-541-2170
McAllen, Texas Office: 4900 North 10th.
Telephone: 956-686-1287.
Telecopier: 956-686-6197.
Harlingen, Texas Office: 402 East Van Buren.
Telephone: 956-423-0216.
Telecopier: 956-423-2035.

(See Next Column)

MEMBERS OF FIRM

Eduardo R. Rodriguez
Norton A. Colvin, Jr.
Mitchell C. Chaney
Marjory Colvin Batsell
Jaime A. Saenz
Joseph A. (Tony) Rodriguez
Alison D. Kennamer

ASSOCIATES

Laura J. Urbis
Lecia L. Chaney
Daniel D. Herink
Robert Patrick Rodriguez
Rosa Maria Villagomez
Vanessa Garza
Teri L. Danish

OF COUNSEL

Orrin W. Johnson (Resident, Harlingen Office)
Benjamin S. Hardy (1912-1993)
Neil E. Norquest (Resident, McAllen Office)
Chris A. Brisack (Resident, McAllen Office)
Raymond A. Cowley

Division Attorneys for: Union Pacific Railroad.
Counsel for: Texas Commerce Bank-Rio Grande Valley, N.A.; Texas Commerce Bancshares, Inc.

For full biographical listings, see the Martindale-Hubbell Law Directory

*CORPUS CHRISTI,** Nueces Co.

BARGER, HERMANSEN, MCKIBBEN & VILLARREAL, L.L.P. (AV)

Formerly Hunt, Hermansen, McKibben & Villarreal, L.L.P.
1100 Tower II, 555 North Carancahua, 78478
Telephone: 512-882-6611
Telecopier: 512-883-8353
Email: hhmv@compuserve.com

MEMBERS OF FIRM

Darrell L. Barger
Tom Hermansen
James F. McKibben, Jr.
Carlos A. Villarreal
Richard C. Woolsey
Matthew B. Cano
David W. Green
Ann Hennis
Thomas A. Silver

ASSOCIATES

Michael B. Anthony
Michael G. Dunnahoo
Patrick M. Martinez
Brian C. Miller
Liza Marie Aguilar
Augustin Rivera, Jr.
Kristina Fernandez
Lane K. Jarvis, Jr.

OF COUNSEL

Lev Hunt

Representative Clients: Reliance Insurance Co.; American States Insurance Group; Medical Protective.

For full biographical listings, see the Martindale-Hubbell Law Directory

CANALES & SIMONSON, P.C. (AV)

2601 Morgan Avenue, P.O. Box 5624, 78465-5624
Telephone: 512-883-0601
Telecopier: 512-884-7023
Email: tonycanales@canalessimonson.com

J. A. "Tony" Canales — Nancy M. Simonson

Barbara Canales Black — Jo Ellen Hewins
Patricia N. Canales

For full biographical listings, see the Martindale-Hubbell Law Directory

DUNN & WEATHERED, P.C. (AV)

611 South Upper Broadway, 78401
Telephone: 512-883-1594
Fax: 512-883-1599

Frank Weathered

Reference: American Bank.

For full biographical listings, see the Martindale-Hubbell Law Directory

*DALLAS,** Dallas Co.

CALHOUN & STACY (AV)

Suite 5700 - Bank of America Plaza, 901 Main Street, 75202-3713
Telephone: 214-748-5000
Facsimile: 214-748-1421
Email: info@calhounstacy.com *URL:* http://www.calhounstacy.com

MEMBER OF FIRM

Shannon B. Schuster

ASSOCIATES

Elizabeth Reding Gambrell — Barbara L. Wohlrabe

For Complete List of Firm Personnel, See General Section

For full biographical listings, see the Martindale-Hubbell Law Directory

Dallas—Continued

CONANT FRENCH & CHANEY, LLP (AV)

3880 Bank One Center, 1717 Main Street, 75201
Telephone: 214-915-0620
Fasimile: 214-915-0634
Email: cfc@cfc-law.com *URL:* http://www.cfc-law.com

A. B. Conant, Jr.
William J. French
William B. Chaney
Linda A. Hale
Glen E. Lavy
Shawn W. Phelan
James D. MacIntyre

For full biographical listings, see the Martindale-Hubbell Law Directory

JACKSON WALKER L.L.P. (AV)

901 Main Street, Suite 6000, 75202-3797
Telephone: 214-953-6000
Fax: 214-953-5822
URL: http://www.jw.com
Austin, Texas Office: 100 Congress Avenue, Suite 1100.
Telephone: 512-236-2000.
Fax: 512-236-2002.
Fort Worth, Texas Office: 301 Commerce Street, Suite 2400.
Telephone: 817-334-7200.
Fax: 817-334-7290.
Houston, Texas Office: 1100 Louisiana, Suite 4200.
Telephone: 713-752-4200.
Fax: 713-752-4221.
Richardson, Texas Office: 2435 North Central Expressway, Suite 600.
Telephone: 972-671-2560.
Fax: 972-671-2566.
San Angelo, Texas Office: 225 West Beauregard Avenue.
Telephone: 915-481-2550.
Fax: 915-481-2552.
San Antonio, Texas Office: 112 E. Pecan Street, Suite 2100.
Telephone: 210-978-7700.
Fax: 210-978-7790.

MEMBERS OF FIRM

David T. Moran
Jack Pew, Jr.
Robert F. Ruckman

Representative Clients Furnished Upon Request.

For Complete List of Firm Personnel, See General Section

For full biographical listings, see the Martindale-Hubbell Law Directory

KRAGE & JANVEY, L.L.P. (AV)

2001 Bryan Tower, Suite 2700, 75201-3059
Telephone: 214-969-7500
Telecopier: 214-220-0230

Ben L. Krage

Representative Client: Regal Capital Co.

For full biographical listings, see the Martindale-Hubbell Law Directory

LAW OFFICES OF LIPPE & ASSOCIATES (AV)

2777 Stemmons Freeway, Suite 925, 75207
Telephone: 214-638-6076
Fax: 214-720-6074
Email: texaslaw@airmail.net *URL:* http://www.texaslaw.com

Emil Lippe, Jr.

OF COUNSEL

Robert B. Buchan

For full biographical listings, see the Martindale-Hubbell Law Directory

THOMAS & CULP, L.L.P. (AV)

2300 Thanksgiving Tower, 1601 Elm Street, 75201-4756
Telephone: 214-953-0000
Facsimile: 214-953-0006

Tom Thomas
Marc S. Culp

ASSOCIATES

Debra Trawick
James Andrew Bench

OF COUNSEL

Fred J. Kolodey

For full biographical listings, see the Martindale-Hubbell Law Directory

THOMPSON & KNIGHT L.L.P. (AV)

(Attorneys and Counselors)
1700 Pacific Avenue Suite 3300, 75201
Telephone: 214-969-1700
Telecopy: 214-969-1751
Telex: 732 298
URL: http://www.tklaw.com
Austin, Texas Office: 1200 San Jacinto Center, 98 San Jacinto Boulevard, 78701.
Telephone: 512-469-6100.
Telecopy: 512-469-6180.
Fort Worth, Texas Office: 801 Cherry Street, Suite 1600, 76102.
Telephone: 817-347-1700.
Telecopy: 817-347-1799.
Houston, Texas Office: Thompson Knight Brown Parker & Leahy L.L.P., 1200 Smith Street, Suite 3600, 77002-4595.
Telephone: 713-654-8111.
Telecopier: 713-654-1871.
San Pedro Garza Garcia, Nuevo León, Mexico Office: Edificio Losoles PD-4, Av. Lázaro Cárdenas No. 2400 Pte., C.P. 66220.
Telephone: (52-8) 363-0096.
Telecopy: (52-8) 363-3067.

PARTNERS

G. Luke Ashley
Beverly Ray Burlingame
Veronica Smith Lewis
Steven W. Sloan
Scott P. Stolley

ASSOCIATE

Bryan P. Neal

For Complete List of Firm Personnel, See General Section

For full biographical listings, see the Martindale-Hubbell Law Directory

TOOLEY & VOSS (AV)

8214 Westchester Drive, Suite 420, 75225
Telephone: 214-368-2224
Fax: 214-368-8307
Email: JCToutfit@aol.com

Joe C. Tooley
Edwin P. Voss Jr.

For full biographical listings, see the Martindale-Hubbell Law Directory

*EDINBURG,** Hidalgo Co.

REED, CARRERA & MCLAIN, L.L.P. (AV)

1 Paseo del Prado, Building 101, 78539
Telephone: 956-631-5444
Fax: 956-631-9187
Mailing Address: P.O. Box 9702, McAllen, Texas, 78502-9702
Email: rcmlaw@compuserve.com

Roger H. Reed
Victor M. Carrera
J. Scott McLain

Ana M. Guerrero
Alberto L. Guerrero

For full biographical listings, see the Martindale-Hubbell Law Directory

*EL PASO,** El Paso Co.

MOUNCE, GREEN, MYERS, SAFI & GALATZAN, A PROFESSIONAL CORPORATION (AV)

100 N. Stanton, Suite 1700, P.O. Box 1977, 79950-1977
Telephone: 915-532-2000
Fax: 915-541-1597
Email: mouncegreenmyers@worldnet.att.net

S. Anthony Safi
H. Keith Myers
Carl H. Green
Barbara Wiederstein
Kurt G. Paxson
Mark C. Walker
Steven L. Hughes
Mark D. Dore
Bruce A. Koehler
Darryl S. Vereen

Carrie D. Helmcamp
James A. Martinez
Hector Andre Beltrán

Attorneys for: El Paso Natural Gas Co.; El Paso Independent School District; Farmers Insurance Group; CGU Insurance; State Farm Mutual Automobile Insurance Co.; Furr's Supermarkets, Inc.; Nationwide Insurance; Scottsdale Insurance Co.

For Complete List of Firm Personnel, See General Section

For full biographical listings, see the Martindale-Hubbell Law Directory

*FORT WORTH,** Tarrant Co.

JOSE, HENRY, BRANTLEY & KELTNER, L.L.P. (AV)

675 North Henderson Street, 76107-8495
Telephone: 817-877-3303
Fax: 817-338-9109

(See Next Column)

JOSE, HENRY, BRANTLEY & KELTNER L.L.P.—*Continued*

John S. Jose
Michael J. Henry
Rickey J. Brantley
David E. Keltner

Karen S. Precella
Scotty MacLean
Anna L. Kingsley
Sara K. Turman-Vedral

For full biographical listings, see the Martindale-Hubbell Law Directory

HARLINGEN, Cameron Co.

ADAMS & GRAHAM, L.L.P. (AV)

222 East Van Buren, West Tower, 78550
Telephone: 956-428-7495
Fax: 956-428-2954
Email: office@adamsgraham.com *URL:* http://www.adamsgraham.com
Affiliate Austin, Texas Office: Hill Gilstrap Adams & Graham, L.L.P., 1005 Congress Avenue, Suite 880, 78701.
Telephone: 512-457-9806.
Fax: 512-457-9066.

John Q. Adams (1900-1968)
Marshall W. Graham (1924-1988)
James S. Graham, Jr. (1922-1990)
Ferriel C. Hamby, Jr.
Tom A. Lockhart
Jim Denison
Leo C. Salzman
Roger W. Hughes
Craig H. Vittitoe
William L. Pope
Patricia Kelly
Jaime Balli
Gina M. Benavides
Charlie J. Cilfone
Juan A. Gonzalez
Barry Ray
Wilbert (Will) Hughes
Trinidad P. Galdean

Representative Clients: The Travelers Insurance Cos.; CIGNA; State Farm Insurance Co.; Valley Baptist Medical Center; McAllen Medical Center; Brownsville Medical Center; Texas Workers' Compensation Insurance Fund; W.R. Grace; American International Companies; Gallagher-Bassett.

For full biographical listings, see the Martindale-Hubbell Law Directory

*HOUSTON,** Harris Co.

BAYKO GIBSON CARNEGIE HAGAN SCHOONMAKER & MEYER LLP (AV)

Chase Tower, 65th Floor, 77002-3008
Telephone: 713-223-0101
Facsimile: 713-223-0042
Email: baykogibson@nol.net

PARTNERS

Tom Bayko
Wendy K. B. Buskop
Jack G. Carnegie
Martin P. Detloff
Larry L. Evans
Michael W. Ford
Michael M. Gibson
John L. Hagan
Robert J. Leidich
M. Michael Meyer
Linda C. Schoonmaker
Leymon Solomon

OF COUNSEL

John T. S. Williams

David M. Bays
Julia Lynn Nye
Ruth E. Piller
Melissa Brook Romine
Lauri De Brie Thanheiser

For full biographical listings, see the Martindale-Hubbell Law Directory

BECK, REDDEN & SECREST (AV)

One Houston Center, 1221 McKinney Street, Suite 4500, 77010
Telephone: 713-951-3700
Telecopier: 713-951-3720
Email: brs@brsfirm.com *URL:* http://www.brsfirm.com

MEMBERS OF FIRM

David J. Beck
Joe W. Redden, Jr.
Ronald Dean Secrest
William Curtis Webb
Eric James Roy Nichols
Alistair Byrne Dawson
Harry P. Weitzel

OF COUNSEL

Keith A. Jones (Not admitted in TX)
Linda K. McCloud
Anne M. Pike
Rufus Wallingford

ASSOCIATES

Jennifer Parker Ainsworth
L. Nicole Batey
Thomas E. Ganucheau
Jeffrey M. Golub
David Watkin Jones
Felicia Harris Kyle
Michael E. Richardson
Jim Taylor

For full biographical listings, see the Martindale-Hubbell Law Directory

COOK, ROACH & LAWLESS, L.L.P. (AV)

1111 Bagby Street, Suite 2650, 77002
Telephone: 713-652-2800
Fax: 713-652-2029
Email: firm@cookroach.com *URL:* http://www.cookroach.com
Austin, Texas Office: 327 Congress Avenue, Suite 490, 78701.
Telephone: 512-472-3067.
Fax: 512-472-3068.

Ronald E. Cook
Robert M. Roach, Jr.
J. Mark Lawless
Dulce M. Stenglein
Robert B. Dubose
Daniel L. McKay

OF COUNSEL

Dana Livingston Cobb

For full biographical listings, see the Martindale-Hubbell Law Directory

GILPIN, PAXSON & BERSCH (AV)

A Registered Limited Liability Partnership
Attorney at Law
1900 West Loop South, Suite 2000, 77027-3259
Telephone: 713-623-8800
Telecopier: 713-993-8451
Email: gpb@gpblaw.com *URL:* http://www.texinslaw.com

PARTNERS

Gary M. Alletag
Timothy R. Bersch
John D. Gilpin
Darryl W. Malone
Michael J. Pappert
Stephen Paxson
Kevin F. Risley

OF COUNSEL

Harless R. Benthul
David F. Webb

ASSOCIATES

Joseph D. Batson
Jeri Pharis Wechsler

Representative Clients: BMW of North America, Inc.; Federal Deposit Insurance Corporation; Greater Houston Builders Association; Owens Corning Fiberglas Corporation; Shaw Industries, Inc.; Southwest Guaranty Trust Company, N.A.; Sprint Communications Company L.P.; Volkswagen of America, Inc.; Volvo North America Corporation; Wells Fargo Bank (Texas), N.A.

For full biographical listings, see the Martindale-Hubbell Law Directory

GLOVER, ANDERSON, LEWIS & PREBEG P.C., PROFESSIONAL CORPORATION (AV)

5599 San Felipe, Suite 1600, 77056
Telephone: 713-621-3306
Facsimile: 713-621-2259

Arthur M. Glover, Jr.
Paul E. Anderson, Jr.
James B. Lewis
Matthew J.M. Prebeg

Scott J. Davenport

For full biographical listings, see the Martindale-Hubbell Law Directory

HOGAN DUBOSE & TOWNSEND, L.L.P. (AV)

1400 Lyric Centre, 440 Louisiana Street, 77002-1635
Telephone: 713-222-8800
Facsimile: 713-222-8810
Email: lawyers@HDTlaw.com

MEMBERS OF FIRM

Richard P. Hogan, Jr.
Jennifer Bruch Hogan
Kevin H. Dubose
Roger D. Townsend
David M. Gunn
Russell S. Post

OF COUNSEL

William Powers, Jr.

For full biographical listings, see the Martindale-Hubbell Law Directory

LANIER, PARKER & SULLIVAN, P.C. (AV)

Four Houston Center, Suite 1550 1331 Lamar Street, 77010
Telephone: 713-659-5200
FAX: 713-659-2204

W. Mark Lanier
Kevin P. Parker
Kent C. Sullivan

Becky J. Lanier
Leslie M. Stewart
Robert E. Leone
Edward W. Fudge
Patrick N. Haines
Dara Grisbee Hegar
Eugene R. Egdorf

For full biographical listings, see the Martindale-Hubbell Law Directory

Houston—Continued

DOUGLAS C. MCNABB (AV)

6200 Chase Tower, 600 Travis Street, 77002
Telephone: 800-870-0828
Fax: 800-679-0679
URL: http://www.lawyers.com/federalcrimes
Email: dmcnabb@mciworld.com *URL:* http://www.federalcrimes.com

For full biographical listings, see the Martindale-Hubbell Law Directory

MOEN, CAIN & O'BRIEN (AV)

1800 Chase Bank Building, 707 Travis, 77002
Telephone: 713-222-9955
Fax: 713-222-6515

Robert A. Moen
Dennis Cain
Douglas M. O'Brien

For full biographical listings, see the Martindale-Hubbell Law Directory

RAMSEY & MURRAY, A PROFESSIONAL CORPORATION (AV)

10000 Memorial Drive, Suite 700, 77024-3412
Telephone: 713-613-5400
Fax: 713-613-5414

Ben Ramsey
John A. Murray, Jr.
Russell J. Ramsey
Mark Ramsey
Curtis D. Collette
Michael Stout Wright
Rick McRory

Joseph W. Gagnon
R. Russell Hollenbeck
Adrian V. Villacorta
Brenda Renee Ferguson

Representative Clients: Great Central Insurance Co.; Republic Insurance Co.

For full biographical listings, see the Martindale-Hubbell Law Directory

SCHWARTZ JUNELL CAMPBELL & OATHOUT, L.L.P. (AV)

Two Houston Center, 909 Fannin, Suite 2000, 77010
Telephone: 713-752-0017
Telecopier: 713-752-0327
Email: dschwartz@schwartz-junell.com

Richard A. Schwartz
William Edward Junell, Jr.
Marshall S. Campbell
Monica F. Oathout
Steven R. Rech

Phillip W. Bechter
J. Parker Fauntleroy, Jr.

OF COUNSEL

Joe H. Reynolds
A. R. Schwartz

LEGAL SUPPORT PERSONNEL

PARALEGALS

Nannette Koger
Maria Woods
Shelly A. Savage, CLA

For full biographical listings, see the Martindale-Hubbell Law Directory

THOMPSON KNIGHT BROWN PARKER & LEAHY L.L.P. (AV)

A Registered Limited Liability Partnership including Professional Corporations
(Attorneys and Counselors)
1200 Smith Street, Suite 3600, 77002-4595
Telephone: 713-654-8111
Telecopier: 713-654-1871
URL: http://www.tklaw.com
Dallas, Texas Office: Thompson & Knight L.L.P., 1700 Pacific Avenue, Suite 3300, 75201.
Telephone: 214-969-1700.
Telecopy: 214-969-1751.
Telex: 732298.
Austin, Texas Office: Thompson & Knight L.L.P., 1200 San Jacinto Center, 98 San Jacinto Boulevard, 78701.
Telephone: 512-469-6100.
Telecopy: 512-469-6180.
Fort Worth, Texas Office: Thompson & Knight L.L.P., 801 Cherry Street, Suite 1600, 76102.
Telephone: 817-347-1700.
Telecopy: 817-347-1799.
San Pedro Garza Garcia, Nuevo León, Mexico Office: Thompson & Knight L.L.P., Edificio Losoles PD-4, Av. Lázaro Cárdenas No. 2400 PTE., C.P. 66220.
Telephone: (52-8) 363-0096.
Telecopy: (52-8) 363-3067.

PARTNERS

Robert L. Galloway
Boris A. Hidalgo

For Complete List of Firm Personnel, See General Section

For full biographical listings, see the Martindale-Hubbell Law Directory

*LUBBOCK,** Lubbock Co.

CARR, HUNT & JOY L.L.P. (AV)

1001 Texas Avenue, P.O. Box 2585, 79408
Telephone: 806-765-7491
Fax: 806-765-0553
Email: info@chjlaw.com
Amarillo, Texas Office: Amarillo National Plaza II, Ste. 509, 500 S. Taylor Street, P.O. Box 989, Amarillo, Texas. 79105.
Telephone: 806-342-3055.
Fax: 806-342-9907.

MEMBERS OF FIRM

Donald M. Hunt
Gary M. Bellair
Charles R. Watson, Jr. (Resident, Amarillo, Texas)
Deborah S. McClure (Resident, Amarillo, Texas)

Representative Clients: Bank of America; Brown-McKee, Inc.; Burk Royalty Co.; Colorado Interstate Gas Co.; Cooper Industries, Inc.; Int'l Bank of Commerce; Motorola, Inc.

For Complete List of Firm Personnel, See General Section

For full biographical listings, see the Martindale-Hubbell Law Directory

MCALLEN, Hidalgo Co.

RODRIGUEZ, COLVIN & CHANEY, L.L.P. (AV)

4900 North 10th Street, 78504
Telephone: 956-686-1287
Telecopier: 956-686-6197
Brownsville, Texas Office: 1201 East Van Buren Street.
Telephone: 956-542-7441.
Telecopier: 956-541-2170.
Harlingen, Texas Office: 402 East Van Buren.
Telephone: 956-423-0216.
Telecopier: 956-423-2035.

OF COUNSEL

Neil E. Norquest
Chris A. Brisack
Raymond A. Cowley

Division Attorneys for: Union Pacific Railroad.
Counsel for: Texas Commerce Bank-Rio Grande Valley, N.A.; Texas Commerce Bancshares, Inc.

For full biographical listings, see the Martindale-Hubbell Law Directory

*SAN ANTONIO,** Bexar Co.

CROFTS, CALLAWAY & JEFFERSON, A PROFESSIONAL CORPORATION (AV)

112 East Pecan Street, Suite 800, 78205-1517
Telephone: 210-225-5551
Telecopier: 210-225-7110
Email: ccj@ccjappeals.com

Thomas H. Crofts, Jr.
Sharon E. Callaway
Wallace B. Jefferson

Ellen B. Mitchell
Nissa Mykleby Sanders
Jacqueline M. Stroh

For full biographical listings, see the Martindale-Hubbell Law Directory

JEFFERS & BANACK, INCORPORATED (AV)

Suite 900, Trinity Plaza II, 745 East Mulberry, 78212-3166
Telephone: 210-736-6600
Telecopier: 210-735-6889
Email: j&b@jeffersbanack.com *URL:* http://www.jeffersbanack.com
Austin Office: 100 Congress, Suite 1050.
Telephone: 512-476-0750.
Telecopier: 512-476-0753.

Emerson Banack, Jr.
William A. Jeffers, Jr.
Charles R. Roberts
Joyce W. Moore
Steven R. Brook
David S. Gragg
William T. Armstrong, III
R. Glen Ayers, Jr.
Joseph D. Martinec
Robert B. Werner
James K. Lowry, Jr.
Peter L. Kilpatrick
William R. Davis, Jr.
Roger D. Kirstein
Steven B. Treu
D. Craig Wood
Robert C. Jones
Deborah A. Bynum
Sherry Rudisell Gonzalez
M. Scott Zimmerer
Juan M. Gonzalez

OF COUNSEL

Ralph Langley

For full biographical listings, see the Martindale-Hubbell Law Directory

*TYLER,** Smith Co.

IRELAND, CARROLL & KELLEY, P.C. (AV)

6101 South Broadway, Suite 500, P.O. Box 7879, 75711
Telephone: 903-561-1600
Fax: 903-581-1071
Email: ICKLAW@AOL.COM

H. Kelly Ireland (Retired)
Donald Carroll (1929-1992)
Otis W. Carroll
Patrick Kelley
Marcus Carroll
Michael G. Carroll

Deborah Race

For full biographical listings, see the Martindale-Hubbell Law Directory

RAMEY & FLOCK, A PROFESSIONAL CORPORATION (AV)

500 First Place, P.O. Box 629, 75710
Telephone: 903-597-3301
Telecopier: 903-597-2413
Email: Ramey@Ramey-Flock.com *URL:* http://www.RameyFlock.com

Thomas B. Ramey (1892-1967)
Jack W. Flock
Tracy Crawford
Glenn Collins
Michael A. Hatchell
Tom Henson
Dennis G. Black
Paul H. Gilliam
R. Brian Craft
Gregory D. Smith
Michael T. Crawford
Mary H. Molly Hatchell
Rosemary Sage Jones
Ronald S. Vickery
John W. Ferguson, Jr.

Deron R. Dacus
Eric H. Findlay
Shannon Dacus
Maria Benecki Sowders
Jamy Mitchell Skaggs

Counsel for: Regions Bank; Exxon Co. U.S.A.; Kelly Springfield Tire Co.; Trinity-Mother Frances Health System; St. Paul Insurance Co.; The Travelers Cos.; Reliance Insurance Co.; Marshall Regional Medical Center.

For full biographical listings, see the Martindale-Hubbell Law Directory

UTAH

*SALT LAKE CITY,** Salt Lake Co.

JOEL M. ALLRED, P.C. (AV)

Suite 800, McIntyre Building, 68 South Main Street, 84101
Telephone: 801-531-8300 (Downtown Office)
801-582-2309 (Home Office)
Fax: 801-533-2463 (Office Hours)
801-363-2420 (After Office Hours)
Email: jallred@vii.com

Joel M. Allred

Amy Allred Dolce

For full biographical listings, see the Martindale-Hubbell Law Directory

VAN COTT, BAGLEY, CORNWALL & MCCARTHY, A PROFESSIONAL CORPORATION (AV)

50 South Main Street, Suite 1600, P.O. Box 45340, 84145-0340
Telephone: 801-532-3333
Telecopier: 801-534-0058
Email: info@vancott.com *URL:* http://www.vancott.com
Ogden, Utah Office: 2404 Washington Boulevard, Suite 900.
Telephone: 801-394-5783.
Park City, Utah Office: 2200 Park Avenue, Suite C200-A.
Telephone: 435-649-3889.

David A. Greenwood
Jeremy M. Hoffman

Jennifer K. Anderson
Stephen K. Christiansen
Tacy A. Hartman
Bradley M. Strassberg

For Complete List of Firm Personnel, See General Section

For full biographical listings, see the Martindale-Hubbell Law Directory

VERMONT

*BURLINGTON,** Chittenden Co.

GRAVEL AND SHEA, A PROFESSIONAL CORPORATION (AV)

Corporate Plaza, 76 St. Paul Street, P.O. Box 369, 05402-0369
Telephone: 802-658-0220
Fax: 802-658-1456

Robert B. Hemley
Dennis R. Pearson

SPECIAL COUNSEL

Norman Williams

For Complete List of Firm Personnel, See General Section

For full biographical listings, see the Martindale-Hubbell Law Directory

*RUTLAND,** Rutland Co.

MILLER FAIGNANT & BEHRENS, P.C. (AV)

36 Merchants Row, P.O. Box 6688, 05702-6688
Telephone: 802-775-2521
Fax: 802-775-8274
Email: lhblaw@aol.com *URL:* http://www.lawyers.com/millerfaignantbehrenslaw

Lawrence Miller
John Paul Faignant
Lawrence H. Behrens

OF COUNSEL

Lisa L. Chalidze

LEGAL SUPPORT PERSONNEL

Marie Peck Fabian
Kim J. Miller

Representative Clients: Travelers Insurance Co.; Government Employees Insurance Co.; Utica Mutual Insurance Co.; Universal Underwriters Insurance Co.; Zurich American Acadia Insurance.
References: Travelers Insurance Co.; Universal Underwriters Insurance Co.

For full biographical listings, see the Martindale-Hubbell Law Directory

VIRGINIA

*ARLINGTON,** Arlington Co.

HENRY ST. JOHN FITZGERALD (AV)

2200 Wilson Boulevard, Suite 800, 22201
Telephone: 703-525-8753
Facsimile: 703-525-2489
Email: hstjf@earthlink.net *URL:* http://www.lawyers.com/henryfitzgerald

For full biographical listings, see the Martindale-Hubbell Law Directory

*FAIRFAX,** (Ind. City; Seat of Fairfax Co.)

CREMINS & ASSOCIATES, P.C. (AV)

Suite 310, 10777 Main Street, 22030-6903
Telephone: 703-352-4800
Fax: 703-352-4805
Email: cremins@bellatlantic.net

William D. Cremins

Jennifer Eileen Cremins
Anisa P. Kelley

For full biographical listings, see the Martindale-Hubbell Law Directory

MCLEAN, Fairfax Co.

VENABLE ATTORNEYS AT LAW VENABLE, BAETJER AND HOWARD, LLP (AV)

A Partnership including Professional Corporations
Suite 400, 2010 Corporate Ridge, 22102
Telephone: 703-760-1600
Fax: 703-821-8949
URL: http://www.venable.com
Baltimore, Maryland Office: 1800 Mercantile Bank & Trust Building, 2 Hopkins Plaza.
Telephone: 410-244-7400.
Fax: 410-244-7742.
Washington, D.C. Office: Venable, Baetjer, Howard & Civiletti LLP, Suite 1000, 1201 New York Avenue, N.W.
Telephone: 202-962-4800.
Fax: 202-962-8300.
Rockville, Maryland Office: Suite 500, One Church Street, P.O. Box 1906.
Telephone: 301-217-5600.
Fax: 301-217-5617.

(See Next Column)

VENABLE ATTORNEYS AT LAW VENABLE, BAETJER AND HOWARD, LLP, *McLean—Continued*

Towson, Maryland Office: 210 Allegheny Avenue, P. O. Box 5517.
Telephone: 410-494-6200.
Fax: 410-821-0147.

MEMBERS OF FIRM

Kenneth C. Bass, III (Also at Washington, D.C. Office)
William D. Dolan, III (P.C.)
J. Scott Hommer, III
David G. Lane
Christine M. McAnney
Michael W. Robinson

ASSOCIATE

Paul N. Wengert

For Complete List of Firm Personnel, See General Section

For full biographical listings, see the Martindale-Hubbell Law Directory

NORFOLK, (Independent City)

SACKS & SACKS, A PROFESSIONAL CORPORATION (AV)

Suite 501 Town Point Center, 150 Boush Street, 23510-1615
Telephone: 757-623-2753
FAX: 757-640-7170
Email: sacks@series2000.com *URL:* http://www.lawyers.com/sacks&sacks-com

Herman A. Sacks (1886-1983)
Stanley E. Sacks
Andrew M. Sacks

LEGAL SUPPORT PERSONNEL

James S. McMahan (Litigation Manager)
Virginia S. McCann (Paralegal)
Maryjane Evans (Paralegal)
Thomas L. Gilchrist (Legal Assistant)
Marshall T. Walker, Jr. (Investigator)

For full biographical listings, see the Martindale-Hubbell Law Directory

RICHMOND, (Independent City)

LECLAIR RYAN, A PROFESSIONAL CORPORATION (AV)

707 East Main Street, 11th Floor, 23219
Telephone: 804-783-2003
Facsmile: 804-783-2294
Email: email@leclairryan.com
Glen Allen, Virginia Office: 4201 Dominion Boulevard, Suite 200, 23060.
Telephone: 804-270-0070.
Facsimile: 804-270-4715.
Blacksburg, Virginia Office: 1872 Pratt Drive, Suite 1865, 24060.
Telephone: 540-961-2762.
Fax: 540-961-2781.
Norfolk, Virginia Office: 999 Waterside Drive, Suite 2025.
Telephone: 757-624-1454.
Facsimile: 757-624-3773.
Alexandria, Virginia Office: 225 Reinekers Lane, Suite 290, 22314.
Telephone: 703-684-8007.
Facsimile: 703-684-8075.
Charlottesville, Virginia Office: 108 S.E. Second Street, P.O. Box 2017, 22902.
Telephone: 804-971-7771.
Facsimile: 804-296-0905.

Lawrence B. Cann, III
Deborah Swindells Donovan (Not admitted in VA)
Laura G. Fox
Grady C. Frank, Jr.
Stephen T. Gannon
Vernon E. Inge, Jr.
Thomas C. Junker
Sharon Maitland Moon
James A. Murphy
David E. Nagle
David G. Shuford
Charles M. Sims

Robert B. Beasley, Jr.

For full biographical listings, see the Martindale-Hubbell Law Directory

VIENNA, Fairfax Co.

BORING & PILGER, P.C. (AV)

307 Maple Avenue West, Suite D, 22180-4307
Telephone: 703-281-2161
Fax: 703-281-9464
URL: http://www.boringandpilger.com

Karl W. Pilger

Sharon C. Williams (Not admitted in VA)

Representative Clients: Hewlett-Packard, Co.; Anthony and Sylvan Pools, Inc.

For full biographical listings, see the Martindale-Hubbell Law Directory

WEST VIRGINIA

*CHARLESTON,** Kanawha Co.

ALLEN GUTHRIE & MCHUGH (AV)

1300 Bank One Center, P.O. Box 3394, 25333
Telephone: 304-345-7250
Telecopier: 304-345-9941
Email: kagwv@kagww.com

George G. Guthrie
Robert B. Allen
Thomas E. McHugh
S. Benjamin Bryant
Wm. Scott Wickline
Pamela Lynn Kandzari
James P. McHugh

Michelle M. Price
John K. McHugh
Nicholas P. Mooney II
Teresa K. Thompson
Charles W. Pace, Jr.

For full biographical listings, see the Martindale-Hubbell Law Directory

SHUMAN ANNAND BAILEY WYANT & EARLES (AV)

Suite 1007, 405 Capitol Street, P.O. Box 3953, 25339
Telephone: 304-345-1400
Telecopier: 304-343-1826
Email: shuman@newwave.net
Wheeling, West Virginia Office: Suite 3002, 1233 Main Street, 26003.
Telephone: 304-233-3100.
Telecopier: 304-233-0201.

MEMBERS OF FIRM

David L. Shuman
Stephen Darley Annand
Charles R. Bailey
Richard L. Earles
David L. Wyant (Resident, Wheeling, West Virginia Office)
Mark William Browning
William R. Slicer
George J. Joseph
Thomas E. Buck (Resident at Wheeling, West Virginia Office)

ASSOCIATES

DesireéHalkias Divita
Roberta F. Green
Paul Kipling Reese
Heidi A. Kossuth (Resident, Wheeling, West Virginia Office)
Lou Ann S. Cassell
Dwayne E. Cyrus
Eric W. Santos (Not admitted in WV; Resident, Wheeling, West Virginia Office)
John T. Molleur
Mark A. Kepple (Resident, Wheeling, West Virginia Office)
David J. Mincer
Karen M. Tracy
Virginia Ann Grottendieck
Arden J. Cogar
Melissa A. Morris
Stacie L. Price (Resident, Wheeling, West Virginia Office)
J. Parker Bazzle
Lisa Bray
Darin C. James
Brian D. Morrison

OF COUNSEL

John F. McCuskey

Representative Clients: American International/Companies (AIG); CNA Insurance Companies; Insurance Corporation of America; Metropolitan Property & Liability Insurance Co.; MMI Companies, Inc.; Motorists Insurance Cos.; Travelers Insurance Cos.; Westfield Companies.
Reference: One Valley Bank.

For full biographical listings, see the Martindale-Hubbell Law Directory

*CLARKSBURG,** Harrison Co.

MCNEER, HIGHLAND, MCMUNN AND VARNER, L.C. (AV)

One Valley Bank Building, P.O. Drawer 2040, 26302-2040
Telephone: 304-626-1100
Facsimile: 304-623-3035
Martinsburg Office: 2520 Aikens Center, P.O. Box 2509.
Telephone: 304-264-4621.
Fax: 304-264-8623.
Parkersburg Office: 404 Market Street, Suite 204, P.O. Box 1507.
Telephone: 304-422-7193.
Facsimile: 304-422-7196.

C. David McMunn
J. Cecil Jarvis
James A. Varner
Robert W. Trumble (Resident, Martinsburg Office)
Catherine D. Munster
James N. Riley
Steven R. Bratke (Resident, Parkersburg Office)
Michael J. Novotny (Resident, Martinsburg Office)
Dennis M. Shreve
Geraldine S. Roberts
William F. Rohrbaugh (Resident, Martinsburg Office)
Gregory H. Schillace
Judy L. Shanholtz
Tiffany R. Durst
Gene W. Bailey, II

(See Next Column)

McNeer, Highland, McMunn and Varner L.C.—*Continued*

OF COUNSEL

James E. McNeer
Cecil B. Highland, Jr.
William L. Fury

Representative Clients: One Valley Bank of Clarksburg, National Assn.; Bruceton Bank; Harrison County Bank; Nationwide Mutual Insurance Cos.; Clarksburg Publishing Co.; C.I.T. Financial Services; State Automobile Mutual Insurance Co.; United Hospital Center, Inc.; West Virginia Coals, Inc.; Swanson Plating Co.

For full biographical listings, see the Martindale-Hubbell Law Directory

WISCONSIN

*MADISON,** Dane Co.

Balisle & Roberson, S.C. (AV)

217 South Hamilton, Suite 302, P.O. Box 870, 53701-0870
Telephone: 608-259-8702
Fax: 608-259-0807
Email: office@mail.b-rlaw.com

Linda S. Balisle
Linda Roberson
Jane Dragisic Clark

ASSOCIATE

Sarah A. Davies

LEGAL SUPPORT PERSONNEL

Diana K. Fleming
Anne C. Harrington (Paralegal)
Laura M. Roenning (Paralegal)

For full biographical listings, see the Martindale-Hubbell Law Directory

*MILWAUKEE,** Milwaukee Co.

Chernov, Stern & Krings, S.C. (AV)

Suite 1275, Two Plaza East, 330 East Kilbourn Avenue, 53202
Telephone: 414-276-4080
Fax: 414-276-4152
Email: mail@chernovlaw.com *URL:* http://www.lawyers.com/chernovlaw

John M. Filachek

For full biographical listings, see the Martindale-Hubbell Law Directory

*RHINELANDER,** Oneida Co.

Eckert Kost & Vocke (AV)

1285 Lincoln Street, P.O. Box 1247, 54501-1247
Telephone: 715-369-1624
FAX: 715-369-1273
Email: ecklaw@newnorth.net *URL:* http://www.ecklaw.com

Michael L. Eckert
Timothy L. Vocke
Keith K. Kost
Mitchell R. Olson

Reference: M & I Merchants Bank.

For full biographical listings, see the Martindale-Hubbell Law Directory

WYOMING

*CASPER,** Natrona Co.

Brown, Drew & Massey, LLP (AV)

Casper Business Center, Suite 800, 123 West First Street, 82601-2486
Telephone: 307-234-1000
800-877-6755
Telefax: 307-265-8025
Email: brwndrew@coffey.com

MEMBERS OF FIRM

Morris R. Massey
J. Kenneth Barbe
Harry B. Durham, III
Jeffrey C. Brinkerhoff
Donn J. McCall
Rex O. Arney
Thomas F. Reese
P. Jaye Rippley
Courtney Robert Kepler

ASSOCIATES

Scott P. Klosterman
Timothy M. Stubson

OF COUNSEL

B. J. Baker
Hampton K. O'Neill

Attorneys for: Norwest Bank Wyoming, N.A.; The CIT Group/Equipment Financing; Aetna Casualty & Surety Co.; The Doctor's Co.; MEDMARC; Westech, Inc.; Chevron USA; Enron Group of Energy Companies; North American Resources Co.

(See Next Column)

For Complete List of Firm Personnel, See General Section

For full biographical listings, see the Martindale-Hubbell Law Directory

VIRGIN ISLANDS

*CHARLOTTE AMALIE, ST. THOMAS,** St. Thomas

Campbell, Arellano & Rich

No. 4 A & B Kongens Gade, P.O. Box 11899, 00801
Telephone: 340-774-4858
Telecopier: 340-776-8442
Email: carvilaw@viaccess.net *URL:* http://www.lawyers.com/lisvilaw
Cruz Bay, St. John, Virgin Islands Office: Scandic Executive Offices, Mongoose Junction, 00831.
Telephone: 304-693-8655.
Telecopier: 304-776-8442.

MEMBERS OF FIRM

Joseph Bruce Wm. Arellano
Carol Ann Rich

ASSOCIATE

W. Mark Hillsman

OF COUNSEL

Roger L. Campbell

Representative Clients: Citibank, N.A.; Cigna Property and Casualty Companies; Royal Insurance.

For full biographical listings, see the Martindale-Hubbell Law Directory

CANADA
ALBERTA

*CALGARY,** Calgary Jud. Dist.

Bennett Jones (AV)

4500 Bankers Hall East, 855-2nd Street S.W., T2P 4K7
Telephone: 403-298-3100
Facsimile: 403-265-7219
Email: firmwatch@bennettjones.ca *URL:* http://www.bennettjones.ca
Edmonton, Alberta Office: 1000, 10035-105 Street.
Telephone: 780-421-8133.
Facsimile: 780-421-7951.
Toronto, Ontario Office: 3400 1 First Canadian Place, P.O. Box 130.
Telephone: 416-863-1200.
Facsimile: 416-863-1716.

MEMBER OF FIRM

John F. Cordeau

For Complete List of Firm Personnel, See General Section

For full biographical listings, see the Martindale-Hubbell Law Directory

*EDMONTON,** Edmonton Jud. Dist.

Parlee McLaws (AV)

15th Floor Manulife Place, 10180 101st Street, T5J 4K1
Telephone: 403-423-8500
Telecopier: 403-423-2870
Email: lawyers@parlee.com *URL:* http://www.parlee.com
Calgary, Alberta Office: 3400 Petro-Canada Centre, 150 - 6th Avenue, SW.
Telephone: 403-294-7000.
Telecopier: 403-265-8263.

MEMBERS OF FIRM

David C. Rolf
Gregory W. Jaycock

ASSOCIATE

Priscilla E. S. J. Kennedy

For Complete List of Firm Personnel, See General Section

For full biographical listings, see the Martindale-Hubbell Law Directory

CANADA NEW BRUNSWICK

*FREDERICTON,** York Co.

COX HANSON O'REILLY MATHESON (AV)

(Formerly Hanson Hashey)
Suite 400, Phoenix Square, P.O. Box 310, E3B 4Y9
Telephone: 506-453-7771
Fax: 506-453-9600
Email: fredericton@coxhanson.ca *URL:* http://www.coxhanson.ca
Halifax, Nova Scotia Office: Suite 1100, Purdy's Wharf Tower 1, P.O. Box 2380 Station Central RPO, B3J 3E5.
Telephone: 902-421-6262.
Fax: 902-421-3130. E-Mail: halifax@coxhanson.ca
Saint John, New Brunswick Office: 1212-One Brunswick Square, 1 Germain St. E2L 4V1.
Telephone: 506-652-7771.
Fax: 506-632-9600.
St. John's, Newfoundland Office: Scotia Centre, 401-235 Water Street, A1C 1B6.
Telephone: 709-726-3321.
Fax: 709-726-2992. E-Mail: stjohns@coxhanson.ca
Charlottetown, Prince Edward Island Office: Queen Square, Suite 202, 119 Queen Street, P.O. Box 875, Station Central, C1A 7L9.
Telephone: 902-894-7051.
Fax: 902-368-3762. E-Mail: charlottetown@coxhanson.ca

MEMBERS OF FIRM

H. A. Hanson, Q.C. (1909-1985)
David T. Hashey, Q.C.
David M. Norman, Q.C.
J. Ian M. Whitcomb, Q.C.
John M. Hanson, Q.C.
Walter D. Vail, Q.C.
Michael E. Bowlin
John D. Larlee, Q.C.
Bruce D. Hatfield, Q.C.
Julian A. G. Dickson, Q.C.
Anne D. Wooder
Terrence J. Morrison
Lucie Richard
Catherine M. Bowlen
J. Marc Richard

ASSOCIATES

Amanda J. Frenette
Monika M. L. Zauhar
Jade A. Spalding
William E. Gould
Christopher R. DeLong
Deborah M. Power
Corinne A. Godbout
Marc-Antoine Chiasson

For full biographical listings, see the Martindale-Hubbell Law Directory

MCINNES COOPER (AV)

Suite 600, 570 Queen Street, P.O. Box 610, E3B 5A6
Telephone: 506-458-8572
Fax: 506-458-9903
Email: mcrfton@mcrlaw.com *URL:* http://www.mcrlaw.com
Halifax, Nova Scotia Office: Summit Place, 1601 Lower Water Street, P.O. Box 730, B3J 2V1.
Telephone: 902-425-6500.
Fax: 902-425-6350. Email: mcrhfx@mcrlaw.com.
St. John's, Newfoundland Office: Baine Johnston Centre, 5th Floor, 10 Fort William Place, P.O. Box 5939, A1C 5X4.
Telephone: 709-722-8735.
Telecopier: 709-722-1763. Email: mcrsj@mcrlaw.com.
Moncton, New Brunswick Office: Place Moncton Place, 655 Main Street, P.O. Box 1368, E1C 8T6.
Telephone: 506-857-8970.
Fax: 506-857-4095. Email: mcrmctn@mcrlaw.com.
Charlottetown, Prince Edward Island Office: BDC Place, Suite 620, 119 Kent Street, C1A 1N3.
Telephone: 902-368-8473.
Fax: 902-368-8346. Email: mcrpei@mcrlaw.com.

PARTNER

David Duncan Young

ASSOCIATE

David D. Eidt

For Complete List of Firm Personnel, See General Section

For full biographical listings, see the Martindale-Hubbell Law Directory

*MONCTON,** Westmorland Co.

MCINNES COOPER (AV)

Barristers, Solicitors & Trade Mark Agents
Place Moncton Place, 655 Main Street, P.O. Box 1368, E1C 8T6
Telephone: 506-857-8970
Fax: 506-857-4095
Email: mcrmctn@mcrlaw.com *URL:* http://www.mcrlaw.com
Halifax, Nova Scotia Office: Summit Place, 1601 Lower Water Street, P.O. Box 730, B3J 2V1.
Telephone: 902-425-6500.
Fax: 902-425-6350. Email: mcrhfx@mcrlaw.com.

(See Next Column)

St. John's, Newfoundland Office: Baine Johnston Centre, 5th Floor, 10 Fort William Place, P.O. Box 5939, A1C 5X4.
Telephone: 709-722-8735.
Telecopier: 709-722-1763. Email: mcrsj@mcrlaw.com.
Charlottetown, Prince Edward Island Office: BDC Place, Suite 620, 119 Kent Street, C1A 1N3.
Telephone: 902-368-8473.
Fax: 902-368-8346. Email: mcrpei@mcrlaw.com.
Fredericton, New Brunswick Office: Suite 600, 570 Queen Street, P.O. Box 610.
Telephone: 506-458-8572.
Fax: 506-458-9903. Email: mcrfton@mcrlaw.com.

ASSOCIATE

John C. Friel, Q.C.

For Complete List of Firm Personnel, See General Section

For full biographical listings, see the Martindale-Hubbell Law Directory

CANADA NEWFOUNDLAND

*ST. JOHN'S,**

MCINNES COOPER (AV)

Barristers, Solicitors & Trade Mark Agents
Baine Johnston Centre, 5th Floor, 10 Fort William Place, P.O. Box 5939, A1C 5X4
Telephone: 709-722-8735
Telecopier: 709-722-1763
Email: mcrsj@mcrlaw.com *URL:* http://www.mcrlaw.com
Halifax, Nova Scotia Office: Summit Place, 1601 Lower Water Street, P.O. Box 730, B3J 2V1.
Telephone: 902-425-6500.
Fax: 902-425-6350. Email: mcrhfx@mcrlaw.com.
Moncton, New Brunswick Office: Place Moncton Place, 655 Main Street, P.O. Box 1368, E1C 8T6.
Telephone: 506-857-8970.
Fax: 506-857-4095. Email: mcrmctn@mcrlaw.com.
Charlottetown, Prince Edward Island Office: BDC Place, Suite 620, 119 Kent Street, C1A 1N3.
Telephone: 902-368-8473.
Fax: 902-368-8346. Email: mcrpei@mcrlaw.com.
Fredericton, New Brunswick Office: Suite 600, 570 Queen Street, P.O. Box 610.
Telephone: 506-458-8572.
Fax: 506-458-9903. Email: mcrfton@mcrlaw.com.

PARTNERS

James R. Chalker, Q.C.
Michael J. Crosbie
J. David B. Eaton
Philip J. Buckingham

For Complete List of Firm Personnel, See General Section

For full biographical listings, see the Martindale-Hubbell Law Directory

CANADA NOVA SCOTIA

*HALIFAX,** Regional Munic. of Halifax

MCINNES COOPER (AV)

Barristers, Solicitors & Trade Mark Agents
Summit Place, 1601 Lower Water Street, P.O. Box 730, B3J 2V1
Telephone: 902-425-6500
Fax: 902-425-6350
Email: mcrhfx@mcrlaw.com *URL:* http://www.mcrlaw.com
St. John's, Newfoundland Office: Baine Johnston Centre, 5th Floor, 10 Fort William Place, P.O. Box 5939, A1C 5X4.
Telephone: 709-722-8735.
Telecopier: 709-722-1763. Email: mcrsj@mcrlaw.com.
Moncton, New Brunswick Office: Place Moncton Place, 655 Main Street, P.O. Box 1368, E1C 8T6.
Telephone: 506-857-8970.
Fax: 506-857-4095. Email: mcrmctn@mcrlaw.com.
Charlottetown, Prince Edward Island Office: BDC Place, Suite 620, 119 Kent Street, C1A 1N3.
Telephone: 902-368-8473.
Fax: 902-368-8346. Email: mcrpei@mcrlaw.com.
Fredericton, New Brunswick Office: Suite 600, 570 Queen Street, P.O. Box 610.
Telephone: 506-458-8572.
Fax: 506-458-9903. Email: mcrfton@mcrlaw.com.

(See Next Column)

McInnes Cooper—*Continued*

PARTNERS

Stewart McInnes, P.C., Q.C.
Eric Durnford, Q.C.
Wylie Spicer, Q.C.
Peter M. S. Bryson
Stephen Kingston
Aidan J. Meade
George W. MacDonald, Q.C.
Robert G. Belliveau, Q.C.
Harvey L. Morrison
Scott C. Norton
John Kulik
Michelle C. Awad

For Complete List of Firm Personnel, See General Section

For full biographical listings, see the Martindale-Hubbell Law Directory

CANADA
PRINCE EDWARD ISLAND

*CHARLOTTETOWN,** Queen's Co.

McInnes Cooper (AV⊕)

Barristers, Solicitors & Trade Mark Agents
BDC Place, Suite 620, 119 Kent Street, C1A 1N3
Telephone: 902-368-8473
Fax: 902-368-8346
Email: mcrpei@mcrlaw.com *URL:* http://www.mcrlaw.com
Halifax, Nova Scotia Office: Summit Place, 1601 Lower Water Street, P.O. Box 730, B3J 2V1.
Telephone: 902-425-6500.
Fax: 902-425-6350. Email: mcrhfx@mcrlaw.com.
St. John's, Newfoundland Office: Baine Johnston Centre, 5th Floor, 10 Fort William Place, P.O. Box 5939, A1C 5X4.
Telephone: 709-722-8735.
Telecopier: 709-722-1763. Email: mcrsj@mcrlaw.com.
Moncton, New Brunswick Office: Place Moncton Place, 655 Main Street, P.O. Box 1368, E1C 8T6.
Telephone: 506-857-8970.
Fax: 506-857-4095. Email: mcrmctn@mcrlaw.com.
Fredericton, New Brunswick Office: Suite 600, 570 Queen Street, P.O. Box 610.
Telephone: 506-458-8572.
Fax: 506-458-9903. Email: mcrfton@mcrlaw.com.

PARTNER

Mark Ledwell

For Complete List of Firm Personnel, See General Section

For full biographical listings, see the Martindale-Hubbell Law Directory

CANADA
SASKATCHEWAN

*REGINA,** Regina Jud. Centre

MacPherson Leslie & Tyerman (AV)

1500-1874 Scarth Street, S4P 4E9
Telephone: 306-347-8000
Telecopier: 306-352-5250
Email: mltreg@mlt.com
Saskatoon, Saskatchewan Office: 1500-410 22nd Street East, S7K 5T6.
Telephone: 306-975-7100.
Telecopier: 306-975-7145.

MEMBERS OF FIRM

Maurice O. Laprairie, Q.C.
Bruce W. Wirth (Resident, Saskatoon Office)
Douglas C. Hodson (Resident, Saskatoon Office)
Kevin C. Wilson (Resident, Saskatoon Office)
Larry B. LeBlanc, Q.C.
Robert G. Richards, Q.C.
Brian J. Kenny
Robert W. Leurer
Jeffrey M. Lee (Resident, Saskatoon Office)
Conrad D. Hadubiak

ASSOCIATES

Kurt G. Wintermute
Heather D. Heavin

For Complete List of Firm Personnel, See General Section

For full biographical listings, see the Martindale-Hubbell Law Directory

ARBITRATION

NEBRASKA

*LINCOLN,** Lancaster Co.

CLINE, WILLIAMS, WRIGHT, JOHNSON & OLDFATHER (AV)

1900 U.S. Bank Building, 233 South 13th Street, 68508
Telephone: 402-474-6900
Fax: 402-474-5393
Email: postmaster@cline-law.com *URL:* http://www.cline-law.com
Omaha, Nebraska Office: Suite 720, One Pacific Place, 1125 South 103rd Street, 68124.
Telephone: 402-397-1700.
Fax: 402-397-1806.

ATTORNEYS

Allen L. Graves
Charles M. Pallesen, Jr.
Fredric H. Kauffman
Donald F. Burt
Alan E. Peterson
Stephen E. Gehring
Robert J. Routh
Kevin Colleran
L. Bruce Wright
James M. Bausch
Larry A. Holle
David R. Buntain
Stephen H. Nelsen
Michael C. Mueller
Lauren W. Wismer
Daniel R. Stogsdill
Scott D. Kelly
Terry R. Wittler
Pamela Hastings Carrier
Mark A. Christensen
Richard P. Garden, Jr.
Shawn D. Renner
John C. Miles
Mary Kay Frank
Thomas C. Huston
Sonya S. Ekart
Don R. Janssen
Susan Kubert Sapp
Kevin J. Schneider
Andrew D. Strotman
Jill Gossin Jensen
Rochelle A. Mullen
John L. Horan
Bryan S. Hatch
Steven C. Likes
Tracy A. Oldemeyer
Jolene M. Papa
Timothy G. Aschoff
Eric N. Bergquist
Janis J. Winterhof
Andrea Dylan Snowden

OF COUNSEL

Charles E. Wright
Richard P. Jeffries
Mary M. Campbell

RETIRED PARTNERS

Flavel A. Wright (Retired)
Warren C. Johnson (Retired)
Charles E. Oldfather (1927-1998)

Representative Clients: U.S. Bank National Association; University of Nebraska; Nebraska Medical Assn.; Saint Elizabeth Regional Medical Center; Media of Nebraska; Cargill Inc.; State Farm Insurance Cos.; Wal-Mart Stores, Inc.; Textron/Cushman; Isco, Inc.

For full biographical listings, see the Martindale-Hubbell Law Directory

*OMAHA,** Douglas Co.

CLINE, WILLIAMS, WRIGHT, JOHNSON & OLDFATHER (AV)

One Pacific Place, 1125 South 103rd Street, Suite 720, 68124
Telephone: 402-397-1700
Fax: 402-397-1806
Email: postmaster@cline-law.com *URL:* http://www.cline-law.com
Lincoln, Nebraska Office: 1900 U.S. Bank Building, 233 South 13th Street, 68508.
Telephone: 402-474-6900.
Fax: 402-474-5393.

ATTORNEYS

Donald F. Burt
Stephen E. Gehring
James M. Bausch
Michael C. Mueller
Daniel R. Stogsdill
Scott D. Kelly
John C. Miles
Mary Kay Frank
Andrew D. Strotman
Rochelle A. Mullen
Steven C. Likes
Tracy A. Oldemeyer
Timothy G. Aschoff

OF COUNSEL

Richard P. Jeffries

Representative Clients: U.S. Bank National Association; University of Nebraska; Nebraska Medical Assn.; Saint Elizabeth Regional Medical Center; Media of Nebraska; Cargill Inc.; State Farm Insurance Cos.; Wal-Mart Stores, Inc.; Textron/Cushman; ISCO, Inc.

For full biographical listings, see the Martindale-Hubbell Law Directory

NEVADA

*RENO,** Washoe Co.

WALTHER, KEY, MAUPIN, OATS, COX & LEGOY, A PROFESSIONAL CORPORATION (AV)

Lakeside Professional Plaza, 3500 Lakeside Court, 89509
Telephone: 775-827-2000
Facsimile: 775-827-2185
Mailing Address: P.O. Box 30000, Reno, Nevada, 89520

Steven T. Walther
Jon J. Key
Ernest J. Maupin
C. Robert Cox
L. Robert LeGoy, Jr.
Michael E. Malloy
G. Barton Mowry
Kim G. Rowe
Procter J. Hug
Donald A. Lattin
Paul J. Anderson
Gustave J. Rossi
Robert A. Winkel
Kurt O. Hunsberger
Michael A. Nivinskus
Christopher D. Jaime

Rick R. Hsu
Michaelle D. Rafferty

Representative Clients: Bank America of Nevada (Trust Dept.); Bechtel Corporations; Bill Pearce Olds, BMW, Volvo; Wells Fargo, N.A. (Trust Dept.); General Motors Acceptance Corp.; Nevada Realtors; Radiation Oncology Associates; The Ralph M. Parsons Corporation; Parsons Corporation; Reno Air, Inc.

For full biographical listings, see the Martindale-Hubbell Law Directory

NEW JERSEY

PARSIPPANY, Morris Co.

CUYLER BURK (AV)

Parsippany Corporate Center, Four Century Drive, 07054-4663
Telephone: 973-734-3200
Telex: 429071
Telecopier: 973-734-3201
Email: Main@Cuyler.com *URL:* http://www.cuyler.com
New York, New York Office: 350 Fifth Avenue, Suite 3304. 10018.
Telephone: 212-645-4039.

MEMBERS OF FIRM

Stephen D. Cuyler
Jo Ann Burk
Stefano Calogero
David L. Menzel
Peter Petrou
Richard A. Crooker
Michael J. Jones

COUNSEL

Anne M. Mohan
Frank J. Miele

ASSOCIATES

Jan C. Walker
Kathleen Jane Olear
Claudia L. Marchese
Mark G. Eliades
Kimberly A. Joel
Christy A. Ramunno
Catherine E. Youngman
Andrew K. Craig
Mark S. Winter
Thomas J. Castano
Hugo A. Hilgendorff, IV

LEGAL SUPPORT PERSONNEL

Frederick M. H. Currie, Jr.

For full biographical listings, see the Martindale-Hubbell Law Directory

PRINCETON, Mercer Co.

BERGMAN & BARRETT (AV)

9 Tamarack Circle, Montgomery Knoll, U.S. Highway 206 North, P.O. Box 1273, 08542
Telephone: 609-921-1502
Fax: 609-683-0288

Edward J. Bergman
Michael T. Barrett

LEGAL SUPPORT PERSONNEL

Kelli E. Murphy (Paralegal)

For full biographical listings, see the Martindale-Hubbell Law Directory

NEW MEXICO

ANGEL FIRE, Colfax Co.

HAWK MESA STORM (AV®)

P.O. Box 314, 87710
Telephone: 505-377-0678
Fax: 505-377-0587
Email: hawk@afweb.com
(Not admitted in NM)

For full biographical listings, see the Martindale-Hubbell Law Directory

NEW YORK

*ALBANY,** Albany Co.

HARVEY AND MUMFORD (AV)

20 Corporate Woods Boulevard, 12211-2396
Telephone: 518-463-4491
Telecopier: 518-463-5665
Email: thefirm@harveyandmumford.com

Arthur J. Harvey (1903-1986)

MEMBERS OF FIRM

Jonathan P. Harvey
Brian F. Mumford

ASSOCIATES

Eva Lynn M. Hayko
Karen Hendricks
Peter Baird Joslin, Jr.
Trudy L. Boulia
Keith J. Starlin

OF COUNSEL

Jack D. Harvey

For full biographical listings, see the Martindale-Hubbell Law Directory

*BINGHAMTON,** Broome Co.

HOGAN & SARZYNSKI, L.L.P. (AV)

20 Hawley Street, P.O. Box 660, 13902-0660
Telephone: 607-723-7413
Fax: 607-723-0129
Email: hsatty@pronetisp.net

MEMBERS OF FIRM

John B. Hogan
Edward J. Sarzynski
John P. Lynch
Michael G. Surowka

Wendy K. DeWind

For full biographical listings, see the Martindale-Hubbell Law Directory

GARDEN CITY, Nassau Co.

EUGENE S. GINSBERG (AV)

300 Garden City Plaza, 11530-3324
Telephone: 516-746-9307
Fax: 516-393-8282

For full biographical listings, see the Martindale-Hubbell Law Directory

*NEW YORK,** New York Co.

ARKIN SCHAFFER & KAPLAN LLP (AV)

590 Madison Avenue, 10022
Telephone: 212-333-0200
Fax: 212-333-2350
Email: info@ARKIN-LAW.com

Stanley S. Arkin
Hyman L. Schaffer
Jeffrey M. Kaplan
Mark S. Cohen
Howard J. Kaplan

ASSOCIATES

Harry B. Feder
Sean R. O'Brien
Robert Pfeffer

OF COUNSEL

Michelle A. Rice

For full biographical listings, see the Martindale-Hubbell Law Directory

PILIERO GOLDSTEIN JENKINS & SULLIVAN, LLP (AV)

292 Madison Avenue, 10017
Telephone: 212-213-8200
Fax: 212-685-2028
Email: lawyers@pgjhlaw.com *URL:* http://www.pgjhlaw.com
Carlstadt, New Jersey Office: One Palmer Terrace.
Telephone: 201-507-5157.
FAX: 201-507-5221.

(See Next Column)

Washington, D.C. Office: 888 17th Street, N.W., Suite 1100.
Telephone: 202-467-6991.
FAX: 202-467-6703.
San Francisco, California Office: 507 Howard Street, Suite 200.
Telephone: 415-281-3631.
Fax: 415-281-3630.

MEMBERS OF FIRM

Kimberlee S. Bogen
Edward J. Goldstein
Jon Mark Jenkins
Marc A. Lebowitz
Robert D. Piliero
George O. Richardson, III
Michael T. Sullivan

ASSOCIATES

Craig Avedisian
Rosemary G. Feit
Eric M. Kogan
Mariano Schwed

OF COUNSEL

Kenneth D. Arbeeny
Christopher P. Hall

For full biographical listings, see the Martindale-Hubbell Law Directory

SALAMANCA, Cattaraugus Co.

BRADY, BROOKS & O'CONNELL, LLP (AV)

41 Main Street, P.O. Box 227, 14779
Telephone: 716-945-2000
Telecopier: 716-945-3566
Email: bbolaw@aol.com *URL:* http://www.lawyers.com/bbolaw
Randolph, New York Office: 165 Main Street.
Telephone: 716-358-6800.
Ellicottville, New York Office: 1887 Building, 1 Washington Street, P.O. Box 550.
Telephone: 716-699-8010.

MEMBERS OF FIRM

Thomas C. Brady
Kameron K. G. Brooks
Brian E. O'Connell, Jr.

Lori Pettit Rieman

For full biographical listings, see the Martindale-Hubbell Law Directory

*WHITE PLAINS,** Westchester Co.

BOEGGEMAN, GEORGE, HODGES & CORDE, P.C. (AV)

11 Martine Avenue, 10606
Telephone: 914-761-2252
Telecopier: 914-761-5211
Email: boeggeman@bghc-law.com *URL:* http://www.bghc-law.com
Albany, New York Office: 46 Columbia Street, 12207-2716.
Telephone: 518-465-1100.
Fax: 518-465-1800.

George S. Hodges
Richard G. Corde
John J. Walsh, II
Harold L. Moroknek
Robert S. Ondrovic
Thomas A. Sica (Resident Managing Attorney, Albany Office)

Karen A.D. Jockimo
William M. Wingertzahn
Elizabeth C. Mirisola
Cynthia Dolan
Marcella M. Green
Paul A. Hurley
Leslie K. Arfine
John T. Holden
James J. Lofrese
Jeanne M. Hurley
Ira H. Lapp
Matt Randolph Belkin
Cynthia K. Messemer

OF COUNSEL

Joseph H. George
John E. Boeggeman (1919-1993)

Representative Clients: American Telephone & Telegraph; Anheuser-Busch Companies, Inc.; Lowe's Home Centers; Great Atlantic & Pacific Tea Company; Reliance National Insurance Company; Metropolitan Property & Casualty Insurance Company; Fisher Price, Inc.; CGU Insurance Company; United Services Automobile Association; New York Central Mutual Fire Insurance Company.

For full biographical listings, see the Martindale-Hubbell Law Directory

OKLAHOMA

*OKLAHOMA CITY,** Oklahoma Co.

DAY, EDWARDS, FEDERMAN, PROPESTER & CHRISTENSEN, P.C. (AV)

Suite 2900 Oklahoma Tower, 210 Park Avenue, 73102-5605
Telephone: 405-239-2121
Telecopier: 405-236-1012
URL: http://lawlinks.com/attys/ok/defpc.html

Bruce W. Day
William B. Federman
Joe E. Edwards
Rodney J. Heggy

(See Next Column)

DAY, EDWARDS, FEDERMAN, PROPESTER & CHRISTENSEN P.C.—*Continued*

Ricki Valerie Sonders

Representative Clients: Applied Thermal Systems, Inc.; BancFirst; Bank One, Oklahoma City; Bank of America, N.A.; CD Warehouse, Inc.; Federal Deposit Insurance Corp.; Fidelity Brokerage Services, Inc.; First Community Bank, Binger; First National Bank and Trust Company of Weatherford; First State Bank & Trust Co., Hollis.

For Complete List of Firm Personnel, See General Section

For full biographical listings, see the Martindale-Hubbell Law Directory

*TULSA,** Tulsa Co.

RHODES, HIERONYMUS, JONES, TUCKER & GABLE, P.L.L.C. (AV)

Oneok Plaza, 100 West 5th Street, Suite 400, P.O. Box 21100, 74121-1100
Telephone: 918-582-1173
Fax: 918-592-3390
URL: http://www.rhodesokla.com

MEMBERS OF FIRM

Richard M. Eldridge
William D. Perrine
Mary Quinn-Cooper
Robert P. Redemann
Chris L. Rhodes, III
Thomas E. Steichen
Catherine C. Taylor
John H. Tucker

Representative Clients: American International Companies; Bechtel; Chubb Group of Insurance Companies; General Motors Corporation; Merrill, Lynch; Nissan Motor Corporation in U.S.A.; Pfizer, Inc.; Volkswagen of America, Volkswagen, A.G.; Zurich U.S.

For full biographical listings, see the Martindale-Hubbell Law Directory

OREGON

*PORTLAND,** Multnomah Co.

JAMES L. KNOLL (AV)

1500 S.W. Taylor Street, 97205
Telephone: 503-222-9000
Fax: 503-226-2801
Email: knolljl@aol.com

For full biographical listings, see the Martindale-Hubbell Law Directory

PENNSYLVANIA

*NORRISTOWN,** Montgomery Co.

THOMAS A. MASTERSON & ASSOCIATES, P.C. (AV)

One Montgomery Plaza, Suite 702, 19401
Telephone: 610-279-6363
Fax: 610-279-6717
Email: mb2@bellatlantic.net *URL:* http://www.lawyers.com/thomasmasterson

Thomas A. Masterson

For full biographical listings, see the Martindale-Hubbell Law Directory

*PHILADELPHIA,** Philadelphia Co.

RALPH D. SAMUEL & CO. A PROFESSIONAL CORPORATION (AV)

225 South 15th Street, Suite 1776, 19102
Telephone: 215-893-9992
Fax: 215-893-9996
Email: RalphSamuel@lawmine.com *URL:* http://www.lawyers.com/ralphdsamuellaw

Ralph David Samuel
Lynn Malmgren

For full biographical listings, see the Martindale-Hubbell Law Directory

VENZIE, PHILLIPS & WARSHAWER, A PROFESSIONAL CORPORATION (AV)

2032 Chancellor Street, 19103
Telephone: 215-567-3322; 647-5121
Telecopier: 215-864-9292
Email: hvenzie@venzie.com *URL:* http://www.venzie.com

Howard D. Venzie, Jr.
Bruce L. Phillips
Sam L. Warshawer, Jr.
K. Gerard Amadio

(See Next Column)

Jeffrey C. Venzie

Representative Clients: Wausau Insurance Cos.; Turner Construction Company; The Hartford Accident & Indemnity Co.

For full biographical listings, see the Martindale-Hubbell Law Directory

SOUTH CAROLINA

*BEAUFORT,** Beaufort Co.

DAVIS, TUPPER & GRIMSLEY, L.L.P. (AV)

611 Bay Street, P.O. Box 2055, 29901-2055
Telephone: 843-524-1116
Facsimile: 843-524-1463
Email: DTGS@Hargray.com

MEMBER OF FIRM

Ralph E. Tupper

For full biographical listings, see the Martindale-Hubbell Law Directory

*COLUMBIA,** Richland Co.

BARNES, ALFORD, STORK & JOHNSON, L.L.P. (AV)

1613 Main Street, P.O. Box 8448, 29202
Telephone: 803-799-1111
Telefax: 803-254-1335
Email: basj@basjlaw.com

Weldon R. Johnson

For Complete List of Firm Personnel, See General Section

For full biographical listings, see the Martindale-Hubbell Law Directory

TENNESSEE

*NASHVILLE,** Davidson Co.

RANDOLPH B. JONES (AV)

3200 West End Avenue, Suite 500, 37203
Telephone: 615-783-1705
Facsimile: 615-783-1606

TEXAS

*DALLAS,** Dallas Co.

HUGHES & LUCE, L.L.P. (AV)

A Registered Limited Liability Partnership including Professional Corporations
1717 Main Street, Suite 2800, 75201
Telephone: 214-939-5500
Fax: 214-939-6100; 214-939-5849
Email: H&L@hughesluce.com *URL:* http://www.hughesluce.com
Austin, Texas Office: 111 Congress, Suite 900.
Telephone: 512-482-6800.
Fax: 512-482-6859.
Houston, Texas Office: 1600 Smith Street, Suite 3550.
Telephone: 713-754-5200.
Fax: 713-754-5270.

MEMBERS OF FIRM

Kim Juanita Askew
James D. McCarthy
Robert H. Mow, Jr. (P.C.)
J. Gregory Taylor

For Complete List of Firm Personnel, See General Section

For full biographical listings, see the Martindale-Hubbell Law Directory

THOMPSON & KNIGHT L.L.P. (AV)

(Attorneys and Counselors)
1700 Pacific Avenue Suite 3300, 75201
Telephone: 214-969-1700
Telecopy: 214-969-1751
Telex: 732 298
URL: http://www.tklaw.com
Austin, Texas Office: 1200 San Jacinto Center, 98 San Jacinto Boulevard, 78701.
Telephone: 512-469-6100.
Telecopy: 512-469-6180.

(See Next Column)

THOMPSON & KNIGHT L.L.P., *Dallas—Continued*

Fort Worth, Texas Office: 801 Cherry Street, Suite 1600, 76102.
Telephone: 817-347-1700.
Telecopy: 817-347-1799.
Houston, Texas Office: Thompson Knight Brown Parker & Leahy L.L.P., 1200 Smith Street, Suite 3600, 77002-4595.
Telephone: 713-654-8111.
Telecopier: 713-654-1871.
San Pedro Garza Garcia, Nuevo León, Mexico Office: Edificio Losoles PD-4, Av. Lázaro Cárdenas No. 2400 Pte., C.P. 66220.
Telephone: (52-8) 363-0096.
Telecopy: (52-8) 363-3067.

PARTNERS

Steven R. Baggett
Frank Finn
Rachelle H. Glazer
Herbert J. Hammond
Molly Steele
Peter J. Thoma

For Complete List of Firm Personnel, See General Section

For full biographical listings, see the Martindale-Hubbell Law Directory

*HOUSTON,** Harris Co.

DAVID T. LOPEZ & ASSOCIATES (AV)

3900 Montrose Boulevard, 77006-4959
Telephone: 713-523-3900
Telecopier: 713-523-3908
Email: david.lopez@lopezlawfirm.com *URL:* http://www.lawyers.com/davidlopezlaw

ASSOCIATE

Christopher D. Yokus

For full biographical listings, see the Martindale-Hubbell Law Directory

RAMSEY & MURRAY, A PROFESSIONAL CORPORATION (AV)

10000 Memorial Drive, Suite 700, 77024-3412
Telephone: 713-613-5400
Fax: 713-613-5414

Ben Ramsey
John A. Murray, Jr.
Russell J. Ramsey
Mark Ramsey
Curtis D. Collette
Michael Stout Wright
Rick McRory

Joseph W. Gagnon
R. Russell Hollenbeck
Adrian V. Villacorta
Brenda Renee Ferguson

Representative Clients: Great Central Insurance Co.; Republic Insurance Co.

For full biographical listings, see the Martindale-Hubbell Law Directory

THOMPSON KNIGHT BROWN PARKER & LEAHY L.L.P. (AV)

A Registered Limited Liability Partnership including Professional Corporations
(Attorneys and Counselors)
1200 Smith Street, Suite 3600, 77002-4595
Telephone: 713-654-8111
Telecopier: 713-654-1871
URL: http://www.tklaw.com
Dallas, Texas Office: Thompson & Knight L.L.P., 1700 Pacific Avenue, Suite 3300, 75201.
Telephone: 214-969-1700.
Telecopy: 214-969-1751.
Telex: 732298.
Austin, Texas Office: Thompson & Knight L.L.P., 1200 San Jacinto Center, 98 San Jacinto Boulevard, 78701.
Telephone: 512-469-6100.
Telecopy: 512-469-6180.
Fort Worth, Texas Office: Thompson & Knight L.L.P., 801 Cherry Street, Suite 1600, 76102.
Telephone: 817-347-1700.
Telecopy: 817-347-1799.
San Pedro Garza Garcia, Nuevo León, Mexico Office: Thompson & Knight L.L.P., Edificio Losoles PD-4, Av. Lázaro Cárdenas No. 2400 PTE., C.P. 66220.
Telephone: (52-8) 363-0096.
Telecopy: (52-8) 363-3067.

PARTNER

Regina Giovannini

For Complete List of Firm Personnel, See General Section

For full biographical listings, see the Martindale-Hubbell Law Directory

UTAH

*SALT LAKE CITY,** Salt Lake Co.

VAN COTT, BAGLEY, CORNWALL & MCCARTHY, A PROFESSIONAL CORPORATION (AV)

50 South Main Street, Suite 1600, P.O. Box 45340, 84145-0340
Telephone: 801-532-3333
Telecopier: 801-534-0058
Email: info@vancott.com *URL:* http://www.vancott.com
Ogden, Utah Office: 2404 Washington Boulevard, Suite 900.
Telephone: 801-394-5783.
Park City, Utah Office: 2200 Park Avenue, Suite C200-A.
Telephone: 435-649-3889.

Robert M. Anderson (President of Firm)
Timothy W. Blackburn (Resident, Ogden, Utah Office)
John L. Young

Sandra L. Crosland

OF COUNSEL

William G. Fowler
Franklin N. Smith

For Complete List of Firm Personnel, See General Section

For full biographical listings, see the Martindale-Hubbell Law Directory

VIRGINIA

SPRINGFIELD, Fairfax Co.

WILLIAM S. COLWELL (AV)

9112 Rockefeller Lane, 22153
Telephone: 703-451-9586
Fax: 703-451-5005
Email: leaderacc@aol.com *URL:* http://www.lawyers.com/wsclaw

For full biographical listings, see the Martindale-Hubbell Law Directory

CANADA BRITISH COLUMBIA

*VANCOUVER,** Vancouver Co.

JENKINS MARZBAN LOGAN (AV)

A Partnership of Law Corporations
Suite 1414, Nelson Square, 808 Nelson Street, P.O. Box 12144, V6Z 2H2
Telephone: 604-681-6564
Facsimile: 604-681-0766
URL: http://www.JML.CA

Robert W. Jenkins

For full biographical listings, see the Martindale-Hubbell Law Directory

CANADA NEWFOUNDLAND

*ST. JOHN'S,**

MCINNES COOPER (AV)

Barristers, Solicitors & Trade Mark Agents
Baine Johnston Centre, 5th Floor, 10 Fort William Place, P.O. Box 5939, A1C 5X4
Telephone: 709-722-8735
Telecopier: 709-722-1763
Email: mcrsj@mcrlaw.com *URL:* http://www.mcrlaw.com
Halifax, Nova Scotia Office: Summit Place, 1601 Lower Water Street, P.O. Box 730, B3J 2V1.
Telephone: 902-425-6500.
Fax: 902-425-6350. Email: mcrhfx@mcrlaw.com.
Moncton, New Brunswick Office: Place Moncton Place, 655 Main Street, P.O. Box 1368, E1C 8T6.
Telephone: 506-857-8970.
Fax: 506-857-4095. Email: mcrmctn@mcrlaw.com.

(See Next Column)

McINNES COOPER—*Continued*

Charlottetown, Prince Edward Island Office: BDC Place, Suite 620, 119 Kent Street, C1A 1N3.
Telephone: 902-368-8473.
Fax: 902-368-8346. Email: mcrpei@mcrlaw.com.
Fredericton, New Brunswick Office: Suite 600, 570 Queen Street, P.O. Box 610.
Telephone: 506-458-8572.
Fax: 506-458-9903. Email: mcrfton@mcrlaw.com.

PARTNER

Christine A. Fagan, Q.C.

For Complete List of Firm Personnel, See General Section

For full biographical listings, see the Martindale-Hubbell Law Directory

CANADA NOVA SCOTIA

*HALIFAX,** Regional Munic. of Halifax

McINNES COOPER (AV)

Barristers, Solicitors & Trade Mark Agents
Summit Place, 1601 Lower Water Street, P.O. Box 730, B3J 2V1
Telephone: 902-425-6500
Fax: 902-425-6350
Email: mcrhfx@mcrlaw.com *URL:* http://www.mcrlaw.com
St. John's, Newfoundland Office: Baine Johnston Centre, 5th Floor, 10 Fort William Place, P.O. Box 5939, A1C 5X4.
Telephone: 709-722-8735.
Telecopier: 709-722-1763. Email: mcrsj@mcrlaw.com.
Moncton, New Brunswick Office: Place Moncton Place, 655 Main Street, P.O. Box 1368, E1C 8T6.
Telephone: 506-857-8970.
Fax: 506-857-4095. Email: mcrmctn@mcrlaw.com.
Charlottetown, Prince Edward Island Office: BDC Place, Suite 620, 119 Kent Street, C1A 1N3.
Telephone: 902-368-8473.
Fax: 902-368-8346. Email: mcrpei@mcrlaw.com.
Fredericton, New Brunswick Office: Suite 600, 570 Queen Street, P.O. Box 610.
Telephone: 506-458-8572.
Fax: 506-458-9903. Email: mcrfton@mcrlaw.com.

PARTNERS

Stewart McInnes, P.C., Q.C.
Eric Durnford, Q.C.
John H. (Jack) Graham
George W. MacDonald, Q.C.
Malcolm D. Boyle
Aidan J. Meade
Michelle C. Awad

ASSOCIATE

Rebecca Saturley

For Complete List of Firm Personnel, See General Section

For full biographical listings, see the Martindale-Hubbell Law Directory

CANADA QUEBEC

*MONTREAL,** Montreal Dist.

McMASTER GERVAIS (AV)

A General Partnership
1000 de La Gauchetière Street West, Suite 900, H3B 5H4
Telephone: 514-879-1212
Fax: 514-954-1905
Email: info@mcmastergervais.com *URL:* http://www.mcmastergervais.com

MEMBERS OF FIRM

Alex K. Paterson, O.C., O.Q., Q.C.
Philippe C. Vachon
Sean J. Harrington
Daniel Ayotte
Thomas M. Davis

COUNSEL

A. Stuart Hyndman, Q.C.
P. André Gervais, Q.C.
Hon. Lawrence A. Poitras, Q.C.
Richard J. Riendeau, Q.C.
Jacques Brien

For Complete List of Firm Personnel, See General Section

For full biographical listings, see the Martindale-Hubbell Law Directory

WOODS & PARTNERS (AV)

2000 McGill College Avenue, Suite 1100, H3A 3H3
Telephone: 514-982-4545
Telecopier: 514-284-2046
Email: general@woods.qc.ca

MEMBERS OF FIRM

James A. Woods
Christian Immer
Julien Cools-Lartigue
Nathalie Chalifour
Christopher Lund Richter
Annie Galarneau
Sébastien Richemont
Kathleen Beaugé
Marjorie Delagrave

For full biographical listings, see the Martindale-Hubbell Law Directory

AVIATION LAW

MINNESOTA

*MINNEAPOLIS,** Hennepin Co.

HUNEGS, STONE, KOENIG, LENEAVE & KVAS, P.A. (AV)

1650 International Center Building, 900 Second Avenue South, 55402
Telephone: 612-339-4511; 800-328-4340
Fax: 612-339-5150
URL: http://hunegslaw.com

Richard Gene Hunegs
Ralph E. Koenig

Reference: National City Bank of Minneapolis.

For full biographical listings, see the Martindale-Hubbell Law Directory

MISSISSIPPI

*JACKSON,** Hinds Co.

WAYNE E. FERRELL, JR. (AV)

405 Tombigbee Street, P.O. Box 24448, 39225-4448
Telephone: 601-969-4700
Fax: 601-969-7514
Email: AIRLAW@MSLAWYER.COM *URL:* http://www.mslawyer.com/ferrell/
(Also Of Counsel, Lundy & Davis, L.L.P., Jackson, Mississippi, Lake Charles, Louisiana and Houston, Texas)

For full biographical listings, see the Martindale-Hubbell Law Directory

MISSOURI

KANSAS CITY, Jackson, Clay, Platte & Cass Cos.

BARTIMUS, FRICKLETON & PRESLEY, A PROFESSIONAL CORPORATION (AV)

23rd Floor City Center Square, 1100 Main Street, 64196
Telephone: 816-842-2300
Fax: 816-421-2111
Email: bfplaw@bfplaw.com *URL:* http://www.bfplaw.com
Jefferson City, Missouri Office: 122 East High, Suite 200, 65101.
Telephone: 573-659-4454.

James R. Bartimus
James P. Frickleton
Kirk R. Presley
Peter S. Obetz

Stephen M. Gorny
Christopher A. Wright

OF COUNSEL

Edward D. Robertson, Jr. (Resident, Jefferson City Office)
Julie C. Frickleton

LEGAL SUPPORT PERSONNEL

LEGAL ASSISTANTS

Tammy J. Gilliams
Laura M. Burbach
Patricia E. Cook
Martha C. Fann

For full biographical listings, see the Martindale-Hubbell Law Directory

COOLING & HERBERS, P.C. (AV)

2400 City Center Square, 1100 Main Street, P.O. Box 26770, 64196
Telephone: 816-474-0777
Telecopier: 816-472-0790
Email: info@coolinglaw.com *URL:* http://www.coolinglaw.com
Merriam (Shawnee Mission), Kansas Office: 7315 Frontage Road, Suite 109.
Telephone: 913-362-9727.
Telecopier: 913-831-2413.
Boulder, Colorado Office: 1942 Broadway Street, Suite 314, 80302.
Telephone: 303-938-6877.
FAX: 303-938-6878.

James E. Cooling
Paul V. Herbers
Joe B. Whisler
Joanne M. Barbera

Susan E. McKeon
James E. Ramsey
Rodney A. Ames

(See Next Column)

OF COUNSEL

Russell C. Leffel (Resident, Merriam, Kansas Office)
Brad Lee Rose (Resident, Boulder, Colorado Office)

Representative Client: Lloyds of London.

For full biographical listings, see the Martindale-Hubbell Law Directory

NEVADA

*LAS VEGAS,** Clark Co.

GARY LOGAN (AV)

Third Floor, 302 East Carson Avenue, 89101
Telephone: 702-385-9900
Telecopier: 702-382-4800
Email: GARYLOGAN@prodigy.net

OF COUNSEL

Richard I. Feinberg

References: Bank of America-Nevada; The Chase Manhattan Bank, N.A.

For full biographical listings, see the Martindale-Hubbell Law Directory

*RENO,** Washoe Co.

BRADLEY, DRENDEL & JEANNEY (AV)

401 Flint Street, P.O. Box 1987, 89505
Telephone: 775-329-2273
Fax: 775-329-6513
Email: bdandj@worldnet.att.net *URL:* http://www.lawyers.com/bd&jlaw

Bill Bradley
Joseph S. Bradley
Thomas E. Drendel
William C. Jeanney

OF COUNSEL

William O. "Bud" Bradley
John Squire Drendel

For full biographical listings, see the Martindale-Hubbell Law Directory

NEW JERSEY

*MORRISTOWN,** Morris Co.

BAUMEISTER & SAMUELS, P.C. (AV®)

1776 On The Green, P.O. Box 1116, 07962-1116
Telephone: 973-267-6666
Telecopier: 973-605-1812
Email: BAUMSAM@AOL.COM
New York, N.Y. Office: One Exchange Plaza, 10006-3008.
Telephone: 212-363-1200.
Telecopier: 212-363-1346.

Michel F. Baumeister
Douglas A. Latto (Not admitted in NJ)
Dorothea M. Capone

OF COUNSEL

Lynn F. Samuels
Robert S. Franklin (Not admitted in NJ)
Marc Z. Edell

For full biographical listings, see the Martindale-Hubbell Law Directory

SPRINGFIELD, Union Co.

McDONOUGH, KORN & EICHHORN, A PROFESSIONAL CORPORATION (AV)

Park Place Legal Center, 959 South Springfield Avenue, P.O. Box 712, 07081-0712
Telephone: 973-912-9099
Fax: 973-912-8604

Matthew S. Schorr

Representative Clients: Yosuda Fire & Marine Insurance Co.; Lurich American Insurance Co.; Chubb Insurance Co.; AIG Insurance Co.; St. Paul Fire & Marine Insurance Co.

For Complete List of Firm Personnel, See General Section

For full biographical listings, see the Martindale-Hubbell Law Directory

NEW MEXICO

*ALBUQUERQUE,** Bernalillo Co.

CARPENTER & CHÁVEZ, LTD. (AV)

1600 University Boulevard, N.E., Suite A, 87102-1711
Telephone: 505-243-1336
Facsimile: 505-243-1339
Email: carpchav@swcp.com *URL:* http://www.carpenter-law.com

William H. Carpenter
Edward L. Chávez
David J. Stout

Reference: Bank of America, Albuquerque, New Mexico.

For full biographical listings, see the Martindale-Hubbell Law Directory

NEW YORK

*NEW YORK,** New York Co.

BADIAK WILL & RUDDY (AV)

Suite 1040, 120 Broadway, 10271
Telephone: 212-376-6767
Telecopier: 212-376-6777
Telex: 6716686 BANDW
Email: admiralaw@aol.com
North Miami Beach, Florida Office: Badiak, Will & Kallen, 17071 West Dixie Highway, P.O. Box 600550.
Telephone: 305-945-1851.

MEMBERS OF FIRM

Roman Badiak
Alfred J. Will
James J. Ruddy
John D. Kallen (Resident, North Miami, Florida Office)
David L. Maloof (1924-1992)

ASSOCIATES

Stephen A. Frank
Nicholas Kalfa
James P. Krauzlis
Martin L. Lindahl
Lisa A. Scognamillo
Deborah R. Reid

OF COUNSEL

Charles C. Goodenough

For full biographical listings, see the Martindale-Hubbell Law Directory

BAUMEISTER & SAMUELS, P.C. (AV)

One Exchange Plaza, 10006-3008
Telephone: 212-363-1200
Telecopier: 212-363-1346
Email: BAUMSAM@AOL.COM
Morristown, New Jersey Office: 1776 On The Green, P.O. Box 1116, 07962-1116.
Telephone: 973-267-6666.
Telecopier: 973-605-1812.

Michel F. Baumeister
Douglas A. Latto
Dorothea M. Capone

OF COUNSEL

Lynn F. Samuels
Robert S. Franklin
Marc Z. Edell

For full biographical listings, see the Martindale-Hubbell Law Directory

KREINDLER & KREINDLER (AV)

100 Park Avenue, 10017
Telephone: 212-687-8181
Telecopier: 212-972-9432
Email: legal@kreindler.com *URL:* http://www.kreindler.com

MEMBERS OF FIRM

Harry E. Kreindler (1896-1983)
Lee S. Kreindler
Marc S. Moller
Francis G. Fleming, Jr.
Steven R. Pounian
James P. Kreindler
David C. Cook
David Beekman
Blanca I. Rodriguez
Noah H. Kushlefsky
Robert J. Spragg

OF COUNSEL

Paul S. Edelman
Milton G. Sincoff
Henry A. Gluckstern

ASSOCIATES

Lori B. Lasson
Susan Friery (Not admitted in NY)
Andrew J. Maloney, III
Brian J. Alexander
David G. Nanz
Justin Timothy Green
Daniel O. Rose
Jacqueline M. James
Victoria J. Maniatis

For full biographical listings, see the Martindale-Hubbell Law Directory

MILBANK, TWEED, HADLEY & MCCLOY LLP (AV)

1 Chase Manhattan Plaza, 10005-1413
Telephone: 212-530-5000
Fax: 212-530-5219
Email: postmaster@milbank.com *URL:* http://www.milbank.com
Midtown Office: 375 Park Avenue, Suite 3601, 10152.
Telephone: 212-530-5800.
Fax: 212-530-0158.
Los Angeles, California Office: 601 South Figueroa Street, 30th Floor, 90017.
Telephone: 213-892-4000.
Fax: 213-629-5063.
Washington, D.C. Office: International Square Building, Suite 1100, 1825 Eye Street, N.W., 20006.
Telephone: 202-835-7500.
Fax: 202-835-7586.
Tokyo, Japan Office: Fukoku Seimei Building, 2-2, Uchisaiwai-cho 2-Chome, Chiyoda-ku, Tokyo 100-0011, Japan.
Telephone: 011-81-3-3504-1050.
Fax: 011-81-3-3595-2790, 011-81-3-3595-2840.
London, England Office: Dashwood House, 69 Old Broad Street, London EC2M 1QS.
Telephone: 011-44-207-448-3000.
Fax: 011-44-207-448-3029.
Hong Kong Office: 3007 Alexandra House, 16 Chater Road.
Telephone: 011-852-2971-4888.
Fax: 011-852-2840-0792; 011-852-2845-9046.
Singapore Office: 14-00 Caltex House, 30 Raffles Place, 048622.
Telephone: 011-65-428-2400.
Fax: 011-65-428-2500.
Moscow, Russia Office: 24/27 Sadovaya-Samotyochnya, Moscow, 103051.
Telephone: 011-7-501-258-5015.
Fax: 011-7-501-258-5014.

MEMBERS OF FIRM

W. Rogers Benson, Jr.
Drew S. Fine
Elliot Gewirtz
Young Joon Kim (Resident, Tokyo, Japan Office)
Elihu F. Robertson
Helfried J. Schwarz

ASSOCIATES

Christopher L. Beers
Christine Luba Carver
James G. Hnat II
Robert S. Kim
Young Il Kim
Ariel Z. Kronman
Thomas C. Lee (Resident, Tokyo, Japan Office)
Alvin K. Leong
Zarrar Sehgal
Robert Sternthal
Susan A. Young (Resident, Tokyo, Japan Office)
Jay S. Zwerling

For Complete List of Firm Personnel, See General Section

For full biographical listings, see the Martindale-Hubbell Law Directory

SPEISER KRAUSE NOLAN & GRANITO, A PROFESSIONAL CORPORATION (AV)

34th Floor, Two Grand Central Tower, 140 East 45th Street, 10017
Telephone: 212-661-0011
Cable Adress: "Speisatt, New York"
Fax: 212-953-6483
URL: http://www.speiserkrause.com
Arlington, Virginia Office: Speiser Krause, A Professional Corporation, 2300 Clarendon Boulevard, Suite 306.
Telephone: 703-522-7500.
Fax: 703-522-7905.
Irvine, California Office: Speiser Krause, A Professional Corporation, One Park Plaza, Suite 470.
Telephone: 949-553-1421.
Fax: 949-553-1346.
Dallas, Texas Office: Speiser Krause, A Professional Corporation, Founders Square, 900 Jackson Street, Suite 750.
Telephone: 214-752-4664.
Fax: 214-752-4774.
Miami, Florida Office: Speiser Krause, A Professional Corporation, Miami Center, 10th Floor, 201 South Biscayne Boulevard.
Telephone: 305-375-9400.
Fax: 305-375-0337.

Kenneth P. Nolan
Frank H. Granito, III
John J. Halloran, Jr.
Gerard R. Lear (Resident, Arlington, Virginia Office)
Juanita M. Madole (Resident, Irvine, California Office)
James Teague Crouse (Resident, Arlington, Virginia Office)
John J. Veth (Resident, Irvine, California Office)
Flor M. Melgar
Thomas A. Frizzell, Jr.

OF COUNSEL

Stuart M. Speiser
Charles F. Krause
Frank H. Granito, Jr.
Joseph T. Cook (Resident, Irvine, California Office)
Richard H. Silver (Not admitted in NY)

For full biographical listings, see the Martindale-Hubbell Law Directory

NORTH CAROLINA

*CHARLOTTE,** Mecklenburg Co.

DEAN & GIBSON, L.L.P. (AV)

Suite 900, Cameron Brown Building, 301 South McDowell Street, 28204-2686
Telephone: 704-372-2700
Facsimile: 704-372-1804
Email: info@deanandgibson.com

Rodney A. Dean
Michael G. Gibson
Brien D. Stockman
Christopher J. Culp

ASSOCIATES

John Whitelaw Ong
Colin E. Scott
Kimberly A. Gossage
Thomas G. Nance, II

OF COUNSEL

Barbara J. Dean

For full biographical listings, see the Martindale-Hubbell Law Directory

*RALEIGH,** Wake Co.

MINEO & WHITTAKER (AV)

First Union Capitol Center, 150 Fayetteville Street, Suite 1700, 27601
Telephone: 919-831-8728
Telecopier: 919-782-5244
Email: NCAIRLAW@AOL.COM
Charlotte, North Carolina Office: 5950 Fairview Road, Suite 622. P.O. Box 10615.
Telephone: 704-571-4022.

MEMBERS OF FIRM

Robert A. Mineo
Malcolm E. Whittaker (Resident, Charlotte Office)
Athena R. Mineo

For full biographical listings, see the Martindale-Hubbell Law Directory

*WINSTON-SALEM,** Forsyth Co.

COMERFORD & BRITT, L.L.P. (AV)

250 West First Street Suite 300, 27101
Telephone: 336-631-8510
Fax: 336-631-8228
Email: @comerfordbritt.com *URL:* http://www.comerfordbritt.com

MEMBERS OF FIRM

W. Thompson Comerford, Jr.
Clifford Britt

ASSOCIATE

Martha Marie Eastman

For full biographical listings, see the Martindale-Hubbell Law Directory

THE LAW OFFICES OF WILLIAM F. MAREADY (AV)

1076 West Fourth Street, Suite 100, 27101-2411
Telephone: 336-722-1027
Fax: 336-722-1028
Email: info@mareadylaw.com *URL:* http://www.mareadylaw.com

ASSOCIATE

Celie Benton Richardson

For full biographical listings, see the Martindale-Hubbell Law Directory

OHIO

*CINCINNATI,** Hamilton Co.

WAITE, SCHNEIDER, BAYLESS & CHESLEY CO., L.P.A. (AV)

1513 Central Trust Tower, Fourth and Vine Streets, 45202
Telephone: 513-621-0267
Fax: 513-381-2375; 621-0262

Stanley M. Chesley

Thomas F. Rehme
Robert A. Steinberg
Fay E. Stilz
Louise M. Roselle
D. Arthur Rabourn
Jerome L. Skinner
Janet G. Abaray
Paul M. De Marco
Terrence L. Goodman
Colleen M. Hegge
Jane H. Walker
Renée Infante
James F. Keller
Jean M. Geoppinger
Robert Heuck II

For full biographical listings, see the Martindale-Hubbell Law Directory

*CLEVELAND,** Cuyahoga Co.

NURENBERG, PLEVIN, HELLER & MCCARTHY CO., L.P.A. (AV)

1370 Ontario Street First Floor, 44113-1792
Telephone: 216-621-2300; Toll Free: 1-800-562-7438
Fax: 216-771-2242
Email: nphm@nphm.com *URL:* http://www.nphm.com

A. H. Dudnik (1905-1963)
S. F. Komito (1902-1984)
Marshall I. Nurenberg
Leon M. Plevin
Maurice L. Heller
John J. McCarthy
Thomas Mester
Harlan M. Gordon
David M. Paris
Richard L. Demsey
Jamie R. Lebovitz
William S. Jacobson
Jeffrey A. Leikin

Robin J. Peterson
Robert S. Zeller
Ellen M. McCarthy
J. Charles Ruiz-Bueno
Kathleen J. St. John
Jonathan D. Mester
Brenda M. Johnson

Reference: Society Key Corp.

For full biographical listings, see the Martindale-Hubbell Law Directory

OKLAHOMA

*OKLAHOMA CITY,** Oklahoma Co.

WILLIAM C. BOSTON, P.L.L.C. (AV)

4005 Northwest Expressway, Suite 600, 73116
Telephone: 405-848-0600
Telefax: 405-848-0655
Email: wcbfirm@ionet.net *URL:* http://www.okaircraftlaw.com

William C. Boston, Jr.

Scott D. McCreary
William Clayton Boston, III
Eric L. Johnson
Lisa Anne Drescher

OF COUNSEL

Donna M. Schmidt (Not admitted in OK)
Willis W. Luttrell (Not admitted in OK)
Joseph T. Brennan (Not admitted in OK)

For full biographical listings, see the Martindale-Hubbell Law Directory

*TULSA,** Tulsa Co.

ATKINSON, HASKINS, NELLIS, BOUDREAUX, HOLEMAN, PHIPPS & BRITTINGHAM, A PROFESSIONAL CORPORATION (AV)

1500 ParkCentre, 525 South Main Street, 74103
Telephone: 918-582-8877
Fax: 918-585-8096
Email: ahnmail@ahn-law.com

Walter D. Haskins, P.C.

Representative Clients: Allstate Insurance Co.; Bayer Corp.; Crum & Forster Insurance Co.; Hartford Insurance Company; National American Insurance Co.; Federated Insurance Co.; Liberty Mutual Insurance Co.; Physicians Liability Insurance Co.; State Farm Mutual Automobile Insurance Co.; United States Aviation Underwriters.

For full biographical listings, see the Martindale-Hubbell Law Directory

RHODES, HIERONYMUS, JONES, TUCKER & GABLE, P.L.L.C. (AV)

Oneok Plaza, 100 West 5th Street, Suite 400, P.O. Box 21100, 74121-1100
Telephone: 918-582-1173
Fax: 918-592-3390
URL: http://www.rhodesokla.com

MEMBERS OF FIRM

Kevin D. Berry
Jo Anne Deaton
Richard M. Eldridge
E. D. Hieronymus (1908 -1994)
Bert M. Jones
William S. Leach
Michael W. McGivern
William D. Perrine
Mary Quinn-Cooper
Robert P. Redemann
David P. Reid
Chris L. Rhodes, III
Thomas E. Steichen
Catherine C. Taylor
John H. Tucker
Wilson T. White
Harold C. Zuckerman

Ann E. Allison
Steven K. Bunting
Robert P. Coffey, Jr.
J. Christopher Davis
Andrew D. Downing
Dana L. Gish
Kerry R. Lewis
Andrew L. Richardson
Michael F. Smith
Leslie J. Southerland
Kimberly E. West
Keith A. Wilkes

(See Next Column)

RHODES, HIERONYMUS, JONES, TUCKER & GABLE P.L.L.C., *Tulsa—Continued*

OF COUNSEL

George W. Gable (Retired Partner)
Larry J. Fulton
Kelly M. Greenough

Representative Clients: American International Companies; Bechtel; Chubb Group of Insurance Companies; General Motors Corporation; Merrill, Lynch; Nissan Motor Corporation in U.S.A.; Pfizer, Inc.; Volkswagen of America, Volkswagen, A.G.; Zurich U.S.

For full biographical listings, see the Martindale-Hubbell Law Directory

PENNSYLVANIA

*PHILADELPHIA,** Philadelphia Co.

McKISSOCK & HOFFMAN, P.C. (AV)

1700 Market Street, Suite 3000, 19103
Telephone: 215-246-2100
Fax: 215-246-2144
Westmont, New Jersey Office: 216 Haddon Avenue, Suite 603.
Telephone: 609-858-1650.
Fax: 609-858-1466.
Doylestown, Pennsylvania Office: 16 North Franklin Street, Suite 300.
Telephone: 215-345-4501.
Fax: 215-246-4503.
Harrisburg, Pennsylvania Office: 105 North Front Street, Suite 205.
Telephone: 717-234-0103.
Fax: 717-234-1350.
West Chester, Pennsylvania Office: 31 South High Street, P.O. Box 3086.
Telephone: 610-738-8850.
Fax: 610-738-9121.

J. Bruce McKissock
Peter J. Hoffman
Leslie Anne Miller
Jeffrey B. Albert
Jill Baratz Clarke
John J. McGrath (Resident, Westmont, New Jersey Office)
Donald J. Brooks, Jr.
William J. Mundy
Bryan Craig Black (Resident, Harrisburg Office)
Eileen Lampe
Christopher Thomson (Resident Shareholder, West Chester Office)
K. Reed Haywood
Maureen P. Fitzgerald

For full biographical listings, see the Martindale-Hubbell Law Directory

WOLK & GENTER (AV)

1710-12 Locust Street, 19103
Telephone: 215-545-4220
Fax: 215-545-5252
Email: airlaw@airlaw.com *URL:* http://www.airlaw.com

MEMBERS OF FIRM

Arthur Alan Wolk
Richard E. Genter

ASSOCIATES

Catherine B. Slavin
Philip J. Ford

For full biographical listings, see the Martindale-Hubbell Law Directory

*WILLIAMSPORT,** Lycoming Co.

MITCHELL, MITCHELL, GRAY & GALLAGHER, A PROFESSIONAL CORPORATION (AV)

10 West Third Street, 17701-6513
Telephone: 570-323-8404
Fax: 570-323-8585
Email: mmggpc@csrlink.net

Jacob Neafie Mitchell (1919-1996)
C. Edward S. Mitchell
Richard A. Gray
Robert A. Gallagher
Gary L. Weber
Bret J. Southard

Darryl R. Wishard

For full biographical listings, see the Martindale-Hubbell Law Directory

SOUTH CAROLINA

*COLUMBIA,** Richland Co.

ROGERS TOWNSEND & THOMAS, PC (AV)

1441 Main Street, 10th Floor, P.O. Box 100200, 29202-3200
Telephone: 803-771-7900
Fax: 803-254-6305; 343-7017; 343-7019
URL: http://www.rtt-law.com

(See Next Column)

Eugene F. Rogers

For Complete List of Firm Personnel, See General Section

For full biographical listings, see the Martindale-Hubbell Law Directory

TENNESSEE

KINGSPORT, Sullivan Co.

WEST & ROSE (AV)

537 East Center Street, P.O. Box 1404, 37660
Telephone: 423-246-8176
Fax: 423-246-4028

MEMBERS OF FIRM

M. Lacy West
Steven C. Rose
Julia C. West

For full biographical listings, see the Martindale-Hubbell Law Directory

*KNOXVILLE,** Knox Co.

GILREATH & ASSOCIATES (AV)

550 Main Avenue, Suite 600, P.O. Box 1270, 37901-1270
Telephone: 423-637-2442
Fax: 423-971-4116
Email: gilknox@sidgilreath.com *URL:* http://www.sidgilreath.com
Nashville, Tennessee Office: 2828 Renaissance Tower, 611 Commerce Street.
Telephone: 615-256-3388.
Memphis, Tennessee Office: 44 North Second Street, Suite 200.
Telephone: 901-527-8288.

MEMBER OF FIRM

Sidney W. Gilreath

ASSOCIATES

Meridith C. Bond
Paul Kaufman
Richard L. Duncan
Dianne E. Lashmit
R. Christopher Gilreath
Patricia Taylor Bruner (Not admitted in TN)

LEGAL SUPPORT PERSONNEL

Tammy Ailshie (Legal Assistant to Senior Partner)
Janie Howerton (Legal Assistant)
Darla R. Johnson (Legal Assistant)
Janet L. Tucker (Legal Assistant to Senior Partner)
Pamela Smith Wise (Senior Legal Assistant)
Susan Stogner (Legal Assistant to Senior Partner)
Bryan L. Capps (Legal Administrator)
Danielle E. Barto (Firm Administrator)

Representative Client: Transportation Communications International Union; Brotherhood of Locomotive Engineers Union.
Reference: Suntrust Bank.

For full biographical listings, see the Martindale-Hubbell Law Directory

TEXAS

*AUSTIN,** Travis Co.

BYRD, DAVIS AND EISENBERG, L.L.P. (AV)

A Partnership including Professional Corporations
707 West 34th Street, 78705
Telephone: 512-454-3751
Fax: 512-451-5857
Email: 70720.3104@compuserve.com

MEMBERS OF FIRM

L. Tonnett Byrd (P.C.)
Don L. Davis
David H. Walter
James H. Furman
Daniel W. Andrews

ASSOCIATE

Derek L. Davis

OF COUNSEL

Jack C. Eisenberg (P.C.)

For full biographical listings, see the Martindale-Hubbell Law Directory

THE ONSTAD LAW FIRM (AV)

907 Ranch Road 620 South, Suite 302, 78734-5609
Telephone: 512-263-7600
Facimile: 512-263-7800
Email: rockonstad@ispchannel.com

(See Next Column)

THE ONSTAD LAW FIRM—*Continued*

Rockne W. Onstad
Blake C. Erskine, Jr.
James Francis Twombly

For full biographical listings, see the Martindale-Hubbell Law Directory

SLACK & DAVIS, L.L.P. (AV)

A Partnership including a Professional Corporation
8911 Capital of Texas Highway Suite 2110, 78759
Telephone: 512-795-8686
Fax: 512-795-8787

MEMBERS OF FIRM

Steven E. Aldous
Mike Davis
Michael L. Slack

ASSOCIATE

Donna J. Bowen

OF COUNSEL

Tom H. Davis, P.C.

For full biographical listings, see the Martindale-Hubbell Law Directory

WHITEHURST, HARKNESS, OZMUN & ARCHULETA, A PROFESSIONAL CORPORATION (AV)

24th Floor, Westgate Building, P.O. Box 1802, 78767
Telephone: 512-476-4346
Fax: 512-476-4400

William O. Whitehurst, Jr.
Thomas R. Harkness
Scott A. Ozmun
Michael E.J. Archuleta
Cynthia K. Stewart
Sally S. Metcalfe
Michelle M. Cheng
Sylvia H. Imhoff

For full biographical listings, see the Martindale-Hubbell Law Directory

*DALLAS,** Dallas Co.

HOWIE & SWEENEY, L.L.P. (AV)

14th Floor, Park Place on Turtle Creek, 2911 Turtle Creek Boulevard, 75219
Telephone: 214-523-8800; 800-523-2339
Telecopier: 214-523-8888
Email: email@howie-sweeney.com *URL:* http://www.howie-sweeney.com

MEMBERS OF FIRM

John R. Howie
Paula Sweeney

Al Ellis
Jon Kettles
Andrew L. Payne
Valerie A. Mosman
Ladd Sanger
Elizabeth A. Florence

For full biographical listings, see the Martindale-Hubbell Law Directory

SIFFORD & ANDERSON, L.L.P. (AV)

A Partnership including Professional Corporations
6300 NationsBank Plaza, 901 Main Street, 75202-3771
Telephone: 214-742-1200
Fax: 214-220-0206

MEMBERS OF FIRM

Lewis R. Sifford (P.C.)
L. W. Anderson
John L. Ratcliffe (P.C.)

Michele A. Ratcliffe
Kevin W. Vice
Ron G. MacFarlane, Jr.

For full biographical listings, see the Martindale-Hubbell Law Directory

SMITH & MOORE (AV)

A Registered Limited Liability Partnership
4242 Lincoln Plaza, 500 N. Akard Street, 75201-6606
Telephone: 214-740-4200
Cable "PALADIN" Telex: 4630225
Facsimile: 214-740-4242
Email: cable_paladin@compuserve.com

Charles H. Smith
John W. Moore
April Robbins

Daniel Lee Alford, IV
Jennifer N. Cook
David Denny
Andrew M. Gilbert
Todd W. Hutton
John J. Reenan

Representative Clients: Associated Aviation Underwriters, Inc.; Aviation & Marine Insurance Group, Inc.; Express One International, Inc.; FlightSafety International, Inc.; Jack Prewitt & Associates, Inc.; Jet Aviation AG, Basel; Jet East, Inc,; National Aircraft Resale Association; United States Aviation Underwriters, Inc.; Tyler-Jet, L.L.C.

For full biographical listings, see the Martindale-Hubbell Law Directory

SPEISER KRAUSE, A PROFESSIONAL CORPORATION (AV)

Founders Square, 900 Jackson Street Suite 750, 75202
Telephone: 214-752-4664
Fax: 214-752-4774
URL: http://www.speiserkrause.com
New York, N.Y. Office: Speiser Krause Nolan & Granito, A Professional Corporation, 34th Floor, Two Grand Central Tower, 140 East 45th Street.
Telephone: 212-661-0011.
Fax: 212-953-6483.
Arlington, Virginia Office: 2300 Clarendon Boulevard, Suite 306.
Telephone: 703-522-7500.
Fax: 703-522-7905.
Irvine, California Office: One Park Plaza, Suite 470.
Telephone: 949-553-1421.
Fax: 949-553-1346.
Miami, Florida Office: Miami Center, 10th Floor, 201 South Biscayne Boulevard.
Telephone: 305-375-9400.
Fax: 305-375-0337.

Charles F. Krause
Kent C. Krause (Resident)
Paula J. Walsh (Resident)
Gerard R. Lear (Resident, Arlington, Virginia Office)
Kenneth P. Nolan (Resident, New York, N.Y. Office)
Juanita M. Madole (Resident, Irvine, California Office)
James Teague Crouse (Resident, Arlington, Virginia Office)

For full biographical listings, see the Martindale-Hubbell Law Directory

THOMPSON & KNIGHT L.L.P. (AV)

(Attorneys and Counselors)
1700 Pacific Avenue Suite 3300, 75201
Telephone: 214-969-1700
Telecopy: 214-969-1751
Telex: 732 298
URL: http://www.tklaw.com
Austin, Texas Office: 1200 San Jacinto Center, 98 San Jacinto Boulevard, 78701.
Telephone: 512-469-6100.
Telecopy: 512-469-6180.
Fort Worth, Texas Office: 801 Cherry Street, Suite 1600, 76102.
Telephone: 817-347-1700.
Telecopy: 817-347-1799.
Houston, Texas Office: Thompson Knight Brown Parker & Leahy L.L.P., 1200 Smith Street, Suite 3600, 77002-4595.
Telephone: 713-654-8111.
Telecopier: 713-654-1871.
San Pedro Garza Garcia, Nuevo León, Mexico Office: Edificio Losoles PD-4, Av. Lázaro Cárdenas No. 2400 Pte., C.P. 66220.
Telephone: (52-8) 363-0096.
Telecopy: (52-8) 363-3067.

PARTNERS

L. James Berglund, II
Michael R. Berry
Stephen F. Fink
Frank Finn
Rachelle H. Glazer
John H. Martin
Maureen A. Murry
Stephen C. Schoettmer
Dawn Marie Wright

For Complete List of Firm Personnel, See General Section

For full biographical listings, see the Martindale-Hubbell Law Directory

LAW OFFICES OF WINDLE TURLEY, P.C. (AV)

1000 University Tower, 6440 North Central Expressway, 75206
Telephone: 214-691-4025
Telefax: 214-361-5802
Telex: 734049
Email: htpillturley@wturley.com *URL:* http://www.wturley.com

Windle Turley
Michael G. Sawicki
R. Christopher Cowan
William J. Dunleavy
Phillip L. Brown

Dale R. Rose
Deana Tunnell
Lori A. Watson
Patrick C. Patterson
Brent Stewart Freefield
Jeffrey T. Embry

For full biographical listings, see the Martindale-Hubbell Law Directory

*FORT WORTH,** Tarrant Co.

THOMPSON & KNIGHT L.L.P. (AV)

(Attorneys and Counselors)
801 Cherry Street, Suite 1600, 76102
Telephone: 817-347-1700
Telecopy: 817-347-1799
URL: http://www.tklaw.com
Dallas, Texas Office: 1700 Pacific Avenue, Suite 3300, 75201.
Telephone: 214-969-1700.
Telecopy: 214-969-1751.
Telex: 732298.

(See Next Column)

THOMPSON & KNIGHT L.L.P., *Fort Worth—Continued*

Austin, Texas Office: 1200 San Jacinto Center, 98 San Jacinto Boulevard, 78701.
Telephone: 512-469-6100.
Telecopy: 512-469-6180.
Houston, Texas Office: Thompson Knight Brown Parker & Leahy L.L.P., 1200 Smith Street, Suite 3600, 77002-4595.
Telephone: 713-654-8111.
Telecopier: 713-654-1871.
San Pedro Garza Garcia, Nuevo León, Mexico Office: Edificio Losoles PD-4, Av. Lázaro Cárdenas No. 2400 Pte., C.P. 66220.
Telephone: (52-8) 363-0096.
Telecopy: (52-8) 363-3067.

PARTNERS

Jennifer Pettijohn Henry
E. Michael Sheehan

For Complete List of Firm Personnel, See General Section

For full biographical listings, see the Martindale-Hubbell Law Directory

*HOUSTON,** Harris Co.

FISHER, BOYD, BROWN, BOUDREAUX & HUGUENARD, L.L.P. (AV)

70th Floor Wells Fargo Plaza, 1000 Louisiana, 77002
Telephone: 713-400-4000
Telefax: 713-400-4050

Wayne Fisher
Larry P. Boyd
Thomas K. Brown
Olan J. Boudreaux
James A. Huguenard

Bernard G. Johnson, III
Kay K. (Daniel) Morgan

For full biographical listings, see the Martindale-Hubbell Law Directory

FLEMING & ASSOCIATES, L.L.P. (AV)

1330 Post Oak Boulevard, Suite 3030, 77056
Telephone: 713-621-7944
Fax: 713-621-9638
URL: http://www.fleming-law.com

George M. Fleming
Robert R. Herring, Jr.
Sylvia Davidow
Bruce B. Kemp
Jim Doyle
Russell T. Abney
D'Lisa R. Simmons
Katrina Von Hedemann
Rand P. Nolen
Christopher A. Kesler
Andres C. Pereira
G. Sean Jez
Anthony E. Farah

For full biographical listings, see the Martindale-Hubbell Law Directory

GALLAGHER, YOUNG, LEWIS, HAMPTON & DOWNEY, L.L.P. (AV)

NationsBank Building, 700 Louisiana, 40th Floor, 77002
Telephone: 713-222-8080
Fax: 713-222-0066

Michael T. Gallagher
William H. Young
Craig Lewis
Hartley Hampton
Daniel M. Downey

Martin John de la Torre
Andrew Sher
Candace Kaiser Eindorf
Scott H. Mclemore
John J. Klevenhagen, III
Araceli E. Flores

OF COUNSEL

Rosemary Conlon McCarthy

For full biographical listings, see the Martindale-Hubbell Law Directory

THOMPSON KNIGHT BROWN PARKER & LEAHY L.L.P. (AV)

A Registered Limited Liability Partnership including Professional Corporations
(Attorneys and Counselors)
1200 Smith Street, Suite 3600, 77002-4595
Telephone: 713-654-8111
Telecopier: 713-654-1871
URL: http://www.tklaw.com
Dallas, Texas Office: Thompson & Knight L.L.P., 1700 Pacific Avenue, Suite 3300, 75201.
Telephone: 214-969-1700.
Telecopy: 214-969-1751.
Telex: 732298.
Austin, Texas Office: Thompson & Knight L.L.P., 1200 San Jacinto Center, 98 San Jacinto Boulevard, 78701.
Telephone: 512-469-6100.
Telecopy: 512-469-6180.
Fort Worth, Texas Office: Thompson & Knight L.L.P., 801 Cherry Street, Suite 1600, 76102.
Telephone: 817-347-1700.
Telecopy: 817-347-1799.

(See Next Column)

San Pedro Garza Garcia, Nuevo León, Mexico Office: Thompson & Knight L.L.P., Edificio Losoles PD-4, Av. Lázaro Cárdenas No. 2400 PTE., C.P. 66220.
Telephone: (52-8) 363-0096.
Telecopy: (52-8) 363-3067.

PARTNERS

J. Michael Bell
Gregory S. Meece
Robert L. Pittsford

For Complete List of Firm Personnel, See General Section

For full biographical listings, see the Martindale-Hubbell Law Directory

*MARSHALL,** Harrison Co.

CURRY, MORIN AND GOUDARZI, P.C. (AV)

201 West Houston Street, P.O. Box 2065, 75671
Telephone: 903-927-2277; 903-935-0797
Fax: 903-935-0799

Doyle W. Curry
James B. Morin (Also practicing in Gilmer, Texas)
J. Brent Goudarzi (Also practicing in Gilmer, Texas)

For full biographical listings, see the Martindale-Hubbell Law Directory

*SAN ANTONIO,** Bexar Co.

GENDRY & SPRAGUE, P.C. (AV)

645 Lockhill Selma, 78216-5057
Telephone: 210-349-0511
Fax: 210-349-2760
Email: genspr@aol.com

Thomas W. Gendry
Ron A. Sprague
Neil H Stone
R. Matt Lair
Blanca P. Galo
Timothy R. Price
Claudia D. Brown

Reference: NCNB Texas National Bank, San Antonio.

For full biographical listings, see the Martindale-Hubbell Law Directory

LANE, GANNON & TALIAFERRO, L.L.P. (AV)

8620 North New Braunfels, Suite 310, 78217
Telephone: 210-829-1545
Telecopier: 210-829-1633
Email: gannon@lgtlaw.com
Austin, Texas Office: 816 Congress Avenue, Suite 1100, 78701.
Telephone: 512-485-4595.
Fax: 512-485-4594.

MEMBERS OF FIRM

Gregory Gannon
John R. Lane, Jr.
William Craig Taliaferro

ASSOCIATES

Sharon Denise Hobbs
Frederick D. Schraub
Georganne G. Leonard
John R. Resendez
Brent Austin Biggs
Alfred Michael Casillas
Christia M. Antolik
Hella V. Caldera

OF COUNSEL

C. Gilbert House
James B. House

For full biographical listings, see the Martindale-Hubbell Law Directory

UTAH

*SALT LAKE CITY,** Salt Lake Co.

JOEL M. ALLRED, P.C. (AV)

Suite 800, McIntyre Building, 68 South Main Street, 84101
Telephone: 801-531-8300 (Downtown Office)
801-582-2309 (Home Office)
Fax: 801-533-2463 (Office Hours)
801-363-2420 (After Office Hours)
Email: jallred@vii.com

Joel M. Allred

Amy Allred Dolce

For full biographical listings, see the Martindale-Hubbell Law Directory

VIRGINIA

*ARLINGTON,** Arlington Co.

SPEISER KRAUSE, A PROFESSIONAL CORPORATION (AV®)

2300 Clarendon Boulevard, Suite 306, 22201-3367
Telephone: 703-522-7500
Fax: 703-522-7905
URL: http://www.speiserkrause.com
New York, N.Y. Office: Speiser Krause Nolan & Granito, A Professional Corporation, 34th Floor, Two Grand Central Tower, 140 East 45th Street.
Telephone: 212-661-0011.
Fax: 212-953-6483.
Irvine, California Office: One Park Plaza, Suite 470.
Telephone: 949-553-1421.
Fax: 949-553-1346.
Dallas, Texas Office: Three Lincoln Centre, 5430 LBJ Freeway - Suite 1575.
Telephone: 972-404-1401.
Fax: 972-404-9797.
Miami, Florida Office: Miami Center, 10th Floor, 201 South Biscayne Boulevard.
Telephone: 305-375-9400.
Fax: 305-375-0337.

Gerard R. Lear (Resident)
James Teague Crouse (Resident)
Kenneth P. Nolan (Resident, New York, N.Y. Office)
Juanita M. Madole (Resident, Irvine, California Office)
Frank H. Granito, III (Resident, New York, N.Y. Office)
John J. Veth (Resident, Irvine, California Office)
John J. Halloran, Jr. (Not admitted in VA)
Leigh J. Ballen (Not admitted in VA)
Daniel D. Barks (Resident)
John A. Boneta (Resident)

OF COUNSEL

Stuart M. Speiser (Not admitted in VA)
Charles F. Krause (Not admitted in VA)
Frank H. Granito, Jr. (Resident, New York, N.Y. Office)
Joseph T. Cook (Resident, Irvine, California Office)

For full biographical listings, see the Martindale-Hubbell Law Directory

NORFOLK, (Independent City)

HARLAN & FLORA, P.C. (AV)

Dominion Tower, 999 Waterside Drive, Suite 1200, 23510
Telephone: 757-625-8300
Fax: 757-625-3714
Email: lawyers@harlan-flora.com *URL:* http://www.harlan-flora.com

Thomas J. Harlan, Jr.
John M. Flora

For full biographical listings, see the Martindale-Hubbell Law Directory

WEST VIRGINIA

*CHARLESTON,** Kanawha Co.

BERTHOLD, TIANO & O'DELL (AV)

208 Capitol Street, P.O. Box 3508, 25335
Telephone: 304-345-5700
Fax: 304-345-5703

Robert V. Berthold, Jr.
William M. Tiano
Tony L. O'Dell

References: Huntington Banks; Bank One; United National Bank.

For full biographical listings, see the Martindale-Hubbell Law Directory

WISCONSIN

*MILWAUKEE,** Milwaukee Co.

KASDORF, LEWIS & SWIETLIK, S.C. (AV)

1551 South 108th Street, 53214
Telephone: 414-257-1055
Facsimile: 414-257-3759
Green Bay, Wisconsin Office: 727 East Walnut Street, 54301.
Telephone: 920-436-0304.
Wausau, Wisconsin Office: 2100 Stewart Avenue, Suite 230, 54401.
Telephone: 715-848-9250.
Facsimile: 715-849-2017.

(See Next Column)

James P. Reardon
Werner E. Scherr
Terrance E. Davczyk
Jeff Schmeckpeper
Gregory J. Cook
Michael J. Cieslewicz
Michael A. Mesirow
Joseph J. Ferris
James J. Kriva
David L. Styer
Robert J. Lauer
James M. Ryan
Robert P. Ochowicz

Michael C. Frohman
Charles G. Maris
Vicki L. Arrowood
Michael S. Murray
Peter J. Eckardt (Resident)
Christine D. Esser
Thomas A. Cabush
John K. Garofani
Bonni D. Fredrick
Christopher A. Duesing
Daniel W. Varline (Resident, Wausau Office)
Jerome A. Long (Resident, Wausau Office)

OF COUNSEL

Clifford C. Kasdorf
John M. Swietlik
Hugh E. Russell
Patti J. Kurth

Representative Clients: Allstate Insurance Co.; State Farm Mutual Automobile; Liberty Mutual Insurance Co.; Shelby Mutual Insurance Co.; Government Employees Insurance Co.
Reference: M & I Marshall & Ilsley Bank.

For full biographical listings, see the Martindale-Hubbell Law Directory

VIRGIN ISLANDS

*CHARLOTTE AMALIE, ST. THOMAS,** St. Thomas

GRUNERT STOUT & BRUCH (BV)

24-25 Kongensgade, P.O. Box 1030, 00804
Telephone: 340-774-1320
Fax: 340-774-7839
Email: gsbusvi@viaccess.net
Affiliated with: Solomon Pearl Blum & Quinn LLP, New York, New York and Denver, Colorado.

MEMBERS OF FIRM

John E. Stout
Susan Bruch Moorehead

ASSOCIATE

Gabriel J. Villegas

OF COUNSEL

William L. Blum

For full biographical listings, see the Martindale-Hubbell Law Directory

CANADA
BRITISH COLUMBIA

*VANCOUVER,** Vancouver Co.

CAMP CHURCH & ASSOCIATES (AV)

4th Floor, The Randall Building, 555 West Georgia Street, V6B 1Z5
Telephone: 604-689-7555
Fax: 604-689-7554
URL: http://www.campchurch.com

MEMBERS OF FIRM

J.J. Camp, Q.C.
David P. Church

Giuseppe (Joe) Fiorante
Andrew J. Pearson
Sharon D. Matthews
Ian G. Schildt

For full biographical listings, see the Martindale-Hubbell Law Directory

CANADA NEWFOUNDLAND

*ST. JOHN'S,**

McINNES COOPER (AV)

Barristers, Solicitors & Trade Mark Agents
Baine Johnston Centre, 5th Floor, 10 Fort William Place, P.O. Box 5939, A1C 5X4
Telephone: 709-722-8735
Telecopier: 709-722-1763
Email: mcrsj@mcrlaw.com *URL:* http://www.mcrlaw.com
Halifax, Nova Scotia Office: Summit Place, 1601 Lower Water Street, P.O. Box 730, B3J 2V1.
Telephone: 902-425-6500.
Fax: 902-425-6350. Email: mcrhfx@mcrlaw.com.
Moncton, New Brunswick Office: Place Moncton Place, 655 Main Street, P.O. Box 1368, E1C 8T6.
Telephone: 506-857-8970.
Fax: 506-857-4095. Email: mcrmctn@mcrlaw.com.
Charlottetown, Prince Edward Island Office: BDC Place, Suite 620, 119 Kent Street, C1A 1N3.
Telephone: 902-368-8473.
Fax: 902-368-8346. Email: mcrpei@mcrlaw.com.
Fredericton, New Brunswick Office: Suite 600, 570 Queen Street, P.O. Box 610.
Telephone: 506-458-8572.
Fax: 506-458-9903. Email: mcrfton@mcrlaw.com.

PARTNER

Thomas R. Kendell

For Complete List of Firm Personnel, See General Section

For full biographical listings, see the Martindale-Hubbell Law Directory

CANADA NOVA SCOTIA

*HALIFAX,** Regional Munic. of Halifax

McINNES COOPER (AV)

Barristers, Solicitors & Trade Mark Agents
Summit Place, 1601 Lower Water Street, P.O. Box 730, B3J 2V1
Telephone: 902-425-6500
Fax: 902-425-6350
Email: mcrhfx@mcrlaw.com *URL:* http://www.mcrlaw.com
St. John's, Newfoundland Office: Baine Johnston Centre, 5th Floor, 10 Fort William Place, P.O. Box 5939, A1C 5X4.
Telephone: 709-722-8735.
Telecopier: 709-722-1763. Email: mcrsj@mcrlaw.com.
Moncton, New Brunswick Office: Place Moncton Place, 655 Main Street, P.O. Box 1368, E1C 8T6.
Telephone: 506-857-8970.
Fax: 506-857-4095. Email: mcrmctn@mcrlaw.com.
Charlottetown, Prince Edward Island Office: BDC Place, Suite 620, 119 Kent Street, C1A 1N3.
Telephone: 902-368-8473.
Fax: 902-368-8346. Email: mcrpei@mcrlaw.com.
Fredericton, New Brunswick Office: Suite 600, 570 Queen Street, P.O. Box 610.
Telephone: 506-458-8572.
Fax: 506-458-9903. Email: mcrfton@mcrlaw.com.

PARTNER

George T. H. Cooper, Q.C.

For Complete List of Firm Personnel, See General Section

For full biographical listings, see the Martindale-Hubbell Law Directory

JAPAN

*TOKYO,**

American Lawyers In Tokyo

MILBANK, TWEED, HADLEY & McCLOY LLP

(Gaikokuho Jimu Bengoshi Jimusho)
Fukoku Seimei Building, 2-2, Uchisaiwai-cho 2-Chome, Chiyoda-ku, Tokyo 100-0011
Telephone: 81-3-3504-1050
Fax: 81-3-3595-2790; 81-3-3595-2840
Email: postmaster@milbank.com *URL:* http://www.milbank.com
New York, New York Office: 1 Chase Manhattan Plaza, 10005-1413.
Telephone: 212-530-5000.
Fax: 212-530-5219.
Midtown Office: 375 Park Avenue, Suite 3601, 10152.
Telephone: 212-530-5800.
Fax: 212-530-0158.
Los Angeles, California Office: 601 South Figueroa Street, 90017.
Telephone: 213-892-4000.
Fax: 213-629-5063.
Washington, D.C. Office: International Square Building, Suite 1100, 1825 Eye Street, N.W., 20006.
Telephone: 202-835-7500.
Fax: 202-835-7586.
London, England Office: Dashwood House, 69 Old Broad Street, London, EC2M 1QS.
Telephone: 44-207-448-3000.
Fax: 44-207-448-3029.
Hong Kong Office: 3007 Alexandra House, 16 Chater Road.
Telephone: 011-852-2971-4888.
Fax: 852-2840-0792; 852-2845-9046.
Singapore Office: 14-00 Caltex House, 30 Raffles Place, 048622.
Telephone: 65-428-2400.
Fax: 65-428-2500.
Moscow, Russia Office: 24/27 Sadovaya-Samotyochnya, Moscow, 103051.
Telephone: 7-501-258-5015.
Fax: 7-501-258-5014.

PARTNER

Young Joon Kim

ASSOCIATES

Thomas C. Lee (Not admitted in Japan)
Susan A. Young (Not admitted in Japan)

For Complete List of Firm Personnel, See General Section

For full biographical listings, see the Martindale-Hubbell Law Directory

BANKING LAW

MINNESOTA

*MINNEAPOLIS,** Hennepin Co.

Oppenheimer Wolff & Donnelly LLP (AV)

3400 Plaza VII, 45 South Seventh Street, 55402
Telephone: 612-607-7000
FAX: 612-607-7100
URL: http://www.owdlaw.com
Amsterdam, The Netherlands Office: Keizergracht 241.
Telephone: 31-20-423-4555.
FAX: 31-20-423-4545.
Brussels, Belgium Office: Avenue Louise 240, Box 5, 1050.
Telephone: 32-2-626-0500.
FAX: 32-2-626-0510.
Geneva, Switzerland Office: Rue Gabriel Eynard, 6, 1205.
Telephone: (41/22) 311-7410.
FAX: (41/22) 311-7407.
New York, N.Y. Office: Citicorp Center, 153 East 53rd Street, 10022.
Telephone: 212-826-5000.
FAX: 212-486-0708.
Newport Beach, California Office: 500 Newport Center Drive, Suite 700, 92660.
Telephone: 949-719-6000.
FAX: 949-719-6020.
Paris, France Office: 53 Avenue Montaigne, 75008.
Telephone: (33/1) 44 95 03 50.
FAX: (33/1) 44 95 03 40.
St. Paul, Minnesota Office: 1700 First National Bank Building, 55101.
Telephone: 651-605-2000.
FAX: 651-605-2100.
Washington, D.C. Office: Oppenheimer Wolff Donnelly & Bayh LLP, 1350 Eye Street, N.W., Suite 200, 20005.
Telephone: 202-312-8000.
FAX: 202-312-8100.
Los Angeles, California Office: 2029 Century Park East, 38th Floor, 90067.
Telephone: 310-788-5000.
FAX: 310-277-1297.
San Jose, California Office: 101 Park Center Plaza, Suite 300, 95113.
Telephone: 408-795-3000.
FAX: 408-795-3100.
Chicago, Illinois Office: Oppenheimer Wolff & Donnelly (Illinois), Two Prudential Plaza, 45th Floor, 180 North Stetson Avenue, 60601.
Telephone: 312-616-1800.
Fax: 312-616-5800.

RESIDENT PARTNERS

Jerome A. Miranowski
Shannon M. O'Toole
Edward T. Wahl
Mark J. Kalla
Steven W. Meyer
Michael B. Fisco
Robert J. McGillivray
Mark G. Rabogliatti

RESIDENT ASSOCIATES

Rikke A. Dierssen-Morice
James M. Jorissen
Anne F. Larsen
Marcus A. Mollison
Patrice H. Kloss
Connie A. Lunceford-Hedtke
Michael F. Cockson
David E. Runck

For Complete List of Firm Personnel, See General Section

For full biographical listings, see the Martindale-Hubbell Law Directory

MISSISSIPPI

BILOXI, Harrison Co.

Rushing & Guice (AV)

683 Water Street, P.O. Box 1925, 39533-1925
Telephone: 228-374-2313
Telecopier: 228-374-8155
Email: rushguice@rushing-guice.com *URL:* http://www.rushing-guice.com

MEMBERS OF FIRM

Charles L. Rushing (1881-1923)
William L. Guice (1887-1971)
William Lee Guice III

OF COUNSEL

Jacob D. Guice

ASSOCIATES

R. Scott Wells
Maria M. Cobb

(See Next Column)

LEGAL SUPPORT PERSONNEL

Antonia Strong

Representative Clients: CBC Gulfport Credit Union; First National Bank of Commerce; Gulfport Veterans Credit Union; Hancock Bank; Hibernia National Bank; Keesler Federal Credit Union; Marine Midland Bank; Secor Bank; SouthTrust Bank, N.A.

For full biographical listings, see the Martindale-Hubbell Law Directory

*BROOKHAVEN,** Lincoln Co.

Allen, Allen, Boerner & Breeland (AV)

214 Justice Street, P.O. Box 751, 39602-0751
Telephone: 601-833-4361
Fax: 601-833-6647
Email: aabblaw@tislink.com

Emmette P. Allen (1915-1999)
Robert O. Allen
William D. Boerner
Durwood J. Breeland

ASSOCIATE

Sally Burchfield Doty

For full biographical listings, see the Martindale-Hubbell Law Directory

*COLUMBIA,** Marion Co.

Aultman, Tyner, Ruffin & Yarborough, Ltd., A Professional Law Corporation (AV)

329 Church Street, P.O. Drawer 707, 39429
Telephone: 601-736-2222
FAX: 601-736-9884
Email: rfyjr@cblink.com
Hattiesburg, Mississippi Office: 315 Hemphill Street, P.O. Drawer 750.
Telephone: 601-583-2671.
FAX: 601-583-2677.
Gulfport, Mississippi Office: 1201 25th Avenue, Suite 300, P.O. Box 607.
Telephone: 228-863-6913.
FAX: 228-868-8505. Email: atmr@digiscape.com.
New Orleans, Louisiana Office: The Texaco Center, 400 Poydras Street, Suite 2250.
Telephone: 504-528-9616.
FAX: 504-528-9640.

Richard F. Yarborough, Jr.

OF COUNSEL

Ernest Ray Duff

Representative Clients: Hercules, Inc.; United States Steel Corp.; Ford Motor Co.; International Paper Co.; Phillips Petroleum Co.; Aetna Casualty & Surety Co.; CNA Group; Liberty Mutual Insurance Co.; St. Paul Fire & Marine Insurance Co.; Fireman's Fund.

For full biographical listings, see the Martindale-Hubbell Law Directory

*GULFPORT,** Harrison Co.

Allen, Vaughn, Cobb & Hood, P.A. (AV)

One Hancock Plaza, Suite 1209, P.O. Drawer 4108, 39502-4108
Telephone: 601-864-4011
Fax: 601-864-4852
Email: avchlaw@sunherald.infinet.com

Harry R. Allen
Thomas E. Vaughn
David L. Cobb
Billy W. Hood
Joy Lambert Phillips
Robert W. Atkinson
Benjamin U. Bowden
Richard B. Tubertini
Rodney Douglas Robinson
E. Colette Towles
David W. Crane
John A. Foxworth, Jr.

J. Adrian Smith
Michael J. Casano

OF COUNSEL

D. Knox White

LEGAL SUPPORT PERSONNEL

Kevin C. Stachowski (Paralegal)

For full biographical listings, see the Martindale-Hubbell Law Directory

Aultman, Tyner, Ruffin & Yarborough, Ltd., A Professional Law Corporation (AV)

1201 25th Avenue, Suite 300, P.O. Box 607, 39502
Telephone: 228-863-6913
FAX: 228-868-8505
Email: atmr@digiscape.com
Hattiesburg, Mississippi Office: 315 Hemphill Street, P.O. Drawer 750.
Telephone: 601-583-2671.
FAX: 601-583-2677.
Columbia, Mississippi Office: 329 Church Street, P.O. Drawer 707.
Telephone: 601-736-2222.
FAX: 601-736-9884. Email: rfyjr@cblink.com.

(See Next Column)

AULTMAN, TYNER, RUFFIN & YARBOROUGH, LTD. A PROFESSIONAL LAW CORPORATION, *Gulfport—Continued*

New Orleans, Louisiana Office: The Texaco Center, 400 Poydras Street, Suite 2250.
Telephone: 504-528-9616.
FAX: 504-528-9640.

Ben E. Sheely — Dorrance (Dee) Aultman, Jr.

Kyle Stuart Moran

For full biographical listings, see the Martindale-Hubbell Law Directory

*HATTIESBURG,** Forrest Co.

AULTMAN, TYNER, RUFFIN & YARBOROUGH, LTD., A PROFESSIONAL LAW CORPORATION (AV)

315 Hemphill Street, P.O. Drawer 750, 39403-0750
Telephone: 601-583-2671
FAX: 601-583-2677
Email: aultyn@c-gate.net
Columbia, Mississippi Office: 329 Church Street, P.O. Drawer 707.
Telephone: 601-736-2222.
FAX: 601-736-9884. Email: rfyjr@cblink.com.
Gulfport, Mississippi Office: 1201 25th Avenue, Suite 300, P.O. Box 607.
Telephone: 228-863-6913.
FAX: 228-868-8505. Email: atmr@digiscape.com.
New Orleans, Louisiana Office: The Texaco Center, 400 Poydras Street, Suite 2250.
Telephone: 504-528-9616.
FAX: 504-528-9640.

Dorrance Aultman
Thomas W. Tyner
Louie F. Ruffin
Richard F. Yarborough, Jr. (Resident, Columbia Office)
Ben E. Sheely (Resident, Gulfport Office)
R. Curtis Smith, II
Dorrance (Dee) Aultman, Jr. (Resident, Gulfport Office)
William Nelson Graham
Glenn L. M. Swetman (Resident, New Orleans, Louisiana Office)
Troy Nathan Bell (Resident, New Orleans, Louisiana Office)

Victor A. DuBose
Daphne M. Lancaster
Jennifer J. Selby
Kyle Stuart Moran (Resident, Gulfport Office)
Jennifer Walley Mozingo
Robert P. Vining (Resident, New Orleans, Louisiana Office)

OF COUNSEL

Ernest Ray Duff (Resident, Columbia Office)

Representative Clients: Hercules, Inc.; U.S. Steel Corp.; Ford Motor Co.; Phillips Petroleum Co.; Aetna Casualty & Surety Co.; CNA Group; Liberty Mutual Insurance Co.; St. Paul Fire & Marine Insurance Co.; Fireman's Fund; L & A Contracting Co.

For full biographical listings, see the Martindale-Hubbell Law Directory

*JACKSON,** Hinds Co.

COPELAND COOK TAYLOR & BUSH, A PROFESSIONAL ASSOCIATION (AV)

200 Concourse, Suite 200, 1062 Highland Colony Parkway, P.O. Box 2132, 39225-2132
Telephone: 601-856-7200
Facsimile: 601-856-7626
Email: mail@cctb.com *URL:* http://www.cctb.com
Ridgeland, Mississippi Office: Post Office Box 6020, 39158.
Telephone: 601-856-7200.
Facsimile: 601-856-7626.

Charles G. Copeland
Thomas A. Cook
Glenn Gates Taylor
C. Glen Bush
Thomas C. Gerity
James T. Knight
James R. Moore, Jr.
J. Tucker Mitchell
Robert P. Thompson
Thomas R. Hudson
R. Nash Neyland
Michael W. Baxter
C. Ted Sanderson, Jr.
Monte L. Barton, Jr.
W. Shan Thompson
C. Dale Shearer
Robert C. Richardson
Lee Howell, III
John M. Breland
Jefferson P.W. Skelton
Patricia H. Cottingham
Samuel S. Goza
Amanda L. Baham
Samuel O. Morris, IV
Michelle C. Partridge
John E. Gough, Jr.
Victor Donald Hunt
Donald J. Blackwood, Jr.
Rhonda Lea McCullough

OF COUNSEL

James P. Knight, Jr. — Robert L. Goza

For full biographical listings, see the Martindale-Hubbell Law Directory

EDMONSON, BIGGS & MOZINGO, P.A. (AV)

Deposit Guaranty Bank Building, 200 East Capitol, Suite 1500, P.O. Box 865, 39205
Telephone: 601-944-1900
Telecopier: 601-944-1906
Email: ebmh@misnet.com *URL:* http://www.ebmh.com

Richard M. Edmonson
Robert A. Biggs, III
James R. Mozingo
Fred W. Johnson, Jr.
Craig D. Smith
Todd A. Coker

Representative Clients: Andover Cos; Combined Insurance Co.; Design Professional Insurance Co.; Bituminous Insurance Co.; Lexington Insurance Co.; Mississippi State Medical Association Benefit Plan; Coregis; USF&G; Utica Mutual Insurance Co.; Trustmark National Bank, Union Planters Bank.

For full biographical listings, see the Martindale-Hubbell Law Directory

WATKINS & EAGER (AV)

A Professional Limited Liability Company
Suite 300 The Emporium Building, 400 East Capitol Street, P.O. Box 650, 39205
Telephone: 601-948-6470
Facsimile: 601-354-3623

MEMBERS OF FIRM

William F. Goodman, Jr.
Thomas R. Crews
George R. Fair
Jamie G. Houston, III
Frank J. Hammond, III
M. Binford Williams, Jr.

Representative Clients: Trustmark National Bank; Merchants & Marine Bank; SouthTrust Bank, National Association; Deposit Guaranty National Bank; Whitney National Bank; Bank One.

For Complete List of Firm Personnel, See General Section

For full biographical listings, see the Martindale-Hubbell Law Directory

*NATCHEZ,** Adams Co.

TRULY, SMITH & LATHAM (AV)

100 South Pearl Street, P.O. Box 1307, 39121-1307
Telephone: 601-442-6495
Telecopier: 601-442-8874
URL: http://www.lawyers.com/trulysmith&latham

George Lawrence Adams (1913-1994)
R. Brent Forman (1917-1994)
E. C. Ward (1928-1994)

MEMBERS OF FIRM

William Marion Smith — Robert C. Latham

OF COUNSEL

Everette Truly

Representative Clients: Deposit Guaranty National Bank; Exxon U.S.A.; Mississippi Power & Light Co.; Southwest Mississippi Electric Power Assn.; South Central Bell Telephone Co.; Sears, Roebuck & Co.; American International Group; Kemper Insurance Co.

For full biographical listings, see the Martindale-Hubbell Law Directory

*OXFORD,** Lafayette Co.

FREELAND & FREELAND (AV)

1013 Jackson Avenue, P.O. Box 269, 38655
Telephone: 662-234-3414
Telecopier: 662-234-0604
Email: thf4@watervalley.net

MEMBERS OF FIRM

T. H. Freeland, III — T. H. Freeland, IV

Representative Clients: The Ohio Casualty Group; Crum & Forester.

For full biographical listings, see the Martindale-Hubbell Law Directory

MISSOURI

KANSAS CITY, Jackson, Clay, Platte & Cass Cos.

SWANSON MIDGLEY, LLC (AV)

Crown Center, 2420 Pershing Road, Suite 400, 64108
Telephone: 816-842-6100
Fax: 816-842-0013
Email: mail@swansonmidgley.com *URL:* http://www.swansonmidgley.com
Overland Park, Kansas Office: Commerce Plaza I, 7th Floor, 7300 W. 110th Street.
Telephone: 913-317-2717.
FAX: 913-317-1505.

Edward M. Dolson — Charles F. Zarter

(See Next Column)

SWANSON MIDGLEY LLC—*Continued*

Richard E. Gier

Counsel for: Unison Bancorp, Inc.; Western National Bank; Douglass National Bank; People's Bank of Burlington; Partners Bank, N.A.; Standard Federal Bank.

For Complete List of Firm Personnel, See General Section

For full biographical listings, see the Martindale-Hubbell Law Directory

MONTANA

*BILLINGS,** Yellowstone Co.

CROWLEY, HAUGHEY, HANSON, TOOLE & DIETRICH, P.L.L.P. (AV)

500 Transwestern II, 490 North 31st Street, P.O. Box 2529, 59103
Telephone: 406-252-3441
Fax: 406-259-4159
Email: crowley@crowleylaw.com
Helena, Montana Office: IBM Building, 100 North Park Avenue, Suite 300, 59601.
Telephone: 406-449-4165.
Fax: 406-449-5149.
Kalispell, Montana Office: 431 1st Avenue West, 59901.
Telephone: 406-752-6644.
Fax: 406-752-5108.
Williston, North Dakota Office: 113 East Broadway, 58801.
Telephone: 701-572-2200.
Fax: 701-572-7072.

OF COUNSEL

John M. Dietrich — Gareld F. Krieg

MEMBERS OF FIRM

Arthur F. Lamey, Jr. — Michael S. Dockery
Terry B. Cosgrove (Resident, Helena, Montana Office) — Mary Scrim Dyre (Resident, Kalispell, Montana Office)
William D. Lamdin, III — Renee L. Coppock

Representative Clients: First Interstate BancSystem of Montana, Inc.; First Interstate Bank of Commerce; Central Montana Bancorporation; Traders State Bank of Poplar; Security Richland Bancorporation; State Bank of Terry; The Bank of Baker; Richland National Bank & Trust.

For Complete List of Firm Personnel, See General Section

For full biographical listings, see the Martindale-Hubbell Law Directory

*BOZEMAN,** Gallatin Co.

KIRWAN & BARRETT, P.C. (AV)

215 West Mendenhall, P.O. Box 1348, 59771-1348
Telephone: 406-586-1553
Fax: 406-586-8971

Stephen M. Barrett

Representative Clients: American Bank; First Interstate Bank of Bozeman; Big Sky Western Bank; Security Bank of Three Forks.

For full biographical listings, see the Martindale-Hubbell Law Directory

NEBRASKA

*OMAHA,** Douglas Co.

FRASER, STRYKER, VAUGHN, MEUSEY, OLSON, BOYER & BLOCH, P.C. (AV)

500 Energy Plaza, 409 South 17th Street, 68102
Telephone: 402-341-6000
Telecopier: 402-341-8290
Email: fraserstryker.com

Thomas F. Flaherty — Robert W. Rieke

For Complete List of Firm Personnel, See General Section

For full biographical listings, see the Martindale-Hubbell Law Directory

MCGILL, GOTSDINER, WORKMAN & LEPP, P.C. (AV)

Suite 500 - First National Plaza, 11404 West Dodge Road, 68154
Telephone: 402-492-9200
Telecopier: 402-492-9222
Email: mgwl@mgwl.com

Gary M. Gotsdiner

(See Next Column)

OF COUNSEL

Richard D. Myers

Representative Clients: Norwest Bank Nebraska N.A.; First National Bank of Omaha; Mutual of Omaha; Nebraska Health Care Assn.; Bethesda Living Centers; Behlen Mfg. Co.; Metz Baking Co.; Lozier Corporation; Service Data Corporation; Slosburg Co.

For Complete List of Firm Personnel, See General Section

For full biographical listings, see the Martindale-Hubbell Law Directory

NEVADA

*LAS VEGAS,** Clark Co.

ALBRIGHT, STODDARD, WARNICK & ALBRIGHT, A PROFESSIONAL CORPORATION (AV)

Quail Park I, Building D-4, 801 South Rancho Drive, 89106
Telephone: 702-384-7111
Fax: 702-384-0605
URL: http://www.aswalaw.com

G. Vern Albright — Whitney B. Warnick
William H. Stoddard — G. Mark Albright

D. Chris Albright — Corey D. Randall (Not admitted in NV)
Tami C. Budo

Representative Clients: Tokio Marine and Fire Insurance Co.; INAPRO, a CIGNA Co.; Nevada Ready Mix; North American Health Care, Inc. (Nursing Home); Royal Insurance; First Security Bank of Utah; Nevada Community Bank; Nationwide Insurance Co.; Liberty Mutual Insurance; CB Commercial.

For full biographical listings, see the Martindale-Hubbell Law Directory

ALVERSON, TAYLOR, MORTENSEN, NELSON & SANDERS (AV)

7401 West Charleston Boulevard, 89117
Telephone: 702-384-7000
FAX: 702-385-7000
Email: alverson@intermind.net
Reno, Nevada Office: 245 East Liberty, Suite 520, 89505.
Telephone: 775-329-0473.
Fax: 775-329-3303.

MEMBERS OF FIRM

J. Bruce Alverson — David J. Mortensen
Eric K. Taylor — Erven T. Nelson
LeAnn Sanders

OF COUNSEL

Jack C. Cherry — Kurt D. Anderson
Philip C. Van Alstyne

ASSOCIATES

Rebecca Hopkins Miller — Darius F. Rafie
Sandra Smagac — Mark J. King, IV
Victoria L. Nelson — Shell L. Mercer
Aaron D. Lovaas — Carrie S. Bourdeau
Diane Obritsch — Jason Lane Earnest
Michael A. Olsen — Nathan R. Reinmiller
Randal D. Shimon — Donn C. Alexander
Catherine A. Olendorff — Afshin Tadayon
Monica L. Pierce — Eric O. Freeman
Gabriel D. Lither — Lindsay L. Stadtlander
Kurt R. Bonds — Julie M. Sueoka

Representative Clients: Citibank; First Interstate Bank; The CIT Group; Norwest Bank; Federal Deposit Insurance Corporation (FDIC); Countrywide Funding Corporation; Overseas Chinese Banking Corporation; Norwest Financial; Colonial Mortgage Company.

For full biographical listings, see the Martindale-Hubbell Law Directory

JOLLEY, URGA, WIRTH & WOODBURY (AV)

3800 Howard Hughes Parkway Suite 1600, 89109
Telephone: 702-699-7500
Facsimile: 702-699-7555
URL: http://www.juww.com
Boulder City, Nevada Office: Suite 105, 1000 Nevada Highway, 89005.
Telephone: 702-293-3674.

MEMBERS OF FIRM

R. Gardner Jolley — Allen D. Emmel

Representative Clients: Wells Fargo Bank and its predecessor, First Interstate Bank of Nevada; Nevada State Bank; Bank of America, Nevada; General Electric Capital Corp.; First Security Bank of Nevada; First Nationwide Bank; Chase Manhattan; Pioneer Citizens Bank.

For Complete List of Firm Personnel, See General Section

For full biographical listings, see the Martindale-Hubbell Law Directory

Las Vegas—Continued

Kolesar & Leatham, Chartered (AV)

Norwest Bank Center, 3320 West Sahara Avenue, Suite 380, 89102
Telephone: 702-362-7800
Telecopier: 702-362-9472

Robert J. Kolesar
Nile Leatham
Elliott R. Eisner
Howard Goldstein
Charles H. Miles, Jr.

Matthew D. Saltzman

Representative Clients: Banc One Financial Services, Inc.; Bank of Hawaii; Colonial Bank of Nevada; Credit Suisse First Boston Mortgage Capital; First Security Bank of Nevada; IBJ Schroeder Bank & Trust Company; Key Bank USA; Marshall & Ilsley Corporation; Old Kent Bank; Silver State Bank.

For full biographical listings, see the Martindale-Hubbell Law Directory

Kravitz, Schnitzer & Sloane, Chartered, A Professional Corporation (AV)

2300 West Sahara Avenue, Suite 500, 89102
Telephone: 702-362-6666
Fax: 702-362-2203
Email: KRAVSCHNIT@AOL.COM

Martin J. Kravitz
Gary E. Schnitzer
Jeffrey G. Sloane
Michael Bradley Johnson
Jane Eberhardy
Marisa C. Guarino

David J. Feldman
Jerry R. Graf

LEGAL SUPPORT PERSONNEL

Sandye Smith (Legal Administrator)

Representative Clients: Bank of America; Norwest Banks; U.S. Bank; Nations Credit; Associates National Bank; Avco Financial Services; HFC Financial Services; West One Bank; Citibank; Allstate Insurance Company.

For full biographical listings, see the Martindale-Hubbell Law Directory

Smith Larsen & Wixom, Chartered (AV)

3360 West Sahara Avenue, Suite 175, 89102
Telephone: 702-252-5002
Fax: 702-252-5006
Email: slwlaw@slwlaw.com

Jay Earl Smith
Kent F. Larsen
Michael B. Wixom

Stewart C. Fitts

Representative Clients: Norwest Bank Nevada, N.A.; Norwest Corporation; Wells Fargo Bank; Bank of New York; Pioneer Citizens Bank; First Security Bank; Commercial Bank of Nevada; Bank Texas; Banc One, Arizona; Bank One, Texas.

For full biographical listings, see the Martindale-Hubbell Law Directory

NEW HAMPSHIRE

*LACONIA,** Belknap Co.

Normandin, Cheney & O'Neil (AV)

Normandin Square, 213 Union Avenue, P.O. Box 575, 03247-0575
Telephone: 603-524-4380
Fax: 603-528-6831
Email: nco@lr.net

MEMBERS OF FIRM

Paul L. Normandin
John D. O'Shea, Jr.
Robert A. Dietz
James F. LaFrance

ASSOCIATES

Susanne M. Weldon
Regina A. Nadeau

Counsel for: Laconia Savings Bank; Lakes Region Mental Health Center; Laconia Airport Authority; Central New Hampshire Realty, Inc.; All Metals Industries, Inc.; Lakes Region Anesthesiology, P.A.; Cormier Corp.; Scotia Technology; Vemaline Products.

For Complete List of Firm Personnel, See General Section

For full biographical listings, see the Martindale-Hubbell Law Directory

NEW JERSEY

ASBURY PARK, Monmouth Co.

Carton, Witt, Arvanitis & Bariscillo, L.L.C. (AV)

(Formerly Durand, Ivins & Carton)
4001 Route 66 At Garden State Parkway, P.O. Box 1229, 07712
Telephone: 732-922-9500
Telecopier: 732-922-1625
Manasquan, New Jersey Office: 40 Union Avenue, P.O. Box 367.
Telephones: 908-223-1800; 449-5311.

MEMBERS OF FIRM

George N. Arvanitis
James D. Carton, III (Manasquan Office)
John C. Carton (Manasquan Office)
Stephen C. Carton
H. Frank Carpentier
Dana C. Argeris
Martin J. McGreevy
Albert A. Zager
Mark R. Aikins
K. Edward Jacobi
Joseph J. Colao, Jr.
James D. Carton (1868-1943)
Forman T. Bailey (1887-1964)
J. Victor Carton (1900-1982)
Thomas D. Nary (1904-1985)
Robert R. Witt (1921-1988)

ASSOCIATES

Thomas F. Heaney, Jr.
Peter V. Koenig
Susan J. F. Weiss
James D. Carton, IV
Aaron J. Rosenfeld
Russell J. Malta
Janice B. Venables
Marc J. Comer

OF COUNSEL

Francis X. Crahay
Henry E. Kordes
George A. Bariscillo, Jr.
Robert V. Carton

Attorneys for: New Jersey Bell Telephone Co.; Garden State Indemnity Co.; Jersey Shore Medical Center, Inc.
Local Attorneys for: Travelers Insurance Co.; Aetna Casualty & Surety Co.; New Jersey Manufacturers Insurance Co.; Liberty Mutual; Prudential Insurance Co.; Chubb & Son.

For full biographical listings, see the Martindale-Hubbell Law Directory

ATLANTIC CITY, Atlantic Co.

Westmoreland, Vesper & Schwartz, A Professional Corporation (AV)

Bayport One, Yacht Club Drive Suite 500, 08232-0034
Telephone: 609-645-1111
Fax: 609-646-2781
URL: http://www.westmorelandvesper.com

Rudolph C. Westmoreland
Thomas J. Vesper
Mark G. Schwartz
Dara A. Quattrone

David I. Sinderbrand
Katherine M. Morris
Carmelo Tony Torraca

Representative Clients: Cape May Foods; The Bank of New York; Title Company of Jersey; Money Store; Re/Max of New Jersey; AT&T Capital; Unitel Cellular; Yank Boat Works; Tomasello Winery.
Reference: Sun National Bank.

For full biographical listings, see the Martindale-Hubbell Law Directory

BERNARDSVILLE, Somerset Co.

Shain, Schaffer & Rafanello, A Professional Corporation (AV)

Plaza 202, 150 Morristown Road, Suite 105, 07924
Telephone: 908-953-9300
Fax: 908-953-2969
Email: ssrpc@aol.com

Joel L. Shain
Marguerite M. Schaffer
Richard A. Rafanello
Gary L. Maher
Robert A. Pinel
Phedra R. Rudell (Not admitted in NJ)

OF COUNSEL

Elliott L. Katz

LEGAL SUPPORT PERSONNEL

Tracy DeWitt (Legal Researcher)

For full biographical listings, see the Martindale-Hubbell Law Directory

FLORHAM PARK, Morris Co.

DRINKER BIDDLE & SHANLEY LLP (AV)

A Pennsylvania Limited Liability Partnership
500 Campus Drive, 07932-1047
Telephone: 973-360-1100
Fax: 973-285-1625; 360-9831
URL: http://www.dbr.com
Philadelphia, Pennsylvania Office: Drinker Biddle & Reath LLP, One Logan Square, 18th & Cherry Streets.
Telephone: 215-988-2700.
Telefax: 215-988-2757.
Cable Address: "Debemac."
Washington, D.C. Office: Drinker Biddle & Reath LLP, 1500 K Street, N.W., Suite 1100.
Telephone: 202-842-8800.
Telefax: 202-842-8465.
Princeton, New Jersey Office: Suite 300, 105 College Road East.
Telephone: 609-716-6500.
Telefax: 609-799-7000.
Berwyn, Pennsylvania Office: Drinker Biddle & Reath LLP, Suite 300, 1000 Westlakes Drive.
Telephone: 610-993-2200.
Telefax: 610-993-8585.
New York, New York Office: Drinker Biddle & Reath LLP, 89th Floor, One World Trade Center.
Telephone: 212-321-1812.
Telecopier: 1-212-466-0569.

John Kandravy
James H. Freis
Lydia C. Stefanowicz
Michael E. Helmer

COUNSEL
Michael J. Nita

For Complete List of Firm Personnel, See General Section

For full biographical listings, see the Martindale-Hubbell Law Directory

*HACKENSACK,** Bergen Co.

CONTANT, SCHERBY & ATKINS (AV)

33 Hudson Street, 07601
Telephone: 201-342-1070
Fax: 201-342-5213
Email: LawfirmCSA@aol.com *URL:* http://www.lawyers.com/csalaw

MEMBERS OF THE FIRM

John M. Contant (1907-1988)
Richard J. Contant
Michael L. Scherby
Bruce L. Atkins
Matthew S. Rogers
Andrew T. Fede
Brian T. Keane
Robert B. Hille

ASSOCIATES

Geraldine E. Beers
Suzanne J. Ryderman
Lisa R. Aljian
Christina A. Stoneburner
Sheila O'Shea

OF COUNSEL
Fenster & Weiss, New City, New York

For full biographical listings, see the Martindale-Hubbell Law Directory

FERRO LABELLA LOGERFO & ZUCKER, A PROFESSIONAL CORPORATION (AV)

The Landmark Building, 27 Warren Street, 07601
Telephone: 201-489-9110
Fax: 201-489-5653

Michael J. Ferro, Jr.
Rocco J. Labella
Michael F. Logerfo
Arthur P. Zucker
Sean M. Aylward
Christopher L. Weiss

Rocio T. Aliaga
Melanie J. Scroble
E. Vicki Arians

Representative Clients: Summit Bank; CoreStates New Jersey National Bank; Bio Medic Corp.; Lab Products, Inc.; COSCO North Americas, Inc.; Thomas J. Lipton Co.

For full biographical listings, see the Martindale-Hubbell Law Directory

JONES AND JONES (AV)

45 Essex Street, 07601
Telephone: 201-487-3600
FAX: 201-487-2826
URL: http://www.lawyers.com/jonesjoneslaw

MEMBER OF FIRM

Graham O. Jones
Walter Henry Jones (1912-1982)
Vincent J. Massa, III

ASSOCIATE
Joyce Wilkins Pollison

OF COUNSEL
Walter Henry Jones, III

For full biographical listings, see the Martindale-Hubbell Law Directory

LAWRENCEVILLE, Mercer Co.

SZAFERMAN, LAKIND, BLUMSTEIN, WATTER & BLADER, P.C. (AV)

Suite 104 Quakerbridge Executive Center, 101 Grovers Mill Road, 08648
Telephone: 609-275-0400
Telefax: 609-275-4511

Arnold C. Lakind
Barry D. Szaferman
Jeffrey P. Blumstein
Paul N. Watter
Steven Blader
Sidney H. Lehmann
Gerald B. Schenkman
David B. Beckett
Scott P. Borsack
Mary Lou Delahanty

Jennifer Weisberg Millner
Cathyanne A. Pisciotta
Jason N. Fruhschein
Demery J. Roberts
Stuart A. Tucker
Brian G. Paul
Victoria Rivera-Cruz
Thomas J. Burns III

LEGAL SUPPORT PERSONNEL

Paula M. Rossi (Office Administrator)
Patricia Hallstrum (Controller)

Representative Clients: Sun National Bank; First Washington Bank; Gilmore Securities & Co.; Communication Workers of America; The Eagle Group; Water's Edge Convalescent Center; Ronson Aviation, Inc.; Holmdel Township Board of Adjustment; Public Service Managers Association; Chemical Leaman Tank Lines.

For full biographical listings, see the Martindale-Hubbell Law Directory

MANASQUAN, Monmouth Co.

CARTON, WITT, ARVANITIS & BARISCILLO, L.L.C. (AV)

(Formerly Durand, Ivins & Carton)
40 Union Avenue, P.O. Box 367, 08736
Telephone: 908-223-1800
Asbury Park, New Jersey Office: 4001 Route 66 at Garden State Parkway, P.O. Box 1229.
Telephone: 732-922-9500.
Telecopier: 732-922-1625.

RESIDENT PARTNERS

James D. Carton, III
John C. Carton

Attorneys for: New Jersey Bell Telephone Co.; Jersey Shore Medical Center, Inc.
Local Attorneys for: Travelers Insurance Co.; Aetna Casualty & Surety Co.; New Jersey Manufacturers Insurance Co.; Liberty Mutual; Prudential Insurance Co.; Chubb & Son.; Princeton Insurance Co.; Garden State Indemnity Co.

For full biographical listings, see the Martindale-Hubbell Law Directory

*MORRISTOWN,** Morris Co.

COLQUHOUN & COLQUHOUN, A PROFESSIONAL CORPORATION (AV)

165 South Street, 07960
Telephone: 973-540-0500
FAX: 973-540-0550
Cable Address: "Lawscot"
URL: http://www.lawyers.com/colqhounlaw

Robert F. Colquhoun
Kevin F. Colquhoun
Robert F. Colquhoun, II
Sean F. Colquhoun
Moira E. Colquhoun

Reference: The Andover Companies.

For full biographical listings, see the Martindale-Hubbell Law Directory

PITNEY, HARDIN, KIPP & SZUCH LLP (AV)

P.O. Box 1945, 07962-1945
Telephone: 973-966-6300
New York City: 212-687-6000
Telex: 642014
Telecopier: 973-966-1550
URL: http://www.phks.com
New York, New York Office: 711 Third Avenue, 10017-4014.
Telephone: 212-687-6000.
Fax: 212-682-3485.

MEMBERS OF FIRM

Joseph Lunin
Warren J. Casey
Ronald H. Janis
Henry Nelson Massey
Michael J. Dunne
Lori J. Braender
Michael W. Zelenty
Joy Harmon Sperling

COUNSEL
Jonathan S. Bristol

Representative Clients: CoreStates Bank, N.A.; HUBCO, Inc.; PNC Bank, N.A., Valley National Bancorp.

(See Next Column)

PITNEY, HARDIN, KIPP & SZUCH LLP, *Morristown—Continued*

For Complete List of Firm Personnel, See General Section

For full biographical listings, see the Martindale-Hubbell Law Directory

*NEWARK,** Essex Co.

CARPENTER, BENNETT & MORRISSEY (AV)

Three Gateway Center, 17th Floor, 100 Mulberry Street, 07102-4079
Telephone: 973-622-7711
New York City: 212-943-6530
Telex: 139405
Telecopier: 973-622-5314
Email: cbm@carpben.com

MEMBERS OF FIRM

Francis X. O'Brien
John D. Goldsmith

OF COUNSEL

Edward F. Day, Jr.

ASSOCIATE

Hans G. Polak

Representative Clients: General Motors Corp.; E. I. du Pont de Nemours and Co.; Texaco Inc.; AT&T; Litton Industries; ITT Industries, Inc.; Johnson & Johnson; International Flavors & Fragrances Inc.; MAN Capital Corp.; Prudential Insurance Company of America; Hartford Insurance Co.

For Complete List of Firm Personnel, See General Section

For full biographical listings, see the Martindale-Hubbell Law Directory

GREENBERG DAUBER EPSTEIN & TUCKER, A PROFESSIONAL CORPORATION (AV)

Suite 600, One Gateway Center, 07102-5311
Telephone: 973-643-3700
Facsimile: 973-643-1218
URL: http://www.greenbergdauber.com

Melvin Greenberg
Edward J. Dauber
Stanley A. Epstein
H. Glenn Tucker
Linda G. Harvey
Russell S. Burnside

Sumeeta A. Gawande
Richard H. Schwartz
Michael H. Freeman
Charles J. Hayden
Scott W. Miller

For full biographical listings, see the Martindale-Hubbell Law Directory

McCARTER & ENGLISH, LLP (AV)

Four Gateway Center, 100 Mulberry Street, P.O. Box 652, 07101-0652
Telephone: 973-622-4444
Telecopier: 973-624-7070
URL: http://www.mccarter.com
Cherry Hill, New Jersey Office: 1820 Chapel Avenue West, Suite 380.
Telephone: 609-662-8444.
Telecopier: 609-662-6203.
New York, New York Office: Suite 2247, One World Trade Center.
Telephone: 212-466-9018.
Telecopier: 212-432-6568.
Boca Raton, Florida Office: 2255 Glades Road, Suite 319-A.
Telephone: 561-994-6262.
Telecopier: 561-241-0798.
Wilmington, Delaware Office: Mellon Bank Center, 919 Market Street.
Telephone: 302-654-8010.
Telecopier: 302-654-0795.
Philadelphia, Pennsylvania Office: One Commerce Square, 2005 Market Street, Suite 3600.
Telephone: 215-557-7700.
Telecopier: 215-557-6544.

MEMBERS OF FIRM

Michael M. Horn
Bart J. Colli
Todd M. Poland
Peter S. Twombly
David F. Broderick

For Complete List of Firm Personnel, See General Section

For full biographical listings, see the Martindale-Hubbell Law Directory

McMANIMON & SCOTLAND, L.L.C. (AV)

One Riverfront Plaza, 4th Floor, 07102-5311
Telephone: 973-622-1800
Fax: 973-622-7333; 973-622-3744

MEMBERS OF FIRM

Joseph P. Baumann, Jr.
John V. Cavaliere
John B. Hall
Glenn F. Scotland
Ronald J. Ianoale
Andrea L. Kahn
Jeffrey G. Kramer
Leslie G. London
Edward J. McManimon, III

OF COUNSEL

Norman M. Robertson
Carla J. Brundage

(See Next Column)

ASSOCIATES

Peter S. Crisafi
Sheila Newsome Maddox
M. Frances Ciesla
Kristin Dwyer Ganley
Joseph C. Jasaitis
Stephen N. Severud
Thomas J. Hastie, Jr.

LEGAL SUPPORT PERSONNEL

Helen Lysaght

PARALEGALS

Sandra Simoes

For full biographical listings, see the Martindale-Hubbell Law Directory

MEYNER AND LANDIS (AV)

One Gateway Center, Suite 2500, 07102-5311
Telephone: 973-624-2800
Fax: 973-624-0356
Email: attys@meyner.com *URL:* http://www.meyner.com

Robert B. Meyner (1908-1990)
Edwin C. Landis, Jr.
John N. Malyska
William J. Fiore
Anthony F. Siliato
Francis R. Perkins
Howard O. Thompson
Scott T. McCleary
Linda Townley Snyder
William H. Schmidt, Jr.
David B. Grantz

For full biographical listings, see the Martindale-Hubbell Law Directory

ST. JOHN & WAYNE, L.L.C. (AV)

Two Penn Plaza East, 07105-2249
Telephone: 973-491-3600
Fax: 973-491-3555
Email: firm@nwk.stjohn-law.com *URL:* http://www.stjohn-law.com
Rochester, New York Office: St. John & Curtin, L.L.C., First Federal Plaza.
Telephone: 716-262-6780.
Fax: 716-262-6755.
New York, New York Office: Heron Tower, 70 East 55th. Street.
Telephone: 212-446-5000.
Fax: 212-446-5055.

Bernard S. Davis
Paul D. Drobbin
John J. Oberdorf
Bryan G. Petkanics (Resident at New York, New York Office)
Robert A. Wayne
E. Kenneth Williams, Jr.

For Complete List of Firm Personnel, See General Section

For full biographical listings, see the Martindale-Hubbell Law Directory

SILLS CUMMIS RADIN TISCHMAN EPSTEIN & GROSS, A PROFESSIONAL CORPORATION (AV)

One Riverfront Plaza, 07102-5400
Telephone: 973-643-7000
Fax: 973-643-6500
Telex: 820630 Sillsbeck Nwk
Email: sillsmail@sillscummis.com *URL:* http://www.sillscummis.com
Atlantic City, New Jersey Office: 17 Gordon's Alley.
Telephone: 609-344-2800.
New York, N.Y. Office: 712 Fifth Avenue.
Telephone: 212-643-7000.
Washington, D.C. Office: 1800 K Street, N.W.
Telephone: 202-296-4750.

MEMBERS OF FIRM

Steven S. Radin
Michael B. Tischman
Steven E. Gross
Jeffrey J. Greenbaum
Morris Yamner
Gerald Span
Noah Bronkesh
Steven M. Goldman
Ira A. Rosenberg
Robert Max Crane
Jack M. Zackin
Jerry Genberg
Margaret F. Black
Brian S. Coven
Trent S. Dickey
Joseph L. Buckley
David J. Rabinowitz
Ronald C. Rak
Victor H. Boyajian
Mark E. Duckstein
Frederic M. Tudor

OF COUNSEL

Diane M. Lavenda

Noel D. Humphreys
Paul F. Doda
Adam J. Kaiser
Lori M. Waldron

Representative Clients: Citibank, N.A.; Credit Lyonnais; Midlantic National Bank; First Fidelity Bancorporation; United Jersey Bank; Emigrant Savings Bank; National Community Bank (Bank of New York); Summit Bancorporation; NatWest; PNC Bank Corp.

For Complete List of Firm Personnel, See General Section

For full biographical listings, see the Martindale-Hubbell Law Directory

Newark—Continued

TOMPKINS, MCGUIRE, WACHENFELD & BARRY (AV)

A New Jersey Limited Liability Partnership including a Professional Association
Four Gateway Center, 100 Mulberry Street, 07102-4070
Telephone: 973-622-3000
Telecopier: 973-623-7780
Email: attorneys@tompkinsmcguire.com
New York, New York Office: 1 Bankers Trust Plaza. 130 Liberty Street, Suite 2707. 10006.
Telephone: 212-714-1720.

OF COUNSEL

Frances S. Margolis

Representative Clients: Corbo Jewelers, Inc.; General Electric Co.; Hartford Insurance Group; Marriott Corp.; National Union Fire Insurance Co.; Summit Bank; Underwriters at Lloyd's, London.

For Complete List of Firm Personnel, See General Section

For full biographical listings, see the Martindale-Hubbell Law Directory

PARSIPPANY, Morris Co.

CUYLER BURK (AV)

Parsippany Corporate Center, Four Century Drive, 07054-4663
Telephone: 973-734-3200
Telex: 429071
Telecopier: 973-734-3201
Email: Main@Cuyler.com *URL:* http://www.cuyler.com
New York, New York Office: 350 Fifth Avenue, Suite 3304. 10018.
Telephone: 212-645-4039.

MEMBERS OF FIRM

Stephen D. Cuyler
Jo Ann Burk
Stefano Calogero
David L. Menzel
Peter Petrou
Richard A. Crooker
Michael J. Jones

COUNSEL

Anne M. Mohan
Frank J. Miele

ASSOCIATES

Jan C. Walker
Kathleen Jane Olear
Claudia L. Marchese
Mark G. Eliades
Kimberly A. Joel
Christy A. Ramunno
Catherine E. Youngman
Andrew K. Craig
Mark S. Winter
Thomas J. Castano
Hugo A. Hilgendorff, IV

LEGAL SUPPORT PERSONNEL

Frederick M. H. Currie, Jr.

For full biographical listings, see the Martindale-Hubbell Law Directory

PRINCETON, Mercer Co.

MCCARTHY AND SCHATZMAN, P.A. (AV)

228 Alexander Street, P.O. Box 2329, 08543-2329
Telephone: 609-924-1199
Fax: 609-683-5251

John F. McCarthy, Jr.
Richard Schatzman
G. Christopher Baker
John F. McCarthy, III
Michael A. Spero
Barbara Strapp Nelson
W. Scott Stoner
James J. Britt, Jr.

Charly Gayden

Representative Clients: Trustees of Princeton University; Carnegie Center Associates; Merrill Lynch Pierce Fenner & Smith, Inc.; Calton Homes, Inc.

For full biographical listings, see the Martindale-Hubbell Law Directory

ROCHELLE PARK, Bergen Co.

FORMAN HOLT & ELIADES LLC (AV)

218 Route 17 North, 07662
Telephone: 201-845-1000
Fax: 201-845-9112
Email: firm@formanlaw.com

Charles M. Forman
Michael E. Holt
Daniel M. Eliades, Jr.
Joseph M. Cerra
Julie L. Singer
Kim R. Lynch

OF COUNSEL

Erin J. Kennedy

For full biographical listings, see the Martindale-Hubbell Law Directory

ROSELAND, Essex Co.

BRACH, EICHLER, ROSENBERG, SILVER, BERNSTEIN, HAMMER & GLADSTONE, A PROFESSIONAL CORPORATION (AV)

101 Eisenhower Parkway, 07068
Telephone: 973-228-5700
Telecopier: 973-228-7852
Email: law@bracheichler.com *URL:* http://www.bracheichler.com

Thomas E. Cohn
Alan R. Hammer
Brian R. Lenker
Robert C. Mignella
Paul F. Rosenberg

Jeffrey H. Itzkowitz
Joseph M. Davis
John P. Inglesino
Allen J. Popowitz
Lisa S. Paye

Representative Clients: Intervest Corporation of New York; National Canada Finance Corp.; NorCrown Bank; Oritani Savings Bank; State Bank of South Orange; Summit Bank; Valley National Bank.

For Complete List of Firm Personnel, See General Section

For full biographical listings, see the Martindale-Hubbell Law Directory

SUMMIT, Union Co.

BOURNE, NOLL & KENYON, A PROFESSIONAL CORPORATION (AV)

382 Springfield Avenue, P.O. Box 690, 07902-0690
Telephone: 908-277-2200
Facsimile: 908-277-6808

Cary R. Hardy
Charles R. Berman
Martin Rubashkin
Roger Mehner
James R. Ottobre
Lawrence A. Rudnick
John F. Kuntz

OF COUNSEL

Edward T. Kenyon
Robert B. Bourne

COUNSEL

Ellyn A. Draikiwicz

Jaime A. O'Brien
Timothy A. Kalas
Alan F. Schwarz
Ross W. Smith

For full biographical listings, see the Martindale-Hubbell Law Directory

VINELAND, Cumberland Co.

GRUCCIO, PEPPER GIOVINAZZI, DESANTO & FARNOLY, P.A. (AV)

817 Landis Avenue, P.O. Box 1501, 08362
Telephone: 856-691-0100
Fax: 856-692-4095
Email: Gruccio1@eticomm.net
Woodbury, New Jersey Office: 21 Delaware Street.
Telephone: 856-848-5558.
Fax: 856-384-1181.
Bridgeton, New Jersey Office: 120 West Broad Street.
Telephone: 856-459-3334.
Fax: 856-692-4095.

James J. Gruccio, Sr.
Lawrence Pepper, Jr.
Cosmo A. Giovinazzi, III
Thomas P. Farnoly

Stephen D. Barse
Judith C. Arnold

OF COUNSEL

Richard M. Milstead

Representative Clients: State Farm Mutual Automobile Insurance Cos.; United States Fidelity & Guaranty Co.; South Jersey Transportation Authority; County of Salem; County of Cape May; Cumberland Mutual Fire Insurance Co.; Farmers and Merchants National Bank of Bridgeton; Newfield National Bank; Sun National Bank of N.J.; Colonial Bank, FSB.

For Complete List of Firm Personnel, See General Section

For full biographical listings, see the Martindale-Hubbell Law Directory

WESTFIELD, Union Co.

LINDABURY, MCCORMICK & ESTABROOK, P.A. (AV)

53 Cardinal Drive, P.O. Box 2369, 07091
Telephone: 908-233-6800
Fax: 908-233-5078
New York, N.Y. Office: 26 Broadway, Suite 2300.
Telephone: 212-742-3390.
Fax: 212-269-5016.

Robert S. Burney

Representative Clients: The Chase Manhattan Bank; Summit Bank; Fleet Bank.

(See Next Column)

LINDABURY, MCCORMICK & ESTABROOK P.A., *Westfield—Continued*

For Complete List of Firm Personnel, See General Section

For full biographical listings, see the Martindale-Hubbell Law Directory

WEST ORANGE, Essex Co.

ALPERT, BUTLER & SANDERS, P.C. (AV)

The Alpert Professional Building, 449 Mount Pleasant Avenue, 07052
Telephone: 973-325-1188
Fax: 973-325-3399
Email: mailbox@abslaw.com *URL:* http://www.abslaw.com
New York, New York Office: 509 Madison Avenue.
Telephone: 212-758-6958.
Fax: 212-758-2817.

Clark E. Alpert
David N. Butler
William D. Sanders

OF COUNSEL

Martin L. Bearg
Ted M. Rosen (Not admitted in NJ)

Elliot L. Lewis
Matthew J. Rice

LEGAL SUPPORT PERSONNEL

PARALEGAL

Robin S. Karpel

For full biographical listings, see the Martindale-Hubbell Law Directory

WOODBRIDGE, Middlesex Co.

WILENTZ, GOLDMAN & SPITZER, A PROFESSIONAL CORPORATION (AV)

90 Woodbridge Center Drive Suite 900, Box 10, 07095
Telephone: 732-636-8000
Telecopier: 732-855-6117
URL: http://www.newjerseylaw.com
Eatontown, New Jersey Office: Meridian Center I, Two Industrial Way West, 07724.
Telephone: 732-542-4500.
Telecopier: 732-493-8387.
New York, New York Office: Wall Street Plaza, 88 Pine Street, 9th Floor, 10005.
Telephone: 212-267-3091.
Telecopier: 212-267-3828.

Stuart A. Hoberman
Peter R. Herman
Sheldon E. Jaffe
Douglas Watson Lubic

Jonathan P. Falk

Representative Clients: Amboy National Bank; Summit Bank; First Union National Bank; Bankers Savings; PNC Bank, National Association; The Trust Company of NJ.

For Complete List of Firm Personnel, See General Section

For full biographical listings, see the Martindale-Hubbell Law Directory

NEW MEXICO

*ALBUQUERQUE,** Bernalillo Co.

EAVES, BARDACKE, BAUGH KIERST & KIERNAN, P.A. (AV)

6400 Uptown Boulevard, N.E., Suite 110-W, P.O. Box 35670, 87176
Telephone: 505-888-4300
Facsimile: 505-883-4406
Email: LGLEAVES@EB-B.com

John M. Eaves
John G. Baugh
Paul Bardacke
Peter S. Kierst
Kerry Kiernan

Derek V. Larson
Karen S. Mendenhall
C. Shannon Bacon

OF COUNSEL

Jennifer J. Pruett

For full biographical listings, see the Martindale-Hubbell Law Directory

MILLER, STRATVERT & TORGERSON, P.A. (AV)

500 Marquette Avenue, N.W., Suite 1100, P.O. Box 25687, 87102
Telephone: 505-842-1950
Facsimile: 505-243-4408
Email: info@mstLAW.com *URL:* http://www.mstLAW.com
Farmington, New Mexico Office: 300 West Arrington, Suite 300, P.O. Box 869.
Telephone: 505-326-4521.
Facsimile: 505-325-5474.
Las Cruces, New Mexico Office: 500 South Main, Suite 800, P.O. Box 1209.
Telephone: 505-523-2481.
Facsimile: 505-526-2215.
Santa Fe, New Mexico Office: 150 Washington Avenue, Suite 300, P.O. Box 1986.
Telephone: 505-989-9614.
Facsimile: 505-989-9857.

Alice Tomlinson Lorenz
Lyman G. Sandy
Sharon P. Gross
Joel T. Newton (Resident at Las Cruces Office)
Thomas M. Domme
Dana M. Kyle (Resident at Las Cruces Office)
Fred Schiller (Resident at Las Cruces Office)
Dean B. Cross (Resident at Las Cruces Office)

COUNSEL

Paul W. Robinson
Ralph Wm. Richards (Resident at Las Cruces Office)
Ross B. Perkal
Bradley D. Tepper

Representative Clients: Bank 1st; Bank of America Trust Department; Citizens Bank of Las Cruces; First Federal Savings Bank of New Mexico; First Security Bank of New Mexico; White Sands Federal Credit Union.

For Complete List of Firm Personnel, See General Section

For full biographical listings, see the Martindale-Hubbell Law Directory

RODEY, DICKASON, SLOAN, AKIN & ROBB, P.A. (AV)

Albuquerque Plaza, Suite 2200, 201 Third Street, N.W., P.O. Box 1888, 87103-1888
Telephone: 505-765-5900
Fax: 505-768-7395
Email: info@rodey.com *URL:* http://www.rodey.com
Santa Fe, New Mexico Office: Suite 101 Marcy Plaza, 123 East Marcy Street, P.O. Box 1357, 87504-1357.
Telephone: 505-984-0100.
Fax: 505-989-9542.

Robert M. St. John
John P. Burton (Resident, Santa Fe Office)
Jonathan W. Hewes
Catherine T. Goldberg
Jo Saxton Brayer
Nancy J. Appleby
Jay D. Hill

COUNSEL

S. I. Betzer, Jr.

For Complete List of Firm Personnel, See General Section

For full biographical listings, see the Martindale-Hubbell Law Directory

*CLOVIS,** Curry Co.

ROWLEY LAW FIRM, P.C. (AV)

305 Pile, P.O. Box 790, 88101
Telephone: 505-763-4457
Fax: 505-763-4450
Email: rowleylaw@3lefties.com

Richard F. Rowley (1908-1980)
Richard F. Rowley, II

Jill Henson

LEGAL SUPPORT PERSONNEL

Antoinette Linder

Representative Clients: Northwestern Mutual Life Insurance Co.; Prudential Insurance Company of America; Equitable Life Assurance Society; Farm Credit Services; Cigna Capitol Advisors, Inc.; New Mexico American Water Co.; Feed Bag, Inc.; Production Credit Association of Eastern New Mexico; Muleshoe State Bank.

For full biographical listings, see the Martindale-Hubbell Law Directory

*LAS CRUCES,** Dona Ana Co.

REEVES, CHAVEZ, GREENFIELD & WALKER, P.A. (AV)

300 South Water Street, P.O. Box 2769, 88004-2769
Telephone: 505-524-9617
Fax: 505-524-1954
Email: rcgw@zianet.com

B. James Reeves
Frank N. Chavez
Charlotte Greenfield
William A. Walker, Jr.
Kelly P. Albers
Joyce A. Montes
William R. Anderson
Carolyn J. Baca

(See Next Column)

REEVES, CHAVEZ, GREENFIELD & WALKER P.A.—*Continued*

Glenn D. Hall CaraLyn Banks

For full biographical listings, see the Martindale-Hubbell Law Directory

*SANTA FE,** Santa Fe Co.

CATRON, CATRON & SAWTELL, A PROFESSIONAL ASSOCIATION (AV)

2006 Botulph Road, P.O. Box 788, 87504-0788
Telephone: 505-982-1947
Telecopier: 505-986-1013
Email: catronlaw@aol.com

Thomas B. Catron III W. Anthony Sawtell

LEGAL SUPPORT PERSONNEL

Peggy L. Feldt (Certified Public Accountant)

For Complete List of Firm Personnel, See General Section

For full biographical listings, see the Martindale-Hubbell Law Directory

SCHEUER, YOST & PATTERSON, A PROFESSIONAL CORPORATION (AV)

125 Lincoln Avenue, Suite 223, P.O. Drawer 9570, 87504
Telephone: 505-982-9911
505-989-7500
Fax: 505-982-1621
Email: firm@santafelawyers.com

Melvin T. Yost (Retired)
Ralph H. Scheuer
Mel E. Yost
John N. Patterson
Byron L. Treaster
Donald A. Walcott
Christopher M. Grimmer
Daniel J. Monte

OF COUNSEL

Reverdy Johnson

Representative Clients: Century Bank, FSB; Chicago Title Insurance Co.; GEICO; Los Alamos National Bank; Manufacturer's Hanover Trust Co.; St. John's College; Sun Loan Companies; Territorial Abstract & Title Co.; Texas Commerce Bank.

For full biographical listings, see the Martindale-Hubbell Law Directory

NEW YORK

*ALBANY,** Albany Co.

McCLUNG, PETERS AND SIMON (AV)

41 State Street, Suite 700, 12207
Telephone: 518-462-7481 Toll Free 1-800-777-7481
Telecopier: 518-462-0112
Email: McClunglaw@aol.com

MEMBERS OF FIRM

Benjamin McClung (1867-1940)
George M. Simon (1909-1981)
Homer E. Peters (1905-1992)
Joseph B. Carr
John W. Scott
Stephen M. Kerwin
Lynda S. Battiste

ASSOCIATES

Marshall A. Courtney Patrick H. Cartwright

OF COUNSEL

Stephen J. Arlington Lawrence E. Becker
David N. Goldin

Representative Clients: Aetna Casualty & Surety Co.; Chemical Bank; Continental Insurance Cos.; Firemen's Insurance Co.; Hartford Insurance Co.; Underwriter's Adjusting Co.

For full biographical listings, see the Martindale-Hubbell Law Directory

*BATH,** Steuben Co.

COLE LAW OFFICES, P.C. (AV)

7 East Steuben Street, P.O. Box 232, 14810
Telephone: 607-776-3306
Fax: 607-776-4189
Email: RCole@LinkNY.Com
Hammondsport, New York Office: Railroad Station Depot, Water Street, P.O. Box 396, 14840.
Telephone: 607-569-2213.
Fax: 607-569-2214,

Robert H. Cole

(See Next Column)

Christine Valkenburgh James H. Burns
William H. Reed

General Counsel for: Bath National Bank; Mercury Aircraft, Inc.
Local Counsel for: Equitable Life Assurance Society of the United States.
Reference: Bath National Bank.

For full biographical listings, see the Martindale-Hubbell Law Directory

BRIDGEHAMPTON, Suffolk Co.

PAYNE, WOOD & LITTLEJOHN (AV)

1936 Montauk Highway, P.O. Box 1980, 11932-1980
Telephone: 516-537-3100
Telefax: 516-537-0560
Email: mail@paynewood.com
Melville, New York Office: 290 Broad Hollow Road.
Telephone: 516-547-8400.
Telefax: 516-547-0501.
Locust Valley, New York Office: 83 Birch Hill Road.
Telephone: 516-676-0700.
Telefax: 516-676-0703.

MEMBER OF FIRM

Alan C. Polacek (Managing Partner)

For full biographical listings, see the Martindale-Hubbell Law Directory

BRONXVILLE, Westchester Co.

GRIFFIN, COOGAN & VENERUSO, P.C. (AV)

51 Pondfield Road, 10708
Telephone: 914-961-1300
Telecopier: 914-961-1476; 914-961-9385

William E. Griffin James M. Coogan
James J. Veneruso

Daniel J. Griffin
Paul R. Herrick
Thomas G. Marzullo
William E. Sulzer
(Not admitted in NY)

Approved Closing Attorneys: Hudson Valley Bank.

For full biographical listings, see the Martindale-Hubbell Law Directory

*BUFFALO,** Erie Co.

BLOCK & COLUCCI, P.C. (AV)

1250 Statler Towers, 14202-3695
Telephone: 716-854-4080; 1-800-388-2595
Fax: 716-854-0059
Litigation Telephone: 716-853-4080
Jupiter, Florida Office: 1001 N. U.S. Highway One, Suite 400.
Telephone: 561-747-0110.
Fax: 561-743-0046.
Clifton Park, New York Office: 9 Executive Park Drive, P.O. Box 5018.
Telephone: 518-348-1000.
Fax: 518-348-2000.
Rochester, New York Office: 311 Alexander Street, Suite 415.
Telephone: 716-454-1660.
Fax: 716-454-7461.

Lester H. Block (1906-1997) Ernest L. Colucci (1909-1989)
Anthony J. Colucci, Jr.

Elpiniki M. Bechakas
Brandi Burns
(Resident, Clifton Park Office)
Heather A. Corey-Mongue
(Resident, Clifton Park Office)
Dennis M. Hyatt
Scott J. Leitten
(Not admitted in NY)
Mark J. Longo
Melanie C. Marotto
Joel P. Peller
Michael W. Schafer
Debra A. Spellman
Jennifer L. Stoeckl
(Resident, Rochester Office)
Kevin P. Wheatley
(Resident, Clifton Park Office)

References: Manufacturers & Traders Trust Co.; Palm Beach National Bank & Trust Co.

For full biographical listings, see the Martindale-Hubbell Law Directory

FARMINGDALE, Nassau Co.

CARMAN, CALLAHAN & INGHAM (AV)

Carman Building, 280 Main Street, 11735
Telephone: 516-249-3450
Telecopier: 516-249-3782

Willis B. Carman, Jr.
Robert M. Callahan
Michael F. Ingham
Gregory W. Carman, Jr.
James M. Carman

ASSOCIATE

Stephanie L. Boden

For full biographical listings, see the Martindale-Hubbell Law Directory

GARDEN CITY, Nassau Co.

O'Reilly, Marsh & Corteselli, P.C. (AV)
1000 Franklin Avenue, 3rd Floor, 11530
Telephone: 516-741-1818

Philip J. O'Reilly — James G. Marsh
Karen P. Corteselli

Richard P. Kirby — Arthur T. Walsh

OF COUNSEL
Robert J. Jordan

For full biographical listings, see the Martindale-Hubbell Law Directory

HUNTINGTON, Suffolk Co.

Smyth & Lack (AV)
143 Main Street, 11743
Telephone: 516-271-7500
Telecopier: 516-271-7504
URL: http://www.lawyers.com/smyth&lacklaw

MEMBERS OF FIRM
Vincent A. Smyth — James J. Lack

ASSOCIATES
Dana M. Barberis — Edmund J.M. Smyth
Karen E. Nora

Reference: Chemical Bank.

For full biographical listings, see the Martindale-Hubbell Law Directory

JERICHO, Nassau Co.

Martin, Van de Walle, Donohue, McGahan, Catalano & Fairgrieve (AV)
555 North Broadway, P.O. Box 350, 11753
Telephone: 516-681-3100
Telecopier: 516-681-5357

MEMBERS OF FIRM
Jules Martin (1928-1995) — James M. McGahan
Charles R. Van de Walle — Thomas C. Catalano, Jr.
Joseph A. Guarino (1946-1991) — Scott Fairgrieve
Nicholas J. Donohue — Michael Belitsis

ASSOCIATES
Randi M. Seidner — Laurie Ann Corallo

Representative Clients: Fidelity National Title Insurance Company of New York; Chase Manhatten Mortgage Corp.; Jones Fund; Festo Corp.; First Investors Corp.; First Financial Savings Bank, S.L.A.; Oppenheimer Funds, Inc.; Capital Trading Corp.; Chase Manhatten Bank, N.A.; Old Republic Republic National Title Insurance Company; New York State Land Title Association, Inc.

For full biographical listings, see the Martindale-Hubbell Law Directory

MELVILLE, Suffolk Co.

Cahn Wishod & Knauer, LLP (AV)
425 Broadhollow Road Suite 315, 11747
Telephone: 631-752-1600
Fax: 631-752-1555
URL: http://www.cahnwishod.com
URL: http://www.lawyers.com/cahnwishod&knauer

MEMBERS OF FIRM
Richard C. Cahn — Eugene L. Wishod
Todd A. Knauer

ASSOCIATES
Brian T. Egan — Patricia A. Rooney

LEGAL SUPPORT PERSONNEL
Susan M. Stonelli (Paralegal)

For full biographical listings, see the Martindale-Hubbell Law Directory

Lamb & Barnosky, LLP (AV)
534 Broadhollow Road-CS 9034, 11747-9034
Telephone: 631-694-2300
Telecopier: 631-694-2309
Email: thefirm@lambbarnosky.com *URL:* http://www.lambbarnosky.com

PARTNERS
Eugene R. Barnosky — Scott M. Karson
Robert H. Cohen — P. L. Lamb
Marcia Lyn Finkelstein — Arthur A. Lane
Michael J. Heller — Joel M. Markowitz
Gary Holman — Gerald P. Rosenberg
Patrice Dowd Shenn

(See Next Column)

OF COUNSEL
Louis E. Black — Howard W. Newman
James F. Gesualdi — Joseph J. Salvatore
Joseph H. Wishod

COUNSEL
Lloyd K. Chanin — Scott P. McBride

ASSOCIATES
Cathleen D. Allen — Rita Fishman Sheena
Catherine Healy Kanzler — Shari Lee Sugarman

For full biographical listings, see the Martindale-Hubbell Law Directory

Payne, Wood & Littlejohn (AV)
290 Broad Hollow Road, 11747-4805
Telephone: 516-547-8400
Telefax: 516-547-0501
Email: mail@paynewood.com
Bridgehampton, New York Office: 1936 Montauk Highway. P.O. Box 1980, 11932.
Telephone: 516-537-3100.
Telefax: 516-537-0560.
Locust Valley, New York Office: 83 Birch Hill Road, 11560.
Telephone: 516-676-0700.
Fax: 516-676-0703.

MEMBERS OF FIRM
Philip C. Kilian — Alan C. Polacek (Managing Partner)

OF COUNSEL
Victor C. McCuaig, Jr. — Warren I. Titus, Jr.

For Complete List of Firm Personnel, See General Section

For full biographical listings, see the Martindale-Hubbell Law Directory

MIDDLETOWN, Orange Co.

MacVean, Lewis, Sherwin & McDermott, P.C. (AV)
34 Grove Street, P.O. Box 310, 10940
Telephone: 914-343-3000
Fax: 914-343-3866

Kermit W. Lewis — Paul T. McDermott
Louis H. Sherwin — Jeffrey D. Sherwin
Thomas P. Clarke, Jr.

SENIOR TRIAL COUNSEL
George F. Roesch, III

Counsel for: Orange County Trust Co.; Middletown Savings Bank; First Federal Savings & Loan Association of Middletown; Goshen Savings Bank; Advest Bank.

For Complete List of Firm Personnel, See General Section

For full biographical listings, see the Martindale-Hubbell Law Directory

*NEW CITY,** Rockland Co.

Freeman, Loftus & Manley (AV)
4 Laurel Road, P.O. Box 629, 10956-0629
Telephone: 914-634-0888
Fax: 914-634-9312
Email: flmattys@aol.com

MEMBERS OF FIRM
James J. Freeman, Jr. — Patrick J. Loftus
Loring K. Manley

OF COUNSEL
James H. Bowers — Ira M. Emanuel
Albert J. Kaiser

For full biographical listings, see the Martindale-Hubbell Law Directory

*NEW YORK,** New York Co.

Blatt, Hammesfahr & Eaton (AV)
45 Broadway 12th Floor, 10006
Telephone: 212-363-1900
Fax: 212-363-2600
Email: bhe@bhelaw.com *URL:* HTTP://WWW.BHELAW.COM
Chicago, Illinois Office: 333 W. Wacker Drive, Suite 1900.
Telephone: 312-849-8000.
FAX: 312-357-0198. Email: BHE@BHELAW.COM. URL: HTTP://WWW.BHELAW.COM.

MEMBERS OF FIRM
Robert W. Hammesfahr — Scott W. Wright

ASSOCIATE
Veronica K. Danko

For full biographical listings, see the Martindale-Hubbell Law Directory

New York—Continued

CORBIN SILVERMAN & SANSEVERINO LLP (AV)

805 Third Avenue, 10022-7513
Telephone: 212-308-5000
Telecopier: 212-308-7189

MEMBERS OF FIRM

Stephen B. Silverman
Raymond A. Sanseverino
Joseph W. Muccia
Richard A. Nardi
Kenneth W. Sold
Marc J. Gottridge
John J. Gallagher, Jr.
James T. Sandnes
Garry C. Berman
Adam H. Schuman
Mary B. Templeton

SENIOR COUNSEL

Sol Neil Corbin

OF COUNSEL

Joseph L. Broadwin

ASSOCIATES

Mark A. Shapiro
Joseph J. Macchiarola
Theodora L. Hunter

For full biographical listings, see the Martindale-Hubbell Law Directory

INGRAM YUZEK GAINEN CARROLL & BERTOLOTTI, LLP (AV)

250 Park Avenue, 10177
Telephone: 212-907-9600
Facsimile: 212-907-9681

MEMBERS OF FIRM

Ernest J. Bertolotti (1942-1999)
Daniel L. Carroll
Roger Cukras
David G. Ebert
Larry F. Gainen
Samuel W. Ingram, Jr.
Paulette Kendler
Steven Mastbaum
Shane O'Neill
Dean G. Yuzek

ASSOCIATES

Warren E. Barrows
Amy Bertolotti
Patricia Hewitt
Theodore M. Kakoyiannis
Jeanne F. Pucci
Leigh A. Roveda
Jennifer E. Schwartz
Paul H. Slaney

OF COUNSEL

Karin J. Barkhorn
Beverly L. Deickler
Mark E. Klein
Paulette Lemay Peters
Cory L. Weiss

For full biographical listings, see the Martindale-Hubbell Law Directory

LOEB & LOEB LLP (AV)

A Limited Liability Partnership including Professional Corporations
345 Park Avenue, 10154-0037
Telephone: 212-407-4000
Facsimile: 212-407-4990
Email: info@loeb.com *URL:* http://www.loeb.com
Los Angeles, California Office: Suite 1800, 1000 Wilshire Boulevard, 90017-2475.
Telephone: 213-688-3400.
Facsimile: 213-688-3460.
Century City (Los Angeles), California Office: Suite 2200, 10100 Santa Monica Boulevard, Los Angeles, 90067-4164.
Telephone: 310-282-2000.
Facsimile: 310-282-2192.
Nashville, Tennessee Office: 45 Music Square West, 37203-3205.
Telephone: 615-749-8300.
Facsimile: 615-749-8308.
Rome, Italy Office: Piazza Digione 1, 00197.
Telephone: 011-3906-808-8456.
Facsimile: 011-3906-808-8288.

MEMBERS OF FIRM

Christopher K. Aidun
David S. Schaefer
Richard P. Streicher

ASSOCIATE

Philippa J. Smith

For Complete List of Firm Personnel, See General Section

For full biographical listings, see the Martindale-Hubbell Law Directory

MILBANK, TWEED, HADLEY & MCCLOY LLP (AV)

1 Chase Manhattan Plaza, 10005-1413
Telephone: 212-530-5000
Fax: 212-530-5219
Email: postmaster@milbank.com *URL:* http://www.milbank.com
Midtown Office: 375 Park Avenue, Suite 3601, 10152.
Telephone: 212-530-5800.
Fax: 212-530-0158.
Los Angeles, California Office: 601 South Figueroa Street, 30th Floor, 90017.
Telephone: 213-892-4000.
Fax: 213-629-5063.

(See Next Column)

Washington, D.C. Office: International Square Building, Suite 1100, 1825 Eye Street, N.W., 20006.
Telephone: 202-835-7500.
Fax: 202-835-7586.
Tokyo, Japan Office: Fukoku Seimei Building, 2-2, Uchisaiwai-cho 2-Chome, Chiyoda-ku, Tokyo 100-0011, Japan.
Telephone: 011-81-3-3504-1050.
Fax: 011-81-3-3595-2790, 011-81-3-3595-2840.
London, England Office: Dashwood House, 69 Old Broad Street, London EC2M 1QS.
Telephone: 011-44-207-448-3000.
Fax: 011-44-207-448-3029.
Hong Kong Office: 3007 Alexandra House, 16 Chater Road.
Telephone: 011-852-2971-4888.
Fax: 011-852-2840-0792; 011-852-2845-9046.
Singapore Office: 14-00 Caltex House, 30 Raffles Place, 048622.
Telephone: 011-65-428-2400.
Fax: 011-65-428-2500.
Moscow, Russia Office: 24/27 Sadovaya-Samotyochnya, Moscow, 103051.
Telephone: 011-7-501-258-5015.
Fax: 011-7-501-258-5014.

MEMBERS OF FIRM

Richard S. Brach
Warren F. Cooke
Glenn S. Gerstell (Resident, Washington, D.C. Office)
Elliot Gewirtz
Richard M. Gray (Resident, Singapore Office)
Mark A. Kantor (Resident, Washington, D.C. Office)
William J. Mahoney
Peter M. Mortimer
Eric K. Moser
Ted Obrzut (Resident, Los Angeles, California Office)
Robert S. O'Hara, Jr.
Frank C. Puleo
Elihu F. Robertson
John E. Shockey (Resident, Washington, D.C. Office)
Robert E. Spring
David A. Stagliano
Tsugumichi D. Watanabe
Richard J. Wight

ASSOCIATES

Suzanne V. Alwan
Katherine Aydin (Resident, Washington, D.C. Office)
Dino Barajas (Resident, Los Angeles, California Office)
Steven Anthony Behar (Not admitted in NY)
Michael J. Bellucci
Michael C. Bisignano (Resident, Washington, D.C. Office)
Barry P. Burland
Kenneth E. Crowell
Joseph K. Falzon
Michael Farrar
Kathryn E. Hoff-Patrinos (Resident, Washington, D.C. Office)
David J. Impastato (Resident, Los Angeles, California Office)
Julie M. Jacobs (Resident, Washington, D.C. Office)
Charlotte J. Kim
Jonathan M. Kohl
Isaac Koyfman
Alex G. Lempiner
Dean A. Manson (Resident, Washington, D.C. Office)
Thomas Christopher Mellor
Geoffrey Peck
Stanford Renas
Raymond R. Richards
Kathleen M. Riester
Matthew D. Royko
Ian W. Sterling
Edward S. Tsai
Blair M. Tyson
Langdon Van Norden
A. Joseph Warburton (Resident, Washington, D.C. Office)
David J. Webb
Thomas R. Wise, III

For Complete List of Firm Personnel, See General Section

For full biographical listings, see the Martindale-Hubbell Law Directory

OPPENHEIMER WOLFF & DONNELLY LLP (AV)

The Chrysler East Building 19th Floor, 666 Third Avenue, 10017
Telephone: 212-826-5000
FAX: 212-486-0708
URL: http://www.oppenheimer.com
Minneapolis, Minnesota Office: 3300 Plaza VII, 45 South Seventh Street, 55402.
Telephone: 612-607-7000.
FAX: 612-607-7100.
Amsterdam, The Netherlands Office: Keizergracht 241.
Telephone: 31-20-423-4555.
FAX: 312-20-423-4545.
Brussels, Belgium Office: Avenue Louise 240, Box 5, 1050.
Telephone: 32-2-626-0500.
FAX: 32-2-626-0510.
Geneva, Switzerland Office: Rue Gabriel Eynard, 6, 1205.
Telephone: (41/22) 311-7410.
FAX: (41/22) 311-4707.
Newport Beach, California Office: 500 Newport Center Drive, Suite 700, 92660.
Telephone: 949-823-6000.
FAX: 949-823-6100.
Paris, France Office: 35 Boulevard des Capucines, 75002.
Telephone: (33/1) 53 45 40 00.
FAX: (33/1) 53 45 40 10.
St. Paul, Minnesota Office: 1700 First National Bank Building, 55101.
Telephone: 651-605-2000.
FAX: 651-605-2100.
Washington, D.C. Office: Oppenheimer Wolff Donnelly & Bayh LLP, 1350 Eye Street, N.W., Suite 200, 20005.
Telephone: 202-312-8000.
FAX: 202-312-8100.

(See Next Column)

OPPENHEIMER WOLFF & DONNELLY LLP, *New York—Continued*

Los Angeles, California Office: 2029 Century Park East, 38th Floor, 90067.
Telephone: 310-788-5000.
FAX: 310-277-1297.
Palo Alto, California Office: 3373 Hillview Avenue, Suite 200, 94304.
Telephone: 650-320-4000.
FAX: 650-320-4100.
Chicago, Illinois Office: Oppenheimer Wolff & Donnelly (Illinois), Two Prudential Plaza, 45th Floor, 180 North Stetson Avenue, 60601.
Telephone: 312-616-1800.
Fax: 312-616-5800.

RESIDENT PARTNERS

Lance Gotthoffer
Thomas M. Gandolfo
Ronald S. Beacher

RESIDENT ASSOCIATES

Teresa J. Olson
Suzanne A. Cruse
Constantine Karides
Ronald J. Kaniuk
Robert M. Hirsh

For full biographical listings, see the Martindale-Hubbell Law Directory

OTTERBOURG, STEINDLER, HOUSTON & ROSEN, P.C. (AV)

230 Park Avenue, 29th Floor, 10169
Telephone: 212-661-9100
Telecopier: 212-682-6104

William M. Silverman
Steven B. Soll
Peter H. Stolzar
Alan Kardon
Alan R. Weiskopf
Mitchell M. Brand
Jonathan N. Helfat
Stanley L. Lane, Jr.
Daniel Wallen
David W. Morse
Glenn B. Rice
Peter L. Feldman
Albert F. Reisman
Richard G. Haddad
Anthony M. Piccione
Andrew M. Kramer

GENERAL COUNSEL

Kurt J. Wolff

COUNSEL

Bernard Beitel
Morton L. Gitter

Lloyd M. Green
Matthew J. Miller
Craig D. Zlotnick
Richard L. Stehl
Stephen H. Alpert
Susan A. Joyce
Lon M. Singer

For Complete List of Firm Personnel, See General Section

For full biographical listings, see the Martindale-Hubbell Law Directory

PARKER CHAPIN LLP (AV)

Chrysler Building, 405 Lexington Avenue, 10017
Telephone: 212-704-6000
Telecopier: 212-704-6288
URL: http://www.parkerchapin.com
Great Neck, New York Office: 175 Great Neck Road.
Telephone: 516-482-4422.
Telecopier: 516-482-4469.
Hackensack, New Jersey: 190 Morre Street, Suite 307.
Telephone: 210-883-6400.
Telecopier: 210-883-6404.
Beverly Hills, California: 9454 Wilshire Boulevard.
Telephone: 310-288-8367.
Telecopier: 310-288-8365.

MEMBERS OF FIRM

Mark Abramowitz
Michael A. Leichtling
Christopher Stewart Auguste
Mitchell P. Portnoy
Aurora Cassirer
Richard A. Rubin
William D. Freedman
Lawrence David Swift
Mark S. Hirsch
Melvin Weinberg
Martin Eric Weisberg

OF COUNSEL

Raymond W. Dusch
Linda R. Giannattasio

For Complete List of Firm Personnel, See General Section

For full biographical listings, see the Martindale-Hubbell Law Directory

PILIERO GOLDSTEIN JENKINS & SULLIVAN, LLP (AV)

292 Madison Avenue, 10017
Telephone: 212-213-8200
Fax: 212-685-2028
Email: lawyers@pgjhlaw.com *URL:* http://www.pgjhlaw.com
Carlstadt, New Jersey Office: One Palmer Terrace.
Telephone: 201-507-5157.
FAX: 201-507-5221.
Washington, D.C. Office: 888 17th Street, N.W., Suite 1100.
Telephone: 202-467-6991.
FAX: 202-467-6703.
San Francisco, California Office: 507 Howard Street, Suite 200.
Telephone: 415-281-3631.
Fax: 415-281-3630.

(See Next Column)

MEMBERS OF FIRM

Kimberlee S. Bogen
Marc A. Lebowitz
Edward J. Goldstein
Robert D. Piliero
Jon Mark Jenkins
George O. Richardson, III
Michael T. Sullivan

ASSOCIATES

Craig Avedisian
Eric M. Kogan
Rosemary G. Feit
Mariano Schwed

OF COUNSEL

Kenneth D. Arbeeny
Christopher P. Hall

For full biographical listings, see the Martindale-Hubbell Law Directory

JEFFREY S. TALLACKSON (AV)

380 Lexington Avenue, Suite 1514, 10168
Telephone: 212-972-1077
Fax: 212-972-1124
Email: jtallack@ix.netcom.com *URL:* http://www.lawyers.com/banklaw

For full biographical listings, see the Martindale-Hubbell Law Directory

WATSON, FARLEY & WILLIAMS (AV)

380 Madison Avenue, 10017
Telephone: 212-922-2200
Telex: 6790626 WFWNY
Fax: 212-922-1512
Email: josborne@wfw.com *URL:* http://www.wfw.com
London, England Office: 15 Appold Street, London EC2A 2HB.
Telephone: (44 171) 814 8000.
Telex: 8955707 WFWLON G.
Fax: (44 171) 814 8141.
Paris, France Office: 47, rue de Monceau, 75008 Paris.
Telephone: (33 1) 53 83 12 12.
Telex: WFWPAR 651096 F.
Fax: (33 1) 45 61 09 01.
Athens, Greece Office: 5th Floor, Alassia Building, Defteras Merarchias 13, 185-35 Piraeus.
Telephone: (30 1) 422 3660.
Telex: 24 1311 WFWGR.
Fax: (30 1) 422 3664.
Singapore Office: 16 Collyer Quay, #12-02 Hitachi Tower, Singapore 049318.
Telephone: (65) 532-5335.
Fax: (65) 532-5454.
Moscow, Russia Office: 16/2 Tverskaya Ulitsa, Business Centre Bldg. 3, The Actor Gallery, Moscow 103009.
Telephone: 7502 237 7770 (international only); 7095 935 7770.
Fax: 7502 237 7771 (international only); 7095 935 7771.
Copenhagen, Denmark Office: Lille Kongensgade 20 DK-1074 Copenhagen K.
Telephone: (45 33) 91 33 03.
Fax: (45 33) 91 49 12.
Associated Office: Abbas F. Ghazzawi Law Firm, Saudi Arabia.

MEMBERS OF FIRM

Leo Chang
Richard L. Jarashow
John S. Osborne, Jr.
William S. Haft
Alfred E. Yudes, Jr.
Caryn Hemsworth
Philip H. Spector
Raymond J. Simon

For Complete List of Firm Personnel, See General Section

For full biographical listings, see the Martindale-Hubbell Law Directory

WINTHROP, STIMSON, PUTNAM & ROBERTS (AV)

One Battery Park Plaza, 10004-1490
Telephone: 212-858-1000
Telex: 62854 WINSTIM
Telefax: 212-858-1500
URL: http://www.winstim.com
Stamford, Connecticut Office: Financial Centre, 695 East Main Street, P.O. Box 6760, 06904-6760.
Telephone: 203-348-2300.
Fax: 203-965-8226.
Washington, D.C. Office: 1133 Connecticut Avenue, N.W., 20036.
Telephone: 202-775-9800.
Fax: 202-833-8491.
Palm Beach, Florida Office: 125 Worth Avenue, Suite 310, 33480.
Telephone: 561-655-7297.
Fax: 561-833-6726.
London Office: 54 Lombard Street, London EC3V 9DH, England.
Telephone: 011-44207-648-9200.
Fax: 011-44207-283-1656.
Tokyo, Japan Office: 608 Atagoyama Bengoshi Building 6-7, Atago 1-chome, Minato-ku, Tokyo 105 Japan.
Telephone: 011-813-3437-9740.
Fax: 011-813-3437-9261.
Hong Kong, China Office: 2505 Asia Pacific Finance Tower, Citibank Plaza, 3 Garden Road, Central.
Telephone: 011-852-2530-3400.
Fax: 011-852-2530-3355.

(See Next Column)

WINTHROP, STIMSON, PUTNAM & ROBERTS—*Continued*

Singapore Office: 6 Battery Road #38-01/B, Singapore 049909.
Telephone: 65-227-4700.
Fax: 65-227-4711.

NEW YORK OFFICE
MEMBERS OF FIRM

Takeo Akiyama
C. Payson Coleman, Jr.
Barton D. Ford
Robert W. Gray
William C. F. Kurz
F. Joseph Owens, Jr.
Michael P. Schumaecker
Leslie E. Shigaki
James R. Silkenat
Jane Wallison Stein
Charles H. Vejvoda
Robert D. Webster
Jonathan B. Whitney

COUNSEL

Glen R. Cuccinello
Ujwala Mahatme

STAMFORD OFFICE
MEMBER OF FIRM

Frode Jensen

TOKYO OFFICE
MEMBER OF FIRM

Jeffrey L. Pote

For Complete List of Firm Personnel, See General Section

For full biographical listings, see the Martindale-Hubbell Law Directory

*PLATTSBURGH,** Clinton Co.

LEWIS, ROGERS & KUDRLE, P.C. (AV)

53 Court Street, 12901-2834
Telephone: 518-561-3700
Fax: 518-561-2080
Email: lrk@westelcom.com *URL:* http://www.lawyers.com/lrklaw

Clyde A. Lewis
Mark J. Rogers
Larry A. Kudrle
Harold A. Jerry (1893-1990)
Robert A. Lyon (1924-1982)

Attorneys for: Graystone Materials, Inc.; Plattsburgh Motor Service Inc.; The Development Corporation, Clinton County, New York.

For full biographical listings, see the Martindale-Hubbell Law Directory

*POUGHKEEPSIE,** Dutchess Co.

VAN DEWATER & VAN DEWATER (AV)

40 Garden Street, P.O. Box 112, 12602
Telephone: 914-452-5900
Fax: 914-452-5848
Pawling, New York Office: 243 Route 22, P.O. Box 668.
Telephone: 914-855-5900.
Fax: 914-855-5945.

MEMBERS OF FIRM

John B. Van DeWater (1892-1968)
Robert B. Van DeWater (1920-1990)
David D. Hagstrom
John K. Gifford
James E. Nelson
Craig T. Digilio
Gerard J. Comatos
Ronald C. Blass, Jr.

OF COUNSEL

Noel deCordova, Jr.
Edward VK. Cunningham, Jr.
James D. Benson
Susanna E. Bedell

ASSOCIATES

Rebecca Supple Mensch
Michael G. Hayes

Counsel for: J. D. Johnson Co., Inc.; The Fishkill National Bank; The Bank of the Hudson; Vassar Brothers Hospital.
Local Counsel for: Vassar College; Chemprene Div. of Witco Chemical Corp.; Gannett Satellite Information Network, Inc.

For full biographical listings, see the Martindale-Hubbell Law Directory

*ROCHESTER,** Monroe Co.

FORSYTH, HOWE, O'DWYER, KALB & MURPHY, P.C. (AV)

Suite 1600, Midtown Tower, 14604
Telephone: 716-325-7515
Fax: 716-325-6407
URL: http://www.forsythhowe.com

Charles B. Forsyth (1890-1968)
C. Benn Forsyth
Gordon A. Howe, II
Duncan W. O'Dwyer
Robert J. Kalb
Gerald N. Murphy

Nancy A. Pappal

OF COUNSEL

John F. Forsyth (Retired)
Allan Wolk
Hoffman Stone
Debra A. Martin
Janice M. Iati
Cathleen W. Smith
Thad F. Sondej

References: The Chase Manhattan Bank; Fleet Bank.

For full biographical listings, see the Martindale-Hubbell Law Directory

LAWRENCE, WERNER, KESSELRING, SWARTOUT & BROWN, LLP (AV)

Formerly Suter Doyle Kesselring Lawrence & Werner
700 First Federal Plaza, 14614-1909
Telephone: 716-325-6446
Fax: 716-262-5185
Email: rochester@lwksb.com *URL:* http://www.lwksb.com
Canandaigua, New York Office: 23 Sly Street, 14424.
Telephone: 716-396-4000.
Fax: 716-396-1210. Email: canandaigua@lwksb.com.
Clifton Springs, New York: 26 East Main Street, P.O. Box 604, 14432.
Telephone: 315-462-3010.
Fax: 315-462-5039. Email: clifton_springs@lwksb.com

Paul J. Suter (1918-1989)

MEMBERS OF FIRM

Leo J. Kesselring
C. Bruce Lawrence
Christopher K. Werner
Colleen A. Brown
Steven H. Swartout
Mary Jo S. Korona

OF COUNSEL

James B. Doyle
Craig J. Doran
John F. Riley

ASSOCIATE

Jeffrey D. Graff

Representative Clients: Canandaigua National Bank; Hadlock Paint Company, Inc.; F.F. Thompson Health Systems, Inc.; Keuka College; Towns of Farmington and Gorham, NY; Toyota Motor Credit Corp.
References: Canandaigua National Bank; Fleet Bank, Rochester; National Association of Credit Manager, Rochester.

For full biographical listings, see the Martindale-Hubbell Law Directory

UNDERBERG & KESSLER LLP (AV)

1800 Chase Square, 14604
Telephone: 716-258-2800
Fax: 716-258-2821
Email: INFO@UNDERBERG-KESSLER.COM
Buffalo, New York Office: 1100 Main Place Tower. 14202.
Telephone: 716-848-9000.
Fax: 716-847-6004.

MEMBERS OF FIRM

Alan J. Underberg (1929-1998)
Irving L. Kessler
Michael J. Beyma
James A. Coniglio
Frank T. Crego
Robert W. Croessmann
John W. Crowe
Patrick L. Cusato
Michael C. Dwyer
Bernard A. Frank
Steven R. Gersz
Katherine Howk Karl
Lawrence P. Keller
Gordon J. Lipson
Anna E. Lynch
Robert F. Mechur
Paul V. Nunes
Terry M. Richman
J. David Sampson (Resident, Buffalo Office)
Sharon P. Stiller
Stephen H. Waite
Russell I. Zuckerman

OF COUNSEL

Andrew M. Greenstein

SENIOR ATTORNEYS

Duncan R. Farney
Ronald G. Hull

ASSOCIATES

James F. Armstrong (Resident, Buffalo Office)
Karen A. DiNardo
Lise C. Hamilton
Jeffrey D. Hummel
Paul F. Keneally
Ella L. Krzanowicz
Maureen E. Mulholland
Suzanne D. Nott
Kelly L. Odorisi
Thomas A. Rall

For full biographical listings, see the Martindale-Hubbell Law Directory

*STATEN ISLAND,** Richmond Co.

HALL & HALL (AV)

57 Beach Street, 10304-0002
Telephone: 718-447-1962
Telecopier: 718-273-3090

MEMBERS OF FIRM

John G. Hall
Thomas J. Hall

ASSOCIATES

John S. Wellekens
Lainie R. Fastman
Julia Hall Perednia
Richard A. Rosenzweig
Joseph G. Battaglia, Jr.
Sabina Dhillon
Kenneth A. Gonzalez
Maria L. Marchiano
Scott M. Schwartz
Kenneth T. Tiangco
Sergio J. Tuero
John Vander Neut
Laura Ciumei
Frank E. Tiernan
John R. Merlino, Jr.

(See Next Column)

HALL & HALL, *Staten Island—Continued*

OF COUNSEL

Charles J. D'Arrigo

References: Staten Island Savings Bank; Chemical Bank.

For full biographical listings, see the Martindale-Hubbell Law Directory

*SYRACUSE,** Onondaga Co.

HISCOCK & BARCLAY, LLP (AV)

Financial Plaza, P.O. Box 4878, 13221
Telephone: 315-422-2131
Fax: 315-472-3059
Email: reachus@hiscockbarclay.com *URL:* http://www.hiscockbarclay.com
Buffalo, New York Office: Suite 301 The Key Bank Towers at Key Center, 50 Fountain Plaza.
Telephone: 716-856-0911.
Fax: 716-856-2567.
Albany, New York Office: 40 Beaver Street.
Telephone: 518-434-2163.
Fax: 518-434-2621.

Frank H. Hiscock (1856-1946)

MEMBERS OF FIRM

H. Douglas Barclay
Taylor H. Obold
David B. Liddell
George S. Deptula
John P. Sindoni
Frederick S. Marty
Richard K. Hughes
J. Eric Charlton
Thomas S. Squire
Clifford H. Wilson
Robert A. Barrer
Christopher J. Bonner
Judith M. Sayles
Peter H. Swartz
John P. Langan
Catherine Keib Johnson
Richard J. Paul
Jon P. Devendorf
Richard R. Capozza

ASSOCIATES

Deborah A. Bentley
Alan R. Peterman
Kathleen M. O'Connor
Jennifer K. Frank
Matthew S. Moses
Christopher J. Centore
Jean K. Sehl
Bonnie Angela Buccina
Joseph P. McRae
Yvonne E. Marciano
Andrew J. Leja
William A. Barclay

OF COUNSEL

Donald M. Mawhinney, Jr.
Roger J. Edinger
Ferdinand L. Picardi
Jan R. Farr

General Counsel for: Syracuse Savings Bank; Key Corp; Key Bank of New York N.A. ; Solvay Bank; Excelsior Insurance Co.; Key Trust Co.; Auburn Steel Co., Inc.
Local Counsel for: Firestone Tire & Rubber Co.; Fidelity & Deposit Company of Maryland.

For full biographical listings, see the Martindale-Hubbell Law Directory

*WHITE PLAINS,** Westchester Co.

DELBELLO DONNELLAN WEINGARTEN & TARTAGLIA, LLP (AV)

One North Lexington Avenue, 10601
Telephone: 914-681-0200
Telecopier: 914-684-0288
Email: general@ddwt.com

Alfred B. DelBello
Alfred E. Donnellan (Managing Partner)
Mark P. Weingarten
Daniel D. Tartaglia
Peter J. Wise
Lee S. Wiederkehr
Patrick M. Reilly
Robert A. Korren

ASSOCIATES

William E. Dumke
Christine Moccia
Suzanne Bogdanoff
Allyse B. Dunefsky
Jerry F. Kebrdle, II
Bradley D. Wank
Ann Farrissey Carlson
Janet J. Giris

OF COUNSEL

J. David Jutkowitz
Andrew J. Balint
Robert C. Epstein

For full biographical listings, see the Martindale-Hubbell Law Directory

SERCHUK & ZELERMYER, LLP (AV)

81 Main Street, 10601
Telephone: 914-761-2100
Telecopier: 914-761-2299
Email: sz@cloud9.net
New York, New York Office: 641 Lexington Avenue.
Telephone: 212-751-7100.

MEMBERS OF FIRM

Ivan Serchuk
Benjamin Zelermyer
Jay L. Hack
Peter A. Meisels
Clifford S. Weber
Wesley Chen

(See Next Column)

ASSOCIATES

Jaine Elkind Eney
Veronica E. Rendón
Kevin P. Sweeny
Jacqueline J. Warner (Not admitted in NY)

OF COUNSEL

David M. Pollack

For full biographical listings, see the Martindale-Hubbell Law Directory

NORTH CAROLINA

*CHARLOTTE,** Mecklenburg Co.

PARHAM, HELMS, HARRIS, BLYTHE & MORTON (AV)

6310 Fairview Road, Suite 200, 28210
Telephone: 704-366-6607
Fax: 704-366-6973
Email: lmbatty@mindspring.com

MEMBERS OF FIRM

Lewis H. Parham, Jr.
Neal G. Helms
Ralph C. Harris, Jr.
Robert B. Blythe
James H. Morton

ASSOCIATE

Lyn Morton Batty

OF COUNSEL

John L. Hazlehurst

For full biographical listings, see the Martindale-Hubbell Law Directory

WOMBLE CARLYLE SANDRIDGE & RICE (AV)

A Professional Limited Liability Company
3300 One First Union Center, 301 South College Street, 28202-6025
Telephone: 704-331-4900
Fax: 704-331-4955
Email: lawyers@wcsr.com *URL:* http://www.wcsr.com
Winston-Salem, North Carolina Office: 200 West Second Street, P.O. Drawer 84.
Telephone: 336-721-3600.
Fax: 336-721-3660.
Raleigh, North Carolina Office: 2100 First Union Capitol Center, 150 Fayetteville Street Mall, P.O. Box 831.
Telephone: 919-755-2100.
Fax: 919-755-2150.
Research Triangle Park, North Carolina Office: 2505 Meridian Parkway, Suite 300 (Durham), 27713.
Telephone: 919-484-2300.
Fax: 919-484-2340.
Atlanta, Georgia Office: One Atlantic Center, 1201 West Peachtree Street, Suite 3500.
Telephone: 404-872-7000.
Fax: 404-888-7490.
Other Atlanta, Georgia Office: Suite 404, 2296 Henderson Mill Road, N.E.
Telephone: 770-492-9030.
Fax: 770-492-9609.
Washington, D.C. Office: 1120 Nineteenth Street, N.W., Eighth Floor.
Telephone: 202-857-4400.
Fax: 202-467-6910.
Greenville, South Carolina Office: 15 South Main Street, Suite 601, P.O. Box 10208.
Telephone: 864-255-5400.
Fax: 864-255-5440.

RESIDENT MEMBERS

Gary D. Chamblee
Bobby D. Hinson
Eugene M. Katz (Not admitted in NC)
William P. McMillan

Representative Clients: Childress Klein Properties, Inc.; Food Lion, Inc.; J.A. Jones Construction Co.; Parkdale Mills, Inc.; Pillowtex; Duke Power Co.; Bowles Hollowell Conner & Co.; ALLTEL Carolina, Inc.; Belk Store Services, Inc.; Philip Holzmann A.G.

For Complete List of Firm Personnel, See General Section

For full biographical listings, see the Martindale-Hubbell Law Directory

*RALEIGH,** Wake Co.

THE SANFORD HOLSHOUSER LAW FIRM PLLC (AV)

219 Fayetteville Street, Suite 1000, P.O. Box 2447, 27602
Telephone: 919-755-1800
Fax: 919-829-0272
Washington, D.C. Office: 901 15th Street, N.W., Suite 470.
Telephone: 202-371-6070.
Fax: 202-371-6279.
Pinehurst, North Carolina Office: 100 Market Square. P.O. Box 1227.
Telephone: 910-295-4250.
Fax: 910-295-2630.

(See Next Column)

THE SANFORD HOLSHOUSER LAW FIRM PLLC—*Continued*

Southern Pines, North Carolina Office: 235 E. Pennsylvania Ave. P.O. Box 1795, 28388.
Telephone: 910-693-0043.
Fax: 910-693-0045.

Terry Sanford (1917-1998)
James E. Holshouser, Jr.
Alfred P. Carlton, Jr.
Ernest C. Pearson
Samuel H. Poole
Reef C. Ivey, II
Ronald D. Raxter
Mark A. Finkelstein

OF COUNSEL

Laurie B. Gengo
Samuel W. Whitt
F. Joseph Diab
Laurence A. Cobb

Sherry E. Tucker
Daniel G. Cahill
Thomas Ashe Lockhart Jr.

For full biographical listings, see the Martindale-Hubbell Law Directory

WOMBLE CARLYLE SANDRIDGE & RICE (AV)

A Professional Limited Liability Company
2100 First Union Capitol Center, 150 Fayetteville Street Mall, P.O. Box 831, 27602
Telephone: 919-755-2100
Fax: 919-755-2150
Email: lawyers@wcsr.com *URL:* http://www.wcsr.com
Charlotte, North Carolina Office: 3300 One First Union Center, 301 South College Street.
Telephone: 704-331-4900.
Fax: 704-331-4955.
Winston-Salem, North Carolina Office: 200 West Second Street, P.O. Drawer 84.
Telephone: 336-721-3600.
Fax: 336-721-3660.
Research Triangle Park, North Carolina Office: 2505 Meridian Parkway, Suite 300 (Durham), 27713.
Telephone: 919-484-2300.
Fax: 919-484-2340.
Atlanta, Georgia Office: One Atlantic Center, 1201 West Peachtree Street, Suite 3500.
Telephone: 404-872-7000.
Fax: 404-888-7490.
Other Atlanta, Georgia Office: Suite 404, 2296 Henderson Mill Road, N.E.
Telephone: 770-492-9030.
Fax: 770-492-9609.
Washington, D.C. Office: 1120 Nineteenth Street, N.W., Eighth Floor.
Telephone: 202-857-4400.
Fax: 202-467-6910.
Greenville, South Carolina Office: 15 South Main Street, Suite 601, P.O. Box 10208.
Telephone: 864-255-5400.
Fax: 864-255-5440.

RESIDENT MEMBERS

Donald A. Donadio
William C. Matthews, Jr.
Stephen A. Yeagy

RESIDENT ASSOCIATE

Nellie Shipley Tomlinson

Representative Clients: Aetna Casualty and Surety Co., Inc.; ALSCO/AmeriMark Building Products, Inc.; Aoki Corporation America, Inc.; Hackney Brothers, Inc.; Lawyers Mutual Liability Insurance Company of North Carolina; Meredith College; Regency Park Corp.; Wachovia Bank, N.A.

For Complete List of Firm Personnel, See General Section

For full biographical listings, see the Martindale-Hubbell Law Directory

*WILMINGTON,** New Hanover Co.

KAUFMAN & GREEN, L.L.P. (AV)

Landfall Park North, 1985 Eastwood Road, Suite 200, 28403
Telephone: 910-256-5135
Fax: 910-256-6451

James J. Kaufman
Michael A. Green

Owen D. Lewis, Jr.

Representative Clients: D.G. Enterprises, Ltd.; Steven P. Braff, M.D. P.C.; Marine Motions; Southeastern Telecom, Inc.; SRS Development Inc.; T.F.S.I.; Eastern Acceptance Corp.; First State Bank of Austin; Hometown Funding, Inc.; Citizens Federal Bank.

For full biographical listings, see the Martindale-Hubbell Law Directory

*WINSTON-SALEM,** Forsyth Co.

WOMBLE CARLYLE SANDRIDGE & RICE (AV)

A Professional Limited Liability Company
200 West Second Street, P.O. Drawer 84, 27102
Telephone: 336-721-3600
Fax: 336-721-3660
Email: lawyers@wcsr.com *URL:* http://www.wcsr.com
Charlotte, North Carolina Office: 3300 One First Union Center, 301 South College Street.
Telephone: 704-331-4900.
Fax: 704-331-4955.
Raleigh, North Carolina Office: 2100 First Union Capitol Center, 150 Fayetteville Street Mall, P.O. Box 831.
Telephone: 919-755-2100.
Fax: 919-755-2150.
Research Triangle Park, North Carolina Office: 2505 Meridian Parkway, Suite 300 (Durham), 27713.
Telephone: 919-484-2300.
Fax: 919-484-2340.
Atlanta, Georgia Office: One Atlantic Center, 1201 West Peachtree Street, Suite 3500.
Telephone: 404-872-7000.
Fax: 404-888-7490.
Other Atlanta, Georgia Office: Suite 404, 2296 Henderson Mill Road, N.E.
Telephone: 770-492-9030.
Fax: 770-492-9609.
Washington, D.C. Office: 1120 Nineteenth Street, N.W., Eighth Floor.
Telephone: 202-857-4400.
Fax: 202-467-6910.
Greenville, South Carolina Office: 15 South Main Street, Suite 601, P.O. Box 10208.
Telephone: 864-255-5400.
Fax: 864-255-5440.

RESIDENT MEMBERS

Leslie E. Browder
Hardin G. Halsey
Christopher E. Leon
Kim Kelly Mann
Dennis W. McNames
Kenneth A. Moser
Robert L. Quick
W. P. Sandridge, Jr.

RESIDENT ASSOCIATE

F. Scott Thomas

Representative Clients: Brad Ragan, Inc.; Brenner Companies; Food Lion, Inc.; Hanes Companies, Inc.; North Carolina Baptist Hospitals, Inc.; R.J. Reynolds Tobacco Co.; Thomasville Furniture Industries, Inc.; Wachovia Corp.; Wake Forest University.

For Complete List of Firm Personnel, See General Section

For full biographical listings, see the Martindale-Hubbell Law Directory

NORTH DAKOTA

*FARGO,** Cass Co.

CONMY, FESTE, HUBBARD, CORWIN & BRUST, LTD. (AV)

200 Norwest Center, 406 Main Avenue, 58126
Telephone: 701-293-9911
Fax: 701-293-3133
URL: http://www.conmylaw.com

Charles A. Feste
Paul M. Hubbard
Wickham Corwin
Kim E. Brust
Michael M. Thomas
Robert J. Schultz
Nancy J. Morris

OF COUNSEL

Lauris N. Molbert
E. T. Conmy, Jr.

Representative Clients: Ford Motor Credit Co.; Norwest Bank, North Dakota, N.A.; Norwest Bank Minnesota West, N.A.; Wells Fargo Bank, N.A.; Bremer Bank, N.A.; Community First Bank, N.A.

For full biographical listings, see the Martindale-Hubbell Law Directory

NILLES, HANSEN & DAVIES, LTD. (AV)

1800 Radisson Tower, P.O. Box 2626, 58108
Telephone: 701-237-5544
Facsimile: 701-280-0762
Williston, North Dakota Office: Energy Resource Building, 504 East Broadway, Suite 101, P.O. Box 1525.
Telephone: 701-572-5544.
Fax: 701-572-5561.

Timothy Q. Davies
Robert L. Stroup, II
Gregory B. Selbo
Andrew L. B. Noah

Representative Clients: U.S. Bank National Association.

For Complete List of Firm Personnel, See General Section

For full biographical listings, see the Martindale-Hubbell Law Directory

Fargo—Continued

VOGEL, WEIR, BYE, HUNKE & MCCORMICK, LTD. (AV)

502 First Avenue North, P.O. Box 1389, 58107
Telephone: 701-237-6983
Facsimile: 701-237-0847
Email: vogellaw@vogellaw.com *URL:* http://www.vogellaw.com

H. Patrick Weir
Kermit Edward Bye
Jon R. Brakke

Representative Clients: Community First National Bank of Fargo; Ramsey National Bank & Trust Co.; Northern Capital Management Co.; Farmers & Merchants Bank of Valley City; First Trust Company of North Dakota; First International Bank & Trust, Fargo; Bremer Financial Corporation; Agri Bank, FCB; AG Services of America, Inc.

For Complete List of Firm Personnel, See General Section

For full biographical listings, see the Martindale-Hubbell Law Directory

OHIO

*CINCINNATI,** Hamilton Co.

FROST & JACOBS LLP (AV)

2500 PNC Center, 201 East Fifth Street, 45202
Telephone: 513-651-6800
Telecopier: 513-651-6981
URL: http://www.frojac.com
Columbus, Ohio Office: One Columbus, 10 West Broad Street, 43215.
Telephone: 614-464-1211.
Telecopier: 614-464-1737.
Lexington, Kentucky Office: 1100 Vine Center Tower, 333 West Vine Street, 40507.
Telephone: 606-254-1100.
Telecopier: 606-253-2990.
Middletown, Ohio Office: 400 First National Bank Building, 2 North Main Street, 45042.
Telephone: 513-422-2001.
Telecopier: 513-422-3010.
Frankfort, Kentucky Office: 201 W. Main Street, 40601.
Telephone: 502-223-1400.
Telecopier: 502-223-1410.

MEMBERS OF FIRM

Edmund J. Adams
Richard J. Erickson
Jeffery R. Rush
E. Richard Oberschmidt
P. Reid Lemasters
Frederick W. Kindel
John C. Krug
Ronald E. Gold
Douglas S. Tripp
David S. Bence

ASSOCIATES

Bryan S. Blade
Douglas L. Lutz
Sandra L. Nunn
Michael J. O'Grady
Christina M. Sprecher
Rita M. Stolper
Colleen M. Haas
Jan R. Wenning
Suzanne Wentzel

OF COUNSEL

Kimberly K. Mauer
Mary Ann Schenk

COLUMBUS, OHIO OFFICE
MEMBER OF FIRM

John I. Cadwallader

COLUMBUS, OHIO OFFICE
ASSOCIATE

Cara E. Gunder

LEXINGTON, KENTUCKY OFFICE
MEMBER OF FIRM

Greg E. Mitchell

MIDDLETOWN, OHIO OFFICE
MEMBER OF FIRM

Thomas A. Swope

MIDDLETOWN, OHIO OFFICE
SENIOR ATTORNEY

Daniel J. Picard

Representative Clients: Bank One, N.A.; Cincinnati Bell, Inc.; Cincinnati Machine; Federated Department Stores; Firstar, National Association; First National Bank of Southwestern Ohio; KeyBank, National Association; PNC Bank, National Association; Turner Construction Co.

For Complete List of Firm Personnel, See General Section

For full biographical listings, see the Martindale-Hubbell Law Directory

KATZ, TELLER, BRANT & HILD A LEGAL PROFESSIONAL ASSOCIATION (AV)

2400 Chemed Center, 255 East Fifth Street, 45202-4724
Telephone: 513-721-4532
Telecopier: 513-721-7120
Email: corp@ktbh.com

Andrew R. Berger
John R. Gierl

For Complete List of Firm Personnel, See General Section

For full biographical listings, see the Martindale-Hubbell Law Directory

KEATING, MUETHING & KLEKAMP, P.L.L. (AV)

1400 Provident Tower, One East Fourth Street, 45202
Telephone: 513-579-6400
Facsimile: 513-579-6457
URL: http://www.kmklaw.com

MEMBERS OF FIRM

Richard D. Siegel
James R. Whitaker
J. David Rosenberg
James M. Jansing
James R. Matthews
Michael F. Bigler

Representative Clients: American Financial Group; BP America Inc.; Chiquita Brands International, Inc.; Cintas Corporation; Comair Holdings, Inc.; Duke Realty Limited Partnership; LSI Industries Inc.; Mosler Inc.; Provident Financial Group Inc.

For Complete List of Firm Personnel, See General Section

For full biographical listings, see the Martindale-Hubbell Law Directory

MASON, SLOVIN & SCHILLING CO., L.P.A. (AV)

11340 Montgomery Road, Suite 210, 45249-2313
Telephone: 513-489-0829
800-840-3514
Fax: 513-489-0834
Email: msscolpa@worldnet.att.net
Covington, Kentucky Office: Heritage International, Suite 203, P.O. Box 2158.
Telephone: 513-489-0829.
Fax: 513-489-0834.
Columbus Office: 10 West Broad Street, Suite 2400 One Columbus.
Telephone: 513-489-0829.
Fax: 513-489-0834.
Dayton Office: 319 Liberty Tower.
Telephone: 513-489-0829.
Fax: 513-489-0834.
Lima Office: 809 West Vine Street, P.O. Box 937.
Telephone: 513-489-0829.
Fax: 513-489-0834.

Jonathan A. Mason
Randy T. Slovin
Richard D. Schilling

David C. Nalley
Joseph Ruwe

OF COUNSEL

Fred H. Summe (Not admitted in OH; Resident, Covington, KY Office)
Richard L. Levine

LEGAL SUPPORT PERSONNEL

Brenda L. Norton (Office Manager and Executive Legal Secretary)
Lisa K. Spencer (Sr. Case Manager; Accounting Manager)
Amy J. Luipold (Sr. Case Manager; Recovery Manager)
William M. Luipold (Manager, Court Administration)
Marilyn E. Mason (Sr. Legal Assistant-Accounting)
Jeremy R. Mason (Sr. Law Clerk)
Rachel J. Mason (Law Clerk)
Sarah Hopkins (Legal Assistant-Recovery)
Becky Grandstaff (Legal Assistant-Claims & Billing)
Connie Shutt (Legal Assistant-Litigation)

For full biographical listings, see the Martindale-Hubbell Law Directory

*CLEVELAND,** Cuyahoga Co.

BAKER & HOSTETLER LLP (AV)

3200 National City Center, 1900 East Ninth Street, 44114-3485
Telephone: 216-621-0200
Telecopier: 216-696-0740
TWX: 810 421 8375
RCA Telex: 215032
To contact an attorney on the Internet use first initial and surname followed by @baker-hostetler.com
URL: http://www.bakerlaw.com
In Cincinnati, Ohio: 312 Walnut Street, Suite 2650.
Telephone: 513-929-3400.
In Columbus, Ohio: Capitol Square, Suite 2100, 65 East State Street.
Telephone: 614-228-1541.
In Denver, Colorado: 303 East 17th Avenue, Suite 1100.
Telephone: 303-861-0600.

(See Next Column)

BAKER & HOSTETLER LLP—*Continued*

In Houston, Texas: 1000 Louisiana, Suite 2000.
Telephone: 713-751-1600.
In Beverly Hills, California: 9150 Wilshire Boulevard, Suite 205.
Telephone: 310-385-7500.
In Long Beach, California: 300 Oceangate, Suite 620.
Telephone: 562-432-2827.
In Los Angeles, California: 600 Wilshire Boulevard.
Telephone: 213-624-2400.
In Orlando, Florida: SunBank Center, Suite 2300, 200 South Orange Avenue.
Telephone: 407-649-4000.
In Washington, D.C.: Washington Square, Suite 1100, 1050 Connecticut Avenue, N.W.
Telephone: 202-861-1500.

PARTNERS

Albert T. Adams
Richard R. Hollington, Jr.
Norman S. Jeavons

OF COUNSEL

Theodore W. Jones

For Complete List of Firm Personnel, See General Section

For full biographical listings, see the Martindale-Hubbell Law Directory

*COLUMBUS,** Franklin Co.

DREHER LANGER & TOMKIES L.L.P. (AV)

2250 Huntington Center, 41 South High Street, 43215
Telephone: 614-628-8000
Facsimile: 614-628-1600
Email: manager@dltlaw.com
Mandeville, Louisiana Office: #1 Sanctuary Boulevard, Suite 303, 70471.
Telephone: 504-727-1664.
Facsimile: 504-727-4388.

MEMBERS OF FIRM

Darrell L. Dreher
Jeffrey I. Langer
Michael C. Tomkies

ASSOCIATES

Elizabeth L. Anstaett
Lisa Kozakowski (Not admitted in OH)
Mary W. Morgan
Judith M. Scheiderer
Jean M. Schwendeman
Margaret M. Stolar

OF COUNSEL

Robin Ronquillo De Leo (Resident, Mandeville, Louisiana Office)
John F. Wyka (Resident, Mandeville, Louisiana Office)

Representative Clients: American Express Company; Associates First Capital Corporation; Banc One Corporation; BankAmerica Corp.; The Chase Manhattan Corporation; Chevron Corporation; General Electric Capital Corporation; Morgan Stanley Dean Witter & Co.; Sears, Roebuck & Co.; Transamerica Corporation.

For full biographical listings, see the Martindale-Hubbell Law Directory

KEGLER, BROWN, HILL & RITTER (AV)

Capitol Square Suite 1800, 65 East State Street, 43215-4294
Telephone: 614-462-5400
Telecopier: 614-464-2634
Cable Address: "Law KBHR"
Telex: 246671
Email: info@kbhr.com *URL:* http://www.kbhr.com
Marion, Ohio Office: 250 Executive Drive, Suite B, P.O. Box 919.
Telephone: 614-387-3501.
Facsimile: 614-387-3630.

Allen L. Handlan
Larry J. McClatchey
Kevin L. Sykes

COUNSEL

John C. Deal

Representative Clients: First Federal Savings and Loan of Galion; National City Bank.

For Complete List of Firm Personnel, See General Section

For full biographical listings, see the Martindale-Hubbell Law Directory

PORTER WRIGHT MORRIS & ARTHUR LLP (AV)

41 South High Street, 43215-6194
Telephone: 614-227-2000; (800-533-2794)
Fax: 614-227-2100
Email: cmh@porterwright.com *URL:* http://www.porterwright.com
Cincinnati, Ohio Office: 250 E. Fifth Street, Suite 2200, 45202-4199.
Telephones: 513-381-4700; (800-582-5813).
Fax: 513-421-0991. Internet: cvg@porterwright.com.
Cleveland, Ohio Office: 925 Euclid Avenue, Suite 1700, 44115-1483.
Telephones: 216-443-9000; (800-824-1980).
Fax: 216-443-9011. Internet: cle@porterwright.com.

(See Next Column)

Dayton, Ohio Office: One Dayton Centre, One South Main Street, Suite 1600, 45402-2028.
Telephones: 937-449-6810; (800-533-4434).
Fax: 937-449-6820. Internet: day@porterwright.com.
Naples, Florida Office: 5801 Pelican Bay Boulevard, Suite 300, 34108-2709.
Telephones: 941-593-2900; (800-876-7962).
Fax: 941-593-2990. Internet: apf@porterwright.com.
Washington, D.C. Office: 1667 K Street, N.W., Suite 1100, 20006-1605.
Telephones: 202-778-3000; (800-456-7962).
Fax: 202-778-3063. Internet: dca@porterwright.com.

MEMBERS OF FIRM
COLUMBUS, OHIO OFFICE

James P. Botti
John E. Brady
S. Ronald Cook, Jr.
Robert E. Fultz
Timothy E. Grady
Polly J. Harris
John C. Hartranft
Donald W. Jordan
Robert C. Kiger
Jennifer T. Mills
Jack R. Pigman
James H. Prior
John B. Rohyans
H. Grant Stephenson
Nancy B. Young

ASSOCIATE
COLUMBUS, OHIO OFFICE

Bradley K. Baker

OF COUNSEL
COLUMBUS, OHIO OFFICE

Norman T. Smith

DAYTON, OHIO OFFICE
RESIDENT MEMBERS

William G. Deas
Walter Reynolds

DAYTON, OHIO OFFICE
RESIDENT ASSOCIATE

N. Robert Goad, Jr.

DAYTON, OHIO OFFICE
RESIDENT OF COUNSEL

Roland F. Eichner
Chester E. Finn
Jeffrey W. Morris

CINCINNATI, OHIO OFFICE
RESIDENT ASSOCIATE

Darryl Mitchell

CLEVELAND, OHIO OFFICE
RESIDENT MEMBERS

Jeffrey Baddeley
Donald J. Fisher
Philip E. Langer

CLEVELAND, OHIO OFFICE
RESIDENT ASSOCIATE

Aimee M. Greenfield

NAPLES, FLORIDA OFFICE
MEMBERS

W. Jeffrey Cecil
Jeffrey S. Kannensohn
Gary K. Wilson

For Complete List of Firm Personnel, See General Section

For full biographical listings, see the Martindale-Hubbell Law Directory

SCHOTTENSTEIN, ZOX & DUNN A LEGAL PROFESSIONAL ASSOCIATION (AV)

The Huntington Center, 41 South High Street, 43215
Telephone: 614-462-2700
Telecopier: 614-462-5135
Telex: 650 24 444 365
URL: http://www.szd.com
Cincinnati, Ohio Office: Bank One Towers, 8044 Montgomery Road, Suite 700, 45236-2926.
Telephone: 513-792-2730.
Cleveland, Ohio Office: One Cleveland Center, 1375 East 9th Street, Suite 950.
Telephone: 216-621-6501.
Fax: 216-621-6502.

Jay R. Dingledy
Herbert R. Godby
Richard A. Barnhart
William F. Simpson
John D. Robinett
Victoria E. Powers
Joanne I. Goldhand

Darrel R. Davison
Marie A. Malloy

Reference: Bank One of Columbus, N.A.

For Complete List of Firm Personnel, See General Section

For full biographical listings, see the Martindale-Hubbell Law Directory

Columbus—Continued

Vorys, Sater, Seymour and Pease LLP (AV)

52 East Gay Street, P.O. Box 1008, 43216-1008
Telephone: 614-464-6400
Telecopier: 614-464-6350
URL: http://www.vssp.com
Washington, D.C. Office: 1828 L Street, N.W., 20036-5109.
Telephone: 202-467-8800.
Telex: 440693.
Telecopier: 202-467-8900.
Cleveland, Ohio Office: 2100 One Cleveland Center, 1375 East Ninth Street, 44114-1724.
Telephone: 216-479-6100.
Telecopier: 216-479-6060.
Cincinnati, Ohio Office: Suite 2100, 221 East Fourth Street, P.O. Box 0236, 45201-0236.
Telephone: 513-723-4000.
Telecopier: 513-723-4056.
Alexandria, Virginia Office: 277 South Washington St., Suite 310, 22314.
Telephone: 703-549-4282.
Telecopier: 703-549-4492.

MEMBERS OF FIRM

Robert W. Werth
James H. Gross
Charles S. DeRousie
James M. Ball
Roger E. Lautzenhiser
Reginald W. Jackson
Elizabeth Turrell Farrar

Representative Client: Bank One State Savings Bank.
Local Counsel: Abbott Laboratories; Anheuser-Busch, Inc.; General Motors Corp.; Household Finance Corporation; National City Corp.; Navistar International Trans.; Ohio Manufacturers' Assn.; Ranco Inc.; Wendy's International, Inc.

For Complete List of Firm Personnel, See General Section

For full biographical listings, see the Martindale-Hubbell Law Directory

*DAYTON,** Montgomery Co.

Conway & Hall A Legal Professional Association (AV)

900 Courthouse Plaza Southwest, 45402
Telephone: 937-228-1111
Facsimile: 937-228-9340
URL: http://www.lawyers.com/conwayhall

Dennis L. Hall
W. Michael Conway

Carolyn L. Mueller

OF COUNSEL

C. Robert Swaninger

For full biographical listings, see the Martindale-Hubbell Law Directory

DUBLIN, Franklin Co.

Blaugrund, Herbert & Martin, Incorporated (AV)

5455 Rings Road, Suite 500, 43017-7517
Telephone: 614-764-0681
Fax: 614-764-0774
Email: bhm@bhmlaw.net

Lawrence H. Cohen
Teri G. Rasmussen

For full biographical listings, see the Martindale-Hubbell Law Directory

*TOLEDO,** Lucas Co.

Eastman & Smith Ltd. (AV)

One Seagate, Twenty-Fourth Floor, P.O. Box 10032, 43699-0032
Telephone: 419-241-6000
Telecopier: 419-247-1777
Columbus, Ohio Office: 65 East State Street, Suite 1000, 43215.
Telephone: 614-460-3556.
Telecopier: 614-228-5371.

MEMBERS OF FIRM

Henry N. Heuerman
Kenneth C. Baker
Steven D. Reinbolt
James L. Rogers

ASSOCIATES

Michael W. Regnier
M. Charles Collins

Representative Clients: The Huntington National Bank; Capital Bank, N.A.; Mid-American National Bank and Trust Co.

For Complete List of Firm Personnel, See General Section

For full biographical listings, see the Martindale-Hubbell Law Directory

OKLAHOMA

*NORMAN,** Cleveland Co.

Crowe & Dunlevy (AV)

A Professional Corporation
2500 South McGee, Suite 140, 73072-6705
Telephone: 405-321-7317
Fax: 405-360-4002
Email: marketing@crowedunlevy.com *URL:* http://www.crowedunlevy.com
Oklahoma City, Oklahoma Office: Crowe & Dunlevy, A Professional Corporation, 1800 Mid-America Tower, 20 North Broadway, 73102-8273.
Telephone: 405-235-7700.
Fax: 405-239-6651.
Tulsa, Oklahoma Office: Crowe & Dunlevy, A Professional Corporation, 500 Kennedy Building, 321 South Boston Avenue, 74103-3313.
Telephone: 918-592-9800.
Fax: 918-592-9801.

Gary C. Rawlinson

Christopher R. Graves

For Complete List of Firm Personnel, See General Section

For full biographical listings, see the Martindale-Hubbell Law Directory

*OKLAHOMA CITY,** Oklahoma Co.

Andrews Davis Legg Bixler Milsten & Price, A Professional Corporation (AV)

500 West Main, Suite 500, 73102
Telephone: 405-272-9241
FAX: 405-235-8786
Email: andrewsdavis@andrewsdavis.com *URL:* http://www.andrewsdavis.com

Charles C. Callaway, Jr.
Alan C. Durbin
John D. Hastie

OF COUNSEL

John P. Roberts

For Complete List of Firm Personnel, See General Section

For full biographical listings, see the Martindale-Hubbell Law Directory

Britton, Gray and Hill, P.C. (AV)

700 Bank of Oklahoma Plaza, 201 Robert S. Kerr, 73102
Telephone: 405-239-2393
Fax: 405-232-5135

James E. Britton
Jackie L. Hill, Jr.

Stephen A. Kepner, Jr.

Representative Clients: BancFirst; Union Bank & Trust Company; Community Action Agency of Oklahoma City and Oklahoma/Canadian Counties, Inc.; NationsBank; Poteau State Bank; Tri Star National Bank; American National Bank of Shawnee; Farmers State Bank, Quinton, Oklahoma; Will Rogers Bank; Tower Tech, Inc.

For full biographical listings, see the Martindale-Hubbell Law Directory

Crowe & Dunlevy, A Professional Corporation (AV)

1800 Mid-America Tower, 20 North Broadway, 73102-8273
Telephone: 405-235-7700
Fax: 405-239-6651
Email: marketing@crowedunlevy.com *URL:* http://www.crowedunlevy.com
Tulsa, Oklahoma Office: 500 Kennedy Building, 321 South Boston Avenue, 74103-3313.
Telephone: 918-592-9800.
Fax: 918-592-9801.
Norman, Oklahoma Office: Crowe & Dunlevy, 2500 South McGee, Suite 140, 73072-6705.
Telephone: 405-321-7317.
Fax: 405-360-4002.

Robert M. Johnson
Harry A. Woods, Jr.
James H. Holloman, Jr.
Michael M. Stewart
Kenni B. Merritt
Michael S. Laird
Reeder E. Ratliff
Roger A. Stong
Robert G. McCampbell

J. Robert Kalsu

For Complete List of Firm Personnel, See General Section

For full biographical listings, see the Martindale-Hubbell Law Directory

Oklahoma City—Continued

DAY, EDWARDS, FEDERMAN, PROPESTER & CHRISTENSEN, P.C. (AV)

Suite 2900 Oklahoma Tower, 210 Park Avenue, 73102-5605
Telephone: 405-239-2121
Telecopier: 405-236-1012
URL: http://lawlinks.com/attys/ok/defpc.html

Joe E. Edwards
Richard P. Propester
J. Clay Christensen
Kent A. Gilliland

Ricki Valerie Sonders
Thomas Pitchlynn Howell, IV
Joel Warren Harmon

Representative Clients: BancFirst; Bank One, Oklahoma City; Bank of America, N.A.; Federal Deposit Insurance Corp.; First Community Bank, Binger; First National Bank and Trust Company of Weatherford; First State Bank & Trust Co., Hollis; Local Oklahoma Bank.

For Complete List of Firm Personnel, See General Section

For full biographical listings, see the Martindale-Hubbell Law Directory

HARTZOG CONGER & CASON, A PROFESSIONAL CORPORATION (AV)

1600 Bank of Oklahoma Plaza 201 Robert S. Kerr, 73102
Telephone: 405-235-7000
Facsimile: 405-235-7329

Larry D. Hartzog
Laura Haag McConnell
J. William Conger
Linda G. Scoggins
Len Cason
Susan B. Shields
James C. Prince
Ryan S. Wilson
Steven C. Davis
Amy J. Sine
Joseph P. Hogsett
Jon H. Trudgeon
John D. Robertson
Charles E. Geister, III
Kurt M. Rupert
Phillip G. Whaley
Armand Paliotta

J. Christian Guzzy
Melissa Beeson Heindselman
Stacey D. Spivey
Christin V. Adkins
Byron K. Linkous

OF COUNSEL

Kent F. Frates
Kenneth R. Davis
Alan Newman

For full biographical listings, see the Martindale-Hubbell Law Directory

PRINGLE & PRINGLE, A PROFESSIONAL CORPORATION (AV)

4101 North Classen Boulevard Suite A, 73118-2432
Telephone: 405-848-4810
Fax: 405-848-4819
Email: pringle@pringleandpringle.com *URL:* http://www.pringleandpringle.com

Lynn A. Pringle
Laura Nan Smith Pringle
Conni L. Allen

OF COUNSEL

Alvin C. Harrell
Michael P. Sullivan

Representative Clients: Bankers Systems, Inc.; Bank of Western Oklahoma, Elk City; The First National Bank and Trust Co., Chickasha; The Farmers Bank, Carnegie; Bank of the Panhandle, Guymon; FirstPlus Financial; Citizens State Bank, Roma, Texas; The Daniluk Corporation; Bank of Union; Pringle Publications Corporation.

For full biographical listings, see the Martindale-Hubbell Law Directory

SELF, GIDDENS & LEES, INC. (AV)

2725 Oklahoma Tower, 210 Park Avenue, 73102-5643
Telephone: 405-232-3001
Telecopier: 405-232-5553

Thomas J. Blalock
C. Ray Lees
Jared D. Giddens
Shannon T. Self
Bryan J. Wells

Michael D. Meleen
John E. Gatliff II

For full biographical listings, see the Martindale-Hubbell Law Directory

*TULSA,** Tulsa Co.

BOESCHE, MCDERMOTT & ESKRIDGE (AV)

Suite 800 Oneok Plaza, 100 West Fifth Street, 74103
Telephone: 918-583-1777
Fax: 918-592-5809
Email: bme@intellex.com
Muskogee, Oklahoma Office: 1111 West Broadway, P.O. Box 2669, 74402.
Telephone: 918-683-6100.
Fax: 918-683-2303.

(See Next Column)

MEMBERS OF FIRM

R. Casey Cooper
Bradley K. Beasley
David B. McKinney
David A. Johnson
Sheila M. Powers

OF COUNSEL

Clifford K. Cate, Jr. (Resident at Muskogee)

Representative Clients: Bank of America; The Chase Manhattan Bank; Community Bank & Trust Co.; Federal Deposit Insurance Corp.; Resolution Trust Corp.; Superior Federal Bank; Union Bank, formerly Security Pacific National Bank; Vian State Bank.

For Complete List of Firm Personnel, See General Section

For full biographical listings, see the Martindale-Hubbell Law Directory

CROWE & DUNLEVY, A PROFESSIONAL CORPORATION (AV)

500 Kennedy Building, 321 South Boston Avenue, 74103-3313
Telephone: 918-592-9800
Fax: 918-592-9801
Email: marketing@crowedunlevy.com *URL:* http://www.crowedunlevy.com
Oklahoma City, Oklahoma Office: 1800 Mid-America Tower, 20 North Broadway, 73102-8273.
Telephone: 405-235-7700.
Fax: 405-239-6651.
Norman, Oklahoma Office: Crowe & Dunlevy, 2500 South McGee, Suite 140, 73072-6705.
Telephone: 405-321-7317.
Fax: 405-360-4002.

Lon Foster, III
Gary L. Betow
Gary R. McSpadden
Malcolm E. Rosser IV
Gary C. Clark
J. Bradford Hammond
W. Kyle Tresch

Terry J. Tarwater

For Complete List of Firm Personnel, See General Section

For full biographical listings, see the Martindale-Hubbell Law Directory

FREDERIC DORWART (AV)

Old City Hall, 124 East Fourth Street, 74103-5010
Telephone: 918-583-9922
Fax: 918-583-8251
Email: fdorwart@fdlaw.kfoc.net

J. Michael Medina
Matthew James Browne, III
Richard J. Cipolla, Jr.
Paul DeMuro
Tamara R. Wagman

OF COUNSEL

John D. Clayman

Representative Clients: BOK Financial Corp.; Bank of Oklahoma, N.A.; Bank of Texas, N.A.; Bank of Albuquerque, N.A.; Kaiser-Francis Oil Co.; The Williford Companies; Williford Energy Co.; Williford Building Corp.; Safety Training Systems, Inc.; Sooner Southwest Bancshares, Inc.

For full biographical listings, see the Martindale-Hubbell Law Directory

SNEED LANG, P.C. (AV)

2300 Williams Center Tower II, Two West Second Street, 74103
Telephone: 918-583-3145
Telecopier: 918-582-0410

James C. Lang
Robbie Emery Burke
D. Faith Orlowski
Patrick O. Waddel
Brian S. Gaskill
Randolph P. Stainer
G. Steven Stidham
Steven K. Balman
Stephen R. McNamara
Brian T. Inbody
Thomas E. Black, Jr.
D. Michael McBride III

OF COUNSEL

James L. Sneed

Representative Clients: Amoco Production Co.; Bank One, Texas; Enron Corp.; Halliburton Energy Services; Helmerich & Payne, Inc.; Shell Oil Co.; State Farm Mutual Automobile Insurance Co.; The Williams Companies.

For full biographical listings, see the Martindale-Hubbell Law Directory

OREGON

*PORTLAND,** Multnomah Co.

BLACK HELTERLINE LLP (AV)

1200 Union Bank of California Tower, 707 S.W. Washington Street, 97205
Telephone: 503-224-5560
Telecopier: 503-224-6148
URL: http://www.bhlaw.com

MEMBERS OF FIRM

Ronald T. Adams
Donald L. Krahmer, Jr.
John M. McGuigan
Michael O. Moran
David P. Roy

ASSOCIATES

Joshua M. Barrett
James R. George

Representative Clients: Union Bank of California, N.A.; Bank of Tokyo-Mitsubishi; Royal Bank of Canada.

For Complete List of Firm Personnel, See General Section

For full biographical listings, see the Martindale-Hubbell Law Directory

PENNSYLVANIA

*HARRISBURG,** Dauphin Co.

METTE, EVANS & WOODSIDE, A PROFESSIONAL CORPORATION (AV)

3401 North Front Street, P.O. Box 5950, 17110-0950
Telephone: 717-232-5000
Fax: 717-236-1816
Email: MEW@Mette.com *URL:* HTTP://WWW.METTE.COM

Howell C. Mette
Peter J. Ressler
Lloyd R. Persun
James A. Ulsh
Elyse E. Rogers
Jeffrey A. Ernico
Thomas F. Smida

Bradley A. Walker
Donna L. Gareis-Smith

For Complete List of Firm Personnel, See General Section

For full biographical listings, see the Martindale-Hubbell Law Directory

RHOADS & SINON LLP (AV)

One South Market Square, 12th Floor, P.O. Box 1146, 17108-1146
Telephone: 717-233-5731
Fax: 717-232-1459
Boca Raton, Florida Affiliated Office: Charles L. Sieck, 1700 South Dixie Highway, Suite 2-C.
Telephone: 561-395-5595.
Fax: 561-395-9497.
York, Pennsylvania Office: 15 North Cherry Lane, Suite 21.
Telephone: 717-843-1718.
Fax: 717-232-1459.

MEMBERS OF FIRM

Henry W. Rhoads
Sherill T. Moyer
J. Bruce Walter
Charles J. Ferry
Stanley A. Smith
Drake D. Nicholas
Dean H. Dusinberre
Donna M. J. Clark
Paul F. Wessell

For Complete List of Firm Personnel, See General Section

For full biographical listings, see the Martindale-Hubbell Law Directory

*PHILADELPHIA,** Philadelphia Co.

BALLARD SPAHR ANDREWS & INGERSOLL, LLP (AV)

1735 Market Street, 51st Floor, 19103-7599
Telephone: 215-665-8500
Fax: 215-864-8999
URL: http://www.ballardspahr.com
Baltimore, Maryland Office: 300 East Lombard Street, 19th Floor.
Telephone: 410-528-5600.
Fax: 410-528-5650.
Camden, New Jersey Office: 800 Hudson Square, 5th Floor.
Telephone: 856-541-5577.
Fax: 856-541-8272.
Denver, Colorado Office: Seventeenth Street Plaza Building, Suite 2300, 1225 17th Street.
Telephone: 303-292-2400.
Fax: 303-296-3956.

(See Next Column)

Salt Lake City, Utah Office: One Utah Center, Suite 1200, 201 South Main Street.
Telephone: 801-531-3000.
Fax: 801-531-3001.
Voorhees, New Jersey Office: Suite 100, 1101 Laurel Oak Drive.
Telephone: 856-627-8555.
Fax: 856-627-1153.
Washington, D.C. Office: Suite 1000 South, 601 13th Street, N.W.
Telephone: 202-661-2200.
Fax: 202-661-2299.

E. Carolan Berkley
Brian D. Doerner
Martha J. Hays
Richard S. Perelman
John L. Culhane, Jr.
Carl H. Fridy
Alan S. Kaplinsky
Jeremy T. Rosenblum
Edward D. Slevin

For Complete List of Firm Personnel, See General Section

For full biographical listings, see the Martindale-Hubbell Law Directory

SILVERMAN FRIMMER BERNHEIM & McDONNELL, A PROFESSIONAL CORPORATION (AV)

Two Penn Center Plaza, Suite 910, 19102
Telephone: 215-569-0000
Fax: 215-636-3999
Email: lawyers@scf-law.com *URL:* http://www.scf-law.com
Westmont, New Jersey Office: Sentry Office Plaza, Suite 704. 216 Haddon Avenue, 08108-2815.
Telephone: 609-858-9499.
Fax: 609-858-4606.

Rick L. Frimmer
Daniel S. Bernheim, 3rd

Jonathan J. Bart
David J. Gaier

OF COUNSEL

Jonathan Saidel

Representative Clients: First Union National Bank; National City Bank; Mellon Bank, N.A.; PNC Bank, National Association; Legg Mason Wood Walker, Incorporated; Independence Blue Cross.

For full biographical listings, see the Martindale-Hubbell Law Directory

WEIR & PARTNERS LLP (AV)

A Pennsylvania Limited Liability Partnership
Suite 500, The Widener Building, 1339 Chestnut Street, 19107
Telephone: 215-665-8181
Telefax: 215-665-8464
Email: info@weirpartners.com
Turnersville, New Jersey Office: 215 Fries Mill Road, 08012.
Telephone: 609-740-1490.
Telefax: 609-740-1491.

MEMBERS OF FIRM

Walter Weir, Jr.
Leonard S. Goodman
Susan Verbonitz
Jeffrey L. Rudnick
Robert D. Sayre
Stephen M. Giroux
Richard P. Coe, Jr.
Brett A. Datto
John B. York
Joseph C. Hare

ASSOCIATES

Bonnie R. Golub
Debra N. Nathanson
Tina L. Colman
Andrew K. Stutzman
Jeffrey A. Guth
Jason M Reiser
Madeline Flanagan

For full biographical listings, see the Martindale-Hubbell Law Directory

*PITTSBURGH,** Allegheny Co.

PLOWMAN, SPIEGEL & LEWIS, P.C. (AV)

Second Floor, The Grant Building, 310 Grant Street, 15219-2201
Telephone: 412-471-8521
Fax: 412-471-4481

Jack W. Plowman
John L. Spiegel
James A. Lewis

Mark A. Griffith
Charles B. Jarrett, Jr.
J. Michael McCague, Jr.

Reference: Pittsburgh National Bank.

For Complete List of Firm Personnel, See General Section

For full biographical listings, see the Martindale-Hubbell Law Directory

YUKEVICH, MARCHETTI, LIEKAR & ZANGRILLI, P.C. (AV)

Sixth Floor, One Gateway Center, 15222-1424
Telephone: 412-261-6777
Fax: 412-261-6789
URL: http://www.ymlz.com

(See Next Column)

YUKEVICH, MARCHETTI, LIEKAR & ZANGRILLI P.C.—*Continued*

Michael Yukevich, Jr.
Christopher J. Marchetti
John P. Liekar, Jr.
Albert J. Zangrilli, Jr.
Mark Fischer
Michael I. Frachioni
Lori Nolan Lindey
Keith J. Rothfus

For full biographical listings, see the Martindale-Hubbell Law Directory

*READING,** Berks Co.

BINGAMAN, HESS, COBLENTZ & BELL, A PROFESSIONAL CORPORATION (AV)

Suite 660, 601 Penn Street, P.O. Box 61, 19603-0061
Telephone: 610-374-8377
Fax: 610-376-3105
URL: http://www.bhcb.com
Cherry Hill, New Jersey Office: Shawn J. Lau, P.C., Building Q, Suite 14B, 1930 East Marlton Pike, 08003-4222.
Telephone: 609-751-4158.
Fax: 609-424-7112.

Llewellyn R. Bingaman (1907-1996)
James F. Bell (1921-1988)
Ralph J. Althouse, Jr. (Retired)

OF COUNSEL

Raymond K. Hess
J. Wendell Coblentz

David E. Turner
Mark G. Yoder
Carl D. Cronrath, Jr.
Kurt Althouse
Harry D. McMunigal
Patrick T. Barrett
Karen Feryo Longenecker
Shawn J. Lau

Lynne K. Beust
Elizabethanne D. McMunigal
Kevin W. Rethore
Eric J. Fabrizio
Elizabeth A. Magovern

General Counsel for: First Union National Bank; Berks Products Corp.; Utilities Employees Credit Union.
Local Counsel for: Erie Insurance Exchange; Liberty Mutual Insurance Co.; Old Guard Mutual Insurance Co.

For full biographical listings, see the Martindale-Hubbell Law Directory

MOGEL, SPEIDEL, BOBB & KERSHNER, A PROFESSIONAL CORPORATION (AV)

520 Walnut Street, P.O. Box 8581, 19603-8581
Telephone: 610-376-1515
Telecopier: 610-372-8710

George B. Balmer (1902-1969)
George A. Kershner (1907-1969)
Carl F. Mogel (1919-1994)
Edwin H. Kershner
Frederick R. Mogel
Michael L. Mixell
George M. Lutz
Paul M. Yatron
Stephen H. Price
Kathryn K. Harenza

Sean J. O'Brien
Matthew Earl Glinn

OF COUNSEL

Harry W. Speidel
Donald K. Bobb
Henry A. Gass

Representative Clients: Great Valley Bank; Union Township, Berks County, Pennsylvania.

For full biographical listings, see the Martindale-Hubbell Law Directory

*SCRANTON,** Lackawanna Co.

KREDER, BROOKS, HAILSTONE & LUDWIG (AV)

Suite 200, 220 Penn Avenue, 18503
Telephone: 570-346-7922
Telecopier: 570-346-3715

Andrew Hailstone
Lawrence M. Ludwig
Michael J. Donohue
David K. Brown
Richard G. Reed
Stephen W. Saunders

ASSOCIATES

Ann Lavelle Powell
Alyce Hailstone Farrell
Robert B. Farrell

OF COUNSEL

Willard M. Henkelman
Joseph C. Kreder

Counsel For: PNC Bank; Citizens Savings Assn.; Corestates Bank; Wayne Bank.

For Complete List of Firm Personnel, See General Section

For full biographical listings, see the Martindale-Hubbell Law Directory

*WEST CHESTER,** Chester Co.

MACELREE, HARVEY, GALLAGHER, FEATHERMAN & SEBASTIAN, LTD. (AV)

17 West Miner Street, P.O. Box 660, 19381-0660
Telephone: 610-436-0100
Fax: 610-430-7885
Kennett Square, Pennsylvania Office: 211 E. State Street, P. O. Box 363. Telephone 610-444-3180.
Fax: 610-444-3270.
Exton, Pennsylvania Office: 740 Springdale Drive, Suite 110.
Telephone: 610-524-7575.
Fax: 610-524-9857.

Randy L. Sebastian (1946-1997)
Joseph F. Harvey (1921-1985)

For full biographical listings, see the Martindale-Hubbell Law Directory

RHODE ISLAND

*PROVIDENCE,** Providence Co.

HINCKLEY, ALLEN & SNYDER LLP (AV)

1500 Fleet Center, 02903-2393
Telephone: 401-274-2000
Fax: 401-277-9600
Email: firm@haslaw.com *URL:* http://www.haslaw.com
Boston, Massachusetts Office: 28 State Street, 30th Floor.
Telephone: 617-345-9000.
Fax: 617-345-9020. URL: http://www.haslaw.com.

MEMBERS OF FIRM

Paula K. Andrews (Not admitted in RI)
David D. Barricelli
E. Jerome Batty
Jonathan Bell
Paul Bork (Not admitted in RI)
Stephen J. Carlotti
David Barry Connolly (Not admitted in RI)
Joseph P. Curran
Michael P. DeFanti
Eric F. Eisenberg (Not admitted in RI)
Malcolm Farmer, III
Margaret D. Farrell
Hugh J. Gorman, III (Not admitted in RI)
Alan P. Gottlieb (Not admitted in RI)
William R. Grimm
Paul A. Hedstrom (Not admitted in RI)
Richard L. E. Jocelyn
Sandra Matrone Mack
Matthew T. Marcello, III
Frederick P. McClure
Elizabeth Murdock Myers
Paul F. O'Donnell, III (Not admitted in RI)
H. Peter Olsen
Julianne Palumbo (Not admitted in RI)
Gerald J. Petros
James O. Reavis
Ralph J. Rivkind (Not admitted in RI)
David J. Rubin
Douglas F. Seaver (Not admitted in RI)
David R. Sullivan (Not admitted in RI)
Robert F. Sylvia (Not admitted in RI)
Howard E. Walker

ASSOCIATES

Mark Bianchi
Alyssa V. Boss
Andrew D. Cummings (Not admitted in RI)
June E. Daniel
Gloria Maria Gutierrez (Not admitted in RI)
Kelley Jordan-Price
Joseph D. Whelan

OF COUNSEL

Willard R. Pope (Not admitted in RI)
Bentley Tobin
Joachim A. Weissfeld

For Complete List of Firm Personnel, See General Section

For full biographical listings, see the Martindale-Hubbell Law Directory

WILLIAM T. MURPHY LAW OFFICES, INC. (AV)

The Calart Tower, 400 Reservoir Avenue, Suite 3L, 02907
Telephone: 401-461-7740
Telecopier: 401-461-7753

William T. Murphy

Charles A. Pisaturo, Jr.
Steven T. Hayes

Reference: Citizens Bank.

For full biographical listings, see the Martindale-Hubbell Law Directory

SOUTH CAROLINA

*COLUMBIA,** Richland Co.

BARNES, ALFORD, STORK & JOHNSON, L.L.P. (AV)

1613 Main Street, P.O. Box 8448, 29202
Telephone: 803-799-1111
Telefax: 803-254-1335
Email: basj@basjlaw.com

William C. Stork
David G. Wolff
James R. Allen

Representative Clients: First Union National Bank; Anchor Bank; BB&T; First Citizens.

For Complete List of Firm Personnel, See General Section

For full biographical listings, see the Martindale-Hubbell Law Directory

HAYNSWORTH, MARION, MCKAY & GUÉRARD, L.L.P. (AV)

Suite 2400 Affinity Building, 1201 Main Street, P.O. Drawer 7157, 29202
Telephone: 803-765-1818
Facsimile: 803-765-2399
Greenville, South Carolina Office: 75 Beattie Place, Eleventh Floor, P.O. Box 2048, 29602.
Telephone: 864-240-3200.
Facsimile: 864-240-3300.
Charleston, South Carolina Office: 134 Meeting Street, P.O. Box 1119, 29402.
Telephone: 843-722-7606.
Facsimile: 843-724-8016.

MEMBERS OF FIRM

Gary W. Morris
Edward G. Kluiters

ASSOCIATE

Shiryl R. Ballard

Counsel for: St. Paul Insurance Group; Allstate Insurance Co.; Fluor-Daniel Corp.; South Carolina Jobs - Economic Development Authority; Anheuser Busch Company; CSX Transportation; Ernst & Young, LLP; Willis Corroon of South Carolina, Inc.; Westinghouse Savannah River Co.; Wachovia Bank of South Carolina, N.A.

For Complete List of Firm Personnel, See General Section

For full biographical listings, see the Martindale-Hubbell Law Directory

RICHARDSON, PLOWDEN, CARPENTER & ROBINSON, P.A. (AV)

1600 Marion Street, P.O. Drawer 7788, 29202
Telephone: 803-771-4400
Telecopy: 803-779-0016
Email: atty@rpcrlaw.com *URL:* http://www.rpcrlaw.com
Myrtle Beach, South Carolina Office: 2103 B Farlow Street, P.O. Box 3646, 29578.
Telephone: 843-448-1008.
FAX: 843-448-1533.

Frank E. Robinson, II
Frederick A. Crawford
S. Nelson Weston Jr.

Stephen C. Lenker, Jr.

For Complete List of Firm Personnel, See General Section

For full biographical listings, see the Martindale-Hubbell Law Directory

SHERRILL & ROOF, L.L.P. (AV)

1122 Lady Street, Suite 1100, P.O. Box 11497, 29211-1497
Telephone: 803-733-3433
Fax: 803-733-2990
Email: info@sherrillandroof.com

Henry F. Sherrill
C. Joseph Roof
Daniel B. Lott, Jr.

Representative Clients: First-Citizens Bank; Wachovia Bank of South Carolina, N.A.

For full biographical listings, see the Martindale-Hubbell Law Directory

TURNER, PADGET, GRAHAM & LANEY, P.A. (AV)

Seventeenth Floor, 1901 Main Street, P.O. Box 1473, 29202
Telephone: 803-254-2200
Telecopy: 803-799-3957
Florence, South Carolina Office: Fourth Floor, 1831 West Evans Street, P.O. Box 5478, 29502.
Telephone: 843-662-9008.
Fax: 843-667-0828.
Charleston, South Carolina Office: 21 Broad Street, 1st Floor, P.O. Box 836, 29402.
Telephone: 843-723-1622.
Fax: 843-577-3369.

(See Next Column)

Ronald E. Boston
W. Duvall Spruill
R. Wayne Byrd (Resident, Florence, SC, Office)
Lanneau William Lambert, Jr.
R. Todd Sherpy
Michael S. Hopewell (Resident, Florence, SC, Office)

OF COUNSEL

Stephen A. Husman

William O. Higgins

For Complete List of Firm Personnel, See General Section

For full biographical listings, see the Martindale-Hubbell Law Directory

WHITENER & WHARTON, P.A. (AV)

2001 Park Street Park at Calhoun, 29201-2006
Telephone: 803-779-7830
Facsimile: 803-765-4649
Email: wwlaw@bellsouth.net

H. Dave Whitener, Jr.
L. Patricia Wharton

Representative Clients: Mortgage Lenders Network; D.R. Horton, Inc.; Torrey Homes; Investors Title Insurance Company of South Carolina; Better Business Bureau of South Carolina; Coastal Federal Savings Bank; Newberry Federal Savings Bank; SouthTrust Bank, N.A., Boyd & Company; Boyd Management Company.
References: NationsBank, N.A., (Carolina); Wachovia Bank.

For full biographical listings, see the Martindale-Hubbell Law Directory

WOODWARD COTHRAN & HERNDON (AV)

1200 Main Street, Suite 600, 29201
Telephone: 803-799-9772
Fax: 803-799-3256
Mailing Address: P.O. Box 12399, Columbia, South Carolina, 29211
Email: wch1@usit.net

OF COUNSEL

Edward M. Woodward, Sr.

General Counsel for: The Columbia College; Sandhills Bank; Heater Utilities.

For full biographical listings, see the Martindale-Hubbell Law Directory

*GREENVILLE,** Greenville Co.

HAYNSWORTH, MARION, MCKAY & GUÉRARD, L.L.P. (AV)

75 Beattie Place, Eleventh Floor, P.O. Box 2048, 29602
Telephone: 864-240-3200
Facsimile: 864-240-3300
Columbia, South Carolina Office: Suite 2400 Affinity Building, 1201 Main Street, P.O. Drawer 7157, 29202
Telephone: 803-765-1818.
Facsimile: 803-765-2399.
Charleston, South Carolina Office: 134 Meeting Street, P.O. Box 1119, 29402.
Telephone: 843-722-7606.
Facsimile: 843-724-8016.

MEMBERS OF FIRM

Jesse C. Belcher
Andrew J. White, Jr.
H. Sam Mabry, III
J. Derrick Quattlebaum

ASSOCIATE

E. Tyler Smith

Counsel for: Wachovia Bank, N.A.; First Union Bank; Branch Banking and Trust Company.

For Complete List of Firm Personnel, See General Section

For full biographical listings, see the Martindale-Hubbell Law Directory

SOUTH DAKOTA

*ABERDEEN,** Brown Co.

BANTZ, GOSCH, CREMER, PETERSON & SOMMERS (AV)

305 Sixth Avenue, S.E., P.O. Box 970, 57402-0970
Telephone: 605-225-2232
Fax: 605-225-2497
Email: bantzlaw@midco.net

MEMBERS OF FIRM

Douglas W. Bantz (1909-1983)
Kennith L. Gosch
James M. Cremer
Greg L. Peterson
Richard A. Sommers
Ronald A. Wager

General Counsel for: Dacotah Banks, Inc.
Attorneys for: Northwestern Mutual Life Insurance Co.; Northwestern National Insurance Group; Transamerica Insurance Group; United Pacific Insurance Co.

For full biographical listings, see the Martindale-Hubbell Law Directory

*RAPID CITY,** Pennington Co.

WHITING, HAGG & HAGG (AV)

1220 Mt. Rushmore Road, Suite Two, P.O. Box 8008, 57701
Telephone: 605-348-1125
Fax: 605-348-9744
URL: http://www.amatteroflaw.com

MEMBERS OF FIRM

Brian D. Hagg
Rexford A. Hagg
John Stanton Dorsey

ASSOCIATES

Kent R. Hagg
Robert J. Hollan
Kevin W. Klapprodt

LEGAL SUPPORT PERSONNEL

Beverly J. McCracken
Becky J. Buhmann

For full biographical listings, see the Martindale-Hubbell Law Directory

*SIOUX FALLS,** Minnehaha Co.

DAVENPORT, EVANS, HURWITZ & SMITH, L.L.P. (AV)

513 South Main Avenue, P.O. Box 1030, 57101-1030
Telephone: 605-336-2880
Telecopier: 605-335-3639
Email: lawyers@dehs.com

MEMBERS OF FIRM

David L. Knudson
Catherine A. Tanck
Robert E. Hayes
Scott Bradley Anderson
Charles D. Gullickson
Dixie K. Hieb

ASSOCIATE

Kim J. Patrick

Counsel for: American Society of Composers, Authors and Publishers (A.S.-C.A.P.); Continental Insurance Cos.; The First National Bank in Sioux Falls; Ford Motor Credit Co.; General Motors Corp.; The St. Paul Cos.; The Travelers.

For Complete List of Firm Personnel, See General Section

For full biographical listings, see the Martindale-Hubbell Law Directory

TENNESSEE

KINGSPORT, Sullivan Co.

HUNTER, SMITH & DAVIS, LLP (AV)

1212 North Eastman Road, P.O. Box 3740, 37664
Telephone: 423-378-8800
Telecopier: 423-378-8801
Email: info@hsdlaw.com *URL:* http://www.hsdlaw.com
Johnson City, Tennessee Office: Suite 500 First American Center, 208 Sunset Drive, 37604.
Telephone: 423-283-6300.
Telecopier: 423-283-6301.

MEMBERS OF FIRM

T. Arthur Scott, Jr.
Mark S. Dessauer
William C. Argabrite
Cynthia S. Kessler

ASSOCIATE

D. Michael Tranum

Representative Clients: First American National Bank; Bank of Tennessee; Banc Tenn Corp.; First Tennessee Bank National Assn.; NationsBank; Carter County Bank; SunTrust Bank, N.A.; Eastman Credit Union; Citizens Bank; First Union National Bank.

For Complete List of Firm Personnel, See General Section

For full biographical listings, see the Martindale-Hubbell Law Directory

*KNOXVILLE,** Knox Co.

EGERTON, MCAFEE, ARMISTEAD & DAVIS, P.C. (AV)

500 First American National Bank Center, P.O. Box 2047, 37901
Telephone: 423-546-0500
Fax: 423-525-5293
URL: http://emadlaw.com

Joe M. McAfee
Herbert H. Slatery III
William W. Davis, Jr.
William E. McClamroch, III

Reese K. Thomas

Representative Clients: First American National Bank of Knoxville; Home Federal Bank of Tennessee, F.S.B.

For full biographical listings, see the Martindale-Hubbell Law Directory

WALKER & WALKER, P.C. (AV)

910 First American Center, P.O. Box 2774, 37901
Telephone: 423-523-0700
Telecopier: 423-523-4990
Email: jwalkerjr@aol.com

John A. Walker, Jr.
Kathryn D. Higginbotham

For full biographical listings, see the Martindale-Hubbell Law Directory

*MEMPHIS,** Shelby Co.

ARMSTRONG ALLEN PREWITT GENTRY JOHNSTON & HOLMES, PLLC (AV)

Brinkley Plaza, Suite 700, 80 Monroe Avenue, 38103-2467
Telephone: 901-523-8211
Facsimile: 901-524-4936
Little Rock, Arkansas Office: Suite 100, 100 Morgan Keegan Drive, 72202.
Telephone: 501-280-0100.
Facsimile: 501-280-0166.
Jackson, Mississippi Office: 2525 Lakeward Drive, Suite 200, 39216.
Telephone: 601-713-1192.
Facsimile: 601-713-2049.
Jackson, Tennessee Office: 464 North Parkway, Suite A, 38305.
Telephone: 901-660-2332.
Facsimile: 901-664-1109.

MEMBERS OF FIRM

Elmore Holmes, III
James Rogers (Josh) Hall, Jr.
Wm. Rowlett Scott
James B. McLaren, Jr.
Paul A. Matthews
Charles R. Crawford
Sidney W. Farnsworth, III

For Complete List of Firm Personnel, See General Section

For full biographical listings, see the Martindale-Hubbell Law Directory

BAKER, DONELSON, BEARMAN & CALDWELL (AV)

20th Floor, First Tennessee Building, 165 Madison, 38103
Telephone: 901-526-2000
Telecopier: 901-577-2303
Email: info@bdbc.com *URL:* http://www.bakerdonelson.com
Nashville, Tennessee Office: 1700 Nashville City Center, 511 Union Street, 37219.
Telephone: 615-726-5600.
Telecopier: 615-726-0464.
Chattanooga, Tennessee Office: 1800 Republic Centre, 633 Chestnut Street, 37450-1800.
Telephone: 423-756-2010.
Telecopier: 423-756-3447.
Knoxville, Tennessee Office: 2200 Riverview Tower, 900 South Gay Street, 37901.
Telephone: 423-549-7000.
Telecopier: 423-525-8569.
Johnson City, Tennessee Office: SunTrust Bank Building, 207 Mockingbird Lane, P.O. Box 3038, 37602.
Telephone: 423-928-0181.
Telecopier: 423-928-5694; 423-928-3654; Kingsport: 423-246-6191.
Huntsville, Tennessee Office: 3 Courthouse Square, 37756.
Telephone: 423-663-2321.
Telecopier: 423-663-2111.
Washington, D.C. Office: Market Square, 801 Pennsylvania Avenue, N.W., 20004.
Telephone: 202-508-3400.
Telecopier: 202-508-3402.
Jackson, Mississippi Office: Suite 500, 700 North State Street, 39202.
Telephone: 601-351-2400.
Telecopier: 601-351-2424.

MANAGING PARTNER

Robert Mark Glover

SHAREHOLDERS

Lewis R. Donelson, III
Charles C. Harrell
Roy Keathley
Stephen D. Goodwin
David G. Williams
George T. Lewis, III
Leo Bearman, Jr.
Ben C. Adams, Jr.
Maurice Wexler
Eugene J. Podesta, Jr.
Frank L. Watson, Jr.
Sam B. Blair, Jr.
Robert Walker
Carla Peacher-Ryan
Boyd L. Rhodes, Jr.
Mary Aronov
W. Michael Richards
Jill M. Steinberg
John C. Speer
Matthew S. Heiter
Charles T. Tuggle, Jr.
Michael C. Patton
Larry E. Killebrew
Janis Wild Kesser
Jerry Stauffer
Stephen William Ragland
Robert C. Liddon
Monique A. Nassar
William H.D. Fones, Jr.
Bradley E. Trammell
William P. Kenworthy
M. Clay Bethell
Allan J. Wade
Desiree M. Franklin
Gregory G. Fletcher
R. Alan Pritchard, Jr.
Peter H. Kesser

(See Next Column)

BAKER, DONELSON, BEARMAN & CALDWELL, *Memphis—Continued*

OF COUNSEL

Frierson M. Graves, Jr.
Donald A. Malmo
Lynn Ackerman Landau
Paul E. Risner (Not admitted in TN)

ASSOCIATES

Paul R. O'Rourke
Anne B. Mathes
Elizabeth Einstman Chance
Frank L. Watson, III
W. Douglas Sweet
Wm. Scott Young
Mary Ann Jackson
Angela R. Merideth
Jackie G. Prester
David L. Bearman
Clarissa M. Cissell
Robert C. McConkey, III
Jennifer R. Keown
Brett T. Parks
Cedric C.Y. Tan
Lang Wiseman
Diane Schratz Holitik
D. Benjamin Bullen
Shannon M. Hernandez
Sylvia Monique Reed
Christopher G. Boling
Louise P. Gaerig
Lori Hackleman Patterson
Lea Hall Speed

For full biographical listings, see the Martindale-Hubbell Law Directory

EVANS & PETREE (AV)

81 Monroe Avenue, 38103
Telephone: 901-525-6781
Telecopier: 901-527-7756

MEMBERS OF FIRM

Marion G. Evans (1877-1957)
Jack Petree (1921-1973)
Charles Pittman Cobb (Retired)
Elwood L. Edwards (Retired)
W. Lytle Nichol IV
John W. McQuiston II
Ernest G. Kelly, Jr.
Michael C. Williams
Joseph W. Barnwell, Jr.
David C. Scruggs
Leonard C. Dunavant, Jr.
E. Woods Weathersby
C. Bradford Foster III
Andrew H. Raines
Frank N. Stockdale Carney
Paul F. T. Edwards
Percy H. Harvey
Katharine A. Jungkind
Scott A. Frick
Michael R. Marshall
Richard E.M. Nichol, Jr.

Karen Baim Reagler

For full biographical listings, see the Martindale-Hubbell Law Directory

FARRIS, MATHEWS, BRANAN & HELLEN, P.L.C. (AV)

One Commerce Square, Suite 2000, 38103
Telephone: 901-259-7100
Fax: 901-259-7150
Email: firm@farris-law.com
East Memphis, Tennessee Office: Suite 400. First Commercial Bank Building. 5384 Poplar Avenue.
Telephone: 901-763-4000.
Fax: 901-763-4095.
Nashville, Tennessee Office: Nashville City Center, 511 Union Street, Suite 2400.
Telephone: 615-726-1200.
Fax: 615-726-1776.

MEMBERS OF FIRM

Robert F. Miller
Robert A. McLean
Anita I. Lotz

For Complete List of Firm Personnel, See General Section

For full biographical listings, see the Martindale-Hubbell Law Directory

*NASHVILLE,** Davidson Co.

CHERNAU, CHAFFIN & BURNSED, PLLC (AV)

SunTrust Center, 424 Church Street, Suite 1750, 37219-2305
Telephone: 615-244-5480
Fax: 615-242-7951
Email: CCBABSMITH@AOL.COM

MEMBERS OF FIRM

Louis Leftwich, Jr. (1910-1960)
Stanley M. Chernau
R. Garry Chaffin
Linda F. Burnsed
Amy Bryson Smith

Representative Clients: SouthTrust Bank National Association; SouthTrust Mortgage Corp.; Chemical Residential Mortgage Corp.; NationsBanc Mortgage Corp.; Southeastern Mortgage of Tennessee, Inc.; First Bank & Trust Company.

For full biographical listings, see the Martindale-Hubbell Law Directory

DANIEL W. SMALL (AV)

323 Union Street, Suite 300, P.O. Box 190608, 37219-0608
Telephone: 615-252-6000
Fax: 615-252-6001
Email: dsmall1@msn.com *URL:* http://www.lawyers.com/danielsmall

Representative Clients: The Bank of Nashville; Bank of Dickson; Capital Bank & Trust Co.; Citizens Community Bank; The Danner Co.; First Bank & Trust; The First National Bank of McMinnville; PFIC Corp.; PFIC Securities Corp.

For full biographical listings, see the Martindale-Hubbell Law Directory

TEXAS

ADDISON, Dallas Co.

BARRETT BURKE WILSON CASTLE DAFFIN & FRAPPIER, L.L.P. (AV)

A Limited Liability Partnership including Professional Corporations
15000 Surveyor Boulevard, Suite 100, 75001
Telephone: 972-386-5040
Fax: 972-386-7673
Houston, Texas Office: 24 Greenway Plaza, Suite 2001.
Telephone: 713-621-8673.
Denver, Colorado Affiliated Office: Castle Barrett Daffin & Frappier, 1099 Eighteenth Street, Suite 2200.
Telephone: 303-299-1800.
Fax: 303-299-1808.
Little Rock, Arkansas Affiliated Office: Wilson & Associates, P.A. 1521 Merrill Drive, Suite D220.
Telephone: 501-219-9388.

Michael C. Barrett

For full biographical listings, see the Martindale-Hubbell Law Directory

*ALICE,** Jim Wells Co.

WARBURTON, ADAMI, MCNEILL, PAISLEY & APPELL, P.C. (AV)

Norwest Bank Building, Fourth Floor, 601 East Main Street, P.O. Box 331, 78333-0331
Telephone: 361-668-8101
Fax: 361-668-8106
Beeville Office: 107 North Washington Street, P.O. Box 278, 78104-0278.
Telephone: 361-358-2525.
Fax: 361-358-2532.

Lawrence H. Warburton, Jr.
Wallis D. McNeill, Jr.
Mark R. Paisley

Representative Clients: Norwest Bank, Alice; Bowden Ford Lincoln Mercury Co.; Brooks County Independent School District; Jim Wells County; Lundells, Inc.; Brush County Bank; Mildred Talbert Estate; Ruth Moos Estate; John G. Kenedy Charitable Trust; San Diego Independent School District.

For Complete List of Firm Personnel, See General Section

For full biographical listings, see the Martindale-Hubbell Law Directory

*AUSTIN,** Travis Co.

BAKER BOTTS L.L.P. (AV)

1600 San Jacinto Center, 98 San Jacinto Boulevard, 78701
Telephone: 512-322-2500
Fax: 512-322-2501
Email: postmaster@bakerbotts.com *URL:* http://www.bakerbotts.com
Houston, Texas Office: One Shell Plaza, 910 Louisiana.
Telephone: 713-229-1234.
Dallas, Texas Office: 2001 Ross Avenue.
Telephone: 214-953-6500.
Washington, D.C. Office: The Warner, 1299 Pennsylvania Avenue, N.W.
Telephone: 202-639-7700.
New York, New York Office: 599 Lexington Avenue.
Telephone: 212-705-5000.
Moscow, Russia Office: 10 ul. Bolshaya Dimitrovka (formerly Pushkinskaya), 103031.
Telephone: 7095/921-5300 (Local); 7501/929-7070 (International).
London, England Office: 45 Ludgate Hill.
Telephone: 0171-778-1400 (Local); 011-44-171-778-1400 (International).
Baku, Azerbaijan Office: 6-10 Vagif Mustafa-zadeh Street, Third Floor, Icheri Sheher, 370004.
Telephone: 994-12-97-63-88 (Local); 011-994-12-97-63-88 (International).
Fax: 994-12-97-63-61 (Local); 011-994-12-97-63-91 (International).

MEMBER OF FIRM

William F. Stutts, Jr.

(See Next Column)

BAKER BOTTS L.L.P.—*Continued*

SPECIAL COUNSEL

Shelley W. Austin

For Complete List of Firm Personnel, See General Section

For full biographical listings, see the Martindale-Hubbell Law Directory

H. GLENN HALL, JR. (AV)

301 Congress Avenue, Suite 2025, 78701
Telephone: 512-236-8955
Fax: 512-320-4162

For full biographical listings, see the Martindale-Hubbell Law Directory

HOHMANN & TAUBE, L.L.P. (AV)

100 Congress Avenue, Suite 1600, 78701-4042
Telephone: 512-472-5997
Fax: 512-472-5248
Email: bille@ht-law.com *URL:* http://www.ht-law.com

Eric J. Taube
Mitchell D. Savrick

Cristina B. McGarr

For full biographical listings, see the Martindale-Hubbell Law Directory

TEMPLE & TEMPLE (AV)

400 West 15th Street, Suite 1510, 78701
Telephone: 512-477-4467
Fax: 512-477-4478

Larry E. Temple
J. Lawrence Temple

For full biographical listings, see the Martindale-Hubbell Law Directory

BEDFORD, Tarrant Co.

ADAMS, LYNCH & LOFTIN, P.C. (AV)

1903 Central Drive, Suite 400, 76021
Telephone: 817-283-7742
Fax: 817-571-2947

Neal W. Adams
John T. Lynch, IV
Stacy B. Loftin

Jon A. McCormick

For full biographical listings, see the Martindale-Hubbell Law Directory

*DALLAS,** Dallas Co.

JOSEPH E. ASHMORE, JR., P.C. (AV)

Regency Plaza, 3710 Rawlins, Suite 1210, LB 84, 75219-4217
Telephone: 214-559-7202
Fax: 214-520-1550

Joseph E. Ashmore, Jr.

C. Gregory Shamoun
Lori Ashmore Peters

For Complete List of Firm Personnel, See General Section

For full biographical listings, see the Martindale-Hubbell Law Directory

BAKER BOTTS L.L.P. (AV)

2001 Ross Avenue, 75201
Telephone: 214-953-6500
Fax: 214-953-6503
Email: postmaster@bakerbotts.com *URL:* http://www.bakerbotts.com
Houston, Texas Office: One Shell Plaza, 910 Louisiana.
Telephone: 713-229-1234.
Washington, D.C. Office: The Warner, 1299 Pennsylvania Avenue, N.W.
Telephone: 202-639-7700.
Austin, Texas Office: 1600 San Jacinto Center, 98 San Jacinto Boulevard.
Telephone: 512-322-2500.
New York, New York Office: 599 Lexington Avenue.
Telephone: 212-705-5000.
Moscow, Russia Office: 10 ul. Bolshaya Dimitrovka (formerly Pushkinskaya), 103031.
Telephone: 7095/921-5300 (Local); 7095/929-7070.
London, England Office: 45 Ludgate Hill.
Telephone: 0171-778-1400 (Local); 011-44-171-778-1400 (International).
Baku, Azerbaijan Office: 6-10 Vagif Mustafa-zadeh Street, Third Floor, Icheri Sheher, 370004.
Telephone: 994-12-97-63-88 (Local); 011-994-12-97-63-88 (International).

MEMBERS OF FIRM

Bryant C. Boren, Jr.
Alison A. Courtwright
Peter B. Dewar
Roderick A. Goyne

(See Next Column)

ASSOCIATE

Christian Brose

For Complete List of Firm Personnel, See General Section

For full biographical listings, see the Martindale-Hubbell Law Directory

CALHOUN & STACY (AV)

Suite 5700 - Bank of America Plaza, 901 Main Street, 75202-3713
Telephone: 214-748-5000
Facsimile: 214-748-1421
Email: info@calhounstacy.com *URL:* http://www.calhounstacy.com

MEMBERS OF FIRM

Mark Alan Calhoun
David W. Elrod
Parker Nelson
Thomas E. Rosen

For Complete List of Firm Personnel, See General Section

For full biographical listings, see the Martindale-Hubbell Law Directory

GODWIN WHITE & GRUBER, A PROFESSIONAL CORPORATION (AV)

Suite 2500, 901 Main Street, 75202-3714
Telephone: 214-939-4400
Fax: 214-760-7332

James F. Bullock
Michael K. Hurst
Christopher L. Kurzner
Steven T. Polino
David J. White

ASSOCIATE

Guy H. Riddle

For Complete List of Firm Personnel, See General Section

For full biographical listings, see the Martindale-Hubbell Law Directory

HUGHES & LUCE, L.L.P. (AV)

A Registered Limited Liability Partnership including Professional Corporations
1717 Main Street, Suite 2800, 75201
Telephone: 214-939-5500
Fax: 214-939-6100; 214-939-5849
Email: H&L@hughesluce.com *URL:* http://www.hughesluce.com
Austin, Texas Office: 111 Congress, Suite 900.
Telephone: 512-482-6800.
Fax: 512-482-6859.
Houston, Texas Office: 1600 Smith Street, Suite 3550.
Telephone: 713-754-5200.
Fax: 713-754-5270.

MEMBERS OF FIRM

Gary G. Null
James W. Sargent
David Weitman

ASSOCIATES

Marc H. Stone
John O. Sutton Jr.
Carlos P. Villota

OF COUNSEL

Paul A. Berry

For Complete List of Firm Personnel, See General Section

For full biographical listings, see the Martindale-Hubbell Law Directory

SMITH, UNDERWOOD & PERKINS, A PROFESSIONAL CORPORATION (AV)

600 Two Lincoln Centre, 5420 LBJ Freeway, 75240
Telephone: 972-661-5114
Telecopier: 972-661-5691
Email: firm@suandp.com *URL:* http://www.suplaw.com

Timothy S. Perkins
David W. Ralston
G. Lynn Smith
William J. Underwood, Jr.

Christine A. McGuire
Amy K. Ratzlaff
P. Theodore Stoinoff, II
Val C. Cronin
Ellen P. Stewart
Todd W. Shadle
Ruth C. Logan
Christina L. Betanzos
Kent D. Williamson

For full biographical listings, see the Martindale-Hubbell Law Directory

Dallas—Continued

THOMPSON & KNIGHT L.L.P. (AV)

(Attorneys and Counselors)
1700 Pacific Avenue Suite 3300, 75201
Telephone: 214-969-1700
Telecopy: 214-969-1751
Telex: 732 298
URL: http://www.tklaw.com
Austin, Texas Office: 1200 San Jacinto Center, 98 San Jacinto Boulevard, 78701.
Telephone: 512-469-6100.
Telecopy: 512-469-6180.
Fort Worth, Texas Office: 801 Cherry Street, Suite 1600, 76102.
Telephone: 817-347-1700.
Telecopy: 817-347-1799.
Houston, Texas Office: Thompson Knight Brown Parker & Leahy L.L.P., 1200 Smith Street, Suite 3600, 77002-4595.
Telephone: 713-654-8111.
Telecopier: 713-654-1871.
San Pedro Garza Garcia, Nuevo León, Mexico Office: Edificio Losoles PD-4, Av. Lázaro Cárdenas No. 2400 Pte., C.P. 66220.
Telephone: (52-8) 363-0096.
Telecopy: (52-8) 363-3067.

PARTNERS

Dorothy H. Bjorck
Paul E. Comeaux
O. Paul Corley, Jr.
James W. McKellar
John W. Rain
Debra J. Villarreal

ASSOCIATES

Heather E. Moulder
Shad E. Sumrow
Kyle S. Volluz

STAFF ATTORNEY

Richard J. Lebos, Jr.

For Complete List of Firm Personnel, See General Section

For full biographical listings, see the Martindale-Hubbell Law Directory

*EL PASO,** El Paso Co.

AINSA PARTNERS, LLP (AV)

5809 Acacia Circle, 79912
Telephone: 915-845-5300
Fax: 915-845-7800
Email: fain@acaciapark.com *URL:* http://www.ainsa.com

Francis S. Ainsa, Jr.
Michael F. Ainsa
David M. Driscoll

For full biographical listings, see the Martindale-Hubbell Law Directory

CROWSON & INGRAM (AV)

Suite 706, The Cortez, 310 North Mesa, P.O. Box 862, 79945
Telephone: 915-533-7717
Telefax: 915-533-1495
Email: crowsing@huntleigh.net

MEMBERS OF FIRM

Harold E. Crowson, Jr.
Temple B. Ingram, Jr.

Reference: Bank of America, N.A.; Norwest Bank, El Paso, N.A.; Bank of the West, El Paso, Texas.

For full biographical listings, see the Martindale-Hubbell Law Directory

JAMES, GOLDMAN & HAUGLAND, P.C. A PROFESSIONAL CORPORATION (AV)

Chase Bank of Texas, 201 East Main, Suite 800, P.O. Box 1770, 79949-1770
Telephone: 915-532-3911
Fax: 915-541-6440

Wiley F. James, III
Merton B. Goldman
Corey W. Haugland
Michael J. Hutson
Victor M. Firth

Attorneys for: Bank of the West; United Investors Realty Trust; Ford Motor Credit Corp.; Financial Federal Credit, Inc.; Mellon Mortgage Company; Wil-Roye Investment Company II, Inc.; First Commonwealth Mortgage Trust; Norwest Mortgage, Inc.

For Complete List of Firm Personnel, See General Section

For full biographical listings, see the Martindale-Hubbell Law Directory

MAYFIELD & PERRENOT, P.C. (AV)

221 N. Kansas, Suite 1600, P.O. Box 2039, 79950
Telephone: 915-533-2468
Telecopier: 915-533-0620
Email: mayper@1eagle1.com

Richard B. Perrenot
Roger C. Davie
James R. Dennis
Jeffery W. McElroy

(See Next Column)

Lisa M. Power
Shelly Weatherly
Marina Mata De La Garza

OF COUNSEL

Ellis O. Mayfield
James B. McIntyre

For full biographical listings, see the Martindale-Hubbell Law Directory

*FORT WORTH,** Tarrant Co.

THOMPSON & KNIGHT L.L.P. (AV)

(Attorneys and Counselors)
801 Cherry Street, Suite 1600, 76102
Telephone: 817-347-1700
Telecopy: 817-347-1799
URL: http://www.tklaw.com
Dallas, Texas Office: 1700 Pacific Avenue, Suite 3300, 75201.
Telephone: 214-969-1700.
Telecopy: 214-969-1751.
Telex: 732298.
Austin, Texas Office: 1200 San Jacinto Center, 98 San Jacinto Boulevard, 78701.
Telephone: 512-469-6100.
Telecopy: 512-469-6180.
Houston, Texas Office: Thompson Knight Brown Parker & Leahy L.L.P., 1200 Smith Street, Suite 3600, 77002-4595.
Telephone: 713-654-8111.
Telecopier: 713-654-1871.
San Pedro Garza Garcia, Nuevo León, Mexico Office: Edificio Losoles PD-4, Av. Lázaro Cárdenas No. 2400 Pte., C.P. 66220.
Telephone: (52-8) 363-0096.
Telecopy: (52-8) 363-3067.

PARTNER

Susan E. Coleman

For Complete List of Firm Personnel, See General Section

For full biographical listings, see the Martindale-Hubbell Law Directory

FRISCO, Collin & Denton Cos.

WINIKATES & WINIKATES (AV)

Prosper State Bank Building, 7700 Main Street, P.O. Box 249, 75034-0249
Telephone: 972-335-1122
Fax: 972-335-1125

MEMBERS OF FIRM

Charles J. Winikates
Charles J. Winikates, Jr.
Regina W. Mentesana
Frances A. Fazio

For full biographical listings, see the Martindale-Hubbell Law Directory

*HOUSTON,** Harris Co.

BAKER BOTTS L.L.P. (AV)

One Shell Plaza, 910 Louisiana, 77002
Telephone: 713-229-1234
Cable Address: "Boterlove"
Fax: 713-229-1522
Email: postmaster@bakerbotts.com *URL:* http://www.bakerbotts.com
Washington, D.C. Office: The Warner, 1299 Pennsylvania Avenue, N.W.
Telephone: 202-639-7700.
New York, New York Office: 599 Lexington Avenue.
Telephone: 212-705-5000.
Austin, Texas Office: 1600 San Jacinto Center, 98 San Jacinto Boulevard.
Telephone: 512-322-2500.
Dallas, Texas Office: 2001 Ross Avenue.
Telephone: 214-953-6500.
Moscow, Russia Office: 10 ul. Bolshaya Dimitrovka (formerly Pushkinskaya), 103031.
Telephone: 7095/921-5300 (Local); 7095/929-7070 (International).
London, England Office: 45 Ludgate Hill.
Telephone: 0171-778-1400 (Local); 011-44-171-778-1400 (International).
Baku, Azerbaijan Office: 6-10 Vagif Mustafa-zadeh Street, Third Floor, Icheri Sheher, 370004.
Telephone: 994-12-97-63-88 (Local); 011-994-12-97-63-88 (International).
Fax: 994-12-97-63-91 (Local); 011-994-12-97-63-91 (International)

MEMBERS OF FIRM

David Alan Burns
Rufus Cormier, Jr.
Pamela B. Ewen
Bill Hart, Jr.
Stephen Krebs
Michael S. Moehlman

ASSOCIATES

Ronald E. Holmes
Denise Dardeau Muller
Wesley P. Shields

For Complete List of Firm Personnel, See General Section

For full biographical listings, see the Martindale-Hubbell Law Directory

Houston—Continued

GILPIN, PAXSON & BERSCH (AV)

A Registered Limited Liability Partnership
Attorney at Law
1900 West Loop South, Suite 2000, 77027-3259
Telephone: 713-623-8800
Telecopier: 713-993-8451
Email: gpb@gpblaw.com *URL:* http://www.texinslaw.com

PARTNERS

Gary M. Alletag
Timothy R. Bersch
John D. Gilpin
Darryl W. Malone
Michael J. Pappert
Stephen Paxson
Kevin F. Risley

OF COUNSEL

Harless R. Benthul
David F. Webb

ASSOCIATES

Joseph D. Batson
Jeri Pharis Wechsler

Representative Clients: BMW of North America, Inc.; Federal Deposit Insurance Corporation; Greater Houston Builders Association; Owens Corning Fiberglas Corporation; Shaw Industries, Inc.; Southwest Guaranty Trust Company, N.A.; Sprint Communications Company L.P.; Volkswagen of America, Inc.; Volvo North America Corporation; Wells Fargo Bank (Texas), N.A.

For full biographical listings, see the Martindale-Hubbell Law Directory

HAYS, MCCONN, RICE & PICKERING (AV)

400 Two Allen Center, 1200 Smith Street, 77002
Telephone: 713-654-1111
Fax: 713-650-0027
Email: HMRP@HaysMcConn.com *URL:* http://www.haysmcconn.com

MEMBERS OF FIRM

Michael S. Hays
James J. McConn, Jr.
B. Stephen Rice
Michael R. Pickering
Mark A. Padon
Bruce Gaible
Susan Crowley Stevenson
Allen Till
Craig S. Wolcott
Naomi S. Ostfeld
Margaret Twomey Brenner
W. Michael Scott
Jeffery Allen Addicks
J. Philip Griffis
A. Scott Kidd
Robert E. Purgatorio
Brian Tew
Steven M. Duble
Lance K. Thomas
Michael W. Magee

ASSOCIATES

Troy A. Williams
Shannon D. Robbie
Staton M. Childers
Timothy R. Hightower
William Jason Walker
Michael A. Durr
Leslie M. Henry
Amanda F. Bell
David Wilson, II

OF COUNSEL

John T. Golden

For full biographical listings, see the Martindale-Hubbell Law Directory

*SAN ANTONIO,** Bexar Co.

BENTON CLARK & TAYLOR, P.C. (AV)

105 South St. Marys Street, Suite 905, 78205
Telephone: 210-472-1800
Fax: 210-472-1872

Barry G. Benton
R. Christopher Clark
Richard M. Taylor, III

Phillip R. Hall

For full biographical listings, see the Martindale-Hubbell Law Directory

COX & SMITH INCORPORATED (AV)

112 East Pecan Street, Suite 1800, 78205-1521
Telephone: 210-554-5500
Fax: 210-226-8395
Email: info@coxsmith.com *URL:* http://www.coxsmith.com

Diann M. Bartek
Cary Plotkin Kavy
David B. West
William J. McDonough, Jr.
Brett W. Schouest
Kerry T. Benedict
Tobin E. Olson
Jonathan A. Nixon

OF COUNSEL

Teresa Ereon Giltner

Representative Clients: Banque Paribas (Suisse) S.A.; Del Rio National Bank; First National Bank of South Texas; First Victoria National Bank; Frost National Bank; International Bancshares Corp.; International Bank of Commerce; NationsBank of Texas, N.A.; Texas Commerce Bank N.A.

For Complete List of Firm Personnel, See General Section

For full biographical listings, see the Martindale-Hubbell Law Directory

*WICHITA FALLS,** Wichita Co.

GIBSON, HOTCHKISS, ROACH & DAVENPORT (AV)

807 8th Street, 8th Floor, 76301
Telephone: 940-322-7856
Fax: 940-322-1204
Email: ed@ghrdlaw.com *URL:* http://www.lawyers.com/ghrdlaw

MEMBER OF FIRM

Charles A. Hotchkiss

ASSOCIATE

Jon P. McGough

Representative Clients: American National Bank, Wichita Falls; First National Bank of Bowie; Wichita Falls PCA; Bennett Production Co.; Red River Authority of Texas; Burcamp Steel Co.

For Complete List of Firm Personnel, See General Section

For full biographical listings, see the Martindale-Hubbell Law Directory

UTAH

*SALT LAKE CITY,** Salt Lake Co.

CALLISTER NEBEKER & MCCULLOUGH, A PROFESSIONAL CORPORATION (AV)

Gateway Tower East, Suite 900, 10 East South Temple, 84133
Telephone: 801-530-7300
Telecopier: 801-364-9127
Email: mjeaston@cnmlaw.com *URL:* http://www.cnmlaw.com

Louis H. Callister
Dorothy C. Pleshe
John A. Beckstead
James R. Holbrook
George R. Sutton
Randall D Benson
George E. Harris, Jr.
John H. Rees
Mark L. Callister
Jan M. Bergeson
Laurie S. Hart
Glen F. Strong
John B. Lindsay
Zachary T. Shields

Representative Clients: Zions First National Bank; Citicorp; Zions Bancorporation; Associates Commercial Corp.; Chrysler Credit Corp.; Merrick Bank Corporation; Wright Express Financial Services Corporation; Key Bank National Association; Federal Land Bank Association of Utah; Utah Production Credit Assn.

For Complete List of Firm Personnel, See General Section

For full biographical listings, see the Martindale-Hubbell Law Directory

RAY, QUINNEY & NEBEKER, A PROFESSIONAL CORPORATION (AV)

79 South Main Street, Suite 400, P.O. Box 45385, 84145-0385
Telephone: 801-532-1500
Fax: 801-532-7543
Email: rqn@rqn.com *URL:* http://www.rqn.com
Provo, Utah Office: 92 North University Avenue, Suite 210, 84601-4420.
Telephone: 801-342-2400.
Fax: 801-375-8379.
Albuquerque, New Mexico Office: Suite 620, 40 First Plaza, N.W.
Telephone: 505-243-6665.
Fax: 505-764-9890.

Alonzo W. Watson, Jr.
Don B. Allen
Scott Hancock Clark
Douglas Matsumori
Larry G. Moore
Douglas M. Monson
Kevin G. Glade
Stephen C. Tingey
Elaine A. Monson
Katie A. Eccles

Michael D. Mayfield

Representative Clients: First Security Bank, N.A.; Borden, Inc.; Salt Lake Organizing Committee for the Winter Olympic Games of 2002; Southern Pacific Transportation; Utah Power & Light Co.; Travelers Insurance Co.; U.S. West.

For Complete List of Firm Personnel, See General Section

For full biographical listings, see the Martindale-Hubbell Law Directory

VAN COTT, BAGLEY, CORNWALL & MCCARTHY, A PROFESSIONAL CORPORATION (AV)

50 South Main Street, Suite 1600, P.O. Box 45340, 84145-0340
Telephone: 801-532-3333
Telecopier: 801-534-0058
Email: info@vancott.com *URL:* http://www.vancott.com
Ogden, Utah Office: 2404 Washington Boulevard, Suite 900.
Telephone: 801-394-5783.
Park City, Utah Office: 2200 Park Avenue, Suite C200-A.
Telephone: 435-649-3889.

(See Next Column)

VAN COTT, BAGLEY, CORNWALL & MCCARTHY A PROFESSIONAL CORPORATION, *Salt Lake City—Continued*

Robert M. Anderson (President of Firm)
Thomas T. Billings
Rand L. Cook
Stephen D. Swindle

Tacy A. Hartman

OF COUNSEL

David E. Salisbury
M. Scott Woodland

For Complete List of Firm Personnel, See General Section

For full biographical listings, see the Martindale-Hubbell Law Directory

VERMONT

*BURLINGTON,** Chittenden Co.

GRAVEL AND SHEA, A PROFESSIONAL CORPORATION (AV)

Corporate Plaza, 76 St. Paul Street, P.O. Box 369, 05402-0369
Telephone: 802-658-0220
Fax: 802-658-1456

Stewart H. McConaughy
Margaret L. Montgomery

For Complete List of Firm Personnel, See General Section

For full biographical listings, see the Martindale-Hubbell Law Directory

VIRGINIA

ALEXANDRIA, (Independent City)

PETER C. WILLIAMS (AV)

510 King Street, Suite 416, 22314
Telephone: 703-684-8813
Fax: 703-548-4742
Email: pcwlaw@erols.com

For full biographical listings, see the Martindale-Hubbell Law Directory

*ARLINGTON,** Arlington Co.

BEAN, KINNEY & KORMAN, A PROFESSIONAL CORPORATION (AV)

2000 North 14th Street, Suite 100, 22201
Telephone: 703-525-4000
Facsimile: 703-525-2207
Email: bkk@beankinney.com

L. Lee Bean (1916-1989)
David B. Kinney (Emeritus)
James W. Korman
Jonathan C. Kinney
Frederick R. Taylor
Leo S. Fisher
James Bruce Davis
James R. Schroll
Carol Schrier-Polak
Joseph P. Corish
Jennifer A. Brust
David C. Canfield
C. Erik Gustafson

OF COUNSEL

John Morland

Marbeth M. Spreyer
Thomas W. Repczynski
Daryl S. Taylor
Christie L. Dowling
Timothy J. McEvoy
William E. Buchanan
Jennifer C. Bier
Leslie J. Long
Lisa J. Tomasseti

Counsel for: First Union National Banks of Virginia; Bank of America.

For full biographical listings, see the Martindale-Hubbell Law Directory

*FAIRFAX,** (Ind. City; Seat of Fairfax Co.)

MCCANDLISH & LILLARD, A PROFESSIONAL CORPORATION (AV)

Fair Oaks Plaza, 11350 Random Hills Road, Suite 500, 22030-7429
Telephone: 703-273-2288
Fax: 703-352-4300
Email: mccand@patriot.net *URL:* http://www.mccandlaw.com
Leesburg, Virginia Office: 305 Harrison Street, S.E., Third Floor.
Telephone: 703-737-0200.
Fax: 703-737-0165.

(See Next Column)

Robert J. McCandlish, Jr. (1909-1996)
Rothwell J. Lillard (1910-1989)
Jesse B. Wilson, III
Peter A. Arntson
Gary W. Brown
Randolph A. Sutliff
Robert H. J. Loftus
William McCauley Arnold
Stephen C. Price
Stephen K. Fox
Douglas J. Sanderson
R. Peyton Mahaffey
William L. Carey
John W. Farrell
Eric J. Berghold
Ralph M. Tener
Vicki L. Layman
Adam W. Smith

Daniel P. Lyon
Lawrence J. McClafferty
Brian R. Sanderson

For full biographical listings, see the Martindale-Hubbell Law Directory

ODIN, FELDMAN & PITTLEMAN, P.C. (AV)

9302 Lee Highway, Suite 1100, 22031
Telephone: 703-218-2100
Facsimile: 703-218-2160
Email: OFP@OFPLAW.COM

David E. Feldman
James B. Pittleman
Donald F. King
David A. Lawrence

OF COUNSEL

Ronald W. Tydings

For Complete List of Firm Personnel, See General Section

For full biographical listings, see the Martindale-Hubbell Law Directory

MCLEAN, Fairfax Co.

VENABLE ATTORNEYS AT LAW VENABLE, BAETJER AND HOWARD, LLP (AV)

A Partnership including Professional Corporations
Suite 400, 2010 Corporate Ridge, 22102
Telephone: 703-760-1600
Fax: 703-821-8949
URL: http://www.venable.com
Baltimore, Maryland Office: 1800 Mercantile Bank & Trust Building, 2 Hopkins Plaza.
Telephone: 410-244-7400.
Fax: 410-244-7742.
Washington, D.C. Office: Venable, Baetjer, Howard & Civiletti LLP, Suite 1000, 1201 New York Avenue, N.W.
Telephone: 202-962-4800.
Fax: 202-962-8300.
Rockville, Maryland Office: Suite 500, One Church Street, P.O. Box 1906.
Telephone: 301-217-5600.
Fax: 301-217-5617.
Towson, Maryland Office: 210 Allegheny Avenue, P. O. Box 5517.
Telephone: 410-494-6200.
Fax: 410-821-0147.

MEMBERS OF FIRM

Lars E. Anderson
Kenneth C. Bass, III (Also at Washington, D.C. Office)
William D. Dolan, III (P.C.)
Ellen F. Dyke

For Complete List of Firm Personnel, See General Section

For full biographical listings, see the Martindale-Hubbell Law Directory

NORFOLK, (Independent City)

PAYNE, GATES, FARTHING & RADD, P.C. (AV)

15th Floor, Dominion Tower, 999 Waterside Drive, Suite 1515, 23510-3309
Telephone: 757-640-1500
Facsimile: 757-627-6583
URL: http://www.paynegates.com

Ronald M. Gates
Philip R. Farthing
Anthony F. Radd
Glen M. Robertson
Brian R. Dinning
Todd J. Preti
Marshall A. Winslow, Jr.

C. Arthur Robinson, II
Stephen E. Heretick
Raymond L. Hogge, Jr.

OF COUNSEL

Charles E. Payne

For full biographical listings, see the Martindale-Hubbell Law Directory

STACKHOUSE, SMITH & NEXSEN (AV)

1600 First Virginia Tower, 555 Main Street, P.O. Box 3640, 23514
Telephone: 757-623-3555
Fax: 757-624-9245

(See Next Column)

STACKHOUSE, SMITH & NEXSEN—*Continued*

MEMBERS OF FIRM

Robert C. Stackhouse
Peter W. Smith, IV
William W. Nexsen
R. Clinton Stackhouse, Jr.
Janice McPherson Doxey
Mary Painter Opitz

ASSOCIATES

J. Derek Turrietta
Michael T. Pangalos

Representative Clients: Heritage Bank & Trust; The Atlantic Group, Inc.; Roughton Pontiac Corp; Federal National Mortgage Association; Kemper National Insurance Cos.; Harleysville Mutual Insurance Co.; Heritage Bankshares, Inc.; Presbyterian League of the Presbytery of Eastern Virginia, Inc.; Oakwood Acceptance Corp.; Sovereign Bank, FSB.

For full biographical listings, see the Martindale-Hubbell Law Directory

TAVSS, FLETCHER, MAIDEN & KING, P.C. (AV)

Fourteenth Floor, 555 Main Street, 23510
Telephone: 757-625-1214
Fax: 757-622-7295
Mailing Address: P.O. Box 3747, 23514
Email: tavss@pilot.infi.net

Richard J. Tavss
John R. Fletcher
Ray W. King
Besianne Tavss Maiden
Michael B. Hamar
Kevin J. O'Leary

Reference: Bank of the Commonwealth.

For Complete List of Firm Personnel, See General Section

For full biographical listings, see the Martindale-Hubbell Law Directory

RICHMOND, (Independent City)

WILLIAMS, MULLEN, CLARK & DOBBINS, A PROFESSIONAL CORPORATION (AV)

Two James Center, 1021 East Cary Street, P.O. Box 1320, 23218-1320
Telephone: 804-643-1991
Fax: 804-783-6507
URL: http://www.wmcd.com
Newport News Office: Harbor Bank Center, Suite 210, One Old Oyster Point Road, 23602-7119.
Telephone: 757-249-5100.
Fax: 757-249-5109.
Virginia Beach Office: One Columbus Center, 23462-6763.
Telephone: 757-499-8800.
Fax: 757-473-0395.
Vienna Office: 1593 Spring Hill Road, Suite 510, 22182.
Telephone: 703-760-5200.
Fax: 703-748-0244.
Washington, D.C. Office: The Farragut Building, 900 17th Street, N.W., Suite 700, 20006.
Telephone: 202-293-0213.
Fax: 804-783-6507. Fax Within D.C.: 202-293-5939.
London, England Office: Blake Lodge, Bridge Lane, SW11 3AD.
Telephone: (011-44-71) 223-2756.
Fax: (011-44-71) 350-0156.
Riyadh, Saudi Arabia Affiliate Office: Saudi-American Legal Consultants Commercial Building #2, Diplomatic Quarter, P.O. Box 57270, 11574.
Telephone: (011-966-1) 488-1563.
Fax: (011-966-1) 488-0542.

Michael C. Buseck
Charles L. Cabell
Howard W. Dobbins
Reginald N. Jones
John M. Mercer
G. Andrew Nea, Jr.
Warren E. Nowlin (Resident, Washington, D.C. Office)
Paul G. Saunders, II
William H. Schwarzschild, III
Wayne A. Whitham, Jr.

Jonathan Aaron Frank

For Complete List of Firm Personnel, See General Section

For full biographical listings, see the Martindale-Hubbell Law Directory

ROANOKE, Roanoke City Co.

WOOTEN & HART, A PROFESSIONAL CORPORATION (AV)

707 Building, Suite 300, P.O. Box 12247, 24024-2247
Telephone: 540-343-2451; 540-342-9672
Telecopier: 540-345-6417
URL: http://www.wootenhart.com

George W. Wooten
David B. Hart
L. Thompson Hanes
Susan A. Waddell
Bradley D. McGraw
John L. Cooley
Thomas W. Farrell
Paul C. Kuhnel
Peter D. Vieth

David W. Hearn
John Mark Cooley
Christopher W. Stevens
Elizabeth D. Guilbert
Eunice Park Austin

(See Next Column)

OF COUNSEL

M. Lanier Woodrum

Representative Clients: Wachovia Bank; St. Paul Insurance Cos.
Approved Attorneys for: Lawyers Title Insurance Corp.
Reference: First Union National Bank.

For full biographical listings, see the Martindale-Hubbell Law Directory

VIRGINIA BEACH, (Independent City)

WOLCOTT, RIVERS, WHEARY, BASNIGHT & KELLY, P.C. (AV)

One Columbus Center, Suite 1100, 23462-6765
Telephone: 757-497-6633
FAX: 757-497-7267
Email: wolriv@series2000.com

Wilson L. Rivers
William A. Wheary, III
W. Brantley Basnight, III
Monroe Kelly, III
Carl A. Eason
Joseph R. Mayes
Samuel W. Meekins, Jr.
Edward W. Wolcott, Jr.
Barry Dorans
Leslie R. Watson
David N. Reda
Richard E. Biemiller
Cheshire I'Anson Eveleigh
M. Powell Peters
Neil L. Rose
Robert D. Marotta

David M. Bastiaans
Deborah Kirkpatrick

Counsel for: Metropolitan Life Insurance Co.; Ford Motor Co.
Approved Attorneys for: Lawyers Title Insurance Corp.

For full biographical listings, see the Martindale-Hubbell Law Directory

WEST VIRGINIA

*BECKLEY,** Raleigh Co.

FILE, PAYNE, SCHERER & FILE (AV)

Law Building, 130 Main Street, P.O. Drawer L, 25802
Telephone: 304-253-3358
Fax: 304-255-5136
Email: filepayne@mtneer.net

MEMBERS OF FIRM

Edward M. Payne, III
John Payne Scherer
Robert N. File
William H. File, III

ASSOCIATE

Floyd M. Sayre, III

OF COUNSEL

William Henry File, Jr.

Representative Clients: City National Bank; City Holding Co.; Norfolk and Western Railway Co.; A. T. Massey Coal Co.; State Automobile Mutual Insurance Co.; Continental Insurance Group; Professional Medical Insurance Co.; Natiowide Insurance Company.

For full biographical listings, see the Martindale-Hubbell Law Directory

*CHARLESTON,** Kanawha Co.

JACKSON & KELLY (AV)

1600 Laidley Tower, P.O. Box 553, 25322
Telephone: 304-340-1000
Fax: 304-340-1130
Email: info@jacksonkelly.com *URL:* http://www.jacksonkelly.com
Martinsburg, West Virginia Office: 300 Foxcroft Avenue, P.O. Box 1068.
Telephone: 304-263-8800.
Fax: 304-263-7110.
Morgantown, West Virginia Office: 6000 Hampton Center, P.O. Box 619.
Telephone: 304-599-3000.
Fax: 304-285-2040.
New Martinsville, West Virginia Office: 256 Russell Avenue, P.O. Box 68.
Telephone: 304-455-1751.
Fax: 304-455-6314.
Parkersburg, West Virginia Office: 412 Market Street, Suite 202, P.O. Box 1144.
Telephone: 304-424-3490.
Fax: 304-424-3499.
Fairmont, West Virginia Office: 1000 Technology Drive, Suite 1310.
Telephone: 304-368-2000.
Fax: 304-368-2020.
Lexington, Kentucky Office: 175 East Main Street, Suite 500, P.O. Box 2150.
Telephone: 606-255-9500.
Fax: 606-281-6478.
Washington, D. C. Office: 2401 Pennsylvania Avenue, N.W., Suite 400.
Telephone: 202-973-0200.
Fax: 202-973-0232.
Denver, Colorado Office: Suite 2710, 1660 Lincoln Street.
Telephone: 303-390-0003.
Fax: 303-390-0040.

(See Next Column)

JACKSON & KELLY, *Charleston—Continued*

Wheeling, West Virginia Office: 1144 Market Street.
Telephone: 304-233-4000.
Fax: 304-233-4077.

MEMBERS OF FIRM

James Knight Brown
John R. Lukens
Taunja Willis Miller
Ellen S. Cappellanti
Mary Clare Eros (Administrative Manager, Martinsburg and Charles Town, West Virginia Offices)
Charles D. Dunbar
Kevin M. McGuire (Resident, Lexington, Kentucky Office)
Charles W. Loeb, Jr.
Eric H. London (Morgantown, West Virginia Office)
Elizabeth Osenton Lord

Representative Clients: One Valley Bancorp of West Virginia Inc.; United National Bank; First Empire Federal; Mellon Bank, N.A.; Horizon Bancorp, Inc.; Potomac Bancshares, Inc.; Bank of Gassaway.

For Complete List of Firm Personnel, See General Section

For full biographical listings, see the Martindale-Hubbell Law Directory

*CLARKSBURG,** Harrison Co.

McNEER, HIGHLAND, McMUNN AND VARNER, L.C. (AV)

One Valley Bank Building, P.O. Drawer 2040, 26302-2040
Telephone: 304-626-1100
Facsimile: 304-623-3035
Martinsburg Office: 2520 Aikens Center, P.O. Box 2509.
Telephone: 304-264-4621.
Fax: 304-264-8623.
Parkersburg Office: 404 Market Street, Suite 204, P.O. Box 1507.
Telephone: 304-422-7193.
Facsimile: 304-422-7196.

C. David McMunn
J. Cecil Jarvis
James A. Varner
Robert W. Trumble (Resident, Martinsburg Office)
Catherine D. Munster
James N. Riley
Steven R. Bratke (Resident, Parkersburg Office)
Michael J. Novotny (Resident, Martinsburg Office)
Dennis M. Shreve
Geraldine S. Roberts
William F. Rohrbaugh (Resident, Martinsburg Office)
Gregory H. Schillace
Judy L. Shanholtz
Tiffany R. Durst
Gene W. Bailey, II

OF COUNSEL

James E. McNeer
Cecil B. Highland, Jr.
William L. Fury

Representative Clients: One Valley Bank of Clarksburg, National Assn.; Bruceton Bank; Harrison County Bank; Nationwide Mutual Insurance Cos.; Clarksburg Publishing Co.; C.I.T. Financial Services; State Automobile Mutual Insurance Co.; United Hospital Center, Inc.; West Virginia Coals, Inc.; Swanson Plating Co.

For full biographical listings, see the Martindale-Hubbell Law Directory

*PRINCETON,** Mercer Co.

GIBSON, LEFLER & ASSOCIATES (AV)

1345 Mercer Street, 24740
Telephone: 304-425-8276
800-742-3545

MEMBERS OF FIRM

Michael F. Gibson
Derrick W. Lefler

LEGAL SUPPORT PERSONNEL

NURSE PARALEGAL

Melody Lambert, RN-RLNC

SOCIAL SECURITY PARALEGAL

Nancy Belcher

PERSONAL INJURY PARALEGAL

Kathy Richards

WORKERS COMPENSATION PARALEGAL

Carol Hylton

MEDICAL NEGLIGENCE PARALEGAL

Deborah Frye

For full biographical listings, see the Martindale-Hubbell Law Directory

*WHEELING,** Ohio Co.

SCHRADER BYRD & COMPANION, PLLC (AV)

(A Professional Limited Liability Company)
The Maxwell Centre, 32-20th Street, Suite 500, P.O. Box 6336, 26003
Telephone: 304-233-3390
Fax: 304-233-2769
URL: http://www.schraderlaw.com
Martins Ferry, Ohio Office: 205 North Fifth Street, P.O. Box 309, 43935.
Telephone: 740-633-9976.
Fax: 740-633-0400.

(See Next Column)

Weirton, West Virginia Office: 3205 Pennsylvania Avenue, Suite 103, Penn Place, P.O. Box 2785, 26062.
Telephone: 304-723-2674.
Fax: 304-723-2876.

MEMBERS

Ray A. Byrd
James F. Companion
Frank X. Duff
Teresa Rieman-Camilletti
Yolonda G. Lambert
Daniel P. Fry (Resident Partner, Martins Ferry, Ohio Office)
James P. Mazzone (Resident Member, Weirton, West Virginia Office)
Sandra K. Law
D. Kevin Coleman

SPECIAL COUNSEL

Thomas B. Miller

ASSOCIATES

Denise D. Klug
Michael A. Adams
John Porco
Aimee Morgan Stern
Kimberly R. Wilson
Christopher J. Adams

OF COUNSEL

James A. Byrum, Jr.

General Counsel: Reynolds Memorial Hospital; WesBanco Bank-Elm Grove.
Representative Clients: American Cyanamid Company; Bank One; Matlack Systems, Inc.; Moutaineer Gas Co.; Ohio County Board of Education; PHICO Insurance Co.; Wheeling Hospital; Wheeling-Pittsburg Steel Corp.

For full biographical listings, see the Martindale-Hubbell Law Directory

WISCONSIN

*MILWAUKEE,** Milwaukee Co.

KOHNER, MANN & KAILAS, S.C. (AV)

1572 East Capitol Drive, P.O. Box 11982, 53211-0982
Telephone: 414-962-5110
Fax: 414-962-8725
Email: kmksc@execpc.com

Marvin L. Kohner (1908-1975)

OF COUNSEL

Robert L. Mann

MEMBERS OF FIRM

Steve Kailas
Mark R. Wolters
Jordan B. Reich
David S. Chartier
Roy Paul Roth
Gary P. Lantzy
Christopher C. Kailas
Matthew P. Gerdisch

Robert E. Nailen
Darrell R. Zall
Daniel J. Flynn
Timothy L. Zuberbier
David M. Henry
Lorinne J Cunningham
Palma M. Forte
Daniel J. Emma

Representative Clients: Ecolab, Inc.; Manpower, Inc.; Abbott Laboratories; Norwest Bank Wisconsin, N.A.; Firstar Bank Corporation; Sysco Food Services; Johnson Controls, Inc.; Worth Inc.; Rayovac, Inc.; York International Corporation.

For full biographical listings, see the Martindale-Hubbell Law Directory

QUARLES & BRADY LLP (AV)

411 East Wisconsin Avenue, 53202-4497
Telephone: 414-277-5000
Fax: 414-271-3552
URL: http://www.quarles.com
Madison, Wisconsin Office: Firstar Plaza, One South Pinckney Street, P.O. Box 2113, 53701-2113.
Telephone: 608-251-5000.
Fax: 608-251-9166.
West Palm Beach, Florida Office: 222 Lakeview Avenue, 4th Floor, 33401.
Telephone: 561-653-5000.
Fax: 561-653-5333.
Naples, Florida Office: Barnett Center, 4501 Tamiami Trail North, Suite 300, 34103-3060.
Telephone: 941-262-5959.
Fax: 941-434-4999.
Phoenix, Arizona Office: One Camelback Building, One East Camelback Road, Suite 400, 85012-1649.
Telephone: 602-230-5500.
Fax: 602-230-5598.
Chicago, Illinois Office: Quarles & Brady LLC, Citicorp Center, 500 West Madison Street, Suite 3700.
Telephone: 312-715-5000.
Fax: 312-715-5155.

(See Next Column)

QUARLES & BRADY LLP—*Continued*

MEMBERS OF FIRM

(ALPHABETICALLY BY YEAR OF ADMISSION TO BAR)

Jeremy C. Shea (Resident, Madison Office)
Arthur B. Harris
Patrick M. Ryan
James D. Friedman
F. Joseph McMackin, III (Resident, Naples, Florida Office)
Andrew M. Barnes
Kenneth V. Hallett
Charles H. McMullen
Elizabeth A. Orelup

OF COUNSEL

James Urdan

For Complete List of Firm Personnel, See General Section

For full biographical listings, see the Martindale-Hubbell Law Directory

WYOMING

*CASPER,** Natrona Co.

BROWN, DREW & MASSEY, LLP (AV)

Casper Business Center, Suite 800, 123 West First Street, 82601-2486
Telephone: 307-234-1000
800-877-6755
Telefax: 307-265-8025
Email: brwndrew@coffey.com

MEMBERS OF FIRM

Morris R. Massey
Donn J. McCall
J. Kenneth Barbe
Courtney Robert Kepler

ASSOCIATE

Timothy M. Stubson

Attorneys for: Norwest Bank Wyoming, N.A.; Wells Fargo Bank, N.A.; The CIT Group/Equipment Financing; The CIT Group/Sales Financing; Chase Manhattan Bank, N.A.; NationsBank; FFCA Mortgage Corp.

For Complete List of Firm Personnel, See General Section

For full biographical listings, see the Martindale-Hubbell Law Directory

*CHEYENNE,** Laramie Co.

HICKEY, MACKEY, EVANS & WALKER (AV)

1800 Carey Avenue, Suite 700, P.O. Drawer 467, 82003
Telephone: 307-634-1525
Telecopier: 307-638-7335
URL: http://www.hickeymackey.com

MEMBERS OF FIRM

Paul J. Hickey
Terry W. Mackey
David F. Evans
John M. Walker
Roger C. Fransen
Richard D. Tim Bush
Mary A. Throne

A List of Representative Clients will be furnished upon request.
Reference: Norwest Bank, Cheyenne, N.A.

For full biographical listings, see the Martindale-Hubbell Law Directory

PUERTO RICO

SAN JUAN, San Juan Dist.

FIDDLER GONZÁLEZ & RODRÍGUEZ, LLP

254 Muñoz Rivera Avenue (Hato Rey), P.O. Box 363507, 00936-3507
Telephone: 787-753-3113
Telecopier: 787-759-3123
Email: fiddler@fgrlaw.com *URL:* http://www.fgrlaw.com

MEMBERS OF FIRM

Rafael Cortés-Dapena
Antonio R. Sifre

Representative Clients: The Chase Manhattan Bank, N.A.; Banco Bilbao Vizcaya; The Bank & Trust Company of Puerto Rico; Shearson, Lehman, Hutton.

For Complete List of Firm Personnel, See General Section

For full biographical listings, see the Martindale-Hubbell Law Directory

GOLDMAN ANTONETTI & CÓRDOVA

American International Plaza Fourteenth & Fifteenth Floors, 250 Muñoz Rivera Avenue (Hato Rey), P.O. Box 70364, 00936-0364
Telephone: 787-759-8000
Telecopiers: 787-767-9333 (Main)
787-767-9177 (Litigation Department)
787-767-8660 (Labor & Corporate Law Departments)
787-767-9325 (Tax & Environmental Law Departments)
URL: http://www.gaclaw.com

MEMBERS OF FIRM

Jorge Souss
Pedro Morell Losada
Thelma Rivera-Miranda
Georgiana S. Colón

SPECIAL COUNSEL

Jaime Morgan-Stubbe

ASSOCIATES

María Patricia Lake
Vanessa Bayonet-Tartak
Maura Santiago-Ducos

Representative Clients: Banque Paribas; The Bank of Nova Scotia; The Royal Bank of Canada; Scotiabank de Puerto Rico.

For Complete List of Firm Personnel, See General Section

For full biographical listings, see the Martindale-Hubbell Law Directory

JORGE R. JIMENEZ LAW OFFICES

Suite 807 IBM Building, 654 Muñoz Rivera Avenue (Hato Rey), 00918
Telephone: 787-763-0106
Fax: 787-763-0574

MEMBERS OF FIRM

Jorge R. Jimenez
Juan F. Doval

For full biographical listings, see the Martindale-Hubbell Law Directory

MARTÍNEZ ODELL & CALABRIA

Banco Popular Center, 209 Muñoz Rivera Avenue, Suite 1600 (Hato Rey), P.O. Box 190998, 00919-0998
Telephone: 787-753-8914
Facsimile: 787-753-8402; 787-759-9075; 787-764-5664
Email: postmaster@mocpr.com

MEMBERS OF FIRM

Lawrence Odell
Juan Ramón Cancio-Ortiz
Luis E. Lopez Correa
Luis Morales-Steinmann
Javier E. Ferrer-Canals
Arnaldo Villamil
Maria del Carmen Garriga
Eric Perez Ochoa
Ramón Eugenio-Meléndez
Rafael Kodesh-Baragaño
Jose Antonio Fernandez-Jaquete
Jose David Medina-Rivera
Carlos P. Santiago-Sarkis

OF COUNSEL

Jose B. Diaz Asencio
Francisco Orsini-Capo

ASSOCIATES

Carmen J. Rocafort
Jorge L. Covas-Mendoza
Jaime L. Vazquez-Bernier
Mariela Garcia-Colberg
Luis A. Hernandez-Vivoni
Gustavo J. Umpierre-Ponton
Brigitte S. Krumhansl
Mario Loyola

Representative Clients: Banco Popular de Puerto Rico; Daewoo Motor Corporation; Eckerd Corporation; Empresas Fonalledas; Hilton International; L'Aire Liquide, S.A.; Loctile Corporation; Lucent Technologies; Lutron Electronics Co., Inc.; Waste Management, Inc.

For Complete List of Firm Personnel, See General Section

For full biographical listings, see the Martindale-Hubbell Law Directory

VIRGIN ISLANDS

*CHARLOTTE AMALIE, ST. THOMAS,** St. Thomas

GRUNERT STOUT & BRUCH

24-25 Kongensgade, P.O. Box 1030, 00804
Telephone: 340-774-1320
Fax: 340-774-7839
Email: gsbusvi@viaccess.net
Affiliated with: Solomon Pearl Blum & Quinn LLP, New York, New York and Denver, Colorado.

MEMBERS OF FIRM

John E. Stout
Susan Bruch Moorehead

ASSOCIATE

Gabriel J. Villegas

OF COUNSEL

William L. Blum

For full biographical listings, see the Martindale-Hubbell Law Directory

CANADA
ALBERTA

*CALGARY,** Calgary Jud. Dist.

BENNETT JONES (AV)

4500 Bankers Hall East, 855-2nd Street S.W., T2P 4K7
Telephone: 403-298-3100
Facsimile: 403-265-7219
Email: firmwatch@bennettjones.ca *URL:* http://www.bennettjones.ca
Edmonton, Alberta Office: 1000, 10035-105 Street.
Telephone: 780-421-8133.
Facsimile: 780-421-7951.
Toronto, Ontario Office: 3400 1 First Canadian Place, P.O. Box 130.
Telephone: 416-863-1200.
Facsimile: 416-863-1716.

MEMBER OF FIRM

Philip D. Backman

For Complete List of Firm Personnel, See General Section

For full biographical listings, see the Martindale-Hubbell Law Directory

PARLEE MCLAWS (AV)

3400 Petro-Canada Centre, 150 - 6th Avenue, SW, T2P 3Y7
Telephone: 403-294-7000
Telecopier: 403-265-8263
Email: lawyers@parlee.com *URL:* http://www.parlee.com
Edmonton, Alberta Office: 15th Floor Manulife Place, 10180 101st Street.
Telephone: 403-423-8500.
Telecopier: 403-423-2870.

MEMBER OF FIRM

Dale R. Spackman, Q.C.

ASSOCIATE

Seema S. Johal

For Complete List of Firm Personnel, See General Section

For full biographical listings, see the Martindale-Hubbell Law Directory

*EDMONTON,** Edmonton Jud. Dist.

PARLEE MCLAWS (AV)

15th Floor Manulife Place, 10180 101st Street, T5J 4K1
Telephone: 403-423-8500
Telecopier: 403-423-2870
Email: lawyers@parlee.com *URL:* http://www.parlee.com
Calgary, Alberta Office: 3400 Petro-Canada Centre, 150 - 6th Avenue, SW.
Telephone: 403-294-7000.
Telecopier: 403-265-8263.

MEMBERS OF FIRM

Colin H. Kerr, Q.C.
Frank J. Niziol
Douglas L. Kennedy
Robert A. Newton, Q.C.
Ian L. MacLachlan
David S. Tam

For Complete List of Firm Personnel, See General Section

For full biographical listings, see the Martindale-Hubbell Law Directory

CANADA
NEW BRUNSWICK

*FREDERICTON,** York Co.

COX HANSON O'REILLY MATHESON (AV)

(Formerly Hanson Hashey)
Suite 400, Phoenix Square, P.O. Box 310, E3B 4Y9
Telephone: 506-453-7771
Fax: 506-453-9600
Email: fredericton@coxhanson.ca *URL:* http://www.coxhanson.ca
Halifax, Nova Scotia Office: Suite 1100, Purdy's Wharf Tower 1, P.O. Box 2380 Station Central RPO, B3J 3E5.
Telephone: 902-421-6262.
Fax: 902-421-3130. E-Mail: halifax@coxhanson.ca
Saint John, New Brunswick Office: 1212-One Brunswick Square, 1 Germain St. E2L 4V1.
Telephone: 506-652-7771.
Fax: 506-632-9600.
St. John's, Newfoundland Office: Scotia Centre, 401-235 Water Street, A1C 1B6.
Telephone: 709-726-3321.
Fax: 709-726-2992. E-Mail: stjohns@coxhanson.ca
Charlottetown, Prince Edward Island Office: Queen Square, Suite 202, 119 Queen Street, P.O. Box 875, Station Central, C1A 7L9.
Telephone: 902-894-7051.
Fax: 902-368-3762. E-Mail: charlottetown@coxhanson.ca

(See Next Column)

MEMBERS OF FIRM

H. A. Hanson, Q.C. (1909-1985)
David T. Hashey, Q.C.
David M. Norman, Q.C.
J. Ian M. Whitcomb, Q.C.
John M. Hanson, Q.C.
Walter D. Vail, Q.C.
Michael E. Bowlin
John D. Larlee, Q.C.
Bruce D. Hatfield, Q.C.
Julian A. G. Dickson, Q.C.
Anne D. Wooder
Terrence J. Morrison
Lucie Richard
Catherine M. Bowlen
J. Marc Richard

ASSOCIATES

Amanda J. Frenette
Monika M. L. Zauhar
Jade A. Spalding
William E. Gould
Christopher R. DeLong
Deborah M. Power
Corinne A. Godbout
Marc-Antoine Chiasson

For full biographical listings, see the Martindale-Hubbell Law Directory

MCINNES COOPER (AV)

Suite 600, 570 Queen Street, P.O. Box 610, E3B 5A6
Telephone: 506-458-8572
Fax: 506-458-9903
Email: mcrfton@mcrlaw.com *URL:* http://www.mcrlaw.com
Halifax, Nova Scotia Office: Summit Place, 1601 Lower Water Street, P.O. Box 730, B3J 2V1.
Telephone: 902-425-6500.
Fax: 902-425-6350. Email: mcrhfx@mcrlaw.com.
St. John's, Newfoundland Office: Baine Johnston Centre, 5th Floor, 10 Fort William Place, P.O. Box 5939, A1C 5X4.
Telephone: 709-722-8735.
Telecopier: 709-722-1763. Email: mcrsj@mcrlaw.com.
Moncton, New Brunswick Office: Place Moncton Place, 655 Main Street, P.O. Box 1368, E1C 8T6.
Telephone: 506-857-8970.
Fax: 506-857-4095. Email: mcrmctn@mcrlaw.com.
Charlottetown, Prince Edward Island Office: BDC Place, Suite 620, 119 Kent Street, C1A 1N3.
Telephone: 902-368-8473.
Fax: 902-368-8346. Email: mcrpei@mcrlaw.com.

PARTNER

David Duncan Young

For Complete List of Firm Personnel, See General Section

For full biographical listings, see the Martindale-Hubbell Law Directory

*MONCTON,** Westmorland Co.

MCINNES COOPER (AV)

Barristers, Solicitors & Trade Mark Agents
Place Moncton Place, 655 Main Street, P.O. Box 1368, E1C 8T6
Telephone: 506-857-8970
Fax: 506-857-4095
Email: mcrmctn@mcrlaw.com *URL:* http://www.mcrlaw.com
Halifax, Nova Scotia Office: Summit Place, 1601 Lower Water Street, P.O. Box 730, B3J 2V1.
Telephone: 902-425-6500.
Fax: 902-425-6350. Email: mcrhfx@mcrlaw.com.
St. John's, Newfoundland Office: Baine Johnston Centre, 5th Floor, 10 Fort William Place, P.O. Box 5939, A1C 5X4.
Telephone: 709-722-8735.
Telecopier: 709-722-1763. Email: mcrsj@mcrlaw.com.
Charlottetown, Prince Edward Island Office: BDC Place, Suite 620, 119 Kent Street, C1A 1N3.
Telephone: 902-368-8473.
Fax: 902-368-8346. Email: mcrpei@mcrlaw.com.
Fredericton, New Brunswick Office: Suite 600, 570 Queen Street, P.O. Box 610.
Telephone: 506-458-8572.
Fax: 506-458-9903. Email: mcrfton@mcrlaw.com.

PARTNER

Bernard F. Miller

ASSOCIATE

Sylvie C. Roussel

For Complete List of Firm Personnel, See General Section

For full biographical listings, see the Martindale-Hubbell Law Directory

*SAINT JOHN,** Saint John Co.

CLARK DRUMMIE (AV)

40 Wellington Row, P.O. Box 6850, E2L 4S3
Telephone: 506-633-3800
Telecopier (Automatic): 506-633-3811
Email: cd@nbnet.nb.ca

MEMBERS OF FIRM

Thomas B. Drummie, Q.C.
Donald F. MacGowan, Q.C.
Willard M. Jenkins

Reference: Royal Bank of Canada.

(See Next Column)

CLARK DRUMMIE—*Continued*

For Complete List of Firm Personnel, See General Section

For full biographical listings, see the Martindale-Hubbell Law Directory

CANADA
NEWFOUNDLAND

*ST. JOHN'S,**

McINNES COOPER (AV)

Barristers, Solicitors & Trade Mark Agents
Baine Johnston Centre, 5th Floor, 10 Fort William Place, P.O. Box 5939, A1C 5X4
Telephone: 709-722-8735
Telecopier: 709-722-1763
Email: mcrsj@mcrlaw.com *URL:* http://www.mcrlaw.com
Halifax, Nova Scotia Office: Summit Place, 1601 Lower Water Street, P.O. Box 730, B3J 2V1.
Telephone: 902-425-6500.
Fax: 902-425-6350. Email: mcrhfx@mcrlaw.com.
Moncton, New Brunswick Office: Place Moncton Place, 655 Main Street, P.O. Box 1368, E1C 8T6.
Telephone: 506-857-8970.
Fax: 506-857-4095. Email: mcrmctn@mcrlaw.com.
Charlottetown, Prince Edward Island Office: BDC Place, Suite 620, 119 Kent Street, C1A 1N3.
Telephone: 902-368-8473.
Fax: 902-368-8346. Email: mcrpei@mcrlaw.com.
Fredericton, New Brunswick Office: Suite 600, 570 Queen Street, P.O. Box 610.
Telephone: 506-458-8572.
Fax: 506-458-9903. Email: mcrfton@mcrlaw.com.

PARTNERS

Deborah L. J. Hutchings
Caroline C. Watton

For Complete List of Firm Personnel, See General Section

For full biographical listings, see the Martindale-Hubbell Law Directory

CANADA
NOVA SCOTIA

*HALIFAX,** Regional Munic. of Halifax

McINNES COOPER (AV)

Barristers, Solicitors & Trade Mark Agents
Summit Place, 1601 Lower Water Street, P.O. Box 730, B3J 2V1
Telephone: 902-425-6500
Fax: 902-425-6350
Email: mcrhfx@mcrlaw.com *URL:* http://www.mcrlaw.com
St. John's, Newfoundland Office: Baine Johnston Centre, 5th Floor, 10 Fort William Place, P.O. Box 5939, A1C 5X4.
Telephone: 709-722-8735.
Telecopier: 709-722-1763. Email: mcrsj@mcrlaw.com.
Moncton, New Brunswick Office: Place Moncton Place, 655 Main Street, P.O. Box 1368, E1C 8T6.
Telephone: 506-857-8970.
Fax: 506-857-4095. Email: mcrmctn@mcrlaw.com.
Charlottetown, Prince Edward Island Office: BDC Place, Suite 620, 119 Kent Street, C1A 1N3.
Telephone: 902-368-8473.
Fax: 902-368-8346. Email: mcrpei@mcrlaw.com.
Fredericton, New Brunswick Office: Suite 600, 570 Queen Street, P.O. Box 610.
Telephone: 506-458-8572.
Fax: 506-458-9903. Email: mcrfton@mcrlaw.com.

PARTNERS

Reginald A. Cluney, Q.C.
David H. Reardon, Q.C.
Lawrence A. Freeman
John D. Stringer, Q.C.
Joseph A. F. Macdonald, Q.C.
Robert G. Belliveau, Q.C.
F. Van W. Penick
Fae J. Shaw
Stephen Kingston

ASSOCIATE

Frank E. Hughes

For Complete List of Firm Personnel, See General Section

For full biographical listings, see the Martindale-Hubbell Law Directory

CANADA
ONTARIO

MISSISSAUGA, Regional Munic. of Peel

KEYSER MASON BALL (AV)

201 City Centre Drive, Suite 701, L5B 2T4
Telephone: 905-276-9111
Fax: 905-276-2298
Email: kmb@kmblaw.com *URL:* http://www.kmblaw.com

MEMBERS OF FIRM

Colin I. Mason, Q.C.
John B. Keyser, Q.C.
John J. Ball
Garth D. Walkden
Eugene J. A. Gierczak
James D. Henderson
M. Lee Stratton
Ruben R. Goulart
Mary J. Main
Robert E. Jarvis, Q.C.
Brian M. Jenkins
Marc S. Tannenbaum
Lorelei G. Graham
Ian J. Wick
Paul M. Demelo
Anthony De Fazekas
Patrizia A. Piccolo
Patrick Thomas Bourk
Jennifer L. Ferguson
Liane LaGroix

COUNSEL

The Honourable B. Barry Shapiro, C.O., Q.C.

For full biographical listings, see the Martindale-Hubbell Law Directory

*TORONTO,** Regional Munic. of Toronto

BORDEN & ELLIOT (AV)

Barristers & Solicitors
Scotia Plaza, 40 King Street West, M5H 3Y4
Telephone: 416-367-6000
Telecopier: 416-367-6749
Email: info@borden.com *URL:* http://www.borden.com
Ottawa, Ontario Office: Borden Elliot Scott & Aylen, 1000-60 Rue Queen Street.
Telephone: 613-237-5160; 800-661-4237. General
Facsimile: 613-230-8842. IP Dept.
Facsimile: 613-787-3558. Email: ottinfo@scottaylen.com. URL: http://www.borden.com.

William S. Robertson

For Complete List of Firm Personnel, See General Section

For full biographical listings, see the Martindale-Hubbell Law Directory

DAVIES, WARD & BECK (AV)

1 First Canadian Place, M5X 1B1
Telephone: 416-863-0900
Fax: 416-863-0871
Email: info@dwb.com *URL:* http://www.dwb.com

PARTNERS AND ASSOCIATES

Mark Q. Connelly
William M. O'Reilly
Robert T. Bauer
Arthur S. Shiff
Gray E. Taylor
Gregory J. Howard
Carol D. Pennycook
Edward C. Hannah
Catherine G. Ross
D. Shawn McReynolds
Michael Creery
James J. Lawson
Carol Hansell
Vincent A. Mercier
Timothy H. Moran
Patrick G. Barry
Gillian R. Stacey
Paolo Boni
Julianna S. Ahn
Delphine Brooker
Andrea E. Daly
Terrance J. Ritchie
Steven M. Harris
Nicholas J. Leblovic
Jay A. Swartz
I. Berl Nadler
Jean-Paul Bisnaire
Michael Disney
William M. Ainley
A. Gerold Goldlist
Jeffrey O. Palmer
Paul M. Kennedy
Kevin J. Thomson
Ian D. Johnson
Thomas A. Smee
Ian R. McBride
Cameron M. Rusaw
Michael W. Clifford
Sarbjit S. Basra
Andrew L. Welsh
Jennifer A. Pfuetzner
Dany H. Assaf
Andrea L. Burke
Sabrina Gherbaz
Paul W. Golding
Christopher H. Jones
Jennifer L. Toone

For Complete List of Firm Personnel, See General Section

For full biographical listings, see the Martindale-Hubbell Law Directory

KELLY AFFLECK GREENE (AV)

One First Canadian Place, Suite 840, P.O. Box 489, M5X 1E5
Telephone: 416-360-2800
Fax: 416-360-5960
Email: info@kag.net *URL:* http://www.kag.net

(See Next Column)

KELLY AFFLECK GREENE, *Toronto—Continued*

MEMBERS OF FIRM

W. Anthony Kelly, Q.C.
Donald S. Affleck, Q.C.
Peter R. Greene
Donald B. Houston
James C. Orr
Peter C. Wardle
Helen A. Daley
Melissa J. Kennedy

ASSOCIATES

Kenneth A. Dekker
W. Michael G. Osborne
Jason C. Markwell
Patrice F. Band

For full biographical listings, see the Martindale-Hubbell Law Directory

CANADA PRINCE EDWARD ISLAND

*CHARLOTTETOWN,** Queen's Co.

MCINNES COOPER (AV®)

Barristers, Solicitors & Trade Mark Agents
BDC Place, Suite 620, 119 Kent Street, C1A 1N3
Telephone: 902-368-8473
Fax: 902-368-8346
Email: mcrpei@mcrlaw.com *URL:* http://www.mcrlaw.com
Halifax, Nova Scotia Office: Summit Place, 1601 Lower Water Street, P.O. Box 730, B3J 2V1.
Telephone: 902-425-6500.
Fax: 902-425-6350. Email: mcrhfx@mcrlaw.com.
St. John's, Newfoundland Office: Baine Johnston Centre, 5th Floor, 10 Fort William Place, P.O. Box 5939, A1C 5X4.
Telephone: 709-722-8735.
Telecopier: 709-722-1763. Email: mcrsj@mcrlaw.com.
Moncton, New Brunswick Office: Place Moncton Place, 655 Main Street, P.O. Box 1368, E1C 8T6.
Telephone: 506-857-8970.
Fax: 506-857-4095. Email: mcrmctn@mcrlaw.com.
Fredericton, New Brunswick Office: Suite 600, 570 Queen Street, P.O. Box 610.
Telephone: 506-458-8572.
Fax: 506-458-9903. Email: mcrfton@mcrlaw.com.

ASSOCIATES

L. Charles Keizer
Kevin J. Kiley

For Complete List of Firm Personnel, See General Section

For full biographical listings, see the Martindale-Hubbell Law Directory

CANADA QUEBEC

*MONTREAL,** Montreal Dist.

GOLDSTEIN, FLANZ & FISHMAN (AV)

Suite 4100, 1250 René-Lévesque Boulevard West, H3B 4W8
Telephone: 514-932-4100
Cable Address: "Meybat"
Telex: 05-24593
Telecopier: 514-932-4170
Email: counsel@gff.qc.ca

MEMBERS OF FIRM

Yoine Goldstein
Leonard W. Flanz
Avram Fishman
Mark Schrager
Gilles Paquin
Mark E. Meland
Ellen Amdursky
Alain Daigle
Cathy Noseworthy
Suzanne Villeneuve

For full biographical listings, see the Martindale-Hubbell Law Directory

MCMASTER GERVAIS (AV)

A General Partnership
1000 de La Gauchetière Street West, Suite 900, H3B 5H4
Telephone: 514-879-1212
Fax: 514-954-1905
Email: info@mcmastergervais.com *URL:* http://www.mcmastergervais.com

MEMBERS OF FIRM

Alexis P. Bergeron
Elizabeth A. Mitchell
Roger P. Simard
D. James Papadimitriou
Patricia Galella
Antoine Leduc
Grégoire Baillargeon
Norman A. Saibil
Benoît M. Provost
Pierre B. Côté
P. Vivian Cyriacopoulos
Gary Rivard
Marc-Antoine La Rochelle
Daniel Ferreira

(See Next Column)

For Complete List of Firm Personnel, See General Section

For full biographical listings, see the Martindale-Hubbell Law Directory

MENDELSOHN ROSENTZVEIG SHACTER (AV)

1000 Sherbrooke Street West, 27th Floor, H3A 3G4
Telephone: 514-987-5000
Telex: 05-27284 Colorlaw
Telecopier: 514-987-1213
Email: mrs@mrslaw.com *URL:* http://www.mrslaw.com

PARTNERS

S. Leon Mendelsohn, Q.C. (1902-1996)
Leo Rosentzveig, Q.C.
Manuel Shacter, Q.C.
Jack C. Shayne
William Levitt
Arthur A. Garvis
Edward E. Aronoff
L. Michael Blumenstein
Max Mendelsohn
Earl S. Cohen
Michael Garonce
Donald M. Devine
Richard S. Uditsky
Joel Weitzman
Ian R. Rudnikoff
Marc I. Leiter
L. B. Erdle
Fredric L. Carsley
Frank Zylberberg
Jules Brossard
David L. Rosentzveig
Judie K. Jokinen
Gilles Seguin
Martin Desrosiers
Andrew Etcovitch
Alain Breault
Jean Carrière
Henri M. Bybelezer
Louis Frédérick Côté
Sandra Abitan

ASSOCIATES

Carl M. Ravinsky
Catherine Muraz
Francine Wiseman
Joelle Sebag
Maria R. Battaglia
Keyvan Nassiry
Linda Schachter
Emmanuelle Saucier
Arnold Cohen
Aaron Makovka
Michel Rochefort
Céline Tessier
Sophie Crevier
Annick Joyal
Francis Desmarais
Nicolas J. Beugnot
Jean-François Brière
Marc-Antoine Deschamps
Philipp F. Duffy
Fred Purkey
Martin Sills
David Tardif-Latourelle

For full biographical listings, see the Martindale-Hubbell Law Directory

POULIOT, MERCURE (AV)

CIBC Tower, 31st Floor, 1155 René-Lévesque Boulevard, West, H3B 3S6
Telephone: 514-875-5210
Telecopier: 514-875-4308
Email: POUMER@CEDEP.COM
Genève, Suisse Office: 8, Rue de la Rôtisserie, 1204 Geneva, Switzerland.
Telephone: +41 22-28 79 40.
Telecopier: +41 22-21 23 67.

MEMBERS OF FIRM

Georges A. Pouliot, Q.C.
Gilles Brunelle
Luc Gratton
Brian Riordan
Pierre Paquet
Anne-Marie Gauthier
Yvon Brizard
Robert Tessier
Daniel Gagné
Lilia Pouliot
Marco Veilleux
Alain Nadon
Jean H. Gagnon
Richard Fontaine
Normand Royal
Gilles Bertrand
Jean Larivière
Louis-Michel Tremblay
David I. Johnston
Stéphane Hébert
Jacques LeBel, Q.C.
Joel A. Silcoff
Ronald M. Auclair
Philippe Roy
Maxime B. Rhéaume
Serge Desrochers
C. Keenan LaPierre
Alain Bond
Louis Coallier
Nicole Chouinard
Stéphane Teasdale

ASSOCIATES

Micheline Perrault
Caroline Lemoine
Béatrice Arronis
Yvan Nantel
Sylvie Boulanger
Vincent Frenette
Robert Cardin
Alexandre Henri
Brent J. Muir
Louise Tremblay
Chantal Joubert
Normand D'Amour
Pascale Cloutier
Eric Couture
Frédéric Chatel
Mary-Lynn Breton
Alexandre Ajami

For full biographical listings, see the Martindale-Hubbell Law Directory

CANADA
SASKATCHEWAN

*REGINA,** Regina Jud. Centre

MacPherson Leslie & Tyerman (AV)

1500-1874 Scarth Street, S4P 4E9
Telephone: 306-347-8000
Telecopier: 306-352-5250
Email: mltreg@mlt.com
Saskatoon, Saskatchewan Office: 1500-410 22nd Street East, S7K 5T6.
Telephone: 306-975-7100.
Telecopier: 306-975-7145.

MEMBERS OF FIRM

Harold H. MacKay, Q.C.
R. Neil MacKay
Donald K. Wilson, Q.C.
John A. Dipple

ASSOCIATES

Michele T. Klebuc-Simes
Aaron D. Runge

For Complete List of Firm Personnel, See General Section

For full biographical listings, see the Martindale-Hubbell Law Directory

BANKRUPTCY LAW

MINNESOTA

*MINNEAPOLIS,** Hennepin Co.

HESSIAN & MCKASY, P.A. (AV)

4700 IDS Center, 80 South Eighth Street, 55402-2228
Telephone: 612-330-3000
Telecopier: 612-371-0653
St. Paul, Minnesota Offices: 2050 Piper Jaffray Plaza, 444 Cedar Street, 55101.
Telephone: 612-330-3071.
Fax: 651-228-9161.

Glen E. Schumann
Jaymes D. Littlejohn
Steven T. Hetland

OF COUNSEL

Darrell B. Johnson

For full biographical listings, see the Martindale-Hubbell Law Directory

HOLPER, WELSH & MITCHELL, LTD. (AV)

10 South Fifth Street, Suite 300, 55402
Telephone: 612-317-1012
Fax: 612-317-0947
Email: rholper@aol.com *URL:* http://www.lawyers.com/holperwelsh&mitchell
Phoenix, Arizona Office: 2415 East Camelback Road, Suite 700, 85016.
Telephone: 602-508-6033.
Fax: 480-483-0269.

Richard D. Holper
Mary Ann Welsh
Ralph V. Mitchell, Jr.

For full biographical listings, see the Martindale-Hubbell Law Directory

THE JOANIS LAW GROUP (AV)

630 Pillsbury Center, 200 South Sixth Street, 55402
Telephone: 612-373-2200
Fax: 612-373-2222
Email: inquiry@joanislaw.com *URL:* http://www.joanislaw.com
Blooming Prairie, Minnesota Office: 236 East Main Street.
Telephone: 507-583-7272.
Fax: 507-583-7343.

Richard M. Bell
William J. Joanis
Eric J. Sherburne

James L. Gunn, IV

For full biographical listings, see the Martindale-Hubbell Law Directory

THOMAS G. LOVETT, JR. (AV)

100 South Fifth Street, Suite 2250, 55402
Telephone: 612-339-4567
Voice Mail: 612-573-4685
Fax: 612-349-6210
Email: LOVET001@tc.UMN.EDU

For full biographical listings, see the Martindale-Hubbell Law Directory

MANSFIELD TANICK & COHEN, P.A. (AV)

1560 International Centre, 900 Second Avenue South, 55402
Telephone: 612-339-4295
Fax: 612-339-3161
Email: tanick@mansfieldtanick.com *URL:* http://www.mansfieldtanick.com

Seymour J. Mansfield
Marshall H. Tanick
Earl H. Cohen
Robert A. Johnson
Teresa J. Ayling
Richard J. Fuller

Phillip J. Trobaugh
Debra S. Lepert
Ann M. Zewiske
V. John Ella

OF COUNSEL

James P. Cullen
Sholly A. Blustin

For full biographical listings, see the Martindale-Hubbell Law Directory

OPPENHEIMER WOLFF & DONNELLY LLP (AV)

3400 Plaza VII, 45 South Seventh Street, 55402
Telephone: 612-607-7000
FAX: 612-607-7100
URL: http://www.owdlaw.com
Amsterdam, The Netherlands Office: Keizergracht 241.
Telephone: 31-20-423-4555.
FAX: 31-20-423-4545.
Brussels, Belgium Office: Avenue Louise 240, Box 5, 1050.
Telephone: 32-2-626-0500.
FAX: 32-2-626-0510.
Geneva, Switzerland Office: Rue Gabriel Eynard, 6, 1205.
Telephone: (41/22) 311-7410.
FAX: (41/22) 311-7407.
New York, N.Y. Office: Citicorp Center, 153 East 53rd Street, 10022.
Telephone: 212-826-5000.
FAX: 212-486-0708.
Newport Beach, California Office: 500 Newport Center Drive, Suite 700, 92660.
Telephone: 949-719-6000.
FAX: 949-719-6020.
Paris, France Office: 53 Avenue Montaigne, 75008.
Telephone: (33/1) 44 95 03 50.
FAX: (33/1) 44 95 03 40.
St. Paul, Minnesota Office: 1700 First National Bank Building, 55101.
Telephone: 651-605-2000.
FAX: 651-605-2100.
Washington, D.C. Office: Oppenheimer Wolff Donnelly & Bayh LLP, 1350 Eye Street, N.W., Suite 200, 20005.
Telephone: 202-312-8000.
FAX: 202-312-8100.
Los Angeles, California Office: 2029 Century Park East, 38th Floor, 90067.
Telephone: 310-788-5000.
FAX: 310-277-1297.
San Jose, California Office: 101 Park Center Plaza, Suite 300, 95113.
Telephone: 408-795-3000.
FAX: 408-795-3100.
Chicago, Illinois Office: Oppenheimer Wolff & Donnelly (Illinois), Two Prudential Plaza, 45th Floor, 180 North Stetson Avenue, 60601.
Telephone: 312-616-1800.
Fax: 312-616-5800.

RESIDENT PARTNERS

Jerome A. Miranowski
Shannon M. O'Toole
Edward T. Wahl
Mark J. Kalla
Steven W. Meyer
Michael B. Fisco
Robert J. McGillivray
Mark G. Rabogliatti

RESIDENT ASSOCIATES

Rikke A. Dierssen-Morice
James M. Jorissen
Anne F. Larsen
Marcus A. Mollison
Patrice H. Kloss
Connie A. Lunceford-Hedtke
Michael F. Cockson
David E. Runck

For Complete List of Firm Personnel, See General Section

For full biographical listings, see the Martindale-Hubbell Law Directory

*ST. PAUL,** Ramsey Co.

STEIN, MOORE & FAY, P.A. (AV)

1010 Minnesota Building, 55101
Telephone: 651-224-9683
Telecopier: 651-223-5212
URL: http://www.steinmoorefay.com

Peter B. Stein
Ralph L. Moore
Jonathan (Jack) R. Fay

Reference: Firstar Bank of Minnesota, N.A.

For full biographical listings, see the Martindale-Hubbell Law Directory

MISSISSIPPI

*ABERDEEN,** Monroe Co.

PATTERSON & PATTERSON (AV)

304 East Jefferson Street, P.O. Box 663, 39730
Telephone: 662-369-2476
Fax: 662-369-9806
Email: JPP@ebicom.net

MEMBERS OF FIRM

Robert D. Patterson
Jan P. Patterson
Peter T. Martin

Local Counsel for: National Bank of Commerce of Mississippi; American Colloid Company; Condea Vista Company; Pruet Production Co.; Arco Oil & Gas Co.; Chemical Corporation; Unimin Corporation; Leggett & Platt; Furst-McNess.
Approved Title Attorneys for: First American Title Insurance Co.

For full biographical listings, see the Martindale-Hubbell Law Directory

*CLEVELAND,** Bolivar Co.

LEVINGSTON & LEVINGSTON (AV)

201 South Pearman Avenue, P.O. Box 1327, 38732-3247
Telephone: 601-843-2791
Fax: 601-843-2797
Email: jleving@tecinfo.com

MEMBERS OF FIRM

Alfred A. Levingston (1917-1997)
Jeffrey A. Levingston

General Counsel for: Bolivar County Drainage Commissioners; Bolivar County Hospital; City of Shelby.
Local Counsel for: Commercial Union; Maryland Casualty Co.; Federated Mutual Implement & Hardware Insurance Co.; Baxter-Travenol Laboratories, Inc.

For full biographical listings, see the Martindale-Hubbell Law Directory

*GULFPORT,** Harrison Co.

DUKES, DUKES, KEATING AND FANECA, P.A. (AV)

2909 13th Street, 6th Floor, P.O. Drawer W, 39501
Telephone: 228-868-1111
Fax: 228-863-2886
Email: ddkf@ddkf.com

Hugh D. Keating

William W. Abbott, Jr.

For Complete List of Firm Personnel, See General Section

For full biographical listings, see the Martindale-Hubbell Law Directory

MEADOWS RILEY LAW FIRM (AV)

1720 23rd Avenue, P.O. Box 550, 39502
Telephone: 601-864-4511
Telecopier: 601-868-2178

Joseph R. Meadows
Donnie D. Riley
Jerry D. Riley
Karen J. Young

Representative Clients: Bubba Oustalat Lincoln Mercury, Inc.; Lee Tractor Co. of Mississippi.
Reference: Hancock Bank.

For full biographical listings, see the Martindale-Hubbell Law Directory

*JACKSON,** Hinds Co.

BENNETT LOTTERHOS SULSER & WILSON, P.A. (AV)

One Jackson Place Suite 1400, 188 East Capitol Street, P.O. Box 98, 39205-0098
Telephone: 601-944-0466
Telecopier: 601-944-0467

Richard T. Bennett
Joseph E. Lotterhos
Marcus M. Wilson
Edward E. Lawler, Jr.
Mary E. McAlister
J. Mark Franklin, III
Ronald Keith Foreman
John L. Pannier

OF COUNSEL

Floyd M. Sulser, Jr.

Representative Clients: Agristor Leasing; Chubb Group of Insurance Companies; 84 Lumber Company; European American Bank; FSLIC; Great Southern Federal Savings; Hibernia National Bank; Holiday Inns, Inc; Masonite Corp.

For full biographical listings, see the Martindale-Hubbell Law Directory

UNDERWOOD LAW FIRM (AV)

340 Edgewood Terrace Drive, P.O. Box 16852, 37206
Telephone: 601-981-7773
Telecopier: 601-362-5673
Email: ulfm@aol.com *URL:* http://www.lawyers.com/underwoodlawfirm

John C. Underwood, Jr.

ASSOCIATES

Catherine W. Underwood
Robert E Moorehead

For full biographical listings, see the Martindale-Hubbell Law Directory

WATKINS & EAGER (AV)

A Professional Limited Liability Company
Suite 300 The Emporium Building, 400 East Capitol Street, P.O. Box 650, 39205
Telephone: 601-948-6470
Facsimile: 601-354-3623

MEMBERS OF FIRM

Thomas R. Crews
John G. Corlew
Jamie G. Houston, III
Frank J. Hammond, III

J. Fred Spencer, Jr.

(See Next Column)

Representative Clients: Federal Deposit Insurance Corp.; Trustmark National Bank; Caterpillar Financial Services, Inc.; Merchants & Marine Bank; Blossman Gas, Inc.

For Complete List of Firm Personnel, See General Section

For full biographical listings, see the Martindale-Hubbell Law Directory

*OXFORD,** Lafayette Co.

FREELAND & FREELAND (AV)

1013 Jackson Avenue, P.O. Box 269, 38655
Telephone: 662-234-3414
Telecopier: 662-234-0604
Email: thf4@watervalley.net

MEMBERS OF FIRM

T. H. Freeland, III
T. H. Freeland, IV

Representative Clients: The Ohio Casualty Group; Crum & Forester.

For full biographical listings, see the Martindale-Hubbell Law Directory

HOLCOMB DUNBAR, A PROFESSIONAL ASSOCIATION (AV)

1217 Jackson Avenue P.O. Drawer 707, 38655
Telephone: 601-234-8775
Facsimile: 601-238-7552
Email: hdccw@holcombdunbar.com *URL:* http://www.holcombdunbar.com
Clarksdale, Mississippi Office: 152 Delta Avenue, P.O. Box 368, 38614.
Telephone: 601-627-2241.
Facsimile: 601-627-9788.
Southaven, Mississippi Office: Suite 1, 728 Goodman Road East, P.O. Box 190, 38671.
Telephone: 601-349-0664.
Facsimile: 601-349-2432.

Thomas J. Suszek

Representative Clients: Union Planters Bank, National Association; Deposit Guaranty National Bank; Trustmark National Bank; Mississippi Power & Light Co.; Mississippi Valley Gas Co.; South Central Bell Telephone Co.; Southern Farm Bureau Casualty Insurance Co.; Bituminous Insurance Co.; State Farm Fire & Casualty Insurance Co.; Fireman's Fund Insurance Cos.

For Complete List of Firm Personnel, See General Section

For full biographical listings, see the Martindale-Hubbell Law Directory

MISSOURI

*JEFFERSON CITY,** Cole Co.

CARSON & COIL, P.C. (AV)

515 East High, P.O. Box 28, 65102
Telephone: 573-636-2177
Telecopier: 573-636-7119
Email: general@carsoncoil.com

Forrest P. Carson (1910-1981)
Cullen Coil (1907-1989)
Michael P. Riley
Ronald R. McMillin
Eugene G. Bushmann
James W. Gallaher
Lori J. Levine
Rudolph L. Veit
Michael Madsen
R. Max Humphreys
Mark A. Ludwig
Dana L. Frese
Edward C. Clausen
Carla G. Holste
Kent L. Brown
Douglas W. Hennon

Charles J. McPheeters

Jack C. Hauser, Jr.
James W. "Jamie" Gallaher, Jr.

General Counsel for: Capital Reserve Life Insurance Co.; Missouri Farm Bureau; Healthcare Services Group.
Reference: Central Trust Bank.

For full biographical listings, see the Martindale-Hubbell Law Directory

KANSAS CITY, Jackson, Clay, Platte & Cass Cos.

GALLAS & SCHULTZ (AV)

9140 Ward Parkway, Suite 225, 64114
Telephone: 816-822-8100
FAX: 816-822-8222

MEMBERS OF FIRM

Alan B. Gallas
Mark J. Schultz

ASSOCIATES

Geoffrey W. Hetley
Jerald S. Enslein
David E. Herron, II
Gwendelyn M Garcia

For full biographical listings, see the Martindale-Hubbell Law Directory

ST. LOUIS, (Independent City)

STONE, LEYTON & GERSHMAN, A PROFESSIONAL CORPORATION (AV)

7733 Forsyth Boulevard, Suite 500, 63105
Telephone: 314-721-7011
Telefax: 314-721-8660

E. Rebecca Case
Howard S. Smotkin

For full biographical listings, see the Martindale-Hubbell Law Directory

MONTANA

*BILLINGS,** Yellowstone Co.

CROWLEY, HAUGHEY, HANSON, TOOLE & DIETRICH, P.L.L.P. (AV)

500 Transwestern II, 490 North 31st Street, P.O. Box 2529, 59103
Telephone: 406-252-3441
Fax: 406-259-4159
Email: crowley@crowleylaw.com
Helena, Montana Office: IBM Building, 100 North Park Avenue, Suite 300, 59601.
Telephone: 406-449-4165.
Fax: 406-449-5149.
Kalispell, Montana Office: 431 1st Avenue West, 59901.
Telephone: 406-752-6644.
Fax: 406-752-5108.
Williston, North Dakota Office: 113 East Broadway, 58801.
Telephone: 701-572-2200.
Fax: 701-572-7072.

MEMBERS OF FIRM

William D. Lamdin, III
Michael S. Dockery
Malcolm H. Goodrich
Renee L. Coppock

Representative Clients: Farm Credit Bank; Northwest Farm Credit Services, ACA; First Interstate Bank of Commerce; General Motors Acceptance Corp.; Manufacturer's Hanover Trust; John Deere Co.; Mutual Life Insurance Co., N.Y.; Connecticut Mutual Life; PLM International; Country Kitchen International, Inc.

For Complete List of Firm Personnel, See General Section

For full biographical listings, see the Martindale-Hubbell Law Directory

WRIGHT, TOLLIVER AND GUTHALS A PROFESSIONAL SERVICE CORPORATION (AV)

Windsor Court, 10 North 27th Street, P.O. Box 1977, 59103-1977
Telephone: 406-245-3071
Telecopier: 406-245-3074
Email: lawfirm@mcn.net

Ralph S. Wright (1939-1985)
Kenneth D. Tolliver
Joel E. Guthals
Virginia A. Bryan
Susan Fisher Stevens
J. Reuss
Jeffery A. Hunnes
James W. Thompson

David Paul Wilkins

For full biographical listings, see the Martindale-Hubbell Law Directory

NEBRASKA

*LINCOLN,** Lancaster Co.

CLINE, WILLIAMS, WRIGHT, JOHNSON & OLDFATHER (AV)

1900 U.S. Bank Building, 233 South 13th Street, 68508
Telephone: 402-474-6900
Fax: 402-474-5393
Email: postmaster@cline-law.com *URL:* http://www.cline-law.com
Omaha, Nebraska Office: Suite 720, One Pacific Place, 1125 South 103rd Street, 68124.
Telephone: 402-397-1700.
Fax: 402-397-1806.

ATTORNEYS

Allen L. Graves
Charles M. Pallesen, Jr.
Fredric H. Kauffman
Donald F. Burt
Alan E. Peterson
Stephen E. Gehring
Robert J. Routh
Kevin Colleran
L. Bruce Wright
James M. Bausch
Larry A. Holle
David R. Buntain
Stephen H. Nelsen
Michael C. Mueller
Lauren W. Wismer
Daniel R. Stogsdill
Scott D. Kelly
Terry R. Wittler

(See Next Column)

ATTORNEYS (Continued)

Pamela Hastings Carrier
Mark A. Christensen
Richard P. Garden, Jr.
Shawn D. Renner
John C. Miles
Mary Kay Frank
Thomas C. Huston
Sonya S. Ekart
Don R. Janssen
Susan Kubert Sapp
Kevin J. Schneider
Andrew D. Strotman
Jill Gossin Jensen
Rochelle A. Mullen
John L. Horan
Bryan S. Hatch
Steven C. Likes
Tracy A. Oldemeyer
Jolene M. Papa
Timothy G. Aschoff
Eric N. Bergquist
Janis J. Winterhof
Andrea Dylan Snowden

OF COUNSEL

Charles E. Wright
Richard P. Jeffries
Mary M. Campbell

RETIRED PARTNERS

Flavel A. Wright (Retired)
Warren C. Johnson (Retired)
Charles E. Oldfather (1927-1998)

Representative Clients: U.S. Bank National Association; University of Nebraska; Nebraska Medical Assn.; Saint Elizabeth Regional Medical Center; Media of Nebraska; Cargill Inc.; State Farm Insurance Cos.; Wal-Mart Stores, Inc.; Textron/Cushman; Isco, Inc.

For full biographical listings, see the Martindale-Hubbell Law Directory

*OMAHA,** Douglas Co.

DWYER, SMITH, GARDNER, LAZER, POHREN, ROGERS & FORREST (AV)

Suite 400, 8712 West Dodge Road, 68114
Telephone: 402-392-0101
Telefax: 402-392-1011
Email: dwyerlaw@dwyer-smith.com *URL:* http://www.dwyer-smith.com

MEMBERS OF FIRM

Clay M. Rogers
Christopher D. Curzon

ASSOCIATE

Patrick Edward Griffin, Jr.

Representative Clients: Ford Motor Credit Company, Dearborn, Michigan; Nebraska Hospital Association subsidiary Bio Electronics, Lincoln, Oak Bancorporation; Lynn Roberts International; Elliot Equipment Co.; Design Plastics, Inc.; Firstar Bank.

For Complete List of Firm Personnel, See General Section

For full biographical listings, see the Martindale-Hubbell Law Directory

ERICKSON & SEDERSTROM, P.C. (AV)

Regency Westpointe, 10330 Regency Parkway Drive, Suite 100, 68114-3761
Telephone: 402-397-2200
Fax: 402-390-7137
Lincoln, Nebraska Office: Suite 400, Cornhusker Plaza, 301 South 13th Street, 68508-2571.
Telephone: 402-476-1000.
Fax: 402-476-6167.

Michael C. Washburn

Representative Clients: Nebraska State Bank of Omaha; Berkshire Hathaway, Inc.; Bozell, Inc.; IBP, Inc. Quaker Oats Co.; United A-G Cooperative, Inc.; Immanuel Medical Center; Cornhusker Casualty Co.; Hartford Accident & Indemnity Co.; Mortgage Guaranty Insurance Corp. (MGIC).

For Complete List of Firm Personnel, See General Section

For full biographical listings, see the Martindale-Hubbell Law Directory

RASMUSSEN & MITCHELL (AV)

11605 Miracle Hills Drive, Suite 205, 68154
Telephone: 402-493-3300
Fax: 402-496-0766
Email: lawman000@aol.com *URL:* http://www.lawyers.com/rasmussen&mitchell

MEMBERS OF FIRM

Wayne S. Rasmussen
James S. Mitchell
Kathryn J. Derr
Shane M. Niebergall

For full biographical listings, see the Martindale-Hubbell Law Directory

NEVADA

*LAS VEGAS,** Clark Co.

ALBRIGHT, STODDARD, WARNICK & ALBRIGHT, A PROFESSIONAL CORPORATION (AV)

Quail Park I, Building D-4, 801 South Rancho Drive, 89106
Telephone: 702-384-7111
Fax: 702-384-0605
URL: http://www.aswalaw.com

G. Vern Albright
William H. Stoddard
Whitney B. Warnick
G. Mark Albright

D. Chris Albright
Tami C. Budo
Corey D. Randall (Not admitted in NV)

Representative Clients: Tokio Marine and Fire Insurance Co.; INAPRO, a CIGNA Co.; Nevada Ready Mix; North American Health Care, Inc. (Nursing Home); Royal Insurance; First Security Bank of Utah; Nevada Community Bank; Nationwide Insurance Co.; Liberty Mutual Insurance; CB Commercial.

For full biographical listings, see the Martindale-Hubbell Law Directory

ALVERSON, TAYLOR, MORTENSEN, NELSON & SANDERS (AV)

7401 West Charleston Boulevard, 89117
Telephone: 702-384-7000
FAX: 702-385-7000
Email: alverson@intermind.net
Reno, Nevada Office: 245 East Liberty, Suite 520, 89505.
Telephone: 775-329-0473.
Fax: 775-329-3303.

MEMBERS OF FIRM

J. Bruce Alverson
Eric K. Taylor
David J. Mortensen
Erven T. Nelson
LeAnn Sanders

OF COUNSEL

Jack C. Cherry
Kurt D. Anderson
Philip C. Van Alstyne

ASSOCIATES

Rebecca Hopkins Miller
Sandra Smagac
Victoria L. Nelson
Aaron D. Lovaas
Diane Obritsch
Michael A. Olsen
Randal D. Shimon
Catherine A. Olendorff
Monica L. Pierce
Gabriel D. Lither
Kurt R. Bonds
Darius F. Rafie
Mark J. King, IV
Shell L. Mercer
Carrie S. Bourdeau
Jason Lane Earnest
Nathan R. Reinmiller
Donn C. Alexander
Afshin Tadayon
Eric O. Freeman
Lindsay L. Stadtlander
Julie M. Sueoka

Representative Clients: Citibank; First Interstate Bank; Federal Deposit Insurance Corporation (FDIC); Norwest Bank; Norwest Financial; The CIT Group; Countrywide Funding Corporation; Overseas Chinese Banking Corporation; Colonial Mortgage Company.

For full biographical listings, see the Martindale-Hubbell Law Directory

LAW OFFICES OF TIMOTHY S. CORY & ASSOCIATES (AV)

520 South Fourth Street, Suite 220, 89101
Telephone: 702-388-1996
Fax: 702-382-7903
Email: cory@epitrustee.com *URL:* http://www.lawyers.com/timothyscory
Affiliated Office: McDowell & Gillman, P.C., Twelfth Floor, 50 West Broadway, Salt Lake City, Utah.
Telephone: 801-359-3500.
Fax: 801-359-3566.

For full biographical listings, see the Martindale-Hubbell Law Directory

EDWARDS & WINTERTON, CHTD. (AV)

401 North Buffalo Drive, Suite 200, 89128
Telephone: 702-363-0317
Telecopier: 702-363-1630
Email: EOWW.LAW@worldnet.att.net

George T. Morse, III (1945-1996)
Douglas M. Edwards
David J. Winterton

Nazario J. Jureidini
Robert B. Gerard
Thomas E. Trojan
Chris A. Beecroft, Jr.

OF COUNSEL

Nicholas A. Boylan (Not admitted in NV)

For full biographical listings, see the Martindale-Hubbell Law Directory

HALE LANE PEEK DENNISON HOWARD AND ANDERSON (AV)

Nevada Financial Center, 2300 West Sahara Avenue, Eighth Floor, Box 8, 89102
Telephone: 702-222-2500
Fax: 702-365-6940
Email: info@halelane.com
Reno, Nevada Office: 100 West Liberty Street, Tenth Floor, P.O. Box 3237.
Telephone: 775-327-3000.
Telefax: 775-786-6179.
Carson City, Nevada Office: 777 East William Street, Suite 200, P.O. Box 2620.
Telephone: 775-684-6000.
Telefax: 775-684-6001.

MEMBER OF FIRM

Lenard E. Schwartzer

ASSOCIATES

Pauline Ng Lee
Jeanette E. McPherson
Michele Eber

Representative Client: Commonwealth Land Title Insurance Co.

For Complete List of Firm Personnel, See General Section

For full biographical listings, see the Martindale-Hubbell Law Directory

JOLLEY, URGA, WIRTH & WOODBURY (AV)

3800 Howard Hughes Parkway Suite 1600, 89109
Telephone: 702-699-7500
Facsimile: 702-699-7555
URL: http://www.juww.com
Boulder City, Nevada Office: Suite 105, 1000 Nevada Highway, 89005.
Telephone: 702-293-3674.

MEMBERS OF FIRM

William R. Urga
Brian E. Holthus
Allen D. Emmel

ASSOCIATE

Kelly J. Brinkman

Representative Clients: Wells Fargo Bank and its predecessor, First Interstate Bank of Nevada; Nevada State Bank; First Nationwide Bank; General Motors Acceptance Corp.; Ford Motor Credit Co.; Nissan Motor Acceptance Corp.; Toyota Motor Credit Corporation; Hyundai Motor Finance Co.; Chase Manhattan.

For Complete List of Firm Personnel, See General Section

For full biographical listings, see the Martindale-Hubbell Law Directory

KOLESAR & LEATHAM, CHARTERED (AV)

Norwest Bank Center, 3320 West Sahara Avenue, Suite 380, 89102
Telephone: 702-362-7800
Telecopier: 702-362-9472

Nile Leatham
Kenneth A. Burns
James D. Greene

Blaine F. Bates
Matthew D. Saltzman

Representative Clients: Alta Gold Co.; Banc One Financial Services, Inc.; Bank of Hawaii; Business Bank of Nevada; Colonial Bank of Nevada; Credit Suisse First Boston Mortgage Capital; First Security Bank of Nevada; Nissan Motor Acceptance Corp.; Silver State Bank; Tom R. Grimmett, Trustee.

For full biographical listings, see the Martindale-Hubbell Law Directory

KRAVITZ, SCHNITZER & SLOANE, CHARTERED, A PROFESSIONAL CORPORATION (AV)

2300 West Sahara Avenue, Suite 500, 89102
Telephone: 702-362-6666
Fax: 702-362-2203
Email: KRAVSCHNIT@AOL.COM

Martin J. Kravitz
Gary E. Schnitzer
Jeffrey G. Sloane
Michael Bradley Johnson
Jane Eberhardy
Marisa C. Guarino

David J. Feldman
Jerry R. Graf

LEGAL SUPPORT PERSONNEL

Sandye Smith (Legal Administrator)

Representative Clients: Ford Motor Credit; Bank of America; U.S. Bank; Nations Credit; Citibank; Norwest Financial Services; Associates Natl. Bank; Avco Financial Services; HFC Financial Services; West One Bank; Allstate Insurance Company.

For full biographical listings, see the Martindale-Hubbell Law Directory

JOHN PETER LEE, LTD. (AV)

830 Las Vegas Boulevard South, 89101
Telephone: 702-382-4044
Telecopier: 702-383-9950

(See Next Column)

JOHN PETER LEE, LTD.—*Continued*

John Peter Lee

Nancy L. Allf
Paul C. Ray
Timothy P. Thomas

For Complete List of Firm Personnel, See General Section

For full biographical listings, see the Martindale-Hubbell Law Directory

LIONEL SAWYER & COLLINS (AV)

1700 Bank of America Plaza, 300 South Fourth Street, 89101
Telephone: 702-383-8888
Fax: 702-383-8845
Email: first initial last@lionelsawyer.com
Reno, Nevada Office: Suite 1100, Bank of America Plaza, 50 West Liberty Street.
Telephone: 702-788-8666.
Fax: 702-788-8682.

MEMBERS OF FIRM

Rodney M. Jean
Laurel Elizabeth Davis
Jennifer A. Smith (Resident, Reno Office)

ASSOCIATES

Michael D. Rawlins
Kenneth Robert Myers

Representative Clients: California Federal Bank; Caterpillar Financial Services, Inc.; City of Las Vegas Downtown Redevelopment Agency; DVI Financial Services, Inc.; Heller Financial, Inc.; Home Federal Bank; ITT Federal Bank; Mercedes-Benz Credit Corporation; U.S. Bancorp Financial; 900 Capital Services, Inc.

For Complete List of Firm Personnel, See General Section

For full biographical listings, see the Martindale-Hubbell Law Directory

SCHRECK MORRIS (AV)

1200 Bank of America Plaza, 300 South Fourth Street, 89101
Telephone: 702-382-2101
Fax: 702-382-8135; 702-474-9422
URL: http://www.schreckmorris.com
Reno, Nevada Office: 100 West Liberty, Suite 940, 89501.
Telephone: 775-322-7777.
Facsimile: 775-322-7791.

MEMBERS OF FIRM

Frank A. Schreck
Steve Morris
Andrew S. Brignone
Leslie Terry Jones
Mary Kristina Pickering
John A. Godfrey
Ann Morgan
Sean T. McGowan
Ellen Schulhofer
James J. Pisanelli
Clark V. Vellis
Todd L. Bice

ASSOCIATES

James R. Chamberlain
Dennis V. Gallagher
Margaret L. Sanner
F. Edward Mulholland, II
Elizabeth M. Fielder
Elayna Youchah
Sonia C. Vermeys
Denise Michaelides
Mary J. Drury
John P. Desmond
Adam P. Segal
Matthew McCaughey
Amelia R. De Los Santos
Wendy Medura
Robert J. Grasso
Shawn G. Pearson
David Dornak
Matthew L. Heinhold
Paul D. Colton

For full biographical listings, see the Martindale-Hubbell Law Directory

*RENO,** Washoe Co.

HALE LANE PEEK DENNISON HOWARD AND ANDERSON (AV)

100 West Liberty Street, Tenth Floor, P.O. Box 3237, 89505
Telephone: 775-327-3000
Telefax: 775-786-6179
Email: info@halelane.com
Las Vegas, Nevada Office: Nevada Financial Center, 2300 West Sahara Avenue, Eighth Floor, Box 8.
Telephone: 702-222-2500.
Fax: 702-365-6940.
Carson City, Nevada Office: 777 East William Street, Suite 200, P.O. Box 2620.
Telephone: 775-684-6000.
Telefax: 775-684-6001.

MEMBER OF FIRM

Lenard E. Schwartzer (Resident, Las Vegas, Nevada)

ASSOCIATE

Timothy A. Lukas

For Complete List of Firm Personnel, See General Section

For full biographical listings, see the Martindale-Hubbell Law Directory

WOODBURN AND WEDGE (AV)

One East First Street, Suite 1600, P.O. Box 2311, 89505
Telephone: 775-688-3000
Telecopier: 775-688-3088
Email: postmaster@woodburnlaw.com *URL:* http://www.woodburnlaw.com
Las Vegas, Nevada Office: Suite 700 Bank of America Plaza, 300 South Fourth Street.
Telephone: 702-387-1000.
Telecopier: 702-387-0024.

MEMBER OF FIRM

John F. Murtha

ASSOCIATE

Louis F. Holland

Representative Clients: Atlantic Richfield Co.; Sierra Pacific Power Co.; The Union Pacific Railroad Co.; Western Union Telegraph Co.; Bank of America; Cyprus Minerals Corp.; The Roman Catholic Bishop of Reno, A Corporation Sole; Shell Oil Co.

For full biographical listings, see the Martindale-Hubbell Law Directory

NEW JERSEY

EDISON, Middlesex Co.

WONG FLEMING, P.C. (AV)

Edison Square West, Suite 1050, 2035 Lincoln Highway, 08817
Telephone: 732-248-4111
Fax: 732-248-8665
Mailing Address: P.O. Box 985, 08818-0985
Email: info@wongfleming.com *URL:* http://www.wongfleming.com
Philadelphia, Pennsylvania Office: 230 South Broad Street, Suite 601, 19102.
Telephone: 215-546-2776.
Fax: 215-546-3206.
New York, New York Office: The Empire State Building, 350 Fifth Avenue, Suite 5411, 10118.
Telephone: 212-643-9668.
Fax: 212-643-9640.

Linda Wong
Daniel C. Fleming
Katherine C. Lee

Andrew J. Bayne
Stephen Tsai
Theresa Homisak
Paul J. Young
Wenjun Zhang (Not admitted in NJ)
Tanya E. Lawrence
Fei F. Lam

For full biographical listings, see the Martindale-Hubbell Law Directory

FLORHAM PARK, Morris Co.

DRINKER BIDDLE & SHANLEY LLP (AV)

A Pennsylvania Limited Liability Partnership
500 Campus Drive, 07932-1047
Telephone: 973-360-1100
Fax: 973-285-1625; 973-360-9831
URL: http://www.dbr.com
Philadelphia, Pennsylvania Office: Drinker Biddle & Reath LLP, One Logan Square, 18th & Cherry Streets.
Telephone: 215-988-2700.
Telefax: 215-988-2757.
Cable Address: "Debemac."
Washington, D.C. Office: Drinker Biddle & Reath LLP, 1500 K Street, N.W., Suite 1100.
Telephone: 202-842-8800.
Telefax: 202-842-8465.
Princeton, New Jersey Office: Suite 300, 105 College Road East.
Telephone: 609-716-6500.
Telefax: 609-799-7000.
Berwyn, Pennsylvania Office: Drinker Biddle & Reath LLP, Suite 300, 1000 Westlakes Drive.
Telephone: 610-993-2200.
Telefax: 610-993-8585.
New York, New York Office: Drinker Biddle & Reath LLP, 89th Floor, One World Trade Center.
Telephone: 212-321-1812.
Telecopier: 1-212-466-0569.

John J. Francis, Jr.
A. Dennis Terrell
Walter J. Fleischer, Jr.
Robert K. Malone

COUNSEL

Lynn Ciolino Boyajian

Michael P. Pompeo
Douglas J. McGill
Christena A. Lambrianakos

For Complete List of Firm Personnel, See General Section

For full biographical listings, see the Martindale-Hubbell Law Directory

Florham Park—Continued

HACK, PIRO, O'DAY, MERKLINGER, WALLACE & MCKENNA, P.A. (AV)

30 Columbia Turnpike, P.O. Box 941, 07932-0941
Telephone: 973-301-6500
Fax: 973-301-0094
Email: hpom@ix.netcom.com

John M. McKenna

Angela J. Mendelsohn

Representative Clients: Cenlar Federal Savings Bank; County Mortgage Company, Inc.; First Fidelity Bank, N.A., N.J.; Citicorp Mortgage, Inc.; Aetna Life & Casualty Co.; Freddie Mac; Marine Midland Bank.

For Complete List of Firm Personnel, See General Section

For full biographical listings, see the Martindale-Hubbell Law Directory

*HACKENSACK,** Bergen Co.

NICOLETTE & PERKINS, P.A. (AV)

3 University Plaza, Fifth Floor, 07601
Telephone: 201-488-9080
Telecopier: 201-488-5580
Email: nicoletteperkins@juno.com *URL:* http://www.lawyers.com/nicolette&perkins

David A. Nicolette, Jr. — Eric R. Perkins

Jeanette A. Odynski — Laura N. Keenan
Toni Marie McPhillips

For full biographical listings, see the Martindale-Hubbell Law Directory

PASHMAN STEIN, A PROFESSIONAL CORPORATION (AV)

45 Essex Street, 07601-5415
Telephone: 201-488-8200
Fax: 201-488-5556
Email: info@pashmanstein.com *URL:* http://www.lawyers.com/pashmanstein

Louis Pashman — Dennis T. Smith
Samuel J. Samaro — Michael S. Stein

Amy E. Whitteaker — John T. Whipple

SPECIAL COUNSEL

Morris Pashman

For full biographical listings, see the Martindale-Hubbell Law Directory

SHAPIRO & CROLAND (AV)

A Partnership including Professional Corporations
Continental Plaza II, 411 Hackensack Avenue, 07601
Telephone: 201-488-3900
Fax: 201-488-9481

Barry I. Croland, P.C. — Meridith J. Bronson
Robert P. Shapiro, P.C. — John P. Di Iorio
Barry L. Baime — David O. Marcus
Jay Rubenstein — Robert F. Green
Kenneth S. Apfel — Lizabeth Sarakin
Kenneth S. Goldrich, P.C. — David Torchin
Bruce J. Ackerman — Robin C. Bogan
Stuart Reiser, P.C. — Craig D. Spector

OF COUNSEL

Harvey R. Sorkow

Donald R. Sorkow (1930-1985)

Reference: Bank of New York-National Community Division.

For full biographical listings, see the Martindale-Hubbell Law Directory

HADDONFIELD, Camden Co.

WEINBERG, MCCORMICK, CHATZINOFF AND PAUL, A PROFESSIONAL ASSOCIATION (AV)

109 Haddon Avenue, 08033
Telephone: 609-795-1600
Telecopier: 609-795-9469

Joseph M. Weinberg — Edward L. Paul
Joseph A. McCormick, Jr. — Donafaye Wilson Zoll
Barry Chatzinoff — Michael A. Weinberg

Representative Clients: Emtec Corp.; John Dere; Aurora Financial Group, Inc.; Case Credit Corp.
Local Counsel for: John Deere Credit Services, Inc.; John Deere Co.; John Deere Industrial Equipment Co.

(See Next Column)

Solicitor for: Berlin Township Planning Board.
Reference: Summit Bank

For full biographical listings, see the Martindale-Hubbell Law Directory

*MORRISTOWN,** Morris Co.

PITNEY, HARDIN, KIPP & SZUCH LLP (AV)

P.O. Box 1945, 07962-1945
Telephone: 973-966-6300
New York City: 212-687-6000
Telex: 642014
Telecopier: 973-966-1550
URL: http://www.phks.com
New York, New York Office: 711 Third Avenue, 10017-4014.
Telephone: 212-687-6000.
Fax: 212-682-3485.

MEMBERS OF FIRM

Peter A. Forgosh — Michael J. Dunne
Roger R. Gottilla — Michael P. Turner

COUNSEL

Linda K. Connolly — Jonathan S. Bristol

Representative Clients: Kentile Floors Inc.; Schering-Plough Corproation; Sterling Optical of Georgia.

For Complete List of Firm Personnel, See General Section

For full biographical listings, see the Martindale-Hubbell Law Directory

*NEWARK,** Essex Co.

HELLRING LINDEMAN GOLDSTEIN & SIEGAL LLP (AV)

One Gateway Center, 07102-5386
Telephone: 973-621-9020
Fax: 973-621-7406
Englewood, New Jersey Office: 32-40 North Dean Street.
Telephone: 201-871-3060.

James A. Scarpone — John A. Adler
Richard B. Honig — Bruce S. Etterman

David Wolff

For Complete List of Firm Personnel, See General Section

For full biographical listings, see the Martindale-Hubbell Law Directory

MCCARTER & ENGLISH, LLP (AV)

Four Gateway Center, 100 Mulberry Street, P.O. Box 652, 07101-0652
Telephone: 973-622-4444
Telecopier: 973-624-7070
URL: http://www.mccarter.com
Cherry Hill, New Jersey Office: 1820 Chapel Avenue West, Suite 380.
Telephone: 609-662-8444.
Telecopier: 609-662-6203.
New York, New York Office: Suite 2247, One World Trade Center.
Telephone: 212-466-9018.
Telecopier: 212-432-6568.
Boca Raton, Florida Office: 2255 Glades Road, Suite 319-A.
Telephone: 561-994-6262.
Telecopier: 561-241-0798.
Wilmington, Delaware Office: Mellon Bank Center, 919 Market Street.
Telephone: 302-654-8010.
Telecopier: 302-654-0795.
Philadelphia, Pennsylvania Office: One Commerce Square, 2005 Market Street, Suite 3600.
Telephone: 215-557-7700.
Telecopier: 215-557-6544.

MEMBERS OF FIRM

Richard W. Hill — Joseph Lubertazzi, Jr.
Hayden Smith, Jr. — William D. Wallach
Theodore D. Moskowitz — Lisa W.S. Bonsall

COUNSEL

Steven A. Beckelman

ASSOCIATES

Kathleen O'Connell Keating — Nancy A. Washington
David J. Adler — Patricia A. Celano
Sheila E. Calello — Clement J. Farley
Eduardo J. Glas

For Complete List of Firm Personnel, See General Section

For full biographical listings, see the Martindale-Hubbell Law Directory

MEYNER AND LANDIS (AV)

One Gateway Center, Suite 2500, 07102-5311
Telephone: 973-624-2800
Fax: 973-624-0356
Email: attys@meyner.com *URL:* http://www.meyner.com

(See Next Column)

MEYNER AND LANDIS—*Continued*

Robert B. Meyner (1908-1990)
Edwin C. Landis, Jr.
John N. Malyska
William J. Fiore
Anthony F. Siliato
Francis R. Perkins
Howard O. Thompson
Scott T. McCleary
Linda Townley Snyder
William H. Schmidt, Jr.
David B. Grantz

For full biographical listings, see the Martindale-Hubbell Law Directory

ST. JOHN & WAYNE, L.L.C. (AV)

Two Penn Plaza East, 07105-2249
Telephone: 973-491-3600
Fax: 973-491-3555
Email: firm@nwk.stjohn-law.com *URL:* http://www.stjohn-law.com
Rochester, New York Office: St. John & Curtin, L.L.C., First Federal Plaza.
Telephone: 716-262-6780.
Fax: 716-262-6755.
New York, New York Office: Heron Tower, 70 East 55th. Street.
Telephone: 212-446-5000.
Fax: 212-446-5055.

Todd Mark Galante

For Complete List of Firm Personnel, See General Section

For full biographical listings, see the Martindale-Hubbell Law Directory

SILLS CUMMIS RADIN TISCHMAN EPSTEIN & GROSS, A PROFESSIONAL CORPORATION (AV)

One Riverfront Plaza, 07102-5400
Telephone: 973-643-7000
Fax: 973-643-6500
Telex: 820630 Sillsbeck Nwk
Email: sillsmail@sillscummis.com *URL:* http://www.sillscummis.com
Atlantic City, New Jersey Office: 17 Gordon's Alley.
Telephone: 609-344-2800.
New York, N.Y. Office: 712 Fifth Avenue.
Telephone: 212-643-7000.
Washington, D.C. Office: 1800 K Street, N.W.
Telephone: 202-296-4750.

MEMBERS OF FIRM

Steven S. Radin
Steven E. Gross
Steven M. Goldman
Ira A. Rosenberg
Robert Max Crane
Jack M. Zackin
Arlene Elgart Mirsky
Brian S. Coven
Philip R. White
Stuart J. Glick
Frederic M. Tudor
Steven R. Kamen

Eric W. Sleeper
Andrew H. Sherman

For Complete List of Firm Personnel, See General Section

For full biographical listings, see the Martindale-Hubbell Law Directory

PARSIPPANY, Morris Co.

MIDDLEBROOKS & SHAPIRO, P.C. (AV)

99 Cherry Hill Road, 07054-0619
Telephone: 973-335-5200
Telecopier: 973-335-5233
Email: ms1093@aol.com *URL:* http://www.lawyers.com/msattorneys

Melinda Dee Middlebrooks
Richard P. Shapiro

Joseph R. Zapata, Jr.
Stephen M. De Luca

LEGAL SUPPORT PERSONNEL

Peter A. Siebel, Jr. (Paralegal)

For full biographical listings, see the Martindale-Hubbell Law Directory

ROCHELLE PARK, Bergen Co.

FORMAN HOLT & ELIADES LLC (AV)

218 Route 17 North, 07662
Telephone: 201-845-1000
Fax: 201-845-9112
Email: firm@formanlaw.com

Charles M. Forman
Michael E. Holt
Daniel M. Eliades, Jr.
Joseph M. Cerra
Julie L. Singer
Kim R. Lynch

OF COUNSEL

Erin J. Kennedy

For full biographical listings, see the Martindale-Hubbell Law Directory

ROSELAND, Essex Co.

RAVIN, GREENBERG & MARKS, A PROFESSIONAL CORPORATION (AV)

101 Eisenhower Parkway, 07068
Telephone: 973-226-1500
Telecopier: 973-226-6888

Morris M. Ravin (1900-1971)
Nathan Ravin
Howard S. Greenberg
Stephen B. Ravin
Gary N. Marks
Bruce J. Wisotsky
Larry Lesnik

Allan M. Harris
Morris S. Bauer
Brian L. Baker

Reference: Hudson United Bank.

For full biographical listings, see the Martindale-Hubbell Law Directory

SADDLE BROOK, Bergen Co.

COHN LIFLAND PEARLMAN HERRMANN & KNOPF LLP (AV)

Park 80 Plaza West-One, 07663
Telephone: 201-845-9600
Telecopier: 201-845-9423
Email: info@njlawfirm.com *URL:* http://www.njlawfirm.com

MEMBERS OF FIRM

Albert L. Cohn
Peter S. Pearlman
Barry A. Knopf
Daniel Crystal (Retired)
Jeffrey W. Herrmann
Robert D. Zatorski
Allen Susser
Mary Ann T. Stokes
Brian D. Zinn
Joshua P. Cohn

ASSOCIATES

Virginia A. Harper
Leonard Z. Kaufmann
Audra DePaolo
Robert Ricci, Jr.
Maurice W. McLaughlin
Andrew C. Abrams
Jessica V. Henry

OF COUNSEL

Sylvia J. Cohn
Jodi B. Scherl

For full biographical listings, see the Martindale-Hubbell Law Directory

*SOMERVILLE,** Somerset Co.

SCHACHTER, TROMBADORE, OFFEN, STANTON & PAVICS, A PROFESSIONAL CORPORATION (AV)

45 East High Street, P.O. Box 520, 08876-0520
Telephone: 908-722-5700
Fax: 908-722-8853

Timothy P. McKeown

For full biographical listings, see the Martindale-Hubbell Law Directory

*TRENTON,** Mercer Co.

TEICH, GROH AND FROST (AV)

691 State Highway 33, 08619-4492
Telephone: 609-890-1500
Fax: 609-890-6961
Email: teich1g2f3@aol.com
Lawrenceville, New Jersey Office: 109 Franklin Corner Road.
Telephone: 609-844-0488.
Fax: 609-844-0784.

MEMBERS OF FIRM

Arthur Teich (1915-1997)
William C. Groh
Barry W. Frost
Carol Oswald
(Also at Lawrenceville Office)
Carol L. Knowlton
Allen I. Gorski
Arthur R. Sypek, Jr.
Dean S. Nalbone

ASSOCIATES

Jill M. Wittenborn
(Also at Lawrenceville Office)
Michael W. Krutman
David A. Martin
Kimberley M. Lake

References: CoreStates/New Jersey National Bank; United National Bank.

For full biographical listings, see the Martindale-Hubbell Law Directory

VINELAND, Cumberland Co.

GRUCCIO, PEPPER GIOVINAZZI, DESANTO & FARNOLY, P.A. (AV)

817 Landis Avenue, P.O. Box 1501, 08362
Telephone: 856-691-0100
Fax: 856-692-4095
Email: Gruccio1@eticomm.net
Woodbury, New Jersey Office: 21 Delaware Street.
Telephone: 856-848-5558.
Fax: 856-384-1181.

(See Next Column)

GRUCCIO, PEPPER GIOVINAZZI, DESANTO & FARNOLY, P.A., *Vineland—Continued*

Bridgeton, New Jersey Office: 120 West Broad Street.
Telephone: 856-459-3334.
Fax: 856-692-4095.

Lawrence Pepper, Jr. — Cosmo A. Giovinazzi, III

Walter F. Gavigan — Stephen D. Barse
Gerald R. Spall — Judith C. Arnold

OF COUNSEL

Richard M. Milstead

Representative Clients: State Farm Mutual Automobile Insurance Cos.; United States Fidelity & Guaranty Co.; South Jersey Transportation Authority; County of Salem; County of Cape May; Cumberland Mutual Fire Insurance Co.; Farmers and Merchants National Bank of Bridgeton; Vineland Board of Education; Southern Intercounty Medical Association; Sun National Bank of N.J.

For Complete List of Firm Personnel, See General Section

For full biographical listings, see the Martindale-Hubbell Law Directory

VOORHEES, Camden Co.

NONA L. OSTROVE (AV)

1307 White Horse Road, Suite F-603, 08043
Telephone: 856-566-4200
Fax: 856-566-4203
URL: http://www.lawyers.com./nonaostrove

For full biographical listings, see the Martindale-Hubbell Law Directory

WEST ORANGE, Essex Co.

RABINOWITZ, TRENK, LUBETKIN & TULLY, P.C. (AV)

200 Executive Drive Suite 225, 07052-3303
Telephone: 973-243-8600
Facsimile: 973-243-8677
URL: http://www.Rabinowitztrenk.com

Jonathan I. Rabinowitz — Jay L. Lubetkin
Richard D. Trenk — Mary Ellen Tully

Joseph J. DiPasquale — Henry M. Karwowski
Joshua H. Raymond — Shoshana Schiff

For full biographical listings, see the Martindale-Hubbell Law Directory

WOODBRIDGE, Middlesex Co.

GREENBAUM, ROWE, SMITH, RAVIN, DAVIS AND HIMMEL LLP (AV)

Metro Corporate Campus I, P.O. Box 5600, 07095-0988
Telephone: 732-549-5600
Fax: 732-549-1881 529
Email: info@greenbaumlaw.com *URL:* http://www.greenbaumlaw.com
Roseland, New Jersey Office: 6 Becker Farm Road.
Telephone: 973-535-1600.
Fax: 973-535-1698.

MEMBERS OF FIRM

David L. Bruck — Lawrence P. Maher

ASSOCIATE

Robert S. Underhill

For Complete List of Firm Personnel, See General Section

For full biographical listings, see the Martindale-Hubbell Law Directory

NEW MEXICO

*ALBUQUERQUE,** Bernalillo Co.

RODEY, DICKASON, SLOAN, AKIN & ROBB, P.A. (AV)

Albuquerque Plaza, Suite 2200, 201 Third Street, N.W., P.O. Box 1888, 87103-1888
Telephone: 505-765-5900
Fax: 505-768-7395
Email: info@rodey.com *URL:* http://www.rodey.com
Santa Fe, New Mexico Office: Suite 101 Marcy Plaza, 123 East Marcy Street, P.O. Box 1357, 87504-1357.
Telephone: 505-984-0100.
Fax: 505-989-9542.

Jo Saxton Brayer

Alice Nystel Page

(See Next Column)

OF COUNSEL

Debra Romero Thal

For Complete List of Firm Personnel, See General Section

For full biographical listings, see the Martindale-Hubbell Law Directory

WATROUS & REARDON (AV)

A Partnership of Professional Associations
3733 Eubank Boulevard, N.E., 87111-3536
Telephone: 505-293-7000
Fax: 505-293-0831

MEMBERS OF FIRM

Thomas S. Watrous (P.A.) — Walter L. Reardon, Jr., (P.A.)

Representative Clients: State Street Bank and Trust Co.; Angel Fire Ski Area and Resort; Air Touch Cellular; American Linen; Rio Pecos Oil Company; First Health Plan (FHP); Albuquerque Title Co.; Melloy Nissan & Jaguar; T.I.W. Manufacturing, Inc.; Kubota Tractor Credit Corp.

For full biographical listings, see the Martindale-Hubbell Law Directory

NEW YORK

EAST MEADOW, Nassau Co.

CERTILMAN BALIN ADLER & HYMAN, LLP (AV)

90 Merrick Avenue, 11554
Telephone: 516-296-7000
Telecopier: 516-296-7111
URL: http://www.cbah.com

MEMBERS OF FIRM

Ira J. Adler — David Z. Herman
Dale Allinson — Richard Herzbach
Michael C. Axelrod — M. Allan Hyman
Herbert M. Balin — Bernard Hyman
Bruce J. Bergman — Donna-Marie Korth
Eileen O'Boyle Bitetto — Steven J. Kuperschmid
Michael D. Brofman — Jeffrey S. Lisabeth
Lewis J. Campanella — Jaspreet S. Mayall
Morton L. Certilman — Richard J. McCord
Robert J. Ciovacco — Thomas J. McNamara
Brian J. Davis — Michael F. O'Shea
Wayne G. Edwards — Marilyn Price
Joseph P. Famighetti — Fred S. Skolnik
Howard R. Gladston — Louis Soloway
Murray Greenberg — Harold Somer
Gavin C. Grusd — Howard M. Stein

Brian K. Ziegler

OF COUNSEL

Daniel S. Cohan — Joseph N. Mondello

ASSOCIATES

Lawrence A. Altholtz — James G. Kapralos
Meredith W. Ayres — Linda P. Manfredi
Daniel J. Baker — Edward G. McCabe
Kimberly I. Berson — Patrick McCormick
Scott B. Black — Susan L. McWalters
Brendan J. DeRiggi — Jothy Narendran
Thomas M. Farrell — James A. Rose
Mary C. Florentz — Wayne J. Schaefer
Candace Reid Gladston — Leslie H. Scharf
Harry P. Greenbaum — Afsheen Ashley Shah
David E. Herold — Victor Spinnelli
Jodi S. Hoffman — Russell H. Stern

Robert G. Wilk

For full biographical listings, see the Martindale-Hubbell Law Directory

GARDEN CITY, Nassau Co.

MORITT, HOCK & HAMROFF, LLP (AV)

400 Garden City Plaza, Suite 202, 11530
Telephone: 516-873-2000
Fax: 516-873-2010
Email: lawyers@mhhlaw.com *URL:* http://www.mhhlaw.com

PARTNERS

Neil J. Moritt — David H. Cohen
Alan S. Hock — Robert M. Tils
Marc L. Hamroff — Gary C. Hisiger

(See Next Column)

MORITT, HOCK & HAMROFF LLP—*Continued*

ASSOCIATES

William P. Laino
Robert S. Cohen
Terese L. Arenth
Leslie A. Berkoff
Michael S. Re
David A. Loglisci
David Z. Ottensoser
Ellen R. Leibowitz
Amy J. Zamir
Michael Cardello, III
Gary E. Ostroff

For full biographical listings, see the Martindale-Hubbell Law Directory

SHAW, LICITRA, BOHNER, ESERNIO & SCHWARTZ, P.C. (AV)

1010 Franklin Avenue, 11530
Telephone: 516-742-0610
Telecopier: 516-742-2670
Email: shaw0610@aol.com

Joseph Licitra (1930-1987)
J. Stanley Shaw
Robert J. Bohner
George P. Esernio
Jeffrey L. Schwartz
Anton J. Borovina
Edward M. Flint
Stuart I. Gordon
John H. Hall, Jr.
Sarah M. Keenan
Frank J. Livoti
Alan E. Marder
Peter Marullo
Roberta L. McManus

David P. Gesser
Steven H. Blatt
Michael Clark

COUNSEL

Victor G. Beaudet (1919-1993)
Alan M. Parente

For full biographical listings, see the Martindale-Hubbell Law Directory

HARRISON, Westchester Co.

RATTET & PASTERNAK, LLP (AV)

550 Mamaroneck Avenue, 10528
Telephone: 914-381-7400; 212-677-6900
Fax: 914-381-7406
URL: http://www.rattetlaw.com
New York, N.Y. Office: 295 Madison Avenue. 19th Floor. 10017.
Telephone: 212-677-6900.

Robert L. Rattet
Jonathan S. Pasternak

Arlene Gordon Oliver
James Glucksman
Jill Allison Abrams
Daniel Scott Alter

OF COUNSEL

Richard J. Rubin

Representative Clients: Pudgies Famous Chicken; Barnett Bank, Di Canio Organization, Inc., RTC Qualified; Circle in the Square, Inc.; Gaseteria Oil Corp.; Business Loan Center.

For full biographical listings, see the Martindale-Hubbell Law Directory

HUNTINGTON, Suffolk Co.

LAW OFFICES OF AVRUM J. ROSEN (AV)

38 New Street, 11743-3327
Telephone: 516-423-8527
Fax: 516-423-4536
Email: ajrlaw@aol.com

For full biographical listings, see the Martindale-Hubbell Law Directory

*NEW YORK,** New York Co.

BERLACK, ISRAELS & LIBERMAN LLP (AV)

120 West 45th Street, 10036
Telephone: 212-704-0100
Cable Address: "Berilib"
Telecopier: 212-704-0196
Email: info@berlack.com
Morristown, New Jersey Office: 65 Madison Avenue.
Telephone: 201-644-3400.
Telecopier: 201-644-3159.

MEMBERS OF FIRM

Harris Berlack (1946-1968)
Carlos L. Israels (1946-1969)
Kenneth R. Asher
Claude A. Baum
Scott M. Berman
Wade M. Boswell
Douglas E. Davidson
Alan N. Forman
Steven E. Greenbaum
Harvey M. Katz
James B. Liberman
Stuart Neuhauser
Robert D. Schmicker
Martin S. Siegel
Steven F. Wasserman
Edward S. Weisfelner

SENIOR ATTORNEYS

Andrew S. Dash
Erica M. Ryland

(See Next Column)

ASSOCIATES

John P. Biedermann
Anne M. Cunningham
Pauline Foley (Resident, Morristown, New Jersey Office)
Julie L. Friedberg (Resident, Morristown, New Jersey Office)
Emilio A. Galván
Linda B. Goebel
Louis Lombardo
Rachel F. Mayerson (Not admitted in NY)
Amy P. K. Motzenbecker (Resident, Morristown, New Jersey Office)
Antonio Peguero, Jr.
Elizabeth Quirk (Resident, Morristown, New Jersey Office)
Marcela M. Sanchez
Melissa Sarubbi

OF COUNSEL

Gerald W. Conway (Not admitted in NY; Resident, Morristown, New Jersey Office)
Marc B. Lasky (Resident, Morristown, New Jersey Office)

For full biographical listings, see the Martindale-Hubbell Law Directory

BRAUNER BARON ROSENZWEIG & KLEIN, L.L.P. (AV)

The Firm of Herman Goldman
61 Broadway, 10006
Telephone: 212-797-9100
Cable Address: "Goldenlaw"
Telecopier: (212) 797-9161
URL: http://www.braunerbaron.com

MEMBERS OF FIRM

Herman Goldman (1880-1968)
Herman M. Brauner (1903-1980)
Stanley Klein (1934-1998)
Raymond S. Baron (1916-1998)
Seymour H. Kligler (1920-1998)
Paul Bauman (1922-1999)
David A. Brauner
David R. Kay
Mel P. Barkan
Christopher C. Schwabacher
Roy M. Sparber
Alan Michigan
Howard L. Simon
Charles A. Damato
Alan Nisselson
Michael J. Clain
Francis P. Manfredi
Nina P. Silfen
Michael J. Weitzner

ASSOCIATES

Christopher L. Chin
Caroline H. Hahn
Stacy M. Modlin
Dina M. Friedman
Margaret A. M. Shearer
Son K. Le
Shalu Rastogi
Sharon I. Farman
Lawrence A. Dunn, Jr.

OF COUNSEL

Jules M. Baron
Norman H. Sparber
Elias Rosenzweig
John J. Bennett, Jr.
Michael L. Goldstein
William L. Kadish
Jon D. Kaplon

For full biographical listings, see the Martindale-Hubbell Law Directory

CURTIS, MALLET-PREVOST, COLT & MOSLE LLP (AV)

101 Park Avenue, 10178-0061
Telephone: 212-696-6000
Telecopier: 212-697-1559
Email: info@cm-p.com *URL:* http://www.cm-p.com
Washington, D.C. Office: Suite 1205L, 1801 K Street, N.W.
Telephone: 202-452-7373.
Telecopier: 202-452-7333.
Newark, New Jersey Office: One Gateway Center, Suite 403.
Telephone: 973-622-0605.
Telecopier: 973-622-5646.
Houston, Texas Office: 2 Houston Center, 909 Fannin Street, Suite 3725.
Telephone: 713-759-9555.
Telecopier: 713-759-0712.
Stamford, Connecticut Office: One Canterbury Green.
Telephone: 203-359-6200.
Telecopier: 203-328-2617.
Mexico City, D.F., Mexico Office: Curtis, Mallet-Prevost, Colt & Mosle, Ruben Dario 281, Piso 9, Col. Bosque de Chapultepec, 11530 Mexico, D.F.
Telephone: 525-282-0444.
Telecopier: 525-282-0637.
Paris, France Office: 15 rue d'Astorg, 75008.
Telephone: +33-1 42-66-39-10.
Telecopier: +33-1 42-66-39-62.
London, England Office: Two Throgmorton Avenue, EC2N 2DL.
Telephone: 0207-638-7957.
Telecopier: 0207-638-5512.
Frankfurt am Main 1, Germany Office: Staufenstrasse 42.
Telephone: +49-69-971-4420.
Telecopier: +49-69-17 33 99.
Muscat, Sultanate of Oman Office: Jewel Beach-134.
Telephone: 968-607-725.
Telecopier: 968-607-724.
Milan, Italy Office: Curtis, Mallet-Prevost & Gilioli, Piazzale Principessa Clotilde 8, 20121.
Telephone: +(39) 02 29 00 29 32.
Telefax: +(39) 02 65 75 969.

(See Next Column)

CURTIS, MALLET-PREVOST, COLT & MOSLE LLP, *New York—Continued*

MEMBERS OF FIRM

Lynn P. Harrison, III
Robert S. Lipton
Steven J. Reisman

COUNSEL

John P. Campbell

ASSOCIATES

Steven Goldberg
Stephen Z. Starr

For full biographical listings, see the Martindale-Hubbell Law Directory

FINKEL GOLDSTEIN BERZOW ROSENBLOOM & NASH, LLP (AV)

26 Broadway, 10004
Telephone: 212-344-2929
Telecopier: 212-422-6836
Email: finkgold@aol.com

MEMBERS OF FIRM

Benjamin Finkel (1905-1986)
Harold S. Berzow
Harvey L. Goldstein
Neal M. Rosenbloom
Kevin J. Nash

ASSOCIATES

Arthur A. Hirschler
Charles Fischer
David J. Ciminesi

For full biographical listings, see the Martindale-Hubbell Law Directory

GRATCH JACOBS & BROZMAN, P.C. (AV)

950 Third Avenue, 10022
Telephone: 212-935-2560
Telecopier: (212) 319-0856

Ariel Gratch
Stephen Wagner
Alan S. Jacobs
Andrew D. Feiner
Andrew P. Brozman
Jennifer C. DeMarco

Holly S. Falkowitz
Robert J. McDermott, Jr.
Nicholas H. Laduzinski
Thomas M. Rao
Mitchell B. Reiter

For full biographical listings, see the Martindale-Hubbell Law Directory

KITTAY, GOLD & GERSHFELD, P.C. (AV)

One Exchange Plaza, Suite 1600, 55 Broadway, 10006
Telephone: 212-768-9500
Email: kittaygoldgershfeld@yahoo.com
White Plains, New York Office: 81 Main Street.
Telephone: 914-686-1900.

David R. Kittay
Barry S. Gold
Michelle Gershfeld

Michael E. Peeples
Judith L. Siegel

For full biographical listings, see the Martindale-Hubbell Law Directory

LOEB & LOEB LLP (AV)

A Limited Liability Partnership including Professional Corporations
345 Park Avenue, 10154-0037
Telephone: 212-407-4000
Facsimile: 212-407-4990
Email: info@loeb.com *URL:* http://www.loeb.com
Los Angeles, California Office: Suite 1800, 1000 Wilshire Boulevard, 90017-2475.
Telephone: 213-688-3400.
Facsimile: 213-688-3460.
Century City (Los Angeles), California Office: Suite 2200, 10100 Santa Monica Boulevard, Los Angeles, 90067-4164.
Telephone: 310-282-2000.
Facsimile: 310-282-2192.
Nashville, Tennessee Office: 45 Music Square West, 37203-3205.
Telephone: 615-749-8300.
Facsimile: 615-749-8308.
Rome, Italy Office: Piazza Digione 1, 00197.
Telephone: 011-3906-808-8456.
Facsimile: 011-3906-808-8288.

MEMBERS OF FIRM

David B. Eizenman
David M. Satnick
Helen Gavaris
P. Gregory Schwed

ASSOCIATE

Paula K. Colbath

For Complete List of Firm Personnel, See General Section

For full biographical listings, see the Martindale-Hubbell Law Directory

NEIMAN GINSBURG & MAIRANZ P.C. (AV)

39 Broadway, 25th Floor, 10006-3003
Telephone: 212-269-1000
Telecopier: 212-635-9302
Email: ngmpc@concentric.net *URL:* http://www.ngmpc.com

Marvin Neiman
Theodore T. Mairanz
Gary Ginsburg

Betsy R. Malik
Susie Chovev

For full biographical listings, see the Martindale-Hubbell Law Directory

OPPENHEIMER WOLFF & DONNELLY LLP (AV)

The Chrysler East Building 19th Floor, 666 Third Avenue, 10017
Telephone: 212-826-5000
FAX: 212-486-0708
URL: http://www.oppenheimer.com
Minneapolis, Minnesota Office: 3300 Plaza VII, 45 South Seventh Street. 55402.
Telephone: 612-607-7000.
FAX: 612-607-7100.
Amsterdam, The Netherlands Office: Keizergracht 241.
Telephone: 31-20-423-4555.
FAX: 312-20-423-4545.
Brussels, Belgium Office: Avenue Louise 240, Box 5, 1050.
Telephone: 32-2-626-0500.
FAX: 32-2-626-0510.
Geneva, Switzerland Office: Rue Gabriel Eynard, 6, 1205.
Telephone: (41/22) 311-7410.
FAX: (41/22) 311-4707.
Newport Beach, California Office: 500 Newport Center Drive, Suite 700, 92660.
Telephone: 949-823-6000.
FAX: 949-823-6100.
Paris, France Office: 35 Boulevard des Capucines, 75002.
Telephone: (33/1) 53 45 40 00.
FAX: (33/1) 53 45 40 10.
St. Paul, Minnesota Office: 1700 First National Bank Building, 55101.
Telephone: 651-605-2000.
FAX: 651-605-2100.
Washington, D.C. Office: Oppenheimer Wolff Donnelly & Bayh LLP, 1350 Eye Street, N.W., Suite 200, 20005.
Telephone: 202-312-8000.
FAX: 202-312-8100.
Los Angeles, California Office: 2029 Century Park East, 38th Floor, 90067.
Telephone: 310-788-5000.
FAX: 310-277-1297.
Palo Alto, California Office: 3373 Hillview Avenue, Suite 200, 94304.
Telephone: 650-320-4000.
FAX: 650-320-4100.
Chicago, Illinois Office: Oppenheimer Wolff & Donnelly (Illinois), Two Prudential Plaza, 45th Floor, 180 North Stetson Avenue, 60601.
Telephone: 312-616-1800.
Fax: 312-616-5800.

RESIDENT PARTNERS

Lance Gotthoffer
Thomas M. Gandolfo
Ronald S. Beacher

RESIDENT ASSOCIATES

Teresa J. Olson
Suzanne A. Cruse
Constantine Karides
Ronald J. Kaniuk
Robert M. Hirsh

For full biographical listings, see the Martindale-Hubbell Law Directory

OTTERBOURG, STEINDLER, HOUSTON & ROSEN, P.C. (AV)

230 Park Avenue, 29th Floor, 10169
Telephone: 212-661-9100
Telecopier: 212-682-6104

William M. Silverman
Glenn B. Rice
Peter H. Stolzar
Albert F. Reisman
Jonathan N. Helfat
Steven B. Soll
Daniel Wallen
Mitchell M. Brand
Scott L. Hazan
Peter L. Feldman
Andrew M. Kramer

GENERAL COUNSEL

Kurt J. Wolff

COUNSEL

Bernard Beitel
Morton L. Gitter

Enid Nagler Stuart
John J. Kenny
Jenette A. Barrow-Bosshart
Richard L. Stehl
Brett H. Miller
Susan A. Joyce
Rosanne A. Finkel

For Complete List of Firm Personnel, See General Section

For full biographical listings, see the Martindale-Hubbell Law Directory

New York—Continued

Parker Chapin LLP (AV)

Chrysler Building, 405 Lexington Avenue, 10017
Telephone: 212-704-6000
Telecopier: 212-704-6288
URL: http://www.parkerchapin.com
Great Neck, New York Office: 175 Great Neck Road.
Telephone: 516-482-4422.
Telecopier: 516-482-4469.
Hackensack, New Jersey: 190 Morre Street, Suite 307.
Telephone: 210-883-6400.
Telecopier: 210-883-6404.
Beverly Hills, California: 9454 Wilshire Boulevard.
Telephone: 310-288-8367.
Telecopier: 310-288-8365.

MEMBERS OF FIRM

Charles P. Greenman
Joel Lewittes
Lee W. Stremba

For Complete List of Firm Personnel, See General Section

For full biographical listings, see the Martindale-Hubbell Law Directory

Skadden, Arps, Slate, Meagher & Flom LLP (AV)

Four Times Square, 10036
Telephone: 212-735-3000
Fax: 212-735-2000
URL: http://www.sasmf.com
Firm/Affiliate Offices:
Boston, Massachusetts: One Beacon Street, 02108.
Telephone: 617-573-4800.
Fax: 617-573-4822.
Washington, D.C.: 1440 New York Avenue, N.W., 20005.
Telephone: 202-371-7000.
Fax: 202-393-5760.
Wilmington, Delaware: One Rodney Square, P.O. Box 636, 19899.
Telephone: 302-651-3000.
Fax: 302-651-3001.
Los Angeles, California: 300 South Grand Avenue, 90071.
Telephone: 213-687-5000.
Fax: 213-687-5600.
Chicago, Illinois: Skadden, Arps, Slate, Meagher & Flom (Illinois), 333 West Wacker Drive, 60606.
Telephone: 312-407-0700.
Fax: 312-407-0411.
San Francisco, California: Four Embarcadero Center, 94111.
Telephone: 415-984-6400.
Fax: 415-984-2698.
Houston, Texas: 1600 Smith Street, Suite 4460, 77002.
Telephone: 713-655-5100.
Fax: 713-655-5181.
Newark, New Jersey: One Newark Center, 07102.
Telephone: 973-639-6800.
Fax: 973-639-6858.
Palo Alto, California: 525 University Avenue, Suite 220, 94301.
Telephone: 650-470-4500.
Fax: 650-470-4570.
Tokyo, Japan: ATT Main Tower 12F, 2-17-22, Akasaka, Minato-ku, 107-0052.
Telephone: 011-813-3568-2600.
Fax: 011-813-3568-2626.
London, England: One Canada Square, Canary Wharf, E14 5DS.
Telephone: 011-44-207-519-7000.
Fax: 011-44-207-519-7070.
Hong Kong, China: 30/F Tower Two, Lippo Centre, 89 Queensway, Central.
Telephone: 011-852-2820-0700.
Fax: 011-852-2820-0727.
Sydney, New South Wales 2000, Australia: Skadden, Arps, Slate, Meagher & Flom (International), Level 13, 131 Macquarie Street.
Telephone: 011-61-2-9253-6000.
Fax: 011-61-2-9253-6044.
Toronto, Ontario, Canada: Suite 1820, North Tower, P.O. Box 189, Royal Bank Plaza, M5J 2J4.
Telephone: 416-777-4700.
Fax: 416-777-4747.
Brussels, Belgium: 523 avenue Louise, Box 30, 1050.
Telephone: 011-32-2-639-0300.
Fax: 011-32-2-639-0339.
Frankfurt am Main, Germany: MesseTurm, 27th Floor, 60308.
Telephone: 011-49-69-742200.
Fax: 011-49-69-74220300.
Paris, France: 68, rue du Faubourg Saint-Honoré, 75008.
Telephone: 011-331-55-27-11-00.
Fax: 011-331-55-27-11-99.
Beijing, China: East Wing Office, Level 4, China World Trade Center, No. 1 Jian Guo Men Wai Avenue, 100004.
Telephone: 011-86-10-6505-5511.
Fax: 011-86-10-6505-5522.
Moscow, Russia: Degtyarniy Pereulok 4, Building 1, 103009.
Telephone: 011-7-501-797-4600.
Fax: 011-7-501-797-4601.

(See Next Column)

Singapore, Singapore: Skadden, Arps, Slate, Meagher & Flom (International), 9 Temasek Boulevard, Suite 29-01, Suntec Tower Two, 038989.
Telephone: 011-65-434-2900.
Fax: 011-65-434-2988.

MEMBERS OF FIRM/AFFILIATES

Michael L. Cook
Alesia Ranney-Marinelli
Kayalyn A. Marafioti
George A. Zimmerman
Sally McDonald Henry
Jay M. Goffman

COUNSEL

Carlene J. Gatting
Stephanie R. Schwartz

CHICAGO, ILLINOIS

PARTNERS

N. Lynn Hiestand
John Wm. Butler, Jr.
J. Eric Ivester
David S. Kurtz

COUNSEL

John K. Lyons

LOS ANGELES, CALIFORNIA

PARTNER

Richard B. Levin

COUNSEL

Peter W. Clapp

WILMINGTON, DELAWARE

PARTNERS

Anthony W. Clark
Gregg M. Galardi

COUNSEL

Mark S. Chehi

NEW YORK, NEW YORK

ASSOCIATES

Giorgio Bovenzi
Alan J. Carr
Steven B. Eichel
Lawrence V. Gelber
Stephen J. Gordon
Neal R. Jacobson
Barbara Krasa Kelly
Jerome J. Lawton
Alexandra Margolis
Shmuel Vasser
Samuel S. Yoo

CHICAGO, ILLINOIS

ASSOCIATES

Robert A. Allison
Amarjeet S. Bhachu
Michael D. Ilagan
Eric W. Kaup
Sherri Morissette
Timothy P. Olson
George N. Panagakis
J. Gregory St. Clair
Stephen D. Williamson

WILMINGTON, DELAWARE

ASSOCIATES

James A. Corrodi
Eric M. Davis
Van C. Durrier, II
Thomas G. Macauley
Cheryl E. Siskin

For Complete List of Firm Personnel, See General Section

For full biographical listings, see the Martindale-Hubbell Law Directory

Stroock & Stroock & Lavan LLP (AV)

180 Maiden Lane, 10038-4982
Telephone: 212-806-5400
Telecopier: 212-806-6006
Telexes: Stroock, UT 177693 and Plastroock NYK 177077 (International)
Email: info@stroock.com *URL:* http://www.stroock.com
New York Conference Center: 767 Third Avenue, New York, N.Y., 10017-2023.
Telephones: 212-806-5767; 5768; 5769; 5770.
Telecopier: 212-421-6234. Email: info@stroock.com
Boston, Massachusetts Office: 100 Federal Street, Boston, MA., 02110-1813 .
Telephone: 617-482-6800.
Fax: 617-330-5111. Email: infoboston@stroock.com
Los Angeles, California Office: 2029 Century Park East, Suite 1800, Los Angeles, CA., 90067-3086.
Telephone: 310-556-5800.
Telecopier: 310-556-5959. Email: infola@stroock.com
Miami, Florida Office: First Union Financial Center, 200 South Biscayne Boulevard, Suite 3300, Miami, FL., 33131-2385.
Telephone: 305-358-9900.
Telecopier: 305-789-9302. Email: infomiami@stroock.com
Washington, D.C. Office: 1150 Seventeenth Street, N.W., Suite 600, Washington, D.C., 20036-4652.
Telephone: 202-452-9250.
Telecopier: 202-293-2293. Email: infodc@stroock.com

MEMBERS OF FIRM

Wendell H. Adair, Jr. (Not admitted in NY)
Lawrence M. Handelsman
Robin E. Keller
Lewis Kruger
Robert A. Raskin
Mark A. Speiser

SPECIAL COUNSEL

Arlene G. Krieger

(See Next Column)

STROOCK & STROOCK & LAVAN LLP, *New York—Continued*

Christopher R. Donoho, III
Kristopher M. Hansen
Steven B. Horowitz
Sherry J. Millman
Harold A. Olsen
Lisa C. Takoudes
Denise K. Wildes

For Complete List of Firm Personnel, See General Section

For full biographical listings, see the Martindale-Hubbell Law Directory

TODTMAN, NACHAMIE, SPIZZ & JOHNS, P.C. (AV)

425 Park Avenue, 10022
Telephone: 212-754-9400
Fax: 212-754-6262
Email: INFO@tnsj-law.com *URL:* http://www.tnsj-law.com
Paris, France Office: 3, rue du Faubourg Saint-Honoré 75008.
Telephone: +33-1 44-71-03-03.
Facsimile: +33-1 44-71-03-04.

Martin Todtman
Barton Nachamie
Alex Spizz
Peter A. Johns (Not admitted in United States)
Robert D. Tolz
Beth S. Barash
Arthur Goldstein
Perry L. Cohen
Mathew E. Hoffman
S. Timothy Ball
Scott S. Markowitz
Gilbert A. Samberg
Alan S. Liebman

Perri E. Frosch
Andrew L. Rosenberg
Richard S. Kanowitz
William A. Palomo
Felipe Montejo
Julie K. Horowitz
Matthew W. Woodruff

OF COUNSEL

Jack Newton Lerner
Harvey I. Sladkus

For full biographical listings, see the Martindale-Hubbell Law Directory

TOGUT, SEGAL & SEGAL (AV)

One Penn Plaza, 10119
Telephone: 212-594-5000
Telecopier: 212-967-4258
Email: email@TeamTogut.com

MEMBERS OF FIRM

Albert Togut
Bernard Segal (1932-1983)
Sidney Segal (1935-1968)
Frank A. Oswald

ASSOCIATES

Neil Berger
Scott E. Ratner

For full biographical listings, see the Martindale-Hubbell Law Directory

TRAUB, BONACQUIST & FOX LLP (AV)

655 Third Avenue, 21st Floor, 10017
Telephone: 212-476-4770
Fax: 212-476-4787
Email: tbfesq@aol.com
Arlington, Texas Office: 433 Washington Drive.
Telephone: 817-794-0667.
Fax: 817-794-0456.

MEMBERS OF FIRM

Paul Traub
Michael S. Fox
Susan F. Balaschak (Resident, Arlington, Texas Office)
Steven E. Fox

ASSOCIATES

Fredrick J. Levy
Wendy G. Marcari
Maura I. Russell

OF COUNSEL

Harold F. Bonacquist
Brian E. Kriger

For full biographical listings, see the Martindale-Hubbell Law Directory

WINTHROP, STIMSON, PUTNAM & ROBERTS (AV)

One Battery Park Plaza, 10004-1490
Telephone: 212-858-1000
Telex: 62854 WINSTIM
Telefax: 212-858-1500
URL: http://www.winstim.com
Stamford, Connecticut Office: Financial Centre, 695 East Main Street, P.O. Box 6760, 06904-6760.
Telephone: 203-348-2300.
Fax: 203-965-8226.
Washington, D.C. Office: 1133 Connecticut Avenue, N.W., 20036.
Telephone: 202-775-9800.
Fax: 202-833-8491.
Palm Beach, Florida Office: 125 Worth Avenue, Suite 310, 33480.
Telephone: 561-655-7297.
Fax: 561-833-6726.
London Office: 54 Lombard Street, London EC3V 9DH, England.
Telephone: 011-44207-648-9200.
Fax: 011-44207-283-1656.

(See Next Column)

Tokyo, Japan Office: 608 Atagoyama Bengoshi Building 6-7, Atago 1-chome, Minato-ku, Tokyo 105 Japan.
Telephone: 011-813-3437-9740.
Fax: 011-813-3437-9261.
Hong Kong, China Office: 2505 Asia Pacific Finance Tower, Citibank Plaza, 3 Garden Road, Central.
Telephone: 011-852-2530-3400.
Fax: 011-852-2530-3355.
Singapore Office: 6 Battery Road #38-01/B, Singapore 049909.
Telephone: 65-227-4700.
Fax: 65-227-4711.

NEW YORK OFFICE
MEMBERS OF FIRM

Richard L. Epling
Barton D. Ford
Robert W. Gray
William C. F. Kurz
F. Joseph Owens, Jr.
John F. Pritchard
Glenn E. Siegel
Charles H. Vejvoda

COUNSEL

Ujwala Mahatme

NEW YORK ASSOCIATES

Karen B. Dine
Margaret V. Malone

For Complete List of Firm Personnel, See General Section

For full biographical listings, see the Martindale-Hubbell Law Directory

*POUGHKEEPSIE,** Dutchess Co.

VAN DEWATER & VAN DEWATER (AV)

40 Garden Street, P.O. Box 112, 12602
Telephone: 914-452-5900
Fax: 914-452-5848
Pawling, New York Office: 243 Route 22, P.O. Box 668.
Telephone: 914-855-5900.
Fax: 914-855-5945.

MEMBERS OF FIRM

John B. Van DeWater (1892-1968)
Robert B. Van DeWater (1920-1990)
David D. Hagstrom
John K. Gifford
James E. Nelson
Craig T. Digilio
Gerard J. Comatos
Ronald C. Blass, Jr.

OF COUNSEL

Noel deCordova, Jr.
Edward VK. Cunningham, Jr.
James D. Benson
Susanna E. Bedell

ASSOCIATES

Rebecca Supple Mensch
Michael G. Hayes

Counsel for: J. D. Johnson Co., Inc.; The Fishkill National Bank; The Bank of the Hudson; Vassar Brothers Hospital.
Local Counsel for: Vassar College; Chemprene Div. of Witco Chemical Corp.; Gannett Satellite Information Network, Inc.

For full biographical listings, see the Martindale-Hubbell Law Directory

*ROCHESTER,** Monroe Co.

FORSYTH, HOWE, O'DWYER, KALB & MURPHY, P.C. (AV)

Suite 1600, Midtown Tower, 14604
Telephone: 716-325-7515
Fax: 716-325-6407
URL: http://www.forsythhowe.com

Charles B. Forsyth (1890-1968)
C. Benn Forsyth
Gordon A. Howe, II
Duncan W. O'Dwyer
Robert J. Kalb
Gerald N. Murphy

Nancy A. Pappal

OF COUNSEL

John F. Forsyth (Retired)
Allan Wolk
Hoffman Stone
Debra A. Martin
Janice M. Iati
Cathleen W. Smith
Thad F. Sondej

References: The Chase Manhattan Bank; Fleet Bank.

For full biographical listings, see the Martindale-Hubbell Law Directory

LACY, KATZEN, RYEN & MITTLEMAN, LLP (AV)

The Granite Building, 130 East Main Street, 14604
Telephone: 716-454-5650
FAX: 716-454-6525
Email: MSS@Frontiernet.net
Charlotte, New York Office: 4292 Lake Avenue.
Telephone: 716-663-4543.
Hilton, New York Office: 20 Main Street.
Telephone: 716-392-2990.
Canandaigua, New York Office: 23 North Main Street.
Telephone: 716-394-5220.
Greece, New York Office: County Village Center, 110 Long Pond Road, Suite 214.
Telephone: 716-225-2470.
Fax: 716-225-5620.

(See Next Column)

LACY, KATZEN, RYEN & MITTLEMAN LLP—*Continued*

Bergen, New York Office: 16 North Lake Street.
Telephone: 716-494-1382.
Ontario, New York Office: 1276 Ridge Road.
Telephone: 315-524-5000.
Roseland, New Jersey Office: 103 Eisenhower Parkway.
Telephone: 201-403-8001.
Penn Yan, New York Office: 116 Main Street, 2nd Floor, P.O. Box 439.
Telephone: 315-536-6281.

MEMBERS OF FIRM

Louis A. Ryen
Ronald A. Mittleman
Michael S. Schnittman
Peter T. Rodgers
Sally A. Smith
Karen Schaefer
Richard G. Curtis
Lawrence J. Schwind
David H. Walsh IV
David E. Anderson
Craig R. Welch
Christopher B. Mumford
Leslie W. Kernan, Jr.

COUNSEL

Leon Katzen
George F. Frey, Jr.
John J. Keigher
Paul A. Sandars, III

ASSOCIATES

David D. MacKnight
Nia J. Nichols
Terrance W. Emmens
Mark H. Stein
Denine K. Carr
Jacqueline M. Thomas
Stephen M. O'Neill
Jennifer Lynn Chadwick
William H. Drumm
Matthew A. Ryen
Roxanne A. Marvasti
Julie E. Meyer

General Counsel for: Village of Bergen, Bergen, New York; Village of Hilton, Hilton, New York; Byron-Bergen Central School District No. 1, Bergen, New York; Ferris Industries, Inc.; L. Woerner, Inc.d/b/a HCR.
Reference: The Chase Manhattan Bank, Rochester, N.Y.

For full biographical listings, see the Martindale-Hubbell Law Directory

LAWRENCE, WERNER, KESSELRING, SWARTOUT & BROWN, LLP (AV)

Formerly Suter Doyle Kesselring Lawrence & Werner
700 First Federal Plaza, 14614-1909
Telephone: 716-325-6446
Fax: 716-262-5185
Email: rochester@lwksb.com *URL:* http://www.lwksb.com
Canandaigua, New York Office: 23 Sly Street, 14424.
Telephone: 716-396-4000.
Fax: 716-396-1210. Email: canandaigua@lwksb.com.
Clifton Springs, New York: 26 East Main Street, P.O. Box 604, 14432.
Telephone: 315-462-3010.
Fax: 315-462-5039. Email: clifton_springs@lwksb.com

Paul J. Suter (1918-1989)

MEMBERS OF FIRM

Leo J. Kesselring
C. Bruce Lawrence
Christopher K. Werner
Colleen A. Brown
Steven H. Swartout
Mary Jo S. Korona

OF COUNSEL

James B. Doyle
Craig J. Doran
John F. Riley

ASSOCIATE

Jeffrey D. Graff

Representative Clients: Canandaigua National Bank; Hadlock Paint Company, Inc.; F.F. Thompson Health Systems, Inc.; Keuka College; Towns of Farmington and Gorham, NY; Toyota Motor Credit Corp.
References: Canandaigua National Bank; Fleet Bank, Rochester; National Association of Credit Manager, Rochester.

For full biographical listings, see the Martindale-Hubbell Law Directory

ROCKVILLE CENTRE, Nassau Co.

BATZAR & WEINBERG, A PROFESSIONAL CORPORATION (AV)

184 Sunrise Highway, P.O. Box 427, 11570
Telephone: 516-766-1860
Telecopier: 516-678-7801
Email: batweinb@aol.com *URL:* http://www.batzarweinberg.com
Edison, New Jersey Office: 86 Hudson Street.
Telephone: 908-653-1797.
Merion, Pennsylvania Office: 405 Andrew Road.
Telephone: 215-568-1060.
West Palm Beach, Florida Office: 3800 Washington Road.
Telephone: 561-659-5881.

Sanford I. Weinberg

Edward J. Damsky
Peter G. Rubin

OF COUNSEL

Norma R. Frank (Not admitted in NY; Resident, Merion, Pennsylvania Office)
Lisa A. Maglone (Not admitted in NY; Resident, Edison, New Jersey Office)

For full biographical listings, see the Martindale-Hubbell Law Directory

*SYRACUSE,** Onondaga Co.

COSTELLO COONEY & FEARON, LLP (AV)

Salina Place, 205 South Salina Street, 13202
Telephone: 315-422-1152
Fax: 315-422-1139
Email: ccf-law.com *URL:* http://www.ccf-law.com

ASSOCIATE

Edmund J. Gegan

General Counsel for: Auburn Memorial Hospital; Crouse Hospital; Health Services Association of Central New York; St. Joseph's Hospital Health Center.
Local Counsel for: Deere & Co.; New York Telephone Co.; Crum & Forster Insurance Co.; The Travelers Insurance Companies; Caterpillar, Inc.; Otis Elevator.

For Complete List of Firm Personnel, See General Section

For full biographical listings, see the Martindale-Hubbell Law Directory

MARTIN, MARTIN & WOODARD, LLP (AV)

Suite 300, One Lincoln Center, 13202-3010
Telephone: 315-478-2222
Fax: 315-478-4318

MEMBERS OF FIRM

Donald J. Martin
David P. Martin
Lee E. Woodard
Harold P. Goldberg
David M. Capriotti

ASSOCIATES

Wendy A. Kinsella
James T. Snyder
Daniel E. Dyer

For full biographical listings, see the Martindale-Hubbell Law Directory

WESTBURY, Nassau Co.

ACKERMAN & TERRY, LLC (AV)

900 Merchants Concourse, Suite 314, 11590
Telephone: 516-228-8245
Fax: 516-228-8249

MEMBERS OF FIRM

Neil H. Ackerman
Gerard Terry
Marianne J. Gallipoli

OF COUNSEL

Karen M. Dowd

ASSOCIATES

Vivek K. Chavan (Not admitted in NY)
Michael G. McAuliffe

For full biographical listings, see the Martindale-Hubbell Law Directory

PRYOR & MANDELUP, L.L.P. (AV)

675 Old Country Road, 11590
Telephone: 516-997-0999
Facsimile: 516-333-7333

Robert L. Pryor
A. Scott Mandelup
Randolph E. White
Eric J. Snyder

Kenneth A. Reynolds
Anthony F. Giuliano
Christopher W. Costello

OF COUNSEL

Michael Salgo
C. Albert Parente

LEGAL SUPPORT PERSONNEL

Gwendolyn V. Myles
Barbara Anson

For full biographical listings, see the Martindale-Hubbell Law Directory

*WHITE PLAINS,** Westchester Co.

POSNER, POSNER & ASSOCIATES, PC (AV)

399 Knollwood Road, 10603
Telephone: 914-948-6620
Telecopier: 914-948-0864
Email: relawyer@aol.com *URL:* http://www.lawyers.com/posner_posner&assoc

Henry A. Greenburg
Martin Louis Posner
Jane Y. Posner

Peter J. McCarthy
Karen Olson

References: Chemical Bank; Citibank.

For full biographical listings, see the Martindale-Hubbell Law Directory

NORTH CAROLINA

ASHEVILLE, * Buncombe Co.

GUM & HILLIER, P.A. (AV)

47 N. Market Street, P.O. Box 3235, 28801
Telephone: 704-258-3368
Fax: 704-252-6721
Email: hgum@interpath.com

David R. Hillier

Representative Client: Shoney's Restaurants.
References: Asheville Savings Bank; Wachovia Bank and Trust Co..

For full biographical listings, see the Martindale-Hubbell Law Directory

CHAPEL HILL, Orange Co.

NORTHEN BLUE, L.L.P. (AV)

Suite 550, 100 Europa Center, P.O. Box 2208, 27515-2208
Telephone: 919-968-4441
Facsimile: 919-942-6603
Email: NBFIRM@aol.com

MEMBERS OF FIRM

John A. Northen
J. William Blue, Jr.
David M. Rooks, III
Charles H. Thibaut
Carol J. Holcomb

ASSOCIATES

James C. Stanford
Cheryl Y. Capron
Margaret W. Holloway

References: Central Carolina Bank; Triangle Bank; Investors Title Insurance Co.; First Union National Bank; Centura Bank; BB&T; Balbirer & Coleman, CPA's.

For full biographical listings, see the Martindale-Hubbell Law Directory

CHARLOTTE, * Mecklenburg Co.

DAVID R. BADGER, P.A. (AV)

Suite 1560 Carillon, 227 West Trade Street, 28202-1625
Telephone: 704-375-8875
FAX: 704-375-8835

David R. Badger

For full biographical listings, see the Martindale-Hubbell Law Directory

CLAWSON & STAUBES, L.L.C. (AV Ⓣ)

756 Tyvola Road, Suite 101, P.O. Box 241352, 29217
Telephone: 843-522-7733
Fax: 843-522-9033
Email: rcraig@clawson&staubes.com
Charleston, South Carolina Office: 304 Meeting Street, 29401.
Telephone: 803-577-2026.
Facsimile: 803-722-2867.

Ronnie F. Craig (Not admitted in NC)
C.O. Ladd Ackerman, Jr.
J. Ronald Jones, Jr.

William Lewis Ellison, Jr.
Jennifer Susan Ahlers

Representative Clients: Chase Financial Corp.; KeyBank USA; Wachovia Bank & Trust, NA.; State Farm Mutual Insurance Co.

For full biographical listings, see the Martindale-Hubbell Law Directory

DOZIER, MILLER, POLLARD & MURPHY (AV)

Cameron Brown Building, 301 South McDowell Street, Suite 700, 28204
Telephone: 704-372-6373
Fax: 704-347-0674
URL: http://www.dmpm.com

MEMBERS OF FIRM

W. Joseph Dozier, Jr.
R. Craig Miller, Jr.
Scott T. Pollard
Gary L. Murphy
William Patrick Hobson
Timothy H. Graham
George N. Miller
Richard S. Gordon
Thomas J. Falish
Kristin L. Smith

For full biographical listings, see the Martindale-Hubbell Law Directory

MITCHELL, RALLINGS, SINGER, MCGIRT & TISSUE, PLLC (AV)

1800 Carillon, 227 West Trade Street, 28202
Telephone: 704-376-6574
FAX: 704-342-1531

MEMBERS OF FIRM

Richard M. Mitchell
Thomas B. Rallings, Jr.
Joseph N. Tissue

(See Next Column)

ASSOCIATES

James L. Fretwell
John W. Taylor
Carl Spencer Alridge, II

Representative Clients: Bonitz Contracting Co.; Captain D's. Inc.; Dyke Industries, Inc.; Edgcomb Metals; Titan Building Products, Inc.
References: Bank of Mecklenburg; Central Carolina Bank ; N.C.N.B.

For full biographical listings, see the Martindale-Hubbell Law Directory

PARHAM, HELMS, HARRIS, BLYTHE & MORTON (AV)

6310 Fairview Road, Suite 200, 28210
Telephone: 704-366-6607
Fax: 704-366-6973
Email: lmbatty@mindspring.com

MEMBERS OF FIRM

Lewis H. Parham, Jr.
Neal G. Helms
Ralph C. Harris, Jr.
Robert B. Blythe
James H. Morton

ASSOCIATE

Lyn Morton Batty

OF COUNSEL

John L. Hazlehurst

Representative Clients: Marsh Associates, Inc.; General Motors Acceptance Corp.; Nations Bank; Pro Credit Corp.
Reference: Nations Bank.

For full biographical listings, see the Martindale-Hubbell Law Directory

GREENSBORO, * Guilford Co.

FOLLIN & OVERFIELD, L.L.P. (AV)

100 South Elm Street, Suite 410, 27401
Telephone: 336-274-6703
Fax: 336-274-0007
Email: jconc@nr.infi.net

MEMBERS OF FIRM

Marion G. Follin III
John Covington Overfield

For full biographical listings, see the Martindale-Hubbell Law Directory

IVEY, MCCLELLAN, GATTON & TALCOTT, L.L.P. (AV)

121 South Elm Street, P.O. Box 3324, 27402
Telephone: 336-274-4658
Telefax: 336-274-4540

MEMBERS OF FIRM

Charles M. Ivey, Jr. (1914-1993)
Charles M. Ivey, III
Robert L. McClellan
Edwin R. Gatton
James K. Talcott
Lillian H. Pinto

ASSOCIATES

John M. Blust
Dirk W. Siegmund
Eric A. Richardson
Mary Beth B. Swecker

Representative Clients: First Home Federal Savings and Loan Assn.; First Citizens Bank & Trust Co.; First National Bank of Randolph Co.; Wachovia Bank and Trust; Friendly Rubber & Seal Co.; Mercedes-Benz Credit Corp.; Norwest Financial, North Carolina.
Approved Attorneys for: Jefferson-Pilot Title Insurance Co.; Lawyers Title Insurance Corp.

For full biographical listings, see the Martindale-Hubbell Law Directory

GERALD S. SCHAFER (AV)

220 Commerce Place, 27401
Telephone: 910-273-9309
Fax: 910-273-2700

Representative Clients: Lewis System & Service, Inc.; Triad Wholesale Lumber, Inc.; Williamson Heating & Cooling, Inc.; Boren Clay Products Co.; Branch Banking & Trust Co.; Regional Acceptance Corp.; Panel of Chapter 7 Trustees; Environmental Air Systems Inc.; Envirotrol Inc.; Rockingham County Tax Collector.
Reference: First Union National Bank.

For full biographical listings, see the Martindale-Hubbell Law Directory

GREENVILLE, * Pitt Co.

EDWARD J. HARPER II ATTORNEY AT LAW (AV)

600 B Country Club Road, P.O. Box 527, 27835
Telephone: 252-215-0200
Fax: 252-215-0222

For full biographical listings, see the Martindale-Hubbell Law Directory

*NEW BERN,** Craven Co.

STUBBS & PERDUE, P.A. (AV)

310 Craven Street, P.O. Box 1654, 28563-1654
Telephone: 252-633-2700
Fax: 252-633-9600
Email: law@stubbsperdue.com
Raleigh, North Carolina Office: Two Hannover Square, 434 Fayetteville Street Mall, Suite 930, P.O. Box 1630, 27602-1630.
Telephone: 919-856-9400.
Fax: 919-856-9300. Email: law@stubbsperdue.com

Gary R. Perdue, Sr. (1947-1997)
Trawick H. Stubbs, Jr.
John W. King, Jr.
David James Haidt
John C. Bircher III

Approved Attorneys For: Lawyers Title Insurance Corp.
References: NationsBank; Wachovia Bank & Trust Co.; Branch Banking & Trust Co.

For full biographical listings, see the Martindale-Hubbell Law Directory

*RALEIGH,** Wake Co.

SMITH DEBNAM NARRON WYCHE STORY & MYERS, L.L.P. (AV)

Hedingham Oaks, 4700 New Bern Avenue, P.O. Box 26268, 27611-6268
Telephone: 919-250-2000
Facsimile: 919-250-2100
Email: smithdebnamlaw.com

MEMBERS OF FIRM

W. Thurston Debnam, Jr.
John W. Narron
Jerry T. Myers
Terri L. Gardner
Byron L. Saintsing
Franklin Drake
Gerald H. Groon, Jr.
Terry M. Kilbride
Elizabeth B. Godfrey
N. Hunter Wyche, Jr.
Ashley H. Story
Bettie Kelley Sousa
Laura K. Howell
Rose H. Stout
Susan Yelton Ellinger
Caren Davis Enloe
Connie E. Carrigan
Jeff D. Rogers
Kevin L. Sink

ASSOCIATES

Melanie J. Hogg
Staci Flaxman Katz
Tabatha L. Cruden
Tracy T. Hyde
Nina L. Gunther
Matthew E. Roehm
Sharon B. Christopher
J. Michael Mackay
Cynthia V. Mcalister

OF COUNSEL

Fred J. Smith, Jr.
Jane Flowers Finch

Representative Clients: Roses Stores, Inc.; Ford Motor Credit Co.; Eastman Kodak Co.; General Electric Capital Corp.

For full biographical listings, see the Martindale-Hubbell Law Directory

*SMITHFIELD,** Johnston Co.

GORDON C. WOODRUFF (AV)

1023 B West Market Street, P.O. Box 708, 27577
Telephone: 919-934-4000
Fax: 919-934-5884

For full biographical listings, see the Martindale-Hubbell Law Directory

*WINSTON-SALEM,** Forsyth Co.

BLANCO TACKABERY COMBS & MATAMOROS, P.A. (AV)

110 S. Stratford Road, 5th Floor, P.O. Drawer 25008, 27114-5008
Telephone: 336-761-1250
Facsimile: 336-761-1530

David B. Blanco
Neal E. Tackabery
Reginald F. Combs
Ronald A. Matamoros
Gene B. Tarr
Michael D. Hurst
Steven C. Garland
Peter J. Juran
Brian L. Herndon
Bowen C. Houff
George E. Hollodick
Charles D. Luckey

Mary Margaret Ogburn
Jeffrey D. Patton
Deborah L. McKenney
Amy L. Schneider
Michelle M. Minnich
Stephen C. Minnich
Jean Sutton Martin

References: Southern Community Bank, Winston-Salem, NC; Premier Federal Credit Union, Greensboro, NC; Reynolds Carolina Federal Credit Union, Winston-Salem, NC; The Community Bank, Mt. Airy, NC.

For full biographical listings, see the Martindale-Hubbell Law Directory

WOMBLE CARLYLE SANDRIDGE & RICE (AV)

A Professional Limited Liability Company
200 West Second Street, P.O. Drawer 84, 27102
Telephone: 336-721-3600
Fax: 336-721-3660
Email: lawyers@wcsr.com *URL:* http://www.wcsr.com
Charlotte, North Carolina Office: 3300 One First Union Center, 301 South College Street.
Telephone: 704-331-4900.
Fax: 704-331-4955.
Raleigh, North Carolina Office: 2100 First Union Capitol Center, 150 Fayetteville Street Mall, P.O. Box 831.
Telephone: 919-755-2100.
Fax: 919-755-2150.
Research Triangle Park, North Carolina Office: 2505 Meridian Parkway, Suite 300 (Durham), 27713.
Telephone: 919-484-2300.
Fax: 919-484-2340.
Atlanta, Georgia Office: One Atlantic Center, 1201 West Peachtree Street, Suite 3500.
Telephone: 404-872-7000.
Fax: 404-888-7490.
Other Atlanta, Georgia Office: Suite 404, 2296 Henderson Mill Road, N.E.
Telephone: 770-492-9030.
Fax: 770-492-9609.
Washington, D.C. Office: 1120 Nineteenth Street, N.W., Eighth Floor.
Telephone: 202-857-4400.
Fax: 202-467-6910.
Greenville, South Carolina Office: 15 South Main Street, Suite 601, P.O. Box 10208.
Telephone: 864-255-5400.
Fax: 864-255-5440.

RESIDENT MEMBERS

Bonnie Kay Donahue
William B. Sullivan
James E. Vaughan

RESIDENT ASSOCIATE

Robyn B. Withrow

Representative Clients: Brad Ragan, Inc.; Brenner Companies; Food Lion, Inc.; Hanes Companies, Inc.; North Carolina Baptist Hospitals, Inc.; R.J. Reynolds Tobacco Co.; Thomasville Furniture Industries, Inc.; Wachovia Corp.; Wake Forest University.

For Complete List of Firm Personnel, See General Section

For full biographical listings, see the Martindale-Hubbell Law Directory

NORTH DAKOTA

*FARGO,** Cass Co.

VOGEL, WEIR, BYE, HUNKE & MCCORMICK, LTD. (AV)

502 First Avenue North, P.O. Box 1389, 58107
Telephone: 701-237-6983
Facsimile: 701-237-0847
Email: vogellaw@vogellaw.com *URL:* http://www.vogellaw.com

William A. Schlossman, Jr.
Jon R. Brakke

For Complete List of Firm Personnel, See General Section

For full biographical listings, see the Martindale-Hubbell Law Directory

OHIO

*AKRON,** Summit Co.

GOLDMAN & ROSEN, LTD. (AV)

12th Floor, One Cascade Plaza, 44308-1196
Telephone: 330-376-8336
Telecopier: 330-376-2522
Email: Goldman@Raex.com

Samuel Goldman
Bernard I. Rosen
George P. Tsarnas
Michael B. Hendler
Marc P. Gertz
Gary M. Rosen
Irving B. Sugerman

Thomas K. Seeker
Stacey Tsarnas Hackenberg

OF COUNSEL

Frank E. Steel, Jr.
Joseph F. Gorman

References: First National Bank of Ohio; National City Bank, Akron.

For full biographical listings, see the Martindale-Hubbell Law Directory

Akron—Continued

Mentzer, Vuillemin and Mygrant Ltd. (AV)

1 Cascade Plaza, 20th Floor, 44308-1114
Telephone: 330-376-7500
Telecopier: 330-376-8018
Email: mvmlaw@juno.com

Howard E. Mentzer
Rajko Radonjich

Reference: National City Bank, Akron, Ohio.

For full biographical listings, see the Martindale-Hubbell Law Directory

*CINCINNATI,** Hamilton Co.

Frost & Jacobs LLP (AV)

2500 PNC Center, 201 East Fifth Street, 45202
Telephone: 513-651-6800
Telecopier: 513-651-6981
URL: http://www.frojac.com
Columbus, Ohio Office: One Columbus, 10 West Broad Street, 43215.
Telephone: 614-464-1211.
Telecopier: 614-464-1737.
Lexington, Kentucky Office: 1100 Vine Center Tower, 333 West Vine Street, 40507.
Telephone: 606-254-1100.
Telecopier: 606-253-2990.
Middletown, Ohio Office: 400 First National Bank Building, 2 North Main Street, 45042.
Telephone: 513-422-2001.
Telecopier: 513-422-3010.
Frankfort, Kentucky Office: 201 W. Main Street, 40601.
Telephone: 502-223-1400.
Telecopier: 502-223-1410.

MEMBERS OF FIRM

Edmund J. Adams
Gerald L. Baldwin
Jeffery R. Rush
Vincent E. Mauer
Ronald E. Gold
Douglas S. Tripp
David S. Bence

ASSOCIATES

Douglas L. Lutz
Michael J. O'Grady
Suzanne Wentzel

OF COUNSEL

Kimberly K. Mauer

COLUMBUS, OHIO OFFICE
OF COUNSEL

Susan L. Rhiel

LEXINGTON, KENTUCKY OFFICE
MEMBER OF FIRM

Greg E. Mitchell

Representative Clients: Champion International Corp.; Cincinnati Machine; Eagle Picher Industries, Inc.; Federated Department Stores; PNC Bank, National Association; Firstar, National Association; KeyBank, National Association; Turner Construction Co.; University of Cincinnati.

For Complete List of Firm Personnel, See General Section

For full biographical listings, see the Martindale-Hubbell Law Directory

Katz, Teller, Brant & Hild A Legal Professional Association (AV)

2400 Chemed Center, 255 East Fifth Street, 45202-4724
Telephone: 513-721-4532
Telecopier: 513-721-7120
Email: corp@ktbh.com

Bradley G. Haas

Wijdan Jreisat

For Complete List of Firm Personnel, See General Section

For full biographical listings, see the Martindale-Hubbell Law Directory

Keating, Muething & Klekamp, P.L.L. (AV)

1400 Provident Tower, One East Fourth Street, 45202
Telephone: 513-579-6400
Facsimile: 513-579-6457
URL: http://www.kmklaw.com

MEMBERS OF FIRM

J. David Rosenberg
J. Neal Gardner
Kevin E. Irwin
Timothy B. Matthews
Robert G. Sanker
Kenneth P. Kreider
Michael L. Scheier

ASSOCIATE

Susan J. Moeller

Representative Clients: American Financial Group; BP America Inc.; Chiquita Brands International, Inc.; Cintas Corporation; Comair Holdings, Inc.; Duke Realty Limited Partnership; LSI Industries Inc.; Mosler Inc.; Provident Financial Group Inc.

(See Next Column)

For Complete List of Firm Personnel, See General Section

For full biographical listings, see the Martindale-Hubbell Law Directory

*CLEVELAND,** Cuyahoga Co.

Baker & Hostetler LLP (AV)

3200 National City Center, 1900 East Ninth Street, 44114-3485
Telephone: 216-621-0200
Telecopier: 216-696-0740
TWX: 810 421 8375
RCA Telex: 215032
To contact an attorney on the Internet use first initial and surname followed by @baker-hostetler.com
URL: http://www.bakerlaw.com
In Cincinnati, Ohio: 312 Walnut Street, Suite 2650.
Telephone: 513-929-3400.
In Columbus, Ohio: Capitol Square, Suite 2100, 65 East State Street.
Telephone: 614-228-1541.
In Denver, Colorado: 303 East 17th Avenue, Suite 1100.
Telephone: 303-861-0600.
In Houston, Texas: 1000 Louisiana, Suite 2000.
Telephone: 713-751-1600.
In Beverly Hills, California: 9150 Wilshire Boulevard, Suite 205.
Telephone: 310-385-7500.
In Long Beach, California: 300 Oceangate, Suite 620.
Telephone: 562-432-2827.
In Los Angeles, California: 600 Wilshire Boulevard.
Telephone: 213-624-2400.
In Orlando, Florida: SunBank Center, Suite 2300, 200 South Orange Avenue.
Telephone: 407-649-4000.
In Washington, D.C.: Washington Square, Suite 1100, 1050 Connecticut Avenue, N.W.
Telephone: 202-861-1500.

PARTNERS

Wendy J. Gibson
Matthew R. Goldman
Thomas R. Lucchesi
Hilary Whipple Rule

ASSOCIATE

R. Timothy Coerdt

RETIRED PARTNER

John S. Hopkins, III

For Complete List of Firm Personnel, See General Section

For full biographical listings, see the Martindale-Hubbell Law Directory

Kelley, McCann & Livingstone, LLP (AV)

3500 BP Tower, 200 Public Square, 44114-2302
Telephone: 216-241-3141
Fax: 216-241-3707
Email: Attorneys@kmlegal.com

MEMBERS OF FIRM

Bruce L. Waterhouse, Jr.
Robert A. Brindza II

ASSOCIATE

Christine A. Allport

For Complete List of Firm Personnel, See General Section

For full biographical listings, see the Martindale-Hubbell Law Directory

*COLUMBUS,** Franklin Co.

Baker & Hostetler LLP (AV)

Capitol Square, Suite 2100, 65 East State Street, 43215-4260
Telephone: 614-228-1541
Telecopier: 614-462-2616
To contact an attorney on the Internet use first initial and surname followed by @baker-hostetler.com
URL: http://www.bakerlaw.com
In Cleveland, Ohio: 3200 National City Center, 1900 East Ninth Street.
Telephone: 216-621-0200.
In Cincinnati, Ohio: 312 Walnut Street, Suite 2650.
Telephone: 513-929-3400.
In Denver, Colorado: 303 East 17th Avenue, Suite 1100.
Telephone: 303-861-0600.
In Houston, Texas: 1000 Louisiana, Suite 2000.
Telephone: 713-751-1600.
In Beverly Hills, California: 9150 Wilshire Boulevard, Suite 205.
Telephone: 310-385-7500.
In Long Beach, California: 300 Oceangate, Suite 620.
Telephone: 562-432-2827.
In Los Angeles, California: 600 Wilshire Boulevard.
Telephone: 213-624-2400.
In Orlando, Florida: SunBank Center, Suite 2300, 200 South Orange Avenue.
Telephone: 407-649-4000.
In Washington, D. C.: Washington Square, Suite 1100, 1050 Connecticut Avenue, N.W.
Telephone: 202-861-1500.

(See Next Column)

BAKER & HOSTETLER LLP—*Continued*

PARTNERS

Henry P. Montgomery, IV — Alec Wightman

For Complete List of Firm Personnel, See General Section

For full biographical listings, see the Martindale-Hubbell Law Directory

CHESTER, WILLCOX AND SAXBE LLP (AV)

17 South High Street, Suite 900, 43215-3413
Telephone: 614-221-4000
Fax: 614-221-4012
Email: cwslaw.com

PARTNERS

James J. Chester
Guy R. Humphrey
J. Anthony Kington
Charles Rockwell Saxbe
Elizabeth Jean Watters
Roderick H. Willcox

ASSOCIATE

Karen S. Hockstad

Representative Clients: American Municipal Power-Ohio, Inc.; The Limited; Scioto Downs, Inc.; Tee Jaye's Country Place Restaurants.

For full biographical listings, see the Martindale-Hubbell Law Directory

KEGLER, BROWN, HILL & RITTER (AV)

Capitol Square Suite 1800, 65 East State Street, 43215-4294
Telephone: 614-462-5400
Telecopier: 614-464-2634
Cable Address: "Law KBHR"
Telex: 246671
Email: info@kbhr.com *URL:* http://www.kbhr.com
Marion, Ohio Office: 250 Executive Drive, Suite B, P.O. Box 919.
Telephone: 614-387-3501.
Facsimile: 614-387-3630.

John P. Brody
Allen L. Handlan
Larry J. McClatchey

Representative Clients: Ashland Chemical Co.; Borden, Inc.; Drug Emporium, Inc.; Farmers Insurance Group; Time Warner Communications.

For Complete List of Firm Personnel, See General Section

For full biographical listings, see the Martindale-Hubbell Law Directory

PORTER WRIGHT MORRIS & ARTHUR LLP (AV)

41 South High Street, 43215-6194
Telephone: 614-227-2000; (800-533-2794)
Fax: 614-227-2100
Email: cmh@porterwright.com *URL:* http://www.porterwright.com
Cincinnati, Ohio Office: 250 E. Fifth Street, Suite 2200, 45202-4199.
Telephones: 513-381-4700; (800-582-5813).
Fax: 513-421-0991. Internet: cvg@porterwright.com.
Cleveland, Ohio Office: 925 Euclid Avenue, Suite 1700, 44115-1483.
Telephones: 216-443-9000; (800-824-1980).
Fax: 216-443-9011. Internet: cle@porterwright.com.
Dayton, Ohio Office: One Dayton Centre, One South Main Street, Suite 1600, 45402-2028.
Telephones: 937-449-6810; (800-533-4434).
Fax: 937-449-6820. Internet: day@porterwright.com.
Naples, Florida Office: 5801 Pelican Bay Boulevard, Suite 300, 34108-2709.
Telephones: 941-593-2900; (800-876-7962).
Fax: 941-593-2990. Internet: apf@porterwright.com.
Washington, D.C. Office: 1667 K Street, N.W., Suite 1100, 20006-1605.
Telephones: 202-778-3000; (800-456-7962).
Fax: 202-778-3063. Internet: dca@porterwright.com.

MEMBERS OF FIRM
COLUMBUS, OHIO OFFICE

James P. Botti
S. Ronald Cook, Jr.
Timothy E. Grady
Polly J. Harris
John C. Hartranft
Jennifer T. Mills
Jack R. Pigman
James H. Prior
H. Grant Stephenson

ASSOCIATE
COLUMBUS, OHIO OFFICE

Bradley K. Baker

DAYTON, OHIO OFFICE
RESIDENT MEMBER

Walter Reynolds

CINCINNATI, OHIO OFFICE
RESIDENT ASSOCIATE

Darryl Mitchell

CLEVELAND, OHIO OFFICE
RESIDENT MEMBERS

Jeffrey Baddeley
Donald J. Fisher
Philip E. Langer

For Complete List of Firm Personnel, See General Section

For full biographical listings, see the Martindale-Hubbell Law Directory

SCHOTTENSTEIN, ZOX & DUNN A LEGAL PROFESSIONAL ASSOCIATION (AV)

The Huntington Center, 41 South High Street, 43215
Telephone: 614-462-2700
Telecopier: 614-462-5135
Telex: 650 24 444 365
URL: http://www.szd.com
Cincinnati, Ohio Office: Bank One Towers, 8044 Montgomery Road, Suite 700, 45236-2926.
Telephone: 513-792-2730.
Cleveland, Ohio Office: One Cleveland Center, 1375 East 9th Street, Suite 950.
Telephone: 216-621-6501.
Fax: 216-621-6502.

E. James Hopple
Victoria E. Powers
Daniel R. Swetnam

Susan K. Cliffel
Daniel M. Anderson

Reference: Bank One of Columbus, N.A.

For Complete List of Firm Personnel, See General Section

For full biographical listings, see the Martindale-Hubbell Law Directory

VORYS, SATER, SEYMOUR AND PEASE LLP (AV)

52 East Gay Street, P.O. Box 1008, 43216-1008
Telephone: 614-464-6400
Telecopier: 614-464-6350
URL: http://www.vssp.com
Washington, D.C. Office: 1828 L Street, N.W., 20036-5109.
Telephone: 202-467-8800.
Telex: 440693.
Telecopier: 202-467-8900.
Cleveland, Ohio Office: 2100 One Cleveland Center, 1375 East Ninth Street, 44114-1724.
Telephone: 216-479-6100.
Telecopier: 216-479-6060.
Cincinnati, Ohio Office: Suite 2100, 221 East Fourth Street, P.O. Box 0236, 45201-0236.
Telephone: 513-723-4000.
Telecopier: 513-723-4056.
Alexandria, Virginia Office: 277 South Washington St., Suite 310, 22314.
Telephone: 703-549-4282.
Telecopier: 703-549-4492.

MEMBERS OF FIRM

Robert W. Werth
James M. Ball
Robert J. Sidman
Reginald W. Jackson
Terry M. Miller
Randall D. LaTour

Representative Client: Honda of America Mfg., Inc.
Local Counsel: Abbott Laboratories; Anheuser-Busch, Inc.; Connecticut General Life Insurance Co.; General Motors Corp.; Navistar International Trans.; Ohio Manufacturers' Assn.; Ranco Inc.; Wendy's International, Inc.

For Complete List of Firm Personnel, See General Section

For full biographical listings, see the Martindale-Hubbell Law Directory

WHITE & FISH, L.P.A., INC. (AV)

1335 Dublin Road Suite 201 (C), 43215
Telephone: 614-485-9300
Fax: 614-485-9462
Email: WFLPA@AOL.COM *URL:* http://www.lawyers.com/white&fish

Arnold S. White
Jeffrey D. Fish

For full biographical listings, see the Martindale-Hubbell Law Directory

*DAYTON,** Montgomery Co.

BOGIN, PATTERSON & BOHMAN LLP (AV)

1200 Talbott Tower, 131 North Ludlow Street, 45402-1135
Telephone: 937-226-1200
FAX: 937-226-1625
Email: BPBLaw1200@aol.com

MEMBERS OF FIRM

Dennis L. Patterson
Jerome B. Bohman
James C. Ellis
Curtis F. Slaton
Randall L. Stump
Asher Bogin (Retired)

For full biographical listings, see the Martindale-Hubbell Law Directory

SEBALY, SHILLITO & DYER A LEGAL PROFESSIONAL ASSOCIATION (AV)

1300 Courthouse Plaza, NE, P.O. Box 220, 45402-0220
Telephone: 937-222-2500
Telefax: 937-222-6554; 222-8279
URL: http://www.ssdlaw.com

(See Next Column)

SEBALY, SHILLITO & DYER A LEGAL PROFESSIONAL ASSOCIATION, *Dayton—Continued*

Martin A. Beyer
Daniel A. Brown
James A. Dyer
Gale S. Finley
John R. Glankler
Deborah D. Hunt
Michael P. Moloney
Jon M. Sebaly
Beverly F. Shillito
Jeffrey B. Shulman
Karl R. Ulrich
Lawrence S. Walter
Nita S. Yates

OF COUNSEL

William W. Lambert

Michael A. Booth
Robert E. Goff, Jr.
Leslie Blair Graden
Joseph V. Hatala
J. David Ruffner, II
Kendra F. Thompson

For full biographical listings, see the Martindale-Hubbell Law Directory

DUBLIN, Franklin Co.

BLAUGRUND, HERBERT & MARTIN, INCORPORATED (AV)

5455 Rings Road, Suite 500, 43017-7517
Telephone: 614-764-0681
Fax: 614-764-0774
Email: bhm@bhmlaw.net

Lawrence H. Cohen
David J. Demers
Steven A. Martin
Teri G. Rasmussen

For full biographical listings, see the Martindale-Hubbell Law Directory

*MANSFIELD,** Richland Co.

WELDON, HUSTON & KEYSER (AV)

Eighth and Ninth Floors, Bank One Building, 28 Park Ave W., 44902-1695
Telephone: 419-524-9811
Fax: 419-522-5758

MEMBERS OF FIRM

William McE. Weldon (1868-1952)
C. H. Huston (1871-1957)
Henry P. Huston (1903-1984)
George H. Keyser (Retired)
George Hall
Richard R. Fowler
John H. Siegenthaler
David D. Carto
John S. Hire
Richard H. Otto

ASSOCIATE

John Allen Holmes

Representative Clients: Bank One, Mansfield; Mansfield General Hospital, Corp.; The Medical Protective Co.; Mechanics Bank; Hi-Stat Manufacturing Co., Inc.; Motorists Insurance Companies; Whitey's Auto Mall; United Telephone Long Distance; Milliron Waste Management; Richland Nursing Homes, Inc.

For full biographical listings, see the Martindale-Hubbell Law Directory

*TOLEDO,** Lucas Co.

MORAN & MORAN (AV)

626 Madison Avenue, Suite 300, 43604
Telephone: 419-241-8171
Fax: Available Upon Request

Wayne R. Peppers (1894-1978)
Peter L. Moran
Mary Beth Moran

Representative Clients: The Exchange Bank; Payak Insurance Agency; Monroe Pharmacy, Inc.
References: Society Bank; The Fifth Third Bank, Toledo, Ohio.

For full biographical listings, see the Martindale-Hubbell Law Directory

*YOUNGSTOWN,** Mahoning Co.

HARRINGTON, HOPPE & MITCHELL, LTD. (AV)

1200 Mahoning Bank Building, 44503-1508
Telephone: 330-744-1111
Telecopier: 330-744-2029
Warren, Ohio Office: 108 Main Avenue, S.W., Suite 500, 44481.
Telephone: 330-392-1541.
Telecopier: 330-394-6890.

Frederick S. Coombs, III
Ralph A. Beard

Representative Clients: Forum Health Hospitals and Medical Centers; Consumers Ohio Water Company (Public Utility); Wilcom Cellular One; SYGNET Communications, Inc.; City of Canfield; The Public Library of Youngstown and Mahoning County; Simon-DeBartolo Group; Office of Attorney General, State of Ohio; Mahoning Valley Economic Development Corporation; National City Bank.

For Complete List of Firm Personnel, See General Section

For full biographical listings, see the Martindale-Hubbell Law Directory

OKLAHOMA

*NORMAN,** Cleveland Co.

CROWE & DUNLEVY (AV)

A Professional Corporation
2500 South McGee, Suite 140, 73072-6705
Telephone: 405-321-7317
Fax: 405-360-4002
Email: marketing@crowedunlevy.com *URL:* http://www.crowedunlevy.com
Oklahoma City, Oklahoma Office: Crowe & Dunlevy, A Professional Corporation, 1800 Mid-America Tower, 20 North Broadway, 73102-8273.
Telephone: 405-235-7700.
Fax: 405-239-6651.
Tulsa, Oklahoma Office: Crowe & Dunlevy, A Professional Corporation, 500 Kennedy Building, 321 South Boston Avenue, 74103-3313.
Telephone: 918-592-9800.
Fax: 918-592-9801.

Christopher R. Graves

For Complete List of Firm Personnel, See General Section

For full biographical listings, see the Martindale-Hubbell Law Directory

*OKLAHOMA CITY,** Oklahoma Co.

ANDREWS DAVIS LEGG BIXLER MILSTEN & PRICE, A PROFESSIONAL CORPORATION (AV)

500 West Main, Suite 500, 73102
Telephone: 405-272-9241
FAX: 405-235-8786
Email: andrewsdavis@andrewsdavis.com *URL:* http://www.andrewsdavis.com

J. Edward Barth

OF COUNSEL

Stephen J. Moriarty

For Complete List of Firm Personnel, See General Section

For full biographical listings, see the Martindale-Hubbell Law Directory

CONNER & WINTERS, A PROFESSIONAL CORPORATION (AV)

One Leadership Square, 211 North Robinson, Suite 1700, 73102-7101
Telephone: 405-272-5711
Facsimile: 405-232-2695
Email: postmaster@cwlaw.com
Tulsa, Oklahoma Office: 3700 First Place Tower, 15 East 5th Street, 74103-4344.
Telephone: 918-586-5711.
Facsimile: 918-586-8982.
Fayetteville, Arkansas Office: Conner & Winters, P.L.L.C., 100 West Center Street, Suite 200, 72701-6081.
Telephone: 501-582-5711.
Facsimile: 501-587-1426.
Washington, D.C. Office: 1050 Seventeenth Street, N.W., Suite 810, 20036-5503.
Telephone: 202-783-5711.
Facsimile: 202-783-5720.

Kiran A. Phansalkar

For Complete List of Firm Personnel, See General Section

For full biographical listings, see the Martindale-Hubbell Law Directory

CROWE & DUNLEVY, A PROFESSIONAL CORPORATION (AV)

1800 Mid-America Tower, 20 North Broadway, 73102-8273
Telephone: 405-235-7700
Fax: 405-239-6651
Email: marketing@crowedunlevy.com *URL:* http://www.crowedunlevy.com
Tulsa, Oklahoma Office: 500 Kennedy Building, 321 South Boston Avenue, 74103-3313.
Telephone: 918-592-9800.
Fax: 918-592-9801.
Norman, Oklahoma Office: Crowe & Dunlevy, 2500 South McGee, Suite 140, 73072-6705.
Telephone: 405-321-7317.
Fax: 405-360-4002.

D. Kent Meyers
Judy Hamilton Morse
Mack J. Morgan III
Roger A. Stong

(See Next Column)

CROWE & DUNLEVY A PROFESSIONAL CORPORATION—*Continued*

William H. Hoch

For Complete List of Firm Personnel, See General Section

For full biographical listings, see the Martindale-Hubbell Law Directory

DAY, EDWARDS, FEDERMAN, PROPESTER & CHRISTENSEN, P.C. (AV)

Suite 2900 Oklahoma Tower, 210 Park Avenue, 73102-5605
Telephone: 405-239-2121
Telecopier: 405-236-1012
URL: http://lawlinks.com/attys/ok/defpc.html

Joe E. Edwards
Richard P. Propester
J. Clay Christensen

Thomas Pitchlynn Howell, IV
Joel Warren Harmon

Representative Clients: BancFirst; Bank One, Oklahoma City; Bank of America, N.A.; Federal Deposit Insurance Corp.; First Community Bank, Binger; First National Bank and Trust Company of Weatherford; First State Bank & Trust Co., Hollis; Local Oklahoma Bank.

For Complete List of Firm Personnel, See General Section

For full biographical listings, see the Martindale-Hubbell Law Directory

NASH, COHENOUR, KELLEY & HUNT, P.C. (AV)

Suite 101, 1001 Northwest 63rd Street, 73116
Telephone: 405-848-7170
Fax: 405-848-1442
Email: NCKHlaw@aol.com *URL:* http://www.law-n-okla.com

Rollin Nash, Jr.
Neal Hunt
Kevin Kelley
Dennis S. Boxeur

For full biographical listings, see the Martindale-Hubbell Law Directory

PRINGLE & PRINGLE, A PROFESSIONAL CORPORATION (AV)

4101 North Classen Boulevard Suite A, 73118-2432
Telephone: 405-848-4810
Fax: 405-848-4819
Email: pringle@pringleandpringle.com *URL:* http://www.pringleandpringle.com

Lynn A. Pringle
Laura Nan Smith Pringle
Conni L. Allen

OF COUNSEL

Alvin C. Harrell
Michael P. Sullivan

Representative Clients: Bankers Systems, Inc.; Bank of Western Oklahoma, Elk City; The First National Bank and Trust Co., Chickasha; The Farmers Bank, Carnegie; Bank of the Panhandle, Guymon; FirstPlus Financial; Citizens State Bank, Roma, Texas; The Daniluk Corporation; Bank of Union; Pringle Publications Corporation.

For full biographical listings, see the Martindale-Hubbell Law Directory

SELF, GIDDENS & LEES, INC. (AV)

2725 Oklahoma Tower, 210 Park Avenue, 73102-5643
Telephone: 405-232-3001
Telecopier: 405-232-5553

Thomas J. Blalock
C. Ray Lees
Jared D. Giddens
Shannon T. Self
Bryan J. Wells

Michael D. Meleen
John E. Gatliff II

For full biographical listings, see the Martindale-Hubbell Law Directory

*TULSA,** Tulsa Co.

ATKINSON, HASKINS, NELLIS, BOUDREAUX, HOLEMAN, PHIPPS & BRITTINGHAM, A PROFESSIONAL CORPORATION (AV)

1500 ParkCentre, 525 South Main Street, 74103
Telephone: 918-582-8877
Fax: 918-585-8096
Email: ahnmail@ahn-law.com

John J. Carwile

Representative Clients: Allstate Insurance Co.; Bayer Corp.; Crum & Forster Insurance Co.; Hartford Insurance Company; National American Insurance Co.; Federated Insurance Co.; Liberty Mutual Insurance Co.; Physicians Liability Insurance Co.; State Farm Mutual Automobile Insurance Co.; United States Aviation Underwriters.

For full biographical listings, see the Martindale-Hubbell Law Directory

BARROW GADDIS GRIFFITH & GRIMM, A PROFESSIONAL CORPORATION (AV)

610 South Main, Suite 300, 74119-1248
Telephone: 918-584-1600
Fax: 918-585-2444
Email: EMAIL@BGGG.com *URL:* http://www.bggg.com

Allen E. Barrow, Jr.
Nancy C. Pruitt
Robert W. Gaddis
Wm. Brad Heckenkemper
David W. Griffith
J. Patrick Mensching, Jr.
William R. Grimm
Robert B. Sartin
William E. Farrior
L. Michele Nelson

Reference: NationsBank.

For full biographical listings, see the Martindale-Hubbell Law Directory

BOESCHE, MCDERMOTT & ESKRIDGE (AV)

Suite 800 Oneok Plaza, 100 West Fifth Street, 74103
Telephone: 918-583-1777
Fax: 918-592-5809
Email: bme@intellex.com
Muskogee, Oklahoma Office: 1111 West Broadway, P.O. Box 2669, 74402.
Telephone: 918-683-6100.
Fax: 918-683-2303.

MEMBERS OF FIRM

R. Casey Cooper
David A. Johnson
Bradley K. Beasley
R. Kevin Layton
Sheila M. Powers

ASSOCIATE

Christopher K. Woosley

OF COUNSEL

Clifford K. Cate, Jr. (Resident at Muskogee)

Representative Clients: Bank of America; The Chase Manhattan Bank; Community Bank & Trust Co.; Federal Deposit Insurance Corp.; Resolution Trust Corp.; Superior Federal Bank; Union Bank, formerly Security Pacific National Bank; Vian State Bank.

For Complete List of Firm Personnel, See General Section

For full biographical listings, see the Martindale-Hubbell Law Directory

CONNER & WINTERS, A PROFESSIONAL CORPORATION (AV)

3700 First Place Tower, 15 East 5th Street, 74103-4344
Telephone: 918-586-5711
Fax: 918-586-8982
Email: postmaster@cwlaw.com
Oklahoma City, Oklahoma Office: One Leadership Square, 211 North Robinson, Suite 1700, 73102-7101.
Telephone: 405-272-5711.
Facsimile: 405-232-2695.
Fayetteville, Arkansas Office: Conner & Winters, P.L.L.C., 100 West Center Street, Suite 200, 72701-6081.
Telephone: 501-582-5711.
Facsimile: 501-587-1426.
Washington, D.C. Office: 1050 Seventeenth Street, N.W., Suite 810, 20036-5503.
Telephone: 202-783-5711.
Facsimile: 202-783-5720.

Andrew R. Turner
Timothy T. Trump

David H. Herrold

For Complete List of Firm Personnel, See General Section

For full biographical listings, see the Martindale-Hubbell Law Directory

CROWE & DUNLEVY, A PROFESSIONAL CORPORATION (AV)

500 Kennedy Building, 321 South Boston Avenue, 74103-3313
Telephone: 918-592-9800
Fax: 918-592-9801
Email: marketing@crowedunlevy.com *URL:* http://www.crowedunlevy.com
Oklahoma City, Oklahoma Office: 1800 Mid-America Tower, 20 North Broadway, 73102-8273.
Telephone: 405-235-7700.
Fax: 405-239-6651.
Norman, Oklahoma Office: Crowe & Dunlevy, 2500 South McGee, Suite 140, 73072-6705.
Telephone: 405-321-7317.
Fax: 405-360-4002.

Gary C. Clark
Terry M. Thomas
Gary L. Betow
Victor E. Morgan

For Complete List of Firm Personnel, See General Section

For full biographical listings, see the Martindale-Hubbell Law Directory

Tulsa—Continued

ENGLISH & WOOD, P.C. (AV)

15 West Sixth Street Suite 1610, 74119-5410
Telephone: 918-582-1564
Telecopier: 918-582-1582

Thomas E. English (1945-1996) | Carol Wood English

For full biographical listings, see the Martindale-Hubbell Law Directory

MAC D. FINLAYSON, P.C. (AV)

115 West 3rd Street, Suite 480, 74103-3410
Telephone: 918-583-2900
Facsimile: 918-583-6811
Email: mdfinlayson@abanet.org

Mac D. Finlayson

For full biographical listings, see the Martindale-Hubbell Law Directory

TODD MAXWELL HENSHAW (AV)

320 South Boston Suite 1130, 74103
Telephone: 918-583-7500
Fax: 918-583-7542
Email: thenshaw@swbell.net

For full biographical listings, see the Martindale-Hubbell Law Directory

RHODES, HIERONYMUS, JONES, TUCKER & GABLE, P.L.L.C. (AV)

Oneok Plaza, 100 West 5th Street, Suite 400, P.O. Box 21100, 74121-1100
Telephone: 918-582-1173
Fax: 918-592-3390
URL: http://www.rhodesokla.com

MEMBERS OF FIRM

Kevin D. Berry
Jo Anne Deaton
Richard M. Eldridge
E. D. Hieronymus (1908 -1994)
Bert M. Jones
William S. Leach
Michael W. McGivern
William D. Perrine
Mary Quinn-Cooper
Robert P. Redemann
David P. Reid
Chris L. Rhodes, III
Thomas E. Steichen
Catherine C. Taylor
John H. Tucker
Wilson T. White
Harold C. Zuckerman

Ann E. Allison
Steven K. Bunting
Robert P. Coffey, Jr.
J. Christopher Davis
Andrew D. Downing
Dana L. Gish
Kerry R. Lewis
Andrew L. Richardson
Michael F. Smith
Leslie J. Southerland
Kimberly E. West
Keith A. Wilkes

OF COUNSEL

George W. Gable (Retired Partner)
Larry J. Fulton
Kelly M. Greenough

Representative Clients: American International Companies; Bechtel; Chubb Group of Insurance Companies; General Motors Corporation; Merrill, Lynch; Nissan Motor Corporation in U.S.A.; Pfizer, Inc.; Volkswagen of America, Volkswagen, A.G.; Zurich U.S.

For full biographical listings, see the Martindale-Hubbell Law Directory

SNEED LANG, P.C. (AV)

2300 Williams Center Tower II, Two West Second Street, 74103
Telephone: 918-583-3145
Telecopier: 918-582-0410

James C. Lang
D. Faith Orlowski
Brian S. Gaskill
G. Steven Stidham
Stephen R. McNamara
Thomas E. Black, Jr.
Robbie Emery Burke
Patrick O. Waddel
Randolph P. Stainer
Steven K. Balman
Brian T. Inbody
D. Michael McBride III

OF COUNSEL

James L. Sneed

Representative Clients: Amoco Production Co.; Bank One, Texas; Enron Corp.; Halliburton Energy Services; Helmerich & Payne, Inc.; Shell Oil Co.; State Farm Mutual Automobile Insurance Co.; The Williams Companies.

For full biographical listings, see the Martindale-Hubbell Law Directory

OREGON

*EUGENE,** Lane Co.

MUHLHEIM PALMER & WADE, A PROFESSIONAL CORPORATION (AV)

U.S. Bank Center, 800 Willamette Street, Suite 700, 97401-2933
Telephone: 541-687-4757
Facsimile: 541-687-4780
Email: mpw-law.com *URL:* http://www.lawyers.com/muhleimpalmer&wade

Wilson C. Muhlheim
R. Scott Palmer
Carolyn G. Wade

Pamela Egan Singer
Stephen C.P. Carroll
Heidi Von Ravensberg
Edward C Singer

LEGAL SUPPORT PERSONNEL

Dawnne L. Linenbrink, CLAS
Fern Puls
Richard Rickson

Representative Clients: Harvest Ford Lincoln Mercury; Georgia Pacific Employees Federal Credit Union; Valley of The Rogue Bank; Bank of Southern Oregon; The Boulders on the River, Inc.; Trans Union Corporation; Heritage Mall, Ltd.; Sandpines Golf Resort; Ariki Co., Ltd.; Water Sports, Inc.; Lowther Assets.

For full biographical listings, see the Martindale-Hubbell Law Directory

*PORTLAND,** Multnomah Co.

BLACK HELTERLINE LLP (AV)

1200 Union Bank of California Tower, 707 S.W. Washington Street, 97205
Telephone: 503-224-5560
Telecopier: 503-224-6148
URL: http://www.bhlaw.com

MEMBERS OF FIRM

Ronald T. Adams | James M. Baumgartner

Representative Client: Union Bank of California, N.A.

For Complete List of Firm Personnel, See General Section

For full biographical listings, see the Martindale-Hubbell Law Directory

COPELAND, LANDYE, BENNETT AND WOLF, LLP (AV)

1300 S.W. 5th Avenue, Suite 3500, 97201
Telephone: 503-224-4100
Facsimile: 503-224-4133
Anchorage, Alaska Office: 701 West Eighth Avenue, Suite 1200, 99501.
Telephone: 907-276-5152.
Facsimile: 907-276-8433.

MEMBERS OF FIRM

J. David Bennett
David L. Blount
David S. Case (Resident, Anchorage, Alaska Office)
Mitchel R. Cohen
Stuart K. Cohen
Mark G. Copeland (Resident, Anchorage, Alaska Office)
James S. Crane
David N. Goulder
Robert B. Hopkins
Robert H. Hume, Jr. (Resident, Anchorage, Alaska Office)
Thomas M. Landye
Jeffrey S. Mutnick
P. Stephen Russell, III
Richard L. Sadler
Thane W. Tienson

ASSOCIATES

Robert P. Owens (Resident, Anchorage, Alaska Office)
Patrick S. Galvin (Resident, Anchorage, Alaska Office)
Karna R. Gustafson
Alison S. Browdie
Katherine A. Dreyfus
David Voluck (Resident, Anchorage, Alaska Office)

For full biographical listings, see the Martindale-Hubbell Law Directory

KELL, ALTERMAN & RUNSTEIN, LLP (AV)

1001 S.W. Fifth Avenue, Suite 1800, 97204
Telephone: 503-222-3531
Telecopier: 503-227-2980
Email: kell@teleport.com

MEMBERS OF FIRM

Raymond M. Kell (1911-1991)
Clifford B. Alterman (1925-1995)
Ted E. Runstein
Lee Davis Kell
Wayne D. Palmer
Lloyd R. Summers
William D. Dickas
Gary P. Compa
Charles R. Williamson
Mary Ellen Page Farr
Eric Sogge
Thomas J. Matsuda
Thomas R. Rask, III
Nicholas S. Fish

(See Next Column)

KELL, ALTERMAN & RUNSTEIN LLP—*Continued*

Dana L. Barnes
Cory Larvik
Robert E. Kabacy
Robin M. Runstein

References: Union Bank of California, N.A. (Portland Branch); The Bank of Tokyo-Mitsubishi, Ltd. (Portland Branch); Bank of America (5th S. Main Branch).

For full biographical listings, see the Martindale-Hubbell Law Directory

VANDEN BOS & CHAPMAN (AV)

Suite 520, The Spalding Building, 319 S.W. Washington Street, 97204-2690
Telephone: 503-241-4869
Fax: 503-241-3731

MEMBERS OF FIRM

Robert J Vanden Bos
Ann K. Chapman

ASSOCIATE

Michelle M. Bertolino

For full biographical listings, see the Martindale-Hubbell Law Directory

PENNSYLVANIA

*ALLENTOWN,** Lehigh Co.

KARL E. FRIEND (AV)

Westfield Corporate Center, Suite 310, 4905 Tilghman Street, 18104
Telephone: 610-391-9878
Telecopier: 610-391-9879
Reading, Pennsylvania Office: 539 Court Street.
Telephone: 610-375-8979.
Telecopier: 610-391-9879.

OF COUNSEL

Stephen J. Palopoli, III

For full biographical listings, see the Martindale-Hubbell Law Directory

WIENER AND WIENER LLP (AV)

Suite 400 Commonwealth Building, 512 Hamilton Street, 18101-1505
Telephone: 610-821-8600
Fax: 610-821-8635
West Palm Beach, Florida Office: Suite 900, 1655 Palm Beach Lakes Boulevard.
Telephone: 561-689-6660.
Fax: 561-683-1559.

MEMBERS OF FIRM

Howard A. Wiener
Joel B. Wiener
Stephen W. Wiener
C. Steven Miller
David C. Schattenstein
John H. McKeever

Representative Clients Available Upon Request.

For full biographical listings, see the Martindale-Hubbell Law Directory

BLUE BELL, Montgomery Co.

KAPLIN STEWART MELOFF REITER & STEIN, PROFESSIONAL CORPORATION (AV)

350 Sentry Parkway, Building 640, P.O. Box 3037, 19422-0765
Telephone: 610-260-6000
Telecopier: 610-260-1240
Cherry Hill, New Jersey Office: 900 Dudley Avenue, #250, 08002-4426.
Telephone: 856-486-1044.
Fax: 856-486-1074.

MEMBER OF FIRM

William J. Levant

For full biographical listings, see the Martindale-Hubbell Law Directory

*HARRISBURG,** Dauphin Co.

PURCELL, KRUG & HALLER (AV)

1719 North Front Street, 17102
Telephone: 717-234-4178
Telefax: 717-233-1149
Email: mortgage@pkh.com
Email: law@pkh.com *URL:* http://www.pkh.com

Joseph Nissley (1910-1982)
John W. Purcell
Howard B. Krug
Leon P. Haller
John W. Purcell, Jr.
Valerie A. Gunn
Jill M. Wineka
Brian Tyler
Nicole Staley

For full biographical listings, see the Martindale-Hubbell Law Directory

*PHILADELPHIA,** Philadelphia Co.

ADELMAN LAVINE GOLD AND LEVIN, A PROFESSIONAL CORPORATION (AV)

Suite 1900, Two Penn Center Plaza, 19102-1799
Telephone: 215-568-7515
Facsimile: 215-557-7922
Wayne Office: 1101 West DeKalb Pike, 2nd Floor, 19087.
Telephone: 610-992-0400.
Facsimile: 610-992-1005.

Lewis H. Gold
Robert H. Levin
Gary M. Schildhorn
Barry D. Kleban
Gary D. Bressler
Steven D. Usdin
Kevin W. Walsh
Raymond H. Lemisch

Douglas N. Candeub
Alan I. Moldoff
Kathleen E. Torbit
Leon R. Barson
Matthew J. Swett
Robert J. Lenahan
Bradford J. Sandler
William R. Hinchman
Victoria M. Endriss
MaryJo Wlazlo
Sebastian Ferrer
Mark W. Drasnin

LEGAL SUPPORT PERSONNEL

Jacqueline Parsio (Paralegal)
Diana J. Papalini (Paralegal)
Wendy A. Raskas (Paralegal)

For full biographical listings, see the Martindale-Hubbell Law Directory

BALLARD SPAHR ANDREWS & INGERSOLL, LLP (AV)

1735 Market Street, 51st Floor, 19103-7599
Telephone: 215-665-8500
Fax: 215-864-8999
URL: http://www.ballardspahr.com
Baltimore, Maryland Office: 300 East Lombard Street. 19th Floor.
Telephone: 410-528-5600.
Fax: 410-528-5650.
Camden, New Jersey Office: 800 Hudson Square, 5th Floor.
Telephone: 856-541-5577.
Fax: 856-541-8272.
Denver, Colorado Office: Seventeenth Street Plaza Building, Suite 2300, 1225 17th Street.
Telephone: 303-292-2400.
Fax: 303-296-3956.
Salt Lake City, Utah Office: One Utah Center, Suite 1200, 201 South Main Street.
Telephone: 801-531-3000.
Fax: 801-531-3001.
Voorhees, New Jersey Office: Suite 100, 1101 Laurel Oak Drive.
Telephone: 856-627-8555.
Fax: 856-627-1153.
Washington, D.C. Office: Suite 1000 South, 601 13th Street, N.W.
Telephone: 202-661-2200.
Fax: 202-661-2299.

Philip B. Korb
Richard S. Perelman
Vincent J. Marriott, III
William A. Slaughter

For Complete List of Firm Personnel, See General Section

For full biographical listings, see the Martindale-Hubbell Law Directory

CIARDI, MASCHMEYER & KARALIS, P.C. (AV)

1900 Spruce Street, 19103
Telephone: 215-546-4500
Fax: 215-985-4175
Cherry Hill, New Jersey Office: 413 Route 70 East, Suite 300, 08034.
Telephone: 609-428-8400.
Telecopier: 609-428-8571.

Albert A. Ciardi, Jr.
Paul Brinton Maschmeyer
Aris J. Karalis
Albert A. Ciardi, III
Camille Spinale
Thomas J. Maiorino
Andrew Henry

Davis A. Schultz

LEGAL SUPPORT PERSONNEL

PARALEGALS

Janice Lazar

For full biographical listings, see the Martindale-Hubbell Law Directory

DIDONATO & WINTERHALTER, P.C. (AV)

1818 Market Street, Suite 3520, 19103-3629
Telephone: 215-564-5050
Telecopier: 215-564-5597
URL: http://www.lawyers.com/didonato
Marlton, New Jersey Office: One Greentree Centre, Route 73 & Greenfield Road, Suite 201, 08053.
Telephone: 609-263-2700.
Telecopier: 609-263-9192.

(See Next Column)

DiDONATO & WINTERHALTER P.C., *Philadelphia—Continued*

Edward J. DiDonato
Paul J. Winterhalter
Eugene Camposano

For full biographical listings, see the Martindale-Hubbell Law Directory

WEIR & PARTNERS LLP (AV)

A Pennsylvania Limited Liability Partnership
Suite 500, The Widener Building, 1339 Chestnut Street, 19107
Telephone: 215-665-8181
Telefax: 215-665-8464
Email: info@weirpartners.com
Turnersville, New Jersey Office: 215 Fries Mill Road, 08012.
Telephone: 609-740-1490.
Telefax: 609-740-1491.

MEMBERS OF FIRM

Walter Weir, Jr.
Leonard S. Goodman
Susan Verbonitz
Jeffrey L. Rudnick
Robert D. Sayre
Stephen M. Giroux
Richard P. Coe, Jr.
Brett A. Datto
John B. York
Joseph C. Hare

ASSOCIATES

Bonnie R. Golub
Debra N. Nathanson
Tina L. Colman
Andrew K. Stutzman
Jeffrey A. Guth
Jason M Reiser
Madeline Flanagan

For full biographical listings, see the Martindale-Hubbell Law Directory

*PITTSBURGH,** Allegheny Co.

APPLE AND APPLE, A PROFESSIONAL CORPORATION (AV)

4650 Baum Boulevard, 15213
Telephone: 412-682-1466; 800-477-APPLE
Fax: 412-682-3138
Email: applelaw@aol.com

Marvin J. Apple
James R. Apple

Charles F. Bennett
Joel E. Hausman
Marylouise Wagner

LEGAL SUPPORT PERSONNEL

Michelle A. Bernard-Danielson (Office Manager)

Representative Clients: Citibank; Bank of America; Providian Financial; PNC Bank; National City Bank; BP Oil; N.A.C.M.; Associates Commercial Corp.; Kemper Insurance; Conrail.

For full biographical listings, see the Martindale-Hubbell Law Directory

CAMPBELL & LEVINE, LLC (AV)

1700 Grant Building, 15219
Telephone: 412-261-0310
Fax: 412-261-5066

MEMBERS OF FIRM

Douglas A. Campbell
Stanley E. Levine
David B. Salzman
Roger M. Bould
Philip E. Milch

ASSOCIATES

Ronald B. Roteman
Michael R. Salzman

OF COUNSEL

Tybe A. Brett

For full biographical listings, see the Martindale-Hubbell Law Directory

GLOSSER & SHREVE (AV)

Suite 200, 213 Smithfield Street, 15222-2224
Telephone: 412-281-6555
FAX: 412-281-6597
Email: mark.glosser@commersel.com *URL:* http://www.lawyers.com/debtorcreditlaw

Mark L. Glosser
Steven T. Shreve

Representative Clients: Crawford Construction Company, Inc.; Franklin & Locust Realty, Inc.; Digital Equipment Corporation, Inc.; Household Financial Corporation; First Union Bank; C.J. Betters Co.

For full biographical listings, see the Martindale-Hubbell Law Directory

MARCUS & SHAPIRA LLP (AV)

35th Floor, One Oxford Centre, 301 Grant Street, 15219-6401
Telephone: 412-471-3490
Telecopier: 412-391-8758
Email: info@marcus-shapira.com *URL:* http://www.marcus-shapira.com

(See Next Column)

MEMBERS OF FIRM

Darlene M. Nowak
Daniel H. Shapira

For Complete List of Firm Personnel, See General Section

For full biographical listings, see the Martindale-Hubbell Law Directory

PLOWMAN, SPIEGEL & LEWIS, P.C. (AV)

Second Floor, The Grant Building, 310 Grant Street, 15219-2201
Telephone: 412-471-8521
Fax: 412-471-4481

Jack W. Plowman
James A. Lewis
J. Michael McCague, Jr.

Reference: Pittsburgh National Bank.

For Complete List of Firm Personnel, See General Section

For full biographical listings, see the Martindale-Hubbell Law Directory

VOLLMER RULONG & KEATING, P.C. (AV)

Suite 1212 Grant Building, 310 Grant Street, 15219
Telephone: 412-391-2121
Telecopier: 412-391-3578
Email: vollmer@vollmerlaw.com *URL:* http://www.vollmerlaw.com

Charles J. Vollmer
Roger G. Rulong, Jr.
John R. Keating

Pamela J. Royesky

For full biographical listings, see the Martindale-Hubbell Law Directory

WEISMAN GOLDMAN BOWEN & GROSS LLP (AV)

310 Grant Street, Suite 420, 15219
Telephone: 412-566-2520
Fax: 412-566-1088

James L. Weisman
S. James Goldman
Alden Earl Bowen
Sanford P. Gross
Barry J. Lipson
Howard J. Schulberg
Christopher J. Klein
Samuel F. Reynolds, Jr.
Frank J. Grzywinski
David J. Brosky
Robert L. Monks

Reference: Pittsburgh National Bank.

For full biographical listings, see the Martindale-Hubbell Law Directory

*READING,** Berks Co.

BINGAMAN, HESS, COBLENTZ & BELL, A PROFESSIONAL CORPORATION (AV)

Suite 660, 601 Penn Street, P.O. Box 61, 19603-0061
Telephone: 610-374-8377
Fax: 610-376-3105
URL: http://www.bhcb.com
Cherry Hill, New Jersey Office: Shawn J. Lau, P.C., Building Q, Suite 14B, 1930 East Marlton Pike, 08003-4222.
Telephone: 609-751-4158.
Fax: 609-424-7112.

Llewellyn R. Bingaman (1907-1996)
James F. Bell (1921-1988)
Ralph J. Althouse, Jr. (Retired)

OF COUNSEL

Raymond K. Hess
J. Wendell Coblentz

David E. Turner
Mark G. Yoder
Carl D. Cronrath, Jr.
Kurt Althouse
Harry D. McMunigal
Patrick T. Barrett
Karen Feryo Longenecker
Shawn J. Lau

Lynne K. Beust
Elizabethanne D. McMunigal
Kevin W. Rethore
Eric J. Fabrizio
Elizabeth A. Magovern

General Counsel for: First Union National Bank; Berks Products Corp.; Utilities Employees Credit Union.
Local Counsel for: Erie Insurance Exchange; Liberty Mutual Insurance Co.; Old Guard Mutual Insurance Co.

For full biographical listings, see the Martindale-Hubbell Law Directory

KARL E. FRIEND (AV)

539 Court Street, 19601
Telephone: 610-375-8979
Telecopier: 610-391-9879
Allentown, Pennsylvania Office: Westfield Corporate Center, Suite 310, 4905 Tilghman Street.
Telephone: 610-391-9878.
Telecopier: 610-391-9879.

(See Next Column)

KARL E. FRIEND—*Continued*

OF COUNSEL

Stephen J. Palopoli, III

For full biographical listings, see the Martindale-Hubbell Law Directory

MOGEL, SPEIDEL, BOBB & KERSHNER, A PROFESSIONAL CORPORATION (AV)

520 Walnut Street, P.O. Box 8581, 19603-8581
Telephone: 610-376-1515
Telecopier: 610-372-8710

George B. Balmer (1902-1969)
George A. Kershner (1907-1969)
Carl F. Mogel (1919-1994)
Edwin H. Kershner
Frederick R. Mogel
Michael L. Mixell
George M. Lutz
Paul M. Yatron
Stephen H. Price
Kathryn K. Harenza

Sean J. O'Brien
Matthew Earl Glinn

OF COUNSEL

Harry W. Speidel
Donald K. Bobb
Henry A. Gass

Representative Clients: Great Valley Bank; Union Township, Berks County, Pennsylvania.

For full biographical listings, see the Martindale-Hubbell Law Directory

*SCRANTON,** Lackawanna Co.

O'MALLEY & HARRIS, P.C. (AV)

345 Wyoming Avenue, 18503
Telephone: 570-348-3711
Fax: 570-348-4092
Email: ohpc@epix.net *URL:* http://www.ohpclaw.com
Stroudsburg, Pennsylvania Office: 111 North Seventh Street.
Telephone: 570-421-2252; 570-422-1280.
FAX: 570-422-1281. Email: cerato@ptdprolog.net.
Wilkes-Barre, Pennsylvania Office: 61 North Washington Street.
Telephone: 570-829-3232.
FAX: 570-829-4418. Email: ohpcwb@epix.net.
Williamsport, Pennsylvania Office: 321 Pine Street, Suite 308.
Telephone: 570-323-4380.

Eugene Nogi (1905-1975)
Henry Nogi (1900-1976)
Russell J. O'Malley, Sr. (1904-1993)
Norman Harris (1907-1998)
William H. Amesbury (Resident, Wilkes-Barre Office)
Paul A. Barrett
Matthew P. Barrett
J. Scott Brady (Resident, Wilkes-Barre Office)
Lori J. Cerato (Resident, Stroudsburg Office)
Bruce L. Coyer
John Q. Durkin
Gerald J. Hanchulak
Richard K. Hodges
Timothy J. Holland (Resident, Wilkes-Barre Office)
John F. Kennedy (Resident, Wilkes-Barre Office)
Daniel Morgan
Michael Perry
James M. Tressler
Joseph Timothy Healey
A. Ruth Whalen (Resident, Wilkes-Barre Office)

Representative Clients: Pennsylvania Hospital Insurance Co.; MMI Systems Agency, Inc.; State Farm Insurance Company; ITT Specialty Risk Services; St. Paul Fire & Marine Insurance Co.; Chubb Group of Insurance Companies; Geisingen System Services; Princeton Insurance Company; Northeastern Pennsylvania Physicians Organization; Catholic Healthcare Partners.

For full biographical listings, see the Martindale-Hubbell Law Directory

*WILKES-BARRE,** Luzerne Co.

DORAN & NOWALIS (AV)

69 Public Square, Suite 700, 18701-2588
Telephone: 570-823-9111
Fax: 570-829-3222

Wm. N. Reynolds (1847-1936)
Wm. N. Reynolds, Jr. (1874-1957)
Robert J. Doran (1895-1962)

MEMBERS OF FIRM

John H. Doran
Robert C. Nowalis

ASSOCIATES

Lisa M. Doran
Brian E. Manning

Reference: Available upon request.

For full biographical listings, see the Martindale-Hubbell Law Directory

DAVID J. HARRIS (AV)

Suite 310, 15 Public Square, 18701
Telephone: 570-823-9400
Fax: 570-820-9600
Email: djhesquire@compuserve.com *URL:* http://www.lawyers.com/davidharrislaw

For full biographical listings, see the Martindale-Hubbell Law Directory

ROSENN, JENKINS & GREENWALD, L.L.P. (AV)

15 South Franklin Street, 18711-0075
Telephone: 570-826-5600
Fax: 570-826-5640
Email: rjg@rjglaw.com *URL:* http://www.rjglaw.com
Hazleton, Pennsylvania Office: P.O. Box 618, 18201-0618.
Telephone: 570-455-7112.
Fax: 570-455-8304.

MEMBERS OF FIRM

Bruce C. Rosenthal
Steven P. Roth

ASSOCIATE

Ernest A. Sposto

Representative Clients: C-TEC Corp.; Chicago Title Insurance Co.; Manufacturers & Traders Trust Company; Guard Insurance Group; May Department Stores Co.; Student Loan Marketing Assn. (Sallie Mae); Penn-State Geisinger Medical Center; Subaru of America, Inc.

For Complete List of Firm Personnel, See General Section

For full biographical listings, see the Martindale-Hubbell Law Directory

WYOMISSING, Berks Co.

LEISAWITZ HELLER ABRAMOWITCH PHILLIPS, P.C. (AV)

2201 Ridgewood Road Suite 400, 19610
Telephone: 610-372-3500
Fax: 610-372-8671
Email: lhap@lhaplaw.com
Reading, Pennsylvania Office: 138 North Fifth Street.
Telephone: 610-372-3500.
Hamburg, Pennsylvania Office: 178 North Third Street.
Telephone: 610-562-4145.

Alan G. Leisawitz
Mervin A. Heller, Jr.
Jay N. Abramowitch
Charles J. Phillips
William R. Blumer
Allen R. Shollenberger

Robert J. Kirwan, II
Kevin A. Moore
Kathleen A. B. Kovach
Douglas Paul Rauch
Kenneth Millman

For full biographical listings, see the Martindale-Hubbell Law Directory

RHODE ISLAND

*PROVIDENCE,** Providence Co.

HINCKLEY, ALLEN & SNYDER LLP (AV)

1500 Fleet Center, 02903-2393
Telephone: 401-274-2000
Fax: 401-277-9600
Email: firm@haslaw.com *URL:* http://www.haslaw.com
Boston, Massachusetts Office: 28 State Street, 30th Floor.
Telephone: 617-345-9000.
Fax: 617-345-9020. URL: http://www.haslaw.com.

MEMBERS OF FIRM

Paula K. Andrews (Not admitted in RI)
Jonathan Bell
Paul Bork (Not admitted in RI)
Stephen J. Carlotti
David Barry Connolly (Not admitted in RI)
Joseph P. Curran
Michael P. DeFanti
Margaret D. Farrell
Hugh J. Gorman, III (Not admitted in RI)
William R. Grimm
Paul A. Hedstrom (Not admitted in RI)
Joel Lewin (Not admitted in RI)
Sandra Matrone Mack
Matthew T. Marcello, III
Frederick P. McClure
Elizabeth Murdock Myers
Paul F. O'Donnell, III (Not admitted in RI)
H. Peter Olsen
James O. Reavis
Robert F. Sylvia (Not admitted in RI)

ASSOCIATES

Mark Bianchi
Alyssa V. Boss
Andrew D. Cummings (Not admitted in RI)
June E. Daniel
Gloria Maria Gutierrez (Not admitted in RI)

For Complete List of Firm Personnel, See General Section

For full biographical listings, see the Martindale-Hubbell Law Directory

WILLIAM T. MURPHY LAW OFFICES, INC. (AV)

The Calart Tower, 400 Reservoir Avenue, Suite 3L, 02907
Telephone: 401-461-7740
Telecopier: 401-461-7753

William T. Murphy

(See Next Column)

WILLIAM T. MURPHY LAW OFFICES, INC., *Providence—Continued*

Charles A. Pisaturo, Jr. Steven T. Hayes

Reference: Citizens Bank.

For full biographical listings, see the Martindale-Hubbell Law Directory

SOUTH CAROLINA

*CHARLESTON,** Charleston Co.

BUIST, MOORE, SMYTHE & MCGEE, P.A. (AV)

Successors to Buist, Buist, Smythe and Smythe and Moore, Mouzon and McGee.
Five Exchange Street, P.O. Box 999, 29402
Telephone: 843-722-3400
Cable Address: "Conferees"
Telex: 57-6488
Telecopier: 843-723-7398
Email: bmsm@lawyer-sc.com *URL:* http://www.lawyer-sc.com

Charles P. Summerall, IV

Representative Clients: Siemens Westinghouse Power Corporation; Metropolitan Life Insurance Co.; Orix Credit Alliance, Inc.; Deere Credit; National Bank of South Carolina; First National Bank of South Carolina; Transport Insurance Co.; SouthTrust Bank; Agricredit Acceptance Corp.; Martin Marietta.

For Complete List of Firm Personnel, See General Section

For full biographical listings, see the Martindale-Hubbell Law Directory

CLAWSON & STAUBES, L.L.C. (AV)

304 Meeting Street, 29401-1544
Telephone: 843-577-2026
Fax: 843-720-0822
Charlotte, North Carolina Office: 756 Tyvola Road, Suite 101, 29217.
Telephone: 704-522-7733.
Facsimile: 704-522-9033.

J. Ronald Jones, Jr. (Also at Charlotte, N.C. Office)
Albert A. Lacour, III

Christopher B. Staubes, III

Representative Clients: Greenpoint Credit Corp.; Carolina Builders; First Federal Savings & Loan of Charleston; Ford Motor Credit Co.

For full biographical listings, see the Martindale-Hubbell Law Directory

*COLUMBIA,** Richland Co.

ANDERSON & ASSOCIATES, P.A. (AV)

208 Candi Lane, Suite B, P.O. Box 76, 29202
Telephone: 803-252-8600
Telefax: 803-256-0950
Email: bnkrtcyl@usit.net

Robert F. Anderson

H. Flynn Griffin, III

References: United States Bankruptcy Court, District of South Carolina; U.S. Trustee's Office for the District of South Carolina.

For full biographical listings, see the Martindale-Hubbell Law Directory

FINKEL & ALTMAN, L.L.C. (AV)

Suite 1800, 1201 Main Street, P.O. Box 1799, 29202
Telephone: 803-765-2935
Fax: 803-252-0786
Email: webmaster@finkellaw.com *URL:* http://www.finkellaw.com
Charleston, South Carolina Office: 12 Exchange Street, P.O. Box 225.
Telephone: 843-577-5460.
Fax: 843-577-5135.

Gerald M. Finkel
Charles S. Altman (Resident, Charleston South Carolina Office)
Harry L. Goldberg
Howard S. Sheftman
Elizabeth Henderson McCullough
Beverly J. Finkel
Richard R. Gleissner

Janet B. Haigler
Laurie Pineau Davidson

(See Next Column)

COUNSEL

Ralph C. McCullough, II
Elizabeth Rhodes

Representative Clients: First Union National Bank; Banc One Mortgage Co.; Motorola Communications & Electronics Corp.; First Union Mortgage Corp.; BancBoston Mortgage Corp.; Dow Chemical Company; S.C. Ports Authority.

For full biographical listings, see the Martindale-Hubbell Law Directory

HAYNSWORTH, MARION, MCKAY & GUÉRARD, L.L.P. (AV)

Suite 2400 Affinity Building, 1201 Main Street, P.O. Drawer 7157, 29202
Telephone: 803-765-1818
Facsimile: 803-765-2399
Greenville, South Carolina Office: 75 Beattie Place, Eleventh Floor, P.O. Box 2048, 29602.
Telephone: 864-240-3200.
Facsimile: 864-240-3300.
Charleston, South Carolina Office: 134 Meeting Street, P.O. Box 1119, 29402.
Telephone: 843-722-7606.
Facsimile: 843-724-8016.

ASSOCIATE

Gina L. Campano

Counsel for: St. Paul Insurance Group; Allstate Insurance Co.; Fluor-Daniel Corp.; South Carolina Jobs - Economic Development Authority; Anheuser Busch Company; CSX Transportation; Ernst & Young, LLP; Willis Corroon of South Carolina, Inc.; Westinghouse Savannah River Co.; Wachovia Bank of South Carolina, N.A.

For Complete List of Firm Personnel, See General Section

For full biographical listings, see the Martindale-Hubbell Law Directory

ROGERS TOWNSEND & THOMAS, PC (AV)

1441 Main Street, 10th Floor, P.O. Box 100200, 29202-3200
Telephone: 803-771-7900
Fax: 803-254-6305; 343-7017; 343-7019
URL: http://www.rtt-law.com

Sherwood M. Cleveland
D. Randolph Whitt

For Complete List of Firm Personnel, See General Section

For full biographical listings, see the Martindale-Hubbell Law Directory

TURNER, PADGET, GRAHAM & LANEY, P.A. (AV)

Seventeenth Floor, 1901 Main Street, P.O. Box 1473, 29202
Telephone: 803-254-2200
Telecopy: 803-799-3957
Florence, South Carolina Office: Fourth Floor, 1831 West Evans Street, P.O. Box 5478, 29502.
Telephone: 843-662-9008.
Fax: 843-667-0828.
Charleston, South Carolina Office: 21 Broad Street, 1st Floor, P.O. Box 836, 29402.
Telephone: 843-723-1622.
Fax: 843-577-3369.

W. Duvall Spruill
Hugh M. Claytor (Resident, Florence, SC, Office)
R. Todd Sherpy
Jeffrey L. Payne (Resident, Florence, SC, Office)
Michael S. Hopewell (Resident, Florence, SC, Office)

OF COUNSEL

Michael S. Church
Stephen A. Husman

For Complete List of Firm Personnel, See General Section

For full biographical listings, see the Martindale-Hubbell Law Directory

*GREENVILLE,** Greenville Co.

HAYNSWORTH, MARION, MCKAY & GUÉRARD, L.L.P. (AV)

75 Beattie Place, Eleventh Floor, P.O. Box 2048, 29602
Telephone: 864-240-3200
Facsimile: 864-240-3300
Columbia, South Carolina Office: Suite 2400 Affinity Building, 1201 Main Street, P.O. Drawer 7157, 29202
Telephone: 803-765-1818.
Facsimile: 803-765-2399.
Charleston, South Carolina Office: 134 Meeting Street, P.O. Box 1119, 29402.
Telephone: 843-722-7606.
Facsimile: 843-724-8016.

MEMBERS OF FIRM

Jesse C. Belcher
Andrew J. White, Jr.

Representative Clients: Wachovia Bank, N.A.; Bank American Housing Services, Inc.; Bergen Acceptance Corp.; Catepillar Financial Corporation.

For Complete List of Firm Personnel, See General Section

For full biographical listings, see the Martindale-Hubbell Law Directory

Greenville—Continued

LEATHERWOOD WALKER TODD & MANN, P.C. (AV)

100 East Coffee Street, P.O. Box 87, 29602
Telephone: 864-242-6440
FAX: 864-240-2477
Email: leatherwood@lwtm.com *URL:* http://www.lwtm.com
Spartanburg, South Carolina Office: 1451 East Main Street, P.O. Box 3188.
Telephone: 864-582-4365.
Telefax: 864-583-8961.

Seann Anderson Gray

COUNSEL

Tara H. Snyder

Representative Clients: Carolina First Bank; Barclay's Business Credit Incorporated; Bank America Housing Services; Ford Motor Credit Company; General Motors Acceptance Corporation; Green Tree Financial Services Corporation; Green Point Credit Corporation; Nissan Motor Acceptance Corporation; Wachovia N.A.

For Complete List of Firm Personnel, See General Section

For full biographical listings, see the Martindale-Hubbell Law Directory

HILTON HEAD ISLAND, Beaufort Co.

BARRY L. JOHNSON, P.A. (AV)

35-A Bow Circle, Palmetto Bay Offices (Suite 35-A), P.O. Box 7261, 29938
Telephone: 843-341-3777
Fax: 843-341-3007
Beaufort, South Carolina Office: 1611 North Street.
Telephone: 843-982-0089.
Fax: 986-9203.

Barry L. Johnson

For full biographical listings, see the Martindale-Hubbell Law Directory

SOUTH DAKOTA

*SIOUX FALLS,** Minnehaha Co.

DAVENPORT, EVANS, HURWITZ & SMITH, L.L.P. (AV)

513 South Main Avenue, P.O. Box 1030, 57101-1030
Telephone: 605-336-2880
Telecopier: 605-335-3639
Email: lawyers@dehs.com

MEMBERS OF FIRM

Robert E. Hayes
Monte R. Walz

Counsel for: American Society of Composers, Authors and Publishers (A.S.-C.A.P.); Continental Insurance Cos.; The First National Bank in Sioux Falls; Ford Motor Credit Co.; General Motors Corp.; The St. Paul Cos.; The Travelers.

For Complete List of Firm Personnel, See General Section

For full biographical listings, see the Martindale-Hubbell Law Directory

TENNESSEE

*CHATTANOOGA,** Hamilton Co.

KENNEDY, FULTON, KOONTZ & FARINASH (AV)

320 North Holtzclaw Avenue, 37404
Telephone: 423-622-4535
Facsimile: 423-622-4583

MEMBERS OF FIRM

Richard C. Kennedy
George E. Koontz
David J. Fulton
Jerrold D. Farinash
James W. Clements, III

ASSOCIATE

Camden Ballard Scearce, Jr.

OF COUNSEL

Richard T. Klingler

For full biographical listings, see the Martindale-Hubbell Law Directory

*KNOXVILLE,** Knox Co.

WALKER & WALKER, P.C. (AV)

910 First American Center, P.O. Box 2774, 37901
Telephone: 423-523-0700
Telecopier: 423-523-4990
Email: jwalkerjr@aol.com

John A. Walker, Jr.
Kathryn D. Higginbotham

For full biographical listings, see the Martindale-Hubbell Law Directory

*MEMPHIS,** Shelby Co.

ARMSTRONG ALLEN PREWITT GENTRY JOHNSTON & HOLMES, PLLC (AV)

Brinkley Plaza, Suite 700, 80 Monroe Avenue, 38103-2467
Telephone: 901-523-8211
Facsimile: 901-524-4936
Little Rock, Arkansas Office: Suite 100, 100 Morgan Keegan Drive, 72202.
Telephone: 501-280-0100.
Facsimile: 501-280-0166.
Jackson, Mississippi Office: 2525 Lakeward Drive, Suite 200, 39216.
Telephone: 601-713-1192.
Facsimile: 601-713-2049.
Jackson, Tennessee Office: 464 North Parkway, Suite A, 38305.
Telephone: 901-660-2332.
Facsimile: 901-664-1109.

MEMBERS OF FIRM

Wm. Rowlett Scott
Paul A. Matthews

For Complete List of Firm Personnel, See General Section

For full biographical listings, see the Martindale-Hubbell Law Directory

BAKER, DONELSON, BEARMAN & CALDWELL (AV)

20th Floor, First Tennessee Building, 165 Madison, 38103
Telephone: 901-526-2000
Telecopier: 901-577-2303
Email: info@bdbc.com *URL:* http://www.bakerdonelson.com
Nashville, Tennessee Office: 1700 Nashville City Center, 511 Union Street, 37219.
Telephone: 615-726-5600.
Telecopier: 615-726-0464.
Chattanooga, Tennessee Office: 1800 Republic Centre, 633 Chestnut Street, 37450-1800.
Telephone: 423-756-2010.
Telecopier: 423-756-3447.
Knoxville, Tennessee Office: 2200 Riverview Tower, 900 South Gay Street, 37901.
Telephone: 423-549-7000.
Telecopier: 423-525-8569.
Johnson City, Tennessee Office: SunTrust Bank Building, 207 Mockingbird Lane, P.O. Box 3038, 37602.
Telephone: 423-928-0181.
Telecopier: 423-928-5694; 423-928-3654; Kingsport: 423-246-6191.
Huntsville, Tennessee Office: 3 Courthouse Square, 37756.
Telephone: 423-663-2321.
Telecopier: 423-663-2111.
Washington, D.C. Office: Market Square, 801 Pennsylvania Avenue, N.W., 20004.
Telephone: 202-508-3400.
Telecopier: 202-508-3402.
Jackson, Mississippi Office: Suite 500, 700 North State Street, 39202.
Telephone: 601-351-2400.
Telecopier: 601-351-2424.

MANAGING PARTNER

Robert Mark Glover

SHAREHOLDERS

Lewis R. Donelson, III
Roy Keathley
David G. Williams
Leo Bearman, Jr.
Maurice Wexler
Frank L. Watson, Jr.
Robert Walker
Boyd L. Rhodes, Jr.
W. Michael Richards
John C. Speer
Charles T. Tuggle, Jr.
Larry E. Killebrew
Jerry Stauffer
Robert C. Liddon
William H.D. Fones, Jr.
William P. Kenworthy
Allan J. Wade
Gregory G. Fletcher
Charles C. Harrell
Stephen D. Goodwin
George T. Lewis, III
Ben C. Adams, Jr.
Eugene J. Podesta, Jr.
Sam B. Blair, Jr.
Carla Peacher-Ryan
Mary Aronov
Jill M. Steinberg
Matthew S. Heiter
Michael C. Patton
Janis Wild Kesser
Stephen William Ragland
Monique A. Nassar
Bradley E. Trammell
M. Clay Bethell
Desiree M. Franklin
R. Alan Pritchard, Jr.
Peter H. Kesser

(See Next Column)

BAKER, DONELSON, BEARMAN & CALDWELL, *Memphis—Continued*

OF COUNSEL

Frierson M. Graves, Jr.
Donald A. Malmo
Lynn Ackerman Landau
Paul E. Risner
(Not admitted in TN)

ASSOCIATES

Paul R. O'Rourke
Anne B. Mathes
Elizabeth Einstman Chance
Frank L. Watson, III
W. Douglas Sweet
Wm. Scott Young
Mary Ann Jackson
Angela R. Merideth
Jackie G. Prester
David L. Bearman
Clarissa M. Cissell
Robert C. McConkey, III
Jennifer R. Keown
Brett T. Parks
Cedric C.Y. Tan
Lang Wiseman
Diane Schratz Holitik
D. Benjamin Bullen
Shannon M. Hernandez
Sylvia Monique Reed
Christopher G. Boling
Louise P. Gaerig
Lori Hackleman Patterson
Lea Hall Speed

For full biographical listings, see the Martindale-Hubbell Law Directory

BOROD & KRAMER, P.C. (AV)

Beale Street Landing, 245 Wagner Place, Suite 350, 38103
Telephone: 901-524-0200
Telecopier: 901-523-0043
Email: administrator@borodankramer.com *URL:* http://www.borodandkramer.com

Bruce S. Kramer

Jeffrey C. Smith
Jeffery D. Parrish

For Complete List of Firm Personnel, See General Section

For full biographical listings, see the Martindale-Hubbell Law Directory

HALE HEADRICK DEWEY & WOLF, PLLC (AV)

One Memphis Place, 200 Jefferson Avenue Suite 1450, 38103
Telephone: 901-523-1123
Fax: 901-523-7472
Nashville, Tennessee Office: Suntrust Bank Building, 201 Fourth Avenue North, Suite 1450, 37219.
Telephone: 615-843-5160.
Fax: 615-843-5165

Stephen P. Hale
S. Russell Headrick
H. Tucker Dewey
Herbert B. Wolf, Jr.
John S. Golwen

OF COUNSEL

Steven L. Gill

Jennifer Ziegenhorn
Wendy A. Geurin
John W. Campbell
Joseph M. Koury
Holly N. Knight
Charles S. Blatteis
Jennifer S. Kiesewetter
J. William Williams

For full biographical listings, see the Martindale-Hubbell Law Directory

KRIVCHER MAGIDS PLC (AV)

International Place II, 6410 Poplar Avenue, Suite 300, 38119-4839
Telephone: 901-682-6431
Facsimile: 901-682-6453
Email: lawfirm@kmplc.com

Henry C. Shelton, III

ASSOCIATE

Rachel L. Hotze

For Complete List of Firm Personnel, See General Section

For full biographical listings, see the Martindale-Hubbell Law Directory

*NASHVILLE,** Davidson Co.

BAKER, DONELSON, BEARMAN & CALDWELL (AV)

1700 Nashville City Center, 511 Union Street, 37219
Telephone: 615-726-5600
Telecopier: 615-726-0464
Email: info@bdbc.com *URL:* http://www.bakerdonelson.com
Memphis, Tennessee Office: 20th Floor, First Tennessee Building, 165 Madison, 38103.
Telephone: 901-526-2000.
Telecopier: 901-577-2303.
Chattanooga, Tennessee Office: 1800 Republic Centre, 633 Chestnut Street, 37450-1800.
Telephone: 423-756-2010.
Telecopier: 423-756-3447.
Knoxville, Tennessee Office: 2200 Riverview Tower, 900 South Gay Street, 37901.
Telephone: 423-549-7000.
Telecopier: 423-525-8569.

(See Next Column)

Johnson City, Tennessee Office: SunTrust Bank Building, 207 Mockingbird Lane, P.O. Box 3038, 37602.
Telephone: 423-928-0181.
Telecopier: 423-928-5694; 423-928-3654; Kingsport: 423-246-6191.
Huntsville, Tennessee Office: 3 Courthouse Square, 37756.
Telephone: 423-663-2321.
Telecopier: 423-663-2111.
Washington, D.C. Office: Market Square, 801 Pennsylvania Avenue, N.W., 20004.
Telephone: 202-508-3400.
Telecopier: 202-508-3402.
Jackson, Mississippi Office: Suite 500, 700 North State Street, 39202.
Telephone: 601-351-2400.
Telecopier: 601-351-2424.

SHAREHOLDERS

Randal S. Mashburn
John H. Rowland

ASSOCIATE

John F. Rogers, Jr.

For Complete List of Firm Personnel, See General Section

For full biographical listings, see the Martindale-Hubbell Law Directory

BASS, BERRY & SIMS PLC (AV)

2700 First American Center, 37238-2700
Telephone: 615-742-6200
Telecopy: 615-742-6293
URL: http://www.bassberry.com
Knoxville, Tennessee Office: 1700 Riverview Tower, 900 S. Gay Street, 37902 and P.O. Box 1509, 37901-1509.
Telephone: 423-521-6200.
Telecopy: 423-521-6234.
Memphis, Tennessee Office: 119 S. Main Street, Suite 500, 38103.
Telephone: 901-312-9100.
Fax: 901-312-9101.

MEMBERS OF FIRM

L. Wearen Hughes
Paul G. Jennings

ASSOCIATE

Beth A. Dunning

Representative Clients: American Healthcorp, Inc.; Arcata Corp.; BellSouth Telecommunications, Inc.; Bowater Incorporated, Southern Division; Comptronix Corp.; First American National Bank; General Electric Capital Corp.; Martin-Marietta; Eastman Chemical Corp.; Securities Investor Protection Corp.

For full biographical listings, see the Martindale-Hubbell Law Directory

GARFINKLE, MCLEMORE & WALKER, PLLC (AV)

2000 Richard Jones Road, P.O. Box 158249, 37215-8249
Telephone: 615-383-9495
Telecopier: 615-292-9848
Email: gmwpllc@sprynet.com *URL:* http://www.citysearch.com/nas/gmwpllc

John C. McLemore
Edwin M. Walker

For full biographical listings, see the Martindale-Hubbell Law Directory

TEXAS

ADDISON, Dallas Co.

BARRETT BURKE WILSON CASTLE DAFFIN & FRAPPIER, L.L.P. (AV)

A Limited Liability Partnership including Professional Corporations
15000 Surveyor Boulevard, Suite 100, 75001
Telephone: 972-386-5040
Fax: 972-386-7673
Houston, Texas Office: 24 Greenway Plaza, Suite 2001.
Telephone: 713-621-8673.
Denver, Colorado Affiliated Office: Castle Barrett Daffin & Frappier, 1099 Eighteenth Street, Suite 2200.
Telephone: 303-299-1800.
Fax: 303-299-1808.
Little Rock, Arkansas Affiliated Office: Wilson & Associates, P.A. 1521 Merrill Drive, Suite D220.
Telephone: 501-219-9388.

Michael C. Barrett
Robert M. Wilson, Jr.
Lawrence E. Castle
(Not admitted in TX)
Robert F. Frappier
(Manager, Houston Office)
Mary A. Daffin (P.C.)
Stephen C. Porter
G. Tommy Bastian
Caren Jacobs Castle (P.C.)
(Not admitted in TX)
Clay A. Cornett (Resident, Dallas, Texas Office)

(See Next Column)

BARRETT BURKE WILSON CASTLE DAFFIN & FRAPPIER L.L.P.—*Continued*

Rosa Jean Bryant
James C. Frappier
Cristina Camarata
Anthony J Flores
Steve M. Cone
Cheryl Hughes Cannon
James L. DeLoach
Erin Archer Rush
Michael Wayne Zientz
David Seybold
Yvonne Renee Knesek
Jennifer Poe Umphress
William "Marty" Ferguson

For full biographical listings, see the Martindale-Hubbell Law Directory

GERARD SINGER & LEVICK, P.C. (AV)

16200 Addison Road Suite 140, 75001-5350
Telephone: 972-380-5533
Fax: 972-380-5748
Email: bcgerard@flash.net

Bretton C. Gerard
Gregory Z. Singer
Larry A. Levick
Michael I. Kahn
Robert J. Mabel
I. Richard Levy

For full biographical listings, see the Martindale-Hubbell Law Directory

*AMARILLO,** Potter Co.

WHITTENBURG WHITTENBURG & SCHACHTER, P.C. (AV)

1010 South Harrison, P.O. Box 31718, 79120
Telephone: 806-372-5700
Facsimile: 806-372-5757
Dallas, Texas Office: 2300 Plaza of the Americas, 600 North Pearl, LB 133.
Telephone: 214-999-5700.
Facsimile: 214-999-5747.

Deborah Ashmore Harris

For Complete List of Firm Personnel, See General Section

For full biographical listings, see the Martindale-Hubbell Law Directory

*AUSTIN,** Travis Co.

BAKER BOTTS L.L.P. (AV)

1600 San Jacinto Center, 98 San Jacinto Boulevard, 78701
Telephone: 512-322-2500
Fax: 512-322-2501
Email: postmaster@bakerbotts.com *URL:* http://www.bakerbotts.com
Houston, Texas Office: One Shell Plaza, 910 Louisiana.
Telephone: 713-229-1234.
Dallas, Texas Office: 2001 Ross Avenue.
Telephone: 214-953-6500.
Washington, D.C. Office: The Warner, 1299 Pennsylvania Avenue, N.W.
Telephone: 202-639-7700.
New York, New York Office: 599 Lexington Avenue.
Telephone: 212-705-5000.
Moscow, Russia Office: 10 ul. Bolshaya Dimitrovka (formerly Pushkinskaya), 103031.
Telephone: 7095/921-5300 (Local); 7501/929-7070 (International).
London, England Office: 45 Ludgate Hill.
Telephone: 0171-778-1400 (Local); 011-44-171-778-1400 (International).
Baku, Azerbaijan Office: 6-10 Vagif Mustafa-zadeh Street, Third Floor, Icheri Sheher, 370004.
Telephone: 994-12-97-63-88 (Local); 011-994-12-97-63-88 (International).
Fax: 994-12-97-63-61 (Local); 011-994-12-97-63-91 (International).

MEMBER OF FIRM

William F. Stutts, Jr.

For Complete List of Firm Personnel, See General Section

For full biographical listings, see the Martindale-Hubbell Law Directory

JAMES V. HOEFFNER (AV)

515 Congress Avenue, Suite 2600, 78701
Telephone: 512-476-9121
Fax: 512-476-8434
Email: jhoeffne@ix.netcom.com

For full biographical listings, see the Martindale-Hubbell Law Directory

HOHMANN & TAUBE, L.L.P. (AV)

100 Congress Avenue, Suite 1600, 78701-4042
Telephone: 512-472-5997
Fax: 512-472-5248
Email: bille@ht-law.com *URL:* http://www.ht-law.com

Eric J. Taube
Mitchell D. Savrick

Cristina B. McGarr
Robert D. Thomas
Neal Meinzer

For full biographical listings, see the Martindale-Hubbell Law Directory

*BROWNSVILLE,** Cameron Co.

RANSOME AND RAY, P.C. (AV)

550 East Levee Street, 78520-5343
Telephone: 956-542-3642
Telecopier: 956-542-3698
Email: ransomeray@aol.com

Marshall R. Ray
Mary Lou Ryan Ray

Cecilia De La Garza De Garcia

OF COUNSEL

C. Fount Ray

For full biographical listings, see the Martindale-Hubbell Law Directory

*CORPUS CHRISTI,** Nueces Co.

JORDAN, HYDEN, WOMBLE & CULBRETH, P.C. (AV)

Suite 900, NationsBank Center North, 500 North Water Street, 78471
Telephone: 512-884-5678
Fax: 512-888-5555
Email: JHWCLAW@AOL.COM

Shelby A. Jordan
Harlin C. Womble

Nathaniel Peter Holzer
Michael J. Urbis

For full biographical listings, see the Martindale-Hubbell Law Directory

*DALLAS,** Dallas Co.

BAKER BOTTS L.L.P. (AV)

2001 Ross Avenue, 75201
Telephone: 214-953-6500
Fax: 214-953-6503
Email: postmaster@bakerbotts.com *URL:* http://www.bakerbotts.com
Houston, Texas Office: One Shell Plaza, 910 Louisiana.
Telephone: 713-229-1234.
Washington, D.C. Office: The Warner, 1299 Pennsylvania Avenue, N.W.
Telephone: 202-639-7700.
Austin, Texas Office: 1600 San Jacinto Center, 98 San Jacinto Boulevard.
Telephone: 512-322-2500.
New York, New York Office: 599 Lexington Avenue.
Telephone: 212-705-5000.
Moscow, Russia Office: 10 ul. Bolshaya Dimitrovka (formerly Pushkinskaya), 103031.
Telephone: 7095/921-5300 (Local); 7095/929-7070.
London, England Office: 45 Ludgate Hill.
Telephone: 0171-778-1400 (Local); 011-44-171-778-1400 (International).
Baku, Azerbaijan Office: 6-10 Vagif Mustafa-zadeh Street, Third Floor, Icheri Sheher, 370004.
Telephone: 994-12-97-63-88 (Local); 011-994-12-97-63-88 (International).

MEMBERS OF FIRM

Jack L. Kinzie
Brenda T. Rhoades
Bobbie T. Shell

ASSOCIATES

David G. Adams
Michael C. Li

For Complete List of Firm Personnel, See General Section

For full biographical listings, see the Martindale-Hubbell Law Directory

CALHOUN & STACY (AV)

Suite 5700 - Bank of America Plaza, 901 Main Street, 75202-3713
Telephone: 214-748-5000
Facsimile: 214-748-1421
Email: info@calhounstacy.com *URL:* http://www.calhounstacy.com

MEMBERS OF FIRM

Rees T. Bowen, III
David W. Elrod
Parker Nelson

ASSOCIATE

Jonathan G. Polak

For Complete List of Firm Personnel, See General Section

For full biographical listings, see the Martindale-Hubbell Law Directory

CAVAZOS, HENDRICKS, POIROT & DEWEY, P.C. (AV)

Suite 570, Founders Square, 900 Jackson Street, 75202-4425
Telephone: 214-748-8171
Facsimile: 214-748-6750
Email: Firm@chfirm.com *URL:* http://www.chfirm.com

Arnaldo N. Cavazos, Jr.
Charles B. Hendricks
Rod L. Poirot
Alicia M. Dewey

Craig H. Smitham

(See Next Column)

CAVAZOS, HENDRICKS, POIROT & DEWEY P.C., *Dallas—Continued*

OF COUNSEL

Frank E. Sheeder, III
R. Matt Dawson
Glenn A. Sodd
Ron Edmondson
Terry L. Jacobson
John Clayton Beard

For full biographical listings, see the Martindale-Hubbell Law Directory

CHARLES R. CHESNUTT (AV)

1600 Pacific Avenue, Suite 2080, 75201
Telephone: 214-965-9599; 800-488-8752
Fax: 214-965-0256
Email: chesnutt@chapter7-11.com *URL:* http://www.lawyers.com/bankruptcy

For full biographical listings, see the Martindale-Hubbell Law Directory

CONANT FRENCH & CHANEY, LLP (AV)

3880 Bank One Center, 1717 Main Street, 75201
Telephone: 214-915-0620
Fasimile: 214-915-0634
Email: cfc@cfc-law.com *URL:* http://www.cfc-law.com

A. B. Conant, Jr.
William J. French
William B. Chaney
Linda A. Hale
Glen E. Lavy
Shawn W. Phelan
James D. MacIntyre

For full biographical listings, see the Martindale-Hubbell Law Directory

GODWIN WHITE & GRUBER, A PROFESSIONAL CORPORATION (AV)

Suite 2500, 901 Main Street, 75202-3714
Telephone: 214-939-4400
Fax: 214-760-7332

Thomas S. Hoekstra

ASSOCIATE

Nick C. Inman

For Complete List of Firm Personnel, See General Section

For full biographical listings, see the Martindale-Hubbell Law Directory

HUGHES & LUCE, L.L.P. (AV)

A Registered Limited Liability Partnership including Professional Corporations
1717 Main Street, Suite 2800, 75201
Telephone: 214-939-5500
Fax: 214-939-6100; 214-939-5849
Email: H&L@hughesluce.com *URL:* http://www.hughesluce.com
Austin, Texas Office: 111 Congress, Suite 900.
Telephone: 512-482-6800.
Fax: 512-482-6859.
Houston, Texas Office: 1600 Smith Street, Suite 3550.
Telephone: 713-754-5200.
Fax: 713-754-5270.

MEMBERS OF FIRM

Craig W. Budner
William B. Finkelstein

ASSOCIATES

James H. Billingsley
Matthew J. Cleaves
Cameron Davis Gray
Christopher Munns
Thomas W. Paxton

OF COUNSEL

Arthur A. Stewart

For Complete List of Firm Personnel, See General Section

For full biographical listings, see the Martindale-Hubbell Law Directory

KANE, RUSSELL, COLEMAN & LOGAN, A PROFESSIONAL CORPORATION (AV)

3700 Thanksgiving Tower, 1601 Elm Street, 75201-7207
Telephone: 214-777-4200
Fax: 214-777-4299
Email: krcl@krcl.com

Raymond J. Kane
Gordon B. Russell
Joseph M. Coleman
Michael A. Logan
Patrick V. Stark
Kenneth W. Biermacher
David N. Condon
Karen A. Cox
William D. Elliott
Joseph A. Friedman
Robert N. LeMay
Michael L. Atchley, II
Margaret M. McLeod Jordan

(See Next Column)

Terry Flett Barakis
Harold R. Busch
Priscilla K. Davenport
Deborah A. DiMarco
Evangelos J. Gegas (Not admitted in TX)
Shelli R. Inmon
Kenneth C. Johnston
Jaqluin M. Bickmore Lloyd
Robert L. Manteuffel
David D. Ritter
Holly J. Roman
Jeffrey S. Seeburger
Jeffrey Charles Tasker
Steven M. Thornton
Karin M. Zaner

For full biographical listings, see the Martindale-Hubbell Law Directory

THOMPSON, COE, COUSINS & IRONS, L.L.P. (AV)

200 Crescent Court, Eleventh Floor, 75201-1853
Telephone: 214-871-8200
Fax: 214-871-8209
Austin, Texas Office: Suite 1500, Austin Centre, 701 Brazos, 78701.
Telephone: 512-708-8200.
Fax: 512-708-8777.

PARTNER

Beth D. Bradley

Representative Clients: Bank One, Texas, N.A.; TIG Insurance Co.; Océ-USA.

For Complete List of Firm Personnel, See General Section

For full biographical listings, see the Martindale-Hubbell Law Directory

THOMPSON & KNIGHT L.L.P. (AV)

(Attorneys and Counselors)
1700 Pacific Avenue Suite 3300, 75201
Telephone: 214-969-1700
Telecopy: 214-969-1751
Telex: 732 298
URL: http://www.tklaw.com
Austin, Texas Office: 1200 San Jacinto Center, 98 San Jacinto Boulevard, 78701.
Telephone: 512-469-6100.
Telecopy: 512-469-6180.
Fort Worth, Texas Office: 801 Cherry Street, Suite 1600, 76102.
Telephone: 817-347-1700.
Telecopy: 817-347-1799.
Houston, Texas Office: Thompson Knight Brown Parker & Leahy L.L.P., 1200 Smith Street, Suite 3600, 77002-4595.
Telephone: 713-654-8111.
Telecopier: 713-654-1871.
San Pedro Garza Garcia, Nuevo León, Mexico Office: Edificio Losoles PD-4, Av. Lázaro Cárdenas No. 2400 Pte., C.P. 66220.
Telephone: (52-8) 363-0096.
Telecopy: (52-8) 363-3067.

PARTNERS

David M. Bennett
Robert W. Jones
James R. Prince
Peter J. Riley
Judith W. Ross

ASSOCIATE

Darin M. Klemchuk

STAFF ATTORNEY

Monica S. Blacker

For Complete List of Firm Personnel, See General Section

For full biographical listings, see the Martindale-Hubbell Law Directory

*EL PASO,** El Paso Co.

CROWSON & INGRAM (AV)

Suite 706, The Cortez, 310 North Mesa, P.O. Box 862, 79945
Telephone: 915-533-7717
Telefax: 915-533-1495
Email: crowsing@huntleigh.net

MEMBERS OF FIRM

Harold E. Crowson, Jr.
Temple B. Ingram, Jr.

Reference: Bank of America, N.A.; Norwest Bank, El Paso, N.A.; Bank of the West, El Paso, Texas.

For full biographical listings, see the Martindale-Hubbell Law Directory

JAMES, GOLDMAN & HAUGLAND, P.C. A PROFESSIONAL CORPORATION (AV)

Chase Bank of Texas, 201 East Main, Suite 800, P.O. Box 1770, 79949-1770
Telephone: 915-532-3911
Fax: 915-541-6440

Wiley F. James, III
Corey W. Haugland
Victor M. Firth
Hector Phillips

(See Next Column)

JAMES, GOLDMAN & HAUGLAND P.C. A PROFESSIONAL CORPORATION—*Continued*

Don W. Minton   Natasha Hazarian

Attorneys for: Bank of the West; Ford Motor Credit Corp.; Financial Federal Credit, Inc.; Mack Massey Motors, Inc.; FCA Corp.; Southwestern General Hospital; Leviton Manufacturing Co., Inc.; Mellon Mortgage Company; Primary Medical Clinic, Inc.; United Investors Realty Trust.

For Complete List of Firm Personnel, See General Section

For full biographical listings, see the Martindale-Hubbell Law Directory

LESLIE & SMITH, P.C. (AV)

2731 A Montana Avenue, 79903
Telephone: 915-565-9000
Fax: 915-565-9191

Donald S. Leslie   Cheryl S. Lay

OF COUNSEL

Nelson Smith

For full biographical listings, see the Martindale-Hubbell Law Directory

*FORT WORTH,** Tarrant Co.

BROUDE, SMITH & JENNINGS, P.C. (AV)

309 West Seventh Street Suite 1100, 76102
Telephone: 817-335-1615
Metro: 817-654-3505
Fax: 817-335-1603

John S. Broude   Cary L. Jennings
Steven M. Smith   Kathryn Durham McGlinchey
Jerry Betsill

OF COUNSEL

Janna Ward Clarke

LEGAL SUPPORT PERSONNEL

Laura deLagerheim (Paralegal).

For full biographical listings, see the Martindale-Hubbell Law Directory

CLIFFORD F. MCMASTER (AV)

1400 Oil & Gas Building, 309 West Seventh Street, 76102
Telephone: 817-335-8080
FAX: 817-429-3371

LEGAL SUPPORT PERSONNEL

Twalla J. Dupriest

For full biographical listings, see the Martindale-Hubbell Law Directory

*HOUSTON,** Harris Co.

BAKER BOTTS L.L.P. (AV)

One Shell Plaza, 910 Louisiana, 77002
Telephone: 713-229-1234
Cable Address: "Boterlove"
Fax: 713-229-1522
Email: postmaster@bakerbotts.com *URL:* http://www.bakerbotts.com
Washington, D.C. Office: The Warner, 1299 Pennsylvania Avenue, N.W.
Telephone: 202-639-7700.
New York, New York Office: 599 Lexington Avenue.
Telephone: 212-705-5000.
Austin, Texas Office: 1600 San Jacinto Center, 98 San Jacinto Boulevard.
Telephone: 512-322-2500.
Dallas, Texas Office: 2001 Ross Avenue.
Telephone: 214-953-6500.
Moscow, Russia Office: 10 ul. Bolshaya Dimitrovka (formerly Pushkinskaya), 103031.
Telephone: 7095/921-5300 (Local); 7095/929-7070 (International).
London, England Office: 45 Ludgate Hill.
Telephone: 0171-778-1400 (Local); 011-44-171-778-1400 (International).
Baku, Azerbaijan Office: 6-10 Vagif Mustafa-zadeh Street, Third Floor, Icheri Sheher, 370004.
Telephone: 994-12-97-63-88 (Local); 011-994-12-97-63-88 (International).
Fax: 994-12-97-63-91 (Local); 011-994-12-97-63-91 (International)

MEMBER OF FIRM

Tony M. Davis

ASSOCIATES

Mary Millwood Gregory   Elizabeth M. Guffy
Denise Dardeau Muller

For Complete List of Firm Personnel, See General Section

For full biographical listings, see the Martindale-Hubbell Law Directory

GILLIS & SLOGAR (AV)

6905 Wells Fargo Plaza, 1000 Louisiana, 77002
Telephone: 713-951-9100
Telecopier: 713-951-9718
Email: gillisslogar@worldnet.att.net

Charles Michael Gillis   John Michael Slogar

OF COUNSEL

Randall W. Heinrich

For full biographical listings, see the Martindale-Hubbell Law Directory

GILPIN, PAXSON & BERSCH (AV)

A Registered Limited Liability Partnership
Attorney at Law
1900 West Loop South, Suite 2000, 77027-3259
Telephone: 713-623-8800
Telecopier: 713-993-8451
Email: gpb@gpblaw.com *URL:* http://www.texinslaw.com

PARTNERS

Gary M. Alletag   Darryl W. Malone
Timothy R. Bersch   Michael J. Pappert
John D. Gilpin   Stephen Paxson
Kevin F. Risley

OF COUNSEL

Harless R. Benthul   David F. Webb

ASSOCIATES

Joseph D. Batson   Jeri Pharis Wechsler

Representative Clients: BMW of North America, Inc.; Federal Deposit Insurance Corporation; Greater Houston Builders Association; Owens Corning Fiberglas Corporation; Shaw Industries, Inc.; Southwest Guaranty Trust Company, N.A.; Sprint Communications Company L.P.; Volkswagen of America, Inc.; Volvo North America Corporation; Wells Fargo Bank (Texas), N.A.

For full biographical listings, see the Martindale-Hubbell Law Directory

KIRKENDALL & ISGUR (AV)

700 Louisiana, Suite 4200, 77002
Telephone: 713-225-4646
Facsimile: 713-230-0016
Data Transfer via computer also available

MEMBERS OF FIRM

Thomas M. Kirkendall   Joseph G. Epstein
Marvin Isgur   David R. Jones
L. Farrell Crane, Jr.

ASSOCIATE

Steven M. Lowenstein

For full biographical listings, see the Martindale-Hubbell Law Directory

LAWRENCE, BACA & DONOHUE PLLC (AV)

5225 Katy Freeway, Suite 350, 77007
Telephone: 713-864-8000
Telecopier: 713-864-0179
Email: lawbacdon@prodigy.net

Paul R. Lawrence   Billy G. Baca
Michael T. Donohue

ASSOCIATE

Libbye C. Howard

For full biographical listings, see the Martindale-Hubbell Law Directory

*SAN ANTONIO,** Bexar Co.

COX & SMITH INCORPORATED (AV)

112 East Pecan Street, Suite 1800, 78205-1521
Telephone: 210-554-5500
Fax: 210-226-8395
Email: info@coxsmith.com *URL:* http://www.coxsmith.com

Diann M. Bartek   Patrick L. Huffstickler
Deborah D. Williamson   H. Joseph Acosta
Douglas B. Kiel

For Complete List of Firm Personnel, See General Section

For full biographical listings, see the Martindale-Hubbell Law Directory

HABBESHAW, KALMANS & SCHWARTZ, P.C. (AV)

The Colonnade, Suite 770, 9901 I.H. 10 West, 78230
Telephone: 210-699-8086
Facsimile: 210-699-3409

Penny K. Habbeshaw   Patricia A. Kalmans
Helen Schwartz

For full biographical listings, see the Martindale-Hubbell Law Directory

*SHERMAN,** Grayson Co.

NIX & WINEGEART, P.C. (AV)

717 North Crockett Street, 75090
Telephone: 903-870-0212
Fax: 903-870-0109
Email: rnix@gte.net

William Riley Nix | Graham C. Winegeart

Representative Clients: American Bank of Texas; Bonham State Bank; BVAC Federal Credit Union; First Bank of Farmersville; First Bank Howe; First National Bank of Durant; First United Bank and Trust Co.; First National Bank of Whitewright; Lamesa National Bank; Security Bank of Whitesboro.

For full biographical listings, see the Martindale-Hubbell Law Directory

TEXARKANA, Bowie Co.

PATTON, HALTOM, ROBERTS, MCWILLIAMS & GREER, L.L.P. (AV)

A Registered Limited Liability Partnership including Professional Corporations
700 Hibernia National Bank Building, P.O. Box 1928, 75504-1928
Telephone: 903-794-3341
Fax: 903-792-6542; 903-792-0448
URL: http://www.pattonhaltom.com

William B. Roberts | Donald W. Capshaw
Phillip N. Cockrell

For Complete List of Firm Personnel, See General Section

For full biographical listings, see the Martindale-Hubbell Law Directory

*TYLER,** Smith Co.

IRELAND, CARROLL & KELLEY, P.C. (AV)

6101 South Broadway, Suite 500, P.O. Box 7879, 75711
Telephone: 903-561-1600
Fax: 903-581-1071
Email: ICKLAW@AOL.COM

H. Kelly Ireland (Retired)
Donald Carroll (1929-1992)
Otis W. Carroll
Patrick Kelley
Marcus Carroll
Michael G. Carroll

Deborah Race

For full biographical listings, see the Martindale-Hubbell Law Directory

UTAH

*SALT LAKE CITY,** Salt Lake Co.

CALLISTER NEBEKER & MCCULLOUGH, A PROFESSIONAL CORPORATION (AV)

Gateway Tower East, Suite 900, 10 East South Temple, 84133
Telephone: 801-530-7300
Telecopier: 801-364-9127
Email: mjeaston@cnmlaw.com *URL:* http://www.cnmlaw.com

Jeffrey L. Shields
Steven E. Tyler
Jan M. Bergeson
Zachary T. Shields

Representative Clients: Zions First National Bank; Citicorp; Federal Land Bank Association of Utah; Chrysler Credit Corp.; Associates Commercial Corp.

For Complete List of Firm Personnel, See General Section

For full biographical listings, see the Martindale-Hubbell Law Directory

PARR WADDOUPS BROWN GEE & LOVELESS, A PROFESSIONAL CORPORATION (AV)

Suite 1300, 185 South State Street, 84111-1537
Telephone: 801-532-7840
Fax: 801-532-7750
URL: http://www.pwlaw.com

Robert B. Lochhead

For Complete List of Firm Personnel, See General Section

For full biographical listings, see the Martindale-Hubbell Law Directory

PARSONS, DAVIES, KINGHORN & PETERS, P.C. (AV)

185 South State Street, Suite 700, 84111
Telephone: 801-363-4300
Facsimile: 801-363-4378
Email: Attorneys@pdkplaw.com

(See Next Column)

Gerald H. Kinghorn | R. Kimball Mosier
Katherine S. Gregory

For Complete List of Firm Personnel, See General Section

For full biographical listings, see the Martindale-Hubbell Law Directory

RAY, QUINNEY & NEBEKER, A PROFESSIONAL CORPORATION (AV)

79 South Main Street, Suite 400, P.O. Box 45385, 84145-0385
Telephone: 801-532-1500
Fax: 801-532-7543
Email: rqn@rqn.com *URL:* http://www.rqn.com
Provo, Utah Office: 92 North University Avenue, Suite 210, 84601-4420.
Telephone: 801-342-2400.
Fax: 801-375-8379.
Albuquerque, New Mexico Office: Suite 620, 40 First Plaza, N.W.
Telephone: 505-243-6665.
Fax: 505-764-9890.

Herschel J. Saperstein
Weston L. Harris
Scott Hancock Clark
Steven H. Gunn
John P. Harrington
Douglas M. Monson
Steven T. Waterman
Steven W. Call

Representative Clients: First Security Bank, N.A.; Borden, Inc.; Salt Lake Organizing Committee for the Winter Olympic Games of 2002; Southern Pacific Transportation; Utah Power & Light Co.; Travelers Insurance Co.; U.S. West.

For Complete List of Firm Personnel, See General Section

For full biographical listings, see the Martindale-Hubbell Law Directory

VAN COTT, BAGLEY, CORNWALL & MCCARTHY, A PROFESSIONAL CORPORATION (AV)

50 South Main Street, Suite 1600, P.O. Box 45340, 84145-0340
Telephone: 801-532-3333
Telecopier: 801-534-0058
Email: info@vancott.com *URL:* http://www.vancott.com
Ogden, Utah Office: 2404 Washington Boulevard, Suite 900.
Telephone: 801-394-5783.
Park City, Utah Office: 2200 Park Avenue, Suite C200-A.
Telephone: 435-649-3889.

Timothy W. Blackburn (Resident, Ogden, Utah Office)
Gerald H. Suniville

Mara A. Brown

OF COUNSEL

William G. Fowler

For Complete List of Firm Personnel, See General Section

For full biographical listings, see the Martindale-Hubbell Law Directory

VERMONT

BETHEL, Windsor Co.

OBUCHOWSKI LAW OFFICE (AV)

Route 107, P.O. Box 60, 05032
Telephone: 802-234-6244
FAX: 802-234-6245
Email: obi@sover.net

MEMBER OF FIRM

Raymond J. Obuchowski

ASSOCIATES

Bernard M. Lewis | Jennifer Emens-Butler

For full biographical listings, see the Martindale-Hubbell Law Directory

VIRGINIA

ALEXANDRIA, (Independent City)

GOLD MORRISON & LAUGHLIN PC (AV)

Third Floor, King Street Station, 1800 Diagonal Road, 22314-2808
Telephone: 703-836-7004
Facsimile: 703-548-9430
Email: gmlmail@goldmorrison.com *URL:* http://www.goldmorrison.com
Washington, D.C. Office: 1200 G Street, N.W., Suite 800, 20003.
Telephone: 703-836-7004.

(See Next Column)

GOLD MORRISON & LAUGHLIN PC—*Continued*

Silver Spring, Maryland Office: 1010 Wayne Avenue, Suite 420.
Telephone: 703-836-7004.

H. Jason Gold — Valerie P. Morrison
Alexander M. Laughlin

William McCarron, Jr. — Adam C. Paul
Raymond R. Pring, Jr. — Kelly M. Call (Not admitted in VA)

For full biographical listings, see the Martindale-Hubbell Law Directory

GORDON P. PEYTON, P.C. (AV)

908 King Street, Suite 201, P.O. Box 25456, 22313
Telephone: 703-549-0200
Facsimile: 703-549-2370
Email: gpeyton.law@worldnet.att.net

Carl Budwesky (1891-1982) — Gordon P. Peyton

References: Burke & Herbert Bank & Trust Co.

For full biographical listings, see the Martindale-Hubbell Law Directory

ROSENBLUM & ROSENBLUM, L.L.C. (AV)

228 South Washington Street, Suite 300, P.O. Box 19110, 22320
Telephone: 703-548-9002
Fax: 703-548-8774
Email: rrlawllc@clark.net *URL:* http://www.lawyers.com/rosenblum&rosenblum

Alan Rosenblum — David Rosenblum

For full biographical listings, see the Martindale-Hubbell Law Directory

TYLER, BARTL, BURKE AND ALBERT, P.L.C. (AV)

206 North Washington Street, Suite 200, 22314
Telephone: 703-549-5000
Fax: 703-549-5011

Robert O. Tyler — Marc E. Albert
Richard A. Bartl — Thomas P. Gorman
Dan Burke — Madeline A. Trainor
Steven B. Ramsdell

ASSOCIATE

Scott J. Newton (Not admitted in VA)

For full biographical listings, see the Martindale-Hubbell Law Directory

*CHARLOTTESVILLE,** Charlottesville City Co.

ROBERT M. MUSSELMAN & ASSOCIATES (AV)

413 7th Street, N.E., P.O. Box 254, 22902
Telephone: 804-977-4500
Fax: 804-293-5727
Email: rmmesquire@aol.com

ASSOCIATES

Carolyn C. Musselman — Douglas E. Little
Jonathan B. Burns

LEGAL SUPPORT PERSONNEL

Eleanor P. Carter (Legal Secretary and Real Estate Paralegal) — Faye M. McBurney (Legal Secretary and Bankruptcy Paralegal)

Representative Clients: Holywell Corporation.

For full biographical listings, see the Martindale-Hubbell Law Directory

NORFOLK, (Independent City)

GOLDBLATT, LIPKIN & COHEN, P.C. (AV)

Suite 300, 415 St. Paul's Boulevard, P.O. Box 3505, 23514
Telephone: 757-627-6225
Telefax: 757-622-3698

Paul M. Lipkin — Steven M. Legum
Robert S. Cohen — Mary G. Commander
Neal C. Schulwolf

For full biographical listings, see the Martindale-Hubbell Law Directory

STACKHOUSE, SMITH & NEXSEN (AV)

1600 First Virginia Tower, 555 Main Street, P.O. Box 3640, 23514
Telephone: 757-623-3555
Fax: 757-624-9245

MEMBERS OF FIRM

Robert C. Stackhouse — R. Clinton Stackhouse, Jr.
Peter W. Smith, IV — Janice McPherson Doxey
William W. Nexsen — Mary Painter Opitz

(See Next Column)

ASSOCIATES

J. Derek Turrietta — Michael T. Pangalos

Representative Clients: Heritage Bank & Trust; The Atlantic Group, Inc.; Roughton Pontiac Corp; Federal National Mortgage Association; Kemper National Insurance Cos.; Harleysville Mutual Insurance Co.; Heritage Bankshares, Inc.; Presbyterian League of the Presbytery of Eastern Virginia, Inc.; Oakwood Acceptance Corp.; Orix Credit Alliance, Inc.

For full biographical listings, see the Martindale-Hubbell Law Directory

VANDEVENTER BLACK LLP (AV)

500 World Trade Center, 23510-1699
Telephone: 757-446-8600
Cable Address: "Hughsvan"
Telecopier: 757-446-8670
URL: http://www.vanblk.com
Kitty Hawk, North Carolina Office: 6 Juniper Trail.
Telephone: 252-261-5055.
Fax: 252-261-8444. E-Mail: nshearin@pinn.net.
London, England Office: Mitre House, 4th Floor, 12-14 Mitre Street.
Telephone: (0171) 623-2081.
Facsimile: (0171) 929-0043.

PARTNERS OF FIRM

Walter B. Martin, Jr. — Michael P. Cotter
Bryant C. McGann

OF COUNSEL

Richard S. Guy

For Complete List of Firm Personnel, See General Section

For full biographical listings, see the Martindale-Hubbell Law Directory

RICHMOND, (Independent City)

LECLAIR RYAN, A PROFESSIONAL CORPORATION (AV)

707 East Main Street, 11th Floor, 23219
Telephone: 804-783-2003
Facsmile: 804-783-2294
Email: email@leclairryan.com
Glen Allen, Virginia Office: 4201 Dominion Boulevard, Suite 200, 23060.
Telephone: 804-270-0070.
Facsimile: 804-270-4715.
Blacksburg, Virginia Office: 1872 Pratt Drive, Suite 1865, 24060.
Telephone: 540-961-2762.
Fax: 540-961-2781.
Norfolk, Virginia Office: 999 Waterside Drive, Suite 2025.
Telephone: 757-624-1454.
Facsimile: 757-624-3773.
Alexandria, Virginia Office: 225 Reinekers Lane, Suite 290, 22314.
Telephone: 703-684-8007.
Facsimile: 703-684-8075.
Charlottesville, Virginia Office: 108 S.E. Second Street, P.O. Box 2017, 22902.
Telephone: 804-971-7771.
Facsimile: 804-296-0905.

Paula Steinhilber Beran — Otto W. Konrad
Vernon E. Inge, Jr. — Bruce H. Matson
Stanley K. Joynes III — E. Duffy Myrtetus
Lynn Lewis Tavenner

Donald F. Lynch, III

For full biographical listings, see the Martindale-Hubbell Law Directory

MALONEY, HUENNEKENS, PARKS, GECKER & PARSONS, A PROFESSIONAL CORPORATION (AV)

Bank of America Center, 1111 East Main Street, Suite 800, 23219-3103
Telephone: 804-644-0313
Telecopier: 804-783-6192

Kevin R. Huennekens — Michael A. Condyles
Daniel A. Gecker — Loc Pfeiffer
Patricia Lea Phillips

Reference: First Union National Bank.

For Complete List of Firm Personnel, See General Section

For full biographical listings, see the Martindale-Hubbell Law Directory

WILLIAMS, MULLEN, CLARK & DOBBINS, A PROFESSIONAL CORPORATION (AV)

Two James Center, 1021 East Cary Street, P.O. Box 1320, 23218-1320
Telephone: 804-643-1991
Fax: 804-783-6507
URL: http://www.wmcd.com
Newport News Office: Harbor Bank Center, Suite 210, One Old Oyster Point Road, 23602-7119.
Telephone: 757-249-5100.
Fax: 757-249-5109.

(See Next Column)

WILLIAMS, MULLEN, CLARK & DOBBINS A PROFESSIONAL CORPORATION, *Richmond—Continued*

Virginia Beach Office: One Columbus Center, 23462-6763.
Telephone: 757-499-8800.
Fax: 757-473-0395.
Vienna Office: 1593 Spring Hill Road, Suite 510, 22182.
Telephone: 703-760-5200.
Fax: 703-748-0244.
Washington, D.C. Office: The Farragut Building, 900 17th Street, N.W., Suite 700, 20006.
Telephone: 202-293-0213.
Fax: 804-783-6507. Fax Within D.C.: 202-293-5939.
London, England Office: Blake Lodge, Bridge Lane, SW11 3AD.
Telephone: (011-44-71) 223-2756.
Fax: (011-44-71) 350-0156.
Riyadh, Saudi Arabia Affiliate Office: Saudi-American Legal Consultants Commercial Building #2, Diplomatic Quarter, P.O. Box 57270, 11574.
Telephone: (011-966-1) 488-1563.
Fax: (011-966-1) 488-0542.

Paul S. Bliley, Jr.
A. Peter Brodell
James J. Burns
Charles L. Cabell
Robert D. Perrow
William H. Schwarzschild, III

Neil E. McCullagh

For Complete List of Firm Personnel, See General Section

For full biographical listings, see the Martindale-Hubbell Law Directory

ROANOKE, Roanoke City Co.

OSTERHOUDT, FERGUSON, NATT, AHERON & AGEE, A PROFESSIONAL CORPORATION (AV)

1919 Electric Road, S.W., 24018
Telephone: 540-774-1197
Telecopier: 540-774-0961
Mailing Address: P.O. Box 20068, Roanoke, 24018
Email: OFNNA@Roanoke.infi.net *URL:* http://www.roanoke.infi.net/~ofnaa

Charles H. Osterhoudt
Michael S. Ferguson
Edward A. Natt
Michael J. Aheron
G. Steven Agee
Mark D. Kidd
Kristen K. Johnstone

For full biographical listings, see the Martindale-Hubbell Law Directory

VIRGINIA BEACH, (Independent City)

WOLCOTT, RIVERS, WHEARY, BASNIGHT & KELLY, P.C. (AV)

One Columbus Center, Suite 1100, 23462-6765
Telephone: 757-497-6633
FAX: 757-497-7267
Email: wolriv@series2000.com

Wilson L. Rivers
William A. Wheary, III
W. Brantley Basnight, III
Monroe Kelly, III
Carl A. Eason
Joseph R. Mayes
Samuel W. Meekins, Jr.
Edward W. Wolcott, Jr.
Barry Dorans
Leslie R. Watson
David N. Reda
Richard E. Biemiller
Cheshire I'Anson Eveleigh
M. Powell Peters
Neil L. Rose
Robert D. Marotta

David M. Bastiaans
Deborah Kirkpatrick

Counsel for: Metropolitan Life Insurance Co.; Ford Motor Co.
Approved Attorneys for: Lawyers Title Insurance Corp.

For full biographical listings, see the Martindale-Hubbell Law Directory

WASHINGTON

*SEATTLE,** King Co.

LANE POWELL SPEARS LUBERSKY LLP (AV)

Limited Liability Partnership composed of Individuals and Professional Service Corporations
1420 Fifth Avenue, Suite 4100, 98101-2338
Telephone: 206-223-7000
Facsimile: 206-223-7107
Email: information@lanepowell.com *URL:* http://www.lanepowell.com
Other Offices at: Portland, Oregon; Anchorage, Alaska; Olympia and Mount Vernon, Washington; London, England.

MEMBERS OF FIRM

Charles R. Ekberg (P.S.)
Bruce W. Leaverton

(See Next Column)

COUNSEL

Mary Jo Heston

Representative Clients: Associates Commercial Corp.; AT&T Commercial Finance Corp.; The Chase Manhattan Bank; Finova Capital Corp.; General Electric Capital Corp.; Heller Financial, Inc.; MONY Life Insurance Co.; Navistar Financial Corp.; Transnation Title Insurance Co.; Wells Fargo Bank.

For Complete List of Firm Personnel, See General Section

For full biographical listings, see the Martindale-Hubbell Law Directory

*SPOKANE,** Spokane Co.

SOUTHWELL & O'ROURKE, P.S. (AV)

Suite 960, Paulsen Center, West 421 Riverside Avenue, 99201
Telephone: 509-624-0159
Fax: 509-624-9231

Daniel O'Rourke

For full biographical listings, see the Martindale-Hubbell Law Directory

WEST VIRGINIA

*CHARLESTON,** Kanawha Co.

JACKSON & KELLY (AV)

1600 Laidley Tower, P.O. Box 553, 25322
Telephone: 304-340-1000
Fax: 304-340-1130
Email: info@jacksonkelly.com *URL:* http://www.jacksonkelly.com
Martinsburg, West Virginia Office: 300 Foxcroft Avenue, P.O. Box 1068.
Telephone: 304-263-8800.
Fax: 304-263-7110.
Morgantown, West Virginia Office: 6000 Hampton Center, P.O. Box 619.
Telephone: 304-599-3000.
Fax: 304-285-2040.
New Martinsville, West Virginia Office: 256 Russell Avenue, P.O. Box 68.
Telephone: 304-455-1751.
Fax: 304-455-6314.
Parkersburg, West Virginia Office: 412 Market Street, Suite 202, P.O. Box 1144.
Telephone: 304-424-3490.
Fax: 304-424-3499.
Fairmont, West Virginia Office: 1000 Technology Drive, Suite 1310.
Telephone: 304-368-2000.
Fax: 304-368-2020.
Lexington, Kentucky Office: 175 East Main Street, Suite 500, P.O. Box 2150.
Telephone: 606-255-9500.
Fax: 606-281-6478.
Washington, D. C. Office: 2401 Pennsylvania Avenue, N.W., Suite 400.
Telephone: 202-973-0200.
Fax: 202-973-0232.
Denver, Colorado Office: Suite 2710, 1660 Lincoln Street.
Telephone: 303-390-0003.
Fax: 303-390-0040.
Wheeling, West Virginia Office: 1144 Market Street.
Telephone: 304-233-4000.
Fax: 304-233-4077.

MEMBERS OF FIRM

William F. Dobbs, Jr.
Ellen S. Cappellanti
Mary Clare Eros (Administrative Manager, Martinsburg and Charles Town, West Virginia Offices)
Stanton L. Cave (Resident, Lexington, Kentucky Office)

Representative Clients: One Valley Bancorp of West Virginia Inc; Navistar Financial Corp.; ORIX Credit Alliance, Inc.; Westmoreland Coal Company; F & M National Bank; Pittston Coal Management Co.; Westvaco Corp.; Electric Fuels Corp.; Kentucky River Coal Corp.; Cypress-AMAX Minerals Co.

For Complete List of Firm Personnel, See General Section

For full biographical listings, see the Martindale-Hubbell Law Directory

*CLARKSBURG,** Harrison Co.

MCNEER, HIGHLAND, MCMUNN AND VARNER, L.C. (AV)

One Valley Bank Building, P.O. Drawer 2040, 26302-2040
Telephone: 304-626-1100
Facsimile: 304-623-3035
Martinsburg Office: 2520 Aikens Center, P.O. Box 2509.
Telephone: 304-264-4621.
Fax: 304-264-8623.
Parkersburg Office: 404 Market Street, Suite 204, P.O. Box 1507.
Telephone: 304-422-7193.
Facsimile: 304-422-7196.

(See Next Column)

McNeer, Highland, McMunn and Varner L.C.—*Continued*

C. David McMunn
J. Cecil Jarvis
James A. Varner
Robert W. Trumble (Resident, Martinsburg Office)
Catherine D. Munster
James N. Riley
Steven R. Bratke (Resident, Parkersburg Office)
Michael J. Novotny (Resident, Martinsburg Office)
Dennis M. Shreve
Geraldine S. Roberts
William F. Rohrbaugh (Resident, Martinsburg Office)
Gregory H. Schillace
Judy L. Shanholtz
Tiffany R. Durst
Gene W. Bailey, II

OF COUNSEL

James E. McNeer
Cecil B. Highland, Jr.
William L. Fury

Representative Clients: One Valley Bank of Clarksburg, National Assn.; Bruceton Bank; Harrison County Bank; Nationwide Mutual Insurance Cos.; Clarksburg Publishing Co.; C.I.T. Financial Services; State Automobile Mutual Insurance Co.; United Hospital Center, Inc.; West Virginia Coals, Inc.; Swanson Plating Co.

For full biographical listings, see the Martindale-Hubbell Law Directory

HUNTINGTON, Cabell & Wayne Cos.

Baker, Lancianese, Campbell & Conaty (AV)

The River Tower, 1108 Third Avenue, Suite 300, 25701-1578
Telephone: 304-522-6906
Facsimile: 304-522-6910
Email: BLCC@BLCCLAW.COM *URL:* http://www.BLCCLAW.COM
Washington, D.C. Office: 1090 Vermont Avenue, N.W. Suite 800.
Telephone: 202-966-1500.
Fax: 202-966-7075. E-Mail: BLCC@BLCCLAW.COM.
Lexington, Kentucky Office: 2265 Harrodsburg Road, Suite 200, 40504-3517.
Telephone: 606-278-0297.
Fax: 206-278-0334. E-Mail: BLCC@BLCCLAW.COM.

Roy D. Baker, Jr.
Richard L. Lancianese
David L. Campbell
Brian P. Conaty
Janice P. Epperly

OF COUNSEL

Margaret M. Brizzolara (Not admitted in WV)

For full biographical listings, see the Martindale-Hubbell Law Directory

*WHEELING,** Ohio Co.

Schrader Byrd & Companion, PLLC (AV)

(A Professional Limited Liability Company)
The Maxwell Centre, 32-20th Street, Suite 500, P.O. Box 6336, 26003
Telephone: 304-233-3390
Fax: 304-233-2769
URL: http://www.schraderlaw.com
Martins Ferry, Ohio Office: 205 North Fifth Street, P.O. Box 309, 43935.
Telephone: 740-633-9976.
Fax: 740-633-0400.
Weirton, West Virginia Office: 3205 Pennsylvania Avenue, Suite 103, Penn Place, P.O. Box 2785, 26062.
Telephone: 304-723-2674.
Fax: 304-723-2876.

MEMBERS

Ray A. Byrd
James F. Companion
Frank X. Duff
Teresa Rieman-Camilletti
Yolonda G. Lambert
Daniel P. Fry (Resident Partner, Martins Ferry, Ohio Office)
James P. Mazzone (Resident Member, Weirton, West Virginia Office)
Sandra K. Law
D. Kevin Coleman

SPECIAL COUNSEL

Thomas B. Miller

ASSOCIATES

Denise D. Klug
Michael A. Adams
John Porco
Aimee Morgan Stern
Kimberly R. Wilson
Christopher J. Adams

OF COUNSEL

James A. Byrum, Jr.

General Counsel: Reynolds Memorial Hospital; WesBanco Bank-Elm Grove.
Representative Clients: American Cyanamid Company; Bank One; Matlack Systems, Inc.; Moutaineer Gas Co.; Ohio County Board of Education; PHICO Insurance Co.; Wheeling Hospital; Wheeling-Pittsburg Steel Corp.

For full biographical listings, see the Martindale-Hubbell Law Directory

WISCONSIN

*MILWAUKEE,** Milwaukee Co.

Kohner, Mann & Kailas, S.C. (AV)

1572 East Capitol Drive, P.O. Box 11982, 53211-0982
Telephone: 414-962-5110
Fax: 414-962-8725
Email: kmksc@execpc.com

Marvin L. Kohner (1908-1975)

OF COUNSEL

Robert L. Mann

MEMBERS OF FIRM

Steve Kailas
Mark R. Wolters
Jordan B. Reich
David S. Chartier
Roy Paul Roth
Gary P. Lantzy
Christopher C. Kailas
Matthew P. Gerdisch

Robert E. Nailen
Darrell R. Zall
Daniel J. Flynn
Timothy L. Zuberbier
David M. Henry
Lorinne J Cunningham
Palma M. Forte
Daniel J. Emma

Representative Clients: Ecolab, Inc.; Manpower, Inc.; Abbott Laboratories; Norwest Bank Wisconsin, N.A.; Firstar Bank Corporation; Sysco Food Services; Johnson Controls, Inc.; Worth Inc.; Rayovac, Inc.; York International Corporation.

For full biographical listings, see the Martindale-Hubbell Law Directory

Quarles & Brady LLP (AV)

411 East Wisconsin Avenue, 53202-4497
Telephone: 414-277-5000
Fax: 414-271-3552
URL: http://www.quarles.com
Madison, Wisconsin Office: Firstar Plaza, One South Pinckney Street, P.O. Box 2113, 53701-2113.
Telephone: 608-251-5000.
Fax: 608-251-9166.
West Palm Beach, Florida Office: 222 Lakeview Avenue, 4th Floor, 33401.
Telephone: 561-653-5000.
Fax: 561-653-5333.
Naples, Florida Office: Barnett Center, 4501 Tamiami Trail North, Suite 300, 34103-3060.
Telephone: 941-262-5959.
Fax: 941-434-4999.
Phoenix, Arizona Office: One Camelback Building, One East Camelback Road, Suite 400, 85012-1649.
Telephone: 602-230-5500.
Fax: 602-230-5598.
Chicago, Illinois Office: Quarles & Brady LLC, Citicorp Center, 500 West Madison Street, Suite 3700.
Telephone: 312-715-5000.
Fax: 312-715-5155.

MEMBERS OF FIRM
(ALPHABETICALLY BY YEAR OF ADMISSION TO BAR)

David E. Jarvis
John A. Casey
Ned R. Nashban (Resident, West Palm Beach, Florida Office)
James J. Gatziolis (Resident, Chicago, Illinois Office)
Andrew M. Barnes
Roy L. Prange, Jr. (Resident, Madison Office)
Thomas J. Magill (Resident, Chicago, Illinois Office)
Alexander Terras (Resident, Chicago, Illinois Office)
James L. Adashek
Ann M. Murphy
Elizabeth A. Orelup
Gerald L. Shelley (Resident, Phoenix, Arizona Office)
Benjamin R. Norris (Resident, Phoenix, Arizona Office)
Nancy Berz Colman (Resident, West Palm Beach, Florida Office)
Timothy S. Harris (Resident, Chicago, Illinois Office)

ASSOCIATES

Patrick J. Schoen
Susan A. Cerbins
David B. Altman (Resident, Chicago, Illinois Office)
Valerie L. Bailey-Rihn (Resident, Madison Office)
Maureen Henry (Resident, Phoenix, Arizona Office)

For Complete List of Firm Personnel, See General Section

For full biographical listings, see the Martindale-Hubbell Law Directory

WYOMING

*CASPER,** Natrona Co.

BROWN, DREW & MASSEY, LLP (AV)

Casper Business Center, Suite 800, 123 West First Street, 82601-2486
Telephone: 307-234-1000
800-877-6755
Telefax: 307-265-8025
Email: brwndrew@coffey.com

MEMBERS OF FIRM

Donn J. McCall
Courtney Robert Kepler

ASSOCIATE

Timothy M. Stubson

Attorneys for: Norwest Bank Wyoming, N.A.; Norwest Mortgage, Inc.; Wells Fargo Bank, N.A.; The CIT Group/Equipment Financing.

For Complete List of Firm Personnel, See General Section

For full biographical listings, see the Martindale-Hubbell Law Directory

PUERTO RICO

SAN JUAN, San Juan Dist.

FIDDLER GONZÁLEZ & RODRÍGUEZ, LLP

254 Muñoz Rivera Avenue (Hato Rey), P.O. Box 363507, 00936-3507
Telephone: 787-753-3113
Telecopier: 787-759-3123
Email: fiddler@fgrlaw.com *URL:* http://www.fgrlaw.com

MEMBERS OF FIRM

Leopoldo J. Cabassa-Sauri
Teodoro Peña-García

Representative Clients: The Chase Manhattan Bank, N.A.; The Equitable Life Assurance Society of the U.S.; Pfizer, Inc.; Merck & Co., Inc.; American Cyanamid Co.; Bacardi Corp.; General Motor Acceptance Corp.; The Bank & Trust of Puerto Rico; Seaboard Surety Co.; Plaza Las Americas, Inc.

For Complete List of Firm Personnel, See General Section

For full biographical listings, see the Martindale-Hubbell Law Directory

INDIANO, WILLIAMS & WEINSTEIN-BACAL

Hato Rey Tower, 21st Floor, 268 Muñoz Rivera Avenue (Hato Rey), 00918
Telephone: 787-754-2323; 763-0485
Fax: 787-766-3366
Email: iww@microjuris.com

MEMBERS OF FIRM

Stuart A. Weinstein-Bacal
David C. Indiano
Jeffrey M. Williams

ASSOCIATES

Peter W. Miller
Edgar A. Lee-Navas
Edward W. Hill Tollinche
Alexander H. Bopp (Not admitted in PR)

For full biographical listings, see the Martindale-Hubbell Law Directory

MARTÍNEZ ODELL & CALABRIA

Banco Popular Center, 209 Muñoz Rivera Avenue, Suite 1600 (Hato Rey), P.O. Box 190998, 00919-0998
Telephone: 787-753-8914
Facsimile: 787-753-8402; 787-759-9075; 787-764-5664
Email: postmaster@mocpr.com

MEMBERS OF FIRM

Luis E. Lopez Correa
Patrick D. O'Neill
Jose David Medina-Rivera

ASSOCIATE

Charles P. Gilmore

Representative Clients: Banco Popular de Puerto Rico; Daewoo Motor Corporation; Eckerd Corporation; Empresas Fonalledas; Hilton International; L'Aire Liquide, S.A.; Loctile Corporation; Lucent Technologies; Lutron Electronics Co., Inc.; Waste Management, Inc.

For Complete List of Firm Personnel, See General Section

For full biographical listings, see the Martindale-Hubbell Law Directory

VIRGIN ISLANDS

*CHARLOTTE AMALIE, ST. THOMAS,** St. Thomas

CAMPBELL, ARELLANO & RICH

No. 4 A & B Kongens Gade, P.O. Box 11899, 00801
Telephone: 340-774-4858
Telecopier: 340-776-8442
Email: carvilaw@viaccess.net *URL:* http://www.lawyers.com/lisvilaw
Cruz Bay, St. John, Virgin Islands Office: Scandic Executive Offices, Mongoose Junction, 00831.
Telephone: 304-693-8655.
Telecopier: 304-776-8442.

MEMBERS OF FIRM

Joseph Bruce Wm. Arellano
Carol Ann Rich

ASSOCIATE

W. Mark Hillsman

OF COUNSEL

Roger L. Campbell

Representative Clients: Citibank, N.A.; Cigna Property and Casualty Companies; Royal Insurance.

For full biographical listings, see the Martindale-Hubbell Law Directory

CANADA ALBERTA

*CALGARY,** Calgary Jud. Dist.

PARLEE MCLAWS (AV)

3400 Petro-Canada Centre, 150 - 6th Avenue, SW, T2P 3Y7
Telephone: 403-294-7000
Telecopier: 403-265-8263
Email: lawyers@parlee.com *URL:* http://www.parlee.com
Edmonton, Alberta Office: 15th Floor Manulife Place, 10180 101st Street.
Telephone: 403-423-8500.
Telecopier: 403-423-2870.

MEMBERS OF FIRM

Gregory D. M. Stirling
G. Scott Watson

ASSOCIATE

Elaine A. Thompson

For Complete List of Firm Personnel, See General Section

For full biographical listings, see the Martindale-Hubbell Law Directory

*EDMONTON,** Edmonton Jud. Dist.

PARLEE MCLAWS (AV)

15th Floor Manulife Place, 10180 101st Street, T5J 4K1
Telephone: 403-423-8500
Telecopier: 403-423-2870
Email: lawyers@parlee.com *URL:* http://www.parlee.com
Calgary, Alberta Office: 3400 Petro-Canada Centre, 150 - 6th Avenue, SW.
Telephone: 403-294-7000.
Telecopier: 403-265-8263.

MEMBER OF FIRM

Jeremy H. H. Hockin

ASSOCIATE

Bryan Maruyama

For Complete List of Firm Personnel, See General Section

For full biographical listings, see the Martindale-Hubbell Law Directory

CANADA NEW BRUNSWICK

*FREDERICTON,** York Co.

COX HANSON O'REILLY MATHESON (AV)

(Formerly Hanson Hashey)
Suite 400, Phoenix Square, P.O. Box 310, E3B 4Y9
Telephone: 506-453-7771
Fax: 506-453-9600
Email: fredericton@coxhanson.ca *URL:* http://www.coxhanson.ca
Halifax, Nova Scotia Office: Suite 1100, Purdy's Wharf Tower 1, P.O. Box 2380 Station Central RPO, B3J 3E5.
Telephone: 902-421-6262.
Fax: 902-421-3130. E-Mail: halifax@coxhanson.ca

(See Next Column)

COX HANSON O'REILLY MATHESON—*Continued*

Saint John, New Brunswick Office: 1212-One Brunswick Square, 1 Germain St. E2L 4V1.
Telephone: 506-652-7771.
Fax: 506-632-9600.
St. John's, Newfoundland Office: Scotia Centre, 401-235 Water Street, A1C 1B6.
Telephone: 709-726-3321.
Fax: 709-726-2992. E-Mail: stjohns@coxhanson.ca
Charlottetown, Prince Edward Island Office: Queen Square, Suite 202, 119 Queen Street, P.O. Box 875, Station Central, C1A 7L9.
Telephone: 902-894-7051.
Fax: 902-368-3762. E-Mail: charlottetown@coxhanson.ca

MEMBERS OF FIRM

H. A. Hanson, Q.C. (1909-1985)
John D. Larlee, Q.C.
David T. Hashey, Q.C.
Bruce D. Hatfield, Q.C.
David M. Norman, Q.C.
Julian A. G. Dickson, Q.C.
J. Ian M. Whitcomb, Q.C.
Anne D. Wooder
John M. Hanson, Q.C.
Terrence J. Morrison
Walter D. Vail, Q.C.
Lucie Richard
Michael E. Bowlin
Catherine M. Bowlen
J. Marc Richard

ASSOCIATES

Amanda J. Frenette
Christopher R. DeLong
Monika M. L. Zauhar
Deborah M. Power
Jade A. Spalding
Corinne A. Godbout
William E. Gould
Marc-Antoine Chiasson

For full biographical listings, see the Martindale-Hubbell Law Directory

MCINNES COOPER (AV)

Suite 600, 570 Queen Street, P.O. Box 610, E3B 5A6
Telephone: 506-458-8572
Fax: 506-458-9903
Email: mcrfton@mcrlaw.com *URL:* http://www.mcrlaw.com
Halifax, Nova Scotia Office: Summit Place, 1601 Lower Water Street, P.O. Box 730, B3J 2V1.
Telephone: 902-425-6500.
Fax: 902-425-6350. Email: mcrhfx@mcrlaw.com.
St. John's, Newfoundland Office: Baine Johnston Centre, 5th Floor, 10 Fort William Place, P.O. Box 5939, A1C 5X4.
Telephone: 709-722-8735.
Telecopier: 709-722-1763. Email: mcrsj@mcrlaw.com.
Moncton, New Brunswick Office: Place Moncton Place, 655 Main Street, P.O. Box 1368, E1C 8T6.
Telephone: 506-857-8970.
Fax: 506-857-4095. Email: mcrmctn@mcrlaw.com.
Charlottetown, Prince Edward Island Office: BDC Place, Suite 620, 119 Kent Street, C1A 1N3.
Telephone: 902-368-8473.
Fax: 902-368-8346. Email: mcrpei@mcrlaw.com.

PARTNER

David Duncan Young

For Complete List of Firm Personnel, See General Section

For full biographical listings, see the Martindale-Hubbell Law Directory

*MONCTON,** Westmorland Co.

MCINNES COOPER (AV)

Barristers, Solicitors & Trade Mark Agents
Place Moncton Place, 655 Main Street, P.O. Box 1368, E1C 8T6
Telephone: 506-857-8970
Fax: 506-857-4095
Email: mcrmctn@mcrlaw.com *URL:* http://www.mcrlaw.com
Halifax, Nova Scotia Office: Summit Place, 1601 Lower Water Street, P.O. Box 730, B3J 2V1.
Telephone: 902-425-6500.
Fax: 902-425-6350. Email: mcrhfx@mcrlaw.com.
St. John's, Newfoundland Office: Baine Johnston Centre, 5th Floor, 10 Fort William Place, P.O. Box 5939, A1C 5X4.
Telephone: 709-722-8735.
Telecopier: 709-722-1763. Email: mcrsj@mcrlaw.com.
Charlottetown, Prince Edward Island Office: BDC Place, Suite 620, 119 Kent Street, C1A 1N3.
Telephone: 902-368-8473.
Fax: 902-368-8346. Email: mcrpei@mcrlaw.com.
Fredericton, New Brunswick Office: Suite 600, 570 Queen Street, P.O. Box 610.
Telephone: 506-458-8572.
Fax: 506-458-9903. Email: mcrfton@mcrlaw.com.

PARTNER

Bernard F. Miller

ASSOCIATES

Christopher A. Borden
Sylvie C. Roussel

For Complete List of Firm Personnel, See General Section

For full biographical listings, see the Martindale-Hubbell Law Directory

*SAINT JOHN,** Saint John Co.

CLARK DRUMMIE (AV)

40 Wellington Row, P.O. Box 6850, E2L 4S3
Telephone: 506-633-3800
Telecopier (Automatic): 506-633-3811
Email: cd@nbnet.nb.ca

MEMBERS OF FIRM

Thomas B. Drummie, Q.C.
Willard M. Jenkins

Reference: Royal Bank of Canada.

For Complete List of Firm Personnel, See General Section

For full biographical listings, see the Martindale-Hubbell Law Directory

CANADA NEWFOUNDLAND

*ST. JOHN'S,**

MCINNES COOPER (AV)

Barristers, Solicitors & Trade Mark Agents
Baine Johnston Centre, 5th Floor, 10 Fort William Place, P.O. Box 5939, A1C 5X4
Telephone: 709-722-8735
Telecopier: 709-722-1763
Email: mcrsj@mcrlaw.com *URL:* http://www.mcrlaw.com
Halifax, Nova Scotia Office: Summit Place, 1601 Lower Water Street, P.O. Box 730, B3J 2V1.
Telephone: 902-425-6500.
Fax: 902-425-6350. Email: mcrhfx@mcrlaw.com.
Moncton, New Brunswick Office: Place Moncton Place, 655 Main Street, P.O. Box 1368, E1C 8T6.
Telephone: 506-857-8970.
Fax: 506-857-4095. Email: mcrmctn@mcrlaw.com.
Charlottetown, Prince Edward Island Office: BDC Place, Suite 620, 119 Kent Street, C1A 1N3.
Telephone: 902-368-8473.
Fax: 902-368-8346. Email: mcrpei@mcrlaw.com.
Fredericton, New Brunswick Office: Suite 600, 570 Queen Street, P.O. Box 610.
Telephone: 506-458-8572.
Fax: 506-458-9903. Email: mcrfton@mcrlaw.com.

PARTNERS

Thomas R. Kendell
Deborah L. J. Hutchings

For Complete List of Firm Personnel, See General Section

For full biographical listings, see the Martindale-Hubbell Law Directory

CANADA NOVA SCOTIA

*HALIFAX,** Regional Munic. of Halifax

MCINNES COOPER (AV)

Barristers, Solicitors & Trade Mark Agents
Summit Place, 1601 Lower Water Street, P.O. Box 730, B3J 2V1
Telephone: 902-425-6500
Fax: 902-425-6350
Email: mcrhfx@mcrlaw.com *URL:* http://www.mcrlaw.com
St. John's, Newfoundland Office: Baine Johnston Centre, 5th Floor, 10 Fort William Place, P.O. Box 5939, A1C 5X4.
Telephone: 709-722-8735.
Telecopier: 709-722-1763. Email: mcrsj@mcrlaw.com.
Moncton, New Brunswick Office: Place Moncton Place, 655 Main Street, P.O. Box 1368, E1C 8T6.
Telephone: 506-857-8970.
Fax: 506-857-4095. Email: mcrmctn@mcrlaw.com.
Charlottetown, Prince Edward Island Office: BDC Place, Suite 620, 119 Kent Street, C1A 1N3.
Telephone: 902-368-8473.
Fax: 902-368-8346. Email: mcrpei@mcrlaw.com.
Fredericton, New Brunswick Office: Suite 600, 570 Queen Street, P.O. Box 610.
Telephone: 506-458-8572.
Fax: 506-458-9903. Email: mcrfton@mcrlaw.com.

PARTNERS

David H. Reardon, Q.C.
Lawrence A. Freeman
John D. Stringer, Q.C.

(See Next Column)

McINNES COOPER, *Halifax—Continued*

ASSOCIATE

Frank E. Hughes

For Complete List of Firm Personnel, See General Section

For full biographical listings, see the Martindale-Hubbell Law Directory

CANADA ONTARIO

*TORONTO,** Regional Munic. of Toronto

BORDEN & ELLIOT (AV)

Barristers & Solicitors
Scotia Plaza, 40 King Street West, M5H 3Y4
Telephone: 416-367-6000
Telecopier: 416-367-6749
Email: info@borden.com *URL:* http://www.borden.com
Ottawa, Ontario Office: Borden Elliot Scott & Aylen, 1000-60 Rue Queen Street.
Telephone: 613-237-5160; 800-661-4237. General
Facsimile: 613-230-8842. IP Dept.
Facsimile: 613-787-3558. Email: ottinfo@scottaylen.com. URL: http://www.borden.com.

Neil C. Saxe

For Complete List of Firm Personnel, See General Section

For full biographical listings, see the Martindale-Hubbell Law Directory

CANADA PRINCE EDWARD ISLAND

*CHARLOTTETOWN,** Queen's Co.

McINNES COOPER (AV(T))

Barristers, Solicitors & Trade Mark Agents
BDC Place, Suite 620, 119 Kent Street, C1A 1N3
Telephone: 902-368-8473
Fax: 902-368-8346
Email: mcrpei@mcrlaw.com *URL:* http://www.mcrlaw.com
Halifax, Nova Scotia Office: Summit Place, 1601 Lower Water Street, P.O. Box 730, B3J 2V1.
Telephone: 902-425-6500.
Fax: 902-425-6350. Email: mcrhfx@mcrlaw.com.
St. John's, Newfoundland Office: Baine Johnston Centre, 5th Floor, 10 Fort William Place, P.O. Box 5939, A1C 5X4.
Telephone: 709-722-8735.
Telecopier: 709-722-1763. Email: mcrsj@mcrlaw.com.
Moncton, New Brunswick Office: Place Moncton Place, 655 Main Street, P.O. Box 1368, E1C 8T6.
Telephone: 506-857-8970.
Fax: 506-857-4095. Email: mcrmctn@mcrlaw.com.
Fredericton, New Brunswick Office: Suite 600, 570 Queen Street, P.O. Box 610.
Telephone: 506-458-8572.
Fax: 506-458-9903. Email: mcrfton@mcrlaw.com.

PARTNER

Michele M. Murphy

For Complete List of Firm Personnel, See General Section

For full biographical listings, see the Martindale-Hubbell Law Directory

CANADA QUEBEC

*MONTREAL,** Montreal Dist.

GOLDSTEIN, FLANZ & FISHMAN (AV)

Suite 4100, 1250 René-Lévesque Boulevard West, H3B 4W8
Telephone: 514-932-4100
Cable Address: "Meybat"
Telex: 05-24593
Telecopier: 514-932-4170
Email: counsel@gff.qc.ca

(See Next Column)

MEMBERS OF FIRM

Yoine Goldstein
Leonard W. Flanz
Avram Fishman
Mark Schrager
Gilles Paquin
Mark E. Meland
Ellen Amdursky
Alain Daigle
Cathy Noseworthy
Suzanne Villeneuve

For full biographical listings, see the Martindale-Hubbell Law Directory

McMASTER GERVAIS (AV)

A General Partnership
1000 de La Gauchetière Street West, Suite 900, H3B 5H4
Telephone: 514-879-1212
Fax: 514-954-1905
Email: info@mcmastergervais.com *URL:* http://www.mcmastergervais.com

MEMBERS OF FIRM

Alexis P. Bergeron
Roger P. Simard
Jacques S. Darche
Virgile A. Buffoni
François Rioux
Gary Rivard
Antoine Leduc

For Complete List of Firm Personnel, See General Section

For full biographical listings, see the Martindale-Hubbell Law Directory

MENDELSOHN ROSENTZVEIG SHACTER (AV)

1000 Sherbrooke Street West, 27th Floor, H3A 3G4
Telephone: 514-987-5000
Telex: 05-27284 Colorlaw
Telecopier: 514-987-1213
Email: mrs@mrslaw.com *URL:* http://www.mrslaw.com

PARTNERS

S. Leon Mendelsohn, Q.C. (1902-1996)
Leo Rosentzveig, Q.C.
Manuel Shacter, Q.C.
Jack C. Shayne
William Levitt
Arthur A. Garvis
Edward E. Aronoff
L. Michael Blumenstein
Max Mendelsohn
Earl S. Cohen
Michael Garonce
Donald M. Devine
Richard S. Uditsky
Joel Weitzman
Ian R. Rudnikoff
Marc I. Leiter
L. B. Erdle
Fredric L. Carsley
Frank Zylberberg
Jules Brossard
David L. Rosentzveig
Judie K. Jokinen
Gilles Seguin
Martin Desrosiers
Andrew Etcovitch
Alain Breault
Jean Carrière
Henri M. Bybelezer
Louis Frédérick Côté
Sandra Abitan

ASSOCIATES

Carl M. Ravinsky
Catherine Muraz
Francine Wiseman
Joelle Sebag
Maria R. Battaglia
Keyvan Nassiry
Linda Schachter
Emmanuelle Saucier
Arnold Cohen
Aaron Makovka
Michel Rochefort
Céline Tessier
Sophie Crevier
Annick Joyal
Francis Desmarais
Nicolas J. Beugnot
Jean-François Brière
Marc-Antoine Deschamps
Philipp F. Duffy
Fred Purkey
Martin Sills
David Tardif-Latourelle

For full biographical listings, see the Martindale-Hubbell Law Directory

POULIOT, MERCURE (AV)

CIBC Tower, 31st Floor, 1155 René-Lévesque Boulevard, West, H3B 3S6
Telephone: 514-875-5210
Telecopier: 514-875-4308
Email: POUMER@CEDEP.COM
Genève, Suisse Office: 8, Rue de la Rôtisserie, 1204 Geneva, Switzerland.
Telephone: +41 22-28 79 40.
Telecopier: +41 22-21 23 67.

MEMBERS OF FIRM

Georges A. Pouliot, Q.C.
Gilles Brunelle
Luc Gratton
Brian Riordan
Pierre Paquet
Anne-Marie Gauthier
Yvon Brizard
Robert Tessier
Daniel Gagné
Lilia Pouliot
Marco Veilleux
Alain Nadon
Jean H. Gagnon
Richard Fontaine
Normand Royal
Gilles Bertrand
Jean Larivière
Louis-Michel Tremblay
David I. Johnston
Stéphane Hébert
Jacques LeBel, Q.C.
Joel A. Silcoff
Ronald M. Auclair
Philippe Roy
Maxime B. Rhéaume
Serge Desrochers
C. Keenan LaPierre
Alain Bond
Louis Coallier
Nicole Chouinard
Stéphane Teasdale

(See Next Column)

POULIOT, MERCURE—*Continued*

ASSOCIATES

Micheline Perrault
Caroline Lemoine
Béatrice Arronis
Yvan Nantel
Sylvie Boulanger
Vincent Frenette
Robert Cardin
Alexandre Henri
Brent J. Muir
Louise Tremblay
Chantal Joubert
Normand D'Amour
Pascale Cloutier
Eric Couture
Frédéric Chatel
Mary-Lynn Breton
Alexandre Ajami

For full biographical listings, see the Martindale-Hubbell Law Directory

CANADA
SASKATCHEWAN

*REGINA,** Regina Jud. Centre

MACPHERSON LESLIE & TYERMAN (AV)

1500-1874 Scarth Street, S4P 4E9
Telephone: 306-347-8000
Telecopier: 306-352-5250
Email: mltreg@mlt.com
Saskatoon, Saskatchewan Office: 1500-410 22nd Street East, S7K 5T6.
Telephone: 306-975-7100.
Telecopier: 306-975-7145.

MEMBERS OF FIRM

R. Neil MacKay (Resident, Saskatoon Office)
Conrad D. Hadubiak
Leonard D. Andrychuk
Jeffrey M. Lee (Resident, Saskatoon Office)

ASSOCIATES

Wendy Y. Martin White
Deron A. Kuski

For Complete List of Firm Personnel, See General Section

For full biographical listings, see the Martindale-Hubbell Law Directory

BUSINESS LAW

MINNESOTA

*MINNEAPOLIS,** Hennepin Co.

ABDO AND ABDO, P.A. (AV)

710 Northstar West 625 Marquette Avenue, 55402
Telephone: 612-333-1526
Fax: 612-342-2608
Email: abdoabdo@aol.com *URL:* http://www.abdo.com.br

E. John Abdo (1912-1993)
Robert P. Abdo
Steven R. Hedges
Keith J. Broady
Kenneth J. Abdo
Daniel M. Satorius
Timothy C. Matson

Representative Client: ADT Security Services, Inc.; Periscope Inc. (Advertising Agency); Bison Instruments, Inc.; Access Cash International, Inc.

For full biographical listings, see the Martindale-Hubbell Law Directory

ARNOLD, ANDERSON & DOVE, P.L.L.P. (AV)

5881 Cedar Lake Road, 55416-1492
Telephone: 612-545-9000
Wats Line: 800-343-4545
Fax: 612-545-1793; 612-542-9210
Email: aad@aadlaw.com
Princeton, Minnesota Office: 501 South Fourth Street.
Telephone: 612-389-2214.
Hutchinson, Minnesota Office: 101 Park Place.
Telephone: 320-587-7575.
Red Wing, Minnesota Office: 481 Fridell Crescent, 55066.
Telephone: 651-388-3454.

MEMBERS OF FIRM

David B. Arnold
Steven A. Anderson
Paul D. Dove

For Complete List of Firm Personnel, See General Section

For full biographical listings, see the Martindale-Hubbell Law Directory

HOLPER, WELSH & MITCHELL, LTD. (AV)

10 South Fifth Street, Suite 300, 55402
Telephone: 612-317-1012
Fax: 612-317-0947
Email: rholper@aol.com *URL:*
http://www.lawyers.com/holperwelsh&mitchell
Phoenix, Arizona Office: 2415 East Camelback Road, Suite 700, 85016.
Telephone: 602-508-6033.
Fax: 480-483-0269.

Richard D. Holper
Mary Ann Welsh
Ralph V. Mitchell, Jr.

For full biographical listings, see the Martindale-Hubbell Law Directory

LOMMEN, NELSON, COLE & STAGEBERG, P.A. (AV)

1800 IDS Center, 80 South 8th Street, 55402
Telephone: 612-339-8131
Fax: 612-339-8064
Email: postmaster@email.lommen.com *URL:* http://www.lommen.com
Hudson, Wisconsin Office: Grandview Professional Building, 400 South Second Street, Suite 210.
Telephones: 715-386-8217 and 612-436-8085.

W. Wyman Smith (1914-1994)
Henry H. Feikema (1926-1996)
V. Owen Nelson (1928-1998)
John P. Lommen (1927-1988)
Michael P. Shroyer (1953-1993)
Leonard T. Juster
Alvin S. Malmon
Ronald L. Haskvitz
Phillip A. Cole
Roger V. Stageberg
Glenn R. Kessel
Thomas R. Jacobson (Resident, Hudson, Wisconsin Office)
John M. Giblin
John R. McBride
J. Christopher Cuneo
Thomas F. Dougherty
Stacey A. DeKalb
Kay N. Hunt
Richard L. Plagens
Ehrich L. Koch
Margie R. Bodas
James M. Lockhart
Stephen C. Rathke
James C. Searls
Paul L. Dinger
Sherri D. Ulland
Reid R. Lindquist
James R. Johnson (Resident, Hudson, Wisconsin Office)
Marc A. Johannsen
Barry A. O'Neil

Scott M. Nelson
Scott N. Ross
Mary I. King
David M. Hudson
Sheila A. Bjorklund
David S. Ezrilov
Susan Hayes Stephan
Geraint D. Powell
Brent R. Johnson (Resident, Hudson, Wisconsin Office)
Laura L. Enga
Christopher R. Grote

(See Next Column)

OF COUNSEL

Thomas F. Miller

Representative Clients: ABRA Auto Body & Glass, Inc.; Associated Bureau; United Rentals, Inc.

For full biographical listings, see the Martindale-Hubbell Law Directory

MARTIN & ASSOCIATES, P.A. (AV)

1650 West 82nd Street, Suite 1460, 55431
Telephone: 612-885-5665
Fax: 612-885-5664
Email: mail@martinandassociates.com

Judith Martin Ventres

Michael J. Zitta
Richard William Van Sickle

For full biographical listings, see the Martindale-Hubbell Law Directory

ZAMANSKY PROFESSIONAL ASSOCIATION (AV)

3901 IDS Tower, 55402
Telephone: 612-340-9720
Fax: 612-340-9662
Email: ZPA4924@aol.com
St. Paul, Minnesota Office: 6 West 5th Street.
Telephone: 612-297-6400.

Ronald A. Zamansky

Matthew B. Cohen

OF COUNSEL

Stephen B. Solomon

Reference: Norwest Bank Minneapolis, N.A.

For full biographical listings, see the Martindale-Hubbell Law Directory

*ST. CLOUD,** Stearns Co.

HUGHES, MATHEWS & DIDIER, P.A. (AV)

110 Sixth Avenue South, Suite 205, P.O. Box 548, 56302-0548
Telephone: 320-251-4399
Fax: 320-251-5781

Kevin J. Hughes
Thomas E. Mathews

Kevin M. O'Driscoll

Representative Clients: The St. Cloud Hospital; CentraCare Health System; St. John's University; College of St. Benedict; Tanner Systems, Inc.; Anderson Trucking Service, Inc.; Wisconsin Fulfillment, Inc.

For full biographical listings, see the Martindale-Hubbell Law Directory

MISSISSIPPI

BILOXI, Harrison Co.

CORBAN & GUNN (AV)

770 Water Street, P.O. Drawer 1916, 39533-1916
Telephone: 228-432-7826
Telecopier: 228-435-5702

MEMBERS OF FIRM

Lawrence C. Corban, Jr.
Clyde H. Gunn, III

Representative Clients: Dees Chevrolet Co.; First Federal Savings & Loan Association of Pascagoula-Moss Point; Frank P. Corso & Co., Inc.; Munro Petroleum & Terminal Corp.; Ship Services Corp.

For full biographical listings, see the Martindale-Hubbell Law Directory

RUSHING & GUICE (AV)

683 Water Street, P.O. Box 1925, 39533-1925
Telephone: 228-374-2313
Telecopier: 228-374-8155
Email: rushguice@rushing-guice.com *URL:* http://www.rushing-guice.com

MEMBERS OF FIRM

Charles L. Rushing (1881-1923)
William L. Guice (1887-1971)
William Lee Guice III

OF COUNSEL

Jacob D. Guice

ASSOCIATES

R. Scott Wells
Maria M. Cobb

(See Next Column)

RUSHING & GUICE, *Biloxi—Continued*

LEGAL SUPPORT PERSONNEL

Antonia Strong

Representative Clients: American Isuzu Motors, Inc.; Butch Oustalet, Inc.; Great Southern Development Co.; Gulf Coast Industries; Gulf Coast Land Co., L.L.C.; Gulf Pride Enterprises, Inc.; R.A. Lesso Seafood; Weems Brothers Seafood; Ocean Springs Lumber, LLC.

For full biographical listings, see the Martindale-Hubbell Law Directory

*GULFPORT,** Harrison Co.

ALLEN, VAUGHN, COBB & HOOD, P.A. (AV)

One Hancock Plaza, Suite 1209, P.O. Drawer 4108, 39502-4108
Telephone: 601-864-4011
Fax: 601-864-4852
Email: avchlaw@sunherald.infinet.com

Harry R. Allen
Thomas E. Vaughn
David L. Cobb
Billy W. Hood
Joy Lambert Phillips
Robert W. Atkinson
Benjamin U. Bowden
Richard B. Tubertini
Rodney Douglas Robinson
E. Colette Towles
David W. Crane
John A. Foxworth, Jr.

J. Adrian Smith
Michael J. Casano

OF COUNSEL

D. Knox White

LEGAL SUPPORT PERSONNEL

Kevin C. Stachowski (Paralegal)

For full biographical listings, see the Martindale-Hubbell Law Directory

DUKES, DUKES, KEATING AND FANECA, P.A. (AV)

2909 13th Street, 6th Floor, P.O. Drawer W, 39501
Telephone: 228-868-1111
Fax: 228-863-2886
Email: ddkf@ddkf.com

Hugh D. Keating
Cy Faneca

William W. Abbott, Jr.

For Complete List of Firm Personnel, See General Section

For full biographical listings, see the Martindale-Hubbell Law Directory

BOYCE HOLLEMAN A PROFESSIONAL CORPORATION (AV)

1913 15th Street, P.O. Drawer 1030, 39502
Telephone: 228-863-3142; 1-800-863-3140
Telecopier: 228-863-9829
Email: boyce1913@aol.com

Boyce Holleman

Timothy C. Holleman
Leslie Dean Holleman
David J. "Jeff" White

References: Hancock Bank, Gulfport; Merchants Bank & Trust Co., Gulfport; Bank of Wiggins, Wiggins, Mississippi.

For full biographical listings, see the Martindale-Hubbell Law Directory

MEADOWS RILEY LAW FIRM (AV)

1720 23rd Avenue, P.O. Box 550, 39502
Telephone: 601-864-4511
Telecopier: 601-868-2178

Joseph R. Meadows
Donnie D. Riley
Jerry D. Riley
Karen J. Young

Representative Clients: Bubba Oustalat Lincoln Mercury, Inc.; Lee Tractor Co. of Mississippi.
Reference: Hancock Bank.

For full biographical listings, see the Martindale-Hubbell Law Directory

NEWTON AND HOFF, L.L.P. (AV)

2019 23rd Avenue, P.O. Box 910, 39502-0910
Telephone: 228-863-8827
Fax: 228-868-6007
Email: newtonhoff@aol.com *URL:* http://www.newtonhoff.com

Paul M. Newton (Resident)
Frederick T. Hoff, Jr. (Resident)
Paul M. Newton, Jr. (Resident)

For full biographical listings, see the Martindale-Hubbell Law Directory

*JACKSON,** Hinds Co.

RHODEN, LACY, DOWNEY & COLBERT (AV)

111 Park Circle Drive, P.O. Box 13762, 39236
Telephone: 601-932-1155
Telecopier: 601-936-2515
Email: rldclaw@netdoor.com *URL:* http://www.Thrhoden-law.com

MEMBERS OF FIRM

Thomas H. Rhoden
William L. Colbert, Jr.

For full biographical listings, see the Martindale-Hubbell Law Directory

MADISON, Madison Co.

BELL & ASSOCIATES, P.A. (AV)

967 Madison Avenue, 39110
Telephone: 601-898-1111
Toll Free: 1-888-898-1600
Fax: 601-898-1102
Mailing Address: P.O. Box 890, Madison, Mississippi, 39130-0890
Email: JamesDBell@aol.com *URL:* http://www.lawyers.com/bell&associates

James D. Bell

Eduardo Alberto Flechas

For full biographical listings, see the Martindale-Hubbell Law Directory

*PASCAGOULA,** Jackson Co.

BRYAN, NELSON, SCHROEDER, CASTIGLIOLA & BANAHAN (AV)

1103 Jackson Avenue, P.O. Drawer 1529, 39568-1529
Telephone: 228-762-6631
Fax: 228-769-6392
Email: bns@datasync.com

MEMBERS OF FIRM

E. S. Ned Nelson (1928-1985)
John F. Bryan, III (1915-1994)
Ernest R. Schroeder
Vincent J. Castigliola, Jr.
John A. Banahan
H. Benjamin Mullen

ASSOCIATES

Melinda O. Johnson
Scott Corlew

For full biographical listings, see the Martindale-Hubbell Law Directory

COLINGO, WILLIAMS, HEIDELBERG, STEINBERGER & McELHANEY, P.A. (AV)

711 Delmas Avenue, P.O. Box 1407, 39568-1407
Telephone: 228-762-8021
FAX: 228-762-7589
Email: info@colingowilliams.com *URL:* http://www.ColingoWilliams.com

John M. Kinard

Representative Clients: International Paper Co.; R.J. Reynolds; CBS Corp.; Kemper Group; Singing River Hospital System; Mississippi Gulf Coast Regional Wastewater Authority; Medical Assurance Company of Mississippi; Mutual Assurance of Alabama; Dole Food Co.

For full biographical listings, see the Martindale-Hubbell Law Directory

MISSOURI

*INDEPENDENCE,** Jackson Co.

WHITE, ALLINDER & GRAHAM, L.L.C. (AV)

Hidden Creek Office Park, 14801 East 42nd Street, 64055
Telephone: 816-373-9080
Fax: 816-373-9319

MEMBERS OF FIRM

Steven W. White
John K. Allinder
Gene P. Graham, Jr.

ASSOCIATE

Mary Beth Clune

For full biographical listings, see the Martindale-Hubbell Law Directory

KANSAS CITY, Jackson, Clay, Platte & Cass Cos.

SWANSON MIDGLEY, LLC (AV)

Crown Center, 2420 Pershing Road, Suite 400, 64108
Telephone: 816-842-6100
Fax: 816-842-0013
Email: mail@swansonmidgley.com *URL:* http://www.swansonmidgley.com
Overland Park, Kansas Office: Commerce Plaza I, 7th Floor, 7300 W. 110th Street.
Telephone: 913-317-2717.
FAX: 913-317-1505.

Robert R. Bartunek
Henry R. Cox
Daniel V. Hiatt
John J. Kitchin
Don R. Lolli
James H. McLarney
Charles F. Zarter

Richard E. Gier

Counsel for: National Collegiate Athletic Assoc.; Pizza Hut; Veterans of Foreign Wars of the U.S.; Danka Business Systems; Physicians Reference Laboratory; National Compressed Steel; Equitable Life Assurance; Mr. Dell Foods, Inc.; Healthcare Medical Solutions, Inc.; Prudential Insurance Co. of America.

For Complete List of Firm Personnel, See General Section
For full biographical listings, see the Martindale-Hubbell Law Directory

LEE'S SUMMIT, Jackson Co.

CARL CHINNERY & ASSOCIATES, P.C. (AV)

200 S.E. Douglas Street, Suite 200, 64063-2375
Telephone: 816-525-2050

Carl L. Chinnery

Nancy E. Blackwell

OF COUNSEL

Elizabeth Unger Carlyle

LEGAL SUPPORT PERSONNEL

PARALEGALS

Jean Wehner Chinnery
Elaine K. Hanrahan
Alicia Hodges
Susan Breitenbach
Pam Kane
Virginia Galate
Alice Mistler

For full biographical listings, see the Martindale-Hubbell Law Directory

ST. LOUIS, (Independent City)

GREEN, SCHAAF & JACOBSON, P.C. (AV)

Suite 700 Pierre Laclede Center, 7733 Forsyth Boulevard (Clayton), 63105
Telephone: 314-862-6800
Telecopier: 314-862-1606
Email: info@stlouislaw.com *URL:* http://www.stlouislaw.com

George E. Schaaf (1930-1995)
Martin M. Green
Joe D. Jacobson
David T. Butsch

Jonathan F. Andres
Allen P. Press
Daniel S. Peters

OF COUNSEL

Howard L. Kanefield

For full biographical listings, see the Martindale-Hubbell Law Directory

JEROME R. MANDELSTAMM (AV)

Suite 1600, 1010 Market Street, 63101-2082
Telephone: 314-621-2261
Fax: 314-436-2303

For full biographical listings, see the Martindale-Hubbell Law Directory

McCARTHY, LEONARD, KAEMMERER, OWEN, LAMKIN & McGOVERN, L.C. (AV)

16141 Swingley Ridge Road (Chesterfield), Suite 300, 63017
Telephone: 636-532-7100
Telecopier: 636-532-0857
Email: info@mlklaw.com

Thomas W. McCarthy, III
Michael E. Kaemmerer
Andrew B. Leonard
James C. Owen
Walter R. Lamkin
Brian E. McGovern
Diana K. Wieland
James P. Towey, Jr.
Todd A. Massa
Paula M. Young
Robert W. Hoffman

(See Next Column)

E. Megan Kinsella
Elaine M. Moss
Katherine S. Walsh
Kevin T. McLaughlin
Tami Zeisler Morrissey
Robert A. Miller
Christopher C. O'Connell
James R. Walsh

For full biographical listings, see the Martindale-Hubbell Law Directory

OTTSEN, MAUZÉ, LEGGAT & BELZ, L.C. (AV)

The Midvale Building, 112 South Hanley Road, 63105-3418
Telephone: 314-726-2800
Telecopier: 314-863-3821

Lamar E. Ottsen
James F. Mauzé
Robert B. Leggat, Jr.
Timothy Belz
Thomas E. Pulliam

For full biographical listings, see the Martindale-Hubbell Law Directory

SCHRAMM & PINES, L.L.C. (AV)

Suite 950 The Bemiston Tower, 231 South Bemiston Avenue, 63105
Telephone: 314-721-5321
Telecopier: 314-721-0790

MEMBERS OF FIRM

Paul H. Schramm
M. Harvey Pines
Daniel R. Schramm

Timothy I. Nicholson
Dean A. Schramm

Reference: Magna Bank.

For full biographical listings, see the Martindale-Hubbell Law Directory

*SPRINGFIELD,** Greene Co.

GREENE & CURTIS, L.L.P. (AV)

1340 East Woodhurst Drive, 65804
Telephone: 417-883-7678
Fax: 417-883-4317
Email: GandClaw@AOL.com

MEMBERS OF FIRM

Joe C. Greene
Arthur E. Curtis
Brett A. Robinson

ASSOCIATES

Jeffery J. Love
Joseph Christopher Greene
Ben K. Upp
Charles R. Greene
Michelle Nahon Leonard

For full biographical listings, see the Martindale-Hubbell Law Directory

MONTANA

*BILLINGS,** Yellowstone Co.

CROWLEY, HAUGHEY, HANSON, TOOLE & DIETRICH, P.L.L.P. (AV)

500 Transwestern II, 490 North 31st Street, P.O. Box 2529, 59103
Telephone: 406-252-3441
Fax: 406-259-4159
Email: crowley@crowleylaw.com
Helena, Montana Office: IBM Building, 100 North Park Avenue, Suite 300, 59601.
Telephone: 406-449-4165.
Fax: 406-449-5149.
Kalispell, Montana Office: 431 1st Avenue West, 59901.
Telephone: 406-752-6644.
Fax: 406-752-5108.
Williston, North Dakota Office: 113 East Broadway, 58801.
Telephone: 701-572-2200.
Fax: 701-572-7072.

OF COUNSEL

John M. Dietrich
Gareld F. Krieg
Myles J. Thomas

MEMBERS OF FIRM

Arthur F. Lamey, Jr.
David L. Johnson
Terry B. Cosgrove (Resident, Helena, Montana Office)
Allan L. Karell
James P. Sites
Daniel N. McLean (Resident, Helena, Montana Office)
Robert G. Michelotti, Jr.
John R. Alexander
William D. Lamdin, III
Michael S. Dockery
Malcolm H. Goodrich
Mary Scrim Dyre (Resident, Kalispell, Montana Office)
Eric K. Anderson
Renee L. Coppock
John R. Lee (Resident, Williston, North Dakota Office)
Scott M. Heard

(See Next Column)

CROWLEY, HAUGHEY, HANSON, TOOLE & DIETRICH P.L.L.P., *Billings—Continued*

Representative Clients: General Motors Acceptance Corporation; Deaconess Medical Center of Billings; Billings Clinic; John Deere Co.; First Interstate Bank of Commerce; Aetna; Montana Livestock Ag Credit, Inc.; Turner Enterprises, Inc.

For Complete List of Firm Personnel, See General Section

For full biographical listings, see the Martindale-Hubbell Law Directory

MURPHY, KIRKPATRICK & FAIN, P.L.L.P. (AV)

Suite 300, Western Security Bank Building, 2929 Third Avenue North, 59101
Telephone: 406-256-9700
Fax: 406-256-9755
Email: mailbox@murphkirk.com *URL:* http://www.murphkirk.com

James P. Murphy
Stewart R. Kirkpatrick
Bruce F. Fain

LEGAL SUPPORT PERSONNEL

Michelle A. Kennedy (Paralegal)

For full biographical listings, see the Martindale-Hubbell Law Directory

*BOZEMAN,** Gallatin Co.

KIRWAN & BARRETT, P.C. (AV)

215 West Mendenhall, P.O. Box 1348, 59771-1348
Telephone: 406-586-1553
Fax: 406-586-8971

Peter M. Kirwan
Stephen M. Barrett

Representative Clients: Boyne USA, Inc.; Kenyon Noble Lumber Company.

For full biographical listings, see the Martindale-Hubbell Law Directory

*MISSOULA,** Missoula Co.

DATSOPOULOS, MACDONALD & LIND, P.C. (AV)

Central Square Building, 201 West Main Street, Suite 201, 59802
Telephone: 406-728-0810
FAX: 406-543-0134
Email: email@dmllaw.com

Milton Datsopoulos
Christopher B. Swartley
Ronald B. MacDonald
William K. VanCanagan
Dennis E. Lind
Rebecca L. Summerville
Darla J. Keck

Edward A. Murphy
Paul N. Tranel
Paul T. Ryan
Susan G. Ridgeway
David M. McLean

For full biographical listings, see the Martindale-Hubbell Law Directory

NEBRASKA

*OMAHA,** Douglas Co.

DWYER, SMITH, GARDNER, LAZER, POHREN, ROGERS & FORREST (AV)

Suite 400, 8712 West Dodge Road, 68114
Telephone: 402-392-0101
Telefax: 402-392-1011
Email: dwyerlaw@dwyer-smith.com *URL:* http://www.dwyer-smith.com

MEMBERS OF FIRM

Robert V. Dwyer, Jr.
John L. Apker
Clay M. Rogers
Christopher D. Curzon
Paul J. Gardner
Bruce J. Goracke

ASSOCIATE

Patrick Edward Griffin, Jr.

Representative Clients: Ford Motor Credit Company, Dearborn, Michigan; Nebraska Hospital Association subsidiary Bio Electronics, Lincoln, Oak Bancorporation; Lynn Roberts International; Elliot Equipment Co.; Design Plastics, Inc.

For Complete List of Firm Personnel, See General Section

For full biographical listings, see the Martindale-Hubbell Law Directory

NEVADA

*CARSON CITY,** (Independent City)

CROWELL, SUSICH, OWEN & TACKES, LTD. A PROFESSIONAL LAW CORPORATION (AV)

510 West Fourth Street, P.O. Box 1000, 89702
Telephone: 775-882-1311; 775-588-5448
Fax: 775-882-0257
Email: thefirm@advocacy.net

William J. Crowell, Jr.
J. Thomas Susich
Robert L. Crowell
Steven E. Tackes
Sandra-Mae Pickens

For full biographical listings, see the Martindale-Hubbell Law Directory

HALE LANE PEEK DENNISON HOWARD AND ANDERSON (AV)

777 East William Street, Suite 200, P.O. Box 2620, 89702
Telephone: 775-684-6000
Telefax: 775-684-6001
Email: info@halelane.com
Reno, Nevada Office: 100 West Liberty Street, Tenth Floor, P.O. Box 3237.
Telephone: 775-327-3000.
Fax: 775-786-6179.
Las Vegas, Nevada Office: Nevada Financial Center, 2300 West Sahara Avenue, Eighth Floor, Box 8.
Telephone: 702-222-2500.
Fax: 702-365-6940.

MEMBERS OF FIRM

Robert C. Anderson
James L. Kelly (Resident, Reno, Nevada)
Richard Bennett (Resident, Reno, Nevada)
David A. Garcia

ASSOCIATES

Richard P. Schulze, III
James Newman (Resident, Reno, Nevada)

OF COUNSEL

Roy L. Farrow
Linda E. Johnson

Representative Clients: Bank of America, N.A.; Scolari's Warehouse Markets, Inc.; Southwest Systems Corporation; American Assay Laboratories, Inc.; Juliet Corporation; Co-Energy Group, Inc.

For Complete List of Firm Personnel, See General Section

For full biographical listings, see the Martindale-Hubbell Law Directory

*ELKO,** Elko Co.

LAW OFFICES GOICOECHEA & DI GRAZIA, LTD. A PROFESSIONAL CORPORATION (AV)

In Association with
Vaughan & Hull, Ltd.
A Professional Corporation
200, Blohm Building, P.O. Box 1358, 89803
Telephone: 775-738-8091
Fax: 775-738-4220
Email: gdclaws@cyberhighway.net

Robert B. Goicoechea
Gary E. Di Grazia
Thomas J. Coyle, Jr.

David M. Stanton

Representative Clients: G & T Construction, Inc.; Alpark Petroleum, Inc.; Nevada Bank & Trust; Metropolitan Life Ins.

For full biographical listings, see the Martindale-Hubbell Law Directory

HENDERSON, Clark Co.

ROOKER & GIBSON (AV)

Suite 105, 701 North Green Valley Parkway, 89014
Telephone: 702-990-8100
Telecopier: 702-932-5266

C. Keith Rooker
James B. Gibson

Reference: BankWest of Nevada.

For full biographical listings, see the Martindale-Hubbell Law Directory

*LAS VEGAS,** Clark Co.

ALVERSON, TAYLOR, MORTENSEN, NELSON & SANDERS (AV)

7401 West Charleston Boulevard, 89117
Telephone: 702-384-7000
FAX: 702-385-7000
Email: alverson@intermind.net
Reno, Nevada Office: 245 East Liberty, Suite 520, 89505.
Telephone: 775-329-0473.
Fax: 775-329-3303.

(See Next Column)

ALVERSON, TAYLOR, MORTENSEN, NELSON & SANDERS—*Continued*

MEMBERS OF FIRM

J. Bruce Alverson
Eric K. Taylor
David J. Mortensen
Erven T. Nelson
LeAnn Sanders

OF COUNSEL

Jack C. Cherry
Kurt D. Anderson
Philip C. Van Alstyne

ASSOCIATES

Rebecca Hopkins Miller
Sandra Smagac
Victoria L. Nelson
Aaron D. Lovaas
Diane Obritsch
Michael A. Olsen
Randal D. Shimon
Catherine A. Olendorff
Monica L. Pierce
Gabriel D. Lither
Kurt R. Bonds
Darius F. Rafie
Mark J. King, IV
Shell L. Mercer
Carrie S. Bourdeau
Jason Lane Earnest
Nathan R. Reinmiller
Donn C. Alexander
Afshin Tadayon
Eric O. Freeman
Lindsay L. Stadtlander
Julie M. Sueoka

Representative Clients: Citibank; First Interstate Bank; General Electric; Southwest Gas Corporation; The CIT Group; Kentucky Fried Chicken; Norwest Bank; Federal Deposit Insurance Corporation (FDIC); Yellow Cab Company.

For full biographical listings, see the Martindale-Hubbell Law Directory

---

JOLLEY, URGA, WIRTH & WOODBURY (AV)

3800 Howard Hughes Parkway Suite 1600, 89109
Telephone: 702-699-7500
Facsimile: 702-699-7555
URL: http://www.juww.com
Boulder City, Nevada Office: Suite 105, 1000 Nevada Highway, 89005. *Telephone:* 702-293-3674.

MEMBERS OF FIRM

R. Gardner Jolley
William R. Urga
Roger A. Wirth
Bruce L. Woodbury
Kathryn Stryker Wirth
Brian E. Holthus
Allen D. Emmel

ASSOCIATES

Gregory G. Gordon
Scott Day Freeman
Mark Rosencrantz
Kelly J. Brinkman
Derek J. Pfaff

Representative Clients: Wells Fargo Bank and its predecessor, First Interstate Bank of Nevada; Nevada State Bank; Chicago Title Insurance Co.; Melvin Simon & Associates, Inc.; General Motors Acceptance Corp.; Toyota Motor Credit Corporation; Champion Home Builders Co.; Circus Circus Casinos, Inc.

For Complete List of Firm Personnel, See General Section

For full biographical listings, see the Martindale-Hubbell Law Directory

---

KEEFER, O'REILLY & FERRARIO (AV)

An Association including a Professional Corporation
Nevada Professional Center, 325 South Maryland Parkway, 89101
Telephone: 702-382-2660; 384-8944
Fax: 702-387-6978
Email: JORAPC@ACCESSWORLDNET.COM

Milton W. Keefer (1914-1999)
John F. O'Reilly (A Professional Corporation)
Mark E. Ferrario

Anita A. Webster
Preston B. Howard
Cynthia Gunther Milanowski
Jennifer A. McGargill
William J. Wray
Glenn F. Meier
Charles W. Simmons
Sandra L. Stewart
Antonia Z. Cowan

Representative Clients: ITT Hartford; MGM Grand Hotel; Aetna Insurance Company; Del Webb Corp.

For full biographical listings, see the Martindale-Hubbell Law Directory

---

KOLESAR & LEATHAM, CHARTERED (AV)

Norwest Bank Center, 3320 West Sahara Avenue, Suite 380, 89102
Telephone: 702-362-7800
Telecopier: 702-362-9472

Robert J. Kolesar
Nile Leatham
Kenneth A. Burns
Elliott R. Eisner
Howard Goldstein
Charles H. Miles, Jr.
Craig S. Newman

Matthew D. Saltzman

Representative Clients: AT&T Corp.; Banc One Financial Services, Inc.; Colonial Bank of Nevada; Credit Suisse First Boston Mortgage Capital; First Security Bank of Nevada; Forest City Enterprises; Marshall & Ilsley Corporation; Old Kent Bank; Sinclair Broadcast Group, Inc.; Weingarten Realty Investments/Management Co.

(See Next Column)

For full biographical listings, see the Martindale-Hubbell Law Directory

---

JOHN PETER LEE, LTD. (AV)

830 Las Vegas Boulevard South, 89101
Telephone: 702-382-4044
Telecopier: 702-383-9950

John Peter Lee

Paul C. Ray
Timothy P. Thomas

For Complete List of Firm Personnel, See General Section

For full biographical listings, see the Martindale-Hubbell Law Directory

---

OSHINS & ASSOCIATES, P.C. (AV)

Suite 170, 1645 Village Center Circle, 89134
Telephone: 702-341-6000
Fax: 702-341-6001
Email: Steveo@wizard.com
Email: Dickoshins@aol.com *URL:* http://firms.findlaw.com/oshins

Richard A. Oshins
Steven J. Oshins

For full biographical listings, see the Martindale-Hubbell Law Directory

---

PICO & MITCHELL (AV)

2000 South Eastern Avenue, 89104
Telephone: 702-457-9099
FAX: 702-457-8451
Email: lawyers@picomitchell.com

MEMBERS OF FIRM

James F. Pico
Bert O. Mitchell
Christy Brad Escobar
James R. Rosenberger
E. Breen Arntz

ASSOCIATES

Michelle Schwarz
Rebecca L. Mastrangelo
Jill M. Chase
Daniel E. Carvalho
Stephen H. Rogers

Representative Clients: Home Insurance Co.; State Farm Mutual Insurance Co.; Industrial Indemnity Insurance Co.; Great American Insurance Co.; Argonaut Insurance Cos.; Clark County Medical Society; Rose de Lima Hospital; Fairway Chevrolet; American States Insurance Co.; The Hartford Insurance Co.

For full biographical listings, see the Martindale-Hubbell Law Directory

---

LAURENCE A. SPEISER, LTD. (AV)

1700 S. Industrial Road, 89102
Telephone: 702-454-9544; 384-6156; 384-6399
Fax: 702-471-0592; 454-9557

Laurence A. Speiser

For full biographical listings, see the Martindale-Hubbell Law Directory

---

*RENO,** Washoe Co.

BIBLE, HOY & TRACHOK, A PROFESSIONAL CORPORATION (AV)

201 West Liberty Street, Third Floor, 89501
Telephone: 775-786-8000
Fax: 775-786-7426
Email: firm@nevadalaw.com *URL:* http://www.nevadalaw.com

Paul A. Bible
David R. Hoy
Richard M. Trachok, II
Michael D. Hoy
Mark S. Sertic
Jon M. Ludwig

Mark F. Bruce
Mark J. Lenz
Andrew Alan List
Ralph A. Fellows (Not admitted in NV)

For full biographical listings, see the Martindale-Hubbell Law Directory

---

ERWIN THOMPSON & HASCHEFF (AV)

A Partnership including Professional Corporations
Suite 424, One East Liberty Street, P.O. Box 40817, 89501-2123
Telephone: 775-786-9494
Facsimile: 775-786-1180
Email: erwin@renolaw.com *URL:* http://www.renolaw.com

Pierre A. Hascheff
Frank W. Thompson
Thomas P. Erwin

Reference: U.S. Bank (Reno, Nevada, Main Office).

For full biographical listings, see the Martindale-Hubbell Law Directory

Reno—Continued

GUILD, RUSSELL, GALLAGHER & FULLER, LTD. (AV)

100 West Liberty, Suite 800, P.O. Box 2838, 89505
Telephone: 775-786-2366
Telecopier: 775-322-9105
Email: attorneys@grgflaw.com

Clark J. Guild (1887-1971)
Clark J. Guild, Jr.
C. David Russell
John K. Gallagher
Gary M. Fuller

Jason J. Freelin

Representative Clients: Caithness Resources, Inc.; Chevron USA, Inc.; Dickson Realty; DRGM Advertising Agency; Federal Deposit Insurance Corp.; Intermountain Power Project; Land Rover North America; Porsche Cars North America; Jones-West Ford; City of Los Angeles, Department of Water & Power; Metropolitan Water District of Southern California; Microsoft Corporation; 100 W. Liberty Ltd. Partnership.

For full biographical listings, see the Martindale-Hubbell Law Directory

HALE LANE PEEK DENNISON HOWARD AND ANDERSON (AV)

100 West Liberty Street, Tenth Floor, P.O. Box 3237, 89505
Telephone: 775-327-3000
Telefax: 775-786-6179
Email: info@halelane.com
Las Vegas, Nevada Office: Nevada Financial Center, 2300 West Sahara Avenue, Eighth Floor, Box 8.
Telephone: 702-222-2500.
Fax: 702-365-6940.
Carson City, Nevada Office: 777 East William Street, Suite 200, P.O. Box 2620.
Telephone: 775-684-6000.
Telefax: 775-684-6001.

MEMBERS OF FIRM

Marilyn L. Skender
Robert C. Anderson
Richard Bennett
James L. Kelly
Kelly Testolin
Matthew E. Woodhead
David A. Garcia

ASSOCIATES

Richard P. Schulze, III
Julia S. Gold (Not admitted in NV)
James Newman

OF COUNSEL

Roy L. Farrow (Resident, Carson City, Nevada)
Linda E. Johnson (Resident, Carson City, Nevada)

Representative Clients: American Assay Laboratories, Inc.; Bank of America, N.A.; Bank of the West; Co-Energy Group, Inc.; Juliet Corporation; Scolari's Warehouse Markets, Inc.; Southwest Systems Corporation.

For Complete List of Firm Personnel, See General Section
For full biographical listings, see the Martindale-Hubbell Law Directory

WALTHER, KEY, MAUPIN, OATS, COX & LEGOY, A PROFESSIONAL CORPORATION (AV)

Lakeside Professional Plaza, 3500 Lakeside Court, 89509
Telephone: 775-827-2000
Facsimile: 775-827-2185
Mailing Address: P.O. Box 30000, Reno, Nevada, 89520

Steven T. Walther
Jon J. Key
Ernest J. Maupin
C. Robert Cox
L. Robert LeGoy, Jr.
Michael E. Malloy
W. Douglass Maupin
G. Barton Mowry
Kim G. Rowe
Procter J. Hug
Donald A. Lattin
Paul J. Anderson
Gustave J. Rossi
Robert A. Winkel
Kurt O. Hunsberger
Michael A. Nivinskus
Christopher D. Jaime

Rick R. Hsu
Michaelle D. Rafferty
Debra O. Waggoner

Representative Clients: Bank America of Nevada (Trust Dept.); Bechtel Corporations; Bill Pearce Olds, BMW, Volvo; Wells Fargo, N.A. (Trust Dept.); General Motors Acceptance Corp.; Nevada Realtors; Radiation Oncology Associates; The Ralph M. Parsons Corporation; Parsons Corporation; Reno Air, Inc.

For full biographical listings, see the Martindale-Hubbell Law Directory

WOODBURN AND WEDGE (AV)

One East First Street, Suite 1600, P.O. Box 2311, 89505
Telephone: 775-688-3000
Telecopier: 775-688-3088
Email: postmaster@woodburnlaw.com *URL:* http://www.woodburnlaw.com
Las Vegas, Nevada Office: Suite 700 Bank of America Plaza, 300 South Fourth Street.
Telephone: 702-387-1000.
Telecopier: 702-387-0024.

MEMBERS OF FIRM

James J. Halley
Richard O. Kwapil
Casey Woodburn Vlautin
John F. Murtha
Kirk S. Schumacher
Don L. Ross
Gregg P. Barnard

Representative Clients: Atlantic Richfield Co.; Sierra Pacific Power Co.; The Union Pacific Railroad Co.; Western Union Telegraph Co.; Bank of America; Cyprus Minerals Corp.; The Roman Catholic Bishop of Reno, A Corporation Sole; Shell Oil Co.

For full biographical listings, see the Martindale-Hubbell Law Directory

NEW JERSEY

BEDMINSTER, Somerset Co.

PURCELL, RIES, SHANNON, MULCAHY & O'NEILL (AV)

One Pluckemin Way, P.O. Box 754, 07921
Telephone: 908-658-3800
Fax: 908-658-4659
Email: general@prsmo.com *URL:* http://www.prsmo.com
Philadelphia, Pennsylvania Office: 12th Floor, East Tower, Centre Square, 1500 Market Square.
Telephone: 215-665-5602.
Fax: 215-569-8228.

MEMBERS OF FIRM

Eugene M. Purcell
William P. Ries
John J. Shannon
Thomas M. Mulcahy
Michael F. O'Neill
David M. Hawkins
Joseph R. Purcell
Kevin R. Brotz
John M. Bowens
Kevin Kovacs
Kenneth D. Merin
Valerie K. Bollheimer
Andrew L. Indeck
Joseph M. Donegan
Mark Mattia

ASSOCIATES

Rita F. Barone
Kathleen J. Devlin
Paul L. Gallagher
Gary Grabas
John R. Haggerty
William T. Hilliard
Eric J. Konecke
Susan Lawless
Michael J. McCaffrey
Kathleen M. Quinn
Thomas Charles Savoth
Donna M. Stephan-Nolan
Barbara C. Zimmerman

OF COUNSEL

David D. Furman
C. Judson Hamlin

LEGAL SUPPORT PERSONNEL

Gary Molloy

Reference: Somerset Trust Co.

For full biographical listings, see the Martindale-Hubbell Law Directory

BERNARDSVILLE, Somerset Co.

SHAIN, SCHAFFER & RAFANELLO, A PROFESSIONAL CORPORATION (AV)

Plaza 202, 150 Morristown Road, Suite 105, 07924
Telephone: 908-953-9300
Fax: 908-953-2969
Email: ssrpc@aol.com

Joel L. Shain
Marguerite M. Schaffer
Richard A. Rafanello
Gary L. Maher
Robert A. Pinel
Phedra R. Rudell (Not admitted in NJ)

OF COUNSEL

Elliott L. Katz

LEGAL SUPPORT PERSONNEL

Tracy DeWitt (Legal Researcher)

For full biographical listings, see the Martindale-Hubbell Law Directory

CHERRY HILL, Camden Co.

FLASTER/GREENBERG, P.C. (AV)

Commerce Center, 1810 Chapel Avenue West, Third Floor, 08002-4609
Telephone: 856-661-1900
Telecopier: 856-661-1919
Email: FIRM@FLASTERGREENBERG.COM *URL:* http://www.flastergreenberg.com

Richard J. Flaster
Stephen M. Greenberg
Laura B. Wallenstein
Allen P. Fineberg
Markley S. Roderick
Peter R. Spirgel
Alan H. Zuckerman
William S. Skinner
J. Philip Kirchner
Paul J. Russoniello
Carl S. Bisgaier
Steven B. Sacharow
E. Richard Dressel
Kenneth S. Goodkind
Frank H. Wisniewski
Alma L. Saravia

OF COUNSEL

Peter M. Dolinger
James J. Binns

Elizabeth J. Hampton
Jeffrey Herskowitz
Christopher E. Kaltenbach
Steven J. Abrams
Julie A. Williamson
Donna T. Urban
Amelia Carolla
Matthew Azoulay
Elaine J. Petruzziello (Not admitted in NJ)
Ann Marie Iannone
Pasquale Guglietta

LEGAL SUPPORT PERSONNEL

PARALEGALS

Ann Gorman
Patricia D'Alessio
Theresa Cooke
Rosemary Dunaif

For full biographical listings, see the Martindale-Hubbell Law Directory

*HACKENSACK,** Bergen Co.

DEENER, FEINGOLD & STERN, A PROFESSIONAL CORPORATION (AV)

2 University Plaza, Suite 503, 07601
Telephone: 201-343-8788
Fax: 201-343-4640
Email: JeromeDeener@DeenerFeingold.com *URL:* http://www.lawyers.com/deenerfeingold&stern

Jerome A. Deener
Cal R. Feingold
Robert A. Stern
David M. Edelblum
Anthony M. Vizzoni

Debra T. Hirsch
Andrew M. Grumet
Ronen Gabbay

References: Hudson United Bank; Commerce Bank.

For full biographical listings, see the Martindale-Hubbell Law Directory

HEIN, SMITH, BEREZIN, MALOOF & JACOBS, L.L.C. (AV)

Court Plaza East, 19 Main Street, 07601-7023
Telephone: 201-487-7400
Telecopier: 201-487-4228
Email: counsel@heinsmith.com

OF COUNSEL

Seymour A. Smith

Reference: Summit Bank.

For Complete List of Firm Personnel, See General Section

For full biographical listings, see the Martindale-Hubbell Law Directory

SHAPIRO & CROLAND (AV)

A Partnership including Professional Corporations
Continental Plaza II, 411 Hackensack Avenue, 07601
Telephone: 201-488-3900
Fax: 201-488-9481

Barry I. Croland, P.C.
Robert P. Shapiro, P.C.
Barry L. Baime
Jay Rubenstein
Kenneth S. Apfel
Kenneth S. Goldrich, P.C.
Bruce J. Ackerman
Stuart Reiser, P.C.
Meridith J. Bronson
John P. Di Iorio
David O. Marcus
Robert F. Green
Lizabeth Sarakin
David Torchin
Robin C. Bogan
Craig D. Spector

OF COUNSEL

Harvey R. Sorkow

Donald R. Sorkow (1930-1985)

Reference: Bank of New York-National Community Division.

For full biographical listings, see the Martindale-Hubbell Law Directory

SOKOL, BEHOT AND FIORENZO (AV)

433 Hackensack Avenue, 07601
Telephone: 201-488-1300
Fax: 201-488-6541

MEMBERS OF FIRM

Leon J. Sokol
Joseph F. Behot, Jr.
Joseph B. Fiorenzo
Jeffrey A. Zenn
Arthur Bergman
Michael P. Feltman

ASSOCIATES

Siobhan Spillane Bailey
Mitchell B. Levine
Steven Seigel
Andrew S. Bosin

COUNSEL

Alan Prigal

For full biographical listings, see the Martindale-Hubbell Law Directory

HAWTHORNE, Passaic Co.

JEFFER, HOPKINSON & VOGEL (AV)

(Formerly Jeffer, Walter, Tierney, DeKorte, Hopkinson & Vogel)
Law Building, 1600 Route 208N, P.O. Box 507, 07507
Telephone: 973-423-0100
Fax: 973-423-5614
Tequesta, Florida Office: Jeffer, Cioffi & Cicalese. 250 Tequesta Drive, 33469.
Telephone: 561-747-6000.
Fax: 561-575-9167.

MEMBERS OF FIRM

Herman M. Jeffer
Reginald F. Hopkinson
Jerome A. Vogel
Peter Hofstra (1886-1961)
George Tierney (1895-1976)
Joseph V. Fumagalli (1901-1965)
Richard W. DeKorte (1936-1975)
Robert Walter (1908-1990)

ASSOCIATES

Melinda B. Maidens
E. David Becker
David H. Altman

LEGAL SUPPORT PERSONNEL

Janet Faber (Office Administrator)

Counsel for: Brioschi, Inc.; Opici Wine Co.; Gas Pumpers of America Corp.; The Paterson Market Growers Assn.; Dowling Fuel Oil Co.; Becton, Dickinson; JFC International, Inc.; Loews Theaters; Christian Health Care Center.

For full biographical listings, see the Martindale-Hubbell Law Directory

LAWRENCEVILLE, Mercer Co.

SZAFERMAN, LAKIND, BLUMSTEIN, WATTER & BLADER, P.C. (AV)

Suite 104 Quakerbridge Executive Center, 101 Grovers Mill Road, 08648
Telephone: 609-275-0400
Telefax: 609-275-4511

Arnold C. Lakind
Barry D. Szaferman
Jeffrey P. Blumstein
Paul N. Watter
Steven Blader
Sidney H. Lehmann
Gerald B. Schenkman
David B. Beckett
Scott P. Borsack
Mary Lou Delahanty

Jennifer Weisberg Millner
Cathyanne A. Pisciotta
Jason N. Fruhschein
Demery J. Roberts
Stuart A. Tucker
Brian G. Paul
Victoria Rivera-Cruz
Thomas J. Burns III

LEGAL SUPPORT PERSONNEL

Paula M. Rossi (Office Administrator)
Patricia Hallstrum (Controller)

Representative Clients: Sun National Bank; First Washington Bank; Gilmore Securities & Co.; Communication Workers of America; The Eagle Group; Water's Edge Convalescent Center; Ronson Aviation, Inc.; Holmdel Township Board of Adjustment; Public Service Managers Association; Chemical Leaman Tank Lines.

For full biographical listings, see the Martindale-Hubbell Law Directory

MONTCLAIR, Essex Co.

MEISLIK & LEVAVY (AV)

66 Park Street, 07042
Telephone: 973-783-3000
Fax: 973-744-5757
Email: meislik@meislik.com *URL:* http://www.meislik.com

MEMBERS OF FIRM

Ira Meislik
Bardin Levavy

For full biographical listings, see the Martindale-Hubbell Law Directory

*MORRISTOWN,** Morris Co.

PITNEY, HARDIN, KIPP & SZUCH LLP (AV)

P.O. Box 1945, 07962-1945
Telephone: 973-966-6300
New York City: 212-687-6000
Telex: 642014
Telecopier: 973-966-1550
URL: http://www.phks.com
New York, New York Office: 711 Third Avenue, 10017-4014.
Telephone: 212-687-6000.
Fax: 212-682-3485.

MEMBERS OF FIRM

Joseph Lunin
Warren J. Casey
Ronald H. Janis
Henry Nelson Massey
Kenneth J. Norcross
Michael J. Dunne
Lori J. Braender
Michael W. Zelenty

COUNSEL

Jonathan S. Bristol
Marjorie F. Chertok

Representaive Clients: Arthur Anderson & Co.; Base Ten Systems, Inc.; HFS, Incorporated; Lucent Technologies; PNC Bank, N.A., Talbots; Warner-Lambert Co.

For Complete List of Firm Personnel, See General Section

For full biographical listings, see the Martindale-Hubbell Law Directory

*NEWARK,** Essex Co.

SILLS CUMMIS RADIN TISCHMAN EPSTEIN & GROSS, A PROFESSIONAL CORPORATION (AV)

One Riverfront Plaza, 07102-5400
Telephone: 973-643-7000
Fax: 973-643-6500
Telex: 820630 Sillsbeck Nwk
Email: sillsmail@sillscummis.com *URL:* http://www.sillscummis.com
Atlantic City, New Jersey Office: 17 Gordon's Alley.
Telephone: 609-344-2800.
New York, N.Y. Office: 712 Fifth Avenue.
Telephone: 212-643-7000.
Washington, D.C. Office: 1800 K Street, N.W.
Telephone: 202-296-4750.

MEMBERS OF FIRM

Michael B. Tischman
Steven E. Gross
Steven M. Goldman
Ira A. Rosenberg
Robert Max Crane
Jerry Genberg
Brian S. Coven
Stanley U. North, III
Victor H. Boyajian
Frederic M. Tudor
Steven R. Kamen

OF COUNSEL

Diane M. Lavenda

Noel D. Humphreys
Gary W. Herschman
Lori M. Waldron
Christian Peter Johnson (Not admitted in NJ)
Jonathan N. Marcus
Joseph A. Becht, Jr.

Representative Clients: Sorin Biomedical Inc.; FIAT (USA); O'Brien Environmental Energy; DiGiorgio Corporation; J. White Rose Foods, Inc.; New Jersey Nets; Bally Entertainment Corp.; Midlantic National Bank; PNC Bank Corp.; Schering AG.

For Complete List of Firm Personnel, See General Section

For full biographical listings, see the Martindale-Hubbell Law Directory

*NEW BRUNSWICK,** Middlesex Co.

HOAGLAND, LONGO, MORAN, DUNST & DOUKAS (AV)

40 Paterson Street, P.O. Box 480, 08903
Telephone: 732-545-4717
Fax: 732-545-4579
Email: info@hlmdd.com

MEMBERS OF FIRM

Bartholomew A. Longo
James B. Moran
Alan I. Dunst
Kenneth J. Doukas, Jr.
Michael John Stone
Donald D. Davidson
Thaddeus J. Hubert, III
Joan Alster Weisblatt
Karen M. Buerle
Robert G. Kenny
Michael J. Baker
Andrew J. Carlowicz, Jr.
Gary J. Hoagland
Jeffrey S. Intravatola
Jamie D. Happas
Thomas J. Walsh, Jr.
Robert S. Helwig
Michael F. Dolan
Douglas M. Fasciale
Marc S. Gaffrey
John Charles Simons
Susan K. O'Connor
Stephen G. Perrella
Jacquelyn L. Poland
Douglas Susan
Patrick J. McDonald

OF COUNSEL

John J. Hoagland
Herman L. Breitkopf
Richard S. Cohen

(See Next Column)

ASSOCIATES

Andrew N. Kessler
John P. Barnes
Christopher M. Longo
Nancy A. Freedman
Tiffany C. Chong
Michael Dermody
Diane Hoagland
Michael T. Kearns
Keith C. Northridge
Andrew J. DiMarsico
Edward J. Rebenack
Paul N. Harris
Denis A. Gooding
Kevin J. Musiakiewicz
Michael N. Porter
Kenneth Sisco
M. Stephanie Beaty

Representative Clients: St. Peters Medical Center; Partners in Care Corp.; MultiMedia Healthcare; Stop & Shop Supermarkets; Poland Springs; Pizza Hut; A.G.S. System Forms; Xerox; McNichols Steel.

For full biographical listings, see the Martindale-Hubbell Law Directory

NORTH BRUNSWICK, Middlesex Co.

BORRUS, GOLDIN, FOLEY, VIGNUOLO, HYMAN, STAHL & CLARKIN, A PROFESSIONAL CORPORATION (AV)

2875 U.S. Highway 1, Route 1 & Finnigans Lane, P.O. Box 7463, 08902
Telephone: 732-422-1000
Fax: 732-422-1016
Email: attys@borrus.com *URL:* http://www.borrus.com

Jack Borrus
Martin S. Goldin
David M. Foley
Anthony B. Vignuolo
Jeffrey M. Hyman
James E. Stahl
James F. Clarkin III
Eileen Mary Foley

Robert C. Nisenson
Rosalind Westlake
Lisa M. Vignuolo
Steven L. Fox
Peter A. Vignuolo
Gerald T. Foley (1903-1976)

Representative Clients: Summit Bank; R. J. Reynolds Tobacco Co.; K. Hovnanian Enterprises, Inc.; Johnson and Johnson; Foster Wheeler, Inc.; Hartz Mountain Industries; Middlesex County Vocational Services Commission; Borough of South Plainfield Board of Adjustment; U-Haul of Northern NJ.

For full biographical listings, see the Martindale-Hubbell Law Directory

BUSCH AND BUSCH, LLP (AV)

215 North Center Drive, Commerce Center - U.S. #1 South, P.O. Box 7448, 08902-7448
Telephone: 732-821-2300
Telecopier: 732-821-5588
Email: busch@ifu.net

MEMBERS OF FIRM

Lewis D. Busch (1901-1986)
Henry Busch (Retired)
Malcolm R. Busch
Ronald J. Busch
Bertram E. Busch
Mark N. Busch
Leonard R. Busch
Steven F. Satz
Donald J. Sears

ASSOCIATE

Paul Alan VanBuskirk

Representative Clients: Utica Mutual Insurance Co.; New Brunswick Tomorrow; Township of South Brunswick; Township of Monroe, Board of Education; Township of East Brunswick; Minnesota Mutual Life Insurance Co.

For full biographical listings, see the Martindale-Hubbell Law Directory

PARSIPPANY, Morris Co.

CUYLER BURK (AV)

Parsippany Corporate Center, Four Century Drive, 07054-4663
Telephone: 973-734-3200
Telex: 429071
Telecopier: 973-734-3201
Email: Main@Cuyler.com *URL:* http://www.cuyler.com
New York, New York Office: 350 Fifth Avenue, Suite 3304. 10018.
Telephone: 212-645-4039.

MEMBERS OF FIRM

Stephen D. Cuyler
Jo Ann Burk
Stefano Calogero
David L. Menzel
Peter Petrou
Richard A. Crooker
Michael J. Jones

COUNSEL

Anne M. Mohan
Frank J. Miele

ASSOCIATES

Jan C. Walker
Kathleen Jane Olear
Claudia L. Marchese
Mark G. Eliades
Kimberly A. Joel
Christy A. Ramunno
Catherine E. Youngman
Andrew K. Craig
Mark S. Winter
Thomas J. Castano
Hugo A. Hilgendorff, IV

LEGAL SUPPORT PERSONNEL

Frederick M. H. Currie, Jr.

For full biographical listings, see the Martindale-Hubbell Law Directory

PRINCETON, Mercer Co.

McCarthy and Schatzman, P.A. (AV)

228 Alexander Street, P.O. Box 2329, 08543-2329
Telephone: 609-924-1199
Fax: 609-683-5251

John F. McCarthy, Jr.
Richard Schatzman
G. Christopher Baker
John F. McCarthy, III
Michael A. Spero
Barbara Strapp Nelson
W. Scott Stoner
James J. Britt, Jr.

Charly Gayden

Representative Clients: Trustees of Princeton University; Carnegie Center Associates; Merrill Lynch Pierce Fenner & Smith, Inc.; Calton Homes, Inc.

For full biographical listings, see the Martindale-Hubbell Law Directory

Stark & Stark, A Professional Corporation (AV)

Princeton Pike Corporate Center, P.O. Box 5315, 08543-5315
Telephone: 609-896-9060
Fax: 609-896-0629
Email: info@stark-stark.com *URL:* http://www.stark-stark.com

Donald B. Brenner
Brian A. Carlis
Timothy P. Duggan
A. Christopher Florio
Steven L. Friedman
Thomas D. Giachetti
Daniel L. Haggerty, III
Richard F. Hamilton
Kevin M. Hart
Craig S. Hilliard
Elizabeth Walsh Kreger
Thomas B. Lewis
Lewis J. Pepperman
Thomas J. Pryor
Allen M. Silk

OF COUNSEL

William H. Brosha
Arthur L. Levy
Amel Stark
Sharon L. Wynn

Mary W. Barrett
Daniel A. Bernstein
David J. Byrne
Brian S. Hamburger
John E. MacDonald
Francis J. McGovern, Jr.
Christopher J. Preate
John Randy Sawyer
Catherine A. Sokoloski
Rachel L. Stark
Susan G. Steinman
Scott I. Unger
George F. Yuska

For full biographical listings, see the Martindale-Hubbell Law Directory

ROSELAND, Essex Co.

Brach, Eichler, Rosenberg, Silver, Bernstein, Hammer & Gladstone, A Professional Corporation (AV)

101 Eisenhower Parkway, 07068
Telephone: 973-228-5700
Telecopier: 973-228-7852
Email: law@bracheichler.com *URL:* http://www.bracheichler.com

Stuart M. Gladstone
Brian R. Lenker
Robert C. Mignella
Stuart L. Pachman
David J. Ritter
Paul F. Rosenberg

Ann D. Stevens
Lisa S. Paye

OF COUNSEL

Harris R. Silver

COUNSEL

Dorothy G. Black (1927-1996)

Representative Clients: Eagle Work Clothes, Inc.; Englehard/Colortronics; Howard Press; Isaac Hazen & Company; I. Epstein, Inc.; Perlmart Shop-Rites; Silver Line Building Products.

For Complete List of Firm Personnel, See General Section

For full biographical listings, see the Martindale-Hubbell Law Directory

Post, Polak, Goodsell & MacNeill, P.A. (AV)

75 Livingston Avenue, 07068-3701
Telephone: 973-994-1100
Telecopier: 973-994-1705
Email: administrator@ppgm.com
New York, New York Office: 575 Madison Avenue, Suite 1006.
Telephone: 212-486-1455.

John N. Post
Robert A. Goodsell
Jay Scott MacNeill
Paul D. Strauchler
Mary H. Post
David L. Epstein

Nilufer O. DeScherer

For Complete List of Firm Personnel, See General Section

For full biographical listings, see the Martindale-Hubbell Law Directory

Walder, Sondak & Brogan, A Professional Corporation (AV)

5 Becker Farm Road, P.O. Box 901, 07068
Telephone: 973-992-5300
Telecopier: 973-992-1505; 992-1006
Email: general@wsbesqs.com *URL:* http://www.wsbesqs.com

Justin P. Walder
John A. Brogan
Thomas J. Spies
Barry A. Kozyra
James A. Plaisted
Heather Grasz Suarez
Michael J. Faul, Jr.
Jeffrey A. Walder

Shalom D. Stone
Judith A. Hartz
Steven D. Grossman
K. Roger Plawker

OF COUNSEL

John H. Skarbnik

For Complete List of Firm Personnel, See General Section

For full biographical listings, see the Martindale-Hubbell Law Directory

SKILLMAN, Somerset Co.

Gerald P. Seid (AV)

144 Tamarack Circle, Montgomery Knoll, U.S. Highway 206 North, 08558
Telephone: 609-921-3747
Fax: 609-921-3936
Email: 72624.2715@compuserve.com

For full biographical listings, see the Martindale-Hubbell Law Directory

*SOMERVILLE,** Somerset Co.

Schachter, Trombadore, Offen, Stanton & Pavics, A Professional Corporation (AV)

45 East High Street, P.O. Box 520, 08876-0520
Telephone: 908-722-5700
Fax: 908-722-8853

Richard J. Schachter
John J. Trombadore
Stephen M. Offen
Michael J. Stanton
Thomas A. Pavics

Timothy P. McKeown
Jerry S. D'Aniello

For full biographical listings, see the Martindale-Hubbell Law Directory

Raymond R. & David W. Trombadore, P.C. A Professional Corporation (AV)

33 East High Street, 08876
Telephone: 908-722-7555
Fax: 908-722-6269
URL: http://www.trombadorelaw.com

Raymond R. Trombadore
David W. Trombadore

OF COUNSEL

Ann W. Trombadore

References: Summit Bank; Somerset Savings & Loan Assn.

For full biographical listings, see the Martindale-Hubbell Law Directory

SPRINGFIELD, Union Co.

Kraemer, Burns, Mytelka, Lovell & Kulka, P.A. (AV)

675 Morris Avenue, 07081
Telephone: 973-912-8700
Telecopier: 973-912-8602

John A. Avery
Douglas E. Burns
Eleonore Kessler Cohen
Wayne D. Greenfeder
Daniel G. Kasen (1905-1990)
Waldron Kraemer
Ellen B. Kulka
Joan A. Lovell
Arnold K. Mytelka

OF COUNSEL

Diane Stolbach
Scott B. Stolbach

For full biographical listings, see the Martindale-Hubbell Law Directory

*TRENTON,** Mercer Co.

Schragger, Lavine & Nagy (AV)

Mountainview Office Park, 840 Bear Tavern Road, Suite 307, 08628
Telephone: 609-771-0700
Fax: 609-771-9535

Bruce M. Schragger
Raymond L. Nagy
James A. Schragger
Jonathan S. Robinson

OF COUNSEL

Henry C. Schragger
Alan S. Lavine
Frank P. Reiche
A. Jerome Moore

(See Next Column)

SCHRAGGER, LAVINE & NAGY, *Trenton—Continued*

LEGAL SUPPORT PERSONNEL

Annemarie Saccani (Office Administrator)

Representative Clients: New Jersey Manufacturers Insurance Co.; Mercer County Community College; Mercer Mutual Insurance Co.; New Jersey Optometric Association; Allentown Caging; Dick Greenfield Dodge.

For Complete List of Firm Personnel, See General Section

For full biographical listings, see the Martindale-Hubbell Law Directory

WESTMONT, Camden Co.

EARP COHN P.C. (AV)

222 Haddon Avenue, 08108
Telephone: 856-854-7100
Fax: 856-854-6434
Email: administrator@earpcohn.com *URL:* http://www.earpcohn.com
Philadelphia, Pennsylvania Office: 2 Penn Center Plaza, Suite 200. 19102-1706.
Telephone: 215-963-9520.
Fax: 215-963-9620.

Thomas L. Earp
Richard B. Cohn
Irving Koffler
Douglas F. Johnson
Kathryn R. Renahan
Carol Schuler Harding
Samantha P. Zazzo
Jeff Schwartz

For full biographical listings, see the Martindale-Hubbell Law Directory

WEST ORANGE, Essex Co.

GOLDBERG, MUFSON & SPAR, A PROFESSIONAL CORPORATION (AV)

200 Executive Drive, 07052
Telephone: 973-736-0100
Telecopier: 973-736-0961
Email: gmspa@chelsea.ios.com

Leonard M. Goldberg
Michael R. Spar
Kenneth J. Isaacson
Jeffrey L. Kantowitz

For full biographical listings, see the Martindale-Hubbell Law Directory

NEW MEXICO

*ALBUQUERQUE,** Bernalillo Co.

KENNETH C. LEACH, P.C. (AV)

1110 Pennsylvania N.E., Suite A, 87110
Telephone: 505-243-3322
Fax: 505-242-1268
URL: http://www.lawyers.com/leachlaw

Kenneth C. Leach

Jonathan Reid Mowrer

LEGAL SUPPORT PERSONNEL

Wayne C. Edwards (CEO)
Marilyn Alires Marsh (Paralegal)
Virginia Bosworth (Paralegal)

For full biographical listings, see the Martindale-Hubbell Law Directory

OMAN, GENTRY & YNTEMA, P.A. (AV)

Suite 201, 215 Gold Avenue, S.W., P.O. Box 1748, 87103
Telephone: 505-843-9565
Fax: 505-242-2879

Kester L. Oman
Hessel E. Yntema, III
Christopher B. Behling

Reference: Norwest Bank.
Representative Clients: S&J Enterprises, Inc.; Educational Assessment Systems, Inc.; Holman's, Inc.; Amfab, Inc.

For full biographical listings, see the Martindale-Hubbell Law Directory

RODEY, DICKASON, SLOAN, AKIN & ROBB, P.A. (AV)

Albuquerque Plaza, Suite 2200, 201 Third Street, N.W., P.O. Box 1888, 87103-1888
Telephone: 505-765-5900
Fax: 505-768-7395
Email: info@rodey.com *URL:* http://www.rodey.com
Santa Fe, New Mexico Office: Suite 101 Marcy Plaza, 123 East Marcy Street, P.O. Box 1357, 87504-1357.
Telephone: 505-984-0100.
Fax: 505-989-9542.

(See Next Column)

Mark K. Adams
John P. Burton (Resident, Santa Fe Office)
Benjamin C. Roybal
Gary D. Eisenberg

Alice Nystel Page

COUNSEL

Richard C. Minzner

For Complete List of Firm Personnel, See General Section

For full biographical listings, see the Martindale-Hubbell Law Directory

TAX, ESTATE & BUSINESS LAW N.A. LLC (AV)

4217 Montgomery Boulevard, N.E., 87109
Telephone: 505-830-2200
Fax: 505-830-4400
Email: tsmidt2@aol.com

Thomas Smidt, II

LEGAL SUPPORT PERSONNEL

William T. Smith

For full biographical listings, see the Martindale-Hubbell Law Directory

NEW YORK

*ALBANY,** Albany Co.

FEATHERSTONHAUGH, CONWAY, WILEY & CLYNE, L.L.P. (AV)

99 Pine Street, Suite 207, 12207
Telephone: 518-436-0786
Fax: 518-427-0452
URL: http://www.fcwc-law.com

MEMBERS OF FIRM

James D. Featherstonhaugh
Thomas A. Conway
Stephen J. Wiley
Elizabeth K. Clyne

ASSOCIATES

Nadine Feiden Shadlock
Denis R. Hurley, Jr.
Andrew W. Kirby
William F. Conway, IV
Gerard L. Conway, Jr.
Steven M. Connolly

OF COUNSEL

William F. Conway
Jeffrey J. Conklin
David Weinraub
Randall J. Ezick

LEGAL SUPPORT PERSONNEL

GOVERNMENTAL RELATIONS

John L. Hardy
Daniel G. Plummer
John P. Griffin
David F. Fleming

For full biographical listings, see the Martindale-Hubbell Law Directory

SEGEL, GOLDMAN & MAZZOTTA, P.C. (AV)

5 Washington Square Washington Avenue Extension, 12205
Telephone: 518-452-0941
Telecopier: 518-452-0417
Email: mazzotta@capital.net

Kenneth B. Segel
Thomas G. Mazzotta
Paul J. Goldman
Jeffrey A. Siegel

Robert J. Koshgarian
Polly J. Feigenbaum
Debra J. Lambek

OF COUNSEL

Peter Bishko
Richard J. Sherwood

For full biographical listings, see the Martindale-Hubbell Law Directory

TABNER, RYAN AND KENIRY (AV)

26 Computer Drive West, P.O. Box 12605, 12212-2605
Telephone: 518-459-9000
Telecopier: 518-459-9165
Email: trk@tabnerryanandkeniry.com

MEMBERS OF FIRM

John W. Tabner
William F. Ryan, Jr.
William J. Keniry

OF COUNSEL

C. Theodore Carlson

ASSOCIATES

Eric N. Dratler
Jennifer K. Corona
Donald W. Biggs

Special Counsel for: Water and Sewer District for Towns of Colonie, Coxsackie, Guilderland, Johnstown, Queensbury, Rotterdam and Village Castleton.

(See Next Column)

TABNER, RYAN AND KENIRY—*Continued*

References: FleetBank; Trustco Bank.

For full biographical listings, see the Martindale-Hubbell Law Directory

BRONXVILLE, Westchester Co.

GRIFFIN, COOGAN & VENERUSO, P.C. (AV)

51 Pondfield Road, 10708
Telephone: 914-961-1300
Telecopier: 914-961-1476; 914-961-9385

William E. Griffin
James M. Coogan
James J. Veneruso

Daniel J. Griffin
Paul R. Herrick
Thomas G. Marzullo
William E. Sulzer (Not admitted in NY)

Approved Closing Attorneys: Hudson Valley Bank.

For full biographical listings, see the Martindale-Hubbell Law Directory

*BUFFALO,** Erie Co.

BROWN & KELLY, L.L.P. (AV)

1500 Liberty Building, 14202-3663
Telephone: 716-854-2620
Fax: 716-854-0082
Email: mail@brownkelly.com *URL:* http://www.brownkelly.com

MEMBERS OF FIRM

Thomas J. Kelly
Rodney O. Personius
Frederick D. Turner
Paul Michael Hassett
Peter E. Klaasesz
Donald B. Eppers
Andrew D. Merrick
William P. Wiles
William D. Harrington
Joseph M. Schnitter
Paula L. Feroleto
Daniel J. Marren
Lisa T. Sofferin

OF COUNSEL

Ogden R. Brown
Charles F. Harrington
James T. Duggan
Karen Cook Serotte
Roland R. Benzow
Philip B. Abramowitz
Elizabeth R. O'Connor
Catherine E. Marra

ASSOCIATES

David S. Zygaj
Olney H. Clowe
Brian M. Melber
David O. Teach
Patricia S. Ciccarelli
Susan J. Schmidt

For full biographical listings, see the Martindale-Hubbell Law Directory

COHEN & LOMBARDO, P.C. (AV)

343 Elmwood Avenue, P.O. Box 5204, 14213-5204
Telephone: 716-881-3010
Fax: 716-881-2755
Email: law@cohenlombardo.com *URL:* http://www.cohenlombardo.com

Joseph Cohen (1909-1966)
Ernest Lombardo (1913-1993)
Richard N. Blewett
Donald A. Fisher
Robert N. Convissar
Rocco Lucente, II
Stuart Brian Shapiro
Neil R. Sherwood
Douglas S. Cream

Robert R. Goods
Katherine J. Bestine
Mark S. Nemeth
Daniel M. Caro
Maria T. Buchanan-Sidorski
Thomas J. Navarro, Jr.
Jennifer D. Bowen
Christopher A. Zampogna

OF COUNSEL

Maryann Saccomando Freedman
Anthony M. Nosek
Dean C. Stathacos
Norman J. Pecora
David R. Koepsell

For full biographical listings, see the Martindale-Hubbell Law Directory

RAICHLE, BANNING, WEISS & STEPHENS (AV)

410 Main Street, 14202
Telephone: 716-852-7587
Telecopier: 716-852-7599
Email: RBWS@MSN.COM

MEMBERS OF FIRM

Frank G. Raichle (1898-1986)
Derrick C. Banning (1916-1995)
Arnold Weiss
R. William Stephens

ASSOCIATES

Lisa Parlato Neff
R. Hugh Stephens

Representative Clients: Cliffstar Corp.; Blue Cross & Blue Shield of Michigan; Superior Jamestown Corp., Adanlock Office Environments Division; Permclip Products Corp.

For full biographical listings, see the Martindale-Hubbell Law Directory

ROLLS KOHN & ASSOCIATES, LLP (AV)

Twenty Court Street, 14202-3201
Telephone: 716-856-2700
Fax: 716-856-2777

MEMBERS OF FIRM

James E. Rolls
Gerald L. Kohn

Robert M. Goldstein

For full biographical listings, see the Martindale-Hubbell Law Directory

GLENS FALLS, Warren Co.

FITZGERALD MORRIS BAKER FIRTH (AV)

One Broad Street Plaza, P.O. Box 2017, 12801
Telephone: 518-745-1400
Fax: 518-745-1576
Email: info@fmbf-law.com

Robert C. Morris
Peter D. FitzGerald
Peter A. Firth
Carl T. Baker
J. Mark Noordsy
Robert P. McNally
Laura V. Nield
Veronica Carrozza O'Dell

Bruce G. Carr
David Gregory Richardson
Kevin O'Shell

Representative Clients: Woodbury Development Group, Ltd.; Homequity; Glens Falls Cement Co., Inc.; Greater Glens Falls Development Corp.; Glens Falls Industrial Development Agency; Torrington Industries, Inc.; Whiteman Chevrolet, Inc.

For full biographical listings, see the Martindale-Hubbell Law Directory

HEMPSTEAD, Nassau Co.

LAWRENCE AND WALSH, P.C. (AV)

215 Hilton Avenue, P.O. Box 1200, 11551-1200
Telephone: 516-538-2400
Telecopier: 516-538-2079
Email: info@lawfirmonline.com *URL:* http://www.lawfirmonline.com

Lawrence S. Lawrence
Edward V. Walsh, Jr.
Michael F. Kennedy
Richard N. Thompson

OF COUNSEL

John S. Wallenstein

For full biographical listings, see the Martindale-Hubbell Law Directory

ISLANDIA, Suffolk Co.

BRACKEN & MARGOLIN, LLP (AV)

One Suffolk Square, Suite 300, 11722
Telephone: 516-234-8585
Telecopier: 516-234-8702
URL: http://www.bracken-margolin.com

MEMBERS OF FIRM

John P. Bracken
Linda U. Margolin

ASSOCIATES

Olympia Gouvis
William J. Graham
Patricia M. Meisenheimer
Ralph J. Reissman
Peter L. Verdon

Representative Clients: Rason Asphalt, Inc.; S & H Building Materials Corp.
Reference: Marine Midland Bank, N.A.

For full biographical listings, see the Martindale-Hubbell Law Directory

LAW OFFICES OF ANDREW D. PRESBERG, P.C. (AV)

100 Corporate Plaza, 11722
Telephone: 516-232-4444
Fax: 516-232-2603
Email: preslaw@erols.com *URL:* http://www.presberg.com

Andrew D. Presberg

For full biographical listings, see the Martindale-Hubbell Law Directory

MELVILLE, Suffolk Co.

CAHN WISHOD & KNAUER, LLP (AV)

425 Broadhollow Road Suite 315, 11747
Telephone: 631-752-1600
Fax: 631-752-1555
URL: http://www.cahnwishod.com
URL: http://www.lawyers.com/cahnwishod&knauer

MEMBERS OF FIRM

Richard C. Cahn
Eugene L. Wishod
Todd A. Knauer

ASSOCIATES

Brian T. Egan
Patricia A. Rooney

(See Next Column)

CAHN WISHOD & KNAUER LLP, *Melville—Continued*

LEGAL SUPPORT PERSONNEL

Susan M. Stonelli (Paralegal)

For full biographical listings, see the Martindale-Hubbell Law Directory

LAMB & BARNOSKY, LLP (AV)

534 Broadhollow Road-CS 9034, 11747-9034
Telephone: 631-694-2300
Telecopier: 631-694-2309
Email: thefirm@lambbarnosky.com *URL:* http://www.lambbarnosky.com

PARTNERS

Eugene R. Barnosky
Robert H. Cohen
Marcia Lyn Finkelstein
Michael J. Heller
Gary Holman
Scott M. Karson
P. L. Lamb
Arthur A. Lane
Joel M. Markowitz
Gerald P. Rosenberg
Patrice Dowd Shenn

OF COUNSEL

Louis E. Black
James F. Gesualdi
Howard W. Newman
Joseph J. Salvatore
Joseph H. Wishod

COUNSEL

Lloyd K. Chanin
Scott P. McBride

ASSOCIATES

Cathleen D. Allen
Catherine Healy Kanzler
Rita Fishman Sheena
Shari Lee Sugarman

For full biographical listings, see the Martindale-Hubbell Law Directory

*MINEOLA,** Nassau Co.

GALLAGHER, WALKER, BIANCO & PLASTARAS (AV)

98 Willis Avenue, 11501
Telephone: 516-248-2002
Fax: 516-248-2394

Gerard M. Gallagher
Robert J. Walker
Dominic P. Bianco
Thomas E. Plastaras

ASSOCIATES

Ann Willoughby
William P. Nolan

OF COUNSEL

Stephen P. Burke

For full biographical listings, see the Martindale-Hubbell Law Directory

NEWBURGH, Orange Co.

RIDER, WEINER, FRANKEL & CALHELHA, P.C. (AV)

655 Little Britain Road, P.O. Box 2280, 12550
Telephone: 914-562-9100
Fax: 914-562-9126
Email: firm@rwfc.com *URL:* http://www.rwfc.com

M.J. Rider (1906-1968)
Elliott M. Weiner (1915-1990)
David L. Rider
Charles E. Frankel
Moacyr R. Calhelha
Maureen Crush
Michael J. Matsler

Donna M. Badura
Mark C. Taylor
Roderick E. de Ramon
Teri L. Shulman

OF COUNSEL

Craig F. Simon
David E. Tower

LEGAL SUPPORT PERSONNEL

Lynn W. Cybulski
Aliza S. D'Agati
Carol E. Garner

For full biographical listings, see the Martindale-Hubbell Law Directory

*NEW YORK,** New York Co.

BAKER BOTTS L.L.P. (AV)

599 Lexington Avenue, 10022-6030 and 30 Rockefeller Plaza, 10112-0228
Telephone: 212-705-5000
Fax: 212-705-5125 (599 Lexington Ave.)
Fax: 212-705-5020 (30 Rockefeller Plaza)
Email: postmaster@bakerbotts.com *URL:* http://www.bakerbotts.com
Washington, D.C. Office: The Warner, 1299 Pennsylvania Avenue, N.W.
Telephone: 202-639-7700.
Austin, Texas Office: 1600 San Jacinto Center, 98 San Jacinto Boulevard.
Telephone: 512-322-2500.
Dallas, Texas Office: 2001 Ross Avenue.
Telephone: 214-953-6500.
Houston, Texas Office: One Shell Plaza, 910 Louisiana.
Telephone: 713-229-1234.
Moscow, Russia Office: 10 ul. Bolshaya Dimitrovka (formerly ul. Pushkinskaya), 103031.
Telephone: 7095/921-5300 (Local); 7095/929-7070 (International).

(See Next Column)

London, England Office: 45 Ludgate Hill.
Telephone: 0171-778-1400 (Local); 011-44-171-778-1400.
Baku, Azerbaijan Office: 6-10 Vagif Mustafa-zadeh Street, Third Floor, Icheri Sheher, 370004.
Telephone: 994-12-97-63-88 (Local); 011-994-12-97-63-88 (International).
Fax: 994-12-97-63-91 (Local); 011-994-12-97-63-61 (International).

MEMBERS OF FIRM

Lee D. Charles
John M. Huggins (Not admitted in NY)
Marc A. Leaf
Elizabeth M. Markowski
Frederick H. McGrath
Robert W. Murray Jr.

SPECIAL COUNSEL

Thomas V. D'Ambrosio

ASSOCIATES

Brayton Dresser
Thomas R. Pappas
Glen W. Roberts II
Craig Troyer (Not admitted in NY)

For Complete List of Firm Personnel, See General Section

For full biographical listings, see the Martindale-Hubbell Law Directory

BECKMAN, MILLMAN & SANDERS, LLP (AV)

116 John Street, 10038
Telephone: 212-406-4700
Telecopier: 212-406-3750
URL: http://www.bmsllp.com

Michael Beckman
Steven A. Sanders
Debra J. Millman
Marc S. Gottlieb

James S. Eisberg
Laurence D. Paredes
William S. Rosenstadt
Rory L. Lubin
Ron S. Berenblatt
Jeffrey R. Miller

For full biographical listings, see the Martindale-Hubbell Law Directory

BERLACK, ISRAELS & LIBERMAN LLP (AV)

120 West 45th Street, 10036
Telephone: 212-704-0100
Cable Address: "Berilib"
Telecopier: 212-704-0196
Email: info@berlack.com
Morristown, New Jersey Office: 65 Madison Avenue.
Telephone: 201-644-3400.
Telecopier: 201-644-3159.

MEMBERS OF FIRM

Harris Berlack (1946-1968)
Carlos L. Israels (1946-1969)
Kenneth R. Asher
Claude A. Baum
Scott M. Berman
Wade M. Boswell
Douglas E. Davidson
Alan N. Forman
Steven E. Greenbaum
Harvey M. Katz
James B. Liberman
Stuart Neuhauser
Robert D. Schmicker
Martin S. Siegel
Steven F. Wasserman
Edward S. Weisfelner

SENIOR ATTORNEYS

Andrew S. Dash
Erica M. Ryland

ASSOCIATES

John P. Biedermann
Anne M. Cunningham
Pauline Foley (Resident, Morristown, New Jersey Office)
Julie L. Friedberg (Resident, Morristown, New Jersey Office)
Emilio A. Galván
Linda B. Goebel
Louis Lombardo
Rachel F. Mayerson (Not admitted in NY)
Amy P. K. Motzenbecker (Resident, Morristown, New Jersey Office)
Antonio Peguero, Jr.
Elizabeth Quirk (Resident, Morristown, New Jersey Office)
Marcela M. Sanchez
Melissa Sarubbi

OF COUNSEL

Gerald W. Conway (Not admitted in NY; Resident, Morristown, New Jersey Office)
Marc B. Lasky (Resident, Morristown, New Jersey Office)

For full biographical listings, see the Martindale-Hubbell Law Directory

BRESLOW & WALKER, LLP (AV)

767 Third Avenue, 10017
Telephone: 212-832-1930
Fax: 212-888-4955
Email: breslow767@aol.com
Jericho, New York Office: 100 Jericho Quadrangle, 11753.
Telephone: 516-822-6505.
Fax: 516-822-6544.

Joel M. Walker
Howard S. Breslow
Leonard J. Breslow

Kevin W. Waite

(See Next Column)

BRESLOW & WALKER LLP—*Continued*

OF COUNSEL

Roy H. Carlin

For full biographical listings, see the Martindale-Hubbell Law Directory

CAPLIN & DRYSDALE, CHARTERED (AV)

399 Park Avenue 36th Floor, 10022
Telephone: 212-319-7125
Fax: 212-644-6755
Washington, D.C. Office: One Thomas Circle, N.W.
Telephone: 202-862-5000.
Fax: 202-429-3301.

Elihu Inselbuch

Rita C. Tobin

For full biographical listings, see the Martindale-Hubbell Law Directory

FORD MARRIN ESPOSITO WITMEYER & GLESER, L.L.P. (AV)

Wall Street Plaza, 10005-1875
Telephone: 212-269-4900
Facsimile: 212-344-4294
Cable Address: "Formarew-New York"
Email: postmaster@fmew.com *URL:* http://www.fmew.com
Montclair, New Jersey Office: 49 Park Street.
Telephone: 973-744-3700.
Facsimile: 973-509-1565.

MEMBERS OF FIRM

James M. Adrian
Michael L. Anania
Charles A. Booth
Cushing O'Malley Condon
Elizabeth M. De Cristofaro
Thomas R. Esposito
William P. Ford
Victor G. Gleser (1948-1992)
Stuart C. Levene
Richard B. Marrin
Edward M. Pinter
Philip S. Plexico (1931-1983)
John J. Witmeyer III

COUNSEL

James F. X. Hiler

ASSOCIATES

Jay R. Alicandri
Jody M. Barringer
David A. Beke
Christopher J. Carney
Todd S. Corey
Joseph D'Ambrosio
Serena C. Hunn
Matthew J. Lasky
Paul V. Majkowski
Michael A. Rowe
Michael J. Tricarico

For full biographical listings, see the Martindale-Hubbell Law Directory

FRIEDMAN KAPLAN & SEILER LLP (AV)

875 Third Avenue, 10022-6225
Telephone: 212-833-1100
Facsimile: 212-355-6401
Email: info@fkslaw.com
Newark, New Jersey Office: One Gateway Center, 25th Floor, 07102-5311.
Telephone: 973-297-4700.
Facsimile: 973-297-4701.

MEMBERS OF FIRM

Bruce S. Kaplan
Edward A. Friedman
Barry A. Adelman
Eric Seiler
Robert D. Kaplan
Gary D. Friedman
Andrew W. Goldwater
Robert J. Lack
Gregg S. Lerner
Hal Neier
Philippe Adler
Matthew S. Haiken
Paul J. Fishman
Richard M. Hoffman
Lance J. Gotko

COUNSEL

Robert D. Wurwarg
Ira A. Freedman

ASSOCIATES

Craig J. Codlin
Michael B. Dorff
Andrew R. Greengrass
Ellen A. Harnick
Sophia S. Hartch
Mishell B. Kneeland
Robert S. Loigman
Craig Nemiroff
Joshua M. Olshin
Katherine L. Pringle
Daniel B. Rapport
Meryl S. Rosenblatt
Robert C. Scherer
Donna Segal
Jonathan M. Silver
Lee D. Sossen
David I. Tanenbaum
Marla J. Wasserman
Sian E. Zelbo

For full biographical listings, see the Martindale-Hubbell Law Directory

GETNICK & GETNICK (AV)

Tower 49, 12 East 49th Street, 31st Floor, 10017-1028
Telephone: 212-376-5666
Telefax: 212-292-3942
Email: info@getnicklaw.com *URL:* http://www.lawyers.com/getnick&getnick

(See Next Column)

MEMBERS OF FIRM

Irving M. Getnick
Neil V. Getnick
Lesley Ann Skillen
Margaret J. Finerty

OF COUNSEL

David A. Koenigsberg
Michael E. Getnick

ASSOCIATE

Richard J. Dircks

For full biographical listings, see the Martindale-Hubbell Law Directory

INGRAM YUZEK GAINEN CARROLL & BERTOLOTTI, LLP (AV)

250 Park Avenue, 10177
Telephone: 212-907-9600
Facsimile: 212-907-9681

MEMBERS OF FIRM

Ernest J. Bertolotti (1942-1999)
Daniel L. Carroll
Roger Cukras
David G. Ebert
Larry F. Gainen
Samuel W. Ingram, Jr.
Paulette Kendler
Steven Mastbaum
Shane O'Neill
Dean G. Yuzek

ASSOCIATES

Warren E. Barrows
Amy Bertolotti
Patricia Hewitt
Theodore M. Kakoyiannis
Jeanne F. Pucci
Leigh A. Roveda
Jennifer E. Schwartz
Paul H. Slaney

OF COUNSEL

Karin J. Barkhorn
Beverly L. Deickler
Mark E. Klein
Paulette Lemay Peters
Cory L. Weiss

For full biographical listings, see the Martindale-Hubbell Law Directory

BUREAU FRANCIS LEFEBVRE (AV)

712 Fifth Avenue, 10019
Telephone: 212-246-8045
Fax: 212-246-2951
Email: clevintoff@bflny.com
Paris, France Office: 1-3, Villa Emile Bergerat, 92522 Neuilly-Sur-Seine, Cedex.
Telephone: +33-1 47 38 55 00.
Fax: +33-1 47 38 55 55. Email: central@bfl-avocats.com.
Barcelona, Spain Office: Rodes y Sala Bureau Francis Lefebvre, Calle Pau Casals 15-3, 08021, Barcelona.
Telephone: +34 93 241 37 40.
Fax: +34 93 209 89 96. Email: rodesysala@bam-bfl.com.
Berlin, Germany Office: Friedrichstrasse 200, D-10117 Berlin.
Telephone: +49 30 2233 11 00.
Fax: +49 30 2233 11 22. Email: bfl-berlin@berlin.sireco.net.
Brussels, Belgium Office: avenue Louise, 523, 1050 Bruxelles.
Telephone: +32-2 644 26 61.
Fax: +32-2 649 68 01. Email: bfl@skynet.be.
Bucharest, Romania Office: 4bd Natiunilor Unite, Bloc 106, sector 5, Bucharest.
Telephone: +40 1 335 15 40.
Fax: +40 1 335 08 74. Email: marcuc@ines.ro.
Buenos Aires, Argentina Office: Paraquay 1132, piso 4°, Buenos Aires, 1057 Capital Federal.
Telephone: +54 11.48.13.64.61.
Fax: +54 11.48.16. 06.08. Email: bfl@ba.net.
Casablanca, Morocco Office: 106 rue Abderrahman Sehraoui, Casablanca 2000.
Telephone: +(212) 2.26.19.92.
Fax: +(212) 2.26.37.61.
Düsseldorf, Germany Office: Immermannstrasse 15, 40210 Düsseldorf.
Telephone: +49 211 17 59 10.
Fax: +49 211 1 64 04 11. Email: bfl-duss@t-online.dc.
Madrid, Spain Office: Briones, Alonso y Martin Bureau Francis Lefebvre, Paseo de la Castellana 20, 28046 Madrid.
Telephone: +34 91 436 45 31.
Fax: +34 91 436 43 02. Email: bam@mx3.rodestb.cs.
Moscow, Russia Office: 10, Uspensky Pereoulok, 103006 Moscow.
Telephone: +7.502.221.49.03.
Fax: +7.095.299.30.24. Email: bflrus@co.ru.

RESIDENT PARTNERS

Carina Levintoff
Edouard Milhac (Not admitted in the United States)

RESIDENT ASSOCIATES

Francine L. Alfandary
Paul Bayle (Not admitted in the United States)

OF COUNSEL

John P. Lowe, Jr.

For full biographical listings, see the Martindale-Hubbell Law Directory

New York—Continued

MORGANROTH & MORGANROTH (AV)
156 W. 56th Street, Suite 1101, 10019
Telephone: 212-586-5905
URL: http://www.lawyers.com/morganroth&morganrothlaw
Southfield, Michigan Office: 3000 Town Center, Suite 1500, 48075.
Telephone: 248-355-3084.
Fax: 248-355-3017.

Mayer Morganroth
Jeffrey B. Morganroth

For full biographical listings, see the Martindale-Hubbell Law Directory

OTTERBOURG, STEINDLER, HOUSTON & ROSEN, P.C. (AV)
230 Park Avenue, 29th Floor, 10169
Telephone: 212-661-9100
Telecopier: 212-682-6104

Donald N. Gellert
William M. Silverman
Peter H. Stolzar
Alan R. Weiskopf
Jonathan N. Helfat
Daniel Wallen
Scott L. Hazan
Glenn B. Rice
Albert F. Reisman
Anthony M. Piccione
Steven B. Soll
Alan Kardon
Mitchell M. Brand
Stanley L. Lane, Jr.
David W. Morse
Peter L. Feldman
Richard G. Haddad
Andrew M. Kramer

GENERAL COUNSEL

Kurt J. Wolff

COUNSEL

Bernard Beitel
Morton L. Gitter

Lloyd M. Green
Enid Nagler Stuart
Craig D. Zlotnick
Stephen H. Alpert
Jenette A. Barrow-Bosshart
Brett H. Miller
Matthew J. Miller
John J. Kenny
Richard L. Stehl
Susan A. Joyce

For Complete List of Firm Personnel, See General Section

For full biographical listings, see the Martindale-Hubbell Law Directory

PILIERO GOLDSTEIN JENKINS & SULLIVAN, LLP (AV)
292 Madison Avenue, 10017
Telephone: 212-213-8200
Fax: 212-685-2028
Email: lawyers@pgjhlaw.com *URL:* http://www.pgjhlaw.com
Carlstadt, New Jersey Office: One Palmer Terrace.
Telephone: 201-507-5157.
FAX: 201-507-5221.
Washington, D.C. Office: 888 17th Street, N.W., Suite 1100.
Telephone: 202-467-6991.
FAX: 202-467-6703.
San Francisco, California Office: 507 Howard Street, Suite 200.
Telephone: 415-281-3631.
Fax: 415-281-3630.

MEMBERS OF FIRM

Kimberlee S. Bogen
Edward J. Goldstein
Jon Mark Jenkins
Marc A. Lebowitz
Robert D. Piliero
George O. Richardson, III
Michael T. Sullivan

ASSOCIATES

Craig Avedisian
Rosemary G. Feit
Eric M. Kogan
Mariano Schwed

OF COUNSEL

Kenneth D. Arbeeny
Christopher P. Hall

For full biographical listings, see the Martindale-Hubbell Law Directory

SEIDMAN, SILVERMAN & SEIDMAN, P.C. (AV)
600 Third Avenue 33rd Floor, 10016-2001
Telephone: 212-922-1900

Irving P. Seidman
Lawrence H. Silverman
Brian William Seidman

Joseph M. Fein

For full biographical listings, see the Martindale-Hubbell Law Directory

TORYS (AV)
237 Park Avenue, 10017
Telephone: 212-880-6000
Facsimile: (212) 682-0200
URL: http://www.toryhaythe.com
Toronto, Ontario Office: Suite 3000, Maritime Life, P.O. Box 270, Toronto-Dominion Centre, M5K 1N2.
Telephones: 416-865-0040; 800-505-8679.
Fax: 416-865-7380.

(See Next Column)

Beijing, China Office: China Merchants Tower, Suite C, 29/F, 2 Dong Huan Nan Lu, Jianguomenwai, Chaoyang District, 100022.
Telephone: 011-8610-6566-9088.
Facsimile: 011-8610-6566-9096.

MEMBERS OF FIRM

Andrew J. Beck
Susan W. Berson
Kimberly S. Blanchard
John J. Butler
Erin T. Cornyn
Bradley P. Cost
Stephen C. Curley
Charles E. Dorkey III
David L. Dubrow
Miroslav M. Fajt
Clinton B. Fisher
Margaret C. Henry
Charles B. Hughes, III
Richard J. Krainin
Jerry E. Muntz
Robert A. Ouimette
Joseph J. Romagnoli
Barbara M. Roth
Steven R. Schoenfeld
Thomas I. Sheridan, III
Mark B Waldstein
David W. R. Wawro
Jun Wei
Richard G. Willoughby (Not admitted in NY)

COUNSEL

Carol L. Divine
Edward J. Henderson
Peter J. Keenan

ASSOCIATES

Stephen J. Adnopoz
Jonathan M. Anderson
Michael H. André
Edward G. Angelini (Not admitted in NY)
Jennifer R. Apiscopa
Linda M. Baldwin
Paula J. Brown
Lina A. Bryan-Toledo
John D. Burton
Dean T. Cho
Daniel P. Conneen (Not admitted in NY)
Michelle Donnay
Linda S. Eliopulos (Not admitted in NY)
William Worth Hatch
Nicomedes Sy Herrera
Lee J. Hirsch
Gail K. Julie
Ronald S. Kornreich
Dong Lan
Timothy J. Mattimore, Jr.
Rachelle A. Peluso
Dominique Proust-Bonnin
Sheree D. Reinbach
Todd L. Schleifstein
I.C. Judy Shen
Evan H. Sils
Marshall A. Sklar
Joseph L. Tambaro
Lee E. Taylor
Piero A. Tozzi
V. Carl Walker (Not admitted in NY)
Lauren Bauer Zinman

For full biographical listings, see the Martindale-Hubbell Law Directory

TRAUB, BONACQUIST & FOX LLP (AV)
655 Third Avenue, 21st Floor, 10017
Telephone: 212-476-4770
Fax: 212-476-4787
Email: tbfesq@aol.com
Arlington, Texas Office: 433 Washington Drive.
Telephone: 817-794-0667.
Fax: 817-794-0456.

MEMBERS OF FIRM

Paul Traub
Michael S. Fox
Susan F. Balaschak (Resident, Arlington, Texas Office)
Steven E. Fox

ASSOCIATES

Fredrick J. Levy
Wendy G. Marcari
Maura I. Russell

OF COUNSEL

Harold F. Bonacquist
Brian E. Kriger

For full biographical listings, see the Martindale-Hubbell Law Directory

*ROCHESTER,** Monroe Co.

UNDERBERG & KESSLER LLP (AV)
1800 Chase Square, 14604
Telephone: 716-258-2800
Fax: 716-258-2821
Email: INFO@UNDERBERG-KESSLER.COM
Buffalo, New York Office: 1100 Main Place Tower. 14202.
Telephone: 716-848-9000.
Fax: 716-847-6004.

MEMBERS OF FIRM

Alan J. Underberg (1929-1998)
Irving L. Kessler
Michael J. Beyma
James A. Coniglio
Frank T. Crego
Robert W. Croessmann
John W. Crowe
Patrick L. Cusato
Michael C. Dwyer
Bernard A. Frank
Steven R. Gersz
Katherine Howk Karl
Lawrence P. Keller
Gordon J. Lipson
Anna E. Lynch
Robert F. Mechur
Paul V. Nunes
Terry M. Richman
J. David Sampson (Resident, Buffalo Office)
Sharon P. Stiller
Stephen H. Waite
Russell I. Zuckerman

OF COUNSEL

Andrew M. Greenstein

(See Next Column)

UNDERBERG & KESSLER LLP—*Continued*

SENIOR ATTORNEYS

Duncan R. Farney
Ronald G. Hull

ASSOCIATES

James F. Armstrong (Resident, Buffalo Office)
Karen A. DiNardo
Lise C. Hamilton
Jeffrey D. Hummel
Paul F. Keneally
Ella L. Krzanowicz
Maureen E. Mulholland
Suzanne D. Nott
Kelly L. Odorisi
Thomas A. Rall

For full biographical listings, see the Martindale-Hubbell Law Directory

*SYRACUSE,** Onondaga Co.

HISCOCK & BARCLAY, LLP (AV)

Financial Plaza, P.O. Box 4878, 13221
Telephone: 315-422-2131
Fax: 315-472-3059
Email: reachus@hiscockbarclay.com *URL:* http://www.hiscockbarclay.com
Buffalo, New York Office: Suite 301 The Key Bank Towers at Key Center, 50 Fountain Plaza.
Telephone: 716-856-0911.
Fax: 716-856-2567.
Albany, New York Office: 40 Beaver Street.
Telephone: 518-434-2163.
Fax: 518-434-2621.

Frank H. Hiscock (1856-1946)

MEMBERS OF FIRM

H. Douglas Barclay
Taylor H. Obold
David B. Liddell
George S. Deptula
John P. Sindoni
Frederick S. Marty
Richard K. Hughes
J. Eric Charlton
Thomas S. Squire
Clifford H. Wilson
Robert A. Barrer
Christopher J. Bonner
Judith M. Sayles
Peter H. Swartz
John P. Langan
Catherine Keib Johnson
Richard J. Paul
Jon P. Devendorf
Richard R. Capozza

ASSOCIATES

Deborah A. Bentley
Alan R. Peterman
Kathleen M. O'Connor
Jennifer K. Frank
Matthew S. Moses
Christopher J. Centore
Jean K. Sehl
Bonnie Angela Buccina
Joseph P. McRae
Yvonne E. Marciano
Andrew J. Leja
William A. Barclay

OF COUNSEL

Donald M. Mawhinney, Jr.
Roger J. Edinger
Ferdinand L. Picardi
Jan R. Farr

General Counsel for: Syracuse Savings Bank; Key Corp; Key Bank of New York N.A. ; Solvay Bank; Excelsior Insurance Co.; Key Trust Co.; Auburn Steel Co., Inc.
Local Counsel for: Firestone Tire & Rubber Co.; Fidelity & Deposit Company of Maryland.

For full biographical listings, see the Martindale-Hubbell Law Directory

UNIONDALE, Nassau Co.

LEHMAN & EILEN LLP (AV)

50 Charles Lindbergh Boulevard, Suite 505, 11553-3600
Telephone: 516-222-0888
Fax: 516-222-0948
Email: info@lehmaneilen.com *URL:* http://www.securitiesattys.com

MEMBERS OF FIRM

Bob E. Lehman
Howard S. Eilen

OF COUNSEL

Hank Gracin
Timothy P. Kebbe

ASSOCIATES

Stephanie G. Senzer
Maureen Ann Porette
Eva M. Possavino
Audrey Blain
Scott D. Stechman
Steven J. Pappas

For full biographical listings, see the Martindale-Hubbell Law Directory

*WHITE PLAINS,** Westchester Co.

ROGAN GUIDA & ORENSTEIN (AV)

235 Mamaroneck Avenue, 10605
Telephone: 1-888-WIN-WITH-US; 914-328-4480
Fax: 914-328-4479
URL: http://www.NYlawyers.com
Email: RoganGO@aol.com *URL:* http://www.lawyers.com/personalinjury

(See Next Column)

Jeffrey P. Rogan
Toni M. Guida
David L. Orenstein

Representative Clients: Recore One Mortgage Corp.; LEASCO; Pappas Enterprises Inc.; Steelcase, Inc.; Printing Center of Westchester Inc.; Corporate Imaging, Inc.; King Jolo's Flowers, Inc.; Systems Exchange, Inc.; Domus Realty.
Reference: Fleet Bank.

For full biographical listings, see the Martindale-Hubbell Law Directory

NORTH CAROLINA

*ASHEVILLE,** Buncombe Co.

VAN WINKLE, BUCK, WALL, STARNES AND DAVIS, P.A. (AV)

11 North Market Street, P.O. Box 7376, 28801
Telephone: 828-258-2991
FAX: 828-255-0255; 257-2767
Hendersonville, North Carolina Office: 422 South Main Street.
Telephone: 828-697-6196.
Fax: 828-693-3999.

Kingsland Van Winkle (1879-1972)
Charles G. Buck (Retired)
Robertson Wall (1913-1996)
O. E. Starnes
Roy W. Davis, Jr.
Brian F. D. Lavelle
Larry S. McDevitt
Philip J. Smith
Barry B. Kempson
Albert L. Sneed, Jr.
Robert H. Haggard (Resident, Hendersonville)
Marla Tugwell Adams
Jones Pharr Byrd
Allan R. Tarleton
Larry C. Harris, Jr.
Michelle Rippon
William Perry Fisher, II
Michael M. Thompson (Resident, Hendersonville, North Carolina Office)
Mark A. Pinkston
Stephen J. Grabenstein
Craig D. Justus
Cynthia W. Eller
Stephen B. Williamson
Adam Langdon Shealy
John G. Kelso
Dale A. Curriden
W. Carleton Metcalf
David G. Redding
W. Kevin McLaughlin, Jr.
Jennifer Wayland Moore
Robert J. Fedder
Juliet M. Sarkessian
Carolyn Lloyd Coward

Western Region General Counsel for: Wachovia Bank & Trust Co.
Attorneys for: Carolina Power & Light Co.; Charles D. Owen Manufacturing Co.; Clyde Savings and Loan Assn.; Continental Telephone Company of N.C.; Gerber Products Co.; Liberty Mutual Insurance Co.; Reliance Insurance Co.; State Farm Mutual Automobile Insurance Co.; United States Fidelity & Guaranty Co.

For full biographical listings, see the Martindale-Hubbell Law Directory

CHAPEL HILL, Orange Co.

NORTHEN BLUE, L.L.P. (AV)

Suite 550, 100 Europa Center, P.O. Box 2208, 27515-2208
Telephone: 919-968-4441
Facsimile: 919-942-6603
Email: NBFIRM@aol.com

MEMBERS OF FIRM

John A. Northen
J. William Blue, Jr.
David M. Rooks, III
Charles H. Thibaut
Carol J. Holcomb

ASSOCIATES

James C. Stanford
Cheryl Y. Capron
Margaret W. Holloway

References: Central Carolina Bank; Triangle Bank; Investors Title Insurance Co.; First Union National Bank; Centura Bank; BB&T; Balbirer & Coleman, CPA's.

For full biographical listings, see the Martindale-Hubbell Law Directory

*CHARLOTTE,** Mecklenburg Co.

CANSLER, LOCKHART, CAMPBELL, EVANS, BRYANT & GARLITZ, P.A. (AV)

2030 The Carillon, 227 West Trade Street, 28202
Telephone: 704-372-1282
Fax: 704-372-1621
URL: http://www.canslerlockhart.com

Hugh B. Campbell, Jr.
George K. Evans, Jr.
Frank L. Bryant
Thomas D. Garlitz
W. Lewis Smith, Jr.
R. Michael Allen
Stacy C. Cordes
Kristin D. Decker

Drupti P. Chauhan

(See Next Column)

CANSLER, LOCKHART, CAMPBELL, EVANS, BRYANT & GARLITZ P.A., *Charlotte—Continued*

OF COUNSEL

Thomas Ashe Lockhart
James B. Craighill

Representative Clients: A.M.E. Zion Church; American National Mortgage, Inc.; The Baldwin Company, Inc.; Con-Way Southern Express, Inc.; Eurotherm Drives, Inc.; InterCon Building Corp.; Megadyne America, LLC; Pavilion Properties, Inc.; Raftelis Financial Consulting, Inc.; Young Ford, Inc.

For full biographical listings, see the Martindale-Hubbell Law Directory

DOZIER, MILLER, POLLARD & MURPHY (AV)

Cameron Brown Building, 301 South McDowell Street, Suite 700, 28204
Telephone: 704-372-6373
Fax: 704-347-0674
URL: http://www.dmpm.com

MEMBERS OF FIRM

W. Joseph Dozier, Jr.
R. Craig Miller, Jr.
Scott T. Pollard
Gary L. Murphy
William Patrick Hobson
Timothy H. Graham
George N. Miller
Richard S. Gordon
Thomas J. Falish
Kristin L. Smith

For full biographical listings, see the Martindale-Hubbell Law Directory

RAYBURN, MOON & SMITH, P.A. (AV)

The Carillon, 227 West Trade Street, Suite 1200, 28202-1675
Telephone: 704-334-0891
Fax: 704-377-1897; 704-377-0395
Email: rmslaw@aol.com

Albert F. Durham
Travis W. Moon
C. Richard Rayburn, Jr.
James C. Smith
W. Scott Cooper
Paul R. Baynard
James B. Gatehouse
G. Kirkland Hardymon
James L. Bagwell
Patricia B. Edmondson
Natalie R. Denton
Robert Aubrey Cox, Jr.
Tricia L. Rolewicz

For full biographical listings, see the Martindale-Hubbell Law Directory

WOMBLE CARLYLE SANDRIDGE & RICE (AV)

A Professional Limited Liability Company
3300 One First Union Center, 301 South College Street, 28202-6025
Telephone: 704-331-4900
Fax: 704-331-4955
Email: lawyers@wcsr.com *URL:* http://www.wcsr.com
Winston-Salem, North Carolina Office: 200 West Second Street, P.O. Drawer 84.
Telephone: 336-721-3600.
Fax: 336-721-3660.
Raleigh, North Carolina Office: 2100 First Union Capitol Center, 150 Fayetteville Street Mall, P.O. Box 831.
Telephone: 919-755-2100.
Fax: 919-755-2150.
Research Triangle Park, North Carolina Office: 2505 Meridian Parkway, Suite 300 (Durham), 27713.
Telephone: 919-484-2300.
Fax: 919-484-2340.
Atlanta, Georgia Office: One Atlantic Center, 1201 West Peachtree Street, Suite 3500.
Telephone: 404-872-7000.
Fax: 404-888-7490.
Other Atlanta, Georgia Office: Suite 404, 2296 Henderson Mill Road, N.E.
Telephone: 770-492-9030.
Fax: 770-492-9609.
Washington, D.C. Office: 1120 Nineteenth Street, N.W., Eighth Floor.
Telephone: 202-857-4400.
Fax: 202-467-6910.
Greenville, South Carolina Office: 15 South Main Street, Suite 601, P.O. Box 10208.
Telephone: 864-255-5400.
Fax: 864-255-5440.

RESIDENT MEMBERS

Joe B. Cogdell, Jr.
J. Carlton Fleming
Cyrus M. Johnson, Jr.
Lesley G. Powell
J. Alexander Salisbury

RESIDENT ASSOCIATES

Douglas A. Mays
Ellen A. Perrin
Daniel G. Schmedlen, Jr.
Todd C. Taylor

RESIDENT OF COUNSEL

Jane Jeffries Jones

Representative Clients: Childress Klein Properties, Inc.; Food Lion, Inc.; J.A. Jones Construction Co.; Parkdale Mills, Inc.; Pillowtex; Duke Power Co.; Bowles Hollowell Conner & Co.; ALLTEL Carolina, Inc.; Belk Store Services, Inc.; Philip Holzmann A.G.

For Complete List of Firm Personnel, See General Section

For full biographical listings, see the Martindale-Hubbell Law Directory

*GREENSBORO,** Guilford Co.

ISAACSON & ISAACSON (AV)

Suite 400 Bank of America Building, 101 West Friendly Avenue, P.O. Box 1888, 27402
Telephone: 336-275-7626
Fax: 336-273-7293
Email: ikeandike@aol.com *URL:* http://www.lawyers.com/isaacson

MEMBERS OF FIRM

Henry H. Isaacson
Marc L. Isaacson

ASSOCIATES

Jennifer N. Fountain
Anna Gregory Wagoner

For full biographical listings, see the Martindale-Hubbell Law Directory

SCHELL BRAY AYCOCK ABEL & LIVINGSTON P.L.L.C. (AV)

1500 Renaissance Plaza, 230 North Elm Street, P.O. Box 21847, 27420
Telephone: 336-370-8800
Fax: 336-370-8830
Email: Info@sbaal.com *URL:* http://www.sbaal.com

MEMBERS OF FIRM

Braxton Schell
Doris R. Bray
William P. Aycock, II
Michael R. Abel
Paul H. Livingston, Jr.
Thomas C. Watkins
Dan T. Barker, Jr.
Barbara R. Christy
John A. McLendon, Jr.

ASSOCIATES

Kathleen A. Kingsbury
Jacqueline E. Camp
A. Nicholas Purrington
Gregory M. Chabon
Jennifer Johnson
Eric M. Braun
Garland V. Gibbes

Representative Clients: The Breakers Palm Beach, Inc.; CBP Resources, Inc. (Carolina By-Products); Cone Mills Corp.; Cornwallis Development Co.; Kenan Transport Co.; Klaussner Furniture Industries, Inc.; North Carolina Trust Co.; Texfi Industries, Inc.; University of North Carolina at Chapel Hill Foundation, Inc.; Vanguard Cellular Systems, Inc.

For full biographical listings, see the Martindale-Hubbell Law Directory

STERN & KLEPFER, L.L.P. (AV)

600 NationsBank Building, P.O. Box 3112, 27402
Telephone: 336-373-1500
Fax: 336-272-8258

Sidney J. Stern, Jr. (1914-1991)
John L. Rendleman (1932-1983)

MEMBERS OF FIRM

Robert O. Klepfer, Jr.
John T. Higgins, Jr.
James W. Miles, Jr.
Brinton D. Wright
William A. Eagles

ASSOCIATES

Melanie H. Rodenbough
Maureen Breen Gerhardt
Ronda Leigh Lowe
Douglas M. Heberle

Representative Clients: Bankers Trust of North Carolina; NationsBank of North Carolina, N.A.; Tannenbaum-Sternberger Foundation; Bennett College; Endura Products, Inc.; Carlyle & Co. Jewelers.

For full biographical listings, see the Martindale-Hubbell Law Directory

*GREENVILLE,** Pitt Co.

GAYLORD, MCNALLY, STRICKLAND & SNYDER, L.L.P. (AV)

498 Red Banks Road, P.O. Drawer 545, 27835-0545
Telephone: 252-321-7111
Fax: 252-321-7112

MEMBERS OF FIRM

Louis W. Gaylord, Jr. (Retired)
Danny D. McNally
D. Michael Strickland
Vernon G. Snyder, III

ASSOCIATE

Emma Stallings Holscher

Representative Clients: Wachovia Bank, N.A.; Nationsbank, N.A.; Garris Evans Lumber Co., Inc.; United States Fidelity and Guaranty Co.; The Daily Reflector, Inc.; Hastings Ford, Inc.; Nationwide Mutual Insurance Co.; U.S. Cellular; Ironwood Development, Inc.

For full biographical listings, see the Martindale-Hubbell Law Directory

*RALEIGH,** Wake Co.

ALLEN & MOORE, L.L.P. (AV)

3700 Computer Drive, Suite 320, 27609-8627
Telephone: 919-783-8023
Fax: 919-783-8282
Email: ALLNMOORE@AOL.COM

(See Next Column)

ALLEN & MOORE L.L.P.—*Continued*

Arch T. Allen, III Joseph C. Moore, III
Ann Strader Hanley

For full biographical listings, see the Martindale-Hubbell Law Directory

EMANUEL AND DUNN (AV)

130 South Salisbury Street, P.O. Box 426, 27602
Telephone: 919-832-0329; 832-0320
Fax: 919-832-6731

MEMBERS OF FIRM

J. L. Emanuel (1894-1968) Robert L. Emanuel
Stephen A. Dunn

Representative Clients: Metropolitan Life Insurance Co.; BellSouth Telecommunications, Inc.; Prudential Insurance Company of America; Cargill, Incorporated.

For full biographical listings, see the Martindale-Hubbell Law Directory

HUTCHISON & MASON PLLC (AV)

4011 Westchase Boulevard, Suite 400, 27607
Telephone: 919-829-9600
Fax: 919-829-9696
URL: http://www.hutchlaw.com

Fred D. Hutchison Merrill McCall Mason

Helga Lura Leftwich Kathleen Nowack Worm
J. Robert Tyler, III Holly Ann Coldiron
E. Christopher Cox

For full biographical listings, see the Martindale-Hubbell Law Directory

MERRITT, WOOTEN & JANVIER, P.A. (AV)

Suite 2010, Two Hannover Square, P.O. Box 3007, 27602-3007
Telephone: 919-834-9160
Facsimile: 919-834-9052

Robert H. Merritt, Jr. Louis E. Wooten, III
William P. Janvier

OF COUNSEL

Alfred L. Purrington, III

Christine H. McCann

For full biographical listings, see the Martindale-Hubbell Law Directory

RAGSDALE LIGGETT, PLLC (AV)

A Professional Limited Liability Company
Suite 400 Crosspointe Plaza, 2840 Plaza Place, P.O. Box 31507, 27612
Telephone: 919-787-5200
Fax: 919-783-8991; 881-2045

MEMBERS OF FIRM

George R. Ragsdale William S. Bost, III
Frank R. Liggett III Dorothy Bass Burch
William A. Mann James Allen Hoffman
Steven I. Reinhard (Not admitted in NC)

OF COUNSEL

Joseph E. Johnson

ASSOCIATES

Kathleen Pepi Southern David K. Liggett
Walter L. Tippett, Jr. Kathleen C. Mcconnell

For full biographical listings, see the Martindale-Hubbell Law Directory

WOMBLE CARLYLE SANDRIDGE & RICE (AV)

A Professional Limited Liability Company
2100 First Union Capitol Center, 150 Fayetteville Street Mall, P.O. Box 831, 27602
Telephone: 919-755-2100
Fax: 919-755-2150
Email: lawyers@wcsr.com *URL:* http://www.wcsr.com
Charlotte, North Carolina Office: 3300 One First Union Center, 301 South College Street.
Telephone: 704-331-4900.
Fax: 704-331-4955.
Winston-Salem, North Carolina Office: 200 West Second Street, P.O. Drawer 84.
Telephone: 336-721-3600.
Fax: 336-721-3660.
Research Triangle Park, North Carolina Office: 2505 Meridian Parkway, Suite 300 (Durham), 27713.
Telephone: 919-484-2300.
Fax: 919-484-2340.
Atlanta, Georgia Office: One Atlantic Center, 1201 West Peachtree Street, Suite 3500.
Telephone: 404-872-7000.
Fax: 404-888-7490.

(See Next Column)

Other Atlanta, Georgia Office: Suite 404, 2296 Henderson Mill Road, N.E.
Telephone: 770-492-9030.
Fax: 770-492-9609.
Washington, D.C. Office: 1120 Nineteenth Street, N.W., Eighth Floor.
Telephone: 202-857-4400.
Fax: 202-467-6910.
Greenville, South Carolina Office: 15 South Main Street, Suite 601, P.O. Box 10208.
Telephone: 864-255-5400.
Fax: 864-255-5440.

RESIDENT MEMBER

Heather K. Mallard

Representative Clients: Aetna Casualty and Surety Co., Inc.; ALSCO/AmeriMark Building Products, Inc.; Aoki Corporation America, Inc.; Hackney Brothers, Inc.; Lawyers Mutual Liability Insurance Company of North Carolina; Meredith College; Regency Park Corp.; Wachovia Bank, N.A.

For Complete List of Firm Personnel, See General Section

For full biographical listings, see the Martindale-Hubbell Law Directory

*WAYNESVILLE,** Haywood Co.

BROWN, WARD & HAYNES, P.A. (AV)

Suite 300 Haywood Savings Bank, 370 North Main Street, P.O. Drawer 928, 28786-0928
Telephone: 828-456-9436
Fax: 828-456-4069

Glenn W. Brown (Retired) Woodrow H. Griffin
H.S. Ward, Jr. (Retired) Michael Bonfoey
David J. Haynes Stephen G. Ellis

General Counsel for: Haywood Savings Bank; Haywood Builders Supply Co., Inc.; Southeastern Jurisdictional Administrative Council, Inc. (f/k/a Lake Junaluska Assembly).
Local Counsel for: Haywood Elect. Membership Corporation.
Approved Attorneys for: Lawyers Title Insurance Corp.; Chicago Title Insurance Co.; Federal Land Bank of Columbia; Lawyers Title of North Carolina; Commonwealth Title Co.

For full biographical listings, see the Martindale-Hubbell Law Directory

*WINSTON-SALEM,** Forsyth Co.

WOMBLE CARLYLE SANDRIDGE & RICE (AV)

A Professional Limited Liability Company
200 West Second Street, P.O. Drawer 84, 27102
Telephone: 336-721-3600
Fax: 336-721-3660
Email: lawyers@wcsr.com *URL:* http://www.wcsr.com
Charlotte, North Carolina Office: 3300 One First Union Center, 301 South College Street.
Telephone: 704-331-4900.
Fax: 704-331-4955.
Raleigh, North Carolina Office: 2100 First Union Capitol Center, 150 Fayetteville Street Mall, P.O. Box 831.
Telephone: 919-755-2100.
Fax: 919-755-2150.
Research Triangle Park, North Carolina Office: 2505 Meridian Parkway, Suite 300 (Durham), 27713.
Telephone: 919-484-2300.
Fax: 919-484-2340.
Atlanta, Georgia Office: One Atlantic Center, 1201 West Peachtree Street, Suite 3500.
Telephone: 404-872-7000.
Fax: 404-888-7490.
Other Atlanta, Georgia Office: Suite 404, 2296 Henderson Mill Road, N.E.
Telephone: 770-492-9030.
Fax: 770-492-9609.
Washington, D.C. Office: 1120 Nineteenth Street, N.W., Eighth Floor
Telephone: 202-857-4400.
Fax: 202-467-6910.
Greenville, South Carolina Office: 15 South Main Street, Suite 601, P.O. Box 10208.
Telephone: 864-255-5400.
Fax: 864-255-5440.

RESIDENT MEMBERS

Linwood L. Davis Murray C. Greason, Jr.
William A. Davis, II Jeffrey C. Howland
Richard N. Drake Robert A. West
John L. W. Garrou Calder W. Womble
William F. Womble

RESIDENT ASSOCIATES

Roger E. Cole Adam B. Hirschfeld
Robert F. Pomper

Representative Clients: Brad Ragan, Inc.; Brenner Companies; Food Lion, Inc.; Hanes Companies, Inc.; North Carolina Baptist Hospitals, Inc.; R.J. Reynolds Tobacco Co.; Thomasville Furniture Industries, Inc.; Wachovia Corp.; Wake Forest University.

(See Next Column)

WOMBLE CARLYLE SANDRIDGE & RICE, *Winston-Salem—Continued*

For Complete List of Firm Personnel, See General Section

For full biographical listings, see the Martindale-Hubbell Law Directory

OHIO

ASHTABULA, Ashtabula Co.

WARREN AND YOUNG PLL (AV)

134 West 46th Street, P.O. Box 2300, 44005-2300
Telephone: 440-997-6175
Facsimile: 440-992-9114
URL: http://www.warrenyoung.com

Stuart W. Cordell

Jeffrey L. Coxon

For Complete List of Firm Personnel, See General Section

For full biographical listings, see the Martindale-Hubbell Law Directory

*CINCINNATI,** Hamilton Co.

BROWN, CUMMINS & BROWN CO., L.P.A. (AV)

3500 Carew Tower, 441 Vine Street, 45202
Telephone: 513-381-2121
Fax: 513-381-2125

Robert S. Brown
James R. Cummins
Donald S. Mendelsohn
Lynne Skilken
Kathryn Knue Przywara
Melanie S. Corwin
JoAnn M. Strasser

Counsel for: Midwest Group of Funds; Eastgate Health Care Center, Inc.; Highlands Health Care Center, Inc.; Clarke Detroit Diesel-Allison; Benson, Inc.; International Theme Park Services, Inc.
Reference: Star Bank of Cincinnati.

For full biographical listings, see the Martindale-Hubbell Law Directory

KATZ, TELLER, BRANT & HILD A LEGAL PROFESSIONAL ASSOCIATION (AV)

2400 Chemed Center, 255 East Fifth Street, 45202-4724
Telephone: 513-721-4532
Telecopier: 513-721-7120
Email: corp@ktbh.com

Reuven J. Katz
Andrew R. Berger
Mark J. Jahnke
John R. Gierl
Bradley G. Haas

Tedd H. Friedman
Robert S. Fletcher

For Complete List of Firm Personnel, See General Section

For full biographical listings, see the Martindale-Hubbell Law Directory

KEPLEY, GILLIGAN & EYRICH A LEGAL PROFESSIONAL ASSOCIATION (AV)

525 Vine Street, Suite 2200, 45202
Telephone: 513-241-5540; 621-1045
Fax: 513-241-8111; 621-0038

James J. Crowe
C. Thomas Dupuis
David J. Eyrich
T. Scott Gilligan
Richard K. Graham
Michael E. Neiheisel
Paul D. Rattermann

Representative Clients and References furnished upon request.

For full biographical listings, see the Martindale-Hubbell Law Directory

STRAUSS & TROY A LEGAL PROFESSIONAL ASSOCIATION (AV)

The Federal Reserve Building, 150 East Fourth Street, 45202-4018
Telephone: 513-621-2120
Telecopier: 513-241-8259
URL: http://www.strauss-troy.com
Northern Kentucky Office: Suite 1400, 50 East Rivercenter Boulevard, Covington, Kentucky, 41011.
Telephone: 513-621-8900; 513-621-2120.
Telecopier: 513-629-9444.

Alan Comstock Rosser
William R. Jacobs
James G. Heldman
Charles Jay Postow
Stuart C. Brinn
Ann W. Gerwin
Timothy B. Theissen (Resident, Covington, Kentucky Office)
Charles C. Ashdown
Shawn M. Young

(See Next Column)

Michael A. Ruh, Jr.

OF COUNSEL

Samuel M. Allen (Resident, Covington, Kentucky Office)
Gordon H. Hood (Resident, Covington, Kentucky Office)
Paul J. Theissen (Resident, Covington, Kentucky Office)

Representative Clients: PNC Bank, N.A. (Ohio and Kentucky); Corporex Companies, Inc.; Mercantile Stores Co., Inc.; Star Bank, N.A. (Ohio and Kentucky).

For Complete List of Firm Personnel, See General Section

For full biographical listings, see the Martindale-Hubbell Law Directory

*CLEVELAND,** Cuyahoga Co.

BERNARD, HAFFEY & BOHNERT CO., L.P.A. (AV)

Jefferson Centre, 5001 Mayfield Road #301, P.O. Box 24005, 44124-0005
Telephone: 216-291-3600
FAX: 216-291-0159
URL: http://www.lawyers.com/bernardhaffey&bohnert

Clifford H. Bernard (1907-1985)
J. Ross Haffey, Jr.
Edward G. Bohnert
Timothy P. Haffey

Reference: KeyBank.

For full biographical listings, see the Martindale-Hubbell Law Directory

CONWAY, MARKEN, WYNER, KURANT & KERN CO., L.P.A. (AV)

30195 Chagrin Boulevard, Pepper Pike Place, Suite 300, 44124
Telephone: 216-292-3300
Telecopier: 216-292-3340

James J. Conway
Howard A. Marken
Jeffrey G. Wyner
Jack Kurant
Keith W. Kern
Peter Turner
Kevin R. Keogh
Peter D. Brosse
Mark Leskovec
Michael R. Stavnicky
Michele R. Yeh
Jennifer A. Corso

For full biographical listings, see the Martindale-Hubbell Law Directory

WILLIAM P. GIBBONS (AV)

1525 Leader Building, 44114-1444
Telephone: 216-623-8000; 241-2500
Facsimile: 216-241-2286
Email: wpgibb1@ibm.net

For full biographical listings, see the Martindale-Hubbell Law Directory

BERNARD S. GOLDFARB (AV)

55 Public Square, Suite 1500, 44113
Telephone: 216-696-0606
Fax: 216-696-0732
Email: resconet@multiverse.com

For full biographical listings, see the Martindale-Hubbell Law Directory

GOODMAN WEISS MILLER LLP (AV)

100 Erieview Plaza, 27th Floor, 44114-1824
Telephone: 216-696-3366
Telecopier: 216-363-5835

Deborah J. Michelson

For full biographical listings, see the Martindale-Hubbell Law Directory

HERMANN, CAHN & SCHNEIDER (AV)

Suite 500, 1301 East Ninth Street, 44114
Telephone: 216-781-5515
Facsimile: 216-781-1030
Email: hcs@en.com

MEMBERS OF FIRM

Gary D. Hermann
James S. Cahn
Kent B. Schneider
Anthony J. Hartman
Robert Warren, Jr.
Kerry S. Volsky
Peter J. Krembs

ASSOCIATES

Jay H. Salamon
Thomas P. Marotta
Romney B. Cullers

Representative Clients: Applied Medical Technology, Inc.; Allen Medical Systems; Cleveland Ear, Nose, Throat and Facial Surgery Group, Inc.; Information Access, Inc.; University Cardiothoracic Surgeons, Inc.; Manfredi Motor Transit Co.

For full biographical listings, see the Martindale-Hubbell Law Directory

Cleveland—Continued

KAUFMAN & CUMBERLAND CO., L.P.A. (AV)

1500 Republic Building, 25 Prospect Avenue, West, 44115-1000
Telephone: 216-861-0707
Telefax: 216-694-6883
TDD: 216-694-6891

Steven S. Kaufman
Frank J. Cumberland, Jr. (Retired)
Frank R. DeSantis
Robert A. Blattner
Gail E. Sindell
William W. Jacobs
Thomas L. Feher
Mitchell Ehrenberg
Douglas P. Whipple

Susan L. Belman
Charles P. Royer
Craig P. Kvale
Kathleen M. Minahan
Robin M. Wilson
Robert J. Patton
Lawrence E. Harkenrider
Scott J. Novak

OF COUNSEL

Jack G. Day (Retired)
Anthony R. Troia
Edda Sara Post

Representative Client: CertainTeed Corp.

For full biographical listings, see the Martindale-Hubbell Law Directory

KELLER AND CURTIN CO., L.P.A. (AV)

Suite 330 The Hanna Building, 44115-1901
Telephone: 216-566-7100
Fax: 216-566-5430
Email: keller@en.com
Akron, Ohio Office: 920 Key Building, 159 South Main Street, 44308-1318.
Telephone: 330-376-7245.
Fax: 330-376-8128. Email: kcakron@en.com.
Elyria, Ohio Office: 120 East Avenue, 44035-5228.
Telephone: 440-323-8662.
Fax: 440-323-6610.

Stanley S. Keller
G. Michael Curtin
Walter H. Krohngold
James M. Johnson
Joseph G. Ritzler
Thomas M. Coughlin, Jr.
John Swansinger
Camille D. Kuri
Franklin C. Malemud
Brian D. Spitz
Deena Charisse Miller

Reference: Bank One, Cleveland.

For full biographical listings, see the Martindale-Hubbell Law Directory

KELLEY, MCCANN & LIVINGSTONE, LLP (AV)

3500 BP Tower, 200 Public Square, 44114-2302
Telephone: 216-241-3141
Fax: 216-241-3707
Email: Attorneys@kmlegal.com

MEMBERS OF FIRM

John D. Brown
Donna M. Flammang
Bruce L. Waterhouse, Jr.
Robert A. Brindza II

OF COUNSEL

George J. Dunn

ASSOCIATES

Gregory J. O'Brien
Christine A. Allport

For Complete List of Firm Personnel, See General Section

For full biographical listings, see the Martindale-Hubbell Law Directory

LOWE • EKLUND • WAKEFIELD CO., L.P.A. (AV)

Tower City Center 610 Skylight Office Tower, 1660 West Second Street, 44113-1454
Telephone: 216-781-2600
Fax: 216-781-2610
Email: lew@lewlaw.com *URL:* http://www.lewlaw.com

James A. Lowe
Claudia Rieth Eklund
Mark L. Wakefield
Dennis P. Mulvihill

Gregory S. Scott
Andrew S. Goldwasser

OF COUNSEL

Donald Cybulski

For full biographical listings, see the Martindale-Hubbell Law Directory

MCDONALD, HOPKINS, BURKE & HABER CO., L.P.A. (AV)

2100 Bank One Center, 600 Superior Avenue, E., 44114-2653
Telephone: 216-348-5400
Telecopier: 216-348-5474
Email: attorney@mhbh.com *URL:* http://www.mhbh.com

(See Next Column)

Patrick J. Berry
Jeffrey P. Consolo
Jerome W. Cook
Richard S. Cooper
Anthony J. DiVenere
Paul N. Edwards
Theodore J. Esborn
Steven L. Gardner
Carl J. Grassi
James A. Griffith
Jeffrey R. Huntsberger
Brian J. Jereb
Bernard L. Karr
Thomas W. Keen
Roger L. Kleinman
Joseph J. LoPresti, Jr.
Dan L. Makee
George L. McGaughey, Jr.
John T. Mulligan
Brian M. O'Neill
William J. O'Neill
Stephen T. Parisi
R. Jeffrey Pollock
Michael G. Riley
Shawn M. Riley
Albert N. Salvatore
Thomas C. Schrader
Roger L. Shumaker
Barbara J. Smith
James M. Stone
Dale R. Vlasek
Kenneth J. Walsh
John M. Wirtshafter
Jane Marie Pine Wood
Charles B. Zellmer

OF COUNSEL

John J. Monroe

Julie A. Callsen
Anne T. Corrigan
Steven A. Eisenberg
G. Andrew Gardner
Anuj Goswami
Donald E. Kacmar
David M. Kall
Jeffrey B. Keiper
Kevin J. Kessinger
Mark D. Klimek
Alan M. Koschik
Deviani M. Kuhar
Paul W. Linehan
Tyler L. Mathews
Jennifer A. Mills
Antoinette K. Palmer
Ketan K. Patel
Sharon Szolosi Regas
Douglas B. Schnee
Michele Smolin
Glenn D. Southworth
Michael R. Spreng

For full biographical listings, see the Martindale-Hubbell Law Directory

MORGANSTERN, MACADAMS & DEVITO CO., L.P.A. (AV)

Burgess Building, Suite 400, 1406 West Sixth Street, 44113
Telephone: 216-621-4244; 216-687-1212
Fax: 216-621-2951
Email: smorgan153@aol.com

Stanley Morganstern
Pamela J. MacAdams
Christopher Michael DeVito

Michael A. Partlow
Cheryl Lukacs
Patrice R. T. Yarham

For full biographical listings, see the Martindale-Hubbell Law Directory

NISCHWITZ, PEMBRIDGE & CHRISZT CO., L.P.A. (AV)

1220 Bond Court Office Building, 1300 East Ninth Street, 44114-1503
Telephone: 216-861-8100
Telecopier: 216-861-8180
Email: dnpc@dnpc.com *URL:* http://www.dnpc.com

Jeffrey L. Nischwitz
D. Timothy Pembridge
James R. Chriszt

Richard J. Ambrose
Timothy L. McGarry

OF COUNSEL

Arthur L. (Tim) Clements, III
Maureen Fiorilli Zito
J. Randall Nye

For full biographical listings, see the Martindale-Hubbell Law Directory

ULMER & BERNE LLP (AV)

Ninth Floor, Bond Court Building, 1300 East Ninth Street, 44114-1583
Telephone: 216-621-8400
FAX: 216-621-7488
Email: infocleveland@ulmer.com
Email: infocolumbus@ulmer.com *URL:* http://www.ulmer.com/
Columbus, Ohio Office: 88 East Broad Street, Suite 1980.
Telephone: 614-228-8400.
FAX: 614-228-8561.

MEMBERS OF FIRM

Lewis T. Barr
Ruth Anna Carlson
Inajo Davis Chappell
Robert A. Fein
Harold E. Friedman
Bill J. Gagliano
A.B. Glickman
Neil W. Gurney
Richard G. Hardy
Donald E. Heiser
Stuart A. Laven
Stephen A. Markus
Christopher C. McCracken
Craig S. Miller
Peter A. Rome
Isaac Schulz

OF COUNSEL

Elliot M. Kaufman

(See Next Column)

ULMER & BERNE LLP, *Cleveland—Continued*

RETIRED MEMBER

Morton L. Stone (Retired)

For Complete List of Firm Personnel, See General Section

For full biographical listings, see the Martindale-Hubbell Law Directory

WEGMAN, HESSLER, VANDERBURG & O'TOOLE A LEGAL PROFESSIONAL ASSOCIATION (AV)

6055 Rockside Woods Boulevard, Suite 200, 44131
Telephone: 216-642-3342
Telecopier: 216-642-8826

Martin J. Wegman (1918-1977)
David J. Hessler
Keith A. Vanderburg
Peter A. Hessler
John K. O'Toole
David R. Knowles
John D. Kedzior
Steven E. Pryatel

Richard T. Coyne
Christopher A. Holecek
Jeffrey W. Krueger
David W. Herrington
Antoinette F. Gideon
David R. Button
Nathan E. Hessler
Lawrence S. Crowther
Derek Kaesgen
David M. Leneghan
Erin M. O'Toole
Elizabeth M. Woda
Dennis J. Siciliano
Tanja M. Holecek
Jeffrey A. Gorski
Diana Delmar Jancura
Anthony N. Palombo
Carl D. Gum, III
Patricia J. Haas

Reference: Key Bank of Cleveland.

For full biographical listings, see the Martindale-Hubbell Law Directory

*COLUMBUS,** Franklin Co.

JOHN F. CASEY (AV)

600 South High Street, 43215-5622
Telephone: 614-228-5711
Fax: 614-228-0982
URL: http://www.lawyers.com/johnfcasey
Email: jfcasey@casey-law.com *URL:* http://www.iwaynet.com/~jfcasey
(Also Of Counsel to Lucas, Prendergast, Albright, Gibson & Newman)

For full biographical listings, see the Martindale-Hubbell Law Directory

CHESTER, WILLCOX AND SAXBE LLP (AV)

17 South High Street, Suite 900, 43215-3413
Telephone: 614-221-4000
Fax: 614-221-4012
Email: cwslaw.com

PARTNERS

Andrew J. Art
John W. Bentine
James J. Chester
John J. Chester
John J. Chester, Jr.
J. Richard Emens
Guy R. Humphrey
J. Anthony Kington
Charles Rockwell Saxbe
Roderick H. Willcox
Beatrice E. Wolper

ASSOCIATES

Maryellen Corna
Karen S. Hockstad
Thomas H. Mallory, Jr.

Representative Clients: American Municipal Power-Ohio, Inc.; Hill Distributing Co.; Ohio Auto Auction; Ohio Federation of Business & Professional Women; Rothschild Berry Farms, Inc.; Scioto Downs, Inc.; Tee Jaye's Country Place Restaurants.

For full biographical listings, see the Martindale-Hubbell Law Directory

KEGLER, BROWN, HILL & RITTER (AV)

Capitol Square Suite 1800, 65 East State Street, 43215-4294
Telephone: 614-462-5400
Telecopier: 614-464-2634
Cable Address: "Law KBHR"
Telex: 246671
Email: info@kbhr.com *URL:* http://www.kbhr.com
Marion, Ohio Office: 250 Executive Drive, Suite B, P.O. Box 919.
Telephone: 614-387-3501.
Facsimile: 614-387-3630.

Donald A. Antrim
Lawrence F. Feheley
Allen L. Handlan
Edward C. Hertenstein
Paul R. Hess
Charles J. Kegler
Paul D. Ritter, Jr.
Kevin L. Sykes
John R. Thomas
Shawnell Williams

COUNSEL

John L. Gray
Ted M. McKinniss (Resident, Marion Office)

(See Next Column)

Greg R. Grabovac
Todd M. Kegler

Representative Clients: Abrasive Technology, Inc.; Donato's Pizza, Inc.; Drug Emporium, Inc.; The Fishel Co.; Spenley Newspapers, Inc.; Warner Cable Communications, Inc.

For Complete List of Firm Personnel, See General Section

For full biographical listings, see the Martindale-Hubbell Law Directory

HARVEY S. MINTON & ASSOCIATES (AV)

6641 North High Street, 43085-4038
Telephone: 614-848-9600
Telecopier: 614-848-9818
URL: http://www.lawyers.com/mintonlaw

OF COUNSEL

Richard E. Gombert
Rainer E. Steinhoff

For full biographical listings, see the Martindale-Hubbell Law Directory

POSTLEWAITE & JORDAN (AV)

3040 Riverside Drive, Suite 122, 43221
Telephone: 614-486-2111
Fax: 614-486-8943

Charles C. Postlewaite
Jeffrey H. Jordan

ASSOCIATE

Holly N. Wolf

For full biographical listings, see the Martindale-Hubbell Law Directory

SCHOTTENSTEIN, ZOX & DUNN A LEGAL PROFESSIONAL ASSOCIATION (AV)

The Huntington Center, 41 South High Street, 43215
Telephone: 614-462-2700
Telecopier: 614-462-5135
Telex: 650 24 444 365
URL: http://www.szd.com
Cincinnati, Ohio Office: Bank One Towers, 8044 Montgomery Road, Suite 700, 45236-2926.
Telephone: 513-792-2730.
Cleveland, Ohio Office: One Cleveland Center, 1375 East 9th Street, Suite 950.
Telephone: 216-621-6501.
Fax: 216-621-6502.

Jay R. Dingledy
Richard A. Barnhart
John D. Robinett
Susan Darnell Rector
Michael R. Becker
Phillip G. Lilly
Robert R. Ouellette

William P. Zox
Marcus D. Dunn
Josef Keglewitsch
Michael S. Jordan
Marie A. Malloy
Kevin R. Fease (Not admitted in OH)

OF COUNSEL

Bryan K. Prosek

Reference: Bank One of Columbus, N.A.

For Complete List of Firm Personnel, See General Section

For full biographical listings, see the Martindale-Hubbell Law Directory

SWEDLOW, BUTLER, LEVINE, LEWIS & DYE CO., L.P.A. (AV)

10 West Broad Street, Suite 2400, 43215-3469
Telephone: 614-461-1100
Telecopier: 614-461-8178
Email: SBILLlaw@aol.com

Gerald H. Swedlow
Jack C. Butler
Richard L. Levine
Jeffrey M. Lewis
David A. Dye
Steven A. Baenen
Todd H. Neuman
Sean M. Gouhin

Reference: National City Bank; Fifth Third Bank.

For full biographical listings, see the Martindale-Hubbell Law Directory

*DAYTON,** Montgomery Co.

BOGIN, PATTERSON & BOHMAN LLP (AV)

1200 Talbott Tower, 131 North Ludlow Street, 45402-1135
Telephone: 937-226-1200
FAX: 937-226-1625
Email: BPBLaw1200@aol.com

MEMBERS OF FIRM

Dennis L. Patterson
Jerome B. Bohman
James C. Ellis
Curtis F. Slaton
Randall L. Stump
Asher Bogin (Retired)

For full biographical listings, see the Martindale-Hubbell Law Directory

Dayton—Continued

FROELICH & WEPRIN CO. LPA (AV)

1812 Kettering Tower, 45423-1812
Telephone: 937-226-1776
Fax: 937-226-1945
Email: froelich4g@aol.com *URL:* http://www.lawyers.com/froelich&weprin

Gary L. Froelich | James I. Weprin

James P. Langendorf

Reference: Key Bank, N.A. of Dayton, Ohio.

For full biographical listings, see the Martindale-Hubbell Law Directory

ROGERS & GREENBERG (AV)

2160 Kettering Tower, 45423
Telephone: 937-223-8171
Fax: 937-223-1649
Email: rgattys@aol.com

MEMBERS OF FIRM

William A. Rogers, Jr.
Stanley Z. Greenberg
John M. Cloud
Barry W. Mancz
Keith R. Kearney
James G. Kordik

L. Anthony Lush
Dawn S. Garrett
Michelle S. Vollmar

General Counsel for: Heartland Federal Credit Union; National Management Association; Moraine Materials Co.; Techway Industries, Inc.; Washington Township Park Board.

For full biographical listings, see the Martindale-Hubbell Law Directory

SEBALY, SHILLITO & DYER A LEGAL PROFESSIONAL ASSOCIATION (AV)

1300 Courthouse Plaza, NE, P.O. Box 220, 45402-0220
Telephone: 937-222-2500
Telefax: 937-222-6554; 222-8279
URL: http://www.ssdlaw.com

Martin A. Beyer
Daniel A. Brown
James A. Dyer
Gale S. Finley
John R. Glankler
Deborah D. Hunt
Michael P. Moloney
Jon M. Sebaly
Beverly F. Shillito
Jeffrey B. Shulman
Karl R. Ulrich
Lawrence S. Walter
Nita S. Yates

OF COUNSEL

William W. Lambert

Michael A. Booth
Robert E. Goff, Jr.
Leslie Blair Graden
Joseph V. Hatala
J. David Ruffner, II
Kendra F. Thompson

For full biographical listings, see the Martindale-Hubbell Law Directory

DUBLIN, Franklin Co.

BLAUGRUND, HERBERT & MARTIN, INCORPORATED (AV)

5455 Rings Road, Suite 500, 43017-7517
Telephone: 614-764-0681
Fax: 614-764-0774
Email: bhm@bhmlaw.net

Christopher T. Cline
Lawrence H. Cohen
Steven A. Martin
Teri G. Rasmussen

Jerry T. Burditt

For full biographical listings, see the Martindale-Hubbell Law Directory

LORAIN, Lorain Co.

COLELLA & KOLCZUN, P.L.L. (AV)

5750 Cooper Foster Park Road Suite 101, 44053
Telephone: 440-988-9000
Telecopier: 440-988-9002
Email: COLELLA@CENTURYINTER.NET

Richard Colella
Lee S. Kolczun
Richard J. Colella
Jeffrey H. Weir II
Scott A. Augustine

References: FirstMerit Bank, N.A.; The Lorain National Bank; FirstMerit Corp.

For full biographical listings, see the Martindale-Hubbell Law Directory

*TOLEDO,** Lucas Co.

DOYLE, LEWIS & WARNER (AV)

202 North Erie Street, P.O. Box 2168, 43603
Telephone: 419-248-1500
Fax: 419-248-2002
Email: dlw1@primenet.com

MEMBERS OF FIRM

Steven Timonere
Richard F. Ellenberger
Michael E. Hyrne
Michael A. Bruno
David W. Doerner

ASSOCIATES

Kevin A. Pituch
Maureen O. Atkins

Counsel for: Consolidated Rail Corp.; The Lakefront Dock & Railroad Terminal Co.; Prudential Insurance Co. of America; Equitable Life Assurance Society of the U.S.; Metropolitan Life Insurance Co.; Greyhound Lines; Fireman's Fund Insurance Cos.

For Complete List of Firm Personnel, See General Section

For full biographical listings, see the Martindale-Hubbell Law Directory

EASTMAN & SMITH LTD. (AV)

One Seagate, Twenty-Fourth Floor, P.O. Box 10032, 43699-0032
Telephone: 419-241-6000
Telecopier: 419-247-1777
Columbus, Ohio Office: 65 East State Street, Suite 1000, 43215.
Telephone: 614-460-3556.
Telecopier: 614-228-5371.

MEMBERS OF FIRM

Frank D. Jacobs
Bruce L. Smith
Henry N. Heuerman
John H. Boggs
David L. Kuhl
Kenneth C. Baker
Ronald J. Tice
Gary M. Harden
Roger Paul Klee
Mark C. Abramson
Steven D. Reinbolt
David C. Krock

OF COUNSEL

Howard M. Friedman
Gerald P. Moran

Counsel for: Marathon Oil Co.; Borg Warner Corp.; McDonalds Corp.; A P Parts Co.; 21 International Holdings, Inc. (f/k/a Knoll International Holdings, Inc.); Master Chemical Co.; Glasstech, Inc.; Omnisource Corporation; North Star BHP Steel.

For Complete List of Firm Personnel, See General Section

For full biographical listings, see the Martindale-Hubbell Law Directory

ROHRBACHERS, LIGHT, CRON, ZMUDA & TRIMBLE CO., L.P.A. (AV)

National City Bank Building 8th Floor, 405 Madison Avenue, 43604-1243
Telephone: 419-248-2600
Telecopier: 419-248-2614
URL: http://www.rlczt.com
URL: http://www.lawyers.com/rlcztcom

Vernon E. Rohrbacher (1920-1978)
David J. Rohrbacher
Matthew J. Rohrbacher
C. Randolph Light
Nicholas J. Cron
Gene A. Zmuda
J. Mark Trimble

Beverly J. St. Clair
Diane J. Knoblauch
Todd M. Zimmerman

OF COUNSEL

Brent B. Nicholson

LEGAL SUPPORT PERSONNEL

PARALEGAL

Anne E. Scott

For full biographical listings, see the Martindale-Hubbell Law Directory

OKLAHOMA

*OKLAHOMA CITY,** Oklahoma Co.

F. SMITH BARNES, P.C. (AV)

1012 Northwest Grand Boulevard, 73118
Telephone: 405-848-1776
Fax: 405-840-1164

F. Smith Barnes

For full biographical listings, see the Martindale-Hubbell Law Directory

Oklahoma City—Continued

BRITTON, GRAY AND HILL, P.C. (AV)

700 Bank of Oklahoma Plaza, 201 Robert S. Kerr, 73102
Telephone: 405-239-2393
Fax: 405-232-5135

James E. Britton
Jackie L. Hill, Jr.
Stephen A. Kepner, Jr.

Representative Clients: BancFirst; Union Bank & Trust Company; Will Rogers Bank; NationsBank; Poteau State Bank; Trigen Energy Corporation, Oklahoma; Marine Recreational Opportunities, Inc.; Visual Image Media Consultants, Inc.; Total Waste Systems, Inc.; Tower Tech, Inc.

For full biographical listings, see the Martindale-Hubbell Law Directory

DAY, EDWARDS, FEDERMAN, PROPESTER & CHRISTENSEN, P.C. (AV)

Suite 2900 Oklahoma Tower, 210 Park Avenue, 73102-5605
Telephone: 405-239-2121
Telecopier: 405-236-1012
URL: http://lawlinks.com/attys/ok/defpc.html

Bruce W. Day
William B. Federman
D. Wade Christensen
Kent A. Gilliland
Joe E. Edwards
Richard P. Propester
J. Clay Christensen
Rodney J. Heggy
Jeanette Cook Timmons

Representative Clients: AIG Aviation, Inc.; Applied Thermal Systems, Inc.; Associates in Occupational Medicine, Inc.; Attorney General of the State of Oklahoma; Attorney General of the State of Texas; Aztec Specialty Co., Inc.; Aztec Rig Equipment Company; Banc One Mortgage Corporation; BancFirst Corporation; Bank One, Oklahoma City.

For Complete List of Firm Personnel, See General Section

For full biographical listings, see the Martindale-Hubbell Law Directory

*TULSA,** Tulsa Co.

ATKINSON, HASKINS, NELLIS, BOUDREAUX, HOLEMAN, PHIPPS & BRITTINGHAM, A PROFESSIONAL CORPORATION (AV)

1500 ParkCentre, 525 South Main Street, 74103
Telephone: 918-582-8877
Fax: 918-585-8096
Email: ahnmail@ahn-law.com

Walter D. Haskins, P.C.
John J. Carwile

Representative Clients: Allstate Insurance Co.; Bayer Corp.; Crum & Forster Insurance Co.; Hartford Insurance Company; National American Insurance Co.; Federated Insurance Co.; Liberty Mutual Insurance Co.; Physicians Liability Insurance Co.; State Farm Mutual Automobile Insurance Co.; United States Aviation Underwriters.

For full biographical listings, see the Martindale-Hubbell Law Directory

BARROW GADDIS GRIFFITH & GRIMM, A PROFESSIONAL CORPORATION (AV)

610 South Main, Suite 300, 74119-1248
Telephone: 918-584-1600
Fax: 918-585-2444
Email: EMAIL@BGGG.com *URL:* http://www.bggg.com

Allen E. Barrow, Jr.
Robert W. Gaddis
David W. Griffith
William R. Grimm
William E. Farrior
Nancy C. Pruitt
Wm. Brad Heckenkemper
J. Patrick Mensching, Jr.
Robert B. Sartin
L. Michele Nelson

Reference: NationsBank.

For full biographical listings, see the Martindale-Hubbell Law Directory

EAGLETON, EAGLETON AND HARRISON, INC. (AV)

Suite 1700, 320 South Boston Avenue, 74103-4706
Telephone: 918-584-0462
Fax: 918-584-3724
Email: eagleton@worldnet.att.net

E. John Eagleton
James R. Eagleton
Charles D. Harrison

OF COUNSEL

Norma Eagleton

For full biographical listings, see the Martindale-Hubbell Law Directory

JAMES, POTTS AND WULFERS, INC. (AV)

2828 Mid-Continent Tower, 401 South Boston Avenue, 74103-4016
Telephone: 918-584-0881
Fax: 918-584-4521

(See Next Column)

David F. James
Thomas G. Potts
David W. Wulfers

For full biographical listings, see the Martindale-Hubbell Law Directory

JONES, GIVENS, GOTCHER & BOGAN, A PROFESSIONAL CORPORATION (AV)

3800 First National Tower, 74103
Telephone: 918-581-8200
Fax: 918-583-1189 or 918-583-6652
URL: http://www.jonesgivens.com

Neil E. Bogan (1945-1990)
William B. Jones
Jack R. Givens
James E. Weger
Thomas L. Vogt
Jack L. Brown
William G. LaSorsa
C. Michael Copeland
Joseph H. Paulk
Marylinn M. Gravis

Robert R. Peters II
Catherine Parker Bollinger
Paul H. Burgess
Thomas H. Dobbs

OF COUNSEL

Deryl Lee Gotcher
Blake R. Givens

Representative Clients: Local America Bank of Tulsa; Tulsa National Bank; BancOklahoma Mortgage Corporation; Kansas City Life Insurance Company; Liberty Mortgage Company; Liberty National Bank. Professional Services: KPMG, Peat Marwick; Williams Bros. Engineering.

For full biographical listings, see the Martindale-Hubbell Law Directory

RONALD MAIN, P.C. (AV)

Center 2800, Suite 821, 2815 East Skelly Drive, 74105-6251
Telephone: 918-742-1990
Fax: 918-742-2004
Email: rmainbtl@aol.com

Ronald Main

Representative Clients: Brumbaugh & Fulton, Co.; Miles Shipping Co.; H.S. Boyd, Co.; Kemco Fuels, Inc.; McDonnell-Douglas Corp.; Oklahoma Bar Professional Liability Insurance Co.; Sawyer Manufacturing Co.
References: Bank of Oklahoma, N.A.; Tulsa National Bank.

For full biographical listings, see the Martindale-Hubbell Law Directory

FREDERICK K. SLICKER (AV)

8908 South Yale Suite 410, 74137-3545
Telephone: 918-496-9020
Facsimile: 918-496-9024
Email: fredslicker@compuserve.com

For full biographical listings, see the Martindale-Hubbell Law Directory

OREGON

*PORTLAND,** Multnomah Co.

BANKS & UNDERHILL, P.C. (AV)

KOIN Center, Suite 1200, 222 S.W. Columbia Street, 97201
Telephone: 503-222-7475
Telecopier: 503-222-7288
URL: http://www.banksunderhill.com
URL: http://www.lawyers.com/banks&underhill

Robert S. Banks, Jr.
Dayna E. Underhill

Reference: Bank of America.

For full biographical listings, see the Martindale-Hubbell Law Directory

ROBERT G. BURT, P.C. (AV)

The 1515 Building, Suite 600, 1515 S.W. Fifth Avenue, 97201-5449
Telephone: 503-223-3600
Fax: 503-274-0778

Robert G. Burt

For full biographical listings, see the Martindale-Hubbell Law Directory

COPELAND, LANDYE, BENNETT AND WOLF, LLP (AV)

1300 S.W. 5th Avenue, Suite 3500, 97201
Telephone: 503-224-4100
Facsimile: 503-224-4133
Anchorage, Alaska Office: 701 West Eighth Avenue, Suite 1200, 99501.
Telephone: 907-276-5152.
Facsimile: 907-276-8433.

(See Next Column)

COPELAND, LANDYE, BENNETT AND WOLF LLP—*Continued*

MEMBERS OF FIRM

J. David Bennett
David L. Blount
David S. Case (Resident, Anchorage, Alaska Office)
Mitchel R. Cohen
Stuart K. Cohen
Mark G. Copeland (Resident, Anchorage, Alaska Office)
James S. Crane
David N. Goulder
Robert B. Hopkins
Robert H. Hume, Jr. (Resident, Anchorage, Alaska Office)
Thomas M. Landye
Jeffrey S. Mutnick
P. Stephen Russell, III
Richard L. Sadler
Thane W. Tienson

ASSOCIATES

Robert P. Owens (Resident, Anchorage, Alaska Office)
Patrick S. Galvin (Resident, Anchorage, Alaska Office)
Karna R. Gustafson
Alison S. Browdie
Katherine A. Dreyfus
David Voluck (Resident, Anchorage, Alaska Office)

For full biographical listings, see the Martindale-Hubbell Law Directory

HAGEN, DYE, HIRSCHY & DILORENZO, P.C. (AV)

888 Southwest 5th Avenue Suite 1000, 97204
Telephone: 503-222-1812
Fax: 503-274-7979

Joseph T. Hagen
Jeffrey L. Dye
John A. Hirschy
John A. DiLorenzo, Jr.
Dana R. Taylor
Mark A. Golding
Kenneth A. Williams
John D. Parsons
David E. Grein

OF COUNSEL

Lewis B. Hampton

Adam S. Rittenberg
Michael E. Farnell
Aaron K. Stuckey
Joel L. Augee
Gretchen M. Ladd
Pamela R. Albee

LEGAL SUPPORT PERSONNEL

Kathryn J. Bell
Gail E. Kuechle
Linda M. Lufkin

For full biographical listings, see the Martindale-Hubbell Law Directory

JAMES, DENECKE, URRUTIA, MARMADUKE & LAWSON, P.C. (AV)

1150 Pioneer Tower, 888 S.W. Fifth Avenue, 97204-2025
Telephone: 503-228-7967
Fax: 503-222-7261
Email: jdum@jdum.com *URL:* http://www.jdum.com

Christopher James
David R. Denecke
J. Richard Urrutia
Susan D. Marmaduke
Jerry L. Lawson, Jr.
Amy J. Carlton

CeeAnn Callahan
Jill D. Laney
Scott N. Steele
C. Robert Steringer

For full biographical listings, see the Martindale-Hubbell Law Directory

KELL, ALTERMAN & RUNSTEIN, LLP (AV)

1001 S.W. Fifth Avenue, Suite 1800, 97204
Telephone: 503-222-3531
Telecopier: 503-227-2980
Email: kell@teleport.com

MEMBERS OF FIRM

Raymond M. Kell (1911-1991)
Clifford B. Alterman (1925-1995)
Ted E. Runstein
Lee Davis Kell
Wayne D. Palmer
Lloyd R. Summers
William D. Dickas
Gary P. Compa
Charles R. Williamson
Mary Ellen Page Farr
Eric Sogge
Thomas J. Matsuda
Thomas R. Rask, III
Nicholas S. Fish

Dana L. Barnes
Cory Larvik
Robert E. Kabacy
Robin M. Runstein

References: Union Bank of California, N.A. (Portland Branch); The Bank of Tokyo-Mitsubishi, Ltd. (Portland Branch); Bank of America (5th S. Main Branch).

For full biographical listings, see the Martindale-Hubbell Law Directory

PENNSYLVANIA

*ALLENTOWN,** Lehigh Co.

WIENER AND WIENER LLP (AV)

Suite 400 Commonwealth Building, 512 Hamilton Street, 18101-1505
Telephone: 610-821-8600
Fax: 610-821-8635
West Palm Beach, Florida Office: Suite 900, 1655 Palm Beach Lakes Boulevard.
Telephone: 561-689-6660.
Fax: 561-683-1559.

MEMBERS OF FIRM

Howard A. Wiener
Joel B. Wiener
Stephen W. Wiener
C. Steven Miller
David C. Schattenstein
John H. McKeever

Representative Clients Available Upon Request.

For full biographical listings, see the Martindale-Hubbell Law Directory

BALA CYNWYD, Montgomery Co.

KANIA, LINDNER, LASAK AND FEENEY (AV)

Suite 525, Two Bala Plaza, 19004
Telephone: 610-667-3240
Fax: 610-668-9676
Email: kllf@aol.com

Arthur J. Kania
Albert A. Lindner
John Lasak
Thomas J. Feeney, III
Robert A. Griffiths

A list of Representative Clients for which the firm serves as General Counsel or Local Counsel will be supplied upon request.

For full biographical listings, see the Martindale-Hubbell Law Directory

MELVIN B. MILLER, LTD. (AV)

191 Presidential Condominium Suite W-8, 19004
Telephone: 610-581-4141
Telecopier: 610-526-9422
Email: buzzmiller@cwix.com

Melvin B. Miller

Representative Clients: Berkshire Investment Corp.; Asbell & Associates; Metropolitan Management Corp.; First Winthrop Corp.; Courthouse Convalescent Center, Inc.; Eastern Shore Nursing and Convalescent Center, Inc.; Drake Tower Limited Partnership; Katz Capital Group.

For full biographical listings, see the Martindale-Hubbell Law Directory

BLUE BELL, Montgomery Co.

GERBER & GERBER (AV)

790 Penllyn-Blue Bell Pike, Suite 100, 19422
Telephone: 610-279-6700; 215-540-9100
Fax: 215-540-9424
Email: grbrlaw@dynanet.com *URL:* http://www.lawyers.com/gerber&gerber

Morris Gerber (1908-1995)

MEMBER OF FIRM

A. Richard Gerber

For full biographical listings, see the Martindale-Hubbell Law Directory

KELLEY & MURPHY (AV)

Union Meeting Corporate Center V, Suite 160 925 Harvest Drive, 19422
Telephone: 215-643-6500
Fax: 215-643-8356
Cable Address: "BIGTIME"
Email: kmlaw@counsel.com

Joseph T. Kelley, Jr.
Patrick G. Murphy
Joseph T. Kelley, III

LEGAL SUPPORT PERSONNEL

Marianne Rowen
Tanja M.Z. Barron

For full biographical listings, see the Martindale-Hubbell Law Directory

*CHAMBERSBURG,** Franklin Co.

BARLEY, SNYDER, SENFT & COHEN, LLC (AV)

247 Lincoln Way East, 17201
Telephone: 717-264-6494
Fax: 717-264-1662
Email: barley@barley.com *URL:* http://www.barley.com
Harrisburg, Pennsylvania Office: 240 North Third Street.
Telephone: 717-238-8263.
Fax: 717-238-8278.

(See Next Column)

BARLEY, SNYDER, SENFT & COHEN LLC, *Chambersburg—Continued*

Lancaster, Pennsylvania Office: 126 East King Street.
Telephone: 717-299-5201.
Fax: 717-291-4660.
York, Pennsylvania Office: 100 East Market Street.
Telephone: 717-846-8888.
Fax: 717-843-8492.
Reading, Pennsylvania Office: 501 Washington Street.
Telephone: 610-376-6651.
Fax: 610-376-5243.
Hanover, Pennsylvania Office: 14 Center Square.
Telephone: 717-637-6239.
Fax: 717-637-5407.
Birdsboro, Pennsylvania Office: 115 E. Main Street.
Telephone: 610-582-2735.
Hamburg, Pennsylvania Office: 239 State Street.
Telephone: 610-562-3721.
Oley, Pennsylvania Office: Route 73 and Main Street.
Telephone: 610-987-6350.
Morgantown, Pennsylvania Office: Route 23.
Telephone: 610-286-5958.

MEMBERS OF FIRM

Martha B. Walker
Christopher W. Mattson
Kathleen Ann Gray
David R. Keller
Carol E. Van Horn
Timothy P. Brown
Lynn Y. MacBride
Michael W. Davis
Melanie A. Zampini

ASSOCIATES

Anne S. Johnson
John W. Venskus

For full biographical listings, see the Martindale-Hubbell Law Directory

*HARRISBURG,** Dauphin Co.

GOLDBERG, KATZMAN & SHIPMAN, P.C. (AV)

320 Market Street - Strawberry Square, P.O. Box 1268, 17108-1268
Telephone: 717-234-4161
Telecopier: 717-234-6808; 717-234-6810
Email: gks@gkslaw.com

Ronald M. Katzman
Neil Hendershot
Jesse Jay Cooper
Thomas J. Weber

Arnold B. Kogan
Steven E. Grubb
John DeLorenzo

Representative Clients: Insource, Inc.; Lemoyne Sleeper; Herre Bros., Inc.; Flight Systems, Inc.; Associated Products, Inc.; Ameralum, Inc.; Plasticert, Inc.; Tressler Lutheran Services; Pennsylvania Dental Association.

For Complete List of Firm Personnel, See General Section

For full biographical listings, see the Martindale-Hubbell Law Directory

PETERS & WASILEFSKI (AV)

2931 North Front Street, 17110
Telephone: 717-238-7555
Fax: 717-238-7750
Email: pwlaw@redrose.net

MEMBERS OF FIRM

William J. Peters
Charles E. Wasilefski
Dennis J. Bonetti
Joseph C. Phillips
Michael R. Bonshock
Thomas A. Lang

ASSOCIATES

Pamela S. Parascandola
Stephen F. Moore
Cindy J. Murphy
James A. Garver

Reference: Commonwealth National Bank.

For full biographical listings, see the Martindale-Hubbell Law Directory

JENKINTOWN, Montgomery Co.

SEMANOFF, ORMSBY & GREENBERG, LLP (AV)

Suite 200 Jenkins Court, 610 Old York Road, 19046
Telephone: 215-887-0200
Fax: 215-884-3500
Email: info@soglaw.com *URL:* http://www.soglaw.com
Philadelphia, Pennsylvania Office: Suite 200, Two Penn Center Plaza.
Telephone: 215-887-2094.

Harold Semanoff
Charles W. Ormsby, Jr.
Howard N. Greenberg
Michael J. Torchia

Michael K. Yarnoff
Peter J. Smith
Claudia M. Becker
Michael B. Dubin
Beth S. Joseph
Joanne M. Murray

OF COUNSEL

David M. Seltzer
Frederick M. Savadove

For full biographical listings, see the Martindale-Hubbell Law Directory

*NORRISTOWN,** Montgomery Co.

MURPHY, OLIVER, CAIOLA & GOWEN, A PROFESSIONAL LAW CORPORATION (AV)

43 East Marshall Street, 19401-4828
Telephone: 610-272-4222; 610-279-3838
Fax: 610-272-2549; 610-275-0140
Email: molaw@injury-law.com *URL:* http://www.injury-law.com
Spring City, Pennsylvania Office: 500 S. Main Street, 19475.
Telephone: 610-948-3770.
Pottstown, Pennsylvania Office: 5 Sunnybrook Road, 19464.
Telephone: 610-323-3480.
West Chester, Pennsylvania Office: 1534 McDaniel Drive, Westtown Business Center, 19250.
Telephone: 610-272-4222.

James J. Oliver
Frank P. Murphy
Frank L. Caiola
Thomas L. Gowen, Jr.
Carla E. Connor
Barbara A. Barnes

John F. Haskins, Jr.
Cynthia Love Dengler
Carol A. Crisci

LEGAL SUPPORT PERSONNEL

Patricia A. Talese (Paralegal)
Kathleen Nicholson

For full biographical listings, see the Martindale-Hubbell Law Directory

*PHILADELPHIA,** Philadelphia Co.

ASTOR WEISS KAPLAN & ROSENBLUM, LLP (AV)

The Bellevue, 6th Floor, 200 South Broad Street, 19102
Telephone: 215-790-0100
Fax: 215-790-0509
Email: lawyers@astorweiss.com
Bala Cynwyd, Pennsylvania Office: 401 City Avenue, Suite 500.
Telephone: 610-667-8660.
Fax: 610-667-2783.

MEMBERS OF FIRM

Alvin M. Weiss (1936-1976)
Paul C. Astor
G. David Rosenblum
Arthur H. Kaplan
Barbara Oaks Silver
David S. Workman
David Gutin
David S. Mandel
Gerald J. Schorr

ASSOCIATES

Christopher P. Flannery
Janet G. Felgoise
Elizabeth F. Warner
Daniel A. Shabel
Frances F. Freedman

SPECIAL COUNSEL

Neil Hurowitz
Jerrold V. Moss
Robert P. Style

OF COUNSEL

Edward W. Silver

For full biographical listings, see the Martindale-Hubbell Law Directory

LAW OFFICES OF JOHN J. GALLAGHER, P.C. (AV)

Suite 1100, 1760 Market Street, 19103
Telephone: 215-963-1555
Fax: 215-963-9104
Email: jjgall@ix.netcom.com *URL:* http://www.lawyers.com/johngallagher

John J. Gallagher

Michael S. Henry
Laura Carberry Muldowney
Joseph H. Meltzer
Larisa Tenberg

LEGAL SUPPORT PERSONNEL

Ronald Winkelvoss
Helene Schramm

For full biographical listings, see the Martindale-Hubbell Law Directory

KLEINBARD, BELL & BRECKER LLP (AV)

Suite 700, 1900 Market Street, 19103
Telephone: 215-568-2000
Facsimile: 215-568-0140
Montclair, New Jersey Office: 240 Claremont Avenue, 07042.
Telephone: 973-233-0600.
Facsimile: 973-233-9390.

Joseph S. Kleinbard (1905-1994)
Robert John Brecker (1916-1996)

COUNSEL TO THE FIRM

Arthur S. Keyser

(See Next Column)

KLEINBARD, BELL & BRECKER LLP—*Continued*

MEMBERS OF FIRM

Paul E. Bomze
Murray I. Blackman
Howard J. Davis
Steven R. Waxman
Steven J. Engelmyer (Resident, Montclair Office)
David L. Hyman (Resident, Montclair Office)
Imogene E. Hughes
John P. Hickey
Jay R. Goldstein
Ralph J. Mauro
Thomas H. Speranza
Lisa E. Brody

ASSOCIATES

Mary Beth H. Gray
Eric J. Rothschild
Mary Vassallo Slinkard
Michael A. Frattone
Benjamin C. Graff (Not admitted in PA)
Ralph F. Salgado

COUNSEL

Joseph Bell

For full biographical listings, see the Martindale-Hubbell Law Directory

SPECTOR GADON & ROSEN, P.C. (AV)

Seven Penn Center, 1635 Market Street, 7th Floor, 19103
Telephone: 215-241-8888
Fax: 215-241-8844
Moorestown, New Jersey Office: Spector, Gadon & Rosen, P.C. 307 Fellowship Road. P.O. Box 1001, 08057.
Telephone: 609-778-8100.
Fax: 609-722-5344.

Paul R. Rosen
Steven F. Gadon
Samuel L. Hirshland
Elliott K. Braverman
Milton H. Cross
Edward G. Fitzgerald, Jr.
Alan B. Epstein
Lary I. Zucker
Bruce L. Thall
Daniel J. Dugan
Alan H. Wallen
David M. Giles
Leslie Beth Baskin
Steven J. Polansky
Stanley Peter Jaskiewicz
Alan J. Mittelman
George M. Vinci, Jr.

OF COUNSEL

Arthur E. Vossberg III

Timothy C. Russell
Peter J. Boyer
Alan M. Rosen
Nancy Abrams
Claudia L. Boyd
Scott A. Burr
Heather M. Eichenbaum
Joshua F. Laff
Kenneth J. LaFiandra
Paul A. Loh
Brooke Caroline Madonna
Lynda M. Miller
David B. Picker
Kelly R. Ramsdell
Thomas Rapp
Suzanne I. Schiller
Michael C. Wagner

For full biographical listings, see the Martindale-Hubbell Law Directory

WEIR & PARTNERS LLP (AV)

A Pennsylvania Limited Liability Partnership
Suite 500, The Widener Building, 1339 Chestnut Street, 19107
Telephone: 215-665-8181
Telefax: 215-665-8464
Email: info@weirpartners.com
Turnersville, New Jersey Office: 215 Fries Mill Road, 08012.
Telephone: 609-740-1490.
Telefax: 609-740-1491.

MEMBERS OF FIRM

Walter Weir, Jr.
Leonard S. Goodman
Susan Verbonitz
Jeffrey L. Rudnick
Robert D. Sayre
Stephen M. Giroux
Richard P. Coe, Jr.
Brett A. Datto
John B. York
Joseph C. Hare

ASSOCIATES

Bonnie R. Golub
Debra N. Nathanson
Tina L. Colman
Andrew K. Stutzman
Jeffrey A. Guth
Jason M Reiser
Madeline Flanagan

For full biographical listings, see the Martindale-Hubbell Law Directory

*PITTSBURGH,** Allegheny Co.

FELDSTEIN GRINBERG STEIN & MCKEE, A PROFESSIONAL CORPORATION (AV)

428 Boulevard of the Allies, 15219
Telephone: 412-471-0677
Fax: 412-263-6129
URL: http://www.fgsmlaw.com
Elizabeth, Pennsylvania Office: 400 Second Street.
Telephone: 412-384-6111.

(See Next Column)

Edwin I. Grinberg
Robert E. McKee, Jr.
Jeffrey B. Balicki

Alison T. Smith
Patricia E. Farrell
Daniel J. McNulty

For full biographical listings, see the Martindale-Hubbell Law Directory

HOGUE & LANNIS (AV)

3400 Gulf Tower, Grant Street at Seventh, 15219
Telephone: 412-263-5650
Fax: 412-263-5660
Email: hllawyers@aol.com

PARTNERS

Jon Geoffrey Hogue
Sandra L. Lannis

ASSOCIATES

Jeannine A. Schuster
George Frank Pomper

For full biographical listings, see the Martindale-Hubbell Law Directory

MOLLICA & MURRAY (AV)

450 Trimont Plaza, 1305 Grandview Avenue, 15211
Telephone: 412-381-7000
Fax: 412-381-7111
Email: firm@mollicamurray.com *URL:* http://www.mollicamurray.com

MEMBERS OF FIRM

James A. Mollica, Jr.
Dr. John E. Murray, Jr.
Cathy Ann Chromulak
Timothy Murray
William J. Moorhead, Jr.

Michael E. Flaherty
Michelle D. Smith

For full biographical listings, see the Martindale-Hubbell Law Directory

WOOD GORDON, P.C. (AV)

Two Chatham Center, Suite 1010, 15219-3499
Telephone: 412-232-3434
Facsimile: 412-232-3498
Email: e.b.wood@worldnet.att.net

Edward B. Wood
James G. Gordon

For full biographical listings, see the Martindale-Hubbell Law Directory

YUKEVICH, MARCHETTI, LIEKAR & ZANGRILLI, P.C. (AV)

Sixth Floor, One Gateway Center, 15222-1424
Telephone: 412-261-6777
Fax: 412-261-6789
URL: http://www.ymlz.com

Michael Yukevich, Jr.
Christopher J. Marchetti
John P. Liekar, Jr.
Albert J. Zangrilli, Jr.
Mark Fischer
Michael I. Frachioni
Lori Nolan Lindey
Keith J. Rothfus

For full biographical listings, see the Martindale-Hubbell Law Directory

*READING,** Berks Co.

MOGEL, SPEIDEL, BOBB & KERSHNER, A PROFESSIONAL CORPORATION (AV)

520 Walnut Street, P.O. Box 8581, 19603-8581
Telephone: 610-376-1515
Telecopier: 610-372-8710

George B. Balmer (1902-1969)
George A. Kershner (1907-1969)
Carl F. Mogel (1919-1994)
Edwin H. Kershner
Frederick R. Mogel
Michael L. Mixell
George M. Lutz
Paul M. Yatron
Stephen H. Price
Kathryn K. Harenza

Sean J. O'Brien
Matthew Earl Glinn

OF COUNSEL

Harry W. Speidel
Donald K. Bobb
Henry A. Gass

Representative Clients: Great Valley Bank; Union Township, Berks County, Pennsylvania.

For full biographical listings, see the Martindale-Hubbell Law Directory

*SCRANTON,** Lackawanna Co.

KREDER, BROOKS, HAILSTONE & LUDWIG (AV)

Suite 200, 220 Penn Avenue, 18503
Telephone: 570-346-7922
Telecopier: 570-346-3715

(See Next Column)

KREDER, BROOKS, HAILSTONE & LUDWIG, *Scranton—Continued*

Andrew Hailstone
Lawrence M. Ludwig
Michael J. Donohue
David K. Brown
Richard G. Reed
Stephen W. Saunders

ASSOCIATES

Ann Lavelle Powell
Alyce Hailstone Farrell
Robert B. Farrell

OF COUNSEL

Willard M. Henkelman
Joseph C. Kreder

Counsel For: NEP Supershooters, Inc.; VNA; WEA Manufacturing, Inc.; Moses Taylor Hospital.

For Complete List of Firm Personnel, See General Section

For full biographical listings, see the Martindale-Hubbell Law Directory

O'MALLEY & HARRIS, P.C. (AV)

345 Wyoming Avenue, 18503
Telephone: 570-348-3711
Fax: 570-348-4092
Email: ohpc@epix.net *URL:* http://www.ohpclaw.com
Stroudsburg, Pennsylvania Office: 111 North Seventh Street.
Telephone: 570-421-2252; 570-422-1280.
FAX: 570-422-1281. Email: cerato@ptdprolog.net.
Wilkes-Barre, Pennsylvania Office: 61 North Washington Street.
Telephone: 570-829-3232.
FAX: 570-829-4418. Email: ohpcwb@epix.net.
Williamsport, Pennsylvania Office: 321 Pine Street, Suite 308.
Telephone: 570-323-4380.

Eugene Nogi (1905-1975)
Henry Nogi (1900-1976)
Russell J. O'Malley, Sr. (1904-1993)
Norman Harris (1907-1998)
William H. Amesbury (Resident, Wilkes-Barre Office)
Paul A. Barrett
Matthew P. Barrett
J. Scott Brady (Resident, Wilkes-Barre Office)
Lori J. Cerato (Resident, Stroudsburg Office)
Bruce L. Coyer
John Q. Durkin
Gerald J. Hanchulak
Richard K. Hodges
Timothy J. Holland (Resident, Wilkes-Barre Office)
John F. Kennedy (Resident, Wilkes-Barre Office)
Daniel Morgan
Michael Perry
James M. Tressler
Joseph Timothy Healey
A. Ruth Whalen (Resident, Wilkes-Barre Office)

Representative Clients: Pennsylvania Hospital Insurance Co.; MMI Systems Agency, Inc.; State Farm Insurance Company; ITT Specialty Risk Services; St. Paul Fire & Marine Insurance Co.; Chubb Group of Insurance Companies; Geisingen System Services; Princeton Insurance Company; Northeastern Pennsylvania Physicians Organization; Catholic Healthcare Partners.

For full biographical listings, see the Martindale-Hubbell Law Directory

WELLES & MCGRATH (AV)

1117 Bank Towers, 321 Spruce Street, 18503
Telephone: 570-348-4951
Fax: 570-348-4954

MEMBERS OF FIRM

Charles H. Welles, Jr. (1876-1962)
Matthew D. Mackie (1897-1965)
Charles H. Welles (1907-1997)
Henry C. McGrath
Charles H. Welles, IV

Counsel For: Grange National Bank; Scranton Industrial Development Co.; Bear Creek Nursing Home; Northeastern Ob-Gyn Associates, P.C.; Metropolitan Life Insurance Co.; New Health Management Systems, Inc.; Chamberlin Insurance Inc.

For full biographical listings, see the Martindale-Hubbell Law Directory

*SUNBURY,** Northumberland Co.

APFELBAUM, APFELBAUM & APFELBAUM (AV)

43 South Fifth Street, 17801
Telephone: 717-286-9421
Fax: 717-286-5349

MEMBERS OF FIRM

Sidney Apfelbaum
Jeffrey Apfelbaum
Michael Morris Apfelbaum

Counsel for: Weis Markets, Inc.; Sunbury Textile Mills, Inc.; Shikellamy School District; City of Sunbury; Borough of Northumberland; Central Builders Supply Co.; The Daily Item.
Agents for: Commonwealth Land Title Insurance Co.
Reference: Snyder County Trust Co.

For full biographical listings, see the Martindale-Hubbell Law Directory

*WASHINGTON,** Washington Co.

PEACOCK KELLER ECKER & CROTHERS, LLP (AV)

East Beau Building, 70 East Beau Street, 15301
Telephone: 724-222-4520
Telefax: 724-222-3318 ABA/NET ABA 34517
Email: peacock@cobweb.net
Waynesburg, Pennsylvania Office: 102 East High Street.
Telephone: 724-627-8331.
Telefax: 724-627-8025.

MEMBERS OF FIRM

Roger J. Ecker
Robert T. Crothers
Kenneth L. Baker
Wesley A. Cramer
Mary Drake Korsmeyer
Richard J. Amrhein
Barbara A. Rizzo
Mary K. Pruss
Jonathan G. Higie
John Allan Rodgers

SENIOR COUNSEL

Charles C. Keller

Representative Clients: Consolidation Coal Co.; Monogahela Valley Hospital, Inc.; Family Health Council, Inc.; Cal-Ed Federal Credit Union; Marianna & Scenery Hill Telephone Co.; Maternal & Family Health Services, Inc.; Sensory Devices, Inc.; Air Products and Chemicals, Inc.

For Complete List of Firm Personnel, See General Section

For full biographical listings, see the Martindale-Hubbell Law Directory

*WEST CHESTER,** Chester Co.

GAWTHROP, GREENWOOD & HALSTED, A PROFESSIONAL CORPORATION (AV)

119 North High Street, P.O. Box 562, 19381-0562
Telephone: 610-696-8225
Fax: 610-344-0922
Email: gghlaw@gawthrop.com *URL:* http://www.gawthrop.com

John S. Halsted
Robert F. Adams
Kevin Holleran
George C. Zumbano
Mark L. Tunnell
Roger N. Huggins
Walter P. Eells

Andrew D.H. Rau
Jeffrey T. Baker
Miguel D. Pena

Counsel for: Chester County Hospital; Tredyffrin Township Municipal Authority; Brandywine Hospital; Penn Mutual Insurance Co.; Wooldridge Construction of Pa.

For full biographical listings, see the Martindale-Hubbell Law Directory

*WILKES-BARRE,** Luzerne Co.

CHARITON & SCHWAGER (AV)

138 South Main Street, P.O. Box 910, 18703-0910
Telephone: 570-824-3511
Fax: 570-824-3580
Email: palaw@charitonschwager.com *URL:* http://www.charitonschwager.com

Jerry B. Chariton
David E. Schwager

For full biographical listings, see the Martindale-Hubbell Law Directory

YOUNGWOOD, Westmoreland Co.

MILLSTEIN & KNUPP (AV)

Cherry Creek Commons Armbrust Road, P.O. Box 467, 15697-0467
Telephone: 724-837-3333
Fax: 724-837-8344

David J. Millstein

For Complete List of Firm Personnel, See General Section

For full biographical listings, see the Martindale-Hubbell Law Directory

(See Next Column)

RHODE ISLAND

*PROVIDENCE,** Providence Co.

CAMERON & MITTLEMAN LLP (AV)

56 Exchange Terrace, 02903
Telephone: 401-331-5700
Telecopier: 401-331-5787

Richard S. Mittleman
E. Colby Cameron
Amy L. Mower
David L. Mayer
Bruce W. Gladstone
Justin T. Shay
Joseph F. Whinery, Jr.
Don E. Wineberg
Robert A. Migliaccio
Karen G. DelPonte

Catherine T. Schneider
John W. Wolfe
Charles S. Beal
Kathy J. Kushnir

Representative Clients: Fleet National Bank; Bank Rhode Island; State Street Bank and Trust; Karvick Enterprises; Fanch Communications, Inc.; United Natural Foods.

For full biographical listings, see the Martindale-Hubbell Law Directory

HINCKLEY, ALLEN & SNYDER LLP (AV)

1500 Fleet Center, 02903-2393
Telephone: 401-274-2000
Fax: 401-277-9600
Email: firm@haslaw.com *URL:* http://www.haslaw.com
Boston, Massachusetts Office: 28 State Street, 30th Floor.
Telephone: 617-345-9000.
Fax: 617-345-9020. URL: http://www.haslaw.com.

MEMBERS OF FIRM

Paula K. Andrews (Not admitted in RI)
David D. Barricelli
E. Jerome Batty
Jonathan Bell
Paul Bork (Not admitted in RI)
Stephen J. Carlotti
David Barry Connolly (Not admitted in RI)
Joseph P. Curran
Michael P. DeFanti
Eric F. Eisenberg (Not admitted in RI)
Malcolm Farmer, III
Margaret D. Farrell
Bruce G. Goodman (Not admitted in RI)
Hugh J. Gorman, III (Not admitted in RI)
Alan P. Gottlieb (Not admitted in RI)
Gerard R. Goulet
William R. Grimm
Paul A. Hedstrom (Not admitted in RI)
Richard L. E. Jocelyn
Michael J. Kelly (Not admitted in RI)
Joel Lewin (Not admitted in RI)
Sandra Matrone Mack
Matthew T. Marcello, III
Frederick P. McClure
Elizabeth Murdock Myers
Paul F. O'Donnell, III (Not admitted in RI)
H. Peter Olsen
Julianne Palumbo (Not admitted in RI)
John J. Pendergast, III
Gerald J. Petros
James O. Reavis
Jeremy Ritzenberg (Not admitted in RI)
Ralph J. Rivkind (Not admitted in RI)
David J. Rubin
Charles E. Schaub, Jr. (Not admitted in RI)
Douglas F. Seaver (Not admitted in RI)
Scott E. Sheridan (Not admitted in RI)
Paul A. Silver
Herman Snyder (Not admitted in RI)
David R. Sullivan (Not admitted in RI)
Robert F. Sylvia (Not admitted in RI)
Howard E. Walker
Richard D. Wayne (Not admitted in RI)

ASSOCIATES

Jessica M. Bettencourt
Mark Bianchi
Alyssa V. Boss
Alexandra K. Callam
Jane E. Cohen (Not admitted in RI)
Andrew D. Cummings (Not admitted in RI)
June E. Daniel
Kim Herman Goslant (Not admitted in RI)
Gloria Maria Gutierrez (Not admitted in RI)
Kelley Jordan-Price
Catherine S. Kim (Not admitted in RI)
Christopher W. Morog (Not admitted in RI)
Elena B. Olson (Not admitted in RI)
Lawrence W. Vernaglia (Not admitted in RI)
Joseph D. Whelan

(See Next Column)

OF COUNSEL

Willard R. Pope (Not admitted in RI)
Bentley Tobin
Joachim A. Weissfeld

For Complete List of Firm Personnel, See General Section

For full biographical listings, see the Martindale-Hubbell Law Directory

MEDEIROS + SANFORD INC. (AV)

One Turks Head Place, Suite 700, 02903-2215
Telephone: 401-831-0700
Fax: 401-274-2752 or 401-861-7249

Matthew F. Medeiros
Paul M. Sanford
Stacey P. Nakasian

Jane E. Brockmann

For full biographical listings, see the Martindale-Hubbell Law Directory

VETTER & WHITE, INCORPORATED (AV)

20 Washington Place, 02903
Telephone: 401-421-3060
Telecopier: 401-272-6803
Email: vetlit@aol.com

Benjamin V. White, III
Gordon P. Cleary
Howard A. Merten, Jr.
Brooks R. Magratten

OF COUNSEL

George Vetter

Kimberly A. Simpson
Michael W. Long

For full biographical listings, see the Martindale-Hubbell Law Directory

SMITHFIELD, Providence Co.

CHARLES S. SOKOLOFF INCORPORATED (AV)

Eleven Thurber Boulevard, 02917-1859
Telephone: 401-233-2800; Toll Free: 888-SOKOLAW
Fax: 401-233-2890
URL: http://www.sokolawyer.com
Email: sokolaw@sokolawyer.com *URL:* http://www.lawyers.com/sokolaw

Charles S. Sokoloff

Anne-Marie Krollman

For full biographical listings, see the Martindale-Hubbell Law Directory

SOUTH CAROLINA

*CHARLESTON,** Charleston Co.

HAYNSWORTH, MARION, MCKAY & GUÉRARD, L.L.P. (AV)

134 Meeting Street, P.O. Box 1119, 29402
Telephone: 843-722-7606
Facsimile: 843-724-8016
Columbia, South Carolina Office: Suite 2400 Affinity Building, 1201 Main Street, P.O. Drawer 7157, 29202.
Telephone: 803-765-1818. Facsimile 803-765-2399.
Greenville, South Carolina Office: 75 Beattie Place, Eleventh Floor, P.O. Box 2048, 29602.
Telephone: 864-240-3200.
Facsimile: 864-240-3300.

MEMBERS OF FIRM

J. Paul Trouche
Samuel W. Howell, IV
Carol L. Clark

Counsel for: Baker Hospital; Healthsource of South Carolina; CSX Corporation; Coward-Hund Construction Co.; South Carolina Public Service Authority; Liberty Property Trust.

For Complete List of Firm Personnel, See General Section

For full biographical listings, see the Martindale-Hubbell Law Directory

WARREN & SINKLER, L.L.P. (AV)

Suite 340 171 Church Street, P.O. Box 1254, 29402
Telephone: 843-577-0660
Fax: 843-577-6843
Email: law@warren-sinkler.com

(See Next Column)

WARREN & SINKLER L.L.P., *Charleston—Continued*

MEMBERS OF FIRM

G. Dana Sinkler
John H. Warren, III
Henry B. Fishburne, Jr.
Scott Y. Barnes
Mark S. Sharpe
Elizabeth W. Settle
Andrea Hall Duenas
William O. Hanahan, III
Holly R. Jensen

For full biographical listings, see the Martindale-Hubbell Law Directory

*COLUMBIA,** Richland Co.

HAYNSWORTH, MARION, MCKAY & GUÉRARD, L.L.P. (AV)

Suite 2400 Affinity Building, 1201 Main Street, P.O. Drawer 7157, 29202
Telephone: 803-765-1818
Facsimile: 803-765-2399
Greenville, South Carolina Office: 75 Beattie Place, Eleventh Floor, P.O. Box 2048, 29602.
Telephone: 864-240-3200.
Facsimile: 864-240-3300.
Charleston, South Carolina Office: 134 Meeting Street, P.O. Box 1119, 29402.
Telephone: 843-722-7606.
Facsimile: 843-724-8016.

MEMBERS OF FIRM

Gary W. Morris
Edward G. Kluiters

ASSOCIATE

Shiryl R. Ballard

Counsel for: St. Paul Insurance Group; Allstate Insurance Co.; Fluor-Daniel Corp.; South Carolina Jobs - Economic Development Authority; Anheuser Busch Company; CSX Transportation; Ernst & Young, LLP; Willis Corroon of South Carolina, Inc.; Westinghouse Savannah River Co.; Wachovia Bank of South Carolina, N.A.

For Complete List of Firm Personnel, See General Section

For full biographical listings, see the Martindale-Hubbell Law Directory

JETER & WILLIAMS, P.A. (AV)

1901 Main Street, Suite 1590, P.O. Box 7425, 29202
Telephone: 803-765-0600
Fax: 803-765-0619
Email: jwpa@mindspring.com

Edwin Russell Jeter
Daryl L. Williams

For full biographical listings, see the Martindale-Hubbell Law Directory

POPE & RODGERS (AV)

Suite 615, 1330 Lady Street, P.O. Box 5907, 29250
Telephone: 803-254-0700
Fax: 803-254-0776

MEMBERS OF FIRM

William L. Pope
Paul B. Rodgers, III

For full biographical listings, see the Martindale-Hubbell Law Directory

QUINN, PATTERSON & WILLARD (AV)

2019 Park Street, P.O. Box 73, 29202
Telephone: 803-779-6365
Telefax: 803-779-6372
Email: qpw@bellsouth.net

MEMBERS OF FIRM

Michael H. Quinn
Grady L. Patterson, III
Theodore DuBose Willard, Jr.

Approved Attorneys for: Lawyers Title Insurance Corp.

For full biographical listings, see the Martindale-Hubbell Law Directory

RICHARDSON, PLOWDEN, CARPENTER & ROBINSON, P.A. (AV)

1600 Marion Street, P.O. Drawer 7788, 29202
Telephone: 803-771-4400
Telecopy: 803-779-0016
Email: atty@rpcrlaw.com *URL:* http://www.rpcrlaw.com
Myrtle Beach, South Carolina Office: 2103 B Farlow Street, P.O. Box 3646, 29578.
Telephone: 843-448-1008.
FAX: 843-448-1533.

Frank E. Robinson, II
Frederick A. Crawford
Douglas C. Baxter
S. Nelson Weston Jr.

Stephen C. Lenker, Jr.

Representative Clients: First Union Bank; Boozer Lumber Co., Inc.; Southern Wine & Spirits of America, Inc.; Cardinal Chemical Co.; Southern National Bank; Victory Savings Bank; Columbia (SC) Teachers Federal Credit Union.

For Complete List of Firm Personnel, See General Section

For full biographical listings, see the Martindale-Hubbell Law Directory

SHERRILL & ROOF, L.L.P. (AV)

1122 Lady Street, Suite 1100, P.O. Box 11497, 29211-1497
Telephone: 803-733-3433
Fax: 803-733-2990
Email: info@sherrillandroof.com

Henry F. Sherrill
C. Joseph Roof
Daniel B. Lott, Jr.

For full biographical listings, see the Martindale-Hubbell Law Directory

TOMPKINS AND MCMASTER (AV)

Palmetto Building, Fourth Floor, 1400 Main Street, P.O. Box 7337, 29202
Telephone: 803-799-4499
Telefax: 803-252-2240

MEMBERS OF FIRM

Frank G. Tompkins (1874-1956)
Frank G. Tompkins, Jr. (1908-1973)
Elizabeth Eldridge (1895-1976)
John Gregg McMaster
Henry Dargan McMaster
George Hunter McMaster
Frank Barnwell McMaster

ASSOCIATE

Bryan P. Stirling
Karl S. Bowers

OF COUNSEL

Joseph D. McMaster

LEGAL SUPPORT PERSONNEL

Martin J. McClellan (Office Manager)

For full biographical listings, see the Martindale-Hubbell Law Directory

TURNER, PADGET, GRAHAM & LANEY, P.A. (AV)

Seventeenth Floor, 1901 Main Street, P.O. Box 1473, 29202
Telephone: 803-254-2200
Telecopy: 803-799-3957
Florence, South Carolina Office: Fourth Floor, 1831 West Evans Street, P.O. Box 5478, 29502.
Telephone: 843-662-9008.
Fax: 843-667-0828.
Charleston, South Carolina Office: 21 Broad Street, 1st Floor, P.O. Box 836, 29402.
Telephone: 843-723-1622.
Fax: 843-577-3369.

Ronald E. Boston
W. Duvall Spruill
R. Wayne Byrd (Resident, Florence, SC, Office)
David G. Fawcett
Lanneau William Lambert, Jr.
Hugh M. Claytor (Resident, Florence, SC, Office)
R. Todd Sherpy
Jeffrey L. Payne (Resident, Florence, SC, Office)
Michael S. Hopewell (Resident, Florence, SC, Office)

OF COUNSEL

Stephen A. Husman

David W. Keller, Jr. (Resident, Florence, SC Office)
William O. Higgins
Julie Jeffords Moose (Resident, Florence, SC, Office)

For Complete List of Firm Personnel, See General Section

For full biographical listings, see the Martindale-Hubbell Law Directory

WOODWARD COTHRAN & HERNDON (AV)

1200 Main Street, Suite 600, 29201
Telephone: 803-799-9772
Fax: 803-799-3256
Mailing Address: P.O. Box 12399, Columbia, South Carolina, 29211
Email: wch1@usit.net

OF COUNSEL

Edward M. Woodward, Sr.

General Counsel for: The Columbia College; Sandhills Bank; Heater Utilities.

For full biographical listings, see the Martindale-Hubbell Law Directory

*GREENVILLE,** Greenville Co.

HAYNSWORTH, MARION, MCKAY & GUÉRARD, L.L.P. (AV)

75 Beattie Place, Eleventh Floor, P.O. Box 2048, 29602
Telephone: 864-240-3200
Facsimile: 864-240-3300
Columbia, South Carolina Office: Suite 2400 Affinity Building, 1201 Main Street, P.O. Drawer 7157, 29202
Telephone: 803-765-1818.
Facsimile: 803-765-2399.
Charleston, South Carolina Office: 134 Meeting Street, P.O. Box 1119, 29402.
Telephone: 843-722-7606.
Facsimile: 843-724-8016.

(See Next Column)

HAYNSWORTH, MARION, MCKAY & GUÉRARD L.L.P.—*Continued*

MEMBERS OF FIRM

Jesse C. Belcher
James B. Pressly, Jr.
Andrew J. White, Jr.
Ellis M. Johnston, II
Joseph J. Blake, Jr.
Bryan Francis Hickey
J. Wesley Crum III
Knox H. White
Arthur Frazier McLean, III
Donna S. Kivett
Frank T. Davis, III

ASSOCIATES

Stephen P. Williams
William David Conner
Jeremy L. Cook
E. Tyler Smith

OF COUNSEL

Maye R. Johnson, Jr.

Representative Clients: Wachovia Bank, N.A.; Willis Corroon Corp. of South Carolina; TNS Mills, Inc.; ACSI, Inc.; Lockheed Martin Aeronautics, Inc.; Insignia Financial Group, Inc.

For Complete List of Firm Personnel, See General Section

For full biographical listings, see the Martindale-Hubbell Law Directory

WILLIAMS & HENRY, PROFESSIONAL ASSOCIATION (AV)

513 East Washington Street, P.O. Box 10307, 29603
Telephone: 864-233-1609
Fax: 864-232-7807
Email: lawfirm@williamshenry.com

Ray R. Williams (1899-1987)
J. A. Henry (1899-1971)
Ray R. Williams, Jr.
Craig H. Allen

For full biographical listings, see the Martindale-Hubbell Law Directory

HILTON HEAD ISLAND, Beaufort Co.

BARRY L. JOHNSON, P.A. (AV)

35-A Bow Circle, Palmetto Bay Offices (Suite 35-A), P.O. Box 7261, 29938
Telephone: 843-341-3777
Fax: 843-341-3007
Beaufort, South Carolina Office: 1611 North Street.
Telephone: 843-982-0089.
Fax: 986-9203.

Barry L. Johnson

For full biographical listings, see the Martindale-Hubbell Law Directory

MYRTLE BEACH, Horry Co.

BELLAMY, RUTENBERG, COPELAND, EPPS, GRAVELY & BOWERS, P.A. (AV)

1000 29th Avenue North, P.O. Box 357, 29578
Telephone: 843-448-2400
Telecopier: 843-448-3022

Howell V. Bellamy, Jr.
John K. Rutenberg
John E. Copeland
Claude M. Epps, Jr.
David R. Gravely
Edward B. Bowers, Jr.
Bradley D. King
Henrietta U. Golding
M. Edwin Hinds, Jr.
Jill F. Griffith
Kathryn M. Cook
David B. Miller
C. Winfield Johnson, III
Sarah A. Johnson
Douglas M. Zayicek
Jeffrey W. King
Mary Anna Malpass
Martin Charles Dawsey

Representative Clients: Dargan Construction Co.; Coastal Federal Savings Bank; Sands Investments; Wachovia Bank of South Carolina; AVX Corp.; Bank of America; Parthenon Insurance Co.; Burroughs & Chapin Co.; International Paper Co.; Hospital Corporation of America.

For full biographical listings, see the Martindale-Hubbell Law Directory

SUMMERVILLE, Dorchester Co.

MICHAEL T. ROSE (AV)

409 Central Avenue, 29483
Telephone: 843-871-1821
Fax: 843-871-2454
Email: senator@excelonline.com

For full biographical listings, see the Martindale-Hubbell Law Directory

SOUTH DAKOTA

*ABERDEEN,** Brown Co.

BANTZ, GOSCH, CREMER, PETERSON & SOMMERS (AV)

305 Sixth Avenue, S.E., P.O. Box 970, 57402-0970
Telephone: 605-225-2232
Fax: 605-225-2497
Email: bantzlaw@midco.net

MEMBERS OF FIRM

Douglas W. Bantz (1909-1983)
Kennith L. Gosch
James M. Cremer
Greg L. Peterson
Richard A. Sommers
Ronald A. Wager

General Counsel for: Dacotah Banks, Inc.
Attorneys for: Northwestern Mutual Life Insurance Co.; Northwestern National Insurance Group; Transamerica Insurance Group; United Pacific Insurance Co.

For full biographical listings, see the Martindale-Hubbell Law Directory

LEAD, Lawrence Co.

FULLER, TELLINGHUISEN, GORDON & PERCY, P.C. (AV)

203 West Main Street, P.O. Box 898, 57754
Telephone: 605-584-2440
Fax: 605-584-1979
Email: leadlaw@mato.com
Spearfish, South Dakota Office: 132 East Illinois, 57783.
Telephone: 605-642-8080.
Fax: 605-642-1756. E-mail: spflaw@mato.com

A. P. Fuller
Roger A. Tellinghuisen
Bradley P. Gordon
Michelle Palmer Percy

Representative Clients: Homestake Mining Co.; Hotel Franklin & Gaming; Black Hills Novelty/Automatic Vending, Inc.; Northern Hills General Hospital; Lantis Enterprises, Inc.; Norwest Bank South Dakota N.A.; Lead-Deadwood Independent School District # 40-1; City of Lead.

For full biographical listings, see the Martindale-Hubbell Law Directory

*SIOUX FALLS,** Minnehaha Co.

DAVENPORT, EVANS, HURWITZ & SMITH, L.L.P. (AV)

513 South Main Avenue, P.O. Box 1030, 57101-1030
Telephone: 605-336-2880
Telecopier: 605-335-3639
Email: lawyers@dehs.com

MEMBERS OF FIRM

P. Daniel Donohue
David L. Knudson
Robert E. Hayes
Charles D. Gullickson
Monte R. Walz
Jonathan P. Brown
Catherine A. Tanck
Scott Bradley Anderson
Dixie K. Hieb
Jean H. Bender

ASSOCIATE

Kim J. Patrick

Counsel for: American Society of Composers, Authors and Publishers (A.S.C.A.P.); Continental Insurance Cos.; The First National Bank in Sioux Falls; Ford Motor Credit Co.; General Motors Corp.; The St. Paul Cos.; The Travelers.

For Complete List of Firm Personnel, See General Section

For full biographical listings, see the Martindale-Hubbell Law Directory

HUGHES LAW OFFICES (AV)

412 West Ninth Street, 57104-3602
Telephone: 605-339-3939
Fax: 605-339-3940

John R. Hughes

LeeAnn Larson LaFave

For full biographical listings, see the Martindale-Hubbell Law Directory

TENNESSEE

BRENTWOOD, Williamson Co.

THRAILKILL, HARRIS & WOOD, PLC (AV)

105 Westpark Drive, Suite 400, P.O. Box 2408, 37024-2408
Telephone: 615-376-3555
Fax: 615-376-3016

Larry T. Thrailkill
Christopher Harris
Steven K. Wood

(See Next Column)

THRAILKILL, HARRIS & WOOD PLC, *Brentwood—Continued*

Angela Humphreys Hamilton

For full biographical listings, see the Martindale-Hubbell Law Directory

*CHATTANOOGA,** Hamilton Co.

GEARHISER, PETERS, LOCKABY & TALLANT, PLLC (AV)

320 McCallie Avenue, 37402-2007
Telephone: 423-756-5171
Fax: 423-266-1605
Email: law@gplt.com

MEMBERS OF FIRM

Charles J. Gearhiser
R. Wayne Peters
Robert L. Lockaby, Jr.
Ralph E. Tallant, Jr.
Terry Atkin Cavett
Sam D. Elliott
Lane C. Avery
Wade K. Cannon

ASSOCIATES

Robin L. Miller
Christopher T. Varner
James C. Davey
Lee Ann Adams
Jeffrey H. Moore
Kevin T. Beck

OF COUNSEL

Richard P. Jahn, Jr.

References: First Tennessee Bank; First American National Bank.

For full biographical listings, see the Martindale-Hubbell Law Directory

JOHNSON CITY, Washington Co.

BRANDT AND BEESON, P.C. (AV)

206 Princeton Road, Suite 25, 37601
Telephone: 423-282-1981
Fax: 423-283-4778
Email: bnb@brandtbeeson.com

Frederic H. Brandt
D. R. Beeson, III
Jack L. Mayfield

For full biographical listings, see the Martindale-Hubbell Law Directory

*KNOXVILLE,** Knox Co.

BERNSTEIN, STAIR & MCADAMS LLP (AV)

Suite 600, 530 South Gay Street, 37902
Telephone: 423-546-8030
Telecopier: 423-522-8879
Effective October 1, 1999 Area Code will change to 865.

MEMBERS OF FIRM

Bernard E. Bernstein
L. Caesar Stair III
Thomas N. McAdams
Doris C. Allen
Celeste H. Herbert
James W. Parris

ASSOCIATES

W. Tyler Chastain
Lauren G. Strange-Boston
Margo J. Maxwell

Representative Clients: ABB Flakt, Inc.; Camel Manufacturing Company; Clayton Homes, Inc.; Horizon Physicians Group, P.C.; Plasti-Line, Inc.; Rafferty's Restaurants; Richardson Turner Construction Co., Inc.; Saks, Inc.; Vanderbilt Mortgage and Finance, Inc.; West Town Mall.

For full biographical listings, see the Martindale-Hubbell Law Directory

LEIBOWITZ & COHEN (AV)

608 Gay Street, S.W., 37902
Telephone: 423-637-1809
FAX: 423-637-9276

MEMBERS OF FIRM

Arnold G. Cohen
Lawrence P. Leibowitz

ASSOCIATE

Melissa A. Ashburn

OF COUNSEL

Russell T. Greene

For full biographical listings, see the Martindale-Hubbell Law Directory

*MEMPHIS,** Shelby Co.

ALLEN, SCRUGGS, SOSSAMAN & THOMPSON, P.C. (AV)

813 Ridge Lake Boulevard, Suite 300, 38120-9409
Telephone: 901-763-4200
Facsimile: 901-684-1768
Mailing Address: P.O. Box 17349, Memphis, TN, 38187-0349
Email: asstlaw@asstlaw.com

(See Next Column)

Richard H. Allen, Jr.
John P. Scruggs
James M. Simpson
Charles R. Keckler, III
M. Blake Barton

For full biographical listings, see the Martindale-Hubbell Law Directory

ARMSTRONG ALLEN PREWITT GENTRY JOHNSTON & HOLMES, PLLC (AV)

Brinkley Plaza, Suite 700, 80 Monroe Avenue, 38103-2467
Telephone: 901-523-8211
Facsimile: 901-524-4936
Little Rock, Arkansas Office: Suite 100, 100 Morgan Keegan Drive, 72202.
Telephone: 501-280-0100.
Facsimile: 501-280-0166.
Jackson, Mississippi Office: 2525 Lakeward Drive, Suite 200, 39216.
Telephone: 601-713-1192.
Facsimile: 601-713-2049.
Jackson, Tennessee Office: 464 North Parkway, Suite A, 38305.
Telephone: 901-660-2332.
Facsimile: 901-664-1109.

MEMBERS OF FIRM

Richard H. Allen
Elmore Holmes, III
Paul A. Matthews
James Rogers (Josh) Hall, Jr.
B. Douglas Earthman
Charles R. Crawford

OF COUNSEL

Edward M. Kaplan

For Complete List of Firm Personnel, See General Section

For full biographical listings, see the Martindale-Hubbell Law Directory

BAKER, DONELSON, BEARMAN & CALDWELL (AV)

20th Floor, First Tennessee Building, 165 Madison, 38103
Telephone: 901-526-2000
Telecopier: 901-577-2303
Email: info@bdbc.com *URL:* http://www.bakerdonelson.com
Nashville, Tennessee Office: 1700 Nashville City Center, 511 Union Street, 37219.
Telephone: 615-726-5600.
Telecopier: 615-726-0464.
Chattanooga, Tennessee Office: 1800 Republic Centre, 633 Chestnut Street, 37450-1800.
Telephone: 423-756-2010.
Telecopier: 423-756-3447.
Knoxville, Tennessee Office: 2200 Riverview Tower, 900 South Gay Street, 37901.
Telephone: 423-549-7000.
Telecopier: 423-525-8569.
Johnson City, Tennessee Office: SunTrust Bank Building, 207 Mockingbird Lane, P.O. Box 3038, 37602.
Telephone: 423-928-0181.
Telecopier: 423-928-5694; 423-928-3654; Kingsport: 423-246-6191.
Huntsville, Tennessee Office: 3 Courthouse Square, 37756.
Telephone: 423-663-2321.
Telecopier: 423-663-2111.
Washington, D.C. Office: Market Square, 801 Pennsylvania Avenue, N.W., 20004.
Telephone: 202-508-3400.
Telecopier: 202-508-3402.
Jackson, Mississippi Office: Suite 500, 700 North State Street, 39202.
Telephone: 601-351-2400.
Telecopier: 601-351-2424.

SHAREHOLDERS

Charles T. Tuggle, Jr.
Ben C. Adams, Jr.

For Complete List of Firm Personnel, See General Section

For full biographical listings, see the Martindale-Hubbell Law Directory

HALE HEADRICK DEWEY & WOLF, PLLC (AV)

One Memphis Place, 200 Jefferson Avenue Suite 1450, 38103
Telephone: 901-523-1123
Fax: 901-523-7472
Nashville, Tennessee Office: Suntrust Bank Building, 201 Fourth Avenue North, Suite 1450, 37219.
Telephone: 615-843-5160.
Fax: 615-843-5165

Stephen P. Hale
S. Russell Headrick
H. Tucker Dewey
Herbert B. Wolf, Jr.
John S. Golwen

OF COUNSEL

Steven L. Gill

Jennifer Ziegenhorn
Wendy A. Geurin
John W. Campbell
Joseph M. Koury
Holly N. Knight
Charles S. Blatteis
Jennifer S. Kiesewetter
J. William Williams

For full biographical listings, see the Martindale-Hubbell Law Directory

Memphis—Continued

HARKAVY, SHAINBERG, KOSTEN, KAPLAN & DUNSTAN, PC (AV)

100 Peabody Place, Suite 1300, 38103
Telephone: 901-761-1263
Telecopier: 901-763-3340
Downtown Telecopier: 901-843-0864
Downtown Office: Memphis, Tennessee, 6060 Poplar Avenue, Suite 140, 38119.

MEMBERS AND ASSOCIATES

Ronald M. Harkavy
Raymond M. Shainberg
Alan L. Kosten
Michael D. Kaplan
Allen C. Dunstan
Neil Harkavy
Jerome A. Broadhurst
Alan M. Harkavy

OF COUNSEL

Ira D. Pruitt, Jr.
Laurie A. Cooper
G. Thomas McPherson

For full biographical listings, see the Martindale-Hubbell Law Directory

*NASHVILLE,** Davidson Co.

DORAMUS, TRAUGER & NEY (AV)

Southern Turf Building, 222 Fourth Avenue North, 37219-2101
Telephone: 615-256-8585
Fax: 615-256-7444
Email: dtnfirm@dtnlaw.com

MEMBERS OF FIRM

Byron R. Trauger
James V. Doramus
Paul C. Ney, Jr.
Anne Sumpter Arney

ASSOCIATE

Jane Hanner Allen

For full biographical listings, see the Martindale-Hubbell Law Directory

TEXAS

ADDISON, Dallas Co.

GERARD SINGER & LEVICK, P.C. (AV)

16200 Addison Road Suite 140, 75001-5350
Telephone: 972-380-5533
Fax: 972-380-5748
Email: bcgerard@flash.net

Bretton C. Gerard
Gregory Z. Singer
Larry A. Levick
Michael I. Kahn
Robert J. Mabel
I. Richard Levy

For full biographical listings, see the Martindale-Hubbell Law Directory

*AUSTIN,** Travis Co.

BAKER BOTTS L.L.P. (AV)

1600 San Jacinto Center, 98 San Jacinto Boulevard, 78701
Telephone: 512-322-2500
Fax: 512-322-2501
Email: postmaster@bakerbotts.com *URL:* http://www.bakerbotts.com
Houston, Texas Office: One Shell Plaza, 910 Louisiana.
Telephone: 713-229-1234.
Dallas, Texas Office: 2001 Ross Avenue.
Telephone: 214-953-6500.
Washington, D.C. Office: The Warner, 1299 Pennsylvania Avenue, N.W.
Telephone: 202-639-7700.
New York, New York Office: 599 Lexington Avenue.
Telephone: 212-705-5000.
Moscow, Russia Office: 10 ul. Bolshaya Dimitrovka (formerly Pushkinskaya), 103031.
Telephone: 7095/921-5300 (Local); 7501/929-7070 (International).
London, England Office: 45 Ludgate Hill.
Telephone: 0171-778-1400 (Local); 011-44-171-778-1400 (International).
Baku, Azerbaijan Office: 6-10 Vagif Mustafa-zadeh Street, Third Floor, Icheri Sheher, 370004.
Telephone: 994-12-97-63-88 (Local); 011-994-12-97-63-88 (International).
Fax: 994-12-97-63-61 (Local); 011-994-12-97-63-91 (International).

MEMBERS OF FIRM

Aileen M. Hooks
Michael X. Marinelli (Not admitted in TX)
William F. Stutts, Jr.

SPECIAL COUNSEL

Shelley W. Austin

OF COUNSEL

E. Scott Lineberry

(See Next Column)

ASSOCIATES

Christopher T. Brown
Jolie M. Howard
Jennifer K. Patterson
Polly F. Powell

For Complete List of Firm Personnel, See General Section

For full biographical listings, see the Martindale-Hubbell Law Directory

JACKSON WALKER L.L.P. (AV)

100 Congress Avenue, Suite 1100, 78701-4099
Telephone: 512-236-2000
Fax: 512-236-2002
Email: hloftin@jw.com *URL:* http://www.jw.com
Dallas, Texas Office: 901 Main Street, Suite 6000.
Telephone: 214-953-6000.
Fax: 214-953-5822.
Fort Worth, Texas Office: 301 Commerce Street, Suite 2400.
Telephone: 817-334-7200.
Fax: 817-334-7290.
Houston, Texas Office: 1100 Louisiana, Suite 4200.
Telephone: 713-752-4200.
Fax: 713-752-4221.
Richardson, Texas Office: 2435 North Central Expressway, Suite 600.
Telephone: 972-671-2560.
Fax: 972-671-2566.
San Angelo, Texas Office: 225 West Beauregard Avenue.
Telephone: 915-481-2550.
Fax: 915-481-2552.
San Antonio, Texas Office: 112 E. Pecan Street, Suite 2100.
Telephone: 210-978-7700.
Fax: 210-978-7790.

MEMBERS OF FIRM

James M. Alsup
Steven R. Martens
William R. McIlhany
Steven D. Moore
James M. Nias
Timothy C. Taylor

For Complete List of Firm Personnel, See General Section

For full biographical listings, see the Martindale-Hubbell Law Directory

SAEGERT, ANGENEND & AUGUSTINE, P.C. (AV)

1145 West Fifth Street, Suite 300, 78703-5341
Telephone: 512-474-6521
Fax: 512-477-4512

Paul D. Angenend

Walter C. Guebert

Representative Clients: The 401(k) Companies, Inc.; Statewide Trucking Corp.; James Transport, Inc.; Merritt Manufacturing, Inc.; PCC Restaurants, Inc.; Paramount Computers Corp.; Spa Ventures, Inc.; SpectraNet, Inc.; Jump Point Communications, Inc.; International Whole Life Expo, Inc.

For full biographical listings, see the Martindale-Hubbell Law Directory

THOMPSON & KNIGHT L.L.P. (AV)

(Attorneys and Counselors)
1200 San Jacinto Center, 98 San Jacinto Boulevard, 78701
Telephone: 512-469-6100
Telecopy: 512-469-6180
URL: http://www.tklaw.com
Dallas, Texas Office: 1700 Pacific Avenue, Suite 3300, 75201.
Telephone: 214-969-1700.
Telecopy: 512-969-1751.
Telex: 732298.
Fort Worth, Texas Office: 801 Cherry Street, Suite 1600, 76102.
Telephone: 817-347-1700.
Telecopy: 817-347-1799.
Houston, Texas Office: Thompson Knight Brown Parker & Leahy L.L.P., 1200 Smith Street, Suite 3600, 77002-4595.
Telephone: 713-654-8111.
Telecopier: 713-654-1871.
San Pedro Garza Garcia, Nuevo León, Mexico Office: Edificio Losoles PD-4, Av. Lázaro Cárdenas No. 2400 Pte., C.P. 66220.
Telephone: (52-8) 363-0096.
Telecopy: (52-8) 363-3067.

PARTNER

Michael L. Bengtson

For Complete List of Firm Personnel, See General Section

For full biographical listings, see the Martindale-Hubbell Law Directory

BEDFORD, Tarrant Co.

ADAMS, LYNCH & LOFTIN, P.C. (AV)

1903 Central Drive, Suite 400, 76021
Telephone: 817-283-7742
Fax: 817-571-2947

(See Next Column)

ADAMS, LYNCH & LOFTIN P.C., *Bedford—Continued*

Neal W. Adams
John T. Lynch, IV
Stacy B. Loftin

Jon A. McCormick

For full biographical listings, see the Martindale-Hubbell Law Directory

*DALLAS,** Dallas Co.

BAKER BOTTS L.L.P. (AV)

2001 Ross Avenue, 75201
Telephone: 214-953-6500
Fax: 214-953-6503
Email: postmaster@bakerbotts.com *URL:* http://www.bakerbotts.com
Houston, Texas Office: One Shell Plaza, 910 Louisiana.
Telephone: 713-229-1234.
Washington, D.C. Office: The Warner, 1299 Pennsylvania Avenue, N.W.
Telephone: 202-639-7700.
Austin, Texas Office: 1600 San Jacinto Center, 98 San Jacinto Boulevard.
Telephone: 512-322-2500.
New York, New York Office: 599 Lexington Avenue.
Telephone: 212-705-5000.
Moscow, Russia Office: 10 ul. Bolshaya Dimitrovka (formerly Pushkinskaya), 103031.
Telephone: 7095/921-5300 (Local); 7095/929-7070.
London, England Office: 45 Ludgate Hill.
Telephone: 0171-778-1400 (Local); 011-44-171-778-1400 (International).
Baku, Azerbaijan Office: 6-10 Vagif Mustafa-zadeh Street, Third Floor, Icheri Sheher, 370004.
Telephone: 994-12-97-63-88 (Local); 011-994-12-97-63-88 (International).

MEMBERS OF FIRM

Andrew M. Baker
Jonathan W. Dunlay
John W. Martin
Geoffrey L. Newton
Sarah M. Rechter (Not admitted in TX)
Patricia M. Stanton
Karen Leslye Wolf

ASSOCIATES

Curtis B. Anderson
Jay Bhattacharya
Lisa DiIorio
Christopher D. Epperson (Not admitted in TX)
Jason D. Krieser (Not admitted in TX)
Thomas J. Masterson
David G. Monk
Royce P. Poinsett
Douglass M. Rayburn
Brenda Levine Sutherland
Arthur C. Swanson

For Complete List of Firm Personnel, See General Section

For full biographical listings, see the Martindale-Hubbell Law Directory

LAW OFFICES OF FRANK L. BRANSON, P.C. (AV)

18th Floor, Highland Park Place, 4514 Cole Avenue, 75205-4185
Telephone: 214-522-0200
Metro: 972-263-7452
Fax: 214-521-5485
URL: http://www.lawyers.com/frankbranson

Frank L. Branson
Debbie D. Branson
George A. Quesada, Jr.
Jerry M. White
Thomas J. Farmer
William B. Curtis
Robert D. Crain
Charles E. Moody

OF COUNSEL

Ted Z. Robertson
J. Hadley Edgar, Jr.

For full biographical listings, see the Martindale-Hubbell Law Directory

CALHOUN & STACY (AV)

Suite 5700 - Bank of America Plaza, 901 Main Street, 75202-3713
Telephone: 214-748-5000
Facsimile: 214-748-1421
Email: info@calhounstacy.com *URL:* http://www.calhounstacy.com

MEMBERS OF FIRM

Rees T. Bowen, III
Mark Alan Calhoun
Dennis D. Conder
LeAnn Wainscott Cross
David W. Elrod
Thomas E. Rosen
Shannon B. Schuster
Michael C. Wright

ASSOCIATES

Joseph G. Barkate, Jr.
Sean P. Fitzgerald
Elizabeth Reding Gambrell
Jonathan G. Polak
Joel W. Reese

For Complete List of Firm Personnel, See General Section

For full biographical listings, see the Martindale-Hubbell Law Directory

CONANT FRENCH & CHANEY, LLP (AV)

3880 Bank One Center, 1717 Main Street, 75201
Telephone: 214-915-0620
Fasimile: 214-915-0634
Email: cfc@cfc-law.com *URL:* http://www.cfc-law.com

(See Next Column)

A. B. Conant, Jr.
William J. French
William B. Chaney
Linda A. Hale
Glen E. Lavy
Shawn W. Phelan
James D. MacIntyre

For full biographical listings, see the Martindale-Hubbell Law Directory

FIGARI DAVENPORT & GRAVES, L.L.P. (AV)

A Partnership including a Professional Corporation
901 Main Street, LB 125, 4800 Bank of America Plaza, 75202-3796
Telephone: 214-939-2000
Fax: 214-939-2090

MEMBERS OF FIRM

Ernest E. Figari, Jr., (P.C.)
Mark T. Davenport
Thomas A. Graves
Doug K. Butler
Donald Colleluori
Gary D. Eisenstat
Andrew G. Jubinsky
Parker D. Young
Michael G. Brown
Timothy A. Daniels
Keith R. Verges
Stephen D. Howen
Monica L. Luebker
Andrew C. Whitaker

Jill B. Davenport
Bill E. Davidoff
Amanda M. Inabnett
Dennis M. Lynch
Melissa A. Mitchell
Katherine S. Rabe
Lisa L. Traylor
Jennifer M. Trulock

For full biographical listings, see the Martindale-Hubbell Law Directory

GOINS, UNDERKOFLER, CRAWFORD & LANGDON, L.L.P. (AV)

3300 Thanksgiving Tower, 1601 Elm Street, 75201
Telephone: 214-969-5454
Fax: 214-969-5902 ABA Net 17432

MEMBERS OF FIRM

Hance W. Burrow, III
Durwood D. Crawford
E. Eldridge Goins, Jr.
John O. Langdon
Ira F. Levy
Paul A. Mohtares
James W. Morris, Jr.
Neil J. Orleans
John D. Rosenberg
Richard E. Schellhammer
John J. Sheedy, Jr.
Paul B. Underkofler
Frank L. Broyles
David L. Paschall

ASSOCIATE

Jeffrey S. Wigder

For full biographical listings, see the Martindale-Hubbell Law Directory

GRIFFITH & NIXON, P.C. (AV)

One Lincoln Center, 5400 LBJ Freeway, Suite 1025, 75240
Telephone: 972-386-8988
Fax: 972-386-8985
Email: griffnix@flash.net

Scott Griffith
Michael S. Nixon

Kimberly A. Davison
Benjamin D. Halpern
L. Christopher Harris
Anthony P. Jach
Jeffery Harold Rusthoven
Scott V. Siddons

For full biographical listings, see the Martindale-Hubbell Law Directory

HUGHES & LUCE, L.L.P. (AV)

A Registered Limited Liability Partnership including Professional Corporations
1717 Main Street, Suite 2800, 75201
Telephone: 214-939-5500
Fax: 214-939-6100; 214-939-5849
Email: H&L@hughesluce.com *URL:* http://www.hughesluce.com
Austin, Texas Office: 111 Congress, Suite 900.
Telephone: 512-482-6800.
Fax: 512-482-6859.
Houston, Texas Office: 1600 Smith Street, Suite 3550.
Telephone: 713-754-5200.
Fax: 713-754-5270.

MEMBERS OF FIRM

David N. Guedry
John E. Howell
David H. Judson

ASSOCIATE

Chad W. King

OF COUNSEL

André J. Brunel
Thomas W. Luce, III
Douglas A. Sorensen
Matthew C. Wood

For Complete List of Firm Personnel, See General Section

For full biographical listings, see the Martindale-Hubbell Law Directory

Dallas—Continued

JACKSON WALKER L.L.P. (AV)

901 Main Street, Suite 6000, 75202-3797
Telephone: 214-953-6000
Fax: 214-953-5822
URL: http://www.jw.com
Austin, Texas Office: 100 Congress Avenue, Suite 1100.
Telephone: 512-236-2000.
Fax: 512-236-2002.
Fort Worth, Texas Office: 301 Commerce Street, Suite 2400.
Telephone: 817-334-7200.
Fax: 817-334-7290.
Houston, Texas Office: 1100 Louisiana, Suite 4200.
Telephone: 713-752-4200.
Fax: 713-752-4221.
Richardson, Texas Office: 2435 North Central Expressway, Suite 600.
Telephone: 972-671-2560.
Fax: 972-671-2566.
San Angelo, Texas Office: 225 West Beauregard Avenue.
Telephone: 915-481-2550.
Fax: 915-481-2552.
San Antonio, Texas Office: 112 E. Pecan Street, Suite 2100.
Telephone: 210-978-7700.
Fax: 210-978-7790.

MEMBERS OF FIRM

Bryan C. Birkeland
Richard F. Dahlson
George L. Diamond
Emily Stacy Donahue
Daniel G. Easley
Byron F. Egan
Charles S. Gilbert
Richard B. Goodner
Michael Patrick Haggerty
Charles D. Maguire, Jr.
Frank P. McEachern
James S. Ryan, III
Joan Sprince Sostek
Bradley L. Whitlock

OF COUNSEL

Roy Howard Baskin, III

Representative Clients Furnished Upon Request.

For Complete List of Firm Personnel, See General Section

For full biographical listings, see the Martindale-Hubbell Law Directory

KRONEY • MINCEY, INC. (AV)

1210 Three Forest Plaza, 12221 Merit Drive, 75251
Telephone: 972-386-8500
FAX: 972-701-0307

Sabina R. Choudhry
H. Kate Hopkins
Robert H. Kroney
Donald P. Lan, Jr.
Taryn N. Milewski
James M. Mincey, Jr.
Stuart A. Morse

For full biographical listings, see the Martindale-Hubbell Law Directory

SMITH, UNDERWOOD & PERKINS, A PROFESSIONAL CORPORATION (AV)

600 Two Lincoln Centre, 5420 LBJ Freeway, 75240
Telephone: 972-661-5114
Telecopier: 972-661-5691
Email: firm@suandp.com *URL:* http://www.suplaw.com

Timothy S. Perkins
David W. Ralston
G. Lynn Smith
William J. Underwood, Jr.

Christine A. McGuire
Amy K. Ratzlaff
P. Theodore Stoinoff, II
Val C. Cronin
Ellen P. Stewart
Todd W. Shadle
Ruth C. Logan
Christina L. Betanzos
Kent D. Williamson

For full biographical listings, see the Martindale-Hubbell Law Directory

THOMPSON, COE, COUSINS & IRONS, L.L.P. (AV)

200 Crescent Court, Eleventh Floor, 75201-1853
Telephone: 214-871-8200
Fax: 214-871-8209
Austin, Texas Office: Suite 1500, Austin Centre, 701 Brazos, 78701.
Telephone: 512-708-8200.
Fax: 512-708-8777.

PARTNERS

Emory L. White, Jr.
Richard S. Geiger
Jack M. Cleaveland, Jr.
Rodney D. Bucker
Beth D. Bradley
James L. Sowder
Michael W. Jones

Representative Clients: Bank One Texas, N.A.; Atlantic Asset Management Company; Compass Bank; PSM International, Inc.; Rigg Group, Inc.; Star Automotive Warehouse, Inc.

For Complete List of Firm Personnel, See General Section

For full biographical listings, see the Martindale-Hubbell Law Directory

THOMPSON & KNIGHT L.L.P. (AV)

(Attorneys and Counselors)
1700 Pacific Avenue Suite 3300, 75201
Telephone: 214-969-1700
Telecopy: 214-969-1751
Telex: 732 298
URL: http://www.tklaw.com
Austin, Texas Office: 1200 San Jacinto Center, 98 San Jacinto Boulevard, 78701.
Telephone: 512-469-6100.
Telecopy: 512-469-6180.
Fort Worth, Texas Office: 801 Cherry Street, Suite 1600, 76102.
Telephone: 817-347-1700.
Telecopy: 817-347-1799.
Houston, Texas Office: Thompson Knight Brown Parker & Leahy L.L.P., 1200 Smith Street, Suite 3600, 77002-4595.
Telephone: 713-654-8111.
Telecopier: 713-654-1871.
San Pedro Garza Garcia, Nuevo León, Mexico Office: Edificio Losoles PD-4, Av. Lázaro Cárdenas No. 2400 Pte., C.P. 66220.
Telephone: (52-8) 363-0096.
Telecopy: (52-8) 363-3067.

PARTNERS

Craig N. Adams
Sam P. Burford, Jr.
Frederick W. Burnett, Jr.
Steven K. Cochran
Joe Dannenmaier
David L. Emmons
James L. Irish, III
Paul M. Johnston
Harold F. Kleinman
C. Neel Lemon III
Jack M. Little
David E. Morrison
James R. Peacock III
William F. Pyne
Norman R. Rogers
William J. Schuerger
Kenn W. Webb
Bill R. Womble
Jeffrey A. Zlotky

ASSOCIATES

Ann Marie Cowdrey
Priscilla Lynn Dunckel
J. Holt Foster, III
Christopher D. Ray

OF COUNSEL

Gayle E. Cannon

For Complete List of Firm Personnel, See General Section

For full biographical listings, see the Martindale-Hubbell Law Directory

*DENTON,** Denton Co.

WOOD, THACKER & WEATHERLY, P.C. (AV)

513 West Oak Street, 76201
Telephone: 817-565-6565
Fax: 817-566-6673

R. William Wood
C. Jane Thacker
Grace A. Weatherly

For full biographical listings, see the Martindale-Hubbell Law Directory

*EL PASO,** El Paso Co.

AINSA PARTNERS, LLP (AV)

5809 Acacia Circle, 79912
Telephone: 915-845-5300
Fax: 915-845-7800
Email: fain@acaciapark.com *URL:* http://www.ainsa.com

Francis S. Ainsa, Jr.
Michael F. Ainsa
David M. Driscoll

For full biographical listings, see the Martindale-Hubbell Law Directory

CROWSON & INGRAM (AV)

Suite 706, The Cortez, 310 North Mesa, P.O. Box 862, 79945
Telephone: 915-533-7717
Telefax: 915-533-1495
Email: crowsing@huntleigh.net

MEMBERS OF FIRM

Harold E. Crowson, Jr.
Temple B. Ingram, Jr.

Reference: Bank of America, N.A.; Norwest Bank, El Paso, N.A.; Bank of the West, El Paso, Texas.

For full biographical listings, see the Martindale-Hubbell Law Directory

*FORT WORTH,** Tarrant Co.

DECKER, JONES, MCMACKIN, MCCLANE, HALL & BATES, A PROFESSIONAL CORPORATION (AV)

2500 Bank One Tower, 500 Throckmorton Street, 76102-3812
Telephone: 817-336-2400; Metro: 817-429-5260
Fax: 817-332-3043; 336-2181
Email: email@deckerjones.com *URL:* http://www.deckerjones.com

(See Next Column)

DECKER, JONES, MCMACKIN, MCCLANE, HALL & BATES A PROFESSIONAL CORPORATION, *Fort Worth—Continued*

Daniel L. Bates
Robert W. Decker
Mark S. Dugan
Janet L. Hahn
Randy J. Hall
Raymond B. Kelly, III
John B. McClane
John W. McMackin
Charles B. Milliken
Gary M. Moates
Bradley H. Rice
Jeffrey W. Storie
James L. Stripling
Brian K. Yost
Tamera H. Bennett
Arthur F. Zobal
Geoffrey A. Mantooth

Representative Clients: Martin-Sprocket and Gear, Inc.; Williamson-Dickie Manufacturing Co.; MICA Corp.; Harbison-Fischer Manufacturing Co.; Employers Insurance of Texas; American International Group; Medical Protective Co.; Redman Homes, Inc.; Texas Medical Liability Trust; MIIX Insurance Group.

For full biographical listings, see the Martindale-Hubbell Law Directory

LAW, SNAKARD & GAMBILL, A PROFESSIONAL CORPORATION (AV)

3200 Bank One Tower, 500 Throckmorton Street, 76102
Telephone: 817-335-7373; Metro: 429-2991
Telecopier: 817-332-7473
Dallas
Dallas, Texas Office: St. Paul Place, 750 North St. Paul, Suite 1350.
Telephone: 214-871-9027; Metro: 429-2991.
Telecopier: 214-954-4476.

Rice M. Tilley (1899-1990)
Robert F. Snakard (1910-1994)
Samuel A. Denny (1937-1995)
Rice M. Tilley, Jr.
Walter S. Fortney
Dennis Swift
Jay Spencer Garrett
William F. McCann
Ed Huddleston
Vernon E. Rew, Jr.
A. Burch Waldron, III
Larry C. Bracken
Pamela Arnold Bassel
Carol Ware Bracken
Dabney D. Bassel
Lynn M. Johnson
Kelley B. Hill
B. Blake Cox
James H. Cheatham, IV
Stephen G. Wilcox
M. W. Cockrell, Jr.
Liane A. Janovsky

Christopher R. Richie
Deborah B. Morton
James O. Wyss
Laurie Dahl Babich
David F. Shurtz
Shoshana L. Thoma-Isgur

OF COUNSEL

Thos. H. Law
Lawton G. Gambill
Robert M. Randolph
Robert F. Watson
Harry Hopkins

Representative Clients: BankOne, Texas, N.A.; Southwestern Bell Telephone Co.; The Perot Group; Ford Motor Credit Co.; Prudential Securities, Inc.; Chrysler Financial Corp.
Attorneys for: Chicago Title Insurance Co.

For full biographical listings, see the Martindale-Hubbell Law Directory

LOE, WARREN, ROSENFIELD, KAITCER & HIBBS, A PROFESSIONAL CORPORATION (AV)

4420 West Vickery Boulevard, P.O. Box 100609, 76185-0609
Telephone: 817-377-0060
Fax: 817-377-1120

H. Joe Loe (1911-1987)
William M. Warren
Mark J. Rosenfield
Jeffrey N. Kaitcer
Kelcie A. Hibbs
M. A. "Mike" Windsor
David E. Kelley, II

General Counsel for: United States Crystal Corp.

For full biographical listings, see the Martindale-Hubbell Law Directory

MICHENER, LARIMORE, SWINDLE, WHITAKER, FLOWERS, SAWYER, REYNOLDS & CHALK, L.L.P. (AV)

3500 City Center Tower II, 301 Commerce Street, 76102
Telephone: 817-335-4417
Telecopy: 817-335-6935

MEMBERS OF FIRM

John W. Michener, Jr.
Tom L. Larimore
Mack Ed Swindle
Wayne M. Whitaker
H. David Flowers
Jerry K. Sawyer
James G. Reynolds
John Allen Chalk, Sr.
Thomas S. Brandon, Jr.
Matthew P. McDonald
Clark R. Cowley
Thomas F. Harkins, Jr.
John A. Chalk, Jr.
Leslie Combs
Robert G. West
Theresa Brewton Lyons
Jonathan K. Henderson
David R. Childress
Harold S. Sparks, III
John M. Cummings
Melinda Watts Smith
Hunter T. McLean

For full biographical listings, see the Martindale-Hubbell Law Directory

THOMPSON & KNIGHT L.L.P. (AV)

(Attorneys and Counselors)
801 Cherry Street, Suite 1600, 76102
Telephone: 817-347-1700
Telecopy: 817-347-1799
URL: http://www.tklaw.com
Dallas, Texas Office: 1700 Pacific Avenue, Suite 3300, 75201.
Telephone: 214-969-1700.
Telecopy: 214-969-1751.
Telex: 732298.
Austin, Texas Office: 1200 San Jacinto Center, 98 San Jacinto Boulevard, 78701.
Telephone: 512-469-6100.
Telecopy: 512-469-6180.
Houston, Texas Office: Thompson Knight Brown Parker & Leahy L.L.P., 1200 Smith Street, Suite 3600, 77002-4595.
Telephone: 713-654-8111.
Telecopier: 713-654-1871.
San Pedro Garza Garcia, Nuevo León, Mexico Office: Edificio Losoles PD-4, Av. Lázaro Cárdenas No. 2400 Pte., C.P. 66220.
Telephone: (52-8) 363-0096.
Telecopy: (52-8) 363-3067.

PARTNER

Stephen B. Norris

For Complete List of Firm Personnel, See General Section

For full biographical listings, see the Martindale-Hubbell Law Directory

*GEORGETOWN,** Williamson Co.

WILLIAM D. BRYCE (AV)

511 Main Street, 78626
Telephone: 512-930-3725
Fax: 512-930-3727

ASSOCIATES

Douglas D. Bryce
David D. Bryce

For full biographical listings, see the Martindale-Hubbell Law Directory

*HOUSTON,** Harris Co.

BAKER BOTTS L.L.P. (AV)

One Shell Plaza, 910 Louisiana, 77002
Telephone: 713-229-1234
Cable Address: "Boterlove"
Fax: 713-229-1522
Email: postmaster@bakerbotts.com *URL:* http://www.bakerbotts.com
Washington, D.C. Office: The Warner, 1299 Pennsylvania Avenue, N.W.
Telephone: 202-639-7700.
New York, New York Office: 599 Lexington Avenue.
Telephone: 212-705-5000.
Austin, Texas Office: 1600 San Jacinto Center, 98 San Jacinto Boulevard.
Telephone: 512-322-2500.
Dallas, Texas Office: 2001 Ross Avenue.
Telephone: 214-953-6500.
Moscow, Russia Office: 10 ul. Bolshaya Dimitrovka (formerly Pushkinskaya), 103031.
Telephone: 7095/921-5300 (Local); 7095/929-7070 (International).
London, England Office: 45 Ludgate Hill.
Telephone: 0171-778-1400 (Local); 011-44-171-778-1400 (International).
Baku, Azerbaijan Office: 6-10 Vagif Mustafa-zadeh Street, Third Floor, Icheri Sheher, 370004.
Telephone: 994-12-97-63-88 (Local); 011-994-12-97-63-88 (International).
Fax: 994-12-97-63-91 (Local); 011-994-12-97-63-91 (International)

MEMBER OF FIRM

Richard C. Johnson

MEMBERS OF FIRM

David F. Asmus
Jonathan T. Bickham
Joseph A. Cialone, II
Joshua Davidson
James A. DeMent, Jr.
Fred H. Dunlop
John D. Geddes
Moulton Goodrum, Jr.
Frank W. R. Hubert, Jr.
J. David Kirkland, Jr.
Paul B. Landen
James L. Leader
Marley Lott
Stephen A. Massad
Roy L. Nolen
Gene J. Oshman
Peter M. Oxman
Theodore William Paris
Joe S. Poff
Kelly Brunetti Rose
Margo S. Scholin
Walter J. Smith
Robert L. Stillwell
R. Joel Swanson
Charles Szalkowski
Darrell W. Taylor
Timothy S. Taylor
Lewis Proctor Thomas
Hugh Tucker
C. Michael Watson
Wade H. Whilden
Robert P. Wright

SPECIAL COUNSEL

W. Brad Bryan
LeAnn Vaughn
Victoria Gardner Wall

OF COUNSEL

James LeGrand Read

(See Next Column)

BAKER BOTTS L.L.P.—*Continued*

ASSOCIATES

Christopher J. Arntzen
Matthew D. Bekerman (Not admitted in TX)
J. Kevin Blodgett
Karen Skeens Caldwell
M. Andrew Chen
Sarah Cooper
Edmund D. Daniels
David Patrick Elder
Brian P. Fenske
Kathleen S. Fenelon
James M. Grace, Jr.
Gregory B. Kopel
James H. Mayor
William S. Moss, III
Denise Dardeau Muller
Michelle A. Neumann
Rebecca Pacholder
Sergio A. Pozzerle
Elizabeth Rose
J. Denmon Sigler
Consuella D. Simmons
Gerald M. Spedale
Stacey F. Tilley
Laura Lanza Tyson

For Complete List of Firm Personnel, See General Section

For full biographical listings, see the Martindale-Hubbell Law Directory

COHEN & SMALL (AV)

2700 Post Oak Boulevard, Suite 950, 77056
Telephone: 713-961-5274
Fax: 713-961-0438
Email: csinfo@cohensmall.com *URL:* http://www.cohensmall.com

MEMBERS OF FIRM

Ronald Cohen
William G. Small

Representative Clients: General Electric Capital Corp.; The Hertz Corp.; Gulf Metals Industries; U.S. Zinc Corp.; Physicians New West Hosp.; United Surgical Assoc.; Sachnowitz & Co.; Brightstar Information Technologies, Inc.; Transcoastal Marine Services, Inc.; Geokinetics, Inc.

For full biographical listings, see the Martindale-Hubbell Law Directory

CORDRAY & GOODRICH, PROFESSIONAL CORPORATION (AV)

3306 Sul Ross, 77098-1808
Telephone: 713-630-0600
Facsimile: 713-630-0017

Howard F. Cordray, Jr.
Christopher M. Goodrich
Richard Alan Tomlin
Gregory A. Goodrich
Glynn D. Nance, Jr.

OF COUNSEL

Ellen M. Lang
Van A. Cates
Robert G. Bailey

For full biographical listings, see the Martindale-Hubbell Law Directory

FARNSWORTH & VONBERG (AV)

A Limited Liability Partnership
333 North Sam Houston Parkway, Suite 300, 77060
Telephone: 281-931-8902
Telecopy: 281-931-6032

T Brooke Farnsworth
Mary Frances vonBerg

ASSOCIATE

Bennett S. Bartlett

For full biographical listings, see the Martindale-Hubbell Law Directory

GILLIS & SLOGAR (AV)

6905 Wells Fargo Plaza, 1000 Louisiana, 77002
Telephone: 713-951-9100
Telecopier: 713-951-9718
Email: gillisslogar@worldnet.att.net

Charles Michael Gillis
John Michael Slogar

OF COUNSEL

Randall W. Heinrich

For full biographical listings, see the Martindale-Hubbell Law Directory

JACKSON WALKER L.L.P. (AV)

1100 Louisiana, Suite 4200, P.O. Box 4771, 77002
Telephone: 713-752-4200
Fax: 713-752-4221
URL: http://www.jw.com
Austin, Texas Office: 100 Congress Avenue, Suite 1100.
Telephone: 512-236-2000.
Fax: 512-236-2002.
Dallas, Texas Office: 901 Main Street, Suite 6000.
Telephone: 214-953-6000.
Fax: 214-953-5822.
Fort Worth, Texas Office: 301 Commerce Street, Suite 2400.
Telephone: 817-334-7200.
Fax: 817-334-7290.
Richardson, Texas Office: 2435 North Central Expressway, Suite 600.
Telephone: 972-671-2560.
Fax: 972-671-2566.

(See Next Column)

San Angelo, Texas Office: 225 West Beauregard Avenue.
Telephone: 915-481-2550.
Fax: 915-481-2552.
San Antonio, Texas Office: 112 E. Pecan Street, Suite 2100.
Telephone: 210-978-7700.
Fax: 210-978-7790.

MEMBERS OF FIRM

Richard L. Burleson
David G. Dunlap
Randal S. Farber
Kurt D. Nondorf
Douglas A. Paisley, II
Michael P. Pearson
Norman T. Reynolds
Richard S. Roth
John B. Scofield

OF COUNSEL

John H. Peper

For Complete List of Firm Personnel, See General Section

For full biographical listings, see the Martindale-Hubbell Law Directory

SCHWARTZ JUNELL CAMPBELL & OATHOUT, L.L.P. (AV)

Two Houston Center, 909 Fannin, Suite 2000, 77010
Telephone: 713-752-0017
Telecopier: 713-752-0327
Email: dschwartz@schwartz-junell.com

Richard A. Schwartz
William Edward Junell, Jr.
Marshall S. Campbell
Monica F. Oathout
Steven R. Rech

Phillip W. Bechter
J. Parker Fauntleroy, Jr.

OF COUNSEL

Joe H. Reynolds
A. R. Schwartz

LEGAL SUPPORT PERSONNEL

PARALEGALS

Nannette Koger
Maria Woods
Shelly A. Savage, CLA

For full biographical listings, see the Martindale-Hubbell Law Directory

THOMPSON KNIGHT BROWN PARKER & LEAHY L.L.P. (AV)

A Registered Limited Liability Partnership including Professional Corporations
(Attorneys and Counselors)
1200 Smith Street, Suite 3600, 77002-4595
Telephone: 713-654-8111
Telecopier: 713-654-1871
URL: http://www.tklaw.com
Dallas, Texas Office: Thompson & Knight L.L.P., 1700 Pacific Avenue, Suite 3300, 75201.
Telephone: 214-969-1700.
Telecopy: 214-969-1751.
Telex: 732298.
Austin, Texas Office: Thompson & Knight L.L.P., 1200 San Jacinto Center, 98 San Jacinto Boulevard, 78701.
Telephone: 512-469-6100.
Telecopy: 512-469-6180.
Fort Worth, Texas Office: Thompson & Knight L.L.P., 801 Cherry Street, Suite 1600, 76102.
Telephone: 817-347-1700.
Telecopy: 817-347-1799.
San Pedro Garza Garcia, Nuevo León, Mexico Office: Thompson & Knight L.L.P., Edificio Losoles PD-4, Av. Lázaro Cárdenas No. 2400 PTE., C.P. 66220.
Telephone: (52-8) 363-0096.
Telecopy: (52-8) 363-3067.

PARTNERS

Debbi M. Johnstone
Michael K. Pierce

For Complete List of Firm Personnel, See General Section

For full biographical listings, see the Martindale-Hubbell Law Directory

*MIDLAND,** Midland Co.

KERR & WARD, L.L.P. (AV)

500 W. Texas, Suite 1310, Drawer 2858, 79702
Telephone: 915-684-9990
Fax: 915-684-9997
Email: info@kerr-ward.com *URL:* http://www.kerr-ward.com

OF COUNSEL

Wm. Monroe Kerr
Theodore M. Kerr

PARTNERS

Harris E. Kerr
William E. Ward
William M. Kerr, Jr.
Brian T. McLaughlin
James Devin Alsup

For full biographical listings, see the Martindale-Hubbell Law Directory

ROUND ROCK, Williamson Co.

STEVEN B. TREDENNICK (AV)

4028 Sable Oaks Drive, 78664-6251
Telephone: 512-246-6865
Fax: 512-246-1094
Email: sbtredennick@email.msn.com
Email: stredennic@aol.com *URL:* http://www.lawyers.com/stevenbtredennick

For full biographical listings, see the Martindale-Hubbell Law Directory

*SAN ANTONIO,** Bexar Co.

COX & SMITH INCORPORATED (AV)

112 East Pecan Street, Suite 1800, 78205-1521
Telephone: 210-554-5500
Fax: 210-226-8395
Email: info@coxsmith.com *URL:* http://www.coxsmith.com

Dan G. Webster, III
James B. Smith, Jr.
William H. Lester, Jr.
Cary Plotkin Kavy
Stephen D. Seidel
James M. McDonough
Steven R. Jacobs
Michael A. Morell
William J. McDonough, Jr.
Robert W. Nelson
Steven A. Elder
R. Bradley Oxford
Harry W. Wolff, Jr.
Elizabeth Johnson Keig
Kerry T. Benedict
David C. Giles
Scott B. Bankler

OF COUNSEL

Teresa Ereon Giltner

Representative Clients: Abraxas Petroleum Corporation; Cancer Therapy and Research Center; Eye Care Centers of America, Inc.; International Bank of Commerce, N.A.; Kinetic Concepts, Inc.; Merrill Lynch, Pierce, Fenner & Smith, Inc.; NationsBank of Texas, N.A.; San Miguel Electric Cooperative, Inc.; Solo Serve Corporation; TETCO, Inc.

For Complete List of Firm Personnel, See General Section

For full biographical listings, see the Martindale-Hubbell Law Directory

SCHOENBAUM, CURPHY & SCANLAN, P.C. (AV)

NationsBank Plaza, Suite 1775, 300 Convent Street, 78205-3744
Telephone: 210-224-4491
Fax: 210-224-7983

Stanley Schoenbaum
R. James Curphy
William Scanlan, Jr.
Alfred G. Holcomb
Banks M. Smith
Darin N. Digby
Patricia Flora Sitchler
Emily Harrison Liljenwall

Stacey Alison Warnix

For full biographical listings, see the Martindale-Hubbell Law Directory

*WICHITA FALLS,** Wichita Co.

GIBSON, HOTCHKISS, ROACH & DAVENPORT (AV)

807 8th Street, 8th Floor, 76301
Telephone: 940-322-7856
Fax: 940-322-1204
Email: ed@ghrdlaw.com *URL:* http://www.lawyers.com/ghrdlaw

MEMBER OF FIRM

Robert K. Roach

ASSOCIATE

Sally E.O. Landback

Representative Clients: American National Bank, Wichita Falls; First National Bank of Bowie; Wichita Falls PCA; Bennett Production Co.; Red River Authority of Texas; Burcamp Steel Co.

For Complete List of Firm Personnel, See General Section

For full biographical listings, see the Martindale-Hubbell Law Directory

UTAH

*SALT LAKE CITY,** Salt Lake Co.

CALLISTER NEBEKER & McCULLOUGH, A PROFESSIONAL CORPORATION (AV)

Gateway Tower East, Suite 900, 10 East South Temple, 84133
Telephone: 801-530-7300
Telecopier: 801-364-9127
Email: mjeaston@cnmlaw.com *URL:* http://www.cnmlaw.com

(See Next Column)

Louis H. Callister
Leland S. McCullough
Dorothy C. Pleshe
John A. Beckstead
Jeffrey N. Clayton
W. Waldan Lloyd
Craig F. McCullough
George E. Harris, Jr.
Damon E. Coombs
Lynda Cook
John H. Rees
Laurie S. Hart
John B. Lindsay
Douglas K. Cummings

Representative Clients: Zions Bancorporation; Utah Automobile Dealers Association; Sinclair Oil (Little America); Keystone Communications; Central Valley Water Reclamation Facility Board; Children's Miracle Network (Osmond Foundation); American Stores; Utah Resources International; Novell, Inc.; Nu Skin International, Inc.; Natures Way; Covel Technologies, Inc.; Fields Aircraft; Plumbers Supply, Inc.; Metrowest, Inc.; Bank of American Fork.

For Complete List of Firm Personnel, See General Section

For full biographical listings, see the Martindale-Hubbell Law Directory

DURHAM JONES & PINEGAR, A PROFESSIONAL CORPORATION (AV)

Key Bank Tower 50 South Main, Suite 800, 84144
Telephone: 801-538-2424
Fax: 801-538-2425
Email: djp@djplaw.com
Ogden Utah Office: The Aerospace Center, Suite 710, 1104 Country Hills Drive, 84403.
Telephone: 801-395-2424.
Fax: 801-395-2430.

Jeffrey M. Jones
Paul M. Durham
Kevin R. Pinegar
David F. Klomp
Robert A. Alsop
Wayne D. Swan
Gregory N. Barrick
S. Robert Bradley
N. Todd Leishman

Tadiana W. Jones
Kyle C. Jones
Alan W. Bell
Christopher D. Trujillo

OF COUNSEL

G. Richard Hill

For full biographical listings, see the Martindale-Hubbell Law Directory

PARSONS, DAVIES, KINGHORN & PETERS, P.C. (AV)

185 South State Street, Suite 700, 84111
Telephone: 801-363-4300
Facsimile: 801-363-4378
Email: Attorneys@pdkplaw.com

John M. Parsons
Glen E. Davies
Gerald H. Kinghorn
Bill Thomas Peters
Langdon T. Owen, Jr.
R. Kimball Mosier
John N. Brems
Ken P. Jones
David W. Scofield
Stuart W. Hinckley
John S. Bradley
Harold L. Reiser
Wm. Shane Topham
J. Scott Brown
Katherine S. Gregory
Paige Bigelow

For full biographical listings, see the Martindale-Hubbell Law Directory

STRONG & HANNI, A PROFESSIONAL CORPORATION (AV)

Sixth Floor Boston Building, 9 Exchange Place, 84111
Telephone: 801-532-7080
Fax: 801-596-1508
Email: pfishler@strongandhanni.com

Gordon R. Strong (1909-1969)
Glenn C. Hanni
Henry E. Heath
Philip R. Fishler
Roger H. Bullock
R. Scott Williams
Dennis M. Astill (Managing Partner)
Stuart H. Schultz
Paul M. Belnap
Stephen J. Trayner
Joseph J. Joyce
Bradley Wm. Bowen
Robert L. Janicki
Elizabeth L. Willey
H. Burt Ringwood
Peter H. Christensen
David R. Nielson

Kevin D. Swenson
Catherine M. Larson
Kristin Van Orman
Darren K. Nelson
Peter H. Barlow
Steven T. Densley
Jennifer C. Polley-Abramson
Shawn T. Welch

OF COUNSEL

Robert A. Burton

Representative Clients: State Farm Mutual Automobile Insurance Co.; Standard Accident Insurance Co.; United Services Automobile Assn.; Western Casualty & Surety Co.; Government Employees Insurance Co.; Guaranty Mutual Life Co.

For full biographical listings, see the Martindale-Hubbell Law Directory

Salt Lake City—Continued

VAN COTT, BAGLEY, CORNWALL & MCCARTHY, A PROFESSIONAL CORPORATION (AV)

50 South Main Street, Suite 1600, P.O. Box 45340, 84145-0340
Telephone: 801-532-3333
Telecopier: 801-534-0058
Email: info@vancott.com *URL:* http://www.vancott.com
Ogden, Utah Office: 2404 Washington Boulevard, Suite 900.
Telephone: 801-394-5783.
Park City, Utah Office: 2200 Park Avenue, Suite C200-A.
Telephone: 435-649-3889.

Robert M. Anderson (President of Firm)
Thomas T. Billings
Rand L. Cook
Matthew F. McNulty, III
Arthur B. Ralph
David J. Smith
Gerald H. Suniville
Stephen D. Swindle
Gregory P. Williams

Kim S Colton
Tacy A. Hartman
Kevin L. Jones

OF COUNSEL

David E. Salisbury
Franklin N. Smith
M. Scott Woodland

For Complete List of Firm Personnel, See General Section

For full biographical listings, see the Martindale-Hubbell Law Directory

WINDER & HASLAM, P.C. (AV)

Suite 4000, 175 West 200 South, P.O. Box 2668, 84110-2668
Telephone: 801-322-2222
Telecopier: 801-532-3706
Email: WINHAS@AROS.NET *URL:* http://www.winhas.com

Donald J. Winder
Robert D. Tingey
John W. Holt

Stewart R. Knight
Gerry B. Holman
Trystan B. Smith

OF COUNSEL

Dennis V. Haslam
William W. Downes, Jr.
Robert K. Rothfeder

Representative Clients: The Utah Jazz (NBA); The Delta Center; Larry H. Miller Group of Automotive Dealerships; Budget Rent-A-Car; Dollar Rent-A-Car; Avis Rent-A-Car; Dick Simon Trucking; United Concerts; Simmons Media Group; KJZZ-TV (Channel 14).

For full biographical listings, see the Martindale-Hubbell Law Directory

VERMONT

*BURLINGTON,** Chittenden Co.

GRAVEL AND SHEA, A PROFESSIONAL CORPORATION (AV)

Corporate Plaza, 76 St. Paul Street, P.O. Box 369, 05402-0369
Telephone: 802-658-0220
Fax: 802-658-1456

Stewart H. McConaughy
William G. Post, Jr.
Margaret L. Montgomery
Stephen P. Magowan

Leigh Polk Cole
Robert H. Rushford

OF COUNSEL

Charles T. Shea

For Complete List of Firm Personnel, See General Section

For full biographical listings, see the Martindale-Hubbell Law Directory

VIRGINIA

ALEXANDRIA, (Independent City)

E. MICHAEL PATURIS (AV)

Lee Street Square, 431 North Lee Street, 22314-2301
Telephone: 703-836-2501
Facsimile: 703-836-4487
Email: paturis@worldweb.net

For full biographical listings, see the Martindale-Hubbell Law Directory

YOUNG, GOLDMAN & VAN BEEK, A PROFESSIONAL CORPORATION (AV)

510 King Street, Suite 416, 22314
Telephone: 703-684-3260
Facsimile: 703-548-4742
Email: YGVB@Erols.com
Washington, D.C. Office: 2000 L Street, N.W. Suite 800.
Telephone: 703-684-3260.

H. Alan Young
Neil D. Goldman
John P. Van Beek

OF COUNSEL

Garrett C. Burke

Representative Clients: Eagle Bancorp, Inc.; National Children's Center, Inc.; Hispanic Scholarship Fund; National Loan Investors, L.P.; Nissan Motor Acceptance Corporation; Trafalgar House Residential Virginia; The Mark Winkler Company; WinStar Communications, Inc.

For full biographical listings, see the Martindale-Hubbell Law Directory

*ARLINGTON,** Arlington Co.

WALSH, COLUCCI, STACKHOUSE, EMRICH & LUBELEY, P.C. (AV)

Courthouse Plaza, Thirteenth Floor, 2200 Clarendon Boulevard, 22201
Telephone: 703-528-4700
Facsimile: 703-525-3197
Email: mdwal@wcsel.com *URL:* http://www.wcsel.com
Woodbridge, Virginia Office: Village Square, 13663 Office Place, Suite 201.
Telephones: 703-680-4664; 690-4647.
Facsimile: 703-690-2412.
Leesburg, Virginia Office: One East Market Street, 3rd Floor, 20176.
Telephone: 703-737-3633.
Fax: 703-737-3632.

Thomas J. Colucci
Peter K. Stackhouse
Michael D. Lubeley (Resident, Woodbridge Office)
Jay du Von (Resident, Woodbridge Office)
William A. Fogarty
David J. Bomgardner (Resident, Woodbridge Office)
Michael L. Murray

For full biographical listings, see the Martindale-Hubbell Law Directory

*FAIRFAX,** (Ind. City; Seat of Fairfax Co.)

MCCANDLISH & LILLARD, A PROFESSIONAL CORPORATION (AV)

Fair Oaks Plaza, 11350 Random Hills Road, Suite 500, 22030-7429
Telephone: 703-273-2288
Fax: 703-352-4300
Email: mccand@patriot.net *URL:* http://www.mccandlaw.com
Leesburg, Virginia Office: 305 Harrison Street, S.E., Third Floor.
Telephone: 703-737-0200.
Fax: 703-737-0165.

Robert J. McCandlish, Jr. (1909-1996)
Rothwell J. Lillard (1910-1989)
Jesse B. Wilson, III
Peter A. Arntson
Gary W. Brown
Randolph A. Sutliff
Robert H. J. Loftus
William McCauley Arnold
Stephen C. Price
Stephen K. Fox
Douglas J. Sanderson
R. Peyton Mahaffey
William L. Carey
John W. Farrell
Eric J. Berghold
Ralph M. Tener
Vicki L. Layman
Adam W. Smith

Daniel P. Lyon
Lawrence J. McClafferty
Brian R. Sanderson

For full biographical listings, see the Martindale-Hubbell Law Directory

MCLEAN, Fairfax Co.

THOMAS M. DAVIDSON (AV Ⓣ)

1750 Tysons Boulevard Suite 240, 22102
Telephone: 703-556-8887
Email: TMD@DAVIDSONCAPITAL.com *URL:* http://www.lawyers.com/davidsonlaw
(Not admitted in VA)

ASSOCIATE

Amy Davidson Bryant (Not admitted in VA)

For full biographical listings, see the Martindale-Hubbell Law Directory

MICHAEL HORWATT & ASSOCIATES P.C. (AV)

8280 Greensboro Drive, Suite 601, 22102
Telephone: 703-749-6060
Fax: 703-749-6063
Email: msh@horwattassoc.com

(See Next Column)

MICHAEL HORWATT & ASSOCIATES P.C., *McLean—Continued*

Michael S. Horwatt

For full biographical listings, see the Martindale-Hubbell Law Directory

TALBOTT AND GALLAGHER, A PROFESSIONAL CORPORATION (AV)

6824 Elm Street, Suite 350, 22101
Telephone: 703-893-6361
Facsimile: 703-893-6825
Email: jct@talbottgallagher.com *URL:* http://www.lawyers.com/talbottgallagher

John C. Talbott
Kathleen G. Gallagher

For full biographical listings, see the Martindale-Hubbell Law Directory

NORFOLK, (Independent City)

PAYNE, GATES, FARTHING & RADD, P.C. (AV)

15th Floor, Dominion Tower, 999 Waterside Drive, Suite 1515, 23510-3309
Telephone: 757-640-1500
Facsimile: 757-627-6583
URL: http://www.paynegates.com

Ronald M. Gates
Philip R. Farthing
Anthony F. Radd
Glen M. Robertson
Brian R. Dinning
Todd J. Preti
Marshall A. Winslow, Jr.

C. Arthur Robinson, II
Stephen E. Heretick
Raymond L. Hogge, Jr.

OF COUNSEL

Charles E. Payne

For full biographical listings, see the Martindale-Hubbell Law Directory

STACKHOUSE, SMITH & NEXSEN (AV)

1600 First Virginia Tower, 555 Main Street, P.O. Box 3640, 23514
Telephone: 757-623-3555
Fax: 757-624-9245

MEMBERS OF FIRM

Robert C. Stackhouse
Peter W. Smith, IV
William W. Nexsen
R. Clinton Stackhouse, Jr.
Janice McPherson Doxey
Mary Painter Opitz

ASSOCIATES

J. Derek Turrietta
Michael T. Pangalos

Representative Clients: Heritage Bank & Trust; The Atlantic Group, Inc.; Roughton Pontiac Corp; Federal National Mortgage Association; Kemper National Insurance Cos.; Harleysville Mutual Insurance Co.; Union Resources, Inc.; Presbyterian League of the Presbytery of Eastern Virginia, Inc.; Oakwood Acceptance Corp.; Virginia Beach Plastic Surgery, L.L.C.

For full biographical listings, see the Martindale-Hubbell Law Directory

TAYLOR & WALKER, P.C. (AV)

1300 First Virginia Tower, 555 Main Street, P.O. Box 3490, 23514-3490
Telephone: 757-625-7300
Telefax: 757-625-1504
URL: http://www.TAYWAL.com
Richmond, Virginia Office: 6802 Paragon Place, Suite 126, 23230.
Telephone: 804-673-0341.
Facsimile: 804-673-2001.

OF COUNSEL

J. Hume Taylor, Jr.

PARTNERS

William C. Walker
Gerard E. W. Voyer
James E. Brydges, Jr.
John Franklin, III
F. Bradford Stillman
Henry M. Massie, Jr.
James E. Vaiden
Brian N. Casey
James C. McCaa, III

Donna White Kearney
Mary Margaret Callahan Lyons
Richard W. Zahn, Jr.
Bradford Clark Jacob
Mark B. Kilduff
Stephen B. Royalty
Patricia C. Arrighi
Douglas Eugene Penner

LEGAL SUPPORT PERSONNEL

Diana L. White (Director of Administration)

For full biographical listings, see the Martindale-Hubbell Law Directory

RICHMOND, (Independent City)

CREWS & HANCOCK, P.L.C. (AV)

Suite 1015, 700 Building, 700 East Main Street, 23219-2693
Telephone: 804-649-9333
Telecopier: 804-783-1759
Email: admin@crewshancock.com
Fairfax, Virginia Office: Flint Hill Centre, Suite 300, 3050 Chain Bridge Road.
Telephone: 703-591-3440.
Telecopier: 703-591-7646.
Roanoke, Virginia Office: P.O. Box 21187.
Telephone: 540-774-6655.
Telecopier: 540-774-7947.
Virginia Beach, Virginia Office: One Columbus Center, Suite 619.
Telephone: 757-490-7802.
Fax: 757-490-7820.

John William Crews
Thomas F. Hancock, III
Martin A. Donlan, Jr.
Karen A. Gould
John A. Blazer (Resident, Fairfax, Virginia Office)
John E. McIntosh, Jr. (Resident, Fairfax, Virginia Office)
Richard W. E. Bland
Judith B. Henry
Peter M. Mellette
Thomas T. Palmer (Resident, Roanoke, Virginia Office)
John R. Redmond
James M. Daniel, Jr.
W. Scott Johnson
B. Page Gravely, Jr.
Thomas L. Appler (Resident, Fairfax, Virginia Office)

Richard L. Nagle (Resident, Fairfax, Virginia Office)
Mary C. Malone (Resident, Virginia Beach, Virginia Office)
Christina S. Yehle (Resident, Fairfax, Virginia Office)
Scott J. Sorkin
Jeannie A. Adams
Elizabeth V. Syer
Martha L. Steele
Andrea L. Bailey
Katherine R. McMillen (Resident, Fairfax, Virginia Office)
Wesley G. Russell, Jr.
William O. Quirey, Jr.
Peter J. Haggerty (Resident, Fairfax, Virginia Office)
Robin M. Vogel
Wirt P. Marks, IV
W. Christopher Shea
Matthew A. Haddad
John B. Mumford, Jr.
William H. Hall, Jr.
Stephanie Lindsey Hiss
Amy M.E. Edwards
Sean P. Byrne
Michael E. Olszewski (Resident, Fairfax, Virginia Office)
Frank J. Russo, III
Maura Jane Brown (Resident, Fairfax, Virginia Office)
Mark D. Epley
Mark Henry Schmidt

For full biographical listings, see the Martindale-Hubbell Law Directory

LECLAIR RYAN, A PROFESSIONAL CORPORATION (AV)

707 East Main Street, 11th Floor, 23219
Telephone: 804-783-2003
Facsmile: 804-783-2294
Email: email@leclairryan.com
Glen Allen, Virginia Office: 4201 Dominion Boulevard, Suite 200, 23060.
Telephone: 804-270-0070.
Facsimile: 804-270-4715.
Blacksburg, Virginia Office: 1872 Pratt Drive, Suite 1865, 24060.
Telephone: 540-961-2762.
Fax: 540-961-2781.
Norfolk, Virginia Office: 999 Waterside Drive, Suite 2025.
Telephone: 757-624-1454.
Facsimile: 757-624-3773.
Alexandria, Virginia Office: 225 Reinekers Lane, Suite 290, 22314.
Telephone: 703-684-8007.
Facsimile: 703-684-8075.
Charlottesville, Virginia Office: 108 S.E. Second Street, P.O. Box 2017, 22902.
Telephone: 804-971-7771.
Facsimile: 804-296-0905.

Alfred J. T. Byrne
Marie D. Carter
Debra J.C. Dowd
Michael P. Drzal
J. Benjamin English
Robert J. Grey, Jr.
Bradley A. Haneberg
Richard L. Hurlbert, Jr.
Steven J. Keeler
Gary D. LeClair
Kurt Robert Magette
Jeffrey K. Mitchell
Dennis M. Ryan
Douglas L. Sbertoli
Andrew W. White
George P. Whitley

Pamela Catania
Scott W. Fancher
Karen S. French
Michael P. Kuhn
Todd Manley Lynn
Nicholas J. Pace
Scott H. Richter
Jeffrey A. Sanborn
Saundra R. Schmidt
Russell J. Singer
Wendy Elizabeth Warren

For full biographical listings, see the Martindale-Hubbell Law Directory

Richmond—Continued

MALONEY, HUENNEKENS, PARKS, GECKER & PARSONS, A PROFESSIONAL CORPORATION (AV)

Bank of America Center, 1111 East Main Street, Suite 800, 23219-3103
Telephone: 804-644-0313
Telecopier: 804-783-6192

Edward F. Parsons
Daniel A. Gecker

Fiona M. Tower

Reference: First Union National Bank.

For Complete List of Firm Personnel, See General Section

For full biographical listings, see the Martindale-Hubbell Law Directory

WILLIAMS, MULLEN, CLARK & DOBBINS, A PROFESSIONAL CORPORATION (AV)

Two James Center, 1021 East Cary Street, P.O. Box 1320, 23218-1320
Telephone: 804-643-1991
Fax: 804-783-6507
URL: http://www.wmcd.com
Newport News Office: Harbor Bank Center, Suite 210, One Old Oyster Point Road, 23602-7119.
Telephone: 757-249-5100.
Fax: 757-249-5109.
Virginia Beach Office: One Columbus Center, 23462-6763.
Telephone: 757-499-8800.
Fax: 757-473-0395.
Vienna Office: 1593 Spring Hill Road, Suite 510, 22182.
Telephone: 703-760-5200.
Fax: 703-748-0244.
Washington, D.C. Office: The Farragut Building, 900 17th Street, N.W., Suite 700, 20006.
Telephone: 202-293-0213.
Fax: 804-783-6507. Fax Within D.C.: 202-293-5939.
London, England Office: Blake Lodge, Bridge Lane, SW11 3AD.
Telephone: (011-44-71) 223-2756.
Fax: (011-44-71) 350-0156.
Riyadh, Saudi Arabia Affiliate Office: Saudi-American Legal Consultants Commercial Building #2, Diplomatic Quarter, P.O. Box 57270, 11574.
Telephone: (011-966-1) 488-1563.
Fax: (011-966-1) 488-0542.

Ralph L. Axselle, Jr.
R. Brian Ball
William J. Benos
Steven D. Brown
Charles L. Cabell
Theodore L. Chandler, Jr.
David L. Dallas, Jr.
Alexander C. Graham, Jr.
A. Brooks Hock
David R. Johnson
Reginald N. Jones
Randolph H. Lickey
Thomas B. McVey (Resident, Washington, D.C. Office)
Robert L. Musick, Jr.
Warren E. Nowlin (Resident, Washington, D.C. Office)
William L. Pitman
Craig L. Rascoe
Malcolm E. Ritsch, Jr.
Robert D. Roseman (Resident, Washington, D.C. Office)
Walter H. Ryland
Paul G. Saunders, II
William H. Schwarzschild, III
Julious P. Smith, Jr.
Robert E. Spicer, Jr.
Andrea Rowse Stiles
W. Scott Street, III
Ian D. Titley
C. William Waechter, Jr.
Charles E. Wall
Wayne A. Whitham, Jr.
Fielding L. Williams, Jr.
Russell Alton Wright

OF COUNSEL

David George Ball (Resident, Washington, D.C. Office)

Wyatt S. Beazley, IV
Judy M. Lin
John M. Oakey, III
Daniel M. Pringle
Kathryn W. Sanborn
Aisha J. Sykes

For Complete List of Firm Personnel, See General Section

For full biographical listings, see the Martindale-Hubbell Law Directory

ROANOKE, Roanoke City Co.

OSTERHOUDT, FERGUSON, NATT, AHERON & AGEE, A PROFESSIONAL CORPORATION (AV)

1919 Electric Road, S.W., 24018
Telephone: 540-774-1197
Telecopier: 540-774-0961
Mailing Address: P.O. Box 20068, Roanoke, 24018
Email: OFNNA@Roanoke.infi.net *URL:* http://www.roanoke.infi.net/~ofnaa

Charles H. Osterhoudt
Michael S. Ferguson
Edward A. Natt
Michael J. Aheron
G. Steven Agee
Mark D. Kidd
Kristen K. Johnstone

For full biographical listings, see the Martindale-Hubbell Law Directory

WOOTEN & HART, A PROFESSIONAL CORPORATION (AV)

707 Building, Suite 300, P.O. Box 12247, 24024-2247
Telephone: 540-343-2451; 540-342-9672
Telecopier: 540-345-6417
URL: http://www.wootenhart.com

George W. Wooten
David B. Hart
L. Thompson Hanes
Susan A. Waddell
Bradley D. McGraw
John L. Cooley
Thomas W. Farrell
Paul C. Kuhnel
Peter D. Vieth

David W. Hearn
John Mark Cooley
Christopher W. Stevens
Elizabeth D. Guilbert
Eunice Park Austin

OF COUNSEL

M. Lanier Woodrum

Representative Clients: Wachovia Bank; St. Paul Insurance Cos.
Approved Attorneys for: Lawyers Title Insurance Corp.
Reference: First Union National Bank.

For full biographical listings, see the Martindale-Hubbell Law Directory

SPRINGFIELD, Fairfax Co.

BECKER, HICKS, IRVING & HADEED, P.C. (AV)

5501 Backlick Road, Suite 220, 22151
Telephone: 703-256-1300
Fax: 703-256-3467
Email: mail@bhihlaw.com *URL:* http://www.bhihlaw.com

Larry E. Becker
B. R. Hicks
James V. Irving
Michael Mitry Hadeed, Jr.
Mark E. Kellogg, P.C.
Lynn E. Berry
Scott R. Sexauer

May Shallal Kheder
Alix L. Mattingly
Ashraf W. Nubani

For full biographical listings, see the Martindale-Hubbell Law Directory

MADIGAN & SCOTT, INC. (AV)

7880 Backlick Road, 22150-2288
Telephone: 703-455-1800; 451-2080
Fax: 703-451-4121
Email: MADSCOTT@EROLS.COM
Manassas, Virginia Office: 9100 Church Street, Suite 107.
Telephone: 703-361-0185. Metro: 631-9193.
Fax: 703-631-9633.

Robert J. Madigan
Paul A. Scott

Mark J. Madigan

OF COUNSEL

Mitchell Komaroff

Richard G. Hornig (1958-1994)

For full biographical listings, see the Martindale-Hubbell Law Directory

VIENNA, Fairfax Co.

GARY & GOODMAN LIMITED (AV)

8500 Leesburg Pike, Suite 7000 (Tysons Corner), 22182
Telephone: 703-848-2828
Facsimile: 703-893-9276
Email: garygoodman@ggllaw.com

Bernard E. Goodman
Stuart H. Gary

Nancy D. Greene

OF COUNSEL

George B. Delta
David E. Sher
Mark D. Cummings
Karen P. Power

For full biographical listings, see the Martindale-Hubbell Law Directory

THE MANDELL LAW FIRM A PROFESSIONAL CORPORATION (AV)

Tysons Office Center, Suite 630 8133 Leesburg Pike, 22182-2706
Telephone: 703-734-9622
Facsimile: 703-356-0005
Email: info@tmlfBizLaw.com
URL: http://www.tmlfBizlaw.com

Steve A. Mandell

(See Next Column)

THE MANDELL LAW FIRM A PROFESSIONAL CORPORATION, *Vienna—Continued*

William J. Bethune
Jerry L. Hall, Jr.
Edward M. McClure (Not admitted in VA)

For full biographical listings, see the Martindale-Hubbell Law Directory

REES, BROOME & DIAZ, P.C. (AV)
Ninth Floor, 8133 Leesburg Pike, 22182
Telephone: 703-790-1911
Telecopier: 703-848-2530
Email: attorney@RBDlaw.com *URL:* http://www.rbdlaw.com

Joel M. Birken
John F. Boland
Michael L. O'Reilly
Andrew B. Golkow
Richard M. Ware, Jr.

For full biographical listings, see the Martindale-Hubbell Law Directory

SMOLEN & PLEVY P.C. (AV)
Seventh Floor 8045 Leesburg Pike, 22182
Telephone: 703-790-1900
Telecopier: 703-790-1754
Email: smolenplevy@smolenplevy.com

Jason D. Smolen
Alan B. Plevy
Daniel H. Ruttenberg

For full biographical listings, see the Martindale-Hubbell Law Directory

WASHINGTON

BELLEVUE, King Co.

PETERSON RUSSELL COFANO PLLC (AV)
870 Skyline Tower, 10900 N.E. Fourth Street, 98004-5873
Telephone: 425-462-4700
Fax: 425-451-0714
Email: grussell@prclegal.com *URL:* http://www.prclegal.com

Peter E. Peterson
Gregory L. Russell
Russell G. Cofano
Patrick M. Moran

ASSOCIATES

David M. Paltzik
John F. Sherwood, Jr.

OF COUNSEL

John F. Sherwood
Michael T. Callan

For full biographical listings, see the Martindale-Hubbell Law Directory

*SEATTLE,** King Co.

BAROKAS, MARTIN, AHLERS & TOMLINSON (AV)
1422 Bellevue Avenue, 98122-3634
Telephone: 206-621-1871
Fax: 206-621-9907
Email: bmlf@aol.com
Anchorage, Alaska Office: 1029 W. Third Avenue, Suite 100.
Telephone: 907-276-8010.
Fax: 907-276-5334.

MEMBERS OF FIRM

Larry L. Barokas
Dale R. Martin
John P. Ahlers
John R. Tomlinson, Jr.
Joseph J. Straus

OF COUNSEL

Rex M. Walker

ASSOCIATES

Scott R. Sleight
John J. Limb
Amanda E. Vedrich
Craig A. Robertson

Reference: Western Bank.

For full biographical listings, see the Martindale-Hubbell Law Directory

THE JOHNSON LAW GROUP (AV)
430 Galland Building, 1221 Second Avenue, 98101-2942
Telephone: 206-344-3085
Fax: 206-344-3087
URL: http://www.lawyers.com/johnsonakyle
URL: http://www.akjlaw.com

A. Kyle Johnson

Molly B. Kenny
Carolann O'Brien Storli
John T. Blanchard
Amanda DuBois

(See Next Column)

OF COUNSEL

Peter S. Lewicki

Representative Clients: Asia-Europe-Americas Bank; BCTS/Acordia Northwest, Inc.; HFI Foods, Inc.; Parker Services, Inc.; Phoenix Savings Bank; TCS/Space Expeditions; U.S. Computer; Washington Hills Cellars.

For full biographical listings, see the Martindale-Hubbell Law Directory

JON G. SCHNEIDLER (AV)
4100 Wells Fargo Center, 999 Third Avenue, 98104
Telephone: 206-624-9400
Telecopier: 206-464-9559
Email: jonandbeth@budsters.com

Reference: Key Bank of Washington.

For full biographical listings, see the Martindale-Hubbell Law Directory

SUMMIT LAW GROUP, PLLC (AV)
1505 Westlake Avenue North, Suite 300, 98109
Telephone: 206-281-9881
Fax: 206-281-9882
Email: info@summitlaw.com *URL:* http://www.summitlaw.com

Karen A. Andersen
Kristin D. Anger
Laura A. Bertin
Lynn M. Engel
Michael J. Erickson
Matthew R. Harris
David M. Heineck
Elizabeth Butler Kennar
Otto G. Klein, III
Lawrence C. Locker
Philip S. McCune
Polly L. McNeill
Ralph H. Palumbo
Bruce L. Schroeder
William R. Squires III
Monika Vasil
Mark F. Worthington
Rodney B. Younker

For full biographical listings, see the Martindale-Hubbell Law Directory

WEST VIRGINIA

*CHARLESTON,** Kanawha Co.

SHUMAN ANNAND BAILEY WYANT & EARLES (AV)
Suite 1007, 405 Capitol Street, P.O. Box 3953, 25339
Telephone: 304-345-1400
Telecopier: 304-343-1826
Email: shuman@newwave.net
Wheeling, West Virginia Office: Suite 3002, 1233 Main Street, 26003.
Telephone: 304-233-3100.
Telecopier: 304-233-0201.

MEMBERS OF FIRM

David L. Shuman
Stephen Darley Annand
Charles R. Bailey
Richard L. Earles
David L. Wyant (Resident, Wheeling, West Virginia Office)
Mark William Browning
William R. Slicer
George J. Joseph
Thomas E. Buck (Resident at Wheeling, West Virginia Office)

ASSOCIATES

DesireéHalkias Divita
Roberta F. Green
Paul Kipling Reese
Heidi A. Kossuth (Resident, Wheeling, West Virginia Office)
Lou Ann S. Cassell
Dwayne E. Cyrus
Eric W. Santos (Not admitted in WV; Resident, Wheeling, West Virginia Office)
John T. Molleur
Mark A. Kepple (Resident, Wheeling, West Virginia Office)
David J. Mincer
Karen M. Tracy
Virginia Ann Grottendieck
Arden J. Cogar
Melissa A. Morris
Stacie L. Price (Resident, Wheeling, West Virginia Office)
J. Parker Bazzle
Lisa Bray
Darin C. James
Brian D. Morrison

OF COUNSEL

John F. McCuskey

Representative Clients: American International/Companies (AIG); CNA Insurance Companies; Insurance Corporation of America; Metropolitan Property & Liability Insurance Co.; MMI Companies, Inc.; Motorists Insurance Cos.; Travelers Insurance Cos.; Westfield Companies.
Reference: One Valley Bank.

For full biographical listings, see the Martindale-Hubbell Law Directory

*CLARKSBURG,** Harrison Co.

McNeer, Highland, McMunn and Varner, L.C. (AV)
One Valley Bank Building, P.O. Drawer 2040, 26302-2040
Telephone: 304-626-1100
Facsimile: 304-623-3035
Martinsburg Office: 2520 Aikens Center, P.O. Box 2509.
Telephone: 304-264-4621.
Fax: 304-264-8623.
Parkersburg Office: 404 Market Street, Suite 204, P.O. Box 1507.
Telephone: 304-422-7193.
Facsimile: 304-422-7196.

C. David McMunn
J. Cecil Jarvis
James A. Varner
Robert W. Trumble (Resident, Martinsburg Office)
Catherine D. Munster
James N. Riley
Steven R. Bratke (Resident, Parkersburg Office)
Michael J. Novotny (Resident, Martinsburg Office)
Dennis M. Shreve
Geraldine S. Roberts
William F. Rohrbaugh (Resident, Martinsburg Office)
Gregory H. Schillace
Judy L. Shanholtz
Tiffany R. Durst
Gene W. Bailey, II

OF COUNSEL

James E. McNeer
Cecil B. Highland, Jr.
William L. Fury

Representative Clients: One Valley Bank of Clarksburg, National Assn.; Bruceton Bank; Harrison County Bank; Nationwide Mutual Insurance Cos.; Clarksburg Publishing Co.; C.I.T. Financial Services; State Automobile Mutual Insurance Co.; United Hospital Center, Inc.; West Virginia Coals, Inc.; Swanson Plating Co.

For full biographical listings, see the Martindale-Hubbell Law Directory

Waters, Warner & Harris, PLLC (AV)
Formerly Stathers & Cantrall
701 Goff Building, P.O. Box 1716, 26301
Telephone: 304-624-5571
Fax: 304-624-7228
Email: wwh.atty@northnap.citynet.net

Birk S. Stathers (1884-1945)
W. G. Stathers (1889-1970)
Arch M. Cantrall (1896-1967)
Stuart R. Waters
Boyd L. Warner
James A. Harris
Scott E. Wilson
James C. Turner
G. Thomas Smith

ASSOCIATES

D. Andrew McMunn
David C. Glover

Representative Clients: Bethlehem Steel Corp.; Davis-Weaver Funeral Home, Inc.; Dowell Schlumberger, Inc.; Grafton Coal Co.; Harry Green Chevrolet, Inc.; Emax Oil Co.; Southern Steel Products Co.; Hartland Planing Mill Co.; Meadowbrook Mail Co.; Household Finance Corp.

For full biographical listings, see the Martindale-Hubbell Law Directory

WISCONSIN

*MADISON,** Dane Co.

Neider & Boucher, S.C. (AV)
440 Science Drive, P.O. Box 5510, 53705-0510
Telephone: 608-661-4500
Facsimile: 608-661-4510
URL: http://www.neiderboucher.com
URL: http://www.lawyers.com/neider&boucher-sc

Ronald C. Berman
Joseph W. Boucher
Charles E. Neider
Steven C. Underwood

Susan M. De Groot
Erik W. Ibele
Rana Kang
Cynthia L. Richson
Matthew L. Schemmel
Kent L. Schlienger
Dean T. Stange

OF COUNSEL

Ralph M. Cagle
Ronald R. Smith

For full biographical listings, see the Martindale-Hubbell Law Directory

Quarles & Brady LLP (AV)
Firstar Plaza, One South Pinckney Street, P.O. Box 2113, 53701-2113
Telephone: 608-251-5000
Fax: 608-251-9166
URL: http://www.quarles.com
Milwaukee, Wisconsin Office: 411 East Wisconsin Avenue, 53202-4497.
Telephone: 414-277-5000.
Fax: 414-271-3552.

(See Next Column)

West Palm Beach, Florida Office: 222 Lakeview Avenue, 4th Floor, 33401.
Telephone: 561-653-5000.
Fax: 561-653-5333.
Naples, Florida Office: Barnett Center, 4501 Tamiami Trail North, Suite 300, 34103-3060.
Telephone: 941-262-5959.
Fax: 941-434-4999.
Phoenix, Arizona Office: One Camelback Building, One East Camelback Road, Suite 400, 85012-1649.
Telephone: 602-230-5500.
Fax: 602-230-5598.
Chicago, Illinois Office: Quarles & Brady LLC, Citicorp Center, 500 West Madison Street, Suite 3700.
Telephone: 312-715-5000.
Fax: 312-715-5155.

PARTNERS

Anthony S. Earl
Jeremy C. Shea
John S. Holbrook, Jr.
Michael L. Zaleski
Jeffrey B. Bartell
James R. Cole
Michael S. Weiden
Anthony H. Driessen
Roy L. Prange, Jr.
Fred Gants
Peter C. Christianson
Nicholas J. Seay
John T. Whiting
Waltraud A. Arts
Donald K. Schott
Ralph V. Topinka
William J. Toman
Jane F. Clokey
Kevin A. Delorey
Kenneth J. Hansen
Jennifer V. Powers
Anthony A. Tomaselli
Jean C. Baker

ASSOCIATES

Lauri D. Morris
Brian W. Blanchard
Gregory T. Everts
Valerie L. Bailey-Rihn
Bennett J. Berson
Sarah Edelman Coyne
Kristin Graham Noel
Thomas N. Shorter
Jill A. Fahrlander
Elizabeth A. Hartman
David M. Kettner

For Complete List of Firm Personnel, See General Section

For full biographical listings, see the Martindale-Hubbell Law Directory

*MILWAUKEE,** Milwaukee Co.

Davis & Kuelthau, S.C. (AV)
111 East Kilbourn Avenue, Suite 1400, 53202-6613
Telephone: 414-276-0200
Facsimile: 414-276-9369
Cable Address: "Shiplaw"
Email: info@daviskuelthau.com *URL:* http://www.daviskuelthau.com
Madison, Wisconsin Office: Ten East Doty Street, Suite 600, P.O. Box 1068, 53703.
Telephone: 608-280-8235.
Fax: 608-280-8231.
Sheboygan, Wisconsin Office: 605 North Eighth, Suite 610, P.O. Box 1287.
Telephone: 920-451-1461.
Fax: 920-451-1465.
Green Bay, Wisconsin Office: 414 East Walnut Street, Suite 240.
Telephone: 920-435-9378.
Fax: 920-435-9391.

Thomas G. Boyer
James A. Brindley
Walter S. Davis
Scott E. Fiducci
Matthew J. Flanary
Robert E. Kuelthau
Harold A. Laufer
Norman J. Matar
Erich Mildenberg
Brett K. Miller
Bradley D. Page
Michael C. Runde
Robert J. Simandl
Amy Klemm Verbos

Stacy Alvarez Delzer
Steven R. Glaser
Shawn D. Guse
Walter Scott Leedom
Eric L. Robinson

For full biographical listings, see the Martindale-Hubbell Law Directory

Ehlinger & Krill, S.C. (AV)
316 North Milwaukee Street, Suite 410, 53202-5803
Telephone: 414-272-8085
Facsimile: 414-272-8290
Email: ehlinger@execpc.com

Ralph J. Ehlinger
R. Jeffrey Krill

For full biographical listings, see the Martindale-Hubbell Law Directory

Kersten & McKinnon, S.C. (AV)
231 West Wisconsin Avenue, Suite 1200, 53203
Telephone: 414-271-0054
Fax: 414-271-7131
Email: Kersten3@ExecPc.com

(See Next Column)

KERSTEN & MCKINNON S.C., *Milwaukee—Continued*

Charles J. Kersten (1929-1972)
Arlo McKinnon (1929-1999)
J. P. McKinnon (1943-1973)
E. Campion Kersten
George P. Kersten
Kenan J. Kersten
Leslie Van Buskirk
Matthew T. Fricker

For full biographical listings, see the Martindale-Hubbell Law Directory

KOHNER, MANN & KAILAS, S.C. (AV)

1572 East Capitol Drive, P.O. Box 11982, 53211-0982
Telephone: 414-962-5110
Fax: 414-962-8725
Email: kmksc@execpc.com

Marvin L. Kohner (1908-1975)

OF COUNSEL

Robert L. Mann

MEMBERS OF FIRM

Steve Kailas
Mark R. Wolters
Jordan B. Reich
David S. Chartier
Roy Paul Roth
Gary P. Lantzy
Christopher C. Kailas
Matthew P. Gerdisch

Robert E. Nailen
Darrell R. Zall
Daniel J. Flynn
Timothy L. Zuberbier
David M. Henry
Lorinne J Cunningham
Palma M. Forte
Daniel J. Emma

Representative Clients: Ecolab, Inc.; Manpower, Inc.; Abbott Laboratories; Norwest Bank Wisconsin, N.A.; Firstar Bank Corporation; Sysco Food Services; Johnson Controls, Inc.; Worth Inc.; Rayovac, Inc.; York International Corporation.

For full biographical listings, see the Martindale-Hubbell Law Directory

MEISSNER TIERNEY FISHER & NICHOLS S.C. (AV)

The Milwaukee Center, 111 East Kilbourn Avenue, 19th Floor, 53202-6622
Telephone: 414-273-1300
Facsimile: 414-273-5840
URL: http://www.mtfn.com

Joseph E. Tierney III
Dennis L. Fisher
Thomas J. Nichols
Randal J. Brotherhood
Michael J. Cohen

Michael A. Kallas
Christopher L. Rexroat
Justin B. Nelsen
William T. Stuart
Jeffrey A. Ellis
Adam J. Tutaj

OF COUNSEL

Paul F. Meissner

For full biographical listings, see the Martindale-Hubbell Law Directory

QUARLES & BRADY LLP (AV)

411 East Wisconsin Avenue, 53202-4497
Telephone: 414-277-5000
Fax: 414-271-3552
URL: http://www.quarles.com
Madison, Wisconsin Office: Firstar Plaza, One South Pinckney Street, P.O. Box 2113, 53701-2113.
Telephone: 608-251-5000.
Fax: 608-251-9166.
West Palm Beach, Florida Office: 222 Lakeview Avenue, 4th Floor, 33401.
Telephone: 561-653-5000.
Fax: 561-653-5333.
Naples, Florida Office: Barnett Center, 4501 Tamiami Trail North, Suite 300, 34103-3060.
Telephone: 941-262-5959.
Fax: 941-434-4999.
Phoenix, Arizona Office: One Camelback Building, One East Camelback Road, Suite 400, 85012-1649.
Telephone: 602-230-5500.
Fax: 602-230-5598.
Chicago, Illinois Office: Quarles & Brady LLC, Citicorp Center, 500 West Madison Street, Suite 3700.
Telephone: 312-715-5000.
Fax: 312-715-5155.

MEMBERS OF FIRM
(ALPHABETICALLY BY YEAR OF ADMISSION TO BAR)

Harry G. Holz
Charles Q. Kamps
Thomas W. Ehrmann
Anthony S. Earl (Resident, Madison Office)
Fred G. Groiss
Richard C. Ninneman
Samuel J. Recht
Jeremy C. Shea (Resident, Madison Office)
Donald S. Taitelman
John A. Hazelwood
John S. Holbrook, Jr. (Resident, Madison Office)
Peter J. Lettenberger
Arthur B. Harris
Richard L. Horn (Resident, Chicago, Illinois Office)
Henry J. Loos
Hugh S. McManus

(See Next Column)

MEMBERS OF FIRM
(ALPHABETICALLY BY YEAR OF ADMISSION TO BAR) (Continued)

Michael J. Spector
George K. Whyte, Jr.
Robert H. Diaz, Jr.
David L. Kinnamon
Gary H. Kline (Resident, Chicago, Illinois Office)
J. Rodman Steele, Jr. (Resident, West Palm Beach, Florida Office)
Michael L. Zaleski (Resident, Madison Office)
Anthony W. Asmuth, III
Wayne E. Babler, Jr.
Thomas E. Maloney (Resident, Naples, Florida Office)
W. Stuart Parsons
Jeffrey B. Bartell (Resident, Madison Office)
Frank J. Daily
Charles W. Herf (Resident, Phoenix, Arizona Office)
David E. Jarvis
Larry J. Martin
Kendall R. Meyer (Resident, Chicago, Illinois Office)
David L. Petersen (Resident, Naples, Florida Office)
Thomas A. Polachek (Resident, Chicago, Illinois Office)
James R. Cole (Resident, Madison Office)
Thomas E. Chomicz (Resident, Chicago, Illinois Office)
Steven R. Duback
Conrad G. Goodkind
Lawrence J. Jost
Patrick M. Ryan
Barry E. Sammons
Ronald L. Wallenfang
Michael S. Weiden (Resident, Madison Office)
John A. Casey
Bruce C. Davidson
Robert F. Forrer (Resident, Chicago, Illinois Office)
P. Robert Moya (Resident, Phoenix, Arizona Office)
Stephen E. Richman
Gerald E. Connolly
Anthony H. Driessen
James D. Friedman
J. Paul Jacobson
Peter C. Karegeannes
John R. Maynard
William M. Shattuck (Resident, Phoenix, Arizona Office)
James H. Baxter III
Quinn W. Martin
Michael J. McGovern
F. Joseph McMackin, III (Resident, Naples, Florida Office)
Ned R. Nashban (Resident, West Palm Beach, Florida Office)
Robert L. Titley
Thomas J. Phillips
James D. Vieregg (Resident, Phoenix, Arizona Office)
Robert T. Bailes (Resident, Phoenix, Arizona Office)
Bruce R. Bauer
Darryl S. Bell
Michael J. Conlan
James F. Daly
John W. Daniels, Jr.
James J. Gatziolis (Resident, Chicago, Illinois Office)
George E. Haas
Timothy G. Hains (Resident, Naples, Florida Office)
Alyce C. Katayama
John H. Lhost
Michael L. Roshar
Peter A. Sarasek (Resident, Chicago, Illinois Office)
Leonard S. Shifflett (Resident, Chicago, Illinois Office)
Thomas Armstrong
Andrew M. Barnes
Robert E. Doyle, Jr. (Resident, Naples, Florida Office)
Matthew J. Flynn
Roy L. Prange, Jr. (Resident, Madison Office)
Michael H. Schaalman
Patrick W. Schmidt
John T. Bannen
Fred Gants (Resident, Madison Office)
Mary Pat Ninneman
Jon E. Pettibone (Resident, Phoenix, Arizona Office)
Phillip E. Recht
Janice E. Rodgers (Resident, Chicago, Illinois Office)
Roger K. Spencer (Resident, Phoenix, Arizona Office)
Eric J. Van Vugt
Patricia K. Ballman
Warren S. Blumenthal
Peter C. Christianson
Patrick J. Goebel
Thomas J. Magill (Resident, Chicago, Illinois Office)
Michael S. McCauley
Nicholas J. Seay (Resident, Madison Office)
Alexander Terras (Resident, Chicago, Illinois Office)
John T. Whiting (Resident, Madison Office)
Joseph D. Masterson
Carl R. Schwartz
Peter A. Terry (Resident, Phoenix, Arizona Office)
Paul J. Tilleman
James L. Adashek
Waltraud A. Arts (Resident, Madison Office)
David B. Kern
Ely A. Leichtling
Jeffrey Morris
Ann M. Murphy
John A. Rothstein
Arthur A. Vogel, Jr.
Kenneth V. Hallett
William H. Harbeck
Charles H. McMullen
Sally C. Merrell
Elizabeth A. Orelup
Gary M. Ruesch
Leo J. Salvatori (Resident, Naples, Florida Office)
Donald K. Schott (Resident, Madison Office)
Ralph V. Topinka (Resident, Madison Office)
John P. Vail (Resident, Chicago, Illinois Office)
David B. Bartel
David G. Beauchamp (Resident, Phoenix, Arizona Office)
David R. Cross
Julianna Ebert
Mary N. Fertl
Glenn Spencer Bacal (Resident, Phoenix, Arizona Office)
Kimberly Leach Johnson (Resident, Naples, Florida Office)
Nancy Meissner Kennedy
Brian G. Lanser
Daniel L. Muchow (Resident, Phoenix, Arizona Office)
Dennis P. Reis
Thomas A. Simonis
David D. Wilmoth
Michael J. Gonring
Kathleen A. Gray
Douglas R. Hoffman (Resident, Chicago, Illinois Office)
Michael A. Levey
Elizabeth G. Nowakowski
David A. Selden (Resident, Phoenix, Arizona Office)
Stephanie B. Shellenback (Resident, Chicago, Illinois Office)

MEMBERS OF FIRM

(See Next Column)

QUARLES & BRADY LLP—*Continued*

(ALPHABETICALLY BY YEAR OF ADMISSION TO BAR) (Continued)

William J. Toman (Resident, Madison Office)
Ann K. Comer
John D. Franzini
Marta S. Levine
Thomas P. McElligott
Gregory A. Nelson (Resident, West Palm Beach, Florida Office)
Nancy K. Peterson
Keith M. Baxter
Jane F. Clokey (Resident, Madison Office)
Robert H. Duffy
Steven P. Emerick
Sarah M. Linsley (Resident, Chicago, Illinois Office)
Dana L. O'Brien
Michael D. Zeka
Mark A. Kircher
Fredrick G. Lautz
David P. Olson
Sheila M. Reynolds
Gerald L. Shelley (Resident, Phoenix, Arizona Office)
Richard P. Blessen (Resident, Chicago, Illinois Office)
Robert S. Bornhoft (Resident, Phoenix, Arizona Office)
Kathryn M. Buono
Daniel E. Conley
Kevin A. Delorey (Resident, Madison Office)
Jeffrey L. Elverman
John D. Humphreville (Resident, Naples, Florida Office)
Scott L. Langlois
Francis H. LoCoco
Jeffrey O. Davis
Kenneth J. Hansen (Resident, Madison, Wisconsin Office)
Benjamin R. Norris (Resident, Phoenix, Arizona Office)
Jennifer V. Powers
Joseph E. Puchner
David L. Bourne
Nancy Berz Colman (Resident, West Palm Beach, Florida Office)
Marie K. Eitrheim (Resident, Chicago, Illinois Office)
Timothy S. Harris (Resident, Chicago, Illinois Office)
Anthony A. Tomaselli (Resident, Madison Office)
Margaret C. Kelsey
Todd A. Rowden (Resident, Chicago, Illinois Office)
Colleen A. Scherkenbach (Resident, Phoenix, Arizona Office)
Jeffrey K. Spoerk
Charles M. Weber
Joseph W. Bain (Resident, West Palm Beach, Florida Office)
Jean C. Baker
Patrick J. Bitterman (Resident, Chicago, Illinois Office)
Michael J. Ostermeyer
George J. Marek
Robert J. Sacco (Resident, West Palm Beach, Florida Office)
Walter J. Skipper
Rebecca A. Speckhard

OF COUNSEL

Paul Noelke
Patrick W. Cotter
A. William Asmuth, Jr.
Richard W. Cutler
James C. Mallien
John T. Harrington
Laurence E. Gooding, Jr.
Elwin J. Zarwell
Neal E. Madisen
Dale L. Sorden
Laurence C. Hammond, Jr.
John S. Sammond (Resident, West Palm Beach, Florida Office)
David L. MacGregor
James Urdan
Roger P. Paulsen
Robert J. Kalupa
Thad F. Kryshak
Thomas O. Kloehn
Thomas W. O'Brien

ASSOCIATES

Neil E. Hamilton
Patrick J. Schoen
Lauri D. Morris (Resident, Madison Office)
Michael G. Galloway (Resident, Phoenix, Arizona Office)
Chris K. Gawart
Brian W. Blanchard (Resident, Madison Office)
Susan A. Cerbins
Michael Aldana
Gregory T. Everts (Resident, Madison Office)
Samara S. Holland (Resident, Naples, Florida Office)
Carmella A. Huser
Catherine Stevens Powell
David B. Altman (Resident, Chicago, Illinois Office)
Valerie L. Bailey-Rihn (Resident, Madison Office)
Mitchell S. Moser
Mark Hubert Muller (Resident, Naples, Florida Office)
David T. Barton (Resident, Phoenix, Arizona Office)
Bennett J. Berson (Resident, Madison, Wisconsin Office)
David G. Bray (Resident, Phoenix, Arizona Office)
Sean D. Garrison (Resident, Phoenix, Arizona Office)
Michael A. Jaskolski
Daniel J. La Fave
Kevin M. Long
Lisa A. Lyons
Mary Beth Miller Orson (Resident, Phoenix, Arizona Office)
Julie A. Pace (Resident, Phoenix, Arizona Office)
Nora M. Platt
David G. Ryser
Kurt T. Temple (Resident, Chicago, Illinois Office)
Guri Ademi
Michael M. Grebe
Daniel M. Janssen
Cheryl A. Johnson
Michael Lappin
Jennifer A. Lazewski
Pamela M. Ploor
Mark K. Briggs (Resident, Phoenix, Arizona Office)
Bonnie J. Buhrow
Maureen Henry (Resident, Phoenix, Arizona Office)
Patricia A. Hintz
Lisa Carozza Lottes (Resident, Naples, Florida Office)
Panna P. Patel (Resident, Chicago, Illinois Office)
Brenda J. Stugelmeyer
Stephen R. White
Joel A. Brodsky (Resident, Chicago, Illinois Office)
James T. Demarest (Resident, Naples, Florida Office)
Sarah Edelman Coyne (Resident, Madison, Wisconsin Office)
Shannon B. Farrell
Michael J. Fischer
Michael A. Hatfield, Jr.
Jason N. Kaplan (Resident, Chicago, Illinois Office)
Susan Kubar (Resident, Naples, Florida Office)

(See Next Column)

ASSOCIATES (Continued)

Douglas P. Martin (Resident, Phoenix, Arizona Office)
Mark D. Passler (Resident, West Palm Beach, Florida Office)
Heidi B. Retzlaff
Steven M. Schindhelm
Gregory J. Stanton (Resident, Phoenix, Arizona Office)
David C. Swanson
C. Christine Burns (Resident, Phoenix, Arizona Office)
Alicia M. Dagosta (Resident, Phoenix, Arizona Office)
Richard G. Frohling
Leezie Kim (Resident, Phoenix, Arizona Office)
Edmond E. Koester (Resident, Naples, Florida Office)
Linda K. Menzel
David P. Muth
Cory L. Nettles
Kristin Graham Noel (Resident, Madison, Wisconsin Office)
Rachel A. Schneider
Thomas N. Shorter (Resident, Madison, Wisconsin Office)
Janice L. Tucker
Brian D. Winters
Paul D. Bauer
Frank C. DeGuire, Jr.
Jill A. Fahrlander (Resident, Madison, Wisconsin Office)
Kelly A. Hardy
Sean D. Johnson (Resident, Phoenix, Arizona Office)
Mireya Castillo Martin (Resident, Phoenix, Arizona Office)
Allen J. Moss (Resident, Phoenix, Arizona Office)
Hoyt R. Stastney
Luis I. Arroyo
Jessamyn L. Bagley (Resident, Chicago, Illinois Office)
Keith A. Bruett
Jennifer Clements
Marcia E. Facey
William B. Gaschler
Elizabeth A. Hartman (Resident, Madison, Wisconsin Office)
Matthew J. Kading
David M. Kettner (Resident, Madison, Wisconsin Office)
Stanley A. Kim (Resident, West Palm Beach, Florida Office)
Scott D. Paul (Resident, West Palm Beach, Florida Office)
Jeffrey D. Peelen
Steven J. Wietrzny
C. Lane Wood (Resident, Naples, Florida Office)
Judith T. Beckler (Resident, Naples, Florida Office)
Nicole E. Dorsey (Resident, Phoenix, Arizona Office)

For Complete List of Firm Personnel, See General Section

For full biographical listings, see the Martindale-Hubbell Law Directory

NEENAH, Winnebago Co.

DI RENZO AND BOMIER, LLC (AV)

231 East Wisconsin Avenue, P.O. Box 788, 54957-0788
Telephone: 920-725-8464
Fax: 920-725-8568
Email: direnzolaw@aol.com

MEMBERS OF FIRM

Robert C. Di Renzo
Roy N. Fine

ASSOCIATES

Denise R. Burkett
Eric S. Gissel

Representative Clients: Bergstrom Chevrolet-Buick-Cadillac, Inc., Neenah and Appleton, WI; Cherokee Park, inc., Madison, WI; Great Northern Corp., Appleton, WI; Kennedy Center for the Hip and Knee, S.C., Neenah, WI; Old Fashioned Foods, Inc., Mayville, WI; Phillips Plastics Corp., Phillips, WI; Watry Industries, Inc., Sheboygan, WI; Clintonville Lumber, Inc., Clintonville, WI; Alexander Eye Institute, S.C., Appleton, WI; TEC Graphics, Inc., Neenah, WI.

For Complete List of Firm Personnel, See General Section

For full biographical listings, see the Martindale-Hubbell Law Directory

*WAUKESHA,** Waukesha Co.

CRAMER, MULTHAUF & HAMMES, LLP (AV)

1601 East Racine Avenue, P.O. Box 558, 53187
Telephone: 414-542-4278
Telecopier: 414-542-4270

MEMBERS OF FIRM

Clayton A. Cramer (1913-1993)
John E. Multhauf
James W. Hammes
Richard R. Kobriger
Peter J. Plaushines
John M. Remmers
Kathryn Sawyer Gutenkunst
Timothy J. Andringa

ASSOCIATES

Suzanne Fischer Lorenz
Philip J. Remmers
Daniel J. Habeck
Jane M. Rolling

Representative Clients: Waukesha State Bank; First Federal Savings Bank of Wisconsin; Bielinski Bros. Builders, Inc.; Dorner Manufacturing Corp.; Towns of Waukesha, Lisbon, Brookfield and Wales; Payco American Corp.; El Rey Mexican Products, Inc.

For full biographical listings, see the Martindale-Hubbell Law Directory

WYOMING

*CASPER,** Natrona Co.

BROWN, DREW & MASSEY, LLP (AV)

Casper Business Center, Suite 800, 123 West First Street, 82601-2486
Telephone: 307-234-1000
800-877-6755
Telefax: 307-265-8025
Email: brwndrew@coffey.com

MEMBERS OF FIRM

Morris R. Massey
Harry B. Durham, III
Donn J. McCall
Thomas F. Reese
J. Kenneth Barbe
Courtney Robert Kepler

ASSOCIATE

Timothy M. Stubson

Attorneys for: Norwest Bank Wyoming, N.A.; The CIT Group/Equipment Financing; Aetna Casualty & Surety Co.; The Doctor's Co.; MEDMARC; Westech, Inc.; Chevron USA; Enron Group of Energy Companies.

For Complete List of Firm Personnel, See General Section

For full biographical listings, see the Martindale-Hubbell Law Directory

SCHWARTZ, BON, WALKER & STUDER, LLC (AV)

141 South Center, Suite 505, 82601
Telephone: 307-235-6681
Fax: 307-234-5099
Email: SBWS@trib.com

William T. Schwartz
William S. Bon
Cameron S. Walker
Judith A. W. Studer
Peter J. Young

Patrick T. Holscher
Rick L. Koehmstedt

Representative Clients: Amoco Production Co.; Equitable Life Assurance Society; ANR Production; Union Carbide Corp.; Hill Top Shopping Center; Exxon Co., U.S.A.; Armco Steel Corp.; USF&G; American States Insurance Co.

For full biographical listings, see the Martindale-Hubbell Law Directory

VIRGIN ISLANDS

*CHARLOTTE AMALIE, ST. THOMAS,** St. Thomas

GRUNERT STOUT & BRUCH

24-25 Kongensgade, P.O. Box 1030, 00804
Telephone: 340-774-1320
Fax: 340-774-7839
Email: gsbusvi@viaccess.net
Affiliated with: Solomon Pearl Blum & Quinn LLP, New York, New York and Denver, Colorado.

MEMBERS OF FIRM

John E. Stout
Susan Bruch Moorehead

ASSOCIATE

Gabriel J. Villegas

OF COUNSEL

William L. Blum

For full biographical listings, see the Martindale-Hubbell Law Directory

DAVID E. NICHOLS, P.C. (AV(T))

100 Blackbeard's Hill, Suite 8E, 00802
Telephone: 340-777-8109
Fax: 340-774-2620
Email: nichols@islands.VI *URL:* http://www.lawyers.com/nicholslaw

David E. Nichols

Representative Clients: First Virgin Islands Federal Savings Bank; Bank of Nova Scotia; McDonald's Corp.; Windward Passage Hotel; McAnderson Real Estate, Inc.; NXP Corp. (A.H. Riise); Shell Seekers, Inc.; McLaughlin Anderson Vacations, Ltd.; Farmers Insurance Group; Morgan Guaranty Bank.

For full biographical listings, see the Martindale-Hubbell Law Directory

CANADA ALBERTA

*CALGARY,** Calgary Jud. Dist.

BENNETT JONES (AV)

4500 Bankers Hall East, 855-2nd Street S.W., T2P 4K7
Telephone: 403-298-3100
Facsimile: 403-265-7219
Email: firmwatch@bennettjones.ca *URL:* http://www.bennettjones.ca
Edmonton, Alberta Office: 1000, 10035-105 Street.
Telephone: 780-421-8133.
Facsimile: 780-421-7951.
Toronto, Ontario Office: 3400 1 First Canadian Place, P.O. Box 130.
Telephone: 416-863-1200.
Facsimile: 416-863-1716.

MEMBER OF FIRM

William S. Rice

For Complete List of Firm Personnel, See General Section

For full biographical listings, see the Martindale-Hubbell Law Directory

*EDMONTON,** Edmonton Jud. Dist.

PARLEE MCLAWS (AV)

15th Floor Manulife Place, 10180 101st Street, T5J 4K1
Telephone: 403-423-8500
Telecopier: 403-423-2870
Email: lawyers@parlee.com *URL:* http://www.parlee.com
Calgary, Alberta Office: 3400 Petro-Canada Centre, 150 - 6th Avenue, SW.
Telephone: 403-294-7000.
Telecopier: 403-265-8263.

MEMBERS OF FIRM

Colin H. Kerr, Q.C.
Terence A. Cockrall, Q.C.
H. Douglas Montemurro
David G. Finlay
Robert A. Newton, Q.C.
Frank J. Niziol
F. Richard Haldane, Q.C.
Ian L. MacLachlan
David S. Tam

ASSOCIATE

George E. Flemming

For Complete List of Firm Personnel, See General Section

For full biographical listings, see the Martindale-Hubbell Law Directory

CANADA MANITOBA

*WINNIPEG,** Eastern Jud. Dist.

AIKINS, MACAULAY & THORVALDSON (AV)

Thirtieth Floor, Commodity Exchange Tower, 360 Main Street, R3C 4G1
Telephone: 204-957-0050
Fax: 204-957-0840
Email: amt@aikins.com *URL:* http://www.aikins.com

MEMBERS OF FIRM

A. Lorne Campbell, O.C., C.D., LL.D., D.C.L., Q.C.
Roger J. Hansell, Q.C.
Michael J. Mercury, Q.C.
Hon. Duncan J. Jessiman, Q.C., LL.D.
A.J. Mercury, Q.C.
Martin H. Freedman, Q.C., C.Arb.
J. Timothy Samson, Q.C.
Larry R. Crane, Q.C.
Bryan D. Klein
Charles L. Chappell
Thomas P. Dooley
Joel A. Weinstein, Q.C.
Edward L. Warkentin
E. Bruce Parker
David L. Voechting
G. Bruce Taylor
Richard L. Yaffe
Frank Lavitt
Herbert J. Peters
David M. Carrick
Barbara M. Shields
J. Douglas Sigurdson
John R. Braun
Brian D. Lerner
James C.R. Ludlow
Michael E. Guttormson
Carmele N. Peter
Robert L. Tyler
Graham E. Robson
David C. Filmon
Steven J. Kohn
Robert C. Lee
Steven M. London
Colin Pewarchuk
Gordon M. Peters
Adam R. Herstein
Marla S. Singer
Todd W. Thomson

Representative Clients: Bank of Montreal; Canada Safeway Ltd.; Co-Operative Credit Society; Great-West Life; Greater Winnipeg Cablevision; National Bank of Canada; New Flyer Industries; Russel Metals Inc.; Standard Aero Limited.

For Complete List of Firm Personnel, See General Section

For full biographical listings, see the Martindale-Hubbell Law Directory

CANADA
NEW BRUNSWICK

*FREDERICTON,** York Co.

McINNES COOPER (AV)

Suite 600, 570 Queen Street, P.O. Box 610, E3B 5A6
Telephone: 506-458-8572
Fax: 506-458-9903
Email: mcrfton@mcrlaw.com *URL:* http://www.mcrlaw.com
Halifax, Nova Scotia Office: Summit Place, 1601 Lower Water Street, P.O. Box 730, B3J 2V1.
Telephone: 902-425-6500.
Fax: 902-425-6350. Email: mcrhfx@mcrlaw.com.
St. John's, Newfoundland Office: Baine Johnston Centre, 5th Floor, 10 Fort William Place, P.O. Box 5939, A1C 5X4.
Telephone: 709-722-8735.
Telecopier: 709-722-1763. Email: mcrsj@mcrlaw.com.
Moncton, New Brunswick Office: Place Moncton Place, 655 Main Street, P.O. Box 1368, E1C 8T6.
Telephone: 506-857-8970.
Fax: 506-857-4095. Email: mcrmctn@mcrlaw.com.
Charlottetown, Prince Edward Island Office: BDC Place, Suite 620, 119 Kent Street, C1A 1N3.
Telephone: 902-368-8473.
Fax: 902-368-8346. Email: mcrpei@mcrlaw.com.

PARTNERS

Leonard T. Hoyt — David Duncan Young

ASSOCIATES

Steven D. Christie — Lise C. Landry

For Complete List of Firm Personnel, See General Section

For full biographical listings, see the Martindale-Hubbell Law Directory

*MONCTON,** Westmorland Co.

McINNES COOPER (AV)

Barristers, Solicitors & Trade Mark Agents
Place Moncton Place, 655 Main Street, P.O. Box 1368, E1C 8T6
Telephone: 506-857-8970
Fax: 506-857-4095
Email: mcrmctn@mcrlaw.com *URL:* http://www.mcrlaw.com
Halifax, Nova Scotia Office: Summit Place, 1601 Lower Water Street, P.O. Box 730, B3J 2V1.
Telephone: 902-425-6500.
Fax: 902-425-6350. Email: mcrhfx@mcrlaw.com.
St. John's, Newfoundland Office: Baine Johnston Centre, 5th Floor, 10 Fort William Place, P.O. Box 5939, A1C 5X4.
Telephone: 709-722-8735.
Telecopier: 709-722-1763. Email: mcrsj@mcrlaw.com.
Charlottetown, Prince Edward Island Office: BDC Place, Suite 620, 119 Kent Street, C1A 1N3.
Telephone: 902-368-8473.
Fax: 902-368-8346. Email: mcrpei@mcrlaw.com.
Fredericton, New Brunswick Office: Suite 600, 570 Queen Street, P.O. Box 610.
Telephone: 506-458-8572.
Fax: 506-458-9903. Email: mcrfton@mcrlaw.com.

ASSOCIATES

Christopher A. Borden — Sylvie C. Roussel

ASSOCIATED ATTORNEY

Robert E. Radford, Q.C.

COUNSEL

Frank J. McKenna

For Complete List of Firm Personnel, See General Section

For full biographical listings, see the Martindale-Hubbell Law Directory

*SAINT JOHN,** Saint John Co.

GILBERT, McGLOAN, GILLIS (AV)

Suite 710, Mercantile Centre, 55 Union Street, P.O. Box 7174, E2L 4S6
Telephone: 506-634-3600
Telecopier: 506-634-3612
Mailing Address: P.O. Box 7174, Station "A", Saint John, New Brunswick, E2L 4S6
Email: gmg@gmglaw.com

T. Louis McGloan, Q.C. (1896-1986) — Adrian B. Gilbert, Q.C. (1895-1986)

MEMBERS OF FIRM

Donald M. Gillis, Q.C.
Thomas L. McGloan, Q.C.
A. G. Warwick Gilbert, Q.C.
Rodney J. Gillis, Q.C.
Douglas A. M. Evans, Q.C.
Brenda J. Lutz, Q.C.
David N. Rogers
Mark A. Canty

(See Next Column)

ASSOCIATES

Edward Veitch
Hugh J. Flemming, Q.C.
Anne F. MacNeill
Nancy E. Forbes
Guy C. Spavold
Claire B.N. Porter
Nathalie L. Godbout
Bruce D. Grant
J. Danie Roy
Catherine A. Fawcett
Danys R.X. Delaquis
James M. Barry

Representative Clients: Bank of Montreal; Canada Packers Ltd.; McCain Foods Ltd.; The Sunderland Steamship Protecting & Indemnity Association; Steamship Mutual Underwriting Association (Bermuda) Limited; Royal Insurance Co.; Wawanesa Mutual Insurance Co.; Dominion of Canada General Insurance Co.; Canadian General Insurance Co.

For full biographical listings, see the Martindale-Hubbell Law Directory

CANADA
NEWFOUNDLAND

*ST. JOHN'S,**

McINNES COOPER (AV)

Barristers, Solicitors & Trade Mark Agents
Baine Johnston Centre, 5th Floor, 10 Fort William Place, P.O. Box 5939, A1C 5X4
Telephone: 709-722-8735
Telecopier: 709-722-1763
Email: mcrsj@mcrlaw.com *URL:* http://www.mcrlaw.com
Halifax, Nova Scotia Office: Summit Place, 1601 Lower Water Street, P.O. Box 730, B3J 2V1.
Telephone: 902-425-6500.
Fax: 902-425-6350. Email: mcrhfx@mcrlaw.com.
Moncton, New Brunswick Office: Place Moncton Place, 655 Main Street, P.O. Box 1368, E1C 8T6.
Telephone: 506-857-8970.
Fax: 506-857-4095. Email: mcrmctn@mcrlaw.com.
Charlottetown, Prince Edward Island Office: BDC Place, Suite 620, 119 Kent Street, C1A 1N3.
Telephone: 902-368-8473.
Fax: 902-368-8346. Email: mcrpei@mcrlaw.com.
Fredericton, New Brunswick Office: Suite 600, 570 Queen Street, P.O. Box 610.
Telephone: 506-458-8572.
Fax: 506-458-9903. Email: mcrfton@mcrlaw.com.

PARTNERS

John M. Green, Q.C.
Thomas R. Kendell
W. Gary Rowe, Q.C.
Christine A. Fagan, Q.C.

For Complete List of Firm Personnel, See General Section

For full biographical listings, see the Martindale-Hubbell Law Directory

CANADA
NOVA SCOTIA

*HALIFAX,** Regional Munic. of Halifax

McINNES COOPER (AV)

Barristers, Solicitors & Trade Mark Agents
Summit Place, 1601 Lower Water Street, P.O. Box 730, B3J 2V1
Telephone: 902-425-6500
Fax: 902-425-6350
Email: mcrhfx@mcrlaw.com *URL:* http://www.mcrlaw.com
St. John's, Newfoundland Office: Baine Johnston Centre, 5th Floor, 10 Fort William Place, P.O. Box 5939, A1C 5X4.
Telephone: 709-722-8735.
Telecopier: 709-722-1763. Email: mcrsj@mcrlaw.com.
Moncton, New Brunswick Office: Place Moncton Place, 655 Main Street, P.O. Box 1368, E1C 8T6.
Telephone: 506-857-8970.
Fax: 506-857-4095. Email: mcrmctn@mcrlaw.com.
Charlottetown, Prince Edward Island Office: BDC Place, Suite 620, 119 Kent Street, C1A 1N3.
Telephone: 902-368-8473.
Fax: 902-368-8346. Email: mcrpei@mcrlaw.com.
Fredericton, New Brunswick Office: Suite 600, 570 Queen Street, P.O. Box 610.
Telephone: 506-458-8572.
Fax: 506-458-9903. Email: mcrfton@mcrlaw.com.

PARTNERS

Lawrence J. Hayes, Q.C.
George T. H. Cooper, Q.C.
F. Van W. Penick
Joseph A. F. Macdonald, Q.C.
Lawrence A. Freeman
Fae J. Shaw

(See Next Column)

McINNES COOPER, *Halifax—Continued*

ASSOCIATES

Frank E. Hughes
Jennifer A. Healy
Jeffrey R. Blucher
Kristi Sebalj

For Complete List of Firm Personnel, See General Section

For full biographical listings, see the Martindale-Hubbell Law Directory

CANADA
ONTARIO

*OTTAWA,** Regional Munic. of Ottawa-Carleton

BORDEN ELLIOT SCOTT & AYLEN (AV)

1000-60 Rue Queen Street, K1P 5Y7
Telephone: 613-237-5160; 800-661-4237
General Facsimile: 613-230-8842
IP Dept. Facsimile: 613-787-3558
Email: ottinfo@scottaylen.com *URL:* http://www.borden.com
Toronto, Ontario Office: Borden & Elliot: Scotia Plaza, 40 King Street West.
Telephone: 416-367-6000.
Telecopier: 416-367-6749. Email: info @borden.com. URL: http://www.borden.com.

John G. Aylen, Q.C.
William C. V. Johnson
Marc Jolicoeur
Walter V. Di Cesare
Yves J. Ménard
Kent D. Howie
Douglas R. Hewson
Laird J. Rasmussen
Thomas J. Marlay
Jeremy Stuart T. Farr
Timothy J. McCunn
Marc A. Babinski
Patricia John
Paule Desjardins-Hageltorn

For full biographical listings, see the Martindale-Hubbell Law Directory

*ST. CATHARINES,** Regional Munic. of Niagara

SULLIVAN, MAHONEY (AV)

40 Queen Street, P.O. Box 1360, L2R 6Z2
Telephone: 905-688-6655
Facsimile: 905-688-5814
Email: lawyers@sullivan-mahoney.com
Niagara Falls, Ontario Office: 4780 Portage Road, L2E 6A8.
Telephone: 905-357-0500.
Fax: 905-357-0501.

MEMBERS OF FIRM

P. H. Sullivan, Q.C. (1909-1988)
Victor F. Muratori, Q.C.
Gordon A. Wiggins
Thomas A. Richardson
Woodward B. McKaig
Douglas A. Goslin
Joseph M. Gottli
J. Rodney Bush
Bruce A. Macdonald
C. H. Mahoney, Q.C.
Peter B. Bedard
Peter T. Banwell, Q.C.
Philip M. Sheehan
Joseph Dallal
Catherine Anne Bain
Robert B. Culliton
Peter A. Mahoney
Michael J. Bonomi
Glen W. McCann

ASSOCIATES

Sara J. Premi
Carmelina D'Angelo
Leanne P. McClay
Rocco Vacca

OF COUNSEL

Marvin D. Kriluck

For full biographical listings, see the Martindale-Hubbell Law Directory

*TORONTO,** Regional Munic. of Toronto

BERESKIN & PARR (AV)

Box 401, 40 King Street West, M5H 3Y2
Telephone: 416-364-7311
Telecopier: 416-361-1398
URL: http://www.bereskinparr.com

MEMBERS AND ASSOCIATES

Daniel R. Bereskin, Q.C.
Richard J. Parr
H. Roger Hart
C. Lloyd Sarginson
Robert H. C. MacFarlane
Cynthia Rowden
Timothy J. Sinnott
Robert B. Storey
Philip C. Mendes da Costa
Jill Diane Jarvis-Tonus
Michael E. Charles
Robin L. Coster
Amalia Trister
Jonathan G. Colombo
Jill M. Holmes
John R. Rudolph
Mark L. Robbins
Justine Wiebe
Andrew I. McIntosh
Shawn D. Jacka
Anita Nador
Todd D. Bailey
Isis E. Caulder
Scott R. Pundsack
Christine M. Pallotta
Tai W. Nahm
Bhupinder S. Randhawa
Lillian Sversky

(See Next Column)

PATENT AND TRADEMARK AGENTS

David W. R. Langton
H. Samuel Frost
Marie E. Manza
Terry Edwards
Jane Sarjeant
Micheline Gravelle
Stephen M. Beney
Janice M. Bereskin
Mark Schisler

For full biographical listings, see the Martindale-Hubbell Law Directory

BORDEN & ELLIOT (AV)

Barristers & Solicitors
Scotia Plaza, 40 King Street West, M5H 3Y4
Telephone: 416-367-6000
Telecopier: 416-367-6749
Email: info@borden.com *URL:* http://www.borden.com
Ottawa, Ontario Office: Borden Elliot Scott & Aylen, 1000-60 Rue Queen Street.
Telephone: 613-237-5160; 800-661-4237. General
Facsimile: 613-230-8842. IP Dept.
Facsimile: 613-787-3558. Email: ottinfo@scottaylen.com. URL: http://www.borden.com.

William T. Pashby

For Complete List of Firm Personnel, See General Section

For full biographical listings, see the Martindale-Hubbell Law Directory

DAVIES, WARD & BECK (AV)

1 First Canadian Place, M5X 1B1
Telephone: 416-863-0900
Fax: 416-863-0871
Email: info@dwb.com *URL:* http://www.dwb.com

PARTNERS AND ASSOCIATES

Mark Q. Connelly
William M. O'Reilly
I. Berl Nadler
Jean-Paul Bisnaire
Michael Disney
William M. Ainley
A. Gerold Goldlist
Jeffrey O. Palmer
Paul M. Kennedy
Kevin J. Thomson
Ian D. Johnson
Carol Hansell
Vincent A. Mercier
Timothy H. Moran
Richard F. D. Corley
Sarbjit S. Basra
Andrew L. Welsh
Julianna S. Ahn
Andrea E. Daly
Terrance J. Ritchie
Warren M. Katz
Steven M. Harris
Jennifer L. Toone
Nicholas J. Leblovic
Jay A. Swartz
Arthur S. Shiff
Gray E. Taylor
Gregory J. Howard
Carol D. Pennycook
Edward C. Hannah
Catherine G. Ross
D. Shawn McReynolds
Michael Creery
Thomas A. Smee
Ian R. McBride
Cameron M. Rusaw
Michael W. Clifford
Patrick G. Barry
Gillian R. Stacey
Paolo Boni
Delphine Brooker
Sabrina Gherbaz
Mitchell P. Finkelstein
Paul W. Golding
Christopher H. Jones
Paul A. Beauregard
Donald S. Harrison

For Complete List of Firm Personnel, See General Section

For full biographical listings, see the Martindale-Hubbell Law Directory

McDONALD & HAYDEN (AV)

One Queen Street East Suite 1500, M5C 2Y3
Telephone: 416-364-3100
Telecopier: 416-601-4100
Email: ddouglas@mchayden.on.ca *URL:* http://www.mchayden.on.ca

MEMBERS OF FIRM

John G. McDonald, Q.C. (1922-1993)
Peter Reginald Hayden, Q.C.
David C. Nathanson, Q.C.
Marvin D. Demone
D. H. Jack
David R. Street
Clifford M. Goldlist
Wendy C. Posluns
Warren S. Rapoport
David H. Goldman
A. Richard Rodier
Mark Adilman
John D. Brunt
Kevin Cai
Jane Southren
Shea T. Small

ASSOCIATE

Bram J. Green

For full biographical listings, see the Martindale-Hubbell Law Directory

CANADA
PRINCE EDWARD ISLAND

*CHARLOTTETOWN,** Queen's Co.

CAMPBELL, LEA, MICHAEL, McCONNELL & PIGOT (AV)

15 Queen Street, P.O. Box 429, C1A 7K7
Telephone: 902-566-3400
Telecopier: 902-566-9266
Email: www.office@campbelllea.com

MEMBERS OF FIRM

Paul D. Michael, Q.C.
Ross D. Pigot
Robert A. McConnell
Kenneth L. Godfrey

General Counsel in Prince Edward Island for: Canadian Imperial Bank of Commerce; Maritime Electric Co., Ltd.; Michelin Tires (Canada) Ltd.; Newsco Investments Ltd. (Dundas Farms); Imperial Oil Limited; General Motors of Canada; Co-op Atlantic; Liberty Mutual; Employers Reinsurance Group.

For Complete List of Firm Personnel, See General Section

For full biographical listings, see the Martindale-Hubbell Law Directory

McINNES COOPER (AV㊉)

Barristers, Solicitors & Trade Mark Agents
BDC Place, Suite 620, 119 Kent Street, C1A 1N3
Telephone: 902-368-8473
Fax: 902-368-8346
Email: mcrpei@mcrlaw.com *URL:* http://www.mcrlaw.com
Halifax, Nova Scotia Office: Summit Place, 1601 Lower Water Street, P.O. Box 730, B3J 2V1.
Telephone: 902-425-6500.
Fax: 902-425-6350. Email: mcrhfx@mcrlaw.com.
St. John's, Newfoundland Office: Baine Johnston Centre, 5th Floor, 10 Fort William Place, P.O. Box 5939, A1C 5X4.
Telephone: 709-722-8735.
Telecopier: 709-722-1763. Email: mcrsj@mcrlaw.com.
Moncton, New Brunswick Office: Place Moncton Place, 655 Main Street, P.O. Box 1368, E1C 8T6.
Telephone: 506-857-8970.
Fax: 506-857-4095. Email: mcrmctn@mcrlaw.com.
Fredericton, New Brunswick Office: Suite 600, 570 Queen Street, P.O. Box 610.
Telephone: 506-458-8572.
Fax: 506-458-9903. Email: mcrfton@mcrlaw.com.

PARTNERS

Mark Ledwell
Michele M. Murphy

ASSOCIATES

Kevin J. Kiley
Paul Kiley

For Complete List of Firm Personnel, See General Section

For full biographical listings, see the Martindale-Hubbell Law Directory

CANADA
QUEBEC

*MONTREAL,** Montreal Dist.

McMASTER GERVAIS (AV)

A General Partnership
1000 de La Gauchetière Street West, Suite 900, H3B 5H4
Telephone: 514-879-1212
Fax: 514-954-1905
Email: info@mcmastergervais.com *URL:* http://www.mcmastergervais.com

MEMBERS OF FIRM

Timothy R. Carsley
Peter C. Casey
Norman A. Saibil
Ian B. Taylor
Raymond Picard
Pierre Gattuso
Michael Patry
Charles P. Marquette
Pierre Trudeau
Sylvie Bouvette
P. Vivian Cyriacopoulos
Michael Bantey
Lise Fortier
Patricia Galella
Catherine Guertin
Roderick Darrock Elliott
Tammy J. Shulman
Lionel J. Blanshay
Paul R. Marchand
Brian M. Schneiderman
Richard W. Shannon
Elizabeth A. Mitchell
Benoît M. Provost
Yves A. Dubois
Janet Casey
André Dufour
François Morin
H. John Godber
Christine Duchaine
Patrice Martin
Virginia Chan
David Torralbo
Sophia Tolias
Sébastien Berthelet

(See Next Column)

COUNSEL

P. André Gervais, Q.C.
Tass G. Grivakes, Q.C.
Richard J. Riendeau, Q.C.

For Complete List of Firm Personnel, See General Section

For full biographical listings, see the Martindale-Hubbell Law Directory

POULIOT, MERCURE (AV)

CIBC Tower, 31st Floor, 1155 René-Lévesque Boulevard, West, H3B 3S6
Telephone: 514-875-5210
Telecopier: 514-875-4308
Email: POUMER@CEDEP.COM
Genève, Suisse Office: 8, Rue de la Rôtisserie, 1204 Geneva, Switzerland.
Telephone: +41 22-28 79 40.
Telecopier: +41 22-21 23 67.

MEMBERS OF FIRM

Georges A. Pouliot, Q.C.
Gilles Brunelle
Luc Gratton
Brian Riordan
Pierre Paquet
Anne-Marie Gauthier
Yvon Brizard
Robert Tessier
Daniel Gagné
Lilia Pouliot
Marco Veilleux
Alain Nadon
Jean H. Gagnon
Richard Fontaine
Normand Royal
Gilles Bertrand
Jean Larivière
Louis-Michel Tremblay
David I. Johnston
Stéphane Hébert
Jacques LeBel, Q.C.
Joel A. Silcoff
Ronald M. Auclair
Philippe Roy
Maxime B. Rhéaume
Serge Desrochers
C. Keenan LaPierre
Alain Bond
Louis Coallier
Nicole Chouinard
Stéphane Teasdale

ASSOCIATES

Micheline Perrault
Caroline Lemoine
Béatrice Arronis
Yvan Nantel
Sylvie Boulanger
Vincent Frenette
Robert Cardin
Alexandre Henri
Brent J. Muir
Louise Tremblay
Chantal Joubert
Normand D'Amour
Pascale Cloutier
Eric Couture
Frédéric Chatel
Mary-Lynn Breton
Alexandre Ajami

For full biographical listings, see the Martindale-Hubbell Law Directory

CANADA
SASKATCHEWAN

*REGINA,** Regina Jud. Centre

MacPHERSON LESLIE & TYERMAN (AV)

1500-1874 Scarth Street, S4P 4E9
Telephone: 306-347-8000
Telecopier: 306-352-5250
Email: mltreg@mlt.com
Saskatoon, Saskatchewan Office: 1500-410 22nd Street East, S7K 5T6.
Telephone: 306-975-7100.
Telecopier: 306-975-7145.

MEMBERS OF FIRM

Harold H. MacKay, Q.C.
Donald K. Wilson, Q.C.
Garret J. Oledzki
Alain J. Gaucher (Resident, Saskatoon Office)
James S. Kerby (Resident, Saskatoon Office)
John A. Dipple
Scott A. Exner
Robert B. Pletch, Q.C.
R. Neil MacKay (Resident, Saskatoon Office)
Douglas A. Ballou
Danny R. Anderson (Resident, Saskatoon Office)
Randy U. Brunet
Curtis R. Stewart (Resident, Saskatoon Office)

ASSOCIATES

David B. Jahnke (Resident, Saskatoon Office)
Grant D. Marshak (Resident, Saskatoon Office)
Kenton J. Gray
Michele T. Klebuc-Simes
Scott D. Whitby
Michael J. Clark (Resident, Saskatoon Office)
R. Allen Kirk (Resident, Saskatoon Office)

COUNSEL

W. Thomas Molloy, O.C., Q.C. (Resident, Saskatoon Office)

For Complete List of Firm Personnel, See General Section

For full biographical listings, see the Martindale-Hubbell Law Directory

MEXICO

GARZA GARCIA, NUEVO LEON,

American Lawyers in Garza Garcia

THOMPSON & KNIGHT L.L.P.

(Attorneys and Counselors)
Edificio Losoles PD-4, Av. Lázaro Cárdenas No. 2400 PTE San Pedro Garza Garcia, Garza Garcia, Nuevo Leon 66220
Telephone: (52-8) 363-0096
Telecopy: (52-8) 363-3067
URL: http://www.tklaw.com
Dallas, Texas Office: 1700 Pacific Avenue, Suite 3300, 75201.
Telephone: 214-969-1700.
Telecopy: 214-969-1751.
Telex: 732298.
Austin, Texas Office: 1200 San Jacinto Center, 98 San Jacinto Boulevard, 78701.
Telephone: 512-469-6100.
Telecopy: 512-469-6180.
Fort Worth, Texas Office: 801 Cherry Street, Suite 1600, 76102.
Telephone: 817-347-1700.
Telecopy: 817-347-1799.
Houston, Texas Office: Thompson Knight Brown Parker & Leahy L.L.P., 1200 Smith Street, Suite 3600.
Telephone: 713-654-8111.
Telecopier: 713-654-1871.

PARTNERS

Joe A. Rudberg | Michael C. Titens

For Complete List of Firm Personnel, See General Section

For full biographical listings, see the Martindale-Hubbell Law Directory

CIVIL RIGHTS

MISSISSIPPI

*CLEVELAND,** Bolivar Co.

GRIFFITH & GRIFFITH (AV)

123 South Court Street, Post Office Drawer 1680, 38732
Telephone: 662-843-6100
Telecopier: 662-843-8153
Email: griffith@tecinfo.com *URL:* http://www.vralitigator.com

MEMBERS OF FIRM

L. Ellis Griffith (1926-1987)
Benjamin E. Griffith
Daniel J. Griffith

Reference: The Cleveland State Bank.

For full biographical listings, see the Martindale-Hubbell Law Directory

NEW JERSEY

EDISON, Middlesex Co.

WONG FLEMING, P.C. (AV)

Edison Square West, Suite 1050, 2035 Lincoln Highway, 08817
Telephone: 732-248-4111
Fax: 732-248-8665
Mailing Address: P.O. Box 985, 08818-0985
Email: info@wongfleming.com *URL:* http://www.wongfleming.com
Philadelphia, Pennsylvania Office: 230 South Broad Street, Suite 601, 19102.
Telephone: 215-546-2776.
Fax: 215-546-3206.
New York, New York Office: The Empire State Building, 350 Fifth Avenue, Suite 5411, 10118.
Telephone: 212-643-9668.
Fax: 212-643-9640.

Linda Wong
Daniel C. Fleming
Katherine C. Lee

Andrew J. Bayne
Stephen Tsai
Theresa Homisak
Paul J. Young
Wenjun Zhang (Not admitted in NJ)
Tanya E. Lawrence
Fei F. Lam

For full biographical listings, see the Martindale-Hubbell Law Directory

*MORRISTOWN,** Morris Co.

RAND, ALGEIER, TOSTI & WOODRUFF, A PROFESSIONAL CORPORATION (AV)

60 Washington Street, 07960
Telephone: 973-539-2600
Telecopier: 973-984-0430
Email: randlaw@bellatlantic.net

Gary C. Algeier
David B. Rand
Robert M. Tosti
Robert B. Woodruff
John F. McDonnell
John E. Croot, Jr.

Kathryn J. Kingree
Deborah A. White

OF COUNSEL

Ronald M. Pflug
Ellen S. Bass
Tamara Krikorian

For full biographical listings, see the Martindale-Hubbell Law Directory

*NEWARK,** Essex Co.

SILLS CUMMIS RADIN TISCHMAN EPSTEIN & GROSS, A PROFESSIONAL CORPORATION (AV)

One Riverfront Plaza, 07102-5400
Telephone: 973-643-7000
Fax: 973-643-6500
Telex: 820630 Sillsbeck Nwk
Email: sillsmail@sillscummis.com *URL:* http://www.sillscummis.com
Atlantic City, New Jersey Office: 17 Gordon's Alley.
Telephone: 609-344-2800.
New York, N.Y. Office: 712 Fifth Avenue.
Telephone: 212-643-7000.
Washington, D.C. Office: 1800 K Street, N.W.
Telephone: 202-296-4750.

(See Next Column)

OF COUNSEL

Cherie L. Maxwell

Representative Clients: Becton Dickinson & Company; Allied Signal; Rutgers University; McKinsey & Co.; Melvin Simon; N.J.. Nets; P.S.E.& G.; Syms; WWOR-TV.

For Complete List of Firm Personnel, See General Section

For full biographical listings, see the Martindale-Hubbell Law Directory

SHORT HILLS, Essex Co.

PETER W. TILL (AV)

820 Morris Turnpike, Suite 201, 07078
Telephone: 973-467-0300
Fax: 973-467-4628
Email: peterwtill@aol.com *URL:* http://www.lawyers.com/peterwtilllaw
(Also Of Counsel, Wilf & Silverman)

For full biographical listings, see the Martindale-Hubbell Law Directory

*TRENTON,** Mercer Co.

NEEDELL, SIEKERKA & CASTELLANI, A PROFESSIONAL CORPORATION (AV)

Quakerbridge Commons, 2681 Quakerbridge Road, 08619-1625
Telephone: 609-584-7700
Fax: 609-584-0123
Email: nsclaw@aol.com

Stanley H. Needell
Michele N. Siekerka
Anthony P. Castellani

John M. Cinti
Dean C. Gresek

LEGAL SUPPORT PERSONNEL

PARALEGALS

Marlene Griesbach
Carolyn D. Shaw
Veronica A. Mitchell

For full biographical listings, see the Martindale-Hubbell Law Directory

NEW MEXICO

*ALBUQUERQUE,** Bernalillo Co.

FREEDMAN BOYD DANIELS HOLLANDER GOLDBERG & CLINE P.A. (AV)

20 First Plaza, Suite 700, 87102
Telephone: 505-842-9960
Fax: 505-842-0761

John W. Boyd

Scott M. Davidson

For full biographical listings, see the Martindale-Hubbell Law Directory

RAY TWOHIG, P.C. (AV)

8998 Rio Grande Boulevard N.W., 87114
Telephone: 505-898-0400
Fax: 505-898-0004
Email: rambaud@flash.net

Ray Twohig

*SANTA FE,** Santa Fe Co.

MONTGOMERY & ANDREWS, PROFESSIONAL ASSOCIATION (AV)

325 Paseo de Peralta, P.O. Box 2307, 87504-2307
Telephone: 505-982-3873
Fax: 505-982-4289
Email: montand@montand.com

Victor R. Ortega
Walter J. Melendres
Bruce Herr
Carolyn Wolf

Representative Clients: State of New Mexico Risk Management Division; Regents of University of California (Los Almos National Laboratory); City of Santa Fe.

For Complete List of Firm Personnel, See General Section

For full biographical listings, see the Martindale-Hubbell Law Directory

NEW YORK

GARDEN CITY, Nassau Co.

MONTFORT, HEALY, MCGUIRE & SALLEY (AV)

1140 Franklin Avenue, 11530
Telephone: 516-747-4082
Telecopier: 516-746-0748

MEMBERS OF FIRM

E. Richard Rimmels, Jr. (1930-1999)
Frank J. Cafaro
Philip J. Catapano
Fredric C. Montfort
Donald S. Neumann, Jr.
James J. Keefe, Jr.
Michael A. Baranowicz
James Michael Murphy

OF COUNSEL

Fredric H. Montfort
Edward M. Salley, Jr.
David J. Fleming
Robert J. Mettalia

ASSOCIATES

Claudia C. Glacken
Marcie K. Glasser
Bruce A. Cook
Jeffrey D. Present
Joan E. Resnik
Susan H. Dempsey
Camille L. Hansen
Christopher T. Cafaro
Kathleen Dumont
Jeffrey B. Siler
Michael G. Kruzynski
Karen J. Cooper

For full biographical listings, see the Martindale-Hubbell Law Directory

*NEW YORK,** New York Co.

BERNSTEIN LITOWITZ BERGER & GROSSMANN LLP (AV)

1285 Avenue of the Americas, 10019
Telephone: 212-554-1400
Telecopier: 212-554-1444
Email: blbg@blbglaw.com *URL:* http://www.blbglaw.com

MEMBERS OF FIRM

Paul M. Bernstein (1929-1990)
Max W. Berger
Edward A. Grossmann
Jeffrey A. Klafter
Daniel L. Berger
Douglas M. McKeige
Seth R. Lesser
John P. Coffey
Robert S. Gans
Darnley Dickinson Stewart

ASSOCIATES

Lisa K. Buckser
Thomas E. Chase
Patricia S. Gillane
Leah Beth Guggenheimer
Rochelle Feder Hansen
Jeffrey N. Leibell
Nancy Bea Lipin
Louis C. Paul
Ryan D. Poliakoff
Robert W. Rodriguez (Not admitted in NY)
Gerald H. Silk
Steven B. Singer

OF COUNSEL

Ronald Litowitz

For full biographical listings, see the Martindale-Hubbell Law Directory

EMERY CUTI BRINCKERHOFF & ABADY PC (AV)

545 Madison Avenue, 3rd Floor, 10022-4219
Telephone: 212-763-5000
Facsimile: 212-763-5001
Email: mail@ecbalaw.com *URL:* http://www.ecbalaw.com

Richard D. Emery
Matthew D. Brinckerhoff
Jonathan S. Abady
John R. Cuti

Ilann M. Maazel
David H. Gans
Alexandra D. Lahav (Not admitted in NY)

For full biographical listings, see the Martindale-Hubbell Law Directory

NORTH CAROLINA

*CHARLOTTE,** Mecklenburg Co.

FERGUSON, STEIN, WALLAS, ADKINS, GRESHAM & SUMTER, P.A. (AV)

741 Kenilworth Avenue, Suite 300, 28204-2828
Telephone: 704-375-8461
Fax: 704-334-5654
Mailing Address: P.O. Box 36486, 28236-6486
Email: FSWAGS@aol.com
Chapel Hill, North Carolina Office: Suite 2, 312 West Franklin Street.
Telephone: 919-933-5300.
Fax: 919-967-4953.

(See Next Column)

James E. Ferguson, II
Adam Stein (Resident, Chapel Hill Office)
Jonathan Wallas
Karl Adkins
John W. Gresham
Geraldine Sumter
Henderson Hill
Thomas M. Stern (Resident, Chapel Hill Office)
C. Margaret Errington
Stephen Luke Largess

Rebecca Ann Thorne
James E. Ferguson, III
Corie Diane Pauling
Ann C. Todd

For full biographical listings, see the Martindale-Hubbell Law Directory

*DURHAM,** Durham Co.

GLENN, MILLS & FISHER, P.A. (AV)

Suite 709, South Bank Building, 400 West Main Street, P.O. Drawer 3865, 27702-3865
Telephone: 919-683-2135
Fax: 919-688-9339

Robert B. Glenn, Jr.
William S. Mills
Stewart W. Fisher

Caitlyn T. Fulghum

For full biographical listings, see the Martindale-Hubbell Law Directory

*WINSTON-SALEM,** Forsyth Co.

WOMBLE CARLYLE SANDRIDGE & RICE (AV)

A Professional Limited Liability Company
200 West Second Street, P.O. Drawer 84, 27102
Telephone: 336-721-3600
Fax: 336-721-3660
Email: lawyers@wcsr.com *URL:* http://www.wcsr.com
Charlotte, North Carolina Office: 3300 One First Union Center, 301 South College Street.
Telephone: 704-331-4900.
Fax: 704-331-4955.
Raleigh, North Carolina Office: 2100 First Union Capitol Center, 150 Fayetteville Street Mall, P.O. Box 831.
Telephone: 919-755-2100.
Fax: 919-755-2150.
Research Triangle Park, North Carolina Office: 2505 Meridian Parkway, Suite 300 (Durham), 27713.
Telephone: 919-484-2300.
Fax: 919-484-2340.
Atlanta, Georgia Office: One Atlantic Center, 1201 West Peachtree Street, Suite 3500.
Telephone: 404-872-7000.
Fax: 404-888-7490.
Other Atlanta, Georgia Office: Suite 404, 2296 Henderson Mill Road, N.E.
Telephone: 770-492-9030.
Fax: 770-492-9609.
Washington, D.C. Office: 1120 Nineteenth Street, N.W., Eighth Floor.
Telephone: 202-857-4400.
Fax: 202-467-6910.
Greenville, South Carolina Office: 15 South Main Street, Suite 601, P.O. Box 10208.
Telephone: 864-255-5400.
Fax: 864-255-5440.

RESIDENT MEMBER

Allan R. Gitter

Representative Clients: Brad Ragan, Inc.; Brenner Companies; Food Lion, Inc.; Hanes Companies, Inc.; North Carolina Baptist Hospitals, Inc.; R.J. Reynolds Tobacco Co.; Thomasville Furniture Industries, Inc.; Wachovia Corp.; Wake Forest University.

For Complete List of Firm Personnel, See General Section

For full biographical listings, see the Martindale-Hubbell Law Directory

OHIO

*CLEVELAND,** Cuyahoga Co.

AVERY S. FRIEDMAN (AV)

701 Citizens Building, 850 Euclid Avenue, 44114
Telephone: 216-621-9282

For full biographical listings, see the Martindale-Hubbell Law Directory

HENNENBERG & ASSOCIATES (AV)

30100 Chagrin Boulevard, Suite 301, 44124-5704
Telephone: 216-765-9600
Fax: 216-765-8292
Email: Hennenberg@aol.com

Michael C. Hennenberg

(See Next Column)

HENNENBERG & ASSOCIATES—*Continued*

ASSOCIATE

John A. Fatica

For full biographical listings, see the Martindale-Hubbell Law Directory

DUBLIN, Franklin Co.

BLAUGRUND, HERBERT & MARTIN, INCORPORATED (AV)

5455 Rings Road, Suite 500, 43017-7517
Telephone: 614-764-0681
Fax: 614-764-0774
Email: bhm@bhmlaw.net

David S. Kessler
Emily J. Lewis

For full biographical listings, see the Martindale-Hubbell Law Directory

OKLAHOMA

*OKLAHOMA CITY,** Oklahoma Co.

MANCHESTER & PIGNATO, P.C. (AV)

Suite 900, Robinson Renaissance Building, 119 North Robinson, 73102
Telephone: 405-235-2222
Fax: 405-235-2204
Email: mplaw@manchesterandpignato.com

Robert Edward Manchester
Gerard F. Pignato
Shannon K. Emmons
Susan Ann Knight

ASSOCIATES

R. Thompson Cooper
Jenny L. Evans

OF COUNSEL

Stacey Haws Felkner

Representative Clients: Electric Mutual Liability Insurance Co.; Otis Elevator Co.; Budget Rent-A-Car Systems, Inc.; Essex Insurance Co.; American Bankers Insurance Company of Florida; Motors Insurance Co.; Lexington Insurance Co.; City of Oklahoma City; Clint Williams Co.

For full biographical listings, see the Martindale-Hubbell Law Directory

THE MILLS LAW FIRM, P.C. (AV)

500 One Leadership Square, 211 North Robinson, 73102
Telephone: 405-239-2501
Fax: 405-239-2575
Email: millsfirm@attymail.com

Robert B. Mills
W. Wayne Mills
Barbara K. Buratti

For full biographical listings, see the Martindale-Hubbell Law Directory

WHITTEN, MCGUIRE, WOOD, TERRY, ROSELIUS & DITTRICH A PROFESSIONAL LIMITED LIABILITY COMPANY (AV)

Suite 400, One Leadership Square, 211 North Robinson, 73102
Telephone: 405-239-2522
Fax: 405-239-2573
Email: whitten@whitten-mcguire.com
Tulsa, Oklahoma Office: 3600 First Place Tower, 15 East Fifth Street.
Telephone: 918-582-9903.

Reggie N. Whitten
Kent R. McGuire
Douglas A. Terry
Jason E. Roselius

Simone Gosnell Fulmer
Philip W. Anderson
R. Gregory Kirby
Derrick T. Dewitt

Representative Clients: Biomet, Inc.; The St. Paul Insurance Cos.; OML Municipal Assurance Group; Progressive Casualty; Shelter Insurance Co.; Fireman's Fund Insurance Co.; Pharmacists Mutual Insurance Co.

For full biographical listings, see the Martindale-Hubbell Law Directory

*TULSA,** Tulsa Co.

ATKINSON, HASKINS, NELLIS, BOUDREAUX, HOLEMAN, PHIPPS & BRITTINGHAM, A PROFESSIONAL CORPORATION (AV)

1500 ParkCentre, 525 South Main Street, 74103
Telephone: 918-582-8877
Fax: 918-585-8096
Email: ahnmail@ahn-law.com

Gregory D. Nellis, P.C.
Paul T. Boudreaux, P.C.
Daniel E. Holeman, P.C.
K. Clark Phipps
Galen Lee Brittingham, P.C.
Marthanda J. Beckworth

Representative Clients: Allstate Insurance Co.; Bayer Corp.; Crum & Forster Insurance Co.; Hartford Insurance Company; National American Insurance Co.; Federated Insurance Co.; Liberty Mutual Insurance Co.; Physicians Liability Insurance Co.; State Farm Mutual Automobile Insurance Co.; United States Aviation Underwriters.

For full biographical listings, see the Martindale-Hubbell Law Directory

RHODES, HIERONYMUS, JONES, TUCKER & GABLE, P.L.L.C. (AV)

Oneok Plaza, 100 West 5th Street, Suite 400, P.O. Box 21100, 74121-1100
Telephone: 918-582-1173
Fax: 918-592-3390
URL: http://www.rhodesokla.com

MEMBERS OF FIRM

Kevin D. Berry
Jo Anne Deaton
Richard M. Eldridge
E. D. Hieronymus (1908 -1994)
Bert M. Jones
William S. Leach
Michael W. McGivern
William D. Perrine
Mary Quinn-Cooper
Robert P. Redemann
David P. Reid
Chris L. Rhodes, III
Thomas E. Steichen
Catherine C. Taylor
John H. Tucker
Wilson T. White
Harold C. Zuckerman

Ann E. Allison
Steven K. Bunting
Robert P. Coffey, Jr.
J. Christopher Davis
Andrew D. Downing
Dana L. Gish
Kerry R. Lewis
Andrew L. Richardson
Michael F. Smith
Leslie J. Southerland
Kimberly E. West
Keith A. Wilkes

OF COUNSEL

George W. Gable (Retired Partner)
Larry J. Fulton
Kelly M. Greenough

Representative Clients: American International Companies; Bechtel; Chubb Group of Insurance Companies; General Motors Corporation; Merrill, Lynch; Nissan Motor Corporation in U.S.A.; Pfizer, Inc.; Volkswagen of America, Volkswagen, A.G.; Zurich U.S.

For full biographical listings, see the Martindale-Hubbell Law Directory

OREGON

*PORTLAND,** Multnomah Co.

BANKS & UNDERHILL, P.C. (AV)

KOIN Center, Suite 1200, 222 S.W. Columbia Street, 97201
Telephone: 503-222-7475
Telecopier: 503-222-7288
URL: http://www.banksunderhill.com
URL: http://www.lawyers.com/banks&underhill

Robert S. Banks, Jr.
Dayna E. Underhill

Reference: Bank of America.

For full biographical listings, see the Martindale-Hubbell Law Directory

PENNSYLVANIA

*PHILADELPHIA,** Philadelphia Co.

MCCOY & ASSOCIATES, P.C. (AV)

The Windsor, Penthouse Suite, 1700 Benjamin Franklin Parkway, 19103
Telephone: 215-587-4322
Fax: 215-587-2110
Email: McCoylaw@msn.com *URL:* http://www.lawyers.com/mccoy&associates
Mount Laurel, New Jersey Office: 534 Charleston Court, 08054.
Telephone: 609-235-7676.
Fax: 609-234-4607.

Edwin F. McCoy

Steven J. Blumenthal
Laura J. Lifsey

For full biographical listings, see the Martindale-Hubbell Law Directory

NEIL A. MORRIS ASSOCIATES, P.C. (AV)

The Widener Building, Suite 1700, One South Penn Square 1339 Chestnut Street, 19107
Telephone: 215-751-0600
Fax: 215-751-1425
URL: http://www.namapc.com
Marlton, New Jersey Office: Ten Lake Center Executive Park, 401 Route 73 North, Suite 204.
Telephone: 609-596-5656.
Telefax: 609-596-6164.

(See Next Column)

NEIL A. MORRIS ASSOCIATES, P.C., *Philadelphia—Continued*

Neil A. Morris

Laurence L. Smith
Richard R. Morris
Daniel F. McLaughlin

OF COUNSEL

Jay H. Rosenfeld

LEGAL SUPPORT PERSONNEL

Jacqueline J. Ben

For full biographical listings, see the Martindale-Hubbell Law Directory

RHODE ISLAND

*PROVIDENCE,** Providence Co.

MANN & MITCHELL (AV)

Suite 501 Turks Head Place, 02903
Telephone: 401-351-5770
Telecopier: 401-521-4305
Email: rmann29@idt.net *URL:* http://www.lawyers.com/mannlaw

MEMBERS OF FIRM

Robert B. Mann
Suzanna J. Mitchell

For full biographical listings, see the Martindale-Hubbell Law Directory

TENNESSEE

KINGSPORT, Sullivan Co.

WEST & ROSE (AV)

537 East Center Street, P.O. Box 1404, 37660
Telephone: 423-246-8176
Fax: 423-246-4028

MEMBERS OF FIRM

M. Lacy West
Steven C. Rose
Julia C. West

For full biographical listings, see the Martindale-Hubbell Law Directory

*KNOXVILLE,** Knox Co.

SOBIESKI, MESSER & ASSOCIATES (AV)

900 South Gay Street, Suite 1801, 37902
Telephone: 423-546-7770
Fax: 423-546-7969
Email: sobilaw@aol.com

Wanda G. Sobieski
Diane M. Messer

ASSOCIATE

R. Richard Carl, II

For full biographical listings, see the Martindale-Hubbell Law Directory

TEXAS

*AUSTIN,** Travis Co.

SCHWARTZ & EICHELBAUM, P.C. (AV)

One Commodore Plaza, 800 Brazos, Suite 870, 78701
Telephone: 512-476-9944
Fax: 512-472-2599
Email: info@edlaw.com
San Antonio, Texas Office: 700 N. St. Mary's, Suite 1850, 78205.
Telephone: 210-228-9944.
Fax: 210-228-9950.
Plano, Texas Office, D/FW Metroplex: P.O. Box 250025, 75025.
Telephone: 972-377-7900.
Fax: 972-377-7277.

Leonard J. Schwartz
Dennis J. Eichelbaum (Resident, D/FW Metroplex, Texas)
Kelli Hamm Karczewski
Robert A. Schulman (Resident, San Antonio, Texas)
Cobby A. Caputo
Stacy C. Ferguson (Resident, San Antonio, Texas)

(See Next Column)

Holly Boyd Wardell
Cheryl Tremaine Mehl
Kaye Knox Feist
Suzanne Stephens Becker (Resident, San Antonio, Texas)
Deirdre Vasquez (Resident, San Antonio, Texas)

For full biographical listings, see the Martindale-Hubbell Law Directory

*DALLAS,** Dallas Co.

TOOLEY & VOSS (AV)

8214 Westchester Drive, Suite 420, 75225
Telephone: 214-368-2224
Fax: 214-368-8307
Email: JCToutfit@aol.com

Joe C. Tooley
Edwin P. Voss Jr.

For full biographical listings, see the Martindale-Hubbell Law Directory

*TYLER,** Smith Co.

RAMEY & FLOCK, A PROFESSIONAL CORPORATION (AV)

500 First Place, P.O. Box 629, 75710
Telephone: 903-597-3301
Telecopier: 903-597-2413
Email: Ramey@Ramey-Flock.com *URL:* http://www.RameyFlock.com

Thomas B. Ramey (1892-1967)
Jack W. Flock
Tracy Crawford
Glenn Collins
Michael A. Hatchell
Tom Henson
Dennis G. Black
Paul H. Gilliam
R. Brian Craft
Gregory D. Smith
Michael T. Crawford
Mary H. Molly Hatchell
Rosemary Sage Jones
Ronald S. Vickery
John W. Ferguson, Jr.

Deron R. Dacus
Eric H. Findlay
Shannon Dacus
Maria Benecki Sowders
Jamy Mitchell Skaggs

Counsel for: Regions Bank; Exxon Co. U.S.A.; Kelly Springfield Tire Co.; Trinity-Mother Frances Health System; St. Paul Insurance Co.; The Travelers Cos.; Reliance Insurance Co.; Marshall Regional Medical Center.

For full biographical listings, see the Martindale-Hubbell Law Directory

VIRGIN ISLANDS

*CHARLOTTE AMALIE, ST. THOMAS,** St. Thomas

GRUNERT STOUT & BRUCH

24-25 Kongensgade, P.O. Box 1030, 00804
Telephone: 340-774-1320
Fax: 340-774-7839
Email: gsbusvi@viaccess.net
Affiliated with: Solomon Pearl Blum & Quinn LLP, New York, New York and Denver, Colorado.

MEMBERS OF FIRM

John E. Stout
Susan Bruch Moorehead

ASSOCIATE

Gabriel J. Villegas

OF COUNSEL

William L. Blum

For full biographical listings, see the Martindale-Hubbell Law Directory

CANADA
NEW BRUNSWICK

*MONCTON,** Westmorland Co.

McINNES COOPER (AV)

Barristers, Solicitors & Trade Mark Agents
Place Moncton Place, 655 Main Street, P.O. Box 1368, E1C 8T6
Telephone: 506-857-8970
Fax: 506-857-4095
Email: mcrmctn@mcrlaw.com *URL:* http://www.mcrlaw.com
Halifax, Nova Scotia Office: Summit Place, 1601 Lower Water Street, P.O. Box 730, B3J 2V1.
Telephone: 902-425-6500.
Fax: 902-425-6350. Email: mcrhfx@mcrlaw.com.

(See Next Column)

McInnes Cooper—*Continued*

St. John's, Newfoundland Office: Baine Johnston Centre, 5th Floor, 10 Fort William Place, P.O. Box 5939, A1C 5X4.
Telephone: 709-722-8735.
Telecopier: 709-722-1763. Email: mcrsj@mcrlaw.com.
Charlottetown, Prince Edward Island Office: BDC Place, Suite 620, 119 Kent Street, C1A 1N3.
Telephone: 902-368-8473.
Fax: 902-368-8346. Email: mcrpei@mcrlaw.com.
Fredericton, New Brunswick Office: Suite 600, 570 Queen Street, P.O. Box 610.
Telephone: 506-458-8572.
Fax: 506-458-9903. Email: mcrfton@mcrlaw.com.

ASSOCIATE

Christa A. Bourque

For Complete List of Firm Personnel, See General Section

For full biographical listings, see the Martindale-Hubbell Law Directory

CANADA
NEWFOUNDLAND

*ST. JOHN'S,**

McInnes Cooper (AV)

Barristers, Solicitors & Trade Mark Agents
Baine Johnston Centre, 5th Floor, 10 Fort William Place, P.O. Box 5939, A1C 5X4
Telephone: 709-722-8735
Telecopier: 709-722-1763
Email: mcrsj@mcrlaw.com *URL:* http://www.mcrlaw.com
Halifax, Nova Scotia Office: Summit Place, 1601 Lower Water Street, P.O. Box 730, B3J 2V1.
Telephone: 902-425-6500.
Fax: 902-425-6350. Email: mcrhfx@mcrlaw.com.
Moncton, New Brunswick Office: Place Moncton Place, 655 Main Street, P.O. Box 1368, E1C 8T6.
Telephone: 506-857-8970.
Fax: 506-857-4095. Email: mcrmctn@mcrlaw.com.
Charlottetown, Prince Edward Island Office: BDC Place, Suite 620, 119 Kent Street, C1A 1N3.
Telephone: 902-368-8473.
Fax: 902-368-8346. Email: mcrpei@mcrlaw.com.
Fredericton, New Brunswick Office: Suite 600, 570 Queen Street, P.O. Box 610.
Telephone: 506-458-8572.
Fax: 506-458-9903. Email: mcrfton@mcrlaw.com.

ASSOCIATES

D. Scott Worsfold
Jennifer Dawn Blackmore

For Complete List of Firm Personnel, See General Section

For full biographical listings, see the Martindale-Hubbell Law Directory

CANADA
NOVA SCOTIA

*HALIFAX,** Regional Munic. of Halifax

McInnes Cooper (AV)

Barristers, Solicitors & Trade Mark Agents
Summit Place, 1601 Lower Water Street, P.O. Box 730, B3J 2V1
Telephone: 902-425-6500
Fax: 902-425-6350
Email: mcrhfx@mcrlaw.com *URL:* http://www.mcrlaw.com
St. John's, Newfoundland Office: Baine Johnston Centre, 5th Floor, 10 Fort William Place, P.O. Box 5939, A1C 5X4.
Telephone: 709-722-8735.
Telecopier: 709-722-1763. Email: mcrsj@mcrlaw.com.
Moncton, New Brunswick Office: Place Moncton Place, 655 Main Street, P.O. Box 1368, E1C 8T6.
Telephone: 506-857-8970.
Fax: 506-857-4095. Email: mcrmctn@mcrlaw.com.
Charlottetown, Prince Edward Island Office: BDC Place, Suite 620, 119 Kent Street, C1A 1N3.
Telephone: 902-368-8473.
Fax: 902-368-8346. Email: mcrpei@mcrlaw.com.
Fredericton, New Brunswick Office: Suite 600, 570 Queen Street, P.O. Box 610.
Telephone: 506-458-8572.
Fax: 506-458-9903. Email: mcrfton@mcrlaw.com.

PARTNER

Eric Durnford, Q.C.

ASSOCIATE

Janet Clark

For Complete List of Firm Personnel, See General Section

For full biographical listings, see the Martindale-Hubbell Law Directory

CIVIL TRIAL PRACTICE

MINNESOTA

*DULUTH,** St. Louis Co.

HANFT, FRIDE, O'BRIEN, HARRIES, SWELBAR & BURNS, P.A. (AV)

1000 U.S. Bank Place, 130 West Superior Street, 55802-2094
Telephone: 218-722-4766
Fax: 218-529-2401
Email: firm@hanftlaw.com

John D. Kelly
John R. Baumgarth
Tim A. Strom
R. Thomas Torgerson
Cheryl M. Prince
Robin C. Merritt
Kathleen S. Bray

OF COUNSEL

Gaylord W. Swelbar

Counsel for: Canadian National Railways; Great American Insurance Cos.; Minnesota Power; Northern Minnesota Utilities; Oglebay Norton Co.; United States Fidelity & Guaranty Co.; U.S. Insurance Group; American International Adjustment Companies; Duluth Transit Authority; LTV Corporation.

For Complete List of Firm Personnel, See General Section

For full biographical listings, see the Martindale-Hubbell Law Directory

MAGIE, ANDRESEN, HAAG, PACIOTTI, BUTTERWORTH & McCARTHY, P.A. (AV)

1000 Alworth Building, P.O. Box 745, 55801
Telephone: 218-722-1411
Telecopier: 218-720-6817
Email: lawduluth@aol.com

Robert H. Magie, III
Michael W. Haag
James P. Paciotti
Brian R. McCarthy
Robert C. Barnes
Steven J. Sheridan

Representative Clients: State Farm Insurance Companies; USX Corporation; Allstate Insurance Company; Cleveland-Cliffs Mining Company; Western National Insurance Company; North Country Equipment; Lakehead Pipe Line, Inc.; Inland Steel Company; AMSOIL, Inc.; Great Lakes Gas Transmission Company.

For Complete List of Firm Personnel, See General Section

For full biographical listings, see the Martindale-Hubbell Law Directory

*GRAND RAPIDS,** Itasca Co.

LANO, NELSON, O'TOOLE & BENGTSON, LTD. (AV)

515 NE 2nd Avenue, 55744
Telephone: 218-326-9603
Fax: 218-326-1565
Email: info@lanolaw.com

Neal Lano
Leif Nelson
Dennis O'Toole
Brian Bengtson

Representative Clients: State Farm Mutual Automobile Insurance Co.; Allstate Insurance Co.; Independent School District No. 316; City of Grand Rapids; Pettibone Corporation; Grand Rapids State Bank; Sandstrom's, Inc.

For full biographical listings, see the Martindale-Hubbell Law Directory

*HALLOCK,** Kittson Co.

BRINK, SOBOLIK, SEVERSON, MALM & ALBRECHT, P.A. (AV)

217 South Birch Avenue, P.O. Box 790, 56728
Telephone: 218-843-3686
FAX: 218-843-2724
Email: brink@rural-access.com

Lyman A. Brink (1909-1972)
Dennis M. Sobolik
Robert K. Severson
Roger C. Malm
Robert M. Albrecht
Blake S. Sobolik
Jeffrey W. Hane

Representative Clients: Northwestern State Bank, Hallock, Minn.; Prime Security Bank, Karlstad, Minn.; Argyle State Bank, Argyle, Minn.; City of Hallock; American Federal Savings & Loan Assn.; State Farm Insurance Co.; Minnesota Rice Growers, Inc.

For full biographical listings, see the Martindale-Hubbell Law Directory

*HASTINGS,** Dakota Co.

SIEBEN, POLK, LAVERDIERE, JONES & HAWN, A PROFESSIONAL ASSOCIATION (AV)

999 Westview Drive, 55033
Telephone: 651-437-3148
Fax: 651-437-2732
St. Paul, Minnesota Office: Galtier Plaza, Suite 550, Box 45, 175 Fifth Street East.
Telephone: 651-222-4146.
Fax: 651-223-8279.

Michael R. Sieben
Michael S. Polk
Harvey N. Jones
Richard A. LaVerdiere
Steven D. Hawn (Resident, St. Paul Office)

Thomas R. Longfellow (Resident, St. Paul Office)
Bernie M. Dusich
Michael R. Strom
John P. Sieben
Scott J. Hertogs
Brian T. Mak (Resident, St. Paul Office)
Lynn A. O'Leary

For full biographical listings, see the Martindale-Hubbell Law Directory

*MANKATO,** Blue Earth Co.

FARRISH, JOHNSON & MASCHKA, P.L.L.P. (AV)

Union Square Business Center, 201 North Broad Street, P.O. Box 550, 56002-0550
Telephone: 507-387-3002
Telecopier: 507-625-4002
Mailing Address: P.O. Box 550, 56002-0550
Email: farrish@mctcnet.net *URL:* http://www.fjm-law.com

MEMBERS OF FIRM

Gerald L. Maschka
John M. Riedy
Scott V. Kelly
William S. Partridge
Kenneth R. White
Mary Anne Wray

ASSOCIATES

Paul J. Simonett
Renee C. Rubish

OF COUNSEL

Robert G. Johnson

Representative Clients: Travelers Insurance Co.; CNA Insurance Co.; Hartford Accident and Indemnity Co.; St. Paul Insurance Cos.; Employers Mutual Companies; State Farm Co.; Federated Insurance Co.; Fireman's Fund Insurance Co.; Maryland Casualty Co.; American Family Insurance Group.

For Complete List of Firm Personnel, See General Section

For full biographical listings, see the Martindale-Hubbell Law Directory

GISLASON & HUNTER LLP (AV)

424 North Riverfront Drive, Suite 250, 56002-4157
Telephone: 507-387-1115
Facsimile: 507-387-4413
Email: mail@gislason.com *URL:* http://www.gislason.com
New Ulm, Minnesota Office: 2700 South Broadway, P.O. Box 458.
Telephone: 507-354-3111.
Facsimile: 507-354-8447.
Minneapolis, Minnesota Office: Opus Center, Suite 215E, 9900 Bren Road East, P.O. Box 5297.
Telephone: 612-933-9900.
Facsimile: 612-933-0242.

MEMBERS OF FIRM

James H. Malecki
Andrew A. Willaert
Steven J. Vatndal
Christopher E. Sandquist

Counsel for: Associated Milk Producers, Inc.
Representative Clients: St. Paul Companies; Farmers Insurance Group; Auto-Owners Insurance Co.; AgriBank, FCB and Farm Credit Services; Wirtz Corporation; Wal-Mart Stores, Inc.; Midwest Medical Insurance Co.; The Travelers Indemnity Co.; Minnesota Lawyers Mutual Insurance Co.

For full biographical listings, see the Martindale-Hubbell Law Directory

*MINNEAPOLIS,** Hennepin Co.

ABDO AND ABDO, P.A. (AV)

710 Northstar West 625 Marquette Avenue, 55402
Telephone: 612-333-1526
Fax: 612-342-2608
Email: abdoabdo@aol.com *URL:* http://www.abdo.com.br

E. John Abdo (1912-1993)
Robert P. Abdo
Steven R. Hedges
Keith J. Broady
Kenneth J. Abdo
Timothy C. Matson

Representative Client: ADT Security Services, Inc.

For Complete List of Firm Personnel, See General Section

For full biographical listings, see the Martindale-Hubbell Law Directory

Minneapolis—Continued

ABRAMS & SMITH, A PROFESSIONAL ASSOCIATION (AV)

700 Northstar West, 55402
Telephone: 612-332-4273; 800-659-2679
Fax: 612-342-2107
Email: abrams@pclink.com

Harold J. Carroll (1901-1978)
Frank X. Cronan (1912-1975)
Jerome B. Abrams
Paul R. Smith
Lauris Heyerdahl
Bradford J. Roegge

Representative Clients: Hawkeye Security Insurance Co.; CNA Insurance; Employer's Mutual Insurance Co.

For full biographical listings, see the Martindale-Hubbell Law Directory

ARNOLD, ANDERSON & DOVE, P.L.L.P. (AV)

5881 Cedar Lake Road, 55416-1492
Telephone: 612-545-9000
Wats Line: 800-343-4545
Fax: 612-545-1793; 612-542-9210
Email: aad@aadlaw.com
Princeton, Minnesota Office: 501 South Fourth Street.
Telephone: 612-389-2214.
Hutchinson, Minnesota Office: 101 Park Place.
Telephone: 320-587-7575.
Red Wing, Minnesota Office: 481 Fridell Crescent, 55066.
Telephone: 651-388-3454.

MEMBERS OF FIRM

David B. Arnold
Laura K. Fretland

ASSOCIATES

Richard G. McGee
James Utley

For Complete List of Firm Personnel, See General Section

For full biographical listings, see the Martindale-Hubbell Law Directory

BASSFORD, LOCKHART, TRUESDELL & BRIGGS, P.A. (AV)

(Formerly Richards, Montgomery, Cobb & Bassford, P.A.)
3550 Multifoods Tower, 55402-3787
Telephone: 612-333-3000
Telecopier: 612-333-8829

Greer E. Lockhart
Frederick E. Finch
John M. Degnan
Lewis A. Remele, Jr.
Kevin P. Keenan
James O. Redman
Rebecca Egge Moos
John M. Anderson
Charles E. Lundberg
Gregory P. Bulinski
Dale M. Wagner
Louis J. Speltz
Laura J. McKnight
Mark P. Hodkinson
Thomas J. Niemiec
Andrew L. Marshall
Michael A. Klutho
Gregory W. Deckert
Kevin P. Hickey
Stanford P. Hill
Mark R. Whitmore
Fred B. Snyder (1859-1951)
Edward C. Gale (1862-1943)
Frank A. Janes (1908-1959)
Nathan A. Cobb, Sr. (1905-1976)
Bergmann Richards (1888-1978)
Edmund T. Montgomery (1904-1987)
Charles A. Bassford (1914-1990)
Jerome C. Briggs (Retired)
Lynn G. Truesdell (Retired)

Dani M. Shimon
Christopher R. Morris
Kelly A. Putney
Jennifer L. Hill
Robin Ann Williams
Michael A. Switzer
Shalanda Denise Ballard

Representative Clients: American States Insurance Co.; Austin Mutual Insurance Co.; Midwest Family Mutual Insurance Co.; Minnesota Lawyers Mutual; National Unim Fire Insurance Company; St. Paul Insurance Cos.; The Travelers Insurance Co.; United States Fidelity & Guaranty Co.; Wausau Insurance.

For full biographical listings, see the Martindale-Hubbell Law Directory

BOWMAN AND BROOKE (AV)

Suite 2600 Fifth Street Towers, 150 South Fifth Street, 55402
Telephone: 612-339-8682
Fax: 612-672-3200
Phoenix, Arizona Office: Phoenix Plaza, Suite 1700, 2929 North Central Avenue.
Telephone: 602-248-0899.
Fax: 602-248-0947.
Detroit, Michigan Office: 1800 Fisher Building, 3011 West Grand Boulevard.
Telephone: 313-871-3000.
Fax: 313-871-3006.
San Jose, California Office: Suite 1150, 160 West Santa Clara Street.
Telephone: 408-279-5393.
Fax: 408-279-5845.
Torrance, California Office: Suite 1000, 19191 South Vermont Avenue.
Telephone: 310-768-3068.
Fax: 310-719-1019.

(See Next Column)

Richmond, Virginia Office: 901 East Byrd Street, Suite 1500.
Telephone: 804-649-8200.
Fax: 804-649-1762.

MEMBERS OF FIRM

Richard A. Bowman
David R. Kelly
David W. Graves, Jr.
George W. Soule
Wayne D. Struble
Thomas B. Heffelfinger
Kenneth Ross
James W. Halbrooks, Jr.
Timothy J. Mattson
Kim M. Schmid
Richard G. Morgan
Daniel C. Adams
David N. Lutz

ASSOCIATES

John D. Sear
Steven L. Reitenour
Bard D. Borkon
C. Paul Carver
Robert M. Lewis
Arlene D. Anderson
Lizzu C. Nasiedlak
Christine Nicole Lindblad
Todd E. Gadtke
Marlene A. Yoder

For full biographical listings, see the Martindale-Hubbell Law Directory

COX, GOUDY, MCNULTY & WALLACE, P.L.L.P. (AV)

100 North Sixth Street, #676A, 55403
Telephone: 612-338-1414
Fax: 612-338-6754
Email: mcwall@bitstream.net
St. Paul Office: 1300 Minnesota Building, 46 East 4th Street.
Telephone: 651-293-9194.

MEMBERS OF FIRM

Charles A. Cox
Craig A. Goudy
Marcy S. Wallace
Charles A. Cox, III

OF COUNSEL

John C. McNulty

For full biographical listings, see the Martindale-Hubbell Law Directory

CULLEN LAW FIRM, LTD. (AV)

1560 International Centre, 900 Second Avenue South, 55402-3383
Telephone: 612-339-4295
Fax: 612-339-3161

James P. Cullen

For full biographical listings, see the Martindale-Hubbell Law Directory

FETTERLY & GORDON, P.A. (AV)

1800 U.S. Bank Place, 650 Third Avenue South, 55402
Telephone: 612-288-2501
800-288-2501
Fax: 612-288-2551
Email: mail@Fetterly.com *URL:* http://www.fetterly.com

James L. Fetterly
Gary J. Gordon
Keith A. Hanson

Stephen G. Lickteig
Diane B. Bratvold
Timothy J. Fetterly
Thomas J. Basting, Jr.
Katherine A. Killen Hall
Christopher J. Sorenson
Stephen M. Warner

Reference: National City Bank.

For full biographical listings, see the Martindale-Hubbell Law Directory

FLYNN & GASKINS, L.L.P. (AV)

29th Floor, Metropolitan Centre, 333 South Seventh Street, 55402
Telephone: 612-333-9500
Fax: 612-333-9579
Email: mail@flynngaskins.com *URL:* http://www.flynngaskins.com

MEMBERS OF FIRM

George W. Flynn
Steve Gaskins
Jeannine L. Lee
Barbara Jean D'Aquila
Thomas Klosowski
Randall J. Pattee
Bradley J. Ayers
Hal A. Shillingstad
David A. Wikoff

ASSOCIATES

Scott M. Rusert
Jennifer F. Rosemark
Karen Reierson
Patrick R. Martin
John J. Laravuso
Gregory J. Wiley
Stephanie D. Sarantopoulos
Cory A. Kallheim
Craig D. Sandok (Not admitted in MN)

For full biographical listings, see the Martindale-Hubbell Law Directory

GARTNER, BENNETT & SCHUPP, P.C. (AV)

One Financial Plaza, Suite 2200, 120 South Sixth Street, 55402-1824
Telephone: 612 333-3839
Telecopier: 612-333-3129

(See Next Column)

GARTNER, BENNETT & SCHUPP P.C.—*Continued*

Ludwig B. Gartner, Jr.
Robert Bennett
Timothy R. Schupp
William J. Tipping
Heidi A. Schneider
Eric William Hageman

Matthew McBride

For full biographical listings, see the Martindale-Hubbell Law Directory

GISLASON & HUNTER LLP (AV)

Opus Center, Suite 215E, 9900 Bren Road East, P.O. Box 5297, 55343-2297
Telephone: 612-933-9900
Facsimile: 612-933-0242
Email: mail@gislason.com *URL:* http://www.gislason.com
New Ulm, Minnesota Office: 2700 South Broadway, P.O. Box 458.
Telephone: 507-354-3111.
Facsimile: 507-354-8447.
Mankato, Minnesota Office: 424 North Riverfront Drive, Suite 250.
Telephone: 507-387-1115.
Facsimile: 507-387-4413.

MEMBERS OF FIRM

Donald F. Hunter
David D. Alsop
Barry G. Vermeer
Timothy P. Tobin
Roger H. Gross
R. Stephen Tillitt
Wade R. Wacholz
Laura L. Myslis
Daniel A. Beckman
Elliot L. Olsen
Gregory A. Wohletz
Cheryl J. Dalby

Counsel for: Associated Milk Producers, Inc.
Representative Clients: St. Paul Companies; Farmers Insurance Group; Auto-Owners Insurance Co.; AgriBank, FCB and Farm Credit Services; Wirtz Corporation; Wal-Mart Stores, Inc.; Midwest Medical Insurance Co.; The Travelers Indemnity Co.; Minnesota Lawyers Mutual Insurance Co.

For full biographical listings, see the Martindale-Hubbell Law Directory

HAGERTY, JOHNSON, ALBRIGHTSON & BEITZ, P.A. (AV)

Suite 901, 701 Fourth Avenue South, 55415
Telephone: 612-349-9000
Telecopier: 612-332-3751
Email: hjab@hjab.com

James A. Beitz

Michael C. Hagerty

Representative Clients: Augustana Care Foundation; Data-Metalcraft,Inc.; Distribution Alternatives, Inc.; Fidelity National Title Insurance Company of New York; Independent Fire Protection, Inc.; PaR Systems Corportion; Universal Hospital Services, Inc.; Nott Co.; Zinpro Corp.
Reference: Norwest Bank of Minnesota, N.A.

For full biographical listings, see the Martindale-Hubbell Law Directory

HANSON MAREK BOLKCOM & GREENE, LTD. (AV)

2200 Rand Tower, 527 Marquette Avenue, 55402
Telephone: 612-342-2880
Fax: 612-342-2899
Email: info@hmbglaw.com *URL:* http://www.hmbglaw.com

Kent B. Hanson
Lezlie Ott Marek
Mary E. Bolkcom
Mickey W. Greene

For full biographical listings, see the Martindale-Hubbell Law Directory

HUNEGS, STONE, KOENIG, LENEAVE & KVAS, P.A. (AV)

1650 International Center Building, 900 Second Avenue South, 55402
Telephone: 612-339-4511; 800-328-4340
Fax: 612-339-5150
URL: http://hunegslaw.com

William H. DeParcq (1905-1988)
Richard Gene Hunegs
Robert N. Stone
Ralph E. Koenig
Randal W. LeNeave
Cortney S. LeNeave
William Kvas
Richard L. Carlson
Steven M. Hunegs
Kermit N. Fruechte

Reference: National City Bank of Minneapolis.

For full biographical listings, see the Martindale-Hubbell Law Directory

LOMMEN, NELSON, COLE & STAGEBERG, P.A. (AV)

1800 IDS Center, 80 South 8th Street, 55402
Telephone: 612-339-8131
Fax: 612-339-8064
Email: postmaster@email.lommen.com *URL:* http://www.lommen.com
Hudson, Wisconsin Office: Grandview Professional Building, 400 South Second Street, Suite 210.
Telephones: 715-386-8217 and 612-436-8085.

(See Next Column)

W. Wyman Smith (1914-1994)
Henry H. Feikema (1926-1996)
V. Owen Nelson (1928-1998)
John P. Lommen (1927-1988)
Michael P. Shroyer (1953-1993)
Leonard T. Juster
Alvin S. Malmon
Ronald L. Haskvitz
Phillip A. Cole
Roger V. Stageberg
Glenn R. Kessel
Thomas R. Jacobson (Resident, Hudson, Wisconsin Office)
John M. Giblin
John R. McBride
J. Christopher Cuneo
Thomas F. Dougherty
Stacey A. DeKalb
Kay N. Hunt
Richard L. Plagens
Ehrich L. Koch
Margie R. Bodas
James M. Lockhart
Stephen C. Rathke
James C. Searls
Paul L. Dinger
Sherri D. Ulland
Reid R. Lindquist
James R. Johnson (Resident, Hudson, Wisconsin Office)
Marc A. Johannsen
Barry A. O'Neil

Scott M. Nelson
Scott N. Ross
Mary I. King
David M. Hudson
Sheila A. Bjorklund
David S. Ezrilov
Susan Hayes Stephan
Geraint D. Powell
Brent R. Johnson (Resident, Hudson, Wisconsin Office)
Laura L. Enga
Christopher R. Grote

OF COUNSEL

Thomas F. Miller

Representative Clients: Midwest Medical Insurance Company; Associated Bureaus, Inc.; Minnesota Lawyers Mutual Insurance Company.

For full biographical listings, see the Martindale-Hubbell Law Directory

MAHONEY, DOUGHERTY AND MAHONEY, P.A. PROFESSIONAL ASSOCIATION (AV)

801 Park Avenue, 55404-1189
Telephone: 612-339-5863; 888-339-5863
Fax: 612-339-1529
Email: mail@mahoney-law.com *URL:* http://www.lawinfo.com/law/mn/mahoney

Richard P. Mahoney
John (Jack) M. Miller
James M. Mahoney
Randee S. Held
Mark J. Manderfeld
Patrick E. Mahoney
James M. Lehman
Gregory A. Zinn
Kelley R. Lorix
Victor E. Lund
Paul E. D. Darsow

Representative Insurance Clients: CGU; Great American Insurance Co.; Guidant Insurance Group (Formerly Preferred Risk Group); John Deere Insurance Co.; Milwaukee Insurance Co.; National Farmers Union Insurance Cos.; Park Glen National Insurance Co.; Preferred Risk Group; Scottsdale Insurance Co.; Wausau Insurance Co.

For full biographical listings, see the Martindale-Hubbell Law Directory

MANSFIELD TANICK & COHEN, P.A. (AV)

1560 International Centre, 900 Second Avenue South, 55402
Telephone: 612-339-4295
Fax: 612-339-3161
Email: tanick@mansfieldtanick.com *URL:* http://www.mansfieldtanick.com

Seymour J. Mansfield
Marshall H. Tanick
Earl H. Cohen
Robert A. Johnson
Teresa J. Ayling
Richard J. Fuller

Phillip J. Trobaugh
Debra S. Lepert
Ann M. Zewiske
V. John Ella

OF COUNSEL

James P. Cullen
Sholly A. Blustin

For full biographical listings, see the Martindale-Hubbell Law Directory

MESHBESHER & SPENCE (AV)

1616 Park Avenue, 55404
Telephone: 612-339-9121
Fax: 612-339-9188
URL: http://www.meshbesher.com
Woodbury, Minnesota Office: 8360 City Centre Drive, 55125.
Telephone: 651-578-8055.
St. Cloud, Minnesota Office: 510 Zapp Bank Plaza, 56301.
Telephone: 320-656-0484.
Rochester, Minnesota Office: 21 SW 2nd Street, 55902.
Telephone: 507-280-8090.
Maplewood, Minnesota Office: 2603 White Bear Avenue, 55109.
Telephone: 651-777-5858.
St. Louis Park, Minnesota Office: 9950 Wayzata Boulevard, 55426.
Telephone: 612-544-5959.

(See Next Column)

MESHBESHER & SPENCE, *Minneapolis—Continued*

MEMBERS OF FIRM

Kenneth Meshbesher
Ronald I. Meshbesher
Russell M. Spence (Resident, Woodbury Office)
John P. Clifford
Dennis R. Johnson
Patrick K. Horan
Michael C. Snyder
John P. Sheehy
Mark D. Streed
Randall Spence
Katherine S. Flom
Jeffrey P. Oistad (Resident, St. Cloud Office)
Anthony J. Nemo
Colleen M. Christianson
Russell Spence, Jr.
Paul Dahlberg (Resident, Rochester Office)
Konstandinos Nicklow

For full biographical listings, see the Martindale-Hubbell Law Directory

SIEGEL, BRILL, GREUPNER, DUFFY & FOSTER, P.A. (AV)

1300 Washington Square, 100 Washington Avenue South, 55401
Telephone: 612-339-7131
Telecopier: 612-339-6591

Gerald S. Duffy
Wood R. Foster, Jr.
Thomas H. Goodman
Wm. Christopher Penwell
Anthony J. Gleekel
Jordan M. Lewis

James A. Yarosh
Steven Weintraut

Representative Clients: Ron-Vik, Inc.; Super America Stations, Inc.; Ashland Oil, Inc.; Applied Spectrum Technology, Inc.; Richard Manufacturing Co.; Mann Theaters; Homecraft Builders, Inc.; New Mech Companies, Inc.; AVR, Inc.; The McNeilus Companies.

For Complete List of Firm Personnel, See General Section

For full biographical listings, see the Martindale-Hubbell Law Directory

WALDECK & LIND, P.A. (AV)

Suite 730, TCF Tower, 121 South Eighth Street, 55402
Telephone: 612-375-1550
Facsimilie: 612-375-0647

Timothy W. Waldeck
Peter E. Lind

Steven D. Pattee

For full biographical listings, see the Martindale-Hubbell Law Directory

ZELLE, HOFMANN, VOELBEL & GETTE, LLP (AV)

33 South Sixth Street, City Center, Suite 4400, 55402
Telephone: 612-339-2020
Telecopier: 612-336-9100
Waltham, Massachusetts Office: 3 University Office Park, 95 Sawyer Road, Suite 500.
Telephone: 781-891-7020.
Dallas, Texas Office: Zelle, Hofmann, Voelbel & Gette, L.L.P., 1201 Main Street, Suite 3000.
Telephone: 214-742-3000.
San Francisco, California Office: 500 Sansome Street, Suite 400.
Telephone: 415-693-0700.
Los Angeles, California Office: 11601 Wilshire Boulevard, Sixth Floor.
Telephone: 310-478-7877.

MEMBERS OF FIRM

Steven J. Badger (Resident, Dallas, Texas Office)
Eric Berg (Resident, Los Angeles, California Office)
Michelle R. Bernard Bitter (Resident, San Francisco, California Office)
Kerry K. Brown (Resident, Dallas, Texas Office)
Michael R. Cashman
Thomas B. Caswell, III
Christopher J. Clifford (Resident, San Francisco, California Office)
Catherine M. Colinvaux (Resident, Waltham, Massachusetts Office)
Thomas M. Darden
Michelle Kathleen Enright
Mark J. Feinberg
H. Jerome Gette (Resident, Dallas, Texas Office)
Rolf E. Gilbertson
Paul L. Gingras
John C. Goodnow
Richard M. Hagstrom
Lawrence T. Hofmann
Ronald S. Kravitz (Resident, San Francisco, California Office)
David S. Markun (Resident, Los Angeles, California Office)
John Buck Massopust
William Gerald McElroy, Jr. (Resident, Waltham, Massachusetts Office)
Terrence C. McRea (Resident, Dallas, Texas Office)
Steven D. Meier (Resident, San Francisco, California Office)
Devera L. Petak (Resident, Los Angeles, California Office)
James S. Reece
Timothy W. Regan
Jeff Ross
Patricia St. Peter
Karl S. Vasiloff (Resident, Waltham, Massachusetts Office)
Richard L. Voelbel
Stephen A. Watson (Resident, Los Angeles, California Office)
Robert M. Wattson
Edward S. Zusman (Resident, San Francisco, California Office)

(See Next Column)

OF COUNSEL

Lawrence Zelle

ASSOCIATES

Brad E. Brewer (Resident, Dallas, Texas Office)
Desiree Brutocao (Resident, Los Angeles, California Office)
David M. Cogliano (Resident, Waltham, Massachusetts Office)
Jeffrey K. Compton (Resident, Los Angeles, California Office)
Thomas H. Cook, Jr. (Resident, Dallas, Texas Office)
Paula R. Domanski (Resident, Waltham, Massachusetts Office)
René I. Gamboa, IV (Resident, San Francisco, California Office)
Shenne J. Hahn (Resident, Los Angeles, California Office)
Lowell H. Haky (Resident, San Francisco, California Office)
Ingrid Hallett
Craig M. Hughes (Resident, San Francisco, California Office)
Dennis J. Kelly (Resident, San Francisco, California Office)
Jonathan H. Koenig (Resident, Waltham, Massachusetts Office)
Aaron B. Latto
Jonathan F. Mack
Dawn Midkiff (Not admitted in MN)
Daniel J. Millea
Jonathan D. Mutch (Resident, Waltham, Massachusetts Office)
Sarah A. Olivier (Resident, Waltham, Massachusetts Office)
M. Anthony Parsons II (Resident, Dallas, Texas Office)
Adam Pollack (Resident, Los Angeles, California Office)
Kendra L. Rubbright (Not admitted in MN)
Jennifer L. Shea
Eugene Sheih
Lee H. Shidlofsky (Resident, Dallas, Texas Office)
Marc J. Shrake
Chad A. Snyder
Richard G. Urquhart (Resident, Dallas, Texas Office)
Daniel S. Weiss
Tricia M. Whitehill

For full biographical listings, see the Martindale-Hubbell Law Directory

*MOORHEAD,** Clay Co.

GUNHUS, GRINNELL, KLINGER, SWENSON & GUY, LTD. (AV)

215 North 30th Street, P.O. Box 1077, 56561-1077
Telephone: 218-236-6462
Telecopier: 218-236-9873
Email: GUNHUSLAW@LINKUP.NET *URL:* http://www.fm-law.com
Fargo, North Dakota Office: 514 Gate City Building, P.O. Box 2783.
Telephone: 701-235-2506.
Telecopier: 701-235-9862.

ATTORNEYS

Gunder Gunhus (1928-1997)
Paul E. Grinnell
Edward F. Klinger
Robert H. Swenson
William L. Guy, III
Craig R. Campbell
Bernard E. Reynolds
Eric K. Fosaaen
Gregory P. Hammes
Steven E. Noack
Michelle Caduff Winkis
Susan E. Johnson-Drenth
Deenelle Ruud Stephenson

Insurance Clients: Aetna Life and Casualty Co.; Crum & Forster; Home Insurance Co.; Sentry Insurance Company; St. Paul Cos.; United States Fidelity and Guaranty Co.
Representative Clients: Certainteed Corp.; Farm Credit Services; Dakota Heartland Health System; U.S. West Communications.

For full biographical listings, see the Martindale-Hubbell Law Directory

JEFFRIES, OLSON, FLOM & BULLIS, P.A. (AV)

403 Center Avenue, P.O. Box 9, 56561-0009
Telephone: 218-233-3222
Fax: 218-233-7065
Fargo, North Dakota Office: 1325 23rd Street SW, 58103.
Telephone: 701-280-2300.
Fax: 701-280-1880.

Richard N. Jeffries
Thomas R. Olson
Joel A. Flom
James R. Bullis
Ronald J. Knoll
Michael S. Montgomery
Michelle M. Donarski

John T. Goff

Representative Clients: American International Adjustment Co.; American States/Western Insurance Co.; Farmers Insurance Group; Federated Mutual Insurance Co.; Hartford Insurance Co.; Midwest Medical Insurance Co.; Nodak Mutual Insurance Co.; St. Paul Fire & Marine Insurance Co.

For full biographical listings, see the Martindale-Hubbell Law Directory

*NEW ULM,** Brown Co.

GISLASON & HUNTER LLP (AV)

2700 South Broadway, P.O. Box 458, 56073-0458
Telephone: 507-354-3111
Facsimile: 507-354-8447
Email: mail@gislason.com *URL:* http://www.gislason.com
Minneapolis, Minnesota Office: Opus Center, Suite 215E, 9900 Bren Road East, P.O. Box 5297.
Telephone: 612-933-9900.
Facsimile: 612-933-0242.
Mankato, Minnesota Office: 424 North Riverfront Drive, Suite 250.
Telephone: 507-387-1115.
Facsimile: 507-387-4413.

MEMBERS OF FIRM

Sidney P. Gislason (1908-1985)
C. Allen Dosland
Daniel A. Gislason
C. Thomas Wilson
Ruth Ann Webster
Gary W. Koch
William A. Moeller
Kurt D. Johnson
David W. Sturges (Not admitted in MN)
Mark S. Ullery
Jeffry C. Braegelmann
Reed H. Glawe
Noel L. Phifer
Michael S. Dove
Dustan J. Cross
Richard F. Prim

Counsel for: Associated Milk Producers, Inc.
Representative Clients: St. Paul Companies; Farmers Insurance Group; Auto-Owners Insurance Co.; AgriBank, FCB and Farm Credit Services; Wirtz Corporation; Wal-Mart Stores, Inc.; Midwest Medical Insurance Co.; The Travelers Indemnity Co.; Minnesota Lawyers Mutual Insurance Co.

For Complete List of Firm Personnel, See General Section

For full biographical listings, see the Martindale-Hubbell Law Directory

*ROCHESTER,** Olmsted Co.

O'BRIEN, EHRICK, WOLF, DEANER & MAUS, L.L.P. (AV)

206 South Broadway, Suite 611, P.O. Box 968, 55903-0968
Telephone: 507-289-4041
Fax: 507-281-4778

MEMBERS OF FIRM

Thomas Wolf
Terence L. Maus
Joseph F. Chase

Representative Clients: City of Rochester; County of Olmsted; Mayo Clinic; U.S. Bank National Association; CNA Insurance.

For Complete List of Firm Personnel, See General Section

For full biographical listings, see the Martindale-Hubbell Law Directory

*ST. CLOUD,** Stearns Co.

HUGHES, MATHEWS & DIDIER, P.A. (AV)

110 Sixth Avenue South, Suite 205, P.O. Box 548, 56302-0548
Telephone: 320-251-4399
Fax: 320-251-5781

Kevin J. Hughes
Paul R. Harris

Kevin M. O'Driscoll

Representative Clients: The St. Cloud Hospital; CentraCare Health System; St. John's University; College of St. Benedict; Tanner Systems, Inc.; Anderson Trucking Service, Inc.; DeZurik, a unit of General Signal; Stearns Bank, N.A.

For full biographical listings, see the Martindale-Hubbell Law Directory

*ST. PAUL,** Ramsey Co.

BANNIGAN & KELLY, P.A. (AV)

Suite 1750, North Central Life Tower, 445 Minnesota Street, 55101
Telephone: 651-224-3781
Fax: 651-223-8019

John F. Bannigan, Jr.
Patrick J. Kelly

Song Lo Fawcett
Stephen Kelly
Sia Lo

JAMES F. DUNN & ASSOCIATES, P.A. (AV)

Suite 100, Shepard Park Office Center, 2177 Youngman Avenue, 55116-3042
Telephone: 612-696-9488
Fax: 612-696-9512
Email: dunnlaw@pclink.com

James F. Dunn

Reference: Firstar Bank.

For full biographical listings, see the Martindale-Hubbell Law Directory

GERAGHTY, O'LOUGHLIN & KENNEY, PROFESSIONAL ASSOCIATION (AV)

1400 Ecolab University Center, 386 North Wabasha Street, 55102-1308
Telephone: 651-291-1177
Fax: 651-291-9477
Email: gok@pclink.com

Terence J. O'Loughlin
Robert M. Mahoney
David C. Hutchinson
William H. Leary, III
Mary H. Alcorn
Matthew J. Hanzel
Ann D. Bray
Jean B. Hoppe
Kyle M. Thomas

OF COUNSEL

James H. Geraghty (Retired)
James W. Kenney (Retired)

Representative Clients: St. Paul Cos.; Allina Health System; Fairview Hospital and Healthcare Services; HealthEast; HealthPartners; MMI Cos.; Midwest Medical Insurance Co.; North Memorial Hospital; Aspen Medical Group.

For full biographical listings, see the Martindale-Hubbell Law Directory

*WILLMAR,** Kandiyohi Co.

SCHNEIDER LAW FIRM (AV)

706 South First Street, P.O. Box 776, 56201
Telephone: 320-235-1902
WATS: 800-242-1902
Fax: 320-235-3611
Email: JSJSJamin@aol.com
St. Cloud, Minnesota Office: 925 South First Street, 56302.
Telephone: 320-253-2007.

Ronald H. Schneider (P.A.)

David W. Schneider
Steven C. Wang

Reference: US Bank Willmar.

For full biographical listings, see the Martindale-Hubbell Law Directory

MISSISSIPPI

*ABERDEEN,** Monroe Co.

PATTERSON & PATTERSON (AV)

304 East Jefferson Street, P.O. Box 663, 39730
Telephone: 662-369-2476
Fax: 662-369-9806
Email: JPP@ebicom.net

MEMBERS OF FIRM

Robert D. Patterson
Jan P. Patterson
Peter T. Martin

Local Counsel for: National Bank of Commerce of Mississippi; American Colloid Company; Condea Vista Company; Pruet Production Co.; Arco Oil & Gas Co.; Chemical Corporation; Unimin Corporation; Leggett & Platt.
Approved Title Attorneys for: First American Title Insurance Co.; Mississippi Valley Title Insurance Co.

For full biographical listings, see the Martindale-Hubbell Law Directory

BILOXI, Harrison Co.

DONALD C. DORNAN, JR. (AV)

771 Water Street, P.O. Box 154, 39533-0154
Telephone: 228-374-2013
Fax: 228-374-3019
Email: ddornan@dornlaw.com *URL:* http://www.lawyers.com/dornlaw
Reference: Coast Community Bank.

For full biographical listings, see the Martindale-Hubbell Law Directory

JUDY M. GUICE A PROFESSIONAL ASSOCIATION (AV)

750 Dr. Martin Luther King Jr. Boulevard, P.O. Box 1919, 39533
Telephone: 228-374-9787
Fax: 228-374-9436
Email: judy@judyguice.com *URL:* http://www.judyguice.com

Judy Guice

For full biographical listings, see the Martindale-Hubbell Law Directory

MINOR AND ASSOCIATES (AV)

A Partnership including a Professional Association
160 Main Street, Drawer 1388, 39533-1388
Telephone: 228-374-5151
Fax: 228-374-6630
Email: pminoratty@aol.com

Paul S. Minor (P.A.)

(See Next Column)

MINOR AND ASSOCIATES, *Biloxi—Continued*

Mark D. Lumpkin James R. Reeves, Jr.
Christopher C. VanCleave

For full biographical listings, see the Martindale-Hubbell Law Directory

RUSHING & GUICE (AV)

683 Water Street, P.O. Box 1925, 39533-1925
Telephone: 228-374-2313
Telecopier: 228-374-8155
Email: rushguice@rushing-guice.com *URL:* http://www.rushing-guice.com

MEMBERS OF FIRM

Charles L. Rushing (1881-1923) William L. Guice (1887-1971)
William Lee Guice III

OF COUNSEL

Jacob D. Guice

ASSOCIATES

R. Scott Wells Maria M. Cobb

LEGAL SUPPORT PERSONNEL

Antonia Strong

Representative Clients: Equitable Life and Casualty Insurance Co.; Firestone Tire and Rubber Co.; Harris Corp.; Hartford Insurance; Hyundai Motor Finance Co.; John Hancock Mutual Life; Keesler Federal Credit Union.

For full biographical listings, see the Martindale-Hubbell Law Directory

*BROOKHAVEN,** Lincoln Co.

ALLEN, ALLEN, BOERNER & BREELAND (AV)

214 Justice Street, P.O. Box 751, 39602-0751
Telephone: 601-833-4361
Fax: 601-833-6647
Email: aabblaw@tislink.com

Emmette P. Allen (1915-1999) William D. Boerner
Robert O. Allen Durwood J. Breeland

ASSOCIATE

Sally Burchfield Doty

For full biographical listings, see the Martindale-Hubbell Law Directory

*CLARKSDALE,** Coahoma Co.

HOLCOMB DUNBAR, A PROFESSIONAL ASSOCIATION (AV)

152 Delta Avenue, P.O. Box 368, 38614
Telephone: 601-627-2241
Facsimile: 601-627-9788
Email: mchaffin@clarksdale.com *URL:* http://www.holcombdunbar.com
Oxford, Mississippi Office: 1217 Jackson Avenue, P.O. Drawer 707, 38655.
Telephone: 601-234-8775.
Facsimile: 601-238-7552.
Southaven, Mississippi Office: Suite 1, 728 Goodman Road East, P.O. Box 190, 38671.
Telephone: 601-349-0664.
Facsimile: 601-349-2432.

William M. Chaffin Edward (Ted) P. Connell, Jr.
Michael K. Graves Daniel M. Czamanske, Jr.

Representative Clients: Union Planters Bank, National Association; Deposit Guaranty National Bank; Trustmark National Bank; Mississippi Power & Light Co.; Southern Farm Bureau Casualty Insurance Co.; Bituminous Insurance Co.; State Farm Fire & Casualty Insurance Co.; Fireman's Fund Insurance Cos.; Atlanta Casualty Insurance Cos.; Drexel Chemical Co.

For Complete List of Firm Personnel, See General Section

For full biographical listings, see the Martindale-Hubbell Law Directory

*CLEVELAND,** Bolivar Co.

GRIFFITH & GRIFFITH (AV)

123 South Court Street, Post Office Drawer 1680, 38732
Telephone: 662-843-6100
Telecopier: 662-843-8153
Email: griffith@tecinfo.com *URL:* http://www.vralitigator.com

MEMBERS OF FIRM

L. Ellis Griffith (1926-1987) Benjamin E. Griffith
Daniel J. Griffith

Reference: The Cleveland State Bank.

For full biographical listings, see the Martindale-Hubbell Law Directory

*COLUMBIA,** Marion Co.

AULTMAN, TYNER, RUFFIN & YARBOROUGH, LTD., A PROFESSIONAL LAW CORPORATION (AV)

329 Church Street, P.O. Drawer 707, 39429
Telephone: 601-736-2222
FAX: 601-736-9884
Email: rfyjr@cblink.com
Hattiesburg, Mississippi Office: 315 Hemphill Street, P.O. Drawer 750.
Telephone: 601-583-2671.
FAX: 601-583-2677.
Gulfport, Mississippi Office: 1201 25th Avenue, Suite 300, P.O. Box 607.
Telephone: 228-863-6913.
FAX: 228-868-8505. Email: atmr@digiscape.com.
New Orleans, Louisiana Office: The Texaco Center, 400 Poydras Street, Suite 2250.
Telephone: 504-528-9616.
FAX: 504-528-9640.

Richard F. Yarborough, Jr.

OF COUNSEL

Ernest Ray Duff

Representative Clients: Hercules, Inc.; United States Steel Corp.; Ford Motor Co.; International Paper Co.; Phillips Petroleum Co.; Aetna Casualty & Surety Co.; CNA Group; Liberty Mutual Insurance Co.; St. Paul Fire & Marine Insurance Co.; Fireman's Fund.

For full biographical listings, see the Martindale-Hubbell Law Directory

*COLUMBUS,** Lowndes Co.

J. RANDOLPH LIPSCOMB (AV)

223 Sixth Street North, 39701
Telephone: 601-328-2100
Facsimile: 601-328-1067
Email: randolph@ebicom.net

For full biographical listings, see the Martindale-Hubbell Law Directory

*GREENWOOD,** Leflore Co.

UPSHAW, WILLIAMS, BIGGERS, BECKHAM & RIDDICK, LLP (AV)

309 Fulton Street, 38930
Telephone: 662-455-1613
Facsimile: 662-453-9245
Mailing Address: P.O. Drawer 8230, Greenwood, Mississippi, 38935-8230
Email: lexgwd@uwbbr.com
Jackson, Mississippi Office: Suite 300 Plaza One, 715 South Pear Orchard Road, P.O. Box 9147, 39286-9147.
Telephone: 601-978-1996.
Facsimile: 601-978-1949. Email: lexjax@uwbbr.com.

MEMBERS OF FIRM

James E. Upshaw
Tommie G. Williams
Marc A. Biggers
Glenn F. Beckham
Roger C. Riddick (Resident, Jackson Office)
F. Ewin Henson III
Lonnie D. Bailey
Robert S. Upshaw
Clinton M. Guenther
Richard C. Williams, Jr. (Resident, Jackson Office)
Richard L. Kimmel
Mark C. Carroll (Resident, Jackson Office)
W. Hugh Gillon IV (Resident, Jackson Office)
Paul L. Goodman
Walter C. Morrison IV (Resident, Jackson Office)

ASSOCIATES

Steven H. Funderburg (Resident, Jackson Office)
Bonnie Bridgers Smith (Resident, Jackson Office)
Patrick M. Tatum (Resident, Jackson Office)
Craig R. Sessums (Resident, Jackson Office)
James K. Warrington
Cecil D. McClellan, III (Resident, Jackson Office)
J. L. Wilson, IV

OF COUNSEL

Ben L. Riddick (Resident, Jackson Office) John R. Countiss III (Resident, Jackson Office)

Representative Clients: United States Fidelity & Guaranty Co.; State Farm Mutual Automobile Insurance Co.; CNA Insurance Cos.; St. Paul Fire & Marine Insurance Co.; Travelers/Aetna Property and Casualty Corp.; Kemper Insurance Co.; Zurich-American Insurance Group; Risk Enterprise Management, Ltd.; Allstate Insurance Co.

For Complete List of Firm Personnel, See General Section

For full biographical listings, see the Martindale-Hubbell Law Directory

*GRENADA,** Grenada Co.

LISTON/LANCASTER

(See Winona)

*GULFPORT,** Harrison Co.

ALLEN, VAUGHN, COBB & HOOD, P.A. (AV)

One Hancock Plaza, Suite 1209, P.O. Drawer 4108, 39502-4108
Telephone: 601-864-4011
Fax: 601-864-4852
Email: avchlaw@sunherald.infinet.com

Harry R. Allen
Thomas E. Vaughn
David L. Cobb
Billy W. Hood
Joy Lambert Phillips
Robert W. Atkinson
Benjamin U. Bowden
Richard B. Tubertini
Rodney Douglas Robinson
E. Colette Towles
David W. Crane
John A. Foxworth, Jr.

J. Adrian Smith
Michael J. Casano

OF COUNSEL

D. Knox White

LEGAL SUPPORT PERSONNEL

Kevin C. Stachowski (Paralegal)

For full biographical listings, see the Martindale-Hubbell Law Directory

AULTMAN, TYNER, RUFFIN & YARBOROUGH, LTD., A PROFESSIONAL LAW CORPORATION (AV)

1201 25th Avenue, Suite 300, P.O. Box 607, 39502
Telephone: 228-863-6913
FAX: 228-868-8505
Email: atmr@digiscape.com
Hattiesburg, Mississippi Office: 315 Hemphill Street, P.O. Drawer 750.
Telephone: 601-583-2671.
FAX: 601-583-2677.
Columbia, Mississippi Office: 329 Church Street, P.O. Drawer 707.
Telephone: 601-736-2222.
FAX: 601-736-9884. Email: rfyjr@cblink.com.
New Orleans, Louisiana Office: The Texaco Center, 400 Poydras Street, Suite 2250.
Telephone: 504-528-9616.
FAX: 504-528-9640.

Ben E. Sheely
Dorrance (Dee) Aultman, Jr.

For Complete List of Firm Personnel, See General Section

For full biographical listings, see the Martindale-Hubbell Law Directory

DUKES, DUKES, KEATING AND FANECA, P.A. (AV)

2909 13th Street, 6th Floor, P.O. Drawer W, 39501
Telephone: 228-868-1111
Fax: 228-863-2886
Email: ddkf@ddkf.com

Walter W. Dukes
Hugh D. Keating
Phillip W. Jarrell

W. Edward Hatten, Jr.
Thomas William Busby
Trace D. McRaney
Stephen M. Cozart

For Complete List of Firm Personnel, See General Section

For full biographical listings, see the Martindale-Hubbell Law Directory

FRANKE, RAINEY & SALLOUM, PLLC (AV)

2605 14th Street, P.O. Drawer 460, 39502
Telephone: 228-868-7070
Telecopier: 228-868-7090
Email: frs@diversicomm.com

Paul M. Franke, Jr.
William M. Rainey
Richard P. Salloum
Paul B. Howell
Fredrick B. Feeney, II
Traci M. Castille
Donald P. Moore

Kaleel G. Salloum, Jr.
Brandi C. Schwartz
James C. Simpson, Jr.

For full biographical listings, see the Martindale-Hubbell Law Directory

BOYCE HOLLEMAN A PROFESSIONAL CORPORATION (AV)

1913 15th Street, P.O. Drawer 1030, 39502
Telephone: 228-863-3142; 1-800-863-3140
Telecopier: 228-863-9829
Email: boyce1913@aol.com

Boyce Holleman

(See Next Column)

Timothy C. Holleman
Leslie Dean Holleman
David J. "Jeff" White

References: Hancock Bank, Gulfport; Merchants Bank & Trust Co., Gulfport; Bank of Wiggins, Wiggins, Mississippi.

For full biographical listings, see the Martindale-Hubbell Law Directory

HOPKINS, CRAWLEY, BAGWELL & UPSHAW, P.L.L.C. (AV)

2701 24th Avenue, P.O. Box 1510, 39501-4941
Telephone: 228-864-2200
Mississippi and USA Wats: 1-800-421-3629
Fax: 228-868-9358; 228-863-4227
Email: Hopkins@MSLawyer.com
Jackson, Mississippi Office: 499 South President Street, Second Floor, Suite 1.
Telephone: 601-355-6510.
Fax: 601-355-6503. Email: TCrawley@MSLawyer.com.

MEMBERS OF FIRM

Alben N. Hopkins
Timothy D. Crawley
Douglas Bagwell
Jessica Sibley Upshaw
Thomas Alan Waller

ASSOCIATES

Raymond D. Carter
Kenneth S. Womack
Mary Benton-Shaw
Pat Sharkey Burke, Jr.
David E. Wilson
Laura Faye Paulk
Ronald C. Small
(Not admitted in MS)

Representative Clients: Coregis Group; General Cable Corp.; Insurance Company of North America; Liberty Mutual Insurance Group; Reliance Insurance Co.; USX Corp.; Employers Insurance of Wausau; American International Group (AIG); Quaker Chemical Corp.

For full biographical listings, see the Martindale-Hubbell Law Directory

MEADOWS RILEY LAW FIRM (AV)

1720 23rd Avenue, P.O. Box 550, 39502
Telephone: 601-864-4511
Telecopier: 601-868-2178

Joseph R. Meadows
Donnie D. Riley
Jerry D. Riley
Karen J. Young

Representative Clients: Bubba Oustalat Lincoln Mercury, Inc.; Lee Tractor Co. of Mississippi.
Reference: Hancock Bank.

For full biographical listings, see the Martindale-Hubbell Law Directory

NEWTON AND HOFF, L.L.P. (AV)

2019 23rd Avenue, P.O. Box 910, 39502-0910
Telephone: 228-863-8827
Fax: 228-868-6007
Email: newtonhoff@aol.com *URL:* http://www.newtonhoff.com

Paul M. Newton (Resident)
Frederick T. Hoff, Jr. (Resident)
Paul M. Newton, Jr. (Resident)

For full biographical listings, see the Martindale-Hubbell Law Directory

*HATTIESBURG,** Forrest Co.

AULTMAN, TYNER, RUFFIN & YARBOROUGH, LTD., A PROFESSIONAL LAW CORPORATION (AV)

315 Hemphill Street, P.O. Drawer 750, 39403-0750
Telephone: 601-583-2671
FAX: 601-583-2677
Email: aultyn@c-gate.net
Columbia, Mississippi Office: 329 Church Street, P.O. Drawer 707.
Telephone: 601-736-2222.
FAX: 601-736-9884. Email: rfyjr@cblink.com.
Gulfport, Mississippi Office: 1201 25th Avenue, Suite 300, P.O. Box 607.
Telephone: 228-863-6913.
FAX: 228-868-8505. Email: atmr@digiscape.com.
New Orleans, Louisiana Office: The Texaco Center, 400 Poydras Street, Suite 2250.
Telephone: 504-528-9616.
FAX: 504-528-9640.

Dorrance Aultman
Thomas W. Tyner
Louie F. Ruffin
Richard F. Yarborough, Jr.
(Resident, Columbia Office)
Ben E. Sheely
(Resident, Gulfport Office)
R. Curtis Smith, II
Dorrance (Dee) Aultman, Jr.
(Resident, Gulfport Office)
William Nelson Graham

Victor A. DuBose

(See Next Column)

AULTMAN, TYNER, RUFFIN & YARBOROUGH, LTD. A PROFESSIONAL LAW CORPORATION, *Hattiesburg—Continued*

OF COUNSEL

Ernest Ray Duff (Resident, Columbia Office)

Representative Clients: Hercules, Inc.; U.S. Steel Corp.; Ford Motor Co.; Phillips Petroleum Co.; Aetna Casualty & Surety Co.; CNA Group; Liberty Mutual Insurance Co.; St. Paul Fire & Marine Insurance Co.; Fireman's Fund; L & A Contracting Co.

For Complete List of Firm Personnel, See General Section

For full biographical listings, see the Martindale-Hubbell Law Directory

*JACKSON,** Hinds Co.

ALSTON & JONES (AV)

A Professional Limited Liability Company
121 North State Street, P.O. Drawer 1532, 39215-1532
Telephone: 601-948-6882
Fax: 601-948-6902
Email: ARVS@Teclink.net

MEMBERS OF FIRM

Alex A. Alston, Jr.
Richard L. Jones
Sheldon G. Alston

Counsel for: Ford Motor Co.; E.I. du Pont de Nemours Co.; Gannett Co., Inc.; Conoco, Inc.; General Electric Company; Jostens, Inc.; Georgia-Pacific Corp.; Dean Witter Reynolds, Inc.; Transcontinental Gas Pipeline, Inc.; Piccadilly Cafeterias.

For Complete List of Firm Personnel, See General Section

For full biographical listings, see the Martindale-Hubbell Law Directory

BAKER, DONELSON, BEARMAN & CALDWELL (AV)

Suite 500, 700 North State Street, 39202
Telephone: 601-351-2400
Telecopier: 601-351-2424
Email: info@bdbc.com *URL:* http://www.bakerdonelson.com
Memphis, Tennessee Office: 20th Floor, First Tennessee Building, 165 Madison, 38103.
Telephone: 901-526-2000.
Telecopier: 901-577-2303.
Nashville, Tennessee Office: 1700 Nashville City Center, 511 Union Street, 37219.
Telephone: 615-726-5600.
Telecopier: 615-726-0464.
Chattanooga, Tennessee Office: 1800 Republic Centre, 633 Chestnut Street, 37450-1800.
Telephone: 423-756-2010.
Telecopier: 423-756-3447.
Knoxville, Tennessee Office: 2200 Riverview Tower, 900 South Gay Street, 37901.
Telephone: 423-549-7000.
Telecopier: 423-525-8569.
Johnson City, Tennessee Office: SunTrust Bank Building, 207 Mockingbird Lane, P.O. Box 3038, 37602.
Telephone: 423-928-0181.
Telecopier: 423-928-5694; 423-928-3654; Kingsport: 423-246-6191.
Huntsville, Tennessee Office: 3 Courthouse Square, 37756.
Telephone: 423-663-2321.
Telecopier: 423-663-2111.
Washington, D.C. Office: Market Square, 801 Pennsylvania Avenue, N.W., 20004.
Telephone: 202-508-3400.
Telecopier: 202-508-3402.

PARTNERS

Robert Engelbrecht Hauberg, Jr.
Walker W. (Bill) Jones, III
James L. Jones

ASSOCIATES

Sheryl Bey
Scott W. Pedigo
Philip W. Thomas
Tiffanee N. Wade
Charles R. Galloway
Scott W. Bates

OF COUNSEL

Karen H. Spencer

For Complete List of Firm Personnel, See General Section

For full biographical listings, see the Martindale-Hubbell Law Directory

COPELAND COOK TAYLOR & BUSH, A PROFESSIONAL ASSOCIATION (AV)

200 Concourse, Suite 200, 1062 Highland Colony Parkway, P.O. Box 2132, 39225-2132
Telephone: 601-856-7200
Facsimile: 601-856-7626
Email: mail@cctb.com *URL:* http://www.cctb.com
Ridgeland, Mississippi Office: Post Office Box 6020, 39158.
Telephone: 601-856-7200.
Facsimile: 601-856-7626.

(See Next Column)

Charles G. Copeland
W. Shan Thompson
Thomas A. Cook
C. Dale Shearer
Glenn Gates Taylor
Robert C. Richardson
C. Glen Bush
Lee Howell, III
Thomas C. Gerity
John M. Breland
James T. Knight
Jefferson P.W. Skelton
James R. Moore, Jr.
Patricia H. Cottingham
J. Tucker Mitchell
Samuel S. Goza
Robert P. Thompson
Amanda L. Baham
Thomas R. Hudson
Samuel O. Morris, IV
R. Nash Neyland
Michelle C. Partridge
Michael W. Baxter
John E. Gough, Jr.
C. Ted Sanderson, Jr.
Victor Donald Hunt
Monte L. Barton, Jr.
Donald J. Blackwood, Jr.
Rhonda Lea McCullough

OF COUNSEL

James P. Knight, Jr.
Robert L. Goza

For full biographical listings, see the Martindale-Hubbell Law Directory

CURRIE JOHNSON GRIFFIN GAINES & MYERS, PLLC (AV)

Mississippi Valley Title Building, 315 Tombigbee Street, P.O. Box 750, 39205-0750
Telephone: 601-969-1010
Telecopier: 601-969-5120
URL: http://www.curriejohnson.com

MEMBERS OF FIRM

Edward J. Currie, Jr.
Philip W. Gaines
Whitman B. Johnson, III
Michael F. Myers
William C. Griffin
Frances R. Shields
William H. Creel, Jr.

Lisa L. Williams
Robert B. Ogletree
James F. Noble, III
James M. Priest, Jr.
William W. McKinley, Jr.
Shelly G. Burns
Timothy D. Moore
Yumeka C. Burt
Trent L. Walker
Kristi A. Duncan

For full biographical listings, see the Martindale-Hubbell Law Directory

JOEL W. HOWELL, III (AV)

5446 Executive Place, P.O. Box 16772, 39236
Telephone: 601-362-8129
Telecopier: 601-362-8419
URL: http://www.lawyers.com/joelhowell

Reference: Deposit Guaranty National Bank, Jackson, Mississippi.

For full biographical listings, see the Martindale-Hubbell Law Directory

LISTON/LANCASTER (AV)

304 North Congress Street, P.O. Box 22983, 39225
Telephone: 601-944-0820
Fax: 601-355-2175
Winona, Mississippi Office: P.O. Box 645, 126 North Quitman Avenue.
Telephone: 662-283-2132.
Fax: 662-283-3742.

William H. Liston
William Liston, III
Alan D. Lancaster
W. Joseph Reid

For full biographical listings, see the Martindale-Hubbell Law Directory

PHELPS DUNBAR, L.L.P. (AV)

Suite 500, SkyTel Centre, 200 South Lamar Street, P.O. Box 23066, 39225-3066
Telephone: 601-352-2300
Telecopier: 601-360-9777
Email: info@phelps.com
New Orleans, Louisiana Office: Texaco Center, 400 Poydras Street.
Telephone: 504-566-1311.
Telecopier: 504-568-9130; 504-568-9007.
Cable Address: "Howspencer."
Telex: 584125 WU.
Telex: 6821155 WUI.
Baton Rouge, Louisiana Office: Suite 701, 445 North Boulevard, P.O. Box 4412.
Telephone: 225-346-0285.
Telecopier: 225-381-9197.
Tupelo, Mississippi Office: Seventh Floor, One Mississippi Plaza, P.O. Box 1220.
Telephone: 662-842-7907.
Telecopier: 662-842-3873.
Houston, Texas Office: Suite 900, 3040 Post Oak Boulevard.
Telephone: 713-626-1386.
Telecopier: 713-626-1388.
London, England Office: Suite 731, Level 7, Lloyd's, 1 Lime Street, London EC3M 7DQ England.
Telephone: 011-44-207-929-4765.
Telecopier: 011-44-207-929-0046.
Telex: 987321.

(See Next Column)

PHELPS DUNBAR L.L.P.—*Continued*

RESIDENT PARTNERS

Reuben V. Anderson	Luther T. Munford
Ross F. Bass, Jr.	James W. O'Mara
William C. Brabec	John W. Robinson, III
James W. Craig	John P. Sneed
E. Clifton Hodge, Jr.	Frank W. Trapp
Stephen H. Leech, Jr.	Michael B. Wallace

RESIDENT ASSOCIATES

Debra M. Brown	Rebecca Hawkins
Heather J. Camp	R. Hayes Johnson, Jr.
Kari L. Foster	Amanda Jones
Christopher R. Green (Not admitted in MS)	J. Douglas Minor, Jr.
	Douglas C. Noble
Eric T. Hamer	James W. Shelson

Representative Clients: Bank of Mississippi; Blue Cross & Blue Shield of Mississippi; CBI Equifax; General Motors Corporation; JESCO, Inc.; The Kroger Co.; Mississippi Municipal Liability Plan; North Mississippi Health Services, Inc. (and affiliated entities); Philip Morris Incorporated; Underwriters at Lloyd's, London.

For Complete List of Firm Personnel, See General Section

For full biographical listings, see the Martindale-Hubbell Law Directory

THOMAS E. ROYALS (AV)

The Plaza Building, Suite 1100, 120 North Congress Street, P.O. Box 22909, 39225-2909
Telephone: 601-948-7777
Telecopier: 601-948-7780
Email: royalslaw@aol.com

For full biographical listings, see the Martindale-Hubbell Law Directory

SHELL, BUFORD, BUFKIN, CALLICUTT & PERRY (AV)

920 Trustmark Building, P.O. Box 157, 39205
Telephone: 601-948-2291
Facsimile: 601-352-6968

MEMBERS OF FIRM

Dan H. Shell (1918-1976)	Douglas R. Duke
Frank T. Williams (1904-1977)	Crane D. Kipp
J. Dudley Buford (1920-1991)	James N. Bullock
Cary E. Bufkin	Ken R. Adcock
Kenneth G. Perry	D. Collier Graham, Jr.

Eugene R. Naylor

ASSOCIATES

E. Frank Goodman	Mark D. Morrison

OF COUNSEL

K. Hayes Callicutt

Representative Clients: Mississippi Baptist Medical Center; Mississippi Chemical Corp.; Aetna Casualty and Surety Co.; American International Group; Atlantic Mutual Insurance Co.; Commercial Union Insurance Co.; United States Fidelity and Guaranty Co.; Home Insurance Co.; The Chubb Group; Trustmark National Bank.

For full biographical listings, see the Martindale-Hubbell Law Directory

STEEN REYNOLDS & DALEHITE, LLP (AV)

Heritage Building, 401 East Capitol Street, Suite 415, P.O. Box 900, 39201
Telephone: 601-969-7054
Telecopier: 601-353-3782
Email: firm@Steenrd.com

Jerome B. Steen (1933-1997)

MEMBERS OF FIRM

Jimmie B. Reynolds, Jr.	Lee Ann Rikard
William M. Dalehite, Jr.	Lanny R. Pace
Michael V. Cory, Jr.	Heather L. Saum

Representative Clients: Allstate Insurance Co.; St. Paul Insurance Cos.; Indiana Lumbermens Mutual Insurance Co.; United Services Automobile Assn.; Empire Fire & Marine Insurance Co.; Sears Roebuck & Co.; State Farm Mutual Co.; State Farm Fire & Casualty Co.
Reference: Trustmark National Bank, Jackson, Mississippi.

For full biographical listings, see the Martindale-Hubbell Law Directory

SULLIVAN AND SULLIVAN (AV)

Suite 200, 5448 I-55 North, 39211
Telephone: 601-952-0799
Facsimile: 601-952-0599;
Cable Address: "Sullaw"

MEMBERS OF FIRM

John C. Sullivan, Sr. (1910-1993)	John C. Sullivan, Jr.

ASSOCIATE

Patricia Alexander Killgore

For full biographical listings, see the Martindale-Hubbell Law Directory

UPSHAW, WILLIAMS, BIGGERS, BECKHAM & RIDDICK, LLP (AV)

Suite 300 Plaza One, 715 South Pear Orchard Road (Ridgeland), 39147
Telephone: 601-978-1996
Facsimile: 601-978-1949
Mailing Address: P.O. Box 9147, Jackson, Mississippi, 39286-9147
Email: lexjax@uwbbr.com
Greenwood, Mississippi Office: 309 Fulton Street, P.O. Drawer 8230, 38935-8230.
Telephone: 662-455-1613.
Facsimile: 662-453-9245. Email: lexgwd@uwbbr.com.

MEMBERS OF FIRM

James E. Upshaw (Resident, Greenwood Office)	Robert S. Upshaw (Resident, Greenwood Office)
Tommie G. Williams (Resident, Greenwood Office)	Clinton M. Guenther (Resident, Greenwood Office)
Marc A. Biggers (Resident, Greenwood Office)	Richard C. Williams, Jr.
	Richard L. Kimmel (Resident, Greenwood Office)
Glenn F. Beckham (Resident, Greenwood Office)	Mark C. Carroll
Roger C. Riddick	W. Hugh Gillon IV
F. Ewin Henson III (Resident, Greenwood Office)	Paul L. Goodman (Resident, Greenwood Office)
Lonnie D. Bailey (Resident, Greenwood Office)	Walter C. Morrison IV

ASSOCIATES

Steven H. Funderburg	James K. Warrington (Resident, Greenwood Office)
Bonnie Bridgers Smith	
Patrick M. Tatum	Cecil D. McClellan, III
Craig R. Sessums	J. L. Wilson, IV (Resident, Greenwood Office)

OF COUNSEL

Ben L. Riddick	John R. Countiss III

Representative Clients: United States Fidelity & Guaranty Co.; State Farm Mutual Automobile Insurance Co.; CNA Insurance Cos.; St. Paul Fire & Marine Insurance Co.; Travelers/Aetna Property and Casualty Corp.; Kemper Insurance Co.; Zurich-America Insurance Group; Risk Enterprise Management, Ltd.; Allstate Insurance Co.

For Complete List of Firm Personnel, See General Section

For full biographical listings, see the Martindale-Hubbell Law Directory

WATKINS & EAGER (AV)

A Professional Limited Liability Company
Suite 300 The Emporium Building, 400 East Capitol Street, P.O. Box 650, 39205
Telephone: 601-948-6470
Facsimile: 601-354-3623

MEMBERS OF FIRM

William H. Cox, Jr.	Paul H. Stephenson, III
P. Nicholas Harkins, III	William F. Goodman, III
John G. Corlew	Douglas J. Gunn
John L. Low, IV	William F. Ray

Representative Clients: Bayer Corp.; Caterpillar Inc.; International Paper Co.; Shell Oil Co.; Toyota Motor Sales, U.S.A., Inc.; Tyson Foods, Inc.

For Complete List of Firm Personnel, See General Section

For full biographical listings, see the Martindale-Hubbell Law Directory

*MERIDIAN,** Lauderdale Co.

GLOVER, YOUNG, WALTON, PHILLIPS & TUCKER, PLLC (AV)

Jefferson Square Office Plaza, 1724-A 23rd Avenue, P.O. Box 5514, 39302-5514
Telephone: 601-693-1301
Telecopy: 601-693-1363
Email: gywptpsp@hotmail.com

H. Wingfield Glover, Jr.	Ronnie L. Walton
Ralph E. Young, Jr.	P. Scott Phillips

Judson T. Tucker

Representative Clients: Alfa Insurance Companies; American States Insurance Co.; Deposit Guaranty National Bank; General Agents Insurance Company of America, Inc.; Great River Insurance; Jeff Anderson Regional Medical Center; Liberty National Life Insurance Co.; Mississippi Power Co.; State Auto Insurance Companies; Universal Underwriters.

For Complete List of Firm Personnel, See General Section

For full biographical listings, see the Martindale-Hubbell Law Directory

*NATCHEZ,** Adams Co.

MULHEARN & MULHEARN (AV)

202 South Wall Street, P.O. Box 967, 39120
Telephone: 601-442-4808
Fax: 601-446-6224
Email: woodland@bkbank.com *URL:* http:/www.lawyers.com/mulhearnlaw

MEMBERS OF FIRM

John E. Mulhearn (1910-1981) John E. Mulhearn, Jr.

LEGAL SUPPORT PERSONNEL

Eva Ruth Seale Judith A. Strickland

Representative Clients: Ashland Plantation; Exxon Corporation; Belle Oil, Inc.; Supermarket Operations, Inc.; Petron, Inc.; Concordia Bank & Trust Co.; Dunleith; J.M. Jones Lumber Co., Inc.; Southwest Mississippi Anesthesia P.A.; Paradise Foods, Inc.

For full biographical listings, see the Martindale-Hubbell Law Directory

TRULY, SMITH & LATHAM (AV)

100 South Pearl Street, P.O. Box 1307, 39121-1307
Telephone: 601-442-6495
Telecopier: 601-442-8874
URL: http://www.lawyers.com/trulysmith&latham

George Lawrence Adams (1913-1994) R. Brent Forman (1917-1994)
E. C. Ward (1928-1994)

MEMBERS OF FIRM

William Marion Smith Robert C. Latham

OF COUNSEL

Everette Truly

Representative Clients: Deposit Guaranty National Bank; Exxon U.S.A.; Mississippi Power & Light Co.; Southwest Mississippi Electric Power Assn.; South Central Bell Telephone Co.; Sears, Roebuck & Co.; American International Group; Kemper Insurance Co.

For full biographical listings, see the Martindale-Hubbell Law Directory

*OXFORD,** Lafayette Co.

FREELAND & FREELAND (AV)

1013 Jackson Avenue, P.O. Box 269, 38655
Telephone: 662-234-3414
Telecopier: 662-234-0604
Email: thf4@watervalley.net

MEMBERS OF FIRM

T. H. Freeland, III T. H. Freeland, IV

Representative Clients: The Ohio Casualty Group; Crum & Forester.

For full biographical listings, see the Martindale-Hubbell Law Directory

HOLCOMB DUNBAR, A PROFESSIONAL ASSOCIATION (AV)

1217 Jackson Avenue P.O. Drawer 707, 38655
Telephone: 601-234-8775
Facsimile: 601-238-7552
Email: hdccw@holcombdunbar.com *URL:* http://www.holcombdunbar.com
Clarksdale, Mississippi Office: 152 Delta Avenue, P.O. Box 368, 38614.
Telephone: 601-627-2241.
Facsimile: 601-627-9788.
Southaven, Mississippi Office: Suite 1, 728 Goodman Road East, P.O. Box 190, 38671.
Telephone: 601-349-0664.
Facsimile: 601-349-2432.

Jack F. Dunbar T. Swayze Alford
Edward A. Moss R. Bradley Best
Thomas J. Suszek Angela M. Spivey
Michael N. Watts Walter Alan Davis
Marjorie T. O'Donnell Mark R. Smith

Representative Clients: Union Planters Bank, National Association; Deposit Guaranty National Bank; Trustmark National Bank; Mississippi Power & Light Co.; Southern Farm Bureau Casualty Insurance Co.; Bituminous Insurance Co.; State Farm Fire & Casualty Insurance Co.; Fireman's Fund Insurance Cos.; Atlanta Casualty Insurance Cos.; Drexel Chemical Co.

For Complete List of Firm Personnel, See General Section

For full biographical listings, see the Martindale-Hubbell Law Directory

RAYBURN & PIERCE (AV)

305 Heritage Drive, P.O. Box 430, 38655
Telephone: 662-234-1400
Fax: 662-234-1999
Email: trayburn@dixie-net.com *URL:* http://www.rayburnlaw.com

MEMBERS OF FIRM

S. T. Rayburn Ronald Henry Pierce
Paige B. Rayburn

(See Next Column)

ASSOCIATE

Victoria Bolling Smith

For full biographical listings, see the Martindale-Hubbell Law Directory

TOLLISON LAW FIRM, P.A. (AV)

100 Courthouse Square, P.O. Box 1216, 38655
Telephone: Telephone: 601-234-7070
Fax: 601-234-7095
Email: tollison@watervalley.net

Grady F. Tollison, Jr. Gray Tollison
Nina Stubblefield Tollison E. Farish Percy
William K. Duke Barbara Miller Dollarhide
J. Rhea Tannehill, Jr.

OF COUNSEL

Edward J. Bogen, Jr.

References: Merchants & Farmers Bank; Pike County National Bank.

For full biographical listings, see the Martindale-Hubbell Law Directory

*PASCAGOULA,** Jackson Co.

BRYAN, NELSON, SCHROEDER, CASTIGLIOLA & BANAHAN (AV)

1103 Jackson Avenue, P.O. Drawer 1529, 39568-1529
Telephone: 228-762-6631
Fax: 228-769-6392
Email: bns@datasync.com

MEMBERS OF FIRM

Ernest R. Schroeder John A. Banahan
Vincent J. Castigliola, Jr. H. Benjamin Mullen

ASSOCIATES

Melinda O. Johnson Scott Corlew

Representative Clients: Allstate Insurance Company; American Tobacco Company; Bethlehem Steel Corporation; Colle Tug & Towing Company, Inc.; Medical Assurance Co. of Mississippi; RYOBI Motor Products Corporation; SAIA Motor Freight Lines, Inc.; South Trust Bank; State Farm Insurance Companies; United Services Automobile Association.

For full biographical listings, see the Martindale-Hubbell Law Directory

COLINGO, WILLIAMS, HEIDELBERG, STEINBERGER & MCELHANEY, P.A. (AV)

711 Delmas Avenue, P.O. Box 1407, 39568-1407
Telephone: 228-762-8021
FAX: 228-762-7589
Email: info@colingowilliams.com *URL:* http://www.ColingoWilliams.com

Roy C. Williams James H. Colmer, Jr.
James H. Heidelberg Brett K. Williams
Stephen W. Burrow

Gina Bardwell Thompkins C. Brice Wiggins
Robert Michael Cunningham, II Kevin C. Bradley

Representative Clients: International Paper Co.; R.J. Reynolds; CBS Corp.; Kemper Group; Singing River Hospital System; Mississippi Gulf Coast Regional Wastewater Authority; Medical Assurance Company of Mississippi; Mutual Assurance of Alabama; Dole Food Co.

For full biographical listings, see the Martindale-Hubbell Law Directory

OSWALD AND REED (AV)

Markland Building, 3106 Canty Street, P.O. Box 1428, 39568-1428
Telephone: 228-769-1027
Telecopier: 228-769-9019

Robert H. Oswald William Townsend Reed

For full biographical listings, see the Martindale-Hubbell Law Directory

SOUTHAVEN, De Soto Co.

BRIDGFORTH & BUNTIN (AV)

1607 State Line Road, P.O. Box 241, 38671
Telephone: 601-393-4450
Fax: 601-342-5646

MEMBERS OF FIRM

Dudley B. Bridgforth, Jr. Taylor D. Buntin, III
Barry W. Bridgforth, Jr.

For full biographical listings, see the Martindale-Hubbell Law Directory

Southaven—Continued

HOLCOMB DUNBAR, A PROFESSIONAL ASSOCIATION (AV)

Suite 1, 728 Goodman Road East, P.O. Box 190, 38671
Telephone: 601-349-0664
Facsimile: 601-349-2432
Email: hdccw@holcombdunbar.com *URL:* http://www.holcombdunbar.com
Clarksdale, Mississippi Office: 152 Delta Avenue, P.O. Box 368, 38614.
Telephone: 601-627-2241.
Facsimile: 601-627-9788.
Oxford, Mississippi Office: 1217 Jackson Avenue, P.O. Drawer 707, 38655.
Telephone: 601-234-8775.
Facsimile: 601-238-7552.

William A. Baskin
John Ramsey McCarroll, III
Billy C. Campbell, Jr.

Representative Clients: Union Planters Bank, National Association; BanCorp South; Trustmark National Bank; Mississippi Power & Light Co.; Southern Farm Bureau Casualty Insurance Co.; Bituminous Insurance Co.; State Farm Fire & Casualty Insurance Co.; Fireman's Fund Insurance Cos.; Atlanta Casualty Insurance Cos.; Drexel Chemical Co.

For Complete List of Firm Personnel, See General Section

For full biographical listings, see the Martindale-Hubbell Law Directory

*TUPELO,** Lee Co.

PHELPS DUNBAR, L.L.P. (AV)

Seventh Floor, One Mississippi Plaza, P.O. Box 1220, 38802-1220
Telephone: 662-842-7907
Telecopier: 662-842-3873
Email: info@phelps.com
New Orleans, Louisiana Office: Texaco Center, 400 Poydras Street.
Telephone: 504-566-1311.
Telecopier: 504-568-9130; 504-568-9007.
Cable Address: "Howspencer."
Telex: 584125 WU.
Telex: 6821155 WUI.
Baton Rouge, Louisiana Office: Suite 701, 445 North Boulevard, P.O. Box 4412.
Telephone: 225-346-0285.
Telecopier: 225-381-9197.
Jackson, Mississippi Office: Suite 500, SkyTel Centre, 200 South Lamar Street, P.O. Box 23066.
Telephone: 601-352-2300.
Telecopier: 601-360-9777.
Houston, Texas Office: Suite 900, 3040 Post Oak Boulevard.
Telephone: 713-626-1386.
Telecopier: 713-626-1388.
London, England Office: Suite 731, Level 7, Lloyd's, 1 Lime Street, London EC3M 7DQ England.
Telephone: 011-44-207-929-4765.
Telecopier: 011-44-207-929-0046.
Telex: 987321.

OF COUNSEL

Fred M. Bush, Jr.

RESIDENT PARTNERS

William M. Beasley
F. M. Bush, III
Jean Magee Hogan
Dinetia M. Newman

COUNSEL

Jeffrey S. Moore
G. Kay L. Trapp

RESIDENT ASSOCIATES

Scott Ellzey
Gregory M. Hunsucker
Mark Stewart Johnson
Mark C. Lewis

Representative Clients: Bank of Mississippi; CBI Equifax; General Motors Corporation; JESCO, Inc.; The Kroger Co.; Lee County, Mississippi; Mississippi Municipal Liability Plan; North Mississippi Health Services, Inc. (and affiliated entities); Philip Morris Incorporated; Underwriters at Lloyd's, London.

For Complete List of Firm Personnel, See General Section

For full biographical listings, see the Martindale-Hubbell Law Directory

WEBB, SANDERS, BALDUCCI & SMITH, P.L.L.C. (AV)

363 North Broadway, P.O. Box 496, 38802-0496
Telephone: 662-844-2137
Fax: 662-842-3863
Email: webbsand@webbsanders.com *URL:* http://www.webbsanders.com
Oxford, Mississippi Office: 405 South Lamar Boulevard, P.O. Box 148, 38655.
Telephone: 662-236-5700.
Fax: 662-236-5800.

Dan W. Webb
Timothy R. Balducci
Kent E. Smith
B. Wayne Williams
Sherrie L. Moore
Sammye S. Tharp
K. Kathy Brown
Guthrie T. Abbott, Jr.
Emily D. Wade

(See Next Column)

OF COUNSEL

Rachael Howell Webb
Benjamin H. Sanders (1942-1999)

Representative Clients: Farm Bureau; Mississippi Farm Bureau; Southern Farm Bureau; GAB Business Services, Inc.; Gulf Guaranty Life Insurance; Phillips and Assocs.; State Farm Fire & Casualty Co.; State Farm Mutual Automobile Insurance Company.

For full biographical listings, see the Martindale-Hubbell Law Directory

*WINONA,** Montgomery Co.

LISTON/LANCASTER (AV)

126 North Quitman Avenue, P.O. Box 645, 38967
Telephone: 662-283-2132
Fax: 662-283-3742
Email: lislan@aol.com
Jackson, Mississippi Office: 304 North Congress Street, P.O. Box 22983, 39225.
Telephone: 601-944-0820.
Fax: 601-355-2175.

William H. Liston
Alan D. Lancaster
William Liston, III
W. Joseph Reid

For full biographical listings, see the Martindale-Hubbell Law Directory

MISSOURI

CAPE GIRARDEAU, Cape Girardeau Co.

OLIVER, OLIVER & WALTZ, P.C. (AV)

400 Broadway, P.O. Box 559, 63702-0559
Telephone: 573-335-8278
Fax: 573-334-6375
Email: oliver@ldd.net

R. B. Oliver (1850-1934)
R. B. Oliver, Jr. (1880-1971)
Allen Laws Oliver (1886-1970)
John (Jack) L. Oliver (1916-1978)
John L. Oliver, Jr.
James Frederick Waltz

Representative Clients: Mercantile Bank of Southern Missouri; Union Electric Co.; Southwestern Bell Corp.; Ford Motor Co.; Consolidated Drainage District; MOMEDICO; The Travelers; The Hartford; The Kemper Group; AAA of Missouri.

For Complete List of Firm Personnel, See General Section

For full biographical listings, see the Martindale-Hubbell Law Directory

THOMASSON, GILBERT, COOK & MAGUIRE, L.C. (AV)

715 Clark Avenue, P.O. Box 1180, 63702-1180
Telephone: 314-335-6651
Fax: 314-335-6182
Email: pgilbert@prodigy.net *URL:* http://pages.prodigy.net/pgilbert

MEMBERS OF FIRM

Donald P. Thomasson
Paul V. Gilbert
John L. Cook
Jeffrey S. Maguire
J. Michael Ponder
Kathleen A. Wolz

Representative Clients: Aetna Life & Casualty; Allstate Insurance Cos.; American Family Insurance; Cameron Mutual Insurance Co.; Farmers Insurance Group; Hospital Services Group; St. Paul Insurance Co.; State Farm Insurance Cos.

For full biographical listings, see the Martindale-Hubbell Law Directory

*COLUMBIA,** Boone Co.

HINDMAN, GOLDSTEIN & HARDER, P.C. (AV)

Suite 300, 1001 East Walnut, 65201-4995
Telephone: 573-443-1602
Fax: 573-449-7678

Darwin A. Hindman, Jr.
Jean E. Goldstein
Janice A. Harder

Cindy S. Kadlec

References: Boone County National Bank; First National Bank and Trust Co.

For full biographical listings, see the Martindale-Hubbell Law Directory

OLIVER, WALKER, WILSON & EHRHARDT, LLC (AV)

Suite 406, 401 Locust Street, P.O. Box 977, 65205
Telephone: 573-443-3134
Telecopier: 573-442-6323
Email: owwe@socket.net

(See Next Column)

OLIVER, WALKER, WILSON & EHRHARDT LLC, *Columbia—Continued*

MEMBERS OF FIRM

David A. Oliver
Roland P. Walker
Betty K. Wilson
Glen R. Ehrhardt
Cynthia Barchet
Ronald N. Sweet

Representative Clients: Aetna Insurance Co.; Allied Group; American Family Insurance Group; Safeco; CNA Insurance; Federated Insurance Co.; Old Republic; Shelter Insurance Cos.

For full biographical listings, see the Martindale-Hubbell Law Directory

RICHARD C. THOMAS (AV)

609 East Broadway, 65201
Telephone: 573-442-3000
Fax: 573-449-1094

References: Boone County National Bank; Mercantile Bank.

For full biographical listings, see the Martindale-Hubbell Law Directory

*HILLSBORO,** Jefferson Co.

THURMAN, HOWALD, WEBER, SENKEL & NORRICK, L.L.C. (AV)

One Thurman Court, 63050
Telephone: 314-789-2601, 797-2601
Telecopier: 314-797-2904
Email: thurmanlaw@theriver.net

MEMBERS OF FIRM

J. W. Thurman (1902-1986)
John W. Howald
Louis J. Weber
David P. Senkel
Floyd T. Norrick

Julianne Platz Hand

For full biographical listings, see the Martindale-Hubbell Law Directory

*JEFFERSON CITY,** Cole Co.

CARSON & COIL, P.C. (AV)

515 East High, P.O. Box 28, 65102
Telephone: 573-636-2177
Telecopier: 573-636-7119
Email: general@carsoncoil.com

Forrest P. Carson (1910-1981)
Cullen Coil (1907-1989)
Michael P. Riley
Ronald R. McMillin
Eugene G. Bushmann
James W. Gallaher
Lori J. Levine
Rudolph L. Veit
Michael Madsen
R. Max Humphreys
Mark A. Ludwig
Dana L. Frese
Edward C. Clausen
Carla G. Holste
Kent L. Brown
Douglas W. Hennon
Charles J. McPheeters
Paul T. Graham

Jack C. Hauser, Jr.
Charles A. "Chip" Gentry
James W. "Jamie" Gallaher, Jr.

General Counsel for: Capital Reserve Life Insurance Co.; Missouri Farm Bureau; Healthcare Services Group.
Reference: Central Trust Bank.

For full biographical listings, see the Martindale-Hubbell Law Directory

INGLISH & MONACO, P.C. (AV)

Monroe House Law Center, 237 East High Street, P.O. Box 67, 65102
Telephone: 573-634-2522
Telecopier: 573-634-4526
Email: inglishmonaco-jc@socket.net
California, Missouri Office: 329 South Oak.
Telephone: 573-796-4333.
Lake Ozark, Missouri Office: Cliffside Office Center, 2140 Bagnell Dam Boulevard, 65049.
Telephone: 573-964-6211.
Telecopier: 573-964-6787.

John W. Inglish
Nicholas M. Monaco
Ann Monaco Warren
Mark G. R. Warren
Lewis Z. Bridges
Timothy R. Cisar
David G. Bandré
Daniel E. Hunt
Daniel C. Mizell
Stephen W. Richey
William Barton
Charles P. Dribben (1929-1991)

OF COUNSEL

Andrew Jackson Higgins

References: Central Trust Bank; Jefferson Bank.

For full biographical listings, see the Martindale-Hubbell Law Directory

KANSAS CITY, Jackson, Clay, Platte & Cass Cos.

BIOFF SINGER AND FINUCANE, LLP (AV)

Suite 400 The Stilwell Building, 104 West Ninth Street, 64105-1718
Telephone: 816-842-8770
Telefax: 816-842-8767

MEMBERS OF FIRM

Allan L. Bioff
Leonard Singer
Brian J. Finucane
J. Randall Coffey

James R. Holland, II
Gregory D. Ballew
Jennifer L. Robinson
Nancy M. Leonard
Jill Waldman (Not admitted in MO)
Von E. Hays
Stacie M. Johnson

OF COUNSEL

Martha A. Halvordson

Representative Clients: United Parcel Service, Inc.; Bunge Corporation; Sprint Corporation; Sutherland Lumber Company; Interstate Brands Corporation; GTE Corporation; Farmers Insurance Group of Companies; Neighbors Construction Company; Hill's Pet Nutrition; Kansas City Southern Industries, Inc.

For full biographical listings, see the Martindale-Hubbell Law Directory

FRANKE & SCHULTZ, A PROFESSIONAL CORPORATION (AV)

1312 Commerce Tower, 911 Main Street, 64105
Telephone: 816-421-7100
Telecopier: 816-421-7915
Email: Franke.Schultz@Micro.com
Springfield, Missouri Office: 300 John Q. Hammons Pkwy., Suite 701, 65806.
Telephone: 417-863-0040.
Fax: 417-863-6286.
Overland Park, Kansas Office: 5340 College, 66211.
Telephone: 913-327-7661.
Fax: 913-327-7669.

John E. Franke
John G. Schultz
John L. Mullen
Bradley C. Nielsen
Ryan E. Karaim
Jill Frost
Keith A. Cary
Wendell E. Koerner, Jr.

Cari F. Walsh
Michael J. Tubbesing
Andrew D. Hennier
Laurel Stevenson
Shawn G. Foster
John H. Kizer
Edward J. Barbosa

For full biographical listings, see the Martindale-Hubbell Law Directory

SHUGHART THOMSON & KILROY, A PROFESSIONAL CORPORATION (AV)

Twelve Wyandotte Plaza, 120 West 12th Street, 64105
Telephone: 816-421-3355
Email: Solutions@KC.STKLAW.COM *URL:* http://www.STKLAW.COM
Overland Park, Kansas Office: Suite 1100, 32 Corporate Woods, 9225 Indian Creek Parkway 66210.
Telephone: 913-451-3355.
Springfield, Missouri Office: Suite 1200, Hammons Tower, 901 St. Louis, 65806.
Telephone: 417-869-3353.
Denver, Colorado Office: 1050 17th Street, Suite 2350. 80265.
Telephone: 303-572-9300.
Fax: 303-572-7883.

R. Lawrence Ward
George E. Leonard
Thomas F. Fisher
Thomas G. Kokoruda
Jack L. Campbell
John M. Kilroy, Jr.
Timothy D. O'Leary
Roy Bash
Dennis D. Palmer
William E. Quirk
Jennifer Gille Bacon
W. Terrence Kilroy
William L. Yocum
Steven D. Ruse
Robert A. Henderson
John S. Conner
P. John Brady
Russell S. Jones, Jr.
Bradley J. Baumgart
James P. O'Hara
Joel R. Mosher
Gregory M. Bentz
Philip W. Bledsoe
Anthony F. Rupp
Gregory L. Musil
Roger P. Wright
Mark A. Olthoff
Thomas J. O'Neal
John R. Cleary
Karen J. Halbrook
G. William Quatman
James C. Sullivan
Andrew L. McMullen
Sheryl Feutz-Harter
David E. Shay

Kurt D. Tilton
Leah M. Gagne
Christopher J. Molzen
Brian D. Malkmus
Linda J. Sheppard
Theodore M. Green
Andrew M. DeMarea
Amy Jurevic Sokol
Heather A. Suve
Leslie A. Greathouse
Lance V. Baughman
Richard M. Paul III

(See Next Column)

SHUGHART THOMSON & KILROY A PROFESSIONAL CORPORATION—*Continued*

J. Calvin Downing, III
Daniel D. Owen
Julie B. Tincknell
Karen M. Gleason
Kelly Anne Kolars
Anne E. Popper
Jamee Maurer Klein
Maureen A. Mannion
Cindy L. Neagle
Jonathan H. Gregor

OF COUNSEL

John M. Kilroy
Thomas J. Leittem
Claudia J. York
William V. North
Robert R. Raymond

For Complete List of Firm Personnel, See General Section

For full biographical listings, see the Martindale-Hubbell Law Directory

SPENCER FANE BRITT & BROWNE LLP (AV)

1000 Walnut Street, Suite 1400, 64106-2140
Telephone: 816-474-8100
URL: http://www.spencerfane.com
Overland Park, Kansas Office: Suite 700, 40 Corporate Woods, 9401 Indian Creek Parkway.
Telephone: 913-345-8100.

MEMBERS OF FIRM

J. Nick Badgerow (Resident, Overland Park, Kansas Office)
Russell W. Baker, Jr.
Gardiner B. Davis
Donald W. Giffin
Carl H. Helmstetter
Michael D. Hockley
Elaine Drodge Koch
William C. Martucci
James R. McKown
Barry L. Pickens
James T. Price
Michael F. Saunders
Terry W. Schackmann
Lowell L. Smithson
Mark A. Thornhill
Michaela M. Warden (Resident, Overland Park, Kansas Office)
Douglas M. Weems
David L. Wing
Teresa A. Woody

OF COUNSEL

Alan R. Clever (Resident, Overland Park, Kansas Office)
John P. Jennings, Jr.
Therese M. Schuele
Jill Galbreath Smith (Resident, Overland Park, Kansas Office)
Jane L. Stafford
Sandra J. Wirtel

ASSOCIATES

Clayton L. Barker
Robert P. Berry
Carol S. Clark (Resident, Overland Park, Kansas Office)
Jeannie M. DeVeney (Resident, Overland Park, Kansas Office)
J. Clayton Johnson
Kristine A. Tidgren
Patrick J. Whalen

Representative Clients: Builders Association of Missouri; Farmland Industries; Graphic Technologies; Heavy Constructors Association; Kansas City Power & Light Company; Lucent; Missouri Hospital Association; TH Agriculture and Nutrition.

For full biographical listings, see the Martindale-Hubbell Law Directory

ARTHUR H. STOUP & ASSOCIATES, P.C. (AV)

1710 Mercantile Tower, 1101 Walnut Street, 64106
Telephone: 816-474-0707; 417-887-3600
Fax: 816-474-0714; 417-887-3600
Email: Stoup@msn.com
Springfield, Missouri Office: 1949 East Sunshine, Suite 1-108.
Telephone: 417-887-3600.

Arthur H. Stoup

Stephen W. Nichols

For full biographical listings, see the Martindale-Hubbell Law Directory

SWANSON MIDGLEY, LLC (AV)

Crown Center, 2420 Pershing Road, Suite 400, 64108
Telephone: 816-842-6100
Fax: 816-842-0013
Email: mail@swansonmidgley.com *URL:* http://www.swansonmidgley.com
Overland Park, Kansas Office: Commerce Plaza I, 7th Floor, 7300 W. 110th Street.
Telephone: 913-317-2717.
FAX: 913-317-1505.

Henry R. Cox
James A. Durbin
W. Ann Hansbrough
Craig T. Kenworthy
John J. Kitchin
Don R. Lolli
James H. McLarney

Rebecca S. Bihr

Counsel for: National Collegiate Athletic Assoc.; Pizza Hut; Veterans of Foreign Wars of the U.S.; Danka Business Systems; Physicians Reference Laboratory; National Compressed Steel; Equitable Life Assurance; Mr. Dell Foods, Inc.; Healthcare Medical Solutions, Inc.; Prudential Insurance Co. of America.

(See Next Column)

For Complete List of Firm Personnel, See General Section

For full biographical listings, see the Martindale-Hubbell Law Directory

WAGSTAFF & CARTMELL, LLP (AV)

Suite 1240, 4520 Main Street, 64111
Telephone: 816-701-1100
Fax: 816-531-2372

Thomas W. Wagstaff
Thomas P. Cartmell
Robert G. Rooney
Jonathan P. Kieffer

Marc K. Erickson
Thomas L. Wagstaff

For full biographical listings, see the Martindale-Hubbell Law Directory

THE WIRKEN GROUP A PROFESSIONAL CORPORATION (AV)

2600 Grand Boulevard, Suite 440, 64108-4600
Telephone: 816-471-0330
Fax: 816-471-3044
Email: wirkengrp@aol.com

James C. Wirken
Michael S. Jones

OF COUNSEL

Troy L. Daugherty

For full biographical listings, see the Martindale-Hubbell Law Directory

WYRSCH HOBBS MIRAKIAN & LEE, P.C. (AV)

1300 Mercantile Tower 1101 Walnut, 64106-2122
Telephone: 816-221-0080
Fax: 816-221-3280
Email: whml@sprintmail.com

James R. Wyrsch
Stephen G. Mirakian
Ronald D. Lee
James R. Hobbs
Keith E. Drill
Jacqueline A. Cook
Charles M. Rogers
Marilyn B. Keller
Cheryl A. Pilate
W. Brian Gaddy

OF COUNSEL

James W. Fletcher

David Andrew Kelly

LEGAL SUPPORT PERSONNEL

Darlene Wyrsch (Paralegal)
Dru A. Colhour (Paralegal)
Katherine Vetsch (Paralegal)
Leslie R. Elkins (Paralegal)
William J. Baltrusaitis, II (Investigator)

For full biographical listings, see the Martindale-Hubbell Law Directory

*KIRKSVILLE,** Adair Co.

OSWALD, COTTEY & TEMPLETON, A PROFESSIONAL CORPORATION (AV)

Suite A, 210 North Elson, P.O. Box K, 63501
Telephone: 660-665-5628
Fax: 660-665-6035
Email: oswaldcotteytempleton@yahoo.com

Louis F. Cottey (1931-1999)
Thomas R. Oswald
Scott L. Templeton

Brenda Wall-Swedberg
Theresa L. Kenney
Susan R. Barrow
David Briggs

For full biographical listings, see the Martindale-Hubbell Law Directory

*LIBERTY,** Clay Co.

WITHERS, BRANT, IGOE & MULLENNIX, P.C. (AV)

Two South Main Street, 64068
Telephone: 816-781-4788
Fax: 816-792-2807
Email: wbimlaw@aol.com

Conn Withers (1907-1993)
Jerome E. Brant
Vincent F. Igoe, Jr.
Ronald C. Mullennix
Steven D. Wolcott
John M. Crossett
Thomas C. Capps
Alison K. Blessing
Mark E. Kelly

Michael S. Shipley
Susan E. Long
Leigh A. Goucher
Joseph F. O'Hara
Duane A. Martin

OF COUNSEL

Nancy A. Norton

For full biographical listings, see the Martindale-Hubbell Law Directory

*MARYVILLE,** Nodaway Co.

STRONG & STRONG, A PROFESSIONAL CORPORATION (AV)

124 East Third Street, 64468
Telephone: 660-582-3133
FAX: 660-582-3145

Frank H. Strong
Frank H. Strong, Jr.

OF COUNSEL

John W. Baker, Jr.

General Counsel for: Bank Midwest N.A., Maryville, Mo.; Dempsey-Hardin L-P Gas; St. Francis Hospital; Loch Sand & Construction Co.
Counsel for: Eveready Battery Co., Inc.; New England Business Services, Inc.; The Daily Forum.
Representative Insurance Client: Farmers Insurance Group.

For full biographical listings, see the Martindale-Hubbell Law Directory

ST. LOUIS, (Independent City)

ANDERSON & GILBERT (AV)

200 S. Hanley, Suite 710, 63105
Telephone: 314-721-2777
Telecopier: 314-721-3515
Email: aglawfirm@brick.net

MEMBERS OF FIRM

Robert G. Burridge
Francis X. Duda
Joel D. Monson
D. Paul Myre

Representative Clients: Medical Defense Associates, Ltd.; Foremost Insurance Co; Schneider Nat'l, Inc.; American Specialty Claims Service; Intermed Insurance Co.; INS Insurance, Inc.; OUM Group; Fireman's Fund Insurance Co.; Wausaw Insurance Cos.; ITT Hartford.

For Complete List of Firm Personnel, See General Section

For full biographical listings, see the Martindale-Hubbell Law Directory

ARMSTRONG TEASDALE LLP (AV)

A Partnership including Professional Corporations
One Metropolitan Square, 63102-2740
Telephone: 314-621-5070
Facsimile: 314-621-5065
Twx: 910 761-2246
Cable: ATKV LAW
Email: armstrongteasdale@armstrongteasdale.com *URL:* http://www.armstrongteasdale.com
Kansas City, Missouri Office: 2345 Grand Boulevard, Suite 2000, 64108.
Telephone: 816-221-3420.
Facsimile: 816-221-0786.
Jefferson City, Missouri Office: 3405 W. Truman Blvd., Suite 210, 65109.
Telephone: 573-636-8394.
Washington, D.C. Office: 1747 Pennsylvania Avenue, N.W., Suite 300, 20006.
Telephone: 202-347-0259.
Belleville, Illinois Office: 23 South First Street, 62220.
Telephone: 618-397-4411.
Olathe, Kansas Office: 100 East Park, 66061.
Telephone: 913-345-0706.
Shanghai, China Office: A-T International Consultants, LLC, Suite 310, No. 12 Zhongshan Road (E1), Shanghai 200002 P.R.C.
Telephone: 86-21-6326-7001.
Facsimile: 86-21-6326-0626.

MEMBERS OF FIRM

Karen A. Baudendistel
Ann E. Buckley
Joan Z. Cohen
Clark H. Cole
William M. Corrigan, Jr.
John F. Cowling
Thomas Cummings (P.C.)
Glenn E. Davis (Assistant Chair, Litigation Department. Chair, Antitrust Trade Regulation and Distribution Law Practice Group)
Raymond R. Fournie
Byron E. Francis (P.C.)
Deirdre C. Gallagher
Frank N. Gundlach (P.C.)
Theodore H. Hellmuth (P.C.)
Mary C. Kickham
Paul E. Kovacs (P.C.)
Peter J. Krane
David G. Loseman
Andrew B. Mayfield
Edwin L. Noel (P.C.)
Daniel K. O'Toole
Thomas L. Orris
David G. Ott (P.C.)
John H. Quinn, III, (P.C.)
Keith A. Rabenberg
Steven P. Sanders
Richard B. Scherrer (P.C.) (Managing Partner)
Mark D. Sophir (P.C.)
James L. Stockberger
Jay A. Summerville
Kenneth F. Teasdale (P.C.)
Wilbur L. Tomlinson (P.C.)
Paul N. Venker
James J. Virtel
George M. von Stamwitz
Thomas B. Weaver (P.C.)
Theodore J. Williams, Jr. (Chair, Transportation Department)
Lisa M. Wood

(See Next Column)

ASSOCIATES

Jennifer Lee Arendes
Mark A. Boatman
Jennifer E. Cook
Timothy J. Gearin
Marshall R. Hoekel
Michael B. Hunter
Patrick J. Kenny
Anita M. Kidd
Lisa A. Larkin
Connie McFarland-Butler
Jeffery T. McPherson
Daniel C. Nelson
Mary Carol Parker
Countess W. Price
Ann E. Verrett

OF COUNSEL

John J. Cole (P.C.)
John P. Emde (P.C.)
Carl R. Gaertner
Frederick H. Mayer (P.C.)
Kevin F. Warren (Not admitted in MO)

Representative Clients: Anheuser-Busch Companies, Inc.; United Missouri Bank; McCarthy Brothers; Lincoln National Life Insurance Company; Avon Products, Inc.; Eli Lilly & Co.; The Coca-Cola Co.; Union Pacific Railroad Company.

For Complete List of Firm Personnel, See General Section

For full biographical listings, see the Martindale-Hubbell Law Directory

BEACH, BURCKE, HELFERS, MITTLEMAN AND STEWART, L.L.C. (AV)

Suite 900, 222 South Central (Clayton), 63105
Telephone: 314-863-8484
Telecopier: 314-863-5312

Douglas R. Beach
Joseph R. Burcke
Mark A. Helfers
Mark D. Mittleman
Allan F. Stewart
Deborah C. M. Henry
Richard Grossman
Robert M. Heggie

Patrick I. Chavez

OF COUNSEL

Joseph R. Niemann

Reference: Boatmen's Bank of St. Louis.

For full biographical listings, see the Martindale-Hubbell Law Directory

EVANS & DIXON, L.L.C. (AV)

1200 Saint Louis Place, 200 North Broadway, 63102-2749
Telephone: 314-621-7755
URL: http://www.evans-dixon.com
Kansas City, Missouri Office: City Center Square, 1100 Main Street, Suite 2000, 64105-2119.
Telephone: 816-472-4600.
Edwardsville, Illinois Office: 17 Ginger Creek Meadows, P.O. Box 405. 62025-3508.
Telephone: 618-656-8505.
Leawood, Kansas Office: 8016 State Line Road, Suite 207. 66208-3713.
Telephone: 913-649-5386.

MEMBERS OF FIRM

Robert W. Wilson (Resident, Edwardsville, Illinois Office)
Sam P. Rynearson
Harvey G. Schneider
Jeffry S. Thomsen
Gerre S. Langton
John A. Michener
Stefan J. Glynias
Edward S. Meyer
Robert J. Krehbiel
Robert P. Numrich (Kansas City, Missouri and Leawood, Kansas Offices)
Carl D. Lothman
Michael Reda (Resident, Edwardsville, Illinois Office)
Brian J. Fowler (Kansas City, Missouri and Leawood, Kansas Offices)
Thomas Clinkenbeard (Resident, Kansas City, Missouri Office)
Priscilla F. Gunn
Jeffrey K. Suess
Kevin P. Schnurbusch
Adrian P. Sulser
Joy Urbom Taylor
Debbie C. Snyder
John S. McCollough

OF COUNSEL

William W. Evans

ASSOCIATES

Christine A. Alsop
Joan B. Bernstein
Joseph F. Callahan
Clinton D. Collier (Resident, Kansas City, Missouri and Leawood, Kansas Offices)
Kristan M. Dames
Raymond B. Flojo
Patricia B. Frank
Mitchell A. Gibson
Lisa A. Green
Cynthia Hamilton
Susan M. Herold
John W. Hoffman (Resident, Edwardsville, Illinois Office)
J. Lee Johnson
John P. Kemppainen, Jr.
Mary Anne Lindsey
Kevin J. Marquitz
Cynthia A. Masterson
Matthew P. O'Grady
James D. O'Leary
David Louis Schrader
David K. Simkins
Dean A. Stark
William B. Starnes, II (Resident, Edwardsville, Illinois Office)
Douglas S. Teasdale
Carol Marie Crandall Van Sambeek
Wendellyn S. Wright

Attorneys for: Allstate Insurance Co.; Chrysler Corp.; Chubb & Son, Inc.; Kemper Insurance Group; Southwestern Bell Telephone Co.; Travelers Insurance Co.; Wal-Mart, Inc.; Zurich Insurance Co.

(See Next Column)

EVANS & DIXON L.L.C.—*Continued*

For full biographical listings, see the Martindale-Hubbell Law Directory

C. MARSHALL FRIEDMAN A PROFESSIONAL CORPORATION (AV)

Thirteenth Floor, 1010 Market Street, 63101
Telephone: 314-621-8400
Fax: 314-621-8843

C. Marshall Friedman
Kenneth E. Rudd
Patrick S. O'Brien
Douglas K. Rush
Thomas P. McDermott
D. Jeffrey Ezra (Not admitted in MO)

Sanjay Agrawal
David M. Dickson
Jeffrey E. Chod

For full biographical listings, see the Martindale-Hubbell Law Directory

THE GRAHAM LAW FIRM (AV)

1015 Locust Street, Suite 700, 63101
Telephone: 314-588-0200
Fax: 314-588-0202
URL: http://www.lawyers.com/grahamlawfirm

MEMBER OF FIRM

Maurice B. Graham

Morry S. Cole

For full biographical listings, see the Martindale-Hubbell Law Directory

HERZOG, CREBS & MCGHEE, LLP (AV)

One City Centre - 24th Floor, 515 North Sixth Street, 63101
Telephone: 314-231-6700
Fax: 314-231-4656
Belleville, Illinois Office: 5111 West Main Street, 62226.
Telephone: 618-235-7656.

MEMBERS OF FIRM

Peter W. Herzog, Jr.
P. Terence Crebs
W. Thomas McGhee
Michael A. Vitale
Edward J. Griesedieck, III
Lawrence E. Evans, Jr.
Daniel G. Donahue
A Fuller Glaser, Jr.
Mark R. Dunn
Mary Ann Hatch (Resident, Bellville, Illinois Office)
James R. Keller

ASSOCIATES

Bryan C. Bacon
Steven B. Beshore
Matthew P. Brookman
Bruce E. Burdick
Dawn T. Christoffersen
David Ross Evelev (Not admitted in MO)
Carol J. Hamilton
Tammy S. King
Patrick N. McHugh
Matthew A. Rosenberg
Mark E. Stallion
Ann Bodewes Stephens
Joan M. Swartz
Lynn M. Thompson
Casper Scott Yost

OF COUNSEL

Gene J. Brockland
Mark S. Hostetler
Raymond C. Loyer
Edward R. Weber

For full biographical listings, see the Martindale-Hubbell Law Directory

LEWIS, RICE & FINGERSH (AV)

A Limited Liability Company
500 North Broadway, Suite 2000, 63102-2147
Telephone: 314-444-7600
Telecopier: 314-241-6056
URL: http://www.lrf.com
Belleville, Illinois Office: 325 South High Street.
Telephone: 618-234-8636.
Leawood, Kansas Office: Suite 375, 8900 State Line Road.
Telephone: 913-381-8898.
Creve Coeur, Missouri Office: 700 Office Parkway, Suite 15.
Telephone: 314-569-2262.
Kansas City, Missouri Office: 1010 Walnut, Suite 500.
Telephone: 816-421-2500.
Washington, Missouri Office: 216 West Main, P.O. Box 1040.
Telephone: 636-239-7747.

RESIDENT MEMBERS

Robert B. Hoemeke
James W. Herron
Michael P. Casey
Allen S. Boston
Barry A. Short
Mark T. Keaney
Andrew Rothschild
John J. Gazzoli, Jr.
Richard A. Ahrens
John J. Moellering
John M. Hessel
Richard A. Wunderlich
James V. O'Brien
Joseph J. Trad
Joseph E. Martineau
Curtis C. Calloway
Richard B. Walsh, Jr.
Jeffrey B. Hunt
David L. Coffman
John E. Hall
Duane L. Coleman
Daniel E. Claggett
Thomas L. Caradonna
Robert J. Golterman
Robert J. Will
Ronald A. Norwood

(See Next Column)

RESIDENT MEMBERS (Continued)

Theodore H. Lucas
Jon A. Santangelo
Gary M. Smith
Benjamin A. Lipman
Jeana D. McFerron
Robert S. Moore
Neal F. Perryman

OF COUNSEL

Robert Smith Allen

ASSOCIATES

Keith J. Grady
Thomas P. Berra, Jr.
Winthrop B. Reed, III
Paul J. Schulte
Shevon L. Harris
Mark N. Light
C. David Goerisch
Christopher C. Swenson

For Complete List of Firm Personnel, See General Section

For full biographical listings, see the Martindale-Hubbell Law Directory

MOSER AND MARSALEK, P.C. (AV)

Suite 700, St. Louis Place, 200 North Broadway, 63102-2730
Telephone: 314-421-5364
Telecopier: 314-421-5640
Email: postmaster@moser.com
Kansas City Office: 1101 Walnut Street, Suite 1510, 64106.
Telephone: 816-471-6060.
Telecopier: 816-471-7744.
Belleville, Illinois Office: 23 South First Street, 62204.
Telephone: 618-234-1408.

W. Edwin Moser (1894-1969)
G. W. Marsalek (1913-1963)
Frank X. Cleary (1900-1975)
John S. Marsalek (1887-1980)
Julian C. Jaeckel (1924-1984)
Joseph H. Mueller
F. Douglas O'Leary
William L. Davis
David L. Zwart
Peter F. Spataro
Brian R. Plegge
Philip L. Willman
Thomas J. Magee
Doreen A. Graham
Kevin M. Leahy
Robyn G. Fox
Brian D. Winer
Jeffrey W. Wright
Terry L. Pijut
Stephen G. Reuter

Ann Gaylor Rucker
Karie E. Casey
Mark A. Cordes
Mark D. Madden
Thomas Edward Fagan
Catherine M. Vale
Neal J. Wallace
Stephen J. Telken
Matthew S. Hendricks

OF COUNSEL

John J. Horgan
Parks G. Carpenter

Representative Clients: Aetna Casualty & Surety; American Indemnity Group; American International Group; Chubb Group Insurance Cos.; Fireman's Fund Insurance Co.; Goodyear Tire & Rubber Co.; Lancer Claims; Medical Protective Insurance Co.; Medical Defense Associates; Tenent.

For full biographical listings, see the Martindale-Hubbell Law Directory

RABBITT, PITZER & SNODGRASS, P.C. (AV)

One NationsBank Plaza, Suite 2300, 800 Market Street, 63101-2608
Telephone: 314-421-5545
Facsimile: 314-421-3144
Email: rps@rabbittlaw.com *URL:* http://www.rabbittlaw.com
Belleville, Illinois Office: 23 South First Street.

Daniel T. Rabbitt
Michael J. Pitzer
Gary E. Snodgrass
Richard J. Zalasky
Peter J. Dunne
Steven J. Hughes
Jerome C. Simon
Donald L. O'Keefe
Seth G. Gausnell
William S. Thomas
Douglas S. Dove
Kimberly Cates Wiseman
James J. Bentivoglio
Jason L. Call
Paula Jane Coughlin
James A. Hansen
Mark M. Anson
Daniel D. Bennett
Elizabeth P. Schott
Christopher J. Lang
J. Phillip Bryant
James Jonathan Rosemergy

For full biographical listings, see the Martindale-Hubbell Law Directory

ROBERTS, PERRYMAN, BOMKAMP & MEIVES, P.C. (AV)

Suite 2300, One Mercantile Center, 63101
Telephone: 314-421-1850
Cable Address: "Henrogo"
Telecopier: 314-421-4346
Email: rpbm@istnet.net
Belleville, Illinois Office: 23 Public Square, Suite 402.
Telephone: 618-277-9955.

Ted L. Perryman
Gary W. Bomkamp
John I. Schaberg
Richard L. Meives
John L. Walker
Thomas J. Kernell
J. Bradley Young
Vickie J. Cochran
Michael P. McDonald, Jr.
Robert C. Anderson
James D. Maschoff

Reference: Boatmen's National Bank.

For full biographical listings, see the Martindale-Hubbell Law Directory

St. Louis—Continued

SCHRAMM & PINES, L.L.C. (AV)

Suite 950 The Bemiston Tower, 231 South Bemiston Avenue, 63105
Telephone: 314-721-5321
Telecopier: 314-721-0790

MEMBERS OF FIRM

Paul H. Schramm
M. Harvey Pines
Daniel R. Schramm

Timothy I. Nicholson
Dean A. Schramm

Reference: Magna Bank.

For full biographical listings, see the Martindale-Hubbell Law Directory

THE SESTRIC LAW FIRM (AV)

801 North Second Street, Suite 401, 63102-2560
Telephone: 314-241-8600
Fax: 314-241-8603
Email: AJSESTRIC@JUNO.COM *URL:* http://www.lawyers.com/thesestriclawfirm

MEMBER OF FIRM

Anthony J. Sestric

ASSOCIATE

Nancy K. Troutman

LEGAL SUPPORT PERSONNEL

Laura A. Schulte

Reference: Mercantile Bank and Trust Co.

For full biographical listings, see the Martindale-Hubbell Law Directory

THOMPSON COBURN LLP (AV)

One Mercantile Center, 63101
Telephone: 314-552-6000
Telecopier: 314-552-7000
Email: info@thompsoncoburn.com *URL:* http://www.thompsoncoburn.com
Belleville, Illinois Office: 525 West Main Street.
Telephone: 618-277-4700.
Telecopier: 618-236-3434.
Washington, D.C. Office: 700 14th Street, N.W., Suite 900.
Telephone: 202-508-1000.
Telecopier: 202-508-1010.
Billings, Montana Office: Norwest Center, 175 North 27th Street, Suite 903, 59101.
Telephone: 406-896-4100.
Fax: 406-896-4199.

MEMBERS OF FIRM

David Wells
Kenneth R. Heineman
J. William Newbold
Gary Mayes

Representative Clients: Emerson Electric Company; General Motors Corp.; GMAC Mortgage Corporation; Mercantile Bank; Monsanto Company; Norwest Business Credit; Peabody Holding Company; Union Pacific Railroad Company; United Industries Corp.

For Complete List of Firm Personnel, See General Section

For full biographical listings, see the Martindale-Hubbell Law Directory

SIKESTON, Scott Co.

DEMENT, VANDIVORT AND DEMENT (AV)

316 South Kingshighway, P.O. Box 158, 63801
Telephone: 573-471-8278
Facsimile: 573-471-8282

MEMBERS OF FIRM

Kenneth L. Dement
William Clayton Vandivort
Kenneth L. Dement, Jr.

References: First Security State Bank, Charleston, Missouri; First National Bank of The Midsouth.

For full biographical listings, see the Martindale-Hubbell Law Directory

DRUMM & THORNTON (AV)

113 West North Street, P.O. Box 40, 63801
Telephone: 573-471-1207
Fax: 573-471-1050

MEMBERS OF FIRM

Manuel Drumm
Fred Howell Thornton, III

Representative Clients: Aetna Casualty & Surety Co.; Cameron Mutual Insurance Co.; Boyer Construction Co.

For full biographical listings, see the Martindale-Hubbell Law Directory

*SPRINGFIELD,** Greene Co.

DANIEL, CLAMPETT, POWELL & CUNNINGHAM, L.L.C. (AV)

A Limited Liability Company
3171 East Sunshine, P.O. Box 10306 G.S., 65808
Telephone: 417-882-9600
Fax: 417-882-7445

MEMBERS OF FIRM

W. Ray Daniel (Retired, 1983)
B. H. Clampett (Retired, 1996)
Max W. Lilley (Retired, 1996)
William D. Powell
Gary R. Cunningham
Patrick K. Roberts
Richard P. Wacker
Charles F. Kiefer, Jr.
M. Douglas Harpool
Michael J. Cordonnier
Patrick J. Platter
Mark L. McQueary
Bryan T. Renfrow
Craig Alden Smith
Paul F. Sherman
Jeffrey L. Groves

ASSOCIATES

Penni Rush Adams
Michael D. Textor
Paul D. Link
Jarrett T. Applegate
Jennifer Ann Headley
Lisa E.Douglass Schrock

OF COUNSEL

James H. Wesley, II

Representative Clients: The Travelers; American Family Insurance Co.; United Services Automobile Assn.; Meadowbrook Claims Service; Chrysler Corporation; Medical Corporation; Medical Protective Company; Missouri Employers Mutual Insurance Co.; Missouri Highway & Transportation Commission.

For full biographical listings, see the Martindale-Hubbell Law Directory

WILLIAM H. MCDONALD & ASSOCIATES, P.C. (AV)

300 South Jefferson, Suite 600, P.O. Box 1245, 65801
Telephone: 417-869-0581
Facsimile: 417-831-7852
Email: mcdassoc@dialnet.net *URL:* http://www.mcdonaldassoc.com

William H. McDonald

William Craig Hosmer
Stuart H. King
James Richard Royce
James A. Endicott
David Andrew Collins
Dana A. Chamblee
Joseph S. Dressner
Eric O. Nau
Venus V. Harry

For full biographical listings, see the Martindale-Hubbell Law Directory

TURNER, REID, DUNCAN, LOOMER & PATTON, P.C. (AV)

Suite A, 1355 East Bradford Parkway, P.O. Box 4043, 65808
Telephone: 417-883-2102
Fax: 417-883-5024

Meredith B. Turner (1913-1993)
Kenneth H. Reid
Donald R. Duncan
Rodney E. Loomer
Michael J. Patton
Sherry Ann Rozell
Joseph P. Winget
Wallace S. Squibb
Steven E. Ward
Jeffrey T. Davis

Representative Clients: General Motors Corp.; Ryder Truck Rental, Inc.; St. John's Regional Health Center; Cox Medical Centers; Allied Groups; CIGNA Ins. Co.; The St. Paul Insurance Cos.; Shelter Insurance Cos; The Cameron Cos.; Employers Reinsurance Corp.

For full biographical listings, see the Martindale-Hubbell Law Directory

MONTANA

*BILLINGS,** Yellowstone Co.

CROWLEY, HAUGHEY, HANSON, TOOLE & DIETRICH, P.L.L.P. (AV)

500 Transwestern II, 490 North 31st Street, P.O. Box 2529, 59103
Telephone: 406-252-3441
Fax: 406-259-4159
Email: crowley@crowleylaw.com
Helena, Montana Office: IBM Building, 100 North Park Avenue, Suite 300, 59601.
Telephone: 406-449-4165.
Fax: 406-449-5149.
Kalispell, Montana Office: 431 1st Avenue West, 59901.
Telephone: 406-752-6644.
Fax: 406-752-5108.
Williston, North Dakota Office: 113 East Broadway, 58801.
Telephone: 701-572-2200.
Fax: 701-572-7072.

OF COUNSEL

Bruce R. Toole
George C. Dalthorp

(See Next Column)

CROWLEY, HAUGHEY, HANSON, TOOLE & DIETRICH P.L.L.P.—*Continued*

MEMBERS OF FIRM

Herbert I. Pierce, III
Terry B. Cosgrove (Resident, Helena, Montana Office)
Ronald R. Lodders
Lawrence B. Cozzens
James P. Sites
Carolyn S. Ostby
Steven J. Lehman
Donald L. Harris
William J. Mattix
Peter F. Habein
Jon T. Dyre (Resident, Kalispell, Montana Office)
Bruce A. Fredrickson
Renee L. Coppock
Janice L. Rehberg
Joe C. Maynard, Jr.
Steven Robert Milch
Leonard H. Smith
Neil G. Westesen
Michael S. Lahr (Resident, Helena, Montana Office)

Representative Clients: Montana Power Company; MDU Resources Group, Inc.; R.J. Reynolds Tobacco Co., Inc.; United Parcel Service; Noranda Minerals Corp.; Connecticut Mutual Life; Metropolitan Life Insurance Co.; Prudential Insurance Co.; Equitable Life Assurance Society of the United States; Washington National Insurance.

For Complete List of Firm Personnel, See General Section

For full biographical listings, see the Martindale-Hubbell Law Directory

*BOZEMAN,** Gallatin Co.

COK, WHEAT, BROWN & MCGARRY, PLLP (AV)

35 North Bozeman Avenue, P.O. Box 1105, 59771-1105
Telephone: 406-587-4445
Facsimile: 406-587-9465
Email: cwblaw@avicom.net

MEMBERS OF FIRM

Michael D. Cok
Michael E. Wheat
John C. Brown
Julieann McGarry

OF COUNSEL

Theodore R. Dunn

A list of Representative Clients will be furnished upon request.
Reference: Valley Bank of Belgrade.

For full biographical listings, see the Martindale-Hubbell Law Directory

KIRWAN & BARRETT, P.C. (AV)

215 West Mendenhall, P.O. Box 1348, 59771-1348
Telephone: 406-586-1553
Fax: 406-586-8971

Peter M. Kirwan
Stephen M. Barrett

For full biographical listings, see the Martindale-Hubbell Law Directory

*GREAT FALLS,** Cascade Co.

JAMES, GRAY, BRONSON & SWANBERG, P.C. (AV)

615 Second Avenue North, P.O. Box 2885, 59403
Telephone: 406-454-5700
Fax: 406-727-0287
URL: http://www.jgbslaw.com

Ted James (1918-1995)
Orville Gray (1920-1993)
Randall H. Gray
Robert F. James
Leslie S. Waite, III
William O. Bronson
Gorham E. Swanberg
Bert A. Fairclough

Nancy Anderson Sinclair
James A. Donahue

Reference: Norwest Bank.

For full biographical listings, see the Martindale-Hubbell Law Directory

*HELENA,** Lewis and Clark Co.

KELLER, REYNOLDS, DRAKE, JOHNSON & GILLESPIE, P.C. (AV)

38 South Last Chance Gulch, 59601
Telephone: 406-442-0230
Fax: 406-449-2256
Email: firm@kellerlawmt.com

P. Keith Keller
Thomas Q. Johnson
Richard E. Gillespie
G. Curt Drake
Jacqueline T. Lenmark
Robert R. Throssell
Charles J. Seifert

Gregory A. Van Horssen
Charles G. Adams

OF COUNSEL

Glen L. Drake

Representative Clients: Northwestern National Insurance Group; Government Employees Insurance Co.; Commercial Union Assurance Cos.; Kemper Insurance Group; Crum and Forster Group; CNA Insurance Cos.; Safeco Insurance; Allstate Insurance Co.; USF&G; American Insurance Assoc.

For full biographical listings, see the Martindale-Hubbell Law Directory

WHITEFISH, Flathead Co.

MORRISONS, MCCARTHY & BARABAN (AV)

236 Wisconsin Avenue, P.O. Box 1090, 59937-1090
Telephone: 406-862-9600
Fax: 406-862-9611
Email: flthdlaw@digisys.net
Claremont, California Office: 401 Harvard Avenue.
Telephone: 909-621-4984.
Fax: 909-621-5757.

Frank B. Morrison, Jr.
Sharon M. Morrison
John C. McCarthy (Resident, Claremont, California Office)
Michael E. Baraban

OF COUNSEL

Frank B. Morrison, Sr.
Larry M. Elison

For full biographical listings, see the Martindale-Hubbell Law Directory

NEBRASKA

*LINCOLN,** Lancaster Co.

CLINE, WILLIAMS, WRIGHT, JOHNSON & OLDFATHER (AV)

1900 U.S. Bank Building, 233 South 13th Street, 68508
Telephone: 402-474-6900
Fax: 402-474-5393
Email: postmaster@cline-law.com *URL:* http://www.cline-law.com
Omaha, Nebraska Office: Suite 720, One Pacific Place, 1125 South 103rd Street, 68124.
Telephone: 402-397-1700.
Fax: 402-397-1806.

ATTORNEYS

Allen L. Graves
Charles M. Pallesen, Jr.
Fredric H. Kauffman
Donald F. Burt
Alan E. Peterson
Stephen E. Gehring
Robert J. Routh
Kevin Colleran
L. Bruce Wright
James M. Bausch
Larry A. Holle
David R. Buntain
Stephen H. Nelsen
Michael C. Mueller
Lauren W. Wismer
Daniel R. Stogsdill
Scott D. Kelly
Terry R. Wittler
Pamela Hastings Carrier
Mark A. Christensen
Richard P. Garden, Jr.
Shawn D. Renner
John C. Miles
Mary Kay Frank
Thomas C. Huston
Sonya S. Ekart
Don R. Janssen
Susan Kubert Sapp
Kevin J. Schneider
Andrew D. Strotman
Jill Gossin Jensen
Rochelle A. Mullen
John L. Horan
Bryan S. Hatch
Steven C. Likes
Tracy A. Oldemeyer
Jolene M. Papa
Timothy G. Aschoff
Eric N. Bergquist
Janis J. Winterhof
Andrea Dylan Snowden

OF COUNSEL

Charles E. Wright
Richard P. Jeffries
Mary M. Campbell

RETIRED PARTNERS

Flavel A. Wright (Retired)
Warren C. Johnson (Retired)
Charles E. Oldfather (1927-1998)

Representative Clients: U.S. Bank National Association; University of Nebraska; Nebraska Medical Assn.; Saint Elizabeth Regional Medical Center; Media of Nebraska; Cargill Inc.; State Farm Insurance Cos.; Wal-Mart Stores, Inc.; Textron/Cushman; Isco, Inc.

For full biographical listings, see the Martindale-Hubbell Law Directory

ERICKSON & SEDERSTROM, P.C. (AV)

Suite 400, Cornhusker Plaza, 301 South 13th Street, 68508
Telephone: 402-476-1000
Fax: 402-476-6167
Omaha, Nebraska Office: Regency Westpointe, 10330 Regency Parkway Drive, Suite 100, 68114-3761.
Telephone: 402-397-2200.
Fax: 402-390-7137.

Charles D. Humble
Linda W. Rohman
David C. Mussman

Representative Clients: Lincoln Electric System; Lincoln General Hospital; Columbia Insurance Group; Cornhusker Casualty Co.

For Complete List of Firm Personnel, See General Section

For full biographical listings, see the Martindale-Hubbell Law Directory

Lincoln—Continued

JOHNSON, FLODMAN, GUENZEL, ESKE & WIDGER (AV)

1227 Lincoln Mall, P.O. Box 81686, 68501-1686
Telephone: 402-475-4240
Fax: 402-475-0329
URL: http://www.linclaw.com

MEMBERS OF FIRM

Robert A. Barlow (1921-1986)
Kile W. Johnson
Steven J. Flodman
Steven E. Guenzel
James A. Eske

Special Counsel: Nebraska Public Power District.
Representative Clients: Atlanta Casualty; Chubb/Pacific Indemnity Group; Citizens State Bank, Polk, Nebraska; Crum & Foster; Federated Rural Electric Insurance Corp.; Runza Drive-Inns of America; State Farm Insurance Cos.; Viking Insurance Company of Wisconsin.

For full biographical listings, see the Martindale-Hubbell Law Directory

*MCCOOK,** Red Willow Co.

BURGER & BENNETT, P.C. (AV)

116 West E Street, P.O. Box 1205, 69001
Telephone: 308-345-7500
Fax: 308-345-7503
Email: ten60w.addison@navix.net

G. Peter Burger
Daylene A. Bennett

For full biographical listings, see the Martindale-Hubbell Law Directory

*OMAHA,** Douglas Co.

BRADFORD, COENEN & WELSH (AV)

1800 First National Center, 1620 Dodge Street, 68102-1500
Telephone: 402-342-4200
Fax: 402-342-4202
URL: http://www.bcwlaw.com

MEMBERS OF FIRM

D.C. "Woody" Bradford
James R. Welsh
Richard J. Coenen

ASSOCIATE

James Polack

Reference: First National Bank of Omaha.

For full biographical listings, see the Martindale-Hubbell Law Directory

CLINE, WILLIAMS, WRIGHT, JOHNSON & OLDFATHER (AV)

One Pacific Place, 1125 South 103rd Street, Suite 720, 68124
Telephone: 402-397-1700
Fax: 402-397-1806
Email: postmaster@cline-law.com *URL:* http://www.cline-law.com
Lincoln, Nebraska Office: 1900 U.S. Bank Building, 233 South 13th Street, 68508.
Telephone: 402-474-6900.
Fax: 402-474-5393.

ATTORNEYS

Donald F. Burt
Stephen E. Gehring
James M. Bausch
Michael C. Mueller
Daniel R. Stogsdill
Scott D. Kelly
John C. Miles
Mary Kay Frank
Andrew D. Strotman
Rochelle A. Mullen
Steven C. Likes
Tracy A. Oldemeyer
Timothy G. Aschoff

OF COUNSEL

Richard P. Jeffries

Representative Clients: U.S. Bank National Association; University of Nebraska; Nebraska Medical Assn.; Saint Elizabeth Regional Medical Center; Media of Nebraska; Cargill Inc.; State Farm Insurance Cos.; Wal-Mart Stores, Inc.; Textron/Cushman; ISCO, Inc.

For full biographical listings, see the Martindale-Hubbell Law Directory

DOMINA LAW PC (AV)

1065 North 115th Street, 68154-4423
Telephone: 402-493-4100
Fax: 402-493-9782
Email: law@dominalaw.com

David A. Domina
Cletus W. Blakeman
Jerold V. Fennell

W. Craig Howell
Pamela J. Dahlquist
Nora M. Kane
James F. Cann

For full biographical listings, see the Martindale-Hubbell Law Directory

DWYER, SMITH, GARDNER, LAZER, POHREN, ROGERS & FORREST (AV)

Suite 400, 8712 West Dodge Road, 68114
Telephone: 402-392-0101
Telefax: 402-392-1011
Email: dwyerlaw@dwyer-smith.com *URL:* http://www.dwyer-smith.com

MEMBERS OF FIRM

Michael L. Lazer
Clay M. Rogers
Bruce H. Abrahamson
H. Daniel Smith
Edward F. Pohren
Christopher D. Curzon

ASSOCIATE

Patrick Edward Griffin, Jr.

Representative Clients: Ford Motor Credit Company, Dearborn, Michigan; Nebraska Hospital Association subsidiary Bio Electronics, Lincoln, Oak Bancorporation; Lynn Roberts International; Elliot Equipment Co.; Design Plastics, Inc.

For Complete List of Firm Personnel, See General Section

For full biographical listings, see the Martindale-Hubbell Law Directory

ERICKSON & SEDERSTROM, P.C. (AV)

Regency Westpointe, 10330 Regency Parkway Drive, Suite 100, 68114-3761
Telephone: 402-397-2200
Fax: 402-390-7137
Lincoln, Nebraska Office: Suite 400, Cornhusker Plaza, 301 South 13th Street, 68508-2571.
Telephone: 402-476-1000.
Fax: 402-476-6167.

Donald H. Erickson
John C. Brownrigg
Thomas J. Culhane
Richard J. Gilloon
Jerald L. Rauterkus

Kevin R. McManaman

OF COUNSEL

Leo Eisenstatt

Representative Clients: Applied Communications, Inc.; Cornhusker Casualty Co.; Hartford Accident & Indemnity Co.; Imperial Casualty & Indemnity Co.; J I Case Co.; Lueder Construction Co.; National American Insurance Company of Nebraska; Pepsico, Inc.; West Telemarketing Corp.

For Complete List of Firm Personnel, See General Section

For full biographical listings, see the Martindale-Hubbell Law Directory

KATSKEE, HENATSCH & SUING (AV)

10404 Essex Court, Suite 100, 68114
Telephone: 402-391-1697
Fax: 402-391-8932
Email: katskee@uswest.net

MEMBERS OF FIRM

Milton A. Katskee
Dean F. Suing
Jerry W. Katskee

ASSOCIATES

Francis T. Belsky
David A. Castello
John B. Henley
Todd W. Weidemann

OF COUNSEL

Harry R. Henatsch

Reference: Mid-City Bank.

For full biographical listings, see the Martindale-Hubbell Law Directory

LAUGHLIN, PETERSON & LANG (AV)

11306 Davenport Street, 68154
Telephone: 402-330-1900
Fax: 402-330-0936
Email: mlaugh43@aol.com

MEMBERS OF FIRM

Mark L. Laughlin
Robert F. Peterson
James E. Lang

Representative Clients: Aliant Communications; General Electric Capital Corp.; Dodge Land Co.; Dodge Development Company; Security Mutual Life Insurance Co. of Lincoln, NE; Century Development Co.; Invesco Realty Advisors; M & S Grading, Inc.

For full biographical listings, see the Martindale-Hubbell Law Directory

MCGILL, GOTSDINER, WORKMAN & LEPP, P.C. (AV)

Suite 500 - First National Plaza, 11404 West Dodge Road, 68154
Telephone: 402-492-9200
Telecopier: 402-492-9222
Email: mgwl@mgwl.com

(See Next Column)

McGILL, GOTSDINER, WORKMAN & LEPP P.C.—*Continued*

Robert L. Lepp
Michael S. Mostek
Paul R. Elofson
Mary L. Hewitt

Representative Clients: Norwest Bank Nebraska N.A.; Metz Baking Company; Vetter Health Services, Inc.; Behlen Mfg. Co.; Mutual of Omaha; Woolworth Corp.; Crawford & Co.

For Complete List of Firm Personnel, See General Section

For full biographical listings, see the Martindale-Hubbell Law Directory

McGRATH, NORTH, MULLIN & KRATZ, P.C. (AV)

Suite 1400, One Central Park Plaza, 68102
Telephone: 402-341-3070
Fax: 402-341-0216

John E. North
Robert D. Mullin, Sr.
James P. Fitzgerald
Leo A. Knowles
Terrence D. O'Hare
John F. Thomas
John P. Passarelli
Mark F. Enenbach
Roger J. Miller
Timothy J. Pugh
Robert D. Mullin, Jr.
Thomas C. McGowan
A. Stevenson Bogue
William F. Hargens
Robert J. Bothe
Edward G. Warin
Michael G. Mullin
Patrick J. Barrett
Steven P. Case
James G. Powers
Ronald L. Comes
Gary F. Wence
Douglas E. Quinn
J. Scott Paul
James J. Frost
Martel J. Bundy
Patrick E. Brookhouser, Jr.
James M. Sulentic
Terry Bauman White
William J. Birkel
John J. Schirger
Aaron A. Clark

General Counsel for: ConAgra, Inc.; InaCom Corp.; Omaha Airport Authority; Physicians Mutual Insurance Co.; Supertel Hospitality, Inc.; Valmont Industries, Inc.
Representative Clients: Clarkson Hospital; Omaha Chamber of Commerce.
Insurance Clients: American Family Insurance Group; Blue Cross-Blue Shield of Nebraska.

For Complete List of Firm Personnel, See General Section

For full biographical listings, see the Martindale-Hubbell Law Directory

NEVADA

*ELKO,** Elko Co.

LAW OFFICES GOICOECHEA & DI GRAZIA, LTD. A PROFESSIONAL CORPORATION (AV)

In Association with
Vaughan & Hull, Ltd.
A Professional Corporation
200, Blohm Building, P.O. Box 1358, 89803
Telephone: 775-738-8091
Fax: 775-738-4220
Email: gdclaws@cyberhighway.net

Robert B. Goicoechea
Gary E. Di Grazia
Thomas J. Coyle, Jr.

David M. Stanton

Representative Clients: Independence Minning Co., Inc.; Alpark Petroleum, Inc.; Nevada Bank & Trust; Metropolitan Life Insurance.

For full biographical listings, see the Martindale-Hubbell Law Directory

PUCCINELLI & PUCCINELLI (AV)

700 Idaho Street, 89801-0130
Telephone: 775-738-7293
FAX: 775-738-0454
Mailing Address: P.O. Box 130, 89803

MEMBERS OF FIRM

Leo J. Puccinelli
Andrew J. Puccinelli

Michael Shurtz

Representative Clients: Credit Bureau of Elko County; Wells Fargo Bank of Nevada; Elko Sanitation Co.; Beehive Telephone Co.; A & E Enterprises, Inc.; Elko Television District.
References: Wells Fargo Bank of Nevada, N.A.; Bank of America.

For full biographical listings, see the Martindale-Hubbell Law Directory

HENDERSON, Clark Co.

ROOKER & GIBSON (AV)

Suite 105, 701 North Green Valley Parkway, 89014
Telephone: 702-990-8100
Telecopier: 702-932-5266

C. Keith Rooker
James B. Gibson

Reference: BankWest of Nevada.

For full biographical listings, see the Martindale-Hubbell Law Directory

*LAS VEGAS,** Clark Co.

ALBRIGHT, STODDARD, WARNICK & ALBRIGHT, A PROFESSIONAL CORPORATION (AV)

Quail Park I, Building D-4, 801 South Rancho Drive, 89106
Telephone: 702-384-7111
Fax: 702-384-0605
URL: http://www.aswalaw.com

G. Vern Albright
William H. Stoddard
Whitney B. Warnick
G. Mark Albright

D. Chris Albright
Tami C. Budo
Corey D. Randall (Not admitted in NV)

Representative Clients: Tokio Marine and Fire Insurance Co.; INAPRO, a CIGNA Co.; Nevada Ready Mix; North American Health Care, Inc. (Nursing Home); Royal Insurance; First Security Bank of Utah; Nevada Community Bank; Nationwide Insurance Co.; Liberty Mutual Insurance; CB Commercial.

For full biographical listings, see the Martindale-Hubbell Law Directory

ALVERSON, TAYLOR, MORTENSEN, NELSON & SANDERS (AV)

7401 West Charleston Boulevard, 89117
Telephone: 702-384-7000
FAX: 702-385-7000
Email: alverson@intermind.net
Reno, Nevada Office: 245 East Liberty, Suite 520, 89505.
Telephone: 775-329-0473.
Fax: 775-329-3303.

MEMBERS OF FIRM

J. Bruce Alverson
Eric K. Taylor
David J. Mortensen
Erven T. Nelson
LeAnn Sanders

OF COUNSEL

Jack C. Cherry
Kurt D. Anderson
Philip C. Van Alstyne

ASSOCIATES

Rebecca Hopkins Miller
Sandra Smagac
Victoria L. Nelson
Aaron D. Lovaas
Diane Obritsch
Michael A. Olsen
Randal D. Shimon
Catherine A. Olendorff
Monica L. Pierce
Gabriel D. Lither
Kurt R. Bonds
Darius F. Rafie
Mark J. King, IV
Shell L. Mercer
Carrie S. Bourdeau
Jason Lane Earnest
Nathan R. Reinmiller
Donn C. Alexander
Afshin Tadayon
Eric O. Freeman
Lindsay L. Stadtlander
Julie M. Sueoka

Representative Clients: Citibank; General Electric Corporation; Kentucky Fried Chicken; Federal Deposit Insurance Corporation (FDIC); American Bonding Company; Southwest Gas Corporation; Decratrend Corporation; ETEC Testing Laboratories; Yellow Cab Company.

For full biographical listings, see the Martindale-Hubbell Law Directory

BARKER, BROWN, BUSBY, CHRISMAN & THOMAS, A PROFESSIONAL CORPORATION (AV)

800 Bank of America Plaza, 300 South Fourth Street, 89101
Telephone: 702-386-1086
Fax: 702-384-5386
Email: BAR-BRO@IX.NETCOM.COM

William S. Barker
Janice J. Brown
Jerry S. Busby
James P. Chrisman
David L. Thomas
Robert A. Winner

Robert D. Tarte
Brent A. Carson
Marino A. Cesaretti
Ann C. Elworth
Michael D. Demman
Curtis J. Busby
J. Scott Ralston

LEGAL SUPPORT PERSONNEL

David A. Ross (Not admitted in NV)
Michael W. Salend
Michael Allen Davis
Britt K. Beckstrom

(See Next Column)

BARKER, BROWN, BUSBY, CHRISMAN & THOMAS A PROFESSIONAL CORPORATION, *Las Vegas—Continued*

Representative Clients: Ford Motor Co.; National Food Processors; Sta-Rite Industries; Albertsons, Inc.; Combustion Engineering; Charter Medical Corp.; Caterpillar, Inc.; Smith's Management Corp.

For full biographical listings, see the Martindale-Hubbell Law Directory

THOMAS D. BEATTY (AV)

601 East Bridger Avenue, 89101
Telephone: 702-382-5111
Facsimile: 702-382-2892

ASSOCIATE

Rena G. Hughes

Reference: Wells Fargo Bank.

For full biographical listings, see the Martindale-Hubbell Law Directory

KENNETH C. CORY A PROFESSIONAL CORPORATION (AV)

626 South Third Street, 89101
Telephone: 702-384-0111
Fax: 702-384-0763
Email: kcory@accessnv.com *URL:* http://www.lawyers.com/kennethcory

Kenneth C. Cory

For full biographical listings, see the Martindale-Hubbell Law Directory

DEANER, DEANER, SCANN, MALAN & LARSEN (AV)

720 South Fourth Street, Suite 300, 89101
Telephone: 702-382-6911
Fax: 702-386-6048
Email: CDeaner@ix.netcom.com *URL:* http://www.lawyers.com/ddsm&lfirm

MEMBERS OF FIRM

Charles W. Deaner
J. Douglas Deaner (1944-1990)
Susan Williams Scann
Douglas R. Malan
Brent A. Larsen

ASSOCIATE

Anthony Ciulla

Representative Clients: California Federal Bank; White Concrete, Inc. Silver State Schools Federal Credit Union.
Reference: First Security Bank.

For full biographical listings, see the Martindale-Hubbell Law Directory

DENTON & LOPEZ (AV)

626 South Seventh Street, 89101
Telephone: 702-384-1723
Fax: 702-384-8019

Ralph L. Denton
Joseph A. Lopez, IV

Representative Clients: Shetakis Wholesalers, Inc.; TRW, Inc.; Leprechaun Mining & Chemical, Inc.; USA Hosts, Ltd; Experian Information Solutions, Inc.
Reference: Bank of America.

For full biographical listings, see the Martindale-Hubbell Law Directory

DICKERSON, DICKERSON, CONSUL & POCKER (AV)

Suite 1130, 330 South Third Street, 89101
Telephone: 702-388-8600
Fax: 702-388-0210

MEMBERS OF FIRM

George M. Dickerson
Robert P. Dickerson
Vincent A. Consul
Richard J. Pocker
Douglass A. Mitchell
Paul J. Lal
Bryce C. Duckworth

ASSOCIATES

Stacie L. Brown
Shann D. Winesett
David F. Sampson

Reference: Citibank.

For full biographical listings, see the Martindale-Hubbell Law Directory

EDWARDS, SOOY & BYRON, A PROFESSIONAL CORPORATION (AV Ⓣ)

3960 Howard Hughes Parkway Fifth Floor, 89109
Telephone: 702-474-0861
Fax: 702-474-4538
Email: esb-legal.com *URL:* http://www.esb-legal.com
San Diego, California Office: 101 West Broadway, Ninth Floor, 92101.
Telephone: 619-231-1500.
Fax: 619-231-1588.

Michael M. Edwards (Not admitted in NV)
Richard R. Sooy
Thomas W. Byron

(See Next Column)

Alfred Paul Centofanti, III
Bart M. Blechschmidt
Michael M. Edwards, Jr.

For full biographical listings, see the Martindale-Hubbell Law Directory

FITZGIBBONS & ANDERSON (AV)

214 South Maryland Parkway, 89101-5319
Telephone: 702-382-2721
FAX: 702-388-4488
Email: FALAWCORP@AOL.COM *URL:* http://www.lawyers.com/fitzgibbons&anderson

MEMBERS OF FIRM

Pat Fitzgibbons
Mark R. Anderson

For full biographical listings, see the Martindale-Hubbell Law Directory

FOLEY & JONES (AV)

850 East Bonneville Avenue, 89101
Telephone: 702-383-9852
Fax: 702-383-8154
Email: FoleyJones@worldnet.att.net *URL:* http://www.lawyers.com/f&jlaw

Joseph M. Foley
Daniel T. Foley
Diana J. Foley
Mark M. Jones

For full biographical listings, see the Martindale-Hubbell Law Directory

GALATZ, EARL, & ASSOCIATES (AV)

710 South Fourth Street, 89101
Telephone: 702-386-0000
Fax: 702-384-0394
Email: neilgalatz@aol.com *URL:* http://www.lawyers.com/galatzlaw

Neil G. Galatz
Allan R. Earl

For full biographical listings, see the Martindale-Hubbell Law Directory

JOEL F. HANSEN & ASSOCIATES (AV)

Suite 200, 415 South Sixth Street, 89101-6937
Telephone: 702-385-5533
Fax: 702-382-8891
Email: HansenLaw@aol.com *URL:* http://www.ins.lawnt.com

LEGAL SUPPORT PERSONNEL

Carole F. Chapman
Karen Quick

Representative Clients: American Drug Stores; Motel 6; Gustin Corporation; Kemper Insurance Group; State Farm Fire and Casualty Company; American National Property and Casualty Company; E & O Professionals; American States Insurance; State Farm Mutual Automobile Insurance Company.

For full biographical listings, see the Martindale-Hubbell Law Directory

JOLLEY, URGA, WIRTH & WOODBURY (AV)

3800 Howard Hughes Parkway Suite 1600, 89109
Telephone: 702-699-7500
Facsimile: 702-699-7555
URL: http://www.juww.com
Boulder City, Nevada Office: Suite 105, 1000 Nevada Highway, 89005.
Telephone: 702-293-3674.

MEMBERS OF FIRM

R. Gardner Jolley
William R. Urga
Roger A. Wirth
Bruce L. Woodbury
Kathryn Stryker Wirth
Brian E. Holthus
Allen D. Emmel

ASSOCIATE

Gregory G. Gordon

Representative Clients: Wells Fargo Bank and its predecessor, First Interstate Bank of Nevada; Nevada State Bank; Citicorp National Services, Inc.; Chicago Title Insurance Co.; National Title Company; Fidelity National Title; First Security Bank of Nevada; General Motors Acceptance Corp.; Ford Motor Credit Co.; Toyota Motor Credit Corporation.

For Complete List of Firm Personnel, See General Section

For full biographical listings, see the Martindale-Hubbell Law Directory

KEEFER, O'REILLY & FERRARIO (AV)

An Association including a Professional Corporation
Nevada Professional Center, 325 South Maryland Parkway, 89101
Telephone: 702-382-2660; 384-8944
Fax: 702-387-6978
Email: JORAPC@ACCESSWORLDNET.COM

Milton W. Keefer (1914-1999)
John F. O'Reilly (A Professional Corporation)
Mark E. Ferrario

(See Next Column)

KEEFER, O'REILLY & FERRARIO—*Continued*

Anita A. Webster
Preston B. Howard
Cynthia Gunther Milanowski
Jennifer A. McGargill
William J. Wray
Glenn F. Meier
Charles W. Simmons
Sandra L. Stewart
Antonia Z. Cowan

Representative Clients: ITT Hartford; MGM Grand Hotel; Aetna Insurance Company; Del Webb Corp.

For full biographical listings, see the Martindale-Hubbell Law Directory

KIRSHMAN, HARRIS & BRANTON, A PROFESSIONAL CORPORATION (AV)

411 East Bonneville Avenue Suite 300, 89101
Telephone: 702-384-3877
Fax: 702-384-7057; 702-384-4250
Email: Kirshman@Juno.com
Beverly Hills, California Office: 315 South Beverly Drive, Suite 315.
Telephone: 310-277-2323.
Telecopier: 310-277-6701.

Norman H. Kirshman
Michael S. Harris
Gary G. Branton
Roger L. Grandgenett, II

Mary F. Chapman

Representative Clients: American Nevada Corp.; City of Henderson; Printronix; Caesars Palace; Nevada Ready Mix; Contractors Wardrobe, Inc; Lewis Homes/Kaufman & Broad; Sands Expo and Convention Center; Republic Silver State Disposal Service, Inc.

For full biographical listings, see the Martindale-Hubbell Law Directory

KRAVITZ, SCHNITZER & SLOANE, CHARTERED, A PROFESSIONAL CORPORATION (AV)

2300 West Sahara Avenue, Suite 500, 89102
Telephone: 702-362-6666
Fax: 702-362-2203
Email: KRAVSCHNIT@AOL.COM

Martin J. Kravitz
Gary E. Schnitzer
Jeffrey G. Sloane
Michael Bradley Johnson
Jane Eberhardy
Marisa C. Guarino

David J. Feldman
Jerry R. Graf

LEGAL SUPPORT PERSONNEL

Sandye Smith (Legal Administrator)

Representative Clients: MGM Grand Hotel & Casino; Circus Circus Enterprises; Hilton Hotels Corporation; State Farm Insurance Companies; John Goodman & Associates; Realty Executives; Makena Development; Realty Executives; Allstate Insurance Company.

For full biographical listings, see the Martindale-Hubbell Law Directory

KUMMER KAEMPFER BONNER & RENSHAW (AV)

Seventh Floor, 3800 Howard Hughes Parkway, 89109-0907
Telephone: 702-792-7000
Fax: 702-796-7181
Email: nvlaw@kkbr.com

MEMBERS OF FIRM

John C. Renshaw
Thomas F. Kummer
Christopher L. Kaempfer
Michael J. Bonner
Kathleen Jane England
John N. Brewer
Gerald D. Waite
Sherwood N. Cook
Shari Cassin Patterson
John C. Jeppsen
Mark H. Fiorentino
John A. Curtas

OF COUNSEL

H. Gregory Nasky
James H. Bilbray
Michael W. Brimley

ASSOCIATES

Thomas D. Amick
Sean L. Anderson
(Not admitted in NV)
Nikki L. Baker
George J. Claseman
L. Joe Coppedge
Gregory S. Gilbert
Robert J. Gronauer
Robert C. Kim
Kurt C. Lambeth
Angela Turriciano Otto
Elizabeth A. Savage
Lyssa M. Simonelli
James E. Smyth II
Gregg R. Vermeys
Anthony A. Zmaila

For full biographical listings, see the Martindale-Hubbell Law Directory

JOHN PETER LEE, LTD. (AV)

830 Las Vegas Boulevard South, 89101
Telephone: 702-382-4044
Telecopier: 702-383-9950

John Peter Lee

(See Next Column)

Nancy L. Allf
Paul C. Ray
Timothy P. Thomas

For Complete List of Firm Personnel, See General Section

For full biographical listings, see the Martindale-Hubbell Law Directory

LEFEBVRE, BARRON & VIVONE, CHTD. (AV)

1404 South Jones Boulevard, 89146-1231
Telephone: 702-383-8668
Facsimile: 702-383-6828
Email: lb@coam.net

Alan J. Lefebvre
David L. Barron
Thomas J. Vivone
Raymond W. Holland
Michelle O. Tobler
William Howard Pruitt
Bradley V. Gibbons
Jared Casper
(Not admitted in NV)
Kevin S. Smith

LEGAL SUPPORT PERSONNEL

Jennifer L. Hageman

For full biographical listings, see the Martindale-Hubbell Law Directory

LIONEL SAWYER & COLLINS (AV)

1700 Bank of America Plaza, 300 South Fourth Street, 89101
Telephone: 702-383-8888
Fax: 702-383-8845
Email: first initial last@lionelsawyer.com
Reno, Nevada Office: Suite 1100, Bank of America Plaza, 50 West Liberty Street.
Telephone: 702-788-8666.
Fax: 702-788-8682.

MEMBERS OF FIRM

Samuel S. Lionel
Paul Hejmanowski
(Managing Partner)
David N. Frederick
Dennis L. Kennedy
Richard W. Horton
(Resident, Reno Office)
Dan C. Bowen
(Resident, Reno Office)
Mark A. Solomon
Rodney M. Jean
Todd M. Touton
Cam Ferenbach
Lynda Sue Mabry
Kirby J. Smith
Jennifer A. Smith
(Resident, Reno Office)
John R. Bailey
Laurel Elizabeth Davis
Dan R. Reaser
(Resident, Reno Office)
Howard E. Cole
Paul E. Larsen
Christopher R. Hooper
(Resident, Reno Office)
Suvinder S. Ahluwalia

OF COUNSEL

Robert M. Buckalew
Ellen F. Whittemore

ASSOCIATES

Jeffrey D. Menicucci
(Resident, Reno Office)
Madelene C. Amendola
(Resident, Reno Office)
Stephen R. Hackett
Robert P. Spretnak
Allen Jay Wilt
(Resident, Reno Office)
Michael D. Rawlins
Etta L. Walker
(Resident, Reno Office)
Nathalie Huynh
(Resident, Reno Office)
Leslie Bryan Hart
(Resident, Reno Office)
David J. Merrill
Todd E. Kennedy
Laura J. Thalacker
Kenneth Robert Myers
James M. Sarnecky
Hector J. Carbajal, II
Janet Sue Bessemer
G. Lance Coburn
Joshua M. Dickey
Christopher M. Strongosky
Shawn A. Mangano
Joanna L. Blake
(Not admitted in NV)
John M. Naylor

Representative Clients: Caesars Palace; Citicorp; Columbia Healthcare Corp.; General Motors Corporation; Humana Inc.; Kerr McGee Corporation; Lewis Homes of Nevada; Sunrise Hospital & Medical Center.

For Complete List of Firm Personnel, See General Section

For full biographical listings, see the Martindale-Hubbell Law Directory

MCDONALD CARANO WILSON MCCUNE BERGIN FRANKOVICH & HICKS LLP (AV)

Suite 1000, 2300 West Sahara Avenue, 89102
Telephone: 702-873-4100
Telecopier: 702-873-9966
URL: http://www.mcdonaldcarano.com
Reno, Nevada Office: 241 Ridge Street.
Telephone: 775-788-2000.
Telecopier: 775-788-2020.

MEMBERS OF FIRM

Thomas R. C. Wilson
James W. Bradshaw
David W. Huston
George F. Ogilvie III
Sylvia L. Harrison
Pat Lundvall
Andrew P. Gordon
Bryan R. Clark

(See Next Column)

McDONALD CARANO WILSON McCUNE BERGIN FRANKOVICH & HICKS LLP, *Las Vegas—Continued*

ASSOCIATES

Anthony D. Guenther
Jeffrey A. Silvestri
David S. Jennings

Representative Clients: AT&T Communications of Nevada; Boomtown, Inc.; Boyd Gaming Corporation; Jackpot Enterprises, Inc.; Q & D Construction, Inc.; Hamilton Group of Companies.

For Complete List of Firm Personnel, See General Section

For full biographical listings, see the Martindale-Hubbell Law Directory

MORSE & MOWBRAY, A PROFESSIONAL CORPORATION (AV)

Suite 1400 Bank of America Plaza, 300 South Fourth Street, 89101
Telephone: 702-384-6340
Telecopier: 702-384-4596
London, England Office: Lamb Building, Temple.
Telephone: 071-353-6701.

William R. Morse
Harold M. Morse
John H. Mowbray
Christopher H. Byrd
Kimberly A. Buchanan

For full biographical listings, see the Martindale-Hubbell Law Directory

PICO & MITCHELL (AV)

2000 South Eastern Avenue, 89104
Telephone: 702-457-9099
FAX: 702-457-8451
Email: lawyers@picomitchell.com

MEMBERS OF FIRM

James F. Pico
Bert O. Mitchell
Christy Brad Escobar
James R. Rosenberger
E. Breen Arntz

ASSOCIATES

Michelle Schwarz
Rebecca L. Mastrangelo
Jill M. Chase
Daniel E. Carvalho
Stephen H. Rogers

Representative Clients: Home Insurance Co.; State Farm Mutual Insurance Co.; Industrial Indemnity Insurance Co.; Great American Insurance Co.; Argonaut Insurance Cos.; Clark County Medical Society; Rose de Lima Hospital; Fairway Chevrolet; American States Insurance Co.; The Hartford Insurance Co.

For full biographical listings, see the Martindale-Hubbell Law Directory

RYAN MARKS JOHNSON TODD & BRODER (AV⓪)

1160 Town Center Drive, Suite 300, 89134
Telephone: 702-341-7870
Facsimile: 702-341-8049
San Diego, California Office: Wingert Grebing Brubaker & Ryan LLP, One America Plaza, Seventh Floor, 600 West Broadway, 92101-3370.
Telephone: 619-232-8151.
Facsimile: 619-232-4665.

MEMBERS OF FIRM

Norman A. Ryan
Eileen Mulligan Marks
Robert L. Johnson
Christopher W. Todd
James P. Broder

ASSOCIATES

Stephen C. Grebing
Jay A. Kenyon

For full biographical listings, see the Martindale-Hubbell Law Directory

SCHRECK MORRIS (AV)

1200 Bank of America Plaza, 300 South Fourth Street, 89101
Telephone: 702-382-2101
Fax: 702-382-8135; 702-474-9422
URL: http://www.schreckmorris.com
Reno, Nevada Office: 100 West Liberty, Suite 940, 89501.
Telephone: 775-322-7777.
Facsimile: 775-322-7791.

MEMBERS OF FIRM

Frank A. Schreck
Steve Morris
Andrew S. Brignone
Leslie Terry Jones
Mary Kristina Pickering
John A. Godfrey
Ann Morgan
Sean T. McGowan
Ellen Schulhofer
James J. Pisanelli
Clark V. Vellis
Todd L. Bice

ASSOCIATES

James R. Chamberlain
Dennis V. Gallagher
Margaret L. Sanner
F. Edward Mulholland, II
Elizabeth M. Fielder
Elayna Youchah
Sonia C. Vermeys
Denise Michaelides
Mary J. Drury
John P. Desmond
Adam P. Segal
Matthew McCaughey
Amelia R. De Los Santos
Wendy Medura

(See Next Column)

ASSOCIATES (Continued)

Robert J. Grasso
Shawn G. Pearson
David Dornak
Matthew L. Heinhold
Paul D. Colton

For full biographical listings, see the Martindale-Hubbell Law Directory

THORNDAL, ARMSTRONG, DELK, BALKENBUSH & EISINGER, A PROFESSIONAL CORPORATION (AV)

1100 East Bridger Avenue, P.O. Box 2070, 89125-2070
Telephone: 702-366-0622
Fax: 702-366-0327
Email: info@thorndal.com *URL:* http://www.thorndal.com
Reno, Nevada Office: Suite 200, 888 West Second Street.
Telephone: 775-786-2882.
Fax: 775-786-8004.
Elko, Nevada Office: 919 Idaho Street, P.O. Box 5508.
Telephone: 775-777-3011.
Fax: 775-786-8004.

John L. Thorndal
James G. Armstrong
Craig R. Delk
Stephen C. Balkenbush (Resident, Reno Office)
Paul F. Eisinger
Charles Lee Burcham (Resident, Reno Office)
Brian K. Terry
Brent Thomas Kolvet (Resident, Reno Office)
Blair C. Parker
William R. Killip, Jr.
Robert F. Balkenbush (Resident, Reno Office)

Michael E. Sullivan (Resident, Reno Office)
Philip Goodhart
Deborah L. Elsasser
James J. Jackson
Gavin C. Jangard
R. Scott Rasmussen
Christopher J. Curtis
Alyssa A. Martini
Susan E. Frasca
Daniel D. Norr
David P. Lane
William R. Jones
Katherine F. Bobier (Resident, Reno Office)
C. Scott Wormsley
Renee E. Jensen
Thierry V. Barkley (Resident, Reno Office)

Representative Clients: Allied Insurance Group; American Hardware; California Casualty; Cigna; Employer's Reinsurance; Farmers Insurance Exchange; Federated Group; Nationwide Insurance; Reliance Insurance Co., Inc.; Zurich-American Insurance.

For full biographical listings, see the Martindale-Hubbell Law Directory

WRIGHT, JUDD & WINCKLER (AV)

302 East Carson Avenue, 3rd Floor, 89101
Telephone: 702-382-4004
FAX: 702-382-4800
Email: wjw@netxs.net

MEMBERS OF FIRM

Richard A. Wright
Bruce M. Judd
Karen C. Winckler

For full biographical listings, see the Martindale-Hubbell Law Directory

*LOVELOCK,** Pershing Co.

BELANGER & PLIMPTON (AV)

1135 Central Avenue, P.O. Box 59, 89419
Telephone: 702-273-2631
Fax: 702-273-2649
Email: todd@todd.lovelock.nv.us

MEMBERS OF FIRM

Roland W. Belanger
Todd A. Plimpton

Representative Clients: Sturgeon's Log Cabin, Inc.; Burns Bros., Inc.; Humboldt River Ranch Homeowner's Association.
Reference: Burns Bros., Inc.

For full biographical listings, see the Martindale-Hubbell Law Directory

*RENO,** Washoe Co.

ERICKSON, THORPE & SWAINSTON, LTD. (AV)

99 West Arroyo Street, P.O. Box 3559, 89505
Telephone: 702-786-3930
Fax: 702-786-4160
Email: etsreno@aol.com

Roger L. Erickson
Donald A. Thorpe
George W. Swainston
William G. Cobb
Gary A. Cardinal
Thomas Peter Beko
John A. Aberasturi
Paul M. Bertone
Lisa E. Bruce
John C. Boyden

Representative Clients: Albertson's, Inc.; Avis Rent-A-Car System; Chrysler Corp.; Airport Authority of Washoe County; Dow Corning; Reno-Sparks Convention and Visitors Authority; Bank of America NT & SA; Brown & Williamson Tobacco Corp.; Crete Carrier Corporation; Sears Roebuck & Co.; Dayton Tire & Rubber Company.

For full biographical listings, see the Martindale-Hubbell Law Directory

Reno—Continued

Erwin Thompson & Hascheff (AV)

A Partnership including Professional Corporations
Suite 424, One East Liberty Street, P.O. Box 40817, 89501-2123
Telephone: 775-786-9494
Facsimile: 775-786-1180
Email: erwin@renolaw.com *URL:* http://www.renolaw.com

Pierre A. Hascheff
Frank W. Thompson
Thomas P. Erwin

Reference: U.S. Bank (Reno, Nevada, Main Office).

For full biographical listings, see the Martindale-Hubbell Law Directory

---

Guild, Russell, Gallagher & Fuller, Ltd. (AV)

100 West Liberty, Suite 800, P.O. Box 2838, 89505
Telephone: 775-786-2366
Telecopier: 775-322-9105
Email: attorneys@grgflaw.com

Clark J. Guild (1887-1971)
C. David Russell
Clark J. Guild, Jr.
John K. Gallagher
Gary M. Fuller

Jason J. Freelin

Representative Clients: Caithness Resources, Inc.; Chevron USA, Inc.; Dickson Realty; DRGM Advertising Agency; Federal Deposit Insurance Corp.; Intermountain Power Project; Land Rover North America; Porsche Cars North America; Jones-West Ford; City of Los Angeles, Department of Water & Power; Metropolitan Water District of Southern California; Microsoft Corporation; 100 W. Liberty Ltd. Partnership.

For full biographical listings, see the Martindale-Hubbell Law Directory

---

Laxalt & Nomura, Ltd. (AV)

50 West Liberty Street Suite 700, 89501
Telephone: 775-322-1170
Facsimile: 775-322-1865
Email: laxalt@juno.com
Las Vegas Office: 201 Las Vegas Boulevard South, Suite 200.
Telephone: 702-388-1551.
Facsimile: 702-388-1559.

Bruce R. Laxalt
Don G. Nomura
Katherine J. MacKenzie
Ellen Jean Winograd
Janice Hodge Jensen
Gregory A. Brower
Robert A. Dotson
Holly S. Stoberski (Resident, Las Vegas Office)
Steven E. Guinn
Daniel T. Hayward
Angela M. Bader
George P. Harris (Resident, Las Vegas Office)
Kristin Darnell Fyda
Stephanie A. Charter (Resident, Las Vegas Office)
Jerry M Snyder
Charles A Jones

Reference: Wells Fargo Bank of Nevada.

For full biographical listings, see the Martindale-Hubbell Law Directory

---

Leverty & Associates Law, Chartered (AV)

Reno Gould House, 832 Willow Street, 89502
Telephone: 775-322-6636
Fax: 775-322-3953
Email: levertyassoc@law.reno.nv.us *URL:* http://www.lawyers.com/levertylaw
San Diego, California Office: 110 West "C" Street. Suite 1300. 92101.
Telephone: 619-234-6636.
Fax: 619-234-6634. Email: levlaw@pacbell.net
Las Vegas, Nevada Office: 2110 East Flamingo Road, Suite 106, 89119.
Telephone: 702-733-0556.
Fax: 702-733-0563.

Vernon E. Leverty
Matthew L. Sharp

Betty C. Baker
Rebecca D. Lack (Not admitted in NV; Resident, San Diego, California Office)

For full biographical listings, see the Martindale-Hubbell Law Directory

---

Marshall Hill Cassas & de Lipkau (AV)

Suite 300 Holcomb Professional Building, 333 Holcomb Avenue, P.O. Box 2790, 89505-2790
Telephone: 775-323-1601
Telecopier: 775-348-7250
Email: general@MHCL-law.com

(See Next Column)

MEMBERS OF FIRM

Robert W. Marshall
Earl M. Hill
Frank Cassas
Ross E. de Lipkau
John P. Fowler
Rew R. Goodenow
Michael R. Kealy
A. Stanyan Peck

For full biographical listings, see the Martindale-Hubbell Law Directory

---

McDonald Carano Wilson McCune Bergin Frankovich & Hicks LLP (AV)

241 Ridge Street, 89501
Telephone: 775-788-2000
Telecopier: 775-788-2020
URL: http://www.mcdonaldcarano.com
Las Vegas, Nevada Office: Suite 1000, 2300 West Sahara Avenue.
Telephone: 702-873-4100.
Telecopier: 702-873-9966.

MEMBERS OF FIRM

John J. McCune
Thomas R. C. Wilson
Leo P. Bergin, III
John J. Frankovich
Larry R. Hicks
Alvin J. (Bud) Hicks
William A. S. Magrath, II
Timothy E. Rowe
James W. Bradshaw
Sylvia L. Harrison
George F. Ogilvie III
James C. Giudici
Pat Lundvall
Andrew P. Gordon
Valerie P. Cooke
Matthew C. Addison
Bryan R. Clark

ASSOCIATES

Paul J. Georgeson
Miranda M. Du

OF COUNSEL

Donald L. Carano
William S. Boyd
Charles E. Huff

Representative Clients: AT&T Communications of Nevada; Associated General Contractors of America; Boyd Gaming Corporation; Eldorado Hotel & Casino; Intermountain Federal Land Bank Association; James Hardie (USA), Inc.; Scolari's Warehouse Markets; Time Oil Co. (Nevada Counsel).

For Complete List of Firm Personnel, See General Section

For full biographical listings, see the Martindale-Hubbell Law Directory

---

Mortimer Sourwine & Sloane, Ltd. (AV)

Sierrawest Bank Building, 4950 Kietzke Lane, Suite 302, P.O. Box 460, 89504-0460
Telephone: 775-828-0200
Facsimile: 775-828-0211

Julien G. Sourwine
Douglas A. Sloane

Representative Clients: American International Group; California Casualty; Capital Ford; General Motors Corp.; Martin Iron Works, Inc.; United States Fidelity and Guaranty Co.; Reliance Insurance Co.; Dean Witter Reynolds, Inc.
Reference: Bank of America, Nevada.

For Complete List of Firm Personnel, See General Section

For full biographical listings, see the Martindale-Hubbell Law Directory

---

Walther, Key, Maupin, Oats, Cox & LeGoy, A Professional Corporation (AV)

Lakeside Professional Plaza, 3500 Lakeside Court, 89509
Telephone: 775-827-2000
Facsimile: 775-827-2185
Mailing Address: P.O. Box 30000, Reno, Nevada, 89520

Steven T. Walther
Jon J. Key
Ernest J. Maupin
C. Robert Cox
L. Robert LeGoy, Jr.
Michael E. Malloy
G. Barton Mowry
Procter J. Hug
Donald A. Lattin
Paul J. Anderson
Gustave J. Rossi
Robert A. Winkel
Kurt O. Hunsberger
Michael A. Nivinskus
Christopher D. Jaime

Rick R. Hsu
Michaelle D. Rafferty
Debra O. Waggoner

Representative Clients: Bank America of Nevada (Trust Dept.); Bechtel Corporations; Bill Pearce Olds, BMW, Volvo; Wells Fargo, N.A. (Trust Dept.); General Motors Acceptance Corp.; Nevada Realtors; Radiation Oncology Associates; The Ralph M. Parsons Corporation; Parsons Corporation; Reno Air, Inc.; Correctional Medical Services, Inc.

For full biographical listings, see the Martindale-Hubbell Law Directory

Reno—Continued

WOODBURN AND WEDGE (AV)

One East First Street, Suite 1600, P.O. Box 2311, 89505
Telephone: 775-688-3000
Telecopier: 775-688-3088
Email: postmaster@woodburnlaw.com *URL:* http://www.woodburnlaw.com
Las Vegas, Nevada Office: Suite 700 Bank of America Plaza, 300 South Fourth Street.
Telephone: 702-387-1000.
Telecopier: 702-387-0024.

MEMBERS OF FIRM

Richard O. Kwapil
Casey Woodburn Vlautin
Gordon H. DePaoli
Suellen Fulstone
John F. Murtha
Stephen S. Kent
W. Chris Wicker
Shawn B Meador
Lynne K. Jones

ASSOCIATES

Dale E. Ferguson
Randy A. Drake
Louis F. Holland

Representative Clients: Atlantic Richfield Co.; Sierra Pacific Power Co.; The Union Pacific Railroad Co.; Western Union Telegraph Co.; Bank of America; Cyprus Minerals Corp.; The Roman Catholic Bishop of Reno, A Corporation Sole; Shell Oil Co.

For full biographical listings, see the Martindale-Hubbell Law Directory

NEW HAMPSHIRE

*CONCORD,** Merrimack Co.

DOUGLAS, ROBINSON, LEONARD & GARVEY, P.C. (AV)

6 Loudon Road Suite 502, 03301
Telephone: 603-224-1988
Fax: 603-229-1988
Email: drlg@grolen.com *URL:* http://www.lawyers.com/drl&glaw

Charles G. Douglas, III
Timothy I. Robinson
C. Kevin Leonard
Carolyn S. Garvey
Susanna G. Robinson

For full biographical listings, see the Martindale-Hubbell Law Directory

RATH, YOUNG AND PIGNATELLI, PROFESSIONAL ASSOCIATION (AV)

One Capital Plaza, P.O. Box 1500, 03302-1500
Telephone: 603-226-2600
Telecopier: 603-226-2700; 228-2294; 225-9774
Email: ryp@rathlaw.com *URL:* http://www.rathlaw.com
Nashua, New Hampshire Office: The Glass Tower, 20 Trafalgar Square.
Telephone: 603-889-9952.
Telecopier: 603-595-7489.

Thomas D. Rath
Michael A. Pignatelli
Andrew W. Serell
Brian T. Tucker

For Complete List of Firm Personnel, See General Section

For full biographical listings, see the Martindale-Hubbell Law Directory

*LACONIA,** Belknap Co.

NORMANDIN, CHENEY & O'NEIL (AV)

Normandin Square, 213 Union Avenue, P.O. Box 575, 03247-0575
Telephone: 603-524-4380
Fax: 603-528-6831
Email: nco@lr.net

MEMBERS OF FIRM

A. Gerard O'Neil
A.G. O'Neil, Jr.
James F. LaFrance

ASSOCIATES

Philip P. Bonafide
Anne Marshall Rice

OF COUNSEL

Duncan J. Farmer

Counsel for: Laconia Savings Bank; Lakes Region Mental Health Center; Laconia Airport Authority; Central New Hampshire Realty, Inc.; All Metals Industries, Inc.; Lakes Region Anesthesiology, P.A.; Cormier Corp.; Scotia Technology; Vemaline Products.

For Complete List of Firm Personnel, See General Section

For full biographical listings, see the Martindale-Hubbell Law Directory

NEW JERSEY

ASBURY PARK, Monmouth Co.

CARTON, WITT, ARVANITIS & BARISCILLO, L.L.C. (AV)

(Formerly Durand, Ivins & Carton)
4001 Route 66 At Garden State Parkway, P.O. Box 1229, 07712
Telephone: 732-922-9500
Telecopier: 732-922-1625
Manasquan, New Jersey Office: 40 Union Avenue, P.O. Box 367.
Telephones: 908-223-1800; 449-5311.

MEMBERS OF FIRM

George N. Arvanitis
James D. Carton, III (Manasquan Office)
John C. Carton (Manasquan Office)
Stephen C. Carton
H. Frank Carpentier
Dana C. Argeris
Martin J. McGreevy
Albert A. Zager
Mark R. Aikins
K. Edward Jacobi
Joseph J. Colao, Jr.
James D. Carton (1868-1943)
Forman T. Bailey (1887-1964)
J. Victor Carton (1900-1982)
Thomas D. Nary (1904-1985)
Robert R. Witt (1921-1988)

ASSOCIATES

Thomas F. Heaney, Jr.
Peter V. Koenig
Susan J. F. Weiss
James D. Carton, IV
Aaron J. Rosenfeld
Russell J. Malta
Janice B. Venables
Marc J. Comer

OF COUNSEL

Francis X. Crahay
Henry E. Kordes
George A. Bariscillo, Jr.
Robert V. Carton

Attorneys for: New Jersey Bell Telephone Co.; Garden State Indemnity Co.; Jersey Shore Medical Center, Inc.
Local Attorneys for: Travelers Insurance Co.; Aetna Casualty & Surety Co.; New Jersey Manufacturers Insurance Co.; Liberty Mutual; Prudential Insurance Co.; Chubb & Son.

For full biographical listings, see the Martindale-Hubbell Law Directory

ATLANTIC CITY, Atlantic Co.

PERSKIE NEHMAD & PERILLO, A PROFESSIONAL CORPORATION (AV)

Suite 711, 1125 Atlantic Avenue, 08401
Telephone: 609-348-1177
Telecopier: 609-348-4219

Stephen R. Nehmad
Philip J. Perskie
Salvatore Perillo
Steven J. Brog

Richard F. DeLucry
Richard S. Mairone
Christopher M. Baylinson

References: Fleet Bank, National Association.

For full biographical listings, see the Martindale-Hubbell Law Directory

DONALD G. TARGAN & ASSOCIATES A PROFESSIONAL CORPORATION (AV)

Suite 212, One South New York Avenue, 08401
Telephone: 609-348-1106
Telefax: 609-345-7330

Donald G. Targan

Leo B. Dubler, III
Michael J. Pender

Reference: Fleet Bank.

For full biographical listings, see the Martindale-Hubbell Law Directory

BEDMINSTER, Somerset Co.

PURCELL, RIES, SHANNON, MULCAHY & O'NEILL (AV)

One Pluckemin Way, P.O. Box 754, 07921
Telephone: 908-658-3800
Fax: 908-658-4659
Email: general@prsmo.com *URL:* http://www.prsmo.com
Philadelphia, Pennsylvania Office: 12th Floor, East Tower, Centre Square, 1500 Market Square.
Telephone: 215-665-5602.
Fax: 215-569-8228.

MEMBERS OF FIRM

Eugene M. Purcell
William P. Ries
John J. Shannon
Thomas M. Mulcahy
Michael F. O'Neill
David M. Hawkins
Joseph R. Purcell
Kevin R. Brotz
John M. Bowens
Kevin Kovacs
Kenneth D. Merin
Valerie K. Bollheimer
Andrew L. Indeck
Joseph M. Donegan
Mark Mattia

(See Next Column)

PURCELL, RIES, SHANNON, MULCAHY & O'NEILL—*Continued*

ASSOCIATES

Rita F. Barone
Kathleen J. Devlin
Paul L. Gallagher
Gary Grabas
John R. Haggerty
William T. Hilliard
Eric J. Konecke
Susan Lawless
Michael J. McCaffrey
Kathleen M. Quinn
Thomas Charles Savoth
Donna M. Stephan-Nolan
Barbara C. Zimmerman

OF COUNSEL

David D. Furman
C. Judson Hamlin

LEGAL SUPPORT PERSONNEL

Gary Molloy

Reference: Somerset Trust Co.

For full biographical listings, see the Martindale-Hubbell Law Directory

*BRIDGETON,** Cumberland Co.

JOHN P. MORRIS (AV)

200 West Commerce Street, P.O. Box 299, 08302
Telephone: 609-453-1000
Fax: 609-453-0200
URL: http://www.lawyers.com/johnpmorris

LEGAL SUPPORT PERSONNEL

Tara Dickson (Paralegal)

For full biographical listings, see the Martindale-Hubbell Law Directory

RITTER AND JESPERSON (AV)

55 Fayette Street, P.O. Box 320, 08302
Telephone: 856-451-3030
Fax: 856-453-0911

MEMBERS OF FIRM

Theodore Henry Ritter
John E. Jesperson

ASSOCIATE

Susan E. Iacovone

OF COUNSEL

Isabella A. Garofola

References: Farmers & Merchants National Bank of Bridgeton; Bridgeton Onized Federal Credit Union.

For full biographical listings, see the Martindale-Hubbell Law Directory

BURLINGTON, Burlington Co.

SMITH, GOLDSTEIN, MAGRAM & BERENATO, A PROFESSIONAL CORPORATION (AV)

415 High Street, P.O. Box 603, 08016-0603
Telephone: 609-386-2633
Fax: 609-386-8674

Louis A. Smith
Jeffrey N. Goldstein
Edward J. Magram
Elizabeth D. Berenato

David C. Michaud

Reference: First Union Bank, Burlington, New Jersey.

For full biographical listings, see the Martindale-Hubbell Law Directory

*CAMDEN,** Camden Co.

BROWN & CONNERY, LLP (AV)

518 Market Street, P.O. Box 1449, 08101
Telephone: 609-365-5100
Facsimile: 609-858-4967
Westmont, New Jersey Office: 360 Haddon Avenue, P.O. Box 539.
Telephone: 609-854-8900.

MEMBERS OF FIRM

Thomas F. Connery, Jr.
Warren W. Faulk
Steven G. Wolschina
Paul Mainardi
Michael J. Vassalotti
Dennis P. Blake
William M. Tambussi
Mark P. Asselta
Stephen J. DeFeo
Joseph M Nardi, III

ASSOCIATES

Joseph A. Zechman
Karen A. McGuinness
Jeffrey E. Ugoretz
Christine O'Hearn
Christine A. Campbell
Joseph T. Carney
Richard C. Belli, Jr.
Stephanie E. Nolan
Shawn C. Huber
Susan M. Leming
Beth L. Marlin
Louis R. Lessig
Kevin C. Heil

Representative Clients: Camden County Health Services Center; Delaware River Port Authority; Federal Deposit Insurance Corp.; Mercedes-Benz Credit Corp.; Philadelphia Newspaper, Inc.; Philip Morris Inc.; Pollution

(See Next Column)

Control Financing Authority of Camden County; Underwood-Memorial Hospital.

For Complete List of Firm Personnel, See General Section

For full biographical listings, see the Martindale-Hubbell Law Directory

CEDAR KNOLLS, Morris Co.

LEARY, BRIDE, TINKER & MORAN, A PROFESSIONAL CORPORATION (AV)

7 Ridgedale Avenue, 07927
Telephone: 973-539-2090
Fax: 973-539-0806

W. Stephen Leary
James D. Bride
John G. Tinker, Jr.
Glenn R. Moran
James T. Gill
William H. Mergner, Jr.
Mark Bongiovanni

Tracey L. VanWiemokly
James P. McHugh III
Brian Peoples
Marguerite Anne Leary
Mark J. Brancato
Wendy Allyson Reek
David J. Dering
Peter M. Bouton
Christopher H. Frick
Mark A. Trudeau

For full biographical listings, see the Martindale-Hubbell Law Directory

CHATHAM, Morris Co.

ARSENEAULT & FASSETT (AV)

560 Main Street, 07928-2119
Telephone: 973-635-3366
Fax: 973-635-0855
Email: www.aklaw.com *URL:* http://www.lawyers.com/arsenaultkrovatinattys

MEMBERS OF FIRM

Jack Arseneault
David W. Fassett

ASSOCIATE

Steven G. Sanders (Not admitted in NJ)

For full biographical listings, see the Martindale-Hubbell Law Directory

O'CONNOR & DEMAS, P.C. (AV)

383 Main Street, 07928
Telephone: 973-635-2210
Fax: 973-635-2622
URL: http://www.lawyers.com/geraldoconnor
Brick, New Jersey Office: 1480 Route 88 West. 08724.
Telephone: 732-836-0770.

Gerald B. O'Connor
Vivian Demas
Paul A. O'Connor, III

Thomas J. Demarest

OF COUNSEL

Patricia J. Cooney

For full biographical listings, see the Martindale-Hubbell Law Directory

ALAN L. ZEGAS (AV)

552 Main Street, 07928
Telephone: 973-701-7080
Fax: 973-701-7081
Email: alanatLaw@aol.com *URL:* http://www.lawyers.com/zegas

Gina L. Mendola
Sharon B. Kean
Patricia A. Lee
Aimee Blakeslee

For full biographical listings, see the Martindale-Hubbell Law Directory

CHERRY HILL, Camden Co.

KENNEY & KEARNEY LLP (AV)

Woodland Falls Corporate Park, Suite 210, 220 Lake Drive East, P.O. Box 5034, 08034-0421
Telephone: 856-779-7000
Telecopier: 856-779-1342

Joseph H. Kenney
John B. Kearney
John A. Miller, Jr.
Allen A. Etish
Michele Mareschi Fox
Thomas J. Hagner
William J. DeSantis
Charles J. Connery
John A. Zohlman, III

ASSOCIATES

John J. Bannan
David A. Haworth
Paul F. Jenkins
Margaret J. Quinn
Laura D. Ruccolo

(See Next Column)

KENNEY & KEARNEY LLP, *Cherry Hill—Continued*

OF COUNSEL

Jane A. Kenney Joel B. Korin

Representative Clients: Acme Markets, Inc.; Diocese of Camden; Eastman Kodak Co.; Hospital of the University of Pennsylvania; Lawson Mardon Wheaton, Inc.; Ryder Truck Rental; Stone & Webster Corp.; Summit Bancorp; The Sherwin Williams Co.; The Travelers Indemnity Co., The Aetna Casualty and Surety Co.

For full biographical listings, see the Martindale-Hubbell Law Directory

MCCARTER & ENGLISH, LLP (AV)

1820 Chapel Avenue West, Suite 380, 08002
Telephone: 609-662-8444
Telecopier: 609-662-6203
URL: http://www.mccarter.com
Newark, New Jersey Office: Four Gateway Center, 100 Mulberry Street. P.O. Box 652.
Telephone: 973-622-4444.
Telecopier: 973-624-7070.
New York, New York Office: Suite 2247, One World Trade Center.
Telephone: 212-466-9018.
Telecopier: 212-432-6568.
Boca Raton, Florida Office: 2255 Glades Road, Suite 319-A.
Telephone: 561-994-6262.
Telecopier: 561-241-0798.
Wilmington, Delaware Office: Mellon Bank Center, 919 Market Street.
Telephone: 302-654-8010
Telecopier: 302-654-0795
Philadelphia, Pennsylvania Office: One Commerce Square, 2005 Market Street, Suite 3600.
Telephone: 215-557-7700.
Telecopier: 215-557-6544.

MEMBERS OF FIRM

James F. Hammill
Glenn P. Callahan
Therese M. Keeley
Nathan A. Schachtman

For Complete List of Firm Personnel, See General Section

For full biographical listings, see the Martindale-Hubbell Law Directory

PARKER, MCCAY & CRISCUOLO, P.A. (AV)

Commerce Atrium, Suite 500, 1701 Route 70 East, P.O. Box 1806, 08034
Telephone: 856-424-4300
Telecopier: 856-424-1006
Email: pmc@pmclaw.com *URL:* http://www.pmclaw.com
Marlton, New Jersey Office: Suite 401 Three Greentree Center, Route 73 & Greentree Road.
Telephone: 856-596-8900.
Telecopier: 856-596-9631.
Lawrenceville, New Jersey Office: Princeton Pike Office Park, 3131 Princeton Pike, Building 4, Room 200.
Telephone: 609-219-0699.
Fax: 609-219-0708.

Robert C. Beck
Richard M. Berman
Emmanuel J. Argentieri

Local Counsel for: Aetna Casualty & Surety Co.; U.S. Fidelity & Guaranty Co.; Keystone Insurance Co.; Zurich-American Insurance Co.; Commerce Bank, N.A.; First Fidelity Bank; Midlantic Bank.

For Complete List of Firm Personnel, See General Section

For full biographical listings, see the Martindale-Hubbell Law Directory

EDISON, Middlesex Co.

HANLON & LAVIGNE, A PROFESSIONAL CORPORATION (AV)

Suite 200, Executive Plaza, 10 Parsonage Road, 08837
Telephone: 732-549-9880
North Jersey Number: 973-808-0186
Fax: 732-549-3068
Email: larry@hlt-law.com *URL:* http://HanlonLavigne.com
New York, New York Office: One Word Trade Center, Suite 7967, 10048.
Telephone: 212-775-7142 and 212-775-7187.
Marysville, Pennsylvania Office: 505 Maple Avenue, P.O. Box 149, 17053-0149.
Telephone: 717-957-4292.
Fax: 717-957-4293.

William F. Hanlon (1901-1972)
Robert M. Hanlon
Lawrence N. Lavigne
Bonnie H. Hanlon

Richard P. Grossman, Jr.
Robert Michael Hanlon, Jr.
Robert M. Cook
Christine Giordano Hanlon

For full biographical listings, see the Martindale-Hubbell Law Directory

ENGLEWOOD CLIFFS, Bergen Co.

BARRY I. FREDERICKS (AV)

560 Sylvan Avenue, 07632
Telephone: 201-871-7484
Telecopier: 201-871-8428
New York, N.Y. Office: Empire State Building, 350 Fifth Avenue, Suite 6011.
Telephone: 212-586-5042.

For full biographical listings, see the Martindale-Hubbell Law Directory

FLORHAM PARK, Morris Co.

CARLIN, MADDOCK, FAY & CERBONE, P.C. (AV)

25 Vreeland Road, P.O. Box 751, 07932
Telephone: 201-377-3350
Fax: 201-377-5626
URL: http://www.lawyers.com/cmfclaw

John J. Carlin, Jr.
Laurence R. Maddock
Donald J. Fay
Richard R. Cerbone

Arthur G. Warden, III

For full biographical listings, see the Martindale-Hubbell Law Directory

D'ALESSANDRO, JACOVINO & GERSON (AV)

147 Columbia Turnpike, 07932
Telephone: 201-966-1910
Fax: 201-966-6774
URL: http://www.lawyers.com/djgattys
New York, N.Y. Office: 321 Broadway, 4th Floor.
Telephone: 212-608-7500.

MEMBERS OF FIRM

Edward G. D'Alessandro
Amedeo C. Jacovino
Frederick E. Gerson

ASSOCIATES

Edward G. D'Alessandro, Jr.
Anthony J. Bianciella

Reference: Midatlantic Bank.

For full biographical listings, see the Martindale-Hubbell Law Directory

DRINKER BIDDLE & SHANLEY LLP (AV)

A Pennsylvania Limited Liability Partnership
500 Campus Drive, 07932-1047
Telephone: 973-360-1100
Fax: 973-285-1625; 360-9831
URL: http://www.dbr.com
Philadelphia, Pennsylvania Office: Drinker Biddle & Reath LLP, One Logan Square, 18th & Cherry Streets.
Telephone: 215-988-2700.
Telefax: 215-988-2757.
Cable Address: "Debemac."
Washington, D.C. Office: Drinker Biddle & Reath LLP, 1500 K Street, N.W., Suite 1100.
Telephone: 202-842-8800.
Telefax: 202-842-8465.
Princeton, New Jersey Office: Suite 300, 105 College Road East.
Telephone: 609-716-6500.
Telefax: 609-799-7000.
Berwyn, Pennsylvania Office: Drinker Biddle & Reath LLP, Suite 300, 1000 Westlakes Drive.
Telephone: 610-993-2200.
Telefax: 610-993-8585.
New York, New York Office: Drinker Biddle & Reath LLP, 89th Floor, One World Trade Center.
Telephone: 212-321-1812.
Telecopier: 1-212-466-0569.

Raymond M. Tierney, Jr.
Arthur R. Schmauder
Thomas F. Campion
John J. Francis, Jr.
A. Dennis Terrell
Richard E. Brennan
Thomas J. Alworth
Jeffrey A. Peck
Matthew Farley
Daniel F. O'Connell
Richard A. Levao
Charles A. Reid, III
Paul G. Nittoly
Walter J. Fleischer, Jr.
Susan M. Sharko
Stephen R. Long (Chairman, Litigation Department, 1995—)
Brian F. McDonough
James M. Altieri
Robert M. Leonard
Theodore S. Smith
Michael O. Adelman
Kenneth J. Wilbur
William T. Corbett, Jr.
Kathleen H. Dooley
Kathleen B. Harden
Michael R. Clarke

COUNSEL

Jodi Sydell Rosenzweig
Bruce L. Shapiro

Maureen Nesbitt Warshaw
Jeffrey S. Lipkin
William J. Mendrzycki
William J. Metcalf
H. Lockwood Miller, III
Laura A. Brady
Robert M. Vinci
Ethan D. Stein
Gregory B. Pasquale
Daniel B. Carroll

(See Next Column)

DRINKER BIDDLE & SHANLEY LLP—*Continued*

Stacey P. Rappaport
Andrew B. Joseph
Melissa L. Klipp
John M. Blumers
Charles J. Falletta
Cheryl Whitney
Rachelle H. Milstein
Michelle M. Bufano
Dana J. Scancarella
Scott C. Carroll
Jennifer La Mont
Marianne Calabrese
Benjamin L. Siegel
Mark C. Errico
Gary J. Hacker
Jeffrey S. Mandel

For Complete List of Firm Personnel, See General Section

For full biographical listings, see the Martindale-Hubbell Law Directory

HACK, PIRO, O'DAY, MERKLINGER, WALLACE & MCKENNA, P.A. (AV)

30 Columbia Turnpike, P.O. Box 941, 07932-0941
Telephone: 973-301-6500
Fax: 973-301-0094
Email: hpom@ix.netcom.com

Peter A. Piro
William J. O'Day
M. Richard Merklinger
Joseph V. Wallace
Peter T. Melnyk
Patrick M. Sages
Bonny G. Rafel
Robert G. Alencewicz
John T. West
Thomas M. Madden

Michael J. Leegan
Stephen DeNaro
Joanne Vos
Peter Nastasi
Carol A. Rankin

For Complete List of Firm Personnel, See General Section

For full biographical listings, see the Martindale-Hubbell Law Directory

RYAN AND GANNON (AV)

Suite 201, 147 Columbia Turnpike, 07932
Telephone: 201-966-1000
Fax: 201-966-6215
URL: http://www.lawyers.com/ryanandgannon

MEMBERS OF FIRM

William J. Gannon
Gerald J. Helfrich

ASSOCIATE

Edward George Fattell, III

OF COUNSEL

George P. Helfrich
Edward V. Ryan
Thomas A. Shepard, Jr.

For full biographical listings, see the Martindale-Hubbell Law Directory

SCHWARTZ SIMON EDELSTEIN CELSO & KESSLER (AV)

A Partnership including a Professional Corporation
Ten James Street, 07932
Telephone: 973-301-0001
Fax: 973-301-0203
Email: sseck1@aol.com

Lawrence S. Schwartz (P.C.)
Stephen J. Edelstein
Nathanya Guritzky Simon
Nicholas Celso, III
Donald A. Kessler
Raymond W. Fisher
Paul H. Green
Allan P. Dzwilewski

Neil H. Braunstein
Marc H. Zitomer
Stefani C Schwartz
Denis G. Murphy

COUNSEL

Jacob Green

OF COUNSEL

Glenn C. Guritzky
Miguel A. Maza
Scott A. Elk (P.A.) (Not admitted in NJ)

For full biographical listings, see the Martindale-Hubbell Law Directory

*FREEHOLD,** Monmouth Co.

CERRATO, DAWES, COLLINS, SAKER & BROWN, A PROFESSIONAL CORPORATION (AV)

Wemrock Professional Mall, 509 Stillwells Corner Road, P.O. Box 6009, 07728
Telephone: 732-431-5000; 462-0480
Fax: 732-462-0483

Dominick A. Cerrato
John I. Dawes
James E. Collins
Mark F. Saker
Sanford D. Brown

Helen M. Wilder

(See Next Column)

OF COUNSEL

Barry William Messinger (Not admitted in NJ)

Representative Clients: Nat West; Freehold Regional High School; New Jersey Conservation Foundation; United Methodist Homes of New Jersey; Southern New Jersey Conference, United Methodist Church; Presbytery of Monmouth; Monmouth Council, Boy Scouts of America; Bayliner Marine Corp.

For full biographical listings, see the Martindale-Hubbell Law Directory

*HACKENSACK,** Bergen Co.

CONTANT, SCHERBY & ATKINS (AV)

33 Hudson Street, 07601
Telephone: 201-342-1070
Fax: 201-342-5213
Email: LawfirmCSA@aol.com *URL:* http://www.lawyers.com/csalaw

MEMBERS OF THE FIRM

John M. Contant (1907-1988)
Richard J. Contant
Michael L. Scherby
Bruce L. Atkins
Matthew S. Rogers
Andrew T. Fede
Brian T. Keane
Robert B. Hille

ASSOCIATES

Geraldine E. Beers
Suzanne J. Ryderman
Lisa R. Aljian
Christina A. Stoneburner
Sheila O'Shea

OF COUNSEL

Fenster & Weiss, New City, New York

For full biographical listings, see the Martindale-Hubbell Law Directory

DEENER, FEINGOLD & STERN, A PROFESSIONAL CORPORATION (AV)

2 University Plaza, Suite 503, 07601
Telephone: 201-343-8788
Fax: 201-343-4640
Email: JeromeDeener@DeenerFeingold.com *URL:* http://www.lawyers.com/deenerfeingold&stern

Jerome A. Deener
Cal R. Feingold
Robert A. Stern
David M. Edelblum
Anthony M. Vizzoni

Debra T. Hirsch
Andrew M. Grumet
Ronen Gabbay

References: Hudson United Bank; Commerce Bank.

For full biographical listings, see the Martindale-Hubbell Law Directory

HEIN, SMITH, BEREZIN, MALOOF & JACOBS, L.L.C. (AV)

Court Plaza East, 19 Main Street, 07601-7023
Telephone: 201-487-7400
Telecopier: 201-487-4228
Email: counsel@heinsmith.com

MEMBERS OF FIRM

Robert J. Maloof
Sidney Berezin
Robert L. Baum
Lawrence H. Jacobs
Ellen W. Smith
Carla H. Madnick

ASSOCIATES

John L. Shanahan
Douglas V. Sanchez
Robert J. Logan

Representative Clients: Bergen County Joint Municipal Insurance Fund; Commercial General Union Insurance Cos. of New York; Crawford & Co.; Health Care Insurance Co.; Princeton Insurance Co.; St. Paul Fire & Marine Insurance Co.; Pro Mutual Insurance Company; NJ Cure.
Reference: Summit Bank.

For Complete List of Firm Personnel, See General Section

For full biographical listings, see the Martindale-Hubbell Law Directory

HERTEN, BURSTEIN, SHERIDAN, CEVASCO, BOTTINELLI & LITT, L.L.C. (AV)

Court Plaza North, 25 Main Street, 07601
Telephone: 201-342-6000
Telecopier: 201-342-6611

Thomas J. Herten
Albert Burstein
Philip F. Sheridan, Jr.
Andrew J. Cevasco
Terry Paul Bottinelli
Arnold D. Litt
Brian T. Campion
Menelaos W. Toskos
Mark P. Marotta
Susan M. Marra
John L. Molinelli
Kevin P. Kelly

ASSOCIATES

Patrick Papalia
Anthony Ronald Suarez
Thomas S. McGuire
Donna T. Tamayne

For full biographical listings, see the Martindale-Hubbell Law Directory

Hackensack—Continued

HOGAN, PALACE & SCULLY (AV)

20 Court Street, 07601
Telephone: 201-342-4422
Fax: 201-342-2554
Email: hpsnj@bellatlantic.net *URL:* http://www.lawyers.com/hogan&palace

MEMBERS OF FIRM

Thomas A. Hogan
Thomas W. Palace
Michael R. Scully

LEGAL SUPPORT PERSONNEL

Shannon S. Casey (Real Estate Paralegal)

Reference: Bergen Commercial Bank, New Jersey.

For full biographical listings, see the Martindale-Hubbell Law Directory

NICOLETTE & PERKINS, P.A. (AV)

3 University Plaza, Fifth Floor, 07601
Telephone: 201-488-9080
Telecopier: 201-488-5580
Email: nicoletteperkins@juno.com *URL:* http://www.lawyers.com/nicolette&perkins

David A. Nicolette, Jr.
Eric R. Perkins

Jeanette A. Odynski
Laura N. Keenan
Toni Marie McPhillips

For full biographical listings, see the Martindale-Hubbell Law Directory

NOWELL AMOROSO KLEIN BIERMAN, P.A. (AV)

155 Polifly Road, 07601
Telephone: 201-343-5001
Facsimile: 201-343-5181
Email: nakb@erols.com
New York, New York Office: 140 Broadway.
Telephone: 212-858-7710.
Facsimile: 212-858-7750.

Daniel C. Nowell
Henry J. Amoroso
Herbert C. Klein
William D. Bierman
Jeanne M. Damgen
Linda Dunne
William R. DeLorenzo, Jr.
Richard J. Kapner
David Edelberg

Craig E. Parles
Andrew A. Elman
Christopher M. McGarry
William T. Curran
Lisa M. Parles
Daniel S. Eichhorn
Brian M. Doyno
Samer E. Khalaf

OF COUNSEL

John J. Cariddi
Barbara L. de Mare
Karen A. Passaro

For full biographical listings, see the Martindale-Hubbell Law Directory

STEPHEN H. ROTH (AV)

62 Summit Avenue, 07601
Telephone: 201-489-3737
Fax: 201-489-0557

ASSOCIATE

Michele M. De Santis

For full biographical listings, see the Martindale-Hubbell Law Directory

SHAPIRO & CROLAND (AV)

A Partnership including Professional Corporations
Continental Plaza II, 411 Hackensack Avenue, 07601
Telephone: 201-488-3900
Fax: 201-488-9481

Barry I. Croland, P.C.
Robert P. Shapiro, P.C.
Barry L. Baime
Jay Rubenstein
Kenneth S. Apfel
Kenneth S. Goldrich, P.C.
Bruce J. Ackerman
Stuart Reiser, P.C.
Meridith J. Bronson
John P. Di Iorio
David O. Marcus
Robert F. Green
Lizabeth Sarakin
David Torchin
Robin C. Bogan
Craig D. Spector

OF COUNSEL

Harvey R. Sorkow

Donald R. Sorkow (1930-1985)

Reference: Bank of New York-National Community Division.

For full biographical listings, see the Martindale-Hubbell Law Directory

SOKOL, BEHOT AND FIORENZO (AV)

433 Hackensack Avenue, 07601
Telephone: 201-488-1300
Fax: 201-488-6541

MEMBERS OF FIRM

Leon J. Sokol
Joseph F. Behot, Jr.
Joseph B. Fiorenzo
Jeffrey A. Zenn
Arthur Bergman
Michael P. Feltman

ASSOCIATES

Siobhan Spillane Bailey
Mitchell B. Levine
Steven Seigel
Andrew S. Bosin

COUNSEL

Alan Prigal

For full biographical listings, see the Martindale-Hubbell Law Directory

STOLDT, HORAN AND KOWAL, A PROFESSIONAL CORPORATION (AV)

Continental Plaza I, 401 Hackensack Avenue, 07601
Telephone: 201-646-9200
Telecopier: 201-646-0167
Email: shlaw@bellatlantic.net *URL:* http://www.lawyers.com/stoldthoran&kowal

Sydney V. Stoldt, Jr.
John D. Horan
Dorothy A. Kowal
Heather A. Gallagher
Brian O'Reilly

OF COUNSEL

Judith R. Levinson

For full biographical listings, see the Martindale-Hubbell Law Directory

THURBER CAPPELL, L.L.C. (AV)

235 Main Street, Suite 300, 07601
Telephone: 201-488-0594
Telecopier: 201-488-5283
Email: thurblaw@aol.com *URL:* http://www.lawyers.com/thurber,cappell,law

Mary F. Thurber
Cynthia A. Cappell

ASSOCIATES

Allison Turley Madden
Anne Marie Fox

OF COUNSEL

Frank Huttle, III

For full biographical listings, see the Martindale-Hubbell Law Directory

JOHN L. WEICHSEL (AV)

79 Main Street, 07601
Telephone: 201-488-1400
Fax: 201-488-3970
URL: http://www.weichlaw.baweb.com
Email: weichlaw@idt.net *URL:* http://www.lawyers.com/weichselatty

Reference: First Union National Bank.

For full biographical listings, see the Martindale-Hubbell Law Directory

HADDONFIELD, Camden Co.

WILBRAHAM, LAWLER & BUBA, A PROFESSIONAL CORPORATION (AV Ⓣ)

24 Kings Highway West, 08033-2122
Telephone: 856-795-4422
Fax: 856-795-4699
Philadelphia, Pennsylvania Office: 1818 Market Street, Suite 3100.
Telephone: 215-564-4141.
Fax: 215-564-4385.
Wilmington, Delaware Office: Stoney Batter Office Building, 5301 Limestone Road, Suite 221.
Telephone: 302-234-8217.
Fax: 302-234-8218.

Edward J. Wilbraham
Michael J. Block
Mary S. Cook

For full biographical listings, see the Martindale-Hubbell Law Directory

HAMILTON SQUARE, Mercer Co.

HARRY HAUSHALTER (AV)

Lexington Square Commons, 2119 Route 33, Suite A, 08690
Telephone: 609-631-7388
Fax: 609-631-7329
Email: harry_haushalter@msn.com *URL:* http://www.lawyers.com/haushaltertaxlawyer

LEGAL SUPPORT PERSONNEL

Jeanie E. Riggio

For full biographical listings, see the Martindale-Hubbell Law Directory

HAWTHORNE, Passaic Co.

JEFFER, HOPKINSON & VOGEL (AV)

(Formerly Jeffer, Walter, Tierney, DeKorte, Hopkinson & Vogel)
Law Building, 1600 Route 208N, P.O. Box 507, 07507
Telephone: 973-423-0100
Fax: 973-423-5614
Tequesta, Florida Office: Jeffer, Cioffi & Cicalese. 250 Tequesta Drive, 33469.
Telephone: 561-747-6000.
Fax: 561-575-9167.

MEMBERS OF FIRM

Herman M. Jeffer — George Tierney (1895-1976)
Reginald F. Hopkinson — Joseph V. Fumagalli (1901-1965)
Jerome A. Vogel — Richard W. DeKorte (1936-1975)
Peter Hofstra (1886-1961)
Robert Walter (1908-1990)

ASSOCIATES

Melinda B. Maidens — E. David Becker
David H. Altman

Counsel for: Brioschi, Inc.; Opici Wine Co.; Gas Pumpers of America Corp.; The Paterson Market Growers Assn.; Dowling Fuel Oil Co.

For Complete List of Firm Personnel, See General Section

For full biographical listings, see the Martindale-Hubbell Law Directory

LAKEWOOD, Ocean Co.

BATHGATE, WEGENER & WOLF, P.C. (AV)

One Airport Road, P.O. Box 2043, 08701
Telephone: 732-363-0666
Telecopier: 732-363-9864
Email: bathweg@idt.net

Lawrence E. Bathgate, II — Ross D. Gertner
Peter H. Wegener — Edward B. Kasselman
William J. Wolf — Dominic J. Aprile
Jan L. Wouters — Nancy G. Wright
Michael M. DiCicco

COUNSEL

Neil Brodsky — Peter A. Valenti

Jonathan S. Fabricant — Peter G. Licata
Robert J. Gillispie, Jr. — Steven E Robertson

For full biographical listings, see the Martindale-Hubbell Law Directory

LAWRENCEVILLE, Mercer Co.

SZAFERMAN, LAKIND, BLUMSTEIN, WATTER & BLADER, P.C. (AV)

Suite 104 Quakerbridge Executive Center, 101 Grovers Mill Road, 08648
Telephone: 609-275-0400
Telefax: 609-275-4511

Arnold C. Lakind — Sidney H. Lehmann
Barry D. Szaferman — Gerald B. Schenkman
Jeffrey P. Blumstein — David B. Beckett
Paul N. Watter — Scott P. Borsack
Steven Blader — Mary Lou Delahanty

Jennifer Weisberg Millner — Stuart A. Tucker
Cathyanne A. Pisciotta — Brian G. Paul
Jason N. Fruhschein — Victoria Rivera-Cruz
Demery J. Roberts — Thomas J. Burns III

LEGAL SUPPORT PERSONNEL

Paula M. Rossi (Office Administrator) — Patricia Hallstrum (Controller)

Representative Clients: Sun National Bank; First Washington Bank; Gilmore Securities & Co.; Communication Workers of America; The Eagle Group; Water's Edge Convalescent Center; Ronson Aviation, Inc.; Holmdel Township Board of Adjustment; Public Service Managers Association; Chemical Leaman Tank Lines.

For full biographical listings, see the Martindale-Hubbell Law Directory

LIVINGSTON, Essex Co.

BRAFF, HARRIS & SUKONECK (AV)

570 West Mount Pleasant Avenue, P.O. Box 657, 07039
Telephone: 973-994-6677
Telefax: 973-994-1296
New York, New York Office: 305 Broadway, Seventh Floor.
Telephone: 212-599-2085.

Joseph N. Braff (1936-1953) — Brian C. Harris
Jerome B. Litvak (1936-1977) — Ira D. Sukoneck
Leo Ertag (1942-1991) — Stephen L. Hopkins

(See Next Column)

Robert J. Gallop — John E. Nolan
Andrew M. Lusskin — Lawrence M. Berkeley
Daniel A. Lynn — Janice Bierman
Stephen Wellinghorst — Albert Wesley McKee
Gloria B. Cherry — Glenn Savarese
Keith Harris — James S. Murphy
Frances M. Wunderlich

OF COUNSEL

Harold I. Braff

Representative Clients: Otis Elevator Co.; Commercial Union Insurance Cos.; American Int'l. Ins. Co.; Harleysville Ins. Co.; Risk Enterprise Mgmt. Co.; Phico CNA; Goodyear Tire & Rubber.

For full biographical listings, see the Martindale-Hubbell Law Directory

GENOVA, BURNS & VERNOIA (AV)

Eisenhower Plaza II, 354 Eisenhower Parkway, 07039
Telephone: 973-533-0777
Facsimile: 973-533-1112
URL: http://www.gbvlaw.com
Trenton, New Jersey Office: The Princeton House, 160 West State Street.
Telephone: 609-393-1131.

MEMBERS OF FIRM

Angelo J. Genova — John C. Petrella
James M. Burns — James J. McGovern, III
Francis J. Vernoia — Carmel Joy Decker

ASSOCIATES

Sandro Polledri — J. Frank Vespa-Papaleo
Celia S. Bosco — Susan B. Burns
Lynn S. Degen — Bruno Genova
Elizabeth A. Daly — Robert C. Gifford, Jr.
Brian O. Lipman — Courtney Gaccione

For full biographical listings, see the Martindale-Hubbell Law Directory

PHILIP M. LUSTBADER & DAVID LUSTBADER A PROFESSIONAL CORPORATION (AV)

615 West Mount Pleasant Avenue, 07039
Telephone: 973-740-1000
Fax: 973-740-1520
URL: http://www.lawyers.com/lustbader,law

Philip M. Lustbader — David Lustbader

John L. Riordan, Jr. — James S. Colavito

For full biographical listings, see the Martindale-Hubbell Law Directory

MANASQUAN, Monmouth Co.

CARTON, WITT, ARVANITIS & BARISCILLO, L.L.C. (AV)

(Formerly Durand, Ivins & Carton)
40 Union Avenue, P.O. Box 367, 08736
Telephone: 908-223-1800
Asbury Park, New Jersey Office: 4001 Route 66 at Garden State Parkway, P.O. Box 1229.
Telephone: 732-922-9500.
Telecopier: 732-922-1625.

RESIDENT PARTNERS

James D. Carton, III — John C. Carton

Attorneys for: New Jersey Bell Telephone Co.; Jersey Shore Medical Center, Inc.
Local Attorneys for: Travelers Insurance Co.; Actna Casualty & Surety Co.; New Jersey Manufacturers Insurance Co.; Liberty Mutual; Prudential Insurance Co.; Chubb & Son.; Princeton Insurance Co.; Garden State Indemnity Co.

For full biographical listings, see the Martindale-Hubbell Law Directory

MAPLEWOOD, Essex Co.

LAW OFFICES OF EMANUEL S. FISH (AV)

2040 Millburn Avenue, 07040
Telephone: 973-763-2001
Fax: 973-763-2832
Email: Afishl@aol.com *URL:* http://www.lawyers.com/esflaw

ASSOCIATE

Thomas J. O'Grady

OF COUNSEL

John D. Kovac

For full biographical listings, see the Martindale-Hubbell Law Directory

MARLTON, Burlington Co.

Parker, McCay & Criscuolo, P.A. (AV)

Suite 401 Three Greentree Centre, Route 73 & Greentree Road, P.O. Box 974, 08053
Telephone: 856-596-8900
Telecopier: 856-596-9631
Email: pmc@pmclaw.com *URL:* http://www.pmclaw.com
Cherry Hill, New Jersey Office: Commerce Atrium, Suite 500, 1701 Route 70 East, P.O. Box 1806.
Telephone: 856-424-4300.
Telecopier: 856-424-1006.
Lawrenceville, New Jersey Office: Princeton Pike Office Park, 3131 Princeton Pike, Building 4, Room 200.
Telephone: 609-219-0699.
Fax: 609-219-0708.

Robert C. Beck (Resident at Cherry Hill, New Jersey Office)
David A. Parker
Robert J. Partlow
Carl J. Gregorio
John Michael Devlin
Yves C. Veenstra
Thomas M. Masick
Marc M. Baldwin
Stephen J. Mushinski
Ronald C. Morgan
Stacy L. Moore, Jr.
Drew J. Parker
Thomas M. Walsh
Gary F. Piserchia
Philip A. Norcross
Carolyn Reinhard Sleeper
Richard M. Berman (Resident at Cherry Hill, New Jersey Office)
Richard W. Hunt
Emmanuel J. Argentieri (Resident at Cherry Hill, New Jersey Office)
Jeanne M. Stiefel
Susan E. Bacso

COUNSEL

Frank P. Cavallo, Jr.

Irving G. Finkel
Victoria C. Fannon
Lynn S. Besancon
Lisa B. Baughman
Francine M. Cracker
J. Brooks DiDonato
Elena B. Zuares
Lora M. Giovacchini
Brad A. Parker
Brooke D. Schmoll
Gene R. Mariano

OF COUNSEL

Barry T. Parker
William V. Webster, Jr.
Richard J. Dill

Representative Clients: Banking: Commerce Bank; Insurance: Aetna Casualty & Surety; Continental Insurance Company; USF&G; Zurich-American Insurance Company; Rider Insurance Company.

For Complete List of Firm Personnel, See General Section

For full biographical listings, see the Martindale-Hubbell Law Directory

MILLBURN, Essex Co.

McDermott & McGee (AV)

75 Main Street, P.O. Box 192, 07041-0192
Telephone: 973-467-8080
Fax: 973-376-8669

MEMBERS OF FIRM

John L. McDermott
John P. McGee
Richard P. Maggi
Thomas A. Wester
Richard M. Tango
Frank P. Leanza
John L. McDermott, Jr.
David J. Dickinson
A. Charles Lorenzo
Robert A. McDermott
Kevin John McGee

ASSOCIATES

Anthony John Verardi
Lindsay K. O'Shaughnessy
Andre L. McGuire

OF COUNSEL

Daniel K. Van Dorn

Representative Clients: Affiliated Building Service, Inc.; Allstate Insurance Co.; General Agents Insurance Company of America; Greater New York Mutual; General Accident Group; ISS International Service System, Inc.; Zurich-American Insurance Co.; Penn National Insurance Co.; Tokio Marine & Fire Insurance Co.; Medical Inter-Insurance Exchange of New Jersey.

For full biographical listings, see the Martindale-Hubbell Law Directory

MONTCLAIR, Essex Co.

Garippa and Davenport, A Professional Corporation (AV)

66 Park Street, 07042
Telephone: 201-744-1688
Telecopier: 201-744-1641
Email: gd@taxappeal.com *URL:* http://www.taxappeal.com

John E. Garippa
Seth I. Davenport
Philip J. Giannuario
Gregory G. Lotz

(See Next Column)

Daniel J. Mulligan

For full biographical listings, see the Martindale-Hubbell Law Directory

MONTVALE, Bergen Co.

Beattie Padovano, LLC (AV)

50 Chestnut Ridge Road, P.O. Box 244, 07645
Telephone: 201-573-1810
Fax: 201-573-9736
Email: beattie-padovano@worldnet.att.net

MEMBERS OF FIRM

James R. Beattie
Ralph J. Padovano
Roger W. Breslin, Jr.
Thomas W. Dunn
Martin W. Kafafian
Adolph A. Romei
Brian R. Martinotti
John J. Lamb
John R. Holsinger
Antimo A. Del Vecchio

SENIOR ASSOCIATES

Emery C. Duell
Brenda J. Stewart
Kathleen S. Cook
Dana B. Cobb
Steven A. Weisfeld
Robert A. Blass
Alan G. White

ASSOCIATES

Gregg A. Padovano
James V. Zarrillo
Andrew D. Hopp
Jennifer Bretz
Matthew T. Rose
Renata A. Helstoski
Maria V. Martin

OF COUNSEL

Ira J. Kaltman
Francis B. Sheehan

For full biographical listings, see the Martindale-Hubbell Law Directory

MOORESTOWN, Burlington Co.

Chierici, Chierici & Smith, A Professional Corporation (AV)

Blason Campus - III, 509 South Lenola Road Building Six, 08057-1561
Telephone: 856-234-6300
Fax: 856-234-9490

Donald R. Chierici, Jr.
Elizabeth Coleman Chierici
Julie C. Smith

Carolyn J. Kornas
Mark G. Esposito
Richard D. DiTomaso
Melvin McDowell
David J. Karbasian
Peter P. Sanchez
Donald R. Chierici, III

For full biographical listings, see the Martindale-Hubbell Law Directory

Estella S. Gold (AV)

Blason II, 505 South Lenola Road, 08057
Telephone: 609-234-1004
Telecopier: 609-234-7836
Email: esglaw@aol.com

Representative Clients: South Jersey Processing, Inc.; OM Assn., Inc.

For full biographical listings, see the Martindale-Hubbell Law Directory

MORRIS PLAINS, Morris Co.

Voorhees & Ouda (AV)

Powder Mill Plaza, 51 Gibraltar Drive, 07950
Telephone: 201-267-6677
Fax: 201-267-9152
Mailing Address: P.O. Box 1236, Morristown, New Jersey, 07962-1236

MEMBERS OF FIRM

William Wolverton Voorhees, Jr.
Peter A. Ouda

For full biographical listings, see the Martindale-Hubbell Law Directory

*MORRISTOWN,** Morris Co.

Baumeister & Samuels, P.C. (AV⊤)

1776 On The Green, P.O. Box 1116, 07962-1116
Telephone: 973-267-6666
Telecopier: 973-605-1812
Email: BAUMSAM@AOL.COM
New York, N.Y. Office: One Exchange Plaza, 10006-3008.
Telephone: 212-363-1200.
Telecopier: 212-363-1346.

Michel F. Baumeister
Douglas A. Latto (Not admitted in NJ)
Dorothea M. Capone

(See Next Column)

BAUMEISTER & SAMUELS P.C.—*Continued*

OF COUNSEL

Lynn F. Samuels
Marc Z. Edell
Robert S. Franklin (Not admitted in NJ)

For full biographical listings, see the Martindale-Hubbell Law Directory

CELLI, SCHLOSSBERG & DIAMOND, L.L.C. (AV)

10 Park Place, Suite 305, 07960
Telephone: 973-292-7500
Fax: 973-539-3359
Email: csdcounsel@aol.com. *URL:* http://www.lawyers.com/csdlaw

Vincent P. Celli
Michael J. Schlossberg
Howard S. Diamond

ASSOCIATES

Shivaun M. McConnell
Antonietta L. Milelli
Hope E. Tuber
Gregory Paul Day

OF COUNSEL

William H. Claxton
Albert B. Jeffers
Joseph A. Molinaro

LEGAL SUPPORT PERSONNEL

Renée Orrico
Debra A. Gerhold

For full biographical listings, see the Martindale-Hubbell Law Directory

MASKALERIS & ASSOCIATES (AV)

30 Court Street, 07960
Telephone: 973-267-0222
Fax: 973-993-1180
Email: maskaleris@erols.com *URL:* http://www.lawyers.com/maskaleris
Athens, Greece Office: Navarinou Street 15. See U.S. Telephone and Fax.

Stephen N. Maskaleris

ASSOCIATES

Peter C. Ioannou
Ronald J. Gregorio

For full biographical listings, see the Martindale-Hubbell Law Directory

MCELROY, DEUTSCH AND MULVANEY (AV)

1300 Mount Kemble Avenue, P.O. Box 2075, 07962-2075
Telephone: 973-993-8100
Fax: 973-425-0161
URL: http://www.MDMlaw.com
Denver, Colorado Office: 1099 18th Street, Suite 3120.
Telephone: 303-293-8800.
Fax: 303-293-3116.
New York, New York Office: Wall Street Plaza, 88 Pine Street.
Telephone: 212-766-1807.
Fax: 212-483-9129.
Ridgewood, New Jersey Office: 40 West Ridgewood Avenue.
Telephone: 201-445-6722.
Fax: 201-445-8075.

MEMBERS OF FIRM

Lorraine M. Armenti (Resident Partner, Denver Colorado Office)
Grace C. Bertone
John P. Beyel
William C. Carey
Stephen H. Cohen (1938-1992)
Kevin T. Coughlin
John F. Darcy (Resident, Ridgewood Office)
Edward B. Deutsch
Timothy I. Duffy
Kevin P. Galvin
Robert J. Kelly
Joseph P. La Sala
James P. Lisovicz
Paul A. Lisovicz
Fred A. Manley, Jr.
Michael J. Marone
Nancy McDonald
William T. McElroy
Laurence M. McHeffey (Resident Partner, Denver, Colorado Office)
Robert W. Muilenburg
James M. Mulvaney
Alfred S. Nugent, Jr. (1925-1989)
Octavius A. Orbe (Resident, Ridgewood Office)
Loren L. Pierce
Warren K. Racusin
Mark A. Rosen
Thomas P. Scrivo
John H. Suminski
Walter F. Timpone
Kevin E. Wolff

COUNSEL TO THE FIRM

Robert L. Clifford

OF COUNSEL

John K. Bradley
John F. Whitteaker

ASSOCIATES

Susan Freeman Anthony
H. George Avery
Elizabeth Addison Barrow
Joseph F. Bermudez
Thomas Richard Calcagni
Patrick J. Casey (Resident Associate, Denver, Colorado Office)
Lisbeth W. Cload (Resident, Ridgewood Office)
Daniel J. Cohen
Craig J. Compoli, Jr.
John P. Cookson (Resident Associate, New York, NY Office)
John Thomas Coyne
Andrew J. D'Arcy
Andrew M. Csaszar
Michael B. Devins
John W. DiNicola, II

(See Next Column)

ASSOCIATES (Continued)

Robin A. Donato
Rebecca Ward Donohue
Steven F. Dorry
Julienne S. Duncan
Brian F. Fowler (Resident, Ridgewood Office)
Aaron C. Foy (Not admitted in NJ; Resident, Denver, Colorado Office)
Christopher S. Frangeš
Lorna A. Friel
Kevin P. Harkins (Resident, Ridgewood Office)
Sarah C. Herzog
Eric J. Hughes
George A. Kelman
Justin N. Kinney
Linda F. Kitz
John P. Leonard
Joseph J. McGlone
Robert McGuire
Kaneez Fatema Madraswalla
Nadine Maleski
Faith Martin
Suzanne Cocco Midlige
Heidi S. Minuskin
Louis A. Modugno
Florina A. Moldovan
John W. Morris
Francis C. Porada (Resident Associate, Denver, Colorado Office)
Robert J. Re
Vincent E. Reilly
Jay R. Ruble
Craig T. Sashihara
Adam R. Schwartz
Peter W. Smith
Timothy P. Smith
Ronnie H. Spring
Michael J. Sullivan
Catharine Acker Vaughan
Meredith A. Walling
Richard J. Williams, Jr.

Representative Clients: ADT Security Systems, Inc.; UpRight, Inc.; Crum & Forster Insurance Co.; Eaton Corp.; Fireman's Fund Insurance Cos.; New Jersey Manufacturers Insurance Co.; The Home Indemnity Co.; The Pittston Company; Security Pacific Finance Corporations; Hyster Co. Inc.

For full biographical listings, see the Martindale-Hubbell Law Directory

MCKIRDY AND RISKIN, A PROFESSIONAL CORPORATION (AV)

136 South Street, 07962-2379
Telephone: 973-539-8900
Fax: 973-984-5529
URL: http://www.lawyers.com/m&rlaw

Edward D. McKirdy
John H. Buonocore, Jr.
Harry J. Riskin
Thomas M. Olson
Anthony F. Della Pelle

Debra L. Kudriavetz

For full biographical listings, see the Martindale-Hubbell Law Directory

PITNEY, HARDIN, KIPP & SZUCH LLP (AV)

P.O. Box 1945, 07962-1945
Telephone: 973-966-6300
New York City: 212-687-6000
Telex: 642014
Telecopier: 973-966-1550
URL: http://www.phks.com
New York, New York Office: 711 Third Avenue, 10017-4014.
Telephone: 212-687-6000.
Fax: 212-682-3485.

MEMBERS OF FIRM

Clyde A. Szuch
Murray J. Laulicht
Richard L. Plotkin
Robert L. Hollingshead
Frederick L. Whitmer
Robert G. Rose
Anthony J. Marchetta
J. Michael Nolan, Jr.
Dennis R. LaFiura
Dennis T. Kearney
Donald W. Kiel
Elizabeth J. Sher
Hope S. Cone
John C. Maloney, Jr.
Benjamin E. Haglund
Joy Harmon Sperling
Christopher John Stracco

Representative Clients: AlliedSignal Inc.; AT&T Corp.; Base Ten Systems, Inc.; Exxon Corp.; Sony Electronics, Inc.; Union Camp Corporation; Union CarbideCorp.; United Parcel Services, Inc.; Volvo North America Corporation; Warner-Lambert Co.

For Complete List of Firm Personnel, See General Section

For full biographical listings, see the Martindale-Hubbell Law Directory

RAND, ALGEIER, TOSTI & WOODRUFF, A PROFESSIONAL CORPORATION (AV)

60 Washington Street, 07960
Telephone: 973-539-2600
Telecopier: 973-984-0430
Email: randlaw@bellatlantic.net

Gary C. Algeier
Robert B. Woodruff
David B. Rand
John F. McDonnell
Robert M. Tosti
John E. Croot, Jr.

Kathryn J. Kingree
Deborah A. White

OF COUNSEL

Ronald M. Pflug
Ellen S. Bass
Tamara Krikorian

For full biographical listings, see the Martindale-Hubbell Law Directory

Morristown—Continued

SCHENCK, PRICE, SMITH & KING, LLP (AV)

10 Washington Street, P.O. Box 905, 07963-0905
Telephone: 973-539-1000
Telecopier: 973-540-7300
Email: SCHENCK@SPSK.COM
New York, New York Office: 261 Madison Avenue, Suite 800.
Telephone: 212-986-6482.

MEMBERS OF FIRM

Clinton J. Curtis
James E. Davidson
Julius J. Denzler
Charles D. LaFiura
William C. Dodd
Willard Bergman, Jr.
Edward W. Ahart
Thomas C. C. Humick
Thomas F. Craig, II
Sidney A. Sayovitz
Douglas S. Brierley
Edward John Trawinski
Roy J. Evans
Howard P. Shaw
Gilbert S. Leeds
Monica E. Peck
Anita Joy Siegel
Lisa K. Pantel
James P. Wyse
Michael K. Mullen
M. Sheilah O'Halloran
Anne E. Aronovitch
John M. DeMarco
Michael A. Moroney
James B. Garland
Joanne L. Butler
Basil F. O'Connor
Patti S. Liberman
Kurt G. Senesky
Gary Mazart
Shirley Berger Whitenack
Richard J. Conway, Jr.

ASSOCIATES

Mary Elizabeth Warner
Barbara W. Stoller
Jeffrey T. LaRosa
Eric A. Inglis
Peter A. Marra
Wynne A. Whitman
Meredith L. Grocott
Karin S. Riecker
Maria A. Volarich
Jason E. Marx

OF COUNSEL

Kenneth J. Quinn
Patrick W. Turner
Douglas S. Zucker
Joseph E. Krakora

For full biographical listings, see the Martindale-Hubbell Law Directory

STEPHEN S. WEINSTEIN A PROFESSIONAL CORPORATION (AV)

20 Park Place, Suite 301, 07960
Telephone: 973-267-5200
Fax: 973-538-1779
Email: skippy@sswpa.com *URL:* http://www.sswpa.com

Stephen S. Weinstein

Gail S. Boertzel
William G. Johnson
Melissa H. Luce

For full biographical listings, see the Martindale-Hubbell Law Directory

*NEWARK,** Essex Co.

ALAN DEXTER BOWMAN, P.A. (AV)

One Gateway Center, Suite 105, 07102
Telephone: 973-622-2225
Fax: 973-242-6768

Alan Dexter Bowman

For full biographical listings, see the Martindale-Hubbell Law Directory

CARPENTER, BENNETT & MORRISSEY (AV)

Three Gateway Center, 17th Floor, 100 Mulberry Street, 07102-4079
Telephone: 973-622-7711
New York City: 212-943-6530
Telex: 139405
Telecopier: 973-622-5314
Email: cbm@carpben.com

MEMBERS OF FIRM

John E. Keale
James J. Crowley, Jr.
John P. Dwyer
Michael S. Waters
James G. Gardner
John F. Lynch, Jr.
Donald A. Romano
Francis X. Dee
Irving L. Hurwitz
Rosemary J. Bruno
William A. Carpenter, Jr.
John J. Peirano
Linda B. Celauro
Patrick G. Brady
Louis M. DeStefano
Thomas F. McGuane
Joseph D. Rasnek
Robert J. Stickles
Robert M. Goodman
Thomas M. Moore
Lois H. Goodman
James Peter Lidon
David J. Reilly
Jane A. Rigby

OF COUNSEL

Thomas L. Morrissey
Edward F. Ryan
John C. Heavey

(See Next Column)

ASSOCIATES

Jennifer L. Kapell
Michelle S. Hydrusko
Jeffrey Bernstein
Joseph Gerard Lee
Daniel J. O'Hern, Jr.
Steven J. Santarsiero
Marc E. Wolin
C. Brian Kornbrek
Melissa B. Popkin
Robert P. McGovern
Claire C. Cecchi
Kenneth B. Rotter
Kerry A. O'Shea
Elizabeth A. Kenny
Deborah A. Young

Representative Clients: General Motors Corp.; E. I. du Pont de Nemours and Co.; Texaco Inc.; Johnson & Johnson; Litton Industries; ITT Industries, Inc. ; International Flavors & Fragrances Inc.; The Boeing Co.; Caterpillar, Inc.; Hartford Insurance Co.

For Complete List of Firm Personnel, See General Section

For full biographical listings, see the Martindale-Hubbell Law Directory

FITZSIMMONS RINGLE & JACOBS, P.C. (AV)

50 Park Place, 07102
Telephone: 973-623-5350
Fax: 973-623-5927
New York, New York: 130 E. 35th Street, 10016.
Telephone: 212-343-0677.

Frank J. Fitzsimmons
Richard Ringle
Andrew R. Jacobs

COUNSEL

Ronald Leibman

Michael E. Coslit
Lisa M. Papp
Martin Trevor Hughes Lyons

For full biographical listings, see the Martindale-Hubbell Law Directory

GREENBERG DAUBER EPSTEIN & TUCKER, A PROFESSIONAL CORPORATION (AV)

Suite 600, One Gateway Center, 07102-5311
Telephone: 973-643-3700
Facsimile: 973-643-1218
URL: http://www.greenbergdauber.com

Melvin Greenberg
Edward J. Dauber
Linda G. Harvey

For Complete List of Firm Personnel, See General Section

For full biographical listings, see the Martindale-Hubbell Law Directory

HELLRING LINDEMAN GOLDSTEIN & SIEGAL LLP (AV)

One Gateway Center, 07102-5386
Telephone: 973-621-9020
Fax: 973-621-7406
Englewood, New Jersey Office: 32-40 North Dean Street.
Telephone: 201-871-3060.

Philip Lindeman, II
Joel D. Siegal
Jonathan L. Goldstein
Margaret Dee Hellring
Richard D. Shapiro
Charles Oransky
Richard B. Honig
Richard K. Coplon
Robert S. Raymar
Ronny Jo Greenwald Siegal
Stephen L. Dreyfuss
John A. Adler
Judah I. Elstein
Bruce S. Etterman
Matthew E. Moloshok
Rachel N. Davidson
David N. Narciso
Ronnie F. Liebowitz
Sheryl E. Koomer

Catherine J. Bick
Joanne M. Frasca

For Complete List of Firm Personnel, See General Section

For full biographical listings, see the Martindale-Hubbell Law Directory

KENNY & STEARNS (AV)

56 Park Place, 07102
Telephone: 201-624-7779
New York, N.Y. Office: 26 Broadway.
Telephone: 212-422-6111.
Fax: 212-422-6544.

PARTNERS IN CHARGE

James M. Kenny
Joseph T. Stearns
Gino A. Zonghetti

ASSOCIATES

Michael C. Mulé
Christina M. Kenny
John D. Blomquist

For full biographical listings, see the Martindale-Hubbell Law Directory

Newark—Continued

Lite, De Palma, Greenberg & Rivas, LLC (AV)

Two Gateway Center, 12th Floor, 07102-5003
Telephone: 973-623-3000
Fax: 973-623-0858

MEMBERS OF FIRM

Allyn Z. Lite
Joseph J. De Palma
Bruce D. Greenberg

For full biographical listings, see the Martindale-Hubbell Law Directory

McCarter & English, LLP (AV)

Four Gateway Center, 100 Mulberry Street, P.O. Box 652, 07101-0652
Telephone: 973-622-4444
Telecopier: 973-624-7070
URL: http://www.mccarter.com
Cherry Hill, New Jersey Office: 1820 Chapel Avenue West, Suite 380.
Telephone: 609-662-8444.
Telecopier: 609-662-6203.
New York, New York Office: Suite 2247, One World Trade Center.
Telephone: 212-466-9018.
Telecopier: 212-432-6568.
Boca Raton, Florida Office: 2255 Glades Road, Suite 319-A.
Telephone: 561-994-6262.
Telecopier: 561-241-0798.
Wilmington, Delaware Office: Mellon Bank Center, 919 Market Street.
Telephone: 302-654-8010.
Telecopier: 302-654-0795.
Philadelphia, Pennsylvania Office: One Commerce Square, 2005 Market Street, Suite 3600.
Telephone: 215-557-7700.
Telecopier: 215-557-6544.

MEMBERS OF FIRM

Andrew T. Berry
Richard C. Cooper
William H. Horton
William J. O'Shaughnessy
Richard M. Eittreim
John E. Flaherty
William T. Reilly
Gita F. Rothschild
David R. Kott
Lanny S. Kurzweil
John F. Brenner
Frank E. Ferruggia
Richard P. O'Leary
Theodore D. Moskowitz
Seth T. Taube
Lisa M. Goldman
Thomas W. Ladd
Patrick J. Perrone
Sherilyn Pastor
Harvey C. Kaish

OF COUNSEL

Thomas F. Daly

COUNSEL

Joseph F. Falgiani
Steven A. Beckelman
Jerry P. Sattin

ASSOCIATE

Cynthia Spera Neff

For Complete List of Firm Personnel, See General Section

For full biographical listings, see the Martindale-Hubbell Law Directory

Meyner and Landis (AV)

One Gateway Center, Suite 2500, 07102-5311
Telephone: 973-624-2800
Fax: 973-624-0356
Email: attys@meyner.com *URL:* http://www.meyner.com

Robert B. Meyner (1908-1990)
Edwin C. Landis, Jr.
John N. Malyska
William J. Fiore
Anthony F. Siliato
Francis R. Perkins
Howard O. Thompson
Scott T. McCleary
Linda Townley Snyder
William H. Schmidt, Jr.
David B. Grantz

For full biographical listings, see the Martindale-Hubbell Law Directory

St. John & Wayne, L.L.C. (AV)

Two Penn Plaza East, 07105-2249
Telephone: 973-491-3600
Fax: 973-491-3555
Email: firm@nwk.stjohn-law.com *URL:* http://www.stjohn-law.com
Rochester, New York Office: St. John & Curtin, L.L.C., First Federal Plaza.
Telephone: 716-262-6780.
Fax: 716-262-6755.
New York, New York Office: Heron Tower, 70 East 55th. Street.
Telephone: 212-446-5000.
Fax: 212-446-5055.

Bruce S. Edington
Peter B. Van Deventer, Jr.

For Complete List of Firm Personnel, See General Section

For full biographical listings, see the Martindale-Hubbell Law Directory

Sills Cummis Radin Tischman Epstein & Gross, A Professional Corporation (AV)

One Riverfront Plaza, 07102-5400
Telephone: 973-643-7000
Fax: 973-643-6500
Telex: 820630 Sillsbeck Nwk
Email: sillsmail@sillscummis.com *URL:* http://www.sillscummis.com
Atlantic City, New Jersey Office: 17 Gordon's Alley.
Telephone: 609-344-2800.
New York, N.Y. Office: 712 Fifth Avenue.
Telephone: 212-643-7000.
Washington, D.C. Office: 1800 K Street, N.W.
Telephone: 202-296-4750.

MEMBERS OF FIRM

Clive S. Cummis
Steven S. Radin
Morton S. Bunis
Barry M. Epstein
Thomas J. Demski
Jeffrey J. Greenbaum
Andrew P. Napolitano
Jeffrey Barton Cahn
Lester Aron
Kenneth F. Oettle
Robert J. Alter
Philip R. Sellinger
Thomas S. Novak
Stuart M. Feinblatt
Trent S. Dickey
Joseph L. Buckley
Kathleen Gengaro
James D. Toll (Resident at Atlantic City, N.J. Office)
James M. Hirschhorn
Ronald C. Rak
Mark S. Olinsky
Richard J. Sapinski
Philip R. White
Alan J. Cohen (Resident at Atlantic City, N.J. Office)
Lori G. Singer
Mark E. Duckstein
Beth S. Rose
Jack Wenik
Jeffrey M. Pollock
A. Ross Pearlson
Linda Badash Katz

OF COUNSEL

Cherie L. Maxwell
Steven R. Rowland

Eric D. Mann (Resident at Atlantic City, N.J. Office)
Bennet Susser
Steven S. Katz
Paul P. Josephson
Paul F. Doda
Helen E. Kleiner
Rhonda Sobral O'Toole
Adam J. Kaiser
Jennifer L. Borofsky
Gwen L. Coleman
Susanne Kaufmann Rosenzweig

Representative Clients: Bristol-Myers Squibb Corporation; Citibank, N.A.; BMW of North America; Circuit City Stores, Inc.; Bellcore; Shortline Bus; Six Flags Corporation; WWOR-TV; Becton Dickinson & Co.; Johnson & Johnson.

For Complete List of Firm Personnel, See General Section

For full biographical listings, see the Martindale-Hubbell Law Directory

Tompkins, McGuire, Wachenfeld & Barry (AV)

A New Jersey Limited Liability Partnership including a Professional Association
Four Gateway Center, 100 Mulberry Street, 07102-4070
Telephone: 973-622-3000
Telecopier: 973-623-7780
Email: attorneys@tompkinsmcguire.com
New York, New York Office: 1 Bankers Trust Plaza. 130 Liberty Street, Suite 2707. 10006.
Telephone: 212-714-1720.

MEMBERS OF FIRM

William F. Tompkins (1913-1989)
William J. Prout, Jr. (1947-1996)
William B. McGuire (P.A.)
Howard G. Wachenfeld
Theodore L. Abeles
John J. Barry
Rex K. Harriott
James F. Flanagan, III
Marianne Espinosa Murphy
Eugene J. Sullivan
Frederic S. Kessler
Michael F. Nestor
Marianne M. DeMarco
Patrick M. Callahan
Paul S. Werther
Mark Falk
Michael S. Miller
Douglas E. Motzenbecker
Evelyn R. Storch
Ellen Nunno Corbo
William H. Trousdale
George G. Campion
Joseph K. Cobuzio
Richard F. Connors, Jr.
Richard A. Ulsamer
Madeline E. Cox
Nadia Walker Brunetto
Angelo R. Giacchi
Adam N. Saravay

OF COUNSEL

Michael F. DeCapua
Frances S. Margolis
Paul B. Thompson
Raymond W. Troy (1911-1992)
William T. Wachenfeld

COUNSEL

Peter A. Bogaard
Brian M. English
Leonore C. Lewis

ASSOCIATES

Christopher A. Barbarisi
Thomas A. Callahan, Jr.
Joann K. Dobransky
Thomas F. Doherty
Robert Leonardo
Stephen C. Matthews
Grant W. McGuire
Matthew P. O'Malley
Michael P. Pasquale
Colleen Duffy Shiarella

(See Next Column)

TOMPKINS, MCGUIRE, WACHENFELD & BARRY, *Newark—Continued*

Representative Clients: Corbo Jewelers, Inc.; General Electric Co.; Hartford Insurance Group; Marriott Corp.; National Union Fire Insurance Co.; Underwriters at Lloyd's, London.

For full biographical listings, see the Martindale-Hubbell Law Directory

ZAZZALI, ZAZZALI, FAGELLA & NOWAK, A PROFESSIONAL CORPORATION (AV)

One Riverfront Plaza, 07102-5410
Telephone: 973-623-1822
Telecopier: 973-623-2209
URL: http://www.lawyers.com/zazzali
Trenton, New Jersey Office: 150 West State Street.
Telephone: 609-392-8172.
Facsimile: 609-392-8933.
New York, New York Office: 15 West 72nd Street.
Telephone: 212-529-3927.
Facsimile: 212-875-8275.

Andrew F. Zazzali (1925-1969)
Andrew F. Zazzali, Jr.
James R. Zazzali
Robert A. Fagella
Kenneth I. Nowak
Paul L. Kleinbaum
Richard A. Friedman

Kathleen Anne Naprstek
Aileen M. O'Driscoll
Edward H. O'Hare
Jason Solowkowski

For full biographical listings, see the Martindale-Hubbell Law Directory

*NEW BRUNSWICK,** Middlesex Co.

HOAGLAND, LONGO, MORAN, DUNST & DOUKAS (AV)

40 Paterson Street, P.O. Box 480, 08903
Telephone: 732-545-4717
Fax: 732-545-4579
Email: info@hlmdd.com

MEMBERS OF FIRM

Bartholomew A. Longo
James B. Moran
Alan I. Dunst
Kenneth J. Doukas, Jr.
Michael John Stone
Donald D. Davidson
Thaddeus J. Hubert, III
Joan Alster Weisblatt
Karen M. Buerle
Robert G. Kenny
Michael J. Baker
Andrew J. Carlowicz, Jr.
Gary J. Hoagland
Jeffrey S. Intravatola
Jamie D. Happas
Thomas J. Walsh, Jr.
Robert S. Helwig
Michael F. Dolan
Douglas M. Fasciale
Marc S. Gaffrey
John Charles Simons
Susan K. O'Connor
Stephen G. Perrella
Jacquelyn L. Poland
Douglas Susan
Patrick J. McDonald

OF COUNSEL

John J. Hoagland
Herman L. Breitkopf
Richard S. Cohen

ASSOCIATES

Andrew N. Kessler
John P. Barnes
Christopher M. Longo
Nancy A. Freedman
Tiffany C. Chong
Michael Dermody
Diane Hoagland
Michael T. Kearns
Keith C. Northridge
Andrew J. DiMarsico
Edward J. Rebenack
Paul N. Harris
Denis A. Gooding
Kevin J. Musiakiewicz
Michael N. Porter
Kenneth Sisco
M. Stephanie Beaty

Representative Clients: CNA/Continental Casualty; National Indemnity Company; Providence Washington Insurance Company; The Mutual Fire, Marine & Inland Insurance Company; INAPRO/CIGNA; Allstate Insurance Company; Home Depot; American Reliance Insurance Company; Shand, Morahan & Company; CPC International.

For full biographical listings, see the Martindale-Hubbell Law Directory

NEW PROVIDENCE, Union Co.

TAFARO & FLYNN, P.A. (AV)

571 Central Avenue, Suite 119, 07974
Telephone: 908-508-0100
Fax: 908-508-0599
Email: tafaroflyn@aol.com

Stephen J. Tafaro
Catherine J. Flynn

Joan Bannan Harris
Eric L. Grogan
Fred J. Hughes
Cheryl M. DeKline
Suellen L. DeBlasio
Marisa R. Kussoy

For full biographical listings, see the Martindale-Hubbell Law Directory

NORTH BRUNSWICK, Middlesex Co.

BORRUS, GOLDIN, FOLEY, VIGNUOLO, HYMAN, STAHL & CLARKIN, A PROFESSIONAL CORPORATION (AV)

2875 U.S. Highway 1, Route 1 & Finnigans Lane, P.O. Box 7463, 08902
Telephone: 732-422-1000
Fax: 732-422-1016
Email: attys@borrus.com *URL:* http://www.borrus.com

Jack Borrus
Martin S. Goldin
David M. Foley
Anthony B. Vignuolo
Jeffrey M. Hyman
James E. Stahl
James F. Clarkin III
Eileen Mary Foley

Robert C. Nisenson
Rosalind Westlake
Lisa M. Vignuolo
Steven L. Fox
Peter A. Vignuolo
Gerald T. Foley (1903-1976)

Representative Clients: Summit Bank; R. J. Reynolds Tobacco Co.; K. Hovnanian Enterprises, Inc.; Johnson and Johnson; Foster Wheeler, Inc.; Hartz Mountain Industries; Middlesex County Vocational Services Commission; Borough of South Plainfield Board of Adjustment; U-Haul of Northern NJ.

For full biographical listings, see the Martindale-Hubbell Law Directory

BUSCH AND BUSCH, LLP (AV)

215 North Center Drive, Commerce Center - U.S. #1 South, P.O. Box 7448, 08902-7448
Telephone: 732-821-2300
Telecopier: 732-821-5588
Email: busch@ifu.net

MEMBERS OF FIRM

Lewis D. Busch (1901-1986)
Henry Busch (Retired)
Malcolm R. Busch
Ronald J. Busch
Bertram E. Busch
Mark N. Busch
Leonard R. Busch
Steven F. Satz
Donald J. Sears

ASSOCIATE

Paul Alan VanBuskirk

Representative Clients: Utica Mutual Insurance Co.; New Brunswick Tomorrow; Township of South Brunswick; Township of Monroe, Board of Education; Township of East Brunswick; Minnesota Mutual Life Insurance Co.

For full biographical listings, see the Martindale-Hubbell Law Directory

LYNCH, MARTIN, KANE, KUPER, KEEFE & BARTELS, LLC (AV)

1368 How Lane, P.O. Box 6022, 08902-6022
Telephone: 732-545-0745
Fax: 732-545-4780
Email: LYNCHMRTN@aol.com

John A. Lynch, Sr. (1908-1978)
John A. Lynch
James D. Martin, Jr.
John J. Kane
Eric Kuper
John E. Keefe, Jr.
Patrick J. Bartels
Carl W. Swanson
James Den Uyl
John W. Harding
Lori A. Dvorak
Bernard P. Hvozdovic, Jr.
Joseph J. LaCosta
Timothy E. Annin

Laura M. Shea
Robyn M. Mitchell
Christine Klimczuk

OF COUNSEL

Robert T. Quackenboss (Retired Superior Court Judge)

LEGAL SUPPORT PERSONNEL

Sharon Stewart (Administrator)

For full biographical listings, see the Martindale-Hubbell Law Directory

NORTHFIELD, Atlantic Co.

MCALLISTER, HYBERG & WHITE (AV)

Executive Plaza, 2111 New Road, Suite 105, 08225
Telephone: 609-407-1000
Fax: 609-407-1010
Email: McAllister-Hyberg@prodigy.net

Robert N. McAllister
Lars S. Hyberg
Joseph B. White

ASSOCIATE

Keith T. Smith

For full biographical listings, see the Martindale-Hubbell Law Directory

OCEAN TOWNSHIP, Monmouth Co.

EVANS, OSBORNE & KREIZMAN (AV)

CN 7808 1500 Lawrence Avenue, 07712-7808
Telephone: 732-643-0300
Fax: 732-643-0340
New York, New York Office: Suite 7967, One World Trade Center.
Telephone: 212-466-1207.

MEMBERS OF FIRM

Harry S. Evans
Harry V. Osborne, II
Joel N. Kreizman
Mary O'Keefe Massey
Kevin E. Hoffman

ASSOCIATES

Marie A. Accardi
James F. McDonough
Kenneth P. Skibinski

Representative Clients: United Kingdom P&I Club (Thomas R. Miller Insurance Services); American Marine Underwriters, Inc.; Continental Insurance Cos.; Hartford Insurance Cos.; CIGNA Cos.; Jersey Central Power & Light Co.; First Union Bank; CNA Insurance Cos.; General Public Utilities, Inc.

For full biographical listings, see the Martindale-Hubbell Law Directory

PARAMUS, Bergen Co.

FINNERTY & LAROCCA, P.C. (AV)

Country Club Plaza, W 115 Century Road, 07652
Telephone: 201-845-4000
Facsimile: 201-845-6799
URL: http://finnertylarocca
URL: http://www.familylaw-nj.com

John E. Finnerty
Frank J. LaRocca

Erin K. Burke
Gina R. Pacinella

OF COUNSEL

Eugenie F. Temmler

For full biographical listings, see the Martindale-Hubbell Law Directory

STRASSER & ASSOCIATES, A PROFESSIONAL CORPORATION (AV)

Paramus Plaza I, 140 Route 17 North, Suite 265, 07652-2816
Telephone: 201-262-7177
Fax: 201-262-3113

William I. Strasser

Conrad M. Olear
Constantinos J. Ballas

Representative Clients: Consumer Value Stores (CVS); Melville Corp.; Melville Realty Corp.; Linens 'N Things, Inc.; This End Up Furniture Co., Inc.; Universal Foods Corp.; Essex Computers, Inc.; Polevoy Associates; Footstar, Inc.; Bob's Stores.

For full biographical listings, see the Martindale-Hubbell Law Directory

PARSIPPANY, Morris Co.

CUYLER BURK (AV)

Parsippany Corporate Center, Four Century Drive, 07054-4663
Telephone: 973-734-3200
Telex: 429071
Telecopier: 973-734-3201
Email: Main@Cuyler.com *URL:* http://www.cuyler.com
New York, New York Office: 350 Fifth Avenue, Suite 3304. 10018.
Telephone: 212-645-4039.

MEMBERS OF FIRM

Stephen D. Cuyler
Jo Ann Burk
Stefano Calogero
David L. Menzel
Peter Petrou
Richard A. Crooker
Michael J. Jones

COUNSEL

Anne M. Mohan
Frank J. Miele

ASSOCIATES

Jan C. Walker
Kathleen Jane Olear
Claudia L. Marchese
Mark G. Eliades
Kimberly A. Joel
Christy A. Ramunno
Catherine E. Youngman
Andrew K. Craig
Mark S. Winter
Thomas J. Castano
Hugo A. Hilgendorff, IV

LEGAL SUPPORT PERSONNEL

Frederick M. H. Currie, Jr.

For full biographical listings, see the Martindale-Hubbell Law Directory

GENNET, KALLMANN, ANTIN & ROBINSON, A PROFESSIONAL CORPORATION (AV)

6 Campus Drive, 07054-4406
Telephone: 973-285-1919
Fax: 973-285-1177
Email: gkar@nac.net
New York, New York Office: Litman Suite, 45 Broadway Atrium, 10006.
Telephone: 212-406-1919.

Stanley W. Kallmann
Mark L. Antin
Harry Robinson, III
Richard S. Nichols

William Gary Hanft
Thomas J. Olsen, IV
Francie E. Joseph
Paul A. Tumbleson

LEGAL SUPPORT PERSONNEL

Eleanor Dawalt (Administrator)

Representative Clients: Aetna Insurance Co.; Hartford Fire; Lloyds of London; New England Mutuals.
Reference: United Jersey Bank.

For full biographical listings, see the Martindale-Hubbell Law Directory

REISEMAN SHARP KELSEY & BROWN LLP (AV)

4 Campus Drive, P.O. Box 431, 07054-0431
Telephone: 973-267-3600
Fax: 973-267-2332

MEMBERS OF FIRM

Neil Reiseman
James B. Sharp
Jane S. Kelsey
Kenneth M. Brown
Sam Rosenberg
Meghan E. Walsh

John C. Macce
Jayne E. Turner
Everett E. Gale, III
Robert T. Gunning
Gregory A. Bush

Representative Clients: Medical Inter-Insurance Exchange of New Jersey; Princeton Insurance Company; Health Care Insurance Company; Home Depot; United Capitol Insurance Company; New Jersey Property-Liability Insurance Guaranty Association; New Jersey Joint Underwriting Association; Franciscan Health Systems; Zurich American; Avis.

For full biographical listings, see the Martindale-Hubbell Law Directory

PRINCETON, Mercer Co.

BERGMAN & BARRETT (AV)

9 Tamarack Circle, Montgomery Knoll, U.S. Highway 206 North, P.O. Box 1273, 08542
Telephone: 609-921-1502
Fax: 609-683-0288

Edward J. Bergman
Michael T. Barrett

LEGAL SUPPORT PERSONNEL

Kelli E. Murphy (Paralegal)

For full biographical listings, see the Martindale-Hubbell Law Directory

MASON, GRIFFIN & PIERSON, A PROFESSIONAL CORPORATION (AV)

101 Poor Farm Road, 08540
Telephone: 609-921-6543
Fax: 609-683-7978
Email: mgp@mgplaw.com *URL:* http://www.mgplaw.com
Flemington, New Jersey, Office: P.O. Box 2420, 151 Main Street, 08822.
Telephone: 908-782-2900.
Fax: 908-782-2428. Email: denilaw@erols.com.

Ralph S. Mason (1913-1988)
Craig H. Davis (1947-1997)
Gordon D. Griffin
Kester R. Pierson
Edwin W. Schmierer
Kristina Pike Hadinger
Donald B. Veix, Jr.
Charles F. Harris
Edmond M. Konin
Shawn M. Neufeld
Valerie L. Howe

Barbara J. Morgan
Christopher H. DeGrezia
F. Clifford Gibbons
Carleen M. Steward
Georgia M. Fraser

OF COUNSEL

William P. Deni, Sr.
Jules Farkas

Representative Clients: Connecticut Indemnity Company; Griffith Electric Supply Company, Inc.; Johnson Controls World Services, Inc.; The Pennington School; Township of Montgomery; Township of Princeton; Management Planning, Inc.

For full biographical listings, see the Martindale-Hubbell Law Directory

MCCARTHY AND SCHATZMAN, P.A. (AV)

228 Alexander Street, P.O. Box 2329, 08543-2329
Telephone: 609-924-1199
Fax: 609-683-5251

(See Next Column)

McCarthy and Schatzman P.A., *Princeton—Continued*

John F. McCarthy, Jr.
Richard Schatzman
G. Christopher Baker
John F. McCarthy, III
Michael A. Spero
Barbara Strapp Nelson
W. Scott Stoner
James J. Britt, Jr.

Charly Gayden

Representative Clients: Trustees of Princeton University; Carnegie Center Associates; Merrill Lynch Pierce Fenner & Smith, Inc.; Calton Homes, Inc.

For full biographical listings, see the Martindale-Hubbell Law Directory

RED BANK, Monmouth Co.

Philip G. Auerbach A Professional Corporation (AV)

231 Maple Avenue, P.O. Box Y, 07701
Telephone: 732-842-6660
Fax: 732-530-7925

Philip G. Auerbach

Edward A. Genz
John J. Ryan
John F. McLaughlin

For full biographical listings, see the Martindale-Hubbell Law Directory

White, Fleischner & Fino (AV)

272 Broad Street, 07701
Telephone: 732-530-7787
Telecopier: 732-530-8552
New York, New York Office: 140 Broadway.
Telephone: 212-487-9700.
Telecopier: 212-487-9777.

Sheri E. Holland

ASSOCIATE

Daniel MacLaren Stewart

Representative Clients: Marriott International; Avis Rent A Car; Empire Fire & Marine Ins. Co.; Raphael & Associates; Interstate Insurance Group.

For full biographical listings, see the Martindale-Hubbell Law Directory

RIDGEFIELD PARK, Bergen Co.

Durkin & Boggia (AV)

71 Mount Vernon Street, P.O. Box 378, 07660
Telephone: 201-641-0006
Fax: 201-641-6649
Email: dnbesqs@aol.com

MEMBERS OF FIRM

Martin T. Durkin
Philip N. Boggia

ASSOCIATES

Priscilla M. Boggia
Michael N. Morea

Reference: First Union National Bank; Village of Ridgefield Park; Borough of Edgewater Planning Board; Borough of Lodi Board of Adjustment; Borough of Moonachie Planning Board; Archdiocese of Newark; Goya Foods, Inc.; Ramsey Outdoor Store; Computer Leasing, Inc.; The Church of the Annunciation of the Blessed Virgin Mary, Paramus, NJ.

For full biographical listings, see the Martindale-Hubbell Law Directory

ROSELAND, Essex Co.

Brach, Eichler, Rosenberg, Silver, Bernstein, Hammer & Gladstone, A Professional Corporation (AV)

101 Eisenhower Parkway, 07068
Telephone: 973-228-5700
Telecopier: 973-228-7852
Email: law@bracheichler.com *URL:* http://www.bracheichler.com

Alan H. Bernstein
William L. Brach
Richard J. Driver
Burton L. Eichler
Charles X. Gormally
Joseph M. Gorrell
Alan S. Pralgever

Stuart Jeffrey Polkowitz
John P. Wyciskala, III
Matthew M. Collins
Carl J. Soranno
Kristine Bogardus Purcell
Christopher A. Erd
Jonathan E. Levitt

OF COUNSEL

Harris R. Silver
Lance A. Posner

COUNSEL

David J. Klein
David S. Bernstein

Representative Clients: Coastal Group, Inc.; Gebroe-Hammer Associates; I. Heller Construction Co. Inc.; M. Epstein, Inc.; Ohio Casualty Insurance Group; R & S Strauss, Inc.; Radiological Society of New Jersey; Saint Barnabas Health Care System; Summit Bank.

(See Next Column)

For Complete List of Firm Personnel, See General Section

For full biographical listings, see the Martindale-Hubbell Law Directory

Connell, Foley & Geiser LLP (AV)

85 Livingston Avenue, 07068
Telephone: 973-535-0500
Telefax: 973-535-9217
Email: info@cfglaw.com *URL:* http://www.cfglaw.com

MEMBERS OF FIRM

George W. Connell
Adrian M. Foley, Jr.
Theodore W. Geiser
John B. La Vecchia
George J. Kenny
Samuel Darrow Lord
Richard D. Catenacci
Richard J. Badolato
Peter D. Manahan
Mark L. Fleder
Linda A. Palazzolo
John F. Neary
Thomas S. Cosma
Kathleen S. Murphy
Patrick J. McAuley
Peter J. Pizzi
Kevin R. Gardner
Robert Emmett Ryan
Michael X. McBride
Jeffrey W. Moryan
Donald S. MacLachlan
Patricia J. Pindar
Peter J. Smith
Brian G. Steller
Judith A. Wahrenberger
Karen Munster Cassidy
Karen Painter Randall
Liza M. Walsh
Timothy E. Corriston
Ernest W. Schoellkopff
Heidi Willis Currier

Representative Clients: Bethlehem Steel Corp.; Borden Inc.; Chase Manhattan Bank; CNA Insurance; Conrail; Hilton Hotels Corp.; Merrill Lynch; Microsoft; New Jersey Manufacturers Insurance.

For Complete List of Firm Personnel, See General Section

For full biographical listings, see the Martindale-Hubbell Law Directory

Post, Polak, Goodsell & MacNeill, P.A. (AV)

75 Livingston Avenue, 07068-3701
Telephone: 973-994-1100
Telecopier: 973-994-1705
Email: administrator@ppgm.com
New York, New York Office: 575 Madison Avenue, Suite 1006.
Telephone: 212-486-1455.

John N. Post
Frederick B. Polak
Robert A. Goodsell
Jay Scott MacNeill
Mary H. Post
David L. Epstein
Lauren Koffler O'Neill

Loretta B. Critchley
Franca D. Maiorano
Joseph Tripodi
Thomas J. Pyle, Jr.
Christopher O. Eriksen

For Complete List of Firm Personnel, See General Section

For full biographical listings, see the Martindale-Hubbell Law Directory

Sellar Richardson, P.C. (AV)

Six Becker Farm Road, 07068-1735
Telephone: 973-535-1400
Fax: 973-535-6522
Email: info@sellarrichardson.com

James P. Richardson
Wendy H. Smith
John M. Kearney
Denise M. Luckenbach
Shawn R. Stowell

Patricia R. Carley
Julia C. Talarick
Deborah M. Taub
Albert N. Montano
Jennifer R. Sentivan
Victoria F. Pratt

OF COUNSEL

Alastair J. Sellar
E. Scott Garrett
Anthony C. Stuart

For full biographical listings, see the Martindale-Hubbell Law Directory

Walder, Sondak & Brogan, A Professional Corporation (AV)

5 Becker Farm Road, P.O. Box 901, 07068
Telephone: 973-992-5300
Telecopier: 973-992-1505; 992-1006
Email: general@wsbesqs.com *URL:* http://www.wsbesqs.com

Justin P. Walder
John A. Brogan
Melvyn H. Bergstein
Thomas J. Spies
Barry A. Kozyra
James A. Plaisted
Michael J. Faul, Jr.
Jeffrey A. Walder
Patricia M. Talbert

John S. Redden
Shalom D. Stone
Judith A. Hartz
Christopher M. Farella
Barbara F. Buchta
Steven D. Grossman
K. Roger Plawker

(See Next Column)

WALDER, SONDAK & BROGAN A PROFESSIONAL CORPORATION—*Continued*

Representative Clients: Hartz Mountain Industries; NEC America, Inc.; Old Republic Insurance Co.; Chicago Underwriting Group; Tuscan/Lehigh Dairies, LP.; Engelhard Corporation; Webcraft Technologies, Inc.; Vermont Teddy Bear Company.

For Complete List of Firm Personnel, See General Section

For full biographical listings, see the Martindale-Hubbell Law Directory

SADDLE BROOK, Bergen Co.

COHN LIFLAND PEARLMAN HERRMANN & KNOPF LLP (AV)

Park 80 Plaza West-One, 07663
Telephone: 201-845-9600
Telecopier: 201-845-9423
Email: info@njlawfirm.com *URL:* http://www.njlawfirm.com

MEMBERS OF FIRM

Albert L. Cohn
Peter S. Pearlman
Barry A. Knopf
Daniel Crystal (Retired)
Jeffrey W. Herrmann
Robert D. Zatorski
Allen Susser
Mary Ann T. Stokes
Brian D. Zinn
Joshua P. Cohn

ASSOCIATES

Virginia A. Harper
Leonard Z. Kaufmann
Audra DePaolo
Robert Ricci, Jr.
Maurice W. McLaughlin
Andrew C. Abrams
Jessica V. Henry

OF COUNSEL

Sylvia J. Cohn
Jodi B. Scherl

For full biographical listings, see the Martindale-Hubbell Law Directory

KRUGMAN & KAILES LLP (AV)

Park 80 West-Plaza Two, 07663-5835
Telephone: 201-845-3434; 212-695-3262
Telecopier: 201-845-9627
Email: counsel@krugmankailes.com
New York, New York Office: 99 Park Avenue, Suite 2200.
Telephone: 212-599-1060.
Telecopier: 212-599-6282.
London, England Office: 90 Fetter Lane, London EC4A-1PT.
Telephone: 011 (44) 171-421-7918.
Telecopier: 011 (44) 171-831-6407.

MEMBERS OF FIRM

Martin Krugman (1916-1994)
Howard Kailes
Thomas J. Goodwin
Ward C. Laracy
Robert I. Wexler
Alan H. Fox
Joy M. Mercer
Kerry B. Flowers

OF COUNSEL

James D. Krugman

COUNSEL

Judith S. Musicant

ASSOCIATES

Anne M. Wallace (Not admitted in NJ)
April A. Savoye
Lisa Ann Miller
Patrizia E. DeBari
David J. Hanley, Jr.
Anjana D. Patel
W. Mark O'Brien

For full biographical listings, see the Martindale-Hubbell Law Directory

SECAUCUS, Hudson Co.

WATERS, MCPHERSON, MCNEILL, P.C. (AV)

300 Lighting Way, 7th Floor, 07096
Telephone: 201-863-4400
Telecopy: 201-863-2866
Email: managingpartner@lawwmm.com *URL:* www.lawwmm.com
Trenton, New Jersey Office: 172 West State Street.
Telephone: 609-599-1000.
New York, N.Y. Office: The Woolworth Building, 233 Broadway, Suite 970.
Telephone: 212-227-7878.

Kenneth D. McPherson
John J. Kot
William J. Ward
Gregory J. Castano
Steven R. Gray
E. Neal Zimmermann
Kenneth D. McPherson, Jr.
Patrick J. Arre

Representative Clients: American Institute of Certified Public Accountants; Crown, Cork & Seal Co., Inc.; Hartz Mountain Industries, Inc.; Liberty Mutual Insurance Co.; Tropicana Products, Inc.

For Complete List of Firm Personnel, See General Section

For full biographical listings, see the Martindale-Hubbell Law Directory

SHIP BOTTOM, Ocean Co.

SHACKLETON, HAZELTINE AND BISHOP (AV)

22nd Street and Long Beach Boulevard, P.O. Box 410, 08008
Telephone: 609-494-2136
Telefax: 609-494-0870
Fairfield, New Jersey Office: One Passaic Avenue.
Telephone: 201-882-4646.
Telefax: 201-882-4620.

MEMBERS OF FIRM

Richard J. Shackleton
Colin R. Hazeltine
James E. Bishop

ASSOCIATES

Laura M. O'Regan
Marc Baden Powell
Robert Emmet Rue

OF COUNSEL

Kenneth L. Leiby, Jr. (Resident, Fairfield Office)

References: Commerce Bank/Shore N/A; Summit Bank Corp.

For full biographical listings, see the Martindale-Hubbell Law Directory

SHORT HILLS, Essex Co.

PETER W. TILL (AV)

820 Morris Turnpike, Suite 201, 07078
Telephone: 973-467-0300
Fax: 973-467-4628
Email: peterwtill@aol.com *URL:* http://www.lawyers.com/peterwtilllaw
(Also Of Counsel, Wilf & Silverman)

For full biographical listings, see the Martindale-Hubbell Law Directory

*SOMERVILLE,** Somerset Co.

SCHACHTER, TROMBADORE, OFFEN, STANTON & PAVICS, A PROFESSIONAL CORPORATION (AV)

45 East High Street, P.O. Box 520, 08876-0520
Telephone: 908-722-5700
Fax: 908-722-8853

Richard J. Schachter
John J. Trombadore
Stephen M. Offen
Michael J. Stanton
Thomas A. Pavics

Timothy P. McKeown
Jerry S. D'Aniello

For full biographical listings, see the Martindale-Hubbell Law Directory

RAYMOND R. & DAVID W. TROMBADORE, P.C. A PROFESSIONAL CORPORATION (AV)

33 East High Street, 08876
Telephone: 908-722-7555
Fax: 908-722-6269
URL: http://www.trombadorelaw.com

Raymond R. Trombadore
David W. Trombadore

OF COUNSEL

Ann W. Trombadore

References: Summit Bank; Somerset Savings & Loan Assn.

For full biographical listings, see the Martindale-Hubbell Law Directory

SPRINGFIELD, Union Co.

HARDIN, KUNDLA, MCKEON, POLETTO & POLIFRONI, P.A., A PROFESSIONAL CORPORATION (AV)

673 Morris Avenue, P.O. Box 730, 07081
Telephone: 973-912-5222
Fax: 973-912-9212
Email: info@HKMPP.com
New York, New York Office: 55 John Street, 10038.
Telephone: 212-571-0111.
Fax: 212-571-1117.

George R. Hardin
Robert L. Polifroni
Janet L. Poletto
Mark S. Kundla
John F. McKeon
James R. Greene
Nicea J. D'Annunzio
John Samuel Favate
Patrick J. Clare
Anna Marie Strand

Jeffrey A. Oshin
Joseph R. Lowicky
Tracy C. Forsyth
Joseph A. DeFuria
John G. Kilbride
Jeffrey H. Goldsmith
Jeffrey Roth
Nora J. Grimbergen
William C. Sullivan, Jr.
Paul Daly
V. Christopher Hirsch
Richard S. Reig
Sam A. Dotro
Brian K. Kaiser
David M. Steiner
Lani M. D'Agostino
Sheila A. Glackin
Michael S. Schwartz
Kirsten L. McCaw
Sanjoy Mukherjee

(See Next Column)

HARDIN, KUNDLA, MCKEON, POLETTO & POLIFRONI, P.A. A PROFESSIONAL CORPORATION, *Springfield—Continued*

Louisa B. Sargent
Michael A. Cifelli
James J. A. Mulhall
Kevin M. Regan
Lisa D. Chanel
Maria-Milagros Herrero
Brian A. King
Christina Fichera Dente
Andrea L. Strack
Roger J. Imhof
John P. Monaghan
Stephen J. Donahue
Cindy L. Thompson
Lisa A. Ganzhorn

Representative Clients: Crum & Forster Insurance; St. Paul Fire and Marine Insurance; Chrysler Corp.; CNA Insurance; McDonald's Corp.; Pepsico; Volvo North America; Xerox Corp.

For full biographical listings, see the Martindale-Hubbell Law Directory

JAVERBAUM WURGAFT HICKS & ZARIN, A PROFESSIONAL CORPORATION (AV)

Park Place Legal Center, 959 South Springfield Avenue, 07081-3555
Telephone: 973-379-4200
Fax: 973-379-7872
Email: javerbaumwurgafthicks@compuserve.com *URL:* http://www.lawyers.com/jwhz,law

Kenneth S. Javerbaum
Jack Wurgaft
Robert G. Hicks
Ira J. Zarin

Anthony P. Valenti
Eric G. Kahn
David L. Wikstrom

OF COUNSEL

Jeffrey E. Strauss

For full biographical listings, see the Martindale-Hubbell Law Directory

KRAEMER, BURNS, MYTELKA, LOVELL & KULKA, P.A. (AV)

675 Morris Avenue, 07081
Telephone: 973-912-8700
Telecopier: 973-912-8602

John A. Avery
Douglas E. Burns
Eleonore Kessler Cohen
Wayne D. Greenfeder
Daniel G. Kasen (1905-1990)
Waldron Kraemer
Ellen B. Kulka
Joan A. Lovell
Arnold K. Mytelka

OF COUNSEL

Diane Stolbach
Scott B. Stolbach

For full biographical listings, see the Martindale-Hubbell Law Directory

MCDONOUGH, KORN & EICHHORN, A PROFESSIONAL CORPORATION (AV)

Park Place Legal Center, 959 South Springfield Avenue, P.O. Box 712, 07081-0712
Telephone: 973-912-9099
Fax: 973-912-8604

Peter L. Korn
R. Scott Eichhorn
James R. Korn
William S. Mezzomo
Timothy J. Jaeger
Wilfred P. Coronato

Julia A. Klubenspies
Matthew S. Schorr
Danielle M. Verrastro
Jeffrey John Berezny

OF COUNSEL

Robert P. McDonough

Representative Clients: Chubb Insurance Co.; The Travelers; Medical Inter-Insurance Exchange of New Jersey; GRE Insurance; New Jersey Property-Liability Insurance Guaranty Association; Medical Liability Mutual Insurance Co.; University of Medicine, Dentistry of New Jersey; Columbia Presbyterian Medical Center; Greater New York Blood Center.
Reference: First Union, Summit, N.J.

For full biographical listings, see the Martindale-Hubbell Law Directory

*TOMS RIVER,** Ocean Co.

LOMELL, MUCCIFORI, ADLER, RAVASCHIERE, AMABILE & PEHLIVANIAN, A PROFESSIONAL CORPORATION (AV)

250 Washington Street, P.O. Box 787, 08754
Telephone: 732-349-2443
Fax: 732-349-6917
Email: thefirm@lomell.com *URL:* http://www.lomell.com

Herman A. Adler
Dominic Ravaschiere
John S. Pehlivanian
Ronald E. Prusek
Jeffrey R. Surenian
James M. McKenna
Teresa K. Gierla
Arthur F. Leyden, III

Marc S. Galella
Robyn A. Belluardo
Janet Zaorski Kalapos
James S. Braaten
Regina M. Butler
Paul J Capotorto

(See Next Column)

For Complete List of Firm Personnel, See General Section

For full biographical listings, see the Martindale-Hubbell Law Directory

NOVINS, YORK & PENTONY, A PROFESSIONAL CORPORATION (AV)

202 Main Street, 08753
Telephone: 732-349-7100
Email: info@nyplaw.com

Robert F. Novins
Kenneth R. Pentony
Ann K. Haskell

Counsel for: Allstate Insurance Co.; Motor Club of America.

For Complete List of Firm Personnel, See General Section

For full biographical listings, see the Martindale-Hubbell Law Directory

STARKEY, KELLY, BLANEY & WHITE (AV)

2 Hooper Avenue, 08753
Telephone: 732-240-3600
Fax: 732-240-3777
Brick, New Jersey Office: 459 Jack Martin Boulevard, 08724.
Telephone: 732-840-5900.
Fax: 732-840-5901.
Manasquan, New Jersey Office: 23 Route 71, 08736.
Telephone: 732-223-7328.
Fax: 732-240-3777.

MEMBERS OF FIRM

Charles E. Starkey
William V. Kelly
James M. Blaney

ASSOCIATES

Natalie Pouch
Anthony Mancuso
Robert A. Bauer
Scott W. Kenneally
Susan K. White
Brent D. Miller

Representative Clients: Hartford Insurance Co.; New Jersey Education Assn.; New Jersey Psychiatric Assn.; Ocean County Utilities Authority; Brick Township Municipal Utilities Authority; Manasquan River Regional Sewerage Authority; Hanover Insurance Co.; John Hancock Insurance Co.; Rider Inc. Co.

For full biographical listings, see the Martindale-Hubbell Law Directory

*TRENTON,** Mercer Co.

BACKES & HILL (AV)

(Originally Backes & Backes)
15 West Front Street, 08608-2098
Telephone: 609-396-8257
Telefax: 609-989-7323

Peter Backes (1858-1941)
Herbert W. Backes (1891-1970)
William Wright Backes (1904-1980)
Michael J. Nizolek (1950-1994)

OF COUNSEL

Robert Maddock Backes

PARTNERS

Harry R. Hill, Jr.
Robert C. Billmeier
Brenda Farr Engel

ASSOCIATES

Robert Carlson Leventhal
Michael B. Roth

LEGAL SUPPORT PERSONNEL

Patricia R. O'Brien (Office Manager)

Representative Clients: New Jersey Manufacturers Insurance Co.; United Services Automobile Association; Mercer Medical Center; Catholic Diocese of Trenton; St. Francis Medical Center; Trenton Savings Bank, FSB; Richie & Page Distributing Co., Inc.; General Sullivan Group, Inc.; Trenton Orthopedic Group; City Beef, Inc..

For full biographical listings, see the Martindale-Hubbell Law Directory

NEEDELL, SIEKERKA & CASTELLANI, A PROFESSIONAL CORPORATION (AV)

Quakerbridge Commons, 2681 Quakerbridge Road, 08619-1625
Telephone: 609-584-7700
Fax: 609-584-0123
Email: nsclaw@aol.com

Stanley H. Needell
Michele N. Siekerka
Anthony P. Castellani

John M. Cinti
Dean C. Gresek

LEGAL SUPPORT PERSONNEL

PARALEGALS

Marlene Griesbach
Carolyn D. Shaw
Veronica A. Mitchell

For full biographical listings, see the Martindale-Hubbell Law Directory

Trenton—Continued

SCHRAGGER, LAVINE & NAGY (AV)

Mountainview Office Park, 840 Bear Tavern Road, Suite 307, 08628
Telephone: 609-771-0700
Fax: 609-771-9535

Bruce M. Schragger
James A. Schragger
Raymond L. Nagy
Jonathan S. Robinson

OF COUNSEL

Henry C. Schragger
Frank P. Reiche
Alan S. Lavine
A. Jerome Moore

LEGAL SUPPORT PERSONNEL

Annemarie Saccani (Office Administrator)

For Complete List of Firm Personnel, See General Section

For full biographical listings, see the Martindale-Hubbell Law Directory

VINELAND, Cumberland Co.

BASILE & TESTA, A PROFESSIONAL CORPORATION (AV)

424 Landis Avenue, P.O. Box 460, 08360
Telephone: 609-691-2300
Telefax: 609-691-5655
Email: LAW424@AOL.COM

Francis G. Basile
Todd W. Heck
Michael L. Testa
Michelle J. Douglass

Michael J. Gruccio
Renee E. Scrocca
Walter A. Schultz, Jr.
Eve-Marie Niskey
Jeffrey A. DiLazzero

OF COUNSEL

Frank J. Testa

Representative Client: U.S. Insurance Group.

For full biographical listings, see the Martindale-Hubbell Law Directory

EISENSTAT, GABAGE, BERMAN & FURMAN, A PROFESSIONAL CORPORATION (AV)

1179 East Landis Avenue, 08360
Telephone: 856-691-1200
Telecopier: 856-691-0414
Mailing Address: P.O. Box 420, Vineland, NJ, 08360-4278

Gerald (Jere) M. Eisenstat
Mitchell S. Berman
Charles W. Gabage
Harry Furman

Patricia Powell

For full biographical listings, see the Martindale-Hubbell Law Directory

JAY H. GREENBLATT & ASSOCIATES A PROFESSIONAL CORPORATION (AV)

200 North Eighth Street, P.O. Box 883, 08360-0883
Telephone: 609-691-0424
Facsimile: 609-696-1010
Email: jhg@algorithms.com *URL:* http://home.earthlink.net/~greenblatt/

M. Joseph Greenblatt (1896-1992)
Jay H. Greenblatt

Bonnie L. Laube
Nicholas Kierniesky

Counsel for: Ware's Van & Storage Co., Inc.; Consolidated Motor Oils, Inc.; Joffe Lumber & Supply Co., Inc.
Local Counsel for: A. O. Smith Corp.; Chance Industries, Inc.; Coca Cola Bottlers' Association; Fireman's Fund Insurance Co.; Ford Motor Co.; Thermadyne Industries; The West Bend Company.

For full biographical listings, see the Martindale-Hubbell Law Directory

GRUCCIO, PEPPER GIOVINAZZI, DESANTO & FARNOLY, P.A. (AV)

817 Landis Avenue, P.O. Box 1501, 08362
Telephone: 856-691-0100
Fax: 856-692-4095
Email: Gruccio1@eticomm.net
Woodbury, New Jersey Office: 21 Delaware Street.
Telephone: 856-848-5558.
Fax: 856-384-1181.
Bridgeton, New Jersey Office: 120 West Broad Street.
Telephone: 856-459-3334.
Fax: 856-692-4095.

James J. Gruccio, Sr.
Thomas P. Farnoly
Robert A. DeSanto
E. Edward Bowman

(See Next Column)

Walter F. Gavigan
Joseph E. Ruth

Representative Clients: State Farm Mutual Automobile Insurance Cos.; United States Fidelity & Guaranty Co.; South Jersey Transportation Authority; County of Salem; County of Cape May; Cumberland Mutual Fire Insurance Co.; Farmers and Merchants National Bank of Bridgeton; Vineland Board of Education; Southern Intercounty Medical Association; Sun National Bank of N.J.

For Complete List of Firm Personnel, See General Section

For full biographical listings, see the Martindale-Hubbell Law Directory

LIPMAN, ANTONELLI, BATT, DUNLAP, WODLINGER & GILSON, A PROFESSIONAL CORPORATION (AV)

110 North Sixth Street, P.O. Box 280, 08360-3703
Telephone: 856-692-8000
Telecopier: 856-692-7580
Email: lipmanlaw@aol.com
Millville, New Jersey Office: 117 Smith Street.
Telephone: 856-825-8800.
Fax: 856-825-3283.

Philip L. Lipman
William M. Gilson
Gerald J. Batt
Robert G. Malestein
Gary D. Wodlinger
Steven L. Rothman
Edward A. Lopez

OF COUNSEL

Marvin M. Wodlinger (Resident, Millville, New Jersey Office)

For full biographical listings, see the Martindale-Hubbell Law Directory

RIESENBURGER & KIZNER, P.C. (AV)

190 South Main Road, P.O. Box 640, 08362-0640
Telephone: 856-691-6200
Telecopier: 856-696-8150
Email: rieskizn@eticomm.net *URL:* http://www.rklawyers.com
Cherry Hill Office: 413 Route 70 East.
Telephone: 609-354-7500.

Franklin J. Riesenburger
Mitchell H. Kizner

Vivian R. Salmon
Robert P. Merenich

For full biographical listings, see the Martindale-Hubbell Law Directory

WALL TOWNSHIP, Monmouth Co.

MAGEE AND ISHERWOOD, L.L.P. (AV)

Mirne & Simmill
Mirne, Nowels, Fundler Magee & Kirschner
1937 Route 35 at Allaire Road, P.O. Box 1200, 07719
Telephone: 732-449-2500
Telecopier: 732-449-4005

MEMBERS OF FIRM

Granville D. Magee
Thomas Isherwood

ASSOCIATE

Granville M. Magee

OF COUNSEL

Michael B. Kirschner

Representative Clients: Royal Insurance Cos.; Township of Upper Freehold.
References: Central Jersey Bank & Trust Co.; Commerce Bank Shore N.A.

For full biographical listings, see the Martindale-Hubbell Law Directory

WAYNE, Passaic Co.

DEYOE HEISSENBUTTEL, L.L.C. (AV)

401 Hamburg Turnpike, P.O. Box 2449, 07474-2449
Telephone: 973-595-6300
Fax: 973-595-0146
Email: deyoelaw@ix.netcom.com *URL:* http://www.deyoe.com

MEMBERS OF FIRM

Charles P. DeYoe (1923-1973)
Frederick C. Heissenbuttel
Wood M. DeYoe
Scott B. Piekarsky

ASSOCIATES

Raymond F. Shenekji
Albert C. Buglione
Anne Hutton
Laureen A. Moloney

LEGAL SUPPORT PERSONNEL

Marilyn Moore (Office Manager)

Representative Clients: Hanover Insurance Inc.; Maryland Casualty Co.; Ohio Casualty Insurance Co.; Motor Club of America; Selective Insurance Co.; Prudential Property & Casualty; Reliance Ins. Co.

For full biographical listings, see the Martindale-Hubbell Law Directory

Wayne—Continued

GERBER & SAMSON, L.L.C. (AV)

155 Willowbrook Boulevard, 07470
Telephone: 973-256-9000
Fax: 973-256-9001
Email: njlaw@gerberlaw.com *URL:* http://www.gerberlaw.com

MEMBERS OF FIRM

Steven Gerber
Linda H. Samson
Mary Patricia Gallagher

ASSOCIATES

Mark J. Semeraro
Patti A. Scott
Keith A. Bregman
N. Noelle Letcher

OF COUNSEL

Richard P. Weiss

For full biographical listings, see the Martindale-Hubbell Law Directory

WESTFIELD, Union Co.

LINDABURY, McCORMICK & ESTABROOK, P.A. (AV)

53 Cardinal Drive, P.O. Box 2369, 07091
Telephone: 908-233-6800
Fax: 908-233-5078
New York, N.Y. Office: 26 Broadway, Suite 2300.
Telephone: 212-742-3390.
Fax: 212-269-5016.

Richard R. Width
Edward J. Frisch
John H. Schmidt, Jr.
Donald F. Nicolai
Bruce P. Ogden
James D. DeRose
Barry J. Donohue
David R. Pierce
Jay Lavroff
Anthony P. Sciarrillo
Richard J. Cino
Stephen A. Santola

Eric B. Levine
Athina Lekas Cornell

OF COUNSEL

Kenneth L. Estabrook

Representative Clients: Alfa Romeo Distributors of N.A.; American Brands, Inc.; BMW of North America, Inc.; Great American Insurance Co.; Handex Environmental Recovery, Inc.; Kuehne Chemical Co., Inc.; Mechanical Contractors Association of New Jersey, Inc.; Saxon Construction and Management Corp.; USF&G; Western Industries, Inc.

For Complete List of Firm Personnel, See General Section

For full biographical listings, see the Martindale-Hubbell Law Directory

WESTMONT, Camden Co.

BROWN & CONNERY, LLP (AV)

360 Haddon Avenue, P.O. Box 539, 08108
Telephone: 609-854-8900
Facsimile: 609-858-4967
Camden, New Jersey Office: 518 Market Street, P.O. Box 1449.
Telephone: 609-365-5100.
Telecopier: 609-858-4967.

MEMBERS OF FIRM

Warren W. Faulk
Steven G. Wolschina
Paul Mainardi
Michael J. Vassalotti
Dennis P. Blake
William M. Tambussi
Mark P. Asselta
Stephen J. DeFeo
Joseph M Nardi, III

ASSOCIATES

Joseph A. Zechman
Karen A. McGuinness
Jeffrey E. Ugoretz
Christine O'Hearn
Christine A. Campbell
Joseph T. Carney
Richard C. Belli, Jr.
Stephanie E. Nolan
Shawn C. Huber
Susan M. Leming
Beth L. Marlin
Louis R. Lessig
Kevin C. Heil

Representative Clients: Camden County Health Services Center; Delaware River Port Authority; Federal Deposit Insurance Corp.; Mercedes-Benz Credit Corp.; Philadelphia Newspaper, Inc.; Philip Morris Inc.; Pollution Control Financing Authority of Camden County; Underwood-Memorial Hospital.

For Complete List of Firm Personnel, See General Section

For full biographical listings, see the Martindale-Hubbell Law Directory

EARP COHN P.C. (AV)

222 Haddon Avenue, 08108
Telephone: 856-854-7100
Fax: 856-854-6434
Email: administrator@earpcohn.com *URL:* http://www.earpcohn.com
Philadelphia, Pennsylvania Office: 2 Penn Center Plaza, Suite 200. 19102-1706.
Telephone: 215-963-9520.
Fax: 215-963-9620.

(See Next Column)

Thomas L. Earp
Richard B. Cohn
Irving Koffler
Douglas F. Johnson
Kathryn R. Renahan
Carol Schuler Harding
Samantha P. Zazzo
Jeff Schwartz

For full biographical listings, see the Martindale-Hubbell Law Directory

MARTIN, GUNN & MARTIN, A PROFESSIONAL CORPORATION (AV)

Sentry Office Plaza, 216 Haddon Avenue, Suite 420, P.O. Box 358, 08108
Telephone: 609-858-0900
Telecopier: 609-858-1278
Email: MARTINGUNN@aol.com

Burchard V. Martin
Bruce M. Gunn
Burchard S. Martin
William J. Martin

Richard C. Bryan

Counsel for: Chubb & Son; Federal Insurance Co.; Liberty Mutual Insurance Co.; Crawford & Co.; Camden County Municipal Joint Insurance Fund; Phico; Township of Cherry Hill; J.C. Penney Co.; Garden State Indemnity.

For full biographical listings, see the Martindale-Hubbell Law Directory

WEST ORANGE, Essex Co.

HOWARD M. DAVIS, P.C. (AV)

743 Northfield Avenue, 07052
Telephone: 201-325-8383
Telefax: 201-325-1159
Email: HMDPC@AOL.COM *URL:* http://www.lawyers.com/davislaw

Howard M. Davis

Howard J. Ehrlich

Reference: PNC Bank, West Orange.

For full biographical listings, see the Martindale-Hubbell Law Directory

GOLDBERG, MUFSON & SPAR, A PROFESSIONAL CORPORATION (AV)

200 Executive Drive, 07052
Telephone: 973-736-0100
Telecopier: 973-736-0961
Email: gmspa@chelsea.ios.com

Leonard M. Goldberg
Michael R. Spar
Kenneth J. Isaacson
Jeffrey L. Kantowitz

Denice P. Gilchrist

For full biographical listings, see the Martindale-Hubbell Law Directory

WOODBRIDGE, Middlesex Co.

GREENBAUM, ROWE, SMITH, RAVIN, DAVIS AND HIMMEL LLP (AV)

Metro Corporate Campus I, P.O. Box 5600, 07095-0988
Telephone: 732-549-5600
Fax: 732-549-1881 529
Email: info@greenbaumlaw.com *URL:* http://www.greenbaumlaw.com
Roseland, New Jersey Office: 6 Becker Farm Road.
Telephone: 973-535-1600.
Fax: 973-535-1698.

MEMBERS OF FIRM

Paul A. Rowe
David L. Bruck
Michael B. Himmel
Dennis A. Estis
William D. Grand
Alan S. Naar
Mark H. Sobel (Resident, Roseland Office)
Barry S. Goodman
Robert S. Goldsmith
John D. North
Margaret Goodzeit
Robert J. Kipnees
Carlton T. Spiller
Sabrina A. Kogel
Jacqueline M. Printz (Resident, Roseland Office)
Lawrence H. Wertheim
David Himelman
Gary Keith Wolinetz
Richard L. Hertzberg
Ellen Ann Silver
Andrea J. Sullivan

ASSOCIATES

Jessica R. Mayer
Christine F. Marks
Jonathan W. Philipp
Marc Jonathan Gross (Resident, Roseland Office)
Luke J. Kealy
Christopher S. Porrino
Jodi L. Rosenberg
Richard L. Elbert
Aaron R. Easley
Jessica L. Kyle
Keita A. Young
Cipora Winters
Marcus A. Banks
Jodi S. Eligberg
Rachel M. Coe
Kelly Michele Brown
Emily A. Kaller
Deirdre Marie Naughton
Brian J. Waters

(See Next Column)

GREENBAUM, ROWE, SMITH, RAVIN, DAVIS AND HIMMEL LLP—*Continued*

OF COUNSEL

Lora L. Fong

For Complete List of Firm Personnel, See General Section

For full biographical listings, see the Martindale-Hubbell Law Directory

WILENTZ, GOLDMAN & SPITZER, A PROFESSIONAL CORPORATION (AV)

90 Woodbridge Center Drive Suite 900, Box 10, 07095
Telephone: 732-636-8000
Telecopier: 732-855-6117
URL: http://www.newjerseylaw.com
Eatontown, New Jersey Office: Meridian Center I, Two Industrial Way West, 07724.
Telephone: 732-542-4500.
Telecopier: 732-493-8387.
New York, New York Office: Wall Street Plaza, 88 Pine Street, 9th Floor, 10005.
Telephone: 212-267-3091.
Telecopier: 212-267-3828.

Warren W. Wilentz
Morris Brown
Frederic K. Becker
Robert J. Cirafesi
Alan M. Darnell
Gordon J. Golum
Frank M. Ciuffani
Marvin J. Brauth
Richard R. Bonamo
Christine D. Petruzzell
Roger B. Kaplan
Philip A. Pahigian
Randall J. Richards
Frederick J. Dennehy
Christopher M. Placitella
Maureen S. Binetti
Michael J. Barrett
Angelo J. Cifaldi
Kevin M. Berry (Resident, New York, N.Y. Office)
Frank M. Ortiz (Resident, New York, N.Y. Office)
Jon G. Kupilik
Edward T. Kole
Lynne M. Kizis

Ruth D. Marcus (Not admitted in NJ)
Richard J. Byrnes
Robert T. Haefele
Donald E. Taylor
Steven P. Knowlton (Resident, New York, N.Y. Office)
Barry R. Sugarman
Alfred M. Anthony

Representative Clients: Amerada Hess Corp.; Chevron, U.S.A.; Co-Steel Raritan; Cumberland Farms, Inc.; Middlesex County Utilities Authority; New Jersey Automobile Dealers Assn.; The Rouse Co.

For Complete List of Firm Personnel, See General Section

For full biographical listings, see the Martindale-Hubbell Law Directory

NEW MEXICO

*ALBUQUERQUE,** Bernalillo Co.

BRANCH LAW FIRM (AV)

Including a Professional Association
2025 Rio Grande Boulevard, N.W., 87104
Telephone: 505-243-3500
Fax: 505-243-3534
New Mexico Toll Free: 1-800-562-3456
Nationwide Toll Free: 1-800-828-4LAW
Email: reception@branchlawfirm.com *URL:* http://www.branchlawfirm.com
Durango, Colorado Office: Suite 205, 102 East Eighth Street.
Telephone: 303-385-7671.
Houston, Texas Office: 808 Travis Street, Suite 1303.
Telephone: 800-243-3545.
Fax: 713-224-1622.

Turner W. Branch (P.A.)
Margaret Moses Branch

Arthur M. Solon
Daniel R. Swiss
Rebecca C. Branch
Justin K. Hall
James P. Lyle
Rhett D. Klok
Suzanne Lafleur Klok
Clyde DeMersseman
Shari D. Thieman

LEGAL SUPPORT PERSONNEL

Krisann Y. Matthes (Office Manager)
Jacqueline Adams
Amy Rigg
Shariesse McCannon
Judi Seff
Daphne Moore (Registered Nurse)
Yvette Rodarte
Shelly Hourani (Houston Office)

For full biographical listings, see the Martindale-Hubbell Law Directory

BUTT, THORNTON & BAEHR, P.C. (AV)

4101 Indian School Road N.E., Suite 300S, P.O. Box 3170, 87190
Telephone: 505-884-0777
Fax: 505-889-8870

J. Duke Thornton
Carlos G. Martinez
Norman L. Gagne
Alfred L. Green, Jr.
James H. Johansen
Rodney L. Schlagel
Martin Diamond
J. Douglas Compton
David N. Whitham
Emily A. Franke
Jane A. Laflin
Paul T. Yarbrough
Glenna Hayes Long
Michael P. Clemens

Sherrill K. Filter
Agnes Fuentevilla Padilla
Gregory P. Williams
Louis N. Colón
Monica R. Garcia
Laura J. Ramos
Robert Tabor Booms
J. Scott Steinberger

OF COUNSEL

Paul L. Butt
Raymond A. Baehr
John A. Klecan

Representative Clients: Ford Motor Co.; Home Insurance Co.; Reliance Insurance Cos.; Royal Insurance Co.; International Harvester/Navistar; FMC Corp.; American Honda Motor; CIGNA; General Tire Company; ARA Spectrum Emergency Care Services.

For full biographical listings, see the Martindale-Hubbell Law Directory

CARPENTER & CHÁVEZ, LTD. (AV)

1600 University Boulevard, N.E., Suite A, 87102-1711
Telephone: 505-243-1336
Facsimile: 505-243-1339
Email: carpchav@swcp.com *URL:* http://www.carpenter-law.com

William H. Carpenter
Edward L. Chávez
David J. Stout

Reference: Bank of America, Albuquerque, New Mexico.

For full biographical listings, see the Martindale-Hubbell Law Directory

CIVEROLO, GRALOW & HILL, A PROFESSIONAL ASSOCIATION (AV)

500 Marquette, N.W., Suite 1400, P.O. Drawer 887, 87103
Telephone: 505-842-8255
Telecopier: 505-764-6099

Richard C. Civerolo
William P. Gralow
Lawrence H. Hill
W. R. Logan
Roberto C. Armijo
Robert J. Curtis
Judith M. Oliva
Lisa Entress Pullen

M. Clea Gutterson
Sandy Henderson Knight
David A. Streubel
Gregory W. MacKenzie
Victor Patrick Montoya
Kerri L. Sanchez
Timothy R. Mortimer

General Counsel for: Western Bank of Albuquerque.
Representative Clients: KPMG Peat Marwick, LLP; M.M.I. Companies, Inc.; Volvo North America Corp.; Western Bank of Albuquerque.

For full biographical listings, see the Martindale-Hubbell Law Directory

EATON, MARTINEZ & HART, P.C. (AV)

3800 Osuna Road N.E., Suite 2, 87109
Telephone: 505-343-1776
Fax: 505-344-7709
URL: http://www.eatonmartinezhart.com
Email: rogeaton@aol.com *URL:* http://www.lawyers.com/eatonmartinez&hart

Roger V. Eaton
David B. Martinez
F. Michael Hart

Gabrielle M. Valdez
Wendy F. Jones

LEGAL SUPPORT PERSONNEL

Laura Paul (Legal Assistant)
Shaylin Buhrle (Legal Assistant)
Angela Stone (Legal Assistant)
Juan Loya (Legal Assistant)
Therse Quetone (Legal Assistant)

For full biographical listings, see the Martindale-Hubbell Law Directory

EAVES, BARDACKE, BAUGH KIERST & KIERNAN, P.A. (AV)

6400 Uptown Boulevard, N.E., Suite 110-W, P.O. Box 35670, 87176
Telephone: 505-888-4300
Facsimile: 505-883-4406
Email: LGLEAVES@EB-B.com

John M. Eaves
Paul Bardacke
John G. Baugh
Peter S. Kierst
Kerry Kiernan

(See Next Column)

EAVES, BARDACKE, BAUGH KIERST & KIERNAN P.A., *Albuquerque—Continued*

Derek V. Larson
Karen S. Mendenhall
C. Shannon Bacon

OF COUNSEL

Jennifer J. Pruett

For full biographical listings, see the Martindale-Hubbell Law Directory

FREEDMAN BOYD DANIELS HOLLANDER GOLDBERG & CLINE P.A. (AV)

20 First Plaza, Suite 700, 87102
Telephone: 505-842-9960
Fax: 505-842-0761

David A. Freedman
Charles W. Daniels
John W. Boyd
Joseph Goldberg

Scott M. Davidson
Eric J. Knapp
K.C. Maxwell

For full biographical listings, see the Martindale-Hubbell Law Directory

LAW OFFICES OF NICHOLAS R. GENTRY, L.L.C. (AV)

902 Roma, N.W., 87102
Telephone: 505-924-1010
Fax: 505-924-1012

Nicholas R. Gentry

For full biographical listings, see the Martindale-Hubbell Law Directory

GUEBERT & YEOMANS, P.C. (AV)

6743 Academy Road NE, Suite A, P.O. Box 93880, 87199-3880
Telephone: 505-823-2300
Fax: 505-823-9600

Terry R. Guebert
Timothy L. Hartley
Richard D. Yeomans
Alysan Boothe Collins
Don Bruckner
Richard F. Rowley, III
RaMona G. Bootes
Patricia M. Monaghan

For full biographical listings, see the Martindale-Hubbell Law Directory

MILLER, STRATVERT & TORGERSON, P.A. (AV)

500 Marquette Avenue, N.W., Suite 1100, P.O. Box 25687, 87102
Telephone: 505-842-1950
Facsimile: 505-243-4408
Email: info@mstLAW.com *URL:* http://www.mstLAW.com
Farmington, New Mexico Office: 300 West Arrington, Suite 300, P.O. Box 869.
Telephone: 505-326-4521.
Facsimile: 505-325-5474.
Las Cruces, New Mexico Office: 500 South Main, Suite 800, P.O. Box 1209.
Telephone: 505-523-2481.
Facsimile: 505-526-2215.
Santa Fe, New Mexico Office: 150 Washington Avenue, Suite 300, P.O. Box 1986.
Telephone: 505-989-9614.
Facsimile: 505-989-9857.

Ranne B. Miller
Alan C. Torgerson
Alice Tomlinson Lorenz
Gregory W. Chase
Lyman G. Sandy
Stephen M. Williams
Stephan M. Vidmar
Robert C. Gutierrez
Seth V. Bingham (Resident at Farmington Office)
James B. Collins (Resident at Farmington Office)
Timothy Ray Briggs
Rudolph A. Lucero
Deborah A. Solove
Gary L. Gordon
Lawrence R. White (Resident at Las Cruces Office)
Virginia Anderman
J. Scott Hall (Resident at Santa Fe Office)
Thomas R. Mack
Terri L. Sauer
Joel T. Newton (Resident at Las Cruces Office)
Thomas M. Domme
Ruth O. Pregenzer
Jeffrey E. Jones (Resident at Santa Fe Office)
Manuel I. Arrieta (Resident at Las Cruces Office)
Robin A. Goble
James R. Wood
Kirk R. Allen
Ruth M. Fuess
Kyle M. Finch (Resident at Farmington Office)
Henry Brook Laskey
Katherine Weeks Hall (Resident at Santa Fe Office)
Lara L. White (Resident at Las Cruces Office)
Paula G. Maynes (Resident at Santa Fe Office)
Dean B. Cross (Resident at Las Cruces Office)
Michael C. Ross
Carla Prando (Resident at Santa Fe Office)
Katherine N. Blackett
Jennifer L. Stone
Andrew M. Sanchez
M. Dylan O'Reilly
Amina Quargnali-Linsley
Beate Boudro

(See Next Column)

COUNSEL

William K. Stratvert
James J. Widland
Ross B. Perkal
Bradley D. Tepper

Representative Clients: BASF Corp.; Massachusetts Mutual Life Insurance; Medical Protective Co.; Mutual Insurance Corp. of America; New Mexico Medical Society; St. Paul Insurance Cos.; State Farm Fire and Casualty Insurance Co.; State Farm Mutual Automobile Insurance Co.; The Travelers; United States Fidelity & Guaranty Co.

For Complete List of Firm Personnel, See General Section

For full biographical listings, see the Martindale-Hubbell Law Directory

SĪLVA, RIEDER & MAESTAS, P.C. (AV)

Albuquerque Plaza, Suite 1700, 201 3rd Street, N.W., P.O. Box 1670, 87103-1670
Telephone: 505-767-9800
Facsimile: 505-767-9807
Email: srmlaw@srmlaw.com *URL:* http://www.lawyers.com/srmlaw

Benjamin Sīlva, Jr.
Geoffrey D. Rieder
Paul Maestas

Wayne R. Suggett
Christopher A. Riehl
Richard A. Allen

Representative Clients: American Contractors Insurance Group, Inc.; CIGNA; GSL Properties, Inc.; Gulf Insurance Company; Honeywell, Inc.; Hospital Services Corporation; Hubbard Broadcasting Company; Intel Corporation; John Q. Hammons, Inc.; KOB-TV, Inc.

For full biographical listings, see the Martindale-Hubbell Law Directory

SIMONE, ROBERTS & WEISS, P.A. (AV)

8102 Menaul Boulevard N.E., 87110
Telephone: 505-298-9400
Fax: 505-298-7070

Stephen M. Simone
Michelle Lalley Blake
Randal W. Roberts
Thomas E. Perkins
Norman F. Weiss
Ashley Gauthier
Megan Day Hill

Representative Clients: Allstate Insurance Co.; Guaranty National Insurance Co.; State Farm Fire and Casualty Co.; State of New Mexico, Risk Management; Liberty Mutual Insurance Company; State Farm Mutual Auto.
Reference: Nationsbank.

For full biographical listings, see the Martindale-Hubbell Law Directory

MARTIN E. THREET & ASSOCIATES (AV)

6400 Uptown Boulevard N.E. Suite 500 West Tower, 87110
Telephone: 505-881-5155
Fax: 505-881-5356
Email: threetlaw@aol.com

MEMBER OF FIRM

Martin E. Threet

ASSOCIATES

Joseph L. Romero
Joey B. Wright

For Complete List of Firm Personnel, See General Section

For full biographical listings, see the Martindale-Hubbell Law Directory

WAYNE C. WOLF (AV)

4159 Montgomery Boulevard, NE, 87109
Telephone: 505-888-6600
Fax: 505-888-6640
Email: wolflaw@bigplanet.com

For full biographical listings, see the Martindale-Hubbell Law Directory

FARMINGTON, San Juan Co.

BRIONES LAW FIRM, A PROFESSIONAL ASSOCIATION (AV)

333 East Main Street, 87401
Telephone: 505-325-0258
Fax: 505-325-3311
Email: brioneslaw@fisi.net

Felix Briones, Jr.
B. Paul Briones

Representative Clients: C.I.P., Inc.; Tech, Inc.; Western Manufacturing & Supply, Inc.; Various General Contractors; A-1 Machine, Inc.; Macaluso Oil Co.; Morningstar Corp.; Calber Corp.; Energy Pump & Supply Inc.

For full biographical listings, see the Martindale-Hubbell Law Directory

GERDING & O'LOUGHLIN, P.C. (AV)

304 North Behrend, P.O. Box 1020, 87499-1020
Telephone: 505-325-1804
Fax: 505-325-4675

(See Next Column)

GERDING & O'LOUGHLIN P.C.—*Continued*

Richard L. Gerding
Michael T. O'Loughlin

For full biographical listings, see the Martindale-Hubbell Law Directory

*LAS CRUCES,** Dona Ana Co.

REEVES, CHAVEZ, GREENFIELD & WALKER, P.A. (AV)

300 South Water Street, P.O. Box 2769, 88004-2769
Telephone: 505-524-9617
Fax: 505-524-1954
Email: rcgw@zianet.com

B. James Reeves
Frank N. Chavez
Charlotte Greenfield
William A. Walker, Jr.
Kelly P. Albers
Joyce A. Montes
William R. Anderson
Carolyn J. Baca

Glenn D. Hall
CaraLyn Banks

For full biographical listings, see the Martindale-Hubbell Law Directory

SANDENAW, CARRILLO & PIAZZA, P.C. (AV)

2951 Roadrunner Parkway, Suite A, 88011
Telephone: 505-522-7500
Fax: 505-522-5544
URL: http://www.lawyers.com/insurancedefenselaw

SHAREHOLDERS

Thomas A. Sandenaw, Jr.
Leonard J. Piazza
Raúl A. Carrillo, Jr.

Carlos M. Quiñones

OF COUNSEL

James T. Martin

For full biographical listings, see the Martindale-Hubbell Law Directory

*SANTA FE,** Santa Fe Co.

CATRON, CATRON & SAWTELL, A PROFESSIONAL ASSOCIATION (AV)

2006 Botulph Road, P.O. Box 788, 87504-0788
Telephone: 505-982-1947
Telecopier: 505-986-1013
Email: catronlaw@aol.com

John S. Catron
W. Anthony Sawtell
Michael T. Pottow
Bryan P. Biedscheid

For Complete List of Firm Personnel, See General Section

For full biographical listings, see the Martindale-Hubbell Law Directory

COMEAU, MALDEGEN, TEMPLEMAN & INDALL, L.L.P. (AV)

Coronado Building, 141 East Palace Avenue, P.O. Box 669, 87504-0669
Telephone: 505-982-4611
Telecopier: 505-988-2987
Email: cmtilaw@earthlink.net

MEMBERS OF FIRM

Michael R. Comeau
Larry D. Maldegen
William P. Templeman
Jon J. Indall
Stephen J. Lauer
Paula Ann Cook
Grey Handy
Joseph E. Manges

Michael C. Smith
Christian A. Hatfield

OF COUNSEL

Jeffrey R. Brannen

Representative Clients: AirTouch Cellular; GTE; Homestake Mining Co.; N.M. Banquest Investors Corp.; United Nuclear Corp.; First National Bank of Santa Fe; Uranium Producers of America; United Van Lines; Mayflower Transit; State of New Mexico.

For full biographical listings, see the Martindale-Hubbell Law Directory

HERRERA, LONG & POUND, P.A. (AV)

2200 Brothers Road, P.O. Box 5098, 87502-5098
Telephone: 505-982-8405
Fax: 505-982-8513
Email: hlplaw@aol.com

Judith C. Herrera
Nancy R. Long
John B. Pound

Mark E. Komer

LEGAL SUPPORT PERSONNEL

Shauna Allen Metzo

Reference: Bank of America.

For full biographical listings, see the Martindale-Hubbell Law Directory

MONTGOMERY & ANDREWS, PROFESSIONAL ASSOCIATION (AV)

325 Paseo de Peralta, P.O. Box 2307, 87504-2307
Telephone: 505-982-3873
Fax: 505-982-4289
Email: montand@montand.com

Victor R. Ortega
Walter J. Melendres
Bruce Herr
Sarah Michael Singleton
Stephen S. Hamilton
Carolyn Wolf
Grace Philips
Jennifer Lynn Weed

Representative Clients: Catholic Mutual Relief Society of America; El Paso Corp.; LAC Minerals (USA) Inc.; Meridian Oil, Inc.; State of Kansas; State of New Mexico, Risk Management Division; St. Vincent Hospital; Travelers Insurance Co.; United States Fidelity and Guaranty Co.; U S WEST Communications, Inc.

For Complete List of Firm Personnel, See General Section

For full biographical listings, see the Martindale-Hubbell Law Directory

ROTHSTEIN, DONATELLI, HUGHES, DAHLSTROM & SCHOENBURG, LLP (AV)

P.O. Box 8180, 87504-8180
Telephone: 505-988-8004
Fax: 505-982-0307
Email: manager@rothsteinlaw.com
Albuquerque Office: 320 Central S.W., Suite 30.
Telephone: 505-243-1443.
Fax: 505-242-7845. Email: ROTHLAWABQ@aol.com.
Phoenix, Arizona Office: 234 North Central, Suite 722.
Telephone: 602-252-3226.
Fax: 602-253-3088. Email: RLAWFPHX@aol.com.

MEMBERS OF FIRM

Robert R. Rothstein
Mark H. Donatelli
Richard W. Hughes
Eric N. Dahlstrom (Not admitted in NM; Resident, Phoenix, AZ Office)
Peter Schoenburg (Resident, Albuquerque Office)

ASSOCIATES

Michael C. Shiel (Not admitted in NM; Resident, Phoenix, AZ Office)
John L. Sullivan

OF COUNSEL

Sarah E. Bennett

For full biographical listings, see the Martindale-Hubbell Law Directory

SCHEUER, YOST & PATTERSON, A PROFESSIONAL CORPORATION (AV)

125 Lincoln Avenue, Suite 223, P.O. Drawer 9570, 87504
Telephone: 505-982-9911
505-989-7500
Fax: 505-982-1621
Email: firm@santafelawyers.com

Melvin T. Yost (Retired)
Ralph H. Scheuer
Mel E. Yost
John N. Patterson
Byron L. Treaster
Donald A. Walcott
Christopher M. Grimmer
Daniel J. Monte

OF COUNSEL

Reverdy Johnson

Representative Clients: Cyprus-AMAX, Inc.; Century Bank, FSB; Chicago Title Insurance Co.; Davis Selected Venture Advisors; St. John's College; Sun Loan Companies; Territorial Abstract & Title Co.; Texas Commerce Bank; Ticor Title Insurance Co.; Union Carbide Corp.

For full biographical listings, see the Martindale-Hubbell Law Directory

NEW YORK

*ALBANY,** Albany Co.

BRENNAN, REHFUSS AND LIGUORI, P.C. (AV)

50 Chapel Street, 12207
Telephone: 518-434-2690
Fax: 518-434-5671
URL: http://www.lawyers.com/brllaw

Joseph M. Brennan
Stephen J. Rehfuss
John W. Liguori

OF COUNSEL

John W. Rehfuss

Representative Clients: Interboro Mutual Indemnity Insurance Co.; Michigan Mutual Insurance Co.

(See Next Column)

Brennan, Rehfuss and Liguori P.C., *Albany—Continued*

Reference: Norstar Bank, Upstate N.Y.

For full biographical listings, see the Martindale-Hubbell Law Directory

Donohue, Sabo, Varley & Armstrong, P.C. (AV)

1 Winner's Circle Drive, P.O. Box 15056, 12212-5056
Telephone: 518-458-8922
Telecopier: 518-438-4349
Email: kvarley@dsvalaw.com

Paul F. Donohue, Sr. (Retired) — Robert J. Armstrong
Alvin O. Sabo — Fred J. Hutchison
Kenneth Varley, Jr. — Bruce S. Huttner
Kathleen L. Werther

Walter M.B. Spiro — Joshua A. Sabo
Andrew R. Ferguson — Gerald D. D'Amelia, Jr.

Representative Clients: CNA Insurance Cos.; Continental Loss Adjusting Services; Electric Insurance Co.; Electric Mutual Insurance Co.; General Accident Assurance Co.; General Electric Co.; NY Central Mutual Fire Insurance Co.; Preferred Mutual Insurance Co.; State Insurance Fund; Zurich-American Insurance Co.

For full biographical listings, see the Martindale-Hubbell Law Directory

Harvey and Mumford (AV)

20 Corporate Woods Boulevard, 12211-2396
Telephone: 518-463-4491
Telecopier: 518-463-5665
Email: thefirm@harveyandmumford.com

Arthur J. Harvey (1903-1986)

MEMBERS OF FIRM

Jonathan P. Harvey — Brian F. Mumford

ASSOCIATES

Eva Lynn M. Hayko — Peter Baird Joslin, Jr.
Karen Hendricks — Trudy L. Boulia
Keith J. Starlin

OF COUNSEL

Jack D. Harvey

For full biographical listings, see the Martindale-Hubbell Law Directory

Iseman, Cunningham, Riester & Hyde, LLP (AV)

9 Thurlow Terrace, 12203
Telephone: 518-462-3000
Telecopier: 518-462-4199
Email: lawfirm@icrh.com *URL:* http://www.icrh.com
Canandaigua, New York Office: 37 East Gibson Street, P.O. Box 179, 14424.
Telephone: 716-394-1450.
Fax: 716-394-5121.

MEMBERS OF FIRM

Frederick C. Riester — Robert Hall Iseman
Michael J. Cunningham — Carol Ann Hyde
Linda J. Clark

Brian M. Culnan — Valerie R. Lape Handy
Kihyun S. Kim — Marcia B. Smith
Richard A. Frankel — Ellen Gillerman Cox
Stephanie E. Moriarty — Jennifer A. Grego
Cara E. Johnson

OF COUNSEL

Michael J. McNeil — Deborah A. Kirby

For full biographical listings, see the Martindale-Hubbell Law Directory

O'Connell and Aronowitz, P.C. (AV)

100 State Street, 12207-1885
Telephone: 518-462-5601
Telecopier: 518-462-2670
Email: info@oalaw.com
Plattsburgh, New York Office: 206 West Bay Plaza.
Telephone: 518-562-0600.
Fax: 518-562-0657.
Saratoga Springs, New York Office: Suite 204, 358 Broadway.
Telephone: 518-587-0425.

Neil H. Rivchin — Stephen R. Coffey
Peter Danziger — Thomas J. DiNovo
Gloria Herron Arthur

Michael L. Koenig — Bradley A. Sherman
Joseph Muia, Jr.

For full biographical listings, see the Martindale-Hubbell Law Directory

Powers & Santola (AV)

39 N. Pearl Street, Suite 2, 12207-2785
Telephone: 518-465-5995; 1-800-540-8742
Fax: 518-426-4012
Email: jpowers@powers-santola.com *URL:* http://www.powers-santola.com

John K. Powers — Daniel R. Santola

ASSOCIATES

Timothy J. Higgins — John H. Fisher
Paul Berne Sherr

Roche Corrigan McCoy & Bush (AV)

The Wilem Van Zandt Building, 36 South Pearl Street, 12207
Telephone: 518-436-9370
Fax: 518-436-8233

MEMBERS OF FIRM

Robert P. Roche — Joseph M. McCoy
Peter J. Corrigan — Scott W. Bush

For full biographical listings, see the Martindale-Hubbell Law Directory

Tabner, Ryan and Keniry (AV)

26 Computer Drive West, P.O. Box 12605, 12212-2605
Telephone: 518-459-9000
Telecopier: 518-459-9165
Email: trk@tabnerryanandkeniry.com

MEMBERS OF FIRM

John W. Tabner — William F. Ryan, Jr.
William J. Keniry

OF COUNSEL

C. Theodore Carlson

ASSOCIATES

Eric N. Dratler — Jennifer K. Corona
Donald W. Biggs

Special Counsel for: Water and Sewer District for Towns of Colonie, Coxsackie, Guilderland, Johnstown, Queensbury, Rotterdam and Village Castleton.
References: FleetBank; Trustco Bank.

For full biographical listings, see the Martindale-Hubbell Law Directory

*AUBURN,** Cayuga Co.

Michaels & Smolak, P.C. (AV)

71 South Street, P.O. Box 308, 13021
Telephone: 315-253-3293
Fax: 315-252-6970
Email: michaels@michaels-smolak.com *URL:* http://www.michaels-smolak.com

Lee S. Michaels — Stephanie Viscelli
Jan M. Smolak — Michael G. Bersani

Reference: Fleet Bank, Auburn, N.Y.

For full biographical listings, see the Martindale-Hubbell Law Directory

BAY SHORE, Suffolk Co.

Long, Tuminello, Besso, Seligman, Quinlan & Werner (AV)

120 Fourth Avenue, P.O. Box 591 P, 11706
Telephone: 516-666-5766; 516-666-2500
Fax: 516-666-8401
Email: bob_quinlan_ltbsqw@msn.com
Naples, Florida Office: 1300 Third Street South, Suite 302 B.
Telephone: 813-262-3377.
Fax: 813-262-0313.

MEMBERS OF FIRM

John E. Long, Jr. (Resident, Naples, Florida Office) — David H. Besso
Barry M. Tuminello — Harold Seligman
Robert F. Quinlan
Kevin J. Werner

ASSOCIATE

Kevin R. Johnston

OF COUNSEL

Hon. Arthur M. Cromarty — Thomas J. Lavallee

For full biographical listings, see the Martindale-Hubbell Law Directory

*BINGHAMTON,** Broome Co.

Aswad & Ingraham (AV)

46 Front Street, 13905
Telephone: 607-722-3495
Fax: 607-722-2566; 607-722-7269
Email: office@AILAW.COM

(See Next Column)

ASWAD & INGRAHAM—*Continued*

MEMBERS OF FIRM

Richard N. Aswad
Charles O. Ingraham
Thomas A. Saitta
James F. Haley, Jr.
Angelina C. Cutrona
William M. Thomas

SPECIAL COUNSEL

James F. Moran

ASSOCIATE

Jeffrey Husisian

Reference: Charter One Bank.

For full biographical listings, see the Martindale-Hubbell Law Directory

COUGHLIN & GERHART, L.L.P. (AV)

20 Hawley Street, P.O. Box 2039, 13902-2039
Telephone: 607-723-9511
Fax: 607-723-1530; 722-6073
Email: info@cglawllp.com
Afton, New York Office: 190 Main Street, 13730.
Telephone: 607-639-2222.
Unadilla, New York Office: 71-73 Main Street, 13849.
Telephone: 607-369-3811.
Owego, New York Office: 32-34 Lake Street, 13827.
Telephone: 607-687-1831.
Deposit, New York Office: 105 Front Street, 13754.
Telephone: 607-467-4010.

MEMBERS OF FIRM

Richard B. Long
Robert J. Smith
Henry J. Rode, II
Peter H. Bouman
Gordon E. Thompson
Mark S. Gorgos
James P. O'Brien (Coughlin & Gerhart, L.L.P., Group Manager, Litigation Group)
Richard W. Mertens
Carl A. Kieper
Joseph J. Steflik, Jr.
Jeffrey A. Brown
David H. Guy
Beth E. Westfall
Gary B. Kline
Susan L. English
Todd D. Kilpatrick
Robert R. Jones
Paul J. Sweeney
Susan A. Inneo

SPECIAL COUNSEL

Brian C. Madigan
Scott B. Anglehart

ASSOCIATES

Keith A. O'Hara
Ann M. Sharpe
Oliver N. Blaise, III
Jennifer C. Ruppel
Noelle M. Long

OF COUNSEL

Eugene C. Gerhart
Edward S. Dermody
George L. Ingalls
Loren W. Guy
Carl R. Gitlitz
Rollin L. Twining
Frank A. Nemia

General Counsel for: Crowley Foods, Inc.; McIntosh Laboratory, Inc.; Azon Corp.; Binghamton City School District; Dover Technologies International, Inc.; Universal Instruments Corp.
Representative Clients: HSBC Bank; NBT Bank, NA; Time Warner Cable; M & T Bank.

For full biographical listings, see the Martindale-Hubbell Law Directory

HINMAN, HOWARD & KATTELL, LLP (AV)

700 Security Mutual Building, 80 Exchange Street, P.O. Box 5250, 13902-5250
Telephone: 607-723-5341
Fax: 607-723-6605
Email: jworband@hhk.com *URL:* http://www.hhk.com
Norwich, New York Office: 48 Hale Street, 13815-2039.
Telephone: 607-334-5896.
Fax: 607-336-1628.
Oneonta, New York Office: 12 South Main Street, 13820-2542.
Telephone: 607-432-5331.
Fax: 607-432-2683.
New York, N.Y. Office: 500 5th Avenue, Suite 1725, 10110.
Telephone: 212-840-3017.
Fax: 212-840-2345.

MEMBERS OF FIRM

James S. Gleason
N. Theodore Sommer
James L. Chivers
James M. Hayes
James F. Lee
Albert J. Millus, Jr.
Paul T. Sheppard
Leslie Prechtl Guy
John M. Keeler

SPECIAL COUNSEL

Brian R. Wright
Amy Shapiro
Lori Grumet Schapiro

ASSOCIATES

Alyssa M. Barreiro
Kathleen S. Campbell
Erik T. Koons

Representative Clients: The Chase Manhattan Bank; BSB Bank & Trust Co.; International Business Machines Corp.; Universal Instruments Corp.; Security Mutual Life Insurance Company of New York; Bell Atlantic; Preferred Mutual Insurance Company; New York State Electric & Gas Corp.; Exxon Corp.

(See Next Column)

For Complete List of Firm Personnel, See General Section

For full biographical listings, see the Martindale-Hubbell Law Directory

*BRONX,** Bronx Co.

MAXWELL S. PFEIFER (AV)

714 East 241st Street, 10470
Telephone: 718-325-5000
Fax: 718-324-0333
Email: mspfeifer@aol.com
New York, New York Office: 18 East 50th Street, 7th Floor, 10022.
Telephone: 212-980-0777.
Fax: 718-324-0333.
Hallandale, Florida Office: 1920 East Hallandale Beach Boulevard, Suite 606.
Telephone: 954-454-1550.

ASSOCIATES

Steven E. Millon
Robert S. Summer

OF COUNSEL

Sandra Krevitsky Janin
Anthony J. Hatab
Hon. Alexander A. Delle Cese (1919-1997)

For full biographical listings, see the Martindale-Hubbell Law Directory

BRONXVILLE, Westchester Co.

GRIFFIN, COOGAN & VENERUSO, P.C. (AV)

51 Pondfield Road, 10708
Telephone: 914-961-1300
Telecopier: 914-961-1476; 914-961-9385

William E. Griffin
James M. Coogan
James J. Veneruso

Daniel J. Griffin
Paul R. Herrick
Thomas G. Marzullo
William E. Sulzer (Not admitted in NY)

Approved Closing Attorneys: Hudson Valley Bank.

For full biographical listings, see the Martindale-Hubbell Law Directory

*BROOKLYN,** Kings Co.

BONINA & BONINA, P.C. (AV)

Suite 1608, 16 Court Street, 11241
Telephone: 718-522-1786
888-MEDLAW-1
Fax: 718-243-0414
URL: http://www.medlaw1.com

John Anthony Bonina
John Bonina, III
Elizabeth Bonina
Andrea E. Bonina

Deborah A. Trerotola
Tyrone Sergio
Amy L. Insler

LEGAL SUPPORT PERSONNEL

Pedro Cintron
Inez M. Diaz
Sandra Ferrari

Reference: Republic Bank of New York.

For full biographical listings, see the Martindale-Hubbell Law Directory

*BUFFALO,** Erie Co.

COHEN & LOMBARDO, P.C. (AV)

343 Elmwood Avenue, P.O. Box 5204, 14213-5204
Telephone: 716-881-3010
Fax: 716-881-2755
Email: law@cohenlombardo.com *URL:* http://www.cohenlombardo.com

Joseph Cohen (1909-1966)
Ernest Lombardo (1913-1993)
Richard N. Blewett
Donald A. Fisher
Robert N. Convissar
Rocco Lucente, II
Stuart Brian Shapiro
Neil R. Sherwood
Douglas S. Cream

Robert R. Goods
Katherine J. Bestine
Mark S. Nemeth
Daniel M. Caro
Maria T. Buchanan-Sidorski
Thomas J. Navarro, Jr.
Jennifer D. Bowen
Christopher A. Zampogna

OF COUNSEL

Maryann Saccomando Freedman
Anthony M. Nosek
Dean C. Stathacos
Norman J. Pecora
David R. Koepsell

For full biographical listings, see the Martindale-Hubbell Law Directory

Buffalo—Continued

CONNORS & VILARDO, LLP (AV)

1020 Liberty Building, 420 Main Street, 14202
Telephone: 716-852-5533
Fax: 716-852-5649
Email: c-v@connors-vilardo.com

MEMBERS OF FIRM

Joseph J. Ricotta (1921-1993)
Terrence M. Connors
Lawrence J. Vilardo
Kevin A. Ricotta
Randall D. White
John T. Loss
Vincent E. Doyle III

ASSOCIATES

Michael J. Roach
Mark R. Uba
Margaret L. Phillips
Henry J. Nowak
Lawlor F. Quinlan III
James W. Grable, Jr.

For full biographical listings, see the Martindale-Hubbell Law Directory

DAMON & MOREY LLP (AV)

(Formerly Damon, Morey, Sawyer & Moot)
1000 Cathedral Place, 298 Main Street, 14202-4096
Telephone: 716-856-5500
Facsimile: 716-856-5510
Email: apinder@damonmorey.com *URL:* http://www.damonmorey.com
Rochester, New York Office: Powers Building, Suite 507, 16 West Main Street, 14614.
Telephone: 716-232-3640.
Fax: 716-232-8448.

MEMBERS OF FIRM

Mason O. Damon (1905-1983)
Robert J. Plache
James N. Schmit
Christopher T. Greene
Franklin W. Heller
Gregory C. Yungbluth
James W. Gormley
James M. Mucklewee
Melinda G. Disare
Robert J. Portin
Joseph J. Schoellkopf, Jr.
William F. Savino
Thomas J. Drury
Patrick B. Curran
Peter S. Marlette
Vincent J. Moore
Gust P. Pullman
Barbara L. Schifeling
Michael J. Willett
Carol Guck Snider
Joseph W. Dunbar
Kenneth W. Africano
Julie M. Bargnesi
Arthur A. Marrapese III (Resident, Rochester Office)
Sharyn G. Rogers
Daniel F. Brown
David L. Edmunds, Jr.
Charles S. Carra
Hedwig Maria Auletta
Marylou K. Roshia
Maryjo C. Falcone
Charles E. Telford, III
Timothy C. Cashmore
Anthony L. Eugeni
Amy Archer Flaherty
Kathleen M. Reilly
Steven I. Rubinstein
Diane C. Zarlock

ASSOCIATES

Brian Alan Birenbach
Daniel T. Cavarello
Michelle A. Crew
Anne C. Evans
Michael Thomas Feeley
Judy S. Hernandez
David S. Kelly
Joseph J. Manna
Rosalie A. Melisz
Mary C. Raymond
Vincent George Saccomando
Allison Fields Stravino
Kellie Muffoletto Ulrich

OF COUNSEL

Joseph H. Morey, Jr.

SPECIAL COUNSEL

Richard E. Moot
George F. Gabel, Jr.
G. Steven Pigeon
Susan A. Benz
Edward Yankelunas

Counsel For: Advanced Refractory Technologies; Catholic Health East; D.A. Elia Construction Corporation; Kaleida Health; Town of Cheektowaga; Bagel Brothers Amherst, Inc.; Burt Rigid Box, Inc.; Lake Shore Health Care Center; County of Cattaraugus; Commonwealth Land Title Insurance; Diocese of Buffalo; Baker Victory Services; Niagara Lutheran Home and Rehabilitation, Inc.; Sheehan Memorial Hospital; Robert James Sales, Inc.; Olean General Hospital; Wendt Corporation; Aria Wireless Systems, Inc.; Buffalo Sewer Authority; City of Tonawanda; Roswell Park Cancer Institute; Ivoclar North America, Inc.; Olean Medical Group; Cold Spring Construction Company; Buffalo Municipal Housing Authority.
Local Counsel For: Healthcare Underwriters Mutual Insurance Company; AIG Companies; Owens-Corning Fiberglas; Unigard Insurance Group; Key Tronic Corporation; Medical Liability Insurance; Risk Enterprise Management Limited; Wintherthur International; Hanover Insurance Company; National Casualty Company; Marine Midland Mortgage Corporation; Acordia Resort Services; Medical Malpractice Insurance Association; OUM & Associates; Ohio Casualty Company; PACCAR, Inc.; Frontier Insurance Company; The Limited, Inc.; Zurich-American Insurance Group; Allstate Insurance Company; Universal Studios, Inc.

For full biographical listings, see the Martindale-Hubbell Law Directory

FELDMAN, KIEFFER & HERMAN, LLP (AV)

110 Pearl Street, Suite 400, 14202
Telephone: 716-852-5875
Fax: 716-852-4253
Email: info@fkhattys.com *URL:* http://www.fkhattys.com

PRINCIPALS OF THE FIRM

Andrew Feldman
James M. Kieffer
Ann W. Herman
Mark F. Scarcello
Gordon D. Tresch
Mary Jo Herrscher

For full biographical listings, see the Martindale-Hubbell Law Directory

J. MICHAEL HAYES (AV)

69 Delaware Avenue, Suite 1111, 14202
Telephone: 716-852-2707
Fax: 716-852-0711
Email: JMHAYES@pcem.net *URL:* http://www.lawyers.com/jmichaelhayes

ASSOCIATES

R. Colin Campbell
Michael A. Riehler
David C. Caywood

For full biographical listings, see the Martindale-Hubbell Law Directory

HODGSON, RUSS, ANDREWS, WOODS & GOODYEAR, LLP (AV)

A Registered Limited Liability Partnership including Professional Associations
One M & T Plaza, Suite 2000, 14203
Telephone: 716-856-4000
Fax: 716-849-0349
Email: info@hodgsonruss.com *URL:* www.hodgsonruss.com
Albany, New York Office: Three City Square, 12207.
Telephone: 518-465-2333.
Fax: 518-465-1567.
Boca Raton, Florida Office: Suite 400, 2000 Glades Road, 33431.
Telephone: 561-394-0500.
Fax: 561-394-3862.
Toronto, Ontario, Canada Office: 150 King Street West, Suite 2309, M5H 1J9, P.O. Box 30.
Telephone: 416-595-5100.
Fax: 416-595-5021.
New York, New York Office: 65 East 55th Street, 10th Floor, 10022.
Telephone: 212-751-4300.
Fax: 212-751-0928.
Gloversville, New York Office: 6 Fremont Street, 12078.
Telephone: 518-725-6347.
Fax: 518-773-7350.
Newark, New Jersey Office: One Gateway Center, Suite 2600, 07102.
Telephone: 973-645-0577.
Fax: 973-645-0551.

MEMBERS OF FIRM
(ALPHABETICALLY BY YEAR OF ADMISSION TO BAR)

William H. Gardner
H. Kenneth Schroeder, Jr.
Michael H. Gora (P.A.)
Robert W. Keller
Robert B. Conklin
Richard A. Goetz (P.A.) (Boca Raton, Florida Office)
Joseph V. Sedita
Jerome D. Schad
Lawrence R. Bailey, Jr. (New York, N.Y. Office)
Garry M. Graber
Richard L. Weisz (Albany Office)
Jerrold S. Brown
Paul I. Perlman
Larry Corman (P.A.) (Boca Raton, Florida Office)
Rick W. Kennedy
Daniel C. Oliverio
Robert J. Lane, Jr.
Benjamin M. Zuffranieri, Jr.
Kevin M. Kearney (Newark, New Jersey and New York, N.Y. Offices)
Michael P. Murphy
Cheryl R. Storie
Deborah L. Kelly (Albany Office)
Hugh M. Russ, III
Michael E. Maxwell
Paul D. Meosky
Lisa A. Coppola
Patrick M. Tomovic
Leecia Roberta Eve
Peter A. Muth

SENIOR COUNSEL

Anna L. Case

COUNSEL

John E. Dickinson

ASSOCIATES
(ALPHABETICALLY BY YEAR OF ADMISSION TO BAR)

Annette M. Tambasco (Albany Office)
Amy J. Vigneron
Stephen A. Aschettino (New York, N.Y. Office)
Diane Nowak Kent (Boca Raton, Florida Office)
Aidan M. McCormack (New York, N.Y. Office)
R. Anthony Rupp III
Daniel A. Spitzer
Stephen L. Yonaty
Jeffrey F. Baase
Julia S. Kreher
Michael V. McLaughlin
James P. Milbrand
Adam W. Perry
Jeffrey S. Geller (Boca Raton, Florida Office)
Mirna E. Martinez (New York, N.Y. Office)
Kevin D. Szczepanski

(See Next Column)

HODGSON, RUSS, ANDREWS, WOODS & GOODYEAR LLP—*Continued*

ASSOCIATES
(ALPHABETICALLY BY YEAR OF ADMISSION TO BAR) (Continued)

Dartaganan L. Jackson
Jason E. Markel
Lorrie Turner-Proulx
Peter R. Keane (Albany Office)
Michael J. Kotin (Albany Office)
David R. Pfalzgraf, Jr.
Kathleen M. Sellers
Jodyann Galvin

For Complete List of Firm Personnel, See General Section

For full biographical listings, see the Martindale-Hubbell Law Directory

MCGEE & GELMAN (AV)

200 Summer Street, 14222-2271
Telephone: 716-883-7272
Fax: 716-883-7084
Email: counsel@mcgee-gelman.com

MEMBERS OF FIRM

Michael R. McGee
Warren B. Gelman
F. Brendan Burke, Jr.
Laura A. Colca
Jennifer L. Friedman

David S. Widenor

For full biographical listings, see the Martindale-Hubbell Law Directory

ROACH, BROWN, MCCARTHY & GRUBER, P.C. (AV)

1620 Liberty Building, 420 Main Street, 14202-3511
Telephone: 716-852-0400
Fax: 716-852-2535
Email: roachbrown@roachbrown.com

Daniel T. Roach
Edmund S. Brown, Jr.
T. Alan Brown
Joseph V. McCarthy
J. Mark Gruber
Mary J. Murray
John P. Danieu
Elizabeth G. Redmond
Gregory T. Miller
Teresa C. Brophy Bair
Jason A. Botticelli
Jennifer L. Noah
Joel J. Java, Jr.

OF COUNSEL

Arthur J. Maloney
John Y. Gallup

Local Attorneys for: American International Group; Chubb Group of Insurance Co.; Healthcare Underwriters Mutual Insurance Co.; Peter J. McBreen and Associates; Frontier Insurance Co.; Medical Liability Mutual Insurance Co.; Medical Malpractice Insurance Assn.; Merrill Dow; Reliance Insurance Group; Travelers Group.

For full biographical listings, see the Martindale-Hubbell Law Directory

RODGERS, MENARD & COPPOLA, LLP (AV)

2020 Liberty Building, 420 Main Street, 14202-3620
Telephone: 716-852-4100
Facsimile: 716-852-0002

MEMBERS OF FIRM

Douglas S. Coppola
Michael Menard
Mark C. Rodgers

ASSOCIATES

Patricia Stroman Walker
William K. Kennedy
Frederick G. Attea

For full biographical listings, see the Martindale-Hubbell Law Directory

STENGER & FINNERTY (AV)

1800 Main Place Tower, 14202
Telephone: 716-849-1700
Fax: 716-849-1717
Email: stenfinn@stenfinn.com *URL:* http://www.stenfinn.com

John H. Stenger
Joseph M. Finnerty

ASSOCIATES

Mitchell M. Stenger
David E. Gutowski

For full biographical listings, see the Martindale-Hubbell Law Directory

SULLIVAN & OLIVERIO (AV)

600 Main Place Tower, 14202-3706
Telephone: 716-854-5300
Telecopier: 716-854-5299
Email: sulliolaw@aol.com

MEMBERS OF FIRM

Richard T. Sullivan
B. P. Oliverio
Bruce W. Hoover

Thomas M. Moll
Michael E. Appelbaum
Kevin M. Carter

OF COUNSEL

Paul D. Pearson

For full biographical listings, see the Martindale-Hubbell Law Directory

WILLIAMS & WILLIAMS (AV)

237 Main Street Suite 1400, 14203
Telephone: 716-856-8200
Fax: 716-856-0559
Email: wmswmsfirm@aol.com

Mark W. Kerwood
Roger J. Edel
Mary Meyer Russo

Robert D. Leary
Lynette M. Gohr
Ellen Shanahan Becker
Boyd L. Earl
Wayne D. Schiffhauer
Julie A. Houghtaling
Melissa A. Day
Dawn M. Netzel
Christina M. Hassler

OF COUNSEL

Clyde M. Williams
Paul D. Williams (1910-1993)

A List of Representative Clients and References will be furnished upon request.

For full biographical listings, see the Martindale-Hubbell Law Directory

ZDARSKY, SAWICKI & AGOSTINELLI (AV)

404 Cathedral Place, 298 Main Street, 14202
Telephone: 716-855-3200
Telecopier: 716-855-3101
Email: zsagtw@buffnet.net

MEMBERS OF FIRM

Joseph E. Zdarsky
K. Michael Sawicki
Guy J. Agostinelli
Gerald T. Walsh
Mark J. Schlant

ASSOCIATES

Patrick A. Dudley
John A. Moscati, Jr.

Reference: Marine Midland Bank, N.A.

For full biographical listings, see the Martindale-Hubbell Law Directory

CARLE PLACE, Nassau Co.

DOLLINGER, GONSKI & GROSSMAN (AV)

One Old Country Road, 11514
Telephone: 516-747-1010
Telecopier: 516-747-2494
Fairfield, New Jersey Office: 710 Route 46 East, Suite 212, 07004.
Telephone: 973-276-0530.
Fax: 973-276-0533.

MEMBERS OF FIRM

Matthew Dollinger
Dennis M. Gonski
Floyd G. Grossman

ASSOCIATES

Leslie Ann Foodim
Michael J. Spithogiannis
Jessica M. Seidman
Bruce N. Roberts
Alicia B. Devins
Mindy Anne Wallach
Joshua N. Krellen

OF COUNSEL

Joseph Goldstein

Reference: Marine Midland National Bank, Carle Place, New York.

For full biographical listings, see the Martindale-Hubbell Law Directory

CEDARHURST, Nassau Co.

NATHANIEL M. SWERGOLD (AV)

124 Cedarhurst Avenue, 11516
Telephone: 516-569-2266
Fax: 516-374-7697
Reference: European American Bank, Cedarhurst Branch.

For full biographical listings, see the Martindale-Hubbell Law Directory

COMMACK, Suffolk Co.

KRAMER, FEINGOLD & CASTROVINCI, PLLC (AV)

Formerly Law Offices of Lynne Adair Kramer
6165 Jericho Turnpike, 11725
Telephone: 516-462-5850
Telecopier: 516-462-5862

Lynne Adair Kramer
Jennifer Feingold
Philip John Castrovinci

Stacy J. Evans

OF COUNSEL

Ruth Sovronsky

For full biographical listings, see the Martindale-Hubbell Law Directory

EAST MEADOW, Nassau Co.

Certilman Balin Adler & Hyman, LLP (AV)

90 Merrick Avenue, 11554
Telephone: 516-296-7000
Telecopier: 516-296-7111
URL: http://www.cbah.com

MEMBERS OF FIRM

Ira J. Adler
Dale Allinson
Michael C. Axelrod
Herbert M. Balin
Bruce J. Bergman
Eileen O'Boyle Bitetto
Michael D. Brofman
Lewis J. Campanella
Morton L. Certilman
Robert J. Ciovacco
Brian J. Davis
Wayne G. Edwards
Joseph P. Famighetti
Howard R. Gladston
Murray Greenberg
Gavin C. Grusd
David Z. Herman
Richard Herzbach
M. Allan Hyman
Bernard Hyman
Donna-Marie Korth
Steven J. Kuperschmid
Jeffrey S. Lisabeth
Jaspreet S. Mayall
Richard J. McCord
Thomas J. McNamara
Michael F. O'Shea
Marilyn Price
Fred S. Skolnik
Louis Soloway
Harold Somer
Howard M. Stein
Brian K. Ziegler

OF COUNSEL

Daniel S. Cohan
Joseph N. Mondello

ASSOCIATES

Lawrence A. Altholtz
Meredith W. Ayres
Daniel J. Baker
Kimberly I. Berson
Scott B. Black
Brendan J. DeRiggi
Thomas M. Farrell
Mary C. Florentz
Candace Reid Gladston
Harry P. Greenbaum
David E. Herold
Jodi S. Hoffman
James G. Kapralos
Linda P. Manfredi
Edward G. McCabe
Patrick McCormick
Susan L. McWalters
Jothy Narendran
James A. Rose
Wayne J. Schaefer
Leslie H. Scharf
Afsheen Ashley Shah
Victor Spinnelli
Russell H. Stern
Robert G. Wilk

For full biographical listings, see the Martindale-Hubbell Law Directory

*ELMIRA,** Chemung Co.

Sayles & Evans (AV)

One West Church Street, 14901
Telephone: 607-734-2271
Fax: 607-734-1754
Email: saylesev@aol.com

Halsey Sayles (1876-1958)
Pierre W. Evans (1895-1982)

COUNSEL

Harry Treinin
Alan Parsons
William C. Ughetta

MEMBERS OF FIRM

Lewis W. Morse, Jr.
J. Philip Hunter
James F. Young
John R. Alexander
Lawrence LeClair
Clover M. Drinkwater
Cynthia S. Hutchinson
Steven E. Agan
Donna M. Hutchison
James D. Young

ASSOCIATES

Jonathan Edward McKeon
Curt N. Meeder
Conrad R. Wolan
Alan R. Hamilton

For full biographical listings, see the Martindale-Hubbell Law Directory

GARDEN CITY, Nassau Co.

Gallagher Gosseen Faller Kaplan & Crowley (AV)

1010 Franklin Avenue, Suite 400, 11530-2927
Telephone: 516-742-2500
Fax: 516-742-2516
Email: GGFKC__Postmaster@GGFKC.com
New York, New York Office: 350 Fifth Avenue, Suite 603.
Telephone: 212-947-5800.
Fax: 212-967-4965.

MEMBERS OF FIRM

James A. Gallagher, Jr.
Robert I. Gosseen (Resident, New York City Office)
Robert A. Faller
Alan D. Kaplan
Michael J. Crowley
William E. Vita
Brian P. Morrissey

ASSOCIATES

David H. Arntsen
Joseph A. Latasso
Amy L. Ruina
Gerald A. Corallo, Jr.

(See Next Column)

OF COUNSEL

John P. Coogan
Peter F. Vetro
William A. Bales, Jr.

For full biographical listings, see the Martindale-Hubbell Law Directory

Law Offices of Stephen Gassman (AV)

666 Old Country Road, 11530
Telephone: 516-228-9181
Telecopier: 516-745-6712

MEMBER OF FIRM

Stephen Gassman

Charlotte Betts
Rosalia Baiamonte

OF COUNSEL

Richard J. Keidel
Timothy M. Tippins
Cynthia J. Cornaire
Mary Sullivan Calabrese

For full biographical listings, see the Martindale-Hubbell Law Directory

Jones & Jones (AV)

1000 Franklin Avenue Suite 302, 11530
Telephone: 516-747-1141
Fax: 516-741-5842
URL: http://www.lawyers.com/jones&joneslaw

MEMBERS OF FIRM

C. H. Tunnicliffe Jones (1900-1991)
Lawrence T. Jones

OF COUNSEL

Howard L. DeMott

Reference: Bank of New York, Long Island Region.

For full biographical listings, see the Martindale-Hubbell Law Directory

Joel S. Kaplan (AV)

585 Stewart Avenue, 11530
Telephone: 516-745-1100
Telecopier: 516-745-6912

For full biographical listings, see the Martindale-Hubbell Law Directory

L'Abbate, Balkan, Colavita & Contini, L.L.P. (AV)

1050 Franklin Avenue, 11530
Telephone: 516-294-8844
Telecopier: 516-294-8202; 742-6563
Email: law@labbatebalkan.com *URL:* http://www.labbatebalkan.com
Livingston, New Jersey Office: 7 Regent Street, Suite 711, 07039.
Telephone: 973-422-0422.
Telecopier: 973-422-0420.

MEMBERS OF FIRM

Donald R. L'Abbate
Anthony P. Colavita
Peter L. Contini
Monte E. Sokol
Douglas L. Pintauro
Richard P. Byrne
Jane M. Myers
Paula M. Gart
Anna M. DiLonardo
David B. Kosakoff
Lewis A. Bartell
Marian C. Rice
Ralph A. Catalano
Douglas R. Halstrom
Steven R. Goldstein
Gary Petropoulos
Domingo R. Gallardo
Mercedes Colwin

COUNSEL TO THE FIRM

Kenneth J. Balkan

SPECIAL COUNSEL

Arthur D. Bromberg (Resident, Livingston, New Jersey Office)
Jonathan M. Kuller (Resident, Livingston, New Jersey Office)

OF COUNSEL

Marianne S. Conklin
Joanne C. Watson
Marie Ann Hoenings

ASSOCIATES

Colleen M. Cronin
Wendy S. Van Dorn
Nicholas Toumbekis
Andrew Marc Warshauer
Michelle J. Simon
Annalee J. Cataldo-Barile
Martin A. Schwartzberg
Louis M. Goldberg
Scott Evan Kossove
Peter D. Rigelhaupt
Orin J. Ketyer
Anthony T. Battaglia
Christopher B. Block (Resident, Livingston, New Jersey Office)
James S. Montano (Resident, Livingston, New Jersey Office)
Maureen E. Scott
John D. McKenna
Michael B. Curan
Jeffrey E. Edelman (Resident, Livingston, New Jersey Office)
Matthew K. Flanagan
Claudia M. Kessler

Representative Clients: Chicago Underwriting Group, Inc.; CNA; DPIC Insurance Cos.; Evanston Insurance Co.; General Accident Insurance Co.; The Home Insurance Co.; Imperial Casualty and Indemnity Co.; Markel American Insurance Co.; Shand, Morahan & Co., Inc.; Utica Mutual Insurance Co.

For full biographical listings, see the Martindale-Hubbell Law Directory

Garden City—Continued

Montfort, Healy, McGuire & Salley (AV)

1140 Franklin Avenue, 11530
Telephone: 516-747-4082
Telecopier: 516-746-0748

MEMBERS OF FIRM

E. Richard Rimmels, Jr. (1930-1999)
Frank J. Cafaro
Philip J. Catapano
Fredric C. Montfort
Donald S. Neumann, Jr.
James J. Keefe, Jr.
Michael A. Baranowicz
James Michael Murphy

OF COUNSEL

Fredric H. Montfort
Edward M. Salley, Jr.
David J. Fleming
Robert J. Mettalia

ASSOCIATES

Claudia C. Glacken
Marcie K. Glasser
Bruce A. Cook
Jeffrey D. Present
Joan E. Resnik
Susan H. Dempsey
Camille L. Hansen
Christopher T. Cafaro
Kathleen Dumont
Jeffrey B. Siler
Michael G. Kruzynski
Karen J. Cooper

For full biographical listings, see the Martindale-Hubbell Law Directory

Moritt, Hock & Hamroff, LLP (AV)

400 Garden City Plaza, Suite 202, 11530
Telephone: 516-873-2000
Fax: 516-873-2010
Email: lawyers@mhhlaw.com *URL:* http://www.mhhlaw.com

PARTNERS

Neil J. Moritt
Alan S. Hock
Marc L. Hamroff
David H. Cohen
Robert M. Tils
Gary C. Hisiger

ASSOCIATES

William P. Laino
Robert S. Cohen
Terese L. Arenth
Leslie A. Berkoff
Michael S. Re
David A. Loglisci
David Z. Ottensoser
Ellen R. Leibowitz
Amy J. Zamir
Michael Cardello, III
Gary E. Ostroff

For full biographical listings, see the Martindale-Hubbell Law Directory

Sawyer, Davis, Halpern & Demetri (AV)

600 Old Country Road, 11530
Telephone: 516-222-4567
Telecopier: 516-222-4585
Email: litlaw@aol.com

MEMBER OF FIRM

James Sawyer

For full biographical listings, see the Martindale-Hubbell Law Directory

Benjamin Vinar (AV)

1050 Franklin Avenue, 11530
Telephone: 516-746-0241
Telecopier: 516-747-9759
Email: BVinar@compuserve.com *URL:* http://www.vinarlaw.com

For full biographical listings, see the Martindale-Hubbell Law Directory

GARRISON, Putnam Co.

Daniel Donnelly (AV)

Garrison's Landing, P.O. Box 253, 10524
Telephone: 914-424-3877
Facsimile: 914-424-3968
Email: danieldonnelly@compuserve.com

For full biographical listings, see the Martindale-Hubbell Law Directory

GLENS FALLS, Warren Co.

Fitzgerald Morris Baker Firth (AV)

One Broad Street Plaza, P.O. Box 2017, 12801
Telephone: 518-745-1400
Fax: 518-745-1576
Email: info@fmbf-law.com

Robert C. Morris
Peter D. FitzGerald
Peter A. Firth
Carl T. Baker
J. Mark Noordsy
Robert P. McNally
Laura V. Nield
Veronica Carrozza O'Dell

(See Next Column)

Bruce G. Carr
David Gregory Richardson
Kevin O'Shell

Representative Clients: Woodbury Development Group, Ltd.; Homequity; Glens Falls Cement Co., Inc.; Greater Glens Falls Development Corp.; Glens Falls Industrial Development Agency; Torrington Industries, Inc.; Whiteman Chevrolet, Inc.

For full biographical listings, see the Martindale-Hubbell Law Directory

HAUPPAUGE, Suffolk Co.

Eric H. Holtzman (AV)

330 Vanderbilt Motor Parkway, P.O. Box 11005, 11788-0903
Telephone: 631-435-8800
Fax: 631-435-8832

Richard E. Trachtenberg
David H. Eisenberg

Reference: European-American Bank & Trust Co.

For full biographical listings, see the Martindale-Hubbell Law Directory

HEMPSTEAD, Nassau Co.

Deegan & Deegan, L.L.P. (AV)

550 Front Street, 11550
Telephone: 516-486-9400
Telecopier: 516-486-8680
Email: deegan550@aol.com

MEMBERS OF FIRM

Donald E. Deegan
James V. Deegan

ASSOCIATES

Michael A. Wolf
James M. Hayes
Robert H. Doud
Mary E. Hayes
Gregg M. McGrath

OF COUNSEL

Diane Klaum Farrell
Thomas G. Nolan
John S. White
George Planos
Donald F. McCarthy
Gregory M. Maurer
George A. Boehling
Theresa Rho

For full biographical listings, see the Martindale-Hubbell Law Directory

Furey & Furey, P.C. (AV)

600 Front Street, 11550-4494
Telephone: 516-538-2500
Telecopier: 516-489-5056
Email: fureyfureypc@mindspring.com

James M. Furey
James M. Furey, Jr.
Thomas G. Leverage
Stuart J. Manzione
Susan B. Williams
Susan W. Darlington

Elena R. Lanza
Christina A. Gulotta
Joseph M. Nador

Reference: Fleet Bank, Hempstead.

For full biographical listings, see the Martindale-Hubbell Law Directory

ISLANDIA, Suffolk Co.

Bracken & Margolin, LLP (AV)

One Suffolk Square, Suite 300, 11722
Telephone: 516-234-8585
Telecopier: 516-234-8702
URL: http://www.bracken-margolin.com

MEMBERS OF FIRM

John P. Bracken
Linda U. Margolin

ASSOCIATES

Olympia Gouvis
William J. Graham
Patricia M. Meisenheimer
Ralph J. Reissman
Peter L. Verdon

Representative Clients: Rason Asphalt, Inc.; S & H Building Materials Corp.
Reference: Marine Midland Bank, N.A.

For full biographical listings, see the Martindale-Hubbell Law Directory

*ITHACA,** Tompkins Co.

Wiggins and Masson, LLP (AV)

308 North Tioga Street, P.O. Box 399, 14851
Telephone: 607-272-0479
Telecopier: 607-273-0502
Email: law@wigginsandmasson.com *URL:* http://www.wigginsandmasson.com

(See Next Column)

WIGGINS AND MASSON LLP, *Ithaca—Continued*

MEMBERS OF FIRM

Walter J. Wiggins
Robin Abrahamson Masson
Erin E. McKinley

Representative Client: Leathers & Associates, Inc.

For Complete List of Firm Personnel, See General Section

For full biographical listings, see the Martindale-Hubbell Law Directory

JAMESTOWN, Chautauqua Co.

BURGETT & ROBBINS (AV)

15 East Fifth Street, P.O. Box 3090, 14702-3090
Telephone: 716-488-3090
Fax: 716-483-3765
1-800-832-6582
Email: help@burgettandrobbins.com *URL:* http://www.burgettandrobbins.com

Dalton J. Burgett
Dale C. Robbins
Kenneth M. Lasker
Mary Speedy Hajdu
Robert A. Liebers
Andrew T. Radack

References: Fleet Bank, Jamestown, New York; Marine Midland Bank, Jamestown, New York; Lake Shore Savings and Loan Association, Jamestown, New York.

For full biographical listings, see the Martindale-Hubbell Law Directory

JERICHO, Nassau Co.

MARTIN, VAN DE WALLE, DONOHUE, MCGAHAN, CATALANO & FAIRGRIEVE (AV)

555 North Broadway, P.O. Box 350, 11753
Telephone: 516-681-3100
Telecopier: 516-681-5357

MEMBERS OF FIRM

Jules Martin (1928-1995)
Charles R. Van de Walle
Joseph A. Guarino (1946-1991)
Nicholas J. Donohue
James M. McGahan
Thomas C. Catalano, Jr.
Scott Fairgrieve
Michael Belitsis

ASSOCIATES

Randi M. Seidner
Laurie Ann Corallo

Representative Clients: Fidelity National Title Insurance Company of New York; Bancker Construction Corp.; Biener Pontiac-Nissan, Inc.; Festo Corp.; First Investors Corp.; First Financial Savings Bank, S.L.A.; Chaminade High School; Oppenheimer Funds, Inc.; Old Republic National Title Insurance Company; New York State Land Title Association, Inc.; The Jones Fund; Carolina Mirror Co.; Genesis Mirror Co.; New York Schools Insurance Reciprocal; New York Municipal Insurance Reciprocal; Liberty Mutual Insurance Company; Long Island Newspapers.

For full biographical listings, see the Martindale-Hubbell Law Directory

KEW GARDENS, Queens Co.

GARY M. DARCHE (AV)

125-10 Queens Boulevard, Suite 223, 11415-1519
Telephone: 718-263-7900
Fax: 718-793-0782
Email: GARYDARCHE@AOL.COM

For full biographical listings, see the Martindale-Hubbell Law Directory

LAKE SUCCESS, Nassau Co.

IVONE, DEVINE & JENSEN, LLP (AV)

2001 Marcus Avenue, Suite N100, 11042
Telephone: 516-326-2400
Telecopier: 516-352-4952
Email: idjlaw@aol.com *URL:* http://www.lawyers.com/idjlaw

MEMBERS OF FIRM

Michael T. Ivone
Robert Devine
Richard C. Jensen
Brian E. Lee
Michael Ferguson

ASSOCIATES

Debora G. Nobel
Ellin M. Regis
Jonathan Rubin
Veronica Henry
Patrick G. Toner
Keith C. Jewell

For full biographical listings, see the Martindale-Hubbell Law Directory

*MALONE,** Franklin Co.

FISCHER, BESSETTE & MULDOWNEY, L.L.P. (AV)

Country Club Road, P.O. Box 420, 12953
Telephone: 518-481-5000
Fax: 518-481-5203
Email: fbm@northnet.org *URL:* http://www.lawyers.com/fb&mlaw

William J. Herron (1905-1993)

(See Next Column)

OF COUNSEL

Henry A. Fischer

MEMBERS OF FIRM

James P. Bessette
John J. Muldowney
Richard F. Hunter

For full biographical listings, see the Martindale-Hubbell Law Directory

MELVILLE, Suffolk Co.

GANDIN, SCHOTSKY, RAPPAPORT, GLASS & GREENE, LLP (AV)

445 Broad Hollow Road, 11747
Telephone: 516-293-2300
Fax: 516-293-2918
Email: gsrmail@gsrlaw.com *URL:* http://www.gsrlaw.com
New York, N.Y. Office: 1212 Avenue of the Americas, 10036.
Telephone: 212-921-5200.
Fax: 212-921-5367.

PARTNERS

Charles J. Rappaport
Arnold M. Schotsky
Michael R. Greene
Michael G. Glass
Kevin E. Balfe
Michael S. Levine

ASSOCIATES

Margery Weinroth
Jonathan H. Freiberger
Brian Robert Gunn
Karen S. Bennett
Kenneth J. Lauri
Matthew J. Zullo
Diane G. Holland
James L. Forde

OF COUNSEL

Michael I. Gandin
Edward Kiley
Charles Krupin

For full biographical listings, see the Martindale-Hubbell Law Directory

LAMB & BARNOSKY, LLP (AV)

534 Broadhollow Road-CS 9034, 11747-9034
Telephone: 631-694-2300
Telecopier: 631-694-2309
Email: thefirm@lambbarnosky.com *URL:* http://www.lambbarnosky.com

PARTNERS

Eugene R. Barnosky
Robert H. Cohen
Marcia Lyn Finkelstein
Michael J. Heller
Gary Holman
Scott M. Karson
P. L. Lamb
Arthur A. Lane
Joel M. Markowitz
Gerald P. Rosenberg
Patrice Dowd Shenn

OF COUNSEL

Louis E. Black
James F. Gesualdi
Howard W. Newman
Joseph J. Salvatore
Joseph H. Wishod

COUNSEL

Lloyd K. Chanin
Scott P. McBride

ASSOCIATES

Cathleen D. Allen
Catherine Healy Kanzler
Rita Fishman Sheena
Shari Lee Sugarman

For full biographical listings, see the Martindale-Hubbell Law Directory

MILLBROOK, Dutchess Co.

WILLIAM E. STANTON (AV)

Merritt Avenue and Elm Drive, P.O. Box 1252, 12545
Telephone: 914-677-9060
FAX: 914-677-9392
Stanfordville, New York Office: Bulls Head Road, 12581.
Telephone: 914-868-7514.
Fax: 914-868-7761.

Representative Clients: Dupont de Nemours & Co.; Millbrook School; New York Telephone Co.
Reference: Pawling Savings Bank.

For full biographical listings, see the Martindale-Hubbell Law Directory

*MINEOLA,** Nassau Co.

FORCHELLI, CURTO, SCHWARTZ, MINEO, CARLINO & COHN, LLP (AV)

330 Old Country Road, P.O. Box 31, 11501
Telephone: 516-248-1700
Telecopier: 516-248-1729
Email: info@fcsmcc.com *URL:* http://fcsmcc.com
Suffolk County Office: One Huntington Quadrangle, Melville, NY 11747.

MEMBERS OF FIRM

Jeffrey D. Forchelli
Anthony V. Curto
Donald Jay Schwartz
Peter R. Mineo
Joseph F. Carlino (Retired)
Barbara Shaheen Alesi
Peter Mills Alpert
Anthony B. Barton
Vincent J. Pizzulli, Jr.
Brian R. Sahn
John V. Terrana

(See Next Column)

FORCHELLI, CURTO, SCHWARTZ, MINEO, CARLINO & COHN LLP—*Continued*

ASSOCIATES

Warren S. Arthur
Richard A. Blumberg
William F. Bonesso
Joseph F. Buzzell
Andrew E. Curto
William A. DiConza
Alicia L. Dvoskin
Diana R. Fantano
Aaron Gershonowitz
Michael J. Greenberg
Janet M. Insardi
Rochelle Laufer
Matthew G. Roseman
Judy Lynn Simoncic

COUNSEL

William S. Cohn
John A. Burns, Jr.
Lester Cooper
Steven G. Gaebler

OF COUNSEL

Robert A. Melillo
Terence E. Smolev

Representative Clients: Dime Savings Bank; Philips International Holding Corp.; The Pep Boys; Cablevision Systems Corp.; Adelphi University; Northrop Grumman Corp.

For full biographical listings, see the Martindale-Hubbell Law Directory

HATTER, DONOVAN & MCFAUL, LLP (AV)

47 Mineola Boulevard, 11501
Telephone: 516-873-8800
Fax: 516-873-1418
Email: law@hdmlaw.com
URL: http://www.hdmlaw.com

MEMBERS OF FIRM

James R. Hatter
Thomas J. Donovan
John M. McFaul

Lawrence J. Freeze, III

For full biographical listings, see the Martindale-Hubbell Law Directory

MURPHY, BARTOL & O'BRIEN, LLP (AV)

Formerly Murphy & Bartol
22 Jericho Turnpike, 11501-2976
Telephone: 516-294-5100
Telecopier: 516-294-5385
Email: mbolegal@aol.com

MEMBERS OF FIRM

Patrick M. Murphy, Jr. (1938-1991)
Ernest T. Bartol
Kevin J. O'Brien

ASSOCIATE

Jeffrey P. Sharkey
Donald N. Mackenzie

OF COUNSEL

Gary F. Musiello (1952-1993)
William L. Maher
Robert M. Stein
Kathleen Godfrey Oldak

References: Republic National Bank, Great Neck, N.Y.; Northfork Bank, Mineola, N.Y.

For full biographical listings, see the Martindale-Hubbell Law Directory

NICOLINI & PARADISE (AV)

114 Old Country Road Suite 500, 11501
Telephone: 516-741-6355

MEMBERS OF FIRM

Anthony J. Nicolini
Vincent J. Paradise

Representative Clients: Long Island Railroad; NYS Liquidation Bureau; Avis Rent-A-Car System, Inc.; County of Nassau; Continental Excess & Select.

For full biographical listings, see the Martindale-Hubbell Law Directory

*MONTICELLO,** Sullivan Co.

LAWRENCE E. LAGARENNÉ (AV)

Successor to Wiess & Costa, Wiess, Ingber & Lagarenné and Ingber & Lagarenné.
230 Broadway, P.O. Box 1265, 12701
Telephone: 914-791-9400
Fax: 914-791-9407

For full biographical listings, see the Martindale-Hubbell Law Directory

NEWBURGH, Orange Co.

RIDER, WEINER, FRANKEL & CALHELHA, P.C. (AV)

655 Little Britain Road, P.O. Box 2280, 12550
Telephone: 914-562-9100
Fax: 914-562-9126
Email: firm@rwfc.com *URL:* http://www.rwfc.com

(See Next Column)

M.J. Rider (1906-1968)
Elliott M. Weiner (1915-1990)
David L. Rider
Charles E. Frankel
Moacyr R. Calhelha
Maureen Crush
Michael J. Matsler

Donna M. Badura
Mark C. Taylor
Roderick E. de Ramon
Teri L. Shulman

OF COUNSEL

Craig F. Simon
David E. Tower

LEGAL SUPPORT PERSONNEL

Lynn W. Cybulski
Aliza S. D'Agati
Carol E. Garner

For full biographical listings, see the Martindale-Hubbell Law Directory

*NEW YORK,** New York Co.

ABRAMS, GORELICK, FRIEDMAN & JACOBSON, P.C. (AV)

120 Wall Street, 10005
Telephone: 212-422-1200
Fax: 212-968-7573
Email: insurancelaw@fgfj.com
Livingston, New Jersey Office: 70 South Orange Avenue, 07039.
Telephone: 973-597-0920.
Fax: 973-535-1760.

Henry H. Abrams (1910-1977)
Mark E. Abrams
Michael E. Gorelick
Daniel J. Friedman
Glenn A. Jacobson

Melvin P. Meyer
Kevin J. Spencer
Pamela R. Wolff Cohen
Martin I. Nagel
Eric E. Rothstein
Jonathan Schaerf
Patrick J. Hayes
Ahmed Elzoghby

OF COUNSEL

Harold A. Craig, Jr.

LEGAL SUPPORT PERSONNEL

Manna Cheng

Representative Clients: Underwriters at Lloyds; New York Property Insurance Underwriting Assn.; American International Group; Jefferson Insurance Co.; Wausau Insurance Co.; Reliance National Insurance Co.; Home Depot, Inc.

For full biographical listings, see the Martindale-Hubbell Law Directory

AHMUTY, DEMERS & MCMANUS (AV)

123 William Street, 10038
Telephone: 212-513-7788
Facsimile: 212-513-7843
Email: Information@admlaw.com
Albertson, New York Office: 200 I.U. Willets Road.
Telephone: 516-294-5433.
Facsimile: 516-294-5387.
Riverhead, New York Office: 750 Roanoke Avenue.
Telephone: 516-727-2340.
Facsimile: 516-727-8198.
White Plains, New York Office: One North Broadway.
Telephone: 914-686-5050.
Facsimile: 914-686-5960.

MEMBERS OF FIRM

William R. Ahmuty, III (Resident, Albertson Office)
Philip J. McManus
Henri A. Demers (Resident, Albertson Office)
Vincent S. Ambrosino
Janice Berkowitz (Resident, Albertson Office)
Peter F. Broderick
Nicholas M. Cardascia (Resident, White Plains Office)
Maureen Casey (Resident, Albertson Office)
Frank A. Cecere (Resident, Albertson Office)
Richard J. DaVolio (Resident, Riverhead Office)
Brian J. Donnelly
James A. Edwards
Robert J. Hindman (Resident, Riverhead Office)
Diane E. Inbody (Resident, Riverhead Office)
Christopher Kendric (Resident, Albertson Office)
Edward G. Lukoski (Resident, Riverhead Office)
Kenneth R. Maguire (Resident, Albertson Office)
Thomas V. McMahon (Resident, Riverhead Office)
Kevin G. McMorrow (Resident, Albertson Office)
John A. McPhilliamy (Resident, Albertson Office)
Gary P. Muhlstock (Resident, Albertson Office)
Frank J. Pecorelli, Jr. (Resident, Albertson Office)
Michael J. Rabus
William E. Rosa
William F. Ryan
Daniel G. Sergiacomi (Resident, Albertson Office)
Robert A. Shaw
Steven L. Sidney (Resident, Albertson Office)
Frederick B. Simpson (Resident, Albertson Office)

COUNSEL

Robert E. Hirsch (Resident, Riverhead Office)
Patrick J. Kenny

(See Next Column)

AHMUTY, DEMERS & MCMANUS, *New York—Continued*

ASSOCIATES

Suzanne J. Adams
Neil H. Angel
(Resident, Albertson Office)
Frederick C. Aranki
Matthew T. Brown
Carmine J. Carolei
(Resident, White Plains Office)
Christopher P. Cartier
(Resident, Albertson Office)
Jennifer A. Casey
(Resident, Albertson Office)
Steven M. Christman
(Resident, Albertson Office)
Thomas J. Colameo
David S. Conklin
(Resident, Albertson Office)
Mark John Connolly
Christopher J. Conover
Patrick J. Cooney
(Resident, Albertson Office)
Deborah A. DelSordo
Michael Gerard Dempsey
Thomas M. DeSimone
(Resident, White Plains Office)
Matthew P. Donohue
(Resident, White Plains Office)
Debra Ann Edwards
(Resident, Albertson Office)
Paul Eschmann
George S. Evans, Jr.
Brendan T. Fitzpatrick
(Resident, Albertson Office)
Emilio F. Grillo
Keith A. Guarnuccio
Michael A. Heran
(Resident, White Plains Office)
Moriah A. Heuer
(Resident, Albertson Office)
Daniel I. Hirsch
Glenn A. Kaminska
(Resident, Albertson Office)
Andria Simone Kelly
(Resident, Albertson Office)
William A. Klaus
Peter G. Lavrenchik
(Resident, Riverhead Office)
Leslie Leonick
(Resident, Albertson Office)
Jeffrey M. Malsch
Matthew J. McDermott
Joseph M. O'Connor
(Resident, Albertson Office)
Erin M. O'Hanlon
Joseph A. Oliva
Sean J. O'Sullivan
(Resident, Albertson Office)
Gary J. Robbins
John J. Ryan
(Resident, Albertson Office)
Michael C. Salvo
Diane R. Silvergleid
John R. Sordi
(Resident, Albertson Office)
Alexandra Vandoros
Cindy Varrecchia

For full biographical listings, see the Martindale-Hubbell Law Directory

ANDERSON KILL & OLICK, P.C. (AV)

1251 Avenue of the Americas, 10020-1182
Telephone: 212-278-1000
Fax: 212-278-1733
Email: AKO@andersonkill.com *URL:* http://www.andersonkill.com
Washington, D.C. Office: Anderson Kill & Olick, L.L.P., 2000 Pennsylvania Avenue, N.W., Suite 7500.
Telephone: 202-728-3100.
Fax: 202-728-3199.
Philadelphia, Pennsylvania Office: 1600 Market Street.
Telephone: 215-568-4202.
Fax: 215-568-4573.
Newark, New Jersey Office: One Gateway Center, Suite 0901.
Telephone: 973-642-5858.
Fax: 973-621-6361.
Chicago, Illinois Office: Anderson Kill & Olick, 227 West Monroe Street, Mezzanine Level.
Telephone: 312-857-2500.
Fax: 312-857-0122.

Eugene R. Anderson
Michael A. Berkowitz
(Not admitted in NY)
John B. Berringer
Malcolm T. Brown
Jeannine W. Chanes
Steven Cooper
John H. Doyle, III
David A. Einhorn
Kirsten M. Eriksson
Jean M. Farrell
Jeremy J. Flanagan
Gloria J. Frank
Mark Garbowski
John P. Gasior
Linda Gerstel
Ann S. Ginsberg
Jeffrey L. Glatzer
Joshua Gold
Finley T. R. Harckham
Robert M. Horkovich
Edward M. Joyce
R. Mark Keenan
Thomas L. Kent
Lawrence Kill
Whitman G.S. Knapp
Ann V. Kramer
Richard P. Lewis
Sandra L. Mallenbaum
John G. Nevius
William G. Passannante
Andrea J. Pincus
Bennett Pine
Anthony Princi
J. Andrew Rahl, Jr.
Maria-Christina Ricarte
David M. Schlecker
David J. Schwartz
Edan Dawn Segal
Jordan W. Siev
Mark D. Silverschotz
Lauren B. Sobel
Edward J. Stein
(Not admitted in NY)
C. Alexander Teu
Irene C. Warshauer
Mark L. Weyman
Judith A. Yavitz
Nicholas J. Zoogman

OF COUNSEL

Roy Babitt
Dona Seeman Kahn
Arthur S. Olick
Melvin Salberg

For full biographical listings, see the Martindale-Hubbell Law Directory

ARKIN SCHAFFER & KAPLAN LLP (AV)

590 Madison Avenue, 10022
Telephone: 212-333-0200
Fax: 212-333-2350
Email: info@ARKIN-LAW.com

Stanley S. Arkin
Hyman L. Schaffer
Jeffrey M. Kaplan
Mark S. Cohen
Howard J. Kaplan

ASSOCIATES

Harry B. Feder
Sean R. O'Brien
Robert Pfeffer

OF COUNSEL

Michelle A. Rice

For full biographical listings, see the Martindale-Hubbell Law Directory

BADIAK WILL & RUDDY (AV)

Suite 1040, 120 Broadway, 10271
Telephone: 212-376-6767
Telecopier: 212-376-6777
Telex: 6716686 BANDW
Email: admiralaw@aol.com
North Miami Beach, Florida Office: Badiak, Will & Kallen, 17071 West Dixie Highway, P.O. Box 600550.
Telephone: 305-945-1851.

MEMBERS OF FIRM

Roman Badiak
Alfred J. Will
James J. Ruddy
John D. Kallen (Resident, North Miami, Florida Office)
David L. Maloof (1924-1992)

ASSOCIATES

Stephen A. Frank
Nicholas Kalfa
James P. Krauzlis
Martin L. Lindahl
Lisa A. Scognamillo
Deborah R. Reid

OF COUNSEL

Charles C. Goodenough

For full biographical listings, see the Martindale-Hubbell Law Directory

BAER MARKS & UPHAM LLP (AV)

A Partnership including a Professional Corporation
805 Third Avenue, 10022
Telephone: 212-702-5700
Fax: 212-702-5941

Howard Graff
Eugene R. Scheiman

For Complete List of Firm Personnel, See General Section

For full biographical listings, see the Martindale-Hubbell Law Directory

BAINTON MCCARTHY & SIEGEL, LLC (AV)

130 East 35th Street, 10016-3815
Telephone: 212-725-7780
Facsimile: 212-725-6920
URL: http://www.baintonlaw.com
Stamford, Connecticut Office: 400 Main Street.
Telephone: 203-323-8080.
Facsimile: 203-323-7298.

J. Joseph Bainton
John G. McCarthy
Ethan D. Siegel

For full biographical listings, see the Martindale-Hubbell Law Directory

BAKER BOTTS L.L.P. (AV)

599 Lexington Avenue, 10022-6030 and 30 Rockefeller Plaza, 10112-0228
Telephone: 212-705-5000
Fax: 212-705-5125 (599 Lexington Ave.)
Fax: 212-705-5020 (30 Rockeffeller Plaza)
Email: postmaster@bakerbotts.com *URL:* http://www.bakerbotts.com
Washington, D.C. Office: The Warner, 1299 Pennsylvania Avenue, N.W.
Telephone: 202-639-7700.
Austin, Texas Office: 1600 San Jacinto Center, 98 San Jacinto Boulevard.
Telephone: 512-322-2500.
Dallas, Texas Office: 2001 Ross Avenue.
Telephone: 214-953-6500.
Houston, Texas Office: One Shell Plaza, 910 Louisiana.
Telephone: 713-229-1234.
Moscow, Russia Office: 10 ul. Bolshaya Dimitrovka (formerly ul. Pushkinskaya), 103031.
Telephone: 7095/921-5300 (Local); 7095/929-7070 (International).
London, England Office: 45 Ludgate Hill.
Telephone: 0171-778-1400 (Local); 011-44-171-778-1400.
Baku, Azerbaijan Office: 6-10 Vagif Mustafa-zadeh Street, Third Floor, Icheri Sheher, 370004.
Telephone: 994-12-97-63-88 (Local); 011-994-12-97-63-88 (International).
Fax: 994-12-97-63-91 (Local); 011-994-12-97-63-61 (International).

MEMBERS OF FIRM

Kenneth M. Bialo
Michael A. Lippert

(See Next Column)

BAKER BOTTS L.L.P.—*Continued*

SPECIAL COUNSEL

Thomas R. Trowbridge, III

OF COUNSEL

Bertram Perkel

ASSOCIATES

Adam Dick
Kristin G. Francis (Not admitted in NY)
Matthew K. McCoy
Anne W. Salisbury
Michael L. Shore

For Complete List of Firm Personnel, See General Section

For full biographical listings, see the Martindale-Hubbell Law Directory

BARRETT GRAVANTE CARPINELLO & STERN LLP (AV)

570 Lexington Avenue, 10022
Telephone: 212-446-2300
Telecopier: 212-446-2350
Albany, New York Office: 100 State Street, 12207.
Telephone: 518-434-0600.
Telecopier: 518-434-0665.
Fort Lauderdale, Florida Office: Barnett Bank Plaza, One East Broward Boulevard, 33301.
Telephone: 954-356-0011.
Telecopier: 954-356-0022.

David A. Barrett
Nicholas A. Gravante, Jr.
George F. Carpinello
Jack G. Stern
Michael I. Endler
Harlan A. Levy
Kathleen M. Franklin
Roland G. Riopelle
Steven I. Froot
Andrew B. Peretz, P.A.
Carla E. Hogan

OF COUNSEL

Michael Straus
Howard A. Wintner
Norman P. Fivel
Karen Martino Valle
Philippa Bainbridge

Jeffrey S. Shelly
Kenneth G. Walsh
Philip J. Iovieno
Evan Glassman
Bradley J. Gross (Resident, Fort Lauderdale, Florida Office)
Jessica M. Tourk
Magda M. Jimenez
Kahlia E. Fisher
Elizabeth Ann Butler
Ryan K. Higgins

For full biographical listings, see the Martindale-Hubbell Law Directory

BARRY, MCTIERNAN & MOORE (AV)

25 Broadway, 10004
Telephone: 212-509-8999
Fax: 212-509-5258
White Plains, New York Office: 175 Main Street.
Telephone: 914-946-1030.
Fax: 914-946-3814.
Jersey City, New Jersey Office: 75 Montgomery Street, 07302.
Telephone: 201-333-0300.
Fax: 201-333-0639.

MEMBERS OF FIRM

Desmond T. Barry (1906-1975)
Roger P. McTiernan
Roger Paul McTiernan, Jr.
Patricia A. Sullivan
James L. Moran
Suzanne M. Halbardier

ASSOCIATES

Katherine Hargas
William E. Fay, III
Kevin Gerard Maguire
Patricia A. McTiernan-Moore
Richard Wayne Wedinger
Dennis A. Breen
John V. Wynne
Regine Dely-Lazard
Mark A. Collesano
Mark P. Hannafey
Suey K. Chung
Michael E. Jones
Diana DeCesare-Treitler
William D. Joyce, III
Jeffrey Miller
Laurel Wedinger-Gyimesi
William A. Cooney
Christopher Sommer
Edwin F. Lambert, Jr.
Anthony J. McNulty

OF COUNSEL

John J. Moore

For full biographical listings, see the Martindale-Hubbell Law Directory

BAUMEISTER & SAMUELS, P.C. (AV)

One Exchange Plaza, 10006-3008
Telephone: 212-363-1200
Telecopier: 212-363-1346
Email: BAUMSAM@AOL.COM
Morristown, New Jersey Office: 1776 On The Green, P.O. Box 1116, 07962-1116.
Telephone: 973-267-6666.
Telecopier: 973-605-1812.

Michel F. Baumeister
Douglas A. Latto
Dorothea M. Capone

(See Next Column)

OF COUNSEL

Lynn F. Samuels
Robert S. Franklin
Marc Z. Edell

For full biographical listings, see the Martindale-Hubbell Law Directory

BEATIE AND OSBORN LLP (AV)

599 Lexington Avenue, 42nd Floor, 10022
Telephone: 212-888-9000
Fax: 212-888-9664
Email: bandolaw@aol.com *URL:* http://www.bandolaw@aol.com

Russel H. Beatie, Jr.
Daniel A. Osborn

ASSOCIATES

Curt D. Marshall
Eduard Korsinsky

OF COUNSEL

Richard M. Cummings

For full biographical listings, see the Martindale-Hubbell Law Directory

BELAIR & EVANS LLP (AV)

61 Broadway Suite 1320, 10006
Telephone: 212-344-3900
Facsimile: 212-514-6661
Cable Address: "Caduceus" New York
Telex: 226000
URL: http://www.belairevans.com
Mineola, New York Office: 136 Willis Avenue.
Telephone: 516-741-4800.

MEMBERS OF FIRM

Raymond W. Belair
John T. Evans
Lawrence W. Burnett
Brian P. Flynn

Jacqueline E. Sheehan-Hemmingson
Robert Radman
Andrew R. Leder
Michael J. Gudzy
Matthew J. Ross
James B. Reich
Robert L. Kerner, Jr.
Michael A. Swimmer
Randall M. Elfenbein
Brian T. Stapleton
Kevin E. Way

For full biographical listings, see the Martindale-Hubbell Law Directory

BELDOCK LEVINE & HOFFMAN LLP (AV)

99 Park Avenue, 10016-1503
Telephone: 212-490-0400
Cable Address: "Telhofflaw, N.Y."
Telecopier: 212-557-0565
URL: http://www.blhny.com

MEMBERS OF FIRM

Lee F. Bantle
Myron Beldock
Karen L. Dippold
Elliot L. Hoffman
Lawrence S. Levine
Jon B. Levison
Brian E. Maas
Cynthia Rollings
Melvin L. Wulf

For full biographical listings, see the Martindale-Hubbell Law Directory

BERLACK, ISRAELS & LIBERMAN LLP (AV)

120 West 45th Street, 10036
Telephone: 212-704-0100
Cable Address: "Berilib"
Telecopier: 212-704-0196
Email: info@berlack.com
Morristown, New Jersey Office: 65 Madison Avenue.
Telephone: 201-644-3400.
Telecopier: 201-644-3159.

MEMBERS OF FIRM

Harris Berlack (1946-1968)
Carlos L. Israels (1946-1969)
Kenneth R. Asher
Claude A. Baum
Scott M. Berman
Wade M. Boswell
Douglas E. Davidson
Alan N. Forman
Steven E. Greenbaum
Harvey M. Katz
James B. Liberman
Stuart Neuhauser
Robert D. Schmicker
Martin S. Siegel
Steven F. Wasserman
Edward S. Weisfelner

SENIOR ATTORNEYS

Andrew S. Dash
Erica M. Ryland

ASSOCIATES

John P. Biedermann
Anne M. Cunningham
Pauline Foley (Resident, Morristown, New Jersey Office)
Julie L. Friedberg (Resident, Morristown, New Jersey Office)
Emilio A. Galván
Linda B. Goebel
Louis Lombardo
Rachel F. Mayerson (Not admitted in NY)
Amy P. K. Motzenbecker (Resident, Morristown, New Jersey Office)
Antonio Peguero, Jr.
Elizabeth Quirk (Resident, Morristown, New Jersey Office)
Marcela M. Sanchez
Melissa Sarubbi

(See Next Column)

BERLACK, ISRAELS & LIBERMAN LLP, *New York—Continued*

OF COUNSEL

Gerald W. Conway (Not admitted in NY; Resident, Morristown, New Jersey Office)
Marc B. Lasky (Resident, Morristown, New Jersey Office)

For full biographical listings, see the Martindale-Hubbell Law Directory

BLATT, HAMMESFAHR & EATON (AV)

45 Broadway 12th Floor, 10006
Telephone: 212-363-1900
Fax: 212-363-2600
Email: bhe@bhelaw.com *URL:* HTTP://WWW.BHELAW.COM
Chicago, Illinois Office: 333 W. Wacker Drive, Suite 1900.
Telephone: 312-849-8000.
FAX: 312-357-0198. Email: BHE@BHELAW.COM. URL: HTTP://WWW.BHELAW.COM.

MEMBERS OF FIRM

Robert W. Hammesfahr
Elliot S. Orol
Scott W. Wright

ASSOCIATES

Veronica K. Danko
Dana Loughran

For full biographical listings, see the Martindale-Hubbell Law Directory

BORSTEIN & SHEINBAUM (AV)

420 Lexington Avenue, Suite 2920, 10170-0002
Telephone: 212-687-1600
Fax: 212-687-8710
URL: http://www.lawyers.com/borsteinsheinbaum
Ghent, New York Office: 2542 Route 66, 12075.
Telephone: 518-392-6276.
Fax: 518-392-6776.

Leon Baer Borstein
James B. Sheinbaum

For full biographical listings, see the Martindale-Hubbell Law Directory

BROWN RAYSMAN MILLSTEIN FELDER & STEINER LLP (AV)

120 West Forty-Fifth Street, 10036
Telephone: 212-944-1515
Fax: 212-840-2429
URL: http://www.brownraysman.com
Los Angeles, California Office: 1880 Century Park East, Suite 711.
Telephone: 310-712-8300.
Fax: 310-712-8383.
Hartford, Connecticut Office: City Place II, 185 Asylum Street, 10th Floor.
Telephone: 860-275-6400.
Fax: 860-275-6410.
Morristown, New Jersey Office: 55 Madison Avenue, Suite 70.
Telephone: 973-285-3222.
Fax: 973-538-0503.
Uniondale, New York Office: EAB Plaza, West Tower, 6th Floor, 11556-0615 (Long Island).
Telephone: 516-522-2520.
Fax: 516-522-2731.

MEMBERS OF FIRM

Richard Raysman
Peter Brown
Julian S. Millstein
Barry G. Felder
Jeffrey B. Steiner
Robert M. Unger
Edward A. Pisacreta
Catherine M. McGrath
Kenneth M. Block
Henry J. Silberberg
Kenneth A. Adler
Rand G. Boyers
Jeffrey D. Neuburger
Norman H. Roos (Resident, Hartford, Connecticut Office)
Benzion J. Westreich (Resident, Los Angeles, California Office)
Monte E. Wetzler (Resident, Hartford, Connecticut Office)
Sarah Hewitt
R. Kenneth MacCallum
Andrew L. Kramer
Jeffrey P. Weingart
J. Christopher Giancarlo
Maureen Massa
Scott A. Weinberg
Seth H. Ostrow
Harold A. Flegelman
Carla E. Craig
William E. Bandon, III
Beverly W. Garofalo (Resident, Hartford, Connecticut Office)
Russell V. D'Italia (Resident, Morristown, New Jersey Office)
Frank J. De Rosa
Stuart Bressman
Robert D. Gilbert (Resident, Hartford, Connecticut Office)
Fredric M. Sanders

COUNSEL

Michael A. Gerber
Yukio Kashiba
H. David Leventhal (Resident, Hartford, Connecticut Office)
Edward P. Tolley, Jr.
Jonathan T. Kaplan

(See Next Column)

ASSOCIATES

Samuel L. Molinari (Resident, Hartford, Connecticut Office)
Shoshana B. Botnick (Resident, Los Angeles, California Office)
James R. Kinyon (Resident, Hartford, Connecticut Office)
M. Lauren McGill
Candace M. Cunningham (Resident, Hartford, Connecticut Office)
Melanie Finkel
Nancy J. Mertzel
Timothy J. Martin (Resident, Los Angeles, California Office)
Louis Greco
Lauren E. McCollester
Frank A. Pugliese
Anthony J. Natoli
Marc S. Roth
Brooks Sandeman Clark
Susan L. Loring Crane
John A. Gliedman
Diane Duhaime (Resident, Hartford, Connecticut Office)
John C. Ohman
Mitchell L. Fishberg (Resident, Hartford, Connecticut Office)
Robert S. Mower
Jeremy Pomeroy
Kevin C. Taylor
Randy Ilene Monkarsh
Jill Amanda Westmoreland
Michael D. Maline
Larry Liberchuk (Not admitted in NY)
Matthew D. Moren
Marc Seewald Brodsky
Jenevra Georgini
Ira Wurcel
John M. Mrsich
Leo K. Chen
Rebecca A. Tapie
Andrew E. Miller
Robert Siedlecki, Jr. (Resident, Hartford, Connecticut Office)
Laura Land Sigal
Irene E. Bassock (Resident, Hartford, Connecticut Office)
Edward J. Leen
Steve A. Semerdjian
Karen D. Nemeth
John M. Strong
Jason R. Goldstein
Jason S. Stevens
Herbert H. Detrick II
Ronald M. Leshnower
Toni S. Jordan
Richard L. Green (Resident, Hartford, Connecticut Office)
Lindsay Mara Schoen
Wayne R. Kaufman
Viktoria Makarevich
John D. Gigante
Vincent Laspisa III
Kristen J. Mathews
Dax Scharfstein
John F. Greco

For full biographical listings, see the Martindale-Hubbell Law Directory

CALLAN, REGENSTREICH, KOSTER & BRADY (AV)

One Whitehall Street 10th Floor, 10004
Telephone: 212-248-8800
Fax: 212-248-6815
Shrewsbury, New Jersey Office: 740 Broad Street.
Telephone: 732-345-9333.
Fax: 732-345-9444.
Garden City, New York Office: 1205 Franklin Avenue.
Telephone: 516-294-4383.
Fax: 516-294-4386.

MEMBERS OF FIRM

Paul F. Callan
Bruce N. Regenstreich
Warren S. Koster
Bruce M. Brady
William L. Brennan
Vincent A. Nagler
Scott W. Bermack

ASSOCIATES

Kenneth S. Merber
Michael P. Kandler
Vincent D. Finnegan
Stephanie Palermo
Walter Paterson Burrell
Beth S. Block
Meredith B. Borg
Pamela Patton Fynes
Mara J. Sibley
Eric A. Wasserfall
Amie Catherine Kalac (Resident, Shrewsbury, New Jersey Office)
Lisa B. Katz

For full biographical listings, see the Martindale-Hubbell Law Directory

CAPLIN & DRYSDALE, CHARTERED (AV)

399 Park Avenue 36th Floor, 10022
Telephone: 212-319-7125
Fax: 212-644-6755
Washington, D.C. Office: One Thomas Circle, N.W.
Telephone: 202-862-5000.
Fax: 202-429-3301.

Elihu Inselbuch

Rita C. Tobin

For full biographical listings, see the Martindale-Hubbell Law Directory

BRUCE G. CLARK & ASSOCIATES (AV)

Room 3600 Woolworth Building, 233 Broadway, 10279
Telephone: 212-227-0020
Fax: 212-233-4247
URL: http://www.medicalmallaw.com
Email: brucegclark@compuserve.com *URL:* http://www.lawyers.com/medmal

Peter L. Gale
Valerie Ullman Taylor
Rhona A. Silverman
Beth Nancy Alson

For full biographical listings, see the Martindale-Hubbell Law Directory

New York—Continued

CLIFFORD CHANCE ROGERS & WELLS LLP (AV)

Two Hundred Park Avenue, 10166-0153
Telephone: 212-878-8000
Facsimile: 212-878-8375
Telex: 234493 RKWUR
URL: http://www.cliffordchance.com
Washington, D.C. Office: 607 Fourteenth Street, N.W., Washington, D.C. 20005-2018.
Telephone: 202-434-0700.
Facsimile: 202-434-0800.
Other Offices: Amsterdam, Bangkok, Barcelona, Berlin, Brussels, Budapest, Dubai, Dusseldorf, Frankfurt, Hanoi, Ho Chi Minh City, Hong Kong, Leipzig, London, Madrid, Milan, Moscow, Munich, Padua, Paris, Prague, Rome, Sao Paulo, Shanghai, Singapore, Tokyo, Warsaw.

PARTNERS

Kevin J. Arquit
Leora Ben-Ami
James N. Benedict
John K. Carroll
Dennis J. Drebsky
Joseph Ferraro
Mark Holland
John E. Kidd
Mark A. Kirsch
C. Joseph Laughon, II
Donald F. Luke
David Meister
James W. Paul
Robert Penchina
Mark F. Pomerantz
James M. Ringer
Philip E. Roux
David A. Schulz
Victor Siber
Margaret Blair Soyster
Craig M. Walker
James B. Weidner
Richard N. Winfield

WASHINGTON, D.C. OFFICE

PARTNERS

Kenneth A. Gallo
Ira D. Hammerman
John Paul Ketels
Steven A. Newborn
Michael A. O'Shea
Joseph J. Simons
Dale C. Turza

For Complete List of Firm Personnel, See General Section

For full biographical listings, see the Martindale-Hubbell Law Directory

COBRIN & GITTES (AV)

750 Lexington Avenue, 10022
Telephone: 212-486-4000
Telecopier: 212-486-4007
Email: cgpats@ix.netcom.com

Peter T. Cobrin
Marvin S. Gittes
Richard M. Lehrer
David W. Denenberg

Robert J. Hess
Michael A. Adler
Gerald J. Cechony (Not admitted in NY)
Oren J. Warshavsky
Clyde Alvin Shuman
Lawrence E. Russ

Representative Clients: Northern Telecom, Inc.; DataPoint Corporation; Magnivision, Inc.; Atico; Global Direct Mail Corporation; MW; Oxigene, Inc.; Horphag Research, LTD.

For full biographical listings, see the Martindale-Hubbell Law Directory

FREDERICK H. COHN (AV)

500 Fifth Avenue, 33rd Floor, 10110
Telephone: 212-768-1110
Fax: 212-764-3701
Email: fcohn@interport.net *URL:* http://www.lawyers.com/frederickcohn

For full biographical listings, see the Martindale-Hubbell Law Directory

COOPERMAN LEVITT WINIKOFF LESTER & NEWMAN, P.C. (AV)

800 Third Avenue, 10022-7601
Telephone: 212-688-7000
Fax: 212-755-2839
URL: http://www.clwln.com
Long Island, New York Office: 1129 Northern Boulevard, Manhasset, 11030.
Telephone: 516-365-1400.
Fax: 516-365-1404.

Robert N. Cooperman
Jack B. Levitt
Robert L. Winikoff
David S. Lester
David B. Newman
Asher H. Miller
H. Frances Kleiner
Harry J. Petchesky
Elliot E. Brecher
Ira I. Roxland
Harris S. Jaffe
Mark L. Lubin
Allen G. Reiter

OF COUNSEL

Vivian L. Dubin

(See Next Column)

Edward J. Reich
Barry A. Cassell
Gary S. Sastow
Susan Denburg Yellin
Joseph H. Schmitt
Stephen Brodsky
Stephen E. Fox
Jill L. Schechterman (Not admitted in NY)
Carol B. Koch
Stephen W. Semian
Helise Harrington

For full biographical listings, see the Martindale-Hubbell Law Directory

THE LAW OFFICES OF MICHAEL E. CURAN, P.C. (AV)

59 John Street, Third Floor, 10038
Telephone: 212-513-1578
Fax: 212-513-1592

Michael E. Curan

Anthony Van Zwaren
Robert J. Callahan
Steven R. Mitlitzky

OF COUNSEL

William H. Maloney, Jr.

For full biographical listings, see the Martindale-Hubbell Law Directory

CURTIS, MALLET-PREVOST, COLT & MOSLE LLP (AV)

101 Park Avenue, 10178-0061
Telephone: 212-696-6000
Telecopier: 212-697-1559
Email: info@cm-p.com *URL:* http://www.cm-p.com
Washington, D.C. Office: Suite 1205L, 1801 K Street, N.W.
Telephone: 202-452-7373.
Telecopier: 202-452-7333.
Newark, New Jersey Office: One Gateway Center, Suite 403.
Telephone: 973-622-0605.
Telecopier: 973-622-5646.
Houston, Texas Office: 2 Houston Center, 909 Fannin Street, Suite 3725.
Telephone: 713-759-9555.
Telecopier: 713-759-0712.
Stamford, Connecticut Office: One Canterbury Green.
Telephone: 203-359-6200.
Telecopier: 203-328-2617.
Mexico City, D.F., Mexico Office: Curtis, Mallet-Prevost, Colt & Mosle, Ruben Dario 281, Piso 9, Col. Bosque de Chapultepec, 11530 Mexico, D.F.
Telephone: 525-282-0444.
Telecopier: 525-282-0637.
Paris, France Office: 15 rue d'Astorg, 75008.
Telephone: +33-1 42-66-39-10.
Telecopier: +33-1 42-66-39-62.
London, England Office: Two Throgmorton Avenue, EC2N 2DL.
Telephone: 0207-638-7957.
Telecopier: 0207-638-5512.
Frankfurt am Main 1, Germany Office: Staufenstrasse 42.
Telephone: +49-69-971-4420.
Telecopier: +49-69-17 33 99.
Muscat, Sultanate of Oman Office: Jewel Beach-134.
Telephone: 968-607-725.
Telecopier: 968-607-724.
Milan, Italy Office: Curtis, Mallet-Prevost & Gilioli, Piazzale Principessa Clotilde 8, 20121.
Telephone: +(39) 02 29 00 29 32.
Telefax: +(39) 02 65 75 969.

MEMBERS OF FIRM

Peter E. Fleming Jr.
T. Barry Kingham
Eliot Lauer
Robert S. Lipton
Joseph D. Pizzurro
Jacques Semmelman
Turner P. Smith
Martin Wendel (Resident Partner, Newark, New Jersey Office)

For full biographical listings, see the Martindale-Hubbell Law Directory

D'AMATO & LYNCH (AV)

70 Pine Street, 10270-0110
Telephone: 212-269-0927
Cable Address: "Damcosh"
Telex: 960085 DCOS UI NYK
Telefax: 212-269-3559

Luke D. Lynch (1921-1999)

MEMBERS OF FIRM

George G. D'Amato
Kenneth A. Sagat
Luke D. Lynch, Jr.
Robert E. Kushner
Richard George
Robert M. Makla
Richard F. Russell
Ronald H. Alenstein
Harry J. Arnold, Jr.
Philip J. Bergan
Robert W. Lang
Neal M. Glazer
Andrew R. Simmonds
John P. Higgins
Thomas F. Breen
Alfred A. D'Agostino, Jr.
William P. Larsen, III
Robert D. Lang
David A. Boyar
Mary Jo Barry
Barbara R. Seymour
Bill V. Kakoullis
Thomas Ward Hanlon, Jr.
John H. FitzSimons

(See Next Column)

D'AMATO & LYNCH, *New York—Continued*

MEMBERS OF FIRM (Continued)

Michael Latham Manire
Kevin J. Windels
Samuel F. Paniccia
William C. Burton
Harvey Barrison

ASSOCIATES

Laurie P. Beatus
Anna E. Bomstein
Frances Buckley
Carla S. Caliendo
Roy T. Caplinger
Kevin P. Carroll
Catherine L. Casavant
Liza A. Chafiian
James D. Christo
Judy Y. Chung
Deborah M. Collins
Mary Lee Cunningham
Daniel J. Curry
Thomas G. Darmody
Michael J. Devereaux
Daniel J. Dolcetti, Jr.
Jan H. Duffalo
Maria T. Ehrlich
Richard F. Ferrigno
Robert S. Fraser
Deeanna M. Galla
Jeffrey R. Gaylord
Lloyd J. Herman
Donna Marie Hughes
David J. Kuffler
Jason M. Lesko
Shari H. Lichtman
Cindy Liu
John J. Maalouf
Annemarie J. Mazzone
Brendon M. McNamara
Neil R. Morrison
Victor F. Mustelier
Anthony C. Pace
John J. Patterson
Edward M. Roth
Sanjit S. Shah
Jennifer G. Smith
Arthur Steinberg
Peter A. Stroili
Maryann Taylor
James E. Tolan, II
Richard S. Trostle
Humphrey O. Uddoh
Johnston de Forest Whitman, Jr
Stephen F. Willig
Robert M. Yellen

COUNSEL

Robert E. Gilroy
Richard G. McGahren
Peter J. Thumser
John J. Cullen
Albert B. Lewis
Charles H. Witherwax
Charles Bramham

For full biographical listings, see the Martindale-Hubbell Law Directory

DANKNER & MILSTEIN, P.C. (AV)

41 East 57th Street, 10022
Telephone: 212-751-8000
Facsimile: 212-751-8091
Email: danmilster@aol.com

Jay W. Dankner
Edward P. Milstein

Edward A. Ruffo
James P. Lundy
Aaron M. Cohen

For full biographical listings, see the Martindale-Hubbell Law Directory

DE BLASIO, FIGMAN, EPSTEIN & LA ROCCA, P.C. (AV)

Woolworth Building, 233 Broadway, 10279
Telephone: 212-732-2620
Fax: 212-571-2045

Peter E. De Blasio
Alan H. Figman
Steven A. Epstein
Stephen S. La Rocca
John A. Orbon

For full biographical listings, see the Martindale-Hubbell Law Directory

DE ORCHIS, WALKER & CORSA, LLP (AV)

One Battery Park Plaza, Second Floor, 10004-1480
Telephone: 212-344-4700
MCI Telex: 673-4608
Telefax: 212-509-7886
Email: DW&C@MCIMAIL.COM *URL:* http://www.marinelex.com
Union, New Jersey Office: 1495 Morris Avenue, P.O. Box 1718.
Telephone: 973-467-4740.
Telefax: 908-687-0255.
Stamford, Connecticut Office: 999 Summer Street.
Telephone: 203-323-9120.
Telefax: 203-323-9015.
Boston, Massachusetts Office: One Boston Place, 5th Floor, 02180.
Telephone: 617-619-3610.
Telefax: 617-619-3924.
Miami, Florida Office: De Orchis, Corsa & Hillerbrand, LLP, 2650 Biscayne Boulevard, 33137.
Telephone: 305-571-9200.
Telefax: 305-571-9250.

PARTNERS

LeRoy S. Corsa
Vincent M. De Orchis
Christopher H. Mansuy
Alexander V. Sansone
John A. Orzel
Michael E. Unger
Cary R. Wiener

ASSOCIATES

R. Brett Kelly
William E. Lakis
Marc I. Kunkin
Francesco A. Di Pietro

(See Next Column)

RESIDENT COUNSEL

M. E. De Orchis

OF COUNSEL

Ara A. Shimshidian
Bruce H. Neuman

For full biographical listings, see the Martindale-Hubbell Law Directory

EMERY CUTI BRINCKERHOFF & ABADY PC (AV)

545 Madison Avenue, 3rd Floor, 10022-4219
Telephone: 212-763-5000
Facsimile: 212-763-5001
Email: mail@ecbalaw.com *URL:* http://www.ecbalaw.com

Richard D. Emery
Matthew D. Brinckerhoff
Jonathan S. Abady
John R. Cuti

Ilann M. Maazel
David H. Gans
Alexandra D. Lahav (Not admitted in NY)

For full biographical listings, see the Martindale-Hubbell Law Directory

FISHER, FISHER & BERGER (AV)

A Partnership including a Professional Corporation
One Whitehall Street, 10004
Telephone: 212-514-8888
Fax: 212-514-9016
Email: fisherberger@earthlink.net

Andrew S. Fisher, P.C.
Henry T. Berger

ASSOCIATES

Melinda H. Vollmer
Eric L. Cooper
Diane C. Lorenc

OF COUNSEL

Harold L. Fisher
Judith E. Held
Gerald A. Resnick
Robert A. Straniere
Stanley Kalmon Schlein
Laurence J. Kaiser

Reference: The Chase Manhattan Bank, N.A.

For full biographical listings, see the Martindale-Hubbell Law Directory

FORD MARRIN ESPOSITO WITMEYER & GLESER, L.L.P. (AV)

Wall Street Plaza, 10005-1875
Telephone: 212-269-4900
Facsimile: 212-344-4294
Cable Address: "Formarew-New York"
Email: postmaster@fmew.com *URL:* http://www.fmew.com
Montclair, New Jersey Office: 49 Park Street.
Telephone: 973-744-3700.
Facsimile: 973-509-1565.

MEMBERS OF FIRM

James M. Adrian
Michael L. Anania
Charles A. Booth
Cushing O'Malley Condon
Elizabeth M. De Cristofaro
Thomas R. Esposito
William P. Ford
Victor G. Gleser (1948-1992)
Stuart C. Levene
Richard B. Marrin
Edward M. Pinter
Philip S. Plexico (1931-1983)
John J. Witmeyer III

COUNSEL

James F. X. Hiler

ASSOCIATES

Jay R. Alicandri
Jody M. Barringer
David A. Beke
Christopher J. Carney
Todd S. Corey
Joseph D'Ambrosio
Serena C. Hunn
Matthew J. Lasky
Paul V. Majkowski
Michael A. Rowe
Michael J. Tricarico

For full biographical listings, see the Martindale-Hubbell Law Directory

FOX HORAN & CAMERINI LLP (AV)

One Broadway, 10004
Telephone: 212-480-4800
Telecopier: 212-269-2383; 212-709-0248
Email: webmaster@foxhoran.com *URL:* http://www.foxhoran.com

MEMBERS OF FIRM

Donald T. Fox
John R. Horan
Ezequiel A. Camerini
Patrick L. Ferriere
Rafael A. Ginebra
Alan R. Johnson
Michael F. Johnston
Kathleen M. Kundar
Robert Courtney Mangone
Edward C. Marschner
Clifford A. Rathkopf, Jr.
Oleg Rivkin
Christopher H. Seymour
Eduardo L. Tabio

OF COUNSEL

Rafael Urquia II

(See Next Column)

FOX HORAN & CAMERINI LLP—*Continued*

ASSOCIATES

David C. Camerini
Drew G.L. Chapman
William S. Kogan
Eric Lindquist
V. David Rivkin

For full biographical listings, see the Martindale-Hubbell Law Directory

FRIEDMAN KAPLAN & SEILER LLP (AV)

875 Third Avenue, 10022-6225
Telephone: 212-833-1100
Facsimile: 212-355-6401
Email: info@fkslaw.com
Newark, New Jersey Office: One Gateway Center, 25th Floor, 07102-5311.
Telephone: 973-297-4700.
Facsimile: 973-297-4701.

MEMBERS OF FIRM

Bruce S. Kaplan
Edward A. Friedman
Barry A. Adelman
Eric Seiler
Robert D. Kaplan
Gary D. Friedman
Andrew W. Goldwater
Robert J. Lack
Gregg S. Lerner
Hal Neier
Philippe Adler
Matthew S. Haiken
Paul J. Fishman
Richard M. Hoffman
Lance J. Gotko

COUNSEL

Robert D. Wurwarg
Ira A. Freedman

ASSOCIATES

Craig J. Codlin
Michael B. Dorff
Andrew R. Greengrass
Ellen A. Harnick
Sophia S. Hartch
Mishell B. Kneeland
Robert S. Loigman
Craig Nemiroff
Joshua M. Olshin
Katherine L. Pringle
Daniel B. Rapport
Meryl S. Rosenblatt
Robert C. Scherer
Donna Segal
Jonathan M. Silver
Lee D. Sossen
David I. Tanenbaum
Marla J. Wasserman
Sian E. Zelbo

For full biographical listings, see the Martindale-Hubbell Law Directory

FRIEDMAN, WITTENSTEIN & HOCHMAN, A PROFESSIONAL CORPORATION (AV)

101 East 52nd Street, 10022
Telephone: 212-750-8700
Telecopier: 212-223-8391
Email: friedwitt@aol.com

Stuart I. Friedman
Andrew A. Wittenstein

COUNSEL

Stephen A. Hochman
John T. McLoughlin (Not admitted in NY)

Mary Hillyer Dontzin
Paul S. Grossman
David O. Lloyd
Gianna M. McCarthy
Allison D. Powell

For full biographical listings, see the Martindale-Hubbell Law Directory

FRYER & ROSS (AV)

551 Fifth Avenue, 10176
Telephone: 212-286-0099
Telecopier: 212-286-0495
Email: geraldross@fryerross.com *URL:* http://www.fryerross.com

MEMBERS OF FIRM

Gerald E. Ross
Hugh N. Fryer

OF COUNSEL

Daniel P. Levitt

For full biographical listings, see the Martindale-Hubbell Law Directory

FUCHSBERG & FUCHSBERG (AV)

100 Church Street, 18th Floor, 10007
Telephone: 212-962-2800
Fax: 212-385-2308

MEMBERS OF FIRM

Abraham Fuchsberg
Seymour Fuchsberg
Preston J. Douglas
Stephen M. Warner

Harvey Goldstein
Irwin M. Berg
Bruce H. Goldstone
Martin Diennor
Maurice Sieradzki
Mordecai T. Schwartz
Frank P. Nervo
Richard Cohen
Iris Claire Finder
Thomas A. Agoglia
Robert M. Futterman
Richard V. Zand
John C. Henninger
Roger N. Lavinsky

(See Next Column)

Joseph Campisi
Devin P. Cohen
David Jacobs
Alan D. Bernstein
Ari Michael Gross

For full biographical listings, see the Martindale-Hubbell Law Directory

GAIR, GAIR, CONASON, STEIGMAN & MACKAUF (AV)

80 Pine Street, 10005
Telephone: 212-943-1090
Fax: 212-425-7513
Email: mail@gairgair.com *URL:* http://www.gairgair.com

MEMBERS OF FIRM

Harry A. Gair (1894-1975)
Robert L. Conason
Seymour Boyers
Ernest R. Steigman
Stephen H. Mackauf
Jerome I. Katz
David G. Miller
Candice Singer Ram
Jeffrey B. Bloom
Anthony H. Gair
Ben B. Rubinowitz
Howard S. Hershenhorn
Mary Nicholls
Rhonda E. Kay

APPELLATE COUNSEL

Herman Schmertz

ASSOCIATES

Herbert H. Hirschhorn
Warren J. Willinger
Ronald Berson
Vincent F. Maher
Daniel A. Gair
Richard M. Steigman
Diana M.A. Carnemolla

COUNSEL

Harriet E. Gair

For full biographical listings, see the Martindale-Hubbell Law Directory

GALLET DREYER & BERKEY, LLP (AV)

845 Third Avenue, 10022-6601
Telephone: 212-935-3131
Telecopier: 212-935-4514
Email: gdb@gdblaw.com *URL:* http://www.gdblaw.com

MEMBERS OF FIRM

Simon Gallet (1914-1974)
Stanley B. Dreyer
David L. Berkey
Ray Beckerman
Benjamin S. Klapper
Seymour D. Reich
Sidney Ingber
John W. Manning
Jerome S. Solomon
Harvey Schwartz
Perry L. Mintz

Beatrice Lesser
Morlan Ty Rogers
Christina M. Ambrosio
Jeffrey S. Harwin
Regina M. Marotti
Natasha Leigh Nordahl
Carole M. Bass

For full biographical listings, see the Martindale-Hubbell Law Directory

GARSON GERSPACH DECORATO & COHEN, LLP (AV)

One Whitehall Street, Tenth Floor, 10004
Telephone: 212-742-8700
Fax: 212-742-1471
Email: ASGGGDC@aol.com *URL:* http://www.MEDILAW@aol.com

Andrew S. Garson
Thomas J. Gerspach
Linda J. DeCorato
Joshua R. Cohen

For full biographical listings, see the Martindale-Hubbell Law Directory

GETNICK & GETNICK (AV)

Tower 49, 12 East 49th Street, 31st Floor, 10017-1028
Telephone: 212-376-5666
Telefax: 212-292-3942
Email: info@getnicklaw.com *URL:* http://www.lawyers.com/getnick&getnick

MEMBERS OF FIRM

Irving M. Getnick
Neil V. Getnick
Lesley Ann Skillen
Margaret J. Finerty

OF COUNSEL

David A. Koenigsberg
Michael E. Getnick

ASSOCIATE

Richard J. Dircks

For full biographical listings, see the Martindale-Hubbell Law Directory

GINSBERG & BROOME (AV)

225 Broadway, Suite 3105, 10007
Telephone: 212-227-4225
Fax: 212-227-4228

Robert M. Ginsberg
Alvin H. Broome

ASSOCIATE

Christopher Jon Longman

(See Next Column)

GINSBERG & BROOME, *New York—Continued*

OF COUNSEL

Jody H. Brackman
Anna Lewis
Simon Ginsberg

For full biographical listings, see the Martindale-Hubbell Law Directory

JAY GOLDBERG, P.C. (AV)

Twentieth Floor, 250 Park Avenue, 10177-2099
Telephone: 212-983-6000
Telecopier: 212-983-6008
Telex: 5101008171

Jay Goldberg

Debra A. Karlstein
Steven D. Isser

OF COUNSEL

Seth Ginsberg

Representative Clients: Donald Trump; Carl Icahn; Willie Nelson; Kris Kristofferson; Riddick Bowe.

For full biographical listings, see the Martindale-Hubbell Law Directory

GOLDMAN & HAFETZ (AV)

500 Fifth Avenue 29th Floor, 10110
Telephone: 212-997-7400
Fax: 212-997-7597
Email: info@goldman-hafetz.com

MEMBERS OF FIRM

Lawrence S. Goldman
Frederick P. Hafetz
Susan R. Necheles

ASSOCIATES

Elizabeth M. Johnson
Jill R. Shellow-Lavine (Not admitted in NY)
William H. Devaney

For full biographical listings, see the Martindale-Hubbell Law Directory

GOLDSTEIN & MORRIS, LLP (AV)

570 Lexington Avenue, 34th Floor, 10022
Telephone: 212-605-0918
Fax: 212-605-0919

Mark L. Goldstein
Francine J. Morris

ASSOCIATE

Andrea H. Stempel

For full biographical listings, see the Martindale-Hubbell Law Directory

GOLENBOCK, EISEMAN, ASSOR & BELL (AV)

437 Madison Avenue, 10022
Telephone: 212-907-7300
Telecopier: 212-754-0330
Email: postmaster@golenbock.com

MEMBERS OF FIRM

Nathan E. Assor
Lawrence M. Bell
David J. Eiseman
Jeffrey T. Golenbock
Andrew C. Peskoe
Richard S. Taffet
Robert B. Goebel
Leonard Eisenberg
Martin S. Hyman
Steven G. Chill
Donald A. Hamburg
Charles D. Schmerler
Jeffrey S. Berger
Lawrence R. Haut
Andrew M. Singer
Janice B. Grubin
Jacqueline G. Veit

OF COUNSEL

William G. Pearlstein
Jonathan S. Hacker

ASSOCIATES

Debra S. Schachtel
Charles B. Rich
Thomas J. Wilson
Elizabeth A. Jaffe
Adam C. Silverstein
Alvin R. Chin
Joel S. Tennenberg
Ruth G. Hirshfeld
Leslie J. Sherman
Hilda B. Gilfillan
David A. Collins
David K. Leitner
Richard S. Kaplan
Aielleen P. Fajardo (Not admitted in NY)
Gioia M. Ligos (Not admitted in NY)
Elaine S. Moshe

For full biographical listings, see the Martindale-Hubbell Law Directory

HARLEY & BROWNE (AV)

18 East 41st Street, 10017
Telephone: 212-545-7900
Email: harleybrowne@worldnet.att.net

MEMBERS OF FIRM

J. Austin Browne
Robert G. Harley

ASSOCIATES

Bradley S. Zimmerman
Enid O-Donnell Joseph
Danielle George

(See Next Column)

OF COUNSEL

Emily K. Harley
Bridget Asaro

Reference: Citibank.

For full biographical listings, see the Martindale-Hubbell Law Directory

HOFFINGER FRIEDLAND DOBRISH & STERN, P.C. (AV)

A Professional Corporation including Professional Corporations
110 East 59th Street, 10022-1392
Telephone: 212-421-4000
Telecopier: 212-223-3857

Jack S. Hoffinger
Lawrence N. Friedland
Robert Z. Dobrish (P.C.)
Stephen R. Stern (P.C.)
Samuel P. Ross
Warren R. Gleicher
Philip S. Ross

Michael J. Sherman
Fran Hoffinger
John H. Friedland
Lydia A. Milone
Devorah S. Weinschneider
Eric I. Wrubel
Nina S. Gross
Scott Lawrence D'Aloise

For full biographical listings, see the Martindale-Hubbell Law Directory

INGRAM YUZEK GAINEN CARROLL & BERTOLOTTI, LLP (AV)

250 Park Avenue, 10177
Telephone: 212-907-9600
Facsimile: 212-907-9681

MEMBERS OF FIRM

Ernest J. Bertolotti (1942-1999)
Daniel L. Carroll
Roger Cukras
David G. Ebert
Larry F. Gainen
Samuel W. Ingram, Jr.
Paulette Kendler
Steven Mastbaum
Shane O'Neill
Dean G. Yuzek

ASSOCIATES

Warren E. Barrows
Amy Bertolotti
Patricia Hewitt
Theodore M. Kakoyiannis
Jeanne F. Pucci
Leigh A. Roveda
Jennifer E. Schwartz
Paul H. Slaney

OF COUNSEL

Karin J. Barkhorn
Beverly L. Deickler
Mark E. Klein
Paulette Lemay Peters
Cory L. Weiss

For full biographical listings, see the Martindale-Hubbell Law Directory

JONES, DAY, REAVIS & POGUE (AV)

599 Lexington Avenue, 10022
Telephone: 212-326-3939
Telecopier: 212-755-7306
Email: counsel@jonesday.com *URL:* http://www.jonesday.com
In Atlanta, Georgia: 3500 SunTrust Plaza, 303 Peachtree Street.
Telephone: 404-521-3939.
Telecopier: 404-581-8330.
In Brussels, Belgium: Avenue Louise 480, 7th Floor, B-1050 Brussels.
Telephone: 32-2-645-14-11.
Telecopier: 32-2-645-14-45.
In Chicago, Illinois: 77 West Wacker.
Telephone: 312-782-3939.
Telecopier: 312-782-8585.
In Cleveland, Ohio: North Point, 901 Lakeside Avenue.
Telephone: 216-586-3939.
Telecopier: 216-579-0212.
In Columbus, Ohio: 1900 Huntington Center.
Telephone: 614-469-3939.
Telecopier: 614-461-4198.
In Dallas, Texas: 2727 North Harwood Street.
Telephone: 214-220-3939.
Telecopier: 214-969-5100.
In Frankfurt, Germany: Hochhaus am Park, Grüneburgweg 102, 60323 Frankfurt am Main.
Telephone: 49-69-9726-3939.
Telecopier: 49-69-9726-3993.
In Geneva, Switzerland: 20, rue de Candolle.
Telephone: 41-22-320-2339.
Telecopier: 41-22-320-1232.
In Hong Kong: 29th Floor, Entertainment Building, 30 Queen's Road Central.
Telephone: 852-2526-6895.
Telecopier: 852-2868-5871.
In Irvine, California: 5 Park Plaza, Suite 1100.
Telephone: 949-851-3939.
Telecopier: 949-553-7539.
In London, England: Bucklersbury House, 3 Queen Victoria Street.
Telephone: 44-20-7236-3939
Telecopier: 44-20-7236-1113.
In Los Angeles, California: 555 West Fifth Street, Suite 4600.
Telephone: 213-489-3939.
Telecopier: 213-243-2539.

(See Next Column)

JONES, DAY, REAVIS & POGUE—*Continued*

In Paris, France: 120, rue du Faubourg Saint-Honoré.
Telephone: 33-1-56-59-39-39.
Telecopier: 33-1-56-59-39-38
In Pittsburgh, Pennsylvania: 500 Grant Street, 31st Floor.
Telephone: 412-391-3939.
Telecopier: 412-394-7959.
In Riyadh, Saudi Arabia: The International Law Firm (In Association with Jones, Day, Reavis & Pogue), Sulaymaniyah, Prince Mishari IBN, Abdulaziz Street, P.O. Box 22166.
Telephone: (966-1) 462-8866.
Telecopier: (966-1) 462-9001.
In Shanghai, China: 2805 Kerry Centre, 1515 Nanjing Road West.
Telephone: 86-21-5298-6568.
Telecopier: 86-21-5298-6569.
In Sydney, Australia: Governor Phillip Tower, Level 38, 1 Farrer Place.
Telephone: 61-2-9210-6921.
Telecopier: 61-2-9210-6926.
In Taipei, Taiwan: 8th Floor, 2 Tun Hwa South Road, Section 2.
Telephone: (886-2) 2704-6808.
Telecopier: (886-2) 2704-6791.
In Tokyo, Japan: Toranomon 45 Mori Building, 3rd Floor, 1-5, Toranomon 5-Chome, Minato-Ku, Tokyo 105, Japan.
Telephone: 81-3-3433-3939.
Telecopier: 81-3-5401-2725.
In Washington, D.C.: 51 Louisiana Avenue, N.W.
Telephone: 202-879-3939.
Telecopier: 202-626-1700.

MEMBER OF FIRM IN NEW YORK

E. Michael Bradley

For Complete List of Firm Personnel, See General Section

For full biographical listings, see the Martindale-Hubbell Law Directory

---

BONNIE P. JOSEPHS (AV)

1414 Avenue of the Americas, 10019
Telephone: 212-644-5712

For full biographical listings, see the Martindale-Hubbell Law Directory

---

JULIEN & SCHLESINGER, P.C. (AV)

150 William Street, 19th Floor, 10038
Telephone: 212-962-8020

Alfred S. Julien (1910-1989)
Stuart A. Schlesinger

Mary Elizabeth Burns
Richard A. Robbins
Michael J. Taub
Marla L. Stein
Adam Schlesinger
Michael S. Schlesinger

For full biographical listings, see the Martindale-Hubbell Law Directory

---

KENNY & STEARNS (AV)

26 Broadway, 10004-1882
Telephone: 212-422-6111
Fax: 212-422-6544
Email: kenny-stearns@erols.com
Newark, New Jersey Office: 56 Park Place.
Telephone: 201-624-7779.

MEMBERS OF FIRM

James M. Kenny
Joseph T. Stearns
Gino A. Zonghetti

ASSOCIATES

Michael C. Mulé
Christina M. Kenny (Not admitted in NY)
John D. Blomquist

For full biographical listings, see the Martindale-Hubbell Law Directory

---

KING, PAGANO & HARRISON (AV)

425 Park Avenue, 10022
Telephone: 212-223-4000
Fax: 212-223-4134
URL: http://www.kph.com
Washington, D.C. Office: 1730 Pennsylvania Avenue, N.W., 20006.
Telephone: 202-371-6800.
FAX: 202-371-6770.

MEMBERS OF FIRM

Jeffrey W. King (Resident, Washington, D.C. Office)
Jeffrey W. Pagano
Keith J. Harrison (Resident, Washington, D.C. Office)
James E. Kellett
Jeffrey L. Poston (Resident, Washington, D.C. Office)
Ira M. Saxe

OF COUNSEL

Herbert I. Meyer

(See Next Column)

ASSOCIATES

Cheryl A. Maier (Resident, Washington, D.C. Office)
Christopher Flynn (Resident, Washington, D.C. Office)
Emily B. Zuckerman
Eric M. Carr

Representative Clients: Brink's, Inc.; The Pittston Co.; BAX Global; GEO Logistics; Air Transport International, L.L.C.; GAB Robbins, Inc.; SGS Control Services, Inc.; Kaiser Permanente; American Association of Health Plans.

For full biographical listings, see the Martindale-Hubbell Law Directory

---

KOSTELANETZ & FINK, LLP (AV)

530 Fifth Avenue, 22nd Floor, 10036
Telephone: 212-808-8100
Fax: 212-808-8108
Email: mail@kostelanetzfink.com

SENIOR COUNSEL

Boris Kostelanetz

MEMBERS OF FIRM

Robert S. Fink
Kevin M. Flynn
Bryan C. Skarlatos

COUNSEL

Norman Sinrich
Theodore F. Dickson
Caroline Rule
Brian C. Wille
William F. Cuozzi, III
Dawn Ngo

For full biographical listings, see the Martindale-Hubbell Law Directory

---

KRAMER, DILLOF, TESSEL, DUFFY & MOORE (AV)

233 Broadway, 45th Floor, 10279-0137
Telephone: 212-267-4177
Fax: 212-233-8525
Email: kdtdm@compuserve.com

Charles Kramer (1916-1988)
Thomas A. Moore
James R. Duffy
Judith A. Livingston
Thomas J. Principe
Matthew Gaier

ASSOCIATES

Andrew S. Targum
William T. Burdo
Carmine Rubino
Anthony DiPietro

OF COUNSEL

Norman Bard
Henry H. Dillof
Stanley Tessel
William R. Dillof

For full biographical listings, see the Martindale-Hubbell Law Directory

---

KRAMER LEVIN NAFTALIS & FRANKEL LLP (AV)

919 Third Avenue, 10022
Telephone: 212-715-9100
Cable Address: "Nickral"
TWX: 710 581-5340
Telex: 645041
Telecopier: 212-715-8000
URL: http://www.kramerlevin.com
Paris, France Office: 47, Avenue Hoche, 75008.
Telephone: +33-1 44 09 46 00.
Telecopier: +33-1 44 09 46 01.

MEMBERS OF FIRM

Arthur H. Aufses III
Philip Bentley
Michael J. Dell
Charlotte Moses Fischman
David S. Frankel
Marvin E. Frankel
Alan R. Friedman
Mark J. Headley
Robert M. Heller
Thomas H. Moreland
Ellen R. Nadler
Gary P. Naftalis
Michael S. Oberman
Jeffrey S. Trachtman
Jonathan M. Wagner
Harold P. Weinberger

SPECIAL COUNSEL

Jeffrey W. Davis
Ronald S. Greenberg

For Complete List of Firm Personnel, See General Section

For full biographical listings, see the Martindale-Hubbell Law Directory

---

LAMBOS & JUNGE (AV)

29 Broadway, 9th Floor, 10006-3101
Telephone: 212-943-2470; 212-269-0061
Telecopiers: 212-797-9213; 212-269-0172
Email: nyoffice@lambosjunge.com *URL:* http://lambosjunge.wld.com
San Francisco, California Office (A California Partnership): Three Embarcadero Center, 28th Floor, 94111.
Telephone: 415-986-7450.
Fax: 415-986-7499.
Tampa, Florida Office: 13992 W. Hillsborough Avenue, 33635.
Telephone: 813-855-5400.
Fax: 813-855-9735.

(See Next Column)

LAMBOS & JUNGE, *New York—Continued*

Bayonne, New Jersey Office: 473 Broadway, Bayonne Plaza, Suite 209, 07002.
Telephone: 201-823-1000.
Fax: 201-823-3097.
Boston, Massachusetts Office: The Vermont Marble Building, 10 Thacher Street, Suite 114, 02113.
Telephone: 617-227-5500.
Fax: 617-227-5500.

MEMBERS OF FIRM

Constantine P. Lambos
Peter A. Junge
Richard P. Lerner
Robert J. Attaway
Donato Caruso
William M. Spelman
Nicholas G. Maglaras
Peter C. Lambos (1945-1991)

SPECIAL COUNSEL

Steven L. Barkan
George W. Sullivan

ASSOCIATES

Ann Marie Flynn
Richard J. Ciampi, Jr.
Armand P. Mele
Carol Notias Lambos
James R. Campbell, Jr.
Robert F. Sloan (Resident Associate, New Jersey Office; Also Practicing Individually in Bayonne, New Jersey)
Daniel Amo Gronda

OF COUNSEL

Edward M. Kovach (Resident California Partner)
Edward J. Heine, Jr.
Vincent De Vito
E. Gordon Cleland

For full biographical listings, see the Martindale-Hubbell Law Directory

LANKLER SIFFERT & WOHL LLP (AV)

33rd Floor, 500 Fifth Avenue, 10110-3398
Telephone: 212-921-8399
Telefax: 212-764-3701
Telex: 4939413 LSWU1
URL: http://www.LSWLAW.com

MEMBERS OF FIRM

Jess Fardella
Helen Gredd
Roderick C. Lankler
John Sand Siffert
Charles T. Spada
Frank H. Wohl

OF COUNSEL

Susan L. Sommer
Peter Herbert

Lisa A. Baroni
Brett S. Deutsch
Brian Fleischer (Not admitted in NY)
Rebecca E. Hollander-Blumoff
Sara Lesch
Ghillaine A Reid
Daniel E. Reynolds
Laura H. Stasior

For full biographical listings, see the Martindale-Hubbell Law Directory

LAVIN, COLEMAN, O'NEIL, RICCI, FINARELLI & GRAY (AV)

7th Floor, 767 Third Avenue, 10017
Telephone: 212-319-6898
Fax: 212-319-6932
Philadelphia, Pennsylvania Office: Suite 1000, 510 Walnut Street.
Telephone: 215-627-0303.
Fax: 215-627-2551.
Mount Laurel, New Jersey Office: 8000 Midlantic Drive, Suite 201 South.
Telephone: 609-778-5544.
Fax: 609-778-3383.

Francis F. Quinn
William J. Ricci
Edward A. Gray
Joseph A. McGinley
Michael D. Brophy

Jessica Faden (Resident, Mount Laurel, New Jersey Office)
Margot L. Ludlam
Leona C. McFadden
Timothy J. McHugh
Michelle S. Regan
Elizabeth A. Weill
Christopher P. Yodice

For full biographical listings, see the Martindale-Hubbell Law Directory

LEAHEY & JOHNSON, P.C. (AV)

Suite 2220, 120 Wall Street, 10005
Telephone: 212-269-7308
Facsimile: 212-422-4751
Email: Leaheylaw@Aol.com

Peter James Johnson
Peter James Johnson, Jr.
William G. Murphy
Kevin Brian Lynch

James P. Tenney
Steven Martin
William J. Gordon
Christopher Delamere Clarke
Vincent L. Gallo, Jr.
Joseph Francis Ferrette
Gregory Wilson
Michael Cannella
James Gerard Mcgovern
Nadine M. Duhamel
Sharon A. Toussaint
Melissa Ann Weinberg

(See Next Column)

Edward J. White
Daniel Michael Sullivan
Lennon C. Edwards
Carmen M. Vasquez
Eric L. Horn
Sean T. O'Leary (Not admitted in NY)

For full biographical listings, see the Martindale-Hubbell Law Directory

LIDDLE & ROBINSON, L.L.P. (AV)

685 Third Avenue, 10017
Telephone: 212-687-8500
Telecopier: 212-687-1505

MEMBERS OF FIRM

Samuel Finkelstein (1906-1996)
Jeffrey L. Liddle
Miriam M. Robinson
Laurence S. Moy
W. Dan Boone
Ethan A. Brecher
James A. Batson
Blaine H. Bortnick
Susan Potter Ellis

ASSOCIATES

Marc A. Susswein
Allan S. Bloom
Michael E. Grenert
Richard B. Palmer, Jr.
Christine A. Palmieri
Keith A. Markel

For full biographical listings, see the Martindale-Hubbell Law Directory

LITMAN, ASCHE & GIOIELLA, LLP (AV)

45 Broadway Atrium, 10006
Telephone: 212-809-4500
Telecopier: GP II, III (212) 509-8403

MEMBERS OF FIRM

Richard M. Asche
Jack T. Litman
Russell M. Gioiella

ASSOCIATES

Thomas H. Burt
Howard Weiner

OF COUNSEL

Stephen Hogan

For full biographical listings, see the Martindale-Hubbell Law Directory

LOCKE & HERBERT (AV)

A Partnership including a Professional Corporation
900 Third Avenue, 10022
Telephone: 212-355-7493
Telecopier: 212-355-7674
Stamford, Connecticut Office: 1100 Summer Street. 06905.
Telephone: 203-969-6030.
Facsimile: 203-324-3607.

MEMBERS OF FIRM

Charles T. Locke (P.C.)
Stephen R. Herbert

Representative Clients: Mutual of Omaha Insurance Co.; National Benefit Life Insurance Co.; Companion Life Insurance Co.
Reference: The Bank of New York.

For full biographical listings, see the Martindale-Hubbell Law Directory

LOEB & LOEB LLP (AV)

A Limited Liability Partnership including Professional Corporations
345 Park Avenue, 10154-0037
Telephone: 212-407-4000
Facsimile: 212-407-4990
Email: info@loeb.com *URL:* http://www.loeb.com
Los Angeles, California Office: Suite 1800, 1000 Wilshire Boulevard, 90017-2475.
Telephone: 213-688-3400.
Facsimile: 213-688-3460.
Century City (Los Angeles), California Office: Suite 2200, 10100 Santa Monica Boulevard, Los Angeles, 90067-4164.
Telephone: 310-282-2000.
Facsimile: 310-282-2192.
Nashville, Tennessee Office: 45 Music Square West, 37203-3205.
Telephone: 615-749-8300.
Facsimile: 615-749-8308.
Rome, Italy Office: Piazza Digione 1, 00197.
Telephone: 011-3906-808-8456.
Facsimile: 011-3906-808-8288.

MEMBERS OF FIRM

David B. Eizenman
Helen Gavaris
John F. Lang
Charles H. Miller
Martin R. Pollner
David M. Satnick
P. Gregory Schwed
Brian R. Socolow
Michael P. Zweig

ASSOCIATES

Christian D. Carbone
Paula K. Colbath
Maria L. Zanfini

For Complete List of Firm Personnel, See General Section

For full biographical listings, see the Martindale-Hubbell Law Directory

New York—Continued

London Fischer LLP (AV)

59 Maiden Lane, 10038
Telephone: 212-972-1000
Facsimile: 212-972-1030
Email: Law@LondonFischer.com

MEMBERS OF FIRM

Bernard London
James L. Fischer
Daniel Zemann, Jr.
John E. Sparling
Richard S. Endres
Leah Campbell
Marvin B. Segal
James Walsh
Anthony F. Tagliagambe

For full biographical listings, see the Martindale-Hubbell Law Directory

Lovell & Stewart, LLP (AV)

A Limited Liability Partnership including a Professional Corporation
500 Fifth Avenue, 10110
Telephone: 212-608-1900
Telefax: 212-719-4677
Email: sklovell@aol.com

Christopher Lovell, P.C.
Victor E. Stewart
Gary S. Jacobson

Peggy J. Wedgworth
Geoffrey M. Horn
William W. Foshay, III
Ian T. Stoll

For full biographical listings, see the Martindale-Hubbell Law Directory

Marx & Marx (AV)

575 Madison Avenue, 10022
Telephone: 212-689-8516
Email: lawmarx@aol.com
Atlanta, Georgia Office: 400 Perimeter Center Terrace, N.E., Suite 900, 30346.
Telephone: 404-261-9559.

MEMBERS OF FIRM

Robert N. Marx
Jean Simonoff Marx (Resident, Atlanta, Georgia Office)

For full biographical listings, see the Martindale-Hubbell Law Directory

Mazur, Carp & Rubin, P.C. (AV)

2 Park Avenue, 10016
Telephone: 212-686-7700
Telecopier: 212-532-1425
Email: mcrlaw@sprynet.com

Gerald I. Carp
Sayward Mazur
Gary L. Rubin
Ira M. Schulman

OF COUNSEL

Charles H. Weinberg

Thomas G. Draper, Jr.
Richard Raab
Frank L. Wagner

For full biographical listings, see the Martindale-Hubbell Law Directory

McAloon & Friedman, P.C. (AV)

116 John Street, 10038
Telephone: 212-732-8700
Fax: 212-227-2903

Edward H. McAloon (1908-1986)
Stanley D. Friedman
Gunther H. Kilsch
Theodore B. Rosenzweig
Gary A. Greenfield
Brendan J. Lantier
Lawrence W. Mumm
Laura R. Shapiro
Lisa B. Goldstein
Thomas Medardo Oliva
Adam R. Goldsmith
Wayne M. Roth
Kenneth S. Oliver
Stephen S. York

Jennifer D. Correale
Mark Gregory Duncan
Kenneth Gordon Ellison
Ilene R. Fish
Gillian Fisher
Kenneth Fox
Evette E. Harrison
Alex Johnson
Ross Katz
Sherry Levin
Robin P. Lorell
Carolan Magnoli
Linda P. McMillan
Douglas M. Nadjari
Timothy O'Shaugnessy
Matthew Luke Prisco
Caryn Rosen
Corey Lee Wishner

LEGAL SUPPORT PERSONNEL

Robyn L. Reyes (Firm Administrator)

For full biographical listings, see the Martindale-Hubbell Law Directory

McGuire, Kehl & Nealon, LLP (AV)

230 Park Avenue, Suite 2830, 10169
Telephone: 212-557-0040
Telecopier: 212-953-0768

MEMBERS OF FIRM

Harold F. McGuire, Jr.
Jeffrey A. Kehl
Arthur V. Nealon

OF COUNSEL

Andrea Green
Marion C. Katzive
Shelley Sanders Kehl
Terri E. Simon

For full biographical listings, see the Martindale-Hubbell Law Directory

Milberg Weiss Bershad Hynes & Lerach LLP (AV)

One Pennsylvania Plaza, 10119
Telephone: 212-594-5300
San Diego, California Office: 600 West Broadway, 1800 One America Plaza.
Telephone: 619-231-1058.
San Francisco, California Office: 100 Pine Street, 26th Floor.
Telephone: 415-288-4545.
Fax: 415-288-4534.
Los Angeles, California Office: 355 South Grand Avenue, Suite 4170, 90071.
Telephone: 213-617-9007.
Fax: 213-617-9185.
Boca Raton, Florida Office: The Plaza, 5355 Town Center Road, Suite 900.
Telephone: 561-361-5000.
Telecopier: 561-367-8400.

MEMBERS OF FIRM

Melvyn I. Weiss (Resident at Boca Raton Office)
Lawrence Milberg (1913-1989)
David J. Bershad
Patricia M. Hynes
Steven G. Schulman
Michael C. Spencer
Keith M. Fleischman
Sol Schreiber
Jerome M. Congress
Arnold N. Bressler
Robert A. Wallner
Sanford P. Dumain
George A. Bauer III
Barry A. Weprin
Richard H. Weiss
Deborah Clark-Weintraub
Joshua H. Vinik
Edith M. Kallas
Janine L. Pollack
Salvatore J. Graziano

ASSOCIATES

Elaine Simek Kusel
U. Seth Ottensoser

OF COUNSEL

Richard M. Meyer
Jared Specthrie

For full biographical listings, see the Martindale-Hubbell Law Directory

Miller, Canfield, Paddock and Stone, P.L.C. (AV®)

A Professional Limited Liability Company
Founded in 1852 by Sidney Davy Miller
1450 Broadway, 41st Floor, 10018
Telephone: 212-704-4400
Fax: 212-704-4410
URL: http://www.millercanfield.com
Detroit, Michigan Office: 150 West Jefferson, Suite 2500, 48226-4415.
Telephone: 313-963-6420.
Fax: 313-496-7500.
Cable Address: "Stem Detroit."
Ann Arbor, Michigan Office: 101 North Main Street, 7th Floor, 48104-1400.
Telephone: 734-663-2445.
Fax: 734-747-7147.
Troy, Michigan Office: 840 West Long Lake Road, Suite 200, 48098.
Telephone: 248-879-2000.
Fax: 248-879-2001.
Grand Rapids, Michigan Office: 99 Monroe, N.W., Suite 1200, 49503-2639.
Telephone: 616-454-8656.
Fax: 616-776-6322.
Howell, Michigan Office: 121 South Barnard Street, Suite 4, 48843-2305.
Telephone: 517-546-7600.
Telecopier: 517-546-6974.
Kalamazoo, Michigan Office: 444 West Michigan Avenue, 49007-3752.
Telephone: 616-381-7030.
Fax: 616-382-0244.
Lansing, Michigan Office: One Michigan Avenue, Suite 900, 48933-1609.
Telephone: 517-487-2070.
Fax: 517-374-6304.
Monroe, Michigan Office: 214 East Elm Avenue, Suite 100, 48162-2682.
Telephone: 734-243-2000.
Fax: 734-243-0901.
Washington, D.C. Office: 1900 K Street, N.W., Suite 1150. 20006.
Telephone: 202-429-5575; 785-0600.
Fax: 202-331-1118; 785-1234.
Pensacola, Florida Office: 25 West Cedar, 32501.
Telephone: 850-469-1088.
Fax: 850-432-0677.

(See Next Column)

MILLER, CANFIELD, PADDOCK AND STONE P.L.C., *New York—Continued*

Gdynia, Poland Office: UL. Slaska 21, 81-319.
Telephone: 011-485-831-2808.
Fax: 011-48-58-628 6411.
Warsaw, Poland Office: UL. Nowogrodzkall, 5th Floor, 00-513.
Telephone: 011-4822 529 0200.
Fax: 011-4822 529 0201.
Katowice, Poland Office: UL. Francuska 35/37, 40-027.
Telephone: 011 (48-32) 757-2414.
Fax: 011 (48-32) 757-2483.

RESIDENT PRINCIPAL

Gregory L. Curtner (Not admitted in NY)

Representative Firm Clients: Chrysler Corp.; Comerica, Inc.; City of Detroit, Mich.; Detroit Tigers, Inc.; First of Michigan; Fretter, Inc.; Ford Motor Co.; Ford Motor Credit Co.; Great Lakes Bancorp; Henry Ford Hospital.

For Complete List of Firm Personnel, See General Section

For full biographical listings, see the Martindale-Hubbell Law Directory

MILLER & WRUBEL P.C. (AV)

250 Park Avenue, 10177-0699
Telephone: 212-336-3500
Facsimile: 212-336-3555

Joel M. Miller
David F. Wrubel
Martin D. Edel
Charles R. Jacob, III

Todd M. Greeley
Dana B. Zimmerman
Adam J. Safer

For full biographical listings, see the Martindale-Hubbell Law Directory

BENEDICT P. MORELLI & ASSOCIATES, P.C. (AV)

950 Third Avenue, 10022
Telephone: 212-751-9800
Fax: 212-751-0046
URL: http://www.alltrials.com
Email: bpmorelli@mindspring.com *URL:* http://www.lawyers.com/alltrials

Benedict P. Morelli

For full biographical listings, see the Martindale-Hubbell Law Directory

MORGANROTH & MORGANROTH (AV)

156 W. 56th Street, Suite 1101, 10019
Telephone: 212-586-5905
URL: http://www.lawyers.com/morganroth&morganrothlaw
Southfield, Michigan Office: 3000 Town Center, Suite 1500, 48075.
Telephone: 248-355-3084.
Fax: 248-355-3017.

Mayer Morganroth
Jeffrey B. Morganroth

For full biographical listings, see the Martindale-Hubbell Law Directory

MORRIS, DUFFY, ALONSO & FALEY, LLP (AV)

170 Broadway, 10038
Telephone: 212-766-1888
Fax: 212-766-3252

John E. Morris (1916-1998)
Kevin G. Faley
Andrea M. Alonso
Barry M. Viuker
Michael B. Titowsky
John J. Duffy

For full biographical listings, see the Martindale-Hubbell Law Directory

MOUND, COTTON & WOLLAN (AV)

One Battery Park Plaza, 10004
Telephone: 212-804-4200
Facsimile: 212-344-8066
San Francisco, California Office: 1700 California Street, Suite 470.
Telephone: 415-434-4301.
Telecopier: 415-434-4303.
London, England Office: Longbow House, 14-20 Chiswell Street.
Telephone: 0071-638-3688.
Newark, New Jersey Office: The Legal Center, One Riverfront Plaza, 8th Floor, 07102-5497.
Telephone: 973-242-2050.
Telecopier: 973-242-4244.

Arthur N. Brook (1933-1997)

MEMBERS OF FIRM

Stuart Cotton
Jeffrey C. Crawford
Leonard S. Dome
Wayne R. Glaubinger
Michael H. Goldstein
Lawrence S. Greengrass
Lloyd A. Gura
Bruce R. Kaliner
Michael R. Koblenz
Daniel Markewich
John C. Mezzacappa
Frederic R. Mindlin
Francis A. Montbach
David A. Silva

(See Next Column)

MEMBERS OF FIRM (Continued)

Philip C. Silverberg
Costantino P. Suriano
James D. Veach
Jeffrey S. Weinstein

COUNSEL

Eugene A. Leiman
Eugene Wollan

RESIDENT OF COUNSEL
SAN FRANCISCO, CALIFORNIA OFFICE

Anna Maria Martin (Not admitted in NY)
Joseph M. Rimac, Jr. (Not admitted in NY)

RESIDENT MEMBER
NEWARK, NEW JERSEY OFFICE

William D. Wilson

ASSOCIATES

Michael Altman
Emilie L. Bakal
Todd A. Bakal
Kevin F. Buckley
Doreen A. Cronin
Frank J. DeAngelis
Alyssa DeSimone
Lauren G. Dome
Douglas K. Eisenstein
Maria Fazzolari
Joseph W. Ferraro
Aaron F. Fishbein
Elisa T. Gilbert
Diana E. Goldberg
Hilary M. Henkind
Mark S. Katz
David W. Kenna
David S. Mahaffey
Mark D. Marino
Catherine F. Megret
Mitchell D. Otto
Albert J. Pinzon
Renee M. Plessner
Jon Quint
Ronnie A. Rifkin
Mark J. Weber
Christina M. Wood

For Complete List of Firm Personnel, See General Section

For full biographical listings, see the Martindale-Hubbell Law Directory

NEWMAN FITCH ALTHEIM MYERS, P.C. (AV)

14 Wall Street, 22nd Floor, 10005
Telephone: 212-619-4350
Fax: 212-619-3622
Email: lawfirm@nfam.com
Newark, New Jersey Office: 744 Broad Street, Suite 2109.
Telephone: 201-824-2600.
Fax: 201-824-2993.

Robert A. Fitch
Abraham S. Altheim
Jan Kevin Myers
Charles W. Kreines
Floyd G. Cottrell (Resident Partner, Newark, New Jersey Office)
Olivia M. Gross
Ian F. Harris

COUNSEL

Laura M. Mattera
Charles Dewey Cole, Jr.
William A. Prinsell

Vanessa M. Corchia
Harry Steinberg
Alex M. Grant
James Sawicki
Jeffrey A. Lesser
Peter C. Bobchin
Elisa Cullen Schorr
Robin B. Baer
Ian R. Grodman (Resident, Newark, New Jersey Office)
Francine Scotto
Susan A. Karp
Jaimi Berliner
John F. Raio Jr.
Rhonda D. Thompson
Steven Bandel
Anita Bowen
Carolyn M. Walsh
Peter DeNoto
Susan A. Romano
Stephanie Monaco (Resident, Newark, New Jersey Office)
Paul Romano (Resident, Newark, New Jersey Office)
Joseph A. Orlando
Lon V. Hughes
Eric Cheng
Richard B. Polner
Colleen A. Tan
Julie C. Chodos
Stephen M. Bigham
Rosario Chetta

Reference: Chase Manhattan Bank, New York.

For full biographical listings, see the Martindale-Hubbell Law Directory

OTTERBOURG, STEINDLER, HOUSTON & ROSEN, P.C. (AV)

230 Park Avenue, 29th Floor, 10169
Telephone: 212-661-9100
Telecopier: 212-682-6104

Donald N. Gellert
William M. Silverman
Peter H. Stolzar
Daniel Wallen
Anthony M. Piccione
Stanley L. Lane, Jr.
Peter L. Feldman
Richard G. Haddad

GENERAL COUNSEL

Kurt J. Wolff

COUNSEL

Bernard Beitel
Morton L. Gitter

Lloyd M. Green

For Complete List of Firm Personnel, See General Section

For full biographical listings, see the Martindale-Hubbell Law Directory

New York—Continued

OWEN & DAVIS PC (AV)

805 Third Avenue, 10022-7513
Telephone: 212-754-1700
Fax: 212-754-1727
Email: odny@owendavis.com

James M. Davis
Robert D. Owen
James H. Neale
Anita Tucker Smith (Not admitted in NY)
Allen Craig Wasserman
India De Carmine
Henry G. Burnett
James L. Fuchs

Lori J. Hoffman

For full biographical listings, see the Martindale-Hubbell Law Directory

PARKER CHAPIN LLP (AV)

Chrysler Building, 405 Lexington Avenue, 10017
Telephone: 212-704-6000
Telecopier: 212-704-6288
URL: http://www.parkerchapin.com
Great Neck, New York Office: 175 Great Neck Road.
Telephone: 516-482-4422.
Telecopier: 516-482-4469.
Hackensack, New Jersey: 190 Morre Street, Suite 307.
Telephone: 210-883-6400.
Telecopier: 210-883-6404.
Beverly Hills, California: 9454 Wilshire Boulevard.
Telephone: 310-288-8367.
Telecopier: 310-288-8365.

MEMBERS OF FIRM

Mark Abramowitz
Barry J. Brett
Robert M. Carmen
Aurora Cassirer
Elliot Cohen
Charles P. Greenman
Stephen F. Harmon
Karen F. Lederer
Stephen G. Rinehart
Will Burt Sandler
Alvin M. Stein
Lee W. Stremba

OF COUNSEL

Katherine Cooney Ash
Richard G. Cushing
Daniel S. Greenfeld
Mark I. Schlesinger
Patricia Lynne Truscelli

For Complete List of Firm Personnel, See General Section

For full biographical listings, see the Martindale-Hubbell Law Directory

PARKER & WAICHMAN (AV)

38th Floor, 233 Broadway, 10279
Telephone: 212-267-6700
URL: http://www.lawyers.com/800lawinfo
Email: INFO@800LAWINFO.COM *URL:* http://www.800lawinfo.com
Long Island Office: 111 Great Neck Road, Great Neck, N.Y. 11021-5042.
Telephone: 516-466-6500.
Newark, New Jersey Office: One Gateway Center, Suite 2500, 07102.
Telephone: 973-297-1020.

PARTNERS

Jerrold S. Parker
Herbert L. Waichman

MANAGING ATTORNEY

Fred R. Rosenthal

ASSOCIATES

Lauren J. Gould
Andres F. Alonso
David J. Broderick
John Andrew Mullan
David B. Krangle

OF COUNSEL

Bruce David Katz
Charles Silverstein
Marc Jay Bern
Benjamin Levine

For full biographical listings, see the Martindale-Hubbell Law Directory

PATTERSON, BELKNAP, WEBB & TYLER LLP (AV)

1133 Avenue of the Americas, 10036-6710
Telephone: 212-336-2000
Fax: 212-336-2222
Email: info@pbwt.com *URL:* http://www.pbwt.com

MEMBERS OF FIRM

William F. Cavanaugh, Jr.
Lisa E. Cleary
John Delli Venneri
John M. DiMatteo
Gregory L. Diskant
David F. Dobbins
Philip R. Forlenza
Eugene M. Gelernter
Kim J. Landsman
Robert W. Lehrburger
Jeffrey I. D. Lewis
Robert P. LoBue
Ellen M. Martin
Thomas C. Morrison
Thomas W. Pippert
Andrew D. Schau
Karl E. Seib, Jr.
Saul B. Shapiro
Frederick B. Warder III
John D. Winter
Stephen P. Younger
Steven A. Zalesin

(See Next Column)

OF COUNSEL

Harold R. Tyler, Jr.
George S. Frazza

COUNSEL

Blair Axel
Cecilia Loving
Christine H. Miller
Robert D. Wilson, Jr.

For Complete List of Firm Personnel, See General Section

For full biographical listings, see the Martindale-Hubbell Law Directory

PILIERO GOLDSTEIN JENKINS & SULLIVAN, LLP (AV)

292 Madison Avenue, 10017
Telephone: 212-213-8200
Fax: 212-685-2028
Email: lawyers@pgjhlaw.com *URL:* http://www.pgjhlaw.com
Carlstadt, New Jersey Office: One Palmer Terrace.
Telephone: 201-507-5157.
FAX: 201-507-5221.
Washington, D.C. Office: 888 17th Street, N.W., Suite 1100.
Telephone: 202-467-6991.
FAX: 202-467-6703.
San Francisco, California Office: 507 Howard Street, Suite 200.
Telephone: 415-281-3631.
Fax: 415-281-3630.

MEMBERS OF FIRM

Kimberlee S. Bogen
Edward J. Goldstein
Jon Mark Jenkins
Marc A. Lebowitz
Robert D. Piliero
George O. Richardson, III
Michael T. Sullivan

ASSOCIATES

Craig Avedisian
Rosemary G. Feit
Eric M. Kogan
Mariano Schwed

OF COUNSEL

Kenneth D. Arbeeny
Christopher P. Hall

For full biographical listings, see the Martindale-Hubbell Law Directory

POSTNER & RUBIN (AV)

17 Battery Place, 10004
Telephone: 212-269-2510
Fax: 212-425-0968
Email: postner@aol.com
Holmdel, New Jersey Office: 42 West Main Street,
Telephone: 732-946-9001.
Fax: 732-946-9005.

Robert A. Rubin
William J. Postner
Robert J. MacPherson
Jeffrey R. Cruz

ASSOCIATES

Patricia M. Caplicki
Dana Wordes
Michael W. Bautz

NEW JERSEY RESIDENT COUNSEL

Sarah B. Biser

For full biographical listings, see the Martindale-Hubbell Law Directory

QUIRK AND BAKALOR, P.C. (AV)

845 Third Avenue, 10022
Telephone: 212-319-1000

Robert E. Quirk
Richard H. Bakalor
Stephen K. Blunda
Jeffrey J. Ellis
Richard M. Freiman
Scott P. Taylor
Henry Nicholas Goodman
Timothy J. Keane

Alice J. Jaffe
Loretta A. Redmond
Michael W. Hecht
Debra E. Seidman
Dominic S. Curcio
A. Lorenzo Bryan
Steven A. Lee
Anoushka Sharifi-Bayley
Brian P. Sexton
Donna Hope Bakalor
Alyssa M. Cohen
James M. Andriola
Liza R. Berliner
Pablo A. Sosa
Christopher J. Gray
Anne E. Pettit
Todd A. Paradeis
Andrew M. Premisler

For full biographical listings, see the Martindale-Hubbell Law Directory

ROSEN, EINBINDER & DUNN, P.C. (AV)

641 Lexington Avenue, 10022
Telephone: 212-888-7717
FAX: 212-980-1444
Email: info@redlawfirm.com *URL:* http://www.redlawfirm.com

Richard L. Rosen
Michael Einbinder
Terrence M. Dunn

Leonardo D'Alessandro

For full biographical listings, see the Martindale-Hubbell Law Directory

New York—Continued

SACKS MONTGOMERY, P.C. (AV)

800 Third Avenue, 10022
Telephone: 212-355-4660
Telecopier: 212-593-7257
Email: sm@sacksmontgomery.com
Westport, Connecticut Office: Sacks, Montgomery, Pastore & Levine, P.C., 1071 Post Road East, Suite 3.
Telephone: 203-291-6844.

Harry P. Sacks
David E. Montgomery
Stuart M. Levine (Resident, Westport, Connecticut Office)
Jeffrey A. Aronson
Frederick R. Rohn
Scott D. St. Marie
Stephen A. Stallings

Thomas F. Giordano
Amy S. Cohen
Kathleen M. Fay

OF COUNSEL

Steven J. Brill

For full biographical listings, see the Martindale-Hubbell Law Directory

JEFFREY SAMEL & PARTNERS (AV)

150 Broadway, 20th Floor, 10038
Telephone: 212-587-9690
Fax: 212-587-9673

Jeffrey Samel
David S. Gary
Dorothy Samel

ASSOCIATES

Robert G. Spevack
David M. Samel
Stacey L. Schwartz

OF COUNSEL

Richard A. Soberman

Representative Clients: New York City Transit Authority; New York City Housing Authority; Empire Insurance Co.; National General Insurance Co.; Federal Express Corp.; Shell Oil Corp.; American Building Maintenance Corp; United Fidelity & Guaranty Corp.; Little Caesar Enterprises, Inc.; Showbiz Pizza Time, Inc.

For full biographical listings, see the Martindale-Hubbell Law Directory

SCHNEIDER, KLEINICK, WEITZ, DAMASHEK & SHOOT (AV)

233 Broadway, Fifth Floor, 10279-0003
Telephone: 212-553-9000
Fax: 212-804-0820
Email: mail@lawyer1.com *URL:* http://www.lawyer1.com

Ivan S. Schneider
Arnold L. Kleinick
Harvey Weitz
Philip M. Damashek
Brian J. Shoot
Robert B. Jackson
Clifford J. Stern
Gregory J. Cannata
Keith A. Kleinick
Richard B. Ancowitz
Charles J. Nolet, Jr.
Leslie Debra Kelmachter
Louis J. Mitchell

John Kieran Daly
Jonathan S. Damashek
Thomas V. Deffina
Dawn S. DeWeil
David W. Druker
Steven Gold
Keith H. Gross
Erin K. Hurley
Judy Keenan
Paul A. Marber
Lloyd M. Roberts
Joseph S. Rosato
Derek S. Sells
Lawrence A. Wilson, II
James M. Lane
Donald D. Casale

For full biographical listings, see the Martindale-Hubbell Law Directory

SCHULTE ROTH & ZABEL LLP (AV)

900 Third Avenue, 10022
Telephone: 212-756-2000; 800-346-9644
Cable Address: "Olympus NewYork"
Telex: 426775
Email: wwwmail@srz.com *URL:* http://www.srz.com

MEMBERS OF FIRM

Robert M. Abrahams
Brooks R. Burdette
Michael S. Feldberg
Alan R. Glickman
Howard O. Godnick
Daniel J. Kramer
Martin L. Perschetz
Frederick P. Schaffer
Irwin J. Sugarman

For Complete List of Firm Personnel, See General Section

For full biographical listings, see the Martindale-Hubbell Law Directory

PAUL A. SCRUDATO (AV)

150 E. 52nd Street, Suite 2700, 10022
Telephone: 212-371-1153
Fax: 212-753-5044
Email: paulscrudato@ibm.net

For full biographical listings, see the Martindale-Hubbell Law Directory

SEIDMAN, SILVERMAN & SEIDMAN, P.C. (AV)

600 Third Avenue 33rd Floor, 10016-2001
Telephone: 212-922-1900

Irving P. Seidman
Lawrence H. Silverman
Brian William Seidman

Joseph M. Fein

For full biographical listings, see the Martindale-Hubbell Law Directory

MARK E. SEITELMAN LAW OFFICES (AV)

Woolworth Building, 233 Broadway, 9th Floor, 10279
Telephone: 212-962-2626
Fax: 212-962-5050

For full biographical listings, see the Martindale-Hubbell Law Directory

SMITH MAZURE DIRECTOR WILKINS YOUNG YAGERMAN & TARALLO, P.C. (AV)

111 John Street, 10038
Telephone: 212-964-7400
Fax: 212-374-1935 (Not for Legal Service)

Gerald Director
David E. Mazure
Stanley Wilkins
Nicholas Tarallo
Jacob J. Young
Mark S. Yagerman

Irwin D. Miller
Marc H. Pillinger
Michael K. Berman
John Kevin Reilly
Cary Maynard
Robert P. Siegel
John Colucci
Haydn J. Brill
Jeffrey T. Miller
Corey A. Tavel
Mark D. Levi
Howard S. Shafer
Peter H. Graber
Irwin Bloom
Michael S. Livow
Steven I. Brizel
Joel M. Simon
Frank J. Keenan
Melissa S. Romano
Paul L. LaClair
Constantine Vlavianos
Joseph A. Schwarzenberg
Stephanie Morfesis
Stacy I. Oberman
Dawn McNamara
David A. Glazer
Lara Jill Miller
Andrew J. Funk
Angela Lurie Milch
Seth M. Katz
Michael G. Brown
Christopher M. FitzPatrick
Neil Thomas Veilleux
Doris M. Carrasquillo
Alan C. Kelhoffer
Howard J. Snyder

For full biographical listings, see the Martindale-Hubbell Law Directory

SOLOVAY, EDLIN & EISEMAN (AV)

845 Third Avenue, Eighth Floor, 10022
Telephone: 212-752-1000
Facsimile: 212-355-4608

Richard A. Edlin
Norman Solovay
Michael B. Solovay
Jonathan Eiseman
Wayne R. Lehrhaupt
Eric R. Levine

OF COUNSEL

Daniel James Cooper
Joseph M. Harary
Stephen L. Weinstein
Peter Kakoyiannis
Sam Schwartz

ASSOCIATES

Murray D. Schneier
Howard S. Roitman

For full biographical listings, see the Martindale-Hubbell Law Directory

SPITZER & FELDMAN, P.C. (AV)

405 Park Avenue, 10022
Telephone: 212-888-6680
Cable Address: "Chastra"
Telecopier: 212-838-7472

M. James Spitzer
Ronald J. Offenkrantz
Leonard Lichter
M. James Spitzer, Jr.
Kenneth Gliedman
Edwin W. Weinberg
Thomas R. Westle

Rita C. Dattola
Michael H. Smith
Charles B. Baron
Lawrence Y. Vincent
Orit Kadosh

For full biographical listings, see the Martindale-Hubbell Law Directory

STILLMAN & FRIEDMAN, P.C. (AV)

425 Park Avenue, 10022
Telephone: 212-223-0200
Telecopier: 212-223-1942

(See Next Column)

STILLMAN & FRIEDMAN P.C.—*Continued*

Charles A. Stillman
Julian W. Friedman
Paul Shechtman
Peter A. Chavkin
Scott M. Himes
Marjorie J. Peerce
John B. Harris
James A. Mitchell
Michael J. Grudberg

Peter E. Dolotta
Sara Beth Savage
Lauren Goldberg
Nathaniel Z. Marmur
Sean T. Haran
Jody L. King
Samantha J. Leventhal

For full biographical listings, see the Martindale-Hubbell Law Directory

SULLIVAN & CROMWELL (AV)

125 Broad Street, 10004-2498
Telephone: 212-558-4000
Telex: 62694
Telecopier: 212-558-3588
URL: http://www.sullcrom.com
Washington, D.C. Office: 1701 Pennsylvania Avenue, N.W., 20006-5805.
Telephone: 202-956-7500.
Telecopier: 202-293-6330.
Los Angeles, California Office: 1888 Century Park East, 90067-1725.
Telephone: 310-712-6600.
Telecopier: 310-712-8800.
Paris Office: 8, Place Vendôme, 75001 Paris, France.
Telephone: (011)(331) 44 50 60 00.
Telex: 240654.
Telecopier: (011)(331) 44 50 60 60 or (011)(331) 42 60 56 36.
London Office: St. Olave's House, 9a Ironmonger Lane, London EC2V 8EY, England.
Telephone: (011)(44207) 710 6500.
Telecopier: (011)(44207) 710 6565.
Melbourne Office: 101 Collins Street, Melbourne, Victoria 3000, Australia.
Telephone: (011)(613) 9635-1500.
Telecopier: (011)(613) 9654-2422.
Tokyo Office: Sullivan & Cromwell, Gaikokuho Jimu Bengoshi Jimusho, Akai Law Offices (Registered Associated Offices), Otemachi First Square East Tower 16F, 5-1, Otemachi 1-chome, Chiyoda-ku, Tokyo 100-0004, Japan.
Telephone: (011)(813) 3213-6140.
Telecopier: (011)(813) 3213-6470 or (011)(813) 3213-6477.
Hong Kong Office: 28th Floor, Nine Queen's Road, Central, Hong Kong.
Telephone: (011)(852) 2826-8688.
Telecopier: (011)(852) 2522-2280.
Frankfurt Office: Neue Mainzer Strasse 52, 60322 Frankfurt, Germany.
Telephone: (011)(4969) 7191 26-0.
Telecopier: (011)(4969) 7191 26-10.
Beijing Office: The Beijing Representative Office of Sullivan & Cromwell, Suite 501, China World Trade Center, No. 1 Jianguo Menwai Avenue, Beijing 100004, P.R.C.
Telephone: (011)(86) 10 6505 6120.
Telecopier: (011)(86) 10 6505 6136.

MEMBERS OF FIRM

Michael A. Cooper
John L. Warden
William R. Norfolk
Robert M. Osgood (London Office)
James H. Carter, Jr.
Philip L. Graham, Jr.
Bruce E. Clark
Richard J. Urowsky
William M. Dallas, Jr.
Margaret K. Pfeiffer * (Washington, D.C. Office)
David B. Tulchin
D. Stuart Meiklejohn
Yvonne S. Quinn
Gandolfo V. DiBlasi
Robinson B. Lacy
Garrard R. Beeney
Richard H. Klapper
Theodore O. Rogers, Jr. *
John L. Hardiman
Robert A. Sacks ** (Los Angeles Office)
Theodore Edelman
Steven L. Holley
Joseph E. Neuhaus
William J. Snipes
David H. Braff
Mark F. Rosenberg
Daryl A. Libow * (Washington, D.C. Office)
Samuel W. Seymour
Michael H. Steinberg (Not admitted in NY; Los Angeles Office)
Michael Lacovara
Robin D. Fessel
Robert J. Giuffra, Jr. *
Michael T. Tomaino, Jr.
Richard C. Pepperman II
Karen Patton Seymour
Penny Shane

OF COUNSEL

Douglas Mark McCall * (Washington, D.C. Office)

SPECIAL COUNSEL

William L. Farris
Thomas R. Leuba * (Washington, D.C. Office)
Michael B. Miller (London Office)
William E. Schroeder
James T. Williams

SENIOR COUNSEL

John F. Cannon
John W. Dickey
Edward W. Keane
Robert MacCrate *
Marvin Schwartz *
William E. Willis

(See Next Column)

ASSOCIATES

Maite Aquino
Michael J. Bowe
Anthony M. Candido
Elizabeth Hughes Carroll (Not admitted in NY; Washington, D.C. Office)
Mark E. Coyne
Marc De Leeuw
John C. L. Dixon
C. Barr Flinn
Brian T. Frawley
David Gaukrodger
Fraser L. Hunter, Jr.
Thomas W. Laryea (London Office)
James V. Masella III
Oliver Metzger
Christine C. Monterosso
Sharon L. Nelles
Jay L. Pomerantz
Alan S. Rabinowitz
Dianne L. Rosky
Samantha Evans Ross * (Washington, D.C. Office)
Megan J. Shafritz
Timothy E. Sheil * (Washington, D.C. Office)
Bradley P. Smith
Daniel E. Sobelsohn (Not admitted in NY; Los Angeles Office)
Rosslyn Coldwell Stevens (Los Angeles Office)
John J. Sullivan
Steven W. Thomas ** (Not admitted in NY; Los Angeles Office)
Dawn M. Wilson

David Liebov (Managing Clerk)

*Attorneys also admitted to the District of Columbia Bar
**Attorneys also admitted to the California Bar

For Complete List of Firm Personnel, See General Section

For full biographical listings, see the Martindale-Hubbell Law Directory

STANLEY A. TEITLER, P.C. (AV)

299 Broadway, Suite 1500, 10007
Telephone: 212-233-8031
Fax: 212-233-8864

Stanley A. Teitler

For full biographical listings, see the Martindale-Hubbell Law Directory

WACHTEL & MASYR, LLP (AV)

110 East 59th Street, 10022
Telephone: 212-909-9500
Telecopier: (212) 371-0320

MEMBERS OF FIRM

Robert W. Berend
Steven J. Cohen
William F. Dowling
Scott J. Lesser
Marvin J. Levine
Jesse Masyr
John H. Reichman
I. Frederick Shotkin
Jeffrey T. Strauss
William B. Wachtel
Morris Missry
Evan S. Weintraub
John W. McConnell
Brian G. Lustbader
Howard J. Goldman

OF COUNSEL

Walter Castore (Legal Consultant on the Laws of Italy)
Walter P. Stasiuk
Robert Stone
Vladimir Zlobinsky
Rosemary Ginty
Francesco Penta (Not admitted in United States)
Maurizio Ulrich-Bansa (Not admitted in United States)
Karen Binder

ASSOCIATES

Aimee Cain
Michele D'Avolio
Howard I. Elman
Aaron D. Greenberg
Avram E. Posner
Allan Joseph Weiss
Anne F. McCaughey

For full biographical listings, see the Martindale-Hubbell Law Directory

WADE CLARK MULCAHY (AV)

111 Broadway, 10006
Telephone: 212-267-1900
Fax: 212-267-9470
Email: info@wcmlaw.com *URL:* http://www.wcmlaw.com
Westfield, New Jersey Office: 211 North Avenue East, 07090.
Telephone: 908-789-1681.
Fax: 908-789-0984.

PARTNERS

Dennis M. Wade
Paul F. Clark
John Mulcahy
Owen B. Carragher, Jr.

ASSOCIATES

Kathleen M. Mulholland
Rose M. McGrinder
Andrea E. Sacco
Christopher C. Mauro
Linda D. Werbel
Nicole Y. Brown
Suzanne M. O'Keefe

For full biographical listings, see the Martindale-Hubbell Law Directory

New York—Continued

RIDLEY M. WHITAKER (AV)

One Rockefeller Plaza, 10020
Telephone: 212-218-5656
Telecopier: 212-218-5665
Email: 74051.3574@compuserve.com

For full biographical listings, see the Martindale-Hubbell Law Directory

WHITE & CASE (AV)

Limited Liability Partnership
1155 Avenue of the Americas, 10036-2787
Telephone: 212-819-8200
Telex: 233188 WHCA UR
Facsimile: 212-354-8113
URL: http://www.whitecase.com
New York, New York: 1140 Avenue of the Americas, New York, NY 10036-6700.
Telephone: 212-819-8900.
New York, New York: Litigation Support Center, 1120 Avenue of the Americas, New York, NY 10036-6700.
Telephone: 212-819-7977.
Facsimile: 212-7970/71.
Los Angeles, California:
Telephone: 213-620-7700.
Facsimile: 213-687-0758; 213-452-2330; 213-452-2331.
Palo Alto, California:
Telephone: 650-213-0300.
Facsimile: 650-213-8158.
San Francisco, California:
Telephone: 415-544-1100.
Facsimile: 415-544-0202.
Miami, Florida:
Telephone: 305-371-2700.
Telephone: 305-358-5744.
Facsimile: 305-358-5766.
Washington, D.C.:
Telephone: 202-626-3600.
Facsimile: 202-639-9355.
Bratislava, Slovak Republic:
Telephone: (421-7) 5441-5100.
Facsimile: (421-7) 5441-6100.
Brussels, Belgium:
Telephone: (32-2) 219-16-20.
Facsimile: (32-2) 219-16-26.
Budapest, Hungary: Réczicza Law Firm White & Case.
Telephone: (36-1) 488-5200.
Facsimile: (36-1) 488-5299.
Frankfurt, Germany: White & Case (Rechtsanwälte).
Telephone: (49-69) 713-77-(0).
Facsimile: (49-69) 713-77-100.
Helsinki, Finland: Asianajotoimisto White & Case Oy.
Telephone: (358-9) 228-641.
Facsimile: (358-9) 228-64228.
Istanbul, Turkey:
Telephone: (90-212) 275-75-33.
Facsimile: (90-212) 275-75-43.
London, England:
Telephone: (44-20) 7600-7300.
Facsimile: (44-20) 7600-7030.
Moscow, Russia:
Telephone: (7-095) 787-3000.
Facsimile: (7-095) 787-3001.
Paris, France:
Telephone: (33-1) 55-04-15-15.
Facsimile: (33-1) 55-04-15-16.
Prague, Czech Republic:
Telephone: (420-2) 2481-0808; 2481-1796.
Facsimile: (420-2) 2481-0330; 2481-0252.
Stockholm, Sweden: White & Case Advokat AB.
Telephone: (46-8) 506-323-00.
Facsimile: (46-8) 611-21-22.
Warsaw, Poland: White & Case (Poland) Sp. z o.o.
Telephone: (48-22) 625-33-33; (48-22) 622-67-67; (48-39) 12-19-06.
Facsimile: (48-22) 628-22-28.
Johannesburg, Republic of South Africa:
Telephone: 27 (11) 884-7689.
Facsimile: 27 (11) 884-7229.
Almaty, Kazakhstan:
Telephone: (7-3272) 50-74-91.
Facsimile: (7-3272) 50-74-93.
Ankara, Turkey:
Telephone: (90-312) 442-5680.
Facsimile: (90-312) 442-5691/4.
Bangkok, Thailand: White & Case (Thailand) Limited.
Telephone: (662) 656-1721 to 32.
Facsimile: (662) 656-1733/34.
Bombay/Mumbai, India: Liaison Office, (91-22) 282-6300/01/02/03.
Facsimile: (91-22) 282-6305.
Hanoi, Vietnam:
Telephone: (84-4) 934-5355.
Facsimile: (84-4) 934-5356.

(See Next Column)

Ho Chi Minh City, Vietnam:
Telephone: (84-8) 821-0888.
Facsimile: (84-8) 823-6902.
Hong Kong:
Telephone: White & Case, Solicitors. (852) 2822-8700.
Facsimile: (852) 2845-9070.
Singapore, Republic of Singapore:
Telephone: (65) 225-6000.
Facsimile: (65) 225-6009.
Tokyo, Japan: White & Case Kandabashi Law Offices.
Telephone: (81-3) 3259-0200.
Facsimile: (81-3) 3259-0150.
Jeddah, Saudi Arabia: Law Office of Hassan Mahassni,
Telephone: (966-2) 665-4353.
Facsimile: (966-2) 669-2996.
Riyadh, Saudi Arabia: Law Office of Hassan Mahassni,
Telephone: (966-1) 464-4006.
Facsimile: (966-1) 465-1348.
Mexico City, Mexico: White & Case, S.C.
Telephone: (52) 5-540-9600.
Facsimile: (52) 5-540-9699.
São Paulo, SP, Brazil:
Telephone: (55-11) 3171-0011.
Facsimile: (55-11) 3171-0041.
Bombay/Mumbai, India: Associated Law Firm; India Law Services (ILS).
Telephones: (91-22) 284-1995; (91-22) 284-1847.
Facsimile: (91-22) 285-0824.
New Delhi, India: Associated Law Firm; India Law Services (ILS).
Telephone: (91-11) 697-1602/3/4.
Facsimile: (91-11) 698-8860.

MEMBERS OF FIRM

Roy M. Bartlett, Jr. (Palo Alto, California Office)
Cyrus Benson III
Steven M. Betensky
J. David Black (Palo Alto, California Office)
Charles N. Brower (Washington, D.C. Office)
William J. Clinton (Washington, D.C. Office)
Christopher F. Corr (Washington, D.C. Office)
Stephen M. Corse (Miami, Florida Office)
Christopher M. Curran (Washington, D.C. Office)
Dimitrios T. Drivas
C. Randolph Fishburn (Los Angeles, California Office)
Paul D. Friedland
J. Mark Gidley (Washington, D.C. Office)
Warren S. Heit (Palo Alto, California Office)
Lawrence M. Hill
Richard J. Holwell
Richard A. Horsch
David P. Houlihan (Washington, D.C. Office)
Marcos D. Jiménez (Miami, Florida Office)
M. Elaine Johnston
Charles C. Kline (Miami, Florida Office)
I. Fred Koenigsberg
Glenn M. Kurtz
Carolyn B. Lamm (Washington, D.C. Office)
Cecilia O'Brien Lofters
Donald T. MacNaughton
Thomas McGanney
James J. McGuire
Bryan A. Merryman (Los Angeles, California Office)
Thomas J. O'Sullivan
Robert D. Paul (Washington, D.C. Office)
Owen C. Pell
Robert L. Raskopf
Michael I. Saltzman
Philip H. Schaeffer
Michael S. Shuster
Gregory J. Spak (Washington, D.C. Office)
Walter J. Spak (Washington, D.C. Office)
John A. Sturgeon (Los Angeles, California Office)
John S. Willems
Carol A. Witschel
Travers D. Wood (Los Angeles, California Office)
Daniel J. Woods (Los Angeles, California Office)

LOCAL PARTNER

PARTNER OF COUNSEL

John Paul Reiner

COUNSEL

Alan Blum
John M. Genova
Dwight A. Healy
Ellen M. Jakovic (Washington, D.C. Office)
Robert M. Kelly
Richard A. Miller
Paul K. Milmed
Anne D. Smith (Washington, D.C. Office)
Mara S. Weissmann

PARTNER
RÉCZICZA LAW FIRM
WHITE & CASE

RESIDENT PARTNERS,
LONDON OFFICE

John M. H. Bellhouse
Margaret R. Cole

RESIDENT PARTNERS,
PARIS OFFICE

Stephen R. Bond
Philippe Métais
Christopher R. Seppala

LOCAL PARTNER
WARSAW OFFICE

Leslaw Z. Kostórkiewicz

RESIDENT PARTNER
JOHANNESBURG OFFICE

Ronald E. M. Goodman

(See Next Column)

WHITE & CASE—*Continued*

JAPANESE COUNSEL
TOKYO OFFICE
Yoshiko Yasuda

For Complete List of Firm Personnel, See General Section

For full biographical listings, see the Martindale-Hubbell Law Directory

WHITE, FLEISCHNER & FINO (AV)

140 Broadway, 10005
Telephone: 212-487-9700
Telecopier: 212-487-9777
Email: infor@wff-law.com
Red Bank, New Jersey Office: 272 Broad Street.
Telephone: 732-530-7787.
Telecopier: 732-530-8552.

MEMBERS OF FIRM

Paul A. Fino, Jr.
Wendy K. Carrano
Sheri E. Holland

ASSOCIATES

Dionne G. Sinclair
Joanne Carlozzi

Representative Clients: Marriott International; Avis Rent A Car; New York Central Ins. Co.; TIG Insurance; Utica Mutual; Empire Fire Mutual Ins. Co.; Acceptance Insurance; Raphael & Assoc.; Interstate Insurance Group; Gerling Insurance Co.

For Complete List of Firm Personnel, See General Section

For full biographical listings, see the Martindale-Hubbell Law Directory

WILLKIE FARR & GALLAGHER (AV)

The Equitable Center, 787 Seventh Avenue, 10019-6099
Telephone: 212-728-8000
Fax: 212-728-8111
Washington, D.C. Office: Three Lafayette Centre, 1155 21st Street, N.W., 20036-3384.
Telephone: 202-328-8000.
Fax: 202-887-8979; 202-331-8187.
Paris, France Office: 21-23 rue de la Ville l'Evêque, 75008.
Telephone: 011-33-1-53-43-45-00.
Fax: 011-33-1-40-06-96-06.
London, England Office: 35 Wilson Street, EC2M 2SJ.
Telephone: 011-44-171-696-9060.
Fax: 011-44-171-417-9191.

MEMBERS OF FIRM

Mitchell J. Auslander
Joseph T. Baio
Kevin B. Clark (Resident Partner, Washington, D.C. Office)
Louis A. Craco
David L. Foster
Stephen W. Greiner
Kelly M. Hnatt
Lawrence O. Kamin
Robert J. Kheel
Richard L. Klein
Martin B. Klotz
Jeanne M. Luboja
Richard Mancino
Francis J. Menton, Jr.
David P. Murray (Resident Partner, Washington, D.C. Office)
Roger D. Netzer
Brian E. O'Connor
John R. Oller
Anthony F. Phillips
Richard L. Posen
Steven H. Reisberg
Benito Romano
William H. Rooney
Philippe M. Salomon
Elizabeth S. Stong
Theodore C. Whitehouse (Resident Partner, Washington, D.C. Office)
Michael R. Young

For Complete List of Firm Personnel, See General Section

For full biographical listings, see the Martindale-Hubbell Law Directory

WILSON, ELSER, MOSKOWITZ, EDELMAN & DICKER LLP (AV)

150 East 42nd Street, 10017-5639
Telephone: 212-490-3000
Telex: 177679
Facsimile: 212-490-3038; 212-557-7810
URL: http://www.wemed.com
Los Angeles, California, San Diego, California, San Francisco, California, Washington, D.C., Newark, New Jersey, Philadelphia, Pennsylvania, Baltimore, Maryland, Miami, Florida, Chicago, Illinois, White Plains, New York, Dallas, Texas, Houston, Texas, Albany, New York, Garden City, New York, London, England.
Affiliates: Paris, France: Honig Buffat Mettetal., Munich, Germany: Bach, Langheid Dallmayr, Cologne, Germany: Bach, Langheid Dallmayr, Frankfurt/Main, Germany: Bach, Langheid Dallmayr, Wiesbaden, Germany: Bach, Langheid Dallmayr, Berlin, Germany: Bach, Langheid Dallmayr.

MEMBERS OF FIRM

Thomas W. Wilson
John T. Elser
Harold J. Moskowitz
Max Edelman (1906-1989)
Herbert Dicker
Michael D. Glatt
Martin M. Ween
Marshal S. Endick
Richard S. Klein
Stephen A. Postelnek
Thomas W. Hyland
Vincent R. Fontana

(See Next Column)

MEMBERS OF FIRM (Continued)

Patrick M. Kelly * (Resident Partner in Charge, Los Angeles Office)
James P. Donovan
Stephen M. Marcellino
Perry I. Kreidman
Philip J. Walsh
Edward J. Boyle
Anthony J. Mercorella
Robert M. Weber
Paul J. Bottari
Michael N. Stevens
Mark K. Anesh
Steven Kent
Harry P. Brett
Glenn J. Fuerth
Phillip A. Tumbarello
Thomas M. Gambardella
Thomas W. Tobin
Robert F. Roarke
Glen S. Feinberg
Arnold Kideckel
Francis P. Manchisi
H. Michael O'Brien
Steven L. Young
Richard H. Rubenstein
Thomas A. Leghorn
Ricki Roer
Thomas R. Manisero
Jerry B. Black
Richard S. Oelsner
Carl J. Pernicone
Carolyn Karp Schwartz
Alan Kaminsky
Robert W. Littleton
Edward A. Taylor
Rosario M. Vignali
James C. Ughetta
Robert L. Joyce
Scott R. Schaffer
Timothy J. Sheehan
John D. Morio
Yongjin Park
Robert T. Adams
Helmut Beron
Michael L. Boulhosa
Brian T. Del Gatto
Julie R. Evans
Lawrence H. Lum
Richard T. Mermelstein
Frederick W. Reif
Carl L. Steccato
Steven Verveniotis
Louis C. Roberts
Eric J. Sauter
David S. Sheiffer
Debra Tama
Lawrence B. Brennan
David A. Jones

*(Not admitted in New York)

For full biographical listings, see the Martindale-Hubbell Law Directory

WINTHROP, STIMSON, PUTNAM & ROBERTS (AV)

One Battery Park Plaza, 10004-1490
Telephone: 212-858-1000
Telex: 62854 WINSTIM
Telefax: 212-858-1500
URL: http://www.winstim.com
Stamford, Connecticut Office: Financial Centre, 695 East Main Street, P.O. Box 6760, 06904-6760.
Telephone: 203-348-2300.
Fax: 203-965-8226.
Washington, D.C. Office: 1133 Connecticut Avenue, N.W., 20036.
Telephone: 202-775-9800.
Fax: 202-833-8491.
Palm Beach, Florida Office: 125 Worth Avenue, Suite 310, 33480.
Telephone: 561-655-7297.
Fax: 561-833-6726.
London Office: 54 Lombard Street, London EC3V 9DH, England.
Telephone: 011-44207-648-9200.
Fax: 011-44207-283-1656.
Tokyo, Japan Office: 608 Atagoyama Bengoshi Building 6-7, Atago 1-chome, Minato-ku, Tokyo 105 Japan.
Telephone: 011-813-3437-9740.
Fax: 011-813-3437-9261.
Hong Kong, China Office: 2505 Asia Pacific Finance Tower, Citibank Plaza, 3 Garden Road, Central.
Telephone: 011-852-2530-3400.
Fax: 011-852-2530-3355.
Singapore Office: 6 Battery Road #38-01/B, Singapore 049909.
Telephone: 65-227-4700.
Fax: 65-227-4711.

NEW YORK OFFICE
MEMBERS OF FIRM

Frederick A. Brodie
Thomas F. Clauss, Jr.
Leo T. Crowley
Philip Le B. Douglas
Mark R. Hellerer
Sutton Keany
David G. Keyko
Susan J. Kohlmann
David M. Lindley
John F. Pritchard
Stephen A. Weiner
Edwin J. Wesely

COUNSEL

Sheila AnnMarie Moeller

SENIOR COUNSEL

Merrell E. Clark, Jr.
William W. Karatz
A. Edward Grashof

STAMFORD OFFICE
MEMBER OF FIRM

Thomas F. Clauss, Jr.

PALM BEACH OFFICE
COUNSEL

John C. Dotterrer

WASHINGTON, D.C. OFFICE
MEMBER OF FIRM

Donald A. Carr

(See Next Column)

WINTHROP, STIMSON, PUTNAM & ROBERTS, *New York—Continued*

WASHINGTON, D.C.
COUNSEL
Aileen Meyer

For Complete List of Firm Personnel, See General Section

For full biographical listings, see the Martindale-Hubbell Law Directory

*POUGHKEEPSIE,** Dutchess Co.

SATZ & KIRSHON, P.C. (AV)

309 Mill Street, 12601
Telephone: 914-454-4040
Fax: 914-454-2938
URL: http://www.lawyers.com/satz&kirshon

Perry Satz

Juliana Muyot Lobiondo

Reference: Premier National Bank.

For full biographical listings, see the Martindale-Hubbell Law Directory

*RIVERHEAD,** Suffolk Co.

ROBERT C. CRIMMINS (AV)

European American Bank Building, 209 West Main Street, P.O. Box 338, 11901
Telephone: 516-369-8448
Telecopier: 516-369-9001

ASSOCIATES

Linda D. Calder
Paula Wetstein
Donna M. Spicer

References: Suffolk County National Bank; European American Bank.

For full biographical listings, see the Martindale-Hubbell Law Directory

SMITH, FINKELSTEIN, LUNDBERG, ISLER AND YAKABOSKI, LLP (AV)

456 Griffing Avenue, P.O. Box 389, 11901
Telephone: 516-727-4100
Telecopier: 516-727-4130
Email: sfliy@peconic.net

Reginald C. Smith (1897-1983)

MEMBERS OF FIRM

Howard M. Finkelstein
Pierre G. Lundberg
Francis J. Yakaboski
Frank A. Isler
Susan Rogers Grun
Gair G. Betts
Matthew M. Finkelstein

ASSOCIATE

Dawn C. Thomas

General Counsel for: Suffolk County National Bank; Riverhead Central, Remsenburg-Speonk, East Moriches and Southampton Union Free School Districts; East Quoque, Flanders and Jamesport Fire Districts.
Local Counsel for: Village of Ocean Beach; Towns of Southhold and Riverhead; American Pulverizer, Inc.; Chips & Bits, Inc.; Reynolds Aluminum, Inc.

For full biographical listings, see the Martindale-Hubbell Law Directory

*ROCHESTER,** Monroe Co.

CONNORS & CORCORAN, L.L.P. (AV)

Suite 250, 45 Exchange Street, 14614-2002
Telephone: 716-232-5885
Fax: 716-546-3631
Email: buholtz@frontiernet.net *URL:* http://www.connorscorcoran.com

MEMBERS OF FIRM

Herbert J. LePage
Roger W. Avery
Joseph G. Fritsch, Jr.
James E. Maslyn
Eileen E. Buholtz
Cheryl Loria-Dinolfo
Gregory T. Phillips

Attorneys for: Allstate Insurance Co.; Continental National American Group; Criterion Insurance Co.; General Accident Group; Ideal Mutual Insurance Co.; Prudential Property & Casualty Co.; SAFECO; Sentry Insurance; Travelers Property Casualty.
Reference: Marine Midland Bank.

For full biographical listings, see the Martindale-Hubbell Law Directory

DOLIN & ASSOCIATES, P.C. (AV)

135 Corporate Woods, 14623
Telephone: 716-272-0540
Telecopier: 716-272-0574
TTY: 716-292-0606
URL: http://www.lawyers.com/dolin

Lonny H. Dolin

(See Next Column)

Donald G. Rehkopf, Jr.

LEGAL SUPPORT PERSONNEL

Dawn M. Stiles (Paralegal)
Laura P. Wagner (Paralegal)

For full biographical listings, see the Martindale-Hubbell Law Directory

HALLENBECK, LASCELL, NORRIS & HELLER (AV)

A Limited Liability Partnership
One Exchange Street, 14614
Telephone: 716-423-5900
Fax: 716-423-5910
Email: HLNZ@hlnz.com

MEMBERS OF FIRM

Alfred M. Hallenbeck
David M. Lascell
Michael D. Norris
Cheryl A. Heller

COUNSEL

Robert A. Feldman
David A. Wier

Daniel P. Purcell
Meghan Mc Manus Di Pasquale
Suzanne E. Ouellette
Andrea F. Basso
Robert S. Attardo

For full biographical listings, see the Martindale-Hubbell Law Directory

ROBERT J. MICHAEL (AV)

39 State Street, Suite 420, 14614
Telephone: 716-232-3460
Fax: 716-232-4583

OF COUNSEL

Mark H. Tiernan

Reference: The Chase Manhattan Bank.

For full biographical listings, see the Martindale-Hubbell Law Directory

TREVETT, LENWEAVER & SALZER, P.C. (AV)

700 Reynolds Arcade, 16 East Main Street, 14614
Telephone: 716-454-2181
Telecopier: 716-454-4026

Oscar J. Brown (1884-1958)
Melvin H. Zurett (1905-1967)
Eric P. Smith (1900-1967)
Thomas W. Sullivan (1916-1981)
William V. Gough (1922-1985)
Walter C. Eves (Retired)
Robert T. Skipworth (Retired)
Ronald James Summers (Retired)
Thomas N. Trevett
Bohdan Wenglowskyj
Thomas E. Lenweaver
Kenneth Bersani
Richard M. Doyle
James A. Valenti
Karl F. Salzer
Peter A. Jacobson
Louis B. Cristo
Cynthia A. Constantino
Henry L. Jesserer, III
Lawrence J. Andolina
James C. Gocker

John C. Palermo
Jon Paul Getz
Nicole L. Black

Representative Clients: American Motorists Insurance Co.; Lumbermens Mutual Casualty Co.; Nationwide Mutual Insurance Co.; Interboro Mutual Indemnity Insurance Co.; Michigan Mutual Liability Insurance Co.; Virginia Surety Co.; Allstate Insurance Co.; American Hardware Insurance Co.; Pearl Assurance Co., Ltd.

For full biographical listings, see the Martindale-Hubbell Law Directory

UNDERBERG & KESSLER LLP (AV)

1800 Chase Square, 14604
Telephone: 716-258-2800
Fax: 716-258-2821
Email: INFO@UNDERBERG-KESSLER.COM
Buffalo, New York Office: 1100 Main Place Tower. 14202.
Telephone: 716-848-9000.
Fax: 716-847-6004.

MEMBERS OF FIRM

Alan J. Underberg (1929-1998)
Irving L. Kessler
Michael J. Beyma
James A. Coniglio
Frank T. Crego
Robert W. Croessmann
John W. Crowe
Patrick L. Cusato
Michael C. Dwyer
Bernard A. Frank
Steven R. Gersz
Katherine Howk Karl
Lawrence P. Keller
Gordon J. Lipson
Anna E. Lynch
Robert F. Mechur
Paul V. Nunes
Terry M. Richman
J. David Sampson (Resident, Buffalo Office)
Sharon P. Stiller
Stephen H. Waite
Russell I. Zuckerman

OF COUNSEL

Andrew M. Greenstein

SENIOR ATTORNEYS

Duncan R. Farney
Ronald G. Hull

(See Next Column)

UNDERBERG & KESSLER LLP—*Continued*

ASSOCIATES

James F. Armstrong (Resident, Buffalo Office)
Karen A. DiNardo
Lise C. Hamilton
Jeffrey D. Hummel
Paul F. Keneally
Ella L. Krzanowicz
Maureen E. Mulholland
Suzanne D. Nott
Kelly L. Odorisi
Thomas A. Rall

For full biographical listings, see the Martindale-Hubbell Law Directory

ROME, Oneida Co.

PAUL L. PILECKAS (AV)

Professional Building, 217 North Washington Street, 13440
Telephone: 315-339-3020
Utica: 315-724-6381
Fax: 315-337-3876

Representative Clients: Don Davidson Motors, Inc.; Rome Rental, Inc.; West Electric, Inc.

For full biographical listings, see the Martindale-Hubbell Law Directory

STONY POINT, Rockland Co.

HURLEY, FOX, SELIG & KELLEHER (AV)

Liberty Building, Route 9 W, 10980
Telephone: 914-942-2222
Fax: 914-942-0378
Email: HFSKlaw@aol.com
New City, New York Office: 60 Pine Street.
Telephone: 614-634-2050.

MEMBERS OF FIRM

Benjamin E. Selig
Glenn W. Kelleher

ASSOCIATES

Steven L. Kahn
Dana Selig Kahn
Bob A. Kramer
Kenneth P. Silver

Representative Clients: Bradlees, Inc.; Stop & Shop Companies; CNA Insurance Cos.; Federal Insurance Co.; Chubb & Son; Commercial Union Group of Insurance Cos.; Empire Insurance Co.; Omaha, N.B.; Excelsior Insurance Co.; Fireman's Insurance Company of Washington, D.C.

For full biographical listings, see the Martindale-Hubbell Law Directory

*SYRACUSE,** Onondaga Co.

ALI, PAPPAS & COX, P.C. (AV)

Syracuse Building, 224 Harrison Street, 13202
Telephone: 315-472-4481
FAX: 315-472-8299
Email: alpaco@dreamscape.com

Lucien Ali
C. Andrew Pappas
Robert B. Cox
Thomas P. Givas
P. Douglas Dodd
David P. Doherty

OF COUNSEL

Edward F. Gerber

LEGAL SUPPORT PERSONNEL

Brenda M. Barch

Representative Clients: Agway, Inc.; Agway Petroleum Corp.; Arcom Labs; Countryside Federal Credit Union; PineCone Federal Credit Union; Oswego City Savings Bank; Telmark, Inc.; Syracuse Executive Air Services, Inc.; Fairbanks Capital Corp.
References: M&T Bank; 1st National Bank of Rochester.

For full biographical listings, see the Martindale-Hubbell Law Directory

ANDREWS LAW OFFICES (AV)

217 South Salina Street, Sixth Floor, 13202
Telephone: 315-471-2413
Telecopier: 315-471-7849
Email: andrews@servtech.com

William S. Andrews

For full biographical listings, see the Martindale-Hubbell Law Directory

CARROLL, CARROLL, DAVIDSON & YOUNG, P.C. (AV)

The Galleries of Syracuse, Second Floor, 441 South Salina Street, 13202-0352
Telephone: 315-474-5356
Fax: 315-474-5451

Lee Carroll
John Benjamin Carroll (P.C.)
Eugene B. Young
J. Alexander Davidson

Woodruff L. Carroll
Sarkis L. Harootunian

For full biographical listings, see the Martindale-Hubbell Law Directory

COSTELLO COONEY & FEARON, LLP (AV)

Salina Place, 205 South Salina Street, 13202
Telephone: 315-422-1152
Fax: 315-422-1139
Email: ccf-law.com *URL:* http://www.ccf-law.com

MEMBERS OF FIRM

Robert J. Smith
James J. Gascon
Paul G. Ferrara
Maureen G. Fatcheric
Daniel Fletcher

ASSOCIATES

Robert W. Connolly
David S. Grasso
Samuel C. Young

OF COUNSEL

Vincent A. O'Neil

General Counsel: Auburn Memorial Hospital; Crouse-Irving Memorial Hospital.
Local Counsel: Caterpillar, Inc.; Otis Elevator; Deere & Co.; New York Telephone Co.; Crum & Forster Insurance Co.; General Motors Acceptance Corp.; American District Telegraph (A&T); Pyramid Brokerage Co.

For Complete List of Firm Personnel, See General Section

For full biographical listings, see the Martindale-Hubbell Law Directory

LYNN LAW OFFICE (AV)

802 M & T Bank Building, 101 S. Salina Street, 13202
Telephone: 315-474-1267
Fax: 315-474-4514
Skaneateles, New York Office: 88 East Genesee Street.
Telephone: 315-685-1207.
Fax: 315-685-1047.

MEMBERS OF FIRM

William F. Lynn
Patricia A. Lynn-Ford
Thomas F. Shannon

For full biographical listings, see the Martindale-Hubbell Law Directory

MARTIN, MARTIN & WOODARD, LLP (AV)

Suite 300, One Lincoln Center, 13202-3010
Telephone: 315-478-2222
Fax: 315-478-4318

MEMBERS OF FIRM

Donald J. Martin
David P. Martin
Lee E. Woodard
Harold P. Goldberg
David M. Capriotti

ASSOCIATES

Wendy A. Kinsella
James T. Snyder
Daniel E. Dyer

For full biographical listings, see the Martindale-Hubbell Law Directory

SUGARMAN, WALLACE, MANHEIM & SCHOENWALD (AV)

HSBC Center, Fifth Floor, 360 South Warren Street, 13202-2680
Telephone: 315-474-2943
Fax: 315-474-0235
URL: http://www.sugarmanlaw.com
Buffalo Office: 1720 Rand Building, 14 Lafayette Square, 14203.
Telephone: 716-847-2523.
Fax: 716-847-2589.

MEMBERS OF FIRM

David B. Sugarman (1885-1968)
Milton Wallace (1917-1985)
George E. DeMore
James G. Stevens, Jr.
Samuel Vulcano
Robert P. Dwyer
Timothy J. Perry
Stephen G. Pesarchick
Charlene E. McGraw
Paul V. Mullin
David A. Kalabanka
Brian Sutter
Kevin T. Hunt
Sherry R. Bruce
Thomas J. Murphy
Sam A. Elbadawi

ASSOCIATES

Matthew D. Gumaer
Keith D. Miller
Brandon R. King
Kevin R. Van Duser
James E. Hanlon
James O. Taylor
Gina M. Panighetti
Gary H Collison
Tasha T. Dandridge

OF COUNSEL

Charles M. Manheim
Alan J. Goldberg
Donald L. Schoenwald

Representative Clients: Allstate Insurance Co.; CNA Insurance Companies; Chubb & Son; Liberty Mutual Insurance Co.; Carpenter Manufacturing Co., Inc.; General Accident Group; Hartford Accident & Indemnity Co.; Firemans Fund; New York Central Mutual; Progressive Insurance Co.
Reference: HSBC.

For full biographical listings, see the Martindale-Hubbell Law Directory

*TROY,** Rensselaer Co.

E. STEWART JONES (AV)

28 Second Street, 12181
Telephone: 518-274-5820
Fax: 518-274-5875
Email: info@esjlaw.com

E. Stewart Jones, Jr. — Jeffrey K. Anderson
W. Farley Jones — David J. Taffany
Peter J. Moschetti, Jr.

OF COUNSEL

E. Stewart Jones — Abbott H. Jones (1873-1939)
Arthur L. Rosen — Charles W. Marshall (1882-1945)

References: Key Bank and On Bank; Troy Savings Bank.

For full biographical listings, see the Martindale-Hubbell Law Directory

UNIONDALE, Nassau Co.

LEHMAN & EILEN LLP (AV)

50 Charles Lindbergh Boulevard, Suite 505, 11553-3600
Telephone: 516-222-0888
Fax: 516-222-0948
Email: info@lehmaneilen.com *URL:* http://www.securitiesattys.com

MEMBERS OF FIRM

Bob E. Lehman — Howard S. Eilen

OF COUNSEL

Hank Gracin — Timothy P. Kebbe

ASSOCIATES

Stephanie G. Senzer — Audrey Blain
Maureen Ann Porette — Scott D. Stechman
Eva M. Possavino — Steven J. Pappas

For full biographical listings, see the Martindale-Hubbell Law Directory

RIVKIN, RADLER & KREMER LLP (AV)

A Partnership including Professional Corporations
EAB Plaza (Long Island), 11556-0111
Telephone: 516-357-3000
Cable Address: "Atlaw"
Telex: 645-074
Telecopier: 516-357-3333
URL: http://www.rivkinradler.com
Chicago, Illinois Office: Suite 4300, 30 North LaSalle Street.
Telephone: 312-782-5680.
Telecopier: 312-782-3112.
New York, New York Office: 275 Madison Avenue.
Telephone: 212-455-9555.
Telecopier: 212-687-9044.
Santa Rosa, California Office: 100 B Street, Suite 300, P.O. Box 14609.
Telephone: 707-525-5400.
Telecopier: 707-576-7955.
Newark, New Jersey Office: One Gateway Center, Suite 1226.
Telephone: 973-622-0900.
Fax: 973-622-7878.

MEMBERS OF FIRM

Arthur J. Kremer — Gary D. Centola
Bruce D. Drucker (P.C.) — Anthony R. Gambardella
William M. Savino — Peter C. Contino
Donald T. McMillan (Resident, Santa Rosa, California Office) — Erica B. Garay
Charlotte Biblow
John L. Rivkin — Steven Brock
Stephen J. Smirti, Jr. (P.C.) — George K. DeHaven
Richard S. Feldman — M. Paul Gorfinkel

OF COUNSEL

William J. Candee, III — Charles H. Reinhardt, Jr.

Representative Clients: Fireman's Fund Insurance Companies; Allstate Insurance Company; Aegis Insurance Services Inc.; Commercial Union Insurance Company; Home Insurance Company; State Farm Insurance Company; Royal Insurance Company; Aetna Property & Casualty; ITT Hartford Insurance Group; Medical Liability Mutual.

For Complete List of Firm Personnel, See General Section

For full biographical listings, see the Martindale-Hubbell Law Directory

*UTICA,** Oneida Co.

GORMAN, WASZKIEWICZ, GORMAN & SCHMITT (AV)

1508 Genesee Street, 13502-5178
Telephone: 315-724-2147
Fax: 315-724-1183
Email: gwgslaw@borg.com

MEMBERS OF FIRM

Bartle Gorman (1897-1974) — Bartle J. Gorman
Edwin A. Waszkiewicz (1917-1998) — William P. Schmitt

(See Next Column)

ASSOCIATE

Darryl B. Rahn

General Counsel for: Carton Foundation, Inc.; T. C. Peters Printing Co., Inc.; Insight House Chemical Dependency Services, Inc.; Town of Whitestown; Village of Clinton.
Local Counsel for: Utica Mutual Insurance Co.; Graphic Arts Mutual Insurance Co.; United National Insurance Co.;
References: Key Bank of N.Y.; Marine Midland Bank.

For full biographical listings, see the Martindale-Hubbell Law Directory

JULIAN & PERTZ, P.C. (AV)

1629 Oneida Street, 13501-4701
Telephone: 315-797-5610
Fax: 315-797-7403

Robert F. Julian — Richard Pertz

LEGAL SUPPORT PERSONNEL

Tracey A. Mills (Paralegal) — Barbara A. Clark (Paralegal)
Nadine J. McIntyre (Paralegal)

For full biographical listings, see the Martindale-Hubbell Law Directory

WESTBURY, Nassau Co.

PRYOR & MANDELUP, L.L.P. (AV)

675 Old Country Road, 11590
Telephone: 516-997-0999
Facsimile: 516-333-7333

Robert L. Pryor — Randolph E. White
A. Scott Mandelup — Eric J. Snyder

Kenneth A. Reynolds — Anthony F. Giuliano
Christopher W. Costello

OF COUNSEL

Michael Salgo — C. Albert Parente

LEGAL SUPPORT PERSONNEL

Gwendolyn V. Myles — Barbara Anson

For full biographical listings, see the Martindale-Hubbell Law Directory

*WHITE PLAINS,** Westchester Co.

BOEGGEMAN, GEORGE, HODGES & CORDE, P.C. (AV)

11 Martine Avenue, 10606
Telephone: 914-761-2252
Telecopier: 914-761-5211
Email: boeggeman@bghc-law.com *URL:* http://www.bghc-law.com
Albany, New York Office: 46 Columbia Street, 12207-2716.
Telephone: 518-465-1100.
Fax: 518-465-1800.

George S. Hodges — Robert S. Ondrovic
Richard G. Corde — Thomas A. Sica (Resident Managing Attorney, Albany Office)
John J. Walsh, II
Harold L. Moroknek

Karen A.D. Jockimo — Leslie K. Arfine
William M. Wingertzahn — John T. Holden
Elizabeth C. Mirisola — James J. Lofrese
Cynthia Dolan — Jeanne M. Hurley
Marcella M. Green — Ira H. Lapp
Paul A. Hurley — Matt Randolph Belkin
Cynthia K. Messemer

OF COUNSEL

Joseph H. George — John E. Boeggeman (1919-1993)

Representative Clients: American Telephone & Telegraph; Anheuser-Busch Companies, Inc.; Lowe's Home Centers; Great Atlantic & Pacific Tea Company; Reliance National Insurance Company; Metropolitan Property & Casualty Insurance Company; Fisher Price, Inc.; CGU Insurance Company; United Services Automobile Association; New York Central Mutual Fire Insurance Company.

For full biographical listings, see the Martindale-Hubbell Law Directory

ANTHONY J. CAPUTO, P.C. (AV)

175 Main Street, 10601
Telephone: 914-948-5151
Fax: 914-761-1246

Anthony J. Caputo

OF COUNSEL

Bruce F. Caputo

References: The Bank of New York; Chemical Bank; Citicorp.

For full biographical listings, see the Martindale-Hubbell Law Directory

White Plains—Continued

CERUSSI & SPRING, A PROFESSIONAL CORPORATION (AV)

One North Lexington Avenue, 10601-1700
Telephone: 914-948-1200
Facsimile: 914-948-1579
Greenwich, Connecticut Office: 66 Field Point Road.
Telephone: 203-661-4000.
Facsimile: 203-661-1197.

MEMBERS OF FIRM

Michael A. Cerussi, Jr. — Ronald G. Crispi
Thomas F. Cerussi — Arthur J. Spring

ASSOCIATES

Laura Morrison Allen — Laura M. Garcia
Donald S. Campbell — Gregg P. Garneau
Michael F. Cavolo (Not admitted in NY) — Thomas M. Giangrande
Lisa Conte — Evy L. Kazansky
Thomas M. Crispi — Peter Riggs
Frank J. DeSalvo, Jr. — John A. Risi
D. Bradford Sessa
Kevin P. Westerman

SENIOR COUNSEL

Richard D. Bentzen

OF COUNSEL

Alfred E. Page, Jr.

For full biographical listings, see the Martindale-Hubbell Law Directory

---

GREENE & ZINNER, P.C. (AV)

202 Mamaroneck Avenue, 10601
Telephone: 914-948-4800
FAX: 914-948-4936

Andrew Greene — Stanley S. Zinner

Arthur M. Neiss — Jarrod S. Schlesinger

For full biographical listings, see the Martindale-Hubbell Law Directory

---

GREENSPAN & GREENSPAN (AV)

34 South Broadway, Suite 605, 10601-4400
Telephone: 914-946-2500
Cable Address: "Gadlex"
Telecopier: 914-946-1432
Email: GandGEsqs@aol.com
Boca Raton, Florida Office: Greenspan & Kane, 301 Yamato Road, Suite 3160.
Telephone: 561-995-8140.
Oradell, New Jersey Office: 690 Kinderkamack Rd., 07649.
Telephone: 201-599-2849; 800-553-6009.

MEMBERS OF FIRM

Leon J. Greenspan — Michael E. Greenspan

For full biographical listings, see the Martindale-Hubbell Law Directory

---

HENDERSON & BRENNAN (AV)

222 Mamaroneck Avenue, 10605
Telephone: 914-761-2700
Telecopier: 914-761-2708
Email: HendBren@interport.net *URL:* http://www.lawyers.com/henderson&grennan

Francis J. Henderson (1929-1994) — John T. Brennan
Brian C. Henderson
Lauren J. De Mase

Reference: Hudson Valley Bank.

For full biographical listings, see the Martindale-Hubbell Law Directory

---

HOFFMAN, WACHTELL, KOSTER & MAIER (AV)

399 Knollwood Road, 10603
Telephone: 914-682-8000
FAX: 914-682-1512
URL: http://www.lawyers.com/hwk&mlaw

MEMBERS OF FIRM

Lee A. Hoffman, Jr. — Eric D. Koster
Marc J. Wachtell — Lynn J. Maier

Representative Clients: Mount Hope Mines, Inc.; Eastern Educational Consortium; Westchester Community College; Prime Office Systems, Inc.; Purchase Environmental Protection Association, Inc.; The Jay Coalition; The Town of Greenburgh; The Town of Mamaroneck; The City of Mt. Vernon.
Reference: Citibank, N.A. (White Plains Branch).

For full biographical listings, see the Martindale-Hubbell Law Directory

---

MCGOVERN AND DAWSON (AV)

50 Main Street, 10606
Telephone: 914-686-1055
Fax: 914-948-4721

(See Next Column)

MEMBERS OF FIRM

Joseph W. McGovern — Lawrence F. McGovern

OF COUNSEL

Philip C. McGovern

For full biographical listings, see the Martindale-Hubbell Law Directory

---

ROBERT G. O'DONNELL (AV)

50 Main Street, Suite 405, 10606
Telephone: 914-761-1600
Fax: 914-761-4016
URL: http://www.lawyers.com/robertgodonnelllaw

For full biographical listings, see the Martindale-Hubbell Law Directory

---

O'KEEFFE & LINDGREN, LLP (AV)

707 Westchester Avenue, 10604
Telephone: 914-948-5300
Fax: 914-948-5399
URL: http://www.lawyers.com/okeeffe&lindgrenlaw

MEMBERS OF FIRM

Richard J. O'Keeffe — Thomas K. Lindgren
Joseph J. Staropoli, Jr.

OF COUNSEL

Robert L. Conkling

LEGAL SUPPORT PERSONNEL

PARALEGAL

Elizabeth M. Cleary

Reference: Chase Bank/NBW.

For full biographical listings, see the Martindale-Hubbell Law Directory

---

STEPHENS, BARONI, REILLY & LEWIS LLP (AV)

Northcourt Building, 175 Main Street, 10601
Telephone: 914-761-0300; 683-5185
Telecopier: 914-761-0995; 683-1323
URL: http://www.lawyers.com/sbrl
Cross River, New York Office: Northern Westchester Office, Old Post Road Professional Building, 10518.
Telephone: 914-763-3232.

MEMBERS OF FIRM

Gerald D. Reilly — Roland A. Baroni, Jr.
Stephen R. Lewis

ASSOCIATE

Roland T. Koke

OF COUNSEL

James R. Caruso (1906-1994)

For full biographical listings, see the Martindale-Hubbell Law Directory

---

VOUTÉ, LOHRFINK, MAGRO & COLLINS, LLP (AV)

170 Hamilton Avenue, 10601-1789
Telephone: 914-946-1400
Facsimile: 914-946-8024

Arthur J. Vouté, Jr. — Charles D. Lohrfink, Jr.
Richard L. Magro — Charles A. Collins, Jr.

Elliot A. Cristantello — Hal Roberts
Stephen F. Fischer — Stephen J. Riebling, Jr.
Ralph F. Schoene — John A. Howard
Kevin P. Fitzpatrick — Michael A. Sonkin
Catherine F. Gale — Kelly E. Cardany

Representative Clients: Aetna Casualty & Surety Co.; Allstate Insurance Co.; Chubb Group; CNA Companies; Medical Liability Mutual Insurance Co.; National Car Rental System, Inc.; Physicians Reciprocal Insurance Co.; Preferred Physicians Medical Insurance Co.; Risk Enterprise Management; St. Josephs Medical Center.

For full biographical listings, see the Martindale-Hubbell Law Directory

---

FRANCIS X. YOUNG (AV)

81 Main Street, 10601
Telephone: 914-285-1500
Fax: 914-285-0055
Email: leighyoung@mindspring.com *URL:* http://www.lawyers.com/fxyounglaw
New York City Office: 67 Wall Street, 24th Floor, 10005.
Telephone: 212-323-8040.
Fax: 212-943-2300.

For full biographical listings, see the Martindale-Hubbell Law Directory

YONKERS, Westchester Co.

ECKER, LOEHR, ECKER & ECKER, L.L.P. (AV)

One Executive Boulevard, 10701
Telephone: 914-968-0500; 914-965-4288
FAX: 914-968-0918
Email: eleellp@aol.com
New York, New York Office: 521 Fifth Avenue, 27th Floor, 10175.
Telephone: 914-965-4288;
Fax: 914-968-0918.

MEMBERS OF FIRM

Gerald E. Loehr
Louis A. Ecker
Lawrence H. Ecker
Robert L. Ecker

OF COUNSEL

Jock Thornton
Iris J. Iler
Tammi L. Blank-Ecker

LEGAL SUPPORT PERSONNEL

Carolyn Caruso

Reference: Hudson Valley National Bank.

For full biographical listings, see the Martindale-Hubbell Law Directory

NORTH CAROLINA

*ASHEVILLE,** Buncombe Co.

LONG, PARKER, WARREN & JONES, P.A. (AV)

Suite 600, 14 South Pack Square, P.O. Box 7216, 28801
Telephone: 828-258-2296
Fax: 828-253-1073

Robert B. Long, Jr.
William A. Parker
Steve Ray Warren
W. Scott Jones

Kimberly A. Lyda
Philip Scott Anderson

For full biographical listings, see the Martindale-Hubbell Law Directory

McGUIRE, WOOD & BISSETTE, P.A. (AV)

Drhumor Building, 48 Patton Avenue, P.O. Box 3180, 28802
Telephone: 828-254-8800
Fax: 828-252-2438
Email: mwb@mwbavl.com

Richard A. Wood, Jr.
W. Louis Bissette, Jr.
Douglas O. Thigpen
Joseph P. McGuire
Doris Phillips Loomis
M. Charles Cloninger
Thomas C. Grella
Grant B. Osborne
T. Douglas Wilson, Jr.
Richard A. Kort
John N. Fleming

Representative Clients: Asheville Citizen-Times Publishing Co.; Dave Steel Co., Inc. (Steel Fabricating); WLOS-TV; The Givens Estates, Inc. (Retirement Community); Hayes & Lunsford Electrical Contractors, Inc.; Wellco Enterprises, Inc.; BASF Corp.; First Union National Bank of North Carolina; St. Joseph's Hospital; Carolina Power & Light Company.

For Complete List of Firm Personnel, See General Section

For full biographical listings, see the Martindale-Hubbell Law Directory

*BEAUFORT,** Carteret Co.

DAVIS, MURRELLE & LUMSDEN, P.A. (AV)

412 Front Street, P.O. Box 819, 28516
Telephone: 252-728-4080
Fax: 252-728-3235
URL: http://www.lawyers.com/dmtlaw

Edward L. Murrelle
Treve B. Lumsden

Janet M. Lyles

OF COUNSEL

Warren J. Davis

Representative Clients: Cooperative Bank for Savings; Roman Catholic Diocese of Raleigh for Carteret County; International Longshoreman's Association Local 1807; Town of Cedar Point; John Yancey Corp.; Morehead City Export Terminal, Inc.; Crow Hill Farms, Inc.; Phoenix Foods, Inc.; Core Sound Waterfowl Museum, Inc.; Northland Ins. Co.

For full biographical listings, see the Martindale-Hubbell Law Directory

CARY, Wake Co.

BROOKS, STEVENS & POPE, P.A. (AV)

2000 Regency Parkway, Suite 150, P.O. Box 1870, 27511-8507
Telephone: 919-481-9103
Fax: 919-481-9137
Email: attys@bsp-pa.com *URL:* http://www.bsp-pa.com

David Victor Brooks
Robert H. Stevens, Jr.
Daniel Carter Pope, Jr.
Jane Kestenbaum
Michael C. Sigmon
Kathlyn Corbett Hobbs
Robert S. Welch

Amy K. Whinery
Ashley B. White
Paul F. Toland
Joy H. Brewer
John Abb Payne
Alicia M. Benson
Matthew P. Blake
Matthew John Dixon

OF COUNSEL

Archie W. Futrell, III
Cathy A. Hinton Pope

For full biographical listings, see the Martindale-Hubbell Law Directory

CHAPEL HILL, Orange Co.

EPTING & HACKNEY (AV)

410 Airport Road, P.O. Box 1329, 27514
Telephone: 919-929-0323
Fax: 919-929-3960

MEMBERS OF FIRM

Robert Epting
Joe Hackney
Elizabeth Lackey Jacobs
Karen P. Davidson
Steve Lackey

For full biographical listings, see the Martindale-Hubbell Law Directory

LONG & LONG (AV)

127 TimberHill Place, 27514
Telephone: 919-929-0408
Fax: 919-929-6819

MEMBERS OF FIRM

Lunsford Long
Florence J. Long

For full biographical listings, see the Martindale-Hubbell Law Directory

RUDOLF & MAHER, P.A. (AV)

312 West Franklin Street, 27516
Telephone: 919-967-4900
Fax: 919-967-4953

David S. Rudolf
Thomas K. Maher

For full biographical listings, see the Martindale-Hubbell Law Directory

BARRY T. WINSTON (AV)

The Center, Suite 300, 1506 East Franklin Street, 27514
Telephone: 919-967-8553
Fax: 919-968-4698

Reference: Village Bank.

For full biographical listings, see the Martindale-Hubbell Law Directory

*CHARLOTTE,** Mecklenburg Co.

BAILEY, PATTERSON, CADDELL, HART, MILLIKEN & BAILEY, P.A. (AV)

Suite 502, Cameron Brown Building, 301 South McDowell Street, 28204
Telephone: 704-333-8612
FAX: 704-333-5279
Email: BaileyPA8@aol.com

Allen A. Bailey
Michael A. Bailey
William J. Patterson
H. Morris Caddell, Jr.
Walter L. Hart, IV
Emery E. Milliken
Martha L. Ramsay
Helen Ruth Harwell

For full biographical listings, see the Martindale-Hubbell Law Directory

CAUDLE & SPEARS, P.A. (AV)

2600 Interstate Tower, 121 West Trade Street, 28202
Telephone: 704-377-1200
Telecopier: 704-338-5858
Email: caudlespears@caudlespears.com

Lloyd C. Caudle
Harold C. Spears
L. Cameron Caudle, Jr.
Timothy T. Leach
Christopher J. Loebsack
Michael J. Selle

Counsel for: Bituminous Casualty Corp.; Baumann Springs A.G.; The A. G. Boone Co.; Capitol Funds, Inc.; Consolidated Freightways; Employers Mutual Casualty Co.; Mark Oil Company, Inc.; Metromont Materials; Otis Elevator Co.; N.C. Farm Bureau Mutual Insurance Co.

(See Next Column)

CAUDLE & SPEARS P.A.—*Continued*

For Complete List of Firm Personnel, See General Section

For full biographical listings, see the Martindale-Hubbell Law Directory

CLAWSON & STAUBES, L.L.C. (AVⓣ)

756 Tyvola Road, Suite 101, P.O. Box 241352, 29217
Telephone: 843-522-7733
Fax: 843-522-9033
Email: rcraig@clawson&staubes.com
Charleston, South Carolina Office: 304 Meeting Street, 29401.
Telephone: 803-577-2026.
Facsimile: 803-722-2867.

Samuel R. Clawson
Ronnie F. Craig
(Not admitted in NC)
C.O. Ladd Ackerman, Jr.

William Lewis Ellison, Jr.
Jennifer Susan Ahlers

Representative Clients: Allstate Insurance Co.; Bituminous Insurance Co.; Catawba Insurance Co.; Nationwide Mutual Insurance Co.; Selective Insurance Co.; State Farm Insurance Co.; Maryland Casualty Co.; Unisun Insurance Co.; Universal Insurance Co.

For full biographical listings, see the Martindale-Hubbell Law Directory

DEAN & GIBSON, L.L.P. (AV)

Suite 900, Cameron Brown Building, 301 South McDowell Street, 28204-2686
Telephone: 704-372-2700
Facsimile: 704-372-1804
Email: info@deanandgibson.com

Rodney A. Dean
Michael G. Gibson
Brien D. Stockman
Christopher J. Culp

ASSOCIATES

John Whitelaw Ong
Colin E. Scott
Kimberly A. Gossage
Thomas G. Nance, II

OF COUNSEL

Barbara J. Dean

For full biographical listings, see the Martindale-Hubbell Law Directory

DOZIER, MILLER, POLLARD & MURPHY (AV)

Cameron Brown Building, 301 South McDowell Street, Suite 700, 28204
Telephone: 704-372-6373
Fax: 704-347-0674
URL: http://www.dmpm.com

MEMBERS OF FIRM

W. Joseph Dozier, Jr.
R. Craig Miller, Jr.
Scott T. Pollard
Gary L. Murphy
William Patrick Hobson
Timothy H. Graham
George N. Miller
Richard S. Gordon
Thomas J. Falish
Kristin L. Smith

For full biographical listings, see the Martindale-Hubbell Law Directory

FERGUSON, STEIN, WALLAS, ADKINS, GRESHAM & SUMTER, P.A. (AV)

741 Kenilworth Avenue, Suite 300, 28204-2828
Telephone: 704-375-8461
Fax: 704-334-5654
Mailing Address: P.O. Box 36486, 28236-6486
Email: FSWAGS@aol.com
Chapel Hill, North Carolina Office: Suite 2, 312 West Franklin Street.
Telephone: 919-933-5300.
Fax: 919-967-4953.

James E. Ferguson, II
Adam Stein
(Resident, Chapel Hill Office)
Jonathan Wallas
Karl Adkins
John W. Gresham
Geraldine Sumter
Henderson Hill
Thomas M. Stern
(Resident, Chapel Hill Office)
C. Margaret Errington
Stephen Luke Largess

Rebecca Ann Thorne
James E. Ferguson, III
Corie Diane Pauling
Ann C. Todd

For full biographical listings, see the Martindale-Hubbell Law Directory

GOLDING HOLDEN COSPER POPE & BAKER, L.L.P. (AV)

Suite 1200, Cameron Brown Building, 301 South McDowell Street, 28204
Telephone: 704-374-1600
Fax: 704-374-1103

MEMBERS OF FIRM

John G. Golding
C. Byron Holden
Harvey L. Cosper, Jr.
James W. Pope
Lawrence M. Baker

(See Next Column)

ASSOCIATES

Chip Holmes, Jr.
Betsy J. Jones
Tricia Y. Morvan
Robert J. Aylward
John H. Beyer
J. Timothy Sparks

Representative Clients: State Farm Insurance Companies; St. Paul Insurance Companies; Allstate Insurance Company; Nationwide Mutual Insurance Companies.

For full biographical listings, see the Martindale-Hubbell Law Directory

MITCHELL, RALLINGS, SINGER, MCGIRT & TISSUE, PLLC (AV)

1800 Carillon, 227 West Trade Street, 28202
Telephone: 704-376-6574
FAX: 704-342-1531

MEMBERS OF FIRM

Richard M. Mitchell
Thomas B. Rallings, Jr.
Joseph N. Tissue

ASSOCIATES

James L. Fretwell
John W. Taylor
Carl Spencer Alridge, II

Representative Clients: Bonitz Contracting Co.; Captain D's. Inc.; Dyke Industries, Inc.; Edgcomb Metals; Titan Building Products, Inc.
References: Bank of Mecklenburg; Central Carolina Bank ; N.C.N.B.

For full biographical listings, see the Martindale-Hubbell Law Directory

RAYBURN, MOON & SMITH, P.A. (AV)

The Carillon, 227 West Trade Street, Suite 1200, 28202-1675
Telephone: 704-334-0891
Fax: 704-377-1897; 704-377-0395
Email: rmslaw@aol.com

Albert F. Durham
Travis W. Moon
C. Richard Rayburn, Jr.
James C. Smith
W. Scott Cooper
Paul R. Baynard
James B. Gatehouse
G. Kirkland Hardymon
James L. Bagwell
Patricia B. Edmondson
Natalie R. Denton
Robert Aubrey Cox, Jr.
Tricia L. Rolewicz

For full biographical listings, see the Martindale-Hubbell Law Directory

WOMBLE CARLYLE SANDRIDGE & RICE (AV)

A Professional Limited Liability Company
3300 One First Union Center, 301 South College Street, 28202-6025
Telephone: 704-331-4900
Fax: 704-331-4955
Email: lawyers@wcsr.com *URL:* http://www.wcsr.com
Winston-Salem, North Carolina Office: 200 West Second Street, P.O. Drawer 84.
Telephone: 336-721-3600.
Fax: 336-721-3660.
Raleigh, North Carolina Office: 2100 First Union Capitol Center, 150 Fayetteville Street Mall, P.O. Box 831.
Telephone: 919-755-2100.
Fax: 919-755-2150.
Research Triangle Park, North Carolina Office: 2505 Meridian Parkway, Suite 300 (Durham), 27713.
Telephone: 919-484-2300.
Fax: 919-484-2340.
Atlanta, Georgia Office: One Atlantic Center, 1201 West Peachtree Street, Suite 3500.
Telephone: 404-872-7000.
Fax: 404-888-7490.
Other Atlanta, Georgia Office: Suite 404, 2296 Henderson Mill Road, N.E.
Telephone: 770-492-9030.
Fax: 770-492-9609.
Washington, D.C. Office: 1120 Nineteenth Street, N.W., Eighth Floor.
Telephone: 202-857-4400.
Fax: 202-467-6910.
Greenville, South Carolina Office: 15 South Main Street, Suite 601, P.O. Box 10208.
Telephone: 864-255-5400.
Fax: 864-255-5440.

RESIDENT MEMBERS

Timothy G. Barber
G. Michael Barnhill
Jim D. Cooley
Bradford A. DeVore
Debbie Weston Harden
Mark P. Henriques
William C. Raper
F. Lane Williamson

RESIDENT ASSOCIATES

Patricia E. Dowds
Steven D. Gardner
W. Clark Goodman
Brian E. Heim

Representative Clients: Childress Klein Properties, Inc.; Food Lion, Inc.; J.A. Jones Construction Co.; Parkdale Mills, Inc.; Pillowtex; Duke Power Co.; Bowles Hollowell Conner & Co.; ALLTEL Carolina, Inc.; Belk Store Services, Inc.; Philip Holzmann A.G.

(See Next Column)

WOMBLE CARLYLE SANDRIDGE & RICE, *Charlotte—Continued*

For Complete List of Firm Personnel, See General Section

For full biographical listings, see the Martindale-Hubbell Law Directory

LAW OFFICES OF JAMES F. WYATT III (AV)

435 East Morehead Street, 28202-2609
Telephone: 704-331-0767
Fax: 704-331-0773
Email: jfwlaw@charlotte.infi.net *URL:* http://www.lawyers.com/jamesfwyatt

ASSOCIATE

Robert A. Blake, Jr.

For full biographical listings, see the Martindale-Hubbell Law Directory

*DURHAM,** Durham Co.

GLENN, MILLS & FISHER, P.A. (AV)

Suite 709, South Bank Building, 400 West Main Street, P.O. Drawer 3865, 27702-3865
Telephone: 919-683-2135
Fax: 919-688-9339

Robert B. Glenn, Jr.
William S. Mills
Stewart W. Fisher

Caitlyn T. Fulghum

For full biographical listings, see the Martindale-Hubbell Law Directory

HAYES HOFLER & ASSOCIATES, P.A. (AV)

1007 Vickers Avenue, 27707-1355
Telephone: 919-682-9663
Fax: 919-682-2016

R. Hayes Hofler

OF COUNSEL

Daniel B. Hill

For full biographical listings, see the Martindale-Hubbell Law Directory

*ELIZABETH CITY,** Pasquotank Co.

HORNTHAL, RILEY, ELLIS & MALAND, L.L.P. (AV)

301 East Main Street, P.O. Box 220, 27909
Telephone: 252-335-0871
Fax: 252-335-4223
URL: http://www.hrem.com
Nags Head, North Carolina Office: 2502 South Croatan Highway, P.O. Box 310, 27959-0310.
Telephone: 252-441-0871.
Telefax: 252-441-8822.

L. P. Hornthal, Jr.
J. Fred Riley
L. Phillip Hornthal III
Thomas L. White, Jr. (Resident, Nags Head Office)
M. H. Hood Ellis
Mark M. Maland
Donald C. Prentiss
Robert B. Hobbs, Jr. (Resident, Nags Head Office)
John D. Leidy
Michael P. Sanders
Lee L. Leidy
David A. Miller

John Charles White

Representative Clients: Elizabeth City-Pasquotank County Board of Education; Kemper Insurance Group; State Farm Mutual; Travelers Insurance Co.; Wachovia Bank of North Carolina, N.A.; Great American Insurance Co.; Horace Mann Insurance Companies; Dare County Airport Authority; N.C. Interlocal Risk Financing Fund; Pennsylvania National Insurance Group.

For full biographical listings, see the Martindale-Hubbell Law Directory

*GREENSBORO,** Guilford Co.

ALEXANDER RALSTON, SPECKHARD & SPECKHARD, L.L.P. (AV)

218 West Friendly Avenue, 27401
Telephone: 336-379-9302
Fax: 336-370-1232
URL: http://www.lawyers.com/aralston,speckhard

Donald K. Speckhard
Stanley E. Speckhard

Representative Clients: Preferred Furniture Components, Inc.; Spring Financial Services, Inc.; Blazer Financial Services; Omega Sports, Inc.; Power & Heat Systems, Inc.; Branch & Company, P.A.; Acme Florist Supply, Inc.

For full biographical listings, see the Martindale-Hubbell Law Directory

BARRON & BERRY, L.L.P. (AV)

301 South Greene Street, Suite 310, 27401
Telephone: 336-274-4782
Fax: 336-379-8592
Mailing Address: P.O. Box 2370, Greensboro, North Carolina, 27402-2370
Email: vbarron@worldnet.att.net *URL:* http://www.lawyers.com/barronberrylaw

Vance Barron, Jr.
Frederick L. Berry

For full biographical listings, see the Martindale-Hubbell Law Directory

BROOKS, PIERCE, MCLENDON, HUMPHREY & LEONARD, L.L.P. (AV)

2000 Renaissance Plaza, 230 North Elm Street (27401), P.O. Box 26000, 27420-6000
Telephone: 336-373-8850
Facsimile: 336-378-1001
Raleigh, North Carolina Office: 1600 First Union Capitol Center, 150 Fayetteville Street Mall, 27601, P.O. Box 1800, 27602-1800.
Telephone: 919-839-0300.
Facsimile: 919-839-0304.

MEMBERS OF FIRM

Aubrey L. Brooks (1872-1958)
William H. Holderness (1904-1965)
Lennox P. McLendon (1890-1968)
Kenneth M. Brim (1898-1974)
C. Theodore Leonard, Jr. (1929-1983)
Claude C. Pierce (1913-1988)
Thornton H. Brooks (1912-1988)
G. Neil Daniels (1911-1997)
Lennox P. McLendon, Jr.
Hubert Humphrey
Edgar B. Fisher, Jr.
W. Erwin Fuller, Jr.
James T. Williams, Jr.
Wade H. Hargrove
M. Daniel McGinn
Michael D. Meeker
William G. McNairy
Edward C. Winslow, III
Howard L. Williams
George W. House
William P. H. Cary
Reid L. Phillips
Robert A. Singer
John H. Small
Randall A. Underwood
S. Leigh Rodenbough, IV
William G. Ross, Jr.
Mark J. Prak
Jill R. Wilson
Marc D. Bishop
Jim W. Phillips, Jr.
Mack Sperling
Jeffrey E. Oleynik
Mark Davidson
James R. Saintsing
John W. Ormand, III
Robert J. King, III
Steven J. Levitas
V. Randall Tinsley
John R. Archambault
S. Kyle Woosley
Daniel M. Sroka
Forrest W. Campbell, Jr.
Marcus W. Trathen
Jean C. Brooks
Ellen P. Hamrick
James C. Adams, II
Allison M. Grimm
Elizabeth S. Brewington

ASSOCIATES

H. Arthur Bolick, II
Natasha Rath Marcus
John M. Cross, Jr.
Jennifer K. Van Zant
Kearns Davis
David W. Sar
Kathleen M. Thornton
Brian J. McMillan
Jennifer L. Bolick
David Kushner
Derek J. Allen
Elizabeth V. LaFollette
Ginger S. Shields
Harold H. Chen
Coe W. Ramsey
Natalie Kay Sanders
Robert W. Saunders
David Shub
Jennifer T. Harrod
Matthew G. Bibbens
Charles E. Coble
John M. DeAngelis
Clinton R. Pinyan
Kathryn V. Purdom
Andrew Kirk Susong

General Counsel for: North Carolina Bankers Association; Trident Securities, Inc.
Division Counsel for: Norfolk Southern Railway Co.
Attorneys for: Burlington Industries, Inc.; Guilford Mills, Inc.; Wachovia Bank, N.A.; PCS Phosphate Company, Inc.; CCB Financial Corporation; Public Service Company of North Carolina.
Labor Counsel for: Lorillard Tobacco Co.

For full biographical listings, see the Martindale-Hubbell Law Directory

BURTON & SUE, L.L.P. (AV)

419 North Elm Street, P.O. Box 20083, 27420
Telephone: 336-275-0512
Facsimile: 336-378-1390

MEMBERS OF FIRM

Gary K. Sue
Walter K. Burton

ASSOCIATES

James D Secor, III
William T. Corbett, Jr.
William L. Hill
Kurt A. Seeber

For full biographical listings, see the Martindale-Hubbell Law Directory

CARRUTHERS & ROTH, P.A. (AV)

235 North Edgeworth Street, P.O. Box 540, 27402
Telephone: 336-379-8651
Fax: 336-273-7885

(See Next Column)

CARRUTHERS & ROTH P.A.—*Continued*

Joseph T. Carruthers, Jr. (1906-1992)
Charles E. Roth (1917-1992)
Walter Rand
Seldon E. Patty
Thomas E. Wagg, III
Kenneth M. Greene
Richard L. Vanore
William L. Tankersley, III
Kenneth R. Keller
L. Worth Holleman, Jr.
Arthur A. Vreeland
Thomas W. Sinks
Jack B. Bayliss, Jr.
Howard L. Borum
J. Scott Dillon
J. Stanley Atwell
Kenneth L. Jones
June L. Basden
Desmond G. Sheridan
Michael J. Allen
Pamela Sarsfield Fox
Gregory S. Williams
John M. Flynn

Keith A. Wood
Christopher J. Vaughn
Norman F. Klick, Jr.
Joe Franklin Teague, Jr.

Representative Clients: AC Corp.; The Bank of New York; First Union Commercial Corp.; Kay Chemical Co.; Kemper Insurance Group; Marine Midland Bank; Metropolitan Life Insurance Co.; Fleet Capital Corp.; Thompson-Arthur Paving Co.

For full biographical listings, see the Martindale-Hubbell Law Directory

CLARK BLOSS & McIVER, PLLC (AV)

600 Dixie Building, 125 South Elm Street, P.O. Box 1349, 27402
Telephone: 336-275-7275
Fax: 336-275-1401
Email: cbm@cbm-law.com

David M. Clark
John F. Bloss
Robert G. McIver
Jonathan Wall

Representative Clients: The Prudential Insurance Company of America (litigation); Johnson Controls, Inc.
Approved Attorneys for: Jefferson-Pilot Insurance Co.

For full biographical listings, see the Martindale-Hubbell Law Directory

HENSON & HENSON, L.L.P. (AV)

Suite 600, The Piedmont Building, 114 North Elm Street, 27401
Telephone: 336-275-0587
Facsimile: 336-273-2585
Mailing Address: P.O. Box 3525, 27402,
Email: hensnlaw@bellsouth.net

MEMBERS OF FIRM

Perry C. Henson
Perry C. Henson, Jr.

ASSOCIATE

Clayton B. Krohn

Representative Clients: Canal Ins. Company; Employers Mutual Insurance Companies; Erie Insurance Group; Fireman's Fund Ins. Company; Frontier Risk Managers; IHDS Corporation; K & K Insurance Group; Kentucky Medical Insurance Company; Kmart Corporation; Lawyers Mutual Liability Ins. Co.

For full biographical listings, see the Martindale-Hubbell Law Directory

HILL, EVANS, DUNCAN, JORDAN & DAVIS (AV)

A Professional Limited Liability Company
1400 Renaissance Plaza, 230 North Elm Street, P.O. Box 989, 27402
Telephone: 336-379-1390
Fax: 336-379-1198
Email: hedjd@worldnet.att.net

MEMBERS OF FIRM

Welch Jordan (1912-1976)
William D. Caffrey (1928-1991)
Karl N. Hill, Jr.
Thomas C. Duncan
William Welch Jordan
Lindsay Reeves Davis, Jr.
Joseph R. Beatty
R. Thompson Wright
Everett B. Saslow, Jr.
Richard J. Votta
Polly D. Sizemore
Charles W. Coltrane
George G. Lockhart

ASSOCIATES

Michele G. Smith
Joseph P. Gram
Elaine Hedrick Ashley
Scott B. Murray (Not admitted in NC)
Richard T. Granowsky

OF COUNSEL

G. Marlin Evans

Representative Clients: Ford Motor Credit Co.; Gilbarco, Inc.; Jefferson-Pilot Corp.; Rheem Manufacturing Co.; Overnight Transportation Co.

For full biographical listings, see the Martindale-Hubbell Law Directory

LAWING SHARPLESS & STAVOLA, P.A. (AV)

826 North Elm Street, P.O. Box 22106, 27420
Telephone: 336-333-6400
Facsimile: 336-333-6399
URL: http://www.elsfirm.com

(See Next Column)

Sally A. Lawing
Brenda S. McClearn
Pamela A. Robertson
Frederick K. Sharpless
Joseph M. Stavola

Joseph P. Booth, III
Eugene E. Lester, III
Marylynn E. Skaggs

Representative Clients: Church Mutual Insurance Co.; CNA Insurance Group; Moses H. Cone Memorial Hospital; High Point Regional Hospital; Jefferson Pilot Corporation.

For full biographical listings, see the Martindale-Hubbell Law Directory

PINTO COATES KYRE & BROWN, PLLC (AV)

3203 Brassfield Road, 27410
Telephone: 336-282-8848
Facsimile: 336-282-8409
Mailing Address: P.O. Box 4848, Greensboro, N.C., 27404
Email: PCKB@Interpath.com

Richard L. Pinto
Paul D. Coates
Kenneth Kyre, Jr.
David L. Brown
Martha P. Brown
Nancy R. Meyers
John I. Malone, Jr.
Deborah J. Bowers

Representative Clients: Travelers; Grain Dealers Mutual Insurance Co.; N.C. Farm Bureau Insurance Co.; Southern Pilot Insurance Co.; Peerless Insurance Co.; Penn National Insurance Co.; Virginia Mutual Insurance Co.; GAB Business Services; Harleysville Mutual Insurance Co.; Selective Insurance.

For full biographical listings, see the Martindale-Hubbell Law Directory

HICKORY, Catawba Co.

SIGMON, CLARK, MACKIE, HUTTON & HANVEY, P.A. (AV)

420 Third Avenue, N.W., P.O. Drawer 1470, 28603
Telephone: 828-328-2596
FAX: 828-328-6876

William R. Sigmon
E. Fielding Clark, II
Jeffrey T. Mackie
Warren A. Hutton
J. Scott Hanvey
Forrest A. Ferrell

Stephen L. Palmer

OF COUNSEL

Marshall V. Yount

Representative Clients: First Union National Bank; Cox Manufacturing Co.
Local Counsel for: The Ohio Casualty Group of Insurance Cos.; United States Fidelity and Guaranty Insurance Co.

For full biographical listings, see the Martindale-Hubbell Law Directory

HIGH POINT, Guilford Co.

WYATT, EARLY, HARRIS & WHEELER, L.L.P. (AV)

1912 Eastchester Drive, Suite 400, P.O. Drawer 2086, 27261
Telephone: 336-884-4444
Fax: 336-889-5232
Email: wyattlaw@northstate.net

MEMBERS OF FIRM

Frank Burkhead Wyatt
William P. Harris
A. Doyle Early, Jr.
William E. Wheeler
David B. Ashcraft
Kim W. Gallimore
Kim R. Bauman
Calvin B. Bryant
R. Bruce Laney
Charles A. Alt
Frederick G. Sawyer
James R. Hundley
Charles L. Cain
Thomas E. Terrell, Jr.
Lee M. Cecil
Ann E. Hanks
John D. Bryson
Stanley F. Hammer
Scott Fitzgerald Wyatt
Debbi L. Aberman (Retired)

Representative Clients: Allstate Insurance Co.; Davis Furniture Industries; First Union National Bank; Dar-Ran Furniture Industries; First Citizens Bank & Trust Co.; Ohio Casualty Insurance Co.; Mid-State Petroleum; Branch Bank & Trust Co.; British Vita.

For full biographical listings, see the Martindale-Hubbell Law Directory

*NEW BERN,** Craven Co.

KELLUM & JONES, P.A. (AV)

219 Broad Street, P.O. Box 866, 28563
Telephone: 919-633-2550
Fax: 919-633-4623
Jacksonville, North Carolina Office: 445-L Western Boulevard.
Telephone: 910-455-4546.
Fax: 910-455-2422.

John W. Beaman (1911-1984)
Norman B. Kellum, Jr.
Douglas M. Jones

(See Next Column)

KELLUM & JONES P.A., *New Bern—Continued*

Michael E. Garland
John T. Briggs
T. Russell Peterman, Jr.
Russell L. Needell
J. Kevin Jones

For full biographical listings, see the Martindale-Hubbell Law Directory

*RALEIGH,** Wake Co.

ALLEN & MOORE, L.L.P. (AV)

3700 Computer Drive, Suite 320, 27609-8627
Telephone: 919-783-8023
Fax: 919-783-8282
Email: ALLNMOORE@AOL.COM

Arch T. Allen, III
Joseph C. Moore, III
Ann Strader Hanley

For full biographical listings, see the Martindale-Hubbell Law Directory

BAILEY & DIXON, L.L.P. (AV)

2500 Two Hannover Square, 434 Fayetteville Street Mall, P.O. Box 1351, 27602
Telephone: 919-828-0731
Facsimile: 919-828-6592
Email: info@bdixon.com *URL:* http://www.bdixon.com

MEMBERS OF FIRM

Ralph McDonald
Gary S. Parsons
Carson Carmichael, III
Alan J. Miles
Patricia P. Kerner
Cathleen M. Plaut
David S. Coats
M. Denise Stanford
Kenyann Brown Stanford

OF COUNSEL

J. Ruffin Bailey
Wright T. Dixon, Jr. (Retired)
James H. Walker (1920-1994)
David M. Britt

ASSOCIATES

David Scott Wisz
Warren Tobin Savage, IV
Rita Lane Hanshumaker
Dayatra T. King
Philip Todd Gray
Ali John Hoomani

Representative Clients: Nationwide Insurance Co.; Lawyers Mutual Liability Insurance Company of North Carolina; Aetna Life and Casualty Insurance Company; Santee Carriers; Abbott Laboratories Inc.; GAB Business Services, Inc.; Sta-Rite Industries, Inc.; Hartford Insurance Group; Interlocal Risk Financing Fund of North Carolina; Erie Insurance Co.; State Auto Insurance Co.

For full biographical listings, see the Martindale-Hubbell Law Directory

MANNING & CROUCH (AV)

133 Fayetteville Street Mall, Suite 210, P.O. Box 350, 27602
Telephone: 919-828-5778
Fax: 919-828-5045
Email: manninglaw@worldnet.att.net

Thomas C. Manning
James A. Crouch

LEGAL SUPPORT PERSONNEL

Janie Riggan (Paralegal)

For full biographical listings, see the Martindale-Hubbell Law Directory

RAGSDALE LIGGETT, PLLC (AV)

A Professional Limited Liability Company
Suite 400 Crosspointe Plaza, 2840 Plaza Place, P.O. Box 31507, 27612
Telephone: 919-787-5200
Fax: 919-783-8991; 881-2045

MEMBERS OF FIRM

George R. Ragsdale
Frank R. Liggett III
William A. Mann
Steven I. Reinhard
William S. Bost, III
Dorothy Bass Burch
James Allen Hoffman (Not admitted in NC)

OF COUNSEL

Joseph E. Johnson

ASSOCIATES

Kathleen Pepi Southern
Walter L. Tippett, Jr.
David K. Liggett
Kathleen C. Mcconnell

For full biographical listings, see the Martindale-Hubbell Law Directory

SMITH DEBNAM NARRON WYCHE STORY & MYERS, L.L.P. (AV)

Hedingham Oaks, 4700 New Bern Avenue, P.O. Box 26268, 27611-6268
Telephone: 919-250-2000
Facsimile: 919-250-2100
Email: smithdebnamlaw.com

(See Next Column)

MEMBERS OF FIRM

W. Thurston Debnam, Jr.
John W. Narron
Jerry T. Myers
Terri L. Gardner
Byron L. Saintsing
Franklin Drake
Gerald H. Groon, Jr.
Terry M. Kilbride
Elizabeth B. Godfrey
N. Hunter Wyche, Jr.
Ashley H. Story
Bettie Kelley Sousa
Laura K. Howell
Rose H. Stout
Susan Yelton Ellinger
Caren Davis Enloe
Connie E. Carrigan
Jeff D. Rogers
Kevin L. Sink

ASSOCIATES

Melanie J. Hogg
Staci Flaxman Katz
Tabatha L. Cruden
Tracy T. Hyde
Nina L. Gunther
Matthew E. Roehm
Sharon B. Christopher
J. Michael Mackay
Cynthia V. Mcalister

OF COUNSEL

Fred J. Smith, Jr.
Jane Flowers Finch

Representative Clients: Eastman Kodak Co.; Hardee's Food Systems; General Electric Capital Corp.; Wal-Mart; Ford Motor Credit Co.

For full biographical listings, see the Martindale-Hubbell Law Directory

TWIGGS, ABRAMS, STRICKLAND & TREHY, P.A. (AV)

First Union Capitol Center, 150 Fayetteville Street Mall, Suite 1100, P.O. Drawer 30, 27602
Telephone: 919-828-4357
Fax: 919-833-7924
Email: tastlaw@tast.com

Howard F. Twiggs
Douglas B. Abrams
Donald R. Strickland
Jerome P. Trehy, Jr.
Karen M. Rabenau

OF COUNSEL

Donald H. Beskind
Margaret Smith Abrams
Jeff Erick Essen

For full biographical listings, see the Martindale-Hubbell Law Directory

WOMBLE CARLYLE SANDRIDGE & RICE (AV)

A Professional Limited Liability Company
2100 First Union Capitol Center, 150 Fayetteville Street Mall, P.O. Box 831, 27602
Telephone: 919-755-2100
Fax: 919-755-2150
Email: lawyers@wcsr.com *URL:* http://www.wcsr.com
Charlotte, North Carolina Office: 3300 One First Union Center, 301 South College Street.
Telephone: 704-331-4900.
Fax: 704-331-4955.
Winston-Salem, North Carolina Office: 200 West Second Street, P.O. Drawer 84.
Telephone: 336-721-3600.
Fax: 336-721-3660.
Research Triangle Park, North Carolina Office: 2505 Meridian Parkway, Suite 300 (Durham), 27713.
Telephone: 919-484-2300.
Fax: 919-484-2340.
Atlanta, Georgia Office: One Atlantic Center, 1201 West Peachtree Street, Suite 3500.
Telephone: 404-872-7000.
Fax: 404-888-7490.
Other Atlanta, Georgia Office: Suite 404, 2296 Henderson Mill Road, N.E.
Telephone: 770-492-9030.
Fax: 770-492-9609.
Washington, D.C. Office: 1120 Nineteenth Street, N.W., Eighth Floor.
Telephone: 202-857-4400.
Fax: 202-467-6910.
Greenville, South Carolina Office: 15 South Main Street, Suite 601, P.O. Box 10208.
Telephone: 864-255-5400.
Fax: 864-255-5440.

RESIDENT MEMBERS

Jerry S. Alvis
Susan Davis Crooks
Charles A. Edwards
Robert E. Fields III
Marilyn R. Forbes
Christopher T. Graebe
Johnny M. Loper
Pressly M. Millen
Robert H. Sasser, III

RESIDENT ASSOCIATES

Coleman M. Cowan
Mark A. Davis
Jeffrey M. Hahn
G. Christopher Olson
M. Todd Sullivan

RESIDENT OF COUNSEL

Elizabeth LeVan Riley

Representative Clients: Aetna Casualty and Surety Co., Inc.; ALSCO/AmeriMark Building Products, Inc.; Aoki Corporation America, Inc.; Hackney Brothers, Inc.; Lawyers Mutual Liability Insurance Company of

(See Next Column)

WOMBLE CARLYLE SANDRIDGE & RICE—*Continued*

North Carolina; Meredith College; Regency Park Corp.; Wachovia Bank, N.A.

For Complete List of Firm Personnel, See General Section

For full biographical listings, see the Martindale-Hubbell Law Directory

YATES, MCLAMB & WEYHER, L.L.P. (AV)

One Hannover Square, 421 Fayetteville Street Mall, Suite 1200, 27601
Telephone: 919-835-0900
Fax: 919-835-0910
Mailing Address: P.O. Box 2889, 27602-2889

MEMBERS OF FIRM

R. Scott Brown
Derek M. Crump
Dan J. McLamb
John W. Minier
Rodney E. Pettey
O. Craig Tierney, Jr.
Andrew A. Vanore, III
Kirk G. Warner
Barbara B. Weyher
Joseph W. Yates, III (Retired)

ASSOCIATES

Virginia Green Adams
Michael J. Byrne
Hunt K. Choi
Barry S. Cobb
Renee Billings Crawford
Susan T. Fountain
Gwenda L. Laws
Michael E. McDaniel
Travis K. Morton
Shirley Maring Pruitt
Beth Y. Smoot
Diane S. Tilley
Michael W. Washburn

OF COUNSEL

Michael C. Hurley

Representative Clients: Aetna Casualty & Surety Co.; CIGNA Cos.; Chrysler Corp.; Ford Motor Co.; General Electric Co.; Nissan Motor Corp.; Sears Roebuck & Co.; Upjohn Co.; Sandoz Pharmaceuticals Corp.; St. Paul Insurance Cos.

For full biographical listings, see the Martindale-Hubbell Law Directory

*SMITHFIELD,** Johnston Co.

GORDON C. WOODRUFF (AV)

1023 B West Market Street, P.O. Box 708, 27577
Telephone: 919-934-4000
Fax: 919-934-5884

For full biographical listings, see the Martindale-Hubbell Law Directory

*SYLVA,** Jackson Co.

COWARD, HICKS & SILER, P.A. (AV)

705 West Main Street, 28779
Telephone: 828-586-2147
Fax: 828-586-2605
Franklin, North Carolina Office: 43 West Main Street, 28734.
Telephone: 828-524-6475.
Fax: 828-524-9833.
Cashiers, North Carolina Office: P.O. Box 1918, 28717.
Telephone: 828-743-2401.
Fax: 828-743-2403.

James Kent Coward (1929-1989)
Orville D. Coward
Ralph L. Hicks (Resident, Cashiers Office)
Robert F. Siler (Resident, Franklin Office)
Orville D. Coward, Jr. (Resident, Franklin Office)
J. K. Coward, Jr.
William H. Coward (Resident, Franklin Office)
Kimberly R. Coward (Resident, Cashiers Office)
Monty C. Beck (Resident, Franklin Office)
Richard K. Walker (Resident at Franklin Office)

Representative Clients: First Union National Bank; Wachovia Bank and Trust Co.; Haywood Savings and Loan Association; NationsBank of North Carolina; Cotton States Mutual Insurance Co.

For full biographical listings, see the Martindale-Hubbell Law Directory

*WILMINGTON,** New Hanover Co.

HOGUE, HILL, JONES, NASH AND LYNCH, L.L.P. (AV)

101 S. Third Street, P.O. Drawer 2178, 28402
Telephone: 910-763-4565
Telecopier: 910-762-6687

MEMBERS OF FIRM

Cyrus D. Hogue (1888-1960)
W. Talmage Jones
David A. Nash
William O. J. Lynch
James B. Snow, III
Wayne A. Bullard

OF COUNSEL

Cyrus D. Hogue, Jr.
William L. Hill, II
Roy C. Bain

(See Next Column)

ASSOCIATE

Stacey L. Fuller

Representative Clients: NationsBank, N.A.; International Paper Company; Kaiser Aluminum & Chemical Corporation; Clancy & Theys Construction Company; New Hanover County Board of Education; El Dorado Chemical Company; Lancer Claims Service; Independence Mall Associates; Wilmington Shipping Company.

For full biographical listings, see the Martindale-Hubbell Law Directory

MARSHALL, WILLIAMS & GORHAM, L.L.P. (AV)

14 South Fifth Street, P.O. Drawer 2088, 28402-2088
Telephone: 910-763-9891
Telecopier: 910-343-8604
URL: http://www.mwglaw.com

MEMBERS OF FIRM

Alan A. Marshall (1908-1979)
Lonnie B. Williams
A. Dumay Gorham, Jr.
Jerry C. Woodell
William Robert Cherry, Jr.
Ronald H. Woodruff
Lonnie B. Williams, Jr.
John Dearman Martin
Charles D. Meier
John L. Coble

Representative Clients: Miller Building Corp.; Kemper Insurance Cos.; State Farm Insurance; K-Mart, Inc.; CNA Insurance Cos.; Aetna/Travelers Insurance Co.; American Continental Insurance Co./MMI; New Hanover Regional Medical Center.

For full biographical listings, see the Martindale-Hubbell Law Directory

MURCHISON, TAYLOR & GIBSON, L.L.P. (AV)

16 North Fifth Avenue, 28401-4593
Telephone: 910-763-2426
Fax: 910-763-6561

MEMBERS OF FIRM

Wallace C. Murchison (Retired)
Joseph O. Taylor, Jr.
Frank B. Gibson, Jr.
Michael Murchison
Nancy M. Guyton
W. Berry Trice
G. Stephen Diab
James W. Latshaw

ASSOCIATE

Frances Youngblood Trask

Representative Clients: BellSouth; Branch Banking & Trust Co.; General Electric Co.; Landfall Assn.; Landmark Organization, Inc.; Lawyer's Mutual Liability Co.; Pharmaceutical Products Development, Inc.; Trustees, Employers-ILA Pension, Welfare and Vacation Fund; Worsley Cos., Inc.

For full biographical listings, see the Martindale-Hubbell Law Directory

ROUNTREE & SEAGLE, L.L.P. (AV)

2419 Market Street, P.O. Box 1409, 28403
Telephone: 910-763-3404
Telecopier: 910-763-0320
URL: http://www.ltinet.com/rountree&seagle

MEMBERS OF FIRM

George Rountree, Jr. (1904-1979)
George Rountree, III
J. Harold Seagle
Geoffrey A. Losee
Charles S. Baldwin, IV
Brian N. Bishop

OF COUNSEL

George K. Freeman, Jr.

ASSOCIATE

J. Mark Seagle

Representative Clients: American International Marine Agency; Fireman's Fund Insurance Cos.; The Japan Shipowners' Mutual Protection & Indemnity Assn., Ltd.; Time Warner Cable - Advance/Newhouse Partnership.
Approved Attorneys for: Chicago Title Insurance Co.; Commonwealth Land Insurance Co.; Investors Title Insurance Co.; Lawyers Title Insurance Corp.
References: Centura Bank; First Union National Bank of North Carolina.

For full biographical listings, see the Martindale-Hubbell Law Directory

*WINSTON-SALEM,** Forsyth Co.

JOHN R. SURRATT, P.A. (AV)

102 West Third Street Suite 700, 27101
Telephone: 336-725-8323
Facsimile: 336-722-5218
Email: surrattpa@aol.com

John R. Surratt
Anita M. Conrad

For full biographical listings, see the Martindale-Hubbell Law Directory

Winston-Salem—Continued

WOMBLE CARLYLE SANDRIDGE & RICE (AV)

A Professional Limited Liability Company
200 West Second Street, P.O. Drawer 84, 27102
Telephone: 336-721-3600
Fax: 336-721-3660
Email: lawyers@wcsr.com *URL:* http://www.wcsr.com
Charlotte, North Carolina Office: 3300 One First Union Center, 301 South College Street.
Telephone: 704-331-4900.
Fax: 704-331-4955.
Raleigh, North Carolina Office: 2100 First Union Capitol Center, 150 Fayetteville Street Mall, P.O. Box 831.
Telephone: 919-755-2100.
Fax: 919-755-2150.
Research Triangle Park, North Carolina Office: 2505 Meridian Parkway, Suite 300 (Durham), 27713.
Telephone: 919-484-2300.
Fax: 919-484-2340.
Atlanta, Georgia Office: One Atlantic Center, 1201 West Peachtree Street, Suite 3500.
Telephone: 404-872-7000.
Fax: 404-888-7490.
Other Atlanta, Georgia Office: Suite 404, 2296 Henderson Mill Road, N.E.
Telephone: 770-492-9030.
Fax: 770-492-9609.
Washington, D.C. Office: 1120 Nineteenth Street, N.W., Eighth Floor.
Telephone: 202-857-4400.
Fax: 202-467-6910.
Greenville, South Carolina Office: 15 South Main Street, Suite 601, P.O. Box 10208.
Telephone: 864-255-5400.
Fax: 864-255-5440.

RESIDENT MEMBERS

Reid C. Adams, Jr.
Conrad C. Baldwin, Jr.
H. Grady Barnhill, Jr.
Jimmy H. Barnhill
S. Fraley Bost
Charles A. Burke
Karen Estelle Carey
Keith A. Clinard
Clayton M. Custer
Tyrus V. Dahl, Jr.
Jeffrey L. Furr
Allan R. Gitter
Ellen M. Gregg
R. Howard Grubbs
Hada V. Haulsee
Lori Privette Hinnant
Martin L. Holton, III
R. Michael Leonard
James R. Morgan, Jr.
Alexander S. Nicholas
Robert S. Pierce
Michael E. Ray
Richard T. Rice
Thomas D. Schroeder
J. Keith Tart
Keith W. Vaughan
G. Criston Windham
Erna A. P. Womble
William F. Womble, Jr.

RESIDENT ASSOCIATES

Kenneth R. Ashford
Amy L. Bircher
John J. Bowers
Ursula M. Henninger
Kenneth R. Michael
John F. Morrow, Jr.
Donald J. Scales

MEMBER OF COUNSEL

W. David Edwards
Kurt C. Stakeman
Dewey W. Wells

Representative Clients: Brad Ragan, Inc.; Brenner Companies; Food Lion, Inc.; Hanes Companies, Inc.; North Carolina Baptist Hospitals, Inc.; R.J. Reynolds Tobacco Co.; Thomasville Furniture Industries, Inc.; Wachovia Corp.; Wake Forest University.

For Complete List of Firm Personnel, See General Section

For full biographical listings, see the Martindale-Hubbell Law Directory

NORTH DAKOTA

*BISMARCK,** Burleigh Co.

PEARCE AND DURICK, PLLP (AV)

314 East Thayer Avenue, P.O. Box 400, 58502
Telephone: 701-223-2890
Fax: 701-223-7865
Email: law.office@pearce-durick.com *URL:* http://www.pearce-durick.com

MEMBERS OF FIRM

Patrick W. Durick
B. Timothy Durick
Gary R. Thune
David E. Reich
Jerome C. Kettleson
Larry L. Boschee
Lawrence Bender

Representative Clients: American Insurance Assn.; Attorneys Liability Protection Society; Deere & Co.; Ford Motor Co.; General Motors Corp.; MDU Resources Group, Inc.; Royal Insurance Co.; Case Corp.; Navistar International Transportation Corp.; North Dakota Insurance Reserve Fund.

(See Next Column)

For Complete List of Firm Personnel, See General Section

For full biographical listings, see the Martindale-Hubbell Law Directory

TSCHIDER & SMITH (AV)

A Partnership including Professional Corporations
Professional Building - Suite 200, 418 East Rosser Avenue, 58501
Telephone: 701-258-4000
Fax: 701-258-4001
Email: ssmith@tschider-smithlaw.com

MEMBERS OF FIRM

Morris A. Tschider (P.C.)
Sean O. Smith (P.C.)
David A. Tschider

Representative Clients: Agri Bank, FCB; Farm Credit Services of Mandan, FLCA; Farm Credit Services of Mandan, P.C.A.; Twin City Implement, Inc.; First Bank Bismarck; N.D. Independent Insurance Agents; Western Steel & Plumbing; Froelich Oil Co.; Bismarck Eagles; St. Alexius Medical Center.

For full biographical listings, see the Martindale-Hubbell Law Directory

ZUGER KIRMIS & SMITH (AV)

A Partnership including Professional Corporations
316 North Fifth Street, P.O. Box 1695, 58502-1695
Telephone: 701-223-2711
Fax: 701-223-7387; 701-223-9619
Email: zkslaw@zkslaw.com *URL:* http://www.zkslaw.com

Lyle W. Kirmis
Thomas O. Smith, P.C.
Lance D. Schreiner, P.C.
James S. Hill, P.C.
Patrick J. Ward
Rebecca S. Thiem, P.C.
Daniel S. Kuntz, P.C.
Brenda L. Blazer, P.C.
Jerry W. Evenson, P.C.
Brent J. Edison, P.C.
Christine A. Hogan
Lawrence A. Dopson
Lawrence E. King

ASSOCIATES

Jodi Billing Bjornson
Tracy Vigness Kolb

OF COUNSEL

John A. Zuger, P.C.

Representative Clients: Burlington Northern Railroad Co.; Continental Western Insurance Company; Coregis, Inc.; Farmers Insurance Group; Nodak Mutual Farm Bureau; PHICO Ins. Co.; St. Paul Cos.; State Farm Insurance Co.; Suzuki Motor Corp.; Williston Basin Interstate Pipeline Company, a wholly-owned subsidiary of Montana Dakota Utilities Resources Group, Inc.

For full biographical listings, see the Martindale-Hubbell Law Directory

*FARGO,** Cass Co.

CONMY, FESTE, HUBBARD, CORWIN & BRUST, LTD. (AV)

200 Norwest Center, 406 Main Avenue, 58126
Telephone: 701-293-9911
Fax: 701-293-3133
URL: http://www.conmylaw.com

Charles A. Feste
Paul M. Hubbard
Wickham Corwin
Kim E. Brust
Michael M. Thomas
Robert J. Schultz
Nancy J. Morris

OF COUNSEL

Lauris N. Molbert
E. T. Conmy, Jr.

Representative Clients: Ford Motor Credit Co.; Norwest Corporation Region VII Banks (North Dakota & Minnesota West); U.S. Gypsum Co.
Insurance: American Hardware Insurance Group; Great American Insurance Companies; Zurich Commercial.

For full biographical listings, see the Martindale-Hubbell Law Directory

JEFFRIES, OLSON, FLOM & BULLIS, P.A. (AV)

1325 23rd Street S.W., 58103
Telephone: 701-280-2300
Fax: 701-280-1880
Moorhead, Minnesota Office: 403 Center Avenue, P.O. Box 9, 56561-0001.
Telephone: 218-233-3222.
Fax: 218-233-7065.

Richard N. Jeffries
Thomas R. Olson
Joel A. Flom
James R. Bullis
Ronald J. Knoll
Michael S. Montgomery
Michelle M. Donarski

John T. Goff

Representative Clients: American International Adjustment Co.; American States Insurance Co.; Farmers Insurance Group; Federated Mutual Insurance Co.; Fireman's Fund Insurance Co.; Hartford Insurance Co.; Midwest Medical Insurance Co.; Nodak Mutual Insurance Co.; St. Paul Fire & Marine Insurance Co.

For full biographical listings, see the Martindale-Hubbell Law Directory

Fargo—Continued

NILLES, HANSEN & DAVIES, LTD. (AV)

1800 Radisson Tower, P.O. Box 2626, 58108
Telephone: 701-237-5544
Facsimile: 701-280-0762
Williston, North Dakota Office: Energy Resource Building, 504 East Broadway, Suite 101, P.O. Box 1525.
Telephone: 701-572-5544.
Fax: 701-572-5561.

Timothy Q. Davies
Duane H. Ilvedson
E. Thomas Conmy, III
Stephen W. Plambeck
Leo F. J. Wilking
Richard Henderson
Daniel J. Crothers
William P. Harrie
Mark R. Hanson
Harry M. Pippin
Douglas W. Gigler
Virginia G. Carter
LaDonne R. Vik

Representative Clients: Burlington Northern; First Bank of North Dakota (NA); Blue Cross/Blue Shield; John Deere Company; Nash Finch Company; National Railroad Passenger Corp. (Amtrak); U.S. Bank National Association; Northern States Power; Lutheran Health Systems.

For Complete List of Firm Personnel, See General Section

For full biographical listings, see the Martindale-Hubbell Law Directory

VOGEL, WEIR, BYE, HUNKE & MCCORMICK, LTD. (AV)

502 First Avenue North, P.O. Box 1389, 58107
Telephone: 701-237-6983
Facsimile: 701-237-0847
Email: vogellaw@vogellaw.com *URL:* http://www.vogellaw.com

H. Patrick Weir
Kermit Edward Bye
Carlton J. Hunke
C. Nicholas Vogel
Maurice G. McCormick
Mart Daniel Vogel
William A. Schlossman, Jr.
Jane C. Voglewede
Jon R. Brakke
W. Todd Haggart

Representative Clients: Associated General Contractors of North Dakota; Blue Shield of North Dakota; Cass County Electric Cooperative, Inc.; Clark Equipment Co.; Forum Communications Company; Merit Care Medical Group; Northern Improvement Co.; Dakota Clinic Ltd.; United Parcel Service; Gateway Chevrolet, Inc.

For Complete List of Firm Personnel, See General Section

For full biographical listings, see the Martindale-Hubbell Law Directory

OHIO

*AKRON,** Summit Co.

OLDHAM & DOWLING (AV)

195 South Main Street Suite 300, 44308
Telephone: 330-762-7377
Telecopier: 330-762-7390
Email: wdowling@oldham-dowling.com *URL:* http://www.lawyers.com/oldham&dowling

William M. Oldham
William D. Dowling, Jr.
Hamilton DeSaussure, Jr.
Martin R. Hulthen
Joseph K. Oldham
Raymond C. Mueller
Blake R. Gerney

Representative Clients: State Farm Mutual Automobile Insurance Co.; State Farm Mutual Fire Insurance Co.; Ohio Casualty Group Insurance Companies; Step II Corp.; WCI Steel Inc.; American States Insurance Co.; Taco Bell Corp.; May Company Department Stores; National City Bank, Masco.
Reference: Key Bank.

For full biographical listings, see the Martindale-Hubbell Law Directory

A. RUSSELL SMITH (AV)

503 Key Building, 159 South Main Street, 44308
Telephone: 330-434-7167; 877-434-7167
Fax: 330-434-7195
Email: smithar@bright.net

A. Russell Smith

R. Bryan Nace

For full biographical listings, see the Martindale-Hubbell Law Directory

BRUCE H. WILSON (AV)

Twin Oaks Estate, 1225 West Market Street, 44313-7188
Telephone: 330-865-1230
Fax: 330-864-7986
Email: wilson@twinoaks.com *URL:* http://www.lawyers.com/bwilsonlaw

(See Next Column)

OF COUNSEL

Terence E. Scanlon

For full biographical listings, see the Martindale-Hubbell Law Directory

A. WILLIAM ZAVARELLO CO., L.P.A. (AV)

313 South High Street, Corner South High and Buchtel, 44308-1532
Telephone: 330-762-9700
Fax: 330-762-1680
Email: RhDavis3205@msn.com
Email: wzavarello@aol.com

A. William Zavarello
Rhonda Gail Davis

References: First National Bank of Ohio; National City Bank, Akron.

For full biographical listings, see the Martindale-Hubbell Law Directory

*BUCYRUS,** Crawford Co.

THE NEFF LAW FIRM, LTD. (AV)

840 South Sandusky Avenue, P.O. Box 406, 44820-0406
Telephone: 419-562-1951
Facsimile: 419-562-1660
Email: nefflaw@cybrtown.com *URL:* http://www.lawyers.com/nefflaw

Robert Clark Neff
Robert Clark Neff, Jr.

For full biographical listings, see the Martindale-Hubbell Law Directory

*CANTON,** Stark Co.

BAKER, DUBLIKAR, BECK, WILEY & MATHEWS (AV)

205 Mellett Building, 115 DeWalt Avenue, N.W., 44702
Telephone: 330-453-4999
Telecopier: 330-455-0333

MEMBERS OF FIRM

Jack R. Baker
Ralph F. Dublikar
Gregory A. Beck
Donald P. Wiley
James F. Mathews
Mel L. Lute, Jr.

ASSOCIATES

Melissa S. Ulrich
Daniel J. Funk
Stephen E. Matasich
Elizabeth Ann Warg

For full biographical listings, see the Martindale-Hubbell Law Directory

BLACK, MCCUSKEY, SOUERS & ARBAUGH A LEGAL PROFESSIONAL ASSOCIATION (AV)

1000 United Bank Plaza, 220 Market Avenue South, 44702
Telephone: 330-456-8341; 877-656-8341
Telecopier: 330-456-5756
Email: info@bmsa.com *URL:* http://www.bmsa.com
Dover Office: 130 West Third Street, P.O. Box 2330, 44622.
Telephone: 330-364-6553; 877-564-6553.
Fax: 330-364-2739.

Ronald K. Bennington
Charles J. Tyburski
Anthony E. Efremoff
Robert I. Friedman
Arnold R. Shifman
Victor R. Marsh
Daniel M. Jonas
Randolph L. Snow (Managing Director)
Stephen D. Thompson
Terrence P. Kessler
James R. Strawn
Joel K. Dayton
Scott P. Sandrock
Gust Callas
Bruce M. Soares
James P. Kamerer
Karen S. Reiland
Richard D. Dodez
Mary E. Randall
John J. Rambacher
Thomas W. Connors
Terrence L. Seeberger
Robert E. Soles, Jr.
Tod T. Morrow
Francis G. Centrone
David M. Hanhart (Resident, Dover Office)
C. Jason Deeds (Resident, Dover Office)
Erick L. Bauer (Resident, Dover Office)

Brenda S. Schwartz
Jane Murphy Timken
Brian C. Cich
Gregory L. Taddonio
Mark E. Owens
Gordon D. Woolbert, II
Edward C. Redder

OF COUNSEL

John D. Jolliffe
Gene Barnhart
Richard M. Hanhart (Resident, Dover Office)

Representative Clients: The Hoover Co.; Diebold, Inc.; Travelers Insurance Co.

For full biographical listings, see the Martindale-Hubbell Law Directory

*CINCINNATI,** Hamilton Co.

BROWN, CUMMINS & BROWN CO., L.P.A. (AV)

3500 Carew Tower, 441 Vine Street, 45202
Telephone: 513-381-2121
Fax: 513-381-2125

(See Next Column)

BROWN, CUMMINS & BROWN CO. L.P.A., *Cincinnati—Continued*

Robert S. Brown
James R. Cummins
Lynne Skilken
Amy G. Applegate
Kathryn Knue Przywara
Melanie S. Corwin

Reference: Star Bank of Cincinnati.

For full biographical listings, see the Martindale-Hubbell Law Directory

FROST & JACOBS LLP (AV)

2500 PNC Center, 201 East Fifth Street, 45202
Telephone: 513-651-6800
Telecopier: 513-651-6981
URL: http://www.frojac.com
Columbus, Ohio Office: One Columbus, 10 West Broad Street, 43215.
Telephone: 614-464-1211.
Telecopier: 614-464-1737.
Lexington, Kentucky Office: 1100 Vine Center Tower, 333 West Vine Street, 40507.
Telephone: 606-254-1100.
Telecopier: 606-253-2990.
Middletown, Ohio Office: 400 First National Bank Building, 2 North Main Street, 45042.
Telephone: 513-422-2001.
Telecopier: 513-422-3010.
Frankfort, Kentucky Office: 201 W. Main Street, 40601.
Telephone: 502-223-1400.
Telecopier: 502-223-1410.

MEMBERS OF FIRM

James R. Adams
Gerald L. Baldwin
Frederick J. McGavran
Joseph J. Dehner
Susan Grogan Faller
Todd H. Bailey
David C. Horn
William H. Hawkins II
Myron L. Dale
David C. Olson
Walter E. Haggerty
Douglas E. Hart
Richard M. Goehler
Beth A. Myers
Grant S. Cowan
Vincent E. Mauer
Beth Schneider Naylor
D. Scott Gurney
Adam P. Hall
Scott D. Phillips

ASSOCIATES

J. Paul Allen
Elizabeth R. Murray
Jack B. Harrison
Lori A. Landrum
Jeffrey R. Teeters
Laurie K. Ahlers
Scott R. Brown
Jill Meyer Vollman
Daniel R. Wireman
Jeffrey S. Rosenstiel
Robert D. Shank
Bill J. Paliobeis
Robert D. Lewis Jr.
Kelly E. Sultzbach
Claire Seltz Eichner

OF COUNSEL

Donald McG. Rose

COLUMBUS, OHIO OFFICE
MEMBER OF FIRM

Michael K. Yarbrough

COLUMBUS, OHIO OFFICE
ASSOCIATE

Jeffrey G. Rupert

LEXINGTON, KENTUCKY OFFICE
MEMBER OF FIRM

Denise H. McClelland

LEXINGTON, KENTUCKY OFFICE
ASSOCIATES

Douglas J. Hallock
D. Eric Lycan

LEXINGTON, KENTUCKY OFFICE
OF COUNSEL

David C. Trimble
Susan C. Sears

MIDDLETOWN, OHIO OFFICE
MEMBERS OF FIRM

Thomas A. Swope
Donald L. Crain

MIDDLETOWN, OHIO OFFICE
ASSOCIATE

Thomas B. Allen

Representative Clients: Armco Inc.; AK Steel Corporation; Arthur Andersen & Co.; Catholic Healthcare Partners; Cincinnati Bell Inc.; Cincinnati Machine; Federated Department Stores Inc.; Mercy Regional Health System-Greater Cincinnati; PNC Bank, National Association; Sencorp.; Champion International.

For Complete List of Firm Personnel, See General Section

For full biographical listings, see the Martindale-Hubbell Law Directory

ROBERT J. GEHRING CO., L.P.A. (AV)

4th Floor, 105 East Fourth Street, 45202
Telephone: 513-721-2758
Fax: 513-621-9285

Robert J. Gehring

For full biographical listings, see the Martindale-Hubbell Law Directory

KATZ, TELLER, BRANT & HILD A LEGAL PROFESSIONAL ASSOCIATION (AV)

2400 Chemed Center, 255 East Fifth Street, 45202-4724
Telephone: 513-721-4532
Telecopier: 513-721-7120
Email: corp@ktbh.com

Robert A. Pitcairn, Jr.
James F. McCarthy, III
Cynthia Loren Gibson

Wijdan Jreisat

For Complete List of Firm Personnel, See General Section

For full biographical listings, see the Martindale-Hubbell Law Directory

KEATING, MUETHING & KLEKAMP, P.L.L. (AV)

1400 Provident Tower, One East Fourth Street, 45202
Telephone: 513-579-6400
Facsimile: 513-579-6457
URL: http://www.kmklaw.com

MEMBERS OF FIRM

Louis F. Gilligan
Joseph L. Trauth, Jr.
Robert W. Maxwell II
Richard L. Creighton, Jr.
Jerome C. Randolph
James E. Burke
Kevin E. Irwin
William A. Posey
Gregory M. Utter
Patrick F. Fischer
David K. Montgomery
James R. Matthews
Robert G. Sanker
W. Keith Noel
Daniel J. Donnellon
Daniel E. Izenson
Pamela Morgan Hodge

ASSOCIATES

Joseph M. Callow Jr.
Rachael A. Rowe
Dwight A. Packard, II
Susan Smith Kost
Peter J. Stautberg

Representative Clients: American Financial Group; BP America Inc.; Chiquita Brands International, Inc.; Cintas Corporation; Comair Holdings, Inc.; Duke Realty Limited Partnership; LSI Industries Inc.; Mosler Inc.; Provident Financial Group Inc.

For Complete List of Firm Personnel, See General Section

For full biographical listings, see the Martindale-Hubbell Law Directory

KEPLEY, GILLIGAN & EYRICH A LEGAL PROFESSIONAL ASSOCIATION (AV)

525 Vine Street, Suite 2200, 45202
Telephone: 513-241-5540; 621-1045
Fax: 513-241-8111; 621-0038

Augustine Giglio
Paul D. Rattermann
Thomas S. Sapinsley

Francis X. Lee

Representative Clients and References furnished upon request.

For full biographical listings, see the Martindale-Hubbell Law Directory

MICHAEL G. KOHN (AV)

2690 Madison Road, P.O. Box 8157, 45208
Telephone: 513-631-6159
Fax: 513-631-8498

For full biographical listings, see the Martindale-Hubbell Law Directory

LINDHORST & DREIDAME CO., L.P.A. (AV)

312 Walnut Street, Suite 2300, 45202-4091
Telephone: 513-421-6630
Telecopier: 513-421-0212

Ambrose H. Lindhorst (1913-1997)
Robert F. Dreidame (1914-1978)
William J. Walsh (1919-1996)

SENIOR COUNSEL

Leo J. Breslin
James L. O'Connell
William M. Cussen
Charles J. Kelly
John A. Goldberg
William N. Kirkham
James M. Moore
James H. ʻmith, III
Jay R. Langenbahn
Thomas E. Martin
James F. Brockman
Michael F. Lyon
Edward S. Dorsey
Harold L. Anness
Dale A. Stalf
Gary F. Franke

Peter C. Newberry

Representative Clients: CNA; CSX Corp.; Fireman's Fund-American Group; Medical Protective Co.; Norfolk Southern Corp.; Roadway Express, Inc.; Sibcy Cline, Inc.; Jewish Hospital; T.W. Smith Aircraft, Inc.; U.S.F.&G.

(See Next Column)

LINDHORST & DREIDAME CO. L.P.A.—*Continued*

For Complete List of Firm Personnel, See General Section

For full biographical listings, see the Martindale-Hubbell Law Directory

GENE MESH & ASSOCIATES (AV)

2605 Burnet Avenue, 45219-2502
Telephone: 513-221-8800
Fax: 513-221-1097
Email: GeneMesh@aol.com

ASSOCIATES

R. Michael Phebus
Michael G. Brautigam (Not admitted in OH)

LEGAL SUPPORT PERSONNEL

Charles H. Short

For full biographical listings, see the Martindale-Hubbell Law Directory

SHEA & ASSOCIATES (AV)

600 Flatiron Building, 401 East Court Street, 45202-1355
Telephone: 513-621-8333
Telecopier: 513-651-3272
Email: SheaLawFrm@aol.com *URL:* http://www.attyfind.com/jwshea

Joseph W. Shea III

ASSOCIATE

Shirley A. Coffey

LEGAL SUPPORT PERSONNEL

Connie DeFillippo

For full biographical listings, see the Martindale-Hubbell Law Directory

SIRKIN PINALES MEZIBOV & SCHWARTZ (AV)

920 Fourth & Race Tower, 105 West Fourth Street, 45202-2776
Telephone: 513-721-4876
Telecopier: 513-721-0876
Email: spms@fuse.net

MEMBERS OF FIRM

H. Louis Sirkin
Martin S. Pinales
Marc D. Mezibov
Howard M. Schwartz

Reference: The Huntington National Bank.

For full biographical listings, see the Martindale-Hubbell Law Directory

STRAUSS & TROY A LEGAL PROFESSIONAL ASSOCIATION (AV)

The Federal Reserve Building, 150 East Fourth Street, 45202-4018
Telephone: 513-621-2120
Telecopier: 513-241-8259
URL: http://www.strauss-troy.com
Northern Kentucky Office: Suite 1400, 50 East Rivercenter Boulevard, Covington, Kentucky, 41011.
Telephone: 513-621-8900; 513-621-2120.
Telecopier: 513-629-9444.

William S. Abernethy, Jr.
William R. Jacobs
Stuart C. Brinn
R. Guy Taft
Richard S. Wayne
Paul B. Calico
Timothy B. Theissen (Resident, Covington, Kentucky Office)
William K. Flynn
Thomas L. Stachler

August T. Janszen
Thomas P. Glass
Michael A. Ruh, Jr.

OF COUNSEL

Charles G. Atkins
Richard D. Heiser
Leon L. Wolf

Representative Clients: BP Oil Company; PNC Bank, N.A.; Corporex Companies, Inc.; Star Bank, N.A. (Ohio and Kentucky); Steinberg's, Inc.

For Complete List of Firm Personnel, See General Section

For full biographical listings, see the Martindale-Hubbell Law Directory

WAITE, SCHNEIDER, BAYLESS & CHESLEY CO., L.P.A. (AV)

1513 Central Trust Tower, Fourth and Vine Streets, 45202
Telephone: 513-621-0267
Fax: 513-381-2375; 621-0262

Stanley M. Chesley

Thomas F. Rehme
Robert A. Steinberg
Fay E. Stilz
Louise M. Roselle
D. Arthur Rabourn
Jerome L. Skinner
Janet G. Abaray
Paul M. De Marco
Terrence L. Goodman
Colleen M. Hegge
Jane H. Walker
Renée Infante

For full biographical listings, see the Martindale-Hubbell Law Directory

*CLEVELAND,** Cuyahoga Co.

BAKER & HOSTETLER LLP (AV)

3200 National City Center, 1900 East Ninth Street, 44114-3485
Telephone: 216-621-0200
Telecopier: 216-696-0740
TWX: 810 421 8375
RCA Telex: 215032
To contact an attorney on the Internet use first initial and surname followed by @baker-hostetler.com
URL: http://www.bakerlaw.com
In Cincinnati, Ohio: 312 Walnut Street, Suite 2650.
Telephone: 513-929-3400.
In Columbus, Ohio: Capitol Square, Suite 2100, 65 East State Street.
Telephone: 614-228-1541.
In Denver, Colorado: 303 East 17th Avenue, Suite 1100.
Telephone: 303-861-0600.
In Houston, Texas: 1000 Louisiana, Suite 2000.
Telephone: 713-751-1600.
In Beverly Hills, California: 9150 Wilshire Boulevard, Suite 205.
Telephone: 310-385-7500.
In Long Beach, California: 300 Oceangate, Suite 620.
Telephone: 562-432-2827.
In Los Angeles, California: 600 Wilshire Boulevard.
Telephone: 213-624-2400.
In Orlando, Florida: SunBank Center, Suite 2300, 200 South Orange Avenue.
Telephone: 407-649-4000.
In Washington, D.C.: Washington Square, Suite 1100, 1050 Connecticut Avenue, N.W.
Telephone: 202-861-1500.

PARTNERS

Diane P. Chapman
Wayne C. Dabb, Jr.
José C. Feliciano
Charles E. Jarrett
Karen B. Newborn
Thomas H. Shunk
Randall L. Solomon

RETIRED PARTNER

H. Stephen Madsen

For Complete List of Firm Personnel, See General Section

For full biographical listings, see the Martindale-Hubbell Law Directory

BERNARD, HAFFEY & BOHNERT CO., L.P.A. (AV)

Jefferson Centre, 5001 Mayfield Road #301, P.O. Box 24005, 44124-0005
Telephone: 216-291-3600
FAX: 216-291-0159
URL: http://www.lawyers.com/bernardhaffey&bohnert

Clifford H. Bernard (1907-1985)
J. Ross Haffey, Jr.
Edward G. Bohnert
Timothy P. Haffey

Reference: KeyBank.

For full biographical listings, see the Martindale-Hubbell Law Directory

BUCKLEY KING & BLUSO A LEGAL PROFESSIONAL ASSOCIATION (AV)

1400 Bank One Center, 44114
Telephone: 216-363-1400
National Watts Line: 800-255-2825
Telecopier: 216-579-1020
Email: bkb@bucklaw.com
Columbus, Ohio Office: One Columbus, 10 West Broad Street, Suite 1300.
Telephone: 614-461-5600.
Telecopier: 614-461-5630.
Akron, Ohio Office: 935 West Market Street.
Telephone: 330-869-8700.
Telecopier: 330-869-4040.
Cincinnati, Ohio Office: 1320 PNC Center, 201 East Fifth Street.
Telephone: 513-412-5400.
Telecopier: 513-412-5401.
Toledo, Ohio Office: 420 Madison Avenue, Suite 1100.
Telephone: 419-254-4300.
Telecopier: 419-249-7383.

Brent M. Buckley
Woods King III
Linda L. Bluso
Rosemary Grdina Gold
William E. Armstrong
Richard J. Disantis
Harry W. Greenfield
Timothy D. Wood
Thomas I. Blackburn (Resident, Columbus Office)
Richard D. Brown (Resident, Columbus Office)
Ray P. Drexel (Resident, Columbus Office)
Robert F. Deacon
Duard D. Bradshaw (Resident, Akron Office)
William G. Chris (Resident, Akron Office)
David C. Engle (Resident, Akron Office)
John J. Lynett (Resident, Akron Office)
Robert J. Walter (Resident, Columbus Office)
James E. Melle (Resident, Columbus Office)
Rosemary Sweeney
Daniel P. Carter (Not admitted in OH)

(See Next Column)

BUCKLEY KING & BLUSO A LEGAL PROFESSIONAL ASSOCIATION, *Cleveland—Continued*

Barbara Lee Armstrong
Gary A. Gillett (Resident, Columbus Office)
Jeffrey C. Toole
R. James Pelstring (Resident, Cincinnati Office)
Richard M. Bain
John F. Bodie, Jr. (Resident, Toledo Office)
Nancy D. Moody (Resident, Toledo Office)
Stephen A. Skiver (Resident, Toledo Office)
Kenneth J. White (Resident, Toledo Office)
Edgar H. Boles
James W. Barnhouse
Theodore M. Dunn, Jr.
Craig P. Burns (Resident, Toledo Office)
Thomas P. Killam (Resident, Toledo Office)
Paul Psota
Harold R. Rauzi

Elizabeth E. Baer (Resident, Toledo Office)
Marci J. Blachman (Resident, Toledo Office)
Ricardo J. Cardenas
Angelica M. Colwell (Resident, Toledo Office)
Thomas C. Drabick, Jr. (Resident, Columbus Office)
Wendy West Feinstein
Jason E. Hickman (Resident, Akron Office)
Matthew M. Mendoza (Resident, Columbus Office)
Erick C. Smith
Christine M.Valera Weaver
Dean E. Weaver (Resident, Toledo Office)
Gary A. Weiss
Timothy J. Weyls, Jr.
Christian M. Williams
M. Scott Young

OF COUNSEL

John A. Hallbauer
Peter R. Harwood
Hylas A. Hilliard (Resident, Columbus Office)
Michael T. Honohan
James Olds, Jr. (Resident, Akron Office)
Eugene B. Schwartz (1909-1997)
Scott F. Sturges (Resident, Columbus Office)

For full biographical listings, see the Martindale-Hubbell Law Directory

DUVIN, CAHN & HUTTON A LEGAL PROFESSIONAL ASSOCIATION (AV)

Erieview Tower, 20th Floor, 1301 East Ninth Street, 44114
Telephone: 216-696-7600
Facsimile: 216-696-2038
Email: attorneys@duvin.com *URL:* http://www.duvinlaw.com
Southfield, Michigan Office: 26211 Central Park Boulevard, Suite 500, 48076.
Telephone: 248-945-1977.
Fax: 248-945-1162.

Robert P. Duvin
Stephen J. Cahn
Lee J. Hutton
Marc J. Bloch
Andrew C. Meyer
Martin S. List
Craig M. Brown
Frank W. Buck
Neal B. Wainblat
Kenneth B. Stark
Martin T. Wymer
Robert M. Wolff
Steven W. Albert
Stephen J. Sferra
Christine C. Covey
Richard C. Hubbard, III
Jon M. Dileno
Suellen Oswald
David A. Posner
Janette McCarthy Louard

Lisa Froimson Mann
David W. Neel
Kathleen M. Kordeleski
Michael T. Pearson
Kenneth D. Schwartz
Brett S. Krantz
Barry Y. Freeman
Bradley A. Sherman
Jonathan S. Forman
Mark F. Humenik
Robert C. Pivonka
Fredrick W Englehart
Jonathan T. Hyman
Latha M. Srinivasan
Shannon K. Patton

OF COUNSEL

Mark V. Webber

Representative Clients: Ameritech; Lincoln Electric; Cleveland-Akron-Canton Supermarket Industry; The Scott Fetzer Co.; Electronic Data Systems Corporation; Cleveland Clinic Foundation; LTV Steel; Steris; CVS/Revco Drug.

For full biographical listings, see the Martindale-Hubbell Law Directory

GALLAGHER, SHARP, FULTON & NORMAN (AV)

(Formerly Hauxhurst, Sharp, Mollison & Gallagher)
Bulkley Building, Seventh Floor, 1501 Euclid Avenue, 44115
Telephone: 216-241-5310
Telecopier: 216-241-1608
Email: gsfn.com *URL:* http://www.gsfn.com

MEMBERS OF FIRM

H. Austin Hauxhurst (1881-1962)
Frank X. Cull (1887-1965)
I. Walter Sharp (1884-1966)
Clarence L. Mollison (1906-1981)
Robert C. Horrigan (1916-1993)
Forrest A. Norman
Edward J. Cass
John B. Robertson
Thomas E. Betz
Alan M. Petrov
Alton L. Stephens, Jr.
Virginia L. Heidloff

(See Next Column)

MEMBERS OF FIRM (Continued)

Jay Clinton Rice
Joseph W. Pappalardo
Thomas E. Dover
James F. Koehler
Robert H. Eddy
Thomas J. Kaiser
D John Travis
Paul J. Schumacher, Jr.
William F. Gibson
Gary L. Nicholson
Lynn L. Moore
Ernest W. Auciello, Jr.
Patrick M. Foy
Kevin C. Alexandersen
Stanley M. Dub
Timothy T. Brick
Sheila A. McKeon
Thomas J. Cabral
Timothy J. Fitzgerald
Mark A. Greer

OF COUNSEL

Michael R. Gallagher
Robert W. Sharp
George W. Stuhldreher
Burt J. Fulton
James F. Sweeney
James G. Gowan
James L. Ryhal, Jr.

Edward G. Kagels
John T. Murphy
M. Terence Cawley
Todd M. Haemmerle
Brian R. McGraw
Timothy P. Whitford
Daniel J. Michalec
Alexander E. Goetsch
Joseph J. Santoro
Monica A. Sansalone
John A. Simon
Dennis G. Rehor
Beth A. Nagel
Timothy Patrick Roth
Gregory K. Boop
Janice Aitken
Gary F. Werner
Mark Joseph Savage
Catherine A. Davis
Charles Allston Bowers
Pamela S. Schremp
James T. Tyminski, Jr.
Matthew J. Hatchadorian

STAFF ATTORNEY

Daniel L. Herak

Counsel for: Associated Aviation Underwriters; Conrail; The Continental Insurance Cos.; Continental National American Group; Fireman's Fund Insurance Cos.; The Home Insurance Co.; Motorist Ins. Co.; Norfolk Southern Corp.; Royal Insurance Co.; United States Aviation Underwriters.

For full biographical listings, see the Martindale-Hubbell Law Directory

GOODMAN WEISS MILLER LLP (AV)

100 Erieview Plaza, 27th Floor, 44114-1824
Telephone: 216-696-3366
Telecopier: 216-363-5835

Deborah J. Michelson

For full biographical listings, see the Martindale-Hubbell Law Directory

HERMANN, CAHN & SCHNEIDER (AV)

Suite 500, 1301 East Ninth Street, 44114
Telephone: 216-781-5515
Facsimile: 216-781-1030
Email: hcs@en.com

MEMBERS OF FIRM

Gary D. Hermann
James S. Cahn
Kent B. Schneider
Anthony J. Hartman
Kerry S. Volsky
Peter J. Krembs

ASSOCIATES

Thomas P. Marotta
Romney B. Cullers

Representative Clients: Allen-Bradley Co.; TRW, Inc.; Pfizer, Inc.; First Nationwide Bank; Prudential Bache Securities; Fleetwood Enterprises, Inc.; Farmers Insurance Companies; Allstate Insurance Company; Sandoz Pharmaceuticals; Pittsburgh Corning Corp.

For full biographical listings, see the Martindale-Hubbell Law Directory

HOFELICH & KING (AV)

BP Tower, 29th Floor, 200 Public Square, 44114
Telephone: 216-344-9999
Fax: 216-344-3999

James A. Hofelich
John F. King

For full biographical listings, see the Martindale-Hubbell Law Directory

JANIK & FORBES (AV)

Building Two, 8223 Brecksville Road, 44141-1371
Telephone: 440-838-7600
Fax: 440-838-7601

MEMBER OF FIRM

Steven G. Janik

For Complete List of Firm Personnel, See General Section

For full biographical listings, see the Martindale-Hubbell Law Directory

Cleveland—Continued

JONES, DAY, REAVIS & POGUE (AV)

North Point, 901 Lakeside Avenue, 44114
Telephone: 216-586-3939
Telecopier: 216-579-0212
Email: counsel@jonesday.com *URL:* http://www.jonesday.com
In Columbus, Ohio: 1900 Huntington Center.
Telephone: 614-469-3939.
Telecopier: 614-461-4198.
In Atlanta, Georgia: 3500 SunTrust Plaza, 303 Peachtree Street.
Telephone: 404-521-3939.
Telecopier: 404-581-8330.
In Brussels, Belgium: Avenue Louise 480, 7th Floor. B-1050 Brussels.
Telephone: 32-2-645-14-11.
Telecopier: 32-2-645-14-45.
In Chicago, Illinois: 77 West Wacker.
Telephone: 312-782-3939.
Telecopier: 312-782-8585.
In Dallas, Texas: 2727 North Harwood Street.
Telephone: 214-220-3939.
Telecopier: 214-969-5100.
In Frankfurt, Germany: Hochhaus am Park, Grüneburgweg 102, 60323 Frankfurt am Main.
Telephone: 49-69-9726-3939.
Telecopier: 49-69-9726-3993.
In Geneva, Switzerland: 20, rue de Candolle.
Telephone: 41-22-320-2339.
Telecopier: 41-22-320-1232.
In Hong Kong, China: 29th Floor, Entertainment Building, 30 Queen's Road Central.
Telephone: 852-2526-6895.
Telecopier: 852-2868-5871 or 852-2868-5699.
In Irvine, California: 5 Park Plaza, Suite 1100.
Telephone: 949-851-3939.
Telecopier: 949-553-7539.
In London, England: Bucklersbury House, 3 Queen Victoria Street.
Telephone: 44-171-236-3939.
Telecopier: 44-171-236-1113.
In Los Angeles, California: 555 West Fifth Street, Suite 4600.
Telephone: 213-489-3939.
Telecopier: 213-243-2539.
In New Delhi, India (Associate Office): Pathak & Associates (an associate firm of Jones, Day, Reavis & Pogue), 1st Floor, Dr. Gopal Das Bhaven, 28 Barakhamba Road.
Telephone: 91-11-373-8793; 91-11-335-7345.
Telecopier: 91-11-335-3761.
In New York, N.Y.: 599 Lexington Avenue.
Telephone: 212-326-3939.
Telecopier: 212-755-7306.
In Paris, France: 120, rue du Faubourg Saint-Honoré.
Telephone: 33-1-56-59-39-39.
Telecopier: 33-1-56-59-39-38
In Pittsburgh, Pennsylvania: 500 Grant Street, 31st Floor.
Telephone: 412-391-3939.
Telecopier: 412-394-7959.
In Riyadh, Saudi Arabia: The International Law Firm (In Association with Jones, Day, Reavis & Pogue), Sulaymaniyah, Prince Mishari IBN, Abdulaziz Street, P.O. Box 22166.
Telephone: (966-1) 462-8866.
Telecopier: (966-1) 462-9001.
In Shanghai, China: 2805 Kerry Centre, 1515 Nanjing Road West.
Telephone: 86-21-5298-6568.
Telecopier: 86-21-5298-6569.
In Sydney, Australia: Governor Phillip Tower, Level 38, 1 Farrer Place.
Telephone: 61-2-9210-6921.
Telecopier: 61-2-9210-6926.
In Taipei, Taiwan: 8th Floor, Tun Hwa South Road, Section 2.
Telephone: (886-2) 2704-6808.
Telecopier: (886-2) 2704-6791.
In Tokyo, Japan: Toranomon MT Building, 4th Floor, 10-3, Toranomon 3-Chome, Minato-ku, Tokyo 105, Japan.
Telephone: 81-3-3433-3939.
Telecopier: 81-3-5401-2725.
In Washington, D.C.: 51 Louisiana Avenue, N.W.
Telephone: 202-879-3939.
Telecopier: 202-626-1700.

MEMBERS OF FIRM IN CLEVELAND

Patrick F. McCartan
John L. Strauch
John M. Newman, Jr.
Robert C. Weber

For Complete List of Firm Personnel, See General Section

For full biographical listings, see the Martindale-Hubbell Law Directory

KAUFMAN & CUMBERLAND CO., L.P.A. (AV)

1500 Republic Building, 25 Prospect Avenue, West, 44115-1000
Telephone: 216-861-0707
Telefax: 216-694-6883
TDD: 216-694-6891

(See Next Column)

Steven S. Kaufman
Frank J. Cumberland, Jr. (Retired)
Frank R. DeSantis
Gail E. Sindell
William W. Jacobs
Thomas L. Feher
Mitchell Ehrenberg
Douglas P. Whipple

Susan L. Belman
Charles P. Royer
Craig P. Kvale
Kathleen M. Minahan
Robin M. Wilson
Robert J. Patton
Lawrence E. Harkenrider
Scott J. Novak

OF COUNSEL

Jack G. Day (Retired)
Edda Sara Post

Representative Clients: CertainTeed Corp.; City of Cleveland; Household Commercial Financial Services, Inc.; International Insurance Co.; International Surplus Lines Insurance Co.; Morgan's Foods, Inc.

For full biographical listings, see the Martindale-Hubbell Law Directory

KELLER AND CURTIN CO., L.P.A. (AV)

Suite 330 The Hanna Building, 44115-1901
Telephone: 216-566-7100
Fax: 216-566-5430
Email: keller@en.com
Akron, Ohio Office: 920 Key Building, 159 South Main Street, 44308-1318.
Telephone: 330-376-7245.
Fax: 330-376-8128. Email: kcakron@en.com.
Elyria, Ohio Office: 120 East Avenue, 44035-5228.
Telephone: 440-323-8662.
Fax: 440-323-6610.

Stanley S. Keller
G. Michael Curtin
Walter H. Krohngold
James M. Johnson
Joseph G. Ritzler
Thomas M. Coughlin, Jr.
John Swansinger
Camille D. Kuri
Franklin C. Malemud
Brian D. Spitz
Deena Charisse Miller

Reference: Bank One, Cleveland.

For full biographical listings, see the Martindale-Hubbell Law Directory

KELLEY, MCCANN & LIVINGSTONE, LLP (AV)

3500 BP Tower, 200 Public Square, 44114-2302
Telephone: 216-241-3141
Fax: 216-241-3707
Email: Attorneys@kmlegal.com

MEMBERS OF FIRM

Stephen M. O'Bryan
John D. Brown
Joel A. Makee
Mark J. Valponi
Thomas J. Lee
Mary Grace Balazs
Carl A. Murway
David H. Wallace
Robert A. Brindza II
Peter M. Poulos

OF COUNSEL

Walter C. Kelley

ASSOCIATES

Timothy J. Duff
Corinne Katz Moore
Colleen G. Treml
Laurie H. Goetz
Gregory J. O'Brien
Andrew Agati
Charles D. Price
Renee B. Weiss
Joshua D. Goldstein
Michelle R. Arendt

For Complete List of Firm Personnel, See General Section

For full biographical listings, see the Martindale-Hubbell Law Directory

KOBLENTZ & KOBLENTZ (AV)

55 Public Square, Suite 1170, 44113
Telephone: 216-621-3012
Fax: 216-621-6567
URL: http://www.lawyers.com/koblentz&koblentz

Richard S. Koblentz

Peter A. Russell
Craig J. Morice
Marvin A. Koblentz (1922-1995)

For full biographical listings, see the Martindale-Hubbell Law Directory

MANSOUR, GAVIN, GERLACK & MANOS CO., L.P.A. (AV)

55 Public Square, Suite 2150, 44113-1994
Telephone: 216-523-1500
Telecopier: 216-523-1705

Ernest P. Mansour
Michael T. Gavin
Julius R. Gerlack
Eli Manos
Dale E. Markworth
Jeffrey M. Embleton

(See Next Column)

MANSOUR, GAVIN, GERLACK & MANOS CO. L.P.A., *Cleveland—Continued*

David B. Cathcart
Samuel R. Martillotta
Jeffrey L. Tasse
Bruce G. Rinker
Anthony J. Coyne
John F. Burke, III
Thomas B. Bralliar, Jr.
Edward O. Patton

Representative Clients: Invacare Corp.; Michigan Mutual Liability Insurance Co.; St Paul Insurance Co; Zurich Insurance Co.

For full biographical listings, see the Martindale-Hubbell Law Directory

MCDONALD, HOPKINS, BURKE & HABER CO., L.P.A. (AV)

2100 Bank One Center, 600 Superior Avenue, E., 44114-2653
Telephone: 216-348-5400
Telecopier: 216-348-5474
Email: attorney@mhbh.com *URL:* http://www.mhbh.com

Patrick J. Berry
Jeffrey P. Consolo
Jerome W. Cook
Richard S. Cooper
Anthony J. DiVenere
Paul N. Edwards
Theodore J. Esborn
Steven L. Gardner
Carl J. Grassi
James A. Griffith
Jeffrey R. Huntsberger
Brian J. Jereb
Bernard L. Karr
Thomas W. Keen
Roger L. Kleinman
Joseph J. LoPresti, Jr.
Dan L. Makee
George L. McGaughey, Jr.
John T. Mulligan
Brian M. O'Neill
William J. O'Neill
Stephen T. Parisi
R. Jeffrey Pollock
Michael G. Riley
Shawn M. Riley
Albert N. Salvatore
Thomas C. Schrader
Roger L. Shumaker
Barbara J. Smith
James M. Stone
Dale R. Vlasek
Kenneth J. Walsh
John M. Wirtshafter
Jane Marie Pine Wood
Charles B. Zellmer

OF COUNSEL

John J. Monroe

Julie A. Callsen
Anne T. Corrigan
Steven A. Eisenberg
G. Andrew Gardner
Anuj Goswami
Donald E. Kacmar
David M. Kall
Jeffrey B. Keiper
Kevin J. Kessinger
Mark D. Klimek
Alan M. Koschik
Deviani M. Kuhar
Paul W. Linehan
Tyler L. Mathews
Jennifer A. Mills
Antoinette K. Palmer
Ketan K. Patel
Sharon Szolosi Regas
Douglas B. Schnee
Michele Smolin
Glenn D. Southworth
Michael R. Spreng

For full biographical listings, see the Martindale-Hubbell Law Directory

MEYERS, HENTEMANN & REA CO., L.P.A. (AV)

21st Floor, Superior Building, 815 Superior Avenue, N.E., 44114
Telephone: 216-241-3435
Telecopier: 216-241-6568
Elyria, Ohio Office: 301 Fifth Street, 44035.
Telephone: 216-323-6920.

John S. Rea
Henry A. Hentemann
Gerald L. Jeppe
Lynn A. Lazzaro

J. Michael Creagan
John J. Reagan
Ronald J. Ziehm
Cornelius J. O'Sullivan, Jr.

OF COUNSEL

Richard C. Talbert
Timothy R. Sweeney
Donald E. Worthing

Representative Clients: State Farm Mutual Insurance Co.; Travelers Insurance Co.; Lloyds Underwriters, London, England; Preferred Risk Mutual Insurance Co.; Detroit Automobile Inter-Insurance Exchange; Electrical Mutual.

For Complete List of Firm Personnel, See General Section

For full biographical listings, see the Martindale-Hubbell Law Directory

NURENBERG, PLEVIN, HELLER & MCCARTHY CO., L.P.A. (AV)

1370 Ontario Street First Floor, 44113-1792
Telephone: 216-621-2300; Toll Free: 1-800-562-7438
Fax: 216-771-2242
Email: nphm@nphm.com *URL:* http://www.nphm.com

(See Next Column)

A. H. Dudnik (1905-1963)
S. F. Komito (1902-1984)
Marshall I. Nurenberg
Leon M. Plevin
Maurice L. Heller
John J. McCarthy
Thomas Mester
Harlan M. Gordon
David M. Paris
Richard L. Demsey
Jamie R. Lebovitz
William S. Jacobson
Jeffrey A. Leikin

Robin J. Peterson
Robert S. Zeller
Ellen M. McCarthy
J. Charles Ruiz-Bueno
Kathleen J. St. John
Jonathan D. Mester
Brenda M. Johnson

Reference: Society Key Corp.

For full biographical listings, see the Martindale-Hubbell Law Directory

QUANDT, GIFFELS & BUCK CO., L.P.A. (AV)

800 Leader Building, 526 Superior Avenue, E., 44114-1460
Telephone: 216-241-2025
Telecopier: 216-241-2080
Email: attys@qgb.com

Robert G. Quandt (1925-1998)
Walter R. Matchinga
Joseph R. Tira
Beth A. Sebaugh
Laurence F. Buzzelli
Larry C. Greathouse
Hunter S. Havens
Timothy G. Sweeney
Richard A. Hoenigman
Jeffrey A. Schenk
Edward J. Stoll, Jr.
Ernest C. Pisanelli
Richard L. Warren, Jr.
Daniel A. Romaine

OF COUNSEL

Stephen D. Richman

Representative Clients: Physicians Insurance Company of Ohio; Royal Insurance; CNA Insurance Co.; Heritage Mutual Insurance Co.; Reliance Insurance Co.; Safeco Insurance Co.; American International Group.

For full biographical listings, see the Martindale-Hubbell Law Directory

RAY, ROBINSON, CARLE & DAVIES P.L.L. (AV)

1650 The East Ohio Building, 1717 East 9th Street, 44114-2898
Telephone: 216-861-4533
Facsimile: 216-861-4568
Email: rayrob@rayrobcle.com

MEMBERS OF FIRM

David G. Davies
Douglas R. Denny
Gene B. George
Julia R. Brouhard
Robert T. Coniam
Sandra Maurer Kelly

ASSOCIATE

Thomas More Wynne

OF COUNSEL

Lucian Y. Ray (1903-1987)
William D. Carle, III (Senior Counsel)
Theodore C. Robinson (Retired)

Representative Clients: The Cleveland-Cliffs Iron Co.; Bethlehem Steel Corp., Great Lakes Steamship Division; Canada Steamship Lines, Ltd.; Canadian Shipowners Assn.; Interlake Steamship Co.; Ispat Inland, Inc.; Amoco Oil Co.; Container Port Group, Inc.; Euclid Universoal Corp.

For full biographical listings, see the Martindale-Hubbell Law Directory

RODGERS AND CO., L.P.A. (AV)

1750 Guildhall, Landmark Office Towers, 45 Prospect Avenue, West, 44115
Telephone: 216-861-6191
Fax: 216-861-4699
Email: attys@rodgers-lpa.com

Walter A. Rodgers

Jeffrey M. Elzeer
Shawn A. Cormier

For full biographical listings, see the Martindale-Hubbell Law Directory

SEELEY, SAVIDGE AND EBERT A LEGAL PROFESSIONAL ASSOCIATION (AV)

800 Bank One Center, 600 Superior Avenue, East, 44114-2655
Telephone: 216-566-8200
Fax-Telecopier: 216-566-0213
URL: http://www.sse-law.com

Keith A. Savidge

Andrew D. Bemer
Matthew K. Seeley
Marc N. Silberman
Michael E. Stinn

Reference: KeyBank.

For Complete List of Firm Personnel, See General Section

For full biographical listings, see the Martindale-Hubbell Law Directory

Cleveland—Continued

TIMOTHY A. SHIMKO & ASSOCIATES A LEGAL PROFESSIONAL ASSOCIATION (AV)

2010 Huntington Building, 925 Euclid Avenue, 44115
Telephone: 216-241-8300
Fax: 216-241-2702
Email: taslaw@ix.netcom.com *URL:* http://www.netcom.com/~taslaw

Timothy A. Shimko

Frank E. Piscitelli, Jr.

Reference: National City Bank, Cleveland.

For full biographical listings, see the Martindale-Hubbell Law Directory

SMITH, MARSHALL, WEAVER AND VERGON (AV)

500 National City East Sixth Building, 1965 East Sixth Street, 44114
Telephone: 216-781-4994
Telecopier: 216-781-9448
Email: smw@multiverse.com.

MEMBERS OF FIRM

Wentworth J. Marshall, Jr.
Philip J. Weaver, Jr.
Frederick P. Vergon, Jr.

ASSOCIATES

R. Eric Smearman
Gretchen A. Hirschauer
Jason W. Richards

Representative Clients: American States Insurance Co.; Federated Mutual Group; Hartford Insurance Group; State Automobile Mutual Insurance Co.

For full biographical listings, see the Martindale-Hubbell Law Directory

SPIETH, BELL, MCCURDY & NEWELL CO., L.P.A. (AV)

2000 Huntington Building, 925 Euclid Avenue, 44115-1496
Telephone: 216-696-4700
Fax: 216-696-2706
Email: law@spiethbell.com

Bruce G. Hearey
Dianne Foley Hearey

Edmund W. Searby
Jennifer Cook Jontz
Jennifer Welfley Nohra

Representative Clients: American Greetings Corp.; Cleveland Cavaliers; Nationwide Advertising Services, Inc.; Independent Steel Co.; Baldwin Wallace College; The Tool-Die Engineering Co.
Representative Labor Relations Clients (Management Only): Parker Hannifin Corp.; Brush Wellman Co.; Elsag Bailey; M.A. Hanna Co.

For Complete List of Firm Personnel, See General Section

For full biographical listings, see the Martindale-Hubbell Law Directory

ULMER & BERNE LLP (AV)

Ninth Floor, Bond Court Building, 1300 East Ninth Street, 44114-1583
Telephone: 216-621-8400
FAX: 216-621-7488
Email: infocleveland@ulmer.com
Email: infocolumbus@ulmer.com *URL:* http://www.ulmer.com/
Columbus, Ohio Office: 88 East Broad Street, Suite 1980.
Telephone: 614-228-8400.
FAX: 614-228-8561.

MEMBERS OF FIRM

Thomas H. Barnard
Steven D. Bell
Barton A. Bixenstine
Kenneth A. Bravo
Robert E. Chudakoff
Maria Del Monaco
Bill J. Gagliano
Ronald H. Isroff
Marvin L. Karp
Mark D. Katz
Murray K. Lenson
David L. Lester
Bruce P. Mandel
Stephen A. Markus
Craig A. Marvinney
Charles R. Olsavsky, Jr.
Brian N. Ramm
Harold (Kip) Reader
Richard E. Rubinstein
Alan S. Sims
Richard D. Sweebe
Stephanie E. Trudeau
Michael N. Ungar
Jeffrey W. Van Wagner
F. Thomas Vickers
Richard G. Witkowski

ATTORNEYS IN COLUMBUS, OHIO OFFICE (SEE LISTING)

MEMBERS OF FIRM

Alexander M. Andrews
Timothy M. Fox
Thomas L. Rosenberg

For Complete List of Firm Personnel, See General Section

For full biographical listings, see the Martindale-Hubbell Law Directory

WALTER & HAVERFIELD, P.L.L. (AV)

1300 Terminal Tower, 44113-2253
Telephone: 216-781-1212
Telecopier: 216-575-0911
Email: law@walterhav.com *URL:* http://www.walterhav.com
Columbus, Ohio Office: 88 East Broad Street.
Telephone: 614-898-1096.

MANAGING PARTNER

Michael T. McMenamin

MEMBERS OF FIRM

Charles T. Riehl, III
John H. Gibbon
Ralph E. Cascarilla
Christopher L. Gibbon
Carl E. Anderson
Frederick W. Whatley
Jonathan D. Greenberg
R. Todd Hunt
Kenneth A. Zirm
W. Mowry Connelly
James D. Wilson

ASSOCIATES

Barbara Rhodes Marburger
Patricia F. Weisberg
Debora S. Lasch
Randal G. Ammons
Katherine A. Friedell
Susan M. Zidek
Vincent L. Cheverine
Darrell A. Clay

For Complete List of Firm Personnel, See General Section

For full biographical listings, see the Martindale-Hubbell Law Directory

WEISS & ASSOCIATES (AV)

1600 Midland Building Landmark Office Towers, 101 Prospect Avenue West, 44115
Telephone: 216-589-9993
Fax: 216-589-9723
Email: jweiss@jweisslaw.com

MEMBERS OF FIRM

Jerome F. Weiss
Robert H. Hanna (Deceased)

For full biographical listings, see the Martindale-Hubbell Law Directory

WESTON HURD FALLON PAISLEY & HOWLEY L.L.P. (AV)

2500 Terminal Tower, 50 Public Square, 44113-2241
Telephone: 216-241-6602;
Ohio Toll Free: 800-336-4952
FAX: 216-621-8369
Email: Hurd2500@westonhurd.com

Joseph Philip Sullivan (1916-1974)
Lee C. Howley (1910-1983)
Harold Fallon (1910-1989)
Frank Seth Hurd (1913-1990)
Lloyd O. Brown (1928-1993)
S. Burns Weston (1904-1994)

MEMBERS OF FIRM

Mark O'Neill
John W. Jeffers
John M. Baker
Ronald A. Rispo
Carolyn M. Cappel
Hilary Sheldon Taylor
Kenneth A. Torgerson
John S. Kluznik
Jeffrey D. Fincun
William H. Baughman, Jr.
Stephen D. Walters
Gary W. Johnson
Deirdre G. Henry
Harry Sigmier
Warren Rosman
Timothy D. Johnson
Dana A. Rose
Hernan N. Visani
John G. Farnan
Gregory E. O'Brien
Scott C. Smith
Timothy P. Ristau
David C. Lamb

OF COUNSEL

Louis Paisley
Norbert F. Werner

ASSOCIATES

Lisa M. Chesler
Maria A. Kortan-Sampson
Daniel A. Richards
John A. Albers
Forrest A. Norman III
Christopher M. Ernst
Marilyn Miller Crisafi
Martin J. Fallon
Mark S. Bennett
Randy L. Taylor
Jeremy R. Sayre
Dennis R. Fogarty
Thomas J. Connick
Jason R. Sussman

For Complete List of Firm Personnel, See General Section

For full biographical listings, see the Martindale-Hubbell Law Directory

*COLUMBUS,** Franklin Co.

BAKER & HOSTETLER LLP (AV)

Capitol Square, Suite 2100, 65 East State Street, 43215-4260
Telephone: 614-228-1541
Telecopier: 614-462-2616
To contact an attorney on the Internet use first initial and surname followed by @baker-hostetler.com
URL: http://www.bakerlaw.com
In Cleveland, Ohio: 3200 National City Center, 1900 East Ninth Street.
Telephone: 216-621-0200.
In Cincinnati, Ohio: 312 Walnut Street, Suite 2650.
Telephone: 513-929-3400.
In Denver, Colorado: 303 East 17th Avenue, Suite 1100.
Telephone: 303-861-0600.

(See Next Column)

BAKER & HOSTETLER LLP, *Columbus—Continued*

In Houston, Texas: 1000 Louisiana, Suite 2000.
Telephone: 713-751-1600.
In Beverly Hills, California: 9150 Wilshire Boulevard, Suite 205.
Telephone: 310-385-7500.
In Long Beach, California: 300 Oceangate, Suite 620.
Telephone: 562-432-2827.
In Los Angeles, California: 600 Wilshire Boulevard.
Telephone: 213-624-2400.
In Orlando, Florida: SunBank Center, Suite 2300, 200 South Orange Avenue.
Telephone: 407-649-4000.
In Washington, D. C.: Washington Square, Suite 1100, 1050 Connecticut Avenue, N.W.
Telephone: 202-861-1500.

OFFICE MANAGING PARTNER

George W. Hairston (Managing Partner-Columbus Office)

PARTNERS

John H. Burtch
Michael D. Dortch
Mark A. Johnson
Robert M. Kincaid, Jr.
Sherri Blank Lazear
David C. Levine
Thomas L. Long
Robert B. McAlister
Randall S. Rabe
Jeffrey T. Williams

ASSOCIATE

Karen E. Sheffer

For Complete List of Firm Personnel, See General Section

For full biographical listings, see the Martindale-Hubbell Law Directory

BRICKER & ECKLER LLP (AV)

100 South Third Street, 43215-4291
Telephone: 614-227-2300
Telecopy: 614-227-2390
Email: info@be.bricker.com *URL:* http://www.bricker.com

Edward A. Matto
John F. Birath, Jr.
Randolph C. Wiseman
Charles H. Walker
Richard S. Lovering
Percy Squire
Quintin F. Lindsmith
Joyce B. Link
Drew H. Campbell

Wendi R. Huntley
Stephen C. Gray
T. Earl LeVere
Matthew J. Arnold
Amy Straker Bartemes
Katherine Spies Giumenti
Nelson M. Reid
Elizabeth H. Watts
Timothy A. Fry

OF COUNSEL

Anne Marie Sferra
Diane Richards Brey

Representative Clients: Consolidated Rail Corp.; Browning Ferris Industries; Waste Technologies Industries; Abbott Foods, Inc.; Westinghouse; IBM; AirTouch Cellular; Nationwide Insurance Companies; Wheeling-Pittsburgh Steel Co.

For Complete List of Firm Personnel, See General Section

For full biographical listings, see the Martindale-Hubbell Law Directory

CHESTER, WILLCOX AND SAXBE LLP (AV)

17 South High Street, Suite 900, 43215-3413
Telephone: 614-221-4000
Fax: 614-221-4012
Email: cwslaw.com

PARTNERS

John W. Bentine
Donald C. Brey
John J. Chester
Stephen C. Fitch
Richard A. Frye
Eugene B. Lewis
Charles Rockwell Saxbe
Elizabeth Jean Watters

ASSOCIATES

David J. Butler
Maryellen Corna
Karen S. Hockstad
Karen A. Hoffman
Sarah D Morrison

OF COUNSEL

J. Craig R. Wright

Representative Clients: American Municipal Power-Ohio, Inc.; Bank One; Franklin County Convention Facilities Authority. The Limited, Inc.; Scioto Downs, Inc.; Tee Jaye's Country Place Restaurants.

For full biographical listings, see the Martindale-Hubbell Law Directory

CRABBE, BROWN, JONES, POTTS & SCHMIDT (AV)

500 South Front Street, Suite 1200, 43215
Telephone: 614-228-5511
Telecopier: 614-229-4559
URL: HTTP://WWW.CBJPS.COM
Cincinnati, Ohio Office: 30 Garfield Place, Suite 940, 45202.
Telephone: 513-784-1525.
Telecopier: 513-784-1250. Email: BHurley@Psinet.com

(See Next Column)

Lancaster, Ohio Office: 111 South Broad Street, Suite 209, 43130.
Telephone: 740-689-1743.
Telecopier: 740-689-1746. Email: sdavis@greenapple.com

MEMBERS OF FIRM

William Page Lewis (1914-1998)
Robert C. Potts (1913-1994)
William T. McCracken (1929-1993)
J. Roth Crabbe (1906-1989)
Charles E. Brown
Theodore D. Sawyer
Vincent J. Lodico
Steven B. Ayers
Keith H. Jung
Jeffrey M. Brown
Larry H. James
Brian E. Hurley (Resident, Cincinnati Office)
Gilbert J. Gradisar
Richard D. Wetzel, Jr.
Jerry A. Eichenberger
James D. Gilbert
Luis M. Alcalde
John C. Albert
George R. McCue, III
Michael R. Henry
Robert C. Buchbinder
Catherine L. Worley
Steven A. Davis (Resident, Lancaster Office)

ASSOCIATES

Francesca Tosi Ward
Todd William Collis
Kristen H. Smith
Daniel J. Hurley
Beth Wayne (Resident, Cincinnati Office)
Heather W. Guthrie
Christina L. Corl
Steven E. Miller
Darlene E. Chavers
Amy M. Fulmer Stevenson
Phillip A. Templeton

OF COUNSEL

William H. Jones
Wilbur W. Jones (1913-1999)
William L. Schmidt

Representative Clients: Allstate Insurance Co.; American States Insurance Co.; General Electric.

For full biographical listings, see the Martindale-Hubbell Law Directory

DENMEAD & MALONEY (AV)

37 West Broad Street, Suite 1150, 43215-4189
Telephone: 614-228-5271
Telecopier: 614-228-7624
Email: cdkmlaw@infinet.com

Craig Denmead
Kevin M. Maloney

Representative Clients: Bode-Finn Co.; Century Surety Co.; COP, Inc.; Inland Products, Inc.; National Head Injury Foundation, Inc., of Washington D.C.; Ohio Head Injury Assn.; Stonhard, Inc.; Sammons Corporate Services, Inc.; Trigg-Hansa Ins. Co., Ltd.; Tuscarawas County, Ohio.

For full biographical listings, see the Martindale-Hubbell Law Directory

GERTNER & GERTNER (AV)

Suite 1780, 88 East Broad Street, 43215
Telephone: 614-463-9393
Fax: 614-463-9669
URL: http://www.lawyers.com/gertner&gertner

MEMBERS OF FIRM

Abraham Gertner (1909-1996)
Michael H. Gertner

For full biographical listings, see the Martindale-Hubbell Law Directory

JONES, DAY, REAVIS & POGUE (AV)

1900 Huntington Center, 43215
Telephone: 614-469-3939
Telecopier: 614-461-4198
Email: counsel@jonesday.com *URL:* http://www.jonesday.com
In Cleveland, Ohio: North Point, 901 Lakeside Avenue.
Telephone: 216-586-3939.
Telecopier: 216-579-0212.
In Atlanta, Georgia: 3500 SunTrust Plaza, 303 Peachtree Street.
Telephone: 404-521-3939.
Telecopier: 404-581-8330.
In Brussels, Belgium: Avenue Louise 480, 7th Floor, B-1050 Brussels.
Telephone: 32-2-645-14-11.
Telecopier: 32-2-645-14-45.
In Chicago, Illinois: 77 West Wacker.
Telephone: 312-782-3939.
Telecopier: 312-782-8585.
In Dallas, Texas: 2727 North Harwood Street.
Telephone: 214-220-3939.
Telecopier: 214-969-5100.
In Frankfurt, Germany: Hochhaus am Park, Grüneburgweg 102, 60323 Frankfurt am Main.
Telephone: 49-69-9726-3939.
Telecopier: 49-69-9726-3993.
In Geneva, Switzerland: 20, rue de Candolle.
Telephone: 41-22-320-2339.
Telecopier: 41-22-320-1232.
In Hong Kong: 29th Floor, Entertainment Building, 30 Queen's Road Central.
Telephone: 852-2526-6895.
Telecopier: 852-2868-5871 or 852-2868-5699.
In Irvine, California: 5 Park Plaza, Suite 1100.
Telephone: 949-851-3939.
Telecopier: 949-553-7539.

(See Next Column)

JONES, DAY, REAVIS & POGUE—*Continued*

In London, England: Bucklersbury House, 3 Queen Victoria Street.
Telephone: 44-171-236-3939.
Telecopier: 44-171-236-1113.
In Los Angeles, California: 555 West Fifth Street, Suite 4600.
Telephone: 213-489-3939.
Telecopier: 213-243-2539.
In New Delhi, India (Associate Office): Pathak & Associates (an associate firm of Jones, Day, Reavis & Pogue), 1st Floor, Dr. Gopal Das Bhaven, 28 Barakhamba Road.
Telephone: 91-11-373-8793; 91-11-335-7345.
Telecopier: 91-11-335-3761.
In New York, New York: 599 Lexington Avenue.
Telephone: 212-326-3939.
Telecopier: 212-755-7306.
In Paris, France: 120, rue du Faubourg Saint-Honoré.
Telephone: 33-1-56-59-39-39.
Telecopier: 33-1-56-59-39-38
In Pittsburgh, Pennsylvania: 500 Grant Street, 31st Floor.
Telephone: 412-391-3939.
Telecopier: 412-394-7959.
In Riyadh, Saudi Arabia: The International Law Firm (In Association with Jones, Day, Reavis & Pogue), Sulaymaniyah, Prince Mishari IBN, Abdulaziz Street, P.O. Box 22166.
Telephone: (966-1) 462-8866.
Telecopier: (966-1) 462-9001.
In Shanghai, China: 2805 Kerry Centre, 1515 Nanjing Road West.
Telephone: 86-21-5298-6568.
Telecopier: 86-21-5298-6569.
In Sydney, Australia: Governor Phillip Tower, Level 38, 1 Farrer Place.
Telephone: 61-2-9210-6921.
Telecopier: 61-2-9210-6926.
In Taipei, Taiwan: 8th Floor, 2 Tun Hwa South Road, Section 2.
Telephone: (886-2) 2704-6808.
Telecopier: (886-2) 2704-6791.
In Tokyo, Japan: Toranomon MT Building, 4th Floor, 10-3, Toranomon 3-Chome, Minato-ku, Tokyo 105, Japan.
Telephone: 81-3-3433-3939.
Telecopier: 81-3-5401-2725.
In Washington, D.C.: 51 Louisiana Avenue, N.W.
Telephone: 202-879-3939.
Telecopier: 202-626-1700.

MEMBER OF FIRM IN COLUMBUS

Fordham E. Huffman

For Complete List of Firm Personnel, See General Section

For full biographical listings, see the Martindale-Hubbell Law Directory

KEENER DOUCHER CURLEY & PATTERSON A LEGAL PROFESSIONAL ASSOCIATION (AV)

88 East Broad Street, Suite 1750, 43215
Telephone: 614-280-1100
Fax: 614-280-9503
Email: KDCP@IWAYNET.NET

Thomas J. Keener
Paul M. Doucher
W. Charles Curley
David T. Patterson
Kevin R. Bush

Michael J. Kelley
Kimberley A. Doucher
Amy K. Schermer

For full biographical listings, see the Martindale-Hubbell Law Directory

KEGLER, BROWN, HILL & RITTER (AV)

Capitol Square Suite 1800, 65 East State Street, 43215-4294
Telephone: 614-462-5400
Telecopier: 614-464-2634
Cable Address: "Law KBHR"
Telex: 246671
Email: info@kbhr.com *URL:* http://www.kbhr.com
Marion, Ohio Office: 250 Executive Drive, Suite B, P.O. Box 919.
Telephone: 614-387-3501.
Facsimile: 614-387-3630.

John P. Brody
William J. Brown
Stephen E. Chappelear
Robert Garrett Cohen
Thomas W. Hill
Gene W. Holliker
R. Kevin Kerns
Ronald L. Mason
Larry J. McClatchey
Richard W. Schuermann, Jr.
Robert G. Schuler
S. Martijn Steger
Roger P. Sugarman
Timothy T. Tullis
Melvin D. Weinstein

COUNSEL

John C. Deal
Ted M. McKinniss (Resident, Marion Office)
S. Noel Melvin

(See Next Column)

Thomas M. L. Metzger
Christopher J. Weber
Anthony C. White

Representative Clients: AT&T Wireless; Borden, Inc.; Columbus Metropolitan Housing Authority; Farmers Insurance Group; Microsoft Corp.; National City Bank; The Ohio State University.

For Complete List of Firm Personnel, See General Section

For full biographical listings, see the Martindale-Hubbell Law Directory

MARK KITRICK CO., L.P.A. (AV)

First Avenue Office Center, 929 Harrison Avenue, Suite 102-103, 43215-6501
Telephone: 614-297-7711
Fax: 614-297-8985
URL: http://www.kitricklaw.com
Email: mkitrick@ljextra.com *URL:* http://www.lawyers.com/markkitrick
Cincinnati, Ohio Office: 6912 Silverton Avenue, P.O. Box 36213, 45236.
Telephone: 513-984-9584

Mark M. Kitrick

Mark D. Lewis

For full biographical listings, see the Martindale-Hubbell Law Directory

LAMKIN, VAN EMAN, TRIMBLE, BEALS & ROURKE (AV)

Suite 200, 500 South Front Street, 43215-5671
Telephone: 614-224-8187
Fax: 614-224-4943
URL: http://www.lawyers.com/lvtb&rlaw

MEMBERS OF FIRM

William W. Lamkin
Timothy L. Van Eman
Thomas W. Trimble
David A. Beals
Michael J. Rourke
Kathy A. Dougherty
Kenneth S. Blumenthal

Reference: Huntington National Bank.

For full biographical listings, see the Martindale-Hubbell Law Directory

MCCARTHY, PALMER, VOLKEMA & THOMAS A LEGAL PROFESSIONAL ASSOCIATION (AV)

140 East Town Street, Suite 1100, 43215
Telephone: Telephone: 614-221-4400
Telecopier: 614-221-6010
URL: http://www.mccarthypalmer.com
Email: attorneys@mccarthypalmer.com *URL:* http://www.lawyers.com/attorneysmccarthy

Dennis M. McCarthy
Robert Gray Palmer
Daniel R. Volkema
Warner M. Thomas, Jr.
Michael S. Miller
Elizabeth Schorpp Burkett
Craig P. Scott
Tony C. Merry

Jennifer K. Thivener

Reference: Huntington National Bank.

For full biographical listings, see the Martindale-Hubbell Law Directory

NEMETH, CABORN & BUTAUSKI (AV)

21 East Frankfort Street, 43206-1069
Telephone: 614-443-4866
Fax: 614-443-4860
URL: http://www.lawyers.com/nemeth
Email: nemeth@nemethlaw.com *URL:* http://www.nemethlaw.com

John C. Nemeth
David A. Caborn
Joseph A. Butauski

ASSOCIATES

David A. Herd
Michael J. Collins

Respresentative Clients: Anheuser-Busch, Inc.; Service Merchandise; Crawford & Co.; Erie Insurance Group; Home Insurance Co.; Safeco Insurance Co.; Mount Carmel Hospital; The Hartford Group; Citizens Insurance Co.; State Farm Insurance Co.; Zurich American Ins. Group.

For full biographical listings, see the Martindale-Hubbell Law Directory

PORTER WRIGHT MORRIS & ARTHUR LLP (AV)

41 South High Street, 43215-6194
Telephone: 614-227-2000; (800-533-2794)
Fax: 614-227-2100
Email: cmh@porterwright.com *URL:* http://www.porterwright.com
Cincinnati, Ohio Office: 250 E. Fifth Street, Suite 2200, 45202-4199.
Telephones: 513-381-4700; (800-582-5813).
Fax: 513-421-0991. Internet: cvg@porterwright.com.
Cleveland, Ohio Office: 925 Euclid Avenue, Suite 1700, 44115-1483.
Telephones: 216-443-9000; (800-824-1980).
Fax: 216-443-9011. Internet: cle@porterwright.com.

(See Next Column)

PORTER WRIGHT MORRIS & ARTHUR LLP, *Columbus—Continued*

Dayton, Ohio Office: One Dayton Centre, One South Main Street, Suite 1600, 45402-2028.
Telephones: 937-449-6810; (800-533-4434).
Fax: 937-449-6820. Internet: day@porterwright.com.
Naples, Florida Office: 5801 Pelican Bay Boulevard, Suite 300, 34108-2709.
Telephones: 941-593-2900; (800-876-7962).
Fax: 941-593-2990. Internet: apf@porterwright.com.
Washington, D.C. Office: 1667 K Street, N.W., Suite 1100, 20006-1605.
Telephones: 202-778-3000; (800-456-7962).
Fax: 202-778-3063. Internet: dca@porterwright.com.

MEMBERS OF FIRM
COLUMBUS, OHIO OFFICE

Marjorie Crowder Briggs, Brian L. Buzby, S. Ronald Cook, Jr., Daniel W. Costello, James D. Curphey, Joyce D. Edelman, Joseph F. Elliott, Lisa L. Eschleman, Mason Evans, IV, R. Leland Evans, Ralph F. Gildehaus, Stuart M. Gordon, Kevin E. Griffith, Brian D. Hall, James A. King, Charles J. Kurtz, III, David A. Laing, John F. Marsh, Alvin J. McKenna, Mark K. Merkle, Jr., Terrance M. Miller, Denise M. Mirman, Scott E. North, Adele E. O'Conner, James S. Oliphant, Fred G. Pressley, Jr., Diane C. Reichwein, Christopher C. Russell, Joseph W. Ryan, Jr., Darrell R. Shepard, David P. Shouvlin, Bradd N. Siegel, Patrick J. Smith, Mark S. Stemm, John M. Stephen, Karl J. Sutter, Kathleen McManus Trafford, Robert W. Trafford, Michael J. Underwood, Charles C. Warner, Franck G. Wobst, Thomas A. Young

ASSOCIATES
COLUMBUS, OHIO OFFICE

Douglas L. Anderson, Daniel A. Bellman, Craig R. Carlson, Gregory B. Foliano, Constance M. Greaney, James B. Hadden, Priscilla Hapner, Barbara A. North, Melissa A. Romig, Sidney L. Williams, Leslie A. Yovan

DAYTON, OHIO OFFICE
RESIDENT MEMBERS

John J. Heron, Jonathan Hollingsworth, R. Bruce Snyder

DAYTON, OHIO OFFICE
RESIDENT ASSOCIATES

Linda S. Holmes, Elizabeth L. Ross

DAYTON, OHIO OFFICE
RESIDENT OF COUNSEL

Richard A. Maresca

CINCINNATI, OHIO OFFICE
RESIDENT MEMBERS

John J. Cruze, Mark E. Elsener, Jerome J. Metz, Jr.

CINCINNATI, OHIO OFFICE
RESIDENT ASSOCIATE

Eric J. Plinke

CLEVELAND, OHIO OFFICE
RESIDENT MEMBERS

Robert D. Anderle, David A. Bell, Paul J. Corrado, Daniel F. Gourash, Margaret M. Koesel, Hugh E. McKay, Patricia A. Screen, Ralph Streza

CLEVELAND, OHIO OFFICE
RESIDENT ASSOCIATES

Mary Kaye Bozza, Laura F. Kenney, Natalie L. Peterson, Eric F. Spade, Leo M. Spellacy, Jr., Tracey L. Turnbull, Alan C. Yarcusko

WASHINGTON, D.C. OFFICE
MEMBERS

David L. Douglass, Alison MacDonald Duncan, Thomas O. Gorman, William P. McGrath, Jr., James E. Pohlman, W. Scott Simmer, Mitchell A. Stearn

WASHINGTON, D.C. OFFICE
RESIDENT ASSOCIATES

Kristie G. Haynes, Claire C. Robinson May, Virginia E. Richards, Heather J. Stewart

WASHINGTON, D.C. OFFICE
RESIDENT OF COUNSEL

Theresa W. Hajost, Alan C. Nessman

NAPLES, FLORIDA OFFICE
MEMBER

Robert C. Gebhardt

(See Next Column)

NAPLES, FLORIDA OFFICE
RESIDENT ASSOCIATES

Margaret Castellana, Jeanette M. Lombardi

For Complete List of Firm Personnel, See General Section
For full biographical listings, see the Martindale-Hubbell Law Directory

---

WALTER W. RECKLESS (AV)

Suite 702, 33 North High Street, 43215-7315
Telephone: 614-221-4740
Fax: Available
Email: wwrlawofc@aol.com *URL:* http://www.lawyers.com/recklesslawoffice

References: Huntington National Bank; National City Bank.

For full biographical listings, see the Martindale-Hubbell Law Directory

---

SCHERNER, HANSON & CORNWELL, LLC (AV)

130 Northwoods Boulevard, 43235-4725
Telephone: 614-431-7200
Fax: 614-431-7262
Delaware, Ohio Office: 5300 David Road.
Telephone: 614-595-3366.
Lima, Ohio Office: 2100 Lost Creek Boulevard.
Telephone: 419-222-1155.
Fax: 419-227-3131.

Hans Scherner, Robert E. Hanson, Ted E. Cornwell

For full biographical listings, see the Martindale-Hubbell Law Directory

---

WHITE & FISH, L.P.A., INC. (AV)

1335 Dublin Road Suite 201 (C), 43215
Telephone: 614-485-9300
Fax: 614-485-9462
Email: WFLPA@AOL.COM *URL:* http://www.lawyers.com/white&fish

Arnold S. White, Jeffrey D. Fish

For full biographical listings, see the Martindale-Hubbell Law Directory

---

*DAYTON,** Montgomery Co.

BIESER, GREER & LANDIS (AV)

400 National City Center, 6 North Main Street, 45402
Telephone: 937-223-3277
Fax: 937-223-6339
Email: bgllaw.com

MEMBERS OF FIRM

David C. Greer, Leo F. Krebs, Howard Penn Krisher, II, Michael W. Krumholtz, John F. Haviland, Jr., David P. Williamson, James H. Greer

ASSOCIATES

Charles F. Shane, Joseph C. Oehlers, Carla J. Morman, Nikki Jo Palmer, James P. Fleisher, Sean P. Donovan, Karen T. Dunlevey

Representative Clients: Medical Protective Company; St. Paul Insurance Company; Crawford & Company; Aetna Life & Casualty Company; Motorists Insurance Company; Travelers Insurance Company; Kettering Medical Center; Good Samaritan Hospital; Miami Valley Hospital; Miami Valley Regional Transit Authority.

For Complete List of Firm Personnel, See General Section
For full biographical listings, see the Martindale-Hubbell Law Directory

---

FREUND, FREEZE & ARNOLD A LEGAL PROFESSIONAL ASSOCIATION (AV)

Suite 1800 One Dayton Centre, One South Main Street, 45402-2017
Telephone: 937-222-2424
Telecopier: 937-222-5369
Email: ffalawda@ffalaw.com *URL:* http://www.ffalaw.com
Cincinnati, Ohio Office: 8805 Governor's Hill Drive, Suite 300, 45249-3313.
Telephone: 513-583-3700.
FAX: 513-583-3703. Email: ffalawci@ffalaw.com.

Neil F. Freund, Stephen V. Freeze, Gordon D. Arnold, Patrick J. Janis, Stephen C. Findley, Robert N. Snyder, Christopher W. Carrigg, Susan Blasik-Miller, Scott F. McDaniel, Wayne E. Waite, Thomas B. Bruns, John G. Witherspoon, Jr., Lisa A. Hesse, Mark L. Schumacher, Shawn M. Blatt, Ray C. Freudiger, Kevin C. Connell, Margaret R. Young, Jennifer L. Kirkpatrick, Lynnette Pisone Ballato

(See Next Column)

FREUND, FREEZE & ARNOLD A LEGAL PROFESSIONAL ASSOCIATION—*Continued*

Timothy B. Schenkel
Daniel D. Ernst
Julie R. Lewis
John J. Garvey, III
David J. Cusack
Marc G. Pera
Julie M. Olson
T. Andrew Vollmar
Robert W. Young

Counsel for: City of Dayton; Dayton Power and Light Co.; Miami Valley Hospital; Children's Medical Center; Baker Concrete Construction; Auto-Owners Insurance Co.; CNA Insurance Co.; Employers Reinsurance Corp.; Farmers Insurance Group; Medical Protective; Midwestern Group; Motorists Mutual Ins.; State Farm Mutual Automobile Insurance Co.

For full biographical listings, see the Martindale-Hubbell Law Directory

SEBALY, SHILLITO & DYER A LEGAL PROFESSIONAL ASSOCIATION (AV)

1300 Courthouse Plaza, NE, P.O. Box 220, 45402-0220
Telephone: 937-222-2500
Telefax: 937-222-6554; 222-8279
URL: http://www.ssdlaw.com

Martin A. Beyer
Daniel A. Brown
James A. Dyer
Gale S. Finley
John R. Glankler
Deborah D. Hunt
Michael P. Moloney
Jon M. Sebaly
Beverly F. Shillito
Jeffrey B. Shulman
Karl R. Ulrich
Lawrence S. Walter
Nita S. Yates

OF COUNSEL

William W. Lambert

Michael A. Booth
Robert E. Goff, Jr.
Leslie Blair Graden
Joseph V. Hatala
J. David Ruffner, II
Kendra F. Thompson

For full biographical listings, see the Martindale-Hubbell Law Directory

DUBLIN, Franklin Co.

BLAUGRUND, HERBERT & MARTIN, INCORPORATED (AV)

5455 Rings Road, Suite 500, 43017-7517
Telephone: 614-764-0681
Fax: 614-764-0774
Email: bhm@bhmlaw.net

Christopher T. Cline
Lawrence H. Cohen
David J. Demers
Beverly J. Farlow
John W. Herbert
John S. Jones
David S. Kessler
Emily J. Lewis
Marc E. Myers
Stephen P. Postalakis
Teri G. Rasmussen

Jerry T. Burditt

For full biographical listings, see the Martindale-Hubbell Law Directory

*EATON,** Preble Co.

BENNETT & BENNETT (AV)

Bennett Law Building, 200 West Main Street, 45320
Telephone: 937-456-5100; 456-4100
Fax: 937-456-4300; 456-7278

MEMBERS OF FIRM

Lloyd B. Bennett (1909-1983)
Herd L. Bennett
Gray W. Bennett

Representative Clients: The National Hummel Foundation and Museum; Star Bank NA, Eaton, Ohio; Eaton National Bank & Trust Co.; First National Bank of Southwestern Ohio; Brookville National Bank; Farm Credit Services of Mid-America, ACA; Miller's Super Markets, Inc.; Northedge Shopping Center, Inc.; Herman M. Brubaker Registered Holstein Cattle; The Eaton Foundation.

For Complete List of Firm Personnel, See General Section

For full biographical listings, see the Martindale-Hubbell Law Directory

*ELYRIA,** Lorain Co.

ZAGRANS LAW FIRM A LEGAL PROFESSIONAL ASSOCIATION (AV)

5338 Meadow Lane Court, 44035-1469
Telephone: 440-934-7000
Facsimile: 440-934-7001
Email: eric@zagrans.com *URL:* http://www.zagrans.com

Eric H. Zagrans

Joshua M. Marks

(See Next Column)

LEGAL SUPPORT PERSONNEL

Jeannette M. Wolff (Legal Assistant)

For full biographical listings, see the Martindale-Hubbell Law Directory

HOLLAND, Lucas Co.

JONES & BAHRET CO., L.P.A. (AV)

Attorneys at Law
7050 Spring Meadows West, 43528
Telephone: 419-861-7800
Fax: 419-861-7808

Willis P. Jones, Jr.
Robert J. Bahret

Keith J. Watkins
Peter C. Munger
Jeffrey B. Charles
Marie E. Findish
Kathleen M Malkoski

LEGAL SUPPORT PERSONNEL

Denise M. Schmidt (Paralegal)
Shannon R. Tilton (Paralegal)
Susan J. Masson (Paralegal)

Representative Clients: American Modern Homes Insurance Company; Auto-Owners Insurance Co.; German Mutual Insurance Company; Michigan Millers Mutual Insurance Company; Motorists Insurance Companies; Podiatry Insurance Co.; Progressive Insurance Co.; Utica National Insurance Group; Western Reserve Mutual Casualty Co.; Westfield Companies.

For full biographical listings, see the Martindale-Hubbell Law Directory

*LIMA,** Allen Co.

GOODING, HUFFMAN, KELLEY & BECKER (AV)

127-129 North Pierce Street, P.O. Box 546, 45802
Telephone: 419-227-3423
Fax: 419-228-1937
URL: http://www.ghkb.com

Lawrence S. Huffman

ASSOCIATES

C. Bradford Kelley
Lawrence A. Huffman
Stephen L. Becker
Matthew C. Huffman
John C. Huffman
T. Blain Brock, II
Craig A. Gottschalk

LEGAL SUPPORT PERSONNEL

Carol L. Swem (Probate Paralegal)

Representative Clients: The Medical Protective Co.; Physicians Insurance Company of Ohio; Hamilton Mutual Insurance Co.; Bank One, Lima, Ohio; Lima Contracting Co.; Otis Wright & Sons Trucking, Inc.; Superior Metal Products; Frontier Insurance Co.; Zurich-American Insurance Group; Urology Assoc. of Ohio, Inc.

For full biographical listings, see the Martindale-Hubbell Law Directory

ROCKY RIVER, Cuyahoga Co.

LAW OFFICES OF JAY MILANO (AV)

2639 Wooster Road, 44116
Telephone: 440-356-2828
Fax: 440-356-2873
Email: milanolaw@aol.com *URL:* http://www.lawyers.com/jmilanolaw
Cleveland Heights, Ohio Office: 3820 Monticello Boulevard, 44121.
Telephone: 216-382-1500.
Fax: 216-382-6843.

ASSOCIATES

Michael P. Mayer
Kathryn Gonser Eloff
Rachel M. Weiser

For full biographical listings, see the Martindale-Hubbell Law Directory

*TOLEDO,** Lucas Co.

FRITZ BYERS (AV)

Suite 824 The Spitzer Building, 43604
Telephone: 419-241-8013
Telecopier: 419-241-4215
Email: fbyers@accesstoledo.com

General Counsel for: Blade Communications, Inc.; Toledo Blade Co.; Buckeye Cablevision, Inc.; Pittsburgh Post Gazette.
Reference: Capital Bank N.A.

For full biographical listings, see the Martindale-Hubbell Law Directory

DOYLE, LEWIS & WARNER (AV)

202 North Erie Street, P.O. Box 2168, 43603
Telephone: 419-248-1500
Fax: 419-248-2002
Email: dlw1@primenet.com

(See Next Column)

DOYLE, LEWIS & WARNER, *Toledo—Continued*

MEMBERS OF FIRM

Steven Timonere
Richard F. Ellenberger
Michael E. Hyrne
Michael A. Bruno
David W. Doerner

ASSOCIATES

Kevin A. Pituch
Maureen O. Atkins

Counsel for: Consolidated Rail Corp.; Lakefront Dock & Terminal Co.; Greyhound Lines; Prudential Insurance Company of America; Equitable Life Assurance Society of U.S.; Metropolitan Life Insurance Co.; Northwestern Mutual Life Insurance Co.; John Hancock Life Insurance Co.

For Complete List of Firm Personnel, See General Section

For full biographical listings, see the Martindale-Hubbell Law Directory

EASTMAN & SMITH LTD. (AV)

One Seagate, Twenty-Fourth Floor, P.O. Box 10032, 43699-0032
Telephone: 419-241-6000
Telecopier: 419-247-1777
Columbus, Ohio Office: 65 East State Street, Suite 1000, 43215.
Telephone: 614-460-3556.
Telecopier: 614-228-5371.

MEMBERS OF FIRM

James F. Nooney
David M. Jones
Henry N. Heuerman
John T. Landwehr
Kenneth C. Baker
Robert J. Gilmer, Jr.
Peter R. Casey, III
David F. Cooper
Rudolph A. Peckinpaugh, Jr.
Thomas A. Dixon
Barry W. Fissel
John D. Willey, Jr.
Joseph A. Gregg
Roger Paul Klee
Stuart J. Goldberg
Thomas J. Gibney
James L. Rogers
David W. Nunn

ASSOCIATES

Timothy C. Kuhlman
Albin Bauer, II
Michael W. Regnier
Margaret A. Mattimoe
M. Charles Collins

OF COUNSEL

Richard E. Antonini
M. Donald Carmin

Representative Clients: Chrysler Corp.; Allstate Insurance Co.; The Medical Protective Co.; Riverside Hospital; Roadway Express, Inc.; Fireman's Fund Insurance Co.; The Travelers Group; Continental Insurance; The Buckeye Union Insurance Company; Physicians Insurance Company of Ohio.

For Complete List of Firm Personnel, See General Section

For full biographical listings, see the Martindale-Hubbell Law Directory

MORAN & MORAN (AV)

626 Madison Avenue, Suite 300, 43604
Telephone: 419-241-8171
Fax: Available Upon Request

Wayne R. Peppers (1894-1978)
Peter L. Moran
Mary Beth Moran

Representative Clients: The Exchange Bank; Payak Insurance Agency; Monroe Pharmacy, Inc.
References: Society Bank; The Fifth Third Bank, Toledo, Ohio.

For full biographical listings, see the Martindale-Hubbell Law Directory

RITTER, ROBINSON, MCCREADY & JAMES (AV)

1850 National City Bank Building, 405 Madison Avenue, 43624
Telephone: 419-241-3213
FAX: 419-241-4925

MEMBERS OF FIRM

Ellis F. Robinson (Retired)
Milton C. Boesel, Jr. (Retired)
William S. McCready
Timothy C. James

Representative Clients: Ohio Casualty Insurance Co.; National Mutual Insurance Co.; Celina Mutual Insurance Co.; Westfield Insurance Co.; Northwestern National Insurance Co.; Midwestern Insurance Co.; United Ohio Insurance Co.

For Complete List of Firm Personnel, See General Section

For full biographical listings, see the Martindale-Hubbell Law Directory

SCHNORF & SCHNORF CO., L.P.A. A PROFESSIONAL CORPORATION (AV)

1400 National City Bank Building, 405 Madison Avenue, 43604
Telephone: 419-248-2646
Facsimile: 419-248-2889

David M. Schnorf
Christopher F. Parker
Johna M. Bella
Barry F. Hudgin

Local Counsel for: Universal Underwriters Group; GRE Insurance Group; Medical Mutual of Ohio; Bankers Multiple Line Insurance Company; Charter One Bank.

(See Next Column)

Representative Clients: American Federation of Teachers, AFL-CIO; Ohio Federation of Teachers, AFL-CIO; Toledo Federation of Teachers, AFL-CIO; Hart Associates, Inc.

For Complete List of Firm Personnel, See General Section

For full biographical listings, see the Martindale-Hubbell Law Directory

TWINSBURG, Summit Co.

WILLIAMS, SENNETT & SCULLY CO., L.P.A. (AV)

2241 Pinnacle Parkway, 44087-2367
Telephone: 330-405-5061
Fax: 330-405-5586
Email: attorneys@wsslaw.com
Cleveland, Ohio Office: 113 St. Clair Building, Suite 430.
Telephone: 216-771-8660.
Fax: 216-771-8831.

Roger H. Williams
James A. Sennett
William F. Scully, Jr.
Adam E. Carr
Louis R. Moliterno
Gina K. Desiderio
Matthew J. Grimm

OF COUNSEL

Charles F. Cichocki

Representative Clients: Allstate Insurance Co.; Giant Eagle, Inc.; Goodyear Tire & Rubber Co.; Nationwide Mutual Insurance Co.; Safeco Insurance Co.; Simon DeBartolo Group, Inc.; State Farm Insurance Cos.; Toys "R" Us; Universal Underwriters Insurance Co.; Senty Insurance Co.;

For full biographical listings, see the Martindale-Hubbell Law Directory

WESTLAKE, Cuyahoga Co.

THOMAS R. SKULINA (AV)

24803 Detroit Road, 44185
Telephone: 440-899-1911
Fax: 440-899-1625
Email: tskulina@msn.com

For full biographical listings, see the Martindale-Hubbell Law Directory

*WOOSTER,** Wayne Co.

KENNEDY, CICCONETTI & KNOWLTON, L.P.A. (AV)

558 North Market Street, 44691-3406
Telephone: 330-262-7555
Telecopier: 330-264-5739

Charles A. Kennedy
Frank Cicconetti
David C. Knowlton
Michael G. Buytendyk

Reference: Wayne County National Bank.

For full biographical listings, see the Martindale-Hubbell Law Directory

*YOUNGSTOWN,** Mahoning Co.

CARLIN & VASVARI, LLC (AV)

62 South Main Street, 44514
Telephone: 330-707-0377
Fax: 330-707-0398
Mailing Address: P.O. Box 5369, Poland, Ohio, 44514-0369

Clair M. Carlin
Thomas M. Vasvari

For full biographical listings, see the Martindale-Hubbell Law Directory

*ZANESVILLE,** Muskingum Co.

MICHELI, BALDWIN, BOPELEY & NORTHRUP CO., L.P.A. (AV)

2806 Bell Street, P.O. Box 788, 43702-0788
Telephone: 614-454-2545
Fax: 614-454-6372

Frank J. Micheli
Michael J. Micheli
James C. Micheli (1956-1992)
Steven R. Baldwin
Thomas R. Bopeley
Michael A. Northrup

Eric D. Martin

Representative Clients: Bank One Cambridge, N.A.; Consolidated Rail Corp.; Medical Protective Co.; Nationwide Insurance Cos.; Continental Insurance Cos.; Motorists Mutual Insurance Co.; Frontier Insurance Co.
Reference: Mutual Federal Savings Bank

For full biographical listings, see the Martindale-Hubbell Law Directory

OKLAHOMA

*ANTLERS,** Pushmataha Co.

STAMPER, HADLEY & REASOR (AV)

112 North High Street, P.O. Box 100, 74523
Telephone: 580-298-3153; 580-298-3332
Fax: 580-298-3263
Email: joestamper@yahoo.com
Atoka, Oklahoma Office: 209 East Court, P.O. Box 393.
Telephone: 580-889-3343.
Fax: 580-889-9334.

MEMBERS OF FIRM

Joe Stamper
Thomas J. Hadley
Shannon Reasor (Resident, Atoka Office)

Representative Clients: Farmers Exchange Bank, Antlers, Okla.; First National Bank at Antlers, Okla.; Town of Antlers; U. S. F. & G. Co.

For full biographical listings, see the Martindale-Hubbell Law Directory

*ARDMORE,** Carter Co.

HARRY L. BICKFORD LAW OFFICE (AV)

29 B Street, S.W., P.O. Box 1027, 73402
Telephone: 580-223-5566
Fax: 580-226-1893
Email: bickford@brightok.net

Local Counsel: Ultramar Diamond Shamrock Corporation (Total Petroleum, Inc. and Total Pipeline Corporation); The Williams Companies, Inc.; Williams Pipe Line Company.
References: American National Bank of Ardmore; BancFirst; Citizens National Bank & Trust Company.

For full biographical listings, see the Martindale-Hubbell Law Directory

*CHANDLER,** Lincoln Co.

R. PATRICK GILMORE (AV)

P.O. Box 9, 74834
Telephone: 405-258-4262
Fax: 405-258-4520
(Also Of Counsel to James, Gilmore & Hodgens, P.A., Stroud, Oklahoma)

For full biographical listings, see the Martindale-Hubbell Law Directory

*EL RENO,** Canadian Co.

FOGG, FOGG & HANDLEY (AV)

421 South Rock Island, P.O. Box 310, 73036
Telephone: 405-262-3502
Fax: 405-262-3531
Email: RMF@IAmerica.net

MEMBERS OF FIRM

Rupert M. Fogg (1914-1989)
Richard M. Fogg
Fletcher Dal Handley, Jr.

ASSOCIATE

Robert E. Grantham

For full biographical listings, see the Martindale-Hubbell Law Directory

*ENID,** Garfield Co.

JONES & WYATT (AV)

Suite 1100 Broadway Tower, 114 East Broadway, P.O. Box 472, 73702
Telephone: 580-242-5500
Fax: 580-242-4556

MEMBERS OF FIRM

Stephen Jones
Robert L. Wyatt, IV

ASSOCIATES

April McCurdy Davis
Leah Fillbach Lenzendorf

Representative Clients: Mesa Limited Partnership; Wells Fargo; City of Enid; Sears & Roebuck, Co.; St. Paul Property and Liability; International Oil, Chemical and Atomic Workers Union; Associated Aviation Underwriters; Independent Petroleum Association of America; Haliburton Industries; Tandy Corp.

For full biographical listings, see the Martindale-Hubbell Law Directory

*GUYMON,** Texas Co.

DAVID K. PETTY A PROFESSIONAL CORPORATION (AV)

301 West Fifth, P.O. Box 1187, 73942
Telephone: 580-338-5484
Fax: 580-338-0066
Email: pettyd@ptsi.net

David K. Petty

(See Next Column)

Jon K. Parsley

Attorney for: First National Bank, Texhoma, Oklahoma; Dorchester Hugoton Ltd.; Town of Hardesty; City of Guymon; Town of Goodwell; Vall Inc.; CJ Nutracon.

For full biographical listings, see the Martindale-Hubbell Law Directory

*MUSKOGEE,** Muskogee Co.

GAGE & WILLIAMS LAW FIRM (AV)

530 Court Street, P.O. Box 87, 74401
Telephone: 918-687-5424
Fax: 918-687-0761

MEMBERS OF FIRM

Edwin L. Gage
Betty Outhier Williams

Edith M. Gregory
Jonathan Heath Lofton

OF COUNSEL

Julian K. Fite

Representative Clients: Nationwide Insurance Co.; Oklahoma Municipal Assurance Group; Golden Rule Insurance Co.; Electronic Data Systems, Inc.; Trucks-For-You, Inc.; First National Bank and Trust Company, Muskogee.

For full biographical listings, see the Martindale-Hubbell Law Directory

*NORMAN,** Cleveland Co.

CROWE & DUNLEVY (AV)

A Professional Corporation
2500 South McGee, Suite 140, 73072-6705
Telephone: 405-321-7317
Fax: 405-360-4002
Email: marketing@crowedunlevy.com *URL:* http://www.crowedunlevy.com
Oklahoma City, Oklahoma Office: Crowe & Dunlevy, A Professional Corporation, 1800 Mid-America Tower, 20 North Broadway, 73102-8273.
Telephone: 405-235-7700.
Fax: 405-239-6651.
Tulsa, Oklahoma Office: Crowe & Dunlevy, A Professional Corporation, 500 Kennedy Building, 321 South Boston Avenue, 74103-3313.
Telephone: 918-592-9800.
Fax: 918-592-9801.

Robert L. Pendarvis
Mary Robertson

For Complete List of Firm Personnel, See General Section

For full biographical listings, see the Martindale-Hubbell Law Directory

*OKLAHOMA CITY,** Oklahoma Co.

ABOWITZ, RHODES & DAHNKE, P.C. (AV)

Tenth Floor 15 North Robinson, P.O. Box 1937, 73101
Telephone: 405-236-4645
Telecopier: 405-239-2843

Murray E. Abowitz
Sarah Jackson Rhodes
George W. Dahnke

Lisa Luschen Dietrich
Janice M. Dansby
Kayce L. Gisinger
Stephen S. Parker
Andrew D. Schwartz
Blake A. Bittel

Representative Clients: Orkin Exterminating, Inc.; Rollins, Inc.; Sofamor Danek Group; Case Corporation; Philip Morris, Inc.; Lorillard Tobacco Company; UNC Lear Siegler, Inc.; Tele-Communications, Inc.; CBS Corporation. Mazda Motors of America, Inc.

For full biographical listings, see the Martindale-Hubbell Law Directory

ADAMS & ASSOCIATES (AV)

City Place Building, 204 North Robinson Twenty-Fifth Floor, 73102
Telephone: 405-232-9100
Fax: 405-232-9114
Email: Adams1@IAmerica.net

R. Scott Adams

ASSOCIATES

Josh T. Welch
Joe Brett Reynolds

OF COUNSEL

O. Clifton Gooding

For full biographical listings, see the Martindale-Hubbell Law Directory

Oklahoma City—Continued

ANDREWS DAVIS LEGG BIXLER MILSTEN & PRICE, A PROFESSIONAL CORPORATION (AV)

500 West Main, Suite 500, 73102
Telephone: 405-272-9241
FAX: 405-235-8786
Email: andrewsdavis@andrewsdavis.com *URL:* http://www.andrewsdavis.com

J. Edward Barth
John J. Breathwit
Gary S. Chilton
James F. Davis
Timothy D. DeGiusti
John F. Fischer, II
Don G. Holladay
Kieran D. Maye, Jr.
Shelia Darling Tims
R. Brown Wallace
William H. Whitehill, Jr.
Elizabeth Brown
Craig L. Cline
Heidi J. Long
Anne E. Zachritz

OF COUNSEL

Carolyn Gregg Hill
Lynn O. Holloman
James C. Peck
William D. Watts

For Complete List of Firm Personnel, See General Section

For full biographical listings, see the Martindale-Hubbell Law Directory

BRITTON, GRAY AND HILL, P.C. (AV)

700 Bank of Oklahoma Plaza, 201 Robert S. Kerr, 73102
Telephone: 405-239-2393
Fax: 405-232-5135

James E. Britton
Michael D. Gray

Stephen A. Kepner, Jr.
Nelson John Christiansen

Representative Clients: BancFirst; Union Bank & Trust Company; Will Rogers Bank; NationsBank; Poteau State Bank; Trigen Energy Corporation; Mitsubishi Acceptance Corporation; Total Waste Systems, Inc.; Marine Recreational Opportunities, Inc.; Tower Tech, Inc.

For full biographical listings, see the Martindale-Hubbell Law Directory

GARY L. BROOKS AND ASSOCIATES (AV)

7100 North Classen Boulevard, Suite 300, 73116-7101
Telephone: 405-840-1066
Fax: 405-843-8446
Email: GLB@medlaws.com *URL:* http://www.medlaws.com

Ann Brooks
Christopher J. Bergin

For full biographical listings, see the Martindale-Hubbell Law Directory

CONNER & WINTERS, A PROFESSIONAL CORPORATION (AV)

One Leadership Square, 211 North Robinson, Suite 1700, 73102-7101
Telephone: 405-272-5711
Facsimile: 405-232-2695
Email: postmaster@cwlaw.com
Tulsa, Oklahoma Office: 3700 First Place Tower, 15 East 5th Street, 74103-4344.
Telephone: 918-586-5711.
Facsimile: 918-586-8982.
Fayetteville, Arkansas Office: Conner & Winters, P.L.L.C., 100 West Center Street, Suite 200, 72701-6081.
Telephone: 501-582-5711.
Facsimile: 501-587-1426.
Washington, D.C. Office: 1050 Seventeenth Street, N.W., Suite 810, 20036-5503.
Telephone: 202-783-5711.
Facsimile: 202-783-5720.

Peter B. Bradford
Raymond E. Tompkins
Timothy J. Bomhoff
Mitchell D. Blackburn

L. Don Smitherman
Laura L. McCasland
Cecily H. Murray

OF COUNSEL

S. Paul Hammons

For Complete List of Firm Personnel, See General Section

For full biographical listings, see the Martindale-Hubbell Law Directory

CROWE & DUNLEVY, A PROFESSIONAL CORPORATION (AV)

1800 Mid-America Tower, 20 North Broadway, 73102-8273
Telephone: 405-235-7700
Fax: 405-239-6651
Email: marketing@crowedunlevy.com *URL:* http://www.crowedunlevy.com
Tulsa, Oklahoma Office: 500 Kennedy Building, 321 South Boston Avenue, 74103-3313.
Telephone: 918-592-9800.
Fax: 918-592-9801.

(See Next Column)

Norman, Oklahoma Office: Crowe & Dunlevy, 2500 South McGee, Suite 140, 73072-6705.
Telephone: 405-321-7317.
Fax: 405-360-4002.

L. E. Stringer
Gary W. Davis
Andrew M. Coats
D. Kent Meyers
Clyde A. Muchmore
William G. Paul
Arlen E. Fielden
Harry A. Woods, Jr.
Jimmy Goodman
Richard C. Ford
John J. Griffin, Jr.
Brooke Smith Murphy
Leonard Court
Judy Hamilton Morse
Kelley C. Callahan
Mark D. Christiansen
Mack J. Morgan III
Anton J. Rupert
Harvey D. Ellis, Jr.
Gayle L. Barrett
L. Mark Walker
Stephen L. DeGiusti
Mark S. Grossman
Kevin D. Gordon
Todd Taylor
Robert G. McCampbell
LeAnne Burnett
Paul D. Trimble
Timila S. Rother
Tamela R. Hughlett
Joseph J. Ferretti
Dana M. Tacker

Rustin J. Strubhar
Mary Hirth Tolbert
C. Robert Stell
William H. Hoch
Jeremy Tubb
Jill F. Padgett
Paige S. Bass
Lance W. Cargill
John M. Thompson
Anthony D. Gould (Not admitted in OK)
Gregory S. Luster
Courtney K. Warmington

OF COUNSEL

Lawrence E. Walsh
Val R. Miller
Ruth Gana Okediji (Not admitted in OK)

For Complete List of Firm Personnel, See General Section

For full biographical listings, see the Martindale-Hubbell Law Directory

DAY, EDWARDS, FEDERMAN, PROPESTER & CHRISTENSEN, P.C. (AV)

Suite 2900 Oklahoma Tower, 210 Park Avenue, 73102-5605
Telephone: 405-239-2121
Telecopier: 405-236-1012
URL: http://lawlinks.com/attys/ok/defpc.html

Bruce W. Day
William B. Federman
D. Wade Christensen
Joe E. Edwards
Richard P. Propester
J. Clay Christensen
Rodney J. Heggy

Ricki Valerie Sonders
Joel Warren Harmon
Bill Powell Guest
Thomas Pitchlynn Howell, IV
Stuart W. Emmons
Gary L. Farnum

OF COUNSEL

Robert S. Baker

Representative Clients: Applied Thermal Systems, Inc.; BancFirst; Bank One, Oklahoma City; Bank of America Corporation; Bank of America, N.A.; CD Warehouse, Inc.; Cole & Reed, P.C.; DeLonghi America, Inc.; Eagle Star Insurance Co., Ltd.; Federal Deposit Insurance Corp.

For Complete List of Firm Personnel, See General Section

For full biographical listings, see the Martindale-Hubbell Law Directory

HARTZOG CONGER & CASON, A PROFESSIONAL CORPORATION (AV)

1600 Bank of Oklahoma Plaza 201 Robert S. Kerr, 73102
Telephone: 405-235-7000
Facsimile: 405-235-7329

Larry D. Hartzog
J. William Conger
Len Cason
James C. Prince
Steven C. Davis
Joseph P. Hogsett
John D. Robertson
Kurt M. Rupert
Laura Haag McConnell
Linda G. Scoggins
Susan B. Shields
Ryan S. Wilson
Amy J. Sine
Jon H. Trudgeon
Charles E. Geister, III
Phillip G. Whaley
Armand Paliotta

J. Christian Guzzy
Stacey D. Spivey
Melissa Beeson Heindselman
Christin V. Adkins
Byron K. Linkous

OF COUNSEL

Kent F. Frates
Kenneth R. Davis
Alan Newman

For full biographical listings, see the Martindale-Hubbell Law Directory

Oklahoma City—Continued

HOLLOWAY, DOBSON, BACHMAN & JENNINGS, A PROFESSIONAL CORPORATION (AV)

Suite 900 One Leadership Square 211 North Robinson, 73102-7102
Telephone: 405-235-8593
Fax: 405-235-1707

Page Dobson
Gary C. Bachman
James A. Jennings, III
Dan L. Holloway
John R. Denneny
Rodney L. Cook
J. William Archibald
Mark E. Duvall
James R. Baker
Stephen D. Bachman

Lu Ann Stout
Margo M. Brown
Carrie Palmer Hoisington
Michael E. Smith
Carolyn Ann Karl
J. Derrick Teague
Bryan G. Garrett
Aleatra Williams
Bret D. Davis

OF COUNSEL

Russell B. Holloway
David H. Dobson
B. Wayne Dabney

Representing: Associated Aviation Underwriters; Chubb Group of Insurance Cos.; Continental Insurance Cos; General Motors Corp.

For full biographical listings, see the Martindale-Hubbell Law Directory

HUCKABY, FLEMING, FRAILEY, CHAFFIN, CORDELL, GREENWOOD & PERRYMAN, L.L.P. (AV)

1215 Classen Drive, P.O. Box 60130, 73146
Telephone: 405-235-6648
Fax: 405-235-1533
URL: http://www.FlemingLaw@aol.com
Chickasha, Oklahoma Office: 201 North 4th, P.O. Box 533.
Telephone: 405-224-0237.
Fax: 405-222-2319.

MEMBERS OF FIRM

Owen Vaughn (1900-1981)
Clarence McElroy (1903-1970)
Steve Stack (1946-1979)
Richard A. Procter (1932-1980)
Kent Fleming
Tom A. Frailey
Michael R. Chaffin
F. Thomas Cordell, Jr.
William D. Greenwood
David L. Perryman
Deborah A. Sterkel
Brently C. Olsson
Stephen R. McCalla

ASSOCIATES

D. Renée Hildebrant
Rodney Dean Fergason
Jason L. West
Jeromy E. Brown

Representative Clients: Amerigas; Atlantic Recording; Baker Hughes; Dallas Carrier Corp.; Scottsdale Insurance Company; Superfos Construction (U.S.) Inc.; Travelers Insurance Company; Time-Warner, Inc.; Wausau Insurance Companies; Yellow Cab.

For full biographical listings, see the Martindale-Hubbell Law Directory

KERR, IRVINE, RHODES & ABLES, A PROFESSIONAL CORPORATION (AV)

201 Robert S. Kerr Avenue, Suite 600, 73102-4267
Telephone: 405-272-9221
Fax: 405-236-3121
Email: kira201@aol.com

J. Angela Ables
James W. Rhodes
R. Thomas Lay

Kevin R. Wisner

Representative Clients: Foundation Health, an Oklahoma Health Plan; Life Assurance Co., Inc.; Directors Life Assurance Co.; Oklahoma Life & Health Guaranty Association; National Organization of Life & Health Guaranty Associations; Farmers New World Life Insurance Co.; Life Assurance Co., Inc.; Wellington Insurance Co.; City of Ada.

For Complete List of Firm Personnel, See General Section

For full biographical listings, see the Martindale-Hubbell Law Directory

KING LAW FIRM (AV)

15 North Robinson, Suite 1100, 73102
Telephone: 405-239-6143
Fax: 405-236-3934
Email: kinglaw@flash.net

Tom L. King

ASSOCIATES

Richard M. Glasgow
Scott F. McKinney
Scott K. Suchy
John J. Foley

(See Next Column)

OF COUNSEL

Donald E. DeSpain

References: BankOne; BancFirst.

For full biographical listings, see the Martindale-Hubbell Law Directory

LEE, DUROCHER, KISNER, WALKER & REID (AV)

An Association of Professional Associations
5532 North Western, 73118
Telephone: 405-848-5532
Facsimile: 405-848-5502

Jim W. Lee
Daniel L. Durocher
David W. Kisner
David A. Walker
James M. Reid

For full biographical listings, see the Martindale-Hubbell Law Directory

LOONEY, NICHOLS & JOHNSON, PLLC (AV)

528 Northwest 12th, 73103
Telephone: 405-235-7641
Fax: 405-239-2050; 239-2052
Email: firm@lnjlaw.com

Ned Looney (1886-1965)
Clyde J. Watts (1907-1975)
Willard R. Bergstrasser (1922-1993)
Robert Dudley Looney
Henry W. Nichols
Burton J. Johnson
Edwin F. Garrison
Robert D. Looney, Jr.
Tenal S. Cooley, III
Timothy L. Martin
Brigid F. Kennedy
H. Grady Parker, Jr.

Bradley K. Donnell
Christian S. Huckaby
James Leo Gaston, Jr.
Shawn E. Harrell

Representative Clients: U.S. Aviation Insurance Underwriters; CNA Insurance Co.; The Goodyear Tire & Rubber Co.; Home Insurance Co.; MEDMARC; The Maryland Insurance Group; Travelers Property & Casualty Co.; Jefferson Insurance Group; Michelin North America, Inc.; TIG Insurance Co.

For full biographical listings, see the Martindale-Hubbell Law Directory

McCAFFREY & TAWWATER (AV)

Suite 1950, One Leadership Square, 211 North Robinson, 73102-7124
Telephone: 405-235-2900
Fax: 405-231-2818
URL: http://www.mccaffreytawwater.com
Other Oklahoma City, Oklahoma Office: 3015 N.W. 59th, 73112.

MEMBERS OF FIRM

George J. McCaffrey
Larry A. Tawwater

ASSOCIATES

Jo Lynn Slama
Loren F. Gibson
Steven R. Davis
Piper E. John
David B. Custar

For full biographical listings, see the Martindale-Hubbell Law Directory

THE MILLS LAW FIRM, P.C. (AV)

500 One Leadership Square, 211 North Robinson, 73102
Telephone: 405-239-2501
Fax: 405-239-2575
Email: millsfirm@attymail.com

Earl D. Mills
Robert B. Mills
W. Wayne Mills

For full biographical listings, see the Martindale-Hubbell Law Directory

MONNET, HAYES, BULLIS, THOMPSON & EDWARDS (AV)

Suite 1719 First National Center West, 120 North Robinson, 73102
Telephone: 405-232-5481
Fax: 405-235-9159
Email: MHBullis@AOL.COM

MEMBERS OF FIRM

John T. Edwards
James M. Peters
Randall A. Breshears
Robert C. Smith, Jr.
Steven K. McKinney
Shannon L. Edwards

Representative Clients: Natural Gas Pipeline Company of America; Chevron USA, Inc.; Firemen's Fund Insurance Co.; Lexington Insurance Co.; United American Insurance; Globe Life & Accident Insurance Company; Chase Manhattan Bank; H & L Operating Company; Oryx Energy Company; OXY USA, Inc.

For Complete List of Firm Personnel, See General Section

For full biographical listings, see the Martindale-Hubbell Law Directory

Oklahoma City—Continued

SELF, GIDDENS & LEES, INC. (AV)

2725 Oklahoma Tower, 210 Park Avenue, 73102-5643
Telephone: 405-232-3001
Telecopier: 405-232-5553

Thomas J. Blalock
Jared D. Giddens
C. Ray Lees
Shannon T. Self
Bryan J. Wells

Michael D. Meleen
John E. Gatliff II

For full biographical listings, see the Martindale-Hubbell Law Directory

WHITE LAW FIRM (AV)

900 N.E. 63rd Street, P.O. Box 18427, 73154
Telephone: 405-858-8899
Fax: 405-858-8844
Email: whitelawok@aol.com

Joe E. White, Jr.

ASSOCIATES

Greg S. Wilson
Derek B. Smith

For full biographical listings, see the Martindale-Hubbell Law Directory

WHITTEN, MCGUIRE, WOOD, TERRY, ROSELIUS & DITTRICH A PROFESSIONAL LIMITED LIABILITY COMPANY (AV)

Suite 400, One Leadership Square, 211 North Robinson, 73102
Telephone: 405-239-2522
Fax: 405-239-2573
Email: whitten@whitten-mcguire.com
Tulsa, Oklahoma Office: 3600 First Place Tower, 15 East Fifth Street.
Telephone: 918-582-9903.

Reggie N. Whitten
Kent R. McGuire
Douglas A. Terry
Jason E. Roselius

Simone Gosnell Fulmer
Philip W. Anderson
R. Gregory Kirby
Derrick T. Dewitt

Representative Clients: The St. Paul Insurance Cos.; Crum & Forster Commercial Insurance Co.; OML Municipal Assurance Group; City of Midwest City of Oklahoma City; City of Oklahoma City.

For full biographical listings, see the Martindale-Hubbell Law Directory

SEMINOLE, Seminole Co.

ELSENER & CADENHEAD, P.C. (AV)

300 East Seminole, P.O. Box 2067, 74818-2067
Telephone: 405-382-6341; 257-2773
Fax: 405-382-5513
Email: elsener@brightok.net

G. Dale Elsener
Ed Cadenhead

References furnished upon request.

For full biographical listings, see the Martindale-Hubbell Law Directory

*TULSA,** Tulsa Co.

ATKINSON, HASKINS, NELLIS, BOUDREAUX, HOLEMAN, PHIPPS & BRITTINGHAM, A PROFESSIONAL CORPORATION (AV)

1500 ParkCentre, 525 South Main Street, 74103
Telephone: 918-582-8877
Fax: 918-585-8096
Email: ahnmail@ahn-law.com

Michael P. Atkinson, P.C.
Walter D. Haskins, P.C.
Gregory D. Nellis, P.C.
Paul T. Boudreaux, P.C.
Daniel E. Holeman, P.C.
K. Clark Phipps
Galen Lee Brittingham, P.C.
John S. Gladd
John J. Carwile
Martha J. Phillips
William A. Fiasco
Jon D. Starr
Mark W. Maguire
Marthanda J. Beckworth
James N. Edmonds

Kirsten E. Pace
Scott R. Hall
Jeffrey L. Wilson
Whitney M. Eschenheimer
Margaret M. Clarke
Margaret A. Nunnery
Jeffrey A. Risch
Jennifer Annis
Eric J. Begin
Roni S. Rierson
Christine M. Benson
Bret A. Sanders

OF COUNSEL

Joseph F. Glass

LEGAL SUPPORT PERSONNEL

Beverly J. Rubino, M.D. (Medical Counsel)

Representative Clients: Allstate Insurance Co.; Bayer Corp.; Crum & Forster Insurance Co.; Hartford Insurance Company; National American Insurance Co.; Federated Insurance Co.; Liberty Mutual Insurance Co.; Physicians Liability Insurance Co.; State Farm Mutual Automobile Insurance Co.; United States Aviation Underwriters.

(See Next Column)

For full biographical listings, see the Martindale-Hubbell Law Directory

BARROW GADDIS GRIFFITH & GRIMM, A PROFESSIONAL CORPORATION (AV)

610 South Main, Suite 300, 74119-1248
Telephone: 918-584-1600
Fax: 918-585-2444
Email: EMAIL@BGGG.com *URL:* http://www.bggg.com

Allen E. Barrow, Jr.
Robert W. Gaddis
David W. Griffith
William R. Grimm
William E. Farrior
Nancy C. Pruitt
Wm. Brad Heckenkemper
J. Patrick Mensching, Jr.
Robert B. Sartin
L. Michele Nelson

Reference: NationsBank.

For full biographical listings, see the Martindale-Hubbell Law Directory

BEST & SHARP, A PROFESSIONAL CORPORATION (AV)

Oneok Plaza, 100 W. 5th, Suite 808, 74103-4225
Telephone: 918-582-1234
Fax: 918-585-9447
Email: Webmaster@BestSharp.com *URL:* http://www.BestSharp.com

Joseph M. Best
Joseph A. Sharp
Timothy G. Best
Daniel S. Sullivan
Amy E. Kempfert
Karen M. Grundy
Terry S. O'Donnell

Catherine L. Campbell
Malcom D. Smith, Jr.
Jeffrey W. Swanson
Dan W. Ernst
Thomas A. Le Blanc

For full biographical listings, see the Martindale-Hubbell Law Directory

BOESCHE, MCDERMOTT & ESKRIDGE (AV)

Suite 800 Oneok Plaza, 100 West Fifth Street, 74103
Telephone: 918-583-1777
Fax: 918-592-5809
Email: bme@intellex.com
Muskogee, Oklahoma Office: 1111 West Broadway, P.O. Box 2669, 74402.
Telephone: 918-683-6100.
Fax: 918-683-2303.

MEMBERS OF FIRM

R. Casey Cooper
David B. McKinney
Bradley K. Beasley
David A. Johnson
R. Kevin Layton
Sheila M. Powers

ASSOCIATES

Byron E. (Rusty) Brown
Christopher K. Woosley

OF COUNSEL

Clifford K. Cate, Jr. (Resident at Muskogee)

Representative Clients: Apache Corporation; Cigna Corp.; Elf Atochem North America, Inc.; General American Life Insurance Company.

For Complete List of Firm Personnel, See General Section

For full biographical listings, see the Martindale-Hubbell Law Directory

CONNER & WINTERS, A PROFESSIONAL CORPORATION (AV)

3700 First Place Tower, 15 East 5th Street, 74103-4344
Telephone: 918-586-5711
Fax: 918-586-8982
Email: postmaster@cwlaw.com
Oklahoma City, Oklahoma Office: One Leadership Square, 211 North Robinson, Suite 1700, 73102-7101.
Telephone: 405-272-5711.
Facsimile: 405-232-2695.
Fayetteville, Arkansas Office: Conner & Winters, P.L.L.C., 100 West Center Street, Suite 200, 72701-6081.
Telephone: 501-582-5711.
Facsimile: 501-587-1426.
Washington, D.C. Office: 1050 Seventeenth Street, N.W., Suite 810, 20036-5503.
Telephone: 202-783-5711.
Facsimile: 202-783-5720.

John T. Schmidt
D. Richard Funk
Randolph L. Jones, Jr.
J. Ronald Petrikin
Larry B. Lipe
James E. Green, Jr.
Andrew R. Turner
Deirdre O'Neil E. Dexter
Tony W. Haynie
Bruce W. Freeman
David R. Cordell
P. Scott Hathaway
John A. Bugg
Timothy T. Trump
Mark E. Dreyer

Rebecca Sellers Woodward
Melodie Freeman-Burney
Jacalyn W. Peter
Robert D. James
David H. Herrold
Fern Holland

(See Next Column)

CONNER & WINTERS A PROFESSIONAL CORPORATION—*Continued*

For Complete List of Firm Personnel, See General Section

For full biographical listings, see the Martindale-Hubbell Law Directory

B. HAYDEN CRAWFORD (AV)

240 Mid-Continent Tower, 401 South Boston Avenue, 74103-4059
Telephone: 918-587-1128
Fax: 918-587-3975

For full biographical listings, see the Martindale-Hubbell Law Directory

CROWE & DUNLEVY, A PROFESSIONAL CORPORATION (AV)

500 Kennedy Building, 321 South Boston Avenue, 74103-3313
Telephone: 918-592-9800
Fax: 918-592-9801
Email: marketing@crowedunlevy.com *URL:* http://www.crowedunlevy.com
Oklahoma City, Oklahoma Office: 1800 Mid-America Tower, 20 North Broadway, 73102-8273.
Telephone: 405-235-7700.
Fax: 405-239-6651.
Norman, Oklahoma Office: Crowe & Dunlevy, 2500 South McGee, Suite 140, 73072-6705.
Telephone: 405-321-7317.
Fax: 405-360-4002.

James L. Kincaid
Craig W. Hoster
Michael J. Gibbens
Terry M. Thomas
Madalene A. B. Witterholt
Randall J. Snapp
Victor E. Morgan
Jeffrey T. Hills

Sarah C. Hartmeyer
Gerald L. Jackson
Timothy F. Sterling
Alexander F. King
Jennifer A. Golm
Kayci Bair Hughes

For Complete List of Firm Personnel, See General Section

For full biographical listings, see the Martindale-Hubbell Law Directory

DOYLE & HARRIS, A PROFESSIONAL CORPORATION (AV)

1350 Boulder, P.O. Box 1679, 74119
Telephone: 918-592-1276
Fax: 918-592-4389
Email: D&H@CommerciaLaw.com *URL:* http://www.CommerciaLaw.com

Stan P. Doyle
Steven M. Harris

Michael D. Davis
Douglas R. Haughey
Bruce A. Spence

Reference: Peoples State Bank.

For full biographical listings, see the Martindale-Hubbell Law Directory

FELDMAN, FRANDEN, WOODARD & FARRIS (AV)

1000 Park Centre, 525 South Main, 74103-4514
Telephone: 918-583-7129
Telecopier: 918-584-3814
Email: feldman@tulsalawyer.com *URL:* http://www.tulsalawyer.com

MEMBERS OF FIRM

W. E. Green (1889-1977)
William S. Hall (1930-1991)
Raymond G. Feldman
Robert A. Franden
John R. Woodard, III
Joseph R. Farris
Victor R. Seagle
Tony M. Graham
J. David Mustain
Jody R. Nathan
R. Jack Freeman
R. Jay McAtee
Paula J. Quillin

ASSOCIATES

Timothy E. Tipton
Kristin Blue Fisher
Cheryl S. Gan
Leah P. Keele
R. Bryan Morrison
Thayla Painter Bohn

Representative Clients: CIGNA; The Equitable Life Assurance Society of the United States; Browning-Ferris Industries, Inc.; American Cyanamid Co.; American Home Assurance Co.; Oklahoma Bar Professional Liability Insurance Co.; American Motors Corp.; Sunbeam Corp.; Aviation Underwriters Inc.; Progressive Casualty Insurance Co.

For full biographical listings, see the Martindale-Hubbell Law Directory

RONALD MAIN, P.C. (AV)

Center 2800, Suite 821, 2815 East Skelly Drive, 74105-6251
Telephone: 918-742-1990
Fax: 918-742-2004
Email: rmainbtl@aol.com

Ronald Main

Representative Clients: Brumbaugh & Fulton, Co.; Miles Shipping Co.; H.S. Boyd, Co.; Kemco Fuels, Inc.; McDonnell-Douglas Corp.; Oklahoma Bar Professional Liability Insurance Co.; Sawyer Manufacturing Co.

(See Next Column)

Approved Attorneys For: Columbia Title Insurance Co.
References: Bank of Oklahoma, N.A.; Tulsa National Bank.

For full biographical listings, see the Martindale-Hubbell Law Directory

PRAY, WALKER, JACKMAN, WILLIAMSON & MARLAR, A PROFESSIONAL CORPORATION (AV)

900 ONEOK Plaza, 100 West 5th Street, 74103-4218
Telephone: 918-581-5500
Fax: 918-581-5599
Oklahoma City, Oklahoma Office: One Leadership Square, 211 North Robinson.
Telephone: 405-236-8911.
Fax: 405-236-0011.

J. Warren Jackman
W. Bland Williamson, Jr.
Donald F. Marlar
William D. Toney
Terry R. Doverspike
John F. McCormick, Jr.
Frank D. Spiegelberg
Ira L. Edwards, Jr.
John L. Randolph, Jr.
William L. Eagleton, IV
Donald S. Smith
Randall G. Vaughan
Charles Bretton Crane
Rita J. Gassaway
Kevin Pierce Doyle
Thomas M. Askew
Robert J. Winter
Steven B. Butterfield
Pamela D. Langston
Ryan G. Cole
Harry A. Parrish
David C. Cameron

OF COUNSEL

Donald E. Pray
Floyd L. Walker
Charles A. Kothe
C. Bruce Jones

OKLAHOMA CITY OFFICE

Henry A. Meyer, III
Wm. Gregory James
Gary Peterson
Georgiana T. Peterson
Gregory J. Crawford
Steven J. Goetzinger (Resident, Oklahoma City Office)

For full biographical listings, see the Martindale-Hubbell Law Directory

RHODES, HIERONYMUS, JONES, TUCKER & GABLE, P.L.L.C. (AV)

Oneok Plaza, 100 West 5th Street, Suite 400, P.O. Box 21100, 74121-1100
Telephone: 918-582-1173
Fax: 918-592-3390
URL: http://www.rhodesokla.com

MEMBERS OF FIRM

Kevin D. Berry
Jo Anne Deaton
Richard M. Eldridge
E. D. Hieronymus (1908 -1994)
Bert M. Jones
William S. Leach
Michael W. McGivern
William D. Perrine
Mary Quinn-Cooper
Robert P. Redemann
David P. Reid
Chris L. Rhodes, III
Thomas E. Steichen
Catherine C. Taylor
John H. Tucker
Wilson T. White
Harold C. Zuckerman

Ann E. Allison
Steven K. Bunting
Robert P. Coffey, Jr.
J. Christopher Davis
Andrew D. Downing
Dana L. Gish
Kerry R. Lewis
Andrew L. Richardson
Michael F. Smith
Leslie J. Southerland
Kimberly E. West
Keith A. Wilkes

OF COUNSEL

George W. Gable (Retired Partner)
Larry J. Fulton
Kelly M. Greenough

Representative Clients: American International Companies; Bechtel; Chubb Group of Insurance Companies; General Motors Corporation; Merrill, Lynch; Nissan Motor Corporation in U.S.A.; Pfizer, Inc.; Volkswagen of America, Volkswagen, A.G.; Zurich U.S.

For full biographical listings, see the Martindale-Hubbell Law Directory

RICHARDS & CONNOR (AV)

9 East 4th Street, Suite 910, 74103-5103
Telephone: 918-585-2394
Fax: 918-585-1449

MEMBERS OF FIRM

Phil R. Richards
James W. Connor, Jr.

ASSOCIATES

Rachel Carver Mathis
Malinda S. Matlock
Thomas D. Hird
Jan L. Heister
Jason Lee Glass
John A.L. Campbell

For full biographical listings, see the Martindale-Hubbell Law Directory

Tulsa—Continued

SHIPLEY, JENNINGS & CHAMPLIN, P.C. (AV)

201 West Fifth Street, Suite 400, 74103-4230
Telephone: 918-582-1720
Fax: 918-584-7681
Email: sjclaw@ionet.net
Oklahoma City, Oklahoma Office: Two Leadership Square, 211 North Robinson, Suite 1300, 73102-7114.
Telephone: 405-235-0808.
Facsimile: 405-232-3746. Email: sjcokc@ionet.net.

Charles W. Shipley
Mark B. Jennings
Blake K. Champlin

Jamie Taylor Boyd

OF COUNSEL

Dee E. Dismukes
Robert D. Kellogg (Resident, Oklahoma City Office)

Reference: Nations Bank.

For full biographical listings, see the Martindale-Hubbell Law Directory

SNEED LANG, P.C. (AV)

2300 Williams Center Tower II, Two West Second Street, 74103
Telephone: 918-583-3145
Telecopier: 918-582-0410

James C. Lang
D. Faith Orlowski
Brian S. Gaskill
G. Steven Stidham
Stephen R. McNamara
Thomas E. Black, Jr.
Robbie Emery Burke
Patrick O. Waddel
Randolph P. Stainer
Steven K. Balman
Brian T. Inbody
D. Michael McBride III

OF COUNSEL

James L. Sneed

Representative Clients: Amoco Production Co.; Bank One, Texas; Enron Corp.; Halliburton Energy Services; Helmerich & Payne, Inc.; Shell Oil Co.; State Farm Mutual Automobile Insurance Co.; The Williams Companies.

For full biographical listings, see the Martindale-Hubbell Law Directory

STRECKER & ASSOCIATES, P.C. (AV)

15 West 6th Street, Suite 1600, 74119-5410
Telephone: 918-582-1716; 918-582-1734
Fax: 918-582-1780
Email: SandK@juno.com *URL:* http://www.lawyers.com/strecker&associates

David E. Strecker

James E. Erwin

For full biographical listings, see the Martindale-Hubbell Law Directory

OREGON

*BEND,** Deschutes Co.

HURLEY, LYNCH & RE, P.C. (AV)

747 S.W. Industrial Way, 97702
Telephone: 541-317-5505
Fax: 541-317-5507

James V. Hurley
Gregory P. Lynch
Daniel C. Re
Kevin J. Keillor
Bryan W. Gruetter

Stanley D. Austin
Christopher D. Hatfield
Kelly L. McDole
Milly Whatley
Troy J. Wood

Representative Clients: Eagle Crest Resort; Sunriver Resort; Jeld-Wen, Inc.; AmeriTitle Co.; Bend Research; Deschutes County; Consep, Inc.; Fuqua Homes, Inc.; Scottsdale Insurance; David Evans and Associates.

For full biographical listings, see the Martindale-Hubbell Law Directory

*PORTLAND,** Multnomah Co.

BLACK HELTERLINE LLP (AV)

1200 Union Bank of California Tower, 707 S.W. Washington Street, 97205
Telephone: 503-224-5560
Telecopier: 503-224-6148
URL: http://www.bhlaw.com

(See Next Column)

MEMBERS OF FIRM

Ronald T. Adams
James M. Baumgartner
Michael B. Merchant
Michael O. Moran

ASSOCIATES

James R. George
Christina L. Haring
Eric J. TenBrook

Representative Clients: Union Bank of California, N.A.; Emergency Medicine Associates, P.S.; McKinstry Co.; Goodyear Rubber and Supply Co.; James River Corp.; Linsco/Private Ledger Corp.; NACCO Materials Handling Group, Inc.; Senco Products, Inc.; Western Council of Industrial Workers--TOC Trust Funds.

For Complete List of Firm Personnel, See General Section

For full biographical listings, see the Martindale-Hubbell Law Directory

BODYFELT, MOUNT, STROUP & CHAMBERLAIN (AV)

300 Powers Building, 65 S.W. Yamhill Street, 97204-3377
Telephone: 503-243-1022
Fax: 503-243-2019
Email: bmsc@bmsc-law.com

MEMBERS OF FIRM

Barry M. Mount
Roger K. Stroup
Peter R. Chamberlain
Richard A. Lee
Mark A. Hiefield

ASSOCIATES

Molly Jo Mullen
Eric "Skip" Winters
Aaron M. Brian

OF COUNSEL

Cathy E. Smith

Representative Clients: American International Group; Catholic Health Initiatives; Chrysler Corp.; Genuine Parts Co.; Georgia-Pacific Corp.; Hartford Insurance Co.; Oregon Mutual Insurance Company; Otis Elevator Co.; Safeway Stores, Inc.; Tokio Marine Insurance Co.

For full biographical listings, see the Martindale-Hubbell Law Directory

JAMES, DENECKE, URRUTIA, MARMADUKE & LAWSON, P.C. (AV)

1150 Pioneer Tower, 888 S.W. Fifth Avenue, 97204-2025
Telephone: 503-228-7967
Fax: 503-222-7261
Email: jdum@jdum.com *URL:* http://www.jdum.com

Christopher James
David R. Denecke
J. Richard Urrutia
Susan D. Marmaduke
Jerry L. Lawson, Jr.

Jill D. Laney
Lee Wyatt
John D. Harrington

For full biographical listings, see the Martindale-Hubbell Law Directory

KELL, ALTERMAN & RUNSTEIN, LLP (AV)

1001 S.W. Fifth Avenue, Suite 1800, 97204
Telephone: 503-222-3531
Telecopier: 503-227-2980
Email: kell@teleport.com

MEMBERS OF FIRM

Raymond M. Kell (1911-1991)
Clifford B. Alterman (1925-1995)
Ted E. Runstein
Lee Davis Kell
Wayne D. Palmer
Lloyd R. Summers
William D. Dickas
Gary P. Compa
Charles R. Williamson
Mary Ellen Page Farr
Eric Sogge
Thomas J. Matsuda
Thomas R. Rask, III
Nicholas S. Fish

Dana L. Barnes
Cory Larvik
Robert E. Kabacy
Robin M. Runstein

References: Union Bank of California, N.A. (Portland Branch); The Bank of Tokyo-Mitsubishi, Ltd. (Portland Branch); Bank of America (5th S. Main Branch).

For full biographical listings, see the Martindale-Hubbell Law Directory

JEROME LABARRE A PROFESSIONAL CORPORATION (AV)

Suite 1800, 101 S.W. Main Street, 97204
Telephone: 503-228-3511
FAX: 503-225-1257
Email: labarre@teleport.com *URL:* http://www.lawyers.com/labarre

Jerome E. LaBarre

Representative Clients: Pacific University; Fone America, Inc.; Pacific X-ray, Inc.; Huntington Bank, Inc. of Kentucky.

For full biographical listings, see the Martindale-Hubbell Law Directory

Portland—Continued

SATHER, BYERLY & HOLLOWAY, LLP (AV)

621 Southwest Morrison Street, Suite 650, 97205
Telephone: 503-225-5858
Fax: 503-721-9272
Email: sbh@teleport.com *URL:* http://www.teleport.com/~sbh/sbh.htm

Deborah L. Sather
Bruce L. Byerly
Ronald C. Holloway
Krishna Balasubramani
Tracy J. White
Constance Lynn Wold

For full biographical listings, see the Martindale-Hubbell Law Directory

ARDEN E. SHENKER (AV)

One World Trade Center, Suite 1480, 121 SW Salmon, 97204-2925
Telephone: 503-294-1118
Fax: 503-294-0015
Email: ashenker@ashenkeresq.com

LEGAL SUPPORT PERSONNEL

Trudy A. Cardoza
Diane L. Thompson

For full biographical listings, see the Martindale-Hubbell Law Directory

*ROSEBURG,** Douglas Co.

DOLE, COALWELL, CLARK, MOUNTAINSPRING & MORNARICH, P.C. (AV)

810 S.E. Douglas Avenue, P.O. Box 1205, 97470
Telephone: 541-673-5541
Fax: 541-673-1156
Email: dcclaw@rosenet.net

George W. Neuner (1914-1985)
Donald A. Dole
Bruce R. Coalwell
Dan W. Clark
Stephen Mountainspring
Jeffrey A. Mornarich

Ronald W. Aitken

Representative Clients: Douglas County Title Co.; C & D Lumber Co.; Herbert Lumber Co.

For full biographical listings, see the Martindale-Hubbell Law Directory

PENNSYLVANIA

*ALLENTOWN,** Lehigh Co.

GROSS, MCGINLEY, LABARRE & EATON, LLP (AV)

33 South Seventh Street, P.O. Box 4060, 18105-4060
Telephone: 610-820-5450
Fax: 610-820-6006
Email: attorney@gmle.com

MEMBERS OF FIRM

Malcolm J. Gross
Paul A. McGinley
Donald L. LaBarre, Jr.
J. Jackson Eaton, III
Michael A. Henry
Patrick J. Reilly
William J. Fries
Anne K. Manley
Susan Ellis Wild

ASSOCIATES

Elizabeth M. Racht
Allen I. Tullar
Sara J. Hogan
John F. Gross
Kimberly Gobla Krupka

For full biographical listings, see the Martindale-Hubbell Law Directory

TALLMAN, HUDDERS & SORRENTINO, P.C. (AV)

Suite 300 The Paragon Centre, 1611 Pond Road, 18104
Telephone: 610-391-1800
Fax: 610-391-1805
Email: info@ths.com *URL:* http://www.thslaw.com

Robert G. Tallman
John R. Hudders (Retired)
Donald H. Lipson
Thomas C. Sadler, Jr.
Donald A. Zamborsky
Oldrich Foucek, III
Matthew R. Sorrentino
Paul McHale, Jr.
Barbara L. Hollenbach
Timothy J. Siegfried
Dolores A. Laputka
Scott B. Allinson

Michael E. Loomis
John K. Baker
Laura J. Herzog
Scott R. Lipson
Theodore J. Zeller, III
Jeffrey A. Durney
Beverly J. Doneker
George C. Hlavac
Douglas G. Cappellini
Ronnie F. Hess
Amy Kohler Howard

OF COUNSEL

Paul J. Schoff

For full biographical listings, see the Martindale-Hubbell Law Directory

BALA CYNWYD, Montgomery Co.

KANIA, LINDNER, LASAK AND FEENEY (AV)

Suite 525, Two Bala Plaza, 19004
Telephone: 610-667-3240
Fax: 610-668-9676
Email: kllf@aol.com

Arthur J. Kania
Albert A. Lindner
John Lasak
Thomas J. Feeney, III
Robert A. Griffiths

A list of Representative Clients for which the firm serves as General Counsel or Local Counsel will be supplied upon request.

For full biographical listings, see the Martindale-Hubbell Law Directory

*BELLEFONTE,** Centre Co.

MILLER, KISTLER, CAMPBELL, MILLER, WILLIAMS & BENSON, INC. (AV)

124 North Allegheny Street, 16823
Telephone: 814-355-5474
Fax: 814-355-5340
State College, Pennsylvania Office: 720 South Atherton Street.
Telephone: 814-234-1500.
Fax: 814-234-1549.

R. Paul Campbell (1908-1988)
Lewis Orvis Harvey (1912-1990)
John R. Miller, Jr.
Richard L. Campbell
John R. Miller, III
Terry James Williams
Tracey G. Benson
Scott C. Etter

Elizabeth A. DuPuis

OF COUNSEL

Robert K. Kistler

General Counsel for: Omega Bank; Glenn O. Hawbaker, Inc.; Cannon Instrument Co.; Hanover Brands.
Local Counsel for: Tele-Media Corp.; Aetna Insurance Co.; Travelers Insurance Co.; The Medical Protective Co.; Corning Glass Works.
Solicitors: Borough of State College.

For full biographical listings, see the Martindale-Hubbell Law Directory

BETHLEHEM, Northampton Co.

O'HARE & HEITCZMAN (AV)

18 East Market Street, P.O. Box 1446, 18018
Telephone: 610-691-5500
Fax: 610-691-7866
Email: heitczman@nni.com *URL:* http://www.heitczman.com

MEMBERS OF FIRM

Bernard V. O'Hare, Jr. (1923-1990)
George A. Heitczman

References: Summit Bank; CoreStates Bank.

For full biographical listings, see the Martindale-Hubbell Law Directory

BLUE BELL, Montgomery Co.

ELLIOTT REIHNER SIEDZIKOWSKI & EGAN, P.C. (AV)

Union Meeting Corporate Center V, 925 Harvest Drive, 19422
Telephone: 215-977-1000
Fax: 215-977-1099
URL: http://www.erse.com
Scranton, Pennsylvania Office:
Telephone: 717-346-7569.
Fax: 717-969-2890.
Harrisburg, Pennsylvania Office:
Telephone: 717-234-8010.
Fax: 717-233-4262.
Reading, Pennsylvania Office:
Telephone: 610-374-6756.
Fax: 610-373-4844.

John M. Elliott
Thomas J. Elliott
Henry F. Siedzikowski
Gerard P. Egan
Douglas R. Blazey (Resident, Reading Office)
James C. Crumlish, III
Mark J. Schwemler
Timothy T. Myers
Mark A. Kearney
Dionysios G. Rassias
Frederick P. Santarelli
Marvin L. Wilenzik
Adam B. Krafczek, Jr. (Resident Managing Partner, Reading Office)
Eric J. Bronstein

COUNSEL

Robert P. Casey

OF COUNSEL

Kevin S. Anderson
Stewart J. Greenleaf
Timothy S. Kerr
Kenneth L. Tepper
Charles M. O'Donnell

(See Next Column)

ELLIOTT REIHNER SIEDZIKOWSKI & EGAN P.C., *Blue Bell—Continued*

Krista Kearns Beatty
Michael A. Bowman
Raymond J. Santarelli
Kathryn M. Schilling
Patricia C. Collins
Brian J. McCormick, Jr.
Eric P. Wilenzik
Meredith T. Shepherd
Brian Richard Elias

For full biographical listings, see the Martindale-Hubbell Law Directory

GERBER & GERBER (AV)
790 Penllyn-Blue Bell Pike, Suite 100, 19422
Telephone: 610-279-6700; 215-540-9100
Fax: 215-540-9424
Email: grbrlaw@dynanet.com *URL:* http://www.lawyers.com/gerber&gerber

Morris Gerber (1908-1995)

MEMBER OF FIRM

A. Richard Gerber

For full biographical listings, see the Martindale-Hubbell Law Directory

KAPLIN STEWART MELOFF REITER & STEIN, PROFESSIONAL CORPORATION (AV)
350 Sentry Parkway, Building 640, P.O. Box 3037, 19422-0765
Telephone: 610-260-6000
Telecopier: 610-260-1240
Cherry Hill, New Jersey Office: 900 Dudley Avenue, #250, 08002-4426.
Telephone: 856-486-1044.
Fax: 856-486-1074.

MEMBERS OF FIRM

David N. Bressler
Michael P. Coughlin
Patricia L. Talcott

OF COUNSEL

Barbara Anisko

ASSOCIATE

Kimberly L. Russell

For full biographical listings, see the Martindale-Hubbell Law Directory

KELLEY & MURPHY (AV)
Union Meeting Corporate Center V, Suite 160 925 Harvest Drive, 19422
Telephone: 215-643-6500
Fax: 215-643-8356
Cable Address: "BIGTIME"
Email: kmlaw@counsel.com

Joseph T. Kelley, Jr.
Patrick G. Murphy
Joseph T. Kelley, III

LEGAL SUPPORT PERSONNEL

Marianne Rowen
Tanja M.Z. Barron

For full biographical listings, see the Martindale-Hubbell Law Directory

SHINGLES & CAPPELLI (AV)
794 Penllyn Blue Bell Pike, Suite 101, 19422
Telephone: 610-941-4444
Fax: 610-941-9880
800-974-9444
URL: http://www.lawyers.com/shingles&cappelli

MEMBERS OF FIRM

Stanley M. Shingles
Joseph J. Cappelli

ASSOCIATES

Elizabeth L. Schmidt
Shawn M. Sassaman

OF COUNSEL

Robert J. F. Brobyn

SPECIAL COUNSEL

Joseph S. Ziccardi

For full biographical listings, see the Martindale-Hubbell Law Directory

BRISTOL, Bucks Co.

BEGLEY, CARLIN & MANDIO (AV)
120 Mill Street, 19007
Telephone: 215-750-0110
Fax: 215-750-0954
Email: bcm@itw.com
Langhorne, Pennsylvania Office: 680 Middletown Boulevard, P.O. Box 308.
Telephone: 215-750-0110.

(See Next Column)

MEMBERS OF FIRM

William J. Carlin
Jeffrey P. Garton
S. Richard Klinges, III
Thomas R. Hecker
Thomas J. Profy, III
James A. Downey, III
Richard M. Snyder
Joseph S. Britton
Charles F. Sampsel
Douglas C. Maloney
John P. Koopman
Thomas J. Profy, IV

ASSOCIATES

Karen Saraco Burns
Randall L. Miller
Timothy J. Duffy
Jennifer L. McGrath

OF COUNSEL

Anthony A. Mandio

For full biographical listings, see the Martindale-Hubbell Law Directory

*BUTLER,** Butler Co.

WARREN D. FERRY, P.C. (AV)
127 South McKean Street, 16001
Telephone: 724-283-7508
Fax: 724-283-8557
Email: wferry1244@aol.com
Pittsburgh, Pennsylvania Office: 500 Four PPG Place.
Telephone: 412-471-9991.
Fax: 412-391-9972.

Warren D. Ferry

For full biographical listings, see the Martindale-Hubbell Law Directory

CAMP HILL, Cumberland Co.

REAGER & ADLER, P.C. (AV)
2331 Market Street, 17011
Telephone: 717-763-1383
Fax: 717-730-7366
Email: reagerpc@epix.net *URL:* http://www.ReagerAdlerPC.com

Theodore A. Adler
Linus E. Fenicle
David W. Reager
Debra Denison Cantor

Thomas O. Williams
Susan H. Confair
Julie A. McConahy

LEGAL SUPPORT PERSONNEL

Monica D. Zercher (Paralegal)

Representative Clients: The Homestead Group, Inc.

For full biographical listings, see the Martindale-Hubbell Law Directory

CLARKS SUMMIT, Lackawanna Co.

BEEMER & BEEMER (AV)
114-116 North Abington Road, 18411
Telephone: 570-587-0188
Facsimile: 570-586-7957
Email: BBeemer123@aol.com *URL:* http://www.lawyers.com/jbbeemer

MEMBERS OF FIRM

Diane F. Beemer (1941-1999)
John Barry Beemer

Reference: Penn Security Bank.

For full biographical listings, see the Martindale-Hubbell Law Directory

*EASTON,** Northampton Co.

PHILIP D. LAUER, P.C. (AV)
704 Washington Street, 18042
Telephone: 610-258-5329
Fax: 610-258-0155
Email: laueresq@enter.net *URL:* http://www.lawyers.com/laueresq

Philip D. Lauer

Robert Einar Sletvold

Reference: Nazareth National Bank.

For full biographical listings, see the Martindale-Hubbell Law Directory

ELKINS PARK, Montgomery Co.

MONAGHAN & GOLD, P.C. (AV)
Manor Professional Building, 7837 Old York Road, 19027
Telephone: 215-782-1800
Fax: 215-782-1010
URL: http://www.MNG-LAW.com

Alan S. Gold
John F. X. Monaghan, Jr.

Murray R. Glickman
Robert F. Fortin
Tanya M. Sweet
Sean Robins
Mitchell K. Brudno
Kenneth W. Taylor
Francis D. Hennessy, Jr.

(See Next Column)

MONAGHAN & GOLD P.C.—*Continued*

OF COUNSEL

Alan L. Butkovitz
Steven M. Zelitch
Barbara Malett Weitz

LEGAL SUPPORT PERSONNEL

Andrew Logan (Paralegal)
Janet McCrossen (Registered Nurse)
Carol Veach (Paralegal)

For full biographical listings, see the Martindale-Hubbell Law Directory

*HARRISBURG,** Dauphin Co.

ANGINO & ROVNER, P.C. (AV)

4503 North Front Street, 17110
Telephone: 717-238-6791
Fax: 717-238-5610
Email: lawfirm@angino-rovner.com *URL:* http://www.angino-rovner.com
Carlisle, Pennsylvania Office: 28 South Pitt Street, 17013.
Telephone: 717-241-2661.

Richard C. Angino
Neil J. Rovner

References: Credit Bureau of Greater Harrisburg; CoreStates.

For full biographical listings, see the Martindale-Hubbell Law Directory

S. WALTER FOULKROD, III & ASSOCIATES (AV)

2215 Forest Hills Drive, Suite 35, P.O. Box 6600, 17112-0600
Telephone: 717-541-0400
Fax: 717-541-1727
Email: law@foulkrod.com *URL:* http://www.foulkrod.com

ASSOCIATES

S. Walter Foulkrod, IV
Andrew H. Foulkrod

Representative Clients: Aegis Security Insurance Company; Allianz Life Insurance Company of North America; Allstate Insurance Co.; ATI Title Co.; Physicians Insurance Company of Ohio; Physicians Mutual Insurance Co.; Pennsylvania Medical Society Liability Insurance Co.; Pennsylvania National Mutual Casualty Insurance Co.; Tighe Industries, Inc.; United Investors Life Insurance Co.

For full biographical listings, see the Martindale-Hubbell Law Directory

GOLDBERG, KATZMAN & SHIPMAN, P.C. (AV)

320 Market Street - Strawberry Square, P.O. Box 1268, 17108-1268
Telephone: 717-234-4161
Telecopier: 717-234-6808; 717-234-6810
Email: gks@gkslaw.com

Ronald M. Katzman
F. Lee Shipman
Jesse Jay Cooper
Thomas E. Brenner
John A. Statler
April L. Strang-Kutay
Guy H. Brooks
Jefferson J. Shipman
Thomas J. Weber

John R. Ninosky

Representative Clients: Cincinnati Insurance Co.; Atlantic Mutual Cos.; Erie Insurance Co.; Gallagher Bassett Company; Merchants & Businessman's Mutual Insurance Co.; State Auto Mutual Insurance Co.; Crawford & Co.; Foremost Insurance Co.; Virginia Mutual Insurance Co.; Zurich Insurance Group.
Reference: Fulton Bank.

For Complete List of Firm Personnel, See General Section

For full biographical listings, see the Martindale-Hubbell Law Directory

KEEFER WOOD ALLEN & RAHAL, LLP (AV)

210 Walnut Street, P.O. Box 11963, 17108-1963
Telephone: 717-255-8000
Telecopier: 717-255-8050
Email: info@keeferwood.com *URL:* http://www.keeferwood.com
Camp Hill, Pennsylvania Office: 415 Fallowfield Road.
Telephone: 717-612-5800.
Telecopier: 717-612-5805.

MEMBERS OF FIRM

Charles W. Rubendall II
Eugene E. Pepinsky, Jr
Thomas E. Wood
Gary E. French
Donna S. Weldon
Bradford Dorrance
Stephen L. Grose

SENIOR ATTORNEY

Donald M. Lewis, III

ASSOCIATES

Brenda L. Gacki
John A. Feichtel

Representative Clients: Case Corp.; Freightliner Corp.; Grove Worldwide; John Hancock Mutual Life Insurance Co.; Highmark, Inc.; PACCAR, Inc.; Revco D.S., Inc.; Tecumsch Products Co.; Texas Eastern Transmission Corp.; TRW, Inc.

(See Next Column)

For Complete List of Firm Personnel, See General Section

For full biographical listings, see the Martindale-Hubbell Law Directory

KILLIAN & GEPHART, LLP (AV)

218 Pine Street, P.O. Box 886, 17108
Telephone: 717-232-1851
Telecopier: 717-238-0592
Email: kg@killiangephart.com *URL:* http://www.killiangephart.com

MEMBERS OF FIRM

John D. Killian
Thomas W. Scott
Paula J. McDermott
J. Paul Helvy

ASSOCIATE

Bradley A. Schutjer

Reference: Fulton Bank.

For full biographical listings, see the Martindale-Hubbell Law Directory

MANCKE, WAGNER, HERSHEY AND TULLY (AV)

2233 North Front Street, 17110
Telephone: 717-234-7051

MEMBERS OF FIRM

John B. Mancke
P. Richard Wagner
David E. Hershey
William T. Tully

For full biographical listings, see the Martindale-Hubbell Law Directory

METTE, EVANS & WOODSIDE, A PROFESSIONAL CORPORATION (AV)

3401 North Front Street, P.O. Box 5950, 17110-0950
Telephone: 717-232-5000
Fax: 717-236-1816
Email: MEW@Mette.com *URL:* HTTP://WWW.METTE.COM

James W. Evans
Craig A. Stone
Daniel L. Sullivan
Steven D. Snyder
Christopher C. Conner
Kathryn Lease Simpson
P. Daniel Altland
Andrew H. Dowling
Michael D. Reed
David A. Fitzsimons
Michael D. Pipa

John F. Yaninek
Kathleen Doyle Yaninek
Elizabeth J. Goldstein
Bryan Scott Megary
John M. Hartzell

For Complete List of Firm Personnel, See General Section

For full biographical listings, see the Martindale-Hubbell Law Directory

METZGER, WICKERSHAM, KNAUSS & ERB, P.C. (AV)

3211 North Front Street, P.O. Box 5300, 17110-0300
Telephone: 717-238-8187
Telefax: 717-234-9478
Other Harrisburg, Pennsylvania Office: 4813 Jonestown Road, P.O. Box 5300, 17110-0300.
Telephone: 717-652-7020.

Maurice R. Metzger (1918-1980)
F. Brewster Wickersham (1918-1974)
Edward E. Knauss, III (Retired)
Christian S. Erb, Jr.
Robert E. Yetter
James F. Carl
Edward E. Knauss, IV
Jered L. Hock
Karl R. Hildabrand
Richard B. Druby
Steven P. Miner

Clark DeVere
Carrie L. Carroll

Representative Clients: Allstate Insurance Co.; Chubb Group of Insurance Companies; Fireman's Fund American Insurance Group; Liberty Mutual Insurance Co.; Crum & Forster; CNA Insurance; Prudential Insurance Co.

For full biographical listings, see the Martindale-Hubbell Law Directory

PETERS & WASILEFSKI (AV)

2931 North Front Street, 17110
Telephone: 717-238-7555
Fax: 717-238-7750
Email: pwlaw@redrose.net

MEMBERS OF FIRM

William J. Peters
Charles E. Wasilefski
Dennis J. Bonetti
Joseph C. Phillips
Michael R. Bonshock
Thomas A. Lang

ASSOCIATES

Pamela S. Parascandola
Stephen F. Moore
Cindy J. Murphy
James A. Garver

Reference: Commonwealth National Bank.

For full biographical listings, see the Martindale-Hubbell Law Directory

Harrisburg—Continued

RHOADS & SINON LLP (AV)

One South Market Square, 12th Floor, P.O. Box 1146, 17108-1146
Telephone: 717-233-5731
Fax: 717-232-1459
Boca Raton, Florida Affiliated Office: Charles L. Sieck, 1700 South Dixie Highway, Suite 2-C.
Telephone: 561-395-5595.
Fax: 561-395-9497.
York, Pennsylvania Office: 15 North Cherry Lane, Suite 21.
Telephone: 717-843-1718.
Fax: 717-232-1459.

OF COUNSEL

John C. Dowling
R. Stephen Shibla

MEMBERS OF FIRM

David B. Dowling
Thomas A. French
Donna M. J. Clark
Dean F. Piermattei

ASSOCIATES

Todd J. Shill
Kevin M. Gold
Stephen Moniak

Representative Clients: Aetna Surety & Casualty Co.; The Coca-Cola Company; Dauphin Deposit Bank & Trust Company; General Motors Corp.; H. J. Heinz Co.; Home Insurance Company; Insurance Company of North America; Weis Markets, Inc.

For Complete List of Firm Personnel, See General Section

For full biographical listings, see the Martindale-Hubbell Law Directory

THOMAS, THOMAS & HAFER, LLP (AV)

305 North Front Street, 6th Floor, P.O. Box 999, 17108
Telephone: 717-237-7100
Fax: 717-237-7105
Verify: 717-255-7642
Bethlehem, Pennsylvania Office: 12 East Market Street, P.O. Box 1172, 12016.
Telephone: 610-868-1675.
Fax: 610-868-1702.

MEMBERS OF FIRM

Joseph P. Hafer
James K. Thomas, II
Robertson B. Taylor
Jeffrey B. Rettig
Peter J. Curry
R. Burke McLemore, Jr.
Edward H. Jordan, Jr.
C. Kent Price
Randall G. Gale
David L. Schwalm
Peter J. Speaker
Douglas B. Marcello
Paul J. Dellasega

OF COUNSEL

James K. Thomas

Timothy I. Mark
Daniel J. Gallagher
Robert A. Taylor
Sarah W. Arosell
Eugene N. McHugh
Stephen E. Geduldig
Karen S. Coates
Gary T. Lathrop
Todd B. Narvol
James J. Dodd-o
Kenneth A. Rapp
Kevin C. McNamara
Brooks R. Foland
John Flounlacker
John M. Popilock
Michele J. Thorp

Representative Clients: Aetna Casualty & Surety Co.; Bethlehem Steel Corp.; Commercial Union Insurance Companies; Geisinger Medical Center; Hartford Insurance Group; Liberty Mutual Insurance Co.; Pennsylvania Hospital Insurance Co.; Pennsylvania Medical Society Liability Insurance Co.; UGI Corp.; Weis Markets, Inc.

For full biographical listings, see the Martindale-Hubbell Law Directory

HAVERFORD, Montgomery & Delaware Cos.

CHIMICLES & TIKELLIS LLP (AV)

One Haverford Centre, 361 West Lancaster Avenue, 19041-0100
Telephone: 610-642-8500
Telecopier: 610-649-3633
Email: chimicles@aol.com *URL:* http://www.chimicles.com
Wilmington, Delaware Office: One Rodney Square, 19801.
Telephone: 302-656-2500.
Telecopier: 302-656-9053.

MEMBERS OF FIRM

Nicholas E. Chimicles
Pamela S. Tikellis (Resident Partner, Wilmington, Delaware Office)
James R. Malone, Jr.
James C. Strum (Resident Partner, Wilmington, Delaware Office)
Michael D. Gottsch
Robert J. Kriner, Jr. (Resident Partner, Wilmington, Delaware Office)
Steven A. Schwartz

OF COUNSEL

Morris M. Shuster
Denise Davis Schwartzman

(See Next Column)

ASSOCIATES

Candice Lea Horn Hegedus
Mary K. Meermans
Pamela Nicolaysen
Ramona Mariani
Andrew Lapat

For full biographical listings, see the Martindale-Hubbell Law Directory

*LANCASTER,** Lancaster Co.

ZIMMERMAN, PFANNEBECKER, NUFFORT & ALBERT, LLP (AV)

22 South Duke Street, 17602
Telephone: 717-299-0711
Fax: 717-299-1092
Columbia, Pennsylvania Office: 342 Walnut Street.
Telephone: 717-684-2665.
Fax: 717-299-1092.
Lititz, Pennsylvania Office: 10 South Broad Street.
Telephone: 717-626-2088.
Quarryville, Pennsylvania Office: 100 East State Street.
Telephone: 717-786-8335.

MEMBERS OF FIRM

S. R. Zimmerman, III
Robert L. Pfannebecker
Richard P. Nuffort
Neil L. Albert
Barry Handwerger

References: First Union Bank, Fulton Bank, Farmers First Bank, all of Lancaster, Pennsylvania.

For full biographical listings, see the Martindale-Hubbell Law Directory

LANGHORNE, Bucks Co.

BEGLEY, CARLIN & MANDIO (AV)

680 Middletown Boulevard, P.O. Box 308, 19047
Telephone: 215-750-0110
Fax: 215-750-0954
Email: BCM@ITW.COM
Bristol, Pennsylvania Office: 120 Mill Street.
Telephone: 215-750-0110.

MEMBERS OF FIRM

William J. Carlin
S. Richard Klinges, III
Thomas J. Profy, III
Richard M. Snyder
Charles F. Sampsel
John P. Koopman
Jeffrey P. Garton
Thomas R. Hecker
James A. Downey, III
Joseph S. Britton
Douglas C. Maloney
Thomas J. Profy, IV

ASSOCIATES

Karen Saraco Burns
Timothy J. Duffy
Randall L. Miller
Jennifer L. McGrath

OF COUNSEL

Anthony A. Mandio
C. David Krewson

Representative Clients: Borough of Bristol; Bristol Borough School Board; Lower Makefield Township; Waste Management, Inc.

For full biographical listings, see the Martindale-Hubbell Law Directory

*LEBANON,** Lebanon Co.

HENRY & BEAVER LLP (AV)

937 Willow Street, P.O. Box 1140, 17042-1140
Telephone: 717-274-3644
Facsimile: 717-274-6782
Email: hblaw@redrose.net

MEMBERS OF FIRM

Charles V. Henry, III
R. Hart Beaver
Frederick S. Wolf
Thomas P. Harlan
Wiley P. Parker
John H. Whitmoyer
Christopher J. Coyle
Kevin M. Richards
Marc A. Hess

ASSOCIATE

Ann E. Endres

Representative Clients: Lebanon Valley Farmers Bank; Cornwall Manor; Medical Protective Company of Fort Wayne; Nationwide Insurance Co.; Liberty Mutual Insurance Co.; Utica Mutual Insurance Co.; CIGNA Insurance Co.; Princeton Insurance Company; The Pennsylvania Sports Hall of Fame; Princeton Insurance Co.

For full biographical listings, see the Martindale-Hubbell Law Directory

*MEDIA,** Delaware Co.

DIORIO & SERENI, LLP (AV)

Front and Plum Streets, P.O. Box 1789, 19063
Telephone: 610-565-5700
Fax: 610-891-0652
Email: info@dioriosereni.com

Robert M. DiOrio
Mark A. Sereni

(See Next Column)

DiOrio & Sereni LLP—*Continued*

ASSOCIATES

Kenneth J. D. Boyden
Christopher R. Mattox

For full biographical listings, see the Martindale-Hubbell Law Directory

*NORRISTOWN,** Montgomery Co.

Creedon & Feliciani, P.C. (AV)

29 East Marshall Street, 19401
Telephone: 610-239-9630
Fax: 610-239-1599
Email: creedon_feliciani@compuserve.com *URL:* http://www.lawyers.com/creedonfeliciani

Michael P. Creedon
Joseph L. Feliciani

For full biographical listings, see the Martindale-Hubbell Law Directory

Murphy, Oliver, Caiola & Gowen, A Professional Law Corporation (AV)

43 East Marshall Street, 19401-4828
Telephone: 610-272-4222; 610-279-3838
Fax: 610-272-2549; 610-275-0140
Email: molaw@injury-law.com *URL:* http://www.injury-law.com
Spring City, Pennsylvania Office: 500 S. Main Street, 19475.
Telephone: 610-948-3770.
Pottstown, Pennsylvania Office: 5 Sunnybrook Road, 19464.
Telephone: 610-323-3480.
West Chester, Pennsylvania Office: 1534 McDaniel Drive, Westtown Business Center, 19250.
Telephone: 610-272-4222.

James J. Oliver
Frank P. Murphy
Frank L. Caiola
Thomas L. Gowen, Jr.
Carla E. Connor
Barbara A. Barnes

John F. Haskins, Jr.
Cynthia Love Dengler
Carol A. Crisci

LEGAL SUPPORT PERSONNEL

Patricia A. Talese (Paralegal)
Kathleen Nicholson

For full biographical listings, see the Martindale-Hubbell Law Directory

OREFIELD, Lehigh Co.

Dimmich, Guldin, Dinkelacker & Brienza, P.C. (AV)

2970 Corporate Court, Suite 1, 18069
Telephone: 610-398-1800
Fax: 610-398-8304
Email: dgdb@erols.com *URL:* http://www.lawyers.com/dgd&b

Jeffrey R. Dimmich
John C. Guldin
Thomas H. Dinkelacker
Gary A. Brienza

For full biographical listings, see the Martindale-Hubbell Law Directory

*PHILADELPHIA,** Philadelphia Co.

Abramson & Freedman, L.L.C. (AV)

2128 Locust Street, 19103
Telephone: 215-545-2400
Telecopier: 215-545-8537
Haddonfield, New Jersey Office: 20 Kings Highway West.
Telephone: 609-795-5363.
Fax: 609-354-0020.

Gilbert B. Abramson
Jeffrey M. Freedman

Michael B. Tolcott
Stanley B. Cheiken (Resident, Haddonfield, New Jersey Office)
Glen L. Abramson

For full biographical listings, see the Martindale-Hubbell Law Directory

Anapol, Schwartz, Weiss, Cohan, Feldman and Smalley, P.C. (AV)

1900 Delancey Place, 19103
Telephone: 215-735-1130
Fax: 215-735-2024
URL: http://www.aswc.net
Other Philadelphia, Pennsylvania Office: 1710 Spruce Street.
Fax: 215-735-2211.
Cherry Hill, New Jersey Office: 402 Park Boulevard, 08002.
Telephone: 1-609-427-9229.
Fax: 609-488-1396.
Fairless Hills, Pennsylvania Office: 920 Trenton Road.
Telephone: 215-945-6799.
Reading, Pennsylvania Office: 146 North 6th Street.
Telephone: 610-375-7488.

(See Next Column)

Media, Pennsylvania Office: 334 W. Front Street, 19063.
Telephone: 610-892-3714.

Alan Schwartz
Sol H. Weiss
Lawrence R. Cohan
Joel D. Feldman
Howard J. Levin
Bernard W. Smalley
Stanton Dubin
Margaret A. Barry
Stephen J. Pokiniewski, Jr.
Sidney M. Grobman
Nelson Levin

Nathaniel E.P. Ehrlich
Thomas R. Anapol
Miriam Benton Barish
Patrice A. Gillotti
Michele Lee Reed
Heather J. Lipson
Michelle L. Altenpohl
Lisa R. Schwartz
Kevin R. Marciano
Brian J. Taylor
Tobias L. Millrood
Tracy A. Finken

OF COUNSEL

Paul R. Anapol
Richard B. Schwartz (Resident, Other Philadelphia Office)
Mark F. Seltzer

Reference: Meridian Bank, Philadelphia, Pennsylvania.

For full biographical listings, see the Martindale-Hubbell Law Directory

Atkins & Cohen (AV)

1430 Land Title Building, 100 South Broad Street, 19110
Telephone: 215-448-3900
Fax: 215-448-3905
Email: a-c@ix.netcom.com *URL:* http://www.lawyers.com/atkins&cohen

MEMBERS OF FIRM

Roland J. Atkins
Robert C. Cohen

ASSOCIATES

D. Pamela Gaines
Michael R. Logue

LEGAL SUPPORT PERSONNEL

Steven D. Anderson (Paralegal)

For full biographical listings, see the Martindale-Hubbell Law Directory

Ballard Spahr Andrews & Ingersoll, LLP (AV)

1735 Market Street, 51st Floor, 19103-7599
Telephone: 215-665-8500
Fax: 215-864-8999
URL: http://www.ballardspahr.com
Baltimore, Maryland Office: 300 East Lombard Street. 19th Floor.
Telephone: 410-528-5600.
Fax: 410-528-5650.
Camden, New Jersey Office: 800 Hudson Square, 5th Floor.
Telephone: 856-541-5577.
Fax: 856-541-8272.
Denver, Colorado Office: Seventeenth Street Plaza Building, Suite 2300, 1225 17th Street.
Telephone: 303-292-2400.
Fax: 303-296-3956.
Salt Lake City, Utah Office: One Utah Center, Suite 1200, 201 South Main Street.
Telephone: 801-531-3000.
Fax: 801-531-3001.
Voorhees, New Jersey Office: Suite 100, 1101 Laurel Oak Drive.
Telephone: 856-627-8555.
Fax: 856-627-1153.
Washington, D.C. Office: Suite 1000 South, 601 13th Street, N.W.
Telephone: 202-661-2200.
Fax: 202-661-2299.

Robert McLaurin Boote
James D. Coleman
Walter M. Einhorn, Jr.
Geoffrey A. Kahn
David H. Pittinsky
Mark S. Stewart
Martin C. Bryce, Jr.
Alan J. Davis
Leslie E. John
Arthur Makadon
Carl G. Roberts
Matthew M. Strickler

For Complete List of Firm Personnel, See General Section

For full biographical listings, see the Martindale-Hubbell Law Directory

Marvin I. Barish Law Offices A Professional Corporation (AV)

6th and Walnut Streets, Suite 801E, 19106-3308
Telephone: 215-923-8900; 800-233-7101
Email: mbarish@aol.com *URL:* http://www.lawyers.com/barishlawoffices
Cherry Hill, New Jersey Office: 1930 East Marlton Pike, Suite Q-38.
Telephone: 609-338-0550.

Marvin I. Barish

Gregory L. Nester

For full biographical listings, see the Martindale-Hubbell Law Directory

Philadelphia—Continued

BILLET & CONNOR (AV)

2000 Market Street Suite 2803, 19103-3201
Telephone: 215-496-7500
Fax: 215-496-7505
Email: BilletandConnor@compuserve.com
Turnersville, New Jersey Office: 4101 South Route 42, P.O. Box 1112, 08012-1112.
Telephone: 609-232-7776.
Fax: 609-232-6720.

MEMBERS OF FIRM

William M. Connor
Robert D. Billet

ASSOCIATES

Michael J. Smith
David K. Brennan
James D. Hicks

OF COUNSEL

Ernest Allen Cohen (Not admitted in PA)

For full biographical listings, see the Martindale-Hubbell Law Directory

BRUCE G. CASSIDY & ASSOCIATES, P.A. (AV)

Suite 1040, 21 South 12th Street, 19107
Telephone: 215-568-6700
Fax: 215-568-4077
Email: bgclaw@aol.com
Princeton, New Jersey Office: 345 Witherspoon Street, 08542.
Telephone: 609-252-9800.
Fax: 609-252-9111.

Bruce G. Cassidy

David E. Breslau

OF COUNSEL

Dr. Peter H. Feuerstein (Not admitted United States)
Halina Pilarska (Not Admitted in United States)

For full biographical listings, see the Martindale-Hubbell Law Directory

LAW OFFICES OF JAMES E. COLLERAN (AV)

1525 Locust Street 18th Floor, 19102
Telephone: 215-790-5500
FAX: 215-790-5509
Email: colleran@colleran.com

James E. Colleran, Jr.
Francis T. Colleran
Teresa Colleran Quinn
Mary T. Colleran
James I. Devine
David C. Devine

For full biographical listings, see the Martindale-Hubbell Law Directory

CONRAD O'BRIEN GELLMAN & ROHN, P.C. (AV)

Sixteenth Floor, 1515 Market Street, 19102-1916
Telephone: 215-864-9600
Fax: 215-864-9620; 864-9621; 864-9622
Email: lawyers@cogr.com *URL:* http://www.COGR.COM
Cherry Hill, New Jersey Office: Woodland Falls Corporate Park, 200 Lake Drive East, Suite 206.
Telephone: 856-665-0888.
Fax: 856-665-5888.
West Chester, Pennsylvania Office: 17 West Gay Street, Suite 100.
Telephone: 610-701-9100.
Fax: 610-701-9195.

K. Robert Conrad
William J. O'Brien
Nancy J. Gellman
James J. Rohn
John (Jack) A. Guernsey
John H. McKeon, Jr.
Howard M. Klein
Robert N. Feltoon
Deborah J. Krabbendam
Patricia M. Hamill
Nicholas M. Centrella

OF COUNSEL

Alan Paul Novak
Robert A. Klein
Stephen Weaver
Clare Keefe Foster

Lisa B. Wershaw
Helen J. Esbenshade
Debra C. Swartz
Thomas W. Blair
Gabriel H. Holdsman
Jonathan K.M. Crawford (Not admitted in PA)
Andrew C. Hanan
Frank R. Emmerich Jr.
Jacquelyn J. Ager
Andrew R. Duffy
Kelly G. Huller
Steven Pachman
Susan L. Bucknum

For full biographical listings, see the Martindale-Hubbell Law Directory

COZEN AND O'CONNOR, A PROFESSIONAL CORPORATION (AV)

1900 Market Street, 19103
Telephone: 215-665-2000
800-523-2900
Fax: 215-665-2013
Email: postmaster@cozen.com *URL:* http://www.cozen.com
Charlotte, North Carolina Office: One First Union Center, Suite 2100, 301 S. College Street, 28202.
Telephones: 704-376-3400; 800-762-3575.
Fax: 704-334-3351.
Dallas, Texas Office: 2300 BankOne Center, 1717 Main Street, 75201.
Telephones: 214-462-3000; 800-448-1207.
Fax: 214-462-3299.
New York, N.Y. Office: 45 Broadway Atrium, 16th Floor, 10006.
Telephones: 212-509-9400; 800-437-7040.
Fax: 212-509-9492.
West Conshohocken, Pennsylvania Office: 200 Four Falls Corporate Center, Suite 400, P.O. Box 800, 19428.
Telephone: 610-941-5400.
Fax: 610-941-0711.
San Diego, California Office: Suite 1610, 501 West Broadway, 92101.
Telephones: 619-234-1700; 800-782-3366.
Fax: 619-234-7831.
Los Angeles, California Office: 777 Tower, 777 South Figueroa Street, Suite 2850, 90017.
Telephones: 213-892-7900; 800-563-1027.
Fax: 213-892-7999.
Seattle, Washington Office: Suite 5200, Washington Mutual Tower, 1201 Third Avenue, 98101.
Telephones: 206-340-1000; 800-423-1950.
Fax: 206-621-8783.
Westmont, New Jersey Office: 316 Haddon Avenue, 08108.
Telephones: 609-854-4900; 800-523-2900.
Fax: 609-854-1782.
Newark, New Jersey Office: One Newark Center, Suite 1900, 1085 Raymond Boulevard, 07102.
Telephone: 973-286-1200; 888-200-9521.
Fax: 973-242-2121.
Atlanta, Georgia Office: Suite 2200, SunTrust Plaza, 303 Peachtree Street, N.E., 30308.
Telephones: 404-572-2000; 800-890-1393.
Fax: 404-572-2199.
London, England Office: Cozen and O'Connor at Radcliffes, 5 Great College Street, Westminster, SW1P 3SJ.
Telephone: 011-44-207-654-7600.
Fax: 011-44-207-654-7613.
Wilmington, Delaware Office: Chase Manhattan Centre, 1201 North Market Street, Suite 1400, 19801.
Telephone: 302-295-2000; 888-207-2440.
Fax: 302-295-2013.
Mt. Laurel, New Jersey Office: 10,000 Midlantic Drive, Suite 301, 08054.

Sydney C. Orlofsky (1936-1968)
Charles A. Fisher, III (1947-1990)

FIRM MEMBERS IN PHILADELPHIA

Stephen A. Cozen
Kevin M. Apollo
A. Richard Bailey
Paul R. Bartolacci
Joseph J. Bellew
Gerard F. Belz, Jr.
Richard C. Bennett
Denise Brinker Bense
James E. Brown
John F. Brown, Jr.
Martin P. Duffey
John Dwyer
Christopher C. Fallon, Jr.
Elliott R. Feldman
Ann Thornton Field
Jim H. Fields, Jr.
William G. Flint
Douglas B. Fox
Eric D. Freed
Thomas F. Gallagher
Joseph A. Gerber
Richard C. Glazer
Lewis A. Grafman
Josh M. Greenbaum
David J. Groth
Dexter R. Hamilton
Ronald B. Hamilton
Daniel Q. Harrington
Robert H. Hawn, Jr.
Robert W. Hayes
Patrick J. O'Connor
James H. Heller
Michael F. Henry
Denise H. Houghton
William H. Howard
Kevin J. Hughes
Michael J. Izzo, Jr.
Miles A. Jellinek
Kathie D. King
Brian L. Lincicome
Richard M. Mackowsky
Michael R. McCarty
Vincent R. McGuinness, Jr.
Deborah Melamut Minkoff
Mark T. Mullen
Jeffrey L. Nash
Mark E. Opalisky
Robert R. Reeder
Thomas M. Regan
Joseph H. Riches
Elaine M. Rinaldi
Peter G. Rossi
John T. Salvucci
Steven L. Smith
William F. Stewart
Jeffrey R. Stoner
John T. Thorn
Joshua Wall
Anita B. Weinstein
Thomas C. Zielinski

Representative Clients: Available upon request.

For Complete List of Firm Personnel, See General Section

For full biographical listings, see the Martindale-Hubbell Law Directory

Philadelphia—Continued

DEASEY, MAHONEY & BENDER, LTD. (AV)

1800 John F. Kennedy Boulevard, Suite 1300, 19103-2978
Telephone: 215-587-9400
Facsimile: 215-587-9456
Email: dmbphila@aol.com
Haddonfield, New Jersey Office: 80 Tanner Street, 08033-2419.
Telephone: 609-429-6331.
Facsimile: 609-429-6562.

William R. Deasey (1917-1993)
James G. Barnes (1961-1997)
Francis J. Deasey
Harry G. Mahoney
James W. Daly, IV

K. Craig McChesney
Gerald J. Valentini
James B. Burns
Jane A. North
Thomas C. Sullivan
John P. Kamstra
Pamela J. Devine
Jane G. O'Donnell
Barbara Corr Morrow
Henri Marcel

OF COUNSEL

Frank C. Bender

For full biographical listings, see the Martindale-Hubbell Law Directory

DESSEN, MOSES & SHEINOFF (AV)

1814 Chestnut Street, 19103-4986
Telephone: 215-564-5600
Fax: 215-564-2879
Email: lawdept@dms-lawyer.com *URL:* http://www.dms-lawyer.com
Jenkintown, Pennsylvania Office: Suite 201, 501 Building, Old York Road and Washington Lane.
Telephone: 215-576-7900.
Fax: 215-576-6219.
Media, Pennsylvania Office: 2nd Floor, 221 North Olive Street.
Telephone: 610-565-8488.
Fax: 610-892-9467.
Chestnut Hill, Pennsylvania Office: 8623 Germantown Avenue, Philadelphia, Pennsylvania.
Telephone: 215-242-3830.
Fax: 215-242-6750.
Cherry Hill, New Jersey Office: Cherry Hill Plaza, 1415 Route 70 East, Suite 102.
Telephone: 856-795-1115.
Fax: 856-795-2066.

MEMBERS OF FIRM

David S. Dessen
Bonnie Smith Moses
Mitchel H. Sheinoff

For full biographical listings, see the Martindale-Hubbell Law Directory

JOHN GERARD DEVLIN & ASSOCIATES, P.C. (AV)

1515 Market Street Suite 2010, 19102
Telephone: 215-564-6740
Telefax: 215-564-6732
Email: devlinlaw@aol.com
Allentown, Pennsylvania Office: The Sovereign Building, Executive Suite 103, 609 Hamilton Mall.
Telephone: 215-820-6422.
Westmont, New Jersey Office: 216 Haddon Avenue, Suite 103.
Telephone: 609-858-1690.
Fax: 609-858-8998.
East Brunswick, New Jersey Office: 190 Route 18, Suite 3000.
Telephone: 908-214-2621.
Fax: 908-246-2917.
Wilkes-Barre, Pennsylvania Office: Cross Creek Pointe, 1065 Hwy 315, Suite H.
Telephone: 610-820-6422.

John Gerard Devlin
James B. Corrigan, Jr.
Joseph T. Murphy, Jr.
Thomas Paschos
Michael Malarick
Suzanne Curran Murphy
Arthur F. Wheeler
Paul A. Lawless, Jr.

Representative Clients: Lloyds of London; Commercial Union; John Hancock Property and Casualty Insurance Co.; Wausau Insurance Co.; Hanseco Insurance Co.; American Family Insurance Co.; Liberty Mutual Insurance Co.; Linberg Adjustment Co.

For full biographical listings, see the Martindale-Hubbell Law Directory

FARAGE, McBRIDE & RUGGIERI (AV)

836 Suburban Station Building, 1617 John F. Kennedy Boulevard, 19103
Telephone: 215-563-3973
Fax: 215-563-3094
URL: http://www.lawyers.com/fmrlaw
Woodbury, New Jersey Office: 9 South Broad Street, 08096.
Telephone: 609-845-9448.
Fax: 606-845-4888.

(See Next Column)

MEMBERS OF FIRM

Donald J. Farage (1909-1998)
James F. McBride
Thomas J. Ruggieri

For full biographical listings, see the Martindale-Hubbell Law Directory

J. MICHAEL FARRELL (AV)

Suite 402 S, 718 Arch Street, 19106
Telephone: 215-925-1105
Fax: 215-925-4099
Woodbury, New Jersey Office: 231 S. Broad Street.
Telephone: 609-848-5801.
Fax: 609-848-0322.

LEGAL SUPPORT PERSONNEL

Marcie Knight

For full biographical listings, see the Martindale-Hubbell Law Directory

F. EMMETT FITZPATRICK, P.C. (AV)

926 Public Ledger Building, 19106
Telephone: 215-925-5200
Fax: 215-925-5991
Email: info@toplaw.com *URL:* http://www.toplaw.com

F. Emmett Fitzpatrick
F. Emmett Fitzpatrick, III

NiaLena Caravasos

LEGAL SUPPORT PERSONNEL

Doreen Howley (Paralegal)

For full biographical listings, see the Martindale-Hubbell Law Directory

FURIA AND TURNER (AV)

1717 Rittenhouse Square, 19103-6109
Telephone: 215-985-4500
Telecopier: 215-985-2824
Email: rfuria1717@aol.com *URL:* http://www.lawyers.com/furiaandturner

MEMBERS OF FIRM

Richard F. Furia
James M. Turner, Jr.

ASSOCIATES

Gina R. Furia
Donna DiPietro-Gerace

For full biographical listings, see the Martindale-Hubbell Law Directory

LAW OFFICES OF JOHN J. GALLAGHER, P.C. (AV)

Suite 1100, 1760 Market Street, 19103
Telephone: 215-963-1555
Fax: 215-963-9104
Email: jjgall@ix.netcom.com *URL:* http://www.lawyers.com/johngallagher

John J. Gallagher

Michael S. Henry
Laura Carberry Muldowney
Joseph H. Meltzer
Larisa Tenberg

LEGAL SUPPORT PERSONNEL

Ronald Winkelvoss
Helene Schramm

For full biographical listings, see the Martindale-Hubbell Law Directory

GOLDFEIN & JOSEPH, A PROFESSIONAL CORPORATION (AV)

1600 Market Street 33rd Floor, 19103-7288
Telephone: 215-979-8200
Fax: 215-979-8201
URL: http://www.goldfeinlaw.com
Princeton, New Jersey Office: Princeton Metro Center, Suite 115, 5 Vaughn Drive.
Telephone: 609-520-0400.
Fax: 609-520-1450.
Wilmington, Delaware Office: PNC Bank Center, Suite 1110, P.O. Box 2206, 222 Delaware Avenue.
Telephone: 302-656-3301.
Fax: 302-656-0643.
New York, New York Office: 150 Broadway, Suite 1212, 10038.
Telephone: 212-791-0340.
Fax: 212-791-0347.

Edward B. Joseph
Fredric L. Goldfein
E. Chandler Hosmer, III
David C. Weinberg
Bernard L. Levinthal
Roseann Lynn Brenner
Gary H. Kaplan
John A. Turlik

Michael A. Billotti
Medford J. Brown, III
Robert P. Coleman
Robert T. Connor
Charles D. Cooper
Kelly A. Costello
Lawrence E. Currier
Janet E. Golup
Christine Renee Guiliano
David M. Katzenstein
Matthew A Kelly, III
Deborah M. Knight

(See Next Column)

GOLDFEIN & JOSEPH A PROFESSIONAL CORPORATION, *Philadelphia—Continued*

Pamela A. Post
Thomas M. Savon
Julie M. Sebring
(Not admitted in PA)
Robert M. Stroh
Marc R. Wilner
Anthony F. Zabicki, Jr.

For full biographical listings, see the Martindale-Hubbell Law Directory

HOHN & SCHEÜERLE (AV)

Eleven Penn Center, Suite 2901, 1835 Market Street, 19103
Telephone: 215-496-9995
Fax: 215-496-9997
URL: http://www.lawyers.com/hohnscheuerle

MEMBERS OF FIRM

Richard K. Hohn
Stephen A. Scheüerle

ASSOCIATES

Maryellen T. Conroy
Stanley S. Frazee, Jr.

For full biographical listings, see the Martindale-Hubbell Law Directory

HOWARD, BRENNER & NASS, P.C. (AV)

(Predecessor firm, George W. Howard, III, P.C.)
Suite 1700, 1608 Walnut Street, 19103
Telephone: 215-546-8200
Fax: 215-545-1591
Westmont, New Jersey Office: 212 Haddon Avenue, 08108.
Telephone: 609-427-9100.
Fax: 609-869-9881.

George W. Howard, III
David E. Brenner
Edward M. Nass
Richard P. Hackman

Robert J. O'Shea, Jr.
Thomas D. Summerville
Michael A. Cancelliere, Jr.
William Charles Bensley

Representative Clients: East Coast Credit; The Republic Bank; The Chestnut Hill Hospital; Heritage Bank; Jakes Bar and Grill; Critiques, Inc.; Mann and Fountain, Inc.; William Austin's Ltd.; Narbeth Presbyterian Church.

For full biographical listings, see the Martindale-Hubbell Law Directory

HOYLE, MORRIS & KERR LLP (AV)

Suite 4900, One Liberty Place, 1650 Market Street, 19103
Telephone: 215-981-5700
Telecopier: 215-981-5959
Email: hoyle@hoylemk.com *URL:* http://www.hoylemk.com

MEMBERS OF FIRM

Lawrence T. Hoyle, Jr.
Alexander Kerr
Bernard J. Smolens (1916-1997)
Susan K. Herschel
Arlene Fickler
F. John Hagele
John Francis Gough
Stephen J. Mathes
Walter M. Phillips, Jr.
Henry H. Janssen
Charles B. Blakinger
Ralph A. Jacobs
Gerald Chalphin
R. Nicholas Gimbel
Bebe H. Kivitz
William R. Herman
Denise D. Colliers
Elizabeth W. Fox
Lisa M. Salazar
R. David Walk, Jr.

OF COUNSEL

Samuel W. Morris, Jr.
Arthur R. Littleton
Nathalie Martin

SENIOR ATTORNEYS

Michael T. Starczewski
Jan Fink Call
Joann M. Lytle

ASSOCIATES

Ellen M. Briggs
Nancy Stuart Portney
George Stephen Bobnak
Kevin J. Kotch
Elliot C. Fertik
Debora C. Fliegelman
Chonda Jordan Nwamu
Michael E. Plunkett
C. Scott Spear
Jeffrey D. Cohen
Todd A. Schoenhaus
Stephen P. McFate
Wendi L. Shohen

For full biographical listings, see the Martindale-Hubbell Law Directory

HWANG & ASSOCIATES, P.C. (AV)

1700 Sansom Street, 12th Floor, 19103
Telephone: 215-972-5100
Fax: 215-972-5110
Email: shwang@HwangLawFirm.com *URL:* http://www.hwanglawfirm.com

Sam Y. Hwang

For full biographical listings, see the Martindale-Hubbell Law Directory

KANE & SILVERMAN, PROFESSIONAL CORPORATION (AV)

The Philadelphian Suite 1C-44, 2401 Pennsylvania Avenue, 19130
Telephone: 215-232-1000
Fax: 215-232-0181
Email: HGS@palegaladvice.com *URL:* http://www.palegaladvice.com

Michael C. Kane
Howard G. Silverman

For full biographical listings, see the Martindale-Hubbell Law Directory

KAUFMAN, COREN, RESS & WEIDMAN, P.C. (AV)

1525 Locust Street, 17th Floor, 19102
Telephone: 215-735-8700
FAX: 215-735-5170

Howard J. Kaufman
Steven M. Coren
Douglas Evan Ress
Peter J. Weidman

OF COUNSEL

Susanna E. Lachs
David Dormont

Peter J. Leyh
Esther L. Hornik
Bruce Bellingham

For full biographical listings, see the Martindale-Hubbell Law Directory

KELLEY, JASONS, MCGUIRE & SPINELLI, L.L.P. (AV)

One Penn Center, Suite 1400, 1617 JFK Boulevard, 19103
Telephone: 215-854-0658
Fax: 215-854-8434; 215-854-0777
Marlton, New Jersey Office: One Greentree Centre, Suite 201, 08053.
Telephone: 609-988-5543.
Fax: 609-988-9165.
Wilmington, Delaware Office: 800 Delaware Avenue, P.O. Box 194, 19899.
Telephone: 302-652-8560.
Fax: 302-652-8405.

MEMBERS OF FIRM

John Patrick Kelley
Catherine N. Jasons
Joseph W. McGuire
Armand J. Della Porta, Jr.
Christopher N. Santoro
Robert N. Spinelli
Thomas P. Hanna
Thomas J. Johanson
Michael L. Turner
Richard L. Walker, II
Timothy McGowan

ASSOCIATES

Neal C. Glenn
W. Matthew Reber
Ann C. Lebowitz
Anthony J. Ryan

OF COUNSEL

Matthew D. Blum

For full biographical listings, see the Martindale-Hubbell Law Directory

KENT & MCBRIDE, P.C. (AV)

Two Logan Square, Suite 600 18th and Arch Streets, 19103
Telephone: 215-568-1800
Fax: 215-568-1830
Cherry Hill, New Jersey Office: 1040 Kings Highway North, Suite 403, 08034.
Telephone: 609-667-3113.
Fax: 609-667-4003.
Wilmington, Delaware Office: Buckner Building, 1308 Delaware Avenue, P.O. Box 2165.
Telephone: 302-777-5477.
Fax: 302-429-8600.

John F. Kent
Denis P. McBride

Kevin G. Dronson
Jack T. Ribble, Jr.
Anne Manero
Jay D. Branderbit
Joseph Andrew Sellitti
John P. Shea
Stephen V. McHugh
Anthony V. Mannino, III
Francis Moritz
Melissa A. Wojtylak
Glenn D. Wattenmaker
Gregory J. Palakow
(Not admitted in PA)
Andrew K. Mitnick
Leonard G. Villari
James L. Moore, Jr.
Thomas T. Booth, Jr.
Evan B. Caplan
Ernest F. Koschineg, III
George T. Lees, III

For full biographical listings, see the Martindale-Hubbell Law Directory

KESSLER, COHEN & ROTH, A PROFESSIONAL CORPORATION (AV)

Two Penn Center Plaza, Suite 1705, 19102
Telephone: 215-567-3500
Fax: 215-567-6019
Email: lawyers@kesslercohen.com

(See Next Column)

KESSLER, COHEN & ROTH A PROFESSIONAL CORPORATION—*Continued*

Arnold M. Kessler
Stewart L. Cohen
Harry M. Roth
Karen R. Bramblett
Stephen R. Kurens
David L. Gordon
William D. Marvin

For full biographical listings, see the Martindale-Hubbell Law Directory

KLINE & SPECTER, P.C. (AV)

The Nineteenth Floor, 1525 Locust Street, 19102
Telephone: 215-772-1000
Fax: 215-772-1359

Thomas R. Kline
Shanin Specter

Joel J. Feller
Derek R. Layser
Robert Ross
Aaron J. Freiwald
Jonathan M. Cohen
Diane L. Hockstein

For full biographical listings, see the Martindale-Hubbell Law Directory

GILDA L. KRAMER (AV)

Suite 1100, 1500 Walnut Street, 19102
Telephone: 215-732-4055
Telecopier: 215-735-9004

For full biographical listings, see the Martindale-Hubbell Law Directory

MARK JAY KRUM (AV)

1515 Market Street, Suite 1100, 19102
Telephone: 215-569-2650
Facsimile: 215-564-3066
Email: markjaykrum@attymail.com

For full biographical listings, see the Martindale-Hubbell Law Directory

LAVIN, COLEMAN, O'NEIL, RICCI, FINARELLI & GRAY (AV)

Suite 1000, 510 Walnut Street, 19106
Telephone: 215-627-0303
Fax: 215-627-2551
Mount Laurel, New Jersey Office: 8000 Midlantic Drive, Suite 201 South.
Telephone: 609-778-5544.
Fax: 609-778-3383.
New York, New York Office: 7th Floor, 767 Third Avenue.
Telephone: 212-319-6898.
Fax: 212-319-6932.

George J. Lavin, Jr.
Thomas Finarelli
William V. Coleman
Francis F. Quinn
Joseph E. O'Neil
Francis P. Burns, III
William J. Ricci
Edward A. Gray
Basil A. DiSipio
Wayne A. Graver
Gerard Cedrone
Mary Grace Maley
Christine O. Boyd
Michael D. Brophy
Joseph A. McGinley
Robert J. Hafner
Robert J. Martin
Susan Ellyn Satkowski
Henry Michael Clinton
Francis J. Grey, Jr.
Richard B. Wickersham, Jr.
John J. Bateman
Ronald W. Boak
Michael T. Droogan, Jr.
Eugene Hamill
Michael P. Kinkopf
Stephen E. Moore
Michael J. Quinn
William E. Staas, III
Denise Carroll Chaplin
Marsha E. Flora
Peter M. Newman
John J. O'Donnell
Jo E. Peifer

Valerie Aabdollah
Lee R. Allman
Jennifer M. Brooks
Jessica Faden (Resident, Mount Laurel, New Jersey Office)
Frank C. B. Friestedt
Julie M. Holland
Leland I. Kellner
George J. Lavin, III
Margot L. Ludlam (Resident, New York, New York Office)
Daniel P. Lynch
Leona C. McFadden
Lorraine B. McGlynn
Henry James Noye
Michael J. O'Neill
Monica Tamar Proffitt
Sheila Marie Raftery
Michelle S. Regan (Resident, New York, New York Office)
Robert L. Sanzo
William E. Schaefer
Richard J. Sexton
Gregory Steven Spizer
Susan L. Troxell
Fiona J. Van Dyck
Anne E. Walters
Dennis P. Ziemba

For full biographical listings, see the Martindale-Hubbell Law Directory

LEVIN, FISHBEIN, SEDRAN & BERMAN (AV)

Suite 500, 510 Walnut Street, 19106-3697
Telephone: 215-592-1500
Fax: 215-592-4663
Email: lfsb@psinet.com

MEMBERS OF FIRM

Arnold Levin
Michael D. Fishbein
Howard J. Sedran
Laurence S. Berman
Frederick S. Longer

(See Next Column)

Craig D. Ginsburg
Cheryl R. Brown Hill
Donald E. Haviland, Jr.
Daniel C. Levin
Terrianne Benedetto
Charles E. Schaffer
Austin B. Cohen

LEGAL SUPPORT PERSONNEL

Lee Ann Fitzpatrick
Cheryl Hesson

For full biographical listings, see the Martindale-Hubbell Law Directory

LEVY, ANGSTREICH, FINNEY, BALDANTE, RUBENSTEIN & COREN, P.C. (AV)

18th Floor, 1616 Walnut Street, 19103
Telephone: 215-735-1616
FAX: 215-545-2642
Email: lafbrc@levyangstreich.com *URL:* http://www.levyangstreich.com
Cherry Hill, New Jersey Office: Woodcrest Pavilion, Suite 100, Ten Melrose Avenue, 08003.
Telephone: 856-424-8967.
Fax: 856-795-7447.

Mark S. Levy
Steven E. Angstreich
Lawrence D. Finney
John W. Baldante
Martin G. Rubenstein
Michael Coren
Carolyn C. Lindheim
Thomas S. Harty

Amy R. Brandt
Melissa T. Herskowitz
Silvia M. Ferri
Beth E. Castelli
Theresa Sweeney Corson
Catherine E. Margolis

LEGAL SUPPORT PERSONNEL

Legal Administrator Michele R. Galasso

For full biographical listings, see the Martindale-Hubbell Law Directory

LIGHTMAN, MANOCHI & KORNILOWICZ (AV)

1520 Locust Street, 12th Floor, 19102-4401
Telephone: 215-545-3000
Telecopy: 215-545-3001
Haddonfield, New Jersey Office: 20 Kings Highway West.
Telephone: 609-795-9669.
Fax: 609-795-9339.

MEMBERS OF FIRM

Gary P. Lightman
Glenn A. Manochi
Marian A. Kornilowicz

ASSOCIATE

Kristine Christensen

For full biographical listings, see the Martindale-Hubbell Law Directory

LOVITZ AND GOLD, P.C. (AV)

Eleven Penn Center, 1835 Market Street Suite 515, 19103
Telephone: 215-569-1999
Fax: 215-569-3870

Hyman Lovitz
Sidney L. Gold
Kevin I. Lovitz

Jennifer L. Myers

OF COUNSEL

Baden Kramer Huffman & Brodsky, P.C., New York, New York

LEGAL SUPPORT PERSONNEL

Christine Johnson (Litigation Paralegal)

For full biographical listings, see the Martindale-Hubbell Law Directory

MARKS, O'NEILL, REILLY, O'BRIEN & COURTNEY, P.C. (AV)

1880 John F. Kennedy Boulevard Suite 1200, 19103
Telephone: 215-564-6688
Fax: 215-564-2526
Email: moro1@morocpa.com
Norristown, Pennsylvania Office: 411 Cherry Street.
Telephone: 215-277-7601.
Pittsburgh, Pennsylvania Office: 707 Grant Street, Gulf Tower, Suite 3200.
Telephone: 412-391-6171.
Fax: 412-391-8804.
Westmont, New Jersey Office: 216 Haddon Avenue, Suite 500.
Telephone: 856-858-6110.
Fax: 856-858-3687. E-Mail: moro1@morocnj.com
Wilmington, Delaware Office: 2004 Foulk Road, Suite 7.
Telephone: 302-475-5500.
Fax: 302-475-5584.

Jerome E. Marks
Joseph M. O'Neill
Vincent F. Reilly
Kevin J. O'Brien
Dawn R. Courtney
Sean Xavier Kelly
Gino P. Mecoli
John J. Repcheck (Resident, Pittsburgh Office)

(See Next Column)

MARKS, O'NEILL, REILLY, O'BRIEN & COURTNEY P.C., *Philadelphia—Continued*

David P. Helwig (Resident, Pittsburgh Office)
Maureen Murray-O'Toole
Patrick C. Lamb
Christine G. Boyle
Nancy E. Mancheski
Michael T. Hamilton
Kelly L. Bracken
Tracey Marie McDevitt
Sharon A. Connors (Resident, Westmont, New Jersey Office)
Malissa A. Richetti
Patricia M. Henrich
Judith H. Ring
Gary Weinberg (Resident, Westmont, New Jersey Office)
Lee J. Janiczek
Wendy D. Testa (Resident, Westmont, New Jersey Office)
Gary F. Sharlock (Resident, Pittsburgh Office)
Robert Dale Leidigh (Resident, Pittsburgh Office)
Joseph L. Orszulak, II (Resident, Pittsburgh Office)
Diane Beckman Carvell
Karen J. Stanzione
Michael A. Kosar
Susan D. Grant (Resident, Westmont, New Jersey Office)
Frances Wang-Deveney (Resident, Westmont, New Jersey)
Courtney E. Passin
Stephanie Victoria Shreibman
Megan Kochell D'Iorio (Resident, Wilmington, Delaware Office)
Megan Trocki Mantzavinos (Resident, Wilmington, Delaware Office)
Toni Anderson Moore
Natalie M. Nugent
Frank Gattuso
Michael A. Ring (Resident, Westmont, New Jersey Office)
Ann M. Madden (Not admitted in PA)
Matthew J. Zamites
Salvatore A. Clemente

LEGAL SUPPORT PERSONNEL
PARALEGALS

Gregory P. Sabo
Elisa LaRosa
Frances P. Rossi
Heather Feenan
Jerry Ezekiel
Steven Randisi
Sharon Williams
Melanie Gaskins

For full biographical listings, see the Martindale-Hubbell Law Directory

MATTIONI, LTD. (AV)

399 Market Street, 2nd Floor, 19106
Telephone: 215-629-1600
Cable Address: "Mattioni"
Fax: 215-923-2227
Email: firmmail@mattioni.com *URL:* http://www.mattioni.com
Westmont, New Jersey Office: Mattioni, LLP, Suite 100, Sentry Office Plaza, 216 Haddon Avenue, 08108.
Telephone: 856-854-6200.
Fax: 856-854-3338.
Montgomery County Office: Suite 200, 1101 Fayette Street, Conshohocken, Pennsylvania, 19428.
Telephone: 610-941-9530.
Fax: 610-940-4489.

Dante Mattioni
Faustino Mattioni
John Mattioni
Blasco Mattioni *
Eugene Mattioni
Francis X. Kelly
George R. Zacharkow
Andrew H. Quinn
Eva Helena Bleich
Robert W. Weidner, Jr.
Scott J. Schwarz
Anthony Granato
Stephen M. Martin
Stephen J. Galati
Joseph F. Bouvier
Michael Mattioni
Bruce A. O'Neill
Alan Mattioni
Itzchak E. Kornfeld
Sarah Wilson Weingast (Not admitted in PA)
Mary Alice Cleve
Paul A. Kettunen
Donald S. Sabatini
Mark David Hasenauer
Bridget C. Sciamanna
Mette Deleuran
Dante C. Rohr

Frank Carano *
Ronald R. Donatucci *
John A. DiPietro **
Kristi L. Treadway **

*Counsel to the Firm
**Of Counsel

For full biographical listings, see the Martindale-Hubbell Law Directory

MCCORMICK & PRIORE, P.C. (AV)

One Penn Square West, 30 S. 15th Street, Suite 1500, 19102
Telephone: 215-972-0161
Fax: 215-972-5580
Email: mccormick5@aol.com
Marlton, New Jersey Office: One Greentree Centre, Suite 201, 08053.
Telephone: 609-988-5452.
Fax: 609-596-8359.

David M. McCormick
Philip D. Priore
Stephen M. McManus

OF COUNSEL

Harry A. Short, Jr.

(See Next Column)

Wendy L. Schmidt-Levin
H. Joseph Byron
Michelle Nick Rossi
Christina A. Toriello
Jill Schneider
John P. Lock

LEGAL SUPPORT PERSONNEL

Deborah Stefan
Jane Coley

For full biographical listings, see the Martindale-Hubbell Law Directory

MCELDREW & FULLAM, P.C. (AV)

Suite 5050 One Liberty Place, 19103
Telephone: 215-563-8300
800-223-3352
Fax: 215-563-6130
URL: http://www.lawyers.com/mceldrew&fullampc
New York, New York Office: McEldrew & Ressler, Suite 2101, 11 Pennsylvania Plaza, 10001.
Telephone: 212-695-6446.
Fax: 212-268-0287.

James J. McEldrew, III
Nancy H. Fullam

Marcella J. Schell
Carol L. Vassallo
Sallie Updyke Mundy
David Felderman

LEGAL SUPPORT PERSONNEL

Christine Doelp (Comptroller)

For full biographical listings, see the Martindale-Hubbell Law Directory

MCKISSOCK & HOFFMAN, P.C. (AV)

1700 Market Street, Suite 3000, 19103
Telephone: 215-246-2100
Fax: 215-246-2144
Westmont, New Jersey Office: 216 Haddon Avenue, Suite 603.
Telephone: 609-858-1650.
Fax: 609-858-1466.
Doylestown, Pennsylvania Office: 16 North Franklin Street, Suite 300.
Telephone: 215-345-4501.
Fax: 215-246-4503.
Harrisburg, Pennsylvania Office: 105 North Front Street, Suite 205.
Telephone: 717-234-0103.
Fax: 717-234-1350.
West Chester, Pennsylvania Office: 31 South High Street, P.O. Box 3086.
Telephone: 610-738-8850.
Fax: 610-738-9121.

J. Bruce McKissock
Peter J. Hoffman
Leslie Anne Miller
Jeffrey B. Albert
Jill Baratz Clarke
John J. McGrath (Resident, Westmont, New Jersey Office)
Donald J. Brooks, Jr.
William J. Mundy
Bryan Craig Black (Resident, Harrisburg Office)
Eileen Lampe
Christopher Thomson (Resident Shareholder, West Chester Office)
K. Reed Haywood
Maureen P. Fitzgerald

For full biographical listings, see the Martindale-Hubbell Law Directory

MCSHEA TECCE, P.C. (AV)

Mellon Bank Center, 26th Floor, 1735 Market Street, 19103
Telephone: 215-599-0800
Fax: 215-599-0888
URL: http://www.mcshea-tecce.com

John P. McShea, III
Frederick A. Tecce

Garen Meguerian
Timothy R. Chapin

For full biographical listings, see the Martindale-Hubbell Law Directory

MULVEY & FLANAGAN, P.C. (AV)

1520 Locust Street, 10th Floor, 19102
Telephone: 215-731-0100
Fax: 215-731-0180
Email: mulvey@ix.netcom.com *URL:* http://www.lawyers.com/mflaw

W. Michael Mulvey
Michael J. Flanagan

Maureen Hope Flanagan
Michael G. Dryden
Richard R. Budney, Jr.

For full biographical listings, see the Martindale-Hubbell Law Directory

Philadelphia—Continued

MURPHY AND O'CONNOR (AV)

Two Penn Center Plaza, Suite 1100, 19102
Telephone: 215-564-0400
Telecopier: 215-564-1973
Email: MRFOCONNJ@AOL.COM
Email: MRFOCONPA@AOL.COM
Haddonfield, New Jersey Office: 65 Haddon Avenue.
Telephone: 609-795-6111.
Telecopier: 609-795-3446.

MEMBERS OF FIRM

Edward R. Murphy
Michael P. O'Connor
Michael J. Dunn
Timothy J. Galanaugh
Kevin P. McCarty (Resident, Haddonfield, New Jersey Office)

ASSOCIATES

David M. Barry
Stephen E. Siegrist (Resident, Haddonfield, New Jersey Office)
Robert E. Smith
Elizabeth A. Dalberth
Kimberly A. Lapworth
Anthony E. Creato, Sr.

OF COUNSEL

Patricia A. Mattern

For full biographical listings, see the Martindale-Hubbell Law Directory

MYLOTTE, DAVID & FITZPATRICK (AV)

7 Penn Center, 1635 Market Street, 9th Floor, 19103
Telephone: 215-751-9450
Facsimile: 215-751-9918
Email: mylottedav@aol.com *URL:* http://www.mylottedavid.com
Voorhees, New Jersey Office: 306 W. Somerdale Road.
Telephone: 609-427-4411.
Wilkes-Barre, Pennsylvania Office: Suite 200, 15 Public Square.
Telephone: 570-824-7739.
Hazleton, Pennsylvania Office: 67 North Church Street.
Telephone: 570-454-5575.

MEMBERS OF FIRM

Joseph P. Mylotte (1939-1991)
Edward J. David
Charles A. Fitzpatrick, III
John A. Fitzpatrick
Robert J. Gillespie, Jr. (Resident, Wilkes-Barre Office)
John C. Janos
Joseph R. Ferdinand (Resident, Hazleton Office)
Daniel A. Miscavige (Resident, Hazleton Office)
William C. McGovern
Bruce K. Anders (Resident, Wilkes-Barre Office)
Martin G. Malloy
Fredrick C. Hanselmann
Christine F. McCafferty
Joseph R. Baranko, Jr. (Resident, Hazleton Office)
Patrice S. O'Brien
Arthur B. Keppel
M. Susan Riley
Edward J. McCarthy
Brian J. Durkin
Kathleen Daily Mock
Peter P. O'Donnell (Resident, Wilkes-Barre Office)
Joseph Zola (Resident, Wilkes-Barre Office)
Brandon G. Johnson
James Hickey
Tyler Tomlinson
Adam D. Wilf
Justin P. McGlynn
James R. Scallion (Resident, Hazleton Office)
Christopher B. Slusser (Resident, Hazleton Office)
Helena M. Quinn
Michael G. Sabo
Sandra L. Jacques

Representative Clients: PENJERDEL Stores Mutual Assn.; Travelers Property & Casualty Co.; Mercy Health Corporation of Southeastern Pennsylvania; Temple University Hospital; Hospital of the University of Pennsylvania.

For full biographical listings, see the Martindale-Hubbell Law Directory

WILLIAM D. PARRY (AV)

Suite 900, 1608 Walnut Street, 19103
Telephone: 215-735-3500
Fax: 215-735-1858
Email: WDPARRY@AOL.COM

For full biographical listings, see the Martindale-Hubbell Law Directory

PERRY, FIALKOWSKI & PERRY (AV)

Suite 1600 One Penn Square West, 30 South 15th Street, 19102
Telephone: 215-561-4110
Fax: 215-561-4177
Email: pfp@pfplaw.com *URL:* http://www.pfplaw.com
Clementon, New Jersey Office: 180 White Horse Pike.
Telephone: 609-627-1005.

MEMBERS OF FIRM

David Perry
Anne E. Fialkowski
Sherryl R. Perry
Marcia F. Rosenbaum

LEGAL SUPPORT PERSONNEL

Lisa Garrett

For full biographical listings, see the Martindale-Hubbell Law Directory

POST & SCHELL, P.C. (AV)

19th Floor, 1800 J. F. K. Boulevard, 19103
Telephone: 215-587-1000
Fax: 215-587-1444
Email: P&S@PostSchell.Com
Allentown, Pennsylvania Office: 1245 South Cedar Crest Boulevard, Suite 300.
Telephone: 610-433-0193.
Fax: 610-433-3972.
Lancaster, Pennsylvania Office: 237 North Prince Street.
Telephone: 717-291-4532.
Fax: 717-291-1609.
Harrisburg, Pennsylvania Office: 240 Grandview Avenue (Camp Hill).
Telephone: 717-731-1970.
Fax: 717-731-1985.
Reading, Pennsylvania Office: The Berkshire, Suite 205, 101-11 N. 11th Street.
Telephone: 610-375-2258.
Fax: 610-375-2263.
Voorhees, New Jersey Office: Adams Place, Suite 3, 701 White Horse Road.
Telephone: 609-627-8900.
Fax: 609-627-4451.

Robert M. Britton
Adrian R. King
David E. Faust
William F. Sutton (Managing Partner)
F. Evan Black (Resident, Camp Hill Office)
Kenneth F. DeMarco
Israel N. Eisenberg (Resident, Voorhees, New Jersey Office)
Brian M. Peters (Managing Partner)
Kenwyn M. Dougherty (Managing Partner)
John R. Sparks, Jr.
Alfred J. Johnston
Allan C. Molotsky
Sharon M. Reiss
Colin M. Vroome
Patrice A. Toland
George M. Nace, III (Resident, Lehigh Valley Office)
John W. Potkai
Joseph F. McNulty, Jr. (Managing Partner, Lehigh Valley Office)
C. Andre Washington
John C. Sullivan
Stephen T. Potako
Donald N. Camhi
Kathleen M. Chancler
Barbara S. Magen
Patrick T. Cusick (Resident, Lancaster Office)
Benjamin A. Post
Peter M. Harrison
Sarah E. Reese
Daniel S. Altschuler
Paul W. Grego (Resident, Camp Hill Office)
Alexander J. Palutis (Managing Partner, Camp Hill Office)
Jonathan B. Sprague
Patrick K. McCoyd
Abbie R. Newman
Barbara L. Young
Deborah L. Hartwell
Richard L. McMonigle
Jay A. Gebauer (Managing Partner, Voorhees, New Jersey Office)
Francis P. Fitzsimmons (Resident, Lancaster Office)
Charles F. McElwee (Resident, Camp Hill Office)
Michael R. Nelson
Georgine A. Olexa (Resident, Lehigh Valley Office)
Steven D. Costello (Resident, Lancaster Office)
Sidney R. Steinberg
Andrew Holbrook Briggs (Resident, Camp Hill Office)
Gregory S. Hirtzel (Resident, Lancaster Office)

Terri L. Ackerman
Jonathan C. Ascher (Resident, Allentown Office)
James S. Bainbridge
David G. Bennett (Resident, Resident Lehigh Office)
Michael A. Boomsma (Resident, Lancaster Office)
Michael P. Broadhurst
Howard J. Burk
Glenn M. Campbell
William H. Catto
Timothy F. Coffey
Andrew J. Connolly
Amy L. Coryer (Resident, Camp Hill Office)
Steven D. Costello (Resident, Lancaster Office)
George Costopoulos
Carol M. Cowhey
Thomas M. Cusack, III
Chester F. Darlington, Jr.
Jennifer Margiotta Davies
Daniel J. de Luca
Jonathan C. Deisher
Shawn M. Dethlefsen (Resident, Allentown Office)
John C. Devine (Resident, Harrisburg Office)
Rebecca L. Dillon (Resident, Lancaster Office)
John W. Dornberger (Resident, Camp Hill Office)
J. Michael Doyle
Ryan J. Durkin
Michael T. Farrell
Tara A. Figore (Resident, Lehigh Office)
Sandra L. Foster (Resident, Lancaster Office)
Joseph R. Fowler
John Gilbert
Jason P. Gosselin
Margret MacGaffey Hagar
Sheila A. Haren
Richard N. Held
Stephanie Lynn Hersperger
Patricia Holden (Resident, Voorhees, New Jersey Office)
Robert T. Horst
Derrick Howard
Amy E. Jackson-Mays (Resident, Lancaster Office)
Maureen A. Jordan (Resident, Allentown Office)
John R. Kantner (Resident, Harrisburg Office)
Kathleen K. Kerns
Hui Yung Kim (Resident, Allentown Office)
Adrian R. King, Jr.
Jennifer R. Kleeman
Geoffrey D. Lawrence
BethAnn Wiley Leaming
Kenneth T. Levine
Valerie H. Lieberman
Colin Kelly Lydon (Resident, Harrisburg Office)
James F. Malloy
Wendy Cherner Maneval
John E. Marquis
Stephan Matanovic

(See Next Column)

POST & SCHELL P.C., *Philadelphia—Continued*

Mark L. Mattioli
Joseph McAleer (Resident, Allentown Office)
Lamont G. McClure (Resident, Lancaster Office)
Richard John McCracken (Resident, Lancaster Office)
Michael E. McGrath (Resident, Harrisburg Office)
Joseph G. McHale
Perry D. Merlo (Resident, Harrisburg Office)
Jonathan C. Meyers (Resident, Allentown Office)
Karen E. Minehan (Resident, Lancaster Office)
Eileen M. Mohrfeld
Monica E. O'Neill
William Dirk Pastorick
Leah B. Perry
Susan B. Pliner
Teresa Reid
Valerie L. Reno
Amalia V. Romanowicz
Regina M. Schluckebier
Lois M. Shenk
Wendy L. Slear
Dolores Marie Spina
Edward J. Stolarski
Stacy A. Tees
Kristin L. Thompson
Mary T. Uhlig
Kenneth L. Voigt
Cindy D. Wager
Walter J. Weinrich
Denise L. Werner (Resident, Voorhees, New Jersey Office)
Leonard A. Windish
Paul Brian Wright
Anne E. Zerbe (Resident, Lancaster Office)

OF COUNSEL

Albert J. Schell, Jr.
Barton L. Post

For full biographical listings, see the Martindale-Hubbell Law Directory

RYAN, BROWN, MCDONNELL, BERGER GIBBONS & LAROCCA, LLP (AV)

1600 Market Street, Suite 2500, 19103-7240
Telephone: 215-564-3800
Facsimile: 215-564-1301
Email: lawfirm@ryanbrown.com
Cherry Hill, New Jersey Office: 500 Kings Highway South, 08034.
Telephone: 609-216-8155.
Facsimile: 609-429-7726.

Daniel J. Ryan
John R. Brown
Michael T. McDonnell, III
Mitchell S. Berger
Patrick J. Gibbons
Robert J. LaRocca

For full biographical listings, see the Martindale-Hubbell Law Directory

RALPH D. SAMUEL & CO. A PROFESSIONAL CORPORATION (AV)

225 South 15th Street, Suite 1776, 19102
Telephone: 215-893-9992
Fax: 215-893-9996
Email: RalphSamuel@lawmine.com *URL:* http://www.lawyers.com/ralphdsamuellaw

Ralph David Samuel
Lynn Malmgren

For full biographical listings, see the Martindale-Hubbell Law Directory

SAVETT FRUTKIN PODELL & RYAN, P.C. (AV)

Suite 700, 325 Chestnut Street, 19106
Telephone: 215-923-5400
FAX: 923-9353
Email: SFPRPC@OP.NET

Stuart H. Savett
Robert P. Frutkin
Barbara A. Podell
Katharine M. Ryan

For full biographical listings, see the Martindale-Hubbell Law Directory

JAMES C. SCHWARTZMAN & ASSOCIATES, P.C. (AV)

1760 Market Street, 12th Floor, 19103
Telephone: 215-563-2233
Fax: 215-563-2134

James C. Schwartzman

Gary Tilles
Dana Pirone Garrity

For full biographical listings, see the Martindale-Hubbell Law Directory

SIDKOFF, PINCUS & GREEN, P.C. (AV)

Aramark Tower, 1101 Market Street, Suite 2700, 19107
Telephone: 215-574-0600
Fax: 215-574-0310
Email: S.P.G.@WORLDNET.ATT.NET

Manuel Sidkoff (1900-1988)
I. David Pincus (1919-1997)
Gary Green
Robert A. Davitch
Larry M. Keller
Steven H. Griffiths

Scott A. George

Reference: PNC Bank.

For full biographical listings, see the Martindale-Hubbell Law Directory

E. ALFRED SMITH & ASSOCIATES (AV)

1333 Race Street, Second Floor, 19107
Telephone: 215-569-8422
Fax: 215-569-8606
Voorhees, New Jersey Office: 41 Arcadia Drive, 08043.
Telephone: 609-751-7077.

ASSOCIATE

Christine L. Serbanic

For full biographical listings, see the Martindale-Hubbell Law Directory

SPECTOR GADON & ROSEN, P.C. (AV)

Seven Penn Center, 1635 Market Street, 7th Floor, 19103
Telephone: 215-241-8888
Fax: 215-241-8844
Moorestown, New Jersey Office: Spector, Gadon & Rosen, P.C. 307 Fellowship Road. P.O. Box 1001, 08057.
Telephone: 609-778-8100.
Fax: 609-722-5344.

Paul R. Rosen
Steven F. Gadon
Samuel L. Hirshland
Elliott K. Braverman
Milton H. Cross
Edward G. Fitzgerald, Jr.
Alan B. Epstein
Lary I. Zucker
Bruce L. Thall
Daniel J. Dugan
Alan H. Wallen
David M. Giles
Leslie Beth Baskin
Steven J. Polansky
Stanley Peter Jaskiewicz
Alan J. Mittelman

George M. Vinci, Jr.

OF COUNSEL

Arthur E. Vossberg III

Timothy C. Russell
Peter J. Boyer
Alan M. Rosen
Nancy Abrams
Claudia L. Boyd
Scott A. Burr
Heather M. Eichenbaum
Joshua F. Laff
Kenneth J. LaFiandra
Paul A. Loh
Brooke Caroline Madonna
Lynda M. Miller
David B. Picker
Kelly R. Ramsdell
Thomas Rapp
Suzanne I. Schiller

Michael C. Wagner

For full biographical listings, see the Martindale-Hubbell Law Directory

SPECTOR & ROSEMAN, A PROFESSIONAL CORPORATION (AV)

1818 Market Street, Suite 2500, 19103
Telephone: 215-496-0300
Telecopier: 215-496-6611
Email: espector@spectorandroseman.com *URL:* http://www.spectorandroseman.com
San Diego, California Office: 600 West Broadway, 1600 One American Plaza, 92101.
Telephone: 619-338-4514.
Telecopier: 619-231-7423.

Eugene A. Spector
Robert M. Roseman
Jeffrey L. Kodroff
Ellen Gusikoff Stewart (Not admitted in PA)

Ronnie D. Seidel
Diane Doherty (Not admitted in PA)
Anthony Chu
Andrew D. Abramowitz (Not admitted in PA)
Joshua H. Grabar
Howard C. Gottlieb
Michael P. Nachman
Beth Mandel Rosenthal

OF COUNSEL

Anthony J. Bolognese

LEGAL SUPPORT PERSONNEL

PARALEGALS

Joseph Morrison
Michelle Adams

Carole Staiger

For full biographical listings, see the Martindale-Hubbell Law Directory

WEIR & PARTNERS LLP (AV)

A Pennsylvania Limited Liability Partnership
Suite 500, The Widener Building, 1339 Chestnut Street, 19107
Telephone: 215-665-8181
Telefax: 215-665-8464
Email: info@weirpartners.com
Turnersville, New Jersey Office: 215 Fries Mill Road, 08012.
Telephone: 609-740-1490.
Telefax: 609-740-1491.

MEMBERS OF FIRM

Walter Weir, Jr.
Leonard S. Goodman
Susan Verbonitz
Jeffrey L. Rudnick
Robert D. Sayre
Stephen M. Giroux
Richard P. Coe, Jr.
Brett A. Datto
John B. York
Joseph C. Hare

(See Next Column)

WEIR & PARTNERS LLP—*Continued*

ASSOCIATES

Bonnie R. Golub
Debra N. Nathanson
Tina L. Colman
Andrew K. Stutzman
Jeffrey A. Guth
Jason M Reiser
Madeline Flanagan

For full biographical listings, see the Martindale-Hubbell Law Directory

WILBRAHAM, LAWLER & BUBA, A PROFESSIONAL CORPORATION (AV)

1818 Market Street, Suite 3100, 19103-3631
Telephone: 215-564-4141
Fax: 215-564-4385
Email: @wlbdeflaw.com
Haddonfield, New Jersey Office: 24 Kings Highway West.
Telephone: 856-795-4422.
Fax: 856-795-4699.
Wilmington, Delaware Office: Stoney Batter Office Building, 5301 Limestone Road, Suite 221.
Telephone: 302-234-8217.
Fax: 302-234-8218.

Edward J. Wilbraham
Robert B. Lawler
Barbara J. Buba
Michael J. Block

R. Erick Chizmar
Kevin J. Maginnis
InSook Kim
Sandra D. Terry-Crawford
John S. Howarth
David M. Maselli
Renee E. Berger
Edward T. Finch
Sean P. Buggy

OF COUNSEL

Walter J. Timby, Jr.
Daniel J. Allan

Representative Clients: GAF Corporation; Armstrong World Industries, Inc.; U.S. Gypsum Company; Georgia-Pacific Corporation; ARCO; Shell; Royal; AIG; Chubb; Keystone.

For full biographical listings, see the Martindale-Hubbell Law Directory

ZARWIN, BAUM, DEVITO, KAPLAN & O'DONNELL, P.C. (AV)

1515 Market Street, Suite 1200, 19102
Telephone: 215-569-2800
Fax: 215-569-1606
Cherry Hill, New Jersey Office: Woodland Falls Corporate Center, Suite 105, 220 Lake Drive East, 08002.
Telephone: 609-667-3434.
Fax: 609-667-2491.
Jersey City, New Jersey Office: 75 Montgomery Street, Suite 200, 07302.
Telephone: 201-432-7840.
Fax: 201-432-3945.

Norman P. Zarwin
E. Harris Baum
John R. O'Donnell
Mitchell S. Kaplan
Gary A. DeVito
Theodore M. Schaer
Lionel A. Prince
Joseph M. Toddy
Kenneth J. Fleisher

Gary Alan Zlotnick
Edward J. McKenna
Jay L. Solnick
Lisa M. Zinn
Michelle R. Sergent
Joseph W. Denneler
Xavier P. Hayden
Mindy L. Feldstein
David R. Joseph
Glori A. Friedman

OF COUNSEL

Joseph F. Busacca
Ronald J. Bayer
Dennis L. Friedman
Mario F. Driggs

For full biographical listings, see the Martindale-Hubbell Law Directory

*PITTSBURGH,** Allegheny Co.

ANSTANDIG, MCDYER, BURDETTE & YURCON, P.C. (AV)

Suite 1300 Gulf Tower, 707 Grant Street, 15219-1911
Telephone: 412-765-3700
Facsimile: 412-765-3730
Email: ambylaw@usaor.net

Louis Anstandig
Daniel P. McDyer
Timothy J. Burdette
Edward A. Yurcon

John F. Deasy
Rebecca Sember
Shawn G. McMahon
Benjamin Marc Mayer

For full biographical listings, see the Martindale-Hubbell Law Directory

JOSEPH WM. CONWAY (AV)

300 Four PPG Place, 15222
Telephone: 412-471-8300
Fax: 412-338-4742
Email: joswconway@aol.com

Reference: Integra Bank/North.

For full biographical listings, see the Martindale-Hubbell Law Directory

DAVIES MCFARLAND & CARROLL, P.C. (AV)

One Gateway Center, Tenth Floor, 15222
Telephone: 412-281-0737
Email: firm@dmcpc.com

Ralph A. Davies
Daniel P. Carroll
William D. Geiger
Francis Garger
Lynn E. Bell
C. Robert Keenan III
M.J. (Jeff) Tindall
Eric K. Falk
David E. Lamm
Clare M. Bello

Howard K. Hilner
Mary Kathleen Coleman
Julie L. Nord
Andrew G. Thiros

Representative Clients: The BOC Group; Cincinnati Insurance Co.; The Goodyear Tire & Rubber Co.; Hobart Brothers Co.; LTV Steel Co.; Medical Protective Co.; Metropolitan Life Insurance Co.; Motorists Insurance Cos.; Premier Auto Insurance Co.

For Complete List of Firm Personnel, See General Section

For full biographical listings, see the Martindale-Hubbell Law Directory

DEFOREST & KOSCELNIK (AV)

3000 Koppers Building, 436 Seventh Avenue, 15219
Telephone: 412-227-3100
Fax: 412-227-3130

Walter P. DeForest, III
Jacqueline A. Koscelnik

ASSOCIATES

David J. Berardinelli
Paul M. Thompson

Representative Clients: Carnegie Mellon University; Ohio Valley Medical Center; Cox Enterprises, Inc.; General Electric Co.; Chancellor Broadcasting; Shooting Star Broadcasting; Leybold Vacuum Products, Inc.; Demegen, Inc.; Emerson Electric Co.; Frank Bryan, Inc.; Rox Trucking, Inc.

For full biographical listings, see the Martindale-Hubbell Law Directory

FECZKO AND SEYMOUR (AV)

520 Grant Building, 15219
Telephone: 412-261-4970
Fax: Available upon Request
Bethel Park, Pennsylvania Office: 3400 South Park Road.
Telephone: 412-833-5554.

MEMBERS OF FIRM

Albert G. Feczko, Jr.
Michael J. Seymour

ASSOCIATE

Michael D. Seymour

Reference: Pittsburgh National Bank.

For full biographical listings, see the Martindale-Hubbell Law Directory

FELDSTEIN GRINBERG STEIN & MCKEE, A PROFESSIONAL CORPORATION (AV)

428 Boulevard of the Allies, 15219
Telephone: 412-471-0677
Fax: 412-263-6129
URL: http://www.fgsmlaw.com
Elizabeth, Pennsylvania Office: 400 Second Street.
Telephone: 412-384-6111.

Jay H. Feldstein
Stanley M. Stein
Gary M. Lang
Francis C. Rapp, Jr.
Jeffrey R. Lalama
Jeffrey B. Balicki

Thomas P. McDermott
James C. Heneghan
Barbara M. Wolvovitz
David S. Bloom
Regis J. Moeller
Beth S. Mills

For full biographical listings, see the Martindale-Hubbell Law Directory

GACA MATIS BAUM & RIZZA, A PROFESSIONAL CORPORATION (AV)

300 Four PPG Place, 15222-5404
Telephone: 412-338-4750
Fax: 412-338-4742
URL: http://www.gaca.com
Wheeling, West Virginia Office: 33 Fifteenth Street, 26003-3535.
Telephone: 304-234-4750.
Fax: 304-234-4742.

(See Next Column)

GACA MATIS BAUM & RIZZA A PROFESSIONAL CORPORATION, *Pittsburgh—Continued*

Erie, Pennsylvania Office: 915 State Street, 16501-1405.
Telephone: 814-451-1147.
Fax: 814-451-1150.

Giles J. Gaca
Thomas A. Matis
Alan S. Baum
Bernard R. Rizza
John W. Jordan IV
Stephen J. Dalesio
M. Brian O'Connor

Marian Patchen Schleppy
Michael R. Lettrich

For full biographical listings, see the Martindale-Hubbell Law Directory

GREENFIELD, BREWER, BAILOR & KAY (AV)

Greenfield Court, 1035-37 Fifth Avenue, 15219
Telephone: 412-261-4466
Fax: 412-261-4408
Email: galaw@nauticom.net *URL:* http://www.lawyers.com/gbbk

Stanley W. Greenfield
Graydon R. Brewer
Martha E. Bailor
Paul G. Kay

For full biographical listings, see the Martindale-Hubbell Law Directory

HEINTZMAN, WARREN, WISE & FORNELLA, P.C. (AV)

The 35th Floor, Gulf Tower, 707 Grant Street, 15219
Telephone: 412-394-7810
Fax: 412-263-5222
Email: hww@hwwlaw.com *URL:* http://www.hwwlaw.com

Michael D. Heintzman
Charles S. Warren
Roger L. Wise
Leonard Fornella
Joseph R. Schaper
Kenneth F. Klanica

Jeanine L. Fonner
Jeanne Welch Sopher
Max T. Busatto

For full biographical listings, see the Martindale-Hubbell Law Directory

JONES, DAY, REAVIS & POGUE (AV)

500 Grant Street 31st Floor, 15219
Telephone: 412-391-3939
Telecopier: 412-394-7959
Email: counsel@jonesday.com *URL:* http://www.jonesday.com
In Atlanta, Georgia: 3500 SunTrust Plaza, 303 Peachtree Street.
Telephone: 404-521-3939.
Telecopier: 404-581-8330.
In Brussels, Belgium: Avenue Louise 480, 7th Floor, B-1050 Brussels.
Telephone: 32-2-645-14-11.
Telecopier: 32-2-645-14-45.
In Chicago, Illinois: 77 West Wacker.
Telephone: 312-782-3939.
Telecopier: 312-782-8585.
In Cleveland, Ohio: North Point, 901 Lakeside Avenue.
Telephone: 216-586-3939.
Telecopier: 216-579-0212.
In Columbus, Ohio: 1900 Huntington Center.
Telephone: 614-469-3939.
Telecopier: 614-461-4198.
In Dallas, Texas: 2727 North Harwood Street.
Telephone: 214-220-3939.
Telecopier: 214-969-5100.
In Frankfurt, Germany: Hochhaus am Park, Grüneburgweg 102, 60323 Frankfurt am Main.
Telephone: 49-69-9726-3939.
Telecopier: 49-69-9726-3993.
In Geneva, Switzerland: 20, rue de Candolle.
Telephone: 41-22-320-2339.
Telecopier: 41-22-320-1232.
In Hong Kong: 29th Floor, Entertainment Building, 30 Queen's Road Central.
Telephone: 852-2526-6895.
Telecopier: 852-2868-5871 or 852-2868-5699.
In Irvine, California: 5 Park Plaza, Suite 1100.
Telephone: 949-851-3939.
Telecopier: 949-553-7539.
In London, England: Bucklersbury House, 3 Queen Victoria Street.
Telephone: 44-171-236-3939.
Telecopier: 44-171-236-1113. 34000 Los Angeles, California: 555 West Fifth Street, Suite 4600.
Telephone: 213-489-3939.
Telecopier: 213-243-2539.
In New Delhi, India (Associate Office): Pathak & Associates (an associate firm of Jones, Day, Reavis & Pogue), 1st Floor, Dr. Gopal Das Bhaven, 28 Barakhamba Road.
Telephone: 91-11-373-8793; 91-11-335-7345.
Telecopier: 91-11-335-3761.
In New York, New York: 599 Lexington Avenue.
Telephone: 212-326-3939.
Telecopier: 212-755-7306.

(See Next Column)

In Paris, France: 120, rue du Faubourg Saint-Honoré.
Telephone: 33-1-56-59-39-39.
Telecopier: 33-1-56-59-39-38
In Riyadh, Saudi Arabia: The International Law Firm (In Association with Jones, Day, Reavis & Pogue), Sulaymaniyah, Prince Mishari IBN, Abdulaziz Street, P.O. Box 22166.
Telephone: (966-1) 462-8866.
Telecopier: (966-1) 462-9001.
In Shanghai, China: 2805 Kerry Centre, 1515 Nanjing Road West.
Telephone: 86-21-5298-6568.
Telecopier: 86-21-5298-6569.
In Sydney, Australia: Governor Phillip Tower, Level 38, 1 Farrer Place.
Telephone: 61-2-9210-6921.
Telecopier: 61-2-9210-6926.
In Taipei, Taiwan: 8th Floor, 2 Tun Hwa South Road, Section 2.
Telephone: (886-2) 2704-6808.
Telecopier: (886-2) 2704-6791.
In Tokyo, Japan: Toranomon MT Building, 4th Floor, 10-3, Toranomon 3-Chome, Minato-Ku, Tokyo 105, Japan.
Telephone: 81-3-3433-3939.
Telecopier: 81-3-5401-2725.
In Washington, D.C.: 51 Louisiana Avenue, N.W.
Telephone: 202-879-3939.
Telecopier: 202-626-1700.

MEMBER OF FIRM IN PITTSBURGH

Paul Michael Pohl

For Complete List of Firm Personnel, See General Section

For full biographical listings, see the Martindale-Hubbell Law Directory

KATARINCIC & SALMON (AV)

2600 CNG Tower, 625 Liberty Avenue, 15222
Telephone: 412-338-2900
Facsimile: 412-261-2212
URL: http://www.kandslaw.com
Wheeling, West Virginia Office: 900 Mull Center, 1025 Main Street.
Telephone: 304-234-6600.
Fax: 304-234-6601.

Joseph A. Katarincic
Kenneth L. Salmon
Robert J. Ridge
Scott W. Irmscher
David A. Borkovic
Richard M. Smith

Theodore N. Black
Kim M. Watterson
Ellen G. McGlone

For full biographical listings, see the Martindale-Hubbell Law Directory

KIGER & ALPERN (AV)

1404 Grant Building, 15219
Telephone: 412-765-1811
Fax: 412-765-0440

MEMBERS OF FIRM

Jerome W. Kiger
Charles H. Alpern

For full biographical listings, see the Martindale-Hubbell Law Directory

LITMAN LITMAN HARRIS & BROWN, P.C. (AV)

An Association of Law Corporations
3600 One Oxford Centre, 15219
Telephone: 412-456-2000
Fax: 412-456-2020
Email: mailbox@Litman-law.com *URL:* http://www.litman-law.com

S. David Litman (1923-1996)
Roslyn M. Litman
Stephen J. Harris
David R. Brown
Martha S. Helmreich
Mark F. Flaherty
Joseph Leibowicz
Robert J. O'Hara, III

For full biographical listings, see the Martindale-Hubbell Law Directory

MARCUS & SHAPIRA LLP (AV)

35th Floor, One Oxford Centre, 301 Grant Street, 15219-6401
Telephone: 412-471-3490
Telecopier: 412-391-8758
Email: info@marcus-shapira.com *URL:* http://www.marcus-shapira.com

MEMBERS OF FIRM

Robert L. Allman, II
Robert M. Barnes
Susan Gromis Flynn
Elly Heller-Toig
James S. Larrimer
Scott D. Livingston
Bernard D. Marcus
Darlene M. Nowak
James F. Rosenberg
Daniel H. Shapira
Stephen S. Zubrow

OF COUNSEL

John M. Burkoff

ASSOCIATES

Henry G. Barr
Moira E. Cain
Traci L. McDonald
Susan H. Snively

(See Next Column)

MARCUS & SHAPIRA LLP—*Continued*

For Complete List of Firm Personnel, See General Section

For full biographical listings, see the Martindale-Hubbell Law Directory

HOWARD F. MESSER, P.C. (AV)

1404 Grant Building, 15219
Telephone: 412-281-7200
FAX: 412-765-0440
URL: http://www.lawyers.com/messerlaw

Howard F. Messer

Philip A. Fabiano

For full biographical listings, see the Martindale-Hubbell Law Directory

PICADIO MCCALL MILLER & NORTON (AV)

4680 USX Tower, 600 Grant Street, 15219-2702
Telephone: 412-288-4000
Fax: 412-288-2405/2409

MEMBERS OF FIRM

C. Robert McCall
Alan S. Miller
Lynette Norton
Anthony P. Picadio
Tracey Garland Vinson

ASSOCIATES

Bridget M. Gillespie
Keith E. Whitson

OF COUNSEL

Kevin J Fiore

Representative Clients: Crum & Forster Commercial Insurance Corp.; Chubb Group of Insurance Companies; Seven Fields Development Company; Massaro Construction Company; Equitable Resources, Inc.; Southwestern Pennsylvania Water Authority; Westchester Specialty Group, Inc.; Pennsylvania Capital Bank; International Fidelity Insurance Company; Manville Sales Corp.

For full biographical listings, see the Martindale-Hubbell Law Directory

PLOWMAN, SPIEGEL & LEWIS, P.C. (AV)

Second Floor, The Grant Building, 310 Grant Street, 15219-2201
Telephone: 412-471-8521
Fax: 412-471-4481

Jack W. Plowman
John L. Spiegel
James A. Lewis

Frank J. Kernan
Kenneth W. Lee

Reference: Pittsburgh National Bank.

For Complete List of Firm Personnel, See General Section

For full biographical listings, see the Martindale-Hubbell Law Directory

RILEY, MCNULTY, HEWITT & SWEITZER, A PROFESSIONAL CORPORATION (AV)

Suite 300, 650 Washingon Road, 15228
Telephone: 412-341-9300
Fax: 412-341-9177
Email: rmhs@nauticom.net

Patrick R. Riley
Sibyl S. McNulty
Patrick A. Hewitt
David E. Sweitzer

William J. Witte

For full biographical listings, see the Martindale-Hubbell Law Directory

ROSE, SCHMIDT, HASLEY & DISALLE, P.C. (AV)

900 Oliver Building, 15222-2310
Telephone: 412-434-8600
Fax: 412-263-2829
Email: rshd@rshdlaw.com
Washington, Pennsylvania Office: 7th Floor, Millcraft Center.
Telephone: 724-228-8883.

Richard DiSalle
Brian W. Ashbaugh
Edmund M. Carney
Kim D. Eaton
Mary Lynch Friedline
Gail L. Gratton
R. Stanley Mitchel
Keithley D. Mulvihill
Steven M. Petrikis

COUNSEL

Raymond G. Hasley

For Complete List of Firm Personnel, See General Section

For full biographical listings, see the Martindale-Hubbell Law Directory

SWENSEN PERER & KONTOS (AV)

Two PNC Plaza, Suite 2710, 15222
Telephone: 412-281-1970
Fax: 412-281-2808
Email: general2@swensenperer.com
Erie, Pennsylvania Office: Swensen Perer & McCandless. 209 Court House Commons.
Telephone: 814-456-0489. Email: erie@swensenperer.com.

MEMBERS OF FIRM

Jan C. Swensen
Alan H. Perer
John W. McCandless (Resident Partner, Erie Office)
George M. Kontos

ASSOCIATES

Anthony C. Mengine
Daniel J. Sinclair

OF COUNSEL

Diane W. Perer
David A. Schroeder
Anthony J. Sciarrino

For full biographical listings, see the Martindale-Hubbell Law Directory

THE TARASI LAW FIRM, P.C. (AV)

510 Third Avenue, 15219
Telephone: 412-391-7135
Fax: 412-471-2673
Email: tarasilaw@aol.com *URL:* http://www.lawyers.com/tarasilaw

Louis M. Tarasi, Jr.

Elizabeth M. Tarasi
Craig L. Fishman
Christina K. Hurnyak

For Complete List of Firm Personnel, See General Section

For full biographical listings, see the Martindale-Hubbell Law Directory

VOLLMER RULONG & KEATING, P.C. (AV)

Suite 1212 Grant Building, 310 Grant Street, 15219
Telephone: 412-391-2121
Telecopier: 412-391-3578
Email: vollmer@vollmerlaw.com *URL:* http://www.vollmerlaw.com

Charles J. Vollmer
Roger G. Rulong, Jr.
John R. Keating

Pamela J. Royesky

For full biographical listings, see the Martindale-Hubbell Law Directory

WEISMAN GOLDMAN BOWEN & GROSS LLP (AV)

310 Grant Street, Suite 420, 15219
Telephone: 412-566-2520
Fax: 412-566-1088

James L. Weisman
S. James Goldman
Alden Earl Bowen
Sanford P. Gross
Barry J. Lipson
Howard J. Schulberg
Christopher J. Klein
Samuel F. Reynolds, Jr.
Frank J. Grzywinski
David J. Brosky
Robert L. Monks

Reference: Pittsburgh National Bank.

For full biographical listings, see the Martindale-Hubbell Law Directory

YUKEVICH, MARCHETTI, LIEKAR & ZANGRILLI, P.C. (AV)

Sixth Floor, One Gateway Center, 15222-1424
Telephone: 412-261-6777
Fax: 412-261-6789
URL: http://www.ymlz.com

Michael Yukevich, Jr.
Christopher J. Marchetti
John P. Liekar, Jr.
Albert J. Zangrilli, Jr.
Mark Fischer
Michael I. Frachioni
Lori Nolan Lindey
Keith J. Rothfus

For full biographical listings, see the Martindale-Hubbell Law Directory

ZIMMER KUNZ, PROFESSIONAL CORPORATION (AV)

3300 USX Tower, 600 Grant Street, 15219
Telephone: 412-281-8000
Fax: 412-281-1765

Harry J. Zimmer
John E. Kunz
Raymond H. Conaway
George N. Stewart
Joni M. Mangino
Joseph W. Selep
Raymond J. Conlon
Edward K. Dixon
Mark R. Hamilton
Alexander P. Bicket
John W. Zotter
Jeffrey A. Ramaley
Thomas P. McGinnis

OF COUNSEL

Andrew J. Banyas, III
Thomas A. Lazaroff

(See Next Column)

ZIMMER KUNZ PROFESSIONAL CORPORATION, *Pittsburgh—Continued*

Dara A. DeCourcy
Robert W. Murdoch
Anthony C. Carone
Timothy R. Smith
Meghan Fawcett Wise
Daniel E. Krauth
George R. Farneth, II
John K. Bryan
Mark T. Caloyer
Christopher T. Yoskosky
Amy J. Brinkos
George W. Boguslawski, Jr.
Carmen A. Martucci
Tracy L. Yaggi
Kurt W. Lenz
Carl Adam Ronald
Claire A. Conaway

Attorneys For: American International Group; Cincinnati Insurance Co.; Equitable Gas Co.; Honda North America; Otis Elevator Co.; Outboard Marine Corp.; Pennsylvania Electric Co.; Travelers Insurance Co.

For full biographical listings, see the Martindale-Hubbell Law Directory

PUNXSUTAWNEY, Jefferson Co.

LORENZO & GIANVITO, P.C. (AV)

410 West Mahoning Street, P.O. Box 495, 15767-1908
Telephone: 814-938-6390
Fax: 814-938-6412
Email: LGPC@Penn.com

Nicholas F. Lorenzo, Jr.
Nicholas A. Gianvito

For full biographical listings, see the Martindale-Hubbell Law Directory

*READING,** Berks Co.

BINGAMAN, HESS, COBLENTZ & BELL, A PROFESSIONAL CORPORATION (AV)

Suite 660, 601 Penn Street, P.O. Box 61, 19603-0061
Telephone: 610-374-8377
Fax: 610-376-3105
URL: http://www.bhcb.com
Cherry Hill, New Jersey Office: Shawn J. Lau, P.C., Building Q, Suite 14B, 1930 East Marlton Pike, 08003-4222.
Telephone: 609-751-4158.
Fax: 609-424-7112.

Llewellyn R. Bingaman (1907-1996)
James F. Bell (1921-1988)
Ralph J. Althouse, Jr. (Retired)

OF COUNSEL

Raymond K. Hess
J. Wendell Coblentz

David E. Turner
Mark G. Yoder
Carl D. Cronrath, Jr.
Kurt Althouse
Harry D. McMunigal
Patrick T. Barrett
Karen Feryo Longenecker
Shawn J. Lau

Lynne K. Beust
Elizabethanne D. McMunigal
Kevin W. Rethore
Eric J. Fabrizio
Elizabeth A. Magovern

General Counsel for: First Union National Bank; Berks Products Corp.; Utilities Employees Credit Union.
Local Counsel for: Erie Insurance Exchange; Liberty Mutual Insurance Co.; Old Guard Mutual Insurance Co.

For full biographical listings, see the Martindale-Hubbell Law Directory

*SCRANTON,** Lackawanna Co.

KREDER, BROOKS, HAILSTONE & LUDWIG (AV)

Suite 200, 220 Penn Avenue, 18503
Telephone: 570-346-7922
Telecopier: 570-346-3715

Cody H. Brooks
Andrew Hailstone
Lawrence M. Ludwig
Lucille Marsh
Michael J. Donohue
Stephen W. Saunders

Counsel For: PNC Bank; U.S. Fidelity & Guaranty Co.; Nationwide Insurance Co.; Liberty Mutual Insurance Co.; Citizens Savings Assn.; NEP Supershooters, Inc.; Moses Taylor Hospital.

For Complete List of Firm Personnel, See General Section

For full biographical listings, see the Martindale-Hubbell Law Directory

LENAHAN & DEMPSEY, A PROFESSIONAL CORPORATION (AV)

116 North Washington Avenue, 18503-0234
Telephone: 717-346-2097; 1-888-LENAHAN
Fax: 717-346-1174
Mailing Address: P.O. Box 234, Scranton, Pennsylvania, 18501-0234

John R. Lenahan, Sr. (1915-1998)
William J. Dempsey (Of Counsel)
John R. Lenahan, Jr.
Joseph P. Lenahan
Kathleen A. Lenahan
David E. Heisler
Timothy G. Lenahan
Matthew D. Dempsey

(See Next Column)

Alan P. Schoen
Brian J. Lenahan
Diane Hepford Lenahan
George E. Mehalchick
Brian Yeager
Thomas R. Daniels
Terrence E. Dempsey
Christine S. Mayernick-Lezinski
John M. Mulcahey
Margaret M. Dempsey
Lisa G. Wilson

Representative Insurance Clients: Allstate Insurance Co.; America Security Insurance Co.; Metropolitan Casualty Insurance Co.; Aetna Insurance Co.; Pennsylvania National Insurance Group; Kemper Insurance Group; American Mutual Insurance Cos.; American States Insurance, Co.

For full biographical listings, see the Martindale-Hubbell Law Directory

MUNLEY, MUNLEY & CARTWRIGHT, P.C. (AV)

205 Madison Avenue, 18503
Telephone: 570-346-7401
Fax: 570-346-3452
URL: http://www.lawyers.com/mmclaw
Email: lawyers@munley.com *URL:* http://www.munley.com

Robert W. Munley
Marion Munley
Matthew A. Cartwright
James Christopher Munley
Daniel W. Munley
Robert W. Munley, III

Reference: First National Bank of Jermyn.

For full biographical listings, see the Martindale-Hubbell Law Directory

MURPHY, PIAZZA & GENELLO, P.C. (AV)

Scranton Life Building, 538 Spruce Street, P.O. Box 909, 18503
Telephone: 570-344-9444
Fax: 570-344-8730
Lancaster, Pennsylvania Office: Franklin Building, 2nd Floor, 604 New Holland Avenue, 17602.
Telephone: 717-394-9448.
Fax: 717-394-9473.

Joseph A. Murphy
Anthony J. Piazza, Jr.
Michael A. Genello

Michael A. Giannetta
Patrick J. Murphy
Kathleen E. Holmes (Resident, Lancaster, Pennsylvania)

Reference: Third National Bank & Trust Co., Scranton, Pa.

For full biographical listings, see the Martindale-Hubbell Law Directory

O'MALLEY & HARRIS, P.C. (AV)

345 Wyoming Avenue, 18503
Telephone: 570-348-3711
Fax: 570-348-4092
Email: ohpc@epix.net *URL:* http://www.ohpclaw.com
Stroudsburg, Pennsylvania Office: 111 North Seventh Street.
Telephone: 570-421-2252; 570-422-1280.
FAX: 570-422-1281. Email: cerato@ptdprolog.net.
Wilkes-Barre, Pennsylvania Office: 61 North Washington Street.
Telephone: 570-829-3232.
FAX: 570-829-4418. Email: ohpcwb@epix.net.
Williamsport, Pennsylvania Office: 321 Pine Street, Suite 308.
Telephone: 570-323-4380.

Eugene Nogi (1905-1975)
Henry Nogi (1900-1976)
Russell J. O'Malley, Sr. (1904-1993)
Norman Harris (1907-1998)
William H. Amesbury (Resident, Wilkes-Barre Office)
Paul A. Barrett
Matthew P. Barrett
J. Scott Brady (Resident, Wilkes-Barre Office)
Lori J. Cerato (Resident, Stroudsburg Office)
Bruce L. Coyer
John Q. Durkin
Gerald J. Hanchulak
Richard K. Hodges
Timothy J. Holland (Resident, Wilkes-Barre Office)
John F. Kennedy (Resident, Wilkes-Barre Office)
Daniel Morgan
Michael Perry
James M. Tressler
Joseph Timothy Healey
A. Ruth Whalen (Resident, Wilkes-Barre Office)

Representative Clients: Pennsylvania Hospital Insurance Co.; MMI Systems Agency, Inc.; State Farm Insurance Company; ITT Specialty Risk Services; St. Paul Fire & Marine Insurance Co.; Chubb Group of Insurance Companies; Geisingen System Services; Princeton Insurance Company; Northeastern Pennsylvania Physicians Organization; Catholic Healthcare Partners.

For full biographical listings, see the Martindale-Hubbell Law Directory

SCANLON, HOWLEY, SCANLON & DOHERTY (AV)

321 Spruce Street, 10th Floor, 18503
Telephone: 570-346-7651
Fax: 570-344-1542

MEMBERS OF FIRM

James M. Howley
James M. Scanlon
James A. Doherty, Jr.
Thomas R. Nealon
Thomas B. Helbig
Patrick R. Casey

(See Next Column)

SCANLON, HOWLEY, SCANLON & DOHERTY—*Continued*

Counsel for: CNA Insurance Company; The Medical Protective Co.; Harleysville Insurance Co.; The Procter & Gamble Co.; Prudential-Bach Securities, Inc.; Zurich-American Insurance Co.; The Keystone Coca-Cola Bottling Co.; The Home Insurance Co.; The Travelers Insurance Co.; Utica First Ins. Co.

For full biographical listings, see the Martindale-Hubbell Law Directory

SHAMOKIN, Northumberland Co.

JACK C. YOUNKIN (AV)

One West Sunbury Street, P.O. Box 552, 17872
Telephone: 717-648-6821
Fax: 717-648-4732
Email: jcy1@Postoffice.ptd.net *URL:* http://www.lawyers.com/younkinlaw
Danville, Pennsylvania Office: 223 Mill Street.
Telephone: 717-275-7742.
Fax: 717-275-7749.

ASSOCIATES

Barbara G. Martin
Todd P. Kerstetter

LEGAL SUPPORT PERSONNEL

Patricia Janovich

For full biographical listings, see the Martindale-Hubbell Law Directory

SOUTHAMPTON, Bucks Co.

MOORE & BERKOWITZ (AV)

A Partnership of Professional Corporations
Suite A-110, 928 Jaymor Road, 18966
Telephone: 215-322-4200
Fax: 215-322-4318
Email: shb@ibob.com

Steven H. Berkowitz (P.C.)
Richard I. Moore (P.C.)

For full biographical listings, see the Martindale-Hubbell Law Directory

STATE COLLEGE, Centre Co.

MILLER, KISTLER, CAMPBELL, MILLER, WILLIAMS & BENSON, INC. (AV)

720 South Atherton Street, 16801
Telephone: 814-234-1500
Fax: 814-234-1549
Bellefonte, Pennsylvania Office: 124 North Allegheny Street.
Telephone: 814-355-5474.
Fax: 814-355-5340.

R. Paul Campbell (1908-1988)
Lewis Orvis Harvey (1912-1990)
John R. Miller, Jr.
Richard L. Campbell
John R. Miller, III
Terry James Williams
Tracey G. Benson
Scott C. Etter

Elizabeth A. DuPuis

OF COUNSEL

Robert K. Kistler

General Counsel for: Omega Bank; Glenn O. Hawbaker, Inc.; Canon Instrument Co.; Hanover Brands.
Local Counsel for: Tele-Media Corp.; Traveler Insurance Co.; The Medical Protective Co.; Corning Glass Works.
Solicitors: Borough of State College.

For full biographical listings, see the Martindale-Hubbell Law Directory

*TUNKHANNOCK,** Wyoming Co.

FARR, DAVIS & FITZE (AV)

7 Marion Street, P.O. Box H, 18657
Telephone: 570-836-3185
Facsimile: 570-836-4991

MEMBERS OF FIRM

John B. Farr (1907-1995)
James E. Davis
Judd B. Fitze

Representative Clients: Community Bank & Trust Co.; Proctor & Gamble Paper Products Co.
Title Agents for: Commonwealth Land Title Insurance Co.
References: Mellon Bank, Tunkhannock, PA Office; First Union Bank (Tunkhannock, PA Office); Community Bank and Trust Co.; Grange National Bank of Wyoming County.

For full biographical listings, see the Martindale-Hubbell Law Directory

WARRINGTON, Bucks Co.

HARRIS AND HARRIS, A PROFESSIONAL CORPORATION (AV)

1760 Bristol Road, P.O. Box 160, 18976
Telephone: 215-343-9000
Fax: 215-343-9012
Email: firmmail@harris-palaw.com

(See Next Column)

Arthur R. Harris
Stephen B. Harris
Gregory L. Sturn
David J. Sander

For full biographical listings, see the Martindale-Hubbell Law Directory

*WASHINGTON,** Washington Co.

PEACOCK KELLER ECKER & CROTHERS, LLP (AV)

East Beau Building, 70 East Beau Street, 15301
Telephone: 724-222-4520
Telefax: 724-222-3318 ABA/NET ABA 34517
Email: peacock@cobweb.net
Waynesburg, Pennsylvania Office: 102 East High Street.
Telephone: 724-627-8331.
Telefax: 724-627-8025.

MEMBERS OF FIRM

Roger J. Ecker
Mary Drake Korsmeyer
Douglas R. Nolin
Mary K. Pruss

ASSOCIATES

Susan T. Roberts
Susan Mondik Key

SENIOR COUNSEL

Charles C. Keller

Representative Clients: Consolidation Coal Co.; Washington School District; Monongahela Valley Hospital, Inc.; Nationwide Insurance Co.; Family Health Council, Inc.; Marianna & Scenery Hill Telephone Co.; Maternal & Family Health Services, Inc.; Pennsylvania Hospital Insurance Co.

For Complete List of Firm Personnel, See General Section

For full biographical listings, see the Martindale-Hubbell Law Directory

*WEST CHESTER,** Chester Co.

MACELREE, HARVEY, GALLAGHER, FEATHERMAN & SEBASTIAN, LTD. (AV)

17 West Miner Street, P.O. Box 660, 19381-0660
Telephone: 610-436-0100
Fax: 610-430-7885
Kennett Square, Pennsylvania Office: 211 E. State Street, P. O. Box 363.
Telephone 610-444-3180.
Fax: 610-444-3270.
Exton, Pennsylvania Office: 740 Springdale Drive, Suite 110.
Telephone: 610-524-7575.
Fax: 610-524-9857.

Randy L. Sebastian (1946-1997)
Joseph F. Harvey (1921-1985)

For full biographical listings, see the Martindale-Hubbell Law Directory

*WILKES-BARRE,** Luzerne Co.

CHARITON & SCHWAGER (AV)

138 South Main Street, P.O. Box 910, 18703-0910
Telephone: 570-824-3511
Fax: 570-824-3580
Email: palaw@charitonschwager.com *URL:* http://www.charitonschwager.com

Jerry B. Chariton
David E. Schwager

For full biographical listings, see the Martindale-Hubbell Law Directory

LARRY S. KEISER (AV)

138 South Main Street, P.O. Box 220, 18703-0220
Telephone: 570-822-2929
Fax: 570-822-2931
Email: keiser@tl.infi.net

For full biographical listings, see the Martindale-Hubbell Law Directory

*WILLIAMSPORT,** Lycoming Co.

MITCHELL, MITCHELL, GRAY & GALLAGHER, A PROFESSIONAL CORPORATION (AV)

10 West Third Street, 17701-6513
Telephone: 570-323-8404
Fax: 570-323-8585
Email: mmggpc@csrlink.net

Jacob Neafie Mitchell (1919-1996)
C. Edward S. Mitchell
Richard A. Gray
Robert A. Gallagher
Gary L. Weber
Bret J. Southard

Darryl R. Wishard

For full biographical listings, see the Martindale-Hubbell Law Directory

YOUNGWOOD, Westmoreland Co.

MILLSTEIN & KNUPP (AV)

Cherry Creek Commons Armbrust Road, P.O. Box 467, 15697-0467
Telephone: 724-837-3333
Fax: 724-837-8344

David J. Millstein

For Complete List of Firm Personnel, See General Section

For full biographical listings, see the Martindale-Hubbell Law Directory

RHODE ISLAND

*PROVIDENCE,** Providence Co.

BLISH & CAVANAGH (AV)

Commerce Center, 30 Exchange Terrace, 02903
Telephone: 401-831-8900
Telecopier: 401-751-7542
Email: BLISHCAV@AOL.COM

MEMBERS OF FIRM

Joseph V. Cavanagh, Jr.
William R. Landry
Edmund L. Alves, Jr.
Stephen J. Reid, Jr.
Karen A. Pelczarski
Scott T. Spear
Raymond A. Marcaccio

Michael W. Carroll
Staci L. Sawyer
Kristin Rodgers Sullivan

OF COUNSEL

John H. Blish

Representative Clients: Providence Journal Co.; Rhode Island Hospital Trust National Bank; Fleet Bank; Metropolitan Insurance Co.; Allstate Insurance Co.; Delta Dental of Rhode Island; Colony Communications; Providence Housing Authority; Textron; A.T. Cross.

For full biographical listings, see the Martindale-Hubbell Law Directory

CARROLL, KELLY & MURPHY (AV)

The Packet Building, 155 South Main Street, 02903
Telephone: 401-331-7272
Telecopier: 401-331-4404

MEMBERS OF FIRM

Joseph A. Kelly
C. Russell Bengtson
Ruth DiMeglio
William H. Jestings

ASSOCIATE

Shannon Gilheeney

Representative Clients: Hartford Accident and Indemnity Co.; Atlantic Mutual Insurance Co.; St. Paul's Insurance Co.; Joint Underwriter's Association; Professional Risk Management Services, Inc.; Norcal Mutual Insurance Company; Prudential Insurance Company of America; Guaranty Fund Management Services; First State Insurance Co.
Reference: Fleet National Bank.

For Complete List of Firm Personnel, See General Section

For full biographical listings, see the Martindale-Hubbell Law Directory

MARTIN K. DONOVAN (AV)

One Park Row, 02903-1235
Telephone: 401-831-2500
Facsimile: 401-751-7830

Reference: Fleet National Bank.

For full biographical listings, see the Martindale-Hubbell Law Directory

EDWARDS & ANGELL, LLP (AV)

A Partnership including Professional Corporations
2800 BankBoston Plaza, 02903
Telephone: 401-274-9200
Telecopier: 401-276-6611
Cable Address: "Edwangle Providence"
Telex: 952001 "E A PVD"
Email: postmaster@ealaw.com *URL:* http://www.ealaw.com
Boston, Massachusetts Office: 101 Federal Street, 02110-1800.
Telephone: 617-439-4444.
Telecopier: 617-439-4170.
New York, New York Office: 750 Lexington Avenue, 10022-1200.
Telephone: 212-308-4411.
Telecopier: 212-308-4844.
Palm Beach, Florida Office: 250 Royal Palm Way, Suite 300, 33480-4356.
Telephone: 561-833-7700.
Telecopier: 561-655-8719.

(See Next Column)

Short Hills, New Jersey Office: 51 John F. Kennedy Parkway, 07078.
Telephone: 973-376-7700.
Telecopier: 973-376-3380.
Hartford, Connecticut Office: 90 State House Square, 06103-2715.
Telephone: 860-525-5065.
Telecopier: 860-527-4198.
Newport, Rhode Island Office: 130 Bellevue Avenue, 02840.
Telephone: 401-849-7800.
Telecopier: 401-849-7887.

MEMBERS OF FIRM

Susan S. Egan (Not admitted in RI; Resident New York, New York Office)
Mark W. Freel
Ira G. Greenberg (Resident, New York, New York Office)
John A. Houlihan (Resident Boston, Massachusetts Office)
Philip D. O'Neill, Jr. (Resident Boston, Massachusetts Office)
Alfred R. Paliani (Not admitted in RI; New York, New York and Newark, New Jersey Offices)
Mark A. Pogue
Stephen M. Prignano
William P. Robinson III
Deming E. Sherman
Patricia A. Sullivan
Gary A. Woodfield (Not admitted in RI; Resident, Palm Beach, Florida Office)

OF COUNSEL

Richard M. Borod
Stephen A. Fanning (Retired)

For Complete List of Firm Personnel, See General Section

For full biographical listings, see the Martindale-Hubbell Law Directory

HANSON, CURRAN, PARKS & WHITMAN (AV)

146 Westminster Street, 02903-2218
Telephone: 401-421-2154
Telecopier: 401-521-7040
URL: http://www.hcpw.com

Kirk Hanson (1948-1991)

MEMBERS OF FIRM

A. Lauriston Parks
David P. Whitman
Michael T. F. Wallor
Dennis J. McCarten
James T. Murphy
Seth E. Bowerman
Thomas R. Bender
Mark W. Dana

ASSOCIATES

Richard H. Burrows
Christopher J. Zangari (Resident)
Wendy J. Taylor

OF COUNSEL

William A. Curran

General Counsel for: Medical Malpractice Joint Underwriting Association of Rhode Island.
Rhode Island Counsel for: Amica Mutual Insurance Co.; CIGNA; St. Paul Insurance Cos.; Occidental Life Insurance Co.; Exchange Mutual Insurance Co.; Aetna Casualty & Surety Co.

For full biographical listings, see the Martindale-Hubbell Law Directory

HIGGINS, CAVANAGH & COONEY (AV)

The Hay Building, Fourth Floor, 123 Dyer Street, 02903
Telephone: 401-272-3500; 800-274-5299
Telecopier: 401-273-8780

James H. Higgins, Jr. (1952-1975)
Joseph V. Cavanagh (1952-1985)
John P. Cooney, Jr. (1960-1981)
Kenneth P. Borden
Gerald C. DeMaria
John T. Walsh, Jr.
Charles A. Hambly, Jr.
Stephen B. Lang
Lawrence P. McCarthy, III
James A. Ruggieri
Michael D. Lynch
James T. Hornstein

ASSOCIATES

John F. Kelleher
Rajaram Suryanarayan
Vivian B. Dogan
Patrick B. Landers
Paul S. Callaghan
Susan Pepin Fay
Peter E. Garvey
Amy C. Vignali
Thomas F. DeVincke

For full biographical listings, see the Martindale-Hubbell Law Directory

HODOSH, SPINELLA & ANGELONE (AV)

128 Dorrance Street, Shakespeare Hall, Suite 450, P.O. Box 1516, 02901-1516
Telephone: 401-274-0200
Fax: 401-274-7538

Thomas C. Angelone

Reference: Fleet National Bank.

For full biographical listings, see the Martindale-Hubbell Law Directory

Providence—Continued

KIERNAN, PLUNKETT & REDIHAN (AV)

The Remington Building, 91 Friendship Street, 02903
Telephone: 401-831-2900
Fax: 401-331-7123

MEMBERS OF FIRM

Leonard A. Kiernan, Jr.
Thomas C. Plunkett
Charles N. Redihan, Jr.
Bernard P. Healy

ASSOCIATES

Michael R. Calise
Michael S. Kiernan
Robert D. Valvo

For full biographical listings, see the Martindale-Hubbell Law Directory

MEDEIROS + SANFORD INC. (AV)

One Turks Head Place, Suite 700, 02903-2215
Telephone: 401-831-0700
Fax: 401-274-2752 or 401-861-7249

Matthew F. Medeiros
Paul M. Sanford
Stacey P. Nakasian

Jane E. Brockmann

For full biographical listings, see the Martindale-Hubbell Law Directory

WILLIAM T. MURPHY LAW OFFICES, INC. (AV)

The Calart Tower, 400 Reservoir Avenue, Suite 3L, 02907
Telephone: 401-461-7740
Telecopier: 401-461-7753

William T. Murphy

Charles A. Pisaturo, Jr.
Steven T. Hayes

Reference: Citizens Bank.

For full biographical listings, see the Martindale-Hubbell Law Directory

ROBERT D. PARRILLO (AV)

128 Dorrance Street Suite 450, P.O. Box 1516, 02901-1516
Telephone: 401-273-3373
Fax: 401-274-7538
Email: RDParrillo@aol.com

For full biographical listings, see the Martindale-Hubbell Law Directory

VETTER & WHITE, INCORPORATED (AV)

20 Washington Place, 02903
Telephone: 401-421-3060
Telecopier: 401-272-6803
Email: vetlit@aol.com

Benjamin V. White, III
Gordon P. Cleary
Howard A. Merten, Jr.
Brooks R. Magratten

OF COUNSEL

George Vetter

Kimberly A. Simpson
Michael W. Long

For full biographical listings, see the Martindale-Hubbell Law Directory

WARWICK, Kent Co.

KIRSHENBAUM LAW ASSOCIATES (AV)

67 Jefferson Boulevard, 02888-1053
Telephone: 401-467-5300
Fax: 401-461-4464

MEMBERS OF FIRM

Allen M. Kirshenbaum
Carolyn R. Barone

Lauri Medwin Fine
Evan M. Kirshenbaum

For full biographical listings, see the Martindale-Hubbell Law Directory

SOUTH CAROLINA

*AIKEN,** Aiken Co.

ROBERT L. BUCHANAN, JR. (AV)

212 Newberry Street, N.W., P.O. Box 463, 29802-0463
Telephone: 803-649-2586
Telefax: 803-649-1392
Email: buchananlawpa@scescape.net

(See Next Column)

OF COUNSEL

Robert E. Johnson

For full biographical listings, see the Martindale-Hubbell Law Directory

*CAMDEN,** Kershaw Co.

SAVAGE, ROYALL AND SHEHEEN, L.L.P. (AV)

1111 Church Street, P.O. Drawer 10, 29020
Telephone: 803-432-4391
Telefax: 803-425-4816

MEMBERS OF FIRM

Edward M. Royall
Robert J. Sheheen
Moultrie B. Burns, Jr.
Dana A. Morris
William David Kelly, III
William B. Cox, Jr.
Vincent Austin Sheheen

Representative Clients: Nations Bank NBSC; First Palmetto Bank; Farmers Bureau Insurance Cos.; Georgia Pacific Corp.; Carolina Power & Light Co.; Cassatt Water Co.; Bowaters Southern Paper Corp.; Kershaw County Medical Center.
Approved Attorneys for: Stewart Title Insurance; Lawyers Title.

For full biographical listings, see the Martindale-Hubbell Law Directory

*CHARLESTON,** Charleston Co.

BARNWELL WHALEY PATTERSON & HELMS, LLC (AV)

134 Meeting Street, Suite 300, P.O. Drawer H, 29402
Telephone: 843-577-7700
Telecopier: 843-577-7708
Email: bwph@barnwell-whaley.com *URL:* http://barnwell-whaley.com

MEMBERS OF FIRM

Robert A. Patterson
William C. Helms, III
M. Dawes Cooke, Jr.
Bruce E. Miller
B. C. Killough
Matthew H. Henrikson
Frank E. Grimball
James E. Reeves

ASSOCIATES

J. Matthew Dillon
James H. Elliott, Jr.
Lucinda Gardner Wichmann
Deborah C. Lacombe (Not admitted in SC)
William E. McIntosh
Wendy Johnson Keefer

SPECIAL COUNSEL

J. Gail Rahn

Representative Clients: General Motors; The Citadel; Carolina Shipping Co.; Design Professionals Ins. Co.; Liberty Mutual Insurance Co.; Royal Insurance Co.; CareAlliance Health Services; General Accident Insurance Co.; U.S. Mineral Products Co.

For full biographical listings, see the Martindale-Hubbell Law Directory

BARR, UNGER AND MCINTOSH, L.L.C. (AV)

11 Broad Street, P.O. Box 1037, 29401
Telephone: 843-577-5083
Fax: 843-723-9039
Walterboro, South Carolina Office: 111A East Washington Street, 29488-3915.
Telephone: 843-549-9406.
Fax: 843-549-1058.
Edisto Island, South Carolina Office: 806 Oyster Park, 29438.
Telephone: 843-869-2389.
Fax: 843-869-0110.

MEMBERS OF FIRM

Capers G. Barr, III
H. Wayne Unger, Jr.
William S. Barr
H. Thomas McIntosh, Jr.
Capers G. Barr, IV

Adam E. Barr

Approved Attorneys for: Lawyers Title Insurance Corp.; Old Republic National Title Insurance Company.
References: NationsBank; Bank of South Carolina.

For full biographical listings, see the Martindale-Hubbell Law Directory

BUIST, MOORE, SMYTHE & MCGEE, P.A. (AV)

Successors to Buist, Buist, Smythe and Smythe and Moore, Mouzon and McGee.
Five Exchange Street, P.O. Box 999, 29402
Telephone: 843-722-3400
Cable Address: "Conferees"
Telex: 57-6488
Telecopier: 843-723-7398
Email: bmsm@lawyer-sc.com *URL:* http://www.lawyer-sc.com

(See Next Column)

BUIST, MOORE, SMYTHE & MCGEE P.A., *Charleston—Continued*

Benjamin Allston Moore, Jr.
Joseph H. McGee
Gordon D. Schreck
Henry B. Smythe, Jr.
Henry E. Grimball
David B. McCormack
C. Allen Gibson, Jr.
Morris A. Ellison
James D. Myrick
Douglas M. Muller
Elizabeth Henry Warner
David S. Yandle

Julius H. Hines
David S. Cox
Jonathan D. Crumly, Sr.
Dwayne M. Green
Cynthia M. Spieth
Margaret O. Dullanty
Gregory Horton

OF COUNSEL

David M. Collins
Charles J. Baker, III

Representative Clients: Metropolitan Life Insurance Co.; E.I. duPont De Nemours & Co.; AIG Aviation, Inc.; ALCOA; Beers Construction Co.; Barton Malow Co.; Pizzagalli Construction; Bridgestone/Firestone, Inc.; Beazer East, Inc.; BP Amoco; CIGNA.

For Complete List of Firm Personnel, See General Section

For full biographical listings, see the Martindale-Hubbell Law Directory

CLAWSON & STAUBES, L.L.C. (AV)

304 Meeting Street, 29401-1544
Telephone: 843-577-2026
Fax: 843-720-0822
Charlotte, North Carolina Office: 756 Tyvola Road, Suite 101, 29217.
Telephone: 704-522-7733.
Facsimile: 704-522-9033.

Robert G. Clawson, Jr.
Christopher B. Staubes, Jr.
Samuel R. Clawson
John L. McDonald, Jr.
J. Ronald Jones, Jr. (Also at Charlotte, N.C. Office)
Matthew J. Story
Albert A. Lacour, III
James A. Atkins
Thomas H. Milligan

Timothy A. Domin
Katherine W. Simons
David C. Cleveland
Christopher B. Staubes, III
William D. Wilson, Jr
Patrick T. Morrissey
Margaret H. McDonald

Representative Clients: Allstate Insurance Co.; Bituminous Insurance Co.; City of Charleston; Greenpoint Credit Corp.; First Federal Savings & Loan Association of Charleston; Maryland Casualty Co.; NationsBank; Nationwide Mutual Insurance Co.; State Farm Mutual Insurance Cos.

For full biographical listings, see the Martindale-Hubbell Law Directory

HALIO & HALIO (AV)

13 North Adgers Wharf, P.O. Box 747, 29402-0747
Telephone: 803-577-5200
Fax: 803-577-7468

MEMBERS OF FIRM

Elliott T. Halio
Andrew S. Halio

Approved Attorneys for: Lawyers Title Insurance Corp.; Chicago Title Insurance Co.; NationsBank; Joint Underwriters Assn.; South Carolina Insurance Reserve Fund; The Doctors Co.; South Carolina Farm Bureau; Cargill, Inc.

For full biographical listings, see the Martindale-Hubbell Law Directory

HAYNSWORTH, MARION, MCKAY & GUÉRARD, L.L.P. (AV)

134 Meeting Street, P.O. Box 1119, 29402
Telephone: 843-722-7606
Facsimile: 843-724-8016
Columbia, South Carolina Office: Suite 2400 Affinity Building, 1201 Main Street, P.O. Drawer 7157, 29202.
Telephone: 803-765-1818. Facsimile 803-765-2399.
Greenville, South Carolina Office: 75 Beattie Place, Eleventh Floor, P.O. Box 2048, 29602.
Telephone: 864-240-3200.
Facsimile: 864-240-3300.

MEMBERS OF FIRM

William C. Cleveland
James J. Hinchey, Jr.
Thomas S. White
James E. Lady

Counsel for: Baker Hospital; Healthsource of South Carolina; Allstate Insurance Co.; CSX Corporation; Lloyd's Underwriters; Coward-Hund Construction Co.; South Carolina Public Service Authority; City of Hanahan.

For Complete List of Firm Personnel, See General Section

For full biographical listings, see the Martindale-Hubbell Law Directory

HOOD LAW FIRM (AV)

172 Meeting Street, P.O. Box 1508, 29402
Telephone: 843-577-4435
Fax: 843-722-1630
Email: hlf@hoodlaw.com *URL:* http://www.hoodlaw.com

(See Next Column)

MEMBERS OF FIRM

Robert H. Hood
Louis P. Herns
G. Mark Phillips
Carl Everette Pierce, II
John K. Blincow, Jr.
James G. Kennedy
Barbara Wynne Showers
Joseph C. Wilson, IV
James Dowell Gandy, III

Dixon F. Pearce, II
Hugh Willcox Buyck
Allan Poe Sloan, III
Mary Agnes Hood Craig
Allison Snead Patrick
P. Gunnar Nistad
Robert H. Hood, Jr.
William Mullins McLeod, Jr.

For full biographical listings, see the Martindale-Hubbell Law Directory

GEDNEY M. HOWE, III, P.A. (AV)

8 Chalmers Street, P.O. Box 1034, 29402
Telephone: 843-722-8048
FAX: 843-722-2140

Gedney M. Howe, Jr. (1914-1981)
Gedney M. Howe, III
Alvin J. Hammer

Caroline M.W. Dillon

For full biographical listings, see the Martindale-Hubbell Law Directory

OBERMAN & OBERMAN (AV)

38 Broad Street, 29401
Telephone: 843-577-7010
Fax: 843-722-7359

MEMBERS OF FIRM

Marvin I. Oberman
Harold A. Oberman

For full biographical listings, see the Martindale-Hubbell Law Directory

SINKLER & BOYD, P.A. (AV)

160 East Bay Street, P.O. Box 340, 29402-0340
Telephone: 843-722-3366
FAX: 843-722-2266
Email: firm@sinklerboyd.com *URL:* http://www.sinklerboyd.com
Columbia, South Carolina Office: Suite 1200 The Palmetto Center, 1426 Main Street, P.O. Box 11889.
Telephone: 803-779-3080.
FAX: 803-765-1243.
Greenville, South Carolina Office: 15 South Main Street, Insignia Financial Center on Main, Suite 500, P.O. Box 275.
Telephone: 864-467-1100.
FAX: 864-467-1521.

H. Simmons Tate, Jr. (Resident, Columbia Office)
William C. Boyd (Resident, Columbia Office)
Francis P. Mood (Resident, Columbia Office)
Bachman S. Smith III
Manton M. Grier (Resident, Columbia Office)
Thomas R. Gottshall (Resident, Columbia Office)
Hamilton Osborne, Jr. (Resident, Columbia Office)
Stephen E. Darling
John P. Linton
Harold E. Trask
Marvin D. Infinger
John C. Bruton, Jr. (Resident, Columbia Office)
Clarke W. DuBose (Resident, Columbia Office)
Terri Morrill Lynch
Robert Y. Knowlton (Resident, Columbia Office)
Thomas C. Hildebrand, Jr.
Robert W. Buffington (Resident, Columbia Office)
Bert Glenn Utsey III
Charles H. Gibbs, Jr.
John H. Tiller
Roy A. Howell III
Edward K. Pritchard III
John F. Emerson (Resident, Columbia Office)

Joseph D. Thompson, III
James L. Ward, Jr. (Resident, Columbia Office)

Representative Clients: Wachovia Bank, N.A.; South Carolina Electric & Gas Co.; AT&T; Westvaco Corp.; ITT Hartford; Pennsylvania National Mutual Casualty Insurance Co.; USF&G; Ohio Casualty Group; Kemper Insurance Group; Liberty Mutual Insurance Co.

For Complete List of Firm Personnel, See General Section

For full biographical listings, see the Martindale-Hubbell Law Directory

SLOTCHIVER & SLOTCHIVER, L.L.P. (AV)

44 State Street, 29401
Telephone: 803-577-6531
Facsimile: 803-577-0261
Email: slotchiver@charleston.net

MEMBERS OF FIRM

Irvin J. Slotchiver
Daniel S. Slotchiver
Stephen M. Slotchiver

For full biographical listings, see the Martindale-Hubbell Law Directory

Charleston—Continued

SOLOMON, BUDMAN, STRICKER & SCHWARTZ, L.L.P. (AV)

Parkshore Centre, 1 Poston Road, Suite 395, P.O. Box 30280, 29417-0280
Telephone: 843-763-1118
Telecopier: 843-763-7518

A. Bernard Solomon
Michael A. Stricker
Donald J. Budman
Lester S. Schwartz

Local Counsel for: Lawyers Title Insurance Corp.

For full biographical listings, see the Martindale-Hubbell Law Directory

URICCHIO, HOWE, KRELL, JACOBSON, TOPOREK & THEOS, P.A. (AV)

17 1/2 Broad Street, 29401
Telephone: 803-723-7491
1-800-899-1683
Fax: 803-577-4179
Mailing Address: P.O. Box 399, Charleston, S.C., 29402-0399
Email: uricchio@ix.netcom.com

Paul N. Uricchio, Jr.
Carl H. Jacobson
Arthur G. Howe
Alan David Toporek
Barry Krell
Jerry N. Theos
Gregory Daulton Keith

For full biographical listings, see the Martindale-Hubbell Law Directory

*COLUMBIA,** Richland Co.

JOSEPH C. COLEMAN (AV)

2312 Beltline Boulevard, Suite 3-B, 29204
Telephone: 803-787-3727
Fax: 803-787-6867

For full biographical listings, see the Martindale-Hubbell Law Directory

COLLINS & LACY, P.C. (AV)

1330 Lady Street, Suite 601, P.O. Box 12487, 29211
Telephone: 803-256-2660
Telefax: 803-771-4484
Email: TheFirm@CollinsandLacy.com *URL:* http://www.collinsandlacy.com

Joel W. Collins, Jr.
Arthur K. Aiken
Stanford E. Lacy
Eric G. Fosmire
Gray Thomas Culbreath
Ellen A. Mercer

Rebecca M. Monroy
Clayton B. McCullough
Joseph S. McCue
Peter H. Dworjanyn

LEGAL SUPPORT PERSONNEL

Joanne B. Moody

LEGAL ASSISTANTS

Jane L. Koon
Leslie Edenfield
Mary D. Malinaroli
M. Larry Nelson
Jeanne S. Volin
Victoria Allen

For full biographical listings, see the Martindale-Hubbell Law Directory

FINKEL & ALTMAN, L.L.C. (AV)

Suite 1800, 1201 Main Street, P.O. Box 1799, 29202
Telephone: 803-765-2935
Fax: 803-252-0786
Email: webmaster@finkellaw.com *URL:* http://www.finkellaw.com
Charleston, South Carolina Office: 12 Exchange Street, P.O. Box 225.
Telephone: 843-577-5460.
Fax: 843-577-5135.

Gerald M. Finkel
Harry L. Goldberg
Charles S. Altman (Resident, Charleston South Carolina Office)
Howard S. Sheftman
Richard R. Gleissner

Michael M. Shetterly

Representative Clients: First Union Mortgage Company; First Union National Bank; Banc One Mortgage Co.; Motorola Communications & Electronics Corp.; BB&T of South Carolina; Dow Chemical Company; Colonia Insurance Company.

For full biographical listings, see the Martindale-Hubbell Law Directory

GLENN MURPHY GRAY & STEPP, L.L.P. (AV)

B B & T Bank Building, Suite 390, 1901 Assembly Street, P.O. Box 1550, 29202-1550
Telephone: 803-765-1100
Telecopy: 803-765-0755

Terrell L. Glenn (1930-1993)

MEMBERS OF FIRM

Peter L. Murphy
Robert E. Stepp
Elizabeth Van Doren Gray
Elizabeth G. Howard

(See Next Column)

Robert C. Rhodes
Roland M. Franklin
Laura W. Robinson
C. Shawn Dryer

Reference: BB&T.

For full biographical listings, see the Martindale-Hubbell Law Directory

GOLDEN, TAYLOR & POTTERFIELD (AV)

A Law Partnership between a Professional Association & Attorneys
1712-1714 Main Street, 29201
Telephone: 803-779-3700
Telefax: 803-779-3422
Email: goldenlaw@worldnett.att.net

Harvey L. Golden
J. Michael Taylor
Ashlin Blanchard Potterfield

ASSOCIATE

Almand James Barron

For full biographical listings, see the Martindale-Hubbell Law Directory

HAYNSWORTH, MARION, MCKAY & GUÉRARD, L.L.P. (AV)

Suite 2400 Affinity Building, 1201 Main Street, P.O. Drawer 7157, 29202
Telephone: 803-765-1818
Facsimile: 803-765-2399
Greenville, South Carolina Office: 75 Beattie Place, Eleventh Floor, P.O. Box 2048, 29602.
Telephone: 864-240-3200.
Facsimile: 864-240-3300.
Charleston, South Carolina Office: 134 Meeting Street, P.O. Box 1119, 29402.
Telephone: 843-722-7606.
Facsimile: 843-724-8016.

MEMBERS OF FIRM

William P. Simpson
Steven Todd Moon
Stephen F. McKinney

ASSOCIATE

Gina L. Campano

OF COUNSEL

Julius W. McKay

Counsel for: St. Paul Insurance Group; Allstate Insurance Co.; Fluor-Daniel Corp.; South Carolina Jobs - Economic Development Authority; Anheuser Busch Company; CSX Transportation; Ernst & Young, LLP; E. I. DuPont de Nemours; Westinghouse Savannah River Co.; Wachovia Bank of South Carolina, N.A.

For Complete List of Firm Personnel, See General Section

For full biographical listings, see the Martindale-Hubbell Law Directory

KING & VERNON, P.A. (AV)

1426 Richland Street, P.O. Box 7667, 29202
Telephone: 803-779-3090
Fax: 803-779-3396
Email: TVernon@usit.net *URL:* http://www.usit.net/users/lawyer/

Kermit S. King
W. Thomas Vernon

For Complete List of Firm Personnel, See General Section

For full biographical listings, see the Martindale-Hubbell Law Directory

LEWIS, BABCOCK & HAWKINS, L.L.P. (AV)

1513 Hampton Street, P.O. Box 11208, 29211
Telephone: 803-771-8000
Telefax: 803-733-3534
Email: FIRM@LBHLAW.com

MEMBERS OF FIRM

A. Camden Lewis
James E. Knight, Jr.
Keith M. Babcock
Mark W. Hardee
Daryl G. Hawkins
Thomas A. Pendarvis
Mary Geiger Lewis
Amy A. Louthian
Ariail E. King

Representative Clients: Southern Bell Telephone and Telegraph Co.; University of South Carolina; Alliance of American Insurers; Wilbur Smith and Associates; Kingdom of Lesotho, Southern Africa.

For full biographical listings, see the Martindale-Hubbell Law Directory

MCANGUS, GOUDELOCK & COURIE, L.L.C. (AV)

1517 Hampton Street, P.O. Box 12519 Capitol Station, 29211-2519
Telephone: 803-779-2300
Telecopier: 803-748-0526
Email: mgc@mgclaw.com *URL:* http://www.mgclaw.com
Charlotte, North Carolina Office: 6101 Carnegie Boulevard, Suite 510. P.O. Box 30307, 28230.
Telephone: 704-940-2300.
Telecopier: 704-643-2376.

(See Next Column)

McANGUS, GOUDELOCK & COURIE L.L.C., *Columbia—Continued*

MEMBERS OF FIRM

W. Hugh McAngus
J. Russell Goudelock, II
James R. Courie
Yolanda C. Courie
Scott B. Garrett
Sterling G. Davies

ASSOCIATES

George D. Gallagher
Anne Marie Partin
A. Mundi Moss
Richard Daniel Addison
Louise M. Boylston
Sean A. Scoopmire
G. Thomas Chase

For full biographical listings, see the Martindale-Hubbell Law Directory

McCUTCHEN, BLANTON, RHODES & JOHNSON, L.L.P. (AV)

1414 Lady Street, P.O. Drawer 11209, 29211
Telephone: 803-799-9791
Telecopier: 803-253-6084
Email: Firm1414@aol.com
Winnsboro, South Carolina Office: 120 West Washington Street, 29180.
Telephone: 803-635-6884.

MEMBERS OF FIRM

Thomas E. McCutchen
Jeter E. Rhodes, Jr.
T. English McCutchen, III
Pope D. Johnson, III
William R. Taylor
Evans Taylor Barnette
G. D. Morgan, Jr.
John C. Bradley, Jr.
Creighton B. Coleman
Ruskin C. Foster
William E. Hopkins, Jr.

ASSOCIATE

Anthony W. Livoti

OF COUNSEL

Hoover C. Blanton

Representative Clients: Liberty Mutual Insurance Co.; Sears; Firemen's Fund; Consolidated Systems, Inc.; State Farm Fire and Casualty Co.; Thurston Motor Lines; Southeastern Freight Lines; Joint Underwriters Assoc.; Allstate; National Indemnity Co.

For full biographical listings, see the Martindale-Hubbell Law Directory

McKAY & McKAY, P.A. (AV)

1325 Laurel Street, P.O. Box 7217, 29202
Telephone: 803-256-4645
FAX: 803-765-1839

Douglas McKay, Jr.
Julius W. McKay, II

Representative Clients: Americlaim Adjustment Corp.; Amoco Oil Co.; Blue Cross & Blue Shield of South Carolina; Britanco Underwriters, Inc.; Browning-Ferris Industries, Inc.; Homestead Insurance Co.; Lincoln National Life Insurance Co.; Pennsylvania Manufacturers' Association Insurance Co. (PMA); Schneider National Carriers; South Carolina Division of General Services-Insurance Reserve Fund (IRF).

For Complete List of Firm Personnel, See General Section

For full biographical listings, see the Martindale-Hubbell Law Directory

ERNEST J. NAUFUL, JR., P.C. (AV)

1321 Lady Street Suite 670, P.O. Box 11866, 29211
Telephone: 803-256-4045
Facsimile: 803-256-7044
Email: nauful@aol.com

Ernest J. Nauful, Jr.

For full biographical listings, see the Martindale-Hubbell Law Directory

POPE & RODGERS (AV)

Suite 615, 1330 Lady Street, P.O. Box 5907, 29250
Telephone: 803-254-0700
Fax: 803-254-0776

MEMBERS OF FIRM

William L. Pope
Paul B. Rodgers, III

For full biographical listings, see the Martindale-Hubbell Law Directory

QUINN, PATTERSON & WILLARD (AV)

2019 Park Street, P.O. Box 73, 29202
Telephone: 803-779-6365
Telefax: 803-779-6372
Email: qpw@bellsouth.net

MEMBERS OF FIRM

Michael H. Quinn
Grady L. Patterson, III
Theodore DuBose Willard, Jr.

Approved Attorneys for: Lawyers Title Insurance Corp.

For full biographical listings, see the Martindale-Hubbell Law Directory

RICHARDSON, PLOWDEN, CARPENTER & ROBINSON, P.A. (AV)

1600 Marion Street, P.O. Drawer 7788, 29202
Telephone: 803-771-4400
Telecopy: 803-779-0016
Email: atty@rpcrlaw.com *URL:* http://www.rpcrlaw.com
Myrtle Beach, South Carolina Office: 2103 B Farlow Street, P.O. Box 3646, 29578.
Telephone: 843-448-1008.
FAX: 843-448-1533.

Charles E. Carpenter, Jr.
Frank E. Robinson, II
George C. Beighley
Frederick A. Crawford
Francis M. Mack
Franklin Jennings Smith, Jr.
Leslie A. Cotter, Jr.
Douglas C. Baxter
Nina Reid Mack
S. Nelson Weston Jr.
Mary Sowell League

Marian Williams Scalise
William C. McDow
Georgia Anna Mitchell
David C. Slough
Stephen C. Lenker, Jr.
David A. Anderson
S. Elizabeth Brosnan

OF COUNSEL

Donald V. Richardson, III
Michael A. Pulliam

Representative Clients: Insurance: CNA Insurance Co.; The Hartford; Kemper Insurance Co.; Pennsylvania National Mutual Casualty Insurance Co.; Wausau Insurance Cos. Construction: S.C. Department of Public Transportation; Northlake Construction Co.

For Complete List of Firm Personnel, See General Section

For full biographical listings, see the Martindale-Hubbell Law Directory

SINKLER & BOYD, P.A. (AV)

Suite 1200 The Palmetto Center, 1426 Main Street, P.O. Box 11889, 29211-1889
Telephone: 803-779-3080
FAX: 803-765-1243
Email: firm@sinklerboyd.com *URL:* http://www.sinklerboyd.com
Charleston, South Carolina Office: 160 East Bay Street, P.O. Box 340.
Telephone: 843-722-3366.
FAX: 843-722-2266.
Greenville, South Carolina Office: 15 South Main Street, Insignia Financial Center on Main, Suite 500, P.O. Box 275.
Telephone: 864-467-1100.
FAX: 864-467-1521.

H. Simmons Tate, Jr.
William C. Boyd
Francis P. Mood
Bachman S. Smith III (Resident, Charleston Office)
Manton M. Grier
Thomas R. Gottshall
Hamilton Osborne, Jr.
Stephen E. Darling (Resident, Charleston Office)
John P. Linton (Resident, Charleston Office)
Harold E. Trask (Resident, Charleston Office)
Marvin D. Infinger (Resident, Charleston Office)
John C. Bruton, Jr.
Clarke W. DuBose
Terri Morrill Lynch (Resident, Charleston Office)
Robert Y. Knowlton
Thomas C. Hildebrand, Jr. (Resident, Charleston Office)
Robert W. Buffington
Bert Glenn Utsey III (Resident, Charleston Office)
Charles H. Gibbs, Jr. (Resident, Charleston Office)
John H. Tiller (Resident, Charleston Office)
Roy A. Howell III (Resident, Charleston Office)
Edward K. Pritchard, III (Resident, Charleston Office)
John F. Emerson

Joseph D. Thompson, III (Resident, Charleston Office)
James L. Ward, Jr.

Representative Clients: Wachovia Bank, N.A.; South Carolina Electric & Gas Co.; The Upjohn Co.; Chrysler Financial Corp.; Exxon Corporation, USA; ; Prudential Bache Securities, Inc.; AT&T; Westvaco Corp.; ITT Hartford.

For Complete List of Firm Personnel, See General Section

For full biographical listings, see the Martindale-Hubbell Law Directory

TOMPKINS AND McMASTER (AV)

Palmetto Building, Fourth Floor, 1400 Main Street, P.O. Box 7337, 29202
Telephone: 803-799-4499
Telefax: 803-252-2240

MEMBERS OF FIRM

Frank G. Tompkins (1874-1956)
Frank G. Tompkins, Jr. (1908-1973)
Elizabeth Eldridge (1895-1976)
John Gregg McMaster
Henry Dargan McMaster
George Hunter McMaster
Frank Barnwell McMaster

ASSOCIATE

Bryan P. Stirling
Karl S. Bowers

OF COUNSEL

Joseph D. McMaster

(See Next Column)

TOMPKINS AND MCMASTER—*Continued*

LEGAL SUPPORT PERSONNEL

Martin J. McClellan (Office Manager)

For full biographical listings, see the Martindale-Hubbell Law Directory

TURNER, PADGET, GRAHAM & LANEY, P.A. (AV)

Seventeenth Floor, 1901 Main Street, P.O. Box 1473, 29202
Telephone: 803-254-2200
Telecopy: 803-799-3957
Florence, South Carolina Office: Fourth Floor, 1831 West Evans Street, P.O. Box 5478, 29502.
Telephone: 843-662-9008.
Fax: 843-667-0828.
Charleston, South Carolina Office: 21 Broad Street, 1st Floor, P.O. Box 836, 29402.
Telephone: 843-723-1622.
Fax: 843-577-3369.

Ronald E. Boston
W. Duvall Spruill
Charles E. Hill
Thomas C. Salane
Danny C. Crowe
R. Wayne Byrd (Resident, Florence, SC, Office)
John S. Wilkerson, III (Resident, Florence, SC, Office)
Steven W. Ouzts
John E. Cuttino
Arthur E. Justice, Jr. (Resident, Florence, SC, Office)
Edward W. Laney, IV
Elbert S. Dorn
Hugh M. Claytor (Resident, Florence, SC, Office)
Vernon F. Dunbar
J. Kenneth Carter, Jr.
O. Carlisle Edwards, Jr.
Richard L. Hinson (Resident, Florence, SC, Office)
Jeffrey L. Payne (Resident, Florence, SC, Office)
Wilson S. Sheldon (Resident, Florence, SC, Office)
Michael S. Hopewell (Resident, Florence, SC, Office)
Teresa A. Arnold

OF COUNSEL

Michael S. Church
Laura Chandler Rublee (Resident, Florence, SC, Office)

David W. Keller, Jr. (Resident, Florence, SC Office)
Jessica C. Moe (Resident, Charleston, SC, Office)
Curtis L. Ott
Michael C. Abbott (Resident, Florence, SC, Office)
David S. Cobb (Resident, Charleston, SC, Office)
Donnell G. Jennings
D. Andrew Williams
William C. Barnes, Jr. (Resident, Florence, SC, Office)
Cynthia C. Dooley
Richard C. Burke (Resident, Florence, SC, Office)
Steven R. LeBlanc
Tiffni Drawdy Shealy (Resident, Florence, SC, Office)
Mark B. Tinsley
Patrick W. Carr (Resident, Florence, SC, Office)
James David Smith, Jr. (Resident, Florence, SC, Office)

For Complete List of Firm Personnel, See General Section

For full biographical listings, see the Martindale-Hubbell Law Directory

WOODWARD COTHRAN & HERNDON (AV)

1200 Main Street, Suite 600, 29201
Telephone: 803-799-9772
Fax: 803-799-3256
Mailing Address: P.O. Box 12399, Columbia, South Carolina, 29211
Email: wch1@usit.net

OF COUNSEL

Edward M. Woodward, Sr.

General Counsel for: The Columbia College; Sandhills Bank; Heater Utilities.

For full biographical listings, see the Martindale-Hubbell Law Directory

*CONWAY,** Horry Co.

MCCUTCHEON, MCCUTCHEON & BAXTER, P.A. (AV)

McCutcheon Building, 208 Elm Street, P.O. Box 1003, 29528
Telephone: 843-248-7225
Telecopier: 843-248-3568
Email: mmb4@gte.net

John Betts McCutcheon (1915-1997)
John Betts McCutcheon, Jr.
Mary Ruth M. Baxter

Lisa A. Thomas
Arrigo P. Carotti

Representative Clients: State of South Carolina, Division of General Services, Insurance Reserve Fund; South Carolina Medical Malpractice Joint Underwriters Assn.; Virginia Professional Underwriters, Inc.; Companion Property and Casualty Co.; Blue Cross and Blue Shield of South Carolina, Inc.; National Indemnity Co.; American Continental Insurance Co.; The Travelers Insurance Group.

For full biographical listings, see the Martindale-Hubbell Law Directory

THE THOMPSON LAW FIRM, P.A. (AV)

1318 Third Avenue, P.O. Box 1533, 29528
Telephone: 843-248-5741
Fax: 843-248-5112
Myrtle Beach, South Carolina Office: 1314 Professional Drive, P.O. Box 1290.
Telephone: 843-692-2628.
Fax: 843-692-0918.

John C. Thompson
John P. Henry
Linda Weeks Gangi
Emma Ruth Brittain
Lynn Gatlin Stevens
Philip C. Thompson
Catherine M. Hedgepath

Representative Clients: NationsBank; Burroughs & Chapin Co., Inc.; Canal Industries, Inc.; State Farm Mutual Automobile Insurance Co.; State Farm Fire and Casualty Insurance Co.; Horry County; Nationwide Insurance Co.; United Carolina Bank; First Union National Bank.
Reference: NationsBank.

For full biographical listings, see the Martindale-Hubbell Law Directory

*GREENVILLE,** Greenville Co.

COVINGTON, PATRICK, HAGINS, STERN & LEWIS, P.A. (AV)

211 Pettigru Street, 29601
Telephone: 864-242-9000
Fax: 864-233-9777
Mailing Address: P.O. Box 2343, 29602
Email: cphsl@mindspring.com

John A. Hagins, Jr.
Douglas F. Patrick
Eugene C. Covington, Jr.
T. S. Stern, Jr.
Stephen R. H. Lewis
Thomas E. Dudley, III

Karen W. Creech

For full biographical listings, see the Martindale-Hubbell Law Directory

GRANT, LEATHERWOOD & PITTS, P.A. (AV)

Palmetto Bank Building, 306 East North Street, 2nd Floor, P.O. Box 10367, 29603-0367
Telephone: 864-242-2300
Facsimile: 864-242-2280
Email: attorneys@grantleatherwood.com

William M. Grant, Jr.
Judith A. Leatherwood
Michael S. Pitts

Langdon Cheves, III
Paul C. Rathke

LEGAL SUPPORT PERSONNEL

Jackie L. Carver (Litigation Paralegal)
Sarah A. Carmichael (Paralegal)
Mary A. Fuller (Paralegal)

For full biographical listings, see the Martindale-Hubbell Law Directory

HAYNSWORTH, MARION, MCKAY & GUÉRARD, L.L.P. (AV)

75 Beattie Place, Eleventh Floor, P.O. Box 2048, 29602
Telephone: 864-240-3200
Facsimile: 864-240-3300
Columbia, South Carolina Office: Suite 2400 Affinity Building, 1201 Main Street, P.O. Drawer 7157, 29202
Telephone: 803-765-1818.
Facsimile: 803-765-2399.
Charleston, South Carolina Office: 134 Meeting Street, P.O. Box 1119, 29402.
Telephone: 843-722-7606.
Facsimile: 843-724-8016.

MEMBERS OF FIRM

G. Dewey Oxner, Jr.
Jesse C. Belcher
James B. Pressly, Jr.
H. Donald Sellers
Andrew J. White, Jr.
Ellis M. Johnston, II
Thomas H. Coker, Jr.
W. Francis Marion, Jr.
John B. McLeod
Bryan Francis Hickey
Edwin Brown Parkinson, Jr.
H. Sam Mabry, III
F. Matlock Elliott
Amy Miller Snyder
Eric Kelly Englebardt
J. Derrick Quattlebaum
Sarah M. (Sally) Purnell

ASSOCIATES

Boyd B. Nicholson, Jr.
Matthew P. Utecht
William David Conner
Sherry L. Boswell
J. Ben Alexander

OF COUNSEL

Julius W. McKay
O. G. Calhoun, Jr.

Representative Clients: Wausau Insurance Co.; Prudential Property & Casualty; The Prudential Insurance Company of America; Fluor-Daniel, Inc.; Ernst & Young, L.L.P.; Owens-Corning Fiberglass Company; Fireman's Fund Insurance Company; Allstate Insurance Company.

For Complete List of Firm Personnel, See General Section

For full biographical listings, see the Martindale-Hubbell Law Directory

Greenville—Continued

LEATHERWOOD WALKER TODD & MANN, P.C. (AV)

100 East Coffee Street, P.O. Box 87, 29602
Telephone: 864-242-6440
FAX: 864-240-2477
Email: leatherwood@lwtm.com *URL:* http://www.lwtm.com
Spartanburg, South Carolina Office: 1451 East Main Street, P.O. Box 3188.
Telephone: 864-582-4365.
Telefax: 864-583-8961.

John E. Johnston
Harvey G. Sanders, Jr.
O. Doyle Martin
Joseph E. Major
Duke K. McCall, Jr.
J. Richard Kelly
Jack H. Tedards, Jr.
F. Marion Hughes
Michael J. Giese
Bradford Neal Martin
Natalma M. McKnew
Steven E. Farrar
Nancy Hyder Robinson
Samuel Wright Outten
Eugene C. McCall, Jr.
James L. Rogers, Jr.
Robert D. Moseley, Jr.
James T. Hewitt

Kurt M. Rozelsky
John Patrick Riordan
Peter A. Rutledge

COUNSEL

Fletcher C. Mann
James H. Watson
Tara H. Snyder
J. Brantley Phillips, Jr.

Counsel for: John D. Hollingsworth on Wheels, Inc.; Platt Saco Lowell Corp.; Canal Insurance Co.; Suitt Construction Co.
Representative Clients: NationsBank; Springs Industries, Inc.; American Federal Bank, F.S.B.; United States Fidelity & Guaranty Co.; Allstate Insurance Co.; Stevens Aviation Inc.

For Complete List of Firm Personnel, See General Section

For full biographical listings, see the Martindale-Hubbell Law Directory

LOVE, THORNTON, ARNOLD & THOMASON, P.A. (AV)

410 East Washington Street, P.O. Box 10045, 29603
Telephone: 864-242-6360
Telefax: 864-271-7972
Email: lovelaw@globalvision.net *URL:* http://www.ltatlaw.com
Greer, South Carolina Office: 1115 West Poinsett Street, P.O. Box 449, 29652-0449.
Telephone: 864-879-0144.
Telefax: 864-879-0149.

Belton O. Thomason, Jr. (1926-1993)
William M. Hagood, III
Theron G. Cochran
Mason A. Goldsmith
Carroll H. Roe, Jr.
Jennings L. Graves, Jr.
Jack D. Griffeth
William A. Coates
David L. Moore, Jr.
James H. Cassidy
V. Clark Price
James A. Blair, III

James Andrew Smith
Amy G. Richmond
Robert Scott Boatwright

Counsel for: Selective Insurance Co.; Risk Enterprise Management (Formerly The Home Insurance Co.); Kemper Insurance Group; Government Employees Insurance Co.; Owens-Corning; American Federal Bank, F.S.B.; Chrysler Corp.; K-Mart Corp.

For Complete List of Firm Personnel, See General Section

For full biographical listings, see the Martindale-Hubbell Law Directory

PARHAM & SMITH, L.L.C. (AV)

Smith Barney Building-Second Floor, 501 River Street, P.O. Box 2800, 29601
Telephone: 864-242-9008
1-800-849-7777
Fax: 864-271-6155
Mailing Address: P.O. Box 2800, Greenville, SC, 29602
Email: mparham@parhamlaw.com *URL:* http://www.lawyers.com/parham&smithlaw

MEMBERS OF FIRM

Michael Parham
Barney O. Smith, Jr. (1952-1996)

Steven Blakely Smith

For full biographical listings, see the Martindale-Hubbell Law Directory

WILKINS & MADDEN, P.A. (AV)

408 East North Street, 29601-3042
Telephone: 864-232-5629
Fax: 864-233-6943

David H. Wilkins
Timothy E. Madden

(See Next Column)

Rochelle Y. Williamson
Joseph M. Ramseur, Jr.

References: Carolina First Bank; The Palmetto Bank.

For full biographical listings, see the Martindale-Hubbell Law Directory

*GREENWOOD,** Greenwood Co.

BURNS, MCDONALD, BRADFORD, PATRICK & TINSLEY, L.L.P. (AV)

414 Main Street, P.O. Box 1547, 29648
Telephone: 864-229-2511
Fax: 864-229-5327
Email: burnslaw@emeraldis.com

Stephen D. Baggett
Roy R. Hemphill
Steven M. Pruitt

Attorneys for: NationsBank; The Greenwood Mills; Geo. W. Park Seed Co.; State Farm Mutual Group; Allstate Insurance Co.; Liberty Mutual Insurance Co.; Nationwide Mutual Insurance Co.; Cincinnati Insurance Co.; South Carolina Insurance Reserve Fund; South Carolina Farm Bureau Insurance Co.

For Complete List of Firm Personnel, See General Section

For full biographical listings, see the Martindale-Hubbell Law Directory

HILTON HEAD ISLAND, Beaufort Co.

LAUGHLIN AND BOWEN (AV)

20 Palmetto Parkway, Suites A & B, Drawer 21119, 29925-1119
Telephone: 843-689-5700
Fax: 843-689-9300
Email: Jazzlaw@Hargray.com

MEMBERS OF FIRM

Drew A. Laughlin
John R. C. Bowen

For full biographical listings, see the Martindale-Hubbell Law Directory

JOHN J. MCKAY, JR., P.A. (AV)

Suite 203 WatersEdge at Shelter Cove, 29928
Telephone: 843-785-7648
Fax: 843-842-2481
Email: jmckay@hargray.com *URL:* http://www.hiltonheadisland.com/jjmckay.htm

John J. McKay, Jr.

For full biographical listings, see the Martindale-Hubbell Law Directory

RUTH & MACNEILLE, PROFESSIONAL ASSOCIATION (AV)

40 Pope Avenue, 29928
Telephone: 843-785-4251
Telex: 988944
Telecopier: 843-686-5404
Mailing Address: P.O. Box 5706, Hilton Head Island, SC, 29938
Bluffton, South Carolina Office: 7 Simmonsville Road, Suite 200.
Telephone: 803-815-5353.
Fax: 803-815-5354.

William A. Ruth
Douglas W. MacNeille
Michael G. Olivetti

Keri A. Jordan
Michael K. Knudsen
Tara Knudsen (Resident, Bluffton Office)

References: NationsBank of South Carolina, N.A.; Anchor Bank; Wachovia Bank, N.A.; Chicago Title Insurance Corp.; First American Title Insurance Co.

For full biographical listings, see the Martindale-Hubbell Law Directory

LORIS, Horry Co.

STEVENS LAW FIRM, P.C. (AV)

3341 Broad Street P.O. Drawer 127, 29569-0127
Telephone: 843-756-7652
Fax: 843-756-3785
E-Mail: RUMMPOLE@AOL.COM
Email: JPKLAW@AOL.COM

James P. Stevens, Jr.
Jonathan P. Kresken

For full biographical listings, see the Martindale-Hubbell Law Directory

MYRTLE BEACH, Horry Co.

BELLAMY, RUTENBERG, COPELAND, EPPS, GRAVELY & BOWERS, P.A. (AV)

1000 29th Avenue North, P.O. Box 357, 29578
Telephone: 843-448-2400
Telecopier: 843-448-3022

(See Next Column)

BELLAMY, RUTENBERG, COPELAND, EPPS, GRAVELY & BOWERS P.A.—*Continued*

Howell V. Bellamy, Jr.
John K. Rutenberg
John E. Copeland
Claude M. Epps, Jr.
David R. Gravely
Edward B. Bowers, Jr.
Bradley D. King
Henrietta U. Golding
M. Edwin Hinds, Jr.
Jill F. Griffith
Kathryn M. Cook
David B. Miller
C. Winfield Johnson, III
Sarah A. Johnson

Representative Clients: Dargan Construction Co.; Coastal Federal Savings Bank; Sands Investments; Wachovia Bank of South Carolina; AVX Corp.; Bank of America; Parthenon Insurance Co.; Burroughs & Chapin Co.; International Paper Co.; Hospital Corporation of America.

For Complete List of Firm Personnel, See General Section

For full biographical listings, see the Martindale-Hubbell Law Directory

FURR AND HENSHAW (AV)

A Partnership of Professional Corporations
1900 Oak Street, P.O. Box 2909, 29578
Telephone: 843-626-7621
Fax: 843-448-6445
Email: f&h@sccoast.net *URL:* http://www.lawyers.com/f&hlaw
Columbia, South Carolina Office: 1534 Blanding Street.
Telephone: 803-252-4050.
FAX: 803-254-7513.

O. Fayrell Furr, Jr. (P.C.)

Karolan F. Ohanesian (Resident)

Reference: Anchor Bank, Myrtle Beach, S.C.

For full biographical listings, see the Martindale-Hubbell Law Directory

THE THOMPSON LAW FIRM, P.A. (AV)

1314 Professional Drive, P.O. Box 1290, 29578-1290
Telephone: 843-692-2628
Fax: 843-692-0918
Conway, South Carolina Office: 1318 Third Avenue, P.O. Box 1533.
Telephone: 843-248-5741.
Fax: 843-248-5112.

J. Jackson Thomas
Clay D. Brittain, III
G. Michael Smith

Russell V. Traw
Thomas C. Stanley
Stacy L. Stanley

Representative Clients: The Citizens and Southern National Bank of South Carolina; Burroughs & Collins Co.; Canal Industries, Inc.; Nationwide Mutual Insurance Co.; State Farm Mutual Automobile Insurance Co.; State Farm Fire and Casualty Insurance Co.; Horry County; United Carolina Bank; First Union National Bank; First Financial Savings Bank, Inc.

For full biographical listings, see the Martindale-Hubbell Law Directory

*ORANGEBURG,** Orangeburg Co.

HÖRGER, HÖRGER, LANIER & KNIGHT, L.L.P. (AV)

160 Centre Street, N.E., P.O. Box 518, 29116-0518
Telephone: 803-531-1700
Fax: 803-531-0160
Summerville, South Carolina Office. 437 A. North Main Street, P.O. Box 280. Telephone: 843-821-9700.
Fax: 843-821-0031.

MEMBERS OF FIRM

William A. Hörger (1922-1998)
Michael P. Hörger
Lewis C. Lanier
Troy G. Knight
Anne Ross Culbreath

Reference: First Union National Bank of South Carolina.

For full biographical listings, see the Martindale-Hubbell Law Directory

*SPARTANBURG,** Spartanburg Co.

JAMES C. COTHRAN, JR. (AV)

Spartan Centre, 101 West St. John Street, Suite 207, P.O. Drawer 2788, 29304-2788
Telephone: 864-591-1996
Fax: 864-591-1017

For full biographical listings, see the Martindale-Hubbell Law Directory

HARRISON, WHITE, SMITH, HAYES & COGGINS, P.A. (AV)

178 West Main Street, 29306
Telephone: 864-542-2990
Fax: 864-542-2994

(See Next Column)

Benjamin C. Harrison
John B. White, Jr.
J. Mark Hayes, II
Danny R. Smith
Donald C. Coggins, Jr.

For full biographical listings, see the Martindale-Hubbell Law Directory

HOLCOMBE, BOMAR, GUNN AND BRADFORD, P.A. (AV)

Advantica Plaza, 203 East Main Street, P.O. Drawer 1897, 29304-1897
Telephone: 864-585-4273
Telecopier: 864-585-3844
Email: hbgb@teleplex.net

William U. Gunn
Perry D. Boulier
William B. Darwin, Jr.

S. Sterling Laney, III
Ginger D. Goforth

Representative Clients: Denny's, Inc.; Advantica Restaurant Group, Inc.; Community Cash Stores; Liberty Mutual Insurance Cos.; Reliance Insurance Cos.; Mary Black Memorial Hospital, Inc.; State Fire and Casualty; S.C. Ins. Res. Fund (State Budget and Control Board).

For Complete List of Firm Personnel, See General Section

For full biographical listings, see the Martindale-Hubbell Law Directory

LEATHERWOOD WALKER TODD & MANN, P.C. (AV)

1451 East Main Street, P.O. Box 3188, 29304-3188
Telephone: 864-582-4365
Telefax: 864-585-8961
Email: leatherwood@lwtm.com *URL:* http://www.lwtm.com
Greenville, South Carolina Office: 100 East Coffee Street, P.O. Box 87.
Telephone: 864-242-6440.
FAX: 864-240-2477.

H. Spencer King

Cathy H. Dunn
Margaret C. McGee

For Complete List of Firm Personnel, See General Section

For full biographical listings, see the Martindale-Hubbell Law Directory

SUMMERVILLE, Dorchester Co.

MICHAEL T. ROSE (AV)

409 Central Avenue, 29483
Telephone: 843-871-1821
Fax: 843-871-2454
Email: senator@excelonline.com

For full biographical listings, see the Martindale-Hubbell Law Directory

*SUMTER,** Sumter Co.

LEE, ERTER, WILSON, HOLLER & SMITH, L.L.C. (AV)

126 North Main Street, P.O. Box 580, 29150
Telephone: 803-778-2471
Telecopier: 803-778-1643

MEMBERS OF FIRM

John Dozier Lee, Jr. (1921-1999)
Jack W. Erter, Jr.
Harry C. Wilson, Jr.
David Cornwell Holler
G. Murrell Smith, Jr.

Representative Clients: South Carolina National Bank; Carolina Power and Light Co.; Peoples Natural Gas Company of South Carolina; BB&T; Allstate Insurance Co.; American Surety Co.; Prudential Insurance Company of America; General Telephone; Korn Industries, Inc.; V-B William Furniture Co., Inc.

For full biographical listings, see the Martindale-Hubbell Law Directory

SURFSIDE BEACH, Horry Co.

KELAHER, CONNELL & CONNOR, P.C. (AV)

Suite 209, The Courtyard, 1500 U.S. Highway 17 North, P.O. Drawer 14547, 29587
Telephone: 843-238-5648
Fax: 843-238-5050

Edward T. Kelaher
Gene M. Connell, Jr.
L. Sidney Connor, IV

Lisa Poe Davis

Representative Clients and References furnished upon request.

For full biographical listings, see the Martindale-Hubbell Law Directory

*WALHALLA,** Oconee Co.

LARRY C. BRANDT, P.A. (AV)

205 West Main Street, P.O. Drawer 738, 29691
Telephone: 864-638-5406
864-638-7873
Email: lbrandt@innova.net

Larry C. Brandt

LEGAL SUPPORT PERSONNEL

Debra C. Miller

For full biographical listings, see the Martindale-Hubbell Law Directory

SOUTH DAKOTA

*BELLE FOURCHE,** Butte Co.

QUINN, DAY & BARKER, P.L.L.C. (AV)

117 Fifth Avenue, P.O. Box 370, 57717-0370
Telephone: 605-892-2743
Fax: 605-892-4273
Email: bfqedb@dtgcom.net
Rapid City, South Dakota Office: 4200 Beach Drive, P.O. Box 9335.
Telephone: 605-343-6400.
Telecopier: 605-343-4841.

Terence R. Quinn
Michael W. Day
Kenneth E. Barker
Robert L. Morris, II
Bradley A. Schreiber
Michael A. Wilson (Resident, Rapid City Office)
Michael P. Reynolds (Resident, Rapid City Office)

ASSOCIATE

Michael C. Loos (Resident, Rapid City Office)

OF COUNSEL

R. E. Brandenburg

Representative Clients: Pioneer Bank & Trust, Belle Fourche, Spearfish and Rapid City Offices; Belle Fourche Irrigation District; Butte-Meade Sanitary Water District; Igloo-Provo Water User Project; Strawberry Hill Mining Co.; American Family Insurance Group.

For full biographical listings, see the Martindale-Hubbell Law Directory

LEAD, Lawrence Co.

FULLER, TELLINGHUISEN, GORDON & PERCY, P.C. (AV)

203 West Main Street, P.O. Box 898, 57754
Telephone: 605-584-2440
Fax: 605-584-1979
Email: leadlaw@mato.com
Spearfish, South Dakota Office: 132 East Illinois, 57783.
Telephone: 605-642-8080.
Fax: 605-642-1756. E-mail: spflaw@mato.com

A. P. Fuller
Roger A. Tellinghuisen
Bradley P. Gordon
Michelle Palmer Percy

Representative Clients: Homestake Mining Co.; Hotel Franklin & Gaming; Black Hills Novelty/Automatic Vending, Inc.; Northern Hills General Hospital; Lantis Enterprises, Inc.; Norwest Bank South Dakota N.A.; Lead-Deadwood Independent School District # 40-1; City of Lead.

For full biographical listings, see the Martindale-Hubbell Law Directory

*RAPID CITY,** Pennington Co.

BANGS, MCCULLEN, BUTLER, FOYE & SIMMONS, L.L.P. (AV)

818 St. Joseph Street, P.O. Box 2670, 57709
Telephone: 605-343-1040
Telecopier: 605-343-1503
URL: http://www.bangsmccullen.com

MEMBERS OF FIRM

Joseph M. Butler
Thomas E. Simmons
Allen G. Nelson
James P. Hurley
Michael M. Hickey
Terry L. Hofer
Rod Schlauger
Daniel F. Duffy
Jeffrey G. Hurd

ASSOCIATES

Veronica L. Bowen
Terry G. Westergaard
Steven R. Nolan
Gregory J. Erlandson

Representative Clients: Norwest Bank South Dakota, N.A., Rapid City, S.D.; Pete Lien & Sons; The Travelers Insurance Co.; Rapid City Regional Hospital; Great American Insurance Co.; Fireman's Fund Insurance; United States Automobile Association; Moyle Petroleum; Rapid City Area School District 51-4; St. Paul Insurance Cos.

For Complete List of Firm Personnel, See General Section

For full biographical listings, see the Martindale-Hubbell Law Directory

DELANEY & SUMNER (AV)

623 Quincy Street Suite 103, 57701
Telephone: 605-388-3153
Fax: 605-388-3155
Mailing Address: P.O. Box 8305, Rapid City, SD, 57709-8305
Email: toogoodoo1@aol.com

MEMBERS OF FIRM

John J. Delaney
Scott Sumner

For full biographical listings, see the Martindale-Hubbell Law Directory

LYNN, JACKSON, SHULTZ & LEBRUN, P.C. (AV)

First National Bank Building Eighth Floor, 909 Saint Joseph Street, P.O. Box 8250, 57709
Telephone: 605-342-2592
Telecopier: 605-342-5185
Email: ljlawrc@lynnjackson.com *URL:* http://www.lynnjackson.com
Sioux Falls, South Dakota Office: U.S. Bank Building, Eighth Floor, P.O. Box 1920.
Telephone: 605-332-5999.
Telecopier: 605-332-4249.

Kelton S. Lynn (1916-1974)
Horace R. Jackson (1907-1987)
Donald R. Shultz
William F. Day, Jr. (Resident, Sioux Falls Office)
Gene N. Lebrun
Thomas G. Fritz
Haven L. Stuck
Lee A. Magnuson (Resident, Sioux Falls Office)
Jay C. Shultz
Jane Wipf Pfeifle
Jon C. Sogn (Resident, Sioux Falls Office)
R. Alan Peterson (Resident, Sioux Falls Office)
Leah J. Jeffries
Craig A. Pfeifle
Steven J. Oberg
David L. Nadolski (Resident, Sioux Falls Office)
Steven J. Morgans (Resident, Sioux Falls Office)
Daniel R. Fritz (Resident, Sioux Falls Office)

Todd L. Brink

Representative Clients: U.S. Bank of South Dakota; Employers Mutual of Wausau; South Dakota School of Mines & Technology; CIGNA Insurance Co.; E.D. Jones & Co.
General Counsel for: Rushmore Electric Power Cooperative; Black Hills Regional Eye Institute.

For Complete List of Firm Personnel, See General Section

For full biographical listings, see the Martindale-Hubbell Law Directory

QUINN, DAY & BARKER, P.L.L.C. (AV)

4200 Beach Drive, P.O. Box 9335, 57709-9335
Telephone: 605-343-6400
Fax: 605-343-4841
Email: rcquedb@dtgcom.net
Belle Fourche, South Dakota Office: 117 Fifth Avenue, P.O. Box 370.
Telephone: 605-892-2743.
Fax: 605-892-4273.

Terence R. Quinn
Michael W. Day
Kenneth E. Barker
Robert L. Morris, II
Bradley A. Schreiber
Michael A. Wilson (Resident)
Michael P. Reynolds (Resident)

ASSOCIATE

Michael C. Loos

OF COUNSEL

R. E. Brandenburg

Representative Clients: Pioneer Bank & Trust, Belle Fourche, Spearfish and Rapid City Offices; Belle Fourche Irrigation District; Butte-Meade Sanitary Water District; Igloo-Provo Water User Project; Strawberry Hill Mining Co.; American Family Insurance Group; State Farm Insurance Companies; Twin City Testing Corp.; Eli Lilly & Co.

For full biographical listings, see the Martindale-Hubbell Law Directory

*SIOUX FALLS,** Minnehaha Co.

DAVENPORT, EVANS, HURWITZ & SMITH, L.L.P. (AV)

513 South Main Avenue, P.O. Box 1030, 57101-1030
Telephone: 605-336-2880
Telecopier: 605-335-3639
Email: lawyers@dehs.com

MEMBERS OF FIRM

Edwin E. Evans
Michael L. Luce
Michael J. Schaffer
Thomas M. Frankman
Rick W. Orr
Timothy M. Gebhart
Susan Brunick Simons
Roberto A. Lange
Cheryle Wiedmeier Gering
Lori Purcell Fossen
Mark W. Haigh
Sandra K. Hoglund

(See Next Column)

DAVENPORT, EVANS, HURWITZ & SMITH L.L.P.—*Continued*

ASSOCIATES

Keith A. Gauer
Melissa C. Hinton
Kristi G. Holm
Dana M. Van Beek

Counsel for: American Society of Composers, Authors and Publishers (A.S.C.A.P.); Continental Insurance Cos.; The First National Bank in Sioux Falls; Ford Motor Credit Co.; General Motors Corp.; The St. Paul Cos.; The Travelers.

For Complete List of Firm Personnel, See General Section

For full biographical listings, see the Martindale-Hubbell Law Directory

HUGHES LAW OFFICES (AV)

412 West Ninth Street, 57104-3602
Telephone: 605-339-3939
Fax: 605-339-3940

John R. Hughes

LeeAnn Larson LaFave

For full biographical listings, see the Martindale-Hubbell Law Directory

TENNESSEE

*CHATTANOOGA,** Hamilton Co.

PHILLIP A. FLEISSNER, PLLC (AV)

600 Georgia Avenue, 37402
Telephone: 423-756-3591
Telecopier: 423-266-5455

Phillip A. Fleissner
David C. Nagle
Christopher Price Butler

For full biographical listings, see the Martindale-Hubbell Law Directory

FOSTER, FOSTER, ALLEN & DURRENCE, P.C. (AV)

Formerly Hall, Haynes, Lusk & Foster
801 Broad Street - Suite 515, 37402
Telephone: 423-266-1141
Telecopier: 423-266-4618
Email: dward@ffadlaw.com

George Lane Foster
Phillip M. Durrence, Jr.
William M. Foster
David J. Ward
Craig R. Allen
Clayton M. Whittaker
John M. Hull

LEGAL SUPPORT PERSONNEL

Peggy Sue Bates

Division Counsel For: Norfolk Southern Railway Co.
Attorneys For: CNA/Insurance; United States Fidelity & Guaranty Co. (USF&G); Bridgestone-Firestone, Inc.; State Volunteer Mutual Insurance Co. (SVMIC); Exxon Corp.; Murphy Oil Corp.; Chicago Title Insurance Co.; Jim Walter Homes; Mid-State Homes, Inc.

For full biographical listings, see the Martindale-Hubbell Law Directory

FRANKLIN, COOPER & MARCUS, PLLC (AV)

837 Fort Wood Street, 37403
Telephone: 423-756-3596
Telecopier: 423-756-3597

David L. Franklin
Gary A. Cooper
H. Richard Marcus

For full biographical listings, see the Martindale-Hubbell Law Directory

GEARHISER, PETERS, LOCKABY & TALLANT, PLLC (AV)

320 McCallie Avenue, 37402-2007
Telephone: 423-756-5171
Fax: 423-266-1605
Email: law@gplt.com

MEMBERS OF FIRM

Charles J. Gearhiser
Terry Atkin Cavett
R. Wayne Peters
Sam D. Elliott
Robert L. Lockaby, Jr.
Lane C. Avery
Ralph E. Tallant, Jr.
Wade K. Cannon

ASSOCIATES

Robin L. Miller
Lee Ann Adams
Christopher T. Varner
Jeffrey H. Moore
James C. Davey
Kevin T. Beck

(See Next Column)

OF COUNSEL

Richard P. Jahn, Jr.

References: First Tennessee Bank; First American National Bank.

For full biographical listings, see the Martindale-Hubbell Law Directory

SUMMERS & WYATT, P.C. (AV)

500 Lindsay Street, 37402
Telephone: 423-265-2385
Fax: 423-266-5211
Email: summers@voy.net

Jerry H. Summers
Thomas L. Wyatt
Jeffrey W. Rufolo

Representative Clients: Glass, Molders, Pottery, Plastics and Allied Workers, International; International Brotherhood of Boilermakers, #656; United Steelworkers, District 35; International Association of Machinists and Aerospace Workers, Local 56; Graphics Communication International Union, Local 394; International Brotherhood of Electrical Workers, Local 175; Chattanooga Building and Construction Trades Council; Carpenters Local 74; Ironworkers Local 704; Ironworkers District Council; Amalgamated Transit Union 1212.

For Complete List of Firm Personnel, See General Section

For full biographical listings, see the Martindale-Hubbell Law Directory

WITT, GAITHER & WHITAKER, P.C. (AV)

1100 SunTrust Bank Building, 37402-2608
Telephone: 423-265-8881
Telefax: 423-266-4138; 423-756-5612

Philip B. Whitaker
K. Stephen Powers
John W. Murrey, III
Rosemarie Luise Bryan
Hugh J. Moore, Jr.
Douglas E. Peck
Frank P. Pinchak
Philip B. Whitaker, Jr.

Ron D. Powers
Cynthia D. Hall
Lisa M. Pate

Representative Clients: Chattanooga Metropolitan Airport Authority; Coca-Cola Bottling Co. Consolidated; Dean Witter Reynolds Inc.; The Dixie Group, Inc.; Ryder Truck Rental, Inc.; Shaw Industries, Inc.; Signal Apparel Company, Inc.; SunTrust Bank, Chattanooga, N.A.; U.S. Xpress Enterprises, Inc.; Vanliner Insurance Co.

For Complete List of Firm Personnel, See General Section

For full biographical listings, see the Martindale-Hubbell Law Directory

*CLEVELAND,** Bradley Co.

JENNE, SCOTT & JENNE (AV)

260 Ocoee Street, P.O. Box 161, 37364-0161
Telephone: 423-476-5506
Fax: 423-476-5058
Email: MichaelJenne@mindspring.com

MEMBERS OF FIRM

Roger E. Jenne
Robert A. Scott (1940-1984)
Michael E. Jenne

For full biographical listings, see the Martindale-Hubbell Law Directory

DENNY E. MOBBS (AV)

55 1/2 First Street, N.E., P.O. Box 192, 37364-0192
Telephone: 423-472-7181
Fax: 423-472-7701

Representative Clients: Liberty Mutual Insurance Co.; Shelby Mutual Insurance Co.; Carolina Casualty Co.; Maytag Corp. (Magic Chef, Inc.-Hardwick Stove Co.); Industrial Development Board of Polk County; Polk County News-Citizen Advance; Ocoee Inn & Marina.

For full biographical listings, see the Martindale-Hubbell Law Directory

*COOKEVILLE,** Putnam Co.

MADEWELL, JARED & HALFACRE (AV)

230 North Washington Avenue, P.O. Box 721, 38501
Telephone: 931-526-6101
Fax: 931-528-1909

MEMBERS OF FIRM

Eugene Jared
James D. Madewell
William E. Halfacre, III

Representative Clients: State of Tennessee; Trial Counsel as Special Assistant to Attorney General; Bank of Putnam County; First Tennessee Bank, N.A. at Cookeville; The Maryland; Transamerica Ins. Group; Home Insurance Co.; Auto Owners Ins. Co.; Insurance Company of North America; Fireman's Fund Insurance Co.

For Complete List of Firm Personnel, See General Section

For full biographical listings, see the Martindale-Hubbell Law Directory

Cookeville—Continued

MOORE, RADER, CLIFT AND FITZPATRICK, P.C. (AV)

46 North Jefferson Avenue, P.O. Box 3347, 38501
Telephone: 615-526-3311
Fax: 615-526-3092

L. Dean Moore
Michael E. Clift
Daniel H. Rader, III
Walter S. Fitzpatrick, III
Richard Lane Moore

General Counsel for: First Tennessee Bank.
Local Counsel for: Heritage Ford-Lincoln-Mercury, Inc.
Representative Clients: Continental Insurance Co.; Kemper Group; U.S.F.&G.; Auto Owners Insurance Co.; Wausau Insurance Cos.

For full biographical listings, see the Martindale-Hubbell Law Directory

*GALLATIN,** Sumner Co.

MCCLELLAN, POWERS, EHMLING & DIX, P.C. (AV)

McClellan Building, 116 Public Square, 37066-2887
Telephone: 615-452-5872
Fax: 615-452-0054
Murfreesboro, Tennessee Office: Suite 201, Court Square Building, 201 West Main Street.
Telephone: 615-895-2529.
FAX: 615-896-7254.

Arthur E. McClellan
Dennis Wade Powers
M. Allen Ehmling

Jade A. Rogers

Representative Clients: First Independent Bank; Tennessee Farmers Mutual Insurance Co.; Travelers Insurance Co.; Blue Cross and Blue Shield of Tennessee; Aetna Casualty & Surety Co.

For full biographical listings, see the Martindale-Hubbell Law Directory

*HUNTSVILLE,** Scott Co.

BAKER, DONELSON, BEARMAN & CALDWELL (AV)

3 Courthouse Square, 37756
Telephone: 423-663-2321
Telecopier: 423-663-2111
Email: infor@bdbc.com *URL:* http://www.bakerdonelson.com
Memphis, Tennessee Office: 20th Floor, First Tennessee Building, 165 Madison, 38103.
Telephone: 901-526-2000.
Telecopier: 901-577-2303.
Nashville, Tennessee Office: 1700 Nashville City Center, 511 Union Street, 37219.
Telephone: 615-726-5600.
Telecopier: 615-726-0464.
Chattanooga, Tennessee Office: 1800 Republic Centre, 633 Chestnut Street, 37450-1800.
Telephone: 423-756-2010.
Telecopier: 423-756-3447.
Knoxville, Tennessee Office: 2200 Riverview Tower, 900 South Gay Street, 37901.
Telephone: 423-549-7000.
Telecopier: 423-525-8569.
Johnson City, Tennessee Office: SunTrust Bank Building, 207 Mockingbird Lane, P.O. Box 3038, 37602.
Telephone: 423-928-0181.
Telecopier: 423-928-5694; 423-928-3654; Kingsport: 423-246-6191.
Washington, D.C. Office: Market Square, 801 Pennsylvania Avenue, N.W., 20004.
Telephone: 202-508-3400.
Telecopier: 202-508-3402.
Jackson, Mississippi Office: Suite 500, 700 North State Street, 39202.
Telephone: 601-351-2400.
Telecopier: 601-351-2424.

MANAGING PARTNER
Ernest A. Petroff, III
PARTNER
Stephen A. Marcum
ASSOCIATE
Mark E. Blakley

For Complete List of Firm Personnel, See General Section

For full biographical listings, see the Martindale-Hubbell Law Directory

*JACKSON,** Madison Co.

MOSS, BENTON & WALLIS, PLLC (AV)

P.O. Box 3897, 38303-3897
Telephone: 901-668-5500
Telecopier: 901-664-2840

(See Next Column)

MEMBERS OF FIRM

William P. Moss (1897-1985)
Edwin E. Wallis, Jr.
William P. Moss, Jr. (1936-1997)
W. Stanworth Harris
Beth H. DuPree

OF COUNSEL
George O. Benton

Attorneys for: First American National Bank of Jackson; Bell South; CSX Transportation, Inc.; The Equitable Life Assurance Society of the United States; Jackson Utility Division; Allied Insurance Companies; United Services Automobile Assn.; Association of Tennessee Cola-Cola Bottlers; Central Distributors, Inc.; Scotsdale Insurance Companies.

For full biographical listings, see the Martindale-Hubbell Law Directory

JOHNSON CITY, Washington Co.

BAKER, DONELSON, BEARMAN & CALDWELL (AV)

SunTrust Bank Building, 207 Mockingbird Lane, P.O. Box 3038, 37602
Telephone: 423-928-0181
Telecopier: 423-928-5694; 928-3654; Kingsport: 423-246-6191
Email: info@bdbc.com *URL:* http://www.bakerdonelson.com
Memphis, Tennessee Office: 20th Floor, First Tennessee Building, 165 Madison, 38103.
Telephone: 901-526-2000.
Telecopier: 901-577-2303.
Nashville, Tennessee Office: 1700 Nashville City Center, 511 Union Street, 37219.
Telephone: 615-726-5600.
Telecopier: 615-726-0464.
Chattanooga, Tennessee Office: 1800 Republic Centre, 633 Chestnut Street, 37450-1800.
Telephone: 423-756-2010.
Telecopier: 423-756-3447.
Knoxville, Tennessee Office: 2200 Riverview Tower, 900 South Gay Street, 37901.
Telephone: 423-549-7000.
Telecopier: 423-525-8569.
Huntsville, Tennessee Office: 3 Courthouse Square, 37756.
Telephone: 615-663-2321.
Telecopier: 615-663-2111.
Washington, D.C. Office: Market Square, 801 Pennsylvania Avenue, N.W., 20004.
Telephone: 202-508-3400.
Telecopier: 202-508-3402.
Jackson, Mississippi Office: Suite 500, 700 North State Street, 39202.
Telephone: 601-351-2400.
Telecopier: 601-351-2424.

MANAGING PARTNER
Robert D. Van de Vuurst

For Complete List of Firm Personnel, See General Section

For full biographical listings, see the Martindale-Hubbell Law Directory

KINGSPORT, Sullivan Co.

HUNTER, SMITH & DAVIS, LLP (AV)

1212 North Eastman Road, P.O. Box 3740, 37664
Telephone: 423-378-8800
Telecopier: 423-378-8801
Email: info@hsdlaw.com *URL:* http://www.hsdlaw.com
Johnson City, Tennessee Office: Suite 500 First American Center, 208 Sunset Drive, 37604.
Telephone: 423-283-6300.
Telecopier: 423-283-6301.

MEMBERS OF FIRM

S. Morris Hadden
Gregory K. Haden
William C. Bovender
Michael L. Forrester
William T. Wray, Jr.
Edward Jennings Webb, Jr.
Jimmie Carpenter Miller
James N. L. Humphreys

ASSOCIATES

K. Jeff Luethke
Suzanne Sweet Cook
Julie Poe Bennett
John C. Bowles
Robert Morris Hadden

COUNSEL
Edwin L. Treadway

Representative Clients: State Farm Insurance Co.; AFG Industries, Inc.; Nationwide Insurance Co.; Home Insurance Co.; Willamette Industries, Inc.; Sprint; Chubb Insurance Co.; Wellmont Health System (Bristol Regional Medical Center/Holston Valley Medical Center/Lonesome Pine Hospital); First American National Bank; Cincinnati Insurance Co.

For Complete List of Firm Personnel, See General Section

For full biographical listings, see the Martindale-Hubbell Law Directory

WEST & ROSE (AV)

537 East Center Street, P.O. Box 1404, 37660
Telephone: 423-246-8176
Fax: 423-246-4028

(See Next Column)

WEST & ROSE—*Continued*

MEMBERS OF FIRM

M. Lacy West
Steven C. Rose
Julia C. West

For full biographical listings, see the Martindale-Hubbell Law Directory

*KNOXVILLE,** Knox Co.

AMBROSE, WILSON, GRIMM & DURAND (AV)

607 Market Street, Ninth Floor, P.O. Box 2466, 37901-2466
Telephone: 423-544-3000
Toll Free: 1-800-242-1709
Facsimile: 423-637-1709
Email: tennlaw@awgd.com

W. L. Ambrose, Jr. (1907-1992)
Wm. C. Wilson (1912-1995)

MEMBERS OF FIRM

Ronald L. Grimm
Philip P. Durand
John B. Fowler

ASSOCIATES

Lars E. Schuller
Robert B. Frost, Jr.
Mary L. Abbott

OF COUNSEL

John M. Smartt
Wallace W. Conaway

Representative Clients: Simon Property Group L.P. (Retail Shopping Mall Devel.); East Tennessee, Automobile Club (AAA); The Toms Foundation; National Association of Credit Management; Teleflex Corp.; Glock, Inc.; H & R 1871 Inc. (New England Firearms Co.); Interarms, Inc.; First Tennessee Bank; Utica Mutual Insurance Co.

For full biographical listings, see the Martindale-Hubbell Law Directory

ARNETT, DRAPER & HAGOOD (AV)

Suite 2300, First Tennessee Plaza, P.O. Box 300, 37901-0300
Telephone: 865-546-7000
Telecopier: 865-546-0423
Email: adandh@aol.com

MEMBERS OF FIRM

Foster D. Arnett
Jack B. Draper
Lewis R. Hagood
Thomas S. Scott, Jr.
William A. Simms
F. Michael Fitzpatrick
Rick L. Powers
Dan D. Rhea
Steven L. Hurdle
Johanna J. McGlothlin
Robert N. Townsend
R. Kim Burnette
John Steven Collins
Keith H. Burroughs
Samuel C. Doak
Thomas M. Cole
Douglas Gerard Brehm
John A. Willis
Donald J. Farinato

Insurance Clients: Allstate Insurance Co.; Associated Aviation Underwriters; Crum & Forster Group; St. Paul Insurance Cos.; State Farm Insurance Cos; United States Aviation Underwriters.
Representative Clients: Covenant Health Systems; Phillips Petroleum Co.; Sea Ray Boats, Inc.; Vinylex Corp.

For full biographical listings, see the Martindale-Hubbell Law Directory

BAKER, DONELSON, BEARMAN & CALDWELL (AV)

2200 Riverview Tower, 900 South Gay Street, 37901
Telephone: 423-549-7000
Telecopier: 423-525-8569
Email: info@bdbc.com *URL:* http://www.bakerdonelson.com
Memphis, Tennessee Office: 20th Floor, First Tennessee Building, 165 Madison, 38103.
Telephone: 901-526-2000.
Telecopier: 901-577-2303.
Nashville, Tennessee Office: 1700 Nashville City Center, 511 Union Street, 37219.
Telephone: 615-726-5600.
Telecopier: 615-726-0464.
Chattanooga, Tennessee Office: 1800 Republic Centre, 633 Chestnut Street, 37450-1800.
Telephone: 423-756-2010.
Telecopier: 423-756-3447.
Johnson City, Tennessee Office: SunTrust Bank Building, 207 Mockingbird Lane, P.O. Box 3038, 37602.
Telephone: 423-928-0181.
Telecopier: 423-928-5694; 423-928-3654; Kingsport: 423-246-6191.
Huntsville, Tennessee Office: 3 Courthouse Square, 37756.
Telephone: 423-663-2321.
Telecopier: 423-663-2111.
Washington, D.C. Office: Market Square, 801 Pennsylvania Avenue, N.W., 20004.
Telephone: 202-508-3400.
Telecopier: 202-508-3402.
Jackson, Mississippi Office: Suite 500, 700 North State Street, 39202.
Telephone: 601-351-2400.
Telecopier: 601-351-2424.

MANAGING PARTNER

Stephen E. Roth

(See Next Column)

PARTNERS

Lewis R. Donelson, III
Howard H. Baker, Jr.
Robert F. Worthington, Jr.
Robert G. McCullough
Richard B. Gossett
James A. McIntosh
Stephen G. Anderson
David E. Fielder
P. Edward Pratt
Mary Dillard Miller
Nelwyn W. Inman
Bruce C. Doeg
Kelli L. Thompson

ASSOCIATES

Wm. Gregory Hall, Jr.
Mary LeAnn Mynatt
Andrew L. Colocotronis
Clarence Risin
Richard D. Plumley
Jason I. Epstein
Suzanne Hefner Bauknight
David L. Morehous (Not admitted in TN)
H. Susanne Bales

For full biographical listings, see the Martindale-Hubbell Law Directory

BERNSTEIN, STAIR & MCADAMS LLP (AV)

Suite 600, 530 South Gay Street, 37902
Telephone: 423-546-8030
Telecopier: 423-522-8879
Effective October 1, 1999 Area Code will change to 865.

MEMBERS OF FIRM

Bernard E. Bernstein
L. Caesar Stair III
Thomas N. McAdams
Doris C. Allen
Celeste H. Herbert
James W. Parris

ASSOCIATES

W. Tyler Chastain
Lauren G. Strange-Boston
Margo J. Maxwell

Representative Clients: ABB Flakt, Inc.; Camel Manufacturing Company; Clayton Homes, Inc.; Metropolotan Life Insurance Company; Modern Supply Co.; Penn - Virginia Corporation; Plasti-Line, Inc.; Saks, Inc.

For full biographical listings, see the Martindale-Hubbell Law Directory

DANIEL & OBERMAN (AV)

An Association including a Professional Corporation
550 West Main Street, Suite 950, 37902
Telephone: 423-546-4292
Fax: 423-546-4294
URL: http://www.daolaw.com
URL: http://www.lawyers.com/daolaw

W. Zane Daniel (P.C.)
Steven Oberman

Jeffrey Zane Daniel
Jonathan D. Cooper
William Todd Daniel

Reference: NationsBank.

For full biographical listings, see the Martindale-Hubbell Law Directory

EGERTON, MCAFEE, ARMISTEAD & DAVIS, P.C. (AV)

500 First American National Bank Center, P.O. Box 2047, 37901
Telephone: 423-546-0500
Fax: 423-525-5293
URL: http://emadlaw.com

Lewis C. Foster, Jr.
William W. Davis, Jr.
Barry K. Maxwell
Stephen A. McSween
Rockforde D. King

Wesley L. Hatmaker
Reese K. Thomas

Representative Clients: First American National Bank of Knoxville; Home Federal Bank of Tennessee, F.S.B.; Bush Bros. & Co.; Johnson & Galyon Contractors; Baptist Hospital of East Tennessee; Revco D.S., Inc.; White Realty Corp.; Dick Broadcasting, Inc.; Institutional Jobbers Companies; The Great American Insurance Companies.

For full biographical listings, see the Martindale-Hubbell Law Directory

FRANTZ, MCCONNELL & SEYMOUR, LLP (AV)

550 Main Avenue, Suite 500, 37902
Telephone: 423-546-9321
Fax: 423-637-5249
Mailing Address: P.O. Box 39, Knoxville, TN, 37901
Email: Lwhitfield@fmsllp.com
Effective October 1, 1999, the Area Code will change to 865.

MEMBERS OF FIRM

Fred H. Cagle, Jr.
Arthur G. Seymour, Jr.
Francis A. Cain
Robert L. Kahn
Reggie E. Keaton
Donald D. Howell
Debra L. Fulton
Michael W. Ewell
Imogene Anderson King
John M. Lawhorn
James E. Wagner

(See Next Column)

FRANTZ, MCCONNELL & SEYMOUR LLP, *Knoxville—Continued*

James D. Moyers | Beverly Dean Nelms
Mary Elizabeth Maddox

Counsel For: ASARCO Incorporated; BellSouth Telecommunications, Inc.; Coca-Cola Enterprises, Inc.; Government Employees Insurance Company; Liberty Mutual Insurance Company; NBC Bank, FSB; Norfolk Southern Railway Company; Prudential Insurance Company of America; The Travelers Insurance Companies; United Services Automobile Association.

For Complete List of Firm Personnel, See General Section

For full biographical listings, see the Martindale-Hubbell Law Directory

LEIBOWITZ & COHEN (AV)

608 Gay Street, S.W., 37902
Telephone: 423-637-1809
FAX: 423-637-9276

MEMBERS OF FIRM

Arnold G. Cohen | Lawrence P. Leibowitz

ASSOCIATE

Melissa A. Ashburn

OF COUNSEL

Russell T. Greene

For full biographical listings, see the Martindale-Hubbell Law Directory

MORTON & MORTON, PLLC (AV)

Suite 620, One Centre Square, 620 Market Street, 37902
Telephone: 423-523-2000
FAX: 423-546-4860
Email: mortonandmorton@msn.com

MEMBERS OF FIRM

G. W. Morton, Jr. | J. Myers Morton

For full biographical listings, see the Martindale-Hubbell Law Directory

NORTON & LUHN, P.C. (AV)

Suite 900, NationsBank Center, 550 Main Avenue, 37902
Telephone: 423-971-4600
Fax: 423-544-0700
Mailing Address: P.O. Box 2467, Knoxville, Tennessee, 37901-2467
Email: nortonluhn@icx.net

R. Franklin Norton | Gary G. Spangler
Warren P. Luhn | Geoffrey D. Kressin

R. David Benner | Jeffrey A. Woods
W. Mitchell Cramer | Lisa A. Webber
Lynn C. Peterson | Steve Erdely (Not admitted in TN)

For full biographical listings, see the Martindale-Hubbell Law Directory

PRYOR, FLYNN, PRIEST & HARBER (AV)

Suite 600 Two Centre Square, 625 Gay Street, P.O. Box 870, 37901
Telephone: 423-522-4191
Telecopier: 423-522-0910

Robert E. Pryor | Timothy A. Priest
Frank L. Flynn, Jr. | John K. Harber

ASSOCIATES

Mark E. Floyd | M. Christopher Coffey
Donald R. Coffey | Robert E. Pryor, Jr.

References: First Vantage Bank; Sun Trust Bank.

For full biographical listings, see the Martindale-Hubbell Law Directory

WAGNER, MYERS & SANGER, A PROFESSIONAL CORPORATION (AV)

1801 First Tennessee Plaza, P.O. Box 1308, 37901-1308
Telephone: 423-525-4600
Fax: 423-524-5731
Email: wms1801@usit.net

Sam F. Fowler, Jr. | Charles A. Wagner III
Herbert S. Sanger, Jr. | William C. Myers, Jr.
Charles W. Van Beke | M. Douglas Campbell, Jr.

Nicholas A. Della Volpe | Robert G. Crane
Ronald D. Garland | John G. Brock
Barbara D. Boulton | Kenneth C. Tucker

Representative Clients: Carolina Power & Light Co.; Cullman Electric Cooperative; Diversified Energy, Inc.; Fort Sanders Health Systems; Gatliff Coal Company, Inc.; Lockheed Martin Energy Systems, Inc.; North American Rayon Corp.; Regal Cinemas, Inc.; Roddy Vending Co.; Sigmon Coal Company, Inc.; Skyline Coal Company.

For full biographical listings, see the Martindale-Hubbell Law Directory

WATSON, HOLLOW & REEVES, P.L.C. (AV)

1700 First Tennessee Plaza, 800 South Gay Street, P.O. Box 131, 37901-0131
Telephone: 423-637-1700
Telecopier: 423-525-2514

MEMBERS OF FIRM

Robert Harmon Watson, Jr. | Jon Gilbert Roach
Richard L. Hollow | John Chapman Duffy
Pamela L. Reeves | John T. Batson, Jr.
Earl Jerome Melson

ASSOCIATES

Nathan D. Rowell | Beverley S. Cornett
Laura C. Webb | Jenny Coques Rogers

For full biographical listings, see the Martindale-Hubbell Law Directory

*MARYVILLE,** Blount Co.

KIZER AND BLACK (AV)

329 Cates Street, 37801
Telephone: 423-982-7650
Fax: 423-982-5776
Email: attorney@usit.com *URL:* http://www.kizer-black.com

MEMBERS OF FIRM

David T. Black | John T. McArthur
Martha S. L. Black | J. Kevin Renfro
Jerry G. Cunningham | Melanie E. Davis

For full biographical listings, see the Martindale-Hubbell Law Directory

NICHOLSON, GARNER & DUGGAN (AV)

250 High Street, P.O. Box 5059, 37802-5059
Telephone: 423-984-1460
Knoxville: 423-637-1970
Telecopier: 423-982-2595
Real Estate Fax: 423-982-2595
Litigation Fax: 423-984-9275
Email: jnicholson@earthlink.net *URL:* http://www.lawyers.com/ngdlaw

MEMBERS OF FIRM

Joe Nicholson | J. Michael Garner
David R. Duggan

ASSOCIATES

Angelia D. Morie | Daphne H. Cornwell

Representative Clients: Will be furnished upon request.

For full biographical listings, see the Martindale-Hubbell Law Directory

*MEMPHIS,** Shelby Co.

ARMSTRONG ALLEN PREWITT GENTRY JOHNSTON & HOLMES, PLLC (AV)

Brinkley Plaza, Suite 700, 80 Monroe Avenue, 38103-2467
Telephone: 901-523-8211
Facsimile: 901-524-4936
Little Rock, Arkansas Office: Suite 100, 100 Morgan Keegan Drive, 72202.
Telephone: 501-280-0100.
Facsimile: 501-280-0166.
Jackson, Mississippi Office: 2525 Lakeward Drive, Suite 200, 39216.
Telephone: 601-713-1192.
Facsimile: 601-713-2049.
Jackson, Tennessee Office: 464 North Parkway, Suite A, 38305.
Telephone: 901-660-2332.
Facsimile: 901-664-1109.

MEMBERS OF FIRM

Thomas R. Prewitt | Paul A. Matthews
Thomas F. Johnston | Randall D. Noel
Carl H. Langschmidt, Jr. | Mark S. Norris
Thomas R. Prewitt, Jr. | Lucian T. Pera
Charles A. Banks (Resident, Little Rock, Arkansas Office) | Robertson M. Leatherman, Jr.
Prince C. Chambliss, Jr. | Cannon F. Allen
Heber S. Simmons III (Resident, Jackson, Mississippi Office)

OF COUNSEL

Gavin M. Gentry

For Complete List of Firm Personnel, See General Section

For full biographical listings, see the Martindale-Hubbell Law Directory

BAKER, DONELSON, BEARMAN & CALDWELL (AV)

20th Floor, First Tennessee Building, 165 Madison, 38103
Telephone: 901-526-2000
Telecopier: 901-577-2303
Email: info@bdbc.com *URL:* http://www.bakerdonelson.com
Nashville, Tennessee Office: 1700 Nashville City Center, 511 Union Street, 37219.
Telephone: 615-726-5600.
Telecopier: 615-726-0464.

(See Next Column)

BAKER, DONELSON, BEARMAN & CALDWELL—*Continued*

Chattanooga, Tennessee Office: 1800 Republic Centre, 633 Chestnut Street, 37450-1800.
Telephone: 423-756-2010.
Telecopier: 423-756-3447.
Knoxville, Tennessee Office: 2200 Riverview Tower, 900 South Gay Street, 37901.
Telephone: 423-549-7000.
Telecopier: 423-525-8569.
Johnson City, Tennessee Office: SunTrust Bank Building, 207 Mockingbird Lane, P.O. Box 3038, 37602.
Telephone: 423-928-0181.
Telecopier: 423-928-5694; 423-928-3654; Kingsport: 423-246-6191.
Huntsville, Tennessee Office: 3 Courthouse Square, 37756.
Telephone: 423-663-2321.
Telecopier: 423-663-2111.
Washington, D.C. Office: Market Square, 801 Pennsylvania Avenue, N.W., 20004.
Telephone: 202-508-3400.
Telecopier: 202-508-3402.
Jackson, Mississippi Office: Suite 500, 700 North State Street, 39202.
Telephone: 601-351-2400.
Telecopier: 601-351-2424.

MANAGING PARTNER

Robert Mark Glover

SHAREHOLDERS

Lewis R. Donelson, III	Charles C. Harrell
Roy Keathley	Stephen D. Goodwin
David G. Williams	George T. Lewis, III
Leo Bearman, Jr.	Ben C. Adams, Jr.
Maurice Wexler	Eugene J. Podesta, Jr.
Frank L. Watson, Jr.	Sam B. Blair, Jr.
Robert Walker	Carla Peacher-Ryan
Boyd L. Rhodes, Jr.	Mary Aronov
W. Michael Richards	Jill M. Steinberg
John C. Speer	Matthew S. Heiter
Charles T. Tuggle, Jr.	Michael C. Patton
Larry E. Killebrew	Janis Wild Kesser
Jerry Stauffer	Stephen William Ragland
Robert C. Liddon	Monique A. Nassar
William H.D. Fones, Jr.	Bradley E. Trammell
William P. Kenworthy	M. Clay Bethell
Allan J. Wade	Desiree M. Franklin
Gregory G. Fletcher	R. Alan Pritchard, Jr.

Peter H. Kesser

OF COUNSEL

Frierson M. Graves, Jr.	Lynn Ackerman Landau
Donald A. Malmo	Paul E. Risner (Not admitted in TN)

ASSOCIATES

Paul R. O'Rourke	Jennifer R. Keown
Anne B. Mathes	Brett T. Parks
Elizabeth Einstman Chance	Cedric C.Y. Tan
Frank L. Watson, III	Lang Wiseman
W. Douglas Sweet	Diane Schratz Holitik
Wm. Scott Young	D. Benjamin Bullen
Mary Ann Jackson	Shannon M. Hernandez
Angela R. Merideth	Sylvia Monique Reed
Jackie G. Prester	Christopher G. Boling
David L. Bearman	Louise P. Gaerig
Clarissa M. Cissell	Lori Hackleman Patterson
Robert C. McConkey, III	Lea Hall Speed

For full biographical listings, see the Martindale-Hubbell Law Directory

BLACK & MCLAREN, A PROFESSIONAL CORPORATION (AV)

530 Oak Court Drive, Suite 310, 38117
Telephone: 901-762-0535
Telecopier: 901-762-0539

Stevan Lenoir Black	Michael G. McLaren

Lynda Wray Spanopoulos	John C. Ryland
Vickie Hardy Jones	Bradley Wayne Eskins

Caren B. Nichol

For full biographical listings, see the Martindale-Hubbell Law Directory

BOROD & KRAMER, P.C. (AV)

Beale Street Landing, 245 Wagner Place, Suite 350, 38103
Telephone: 901-524-0200
Telecopier: 901-523-0043
Email: administrator@borodandkramer.com *URL:* http://www.borodandkramer.com

Bruce S. Kramer

Jeffrey C. Smith	Elaine Sheng
Jeffery D. Parrish	P. Bryan Mauldin

(See Next Column)

For Complete List of Firm Personnel, See General Section

For full biographical listings, see the Martindale-Hubbell Law Directory

EVANS & PETREE (AV)

81 Monroe Avenue, 38103
Telephone: 901-525-6781
Telecopier: 901-527-7756

MEMBERS OF FIRM

Marion G. Evans (1877-1957)	Leonard C. Dunavant, Jr.
Jack Petree (1921-1973)	E. Woods Weathersby
Charles Pittman Cobb (Retired)	C. Bradford Foster III
Elwood L. Edwards (Retired)	Andrew H. Raines
W. Lytle Nichol IV	Frank N. Stockdale Carney
John W. McQuiston II	Paul F. T. Edwards
Ernest G. Kelly, Jr.	Percy H. Harvey
Michael C. Williams	Katharine A. Jungkind
Joseph W. Barnwell, Jr.	Scott A. Frick
David C. Scruggs	Michael R. Marshall

Richard E.M. Nichol, Jr.

Karen Baim Reagler

For full biographical listings, see the Martindale-Hubbell Law Directory

FARRIS, MATHEWS, BRANAN & HELLEN, P.L.C. (AV)

One Commerce Square, Suite 2000, 38103
Telephone: 901-259-7100
Fax: 901-259-7150
Email: firm@farris-law.com
East Memphis, Tennessee Office: Suite 400. First Commercial Bank Building. 5384 Poplar Avenue.
Telephone: 901-763-4000.
Fax: 901-763-4095.
Nashville, Tennessee Office: Nashville City Center, 511 Union Street, Suite 2400.
Telephone: 615-726-1200.
Fax: 615-726-1776.

MEMBERS OF FIRM

Tim Wade Hellen	D. Edward Harvey (Resident, Nashville Office)
Edwin Dean White, III	Rebecca Pearson Tuttle
Charles B. Welch, Jr. (Resident, Nashville Office)	Eugene Stone Forrester, Jr.
G. Ray Bratton	Dedrick Brittenum, Jr.
John M. Farris	Robert F. Miller

Robert A. McLean

ASSOCIATES

Gregory W. O'Neal	Pamela Haddock Klavon
Steven Caines Brammer	Paul C. Peel
Harold W. Fonville, II	Garrett M. Estep

For Complete List of Firm Personnel, See General Section

For full biographical listings, see the Martindale-Hubbell Law Directory

GLASSMAN, JETER, EDWARDS & WADE, P.C. (AV)

26 North Second Street Building, 38103
Telephone: 901-527-4673
Telecopier: 901-521-0940
Email: GJEWW@Memphisonline.com

Richard Glassman	John Barry Burgess
William M. Jeter	Robert A. Cox
Tim Edwards	Rebecca Adelman
B. J. Wade	Lori J. Keen
Carl K. Wyatt, Jr.	James F. Horner, Jr.
Dale H. Tuttle	Richard E. Sorin

Todd Britton Murrah	Heather Walters Thompson

For full biographical listings, see the Martindale-Hubbell Law Directory

SMITH, SABBATINI & MCLEARY, PLLC (AV)

100 Peabody Place Suite 1250, 38103
Telephone: 901-312-5555
Fax: 901-312-5667
Mailing Address: P.O. Box 3582, Memphis, TN, 38173
URL: http://www.smithlawetal.com

Gary K. Smith	James F. Kyle
Robert L. Sabbatini	James T. McColgan, III
Harold W. McLeary, Jr.	G. Edward Coleman, III
William D. Domico	Bryant C. Witt

Representative Clients: Premier RRG Insurance; Illinois Central Railroad; Medical Assurance; Albertson's, Inc.; Med. Marc (Chiro Co.); Medical Protective Co.; Methodist Health Systems; Hartford Insurance Co.; Sentry Insurance; State Farm Insurance.

For full biographical listings, see the Martindale-Hubbell Law Directory

Memphis—Continued

WARING COX, PLC (AV)

Morgan Keegan Tower, 50 North Front Street, Suite 1300, 38103-1190
Telephone: 901-543-8000
Telecopy: 901-543-8030
Email: Desk@waringcox.com

Louis F. Allen
Saul C. Belz
William E. Frulla
Louis J. Miller
Charles W. Hill
Earle J. Schwarz
Robert B.C. Hale

OF COUNSEL

Roane Waring, Jr.

Representative Clients: Federal Express Corp.; South Central Bell Telephone Co.; Cook International, Inc.; Express Airlines I, Inc.; Flavorite Laboratories, Inc.; MobileComm; Osceola Foods, Inc.; Perkins Family Restaurants.

For Complete List of Firm Personnel, See General Section

For full biographical listings, see the Martindale-Hubbell Law Directory

*MURFREESBORO,** Rutherford Co.

WILLIAM KENNERLY BURGER (AV)

SunTrust Bank Building, 201 East Main Street, Suite 306, P.O. Box 1969, 37133-1969
Telephone: 615-893-8933
Fax: 615-893-5333

For full biographical listings, see the Martindale-Hubbell Law Directory

*NASHVILLE,** Davidson Co.

BAKER, DONELSON, BEARMAN & CALDWELL (AV)

1700 Nashville City Center, 511 Union Street, 37219
Telephone: 615-726-5600
Telecopier: 615-726-0464
Email: info@bdbc.com *URL:* http://www.bakerdonelson.com
Memphis, Tennessee Office: 20th Floor, First Tennessee Building, 165 Madison, 38103.
Telephone: 901-526-2000.
Telecopier: 901-577-2303.
Chattanooga, Tennessee Office: 1800 Republic Centre, 633 Chestnut Street, 37450-1800.
Telephone: 423-756-2010.
Telecopier: 423-756-3447.
Knoxville, Tennessee Office: 2200 Riverview Tower, 900 South Gay Street, 37901.
Telephone: 423-549-7000.
Telecopier: 423-525-8569.
Johnson City, Tennessee Office: SunTrust Bank Building, 207 Mockingbird Lane, P.O. Box 3038, 37602.
Telephone: 423-928-0181.
Telecopier: 423-928-5694; 423-928-3654; Kingsport: 423-246-6191.
Huntsville, Tennessee Office: 3 Courthouse Square, 37756.
Telephone: 423-663-2321.
Telecopier: 423-663-2111.
Washington, D.C. Office: Market Square, 801 Pennsylvania Avenue, N.W., 20004.
Telephone: 202-508-3400.
Telecopier: 202-508-3402.
Jackson, Mississippi Office: Suite 500, 700 North State Street, 39202.
Telephone: 601-351-2400.
Telecopier: 601-351-2424.

MANAGING PARTNER

Laurence M. Papel

SHAREHOLDERS

Lewis R. Donelson, III
Howard H. Baker, Jr.
Robert F. Worthington, Jr.
Robert G. McCullough
Richard D. Bird
Thomas O. Helton
Richard B. Gossett
Robert L. Baker
Robert G. McDowell
Carl E. Hartley
William S. Painter (Not admitted in TN)
John A. Gupton, III
Claudia W. Dickerson
James A. DeLanis
Richard G. Cowart
Kenneth P. Ezell, Jr.
James L. McElroy
Robert M. Steele
Gary C. Shockley
Randal S. Mashburn
Steven J. Eisen
John S. Hicks
J. Porter Durham, Jr.
M. Kevin Outterson
J. Steven Kirkham
John H. Rowland
Philip Stuart McSween
Thomas E. Bartrum (Not admitted in TN)

ASSOCIATES

Claire F. Miley
Barbara A. Rose
John F. Rogers, Jr.
Scott D. Carey
John M. Bryant, Jr.
Kenneth A. Weber
Darwin A. Hindman III
Ann Duncan Jarvis
Lawrence S. Eastwood, Jr.
Jonathan Cole
Christopher R. Kelly
Brigid T. Miller
Christy Tosh Crider
Kelley Taylor Oliver

(See Next Column)

ASSOCIATES (Continued)

Richard H. Stout
J. Adin Lara
Tonya Mitchem Grindon (Not admitted in TN)
Jennifer Lynch Butler

OF COUNSEL

Peter C. Ward (Not admitted in TN)
Thomas H. Holter (Not admitted in TN)
Christy F. Batts

For full biographical listings, see the Martindale-Hubbell Law Directory

CHERNAU, CHAFFIN & BURNSED, PLLC (AV)

SunTrust Center, 424 Church Street, Suite 1750, 37219-2305
Telephone: 615-244-5480
Fax: 615-242-7951
Email: CCBABSMITH@AOL.COM

MEMBERS OF FIRM

Louis Leftwich, Jr. (1910-1960)
Stanley M. Chernau
R. Garry Chaffin
Linda F. Burnsed
Amy Bryson Smith

Representative Clients: A.G. Edwards & Sons, Inc.; Belz Enterprises; B & G Wholesalers, Inc.; SouthTrust Bank National Association; Edwin B. Raskins Co.

For full biographical listings, see the Martindale-Hubbell Law Directory

CORNELIUS & COLLINS, LLP (AV)

Suite 2700 Nashville City Center, P.O. Box 190695, 37219-0695
Telephone: 615-244-1440
Facsimile: 615-254-9477

Charles L. Cornelius (1888-1968)
Charles L. Cornelius, Jr.
William Ovid Collins, Jr.
Charles Hampton White
Thomas I. Carlton, Jr.
Charles G. Cornelius
Noel F. Stahl
C. Bennett Harrison, Jr.
David L. Steed
Richard L. Colbert
David A. King
Blakeley D. Matthews
Joseph R. Wheeler
Kurtis J. Winstead
Rebecca Wells Demaree
Daniel P. Berexa
Jay Nelson Chamness
Leigh Ann Buckley
E. Todd Presnell
Christopher S. Dunn
J. Frank Rudy, Jr.
Beth C. Baggett

Bryan K. Williams

Representative Clients: General Motors Corp.; Tennessee Medical Assn; Tennessee Education Assn.; United Parcel Service; Hartford Insurance Group; State Volunteer Mutual Insurance Co.; Johnson & Johnson Inc.; Mercedes Benz of North American, Inc.; BIC Corp.; Pirelli Armstrong Tire Corporation.

For full biographical listings, see the Martindale-Hubbell Law Directory

DORAMUS, TRAUGER & NEY (AV)

Southern Turf Building, 222 Fourth Avenue North, 37219-2101
Telephone: 615-256-8585
Fax: 615-256-7444
Email: dtnfirm@dtnlaw.com

MEMBERS OF FIRM

Byron R. Trauger
James V. Doramus
Paul C. Ney, Jr.

ASSOCIATES

Gregory Mitchell
Jane Hanner Allen
Leesa A. Hinson

For full biographical listings, see the Martindale-Hubbell Law Directory

HOLLINS, WAGSTER & YARBROUGH, P.C. (AV)

22nd Floor SunTrust Center, 424 Church Street, 37219
Telephone: 615-256-6666
Telecopier: 615-254-4254

John J. Hollins
John W. Wagster
Edward M. Yarbrough
John L. Norris
David L. Raybin
James L. Weatherly, Jr.
John J. Hollins, Jr.
Patrick T. McNally

Jacqueline B. Dixon

References: First American National Bank; Sun Trust Bank.

For full biographical listings, see the Martindale-Hubbell Law Directory

KING & BALLOW (AV)

Union Street Plaza, 315 Union Street, Suite 1100, 37201
Telephone: 615-259-3456
Fax: 615-254-7907
Email: lawfirm@king-ballow.com *URL:* http://www.king-ballow.com
San Diego, California Office: 2700 Symphony Towers, 750 B Street, 92101.
Telephone: 619-236-9401.
Fax: 619-236-9437.

(See Next Column)

KING & BALLOW—*Continued*

MEMBERS OF FIRM

Frank S. King, Jr.
Robert L. Ballow
Richard C. Lowe
R. Eddie Wayland
Larry D. Crabtree
Alan L. Marx
Paul H. Duvall (Resident, San Diego, California Office)
Steven C. Douse
Douglas R. Pierce
Howard M. Kastrinsky
Mark E. Hunt
John J. Matchulat
M. Kim Vance
R. Brent Ballow
Michael D. Oesterle
Richard S. Busch

ASSOCIATES

James P. Thompson
Patrick M. Thomas
D'Lesli M. Davis
Andrew S. Naylor
Nels Jacobson
Marcus M. Crider
Alexander J. Passantino
B. Todd Vinson
David L. Wiley
James A. Crumlin, Jr.
Elizabeth S. Washko (Not admitted in TN)
Douglas B. Janney, III
Amy C. Martin (Not admitted in TN)
Abraham F. Barker (Not admitted in TN)

Representative Clients: American Airlines, Nashville, Tennessee; Cooper Industries, Inc., Houston, TX; Dollar General Corp.; Ingram, Industries, Inc., Nashville, Tennessee; Ingram Micro, Inc., Santa Ana, CA; Kroger Co., Cincinnati, Ohio; O'Charley's, Inc., Nashville, TN; Opryland USA, Inc.; Roadway Express, Inc., Akron, OH; Scene Three, Inc., Nashville, TN.

For Complete List of Firm Personnel, See General Section

For full biographical listings, see the Martindale-Hubbell Law Directory

LACKEY, RODGERS, PRICE AND SNEDEKER (AV)

Suite 1230, First American Center, 37238-1230
Telephone: 615-244-5772
Fax: 615-244-5821

MEMBERS OF FIRM

Joseph L. Lackey, Jr.
John E. Rodgers
James W. Price, Jr.
Larry H. Snedeker
John E. Rodgers, Jr.
William Timothy Hill
Robert E. Kolarich, Jr.
Joyce M. Grimes

For full biographical listings, see the Martindale-Hubbell Law Directory

MINK & BLAIR (AV)

Suite 400, 219 Second Avenue, North, P.O. Box 190584, 37219-0584
Telephone: 615-256-0138
Fax: 615-726-8796
Lawrenceburg, Tennessee Office: 316 Waterloo Street, P.O. Box 707.
Telephone: 931-762-7112.
Fax: 931-762-1318. Email: tmink@lorettotel.net.
Smithville, Tennessee Office: 110 Market Street, 37166.
Telephone: 615-597-3065.
Fax: 615-597-3066.

MEMBERS OF FIRM

Thomas F. Mink, II
Keith W. Blair

M. Wallace Coleman

For full biographical listings, see the Martindale-Hubbell Law Directory

PARKER, LAWRENCE, CANTRELL & DEAN (AV)

Fifth Floor, 200 Fourth Avenue North, 37219
Telephone: 615-255-7500
Telecopy: 615-242-1515
Email: plcd@plcd.com *URL:* http://www.plcd.com

MEMBERS OF FIRM

Robert E. Parker
Thomas W. Lawrence, Jr.
Rose Park Cantrell
George A. Dean
Richard K. Smith
Louis Marshall Albritton
M. Bradley Gilmore
Garrett E. Asher
R. Blake Menzel

ASSOCIATE

Richard F. Russell

Representative Clients: Regions Bank; Wal-Mart Stores, Inc.; State Volunteer Mutual Insurance Co.; Harpeth Valley Utility District; Steinhouse Supply Co.

For full biographical listings, see the Martindale-Hubbell Law Directory

GAIL P. PIGG (AV)

219 Second Avenue North, 37201
Telephone: 615-244-0001
Fax: 615-244-0003

References: Nations Bank.

For full biographical listings, see the Martindale-Hubbell Law Directory

PRINCE & HELLINGER, P.C. (AV)

150 Second Avenue North, Suite 300, 37201-1902
Telephone: 615-244-8630
Fax: 615-244-8644

Raymond G. Prince
John R. Hellinger

For full biographical listings, see the Martindale-Hubbell Law Directory

DAVID RANDOLPH SMITH & ASSOCIATES (AV)

611 Commerce Street, 3121 Renaissance Tower, 37203
Telephone: 615-742-1775; 800-394-2119
Fax: 615-742-1223
URL: http://www.lawyers.com/drs&associates
Email: info@drslawfirm.com *URL:* http://www.drslawfirm.com

For full biographical listings, see the Martindale-Hubbell Law Directory

TEXAS

ADDISON, Dallas Co.

BARRETT BURKE WILSON CASTLE DAFFIN & FRAPPIER, L.L.P. (AV)

A Limited Liability Partnership including Professional Corporations
15000 Surveyor Boulevard, Suite 100, 75001
Telephone: 972-386-5040
Fax: 972-386-7673
Houston, Texas Office: 24 Greenway Plaza, Suite 2001.
Telephone: 713-621-8673.
Denver, Colorado Affiliated Office: Castle Barrett Daffin & Frappier, 1099 Eighteenth Street, Suite 2200.
Telephone: 303-299-1800.
Fax: 303-299-1808.
Little Rock, Arkansas Affiliated Office: Wilson & Associates, P.A. 1521 Merrill Drive, Suite D220.
Telephone: 501-219-9388.

Michael C. Barrett

For full biographical listings, see the Martindale-Hubbell Law Directory

GERARD SINGER & LEVICK, P.C. (AV)

16200 Addison Road Suite 140, 75001-5350
Telephone: 972-380-5533
Fax: 972-380-5748
Email: bcgerard@flash.net

Bretton C. Gerard
Gregory Z. Singer
Larry A. Levick
Michael I. Kahn
Robert J. Mabel
I. Richard Levy

For full biographical listings, see the Martindale-Hubbell Law Directory

*AMARILLO,** Potter Co.

GARNER & STEIN, LLP (AV)

777 Amarillo National Plaza/Two, 500 South Taylor, LB #233, 79101-2446
Telephone: 806-373-0505
Telecopier: 806-379-8056
Email: regarner@tcac.net

MEMBERS OF FIRM

Robert E. Garner
Sam L. Stein

ASSOCIATE

Ana E. Estevez

LEGAL SUPPORT PERSONNEL

PARALEGALS

Michele Kindle
Roxann Sillivent

Representative Clients: Panhandle Capitol Corp.; Friona Industries, L.P.; Page and Associates, Contractors; Hereford Bi-Products, Inc.; Amarillo National Bank.

For full biographical listings, see the Martindale-Hubbell Law Directory

ART B. LARA, JR. (AV)

PRPC Building, Suite 30, 415 West 8th Street, 79101
Telephone: 806-358-8773
Fax: 806-376-6437
Email: abllaw@arn.net *URL:* http://www.lawyers.com/artblara

For full biographical listings, see the Martindale-Hubbell Law Directory

Amarillo—Continued

NANCY J. STONE (AV)

Maxor Building, Suite 820, 320 South Polk Street, Lobby Box 32, 79101
Telephone: 806-374-9300
Fax: 806-373-3008
Email: nstone@arn.net *URL:* http://www.nancyjstone.com/806-374-9300/2-1.html

For full biographical listings, see the Martindale-Hubbell Law Directory

WHITTENBURG WHITTENBURG & SCHACHTER, P.C. (AV)

1010 South Harrison, P.O. Box 31718, 79120
Telephone: 806-372-5700
Facsimile: 806-372-5757
Dallas, Texas Office: 2300 Plaza of the Americas, 600 North Pearl, LB 133.
Telephone: 214-999-5700.
Facsimile: 214-999-5747.

Deborah Ashmore Harris

For Complete List of Firm Personnel, See General Section

For full biographical listings, see the Martindale-Hubbell Law Directory

*AUSTIN,** Travis Co.

BAKER BOTTS L.L.P. (AV)

1600 San Jacinto Center, 98 San Jacinto Boulevard, 78701
Telephone: 512-322-2500
Fax: 512-322-2501
Email: postmaster@bakerbotts.com *URL:* http://www.bakerbotts.com
Houston, Texas Office: One Shell Plaza, 910 Louisiana.
Telephone: 713-229-1234.
Dallas, Texas Office: 2001 Ross Avenue.
Telephone: 214-953-6500.
Washington, D.C. Office: The Warner, 1299 Pennsylvania Avenue, N.W.
Telephone: 202-639-7700.
New York, New York Office: 599 Lexington Avenue.
Telephone: 212-705-5000.
Moscow, Russia Office: 10 ul. Bolshaya Dimitrovka (formerly Pushkinskaya), 103031.
Telephone: 7095/921-5300 (Local); 7501/929-7070 (International).
London, England Office: 45 Ludgate Hill.
Telephone: 0171-778-1400 (Local); 011-44-171-778-1400 (International).
Baku, Azerbaijan Office: 6-10 Vagif Mustafa-zadeh Street, Third Floor, Icheri Sheher, 370004.
Telephone: 994-12-97-63-88 (Local); 011-994-12-97-63-88 (International).
Fax: 994-12-97-63-61 (Local); 011-994-12-97-63-91 (International).

MEMBERS OF FIRM

Robert I. Howell
Patrick O. Keel
Joseph R. Knight
Mark R. Robeck
Kevin M. Sadler
Robert T. Stewart
Robb L. Voyles
Larry F. York

OF COUNSEL

Joe R. Greenhill
Bob E. Shannon

ASSOCIATES

David T. Arlington
Julie K. Buchanan
Scott King Field
Daniel S. Floyd
Susan Denmon Gusky
Sofia Harber
Derek R. McDonald
Gavin R. Villareal
Kelly Diane Walton
Rebecca S. Whitehouse

For Complete List of Firm Personnel, See General Section

For full biographical listings, see the Martindale-Hubbell Law Directory

BANKSTON & RICHARDSON, L.L.P. (AV)

400 West 15th Street, Suite 710, 78701
Telephone: 512-499-8855
Fax: 512-499-8886
Email: brmlaw@brmlaw.com

Milton L. Bankston
James M. Richardson

Representative Clients: H.B. Fuller; University Co-operative Society; Coca-Cola Enterprises, Inc.; BDO Seidman; Wesson International; Texas Lawyers Insurance Exchange; Mercantile Financial Corp.; Benarides Investment Group.

For full biographical listings, see the Martindale-Hubbell Law Directory

KARL BAYER (AV)

900 Norwood Tower, 114 West Seventh Street, 78701
Telephone: 512-476-1226
Fax: 512-476-1280
Email: karl@karlbayer.com

Karl Bayer

For full biographical listings, see the Martindale-Hubbell Law Directory

BROYLES & PRATT, A PROFESSIONAL CORPORATION (AV)

One Northpoint Centre, Suite 250, 6836 Austin Center Boulevard, 78731
Telephone: 361-886 6200
Fax: 361-886 6262
Corpus Christi, Texas Office: 1001 Bank of America Center North. 500 North Shoreline Boulevard, 78471.
Telephone: 361-886-6200.
Fax: 361-886-6262.

R. Michael Anderson
Larry W. Brewer
Mark Held
Joe N. Pratt
Davison W. Grant
Mason L. Terry

Dudley McClellan

OF COUNSEL

Richard H. Cory

For full biographical listings, see the Martindale-Hubbell Law Directory

THE BURK LAW FIRM A PROFESSIONAL CORPORATION (AV)

The Bremond House, 711 San Antonio Street, 78701
Telephone: 512-476-8350; 888-476-9210
Fax: 512-476-8360
Email: firm@burklawtx.com *URL:* http://www.lawyers.com/theburklawfirm

Michael G. Burk

OF COUNSEL

Colten Wade Smith
Hollis W. Burklund

For full biographical listings, see the Martindale-Hubbell Law Directory

DAVIS & DAVIS, P.C. (AV)

Arboretum Plaza One, 9th Floor, 9442 Capital of Texas Highway, P.O. Box 1588, 78759
Telephone: 512-343-6248
Fax: 512-343-0121
Mailing Address: P.O. Box 1588, Austin, Texas, 78767

C. Dean Davis
Fred E. Davis
Alexis J. Fuller, Jr.
Ruth Russell-Schafer
Michael L. Neely
Brian Gregory Jackson
Monte F. James

Bill Cline, Jr.
Mark Alan Keene
Kenda B. Dalrymple
Marian J. Wu
Mark S. La Spina

For Complete List of Firm Personnel, See General Section

For full biographical listings, see the Martindale-Hubbell Law Directory

DAVIS & WILKERSON, P.C. (AV)

1801 South Mopac, Suite 300, P.O. Box 2283, 78768-2283
Telephone: 512-482-0614
Fax: 512-482-0342
Email: dwlaw@dwlaw.com *URL:* http://www.dwlaw.com
Alpine Office: 1110 East Holland, P.O. Box 777.
Telephone: 915-837-5547.

David M. Davis
Steven R. Welch
Glen Wilkerson
David A. Wright
Leonard W. Woods
Kevin A. Reed
J. Mark Holbrook
Brian E. Riewe
Brian McElroy
Robert L. Hargett
Michael Wilson
Frances W. Hamermesh
Fletcher H. Brown

Jennifer B. Claymon
David M. Coffey
Hollis Hudson Gaston
Steven C. Levatino
Diana Maldonado
Erin E. Matherne
Joel S. Pace
Stephen G. Wohleb
Michael P. Young

OF COUNSEL

Pete P. Gallego (Resident, Alpine Office)
Peter R. Meeker

For full biographical listings, see the Martindale-Hubbell Law Directory

DELEON, BOGGINS & ICENOGLE, A PROFESSIONAL CORPORATION (AV)

Bank One Tower, 221 West 6th Street, Suite 1050, 78701
Telephone: 512-478-5308
Fax: 512-482-8628
Email: deleon@dandb.com

Hector DeLeon
Anthony Icenogle
Thomas P. Washburn

(See Next Column)

DeLeon, Boggins & Icenogle A Professional Corporation—*Continued*

OF COUNSEL

Joseph C. Boggins
Waggoner Carr
L. Dean Coff

Reference: Bank One, Austin.

For full biographical listings, see the Martindale-Hubbell Law Directory

Franklin W. Denius (AV)

700 Chase Bank Building, 700 Lavaca, 78701-3102
Telephone: 512-472-9840
Fax: 512-472-9870

Reference: Chase Bank of Texas.

For full biographical listings, see the Martindale-Hubbell Law Directory

Gary F. DeShazo & Associates (AV)

823 Congress Avenue, Suite 1550, 78701
Telephone: 512-476-3800
Fax: 512-476-0435
Email: Deshazo@worldnet.att.net *URL:* http://www.lawyers.com/deshazolaw

OF COUNSEL

Jerome J. Schielfelbein (Not admitted in TX)

For full biographical listings, see the Martindale-Hubbell Law Directory

George & Donaldson, L.L.P. (AV)

1100 Norwood Tower, 114 West 7th Street, 78701
Telephone: 512-495-1400
Facsimile: 512-499-0094
Email: gdf@gdf.com *URL:* http://www.gdf.com

MEMBERS OF FIRM

R. James George, Jr.
David H. Donaldson, Jr.
Ben J. Cunningham
Renea Hicks
Peter D. Kennedy
J. Roger Williams, Jr.
Gary L. Lewis
James A. Hemphill

ASSOCIATES

Todd S. George
Paul Vigushin

For full biographical listings, see the Martindale-Hubbell Law Directory

Thomas George, P.C. (AV)

2310 Westgate Building, 1122 Colorado Street, 78701
Telephone: 512-477-9651
Fax: 512-477-6586
Email: tomwgeorge@aol.com

Thomas William George

For full biographical listings, see the Martindale-Hubbell Law Directory

Harris & Harris (AV)

Building III, 5300 Bee Cave Road, Suite 200, 78746
Telephone: 512-346-5533
Fax: 512-346-2539
Email: info@harriswc.com *URL:* http://www.harriswc.com

MEMBERS OF FIRM

H. S. Harris, Jr. (1916-1991)
H. S. Harris, III
Christopher J. Ameel
Charles E. Morse, Jr.
Frances A. Lout
William J. Grove, Jr.

ASSOCIATES

Camille L. Espey
Janice G. Menzies
Stuart Colburn
Ricky D. Green
LeeAnna Gainer
Paul Kelley
Jessica Mendes Warren
Robert F. Josey
Mark H. Sickles

For full biographical listings, see the Martindale-Hubbell Law Directory

Hearne, Eppright & Gest, A Professional Corporation (AV)

700 Lavaca, Suite 1500, P.O. Box 1687, 78767
Telephone: 512-478-1500
Telecopier: 512-478-2906

Douglass D. Hearne
Charles L. Eppright
Darrell D. Gest

Douglass D. Hearne, Jr.
Allen Halbrook, Jr.
Ann R. Powers
Roger B. Williams

(See Next Column)

OF COUNSEL

Nola White

Representative Clients: Dahlstrom Corporation; EZ Pipe Paddler; Faison Stone, Inc.; Gilbane Building Supply Company; Guarantee Federal Savings; Midland Independent School District; Texas A & M University System; Temple-Inland Mortgage Corporation; University of Texas System.

For full biographical listings, see the Martindale-Hubbell Law Directory

Herman & Howry, L.L.P. (AV)

1900 Pearl Street, 78705-5408
Telephone: 512-474-7300
Fax: 512-474-8557
URL: http://www.hermanhowry.com

Timothy J. Herman
Randy R. Howry
Sean E. Breen
Matthew R. Beatty
Thomas H. Daniel
Melissa C. Hill

For full biographical listings, see the Martindale-Hubbell Law Directory

Hohmann & Taube, L.L.P. (AV)

100 Congress Avenue, Suite 1600, 78701-4042
Telephone: 512-472-5997
Fax: 512-472-5248
Email: bille@ht-law.com *URL:* http://www.ht-law.com

Guy M. Hohmann
Eric J. Taube
Robert Summers
Mitchell D. Savrick
Gary N. Schumann

Cristina B. McGarr
Robert D. Thomas
T. Wade Jefferies
Neal Meinzer
Scott B. Herlihy

For full biographical listings, see the Martindale-Hubbell Law Directory

Minton, Burton, Foster & Collins, A Professional Corporation (AV)

1100 Guadalupe Street, 78701-2198
Telephone: 512-476-4873
Fax: 512-479-8315

Perry L. Jones (1908-1969)
J. Travis Blakeslee (1919-1990)
Paul T. Holt (1906-1995)
Roy Q. Minton
Charles R. Burton
John L. Foster
Warren L. (Rip) Collins, Jr.
Randy T. Leavitt
Martha S. Dickie
Scott A. Young
John C. Carsey
David F. Minton
Jennifer Ramsey
Michael L.R. Burnett
Jeffrey David Miller

Representative Clients: South Texas Nuclear Operating Project; Reliant Energy; Stratus Properties; City of Cedar Park; Eco Resources, Inc.; International Game Technology; Texas Department of Public Safety; Texas Instruments; Intel, Inc.; Southern Union Gas Company.

For full biographical listings, see the Martindale-Hubbell Law Directory

Mithoff & Jacks, L.L.P. (AV)

Suite 1010, Franklin Plaza, 111 Congress Avenue, 78701
Telephone: 512-478-4422
Telecopier: 512-478-5015
Houston, Texas Office: Penthouse, 3450 One Allen Center.
Telephone: 713-654-1122.
Fax: 713-739-8085.

Richard Warren Mithoff
Tommy Jacks

James L. Wright
Belinda Manning Howell
Mark George Einfalt
Greig W. Coates
David Drew Wright

For full biographical listings, see the Martindale-Hubbell Law Directory

Saegert, Angenend & Augustine, P.C. (AV)

1145 West Fifth Street, Suite 300, 78703-5341
Telephone: 512-474-6521
Fax: 512-477-4512

John C. Augustine

Rebecca K. Knapik
Amy Jeanne Welton
Elizabeth Fuller
David M. Dillon

Representative Clients: Mayflower Transit; Acme Truck Line; Southern Union; OmniTRAX, Inc.; Statewide Trucking Corp.

For full biographical listings, see the Martindale-Hubbell Law Directory

Austin—Continued

THOMPSON & KNIGHT L.L.P. (AV)

(Attorneys and Counselors)
1200 San Jacinto Center, 98 San Jacinto Boulevard, 78701
Telephone: 512-469-6100
Telecopy: 512-469-6180
URL: http://www.tklaw.com
Dallas, Texas Office: 1700 Pacific Avenue, Suite 3300, 75201.
Telephone: 214-969-1700.
Telecopy: 512-969-1751.
Telex: 732298.
Fort Worth, Texas Office: 801 Cherry Street, Suite 1600, 76102.
Telephone: 817-347-1700.
Telecopy: 817-347-1799.
Houston, Texas Office: Thompson Knight Brown Parker & Leahy L.L.P., 1200 Smith Street, Suite 3600, 77002-4595.
Telephone: 713-654-8111.
Telecopier: 713-654-1871.
San Pedro Garza Garcia, Nuevo León, Mexico Office: Edificio Losoles PD-4, Av. Lázaro Cárdenas No. 2400 Pte., C.P. 66220.
Telephone: (52-8) 363-0096.
Telecopy: (52-8) 363-3067.

PARTNERS

Debora Beck Alsup
Jeffrey S. Boyd
Eugene W. Brees, II
James E. Cousar
Frank L. Hill

ASSOCIATES

Matthew J. Knifton
Peter A. Vermillion

OF COUNSEL

Raymond M. Galasso (Not admitted in TX)
Mark L. Murdock

For Complete List of Firm Personnel, See General Section

For full biographical listings, see the Martindale-Hubbell Law Directory

VINSON & ELKINS L.L.P. (AV)

One American Center, Suite 2700, 600 Congress Avenue, 78701-3200
Telephone: 512-495-8400
Fax: 512-495-8612
URL: http://www.velaw.com
Beijing, China Office: 20/F, Beijing Silver Tower, No. 2, Dong San Huan Bei Lu, Chaoyang District, 100027.
Telephone: +86-10-6410-6300.
Fax: +86-10-6410-6360.
Dallas, Texas Office: 3700 Trammell Crow Center, 2001 Ross Avenue, Dallas, Texas, 75201-2975.
Telephone: 214-220-7700.
Fax: 214-220-7716.
Houston, Texas Office: 2300 First City Tower, 1001 Fannin, Houston, Texas, 77002-6760.
Telephone: 713-758-2222.
Fax: 713-758-2346.
London, England Office: Regis House, 8th Floor, 45 King William Street, London, EC4R 9AN, England.
Telephone: (44-171) 618-6000.
Fax: (44-171) 618-6001.
Moscow, Russia Office: 16 Ulitsa Spiridonovka, Second Floor, 103001 Moscow, Russia.
Telephone: (7-095) 956-1995. Local
Fax: (7-095) 956-1996. U.S. Satellite
Fax: (212) 803-0142.
New York, N.Y. Office: 1325 Avenue of the Americas, 17th Floor, New York, N.Y., 10019.
Telephone: 917-206-8000.
Fax: 917-206-8100.
Singapore Office: 6 Battery Road, #39-01, Singapore, 049909.
Telephone: (65) 536-8300.
Fax: (65) 536-8311.
Washington, D.C. Office: The Willard Office Building, 1455 Pennsylvania Avenue, N.W., Washington, D.C., 20004-1008.
Telephone: 202-639-6500.
Fax: 202-639-6604.

RESIDENT PARTNERS

Kim Edward Brightwell
Richard D. Milvenan
Beverly G. Reeves

OF COUNSEL

Spikes Kangerga

RESIDENT ASSOCIATES

J. David Bickham, Jr.
William J. Cobb III
Dean W. Harvey
Robbi B. Hull
Katherine D. Jordan
Michael Dennis Marin
Jennifer Barrett Poppe
Spencer Smith
James M. Vickery

For Complete List of Firm Personnel, See General Section

For full biographical listings, see the Martindale-Hubbell Law Directory

WALSH, ANDERSON, BROWN, SCHULZE & ALDRIDGE, P.C. (AV)

La Costa Centre, 6300 La Calma, Suite 200, P.O. Box 2156, 78768
Telephone: 512-454-6864
Fax: 512-467-9318
San Antonio, Texas Office: Renaissance Plaza, Suite 800, 70 N.E. Loop 410. P.O. Box 460606, 78246-0606.
Telephone: 210-979-6633.
Fax: 210-979-7024.
Irving, Texas Office: 511 E. John Carpenter Freeway, Suite 430, P.O. Box 168046, 75062.
Telephone: 214-574-8800.
Fax: 214-574-8801.

Jim Walsh
Denise Howell Anderson
Judy Brown
Eric W. Schulze
John S. Aldridge
Paul William Hunn
Elena M. Gallegos
Nan Porett Hundere (Resident, San Antonio Office)
Joe B. Hairston
Dorcas A. Green
Therold I. Farmer
Robert Russo (Resident, San Antonio Office)
Paige C. Kyle (Resident, San Antonio Office)
Oscar G. Treviño
Bridget R. Robinson
Mark C. Goulet
Susan B. Graham (Resident, Irving Office)

Nona C. Matthews (Resident, Irving Office)
Denise Hays
Paula Maddox Roalson (Resident, San Antonio Office)
Daniel M. (Matt) Burns
Terry L. Kyle (Resident, San Antonio Office)
JoAnn S. Wright (Resident, Irving Office)
Liza M. Crow (Resident, San Antonio Office)
Stacy Tuer Castillo (Resident, San Antonio Office)
Jennifer A. Childress
Joe A. De Los Santos
Marie K. Williams
George E. Grimes, Jr. (Resident, San Antonio Office)
Sharon E. Ramage (Resident, Irving, Texas Office)
Yvonnilda G. Muñiz
Marquette M. Maresh

LEGAL SUPPORT PERSONNEL

Diana Stangl (Office Manager)

For full biographical listings, see the Martindale-Hubbell Law Directory

WATSON, BISHOP, LONDON, GALOW, P.C. (AV)

The Littlefield Building, 106 East Sixth Street, Suite 700, 78701
Telephone: 512-479-5900
Telefax: 512-479-5934

Kirk P. Watson
Daniel W. Bishop, II
Alice London
Jerry Galow

Christina Carlson Dodds
Phillip H. Schmandt
Joseph F. Brophy
Cory W. Smith

For full biographical listings, see the Martindale-Hubbell Law Directory

LAW OFFICES OF JOSEPH P. WEBBER (AV)

Frost Bank Plaza, Suite 1100, 816 Congress Avenue, 78701
Telephone: 512-472-1131
Telecopier: 512-479-8977

For full biographical listings, see the Martindale-Hubbell Law Directory

*BEAUMONT,** Jefferson Co.

BENCKENSTEIN, NORVELL & NATHAN, L.L.P. (AV)

550 Fannin, Suite 200, P.O. Box 551, 77704
Telephone: 409-833-4309
Telecopier: 409-833-9558
Email: bmtlaw@aol.com
Houston, Texas Office: One Riverway, Suite 100
Telephone: 713-871-8081.
Fax: 713-871-1509.

MEMBERS OF FIRM

Lipscomb Norvell, Jr.
Gerald W. Riedmueller
Michael J. Reviere (Resident, Houston Office)
Paul A. Scheurich
Craig H. Clendenin (Resident, Houston Office)

ASSOCIATES

Floyd F. McSpadden, Jr.
Dennis S. Dresden (Resident, Houston Office)
David A. Oubre (Resident, Houston Office)
J. Keith Stanley

OF COUNSEL

Jerry J. Nathan

Representative Clients: Chubb/Pacific Indemnity Group; Mobil Oil Corp.; Travelers; Wausau; American International Group; CNA; Kemper Insurance Group; E.I. DuPont; Zurich American; Fina Oil & Chemical Co.

For full biographical listings, see the Martindale-Hubbell Law Directory

Beaumont—Continued

BENCKENSTEIN & OXFORD, L.L.P. (AV)

Community Bank Building, P.O. Box 150, 77704
Telephone: 409-833-9182
Cable Address: "Bmor"
Telex: 779485
Telefax: 409-833-8819
Email: lawfirm@benoxford.com
Houston, Texas Office: Two Post Oak Central, 1980 Post Oak Boulevard, Suite 1600, 77056.
Telephone: 713-629-0345.
Fax: 713-629-0614.

MEMBERS OF FIRM

L. J. Benckenstein (1894-1966)
F. L. Benckenstein (1918-1987)
Hubert Oxford, III
Alan G. Sampson
Frank D. Calvert
Dana Timaeus
Frances Blair Bethea
Robert J. Rose, Sr.

ASSOCIATES

F. Blair Clarke
Michael K. Eaves
Alex J. Stelly, Jr.
Robert W. Craft
Lauren Miller Robbins (Resident, Houston Office)

Representative Clients: Marine Office of American Corp. (MOAC); Moran Towing and Transportation Co., Inc.

For full biographical listings, see the Martindale-Hubbell Law Directory

LEWIS & ASSOCIATES (AV)

The Courtyard, 4180 Delaware, Suite 402, 77706
Telephone: 409-899-5600
Fax: 409-899-5682

Clint W. Lewis

Edward B. Chatelain, III
James W. Henges

For full biographical listings, see the Martindale-Hubbell Law Directory

MICHAEL R. MCGOWN (AV)

2615 Calder Street, Suite 300, P.O. Box 5876, 77726-5876
Telephone: 409-839-8389
Fax: 409-839-8387
Email: mcgown@ih2000.net *URL:* http://www.mcgown@ih2000.net

For full biographical listings, see the Martindale-Hubbell Law Directory

MEHAFFY & WEBER, A PROFESSIONAL CORPORATION (AV)

2615 Calder Avenue, Suite 800, P.O. Box 16, 77704
Telephone: 409-835-5011
Fax: 409-835-5729; 835-5177
Email: MehaffyWeber.com
Orange, Texas Office: 1006 Green Avenue, P.O. Drawer 189.
Telephone: 409-886-7766.
Houston, Texas Office: One Allen Center, 500 Dallas, Suite 1200.
Telephone: 713-655-1200.

James W. Mehaffy (1914-1985)
Roger S. McCabe
Jim I. Graves
John Cash Smith
Arthur R. Almquist
Louis M. Scofield
Patricia Chamblin
Gene M. Williams
David B. Gaultney
Robert A. Black
Sandra F. Clark
M. C. Carrington
Barbara J. Barron
Elizabeth Brandes Pratt
John E. Haught
Keith W. Foley
Charles Stanton Perry
Ernest W. Boyd
Michele Y. Smith

Vickie R. Thompson
Paul R. Heyburn
James G. Martingano
Debra N. Bigler
Charles W. Goehringer, Jr.
Elizabeth C. Turley
Peter T. Gregg
E. Wade Carpenter
Nikkee E. Rutherford
Bridget M. Fuselier
Jonathan C. Allen
Chris H. Booth
Maryalyce W. Cox
Timothy A. Gasaway
Elna Nguyen Griggs
Sean Stotsky

OF COUNSEL

Otto J. Weber, Jr.
Dewey J. Gonsoulin
John J. Durkay

Representative Clients: E.I. du Pont de Nemours and Co.; Eli Lilly & Co.; Merrell Dow; Jefferson County Tax Appraisal District; W.R. Grace & Co.-Conn.; Bank of America; Christus Health; Christus St. Elizabeth; Christus St. Mary; Burlington Northern Santa Fe Railway.
Approved Attorneys for: Stewart Title Guaranty Co.

For Complete List of Firm Personnel, See General Section

For full biographical listings, see the Martindale-Hubbell Law Directory

BEDFORD, Tarrant Co.

RONALD D. WREN (AV)

1244 Harwood Road, Suite 220, 76021
Telephone: 817-540-6522 (Metro)
Fax: 817-540-0650 (Metro)
Email: ronaldwren@airmail.net

For full biographical listings, see the Martindale-Hubbell Law Directory

*BROWNSVILLE,** Cameron Co.

GARZA & GARZA, L.L.P. (AV)

680 East St. Charles, Suite 300, 78520
Telephone: 956-541-4914
Fax: 956-542-7403

Reynaldo G. Garza, Jr.
David C. Garza

For full biographical listings, see the Martindale-Hubbell Law Directory

RILEY & HARRIS, L.L.P. (AV)

845 E. Harrison, Suite A, 78520-7120
Telephone: 956-550-8825
Fax: 956-550-8854
Email: txlaw@riley-harris.com *URL:* http://www.riley-harris.com
Houston, Texas Office: One Houston Center, 1221 Mckinney, Suite 3000, 77010-2023.
Telephone: 713-646-1000.
Fax: 713-646-1036. Email: txlaw@riley-harris.com.

MEMBER OF FIRM

Timothy D. Riley

For full biographical listings, see the Martindale-Hubbell Law Directory

RODRIGUEZ, COLVIN & CHANEY, L.L.P. (AV)

1201 East Van Buren, P.O. Box 2155, 78520
Telephone: 956-542-7441
Fax: 956-541-2170
McAllen, Texas Office: 4900 North 10th.
Telephone: 956-686-1287.
Telecopier: 956-686-6197.
Harlingen, Texas Office: 402 East Van Buren.
Telephone: 956-423-0216.
Telecopier: 956-423-2035.

MEMBERS OF FIRM

Eduardo R. Rodriguez
Norton A. Colvin, Jr.
Mitchell C. Chaney
Marjory Colvin Batsell
Jaime A. Saenz
Joseph A. (Tony) Rodriguez
Alison D. Kennamer

ASSOCIATES

Laura J. Urbis
Lecia L. Chaney
Daniel D. Herink
Robert Patrick Rodriguez
Rosa Maria Villagomez
Vanessa Garza
Teri L. Danish

OF COUNSEL

Orrin W. Johnson (Resident, Harlingen Office)
Benjamin S. Hardy (1912-1993)
Neil E. Norquest (Resident, McAllen Office)
Chris A. Brisack (Resident, McAllen Office)
Raymond A. Cowley

Division Attorneys for: Union Pacific Railroad.
Counsel for: Texas Commerce Bank-Rio Grande Valley, N.A.; Texas Commerce Bancshares, Inc.

For full biographical listings, see the Martindale-Hubbell Law Directory

WILLETTE & GUERRA, L.L.P. (AV)

International Plaza, 3505 Boca Chica Boulevard Suite 460, 78521
Telephone: 956-541-1846
Fax: 956-541-1893
McAllen, Texas Office: 801 Nolana, Suite, 320-A.
Telephone: 956-686-2266.

Charles Willette, Jr.
Roberto (Bobby) D. Guerra (Resident, McAllen Office)
Mark Sossi
Hugh P. Touchy
Eileen M. Leeds

ASSOCIATES

Joe D. Garcia (Resident, McAllen Office)
Eduardo G. Garza
Ryan Henry
George C. Kraehe
Ilene S. Peralez (Resident, McAllen, Texas Office)
Lawrence J. Rabb
Elizabeth Sandoval (Resident, McAllen, Texas Office)

For full biographical listings, see the Martindale-Hubbell Law Directory

CARROLLTON, Dallas & Denton Cos.

LAW OFFICES OF FRANK SHOR (AV)

Herald Hall, 1620 East Belt Line Road, 75006
Telephone: 972-242-8887
Fax: 972-446-7976

Representative Clients: Dallas Police Patrolman's Union; Lake Point Medical Center; Rudy's Tortillas; The Gas Pipe.
References: Fuller & Parker Court Reporters; Professional Civil Process.

For full biographical listings, see the Martindale-Hubbell Law Directory

*CORPUS CHRISTI,** Nueces Co.

BARGER, HERMANSEN, MCKIBBEN & VILLARREAL, L.L.P. (AV)

Formerly Hunt, Hermansen, McKibben & Villarreal, L.L.P.
1100 Tower II, 555 North Carancahua, 78478
Telephone: 512-882-6611
Telecopier: 512-883-8353
Email: hhmv@compuserve.com

MEMBERS OF FIRM

Darrell L. Barger
Tom Hermansen
James F. McKibben, Jr.
Carlos A. Villarreal
Richard C. Woolsey
Matthew B. Cano
David W. Green
Ann Hennis
Thomas A. Silver

ASSOCIATES

Michael B. Anthony
Michael G. Dunnahoo
Patrick M. Martinez
Brian C. Miller
Liza Marie Aguilar
Augustin Rivera, Jr.
Kristina Fernandez
Lane K. Jarvis, Jr.

OF COUNSEL

Lev Hunt

Representative Clients: Reliance Insurance Co.; American States Insurance Group; Medical Protective.

For full biographical listings, see the Martindale-Hubbell Law Directory

BROYLES & PRATT, A PROFESSIONAL CORPORATION (AV)

1001 Bank of America Center North, 500 North Shoreline Boulevard, 78471
Telephone: 361-886-6200
Fax: 361-886-6262
Austin, Texas Office: One Northpoint Centre, Suite 250, 6836 Austin Center Boulevard, 78731.
Telephone: 512-794-2100.
Fax: 512-794-2111.

Gaston M. Broyles, Jr.
Hal George
Milton E. Lorenz, Jr.
Richard A. Houston

For full biographical listings, see the Martindale-Hubbell Law Directory

CANALES & SIMONSON, P.C. (AV)

2601 Morgan Avenue, P.O. Box 5624, 78465-5624
Telephone: 512-883-0601
Telecopier: 512-884-7023
Email: tonycanales@canalessimonson.com

J. A. "Tony" Canales
Nancy M. Simonson

Barbara Canales Black
Jo Ellen Hewins
Patricia N. Canales

For full biographical listings, see the Martindale-Hubbell Law Directory

LAW OFFICES OF WILLIAM J. CHRISS, P.C. (AV)

719 South Shoreline, Suite 100, P.O. Box 2946, 78403
Telephone: 361-884-3330
Facsimile: 361-883-9187

William J. Chriss

Michael Nored

For full biographical listings, see the Martindale-Hubbell Law Directory

DUNN & WEATHERED, P.C. (AV)

611 South Upper Broadway, 78401
Telephone: 512-883-1594
Fax: 512-883-1599

David J. Dunn
Frank Weathered
John A. Smith, III
L. Nelson Hall
Lawrence A. Coffey

Reference: American Bank.

For full biographical listings, see the Martindale-Hubbell Law Directory

FRANCIS I. GANDY, JR. (AV)

148 American Bank Plaza, P.O. Box 1316, 78475-1197
Telephone: 361-883-6333
Fax: 361-883-0148
Email: gandyslaw@aol.com

For full biographical listings, see the Martindale-Hubbell Law Directory

JAMES M. WHITTEN (AV)

540 Frost Bank Plaza, 802 North Carancahua Street, 78470
Telephone: 361-881-8000
FAX: 361-887-9103
Sinton, Texas Office: 401 West Fulton St., P.O. Box 760.
Telephone: 361-364-3000.
Fax: 361-364-5911.

For full biographical listings, see the Martindale-Hubbell Law Directory

*CORSICANA,** Navarro Co.

DAWSON, SODD & BEARD, P.C. (AV)

121 North Main, P.O. Box 837, 75151
Telephone: 903-872-8181
Fax: 903-872-3654
Email: dawsonsodd@icountry.net

R. Matt Dawson
Glenn A. Sodd
John Clayton Beard
Micah Cade Haden

For full biographical listings, see the Martindale-Hubbell Law Directory

*DALLAS,** Dallas Co.

BAKER BOTTS L.L.P. (AV)

2001 Ross Avenue, 75201
Telephone: 214-953-6500
Fax: 214-953-6503
Email: postmaster@bakerbotts.com *URL:* http://www.bakerbotts.com
Houston, Texas Office: One Shell Plaza, 910 Louisiana.
Telephone: 713-229-1234.
Washington, D.C. Office: The Warner, 1299 Pennsylvania Avenue, N.W.
Telephone: 202-639-7700.
Austin, Texas Office: 1600 San Jacinto Center, 98 San Jacinto Boulevard.
Telephone: 512-322-2500.
New York, New York Office: 599 Lexington Avenue.
Telephone: 212-705-5000.
Moscow, Russia Office: 10 ul. Bolshaya Dimitrovka (formerly Pushkinskaya), 103031.
Telephone: 7095/921-5300 (Local); 7095/929-7070.
London, England Office: 45 Ludgate Hill.
Telephone: 0171-778-1400 (Local); 011-44-171-778-1400 (International).
Baku, Azerbaijan Office: 6-10 Vagif Mustafa-zadeh Street, Third Floor, Icheri Sheher, 370004.
Telephone: 994-12-97-63-88 (Local); 011-994-12-97-63-88 (International).

MEMBERS OF FIRM

Earl B. Austin
Van H. Beckwith
Bryant C. Boren, Jr.
Larry D. Carlson
Timothy S. Durst
Dan Hartsfield
Robert W. Jordan
Robert W. Kantner
George C. Lamb III
Peter A. Moir
Timothy W. Mountz
Ronald L. Palmer
Rod Phelan
Eric J. Senske
Don C. Stephenson

SPECIAL COUNSEL

Nanette Rutka Everson (Not admitted in TX)
Mary L. Scott
Kenneth B. Tomlinson

ASSOCIATES

Randolph L. Burns
Aaron D. Davidson
David M. Genender
Karen E. Griffin
Kelly D. Hine
William Johnson
Samara Lackman Kline
Jose M. Luzarraga
Cheryl L. Mann
Tyler L. Murray
Colleen B. Nabhan
K. Alan Parry
Karen B. Peck
Pamela B. Peck
Pennie Peck
Chad M. Pinson
Tracy L. S. Pylant
Adolfo R. Rodriguez, Jr.
Fernando Rodriguez, Jr.
Andy D. Sarwal
J. Kemp Sawers
Katrin U. Schatz
Steven G. Schortgen
Carol R. Young

For Complete List of Firm Personnel, See General Section

For full biographical listings, see the Martindale-Hubbell Law Directory

BICKEL & BREWER (AV)

4800 Bank One Center, 1717 Main Street, 75201
Telephone: 214-653-4000
Fax: 214-653-1015
Email: counsel@bickelbrewer.com *URL:* http://www.bickelbrewer.com
Chicago, Illinois Office: 35 W. Wacker Drive, Suite 3830, 60601.
Telephone: 312-855-9200.
Fax: 312-855-1234.

(See Next Column)

BICKEL & BREWER—*Continued*

New York, New York Office: 885 Third Avenue, Suite 3040, 10022.
Telephone: 212-489-1400.
Fax: 212-758-6468.

MEMBERS OF FIRM

John W. Bickel II
William A. Brewer III
Thomas C. Cronin (Not admitted in TX)
Robert P. Cummins (Not admitted in TX; Resident, Chicago, Illinois Office)
Deborah Deitsch-Perez (Resident, New York, N.Y. Office)
Porter F. Fleming (Resident, New York, N.Y. Office)
Joyce M. Hellstern
Scott S. Hershman
Paul B. Lackey
James S. Renard
William G. Todd (Resident, New York, N.Y. Office)

SENIOR ASSOCIATES

Wayne S. Ball
Kennedy Barnes
Michael S. Gardner
Jo Esta Hartwick
Kelly D. Hollingsworth
Bryan J. Wick

ASSOCIATES

Richard W. Barrett
Scott J. Bornstein (Resident, New York, N.Y. Office)
Daniel L. Brown (Resident, New York, N.Y. Office)
D. Wade Carvell
Carmela DeGruttola (Resident, New York, N.Y. Office)
Marsha L. Foulks

OF COUNSEL

Camille Reid McLeod

For full biographical listings, see the Martindale-Hubbell Law Directory

LAW OFFICES OF FRANK L. BRANSON, P.C. (AV)

18th Floor, Highland Park Place, 4514 Cole Avenue, 75205-4185
Telephone: 214-522-0200
Metro: 972-263-7452
Fax: 214-521-5485
URL: http://www.lawyers.com/frankbranson

Frank L. Branson
Debbie D. Branson
George A. Quesada, Jr.
Jerry M. White
Thomas J. Farmer
William B. Curtis
Robert D. Crain
Charles E. Moody

OF COUNSEL

Ted Z. Robertson
J. Hadley Edgar, Jr.

For full biographical listings, see the Martindale-Hubbell Law Directory

BUSH CRADDOCK & RENEKER, L.L.P. (AV)

Chase Bank Building, 6517 Hillcrest Avenue, Suite 110, 75205-1857
Telephone: 214-750-3550
Fax: 214-750-3551
Email: info@bcrlaw.com *URL:* http://www.bcrlaw.com
Marshall, Texas Office: 201 W. Grand.
Telephone: 903-935-9700.
Fax: 903-935-9743.

MEMBERS OF FIRM

Don D. Bush
Michael J. Craddock
D. Ronald Reneker
Douglas J. Buncher
Craig M. Patrick
Katherine Kolenberg Miracle
Kevin T. White

OF COUNSEL

Richard K. Berger

Representative Clients: AAF McQuay, Inc.; CSX Transportation, Inc.; Fleetwood Enterprises, Inc.; Ford Motor Co.; Fresenius Medical Care-North America; General Motors Corp.; Monumental Life Insurance Company; Palm Harbor Homes, Inc.; Sun Life Assurance Company of Canada; Union Pacific Railroad Co.

For full biographical listings, see the Martindale-Hubbell Law Directory

CALHOUN & STACY (AV)

Suite 5700 - Bank of America Plaza, 901 Main Street, 75202-3713
Telephone: 214-748-5000
Facsimile: 214-748-1421
Email: info@calhounstacy.com *URL:* http://www.calhounstacy.com

MEMBERS OF FIRM

Mark Alan Calhoun
LeAnn Wainscott Cross
David W. Elrod
Shannon B. Schuster
Roy L. Stacy
Pamela J. Touchstone
Michael C. Wright

ASSOCIATES

David G. Allen
Joseph G. Barkate, Jr.
Scott S. Crocker
Sean P. Fitzgerald
Elizabeth Reding Gambrell
Leanne Capps Medford
Jonathan G. Polak
Joel W. Reese
Barbara L. Wohlrabe

For Complete List of Firm Personnel, See General Section

For full biographical listings, see the Martindale-Hubbell Law Directory

CLARK, WEST, KELLER, BUTLER & ELLIS, L.L.P. (AV)

4800 Renaissance Tower, 1201 Elm Street, 75270-2146
Telephone: 214-741-1001
Telecopier: 214-760-9812

MEMBERS OF FIRM

William H. Clark (1861-1931)
William H. Clark, Jr. (1895-1943)
Robert L. Clark (1903-1963)
William L. Keller
Allen Butler
David M. Ellis
Melvyn L. Douglas
Mike M. Tabor
Mark A. Shank
Michael P. Maslanka
Kervyn B. Altaffer, Jr.
Kelly Gaffney McClure

ASSOCIATES

Veronica Cuadra
Melinda L. Eitzen
Wade A. Forsman
Theresa M. Gegen
M. Brenk Johnson
Christie A. Newkirk
Robert J. Wood, Jr.
John Peter Hagan
Sonja J. McGill

For full biographical listings, see the Martindale-Hubbell Law Directory

COHEN DARNELL & COHEN (AV)

A Professional Limited Liability Company
302 North Market Street, Suite 200, 75202
Telephone: 214-655-2600
Telecopier: 214-655-2601
Email: cdc@cohen-law.com *URL:* http://www.connect.net/cdc
Oklahoma City, Oklahoma Office: 5530 N. Western.
Telephone: 405-840-9049.
Fax: 405-840-9187.

Mark A. Cohen
Jim Darnell
Michael Lee Cohen

OF COUNSEL

Murray Cohen (Not admitted in TX)
Simon Jenour (Not admitted in the United States)
David E. Charney (Not admitted in TX)

For full biographical listings, see the Martindale-Hubbell Law Directory

CONANT FRENCH & CHANEY, LLP (AV)

3880 Bank One Center, 1717 Main Street, 75201
Telephone: 214-915-0620
Fasimile: 214-915-0634
Email: cfc@cfc-law.com *URL:* http://www.cfc-law.com

A. B. Conant, Jr.
William J. French
William B. Chaney
Linda A. Hale
Glen E. Lavy
Shawn W. Phelan
James D. MacIntyre

For full biographical listings, see the Martindale-Hubbell Law Directory

COWLES & THOMPSON, A PROFESSIONAL CORPORATION (AV)

901 Main Street Suite 4000, 75202
Telephone: 214-672-2000
Metro: 972-263-0005
Fax: 214-672-2020
URL: http://www.cowlesthompson.com
McKinney, Texas Office: 307 S. McDonald St., 75069-5659.
Telephone: 972-542-5000. Metro: 972-562-2270.
Fax: 972-542-5040.
Tyler, Texas Office: 1103 First Place, P.O. Box 239, 75710-0239.
Telephone: 903-593-7508.
Fax: 903-593-4057.

Jim E. Cowles
Hardy E. Thompson, III
Charles A. Green
William D. Cobb, Jr.
Auston Cherry
Dwayne J. Hermes
Michael L. Hurst
Charles T. Frazier, Jr.
Robert G. Buchanan, Jr.
David R. Woodward
B. Michael Bennett
Susan J. Snare
Mickie S. Bragalone
Warren Austin Gage
Sim Israeloff
David M. Hymer
Daniel D. Tostrud
Nancy Forbis Carnahan
Veronica M. Bates
Julia F. Pendery
Ramona Martinez

OF COUNSEL

Kenneth J. Mighell

For Complete List of Firm Personnel, See General Section

For full biographical listings, see the Martindale-Hubbell Law Directory

CRACKEN, HARKEY & PAYNE, LLP (AV)

5956 Sherry Lane, Suite 1401, 75225
Telephone: 214-750-1855
Fax: 214-750-7086
Email: info@cracken-harkey.com *URL:* http://www.cracken-harkey.com

(See Next Column)

CRACKEN, HARKEY & PAYNE LLP, *Dallas—Continued*

John R. W. Cracken
John D. Harkey, Jr.
Christopher A. Payne
James R. Snell

For full biographical listings, see the Martindale-Hubbell Law Directory

DEHAY & ELLISTON, L.L.P. (AV)

3500 NationsBank Plaza, 901 Main Street, 75202-3736
Telephone: 214-210-2400
Facsimile: 214-210-2500
Beaumont, Texas Office: 215 Orleans Street, 77701.
Telephone: 409-833-0900.
Facsimile: 409-833-0964.

J. Carlisle DeHay, Jr. (1922-1991)

PARTNERS

Gary D. Elliston
David W. Crowe
Mel D. Bailey
Eric D. Wewers
Christopher P. Manning
Paul E. Hamilton
Laura E. Kugler
Melinda S. Huff
Charlene R. Echols

OF COUNSEL

W. Scott Berry
Kathryn O. Hermes

Brent M. Karren
Stuart G. Brooks
Anthony S. Miller
Todd D. Ogden
William C. Arnold
Todd J. Suddleson (Not admitted in TX)
Kyle Christophen Steele
Lily Chang Myers
Kirsten L. Alessio
Russell J. DePalma
Tandy V. Jouret
M. Lauren Mathews
Jill G. Adams
John W. Arnold
William A. Fynes
Jeffrey M. Marosz
Kenneth D. Morris
Todd H. Ramsey
Mitzi S. Wallace
Susan Chapman

For full biographical listings, see the Martindale-Hubbell Law Directory

ELLISTON & ORMESHER, L.L.P. (AV)

1401 Elm Street, Suite 4585, 75202-2953
Telephone: 214-752-0400
Fax: 214-752-0404
URL: http://www.lawyers.com/elliston&ormesher

PARTNERS

D. Mark Elliston
J. Russell Ormesher

OF COUNSEL

Susan R. Patterson

For full biographical listings, see the Martindale-Hubbell Law Directory

ERHARD, RUEBEL & JENNINGS, A PROFESSIONAL CORPORATION (AV)

1600 Pacific Avenue, 75201-3509
Telephone: 214-720-4001, 741-6201
Fax: 214-871-1655
Email: erjennings@compuserve.com *URL:* http://www.lawyers.com/erruje

James Albert Jennings
W. Christopher W. Haynes

Representative Client: Halliburton Co./Halliburton Energy Services.

For full biographical listings, see the Martindale-Hubbell Law Directory

FERNANDEZ & KNEBEL, A PROFESSIONAL CORPORATION (AV)

Bank One Center, 1717 Main Street, Suite 2100, 75201
Telephone: 214-747-2100
Fax: 214-747-2144

Bennett I. Abramowitz
Clint A. Corrie
Raymond R. Fernandez, Jr.
Delbert L. Gibbs
Robert L. Knebel, Jr.
Mary Jo Vida

Barbara F. Blaylock
Herbert J. Gilles
Maria Isabel Roman
Jon M. Payne
Joseph L. Mira

For full biographical listings, see the Martindale-Hubbell Law Directory

FIGARI DAVENPORT & GRAVES, L.L.P. (AV)

A Partnership including a Professional Corporation
901 Main Street, LB 125, 4800 Bank of America Plaza, 75202-3796
Telephone: 214-939-2000
Fax: 214-939-2090

(See Next Column)

MEMBERS OF FIRM

Ernest E. Figari, Jr., (P.C.)
Mark T. Davenport
Thomas A. Graves
Doug K. Butler
Donald Colleluori
Gary D. Eisenstat
Andrew G. Jubinsky
Parker D. Young
Michael G. Brown
Timothy A. Daniels
Keith R. Verges
Stephen D. Howen
Monica L. Luebker
Andrew C. Whitaker

Jill B. Davenport
Bill E. Davidoff
Amanda M. Inabnett
Dennis M. Lynch
Melissa A. Mitchell
Katherine S. Rabe
Lisa L. Traylor
Jennifer M. Trulock

For full biographical listings, see the Martindale-Hubbell Law Directory

FRALEY & FRALEY, L.L.P. (AV)

901 Main Street, Suite 6510, 75202
Telephone: 214-761-6460
Fax: 214-761-6469
Email: info@fraleyandfraley.com *URL:* http://www.fraleyandfraley.com

R. Scott Fraley
Elizabeth Masters Fraley
J. Patrick Bredehoft

J. David Criss

For full biographical listings, see the Martindale-Hubbell Law Directory

GEARY, PORTER & DONOVAN, P.C. (AV)

One Bent Tree Tower, 16475 Dallas Parkway, Suite 500, 75001-6837
Telephone: 972-931-9901
Facsimile: 972-931-9208
Mailing Address: P.O. Box 700248, Dallas, Texas, 75370-0248
Email: firm@gpd.com *URL:* http://www.gpd.com

Bruce W. Claycombe
Daniel P. Donovan
Joseph W. Geary
Ronald D. Gray
David J. Kaplan
Catherine C. Kays
Nicole T. LeBoeuf
Larry L. Martin
Theodore J. Riney

For full biographical listings, see the Martindale-Hubbell Law Directory

GIBSON, MCCLURE & WALLACE, L.L.P. (AV)

8080 North Central Expressway, Suite 1300, LB50, 75206
Telephone: 214-891-8040
Fax: 214-891-8010

MEMBERS OF FIRM

Dennis D. Gibson
Wade L. McClure
Jay M. Wallace
Gabrielle Honore Kickham
Ruth Ann Norton Daniels
James M. McCoy
Alan L. Rucker
Bryan D. Perkins

Evelyn A. Yeager
Connie Kay Wilhite

For full biographical listings, see the Martindale-Hubbell Law Directory

GODWIN WHITE & GRUBER, A PROFESSIONAL CORPORATION (AV)

Suite 2500, 901 Main Street, 75202-3714
Telephone: 214-939-4400
Fax: 214-760-7332

Lawrence W. Bailey
Susan Barilich
Danny C. Garner
Donald E. Godwin
G. Michael Gruber
Brian N. Hail
Thomas S. Hoekstra
Michael K. Hurst
Christopher L. Kurzner
David L. Patterson
Steven T. Polino
Harvey M. Shapan
David J. White

ASSOCIATES

Paul M. Bass, III
Mary A. Goodrich
John F. Martin
Tonya L. Meier
Guy H. Riddle
Kenneth W. Rockenbach
Robert C. Wiegand

For Complete List of Firm Personnel, See General Section

For full biographical listings, see the Martindale-Hubbell Law Directory

HUGHES & LUCE, L.L.P. (AV)

A Registered Limited Liability Partnership including Professional Corporations
1717 Main Street, Suite 2800, 75201
Telephone: 214-939-5500
Fax: 214-939-6100; 214-939-5849
Email: H&L@hughesluce.com *URL:* http://www.hughesluce.com
Austin, Texas Office: 111 Congress, Suite 900.
Telephone: 512-482-6800.
Fax: 512-482-6859.

(See Next Column)

HUGHES & LUCE L.L.P.—*Continued*

Houston, Texas Office: 1600 Smith Street, Suite 3550.
Telephone: 713-754-5200.
Fax: 713-754-5270.

MEMBERS OF FIRM

Danny S. Ashby
Kim Juanita Askew
Bert Black
David Bryant
Douglas A. Cawley
Robert Edwin Davis
Allan B. Diamond
Stephen G. Gleboff
Clifton T. Hutchinson
MaryAnn Joerres
Darrell E. Jordan
David C. Kent
Jeffrey C. King
Paul M. Koning
Weston C. Loegering
James D. McCarthy
R. Matthew Molash
Robert H. Mow, Jr. (P.C.)
Walter G. Pettey, III
Bobby M. Rubarts
Mark K. Sales
Theodore Stevenson, III
J. Gregory Taylor

ASSOCIATES

Gregory M. Bair
Beth W. Bivans
Julie Edwards Blend
Christopher T. Bovenkamp
H. Esther Cochran (Not admitted in TX)
Joseph M. Cox
Courtney J. Dreslin
John E. Garda
Derek S. Hollingsworth
James W. Hryekewicz
Price L. Johnson
Samuel V. Jones
John W. Patton
Aubrey Nick Pittman
Brooke Leslie Rollins
David J. Schenck
Bart Sloan
Catherine C. Theisen
Marion Turner (Van) Van Bebber

For Complete List of Firm Personnel, See General Section

For full biographical listings, see the Martindale-Hubbell Law Directory

JACKSON WALKER L.L.P. (AV)

901 Main Street, Suite 6000, 75202-3797
Telephone: 214-953-6000
Fax: 214-953-5822
URL: http://www.jw.com
Austin, Texas Office: 100 Congress Avenue, Suite 1100.
Telephone: 512-236-2000.
Fax: 512-236-2002.
Fort Worth, Texas Office: 301 Commerce Street, Suite 2400.
Telephone: 817-334-7200.
Fax: 817-334-7290.
Houston, Texas Office: 1100 Louisiana, Suite 4200.
Telephone: 713-752-4200.
Fax: 713-752-4221.
Richardson, Texas Office: 2435 North Central Expressway, Suite 600.
Telephone: 972-671-2560.
Fax: 972-671-2566.
San Angelo, Texas Office: 225 West Beauregard Avenue.
Telephone: 915-481-2550.
Fax: 915-481-2552.
San Antonio, Texas Office: 112 E. Pecan Street, Suite 2100.
Telephone: 210-978-7700.
Fax: 210-978-7790.

MEMBERS OF FIRM

Carl C. Butzer
E. Leon Carter
H. Dudley Chambers
Alan N. Greenspan
Robert F. Henderson
Mark T. Josephs
Michael L. Knapek
John L. Lancaster, III
Robert P. Latham
Billy R. McGill
Retta A. Miller
David T. Moran
David C. Myers
Jack Pew, Jr.
Robert F. Ruckman
Gordon M. Shapiro
Frank C. Vecella
Troy Michael Wilson

OF COUNSEL

Mary Emma Ackels Karam

SENIOR COUNSEL

James D. Struble

Representative Clients Furnished Upon Request.

For Complete List of Firm Personnel, See General Section

For full biographical listings, see the Martindale-Hubbell Law Directory

JONES, DAY, REAVIS & POGUE (AV)

2727 North Harwood Street, 75201-1515
Telephone: 214-220-3939
Telecopier: 214-969-5100
Email: counsel@jonesday.com *URL:* http://www.jonesday.com
In Atlanta, Georgia: 3500 SunTrust Plaza, 303 Peachtree Street.
Telephone: 404-521-3939.
Telecopier: 404-581-8330.
In Brussels, Belgium: Avenue Louise 480, 7th Floor, B-1050 Brussels.
Telephone: 32-2-645-14-11.
Telecopier: 32-2-645-14-45.
In Chicago, Illinois: 77 West Wacker.
Telephone: 312-782-3939.
Telecopier: 312-782-8585.

(See Next Column)

In Cleveland, Ohio: North Point, 901 Lakeside Avenue.
Telephone: 216-586-3939.
Telecopier: 216-579-0212.
In Columbus, Ohio: 1900 Huntington Center.
Telephone: 614-469-3939.
Telecopier: 614-461-4198.
In Frankfurt, Germany: Hochhaus am Park, Grüneburgweg 102, 60323 Frankfurt am Main.
Telephone: 49-69-9726-3939.
Telecopier: 49-69-9726-3993.
In Geneva, Switzerland: 20, rue de Candolle.
Telephone: 41-22-320-2339.
Telecopier: 41-22-320-1232.
In Hong Kong: 29th Floor, Entertainment Building, 30 Queen's Road Central.
Telephone: 852-2526-6895.
Telecopier: 852-2868-5871.
In Irvine, California: 5 Park Plaza, Suite 1100.
Telephone: 949-851-3939.
Telecopier: 949-553-7539.
In London, England: Bucklersbury House, 3 Queen Victoria Street.
Telephone: 44-20-7236-3939.
Telecopier: 44-20-7236-1113.
In Los Angeles, California: 555 West Fifth Street, Suite 4600.
Telephone: 213-489-3939.
Telecopier: 213-243-2539.
In New York, New York: 599 Lexington Avenue.
Telephone: 212-326-3939.
Telecopier: 212-755-7306.
In Paris, France: 120, rue du Faubourg Saint-Honoré.
Telephone: 33-1-56-59-39-39.
Telecopier: 33-1-56-59-39-38
In Pittsburgh, Pennsylvania: 500 Grant Street, 31st Floor.
Telephone: 412-391-3939.
Telecopier: 412-394-7959.
Riyadh, Saudi Arabia: The International Law Firm (In Association with Jones, Day, Reavis & Pogue), Sulaymaniyah, Prince Mishari IBN, Addulaziz Street, P.O. Box 22166.
Telephone: (966-1) 462-8866.
Telecopier: (966-1) 462-9001.
In Shanghai, China: 2805 Kerry Centre, 1515 Nanjing Road West.
Telephone: 86-21-5298-6568.
Telecopier: 86-21-5298-6569.
In Sydney, Australia: Governor Phillip Tower, Level 38, 1 Farrer Place.
Telephone: 61-2-9210-6921.
Telecopier: 61-2-9210-6926.
In Taipei, Taiwan: 8th Floor, 2 Tun Hwa South Road, Section 2.
Telephone: (886-2) 2704-6808.
Telecopier: (886-2) 2704-6791.
In Tokyo, Japan: Toranomon 45 Mori Building, 3rd Floor, 1-5, Toranomon, 5-Chome, Minato-ku, Tokyo 105, Japan.
Telephone: 81-3-3433-3939.
Telecopier: 81-3-5401-2725.
In Washington, D.C.: 51 Louisiana Avenue, N.W.
Telephone: 202-879-3939.
Telecopier: 202-626-1700.

MEMBERS OF FIRM IN DALLAS

Terence M. Murphy
Joseph L. McEntee

For Complete List of Firm Personnel, See General Section

For full biographical listings, see the Martindale-Hubbell Law Directory

KANE, RUSSELL, COLEMAN & LOGAN, A PROFESSIONAL CORPORATION (AV)

3700 Thanksgiving Tower, 1601 Elm Street, 75201-7207
Telephone: 214-777-4200
Fax: 214-777-4299
Email: krcl@krcl.com

Raymond J. Kane
Gordon B. Russell
Joseph M. Coleman
Michael A. Logan
Patrick V. Stark
Kenneth W. Biermacher
David N. Condon
Karen A. Cox
William D. Elliott
Joseph A. Friedman
Robert N. LeMay
Michael L. Atchley, II
Margaret M. McLeod Jordan

Terry Flett Barakis
Harold R. Busch
Priscilla K. Davenport
Deborah A. DiMarco
Evangelos J. Gegas (Not admitted in TX)
Shelli R. Inmon
Kenneth C. Johnston
Jaqluin M. Bickmore Lloyd
Robert L. Manteuffel
David D. Ritter
Holly J. Roman
Jeffrey S. Seeburger
Jeffrey Charles Tasker
Steven M. Thornton
Karin M. Zaner

For full biographical listings, see the Martindale-Hubbell Law Directory

KILGORE & KILGORE, A PROFESSIONAL CORPORATION (AV)

700 McKinney Place, 3131 McKinney Avenue - LB 103, 75204-2471
Telephone: 214-969-9099
Fax: 214-953-0133; 214-953-0242; 214-953-0677

(See Next Column)

KILGORE & KILGORE A PROFESSIONAL CORPORATION, *Dallas—Continued*

Wilmer D. Masterson, III
W. Stephen Swayze
Robert M. Thornton
Theodore C. Anderson, III

For Complete List of Firm Personnel, See General Section

For full biographical listings, see the Martindale-Hubbell Law Directory

---

KRAGE & JANVEY, L.L.P. (AV)

2001 Bryan Tower, Suite 2700, 75201-3059
Telephone: 214-969-7500
Telecopier: 214-220-0230

Ben L. Krage

Representative Client: Regal Capital Co.

For full biographical listings, see the Martindale-Hubbell Law Directory

---

LAW OFFICES OF LIPPE & ASSOCIATES (AV)

2777 Stemmons Freeway, Suite 925, 75207
Telephone: 214-638-6076
Fax: 214-720-6074
Email: texaslaw@airmail.net *URL:* http://www.texaslaw.com

Emil Lippe, Jr.

OF COUNSEL

Robert B. Buchan

For full biographical listings, see the Martindale-Hubbell Law Directory

---

MCKOOL SMITH, A PROFESSIONAL CORPORATION (AV)

300 Crescent Court, Suite 1500, 75201
Telephone: 214-978-4000
Fax: 214-978-4044
Email: mckool@mckoolsmith.com *URL:* http://www.mckoolsmith.com
Marshall, Texas Office: 505 East Travis Street, Suite 105.
Telephone: 903-927-2111.

Sam F. Baxter
Jeffrey R. Bragalone
Eric W. Buether
Jeffrey A. Carter
Gary Cruciani
Charles W. Cunningham
Robert Elkin
Richard A. Lempert
Lewis Titus LeClair
Mike McKool, Jr.
Phillip N. Smith, Jr.

SENIOR COUNSEL

Randy J. Carter
Mark L. Mathie
Kevin C. Nash
Rosemary T. Snider

ASSOCIATES

Monte M. Bond
Ruben Brochner, Jr.
Brent N. Bumgardner
R. Darryl Burke
Garret Wesley Chambers
John Sabine DeGroote
Thomas G. Fasone, III
Christopher J. Harrington
James T. Harris
Angela A. Hunt
Christopher M. Joe
Caroline Jordan
Jill F. Keenom
Kenneth P. Kula
Robert C. W. Lamb
Valerie L. Leatherwood (Not admitted in TX)
Anthony J. Magee
Robert M. Manley
Michael V. Marconi
Angela D. McKee (Not admitted in TX)
Mark Andrew Tatkenhorst
John Tyson
Tina J. Wysk
Jennifer L. Yelton

For full biographical listings, see the Martindale-Hubbell Law Directory

---

MIDDLEBERG, RIDDLE & GIANNA (AV)

2323 Bryan Street, Suite 1600, 75201
Telephone: 214-220-6300
Telecopier: 214-220-2785
New Orleans, Louisiana Office: 201 St. Charles Avenue, Suite 3100.
Telephone: 504-525-7200.
Telecopier: 504-581-5983.
Austin, Texas Office: 1300 South Mopac Expressway, First Floor.
Telephone: 512-434-8334.
Houston, Texas Office: 7676 Woodway, Suite 325.
Telephone: 713-430-5000.
Telecopier: 713-430-5090.

Ira Joel Middleberg (Not admitted in TX)
Michael Lee Riddle
Dominic J. Gianna (Not admitted in TX)

Kay A. King
Laura C. LaRaia
Angela R. Maverick
Lisa E. Minkoff
Carol J. Riddle
Robert A. Schlanger
Alexandra Smith
Marsha L. Williams
Christina R. Wommack

(See Next Column)

OF COUNSEL

Richard S. Wilensky
Robert M. Duval

For full biographical listings, see the Martindale-Hubbell Law Directory

---

MILLS PRESBY AND ASSOCIATES, L.L.P. (AV)

5910 North Central Expressway Premier Place Suite 900, 75206-5141
Telephone: 214-265-9265
Fax: 214-363-3167
URL: http://www.millspresby.com

Thomas W. Mills, Jr.
Ellen A. Presby
John M. Frick
Lisa A. Schumacher

David S. Weber
Jonathan Mark Spigel
Joseph D. Cohen

For full biographical listings, see the Martindale-Hubbell Law Directory

---

OWENS, CLARY & AIKEN, L.L.P. (AV)

1717 Main Street, Suite 2400, 75201
Telephone: 214-698-2100
Facsimile: 214-698-2121

MEMBERS OF FIRM

Leighton Aiken
Dana Mark Campbell
Robert J. Clary
Charles R. Haworth
Robert L. Owens
Leon G. Scroggins, II

ASSOCIATES

Jamie King Harrison
Mary T. Ritter

For full biographical listings, see the Martindale-Hubbell Law Directory

---

PAYNE & BLANCHARD, L.L.P. (AV)

Plaza of the Americas, 700 North Pearl Street Suite 500, LB 393, 75201-7424
Telephone: 214-953-1313
Telecopier: 214-220-0439
Email: pblaw@flash.net

MEMBERS OF FIRM

Arthur Blanchard (Retired)
James C. Allums, Jr.
John William Payne
Charles A. Girand
Bobby D. Dyess
Kevin J. Cook
Gary W. Maxfield
Jonathan A. Manning
Harold R. McKeever, Jr.

ASSOCIATES

Samuel J. Polak
David M. Walsh, IV

OF COUNSEL

Robert S. Addison

Representative Clients: AIG; American Home Products Corp.; American National Property and Casualty Co.; Liberty Mutual Insurance Co.; Maryland Casualty Co.; Mutual and United of Omaha Insurance Co.; Nationwide Insurance Cos.; Preston Chrysler-Plymouth; Texas Association of Counties; Travelers Insurance Co.; Tyler Ford, Inc.

For full biographical listings, see the Martindale-Hubbell Law Directory

---

THE SCHMIDT FIRM (AV)

3102 Oak Lawn, Suite 730, LB 158, 75219
Telephone: 214-521-4898
Toll Free No. 1-800-745-1372, x4898
Fax: 214-521-9995
Email: schmidt@schmidtlaw.com *URL:* http://www.schmidtlaw.com

C. L. Mike Schmidt

For full biographical listings, see the Martindale-Hubbell Law Directory

---

SMITH, UNDERWOOD & PERKINS, A PROFESSIONAL CORPORATION (AV)

600 Two Lincoln Centre, 5420 LBJ Freeway, 75240
Telephone: 972-661-5114
Telecopier: 972-661-5691
Email: firm@suandp.com *URL:* http://www.suplaw.com

Timothy S. Perkins
David W. Ralston
G. Lynn Smith
William J. Underwood, Jr.

Christine A. McGuire
Amy K. Ratzlaff
P. Theodore Stoinoff, II
Val C. Cronin
Ellen P. Stewart
Todd W. Shadle
Ruth C. Logan
Christina L. Betanzos
Kent D. Williamson

For full biographical listings, see the Martindale-Hubbell Law Directory

Dallas—Continued

SUSMAN GODFREY L.L.P. (AV)

A Registered Limited Liability Partnership including Professional Corporations
Suite 1400 2323 Bryan Street, 75201-2663
Telephone: 214-754-1900
Fax: 214-754-1933
URL: http://www.susmangodfrey.com
Houston, Texas Office: Suite 5100, 1000 Louisiana Street.
Telephone: 713-651-9366.
Telecopy: 713-653-7897.
Seattle, Washington Office: Suite 3090, 1201 Third Avenue.
Telephone: 206-516-3880.
Telecopy: 206-516-3883.
Los Angeles, California Office: Suite 950, 1880 Century Park East.
Telephone: 310-789-3100.
Fax: 310-789-3150.
New address effective March, 2000: Suite 4100, 901 Main Street, 75202.

MEMBERS OF FIRM

Stephen D. Susman (P.C.)
Terrell W. Oxford (P.C.) (Resident)
Barry C. Barnett (Resident)
Ophelia F. Camiña (Resident)
John M. Helms (Resident)

ASSOCIATES

Kenneth E. Gardner (Resident)
Mark A. Evetts (Resident)
Jason Rodgers (Resident)
Talcott J. Franklin (Resident)
Andrew W. Yung

STAFF ATTORNEY

Martha A. Evans

OF COUNSEL

E. Lawrence Vincent, Jr. (Resident)

Reference: Laredo National Bank, Houston.

For full biographical listings, see the Martindale-Hubbell Law Directory

THOMAS & CULP, L.L.P. (AV)

2300 Thanksgiving Tower, 1601 Elm Street, 75201-4756
Telephone: 214-953-0000
Facsimile: 214-953-0006

Tom Thomas
Marc S. Culp

ASSOCIATES

Debra Trawick
James Andrew Bench

OF COUNSEL

Fred J. Kolodey

For full biographical listings, see the Martindale-Hubbell Law Directory

THOMAS, FELDMAN & WILSHUSEN, L.L.P. (AV)

9400 NCX Tower, 9400 North Central Expressway, Suite 900, 75231
Telephone: 214-369-3008
Facsimile: 214-369-8393

MEMBERS OF FIRM

Richard Gary Thomas
Robert L. Feldman
Fred D. Wilshusen

ASSOCIATES

Regan Gayle O'Steen
Trice Ragon Richey
Edward (Ted) J. Laperouse, II

OF COUNSEL

Joseph M. Stuhl

Representative Clients: Baker Drywall Co.; CMC Steel Group; Dallas Door and Supply Co.; Dallas Fire Insurance Company; Fischbach & Moore, Inc.; Mills Electrical Contractors, Inc.; Spaw Glass General Contractors, Inc.; TAS Construction, Inc; Texas Air Systems, Inc.; United Dominion Realty Trust.

For full biographical listings, see the Martindale-Hubbell Law Directory

THOMAS & SELF, A PROFESSIONAL CORPORATION (AV)

5339 Spring Valley Road, 75240-3009
Telephone: 972-991-2121
Telecopier: 972-991-3220

David E. Thomas
Rudolf W. Beuttenmuller
Richard J. Cinclair, Jr.

OF COUNSEL

Thomas C. Self

For full biographical listings, see the Martindale-Hubbell Law Directory

THOMPSON, COE, COUSINS & IRONS, L.L.P. (AV)

200 Crescent Court, Eleventh Floor, 75201-1853
Telephone: 214-871-8200
Fax: 214-871-8209
Austin, Texas Office: Suite 1500, Austin Centre, 701 Brazos, 78701.
Telephone: 512-708-8200.
Fax: 512-708-8777.

(See Next Column)

PARTNERS

Franklin H. Perry
Randy A. Nelson
David M. Taylor
Robert B. Wellenberger
Rhonda Johnson Byrd
Roger D. Higgins
Richard M. Mosher
Jennifer D. Aufricht
James L. Sowder
John B. Kronenberger
David F. Eriksen
James Richard Harmon
Thomas A. Culpepper
Wade C. Crosnoe

Representative Clients: Frontier Financial Services Corp.; Capital Technologies (B.V.I.); TIG Holdings.

For Complete List of Firm Personnel, See General Section

For full biographical listings, see the Martindale-Hubbell Law Directory

THOMPSON & KNIGHT L.L.P. (AV)

(Attorneys and Counselors)
1700 Pacific Avenue Suite 3300, 75201
Telephone: 214-969-1700
Telecopy: 214-969-1751
Telex: 732 298
URL: http://www.tklaw.com
Austin, Texas Office: 1200 San Jacinto Center, 98 San Jacinto Boulevard, 78701.
Telephone: 512-469-6100.
Telecopy: 512-469-6180.
Fort Worth, Texas Office: 801 Cherry Street, Suite 1600, 76102.
Telephone: 817-347-1700.
Telecopy: 817-347-1799.
Houston, Texas Office: Thompson Knight Brown Parker & Leahy L.L.P., 1200 Smith Street, Suite 3600, 77002-4595.
Telephone: 713-654-8111.
Telecopier: 713-654-1871.
San Pedro Garza Garcia, Nuevo León, Mexico Office: Edificio Losoles PD-4, Av. Lázaro Cárdenas No. 2400 Pte., C.P. 66220.
Telephone: (52-8) 363-0096.
Telecopy: (52-8) 363-3067.

PARTNERS

G. Luke Ashley
Steven R. Baggett
P. Jefferson Ballew
William L. Banowsky
L. James Berglund, II
Michael R. Berry
Jane Politz Brandt
Beverly Ray Burlingame
George C. Chapman
Greg W. Curry
F. Barrett Davis
Cheryl E. Diaz
Frank Finn
Rachelle H. Glazer
Herbert J. Hammond
Craig A. Haynes
Gregory S. C. Huffman
Veronica Smith Lewis
Stephen S. Livingston
John A. Mackintosh, Jr.
Timothy R. McCormick
Maureen A. Murry
Joseph S. Pevsner
Stephen C. Rasch
A. Kay Roska
Stephen C. Schoettmer
Michael E. Schonberg
Bruce S. Sostek
Molly Steele
Scott P. Stolley
Peter J. Thoma
Dawn Marie Wright

SENIOR ATTORNEY

David S. White

ASSOCIATES

Cindy W. Andrew
Christopher Lee Barnes
James S. Bowie, II
Amy Brimmage
J. Jeffrey Cash
Kelley Cash
Adrienne E. Dominguez
Aditi Dravid
Lauren C. Felts
Marcie Y. Flores
Julia Elizabeth Jones
William M. Katz, Jr.
Anna E. Marple
Matthew P. Nugent
G. Dawn Shawger
Deborah Lin Whalen
Richard L. Wynne, Jr.

OF COUNSEL

Laura Peterson Elkind
Jerry P. Jones
David S. Kidder

For Complete List of Firm Personnel, See General Section

For full biographical listings, see the Martindale-Hubbell Law Directory

TOOLEY & VOSS (AV)

8214 Westchester Drive, Suite 420, 75225
Telephone: 214-368-2224
Fax: 214-368-8307
Email: JCToutfit@aol.com

Joe C. Tooley
Edwin P. Voss Jr.

For full biographical listings, see the Martindale-Hubbell Law Directory

LAW OFFICES OF WINDLE TURLEY, P.C. (AV)

1000 University Tower, 6440 North Central Expressway, 75206
Telephone: 214-691-4025
Telefax: 214-361-5802
Telex: 734049
Email: htpillturley@wturley.com *URL:* http://www.wturley.com

(See Next Column)

LAW OFFICES OF WINDLE TURLEY, P.C., *Dallas—Continued*

Windle Turley
Michael G. Sawicki
R. Christopher Cowan
William J. Dunleavy
Phillip L. Brown

Dale R. Rose
Deana Tunnell
Lori A. Watson
Patrick C. Patterson
Brent Stewart Freefield
Jeffrey T. Embry

For full biographical listings, see the Martindale-Hubbell Law Directory

LAW OFFICES OF EDDIE VASSALLO, P.C. (AV)

Regency Plaza, 3710 Rawlins, Suite 1200, 75219-4217
Telephone: 214-559-7200
Fax: 214-559-7209
Email: mikkiwes@aol.com *URL:* http://www.lawyers.com/vassallolaw

Edward DiMare Vassallo, Jr.

Charles A. Salazar
Christene Jones
Scott T. Doggett

For full biographical listings, see the Martindale-Hubbell Law Directory

VINSON & ELKINS L.L.P. (AV)

3700 Trammell Crow Center, 2001 Ross Avenue, 75201-2975
Telephone: 214-220-7700
Fax: 214-220-7716
URL: http://www.velaw.com
Austin, Texas Office: One American Center Suite 2700, 600 Congress Avenue, Austin, Texas, 78701-3200.
Telephone: 512-495-8400.
Fax: 512-495-8612.
Beijing, China Office: 20/F, Beijing Silver Tower, No. 2, Dong San Huan Bei Lu, Chaoyang District, 100027.
Telephone: +86-10-6410-6300.
Fax: +86-10-6410-6360.
Houston, Texas Office: 2300 First City Tower, 1001 Fannin, Houston, Texas, 77002-6760.
Telephone: 713-758-2222.
Fax: 713-758-2346.
London, England Office: Regis House, 8th Floor, 45 King William Street, London, EC4R 9AN, England.
Telephone: (44-171) 618-6000.
Fax: (44-171) 618-6001.
Moscow, Russia Office: 16 Ulitsa Spiridonovka, Second Floor, 103001 Moscow, Russia.
Telephone: (7-095) 956-1995. Local
Fax: (7-095) 956-1996. U.S. Satellite
Fax: (212) 803-0142.
New York, N.Y. Office: 1325 Avenue of the Americas, 17th Floor, New York, N.Y., 10019.
Telephone: 917-206-8000.
Fax: 917-206-8100.
Singapore Office: 6 Battery Road, #39-01, Singapore, 049909.
Telephone: (65) 536-8300.
Fax: (65) 536-8311.
Washington, D.C. Office: The Willard Office Building, 1455 Pennsylvania Avenue, N.W., Washington, D.C., 20004-1008.
Telephone: 202-639-6500.
Fax: 202-639-6604.

RESIDENT PARTNERS

David P. Blanke
William H. Church, Jr.
Samuel Poage Dalton
William B. Dawson
Orrin L. Harrison, III
Karen L. Hirschman
George M. Kryder III
Thomas S. Leatherbury
Dale Gene Markland
Russell L. Reid, Jr.
William D. Sims, Jr.
Robert C. Walters
Russell Yager

OF COUNSEL

Sheryl L. Hopkins
J. Stuart Tonkinson

RESIDENT ASSOCIATES

Keefe M. Bernstein
Scott W. Breedlove
Scott L. Cole
Alexis R. Connally
Toni N. Dinh
Stacey H. Dore
Delwin E. Hervey
Todd A. Murray
Walter R. Owens, Jr.
Carol Collins Payne
Michael L. Raiff
Tara H. Reynolds
Brian E. Robison
Eric Stahl
Matthew R. Stammel
John C. Wander

For Complete List of Firm Personnel, See General Section

For full biographical listings, see the Martindale-Hubbell Law Directory

WEIL & PETROCCHI, A PROFESSIONAL CORPORATION (AV)

1900 Thanksgiving Tower, 1601 Elm Street, L.B. 100, 75201
Telephone: 214-969-7272
Facsimile Copier: 214-880-7402

(See Next Column)

Christopher M. Weil
Anthony A. Petrocchi

Jeffrey W. Hellberg, Jr.

For full biographical listings, see the Martindale-Hubbell Law Directory

WHITTENBURG WHITTENBURG & SCHACHTER, P.C. (AV)

2300 Plaza of the Americas, 600 North Pearl, LB 133, 75201
Telephone: 214-999-5700
Facsimile: 214-999-5747
Amarillo, Texas Office: 1010 South Harrison.
Telephone: 806-372-5700.
Facsimile: 806-372-5757.

Deborah Ashmore Harris

For Complete List of Firm Personnel, See General Section

For full biographical listings, see the Martindale-Hubbell Law Directory

*DECATUR,** Wise Co.

SIMPSON & BOYD, P.L.L.C. (AV)

105 North State Street, Suite B, P.O. Box 957, 76234
Telephone: 940-627-8308
Fax: 940-627-8092
Email: Derrick@wf.net
Email: sbblo@wf.net *URL:* http://www.lawyers.com/simpson&boydpllc
Bridgeport, Texas Office: 1119 Halsell Street, P.O. Box 685, 76426.
Telephone: 940-683-4098.
Fax: 940-683-3122.

Michael A. Simpson
Ross M. Simpson
Derrick S. Boyd

G. Alan Powers
J. Michael Carrillo

For full biographical listings, see the Martindale-Hubbell Law Directory

*DENTON,** Denton Co.

PHILIPS, HOPKINS, EAMES & COBB, P.C. (AV)

525 North Locust, P.O. Box 2027, 76202-2027
Telephone: 940-566-7010; Metro 940-243-0946
Facsimile: 940-898-0502
Email: dentonlaw.com

Brian T. Cartwright
Gerald W. Cobb
Lawrence C. Collister

OF COUNSEL

George Hopkins

Representative Clients: First Federal Bank of North Texas; First State Bank of Texas, Denton, Texas; Sanger Bank, Sanger, Texas; BankOne, Texas, N.A.; Provident Bank, Denton, Texas; Dentex Title Co., Denton, Texas.

For full biographical listings, see the Martindale-Hubbell Law Directory

WOOD, THACKER & WEATHERLY, P.C. (AV)

513 West Oak Street, 76201
Telephone: 817-565-6565
Fax: 817-566-6673

R. William Wood
C. Jane Thacker
Grace A. Weatherly

For full biographical listings, see the Martindale-Hubbell Law Directory

*EDINBURG,** Hidalgo Co.

REED, CARRERA & MCLAIN, L.L.P. (AV)

1 Paseo del Prado, Building 101, 78539
Telephone: 956-631-5444
Fax: 956-631-9187
Mailing Address: P.O. Box 9702, McAllen, Texas, 78502-9702
Email: rcmlaw@compuserve.com

Roger H. Reed
Victor M. Carrera
J. Scott McLain

Ana M. Guerrero
Alberto L. Guerrero

For full biographical listings, see the Martindale-Hubbell Law Directory

*EL PASO,** El Paso Co.

CROWSON & INGRAM (AV)

Suite 706, The Cortez, 310 North Mesa, P.O. Box 862, 79945
Telephone: 915-533-7717
Telefax: 915-533-1495
Email: crowsing@huntleigh.net

(See Next Column)

CROWSON & INGRAM—*Continued*

MEMBERS OF FIRM

Harold E. Crowson, Jr. Temple B. Ingram, Jr.

Reference: Bank of America, N.A.; Norwest Bank, El Paso, N.A.; Bank of the West, El Paso, Texas.

For full biographical listings, see the Martindale-Hubbell Law Directory

DIAMOND RASH GORDON & JACKSON, P.C. (AV)

300 East Main Drive, 7th Floor, 79901
Telephone: 915-533-2277
Fax: 915-545-4623

Tom Diamond
Alan V. Rash
Norman J. Gordon
Ronald L. Jackson
John R. Batoon
Robert J. Truhill
Russell D. Leachman

Representative Clients: City of El Paso; El Paso Housing Finance Corp.; City of El Paso Industrial Development Authority; Ysleta del sur Pueblo Indian Tribe; Alabama and Coushatta Indian Tribe of Texas; Metropolitan Life Insurance Co.

For full biographical listings, see the Martindale-Hubbell Law Directory

HICKS & LUCKY, A PROFESSIONAL CORPORATION (AV)

5812 Cromo Drive, 79912-5502
Telephone: 915-834-8400
Fax: 915-587-8401
Toll Free: 888-738-8401
Email: info@hicksandlucky.com *URL:* http://www.hicksandlucky.com

Larry W. Hicks
Jeffrey T. Lucky
Hadley A. Huchton

John Scott Mann
Cynthia C. Llamas
Jennifer F. Callan
Melissa A. Dorman
Laura Montalvo

For full biographical listings, see the Martindale-Hubbell Law Directory

RAY, MCCHRISTIAN & JEANS, A PROFESSIONAL CORPORATION (AV)

5822 Cromo Drive, Suite 400, 79912
Telephone: 915-832-7200
Fax: 915-832-7333
Email: rmj@rmjfirm.com

Jeff Ray
John W. McChristian, Jr.
David S. Jeans
James A. Mounts, III
Eduardo Miranda
Robin Collins
Leticia Nuñez

Daniel H. Hernandez
Michael K. Dean
Angelica B. Carreon
Todd E. Marshall
Stacy Bearden Zavala

Representative Clients: St. Paul Insurance Cos.; Texas Medical Liability Trust; Union Pacific Railroad; Kemper National Insurance Cos.; Cigna Property and Casualty Co.; The Travelers Indemnity Co. and Aetna Casualty & Surety Co.; USAA Property and Casualty Co.; Wal-Mart Stores, Inc.; State Farm Insurance Cos.; Professional Liability Insurance Co.

For full biographical listings, see the Martindale-Hubbell Law Directory

*FORT WORTH,** Tarrant Co.

BISHOP, PAYNE, HARVARD & KAITCER, L.L.P. (AV)

Eighteenth Floor, 500 West Seventh Street, 76102
Telephone: 817-335-4911
Telecopier: 817-870-2631
Email: BishopPayne@BishopPayne.com

Philip R. Bishop
Hershel R. Payne
Timothy J. Harvard
Michael D. Kaitcer

Andrew S. Jones
Jonathan S. Hyman

OF COUNSEL

Richard L. Brown

For full biographical listings, see the Martindale-Hubbell Law Directory

CHAPPELL, PARMELEE, JOHNSON & HILL, P.C. (AV)

1800 City Center Tower II, 301 Commerce Street, 76102-4118
Telephone: 817-332-1800
Metro: 817-654-2140
Telecopy: 817-332-1956
Email: cpjh@cmlaw.com *URL:* http://www.cmlaw.com

David F. Chappell
Robert A. Parmelee
Robert S. Johnson
Cynthia L. Hill

(See Next Column)

Suzanne K. Rosen
William F. Peters, Jr.

OF COUNSEL

James L. Williams, Jr.
Carolyn Mitchell
Christopher Cooke
C.C. "Kit" Cooke, III

For full biographical listings, see the Martindale-Hubbell Law Directory

DECKER, JONES, MCMACKIN, MCCLANE, HALL & BATES, A PROFESSIONAL CORPORATION (AV)

2500 Bank One Tower, 500 Throckmorton Street, 76102-3812
Telephone: 817-336-2400; Metro: 817-429-5260
Fax: 817-332-3043; 336-2181
Email: email@deckerjones.com *URL:* http://www.deckerjones.com

Daniel L. Bates
Robert W. Decker
Mark S. Dugan
Janet L. Hahn
Randy J. Hall
Raymond B. Kelly, III
John B. McClane
John W. McMackin
Charles B. Milliken
Gary M. Moates
Bradley H. Rice
Jeffrey W. Storie
James L. Stripling
Brian K. Yost
Tamera H. Bennett
Arthur F. Zobal
Geoffrey A. Mantooth

Representative Clients: Martin-Sprocket and Gear, Inc.; Williamson-Dickie Manufacturing Co.; MICA Corp.; Harbison-Fischer Manufacturing Co.; Employers Insurance of Texas; American International Group; Medical Protective Co.; Redman Homes, Inc.; Liberty Mutual Insurance; Texas Medical Liability Trust.

For full biographical listings, see the Martindale-Hubbell Law Directory

THE HASLAM FIRM (AV)

555 South Summit Avenue, 76104-2004
Telephone: 817-332-3115
Fax: 817-332-3148
Email: rhaslam@flash.net

Robert E. Haslam

For full biographical listings, see the Martindale-Hubbell Law Directory

JACKSON WALKER L.L.P. (AV)

301 Commerce Street, Suite 2400, 76102
Telephone: 817-334-7200
Fax: 817-334-7290
URL: http://www.jw.com
Austin, Texas Office: 100 Congress Avenue, Suite 1100.
Telephone: 512-236-2000.
Fax: 512-236-2002.
Dallas, Texas Office: 901 Main Street, Suite 6000.
Telephone: 214-953-6000.
Fax: 214-953-5822.
Houston, Texas Office: 1100 Louisiana, Suite 4200.
Telephone: 713-752-4200.
Fax: 713-752-4221.
Richardson, Texas Office: 2435 North Central Expressway, Suite 600.
Telephone: 972-671-2560.
Fax: 972-671-2566.
San Angelo, Texas Office: 225 West Beauregard Avenue.
Telephone: 915-481-2550.
Fax: 915-481-2552.
San Antonio, Texas Office: 112 E. Pecan Street, Suite 2100.
Telephone: 210-978-7700.
Fax: 210-978-7790.

MEMBERS OF FIRM

Sheldon Anisman
Albon O. Head, Jr.
Jeffrey J. Wolf

For Complete List of Firm Personnel, See General Section

For full biographical listings, see the Martindale-Hubbell Law Directory

JOSE, HENRY, BRANTLEY & KELTNER, L.L.P. (AV)

675 North Henderson Street, 76107-8495
Telephone: 817-877-3303
Fax: 817-338-9109

John S. Jose
Michael J. Henry
Rickey J. Brantley
David E. Keltner

Karen S. Precella
Scotty MacLean
Anna L. Kingsley
Sara K. Turman-Vedral

For full biographical listings, see the Martindale-Hubbell Law Directory

MCMULLEN LAW FIRM (AV)

6300 Ridglea Place Suite 509, 76116-5731
Telephone: 817-731-4163
Fax: 817-731-4340
Email: wademcmullen@msn.com

(See Next Column)

McMullen Law Firm, *Fort Worth—Continued*

Wade H. McMullen

For full biographical listings, see the Martindale-Hubbell Law Directory

Law Offices of Patrick H. O'Neill (AV)

110 West 7th Street, Suite 1100, 76102
Telephone: 817-878-3333
Fax: 817-878-3672

Patrick H. O'Neill

James L. Jackson, Jr. Glenn T. Lupo

For full biographical listings, see the Martindale-Hubbell Law Directory

Russell, Turner, Laird & Jones, L.L.P. (AV)

One Colonial Place, 2400 Scott Avenue, 76103-2200
Telephone: 817-531-3000; 1-800-448-2889
Fax: 817-535-3046
Irving, Texas Office: Williams Square, Central Tower, Suite 700, 5215 North O'Connor Boulevard, Las Colinas Urban Center.
Telephone: 972-444-0444; 1-800-448-2889.

Wm. Greg Russell
Steven C. Laird
Randall E. Turner
Gregory G. Jones

For full biographical listings, see the Martindale-Hubbell Law Directory

Thompson & Knight L.L.P. (AV)

(Attorneys and Counselors)
801 Cherry Street, Suite 1600, 76102
Telephone: 817-347-1700
Telecopy: 817-347-1799
URL: http://www.tklaw.com
Dallas, Texas Office: 1700 Pacific Avenue, Suite 3300, 75201.
Telephone: 214-969-1700.
Telecopy: 214-969-1751.
Telex: 732298.
Austin, Texas Office: 1200 San Jacinto Center, 98 San Jacinto Boulevard, 78701.
Telephone: 512-469-6100.
Telecopy: 512-469-6180.
Houston, Texas Office: Thompson Knight Brown Parker & Leahy L.L.P., 1200 Smith Street, Suite 3600, 77002-4595.
Telephone: 713-654-8111.
Telecopier: 713-654-1871.
San Pedro Garza Garcia, Nuevo León, Mexico Office: Edificio Losoles PD-4, Av. Lázaro Cárdenas No. 2400 Pte., C.P. 66220.
Telephone: (52-8) 363-0096.
Telecopy: (52-8) 363-3067.

PARTNERS

Lonnie J. Copps
Jennifer Pettijohn Henry
E. Michael Sheehan

ASSOCIATES

Monty B. Moncrief
Jason Wylie

For Complete List of Firm Personnel, See General Section

For full biographical listings, see the Martindale-Hubbell Law Directory

FRISCO, Collin & Denton Cos.

Winikates & Winikates (AV)

Prosper State Bank Building, 7700 Main Street, P.O. Box 249, 75034-0249
Telephone: 972-335-1122
Fax: 972-335-1125

MEMBERS OF FIRM

Charles J. Winikates
Regina W. Mentesana
Charles J. Winikates, Jr.
Frances A. Fazio

For full biographical listings, see the Martindale-Hubbell Law Directory

HARLINGEN, Cameron Co.

Adams & Graham, L.L.P. (AV)

222 East Van Buren, West Tower, 78550
Telephone: 956-428-7495
Fax: 956-428-2954
Email: office@adamsgraham.com *URL:* http://www.adamsgraham.com
Affiliate Austin, Texas Office: Hill Gilstrap Adams & Graham, L.L.P., 1005 Congress Avenue, Suite 880, 78701.
Telephone: 512-457-9806.
Fax: 512-457-9066.

John Q. Adams (1900-1968)
Marshall W. Graham (1924-1988)
James S. Graham, Jr. (1922-1990)
Ferriel C. Hamby, Jr.
Tom A. Lockhart
Jim Denison
Leo C. Salzman
Roger W. Hughes

(See Next Column)

Craig H. Vittitoe
Charlie J. Cilfone
William L. Pope
Juan A. Gonzalez
Patricia Kelly
Barry Ray
Jaime Balli
Wilbert (Will) Hughes
Gina M. Benavides
Trinidad P. Galdean

Representative Clients: The Travelers Insurance Cos.; State Farm Insurance Co.; W.R. Grace; American International Companies; Gallagher-Bassett; Texas Workers' Compensation Insurance Fund; Coca-Cola; Texas Municipal League; Highlands Insurance Co.; Farmers Insurance Co.

For full biographical listings, see the Martindale-Hubbell Law Directory

The Fleuriet Schell Law Firm LLP (AV)

621 East Tyler, 78550
Telephone: 956-428-3030
Fax: 956-421-4339
Email: mail@fleurietschell.com *URL:* http://www.fleurietschell.com

MEMBERS OF FIRM

Edwin Randolph Fleuriet
Richard D. Schell
Edward E. Robinson

For full biographical listings, see the Martindale-Hubbell Law Directory

*HOUSTON,** Harris Co.

Tom Alexander & Associates (AV)

Bank of America Center, 37th Floor, 700 Louisiana, 77002
Telephone: 713-439-0000
Telecopy: 713-963-8478

Tom Alexander

References: American Bank; Chasewood Bank; Southwest Bank of Texas.

For full biographical listings, see the Martindale-Hubbell Law Directory

Baker Botts L.L.P. (AV)

One Shell Plaza, 910 Louisiana, 77002
Telephone: 713-229-1234
Cable Address: "Boterlove"
Fax: 713-229-1522
Email: postmaster@bakerbotts.com *URL:* http://www.bakerbotts.com
Washington, D.C. Office: The Warner, 1299 Pennsylvania Avenue, N.W.
Telephone: 202-639-7700.
New York, New York Office: 599 Lexington Avenue.
Telephone: 212-705-5000.
Austin, Texas Office: 1600 San Jacinto Center, 98 San Jacinto Boulevard.
Telephone: 512-322-2500.
Dallas, Texas Office: 2001 Ross Avenue.
Telephone: 214-953-6500.
Moscow, Russia Office: 10 ul. Bolshaya Dimitrovka (formerly Pushkinskaya), 103031.
Telephone: 7095/921-5300 (Local); 7095/929-7070 (International).
London, England Office: 45 Ludgate Hill.
Telephone: 0171-778-1400 (Local); 011-44-171-778-1400 (International).
Baku, Azerbaijan Office: 6-10 Vagif Mustafa-zadeh Street, Third Floor, Icheri Sheher, 370004.
Telephone: 994-12-97-63-88 (Local); 011-994-12-97-63-88 (International).
Fax: 994-12-97-63-91 (Local); 011-994-12-97-63-91 (International)

MEMBERS OF FIRM

Thomas H. Adolph
Louis Lee Bagwell
J. Michael Baldwin
Maria Wyckoff Boyce
Richard R. Brann
Michael Lamar Brem
B. Daryl Bristow
Charles Tynan Buthod
Joseph D. Cheavens
F. Walter Conrad, Jr.
Paul R. Elliott
Larry B. Feldcamp
Michael S. Goldberg
Michael Paul Graham
Philip J. John, Jr.
Richard L. Josephson
William Karl Kroger
Matthew L. Kuryla
Ronald C. Lewis
Mitchell D. Lukin
James Edward Maloney
Karen Kay Maston
J. Bruce McDonald
Rufus W. Oliver, III
Scott F. Partridge
David R. Poage
Bradley I. Raffle
Tony P. Rosenstein
Travis James Sales
George T. Shipley
L. Chapman Smith
David D. Sterling
G. Irvin Terrell
Stephen Gillham Tipps
Teresa S. Valderrama
Allister M. Waldrop, Jr.
Michael E. Wilson

SPECIAL COUNSEL

Carolyn Brostad Southerland

ASSOCIATES

Timothy Craig Allen, M.D.
Jed P. Anderson
Michael B. Bennett
Katherine Butler Brem
Richard A. Brooks
Michael L. Calhoon
Samuel W. Cooper
Cynthia Crawford
Sandra K. Elzerman
Nellie Agah Fisher
Roger J. Fulghum
David George
Carey Jordan Hetherington
Seshasayee Kalapatapu
Alan F. Kansas
M. Shane Kimzey

(See Next Column)

BAKER BOTTS L.L.P.—*Continued*

ASSOCIATES (Continued)

Sandra Thourot Krider
Pamela Roger Laborde
Michael P. Lennon, Jr.
Judy Y. Liu
Maryanne Lyons
Amy Douthitt Maddux
Robin Lightner Maisashvili (Not admitted in TX)
Njeri I. Mathis
Laura B. Medina
Joel Z. Montgomery
Beth K. Neese
Kay M. Peterson
Teresa M. Potter
David M. Rodi
Kathryn Stegall Schueler
D'Andra Millsap Shu
Amy L. Snell
Jonathan E. Sommer
James R. Staley
Paul J. Stancil
Lori D. Stiffler
Macey Reasoner Stokes
Kathryn S. Vaughn
Mark L. Walters
Shelley L. Ward
Gerard Alan Witte
Shira R. Yoshor

For Complete List of Firm Personnel, See General Section

For full biographical listings, see the Martindale-Hubbell Law Directory

BAKER & HOSTETLER LLP (AV)

1000 Louisiana, Suite 2000, 77002-5008
Telephone: 713-751-1600
FAX: 713-751-1717
To contact an attorney on the Internet use first initial and surname followed by @baker-hostetler.com
URL: http://www.bakerlaw.com
In Cleveland, Ohio: 3200 National City Center, 1900 East Ninth Street.
Telephone: 216-621-0200.
In Cincinnati, Ohio: 312 Walnut Street, Suite 2650.
Telephone: 513-929-3400.
In Columbus, Ohio: Capitol Square, Suite 2100, 65 East State Street.
Telephone: 614-228-1541.
In Denver, Colorado: 303 East 17th Avenue, Suite 1100.
Telephone: 303-861-0600.
In Beverly Hills, California: 9150 Wilshire Boulevard, Suite 205.
Telephone: 310-385-7500.
In Long Beach, California: 300 Oceangate, Suite 620.
Telephone: 562-432-2827.
In Los Angeles, California: 600 Wilshire Boulevard.
Telephone: 213-624-2400.
In Orlando, Florida: SunBank Center, Suite 2300, 200 South Orange Avenue.
Telephone: 407-649-4000.
In Washington, D. C.: Washington Square, Suite 1100, 1050 Connecticut Avenue, N.W.
Telephone: 202-861-1500.

OFFICE MANAGING PARTNER

Kenneth R. Valka (Managing Partner-Houston Office)

PARTNERS

Hurlie H. Collier
Jon David Ivey
Lisa H. Pennington

ASSOCIATE

Lilly E. Thrower

For Complete List of Firm Personnel, See General Section

For full biographical listings, see the Martindale-Hubbell Law Directory

BAYKO GIBSON CARNEGIE HAGAN SCHOONMAKER & MEYER LLP (AV)

Chase Tower, 65th Floor, 77002-3008
Telephone: 713-223-0101
Facsimile: 713-223-0042
Email: baykogibson@nol.net

PARTNERS

Tom Bayko
Wendy K. B. Buskop
Jack G. Carnegie
Martin P. Detloff
Larry L. Evans
Michael W. Ford
Michael M. Gibson
John L. Hagan
Robert J. Leidich
M. Michael Meyer
Linda C. Schoonmaker
Leymon Solomon

OF COUNSEL

John T. S. Williams

David M. Bays
Julia Lynn Nye
Ruth E. Piller
Melissa Brook Romine
Lauri De Brie Thanheiser

For full biographical listings, see the Martindale-Hubbell Law Directory

BAYLESS & STOKES (AV)

2931 Ferndale Street, 77098
Telephone: 713-522-2224
Fax: 713-522-2218
Email: bayless@baylessstokes.com

MEMBER OF FIRM

Bobbie G. Bayless

(See Next Column)

ASSOCIATE

Spencer W. Creed

For full biographical listings, see the Martindale-Hubbell Law Directory

BECK, REDDEN & SECREST (AV)

One Houston Center, 1221 McKinney Street, Suite 4500, 77010
Telephone: 713-951-3700
Telecopier: 713-951-3720
Email: brs@brsfirm.com *URL:* http://www.brsfirm.com

MEMBERS OF FIRM

David J. Beck
Joe W. Redden, Jr.
Ronald Dean Secrest
William Curtis Webb
Eric James Roy Nichols
Alistair Byrne Dawson
Harry P. Weitzel

OF COUNSEL

Keith A. Jones (Not admitted in TX)
Linda K. McCloud
Anne M. Pike
Rufus Wallingford

ASSOCIATES

Jennifer Parker Ainsworth
L. Nicole Batey
Thomas E. Ganucheau
Jeffrey M. Golub
David Watkin Jones
Felicia Harris Kyle
Michael E. Richardson
Jim Taylor

For full biographical listings, see the Martindale-Hubbell Law Directory

BEIRNE, MAYNARD & PARSONS, L.L.P. (AV)

Wells Fargo Bank Tower 25th Floor, 1300 Post Oak Boulevard, 77056-3000
Telephone: 713-623-0887
Fax: 713-960-1527
Email: info@bmpllp.com *URL:* http://www.bmpllp.com

MEMBER OF FIRM

Gene F. Creely, II

For Complete List of Firm Personnel, See General Section

For full biographical listings, see the Martindale-Hubbell Law Directory

BERG & ANDROPHY (AV)

3704 Travis, 77002-9550
Telephone: 713-529-5622
Fax: 713-529-3785
URL: http://www.lawyers.com/b&alaw
Email: mail@bahou.com *URL:* http://www.bafirm.com
New York, New York Office: 230 Park Avenue, Suite 1000, 10169-1099.
Telephone: 212-808-6580.
Fax: 212-808-3020.

David H. Berg (P.C.)
Joel M. Androphy
Cynthia R. Levin Moulton

Wade T. Howard
Geoffrey A. Berg
Gabriel A. Berg (Not admitted in TX)

For full biographical listings, see the Martindale-Hubbell Law Directory

JOHN GORDON BOCK (AV)

The Lyric Centre, 440 Louisiana, Suite 850, 77002
Telephone: 713-739-0902
Fax: 713-650-3816
Email: Bocklaw@aol.com

For full biographical listings, see the Martindale-Hubbell Law Directory

BURROW & PARROTT, L.L.P. (AV)

A Registered Limited Liability Partnership
3500 Chevron Tower, 1301 McKinney, 77010-3092
Telephone: 713-222-6333
Fax: 713-650-6333
Email: bpfirm@bpcd.com *URL:* http://www.lawyers.com/burrowlaw

David H. Burrow
Alice Oliver-Parrott

Philip Brashier
Randall R. Smidt

OF COUNSEL

Robert H. Walker

For full biographical listings, see the Martindale-Hubbell Law Directory

CARPENTER & ASSOCIATES (AV)

Suite 604, River Oaks Bank Building, 2001 Kirby Drive, 77019
Telephone: 713-528-3118
Facsimile: 713-528-3198
Email: wscarpenter@juno.com

W. Scott Carpenter

For full biographical listings, see the Martindale-Hubbell Law Directory

Houston—Continued

CASH JONES, L.L.P. (AV)

Chase Tower, 600 Travis, Suite 6710, 77002
Telephone: 713-224-6767
Telecopier: 713-227-6222

MEMBERS OF FIRM

Michael P. Cash
Bill Jones

ASSOCIATES

Susan E. Kinkaid
John D. Walker
Robert J. Montoya
Eleanor H. Hodges
R. Bryant Siddoway

OF COUNSEL

David A. Springhetti
Denice Smith

For full biographical listings, see the Martindale-Hubbell Law Directory

CLEMENTS, O'NEILL, PIERCE NICKENS & WILSON, L.L.P. (AV)

Wells Fargo Plaza, 1000 Louisiana, Suite 1800, 77002-5009
Telephone: 713-654-7600
Fax: 713-654-7690
Email: mail@copn.com
Dallas, Texas Office: 3405 Oak Grove Avenue, 75204-2332.
Telephone: 214-953-0192.
Fax: 214-871-9015.

PARTNERS

J. Eugene Clements (1941-1999)
Paul D. Flack
Thomas M. Fulkerson
Byron C. Keeling
Evelyn V. Keyes
Michael D. Kirby
Kelly J. Kirkland
Tex Lezar (P.C.) (Resident at Dallas, Texas Office)
Ralph A. Midkiff
Jacks C. Nickens
Edward J. O'Neill, Jr.
John E. O'Neill
Jesse R. Pierce
Michael M. Wilson

ASSOCIATES

James M. Baker
Kelly Michelle Battle
Alice M. Bragg
Barbara A. Clark
Ruth B. Downes
Neil E. Giles
Linda Gordon Hester
Craig S. Miles
Molly D. Naylor
Karolyn King Nelson (Not admitted in TX)
Tara Porterfield
Reagan D. Pratt
Katherine McIlroy Shoebotham
Mark A. White

For full biographical listings, see the Martindale-Hubbell Law Directory

COOK, ROACH & LAWLESS, L.L.P. (AV)

1111 Bagby Street, Suite 2650, 77002
Telephone: 713-652-2800
Fax: 713-652-2029
Email: firm@cookroach.com *URL:* http://www.cookroach.com
Austin, Texas Office: 327 Congress Avenue, Suite 490, 78701.
Telephone: 512-472-3067.
Fax: 512-472-3068.

Ronald E. Cook
Robert M. Roach, Jr.
J. Mark Lawless
Dulce M. Stenglein
Robert B. Dubose
Daniel L. McKay

OF COUNSEL

Dana Livingston Cobb

For full biographical listings, see the Martindale-Hubbell Law Directory

CRUSE, SCOTT, HENDERSON & ALLEN, L.L.P. (AV)

Chase Tower, 600 Travis, Suite 3900, 77002-2910
Telephone: 713-650-6600
Fax: 713-650-1720

Sam W. Cruse, Jr.
John P. Scott
Jay H. Henderson
T. Scott Allen, Jr.
Samuel A. Houston
George W. (Billy) Shepherd, III
John R. Strawn, Jr.
Stephen R. Bailey
John D. Vogel
Wayne Clawater

ASSOCIATES

Debra L. Elmore
Merritt McReynolds Marinelli
David J. McTaggart
Matthew M. Prewett

For full biographical listings, see the Martindale-Hubbell Law Directory

PATRICIA KAY DUBE, P.C. (AV)

4140 Bank of America Center, 700 Louisiana Street, 77002
Telephone: 713-225-2297
Facsimile: 713-225-2298
Email: pkdube@wt.net *URL:* http://www.lawyers.com/dubelaw

Patricia Kay Dube
Clare I. Vetters
Lee Broze

(See Next Column)

OF COUNSEL

Alan J. Winters
Harold J. Eisenman

For full biographical listings, see the Martindale-Hubbell Law Directory

DUNN, KACAL, ADAMS, PAPPAS & LAW, A PROFESSIONAL CORPORATION (AV)

2600 America Tower, 2929 Allen Parkway at Waugh, 77019-2151
Telephone: 713-529-3992
Telefax: 713-529-8161
Email: DKAPL@worldnet.att.net

Charles R. Dunn
Jerry Kacal
Robert L. Adams
Christopher C. Pappas
Richard M. Law
Gordon M. Carver, III
Michael C. Feehan
Daniel D. King
Kenneth D. Rhodes
Frances Moore
A.M. "Andy" Landry, III
Robert Scherrer
James D. Smith

Karen M. Alvarado
Darrell R. Greer
Lucille Anderson Reiter
Andrew J. Sarne
J. Christopher Dean
Daniel F. Crowder
Laurel A. Agris
Tamara L. Sheffield
M. Laura Lopez
Karen R. Dow
Kevin Douglas Bowie
Melanie A. Rubinsky

For full biographical listings, see the Martindale-Hubbell Law Directory

JACK H. EMMOTT III & ASSOCIATES, P.C. (AV)

5120 Woodway Suite 10002, 77056
Telephone: 713-840-1300
Fax: 713-840-1303
Email: jemmott@net1.net *URL:* http://www.j-emmott.com

Jack H. Emmott III

For full biographical listings, see the Martindale-Hubbell Law Directory

FJELDAL & ASSOCIATES, A PROFESSIONAL CORPORATION (AV)

1225 North Loop West, Suite 1111, 77008
Telephone: 713-869-9690
Fax: 713-869-6777
Email: fjeldlaw@aol.com

Timothy A. Fjeldal

Scott T. Burkett

For full biographical listings, see the Martindale-Hubbell Law Directory

FRANKLIN, CARDWELL & JONES (AV)

Chase Tower, 24th Floor, 600 Travis Street, 77002-2910
Telephone: 713-222-6025
Fax: 713-222-0938
Email: attorneys@fcj.com *URL:* http://www.fcj.com

Ronald G. Franklin
Suzan K. Cardwell
Gregory N. Jones
Scott G. Burdine
Carlton D. Wilde, Jr.
A. Scott Alford
Mary Angela Meyer
Jeffrey D. Meyer
Joseph A. Fischer, III
Sheila Wollam

For full biographical listings, see the Martindale-Hubbell Law Directory

GALLAGHER, YOUNG, LEWIS, HAMPTON & DOWNEY, L.L.P. (AV)

NationsBank Building, 700 Louisiana, 40th Floor, 77002
Telephone: 713-222-8080
Fax: 713-222-0066

Michael T. Gallagher
William H. Young
Craig Lewis
Hartley Hampton
Daniel M. Downey

Martin John de la Torre
Andrew Sher
Candace Kaiser Eindorf
Scott H. Mclemore
John J. Klevenhagen, III
Araceli E. Flores

OF COUNSEL

Rosemary Conlon McCarthy

For full biographical listings, see the Martindale-Hubbell Law Directory

GIBBS & BRUNS, L.L.P. (AV)

1100 Louisiana, Suite 5300, 77002
Telephone: 713-650-8805
Fax: 713-750-0903

(See Next Column)

GIBBS & BRUNS L.L.P.—*Continued*

PARTNERS

Robin C. Gibbs
Phillip T. Bruns
J. Christopher Reynolds
Kathy D. Patrick
Jeffrey C. Alexander
Robert R. Burford
Jean C. Frizzell
Grant J. Harvey
Barrett H. Reasoner
Robert J. Madden
Jeffry J. Cotner
Jennifer Horan Greer

ASSOCIATES

Andrew L. Pickens
John A. Basinger
Scott A. Humphries
Michael K. Oldham
Caren Schmulen Sweetland
John Scott Black
Jeremy L. Doyle
Brandon T. Allen

For full biographical listings, see the Martindale-Hubbell Law Directory

GILLIS & SLOGAR (AV)

6905 Wells Fargo Plaza, 1000 Louisiana, 77002
Telephone: 713-951-9100
Telecopier: 713-951-9718
Email: gillisslogar@worldnet.att.net

Charles Michael Gillis
John Michael Slogar

OF COUNSEL

Randall W. Heinrich

For full biographical listings, see the Martindale-Hubbell Law Directory

GILPIN, PAXSON & BERSCH (AV)

A Registered Limited Liability Partnership
Attorney at Law
1900 West Loop South, Suite 2000, 77027-3259
Telephone: 713-623-8800
Telecopier: 713-993-8451
Email: gpb@gpblaw.com *URL:* http://www.texinslaw.com

PARTNERS

Gary M. Alletag
Timothy R. Bersch
John D. Gilpin
Darryl W. Malone
Michael J. Pappert
Stephen Paxson
Kevin F. Risley

OF COUNSEL

Harless R. Benthul
David F. Webb

ASSOCIATES

Joseph D. Batson
Jeri Pharis Wechsler

Representative Clients: BMW of North America, Inc.; Federal Deposit Insurance Corporation; Greater Houston Builders Association; Owens Corning Fiberglas Corporation; Shaw Industries, Inc.; Southwest Guaranty Trust Company, N.A.; Sprint Communications Company L.P.; Volkswagen of America, Inc.; Volvo North America Corporation; Wells Fargo Bank (Texas), N.A.

For full biographical listings, see the Martindale-Hubbell Law Directory

GLOVER, ANDERSON, LEWIS & PREBEG P.C., PROFESSIONAL CORPORATION (AV)

5599 San Felipe, Suite 1600, 77056
Telephone: 713-621-3306
Facsimile: 713-621-2259

Arthur M. Glover, Jr.
Paul E. Anderson, Jr.
James B. Lewis
Matthew J.M. Prebeg

Scott J. Davenport

For full biographical listings, see the Martindale-Hubbell Law Directory

GREGG & GREGG, P.C. (AV)

16055 Space Center Boulevard Suite 150, 77062
Telephone: 281-480-1211
Fax: 281-480-1210
Email: dhgregg3@flash.net

Dick H. Gregg, Jr.
Dick H. Gregg, III

For full biographical listings, see the Martindale-Hubbell Law Directory

HANEN, ALEXANDER, JOHNSON & SPALDING, L.L.P. (AV)

910 Travis, Suite 1700, 77002
Telephone: 713-222-2323
Fax: 713-222-2226

Andrew S. Hanen
Joseph R. Alexander, Jr.
Brian P. Johnson
John E. Spalding
Frank A. Doyle
Lawrence J. West
T. Christopher Trent

(See Next Column)

Geoffrey C. Guill
Tamara M. Madden
Richard Todd Marshall
Raphael (Rafe) Taylor
Lisa M. Moran
Shashi Patel
Annette Sepulveda Kenefick
Craig A. Choate

For full biographical listings, see the Martindale-Hubbell Law Directory

G.P. HARDY III, P.C. (AV)

500 Two Houston Center, 909 Fannin at McKinney, 77010
Telephone: 713-222-0381
Fax: 713-759-9650
Bay City, Texas Office: 2042 Avenue F.
Telephone: 409-245-3797.
Fax: 409-245-4713.

G. P. Hardy, Jr. (1913-1988)
G. P. Hardy, III
Gail Johns

Timothy M. Purcell
Mark G. Cypert
Patricia Haylon

References: Southwest Bank of Texas; International Bank of Commerce.

For full biographical listings, see the Martindale-Hubbell Law Directory

HAYS, MCCONN, RICE & PICKERING (AV)

400 Two Allen Center, 1200 Smith Street, 77002
Telephone: 713-654-1111
Fax: 713-650-0027
Email: HMRP@HaysMcConn.com *URL:* http://www.haysmcconn.com

MEMBERS OF FIRM

Michael S. Hays
James J. McConn, Jr.
B. Stephen Rice
Michael R. Pickering
Mark A. Padon
Bruce Gaible
Susan Crowley Stevenson
Allen Till
Craig S. Wolcott
Naomi S. Ostfeld
Margaret Twomey Brenner
W. Michael Scott
Jeffery Allen Addicks
J. Philip Griffis
A. Scott Kidd
Robert E. Purgatorio
Brian Tew
Steven M. Duble
Lance K. Thomas
Michael W. Magee

ASSOCIATES

Troy A. Williams
Shannon D. Robbie
Staton M. Childers
Timothy R. Hightower
William Jason Walker
Michael A. Durr
Leslie M. Henry
Amanda F. Bell
David Wilson, II

OF COUNSEL

John T. Golden

For full biographical listings, see the Martindale-Hubbell Law Directory

HILL & PARKER, A PROFESSIONAL CORPORATION (AV)

5300 Memorial, Suite 700, 77007-8292
Telephone: 713-868-5581
Telefax: 713-868-1275
Email: hillparker@compuserve.com *URL:* http://www.hillparker.com

John Graham Hill
Charles R. Parker
Brian Q. Carmichael
John Roberson
Hector A. Canales

Reference: Chase Texas Bank, N.A.

For full biographical listings, see the Martindale-Hubbell Law Directory

HOGAN DUBOSE & TOWNSEND, L.L.P. (AV)

1400 Lyric Centre, 440 Louisiana Street, 77002-1635
Telephone: 713-222-8800
Facsimile: 713-222-8810
Email: lawyers@HDTlaw.com

MEMBERS OF FIRM

Richard P. Hogan, Jr.
Jennifer Bruch Hogan
Kevin H. Dubose
Roger D. Townsend
David M. Gunn
Russell S. Post

OF COUNSEL

William Powers, Jr.

For full biographical listings, see the Martindale-Hubbell Law Directory

HOLLOWAY & ROWLEY, P.C. (AV)

1415 Louisiana Street, Suite 2550, 77002
Telephone: 713-751-0055
Telecopier: 713-751-0057

Gordon A. Holloway
Kyle M. Rowley

For full biographical listings, see the Martindale-Hubbell Law Directory

Houston—Continued

JACKSON WALKER L.L.P. (AV)

1100 Louisiana, Suite 4200, P.O. Box 4771, 77002
Telephone: 713-752-4200
Fax: 713-752-4221
URL: http://www.jw.com
Austin, Texas Office: 100 Congress Avenue, Suite 1100.
Telephone: 512-236-2000.
Fax: 512-236-2002.
Dallas, Texas Office: 901 Main Street, Suite 6000.
Telephone: 214-953-6000.
Fax: 214-953-5822.
Fort Worth, Texas Office: 301 Commerce Street, Suite 2400.
Telephone: 817-334-7200.
Fax: 817-334-7290.
Richardson, Texas Office: 2435 North Central Expressway, Suite 600.
Telephone: 972-671-2560.
Fax: 972-671-2566.
San Angelo, Texas Office: 225 West Beauregard Avenue.
Telephone: 915-481-2550.
Fax: 915-481-2552.
San Antonio, Texas Office: 112 E. Pecan Street, Suite 2100.
Telephone: 210-978-7700.
Fax: 210-978-7790.

MEMBERS OF FIRM

Charles L. Babcock
W. Todd Barnett
Janet Douvas Chafin
John R. Clayton
Linda J. Cole
Anne Marie Finch
Richard Earl Griffin
Nancy Wells Hamilton
Mollie Cohn Lambert
Lisa A. Powell
Fred A. Simpson

OF COUNSEL

Laurie B. Easter
Mary Lou Flynn-DuPart
Randall L. Smith

For Complete List of Firm Personnel, See General Section

For full biographical listings, see the Martindale-Hubbell Law Directory

KILBURN, JONES, GILL & CAMPBELL, L.L.P. (AV)

1100 Louisiana, Suite 3400, 77002-5234
Telephone: 713-652-4068
Fax: 713-652-4078
Email: info@kjgc.com *URL:* http://www.kjgc.com

Kerry A. Kilburn
Michael D. Jones
Lee S. Gill
K. Ray Campbell

David A. Birchall
K. Anne Bullen
Jeffery Robin Koch
Debra D. Sandefer

OF COUNSEL

Lynn C. Woods, Jr.

For full biographical listings, see the Martindale-Hubbell Law Directory

KILLEEN & FIERRO (AV)

1717 St. James Place, Suite 620, 77056
Telephone: 713-626-5100
Facsimile: 713-626-4545

Robert Joseph Killeen, Jr.
John M. Longoria
L. Byron Wilson

Candace A. Ourso

OF COUNSEL

Gerald M. Johnson, III

For full biographical listings, see the Martindale-Hubbell Law Directory

THE KRIST LAW FIRM, P.C. (AV)

17555 El Camino Real (Clear Lake City), 77058
Telephone: 281-283-8500
Fax: 281-488-3489
URL: http://www.lawyers.com/kristlaw

Ronald D. Krist
Kevin D. Krist
Scott C. Krist
Perry O. Barber Jr. (1938-1992)

Reference: Horizon Capital Bank, Webster, Texas.

For full biographical listings, see the Martindale-Hubbell Law Directory

MATTHIESEN, CHASE & ERWIN, L.L.P. (AV)

3003 Eleven Greenway Plaza, 77046
Telephone: 713-877-8522
Fax: 713-877-8822

David G. Matthiesen
A. Scot Chase
R. Harding Erwin, Jr.
Aaron Pool

(See Next Column)

R. Todd Carpenter
Trevor R. Jefferies
Deborah M. Wotring Landis
Ronald A. Wasinger

For full biographical listings, see the Martindale-Hubbell Law Directory

MCDADE, FOGLER, MAINES & LOHSE, L.L.P. (AV)

Two Houston Center, 909 Fannin, Suite 1200, 77010-1006
Telephone: 713-654-4300
Fax: 713-654-4343

Thomas R. McDade
Murray J. Fogler
William P. Maines
Albert R. Lohse

ASSOCIATE

Lesa A. Nickelson

OF COUNSEL

Paula K. Hutchinson

For full biographical listings, see the Martindale-Hubbell Law Directory

MEHAFFY & WEBER, A PROFESSIONAL CORPORATION (AV)

One Allen Center, 500 Dallas, Suite 1200, 77002
Telephone: 713-655-1200
Fax: 713-655-0222
Email: MehaffyWeber.com
Beaumont, Texas Office: 2615 Calder Avenue, Suite 800, P.O. Box 16.
Telephone: 409-835-5011.
Orange, Texas Office: 1006 Green Avenue, P.O. Drawer 189.
Telephone: 409-886-7766.

Jim I. Graves
Arthur R. Almquist
Charles Stanton Perry

Paul R. Heyburn
James G. Martingano
Debra N. Bigler
Peter T. Gregg
Elna Nguyen Griggs

Representative Clients: E.I. duPont de Nemours and Co.; W.R. Grace & Co.-Conn.; Merrill Dow; Eli Lilly & Company; Burlington, Northen, Santa Fe Railway Company; Christus Health.

For full biographical listings, see the Martindale-Hubbell Law Directory

PHELPS DUNBAR, L.L.P. (AV)

Suite 900, 3040 Post Oak Boulevard, 77056
Telephone: 713-626-1386
Telecopier: 713-626-1388
Email: info@phelps.com
New Orleans, Louisiana Office: Texaco Center, 400 Poydras Street.
Telephone: 504-566-1311.
Telecopier: 504-568-9130, 504-568-9007.
Cable Address: "Howspencer."
Telex: 584125 WU.
Telex: 6821155 WUI.
Baton Rouge, Louisiana Office: Suite 701, 445 North Boulevard, P.O. Box 4412.
Telephone: 225-346-0285.
Telecopier: 225-381-9197.
Jackson, Mississippi Office: Suite 500, SkyTel Centre, 200 South Lamar Street, P.O. Box 23066.
Telephone: 601-352-2300.
Telecopier: 601-360-9777.
Tupelo, Mississippi Office: Seventh Floor, One Mississippi Plaza, P.O. Box 1220.
Telephone: 662-842-7907.
Telecopier: 662-842-3873.
London, England Office: Suite 731, Level 7, Lloyd's, 1 Lime Street, London EC3M 7DQ England.
Telephone: 011-44-207-929-4765.
Telecopier: 011-44-207-929-0046.
Telex: 987321.

RESIDENT PARTNERS

Julia Marie Adams
David Lee Crawford
J. Clifton Hall III (Also at London, England Office)
Matthew R. Muth
Deborah A. Newman
Claude LeRoy Stuart, III
Kent E. Westmoreland (Also at London, England Office)
Joseph A. Ziemianski

COUNSEL

Peter B. Magnuson

RESIDENT ASSOCIATES

Jennifer M. Benson
Wendy T. Blanchard
N. Jerae Carlson
Mary A. Cazes
Patrick W. Drouilhet
Laura Schuler Favaloro
Marilee R. Kainer
Clint E. McGuire
Karen Klaas Milhollin
Debra S. Noll
Stanley T. Proctor
Mark B. Schaffer
John L. Schouest
Bryan P. Vezey
April M. Zubizarreta

Representative Clients: Aluminum Company of America; Atlantic Mutual Insurance Co.; Commercial Union Assurance, PLC; Entex; GATX Terminals Corp.; General Star Management Company; Terra Nova Insurance

(See Next Column)

PHELPS DUNBAR L.L.P.—*Continued*

Company, Ltd.; Underwriters at Lloyd's, London; Union Pacific Railroad Company; Zurich (U.K.).

For full biographical listings, see the Martindale-Hubbell Law Directory

PLUMMER & FARMER (AV)

Formerly: Bradshaw & Plummer, 1979-1990
Brown, Bradshaw & Plummer, 1974-1979
Brown & Bradshaw, 1963-1974
3000 Smith, 77006
Telephone: 713-524-2400
Fax: 713-524-6371

MEMBERS OF FIRM

Hugh J. Plummer
Michael D. Farmer

For full biographical listings, see the Martindale-Hubbell Law Directory

RAMSEY & MURRAY, A PROFESSIONAL CORPORATION (AV)

10000 Memorial Drive, Suite 700, 77024-3412
Telephone: 713-613-5400
Fax: 713-613-5414

Ben Ramsey
John A. Murray, Jr.
Russell J. Ramsey
Mark Ramsey
Curtis D. Collette
Michael Stout Wright
Rick McRory

Joseph W. Gagnon
R. Russell Hollenbeck
Adrian V. Villacorta
Brenda Renee Ferguson

Representative Clients: Great Central Insurance Co.; Republic Insurance Co.

For full biographical listings, see the Martindale-Hubbell Law Directory

RILEY & HARRIS, L.L.P. (AV)

One Houston Center, 1221 McKinney, Suite 3000, 77010-2023
Telephone: 713-646-1000
Fax: 713-646-1036
Email: txlaw@riley-harris.com *URL:* http://www.riley-harris.com
Brownsville, Texas Office: 845 E. Harrison, Suite A, 78520-7120.
Telephone: 956-550-8825.
Fax: 956-550-8854.

MEMBERS OF FIRM

Timothy D. Riley
Britton B. Harris
Patrick W. O'Briant

Brett J. Sileo
Matthew T. Heffner
Jill Ellen Ferguson

For full biographical listings, see the Martindale-Hubbell Law Directory

SCHWARTZ JUNELL CAMPBELL & OATHOUT, L.L.P. (AV)

Two Houston Center, 909 Fannin, Suite 2000, 77010
Telephone: 713-752-0017
Telecopier: 713-752-0327
Email: dschwartz@schwartz-junell.com

Richard A. Schwartz
William Edward Junell, Jr.
Marshall S. Campbell
Monica F. Oathout
Steven R. Rech

Phillip W. Bechter
J. Parker Fauntleroy, Jr.

OF COUNSEL

Joe H. Reynolds
A. R. Schwartz

LEGAL SUPPORT PERSONNEL

PARALEGALS

Nannette Koger
Maria Woods
Shelly A. Savage, CLA

For full biographical listings, see the Martindale-Hubbell Law Directory

STEPP & SULLIVAN, P.C. (AV)

Three Allen Center, 333 Clay Street, Suite 4750, 77002
Telephone: 713-336-7200
Fax: 713-336-7250
URL: http://www.ss-pc.com

Jad J. Stepp
Dennis J. Sullivan

Mark H. Barber
Richard C. Brister
Kimberly Y. Delaney
Kevin Troy Dossett

For full biographical listings, see the Martindale-Hubbell Law Directory

SUSMAN GODFREY L.L.P. (AV)

A Registered Limited Liability Partnership including Professional Corporations
Suite 5100 1000 Louisiana Street, 77002-5096
Telephone: 713-651-9366
Telecopy: 713-653-7897
URL: http://www.susmangodfrey
Dallas, Texas Office: Suite 1400, 2323 Bryan Street.
Telephone: 214-754-1900.
Fax: 214-754-1933. New address effective March, 2000: Suite 4100, 901 Main Street, 75202.
Seattle, Washington Office: Suite 3090, 1201 Third Avenue.
Telephone: 206-516-3880.
Telecopy: 206-516-3883.
Los Angeles, California Office: Suite 950, 1880 Century Park East.
Telephone: 310-789-3100.
Fax: 310-789-3150.

MEMBERS OF FIRM

Stephen D. Susman (P.C.)
H. Lee Godfrey (P.C.) (Resident)
Randall W. Wilson (Resident)
Franci Neely Crane (Resident)
Mark L. D. Wawro (Resident)
Kenneth E. McNeil (Resident)
Kenneth S. Marks (Resident)
Thomas W. Paterson (Resident)
Neal S. Manne (Resident)
Eric J. Mayer (Resident)
Mary Kathryn Sammons (Resident)
Max LaLon Tribble, Jr. (Resident)
Michael A. Lee (Resident)
Cyrus D. Marter IV (Resident)
Robert Rivera, Jr. (Resident)
J. Hoke Peacock III (Resident)
Karen A. Oshman (Resident)
Geoffrey L. Harrison (Resident)
Charles R. Eskridge, III (Resident)
Vineet Bhatia (Resident)
Jonathan J. Ross (Resident)

OF COUNSEL

Stuart V. Kusin (Resident)

ASSOCIATES

Katherine G. Treistman (Resident)
James T. Southwick (Resident)
Erica W. Harris (Resident)
Carolyn P. Courville (Resident)
Joseph S. Grinstein (Resident)
Johnny W. Carter (Resident)
Harry P. Susman (Resident)
William R.H. Merrill (Resident)

STAFF ATTORNEY

Shannon L. Rankin

Reference: Laredo National Bank, Houston.

For full biographical listings, see the Martindale-Hubbell Law Directory

TAYLOR & CIRE (AV)

An Assumed Name of a Professional Corporation
One Allen Center, 3400 Penthouse, 77002
Telephone: 713-654-7799
Fax: 713-654-7814
Email: tc3400@aol.com
Galveston, Texas Office: 1721 Broadway, 77550.
Telephone: 409-762-8914.

Robert G. Taylor II, (P.C.)
George E. (Buck) Cire, Jr.

J. Robert Davis, Jr.
Cletus P. Ernster, III

For full biographical listings, see the Martindale-Hubbell Law Directory

TEKELL, BOOK, MATTHEWS & LIMMER, L.L.P. (AV)

4300 One Houston Center, 1221 McKinney, 77010
Telephone: 713-222-9542
Fax: 713-655-7727
Email: tbml@tbml.com
Corpus Christi, Texas Office: 711 North Carancahua, Suite 902, 78475.
Telephone: 361-883-6100.
Fax: 361-883-6103. Email: cctbml@swbell.net.

Kenneth Tekell
William Book
Raymond T. Matthews
James H. Limmer
Mark K. Allen
Michael P. Morris
Todd A. Kissner
Matt W. Childs
Jeff Murphrey

Michele E. Taylor
David W. Burns
Kevin D. Didway
Kathleen Carney
WC "Trey" Book
Kenneth L. Tekell, Jr.
J. Gregory McEldowney
Robin T. Balette

OF COUNSEL

Danny L. Van Winkle

Representative Clients: Royal-Globe Insurance Group; Minnesota Mining and Manufacturing; Chubb Insurance Co.; CIGNA Companies; Fireman's Fund; Mobil Oil Co.; Arco Oil Co.

For full biographical listings, see the Martindale-Hubbell Law Directory

Houston—Continued

THOMPSON KNIGHT BROWN PARKER & LEAHY L.L.P. (AV)

A Registered Limited Liability Partnership including Professional Corporations
(Attorneys and Counselors)
1200 Smith Street, Suite 3600, 77002-4595
Telephone: 713-654-8111
Telecopier: 713-654-1871
URL: http://www.tklaw.com
Dallas, Texas Office: Thompson & Knight L.L.P., 1700 Pacific Avenue, Suite 3300, 75201.
Telephone: 214-969-1700.
Telecopy: 214-969-1751.
Telex: 732298.
Austin, Texas Office: Thompson & Knight L.L.P., 1200 San Jacinto Center, 98 San Jacinto Boulevard, 78701.
Telephone: 512-469-6100.
Telecopy: 512-469-6180.
Fort Worth, Texas Office: Thompson & Knight L.L.P., 801 Cherry Street, Suite 1600, 76102.
Telephone: 817-347-1700.
Telecopy: 817-347-1799.
San Pedro Garza Garcia, Nuevo León, Mexico Office: Thompson & Knight L.L.P., Edificio Losoles PD-4, Av. Lázaro Cárdenas No. 2400 PTE., C.P. 66220.
Telephone: (52-8) 363-0096.
Telecopy: (52-8) 363-3067.

PARTNERS

Roxella T. Cavazos
Gregory S. Meece
David R. Noteware

ASSOCIATES

Jai-Prakash (J.P.) Philip Kumar
Kevin J. Parks

For Complete List of Firm Personnel, See General Section

For full biographical listings, see the Martindale-Hubbell Law Directory

VINSON & ELKINS L.L.P. (AV)

2300 First City Tower, 1001 Fannin, 77002-6760
Telephone: 713-758-2222
Fax: 713-758-2346
Email: info@velaw.com *URL:* http://www.velaw.com
Austin, Texas Office: One American Center Suite 2700, 600 Congress Avenue, Austin, Texas, 78701-3200.
Telephone: 512-495-8400.
Fax: 512-495-8612.
Beijing, China Office: 20/F, Beijing Silver Tower, No. 2, Dong San Huan Bei Lu, Chaoyang District, 100027.
Telephone: +86-10-6410-6300.
Fax: +86-10-6410-6360.
Dallas, Texas Office: 3700 Trammell Crow Center, 2001 Ross Avenue, Dallas, Texas, 75201-2975.
Telephone: 214-220-7700.
Fax: 214-220-7716.
London, England Office: Regis House, 8th Floor, 45 King William Street, London, EC4R 9AN, England.
Telephone: (44-171) 618-6000.
Fax: (44-171) 618-6001.
Moscow, Russia Office: 16 Ulitsa Spiridonovka, Second Floor, 103001 Moscow, Russia.
Telephone: (7-095) 956-1995. Local
Fax: (7-095) 956-1996. U.S. Satellite
Fax: (212) 803-0142.
New York, N.Y. Office: 1325 Avenue of the Americas, 17th Floor, New York, N.Y., 10019.
Telephone: 917-206-8000.
Fax: 917-206-8100.
Singapore Office: 6 Battery Road, #39-01, Singapore, 049909.
Telephone: (65) 536-8300.
Fax: (65) 536-8311.
Washington, D.C. Office: The Willard Office Building, 1455 Pennsylvania Avenue, N.W., Washington, D.C., 20004-1008.
Telephone: 202-639-6500.
Fax: 202-639-6604.

MEMBER OF FIRM

Harry M. Reasoner (Managing Partner)

MEMBERS OF FIRM

Scott J. Atlas
Walker W. Beavers
David M. Bond
David H. Brown
Christopher W. Byrd
Edward A. Carr
John L. Carter
Morgan Lee Copeland, Jr.
Thad T. Dameris
Elena-Faye DiIorio
Sarah A. Duckers
Phillip B. Dye, Jr.
Billy Coe Dyer
Harrell Feldt
N. Scott Fletcher
Lawrence J. Fossi
Kathleen A. Gallagher
Celso M. Gonzalez-Falla
David T. Harvin
David T. Hedges, Jr.
Max Hendrick, III
John B. Holstead
Daniel A. Hyde
Karen Jewell
Erica L. Krennerich
Guy S. Lipe
Louis E. McCarter
Andrew McCollam III

(See Next Column)

MEMBERS OF FIRM (Continued)

D. Ferguson McNiel, III
Clara L. Meek
Michael W. Mengis
H. Dixon Montague
John L. Murchison, Jr.
Charles T. Newton, Jr.
Penelope E. Nicholson
D. Bobbitt Noel, Jr.
Knox D. Nunnally
Harold A. Odom III
Betty R. Owens
Richard H. Page
Barbara A. Radnofsky
James Arthur Reeder, Jr.
R. Glen Rigby
Robert M. Schick
Adam P. Schiffer
Charles W. Schwartz
Russell B. Serafin
Ben H. Sheppard, Jr.
Eugene J. Silva
Alison L. Smith
L. Boyd Smith, Jr.
Paul E. Stallings
Scott Statham
Karl S. Stern
Mary Lou Strange
Walter B. Stuart IV
James D. Thompson III
Lisa Lepow Turboff
Allan Van Fleet
D. Gibson Walton
Paul S. Wells
H. Ronald Welsh
Marie R. Yeates

HOUSTON OF COUNSEL

Hollis A. Hubenak
John H. Kyles
John E. West
Julie P. Woody

ASSOCIATES

Demetrios Anaipakos
Joël Elaine Baird
C. Dennis Barrow, Jr.
Walter Moreau Berger
Bruce A. Blefeld
Derek Chan
Stephanie Crain
Anissa J. Crumley
Oscar L. De la Rosa
John P. DeGeeter
Elizabeth L. Dodge
John F. Easton
Matthew D. Eisele
Clayton R. Gollnick
Don C. Griffin, Jr.
Carolyn R. Guest
Wallis M. Hampton
Kathryn L. Hays
Lisa R. Helgoe
Karl K. Hennessee
Michael C. Holmes
Tracy L. Howard
Jeffrey S. Johnston
Lauren J. Kares
(Not admitted in TX)
Jared I. Levinthal
Barbara Popper Lipshultz
Charles B. McFarland
Christopher H. Meakin
George Robertson Murphy, III
D. John Neese, Jr.
Kevin Michael O'Gorman
Matthew S. Okin
Paige C. Patton
Jason M. Powers
S. Douglas Pritchett, Jr.
Jeffrey L. Raizner
Sean Alan Roberts
Mark C. Rodriguez
Sandra Garza Rodriguez
Gwen J. Samora
Mary M. Schill
Daniel B. Shilliday
Tomasz J. Sikora
Catherine Bukowski Smith
Kathleen Bone Spangler
Fred I. Williams
Richard C. Williams
Rhonda Hunter Wills
Michael J. Yanochik

For Complete List of Firm Personnel, See General Section

For full biographical listings, see the Martindale-Hubbell Law Directory

WILSHIRE SCOTT & DYER, A PROFESSIONAL CORPORATION (AV)

4550 One Houston Center, 1221 McKinney, 77010
Telephone: 713-651-1221
Telefax: 713-651-0020
Email: wsd@wsd-law.com

Eugene B. Wilshire, Jr.
Jacalyn D Scott
Patrick J. Dyer
Keavin D. McDonald

Christopher A. Artzer

For full biographical listings, see the Martindale-Hubbell Law Directory

IRVING, Dallas Co.

BREWER, BREWER, ANTHONY & MIDDLEBROOK (AV)

A Professional Legal Corporation
1159 Cottonwood Lane, Suite 150, 75038
Telephone: 972-870-9898; Metro: 972-953-0533
FAX: 972-870-9053
Email: brewer10@airmail.net

MEMBERS OF FIRM

Dennis G. Brewer, Sr.
Dennis G. Brewer, Jr. (P.C.)
John Matthew Anthony
David O. Middlebrook

ASSOCIATES

Cynthia Bullock Dunn
Monika L. Manor
David R. Joe
Jenny L. Womack

OF COUNSEL

Cary Jay Cross

For full biographical listings, see the Martindale-Hubbell Law Directory

*KERRVILLE,** Kerr Co.

LAVERN D. HARRIS ATTORNEY AT LAW, P.C. (AV)
815 Jefferson Street, Suite C, 78028-4558
Telephone: 830-896-2711
Fax: 830-792-3323
Email: ldharris@ktc.com *URL:* http://www.lawyers.com/ldharris

Lavern D. Harris

For full biographical listings, see the Martindale-Hubbell Law Directory

*LAMESA,** Dawson Co.

JOHN SALEH (AV)
502 North First Street, 79331
Telephone: 806-872-2171; 806-872-2172
Fax: 806-872-2002

For full biographical listings, see the Martindale-Hubbell Law Directory

*LUBBOCK,** Lubbock Co.

MCWHORTER, COBB & JOHNSON, L.L.P. (AV)
1722 Broadway, 79401
Telephone: 806-762-0214
Fax: 806-762-8014
Mailing Address: P.O. Box 2547, Lubbock, TX, 79408
Email: mcj@mcjllp.com

Owen W. McWhorter (1897-1986)
J. R. Blumrosen (1925-1996)
D. Thomas Johnson
Jack P. Driskill
D. Murray Hensley
Don R. Richards
Dulan D. Elder
Ann Manning
Sabra J. Srader
Timothy T. Pridmore

ASSOCIATES

Jamey Laney Phillips
Gary R. McLaren
R. Michael McCauley, Jr.
Gwynn P. Key

OF COUNSEL

Charles L. Cobb
Dale H. Johnson
Owen W. McWhorter, Jr.

Representative Clients: American State Bank; South Plains Electric Cooperative; Plains Cotton Cooperative Association; Plains Cooperative Oil Mill; Farmers Cooperative Compress; Lubbock Independent School District; Lubbock Avalanche Journal Newspaper; Texas Statewide Telephone Cooperatives Assn.

For full biographical listings, see the Martindale-Hubbell Law Directory

MIKE MILLSAP (AV)
1116A Broadway, 79401
Telephone: 806-747-0264
Fax: 806-747-0292
Email: mikemillsap@msn.com

Reference: Norwest Bank.

For full biographical listings, see the Martindale-Hubbell Law Directory

*MARSHALL,** Harrison Co.

CURRY, MORIN AND GOUDARZI, P.C. (AV)
201 West Houston Street, P.O. Box 2065, 75671
Telephone: 903-927-2277; 903-935-0797
Fax: 903-935-0799

Doyle W. Curry
James B. Morin (Also practicing in Gilmer, Texas)
J. Brent Goudarzi (Also practicing in Gilmer, Texas)

For full biographical listings, see the Martindale-Hubbell Law Directory

JONES & JONES, INC., A PROFESSIONAL CORPORATION (AV)
201 West Houston Street, P.O. Drawer 1249, 75671-1249
Telephone: 903-938-4395
Fax: 903-938-3360

Franklin Jones (1903-1996)
Franklin Jones, Jr.

References: Bank One Marshall; First National Bank.

For full biographical listings, see the Martindale-Hubbell Law Directory

MCALLEN, Hidalgo Co.

DALE & KLEIN, L.L.P. (AV)
A Partnership including Professional Corporations
6301 North Tenth Street, 78504
Telephone: 956-687-8700
FAX: 956-687-2416
Brownsville Office: 815 Ridgewood.
Telephone: 956-546-5100.

(See Next Column)

Roy S. Dale (P.C.)
Katie Pearson Klein (P.C.)
Martin E. Morris
William D. Mount, Jr.

A. Peter Thaddeus, Jr.
Kathryn M. Flagg
Catherine Anderson Garcia
Marina Garcia

For full biographical listings, see the Martindale-Hubbell Law Directory

RODRIGUEZ, COLVIN & CHANEY, L.L.P. (AV)
4900 North 10th Street, 78504
Telephone: 956-686-1287
Telecopier: 956-686-6197
Brownsville, Texas Office: 1201 East Van Buren Street.
Telephone: 956-542-7441.
Telecopier: 956-541-2170.
Harlingen, Texas Office: 402 East Van Buren.
Telephone: 956-423-0216.
Telecopier: 956-423-2035.

OF COUNSEL

Neil E. Norquest
Chris A. Brisack
Raymond A. Cowley

Division Attorneys for: Union Pacific Railroad.
Counsel for: Texas Commerce Bank-Rio Grande Valley, N.A.; Texas Commerce Bancshares, Inc.

For full biographical listings, see the Martindale-Hubbell Law Directory

*MIDLAND,** Midland Co.

KERR & WARD, L.L.P. (AV)
500 W. Texas, Suite 1310, Drawer 2858, 79702
Telephone: 915-684-9990
Fax: 915-684-9997
Email: info@kerr-ward.com *URL:* http://www.kerr-ward.com

OF COUNSEL

Wm. Monroe Kerr
Theodore M. Kerr

PARTNERS

Harris E. Kerr
William E. Ward
William M. Kerr, Jr.
Brian T. McLaughlin
James Devin Alsup

For full biographical listings, see the Martindale-Hubbell Law Directory

LESLIE G. MCLAUGHLIN (AV)
1209 West Texas Avenue, 79701
Telephone: 915-687-1331
Fax: 915-687-1336

For full biographical listings, see the Martindale-Hubbell Law Directory

*ORANGE,** Orange Co.

MEHAFFY & WEBER, A PROFESSIONAL CORPORATION (AV)
1006 Green Avenue, P.O. Drawer 189, 77630
Telephone: 409-886-7766
Fax: 409-886-7790
Email: MehaffyWeber.com
Beaumont, Texas Office: 2615 Calder Avenue, Suite 800, P.O. Box 16.
Telephone: 409-835-5011.
Houston, Texas Office: One Allen Center, 500 Dallas, Suite 1200.
Telephone: 713-655-1200.

John Cash Smith

Representative Clients: Sabine River Authority of Texas; Equitable Bag Co., Southern Division; Texas Farm Bureau; City of Orange; CNA Insurance, Maryland Casualty/Zurich Insurance Co.

For full biographical listings, see the Martindale-Hubbell Law Directory

*PERRYTON,** Ochiltree Co.

LEMON, SHEARER, EHRLICH, PHILLIPS & GOOD, A PROFESSIONAL CORPORATION (AV)
311 South Main Street, P.O. Box 1066, 79070
Telephone: 806-435-6544
FAX: 806-435-4377
Email: lsepglaw@ren.net
Booker, Texas Office: 122 South Main Street, P.O. Box 348.
Telephone: 806-658-4545.
FAX: 806-658-4524.

Robert D. Lemon
Otis C. Shearer
Mitchell Ehrlich
Randall M. Phillips
F. Keith Good

Representative Clients: The Perryton National Bank; The Perryton Equity Exchange; The North Plains Ground Water Conservation District; Natural Gas Anadarko Co.; Courson Oil & Gas, Inc.; The City of Perryton; The Booker Equity Exchange; The Follett National Bank; Unit Petroleum Co.

For full biographical listings, see the Martindale-Hubbell Law Directory

PLANO, Collin Co.

GOLD & GOLD (AV)

Harrington Place, Suite 300, 1700 Alma Drive, 75075-6936
Telephone: 972-578-1050
Fax: 972-578-1555
Email: goldlaw@flash.net

Jacob M. Gold

For full biographical listings, see the Martindale-Hubbell Law Directory

*SAN ANGELO,** Tom Green Co.

JACKSON WALKER L.L.P. (AV)

225 West Beauregard Avenue, 76903
Telephone: 915-481-2550
Fax: 915-481-2552
Email: hloftin@jw.com *URL:* http://www.jw.com
Austin, Texas Office: 100 Congress Avenue, Suite 1100.
Telephone: 512-236-2000.
Fax: 512-236-2002.
Dallas, Texas Office: 901 Main Street, Suite 6000.
Telephone: 214-953-6000.
Fax: 214-953-5822.
Fort Worth, Texas Office: 301 Commerce Street, Suite 2400.
Telephone: 817-334-7200.
Fax: 817-334-7290.
Houston, Texas Office: 1100 Louisiana, Suite 4200.
Telephone: 713-752-4200.
Fax: 713-752-4221.
Richardson, Texas Office: 2435 North Central Expressway, Suite 600.
Telephone: 972-671-2560.
Fax: 972-671-2566.
San Antonio, Texas Office: 112 E. Pecan Street, Suite 2100.
Telephone: 210-978-7700.
Fax: 210-978-7790.

MEMBER OF FIRM

Donald W. Griffis

OF COUNSEL

Robert A. Junell

For Complete List of Firm Personnel, See General Section

For full biographical listings, see the Martindale-Hubbell Law Directory

*SAN ANTONIO,** Bexar Co.

JEFFREY R. AKINS (AV)

Suite 700 Camino Real Bank Building, 13750 San Pedro Avenue, 78232-4370
Telephone: 210-599-4905
Fax: 210-496-4746

Reference: Chase Bank of Texas.

For full biographical listings, see the Martindale-Hubbell Law Directory

LAW OFFICES OF JAMES R. BASS, INC. (AV)

9002 Wurzbach Road, 78240
Telephone: 210-614-4444
Fax: 210-614-7737
Email: JBASSLAW@AOL.COM *URL:* http://www.lawyers.com/basslaw

James R. Bass

Michele Kay Jura

Reference: Frost National Bank.

For full biographical listings, see the Martindale-Hubbell Law Directory

COX & SMITH INCORPORATED (AV)

112 East Pecan Street, Suite 1800, 78205-1521
Telephone: 210-554-5500
Fax: 210-226-8395
Email: info@coxsmith.com *URL:* http://www.coxsmith.com

John J. Cox (1905-1971)
J. Burleson Smith
Keith E. Kaiser
Diann M. Bartek
A. Michael Ferrill
Deborah D. Williamson
David B. West
Donna K. McElroy
J. Daniel Harkins
Gardner S. Kendrick
Margaret Pedrick Sullivan
Patrick L. Huffstickler
Brett W. Schouest
James K. Spivey
James M. Truss
Leslie S. Hyman
W. Bradley Barnes
David C. Giles
Lauren R. Huckaby
John M. Black
William ("Butch") F. Hulse, IV

(See Next Column)

OF COUNSEL

Stephen M. Marceau

Representative Clients: Abraxas Petroleum Corporation; Bally Total Fitness Corporation; Banque Paribas (Suisse) S.A.; Dain Rauscher Incorporated; Eastman Kodak Company; International Bancshares Corporation; Merrill, Lynch, Pierce, Fenner & Smith, Inc.; Miller Brewing Company; NationsBank of Texas, N.A.; Phillip Morris, Inc.

For Complete List of Firm Personnel, See General Section

For full biographical listings, see the Martindale-Hubbell Law Directory

JACKSON WALKER L.L.P. (AV)

112 E. Pecan Street, Suite 2100, 78205-1521
Telephone: 210-978-7700
Fax: 210-978-7790
URL: http://www.jw.com
Austin, Texas Office: 100 Congress Avenue, Suite 1100.
Telephone: 512-236-2000.
Fax: 512-236-2002.
Dallas, Texas Office: 901 Main Street, Suite 6000.
Telephone: 214-953-6000.
Fax: 214-953-5822.
Fort Worth, Texas Office: 301 Commerce Street, Suite 2400.
Telephone: 817-334-7200.
Fax: 817-334-7290.
Houston, Texas Office: 1100 Louisiana, Suite 4200.
Telephone: 713-752-4200.
Fax: 713-752-4221.
Richardson, Texas Office: 2435 North Central Expressway, Suite 600.
Telephone: 972-671-2560.
Fax: 972-671-2566.
San Angelo, Texas Office: 225 West Beauregard Avenue.
Telephone: 915-481-2550.
Fax: 915-481-2552.

MEMBERS OF FIRM

Leo D. Figueroa
Stephen R. Fogle
Jeffrey T. Harvey
Robert F. Scheihing
James L. Walker

For Complete List of Firm Personnel, See General Section

For full biographical listings, see the Martindale-Hubbell Law Directory

RAY LEACH (AV)

3737 Broadway, Suite 310, 78209-6547
Telephone: 210-820-3737
Facsimile: 210-820-0971
Email: advocate@txdirect.net
(Also Of Counsel to Heard & Smith)

OF COUNSEL

John R. Heard

For full biographical listings, see the Martindale-Hubbell Law Directory

LEON, AMBERSON & CARROLL, L.L.P. (AV)

500 Lexington, 78215
Telephone: 210-223-4254
Fax: 210-227-7721

Jack Paul Leon
Jon Christian Amberson

OF COUNSEL

Gilbert Lang Mathews

For full biographical listings, see the Martindale-Hubbell Law Directory

ROBERT J. MYERS & ASSOCIATES (AV)

3838 Medical Drive, Suite 100, 78229
Telephone: 210-615-6633
Telecopier: 210-615-1852
Email: rojomy@aol.com

Robert J. Myers

For full biographical listings, see the Martindale-Hubbell Law Directory

O'CONNELL, BENJAMIN & COGHLAN, L.L.P. (AV)

153 Treeline Park, Suite 200, 78209
Telephone: 210-824-0009
Fax: 210-824-9429
Email: obcllp@oconben.com

Keith B. O'Connell
David P. Benjamin
G. Thomas Coghlan
Ernest F. Avery
Les Katona, Jr.
Dan Vana

Gayla S. Corley
Cathrin J. Martinez

For full biographical listings, see the Martindale-Hubbell Law Directory

San Antonio—Continued

PLUNKETT & GIBSON, INC. (AV)

6243 IH-10 West, Suite 600, P.O. Box BH002, 78201
Telephone: 210-734-7092
Telecopier: 210-734-0379

Laura A. Cavaretta
D. Ann Comerio
Richard B. Copeland
Joseph C. Elliott
Richard N. Francis, Jr.
Jerry A. Gibson
Tim T. Griesenbeck, Jr.
John A. Heller
Nina E. Henderson
Ronald Hornberger
Lewin Plunkett
Cathy J. Sheehan

OF COUNSEL

Daniel Diaz, Jr.
Marilyn G. Eades
Robert D. Reed
F. Beth Morgan

William J. Baine
Charles L. Fridge, III
Gary B. Gibson
Erik V. Larson

Representative Clients: St. Paul Insurance Co.; Toyota Motor Sales, Inc.; Travelers Insurance Co.; Transport Insurance Co.; CIGNA Insurance Co.; Mazda Motor Co.; Pacificare of Texas Inc; Santa Rosa Health Care Corp.; Sisters of Mercy Health System; ANPAC.

For full biographical listings, see the Martindale-Hubbell Law Directory

SHELTON & VALADEZ, P.C. (AV)

112 East Pecan Street, Suite 2600, 78205
Telephone: 210-349-0515
Facsimile: 210-349-3666
Email: shelton-valadez.com

Wade B. Shelton
Robert A. Valadez
Mark A. Giltner
Robert J. Perez

Stephen D. Navarro
Brandon T. Hudson
Michael I. Ramirez

OF COUNSEL

K. Blake Coffee

For full biographical listings, see the Martindale-Hubbell Law Directory

TINSMAN & HOUSER, INC. (AV)

One Riverwalk Place, 14th Floor, 700 North St. Mary's Street, 78205
Telephone: 210-225-3121
U.S. Wats: 1-800-292-9999
Fax: 210-225-6235
Email: info@thlaw.com *URL:* http://www.thlaw.com

Richard Tinsman
Franklin D. Houser
Margaret M. Maisel
David G. Jayne
Robert C. Scott
Daniel J. T. Sciano
Rey Perez
Bernard Wm. Fischman
Sharon L. Savage
Ronald J. Salazar
Sue Dodson
Dennis P. Bujnoch

For full biographical listings, see the Martindale-Hubbell Law Directory

WEIR & ALVARADO, P.C. (AV)

115 Camaron Street, Suite 100, 78205
Telephone: 210-223-2685
Fax: 210-223-9464

Warren Weir
Leo Alvarado, Jr.

For full biographical listings, see the Martindale-Hubbell Law Directory

TEXARKANA, Bowie Co.

ATCHLEY, RUSSELL, WALDROP & HLAVINKA, L.L.P. (AV)

1710 Moores Lane, P.O. Box 5517, 75505-5517
Telephone: 903-792-8246
Fax: 903-792-5801
Email: arwh@compuserve.com

MEMBERS OF FIRM

Otto H. Atchley (1904-1989)
Norman C. Russell (1915-1996)
Howard Waldrop
Charles J. Hlavinka
Victor F. Hlavinka
Stephen Oden
J. Dennis Chambers
Robert W. Weber
Alan D. Harrel
Josh R. Morriss, III
John R. Mercy
J. Michael Smith
Jeffrey C. Elliott
William Howard Mowery
Louise E. Tausch
Kenneth Dale Edwards (1940-1976)
Robert W. Littrell (1953-1983)
Jeffery C. Lewis

ASSOCIATES

John L. Tidwell
Shawn M. Morgan

Representative Clients: United States Fidelity & Guaranty Co.; Employer's Casualty Co.; Liberty Mutual Insurance Co.; The Home Co.; Missouri-Pacific Railway Co.; St. Louis Southwestern Railway Co.; State First National Bank in Texas; State Bank of DeKalb; St. Paul Insurance Co.; First-Bank.

(See Next Column)

For full biographical listings, see the Martindale-Hubbell Law Directory

LAW OFFICES OF E. BEN FRANKS (AV)

8 Woodmont Crossing, 75503
Telephone: 903-792-3215
Fax: 903-792-4531
Email: riataland@aol.com *URL:* http://www.lawyers.com/frankslaw

For full biographical listings, see the Martindale-Hubbell Law Directory

GOODING & DODSON, P.C. (AV)

300 Hibernia National Bank Building, P.O. Box 1877, 75504
Telephone: 903-794-3121
Fax: 903-793-4801
Email: GandDLaw@cs.com

William C. Gooding
Robert E. Dodson
Robert S. McGinnis, Jr.
Michael F. Jones
Lisa R. Crittenden

Jeffrey S. Young

Representative Clients: American General Insurance Co.; Kansas City Southern Railway Co.; Maryland Casualty Co.; North Texas Production Credit Assn.; The Travelers Indemnity Company/The Aetna Casualty; Wadely Regional Medical Center; Hibernia National Bank; Resolution Trust Corp.

For full biographical listings, see the Martindale-Hubbell Law Directory

PATTON, HALTOM, ROBERTS, MCWILLIAMS & GREER, L.L.P. (AV)

A Registered Limited Liability Partnership including Professional Corporations
700 Hibernia National Bank Building, P.O. Box 1928, 75504-1928
Telephone: 903-794-3341
Fax: 903-792-6542; 903-792-0448
URL: http://www.pattonhaltom.com

James N. Haltom (P.C.)
George L. McWilliams (P.C.)
John B. Greer, III, (P.C.)
Kristi I. McCasland
Jennifer Haltom Doan

ASSOCIATES

William W. Miller, Jr.
David P. Cotten

Representative Clients: Allstate Insurance Co.; Royal Insurance Group; Continental Insurance Group; Ranger/Pan American Insurance Cos.; The Hanover Insurance Group; American Mutual Liability Insurance Co.; American Hardware Mutual Insurance Co.; Kemper Insurance Co.

For Complete List of Firm Personnel, See General Section

For full biographical listings, see the Martindale-Hubbell Law Directory

PATTON, TIDWELL & SANDEFUR, L.L.P. (AV)

4605 Texas Boulevard, P.O. Box 5398, 75505-5398
Telephone: 903-792-7080; 903-792-5859
Fax: 903-792-8233
Email: KTIDW87157@aol.com

Nicholas H. Patton
Kelly B. Tidwell
Gregory C. Sandefur

Christie G. Adams

For full biographical listings, see the Martindale-Hubbell Law Directory

YOUNG & PICKETT (AV)

4122 Texas Boulevard, P.O. Box 1897, 75504
Telephone: 870-774-3206; 903-794-1303
Facsimile: 903-792-5098; 903-794-5098
Email: YP1303@aol.com

Damon Young
John M. Pickett

ASSOCIATE

Lance Lee

Representative Clients: AT&T Corporation; AmeriSource Corporation; Bridgestone/Firestone, Inc.; Exxon Chemical Americas; Century Bank of New Boston, Texas; International Paper Company, Inc.; Lucent Technologies, Inc.; Medtronic, Inc.; Michelin North America; SmithKline Beecham Corporation.

For full biographical listings, see the Martindale-Hubbell Law Directory

*TYLER,** Smith Co.

IRELAND, CARROLL & KELLEY, P.C. (AV)
6101 South Broadway, Suite 500, P.O. Box 7879, 75711
Telephone: 903-561-1600
Fax: 903-581-1071
Email: ICKLAW@AOL.COM

H. Kelly Ireland (Retired)
Donald Carroll (1929-1992)
Otis W. Carroll
Patrick Kelley
Marcus Carroll
Michael G. Carroll

Deborah Race

For full biographical listings, see the Martindale-Hubbell Law Directory

RAMEY & FLOCK, A PROFESSIONAL CORPORATION (AV)
500 First Place, P.O. Box 629, 75710
Telephone: 903-597-3301
Telecopier: 903-597-2413
Email: Ramey@Ramey-Flock.com *URL:* http://www.RameyFlock.com

Thomas B. Ramey (1892-1967)
Jack W. Flock
Tracy Crawford
Glenn Collins
Michael A. Hatchell
Tom Henson
Dennis G. Black
Paul H. Gilliam
R. Brian Craft
Gregory D. Smith
Michael T. Crawford
Mary H. Molly Hatchell
Rosemary Sage Jones
Ronald S. Vickery
John W. Ferguson, Jr.

Deron R. Dacus
Eric H. Findlay
Shannon Dacus
Maria Benecki Sowders
Jamy Mitchell Skaggs

Counsel for: Regions Bank; Exxon Co. U.S.A.; Kelly Springfield Tire Co.; Trinity-Mother Frances Health System; St. Paul Insurance Co.; The Travelers Cos.; Reliance Insurance Co.; Marshall Regional Medical Center.

For full biographical listings, see the Martindale-Hubbell Law Directory

SAMMONS & PARKER, A PROFESSIONAL CORPORATION (AV)
218 North College, 75702
Telephone: 903-595-4541
FAX: 903-595-2864

Martin Z. Sammons, Jr.
Jerry C. Parker
Clay M. White
Jeffery J. Shaver
Reid Wm. Martin
J. Chad Parker

W. Todd Parker
Alan D. Wharton
John F. (Jack) Walker, III
Vanessa L. Vance

Representative Clients: A list of Representative Clients will be furnished upon request.

For full biographical listings, see the Martindale-Hubbell Law Directory

*VICTORIA,** Victoria Co.

LAW OFFICE OF O. F. JONES, III (AV)
109 West Santa Rosa Street, P.O. Drawer E, 77902
Telephone: 361-573-6381
Fax: 361-576-4607
Email: OFJ@VIPTX.NET

For full biographical listings, see the Martindale-Hubbell Law Directory

*WACO,** McLennan Co.

DUNNAM & DUNNAM, L.L.P. (AV)
4125 West Waco Drive, P.O. Box 8418, 76714-8418
Telephone: 254-753-6437
Fax: 254-753-7434

MEMBERS OF FIRM

W. V. Dunnam (1891-1974)
W. V. Dunnam, Jr.
Vance Dunnam
Vance Dunnam, Jr.
James R. Dunnam

ASSOCIATES

Alan Stucky
John Porter Mabry, Jr.
James Robert Angel

For full biographical listings, see the Martindale-Hubbell Law Directory

JIM MEYER & ASSOCIATES, P.C. (AV)
4734 West Waco Drive, P.O. Box 21957, 76710
Telephone: 817-772-9255
Fax: 817-776-9110
Email: jmeyer@calpha.com

Jim Meyer

For full biographical listings, see the Martindale-Hubbell Law Directory

SHEEHY, LOVELACE & MAYFIELD, P.C. A PROFESSIONAL CORPORATION (AV)
510 North Valley Mills Drive, Suite 500, 76710
Telephone: 254-772-8022
Fax: 254-772-9297
Email: sheehy@slmpc.com *URL:* http://www.slmpc.com

John F. Sheehy (1898-1979)
J. Henry Lovelace (1926-1992)
John F. Sheehy, Jr.
Dan E. Mayfield
Henry W. Fielder
Philip E. McCleery
Gary K. Jordan
G. Maynard Green
Robert A. Watson
L. Hayes Fuller, III
J. David Dickson
Peter K. Rusek
Jeffrey R. Cox
John O'Herren
J. Patrick Atkins

Elisa Dillard Rainey
Erin B. Shank
Steven M. Burton
Scott V. Allen

OF COUNSEL

Michael J. Gulig

General Counsel for: American-Amicable Life Insurance Company of Texas; Community Bank & Trust; Waco Independent School District; McLennan Community College; Waco Board of REALTORS; Housing Authority of the City of Waco.
Local Counsel for: Kemper Insurance Group; United States Fidelity & Guaranty Co.; Fleetwood Enterprises, Inc.; USAA.

For full biographical listings, see the Martindale-Hubbell Law Directory

WILLIAMS, PATTILLO, SQUIRES & WREN, L.L.P. (AV)
Bridgeview Center, 2nd Floor, 7901 Fish Pond Road, 76710
Telephone: 254-741-6200
Fax: 254-741-6300
Email: lawyers@trialfirm.com *URL:* http://www.trialfirm.com

Dale D. Williams
R. D. (Spike) Pattillo, III
Rod S. Squires
James E. Wren

ASSOCIATES

Fadra LeBlanc Day
John H. McLeod

For full biographical listings, see the Martindale-Hubbell Law Directory

WESLACO, Hidalgo Co.

JONES, GALLIGAN, KEY & LOZANO, L.L.P. (AV)
Town Center Tower, 3300 W. Pike, Suite #300, P.O. Drawer 1247, 78599-1247
Telephone: 956-968-5402
Fax: 956-968-6089; 956-969-9402
Email: jones4@hiline.net

MEMBERS OF FIRM

Forrest L. Jones
Robert L. Galligan
Terry D. Key
Anita G. Lozano

Julie Crockett Graham
Mark W. Farris
Matthew Lee Jones
Lance Alan Kirby
Rebecca Gay Jones
Alan Troy Ozuna

For full biographical listings, see the Martindale-Hubbell Law Directory

*WICHITA FALLS,** Wichita Co.

GIBSON, HOTCHKISS, ROACH & DAVENPORT (AV)
807 8th Street, 8th Floor, 76301
Telephone: 940-322-7856
Fax: 940-322-1204
Email: ed@ghrdlaw.com *URL:* http://www.lawyers.com/ghrdlaw

MEMBER OF FIRM

Robert K. Roach

ASSOCIATE

John D. Rosentreter

Representative Clients: American National Bank, Wichita Falls; First National Bank of Bowie; Wichita Falls PCA; Bennett Production Co.; Red River Authority of Texas; Burcamp Steel Co.

For Complete List of Firm Personnel, See General Section
For full biographical listings, see the Martindale-Hubbell Law Directory

MORRISON & SHELTON, A PROFESSIONAL CORPORATION (AV)
City National Building, 807 Eighth Street, Suite 400, 76301-3316
Telephone: 940-322-2929
Telecopier: 940-322-7463

Lonny D. Morrison
Stephen R. Shelton

For full biographical listings, see the Martindale-Hubbell Law Directory

UTAH

*SALT LAKE CITY,** Salt Lake Co.

JOEL M. ALLRED, P.C. (AV)

Suite 800, McIntyre Building, 68 South Main Street, 84101
Telephone: 801-531-8300 (Downtown Office)
801-582-2309 (Home Office)
Fax: 801-533-2463 (Office Hours)
801-363-2420 (After Office Hours)
Email: jallred@vii.com

Joel M. Allred

Amy Allred Dolce

For full biographical listings, see the Martindale-Hubbell Law Directory

BERMAN, GAUFIN, TOMSIC, SAVAGE & CAMPBELL, A PROFESSIONAL CORPORATION (AV)

Suite 1250, 50 South Main Street, 84144
Telephone: 801-328-2200
Fax: 801-531-9926
Email: mailbox@bgtslaw.com *URL:* http://www.bgtslaw.com

Daniel L. Berman
Robert S. Campbell, Jr.
E. Scott Savage
Jay D. Gurmankin
Samuel O. Gaufin
Peggy A. Tomsic
Casey K. McGarvey
Stephen R. Waldron
Tony J. Rudman
David P. Williams
Chris R. Hogle
James E. Magleby
Richard D. Flint
Sheleigh Chalkley
David R. Parkinson

OF COUNSEL

D. Frank Wilkins

For full biographical listings, see the Martindale-Hubbell Law Directory

CALLISTER NEBEKER & McCULLOUGH, A PROFESSIONAL CORPORATION (AV)

Gateway Tower East, Suite 900, 10 East South Temple, 84133
Telephone: 801-530-7300
Telecopier: 801-364-9127
Email: mjeaston@cnmlaw.com *URL:* http://www.cnmlaw.com

Gary R. Howe
John A. Beckstead
James R. Holbrook
Steven E. Tyler
Randall D Benson
T. Richard Davis
Cass C. Butler
Mark L. Callister
P. Bryan Fishburn
Martin R. Denney
William H. Christensen
James D. Gilson
Craig T. Jacobsen
Zachary T. Shields

Jennifer Ward

Representative Clients: Zions First National Bank; Chrysler Credit Corp.; Citicorp; Associates Commercial Corp.; Federal Land Bank Association of Utah; Sinclair Oil (Little America).

For Complete List of Firm Personnel, See General Section

For full biographical listings, see the Martindale-Hubbell Law Directory

DURHAM JONES & PINEGAR, A PROFESSIONAL CORPORATION (AV)

Key Bank Tower 50 South Main, Suite 800, 84144
Telephone: 801-538-2424
Fax: 801-538-2425
Email: djp@djplaw.com
Ogden Utah Office: The Aerospace Center, Suite 710, 1104 Country Hills Drive, 84403.
Telephone: 801-395-2424.
Fax: 801-395-2430.

Jeffrey M. Jones
Paul M. Durham
R. Stephen Marshall
David L. Arrington
J. Mark Gibb
Steven K. Gordon

David W. Tufts (Not admitted in UT)
Timothy M. Wheelwright (Resident, in Ogden Office)

OF COUNSEL

G. Richard Hill

For full biographical listings, see the Martindale-Hubbell Law Directory

KIPP AND CHRISTIAN, P.C. (AV)

10 Exchange Place, Fourth Floor, 84111
Telephone: 801-521-3773
Fax: 801-359-9004
Email: kc1gsb@inquo.net

(See Next Column)

Carman E. Kipp
J. Anthony Eyre
Gregory J. Sanders
Heinz J. Mahler
Michael F. Skolnick
Shawn McGarry
Kirk G. Gibbs

OF COUNSEL

D. Gary Christian

Representative Clients: CNA Insurance Co; Coregis; Utah State Bar; Reliance Insurance Co.; National Farmers Union Insurance Co.; Utah Medical Insurance Association (UMIA); Utah Paper Box; Skivations, Condominium & Land Developers; Montgomery Elevators; Tim Dahle Imports/Nissan.

For Complete List of Firm Personnel, See General Section

For full biographical listings, see the Martindale-Hubbell Law Directory

KIRTON & McCONKIE, A PROFESSIONAL CORPORATION (AV)

1800 Eagle Gate Tower, 60 East South Temple, 84111
Telephone: 801-328-3600
Telecopier: 801-321-4893

Randy T. Austin
Lorin C. Barker
Anthony I. Bentley, Jr.
Rolf H. Berger
Berne S. Broadbent
Charles W. Dahlquist, II
Jerry W. Dearinger
Robert W. Edwards
James E. Ellsworth
Fred D. Essig
Wallace O. Felsted
Clark B. Fetzer
R. Bruce Findlay
David J. Hardy
Keith L. Hargrove
Read R. Hellewell
Dale E. Hulse
Lee Ford Hunter
Richard G. Johnson, Jr.
Von G. Keetch
Raeburn G. Kennard
Wilford W. Kirton, Jr.
Michael F. Krieger
Paul H. Matthews
Daniel S. McConkie
David M. McConkie
Oscar W. McConkie, III
Oscar W. McConkie, Jr.
Samuel D. McVey
William A. Meaders, Jr.
Thomas L. Monson
Denis Roy Morrill
Merrill F. Nelson
Richard R. Neslen
Eric C. Olson
R. Willis Orton
B. Lloyd Poelman
Robert S. Prince
Gregory M. Simonsen
Robert T. Smith (Not admitted in UT)
Myron L. Sorensen
Jon E. Waddoups
David M. Wahlquist
Thomas D. Walk
Stuart F. Weed
David A. Westerby
Todd E. Zenger

Randall C. Allen
Bryan H. Booth
Michael M. Conger
David S. Doty
Alexander Dushku
Scott C. Krieger
Melinda R. Porter
Matthew K. Richards
Dorany Rodriguez-Baltazar (Not admitted in UT)
Jeffrey Dean Stevens
Amy S. Thomas
Steven L. Whitehead

For full biographical listings, see the Martindale-Hubbell Law Directory

MORGAN, MEYER & RICE, L.C. (AV)

Kearns Building, Eighth Floor, 136 South Main Street, 84101
Telephone: 801-531-7888
Telefax: 801-531-9732
Email: morgan@inquo.net

MEMBERS OF FIRM

Stephen G. Morgan
Cynthia K.C. Meyer
Mitchel T. Rice
Joseph E. Minnock
Jeffrey C. Miner

Representative Clients: Albertson's, Inc.; Smith Food and Drug Centers, Inc.; Colorado Casualty; Farmers Insurance Group; SLC Airport Authority; St. Paul Fire and Marine Insurance Co.; State Farm Fire and Casualty; State Farm Mutual Automobile Insurance Co.; Utah Farm Bureau Insurance Co.; Utah Local Government's Insurance Trust.

For full biographical listings, see the Martindale-Hubbell Law Directory

PARR WADDOUPS BROWN GEE & LOVELESS, A PROFESSIONAL CORPORATION (AV)

Suite 1300, 185 South State Street, 84111-1537
Telephone: 801-532-7840
Fax: 801-532-7750
URL: http://www.pwlaw.com

Clark Waddoups
Patricia W. Christensen
Robert B. Lochhead
Gary A. Dodge
Robert S. Clark
Carolyn B. McHugh
Ronald G. Russell
Brian J. Romriell
Heidi E. C. Leithead
Stephen E. W. Hale
Daniel A. Jensen
Gregory M. Hess
Terry E. Welch
Jeffrey J. Hunt
Jonathan O. Hafen
Mark A. Wagner
Bentley J. Tolk
D. Craig Parry
Steven E. Hugie

(See Next Column)

PARR WADDOUPS BROWN GEE & LOVELESS A PROFESSIONAL CORPORATION, *Salt Lake City—Continued*

OF COUNSEL

Bruce A. Maak

For Complete List of Firm Personnel, See General Section

For full biographical listings, see the Martindale-Hubbell Law Directory

PARSONS BEHLE & LATIMER, A PROFESSIONAL CORPORATION (AV)

One Utah Center, 201 South Main Street, Suite 1800, P.O. Box 45898, 84145-0898
Telephone: 801-532-1234
Telecopy: 801-536-6111
Email: pbl@pblutah.com *URL:* http://www.pblutah.com

James B. Lee
Gordon L. Roberts
Lawrence E. Stevens
Daniel M. Allred
Barbara K. Polich
Randy L. Dryer
Charles H. Thronson
Raymond J. Etcheverry
Francis M. Wikstrom
Chris Wangsgard
Val R. Antczak
Spencer E. Austin
John B. Wilson
David A. Anderson
Kent O. Roche
Paul D. Veasy
Daniel W. Hindert
Lois A. Baar
Michael L. Larsen
David G. Mangum
Derek Langton
W. Mark Gavre
J. Michael Bailey
J. Thomas Beckett
Elizabeth S. Conley
Elizabeth S. Whitney
Matthew J. Harmer
Laura S. Scott
Kristine M. Edde
Ellen Kitzmiller
Dianna M. Gibson
Angie Nelson
Shane D. Hillman
Lara A. Reymann

OF COUNSEL

Keith E. Taylor
Roy G. Haslam

Representative Clients: Alliant Techsystems, Inc.; Barrick Gold Corp.; Coastal States Energy Co.; DYNO NOBEL INC.; Energy Fuels Nuclear Inc.; Kennecott Corp.; NERCO, Inc.; Questar Corp.; Rio Algom Mining Corp.

For Complete List of Firm Personnel, See General Section

For full biographical listings, see the Martindale-Hubbell Law Directory

RAY, QUINNEY & NEBEKER, A PROFESSIONAL CORPORATION (AV)

79 South Main Street, Suite 400, P.O. Box 45385, 84145-0385
Telephone: 801-532-1500
Fax: 801-532-7543
Email: rqn@rqn.com *URL:* http://www.rqn.com
Provo, Utah Office: 92 North University Avenue, Suite 210, 84601-4420.
Telephone: 801-342-2400.
Fax: 801-375-8379.
Albuquerque, New Mexico Office: Suite 620, 40 First Plaza, N.W.
Telephone: 505-243-6665.
Fax: 505-764-9890.

Stephen B. Nebeker
Paul S. Felt
Jonathan A. Dibble
Steven H. Gunn
James S. Jardine
Janet Hugie Smith
A. Robert Thorup
John P. Harrington
John A. Adams
Keith A. Kelly
Mark M. Bettilyon
Rick L. Rose
Rick B. Hoggard
Lisa A. Yerkovich
Brent D. Wride
Michael E. Blue
Scott A. Hagen
Steven W. Call
Cameron M. Hancock
Elaine A. Monson
Arthur B. Berger

John W. Mackay
Eric D. Barton
Mark W. Pugsley
Joni J. Jones
Daniel W. Walker
Samuel C. Straight
Paul C. Burke
Elaina M. Maragakis
Joan M. Andrews
Melissa Herring Bailey
D. Zachary Wiseman
David O. Gibbon

Representative Clients: First Security Bank, N.A.; Borden, Inc.; Salt Lake Organizing Committee for the Winter Olympic Games of 2002; Southern Pacific Transportation; Utah Power & Light Co.; Travelers Insurance Co.; U.S. West.

For Complete List of Firm Personnel, See General Section

For full biographical listings, see the Martindale-Hubbell Law Directory

VAN COTT, BAGLEY, CORNWALL & MCCARTHY, A PROFESSIONAL CORPORATION (AV)

50 South Main Street, Suite 1600, P.O. Box 45340, 84145-0340
Telephone: 801-532-3333
Telecopier: 801-534-0058
Email: info@vancott.com *URL:* http://www.vancott.com
Ogden, Utah Office: 2404 Washington Boulevard, Suite 900.
Telephone: 801-394-5783.
Park City, Utah Office: 2200 Park Avenue, Suite C200-A.
Telephone: 435-649-3889.

Robert M. Anderson (President of Firm)
Timothy W. Blackburn (Resident, Ogden, Utah Office)
David A. Greenwood
Jeremy M. Hoffman
Gerald H. Suniville
Kenneth W. Yeates
John L. Young

Jennifer K. Anderson
Stephen K. Christiansen
Sandra L. Crosland
Kevin M. Sheff
Bradley M. Strassberg
Evan S. Strassberg
Justin Toth (Not admitted in UT)

OF COUNSEL

Clifford L. Ashton
Cecil R. Hedger

For Complete List of Firm Personnel, See General Section

For full biographical listings, see the Martindale-Hubbell Law Directory

WEISS BERRETT PETTY, L.C. (AV)

Key Bank Tower, 50 South Main Street, Suite 530, 84144
Telephone: 801-531-7733
Facsimile: 801-531-7711

Loren E. Weiss
Barbara K. Berrett
Ralph C. Petty

Bret M. Hanna

OF COUNSEL

Charles F. Loyd

For full biographical listings, see the Martindale-Hubbell Law Directory

WINDER & HASLAM, P.C. (AV)

Suite 4000, 175 West 200 South, P.O. Box 2668, 84110-2668
Telephone: 801-322-2222
Telecopier: 801-532-3706
Email: WINHAS@AROS.NET *URL:* http://www.winhas.com

Donald J. Winder
Robert D. Tingey
John W. Holt

Stewart R. Knight
Gerry B. Holman
Trystan B. Smith

OF COUNSEL

Dennis V. Haslam
William W. Downes, Jr.
Robert K. Rothfeder

Representative Clients: The Utah Jazz (NBA); The Delta Center: Larry H. Miller Group of Automotive Dealerships; Budget Rent-A-Car; Avis Rent-A-Car; Dollar Rent-A-Car; Dick Simon Trucking; United Concerts; Simmons Media Group; KJZZ-TV (Channel 14).

For full biographical listings, see the Martindale-Hubbell Law Directory

VERMONT

*BURLINGTON,** Chittenden Co.

DINSE, KNAPP & MCANDREW, P.C. (AV)

209 Battery Street, P.O. Box 988, 05402-0988
Telephone: 802-864-5751
Fax: 802-862-6409
URL: http://www.dinse.com

COUNSEL

John M. Dinse

MEMBERS OF FIRM

Spencer R. Knapp
Karen McAndrew
Barbara E. Cory
Robert R. McKearin
James W. Spink
John D. Monahan, Jr.
Emily R. Morrow
Ritchie E. Berger
Austin D. Hart
Samuel Hoar, Jr.
Steven L. Knudson
Sandra A. Strempel
Molly K. Lebowitz
Pietro J. Lynn
Philip C. Woodward
Jeffrey J. Nolan
Mark A. Langan

(See Next Column)

DINSE, KNAPP & MCANDREW P.C.—*Continued*

ASSOCIATES

Douglas D. Le Brun
Craig S. Nolan
Shapleigh Smith, Jr.
Elizabeth H. Miller
Heather E. Thomas

Representative Clients: Chittenden Trust Co.; Vermont Transit Co., Inc.; Sears, Roebuck & Co.; Ford Motor Co.; Inc.; Middlebury College; Vt. Teddy Bear Co., Inc.; Key Bank.

For full biographical listings, see the Martindale-Hubbell Law Directory

GRAVEL AND SHEA, A PROFESSIONAL CORPORATION (AV)

Corporate Plaza, 76 St. Paul Street, P.O. Box 369, 05402-0369
Telephone: 802-658-0220
Fax: 802-658-1456

Robert B. Hemley
Dennis R. Pearson
Craig Weatherly
Robert F. O'Neill

Erik B. FitzPatrick
Leigh Polk Cole

SPECIAL COUNSEL

Norman Williams
Lucy T. Brown

For Complete List of Firm Personnel, See General Section

For full biographical listings, see the Martindale-Hubbell Law Directory

MANCHESTER LAW OFFICES, PROFESSIONAL CORPORATION (AV)

One Lawson Lane, P.O. Box 1459, 05402-1459
Telephone: 802-658-7444
Fax: 802-658-2078
Email: mlo@together.net *URL:* http://www.lawyers.com/manchesterlaw

Robert E. Manchester

Tina L. Shoup
George N. Collias

LEGAL SUPPORT PERSONNEL

Maureen P. Neacy (Legal Nurse Consultant)

For full biographical listings, see the Martindale-Hubbell Law Directory

MILLER, EGGLESTON & CRAMER, LTD. (AV)

150 South Champlain Street, P.O. Box 1489, 05402-1489
Telephone: 802-864-0880
Telecopier: 802-864-0328

Martin K. Miller
Scot L. Kline
Peter F. Young

For Complete List of Firm Personnel, See General Section

For full biographical listings, see the Martindale-Hubbell Law Directory

SYLVESTER & MALEY, INC. (AV)

78 Pine Street, P.O. Box 1053, 05402-1053
Telephone: 802-864-5722
Fax: 802-658-6124
Email: sylvester-maley@worldnet.att.net

Alan F. Sylvester
Michael S. Brow
John P. Maley
Amy E. Sylvester

For full biographical listings, see the Martindale-Hubbell Law Directory

*RUTLAND,** Rutland Co.

MILLER FAIGNANT & BEHRENS, P.C. (AV)

36 Merchants Row, P.O. Box 6688, 05702-6688
Telephone: 802-775-2521
Fax: 802-775-8274
Email: lhblaw@aol.com *URL:* http://www.lawyers.com/millerfaignantbehrenslaw

Lawrence Miller
John Paul Faignant
Lawrence H. Behrens

OF COUNSEL

Lisa L. Chalidze

LEGAL SUPPORT PERSONNEL

Marie Peck Fabian
Kim J. Miller

Representative Clients: Travelers Insurance Co.; Government Employees Insurance Co.; Utica Mutual Insurance Co.; Universal Underwriters Insurance Co.; Zurich American Acadia Insurance.
References: Travelers Insurance Co.; Universal Underwriters Insurance Co.

For full biographical listings, see the Martindale-Hubbell Law Directory

VIRGINIA

ALEXANDRIA, (Independent City)

CARTER & COLEMAN (AV)

602 Cameron Street, 22314
Telephone: 703-739-4200
Fax: 703-739-4210
Email: rcarter@cartercoleman.com *URL:* http://www.lawyers.com/carter&coleman
Washington, D.C. Office: 900 Seventeenth Street, N.W., Suite 900, 20006.
Telephone: 202-326-8600.
Fax: 202-289-0184.

Richard D. Carter
James M. Loots (Not admitted in VA)
Douglas M. Coleman
David C. Simmons (Not admitted in VA)

ASSOCIATES

Juliane C. Miller
Paul A. Daniels
Mercedes Madole (Not admitted in VA)

For full biographical listings, see the Martindale-Hubbell Law Directory

GANNON, COTTRELL & WARD, P.C. (AV)

411 North Washington Street, P.O. Box 1286, 22313
Telephone: 703-836-2770
FAX: 703-836-9086
Fairfax, Virginia Office: Suite 203, The Equity Building, 4085 Chain Bridge Road, Fairfax, Virginia, 20030.
Telephone: 703-591-7700.

Martin A. Gannon
James Ray Cottrell
Michael A. Ward

David H. Fletcher
Kyle F. Bartol
Christopher W. Schinstock

LEGAL SUPPORT PERSONNEL

Laurie Lee Sheldon
Carla A. Drew

For full biographical listings, see the Martindale-Hubbell Law Directory

HARRISON & HUGHES, P.C. (AV)

221 North Washington Street, 22314-2520
Telephone: 703-519-0111
FAX: 703-519-0814

John Edwards Harrison
Sandra L. Hughes

For full biographical listings, see the Martindale-Hubbell Law Directory

HUDGINS LAW FIRM (AV)

515 King Street, Suite 400, 22314
Telephone: 703-739-3300
Telefax: 703-739-3700
URL: http://www.hudginslawfirm.com
Norfolk, Virginia Office: 125 Saint Paul's Boulevard, Suite 600, 23510.
Washington, D.C. Office: 1510 H Street, N.W., 4th Floor, 20005.
Baltimore, Maryland Office: 201 North Charles Street, Suite 600, 21201-4110.

PARTNERS

David D. Hudgins
Mary K. Gogoel

ASSOCIATES

Ann S. Hudgins
Paul T. Emerick
John Christopher McDonough
Kevin A. Kernan
Sean C. E. McDonough

OF COUNSEL

Robert B. Scarlett (Not admitted in VA; Resident, Baltimore, Maryland Office)

For full biographical listings, see the Martindale-Hubbell Law Directory

PARKHURST & WENDEL, L.L.P. (AV)

Suite 210, 1421 Prince Street, 22314-2805
Telephone: 703-739-0220
Facsimile: 703-739-0229
Email: 701-4718@mcimail.com

MEMBERS OF FIRM

Roger W. Parkhurst
Charles A. Wendel

ASSOCIATES

Janet G. Ricciuti
Bradley Dale Goldizen

OF COUNSEL

Gerald E. Battist

For full biographical listings, see the Martindale-Hubbell Law Directory

ALTAVISTA, Campbell Co.

DAVID WILLIAM SHREVE (AV)

Seventh and Franklin Streets, P.O. Box 547, 24517-0547
Telephone: 804-369-6621
FAX: 804-369-5971
Email: DWSLAW@AOL.COM *URL:* http://www.lawyers.com/dwslaw

For full biographical listings, see the Martindale-Hubbell Law Directory

*ARLINGTON,** Arlington Co.

COHEN, GETTINGS & DUNHAM, P.C. (AV)

2200 Wilson Boulevard, Suite 800, 22201
Telephone: 703-525-2260
Fax: 703-525-2489
Email: info@cohengettings.com *URL:* http://www.cohengettings.com
Alexandria, Virginia Office: 211 North Union Street, Suite 350.
Telephone: 703-525-2260.
Washington, D.C. Office: 1225 19th Street, N.W., 7th Floor.
Silver Spring, Maryland Office: Suite 700, 8701 Georgia Avenue.
Telephone: 301-589-6072.

Harvey B. Cohen
Brian P. Gettings (1933-1995)
Frank W. Dunham, Jr.
R. Scott Caulkins
Joel L. Dahnke
John E. Gagliano
Manuel A. Capsalis
John C. Pasierb

Carole H. Capsalis
Michael S. Nachmanoff
Kristen L. Loesch

OF COUNSEL

Carroll E. Dubuc
Joseph A. Fisher, III
Nancy Lee Feldman

References: First Virginia Bank; Virginia Commerce Bank; Crestar Bank; United Bank.

For full biographical listings, see the Martindale-Hubbell Law Directory

SCHWARTZ AND ELLIS, LTD. (AV)

6950 North Fairfax Drive, 22213
Telephone: 703-532-9300
Telex: 892320
Facsimile: 703-534-0329
Email: schwellis@aol.com *URL:* http://www.lawyers.com/schwartzandellis

Philip Schwartz
John P. Ellis

John S. Petrillo

References: First Virginia Bank; Bank of America; First Union National Bank.

For full biographical listings, see the Martindale-Hubbell Law Directory

WALSH, COLUCCI, STACKHOUSE, EMRICH & LUBELEY, P.C. (AV)

Courthouse Plaza, Thirteenth Floor, 2200 Clarendon Boulevard, 22201
Telephone: 703-528-4700
Facsimile: 703-525-3197
Email: mdwal@wcsel.com *URL:* http://www.wcsel.com
Woodbridge, Virginia Office: Village Square, 13663 Office Place, Suite 201.
Telephones: 703-680-4664; 690-4647.
Facsimile: 703-690-2412.
Leesburg, Virginia Office: One East Market Street, 3rd Floor, 20176.
Telephone: 703-737-3633.
Fax: 703-737-3632.

Peter K. Stackhouse
Jerry K. Emrich
William A. Fogarty
John E. Rinaldi (Resident, Woodbridge Office)
Michael L. Murray
Timothy S. Sampson

For full biographical listings, see the Martindale-Hubbell Law Directory

BIG STONE GAP, Wise Co.

KEULING-STOUT, P.C. (AV)

125 Clinton Avenue East, P.O. Box 400, 24219
Telephone: 540-523-1676
Fax: 540-523-1608

Henry S. Keuling-Stout

For full biographical listings, see the Martindale-Hubbell Law Directory

*CHARLOTTESVILLE,** Charlottesville City Co.

HAUGH & HAUGH, P.C. (AV)

435 Park Street, 22901
Telephone: 804-296-0185
Fax: 804-296-1146

(See Next Column)

Charles R. Haugh
Lair Dayton Haugh

For full biographical listings, see the Martindale-Hubbell Law Directory

TREMBLAY & SMITH, LLP (AV)

105-109 East High Street, P.O. Box 1585, 22902
Telephone: 804-977-4455
Fax: 804-979-1221
Email: tslaw@esinet.net

MEMBERS OF FIRM

John K. Taggart, III
Melvin E. Gibson, Jr.
Thomas E. Albro
Christine Thomson
Patricia D. McGraw

ASSOCIATES

R. Lee Livingston
Heidi Parker
Rachel L. Rust
Christopher J. Robinette
Peter J. Caramanis

Representative Clients: Central; Sieg Distributing Co. (Anheuser-Busch Distributors); Kloeckner Pentaplast of America, Inc.; Virginia Broadcasting Corp.; Farmington Country Club; Management Services Corporation of Charlottesville; Intertrans Carrier Co.; 360° Communications.

For full biographical listings, see the Martindale-Hubbell Law Directory

CHESTER, Chesterfield Co.

HOPSON AND HABENICHT, LTD. (AV)

5601 Ironbridge Parkway, Suite 102, 23831
Telephone: 804-748-3381
Fax: 804-748-5386

R. Craig Hopson
Christopher J. Habenicht

Reference: First Virginia Bank-Colonial, Chesterfield, VA.

For full biographical listings, see the Martindale-Hubbell Law Directory

DANVILLE, (Independent City)

LAW OFFICES OF MICHAEL P. REGAN, P.C. (AV)

703 Patton Street, 24541
Telephone: 804-793-9670; 793-1622
Telecopier: 804-793-6647
Email: MPRlaw@gamewood.net *URL:* http://www.lawyers.com/reganlaw

Michael P. Regan

LEGAL SUPPORT PERSONNEL

Fred N. Fitzgerald (Tax and Financial Assistant)
Janet E. Hylton (Legal Assistant)

References: First Citizens Bank; Bank of America; Virginia Bank & Trust.

For full biographical listings, see the Martindale-Hubbell Law Directory

*FAIRFAX,** (Ind. City; Seat of Fairfax Co.)

BRAULT, PALMER, GROVE, ZIMMERMAN, WHITE & STEINHILBER (AV)

10533 Main Street, P.O. Box 1010, 22030-1010
Telephone: 703-273-6400
Fax: 703-273-3514
Manassas, Virginia Office: 8567-D Sudley Road, 20110. Mailing Address: P.O. Box 534, Manassas, VA 20108.
Telephone: 703-369-7500; 631-9727.
Fax: 703-369-2285.

MEMBERS OF FIRM

Adelard L. Brault (Emeritus)
Thomas C. Palmer, Jr. (Resident, Manassas Office)
Edward H. Grove, III
Michael L. Zimmerman
Bruce D. White
August W. Steinhilber, III

ASSOCIATES

Jack A. Robbins, Jr. (Resident, Manassas Office)
C. Mark Whittington
Craig J. Franco
Bobby Puri (Resident, Manassas Office)

Representative Clients: Alamo Rent-A-Car, Inc.; CNA Insurance Companies; E.I. du Pont de Nemours and Company; Erie Insurance Group; Fidelity & Deposit Company of Maryland; Hanover Insurance Company; Harleysville Insurance Companies; Home Insurance Company; J.B. Hunt Transport, Inc.; Kemper Insurance Group.

For full biographical listings, see the Martindale-Hubbell Law Directory

CREMINS & ASSOCIATES, P.C. (AV)

Suite 310, 10777 Main Street, 22030-6903
Telephone: 703-352-4800
Fax: 703-352-4805
Email: cremins@bellatlantic.net

William D. Cremins

(See Next Column)

CREMINS & ASSOCIATES P.C.—*Continued*

Jennifer Eileen Cremins | Anisa P. Kelley

For full biographical listings, see the Martindale-Hubbell Law Directory

ROBERT W. DOWLER (AV)

3900 University Drive Suite 200, 22030
Telephone: 703-352-3584
Fax: 703-385-9162

Representative Clients: Montgomery Mutual Insurance Co.; Haulers Insurance Co.; Barber-Curran Elevator Co.

For full biographical listings, see the Martindale-Hubbell Law Directory

PETER D. GREENSPUN & ASSOCIATES, P.C. (AV)

Building A-5, 10605 Judicial Drive, 22030-5167
Telephone: 703-352-0100
Fax: 703-591-7268
Email: G&A@Greenspunlaw.com

Peter D. Greenspun

Thomas Peter Mann | Cynthia Ann Bailey
Vladimir I. Arezina

Representative Client: Moore Cadillac Co.

For full biographical listings, see the Martindale-Hubbell Law Directory

LAWSON, KIPP, FORBES & AYRES (AV)

Suite 200, 10805 Main Street, 22030
Telephone: 703-352-2600
Fax: 703-352-4190
Email: lforbes@lkf-law.com *URL:* http://www.lkf-law.com

MEMBERS OF FIRM

Thomas O. Lawson | Laurie E. Forbes
Ralph E. Kipp | Beth S. Ayres

Representative Client: Fairfax County Economic Development Authority.

For full biographical listings, see the Martindale-Hubbell Law Directory

LEFFLER, HYLAND & THOMPSON, A PROFESSIONAL CORPORATION (AV)

Inns of Court, 4163 Chain Bridge Road, 22030-4102
Telephone: 703-293-9300
Facsimile: 703-293-9301
Email: mail@lefflerhyland.com *URL:* http://www.lefflerhyland.com

Rodney G. Leffler | Timothy B. Hyland
Sharon E. Thompson

For full biographical listings, see the Martindale-Hubbell Law Directory

MCCANDLISH & LILLARD, A PROFESSIONAL CORPORATION (AV)

Fair Oaks Plaza, 11350 Random Hills Road, Suite 500, 22030-7429
Telephone: 703-273-2288
Fax: 703-352-4300
Email: mccand@patriot.net *URL:* http://www.mccandlaw.com
Leesburg, Virginia Office: 305 Harrison Street, S.E., Third Floor.
Telephone: 703-737-0200.
Fax: 703-737-0165.

Robert J. McCandlish, Jr. (1909-1996)
Rothwell J. Lillard (1910-1989)
Jesse B. Wilson, III
Peter A. Arntson
Gary W. Brown
Randolph A. Sutliff
Robert H. J. Loftus
William McCauley Arnold
Stephen C. Price
Stephen K. Fox
Douglas J. Sanderson
R. Peyton Mahaffey
William L. Carey
John W. Farrell
Eric J. Berghold
Ralph M. Tener
Vicki L. Layman
Adam W. Smith

Daniel P. Lyon | Lawrence J. McClafferty
Brian R. Sanderson

For full biographical listings, see the Martindale-Hubbell Law Directory

ODIN, FELDMAN & PITTLEMAN, P.C. (AV)

9302 Lee Highway, Suite 1100, 22031
Telephone: 703-218-2100
Facsimile: 703-218-2160
Email: OFP@OFPLAW.COM

(See Next Column)

Dexter S. Odin
Robert K. Richardson
Donald F. King
F. Douglas Ross
Bruce M. Blanchard
Sally Ann Hostetler
Frances P. Dwornik
Edward W. Cameron
Robert G. Nath
Kevin Thomas Oliveira

Matthew J. Britton | Timothy S. Bird
Jonathan D. Frieden | Richard D. Martindale
Matthew Anthony Rizzo

OF COUNSEL

Stephen J. O'Brien | Robert C. Adams

For Complete List of Firm Personnel, See General Section

For full biographical listings, see the Martindale-Hubbell Law Directory

TRICHILO, BANCROFT, MCGAVIN, HORVATH & JUDKINS, P.C. (AV)

F & M Bank Building, Suite 400, 4117 Chain Bridge Road, P.O. Box 22, 22030-0022
Telephone: 703-385-1000
Telecopier: 703-385-1555

Benjamin J. Trichilo
Steven W. Bancroft
John D. McGavin
Stephen A. Horvath
Julia B. Judkins
Melissa Hogue Katz
Dawn E. Boyce

Heather Kathleen Bardot | Michael Earle Thorsen
Michael J. Carita | Barry J. Waldman

Representative Clients: Virginia Farm Bureau Insurance Cos.; Amoco Oil Co.; Erie Insurance Exchange; The Hartford; State Farm Insurance Cos.; Ohio Casualty Group; Chubb Group of Insurance Companies; Atlantic Mutual Insurance Co.; USSA; Allstate Insurance Co.; CNA; Reliance Insurance Co.; K-Mart Corp.; Farmer's Insurance Co.; CIGNA Insurance Co.

For full biographical listings, see the Martindale-Hubbell Law Directory

*LEESBURG,** Loudoun Co.

SEVILA, SAUNDERS, HUDDLESTON & WHITE, A PROFESSIONAL CORPORATION (AV)

30 North King Street, 20176
Telephone: 703-777-5700
Metro: 471-9800; Fax: 703-771-4161

Robert E. Sevila | Jon D. Huddleston
Richard R. Saunders, Jr. | Craig E. White

Jeffrey A. Tuten | Jeanine M. Irving

LEGAL SUPPORT PERSONNEL

Joan Rust

For full biographical listings, see the Martindale-Hubbell Law Directory

MCLEAN, Fairfax Co.

PLEDGER & FEORD P.L.C. (AV)

Suite 204, 1489 Chain Bridge Road, 22101
Telephone: 703-821-1250
Fax: 703-790-7250
Email: Pledger@his.com *URL:* http://www.lawyers.com/pledgerlaw

R. Harrison Pledger, Jr. | Bernard G. Feord, Jr.

Kevin D. Pledger

For full biographical listings, see the Martindale-Hubbell Law Directory

VENABLE ATTORNEYS AT LAW VENABLE, BAETJER AND HOWARD, LLP (AV)

A Partnership including Professional Corporations
Suite 400, 2010 Corporate Ridge, 22102
Telephone: 703-760-1600
Fax: 703-821-8949
URL: http://www.venable.com
Baltimore, Maryland Office: 1800 Mercantile Bank & Trust Building, 2 Hopkins Plaza.
Telephone: 410-244-7400.
Fax: 410-244-7742.
Washington, D.C. Office: Venable, Baetjer, Howard & Civiletti LLP, Suite 1000, 1201 New York Avenue, N.W.
Telephone: 202-962-4800.
Fax: 202-962-8300.
Rockville, Maryland Office: Suite 500, One Church Street, P.O. Box 1906.
Telephone: 301-217-5600.
Fax: 301-217-5617.
Towson, Maryland Office: 210 Allegheny Avenue, P. O. Box 5517.
Telephone: 410-494-6200.
Fax: 410-821-0147.

(See Next Column)

VENABLE ATTORNEYS AT LAW VENABLE, BAETJER AND HOWARD, LLP, *McLean—Continued*

MEMBERS OF FIRM

Kenneth C. Bass, III (Also at Washington, D.C. Office)
William D. Dolan, III (P.C.)
J. Scott Hommer, III
David G. Lane
Christine M. McAnney
Michael W. Robinson

ASSOCIATE

Paul N. Wengert

For Complete List of Firm Personnel, See General Section

For full biographical listings, see the Martindale-Hubbell Law Directory

NEWPORT NEWS, (Independent City)

WILLIAM V. HOYLE JR., P.C. (AV)

10401 Warwick Boulevard, 23601
Telephone: 757-596-1850
Fax: 757-596-1925
Email: habeas@erols.com *URL:* http://www.lawyers.com/williamhoyle

William V. Hoyle, Jr.

For full biographical listings, see the Martindale-Hubbell Law Directory

NORFOLK, (Independent City)

BREEDEN, MACMILLAN & GREEN, P.L.C. (AV)

1700 First Virginia Tower, 555 Main Street, 23510-2230
Telephone: 757-622-1111
Telecopier: 757-622-4049
Email: BMGPLC@AOL.COM *URL:* http://www.hometown.aol.com/bmgplc/bmg.html

Edward L. Breeden (1905-1990)
Robert R. MacMillan (1923-1990)
Berryman Green, IV (1926-1999)
Edward L. Breeden, III
T. Jeffrey Salb
Allen W. Beasley
Darlene P. Bradberry

Cameron S. Meals

OF COUNSEL

Michael T. Zugelder

Representative Clients: First Virginia Bank of Tidewater; A.S.C.A.P.; Metropolitan Property & Casualty Co.; Progressive Insurance Co.; Reliance Insurance Co.

For full biographical listings, see the Martindale-Hubbell Law Directory

PAYNE, GATES, FARTHING & RADD, P.C. (AV)

15th Floor, Dominion Tower, 999 Waterside Drive, Suite 1515, 23510-3309
Telephone: 757-640-1500
Facsimile: 757-627-6583
URL: http://www.paynegates.com

Ronald M. Gates
Philip R. Farthing
Anthony F. Radd
Glen M. Robertson
Todd J. Preti
Marshall A. Winslow, Jr.

Stephen E. Heretick
Raymond L. Hogge, Jr.

OF COUNSEL

Charles E. Payne

For full biographical listings, see the Martindale-Hubbell Law Directory

SACKS & SACKS, A PROFESSIONAL CORPORATION (AV)

Suite 501 Town Point Center, 150 Boush Street, 23510-1615
Telephone: 757-623-2753
FAX: 757-640-7170
Email: sacks@series2000.com *URL:* http://www.lawyers.com/sacks&sacks-com

Herman A. Sacks (1886-1983)
Stanley E. Sacks
Andrew M. Sacks

LEGAL SUPPORT PERSONNEL

James S. McMahan (Litigation Manager)
Virginia S. McCann (Paralegal)
Maryjane Evans (Paralegal)
Thomas L. Gilchrist (Legal Assistant)
Marshall T. Walker, Jr. (Investigator)

For full biographical listings, see the Martindale-Hubbell Law Directory

STACKHOUSE, SMITH & NEXSEN (AV)

1600 First Virginia Tower, 555 Main Street, P.O. Box 3640, 23514
Telephone: 757-623-3555
Fax: 757-624-9245

(See Next Column)

MEMBERS OF FIRM

Robert C. Stackhouse
Peter W. Smith, IV
William W. Nexsen
R. Clinton Stackhouse, Jr.
Janice McPherson Doxey
Mary Painter Opitz

ASSOCIATES

J. Derek Turrietta
Michael T. Pangalos

Representative Clients: Heritage Bank & Trust; The Atlantic Group, Inc.; Roughton Pontiac Corp; Federal National Mortgage Association; Kemper National Insurance Cos.; Harleysville Mutual Insurance Co.; McDonald's Corporation; Presbyterian League of the Presbytery of Eastern Virginia, Inc.; Oakwood Acceptance Corp.; Taylor Freezer Sales Co., Inc.

For full biographical listings, see the Martindale-Hubbell Law Directory

TAVSS, FLETCHER, MAIDEN & KING, P.C. (AV)

Fourteenth Floor, 555 Main Street, 23510
Telephone: 757-625-1214
Fax: 757-622-7295
Mailing Address: P.O. Box 3747, 23514
Email: tavss@pilot.infi.net

Richard J. Tavss
John R. Fletcher
Ray W. King
Besianne Tavss Maiden
Michael B. Hamar
Kevin J. O'Leary

LEGAL SUPPORT PERSONNEL

Maurice J. O'Connor
Retha Rish (Paralegal)

Reference: Bank of the Commonwealth.

For full biographical listings, see the Martindale-Hubbell Law Directory

VANDEVENTER BLACK LLP (AV)

500 World Trade Center, 23510-1699
Telephone: 757-446-8600
Cable Address: "Hughsvan"
Telecopier: 757-446-8670
URL: http://www.vanblk.com
Kitty Hawk, North Carolina Office: 6 Juniper Trail.
Telephone: 252-261-5055.
Fax: 252-261-8444. E-Mail: nshearin@pinn.net.
London, England Office: Mitre House, 4th Floor, 12-14 Mitre Street.
Telephone: (0171) 623-2081.
Facsimile: (0171) 929-0043.

PARTNERS OF FIRM

Walter B. Martin, Jr.
Morton H. Clark
John M. Ryan
James S. Mathews
Geoffrey F. Birkhead
Robert L. O'Donnell
Deborah Mancoll Casey

For Complete List of Firm Personnel, See General Section

For full biographical listings, see the Martindale-Hubbell Law Directory

*ORANGE,** Orange Co.

SHACKELFORD, HONENBERGER, THOMAS, WILLIS & GREGG, P.L.C. (AV)

149 West Main Street, P.O. Box 871, 22960
Telephone: 540-672-2711
Fax: 540-672-2714
Email: shtwg1@ns.gemlink.com
Culpeper, Virginia Office: 147 West Davis Street, P.O. Box 1002.
Telephone: 540-825-0305.

OF COUNSEL

Virginius R. Shackelford, Jr.

MEMBERS OF FIRM

Virginius R. Shackelford, III
Christopher J. Honenberger
Frank A. Thomas, III
Jere M. H. Willis, III (Resident, Culpeper, Virginia Office)
Sarah Collins Honenberger
Sean D. Gregg

For full biographical listings, see the Martindale-Hubbell Law Directory

PORTSMOUTH, (Independent City)

MOODY, STROPLE & KLOEPPEL, INC. (AV)

500 Crawford Street, Suite 300, P.O. Box 1138, 23705-1138
Telephone: 757-393-4093
Fax: 757-397-7257
URL: http://www.moodyrrlaw.com
Tampa, Florida Office: 9280 Bay Plaza Boulevard, Suite 714, 33619.
Telephone 813-627-9202.
Fax: 813-627-9423.

Willard J. Moody, Sr.

(See Next Column)

MOODY, STROPLE & KLOEPPEL INC.—*Continued*

Willard J. Moody, Jr.
Raymond H. Strople
Robert A. Small
John E. Basilone
Joseph J. Perez
Thomas F. Burris, III
E. Stanley Murphy
John C. Henry
Steven S. Nelson
Andrew K. Chafin
Claude W. Anderson, Jr.
John W. Hall
Kenneth C. Whalen (Resident, Tampa, Florida Office)

OF COUNSEL

Byron P. Kloeppel, Retired

Reference: BB&T Bank.

For full biographical listings, see the Martindale-Hubbell Law Directory

RESTON, Fairfax Co.

GARVER LAW OFFICES, P.C. (AV)

11702 Bowman Green Drive, P.O. Box 2430, 20195
Telephone: 703-471-1090; 800-440-8605
Fax: 703-471-1095
Email: GLAW@Erols.com *URL:* http://www.lawyers.com/stevengarver

Steven M. Garver
Cheryl Gilley Rice

For full biographical listings, see the Martindale-Hubbell Law Directory

RICHMOND, (Independent City)

BOWLES AND BOWLES (AV)

Two North Fifth Street, 23219-2218
Telephone: 804-643-6768
Fax: 804-648-8134

Aubrey Russell Bowles, Jr. (1896-1984)
Aubrey Russell Bowles, III
Aubrey R. Bowles, IV

For full biographical listings, see the Martindale-Hubbell Law Directory

FRAMME LAW FIRM, PLC (AV)

830 East Main Street, 19th Floor, 23219
Telephone: 804-649-3159
Facsimile: 804-649-3247
Email: LFRAMME@FRAMMELAW.COM *URL:* http://www.FRAMMELAW.COM

Lawrence H. Framme, III

Joseph A. Romito
Susan H. Call
Audria Marie Frazier
Adam E. Strauchler
Mark K. Ames
Charles A. Hartz, Jr.
Charlie P. Phelps
Stuart R. Kaplan

LEGAL SUPPORT PERSONNEL

Maria S. Lavin

PARALEGALS

Thomas W. Wright, Sr.
Sheila Martin Berry
Sharon K. Rideout

For full biographical listings, see the Martindale-Hubbell Law Directory

LECLAIR RYAN, A PROFESSIONAL CORPORATION (AV)

707 East Main Street, 11th Floor, 23219
Telephone: 804-783-2003
Facsmile: 804-783-2294
Email: email@leclairryan.com
Glen Allen, Virginia Office: 4201 Dominion Boulevard, Suite 200, 23060.
Telephone: 804-270-0070.
Facsimile: 804-270-4715.
Blacksburg, Virginia Office: 1872 Pratt Drive, Suite 1865, 24060.
Telephone: 540-961-2762.
Fax: 540-961-2781.
Norfolk, Virginia Office: 999 Waterside Drive, Suite 2025.
Telephone: 757-624-1454.
Facsimile: 757-624-3773.
Alexandria, Virginia Office: 225 Reinekers Lane, Suite 290, 22314.
Telephone: 703-684-8007.
Facsimile: 703-684-8075.
Charlottesville, Virginia Office: 108 S.E. Second Street, P.O. Box 2017, 22902.
Telephone: 804-971-7771.
Facsimile: 804-296-0905.

Rodney K. Adams
William W. Belt, Jr.
Paula Steinhilber Beran
Lawrence B. Cann, III
Deborah Swindells Donovan (Not admitted in VA)
John M. Fitzpatrick
Laura G. Fox
Stephen T. Gannon
Sharon J. Glover
Jonathan M. Harris (Not admitted in VA)
Ronald P. Herbert
Vernon E. Inge, Jr.
Sharon Maitland Moon
James A. Murphy
Kelvin L. Newsome
Robert F. Redmond, Jr.

(See Next Column)

Anne G. Scher
David G. Shuford
Charles M. Sims
Lynn Lewis Tavenner

Robert B. Beasley, Jr.
Lynn S. Brice
Anne M. Glenn
Michael J. Hudak
Harris L. Kay
Michael Liberman
Donald F. Lynch, III
Mike F. Melis
Charles G. Meyer, III
Christopher L. Perkins
Patricia M. Powis
Andrea Lynn White

For full biographical listings, see the Martindale-Hubbell Law Directory

WILLIAMS, MULLEN, CLARK & DOBBINS, A PROFESSIONAL CORPORATION (AV)

Two James Center, 1021 East Cary Street, P.O. Box 1320, 23218-1320
Telephone: 804-643-1991
Fax: 804-783-6507
URL: http://www.wmcd.com
Newport News Office: Harbor Bank Center, Suite 210, One Old Oyster Point Road, 23602-7119.
Telephone: 757-249-5100.
Fax: 757-249-5109.
Virginia Beach Office: One Columbus Center, 23462-6763.
Telephone: 757-499-8800.
Fax: 757-473-0395.
Vienna Office: 1593 Spring Hill Road, Suite 510, 22182.
Telephone: 703-760-5200.
Fax: 703-748-0244.
Washington, D.C. Office: The Farragut Building, 900 17th Street, N.W., Suite 700, 20006.
Telephone: 202-293-0213.
Fax: 804-783-6507. Fax Within D.C.: 202-293-5939.
London, England Office: Blake Lodge, Bridge Lane, SW11 3AD.
Telephone: (011-44-71) 223-2756.
Fax: (011-44-71) 350-0156.
Riyadh, Saudi Arabia Affiliate Office: Saudi-American Legal Consultants Commercial Building #2, Diplomatic Quarter, P.O. Box 57270, 11574.
Telephone: (011-966-1) 488-1563.
Fax: (011-966-1) 488-0542.

Stephen E. Baril
William D. Bayliss
A. Peter Brodell
James J. Burns
Donald H. Clark (Resident, Virginia Beach Office)
Howard W. Dobbins
Theodore J. Edlich, IV
Robert E. Eicher
Calvin W. Fowler, Jr.
Michael J. Gardner (Resident, Virginia Beach Office)
Curtis M. Hairston, Jr.
Samuel W. Hixon, III
William R. Mauck, Jr.
Dana D. McDaniel
James V. Meath
Robert D. Perrow
Robert L. Samuel, Jr. (Resident, Virginia Beach Office)
Andrea Rowse Stiles
W. Scott Street, III
Stephen C. Swain (Resident, Virginia Beach Office)
Stephen G. Test (Resident, Virginia Beach Office)
Sandy T. Tucker
Abram W. VanderMeer, Jr. (Resident, Virginia Beach Office)
John L. Walker, III

Lynn K. Brugh, IV
Megan E. Burns (Resident, Virginia Beach Office)
David C. Burton
David A. Cardon (Resident, Virginia Beach Office)
Timothy W. Dorsey (Resident, Virginia Beach Office)
Ann Mayhew Golski (Resident, Virginia Beach Office)
Mary Eve Grandis (Resident, Virginia Beach Office)
Patrick R. Hanes
Elizabeth Mason Horsley
Michelle A. Hughes (Resident, Virginia Beach Office)
William F. Jones
James Scott Kulp
Kevin C. Nunnally
Dana C. M. Peluso
Donald J. Richardson
Frances W. Russell (Resident, Virginia Beach Office)
Kimberly A. Satterwhite

For Complete List of Firm Personnel, See General Section

For full biographical listings, see the Martindale-Hubbell Law Directory

ROANOKE, Roanoke City Co.

WOOTEN & HART, A PROFESSIONAL CORPORATION (AV)

707 Building, Suite 300, P.O. Box 12247, 24024-2247
Telephone: 540-343-2451; 540-342-9672
Telecopier: 540-345-6417
URL: http://www.wootenhart.com

George W. Wooten
David B. Hart
L. Thompson Hanes
Susan A. Waddell
Bradley D. McGraw
John L. Cooley
Thomas W. Farrell
Paul C. Kuhnel
Peter D. Vieth

David W. Hearn
John Mark Cooley
Christopher W. Stevens
Elizabeth D. Guilbert
Eunice Park Austin

(See Next Column)

WOOTEN & HART A PROFESSIONAL CORPORATION, *Roanoke—Continued*

OF COUNSEL

M. Lanier Woodrum

Representative Clients: Wachovia Bank; St. Paul Insurance Cos.
Approved Attorneys for: Lawyers Title Insurance Corp.
Reference: First Union National Bank.

For full biographical listings, see the Martindale-Hubbell Law Directory

*RUSTBURG,** Campbell Co.

OVERBEY, HAWKINS & SELZ (AV)

Court House Square, P.O. Box 38, 24588
Telephone: 804-332-5155
FAX: 804-332-5143

W. Hutchings Overbey (1906-1991)
A. David Hawkins
Bryan K. Selz

ASSOCIATE

Frank A. Wright, Jr.

OF COUNSEL

W. Hutchings Overbey, Jr.

Local Counsel for: First Virginia Bank, Piedmont; Colonial Farm Credit, ACA; Browning-Ferris Industries; WESTVACO; Truck Body Corp.; Falwell Aviation, Inc.; Campbell County School Board; Bedford County School Board; Industrial Development Authority of the County of Campbell; Modern Home Construction, Inc.

For full biographical listings, see the Martindale-Hubbell Law Directory

SPRINGFIELD, Fairfax Co.

BECKER, HICKS, IRVING & HADEED, P.C. (AV)

5501 Backlick Road, Suite 220, 22151
Telephone: 703-256-1300
Fax: 703-256-3467
Email: mail@bhihlaw.com *URL:* http://www.bhihlaw.com

Larry E. Becker
B. R. Hicks
James V. Irving
Michael Mitry Hadeed, Jr.
Mark E. Kellogg, P.C.
Lynn E. Berry
Scott R. Sexauer

May Shallal Kheder
Alix L. Mattingly
Ashraf W. Nubani

For full biographical listings, see the Martindale-Hubbell Law Directory

MADIGAN & SCOTT, INC. (AV)

7880 Backlick Road, 22150-2288
Telephone: 703-455-1800; 451-2080
Fax: 703-451-4121
Email: MADSCOTT@EROLS.COM
Manassas, Virginia Office: 9100 Church Street, Suite 107.
Telephone: 703-361-0185. Metro: 631-9193.
Fax: 703-631-9633.

Robert J. Madigan
Paul A. Scott
Mark J. Madigan

OF COUNSEL

Mitchell Komaroff

Richard G. Hornig (1958-1994)

For full biographical listings, see the Martindale-Hubbell Law Directory

*TAZEWELL,** Tazewell Co.

DUDLEY, GALUMBECK & NECESSARY (AV)

104 West Main Street, P.O. Box 626, 24651
Telephone: 540-988-9436; 988-6561
Telecopier: 540-988-2921
Bluefield, Virginia Office: 728 Virginia Avenue, P.O. Box 468, 24605.
Telephone: 540-322-3454; 540-988-6590; 1-800-580-6590.
Telecopier: 540-322-4420.
Wytheville, Virginia Office: 100 West Main Street, Suite 201, 24382.
Telephone: 540-228-6060.
Fax: 540-228-7573.

MEMBERS OF FIRM

James W. Dudley (Resident, Bluefield Office)
Robert M. Galumbeck (Resident)
Kelly Combs Necessary (Resident)
Charles A. Stacy (Resident, Bluefield Office)
Clinton Sherwood Kegley (Resident, Wytheville Office)

References: Lawyers Title Insurance; Bank of Tazewell County.

For full biographical listings, see the Martindale-Hubbell Law Directory

VIENNA, Fairfax Co.

BORING & PILGER, P.C. (AV)

307 Maple Avenue West, Suite D, 22180-4307
Telephone: 703-281-2161
Fax: 703-281-9464
URL: http://www.boringandpilger.com

Karl W. Pilger

Sharon C. Williams (Not admitted in VA)

Representative Clients: Hewlett-Packard Co.; Toshiba America Information Systems, Inc.; Anthony and Sylvan Pools, Inc.

For full biographical listings, see the Martindale-Hubbell Law Directory

VIRGINIA BEACH, (Independent City)

BRYDGES, MAHAN, O'BRIEN & FRUCCI, P.C. (AV)

Professional Building, 1369 Laskin Road, 23451
Telephone: 757-428-6021
Fax: 757-491-7634

Richard G. Brydges
Stephen C. Mahan
William R. "Buster" O'Brien
Steven C. Frucci

Approved Mediators/Arbitrators for: United States Arbitration and Mediation, Inc.; Arbitration Associates, Inc.- Jams/Endispute.
Reference: The Bank of Tidewater.

For full biographical listings, see the Martindale-Hubbell Law Directory

WHITE STONE, Lancaster Co.

DUNTON, SIMMONS & DUNTON, L.L.P (AV)

678 Rappahannock Drive, 22578
Telephone: 804-435-4000
Telecopier: 804-435-1614
Email: dsd@crosslink.net

MEMBERS OF FIRM

Ammon G. Dunton, Jr.
Craig H. Smith
William R. Curdts
John S. Martin
J. Rawleigh Simmons
Morgan Wade Alley

ASSOCIATE

John Christian Hodges

General Counsel: Bay Banks of Virginia; Bay Trust Company; Bank of Lancaster; Northern Neck Insurance Co.; Virginia Health and Accident Assn.

For full biographical listings, see the Martindale-Hubbell Law Directory

WASHINGTON

KENNEWICK, Benton Co.

RETTIG, OSBORNE, FORGETTE, O'DONNELL, ILLER & ADAMSON, LLP (AV)

6725 West Clearwater Avenue, 99336
Telephone: 509-783-6154
Fax: 509-783-0858
Email: rettlaw@ix.netcom.com

MEMBERS OF FIRM

Diehl R. Rettig
Stephen T. Osborne
Francois X. Forgette
Michael L. O'Donnell
Brian J. Iller
Cheryl R.G. Adamson

John P. Raekes
Jeffrey T. Sperline
Stella J. Edens

Representative Clients: Columbia School District; Chevron Pipeline Co.; Federal Land Bank.
Insurance Clients: Farmers Insurance Group; American States Insurance Co.; Continental Insurance Co.; Cigna Insurance Co.; Mutual of Enumclaw.

For full biographical listings, see the Martindale-Hubbell Law Directory

PUYALLUP, Pierce Co.

CAMPBELL, DILLE AND BARNETT P.L.L.C. (AV)

A Professional Limited Liability Company including Professional Service Corporations
317 South Meridian Street, 98371
Telephone: 253-848-3513
Fax: 253-845-4941
Email: hbarnett@cdb-law.com

(See Next Column)

CAMPBELL, DILLE AND BARNETT P.L.L.C.—*Continued*

MEMBERS OF FIRM

Robert D. Campbell (Retired)
Bryce H. Dille (P.S.)
Hollis H. Barnett (P.S.)
Daniel W. Smith
Boyd S. Wiley

Patricia J. Barnett
Gilbert J. Price
Shannon R. Jones

OF COUNSEL

Charles W. Dent

Representative Clients: Fors Farms, Inc.; Puyallup School District No. 3; Puyallup Valley Bank; Town of Eatonville; McMullen Electric Co.; Larson Glass Co.; Girard Wood Products; Uniland, Inc.; Western Washington Fair; Good Samaritan Community Health Care.

For full biographical listings, see the Martindale-Hubbell Law Directory

*SEATTLE,** King Co.

ADOLPH & BINTINGER, P.S. (AV)

7100 Columbia Center, 701 Fifth Avenue, 98104
Telephone: 206-621-7900
Telefax: 206-682-3203
Email: rjadolph@msn.com

Robert J. Adolph
Paul M. Bintinger
Christina B. Gamache

Representative Clients: Ocean Beauty Seafoods, Inc.; Philip Environmental Company; Seattle First National Bank; Conover Insurance, Inc.; The Research Group; CAPCO Financial Co.; Bruce Blume and Company (real estate holdings); R.H. Conner, Inc. (real estate holdings).
Reference: Seattle First National Bank.

For full biographical listings, see the Martindale-Hubbell Law Directory

DANIELSON HARRIGAN & TOLLEFSON, LLP (AV)

A Limited Liability Partnership including a Professional Service Corporation
999 Third Avenue, 44th Floor, 98104
Telephone: 206-623-1700
Facsimile: 206-623-8717
Email: lawfirm@dh-t.com

David Danielson (P.S.)
Arthur W. Harrigan, Jr.
G. Val Tollefson
Timothy G. Leyh
Michelle Buhler
Karl F. Oles
Charles Jordan

COUNSEL

Richard H. Holmquist
Katherine See Kennedy
Matthew R. Kenney
Terence K. McGee

ASSOCIATES

Randall Thomsen
Michael M.K. Hemphill

For full biographical listings, see the Martindale-Hubbell Law Directory

LANE POWELL SPEARS LUBERSKY LLP (AV)

Limited Liability Partnership composed of Individuals and Professional Service Corporations
1420 Fifth Avenue, Suite 4100, 98101-2338
Telephone: 206-223-7000
Facsimile: 206-223-7107
Email: information@lanepowell.com *URL:* http://www.lanepowell.com
Other Offices at: Portland, Oregon; Anchorage, Alaska; Olympia and Mount Vernon, Washington; London, England.

MANAGING PARTNER

James L. Robart

MEMBERS OF FIRM

Randall P. Beighle
Rudy A. Englund
Larry S. Gangnes
Kenneth B. Kaplan
Dale E. Kremer
Gail E. Mautner
John R. Neeleman
Christian N. Oldham
Mark A. Rossi
Richard C. Siefert
Douglas E. Smith
H. Peter Sorg, Jr.
Christopher B. Wells

Representative Clients: Brunswick Corp.; Equire Services LLC; Fred Hutchinson Cancer Research Center; The Hillhaven Corp.; Litton Industries; Mitsui & Co., Ltd.; Morgan Stanley Dean Witter; Nordstrom, Inc.; Prudential Securities; Simpson Investment Co. and Affiliates; Texaco Inc.; Wells Fargo Bank.

For Complete List of Firm Personnel, See General Section

For full biographical listings, see the Martindale-Hubbell Law Directory

MCNAUL EBEL NAWROT HELGREN & VANCE P.L.L.C. (AV)

600 University Street, Suite 2700, 98101-3143
Telephone: 206-467-1816
Facsimile: 206-624-5128
Email: info@mcnaul.com *URL:* http://www.mcnaul.com

MEMBERS OF FIRM

John S. Ebel
Tyler B. Ellrodt
Barbara Hallowell
Michael D. Helgren
Jerry R. McNaul
Matthew N. Menzer
Louis F. Nawrot, Jr.
Robert D. Stewart
Robert M. Sulkin
Cyrus R. Vance, Jr.
Peter M. Vial
Marc O. Winters

OF COUNSEL

Murray B. Guterson
Barbara H. Schuknecht

RETIRED

George L. Grader

ASSOCIATES

Steven J.S. Christophersen
Gregory J. Hollon
Johnathan E. Mansfield
Ann Marie Schwartz
Nancy G. Stephenson
Christopher E. Tucker

For full biographical listings, see the Martindale-Hubbell Law Directory

JEFFREY A. SMYTH, P.S. (AV)

7100 Columbia Center, 701 Fifth Avenue, 98104
Telephone: 206-621-7100
Telefax: 206-682-3203
Email: jsmythps@smythlaw.com *URL:* http://www.smythlaw.com

Jeffrey A. Smyth

Representative Clients: The Monier Roof Tile Co.; Alper Northwest (First City); Alistar Capital Corp.; Kodiak & Western Trawler Group; Coregis Group.

For full biographical listings, see the Martindale-Hubbell Law Directory

SUSMAN GODFREY L.L.P. (AV Ⓣ)

A Registered Limited Liability Partnership including Professional Corporations
Suite 3090, 1201 Third Avenue, 98101-3000
Telephone: 206-516-3880
Telecopy: 206-516-3883
URL: http://www.susmangodfrey.com
Houston, Texas Office: Suite 5100, 1000 Louisiana Street.
Telephone: 713-651-9366.
Telecopy: 713-653-7897.
Dallas, Texas Office: Suite 1400, 2323 Bryan Street.
Telephone: 214-754-1900.
Fax: 214-754-1933.
Los Angeles, California Office: Suite 950, 1880 Century Park East.
Telephone: 310-789-3100.
Fax: 310-789-3150.

MEMBER OF FIRM

Parker C. Folse, III (Resident)

OF COUNSEL

Timothy K. Borchers (Resident)

ASSOCIATE

Jonathan M. Shaw (Not admitted in WA; Resident)

Reference: Laredo National Bank, Houston.

For full biographical listings, see the Martindale-Hubbell Law Directory

WEST VIRGINIA

*CHARLESTON,** Kanawha Co.

ALLEN GUTHRIE & MCHUGH (AV)

1300 Bank One Center, P.O. Box 3394, 25333
Telephone: 304-345-7250
Telecopier: 304-345-9941
Email: kagwv@kagww.com

George G. Guthrie
Robert B. Allen
Thomas E. McHugh
R. Terrance Rodgers
S. Benjamin Bryant
Wm. Scott Wickline
Pamela Lynn Kandzari
James P. McHugh

Michelle M. Price
John K. McHugh
Nicholas P. Mooney II
Teresa K. Thompson
Charles W. Pace, Jr.

For full biographical listings, see the Martindale-Hubbell Law Directory

Charleston—Continued

BOWLES RICE MCDAVID GRAFF & LOVE, PLLC (AV)

600 Quarrier Street, P.O. Box 1386, 25325-1386
Telephone: 304-347-1100
Fax: 304-343-2867
Email: bowles@bowlesrice.com *URL:* http://www.bowlesrice.com
Fairmont, West Virginia Office: 1000 Technology Drive, Suite 2310.
Telephone: 304-368-4000.
Fax: 304-368-4040.
Martinsburg, West Virginia Office: (Serves Berkeley Springs and Charles Town, West Virginia). 105 West Burke Street, P.O. Drawer 1419.
Telephone: 304-263-0836.
Fax: 304-267-3822.
Morgantown, West Virginia Office: 7000 Hampton Center, Suite K.
Telephone: 304-599-1390.
Fax: 304-599-1308.
Parkersburg, West Virginia Office: 501 Avery Street, Fifth Floor, P.O. Box 49.
Telephone: 304-485-8500.
Fax: 304-485-7973.
Lexington, Kentucky Office: 1200 World Trade Center, 333 West Vine Street.
Telephone: 606-225-8700.
Fax: 606-225-8418.

MEMBERS OF FIRM

Paul N. Bowles (1921-1986)
F. Thomas Graff, Jr.
Charles M. Love, III
P. Michael Pleska
Gary G. Markham
Carl D. Andrews
Edward D. McDevitt
Ricklin Brown
J. Thomas Lane
Gerard R. Stowers
P. Nathan Bowles, Jr.
Sarah E. Smith
Richard M. Francis
George A. Patterson, III
Phyllis M. Potterfield
John W. Woods, III
Thomas A. Heywood
Camden P. Siegrist
Sandra M. Murphy
Julia A. Chincheck
Leonard Knee
Marc A. Monteleone
Lesley A. Russo
Ellen Maxwell-Hoffman
Lynn Photiadis
Fazal A. Shere
Charles B. Dollison
Kenneth E. Webb, Jr.
Michael J. Schessler
John R. Teare, Jr.
Elizabeth D. Harter
Joseph J. Starsick, Jr.

ASSOCIATES

Ronda L. Harvey
Stuart A. McMillan
Geoffry Alan Haddad

SPECIAL COUNSEL

Giles D. H. Snyder

OF COUNSEL

William R. McDavid

For Complete List of Firm Personnel, See General Section

For full biographical listings, see the Martindale-Hubbell Law Directory

FLAHERTY, SENSABAUGH & BONASSO, P.L.L.C. (AV)

200 Capitol Street, P.O. Box 3843, 25301
Telephone: 304-345-0200
Telecopier: 304-345-0260
Email: ralphj@fsbwv.com *URL:* http://www.fsbwv.com
Morgantown, West Virginia Office: 7000 Hampton Center, Suite I.
Telephone: 304-598-0788.
Fax: 304-598-0790.
Wheeling, West Virginia Office: 1031 National Road, P.O. Box 6545.
Telephone: 304-242-3941.
Fax: 304-242-3944.

MEMBERS

Thomas V. Flaherty
Don R. Sensabaugh, Jr.
Michael Bonasso
Jeffrey M. Wakefield
Richard D. Jones
Michele Grinberg
Edward C. Martin
W. E. Sam Fox, II
Christine S. Vaglienti (Resident, Morgantown Office)
Patrick S. Casey (Resident, Wheeling Office)
John D. Hoffman
William Jay Cooper
J. Tyler Dinsmore
William J. Hanna
Pamela Dawn Tarr

OF COUNSEL

Fred B. Westfall, Jr.
Sandra M. Chapman (Resident, Wheeling Office)

ASSOCIATES

David Straley Givens
Andrew B. Cooke
Amberly A. Warner
Mark A. Robinson
Carol Ann Marunich (Resident, Morgantown Office)
Erica M. Baumgras
Elizabeth S. Cimino
Keith M. Kodosky
Robert P. Lorea
Amy R. Humphreys
Michelle Lee Marinacci
Quan S. Le (Resident, Wheeling Office)

(See Next Column)

ASSOCIATES (Continued)

Christopher A. Brumley
Salem C. Smith
Scott H. Kaminski
C. Benjamin Salango
Mark Allen Glover

For full biographical listings, see the Martindale-Hubbell Law Directory

GOODWIN & GOODWIN (AV)

1500 One Valley Square, 25301
Telephone: 304-346-7000
Fax: 304-344-9692
Email: g&glaw@goodwin.goodwin.com *URL:* http://www.goodwingoodwin.com
Ripley, West Virginia Office: 500 Church Street, P.O. Box 349.
Telephone: 304-372-2651.
Parkersburg, West Virginia Office: 201 Third Street, Town Square.
Telephone: 304-485-2345.
Fax: 304-485-3459.

Robert B. Goodwin (1909-1955)

OF COUNSEL

C. E. Goodwin

MEMBERS OF FIRM

Thomas R. Goodwin
Stephen P. Goodwin
Michael I. Spiker
Richard E. Rowe
Susan C. Wittemeier
Robert W. Full (Resident at Parkersburg Office)
Richard D. Owen

ASSOCIATE

Suzanne Jett Trowbridge

Representative Clients: Bucyrus-Erie Co.; CSX Corp.; Eastern American Energy Corp.; The Eureka Pipe Line Co.

For Complete List of Firm Personnel, See General Section

For full biographical listings, see the Martindale-Hubbell Law Directory

JACKSON & KELLY (AV)

1600 Laidley Tower, P.O. Box 553, 25322
Telephone: 304-340-1000
Fax: 304-340-1130
Email: info@jacksonkelly.com *URL:* http://www.jacksonkelly.com
Martinsburg, West Virginia Office: 300 Foxcroft Avenue, P.O. Box 1068.
Telephone: 304-263-8800.
Fax: 304-263-7110.
Morgantown, West Virginia Office: 6000 Hampton Center, P.O. Box 619.
Telephone: 304-599-3000.
Fax: 304-285-2040.
New Martinsville, West Virginia Office: 256 Russell Avenue, P.O. Box 68.
Telephone: 304-455-1751.
Fax: 304-455-6314.
Parkersburg, West Virginia Office: 412 Market Street, Suite 202, P.O. Box 1144.
Telephone: 304-424-3490.
Fax: 304-424-3499.
Fairmont, West Virginia Office: 1000 Technology Drive, Suite 1310.
Telephone: 304-368-2000.
Fax: 304-368-2020.
Lexington, Kentucky Office: 175 East Main Street, Suite 500, P.O. Box 2150.
Telephone: 606-255-9500.
Fax: 606-281-6478.
Washington, D. C. Office: 2401 Pennsylvania Avenue, N.W., Suite 400.
Telephone: 202-973-0200.
Fax: 202-973-0232.
Denver, Colorado Office: Suite 2710, 1660 Lincoln Street.
Telephone: 303-390-0003.
Fax: 303-390-0040.
Wheeling, West Virginia Office: 1144 Market Street.
Telephone: 304-233-4000.
Fax: 304-233-4077.

MEMBERS OF FIRM

W. Warren Upton
John M. Slack, III
Stephen R. Crislip
W. Henry Jernigan, Jr.
A. L. Emch
William A. Hoskins, III (Administrative Manager, Lexington, Kentucky Office)
Dennis C. Sauter
Larry W. Blalock (Administrative Manager, New Martinsville and Wheeling, West Virginia Offices)
Gary W. Hart
Thomas J. Hurney, Jr.
Lynn Oliver Frye
Gale Reddie Lea
Stephen M. LaCagnin (Administrative Manager, Morgantown, West Virginia Office)
G. Lindsay Simmons (Resident, Washington, D.C. Office)
William J. Powell
Stanton L. Cave (Resident, Lexington, Kentucky Office)
William Prentice Young (Martinsburg and Charles Town, West Virginia Offices)
Julia M. Chico (Resident, Morgantown, West Virginia Office)
J. Rudy Martin

(See Next Column)

JACKSON & KELLY—*Continued*

ASSOCIATES

Jennifer Z. Cain (Resident, Parkersburg, West Virginia Office)
Mychal S. Schulz
Michael T. Cimino
Katherine Venti

OF COUNSEL

Katherine Shand Larkin (Resident, Denver, Colorado Office)

Representative Clients: Rhone-Poulenc Ag Company; Caterpillar Inc.; Union Carbide Corp.; Pittston Coal Management Co.; General Motors Corp.; Bayer Corporation; Cypress-AMAX Minerals Company; CONSOL Inc.; Monongahela Power Co.; Thomas Memorial Hospital.

For Complete List of Firm Personnel, See General Section

For full biographical listings, see the Martindale-Hubbell Law Directory

KAY CASTO & CHANEY PLLC (AV)

1600 Bank One Center, P.O. Box 2031, 25327
Telephone: 304-345-8900
Telefax: 304-345-8909; 304-343-9833
Email: kcc@kaycasto.com *URL:* http://www.kaycasto.com
Morgantown, West Virginia Office: Suite C, 3000 Hampton Center.
Telephone: 304-599-8900.
Telefax: 304-599-8901.

OF COUNSEL

John B. Carrico
John O. Kizer

MEMBERS OF FIRM

Michael T. Chaney
Barney W. Frazier, Jr.
George W. S. Grove, Jr.
Ann L. Haight
Steven C. Hanley
Elliot G. Hicks
John R. Hoblitzell
John R. McGhee, Jr.
Dina M. Mohler
W. Michael Moore
Kevin A. Nelson
Harry M. Rubenstein (Morgantown, West Virginia Office)

ASSOCIATE

Daniel A. Oliver (Morgantown, West Virginia Office)

Attorneys for: Bank One, West Virginia; Wausau Insurance Cos,; West Virginia Contractors Bargaining Assn.; Charleston Area Medical Center, Inc.; Wal-Mart Stores, Inc.; University of Charleston; Ford Motor Credit Co.; The Huntington National Bank; West Virginia Hospital Assn.; Appalachian Regional Healthcare, Inc.

For Complete List of Firm Personnel, See General Section

For full biographical listings, see the Martindale-Hubbell Law Directory

SALSBERY & DRUCKMAN (AV)

606 Virginia Street East, Suite 100, 25305
Telephone: 304-343-0075
Fax: 304-343-0099
Email: salsdruck@citynet.net

H. F. Salsbery
William S. Druckman
Madonna C. Estep

OF COUNSEL

Anne E. Shaffer

For full biographical listings, see the Martindale-Hubbell Law Directory

*CLARKSBURG,** Harrison Co.

JOHNSON, SIMMERMAN & BROUGHTON, L.C. (AV)

Ogden Building, 203 West Main Street, 26301
Telephone: 304-624-6555; 304-623-4900
Telecopier: 304-623-4933
Mailing Address: P.O. Box 150, Clarksburg, West Virginia, 26302-0150

Charles G. Johnson
Frank E. Simmerman, Jr.
Marcia Allen Broughton
Bridget D. Furbee
Robin Queen Triplett

For full biographical listings, see the Martindale-Hubbell Law Directory

MCNEER, HIGHLAND, MCMUNN AND VARNER, L.C. (AV)

One Valley Bank Building, P.O. Drawer 2040, 26302-2040
Telephone: 304-626-1100
Facsimile: 304-623-3035
Martinsburg Office: 2520 Aikens Center, P.O. Box 2509.
Telephone: 304-264-4621.
Fax: 304-264-8623.
Parkersburg Office: 404 Market Street, Suite 204, P.O. Box 1507.
Telephone: 304-422-7193.
Facsimile: 304-422-7196.

C. David McMunn
J. Cecil Jarvis
James A. Varner
Robert W. Trumble (Resident, Martinsburg Office)
Catherine D. Munster
James N. Riley
Steven R. Bratke (Resident, Parkersburg Office)

(See Next Column)

Michael J. Novotny (Resident, Martinsburg Office)
Dennis M. Shreve
Geraldine S. Roberts
William F. Rohrbaugh (Resident, Martinsburg Office)
Gregory H. Schillace
Judy L. Shanholtz
Tiffany R. Durst
Gene W. Bailey, II

OF COUNSEL

James E. McNeer
Cecil B. Highland, Jr.
William L. Fury

Representative Clients: Nationwide Insurance Group; State Automobile Insurance Co.; Insurance Company of North America (CIGNA); Home Insurance Co.; Westfield Insurance Co.; St. Paul Insurance Co.; West Virginia Fire and Casualty; United Hospital Center; One Valley Bank; Clarksburg Publishing Co.

For full biographical listings, see the Martindale-Hubbell Law Directory

WATERS, WARNER & HARRIS, PLLC (AV)

Formerly Stathers & Cantrall
701 Goff Building, P.O. Box 1716, 26301
Telephone: 304-624-5571
Fax: 304-624-7228
Email: wwh.atty@northnap.citynet.net

Birk S. Stathers (1884-1945)
W. G. Stathers (1889-1970)
Arch M. Cantrall (1896-1967)
Stuart R. Waters
Boyd L. Warner
James A. Harris
Scott E. Wilson
James C. Turner
G. Thomas Smith

ASSOCIATES

D. Andrew McMunn
David C. Glover

Representative Clients: United States Fidelity and Guaranty Co.; State Farm Insurance Companies; The Shelby Mutual Insurance Co.; Westfield Insurance Company; Bethlehem Steel Corp.; The Cafaro Co.

For full biographical listings, see the Martindale-Hubbell Law Directory

*FAIRMONT,** Marion Co.

BOWLES RICE MCDAVID GRAFF & LOVE, PLLC (AV)

Alan B. Mollohan Innovation Center, 1000 Technology Drive, Suite 2310, 26554
Telephone: 304-368-4000
Fax: 304-368-4040
Email: bowles@bowlesrice.com *URL:* http://www.bowlesrice.com
Charleston, West Virginia Office: 600 Quarrier Street, P.O. Box 1386.
Telephone: 304-347-1100.
Fax: 304-343-2867.
Martinsburg, West Virginia Office: (Serves Berkeley Springs and Charles Town, West Virginia). 105 West Burke Street, P.O. Drawer 1419.
Telephone: 304-263-0836.
Fax: 304-267-3822.
Morgantown, West Virginia Office: 7000 Hampton Center, Suite K.
Telephone: 304-599-1390.
Fax: 304-599-1308.
Parkersburg, West Virginia Office: 501 Avery Street, Fifth Floor, P.O. Box 49.
Telephone: 304-485-7973.
Fax: 304-485-7973.
Lexington, Kentucky Office: 1200 World Trade Center, 333 West Vine Street.
Telephone: 606-225-8700.
Fax: 606-225-8418.

MEMBERS OF FIRM

Paul E. Frampton (Resident)
Charles C. Wise, III (Resident)

For Complete List of Firm Personnel, See General Section

For full biographical listings, see the Martindale-Hubbell Law Directory

FURBEE, AMOS, WEBB & CRITCHFIELD (AV)

132 Adams Street, P.O. Box 1189, 26555
Telephone: 304-363-8800
Telecopier: 304-366-3783
Morgantown, West Virginia Office: 5000 Hampton Center, Suite 4.
Telephone: 304-598-0900.
Telecopier: 304-598-2712.

MEMBERS OF FIRM

Russell L. Furbee (1898-1978)
John D. Amos
Benjamin Hays Webb
Charles Vincent Critchfield
Alfred J. Lemley
Billy Atkins
Kenneth R. Miller
Stephen R. Brooks
William T. Holmes
Debra Hodges Scudiere (Resident at Morgantown Office)
Rebecca J. Zuleski
Tamara J. DeFazio

(See Next Column)

FURBEE, AMOS, WEBB & CRITCHFIELD, *Fairmont—Continued*

ASSOCIATE

Peter T. DeMasters

Attorneys for: Consolidation Coal Co.; Westinghouse Electric Co.; Monongahela Power Co.; Eastern Associated Coal Corp.; West Virginia Community Television Association; Continental Casualty Co.; State Farm Insurance Co.; Nationwide Insurance Co.

For full biographical listings, see the Martindale-Hubbell Law Directory

*MARTINSBURG,** Berkeley Co.

BOWLES RICE MCDAVID GRAFF & LOVE, PLLC (AV)

(Formerly Rice, Douglas & Shingleton)
105 West Burke Street, P.O. Drawer 1419, 25401
Telephone: 304-263-0836
Fax: 304-267-3822
Email: bowles@bowlesrice.com *URL:* http://www.bowlesrice.com
Charleston, West Virginia Office: 600 Quarrier Street, P.O. Box 1386.
Telephone: 304-347-1100.
Fax: 304-343-2867.
Fairmont, West Virginia Office: 1000 Technology Drive, Suite 2310.
Telephone: 304-368-4000.
Fax: 304-368-4040.
Morgantown, West Virginia Office: 7000 Hampton Center, Suite K.
Telephone: 304-599-1390.
Fax: 304-599-1308.
Parkersburg, West Virginia Office: 501 Avery Street, Fifth Floor, P.O. Box 49.
Telephone: 304-485-7973.
Fax: 304-485-7973.
Lexington, Kentucky Office: 1200 World Trade Center, 333 West Vine Street.
Telephone: 606-225-8700.
Fax: 606-225-8418.

MEMBERS OF FIRM

Lacy I. Rice (1901-1974)
J. Oakley Seibert (Resident)
Michael B. Keller (Resident)
Michael E. Caryl
Charles F. Printz, Jr. (Resident)
Michael D. Lorensen (Resident)
M. Shannon Brown (Resident)
Norwood Bentley (Resident)
Claudia W. Bentley (Resident)
David A. DeJarnett (Resident)
Curtis G. Power III (Resident)
Stephen McDowell Mathias

RESIDENT ASSOCIATES

Amy R. Lamp
Susan Mosser Caperton
Brian M. Peterson
Tracey A. Rohrbaugh

RESIDENT OF COUNSEL

Lacy I. Rice, Jr.

For full biographical listings, see the Martindale-Hubbell Law Directory

*MORGANTOWN,** Monongalia Co.

BOWLES RICE MCDAVID GRAFF & LOVE, PLLC (AV)

7000 Hampton Center, Suite K, 26505
Telephone: 304-599-1390
Fax: 304-599-1308
Email: bowles@bowlesrice.com *URL:* http://www.bowlesrice.com
Charleston, West Virginia Office: 600 Quarrier Street, P.O. Box 1386.
Telephone: 304-347-1100.
Fax: 304-343-2867.
Fairmont, West Virginia Office: 1000 Technology Drive, Suite 2310.
Telephone: 304-368-4000.
Fax: 304-368-4040.
Martinsburg, West Virginia Office: (Serves Berkeley Springs and Charles Town, West Virginia). 105 West Burke Street, P.O. Drawer 1419.
Telephone: 304-263-0836.
Fax: 304-267-3822.
Parkersburg, West Virginia Office: 501 Avery Street, Fifth Floor, P.O. Box 49.
Telephone: 304-485-8500.
Fax: 304-485-7973.
Lexington, Kentucky Office: 1200 World Trade Center, 333 West Vine Street.
Telephone: 606-225-8700.
Fax: 606-225-8418.

MEMBER OF FIRM

Robert W. Dinsmore
Kimberly S. Croyle

For full biographical listings, see the Martindale-Hubbell Law Directory

THE FUSCO LEGAL GROUP, L.C. (AV)

2400 Cranberry Square, 26505-9209
Telephone: 304-594-1000
Telecopier: 304-594-1181
URL: http://www.fuscolegalgroup.com
Email: fnlaw@wvlaw.com *URL:* http://www.wvlaw.com

Andrew G. Fusco

(See Next Column)

William J. Leon, Jr.
Steven M. Prunty
Jeffrey A. Ray

For full biographical listings, see the Martindale-Hubbell Law Directory

*PARKERSBURG,** Wood Co.

BOWLES RICE MCDAVID GRAFF & LOVE, PLLC (AV)

(Formerly Davis, Bailey, Pfalzgraf & Hall)
501 Avery Street, Fifth Floor, P.O. Box 49, 26102-0048
Telephone: 304-485-8500
Fax: 304-485-7973
Email: bowles@bowlesrice.com *URL:* http://www.bowlesrice.com
Charleston, West Virginia Office: 600 Quarrier Street, P.O. Box 1386.
Telephone: 304-347-1100.
Fax: 304-343-2867.
Fairmont, West Virginia Office: 1000 Technology Drive, Suite 2310.
Telephone: 304-368-4000.
Fax: 304-368-4040.
Martinsburg, West Virginia Office (Serves Berkeley Springs and Charles Town, West Virginia): 105 West Burke Street, P.O. Drawer 1419.
Telephone: 304-263-0836.
Fax: 304-267-3822.
Morgantown, West Virginia Office: 7000 Hampton Center, Suite K.
Telephone: 304-599-1390.
Fax: 304-599-1308.
Lexington, Kentucky Office: 1200 World Trade Center, 333 West Vine Street.
Telephone: 606-225-8700.
Fax: 606-225-8418.

MEMBERS OF FIRM

Howard E. Seufer, Jr. (Resident)
Robert J. Kent (Resident)
Steven R. Hardman (Resident)
Robert L. Bays (Resident)

RESIDENT ASSOCIATES

Ellen L. Medaglio
Kevin A. Rings
Charles E. McDonough

RESIDENT OF COUNSEL

John S. Bailey, Jr.

For full biographical listings, see the Martindale-Hubbell Law Directory

*PARSONS,** Tucker Co.

COOPER & PRESTON (AV)

333 Second Street, P.O. Box 365, 26287
Telephone: 304-478-4600
Fax: 304-478-4601

MEMBERS OF FIRM

John W. Cooper
Janet D. Preston

ASSOCIATE

Jodi K. Douglas

For full biographical listings, see the Martindale-Hubbell Law Directory

*PRINCETON,** Mercer Co.

GIBSON, LEFLER & ASSOCIATES (AV)

1345 Mercer Street, 24740
Telephone: 304-425-8276
800-742-3545

MEMBERS OF FIRM

Michael F. Gibson
Derrick W. Lefler

LEGAL SUPPORT PERSONNEL

NURSE PARALEGAL

Melody Lambert, RN-RLNC

SOCIAL SECURITY PARALEGAL

Nancy Belcher

PERSONAL INJURY PARALEGAL

Kathy Richards

WORKERS COMPENSATION PARALEGAL

Carol Hylton

MEDICAL NEGLIGENCE PARALEGAL

Deborah Frye

For full biographical listings, see the Martindale-Hubbell Law Directory

SANDERS, AUSTIN, SWOPE & FLANIGAN (AV)

Hunter Park, 320 Courthouse Road, 24740-2421
Telephone: 304-425-8125
FAX: 304-425-4155
Email: sasf@inetone.net

MEMBERS OF FIRM

Hartley Sanders (1879-1952)
Lane O. Austin
Derek C. Swope
William H. Sanders, III
William B. Flanigan
Gregory S. Prudich

(See Next Column)

SANDERS, AUSTIN, SWOPE & FLANIGAN—*Continued*

ASSOCIATES

S. Paige Burress
Omar J. Aboulhosn

OF COUNSEL

William H. Sanders, II

References: First Community Bank-Princeton; One Valley Bank-Princeton.

For full biographical listings, see the Martindale-Hubbell Law Directory

*WESTON,** Lewis Co.

WEBER & WEBER (AV)

208 Main Avenue, P.O. Box 270, 26452
Telephone: 304-269-2228
Fax: 304-269-7938
URL: http://www.lawyers.com/webercom

W. T. Weber, Jr.
W. T. Weber, III

LEGAL SUPPORT PERSONNEL

Greta Wade
Carla Kemper
Stephanie Frazier

Reference: The Citizens Bank Of Weston, Inc.

For full biographical listings, see the Martindale-Hubbell Law Directory

*WHEELING,** Ohio Co.

CASSIDY, MYERS, COGAN, VOEGELIN & TENNANT, L.C. (AV)

The First State Capitol, 1413 Eoff Street, 26003-3582
Telephone: 304-232-8100
Fax: 304-232-8200
St. Clairsville, Ohio Office: 126 E. Main Street.
Telephone: 740-695-1350.
Fax: 740-695-1356.

Frank A. O'Brien, Jr.
Patrick S. Cassidy
William C. Gallagher
Thomas M. Myers (Resident at St. Clairsville, Ohio, Office)
Timothy F. Cogan
Wray V. Voegelin
Donald James Tennant, Jr.
Thomas M. Cunningham

Representative Clients: United Steel Workers of America AFL, CIO, CLC; District 6 United Mine Workers of America; District 23 United Food and Commercial Workers; Local 1149 Laborers National Union of North America; West Virginia Education Association; International Union of Oil, Chemical & Atomic Workers; International Union of Electrical, Radio & Machine Workers; Local 83 United Association of Plumbers and Steamfitters; Local 549, International Association of Bridge, Structural and Ornamental Iron Workers of Wheeling, WV.

For full biographical listings, see the Martindale-Hubbell Law Directory

SCHRADER BYRD & COMPANION, PLLC (AV)

(A Professional Limited Liability Company)
The Maxwell Centre, 32-20th Street, Suite 500, P.O. Box 6336, 26003
Telephone: 304-233-3390
Fax: 304-233-2769
URL: http://www.schraderlaw.com
Martins Ferry, Ohio Office: 205 North Fifth Street, P.O. Box 309, 43935.
Telephone: 740-633-9976.
Fax: 740-633-0400.
Weirton, West Virginia Office: 3205 Pennsylvania Avenue, Suite 103, Penn Place, P.O. Box 2785, 26062.
Telephone: 304-723-2674.
Fax: 304-723-2876.

MEMBERS

Ray A. Byrd
James F. Companion
Frank X. Duff
Teresa Rieman-Camilletti
Yolonda G. Lambert
Daniel P. Fry (Resident Partner, Martins Ferry, Ohio Office)
James P. Mazzone (Resident Member, Weirton, West Virginia Office)
Sandra K. Law
D. Kevin Coleman

SPECIAL COUNSEL

Thomas B. Miller

ASSOCIATES

Denise D. Klug
Michael A. Adams
John Porco
Aimee Morgan Stern
Kimberly R. Wilson
Christopher J. Adams

OF COUNSEL

James A. Byrum, Jr.

General Counsel: Reynolds Memorial Hospital; WesBanco Bank-Elm Grove.
Representative Clients: American Cyanamid Company; Bank One; Matlack Systems, Inc.; Moutaineer Gas Co.; Ohio County Board of Education; PHICO Insurance Co.; Wheeling Hospital; Wheeling-Pittsburg Steel Corp.

For full biographical listings, see the Martindale-Hubbell Law Directory

WISCONSIN

*APPLETON,** Outagamie Co.

MCCANNA, KONZ, DUDAS, KEWLEY & PAPENDORF, S.C. (AV)

Forty Seven Park Place, P.O. Box 1857, 54913-1857
Telephone: 920-734-2825
Fax: 920-734-9770
Email: mkdlegal@aol.com

Michael R. McCanna
Michael P. Konz
David G. Dudas
Richard Kewley, Jr.
Jarrod J. Papendorf

Representative Clients: American States Insurance Co.; Auto Owners Insurance Co.; Custom Marine Engineering, Inc.; Economy Fire & Casualty Co.; C. R. Meyer & Sons Company; Northbrook Property & Casualty Co.; West Bend Mutual Insurance Co.; St. Paul Companies; National Union Fine Ins Co.

For full biographical listings, see the Martindale-Hubbell Law Directory

BROOKFIELD, Waukesha Co.

NELSON, DRIES, CONNELL & KRAMER, S.C. (AV)

150 North Sunnyslope Road, Suite 305, 53005
Telephone: 262-789-5880
Facsimile: 262-789-5888
Email: ndck@execpc.com

Christine K. Nelson
Craig W. Nelson
James J. Dries
Robert W. Connell
Mark S. Nelson
Mark R. Kramer
Christopher J. Conrad
Philip J. Tallmadge
Jennifer C. Tierney

For full biographical listings, see the Martindale-Hubbell Law Directory

*EAU CLAIRE,** Eau Claire Co.

WILCOX, WILCOX, ENRIGHT, HALLSTEIN, MCMAHON & ADLER, LLC (AV)

Limited Liability Company
1030 Regis Court, P.O. Box 128, 54701
Telephone: 715-832-6645
Fax: 715-832-8438
Email: willaw@win.bright.net

MEMBERS OF FIRM

Roy P. Wilcox (1873-1946)
Francis J. Wilcox
Roy S. Wilcox
Daniel A. Enright
John F. Wilcox
Howard G. McMahon
George W. Hallstein
Timothy J. Adler

Attorneys for: St. Paul Fire & Marine Insurance; Wisconsin Health Care Liability Insurance Health Plan; Allstate Insurance; Rural Insurance Co.; Farmers Insurance; Federated Insurance.

For full biographical listings, see the Martindale-Hubbell Law Directory

LAKE GENEVA, Walworth Co.

BRADEN & OLSON (AV)

716 Wisconsin Street, P.O. Box 940, 53147
Telephone: 414-248-6636
Fax: 414-248-2901
Email: bando@genevaonline.com

MEMBERS OF FIRM

Berwyn B. Braden
John O. Olson

ASSOCIATES

Christine Tomas
Daniel S. Draper

For full biographical listings, see the Martindale-Hubbell Law Directory

*MADISON,** Dane Co.

AXLEY BRYNELSON, LLP (AV)

(Formerly Brynelson, Herrick, Bucaida, Dorschel & Armstrong Including the former Easton & Assoc., S.C.)
2 East Mifflin Street, P.O. Box 1767, 53701-1767
Telephone: 608-257-5661
Fax: 608-257-5444
Email: law@axley.com *URL:* http://www.axley.com

MEMBERS OF FIRM

Bradley D. Armstrong
John H. Schmid, Jr.
Timothy D. Fenner
John C. Mitby
Daniel T. Hardy
John Walsh
Bruce L. Harms
David Easton
Curtis C. Swanson
Michael S. Anderson
Patricia M. Gibeault
Michael J. Westcott
Larry K. Libman
Richard E. Petershack
Steven A. Brezinski
Steven M. Streck

(See Next Column)

AXLEY BRYNELSON LLP, *Madison—Continued*

MEMBERS OF FIRM (Continued)

Joy L. O'Grosky
Edith F. Merila
Arthur E. Kurtz
Michael J. Modl

OF COUNSEL

Ralph E. Axley (1902-1995)
James C. Herrick
Floyd A. Brynelson (1914-1998)
Frank J. Bucaida
Griffin G. Dorschel

For Complete List of Firm Personnel, See General Section

For full biographical listings, see the Martindale-Hubbell Law Directory

COYNE, NIESS, SCHULTZ, BECKER & BAUER, S.C. (AV)

150 East Gilman Street Suite 1000, 53703
Telephone: 608-255-1388
Facsimile: 608-255-8592
Affiliate: Daar, Fisher, Kanaris & Vanek, P.C., 200 South Wacker Drive, Suite 3350.

SHAREHOLDERS

Richard G. Niess
Todd A. Becker
Bruce A. Schultz
William F. Bauer
Ronald S. Aplin

ASSOCIATES

Karen Gallagher
Laura N. Whipple
Amy F. Scholl
Jeremy L. Resar

OF COUNSEL

Frank M. Coyne
Eugene O. Gehl

Representative Clients: Alliant Energy; Allstate Insurance Co.; CNA Group of Insurance Companies; General Casualty Company of Wisconsin, Inc.; Grinnell Mutual Reinsurance Company; Heritage Insurance Co.; Kraft Foods, Inc.; Oscar Mayer Foods Corporation; Stoughton Trailers, Inc.; Eli Lilly & Company.

For full biographical listings, see the Martindale-Hubbell Law Directory

KAY & ANDERSEN, S.C. (AV)

One Point Place, Suite 201, 53719
Telephone: 608-833-0077
Fax: 608-833-3901
Email: KandA@execpc.com

Robert J. Kay
Randall J. Andersen

James N. Graham
Robert A. Mich, Jr.

For full biographical listings, see the Martindale-Hubbell Law Directory

LAWTON & CATES, S.C. (AV)

10 East Doty Street Suite 400, P.O. Box 2965, 53701-2965
Telephone: 608-282-6200
Fax: 608-282-6252
Email: lawcat@madison.tds.net *URL:* http://www.lawtoncates.com

John C. Carlson
James W. Gardner
James A. Olson
Kent I. Carnell

Reference: Bank One, Madison.

For full biographical listings, see the Martindale-Hubbell Law Directory

QUARLES & BRADY LLP (AV)

Firstar Plaza, One South Pinckney Street, P.O. Box 2113, 53701-2113
Telephone: 608-251-5000
Fax: 608-251-9166
URL: http://www.quarles.com
Milwaukee, Wisconsin Office: 411 East Wisconsin Avenue, 53202-4497.
Telephone: 414-277-5000.
Fax: 414-271-3552.
West Palm Beach, Florida Office: 222 Lakeview Avenue, 4th Floor, 33401.
Telephone: 561-653-5000.
Fax: 561-653-5333.
Naples, Florida Office: Barnett Center, 4501 Tamiami Trail North, Suite 300, 34103-3060.
Telephone: 941-262-5959.
Fax: 941-434-4999.
Phoenix, Arizona Office: One Camelback Building, One East Camelback Road, Suite 400, 85012-1649.
Telephone: 602-230-5500.
Fax: 602-230-5598.
Chicago, Illinois Office: Quarles & Brady LLC, Citicorp Center, 500 West Madison Street, Suite 3700.
Telephone: 312-715-5000.
Fax: 312-715-5155.

PARTNERS

Michael L. Zaleski
Waltraud A. Arts
James R. Cole
Donald K. Schott
Michael S. Weiden
Ralph V. Topinka
Roy L. Prange, Jr.
Jane F. Clokey
Fred Gants
Anthony A. Tomaselli

(See Next Column)

ASSOCIATES

Lauri D. Morris
Valerie L. Bailey-Rihn
Brian W. Blanchard
Sarah Edelman Coyne
Gregory T. Everts
Elizabeth A. Hartman
David M. Kettner

For Complete List of Firm Personnel, See General Section

For full biographical listings, see the Martindale-Hubbell Law Directory

*MILWAUKEE,** Milwaukee Co.

EHLINGER & KRILL, S.C. (AV)

316 North Milwaukee Street, Suite 410, 53202-5803
Telephone: 414-272-8085
Facsimile: 414-272-8290
Email: ehlinger@execpc.com

Ralph J. Ehlinger
R. Jeffrey Krill

For full biographical listings, see the Martindale-Hubbell Law Directory

KERSTEN & MCKINNON, S.C. (AV)

231 West Wisconsin Avenue, Suite 1200, 53203
Telephone: 414-271-0054
Fax: 414-271-7131
Email: Kersten3@ExecPc.com

Charles J. Kersten (1929-1972)
George P. Kersten
Arlo McKinnon (1929-1999)
Kenan J. Kersten
J. P. McKinnon (1943-1973)
Leslie Van Buskirk
E. Campion Kersten
Matthew T. Fricker

For full biographical listings, see the Martindale-Hubbell Law Directory

KOHNER, MANN & KAILAS, S.C. (AV)

1572 East Capitol Drive, P.O. Box 11982, 53211-0982
Telephone: 414-962-5110
Fax: 414-962-8725
Email: kmksc@execpc.com

Marvin L. Kohner (1908-1975)

OF COUNSEL

Robert L. Mann

MEMBERS OF FIRM

Steve Kailas
Roy Paul Roth
Mark R. Wolters
Gary P. Lantzy
Jordan B. Reich
Christopher C. Kailas
David S. Chartier
Matthew P. Gerdisch

Robert E. Nailen
David M. Henry
Darrell R. Zall
Lorinne J Cunningham
Daniel J. Flynn
Palma M. Forte
Timothy L. Zuberbier
Daniel J. Emma

Representative Clients: Ecolab, Inc.; Manpower, Inc.; Abbott Laboratories; Norwest Bank Wisconsin, N.A.; Firstar Bank Corporation; Sysco Food Services; Johnson Controls, Inc.; Worth Inc.; Rayovac, Inc.; York International Corporation.

For full biographical listings, see the Martindale-Hubbell Law Directory

LEIB & KATT, S.C. (AV)

Suite 600, 740 N. Plankinton Avenue, 53203
Telephone: 414-276-8816
Fax: 414-276-8819
Email: leibkatt@liebkatt.com

Samuel J. Leib
Cecilia M. McCormack
William J. Katt
Rebecca E. Cline
Kevin A. Christensen
Ava M. Bortin
Douglas S. Knott
Rosalie Leib

For full biographical listings, see the Martindale-Hubbell Law Directory

MURPHY, GILLICK, WICHT & PRACHTHAUSER (AV)

Suite 1200, 330 East Kilbourn Avenue, 53202
Telephone: 414-271-1011
Milwaukee: 800-942-2880
Fax: 414-271-9987
Email: mail@murphygillick.com *URL:* http://www.murphygillick.com
South Office: State Financial Bank Building, 4811 South 76th Street.
Telephone: 414-281-5700.
North Office: M&I Bank Building, 9001 North 76th Street.
Telephone: 414-354-5051.
Brookfield, Wisconsin Office: Brookfield Lakes Corporate Center, Suite 260, 300 North Corporate Drive (180th Street and Blue Mound Road).
Telephone: 414-792-0888.
Racine, Wisconsin Office: 4701 Washington Avenue.
Telephone: 414-635-8967.
Mequon, Wisconsin Office: 1496 West Mequon Road.
Telephone: 414-240-1138.

(See Next Column)

MURPHY, GILLICK, WICHT & PRACHTHAUSER—*Continued*

MEMBERS OF FIRM

Lawrence D. Gillick (1914-1984)
James J. Murphy
Michael H. Gillick
Dennis H. Wicht
Don C. Prachthauser
George F. Graf (Resident, Brookfield and Racine Offices)
Patrick J. Gillick
Melita M. Biese
Kevin J. Kukor

ASSOCIATES

Keith R. Stachowiak
Thadd J. Llaurado
Mark D. Baus
Sandra K. Graf
Frank T. Pasternak
Charles J. Graf

OF COUNSEL

M. Josef Zimmermann

For full biographical listings, see the Martindale-Hubbell Law Directory

QUARLES & BRADY LLP (AV)

411 East Wisconsin Avenue, 53202-4497
Telephone: 414-277-5000
Fax: 414-271-3552
URL: http://www.quarles.com
Madison, Wisconsin Office: Firstar Plaza, One South Pinckney Street, P.O. Box 2113, 53701-2113.
Telephone: 608-251-5000.
Fax: 608-251-9166.
West Palm Beach, Florida Office: 222 Lakeview Avenue, 4th Floor, 33401.
Telephone: 561-653-5000.
Fax: 561-653-5333.
Naples, Florida Office: Barnett Center, 4501 Tamiami Trail North, Suite 300, 34103-3060.
Telephone: 941-262-5959.
Fax: 941-434-4999.
Phoenix, Arizona Office: One Camelback Building, One East Camelback Road, Suite 400, 85012-1649.
Telephone: 602-230-5500.
Fax: 602-230-5598.
Chicago, Illinois Office: Quarles & Brady LLC, Citicorp Center, 500 West Madison Street, Suite 3700.
Telephone: 312-715-5000.
Fax: 312-715-5155.

MEMBERS OF FIRM
(ALPHABETICALLY BY YEAR OF ADMISSION TO BAR)

Richard C. Ninneman
Samuel J. Recht
Michael J. Spector
George K. Whyte, Jr.
Michael L. Zaleski (Resident, Madison Office)
Wayne E. Babler, Jr.
W. Stuart Parsons
Frank J. Daily
Charles W. Herf (Resident, Phoenix, Arizona Office)
David E. Jarvis
Larry J. Martin
James R. Cole (Resident, Madison Office)
Ronald L. Wallenfang
Michael S. Weiden (Resident, Madison Office)
John A. Casey
Peter C. Karegeannes
William M. Shattuck (Resident, Phoenix, Arizona Office)
James H. Baxter III
Quinn W. Martin
Michael J. McGovern
Robert L. Titley
James D. Vieregg (Resident, Phoenix, Arizona Office)
Thomas Armstrong
Matthew J. Flynn
Roy L. Prange, Jr. (Resident, Madison Office)
Michael H. Schaalman
Patrick W. Schmidt
Fred Gants (Resident, Madison Office)
Mary Pat Ninneman
Eric J. Van Vugt
Patricia K. Ballman
Michael S. McCauley
David B. Kern
Ely A. Leichtling
Jeffrey Morris
John A. Rothstein
William H. Harbeck
Donald K. Schott (Resident, Madison Office)
Ralph V. Topinka (Resident, Madison Office)
David B. Bartel
David R. Cross
Michael J. Gonring
John D. Franzini
Nancy K. Peterson
Robert H. Duffy
Mark A. Kircher
Daniel E. Conley
Francis H. LoCoco
Jeffrey O. Davis
Benjamin R. Norris (Resident, Phoenix, Arizona Office)
Jennifer V. Powers
Nancy Berz Colman (Resident, West Palm Beach, Florida Office)
Anthony A. Tomaselli (Resident, Madison Office)
Margaret C. Kelsey
Colleen A. Scherkenbach (Resident, Phoenix, Arizona Office)
Jeffrey K. Spoerk

OF COUNSEL

Laurence C. Hammond, Jr.

ASSOCIATES

Michael G. Galloway (Resident, Phoenix, Arizona Office)
Carmella A. Huser
Valerie L. Bailey-Rihn (Resident, Madison Office)
Mitchell S. Moser
Mark Hubert Muller (Resident, Naples, Florida Office)
Sean D. Garrison (Resident, Phoenix, Arizona Office)
Nora M. Platt
Pamela M. Ploor
Sarah Edelman Coyne (Resident, Madison, Wisconsin Office)

(See Next Column)

For Complete List of Firm Personnel, See General Section

For full biographical listings, see the Martindale-Hubbell Law Directory

*OSHKOSH,** Winnebago Co.

CURTIS LAW OFFICE (AV)

2905 Universal Street, P.O. Box 2845, 54903-2845
Telephone: 920-233-1010
Fax: 920-233-8053
Email: osowski@execpc.com

George W. Curtis

Scott C. Woldt
Beth Driscoll Osowski

Reference: M & I Bank.

For full biographical listings, see the Martindale-Hubbell Law Directory

*RACINE,** Racine Co.

JEFFREY LEAVELL, S.C. (AV)

723 South Main Street, 53403
Telephone: 414-633-7322
Fax: 414-633-7323
Email: 102661.3312@compuserve.com

Jeffrey L. Leavell

ASSOCIATES

Michael R. Vescio
Christine M. Genthner

For full biographical listings, see the Martindale-Hubbell Law Directory

*RHINELANDER,** Oneida Co.

ECKERT KOST & VOCKE (AV)

1285 Lincoln Street, P.O. Box 1247, 54501-1247
Telephone: 715-369-1624
FAX: 715-369-1273
Email: ecklaw@newnorth.net *URL:* http://www.ecklaw.com

Michael L. Eckert
Keith K. Kost
Timothy L. Vocke
Mitchell R. Olson

Reference: M & I Merchants Bank.

For full biographical listings, see the Martindale-Hubbell Law Directory

*WAUSAU,** Marathon Co.

KELLEY, WEBER, PIETZ & SLATER, S.C. (AV)

530 Jackson Street, 54403-5589
Telephone: 715-845-9211; New York Tie Line: 212-690-7830
FAX: 715-842-9317
Email: kwpslaw@kwpslaw.com

Richard J. Weber
Colin D. Pietz
Jerry W. Slater
Shane J. VanderWaal
Patrick H. Finlan

Peter C. Gunther

OF COUNSEL

John W. Kelley

Representative Client: Associated Bank North, Wausau.
Reference: Associated Bank North, Wausau.

For full biographical listings, see the Martindale-Hubbell Law Directory

WYOMING

*CASPER,** Natrona Co.

BROWN, DREW & MASSEY, LLP (AV)

Casper Business Center, Suite 800, 123 West First Street, 82601-2486
Telephone: 307-234-1000
800-877-6755
Telefax: 307-265-8025
Email: brwndrew@coffey.com

MEMBERS OF FIRM

Morris R. Massey
Harry B. Durham, III
Donn J. McCall
Thomas F. Reese
J. Kenneth Barbe
Jeffrey C. Brinkerhoff
Rex O. Arney
P. Jaye Rippley
Courtney Robert Kepler

ASSOCIATES

Scott P. Klosterman
Timothy M. Stubson

(See Next Column)

BROWN, DREW & MASSEY LLP, *Casper—Continued*

OF COUNSEL

B. J. Baker
Hampton K. O'Neill

Attorneys for: Norwest Bank Wyoming, N.A.; Aetna Casualty & Surety Co.; Commercial Union Insurance Co.; The Doctor's Co.; MEDMARC; Westech, Inc.; Chevron USA; Enron Group of Energy Companies; North American Resources Co.

For Complete List of Firm Personnel, See General Section

For full biographical listings, see the Martindale-Hubbell Law Directory

DALLAS J. LAIRD (AV)

The Ormsby Mansion, 536 South Center Street, 82601
Telephone: 307-265-6352
Fax: 307-237-1570
Email: mary825@aol.com

For full biographical listings, see the Martindale-Hubbell Law Directory

WILLIAMS, PORTER, DAY & NEVILLE, P.C. (AV)

159 North Wolcott Street Suite 400, P.O. Box 10700, 82602
Telephone: 307-265-0700
Fax: 307-266-2306
Email: wpdn@trib.com

Houston G. Williams
Richard E. Day
Frank D. Neville
Barry G. Williams
Patrick J. Murphy
Stuart R. Day
Ann M. Rochelle
Mark L. Carman
Stephenson D. Emery
Scott E. Ortiz
Margo Harlan Sabec
Scott W. Skavdahl
Kevin D. Huber
Susan Chapin Stubson

Representative Clients: True Industries; PacifiCorp; Amoco Oil Co.; Conoco, Inc.; Marathon Oil Co.; Mobil Exploration and Production; Phillips Petroleum Co.; Casper College; Wyoming Medical Center; First American Title Insurance Company.

For full biographical listings, see the Martindale-Hubbell Law Directory

*CHEYENNE,** Laramie Co.

BAILEY & STOCK (AV)

221 East 21st Street, P.O. Box 1557, 82001
Telephone: 307-638-7745
Fax: 307-638-7749
URL: http://www.lawyers.com/b&slaw

MEMBERS OF FIRM

Henry F. Bailey, Jr.
Wallace L. Stock

For full biographical listings, see the Martindale-Hubbell Law Directory

THE FITZGERALD LAW FIRM (AV)

A Partnership of Professional Corporations
2108 Warren Avenue, 82001-3740
Telephone: 307-634-4000
Telecopier: 307-635-2391
Email: lawyers@fitzgeraldlaw.com *URL:* http://www.fitzgeraldlaw.com

MEMBERS OF FIRM

James E. Fitzgerald (P.C.)
Sharon A. Fitzgerald (P.C.)

OF COUNSEL

A. G. McClintock

For full biographical listings, see the Martindale-Hubbell Law Directory

HICKEY, MACKEY, EVANS & WALKER (AV)

1800 Carey Avenue, Suite 700, P.O. Drawer 467, 82003
Telephone: 307-634-1525
Telecopier: 307-638-7335
URL: http://www.hickeymackey.com

MEMBERS OF FIRM

Paul J. Hickey
Terry W. Mackey
David F. Evans
John M. Walker
Roger C. Fransen
Richard D. Tim Bush
Mary A. Throne

A List of Representative Clients will be furnished upon request.
Reference: Norwest Bank, Cheyenne, N.A.

For full biographical listings, see the Martindale-Hubbell Law Directory

HIRST & APPLEGATE, A PROFESSIONAL CORPORATION (AV)

1720 Carey Avenue, Suite 200, P.O. Box 1083, 82003-1083
Telephone: 307-632-0541
Telefax: 307-632-4999
Email: attorneys@hirstapplegate.com *URL:* http://hirstapplegate.com

(See Next Column)

James L. Applegate
Thomas G. Gorman
Thomas A. Nicholas III
Gary R. Scott
John J. Metzke
Dale W. Cottam

Richard A. Mincer
Misha E. Westby
Boyd M. McMaster
Ryan T. Schelhaas

Representative Clients: American Insurance Group; ARCO; Ford Motor Company; Scottsdale Insurance Co.; The Doctors Company; Copley Pharmaceutical, Inc.; Royal Insurance Co.; Wyoming Stock Growers Assn.; General Motors Corp.; Fassett-Nickel, Inc.
Reference: Norwest Bank Wyoming Cheyenne, N.A.

For full biographical listings, see the Martindale-Hubbell Law Directory

LATHROP & RUTLEDGE, A PROFESSIONAL CORPORATION (AV)

Suite 500 City Center Building, 1920 Thomes Avenue, P.O. Box 4068, 82003-4068
Telephone: 307-632-0554
Telecopier: 307-635-4502
Email: mail@lathropandrutledge.com

Carl L. Lathrop
J. Kent Rutledge
Corinne E. Rutledge
James T. Dinneen

Lou Piccioni
Scott W. Meier
Kevin C. Cook

General Counsel for: Laramie County School District No. 2; Cheyenne Newspapers, Inc.; Wyoming Hospital Assn.; Cheyenne Medical Specialists, P.C.; Emergency Medical Physicians.
Insurance Clients: The Doctor's Company; CUMIS Insurance Society; Gainsco, Inc.; The St. Paul Companies; Infinity Insurance Co.

For full biographical listings, see the Martindale-Hubbell Law Directory

SUNDAHL, POWERS, KAPP & MARTIN, L.L.C. (AV)

1725 Carey Avenue, P.O. Box 328, 82001
Telephone: 307-632-6421
Fax: 307-632-7216
Email: atty@spkm.org

MEMBERS OF FIRM

John Alan Sundahl
George E. Powers, Jr.
Paul Kapp
Raymond W. Martin

ASSOCIATES

John A. Coppede
Kay Lynn Bestol
Deborah G. M. Kellam
Brian J. Hanify

A list of Representative Clients will be furnished upon request.

For full biographical listings, see the Martindale-Hubbell Law Directory

*JACKSON,** Teton Co.

KING AND KING, L.L.C. (AV)

Suite 201 Centennial Building, 610 West Broadway, P.O. Box 40, 83001
Telephone: 307-733-2904
Fax: 307-733-1058
Email: kinglaw@blissnet.com *URL:* http://www.lawyers.com/kingandking

Floyd R. King
Bret F. King

Kyra Knapp

Reference: Community First Bank, Jackson, Wyoming.

For full biographical listings, see the Martindale-Hubbell Law Directory

SPENCE, MORIARITY & SCHUSTER, LLC (AV)

15 South Jackson Street, P.O. Box 548, 83001
Telephone: 307-733-7290
Fax: 307-733-5248
Salt Lake City, Utah Office: 39 Exchange Place, Suite 101, 84111.
Telephone: 801-521-0811.
Fax: 801-521-0437.

MEMBERS OF FIRM

Gerry L. Spence, P.C.
Edward P. Moriarity
Robert P. Schuster
Gary L. Shockey
J. Douglas McCalla
Roy A. Jacobson, Jr.
Kent W. Spence
Robert A. Krause

ASSOCIATES

Glen G. Debroder
R. Daniel Fleck
G. Bryan Ulmer, III
Laura N. MacPherson (Not admitted in WY)
David M. Gosar
Gerard R. Bosch
Jeffrey Gooch

Reference: First Interstate Bank, Casper, Wyoming.

For full biographical listings, see the Martindale-Hubbell Law Directory

ROCK SPRINGS, Sweetwater Co.

BUSSART, WEST, ROSSETTI, PIAIA & TYLER, P.C. (AV)

Suite A, 409 Broadway, P.O. Box 1020, 82902-1020
Telephone: 307-362-3300; 307-875-4080
Telecopier: 307-362-3309

Ford T. Bussart
L. Galen West
John D. Rossetti
Marvin L. Tyler
David M. Piaia

Representative Clients: Memorial Hospital of Sweetwater Co.; Horace Mann Insurance; American Hardware Insurance; Lancer Claims; The Home Insurance; Black Butte Coal Co.; Bridger Coal Co.; Castle Rock Hospital District; City of Green River, Wyoming; State Farm Insurance.

For full biographical listings, see the Martindale-Hubbell Law Directory

*SHERIDAN,** Sheridan Co.

DAVIS & CANNON (AV)

Formerly Burgess, Davis & Cannon
40 South Main Street, P.O. Box 728, 82801
Telephone: 307-672-7491
Fax: 307-672-8955
Cheyenne, Wyoming Office: 2710 Thomes Avenue, P.O. Box 43, 82003.
Telephone: 307-634-3210.
Fax: 307-778-7118.

MEMBERS OF FIRM

Henry A. Burgess (deceased, 1918-1995)
Richard M. Davis, Jr.
Kim D. Cannon
Hayden F. Heaphy, Jr.
Anthony T. Wendtland
Kate M. Fox
John C. McKinley
Nancy D. Freudenthal

ASSOCIATES

Kathleen G. Healy
Debra J. Wendtland

Representative Clients: Consol, Inc.; Hesston Corp.; Mutual of New York; Peter Kiewit Sons, Inc.; Life Care Centers of America, Inc.; Montana-Dakota Utilities Co.; First Interstate Bank of Commerce (Sheridan and Gillette); Memorial Hospital of Sheridan County; Philip Morris, Inc.; American Home Products, Inc. (Pondimin and Redux litigation).

For full biographical listings, see the Martindale-Hubbell Law Directory

PUERTO RICO

SAN JUAN, San Juan Dist.

DEL TORO & SANTANA

Plaza Scotiabank, 6th Floor, 273 Ponce de Leon Avenue, 00917-1902
Telephone: 787-754-8700
Telecopier: 787-756-6677
Email: robsant@coqui.net
Email: russell@prtc.net

MEMBERS OF FIRM

Russell A. Del Toro
Roberto Santana Aparicio

ASSOCIATES

Giancarlo Font
Camelia Fernandez Romeu
Marisol Vega Couto
Miriam Waleska Sanchez-Arroyo

For full biographical listings, see the Martindale-Hubbell Law Directory

FIDDLER GONZÁLEZ & RODRÍGUEZ, LLP

254 Muñoz Rivera Avenue (Hato Rey), P.O. Box 363507, 00936-3507
Telephone: 787-753-3113
Telecopier: 787-759-3123
Email: fiddler@fgrlaw.com *URL:* http://www.fgrlaw.com

MEMBERS OF FIRM

Rafael R. Vizcarrondo
Salvador Antonetti-Zequeira
Diego A. Ramos
Ricardo F. Casellas

Representative Clients: The Chase Manhattan Bank, N.A.; General Motors Corp.; Pfizer, Inc.; Merck & Co., Inc.; Bacardi Corp.; U.S. Aviation Insurance Group.

For Complete List of Firm Personnel, See General Section

For full biographical listings, see the Martindale-Hubbell Law Directory

GOLDMAN ANTONETTI & CÓRDOVA

American International Plaza Fourteenth & Fifteenth Floors, 250 Muñoz Rivera Avenue (Hato Rey), P.O. Box 70364, 00936-0364
Telephone: 787-759-8000
Telecopiers: 787-767-9333 (Main)
787-767-9177 (Litigation Department)
787-767-8660 (Labor & Corporate Law Departments)
787-767-9325 (Tax & Environmental Law Departments)
URL: http://www.gaclaw.com

(See Next Column)

MEMBERS OF FIRM

Edgar Cartagena-Santiago
Ramón E. Dapena
Jorge L. Martinez
Carlos A. Rodríguez-Vidal
Jorge Segurola
Edgardo Colón Arrarás
Jesús E. Cuza

OF COUNSEL

Fernando Castro

ASSOCIATES

Mildred Cabán
Wilda Rodriguez Plaza
Ina M. Berlingeri Vincenty
Joanna Bocanegra Ocasio
Veronica Olivieri-Barreto
Edna E. Perez-Roman
Michelle Feria-Cestero
Lizzie M. Padro
Rosalie Irizarry-Silvestrini

Representative Clients: American Airlines Employees Credit Union; Oliver & Company; New England Life Insurance Co.; United Healthcare Corp.; Xerox Corp.; McDonald's Corporation; Metropolitan Life Insurance Company.

For Complete List of Firm Personnel, See General Section

For full biographical listings, see the Martindale-Hubbell Law Directory

INDIANO, WILLIAMS & WEINSTEIN-BACAL

Hato Rey Tower, 21st Floor, 268 Muñoz Rivera Avenue (Hato Rey), 00918
Telephone: 787-754-2323; 763-0485
Fax: 787-766-3366
Email: iww@microjuris.com

MEMBERS OF FIRM

Stuart A. Weinstein-Bacal
David C. Indiano
Jeffrey M. Williams

ASSOCIATES

Peter W. Miller
Edgar A. Lee-Navas
Edward W. Hill Tollinche
Alexander H. Bopp (Not admitted in PR)

For full biographical listings, see the Martindale-Hubbell Law Directory

JIMÉNEZ, GRAFFAM & LAUSELL

Suite 505, Midtown Building, 421 Muñoz Rivera Avenue, Hato Rey, P.O. Box 366104, 00936-6104
Telephone: 787-767-1030; 767-1000; 767-1061; 767-1064
Telefax: 787-751-4068;
Cable: "Nezte"
RCA Telex: 325-2730
Email: manager@jgl.com *URL:* http://www.jgl.com

MEMBERS OF FIRM

William A. Graffam
Steven C. Lausell
J. Ramón Rivera-Morales
José Juan Torres-Escalera
Raquel M. Dulzaides
Manolo T. Rodríguez-Bird

ASSOCIATES

Patricia A. Garrity
Isabel J. Vélez-Serrano
Edgardo A. Vega-López
José Luis Suárez-Villafañe
Jorge F. Blasini
Ruy V. Díaz-Díaz
Rafael A. Rosado-Marrero

Representative Clients: Sea-Land Service, Inc.; McAllister Brothers, Inc.; Crowley Maritime Corp.; Puerto Rico Sun Oil; General Motors Overseas Distribution Corp.; Bristol Myers Squibb Co.; The United Kingdom Steamship P & I Association; The Britannia Steamship Insurance Association.

For Complete List of Firm Personnel, See General Section

For full biographical listings, see the Martindale-Hubbell Law Directory

JORGE R. JIMENEZ LAW OFFICES

Suite 807 IBM Building, 654 Muñoz Rivera Avenue (Hato Rey), 00918
Telephone: 787-763-0106
Fax: 787-763-0574

MEMBERS OF FIRM

Jorge R. Jimenez
Juan F. Doval

For full biographical listings, see the Martindale-Hubbell Law Directory

MARTÍNEZ ODELL & CALABRIA

Banco Popular Center, 209 Muñoz Rivera Avenue, Suite 1600 (Hato Rey), P.O. Box 190998, 00919-0998
Telephone: 787-753-8914
Facsimile: 787-753-8402; 787-759-9075; 787-764-5664
Email: postmaster@mocpr.com

MEMBERS OF FIRM

Francisco M. Ramirez-Rivera
Luis E. Lopez Correa
Patrick D. O'Neill
Graciela J. Belaval
Anabelle Rodriguez-Rodriguez
Fernando A. Pérez-Colon
Alberto Rodríguez-Ramos
Roberto E. Vega Pacheco
Francisco L. Acevedo-Nogueras
Carlos Berreteaga
Maria del Carmen Garriga
Eric Perez Ochoa
Ramón Eugenio-Meléndez
Rafael Kodesh-Baragaño
Manuel E. Lopez-Fernandez
Ivonne Palerm-Cruz
Jose G. Fagot-Diaz
Jose David Medina-Rivera

(See Next Column)

MARTÍNEZ ODELL & CALABRIA, *San Juan—Continued*

OF COUNSEL

Jose B. Diaz Asencio
Dominic T. Longo
Francisco Orsini-Capo

ASSOCIATES

Amelia Fortuño-Ruiz
Fernando J. Gierbolini-Gonzalez
Charles P. Gilmore
Dora L. Monserrate-Peñagaricano
Carmen T. Ubarri-Nevares
Jaime L. Vazquez-Bernier
Jennifer Odell-Gonzalez
Mariela Garcia-Colberg
Juan A. Frau-Escudero
Jose Luis Baez-Rivera
Julio D. Vazquez-Rodriguez
Mildred L. Santana-Mejias
Jose Carlos Diaz-Vega
Jose G. Diaz-Tejera
Roxana M. Viera-Canales

Representative Clients: Banco Popular de Puerto Rico; Daewoo Motor Corporation; Eckerd Corporation; Empresas Fonalledas; Hilton International; L'Aire Liquide, S.A.; Loctile Corporation; Lucent Technologies; Lutron Electronics Co., Inc.; Waste Management, Inc.

For Complete List of Firm Personnel, See General Section

For full biographical listings, see the Martindale-Hubbell Law Directory

VIRGIN ISLANDS

*CHRISTIANSTED, ST. CROIX,** St. Croix

ALKON, RHEA & HART (AV)

2115 Queen Street, 00820
Telephone: 340-773-3305
Fax: 340-773-4491
URL: http://www.lawyers.com/ar&hlaw

Gordon C. Rhea
Thomas H. Hart, III

ASSOCIATES

Maxwell D. McIntosh
James A. Meaney

OF COUNSEL

Thomas Alkon

For full biographical listings, see the Martindale-Hubbell Law Directory

R. ERIC MOORE (AV)

2108 Company Street, P.O. Box 3086, 00822
Telephone: 340-773-4150
Fax: 340-778-7168
Email: rericmoore@worldnet.att.net

ASSOCIATES

Edgar A. Christensen
Ivan A. Guzman
Odis Simpson Mingus, II
Franklin G. Quow

For full biographical listings, see the Martindale-Hubbell Law Directory

*CHARLOTTE AMALIE, ST. THOMAS,** St. Thomas

GRUNERT STOUT & BRUCH

24-25 Kongensgade, P.O. Box 1030, 00804
Telephone: 340-774-1320
Fax: 340-774-7839
Email: gsbusvi@viaccess.net
Affiliated with: Solomon Pearl Blum & Quinn LLP, New York, New York and Denver, Colorado.

MEMBERS OF FIRM

John E. Stout
Susan Bruch Moorehead

ASSOCIATE

Gabriel J. Villegas

OF COUNSEL

William L. Blum

For full biographical listings, see the Martindale-Hubbell Law Directory

CANADA
ALBERTA

*CALGARY,** Calgary Jud. Dist.

BENNETT JONES (AV)

4500 Bankers Hall East, 855-2nd Street S.W., T2P 4K7
Telephone: 403-298-3100
Facsimile: 403-265-7219
Email: firmwatch@bennettjones.ca *URL:* http://www.bennettjones.ca
Edmonton, Alberta Office: 1000, 10035-105 Street.
Telephone: 780-421-8133.
Facsimile: 780-421-7951.

(See Next Column)

Toronto, Ontario Office: 3400 1 First Canadian Place, P.O. Box 130.
Telephone: 416-863-1200.
Facsimile: 416-863-1716.

MEMBER OF FIRM

John F. Cordeau

For Complete List of Firm Personnel, See General Section

For full biographical listings, see the Martindale-Hubbell Law Directory

MCLENNAN ROSS (AV)

1801 Altius Centre, 500 - 4th Avenue S.W., T2P 2V6
Telephone: 403-543-9120
Fax: 403-543-9150
Email: calgary@mross.com *URL:* http://www.mross.com
Edmonton, Alberta Office: 600 West Chambers, 12220 Stony Plain Road.
Telephone: 780-482-9200.
Fax: 780-482-9100; 780-482-9101; 780-482-9102. Email: edmonton@mross.com
Yellowknife, Northwest Territories Office: 802 Precambrian Building, 4920-52nd Street, X1A 3T1.
Telephone: 867-873-5968.
Fax: 867-873-5972

Philip G. Ponting, Q.C.
Joel S. Shortt
Laurie M. Ziola
Donald W. Dear
Damon S. Bailey
Thomas W. R. Ross

For full biographical listings, see the Martindale-Hubbell Law Directory

PARLEE MCLAWS (AV)

3400 Petro-Canada Centre, 150 - 6th Avenue, SW, T2P 3Y7
Telephone: 403-294-7000
Telecopier: 403-265-8263
Email: lawyers@parlee.com *URL:* http://www.parlee.com
Edmonton, Alberta Office: 15th Floor Manulife Place, 10180 101st Street.
Telephone: 403-423-8500.
Telecopier: 403-423-2870.

MEMBERS OF FIRM

Everett L. Bunnell, Q.C.
Patrick J. McGovern
Bruce Churchill-Smith
G. Scott Watson
Nancy M. Carruthers

ASSOCIATES

Donald A. Young
Alec N. Silenzi
Peter W. Cline
Kathryn Trenerry-Harker
Brenda M. Tsukishima
Morey D. Sair
H. David McLellan
Jon W. Arnott

For Complete List of Firm Personnel, See General Section

For full biographical listings, see the Martindale-Hubbell Law Directory

*EDMONTON,** Edmonton Jud. Dist.

EMERY JAMIESON (AV)

1700 Oxford Tower, 10235 - 101 Street, T5J 3G1
Telephone: 780-426-5220
Fax: 780-420-6277
Email: general@emeryjamieson.com *URL:* http://www.emeryjamieson.com
Calgary, Alberta Office: 206 Kensington House, 1167 Kensington Crescent, N.W., T2N 1X7.
Telephone: 403-543-6010.
Fax: 403-270-8080. E-mail: ejcalg@emeryjamieson.com

MEMBERS OF FIRM

Howard T. Emery, Q.C. (1899-1990)
John H. Jamieson, Q.C. (Retired)
Sydney A. Bercov, Q.C.
Henry B. Martin, Q.C.
Richard B. Drewry
W. Paul Sharek, Q.C.
Robert W. Thompson
Phyllis A. Smith, Q.C.
Gordon D. Sustrik
Shirley A. McNeilly
Michael J. Penny
G. Bruce Comba
Rex M. Nielsen
Donna Carson Read
Susan L. Bercov
Bruce F. Hughson
Murray F. Tait
Robert D. McDonald
Jeffrey K. Friesen
Blair E. Maxston
Frederica L. Schutz
Janet N. Alexander-Smith
Claire M. Klassen
Earl J. Evaniew

ASSOCIATES

Regina M. Corrigan (Resident, Calgary Office)
Stuart J. Weatherill
Scott H. Chen
Michael D. Cooper (Resident at Calgary Office)
Patrick G. Nugent
Heidi K. Robinson
Christopher R. Ontkean

Reference: Canadian Imperial Bank of Commerce.

For full biographical listings, see the Martindale-Hubbell Law Directory

Edmonton—Continued

LUCAS BOWKER & WHITE (AV)

Scotia 2 Tower - Scotia Place, 1201-10060 Jasper Avenue, T5J 4E5
Telephone: 780-426-5330
Fax: 780-428-1066
Email: Lucas@lbw.ab.ca *URL:* http://www.lbw.ab.ca
Calgary, Alberta Office: Suite 3800, Bankers Hall, 855 2nd Street S.W., T2P 4J8.
Telephone: 403-218-1795.
Fax: 403-264-2993. Email: Lucas@lbw.ab.ca. URL: http://www.lbw.ab.ca

MEMBERS OF FIRM

George E. Bowker, Q.C.
Robert B. White, Q.C.
Norman J. Pollock, Q.C.
Robert C. Dunseith
Kent H. Davidson
Alan R. Gray
David J. Stam
Donald J. Wilson

Reference: Canadian Imperial Bank of Commerce.

For Complete List of Firm Personnel, See General Section

For full biographical listings, see the Martindale-Hubbell Law Directory

MCLENNAN ROSS (AV)

A Partnership including Professional Corporations
600 West Chambers, 12220 Stony Plain Road, T5N 3Y4
Telephone: 780-482-9200
Fax: 780-482-9100; 780-482-9101; 780-482-9102
Email: edmonton@mross.com *URL:* http://www.mross.com
Calgary, Alberta Office: 1801 Altius Centre, 500 - 4th Avenue S.W, T2P 2V6.
Telephone: 403-543-9120.
Fax: 403-543-9150. Email: calgary@mross.com
Yellowknife, Northwest Territory Office: 802 Precambrian Building, 4920-52nd Street, X1A 3T1.
Telephone: 867-873-5968.
Fax: 867-873-5972

Roderick A. McLennan, Q.C. *
David J. Ross, Q.C.
Peter P. Taschuk, Q.C.
Havelock B. Madill, Q.C.
Darren B. Becker, Q.C. *
Frederick A. Day, Q.C. *
Hugh J. D. McPhail
Charles P. Russell *
Karen A. Platten
Jonathan P. Rossall *
Graham McLennan
Glenn D. Tait
William S. Rosser *
Yolanda S. Van Wachem
Ronald M. Kruhlak
Michelle G. Crighton
Gerhard J. Seifner
Rodney R. Neys
Donald J. McGarvey
Christopher J. Lane
Shawn W. McLeod
Clay K. Hamdon
Stephen J. Livingstone
Sandra J. Weber
Robert R. Chappell
Doreen C. Mueller
Karen J. A. Metcalfe
David D. Risling
Corbin D. Devlin
Andrew J. Haynes
Charles R. Dalton
Kenneth W. Fitz
Vicki L. Giles
Neal A. McLennan
Bernard C. Grenon
Carole P. Karbonik
Pierre R. Dagenais
J. Jay Haugen
Stuart W. Chambers

*Denotes Lawyer Whose Professional Corporation is a Member of the Partnership.

For full biographical listings, see the Martindale-Hubbell Law Directory

PARLEE MCLAWS (AV)

15th Floor Manulife Place, 10180 101st Street, T5J 4K1
Telephone: 403-423-8500
Telecopier: 403-423-2870
Email: lawyers@parlee.com *URL:* http://www.parlee.com
Calgary, Alberta Office: 3400 Petro-Canada Centre, 150 - 6th Avenue, SW.
Telephone: 403-294-7000.
Telecopier: 403-265-8263.

MEMBERS OF FIRM

Michael D. MacDonald
Roderick B. Davison, Q.C.
James K. McFadyen
David C. Rolf
Allan A. Garber
Robert P. James
Anthony W. Slemko
R. Johnson Billingsley
Karen A. Smith
Kenneth F. Bailey, Q.C.
Richard W. Wilson
James T. Neilson
James F. McGinnis
Gregory W. Jaycock
Jerri L. Cairns
Marco S. Poretti
Paul A. Shenher
Galan T. Lund

ASSOCIATES

Priscilla E. S. J. Kennedy
Sandra L. Corbett
Thomas L.B. Carbone
Kim D. Watamaniuk
David L. Sharko
Diana W. Kwan
Norah B. Ramsay
Jamie E. Pytel
Shawn M. Johanson
Carla L. Lamash
Donn MacDougall
Sean P. Tindale
Randy S. Shapiro

(See Next Column)

COUNSEL

Edward H. Molstad, Q.C.

For Complete List of Firm Personnel, See General Section

For full biographical listings, see the Martindale-Hubbell Law Directory

SPITZ & CARR (AV)

1870 Canadian Western Bank Place, 10303 Jasper Avenue, T5J 3N6
Telephone: 780-428-0792
Fax: 780-424-7130
Email: spitzcar@telusplanet.net

MEMBERS OF FIRM

Derek Spitz, Q.C. *
James W. Carr *

ASSOCIATE

Michael Kraus

*Denotes Lawyer Whose Professional Corporation is a Member of the Partnership

For full biographical listings, see the Martindale-Hubbell Law Directory

CANADA BRITISH COLUMBIA

*VANCOUVER,** Vancouver Co.

JENKINS MARZBAN LOGAN (AV)

A Partnership of Law Corporations
Suite 1414, Nelson Square, 808 Nelson Street, P.O. Box 12144, V6Z 2H2
Telephone: 604-681-6564
Facsimile: 604-681-0766
URL: http://www.JML.CA

Dinyar Marzban

For full biographical listings, see the Martindale-Hubbell Law Directory

CANADA MANITOBA

*WINNIPEG,** Eastern Jud. Dist.

AIKINS, MACAULAY & THORVALDSON (AV)

Thirtieth Floor, Commodity Exchange Tower, 360 Main Street, R3C 4G1
Telephone: 204-957-0050
Fax: 204-957-0840
Email: amt@aikins.com *URL:* http://www.aikins.com

MEMBERS OF FIRM

John S. Lamont, Q.C.
Roger J. Hansell, Q.C.
Michael J. Mercury, Q.C.
James E. Foran, Q.C.
Knox B. Foster, Q.C.
Raymond H.G. Flett, Q.C.
Winston F. Smith, Q.C.
Cyril G. Labman
Colin R. MacArthur, Q.C.
Rod E. Stephenson, Q.C.
Daryl J. Rosin
G. Todd Campbell
Lori T. Spivak
Betty A. Johnstone
L. William Bowles
Jonathan B. Kroft
William K.A. Emslie
Allan F. Foran
Keith Ferbers
Thor J. Hansell
Marianne Rivoalen
Theodor E. Bock
Helga D. Van Iderstine
Barbara S. MacDonald
Philip T. Samyn
Tyler J. Kochanski
R. Reis Pagtakhan
David M. Wright
Kathryn J. Durkin
Jennifer (JJ) Burnell
Gregory M. Fleetwood
Rachel E. R. Margolis
Lucia M. Stuhldreier
Brent C. Ross
Curtis M. Unfried
Keith C. Eyrikson

Counsel for: Air Canada; Bank of Montreal; Boeing of Canada; Canada Safeway Limited; Canadian Medical Protective Assn.; The Great West Life Assurance Co.; John Labatt Limited; Russel Metals Inc.; Winnipeg Free Press.

For Complete List of Firm Personnel, See General Section

For full biographical listings, see the Martindale-Hubbell Law Directory

CANADA NEW BRUNSWICK

*FREDERICTON,** York Co.

COX HANSON O'REILLY MATHESON (AV)

(Formerly Hanson Hashey)
Suite 400, Phoenix Square, P.O. Box 310, E3B 4Y9
Telephone: 506-453-7771
Fax: 506-453-9600
Email: fredericton@coxhanson.ca *URL:* http://www.coxhanson.ca
Halifax, Nova Scotia Office: Suite 1100, Purdy's Wharf Tower 1, P.O. Box 2380 Station Central RPO, B3J 3E5.
Telephone: 902-421-6262.
Fax: 902-421-3130. E-Mail: halifax@coxhanson.ca
Saint John, New Brunswick Office: 1212-One Brunswick Square, 1 Germain St. E2L 4V1.
Telephone: 506-652-7771.
Fax: 506-632-9600.
St. John's, Newfoundland Office: Scotia Centre, 401-235 Water Street, A1C 1B6.
Telephone: 709-726-3321.
Fax: 709-726-2992. E-Mail: stjohns@coxhanson.ca
Charlottetown, Prince Edward Island Office: Queen Square, Suite 202, 119 Queen Street, P.O. Box 875, Station Central, C1A 7L9.
Telephone: 902-894-7051.
Fax: 902-368-3762. E-Mail: charlottetown@coxhanson.ca

MEMBERS OF FIRM

H. A. Hanson, Q.C. (1909-1985)
David T. Hashey, Q.C.
David M. Norman, Q.C.
J. Ian M. Whitcomb, Q.C.
John M. Hanson, Q.C.
Walter D. Vail, Q.C.
Michael E. Bowlin
John D. Larlee, Q.C.
Bruce D. Hatfield, Q.C.
Julian A. G. Dickson, Q.C.
Anne D. Wooder
Terrence J. Morrison
Lucie Richard
Catherine M. Bowlen
J. Marc Richard

ASSOCIATES

Amanda J. Frenette
Monika M. L. Zauhar
Jade A. Spalding
William E. Gould
Christopher R. DeLong
Deborah M. Power
Corinne A. Godbout
Marc-Antoine Chiasson

For full biographical listings, see the Martindale-Hubbell Law Directory

MCINNES COOPER (AV)

Suite 600, 570 Queen Street, P.O. Box 610, E3B 5A6
Telephone: 506-458-8572
Fax: 506-458-9903
Email: mcrfton@mcrlaw.com *URL:* http://www.mcrlaw.com
Halifax, Nova Scotia Office: Summit Place, 1601 Lower Water Street, P.O. Box 730, B3J 2V1.
Telephone: 902-425-6500.
Fax: 902-425-6350. Email: mcrhfx@mcrlaw.com.
St. John's, Newfoundland Office: Baine Johnston Centre, 5th Floor, 10 Fort William Place, P.O. Box 5939, A1C 5X4.
Telephone: 709-722-8735.
Telecopier: 709-722-1763. Email: mcrsj@mcrlaw.com.
Moncton, New Brunswick Office: Place Moncton Place, 655 Main Street, P.O. Box 1368, E1C 8T6.
Telephone: 506-857-8970.
Fax: 506-857-4095. Email: mcrmctn@mcrlaw.com.
Charlottetown, Prince Edward Island Office: BDC Place, Suite 620, 119 Kent Street, C1A 1N3.
Telephone: 902-368-8473.
Fax: 902-368-8346. Email: mcrpei@mcrlaw.com.

PARTNER

David Duncan Young

ASSOCIATES

David D. Eidt
Patrick V. Windle

For Complete List of Firm Personnel, See General Section

For full biographical listings, see the Martindale-Hubbell Law Directory

*MONCTON,** Westmorland Co.

MCINNES COOPER (AV)

Barristers, Solicitors & Trade Mark Agents
Place Moncton Place, 655 Main Street, P.O. Box 1368, E1C 8T6
Telephone: 506-857-8970
Fax: 506-857-4095
Email: mcrmctn@mcrlaw.com *URL:* http://www.mcrlaw.com
Halifax, Nova Scotia Office: Summit Place, 1601 Lower Water Street, P.O. Box 730, B3J 2V1.
Telephone: 902-425-6500.
Fax: 902-425-6350. Email: mcrhfx@mcrlaw.com.

(See Next Column)

St. John's, Newfoundland Office: Baine Johnston Centre, 5th Floor, 10 Fort William Place, P.O. Box 5939, A1C 5X4.
Telephone: 709-722-8735.
Telecopier: 709-722-1763. Email: mcrsj@mcrlaw.com.
Charlottetown, Prince Edward Island Office: BDC Place, Suite 620, 119 Kent Street, C1A 1N3.
Telephone: 902-368-8473.
Fax: 902-368-8346. Email: mcrpei@mcrlaw.com.
Fredericton, New Brunswick Office: Suite 600, 570 Queen Street, P.O. Box 610.
Telephone: 506-458-8572.
Fax: 506-458-9903. Email: mcrfton@mcrlaw.com.

ASSOCIATE

John C. Friel, Q.C.

For Complete List of Firm Personnel, See General Section

For full biographical listings, see the Martindale-Hubbell Law Directory

*SAINT JOHN,** Saint John Co.

CLARK DRUMMIE (AV)

40 Wellington Row, P.O. Box 6850, E2L 4S3
Telephone: 506-633-3800
Telecopier (Automatic): 506-633-3811
Email: cd@nbnet.nb.ca

MEMBERS OF FIRM

Thomas B. Drummie, Q.C.
M. Robert Jette
Norman J. Bossé
William B. Richards
Deno P. Pappas, Q.C.
Barry R. Morrison, Q.C.
J. George Byrne
Peter H. MacPhail

Reference: Royal Bank of Canada.

For Complete List of Firm Personnel, See General Section

For full biographical listings, see the Martindale-Hubbell Law Directory

GILBERT, MCGLOAN, GILLIS (AV)

Suite 710, Mercantile Centre, 55 Union Street, P.O. Box 7174, E2L 4S6
Telephone: 506-634-3600
Telecopier: 506-634-3612
Mailing Address: P.O. Box 7174, Station "A", Saint John, New Brunswick, E2L 4S6
Email: gmg@gmglaw.com

T. Louis McGloan, Q.C. (1896-1986)
Adrian B. Gilbert, Q.C. (1895-1986)

MEMBERS OF FIRM

Donald M. Gillis, Q.C.
Thomas L. McGloan, Q.C.
A. G. Warwick Gilbert, Q.C.
Rodney J. Gillis, Q.C.
Douglas A. M. Evans, Q.C.
Brenda J. Lutz, Q.C.
David N. Rogers
Mark A. Canty

ASSOCIATES

Edward Veitch
Hugh J. Flemming, Q.C.
Anne F. MacNeill
Nancy E. Forbes
Guy C. Spavold
Claire B.N. Porter
Nathalie L. Godbout
Bruce D. Grant
J. Danie Roy
Catherine A. Fawcett
Danys R.X. Delaquis
James M. Barry

Representative Clients: Bank of Montreal; Canada Packers Ltd.; McCain Foods Ltd.; The Sunderland Steamship Protecting & Indemnity Association; Steamship Mutual Underwriting Association (Bermuda) Limited; Royal Insurance Co.; Wawanesa Mutual Insurance Co.; Dominion of Canada General Insurance Co.; Canadian General Insurance Co.

For full biographical listings, see the Martindale-Hubbell Law Directory

CANADA NEWFOUNDLAND

*ST. JOHN'S,**

MCINNES COOPER (AV)

Barristers, Solicitors & Trade Mark Agents
Baine Johnston Centre, 5th Floor, 10 Fort William Place, P.O. Box 5939, A1C 5X4
Telephone: 709-722-8735
Telecopier: 709-722-1763
Email: mcrsj@mcrlaw.com *URL:* http://www.mcrlaw.com
Halifax, Nova Scotia Office: Summit Place, 1601 Lower Water Street, P.O. Box 730, B3J 2V1.
Telephone: 902-425-6500.
Fax: 902-425-6350. Email: mcrhfx@mcrlaw.com.
Moncton, New Brunswick Office: Place Moncton Place, 655 Main Street, P.O. Box 1368, E1C 8T6.
Telephone: 506-857-8970.
Fax: 506-857-4095. Email: mcrmctn@mcrlaw.com.

(See Next Column)

McInnes Cooper—Continued

Charlottetown, Prince Edward Island Office: BDC Place, Suite 620, 119 Kent Street, C1A 1N3.
Telephone: 902-368-8473.
Fax: 902-368-8346. Email: mcrpei@mcrlaw.com.
Fredericton, New Brunswick Office: Suite 600, 570 Queen Street, P.O. Box 610.
Telephone: 506-458-8572.
Fax: 506-458-9903. Email: mcrfton@mcrlaw.com.

PARTNERS

James R. Chalker, Q.C. — J. David B. Eaton
Michael J. Crosbie — Philip J. Buckingham

ASSOCIATES

Genevieve M. Dawson — D. Scott Worsfold

For Complete List of Firm Personnel, See General Section

For full biographical listings, see the Martindale-Hubbell Law Directory

CANADA NOVA SCOTIA

*HALIFAX,** Regional Munic. of Halifax

McInnes Cooper (AV)

Barristers, Solicitors & Trade Mark Agents
Summit Place, 1601 Lower Water Street, P.O. Box 730, B3J 2V1
Telephone: 902-425-6500
Fax: 902-425-6350
Email: mcrhfx@mcrlaw.com *URL:* http://www.mcrlaw.com
St. John's, Newfoundland Office: Baine Johnston Centre, 5th Floor, 10 Fort William Place, P.O. Box 5939, A1C 5X4.
Telephone: 709-722-8735.
Telecopier: 709-722-1763. Email: mcrsj@mcrlaw.com.
Moncton, New Brunswick Office: Place Moncton Place, 655 Main Street, P.O. Box 1368, E1C 8T6.
Telephone: 506-857-8970.
Fax: 506-857-4095. Email: mcrmctn@mcrlaw.com.
Charlottetown, Prince Edward Island Office: BDC Place, Suite 620, 119 Kent Street, C1A 1N3.
Telephone: 902-368-8473.
Fax: 902-368-8346. Email: mcrpei@mcrlaw.com.
Fredericton, New Brunswick Office: Suite 600, 570 Queen Street, P.O. Box 610.
Telephone: 506-458-8572.
Fax: 506-458-9903. Email: mcrfton@mcrlaw.com.

PARTNERS

Reginald A. Cluney, Q.C. — Harry E. Wrathall, Q.C.
Stewart McInnes, P.C., Q.C. — Alan J. Stern, Q.C.
James E. Gould, Q.C. — George W. MacDonald, Q.C.
Robert G. Belliveau, Q.C. — Thomas E. Hart
David A. Graves — Scott C. Norton
Deborah K. Smith — Stephen Kingston
John Kulik — Aidan J. Meade
G. Grant Machum — Michelle C. Awad

ASSOCIATES

Paul McLean — Tara A. Miller
Janet Clark

For Complete List of Firm Personnel, See General Section

For full biographical listings, see the Martindale-Hubbell Law Directory

CANADA ONTARIO

*HAMILTON,** Regional Munic. of Hamilton-Wentworth

John F. Evans & Associates (AV)

Suite 1201, One King Street West, L8P 1A4
Telephone: 905-523-5666
Fax: 905-523-8098

John F. Evans, Q.C.

ASSOCIATES

Liza C. Sheard — Paul Richard Sweeny
Sean Philip Lawler

For full biographical listings, see the Martindale-Hubbell Law Directory

Thoman Soule Gage (AV)

46 Jackson Street East, P.O. Box 187, L8N 3C5
Telephone: 905-529-8195
Fax: 905-529-7906

J. Douglas Thoman, Q.C. — David J. Sherman
John A. Soule — Lesley G. Matthewson
George S. Gage — William F. Bastien
J. Neil Smith — James Scott Greve
S. Stuart Aird — Catherine A. Korte

For full biographical listings, see the Martindale-Hubbell Law Directory

KITCHENER, Regional Munic. of Waterloo

Giffen Lee (AV)

50 Queen Street North, P.O. Box 2396, N2H 6M3
Telephone: 519-578-4150
Fax: 519-578-8740
Email: info@GiffenLeeLaw.com *URL:* http://www.GiffenLeeLaw.com

MEMBERS OF FIRM

J. Peter Giffen, Q.C. — Brian R. Wagner
Bruce L. Lee — Philip A. Garbutt
J. Scott Morley — Daniel J. Fife

ASSOCIATES

(Ms.) Milena Protich — Graham M. Bennett
Cindy L. Dickinson — Mitra Golnaraghi
Edward J. Vanderkloet — Donald C. Olson

For full biographical listings, see the Martindale-Hubbell Law Directory

*OTTAWA,** Regional Munic. of Ottawa-Carleton

Borden Elliot Scott & Aylen (AV)

1000-60 Rue Queen Street, K1P 5Y7
Telephone: 613-237-5160; 800-661-4237
General Facsimile: 613-230-8842
IP Dept. Facsimile: 613-787-3558
Email: ottinfo@scottaylen.com *URL:* http://www.borden.com
Toronto, Ontario Office: Borden & Elliot: Scotia Plaza, 40 King Street West.
Telephone: 416-367-6000.
Telecopier: 416-367-6749. Email: info @borden.com. URL: http://www.borden.com.

David W. Scott, Q.C. — Peter C. P. Thompson, Q.C.
Bryan A. Carroll — Peter B. Annis
George D. Hunter — James I. Minnes
J. Bruce Carr-Harris — Marc Jolicoeur
Peter K. Doody — Carole J. Brown
Kevin P. Nearing — Fay Kathleen Brunning-Howard
Martine M. Richard — Pierre E. Roger
David Sherriff-Scott — Jane M. Bachynski
Lawrence A. Elliot — Brian Saunderson
Matthew H. Williams — Johanne M. Asselin

For full biographical listings, see the Martindale-Hubbell Law Directory

*TORONTO,** Regional Munic. of Toronto

Borden & Elliot (AV)

Barristers & Solicitors
Scotia Plaza, 40 King Street West, M5H 3Y4
Telephone: 416-367-6000
Telecopier: 416-367-6749
Email: info@borden.com *URL:* http://www.borden.com
Ottawa, Ontario Office: Borden Elliot Scott & Aylen, 1000-60 Rue Queen Street.
Telephone: 613-237-5160; 800-661-4237. General *Facsimile:* 613-230-8842. IP Dept.
Facsimile: 613-787-3558. Email: ottinfo@scottaylen.com. URL: http://www.borden.com.

Edward A. Ayers, Q.C.

For Complete List of Firm Personnel, See General Section

For full biographical listings, see the Martindale-Hubbell Law Directory

Davies, Ward & Beck (AV)

1 First Canadian Place, M5X 1B1
Telephone: 416-863-0900
Fax: 416-863-0871
Email: info@dwb.com *URL:* http://www.dwb.com

PARTNERS AND ASSOCIATES

Neil Finkelstein — Jeremy M. Freedman
Matthew P. Gottlieb — James W. E. Doris
Sandra A. Forbes — Melanie L. Aitken
Andrea L. Burke — Russell Cohen
David Stevens — Rachel J. Urman

For Complete List of Firm Personnel, See General Section

For full biographical listings, see the Martindale-Hubbell Law Directory

Toronto—Continued

KELLY AFFLECK GREENE (AV)

One First Canadian Place, Suite 840, P.O. Box 489, M5X 1E5
Telephone: 416-360-2800
Fax: 416-360-5960
Email: info@kag.net *URL:* http://www.kag.net

MEMBERS OF FIRM

W. Anthony Kelly, Q.C.
Donald S. Affleck, Q.C.
Peter R. Greene
Donald B. Houston
James C. Orr
Peter C. Wardle
Helen A. Daley
Melissa J. Kennedy

ASSOCIATES

Kenneth A. Dekker
W. Michael G. Osborne
Jason C. Markwell
Patrice F. Band

For full biographical listings, see the Martindale-Hubbell Law Directory

STOCKWOOD SPIES (AV)

Suite 2512 The Sun Life Tower, 150 King Street West, M5H 1J9
Telephone: 416-593-7200
Fax: 416-593-9345
Email: stospies@istar.ca

David T. Stockwood, Q.C.
Nancy J. Spies
Paul H. Le Vay
Brian J. Gover
Christopher H. Wirth
Elaine Shin
Johanna Braden

LEGAL SUPPORT PERSONNEL

Ephry Mudryk

For full biographical listings, see the Martindale-Hubbell Law Directory

*WINDSOR,** Essex Co.

MCTAGUE LAW FIRM (AV)

455 Pelissier Street, N9A 6Z9
Telephone: 519-255-4300
Detroit, Michigan Telephone: 313-965-1332
Fax: 519-255-4360(Corporate/Labor)
Fax: 519-255-4384 (Litigation/Real Estate)

MEMBERS OF FIRM

J. Douglas Lawson, Q.C.
Alexander R. Szalkai, Q.C.
Peter J. Kuker
George W. King
Josephine Stark
Tom Serafimovski
Roger A. Skinner
Daniel K. Moorhouse
Jerry B. Udell
Michael K. Coughlin
John D. Leslie
Marilee Marcotte

ASSOCIATES

Kevin G. Fanick
Michael A. Wills
Dana J. Young
Jeffrey W. MacKinnon
Brian L. Chillman

For Complete List of Firm Personnel, See General Section

For full biographical listings, see the Martindale-Hubbell Law Directory

SUTTS, STROSBERG LLP (AV)

600 Westcourt Place, 251 Goyeau Street, P.O. Box 670, N9A 6V4
Telephone: 519-258-9333
Detroit Michigan: 313-962-0137
Facsimile: Windsor 519-258-9527
Detroit 313-962-0139

MEMBERS OF FIRM

Achille F. Gignac, Q.C. (1902-1984)
Robert E. Barnes, Q.C.
Clifford N. Sutts, Q.C.
Harvey T. Strosberg, Q.C.
Gary V. Wortley
James K. Ball
John C. Holland
Mary M. S. Fox
William C. Chapman
Donald M. Gordon
Paul C. Nesseth
Heather Rumble Peterson
Patricia A. Speight
Edward W. Ducharme
Michelle A. Gagnon
Craig J. Allen
Werner H. Keller
Francine A. Herlehy
Paul Simard
Jasminka Kalajdzic

COUNSEL FOR CRIMINAL MATTERS

Patrick J. Ducharme

For full biographical listings, see the Martindale-Hubbell Law Directory

CANADA
PRINCE EDWARD ISLAND

*CHARLOTTETOWN,** Queen's Co.

CAMPBELL, LEA, MICHAEL, MCCONNELL & PIGOT (AV)

15 Queen Street, P.O. Box 429, C1A 7K7
Telephone: 902-566-3400
Telecopier: 902-566-9266
Email: www.office@campbelllea.com

MEMBERS OF FIRM

William G. Lea, Q.C.
Robert A. McConnell
Paul D. Michael, Q.C.
Kenneth L. Godfrey

General Counsel in Prince Edward Island for: Canadian Imperial Bank of Commerce; Maritime Electric Co., Ltd.; Michelin Tires (Canada) Ltd.; Newsco Investments Ltd. (Dundas Farms); Imperial Oil Limited; General Motors of Canada; Co-op Atlantic; Liberty Mutual; Employers Reinsurance Group.

For Complete List of Firm Personnel, See General Section

For full biographical listings, see the Martindale-Hubbell Law Directory

MCINNES COOPER (AV Ⓣ)

Barristers, Solicitors & Trade Mark Agents
BDC Place, Suite 620, 119 Kent Street, C1A 1N3
Telephone: 902-368-8473
Fax: 902-368-8346
Email: mcrpei@mcrlaw.com *URL:* http://www.mcrlaw.com
Halifax, Nova Scotia Office: Summit Place, 1601 Lower Water Street, P.O. Box 730, B3J 2V1.
Telephone: 902-425-6500.
Fax: 902-425-6350. Email: mcrhfx@mcrlaw.com.
St. John's, Newfoundland Office: Baine Johnston Centre, 5th Floor, 10 Fort William Place, P.O. Box 5939, A1C 5X4.
Telephone: 709-722-8735.
Telecopier: 709-722-1763. Email: mcrsj@mcrlaw.com.
Moncton, New Brunswick Office: Place Moncton Place, 655 Main Street, P.O. Box 1368, E1C 8T6.
Telephone: 506-857-8970.
Fax: 506-857-4095. Email: mcrmctn@mcrlaw.com.
Fredericton, New Brunswick Office: Suite 600, 570 Queen Street, P.O. Box 610.
Telephone: 506-458-8572.
Fax: 506-458-9903. Email: mcrfton@mcrlaw.com.

ASSOCIATES

Kevin J. Kiley
Murray L. Murphy
Kim Petrie

For Complete List of Firm Personnel, See General Section

For full biographical listings, see the Martindale-Hubbell Law Directory

CANADA
QUEBEC

*MONTREAL,** Montreal Dist.

DE GRANDPRÉ CHAIT (AV)

1000, De La Gauchetière Street West, Suite 2900, H3B 4W5
Telephone: 514-878-4311
Fax: 514-878-4333
Email: info@degrandpre-chait.com

PARTNER OF FIRM

Founding Partner Samuel Chait, Q.C. (1904-1982)

Christiane Alary
Normand Amyot
Jacques L. Archambault
André P. Asselin
François Beauchamp
Marc Beauchemin
Jean Benoît
Jacques Bourque
Arthur I. Bronstein
Pierre Brossoit
J. Brian Cornish
Louis Demers
Jean-Pierre Desmarais
Gilles Fafard
Jean-Jacques Gagnon
Guy Gilain
Jean François Giroux
Gilles Godin, Q.C.
Andrée Gosselin
Frederica Jacobs
David H. Kauffman
Sandor J. Klein
Gabriel Kordovi
Pierre Labelle
Diane Lajeunesse
Eric Lalanne
Virginia K. H. Lam
Benoît Larose
Philippe Leclercq
Daniel Lessard
Ronald H. Levy
C. Ralph Lipper
Jean-François Ménard
Pierre Mercille

(See Next Column)

de Grandpré Chait—*Continued*

(Continued)

Benoît Pelchat	Marc J. Rubin
Yves Poirier	Louis Samuel
Olivier Prat, Q.C.	Ronald L. Stein
Alain Robichaud	Mark E. Turcot

For full biographical listings, see the Martindale-Hubbell Law Directory

Goldstein, Flanz & Fishman (AV)

Suite 4100, 1250 René-Lévesque Boulevard West, H3B 4W8
Telephone: 514-932-4100
Cable Address: "Meybat"
Telex: 05-24593
Telecopier: 514-932-4170
Email: counsel@gff.qc.ca

MEMBERS OF FIRM

Yoine Goldstein	Mark E. Meland
Leonard W. Flanz	Ellen Amdursky
Avram Fishman	Alain Daigle
Mark Schrager	Cathy Noseworthy
Gilles Paquin	Suzanne Villeneuve

For full biographical listings, see the Martindale-Hubbell Law Directory

McMaster Gervais (AV)

A General Partnership
1000 de La Gauchetière Street West, Suite 900, H3B 5H4
Telephone: 514-879-1212
Fax: 514-954-1905
Email: info@mcmastergervais.com *URL:* http://www.mcmastergervais.com

MEMBERS OF FIRM

Alex K. Paterson, O.C., O.Q., Q.C.	Alexis P. Bergeron
	Daniel Ayotte
Georges R. Thibaudeau	Peter Richardson
Robert E. Charbonneau	Virgile A. Buffoni
Roger P. Simard	Jacques Gauthier
Bruno Duguay	Yvan Houle
John G. Murphy	Christine Duchaine
Jacques S. Darche	Marie Audren
Julie Normand	Caroline Matte
Stéphanie Moffatt	Patrice Morin
Robert Fosco	Gary Rivard
Manon Gauthier	Antoine Leduc

COUNSEL

Jacques Brien

For Complete List of Firm Personnel, See General Section

For full biographical listings, see the Martindale-Hubbell Law Directory

Pouliot, Mercure (AV)

CIBC Tower, 31st Floor, 1155 René-Lévesque Boulevard, West, H3B 3S6
Telephone: 514-875-5210
Telecopier: 514-875-4308
Email: POUMER@CEDEP.COM
Genève, Suisse Office: 8, Rue de la Rôtisserie, 1204 Geneva, Switzerland.
Telephone: +41 22-28 79 40.
Telecopier: +41 22-21 23 67.

MEMBERS OF FIRM

Georges A. Pouliot, Q.C.	Gilles Bertrand
Gilles Brunelle	Jean Larivière
Luc Gratton	Louis-Michel Tremblay
Brian Riordan	David I. Johnston
Pierre Paquet	Stéphane Hébert
Anne-Marie Gauthier	Jacques LeBel, Q.C.
Yvon Brizard	Joel A. Silcoff
Robert Tessier	Ronald M. Auclair
Daniel Gagné	Philippe Roy
Lilia Pouliot	Maxime B. Rhéaume
Marco Veilleux	Serge Desrochers
Alain Nadon	C. Keenan LaPierre
Jean H. Gagnon	Alain Bond
Richard Fontaine	Louis Coallier
Normand Royal	Nicole Chouinard

Stéphane Teasdale

ASSOCIATES

Micheline Perrault	Brent J. Muir
Caroline Lemoine	Louise Tremblay
Béatrice Arronis	Chantal Joubert
Yvan Nantel	Normand D'Amour
Sylvie Boulanger	Pascale Cloutier
Vincent Frenette	Eric Couture
Robert Cardin	Frédéric Chatel
Alexandre Henri	Mary-Lynn Breton

Alexandre Ajami

For full biographical listings, see the Martindale-Hubbell Law Directory

Woods & Partners (AV)

2000 McGill College Avenue, Suite 1100, H3A 3H3
Telephone: 514-982-4545
Telecopier: 514-284-2046
Email: general@woods.qc.ca

MEMBERS OF FIRM

James A. Woods	Christopher Lund Richter
Christian Immer	Annie Galarneau
Julien Cools-Lartigue	Sébastien Richemont
Nathalie Chalifour	Kathleen Beaugé

Marjorie Delagrave

For full biographical listings, see the Martindale-Hubbell Law Directory

CANADA SASKATCHEWAN

*REGINA,** Regina Jud. Centre

Balfour Moss (AV)

Bank of Montreal Building, 700-2103 11th Avenue, S4P 4G1
Telephone: 306-347-8300
Fax: 306-347-8350
Email: balfourmoss.regina@dlcwest.com *URL:* http://www.dlcwest.com/~balfourmoss
Saskatoon, Saskatchewan Office: #600-123-2nd Avenue South.
Telephone: 306-665-7844.
Fax: 306-652-1586.

PARTNERS

A. John Beke, Q.C.	Rick M. Van Beselaere
Fredrick C. McBeth	George E. Nystrom
Brian J. Scherman (Resident Saskatoon)	Jeff N. Grubb
	David G. Gerecke (Resident Saskatoon)
Roger J.F. Lepage	Raymond J. Dean
Reginald A. Watson	Bob P. Hrycan
Glen S. Lekach	

COUNSEL

E. John Moss, Q.C.	Robert A. Milliken, Q.C.
Hon. R. James Balfour, Q.C.	Roy B. Laschuk, Q.C.

ASSOCIATES

Michael D. Crosbie	Kathleen A. Richardson
Peter T. Bergbusch	Stewart J.O. Berringer
Kerri A. Froc	Yens Pedersen
Heather MacMillan-Brown (Resident, Saskatoon Office)	

Representative Clients: Saskatchewan Government Insurance; Walmart Canada Limited; Saskatchewan Wheat Pool; Bank of Montreal; Saskatchewan Registered Nurses Association; Regina Regional Health District; Rolls-Royce Canada Limited; Insurance Brokers of Saskatchewan; Saskatchewan Lawyers Insurance Association; Encon Insurance Managers Inc.

For full biographical listings, see the Martindale-Hubbell Law Directory

MacPherson Leslie & Tyerman (AV)

1500-1874 Scarth Street, S4P 4E9
Telephone: 306-347-8000
Telecopier: 306-352-5250
Email: mltreg@mlt.com
Saskatoon, Saskatchewan Office: 1500-410 22nd Street East, S7K 5T6.
Telephone: 306-975-7100.
Telecopier: 306-975-7145.

MEMBERS OF FIRM

Maurice O. Laprairie, Q.C.	Larry B. LeBlanc, Q.C.
Bruce W. Wirth (Resident, Saskatoon Office)	Robert G. Richards, Q.C.
	Brian J. Kenny
Douglas C. Hodson (Resident, Saskatoon Office)	Robert W. Leurer
	Jeffrey M. Lee (Resident, Saskatoon Office)
Conrad D. Hadubiak	

Eileen V. Libby

ASSOCIATES

R. M. Louise Simard, Q.C.	F. Neil Turcotte (Resident, Saskatoon Office)
Paul A. Beke (Resident, Saskatoon Office)	Vanessa Monar Enweani (Resident, Saskatoon Office)
M. Jean Torrens (Resident, Saskatoon Office)	Jordan P. Hardy
Kurt G. Wintermute (Resident, Saskatoon Office)	Dana D.J. Schindelka
	Heather D. Heavin
Charita N. Parchewsky	Deron A. Kuski

For Complete List of Firm Personnel, See General Section

For full biographical listings, see the Martindale-Hubbell Law Directory

*SASKATOON,** Saskatoon Jud. Centre

Gauley & Co. (AV)

701 Broadway Avenue, P.O. Box 638, S7K 3L7
Telephone: 306-653-1212
Telecopier: 306-652-1323
Email: gauleyco@gauleyco.com
Regina, Saskatchewan Office: Suite 400, 2201 11th Avenue S4P 0J8.
Telephone: 306-352-1643.
Telecopier: 306-525-8499.

MEMBERS OF FIRM

David E. "Tom" Gauley, Q.C.
Pat A. Kelly, Q.C. (Resident, Regina Office)
Peter Foley, Q.C.
Gary A. Zabos

Reference: Royal Bank of Canada.

For Complete List of Firm Personnel, See General Section

For full biographical listings, see the Martindale-Hubbell Law Directory

COMMERCIAL LAW

MINNESOTA

*MINNEAPOLIS,** Hennepin Co.

COX, GOUDY, MCNULTY & WALLACE, P.L.L.P. (AV)

100 North Sixth Street, #676A, 55403
Telephone: 612-338-1414
Fax: 612-338-6754
Email: mcwall@bitstream.net
St. Paul Office: 1300 Minnesota Building, 46 East 4th Street.
Telephone: 651-293-9194.

MEMBERS OF FIRM

Charles A. Cox
Craig A. Goudy
Marcy S. Wallace
Charles A. Cox, III

OF COUNSEL

John C. McNulty

For full biographical listings, see the Martindale-Hubbell Law Directory

*ST. CLOUD,** Stearns Co.

HUGHES, MATHEWS & DIDIER, P.A. (AV)

110 Sixth Avenue South, Suite 205, P.O. Box 548, 56302-0548
Telephone: 320-251-4399
Fax: 320-251-5781

Kevin J. Hughes
Thomas E. Mathews

Kevin M. O'Driscoll
Suzanne M. Johnson

Representative Clients: The St. Cloud Hospital; CentraCare Health System; St. John's University; College of St. Benedict; Tanner Systems, Inc.; Anderson Trucking Service, Inc.; DeZurik, a unit of General Signal; Stearns Bank, N.A.

For full biographical listings, see the Martindale-Hubbell Law Directory

MISSISSIPPI

*BROOKHAVEN,** Lincoln Co.

ALLEN, ALLEN, BOERNER & BREELAND (AV)

214 Justice Street, P.O. Box 751, 39602-0751
Telephone: 601-833-4361
Fax: 601-833-6647
Email: aabblaw@tislink.com

Emmette P. Allen (1915-1999)
Robert O. Allen
William D. Boerner
Durwood J. Breeland

ASSOCIATE

Sally Burchfield Doty

For full biographical listings, see the Martindale-Hubbell Law Directory

*CLARKSDALE,** Coahoma Co.

HOLCOMB DUNBAR, A PROFESSIONAL ASSOCIATION (AV)

152 Delta Avenue, P.O. Box 368, 38614
Telephone: 601-627-2241
Facsimile: 601-627-9788
Email: mchaffin@clarksdale.com *URL:* http://www.holcombdunbar.com
Oxford, Mississippi Office: 1217 Jackson Avenue, P.O. Drawer 707, 38655.
Telephone: 601-234-8775.
Facsimile: 601-238-7552.
Southaven, Mississippi Office: Suite 1, 728 Goodman Road East, P.O. Box 190, 38671.
Telephone: 601-349-0664.
Facsimile: 601-349-2432.

William M. Chaffin
Michael K. Graves
Edward (Ted) P. Connell, Jr.
Daniel M. Czamanske, Jr.

Representative Clients: Union Planters Bank, National Association; Bank of Mississippi; Deposit Guaranty National Bank; Trustmark National Bank; Citibank; Mississippi Power & Light Co.; Mississippi Valley Gas Co.; South Central Bell Telephone Co.; Bituminous Insurance Co.; State Farm Fire & Casualty Co.

For Complete List of Firm Personnel, See General Section

For full biographical listings, see the Martindale-Hubbell Law Directory

*COLUMBIA,** Marion Co.

AULTMAN, TYNER, RUFFIN & YARBOROUGH, LTD., A PROFESSIONAL LAW CORPORATION (AV)

329 Church Street, P.O. Drawer 707, 39429
Telephone: 601-736-2222
FAX: 601-736-9884
Email: rfyjr@cblink.com
Hattiesburg, Mississippi Office: 315 Hemphill Street, P.O. Drawer 750.
Telephone: 601-583-2671.
FAX: 601-583-2677.
Gulfport, Mississippi Office: 1201 25th Avenue, Suite 300, P.O. Box 607.
Telephone: 228-863-6913.
FAX: 228-868-8505. Email: atmr@digiscape.com.
New Orleans, Louisiana Office: The Texaco Center, 400 Poydras Street, Suite 2250.
Telephone: 504-528-9616.
FAX: 504-528-9640.

Richard F. Yarborough, Jr.

OF COUNSEL

Ernest Ray Duff

Representative Clients: Hercules, Inc.; United States Steel Corp.; Ford Motor Co.; International Paper Co.; Phillips Petroleum Co.; Aetna Casualty & Surety Co.; CNA Group; Liberty Mutual Insurance Co.; St. Paul Fire & Marine Insurance Co.; Fireman's Fund.

For full biographical listings, see the Martindale-Hubbell Law Directory

*GULFPORT,** Harrison Co.

AULTMAN, TYNER, RUFFIN & YARBOROUGH, LTD., A PROFESSIONAL LAW CORPORATION (AV)

1201 25th Avenue, Suite 300, P.O. Box 607, 39502
Telephone: 228-863-6913
FAX: 228-868-8505
Email: atmr@digiscape.com
Hattiesburg, Mississippi Office: 315 Hemphill Street, P.O. Drawer 750.
Telephone: 601-583-2671.
FAX: 601-583-2677.
Columbia, Mississippi Office: 329 Church Street, P.O. Drawer 707.
Telephone: 601-736-2222.
FAX: 601-736-9884. Email: rfyjr@cblink.com.
New Orleans, Louisiana Office: The Texaco Center, 400 Poydras Street, Suite 2250.
Telephone: 504-528-9616.
FAX: 504-528-9640.

Ben E. Sheely
Dorrance (Dee) Aultman, Jr.

For Complete List of Firm Personnel, See General Section

For full biographical listings, see the Martindale-Hubbell Law Directory

DUKES, DUKES, KEATING AND FANECA, P.A. (AV)

2909 13th Street, 6th Floor, P.O. Drawer W, 39501
Telephone: 228-868-1111
Fax: 228-863-2886
Email: ddkf@ddkf.com

Hugh D. Keating
Cy Faneca

William W. Abbott, Jr.

For Complete List of Firm Personnel, See General Section

For full biographical listings, see the Martindale-Hubbell Law Directory

FRANKE, RAINEY & SALLOUM, PLLC (AV)

2605 14th Street, P.O. Drawer 460, 39502
Telephone: 228-868-7070
Telecopier: 228-868-7090
Email: frs@diversicomm.com

Paul M. Franke, Jr.
William M. Rainey
Richard P. Salloum
Paul B. Howell
Fredrick B. Feeney, II
Traci M. Castille
Donald P. Moore

Kaleel G. Salloum, Jr.
Brandi C. Schwartz
James C. Simpson, Jr.

For full biographical listings, see the Martindale-Hubbell Law Directory

*HATTIESBURG,** Forrest Co.

AULTMAN, TYNER, RUFFIN & YARBOROUGH, LTD., A PROFESSIONAL LAW CORPORATION (AV)

315 Hemphill Street, P.O. Drawer 750, 39403-0750
Telephone: 601-583-2671
FAX: 601-583-2677
Email: aultyn@c-gate.net
Columbia, Mississippi Office: 329 Church Street, P.O. Drawer 707.
Telephone: 601-736-2222.
FAX: 601-736-9884. Email: rfyjr@cblink.com.
Gulfport, Mississippi Office: 1201 25th Avenue, Suite 300, P.O. Box 607.
Telephone: 228-863-6913.
FAX: 228-868-8505. Email: atmr@digiscape.com.
New Orleans, Louisiana Office: The Texaco Center, 400 Poydras Street, Suite 2250.
Telephone: 504-528-9616.
FAX: 504-528-9640.

Dorrance Aultman
Thomas W. Tyner
Louie F. Ruffin
Richard F. Yarborough, Jr. (Resident, Columbia Office)
Ben E. Sheely (Resident, Gulfport Office)
R. Curtis Smith, II
Dorrance (Dee) Aultman, Jr. (Resident, Gulfport Office)
William Nelson Graham

Victor A. DuBose

OF COUNSEL

Ernest Ray Duff (Resident, Columbia Office)

Representative Clients: Hercules, Inc.; U.S. Steel Corp.; Ford Motor Co.; Phillips Petroleum Co.; Aetna Casualty & Surety Co.; CNA Group; Liberty Mutual Insurance Co.; St. Paul Fire & Marine Insurance Co.; Fireman's Fund; L & A Contracting Co.

For Complete List of Firm Personnel, See General Section

For full biographical listings, see the Martindale-Hubbell Law Directory

*JACKSON,** Hinds Co.

COPELAND COOK TAYLOR & BUSH, A PROFESSIONAL ASSOCIATION (AV)

200 Concourse, Suite 200, 1062 Highland Colony Parkway, P.O. Box 2132, 39225-2132
Telephone: 601-856-7200
Facsimile: 601-856-7626
Email: mail@cctb.com *URL:* http://www.cctb.com
Ridgeland, Mississippi Office: Post Office Box 6020, 39158.
Telephone: 601-856-7200.
Facsimile: 601-856-7626.

Charles G. Copeland
Thomas A. Cook
Glenn Gates Taylor
C. Glen Bush
Thomas C. Gerity
James T. Knight
James R. Moore, Jr.
J. Tucker Mitchell
Robert P. Thompson
Thomas R. Hudson
R. Nash Neyland
Michael W. Baxter
C. Ted Sanderson, Jr.
Monte L. Barton, Jr.
W. Shan Thompson
C. Dale Shearer
Robert C. Richardson
Lee Howell, III
John M. Breland
Jefferson P.W. Skelton
Patricia H. Cottingham
Samuel S. Goza
Amanda L. Baham
Samuel O. Morris, IV
Michelle C. Partridge
John E. Gough, Jr.
Victor Donald Hunt
Donald J. Blackwood, Jr.
Rhonda Lea McCullough

OF COUNSEL

James P. Knight, Jr.
Robert L. Goza

For full biographical listings, see the Martindale-Hubbell Law Directory

EDMONSON, BIGGS & MOZINGO, P.A. (AV)

Deposit Guaranty Bank Building, 200 East Capitol, Suite 1500, P.O. Box 865, 39205
Telephone: 601-944-1900
Telecopier: 601-944-1906
Email: ebmh@misnet.com *URL:* http://www.ebmh.com

Richard M. Edmonson
Robert A. Biggs, III
James R. Mozingo
Fred W. Johnson, Jr.
Craig D. Smith
Todd A. Coker

Representative Clients: Andover Cos; Combined Insurance Co.; Design Professional Insurance Co.; Bituminous Insurance Co.; Lexington Insurance Co.; Mississippi State Medical Association Benefit Plan; Coregis; USF&G; Utica Mutual Insurance Co.; Trustmark National Bank, Union Planters Bank.

For full biographical listings, see the Martindale-Hubbell Law Directory

WATKINS & EAGER (AV)

A Professional Limited Liability Company
Suite 300 The Emporium Building, 400 East Capitol Street, P.O. Box 650, 39205
Telephone: 601-948-6470
Facsimile: 601-354-3623

MEMBERS OF FIRM

William F. Goodman, Jr.
John G. Corlew
George R. Fair
Frank J. Hammond, III
M. Binford Williams, Jr.

ASSOCIATES

Joe D. Nosef, III
Martin E. Willoughby, Jr.
Jesse M. Harrington

Representative Clients: Willmut Gas Co.; Pavco Industries, Inc.; Trustmark National Bank; Merchants & Marine Bank; Millsaps College; Dollar General Corp.; Chesapeake Corp.; Delta Industries, Inc.; Freide Goldman International, Inc; Whitney National Bank.

For Complete List of Firm Personnel, See General Section

For full biographical listings, see the Martindale-Hubbell Law Directory

*OXFORD,** Lafayette Co.

FREELAND & FREELAND (AV)

1013 Jackson Avenue, P.O. Box 269, 38655
Telephone: 662-234-3414
Telecopier: 662-234-0604
Email: thf4@watervalley.net

MEMBERS OF FIRM

T. H. Freeland, III
T. H. Freeland, IV

Representative Clients: The Ohio Casualty Group; Crum & Forester.

For full biographical listings, see the Martindale-Hubbell Law Directory

HOLCOMB DUNBAR, A PROFESSIONAL ASSOCIATION (AV)

1217 Jackson Avenue P.O. Drawer 707, 38655
Telephone: 601-234-8775
Facsimile: 601-238-7552
Email: hdccw@holcombdunbar.com *URL:* http://www.holcombdunbar.com
Clarksdale, Mississippi Office: 152 Delta Avenue, P.O. Box 368, 38614.
Telephone: 601-627-2241.
Facsimile: 601-627-9788.
Southaven, Mississippi Office: Suite 1, 728 Goodman Road East, P.O. Box 190, 38671.
Telephone: 601-349-0664.
Facsimile: 601-349-2432.

Jack F. Dunbar
Thomas J. Suszek
T. Swayze Alford

Representative Clients: Union Planters Bank, National Association; Bank of Mississippi; Deposit Guaranty National Bank; Trustmark National Bank; Citibank; Mississippi Power & Light Co.; Mississippi Valley Gas Co.; South Central Bell Telephone Co.; Bituminous Insurance Co.; State Farm Fire & Casualty Insurance Co.

For Complete List of Firm Personnel, See General Section

For full biographical listings, see the Martindale-Hubbell Law Directory

SOUTHAVEN, De Soto Co.

HOLCOMB DUNBAR, A PROFESSIONAL ASSOCIATION (AV)

Suite 1, 728 Goodman Road East, P.O. Box 190, 38671
Telephone: 601-349-0664
Facsimile: 601-349-2432
Email: hdccw@holcombdunbar.com *URL:* http://www.holcombdunbar.com
Clarksdale, Mississippi Office: 152 Delta Avenue, P.O. Box 368, 38614.
Telephone: 601-627-2241.
Facsimile: 601-627-9788.
Oxford, Mississippi Office: 1217 Jackson Avenue, P.O. Drawer 707, 38655.
Telephone: 601-234-8775.
Facsimile: 601-238-7552.

William A. Baskin
Billy C. Campbell, Jr.
Mary Launa Gray

Representative Clients: Union Planters Bank, National Association; BanCorp South; Trustmark National Bank; Citibank; Mississippi Power & Light Co.; Mississippi Valley Gas Co.; South Central Bell Telephone Co.; Bituminous Insurance Co.; State Farm Fire & Casualty Insurance Co.; Atlanta Casualty Insurance Company.

For Complete List of Firm Personnel, See General Section

For full biographical listings, see the Martindale-Hubbell Law Directory

MISSOURI

KANSAS CITY, Jackson, Clay, Platte & Cass Cos.

KURLBAUM STOLL SEAMAN & MUSTOE, P.C. (AV)

City Center Square, 1100 Main Street, Suite 2001, 64105
Telephone: 816-221-5444
Telecopy: 816-474-6822
Email: kssrsm@micro.com

Scuyler M. P. Kurlbaum
Steven H. Mustoe
James M. Seaman
Thomas G. Stoll
Roger K. McCrummen
Jeffrey M. Rinne

Theodore M. Meierotto
Eric C. Carter (Not admitted in MO)

For full biographical listings, see the Martindale-Hubbell Law Directory

ST. LOUIS, (Independent City)

THOMPSON COBURN LLP (AV)

One Mercantile Center, 63101
Telephone: 314-552-6000
Telecopier: 314-552-7000
Email: info@thompsoncoburn.com *URL:* http://www.thompsoncoburn.com
Belleville, Illinois Office: 525 West Main Street.
Telephone: 618-277-4700.
Telecopier: 618-236-3434.
Washington, D.C. Office: 700 14th Street, N.W., Suite 900.
Telephone: 202-508-1000.
Telecopier: 202-508-1010.
Billings, Montana Office: Norwest Center, 175 North 27th Street, Suite 903, 59101.
Telephone: 406-896-4100.
Fax: 406-896-4199.

MEMBERS OF FIRM

Donald B. Dorwart
Thomas J. Minogue

Representative Clients: Enterprise Rent-A-Car; Mercantile Bancorporation, Inc.; Mills Group, Inc.; Monsanto Company; Nine West Group, Inc.; RehabCare Corporation, Inc.; Stifel, Nicolaus & Company.

For Complete List of Firm Personnel, See General Section

For full biographical listings, see the Martindale-Hubbell Law Directory

*SPRINGFIELD,** Greene Co.

WILLIAM H. MCDONALD & ASSOCIATES, P.C. (AV)

300 South Jefferson, Suite 600, P.O. Box 1245, 65801
Telephone: 417-869-0581
Facsimile: 417-831-7852
Email: mcdassoc@dialnet.net *URL:* http://www.mcdonaldassoc.com

William H. McDonald

William Craig Hosmer
Stuart H. King
James Richard Royce
James A. Endicott
David Andrew Collins
Dana A. Chamblee
Joseph S. Dressner
Eric O. Nau
Venus V. Harry

For full biographical listings, see the Martindale-Hubbell Law Directory

MONTANA

*BILLINGS,** Yellowstone Co.

CROWLEY, HAUGHEY, HANSON, TOOLE & DIETRICH, P.L.L.P. (AV)

500 Transwestern II, 490 North 31st Street, P.O. Box 2529, 59103
Telephone: 406-252-3441
Fax: 406-259-4159
Email: crowley@crowleylaw.com
Helena, Montana Office: IBM Building, 100 North Park Avenue, Suite 300, 59601.
Telephone: 406-449-4165.
Fax: 406-449-5149.
Kalispell, Montana Office: 431 1st Avenue West, 59901.
Telephone: 406-752-6644.
Fax: 406-752-5108.
Williston, North Dakota Office: 113 East Broadway, 58801.
Telephone: 701-572-2200.
Fax: 701-572-7072.

(See Next Column)

OF COUNSEL

John M. Dietrich
Gareld F. Krieg
Myles J. Thomas

MEMBERS OF FIRM

Arthur F. Lamey, Jr.
David L. Johnson
Terry B. Cosgrove (Resident, Helena, Montana Office)
Allan L. Karell
James P. Sites
Daniel N. McLean (Resident, Helena, Montana Office)
Robert G. Michelotti, Jr.
John R. Alexander
William D. Lamdin, III
Michael S. Dockery
Malcolm H. Goodrich
Mary Scrim Dyre (Resident, Kalispell, Montana Office)
Eric K. Anderson
Renee L. Coppock
John R. Lee (Resident, Williston, North Dakota Office)
Scott M. Heard

Representative Clients: General Motors Acceptance Corporation; Deaconess Medical Center of Billings; Billings Clinic; John Deere Co.; First Interstate Bank of Commerce; Aetna; Montana Livestock Ag Credit, Inc.; Turner Enterprises, Inc.

For Complete List of Firm Personnel, See General Section

For full biographical listings, see the Martindale-Hubbell Law Directory

WRIGHT, TOLLIVER AND GUTHALS A PROFESSIONAL SERVICE CORPORATION (AV)

Windsor Court, 10 North 27th Street, P.O. Box 1977, 59103-1977
Telephone: 406-245-3071
Telecopier: 406-245-3074
Email: lawfirm@mcn.net

Ralph S. Wright (1939-1985)
Kenneth D. Tolliver
Joel E. Guthals
Virginia A. Bryan
Susan Fisher Stevens
J. Reuss
Jeffery A. Hunnes
James W. Thompson

David Paul Wilkins

For full biographical listings, see the Martindale-Hubbell Law Directory

*BOZEMAN,** Gallatin Co.

KIRWAN & BARRETT, P.C. (AV)

215 West Mendenhall, P.O. Box 1348, 59771-1348
Telephone: 406-586-1553
Fax: 406-586-8971

Peter M. Kirwan
Stephen M. Barrett

Representative Clients: Boyne USA, Inc.; Kenyon Noble Lumber Company; American Bank; First Interstate Bank; Big Sky Western Bank; Security Bank of Three Forks.

For full biographical listings, see the Martindale-Hubbell Law Directory

*HELENA,** Lewis and Clark Co.

BROWNING, KALECZYC, BERRY & HOVEN, P.C. (AV)

139 North Last Chance Gulch, P.O. Box 1697, 59624
Telephone: 406-443-6820
Telefax: 406-443-6882
Email: BKBH@BKBH.COM *URL:* http://www.BKBH.com

Stanley T. Kaleczyc
Katharine S. Donnelley

Kimberly A. Beatty
Mary K. Giddings
Steven T. Wade
Mark R. Taylor

Representative Clients: The Burlington Northern Santa Fe Railway Co.; Columbia Falls Aluminum Company; U.S. West; Crane Company; Watkins and Shepard Trucking, Inc.; Rhone-Poulene.

For full biographical listings, see the Martindale-Hubbell Law Directory

NEBRASKA

*LINCOLN,** Lancaster Co.

CLINE, WILLIAMS, WRIGHT, JOHNSON & OLDFATHER (AV)

1900 U.S. Bank Building, 233 South 13th Street, 68508
Telephone: 402-474-6900
Fax: 402-474-5393
Email: postmaster@cline-law.com *URL:* http://www.cline-law.com
Omaha, Nebraska Office: Suite 720, One Pacific Place, 1125 South 103rd Street, 68124.
Telephone: 402-397-1700.
Fax: 402-397-1806.

(See Next Column)

CLINE, WILLIAMS, WRIGHT, JOHNSON & OLDFATHER, *Lincoln—Continued*

ATTORNEYS

Allen L. Graves
Charles M. Pallesen, Jr.
Fredric H. Kauffman
Donald F. Burt
Alan E. Peterson
Stephen E. Gehring
Robert J. Routh
Kevin Colleran
L. Bruce Wright
James M. Bausch
Larry A. Holle
David R. Buntain
Stephen H. Nelsen
Michael C. Mueller
Lauren W. Wismer
Daniel R. Stogsdill
Scott D. Kelly
Terry R. Wittler
Pamela Hastings Carrier
Mark A. Christensen
Richard P. Garden, Jr.
Shawn D. Renner
John C. Miles
Mary Kay Frank
Thomas C. Huston
Sonya S. Ekart
Don R. Janssen
Susan Kubert Sapp
Kevin J. Schneider
Andrew D. Strotman
Jill Gossin Jensen
Rochelle A. Mullen
John L. Horan
Bryan S. Hatch
Steven C. Likes
Tracy A. Oldemeyer
Jolene M. Papa
Timothy G. Aschoff
Eric N. Bergquist
Janis J. Winterhof
Andrea Dylan Snowden

OF COUNSEL

Charles E. Wright
Richard P. Jeffries
Mary M. Campbell

RETIRED PARTNERS

Flavel A. Wright (Retired)
Warren C. Johnson (Retired)
Charles E. Oldfather (1927-1998)

Representative Clients: U.S. Bank National Association; University of Nebraska; Nebraska Medical Assn.; Saint Elizabeth Regional Medical Center; Media of Nebraska; Cargill Inc.; State Farm Insurance Cos.; Wal-Mart Stores, Inc.; Textron/Cushman; Isco, Inc.

For full biographical listings, see the Martindale-Hubbell Law Directory

*OMAHA,** Douglas Co.

DWYER, SMITH, GARDNER, LAZER, POHREN, ROGERS & FORREST (AV)

Suite 400, 8712 West Dodge Road, 68114
Telephone: 402-392-0101
Telefax: 402-392-1011
Email: dwyerlaw@dwyer-smith.com *URL:* http://www.dwyer-smith.com

MEMBERS OF FIRM

Michael L. Lazer
Clay M. Rogers
Edward F. Pohren
John L. Apker
Christopher D. Curzon

ASSOCIATE

Patrick Edward Griffin, Jr.

Representative Clients: Ford Motor Credit Company, Dearborn, Michigan; Nebraska Hospital Association subsidiary Bio Electronics, Lincoln, Oak Bancorporation; Lynn Roberts International; Elliot Equipment Co.; Design Plastics, Inc.

For Complete List of Firm Personnel, See General Section

For full biographical listings, see the Martindale-Hubbell Law Directory

FRASER, STRYKER, VAUGHN, MEUSEY, OLSON, BOYER & BLOCH, P.C. (AV)

500 Energy Plaza, 409 South 17th Street, 68102
Telephone: 402-341-6000
Telecopier: 402-341-8290
Email: fraserstryker.com

Steven Bloch
Robert L. Freeman
Robert W. Rieke

For Complete List of Firm Personnel, See General Section

For full biographical listings, see the Martindale-Hubbell Law Directory

NEVADA

HENDERSON, Clark Co.

ROOKER & GIBSON (AV)

Suite 105, 701 North Green Valley Parkway, 89014
Telephone: 702-990-8100
Telecopier: 702-932-5266

C. Keith Rooker
James B. Gibson

Reference: BankWest of Nevada.

For full biographical listings, see the Martindale-Hubbell Law Directory

*LAS VEGAS,** Clark Co.

ALBRIGHT, STODDARD, WARNICK & ALBRIGHT, A PROFESSIONAL CORPORATION (AV)

Quail Park I, Building D-4, 801 South Rancho Drive, 89106
Telephone: 702-384-7111
Fax: 702-384-0605
URL: http://www.aswalaw.com

G. Vern Albright
William H. Stoddard
Whitney B. Warnick
G. Mark Albright

D. Chris Albright
Tami C. Budo
Corey D. Randall (Not admitted in NV)

Representative Clients: Tokio Marine and Fire Insurance Co.; INAPRO, a CIGNA Co.; Nevada Ready Mix; North American Health Care, Inc. (Nursing Home); Royal Insurance; First Security Bank of Utah; Nevada Community Bank; Nationwide Insurance Co.; Liberty Mutual Insurance; CB Commercial.

For full biographical listings, see the Martindale-Hubbell Law Directory

ALVERSON, TAYLOR, MORTENSEN, NELSON & SANDERS (AV)

7401 West Charleston Boulevard, 89117
Telephone: 702-384-7000
FAX: 702-385-7000
Email: alverson@intermind.net
Reno, Nevada Office: 245 East Liberty, Suite 520, 89505.
Telephone: 775-329-0473.
Fax: 775-329-3303.

MEMBERS OF FIRM

J. Bruce Alverson
Eric K. Taylor
David J. Mortensen
Erven T. Nelson
LeAnn Sanders

OF COUNSEL

Jack C. Cherry
Kurt D. Anderson
Philip C. Van Alstyne

ASSOCIATES

Rebecca Hopkins Miller
Sandra Smagac
Victoria L. Nelson
Aaron D. Lovaas
Diane Obritsch
Michael A. Olsen
Randal D. Shimon
Catherine A. Olendorff
Monica L. Pierce
Gabriel D. Lither
Kurt R. Bonds
Darius F. Rafie
Mark J. King, IV
Shell L. Mercer
Carrie S. Bourdeau
Jason Lane Earnest
Nathan R. Reinmiller
Donn C. Alexander
Afshin Tadayon
Eric O. Freeman
Lindsay L. Stadtlander
Julie M. Sueoka

Representative Clients: Citibank; First Interstate Bank; General Electric; Southwest Gas Corporation; The CIT Group; Kentucky Fried Chicken; Norwest Bank; Federal Deposit Insurance Corporation (FDIC); Yellow Cab Company.

For full biographical listings, see the Martindale-Hubbell Law Directory

GOOLD PATTERSON DEVORE ALES & ROADHOUSE (AV)

4496 South Pecos Road, 89121
Telephone: 702-436-2600
Telecopier: 702-436-2650
URL: http://www.gooldpatterson.com

Barry Stephen Goold
Jeffrey D. Patterson
Thomas J. DeVore
Barney C. Ales
Wilbur M. Roadhouse

ASSOCIATES

Bryan K. Day
E. Bruce Jorgensen
James A. Kohl

Representative Clients: Adams Management; The Allen Group; Archon Financial, L.P.; Desert Oak Development; Lockheed Martin Corporation; Newcourt Financial Corporation; Olympic Land Corporation; Presley Homes; Red Rock Land, LLC; Sunrise Company.

For full biographical listings, see the Martindale-Hubbell Law Directory

JOLLEY, URGA, WIRTH & WOODBURY (AV)

3800 Howard Hughes Parkway Suite 1600, 89109
Telephone: 702-699-7500
Facsimile: 702-699-7555
URL: http://www.juww.com
Boulder City, Nevada Office: Suite 105, 1000 Nevada Highway, 89005.
Telephone: 702-293-3674.

MEMBERS OF FIRM

R. Gardner Jolley
William R. Urga
Roger A. Wirth
Brian E. Holthus
Allen D. Emmel

(See Next Column)

JOLLEY, URGA, WIRTH & WOODBURY—*Continued*

ASSOCIATE

Scott Day Freeman

Representative Clients: Wells Fargo Bank and its predecessor, First Interstate Bank of Nevada; Nevada State Bank; General Electric Capital Corp.; First Security Bank of Nevada; First Nationwide Bank; General Motors Acceptance Corp.; Ford Motor Credit Co.; Nissan Motor Acceptance Corp.; Toyota Motor Credit Corporation; Chase Manhattan.

For Complete List of Firm Personnel, See General Section

For full biographical listings, see the Martindale-Hubbell Law Directory

KUMMER KAEMPFER BONNER & RENSHAW (AV)

Seventh Floor, 3800 Howard Hughes Parkway, 89109-0907
Telephone: 702-792-7000
Fax: 702-796-7181
Email: nvlaw@kkbr.com

MEMBERS OF FIRM

John C. Renshaw
Thomas F. Kummer
Christopher L. Kaempfer
Michael J. Bonner
Kathleen Jane England
John N. Brewer
Gerald D. Waite
Sherwood N. Cook
Shari Cassin Patterson
John C. Jeppsen
Mark H. Fiorentino
John A. Curtas

OF COUNSEL

H. Gregory Nasky
James H. Bilbray
Michael W. Brimley

ASSOCIATES

Thomas D. Amick
Sean L. Anderson (Not admitted in NV)
Nikki L. Baker
George J. Claseman
L. Joe Coppedge
Gregory S. Gilbert
Robert J. Gronauer
Robert C. Kim
Kurt C. Lambeth
Angela Turriciano Otto
Elizabeth A. Savage
Lyssa M. Simonelli
James E. Smyth II
Gregg R. Vermeys
Anthony A. Zmaila

For full biographical listings, see the Martindale-Hubbell Law Directory

MCDONALD CARANO WILSON MCCUNE BERGIN FRANKOVICH & HICKS LLP (AV)

Suite 1000, 2300 West Sahara Avenue, 89102
Telephone: 702-873-4100
Telecopier: 702-873-9966
URL: http://www.mcdonaldcarano.com
Reno, Nevada Office: 241 Ridge Street.
Telephone: 775-788-2000.
Telecopier: 775-788-2020.

MEMBERS OF FIRM

Thomas R. C. Wilson
Alvin J. (Bud) Hicks
Robert E. Armstrong
David W. Huston
George F. Ogilvie III
Scott A. Swain
Andrew P. Gordon
Bryan R. Clark

ASSOCIATES

Andrew S. Gabriel
Anthony D. Guenther
Jeffrey A. Silvestri
Donald G. Martin

Representative Clients: Boyd Gaming Corporation; Clark & Sullivan Constructors, Inc.; Colorite Plastics; First Security Bank of Nevada; Intermountain Federal Land Bank Association; Jackpot Enterprises, Inc.; Nevada State Bank; Valley National Financial Services Co.

For Complete List of Firm Personnel, See General Section

For full biographical listings, see the Martindale-Hubbell Law Directory

PICO & MITCHELL (AV)

2000 South Eastern Avenue, 89104
Telephone: 702-457-9099
FAX: 702-457-8451
Email: lawyers@picomitchell.com

MEMBERS OF FIRM

James F. Pico
Bert O. Mitchell
Christy Brad Escobar
James R. Rosenberger
E. Breen Arntz

ASSOCIATES

Michelle Schwarz
Rebecca L. Mastrangelo
Jill M. Chase
Daniel E. Carvalho
Stephen H. Rogers

Representative Clients: Home Insurance Co.; State Farm Mutual Insurance Co.; Industrial Indemnity Insurance Co.; Great American Insurance Co.; Argonaut Insurance Cos.; Clark County Medical Society; Rose de Lima Hospital; Fairway Chevrolet; American States Insurance Co.; The Hartford Insurance Co.

For full biographical listings, see the Martindale-Hubbell Law Directory

SCHRECK MORRIS (AV)

1200 Bank of America Plaza, 300 South Fourth Street, 89101
Telephone: 702-382-2101
Fax: 702-382-8135; 702-474-9422
URL: http://www.schreckmorris.com
Reno, Nevada Office: 100 West Liberty, Suite 940, 89501.
Telephone: 775-322-7777.
Facsimile: 775-322-7791.

MEMBERS OF FIRM

Frank A. Schreck
Steve Morris
Andrew S. Brignone
Leslie Terry Jones
Mary Kristina Pickering
John A. Godfrey
Ann Morgan
Sean T. McGowan
Ellen Schulhofer
James J. Pisanelli
Clark V. Vellis
Todd L. Bice

ASSOCIATES

James R. Chamberlain
Dennis V. Gallagher
Margaret L. Sanner
F. Edward Mulholland, II
Elizabeth M. Fielder
Elayna Youchah
Sonia C. Vermeys
Denise Michaelides
Mary J. Drury
John P. Desmond
Adam P. Segal
Matthew McCaughey
Amelia R. De Los Santos
Wendy Medura
Robert J. Grasso
Shawn G. Pearson
David Dornak
Matthew L. Heinhold
Paul D. Colton

For full biographical listings, see the Martindale-Hubbell Law Directory

*RENO,** Washoe Co.

MCDONALD CARANO WILSON MCCUNE BERGIN FRANKOVICH & HICKS LLP (AV)

241 Ridge Street, 89501
Telephone: 775-788-2000
Telecopier: 775-788-2020
URL: http://www.mcdonaldcarano.com
Las Vegas, Nevada Office: Suite 1000, 2300 West Sahara Avenue.
Telephone: 702-873-4100.
Telecopier: 702-873-9966.

MEMBERS OF FIRM

John J. McCune
Thomas R. C. Wilson
Leo P. Bergin, III
John J. Frankovich
Alvin J. (Bud) Hicks
Robert E. Armstrong
William A. S. Magrath, II
James W. Bradshaw
John B. Galvin
George F. Ogilvie III
James C. Giudici
Scott A. Swain
Andrew P. Gordon
Valerie P. Cooke
Bryan R. Clark

ASSOCIATES

Paul J. Georgeson
Bonnie Fleischer Drinkwater
Jane M. Long (Not admitted in NV)

Representative Clients: Associated General Contractors of America; Clark & Sullivan Constructors, Inc.; Eldorado Hotel & Casino; Hamilton Group of Companies; Jackpot Enterprises, Inc. ; James Hardie (USA), Inc.; Q & D Construction Company; Regional Emergency Medical Services Authority; Scolari's Warehouse Markets, Inc.; Sierra Nevada Production Credit Association.

For Complete List of Firm Personnel, See General Section

For full biographical listings, see the Martindale-Hubbell Law Directory

WOODBURN AND WEDGE (AV)

One East First Street, Suite 1600, P.O. Box 2311, 89505
Telephone: 775-688-3000
Telecopier: 775-688-3088
Email: postmaster@woodburnlaw.com *URL:* http://www.woodburnlaw.com
Las Vegas, Nevada Office: Suite 700 Bank of America Plaza, 300 South Fourth Street.
Telephone: 702-387-1000.
Telecopier: 702-387-0024.

MEMBERS OF FIRM

Richard O. Kwapil
Kirk S. Schumacher
Gregg P. Barnard

Representative Clients: Atlantic Richfield Co.; Sierra Pacific Power Co.; The Union Pacific Railroad Co.; Pacific Telesis Group; The Hillhave Corp.; National Medical Enterprises; Western Union Telegraph Co.; Bank of America; Cyprus Minerals Corp.; The Roman Catholic Bishop of Reno, A Corporation Sole.

For full biographical listings, see the Martindale-Hubbell Law Directory

NEW HAMPSHIRE

*LACONIA,** Belknap Co.

NORMANDIN, CHENEY & O'NEIL (AV)

Normandin Square, 213 Union Avenue, P.O. Box 575, 03247-0575
Telephone: 603-524-4380
Fax: 603-528-6831
Email: nco@lr.net

MEMBERS OF FIRM

Paul L. Normandin
Robert A. Dietz

ASSOCIATE

Regina A. Nadeau

OF COUNSEL

Duncan J. Farmer

Counsel for: Laconia Savings Bank; Lakes Region Mental Health Center; Laconia Airport Authority; Central New Hampshire Realty, Inc.; All Metals Industries, Inc.; Lakes Region Anesthesiology, P.A.; Cormier Corp.; Scotia Technology; Vemaline Products.

For Complete List of Firm Personnel, See General Section

For full biographical listings, see the Martindale-Hubbell Law Directory

*MANCHESTER,** Hillsborough Co.

SHEEHAN PHINNEY BASS + GREEN, PROFESSIONAL ASSOCIATION (AV)

Hampshire Plaza, 1000 Elm Street, P.O. Box 3701, 03105-3701
Telephone: 603-668-0300
800-625-SPBG
Fax: 603-627-8121
Email: postmaster@sheehan.com *URL:* http://www.sheehan.com
Portsmouth, New Hampshire Office: Old City Hall, 126 Daniel Street.
Telephone: 603-433-2111.
Fax: 603-433-3126.
Concord, New Hampshire Office: 143 North Main Street.
Telephone: 603-223-2020.
Fax: 603-224-8899.

James E. Higgins
Peter F. Kearns
James Q. Shirley
William J. Donovan
Edward A. Haffer
Michael C. Harvell
Stephen E. Weyl
Peter S. Cowan
Katherine M. Hanna
Douglas G. Verge
Christopher Cole
David W. McGrath
James F. Ogorchock

Representative Clients: Anheuser-Busch, Inc.; Bank of New Hampshire Corp.; The Elliot Hospital of Manchester; Granite State Packing Co.; Moore Business Forms, Inc.; New Hampshire College; New Hampshire Dental Service Corp.; New Hampshire Yankee Electric Corp.; Numerica Financial Corp.

For Complete List of Firm Personnel, See General Section

For full biographical listings, see the Martindale-Hubbell Law Directory

NEW JERSEY

CHERRY HILL, Camden Co.

FLASTER/GREENBERG, P.C. (AV)

Commerce Center, 1810 Chapel Avenue West, Third Floor, 08002-4609
Telephone: 856-661-1900
Telecopier: 856-661-1919
Email: FIRM@FLASTERGREENBERG.COM *URL:* http://www.flastergreenberg.com

Richard J. Flaster
Stephen M. Greenberg
Laura B. Wallenstein
Allen P. Fineberg
Markley S. Roderick
Peter R. Spirgel
Alan H. Zuckerman
William S. Skinner
J. Philip Kirchner
Paul J. Russoniello
Carl S. Bisgaier
Steven B. Sacharow
E. Richard Dressel
Kenneth S. Goodkind
Frank H. Wisniewski
Alma L. Saravia

OF COUNSEL

Peter M. Dolinger
James J. Binns

Elizabeth J. Hampton
Jeffrey Herskowitz
Christopher E. Kaltenbach
Steven J. Abrams
Julie A. Williamson
Donna T. Urban
Amelia Carolla
Matthew Azoulay
Elaine J. Petruzziello (Not admitted in NJ)
Ann Marie Iannone
Pasquale Guglietta

(See Next Column)

LEGAL SUPPORT PERSONNEL

PARALEGALS

Ann Gorman
Patricia D'Alessio
Theresa Cooke
Rosemary Dunaif

For full biographical listings, see the Martindale-Hubbell Law Directory

FLORHAM PARK, Morris Co.

SCHWARTZ SIMON EDELSTEIN CELSO & KESSLER (AV)

A Partnership including a Professional Corporation
Ten James Street, 07932
Telephone: 973-301-0001
Fax: 973-301-0203
Email: sseck1@aol.com

Lawrence S. Schwartz (P.C.)
Stephen J. Edelstein
Donald A. Kessler
John B. Mariano, Jr.
Raymond W. Fisher
Burton Zitomer
Joseph Richard Morano

Neil H. Braunstein
Marc H. Zitomer
Stefani C Schwartz
Denis G. Murphy

COUNSEL

Jacob Green

OF COUNSEL

Glenn C. Guritzky
Miguel A. Maza
Scott A. Elk (P.A.) (Not admitted in NJ)

For full biographical listings, see the Martindale-Hubbell Law Directory

*HACKENSACK,** Bergen Co.

CONTANT, SCHERBY & ATKINS (AV)

33 Hudson Street, 07601
Telephone: 201-342-1070
Fax: 201-342-5213
Email: LawfirmCSA@aol.com *URL:* http://www.lawyers.com/csalaw

MEMBERS OF THE FIRM

John M. Contant (1907-1988)
Richard J. Contant
Michael L. Scherby
Bruce L. Atkins
Matthew S. Rogers
Andrew T. Fede
Brian T. Keane
Robert B. Hille

ASSOCIATES

Geraldine E. Beers
Suzanne J. Ryderman
Lisa R. Aljian
Christina A. Stoneburner
Sheila O'Shea

OF COUNSEL

Fenster & Weiss, New City, New York

For full biographical listings, see the Martindale-Hubbell Law Directory

DEENER, FEINGOLD & STERN, A PROFESSIONAL CORPORATION (AV)

2 University Plaza, Suite 503, 07601
Telephone: 201-343-8788
Fax: 201-343-4640
Email: JeromeDeener@DeenerFeingold.com *URL:* http://www.lawyers.com/deenerfeingold&stern

Jerome A. Deener
Cal R. Feingold
Robert A. Stern
David M. Edelblum
Anthony M. Vizzoni

Debra T. Hirsch
Andrew M. Grumet
Ronen Gabbay

References: Hudson United Bank; Commerce Bank.

For full biographical listings, see the Martindale-Hubbell Law Directory

FERRO LABELLA LOGERFO & ZUCKER, A PROFESSIONAL CORPORATION (AV)

The Landmark Building, 27 Warren Street, 07601
Telephone: 201-489-9110
Fax: 201-489-5653

Michael J. Ferro, Jr.
Rocco J. Labella
Michael F. Logerfo
Arthur P. Zucker
Sean M. Aylward
Christopher L. Weiss

Rocio T. Aliaga
Melanie J. Scroble
E. Vicki Arians

Representative Clients: Summit Bank; CoreStates New Jersey National Bank; Bio Medic Corp.; Lab Products, Inc.; COSCO North Americas, Inc.; Thomas J. Lipton Co.

For full biographical listings, see the Martindale-Hubbell Law Directory

Hackensack—Continued

Hein, Smith, Berezin, Maloof & Jacobs, L.L.C. (AV)

Court Plaza East, 19 Main Street, 07601-7023
Telephone: 201-487-7400
Telecopier: 201-487-4228
Email: counsel@heinsmith.com

OF COUNSEL

Seymour A. Smith

For Complete List of Firm Personnel, See General Section

For full biographical listings, see the Martindale-Hubbell Law Directory

Jones and Jones (AV)

45 Essex Street, 07601
Telephone: 201-487-3600
FAX: 201-487-2826
URL: http://www.lawyers.com/jonesjoneslaw

MEMBER OF FIRM

Graham O. Jones
Walter Henry Jones (1912-1982)
Vincent J. Massa, III

ASSOCIATE

Joyce Wilkins Pollison

OF COUNSEL

Walter Henry Jones, III

For full biographical listings, see the Martindale-Hubbell Law Directory

Nicolette & Perkins, P.A. (AV)

3 University Plaza, Fifth Floor, 07601
Telephone: 201-488-9080
Telecopier: 201-488-5580
Email: nicoletteperkins@juno.com *URL:* http://www.lawyers.com/nicolette&perkins

David A. Nicolette, Jr.
Eric R. Perkins

Jeanette A. Odynski
Laura N. Keenan
Toni Marie McPhillips

For full biographical listings, see the Martindale-Hubbell Law Directory

Pashman Stein, A Professional Corporation (AV)

45 Essex Street, 07601-5415
Telephone: 201-488-8200
Fax: 201-488-5556
Email: info@pashmanstein.com *URL:* http://www.lawyers.com/pashmanstein

Louis Pashman
Samuel J. Samaro
Dennis T. Smith
Michael S. Stein

Amy E. Whitteaker
John T. Whipple

SPECIAL COUNSEL

Morris Pashman

For full biographical listings, see the Martindale-Hubbell Law Directory

Stephen H. Roth (AV)

62 Summit Avenue, 07601
Telephone: 201-489-3737
Fax: 201-489-0557

ASSOCIATE

Michele M. De Santis

For full biographical listings, see the Martindale-Hubbell Law Directory

Sokol, Behot and Fiorenzo (AV)

433 Hackensack Avenue, 07601
Telephone: 201-488-1300
Fax: 201-488-6541

MEMBERS OF FIRM

Leon J. Sokol
Joseph F. Behot, Jr.
Joseph B. Fiorenzo
Jeffrey A. Zenn
Arthur Bergman
Michael P. Feltman

ASSOCIATES

Siobhan Spillane Bailey
Mitchell B. Levine
Steven Seigel
Andrew S. Bosin

COUNSEL

Alan Prigal

For full biographical listings, see the Martindale-Hubbell Law Directory

LIBERTY CORNER, Somerset Co.

Apruzzese, McDermott, Mastro & Murphy, A Professional Corporation (AV)

25 Independence Boulevard, P.O. Box 112, 07938
Telephone: 908-580-1776
Fax: 908-647-1492
Email: firmmail@ammm.com *URL:* http://www.firmmail@ammm.com

OF COUNSEL

Vincent J. Apruzzese
Frank X. McDermott

Francis A. Mastro
James F. Murphy (1938-1990)
Frederick T. Danser, III
Maurice J. Nelligan, Jr.
Barry Marell
Robert T. Clarke
Mark J. Blunda
James L. Plosia, Jr.

J. Andrew Kinsey
John P. Harrington
Robert J. Merryman
Kathleen Barnett Einhorn
Joseph C. DeBlasio

COUNSEL

Lisa Barré-Quick

Representative Clients: General Public Utilities Corp.; Public Service Electric & Gas Co.; Jersey Central Power & Light Co.; Saint Barnabas Health Care System; Schering Plough Corp.; New Jersey Transit Corporations; Smith-Kline Beecham; U.S. Metals & Refining Co.; Asea Brown-Boveri; Foster Wheeler Corp.

For full biographical listings, see the Martindale-Hubbell Law Directory

MONTVALE, Bergen Co.

Beattie Padovano, LLC (AV)

50 Chestnut Ridge Road, P.O. Box 244, 07645
Telephone: 201-573-1810
Fax: 201-573-9736
Email: beattie-padovano@worldnet.att.net

MEMBERS OF FIRM

James R. Beattie
Ralph J. Padovano
Roger W. Breslin, Jr.
Thomas W. Dunn
Martin W. Kafafian
Adolph A. Romei
Brian R. Martinotti
John J. Lamb
John R. Holsinger
Antimo A. Del Vecchio

SENIOR ASSOCIATES

Emery C. Duell
Brenda J. Stewart
Kathleen S. Cook
Dana B. Cobb
Steven A. Weisfeld
Robert A. Blass
Alan G. White

ASSOCIATES

Gregg A. Padovano
James V. Zarrillo
Andrew D. Hopp
Jennifer Bretz
Matthew T. Rose
Renata A. Helstoski
Maria V. Martin

OF COUNSEL

Ira J. Kaltman
Francis B. Sheehan

For full biographical listings, see the Martindale-Hubbell Law Directory

*MORRISTOWN,** Morris Co.

Edwards & Antholis, P.C. (AV)

22 Pine Street, 07960-6092
Telephone: 973-540-0050; 800-464-9608
Fax: 973-292-1889
Email: eandapc@aol.com *URL:* http://www.lawyers.com/eandapc

David F. Edwards (1908-1983)
John K. Antholis

For full biographical listings, see the Martindale-Hubbell Law Directory

McElroy, Deutsch and Mulvaney (AV)

1300 Mount Kemble Avenue, P.O. Box 2075, 07962-2075
Telephone: 973-993-8100
Fax: 973-425-0161
URL: http://www.MDMlaw.com
Denver, Colorado Office: 1099 18th Street, Suite 3120.
Telephone: 303-293-8800.
Fax: 303-293-3116.
New York, New York Office: Wall Street Plaza, 88 Pine Street.
Telephone: 212-766-1807.
Fax: 212-483-9129.
Ridgewood, New Jersey Office: 40 West Ridgewood Avenue.
Telephone: 201-445-6722.
Fax: 201-445-8075.

MEMBERS OF FIRM

Lorraine M. Armenti (Resident Partner, Denver Colorado Office)
Grace C. Bertone
John P. Beyel
William C. Carey
Stephen H. Cohen (1938-1992)
Kevin T. Coughlin

(See Next Column)

McElroy, Deutsch and Mulvaney, *Morristown—Continued*

MEMBERS OF FIRM (Continued)

John F. Darcy (Resident, Ridgewood Office)
Edward B. Deutsch
Timothy I. Duffy
Kevin P. Galvin
Robert J. Kelly
Joseph P. La Sala
James P. Lisovicz
Paul A. Lisovicz
Fred A. Manley, Jr.
Michael J. Marone
Nancy McDonald
William T. McElroy
Laurence M. McHeffey (Resident Partner, Denver, Colorado Office)
Robert W. Muilenburg
James M. Mulvaney
Alfred S. Nugent, Jr. (1925-1989)
Octavius A. Orbe (Resident, Ridgewood Office)
Loren L. Pierce
Warren K. Racusin
Mark A. Rosen
Thomas P. Scrivo
John H. Suminski
Walter F. Timpone
Kevin E. Wolff

COUNSEL TO THE FIRM

Robert L. Clifford

OF COUNSEL

John K. Bradley
John F. Whitteaker

ASSOCIATES

Susan Freeman Anthony
H. George Avery
Elizabeth Addison Barrow
Joseph F. Bermudez
Thomas Richard Calcagni
Patrick J. Casey (Resident Associate, Denver, Colorado Office)
Lisbeth W. Cload (Resident, Ridgewood Office)
Daniel J. Cohen
Craig J. Compoli, Jr.
John P. Cookson (Resident Associate, New York, NY Office)
John Thomas Coyne
Andrew J. D'Arcy
Andrew M. Csaszar
Michael B. Devins
John W. DiNicola, II
Robin A. Donato
Rebecca Ward Donohue
Steven F. Dorry
Julienne S. Duncan
Brian F. Fowler (Resident, Ridgewood Office)
Aaron C. Foy (Not admitted in NJ; Resident, Denver, Colorado Office)
Christopher S. Frangeš
Lorna A. Friel
Kevin P. Harkins (Resident, Ridgewood Office)
Sarah C. Herzog
Eric J. Hughes
George A. Kelman
Justin N. Kinney
Linda F. Kitz
John P. Leonard
Joseph J. McGlone
Robert McGuire
Kaneez Fatema Madraswalla
Nadine Maleski
Faith Martin
Suzanne Cocco Midlige
Heidi S. Minuskin
Louis A. Modugno
Florina A. Moldovan
John W. Morris
Francis C. Porada (Resident Associate, Denver, Colorado Office)
Robert J. Re
Vincent E. Reilly
Jay R. Ruble
Craig T. Sashihara
Adam R. Schwartz
Peter W. Smith
Timothy P. Smith
Ronnie H. Spring
Michael J. Sullivan
Catharine Acker Vaughan
Meredith A. Walling
Richard J. Williams, Jr.

Representative Clients: ADT Security Systems, Inc.; Grove Bank; Crum & Forster Insurance Co.; Eaton Corp.; Fireman's Fund Insurance Cos.; New Jersey Manufacturers Insurance Co.; The Home Indemnity Co.; The Pittston Company; Security Pacific Finance Corporation; American Honda Motor Co., Inc.

For full biographical listings, see the Martindale-Hubbell Law Directory

---

Rand, Algeier, Tosti & Woodruff, A Professional Corporation (AV)

60 Washington Street, 07960
Telephone: 973-539-2600
Telecopier: 973-984-0430
Email: randlaw@bellatlantic.net

Gary C. Algeier
David B. Rand
Robert M. Tosti
Robert B. Woodruff
John F. McDonnell
John E. Croot, Jr.

Kathryn J. Kingree
Deborah A. White

OF COUNSEL

Ronald M. Pflug
Ellen S. Bass
Tamara Krikorian

For full biographical listings, see the Martindale-Hubbell Law Directory

*NEWARK,** Essex Co.

Apruzzese, McDermott, Mastro & Murphy, A Professional Corporation

(See Liberty Corner)

Carpenter, Bennett & Morrissey (AV)

Three Gateway Center, 17th Floor, 100 Mulberry Street, 07102-4079
Telephone: 973-622-7711
New York City: 212-943-6530
Telex: 139405
Telecopier: 973-622-5314
Email: cbm@carpben.com

MEMBERS OF FIRM

Laurence Reich
Michael S. Waters
James G. Gardner
John D. Goldsmith
Joseph D. Rasnek
Robert J. Stickles
Lois H. Goodman

OF COUNSEL

Edward F. Day, Jr.

ASSOCIATES

Hans G. Polak
Michelle S. Hydrusko
Jeffrey Bernstein
Daniel J. O'Hern, Jr.
Marc E. Wolin
Melissa B. Popkin
Marny Lundy Solazzo

Representative Clients: General Motors Corp.; E. I. du Pont de Nemours and Co.; Texaco Inc.; AT&T; Litton Industries; ITT Industries, Inc.; Johnson & Johnson; International Flavors & Fragrances Inc.; MAN Capital Corp.; Prudential Insurance Company of America; Hartford Insurance Co.

For Complete List of Firm Personnel, See General Section

For full biographical listings, see the Martindale-Hubbell Law Directory

---

Greenberg Dauber Epstein & Tucker, A Professional Corporation (AV)

Suite 600, One Gateway Center, 07102-5311
Telephone: 973-643-3700
Facsimile: 973-643-1218
URL: http://www.greenbergdauber.com

Melvin Greenberg
Edward J. Dauber
Stanley A. Epstein
H. Glenn Tucker
Linda G. Harvey
Russell S. Burnside

Sumeeta A. Gawande
Richard H. Schwartz
Michael H. Freeman
Charles J. Hayden
Scott W. Miller

For full biographical listings, see the Martindale-Hubbell Law Directory

McCarter & English, LLP (AV)

Four Gateway Center, 100 Mulberry Street, P.O. Box 652, 07101-0652
Telephone: 973-622-4444
Telecopier: 973-624-7070
URL: http://www.mccarter.com
Cherry Hill, New Jersey Office: 1820 Chapel Avenue West, Suite 380.
Telephone: 609-662-8444.
Telecopier: 609-662-6203.
New York, New York Office: Suite 2247, One World Trade Center.
Telephone: 212-466-9018.
Telecopier: 212-432-6568.
Boca Raton, Florida Office: 2255 Glades Road, Suite 319-A.
Telephone: 561-994-6262.
Telecopier: 561-241-0798.
Wilmington, Delaware Office: Mellon Bank Center, 919 Market Street.
Telephone: 302-654-8010.
Telecopier: 302-654-0795.
Philadelphia, Pennsylvania Office: One Commerce Square, 2005 Market Street, Suite 3600.
Telephone: 215-557-7700.
Telecopier: 215-557-6544.

MEMBERS OF FIRM

Alfred L. Ferguson
Andrew T. Berry
Richard W. Hill
William H. Horton
Bart J. Colli
Richard M. Eittreim
William T. Reilly
Hayden Smith, Jr.
Todd M. Poland
Roslyn S. Harrison
Gita F. Rothschild
David R. Kott
Lanny S. Kurzweil
Frank E. Ferruggia
Michael A. Tanenbaum
Richard P. O'Leary
Theodore D. Moskowitz
Myrna L. Wigod
Joseph Lubertazzi, Jr.
Peter S. Twombly
David F. Broderick
William D. Wallach
Lisa W.S. Bonsall
Sherilyn Pastor

OF COUNSEL

Peter C. Aslanides

COUNSEL

Joseph F. Falgiani
Steven A. Beckelman
Jerry P. Sattin

For Complete List of Firm Personnel, See General Section

For full biographical listings, see the Martindale-Hubbell Law Directory

Newark—Continued

McManimon & Scotland, L.L.C. (AV)

One Riverfront Plaza, 4th Floor, 07102-5311
Telephone: 973-622-1800
Fax: 973-622-7333; 973-622-3744

MEMBERS OF FIRM

Joseph P. Baumann, Jr.
John V. Cavaliere
John B. Hall
Glenn F. Scotland
Ronald J. Ianoale
Andrea L. Kahn
Jeffrey G. Kramer
Leslie G. London
Edward J. McManimon, III

OF COUNSEL

Norman M. Robertson
Carla J. Brundage

ASSOCIATES

Peter S. Crisafi
Sheila Newsome Maddox
M. Frances Ciesla
Kristin Dwyer Ganley
Joseph C. Jasaitis
Stephen N. Severud
Thomas J. Hastie, Jr.

LEGAL SUPPORT PERSONNEL

Helen Lysaght

PARALEGALS

Sandra Simoes

For full biographical listings, see the Martindale-Hubbell Law Directory

Meyner and Landis (AV)

One Gateway Center, Suite 2500, 07102-5311
Telephone: 973-624-2800
Fax: 973-624-0356
Email: attys@meyner.com *URL:* http://www.meyner.com

Robert B. Meyner (1908-1990)
Edwin C. Landis, Jr.
John N. Malyska
William J. Fiore
Anthony F. Siliato
Francis R. Perkins
Howard O. Thompson
Scott T. McCleary
Linda Townley Snyder
William H. Schmidt, Jr.
David B. Grantz

For full biographical listings, see the Martindale-Hubbell Law Directory

St. John & Wayne, L.L.C. (AV)

Two Penn Plaza East, 07105-2249
Telephone: 973-491-3600
Fax: 973-491-3555
Email: firm@nwk.stjohn-law.com *URL:* http://www.stjohn-law.com
Rochester, New York Office: St. John & Curtin, L.L.C., First Federal Plaza.
Telephone: 716-262-6780.
Fax: 716-262-6755.
New York, New York Office: Heron Tower, 70 East 55th. Street.
Telephone: 212-446-5000.
Fax: 212-446-5055.

Paul D. Drobbin
Bruce S. Edington
David C. Freinberg
David W. Phillips
Thomas D. Ruane (Resident, New York, New York Office)
Peter B. Van Deventer, Jr.
Robert A. Wayne

Bryant Kenneth Aaron
Douglas H. Amster
Robyn M. Gnudi

For Complete List of Firm Personnel, See General Section

For full biographical listings, see the Martindale-Hubbell Law Directory

Sills Cummis Radin Tischman Epstein & Gross, A Professional Corporation (AV)

One Riverfront Plaza, 07102-5400
Telephone: 973-643-7000
Fax: 973-643-6500
Telex: 820630 Sillsbeck Nwk
Email: sillsmail@sillscummis.com *URL:* http://www.sillscummis.com
Atlantic City, New Jersey Office: 17 Gordon's Alley.
Telephone: 609-344-2800.
New York, N.Y. Office: 712 Fifth Avenue.
Telephone: 212-643-7000.
Washington, D.C. Office: 1800 K Street, N.W.
Telephone: 202-296-4750.

MEMBERS OF FIRM

Clive S. Cummis
Michael B. Tischman
Steven E. Gross
Simon Levin
Andrew P. Napolitano
William J. Martini
Noah Bronkesh
Steven M. Goldman
Ira A. Rosenberg
Robert Max Crane
Jerry Genberg
Brian S. Coven
Stanley U. North, III
James D. Toll (Resident at Atlantic City, N.J. Office)
Victor H. Boyajian
Alan J. Cohen (Resident at Atlantic City, N.J. Office)
Frederic M. Tudor
Steven R. Kamen

(See Next Column)

OF COUNSEL

Diane M. Lavenda

Noel D. Humphreys
Eric D. Mann (Resident at Atlantic City, N.J. Office)
Rhonda Sobral O'Toole
Lori M. Waldron

Representative Clients: WWOR-TV, Inc.; Midlantic National Bank; Foods, Inc.; Jersey City Medical Center; Bally's Entertainment Corp.; BMW North America; Motor Club of America; GAF Corporation; Maidenform, Inc.; Exxon Company, U.S.A.; PNC Bank Corp.

For Complete List of Firm Personnel, See General Section

For full biographical listings, see the Martindale-Hubbell Law Directory

NORTH BRUNSWICK, Middlesex Co.

Borrus, Goldin, Foley, Vignuolo, Hyman, Stahl & Clarkin, A Professional Corporation (AV)

2875 U.S. Highway 1, Route 1 & Finnigans Lane, P.O. Box 7463, 08902
Telephone: 732-422-1000
Fax: 732-422-1016
Email: attys@borrus.com *URL:* http://www.borrus.com

Jack Borrus
Martin S. Goldin
David M. Foley
Anthony B. Vignuolo
Jeffrey M. Hyman
James E. Stahl
James F. Clarkin III
Eileen Mary Foley

Robert C. Nisenson
Rosalind Westlake
Lisa M. Vignuolo
Steven L. Fox
Peter A. Vignuolo
Gerald T. Foley (1903-1976)

Representative Clients: Summit Bank; R. J. Reynolds Tobacco Co.; K. Hovnanian Enterprises, Inc.; Johnson and Johnson; Foster Wheeler, Inc.; Hartz Mountain Industries; Middlesex County Vocational Services Commission; Borough of South Plainfield Board of Adjustment; U-Haul of Northern NJ.

For full biographical listings, see the Martindale-Hubbell Law Directory

PARAMUS, Bergen Co.

Strasser & Associates, A Professional Corporation (AV)

Paramus Plaza I, 140 Route 17 North, Suite 265, 07652-2816
Telephone: 201-262-7177
Fax: 201-262-3113

William I. Strasser

Conrad M. Olear
Constantinos J. Ballas

Representative Clients: Consumer Value Stores (CVS); Melville Corp.; Melville Realty Corp.; Linens 'N Things, Inc.; This End Up Furniture Co., Inc.; Universal Foods Corp.; Essex Computers, Inc.; Polevoy Associates; Footstar, Inc.; Bob's Stores.

For full biographical listings, see the Martindale-Hubbell Law Directory

PRINCETON, Mercer Co.

Bergman & Barrett (AV)

9 Tamarack Circle, Montgomery Knoll, U.S. Highway 206 North, P.O. Box 1273, 08542
Telephone: 609-921-1502
Fax: 609-683-0288

Edward J. Bergman
Michael T. Barrett

LEGAL SUPPORT PERSONNEL

Kelli E. Murphy (Paralegal)

For full biographical listings, see the Martindale-Hubbell Law Directory

McCarthy and Schatzman, P.A. (AV)

228 Alexander Street, P.O. Box 2329, 08543-2329
Telephone: 609-924-1199
Fax: 609-683-5251

John F. McCarthy, Jr.
Richard Schatzman
G. Christopher Baker
John F. McCarthy, III
Michael A. Spero
Barbara Strapp Nelson
W. Scott Stoner
James J. Britt, Jr.

Charly Gayden

Representative Clients: Trustees of Princeton University; Carnegie Center Associates; Merrill Lynch Pierce Fenner & Smith, Inc.; Calton Homes, Inc.

For full biographical listings, see the Martindale-Hubbell Law Directory

ROSELAND, Essex Co.

POST, POLAK, GOODSELL & MACNEILL, P.A. (AV)

75 Livingston Avenue, 07068-3701
Telephone: 973-994-1100
Telecopier: 973-994-1705
Email: administrator@ppgm.com
New York, New York Office: 575 Madison Avenue, Suite 1006.
Telephone: 212-486-1455.

John N. Post
Frederick B. Polak
Robert A. Goodsell
Jay Scott MacNeill
Paul D. Strauchler
Mary H. Post
David L. Epstein

Loretta B. Critchley
Nilufer O. DeScherer

For Complete List of Firm Personnel, See General Section

For full biographical listings, see the Martindale-Hubbell Law Directory

CHARLES A. ROSEN (AV)

280 Corporate Center, 5 Becker Farm Road, 07068
Telephone: 973-535-2800
Telecopier: 973-535-9777
New York, New York Office: 60 East 42nd Street, Suite 1217.
Telephone: 212-921-2236.

ASSOCIATE

Cecilia M.E. Lindenfelser

Reference: Summit Bank.

For full biographical listings, see the Martindale-Hubbell Law Directory

WALDER, SONDAK & BROGAN, A PROFESSIONAL CORPORATION (AV)

5 Becker Farm Road, P.O. Box 901, 07068
Telephone: 973-992-5300
Telecopier: 973-992-1505; 992-1006
Email: general@wsbesqs.com *URL:* http://www.wsbesqs.com

Justin P. Walder
Thomas J. Spies
Barry A. Kozyra
James A. Plaisted
Heather Grasz Suarez
Michael J. Faul, Jr.
Jeffrey A. Walder
Patricia M. Talbert

John S. Redden
Shalom D. Stone
Christopher M. Farella
Barbara F. Buchta
Steven D. Grossman
K. Roger Plawker

Representative Clients: Hartz Mountain Industries; NEC America, Inc.; Old Republic Insurance Co.; Chicago Underwriting Group; Tuscan/Lehigh Dairies, LP.; Engelhard Corporation; Webcraft Technologies, Inc.; Vermont Teddy Bear Company.

For Complete List of Firm Personnel, See General Section

For full biographical listings, see the Martindale-Hubbell Law Directory

SADDLE BROOK, Bergen Co.

COHN LIFLAND PEARLMAN HERRMANN & KNOPF LLP (AV)

Park 80 Plaza West-One, 07663
Telephone: 201-845-9600
Telecopier: 201-845-9423
Email: info@njlawfirm.com *URL:* http://www.njlawfirm.com

MEMBERS OF FIRM

Albert L. Cohn
Peter S. Pearlman
Barry A. Knopf
Daniel Crystal (Retired)
Jeffrey W. Herrmann
Robert D. Zatorski
Allen Susser
Mary Ann T. Stokes
Brian D. Zinn
Joshua P. Cohn

ASSOCIATES

Virginia A. Harper
Leonard Z. Kaufmann
Audra DePaolo
Robert Ricci, Jr.
Maurice W. McLaughlin
Andrew C. Abrams
Jessica V. Henry

OF COUNSEL

Sylvia J. Cohn
Jodi B. Scherl

For full biographical listings, see the Martindale-Hubbell Law Directory

KRUGMAN & KAILES LLP (AV)

Park 80 West-Plaza Two, 07663-5835
Telephone: 201-845-3434; 212-695-3262
Telecopier: 201-845-9627
Email: counsel@krugmankailes.com
New York, New York Office: 99 Park Avenue, Suite 2200.
Telephone: 212-599-1060.
Telecopier: 212-599-6282.

(See Next Column)

London, England Office: 90 Fetter Lane, London EC4A-1PT.
Telephone: 011 (44) 171-421-7918.
Telecopier: 011 (44) 171-831-6407.

MEMBERS OF FIRM

Martin Krugman (1916-1994)
Howard Kailes
Thomas J. Goodwin
Ward C. Laracy
Robert I. Wexler
Alan H. Fox
Joy M. Mercer
Kerry B. Flowers

OF COUNSEL

James D. Krugman

COUNSEL

Judith S. Musicant

ASSOCIATES

Anne M. Wallace (Not admitted in NJ)
April A. Savoye
Lisa Ann Miller
Patrizia E. DeBari
David J. Hanley, Jr.
Anjana D. Patel
W. Mark O'Brien

For full biographical listings, see the Martindale-Hubbell Law Directory

SHORT HILLS, Essex Co.

EDWIN R. MATTHEWS, P.C. (AV)

150 John F. Kennedy Parkway CN 5008, 07078-2707
Telephone: 973-912-9500
Telecopier: 973-912-9411
Email: mwgf@mail.att.net

Edwin R. Matthews

Robert J. Pansulla
Daniel J. Bonner
Drew D. Krause
Lisa A. Grattan

For full biographical listings, see the Martindale-Hubbell Law Directory

*SOMERVILLE,** Somerset Co.

SCHACHTER, TROMBADORE, OFFEN, STANTON & PAVICS, A PROFESSIONAL CORPORATION (AV)

45 East High Street, P.O. Box 520, 08876-0520
Telephone: 908-722-5700
Fax: 908-722-8853

Richard J. Schachter
Stephen M. Offen

For full biographical listings, see the Martindale-Hubbell Law Directory

RAYMOND R. & DAVID W. TROMBADORE, P.C. A PROFESSIONAL CORPORATION (AV)

33 East High Street, 08876
Telephone: 908-722-7555
Fax: 908-722-6269
URL: http://www.trombadorelaw.com

Raymond R. Trombadore
David W. Trombadore

OF COUNSEL

Ann W. Trombadore

References: Summit Bank; Somerset Savings & Loan Assn.

For full biographical listings, see the Martindale-Hubbell Law Directory

SOUTH ORANGE, Essex Co.

LAW OFFICE OF CHARLES B. TURNER (AV)

76 South Orange Avenue, P.O. Box 526, 07079
Telephone: 973-763-5000
Fax: 973-763-0568

ASSOCIATES

Marcia Klosk Graydon
Andrew R. Turner

For full biographical listings, see the Martindale-Hubbell Law Directory

SPRINGFIELD, Union Co.

APRUZZESE, MCDERMOTT, MASTRO & MURPHY, A PROFESSIONAL CORPORATION

(See Liberty Corner)

SUMMIT, Union Co.

BOURNE, NOLL & KENYON, A PROFESSIONAL CORPORATION (AV)

382 Springfield Avenue, P.O. Box 690, 07902-0690
Telephone: 908-277-2200
Facsimile: 908-277-6808

(See Next Column)

BOURNE, NOLL & KENYON A PROFESSIONAL CORPORATION—*Continued*

Cary R. Hardy
Charles R. Berman
Martin Rubashkin
Roger Mehner
James R. Ottobre
Lawrence A. Rudnick
John F. Kuntz

OF COUNSEL

Edward T. Kenyon
Robert B. Bourne

COUNSEL

Ellyn A. Draikiwicz

Jaime A. O'Brien
Timothy A. Kalas
Alan F. Schwarz
Ross W. Smith

For full biographical listings, see the Martindale-Hubbell Law Directory

*TRENTON,** Mercer Co.

NEEDELL, SIEKERKA & CASTELLANI, A PROFESSIONAL CORPORATION (AV)

Quakerbridge Commons, 2681 Quakerbridge Road, 08619-1625
Telephone: 609-584-7700
Fax: 609-584-0123
Email: nsclaw@aol.com

Stanley H. Needell
Michele N. Siekerka
Anthony P. Castellani

John M. Cinti
Dean C. Gresek

LEGAL SUPPORT PERSONNEL

PARALEGALS

Marlene Griesbach
Carolyn D. Shaw
Veronica A. Mitchell

For full biographical listings, see the Martindale-Hubbell Law Directory

TEICH, GROH AND FROST (AV)

691 State Highway 33, 08619-4492
Telephone: 609-890-1500
Fax: 609-890-6961
Email: teich1g2f3@aol.com
Lawrenceville, New Jersey Office: 109 Franklin Corner Road.
Telephone: 609-844-0488.
Fax: 609-844-0784.

MEMBERS OF FIRM

Arthur Teich (1915-1997)
William C. Groh
Barry W. Frost
Carol Oswald
(Also at Lawrenceville Office)
Carol L. Knowlton
Allen I. Gorski
Arthur R. Sypek, Jr.
Dean S. Nalbone

ASSOCIATES

Jill M. Wittenborn
(Also at Lawrenceville Office)
Michael W. Krutman
David A. Martin
Kimberley M. Lake

References: CoreStates/New Jersey National Bank; United National Bank.

For full biographical listings, see the Martindale-Hubbell Law Directory

WESTFIELD, Union Co.

LINDABURY, MCCORMICK & ESTABROOK, P.A. (AV)

53 Cardinal Drive, P.O. Box 2369, 07091
Telephone: 908-233-6800
Fax: 908-233-5078
New York, N.Y. Office: 26 Broadway, Suite 2300.
Telephone: 212-742-3390.
Fax: 212-269-5016.

Richard R. Width
William R. Watkins
John R. Blasi
Donald F. Nicolai
James D. DeRose
Robert S. Burney
David R. Pierce
Jay Lavroff
Robert W. Anderson
Robert S. Schwartz
Richard J. Cino

Kelly A. Briganti
Jennifer F. Barry

OF COUNSEL

Kenneth L. Estabrook

Representative Clients: Furnished Upon Request.

For Complete List of Firm Personnel, See General Section

For full biographical listings, see the Martindale-Hubbell Law Directory

WEST ORANGE, Essex Co.

HOWARD M. DAVIS, P.C. (AV)

743 Northfield Avenue, 07052
Telephone: 201-325-8383
Telefax: 201-325-1159
Email: HMDPC@AOL.COM *URL:* http://www.lawyers.com/davislaw

Howard M. Davis

Howard J. Ehrlich

Reference: PNC Bank, West Orange.

For full biographical listings, see the Martindale-Hubbell Law Directory

WOODBRIDGE, Middlesex Co.

WILENTZ, GOLDMAN & SPITZER, A PROFESSIONAL CORPORATION (AV)

90 Woodbridge Center Drive Suite 900, Box 10, 07095
Telephone: 732-636-8000
Telecopier: 732-855-6117
URL: http://www.newjerseylaw.com
Eatontown, New Jersey Office: Meridian Center I, Two Industrial Way West, 07724.
Telephone: 732-542-4500.
Telecopier: 732-493-8387.
New York, New York Office: Wall Street Plaza, 88 Pine Street, 9th Floor, 10005.
Telephone: 212-267-3091.
Telecopier: 212-267-3828.

Francis V. Bonello
Stuart A. Hoberman
Sheldon E. Jaffe
Anthony J. Pannella, Jr.
Michael F. Schaff
Louis T. DeLucia
Peter R. Herman
Robert C. Kautz
Steven P. Marshall
Douglas Watson Lubic

Jonathan P. Falk

Representative Clients: Amerada Hess Corp.; Chevron, U.S.A.; Cumberland Farms, Inc.; Middlesex County Utilities Co.; New Jersey Automobile Dealers Assn.; Co-Steel Raritan; The Rouse Co.

For Complete List of Firm Personnel, See General Section

For full biographical listings, see the Martindale-Hubbell Law Directory

NEW MEXICO

*ALBUQUERQUE,** Bernalillo Co.

EAVES, BARDACKE, BAUGH KIERST & KIERNAN, P.A. (AV)

6400 Uptown Boulevard, N.E., Suite 110-W, P.O. Box 35670, 87176
Telephone: 505-888-4300
Facsimile: 505-883-4406
Email: LGLEAVES@EB-B.com

John M. Eaves
Paul Bardacke
John G. Baugh
Peter S. Kierst
Kerry Kiernan

Derek V. Larson
Karen S. Mendenhall
C. Shannon Bacon

OF COUNSEL

Jennifer J. Pruett

For full biographical listings, see the Martindale-Hubbell Law Directory

KREHBIEL, BANNERMAN & HORN, P.A. (AV)

6400 Uptown Boulevard, N.E., Suite 310 East, 87110
Telephone: 505-837-1900
Fax: 505-837-1800
Email: kbh@kbh-lawfirm.com *URL:* http://www.kbh-lawfirm.com

Phil Krehbiel
John A. Bannerman
Barry D. Williams

Rikki L. Quintana
Carol Lisa Smith
David H. Johnson
Lucinda R. Bovee

OF COUNSEL

Ronald F. Horn

For full biographical listings, see the Martindale-Hubbell Law Directory

Albuquerque—Continued

MILLER, STRATVERT & TORGERSON, P.A. (AV)

500 Marquette Avenue, N.W., Suite 1100, P.O. Box 25687, 87102
Telephone: 505-842-1950
Facsimile: 505-243-4408
Email: info@mstLAW.com *URL:* http://www.mstLAW.com
Farmington, New Mexico Office: 300 West Arrington, Suite 300, P.O. Box 869.
Telephone: 505-326-4521.
Facsimile: 505-325-5474.
Las Cruces, New Mexico Office: 500 South Main, Suite 800, P.O. Box 1209.
Telephone: 505-523-2481.
Facsimile: 505-526-2215.
Santa Fe, New Mexico Office: 150 Washington Avenue, Suite 300, P.O. Box 1986.
Telephone: 505-989-9614.
Facsimile: 505-989-9857.

Seth V. Bingham (Resident at Farmington Office)
Lawrence R. White (Resident at Las Cruces Office)
Sharon P. Gross
J. Scott Hall (Resident at Santa Fe Office)
Joel T. Newton (Resident at Las Cruces Office)
Thomas M. Domme
Dana M. Kyle (Resident at Las Cruces Office)
Kyle M. Finch (Resident at Farmington Office)
Fred Schiller (Resident at Las Cruces Office)
Dean B. Cross (Resident at Las Cruces Office)

COUNSEL

Paul W. Robinson
Ralph Wm. Richards (Resident at Las Cruces Office)
Ross B. Perkal
James J. Widland
Bradley D. Tepper

Representative Clients: CDK Contracting Co.; Citizens Bank of Las Cruces; Dominos Pizza, Inc.; Ellen Equipment Corp.; Farmers Insurance Group; Mutual Insurance Corp. of America; St. Paul Insurance Cos.; Stahman Farms, Inc.; Star Construction; State Farm Mutual Automobile Insurance Co.

For Complete List of Firm Personnel, See General Section

For full biographical listings, see the Martindale-Hubbell Law Directory

RODEY, DICKASON, SLOAN, AKIN & ROBB, P.A. (AV)

Albuquerque Plaza, Suite 2200, 201 Third Street, N.W., P.O. Box 1888, 87103-1888
Telephone: 505-765-5900
Fax: 505-768-7395
Email: info@rodey.com *URL:* http://www.rodey.com
Santa Fe, New Mexico Office: Suite 101 Marcy Plaza, 123 East Marcy Street, P.O. Box 1357, 87504-1357.
Telephone: 505-984-0100.
Fax: 505-989-9542.

Robert M. St. John
John P. Burton (Resident, Santa Fe Office)
Catherine T. Goldberg
Jo Saxton Brayer
Nancy J. Appleby
Mark A. Smith
Jay D. Hill

COUNSEL

Richard C. Minzner
S. I. Betzer, Jr.

OF COUNSEL

John D. Robb
Debra Romero Thal

For Complete List of Firm Personnel, See General Section

For full biographical listings, see the Martindale-Hubbell Law Directory

*SANTA FE,** Santa Fe Co.

CATRON, CATRON & SAWTELL, A PROFESSIONAL ASSOCIATION (AV)

2006 Botulph Road, P.O. Box 788, 87504-0788
Telephone: 505-982-1947
Telecopier: 505-986-1013
Email: catronlaw@aol.com

Thomas B. Catron III
John S. Catron
Fletcher R. Catron
W. Anthony Sawtell

LEGAL SUPPORT PERSONNEL

Peggy L. Feldt (Certified Public Accountant)

For Complete List of Firm Personnel, See General Section

For full biographical listings, see the Martindale-Hubbell Law Directory

COMEAU, MALDEGEN, TEMPLEMAN & INDALL, L.L.P. (AV)

Coronado Building, 141 East Palace Avenue, P.O. Box 669, 87504-0669
Telephone: 505-982-4611
Telecopier: 505-988-2987
Email: cmtilaw@earthlink.net

(See Next Column)

MEMBERS OF FIRM

Michael R. Comeau
Larry D. Maldegen
William P. Templeman
Jon J. Indall
Stephen J. Lauer
Paula Ann Cook
Grey Handy
Joseph E. Manges

Michael C. Smith
Christian A. Hatfield

OF COUNSEL

Jeffrey R. Brannen

Representative Clients: AirTouch Cellular; GTE; Homestake Mining Co.; N.M. Banquest Investors Corp.; United Nuclear Corp.; First National Bank of Santa Fe; Uranium Producers of America; United Van Lines; Mayflower Transit; State of New Mexico.

For full biographical listings, see the Martindale-Hubbell Law Directory

WHITE, KOCH, KELLY & MCCARTHY, A PROFESSIONAL ASSOCIATION (AV)

433 Paseo De Peralta, P.O. Box 787, 87504-0787
Telephone: 505-982-4374
ABA/NET: 1154
Fax: 505-982-0350; 984-8631
Email: WKKM@NM.NET

John F. McCarthy, Jr.
Charles W. N. Thompson, Jr.
M. Karen Kilgore

OF COUNSEL

John M. Hickey

Suzanne C. Odom (Not admitted in NM)

Representative Clients: Hilton Hotel; Sprint Communications; Gateway 2000, Inc.; El Paso Electric Company; Thornburg Investment Trust; Thornburg Limited Term Municipal Fund, Inc.; First National Bank of Santa Fe; Hibernia National Bank; Noble House.

For Complete List of Firm Personnel, See General Section

For full biographical listings, see the Martindale-Hubbell Law Directory

NEW YORK

*BUFFALO,** Erie Co.

RAICHLE, BANNING, WEISS & STEPHENS (AV)

410 Main Street, 14202
Telephone: 716-852-7587
Telecopier: 716-852-7599
Email: RBWS@MSN.COM

MEMBERS OF FIRM

Frank G. Raichle (1898-1986)
Derrick C. Banning (1916-1995)
Arnold Weiss
R. William Stephens

ASSOCIATES

Lisa Parlato Neff
R. Hugh Stephens

Representative Clients: General Motors Corp.; Cliffstar Corp.; Blue Cross & Blue Shield of Michigan; Sony Picture Releasing Inc.; Superior Jamestown Corp., Adanlock Office Environments Division; Permclip Products Corp.; Living Monuments Inc.

For full biographical listings, see the Martindale-Hubbell Law Directory

SULLIVAN & OLIVERIO (AV)

600 Main Place Tower, 14202-3706
Telephone: 716-854-5300
Telecopier: 716-854-5299
Email: sulliolaw@aol.com

MEMBERS OF FIRM

Richard T. Sullivan
B. P. Oliverio
Bruce W. Hoover

Thomas M. Moll
Michael E. Appelbaum
Kevin M. Carter

OF COUNSEL

Paul D. Pearson

For full biographical listings, see the Martindale-Hubbell Law Directory

CARLE PLACE, Nassau Co.

Dollinger, Gonski & Grossman (AV)

One Old Country Road, 11514
Telephone: 516-747-1010
Telecopier: 516-747-2494
Fairfield, New Jersey Office: 710 Route 46 East, Suite 212, 07004.
Telephone: 973-276-0530.
Fax: 973-276-0533.

MEMBERS OF FIRM

Matthew Dollinger
Dennis M. Gonski
Floyd G. Grossman

ASSOCIATES

Leslie Ann Foodim
Michael J. Spithogiannis
Jessica M. Seidman
Bruce N. Roberts
Alicia B. Devins
Mindy Anne Wallach
Joshua N. Krellen

OF COUNSEL

Joseph Goldstein

Reference: Marine Midland National Bank, Carle Place, New York.

For full biographical listings, see the Martindale-Hubbell Law Directory

FARMINGDALE, Nassau Co.

Carman, Callahan & Ingham (AV)

Carman Building, 280 Main Street, 11735
Telephone: 516-249-3450
Telecopier: 516-249-3782

Willis B. Carman, Jr.
Robert M. Callahan
Michael F. Ingham
Gregory W. Carman, Jr.
James M. Carman

ASSOCIATE

Stephanie L. Boden

For full biographical listings, see the Martindale-Hubbell Law Directory

GARDEN CITY, Nassau Co.

Moritt, Hock & Hamroff, LLP (AV)

400 Garden City Plaza, Suite 202, 11530
Telephone: 516-873-2000
Fax: 516-873-2010
Email: lawyers@mhhlaw.com *URL:* http://www.mhhlaw.com

PARTNERS

Neil J. Moritt
Alan S. Hock
Marc L. Hamroff
David H. Cohen
Robert M. Tils
Gary C. Hisiger

ASSOCIATES

William P. Laino
Robert S. Cohen
Terese L. Arenth
Leslie A. Berkoff
Michael S. Re
David A. Loglisci
David Z. Ottensoser
Ellen R. Leibowitz
Amy J. Zamir
Michael Cardello, III
Gary E. Ostroff

For full biographical listings, see the Martindale-Hubbell Law Directory

GREAT NECK, Nassau Co.

Steven Wimpfheimer (AV)

8 Bond Street, Suite 203, 11021
Telephone: 516-504-8585
Telecopier: 516-504-1003
Email: WIMPF@WORLDNET.ATT.NET *URL:*
http://www.lawyers.com/wimpfheimer

For full biographical listings, see the Martindale-Hubbell Law Directory

HAUPPAUGE, Suffolk Co.

Eric H. Holtzman (AV)

330 Vanderbilt Motor Parkway, P.O. Box 11005, 11788-0903
Telephone: 631-435-8800
Fax: 631-435-8832

Richard E. Trachtenberg
David H. Eisenberg

Reference: European-American Bank & Trust Co.

For full biographical listings, see the Martindale-Hubbell Law Directory

MELVILLE, Suffolk Co.

Lamb & Barnosky, LLP (AV)

534 Broadhollow Road-CS 9034, 11747-9034
Telephone: 631-694-2300
Telecopier: 631-694-2309
Email: thefirm@lambbarnosky.com *URL:* http://www.lambbarnosky.com

(See Next Column)

PARTNERS

Eugene R. Barnosky
Robert H. Cohen
Marcia Lyn Finkelstein
Michael J. Heller
Gary Holman
Scott M. Karson
P. L. Lamb
Arthur A. Lane
Joel M. Markowitz
Gerald P. Rosenberg
Patrice Dowd Shenn

OF COUNSEL

Louis E. Black
James F. Gesualdi
Howard W. Newman
Joseph J. Salvatore
Joseph H. Wishod

COUNSEL

Lloyd K. Chanin
Scott P. McBride

ASSOCIATES

Cathleen D. Allen
Catherine Healy Kanzler
Rita Fishman Sheena
Shari Lee Sugarman

For full biographical listings, see the Martindale-Hubbell Law Directory

*MINEOLA,** Nassau Co.

Gutman & Gutman LLP (AV)

Gutman Building, 19 Roslyn Road, 11501-4521
Telephone: 516-248-0470
Telecopier: 516-746-6997
Email: aegutman@aol.com *URL:*
http://www.lawyers.com/gutman,gutman&gutman

MEMBERS OF FIRM

Lawrence C. Gutman
Elizabeth A. Gutman
Andrew E. Gutman

References: United Mercantile Agencies, Inc.; Commercial Law League of America, CST Co. Inc.; Fleet Bank; Kohner Mann, and Kailas.

For full biographical listings, see the Martindale-Hubbell Law Directory

*NEW YORK,** New York Co.

Baker Botts L.L.P. (AV)

599 Lexington Avenue, 10022-6030 and 30 Rockefeller Plaza, 10112-0228
Telephone: 212-705-5000
Fax: 212-705-5125 (599 Lexington Ave.)
Fax: 212-705-5020 (30 Rockeffeller Plaza)
Email: postmaster@bakerbotts.com *URL:* http://www.bakerbotts.com
Washington, D.C. Office: The Warner, 1299 Pennsylvania Avenue, N.W.
Telephone: 202-639-7700.
Austin, Texas Office: 1600 San Jacinto Center, 98 San Jacinto Boulevard.
Telephone: 512-322-2500.
Dallas, Texas Office: 2001 Ross Avenue.
Telephone: 214-953-6500.
Houston, Texas Office: One Shell Plaza, 910 Louisiana.
Telephone: 713-229-1234.
Moscow, Russia Office: 10 ul. Bolshaya Dimitrovka (formerly ul. Pushkinskaya), 103031.
Telephone: 7095/921-5300 (Local); 7095/929-7070 (International).
London, England Office: 45 Ludgate Hill.
Telephone: 0171-778-1400 (Local); 011-44-171-778-1400.
Baku, Azerbaijan Office: 6-10 Vagif Mustafa-zadeh Street, Third Floor, Icheri Sheher, 370004.
Telephone: 994-12-97-63-88 (Local); 011-994-12-97-63-88 (International).
Fax: 994-12-97-63-91 (Local); 011-994-12-97-63-61 (International).

MEMBERS OF FIRM

Lee D. Charles
John M. Huggins (Not admitted in NY)
Marc A. Leaf
Elizabeth M. Markowski
Frederick H. McGrath
Robert W. Murray Jr.

SPECIAL COUNSEL

Thomas V. D'Ambrosio

ASSOCIATES

Brayton Dresser
Thomas R. Pappas
Glen W. Roberts II
Craig Troyer (Not admitted in NY)

For Complete List of Firm Personnel, See General Section

For full biographical listings, see the Martindale-Hubbell Law Directory

Beatie and Osborn LLP (AV)

599 Lexington Avenue, 42nd Floor, 10022
Telephone: 212-888-9000
Fax: 212-888-9664
Email: bandolaw@aol.com *URL:* http://www.bandolaw@aol.com

Russel H. Beatie, Jr.
Daniel A. Osborn

ASSOCIATES

Curt D. Marshall
Eduard Korsinsky

OF COUNSEL

Richard M. Cummings

For full biographical listings, see the Martindale-Hubbell Law Directory

New York—Continued

DE ORCHIS, WALKER & CORSA, LLP (AV)

One Battery Park Plaza, Second Floor, 10004-1480
Telephone: 212-344-4700
MCI Telex: 673-4608
Telefax: 212-509-7886
Email: DW&C@MCIMAIL.COM *URL:* http://www.marinelex.com
Union, New Jersey Office: 1495 Morris Avenue, P.O. Box 1718.
Telephone: 973-467-4740.
Telefax: 908-687-0255.
Stamford, Connecticut Office: 999 Summer Street.
Telephone: 203-323-9120.
Telefax: 203-323-9015.
Boston, Massachusetts Office: One Boston Place, 5th Floor, 02180.
Telephone: 617-619-3610.
Telefax: 617-619-3924.
Miami, Florida Office: De Orchis, Corsa & Hillerbrand, LLP, 2650 Biscayne Boulevard, 33137.
Telephone: 305-571-9200.
Telefax: 305-571-9250.

PARTNERS

LeRoy S. Corsa — Alexander V. Sansone
Vincent M. De Orchis — John A. Orzel
Christopher H. Mansuy — Michael E. Unger
Cary R. Wiener

ASSOCIATES

R. Brett Kelly — Marc I. Kunkin
William E. Lakis — Francesco A. Di Pietro

RESIDENT COUNSEL

M. E. De Orchis

OF COUNSEL

Ara A. Shimshidian — Bruce H. Neuman

For full biographical listings, see the Martindale-Hubbell Law Directory

FISHBACH, HERTAN & IVES (AV)

767 Third Avenue, 10017
Telephone: 212-752-4433

MEMBERS OF FIRM

Myron Fishbach — Ira J. Hertan (1931-1988)
Garrison Ives

For full biographical listings, see the Martindale-Hubbell Law Directory

GOLENBOCK, EISEMAN, ASSOR & BELL (AV)

437 Madison Avenue, 10022
Telephone: 212-907-7300
Telecopier: 212-754-0330
Email: postmaster@golenbock.com

MEMBERS OF FIRM

Nathan E. Assor — Martin S. Hyman
Lawrence M. Bell — Steven G. Chill
David J. Eiseman — Donald A. Hamburg
Jeffrey T. Golenbock — Charles D. Schmerler
Andrew C. Peskoe — Jeffrey S. Berger
Richard S. Taffet — Lawrence R. Haut
Robert B. Goebel — Andrew M. Singer
Leonard Eisenberg — Janice B. Grubin
Jacqueline G. Veit

OF COUNSEL

William G. Pearlstein — Jonathan S. Hacker

ASSOCIATES

Debra S. Schachtel — Hilda B. Gilfillan
Charles B. Rich — David A. Collins
Thomas J. Wilson — David K. Leitner
Elizabeth A. Jaffe — Richard S. Kaplan
Adam C. Silverstein — Aielleen P. Fajardo (Not admitted in NY)
Alvin R. Chin
Joel S. Tennenberg — Gioia M. Ligos (Not admitted in NY)
Ruth G. Hirshfeld
Leslie J. Sherman — Elaine S. Moshe

For full biographical listings, see the Martindale-Hubbell Law Directory

H. MELVILLE HICKS, JR. (AV)

551 5th Avenue, Room 1625, 10176-1699
Telephone: 212-655-5944
Fax: 212-655-5943
Email: ighs@idt.net

For full biographical listings, see the Martindale-Hubbell Law Directory

INGRAM YUZEK GAINEN CARROLL & BERTOLOTTI, LLP (AV)

250 Park Avenue, 10177
Telephone: 212-907-9600
Facsimile: 212-907-9681

(See Next Column)

MEMBERS OF FIRM

Ernest J. Bertolotti (1942-1999) — Samuel W. Ingram, Jr.
Daniel L. Carroll — Paulette Kendler
Roger Cukras — Steven Mastbaum
David G. Ebert — Shane O'Neill
Larry F. Gainen — Dean G. Yuzek

ASSOCIATES

Warren E. Barrows — Jeanne F. Pucci
Amy Bertolotti — Leigh A. Roveda
Patricia Hewitt — Jennifer E. Schwartz
Theodore M. Kakoyiannis — Paul H. Slaney

OF COUNSEL

Karin J. Barkhorn — Mark E. Klein
Beverly L. Deickler — Paulette Lemay Peters
Cory L. Weiss

For full biographical listings, see the Martindale-Hubbell Law Directory

LOVELL & STEWART, LLP (AV)

A Limited Liability Partnership including a Professional Corporation
500 Fifth Avenue, 10110
Telephone: 212-608-1900
Telefax: 212-719-4677
Email: sklovell@aol.com

Christopher Lovell, P.C. — Victor E. Stewart
Gary S. Jacobson

Peggy J. Wedgworth — William W. Foshay, III
Geoffrey M. Horn — Ian T. Stoll

For full biographical listings, see the Martindale-Hubbell Law Directory

MILLER & WRUBEL P.C. (AV)

250 Park Avenue, 10177-0699
Telephone: 212-336-3500
Facsimile: 212-336-3555

Joel M. Miller — Martin D. Edel
David F. Wrubel — Charles R. Jacob, III

Todd M. Greeley — Dana B. Zimmerman
Adam J. Safer

For full biographical listings, see the Martindale-Hubbell Law Directory

MORGANROTH & MORGANROTH (AV)

156 W. 56th Street, Suite 1101, 10019
Telephone: 212-586-5905
URL: http://www.lawyers.com/morganroth&morganrothlaw
Southfield, Michigan Office: 3000 Town Center, Suite 1500, 48075.
Telephone: 248-355-3084.
Fax: 248-355-3017.

Mayer Morganroth — Jeffrey B. Morganroth

For full biographical listings, see the Martindale-Hubbell Law Directory

OTTERBOURG, STEINDLER, HOUSTON & ROSEN, P.C. (AV)

230 Park Avenue, 29th Floor, 10169
Telephone: 212-661-9100
Telecopier: 212-682-6104

Donald N. Gellert — Anthony M. Piccione
William M. Silverman — Steven B. Soll
Peter H. Stolzar — Alan Kardon
Alan R. Weiskopf — Mitchell M. Brand
Jonathan N. Helfat — Stanley L. Lane, Jr.
Daniel Wallen — David W. Morse
Scott L. Hazan — Peter L. Feldman
Glenn B. Rice — Richard G. Haddad
Albert F. Reisman — Andrew M. Kramer

GENERAL COUNSEL

Kurt J. Wolff

COUNSEL

Bernard Beitel — Morton L. Gitter

Lloyd M. Green — Brett H. Miller
Enid Nagler Stuart — Matthew J. Miller
Craig D. Zlotnick — John J. Kenny
Stephen H. Alpert — Richard L. Stehl
Jenette A. Barrow-Bosshart — Susan A. Joyce

For Complete List of Firm Personnel, See General Section

For full biographical listings, see the Martindale-Hubbell Law Directory

New York—Continued

PARKER CHAPIN LLP (AV)

Chrysler Building, 405 Lexington Avenue, 10017
Telephone: 212-704-6000
Telecopier: 212-704-6288
URL: http://www.parkerchapin.com
Great Neck, New York Office: 175 Great Neck Road.
Telephone: 516-482-4422.
Telecopier: 516-482-4469.
Hackensack, New Jersey: 190 Morre Street, Suite 307.
Telephone: 210-883-6400.
Telecopier: 210-883-6404.
Beverly Hills, California: 9454 Wilshire Boulevard.
Telephone: 310-288-8367.
Telecopier: 310-288-8365.

MEMBERS OF FIRM

Mark Abramowitz
James Alterbaum
Christopher Stewart Auguste
Aurora Cassirer
Lloyd Frank
Michael D. Friedman
James D. Garbus
Charles P. Greenman
Mark S. Hirsch
Jordan A. Horvath
Timothy I. Kahler
Michael A. Leichtling
Edward R. Mandell
Mitchell P. Portnoy
Stephen G. Rinehart
Henry I. Rothman
Richard A. Rubin
Michael J. Shef
Gary J. Simon
Alvin M. Stein
Lawrence David Swift
Melvin Weinberg
Michael Weinsier
Martin Eric Weisberg

OF COUNSEL

Raymond W. Dusch
Linda R. Giannattasio
Allan Grauberd
Herbert L. Rosedale

For Complete List of Firm Personnel, See General Section

For full biographical listings, see the Martindale-Hubbell Law Directory

PILIERO GOLDSTEIN JENKINS & SULLIVAN, LLP (AV)

292 Madison Avenue, 10017
Telephone: 212-213-8200
Fax: 212-685-2028
Email: lawyers@pgjhlaw.com *URL:* http://www.pgjhlaw.com
Carlstadt, New Jersey Office: One Palmer Terrace.
Telephone: 201-507-5157.
FAX: 201-507-5221.
Washington, D.C. Office: 888 17th Street, N.W., Suite 1100.
Telephone: 202-467-6991.
FAX: 202-467-6703.
San Francisco, California Office: 507 Howard Street, Suite 200.
Telephone: 415-281-3631.
Fax: 415-281-3630.

MEMBERS OF FIRM

Kimberlee S. Bogen
Edward J. Goldstein
Jon Mark Jenkins
Marc A. Lebowitz
Robert D. Piliero
George O. Richardson, III
Michael T. Sullivan

ASSOCIATES

Craig Avedisian
Rosemary G. Feit
Eric M. Kogan
Mariano Schwed

OF COUNSEL

Kenneth D. Arbeeny
Christopher P. Hall

For full biographical listings, see the Martindale-Hubbell Law Directory

JEFFREY S. TALLACKSON (AV)

380 Lexington Avenue, Suite 1514, 10168
Telephone: 212-972-1077
Fax: 212-972-1124
Email: jtallack@ix.netcom.com *URL:* http://www.lawyers.com/banklaw

For full biographical listings, see the Martindale-Hubbell Law Directory

*ROCHESTER,** Monroe Co.

FORSYTH, HOWE, O'DWYER, KALB & MURPHY, P.C. (AV)

Suite 1600, Midtown Tower, 14604
Telephone: 716-325-7515
Fax: 716-325-6407
URL: http://www.forsythhowe.com

Charles B. Forsyth (1890-1968)
C. Benn Forsyth
Gordon A. Howe, II
Duncan W. O'Dwyer
Robert J. Kalb
Gerald N. Murphy

Nancy A. Pappal

OF COUNSEL

John F. Forsyth (Retired)
Allan Wolk
Hoffman Stone
Debra A. Martin
Janice M. Iati
Cathleen W. Smith
Thad F. Sondej

(See Next Column)

References: The Chase Manhattan Bank; Fleet Bank.

For full biographical listings, see the Martindale-Hubbell Law Directory

LAWRENCE, WERNER, KESSELRING, SWARTOUT & BROWN, LLP (AV)

Formerly Suter Doyle Kesselring Lawrence & Werner
700 First Federal Plaza, 14614-1909
Telephone: 716-325-6446
Fax: 716-262-5185
Email: rochester@lwksb.com *URL:* http://www.lwksb.com
Canandaigua, New York Office: 23 Sly Street, 14424.
Telephone: 716-396-4000.
Fax: 716-396-1210. Email: canandaigua@lwksb.com.
Clifton Springs, New York: 26 East Main Street, P.O. Box 604, 14432.
Telephone: 315-462-3010.
Fax: 315-462-5039. Email: clifton_springs@lwksb.com

Paul J. Suter (1918-1989)

MEMBERS OF FIRM

Leo J. Kesselring
C. Bruce Lawrence
Christopher K. Werner
Colleen A. Brown
Steven H. Swartout
Mary Jo S. Korona

OF COUNSEL

James B. Doyle
Craig J. Doran
John F. Riley

ASSOCIATE

Jeffrey D. Graff

Representative Clients: Canandaigua National Bank; Hadlock Paint Company, Inc.; F.F. Thompson Health Systems, Inc.; Keuka College; Towns of Farmington and Gorham, NY; Toyota Motor Credit Corp.
References: Canandaigua National Bank; Fleet Bank, Rochester; National Association of Credit Manager, Rochester.

For full biographical listings, see the Martindale-Hubbell Law Directory

ROCKVILLE CENTRE, Nassau Co.

BATZAR & WEINBERG, A PROFESSIONAL CORPORATION (AV)

184 Sunrise Highway, P.O. Box 427, 11570
Telephone: 516-766-1860
Telecopier: 516-678-7801
Email: batweinb@aol.com *URL:* http://www.batzarweinberg.com
Edison, New Jersey Office: 86 Hudson Street.
Telephone: 908-653-1797.
Merion, Pennsylvania Office: 405 Andrew Road.
Telephone: 215-568-1060.
West Palm Beach, Florida Office: 3800 Washington Road.
Telephone: 561-659-5881.

Sanford I. Weinberg

Edward J. Damsky
Peter G. Rubin

OF COUNSEL

Norma R. Frank (Not admitted in NY; Resident, Merion, Pennsylvania Office)
Lisa A. Maglone (Not admitted in NY; Resident, Edison, New Jersey Office)

For full biographical listings, see the Martindale-Hubbell Law Directory

STONY POINT, Rockland Co.

HURLEY, FOX, SELIG & KELLEHER (AV)

Liberty Building, Route 9 W, 10980
Telephone: 914-942-2222
Fax: 914-942-0378
Email: HFSKlaw@aol.com
New City, New York Office: 60 Pine Street.
Telephone: 614-634-2050.

MEMBERS OF FIRM

Benjamin E. Selig
Glenn W. Kelleher

ASSOCIATES

Steven L. Kahn
Dana Selig Kahn
Bob A. Kramer
Kenneth P. Silver

Representative Clients: Bradlees, Inc.; Stop & Shop Companies; CNA Insurance Cos.; Federal Insurance Co.; Chubb & Son; Commercial Union Group of Insurance Cos.; Empire Insurance Co.; Omaha, N.B.; Excelsior Insurance Co.; Fireman's Insurance Company of Washington, D.C.

For full biographical listings, see the Martindale-Hubbell Law Directory

*SYRACUSE,** Onondaga Co.

MARTIN, MARTIN & WOODARD, LLP (AV)

Suite 300, One Lincoln Center, 13202-3010
Telephone: 315-478-2222
Fax: 315-478-4318

(See Next Column)

MARTIN, MARTIN & WOODARD LLP, *Syracuse—Continued*

MEMBERS OF FIRM

Donald J. Martin
Lee E. Woodard
David P. Martin
Harold P. Goldberg
David M. Capriotti

ASSOCIATES

Wendy A. Kinsella
James T. Snyder
Daniel E. Dyer

For full biographical listings, see the Martindale-Hubbell Law Directory

*TROY,** Rensselaer Co.

MARTIN, SHUDT, WALLACE, DILORENZO & JOHNSON (AV)

The Dauchy Building, 279 River Street, P.O. Box 1530, 12181
Telephone: 518-272-6565
Fax: 518-272-5573
URL: http://www.estateplanning.com/martinlawfirm

Carl E. Martin (1902-1988)
Robert Wm. Johnson, III
Edwyn L. Shudt
James E. Prout
Richard P. Wallace
Frank C. Sarratori
Kirby W. DiLorenzo
Paul M. Macari

ASSOCIATES

Jennifer A. Cusack
Matthew L. Hosford
Jaime B. Thomas
Ronald J. Moss

OF COUNSEL

Thomas B. Hunt (Not admitted in NY)

For full biographical listings, see the Martindale-Hubbell Law Directory

*WHITE PLAINS,** Westchester Co.

KEANE & BEANE, P.C. (AV)

One North Broadway, 10601
Telephone: 914-946-4777
Telecopier: 914-946-6868
Rye, New York Office: 15 Elm Place.
Telephone: 914-967-3936.

Thomas F. Keane, Jr. (1932-1991)
Ronald A. Longo
Richard L. O'Rourke
Edward F. Beane
Lawrence Praga
Donna E. Frosco
Joel H. Sachs
David Glasser
Steven A. Schurkman
Lance H. Klein
Judson K. Siebert

Stephanie L. Burns
Stephanie M. Orefice
Eric L. Gordon
Patrick J. O'Sullivan
Jonathan Kornblatt
Frances M. Pantaleo
Nicholas M. Ward-Willis

OF COUNSEL

Peter A. Borrok
John F. Burkhardt
Eric F. Jensen

LEGAL SUPPORT PERSONNEL

Lenny Amodeo (Legal Assistant)
Sylvia J. Zuckerman (Legal Assistant)
Barbara S. Durkin (Office Manager)

For full biographical listings, see the Martindale-Hubbell Law Directory

POSNER, POSNER & ASSOCIATES, PC (AV)

399 Knollwood Road, 10603
Telephone: 914-948-6620
Telecopier: 914-948-0864
Email: relawyer@aol.com *URL:* http://www.lawyers.com/posner__posner&assoc

Henry A. Greenburg
Martin Louis Posner
Jane Y. Posner

Peter J. McCarthy
Karen Olson

References: Chemical Bank; Citibank.

For full biographical listings, see the Martindale-Hubbell Law Directory

NORTH CAROLINA

*CHARLOTTE,** Mecklenburg Co.

MITCHELL, RALLINGS, SINGER, MCGIRT & TISSUE, PLLC (AV)

1800 Carillon, 227 West Trade Street, 28202
Telephone: 704-376-6574
FAX: 704-342-1531

(See Next Column)

MEMBERS OF FIRM

Richard M. Mitchell
Thomas B. Rallings, Jr.
Joseph N. Tissue

ASSOCIATES

James L. Fretwell
John W. Taylor
Carl Spencer Alridge, II

Representative Clients: Bonitz Contracting Co.; Captain D's. Inc.; Dyke Industries, Inc.; Edgcomb Metals; Titan Building Products, Inc.
References: Bank of Mecklenburg; Central Carolina Bank ; N.C.N.B.

For full biographical listings, see the Martindale-Hubbell Law Directory

WOMBLE CARLYLE SANDRIDGE & RICE (AV)

A Professional Limited Liability Company
3300 One First Union Center, 301 South College Street, 28202-6025
Telephone: 704-331-4900
Fax: 704-331-4955
Email: lawyers@wcsr.com *URL:* http://www.wcsr.com
Winston-Salem, North Carolina Office: 200 West Second Street, P.O. Drawer 84.
Telephone: 336-721-3600.
Fax: 336-721-3660.
Raleigh, North Carolina Office: 2100 First Union Capitol Center, 150 Fayetteville Street Mall, P.O. Box 831.
Telephone: 919-755-2100.
Fax: 919-755-2150.
Research Triangle Park, North Carolina Office: 2505 Meridian Parkway, Suite 300 (Durham), 27713.
Telephone: 919-484-2300.
Fax: 919-484-2340.
Atlanta, Georgia Office: One Atlantic Center, 1201 West Peachtree Street, Suite 3500.
Telephone: 404-872-7000.
Fax: 404-888-7490.
Other Atlanta, Georgia Office: Suite 404, 2296 Henderson Mill Road, N.E.
Telephone: 770-492-9030.
Fax: 770-492-9609.
Washington, D.C. Office: 1120 Nineteenth Street, N.W., Eighth Floor.
Telephone: 202-857-4400.
Fax: 202-467-6910.
Greenville, South Carolina Office: 15 South Main Street, Suite 601, P.O. Box 10208.
Telephone: 864-255-5400.
Fax: 864-255-5440.

RESIDENT MEMBERS

Gary D. Chamblee
Cyrus M. Johnson, Jr.
Joe B. Cogdell, Jr.
William P. McMillan
J. Carlton Fleming
Lesley G. Powell
Bobby D. Hinson
J. Alexander Salisbury

RESIDENT ASSOCIATES

Douglas A. Mays
Daniel G. Schmedlen, Jr.
Ellen A. Perrin
Todd C. Taylor

RESIDENT OF COUNSEL

Jane Jeffries Jones

Representative Clients: Childress Klein Properties, Inc.; Food Lion, Inc.; J.A. Jones Construction Co.; Parkdale Mills, Inc.; Pillowtex; Duke Power Co.; Bowles Hollowell Conner & Co.; ALLTEL Carolina, Inc.; Belk Store Services, Inc.; Philip Holzmann A.G.

For Complete List of Firm Personnel, See General Section

For full biographical listings, see the Martindale-Hubbell Law Directory

*GREENSBORO,** Guilford Co.

ALEXANDER RALSTON, SPECKHARD & SPECKHARD, L.L.P. (AV)

218 West Friendly Avenue, 27401
Telephone: 336-379-9302
Fax: 336-370-1232
URL: http://www.lawyers.com/aralston,speckhard

Donald K. Speckhard
Stanley E. Speckhard

Representative Clients: Preferred Furniture Components, Inc.; Spring Financial Services, Inc.; Blazer Financial Services; Omega Sports, Inc.; Power & Heat Systems, Inc.; Branch & Company, P.A.; Acme Florist Supply, Inc.

For full biographical listings, see the Martindale-Hubbell Law Directory

ISAACSON & ISAACSON (AV)

Suite 400 Bank of America Building, 101 West Friendly Avenue, P.O. Box 1888, 27402
Telephone: 336-275-7626
Fax: 336-273-7293
Email: ikeandike@aol.com *URL:* http://www.lawyers.com/isaacson

MEMBERS OF FIRM

Henry H. Isaacson
Marc L. Isaacson

(See Next Column)

ISAACSON & ISAACSON—*Continued*

ASSOCIATES

Jennifer N. Fountain | Anna Gregory Wagoner

For full biographical listings, see the Martindale-Hubbell Law Directory

STERN & KLEPFER, L.L.P. (AV)

600 NationsBank Building, P.O. Box 3112, 27402
Telephone: 336-373-1500
Fax: 336-272-8258

Sidney J. Stern, Jr. (1914-1991) | John L. Rendleman (1932-1983)

MEMBERS OF FIRM

Robert O. Klepfer, Jr. | James W. Miles, Jr.
John T. Higgins, Jr. | Brinton D. Wright
William A. Eagles

ASSOCIATES

Melanie H. Rodenbough | Ronda Leigh Lowe
Maureen Breen Gerhardt | Douglas M. Heberle

Representative Clients: Bankers Trust of North Carolina; NationsBank of North Carolina, N.A.; Tannenbaum-Sternberger Foundation; Bennett College; Endura Products, Inc.; Carlyle & Co. Jewelers.

For full biographical listings, see the Martindale-Hubbell Law Directory

*RALEIGH,** Wake Co.

SMITH DEBNAM NARRON WYCHE STORY & MYERS, L.L.P. (AV)

Hedingham Oaks, 4700 New Bern Avenue, P.O. Box 26268, 27611-6268
Telephone: 919-250-2000
Facsimile: 919-250-2100
Email: smithdebnamlaw.com

MEMBERS OF FIRM

W. Thurston Debnam, Jr. | N. Hunter Wyche, Jr.
John W. Narron | Ashley H. Story
Jerry T. Myers | Bettie Kelley Sousa
Terri L. Gardner | Laura K. Howell
Byron L. Saintsing | Rose H. Stout
Franklin Drake | Susan Yelton Ellinger
Gerald H. Groon, Jr. | Caren Davis Enloe
Terry M. Kilbride | Connie E. Carrigan
Elizabeth B. Godfrey | Jeff D. Rogers
Kevin L. Sink

ASSOCIATES

Melanie J. Hogg | Nina L. Gunther
Staci Flaxman Katz | Matthew E. Roehm
Tabatha L. Cruden | Sharon B. Christopher
Tracy T. Hyde | J. Michael Mackay
Cynthia V. Mcalister

OF COUNSEL

Fred J. Smith, Jr. | Jane Flowers Finch

Representative Clients: Eastman Kodak Co.; Bell Atlantic Tricon Leasing Corp.; Ford Motor Credit Co.; Advanta Leasing Corp.; Handy Company; Hertz Equipment Rental Corp.

For full biographical listings, see the Martindale-Hubbell Law Directory

WOMBLE CARLYLE SANDRIDGE & RICE (AV)

A Professional Limited Liability Company
2100 First Union Capitol Center, 150 Fayetteville Street Mall, P.O. Box 831, 27602
Telephone: 919-755-2100
Fax: 919-755-2150
Email: lawyers@wcsr.com *URL:* http://www.wcsr.com
Charlotte, North Carolina Office: 3300 One First Union Center, 301 South College Street.
Telephone: 704-331-4900.
Fax: 704-331-4955.
Winston-Salem, North Carolina Office: 200 West Second Street, P.O. Drawer 84.
Telephone: 336-721-3600.
Fax: 336-721-3660.
Research Triangle Park, North Carolina Office: 2505 Meridian Parkway, Suite 300 (Durham), 27713.
Telephone: 919-484-2300.
Fax: 919-484-2340.
Atlanta, Georgia Office: One Atlantic Center, 1201 West Peachtree Street, Suite 3500.
Telephone: 404-872-7000.
Fax: 404-888-7490.
Other Atlanta, Georgia Office: Suite 404, 2296 Henderson Mill Road, N.E.
Telephone: 770-492-9030.
Fax: 770-492-9609.
Washington, D.C. Office: 1120 Nineteenth Street, N.W., Eighth Floor.
Telephone: 202-857-4400.
Fax: 202-467-6910.

(See Next Column)

Greenville, South Carolina Office: 15 South Main Street, Suite 601, P.O. Box 10208.
Telephone: 864-255-5400.
Fax: 864-255-5440.

RESIDENT MEMBER

Heather K. Mallard

Representative Clients: Aetna Casualty and Surety Co., Inc.; ALSCO/AmeriMark Building Products, Inc.; Aoki Corporation America, Inc.; Hackney Brothers, Inc.; Lawyers Mutual Liability Insurance Company of North Carolina; Meredith College; Regency Park Corp.; Wachovia Bank, N.A.

For Complete List of Firm Personnel, See General Section

For full biographical listings, see the Martindale-Hubbell Law Directory

*WILMINGTON,** New Hanover Co.

MURCHISON, TAYLOR & GIBSON, L.L.P. (AV)

16 North Fifth Avenue, 28401-4593
Telephone: 910-763-2426
Fax: 910-763-6561

MEMBERS OF FIRM

Wallace C. Murchison (Retired) | Nancy M. Guyton
Joseph O. Taylor, Jr. | W. Berry Trice
Frank B. Gibson, Jr. | G. Stephen Diab
Michael Murchison | James W. Latshaw

ASSOCIATE

Frances Youngblood Trask

Representative Clients: Bell South; Branch Banking & Trust Co.; First National Bank, Southeast; General Electric Co.; Interroll Corp.; Landfall Assn.; Landmark Organization, Inc.; Telechron, Inc.; Trustees, Employers-ILA Pension, Welfare and Vacation Fund; Worsley Cos., Inc.

For full biographical listings, see the Martindale-Hubbell Law Directory

SHANKLIN & MCDANIEL, L.L.P. (AV)

214 Market Street, P.O. Box 1347, 28402-1347
Telephone: 910-762-9400
Fax: 910-251-1773
Email: shanklaw@wilmington.net

Kenneth A. Shanklin | Susan J. McDaniel

ASSOCIATE

G. Grady Richardson, Jr.

For full biographical listings, see the Martindale-Hubbell Law Directory

*WINSTON-SALEM,** Forsyth Co.

BLANCO TACKABERY COMBS & MATAMOROS, P.A. (AV)

110 S. Stratford Road, 5th Floor, P.O. Drawer 25008, 27114-5008
Telephone: 336-761-1250
Facsimile: 336-761-1530

David B. Blanco | Steven C. Garland
Neal E. Tackabery | Peter J. Juran
Reginald F. Combs | Brian L. Herndon
Ronald A. Matamoros | Bowen C. Houff
Gene B. Tarr | George E. Hollodick
Michael D. Hurst | Charles D. Luckey

Mary Margaret Ogburn | Amy L. Schneider
Jeffrey D. Patton | Michelle M. Minnich
Deborah L. McKenney | Stephen C. Minnich
Jean Sutton Martin

Reference: Branch Banking and Trust Company, Winston-Salem, North Carolina.

For full biographical listings, see the Martindale-Hubbell Law Directory

JOHN R. SURRATT, P.A. (AV)

102 West Third Street Suite 700, 27101
Telephone: 336-725-8323
Facsimile: 336-722-5218
Email: surrattpa@aol.com

John R. Surratt | Anita M. Conrad

For full biographical listings, see the Martindale-Hubbell Law Directory

WOMBLE CARLYLE SANDRIDGE & RICE (AV)

A Professional Limited Liability Company
200 West Second Street, P.O. Drawer 84, 27102
Telephone: 336-721-3600
Fax: 336-721-3660
Email: lawyers@wcsr.com *URL:* http://www.wcsr.com
Charlotte, North Carolina Office: 3300 One First Union Center, 301 South College Street.
Telephone: 704-331-4900.
Fax: 704-331-4955.

(See Next Column)

WOMBLE CARLYLE SANDRIDGE & RICE, *Winston-Salem—Continued*

Raleigh, North Carolina Office: 2100 First Union Capitol Center, 150 Fayetteville Street Mall, P.O. Box 831.
Telephone: 919-755-2100.
Fax: 919-755-2150.
Research Triangle Park, North Carolina Office: 2505 Meridian Parkway, Suite 300 (Durham), 27713.
Telephone: 919-484-2300.
Fax: 919-484-2340.
Atlanta, Georgia Office: One Atlantic Center, 1201 West Peachtree Street, Suite 3500.
Telephone: 404-872-7000.
Fax: 404-888-7490.
Other Atlanta, Georgia Office: Suite 404, 2296 Henderson Mill Road, N.E.
Telephone: 770-492-9030.
Fax: 770-492-9609.
Washington, D.C. Office: 1120 Nineteenth Street, N.W., Eighth Floor.
Telephone: 202-857-4400.
Fax: 202-467-6910.
Greenville, South Carolina Office: 15 South Main Street, Suite 601, P.O. Box 10208.
Telephone: 864-255-5400.
Fax: 864-255-5440.

RESIDENT MEMBERS

Linwood L. Davis
William A. Davis, II
Richard N. Drake
John L. W. Garrou
Murray C. Greason, Jr.
Hardin G. Halsey
Jeffrey C. Howland
Kenneth A. Moser
W. P. Sandridge, Jr.
Robert A. West
Calder W. Womble
William F. Womble

RESIDENT ASSOCIATES

Roger E. Cole
Adam B. Hirschfeld
Robert F. Pomper

Representative Clients: Brad Ragan, Inc.; Brenner Companies; Food Lion, Inc.; Hanes Companies, Inc.; North Carolina Baptist Hospitals, Inc.; R.J. Reynolds Tobacco Co.; Thomasville Furniture Industries, Inc.; Wachovia Corp.; Wake Forest University.

For Complete List of Firm Personnel, See General Section

For full biographical listings, see the Martindale-Hubbell Law Directory

NORTH DAKOTA

*BISMARCK,** Burleigh Co.

MALCOLM H. BROWN, P.C. (AV)

209 East Broadway Avenue, P.O. Box 2692, 58502-2692
Telephone: 701-224-8825
Fax: 701-224-8820
Email: mhblaw@btigate.com

Malcolm H. Brown

For full biographical listings, see the Martindale-Hubbell Law Directory

PEARCE AND DURICK, PLLP (AV)

314 East Thayer Avenue, P.O. Box 400, 58502
Telephone: 701-223-2890
Fax: 701-223-7865
Email: law.office@pearce-durick.com *URL:* http://www.pearce-durick.com

MEMBERS OF FIRM

William P. Pearce
Patrick W. Durick

ASSOCIATE

Jonathan P. Sanstead

Representative Clients: Bank Center First; BNC National Bank; Federal Deposit Insurance Corp.; MDU Resources Group, Inc.; North Dakota Development Fund; USBank.

For Complete List of Firm Personnel, See General Section

For full biographical listings, see the Martindale-Hubbell Law Directory

*FARGO,** Cass Co.

NILLES, HANSEN & DAVIES, LTD. (AV)

1800 Radisson Tower, P.O. Box 2626, 58108
Telephone: 701-237-5544
Facsimile: 701-280-0762
Williston, North Dakota Office: Energy Resource Building, 504 East Broadway, Suite 101, P.O. Box 1525.
Telephone: 701-572-5544.
Fax: 701-572-5561.

Timothy Q. Davies
Russell F. Freeman
Gregory B. Selbo
Daniel J. Crothers
Harry M. Pippin
Andrew L. B. Noah

(See Next Column)

Representative Clients: Blue Cross/Blue Shield; U.S. Bank National Association; Burlington Northern.

For Complete List of Firm Personnel, See General Section

For full biographical listings, see the Martindale-Hubbell Law Directory

VOGEL, WEIR, BYE, HUNKE & MCCORMICK, LTD. (AV)

502 First Avenue North, P.O. Box 1389, 58107
Telephone: 701-237-6983
Facsimile: 701-237-0847
Email: vogellaw@vogellaw.com *URL:* http://www.vogellaw.com

Kermit Edward Bye
Maurice G. McCormick
William A. Schlossman, Jr.
Jon R. Brakke
Frank G. Gokey
Steven A. Johnson

Representative Clients: Associated General Contractors of North Dakota; Blue Shield of North Dakota; Cass County Electric Cooperative, Inc.; Clark Equipment Co.; Forum Communications Company; Merit Care Medical Group; Northern Improvement Co.; Dakota Clinic Ltd.; United Parcel Service; Gateway Chevrolet, Inc.

For Complete List of Firm Personnel, See General Section

For full biographical listings, see the Martindale-Hubbell Law Directory

OHIO

*AKRON,** Summit Co.

MENTZER, VUILLEMIN AND MYGRANT LTD. (AV)

1 Cascade Plaza, 20th Floor, 44308-1114
Telephone: 330-376-7500
Telecopier: 330-376-8018
Email: mvmlaw@juno.com

Howard E. Mentzer
Rajko Radonjich

Reference: National City Bank, Akron, Ohio.

For full biographical listings, see the Martindale-Hubbell Law Directory

*CINCINNATI,** Hamilton Co.

FROST & JACOBS LLP (AV)

2500 PNC Center, 201 East Fifth Street, 45202
Telephone: 513-651-6800
Telecopier: 513-651-6981
URL: http://www.frojac.com
Columbus, Ohio Office: One Columbus, 10 West Broad Street, 43215.
Telephone: 614-464-1211.
Telecopier: 614-464-1737.
Lexington, Kentucky Office: 1100 Vine Center Tower, 333 West Vine Street, 40507.
Telephone: 606-254-1100.
Telecopier: 606-253-2990.
Middletown, Ohio Office: 400 First National Bank Building, 2 North Main Street, 45042.
Telephone: 513-422-2001.
Telecopier: 513-422-3010.
Frankfort, Kentucky Office: 201 W. Main Street, 40601.
Telephone: 502-223-1400.
Telecopier: 502-223-1410.

MEMBERS OF FIRM

Edmund J. Adams
Lawrence H. Kyte, Jr.
Richard J. Erickson
Jeffery R. Rush
E. Richard Oberschmidt
P. Reid Lemasters
Frederick W. Kindel
John C. Krug
Ronald E. Gold
Douglas S. Tripp
David S. Bence

ASSOCIATES

Bryan S. Blade
Douglas L. Lutz
Sandra L. Nunn
Michael J. O'Grady
Christina M. Sprecher
Rita M. Stolper
Colleen M. Haas
Jan R. Wenning
Suzanne Wentzel

OF COUNSEL

Kimberly K. Mauer
Mary Ann Schenk

COLUMBUS, OHIO OFFICE
MEMBER OF FIRM

John I. Cadwallader

COLUMBUS, OHIO OFFICE
ASSOCIATE

Cara E. Gunder

LEXINGTON, KENTUCKY OFFICE
MEMBER OF FIRM

Greg E. Mitchell

(See Next Column)

FROST & JACOBS LLP—*Continued*

LEXINGTON, KENTUCKY OFFICE
ASSOCIATE
David L. Kinsella

MIDDLETOWN, OHIO OFFICE
MEMBER OF FIRM
Thomas A. Swope

MIDDLETOWN, OHIO OFFICE
SENIOR ATTORNEY
Daniel J. Picard

Representative Clients: Bank One, Cincinnati, N.A.; Cincinnati Bell, Inc.; Cincinnati Machine; Federated Department Stores; First National Bank of Southwestern Ohio; Firstar, National Association; Key Bank, National Association; PNC Bank, National Association; Turner Construction Co.

For Complete List of Firm Personnel, See General Section

For full biographical listings, see the Martindale-Hubbell Law Directory

MASON, SLOVIN & SCHILLING CO., L.P.A. (AV)

11340 Montgomery Road, Suite 210, 45249-2313
Telephone: 513-489-0829
800-840-3514
Fax: 513-489-0834
Email: msscolpa@worldnet.att.net
Covington, Kentucky Office: Heritage International, Suite 203, P.O. Box 2158.
Telephone: 513-489-0829.
Fax: 513-489-0834.
Columbus Office: 10 West Broad Street, Suite 2400 One Columbus.
Telephone: 513-489-0829.
Fax: 513-489-0834.
Dayton Office: 319 Liberty Tower.
Telephone: 513-489-0829.
Fax: 513-489-0834.
Lima Office: 809 West Vine Street, P.O. Box 937.
Telephone: 513-489-0829.
Fax: 513-489-0834.

Jonathan A. Mason
Randy T. Slovin
Richard D. Schilling

David C. Nalley
Joseph Ruwe

OF COUNSEL

Fred H. Summe (Not admitted in OH; Resident, Covington, KY Office)
Richard L. Levine

LEGAL SUPPORT PERSONNEL

Brenda L. Norton (Office Manager and Executive Legal Secretary)
Lisa K. Spencer (Sr. Case Manager; Accounting Manager)
Amy J. Luipold (Sr. Case Manager; Recovery Manager)
William M. Luipold (Manager, Court Administration)
Marilyn E. Mason (Sr. Legal Assistant-Accounting)
Jeremy R. Mason (Sr. Law Clerk)
Rachel J. Mason (Law Clerk)
Sarah Hopkins (Legal Assistant-Recovery)
Becky Grandstaff (Legal Assistant-Claims & Billing)
Connie Shutt (Legal Assistant-Litigation)

For full biographical listings, see the Martindale-Hubbell Law Directory

*DAYTON,** Montgomery Co.

FREUND, FREEZE & ARNOLD A LEGAL PROFESSIONAL ASSOCIATION (AV)

Suite 1800 One Dayton Centre, One South Main Street, 45402-2017
Telephone: 937-222-2424
Telecopier: 937-222-5369
Email: ffalawda@ffalaw.com *URL:* http://www.ffalaw.com
Cincinnati, Ohio Office: 8805 Governor's Hill Drive, Suite 300, 45249-3313.
Telephone: 513-583-3700.
FAX: 513-583-3703. Email: ffalawci@ffalaw.com.

Neil F. Freund
Susan Blasik-Miller
Wayne E. Waite
John G. Witherspoon, Jr.
T. Andrew Vollmar

Representative Clients: Dayton Power and Light Company; Baker Concrete Construction; Bottlers Services, Inc.; Elder-Beerman Stores Corporation; Walgreen's.

For full biographical listings, see the Martindale-Hubbell Law Directory

*SANDUSKY,** Erie Co.

BUCKINGHAM, HOLZAPFEL, ZEIHER, WALDOCK & SCHELL CO., L.P.A. (AV)

414 Wayne Street, P.O. Box 929, 44870
Telephone: 419-627-0414
Fax: 419-627-0009
Vermilion, Ohio Office: 678 Main Street.
Telephone: 216-967-6136.
Fax: 216-967-8541.

F. H. Buckingham (1901-1971)
George C. Steinemann (Retired)
Richard D. Holzapfel (Retired)
Arthur W. Zeiher (Retired)
Thomas S. Buckingham
Frederick D. Waldock
Lawrence H. Schell *
Maurice L. McDermond, Jr.
Kevin J. Zeiher
John D. Frankel
W. Zack Dolyk *

Troy Wisehart
John R. Ball
Linda Fritz-Gasteier

Local Counsel: Erie County Cablevision, Inc.
General Counsel: Sandusky Newspapers, Inc.; The Cooke Properties; Firelands Community Hospital.
*Sandusky and Vermilion, Ohio Offices

For full biographical listings, see the Martindale-Hubbell Law Directory

OKLAHOMA

*NORMAN,** Cleveland Co.

CROWE & DUNLEVY (AV)

A Professional Corporation
2500 South McGee, Suite 140, 73072-6705
Telephone: 405-321-7317
Fax: 405-360-4002
Email: marketing@crowedunlevy.com *URL:* http://www.crowedunlevy.com
Oklahoma City, Oklahoma Office: Crowe & Dunlevy, A Professional Corporation, 1800 Mid-America Tower, 20 North Broadway, 73102-8273.
Telephone: 405-235-7700.
Fax: 405-239-6651.
Tulsa, Oklahoma Office: Crowe & Dunlevy, A Professional Corporation, 500 Kennedy Building, 321 South Boston Avenue, 74103-3313.
Telephone: 918-592-9800.
Fax: 918-592-9801.

Gary C. Rawlinson
Mary Robertson

Christopher R. Graves

For Complete List of Firm Personnel, See General Section

For full biographical listings, see the Martindale-Hubbell Law Directory

*OKLAHOMA CITY,** Oklahoma Co.

WILLIAM C. BOSTON, P.L.L.C. (AV)

4005 Northwest Expressway, Suite 600, 73116
Telephone: 405-848-0600
Telefax: 405-848-0655
Email: wcbfirm@ionet.net *URL:* http://www.okaircraftlaw.com

William C. Boston, Jr.

Scott D. McCreary
William Clayton Boston, III
Eric L. Johnson
Lisa Anne Drescher

OF COUNSEL

Donna M. Schmidt (Not admitted in OK)
Willis W. Luttrell (Not admitted in OK)
Joseph T. Brennan (Not admitted in OK)

For full biographical listings, see the Martindale-Hubbell Law Directory

CROWE & DUNLEVY, A PROFESSIONAL CORPORATION (AV)

1800 Mid-America Tower, 20 North Broadway, 73102-8273
Telephone: 405-235-7700
Fax: 405-239-6651
Email: marketing@crowedunlevy.com *URL:* http://www.crowedunlevy.com
Tulsa, Oklahoma Office: 500 Kennedy Building, 321 South Boston Avenue, 74103-3313.
Telephone: 918-592-9800.
Fax: 918-592-9801.

(See Next Column)

CROWE & DUNLEVY A PROFESSIONAL CORPORATION, *Oklahoma City—Continued*

Norman, Oklahoma Office: Crowe & Dunlevy, 2500 South McGee, Suite 140, 73072-6705.
Telephone: 405-321-7317.
Fax: 405-360-4002.

Robert M. Johnson
James F. Hartmann, Jr.
Michael M. Stewart
Kenni B. Merritt
Michael S. Laird
Stephen L. DeGiusti
Todd Taylor
Roger A. Stong

William H. Hoch

OF COUNSEL

Val R. Miller

For Complete List of Firm Personnel, See General Section

For full biographical listings, see the Martindale-Hubbell Law Directory

DAY, EDWARDS, FEDERMAN, PROPESTER & CHRISTENSEN, P.C. (AV)

Suite 2900 Oklahoma Tower, 210 Park Avenue, 73102-5605
Telephone: 405-239-2121
Telecopier: 405-236-1012
URL: http://lawlinks.com/attys/ok/defpc.html

Joe E. Edwards
J. Clay Christensen
Richard P. Propester
Kent A. Gilliland

Ricki Valerie Sonders
Thomas Pitchlynn Howell, IV
Joel Warren Harmon

Representative Clients: Applied Thermal Systems, Inc.; BancFirst; Bank One, Oklahoma City; Bank of America, N.A.; CD Warehouse, Inc.; First Community Bank, Binger; First National Bank and Trust Company of Weatherford; First State Bank & Trust Co., Hollis; Local Oklahoma Bank; LSB Industries, Inc.

For Complete List of Firm Personnel, See General Section

For full biographical listings, see the Martindale-Hubbell Law Directory

DURBIN, LARIMORE & BIALICK, P.C. (AV)

920 North Harvey, 73102-2610
Telephone: 405-235-9584
Fax: 405-235-0551
Email: DLB@Telepath.com

Gerald E. Durbin, II
James K. Larimore
Mark E. Bialick
Jerry John Hager, Jr.
David B. Donchin
Micheal L. Darrah

Rodney D. Stewart
Bill M. Roberts
Katherine Taylor Loy
J. Logan Johnson
Hilary S. Allen
Frances J. Stanton
Amy L. Alden
R. Brad Miller
Susanna M. Gattoni

For full biographical listings, see the Martindale-Hubbell Law Directory

HARTZOG CONGER & CASON, A PROFESSIONAL CORPORATION (AV)

1600 Bank of Oklahoma Plaza 201 Robert S. Kerr, 73102
Telephone: 405-235-7000
Facsimile: 405-235-7329

Larry D. Hartzog
J. William Conger
Len Cason
James C. Prince
Steven C. Davis
Joseph P. Hogsett
John D. Robertson
Kurt M. Rupert
Laura Haag McConnell
Linda G. Scoggins
Susan B. Shields
Ryan S. Wilson
Amy J. Sine
Jon H. Trudgeon
Charles E. Geister, III
Phillip G. Whaley
Armand Paliotta

J. Christian Guzzy
Stacey D. Spivey
Melissa Beeson Heindselman
Christin V. Adkins
Byron K. Linkous

OF COUNSEL

Kent F. Frates
Kenneth R. Davis
Alan Newman

For full biographical listings, see the Martindale-Hubbell Law Directory

NASH, COHENOUR, KELLEY & HUNT, P.C. (AV)

Suite 101, 1001 Northwest 63rd Street, 73116
Telephone: 405-848-7170
Fax: 405-848-1442
Email: NCKHlaw@aol.com *URL:* http://www.law-n-okla.com

(See Next Column)

Rollin Nash, Jr.
Kevin Kelley
Neal Hunt
Dennis S. Boxeur

For full biographical listings, see the Martindale-Hubbell Law Directory

SELF, GIDDENS & LEES, INC. (AV)

2725 Oklahoma Tower, 210 Park Avenue, 73102-5643
Telephone: 405-232-3001
Telecopier: 405-232-5553

Thomas J. Blalock
Jared D. Giddens
C. Ray Lees
Shannon T. Self
Bryan J. Wells

Michael D. Meleen
John E. Gatliff II

For full biographical listings, see the Martindale-Hubbell Law Directory

STEPHEN A. SHERMAN & ASSOCIATES (AV)

117 Park Avenue Building, Fourth Floor, 73102
Telephone: 405-235-0707
Fax: 405-235-0712
Email: ssherman@shermanfirm.com

Stephen A. Sherman

Representative Clients: Insignia Commercial Investments Group, Inc.; Kaiser-Francis Oil Co.; U.S. Foodservice, Inc.; B.F. Saul Co.; Irish Realty Corp.; Hogan Property Corp.; Western Industries, Inc.; ISC Telecom, Inc.; Rockcity.com, L.L.C.

For full biographical listings, see the Martindale-Hubbell Law Directory

WILLIAMS, BOX, FORSHEE & BULLARD, P.C. (AV)

522 Colcord Drive, 73102-2202
Telephone: 405-232-0080
Telecopier: 405-236-5814

John Michael Williams
Dennis R. Box
Richard D. Forshee
William J. Bullard
Keith R. Gibson
Paul E. Lefebvre

Kimberly K. Brown

For full biographical listings, see the Martindale-Hubbell Law Directory

*STILLWATER,** Payne Co.

ELLIS & MORGAN (AV)

711 South Husband Street, P.O. Box 1507, 74076
Telephone: 405-743-3770
Fax: 405-743-3773

MEMBERS OF FIRM

Hal Wm. Ellis
Michael S. Morgan
Tracy Emmet Morgan
G. Michael Solomon

For full biographical listings, see the Martindale-Hubbell Law Directory

*TULSA,** Tulsa Co.

CROWE & DUNLEVY, A PROFESSIONAL CORPORATION (AV)

500 Kennedy Building, 321 South Boston Avenue, 74103-3313
Telephone: 918-592-9800
Fax: 918-592-9801
Email: marketing@crowedunlevy.com *URL:* http://www.crowedunlevy.com
Oklahoma City, Oklahoma Office: 1800 Mid-America Tower, 20 North Broadway, 73102-8273.
Telephone: 405-235-7700.
Fax: 405-239-6651.
Norman, Oklahoma Office: Crowe & Dunlevy, 2500 South McGee, Suite 140, 73072-6705.
Telephone: 405-321-7317.
Fax: 405-360-4002.

Lon Foster, III
Gary R. McSpadden
Gary C. Clark
Gary L. Betow
Malcolm E. Rosser IV
Michael J. Gibbens
Terry M. Thomas
J. Bradford Hammond
Victor E. Morgan
Jeffrey T. Hills
W. Kyle Tresch

Nancy Lynn Roberts
Timothy F. Sterling
Elizabeth Moseley Guse
David G. Harris
J. Ryan Sacra

For Complete List of Firm Personnel, See General Section

For full biographical listings, see the Martindale-Hubbell Law Directory

Tulsa—Continued

JAMES, POTTS AND WULFERS, INC. (AV)

2828 Mid-Continent Tower, 401 South Boston Avenue, 74103-4016
Telephone: 918-584-0881
Fax: 918-584-4521

David F. James
Thomas G. Potts
David W. Wulfers

For full biographical listings, see the Martindale-Hubbell Law Directory

SNEED LANG, P.C. (AV)

2300 Williams Center Tower II, Two West Second Street, 74103
Telephone: 918-583-3145
Telecopier: 918-582-0410

James C. Lang
D. Faith Orlowski
Brian S. Gaskill
G. Steven Stidham
Stephen R. McNamara
Thomas E. Black, Jr.
Robbie Emery Burke
Patrick O. Waddel
Randolph P. Stainer
Steven K. Balman
Brian T. Inbody
D. Michael McBride III

OF COUNSEL

James L. Sneed

Representative Clients: Amoco Production Co.; Bank One, Texas; Enron Corp.; Halliburton Energy Services; Helmerich & Payne, Inc.; Shell Oil Co.; State Farm Mutual Automobile Insurance Co.; The Williams Companies.

For full biographical listings, see the Martindale-Hubbell Law Directory

OREGON

*EUGENE,** Lane Co.

MUHLHEIM PALMER & WADE, A PROFESSIONAL CORPORATION (AV)

U.S. Bank Center, 800 Willamette Street, Suite 700, 97401-2933
Telephone: 541-687-4757
Facsimile: 541-687-4780
Email: mpw-law.com *URL:* http://www.lawyers.com/muhleimpalmer&wade

Wilson C. Muhlheim
R. Scott Palmer
Carolyn G. Wade

Pamela Egan Singer
Stephen C.P. Carroll
Heidi Von Ravensberg
Edward C Singer

LEGAL SUPPORT PERSONNEL

Dawnne L. Linenbrink, CLAS
Fern Puls
Richard Rickson

Representative Clients: Harvest Ford Lincoln Mercury; Georgia Pacific Employees Federal Credit Union; Valley of The Rogue Bank; Bank of Southern Oregon; The Boulders on the River, Inc.; Trans Union Corporation; Heritage Mall, Ltd.; Sandpines Golf Resort; Ariki Co., Ltd.; Water Sports, Inc.; Lowther Assets.

For full biographical listings, see the Martindale-Hubbell Law Directory

*PORTLAND,** Multnomah Co.

BLACK HELTERLINE LLP (AV)

1200 Union Bank of California Tower, 707 S.W. Washington Street, 97205
Telephone: 503-224-5560
Telecopier: 503-224-6148
URL: http://www.bhlaw.com

MEMBERS OF FIRM

Ronald T. Adams
James M. Baumgartner
John M. McGuigan
Michael O. Moran
David P. Roy

ASSOCIATES

Amy P. Alexander
James R. George

OF COUNSEL

Robert E. Glasgow

Representative Clients: Union Bank of California, N.A.; Bank of Tokyo-Mitsubishi; First Nationwide Automotive Acceptance, Inc.; Fleming Companies, Inc.; NACCO Materials Handling Group, Inc.; Royal Bank of Canada.

For Complete List of Firm Personnel, See General Section

For full biographical listings, see the Martindale-Hubbell Law Directory

HAGEN, DYE, HIRSCHY & DILORENZO, P.C. (AV)

888 Southwest 5th Avenue Suite 1000, 97204
Telephone: 503-222-1812
Fax: 503-274-7979

(See Next Column)

Joseph T. Hagen
Jeffrey L. Dye
John A. Hirschy
John A. DiLorenzo, Jr.
Dana R. Taylor
Mark A. Golding
Kenneth A. Williams
John D. Parsons
David E. Grein

OF COUNSEL

Lewis B. Hampton

Adam S. Rittenberg
Michael E. Farnell
Aaron K. Stuckey
Joel L. Augee
Gretchen M. Ladd
Pamela R. Albee

LEGAL SUPPORT PERSONNEL

Kathryn J. Bell
Gail E. Kuechle
Linda M. Lufkin

For full biographical listings, see the Martindale-Hubbell Law Directory

PENNSYLVANIA

BALA CYNWYD, Montgomery Co.

KANIA, LINDNER, LASAK AND FEENEY (AV)

Suite 525, Two Bala Plaza, 19004
Telephone: 610-667-3240
Fax: 610-668-9676
Email: kllf@aol.com

Arthur J. Kania
Albert A. Lindner
John Lasak
Thomas J. Feeney, III
Robert A. Griffiths

A list of Representative Clients for which the firm serves as General Counsel or Local Counsel will be supplied upon request.

For full biographical listings, see the Martindale-Hubbell Law Directory

BLUE BELL, Montgomery Co.

ELLIOTT REIHNER SIEDZIKOWSKI & EGAN, P.C. (AV)

Union Meeting Corporate Center V, 925 Harvest Drive, 19422
Telephone: 215-977-1000
Fax: 215-977-1099
URL: http://www.erse.com
Scranton, Pennsylvania Office:
Telephone: 717-346-7569.
Fax: 717-969-2890.
Harrisburg, Pennsylvania Office:
Telephone: 717-234-8010.
Fax: 717-233-4262.
Reading, Pennsylvania Office:
Telephone: 610-374-6756.
Fax: 610-373-4844.

John M. Elliott
Thomas J. Elliott
Henry F. Siedzikowski
Gerard P. Egan
Douglas R. Blazey (Resident, Reading Office)
James C. Crumlish, III
Mark J. Schwemler
Timothy T. Myers
Mark A. Kearney
Dionysios G. Rassias
Frederick P. Santarelli
Marvin L. Wilenzik
Adam B. Krafczek, Jr. (Resident Managing Partner, Reading Office)
Eric J. Bronstein

COUNSEL

Robert P. Casey

OF COUNSEL

Kevin S. Anderson
Stewart J. Greenleaf
Timothy S. Kerr
Kenneth L. Tepper
Charles M. O'Donnell

Krista Kearns Beatty
Raymond J. Santarelli
Patricia C. Collins
Eric P. Wilenzik
Michael A. Bowman
Kathryn M. Schilling
Brian J. McCormick, Jr.
Meredith T. Shepherd
Brian Richard Elias

For full biographical listings, see the Martindale-Hubbell Law Directory

KAPLIN STEWART MELOFF REITER & STEIN, PROFESSIONAL CORPORATION (AV)

350 Sentry Parkway, Building 640, P.O. Box 3037, 19422-0765
Telephone: 610-260-6000
Telecopier: 610-260-1240
Cherry Hill, New Jersey Office: 900 Dudley Avenue, #250, 08002-4426.
Telephone: 856-486-1044.
Fax: 856-486-1074.

MEMBERS OF FIRM

William K. Stewart, Jr.
L. Leonard Lundy

(See Next Column)

KAPLIN STEWART MELOFF REITER & STEIN PROFESSIONAL CORPORATION, *Blue Bell—Continued*

ASSOCIATE

Scott C. Butler

For full biographical listings, see the Martindale-Hubbell Law Directory

KELLEY & MURPHY (AV)

Union Meeting Corporate Center V, Suite 160 925 Harvest Drive, 19422
Telephone: 215-643-6500
Fax: 215-643-8356
Cable Address: "BIGTIME"
Email: kmlaw@counsel.com

Joseph T. Kelley, Jr.
Patrick G. Murphy
Joseph T. Kelley, III

LEGAL SUPPORT PERSONNEL

Marianne Rowen
Tanja M.Z. Barron

For full biographical listings, see the Martindale-Hubbell Law Directory

*CARLISLE,** Cumberland Co.

FISHMAN & MORGENTHAL (AV)

95 Alexander Spring Road, 17013
Telephone: 717-249-6333
Fax: 717-249-7334
Email: info@carlislelaw.com *URL:* http://www.carlislelaw.com

MEMBERS OF FIRM

Steven J. Fishman
Roger M. Morgenthal

For full biographical listings, see the Martindale-Hubbell Law Directory

ELKINS PARK, Montgomery Co.

MONAGHAN & GOLD, P.C. (AV)

Manor Professional Building, 7837 Old York Road, 19027
Telephone: 215-782-1800
Fax: 215-782-1010
URL: http://www.MNG-LAW.com

Alan S. Gold
John F. X. Monaghan, Jr.

Murray R. Glickman
Tanya M. Sweet
Mitchell K. Brudno
Robert F. Fortin
Sean Robins
Kenneth W. Taylor
Francis D. Hennessy, Jr.

OF COUNSEL

Alan L. Butkovitz
Steven M. Zelitch
Barbara Malett Weitz

LEGAL SUPPORT PERSONNEL

Andrew Logan (Paralegal)
Carol Veach (Paralegal)
Janet McCrossen (Registered Nurse)

For full biographical listings, see the Martindale-Hubbell Law Directory

*HARRISBURG,** Dauphin Co.

GOLDBERG, KATZMAN & SHIPMAN, P.C. (AV)

320 Market Street - Strawberry Square, P.O. Box 1268, 17108-1268
Telephone: 717-234-4161
Telecopier: 717-234-6808; 717-234-6810
Email: gks@gkslaw.com

Ronald M. Katzman
Neil Hendershot
Jesse Jay Cooper
Thomas J. Weber

Arnold B. Kogan
Steven E. Grubb
John DeLorenzo

Representative Clients: Insource, Inc.; Lemoyne Sleeper; Herre Bros., Inc.; Flight Systems, Inc.; Associated Products Inc.; Ameralum, Inc.; Plasticert, Inc.; Tressler Lutheran Services; Pennsylvania Dental Association.
Reference: Fulton Bank.

For Complete List of Firm Personnel, See General Section

For full biographical listings, see the Martindale-Hubbell Law Directory

METTE, EVANS & WOODSIDE, A PROFESSIONAL CORPORATION (AV)

3401 North Front Street, P.O. Box 5950, 17110-0950
Telephone: 717-232-5000
Fax: 717-236-1816
Email: MEW@Mette.com *URL:* HTTP://WWW.METTE.COM

(See Next Column)

Howell C. Mette
Robert Moore
Charles B. Zwally
Lloyd R. Persun
James A. Ulsh
Elyse E. Rogers
Jeffrey A. Ernico
P. Daniel Altland
Paula J. Leicht
Guy P. Beneventano
Thomas F. Smida

Vicky Ann Trimmer
Bradley A. Walker
Donna L. Gareis-Smith

For Complete List of Firm Personnel, See General Section

For full biographical listings, see the Martindale-Hubbell Law Directory

*PHILADELPHIA,** Philadelphia Co.

BALLARD SPAHR ANDREWS & INGERSOLL, LLP (AV)

1735 Market Street, 51st Floor, 19103-7599
Telephone: 215-665-8500
Fax: 215-864-8999
URL: http://www.ballardspahr.com
Baltimore, Maryland Office: 300 East Lombard Street. 19th Floor.
Telephone: 410-528-5600.
Fax: 410-528-5650.
Camden, New Jersey Office: 800 Hudson Square, 5th Floor.
Telephone: 856-541-5577.
Fax: 856-541-8272.
Denver, Colorado Office: Seventeenth Street Plaza Building, Suite 2300, 1225 17th Street.
Telephone: 303-292-2400.
Fax: 303-296-3956.
Salt Lake City, Utah Office: One Utah Center, Suite 1200, 201 South Main Street.
Telephone: 801-531-3000.
Fax: 801-531-3001.
Voorhees, New Jersey Office: Suite 100, 1101 Laurel Oak Drive.
Telephone: 856-627-8555.
Fax: 856-627-1153.
Washington, D.C. Office: Suite 1000 South, 601 13th Street, N.W.
Telephone: 202-661-2200.
Fax: 202-661-2299.

Raymond D. Agran
E. Carolan Berkley
C. Baird Brown
Carl H. Fridy
Gerald J. Guarcini
Cathleen C. Judge
William H. Rheiner
Edward D. Slevin
John N. Ake
Richard J. Braemer
Morris Cheston, Jr.
Robert C. Gerlach
Martha J. Hays
Justin P. Klein
J. Douglas Rollow, III
William Y. Webb

Michael J. Konowal

For Complete List of Firm Personnel, See General Section

For full biographical listings, see the Martindale-Hubbell Law Directory

COZEN AND O'CONNOR, A PROFESSIONAL CORPORATION (AV)

1900 Market Street, 19103
Telephone: 215-665-2000
800-523-2900
Fax: 215-665-2013
Email: postmaster@cozen.com *URL:* http://www.cozen.com
Charlotte, North Carolina Office: One First Union Center, Suite 2100, 301 S. College Street, 28202.
Telephones: 704-376-3400; 800-762-3575.
Fax: 704-334-3351.
Dallas, Texas Office: 2300 BankOne Center, 1717 Main Street, 75201.
Telephones: 214-462-3000; 800-448-1207.
Fax: 214-462-3299.
New York, N.Y. Office: 45 Broadway Atrium, 16th Floor, 10006.
Telephones: 212-509-9400; 800-437-7040.
Fax: 212-509-9492.
West Conshohocken, Pennsylvania Office: 200 Four Falls Corporate Center, Suite 400, P.O. Box 800, 19428.
Telephone: 610-941-5400.
Fax: 610-941-0711.
San Diego, California Office: Suite 1610, 501 West Broadway, 92101.
Telephones: 619-234-1700; 800-782-3366.
Fax: 619-234-7831.
Los Angeles, California Office: 777 Tower, 777 South Figueroa Street, Suite 2850, 90017.
Telephones: 213-892-7900; 800-563-1027.
Fax: 213-892-7999.
Seattle, Washington Office: Suite 5200, Washington Mutual Tower, 1201 Third Avenue, 98101.
Telephones: 206-340-1000; 800-423-1950.
Fax: 206-621-8783.
Westmont, New Jersey Office: 316 Haddon Avenue, 08108.
Telephones: 609-854-4900; 800-523-2900.
Fax: 609-854-1782.

(See Next Column)

COZEN AND O'CONNOR A PROFESSIONAL CORPORATION—*Continued*

Newark, New Jersey Office: One Newark Center, Suite 1900, 1085 Raymond Boulevard, 07102.
Telephone: 973-286-1200; 888-200-9521.
Fax: 973-242-2121.
Atlanta, Georgia Office: Suite 2200, SunTrust Plaza, 303 Peachtree Street, N.E., 30308.
Telephones: 404-572-2000; 800-890-1393.
Fax: 404-572-2199.
London, England Office: Cozen and O'Connor at Radcliffes, 5 Great College Street, Westminster, SW1P 3SJ.
Telephone: 011-44-207-654-7600.
Fax: 011-44-207-654-7613.
Wilmington, Delaware Office: Chase Manhattan Centre, 1201 North Market Street, Suite 1400, 19801.
Telephone: 302-295-2000; 888-207-2440.
Fax: 302-295-2013.
Mt. Laurel, New Jersey Office: 10,000 Midlantic Drive, Suite 301, 08054.

FIRM MEMBER IN PHILADELPHIA

Stephen A. Cozen

Kevin M. Apollo
Richard C. Bennett
James E. Brown
Martin P. Duffey
Lewis A. Grafman
Robert W. Hayes
Kathie D. King
Thomas C. Zielinski

Representative Clients: Available upon request.

For Complete List of Firm Personnel, See General Section

For full biographical listings, see the Martindale-Hubbell Law Directory

DiDONATO & WINTERHALTER, P.C. (AV)

1818 Market Street, Suite 3520, 19103-3629
Telephone: 215-564-5050
Telecopier: 215-564-5597
URL: http://www.lawyers.com/didonato
Marlton, New Jersey Office: One Greentree Centre, Route 73 & Greenfield Road, Suite 201, 08053.
Telephone: 609-263-2700.
Telecopier: 609-263-9192.

Edward J. DiDonato
Paul J. Winterhalter
Eugene Camposano

For full biographical listings, see the Martindale-Hubbell Law Directory

F. EMMETT FITZPATRICK, P.C. (AV)

926 Public Ledger Building, 19106
Telephone: 215-925-5200
Fax: 215-925-5991
Email: info@toplaw.com *URL:* http://www.toplaw.com

F. Emmett Fitzpatrick
F. Emmett Fitzpatrick, III

NiaLena Caravasos

LEGAL SUPPORT PERSONNEL

Doreen Howley (Paralegal)

For full biographical listings, see the Martindale-Hubbell Law Directory

KELLEY, JASONS, McGUIRE & SPINELLI, L.L.P. (AV)

One Penn Center, Suite 1400, 1617 JFK Boulevard, 19103
Telephone: 215-854-0658
Fax: 215-854-8434; 215-854-0777
Marlton, New Jersey Office: One Greentree Centre, Suite 201, 08053.
Telephone: 609-988-5543.
Fax: 609-988-9165.
Wilmington, Delaware Office: 800 Delaware Avenue, P.O. Box 194, 19899.
Telephone: 302-652-8560.
Fax: 302-652-8405.

MEMBERS OF FIRM

John Patrick Kelley
Catherine N. Jasons
Joseph W. McGuire
Armand J. Della Porta, Jr.
Christopher N. Santoro
Robert N. Spinelli
Thomas P. Hanna
Thomas J. Johanson
Michael L. Turner
Richard L. Walker, II
Timothy McGowan

ASSOCIATES

Neal C. Glenn
W. Matthew Reber
Ann C. Lebowitz
Anthony J. Ryan

OF COUNSEL

Matthew D. Blum

For full biographical listings, see the Martindale-Hubbell Law Directory

MANTA AND WELGE, A PROFESSIONAL CORPORATION (AV)

2000 Market Street, 6th Floor, 19103
Telephone: 215-851-6600
Telecopy: 215-851-6644
URL: http://www.mantalaw.com
Allentown, Pennsylvania Office: Suite 204, 5000 Tilghman Street.
Telephone: 610-395-7499.
Fax: 610-366-5096.
Harrisburg, Pennsylvania Office: Governors Row, 27 North Front Street.
Telephone: 717-236-8420.
West Trenton, New Jersey Office: 810 Bear Tavern Road, Suite 301.
Telephone: 609-883-6990.
Fax: 609-883-7730.
Wilmington, Delaware Office: Suite 1400, Mellon Bank Center, 919 Market Street.
Telephone: 302-655-7460.
Fax: 302-655-7004.

MEMBERS OF FIRM

Kathleen Misturak-Gingrich
Thomas B. O'Brien, Jr.
Francis G. X. Pileggi (Resident, Wilmington, Delaware Office)

Joseph B. Silverstein
Yasmeen Sabina Khaleel
Denise Adamucci
Jennifer M. Welding
Michael A. Green

For full biographical listings, see the Martindale-Hubbell Law Directory

McKISSOCK & HOFFMAN, P.C. (AV)

1700 Market Street, Suite 3000, 19103
Telephone: 215-246-2100
Fax: 215-246-2144
Westmont, New Jersey Office: 216 Haddon Avenue, Suite 603.
Telephone: 609-858-1650.
Fax: 609-858-1466.
Doylestown, Pennsylvania Office: 16 North Franklin Street, Suite 300.
Telephone: 215-345-4501.
Fax: 215-246-4503.
Harrisburg, Pennsylvania Office: 105 North Front Street, Suite 205.
Telephone: 717-234-0103.
Fax: 717-234-1350.
West Chester, Pennsylvania Office: 31 South High Street, P.O. Box 3086.
Telephone: 610-738-8850.
Fax: 610-738-9121.

J. Bruce McKissock
Peter J. Hoffman
Leslie Anne Miller
Jeffrey B. Albert
Jill Baratz Clarke
John J. McGrath (Resident, Westmont, New Jersey Office)
Donald J. Brooks, Jr.
William J. Mundy
Bryan Craig Black (Resident, Harrisburg Office)
Eileen Lampe
Christopher Thomson (Resident Shareholder, West Chester Office)
K. Reed Haywood
Maureen P. Fitzgerald

For full biographical listings, see the Martindale-Hubbell Law Directory

WEIR & PARTNERS LLP (AV)

A Pennsylvania Limited Liability Partnership
Suite 500, The Widener Building, 1339 Chestnut Street, 19107
Telephone: 215-665-8181
Telefax: 215-665-8464
Email: info@weirpartners.com
Turnersville, New Jersey Office: 215 Fries Mill Road, 08012.
Telephone: 609-740-1490.
Telefax: 609-740-1491.

MEMBERS OF FIRM

Walter Weir, Jr.
Leonard S. Goodman
Susan Verbonitz
Jeffrey L. Rudnick
Robert D. Sayre
Stephen M. Giroux
Richard P. Coe, Jr.
Brett A. Datto
John B. York
Joseph C. Hare

ASSOCIATES

Bonnie R. Golub
Debra N. Nathanson
Tina L. Colman
Andrew K. Stutzman
Jeffrey A. Guth
Jason M Reiser
Madeline Flanagan

For full biographical listings, see the Martindale-Hubbell Law Directory

*PITTSBURGH,** Allegheny Co.

APPLE AND APPLE, A PROFESSIONAL CORPORATION (AV)

4650 Baum Boulevard, 15213
Telephone: 412-682-1466; 800-477-APPLE
Fax: 412-682-3138
Email: applelaw@aol.com

Marvin J. Apple
James R. Apple

Charles F. Bennett
Joel E. Hausman
Marylouise Wagner

(See Next Column)

APPLE AND APPLE A PROFESSIONAL CORPORATION, *Pittsburgh—Continued*

LEGAL SUPPORT PERSONNEL

Michelle A. Bernard-Danielson (Office Manager)

Representative Clients: Citibank; Bank of America; Providian Financial; PNC Bank; National City Bank; BP Oil; N.A.C.M.; Associates Commercial Corp.; Kemper Insurance; Conrail.

For full biographical listings, see the Martindale-Hubbell Law Directory

BABST, CALLAND, CLEMENTS AND ZOMNIR, A PROFESSIONAL CORPORATION (AV)

Two Gateway Center, 15222
Telephone: 412-394-5400
Fax: 412-394-6576
Email: BCCZ@BCCZ.com
Philadelphia, Pennsylvania Office: The Widener Building, Suite 1700, One South Penn Square.
Telephone: 215-567-1020.
Fax: 215-751-1425.

Frank J. Clements
R. Douglas DeNardo
James A. Escovitz
Ronald W. Frank
Michael A. Snyder
James W. Ummer
Ted Wesolowski

Richard M. Albert
Carla E. Charlton
Christian A. Farmakis
Joseph S. Koscinski
Paul H. Minton
Alexander J. Simakas

For full biographical listings, see the Martindale-Hubbell Law Directory

CAMPBELL & LEVINE, LLC (AV)

1700 Grant Building, 15219
Telephone: 412-261-0310
Fax: 412-261-5066

MEMBERS OF FIRM

Douglas A. Campbell
Stanley E. Levine
David B. Salzman
Roger M. Bould
Philip E. Milch

ASSOCIATES

Ronald B. Roteman
Michael R. Salzman

OF COUNSEL

Tybe A. Brett

For full biographical listings, see the Martindale-Hubbell Law Directory

DEFOREST & KOSCELNIK (AV)

3000 Koppers Building, 436 Seventh Avenue, 15219
Telephone: 412-227-3100
Fax: 412-227-3130

Walter P. DeForest, III
Jacqueline A. Koscelnik

ASSOCIATES

David J. Berardinelli
Paul M. Thompson

Representative Clients: Carnegie Mellon University; Ohio Valley Medical Center; Cox Enterprises, Inc.; General Electric Co.; Chancellor Broadcasting; Shooting Star Broadcasting; Leybold Vacuum Products, Inc.; Demegen, Inc.; Emerson Electric Co.; Frank Bryan, Inc.; Rox Trucking, Inc.

For full biographical listings, see the Martindale-Hubbell Law Directory

GLOSSER & SHREVE (AV)

Suite 200, 213 Smithfield Street, 15222-2224
Telephone: 412-281-6555
FAX: 412-281-6597
Email: mark.glosser@commersel.com *URL:* http://www.lawyers.com/debtorcreditlaw

Mark L. Glosser
Steven T. Shreve

Representative Clients: Crawford Construction Company, Inc.; Franklin & Locust Realty, Inc.; Digital Equipment Corporation, Inc.; Household Financial Corporation; First Union Bank; C.J. Betters Co.

For full biographical listings, see the Martindale-Hubbell Law Directory

MARCUS & SHAPIRA LLP (AV)

35th Floor, One Oxford Centre, 301 Grant Street, 15219-6401
Telephone: 412-471-3490
Telecopier: 412-391-8758
Email: info@marcus-shapira.com *URL:* http://www.marcus-shapira.com

(See Next Column)

MEMBERS OF FIRM

Robert L. Allman, II
Joseph J. Barnes
Robert M. Barnes
Sylvester A. Beozzo
Estelle F. Comay
Elly Heller-Toig
Charles G. Knox
Carrie Kochenbach
James S. Larrimer
Scott D. Livingston
Bernard D. Marcus
Darlene M. Nowak
James F. Rosenberg
Daniel H. Shapira
Stephen S. Zubrow

OF COUNSEL

John M. Burkoff

ASSOCIATES

Henry G. Barr
Moira E. Cain
Traci L. McDonald

For Complete List of Firm Personnel, See General Section

For full biographical listings, see the Martindale-Hubbell Law Directory

PLOWMAN, SPIEGEL & LEWIS, P.C. (AV)

Second Floor, The Grant Building, 310 Grant Street, 15219-2201
Telephone: 412-471-8521
Fax: 412-471-4481

Jack W. Plowman
John L. Spiegel
James A. Lewis

Mark A. Griffith
Charles B. Jarrett, Jr.
J. Michael McCague, Jr.

Reference: Pittsburgh National Bank.

For Complete List of Firm Personnel, See General Section

For full biographical listings, see the Martindale-Hubbell Law Directory

RILEY, MCNULTY, HEWITT & SWEITZER, A PROFESSIONAL CORPORATION (AV)

Suite 300, 650 Washingon Road, 15228
Telephone: 412-341-9300
Fax: 412-341-9177
Email: rmhs@nauticom.net

Patrick R. Riley
Sibyl S. McNulty
Patrick A. Hewitt
David E. Sweitzer

William J. Witte

For full biographical listings, see the Martindale-Hubbell Law Directory

WEISMAN GOLDMAN BOWEN & GROSS LLP (AV)

310 Grant Street, Suite 420, 15219
Telephone: 412-566-2520
Fax: 412-566-1088

James L. Weisman
S. James Goldman
Alden Earl Bowen
Sanford P. Gross
Barry J. Lipson
Howard J. Schulberg
Christopher J. Klein
Samuel F. Reynolds, Jr.
Frank J. Grzywinski
David J. Brosky
Robert L. Monks

Reference: Pittsburgh National Bank.

For full biographical listings, see the Martindale-Hubbell Law Directory

*READING,** Berks Co.

MOGEL, SPEIDEL, BOBB & KERSHNER, A PROFESSIONAL CORPORATION (AV)

520 Walnut Street, P.O. Box 8581, 19603-8581
Telephone: 610-376-1515
Telecopier: 610-372-8710

George B. Balmer (1902-1969)
George A. Kershner (1907-1969)
Carl F. Mogel (1919-1994)
Edwin H. Kershner
Frederick R. Mogel
Michael L. Mixell
George M. Lutz
Paul M. Yatron
Stephen H. Price
Kathryn K. Harenza

Sean J. O'Brien
Matthew Earl Glinn

OF COUNSEL

Harry W. Speidel
Donald K. Bobb
Henry A. Gass

Representative Clients: Great Valley Bank; Union Township, Berks County, Pennsylvania.

For full biographical listings, see the Martindale-Hubbell Law Directory

*SCRANTON,** Lackawanna Co.

WELLES & MCGRATH (AV)

1117 Bank Towers, 321 Spruce Street, 18503
Telephone: 570-348-4951
Fax: 570-348-4954

MEMBERS OF FIRM

Charles H. Welles, Jr. (1876-1962)
Matthew D. Mackie (1897-1965)
Charles H. Welles (1907-1997)
Henry C. McGrath
Charles H. Welles, IV

Counsel For: Grange National Bank; Scranton Industrial Development Co.; Bear Creek Nursing Home; Northeastern Ob-Gyn Associates, P.C.; Metropolitan Life Insurance Co.; New Health Management Systems, Inc.; Chamberlin Insurance Inc.

For full biographical listings, see the Martindale-Hubbell Law Directory

RHODE ISLAND

*PROVIDENCE,** Providence Co.

BLISH & CAVANAGH (AV)

Commerce Center, 30 Exchange Terrace, 02903
Telephone: 401-831-8900
Telecopier: 401-751-7542
Email: BLISHCAV@AOL.COM

MEMBERS OF FIRM

Joseph V. Cavanagh, Jr.
William R. Landry
Edmund L. Alves, Jr.
Stephen J. Reid, Jr.
Karen A. Pelczarski
Scott T. Spear
Raymond A. Marcaccio

Michael W. Carroll
Staci L. Sawyer
Kristin Rodgers Sullivan

OF COUNSEL

John H. Blish

Representative Clients: Providence Journal Co.; Rhode Island Hospital Trust National Bank; Fleet Bank; Metropolitan Insurance Co.; Allstate Insurance Co.; Delta Dental of Rhode Island; Colony Communications; Providence Housing Authority; Textron; A.T. Cross.

For full biographical listings, see the Martindale-Hubbell Law Directory

HINCKLEY, ALLEN & SNYDER LLP (AV)

1500 Fleet Center, 02903-2393
Telephone: 401-274-2000
Fax: 401-277-9600
Email: firm@haslaw.com *URL:* http://www.haslaw.com
Boston, Massachusetts Office: 28 State Street, 30th Floor.
Telephone: 617-345-9000.
Fax: 617-345-9020. URL: http://www.haslaw.com.

MEMBERS OF FIRM

Paula K. Andrews (Not admitted in RI)
David D. Barricelli
E. Jerome Batty
Jonathan Bell
Paul Bork (Not admitted in RI)
Stephen J. Carlotti
David Barry Connolly (Not admitted in RI)
Joseph P. Curran
Michael P. DeFanti
Eric F. Eisenberg (Not admitted in RI)
Malcolm Farmer, III
Margaret D. Farrell
Bruce G. Goodman (Not admitted in RI)
Hugh J. Gorman, III (Not admitted in RI)
Alan P. Gottlieb (Not admitted in RI)
Gerard R. Goulet
William R. Grimm
Paul A. Hedstrom (Not admitted in RI)
Richard L. E. Jocelyn
Michael J. Kelly (Not admitted in RI)
Joel Lewin (Not admitted in RI)
Sandra Matrone Mack
Matthew T. Marcello, III
Frederick P. McClure
Elizabeth Murdock Myers
Paul F. O'Donnell, III (Not admitted in RI)
H. Peter Olsen
Julianne Palumbo (Not admitted in RI)
John J. Pendergast, III
Gerald J. Petros
James O. Reavis
Jeremy Ritzenberg (Not admitted in RI)
Ralph J. Rivkind (Not admitted in RI)
David J. Rubin
Charles E. Schaub, Jr. (Not admitted in RI)
Douglas F. Seaver (Not admitted in RI)
Scott E. Sheridan (Not admitted in RI)
Herman Snyder (Not admitted in RI)
David R. Sullivan (Not admitted in RI)
Robert F. Sylvia (Not admitted in RI)
Howard E. Walker
Richard D. Wayne (Not admitted in RI)

(See Next Column)

ASSOCIATES

Jessica M. Bettencourt
Mark Bianchi
Alyssa V. Boss
Alexandra K. Callam
Jane E. Cohen (Not admitted in RI)
Andrew D. Cummings (Not admitted in RI)
June E. Daniel
Kim Herman Goslant (Not admitted in RI)
Gloria Maria Gutierrez (Not admitted in RI)
Kelley Jordan-Price
Catherine S. Kim (Not admitted in RI)
Christopher W. Morog (Not admitted in RI)
Elena B. Olson (Not admitted in RI)
Lawrence W. Vernaglia (Not admitted in RI)
Joseph D. Whelan

OF COUNSEL

Willard R. Pope (Not admitted in RI)
Bentley Tobin
Joachim A. Weissfeld

For Complete List of Firm Personnel, See General Section

For full biographical listings, see the Martindale-Hubbell Law Directory

WILLIAM T. MURPHY LAW OFFICES, INC. (AV)

The Calart Tower, 400 Reservoir Avenue, Suite 3L, 02907
Telephone: 401-461-7740
Telecopier: 401-461-7753

William T. Murphy

Charles A. Pisaturo, Jr.
Steven T. Hayes

Reference: Citizens Bank.

For full biographical listings, see the Martindale-Hubbell Law Directory

SOUTH CAROLINA

*CHARLESTON,** Charleston Co.

BUIST, MOORE, SMYTHE & MCGEE, P.A. (AV)

Successors to Buist, Buist, Smythe and Smythe and Moore, Mouzon and McGee.
Five Exchange Street, P.O. Box 999, 29402
Telephone: 843-722-3400
Cable Address: "Conferees"
Telex: 57-6488
Telecopier: 843-723-7398
Email: bmsm@lawyer-sc.com *URL:* http://www.lawyer-sc.com

Susan M. Smythe
W. Foster Gaillard
Henry E. Grimball
Morris A. Ellison
Charles P. Summerall, IV
David H. Crawford

Thomas L. Harper, Jr.
Gregory Horton

Representative Clients: NationsBank; Metropolitan Life Insurance Co.; Independent Life & Accident Co.; National Bank of South Carolina; SouthTrust; The Bennett-Hofford Co.; Ziff Properties; The InterTech Group; ECDC d/b/a East Coast Development Co.; National Car Rental System, Inc.

For Complete List of Firm Personnel, See General Section

For full biographical listings, see the Martindale-Hubbell Law Directory

*COLUMBIA,** Richland Co.

BEACH LAW FIRM, P.A. (AV)

1321 Lady Street, Suite 310, 29211-1547
Telephone: 803-779-0066
Fax: 803-799-8479
Mailing Address: P.O. Box 11547, Columbia, South Carolina, 29211-1547
Email: firm@beachlaw.net

John F. Beach

John J. Pringle, Jr.

For full biographical listings, see the Martindale-Hubbell Law Directory

FINKEL & ALTMAN, L.L.C. (AV)

Suite 1800, 1201 Main Street, P.O. Box 1799, 29202
Telephone: 803-765-2935
Fax: 803-252-0786
Email: webmaster@finkellaw.com *URL:* http://www.finkellaw.com
Charleston, South Carolina Office: 12 Exchange Street, P.O. Box 225.
Telephone: 843-577-5460.
Fax: 843-577-5135.

(See Next Column)

FINKEL & ALTMAN L.L.C., *Columbia—Continued*

Gerald M. Finkel
Charles S. Altman (Resident, Charleston South Carolina Office)
Beverly J. Finkel

Janet B. Haigler

Representative Clients: First Union Mortgage Company; First Union National Bank; Banc One Mortgage Co.; Motorola Communications & Electronics Corp.; The Columbia Company, Inc.

For full biographical listings, see the Martindale-Hubbell Law Directory

RICHARDSON, PLOWDEN, CARPENTER & ROBINSON, P.A. (AV)

1600 Marion Street, P.O. Drawer 7788, 29202
Telephone: 803-771-4400
Telecopy: 803-779-0016
Email: atty@rpcrlaw.com *URL:* http://www.rpcrlaw.com
Myrtle Beach, South Carolina Office: 2103 B Farlow Street, P.O. Box 3646, 29578.
Telephone: 843-448-1008.
FAX: 843-448-1533.

Frank E. Robinson, II
Frederick A. Crawford
S. Nelson Weston Jr.

Stephen C. Lenker, Jr.

For Complete List of Firm Personnel, See General Section

For full biographical listings, see the Martindale-Hubbell Law Directory

TURNER, PADGET, GRAHAM & LANEY, P.A. (AV)

Seventeenth Floor, 1901 Main Street, P.O. Box 1473, 29202
Telephone: 803-254-2200
Telecopy: 803-799-3957
Florence, South Carolina Office: Fourth Floor, 1831 West Evans Street, P.O. Box 5478, 29502.
Telephone: 843-662-9008.
Fax: 843-667-0828.
Charleston, South Carolina Office: 21 Broad Street, 1st Floor, P.O. Box 836, 29402.
Telephone: 843-723-1622.
Fax: 843-577-3369.

W. Duvall Spruill
R. Wayne Byrd (Resident, Florence, SC, Office)
David G. Fawcett
Lanneau William Lambert, Jr.
Hugh M. Claytor (Resident, Florence, SC, Office)
R. Todd Sherpy
Jeffrey L. Payne (Resident, Florence, SC, Office)
Michael S. Hopewell (Resident, Florence, SC, Office)

OF COUNSEL

Stephen A. Husman

David W. Keller, Jr. (Resident, Florence, SC Office)
William O. Higgins
Julie Jeffords Moose (Resident, Florence, SC, Office)

For Complete List of Firm Personnel, See General Section

For full biographical listings, see the Martindale-Hubbell Law Directory

TYLER, CASSELL, JACKSON, PEACE & SILVER, L.L.P. (AV)

1331 Elmwood Avenue, Suite 300, P.O. Box 11656, 29211-1656
Telephone: 803-779-4997
Telecopier: 803-765-2468

MEMBERS OF FIRM

Donald W. Tyler
Herbert C. Cassell, Jr.
Thomas B. Jackson, III
M. Alan Peace
Jeffrey L. Silver

OF COUNSEL

Eugene L. Brantley

References: SouthTrust Bank; Branch Banking and Trust Company; Bank of Columbia; McDonald's Corp.; Centex Real Estate Corp.; Commercial Credit Corp.; Merrill Lynch Credit Corporation.

For full biographical listings, see the Martindale-Hubbell Law Directory

*GREENVILLE,** Greenville Co.

WILLIAMS & HENRY, PROFESSIONAL ASSOCIATION (AV)

513 East Washington Street, P.O. Box 10307, 29603
Telephone: 864-233-1609
Fax: 864-232-7807
Email: lawfirm@williamshenry.com

(See Next Column)

Ray R. Williams (1899-1987)
J. A. Henry (1899-1971)
Ray R. Williams, Jr.
Craig H. Allen

For full biographical listings, see the Martindale-Hubbell Law Directory

MYRTLE BEACH, Horry Co.

BELLAMY, RUTENBERG, COPELAND, EPPS, GRAVELY & BOWERS, P.A. (AV)

1000 29th Avenue North, P.O. Box 357, 29578
Telephone: 843-448-2400
Telecopier: 843-448-3022

Howell V. Bellamy, Jr.
John K. Rutenberg
John E. Copeland
Claude M. Epps, Jr.
David R. Gravely
Edward B. Bowers, Jr.
Bradley D. King
Henrietta U. Golding
M. Edwin Hinds, Jr.
Jill F. Griffith
Kathryn M. Cook
David B. Miller
C. Winfield Johnson, III
Sarah A. Johnson
Douglas M. Zayicek
Jeffrey W. King
Mary Anna Malpass
Martin Charles Dawsey

Representative Clients: Dargan Construction Co.; Coastal Federal Savings Bank; Sands Investments; Wachovia Bank of South Carolina; AVX Corp.; Bank of America; Parthenon Insurance Co.; Burroughs & Chapin Co.; International Paper Co.; Hospital Corporation of America.

For full biographical listings, see the Martindale-Hubbell Law Directory

*SPARTANBURG,** Spartanburg Co.

PERRIN, PERRIN, MANN & PATTERSON, L.L.P. (AV)

200 Library Street, P.O. Box 1655, 29304
Telephone: 864-582-5461
Fax: 864-583-5235
Email: ppm&p@teleplex.net

L. W. Perrin (1918-1980)

OF COUNSEL

Edward P. Perrin

MEMBERS OF FIRM

Franklin M. Mann
Dwight F. Patterson, Jr.
Lawrence E. Flynn, Jr.
William O. Pressley, Jr.

General Counsel for: Carolina Cash Co.; Spartanburg Sanitary Sewer District.

For full biographical listings, see the Martindale-Hubbell Law Directory

SOUTH DAKOTA

*RAPID CITY,** Pennington Co.

JOHNSON EIESLAND HUFFMAN & CLAYBORNE LAW FIRM, LLP (AV)

2201 Jackson Boulevard, Suite 200, P.O. Box 6900, 57709-6900
Telephone: 605-348-7300; 800-998-3998
FAX: 605-348-4757
Email: jehc22@aol.com *URL:* http://www.jehc-law.com

Glen H. Johnson
Gregory A. Eiesland
Richard E. Huffman
Courtney R. Clayborne

Kristi K. Wammen

For full biographical listings, see the Martindale-Hubbell Law Directory

TENNESSEE

*DYERSBURG,** Dyer Co.

PALMER LAW FIRM (AV)

116 West Court Street, P.O. Box 746, 38024
Telephone: 901-285-7382
Fax: 901-286-6537

MEMBERS OF FIRM

E. T. "Rocky" Palmer (1907-1986)
John W. Palmer

ASSOCIATE

Earl F. Johnson

For full biographical listings, see the Martindale-Hubbell Law Directory

*MEMPHIS,** Shelby Co.

ARMSTRONG ALLEN PREWITT GENTRY JOHNSTON & HOLMES, PLLC (AV)

Brinkley Plaza, Suite 700, 80 Monroe Avenue, 38103-2467
Telephone: 901-523-8211
Facsimile: 901-524-4936
Little Rock, Arkansas Office: Suite 100, 100 Morgan Keegan Drive, 72202.
Telephone: 501-280-0100.
Facsimile: 501-280-0166.
Jackson, Mississippi Office: 2525 Lakeward Drive, Suite 200, 39216.
Telephone: 601-713-1192.
Facsimile: 601-713-2049.
Jackson, Tennessee Office: 464 North Parkway, Suite A, 38305.
Telephone: 901-660-2332.
Facsimile: 901-664-1109.

MEMBERS OF FIRM

Paul A. Matthews
B. Douglas Earthman
James B. McLaren, Jr.
Charles R. Crawford
David A. Thornton

For Complete List of Firm Personnel, See General Section

For full biographical listings, see the Martindale-Hubbell Law Directory

EVANS & PETREE (AV)

81 Monroe Avenue, 38103
Telephone: 901-525-6781
Telecopier: 901-527-7756

MEMBERS OF FIRM

Marion G. Evans (1877-1957)
Jack Petree (1921-1973)
Charles Pittman Cobb (Retired)
Elwood L. Edwards (Retired)
W. Lytle Nichol IV
John W. McQuiston II
Ernest G. Kelly, Jr.
Michael C. Williams
Joseph W. Barnwell, Jr.
David C. Scruggs
Leonard C. Dunavant, Jr.
E. Woods Weathersby
C. Bradford Foster III
Andrew H. Raines
Frank N. Stockdale Carney
Paul F. T. Edwards
Percy H. Harvey
Katharine A. Jungkind
Scott A. Frick
Michael R. Marshall
Richard E.M. Nichol, Jr.

Karen Baim Reagler

For full biographical listings, see the Martindale-Hubbell Law Directory

KRIVCHER MAGIDS PLC (AV)

International Place II, 6410 Poplar Avenue, Suite 300, 38119-4839
Telephone: 901-682-6431
Facsimile: 901-682-6453
Email: lawfirm@kmplc.com

L. Don Campbell, Jr.
Charles C. Cottam
Jack Steven Magids
Michael B. Neal

ASSOCIATES

Rachel L. Hotze
Shawn A. Tidwell
Elizabeth J. Landrigan
Geoffrey M. Hirsch

For Complete List of Firm Personnel, See General Section

For full biographical listings, see the Martindale-Hubbell Law Directory

MERRILL, MULLINS & SPEARS, A PROFESSIONAL ASSOCIATION (AV)

1075 Morgan Keegan Tower, 50 North Front Street, 38103
Telephone: 901-526-6464
Telecopier: 901-526-6467

Erich W. Merrill
Irma W. Merrill
Kimbrough Brown Mullins
Diane C. Spears

For full biographical listings, see the Martindale-Hubbell Law Directory

*NASHVILLE,** Davidson Co.

CORBETT CROCKETT & LECKRONE (AV)

An Association of Attorneys including a Professional Corporation
Suite 1050, American Center, 3100 West End Avenue, 37203
Telephone: 615-383-0500
Facsimile: 615-383-5556
Email: counsel@ccllaw.com *URL:* http://www.lawyers.com/ccl

W. Lee Corbett (P.C.)
Joe Vaulx Crockett, III
James David Leckrone
David F. Lewis
Robert H. Turner, III

For full biographical listings, see the Martindale-Hubbell Law Directory

RANDOLPH B. JONES (AV)

3200 West End Avenue, Suite 500, 37203
Telephone: 615-783-1705
Facsimile: 615-783-1606

GAIL P. PIGG (AV)

219 Second Avenue North, 37201
Telephone: 615-244-0001
Fax: 615-244-0003

References: Nations Bank.

For full biographical listings, see the Martindale-Hubbell Law Directory

TEXAS

*ABILENE,** Taylor Co.

WHITTEN & YOUNG, P.C. (AV)

500 Chestnut, Suite 1402, P.O. Box 208, 79602
Telephone: 915-672-7824
Fax: 915-672-2158
Email: wypc@camalott.com

O. Henry (Mike) Young
Gary L. Hacker
C. Terry Hagin
Donald L. Anderson, Jr.
Cynthia Rucker Allen
Charles C. Self, III

Paul R. Rotenberry

OF COUNSEL

C. G. Whitten

For full biographical listings, see the Martindale-Hubbell Law Directory

*AMARILLO,** Potter Co.

GARNER & STEIN, LLP (AV)

777 Amarillo National Plaza/Two, 500 South Taylor, LB #233, 79101-2446
Telephone: 806-373-0505
Telecopier: 806-379-8056
Email: regarner@tcac.net

MEMBERS OF FIRM

Robert E. Garner
Sam L. Stein

ASSOCIATE

Ana E. Estevez

LEGAL SUPPORT PERSONNEL

PARALEGALS

Michele Kindle
Roxann Sillivent

Representative Clients: Panhandle Capitol Corp.; Friona Industries, L.P.; Page and Associates, Contractors; Hereford Bi-Products, Inc.; Amarillo National Bank.

For full biographical listings, see the Martindale-Hubbell Law Directory

*AUSTIN,** Travis Co.

BAKER BOTTS L.L.P. (AV)

1600 San Jacinto Center, 98 San Jacinto Boulevard, 78701
Telephone: 512-322-2500
Fax: 512-322-2501
Email: postmaster@bakerbotts.com *URL:* http://www.bakerbotts.com
Houston, Texas Office: One Shell Plaza, 910 Louisiana.
Telephone: 713-229-1234.
Dallas, Texas Office: 2001 Ross Avenue.
Telephone: 214-953-6500.
Washington, D.C. Office: The Warner, 1299 Pennsylvania Avenue, N.W.
Telephone: 202-639-7700.
New York, New York Office: 599 Lexington Avenue.
Telephone: 212-705-5000.
Moscow, Russia Office: 10 ul. Bolshaya Dimitrovka (formerly Pushkinskaya), 103031.
Telephone: 7095/921-5300 (Local); 7501/929-7070 (International).
London, England Office: 45 Ludgate Hill.
Telephone: 0171-778-1400 (Local); 011-44-171-778-1400 (International).
Baku, Azerbaijan Office: 6-10 Vagif Mustafa-zadeh Street, Third Floor, Icheri Sheher, 370004.
Telephone: 994-12-97-63-88 (Local); 011-994-12-97-63-88 (International).
Fax: 994-12-97-63-61 (Local); 011-994-12-97-63-91 (International).

MEMBER OF FIRM

William F. Stutts, Jr.

SPECIAL COUNSEL

Shelley W. Austin

For Complete List of Firm Personnel, See General Section

For full biographical listings, see the Martindale-Hubbell Law Directory

*BEAUMONT,** Jefferson Co.

REAUD, MORGAN & QUINN (AV)

801 Laurel, 77701
Telephone: 409-838-1000
Fax: 409-833-8236

MEMBERS OF FIRM

Wayne A. Reaud
Glen W. Morgan
Cris Quinn
Richard J. Clarkson
Bob Wortham
Curtis W. Leister
Gary T. Cornwell

ASSOCIATES

Mary Ferguson Bradford
John Werner
David W. Ferrell
J. Trenton Bond
Sally A. Gary

For full biographical listings, see the Martindale-Hubbell Law Directory

THOMAS J. SIBLEY, P.C. (AV)

304 Pearl Street, First Floor, P.O. Box 3945, 77704-3945
Telephone: 409-835-9944
Fax: 409-838-4741
Email: tsibley@earthlink.net

Thomas J. Sibley
Kathleen Quick Sibley

Sara McDonald McElroy

Reference: Texas Commerce Bank-Beaumont.

For full biographical listings, see the Martindale-Hubbell Law Directory

*DALLAS,** Dallas Co.

BAKER BOTTS L.L.P. (AV)

2001 Ross Avenue, 75201
Telephone: 214-953-6500
Fax: 214-953-6503
Email: postmaster@bakerbotts.com *URL:* http://www.bakerbotts.com
Houston, Texas Office: One Shell Plaza, 910 Louisiana.
Telephone: 713-229-1234.
Washington, D.C. Office: The Warner, 1299 Pennsylvania Avenue, N.W.
Telephone: 202-639-7700.
Austin, Texas Office: 1600 San Jacinto Center, 98 San Jacinto Boulevard.
Telephone: 512-322-2500.
New York, New York Office: 599 Lexington Avenue.
Telephone: 212-705-5000.
Moscow, Russia Office: 10 ul. Bolshaya Dimitrovka (formerly Pushkinskaya), 103031.
Telephone: 7095/921-5300 (Local); 7095/929-7070.
London, England Office: 45 Ludgate Hill.
Telephone: 0171-778-1400 (Local); 011-44-171-778-1400 (International).
Baku, Azerbaijan Office: 6-10 Vagif Mustafa-zadeh Street, Third Floor, Icheri Sheher, 370004.
Telephone: 994-12-97-63-88 (Local); 011-994-12-97-63-88 (International).

MEMBERS OF FIRM

Andrew M. Baker
Jonathan W. Dunlay
John W. Martin
Geoffrey L. Newton
Patricia M. Stanton
Karen Leslye Wolf

ASSOCIATES

Curtis B. Anderson
Jay Bhattacharya
Lisa DiIorio
Christopher D. Epperson (Not admitted in TX)
Jason D. Krieser (Not admitted in TX)
Thomas J. Masterson
David G. Monk
Joel M. Overton, Jr.
Royce P. Poinsett
Douglass M. Rayburn
Brenda Levine Sutherland
Arthur C. Swanson

For Complete List of Firm Personnel, See General Section

For full biographical listings, see the Martindale-Hubbell Law Directory

CALHOUN & STACY (AV)

Suite 5700 - Bank of America Plaza, 901 Main Street, 75202-3713
Telephone: 214-748-5000
Facsimile: 214-748-1421
Email: info@calhounstacy.com *URL:* http://www.calhounstacy.com

MEMBERS OF FIRM

Mark Alan Calhoun
LeAnn Wainscott Cross
David W. Elrod
Thomas E. Rosen
Shannon B. Schuster
Roy L. Stacy
Michael C. Wright

ASSOCIATES

David G. Allen
Joseph G. Barkate, Jr.
Scott S. Crocker
Sean P. Fitzgerald
Elizabeth Reding Gambrell
Leanne Capps Medford
Jonathan G. Polak
Joel W. Reese
Barbara L. Wohlrabe

(See Next Column)

For Complete List of Firm Personnel, See General Section

For full biographical listings, see the Martindale-Hubbell Law Directory

COWLES & THOMPSON, A PROFESSIONAL CORPORATION (AV)

901 Main Street Suite 4000, 75202
Telephone: 214-672-2000
Metro: 972-263-0005
Fax: 214-672-2020
URL: http://www.cowlesthompson.com
McKinney, Texas Office: 307 S. McDonald St., 75069-5659.
Telephone: 972-542-5000. Metro: 972-562-2270.
Fax: 972-542-5040.
Tyler, Texas Office: 1103 First Place, P.O. Box 239, 75710-0239.
Telephone: 903-593-7508.
Fax: 903-593-4057.

Hardy E. Thompson, III
Melissa J. Pegram
Glenda O. Brewer
William D. Cobb, Jr.
Robert G. Buchanan, Jr.
David R. Woodward
B. Michael Bennett
Susan J. Snare
Sim Israeloff
Daniel D. Tostrud

For Complete List of Firm Personnel, See General Section

For full biographical listings, see the Martindale-Hubbell Law Directory

GODWIN WHITE & GRUBER, A PROFESSIONAL CORPORATION (AV)

Suite 2500, 901 Main Street, 75202-3714
Telephone: 214-939-4400
Fax: 214-760-7332

James F. Bullock
Thomas S. Hoekstra
James G. Vetter, Jr.
David J. White

OF COUNSEL

Joshua Mond

ASSOCIATE

Guy H. Riddle

For Complete List of Firm Personnel, See General Section

For full biographical listings, see the Martindale-Hubbell Law Directory

HUGHES & LUCE, L.L.P. (AV)

A Registered Limited Liability Partnership including Professional Corporations
1717 Main Street, Suite 2800, 75201
Telephone: 214-939-5500
Fax: 214-939-6100; 214-939-5849
Email: H&L@hughesluce.com *URL:* http://www.hughesluce.com
Austin, Texas Office: 111 Congress, Suite 900.
Telephone: 512-482-6800.
Fax: 512-482-6859.
Houston, Texas Office: 1600 Smith Street, Suite 3550.
Telephone: 713-754-5200.
Fax: 713-754-5270.

MEMBERS OF FIRM

Alan J. Bogdanow
Kenneth G. Hawari
Glen J. Hettinger
John B. Holden, Jr., (P.C.)
Mont P. Hoyt
David G. Luther, Jr.
William A. McCormack
Ross Clayton Mulford
Dudley W. Murrey

ASSOCIATES

Joanna H. Buck
James E. Cahill, III
Robert B. Hale
Gary W. Hays
Laura M. Kalesnik
Michael S.J. Lozich
Richard H. Mains
Bliss Burdett Pak
Anne-Marie Roy
Morgan A. Ryder
John Sepehri
John R. Wilcox III
Scott M. Wilson

OF COUNSEL

Nancy Figg Duessel

For Complete List of Firm Personnel, See General Section

For full biographical listings, see the Martindale-Hubbell Law Directory

LYNN STODGHILL MELSHEIMER & TILLOTSON, L.L.P. (AV)

A Partnership including a Professional Corporation
750 N. St. Paul Street, Suite 1400, 75201
Telephone: 214-981-3800
Fax: 214-981-3839
Email: mlynn@lsmt.com

Michael P. Lynn (P.C.)
Steven H. Stodghill (P.C.)
Thomas M. Melsheimer (P.C.)
Jeffrey M. Tillotson (P.C.)
Eric W. Pinker, P.C.

(See Next Column)

LYNN STODGHILL MELSHEIMER & TILLOTSON L.L.P.—*Continued*

ASSOCIATES

Nancy Horton Burke
Thomas B. Walsh, IV
Eric N. Whitney
M. Brett Johnson
Renée Skinner
John T. Cox, III
Geoffrey S. Harper
Mark E. Turk
Thomas E. Gavigan

OF COUNSEL

Robert E. Goodfriend, P.C.

For full biographical listings, see the Martindale-Hubbell Law Directory

MIDDLEBERG, RIDDLE & GIANNA (AV)

2323 Bryan Street, Suite 1600, 75201
Telephone: 214-220-6300
Telecopier: 214-220-2785
New Orleans, Louisiana Office: 201 St. Charles Avenue, Suite 3100.
Telephone: 504-525-7200.
Telecopier: 504-581-5983.
Austin, Texas Office: 1300 South Mopac Expressway, First Floor.
Telephone: 512-434-8334.
Houston, Texas Office: 7676 Woodway, Suite 325.
Telephone: 713-430-5000.
Telecopier: 713-430-5090.

Ira Joel Middleberg (Not admitted in TX)
Michael Lee Riddle
Dominic J. Gianna (Not admitted in TX)

Kay A. King
Laura C. LaRaia
Angela R. Maverick
Lisa E. Minkoff
Carol J. Riddle
Robert A. Schlanger
Alexandra Smith
Marsha L. Williams
Christina R. Wommack

OF COUNSEL

Richard S. Wilensky
Robert M. Duval

For full biographical listings, see the Martindale-Hubbell Law Directory

SMITH, UNDERWOOD & PERKINS, A PROFESSIONAL CORPORATION (AV)

600 Two Lincoln Centre, 5420 LBJ Freeway, 75240
Telephone: 972-661-5114
Telecopier: 972-661-5691
Email: firm@suandp.com *URL:* http://www.suplaw.com

Timothy S. Perkins
David W. Ralston
G. Lynn Smith
William J. Underwood, Jr.

Christine A. McGuire
Amy K. Ratzlaff
P. Theodore Stoinoff, II
Val C. Cronin
Ellen P. Stewart
Todd W. Shadle
Ruth C. Logan
Christina L. Betanzos
Kent D. Williamson

For full biographical listings, see the Martindale-Hubbell Law Directory

THOMPSON & KNIGHT L.L.P. (AV)

(Attorneys and Counselors)
1700 Pacific Avenue Suite 3300, 75201
Telephone: 214-969-1700
Telecopy: 214-969-1751
Telex: 732 298
URL: http://www.tklaw.com
Austin, Texas Office: 1200 San Jacinto Center, 98 San Jacinto Boulevard, 78701.
Telephone: 512-469-6100.
Telecopy: 512-469-6180.
Fort Worth, Texas Office: 801 Cherry Street, Suite 1600, 76102.
Telephone: 817-347-1700.
Telecopy: 817-347-1799.
Houston, Texas Office: Thompson Knight Brown Parker & Leahy L.L.P., 1200 Smith Street, Suite 3600, 77002-4595.
Telephone: 713-654-8111.
Telecopier: 713-654-1871.
San Pedro Garza Garcia, Nuevo León, Mexico Office: Edificio Losoles PD-4, Av. Lázaro Cárdenas No. 2400 Pte., C.P. 66220.
Telephone: (52-8) 363-0096.
Telecopy: (52-8) 363-3067.

PARTNERS

P. Jefferson Ballew
Beverly Ray Burlingame
Veronica Smith Lewis

For Complete List of Firm Personnel, See General Section

For full biographical listings, see the Martindale-Hubbell Law Directory

*EL PASO,** El Paso Co.

CROWSON & INGRAM (AV)

Suite 706, The Cortez, 310 North Mesa, P.O. Box 862, 79945
Telephone: 915-533-7717
Telefax: 915-533-1495
Email: crowsing@huntleigh.net

MEMBERS OF FIRM

Harold E. Crowson, Jr.
Temple B. Ingram, Jr.

Reference: Bank of America, N.A.; Norwest Bank, El Paso, N.A.; Bank of the West, El Paso, Texas.

For full biographical listings, see the Martindale-Hubbell Law Directory

*FORT WORTH,** Tarrant Co.

RUSSELL, TURNER, LAIRD & JONES, L.L.P. (AV)

One Colonial Place, 2400 Scott Avenue, 76103-2200
Telephone: 817-531-3000; 1-800-448-2889
Fax: 817-535-3046
Irving, Texas Office: Williams Square, Central Tower, Suite 700, 5215 North O'Connor Boulevard, Las Colinas Urban Center.
Telephone: 972-444-0444; 1-800-448-2889.

Wm. Greg Russell
Randall E. Turner
Steven C. Laird
Gregory G. Jones

For full biographical listings, see the Martindale-Hubbell Law Directory

*HENDERSON,** Rusk Co.

WELLBORN, HOUSTON, ADKISON, MANN, SADLER & HILL, L.L.P. (AV)

300 West Main Street, P.O. Box 1109, 75653-1109
Telephone: 903-657-8544; 903-657-7227
Fax: 903-657-6108
Email: FD@whamsh.com *URL:* http://www.whamsh.com

MEMBER OF FIRM

Ron Adkison

For full biographical listings, see the Martindale-Hubbell Law Directory

*HOUSTON,** Harris Co.

BAKER BOTTS L.L.P. (AV)

One Shell Plaza, 910 Louisiana, 77002
Telephone: 713-229-1234
Cable Address: "Boterlove"
Fax: 713-229-1522
Email: postmaster@bakerbotts.com *URL:* http://www.bakerbotts.com
Washington, D.C. Office: The Warner, 1299 Pennsylvania Avenue, N.W.
Telephone: 202-639-7700.
New York, New York Office: 599 Lexington Avenue.
Telephone: 212-705-5000.
Austin, Texas Office: 1600 San Jacinto Center, 98 San Jacinto Boulevard.
Telephone: 512-322-2500.
Dallas, Texas Office: 2001 Ross Avenue.
Telephone: 214-953-6500.
Moscow, Russia Office: 10 ul. Bolshaya Dimitrovka (formerly Pushkinskaya), 103031.
Telephone: 7095/921-5300 (Local); 7095/929-7070 (International).
London, England Office: 45 Ludgate Hill.
Telephone: 0171-778-1400 (Local); 011-44-171-778-1400 (International).
Baku, Azerbaijan Office: 6-10 Vagif Mustafa-zadeh Street, Third Floor, Icheri Sheher, 370004.
Telephone: 994-12-97-63-88 (Local); 011-994-12-97-63-88 (International).
Fax: 994-12-97-63-91 (Local); 011-994-12-97-63-91 (International)

MEMBER OF FIRM

Richard C. Johnson

MEMBERS OF FIRM

David F. Asmus
Jonathan T. Bickham
David Alan Burns
Joseph A. Cialone, II
Rufus Cormier, Jr.
Joshua Davidson
Tony M. Davis
James A. DeMent, Jr.
Fred H. Dunlop
Pamela B. Ewen
John D. Geddes
Moulton Goodrum, Jr.
Bill Hart, Jr.
Frank W. R. Hubert, Jr.
J. David Kirkland, Jr.
Stephen Krebs
Paul B. Landen
James L. Leader
Marley Lott
Stephen A. Massad
Michael S. Moehlman
Roy L. Nolen
Gene J. Oshman
Peter M. Oxman
Theodore William Paris
Joe S. Poff
Kelly Brunetti Rose
Margo S. Scholin
Walter J. Smith
Robert L. Stillwell
R. Joel Swanson
Charles Szalkowski
Darrell W. Taylor
Timothy S. Taylor
Lewis Proctor Thomas
Hugh Tucker
C. Michael Watson
Wade H. Whilden
Robert P. Wright

(See Next Column)

BAKER BOTTS L.L.P., *Houston—Continued*

SPECIAL COUNSEL

W. Brad Bryan
LeAnn Vaughn
Victoria Gardner Wall

OF COUNSEL

Greg N. Martin
James LeGrand Read

ASSOCIATES

Christopher J. Arntzen
Matthew D. Bekerman (Not admitted in TX)
J. Kevin Blodgett
Deidre Sullivan Brod
Karen Skeens Caldwell
M. Andrew Chen
Sarah Cooper
Edmund D. Daniels
David Patrick Elder
Brian P. Fenske
Kathleen S. Fenelon
Mary Millwood Gregory
Elizabeth M. Guffy
Ronald E. Holmes
Gregory B. Kopel
James H. Mayor
William S. Moss, III
Denise Dardeau Muller
Michelle A. Neumann
Rebecca Pacholder
Sergio A. Pozzerle
Elizabeth Rose
Wesley P. Shields
J. Denmon Sigler
Consuella D. Simmons
Gerald M. Spedale
Stacey F. Tilley
Laura Lanza Tyson

For Complete List of Firm Personnel, See General Section

For full biographical listings, see the Martindale-Hubbell Law Directory

FARNSWORTH & VONBERG (AV)

A Limited Liability Partnership
333 North Sam Houston Parkway, Suite 300, 77060
Telephone: 281-931-8902
Telecopy: 281-931-6032

T Brooke Farnsworth
Mary Frances vonBerg

ASSOCIATE

Bennett S. Bartlett

For full biographical listings, see the Martindale-Hubbell Law Directory

GALLAGHER, YOUNG, LEWIS, HAMPTON & DOWNEY, L.L.P. (AV)

NationsBank Building, 700 Louisiana, 40th Floor, 77002
Telephone: 713-222-8080
Fax: 713-222-0066

Michael T. Gallagher
William H. Young
Craig Lewis
Hartley Hampton
Daniel M. Downey

Martin John de la Torre
Andrew Sher
Candace Kaiser Eindorf
Scott H. Mclemore
John J. Klevenhagen, III
Araceli E. Flores

OF COUNSEL

Rosemary Conlon McCarthy

For full biographical listings, see the Martindale-Hubbell Law Directory

GIBBS & BRUNS, L.L.P. (AV)

1100 Louisiana, Suite 5300, 77002
Telephone: 713-650-8805
Fax: 713-750-0903

PARTNERS

Robin C. Gibbs
Phillip T. Bruns
J. Christopher Reynolds
Kathy D. Patrick
Jeffrey C. Alexander
Robert R. Burford
Jean C. Frizzell
Grant J. Harvey
Barrett H. Reasoner
Robert J. Madden
Jeffry J. Cotner
Jennifer Horan Greer

ASSOCIATES

Andrew L. Pickens
John A. Basinger
Scott A. Humphries
Michael K. Oldham
Caren Schmulen Sweetland
John Scott Black
Jeremy L. Doyle
Brandon T. Allen

For full biographical listings, see the Martindale-Hubbell Law Directory

GILLIS & SLOGAR (AV)

6905 Wells Fargo Plaza, 1000 Louisiana, 77002
Telephone: 713-951-9100
Telecopier: 713-951-9718
Email: gillisslogar@worldnet.att.net

Charles Michael Gillis
John Michael Slogar

OF COUNSEL

Randall W. Heinrich

For full biographical listings, see the Martindale-Hubbell Law Directory

G.P. HARDY III, P.C. (AV)

500 Two Houston Center, 909 Fannin at McKinney, 77010
Telephone: 713-222-0381
Fax: 713-759-9650
Bay City, Texas Office: 2042 Avenue F.
Telephone: 409-245-3797.
Fax: 409-245-4713.

G. P. Hardy, Jr. (1913-1988)
G. P. Hardy, III
Gail Johns

Timothy M. Purcell
Mark G. Cypert
Patricia Haylon

References: Southwest Bank of Texas; International Bank of Commerce.

For full biographical listings, see the Martindale-Hubbell Law Directory

LIPSTET & HIRSCH, L.L.P. (AV)

A Partnership including a Professional Corporation
Suite 1780, Two Post Oak Central, 1980 Post Oak Boulevard, 77056
Telephone: 713-961-7800
Fax: 713-961-3453

MEMBERS OF FIRM

Robert Leighton Lipstet (P.C.)
Reginald A. Hirsch

For full biographical listings, see the Martindale-Hubbell Law Directory

SCHWARTZ JUNELL CAMPBELL & OATHOUT, L.L.P. (AV)

Two Houston Center, 909 Fannin, Suite 2000, 77010
Telephone: 713-752-0017
Telecopier: 713-752-0327
Email: dschwartz@schwartz-junell.com

Richard A. Schwartz
William Edward Junell, Jr.
Marshall S. Campbell
Monica F. Oathout
Steven R. Rech

Phillip W. Bechter
J. Parker Fauntleroy, Jr.

OF COUNSEL

Joe H. Reynolds
A. R. Schwartz

LEGAL SUPPORT PERSONNEL

PARALEGALS

Nannette Koger
Maria Woods
Shelly A. Savage, CLA

For full biographical listings, see the Martindale-Hubbell Law Directory

*LUBBOCK,** Lubbock Co.

CARR, HUNT & JOY L.L.P. (AV)

1001 Texas Avenue, P.O. Box 2585, 79408
Telephone: 806-765-7491
Fax: 806-765-0553
Email: info@chjlaw.com
Amarillo, Texas Office: Amarillo National Plaza II, Ste. 509, 500 S. Taylor Street, P.O. Box 989, Amarillo, Texas. 79105.
Telephone: 806-342-3055.
Fax: 806-342-9907.

MEMBERS OF FIRM

Marvin Warlick Carr
Latrelle Bright Joy
Gary M. Bellair
Deborah S. McClure (Resident, Amarillo, Texas)

Representative Clients: Bank of America; Beef Products, Inc.; Brown-McKee, Inc.; Burk Royalty Co.; Colorado Interstate Gas Co.; Cooper Industries, Inc.; Int'l Bank of Commerce; Motorola, Inc.; Petrosurance.

For Complete List of Firm Personnel, See General Section

For full biographical listings, see the Martindale-Hubbell Law Directory

*SAN ANTONIO,** Bexar Co.

JOEL KLEIN & ASSOCIATES (AV)

6800 Park Ten Boulevard, Suite 264S, 78213-4204
Telephone: 210-734-4488
Fax: 210-734-4482
Email: joel@joelklein.com *URL:* http://www.joelklein.com

Joel H. Klein

OF COUNSEL

Lester L. Klein

For full biographical listings, see the Martindale-Hubbell Law Directory

TINSMAN & HOUSER, INC. (AV)

One Riverwalk Place, 14th Floor, 700 North St. Mary's Street, 78205
Telephone: 210-225-3121
U.S. Wats: 1-800-292-9999
Fax: 210-225-6235
Email: info@thlaw.com *URL:* http://www.thlaw.com

(See Next Column)

TINSMAN & HOUSER INC.—*Continued*

Richard Tinsman
Franklin D. Houser
Margaret M. Maisel
David G. Jayne
Robert C. Scott
Daniel J. T. Sciano
Rey Perez
Bernard Wm. Fischman
Sharon L. Savage
Ronald J. Salazar
Sue Dodson
Dennis P. Bujnoch

For full biographical listings, see the Martindale-Hubbell Law Directory

*TYLER,** Smith Co.

RAMEY & FLOCK, A PROFESSIONAL CORPORATION (AV)

500 First Place, P.O. Box 629, 75710
Telephone: 903-597-3301
Telecopier: 903-597-2413
Email: Ramey@Ramey-Flock.com *URL:* http://www.RameyFlock.com

Thomas B. Ramey (1892-1967)
Jack W. Flock
Tracy Crawford
Glenn Collins
Michael A. Hatchell
Tom Henson
Dennis G. Black
Paul H. Gilliam
R. Brian Craft
Gregory D. Smith
Michael T. Crawford
Mary H. Molly Hatchell
Rosemary Sage Jones
Ronald S. Vickery
John W. Ferguson, Jr.

Deron R. Dacus
Eric H. Findlay
Shannon Dacus
Maria Benecki Sowders
Jamy Mitchell Skaggs

Counsel for: Regions Bank; Exxon Co. U.S.A.; Kelly Springfield Tire Co.; Trinity-Mother Frances Health System; St. Paul Insurance Co.; The Travelers Cos.; Reliance Insurance Co.; Marshall Regional Medical Center.

For full biographical listings, see the Martindale-Hubbell Law Directory

UTAH

*SALT LAKE CITY,** Salt Lake Co.

CALLISTER NEBEKER & MCCULLOUGH, A PROFESSIONAL CORPORATION (AV)

Gateway Tower East, Suite 900, 10 East South Temple, 84133
Telephone: 801-530-7300
Telecopier: 801-364-9127
Email: mjeaston@cnmlaw.com *URL:* http://www.cnmlaw.com

Louis H. Callister
Dorothy C. Pleshe
John A. Beckstead
James R. Holbrook
Jeffrey L. Shields
Randall D Benson
George E. Harris, Jr.
John H. Rees
Jan M. Bergeson
John B. Lindsay

Representative Clients: Zions First National Bank; Zions Credit Corporation; Chrysler Credit Corp.; Associates Commercial Corp.; Federal Land Bank Association of Utah; Altres Financial, L.P.; Utah Technology Finance Corporation.

For Complete List of Firm Personnel, See General Section

For full biographical listings, see the Martindale-Hubbell Law Directory

GIAUQUE, CROCKETT, BENDINGER & PETERSON, A PROFESSIONAL CORPORATION (AV)

Wells Fargo Plaza, 170 South Main, Suite 400, 84101-1664
Telephone: 801-533-8383
Fax: 801-531-1486
Email: gcbp@xmission.com

PARTNERS

Stephen G. Crockett
Gary F. Bendinger
Robert A. Peterson
Richard W. Casey
Stephen T. Hard
Milo Steven Marsden
Jeffery S. Williams

OF COUNSEL

Richard W. Giauque
Roger D. Sandack
Kevin M. McDonough
Robert J. Moore
Patricia A. O'Rorke

Sean N. Egan
Wesley D. Felix
Rebecca S. Parr
John H. Bogart
Lisa R. Petersen
J. Robert Sonne
Karen L. Martinez
Andrew G. Deiss (On Leave)

For full biographical listings, see the Martindale-Hubbell Law Directory

KIRTON & MCCONKIE, A PROFESSIONAL CORPORATION (AV)

1800 Eagle Gate Tower, 60 East South Temple, 84111
Telephone: 801-328-3600
Telecopier: 801-321-4893

Randy T. Austin
Lorin C. Barker
Anthony I. Bentley, Jr.
Rolf H. Berger
Berne S. Broadbent
Charles W. Dahlquist, II
Jerry W. Dearinger
Robert W. Edwards
James E. Ellsworth
Fred D. Essig
Wallace O. Felsted
Clark B. Fetzer
R. Bruce Findlay
David J. Hardy
Keith L. Hargrove
Read R. Hellewell
Dale E. Hulse
Lee Ford Hunter
Richard G. Johnson, Jr.
Von G. Keetch
Raeburn G. Kennard
Wilford W. Kirton, Jr.
Michael F. Krieger
Paul H. Matthews
Daniel S. McConkie
David M. McConkie
Oscar W. McConkie, III
Oscar W. McConkie, Jr.
Samuel D. McVey
William A. Meaders, Jr.
Thomas L. Monson
Denis Roy Morrill
Merrill F. Nelson
Richard R. Neslen
Eric C. Olson
R. Willis Orton
B. Lloyd Poelman
Robert S. Prince
Gregory M. Simonsen
Robert T. Smith
(Not admitted in UT)
Myron L. Sorensen
Jon E. Waddoups
David M. Wahlquist
Thomas D. Walk
Stuart F. Weed
David A. Westerby
Todd E. Zenger

Randall C. Allen
Bryan H. Booth
Michael M. Conger
David S. Doty
Alexander Dushku
Scott C. Krieger
Melinda R. Porter
Matthew K. Richards
Dorany Rodriguez-Baltazar
(Not admitted in UT)
Jeffrey Dean Stevens
Amy S. Thomas
Steven L. Whitehead

For full biographical listings, see the Martindale-Hubbell Law Directory

PARSONS, DAVIES, KINGHORN & PETERS, P.C. (AV)

185 South State Street, Suite 700, 84111
Telephone: 801-363-4300
Facsimile: 801-363-4378
Email: Attorneys@pdkplaw.com

John M. Parsons
Glen E. Davies
Gerald H. Kinghorn
Bill Thomas Peters
Langdon T. Owen, Jr.
R. Kimball Mosier
John N. Brems
Ken P. Jones
David W. Scofield
Stuart W. Hinckley
John S. Bradley
Harold L. Reiser
Wm. Shane Topham
J. Scott Brown
Katherine S. Gregory
Paige Bigelow

For full biographical listings, see the Martindale-Hubbell Law Directory

RAY, QUINNEY & NEBEKER, A PROFESSIONAL CORPORATION (AV)

79 South Main Street, Suite 400, P.O. Box 45385, 84145-0385
Telephone: 801-532-1500
Fax: 801-532-7543
Email: rqn@rqn.com *URL:* http://www.rqn.com
Provo, Utah Office: 92 North University Avenue, Suite 210, 84601-4420.
Telephone: 801-342-2400.
Fax: 801-375-8379.
Albuquerque, New Mexico Office: Suite 620, 40 First Plaza, N.W.
Telephone: 505-243-6665.
Fax: 505-764-9890.

Don B. Allen
Scott Hancock Clark
Allan T. Brinkerhoff
Douglas Matsumori
Steven T. Waterman
Gregory E. Lindley
Stephen C. Tingey
Michael W. Spence
Lorin E. Patterson
Steven W. Call
Katie A. Eccles
Mark A. Cotter
R. Gary Winger

Michael D. Creer

Representative Clients: First Security Bank, N.A.; Borden, Inc.; Salt Lake Organizing Committee for the Winter Olympic Games of 2002; Southern Pacific Transportation; Utah Power & Light Co.; Travelers Insurance Co.; U.S. West.

For Complete List of Firm Personnel, See General Section

For full biographical listings, see the Martindale-Hubbell Law Directory

Salt Lake City—Continued

VAN COTT, BAGLEY, CORNWALL & MCCARTHY, A PROFESSIONAL CORPORATION (AV)

50 South Main Street, Suite 1600, P.O. Box 45340, 84145-0340
Telephone: 801-532-3333
Telecopier: 801-534-0058
Email: info@vancott.com *URL:* http://www.vancott.com
Ogden, Utah Office: 2404 Washington Boulevard, Suite 900.
Telephone: 801-394-5783.
Park City, Utah Office: 2200 Park Avenue, Suite C200-A.
Telephone: 435-649-3889.

Thomas T. Billings
Timothy W. Blackburn (Resident, Ogden, Utah Office)
Rand L. Cook
Arthur B. Ralph
David J. Smith
Gerald H. Suniville
Stephen D. Swindle
John L. Young

Tacy A. Hartman

OF COUNSEL

William G. Fowler
David E. Salisbury
M. Scott Woodland

For Complete List of Firm Personnel, See General Section

For full biographical listings, see the Martindale-Hubbell Law Directory

VERMONT

*BURLINGTON,** Chittenden Co.

GRAVEL AND SHEA, A PROFESSIONAL CORPORATION (AV)

Corporate Plaza, 76 St. Paul Street, P.O. Box 369, 05402-0369
Telephone: 802-658-0220
Fax: 802-658-1456

Stephen R. Crampton
Stewart H. McConaughy
William G. Post, Jr.
Craig Weatherly
James E. Knapp
John R. Ponsetto
Peter S. Erly
Margaret L. Montgomery
Stephen P. Magowan

Leigh Polk Cole

OF COUNSEL

Charles T. Shea

For Complete List of Firm Personnel, See General Section

For full biographical listings, see the Martindale-Hubbell Law Directory

MANCHESTER LAW OFFICES, PROFESSIONAL CORPORATION (AV)

One Lawson Lane, P.O. Box 1459, 05402-1459
Telephone: 802-658-7444
Fax: 802-658-2078
Email: mlo@together.net *URL:* http://www.lawyers.com/manchesterlaw

Robert E. Manchester

Tina L. Shoup
George N. Collias

LEGAL SUPPORT PERSONNEL

Maureen P. Neacy (Legal Nurse Consultant)

For full biographical listings, see the Martindale-Hubbell Law Directory

VIRGINIA

*FAIRFAX,** (Ind. City; Seat of Fairfax Co.)

ODIN, FELDMAN & PITTLEMAN, P.C. (AV)

9302 Lee Highway, Suite 1100, 22031
Telephone: 703-218-2100
Facsimile: 703-218-2160
Email: OFP@OFPLAW.COM

Dexter S. Odin
James B. Pittleman
John S. Wisiackas
David J. Brewer
David A. Lawrence
Frances P. Dwornik
John P. Dedon
Harry N. Lowe, III
Robert G. Nath
Kevin Thomas Oliveira

Misti Mukherjee
Eric F. Horvitz
Thomas F. Quinn, III

(See Next Column)

OF COUNSEL

Ronald W. Tydings

For Complete List of Firm Personnel, See General Section

For full biographical listings, see the Martindale-Hubbell Law Directory

HERNDON, Fairfax Co.

JEFFREY J. FAIRFIELD, P.C. (AV)

1175 Herndon Parkway, Suite 300, 20170
Telephone: 703-437-9200
Fax: 703-481-3765
Email: JJFPC@ALMA.NET

Jeffrey J. Fairfield

For full biographical listings, see the Martindale-Hubbell Law Directory

MCLEAN, Fairfax Co.

MICHAEL HORWATT & ASSOCIATES P.C. (AV)

8280 Greensboro Drive, Suite 601, 22102
Telephone: 703-749-6060
Fax: 703-749-6063
Email: msh@horwattassoc.com

Michael S. Horwatt

For full biographical listings, see the Martindale-Hubbell Law Directory

VENABLE ATTORNEYS AT LAW VENABLE, BAETJER AND HOWARD, LLP (AV)

A Partnership including Professional Corporations
Suite 400, 2010 Corporate Ridge, 22102
Telephone: 703-760-1600
Fax: 703-821-8949
URL: http://www.venable.com
Baltimore, Maryland Office: 1800 Mercantile Bank & Trust Building, 2 Hopkins Plaza.
Telephone: 410-244-7400.
Fax: 410-244-7742.
Washington, D.C. Office: Venable, Baetjer, Howard & Civiletti LLP, Suite 1000, 1201 New York Avenue, N.W.
Telephone: 202-962-4800.
Fax: 202-962-8300.
Rockville, Maryland Office: Suite 500, One Church Street, P.O. Box 1906.
Telephone: 301-217-5600.
Fax: 301-217-5617.
Towson, Maryland Office: 210 Allegheny Avenue, P. O. Box 5517.
Telephone: 410-494-6200.
Fax: 410-821-0147.

MEMBERS OF FIRM

Kenneth C. Bass, III (Also at Washington, D.C. Office)
William D. Dolan, III (P.C.)
David G. Lane
David C. Mancini
Michael W. Robinson

ASSOCIATE

Charles W. Durant

For Complete List of Firm Personnel, See General Section

For full biographical listings, see the Martindale-Hubbell Law Directory

NORFOLK, (Independent City)

GOLDBLATT, LIPKIN & COHEN, P.C. (AV)

Suite 300, 415 St. Paul's Boulevard, P.O. Box 3505, 23514
Telephone: 757-627-6225
Telefax: 757-622-3698

Paul M. Lipkin
Robert S. Cohen
Steven M. Legum
Mary G. Commander
Neal C. Schulwolf

For full biographical listings, see the Martindale-Hubbell Law Directory

PAYNE, GATES, FARTHING & RADD, P.C. (AV)

15th Floor, Dominion Tower, 999 Waterside Drive, Suite 1515, 23510-3309
Telephone: 757-640-1500
Facsimile: 757-627-6583
URL: http://www.paynegates.com

Ronald M. Gates
Philip R. Farthing
Anthony F. Radd
Glen M. Robertson
Brian R. Dinning
Todd J. Preti
Marshall A. Winslow, Jr.

C. Arthur Robinson, II
Stephen E. Heretick
Raymond L. Hogge, Jr.

(See Next Column)

PAYNE, GATES, FARTHING & RADD P.C.—*Continued*

OF COUNSEL

Charles E. Payne

For full biographical listings, see the Martindale-Hubbell Law Directory

TAYLOR & WALKER, P.C. (AV)

1300 First Virginia Tower, 555 Main Street, P.O. Box 3490, 23514-3490
Telephone: 757-625-7300
Telefax: 757-625-1504
URL: http://www.TAYWAL.com
Richmond, Virginia Office: 6802 Paragon Place, Suite 126, 23230.
Telephone: 804-673-0341.
Facsimile: 804-673-2001.

OF COUNSEL

J. Hume Taylor, Jr.

PARTNERS

William C. Walker
Gerard E. W. Voyer
James E. Brydges, Jr.
John Franklin, III
F. Bradford Stillman
Henry M. Massie, Jr.
James E. Vaiden
Brian N. Casey
James C. McCaa, III

Donna White Kearney
Mary Margaret Callahan Lyons
Richard W. Zahn, Jr.
Bradford Clark Jacob
Mark B. Kilduff
Stephen B. Royalty
Patricia C. Arrighi
Douglas Eugene Penner

LEGAL SUPPORT PERSONNEL

Diana L. White (Director of Administration)

For full biographical listings, see the Martindale-Hubbell Law Directory

PORTSMOUTH, (Independent City)

DONALD C. KILGORE (AV)

Suite 302 Wachovia Bank Building, P.O. Box 1051, 23705
Telephone: 757-397-7955
Fax: 757-393-3647

Reference: Wachovia Bank.

For full biographical listings, see the Martindale-Hubbell Law Directory

RICHMOND, (Independent City)

CREWS & HANCOCK, P.L.C. (AV)

Suite 1015, 700 Building, 700 East Main Street, 23219-2693
Telephone: 804-649-9333
Telecopier: 804-783-1759
Email: admin@crewshancock.com
Fairfax, Virginia Office: Flint Hill Centre, Suite 300, 3050 Chain Bridge Road.
Telephone: 703-591-3440.
Telecopier: 703-591-7646.
Roanoke, Virginia Office: P.O. Box 21187.
Telephone: 540-774-6655.
Telecopier: 540-774-7947.
Virginia Beach, Virginia Office: One Columbus Center, Suite 619.
Telephone: 757-490-7802.
Fax: 757-490-7820.

John William Crews
Thomas F. Hancock, III
Martin A. Donlan, Jr.
Karen A. Gould
John A. Blazer (Resident, Fairfax, Virginia Office)
John E. McIntosh, Jr. (Resident, Fairfax, Virginia Office)
Richard W. E. Bland
Judith B. Henry
Peter M. Mellette
Thomas T. Palmer (Resident, Roanoke, Virginia Office)
John R. Redmond
James M. Daniel, Jr.
W. Scott Johnson
B. Page Gravely, Jr.
Thomas L. Appler (Resident, Fairfax, Virginia Office)

Richard L. Nagle (Resident, Fairfax, Virginia Office)
Mary C. Malone (Resident, Virginia Beach, Virginia Office)
Christina S. Yehle (Resident, Fairfax, Virginia Office)
Scott J. Sorkin
Jeannie A. Adams
Elizabeth V. Syer
Martha L. Steele
Andrea L. Bailey
Katherine R. McMillen (Resident, Fairfax, Virginia Office)
Wesley G. Russell, Jr.
William O. Quirey, Jr.
Peter J. Haggerty (Resident, Fairfax, Virginia Office)
Robin M. Vogel
Wirt P. Marks, IV
W. Christopher Shea
Matthew A. Haddad
John B. Mumford, Jr.
William H. Hall, Jr.
Stephanie Lindsey Hiss
Amy M.E. Edwards
Sean P. Byrne
Michael E. Olszewski (Resident, Fairfax, Virginia Office)

(See Next Column)

Frank J. Russo, III
Maura Jane Brown (Resident, Fairfax, Virginia Office)
Mark D. Epley
Mark Henry Schmidt

For full biographical listings, see the Martindale-Hubbell Law Directory

MALONEY, HUENNEKENS, PARKS, GECKER & PARSONS, A PROFESSIONAL CORPORATION (AV)

Bank of America Center, 1111 East Main Street, Suite 800, 23219-3103
Telephone: 804-644-0313
Telecopier: 804-783-6192

Edward F. Parsons
Daniel A. Gecker
Patricia Lea Phillips
Christopher A. Jones

Fiona M. Tower

Reference: First Union National Bank.

For Complete List of Firm Personnel, See General Section

For full biographical listings, see the Martindale-Hubbell Law Directory

WILLIAMS, MULLEN, CLARK & DOBBINS, A PROFESSIONAL CORPORATION (AV)

Two James Center, 1021 East Cary Street, P.O. Box 1320, 23218-1320
Telephone: 804-643-1991
Fax: 804-783-6507
URL: http://www.wmcd.com
Newport News Office: Harbor Bank Center, Suite 210, One Old Oyster Point Road, 23602-7119.
Telephone: 757-249-5100.
Fax: 757-249-5109.
Virginia Beach Office: One Columbus Center, 23462-6763.
Telephone: 757-499-8800.
Fax: 757-473-0395.
Vienna Office: 1593 Spring Hill Road, Suite 510, 22182.
Telephone: 703-760-5200.
Fax: 703-748-0244.
Washington, D.C. Office: The Farragut Building, 900 17th Street, N.W., Suite 700, 20006.
Telephone: 202-293-0213.
Fax: 804-783-6507. Fax Within D.C.: 202-293-5939.
London, England Office: Blake Lodge, Bridge Lane, SW11 3AD.
Telephone: (011-44-71) 223-2756.
Fax: (011-44-71) 350-0156.
Riyadh, Saudi Arabia Affiliate Office: Saudi-American Legal Consultants Commercial Building #2, Diplomatic Quarter, P.O. Box 57270, 11574.
Telephone: (011-966-1) 488-1563.
Fax: (011-966-1) 488-0542.

William J. Benos
Paul S. Bliley, Jr.
A. Peter Brodell
Charles L. Cabell
David L. Dallas, Jr.
Howard W. Dobbins
Robert E. Eicher
Calvin W. Fowler, Jr.
A. Brooks Hock
David R. Johnson
Randolph H. Lickey
Dana D. McDaniel
Robert D. Perrow
William L. Pitman
Paul G. Saunders, II
William H. Schwarzschild, III
Andrea Rowse Stiles
W. Scott Street, III
John L. Walker, III
Charles E. Wall

Andrew M. Condlin

For Complete List of Firm Personnel, See General Section

For full biographical listings, see the Martindale-Hubbell Law Directory

VIENNA, Fairfax Co.

BORING & PILGER, P.C. (AV)

307 Maple Avenue West, Suite D, 22180-4307
Telephone: 703-281-2161
Fax: 703-281-9464
URL: http://www.boringandpilger.com

James L. Boring
Karl W. Pilger

Sharon C. Williams (Not admitted in VA)

Representative Clients: Balmar, Inc.; Hewlett-Packard Co.; Toshiba America Information Systems, Inc.; King Wholesale, Inc.; Anthony and Sylvan Pools, Inc.; Northern Virginia Surgical Associates, P.C.

For full biographical listings, see the Martindale-Hubbell Law Directory

GARY & GOODMAN LIMITED (AV)

8500 Leesburg Pike, Suite 7000 (Tysons Corner), 22182
Telephone: 703-848-2828
Facsimile: 703-893-9276
Email: garygoodman@ggllaw.com

Bernard E. Goodman
Stuart H. Gary

(See Next Column)

GARY & GOODMAN LIMITED, *Vienna—Continued*

Nancy D. Greene
OF COUNSEL
George B. Delta

For full biographical listings, see the Martindale-Hubbell Law Directory

WASHINGTON

*SEATTLE,** King Co.

BUCKNELL STEHLIK (AV)

1201 Third Avenue, Suite 3150, 98101
Telephone: 206-587-0144
Telecopier: 206-587-0277
Email: cpercy@bsss-law.com

MEMBERS OF FIRM

Thomas N. Bucknell
Jerry N. Stehlik
Edwin K. Sato
James W. Stubner, Jr.

For full biographical listings, see the Martindale-Hubbell Law Directory

THE JOHNSON LAW GROUP (AV)

430 Galland Building, 1221 Second Avenue, 98101-2942
Telephone: 206-344-3085
Fax: 206-344-3087
URL: http://www.lawyers.com/johnsonakyle
URL: http://www.akjlaw.com

A. Kyle Johnson

Molly B. Kenny
Carolann O'Brien Storli
John T. Blanchard
Amanda DuBois

OF COUNSEL
Peter S. Lewicki

Representative Clients: Asia-Europe-Americas Bank; BCTS/Acordia Northwest, Inc.; HFI Foods, Inc.; Parker Services, Inc.; Phoenix Savings Bank; TCS/Space Expeditions; U.S. Computer; Washington Hills Cellars.

For full biographical listings, see the Martindale-Hubbell Law Directory

SCHIFFRIN OLSON SCHLEMLEIN & HOPKINS, P.L.L.C. (AV)

First and Cedar Building Suite 300, 2701 First Avenue, 98121
Telephone: 206-448-8100
Telecopier: 206-448-8514
URL: http://www.soslaw.com

David W. Schiffrin
James T. Hopkins
Robert L. Olson
Garth A. Schlemlein
Theresa A. Goetz

Representative Clients: Alaska Petroleum Contractors; The Evans Company; Fluor Daniel; Murray-Franklyn Cos.; Sanken, USA; Seamark Properties; Talking Rain Beverage Co.; Coca Cola Bottling; Nordic Cold Storage; OPUS N.W., LLC.

For full biographical listings, see the Martindale-Hubbell Law Directory

WEST VIRGINIA

*CHARLESTON,** Kanawha Co.

JACKSON & KELLY (AV)

1600 Laidley Tower, P.O. Box 553, 25322
Telephone: 304-340-1000
Fax: 304-340-1130
Email: info@jacksonkelly.com *URL:* http://www.jacksonkelly.com
Martinsburg, West Virginia Office: 300 Foxcroft Avenue, P.O. Box 1068.
Telephone: 304-263-8800.
Fax: 304-263-7110.
Morgantown, West Virginia Office: 6000 Hampton Center, P.O. Box 619.
Telephone: 304-599-3000.
Fax: 304-285-2040.
New Martinsville, West Virginia Office: 256 Russell Avenue, P.O. Box 68.
Telephone: 304-455-1751.
Fax: 304-455-6314.
Parkersburg, West Virginia Office: 412 Market Street, Suite 202, P.O. Box 1144.
Telephone: 304-424-3490.
Fax: 304-424-3499.
Fairmont, West Virginia Office: 1000 Technology Drive, Suite 1310.
Telephone: 304-368-2000.
Fax: 304-368-2020.

(See Next Column)

Lexington, Kentucky Office: 175 East Main Street, Suite 500, P.O. Box 2150.
Telephone: 606-255-9500.
Fax: 606-281-6478.
Washington, D. C. Office: 2401 Pennsylvania Avenue, N.W., Suite 400.
Telephone: 202-973-0200.
Fax: 202-973-0232.
Denver, Colorado Office: Suite 2710, 1660 Lincoln Street.
Telephone: 303-390-0003.
Fax: 303-390-0040.
Wheeling, West Virginia Office: 1144 Market Street.
Telephone: 304-233-4000.
Fax: 304-233-4077.

MEMBERS OF FIRM

James Knight Brown
Thomas E. Potter
John R. Lukens
Louis S. Southworth, II
Charles Q. Gage
Michael A. Albert
William F. Dobbs, Jr.
David Allen Barnette
Ellen S. Cappellanti
Mary Clare Eros (Administrative Manager, Martinsburg and Charles Town, West Virginia Offices)
Charles D. Dunbar
Thad S. Huffman (Administrative Manager, Washington, D.C. Office)
Charles W. Loeb, Jr.
Eric H. London (Morgantown, West Virginia Office)
Elizabeth Osenton Lord
Anthony J. Ferrise

ASSOCIATES

William C. Miller, II
Robert G. Tweel
Steven M. Condaras

Representative Clients: One Valley Bancorp of West Virginia, Inc.; West Virginia Housing Development Fund; Go-Mart, Inc.; Provident National Bank; Chase Manhattan Bank; Shoney's, Inc.; Park Corp.; Jim Walter Homes, Inc.; Gabriel Brothers, Inc.; United Parcel Service.

For Complete List of Firm Personnel, See General Section

For full biographical listings, see the Martindale-Hubbell Law Directory

*CLARKSBURG,** Harrison Co.

MCNEER, HIGHLAND, MCMUNN AND VARNER, L.C. (AV)

One Valley Bank Building, P.O. Drawer 2040, 26302-2040
Telephone: 304-626-1100
Facsimile: 304-623-3035
Martinsburg Office: 2520 Aikens Center, P.O. Box 2509.
Telephone: 304-264-4621.
Fax: 304-264-8623.
Parkersburg Office: 404 Market Street, Suite 204, P.O. Box 1507.
Telephone: 304-422-7193.
Facsimile: 304-422-7196.

C. David McMunn
J. Cecil Jarvis
James A. Varner
Robert W. Trumble (Resident, Martinsburg Office)
Catherine D. Munster
James N. Riley
Steven R. Bratke (Resident, Parkersburg Office)
Michael J. Novotny (Resident, Martinsburg Office)
Dennis M. Shreve
Geraldine S. Roberts
William F. Rohrbaugh (Resident, Martinsburg Office)
Gregory H. Schillace
Judy L. Shanholtz
Tiffany R. Durst
Gene W. Bailey, II

OF COUNSEL

James E. McNeer
Cecil B. Highland, Jr.
William L. Fury

Representative Clients: One Valley Bank of Clarksburg, National Assn.; Bruceton Bank; Harrison County Bank; Nationwide Mutual Insurance Cos.; Clarksburg Publishing Co.; C.I.T. Financial Services; State Automobile Mutual Insurance Co.; United Hospital Center, Inc.; West Virginia Coals, Inc.; Swanson Plating Co.

For full biographical listings, see the Martindale-Hubbell Law Directory

WISCONSIN

*MADISON,** Dane Co.

AXLEY BRYNELSON, LLP (AV)

(Formerly Brynelson, Herrick, Bucaida, Dorschel & Armstrong Including the former Easton & Assoc., S.C.)
2 East Mifflin Street, P.O. Box 1767, 53701-1767
Telephone: 608-257-5661
Fax: 608-257-5444
Email: law@axley.com *URL:* http://www.axley.com

MEMBERS OF FIRM

Timothy D. Fenner
Bruce L. Harms
Patricia M. Gibeault
Michael J. Westcott
Larry K. Libman
Richard E. Petershack

(See Next Column)

AXLEY BRYNELSON LLP—*Continued*

OF COUNSEL

Frank J. Bucaida

For Complete List of Firm Personnel, See General Section

For full biographical listings, see the Martindale-Hubbell Law Directory

*MILWAUKEE,** Milwaukee Co.

CHERNOV, STERN & KRINGS, S.C. (AV)

Suite 1275, Two Plaza East, 330 East Kilbourn Avenue, 53202
Telephone: 414-276-4080
Fax: 414-276-4152
Email: mail@chernovlaw.com *URL:* http://www.lawyers.com/chernovlaw

Benjamin S. Stern
Jerome D. Krings

OF COUNSEL

Ben L. Chernov

For full biographical listings, see the Martindale-Hubbell Law Directory

KOHNER, MANN & KAILAS, S.C. (AV)

1572 East Capitol Drive, P.O. Box 11982, 53211-0982
Telephone: 414-962-5110
Fax: 414-962-8725
Email: kmksc@execpc.com

Marvin L. Kohner (1908-1975)

OF COUNSEL

Robert L. Mann

MEMBERS OF FIRM

Steve Kailas
Mark R. Wolters
Jordan B. Reich
David S. Chartier
Roy Paul Roth
Gary P. Lantzy
Christopher C. Kailas
Matthew P. Gerdisch

Robert E. Nailen
Darrell R. Zall
Daniel J. Flynn
Timothy L. Zuberbier
David M. Henry
Lorinne J Cunningham
Palma M. Forte
Daniel J. Emma

Representative Clients: Ecolab, Inc.; Manpower, Inc.; Abbott Laboratories; Norwest Bank Wisconsin, N.A.; Firstar Bank Corporation; Sysco Food Services; Johnson Controls, Inc.; Worth Inc.; Rayovac, Inc.; York International Corporation.

For full biographical listings, see the Martindale-Hubbell Law Directory

QUARLES & BRADY LLP (AV)

411 East Wisconsin Avenue, 53202-4497
Telephone: 414-277-5000
Fax: 414-271-3552
URL: http://www.quarles.com
Madison, Wisconsin Office: Firstar Plaza, One South Pinckney Street, P.O. Box 2113, 53701-2113.
Telephone: 608-251-5000.
Fax: 608-251-9166.
West Palm Beach, Florida Office: 222 Lakeview Avenue, 4th Floor, 33401.
Telephone: 561-653-5000.
Fax: 561-653-5333.
Naples, Florida Office: Barnett Center, 4501 Tamiami Trail North, Suite 300, 34103-3060.
Telephone: 941-262-5959.
Fax: 941-434-4999.
Phoenix, Arizona Office: One Camelback Building, One East Camelback Road, Suite 400, 85012-1649.
Telephone: 602-230-5500.
Fax: 602-230-5598.
Chicago, Illinois Office: Quarles & Brady LLC, Citicorp Center, 500 West Madison Street, Suite 3700.
Telephone: 312-715-5000.
Fax: 312-715-5155.

MEMBERS OF FIRM

(ALPHABETICALLY BY YEAR OF ADMISSION TO BAR)

Arthur B. Harris
David L. Petersen (Resident, Naples, Florida Office)
Stephen E. Richman
John R. Maynard
Robert T. Bailes (Resident, Phoenix, Arizona Office)
John W. Daniels, Jr.
Andrew M. Barnes
Matthew J. Flynn
Roger K. Spencer (Resident, Phoenix, Arizona Office)
Patrick J. Goebel
Peter A. Terry (Resident, Phoenix, Arizona Office)
Ann M. Murphy
John A. Rothstein
Elizabeth A. Orelup
Leo J. Salvatori (Resident, Naples, Florida Office)
David R. Cross
Ann K. Comer
Marta S. Levine
Robert S. Bornhoft (Resident, Phoenix, Arizona Office)
Jeffrey O. Davis
Benjamin R. Norris (Resident, Phoenix, Arizona Office)
David L. Bourne
Nancy Berz Colman (Resident, West Palm Beach, Florida Office)

(See Next Column)

ASSOCIATES

Valerie L. Bailey-Rihn (Resident, Madison Office)
Mark Hubert Muller (Resident, Naples, Florida Office)
Sean D. Garrison (Resident, Phoenix, Arizona Office)

For Complete List of Firm Personnel, See General Section

For full biographical listings, see the Martindale-Hubbell Law Directory

WALSH & KEATING, S.C. (AV)

1505 Wawatosa Avenue, 53213
Telephone: 414-257-9929
Fax: 414-257-9959
URL: http://www.lawyers.com/walshandkeating

Gerald S. Walsh
David C. Keating

ASSOCIATE

Peter J. Walsh

OF COUNSEL

Lloyd W. Herrold

Representative Clients: Immtech International, Inc.; Howard Precision Metals Inc.; James L. Callan Inc.; Milwaukee Chaplet & Mfg. Co., Inc.; Milwaukee Envelope, Inc.; Stearns Foundation, Inc.; Wausau Tile, Inc.; August Urbanek Investments, Inc.; Germantown Market Place, Inc.; Precision Metrology, Inc.

For full biographical listings, see the Martindale-Hubbell Law Directory

WYOMING

*CASPER,** Natrona Co.

BROWN, DREW & MASSEY, LLP (AV)

Casper Business Center, Suite 800, 123 West First Street, 82601-2486
Telephone: 307-234-1000
800-877-6755
Telefax: 307-265-8025
Email: brwndrew@coffey.com

MEMBERS OF FIRM

Morris R. Massey
Harry B. Durham, III
Donn J. McCall
Thomas F. Reese
J. Kenneth Barbe
Jeffrey C. Brinkerhoff
P. Jaye Rippley
Courtney Robert Kepler

ASSOCIATE

Timothy M. Stubson

Attorneys for: Norwest Bank Wyoming, N.A.; The CIT Group/Equipment Financing; Aetna Casualty & Surety Co.; The Doctor's Co.; MEDMARC; Westech, Inc.; Chevron USA; Enron Group of Energy Companies; North American Resources Co.

For Complete List of Firm Personnel, See General Section

For full biographical listings, see the Martindale-Hubbell Law Directory

*CHEYENNE,** Laramie Co.

HICKEY, MACKEY, EVANS & WALKER (AV)

1800 Carey Avenue, Suite 700, P.O. Drawer 467, 82003
Telephone: 307-634-1525
Telecopier: 307-638-7335
URL: http://www.hickeymackey.com

MEMBERS OF FIRM

Paul J. Hickey
Terry W. Mackey
David F. Evans
John M. Walker
Roger C. Fransen
Richard D. Tim Bush
Mary A. Throne

A List of Representative Clients will be furnished upon request.
Reference: Norwest Bank, Cheyenne, N.A.

For full biographical listings, see the Martindale-Hubbell Law Directory

PUERTO RICO

SAN JUAN, San Juan Dist.

FIDDLER GONZÁLEZ & RODRÍGUEZ, LLP

254 Muñoz Rivera Avenue (Hato Rey), P.O. Box 363507, 00936-3507
Telephone: 787-753-3113
Telecopier: 787-759-3123
Email: fiddler@fgrlaw.com *URL:* http://www.fgrlaw.com

OF COUNSEL

Ileana Fernández-Buitrago

(See Next Column)

FIDDLER GONZÁLEZ & RODRÍGUEZ LLP, *San Juan—Continued*

MEMBERS OF FIRM

Rafael Cortés-Dapena
Aurelio Emanuelli-Belaval
Antonio R. Sifre
Leopoldo J. Cabassa-Sauri

For Complete List of Firm Personnel, See General Section

For full biographical listings, see the Martindale-Hubbell Law Directory

GOLDMAN ANTONETTI & CÓRDOVA

American International Plaza Fourteenth & Fifteenth Floors, 250 Muñoz Rivera Avenue (Hato Rey), P.O. Box 70364, 00936-0364
Telephone: 787-759-8000
Telecopiers: 787-767-9333 (Main)
787-767-9177 (Litigation Department)
787-767-8660 (Labor & Corporate Law Departments)
787-767-9325 (Tax & Environmental Law Departments)
URL: http://www.gaclaw.com

MEMBERS OF FIRM

Vicente J. Antonetti
Roberto Montalvo Carbia
Luis F. Antonetti
Jorge Souss
Francisco de Jesús-Schuck
Luis D. Ortiz-Abreu
Edgar Cartagena-Santiago
Pedro Morell Losada
Ramón E. Dapena
Francis Torres-Fernández
Jorge L. Martinez
Carlos A. Rodríguez-Vidal
Thelma Rivera-Miranda
Jorge Segurola
Edgardo Colón Arrarás
Jesús E. Cuza
Howard Pravda
Braulio García Jiménez
Karín G. Díaz-Toro
Jorge R. Rodriguez-Micheo
Georgiana S. Colón
Migdalia Davila-Garcia

OF COUNSEL

Max Goldman
Charles P. Adams
Heber E. Lugo-Rigau
Fernando Castro

SPECIAL COUNSEL

Jaime Morgan-Stubbe

ASSOCIATES

Mildred Cabán
Wilda Rodriguez Plaza
Gretchen M. Mendez-Vilella
María Patricia Lake
Ina M. Berlingeri Vincenty
Mayra Del C. Doble-Ruiz
Vivian Nuñez
Hector Perez
Claribel Ortiz-Rodríguez
Joanna Bocanegra Ocasio
Vanessa Bayonet-Tartak
Raul Negron Casasnovas
Guillermo J. Silva-Wiscovich
Frances R. Colon-Rivera
Veronica Olivieri-Barreto
Aida Barrios-Castellanos
Edna E. Perez-Roman
Michelle Feria-Cestero
Nilsa Flores-Sola
Eugenia I. Orsini-Herencia
Yvette De Luna-Colon
Ricardo Pizarro
Ruben Rivera-Rosa
Maura Santiago-Ducos
Lizzie M. Padro
Rosalie Irizarry-Silvestrini
Alicia Lamboy
Angel Berberena
Sara Vazquez
Rebeca Vargas-Ruiz

Representative Clients: Borden, Inc.; Crown Cork de Puerto Rico, Inc.; Maidenform, Inc.; Philip Morris, Inc.; Seven Up Flavors Mfg. Co.; Xerox Corp.

For Complete List of Firm Personnel, See General Section

For full biographical listings, see the Martindale-Hubbell Law Directory

NOEL S. GONZALEZ-MIRANDA

252 Ponce De Leon Avenue, Suite 1101 Citibank Towers, 00918
Telephone: 787-767-9494
Fax: 787-281-6585
Email: nsgonzalez@micrjuris.com *URL:* http://www.lawyers.com/nsgmlaw

ASSOCIATE

Celeste Abella-Padilla

For full biographical listings, see the Martindale-Hubbell Law Directory

INDIANO, WILLIAMS & WEINSTEIN-BACAL

Hato Rey Tower, 21st Floor, 268 Muñoz Rivera Avenue (Hato Rey), 00918
Telephone: 787-754-2323; 763-0485
Fax: 787-766-3366
Email: iww@microjuris.com

MEMBERS OF FIRM

Stuart A. Weinstein-Bacal
David C. Indiano
Jeffrey M. Williams

ASSOCIATES

Peter W. Miller
Edgar A. Lee-Navas
Edward W. Hill Tollinche
Alexander H. Bopp (Not admitted in PR)

For full biographical listings, see the Martindale-Hubbell Law Directory

JORGE R. JIMENEZ LAW OFFICES

Suite 807 IBM Building, 654 Muñoz Rivera Avenue (Hato Rey), 00918
Telephone: 787-763-0106
Fax: 787-763-0574

(See Next Column)

MEMBERS OF FIRM

Jorge R. Jimenez
Juan F. Doval

For full biographical listings, see the Martindale-Hubbell Law Directory

MARTÍNEZ ODELL & CALABRIA

Banco Popular Center, 209 Muñoz Rivera Avenue, Suite 1600 (Hato Rey), P.O. Box 190998, 00919-0998
Telephone: 787-753-8914
Facsimile: 787-753-8402; 787-759-9075; 787-764-5664
Email: postmaster@mocpr.com

MEMBERS OF FIRM

Patrick D. O'Neill
Anabelle Rodriguez-Rodriguez
Alberto Rodríguez-Ramos
Humberto Guzmán-Rodríguez
Maria del Carmen Garriga
Eric Perez Ochoa
Ramón Eugenio-Meléndez
Jose Antonio Fernandez-Jaquete
Ivonne Palerm-Cruz
Jose David Medina-Rivera

OF COUNSEL

Hernan R. Franco
Francisco Orsini-Capo

ASSOCIATES

Fernando J. Gierbolini-Gonzalez
Dora L. Monserrate-Peñagaricano
Carmen T. Ubarri-Nevares
Jaime L. Vazquez-Bernier
Jennifer Odell-Gonzalez
Mariela Garcia-Colberg
Juan A. Frau-Escudero
Jose G. Diaz-Tejera

Representative Clients: Banco Popular de Puerto Rico; Daewoo Motor Corporation; Eckerd Corporation; Empresas Fonalledas; Hilton International; L'Aire Liquide, S.A.; Loctile Corporation; Lucent Technologies; Lutron Electronics Co., Inc.; Waste Management, Inc.

For Complete List of Firm Personnel, See General Section

For full biographical listings, see the Martindale-Hubbell Law Directory

VIRGIN ISLANDS

*CHARLOTTE AMALIE, ST. THOMAS,** St. Thomas

GRUNERT STOUT & BRUCH

24-25 Kongensgade, P.O. Box 1030, 00804
Telephone: 340-774-1320
Fax: 340-774-7839
Email: gsbusvi@viaccess.net
Affiliated with: Solomon Pearl Blum & Quinn LLP, New York, New York and Denver, Colorado.

MEMBERS OF FIRM

John E. Stout
Susan Bruch Moorehead

ASSOCIATE

Gabriel J. Villegas

OF COUNSEL

William L. Blum

For full biographical listings, see the Martindale-Hubbell Law Directory

CANADA
ALBERTA

*CALGARY,** Calgary Jud. Dist.

BENNETT JONES (AV)

4500 Bankers Hall East, 855-2nd Street S.W., T2P 4K7
Telephone: 403-298-3100
Facsimile: 403-265-7219
Email: firmwatch@bennettjones.ca *URL:* http://www.bennettjones.ca
Edmonton, Alberta Office: 1000, 10035-105 Street.
Telephone: 780-421-8133.
Facsimile: 780-421-7951.
Toronto, Ontario Office: 3400 1 First Canadian Place, P.O. Box 130.
Telephone: 416-863-1200.
Facsimile: 416-863-1716.

MEMBERS OF FIRM

Walter B. O'Donoghue, Q.C.
William S. Rice

For Complete List of Firm Personnel, See General Section

For full biographical listings, see the Martindale-Hubbell Law Directory

Calgary—Continued

PARLEE MCLAWS (AV)

3400 Petro-Canada Centre, 150 - 6th Avenue, SW, T2P 3Y7
Telephone: 403-294-7000
Telecopier: 403-265-8263
Email: lawyers@parlee.com *URL:* http://www.parlee.com
Edmonton, Alberta Office: 15th Floor Manulife Place, 10180 101st Street.
Telephone: 403-423-8500.
Telecopier: 403-423-2870.

MEMBERS OF FIRM

Dale R. Spackman, Q.C. — Richard B. Mask

ASSOCIATES

Angela M. Tripathy — Seema S. Johal

For Complete List of Firm Personnel, See General Section

For full biographical listings, see the Martindale-Hubbell Law Directory

*EDMONTON,** Edmonton Jud. Dist.

LUCAS BOWKER & WHITE (AV)

Scotia 2 Tower - Scotia Place, 1201-10060 Jasper Avenue, T5J 4E5
Telephone: 780-426-5330
Fax: 780-428-1066
Email: Lucas@lbw.ab.ca *URL:* http://www.lbw.ab.ca
Calgary, Alberta Office: Suite 3800, Bankers Hall, 855 2nd Street S.W., T2P 4J8.
Telephone: 403-218-1795.
Fax: 403-264-2993. Email: Lucas@lbw.ab.ca. URL: http://www.lbw.ab.ca

MEMBERS OF FIRM

Gerald A. I. Lucas, Q.C.
David J. Stratton, Q.C.
John Reginald Day, Q.C.
Robert C. Dunseith
Douglas H. Shell
Kent H. Davidson
Robert A. Seidel, Q.C.
Robert P. Bruce
Kevin J. Smith
Gordon V. Garside
Debbie L. Hughes
Douglas A. Bodner

Reference: Canadian Imperial Bank of Commerce.

For Complete List of Firm Personnel, See General Section

For full biographical listings, see the Martindale-Hubbell Law Directory

PARLEE MCLAWS (AV)

15th Floor Manulife Place, 10180 101st Street, T5J 4K1
Telephone: 403-423-8500
Telecopier: 403-423-2870
Email: lawyers@parlee.com *URL:* http://www.parlee.com
Calgary, Alberta Office: 3400 Petro-Canada Centre, 150 - 6th Avenue, SW.
Telephone: 403-294-7000.
Telecopier: 403-265-8263.

MEMBERS OF FIRM

Colin H. Kerr, Q.C.
Frank J. Niziol
Ian L. MacLachlan
Brian J. Curial
Robert A. Newton, Q.C.
David G. Finlay
Douglas L. Kennedy
Kevin L. Lynch
David S. Tam

ASSOCIATES

Lorne J. Ruzicka — Gregory P. Nakonechny

For Complete List of Firm Personnel, See General Section

For full biographical listings, see the Martindale-Hubbell Law Directory

CANADA
NEW BRUNSWICK

*FREDERICTON,** York Co.

COX HANSON O'REILLY MATHESON (AV)

(Formerly Hanson Hashey)
Suite 400, Phoenix Square, P.O. Box 310, E3B 4Y9
Telephone: 506-453-7771
Fax: 506-453-9600
Email: fredericton@coxhanson.ca *URL:* http://www.coxhanson.ca
Halifax, Nova Scotia Office: Suite 1100, Purdy's Wharf Tower 1, P.O. Box 2380 Station Central RPO, B3J 3E5.
Telephone: 902-421-6262.
Fax: 902-421-3130. E-Mail: halifax@coxhanson.ca
Saint John, New Brunswick Office: 1212-One Brunswick Square, 1 Germain St. E2L 4V1.
Telephone: 506-652-7771.
Fax: 506-632-9600.
St. John's, Newfoundland Office: Scotia Centre, 401-235 Water Street, A1C 1B6.
Telephone: 709-726-3321.
Fax: 709-726-2992. E-Mail: stjohns@coxhanson.ca

(See Next Column)

Charlottetown, Prince Edward Island Office: Queen Square, Suite 202, 119 Queen Street, P.O. Box 875, Station Central, C1A 7L9.
Telephone: 902-894-7051.
Fax: 902-368-3762. E-Mail: charlottetown@coxhanson.ca

MEMBERS OF FIRM

H. A. Hanson, Q.C. (1909-1985)
David T. Hashey, Q.C.
David M. Norman, Q.C.
J. Ian M. Whitcomb, Q.C.
John M. Hanson, Q.C.
Walter D. Vail, Q.C.
Michael E. Bowlin
John D. Larlee, Q.C.
Bruce D. Hatfield, Q.C.
Julian A. G. Dickson, Q.C.
Anne D. Wooder
Terrence J. Morrison
Lucie Richard
Catherine M. Bowlen
J. Marc Richard

ASSOCIATES

Amanda J. Frenette
Monika M. L. Zauhar
Jade A. Spalding
William E. Gould
Christopher R. DeLong
Deborah M. Power
Corinne A. Godbout
Marc-Antoine Chiasson

For full biographical listings, see the Martindale-Hubbell Law Directory

MCINNES COOPER (AV)

Suite 600, 570 Queen Street, P.O. Box 610, E3B 5A6
Telephone: 506-458-8572
Fax: 506-458-9903
Email: mcrfton@mcrlaw.com *URL:* http://www.mcrlaw.com
Halifax, Nova Scotia Office: Summit Place, 1601 Lower Water Street, P.O. Box 730, B3J 2V1.
Telephone: 902-425-6500.
Fax: 902-425-6350. Email: mcrhfx@mcrlaw.com.
St. John's, Newfoundland Office: Baine Johnston Centre, 5th Floor, 10 Fort William Place, P.O. Box 5939, A1C 5X4.
Telephone: 709-722-8735.
Telecopier: 709-722-1763. Email: mcrsj@mcrlaw.com
Moncton, New Brunswick Office: Place Moncton Place, 655 Main Street, P.O. Box 1368, E1C 8T6.
Telephone: 506-857-8970.
Fax: 506-857-4095. Email: mcrmctn@mcrlaw.com.
Charlottetown, Prince Edward Island Office: BDC Place, Suite 620, 119 Kent Street, C1A 1N3.
Telephone: 902-368-8473.
Fax: 902-368-8346. Email: mcrpei@mcrlaw.com.

PARTNERS

Leonard T. Hoyt — Carol J. Downs

ASSOCIATE

Alan Rockwell

For Complete List of Firm Personnel, See General Section

For full biographical listings, see the Martindale-Hubbell Law Directory

*MONCTON,** Westmorland Co.

MCINNES COOPER (AV)

Barristers, Solicitors & Trade Mark Agents
Place Moncton Place, 655 Main Street, P.O. Box 1368, E1C 8T6
Telephone: 506-857-8970
Fax: 506-857-4095
Email: mcrmctn@mcrlaw.com *URL:* http://www.mcrlaw.com
Halifax, Nova Scotia Office: Summit Place, 1601 Lower Water Street, P.O. Box 730, B3J 2V1.
Telephone: 902-425-6500.
Fax: 902-425-6350. Email: mcrhfx@mcrlaw.com.
St. John's, Newfoundland Office: Baine Johnston Centre, 5th Floor, 10 Fort William Place, P.O. Box 5939, A1C 5X4.
Telephone: 709-722-8735.
Telecopier: 709-722-1763. Email: mcrsj@mcrlaw.com.
Charlottetown, Prince Edward Island Office: BDC Place, Suite 620, 119 Kent Street, C1A 1N3.
Telephone: 902-368-8473.
Fax: 902-368-8346. Email: mcrpei@mcrlaw.com.
Fredericton, New Brunswick Office: Suite 600, 570 Queen Street, P.O. Box 610.
Telephone: 506-458-8572.
Fax: 506-458-9903. Email: mcrfton@mcrlaw.com.

PARTNER

Bernard F. Miller

ASSOCIATES

Christopher A. Borden — Sylvie C. Roussel

ASSOCIATED ATTORNEY

Robert E. Radford, Q.C.

For Complete List of Firm Personnel, See General Section

For full biographical listings, see the Martindale-Hubbell Law Directory

*SAINT JOHN,** Saint John Co.

CLARK DRUMMIE (AV)

40 Wellington Row, P.O. Box 6850, E2L 4S3
Telephone: 506-633-3800
Telecopier (Automatic): 506-633-3811
Email: cd@nbnet.nb.ca

MEMBERS OF FIRM

Thomas B. Drummie, Q.C.
Terrence W. Hutchinson
Donald F. MacGowan, Q.C.
Ross A. Pierce
William C. Kean

OF COUNSEL

Richard W. Bird, Q.C.

Reference: Royal Bank of Canada.

For Complete List of Firm Personnel, See General Section

For full biographical listings, see the Martindale-Hubbell Law Directory

CANADA NEWFOUNDLAND

*ST. JOHN'S,**

MCINNES COOPER (AV)

Barristers, Solicitors & Trade Mark Agents
Baine Johnston Centre, 5th Floor, 10 Fort William Place, P.O. Box 5939, A1C 5X4
Telephone: 709-722-8735
Telecopier: 709-722-1763
Email: mcrsj@mcrlaw.com *URL:* http://www.mcrlaw.com
Halifax, Nova Scotia Office: Summit Place, 1601 Lower Water Street, P.O. Box 730, B3J 2V1.
Telephone: 902-425-6500.
Fax: 902-425-6350. Email: mcrhfx@mcrlaw.com.
Moncton, New Brunswick Office: Place Moncton Place, 655 Main Street, P.O. Box 1368, E1C 8T6.
Telephone: 506-857-8970.
Fax: 506-857-4095. Email: mcrmctn@mcrlaw.com.
Charlottetown, Prince Edward Island Office: BDC Place, Suite 620, 119 Kent Street, C1A 1N3.
Telephone: 902-368-8473.
Fax: 902-368-8346. Email: mcrpei@mcrlaw.com.
Fredericton, New Brunswick Office: Suite 600, 570 Queen Street, P.O. Box 610.
Telephone: 506-458-8572.
Fax: 506-458-9903. Email: mcrfton@mcrlaw.com.

PARTNERS

James R. Chalker, Q.C.
W. Gary Rowe, Q.C.
Michael J. Crosbie
John M. Green, Q.C.
Christine A. Fagan, Q.C.
Deborah L. J. Hutchings
Caroline C. Watton

ASSOCIATE

Dennis N. Clarke

For Complete List of Firm Personnel, See General Section

For full biographical listings, see the Martindale-Hubbell Law Directory

CANADA NOVA SCOTIA

*HALIFAX,** Regional Munic. of Halifax

MCINNES COOPER (AV)

Barristers, Solicitors & Trade Mark Agents
Summit Place, 1601 Lower Water Street, P.O. Box 730, B3J 2V1
Telephone: 902-425-6500
Fax: 902-425-6350
Email: mcrhfx@mcrlaw.com *URL:* http://www.mcrlaw.com
St. John's, Newfoundland Office: Baine Johnston Centre, 5th Floor, 10 Fort William Place, P.O. Box 5939, A1C 5X4.
Telephone: 709-722-8735.
Telecopier: 709-722-1763. Email: mcrsj@mcrlaw.com.
Moncton, New Brunswick Office: Place Moncton Place, 655 Main Street, P.O. Box 1368, E1C 8T6.
Telephone: 506-857-8970.
Fax: 506-857-4095. Email: mcrmctn@mcrlaw.com.
Charlottetown, Prince Edward Island Office: BDC Place, Suite 620, 119 Kent Street, C1A 1N3.
Telephone: 902-368-8473.
Fax: 902-368-8346. Email: mcrpei@mcrlaw.com.

(See Next Column)

Fredericton, New Brunswick Office: Suite 600, 570 Queen Street, P.O. Box 610.
Telephone: 506-458-8572.
Fax: 506-458-9903. Email: mcrfton@mcrlaw.com.

PARTNERS

Stewart McInnes, P.C., Q.C.
Alan J. Stern, Q.C.
George T. H. Cooper, Q.C.
Robert G. Belliveau, Q.C.
F. Van W. Penick
Lawrence J. Hayes, Q.C.
Joseph A. F. Macdonald, Q.C.
David H. Reardon, Q.C.
Lawrence A. Freeman
Marcia L. Brennan
Fae J. Shaw

ASSOCIATES

Frank E. Hughes
Jennifer A. Healy
Jeffrey R. Blucher
Kristi Sebalj

For Complete List of Firm Personnel, See General Section

For full biographical listings, see the Martindale-Hubbell Law Directory

CANADA ONTARIO

*TORONTO,** Regional Munic. of Toronto

BORDEN & ELLIOT (AV)

Barristers & Solicitors
Scotia Plaza, 40 King Street West, M5H 3Y4
Telephone: 416-367-6000
Telecopier: 416-367-6749
Email: info@borden.com *URL:* http://www.borden.com
Ottawa, Ontario Office: Borden Elliot Scott & Aylen, 1000-60 Rue Queen Street.
Telephone: 613-237-5160; 800-661-4237. General
Facsimile: 613-230-8842. IP Dept.
Facsimile: 613-787-3558. Email: ottinfo@scottaylen.com. URL: http://www.borden.com.

Simon B. Scott, Q.C.

For Complete List of Firm Personnel, See General Section

For full biographical listings, see the Martindale-Hubbell Law Directory

DAVIES, WARD & BECK (AV)

1 First Canadian Place, M5X 1B1
Telephone: 416-863-0900
Fax: 416-863-0871
Email: info@dwb.com *URL:* http://www.dwb.com

PARTNERS AND ASSOCIATES

Mark Q. Connelly
William M. O'Reilly
Robert T. Bauer
Arthur S. Shiff
Patricia L. Olasker
Michael Disney
William M. Ainley
Neil Finkelstein
Edward C. Hannah
Catherine G. Ross
Paul M. Kennedy
Kevin J. Thomson
Ian D. Johnson
Thomas A. Smee
Ian R. McBride
Cameron M. Rusaw
Michael W. Clifford
David A. Dell
Sarbjit S. Basra
Christine J. Prudham
Andrew L. Welsh
Gabriella Lombardi
Delphine Brooker
Sabrina Gherbaz
Mitchell P. Finkelstein
Paul W. Golding
Christopher H. Jones
Richard J. Fullerton
Patrick E. Moyer
James R. Reid
Robin G. Tessier
Tarne P. Whiteley
Andrée M. Blais
Michael S. Brown
Robert S. Murphy
Lori K. Sullivan
Nicholas J. Leblovic
Jay A. Swartz
I. Berl Nadler
Jean-Paul Bisnaire
Gray E. Taylor
Gregory J. Howard
Carol D. Pennycook
A. Gerold Goldlist
Jeffrey O. Palmer
Jeremy M. Freedman
D. Shawn McReynolds
Michael Creery
James J. Lawson
Carol Hansell
Vincent A. Mercier
Timothy H. Moran
Richard F. D. Corley
Patrick G. Barry
Kent F. Beattie
Gillian R. Stacey
Paolo Boni
Julianna S. Ahn
Andrea E. Daly
Terrance J. Ritchie
Warren M. Katz
Steven M. Harris
Jennifer L. Toone
Alana G. McPhee
Rosemary A. Newman
Gregory G. Southam
Derek R. G. Vesey
Paul A. Beauregard
R. Michael Brisson
Donald S. Harrison
Erinn E. Somerville
John M. Walsh

For Complete List of Firm Personnel, See General Section

For full biographical listings, see the Martindale-Hubbell Law Directory

*WINDSOR,** Essex Co.

McTague Law Firm (AV)

455 Pelissier Street, N9A 6Z9
Telephone: 519-255-4300
Detroit, Michigan Telephone: 313-965-1332
Fax: 519-255-4360(Corporate/Labor)
Fax: 519-255-4384 (Litigation/Real Estate)

MEMBERS OF FIRM

J. Douglas Lawson, Q.C.
Alexander R. Szalkai, Q.C.
Peter J. Kuker
George W. King
Josephine Stark
Tom Serafimovski
Roger A. Skinner
Daniel K. Moorhouse
Jerry B. Udell
Michael K. Coughlin
John D. Leslie
Marilee Marcotte

ASSOCIATES

Kevin G. Fanick
Michael A. Wills
Dana J. Young
Jeffrey W. MacKinnon
Brian L. Chillman

For Complete List of Firm Personnel, See General Section

For full biographical listings, see the Martindale-Hubbell Law Directory

Sutts, Strosberg LLP (AV)

600 Westcourt Place, 251 Goyeau Street, P.O. Box 670, N9A 6V4
Telephone: 519-258-9333
Detroit Michigan: 313-962-0137
Facsimile: Windsor 519-258-9527
Detroit 313-962-0139

MEMBERS OF FIRM

Achille F. Gignac, Q.C. (1902-1984)
Robert E. Barnes, Q.C.
Clifford N. Sutts, Q.C.
Harvey T. Strosberg, Q.C.
Gary V. Wortley
James K. Ball
John C. Holland
Mary M. S. Fox
William C. Chapman
Donald M. Gordon
Paul C. Nesseth
Heather Rumble Peterson
Patricia A. Speight
Edward W. Ducharme
Michelle A. Gagnon
Craig J. Allen
Werner H. Keller
Francine A. Herlehy
Paul Simard
Jasminka Kalajdzic

COUNSEL FOR CRIMINAL MATTERS

Patrick J. Ducharme

For full biographical listings, see the Martindale-Hubbell Law Directory

CANADA PRINCE EDWARD ISLAND

*CHARLOTTETOWN,** Queen's Co.

McInnes Cooper (AVⓣ)

Barristers, Solicitors & Trade Mark Agents
BDC Place, Suite 620, 119 Kent Street, C1A 1N3
Telephone: 902-368-8473
Fax: 902-368-8346
Email: mcrpei@mcrlaw.com *URL:* http://www.mcrlaw.com
Halifax, Nova Scotia Office: Summit Place, 1601 Lower Water Street, P.O. Box 730, B3J 2V1.
Telephone: 902-425-6500.
Fax: 902-425-6350. Email: mcrhfx@mcrlaw.com.
St. John's, Newfoundland Office: Baine Johnston Centre, 5th Floor, 10 Fort William Place, P.O. Box 5939, A1C 5X4.
Telephone: 709-722-8735.
Telecopier: 709-722-1763. Email: mcrsj@mcrlaw.com.
Moncton, New Brunswick Office: Place Moncton Place, 655 Main Street, P.O. Box 1368, E1C 8T6.
Telephone: 506-857-8970.
Fax: 506-857-4095. Email: mcrmctn@mcrlaw.com.
Fredericton, New Brunswick Office: Suite 600, 570 Queen Street, P.O. Box 610.
Telephone: 506-458-8572.
Fax: 506-458-9903. Email: mcrfton@mcrlaw.com.

PARTNERS

Horace B. Carver, Q.C.
Michele M. Murphy

ASSOCIATES

L. Charles Keizer
Murray L. Murphy
Kevin J. Kiley
Paul Kiley

For Complete List of Firm Personnel, See General Section

For full biographical listings, see the Martindale-Hubbell Law Directory

CANADA QUEBEC

*MONTREAL,** Montreal Dist.

Goldstein, Flanz & Fishman (AV)

Suite 4100, 1250 René-Lévesque Boulevard West, H3B 4W8
Telephone: 514-932-4100
Cable Address: "Meybat"
Telex: 05-24593
Telecopier: 514-932-4170
Email: counsel@gff.qc.ca

MEMBERS OF FIRM

Yoine Goldstein
Leonard W. Flanz
Avram Fishman
Mark Schrager
Gilles Paquin
Mark E. Meland
Ellen Amdursky
Alain Daigle
Cathy Noseworthy
Suzanne Villeneuve

For full biographical listings, see the Martindale-Hubbell Law Directory

McMaster Gervais (AV)

A General Partnership
1000 de La Gauchetière Street West, Suite 900, H3B 5H4
Telephone: 514-879-1212
Fax: 514-954-1905
Email: info@mcmastergervais.com *URL:* http://www.mcmastergervais.com

MEMBERS OF FIRM

William E. Stavert
Lionel J. Blanshay
Paul R. Marchand
Brian M. Schneiderman
Richard W. Shannon
Elizabeth A. Mitchell
Johanne Thomas
Michael Patry
Charles P. Marquette
Pierre Trudeau
Sylvie Bouvette
P. Vivian Cyriacopoulos
Michael Bantey
Lise Fortier
Patrice Martin
Avi Levy
Catherine Guertin
Geneviève Bergeron
Sophia Tolias
Sébastien Lormeau
Sébastien Berthelet
Daniel Ferreira
Timothy R. Carsley
Peter C. Casey
Norman A. Saibil
Ian B. Taylor
Raymond Picard
Pierre Gattuso
Benoît M. Provost
Yves A. Dubois
Janet Casey
André Dufour
François Morin
H. John Godber
Christine Duchaine
Elana Weissbach
Patricia Galella
Virginia Chan
David Torralbo
Roderick Darrock Elliott
Tammy J. Shulman
Joel M. Cabelli
Grégoire Baillargeon
Rhonda Friesen

COUNSEL

Thomas C. Camp, Q.C.
Tass G. Grivakes, Q.C.
P. André Gervais, Q.C.
Richard J. Riendeau, Q.C.
Bartha M. Knoppers

For Complete List of Firm Personnel, See General Section

For full biographical listings, see the Martindale-Hubbell Law Directory

Mendelsohn Rosentzveig Shacter (AV)

1000 Sherbrooke Street West, 27th Floor, H3A 3G4
Telephone: 514-987-5000
Telex: 05-27284 Colorlaw
Telecopier: 514-987-1213
Email: mrs@mrslaw.com *URL:* http://www.mrslaw.com

PARTNERS

S. Leon Mendelsohn, Q.C. (1902-1996)
Leo Rosentzveig, Q.C.
Manuel Shacter, Q.C.
Jack C. Shayne
William Levitt
Arthur A. Garvis
Edward E. Aronoff
L. Michael Blumenstein
Max Mendelsohn
Earl S. Cohen
Michael Garonce
Donald M. Devine
Richard S. Uditsky
Joel Weitzman
Ian R. Rudnikoff
Marc I. Leiter
L. B. Erdle
Fredric L. Carsley
Frank Zylberberg
Jules Brossard
David L. Rosentzveig
Judie K. Jokinen
Gilles Seguin
Martin Desrosiers
Andrew Etcovitch
Alain Breault
Jean Carrière
Henri M. Bybelezer
Louis Frédérick Côté
Sandra Abitan

(See Next Column)

MENDELSOHN ROSENTZVEIG SHACTER, *Montreal—Continued*

ASSOCIATES

Carl M. Ravinsky
Catherine Muraz
Francine Wiseman
Joelle Sebag
Maria R. Battaglia
Keyvan Nassiry
Linda Schachter
Emmanuelle Saucier
Arnold Cohen
Aaron Makovka
Michel Rochefort
Céline Tessier
Sophie Crevier
Annick Joyal
Francis Desmarais
Nicolas J. Beugnot
Jean-François Brière
Marc-Antoine Deschamps
Philipp F. Duffy
Fred Purkey
Martin Sills
David Tardif-Latourelle

For full biographical listings, see the Martindale-Hubbell Law Directory

CANADA
SASKATCHEWAN

*REGINA,** Regina Jud. Centre

BALFOUR MOSS (AV)

Bank of Montreal Building, 700-2103 11th Avenue, S4P 4G1
Telephone: 306-347-8300
Fax: 306-347-8350
Email: balfourmoss.regina@dlcwest.com *URL:* http://www.dlcwest.com/~balfourmoss
Saskatoon, Saskatchewan Office: #600-123-2nd Avenue South.
Telephone: 306-665-7844.
Fax: 306-652-1586.

PARTNERS

A. John Beke, Q.C.
Fredrick C. McBeth
Brian J. Scherman (Resident Saskatoon)
Roger J.F. Lepage
Reginald A. Watson
Glen S. Lekach
Rick M. Van Beselaere
George E. Nystrom
Jeff N. Grubb
David G. Gerecke (Resident Saskatoon)
Raymond J. Dean
Bob P. Hrycan

COUNSEL

E. John Moss, Q.C.
Hon. R. James Balfour, Q.C.
Robert A. Milliken, Q.C.
Roy B. Laschuk, Q.C.

ASSOCIATES

Michael D. Crosbie
Peter T. Bergbusch
Kerri A. Froc
Heather MacMillan-Brown (Resident, Saskatoon Office)
Kathleen A. Richardson
Stewart J.O. Berringer
Yens Pedersen

Representative Clients: Saskatchewan Wheat Pool; Bank of Montreal; Cable Regina; Cameco; Canadian Western Bank; Hongkong Bank of Canada; The Canada Trust Company; Thyssen Mining Construction of Canada; Canadian National; Canadian Pacific Limited.

For full biographical listings, see the Martindale-Hubbell Law Directory

MACPHERSON LESLIE & TYERMAN (AV)

1500-1874 Scarth Street, S4P 4E9
Telephone: 306-347-8000
Telecopier: 306-352-5250
Email: mltreg@mlt.com
Saskatoon, Saskatchewan Office: 1500-410 22nd Street East, S7K 5T6.
Telephone: 306-975-7100.
Telecopier: 306-975-7145.

MEMBERS OF FIRM

Harold H. MacKay, Q.C.
A. Robson Garden, Q.C. (Resident, Saskatoon Office)
Leonard D. Andrychuk
Garret J. Oledzki
Douglas A. Ballou
Danny R. Anderson (Resident, Saskatoon Office)
Randy U. Brunet
Scott A. Exner
Robert B. Pletch, Q.C.
Donald K. Wilson, Q.C.
R. Neil MacKay (Resident, Saskatoon Office)
Alain J. Gaucher (Resident, Saskatoon Office)
James S. Kerby (Resident, Saskatoon Office)
John A. Dipple
Todd M. Rosenberg (Resident, Saskatoon Office)

ASSOCIATES

Michele T. Klebuc-Simes
Grant D. Marshak (Resident, Saskatoon Office)
Aaron D. Runge
Michael J. Clark (Resident, Saskatoon Office)
Crystal L. Taylor (Resident, Saskatoon Office)
Scott D. Whitby
Barclay A. Laughland (Resident, Saskatoon Office)
Rachelle M. Verret
Kenton J. Gray
R. Allen Kirk (Resident, Saskatoon Office)
Bradley N. Vance

COUNSEL

W. Thomas Molloy, O.C., Q.C. (Resident, Saskatoon Office)

For Complete List of Firm Personnel, See General Section

For full biographical listings, see the Martindale-Hubbell Law Directory

*SASKATOON,** Saskatoon Jud. Centre

GAULEY & CO. (AV)

701 Broadway Avenue, P.O. Box 638, S7K 3L7
Telephone: 306-653-1212
Telecopier: 306-652-1323
Email: gauleyco@gauleyco.com
Regina, Saskatchewan Office: Suite 400, 2201 11th Avenue S4P 0J8.
Telephone: 306-352-1643.
Telecopier: 306-525-8499.

MEMBERS OF FIRM

Nancy E. Hopkins, Q.C. (Hon.) C.A.
James Russell
Ian A. Sutherland
J. J. (Joe) Dierker, Q.C.
William J. Shaw
David J. McKeague, Q.C.

Reference: Royal Bank of Canada.

For Complete List of Firm Personnel, See General Section

For full biographical listings, see the Martindale-Hubbell Law Directory

COMMERCIAL LITIGATION

MINNESOTA

*MINNEAPOLIS,** Hennepin Co.

BRIOL & ASSOCIATES (AV)

3905 IDS Center, 80 South Eighth Street, 55402
Telephone: 612-337-8410
Fax: 612-337-5151
Email: briol@mm.com

Mark J. Briol

ASSOCIATES

Amy J. Ihlan
Mary E. Briol
Scott A. Benson
Ellen R. Brostrom

For full biographical listings, see the Martindale-Hubbell Law Directory

COLEMAN, HULL & VAN VLIET, P.L.L.P. (AV)

8500 Normandale Lake Boulevard Suite 2110, 55437
Telephone: 612-841-0001
Fax: 612-841-0041
URL: http://www.chvv.com

Willem F. van Vliet (1924-1996)
Timothy R. Duncan
Katherine M. Bergenthal
William D. Hull
Michael P. Coaty
Marcia B. Haffmans
Jeffrey W. Coleman
Eric R. Heiberg

Reference: Richfield Bank & Trust Co.

For full biographical listings, see the Martindale-Hubbell Law Directory

HEAD, SEIFERT & VANDER WEIDE, A PROFESSIONAL ASSOCIATION (AV)

One Financial Plaza, Suite 2400, 120 South Sixth Street, 55402
Telephone: 612-339-1601
Fax: 612-339-3372
Email: hsvw@wavefront.com

Jerome Truhn (1940-1982)
Howard J. Kauffman
Douglas M. Head
Kenneth A. Larson
Thomas V. Seifert
Marianne E. Durkin
Vernon J. Vander Weide
Charles H. Clay
Aaron F. Biber

For full biographical listings, see the Martindale-Hubbell Law Directory

HENSON & EFRON, P.A. (AV)

400 Second Avenue South, Suite 1200, 55401-2496
Telephone: 612-339-2500
Fax: 612-339-6364
Email: firm@hensonefron.com

Joseph T. Dixon, Jr.
Stuart T. Williams
William F. Forsyth
Bruce C. Recher
David Bradley Olsen

Scott A. Neilson
Neil M. Kliebenstein

Representative Clients: ACandS, Inc.; Pentair, Inc.; Hawkins Chemical, Inc.; Medtronic Sofamor Danek.

For Complete List of Firm Personnel, See General Section

For full biographical listings, see the Martindale-Hubbell Law Directory

HOLPER, WELSH & MITCHELL, LTD. (AV)

10 South Fifth Street, Suite 300, 55402
Telephone: 612-317-1012
Fax: 612-317-0947
Email: rholper@aol.com *URL:* http://www.lawyers.com/holperwelsh&mitchell
Phoenix, Arizona Office: 2415 East Camelback Road, Suite 700, 85016.
Telephone: 602-508-6033.
Fax: 480-483-0269.

Richard D. Holper
Mary Ann Welsh
Ralph V. Mitchell, Jr.

For full biographical listings, see the Martindale-Hubbell Law Directory

OPPENHEIMER WOLFF & DONNELLY LLP (AV)

3400 Plaza VII, 45 South Seventh Street, 55402
Telephone: 612-607-7000
FAX: 612-607-7100
URL: http://www.owdlaw.com
Amsterdam, The Netherlands Office: Keizergracht 241.
Telephone: 31-20-423-4555.
FAX: 31-20-423-4545.
Brussels, Belgium Office: Avenue Louise 240, Box 5, 1050.
Telephone: 32-2-626-0500.
FAX: 32-2-626-0510.
Geneva, Switzerland Office: Rue Gabriel Eynard, 6, 1205.
Telephone: (41/22) 311-7410.
FAX: (41/22) 311-7407.
New York, N.Y. Office: Citicorp Center, 153 East 53rd Street, 10022.
Telephone: 212-826-5000.
FAX: 212-486-0708.
Newport Beach, California Office: 500 Newport Center Drive, Suite 700, 92660.
Telephone: 949-719-6000.
FAX: 949-719-6020.
Paris, France Office: 53 Avenue Montaigne, 75008.
Telephone: (33/1) 44 95 03 50.
FAX: (33/1) 44 95 03 40.
St. Paul, Minnesota Office: 1700 First National Bank Building, 55101.
Telephone: 651-605-2000.
FAX: 651-605-2100.
Washington, D.C. Office: Oppenheimer Wolff Donnelly & Bayh LLP, 1350 Eye Street, N.W., Suite 200, 20005.
Telephone: 202-312-8000.
FAX: 202-312-8100.
Los Angeles, California Office: 2029 Century Park East, 38th Floor, 90067.
Telephone: 310-788-5000.
FAX: 310-277-1297.
San Jose, California Office: 101 Park Center Plaza, Suite 300, 95113.
Telephone: 408-795-3000.
FAX: 408-795-3100.
Chicago, Illinois Office: Oppenheimer Wolff & Donnelly (Illinois), Two Prudential Plaza, 45th Floor, 180 North Stetson Avenue, 60601.
Telephone: 312-616-1800.
Fax: 312-616-5800.

RESIDENT PARTNERS

Harold D. Jastram
Cynthia J. Atsatt
Craig W. Gagnon
Mary E. Senkus
William P. Studer
Edward T. Wahl
Edward J. Hayward
Mark J. Kalla
Richard J. Wegener
Steven W. Meyer
Gary Hansen
Gary P. Gengel II
Edward M. Laine
Jeffrey J. Bouslog
William L. Sippel
Michael B. Fisco
W. C. Blanton
Cary B. Johnson
Michael J. Bleck
David P. Graham
Bradley G. Clary
Jonathon H. Bloomberg
Mark S. Olson
Michael E. Keyes
Paula D. Osborn
Thaddeus R. Lightfoot
Edward F. Fox
Robert J. McGillivray
Jerome A. Miranowski
Jake M. Holdreith
David B. Potter
Mark G. Rabogliatti
Shannon M. O'Toole
Craig J. Lervick
James A. Mennell

RESIDENT ASSOCIATES

James C. Zacharski
Elizabeth A. Wefel
Elliott M. Fliés
Ernest W. Grumbles, III
Erika S. Koster
Marcus A. Mollison
Michael C. Zender
Patrice H. Kloss
Rikke A. Dierssen-Morice
Vanessa L. Parvin
Rachel A. Igel
Seth J. Sergent-Leventhal
James M. Jorissen
Carey Sirota Meyer
Anne F. Larsen
Bridget A. Sullivan
Jacqueline M. Moen
Bliss A. Baldwin
J. Aron Allen
Ranelle A. Leier
Jennifer K. Eggers
Chad D. Striker
Jason S. Kilene
David E. Runck
Timothy C. Krsul
Kari L. Wraspir
Thomas E. Ring
Andrew S. Hansen
Lowell M. Rothschild
Cyrus A. Morton

For Complete List of Firm Personnel, See General Section

For full biographical listings, see the Martindale-Hubbell Law Directory

*ST. PAUL,** Ramsey Co.

JOHN MURRAY & ASSOCIATES, LTD. (AV)

Suite 920 Piper Jaffray Plaza, 444 Cedar Street, 55101
Telephone: 651-227-8820
Telecopier: 651-223-5332
Email: jmurray@abanet.org

John A. Murray

Reference: American National (Firstar) Bank, St. Paul.

For full biographical listings, see the Martindale-Hubbell Law Directory

St. Paul—Continued

OPPENHEIMER WOLFF & DONNELLY LLP (AV)

1700 First National Bank Building, 55101
Telephone: 651-605-2000
FAX: 651-605-2100
URL: http://www.owdlaw.com
Minneapolis, Minnesota Office: 3400 Plaza VII, 45 South Seventh Street. 55402.
Telephone: 612-607-7000.
FAX: 612-607-7100.
Amsterdam, The Netherlands Office: Keizergracht 241.
Telephone: 31-20-423-4555.
FAX: 31-20-423-4545.
Brussels, Belgium Office: Avenue Louise 240, Box 5, 1050.
Telephone: 32-2-626-0500.
FAX: 32-2-626-0510.
Geneva, Switzerland Office: Rue Gabriel Eynard, 6, 1205.
Telephone: (41/22) 311-7410.
FAX: (41/22) 311-7407.
Newport Beach, California Office: 500 Newport Center Drive, Suite 700, 92660.
Telephone: 949-719-6000.
FAX: 949-719-6020.
New York, N.Y. Office: Citicorp Center, 153 East 53rd Street, 10022.
Telephone: 212-826-5000.
FAX: 212-486-0708.
Paris, France Office: 53 Avenue Montaigne, 75008.
Telephone: (33/1) 44 95 03 50.
FAX: (33/1) 44 95 03 40.
Washington, D.C. Office: Oppenheimer Wolff Donnelly & Bayh LLP, 1350 Eye Street, N.W., Suite 200, 20005.
Telephone: 202-312-8000.
FAX: 202-312-8100.
Los Angeles, California Office: 2029 Century Park East, 38th Floor, 90067.
Telephone: 310-788-5000.
FAX: 310-277-1297.
San Jose, California Office: 101 Park Center Plaza, Suite 300, 95113.
Telephone: 408-795-3000.
FAX: 408-795-3100.
Chicago, Illinois Office: Oppenheimer Wolff & Donnelly (Illinois), Two Prudential Plaza, 45th Floor, 180 North Stetson Avenue, 60601.
Telephone: 312-616-1800.
FAX: 312-616-5800.

RESIDENT PARTNERS

Leon R. Goodrich
Thomas P. Kane
Kathleen M. Mahoney
Bethany K. Culp
David M. Wilk

RESIDENT ASSOCIATES

Terrance C. Newby
David L. Jordan-Huffman
Jeffrey P. Diebel

Representative Clients: American Motors Corp.; Control Data Corp.; Minneapolis-Saint Paul Metropolitan Airports Commission; St. Paul Companies (St. Paul Fire & Marine Insurance); 3M.

For full biographical listings, see the Martindale-Hubbell Law Directory

MISSISSIPPI

BILOXI, Harrison Co.

RUSHING & GUICE (AV)

683 Water Street, P.O. Box 1925, 39533-1925
Telephone: 228-374-2313
Telecopier: 228-374-8155
Email: rushguice@rushing-guice.com *URL:* http://www.rushing-guice.com

MEMBERS OF FIRM

Charles L. Rushing (1881-1923)
William L. Guice (1887-1971)
William Lee Guice III

OF COUNSEL

Jacob D. Guice

ASSOCIATES

R. Scott Wells
Maria M. Cobb

LEGAL SUPPORT PERSONNEL

Antonia Strong

Representative Clients: American Isuzu Motors, Inc.; AT&T; Credit Acceptance Corp.; Davison Oil Co.; First National Bank of Commerce; Gulf Coast Industries; Harris Corp.; Hibernia National Bank; Phillips Supply of Gulfport, Inc.; SECOR Bank.

For full biographical listings, see the Martindale-Hubbell Law Directory

*GULFPORT,** Harrison Co.

DUKES, DUKES, KEATING AND FANECA, P.A. (AV)

2909 13th Street, 6th Floor, P.O. Drawer W, 39501
Telephone: 228-868-1111
Fax: 228-863-2886
Email: ddkf@ddkf.com

Hugh D. Keating
Cy Faneca

William W. Abbott, Jr.

For Complete List of Firm Personnel, See General Section

For full biographical listings, see the Martindale-Hubbell Law Directory

*JACKSON,** Hinds Co.

BAKER, DONELSON, BEARMAN & CALDWELL (AV)

Suite 500, 700 North State Street, 39202
Telephone: 601-351-2400
Telecopier: 601-351-2424
Email: info@bdbc.com *URL:* http://www.bakerdonelson.com
Memphis, Tennessee Office: 20th Floor, First Tennessee Building, 165 Madison, 38103.
Telephone: 901-526-2000.
Telecopier: 901-577-2303.
Nashville, Tennessee Office: 1700 Nashville City Center, 511 Union Street, 37219.
Telephone: 615-726-5600.
Telecopier: 615-726-0464.
Chattanooga, Tennessee Office: 1800 Republic Centre, 633 Chestnut Street, 37450-1800.
Telephone: 423-756-2010.
Telecopier: 423-756-3447.
Knoxville, Tennessee Office: 2200 Riverview Tower, 900 South Gay Street, 37901.
Telephone: 423-549-7000.
Telecopier: 423-525-8569.
Johnson City, Tennessee Office: SunTrust Bank Building, 207 Mockingbird Lane, P.O. Box 3038, 37602.
Telephone: 423-928-0181.
Telecopier: 423-928-5694; 423-928-3654; Kingsport: 423-246-6191.
Huntsville, Tennessee Office: 3 Courthouse Square, 37756.
Telephone: 423-663-2321.
Telecopier: 423-663-2111.
Washington, D.C. Office: Market Square, 801 Pennsylvania Avenue, N.W., 20004.
Telephone: 202-508-3400.
Telecopier: 202-508-3402.

PARTNERS

Walker W. (Bill) Jones, III
James L. Jones

ASSOCIATES

Sheryl Bey
Philip W. Thomas
Charles R. Galloway
Scott W. Pedigo
Tiffanee N. Wade
Scott W. Bates

OF COUNSEL

Karen H. Spencer

For Complete List of Firm Personnel, See General Section

For full biographical listings, see the Martindale-Hubbell Law Directory

BENNETT LOTTERHOS SULSER & WILSON, P.A. (AV)

One Jackson Place Suite 1400, 188 East Capitol Street, P.O. Box 98, 39205-0098
Telephone: 601-944-0466
Telecopier: 601-944-0467

Richard T. Bennett
Joseph E. Lotterhos
Marcus M. Wilson
Edward E. Lawler, Jr.
Mary E. McAlister
J. Mark Franklin, III
Ronald Keith Foreman
John L. Pannier

OF COUNSEL

Floyd M. Sulser, Jr.

Representative Clients: Agristor Leasing; Chubb Group of Insurance Companies; 84 Lumber Company; European American Bank; FSLIC; Great Southern Federal Savings; Hibernia National Bank; Holiday Inns, Inc; Masonite Corp.

For full biographical listings, see the Martindale-Hubbell Law Directory

SULLIVAN AND SULLIVAN (AV)

Suite 200, 5448 I-55 North, 39211
Telephone: 601-952-0799
Facsimile: 601-952-0599;
Cable Address: "Sullaw"

MEMBERS OF FIRM

John C. Sullivan, Sr. (1910-1993)
John C. Sullivan, Jr.

(See Next Column)

SULLIVAN AND SULLIVAN—*Continued*

ASSOCIATE

Patricia Alexander Killgore

For full biographical listings, see the Martindale-Hubbell Law Directory

WATKINS & EAGER (AV)

A Professional Limited Liability Company
Suite 300 The Emporium Building, 400 East Capitol Street, P.O. Box 650, 39205
Telephone: 601-948-6470
Facsimile: 601-354-3623

MEMBERS OF FIRM

Thomas R. Crews
Paul H. Stephenson, III
John L. Low, IV
Lewis W. Bell

Representative Clients: Chevron U.S.A. Inc.; McDonald's Corp.; New Holland North America, Inc.; Pavco Industries, Inc.; Trustmark National Bank; Texaco Inc.

For Complete List of Firm Personnel, See General Section

For full biographical listings, see the Martindale-Hubbell Law Directory

*OXFORD,** Lafayette Co.

FREELAND & FREELAND (AV)

1013 Jackson Avenue, P.O. Box 269, 38655
Telephone: 662-234-3414
Telecopier: 662-234-0604
Email: thf4@watervalley.net

MEMBERS OF FIRM

T. H. Freeland, III
T. H. Freeland, IV

Representative Clients: The Ohio Casualty Group; Crum & Forester.

For full biographical listings, see the Martindale-Hubbell Law Directory

*PASCAGOULA,** Jackson Co.

COLINGO, WILLIAMS, HEIDELBERG, STEINBERGER & McELHANEY, P.A. (AV)

711 Delmas Avenue, P.O. Box 1407, 39568-1407
Telephone: 228-762-8021
FAX: 228-762-7589
Email: info@colingowilliams.com *URL:* http://www.ColingoWilliams.com

Joe R. Colingo
Karl R. Steinberger
Roy C. Williams
James H. Colmer, Jr.
James H. Heidelberg
Brett K. Williams
Stephen W. Burrow

C. Brice Wiggins
Kevin C. Bradley

Representative Clients: International Paper Co.; R.J. Reynolds; CBS Corp.; Kemper Group; Singing River Hospital System; Mississippi Gulf Coast Regional Wastewater Authority; Medical Assurance Company of Mississippi; Mutual Assurance of Alabama; Dole Food Co.

For full biographical listings, see the Martindale-Hubbell Law Directory

MISSOURI

*CLAYTON,** St. Louis Co.

THEODORE F. SCHWARTZ (AV)

130 South Bemiston, Suite 700, 63105
Telephone: 314-863-4654
Telecopier: 314-862-4357
Email: schwartz@primary.net
Santa Monica, California Office: Suite 1400, 100 Wilshire Boulevard, 90401.
Telephone: 310-458-0202.
San Francisco, California Office: One Embarcadero Center, 40th Floor, 94111.
Telephone: 415-434-8900.

Barry S. Ginsburg
Kenneth R. Schwartz

Reference: First National Bank of St. Louis County, Clayton, Missouri.

For full biographical listings, see the Martindale-Hubbell Law Directory

*INDEPENDENCE,** Jackson Co.

WHITE, ALLINDER & GRAHAM, L.L.C. (AV)

Hidden Creek Office Park, 14801 East 42nd Street, 64055
Telephone: 816-373-9080
Fax: 816-373-9319

(See Next Column)

MEMBERS OF FIRM

Steven W. White
John K. Allinder
Gene P. Graham, Jr.

ASSOCIATE

Mary Beth Clune

For full biographical listings, see the Martindale-Hubbell Law Directory

KANSAS CITY, Jackson, Clay, Platte & Cass Cos.

MILLER LAW FIRM, A PROFESSIONAL CORPORATION (AV)

4310 Madison Avenue, 64111
Telephone: 816-531-0755
Telefax: 816-561-6361
Email: MLFIRM@aol.com

Richard W. Miller
Andrew C. Gately
Stephen R. Miller
Danne W. Webb
Weston A. Sechtem
Michael T. Metcalf

Jennifer V. Ballengee
Scott H. Murphy
David R. Vandeginste

For full biographical listings, see the Martindale-Hubbell Law Directory

WAGSTAFF & CARTMELL, LLP (AV)

Suite 1240, 4520 Main Street, 64111
Telephone: 816-701-1100
Fax: 816-531-2372

Thomas W. Wagstaff
Robert G. Rooney
Thomas P. Cartmell
Jonathan P. Kieffer

Marc K. Erickson
Thomas L. Wagstaff

For full biographical listings, see the Martindale-Hubbell Law Directory

ST. LOUIS, (Independent City)

DEVEREUX, MURPHY, STRILER, BRICKEY & SHER, L.L.C. (AV)

10 South Brentwood Boulevard (Clayton), 63105
Telephone: 314-721-1516
FAX: 314-721-4434

Joseph F. Devereux, Jr.
James N. Brickey
Robert L. Devereux

For full biographical listings, see the Martindale-Hubbell Law Directory

ALAN E. DEWOSKIN, P.C. (AV)

Suite 426 T, 225 South Meramec Avenue, 63105
Telephone: 314-727-6330
Telecopier: 314-727-5297
URL: http://www.lawyers.com/dewoskinlaw

Alan E. DeWoskin
Henry M. DeWoskin

For full biographical listings, see the Martindale-Hubbell Law Directory

GREEN, SCHAAF & JACOBSON, P.C. (AV)

Suite 700 Pierre Laclede Center, 7733 Forsyth Boulevard (Clayton), 63105
Telephone: 314-862-6800
Telecopier: 314-862-1606
Email: info@stlouislaw.com *URL:* http://www.stlouislaw.com

George E. Schaaf (1930-1995)
Joe D. Jacobson
Martin M. Green
David T. Butsch

Jonathan F. Andres
Allen P. Press
Daniel S. Peters

OF COUNSEL

Howard L. Kanefield

For full biographical listings, see the Martindale-Hubbell Law Directory

KRAMER & FRANK, P.C. (AV)

9666 Olive Boulevard, Suite 450, 63132
Telephone: 314-991-1177; 800-288-5437
Telecopier: 314-991-0485
Email: george@lawusa.com *URL:* http://www.lawusa.com
Kansas City, Missouri Office: 1101 Walnut, Suite 1202, 64106.
Telephone: 816-471-0030.
Fax: 816-472-0963.

Donald B. Kramer
Timothy M. Bosslet
I. James Frankel
Jay B. Umansky
George J. Skupnik, Jr.
David L. Smith
David J. Kozeny
Bradley D. Pierce

(See Next Column)

KRAMER & FRANK P.C., *St. Louis—Continued*

Pamela P. Floro
Tammy F. Wool
D. Jay Cohen
Diane W. Ortlip
Janice Valdez

For full biographical listings, see the Martindale-Hubbell Law Directory

THE LOWENBAUM PARTNERSHIP, L.L.C. (AV)

222 South Central Avenue, Suite 901 (Clayton), 63105
Telephone: 314-863-0092
Facsimile: 314-746-4848
Email: rml@lowenbaumlaw.com

Gerald M. Richardson

Representative Clients: Drury Inns, Inc.; Unity Health; Color Art, Inc.; American Optometric Assn.

For full biographical listings, see the Martindale-Hubbell Law Directory

NEWMAN, FREYMAN, KLEIN & GAMACHE, P.C. (AV)

7777 Bonhomme, 24th Floor, 63105
Telephone: 314-727-0220
Telecopier: 314-727-9246
URL: http://www.nfk-law.com

Mayer S. Klein
Robert A. Margulis
John E. Toma, Jr.
Edward J. Myers

Eileen M. Love
John P. Lavey
Scott D. Levine
Richard L. Saville, Jr.
Steven M. Aroesty

For full biographical listings, see the Martindale-Hubbell Law Directory

REINERT & ROURKE, P.C. (AV)

812 North Collins Laclede's Landing, 63102
Telephone: 314-621-5743
Telecopier: 314-621-8071
Email: reinertrourke@reinertrourke.com *URL:* http://www.reinertrourke.com

Bernard A. Reinert
John W. Rourke

OF COUNSEL

Nicholas B. Carter

For full biographical listings, see the Martindale-Hubbell Law Directory

ROSENBLUM, GOLDENHERSH, SILVERSTEIN & ZAFFT, P.C. (AV)

Fourth Floor, 7733 Forsyth Boulevard, 63105
Telephone: 314-726-6868
Telecopier: 314-726-6786
Belleville, Illinois Office: 2 Park Place Professional Centre, 62221.
Telephone: 618-234-9900.
Columbia, Missouri Office: 3201 South Providence, Suite 101, 65205-4000.
Telephone: 573-441-8686.

Stanley M. Rosenblum
Robert S. Goldenhersh
Merle L. Silverstein
Gene M. Zafft
Carl C. Lang
Richard S. Bender
Michael A. Markenson
David V. Capes
Mark E. Goodman
Jay A. Nathanson
Richard Greenberg
Bennett S. Keller
Leonard D. Vines
Roger M. Herman
Thomas A. Duda
Paul G. Klug
Ira L. Blank
Ellen Levy Siwak
Joshua M. Schindler
Sanford J. Boxerman
Carl R. Desenberg
Scott H. Malin

Jeffrey Alan Cohen
Kristen L. Maly
Todd C. Brockmann
Marilyn Eichler Nathanson
Shelley H. Koren
Jared M. Minkoff

For full biographical listings, see the Martindale-Hubbell Law Directory

SCHRAMM & PINES, L.L.C. (AV)

Suite 950 The Bemiston Tower, 231 South Bemiston Avenue, 63105
Telephone: 314-721-5321
Telecopier: 314-721-0790

MEMBERS OF FIRM

Paul H. Schramm
M. Harvey Pines
Daniel R. Schramm

Timothy I. Nicholson
Dean A. Schramm

Reference: Magna Bank.

For full biographical listings, see the Martindale-Hubbell Law Directory

SEIGEL & WOLFF, P.C. (AV)

Pierre Laclede Center, 7701 Forsyth Boulevard, Suite 950, 63105
Telephone: 314-726-0009
FAX: 314-726-5809
Email: seigelwolf@stlnet.com *URL:* http://www.lawyers.com/seigel&wolff

Charles A. Seigel, III
Michael A. Wolff

For full biographical listings, see the Martindale-Hubbell Law Directory

STONE, LEYTON & GERSHMAN, A PROFESSIONAL CORPORATION (AV)

7733 Forsyth Boulevard, Suite 500, 63105
Telephone: 314-721-7011
Telefax: 314-721-8660

Steven M. Stone
Steven H. Leyton
Jeffrey S. Gershman
Thomas P. Rosenfeld
Paul J. Puricelli

Amy M. Sneirson

For full biographical listings, see the Martindale-Hubbell Law Directory

MONTANA

*BILLINGS,** Yellowstone Co.

MURPHY, KIRKPATRICK & FAIN, P.L.L.P. (AV)

Suite 300, Western Security Bank Building, 2929 Third Avenue North, 59101
Telephone: 406-256-9700
Fax: 406-256-9755
Email: mailbox@murphkirk.com *URL:* http://www.murphkirk.com

James P. Murphy
Stewart R. Kirkpatrick
Bruce F. Fain

LEGAL SUPPORT PERSONNEL

Michelle A. Kennedy (Paralegal)

For full biographical listings, see the Martindale-Hubbell Law Directory

*MISSOULA,** Missoula Co.

DATSOPOULOS, MACDONALD & LIND, P.C. (AV)

Central Square Building, 201 West Main Street, Suite 201, 59802
Telephone: 406-728-0810
FAX: 406-543-0134
Email: email@dmllaw.com

Milton Datsopoulos
Ronald B. MacDonald
Dennis E. Lind
Christopher B. Swartley
William K. VanCanagan
Rebecca L. Summerville
Darla J. Keck

Edward A. Murphy
Paul T. Ryan
Paul N. Tranel
Susan G. Ridgeway
David M. McLean

For full biographical listings, see the Martindale-Hubbell Law Directory

PHILLIPS & BOHYER, P.C. (AV)

Suite 301 River Front Place, 283 W. Front Street, P.O. Box 8569, 59807-8569
Telephone: 406-721-7880
Telecopier: 406-549-2253
Email: phillips@montana.com

Robert J. Phillips
John E. Bohyer
Tammy Wyatt-Shaw
Fred Simpson, Jr.
John F. Jenks

LEGAL SUPPORT PERSONNEL

Mary J. Maynard
Elaine LaPointe-Vetter
Martin Suda

For full biographical listings, see the Martindale-Hubbell Law Directory

NEBRASKA

*LINCOLN,** Lancaster Co.

CLINE, WILLIAMS, WRIGHT, JOHNSON & OLDFATHER (AV)

1900 U.S. Bank Building, 233 South 13th Street, 68508
Telephone: 402-474-6900
Fax: 402-474-5393
Email: postmaster@cline-law.com *URL:* http://www.cline-law.com
Omaha, Nebraska Office: Suite 720, One Pacific Place, 1125 South 103rd Street, 68124.
Telephone: 402-397-1700.
Fax: 402-397-1806.

ATTORNEYS

Allen L. Graves
Charles M. Pallesen, Jr.
Fredric H. Kauffman
Donald F. Burt
Alan E. Peterson
Stephen E. Gehring
Robert J. Routh
Kevin Colleran
L. Bruce Wright
James M. Bausch
Larry A. Holle
David R. Buntain
Stephen H. Nelsen
Michael C. Mueller
Lauren W. Wismer
Daniel R. Stogsdill
Scott D. Kelly
Terry R. Wittler
Pamela Hastings Carrier
Mark A. Christensen
Richard P. Garden, Jr.
Shawn D. Renner
John C. Miles
Mary Kay Frank
Thomas C. Huston
Sonya S. Ekart
Don R. Janssen
Susan Kubert Sapp
Kevin J. Schneider
Andrew D. Strotman
Jill Gossin Jensen
Rochelle A. Mullen
John L. Horan
Bryan S. Hatch
Steven C. Likes
Tracy A. Oldemeyer
Jolene M. Papa
Timothy G. Aschoff
Eric N. Bergquist
Janis J. Winterhof
Andrea Dylan Snowden

OF COUNSEL

Charles E. Wright
Richard P. Jeffries
Mary M. Campbell

RETIRED PARTNERS

Flavel A. Wright (Retired)
Warren C. Johnson (Retired)
Charles E. Oldfather (1927-1998)

Representative Clients: U.S. Bank National Association; University of Nebraska; Nebraska Medical Assn.; Saint Elizabeth Regional Medical Center; Media of Nebraska; Cargill Inc.; State Farm Insurance Cos.; Wal-Mart Stores, Inc.; Textron/Cushman; Isco, Inc.

For full biographical listings, see the Martindale-Hubbell Law Directory

*OMAHA,** Douglas Co.

BETTERMAN & DIXON (AV)

2868 Woodmen Tower, 1700 Farnam Street, 68102
Telephone: 402-345-3900
Fax: 402-345-3341

MEMBERS OF FIRM

W. Patrick Betterman
Joyce A. Dixon

ASSOCIATES

Deana K. Meisinger
David J. Skalka

For full biographical listings, see the Martindale-Hubbell Law Directory

CLINE, WILLIAMS, WRIGHT, JOHNSON & OLDFATHER (AV)

One Pacific Place, 1125 South 103rd Street, Suite 720, 68124
Telephone: 402-397-1700
Fax: 402-397-1806
Email: postmaster@cline-law.com *URL:* http://www.cline-law.com
Lincoln, Nebraska Office: 1900 U.S. Bank Building, 233 South 13th Street, 68508.
Telephone: 402-474-6900.
Fax: 402-474-5393.

ATTORNEYS

Donald F. Burt
Stephen E. Gehring
James M. Bausch
Michael C. Mueller
Daniel R. Stogsdill
Scott D. Kelly
John C. Miles
Mary Kay Frank
Andrew D. Strotman
Rochelle A. Mullen
Steven C. Likes
Tracy A. Oldemeyer
Timothy G. Aschoff

OF COUNSEL

Richard P. Jeffries

Representative Clients: U.S. Bank National Association; University of Nebraska; Nebraska Medical Assn.; Saint Elizabeth Regional Medical Center; Media of Nebraska; Cargill Inc.; State Farm Insurance Cos.; Wal-Mart Stores, Inc.; Textron/Cushman; ISCO, Inc.

For full biographical listings, see the Martindale-Hubbell Law Directory

McGILL, GOTSDINER, WORKMAN & LEPP, P.C. (AV)

Suite 500 - First National Plaza, 11404 West Dodge Road, 68154
Telephone: 402-492-9200
Telecopier: 402-492-9222
Email: mgwl@mgwl.com

Robert L. Lepp
Paul R. Elofson
Alan E. Pedersen

Representative Clients: Metz Baking Company; Service Data Corporation; Heartland Beef, Inc.

For Complete List of Firm Personnel, See General Section

For full biographical listings, see the Martindale-Hubbell Law Directory

RASMUSSEN & MITCHELL (AV)

11605 Miracle Hills Drive, Suite 205, 68154
Telephone: 402-493-3300
Fax: 402-496-0766
Email: lawman000@aol.com *URL:* http://www.lawyers.com/rasmussen&mitchell

MEMBERS OF FIRM

Wayne S. Rasmussen
James S. Mitchell
Kathryn J. Derr
Shane M. Niebergall

For full biographical listings, see the Martindale-Hubbell Law Directory

SCOTTSBLUFF, Scotts Bluff Co.

VAN STEENBERG, CHALOUPKA, MULLIN, HOLYOKE, PAHLKE, SMITH, SNYDER & HOFMEISTER, P.C. (AV)

1904 1st Avenue, P.O. Box 2424, 69363-2424
Telephone: 308-635-3161
Telecopier: 308-632-3128
Email: vanlaw@prairieweb.com

Richard M. Van Steenberg (1917-1997)
Robert Paul Chaloupka
Robert W. Mullin
Thomas T. Holyoke
Robert G. Pahlke
Steven C. Smith
Paul W. Snyder
Paul E. Hofmeister

Tylor J. Petitt
David B. Eubanks
Andrew W. Snyder
Maren Lynn Chaloupka

For full biographical listings, see the Martindale-Hubbell Law Directory

NEVADA

*LAS VEGAS,** Clark Co.

ALVERSON, TAYLOR, MORTENSEN, NELSON & SANDERS (AV)

7401 West Charleston Boulevard, 89117
Telephone: 702-384-7000
FAX: 702-385-7000
Email: alverson@intermind.net
Reno, Nevada Office: 245 East Liberty, Suite 520, 89505.
Telephone: 775-329-0473.
Fax: 775-329-3303.

MEMBERS OF FIRM

J. Bruce Alverson
Eric K. Taylor
David J. Mortensen
Erven T. Nelson
LeAnn Sanders

OF COUNSEL

Jack C. Cherry
Kurt D. Anderson
Philip C. Van Alstyne

ASSOCIATES

Rebecca Hopkins Miller
Sandra Smagac
Victoria L. Nelson
Aaron D. Lovaas
Diane Obritsch
Michael A. Olsen
Randal D. Shimon
Catherine A. Olendorff
Monica L. Pierce
Gabriel D. Lither
Kurt R. Bonds
Darius F. Rafie
Mark J. King, IV
Shell L. Mercer
Carrie S. Bourdeau
Jason Lane Earnest
Nathan R. Reinmiller
Donn C. Alexander
Afshin Tadayon
Eric O. Freeman
Lindsay L. Stadtlander
Julie M. Sueoka

Representative Clients: Citibank (Nevada), N.A.; First Interstate Bank of Nevada; The CIT Group; Federal Deposit Insurance Corporation/Resolution Trust Corporation (TRTC); General Electric Company; St. Paul Fire & Marine Insurance Co.; The Doctors Company; University Medical Center of So. Nevada; Chubb Group of Insurance Companies.

For full biographical listings, see the Martindale-Hubbell Law Directory

Las Vegas—Continued

BARKER, BROWN, BUSBY, CHRISMAN & THOMAS, A PROFESSIONAL CORPORATION (AV)

800 Bank of America Plaza, 300 South Fourth Street, 89101
Telephone: 702-386-1086
Fax: 702-384-5386
Email: BAR-BRO@IX.NETCOM.COM

William S. Barker — James P. Chrisman
Janice J. Brown — David L. Thomas
Jerry S. Busby — Robert A. Winner

Robert D. Tarte — Ann C. Elworth
Brent A. Carson — Michael D. Demman
Marino A. Cesaretti — Curtis J. Busby
J. Scott Ralston

LEGAL SUPPORT PERSONNEL

David A. Ross (Not admitted in NV) — Michael W. Salend
Michael Allen Davis
Britt K. Beckstrom

Representative Clients: Fireman's Fund; Liberty Mutual; Southwest Airlines; Colonial Penn; Metropolitan, Inc.; Uniroyal Tire; Del E. Webb Corp.

For full biographical listings, see the Martindale-Hubbell Law Directory

DEANER, DEANER, SCANN, MALAN & LARSEN (AV)

720 South Fourth Street, Suite 300, 89101
Telephone: 702-382-6911
Fax: 702-386-6048
Email: CDeaner@ix.netcom.com *URL:* http://www.lawyers.com/ddsm&lfirm

MEMBERS OF FIRM

Charles W. Deaner — Susan Williams Scann
J. Douglas Deaner (1944-1990) — Douglas R. Malan
Brent A. Larsen

ASSOCIATE

Anthony Ciulla

Representative Clients: California Federal Bank; White Concrete, Inc. Silver State Schools Federal Credit Union.
Reference: First Security Bank.

For full biographical listings, see the Martindale-Hubbell Law Directory

DELANOY, ENGLISH, SCHUETZE & MCGAHA, A PROFESSIONAL CORPORATION (AV)

Suite One, 1000 East Sahara Avenue, 89104
Telephone: 702-369-3225
Fax: 702-369-2110
Email: motovegas@aol.com

Drake DeLanoy — Damon A. Schuetze
William W. McGaha

For full biographical listings, see the Martindale-Hubbell Law Directory

DICKERSON, DICKERSON, CONSUL & POCKER (AV)

Suite 1130, 330 South Third Street, 89101
Telephone: 702-388-8600
Fax: 702-388-0210

MEMBERS OF FIRM

George M. Dickerson — Richard J. Pocker
Robert P. Dickerson — Douglass A. Mitchell
Vincent A. Consul — Paul J. Lal
Bryce C. Duckworth

ASSOCIATES

Stacie L. Brown — Shann D. Winesett
David F. Sampson

Reference: Citibank.

For full biographical listings, see the Martindale-Hubbell Law Directory

EDWARDS, SOOY & BYRON, A PROFESSIONAL CORPORATION (AV®)

3960 Howard Hughes Parkway Fifth Floor, 89109
Telephone: 702-474-0861
Fax: 702-474-4538
Email: esb-legal.com *URL:* http://www.esb-legal.com
San Diego, California Office: 101 West Broadway, Ninth Floor, 92101.
Telephone: 619-231-1500.
Fax: 619-231-1588.

Michael M. Edwards (Not admitted in NV) — Richard R. Sooy
Thomas W. Byron

Alfred Paul Centofanti, III — Bart M. Blechschmidt
Michael M. Edwards, Jr.

For full biographical listings, see the Martindale-Hubbell Law Directory

EDWARDS & WINTERTON, CHTD. (AV)

401 North Buffalo Drive, Suite 200, 89128
Telephone: 702-363-0317
Telecopier: 702-363-1630
Email: EOWW.LAW@worldnet.att.net

George T. Morse, III (1945-1996) — Douglas M. Edwards
David J. Winterton

Nazario J. Jureidini — Thomas E. Trojan
Robert B. Gerard — Chris A. Beecroft, Jr.

OF COUNSEL

Nicholas A. Boylan (Not admitted in NV)

For full biographical listings, see the Martindale-Hubbell Law Directory

GOOLD PATTERSON DEVORE ALES & ROADHOUSE (AV)

4496 South Pecos Road, 89121
Telephone: 702-436-2600
Telecopier: 702-436-2650
URL: http://www.gooldpatterson.com

Barry Stephen Goold — Thomas J. DeVore
Jeffrey D. Patterson — Barney C. Ales
Wilbur M. Roadhouse

ASSOCIATES

Bryan K. Day — E. Bruce Jorgensen
James A. Kohl

Representative Clients: Adams Management; The Allen Group; Archon Financial, L.P.; Desert Oak Development; Lockheed Martin Corporation; Newcourt Financial Corporation; Olympic Land Corporation; Presley Homes; Red Rock Land, LLC; Sunrise Company.

For full biographical listings, see the Martindale-Hubbell Law Directory

HALE LANE PEEK DENNISON HOWARD AND ANDERSON (AV)

Nevada Financial Center, 2300 West Sahara Avenue, Eighth Floor, Box 8, 89102
Telephone: 702-222-2500
Fax: 702-365-6940
Email: info@halelane.com
Reno, Nevada Office: 100 West Liberty Street, Tenth Floor, P.O. Box 3237.
Telephone: 775-327-3000.
Telefax: 775-786-6179.
Carson City, Nevada Office: 777 East William Street, Suite 200, P.O. Box 2620.
Telephone: 775-684-6000.
Telefax: 775-684-6001.

MEMBERS OF FIRM

Steve Lane — Robert D. Martin
J. Stephen Peek — Michelle D. Mullins
Lenard E. Schwartzer — Lance C. Earl
Fred D. Gibson, III

ASSOCIATES

Elissa F. Cadish — Patrick J. Reilly
Pauline Ng Lee — Noah G. Allison
Michele Eber — Michael C. Mathis (Not admitted in NV)
W. West Allen — Christopher T. Byrd
Torry R. Somers

Representative Clients: Lenders: Bank of America, N.A.; U.S. Bank National Association; Wells Fargo Bank. Title Companies: Chicago Title Insurance Co. General: Lake at Las Vegas Joint Venture; United Coin Machine Co.; Alliance Gaming.

For Complete List of Firm Personnel, See General Section

For full biographical listings, see the Martindale-Hubbell Law Directory

JOLLEY, URGA, WIRTH & WOODBURY (AV)

3800 Howard Hughes Parkway Suite 1600, 89109
Telephone: 702-699-7500
Facsimile: 702-699-7555
URL: http://www.juww.com
Boulder City, Nevada Office: Suite 105, 1000 Nevada Highway, 89005.
Telephone: 702-293-3674.

MEMBERS OF FIRM

R. Gardner Jolley — Bruce L. Woodbury
William R. Urga — Kathryn Stryker Wirth
Roger A. Wirth — Brian E. Holthus
Allen D. Emmel

ASSOCIATES

Gregory G. Gordon — Mark Rosencrantz
Scott Day Freeman — Kelly J. Brinkman
Derek J. Pfaff

Representative Clients: Wells Fargo Bank and its predecessor, First Interstate Bank of Nevada; Nevada State Bank; Chicago Title Insurance Co.; Melvin Simon & Associates, Inc.; General Motors Acceptance Corp.; Toyota Motor

(See Next Column)

JOLLEY, URGA, WIRTH & WOODBURY—*Continued*

Credit Corporation; Champion Home Builders Co.; Circus Circus Casinos, Inc.

For Complete List of Firm Personnel, See General Section

For full biographical listings, see the Martindale-Hubbell Law Directory

KOLESAR & LEATHAM, CHARTERED (AV)

Norwest Bank Center, 3320 West Sahara Avenue, Suite 380, 89102
Telephone: 702-362-7800
Telecopier: 702-362-9472

Nile Leatham
James D. Greene
Charles H. Miles, Jr.
Craig S. Newman

David W. Dachelet
Margaret E. Kerr
Dana Earl Morris
Mark W. Patterson

Representative Clients: Agassi Enterprises, Inc.; AT&T Corp.; Business Bank of Nevada; Commonwealth Land Title Insurance Company; Enterprise Auto Leasing; First Security Bank of Nevada; Forest City Enterprises; Nissan Motor Acceptance Corp.; Silver State Bank; Young Electric Sign Co.

For full biographical listings, see the Martindale-Hubbell Law Directory

KRAVITZ, SCHNITZER & SLOANE, CHARTERED, A PROFESSIONAL CORPORATION (AV)

2300 West Sahara Avenue, Suite 500, 89102
Telephone: 702-362-6666
Fax: 702-362-2203
Email: KRAVSCHNIT@AOL.COM

Martin J. Kravitz
Gary E. Schnitzer
Jeffrey G. Sloane
Michael Bradley Johnson
Jane Eberhardy
Marisa C. Guarino

David J. Feldman
Jerry R. Graf

LEGAL SUPPORT PERSONNEL

Sandye Smith (Legal Administrator)

References: Bank of America; U.S. Bank.

For full biographical listings, see the Martindale-Hubbell Law Directory

JOHN PETER LEE, LTD. (AV)

830 Las Vegas Boulevard South, 89101
Telephone: 702-382-4044
Telecopier: 702-383-9950

John Peter Lee

Paul C. Ray
Timothy P. Thomas

For Complete List of Firm Personnel, See General Section

For full biographical listings, see the Martindale-Hubbell Law Directory

SHIRINIAN & ROITMAN (AV)

333 North Rancho Drive, Suite 520, 89106
Telephone: 702-631-5650
Fax: 702-631-5603
Email: ashirinian@aol.com *URL:* http://www.lawyers.com/shirinian&roitman
San Francisco, California Office: 44 Montgomery Street, Suite 1500, 94104.
Telephone: 415-788-1771.
Fax: 415-788-1744.

Ara H. Shirinian
Howard Roitman

For full biographical listings, see the Martindale-Hubbell Law Directory

SMITH LARSEN & WIXOM, CHARTERED (AV)

3360 West Sahara Avenue, Suite 175, 89102
Telephone: 702-252-5002
Fax: 702-252-5006
Email: slwlaw@slwlaw.com

Jay Earl Smith
Kent F. Larsen
Michael B. Wixom

Stewart C. Fitts

Representative Clients: Norwest Bank Nevada, N.A.; Wells Fargo Bank; Chicago Title Comapny; Mellon Mortgage Company; Luxor Hotel & Casino; Excalibur Hotel & Casino; Pioneer Citizens Bank; The Archon Group; AMRESCO Capital Corporation.

For full biographical listings, see the Martindale-Hubbell Law Directory

WRIGHT, JUDD & WINCKLER (AV)

302 East Carson Avenue, 3rd Floor, 89101
Telephone: 702-382-4004
FAX: 702-382-4800
Email: wjw@netxs.net

MEMBERS OF FIRM

Richard A. Wright
Bruce M. Judd
Karen C. Winckler

For full biographical listings, see the Martindale-Hubbell Law Directory

*RENO,** Washoe Co.

BIBLE, HOY & TRACHOK, A PROFESSIONAL CORPORATION (AV)

201 West Liberty Street, Third Floor, 89501
Telephone: 775-786-8000
Fax: 775-786-7426
Email: firm@nevadalaw.com *URL:* http://www.nevadalaw.com

Paul A. Bible
David R. Hoy
Richard M. Trachok, II
Michael D. Hoy
Mark S. Sertic
Jon M. Ludwig

Mark F. Bruce
Mark J. Lenz
Andrew Alan List
Ralph A. Fellows (Not admitted in NV)

For full biographical listings, see the Martindale-Hubbell Law Directory

HALE LANE PEEK DENNISON HOWARD AND ANDERSON (AV)

100 West Liberty Street, Tenth Floor, P.O. Box 3237, 89505
Telephone: 775-327-3000
Telefax: 775-786-6179
Email: info@halelane.com
Las Vegas, Nevada Office: Nevada Financial Center, 2300 West Sahara Avenue, Eighth Floor, Box 8.
Telephone: 702-222-2500.
Fax: 702-365-6940.
Carson City, Nevada Office: 777 East William Street, Suite 200, P.O. Box 2620.
Telephone: 775-684-6000.
Telefax: 775-684-6001.

MEMBERS OF FIRM

J. Stephen Peek
Richard L. Elmore
Alex J. Flangas
James M. Walsh
Norman Patrick Flanagan
Roger W. Jeppson
Jeremy J. Nork

ASSOCIATES

Robert C. Vohl
Timothy A. Lukas
Dania M. Severson

Representative Clients: Lenders: Bank of America, N.A.; U.S. Bank National Association. Title Companies: Stewart Title Co. of Northern Nevada; Chicago Title Insurance Co. Construction and Development: Centex Homes; Caughlin Ranch.

For Complete List of Firm Personnel, See General Section

For full biographical listings, see the Martindale-Hubbell Law Directory

WALTHER, KEY, MAUPIN, OATS, COX & LEGOY, A PROFESSIONAL CORPORATION (AV)

Lakeside Professional Plaza, 3500 Lakeside Court, 89509
Telephone: 775-827-2000
Facsimile: 775-827-2185
Mailing Address: P.O. Box 30000, Reno, Nevada, 89520

Steven T. Walther
Jon J. Key
Ernest J. Maupin
C. Robert Cox
L. Robert LeGoy, Jr.
Michael E. Malloy
G. Barton Mowry
Procter J. Hug
Donald A. Lattin
Paul J. Anderson
Gustave J. Rossi
Robert A. Winkel
Kurt O. Hunsberger
Michael A. Nivinskus
Christopher D. Jaime

Rick R. Hsu
Michaelle D. Rafferty
Debra O. Waggoner

Representative Clients: Bank America of Nevada (Trust Dept.); Bechtel Corporations; Bill Pearce Olds, BMW, Volvo; Wells Fargo, N.A. (Trust Dept.); General Motors Acceptance Corp.; Nevada Realtors; Radiation Oncology Associates; The Ralph M. Parsons Corporation; Parsons Corporation; Reno Air, Inc.

For full biographical listings, see the Martindale-Hubbell Law Directory

NEW JERSEY

ATLANTIC CITY, Atlantic Co.

WESTMORELAND, VESPER & SCHWARTZ, A PROFESSIONAL CORPORATION (AV)

Bayport One, Yacht Club Drive Suite 500, 08232-0034
Telephone: 609-645-1111
Fax: 609-646-2781
URL: http://www.westmorelandvesper.com

Rudolph C. Westmoreland
Thomas J. Vesper
Mark G. Schwartz
Dara A. Quattrone

David I. Sinderbrand
Katherine M. Morris
Carmelo Tony Torraca

Representative Clients: Cape May Foods; The Bank of New York; Title Company of Jersey; Money Store; Re/Max of New Jersey; AT&T Capital; Unitel Cellular; Yank Boat Works; Tomasello Winery.
Reference: Sun National Bank.

For full biographical listings, see the Martindale-Hubbell Law Directory

CHATHAM, Morris Co.

ALAN L. ZEGAS (AV)

552 Main Street, 07928
Telephone: 973-701-7080
Fax: 973-701-7081
Email: alanatLaw@aol.com *URL:* http://www.lawyers.com/zegas

Gina L. Mendola
Sharon B. Kean
Patricia A. Lee
Aimee Blakeslee

For full biographical listings, see the Martindale-Hubbell Law Directory

CHERRY HILL, Camden Co.

FLASTER/GREENBERG, P.C. (AV)

Commerce Center, 1810 Chapel Avenue West, Third Floor, 08002-4609
Telephone: 856-661-1900
Telecopier: 856-661-1919
Email: FIRM@FLASTERGREENBERG.COM *URL:* http://www.flastergreenberg.com

Richard J. Flaster
Stephen M. Greenberg
Laura B. Wallenstein
Allen P. Fineberg
Markley S. Roderick
Peter R. Spirgel
Alan H. Zuckerman
William S. Skinner
J. Philip Kirchner
Paul J. Russoniello
Carl S. Bisgaier
Steven B. Sacharow
E. Richard Dressel
Kenneth S. Goodkind
Frank H. Wisniewski
Alma L. Saravia

OF COUNSEL

Peter M. Dolinger
James J. Binns

Elizabeth J. Hampton
Jeffrey Herskowitz
Christopher E. Kaltenbach
Steven J. Abrams
Julie A. Williamson
Donna T. Urban
Amelia Carolla
Matthew Azoulay
Elaine J. Petruzziello
(Not admitted in NJ)
Ann Marie Iannone
Pasquale Guglietta

LEGAL SUPPORT PERSONNEL

PARALEGALS

Ann Gorman
Patricia D'Alessio
Theresa Cooke
Rosemary Dunaif

For full biographical listings, see the Martindale-Hubbell Law Directory

KENNEY & KEARNEY LLP (AV)

Woodland Falls Corporate Park, Suite 210, 220 Lake Drive East, P.O. Box 5034, 08034-0421
Telephone: 856-779-7000
Telecopier: 856-779-1342

Joseph H. Kenney
John B. Kearney
John A. Miller, Jr.
Allen A. Etish
Michele Mareschi Fox
Thomas J. Hagner
William J. DeSantis
Charles J. Connery
John A. Zohlman, III

ASSOCIATES

John J. Bannan
David A. Haworth
Paul F. Jenkins
Margaret J. Quinn
Laura D. Ruccolo

OF COUNSEL

Jane A. Kenney
Joel B. Korin

For full biographical listings, see the Martindale-Hubbell Law Directory

EDISON, Middlesex Co.

WONG FLEMING, P.C. (AV)

Edison Square West, Suite 1050, 2035 Lincoln Highway, 08817
Telephone: 732-248-4111
Fax: 732-248-8665
Mailing Address: P.O. Box 985, 08818-0985
Email: info@wongfleming.com *URL:* http://www.wongfleming.com
Philadelphia, Pennsylvania Office: 230 South Broad Street, Suite 601, 19102.
Telephone: 215-546-2776.
Fax: 215-546-3206.
New York, New York Office: The Empire State Building, 350 Fifth Avenue, Suite 5411, 10118.
Telephone: 212-643-9668.
Fax: 212-643-9640.

Linda Wong
Daniel C. Fleming
Katherine C. Lee

Andrew J. Bayne
Stephen Tsai
Theresa Homisak
Paul J. Young
Wenjun Zhang
(Not admitted in NJ)
Tanya E. Lawrence
Fei F. Lam

For full biographical listings, see the Martindale-Hubbell Law Directory

FLORHAM PARK, Morris Co.

CARLIN, MADDOCK, FAY & CERBONE, P.C. (AV)

25 Vreeland Road, P.O. Box 751, 07932
Telephone: 201-377-3350
Fax: 201-377-5626
URL: http://www.lawyers.com/cmfclaw

John J. Carlin, Jr.
Laurence R. Maddock
Donald J. Fay
Richard R. Cerbone

Arthur G. Warden, III

For full biographical listings, see the Martindale-Hubbell Law Directory

*HACKENSACK,** Bergen Co.

ARONSOHN WEINER, A PROFESSIONAL CORPORATION (AV)

263 Main Street, 07601
Telephone: 201-487-4747
Telecopier: 201-487-7601

Richard F. Aronsohn (1938-1996)
Richard H. Weiner
John E. Selser, III
Gerald R. Salerno

Patrick W. Harrington
Gaiana S. Flynn

For full biographical listings, see the Martindale-Hubbell Law Directory

HOGAN, PALACE & SCULLY (AV)

20 Court Street, 07601
Telephone: 201-342-4422
Fax: 201-342-2554
Email: hpsnj@bellatlantic.net *URL:* http://www.lawyers.com/hogan&palace

MEMBERS OF FIRM

Thomas A. Hogan
Thomas W. Palace
Michael R. Scully

LEGAL SUPPORT PERSONNEL

Shannon S. Casey (Real Estate Paralegal)

Reference: Bergen Commercial Bank, New Jersey.

For full biographical listings, see the Martindale-Hubbell Law Directory

SHAPIRO & CROLAND (AV)

A Partnership including Professional Corporations
Continental Plaza II, 411 Hackensack Avenue, 07601
Telephone: 201-488-3900
Fax: 201-488-9481

Barry I. Croland, P.C.
Robert P. Shapiro, P.C.
Barry L. Baime
Jay Rubenstein
Kenneth S. Apfel
Kenneth S. Goldrich, P.C.
Bruce J. Ackerman
Stuart Reiser, P.C.
Meridith J. Bronson
John P. Di Iorio
David O. Marcus
Robert F. Green
Lizabeth Sarakin
David Torchin
Robin C. Bogan
Craig D. Spector

OF COUNSEL

Harvey R. Sorkow

(See Next Column)

SHAPIRO & CROLAND—*Continued*

Donald R. Sorkow (1930-1985)

Reference: Bank of New York-National Community Division.

For full biographical listings, see the Martindale-Hubbell Law Directory

LAWRENCEVILLE, Mercer Co.

SZAFERMAN, LAKIND, BLUMSTEIN, WATTER & BLADER, P.C. (AV)

Suite 104 Quakerbridge Executive Center, 101 Grovers Mill Road, 08648
Telephone: 609-275-0400
Telefax: 609-275-4511

Arnold C. Lakind
Barry D. Szaferman
Jeffrey P. Blumstein
Paul N. Watter
Steven Blader
Sidney H. Lehmann
Gerald B. Schenkman
David B. Beckett
Scott P. Borsack
Mary Lou Delahanty

Jennifer Weisberg Millner
Cathyanne A. Pisciotta
Jason N. Fruhschein
Demery J. Roberts
Stuart A. Tucker
Brian G. Paul
Victoria Rivera-Cruz
Thomas J. Burns III

LEGAL SUPPORT PERSONNEL

Paula M. Rossi (Office Administrator)
Patricia Hallstrum (Controller)

Representative Clients: Sun National Bank; First Washington Bank; Gilmore Securities & Co.; Communication Workers of America; The Eagle Group; Water's Edge Convalescent Center; Ronson Aviation, Inc.; Holmdel Township Board of Adjustment; Public Service Managers Association; Chemical Leaman Tank Lines.

For full biographical listings, see the Martindale-Hubbell Law Directory

MOORESTOWN, Burlington Co.

CHIERICI, CHIERICI & SMITH, A PROFESSIONAL CORPORATION (AV)

Blason Campus - III, 509 South Lenola Road Building Six, 08057-1561
Telephone: 856-234-6300
Fax: 856-234-9490

Donald R. Chierici, Jr.
Elizabeth Coleman Chierici
Julie C. Smith

Carolyn J. Kornas
Mark G. Esposito
Richard D. DiTomaso
Melvin McDowell
David J. Karbasian
Peter P. Sanchez
Donald R. Chierici, III

For full biographical listings, see the Martindale-Hubbell Law Directory

*MORRISTOWN,** Morris Co.

DAVID C. BERMAN A PROFESSIONAL CORPORATION (AV)

64 MacCulloch Avenue, P.O. Box 111, 07963-0111
Telephone: 973-631-1000
Fax: 973-631-1111

David Charles Berman

OF COUNSEL

Diane Levine (Not admitted in NJ)

LEGAL SUPPORT PERSONNEL

Debbie Lee Russo (Paralegal)

For full biographical listings, see the Martindale-Hubbell Law Directory

STEPHEN S. WEINSTEIN A PROFESSIONAL CORPORATION (AV)

20 Park Place, Suite 301, 07960
Telephone: 973-267-5200
Fax: 973-538-1779
Email: skippy@sswpa.com *URL:* http://www.sswpa.com

Stephen S. Weinstein

Gail S. Boertzel
William G. Johnson
Melissa H. Luce

For full biographical listings, see the Martindale-Hubbell Law Directory

*NEWARK,** Essex Co.

HELLRING LINDEMAN GOLDSTEIN & SIEGAL LLP (AV)

One Gateway Center, 07102-5386
Telephone: 973-621-9020
Fax: 973-621-7406
Englewood, New Jersey Office: 32-40 North Dean Street.
Telephone: 201-871-3060.

(See Next Column)

Bernard Hellring (1916-1991)
Philip Lindeman, II
Joel D. Siegal
Jonathan L. Goldstein
Barry H. Evenchick
James A. Scarpone
Michael Edelson
Margaret Dee Hellring
Richard D. Shapiro
Charles Oransky
Richard B. Honig
Richard K. Coplon
Robert S. Raymar
Ronny Jo Greenwald Siegal
Stephen L. Dreyfuss
John A. Adler
Judah I. Elstein
Bruce S. Etterman
Matthew E. Moloshok
Rachel N. Davidson
David N. Narciso
Ronnie F. Liebowitz
Robert B. Rosen
Sheryl E. Koomer

David Wolff
Lisa P. Parker
Jonathan Wayne
Catherine J. Bick
Joanne M. Frasca

For full biographical listings, see the Martindale-Hubbell Law Directory

SILLS CUMMIS RADIN TISCHMAN EPSTEIN & GROSS, A PROFESSIONAL CORPORATION (AV)

One Riverfront Plaza, 07102-5400
Telephone: 973-643-7000
Fax: 973-643-6500
Telex: 820630 Sillsbeck Nwk
Email: sillsmail@sillscummis.com *URL:* http://www.sillscummis.com
Atlantic City, New Jersey Office: 17 Gordon's Alley.
Telephone: 609-344-2800.
New York, N.Y. Office: 712 Fifth Avenue.
Telephone: 212-643-7000.
Washington, D.C. Office: 1800 K Street, N.W.
Telephone: 202-296-4750.

MEMBERS OF FIRM

Steven S. Radin
Morton S. Bunis
Barry M. Epstein
Thomas J. Demski
Jeffrey J. Greenbaum
Jeffrey Barton Cahn
Noah Bronkesh
Kenneth F. Oettle
Philip R. Sellinger
Jack M. Zackin
Thomas S. Novak
Stuart M. Feinblatt
Trent S. Dickey
Joseph L. Buckley
Kathleen Gengaro
James D. Toll (Resident at Atlantic City, N.J. Office)
James M. Hirschhorn
Ronald C. Rak
Mark S. Olinsky
Philip R. White
Alan J. Cohen (Resident at Atlantic City, N.J. Office)
Lori G. Singer
Mark E. Duckstein
Beth S. Rose
Jack Wenik
Ted Zangari
A. Ross Pearlson
Linda Badash Katz

OF COUNSEL

Mitchel E. Ostrer
Steven R. Rowland

James E. Brandt (Not admitted in NJ)
Eric D. Mann (Resident at Atlantic City, N.J. Office)
Bennet Susser
Steven S. Katz
Paul P. Josephson
Paul F. Doda
Adam J. Kaiser
Robert I. Siegel
Jennifer L. Borofsky
Gwen L. Coleman
Susanne Kaufmann Rosenzweig
Derrick R. Freijomil

Representative Clients: WWOR-TV, Inc.; Midlantic National Bank; Foods, Inc.; Jersey City Medical Center; Bally's Entertainment Corp.; BMW North America; Motor Club of America; GAF Corporation; Maidenform, Inc.; Exxon Company, U.S.A.; PNC Bank Corp.

For Complete List of Firm Personnel, See General Section

For full biographical listings, see the Martindale-Hubbell Law Directory

PARSIPPANY, Morris Co.

CUYLER BURK (AV)

Parsippany Corporate Center, Four Century Drive, 07054-4663
Telephone: 973-734-3200
Telex: 429071
Telecopier: 973-734-3201
Email: Main@Cuyler.com *URL:* http://www.cuyler.com
New York, New York Office: 350 Fifth Avenue, Suite 3304. 10018.
Telephone: 212-645-4039.

MEMBERS OF FIRM

Stephen D. Cuyler
Jo Ann Burk
Stefano Calogero
David L. Menzel
Peter Petrou
Richard A. Crooker
Michael J. Jones

COUNSEL

Anne M. Mohan
Frank J. Miele

(See Next Column)

CUYLER BURK, *Parsippany—Continued*

ASSOCIATES

Jan C. Walker
Kathleen Jane Olear
Claudia L. Marchese
Mark G. Eliades
Kimberly A. Joel
Christy A. Ramunno
Catherine E. Youngman
Andrew K. Craig
Mark S. Winter
Thomas J. Castano
Hugo A. Hilgendorff, IV

LEGAL SUPPORT PERSONNEL

Frederick M. H. Currie, Jr.

For full biographical listings, see the Martindale-Hubbell Law Directory

MIDDLEBROOKS & SHAPIRO, P.C. (AV)

99 Cherry Hill Road, 07054-0619
Telephone: 973-335-5200
Telecopier: 973-335-5233
Email: ms1093@aol.com *URL:* http://www.lawyers.com/msattorneys

Melinda Dee Middlebrooks
Richard P. Shapiro

Joseph R. Zapata, Jr.
Stephen M. De Luca

LEGAL SUPPORT PERSONNEL

Peter A. Siebel, Jr. (Paralegal)

For full biographical listings, see the Martindale-Hubbell Law Directory

PRINCETON, Mercer Co.

BERGMAN & BARRETT (AV)

9 Tamarack Circle, Montgomery Knoll, U.S. Highway 206 North, P.O. Box 1273, 08542
Telephone: 609-921-1502
Fax: 609-683-0288

Edward J. Bergman
Michael T. Barrett

LEGAL SUPPORT PERSONNEL

Kelli E. Murphy (Paralegal)

For full biographical listings, see the Martindale-Hubbell Law Directory

STARK & STARK, A PROFESSIONAL CORPORATION (AV)

Princeton Pike Corporate Center, P.O. Box 5315, 08543-5315
Telephone: 609-896-9060
Fax: 609-896-0629
Email: info@stark-stark.com *URL:* http://www.stark-stark.com

Donald B. Brenner
Brian A. Carlis
Timothy P. Duggan
Kevin M. Hart
Craig S. Hilliard
Thomas B. Lewis
Lewis J. Pepperman
Thomas J. Pryor

OF COUNSEL

William H. Brosha

Brian S. Hamburger
John E. MacDonald
John Randy Sawyer
Catherine A. Sokoloski
Susan G. Steinman
Scott I. Unger
George F. Yuska

For full biographical listings, see the Martindale-Hubbell Law Directory

ROCHELLE PARK, Bergen Co.

FORMAN HOLT & ELIADES LLC (AV)

218 Route 17 North, 07662
Telephone: 201-845-1000
Fax: 201-845-9112
Email: firm@formanlaw.com

Charles M. Forman
Michael E. Holt
Daniel M. Eliades, Jr.
Joseph M. Cerra
Julie L. Singer
Kim R. Lynch

OF COUNSEL

Erin J. Kennedy

For full biographical listings, see the Martindale-Hubbell Law Directory

ROSELAND, Essex Co.

BRACH, EICHLER, ROSENBERG, SILVER, BERNSTEIN, HAMMER & GLADSTONE, A PROFESSIONAL CORPORATION (AV)

101 Eisenhower Parkway, 07068
Telephone: 973-228-5700
Telecopier: 973-228-7852
Email: law@bracheichler.com *URL:* http://www.bracheichler.com

Alan H. Bernstein
William L. Brach
Alan S. Pralgever

(See Next Column)

Carl J. Soranno

Representative Clients: Vanstar Corporation; Vivetone Corporation; Bridgewater/Raritan Regional School District; Davidoff of Geneva, Inc.; Kushner Companies; Power Dynamics; Silverline Building Products, Inc.; Glass Gardens ShopRite, Inc.; CMI Marketing Consultants, Inc.; First Tennessee National Bank Corporation; Sparta Steel Corporation; Protameen Chemicals, Inc.; United CompuPham, Inc.; Cerebal Palsy of North Jersey, Inc.

For Complete List of Firm Personnel, See General Section

For full biographical listings, see the Martindale-Hubbell Law Directory

POST, POLAK, GOODSELL & MACNEILL, P.A. (AV)

75 Livingston Avenue, 07068-3701
Telephone: 973-994-1100
Telecopier: 973-994-1705
Email: administrator@ppgm.com
New York, New York Office: 575 Madison Avenue, Suite 1006.
Telephone: 212-486-1455.

John N. Post
Frederick B. Polak
Robert A. Goodsell
Jay Scott MacNeill
Paul D. Strauchler
Mary H. Post
David L. Epstein
Lauren Koffler O'Neill

Loretta B. Critchley
Franca D. Maiorano
Nilufer O. DeScherer
Joseph Tripodi
Thomas J. Pyle, Jr.
Christopher O. Eriksen
Kelly Mack Carey

LEGAL SUPPORT PERSONNEL

Charles A. Tamasaukas (Firm Administrator)

PARALEGALS

Nancy Mendelsohn
Glenn A. Harris
Susan B. Cobb
Nancy G. Barrett

For full biographical listings, see the Martindale-Hubbell Law Directory

SADDLE BROOK, Bergen Co.

KRUGMAN & KAILES LLP (AV)

Park 80 West-Plaza Two, 07663-5835
Telephone: 201-845-3434; 212-695-3262
Telecopier: 201-845-9627
Email: counsel@krugmankailes.com
New York, New York Office: 99 Park Avenue, Suite 2200.
Telephone: 212-599-1060.
Telecopier: 212-599-6282.
London, England Office: 90 Fetter Lane, London EC4A-1PT.
Telephone: 011 (44) 171-421-7918.
Telecopier: 011 (44) 171-831-6407.

MEMBERS OF FIRM

Martin Krugman (1916-1994)
Howard Kailes
Thomas J. Goodwin
Ward C. Laracy
Robert I. Wexler
Alan H. Fox
Joy M. Mercer
Kerry B. Flowers

OF COUNSEL

James D. Krugman

COUNSEL

Judith S. Musicant

ASSOCIATES

Anne M. Wallace (Not admitted in NJ)
April A. Savoye
Lisa Ann Miller
Patrizia E. DeBari
David J. Hanley, Jr.
Anjana D. Patel
W. Mark O'Brien

For full biographical listings, see the Martindale-Hubbell Law Directory

*SOMERVILLE,** Somerset Co.

SCHACHTER, TROMBADORE, OFFEN, STANTON & PAVICS, A PROFESSIONAL CORPORATION (AV)

45 East High Street, P.O. Box 520, 08876-0520
Telephone: 908-722-5700
Fax: 908-722-8853

Richard J. Schachter
John J. Trombadore
Stephen M. Offen
Michael J. Stanton
Thomas A. Pavics

Timothy P. McKeown
Jerry S. D'Aniello

For full biographical listings, see the Martindale-Hubbell Law Directory

SPRINGFIELD, Union Co.

HARDIN, KUNDLA, MCKEON, POLETTO & POLIFRONI, P.A., A PROFESSIONAL CORPORATION (AV)

673 Morris Avenue, P.O. Box 730, 07081
Telephone: 973-912-5222
Fax: 973-912-9212
Email: info@HKMPP.com
New York, New York Office: 55 John Street, 10038.
Telephone: 212-571-0111.
Fax: 212-571-1117.

George R. Hardin
Robert L. Polifroni
Janet L. Poletto
Mark S. Kundla
John F. McKeon
James R. Greene
Nicea J. D'Annunzio
John Samuel Favate
Patrick J. Clare
Anna Marie Strand

Jeffrey A. Oshin
Joseph R. Lowicky
Tracy C. Forsyth
Joseph A. DeFuria
John G. Kilbride
Jeffrey H. Goldsmith
Jeffrey Roth
Nora J. Grimbergen
William C. Sullivan, Jr.
Paul Daly
V. Christopher Hirsch
Richard S. Reig
Sam A. Dotro
Brian K. Kaiser
David M. Steiner
Lani M. D'Agostino
Sheila A. Glackin
Michael S. Schwartz
Kirsten L. McCaw
Sanjoy Mukherjee
Louisa B. Sargent
Michael A. Cifelli
James J. A. Mulhall
Kevin M. Regan
Lisa D. Chanel
Maria-Milagros Herrero
Brian A. King
Christina Fichera Dente
Andrea L. Strack
Roger J. Imhof
John P. Monaghan
Stephen J. Donahue
Cindy L. Thompson
Lisa A. Ganzhorn

Representative Clients: Crum & Forster Insurance; Wausau Insurance Cos.; A.M. Best Co.; Chrysler Corp.; CNA Insurance; McDonald's Corp.; Pepsico; Xerox Corp.

For full biographical listings, see the Martindale-Hubbell Law Directory

JAVERBAUM WURGAFT HICKS & ZARIN, A PROFESSIONAL CORPORATION (AV)

Park Place Legal Center, 959 South Springfield Avenue, 07081-3555
Telephone: 973-379-4200
Fax: 973-379-7872
Email: javerbaumwurgafthicks@compuserve.com *URL:* http://www.lawyers.com/jwhz,law

Kenneth S. Javerbaum
Jack Wurgaft
Robert G. Hicks
Ira J. Zarin

Anthony P. Valenti
Eric G. Kahn
David L. Wikstrom

OF COUNSEL

Jeffrey E. Strauss

For full biographical listings, see the Martindale-Hubbell Law Directory

KRAEMER, BURNS, MYTELKA, LOVELL & KULKA, P.A. (AV)

675 Morris Avenue, 07081
Telephone: 973-912-8700
Telecopier: 973-912-8602

John A. Avery
Douglas E. Burns
Eleonore Kessler Cohen
Wayne D. Greenfeder
Daniel G. Kasen (1905-1990)
Waldron Kraemer
Ellen B. Kulka
Joan A. Lovell
Arnold K. Mytelka

OF COUNSEL

Diane Stolbach
Scott B. Stolbach

For full biographical listings, see the Martindale-Hubbell Law Directory

WEST ORANGE, Essex Co.

ALPERT, BUTLER & SANDERS, P.C. (AV)

The Alpert Professional Building, 449 Mount Pleasant Avenue, 07052
Telephone: 973-325-1188
Fax: 973-325-3399
Email: mailbox@abslaw.com *URL:* http://www.abslaw.com
New York, New York Office: 509 Madison Avenue.
Telephone: 212-758-6958.
Fax: 212-758-2817.

Clark E. Alpert
David N. Butler
William D. Sanders

OF COUNSEL

Martin L. Bearg
Ted M. Rosen (Not admitted in NJ)

(See Next Column)

Elliot L. Lewis
Matthew J. Rice

LEGAL SUPPORT PERSONNEL

PARALEGAL

Robin S. Karpel

For full biographical listings, see the Martindale-Hubbell Law Directory

RABINOWITZ, TRENK, LUBETKIN & TULLY, P.C. (AV)

200 Executive Drive Suite 225, 07052-3303
Telephone: 973-243-8600
Facsimile: 973-243-8677
URL: http://www.Rabinowitztrenk.com

Jonathan I. Rabinowitz
Richard D. Trenk
Jay L. Lubetkin
Mary Ellen Tully
Richard S. Schkolnick

Joseph J. DiPasquale
Joshua H. Raymond
Henry M. Karwowski
Shoshana Schiff

For full biographical listings, see the Martindale-Hubbell Law Directory

NEW MEXICO

*ALBUQUERQUE,** Bernalillo Co.

EAVES, BARDACKE, BAUGH KIERST & KIERNAN, P.A. (AV)

6400 Uptown Boulevard, N.E., Suite 110-W, P.O. Box 35670, 87176
Telephone: 505-888-4300
Facsimile: 505-883-4406
Email: LGLEAVES@EB-B.com

John M. Eaves
Paul Bardacke
John G. Baugh
Peter S. Kierst
Kerry Kiernan

Derek V. Larson
Karen S. Mendenhall
C. Shannon Bacon

OF COUNSEL

Jennifer J. Pruett

For full biographical listings, see the Martindale-Hubbell Law Directory

FAIRFIELD, FARROW, FLOWERS, PIERSON & STROTZ, P.C. (AV)

2400 Louisiana N.E., AFC 3, Suite 100, P.O. Box 35400, 87176-5400
Telephone: 505-881-8300
Fax: 505-889-0553
Email: fairlaw@nm.net

Raymond R. (Dick) Flowers, Jr.
Michael W. Pierson
Bruce H. Strotz

Representative Clients: New Mexico Casualty; USF&G; Public Service Co. of NM; Alliant Food Services; First American Title Co.; Albuquerque Title Co.; Travelers Insurance Co.; Commodore Advanced Sciences, Inc.

For full biographical listings, see the Martindale-Hubbell Law Directory

FREEDMAN BOYD DANIELS HOLLANDER GOLDBERG & CLINE P.A. (AV)

20 First Plaza, Suite 700, 87102
Telephone: 505-842-9960
Fax: 505-842-0761

David A. Freedman
John W. Boyd
Joseph Goldberg

Scott M. Davidson

For full biographical listings, see the Martindale-Hubbell Law Directory

GUEBERT & YEOMANS, P.C. (AV)

6743 Academy Road NE, Suite A, P.O. Box 93880, 87199-3880
Telephone: 505-823-2300
Fax: 505-823-9600

Terry R. Guebert
Richard D. Yeomans
Don Bruckner
RaMona G. Bootes
Timothy L. Hartley
Alysan Boothe Collins
Richard F. Rowley, III
Patricia M. Monaghan

Representative Clients: ABN-AMRO Bank, N.V.; Greek Orthodox Archdiocese of North and South America; Resolution Trust Corporation; Carvel Corporation; McNeil Real Estate Management, Inc.; Confederated Leasing, Ltd.; AMREP; Environmental Specialists, Inc.; World's Finest Chocolate; Yellow Checker Cab.

For full biographical listings, see the Martindale-Hubbell Law Directory

Albuquerque—Continued

HUFFAKER & CONWAY, A PROFESSIONAL CORPORATION (AV)

201 Third Street, N.W., Suite 1910, 87103-1190
Telephone: 505-244-0021
Facsimile: 505-244-1372
Email: albstaff@sisna.com
Santa Fe, New Mexico Office: 155 Grant Avenue, P.O. Box 1868.
Telephone: 505-988-8921.
Fax: 505-983-3927.

Gregory D. Huffaker, Jr.
Ann Maloney Conway
Lisa A. Joynes
Seth L. Sparks
Edward C. Bagley

Representative Clients: Chevron Products Co.; Federal Deposit Insurance Corp.; State Farm Insurance Cos.; St. Paul Cos.; National Federation of the Blind; Insurance Company of the West Group.

For full biographical listings, see the Martindale-Hubbell Law Directory

KREHBIEL, BANNERMAN & HORN, P.A. (AV)

6400 Uptown Boulevard, N.E., Suite 310 East, 87110
Telephone: 505-837-1900
Fax: 505-837-1800
Email: kbh@kbh-lawfirm.com *URL:* http://www.kbh-lawfirm.com

Phil Krehbiel
John A. Bannerman
Barry D. Williams

Rikki L. Quintana
Carol Lisa Smith
David H. Johnson
Lucinda R. Bovee

OF COUNSEL

Ronald F. Horn

For full biographical listings, see the Martindale-Hubbell Law Directory

MADISON, HARBOUR, MROZ & BRENNAN, P.A. (AV)

Suite 1800 Albuquerque Plaza, 201 Third Street, N.W., P.O. Box 25467, 87102
Telephone: 505-242-2177
Fax: 505-242-7184
URL: http://www.madisonlaw.com
Santa Fe, New Mexico Office: Coronado Building, 2nd Floor, 141 East Palace Avenue, P.O. Box 1234.
Telephone: 505-992-8933.
Facsimile: 505-988-2987.

William C. Madison
Michael W. Brennan
Michael H. Harbour
Robert J. Mroz
Neils L. Thompson
M. Eliza Stewart
Lorri Krehbiel
Gregory D. Steinman

Michael Joseph Dekleva
Michele U. Estrada
Scott E. Turner
Shannon A. Parden
Corey A. Goldsand
Jude A. Cisneros

For full biographical listings, see the Martindale-Hubbell Law Directory

SÍLVA, RIEDER & MAESTAS, P.C. (AV)

Albuquerque Plaza, Suite 1700, 201 3rd Street, N.W., P.O. Box 1670, 87103-1670
Telephone: 505-767-9800
Facsimile: 505-767-9807
Email: srmlaw@srmlaw.com *URL:* http://www.lawyers.com/srmlaw

Benjamin Sílva, Jr.
Geoffrey D. Rieder
Paul Maestas

Wayne R. Suggett
Christopher A. Riehl
Richard A. Allen

Representative Clients: American Contractors Insurance Group, Inc.; CIGNA; GSL Properties, Inc.; Gulf Insurance Company; Honeywell, Inc.; Hospital Services Corporation; Hubbard Broadcasting Company; Intel Corporation; John Q. Hammons, Inc.; KOB-TV, Inc.

For full biographical listings, see the Martindale-Hubbell Law Directory

WATROUS & REARDON (AV)

A Partnership of Professional Associations
3733 Eubank Boulevard, N.E., 87111-3536
Telephone: 505-293-7000
Fax: 505-293-0831

MEMBERS OF FIRM

Thomas S. Watrous (P.A.)
Walter L. Reardon, Jr., (P.A.)

Representative Clients: U.S. West, Inc.; State Street Bank and Trust Co.; Angel Fire Ski Area and Resort; Air Touch Cellular; American Linen; Rio Pecos Oil Company; First Health Plan (FHP); Albuquerque Title Co.; Furrow Building materials; Melloy Nissan.

For full biographical listings, see the Martindale-Hubbell Law Directory

*LAS CRUCES,** Dona Ana Co.

REEVES, CHAVEZ, GREENFIELD & WALKER, P.A. (AV)

300 South Water Street, P.O. Box 2769, 88004-2769
Telephone: 505-524-9617
Fax: 505-524-1954
Email: rcgw@zianet.com

B. James Reeves
Frank N. Chavez
Charlotte Greenfield
William A. Walker, Jr.
Kelly P. Albers
Joyce A. Montes
William R. Anderson
Carolyn J. Baca

Glenn D. Hall
CaraLyn Banks

For full biographical listings, see the Martindale-Hubbell Law Directory

*SANTA FE,** Santa Fe Co.

HUFFAKER & CONWAY, A PROFESSIONAL CORPORATION (AV)

155 Grant Avenue, P.O. Box 1868, 87504-1868
Telephone: 505-988-8921
Fax: 505-983-3927
Email: sfstaff@sisna.com
Albuquerque, New Mexico Office: 201 Third Street, N.W., Suite 1910.
Telephone: 505-244-0021.
Facsimile: 505-244-1372.

Gregory D. Huffaker, Jr.
Ann Maloney Conway
Lisa A. Joynes
Seth L. Sparks
Edward C. Bagley

Representative Clients: Chevron Products Co.; Federal Deposit Insurance Corp.; The St. Paul Companies; Insurance Company of the West; National Federation of the Blind.

For full biographical listings, see the Martindale-Hubbell Law Directory

JONES, SNEAD, WERTHEIM, WENTWORTH & JARAMILLO, P.A. (AV)

215 Lincoln Avenue, P.O. Box 2228, 87504-2228
Telephone: 505-982-0011
Fax: 505-989-6288

O. Russell Jones (1912-1978)
James E. Snead
Jerry Wertheim
John Wentworth
Arturo L. Jaramillo
Francis J. Mathew
Jerry Todd Wertheim
Carol A. Clifford
John V. Wertheim
Lisa N. Cassidy

General Counsel for: Bank of Santa Fe; Charter Bank for Savings, F.S.B.; National Education Association of New Mexico.
Representative Clients: Century Bank, F.S.B.; Minnesota Mining & Manufacturing Co.; Abbott Laboratories; Merchants Fast Motor Lines; Billy Walker Trucking, Inc.; 360 Communications Co.
Reference: Bank of Santa Fe.

For full biographical listings, see the Martindale-Hubbell Law Directory

WHITE, KOCH, KELLY & MCCARTHY, A PROFESSIONAL ASSOCIATION (AV)

433 Paseo De Peralta, P.O. Box 787, 87504-0787
Telephone: 505-982-4374
ABA/NET: 1154
Fax: 505-982-0350; 984-8631
Email: WKKM@NM.NET

John F. McCarthy, Jr.
Benjamin J. Phillips
David F. Cunningham
Albert V. Gonzales
Kevin V. Reilly
M. Karen Kilgore
Aaron J. Wolf
Mary E. Walta
Rebecca A. Dempsey

Suzanne C. Odom (Not admitted in NM)

Representative Clients: Public Service Company of New Mexico; Northern Trust Bank of Texas; Hagood New Mexico Trust; Rockwell; Johnson & Johnson; Fahnestock & Co., Inc.

For Complete List of Firm Personnel, See General Section

For full biographical listings, see the Martindale-Hubbell Law Directory

NEW YORK

*ALBANY,** Albany Co.

FEATHERSTONHAUGH, CONWAY, WILEY & CLYNE, L.L.P. (AV)

99 Pine Street, Suite 207, 12207
Telephone: 518-436-0786
Fax: 518-427-0452
URL: http://www.fcwc-law.com

MEMBERS OF FIRM

James D. Featherstonhaugh, Stephen J. Wiley, Thomas A. Conway, Elizabeth K. Clyne

ASSOCIATES

Nadine Feiden Shadlock, William F. Conway, IV, Denis R. Hurley, Jr., Gerard L. Conway, Jr., Andrew W. Kirby, Steven M. Connolly

OF COUNSEL

William F. Conway, David Weinraub, Jeffrey J. Conklin, Randall J. Ezick

LEGAL SUPPORT PERSONNEL

GOVERNMENTAL RELATIONS

John L. Hardy, John P. Griffin, Daniel G. Plummer, David F. Fleming

For full biographical listings, see the Martindale-Hubbell Law Directory

HARVEY AND MUMFORD (AV)

20 Corporate Woods Boulevard, 12211-2396
Telephone: 518-463-4491
Telecopier: 518-463-5665
Email: thefirm@harveyandmumford.com

Arthur J. Harvey (1903-1986)

MEMBERS OF FIRM

Jonathan P. Harvey, Brian F. Mumford

ASSOCIATES

Eva Lynn M. Hayko, Peter Baird Joslin, Jr., Karen Hendricks, Trudy L. Boulia, Keith J. Starlin

OF COUNSEL

Jack D. Harvey

For full biographical listings, see the Martindale-Hubbell Law Directory

ISEMAN, CUNNINGHAM, RIESTER & HYDE, LLP (AV)

9 Thurlow Terrace, 12203
Telephone: 518-462-3000
Telecopier: 518-462-4199
Email: lawfirm@icrh.com *URL:* http://www.icrh.com
Canandaigua, New York Office: 37 East Gibson Street, P.O. Box 179, 14424.
Telephone: 716-394-1450.
Fax: 716-394-5121.

MEMBERS OF FIRM

Frederick C. Riester, Robert Hall Iseman, Michael J. Cunningham, Carol Ann Hyde, Linda J. Clark

Brian M. Culnan, Valerie R. Lape Handy, Kihyun S. Kim, Marcia B. Smith, Richard A. Frankel, Ellen Gillerman Cox, Stephanie E. Moriarty, Jennifer A. Grego, Cara E. Johnson

OF COUNSEL

Michael J. McNeil, Deborah A. Kirby

For full biographical listings, see the Martindale-Hubbell Law Directory

McCLUNG, PETERS AND SIMON (AV)

41 State Street, Suite 700, 12207
Telephone: 518-462-7481 Toll Free 1-800-777-7481
Telecopier: 518-462-0112
Email: McClunglaw@aol.com

MEMBERS OF FIRM

Benjamin McClung (1867-1940), Joseph B. Carr, George M. Simon (1909-1981), John W. Scott, Homer E. Peters (1905-1992), Stephen M. Kerwin, Lynda S. Battiste

ASSOCIATES

Marshall A. Courtney, Patrick H. Cartwright

(See Next Column)

OF COUNSEL

Stephen J. Arlington, Lawrence E. Becker, David N. Goldin

Representative Clients: Aetna Casualty & Surety Co.; Chemical Bank; Continental Insurance Cos.; Firemen's Insurance Co.; Hartford Insurance Co.; Underwriter's Adjusting Co.

For full biographical listings, see the Martindale-Hubbell Law Directory

O'CONNOR, O'CONNOR, MAYBERGER & FIRST, P.C. (AV)

20 Corporate Woods Boulevard, 12211-0400
Telephone: 518-465-0400
Facsimile: 518-465-0015
Email: info@1stlaw.com *URL:* http://www.1stlaw.com

Michael J. O'Connor, Dennis A. First, Terence P. O'Connor, Michele M. Monserrate, Dianne Bresee Mayberger, Cynthia Ann Platt

Justin O. Corcoran, Eugene N. Sarfoh, Michael P. Cavanagh, Francis J. Brennan, Christopher D. Drake, Colleen D. Galligan

For full biographical listings, see the Martindale-Hubbell Law Directory

SHANLEY, SWEENEY, REILLY & ALLEN, P.C. (AV)

The Castle at Ten Thurlow Terrace, 12203
Telephone: 518-463-1415
Fax: 518-463-3210
Email: lawyers@shanleysweeney.com *URL:* http://www.shanleysweeney.com

Michael P. Shanley, Jr., Steven S. Heyman, Robert L. Sweeney, Scott P. Olson, J. Stephen Reilly, David C. Kuracina, John L. Allen, Thomas A. Shepardson, Gregory D. Faucher, Melissa M. Beskid, J. Michael Naughton, Mark T. Sweeney

Christopher E. Buckey, Stacey Weisenfeld

For full biographical listings, see the Martindale-Hubbell Law Directory

*BATH,** Steuben Co.

COLE LAW OFFICES, P.C. (AV)

7 East Steuben Street, P.O. Box 232, 14810
Telephone: 607-776-3306
Fax: 607-776-4189
Email: RCole@LinkNY.Com
Hammondsport, New York Office: Railroad Station Depot, Water Street, P.O. Box 396, 14840.
Telephone: 607-569-2213.
Fax: 607-569-2214.

Robert H. Cole

Christine Valkenburgh, James H. Burns, William H. Reed

General Counsel for: Bath National Bank; Mercury Aircraft, Inc.
Local Counsel for: Equitable Life Assurance Society of the United States.
Reference: Bath National Bank.

For full biographical listings, see the Martindale-Hubbell Law Directory

*BUFFALO,** Erie Co.

BROWN & KELLY, L.L.P. (AV)

1500 Liberty Building, 14202-3663
Telephone: 716-854-2620
Fax: 716-854-0082
Email: mail@brownkelly.com *URL:* http://www.brownkelly.com

MEMBERS OF FIRM

Thomas J. Kelly, Andrew D. Merrick, Rodney O. Personius, William P. Wiles, Frederick D. Turner, William D. Harrington, Paul Michael Hassett, Joseph M. Schnitter, Peter E. Klaasesz, Paula L. Feroleto, Donald B. Eppers, Daniel J. Marren, Lisa T. Sofferin

OF COUNSEL

Ogden R. Brown, Roland R. Benzow, Charles F. Harrington, Philip B. Abramowitz, James T. Duggan, Elizabeth R. O'Connor, Karen Cook Serotte, Catherine E. Marra

ASSOCIATES

David S. Zygaj, David O. Teach, Olney H. Clowe, Patricia S. Ciccarelli, Brian M. Melber, Susan J. Schmidt

For full biographical listings, see the Martindale-Hubbell Law Directory

Buffalo—Continued

DAMON & MOREY LLP (AV)

(Formerly Damon, Morey, Sawyer & Moot)
1000 Cathedral Place, 298 Main Street, 14202-4096
Telephone: 716-856-5500
Facsimile: 716-856-5510
Email: apinder@damonmorey.com *URL:* http://www.damonmorey.com
Rochester, New York Office: Powers Building, Suite 507, 16 West Main Street, 14614.
Telephone: 716-232-3640.
Fax: 716-232-8448.

MEMBERS OF FIRM

Mason O. Damon (1905-1983)
Robert J. Plache
James N. Schmit
Christopher T. Greene
Franklin W. Heller
Gregory C. Yungbluth
James W. Gormley
James M. Mucklewee
Melinda G. Disare
Robert J. Portin
Joseph J. Schoellkopf, Jr.
William F. Savino
Thomas J. Drury
Patrick B. Curran
Peter S. Marlette
Vincent J. Moore
Gust P. Pullman
Barbara L. Schifeling
Michael J. Willett
Carol Guck Snider
Joseph W. Dunbar
Kenneth W. Africano
Julie M. Bargnesi
Arthur A. Marrapese III (Resident, Rochester Office)
Sharyn G. Rogers
Daniel F. Brown
David L. Edmunds, Jr.
Charles S. Carra
Hedwig Maria Auletta
Marylou K. Roshia
Maryjo C. Falcone
Charles E. Telford, III
Timothy C. Cashmore
Anthony L. Eugeni
Amy Archer Flaherty
Kathleen M. Reilly
Steven I. Rubinstein
Diane C. Zarlock

ASSOCIATES

Brian Alan Birenbach
Daniel T. Cavarello
Michelle A. Crew
Anne C. Evans
Michael Thomas Feeley
Judy S. Hernandez
David S. Kelly
Joseph J. Manna
Rosalie A. Melisz
Mary C. Raymond
Vincent George Saccomando
Allison Fields Stravino
Kellie Muffoletto Ulrich

OF COUNSEL

Joseph H. Morey, Jr.

SPECIAL COUNSEL

Richard E. Moot
George F. Gabel, Jr.
G. Steven Pigeon
Susan A. Benz
Edward Yankelunas

Counsel For: Advanced Refractory Technologies; Catholic Health East; D.A. Elia Construction Corporation; Kaleida Health; Town of Cheektowaga; Bagel Brothers Amherst, Inc.; Burt Rigid Box, Inc.; Lake Shore Health Care Center; County of Cattaraugus; Commonwealth Land Title Insurance; Diocese of Buffalo; Baker Victory Services; Niagara Lutheran Home and Rehabilitation, Inc.; Sheehan Memorial Hospital; Robert James Sales, Inc.; Olean General Hospital; Wendt Corporation; Aria Wireless Systems, Inc.; Buffalo Sewer Authority; City of Tonawanda; Roswell Park Cancer Institute; Ivoclar North America, Inc.; Olean Medical Group; Cold Spring Construction Company; Buffalo Municipal Housing Authority.
Local Counsel For: Healthcare Underwriters Mutual Insurance Company; AIG Companies; Owens-Corning Fiberglas; Unigard Insurance Group; Key Tronic Corporation; Medical Liability Insurance; Risk Enterprise Management Limited; Wintherthur International; Hanover Insurance Company; National Casualty Company; Marine Midland Mortgage Corporation; Acordia Resort Services; Medical Malpractice Insurance Association; OUM & Associates; Ohio Casualty Company; PACCAR, Inc.; Frontier Insurance Company; The Limited, Inc.; Zurich-American Insurance Group; Allstate Insurance Company; Universal Studios, Inc.

For full biographical listings, see the Martindale-Hubbell Law Directory

GRESENS & GILLEN LLP (AV)

510 Fleet Building, 12 Fountain Plaza, 14202-2292
Telephone: 716-842-1600
Fax: 716-842-6161
Email: greslaw@pcom.net *URL:* http://www.greslaw.com

James W. Gresens
Patricia Gillen

Andrew B. Isenberg
Peter L. Powers

For full biographical listings, see the Martindale-Hubbell Law Directory

STENGER & FINNERTY (AV)

1800 Main Place Tower, 14202
Telephone: 716-849-1700
Fax: 716-849-1717
Email: stenfinn@stenfinn.com *URL:* http://www.stenfinn.com

John H. Stenger
Joseph M. Finnerty

(See Next Column)

ASSOCIATES

Mitchell M. Stenger
David E. Gutowski

For full biographical listings, see the Martindale-Hubbell Law Directory

SULLIVAN & OLIVERIO (AV)

600 Main Place Tower, 14202-3706
Telephone: 716-854-5300
Telecopier: 716-854-5299
Email: sulliolaw@aol.com

MEMBERS OF FIRM

Richard T. Sullivan
B. P. Oliverio
Bruce W. Hoover

Thomas M. Moll
Michael E. Appelbaum
Kevin M. Carter

OF COUNSEL

Paul D. Pearson

For full biographical listings, see the Martindale-Hubbell Law Directory

ZDARSKY, SAWICKI & AGOSTINELLI (AV)

404 Cathedral Place, 298 Main Street, 14202
Telephone: 716-855-3200
Telecopier: 716-855-3101
Email: zsagtw@buffnet.net

MEMBERS OF FIRM

Joseph E. Zdarsky
K. Michael Sawicki
Guy J. Agostinelli
Gerald T. Walsh
Mark J. Schlant

ASSOCIATES

Patrick A. Dudley
John A. Moscati, Jr.

Reference: Marine Midland Bank, N.A.

For full biographical listings, see the Martindale-Hubbell Law Directory

GARDEN CITY, Nassau Co.

MORITT, HOCK & HAMROFF, LLP (AV)

400 Garden City Plaza, Suite 202, 11530
Telephone: 516-873-2000
Fax: 516-873-2010
Email: lawyers@mhhlaw.com *URL:* http://www.mhhlaw.com

PARTNERS

Neil J. Moritt
Alan S. Hock
Marc L. Hamroff
David H. Cohen
Robert M. Tils
Gary C. Hisiger

ASSOCIATES

William P. Laino
Robert S. Cohen
Terese L. Arenth
Leslie A. Berkoff
Michael S. Re
David A. Loglisci
David Z. Ottensoser
Ellen R. Leibowitz
Amy J. Zamir
Michael Cardello, III
Gary E. Ostroff

For full biographical listings, see the Martindale-Hubbell Law Directory

TRYON & ASSOCIATES, P.C. (AV)

1325 Franklin Avenue, Suite 325, P.O. Box 8022, 11530
Telephone: 516-746-3400
Fax: 516-746-5756
URL: http://www.lawyers.com/tryon&associates

Michael D. Tryon

Susan Marie Pascale

For full biographical listings, see the Martindale-Hubbell Law Directory

HAUPPAUGE, Suffolk Co.

LAW OFFICES OF HARVEY B. BESUNDER (AV)

The Woodlands, 700 Veterans Memorial Highway, Suite 310, 11788
Telephone: 516-361-5131
Fax: 516-361-5134

For full biographical listings, see the Martindale-Hubbell Law Directory

ERIC H. HOLTZMAN (AV)

330 Vanderbilt Motor Parkway, P.O. Box 11005, 11788-0903
Telephone: 631-435-8800
Fax: 631-435-8832

Richard E. Trachtenberg
David H. Eisenberg

Reference: European-American Bank & Trust Co.

For full biographical listings, see the Martindale-Hubbell Law Directory

ISLANDIA, Suffolk Co.

LAW OFFICES OF ANDREW D. PRESBERG, P.C. (AV)

100 Corporate Plaza, 11722
Telephone: 516-232-4444
Fax: 516-232-2603
Email: preslaw@erols.com *URL:* http://www.presberg.com

Andrew D. Presberg

For full biographical listings, see the Martindale-Hubbell Law Directory

JERICHO, Nassau Co.

MARTIN, VAN DE WALLE, DONOHUE, MCGAHAN, CATALANO & FAIRGRIEVE (AV)

555 North Broadway, P.O. Box 350, 11753
Telephone: 516-681-3100
Telecopier: 516-681-5357

MEMBERS OF FIRM

Jules Martin (1928-1995)
Charles R. Van de Walle
Joseph A. Guarino (1946-1991)
Nicholas J. Donohue
James M. McGahan
Thomas C. Catalano, Jr.
Scott Fairgrieve
Michael Belitsis

ASSOCIATES

Randi M. Seidner
Laurie Ann Corallo

Representative Clients: Fidelity National Title Insurance Company of New York; Bancker Construction Corp.; Biener Pontiac-Nissan, Inc.; Festo Corp.; First Investors Corp.; First Financial Savings Bank, S.L.A.; Chaminade High School; Oppenheimer Funds, Inc.; Old Republic National Title Insurance Company; New York State Land Title Association, Inc.; Chase Manhatten Mortgage Corp.; First Investors Corp.; Leaseway Transportation Corp.; Jones Fund; Northeast Adjustment Co., Inc.; Capital Trading Corp.; Leo and Arnstein Agency; Chase Manhattan Bank, N.A.; Long Island Community Newspapers.

For full biographical listings, see the Martindale-Hubbell Law Directory

MELVILLE, Suffolk Co.

CAHN WISHOD & KNAUER, LLP (AV)

425 Broadhollow Road Suite 315, 11747
Telephone: 631-752-1600
Fax: 631-752-1555
URL: http://www.cahnwishod.com
URL: http://www.lawyers.com/cahnwishod&knauer

MEMBERS OF FIRM

Richard C. Cahn
Eugene L. Wishod
Todd A. Knauer

ASSOCIATES

Brian T. Egan
Patricia A. Rooney

LEGAL SUPPORT PERSONNEL

Susan M. Stonelli (Paralegal)

For full biographical listings, see the Martindale-Hubbell Law Directory

*MINEOLA,** Nassau Co.

GUTMAN & GUTMAN LLP (AV)

Gutman Building, 19 Roslyn Road, 11501-4521
Telephone: 516-248-0470
Telecopier: 516-746-6997
Email: aegutman@aol.com *URL:* http://www.lawyers.com/gutman,gutman&gutman

MEMBERS OF FIRM

Lawrence C. Gutman
Elizabeth A. Gutman
Andrew E. Gutman

References: United Mercantile Agencies, Inc.; Commercial Law League of America, CST Co. Inc.; Fleet Bank; Kohner Mann, and Kailas.

For full biographical listings, see the Martindale-Hubbell Law Directory

*NEW YORK,** New York Co.

BEATIE AND OSBORN LLP (AV)

599 Lexington Avenue, 42nd Floor, 10022
Telephone: 212-888-9000
Fax: 212-888-9664
Email: bandolaw@aol.com *URL:* http://www.bandolaw@aol.com

Russel H. Beatie, Jr.
Daniel A. Osborn

ASSOCIATES

Curt D. Marshall
Eduard Korsinsky

OF COUNSEL

Richard M. Cummings

For full biographical listings, see the Martindale-Hubbell Law Directory

CARB, LURIA, COOK & KUFELD, LLP (AV)

521 Fifth Avenue, 10175
Telephone: 212-986-3131
Telecopier: 212-682-2682
Email: mail@carbluria.com *URL:* http://www.carbluria.com

MEMBERS OF FIRM

Alfred B. Carb (1902-1963)
George Cook, III (1915-1994)
William M. Kufeld (1922-1998)
Stephen A. Carb
Daniel Scheyer
Geoffrey P. Picket
Leonard H. Carter
Stephen J. Fallis
M. William Scherer
Linda T. Newman
Edwin A. Novak
Carol Wallis Duffy
James E. Schwartz
Kenneth Richter

ASSOCIATES

Jonathan K. Bright
Janet M. Joyce
Jay A. Lang
Peter L. Lese
Andrew G. Lipkin
David L. Paldy
Jeffrey A. Samuels

COUNSEL

Sydney A. Luria
Gerald J. Robinson

SPECIAL COUNSEL

David K. Ford

For full biographical listings, see the Martindale-Hubbell Law Directory

COLUCCI & UMANS (AV)

Manhattan Tower, 101 East 52nd Street, 10022
Telephone: 212-935-5700
Facsimile: 212-935-5728
Telex: 661503 WUI
Email: emial@colucci-umans.com
Westchester County, Scarsdale, New York Office: 670 White Plains Road, Scarsdale.
Telephone: 914-472-1500.
Facsimile: 914-472-1551.

MEMBERS OF FIRM

Frank J. Colucci
Courtney Wilson Monahan

Thomas A. Kain
Raymond J. Glynn
W. Brant Mossop
Susan B. Jacobson
Gregory J. Colucci (Resident, Scarsdale Office)
Richard P. Jacobson
David M. Dahan
Katherine Beecher Carlburg
Kathleen M. McGann
Renée L. Duff (Resident, Scarsdale Office)

OF COUNSEL

Angelo Notaro

For full biographical listings, see the Martindale-Hubbell Law Directory

EMERY CUTI BRINCKERHOFF & ABADY PC (AV)

545 Madison Avenue, 3rd Floor, 10022-4219
Telephone: 212-763-5000
Facsimile: 212-763-5001
Email: mail@ecbalaw.com *URL:* http://www.ecbalaw.com

Richard D. Emery
Matthew D. Brinckerhoff
Jonathan S. Abady
John R. Cuti

Ilann M. Maazel
David H. Gans
Alexandra D. Lahav (Not admitted in NY)

For full biographical listings, see the Martindale-Hubbell Law Directory

FABRICANT & YESKOO, LLP (AV)

535 Fifth Avenue, 10017
Telephone: 212-983-0900
Telecopier: 212-983-0907
Hoboken, New Jersey Office: Hudson Legal Center, 86 Hudson Street.
Telephone: 201-420-8650.

Alfred R. Fabricant
Richard C. Yeskoo

Thomas T. Tamlyn, Jr.
Elénee Argentinis

For full biographical listings, see the Martindale-Hubbell Law Directory

FINKEL GOLDSTEIN BERZOW ROSENBLOOM & NASH, LLP (AV)

26 Broadway, 10004
Telephone: 212-344-2929
Telecopier: 212-422-6836
Email: finkgold@aol.com

MEMBERS OF FIRM

Benjamin Finkel (1905-1986)
Harvey L. Goldstein
Harold S. Berzow
Neal M. Rosenbloom
Kevin J. Nash

(See Next Column)

FINKEL GOLDSTEIN BERZOW ROSENBLOOM & NASH LLP, *New York—Continued*

ASSOCIATES

Arthur A. Hirschler
Charles Fischer
David J. Ciminesi

For full biographical listings, see the Martindale-Hubbell Law Directory

FISHBACH, HERTAN & IVES (AV)

767 Third Avenue, 10017
Telephone: 212-752-4433

MEMBERS OF FIRM

Myron Fishbach
Ira J. Hertan (1931-1988)
Garrison Ives

For full biographical listings, see the Martindale-Hubbell Law Directory

FISHER, FISHER & BERGER (AV)

A Partnership including a Professional Corporation
One Whitehall Street, 10004
Telephone: 212-514-8888
Fax: 212-514-9016
Email: fisherberger@earthlink.net

Andrew S. Fisher, P.C.
Henry T. Berger

ASSOCIATES

Melinda H. Vollmer
Eric L. Cooper
Diane C. Lorenc

OF COUNSEL

Harold L. Fisher
Judith E. Held
Gerald A. Resnick
Robert A. Straniere
Stanley Kalmon Schlein
Laurence J. Kaiser

Reference: The Chase Manhattan Bank, N.A.

For full biographical listings, see the Martindale-Hubbell Law Directory

FRIEDMAN KAPLAN & SEILER LLP (AV)

875 Third Avenue, 10022-6225
Telephone: 212-833-1100
Facsimile: 212-355-6401
Email: info@fkslaw.com
Newark, New Jersey Office: One Gateway Center, 25th Floor, 07102-5311.
Telephone: 973-297-4700.
Facsimile: 973-297-4701.

MEMBERS OF FIRM

Bruce S. Kaplan
Edward A. Friedman
Barry A. Adelman
Eric Seiler
Robert D. Kaplan
Gary D. Friedman
Andrew W. Goldwater
Robert J. Lack
Gregg S. Lerner
Hal Neier
Philippe Adler
Matthew S. Haiken
Paul J. Fishman
Richard M. Hoffman
Lance J. Gotko

COUNSEL

Robert D. Wurwarg
Ira A. Freedman

ASSOCIATES

Craig J. Codlin
Michael B. Dorff
Andrew R. Greengrass
Ellen A. Harnick
Sophia S. Hartch
Mishell B. Kneeland
Robert S. Loigman
Craig Nemiroff
Joshua M. Olshin
Katherine L. Pringle
Daniel B. Rapport
Meryl S. Rosenblatt
Robert C. Scherer
Donna Segal
Jonathan M. Silver
Lee D. Sossen
David I. Tanenbaum
Marla J. Wasserman
Sian E. Zelbo

For full biographical listings, see the Martindale-Hubbell Law Directory

FROMME SCHWARTZ NEWMAN & CORNICELLO, LLP (AV)

The Woolworth Building, 233 Broadway, Suite 2702, 10279-2799
Telephone: 212-267-8100
Fax: 212-406-2222
Email: attorneys@fsnc.com *URL:* http://www.fsnc.com

Martin D. Newman
Peter A. Schwartz
Anthony J. Cornicello
Eric F. Fromme
Paul F. Peragine

ASSOCIATES

Robert David Werth
David Tendler
Charlotte G. Anderson-Bedford
John Pizzano

COUNSEL

Michael B. Rosenblatt

For full biographical listings, see the Martindale-Hubbell Law Directory

GETNICK & GETNICK (AV)

Tower 49, 12 East 49th Street, 31st Floor, 10017-1028
Telephone: 212-376-5666
Telefax: 212-292-3942
Email: info@getnicklaw.com *URL:* http://www.lawyers.com/getnick&getnick

MEMBERS OF FIRM

Irving M. Getnick
Neil V. Getnick
Lesley Ann Skillen
Margaret J. Finerty

OF COUNSEL

David A. Koenigsberg
Michael E. Getnick

ASSOCIATE

Richard J. Dircks

For full biographical listings, see the Martindale-Hubbell Law Directory

GOLDSTEIN & MORRIS, LLP (AV)

570 Lexington Avenue, 34th Floor, 10022
Telephone: 212-605-0918
Fax: 212-605-0919

Mark L. Goldstein
Francine J. Morris

ASSOCIATE

Andrea H. Stempel

For full biographical listings, see the Martindale-Hubbell Law Directory

GRATCH JACOBS & BROZMAN, P.C. (AV)

950 Third Avenue, 10022
Telephone: 212-935-2560
Telecopier: (212) 319-0856

Ariel Gratch
Alan S. Jacobs
Andrew P. Brozman
Stephen Wagner
Andrew D. Feiner
Jennifer C. DeMarco

Holly S. Falkowitz
Nicholas H. Laduzinski
Robert J. McDermott, Jr.
Thomas M. Rao
Mitchell B. Reiter

For full biographical listings, see the Martindale-Hubbell Law Directory

GARY J. GREENBERG (AV)

Suite 906, 12 West 57th Street, 10019
Telephone: 212-246-1222
Fax: 212-265-5379
Email: garyjgreenberg@mginewyork.com

ASSOCIATE

Claudia Beth Gross

For full biographical listings, see the Martindale-Hubbell Law Directory

HOFFINGER FRIEDLAND DOBRISH & STERN, P.C. (AV)

A Professional Corporation including Professional Corporations
110 East 59th Street, 10022-1392
Telephone: 212-421-4000
Telecopier: 212-223-3857

Jack S. Hoffinger
Lawrence N. Friedland
Robert Z. Dobrish (P.C.)
Stephen R. Stern (P.C.)
Samuel P. Ross
Warren R. Gleicher
Philip S. Ross

Michael J. Sherman
Fran Hoffinger
John H. Friedland
Lydia A. Milone
Devorah S. Weinschneider
Eric I. Wrubel
Nina S. Gross
Scott Lawrence D'Aloise

For full biographical listings, see the Martindale-Hubbell Law Directory

KITTAY, GOLD & GERSHFELD, P.C. (AV)

One Exchange Plaza, Suite 1600, 55 Broadway, 10006
Telephone: 212-768-9500
Email: kittaygoldgershfeld@yahoo.com
White Plains, New York Office: 81 Main Street.
Telephone: 914-686-1900.

David R. Kittay
Barry S. Gold
Michelle Gershfeld

Michael E. Peeples
Judith L. Siegel

For full biographical listings, see the Martindale-Hubbell Law Directory

KOSTELANETZ & FINK, LLP (AV)

530 Fifth Avenue, 22nd Floor, 10036
Telephone: 212-808-8100
Fax: 212-808-8108
Email: mail@kostelanetzfink.com

(See Next Column)

KOSTELANETZ & FINK LLP—*Continued*

SENIOR COUNSEL

Boris Kostelanetz

MEMBERS OF FIRM

Robert S. Fink
Kevin M. Flynn
Bryan C. Skarlatos

COUNSEL

Norman Sinrich
Theodore F. Dickson
Caroline Rule
Brian C. Wille
William F. Cuozzi, III
Dawn Ngo

For full biographical listings, see the Martindale-Hubbell Law Directory

LANKLER SIFFERT & WOHL LLP (AV)

33rd Floor, 500 Fifth Avenue, 10110-3398
Telephone: 212-921-8399
Telefax: 212-764-3701
Telex: 4939413 LSWU1
URL: http://www.LSWLAW.com

MEMBERS OF FIRM

Jess Fardella
Helen Gredd
Roderick C. Lankler
John Sand Siffert
Charles T. Spada
Frank H. Wohl

OF COUNSEL

Susan L. Sommer
Peter Herbert

Lisa A. Baroni
Brett S. Deutsch
Brian Fleischer (Not admitted in NY)
Rebecca E. Hollander-Blumoff
Sara Lesch
Ghillaine A Reid
Daniel E. Reynolds
Laura H. Stasior

For full biographical listings, see the Martindale-Hubbell Law Directory

MILBANK, TWEED, HADLEY & McCLOY LLP (AV)

1 Chase Manhattan Plaza, 10005-1413
Telephone: 212-530-5000
Fax: 212-530-5219
Email: postmaster@milbank.com *URL:* http://www.milbank.com
Midtown Office: 375 Park Avenue, Suite 3601, 10152.
Telephone: 212-530-5800.
Fax: 212-530-0158.
Los Angeles, California Office: 601 South Figueroa Street, 30th Floor, 90017.
Telephone: 213-892-4000.
Fax: 213-629-5063.
Washington, D.C. Office: International Square Building, Suite 1100, 1825 Eye Street, N.W., 20006.
Telephone: 202-835-7500.
Fax: 202-835-7586.
Tokyo, Japan Office: Fukoku Seimei Building, 2-2, Uchisaiwai-cho 2-Chome, Chiyoda-ku, Tokyo 100-0011, Japan.
Telephone: 011-81-3-3504-1050.
Fax: 011-81-3-3595-2790, 011-81-3-3595-2840.
London, England Office: Dashwood House, 69 Old Broad Street, London EC2M 1QS.
Telephone: 011-44-207-448-3000.
Fax: 011-44-207-448-3029.
Hong Kong Office: 3007 Alexandra House, 16 Chater Road.
Telephone: 011-852-2971-4888.
Fax: 011-852-2840-0792; 011-852-2845-9046.
Singapore Office: 14-00 Caltex House, 30 Raffles Place, 048622.
Telephone: 011-65-428-2400.
Fax: 011-65-428-2500.
Moscow, Russia Office: 24/27 Sadovaya-Samotyochnya, Moscow, 103051.
Telephone: 011-7-501-258-5015.
Fax: 011-7-501-258-5014.

MEMBERS OF FIRM

Parker H. Bagley
Jeffrey Barist
Devan D. Beck (Resident, Los Angeles, California Office)
Russell E. Brooks
Christopher E. Chalsen
Linda Dakin-Grimm (Resident, Los Angeles, California Office)
Scott A. Edelman
David R. Gelfand
Joseph S. Genova
Michael L. Hirschfeld
C. Stephen Howard (Resident, Los Angeles, California Office)
Toni C. Lichstein
Michael D. Nolan
Andrew E. Tomback
Richard C. Tufaro (Resident, Washington, D.C. Office)
William H. Webster (Resident, Washington, D.C. Office)

OF COUNSEL

Jane L. Hanson
Fred W. Reinke (Resident, Washington, D.C. Office)

SENIOR ATTORNEY

Charles W. Westland

(See Next Column)

ASSOCIATES

Sally Agel (Resident, Los Angeles, California Office)
Thomas A. Arena
John C. Ashby (Resident, Los Angeles, California Office)
Aaron J. Benjamin (Not admitted in NY; Not admitted in United States) (Legal Consultant)
Sabina Bhalla (Resident, Los Angeles, California Office)
Richard M. Campo
Keri A. Christ
David S. Cohen (Resident, Washington, D.C. Office)
Douglas N. Cohen
Hillary S. DeNigro (Resident, Washington, D.C. Office)
Anne K. DeSimone
Uttam Dhillon (Resident, Los Angeles, California Office)
Mitchell E. Epner
Seth D. Garland (Resident, Washington, D.C. Office)
Teresa A. Gonsalves
Chandra L. Gooding (Resident, Los Angeles, California Office)
John M. Griem, Jr.
Brian D. Hail
Douglas W. Henkin
David H. Hwang
Kelly S. Kibbie
James R. Klaiber
Duncan J. Logan
William Jackson Matney, Jr. (Resident, Washington, D.C. Office)
Aline Matta
Alison Naidech
Fred Neufeld (Resident, Los Angeles, California Office)
Elizabeth Noyes
Janice Payne
David A. Pawlak
Lara M. Posner
Stacey J. Rappaport
Felice Roggen (Resident, Washington, D.C. Office)
Richard E. Rosberger
Nicholas Smithberg
William R. Spiegelberger
Allana F. Stark
Roland K. Tellis (Resident, Los Angeles, California Office)
M. Benjamin Valerio (Resident, Los Angeles, California Office)
Tedd W. VanBuskirk
Scott Vick (Resident, Los Angeles, California Office)
Timothy P. Wei
Mathew B. West

For Complete List of Firm Personnel, See General Section

For full biographical listings, see the Martindale-Hubbell Law Directory

MOUND, COTTON & WOLLAN (AV)

One Battery Park Plaza, 10004
Telephone: 212-804-4200
Facsimile: 212-344-8066
San Francisco, California Office: 1700 California Street, Suite 470.
Telephone: 415-434-4301.
Telecopier: 415-434-4303.
London, England Office: Longbow House, 14-20 Chiswell Street.
Telephone: 0071-638-3688.
Newark, New Jersey Office: The Legal Center, One Riverfront Plaza, 8th Floor, 07102-5497.
Telephone: 973-242-2050.
Telecopier: 973-242-4244.

Arthur N. Brook (1933-1997)
Bert Cotton (1911-1981)
Maurice Mound (1907-1994)
Ernest E. Rosenberg (1924-1983)

MEMBERS OF FIRM

Stuart Cotton
Jeffrey C. Crawford
Leonard S. Dome
Wayne R. Glaubinger
Michael H. Goldstein
Lawrence S. Greengrass
Lloyd A. Gura
Bruce R. Kaliner
Michael R. Koblenz
Daniel Markewich
John C. Mezzacappa
Frederic R. Mindlin
Francis A. Montbach
David A. Silva
Philip C. Silverberg
Costantino P. Suriano
James D. Veach
Jeffrey S. Weinstein

COUNSEL

Eugene A. Leiman
Eugene Wollan

RESIDENT OF COUNSEL
SAN FRANCISCO, CALIFORNIA OFFICE

Anna Maria Martin (Not admitted in NY)
Joseph M. Rimac, Jr. (Not admitted in NY)

RESIDENT MEMBER
NEWARK, NEW JERSEY OFFICE

William D. Wilson

ASSOCIATES

Michael Altman
Emilie L. Bakal
Todd A. Bakal
Kevin F. Buckley
Doreen A. Cronin
Frank J. DeAngelis
Alyssa DeSimone
Lauren G. Dome
Douglas K. Eisenstein
Maria Fazzolari
Joseph W. Ferraro
Aaron F. Fishbein
Elisa T. Gilbert
Diana E. Goldberg
Hilary M. Henkind
Mark S. Katz
David W. Kenna
David S. Mahaffey
Mark D. Marino
Catherine F. Megret
Mitchell D. Otto
Albert J. Pinzon
Renee M. Plessner
Jon Quint
Ronnie A. Rifkin
Mark J. Weber
Christina M. Wood

For Complete List of Firm Personnel, See General Section

For full biographical listings, see the Martindale-Hubbell Law Directory

New York—Continued

NEIMAN GINSBURG & MAIRANZ P.C. (AV)

39 Broadway, 25th Floor, 10006-3003
Telephone: 212-269-1000
Telecopier: 212-635-9302
Email: ngmpc@concentric.net *URL:* http://www.ngmpc.com

Marvin Neiman
Theodore T. Mairanz
Gary Ginsburg

Betsy R. Malik
Susie Chovev

For full biographical listings, see the Martindale-Hubbell Law Directory

OPPENHEIMER WOLFF & DONNELLY LLP (AV)

The Chrysler East Building 19th Floor, 666 Third Avenue, 10017
Telephone: 212-826-5000
FAX: 212-486-0708
URL: http://www.oppenheimer.com
Minneapolis, Minnesota Office: 3300 Plaza VII, 45 South Seventh Street. 55402.
Telephone: 612-607-7000.
FAX: 612-607-7100.
Amsterdam, The Netherlands Office: Keizergracht 241.
Telephone: 31-20-423-4555.
FAX: 312-20-423-4545.
Brussels, Belgium Office: Avenue Louise 240, Box 5, 1050.
Telephone: 32-2-626-0500.
FAX: 32-2-626-0510.
Geneva, Switzerland Office: Rue Gabriel Eynard, 6, 1205.
Telephone: (41/22) 311-7410.
FAX: (41/22) 311-4707.
Newport Beach, California Office: 500 Newport Center Drive, Suite 700, 92660.
Telephone: 949-823-6000.
FAX: 949-823-6100.
Paris, France Office: 35 Boulevard des Capucines, 75002.
Telephone: (33/1) 53 45 40 00.
FAX: (33/1) 53 45 40 10.
St. Paul, Minnesota Office: 1700 First National Bank Building, 55101.
Telephone: 651-605-2000.
FAX: 651-605-2100.
Washington, D.C. Office: Oppenheimer Wolff Donnelly & Bayh LLP, 1350 Eye Street, N.W., Suite 200, 20005.
Telephone: 202-312-8000.
FAX: 202-312-8100.
Los Angeles, California Office: 2029 Century Park East, 38th Floor, 90067.
Telephone: 310-788-5000.
FAX: 310-277-1297.
Palo Alto, California Office: 3373 Hillview Avenue, Suite 200, 94304.
Telephone: 650-320-4000.
FAX: 650-320-4100.
Chicago, Illinois Office: Oppenheimer Wolff & Donnelly (Illinois), Two Prudential Plaza, 45th Floor, 180 North Stetson Avenue, 60601.
Telephone: 312-616-1800.
Fax: 312-616-5800.

RESIDENT PARTNERS

Joseph J. Vicinanza (Resident Managing Partner)
P. Jay Wilker
Lance Gotthoffer
Herbert C. Ross, Jr.
Ted G. Semaya
Christopher W. Jones
Robert J. Tracy
Thomas M. Gandolfo
Ronald S. Beacher

RESIDENT ASSOCIATES

Ranfi R. Rivera
Edward K. Lenci
Constantine Karides
Ronald J. Kaniuk
Nicholas A. Ritrivi
Robert M. Hirsh

For full biographical listings, see the Martindale-Hubbell Law Directory

PILIERO GOLDSTEIN JENKINS & SULLIVAN, LLP (AV)

292 Madison Avenue, 10017
Telephone: 212-213-8200
Fax: 212-685-2028
Email: lawyers@pgjhlaw.com *URL:* http://www.pgjhlaw.com
Carlstadt, New Jersey Office: One Palmer Terrace.
Telephone: 201-507-5157.
FAX: 201-507-5221.
Washington, D.C. Office: 888 17th Street, N.W., Suite 1100.
Telephone: 202-467-6991.
FAX: 202-467-6703.
San Francisco, California Office: 507 Howard Street, Suite 200.
Telephone: 415-281-3631.
Fax: 415-281-3630.

MEMBERS OF FIRM

Kimberlee S. Bogen
Edward J. Goldstein
Jon Mark Jenkins
Marc A. Lebowitz
Robert D. Piliero
George O. Richardson, III
Michael T. Sullivan

(See Next Column)

ASSOCIATES

Craig Avedisian
Rosemary G. Feit
Eric M. Kogan
Mariano Schwed

OF COUNSEL

Kenneth D. Arbeeny
Christopher P. Hall

For full biographical listings, see the Martindale-Hubbell Law Directory

PLUNKETT & JAFFE, P.C. (AV)

230 Park Avenue, Suite 1847, 10169
Telephone: 212-922-1800
Facsimile: 212-922-1819
Email: plunkettjaffe.com
White Plains, New York Office: 1 North Broadway.
Telephone: 914-948-7722.
Facsimile: 914-948-7603.
Albany, New York Office: 111 Washington Avenue.
Telephone: 518-462-1800.
Facsimile: 518-462-4875.

William F. Plunkett, Jr.
Kevin J. Plunkett
Justin E. Driscoll, III
Robert H. Hermann
Kerry A. Lawrence
Gary I. Selinger
Josephine Trovini
Lino J. Sciarretta
Susannah Cahill
Francis J. Earley

For Complete List of Firm Personnel, See General Section

For full biographical listings, see the Martindale-Hubbell Law Directory

SACKS MONTGOMERY, P.C. (AV)

800 Third Avenue, 10022
Telephone: 212-355-4660
Telecopier: 212-593-7257
Email: sm@sacksmontgomery.com
Westport, Connecticut Office: Sacks, Montgomery, Pastore & Levine, P.C., 1071 Post Road East, Suite 3.
Telephone: 203-291-6844.

Harry P. Sacks
David E. Montgomery
Stuart M. Levine (Resident, Westport, Connecticut Office)
Jeffrey A. Aronson
Frederick R. Rohn
Scott D. St. Marie
Stephen A. Stallings

Thomas F. Giordano
Amy S. Cohen
Kathleen M. Fay

OF COUNSEL

Steven J. Brill

For full biographical listings, see the Martindale-Hubbell Law Directory

PAUL A. SCRUDATO (AV)

150 E. 52nd Street, Suite 2700, 10022
Telephone: 212-371-1153
Fax: 212-753-5044
Email: paulscrudato@ibm.net

For full biographical listings, see the Martindale-Hubbell Law Directory

SLADE & ASSOCIATES, P.C. (AV)

11 Vestry Street, 5th Floor, 10013
Telephone: 212-226-8787
Fax: 212-226-3619
URL: http://www.lawyers.com/slade&associatespc

Jeffrey C. Slade

Marianne Yen
Bridget Connolly

OF COUNSEL

Douglas E. Grover
Norman A. Bloch

For full biographical listings, see the Martindale-Hubbell Law Directory

SOLOVAY, EDLIN & EISEMAN (AV)

845 Third Avenue, Eighth Floor, 10022
Telephone: 212-752-1000
Facsimile: 212-355-4608

Richard A. Edlin
Norman Solovay
Michael B. Solovay
Jonathan Eiseman
Wayne R. Lehrhaupt
Eric R. Levine

OF COUNSEL

Daniel James Cooper
Joseph M. Harary
Stephen L. Weinstein
Peter Kakoyiannis
Sam Schwartz

ASSOCIATES

Murray D. Schneier
Howard S. Roitman

For full biographical listings, see the Martindale-Hubbell Law Directory

New York—Continued

WAGNER, DAVIS & GOLD, P.C. (AV)

99 Madison Avenue, 10016
Telephone: 212-481-9600
Telefax: 212-481-8245

Steven R. Wagner
John R. Wagner
Ronald Jay Gold
Bonnie Reid Berkow
William R. Fried

OF COUNSEL

Deborah Lynn Davis

Adam D. Finkelstein
Glen C. Rosenberg
Keith L. Woodside
Mikelle V. Lipsius (Not admitted in NY)
Robert J. Patchen

LEGAL SUPPORT PERSONNEL

Nicole J. Ottley (Paralegal)
Tracey A. Lewis (Paralegal)
Steven Henderson (Paralegal)
Karen Chin (Paralegal)
Daniel E. Glatter (Law Clerk)

For full biographical listings, see the Martindale-Hubbell Law Directory

---

WHITE, FLEISCHNER & FINO (AV)

140 Broadway, 10005
Telephone: 212-487-9700
Telecopier: 212-487-9777
Email: infor@wff-law.com
Red Bank, New Jersey Office: 272 Broad Street.
Telephone: 732-530-7787.
Telecopier: 732-530-8552.

MEMBER OF FIRM

Allan P. White

OF COUNSEL

Gil M. Coogler

Representative Client: Island Construction Company.

For Complete List of Firm Personnel, See General Section

For full biographical listings, see the Martindale-Hubbell Law Directory

---

ZANE AND RUDOFSKY (AV)

A Partnership including Professional Corporations
Carnegie Hall Tower, 152 West 57th Street, 10019
Telephone: 212-245-2222
Fax: (212) 541-5555 and (212) 541-6666
Easylink: 6284-5474
MCI Mail: 258-4388
Telex: 31-7465
Cable Address: "Zanelex"
Voice Mail: 212-541-4444
Email: info@zrlex.com *URL:* http://www.zrlex.com

MEMBERS OF FIRM

James B. Zane (P.C.)
Edward S. Rudofsky (P.C.)
Eric S. Horowitz

COUNSEL

Arlene H. Schechter

For full biographical listings, see the Martindale-Hubbell Law Directory

---

*RIVERHEAD,** Suffolk Co.

ROBERT C. CRIMMINS (AV)

European American Bank Building, 209 West Main Street, P.O. Box 338, 11901
Telephone: 516-369-8448
Telecopier: 516-369-9001

ASSOCIATES

Linda D. Calder
Paula Wetstein
Donna M. Spicer

References: Suffolk County National Bank; European American Bank.

For full biographical listings, see the Martindale-Hubbell Law Directory

---

*ROCHESTER,** Monroe Co.

ERNSTROM & DRESTE, LLP (AV)

Crossbridge Office Park, 2000 Winton Road South Building One, Suite 300, 14618-3922
Telephone: 716-473-3100
Fax: 716-473-3113
URL: http://www.ernstromdreste.com
New York, N.Y. Office: 317 Madison Avenue, Suite 703, 10017-5201.
Telephone: 212-687-0303.
Fax: 212-687-1597.

MEMBERS OF FIRM

J. William Ernstrom
Theodore M. B. Baum
John W. Dreste
Todd R. Braggins

(See Next Column)

ASSOCIATES

Martha A. Connolly
Kevin F. Peartree
Michael F. Dehmler

COUNSEL

William E. Brueckner, III
Michael E. O'Neill

For full biographical listings, see the Martindale-Hubbell Law Directory

---

HALLENBECK, LASCELL, NORRIS & HELLER (AV)

A Limited Liability Partnership
One Exchange Street, 14614
Telephone: 716-423-5900
Fax: 716-423-5910
Email: HLNZ@hlnz.com

MEMBERS OF FIRM

Alfred M. Hallenbeck
Michael D. Norris
David M. Lascell
Cheryl A. Heller

COUNSEL

Robert A. Feldman
David A. Wier

Daniel P. Purcell
Suzanne E. Ouellette
Meghan Mc Manus Di Pasquale
Andrea F. Basso
Robert S. Attardo

For full biographical listings, see the Martindale-Hubbell Law Directory

---

LAWRENCE, WERNER, KESSELRING, SWARTOUT & BROWN, LLP (AV)

Formerly Suter Doyle Kesselring Lawrence & Werner
700 First Federal Plaza, 14614-1909
Telephone: 716-325-6446
Fax: 716-262-5185
Email: rochester@lwksb.com *URL:* http://www.lwksb.com
Canandaigua, New York Office: 23 Sly Street, 14424.
Telephone: 716-396-4000.
Fax: 716-396-1210. Email: canandaigua@lwksb.com.
Clifton Springs, New York: 26 East Main Street, P.O. Box 604, 14432.
Telephone: 315-462-3010.
Fax: 315-462-5039. Email: clifton_springs@lwksb.com

Paul J. Suter (1918-1989)

MEMBERS OF FIRM

Leo J. Kesselring
Colleen A. Brown
C. Bruce Lawrence
Steven H. Swartout
Christopher K. Werner
Mary Jo S. Korona

OF COUNSEL

James B. Doyle
Craig J. Doran
John F. Riley

ASSOCIATE

Jeffrey D. Graff

Representative Clients: Canandaigua National Bank; Hadlock Paint Company, Inc.; F.F. Thompson Health Systems, Inc.; Keuka College; Towns of Farmington and Gorham, NY; Toyota Motor Credit Corp.
References: Canandaigua National Bank; Fleet Bank, Rochester; National Association of Credit Manager, Rochester.

For full biographical listings, see the Martindale-Hubbell Law Directory

---

ROCKVILLE CENTRE, Nassau Co.

BATZAR & WEINBERG, A PROFESSIONAL CORPORATION (AV)

184 Sunrise Highway, P.O. Box 427, 11570
Telephone: 516-766-1860
Telecopier: 516-678-7801
Email: batweinb@aol.com *URL:* http://www.batzarweinberg.com
Edison, New Jersey Office: 86 Hudson Street.
Telephone: 908-653-1797.
Merion, Pennsylvania Office: 405 Andrew Road.
Telephone: 215-568-1060.
West Palm Beach, Florida Office: 3800 Washington Road.
Telephone: 561-659-5881.

Sanford I. Weinberg

Edward J. Damsky
Peter G. Rubin

OF COUNSEL

Norma R. Frank (Not admitted in NY; Resident, Merion, Pennsylvania Office)
Lisa A. Maglone (Not admitted in NY; Resident, Edison, New Jersey Office)

For full biographical listings, see the Martindale-Hubbell Law Directory

ROSLYN, Nassau Co.

CARL S. LEVINE & ASSOCIATES, P.C. (AV)

1800 Northern Boulevard, 11576
Telephone: 516-621-5380
Fax: 516-621-5388
Email: cslpcesq@aol.com *URL:* http://www.lawyers.com/carllevinelaw

Carl S. Levine

Diane J. Moffet

For full biographical listings, see the Martindale-Hubbell Law Directory

ROSLYN HEIGHTS, Nassau Co.

NATISS, NATISS & GORDON, P.C. (AV)

277 Willis Avenue, 11577
Telephone: 516-621-0900
Telecopier: 516-621-1304
Email: MNatisslaw@aol.com

Marvin Natiss
Gary M. Natiss
Stacey Natiss Gordon

Sharon G. Haut

For full biographical listings, see the Martindale-Hubbell Law Directory

SALAMANCA, Cattaraugus Co.

BRADY, BROOKS & O'CONNELL, LLP (AV)

41 Main Street, P.O. Box 227, 14779
Telephone: 716-945-2000
Telecopier: 716-945-3566
Email: bbolaw@aol.com *URL:* http://www.lawyers.com/bbolaw
Randolph, New York Office: 165 Main Street.
Telephone: 716-358-6800.
Ellicottville, New York Office: 1887 Building, 1 Washington Street, P.O. Box 550.
Telephone: 716-699-8010.

MEMBERS OF FIRM

Thomas C. Brady
Kameron K. G. Brooks
Brian E. O'Connell, Jr.

Lori Pettit Rieman

For full biographical listings, see the Martindale-Hubbell Law Directory

*SYRACUSE,** Onondaga Co.

ALI, PAPPAS & COX, P.C. (AV)

Syracuse Building, 224 Harrison Street, 13202
Telephone: 315-472-4481
FAX: 315-472-8299
Email: alpaco@dreamscape.com

Lucien Ali
C. Andrew Pappas
Robert B. Cox
Thomas P. Givas
P. Douglas Dodd
David P. Doherty

OF COUNSEL

Edward F. Gerber

LEGAL SUPPORT PERSONNEL

Brenda M. Barch

Representative Clients: Agway, Inc.; Agway Petroleum Corp.; Arcom Labs; Countryside Federal Credit Union; PineCone Federal Credit Union; Oswego City Savings Bank; Telmark, Inc.; Syracuse Executive Air Services, Inc.; Fairbanks Capital Corp.
References: M&T Bank; 1st National Bank of Rochester.

For full biographical listings, see the Martindale-Hubbell Law Directory

HISCOCK & BARCLAY, LLP (AV)

Financial Plaza, P.O. Box 4878, 13221
Telephone: 315-422-2131
Fax: 315-472-3059
Email: reachus@hiscockbarclay.com *URL:* http://www.hiscockbarclay.com
Buffalo, New York Office: Suite 301 The Key Bank Towers at Key Center, 50 Fountain Plaza.
Telephone: 716-856-0911.
Fax: 716-856-2567.
Albany, New York Office: 40 Beaver Street.
Telephone: 518-434-2163.
Fax: 518-434-2621.

Frank H. Hiscock (1856-1946)

(See Next Column)

MEMBERS OF FIRM

H. Douglas Barclay
Taylor H. Obold
David B. Liddell
George S. Deptula
John P. Sindoni
Frederick S. Marty
Richard K. Hughes
J. Eric Charlton
Thomas S. Squire
Clifford H. Wilson
Robert A. Barrer
Christopher J. Bonner
Judith M. Sayles
Peter H. Swartz
John P. Langan
Catherine Keib Johnson
Richard J. Paul
Jon P. Devendorf
Richard R. Capozza

ASSOCIATES

Deborah A. Bentley
Alan R. Peterman
Kathleen M. O'Connor
Jennifer K. Frank
Matthew S. Moses
Christopher J. Centore
Jean K. Sehl
Bonnie Angela Buccina
Joseph P. McRae
Yvonne E. Marciano
Andrew J. Leja
William A. Barclay

OF COUNSEL

Donald M. Mawhinney, Jr.
Roger J. Edinger
Ferdinand L. Picardi
Jan R. Farr

General Counsel for: Syracuse Savings Bank; Key Corp; Key Bank of New York N.A. ; Solvay Bank; Excelsior Insurance Co.; Key Trust Co.; Auburn Steel Co., Inc.
Local Counsel for: Firestone Tire & Rubber Co.; Fidelity & Deposit Company of Maryland.

For full biographical listings, see the Martindale-Hubbell Law Directory

WESTBURY, Nassau Co.

ACKERMAN & TERRY, LLC (AV)

900 Merchants Concourse, Suite 314, 11590
Telephone: 516-228-8245
Fax: 516-228-8249

MEMBERS OF FIRM

Neil H. Ackerman
Gerard Terry
Marianne J. Gallipoli

OF COUNSEL

Karen M. Dowd

ASSOCIATES

Vivek K. Chavan (Not admitted in NY)
Michael G. McAuliffe

For full biographical listings, see the Martindale-Hubbell Law Directory

PRYOR & MANDELUP, L.L.P. (AV)

675 Old Country Road, 11590
Telephone: 516-997-0999
Facsimile: 516-333-7333

Robert L. Pryor
A. Scott Mandelup
Randolph E. White
Eric J. Snyder

Kenneth A. Reynolds
Anthony F. Giuliano
Christopher W. Costello

OF COUNSEL

Michael Salgo
C. Albert Parente

LEGAL SUPPORT PERSONNEL

Gwendolyn V. Myles
Barbara Anson

For full biographical listings, see the Martindale-Hubbell Law Directory

*WHITE PLAINS,** Westchester Co.

BOEGGEMAN, GEORGE, HODGES & CORDE, P.C. (AV)

11 Martine Avenue, 10606
Telephone: 914-761-2252
Telecopier: 914-761-5211
Email: boeggeman@bghc-law.com *URL:* http://www.bghc-law.com
Albany, New York Office: 46 Columbia Street, 12207-2716.
Telephone: 518-465-1100.
Fax: 518-465-1800.

George S. Hodges
Richard G. Corde
John J. Walsh, II
Harold L. Moroknek
Robert S. Ondrovic
Thomas A. Sica (Resident Managing Attorney, Albany Office)

Karen A.D. Jockimo
William M. Wingertzahn
Elizabeth C. Mirisola
Cynthia Dolan
Marcella M. Green
Paul A. Hurley
Leslie K. Arfine
John T. Holden
James J. Lofrese
Jeanne M. Hurley
Ira H. Lapp
Matt Randolph Belkin
Cynthia K. Messemer

(See Next Column)

BOEGGEMAN, GEORGE, HODGES & CORDE P.C.—*Continued*

OF COUNSEL

Joseph H. George — John E. Boeggeman (1919-1993)

Representative Clients: American Telephone & Telegraph; Anheuser-Busch Companies, Inc.; Lowe's Home Centers; Great Atlantic & Pacific Tea Company; Reliance National Insurance Company; Metropolitan Property & Casualty Insurance Company; Fisher Price, Inc.; CGU Insurance Company; United Services Automobile Association; New York Central Mutual Fire Insurance Company.

For full biographical listings, see the Martindale-Hubbell Law Directory

DELBELLO DONNELLAN WEINGARTEN & TARTAGLIA, LLP (AV)

One North Lexington Avenue, 10601
Telephone: 914-681-0200
Telecopier: 914-684-0288
Email: general@ddwt.com

Alfred B. DelBello
Alfred E. Donnellan (Managing Partner)
Mark P. Weingarten
Daniel D. Tartaglia
Peter J. Wise
Lee S. Wiederkehr
Patrick M. Reilly
Robert A. Korren

ASSOCIATES

William E. Dumke
Christine Moccia
Suzanne Bogdanoff
Allyse B. Dunefsky
Jerry F. Kebrdle, II
Bradley D. Wank
Ann Farrissey Carlson
Janet J. Giris

OF COUNSEL

J. David Jutkowitz
Andrew J. Balint
Robert C. Epstein

For full biographical listings, see the Martindale-Hubbell Law Directory

FARBER, SEGALL & PAPPALARDO (AV)

200 East Post Road, 10601
Telephone: 914-761-9400; 212-752-3396
Fax: 914-761-0747
Email: segallaw@prodigy.net
Roseland, New Jersey Office: 204 Eagle Rock Avenue.

MEMBERS OF FIRM

Eugene I. Farber
Steven L. Segall
John A. Pappalardo

ASSOCIATE

Hinda Keller Farber

For full biographical listings, see the Martindale-Hubbell Law Directory

JOSEPH P. GOVERNALI (AV)

Inns of Court, North Suite, 99 Court Street, 10601
Telephone: 914-946-5300
Telecopier: 914-946-1058

For full biographical listings, see the Martindale-Hubbell Law Directory

GREENE & ZINNER, P.C. (AV)

202 Mamaroneck Avenue, 10601
Telephone: 914-948-4800
FAX: 914-948-4936

Andrew Greene
Stanley S. Zinner

Arthur M. Neiss
Jarrod S. Schlesinger

For full biographical listings, see the Martindale-Hubbell Law Directory

MARCUS, GOULD & SUSSMAN, LLP (AV)

222 Bloomingdale Road, 10605
Telephone: 914-683-0090
Telecopier: 914-683-0098
Email: firm@marcus-gould-sussman.com *URL:* http://www.lawyers.com/marcusgould&sussman

MEMBERS OF FIRM

Myron Marcus
Kenneth J. Gould
Marianne L. Sussman

References: Bennett, Kielson & Co.; Citibank, N.A.; Chemical Bank.

For full biographical listings, see the Martindale-Hubbell Law Directory

ROBERT G. O'DONNELL (AV)

50 Main Street, Suite 405, 10606
Telephone: 914-761-1600
Fax: 914-761-4016
URL: http://www.lawyers.com/robertgodonnelllaw

For full biographical listings, see the Martindale-Hubbell Law Directory

ROGAN GUIDA & ORENSTEIN (AV)

235 Mamaroneck Avenue, 10605
Telephone: 1-888-WIN-WITH-US; 914-328-4480
Fax: 914-328-4479
URL: http://www.NYlawyers.com
Email: RoganGO@aol.com *URL:* http://www.lawyers.com/personalinjury

Jeffrey P. Rogan
Toni M. Guida
David L. Orenstein

Representative Clients: Recore One Mortgage Corp.; LEASCO; Pappas Enterprises Inc.; Steelcase, Inc.; Printing Center of Westchester Inc.; Corporate Imaging, Inc.; King Jolo's Flowers, Inc.; Systems Exchange, Inc.; Domus Realty.
Reference: Fleet Bank.

For full biographical listings, see the Martindale-Hubbell Law Directory

SMITH, RANSCHT, CONNORS, MUTINO, NORDELL & SIRIGNANO, P.C. (AV)

235 Main Street, 10601
Telephone: 914-946-8800
Telecopier: 914-946-8861
Cable Address: "Smiran" White Plains, New York

James P. Connors, Jr.
Peter J. Mutino
Michael Nordell
George A. Sirignano, Jr.

Counsel for: Universal Builders Supply, Inc.; The Walter Karl Cos.; Hartsdale Canine Cemetery; Wise Components, Inc.; Facsimile Communications Industries, Inc.; Carlcraft Knit Sales, Inc.
Closing Attorney for: First Union Mortgage Corp.
Representative Client: United Airlines, Corporate Express, Inc.

For full biographical listings, see the Martindale-Hubbell Law Directory

NORTH CAROLINA

*CHARLOTTE,** Mecklenburg Co.

BLAIR CONAWAY BOGRAD & MARTIN, P.A.

(See Shumaker, Loop & Kendrick, LLP)

CANSLER, LOCKHART, CAMPBELL, EVANS, BRYANT & GARLITZ, P.A. (AV)

2030 The Carillon, 227 West Trade Street, 28202
Telephone: 704-372-1282
Fax: 704-372-1621
URL: http://www.canslerlockhart.com

Hugh B. Campbell, Jr.
George K. Evans, Jr.
Frank L. Bryant
Thomas D. Garlitz
W. Lewis Smith, Jr.
R. Michael Allen
Stacy C. Cordes
Kristin D. Decker

Drupti P. Chauhan

OF COUNSEL

Thomas Ashe Lockhart
James B. Craighill

Representative Clients: American Honda Finance Corp.; Blue Cross/Blue Shield of North Carolina, Inc.; Branch Banking & Trust Co.; Ford Motor Credit Co.; Mellon US Leasing; New York Life Insurance Co.; Wal Mart Stores, Inc.; Watkins Motor Lines, Inc.; Westinghouse Electric Corp.; Young Ford, Inc.

For full biographical listings, see the Martindale-Hubbell Law Directory

CAUDLE & SPEARS, P.A. (AV)

2600 Interstate Tower, 121 West Trade Street, 28202
Telephone: 704-377-1200
Telecopier: 704-338-5858
Email: caudlespears@caudlespears.com

Lloyd C. Caudle
Harold C. Spears
L. Cameron Caudle, Jr.
Timothy T. Leach
Michael J. Selle

Counsel for: Bituminous Casualty Corp.; Baumann Springs A.G.; The A. G. Boone Co.; Capitol Funds, Inc.; Consolidated Freightways; Employers Mutual Casualty Co.; Metromont Materials; Otis Elevator Co.; N.C. Farm Bureau Mutual Insurance Co.; Royster Transport Co.

For Complete List of Firm Personnel, See General Section

For full biographical listings, see the Martindale-Hubbell Law Directory

Charlotte—Continued

DEAN & GIBSON, L.L.P. (AV)

Suite 900, Cameron Brown Building, 301 South McDowell Street, 28204-2686
Telephone: 704-372-2700
Facsimile: 704-372-1804
Email: info@deanandgibson.com

Rodney A. Dean
Michael G. Gibson
Brien D. Stockman
Christopher J. Culp

ASSOCIATES

John Whitelaw Ong
Colin E. Scott
Kimberly A. Gossage
Thomas G. Nance, II

OF COUNSEL

Barbara J. Dean

For full biographical listings, see the Martindale-Hubbell Law Directory

*GREENVILLE,** Pitt Co.

GAYLORD, MCNALLY, STRICKLAND & SNYDER, L.L.P. (AV)

498 Red Banks Road, P.O. Drawer 545, 27835-0545
Telephone: 252-321-7111
Fax: 252-321-7112

MEMBERS OF FIRM

Louis W. Gaylord, Jr. (Retired)
Danny D. McNally
D. Michael Strickland
Vernon G. Snyder, III

ASSOCIATE

Emma Stallings Holscher

Representative Clients: Wachovia Bank, N.A.; Nationsbank, N.A.; Garris Evans Lumber Co., Inc.; United States Fidelity and Guaranty Co.; The Daily Reflector, Inc.; Hastings Ford, Inc.; Nationwide Mutual Insurance Co.; U.S. Cellular; Ironwood Development, Inc.

For full biographical listings, see the Martindale-Hubbell Law Directory

EDWARD J. HARPER II ATTORNEY AT LAW (AV)

600 B Country Club Road, P.O. Box 527, 27835
Telephone: 252-215-0200
Fax: 252-215-0222

For full biographical listings, see the Martindale-Hubbell Law Directory

*WILMINGTON,** New Hanover Co.

STEVENS, MCGHEE, MORGAN, LENNON, O'QUINN & TOLL (AV)

409 Wachovia Bank Building, 101 North Front Street, P.O. Drawer 59, 28402
Telephone: 910-763-3666
Fax: 910-251-9562
Email: smmlo@Wilmington.net

MEMBERS OF FIRM

John A. Stevens (1895-1990)
Karl W. McGhee (1923-1981)
Richard M. Morgan
Alton Y. Lennon
Robert A. O'Quinn
Alan E. Toll
J. Layne McNeill

ASSOCIATE

Maria D. McIntyre

Representative Clients: Hanover Iron Works, Inc.; Queensboro Steel Corp.; Star-News Newspapers Co.; The Pillsbury Co.; Wachovia Bank & Trust Co.; Wertheimer Bag Co.

For full biographical listings, see the Martindale-Hubbell Law Directory

*WINSTON-SALEM,** Forsyth Co.

BENNETT & GUTHRIE, P.L.L.C. (AV)

3334 Healy Drive, Suite 203, 27103-1476
Telephone: 336-765-3121
Fax: 336-765-8622

Richard V. Bennett
Rodney A. Guthrie
Stanley P. Dean

Kevin J. Williams

Representative Clients: American Continental Insurance Company; Commercial Union Insurance Company; Integon Insurance; Kentucky Medical Insurance Company; Medtronic, Inc.; Montgomery Mutual Insurance Company; Novant Health, Inc.; Pennsylvania Lumberman's Mutual Insurance Company; St. Paul Fire & Marine Insurance Company; Zurich Insurance Company.

For full biographical listings, see the Martindale-Hubbell Law Directory

JOHN R. SURRATT, P.A. (AV)

102 West Third Street Suite 700, 27101
Telephone: 336-725-8323
Facsimile: 336-722-5218
Email: surrattpa@aol.com

John R. Surratt
Anita M. Conrad

For full biographical listings, see the Martindale-Hubbell Law Directory

NORTH DAKOTA

*BISMARCK,** Burleigh Co.

PEARCE AND DURICK, PLLP (AV)

314 East Thayer Avenue, P.O. Box 400, 58502
Telephone: 701-223-2890
Fax: 701-223-7865
Email: law.office@pearce-durick.com *URL:* http://www.pearce-durick.com

MEMBERS OF FIRM

Patrick W. Durick
Jerome C. Kettleson
Lawrence Bender

ASSOCIATE

Jonathan P. Sanstead

Representative Clients: BNC National Bank; MDU Resources Group; Meyer Broadcasting Co.; Montana Power Company.

For Complete List of Firm Personnel, See General Section

For full biographical listings, see the Martindale-Hubbell Law Directory

OHIO

*AKRON,** Summit Co.

MENTZER, VUILLEMIN AND MYGRANT LTD. (AV)

1 Cascade Plaza, 20th Floor, 44308-1114
Telephone: 330-376-7500
Telecopier: 330-376-8018
Email: mvmlaw@juno.com

Howard E. Mentzer
John W. Mygrant
Rajko Radonjich

Reference: National City Bank, Akron, Ohio.

For full biographical listings, see the Martindale-Hubbell Law Directory

*CINCINNATI,** Hamilton Co.

GENE MESH & ASSOCIATES (AV)

2605 Burnet Avenue, 45219-2502
Telephone: 513-221-8800
Fax: 513-221-1097
Email: GeneMesh@aol.com

ASSOCIATES

R. Michael Phebus
Michael G. Brautigam (Not admitted in OH)

LEGAL SUPPORT PERSONNEL

Charles H. Short

For full biographical listings, see the Martindale-Hubbell Law Directory

*CLEVELAND,** Cuyahoga Co.

BERNARD, HAFFEY & BOHNERT CO., L.P.A. (AV)

Jefferson Centre, 5001 Mayfield Road #301, P.O. Box 24005, 44124-0005
Telephone: 216-291-3600
FAX: 216-291-0159
URL: http://www.lawyers.com/bernardhaffey&bohnert

Clifford H. Bernard (1907-1985)
J. Ross Haffey, Jr.
Edward G. Bohnert
Timothy P. Haffey

Reference: KeyBank.

For full biographical listings, see the Martindale-Hubbell Law Directory

CHATTMAN, GAINES & STERN (AV)

1400 Renaissance Center, 1350 Euclid Avenue, 44115-1817
Telephone: 216-781-1700; 800-321-1700
Telecopier: 216-781-1972
Lorain, Ohio Office: 5300 Baumhart Road.
Telephone: 216-282-4598.
Fax: 216-960-1298.

(See Next Column)

CHATTMAN, GAINES & STERN—*Continued*

Gerald B. Chattman
Roger W. Van Deusen
Michael B. Michelson
Douglas J. Paul
John V. Scharon, Jr.
Thomas C. Wagner
Loreen M. Robinson

Dale A. Nowak
John Patrick

For full biographical listings, see the Martindale-Hubbell Law Directory

CONWAY, MARKEN, WYNER, KURANT & KERN CO., L.P.A. (AV)

30195 Chagrin Boulevard, Pepper Pike Place, Suite 300, 44124
Telephone: 216-292-3300
Telecopier: 216-292-3340

James J. Conway
Howard A. Marken
Jeffrey G. Wyner
Jack Kurant
Keith W. Kern
Peter Turner
Kevin R. Keogh
Peter D. Brosse
Mark Leskovec
Michael R. Stavnicky
Michele R. Yeh
Jennifer A. Corso

For full biographical listings, see the Martindale-Hubbell Law Directory

BERNARD S. GOLDFARB (AV)

55 Public Square, Suite 1500, 44113
Telephone: 216-696-0606
Fax: 216-696-0732
Email: resconet@multiverse.com

For full biographical listings, see the Martindale-Hubbell Law Directory

KAUFMAN & CUMBERLAND CO., L.P.A. (AV)

1500 Republic Building, 25 Prospect Avenue, West, 44115-1000
Telephone: 216-861-0707
Telefax: 216-694-6883
TDD: 216-694-6891

Steven S. Kaufman
Frank J. Cumberland, Jr. (Retired)
Frank R. DeSantis
Robert A. Blattner
Gail E. Sindell
William W. Jacobs
Thomas L. Feher
Mitchell Ehrenberg
Douglas P. Whipple

Susan L. Belman
Charles P. Royer
Craig P. Kvale
Kathleen M. Minahan
Robin M. Wilson
Robert J. Patton
Lawrence E. Harkenrider
Scott J. Novak

OF COUNSEL

Jack G. Day (Retired)
Anthony R. Troia
Edda Sara Post

Representative Clients: CertainTeed Corp.; City of Cleveland; Household Commercial Financial Services, Inc.

For full biographical listings, see the Martindale-Hubbell Law Directory

KREMBS & ALKIRE LLP (AV)

750 Courthouse Square, 310 West Lakeside Avenue, 44113-1021
Telephone: 216-875-7500
Fax: 216-875-7501
URL: http://www.krembs-alkire.com

Andrew P. Krembs
Richard C. Alkire
Dean C. Nieding

For full biographical listings, see the Martindale-Hubbell Law Directory

LEVIN, MARMAROS & CHARMS CO., L.P.A. (AV)

2970 BP Tower, 200 Public Square, 44114
Telephone: 216-781-4900
Fax: 216-787-0330
URL: http://www.lawyers.com/lmc

Joel Levin
Peter W. Marmaros
Stephen J. Charms

Anthony R. Brighton

For full biographical listings, see the Martindale-Hubbell Law Directory

LOWE • EKLUND • WAKEFIELD CO., L.P.A. (AV)

Tower City Center 610 Skylight Office Tower, 1660 West Second Street, 44113-1454
Telephone: 216-781-2600
Fax: 216-781-2610
Email: lew@lewlaw.com *URL:* http://www.lewlaw.com

(See Next Column)

James A. Lowe
Claudia Rieth Eklund
Mark L. Wakefield
Dennis P. Mulvihill

Gregory S. Scott
Andrew S. Goldwasser

OF COUNSEL

Donald Cybulski

For full biographical listings, see the Martindale-Hubbell Law Directory

MCDONALD, HOPKINS, BURKE & HABER CO., L.P.A. (AV)

2100 Bank One Center, 600 Superior Avenue, E., 44114-2653
Telephone: 216-348-5400
Telecopier: 216-348-5474
Email: attorney@mhbh.com *URL:* http://www.mhbh.com

Patrick J. Berry
Jeffrey P. Consolo
Jerome W. Cook
Richard S. Cooper
Anthony J. DiVenere
Paul N. Edwards
Theodore J. Esborn
Steven L. Gardner
Carl J. Grassi
James A. Griffith
Jeffrey R. Huntsberger
Brian J. Jereb
Bernard L. Karr
Thomas W. Keen
Roger L. Kleinman
Joseph J. LoPresti, Jr.
Dan L. Makee
George L. McGaughey, Jr.
John T. Mulligan
Brian M. O'Neill
William J. O'Neill
Stephen T. Parisi
R. Jeffrey Pollock
Michael G. Riley
Shawn M. Riley
Albert N. Salvatore
Thomas C. Schrader
Roger L. Shumaker
Barbara J. Smith
James M. Stone
Dale R. Vlasek
Kenneth J. Walsh
John M. Wirtshafter
Jane Marie Pine Wood
Charles B. Zellmer

OF COUNSEL

John J. Monroe

Julie A. Callsen
Anne T. Corrigan
Steven A. Eisenberg
G. Andrew Gardner
Anuj Goswami
Donald E. Kacmar
David M. Kall
Jeffrey B. Keiper
Kevin J. Kessinger
Mark D. Klimek
Alan M. Koschik
Deviani M. Kuhar
Paul W. Linehan
Tyler L. Mathews
Jennifer A. Mills
Antoinette K. Palmer
Ketan K. Patel
Sharon Szolosi Regas
Douglas B. Schnee
Michele Smolin
Glenn D. Southworth
Michael R. Spreng

For full biographical listings, see the Martindale-Hubbell Law Directory

MORGANSTERN, MACADAMS & DEVITO CO., L.P.A. (AV)

Burgess Building, Suite 400, 1406 West Sixth Street, 44113
Telephone: 216-621-4244; 216-687-1212
Fax: 216-621-2951
Email: smorgan153@aol.com

Stanley Morganstern
Pamela J. MacAdams
Christopher Michael DeVito

Michael A. Partlow
Cheryl Lukacs
Patrice R. T. Yarham

For full biographical listings, see the Martindale-Hubbell Law Directory

NISCHWITZ, PEMBRIDGE & CHRISZT CO., L.P.A. (AV)

1220 Bond Court Office Building, 1300 East Ninth Street, 44114-1503
Telephone: 216-861-8100
Telecopier: 216-861-8180
Email: dnpc@dnpc.com *URL:* http://www.dnpc.com

Jeffrey L. Nischwitz
D. Timothy Pembridge
James R. Chriszt

Richard J. Ambrose
Timothy L. McGarry

OF COUNSEL

Arthur L. (Tim) Clements, III
Maureen Fiorilli Zito
J. Randall Nye

For full biographical listings, see the Martindale-Hubbell Law Directory

NURENBERG, PLEVIN, HELLER & MCCARTHY CO., L.P.A. (AV)

1370 Ontario Street First Floor, 44113-1792
Telephone: 216-621-2300; Toll Free: 1-800-562-7438
Fax: 216-771-2242
Email: nphm@nphm.com *URL:* http://www.nphm.com

(See Next Column)

NURENBERG, PLEVIN, HELLER & McCARTHY CO. L.P.A., *Cleveland—Continued*

A. H. Dudnik (1905-1963)
S. F. Komito (1902-1984)
Marshall I. Nurenberg
Leon M. Plevin
Maurice L. Heller
John J. McCarthy
Thomas Mester
Harlan M. Gordon
David M. Paris
Richard L. Demsey
Jamie R. Lebovitz
William S. Jacobson
Jeffrey A. Leikin

Robin J. Peterson
Robert S. Zeller
Ellen M. McCarthy
J. Charles Ruiz-Bueno
Kathleen J. St. John
Jonathan D. Mester
Brenda M. Johnson

Reference: Society Key Corp.

For full biographical listings, see the Martindale-Hubbell Law Directory

RODGERS AND CO., L.P.A. (AV)

1750 Guildhall, Landmark Office Towers, 45 Prospect Avenue, West, 44115
Telephone: 216-861-6191
Fax: 216-861-4699
Email: attys@rodgers-lpa.com

Walter A. Rodgers

Jeffrey M. Elzeer
Shawn A. Cormier

For full biographical listings, see the Martindale-Hubbell Law Directory

TRACI & MARX CO., L.P.A. (AV)

55 Public Square, Suite 1550, 44113
Telephone: 216-623-8010
Fax: 216-623-8012
Email: lawyers@tracimarx.com

Robert V. Traci
James A. Marx

For full biographical listings, see the Martindale-Hubbell Law Directory

*COLUMBUS,** Franklin Co.

BRICKER & ECKLER LLP (AV)

100 South Third Street, 43215-4291
Telephone: 614-227-2300
Telecopy: 614-227-2390
Email: info@be.bricker.com *URL:* http://www.bricker.com

Randolph C. Wiseman
Charles H. Walker
Quintin F. Lindsmith
Drew H. Campbell

Stephen C. Gray
T. Earl LeVere
Amy Straker Bartemes
Timothy A. Fry

For Complete List of Firm Personnel, See General Section

For full biographical listings, see the Martindale-Hubbell Law Directory

HAMMOND & SEWARDS (AV)

22 East Gay Street - Suite 700, 43215
Telephone: 614-461-5300
Telephone: 1-800-842-5475
Fax: 614-461-8285
Email: pmartz@hammondsewards.com *URL:* http://www.lawyers.com/hammondlawoffice

MEMBERS OF FIRM

Gary W. Hammond
Frederick A. Sewards

ASSOCIATE

Scott E. Williams

LEGAL SUPPORT PERSONNEL

Heather Vekasy (Secretary to Attorney Williams and Attorney Sewards)
Heather Rodgers (Secretary to Attorney Hammond)
Prindall H. Martz (Office Manager)

For full biographical listings, see the Martindale-Hubbell Law Directory

POSTLEWAITE & JORDAN (AV)

3040 Riverside Drive, Suite 122, 43221
Telephone: 614-486-2111
Fax: 614-486-8943

Charles C. Postlewaite
Jeffrey H. Jordan

ASSOCIATE

Holly N. Wolf

For full biographical listings, see the Martindale-Hubbell Law Directory

SWEDLOW, BUTLER, LEVINE, LEWIS & DYE CO., L.P.A. (AV)

10 West Broad Street, Suite 2400, 43215-3469
Telephone: 614-461-1100
Telecopier: 614-461-8178
Email: SBILLlaw@aol.com

Gerald H. Swedlow
Jack C. Butler
Richard L. Levine
Jeffrey M. Lewis
David A. Dye
Steven A. Baenen
Todd H. Neuman
Sean M. Gouhin

Reference: National City Bank; Fifth Third Bank.

For full biographical listings, see the Martindale-Hubbell Law Directory

ZEIGER & CARPENTER (AV)

1600 Huntington Center, 41 South High Street, 43215
Telephone: 614-365-4100
Facsimile: 614-365-9145

MEMBERS OF FIRM

John W. Zeiger
Michael H. Carpenter
Jeffrey A. Lipps
Steven W. Tigges
David A. Wallace
Marion H. Little, Jr.
Michael Romanello

ASSOCIATES

Timothy R. Bricker
Daniel R. Mordarski
Joseph T. Olecki
Michael N. Beekhuizen
Ronald E. Laymon
Angela Paul
Craig Calcaterra
John J. Todor

OF COUNSEL

Daniel R. Freytag
Mary R. True
Douglas R. Cole (Not admitted in OH)
Stuart G. Parsell

For full biographical listings, see the Martindale-Hubbell Law Directory

*DAYTON,** Montgomery Co.

FARUKI GILLIAM & IRELAND P.L.L. (AV)

600 Courthouse Plaza, S.W., 10 North Ludlow Street, 45402
Telephone: 937-227-3700
Fax: 937-227-3717
Email: admin@fgilaw.com *URL:* http://www.fgilaw.com

MEMBERS OF FIRM

Charles J. Faruki
D. Jeffrey Ireland
Paul L. Horstman
Ann Wightman
Paul G. Hallinan
Mary L. Wiseman

Daniel H. Binegar
Donald E. Burton
Jeffrey T. Cox
James A. Dearie (Not admitted in OH)
John A. Fischer
Martin A. Foos
Caroline H. Gentry
Diane M. Goderre
Scott K. Jones
Michele L. King
Thomas R. Kraemer
Bryce A. Lenox
Lisa M. Parilo
Bryan M. Perrero
Ronald I. Raether, Jr.
Shaun A. Roberts
Laura A. Sanom
Jeffrey S. Sharkey

For full biographical listings, see the Martindale-Hubbell Law Directory

*TOLEDO,** Lucas Co.

MANAHAN, PIETRYKOWSKI, BAMMAN & DELANEY (AV)

(Formerly Finn, Manahan & Pietrykowski)
414 North Erie Street, P.O. Box 2328, 43603-2328
Telephone: 419-243-6148
Fax: 419-241-7759
Email: mpbd@mindspring.com
Port Clinton Office: 125 Jefferson Street.
Telephone: 419-734-5516.
Fax: 419-732-8246.

MEMBERS OF FIRM

William A. Finn (1898-1980)
Thomas J. Manahan (1923-1988)
John A. Pietrykowski (1931-1993)
Cormac B. DeLaney
George C. Ward
Stephen F. Ahern
Gerald R. Kowalski
Michael J. Manahan
Glenn E. Wasielewski
William F. Pietrykowski (Resident, Port Clinton Office)
Larry P. Meyer
Ted B. Riley

ASSOCIATES

Jeffrey Jon Madrzykowski
Stephen E. House

OF COUNSEL

H. William Bamman (Retired)

For full biographical listings, see the Martindale-Hubbell Law Directory

Toledo—Continued

SHUMAKER, LOOP & KENDRICK, LLP (AV)

North Courthouse Square, 1000 Jackson, 43624-1573
Telephone: 419-241-9000
Fax: 419-241-6894
Tampa, Florida Office: Barnett Plaza, Suite 2800, 101 East Kennedy Boulevard, 33602-5151,
Telephone: 813-229-7600.
Fax: 813-229-1660.
Charlotte, North Carolina Office: 128 South Tryon Street, Suite 1800, 28202.
Telephone: 704-375-0057.
Fax: 704-332-1197.
Columbus, Ohio Office: Huntington Center, 41 South High Street, Suite 2210, 43215.
Telephone: 614-463-9441.
Fax: 614-463-1108.

MEMBERS OF FIRM

John C. Barron
Larry A. Becker
Edward Bograd (Resident, Charlotte, North Carolina Office)
Aleta M. Bonini
Michael E. Born (Resident, Columbus, Ohio Office)
Michael M. Briley
Eric D. Britton
John H. Burson
C. Philip Campbell, Jr. (Resident, Tampa, Florida Office)
Philip S. Chubb (Resident, Charlotte, North Carolina Office)
David Harris Conaway (Resident, Charlotte, North Carolina Office)
Thomas A. Cotter (Resident, Tampa, Florida Office)
Marlene (Neema) M. Cottrill-Bell
David J. Coyle
Jeffrey S. Creamer
William E. Curphey (Resident, Tampa, Florida Office)
Joseph A. D'Amico (Resident, Charlotte, North Carolina Office)
Diane Vulich Davis
Terrance K. Davis
Scott G. Deller
Gary R. Diesing
Thomas P. Dillon
Victoria J. Elliot (Resident, Tampa, Florida Office)
Edwin G. Emerson
William G. Fischer
Vivian C. Folk
Jeffrey E. Fort
Jack G. Fynes
Marc Gertner
Bruce H. Gordon (Resident, Tampa, Florida Office)
William H. Gosline
Kevin H. Graham (Resident, Tampa, Florida Office)
David M. Grogan (Resident, Charlotte, North Carolina Office)
Douglas G. Haynam
John F. Hayward
William H. Heywood, III
John W. Hilbert, II
Charles W. Hiller
John S. Inglis (Resident, Tampa, Florida Office)
Regina M. Joseph
Robert A. Koenig
Kathleen A. Kress
Gregory T. Lodge
Oksana M. Ludd
Moses Luski (Resident, Charlotte, North Carolina Office)
Paul R. Lynch (Resident, Tampa, Florida Office)
John N. MacKay
Maria Maistrellis (Resident, Tampa, Florida Office)
Bentford E. Martin (Resident, Charlotte, North Carolina Office)
Timothy C. McCarthy
Susan D. McClay
Michael S. McGowan
Brian N. McMahon
William H. McNair (Resident, Charlotte, North Carolina Office)
Donald M. Mewhort, Jr.
Jeffrey H. Miller
Richard A. Mitchell
Michael J. O'Callaghan (Resident, Columbus, Ohio Office)
Barbara R. Pankau (Resident, Tampa, Florida Office)
William L. Patberg
Mary Ellen Pisanelli
Thomas G. Pletz
David J. Rectenwald
Cynthia L. Rerucha
Edward J. Richardson (Resident, Tampa, Florida Office)
Joseph A. Rideout
Stephen A. Rothschild
Michael G. Sanderson
Rolf H. Scheidel
Steven G. Schember (Resident, Tampa, Florida Office)
Gregory S. Shumaker
John J. Siciliano
Peter R. Silverman
Joseph S. Simpson
Darrell C. Smith (Resident, Tampa, Florida Office)
Lyman F. Spitzer
Harry J. Stathopoulos (Resident, Charlotte, North Carolina Office)
Mark C. Stewart
John L. Straub
William H. Sturges (Resident, Charlotte, North Carolina Office)
John B. Taylor (Resident, Charlotte, North Carolina Office)
W. Thompson Thorn, III (Resident, Tampa, Florida Office)
Louis E. Tosi
Michael T. Trocke (Resident, Tampa, Florida Office)
Barton L. Wagenman
David F. Waterman
Thomas I. Webb, Jr.
David W. Wicklund
Dennis P. Witherell
Thomas M. Wood (Resident, Tampa, Florida Office)
Kathryn J. Woodward
Gregory C. Yadley (Resident, Tampa, Florida Office)

(See Next Column)

ASSOCIATES

M. Scott Aubry
Stacy Solochek Beckman (Resident, Columbus, Ohio Office)
Jenifer A. Belt
Stefanie E. Berk
Eileen M. Best
Kathleen M. Bickelhaupt (Resident, Tampa, Florida Office)
C. Graham Carothers, Jr. (Resident, Tampa, Florida Office)
Mark A. Catchur (Resident, Tampa, Florida Office)
Emily K. Cooper
Julio C. Esquivel (Resident, Tampa, Florida Office)
Sharon M. Fulop
Tammy N. Giroux (Resident, Tampa, Florida Office)
Daniel R. Hansen (Resident, Charlotte, North Carolina Office)
D. Scott Harves
W. Reed Hauptman
Lynn M. Hoover
John V. Ivsan
Ernest J. Marquart (Resident, Tampa, Florida Office)
Darrick M Mix
Daniel G. Musca (Resident, Tampa, Florida Office)
Christian A. Petersen (Resident, Tampa, Florida Office)
Christopher J. Pooley
Joseph A. Porrello (Resident, Tampa, Florida Office)
Brian Wayne Prewitt (Resident, Charlotte, North Carolina Office)
Eugene F. Rash (Resident, Charlotte, North Carolina Office)
Brenda A. Ray
Michael H. Robbins (Resident, Tampa, Florida Office)
James I. Rothschild
Joseph J. Santaniello (Resident, Charlotte, North Carolina Office)
Gregory L. Shelton (Resident, Tampa, Florida Office)
Angelina M. Stayton (Resident, Tampa, Florida Office)
Karen M. Steffens (Resident, Charlotte, North Carolina Office)
Frederick M. Thurman, Jr. (Resident, Charlotte, North Carolina Office)
J. Todd Timmerman (Resident, Tampa, Florida Office)
Mark D. Wagoner, Jr.

COUNSEL

James F. White, Jr.

OF COUNSEL

Gregory G. Alexander
Mary Li Creasy (Resident, Tampa, Florida Office)
Robert R. Warchola (Resident, Tampa, Florida Office)
George O. Wilson, III (Resident, Tampa, Florida Office)

For full biographical listings, see the Martindale-Hubbell Law Directory

OKLAHOMA

*OKLAHOMA CITY,** Oklahoma Co.

CROWE & DUNLEVY, A PROFESSIONAL CORPORATION (AV)

1800 Mid-America Tower, 20 North Broadway, 73102-8273
Telephone: 405-235-7700
Fax: 405-239-6651
Email: marketing@crowedunlevy.com *URL:* http://www.crowedunlevy.com
Tulsa, Oklahoma Office: 500 Kennedy Building, 321 South Boston Avenue, 74103-3313.
Telephone: 918-592-9800.
Fax: 918-592-9801.
Norman, Oklahoma Office: Crowe & Dunlevy, 2500 South McGee, Suite 140, 73072-6705.
Telephone: 405-321-7317.
Fax: 405-360-4002.

Gary W. Davis
D. Kent Meyers
Jimmy Goodman
John J. Griffin, Jr.
Brooke Smith Murphy
Judy Hamilton Morse
Mack J. Morgan III
Mark S. Grossman
Kevin D. Gordon
Todd Taylor
Robert G. McCampbell
Tamela R. Hughlett
Joseph J. Ferretti

Lance W. Cargill
Brian C. Henderson
John M. Thompson

For Complete List of Firm Personnel, See General Section

For full biographical listings, see the Martindale-Hubbell Law Directory

DAY, EDWARDS, FEDERMAN, PROPESTER & CHRISTENSEN, P.C. (AV)

Suite 2900 Oklahoma Tower, 210 Park Avenue, 73102-5605
Telephone: 405-239-2121
Telecopier: 405-236-1012
URL: http://lawlinks.com/attys/ok/defpc.html

Bruce W. Day
William B. Federman
Joe E. Edwards
Richard P. Propester
J. Clay Christensen

(See Next Column)

DAY, EDWARDS, FEDERMAN, PROPESTER & CHRISTENSEN P.C., *Oklahoma City—Continued*

Ricki Valerie Sonders
Thomas Pitchlynn Howell, IV
Joel Warren Harmon
Gary L. Farnum

Representative Clients: Applied Thermal Systems, Inc.; BancFirst; Bank One, Oklahoma City; Bank of America, N.A.; Federal Deposit Insurance Corp.; Fidelity Brokerage Services, Inc.; First Community Bank, Binger; First National Bank and Trust Company of Weatherford; First State Bank & Trist Co., Hollis; Local Oklahoma Bank.

For Complete List of Firm Personnel, See General Section

For full biographical listings, see the Martindale-Hubbell Law Directory

PRINGLE & PRINGLE, A PROFESSIONAL CORPORATION (AV)

4101 North Classen Boulevard Suite A, 73118-2432
Telephone: 405-848-4810
Fax: 405-848-4819
Email: pringle@pringleandpringle.com *URL:* http://www.pringleandpringle.com

Lynn A. Pringle
Laura Nan Smith Pringle
Conni L. Allen

OF COUNSEL

Alvin C. Harrell
Michael P. Sullivan

Representative Clients: Bankers Systems, Inc.; Bank of Western Oklahoma, Elk City; The First National Bank and Trust Co., Chickasha; The Farmers Bank, Carnegie; Bank of the Panhandle, Guymon; FirstPlus Financial; Citizens State Bank, Roma, Texas; The Daniluk Corporation; Bank of Union; Pringle Publications Corporation.

For full biographical listings, see the Martindale-Hubbell Law Directory

JAYNE JARNIGAN ROBERTSON, P.C. (AV)

119 North Robinson, Suite 825, 73102
Telephone: 405-319-0400
Fax: 405-319-0404
Email: jaynerobertson@compuserve.com

Jayne J. Robertson

For full biographical listings, see the Martindale-Hubbell Law Directory

*TULSA,** Tulsa Co.

ATKINSON, HASKINS, NELLIS, BOUDREAUX, HOLEMAN, PHIPPS & BRITTINGHAM, A PROFESSIONAL CORPORATION (AV)

1500 ParkCentre, 525 South Main Street, 74103
Telephone: 918-582-8877
Fax: 918-585-8096
Email: ahnmail@ahn-law.com

Michael P. Atkinson, P.C.
Walter D. Haskins, P.C.
John J. Carwile

Representative Clients: Allstate Insurance Co.; Bayer Corp.; Crum & Forster Insurance Co.; Hartford Insurance Company; National American Insurance Co.; Federated Insurance Co.; Liberty Mutual Insurance Co.; Physicians Liability Insurance Co.; State Farm Mutual Automobile Insurance Co.; United States Aviation Underwriters.

For full biographical listings, see the Martindale-Hubbell Law Directory

BOESCHE, MCDERMOTT & ESKRIDGE (AV)

Suite 800 Oneok Plaza, 100 West Fifth Street, 74103
Telephone: 918-583-1777
Fax: 918-592-5809
Email: bme@intellex.com
Muskogee, Oklahoma Office: 1111 West Broadway, P.O. Box 2669, 74402.
Telephone: 918-683-6100.
Fax: 918-683-2303.

MEMBERS OF FIRM

R. Casey Cooper
David B. McKinney
Bradley K. Beasley
David A. Johnson
R. Kevin Layton
Sheila M. Powers

ASSOCIATES

Byron E. (Rusty) Brown
Christopher K. Woosley

OF COUNSEL

Clifford K. Cate, Jr. (Resident at Muskogee)

Representative Clients: Apache Corporation; Cigna Corp.; Elf Atochem North America, Inc.; General American Life Insurance Company.

For Complete List of Firm Personnel, See General Section

For full biographical listings, see the Martindale-Hubbell Law Directory

CROWE & DUNLEVY, A PROFESSIONAL CORPORATION (AV)

500 Kennedy Building, 321 South Boston Avenue, 74103-3313
Telephone: 918-592-9800
Fax: 918-592-9801
Email: marketing@crowedunlevy.com *URL:* http://www.crowedunlevy.com
Oklahoma City, Oklahoma Office: 1800 Mid-America Tower, 20 North Broadway, 73102-8273.
Telephone: 405-235-7700.
Fax: 405-239-6651.
Norman, Oklahoma Office: Crowe & Dunlevy, 2500 South McGee, Suite 140, 73072-6705.
Telephone: 405-321-7317.
Fax: 405-360-4002.

Michael J. Gibbens
Terry M. Thomas

Timothy F. Sterling

For Complete List of Firm Personnel, See General Section

For full biographical listings, see the Martindale-Hubbell Law Directory

CRUMP, TOLSON & PAGE LLP (AV)

1516 South Boston Avenue, Suite 310, 74119-4019
Telephone: 918-583-2393
Fax: 918-583-2394
Email: kcrump@crumptolson.com *URL:* http://www.lawyers.com/crumplaw

MEMBERS OF FIRM

Kenneth E. Crump Jr.
Michael B. Tolson
David P. Page (Resident)

ASSOCIATE

Rodney H. Dusinberre

For full biographical listings, see the Martindale-Hubbell Law Directory

SNEED LANG, P.C. (AV)

2300 Williams Center Tower II, Two West Second Street, 74103
Telephone: 918-583-3145
Telecopier: 918-582-0410

James C. Lang
D. Faith Orlowski
Brian S. Gaskill
G. Steven Stidham
Stephen R. McNamara
Thomas E. Black, Jr.
Robbie Emery Burke
Patrick O. Waddel
Randolph P. Stainer
Steven K. Balman
Brian T. Inbody
D. Michael McBride III

OF COUNSEL

James L. Sneed

Representative Clients: Amoco Production Co.; Bank One, Texas; Enron Corp.; Halliburton Energy Services; Helmerich & Payne, Inc.; Shell Oil Co.; State Farm Mutual Automobile Insurance Co.; The Williams Companies.

For full biographical listings, see the Martindale-Hubbell Law Directory

OREGON

*EUGENE,** Lane Co.

MUHLHEIM PALMER & WADE, A PROFESSIONAL CORPORATION (AV)

U.S. Bank Center, 800 Willamette Street, Suite 700, 97401-2933
Telephone: 541-687-4757
Facsimile: 541-687-4780
Email: mpw-law.com *URL:* http://www.lawyers.com/muhleimpalmer&wade

Wilson C. Muhlheim
R. Scott Palmer
Carolyn G. Wade

Pamela Egan Singer
Stephen C.P. Carroll
Heidi Von Ravensberg
Edward C Singer

LEGAL SUPPORT PERSONNEL

Dawnne L. Linenbrink, CLAS
Fern Puls
Richard Rickson

Representative Clients: Harvest Ford Lincoln Mercury; Georgia Pacific Employees Federal Credit Union; Valley of The Rogue Bank; Bank of Southern Oregon; The Boulders on the River, Inc.; Trans Union Corporation; Heritage Mall, Ltd.; Sandpines Golf Resort; Ariki Co., Ltd.; Water Sports, Inc.; Lowther Assets.

For full biographical listings, see the Martindale-Hubbell Law Directory

*MEDFORD,** Jackson Co.

FROHNMAYER, DEATHERAGE, PRATT, JAMIESON, CLARKE & MOORE, P.C. (AV)

Larson Creek Professional Center, 2592 E. Barnett Road, 97504
Telephone: 541-779-2333
Fax: 541-779-6379
Email: fdfirm@internetcds.com

Otto J. Frohnmayer
William V. Deatherage
Steven H. Pratt
Stephen G. Jamieson
Mark D. Clarke
Bernard S. Moore
Thomas F. Armosino, Jr.

Tracy M. McGovern
Frederick H. Lundblade
Christian Oelke

Local Counsel for: Allstate Insurance Company; CNA; Farmers Insurance Group; Northwest Physicians Mutual Insurance Company; Professional Liability Fund.
General Counsel for: Lithia Motors, Inc.

For full biographical listings, see the Martindale-Hubbell Law Directory

PENNSYLVANIA

BALA CYNWYD, Montgomery Co.

KANIA, LINDNER, LASAK AND FEENEY (AV)

Suite 525, Two Bala Plaza, 19004
Telephone: 610-667-3240
Fax: 610-668-9676
Email: kllf@aol.com

Arthur J. Kania
Albert A. Lindner
John Lasak
Thomas J. Feeney, III
Robert A. Griffiths

A list of Representative Clients for which the firm serves as General Counsel or Local Counsel will be supplied upon request.

For full biographical listings, see the Martindale-Hubbell Law Directory

BENSALEM, Bucks Co.

RUDOLPH, DORIAN, GOLDSTEIN, ROCHESTIE, WISNIEWSKI & TAYLOR, P.C. (AV)

Neshaminy Valley Commons, 2410 Bristol Road, 19020
Telephone: 215-750-7200
Fax: 215-750-9294
Email: admin@rudolphdorian.com *URL:* http://www.palaw.lawoffice.com
Philadelphia, Pennsylvania Office: 1818 Market Street, Suite 2300, 19103.
Telephone: 215-299-9900.
Fax: 215-299-9910.

Edward Rudolph
Harry A. Dorian, Jr.
Stephan H. Goldstein
Gary A. Rochestie
Mark A. Wisniewski
John J. Taylor
Jeffrey S. Orchinik
Kim A. Piermattei
Michael Parlow
Lawrence P. Kempner
Nancy M. Bonner

For full biographical listings, see the Martindale-Hubbell Law Directory

BLUE BELL, Montgomery Co.

KELLEY & MURPHY (AV)

Union Meeting Corporate Center V, Suite 160 925 Harvest Drive, 19422
Telephone: 215-643-6500
Fax: 215-643-8356
Cable Address: "BIGTIME"
Email: kmlaw@counsel.com

Joseph T. Kelley, Jr.
Patrick G. Murphy
Joseph T. Kelley, III

LEGAL SUPPORT PERSONNEL

Marianne Rowen
Tanja M.Z. Barron

For full biographical listings, see the Martindale-Hubbell Law Directory

*EASTON,** Northampton Co.

COHEN & FEELEY, P.C. (AV)

2940 William Penn Highway, 18045
Telephone: 610-258-0111
Fax: 610-258-8095
Email: cohenfeeley@enter.net *URL:* http://www.seriouslyinjured.com
Allentown, Pennsylvania Office: 1405 North Cedar Crest Boulevard, Suite 205, 18104.
Telephone: 610-821-7702.
Fax: 610-821-9067.

(See Next Column)

Martin D. Cohen
Dennis F. Feeley

For full biographical listings, see the Martindale-Hubbell Law Directory

FORT WASHINGTON, Montgomery Co.

DALLER GREENBERG & DIETRICH, LLP (AV)

Valley Green Corporate Center, 7111 Valley Green Road, 19034
Telephone: 215-836-1100
Facsimile: 215-836-2845
URL: http://www.dallergreenberg.com
Haddon Heights, New Jersey Office: 2 White Horse Pike.
Telephone: 856-547-9068.
Facsimile: 856-547-2391.

PARTNERS

Morton F. Daller
Edward A. Greenberg
Gerhard P. Dietrich
Eileen M. Johnson
Dennis R. Callahan

ASSOCIATES

Tracy Canuso Nugent (Resident, Haddon Heights, New Jersey Office)
Catherine N. Walto
Mark S. Kirby
Marie Handrich Kramer
Alison R. Rohmer

For full biographical listings, see the Martindale-Hubbell Law Directory

HANOVER, York Co.

BARLEY, SNYDER, SENFT & COHEN, LLC (AV)

Formerly: Daniel M. Frey & Associates, P.C.
14 Center Square, 17331
Telephone: 717-637-6239
Fax: 717-637-5407
Email: barley@barley.com *URL:* http://www.barley.com
Lancaster, Pennsylvania Office: 126 East King Street.
Telephone: 717-299-5201.
Fax: 717-291-4660.
Harrisburg, Pennsylvania Office: 240 North Third Street.
Telephone: 717-238-8263.
Fax: 717-238-8278.
York, Pennsylvania Office: 100 East Market Street.
Telephone: 717-846-8888.
Fax: 717-843-8492.
Chambersburg, Pennsylvania Office: 247 Lincoln Way East.
Telephone: 717-264-6494.
Fax: 717-264-1662.
Reading, Pennsylvania Office: 501 Washington Street.
Telephone: 610-376-6651.
Fax: 610-376-5243.
Birdsboro, Pennsylvania Office: 115 E. Main Street.
Telephone: 610-582-2735.
Hamburg, Pennsylvania Office: 239 State Street.
Telephone: 610-562-3721.
Oley, Pennsylvania Office: Route 73 and Main Street.
Telephone: 610-987-6350.
Morgantown, Pennsylvania Office: Route 23.
Telephone: 610-286-5958.

MEMBERS OF FIRM

Daniel M. Frey
David R. Keller
Jeffrey D. Lobach
Paul G. Mattaini
Timothy P. Brown
Deborah A. Datte
Michael W. Davis

ASSOCIATES

Craig T. Trebilcock
John L. Senft
Kimberly J. Decker
Andrew T. Kravitz

Representative Clients: Bank of Hanover and Trust Co.; J.A. Myers Building and Development Inc.; Snyders of Hanover; Sheppard Enterprises; D.F. Stauffer Biscuit; Fulton Bank/Fulton Financial Corp.; Summit Health; South Central Community Health.

For Complete List of Firm Personnel, See General Section

For full biographical listings, see the Martindale-Hubbell Law Directory

*HARRISBURG,** Dauphin Co.

BARLEY, SNYDER, SENFT & COHEN, LLC (AV)

240 North Third Street, P.O. Box 1129, 17108
Telephone: 717-238-8263
Fax: 717-238-8278
Email: barley@barley.com *URL:* http://www.barley.com
Lancaster, Pennsylvania Office: 126 East King Street.
Telephone: 717-299-5201.
Fax: 717-291-4660.
York, Pennsylvania Office: 100 East Market Street.
Telephone: 717-846-8888.
Fax: 717-843-8492.
Chambersburg, Pennsylvania Office: 247 Lincoln Way East.
Telephone: 717-264-6494.
Fax: 717-264-1662.

(See Next Column)

BARLEY, SNYDER, SENFT & COHEN LLC, *Harrisburg—Continued*

Reading, Pennsylvania Office: 501 Washington Street.
Telephone: 610-376-6651.
Fax: 610-376-5243.
Hanover, Pennsylvania Office: 14 Center Square.
Telephone: 717-637-6239.
Fax: 717-637-5407.
Birdsboro, Pennsylvania Office: 115 E. Main Street.
Telephone: 610-582-2735.
Hamburg, Pennsylvania Office: 239 State Street.
Telephone: 610-562-3721.
Oley, Pennsylvania Office: Route 73 and Main Street.
Telephone: 610-987-6350.
Morgantown, Pennsylvania Office: Route 23.
Telephone: 610-286-5958.

MEMBERS OF FIRM

Harry J. Rubin
David R. Keller
Brian R. Ott
Michael S. Butler
Michael W. Davis

ASSOCIATE

Robert Freedenberg

RETIRED

H. Robert Lasday

For full biographical listings, see the Martindale-Hubbell Law Directory

MCNEES, WALLACE & NURICK (AV)

100 Pine Street, P.O. Box 1166, 17108-1166
Telephone: 717-232-8000
Fax: 717-237-5300
Email: info@mwn.com *URL:* http://www.mwn.com
Columbus, Ohio Office: 21 East State Street, Suite 1700, 43215.
Telephone: 614-469-8000.
Fax: 614-469-4653.
Washington, D.C. Office: 1200 G Street, N.W., 20005.
Telephone: 202-434-8991.
Fax: 202-434-8707.
Hazleton, Pennsylvania Office: 1 South Church Street, Suite 302, 18201.
Telephone: 570-455-8300.
Fax: 570-455-8390.

MEMBERS OF THE FIRM

Alan R. Boynton, Jr.
Harvey Freedenberg
Donald B. Kaufman
James W. Kutz
Delano M. Lantz
David E. Lehman
Elizabeth A. Maguschak (Resident, Hazleton Office)
Robert A. Mills
Nedric L. Nissly
Dana Stevens Scaduto
Diane M. Tokarsky
Lawrence R. Wieder
William M. Young, Jr.

OF COUNSEL

Jonathan H. Rudd
Carol A. Steinour

ASSOCIATES

Jeffrey F. Champagne
James P. DeAngelo
Debra P. Fourlas
Helen L. Gemmill
Scott A. Gould
Brian F. Jackson
Michael R. Kelley
Curtis N. Stambaugh
Charles T. Young, Jr.

For Complete List of Firm Personnel, See General Section

For full biographical listings, see the Martindale-Hubbell Law Directory

*LANCASTER,** Lancaster Co.

BARLEY, SNYDER, SENFT & COHEN, LLC (AV)

126 East King Street, 17602-2893
Telephone: 717-299-5201
Fax: 717-291-4660
Email: barley@barley.com *URL:* http://www.barley.com
Reading, Pennsylvania Office: 501 Washington Street.
Telephone: 610-376-6651.
Fax: 610-376-5243.
Harrisburg, Pennsylvania Office: 240 North Third Street.
Telephone: 717-238-8263.
Fax: 717-238-8278.
York, Pennsylvania Office: 100 East Market Street.
Telephone: 717-846-8888.
Fax: 717-843-8492.
Chambersburg, Pennsylvania Office: 247 Lincoln Way East.
Telephone: 717-264-6494.
Fax: 717-264-1662.
Hanover, Pennsylvania Office: 14 Center Square.
Telephone: 717-637-6239.
Fax: 717-637-5407.
Birdsboro, Pennsylvania Office: 115 E. Main Street.
Telephone: 610-582-2735.
Hamburg, Pennsylvania Office: 239 State Street.
Telephone: 610-562-3721.
Oley, Pennsylvania Office: Route 73 and Main Street.
Telephone: 610-987-6350.

(See Next Column)

Morgantown, Pennsylvania Office: Route 23.
Telephone: 610-286-5958.

MEMBERS OF FIRM

John O. Shirk
James R. Adams
W. Jeffrey Sidebottom
Christopher W. Mattson
Jesse C. Robinson
Paul M. Browning
Kathleen Ann Gray
George C. Werner, Jr.
David R. Keller
Caroline M. Hoffer
Paul G. Mattaini
Elaine Pennington Stanko
Paul D. Clouser
Michael A. Moore
Kendra D. McGuire
Anne E. Doliner
Timothy P. Brown
Deborah A. Datte
Ronald H. Pollock, Jr.
Michael S. Butler
Michael W. Davis
Katherine Betz Kravitz
Bruce J. Wolstoncroft

ASSOCIATES

Nancy Mayer Hughes
Craig T. Trebilcock
Leigh A. J. Ellis
Hanna-Aurelia Dunlap
Barbara M. Boben
Jennifer L. Craighead
Scott F. Landis
Robert A. Evarts
James F. Devine, III
Philip A. Wolgemuth
Theresa M. Melchiorre
John T. Reed
Gene P. Otto
Cynthia A. Otto
Stephanie Carfley
Kurt W. McCabe
Daniel M. Lieberman

RETIRED

Paul A. Mueller, Jr.
Charles R. Cooper, Jr.
John T. Barber

Counsel for: Franklin & Marshall College; Fulton Bank/Fulton Financial Corp.; Lancaster Chamber of Commerce and Industry; Lancaster General Hospital; Robert A. Kinsley, Inc.
Local Counsel for: Armstrong World Industries; Susquehanna Pfaltzgraff Co.; Graham Packaging.
Insurance Defense Counsel for: Medical Protective Co.; The PMA Group.

For full biographical listings, see the Martindale-Hubbell Law Directory

*NORRISTOWN,** Montgomery Co.

MURPHY, OLIVER, CAIOLA & GOWEN, A PROFESSIONAL LAW CORPORATION (AV)

43 East Marshall Street, 19401-4828
Telephone: 610-272-4222; 610-279-3838
Fax: 610-272-2549; 610-275-0140
Email: molaw@injury-law.com *URL:* http://www.injury-law.com
Spring City, Pennsylvania Office: 500 S. Main Street, 19475.
Telephone: 610-948-3770.
Pottstown, Pennsylvania Office: 5 Sunnybrook Road, 19464.
Telephone: 610-323-3480.
West Chester, Pennsylvania Office: 1534 McDaniel Drive, Westtown Business Center, 19250.
Telephone: 610-272-4222.

James J. Oliver
Frank P. Murphy
Frank L. Caiola
Thomas L. Gowen, Jr.
Carla E. Connor
Barbara A. Barnes

John F. Haskins, Jr.
Cynthia Love Dengler
Carol A. Crisci

LEGAL SUPPORT PERSONNEL

Patricia A. Talese (Paralegal)
Kathleen Nicholson

For full biographical listings, see the Martindale-Hubbell Law Directory

*PHILADELPHIA,** Philadelphia Co.

ABRAMSON & FREEDMAN, L.L.C. (AV)

2128 Locust Street, 19103
Telephone: 215-545-2400
Telecopier: 215-545-8537
Haddonfield, New Jersey Office: 20 Kings Highway West.
Telephone: 609-795-5363.
Fax: 609-354-0020.

Gilbert B. Abramson
Jeffrey M. Freedman

Michael B. Tolcott
Stanley B. Cheiken (Resident, Haddonfield, New Jersey Office)
Glen L. Abramson

For full biographical listings, see the Martindale-Hubbell Law Directory

ANAPOL, SCHWARTZ, WEISS, COHAN, FELDMAN AND SMALLEY, P.C. (AV)

1900 Delancey Place, 19103
Telephone: 215-735-1130
Fax: 215-735-2024
URL: http://www.aswc.net
Other Philadelphia, Pennsylvania Office: 1710 Spruce Street.
Fax: 215-735-2211.

(See Next Column)

ANAPOL, SCHWARTZ, WEISS, COHAN, FELDMAN AND SMALLEY P.C.—*Continued*

Cherry Hill, New Jersey Office: 402 Park Boulevard, 08002.
Telephone: 1-609-427-9229.
Fax: 609-488-1396.
Fairless Hills, Pennsylvania Office: 920 Trenton Road.
Telephone: 215-945-6799.
Reading, Pennsylvania Office: 146 North 6th Street.
Telephone: 610-375-7488.
Media, Pennsylvania Office: 334 W. Front Street, 19063.
Telephone: 610-892-3714.

Alan Schwartz
Sol H. Weiss
Lawrence R. Cohan
Joel D. Feldman
Howard J. Levin
Bernard W. Smalley
Stanton Dubin
Margaret A. Barry
Stephen J. Pokiniewski, Jr.
Sidney M. Grobman
Nelson Levin

Nathaniel E.P. Ehrlich
Thomas R. Anapol
Miriam Benton Barish
Patrice A. Gillotti
Michele Lee Reed
Heather J. Lipson
Michelle L. Altenpohl
Lisa R. Schwartz
Kevin R. Marciano
Brian J. Taylor
Tobias L. Millrood
Tracy A. Finken

OF COUNSEL

Paul R. Anapol
Richard B. Schwartz (Resident, Other Philadelphia Office)
Mark F. Seltzer

Reference: Meridian Bank, Philadelphia, Pennsylvania.

For full biographical listings, see the Martindale-Hubbell Law Directory

---

ASTOR WEISS KAPLAN & ROSENBLUM, LLP (AV)

The Bellevue, 6th Floor, 200 South Broad Street, 19102
Telephone: 215-790-0100
Fax: 215-790-0509
Email: lawyers@astorweiss.com
Bala Cynwyd, Pennsylvania Office: 401 City Avenue, Suite 500.
Telephone: 610-667-8660.
Fax: 610-667-2783.

MEMBERS OF FIRM

Alvin M. Weiss (1936-1976)
Paul C. Astor
G. David Rosenblum
Arthur H. Kaplan
Barbara Oaks Silver
David S. Workman
David Gutin
David S. Mandel
Gerald J. Schorr

ASSOCIATES

Christopher P. Flannery
Janet G. Felgoise
Elizabeth F. Warner
Daniel A. Shabel
Frances F. Freedman

SPECIAL COUNSEL

Neil Hurowitz
Jerrold V. Moss
Robert P. Style

OF COUNSEL

Edward W. Silver

For full biographical listings, see the Martindale-Hubbell Law Directory

---

CONRAD O'BRIEN GELLMAN & ROHN, P.C. (AV)

Sixteenth Floor, 1515 Market Street, 19102-1916
Telephone: 215-864-9600
Fax: 215-864-9620; 864-9621; 864-9622
Email: lawyers@cogr.com *URL:* http://www.COGR.COM
Cherry Hill, New Jersey Office: Woodland Falls Corporate Park, 200 Lake Drive East, Suite 206.
Telephone: 856-665-0888.
Fax: 856-665-5888.
West Chester, Pennsylvania Office: 17 West Gay Street, Suite 100.
Telephone: 610-701-9100.
Fax: 610-701-9195.

K. Robert Conrad
William J. O'Brien
Nancy J. Gellman
James J. Rohn
John (Jack) A. Guernsey
John H. McKeon, Jr.
Howard M. Klein
Robert N. Feltoon
Deborah J. Krabbendam
Patricia M. Hamill
Nicholas M. Centrella

OF COUNSEL

Alan Paul Novak
Robert A. Klein
Stephen Weaver
Clare Keefe Foster

(See Next Column)

Lisa B. Wershaw
Helen J. Esbenshade
Debra C. Swartz
Thomas W. Blair
Gabriel H. Holdsman
Jonathan K.M. Crawford (Not admitted in PA)
Andrew C. Hanan
Frank R. Emmerich Jr.
Jacquelyn J. Ager
Andrew R. Duffy
Kelly G. Huller
Steven Pachman
Susan L. Bucknum

For full biographical listings, see the Martindale-Hubbell Law Directory

---

DIDONATO & WINTERHALTER, P.C. (AV)

1818 Market Street, Suite 3520, 19103-3629
Telephone: 215-564-5050
Telecopier: 215-564-5597
URL: http://www.lawyers.com/didonato
Marlton, New Jersey Office: One Greentree Centre, Route 73 & Greenfield Road, Suite 201, 08053.
Telephone: 609-263-2700.
Telecopier: 609-263-9192.

Edward J. DiDonato
Paul J. Winterhalter
Eugene Camposano

For full biographical listings, see the Martindale-Hubbell Law Directory

---

F. EMMETT FITZPATRICK, P.C. (AV)

926 Public Ledger Building, 19106
Telephone: 215-925-5200
Fax: 215-925-5991
Email: info@toplaw.com *URL:* http://www.toplaw.com

F. Emmett Fitzpatrick
F. Emmett Fitzpatrick, III

NiaLena Caravasos

LEGAL SUPPORT PERSONNEL

Doreen Howley (Paralegal)

For full biographical listings, see the Martindale-Hubbell Law Directory

---

LAW OFFICES OF JOHN J. GALLAGHER, P.C. (AV)

Suite 1100, 1760 Market Street, 19103
Telephone: 215-963-1555
Fax: 215-963-9104
Email: jjgall@ix.netcom.com *URL:* http://www.lawyers.com/johngallagher

John J. Gallagher

Michael S. Henry
Laura Carberry Muldowney
Joseph H. Meltzer
Larisa Tenberg

LEGAL SUPPORT PERSONNEL

Ronald Winkelvoss
Helene Schramm

For full biographical listings, see the Martindale-Hubbell Law Directory

---

GOLDFEIN & JOSEPH, A PROFESSIONAL CORPORATION (AV)

1600 Market Street 33rd Floor, 19103-7288
Telephone: 215-979-8200
Fax: 215-979-8201
URL: http://www.goldfeinlaw.com
Princeton, New Jersey Office: Princeton Metro Center, Suite 115, 5 Vaughn Drive.
Telephone: 609-520-0400.
Fax: 609-520-1450.
Wilmington, Delaware Office: PNC Bank Center, Suite 1110, P.O. Box 2206, 222 Delaware Avenue.
Telephone: 302-656-3301.
Fax: 302-656-0643.
New York, New York Office: 150 Broadway, Suite 1212, 10038.
Telephone: 212-791-0340.
Fax: 212-791-0347.

Edward B. Joseph
Fredric L. Goldfein
E. Chandler Hosmer, III
David C. Weinberg
Bernard L. Levinthal
Roseann Lynn Brenner
Gary H. Kaplan
John A. Turlik

Michael A. Billotti
Medford J. Brown, III
Robert P. Coleman
Robert T. Connor
Charles D. Cooper
Kelly A. Costello
Lawrence E. Currier
Janet E. Golup
Christine Renee Guiliano
David M. Katzenstein
Matthew A Kelly, III
Deborah M. Knight
Pamela A. Post
Thomas M. Savon
Julie M. Sebring (Not admitted in PA)
Robert M. Stroh
Marc R. Wilner
Anthony F. Zabicki, Jr.

For full biographical listings, see the Martindale-Hubbell Law Directory

Philadelphia—Continued

HOLLSTEIN KEATING CATTELL JOHNSON & GOLDSTEIN, P.C. (AV)
Suite 1602 1608 Walnut Street, 19103
Telephone: 215-893-9488
Fax: 215-893-9480
Email: JFJ@HKCJG.com
Voorhees, New Jersey Office: 1016 Laurel Oak Road, Suite 2, 08043.
Telephone: 609-309-9000.
Fax: 609-309-0337.
Wilmington, Delaware Office: One Commerce Center, Suite 730, 12th and Orange Streets, 19801.
Telephone: 302-884-6700.
Fax: 302-573-2507.

Richard W. Hollstein
E. Michael Keating, III
Edward V. Cattell, Jr.
James W. Johnson
Stuart M. Goldstein (Resident, Voorhees, New Jersey Office)
Mark G. Lionetti
John E. Tyrrell
Lynne M. Parker (at Voorhees, New Jersey and Wilmington, Delaware Offices)
Paul F. Weisbein
James D. Lloyd
Nancy D. Wagman
Margaret M. Grasso

LEGAL SUPPORT PERSONNEL

Nancy Hevener (Paralegal)
Libby Carrol (Paralegal)

For full biographical listings, see the Martindale-Hubbell Law Directory

KAUFMAN, COREN, RESS & WEIDMAN, P.C. (AV)
1525 Locust Street, 17th Floor, 19102
Telephone: 215-735-8700
FAX: 215-735-5170

Howard J. Kaufman
Steven M. Coren
Douglas Evan Ress
Peter J. Weidman

OF COUNSEL

Susanna E. Lachs
David Dormont

Peter J. Leyh
Esther L. Hornik
Bruce Bellingham

For full biographical listings, see the Martindale-Hubbell Law Directory

KITTREDGE, DONLEY, ELSON, FULLEM & EMBICK, LLP (AV)
Fifth Floor, The Bank Building, 421 Chestnut Street, 19106-2416
Telephone: 215-829-9900
Fax: 215-829-9888
Email: lawoffice@kdefe.com *URL:* http://www.kdefe.com

MEMBERS OF FIRM

Patrick W. Kittredge
Joseph M. Donley
Barry R. Elson
Joseph W. Fullem, Jr.
John R. Embick
Keith E. Johnston

ASSOCIATES

Glenn E. Davis
Michael S. Soule
Patricia Powers
Brendan P. McGlynn
Lisa G. Miller
Edward Bigham
Michael K. Smith (1963-1995)

OF COUNSEL

Richard B. Pearl

For full biographical listings, see the Martindale-Hubbell Law Directory

KLEINBARD, BELL & BRECKER LLP (AV)
Suite 700, 1900 Market Street, 19103
Telephone: 215-568-2000
Facsimile: 215-568-0140
Montclair, New Jersey Office: 240 Claremont Avenue, 07042.
Telephone: 973-233-0600.
Facsimile: 973-233-9390.

Joseph S. Kleinbard (1905-1994)
Robert John Brecker (1916-1996)

COUNSEL TO THE FIRM

Arthur S. Keyser

MEMBERS OF FIRM

Paul E. Bomze
Murray I. Blackman
Howard J. Davis
Steven R. Waxman
Steven J. Engelmyer (Resident, Montclair Office)
David L. Hyman (Resident, Montclair Office)
Imogene E. Hughes
John P. Hickey
Jay R. Goldstein
Ralph J. Mauro
Thomas H. Speranza
Lisa E. Brody

ASSOCIATES

Mary Beth H. Gray
Eric J. Rothschild
Mary Vassallo Slinkard
Michael A. Frattone
Benjamin C. Graff (Not admitted in PA)
Ralph F. Salgado

(See Next Column)

COUNSEL

Joseph Bell

For full biographical listings, see the Martindale-Hubbell Law Directory

LEVIN, FISHBEIN, SEDRAN & BERMAN (AV)
Suite 500, 510 Walnut Street, 19106-3697
Telephone: 215-592-1500
Fax: 215-592-4663
Email: lfsb@psinet.com

MEMBERS OF FIRM

Arnold Levin
Michael D. Fishbein
Howard J. Sedran
Laurence S. Berman
Frederick S. Longer

Craig D. Ginsburg
Cheryl R. Brown Hill
Donald E. Haviland, Jr.
Daniel C. Levin
Terrianne Benedetto
Charles E. Schaffer
Austin B. Cohen

LEGAL SUPPORT PERSONNEL

Lee Ann Fitzpatrick
Cheryl Hesson

For full biographical listings, see the Martindale-Hubbell Law Directory

LEVY, ANGSTREICH, FINNEY, BALDANTE, RUBENSTEIN & COREN, P.C. (AV)
18th Floor, 1616 Walnut Street, 19103
Telephone: 215-735-1616
FAX: 215-545-2642
Email: lafbrc@levyangstreich.com *URL:* http://www.levyangstreich.com
Cherry Hill, New Jersey Office: Woodcrest Pavilion, Suite 100, Ten Melrose Avenue, 08003.
Telephone: 856-424-8967.
Fax: 856-795-7447.

Mark S. Levy
Steven E. Angstreich
Lawrence D. Finney
John W. Baldante
Martin G. Rubenstein
Michael Coren
Carolyn C. Lindheim
Thomas S. Harty

Amy R. Brandt
Melissa T. Herskowitz
Silvia M. Ferri
Beth E. Castelli
Theresa Sweeney Corson
Catherine E. Margolis

LEGAL SUPPORT PERSONNEL

Legal Administrator Michele R. Galasso

For full biographical listings, see the Martindale-Hubbell Law Directory

HENRY C. LUCAS, III (AV)
2000 Market Street, 6th Floor, 19103
Telephone: 215-851-6620
Fax: 215-851-6644
Email: 6762434@mcimail.com *URL:* http://www.lawyers.com/henryclucas111

For full biographical listings, see the Martindale-Hubbell Law Directory

MANTA AND WELGE, A PROFESSIONAL CORPORATION (AV)
2000 Market Street, 6th Floor, 19103
Telephone: 215-851-6600
Telecopy: 215-851-6644
URL: http://www.mantalaw.com
Allentown, Pennsylvania Office: Suite 204, 5000 Tilghman Street.
Telephone: 610-395-7499.
Fax: 610-366-5096.
Harrisburg, Pennsylvania Office: Governors Row, 27 North Front Street.
Telephone: 717-236-8420.
West Trenton, New Jersey Office: 810 Bear Tavern Road, Suite 301.
Telephone: 609-883-6990.
Fax: 609-883-7730.
Wilmington, Delaware Office: Suite 1400, Mellon Bank Center, 919 Market Street.
Telephone: 302-655-7460.
Fax: 302-655-7004.

MEMBERS OF FIRM

Mark A. Welge
Albert L. Piccerilli
Kathleen Misturak-Gingrich
Thomas B. O'Brien, Jr.
Francis G. X. Pileggi (Resident, Wilmington, Delaware Office)

Joseph B. Silverstein
Yasmeen Sabina Khaleel
Janelle E. Fulton
Denise Adamucci
Jennifer M. Welding
Michael A. Green

For full biographical listings, see the Martindale-Hubbell Law Directory

Philadelphia—Continued

McKissock & Hoffman, P.C. (AV)

1700 Market Street, Suite 3000, 19103
Telephone: 215-246-2100
Fax: 215-246-2144
Westmont, New Jersey Office: 216 Haddon Avenue, Suite 603.
Telephone: 609-858-1650.
Fax: 609-858-1466.
Doylestown, Pennsylvania Office: 16 North Franklin Street, Suite 300.
Telephone: 215-345-4501.
Fax: 215-246-4503.
Harrisburg, Pennsylvania Office: 105 North Front Street, Suite 205.
Telephone: 717-234-0103.
Fax: 717-234-1350.
West Chester, Pennsylvania Office: 31 South High Street, P.O. Box 3086.
Telephone: 610-738-8850.
Fax: 610-738-9121.

J. Bruce McKissock
Peter J. Hoffman
Leslie Anne Miller
Jeffrey B. Albert
Jill Baratz Clarke
John J. McGrath (Resident, Westmont, New Jersey Office)
Donald J. Brooks, Jr.
William J. Mundy
Bryan Craig Black (Resident, Harrisburg Office)
Eileen Lampe

OF COUNSEL

Marybeth Stanton Christiansen

For full biographical listings, see the Martindale-Hubbell Law Directory

---

Ralph D. Samuel & Co. A Professional Corporation (AV)

225 South 15th Street, Suite 1776, 19102
Telephone: 215-893-9992
Fax: 215-893-9996
Email: RalphSamuel@lawmine.com *URL:* http://www.lawyers.com/ralphdsamuellaw

Ralph David Samuel
Lynn Malmgren

For full biographical listings, see the Martindale-Hubbell Law Directory

---

Sandals, Langer & Taylor, LLP (AV)

One Liberty Place 50th Floor, 1650 Market Street, 19103-7301
Telephone: 215-419-6500
Fax: 215-419-6501
Email: Main@SLT-LAW.COM *URL:* http://www.slt-law.com

Howard I. Langer
Alan M. Sandals
John R. Taylor

Scott M. Lempert
Kay E. Sickles

For full biographical listings, see the Martindale-Hubbell Law Directory

---

Savett Frutkin Podell & Ryan, P.C. (AV)

Suite 700, 325 Chestnut Street, 19106
Telephone: 215-923-5400
FAX: 923-9353
Email: SFPRPC@OP.NET

Stuart H. Savett
Robert P. Frutkin
Barbara A. Podell
Katharine M. Ryan

For full biographical listings, see the Martindale-Hubbell Law Directory

---

Schwartz & Blackman (AV)

Washington West Building, 235 South 8th Street, 19106-3593
Telephone: 215-925-5800
Fax: 215-925-1590
Cherry Hill, New Jersey Office: 411 East Route 70, Suite 200 A, 08034.
Telephone: 609-427-0614.

Stacey L. Schwartz
Philip L. Blackman

For full biographical listings, see the Martindale-Hubbell Law Directory

---

James C. Schwartzman & Associates, P.C. (AV)

1760 Market Street, 12th Floor, 19103
Telephone: 215-563-2233
Fax: 215-563-2134

James C. Schwartzman

Gary Tilles
Dana Pirone Garrity

For full biographical listings, see the Martindale-Hubbell Law Directory

---

Spector Gadon & Rosen, P.C. (AV)

Seven Penn Center, 1635 Market Street, 7th Floor, 19103
Telephone: 215-241-8888
Fax: 215-241-8844
Moorestown, New Jersey Office: Spector, Gadon & Rosen, P.C. 307 Fellowship Road. P.O. Box 1001, 08057.
Telephone: 609-778-8100.
Fax: 609-722-5344.

Paul R. Rosen
Steven F. Gadon
Samuel L. Hirshland
Elliott K. Braverman
Milton H. Cross
Edward G. Fitzgerald, Jr.
Alan B. Epstein
Lary I. Zucker
Bruce L. Thall
Daniel J. Dugan
Alan H. Wallen
David M. Giles
Leslie Beth Baskin
Steven J. Polansky
Stanley Peter Jaskiewicz
Alan J. Mittelman
George M. Vinci, Jr.

OF COUNSEL

Arthur E. Vossberg III

Timothy C. Russell
Peter J. Boyer
Alan M. Rosen
Nancy Abrams
Claudia L. Boyd
Scott A. Burr
Heather M. Eichenbaum
Joshua F. Laff
Kenneth J. LaFiandra
Paul A. Loh
Brooke Caroline Madonna
Lynda M. Miller
David B. Picker
Kelly R. Ramsdell
Thomas Rapp
Suzanne I. Schiller
Michael C. Wagner

For full biographical listings, see the Martindale-Hubbell Law Directory

---

Spector & Roseman, A Professional Corporation (AV)

1818 Market Street, Suite 2500, 19103
Telephone: 215-496-0300
Telecopier: 215-496-6611
Email: espector@spectorandroseman.com *URL:* http://www.spectorandroseman.com
San Diego, California Office: 600 West Broadway, 1600 One American Plaza, 92101.
Telephone: 619-338-4514.
Telecopier: 619-231-7423.

Eugene A. Spector
Robert M. Roseman
Jeffrey L. Kodroff
Ellen Gusikoff Stewart (Not admitted in PA)

Ronnie D. Seidel
Diane Doherty (Not admitted in PA)
Anthony Chu
Andrew D. Abramowitz (Not admitted in PA)
Joshua H. Grabar
Howard C. Gottlieb
Michael P. Nachman
Beth Mandel Rosenthal

OF COUNSEL

Anthony J. Bolognese

LEGAL SUPPORT PERSONNEL

PARALEGALS

Joseph Morrison
Michelle Adams
Carole Staiger

For full biographical listings, see the Martindale-Hubbell Law Directory

---

Weir & Partners LLP (AV)

A Pennsylvania Limited Liability Partnership
Suite 500, The Widener Building, 1339 Chestnut Street, 19107
Telephone: 215-665-8181
Telefax: 215-665-8464
Email: info@weirpartners.com
Turnersville, New Jersey Office: 215 Fries Mill Road, 08012.
Telephone: 609-740-1490.
Telefax: 609-740-1491.

MEMBERS OF FIRM

Walter Weir, Jr.
Leonard S. Goodman
Susan Verbonitz
Jeffrey L. Rudnick
Robert D. Sayre
Stephen M. Giroux
Richard P. Coe, Jr.
Brett A. Datto
John B. York
Joseph C. Hare

ASSOCIATES

Bonnie R. Golub
Debra N. Nathanson
Tina L. Colman
Andrew K. Stutzman
Jeffrey A. Guth
Jason M Reiser
Madeline Flanagan

For full biographical listings, see the Martindale-Hubbell Law Directory

*PITTSBURGH,** Allegheny Co.

HOGUE & LANNIS (AV)

3400 Gulf Tower, Grant Street at Seventh, 15219
Telephone: 412-263-5650
Fax: 412-263-5660
Email: hllawyers@aol.com

PARTNERS

Jon Geoffrey Hogue — Sandra L. Lannis

ASSOCIATES

Jeannine A. Schuster — George Frank Pomper

For full biographical listings, see the Martindale-Hubbell Law Directory

VOLLMER RULONG & KEATING, P.C. (AV)

Suite 1212 Grant Building, 310 Grant Street, 15219
Telephone: 412-391-2121
Telecopier: 412-391-3578
Email: vollmer@vollmerlaw.com *URL:* http://www.vollmerlaw.com

Charles J. Vollmer — Roger G. Rulong, Jr.
John R. Keating

Pamela J. Royesky

For full biographical listings, see the Martindale-Hubbell Law Directory

PUNXSUTAWNEY, Jefferson Co.

LORENZO & GIANVITO, P.C. (AV)

410 West Mahoning Street, P.O. Box 495, 15767-1908
Telephone: 814-938-6390
Fax: 814-938-6412
Email: LGPC@Penn.com

Nicholas F. Lorenzo, Jr. — Nicholas A. Gianvito

For full biographical listings, see the Martindale-Hubbell Law Directory

*SCRANTON,** Lackawanna Co.

MUNLEY, MUNLEY & CARTWRIGHT, P.C. (AV)

205 Madison Avenue, 18503
Telephone: 570-346-7401
Fax: 570-346-3452
URL: http://www.lawyers.com/mmclaw
Email: lawyers@munley.com *URL:* http://www.munley.com

Robert W. Munley — James Christopher Munley
Marion Munley — Daniel W. Munley
Matthew A. Cartwright — Robert W. Munley, III

Reference: First National Bank of Jermyn.

For full biographical listings, see the Martindale-Hubbell Law Directory

O'MALLEY & HARRIS, P.C. (AV)

345 Wyoming Avenue, 18503
Telephone: 570-348-3711
Fax: 570-348-4092
Email: ohpc@epix.net *URL:* http://www.ohpclaw.com
Stroudsburg, Pennsylvania Office: 111 North Seventh Street.
Telephone: 570-421-2252; 570-422-1280.
FAX: 570-422-1281. Email: cerato@ptdprolog.net.
Wilkes-Barre, Pennsylvania Office: 61 North Washington Street.
Telephone: 570-829-3232.
FAX: 570-829-4418. Email: ohpcwb@epix.net.
Williamsport, Pennsylvania Office: 321 Pine Street, Suite 308.
Telephone: 570-323-4380.

Eugene Nogi (1905-1975)
Henry Nogi (1900-1976)
Russell J. O'Malley, Sr. (1904-1993)
Norman Harris (1907-1998)
William H. Amesbury (Resident, Wilkes-Barre Office)
Paul A. Barrett
Matthew P. Barrett
J. Scott Brady (Resident, Wilkes-Barre Office)
Lori J. Cerato (Resident, Stroudsburg Office)
Bruce L. Coyer
John Q. Durkin
Gerald J. Hanchulak
Richard K. Hodges
Timothy J. Holland (Resident, Wilkes-Barre Office)
John F. Kennedy (Resident, Wilkes-Barre Office)
Daniel Morgan
Michael Perry
James M. Tressler
Joseph Timothy Healey
A. Ruth Whalen (Resident, Wilkes-Barre Office)

Representative Clients: Pennsylvania Hospital Insurance Co.; MMI Systems Agency, Inc.; State Farm Insurance Company; ITT Specialty Risk Services; St. Paul Fire & Marine Insurance Co.; Chubb Group of Insurance Companies; Geisingen System Services; Princeton Insurance Company; Northeastern Pennsylvania Physicians Organization; Catholic Healthcare Partners.

For full biographical listings, see the Martindale-Hubbell Law Directory

WYOMISSING, Berks Co.

LEISAWITZ HELLER ABRAMOWITCH PHILLIPS, P.C. (AV)

2201 Ridgewood Road Suite 400, 19610
Telephone: 610-372-3500
Fax: 610-372-8671
Email: lhap@lhaplaw.com
Reading, Pennsylvania Office: 138 North Fifth Street.
Telephone: 610-372-3500.
Hamburg, Pennsylvania Office: 178 North Third Street.
Telephone: 610-562-4145.

Alan G. Leisawitz — Charles J. Phillips
Mervin A. Heller, Jr. — William R. Blumer
Jay N. Abramowitch — Allen R. Shollenberger

Robert J. Kirwan, II — Kathleen A. B. Kovach
Kevin A. Moore — Douglas Paul Rauch
Kenneth Millman

For full biographical listings, see the Martindale-Hubbell Law Directory

*YORK,** York Co.

BARLEY, SNYDER, SENFT & COHEN, LLC (AV)

100 East Market Street, P.O. Box 15012, 17405-7012
Telephone: 717-846-8888
Fax: 717-843-8492
Email: barley@barley.com *URL:* http://www.barley.com
Lancaster, Pennsylvania Office: 126 East King Street.
Telephone: 717-299-5201.
Fax: 717-291-4660.
Harrisburg, Pennsylvania Office: 240 North Third Street.
Telephone: 717-238-8263.
Fax: 717-238-8278.
Chambersburg, Pennsylvania Office: 247 Lincoln Way East.
Telephone: 717-264-6494.
Fax: 717-264-1662.
Reading, Pennsylvania Office: 501 Washington Street.
Telephone: 610-376-6651.
Fax: 610-376-5243.
Hanover, Pennsylvania Office: 14 Center Square.
Telephone: 717-637-6239.
Fax: 717-637-5407.
Birdsboro, Pennsylvania Office: 115 E. Main Street.
Telephone: 610-582-2735.
Hamburg, Pennsylvania Office: 239 State Street.
Telephone: 610-562-3721.
Oley, Pennsylvania Office: Route 73 and Main Street.
Telephone: 610-987-6350.
Morgantown, Pennsylvania Office: Route 23.
Telephone: 610-286-5958.

MEMBERS OF FIRM

Harry J. Rubin — Steven J. Koehler
Christopher W. Mattson — Val E. Winter
Frederick S. Spangler — Deborah A. Datte
Rees Griffiths — Michael W. Davis
David R. Keller — Melanie A. Zampini
Jeffrey D. Lobach — Bruce J. Wolstoncroft

ASSOCIATES

Craig T. Trebilcock — Paul W. Minnich
Beverly J. Points — Robert J. Schefter
John L. Senft — Kimberly J. Decker
John W. Venskus

COUNSEL

Robert J. Stewart — Lavere C. Senft

RETIRED

Donn I. Cohen

Counsel for: Franklin & Marshall College; Fulton Bank/Fulton Financial Corp.; Graham Packaging; Lancaster General Hospital; Robert A. Kinsley, Inc.; D.F. Stauffer Biscuit.
Local Counsel for: Armstrong World Industries; Susquehanna Pfaltzgraff Co.
Insurance Defense Counsel for: Medical Protective Co.; The PMA Group.

For full biographical listings, see the Martindale-Hubbell Law Directory

RHODE ISLAND

*PROVIDENCE,** Providence Co.

BLISH & CAVANAGH (AV)

Commerce Center, 30 Exchange Terrace, 02903
Telephone: 401-831-8900
Telecopier: 401-751-7542
Email: BLISHCAV@AOL.COM

(See Next Column)

BLISH & CAVANAGH—*Continued*

MEMBERS OF FIRM

Joseph V. Cavanagh, Jr.
William R. Landry
Edmund L. Alves, Jr.
Stephen J. Reid, Jr.
Karen A. Pelczarski
Scott T. Spear
Raymond A. Marcaccio

Michael W. Carroll
Staci L. Sawyer
Kristin Rodgers Sullivan

OF COUNSEL

John H. Blish

Representative Clients: Providence Journal Co.; ABC-6; Fleet Bank; Metropolitan Insurance Co.; Delta Dental of Rhode Island; Textron; A.T. Cross; Citizens Bank.

For full biographical listings, see the Martindale-Hubbell Law Directory

HINCKLEY, ALLEN & SNYDER LLP (AV)

1500 Fleet Center, 02903-2393
Telephone: 401-274-2000
Fax: 401-277-9600
Email: firm@haslaw.com *URL:* http://www.haslaw.com
Boston, Massachusetts Office: 28 State Street, 30th Floor.
Telephone: 617-345-9000.
Fax: 617-345-9020. URL: http://www.haslaw.com.

MEMBERS OF FIRM

David D. Barricelli
E. Jerome Batty
Jonathan Bell
Leon C. Boghossian III
Paul Bork (Not admitted in RI)
Stephen J. Carlotti
David Barry Connolly (Not admitted in RI)
Michael J. Connolly (Not admitted in RI)
Robert Corrente
Eric F. Eisenberg (Not admitted in RI)
Malcolm Farmer, III
Margaret D. Farrell
Hugh J. Gorman, III (Not admitted in RI)
Gerard R. Goulet
William R. Grimm
Paul A. Hedstrom (Not admitted in RI)
Richard L. E. Jocelyn
Joel Lewin (Not admitted in RI)
Sandra Matrone Mack
Matthew T. Marcello, III
Frederick P. McClure
Paul F. O'Donnell, III (Not admitted in RI)
H. Peter Olsen
Julianne Palumbo (Not admitted in RI)
John J. Pendergast, III
Gerald J. Petros
Jeremy Ritzenberg (Not admitted in RI)
Charles E. Schaub, Jr. (Not admitted in RI)
Douglas F. Seaver (Not admitted in RI)
Herman Snyder (Not admitted in RI)
David R. Sullivan (Not admitted in RI)
Robert F. Sylvia (Not admitted in RI)
Howard E. Walker
Richard D. Wayne (Not admitted in RI)
John R. Allen (Retired)
Richard W. Billings (Retired)
Thomas J. Hogan (Retired)
Jacques V. Hopkins (Retired)
James A. Jackson (Retired)
James E. Keeley (Retired)
Robert F. Pickard (Retired)
Robert W. Shadd (Retired)
Richard F. Staples (Retired)
Edwin G. Torrance (Retired)

ASSOCIATES

Jessica M. Bettencourt
Mark Bianchi
Charles D. Blackman
Alexandra K. Callam
Brent R. Canning
Jane E. Cohen (Not admitted in RI)
Andrew D. Cummings (Not admitted in RI)
June E. Daniel
Kim Herman Goslant (Not admitted in RI)
Gloria Maria Gutierrez (Not admitted in RI)
Kelley Jordan-Price
Catherine S. Kim (Not admitted in RI)
Christopher W. Morog (Not admitted in RI)
Elena B. Olson (Not admitted in RI)
Timothy J. Perry (Not admitted in RI)
Michael J. Pisaturo
Leah A. Rochwarg (Not admitted in RI)
Lawrence W. Vernaglia (Not admitted in RI)
Joseph D. Whelan

OF COUNSEL

Willard R. Pope (Not admitted in RI)
Bentley Tobin
Joachim A. Weissfeld

For Complete List of Firm Personnel, See General Section

For full biographical listings, see the Martindale-Hubbell Law Directory

MEDEIROS + SANFORD INC. (AV)

One Turks Head Place, Suite 700, 02903-2215
Telephone: 401-831-0700
Fax: 401-274-2752 or 401-861-7249

Matthew F. Medeiros
Paul M. Sanford
Stacey P. Nakasian

Jane E. Brockmann

For full biographical listings, see the Martindale-Hubbell Law Directory

SMITHFIELD, Providence Co.

CHARLES S. SOKOLOFF INCORPORATED (AV)

Eleven Thurber Boulevard, 02917-1859
Telephone: 401-233-2800; Toll Free: 888-SOKOLAW
Fax: 401-233-2890
URL: http://www.sokolawyer.com
Email: sokolaw@sokolawyer.com *URL:* http://www.lawyers.com/sokolaw

Charles S. Sokoloff

Anne-Marie Krollman

For full biographical listings, see the Martindale-Hubbell Law Directory

SOUTH CAROLINA

*BEAUFORT,** Beaufort Co.

HARVEY & BATTEY, P.A. (AV)

1001 Craven Street, P.O. Drawer 1107, 29902
Telephone: 843-524-3109
Telefax: 843-524-6973

W. Brantley Harvey, Jr.
Colden R. Battey, Jr.
William B. Harvey, III
John M. Tatum, III
Thomas A. Holloway

Approved Attorneys for: Lawyers Title Insurance Corp.; Chicago Title Insurance Corp.
Representative Clients: Nations Bank; First Bank, F.S.B.; Pleasant Point Plantation Associates; Century 21-Carolina Realty, Inc.; Lobeco Products, Inc.; Beaufort County Association of Realtors; The Fripp Company.

For Complete List of Firm Personnel, See General Section

For full biographical listings, see the Martindale-Hubbell Law Directory

*COLUMBIA,** Richland Co.

GLENN MURPHY GRAY & STEPP, L.L.P. (AV)

B B & T Bank Building, Suite 390, 1901 Assembly Street, P.O. Box 1550, 29202-1550
Telephone: 803-765-1100
Telecopy: 803-765-0755

Terrell L. Glenn (1930-1993)

MEMBERS OF FIRM

Peter L. Murphy
Elizabeth Van Doren Gray
Robert E. Stepp
Elizabeth G. Howard

Robert C. Rhodes
Laura W. Robinson
Roland M. Franklin
C. Shawn Dryer

Reference: BB&T.

For full biographical listings, see the Martindale-Hubbell Law Directory

NEXSEN PRUET JACOBS & POLLARD, LLP (AV)

1441 Main Street, 15th Floor, P.O. Drawer 2426, 29202
Telephone: 803-771-8900
Facsimile: 803-253-8277
Email: NPJP@NPJP.COM *URL:* HTTP://WWW.NPJP.COM
Charleston, South Carolina Office: 200 Meeting Street, Suite 301. P.O. Box 486.
Telephone: 803-577-9440.
Facsimile: 803-720-1777.
Greenville, South Carolina Office: 201 West McBee Avenue, Fourth Floor, P.O. Box 10648.
Telephone: 864-370-2211.
Facsimile: 864-282-1177.
Myrtle Beach, South Carolina Office: 2411 Oak Street, Suite 105.
Telephone: 843-445-9688.
Facsimile: 843-445-9949.
Charlotte, North Carolina Office: 212 South Tryon Street, Suite 1700.
Telephone: 704-339-0304.
Facsimile: 704-338-5377.

MEMBERS OF FIRM

Wilburn Brewer, Jr.
Russell T. Burke
Harold W. Jacobs
Susan Batten Lipscomb
Susan Taylor Wall (Resident, Charleston, SC Office)

ASSOCIATES

Elizabeth Herlong Campbell
David J. Parrish (Resident, Charleston, SC Office)

For Complete List of Firm Personnel, See General Section

For full biographical listings, see the Martindale-Hubbell Law Directory

Columbia—Continued

TODD, HOLLOWAY & WARD, P.C. (AV)

1709 Devonshire Drive, P.O. Box 1549, 29202
Telephone: 803-779-4383
Fax: 803-799-7604
Email: thandw@alltel.net

Walter B. Todd, Jr.
Carl L. Holloway, Jr.
Tobias G. Ward, Jr.

J. Derrick Jackson

Approved Attorneys for: Lawyers Title Insurance Corp.

For full biographical listings, see the Martindale-Hubbell Law Directory

*GREENVILLE,** Greenville Co.

CLARKSON, FORTSON, WALSH & RHENEY, P.A. (AV)

117 Manly Street, P.O. Box 6186, 29606
Telephone: 864-232-4400
Fax: 864-235-4399
Email: cfwr@cfwr.com

Rebecca R. Wray
Samuel C. Weldon

For full biographical listings, see the Martindale-Hubbell Law Directory

GRANT, LEATHERWOOD & PITTS, P.A. (AV)

Palmetto Bank Building, 306 East North Street, 2nd Floor, P.O. Box 10367, 29603-0367
Telephone: 864-242-2300
Facsimile: 864-242-2280
Email: attorneys@grantleatherwood.com

William M. Grant, Jr.
Judith A. Leatherwood
Michael S. Pitts

Langdon Cheves, III
Paul C. Rathke

LEGAL SUPPORT PERSONNEL

Jackie L. Carver (Litigation Paralegal)
Sarah A. Carmichael (Paralegal)
Mary A. Fuller (Paralegal)

For full biographical listings, see the Martindale-Hubbell Law Directory

THE HARPER LAW FIRM, P.A. (AV)

Old Chamber Building, 6th Floor, 135 South Main Street, P.O. Box 908, 29602
Telephone: 864-235-5535
Fax: 864-235-6866
Email: HARPERFIRM@aol.com

Donald A. Harper
Norman Ward Lambert
Cynthia Buck Brown

For full biographical listings, see the Martindale-Hubbell Law Directory

WILLIAMS & HENRY, PROFESSIONAL ASSOCIATION (AV)

513 East Washington Street, P.O. Box 10307, 29603
Telephone: 864-233-1609
Fax: 864-232-7807
Email: lawfirm@williamshenry.com

Ray R. Williams (1899-1987)
J. A. Henry (1899-1971)
Ray R. Williams, Jr.
Craig H. Allen

For full biographical listings, see the Martindale-Hubbell Law Directory

HILTON HEAD ISLAND, Beaufort Co.

BARRY L. JOHNSON, P.A. (AV)

35-A Bow Circle, Palmetto Bay Offices (Suite 35-A), P.O. Box 7261, 29938
Telephone: 843-341-3777
Fax: 843-341-3007
Beaufort, South Carolina Office: 1611 North Street.
Telephone: 843-982-0089.
Fax: 986-9203.

Barry L. Johnson

For full biographical listings, see the Martindale-Hubbell Law Directory

TENNESSEE

*CHATTANOOGA,** Hamilton Co.

BAKER, DONELSON, BEARMAN & CALDWELL (AV)

1800 Republic Centre, 633 Chestnut Street, 37450-1800
Telephone: 423-756-2010
Telecopier: 423-756-3447
Email: info@bdbc.com *URL:* http://www.bakerdonelson.com
Memphis, Tennessee Office: 20th Floor, First Tennessee Building, 165 Madison, 38103.
Telephone: 901-526-2000.
Telecopier: 901-577-2303.
Nashville, Tennessee Office: 1700 Nashville City Center, 511 Union Street, 37219.
Telephone: 615-726-5600.
Telecopier: 615-726-0464.
Knoxville, Tennessee Office: 2200 Riverview Tower, 900 South Gay Street, 37901.
Telephone: 423-549-7000.
Telecopier: 423-525-8569.
Johnson City, Tennessee Office: SunTrust Bank Building, 207 Mockingbird Lane, P.O. Box 3038, 37602.
Telephone: 423-928-0181.
Telecopier: 423-928-5694; 423-928-3654; Kingsport: 423-246-6191.
Huntsville, Tennessee Office: 3 Courthouse Square, 37756.
Telephone: 423-663-2321.
Telecopier: 423-663-2111.
Washington, D.C. Office: Market Square, 801 Pennsylvania Avenue, N.W., 20004.
Telephone: 202-508-3400.
Telecopier: 202-508-3402.
Jackson, Mississippi Office: Suite 500, 700 North State Street, 39202.
Telephone: 601-351-2400.
Telecopier: 601-351-2424.

SHAREHOLDERS

Thomas O. Helton
Richard J. McAfee
Joe A. Conner

OF COUNSEL

Robert W. Sauser

For Complete List of Firm Personnel, See General Section

For full biographical listings, see the Martindale-Hubbell Law Directory

*CLARKSVILLE,** Montgomery Co.

BATSON, NOLAN, BRICE, HARVEY & WILLIAMSON, PLLC (AV)

622 Madison, P.O. Box 0, 37041-1334
Telephone: 931-647-1501
Fax: 931-553-0153

Richard H. Batson
Dan L. Nolan, Jr.
John R. Brice
W. Timothy Harvey
Michael K. Williamson
Steven C. Girsky
Daniel Mark Nolan
Jill Bartee Nolan

Joel D. Ragland
Suzanne Marsh Pearson
Christopher J. Pittman
David J. Silvus
Craig Hargrow
Marie Antoinette Joiner
Carol M. Joiner
J. Matthew Miller

LEGAL SUPPORT PERSONEL

Teri Blackburn (Office Legal Administrator)

Representative Clients: The City of Clarksville; Montgomery County, Tennessee; Cafaro Company; Clarksville Memorial Hospital; Farmers & Merchants Bank; First American National Bank; First Federal Savings Bank of Clarksville; Savage Zinc; Sears, Roebuck and Company; Shoney's Inc.; South Central Bell; Trans Financial Bank; The Industrial Development Board of the County of Montgomery.

For full biographical listings, see the Martindale-Hubbell Law Directory

JOHNSON CITY, Washington Co.

BAKER, DONELSON, BEARMAN & CALDWELL (AV)

SunTrust Bank Building, 207 Mockingbird Lane, P.O. Box 3038, 37602
Telephone: 423-928-0181
Telecopier: 423-928-5694; 928-3654; Kingsport: 423-246-6191
Email: info@bdbc.com *URL:* http://www.bakerdonelson.com
Memphis, Tennessee Office: 20th Floor, First Tennessee Building, 165 Madison, 38103.
Telephone: 901-526-2000.
Telecopier: 901-577-2303.
Nashville, Tennessee Office: 1700 Nashville City Center, 511 Union Street, 37219.
Telephone: 615-726-5600.
Telecopier: 615-726-0464.
Chattanooga, Tennessee Office: 1800 Republic Centre, 633 Chestnut Street, 37450-1800.
Telephone: 423-756-2010.
Telecopier: 423-756-3447.

(See Next Column)

BAKER, DONELSON, BEARMAN & CALDWELL—*Continued*

Knoxville, Tennessee Office: 2200 Riverview Tower, 900 South Gay Street, 37901.
Telephone: 423-549-7000.
Telecopier: 423-525-8569.
Huntsville, Tennessee Office: 3 Courthouse Square, 37756.
Telephone: 615-663-2321.
Telecopier: 615-663-2111.
Washington, D.C. Office: Market Square, 801 Pennsylvania Avenue, N.W., 20004.
Telephone: 202-508-3400.
Telecopier: 202-508-3402.
Jackson, Mississippi Office: Suite 500, 700 North State Street, 39202.
Telephone: 601-351-2400.
Telecopier: 601-351-2424.

MANAGING PARTNER

Robert D. Van de Vuurst

For Complete List of Firm Personnel, See General Section

For full biographical listings, see the Martindale-Hubbell Law Directory

*KNOXVILLE,** Knox Co.

BERNSTEIN, STAIR & MCADAMS LLP (AV)

Suite 600, 530 South Gay Street, 37902
Telephone: 423-546-8030
Telecopier: 423-522-8879
Effective October 1, 1999 Area Code will change to 865.

MEMBERS OF FIRM

Bernard E. Bernstein
L. Caesar Stair III
Doris C. Allen
Celeste H. Herbert

Representative Clients: ABB Flakt, Inc.; Camel Manufacturing Company; Clayton Homes, Inc.; Modern Supply Co.; Plasti-Line, Inc.; Rafferty's Restaurants; Saks, Inc.; Union Planters Bank of East Tennessee, N.A.; Vanderbilt Mortgage and Finance, Inc.; West Town Mall.

For Complete List of Firm Personnel, See General Section

For full biographical listings, see the Martindale-Hubbell Law Directory

FRANTZ, MCCONNELL & SEYMOUR, LLP (AV)

550 Main Avenue, Suite 500, 37902
Telephone: 423-546-9321
Fax: 423-637-5249
Mailing Address: P.O. Box 39, Knoxville, TN, 37901
Email: Lwhitfield@fmsllp.com
Effective October 1, 1999, the Area Code will change to 865.

MEMBERS OF FIRM

Fred H. Cagle, Jr.
Arthur G. Seymour, Jr.
Francis A. Cain
Robert L. Kahn
Reggie E. Keaton
Donald D. Howell
Debra L. Fulton
Michael W. Ewell
Imogene Anderson King
John M. Lawhorn
James E. Wagner

Counsel For: ASARCO Incorporated; BellSouth Telecommunications, Inc.; Coca-Cola Enterprises, Inc.; Government Employees Insurance Company; Liberty Mutual Insurance Company; NBC Bank, FSB; Norfolk Southern Railway Company; Prudential Insurance Company of America; The Travelers Insurance Companies; United Services Automobile Association.

For Complete List of Firm Personnel, See General Section

For full biographical listings, see the Martindale-Hubbell Law Directory

*MARYVILLE,** Blount Co.

NICHOLSON, GARNER & DUGGAN (AV)

250 High Street, P.O. Box 5059, 37802-5059
Telephone: 423-984-1460
Knoxville: 423-637-1970
Telecopier: 423-982-2595
Real Estate Fax: 423-982-2595
Litigation Fax: 423-984-9275
Email: jnicholson@earthlink.net *URL:* http://www.lawyers.com/ngdlaw

MEMBERS OF FIRM

Joe Nicholson
J. Michael Garner
David R. Duggan

ASSOCIATES

Angelia D. Morie
Daphne H. Cornwell

Representative Clients: 1st American National Bank; Citizens Bank of Blount County.

For full biographical listings, see the Martindale-Hubbell Law Directory

*MEMPHIS,** Shelby Co.

ARMSTRONG ALLEN PREWITT GENTRY JOHNSTON & HOLMES, PLLC (AV)

Brinkley Plaza, Suite 700, 80 Monroe Avenue, 38103-2467
Telephone: 901-523-8211
Facsimile: 901-524-4936
Little Rock, Arkansas Office: Suite 100, 100 Morgan Keegan Drive, 72202.
Telephone: 501-280-0100.
Facsimile: 501-280-0166.
Jackson, Mississippi Office: 2525 Lakeward Drive, Suite 200, 39216.
Telephone: 601-713-1192.
Facsimile: 601-713-2049.
Jackson, Tennessee Office: 464 North Parkway, Suite A, 38305.
Telephone: 901-660-2332.
Facsimile: 901-664-1109.

MEMBERS OF FIRM

Thomas F. Johnston
Charles A. Banks (Resident, Little Rock, Arkansas Office)
Paul A. Matthews
Mark S. Norris
Lucian T. Pera
Cannon F. Allen

OF COUNSEL

Gavin M. Gentry

For Complete List of Firm Personnel, See General Section

For full biographical listings, see the Martindale-Hubbell Law Directory

HALE HEADRICK DEWEY & WOLF, PLLC (AV)

One Memphis Place, 200 Jefferson Avenue Suite 1450, 38103
Telephone: 901-523-1123
Fax: 901-523-7472
Nashville, Tennessee Office: Suntrust Bank Building, 201 Fourth Avenue North, Suite 1450, 37219.
Telephone: 615-843-5160.
Fax: 615-843-5165

Stephen P. Hale
S. Russell Headrick
H. Tucker Dewey
Herbert B. Wolf, Jr.
John S. Golwen

OF COUNSEL

Steven L. Gill

Jennifer Ziegenhorn
Wendy A. Geurin
John W. Campbell
Joseph M. Koury
Holly N. Knight
Charles S. Blatteis
Jennifer S. Kiesewetter
J. William Williams

For full biographical listings, see the Martindale-Hubbell Law Directory

SMITH, SABBATINI & MCLEARY, PLLC (AV)

100 Peabody Place Suite 1250, 38103
Telephone: 901-312-5555
Fax: 901-312-5667
Mailing Address: P.O. Box 3582, Memphis, TN, 38173
URL: http://www.smithlawetal.com

Gary K. Smith
Robert L. Sabbatini
Harold W. McLeary, Jr.
William D. Domico
James F. Kyle
James T. McColgan, III
G. Edward Coleman, III
Bryant C. Witt

Representative Clients: Premier RRG Insurance; Illinois Central Railroad; Medical Assurance; Albertson's, Inc.; Med. Marc (Chiro Co.); Medical Protective Co.; Methodist Health Systems; Hartford Insurance Co.; Sentry Insurance; State Farm Insurance.

For full biographical listings, see the Martindale-Hubbell Law Directory

*NASHVILLE,** Davidson Co.

CHEADLE & CHEADLE (AV)

An Association of Attorneys
129 Second Avenue, North, 37201-1998
Telephone: 615-254-1009
Facsimile: 615-242-7378
Email: cheadle@edgenet.com
Knoxville, Tennessee Office: One Centre Square, 620 Market Street, Suite 260. 37902.
Telephone: 423-522-8440.
Facsimile: 423-522-8102.

John R. Cheadle, Sr. (1930-1997)
John R. Cheadle, Jr.
Evalina C. Cheadle

LEGAL SUPPORT PERSONNEL

Gail A. Dodd (Office Manager)
Wendy H. Williams (Paralegal)
Joy Westerbeck (Paralegal)
Michelle Primm (Paralegal)

References: First American National Bank of Nashville, Nashville, Tennessee; NationsBank, Nashville, Tennessee.

For full biographical listings, see the Martindale-Hubbell Law Directory

Nashville—Continued

CORBETT CROCKETT & LECKRONE (AV)

An Association of Attorneys including a Professional Corporation
Suite 1050, American Center, 3100 West End Avenue, 37203
Telephone: 615-383-0500
Facsimile: 615-383-5556
Email: counsel@ccllaw.com *URL:* http://www.lawyers.com/ccl

W. Lee Corbett (P.C.) David F. Lewis

For full biographical listings, see the Martindale-Hubbell Law Directory

DANIEL W. SMALL (AV)

323 Union Street, Suite 300, P.O. Box 190608, 37219-0608
Telephone: 615-252-6000
Fax: 615-252-6001
Email: dsmall1@msn.com *URL:* http://www.lawyers.com/danielsmall

Representative Clients: The Bank of Nashville; Bank of Dickson; Capital Bank & Trust Co.; Citizens Community Bank; The Danner Co.; First Bank & Trust; The First National Bank of McMinnville; PFIC Corp.; PFIC Securities Corp.

For full biographical listings, see the Martindale-Hubbell Law Directory

SMITH & CASHION, PLC (AV)

Suite 1200, Suntrust Center, 424 Church Street, 37219-2306
Telephone: 615-742-8555
Telecopier: 615-742-8556
Email: sclaw@bellsouth.net

Don L. Smith
Gregory L. Cashion
Richard McCallister Smith
Jefferson C. Orr
Lawrence B. Hammet II
O. Wade Nelson
Kenneth S. Schrupp

Carol Rose Dunn
H. Brent Patrick
Vic L. McConnell

For full biographical listings, see the Martindale-Hubbell Law Directory

TUKE YOPP & SWEENEY, PLC (AV)

NationsBank Plaza Suite 1100, 414 Union Street, 37219
Telephone: 615-313-3300
Fax: 615-313-3310

MEMBERS OF FIRM

Robert D. Tuke
G. Michael Yopp
Matthew J. Sweeney, III
Lawrence C. Maxwell
Peter H. Curry
Barrett B. Sutton, Jr.
John W. Stone, III
Gary M. Brown
David J. White
Robert P. Felber, Jr.
Robb S. Harvey
Gerald F. Mace
Kathryn A. Stephenson
John C. Tishler

ASSOCIATES

W. Edward Ramage
Lisa L. Collins
Theresa M. Costonis
E. Blaine Sprouse
Warren A. Jasper
Mark W. Miller
Elizabeth A. Carnahan
Richard L. Pensinger

OF COUNSEL

Kenneth E. Douthat
William B. Drescher
Michael T. Folks (Not admitted in TN)
Larry D. Soderquist
Charles K. Grant

For full biographical listings, see the Martindale-Hubbell Law Directory

TEXAS

*ABILENE,** Taylor Co.

RUSSELL C. (RUSTY) BEARD (AV)

Bank of America Tower, 500 Chestnut Street, Suite 1716, P.O. Box 1401, 79604
Telephone: 915-670-9011
Fax: 915-670-9525
Email: rustybeardattorney@abilene.com

ASSOCIATES

Tami Ratliff Morris
Tami Ratliff Morris

For full biographical listings, see the Martindale-Hubbell Law Directory

ADDISON, Dallas Co.

GERARD SINGER & LEVICK, P.C. (AV)

16200 Addison Road Suite 140, 75001-5350
Telephone: 972-380-5533
Fax: 972-380-5748
Email: bcgerard@flash.net

Bretton C. Gerard
Gregory Z. Singer
Larry A. Levick
Michael I. Kahn
Robert J. Mabel
I. Richard Levy

For full biographical listings, see the Martindale-Hubbell Law Directory

*AMARILLO,** Potter Co.

NANCY J. STONE (AV)

Maxor Building, Suite 820, 320 South Polk Street, Lobby Box 32, 79101
Telephone: 806-374-9300
Fax: 806-373-3008
Email: nstone@arn.net *URL:* http://www.nancyjstone.com/806-374-9300/2-1.html

For full biographical listings, see the Martindale-Hubbell Law Directory

*AUSTIN,** Travis Co.

BASKIN, BENNETT & KOMKOV, L.L.P. (AV)

919 Congress Avenue, Suite 1000, 78701
Telephone: 512-322-9250
Fax: 512-322-9280
URL: http://www.baskin.com

James D. Baskin, III
J. Bruce Bennett
Leon V. Komkov

For full biographical listings, see the Martindale-Hubbell Law Directory

THE BURK LAW FIRM A PROFESSIONAL CORPORATION (AV)

The Bremond House, 711 San Antonio Street, 78701
Telephone: 512-476-8350; 888-476-9210
Fax: 512-476-8360
Email: firm@burklawtx.com *URL:* http://www.lawyers.com/theburklawfirm

Michael G. Burk

OF COUNSEL

Colten Wade Smith
Hollis W. Burklund

For full biographical listings, see the Martindale-Hubbell Law Directory

DAVIS & WILKERSON, P.C. (AV)

1801 South Mopac, Suite 300, P.O. Box 2283, 78768-2283
Telephone: 512-482-0614
Fax: 512-482-0342
Email: dwlaw@dwlaw.com *URL:* http://www.dwlaw.com
Alpine Office: 1110 East Holland, P.O. Box 777.
Telephone: 915-837-5547.

David M. Davis
Steven R. Welch
Glen Wilkerson
David A. Wright
Leonard W. Woods
Kevin A. Reed
J. Mark Holbrook
Brian E. Riewe
Brian McElroy
Robert L. Hargett
Michael Wilson
Frances W. Hamermesh
Fletcher H. Brown

Jennifer B. Claymon
David M. Coffey
Hollis Hudson Gaston
Steven C. Levatino
Diana Maldonado
Erin E. Matherne
Joel S. Pace
Stephen G. Wohleb
Michael P. Young

OF COUNSEL

Pete P. Gallego (Resident, Alpine Office)
Peter R. Meeker

For full biographical listings, see the Martindale-Hubbell Law Directory

HARRISON & RIAL, L.L.P. (AV)

100 Congress Avenue, Suite 1550, 78701
Telephone: 512-472-6900
Facsimile: 512-477-8480

Richard W. Harrison
J. Hamilton Rial, III

Kelli A. N. Carlton

Representative Clients: General Motors Corporation; Union Pacific Resources Company; Eaton Corporation; U.S. TeleCoin Corp.; Bay Maintenance Company, Inc.

For full biographical listings, see the Martindale-Hubbell Law Directory

Austin—Continued

HERMAN & HOWRY, L.L.P. (AV)

1900 Pearl Street, 78705-5408
Telephone: 512-474-7300
Fax: 512-474-8557
URL: http://www.hermanhowry.com

Timothy J. Herman
Randy R. Howry
Sean E. Breen
Matthew R. Beatty
Thomas H. Daniel
Melissa C. Hill

For full biographical listings, see the Martindale-Hubbell Law Directory

SAPP, SAPP & WHITE, P.C. (AV)

710 West Avenue, 78701
Telephone: 512-474-1801
Facsimile: 512-474-8230
URL: http://sapplaw.wld.com
URL: http://www.lawyers.com/sapplaw
Affiliated Office: Gay N. Sapp, 703 West 10th Street, Austin, Texas, 78701.
Telephone: 512-481-9401.
Facsimile: 512-478-9882.

David R. Sapp
Gay N. Sapp
Susan G. White

James "Beau" Eccles

OF COUNSEL

Russell Harding

For full biographical listings, see the Martindale-Hubbell Law Directory

SLACK & DAVIS, L.L.P. (AV)

A Partnership including a Professional Corporation
8911 Capital of Texas Highway Suite 2110, 78759
Telephone: 512-795-8686
Fax: 512-795-8787

MEMBERS OF FIRM

Steven E. Aldous
Mike Davis
Michael L. Slack

ASSOCIATE

Donna J. Bowen

OF COUNSEL

Tom H. Davis, P.C.

For full biographical listings, see the Martindale-Hubbell Law Directory

WATSON, BISHOP, LONDON, GALOW, P.C. (AV)

The Littlefield Building, 106 East Sixth Street, Suite 700, 78701
Telephone: 512-479-5900
Telefax: 512-479-5934

Kirk P. Watson
Daniel W. Bishop, II
Alice London
Jerry Galow

Christina Carlson Dodds
Phillip H. Schmandt
Joseph F. Brophy
Cory W. Smith

For full biographical listings, see the Martindale-Hubbell Law Directory

LAW OFFICES OF JOSEPH P. WEBBER (AV)

Frost Bank Plaza, Suite 1100, 816 Congress Avenue, 78701
Telephone: 512-472-1131
Telecopier: 512-479-8977

For full biographical listings, see the Martindale-Hubbell Law Directory

*BEAUMONT,** Jefferson Co.

PATE & DODSON (AV)

470 Orleans Building, Suite 1201, 77701
Telephone: 409-838-6578
Fax: 409-838-6922

MEMBERS OF FIRM

Gordon R. Pate
Joe Michael Dodson
Karen L. Spivey
Christy Amuny

ASSOCIATE

Mark William Frasher

Representative Clients: The Travelers Insurance Co.; Universal Underwriters Insurance Co.; Allstate Insurance Co.; City Coach Lines, Inc.; Commercial Union Insurance Co.; Scottsdale Insurance Co.; GAINSCO; Hartford Insurance Co.; American International Adjustment Co., Inc.; Fidelity and Deposit Company of Maryland.

For full biographical listings, see the Martindale-Hubbell Law Directory

*CORPUS CHRISTI,** Nueces Co.

CANALES & SIMONSON, P.C. (AV)

2601 Morgan Avenue, P.O. Box 5624, 78465-5624
Telephone: 512-883-0601
Telecopier: 512-884-7023
Email: tonycanales@canalessimonson.com

J. A. "Tony" Canales
Nancy M. Simonson

Barbara Canales Black
Jo Ellen Hewins
Patricia N. Canales

For full biographical listings, see the Martindale-Hubbell Law Directory

LAW OFFICES OF WILLIAM J. CHRISS, P.C. (AV)

719 South Shoreline, Suite 100, P.O. Box 2946, 78403
Telephone: 361-884-3330
Facsimile: 361-883-9187

William J. Chriss

Michael Nored

For full biographical listings, see the Martindale-Hubbell Law Directory

JORDAN, HYDEN, WOMBLE & CULBRETH, P.C. (AV)

Suite 900, NationsBank Center North, 500 North Water Street, 78471
Telephone: 512-884-5678
Fax: 512-888-5555
Email: JHWCLAW@AOL.COM

Larry G. Hyden
Kenneth M. Culbreth, Jr.

For full biographical listings, see the Martindale-Hubbell Law Directory

LAW OFFICES OF PAUL G. KRATZIG (AV)

600 Leopard Street, Suite 2100, 78473
Telephone: 361-883-3563
Telecopier: 361-883-0210
Email: kratzig@flash.net

For full biographical listings, see the Martindale-Hubbell Law Directory

*DALLAS,** Dallas Co.

CALHOUN & STACY (AV)

Suite 5700 - Bank of America Plaza, 901 Main Street, 75202-3713
Telephone: 214-748-5000
Facsimile: 214-748-1421
Email: info@calhounstacy.com *URL:* http://www.calhounstacy.com

MEMBERS OF FIRM

Rees T. Bowen, III
Mark Alan Calhoun
LeAnn Wainscott Cross
David W. Elrod
Parker Nelson
Shannon B. Schuster
Roy L. Stacy
Pamela J. Touchstone
Michael C. Wright

ASSOCIATES

David G. Allen
Joseph G. Barkate, Jr.
Scott S. Crocker
Sean P. Fitzgerald
Elizabeth Reding Gambrell
Leanne Capps Medford
Jonathan G. Polak
Joel W. Reese
Barbara L. Wohlrabe

For Complete List of Firm Personnel, See General Section

For full biographical listings, see the Martindale-Hubbell Law Directory

COHAN, SIMPSON, COWLISHAW & WULFF, L.L.P. (AV)

2700 One Dallas Centre, 350 North St. Paul Street, 75201-4283
Telephone: 214-754-0100
Telecopier: 214-754-0225

Linda S. Althoff
Michael Byrd
Robert M. Cohan
Patrick R. Cowlishaw
James A. Holmes (Resident)
Elizabeth Hawkins Hosch
John Martin Jackson
Kathleen M. LaValle
Ella J. Martinez
Scott M. McElhaney
Susan J. Sandidge
Kurt A. Schwarz
Lee M. Simpson
Mark R. Steiner
Shirley A. Stover
Bart Wulff

For full biographical listings, see the Martindale-Hubbell Law Directory

CONANT FRENCH & CHANEY, LLP (AV)

3880 Bank One Center, 1717 Main Street, 75201
Telephone: 214-915-0620
Fasimile: 214-915-0634
Email: cfc@cfc-law.com *URL:* http://www.cfc-law.com

(See Next Column)

CONANT FRENCH & CHANEY LLP, *Dallas—Continued*

A. B. Conant, Jr.
William J. French
William B. Chaney
Linda A. Hale
Glen E. Lavy
Shawn W. Phelan
James D. MacIntyre

For full biographical listings, see the Martindale-Hubbell Law Directory

FERNANDEZ & KNEBEL, A PROFESSIONAL CORPORATION (AV)

Bank One Center, 1717 Main Street, Suite 2100, 75201
Telephone: 214-747-2100
Fax: 214-747-2144

Bennett I. Abramowitz
Clint A. Corrie
Raymond R. Fernandez, Jr.
Delbert L. Gibbs
Robert L. Knebel, Jr.
Mary Jo Vida

Barbara F. Blaylock
Herbert J. Gilles
Maria Isabel Roman
Jon M. Payne
Joseph L. Mira

For full biographical listings, see the Martindale-Hubbell Law Directory

FRALEY & FRALEY, L.L.P. (AV)

901 Main Street, Suite 6510, 75202
Telephone: 214-761-6460
Fax: 214-761-6469
Email: info@fraleyandfraley.com *URL:* http://www.fraleyandfraley.com

R. Scott Fraley
Elizabeth Masters Fraley
J. Patrick Bredehoft

J. David Criss

For full biographical listings, see the Martindale-Hubbell Law Directory

GIBSON, MCCLURE & WALLACE, L.L.P. (AV)

8080 North Central Expressway, Suite 1300, LB50, 75206
Telephone: 214-891-8040
Fax: 214-891-8010

MEMBERS OF FIRM

Dennis D. Gibson
Wade L. McClure
Jay M. Wallace
Gabrielle Honore Kickham
Ruth Ann Norton Daniels
James M. McCoy
Alan L. Rucker
Bryan D. Perkins

Evelyn A. Yeager
Connie Kay Wilhite

For full biographical listings, see the Martindale-Hubbell Law Directory

ANDREW R. KORN, P.C. (AV)

900 Jackson Street, 470 Founders Square, 75202
Telephone: 214-748-5255
Facsimile: 214-748-7104
Email: arkpc@kornlaw.com *URL:* http://www.lawyers.com/andrewrkorn

Andrew R. Korn

David M. Diaz
Tanya M. Henkels

For full biographical listings, see the Martindale-Hubbell Law Directory

KRAGE & JANVEY, L.L.P. (AV)

2001 Bryan Tower, Suite 2700, 75201-3059
Telephone: 214-969-7500
Telecopier: 214-220-0230

Ben L. Krage

Representative Client: Regal Capital Co.

For full biographical listings, see the Martindale-Hubbell Law Directory

THE SEIB LAW FIRM A PROFESSIONAL CORPORATION (AV)

350 Founders Square, 900 Jackson Street, 75202
Telephone: 214-752-1234
Fax: 214-752-1212

John A. Seib, Jr. (P.C.)

Gregory T. Pratt

For full biographical listings, see the Martindale-Hubbell Law Directory

SMITH, UNDERWOOD & PERKINS, A PROFESSIONAL CORPORATION (AV)

600 Two Lincoln Centre, 5420 LBJ Freeway, 75240
Telephone: 972-661-5114
Telecopier: 972-661-5691
Email: firm@suandp.com *URL:* http://www.suplaw.com

(See Next Column)

Timothy S. Perkins
David W. Ralston
G. Lynn Smith
William J. Underwood, Jr.

Christine A. McGuire
Amy K. Ratzlaff
P. Theodore Stoinoff, II
Val C. Cronin
Ellen P. Stewart
Todd W. Shadle
Ruth C. Logan
Christina L. Betanzos
Kent D. Williamson

For full biographical listings, see the Martindale-Hubbell Law Directory

SOPUCH NOUHAN HIGGINS & ARNETT, L.L.P. (AV)

400 North St. Paul Street Suite 840, 75201
Telephone: 214-760-0900
Fax: 214-760-0905
Email: SNHADALLAS@aol.com *URL:* http://www.SNHA.com
Chicago, Illinois Office: 311 South Wacker Drive, Suite 5600.
Telephone: 312-922-0900.
Fax: 312-922-2255. Email: SNHACHGO@aol.com

James Robert Arnett, II
Michael L. Gaubert
Jamil N. Alibhai

For full biographical listings, see the Martindale-Hubbell Law Directory

THOMAS, FELDMAN & WILSHUSEN, L.L.P. (AV)

9400 NCX Tower, 9400 North Central Expressway, Suite 900, 75231
Telephone: 214-369-3008
Facsimile: 214-369-8393

MEMBERS OF FIRM

Richard Gary Thomas
Robert L. Feldman
Fred D. Wilshusen

ASSOCIATES

Regan Gayle O'Steen
Trice Ragon Richey
Edward (Ted) J. Laperouse, II

OF COUNSEL

Joseph M. Stuhl

Representative Clients: Baker Drywall Co., Inc.; CMC Steel Group; Dallas Door and Supply Co.; Dallas Fire Insurance Company; Fischbach & Moore, Inc.; Mills Electrical Contractors, Inc.; SGB Construction Services, Inc.; TD Mechanical; Spaw Glass General Contractors, Inc.; TAS Construction, Inc.

For full biographical listings, see the Martindale-Hubbell Law Directory

WEIL & PETROCCHI, A PROFESSIONAL CORPORATION (AV)

1900 Thanksgiving Tower, 1601 Elm Street, L.B. 100, 75201
Telephone: 214-969-7272
Facsimile Copier: 214-880-7402

Christopher M. Weil
Anthony A. Petrocchi

Jeffrey W. Hellberg, Jr.

For full biographical listings, see the Martindale-Hubbell Law Directory

*DECATUR,** Wise Co.

SIMPSON & BOYD, P.L.L.C. (AV)

105 North State Street, Suite B, P.O. Box 957, 76234
Telephone: 940-627-8308
Fax: 940-627-8092
Email: Derrick@wf.net
Email: sbblo@wf.net *URL:* http://www.lawyers.com/simpson&boydpllc
Bridgeport, Texas Office: 1119 Halsell Street, P.O. Box 685, 76426.
Telephone: 940-683-4098.
Fax: 940-683-3122.

Michael A. Simpson
Ross M. Simpson
Derrick S. Boyd

G. Alan Powers
J. Michael Carrillo

For full biographical listings, see the Martindale-Hubbell Law Directory

*EDINBURG,** Hidalgo Co.

HOCKEMA, TIPPIT & ESCOBEDO, L.L.P. (AV)

Building 101, 1 Paseo del Prado, 78539-9672
Telephone: 956-631-9112; 800-966-9112
Fax: 956-630-9472
Mailing Address: P.O. Box 720540, McAllen, Texas, 78504-0540
Email: htelaw@ibm.net

David H. Hockema
John L. Tippit, III
Jose Escobedo, Jr.

ASSOCIATE

Michael L. Young

For full biographical listings, see the Martindale-Hubbell Law Directory

*EL PASO,** El Paso Co.

AINSA PARTNERS, LLP (AV)

5809 Acacia Circle, 79912
Telephone: 915-845-5300
Fax: 915-845-7800
Email: fain@acaciapark.com *URL:* http://www.ainsa.com

Francis S. Ainsa, Jr.
Michael F. Ainsa
David M. Driscoll

For full biographical listings, see the Martindale-Hubbell Law Directory

CROWSON & INGRAM (AV)

Suite 706, The Cortez, 310 North Mesa, P.O. Box 862, 79945
Telephone: 915-533-7717
Telefax: 915-533-1495
Email: crowsing@huntleigh.net

MEMBERS OF FIRM

Harold E. Crowson, Jr.
Temple B. Ingram, Jr.

Reference: Bank of America, N.A.; Norwest Bank, El Paso, N.A.; Bank of the West, El Paso, Texas.

For full biographical listings, see the Martindale-Hubbell Law Directory

RAY, MCCHRISTIAN & JEANS, A PROFESSIONAL CORPORATION (AV)

5822 Cromo Drive, Suite 400, 79912
Telephone: 915-832-7200
Fax: 915-832-7333
Email: rmj@rmjfirm.com

Jeff Ray
John W. McChristian, Jr.
David S. Jeans
James A. Mounts, III
Eduardo Miranda
Robin Collins
Leticia Nuñez

Daniel H. Hernandez
Michael K. Dean
Angelica B. Carreon
Todd E. Marshall
Stacy Bearden Zavala

Representative Clients: Carolina Casualty Insurance Co.; Cigna Property and Casualty Insurance Co.; CNA Insurance Cos.; Commercial Union Insurance Cos; Houston General Insurance Co.; Kemper National Insurance Cos.; Occidental Fire and Casualty Company of North Carolina; Reliance Insurance Co.; St. Paul Fire & Marine Insurance Co.; Travelers Indemnity Co. and Aetna Casualty & Surety Co.

For full biographical listings, see the Martindale-Hubbell Law Directory

*FORT WORTH,** Tarrant Co.

DECKER, JONES, MCMACKIN, MCCLANE, HALL & BATES, A PROFESSIONAL CORPORATION (AV)

2500 Bank One Tower, 500 Throckmorton Street, 76102-3812
Telephone: 817-336-2400; Metro: 817-429-5260
Fax: 817-332-3043; 336-2181
Email: email@deckerjones.com *URL:* http://www.deckerjones.com

Daniel L. Bates
Robert W. Decker
Mark S. Dugan
Janet L. Hahn
Randy J. Hall
Raymond B. Kelly, III
John B. McClane
John W. McMackin
Charles B. Milliken
Gary M. Moates
Bradley H. Rice
Jeffrey W. Storie
James L. Stripling
Brian K. Yost
Tamera H. Bennett
Arthur F. Zobal
Geoffrey A. Mantooth

Representative Clients: Martin-Sprocket and Gear, Inc.; Williamson-Dickie Manufacturing Co.; MICA Corp.; Ibertech, Inc.; Harbison-Fischer Manufacturing Co.; Employers Insurance of Texas; American International Group; Medical Protective Co.; Redman Homes, Inc.; Liberty Mutual Insurance.

For full biographical listings, see the Martindale-Hubbell Law Directory

LAW, SNAKARD & GAMBILL, A PROFESSIONAL CORPORATION (AV)

3200 Bank One Tower, 500 Throckmorton Street, 76102
Telephone: 817-335-7373; Metro: 429-2991
Telecopier: 817-332-7473
Dallas
Dallas, Texas Office: St. Paul Place, 750 North St. Paul, Suite 1350.
Telephone: 214-871-9027; Metro: 429-2991.
Telecopier: 214-954-4476.

Rice M. Tilley (1899-1990)
Robert F. Snakard (1910-1994)
Samuel A. Denny (1937-1995)
Rice M. Tilley, Jr.
Walter S. Fortney
Dennis Swift
Jay Spencer Garrett
William F. McCann
Ed Huddleston
Vernon E. Rew, Jr.

(See Next Column)

A. Burch Waldron, III
Larry C. Bracken
Pamela Arnold Bassel
Carol Ware Bracken
Dabney D. Bassel
Lynn M. Johnson
Kelley B. Hill
B. Blake Cox
James H. Cheatham, IV
Stephen G. Wilcox
M. W. Cockrell, Jr.
Liane A. Janovsky

Christopher R. Richie
Deborah B. Morton
James O. Wyss
Laurie Dahl Babich
David F. Shurtz
Shoshana L. Thoma-Isgur

OF COUNSEL

Thos. H. Law
Lawton G. Gambill
Robert M. Randolph
Robert F. Watson
Harry Hopkins

Representative Clients: BankOne, Texas, N.A.; Southwestern Bell Telephone Co.; The Perot Group; Ford Motor Credit Co.; Prudential Securities, Inc.; Chrysler Financial Corp.
Attorneys for: Chicago Title Insurance Co.

For full biographical listings, see the Martindale-Hubbell Law Directory

MCMULLEN LAW FIRM (AV)

6300 Ridglea Place Suite 509, 76116-5731
Telephone: 817-731-4163
Fax: 817-731-4340
Email: wademcmullen@msn.com

Wade H. McMullen

For full biographical listings, see the Martindale-Hubbell Law Directory

LAW OFFICES OF PATRICK H. O'NEILL (AV)

110 West 7th Street, Suite 1100, 76102
Telephone: 817-878-3333
Fax: 817-878-3672

Patrick H. O'Neill

James L. Jackson, Jr.
Glenn T. Lupo

For full biographical listings, see the Martindale-Hubbell Law Directory

*GALVESTON,** Galveston Co.

GREER, HERZ & ADAMS, L.L.P. (AV)

A Partnership including Professional Corporations
(Formerly Dibrell & Greer)
One Moody Plaza, 18th Floor, 77550
Telephone: 409-797-3200; Houston Line: 281-480-5278
Telecopier: 409-766-6424
League City
URL: http://www.greerherz.com
League City Office: 2525 South Shore Boulevard, Suite 203, 77573.
Telephone: 281-480-5278.
Fax: 281-538-3791.

MEMBERS OF FIRM

W. E. Greer (1901-1996)
Irwin M. Herz, Jr. (P.C.)
Jerry L. Adams (P.C.)
Stephen G. Schulz (P.C.)
Debra G. James
John A. Buckley, Jr. (P.C.)
Andrew J. Mytelka
Darryl H. Levy
Frederick E. Black
Janet L. Rushing
Marilyn L. Soloway
Gregory S. Garrison
Scott D. Daniel
Joseph A. C. Fulcher
Jim Itin

ASSOCIATES

Tara B. Annweiler
Michael G. Adams
David Le Blanc
Joseph Russo, Jr.
Steve Windsor
Melissa E. Palmer
William J. Hogan
Sean Monticello

OF COUNSEL

Frank T. Crews, Jr. (P.C.)
John S. McEldowney
Charles Brown (P.C.)

General Counsel for: American National Insurance Co.; The Moody National Bank of Galveston; United States National Bank of Galveston; Transitional Learning Community of Galveston; Securities Management & Research, Inc.; American National Growth Fund, Inc.; Kempner Capital Management, Inc.; The Moody Endowment.
Counsel for: National Western Life Insurance Co.

For full biographical listings, see the Martindale-Hubbell Law Directory

*HOUSTON,** Harris Co.

BAYLESS & STOKES (AV)

2931 Ferndale Street, 77098
Telephone: 713-522-2224
Fax: 713-522-2218
Email: bayless@baylessstokes.com

MEMBER OF FIRM

Bobbie G. Bayless

(See Next Column)

BAYLESS & STOKES, *Houston—Continued*

ASSOCIATE

Spencer W. Creed

For full biographical listings, see the Martindale-Hubbell Law Directory

BECK, REDDEN & SECREST (AV)

One Houston Center, 1221 McKinney Street, Suite 4500, 77010
Telephone: 713-951-3700
Telecopier: 713-951-3720
Email: brs@brsfirm.com *URL:* http://www.brsfirm.com

MEMBERS OF FIRM

David J. Beck
Joe W. Redden, Jr.
Ronald Dean Secrest
William Curtis Webb
Eric James Roy Nichols
Alistair Byrne Dawson
Harry P. Weitzel

OF COUNSEL

Keith A. Jones (Not admitted in TX)
Linda K. McCloud
Anne M. Pike
Rufus Wallingford

ASSOCIATES

Jennifer Parker Ainsworth
L. Nicole Batey
Thomas E. Ganucheau
Jeffrey M. Golub
David Watkin Jones
Felicia Harris Kyle
Michael E. Richardson
Jim Taylor

For full biographical listings, see the Martindale-Hubbell Law Directory

BERG & ANDROPHY (AV)

3704 Travis, 77002-9550
Telephone: 713-529-5622
Fax: 713-529-3785
URL: http://www.lawyers.com/b&alaw
Email: mail@bahou.com *URL:* http://www.bafirm.com
New York, New York Office: 230 Park Avenue, Suite 1000, 10169-1099.
Telephone: 212-808-6580.
Fax: 212-808-3020.

David H. Berg (P.C.)
Joel M. Androphy
Cynthia R. Levin Moulton

Wade T. Howard
Geoffrey A. Berg
Gabriel A. Berg (Not admitted in TX)

For full biographical listings, see the Martindale-Hubbell Law Directory

COHEN & SMALL (AV)

2700 Post Oak Boulevard, Suite 950, 77056
Telephone: 713-961-5274
Fax: 713-961-0438
Email: csinfo@cohensmall.com *URL:* http://www.cohensmall.com

MEMBERS OF FIRM

Ronald Cohen
William G. Small

Representative Clients: General Electric Capital Corp.; The Hertz Corp.; Gulf Metals Industries; U.S. Zinc Corp.; Texas Outpatient Surgicare; Metroplex Industries, Inc.; Sachnowitz & Co.; U.S. Zinc Incorporated; Midway Petroleum, Ltd.

For full biographical listings, see the Martindale-Hubbell Law Directory

CUNNINGHAM, DARLOW, ZOOK & CHAPOTON, LLP (AV)

1000 Louisiana, Suite 6900, 77002
Telephone: 713-659-5522
Fax: 713-659-4466
Email: sgosslee@cdzc.com

Tom Alan Cunningham
Debbie Crupain Darlow
Richard J. Zook
John E. Chapoton, Jr.

ASSOCIATES

Kelley M. Keller
Jon T. Powell

For full biographical listings, see the Martindale-Hubbell Law Directory

DAVIS, ORETSKY & GUILFOYLE, P.C. (AV)

1415 Louisiana, Suite 4200, 77002
Telephone: 713-659-1010
Facsimile: 713-659-1122
Email: doglawfirm@dog.pc *URL:* http://www.dogpc.com
Affiliated Law Firm: Wommack Law Firm, P.C., 7 West Way Court, Suite A, P.O. Box 420, Lake Jackson, Texas 77566.
Telephone: 409-297-9755. Houston
Telephone: 713-355-5737.
Fax: 409-297-9761. Email: wdm-george@computron.net.

Tom M. Davis, Jr.
Andrew S. Oretsky
Matthew C. Guilfoyle
Juliann H. Panagos
Curt M. Langley
George T. Wommack, Jr.
David C. Redford

(See Next Column)

M. Lucille Anderson
Kristin Bauer
Robert M. Browning
Paige Black Larrabee
Norman W. Peters, Jr.
Jonathan L. Phillips
William R. Pilat

For full biographical listings, see the Martindale-Hubbell Law Directory

FISHER, BOYD, BROWN, BOUDREAUX & HUGUENARD, L.L.P. (AV)

70th Floor Wells Fargo Plaza, 1000 Louisiana, 77002
Telephone: 713-400-4000
Telefax: 713-400-4050

Wayne Fisher
Larry P. Boyd
Thomas K. Brown
Olan J. Boudreaux
James A. Huguenard

Bernard G. Johnson, III
Kay K. (Daniel) Morgan

For full biographical listings, see the Martindale-Hubbell Law Directory

FRANKLIN, CARDWELL & JONES (AV)

Chase Tower, 24th Floor, 600 Travis Street, 77002-2910
Telephone: 713-222-6025
Fax: 713-222-0938
Email: attorneys@fcj.com *URL:* http://www.fcj.com

Ronald G. Franklin
Gregory N. Jones
Scott G. Burdine
Carlton D. Wilde, Jr.
Jeffrey D. Meyer
Joseph A. Fischer, III

For full biographical listings, see the Martindale-Hubbell Law Directory

HANEN, ALEXANDER, JOHNSON & SPALDING, L.L.P. (AV)

910 Travis, Suite 1700, 77002
Telephone: 713-222-2323
Fax: 713-222-2226

Andrew S. Hanen
Joseph R. Alexander, Jr.
Brian P. Johnson
John E. Spalding
Frank A. Doyle
Lawrence J. West
T. Christopher Trent

Geoffrey C. Guill
Tamara M. Madden
Richard Todd Marshall
Raphael (Rafe) Taylor
Lisa M. Moran
Shashi Patel
Annette Sepulveda Kenefick
Craig A. Choate

For full biographical listings, see the Martindale-Hubbell Law Directory

LANIER, PARKER & SULLIVAN, P.C. (AV)

Four Houston Center, Suite 1550 1331 Lamar Street, 77010
Telephone: 713-659-5200
FAX: 713-659-2204

W. Mark Lanier
Kevin P. Parker
Kent C. Sullivan

Becky J. Lanier
Leslie M. Stewart
Robert E. Leone
Edward W. Fudge
Patrick N. Haines
Dara Grisbee Hegar
Eugene R. Egdorf

For full biographical listings, see the Martindale-Hubbell Law Directory

KATHLEEN AMELIA SLAYDON, P.C. (AV)

The Niels Esperson Building, 808 Travis Street, 23rd Floor, 77002-5704
Telephone: 713-221-5444
Fax: 713-221-5445
Email: Lawfirm@slaydon.com *URL:* http://www.slaydon.com

Kathleen Amelia Slaydon

For full biographical listings, see the Martindale-Hubbell Law Directory

RUSSELL B. STARBIRD, P.C. (AV)

1111 Bagby, Suite 2450, 77002
Telephone: 713-652-0652
Fax: 713-652-0653
URL: http://www.lawyers.com/starbirdlaw

Russell B. Starbird

For full biographical listings, see the Martindale-Hubbell Law Directory

Houston—Continued

STUMPF CRADDOCK MASSEY & PULMAN, A PROFESSIONAL CORPORATION (AV)

1400 Post Oak Boulevard Suite 400, 77056
Telephone: 713-871-0919
Fax: 713-871-0408
URL: http://www.sfcm.com
San Antonio, Texas Office: One Riverwalk Place, 700 North St. Mary's, Suite 1150, 78205.
Telephone: 210-231-0919.
Fax: 210-231-0004.
Beaumont, Texas Office: 550 Fannin, Suite 230, 77701.
Telephone: 409-813-1761.
Fax: 409-813-1786.

Frederick W. Stumpf
Daniel K. Craddock
Michael B. Massey
Clayton C. Cannon
John M. Castillo (Resident, San Antonio Office)
Scott A. Farrimond (Resident, San Antonio Office)
Henry J. Fasthoff, IV (Resident, San Antonio Office)
Lawrence J. Fontana
Robert F. Maher (P.C.)
Randall A. Pulman (Resident, San Antonio Office)
Shari Pullen Pulman (Resident, San Antonio Office)
Douglas S. Sandage (P.C.)
Ray B. Jeffrey

OF COUNSEL

Tilman J. Falgout, III
John H. Marshall

For full biographical listings, see the Martindale-Hubbell Law Directory

RONALD J. WASKA A PROFESSIONAL CORPORATION (AV)

952 Echo Lane, Suite 180, 77024-2783
Telephone: 713-461-8181
Fax: 713-461-8186
Email: rjwaska@worldnet.att.net

Ronald J. Waska

For full biographical listings, see the Martindale-Hubbell Law Directory

*LUBBOCK,** Lubbock Co.

THOMPSON & THOMAS, A PROFESSIONAL CORPORATION (AV)

4412 74th Street, Suite A-100, P.O. Box 65150, 79464
Telephone: 806-793-7600
Fax: 806-793-6882

George L. Thompson, III
Michael A. Thomas

Molly Forsyth

For full biographical listings, see the Martindale-Hubbell Law Directory

*MIDLAND,** Midland Co.

TURNER & DAVIS, A PROFESSIONAL CORPORATION (AV)

400 West Illinois, Suite 1400, P.O. Box 2796, 79701
Telephone: 915-687-0011
Fax: 915-687-1735
Email: turdavpc@iglobal.net

J. Randy Turner
John Allen "Jad" Davis, Jr.
Frank N. Cremer, Jr.
James R. "Rusty" Fuller
Patrick S. Gerald
Holly B. Williams

Robert P. Crumpler, Jr.
David H. Smith

For full biographical listings, see the Martindale-Hubbell Law Directory

*SAN ANTONIO,** Bexar Co.

DAVIS, CEDILLO & MENDOZA, INCORPORATED (AV)

Harte-Hanks Tower, Suite 400, 7710 Jones-Maltsberger, 78216
Telephone: 210-822-6666
Telecopier: 210-822-1151
URL: http://www.dcm.com

Ricardo G. Cedillo
J. Russell Davis
Richard W. Espey
Marlise Aimone Kercheville
Ronald E. Mendoza

Velma Garza Anderson
David S. Angulo
David C. Badger
Steve Alfonso Chiscano
Jason R. Cliffe
Troy A. Glander
Henry B. Gonzalez, III
Nancy J. Meyers-Harvey
Derick J. Rodgers

OF COUNSEL

Norman S. Davis

For full biographical listings, see the Martindale-Hubbell Law Directory

HABBESHAW, KALMANS & SCHWARTZ, P.C. (AV)

The Colonnade, Suite 770, 9901 I.H. 10 West, 78230
Telephone: 210-699-8086
Facsimile: 210-699-3409

Penny K. Habbeshaw
Patricia A. Kalmans
Helen Schwartz

For full biographical listings, see the Martindale-Hubbell Law Directory

LANE, GANNON & TALIAFERRO, L.L.P. (AV)

8620 North New Braunfels, Suite 310, 78217
Telephone: 210-829-1545
Telecopier: 210-829-1633
Email: gannon@lgtlaw.com
Austin, Texas Office: 816 Congress Avenue, Suite 1100, 78701.
Telephone: 512-485-4595.
Fax: 512-485-4594.

MEMBERS OF FIRM

Gregory Gannon
John R. Lane, Jr.
William Craig Taliaferro

ASSOCIATES

Sharon Denise Hobbs
Frederick D. Schraub
Georganne G. Leonard
John R. Resendez
Brent Austin Biggs
Alfred Michael Casillas
Christia M. Antolik
Hella V. Caldera

OF COUNSEL

C. Gilbert House
James B. House

For full biographical listings, see the Martindale-Hubbell Law Directory

O'CONNELL, BENJAMIN & COGHLAN, L.L.P. (AV)

153 Treeline Park, Suite 200, 78209
Telephone: 210-824-0009
Fax: 210-824-9429
Email: obcllp@oconben.com

Keith B. O'Connell
David P. Benjamin
G. Thomas Coghlan
Ernest F. Avery
Les Katona, Jr.
Dan Vana

Gayla S. Corley
Cathrin J. Martinez

For full biographical listings, see the Martindale-Hubbell Law Directory

TEXARKANA, Bowie Co.

YOUNG & PICKETT (AV)

4122 Texas Boulevard, P.O. Box 1897, 75504
Telephone: 870-774-3206; 903-794-1303
Facsimile: 903-792-5098; 903-794-5098
Email: YP1303@aol.com

Damon Young
John M. Pickett

ASSOCIATE

Lance Lee

Representative Clients: AT&T Corporation; AmeriSource Corporation; Bridgestone/Firestone, Inc.; Exxon Chemical Americas; Century Bank of New Boston, Texas; International Paper Company, Inc.; Lucent Technologies, Inc.; Medtronic, Inc.; Michelin North America; SmithKline Beecham Corporation.

For full biographical listings, see the Martindale-Hubbell Law Directory

UTAH

*SALT LAKE CITY,** Salt Lake Co.

BURBIDGE AND MITCHELL (AV)

Suite 2001, 139 East South Temple, 84111
Telephone: 801-355-6677
Fax: 801-355-2341
Email: Burbidge@xmission.com

Richard D. Burbidge
Stephen B. Mitchell

ASSOCIATES

Jefferson W. Gross
Jason D. Boren

For full biographical listings, see the Martindale-Hubbell Law Directory

DART ADAMSON DONOVAN & HANSON (AV)

A Partnership of Professional Corporations
370 E. South Temple, Suite 400, 84111
Telephone: 801-521-6383
Telefax: 801-355-2513

Craig G. Adamson (P.C.)

(See Next Column)

DART ADAMSON DONOVAN & HANSON, *Salt Lake City—Continued*

ASSOCIATES

Eric P. Lee (P.C.) | Cameron S. Denning

A list of References will be furnished upon request.

For full biographical listings, see the Martindale-Hubbell Law Directory

DAVID K. ISOM LAW OFFICES (AV)

60 East South Temple, Suite 1680, 84111
Telephone: 801-366-6000
Fax: 801-366-6010
Email: isomoff@inconnect.com

ASSOCIATES

J. Preston Stieff | Matthew R. Howell

For full biographical listings, see the Martindale-Hubbell Law Directory

PARSONS, DAVIES, KINGHORN & PETERS, P.C. (AV)

185 South State Street, Suite 700, 84111
Telephone: 801-363-4300
Facsimile: 801-363-4378
Email: Attorneys@pdkplaw.com

Glen E. Davies
Gerald H. Kinghorn
Bill Thomas Peters
R. Kimball Mosier
David W. Scofield
Stuart W. Hinckley
Harold L. Reiser
J. Scott Brown
Katherine S. Gregory
Paige Bigelow

For Complete List of Firm Personnel, See General Section

For full biographical listings, see the Martindale-Hubbell Law Directory

VAN COTT, BAGLEY, CORNWALL & McCARTHY, A PROFESSIONAL CORPORATION (AV)

50 South Main Street, Suite 1600, P.O. Box 45340, 84145-0340
Telephone: 801-532-3333
Telecopier: 801-534-0058
Email: info@vancott.com *URL:* http://www.vancott.com
Ogden, Utah Office: 2404 Washington Boulevard, Suite 900.
Telephone: 801-394-5783.
Park City, Utah Office: 2200 Park Avenue, Suite C200-A.
Telephone: 435-649-3889.

Robert M. Anderson (President of Firm)
Thomas T. Billings
Timothy W. Blackburn (Resident, Ogden, Utah Office)
David A. Greenwood
Jeremy M. Hoffman
Gerald H. Suniville
Kenneth W. Yeates
John L. Young

Jennifer K. Anderson
Stephen K. Christiansen
Sandra L. Crosland
Kevin M. Sheff
Bradley M. Strassberg
Evan S. Strassberg
Justin Toth (Not admitted in UT)

OF COUNSEL

Cecil R. Hedger

For Complete List of Firm Personnel, See General Section

For full biographical listings, see the Martindale-Hubbell Law Directory

WOOD CRAPO LLC (AV)

60 E. South Temple, Suite 500, 84111
Telephone: 801-366-6060
Fax: 801-366-6061

Mary Anne Q. Wood
David J. Crapo
Larry Stuart Jenkins
Darryl J. Lee

Susan J. Mueller
Eric T. Johnson
Richard J. Armstrong
Joi Gardner Pearson

OF COUNSEL

Kathryn Ogden Balmforth
James W. Stewart
Richard L. Evans
Pamela B. Hunsaker
Sheri Ann Mower
Stephen G. Wood

For full biographical listings, see the Martindale-Hubbell Law Directory

VERMONT

*BURLINGTON,** Chittenden Co.

O'NEILL CRAWFORD & GREEN, P.C. (AV)

159 Bank Street, P.O. Box 5359, 05402-5359
Telephone: 802-865-4700
Fax: 802-865-4778

(See Next Column)

Jerome F. O'Neill
Geoffrey W. Crawford
Michael I. Green

Samantha W. Foxen

For full biographical listings, see the Martindale-Hubbell Law Directory

VIRGINIA

*ABINGDON,** Washington Co.

THE TATE LAW FIRM (AV)

Abingdon Professional Centre, 110 Abingdon Place, 24211
Telephone: 540-628-5185
Telecopier: 540-628-5045
Email: lynntate@naxs.com *URL:* http://www.tatelaw.com

Mary Lynn Tate

OF COUNSEL

Olen G. Haynes (Not admitted in VA)

LEGAL SUPPORT PERSONNEL

Rebecca A. Wyatt | Teresa L. Brown

For full biographical listings, see the Martindale-Hubbell Law Directory

ALEXANDRIA, (Independent City)

BLANKINGSHIP & KOOMEY, P.C. (AV)

516 1/2 Oronoco Street, 22314
Telephone: 703-739-7621
Fax: 703-739-7622
URL: http://www.valawyer.net
Email: ahblaw@ziplink.net *URL:* http://www.lawyers.com/valawyers

A. Hugo Blankingship, III | Christopher Koomey

OF COUNSEL

Douglas A. Anderson

For full biographical listings, see the Martindale-Hubbell Law Directory

DIMURO, GINSBERG & MOOK, P.C. (AV)

908 King Street, Suite 200, 22314
Telephone: 703-684-4333
Telecopier: 703-548-3181
Email: dimuro@dimuro.com *URL:* http://www.dimuro.com

Bernard J. DiMuro
Nina J. Ginsberg
Jonathan R. Mook
Michael E. Barnsback

David J. Duffett

OF COUNSEL

Michael S. Lieberman

Representative Clients: Sun Healthcare Group; Ridgways, Inc.; Medtronic, Inc.; Prince William County Police; OKi Telecom.

For full biographical listings, see the Martindale-Hubbell Law Directory

*ARLINGTON,** Arlington Co.

COHEN, GETTINGS & DUNHAM, P.C. (AV)

2200 Wilson Boulevard, Suite 800, 22201
Telephone: 703-525-2260
Fax: 703-525-2489
Email: info@cohengettings.com *URL:* http://www.cohengettings.com
Alexandria, Virginia Office: 211 North Union Street, Suite 350.
Telephone: 703-525-2260.
Washington, D.C. Office: 1225 19th Street, N.W., 7th Floor.
Silver Spring, Maryland Office: Suite 700, 8701 Georgia Avenue.
Telephone: 301-589-6072.

Harvey B. Cohen
Brian P. Gettings (1933-1995)
Frank W. Dunham, Jr.
R. Scott Caulkins
Joel L. Dahnke
John E. Gagliano
Manuel A. Capsalis
John C. Pasierb

Carole H. Capsalis
Michael S. Nachmanoff
Kristen L. Loesch

OF COUNSEL

Carroll E. Dubuc
Joseph A. Fisher, III
Nancy Lee Feldman

References: First Virginia Bank; Virginia Commerce Bank; Crestar Bank; United Bank.

For full biographical listings, see the Martindale-Hubbell Law Directory

Arlington—Continued

HENRY ST. JOHN FITZGERALD (AV)

2200 Wilson Boulevard, Suite 800, 22201
Telephone: 703-525-8753
Facsimile: 703-525-2489
Email: hstjf@earthlink.net *URL:* http://www.lawyers.com/henryfitzgerald

For full biographical listings, see the Martindale-Hubbell Law Directory

*FAIRFAX,** (Ind. City; Seat of Fairfax Co.)

MCCANDLISH & LILLARD, A PROFESSIONAL CORPORATION (AV)

Fair Oaks Plaza, 11350 Random Hills Road, Suite 500, 22030-7429
Telephone: 703-273-2288
Fax: 703-352-4300
Email: mccand@patriot.net *URL:* http://www.mccandlaw.com
Leesburg, Virginia Office: 305 Harrison Street, S.E., Third Floor.
Telephone: 703-737-0200.
Fax: 703-737-0165.

Robert J. McCandlish, Jr. (1909-1996)
Rothwell J. Lillard (1910-1989)
Jesse B. Wilson, III
Peter A. Arntson
Gary W. Brown
Randolph A. Sutliff
Robert H. J. Loftus
William McCauley Arnold
Stephen C. Price
Stephen K. Fox
Douglas J. Sanderson
R. Peyton Mahaffey
William L. Carey
John W. Farrell
Eric J. Berghold
Ralph M. Tener
Vicki L. Layman
Adam W. Smith

Daniel P. Lyon
Lawrence J. McClafferty
Brian R. Sanderson

For full biographical listings, see the Martindale-Hubbell Law Directory

MICHAEL C. MONTAVON, P.C. (AV)

3975 Fair Ridge Drive, Suite 150, 22033
Telephone: 703-352-2550
Fax: 703-352-3466

Michael C. Montavon

For full biographical listings, see the Martindale-Hubbell Law Directory

SILVER & BROWN, A PROFESSIONAL CORPORATION (AV)

10621 Jones Street, Suite 101, P.O. Box 1108, 22030
Telephone: 703-591-6666
Facsimile: 703-591-5618
Email: ctbghs@aol.com

Glenn H. Silver
C. Thomas Brown

For full biographical listings, see the Martindale-Hubbell Law Directory

*MANASSAS,** Prince William Co.

MCCARTHY & MASSEY, P.C. (AV)

9315 Center Street, Suite 104, 20110
Telephone: 703-330-2726; Metro: 703-551-2146
Fax: 703-330-2429

Tara M. McCarthy
Joyce A. Naumann Massey

Susan L. Mitchell
Marian L. Beckett

For full biographical listings, see the Martindale-Hubbell Law Directory

NORFOLK, (Independent City)

PAYNE, GATES, FARTHING & RADD, P.C. (AV)

15th Floor, Dominion Tower, 999 Waterside Drive, Suite 1515, 23510-3309
Telephone: 757-640-1500
Facsimile: 757-627-6583
URL: http://www.paynegates.com

Ronald M. Gates
Philip R. Farthing
Anthony F. Radd
Glen M. Robertson
Brian R. Dinning
Todd J. Preti
Marshall A. Winslow, Jr.

C. Arthur Robinson, II
Stephen E. Heretick
Raymond L. Hogge, Jr.

OF COUNSEL

Charles E. Payne

For full biographical listings, see the Martindale-Hubbell Law Directory

RICHMOND, (Independent City)

MALONEY, HUENNEKENS, PARKS, GECKER & PARSONS, A PROFESSIONAL CORPORATION (AV)

Bank of America Center, 1111 East Main Street, Suite 800, 23219-3103
Telephone: 804-644-0313
Telecopier: 804-783-6192

Kevin R. Huennekens
Daniel A. Gecker
Yvonne Steenstra Wellford
Christopher A. Jones

Reference: First Union National Bank.

For Complete List of Firm Personnel, See General Section

For full biographical listings, see the Martindale-Hubbell Law Directory

ROANOKE, Roanoke City Co.

WOOTEN & HART, A PROFESSIONAL CORPORATION (AV)

707 Building, Suite 300, P.O. Box 12247, 24024-2247
Telephone: 540-343-2451; 540-342-9672
Telecopier: 540-345-6417
URL: http://www.wootenhart.com

George W. Wooten
David B. Hart
L. Thompson Hanes
Susan A. Waddell
Bradley D. McGraw
John L. Cooley
Thomas W. Farrell
Paul C. Kuhnel
Peter D. Vieth

David W. Hearn
John Mark Cooley
Christopher W. Stevens
Elizabeth D. Guilbert
Eunice Park Austin

OF COUNSEL

M. Lanier Woodrum

Representative Clients: Wachovia Bank; St. Paul Insurance Cos.
Approved Attorneys for: Lawyers Title Insurance Corp.
Reference: First Union National Bank.

For full biographical listings, see the Martindale-Hubbell Law Directory

VIENNA, Fairfax Co.

BORING & PILGER, P.C. (AV)

307 Maple Avenue West, Suite D, 22180-4307
Telephone: 703-281-2161
Fax: 703-281-9464
URL: http://www.boringandpilger.com

Karl W. Pilger

Sharon C. Williams (Not admitted in VA)

Representative Clients: Hewlett-Packard, Co.; Anthony and Sylvan Pools, Inc.; Toshiba America Information Services, Inc.

For full biographical listings, see the Martindale-Hubbell Law Directory

WASHINGTON

*SEATTLE,** King Co.

BADGLEY - MULLINS (AV)

5100 Washington Mutual Tower, 1201 Third Avenue, 98101
Telephone: 206-621-6566
Fax: 206-621-9686

MEMBERS OF FIRM

Don Paul Badgley
Donald H. Mullins
Duncan C. Turner
Diana P. Danzberger

ASSOCIATES

Michael G. Atkins
Sandrin B. Rasmussen
John J. Chihak, Jr.

OF COUNSEL

Lish Whitson

For full biographical listings, see the Martindale-Hubbell Law Directory

BARRETT GILMAN & ZIKER (AV)

A Partnership including Professional Service Corporations
1000 Second Avenue, Suite 3500, 98104-1063
Telephone: 206-464-1900
Fax: 206-667-9087
Email: bgz@bgz.com *URL:* http://www.bgz.com

MEMBERS OF FIRM

Paul A. Barrett (P.S.)
Thomas L. Gilman (P.S.)
Barry G. Ziker (P.S.)
Thomas A. Carr (P.S.)

(See Next Column)

BARRETT GILMAN & ZIKER, *Seattle—Continued*

ASSOCIATE

Amy C. Hevly

OF COUNSEL

David A. Shaw

Reference: U.S. Bank, Seattle, Washington.

For full biographical listings, see the Martindale-Hubbell Law Directory

BERESFORD, BOOTH, DEMARAY & TROMPETER, INC., P.S. (AV)

1420 5th Avenue, Suite 3650, 98101
Telephone: 206-682-4000
Telecopier: 206-682-4004
Email: B11SULAW@AOL.COM

William Beresford
Richard R. Beresford
Mark M. Demaray
Ronald J. Trompeter
David Tingstad

OF COUNSEL

Wayne C. Booth, Sr.
Susan L. Samuelson

Representative Clients: Frontier Bank; AT&T Commercial Finance; Production Supply Corp.; Washington State Adoption Council; WARM; Bank of America; United States Shippers, Inc.; World Point Logistics, Inc.; Midwest Specialty Steel, LLC; Ivar's.

For full biographical listings, see the Martindale-Hubbell Law Directory

DANIELSON HARRIGAN & TOLLEFSON, LLP (AV)

A Limited Liability Partnership including a Professional Service Corporation
999 Third Avenue, 44th Floor, 98104
Telephone: 206-623-1700
Facsimile: 206-623-8717
Email: lawfirm@dh-t.com

David Danielson (P.S.)
Arthur W. Harrigan, Jr.
G. Val Tollefson
Timothy G. Leyh
Michelle Buhler
Karl F. Oles
Charles Jordan

COUNSEL

Richard H. Holmquist
Katherine See Kennedy
Matthew R. Kenney
Terence K. McGee

ASSOCIATES

Randall Thomsen
Michael M.K. Hemphill

For full biographical listings, see the Martindale-Hubbell Law Directory

ELLIS, LI & MCKINSTRY PLLC (AV)

Two Union Square, 601 Union Street, Suite 4900, 98101-3906
Telephone: 206-682-0565
Telecopier: 206-625-1052
Email: elm@elmlaw.com *URL:* http://www.elmlaw.com

MEMBERS OF FIRM

William H. Ellis, Jr. (1932-1994)
Ronald E. McKinstry
Chi-Dooh Li
Michael R. McKinstry
Jan P. Olson
Daniel J. Ichinaga
Steven T. O'Ban
Keith A. Kemper

ASSOCIATES

Heidi J. Abrams
Andrew J. Toles
Troy S. Anderson
Kyle D. J. Netterfield
Nathaniel L. Taylor
Kristen K. Waggoner
A. Chad Allred

Reference: U.S. Bank of Washington, N.A.

For full biographical listings, see the Martindale-Hubbell Law Directory

SUMMIT LAW GROUP, PLLC (AV)

1505 Westlake Avenue North, Suite 300, 98109
Telephone: 206-281-9881
Fax: 206-281-9882
Email: info@summitlaw.com *URL:* http://www.summitlaw.com

Karen A. Andersen
Kristin D. Anger
Laura A. Bertin
Lynn M. Engel
Michael J. Erickson
Matthew R. Harris
David M. Heineck
Elizabeth Butler Kennar
Otto G. Klein, III
Lawrence C. Locker
Philip S. McCune
Polly L. McNeill
Ralph H. Palumbo
Bruce L. Schroeder
William R. Squires III
Monika Vasil
Mark F. Worthington
Rodney B. Younker

For full biographical listings, see the Martindale-Hubbell Law Directory

WEST VIRGINIA

*CHARLESTON,** Kanawha Co.

SALSBERY & DRUCKMAN (AV)

606 Virginia Street East, Suite 100, 25305
Telephone: 304-343-0075
Fax: 304-343-0099
Email: salsdruck@citynet.net

H. F. Salsbery
William S. Druckman
Madonna C. Estep

OF COUNSEL

Anne E. Shaffer

For full biographical listings, see the Martindale-Hubbell Law Directory

*CLARKSBURG,** Harrison Co.

MCNEER, HIGHLAND, MCMUNN AND VARNER, L.C. (AV)

One Valley Bank Building, P.O. Drawer 2040, 26302-2040
Telephone: 304-626-1100
Facsimile: 304-623-3035
Martinsburg Office: 2520 Aikens Center, P.O. Box 2509.
Telephone: 304-264-4621.
Fax: 304-264-8623.
Parkersburg Office: 404 Market Street, Suite 204, P.O. Box 1507.
Telephone: 304-422-7193.
Facsimile: 304-422-7196.

C. David McMunn
J. Cecil Jarvis
James A. Varner
Robert W. Trumble (Resident, Martinsburg Office)
Catherine D. Munster
James N. Riley
Steven R. Bratke (Resident, Parkersburg Office)
Michael J. Novotny (Resident, Martinsburg Office)
Dennis M. Shreve
Geraldine S. Roberts
William F. Rohrbaugh (Resident, Martinsburg Office)
Gregory H. Schillace
Judy L. Shanholtz
Tiffany R. Durst
Gene W. Bailey, II

OF COUNSEL

James E. McNeer
Cecil B. Highland, Jr.
William L. Fury

Representative Clients: One Valley Bank of Clarksburg, National Assn.; Bruceton Bank; Harrison County Bank; Nationwide Mutual Insurance Cos.; Clarksburg Publishing Co.; C.I.T. Financial Services; State Automobile Mutual Insurance Co.; United Hospital Center, Inc.; West Virginia Coals, Inc.; Swanson Plating Co.

For full biographical listings, see the Martindale-Hubbell Law Directory

WATERS, WARNER & HARRIS, PLLC (AV)

Formerly Stathers & Cantrall
701 Goff Building, P.O. Box 1716, 26301
Telephone: 304-624-5571
Fax: 304-624-7228
Email: wwh.atty@northnap.citynet.net

Birk S. Stathers (1884-1945)
W. G. Stathers (1889-1970)
Arch M. Cantrall (1896-1967)
Stuart R. Waters
Boyd L. Warner
James A. Harris
Scott E. Wilson
James C. Turner
G. Thomas Smith

ASSOCIATES

D. Andrew McMunn
David C. Glover

Representative Clients: Bethlehem Steel Corp.; Davis-Weaver Funeral Home, Inc.; Dowell Schlumberger, Inc.; Grafton Coal Co.; Harry Green Chevrolet, Inc.; Emax Oil Co.; Southern Steel Products Co.; Hartland Planing Mill Co.; Household Finance Corportion; Meadowbrook Mail Co.

For full biographical listings, see the Martindale-Hubbell Law Directory

*FAIRMONT,** Marion Co.

FURBEE, AMOS, WEBB & CRITCHFIELD (AV)

132 Adams Street, P.O. Box 1189, 26555
Telephone: 304-363-8800
Telecopier: 304-366-3783
Morgantown, West Virginia Office: 5000 Hampton Center, Suite 4.
Telephone: 304-598-0900.
Telecopier: 304-598-2712.

MEMBERS OF FIRM

Russell L. Furbee (1898-1978)
John D. Amos
Benjamin Hays Webb
Charles Vincent Critchfield
Alfred J. Lemley
Billy Atkins
Kenneth R. Miller
Stephen R. Brooks
William T. Holmes
Debra Hodges Scudiere (Resident at Morgantown Office)
Rebecca J. Zuleski
Tamara J. DeFazio

(See Next Column)

FURBEE, AMOS, WEBB & CRITCHFIELD—*Continued*

ASSOCIATE
Peter T. DeMasters

Attorneys for: Consolidation Coal Co.; Westinghouse Electric Co.; Monongahela Power Co.; Eastern Associated Coal Corp.; West Virginia Community Television Association; Continental Casualty Co.; State Farm Insurance Co.; Nationwide Insurance Co.

For full biographical listings, see the Martindale-Hubbell Law Directory

HUNTINGTON, Cabell & Wayne Cos.

FARRELL, FARRELL & FARRELL, L.C. (AV)

The Farrell Building, 914 Fifth Avenue, P.O. Box 6457, 25772-6457
Telephone: 304-522-9100
Facsimile: 304-522-9162
Email: lawyers@farrell3.com

Michael J. Farrell
Joseph M. Farrell, Jr.
Paul T. Farrell
Charlotte A. Hoffman
Tamela J. White

Robert L. Hogan
Paul T. Farrell, Jr.

OF COUNSEL
Lionel D. Egnor

For full biographical listings, see the Martindale-Hubbell Law Directory

OFFUTT, FISHER & NORD (AV)

949 Third Avenue, Suite 300, P.O. Box 2868, 25728-2868
Telephone: 304-529-2868; Toll Free: 1-800-529-2868
Fax: 304-529-2999
Charleston
Email: oefn@earthlink.net
Charleston, West Virginia Office: 208 Capitol Street, Suite 400, 25530.
Telephone: 304-343-2869.
Fax: 304-343-3053.

MEMBERS OF FIRM
D. C. Offutt, Jr.
Michael M. Fisher
Steven K. Nord

ASSOCIATES
Scott W. Andrews
Perry W. Oxley
Sonja L. Carpenter
Tammy R. Harvey
Monica L. Robinson

Representative Clients: St. Paul Insurance Co.; Home Insurance Co.; Federal Kemper Insurance Co.; Insurance Corporation of America; Erie Insurance Co.; Continental Insurance Co.; Liberty Mutual Insurance Co.; Colonial Insurance Company of California; CIGNA Insurance Cos.; Westfield Insurance Co.

For full biographical listings, see the Martindale-Hubbell Law Directory

*MORGANTOWN,** Monongalia Co.

THE FUSCO LEGAL GROUP, L.C. (AV)

2400 Cranberry Square, 26505-9209
Telephone: 304-594-1000
Telecopier: 304-594-1181
URL: http://www.fuscolegalgroup.com
Email: fnlaw@wvlaw.com *URL:* http://www.wvlaw.com

Andrew G. Fusco

William J. Leon, Jr.
Steven M. Prunty
Jeffrey A. Ray

For full biographical listings, see the Martindale-Hubbell Law Directory

*WHEELING,** Ohio Co.

SCHRADER BYRD & COMPANION, PLLC (AV)

(A Professional Limited Liability Company)
The Maxwell Centre, 32-20th Street, Suite 500, P.O. Box 6336, 26003
Telephone: 304-233-3390
Fax: 304-233-2769
URL: http://www.schraderlaw.com
Martins Ferry, Ohio Office: 205 North Fifth Street, P.O. Box 309, 43935.
Telephone: 740-633-9976.
Fax: 740-633-0400.
Weirton, West Virginia Office: 3205 Pennsylvania Avenue, Suite 103, Penn Place, P.O. Box 2785, 26062.
Telephone: 304-723-2674.
Fax: 304-723-2876.

MEMBERS
Ray A. Byrd
Daniel P. Fry (Resident Partner, Martins Ferry, Ohio Office)
James F. Companion
Frank X. Duff
James P. Mazzone (Resident Member, Weirton, West Virginia Office)
Teresa Rieman-Camilletti
Yolonda G. Lambert
Sandra K. Law
D. Kevin Coleman

(See Next Column)

SPECIAL COUNSEL
Thomas B. Miller

ASSOCIATES
Denise D. Klug
Aimee Morgan Stern
Michael A. Adams
Kimberly R. Wilson
John Porco
Christopher J. Adams

OF COUNSEL
James A. Byrum, Jr.

General Counsel: Reynolds Memorial Hospital; WesBanco Bank-Elm Grove.
Representative Clients: American Cyanamid Company; Bank One; Matlack Systems, Inc.; Moutaineer Gas Co.; Ohio County Board of Education; PHICO Insurance Co.; Wheeling Hospital; Wheeling-Pittsburg Steel Corp.

For full biographical listings, see the Martindale-Hubbell Law Directory

WISCONSIN

*MILWAUKEE,** Milwaukee Co.

CHERNOV, STERN & KRINGS, S.C. (AV)

Suite 1275, Two Plaza East, 330 East Kilbourn Avenue, 53202
Telephone: 414-276-4080
Fax: 414-276-4152
Email: mail@chernovlaw.com *URL:* http://www.lawyers.com/chernovlaw

Benjamin S. Stern

OF COUNSEL
Ben L. Chernov

For full biographical listings, see the Martindale-Hubbell Law Directory

HALE & WAGNER, S.C. (AV)

(formerly known as Hale & Lein, S.C.)
205 East Wisconsin Avenue Suite 300, 53202
Telephone: 414-278-7000
Fax: 414-278-7590
URL: http://www.lawyers.com/halewagner

Christopher T. Hale
Amy V. Kossoris
K. Scott Wagner
John J. Slein

OF COUNSEL
Russell M. Lein

For full biographical listings, see the Martindale-Hubbell Law Directory

KOHNER, MANN & KAILAS, S.C. (AV)

1572 East Capitol Drive, P.O. Box 11982, 53211-0982
Telephone: 414-962-5110
Fax: 414-962-8725
Email: kmksc@execpc.com

Marvin L. Kohner (1908-1975)

OF COUNSEL
Robert L. Mann

MEMBERS OF FIRM
Steve Kailas
Roy Paul Roth
Mark R. Wolters
Gary P. Lantzy
Jordan B. Reich
Christopher C. Kailas
David S. Chartier
Matthew P. Gerdisch

Robert E. Nailen
David M. Henry
Darrell R. Zall
Lorinne J Cunningham
Daniel J. Flynn
Palma M. Forte
Timothy L. Zuberbier
Daniel J. Emma

Representative Clients: Ecolab, Inc.; Manpower, Inc.; Abbott Laboratories; Norwest Bank Wisconsin, N.A.; Firstar Bank Corporation; Sysco Food Services; Johnson Controls, Inc.; Worth Inc.; Rayovac, Inc.; York International Corporation.

For full biographical listings, see the Martindale-Hubbell Law Directory

MEISSNER TIERNEY FISHER & NICHOLS S.C. (AV)

The Milwaukee Center, 111 East Kilbourn Avenue, 19th Floor, 53202-6622
Telephone: 414-273-1300
Facsimile: 414-273-5840
URL: http://www.mtfn.com

Dennis L. Fisher
Michael J. Cohen

(See Next Column)

MEISSNER TIERNEY FISHER & NICHOLS S.C., *Milwaukee—Continued*

Christopher L. Rexroat
Justin B. Nelsen
William T. Stuart

For full biographical listings, see the Martindale-Hubbell Law Directory

PETRIE & STOCKING S.C. (AV)

111 East Wisconsin Avenue, Suite 1500, 53202
Telephone: 414-276-2850
Facsimile: 414-276-0731
Email: info@petriestocking.com *URL:* http://www.petriestocking.com

James R. Petrie
John A. Stocking
Roger L. Pettit
John R. Nelson
Gregg E. Bridge
Roy H. Nelson
Thomas L. Frenn
Mark E. Sostarich
Daniel J. Miske
Laura J. Petrie
Shawn M. Govern
Tristan R. Pettit

For full biographical listings, see the Martindale-Hubbell Law Directory

WYOMING

*CASPER,** Natrona Co.

SCHWARTZ, BON, WALKER & STUDER, LLC (AV)

141 South Center, Suite 505, 82601
Telephone: 307-235-6681
Fax: 307-234-5099
Email: SBWS@trib.com

William T. Schwartz
William S. Bon
Cameron S. Walker
Judith A. W. Studer
Peter J. Young

Patrick T. Holscher
Rick L. Koehmstedt

For full biographical listings, see the Martindale-Hubbell Law Directory

VIRGIN ISLANDS

*CHARLOTTE AMALIE, ST. THOMAS,** St. Thomas

CAMPBELL, ARELLANO & RICH

No. 4 A & B Kongens Gade, P.O. Box 11899, 00801
Telephone: 340-774-4858
Telecopier: 340-776-8442
Email: carvilaw@viaccess.net *URL:* http://www.lawyers.com/lisvilaw
Cruz Bay, St. John, Virgin Islands Office: Scandic Executive Offices, Mongoose Junction, 00831.
Telephone: 304-693-8655.
Telecopier: 304-776-8442.

MEMBERS OF FIRM

Joseph Bruce Wm. Arellano
Carol Ann Rich

ASSOCIATE

W. Mark Hillsman

OF COUNSEL

Roger L. Campbell

Representative Clients: Citibank, N.A.; Cigna Property and Casualty Companies; Royal Insurance.

For full biographical listings, see the Martindale-Hubbell Law Directory

CANADA
BRITISH COLUMBIA

*VANCOUVER,** Vancouver Co.

CAMP CHURCH & ASSOCIATES (AV)

4th Floor, The Randall Building, 555 West Georgia Street, V6B 1Z5
Telephone: 604-689-7555
Fax: 604-689-7554
URL: http://www.campchurch.com

MEMBERS OF FIRM

J.J. Camp, Q.C.
David P. Church

(See Next Column)

Giuseppe (Joe) Fiorante
Andrew J. Pearson
Sharon D. Matthews
Ian G. Schildt

For full biographical listings, see the Martindale-Hubbell Law Directory

JENKINS MARZBAN LOGAN (AV)

A Partnership of Law Corporations
Suite 1414, Nelson Square, 808 Nelson Street, P.O. Box 12144, V6Z 2H2
Telephone: 604-681-6564
Facsimile: 604-681-0766
URL: http://www.JML.CA

Dinyar Marzban
John S. Logan

Scott Booth

For full biographical listings, see the Martindale-Hubbell Law Directory

CANADA
NEW BRUNSWICK

*FREDERICTON,** York Co.

MCINNES COOPER (AV)

Suite 600, 570 Queen Street, P.O. Box 610, E3B 5A6
Telephone: 506-458-8572
Fax: 506-458-9903
Email: mcrfton@mcrlaw.com *URL:* http://www.mcrlaw.com
Halifax, Nova Scotia Office: Summit Place, 1601 Lower Water Street, P.O. Box 730, B3J 2V1.
Telephone: 902-425-6500.
Fax: 902-425-6350. Email: mcrhfx@mcrlaw.com.
St. John's, Newfoundland Office: Baine Johnston Centre, 5th Floor, 10 Fort William Place, P.O. Box 5939, A1C 5X4.
Telephone: 709-722-8735.
Telecopier: 709-722-1763. Email: mcrsj@mcrlaw.com.
Moncton, New Brunswick Office: Place Moncton Place, 655 Main Street, P.O. Box 1368, E1C 8T6.
Telephone: 506-857-8970.
Fax: 506-857-4095. Email: mcrmctn@mcrlaw.com.
Charlottetown, Prince Edward Island Office: BDC Place, Suite 620, 119 Kent Street, C1A 1N3.
Telephone: 902-368-8473.
Fax: 902-368-8346. Email: mcrpei@mcrlaw.com.

PARTNER

David Duncan Young

ASSOCIATES

David D. Eidt
Patrick V. Windle

For Complete List of Firm Personnel, See General Section

For full biographical listings, see the Martindale-Hubbell Law Directory

*MONCTON,** Westmorland Co.

MCINNES COOPER (AV)

Barristers, Solicitors & Trade Mark Agents
Place Moncton Place, 655 Main Street, P.O. Box 1368, E1C 8T6
Telephone: 506-857-8970
Fax: 506-857-4095
Email: mcrmctn@mcrlaw.com *URL:* http://www.mcrlaw.com
Halifax, Nova Scotia Office: Summit Place, 1601 Lower Water Street, P.O. Box 730, B3J 2V1.
Telephone: 902-425-6500.
Fax: 902-425-6350. Email: mcrhfx@mcrlaw.com.
St. John's, Newfoundland Office: Baine Johnston Centre, 5th Floor, 10 Fort William Place, P.O. Box 5939, A1C 5X4.
Telephone: 709-722-8735.
Telecopier: 709-722-1763. Email: mcrsj@mcrlaw.com.
Charlottetown, Prince Edward Island Office: BDC Place, Suite 620, 119 Kent Street, C1A 1N3.
Telephone: 902-368-8473.
Fax: 902-368-8346. Email: mcrpei@mcrlaw.com.
Fredericton, New Brunswick Office: Suite 600, 570 Queen Street, P.O. Box 610.
Telephone: 506-458-8572.
Fax: 506-458-9903. Email: mcrfton@mcrlaw.com.

PARTNER

Eric LeDrew

ASSOCIATES

John C. Friel, Q.C.
Christa A. Bourque

For Complete List of Firm Personnel, See General Section

For full biographical listings, see the Martindale-Hubbell Law Directory

CANADA NEWFOUNDLAND

*ST. JOHN'S,**

McInnes Cooper (AV)

Barristers, Solicitors & Trade Mark Agents
Baine Johnston Centre, 5th Floor, 10 Fort William Place, P.O. Box 5939, A1C 5X4
Telephone: 709-722-8735
Telecopier: 709-722-1763
Email: mcrsj@mcrlaw.com *URL:* http://www.mcrlaw.com
Halifax, Nova Scotia Office: Summit Place, 1601 Lower Water Street, P.O. Box 730, B3J 2V1.
Telephone: 902-425-6500.
Fax: 902-425-6350. Email: mcrhfx@mcrlaw.com.
Moncton, New Brunswick Office: Place Moncton Place, 655 Main Street, P.O. Box 1368, E1C 8T6.
Telephone: 506-857-8970.
Fax: 506-857-4095. Email: mcrmctn@mcrlaw.com.
Charlottetown, Prince Edward Island Office: BDC Place, Suite 620, 119 Kent Street, C1A 1N3.
Telephone: 902-368-8473.
Fax: 902-368-8346. Email: mcrpei@mcrlaw.com.
Fredericton, New Brunswick Office: Suite 600, 570 Queen Street, P.O. Box 610.
Telephone: 506-458-8572.
Fax: 506-458-9903. Email: mcrfton@mcrlaw.com.

PARTNERS

James R. Chalker, Q.C.
Thomas R. Kendell
Deborah L. J. Hutchings
W. Gary Rowe, Q.C.
Michael J. Crosbie
Philip J. Buckingham

For Complete List of Firm Personnel, See General Section

For full biographical listings, see the Martindale-Hubbell Law Directory

CANADA NOVA SCOTIA

*HALIFAX,** Regional Munic. of Halifax

McInnes Cooper (AV)

Barristers, Solicitors & Trade Mark Agents
Summit Place, 1601 Lower Water Street, P.O. Box 730, B3J 2V1
Telephone: 902-425-6500
Fax: 902-425-6350
Email: mcrhfx@mcrlaw.com *URL:* http://www.mcrlaw.com
St. John's, Newfoundland Office: Baine Johnston Centre, 5th Floor, 10 Fort William Place, P.O. Box 5939, A1C 5X4.
Telephone: 709-722-8735.
Telecopier: 709-722-1763. Email: mcrsj@mcrlaw.com.
Moncton, New Brunswick Office: Place Moncton Place, 655 Main Street, P.O. Box 1368, E1C 8T6.
Telephone: 506-857-8970.
Fax: 506-857-4095. Email: mcrmctn@mcrlaw.com.
Charlottetown, Prince Edward Island Office: BDC Place, Suite 620, 119 Kent Street, C1A 1N3.
Telephone: 902-368-8473.
Fax: 902-368-8346. Email: mcrpei@mcrlaw.com.
Fredericton, New Brunswick Office: Suite 600, 570 Queen Street, P.O. Box 610.
Telephone: 506-458-8572.
Fax: 506-458-9903. Email: mcrfton@mcrlaw.com.

PARTNERS

Reginald A. Cluney, Q.C.
Stewart McInnes, P.C., Q.C.
George W. MacDonald, Q.C.
Wylie Spicer, Q.C.
David A. Graves
Scott C. Norton
G. Grant Machum
Harry E. Wrathall, Q.C.
David H. Reardon, Q.C.
Robert G. Belliveau, Q.C.
Christopher C. Robinson, Q.C.
Peter M. S. Bryson
Stephen Kingston
Michelle C. Awad

ASSOCIATE

Hugh Wright

For Complete List of Firm Personnel, See General Section

For full biographical listings, see the Martindale-Hubbell Law Directory

CANADA ONTARIO

*OTTAWA,** Regional Munic. of Ottawa-Carleton

Borden Elliot Scott & Aylen (AV)

1000-60 Rue Queen Street, K1P 5Y7
Telephone: 613-237-5160; 800-661-4237
General Facsimile: 613-230-8842
IP Dept. Facsimile: 613-787-3558
Email: ottinfo@scottaylen.com *URL:* http://www.borden.com
Toronto, Ontario Office: Borden & Elliot: Scotia Plaza, 40 King Street West.
Telephone: 416-367-6000.
Telecopier: 416-367-6749. Email: info @borden.com. URL: http://www.borden.com.

Laird J. Rasmussen
Bryan A. Carroll
J. Bruce Carr-Harris
Kevin LaRoche
Jane M. Bachynski
Lawrence A. Elliot
Peter C. P. Thompson, Q.C.
George D. Hunter
Guy J. Pratte
Pierre E. Roger
Noëlle Caloren
Matthew H. Williams
Johanne M. Asselin

For full biographical listings, see the Martindale-Hubbell Law Directory

*TORONTO,** Regional Munic. of Toronto

Kelly Affleck Greene (AV)

One First Canadian Place, Suite 840, P.O. Box 489, M5X 1E5
Telephone: 416-360-2800
Fax: 416-360-5960
Email: info@kag.net *URL:* http://www.kag.net

MEMBERS OF FIRM

W. Anthony Kelly, Q.C.
Donald S. Affleck, Q.C.
Peter R. Greene
Donald B. Houston
James C. Orr
Peter C. Wardle
Helen A. Daley
Melissa J. Kennedy

ASSOCIATES

Kenneth A. Dekker
W. Michael G. Osborne
Jason C. Markwell
Patrice F. Band

For full biographical listings, see the Martindale-Hubbell Law Directory

CANADA PRINCE EDWARD ISLAND

*CHARLOTTETOWN,** Queen's Co.

McInnes Cooper (AV Ⓣ)

Barristers, Solicitors & Trade Mark Agents
BDC Place, Suite 620, 119 Kent Street, C1A 1N3
Telephone: 902-368-8473
Fax: 902-368-8346
Email: mcrpei@mcrlaw.com *URL:* http://www.mcrlaw.com
Halifax, Nova Scotia Office: Summit Place, 1601 Lower Water Street, P.O. Box 730, B3J 2V1.
Telephone: 902-425-6500.
Fax: 902-425-6350. Email: mcrhfx@mcrlaw.com.
St. John's, Newfoundland Office: Baine Johnston Centre, 5th Floor, 10 Fort William Place, P.O. Box 5939, A1C 5X4.
Telephone: 709-722-8735.
Telecopier: 709-722-1763. Email: mcrsj@mcrlaw.com.
Moncton, New Brunswick Office: Place Moncton Place, 655 Main Street, P.O. Box 1368, E1C 8T6.
Telephone: 506-857-8970.
Fax: 506-857-4095. Email: mcrmctn@mcrlaw.com.
Fredericton, New Brunswick Office: Suite 600, 570 Queen Street, P.O. Box 610.
Telephone: 506-458-8572.
Fax: 506-458-9903. Email: mcrfton@mcrlaw.com.

PARTNER

Mark Ledwell

ASSOCIATES

Kevin J. Kiley
Murray L. Murphy
Paul Kiley

For Complete List of Firm Personnel, See General Section

For full biographical listings, see the Martindale-Hubbell Law Directory

CANADA QUEBEC

*MONTREAL,** Montreal Dist.

McMaster Gervais (AV)

A General Partnership
1000 de La Gauchetière Street West, Suite 900, H3B 5H4
Telephone: 514-879-1212
Fax: 514-954-1905
Email: info@mcmastergervais.com *URL:* http://www.mcmastergervais.com

MEMBERS OF FIRM

Alex K. Paterson, O.C., O.Q., Q.C.
Georges R. Thibaudeau
Robert E. Charbonneau
Roger P. Simard
Jacques Gauthier
Yvan Houle
Christine Duchaine
Marie Audren
Caroline Matte
Patrice Morin
Antoine Leduc
Alexis P. Bergeron
Daniel Ayotte
Peter Richardson
Virgile A. Buffoni
François Rioux
Bruno Duguay
John G. Murphy
Jacques S. Darche
Julie Normand
Stéphanie Moffatt
Manon Gauthier
Stéphane Pitre

COUNSEL

Hon. Lawrence A. Poitras, Q.C.
Jacques Brien

For Complete List of Firm Personnel, See General Section

For full biographical listings, see the Martindale-Hubbell Law Directory

Mendelsohn Rosentzveig Shacter (AV)

1000 Sherbrooke Street West, 27th Floor, H3A 3G4
Telephone: 514-987-5000
Telex: 05-27284 Colorlaw
Telecopier: 514-987-1213
Email: mrs@mrslaw.com *URL:* http://www.mrslaw.com

PARTNERS

S. Leon Mendelsohn, Q.C. (1902-1996)
Leo Rosentzveig, Q.C.
Manuel Shacter, Q.C.
Jack C. Shayne
William Levitt
Arthur A. Garvis
Edward E. Aronoff
L. Michael Blumenstein
Max Mendelsohn
Earl S. Cohen
Michael Garonce
Donald M. Devine
Richard S. Uditsky
Joel Weitzman
Ian R. Rudnikoff
Marc I. Leiter
L. B. Erdle
Fredric L. Carsley
Frank Zylberberg
Jules Brossard
David L. Rosentzveig
Judie K. Jokinen
Gilles Seguin
Martin Desrosiers
Andrew Etcovitch
Alain Breault
Jean Carrière
Henri M. Bybelezer
Louis Frédérick Côté
Sandra Abitan

ASSOCIATES

Carl M. Ravinsky
Catherine Muraz
Francine Wiseman
Joelle Sebag
Maria R. Battaglia
Keyvan Nassiry
Linda Schachter
Emmanuelle Saucier
Arnold Cohen
Aaron Makovka
Michel Rochefort
Céline Tessier
Sophie Crevier
Annick Joyal
Francis Desmarais
Nicolas J. Beugnot
Jean-François Brière
Marc-Antoine Deschamps
Philipp F. Duffy
Fred Purkey
Martin Sills
David Tardif-Latourelle

For full biographical listings, see the Martindale-Hubbell Law Directory

Pouliot, Mercure (AV)

CIBC Tower, 31st Floor, 1155 René-Lévesque Boulevard, West, H3B 3S6
Telephone: 514-875-5210
Telecopier: 514-875-4308
Email: POUMER@CEDEP.COM
Genève, Suisse Office: 8, Rue de la Rôtisserie, 1204 Geneva, Switzerland.
Telephone: +41 22-28 79 40.
Telecopier: +41 22-21 23 67.

MEMBERS OF FIRM

Georges A. Pouliot, Q.C.
Gilles Brunelle
Luc Gratton
Brian Riordan
Pierre Paquet
Anne-Marie Gauthier
Yvon Brizard
Robert Tessier
Daniel Gagné
Gilles Bertrand
Jean Larivière
Louis-Michel Tremblay
David I. Johnston
Stéphane Hébert
Jacques LeBel, Q.C.
Joel A. Silcoff
Ronald M. Auclair
Philippe Roy

MEMBERS OF FIRM (Continued)

Lilia Pouliot
Marco Veilleux
Alain Nadon
Jean H. Gagnon
Richard Fontaine
Normand Royal
Maxime B. Rhéaume
Serge Desrochers
C. Keenan LaPierre
Alain Bond
Louis Coallier
Nicole Chouinard
Stéphane Teasdale

ASSOCIATES

Micheline Perrault
Caroline Lemoine
Béatrice Arronis
Yvan Nantel
Sylvie Boulanger
Vincent Frenette
Robert Cardin
Alexandre Henri
Brent J. Muir
Louise Tremblay
Chantal Joubert
Normand D'Amour
Pascale Cloutier
Eric Couture
Frédéric Chatel
Mary-Lynn Breton
Alexandre Ajami

For full biographical listings, see the Martindale-Hubbell Law Directory

Woods & Partners (AV)

2000 McGill College Avenue, Suite 1100, H3A 3H3
Telephone: 514-982-4545
Telecopier: 514-284-2046
Email: general@woods.qc.ca

MEMBERS OF FIRM

James A. Woods
Christian Immer
Julien Cools-Lartigue
Nathalie Chalifour
Christopher Lund Richter
Annie Galarneau
Sébastien Richemont
Kathleen Beaugé
Marjorie Delagrave

For full biographical listings, see the Martindale-Hubbell Law Directory

CANADA SASKATCHEWAN

*REGINA,** Regina Jud. Centre

MacPherson Leslie & Tyerman (AV)

1500-1874 Scarth Street, S4P 4E9
Telephone: 306-347-8000
Telecopier: 306-352-5250
Email: mltreg@mlt.com
Saskatoon, Saskatchewan Office: 1500-410 22nd Street East, S7K 5T6.
Telephone: 306-975-7100.
Telecopier: 306-975-7145.

MEMBERS OF FIRM

Maurice O. Laprairie, Q.C.
Bruce W. Wirth (Resident, Saskatoon Office)
Robert W. Leurer
Leonard D. Andrychuk
Douglas C. Hodson (Resident, Saskatoon Office)
Jeffrey M. Lee (Resident, Saskatoon Office)

ASSOCIATES

Wendy Y. Martin White (Resident, Saskatoon Office)
Kurt G. Wintermute (Resident, Saskatoon Office)
Heather D. Heavin

COUNSEL

William M. Elliott, Q.C.

For Complete List of Firm Personnel, See General Section

For full biographical listings, see the Martindale-Hubbell Law Directory

COMMUNICATIONS LAW

MISSISSIPPI

*JACKSON,** Hinds Co.

ALSTON & JONES (AV)

A Professional Limited Liability Company
121 North State Street, P.O. Drawer 1532, 39215-1532
Telephone: 601-948-6882
Fax: 601-948-6902
Email: ARVS@Teclink.net

MEMBER OF FIRM
Alex A. Alston, Jr.

Counsel for: Gannett Co., Inc. (Jackson Clarion-Ledger); TV-3, Inc. (WLBT); North Star Television of Jackson, Inc. (WAPT); Newsweek; Motion Picture Association of America, Inc.; Paramount Pictures Corp.; Memphis Publishing Co. (Commercial-Appeal); Society of Professional Journalists.

For Complete List of Firm Personnel, See General Section

For full biographical listings, see the Martindale-Hubbell Law Directory

NEW JERSEY

*NEWARK,** Essex Co.

McCARTER & ENGLISH, LLP (AV)

Four Gateway Center, 100 Mulberry Street, P.O. Box 652, 07101-0652
Telephone: 973-622-4444
Telecopier: 973-624-7070
URL: http://www.mccarter.com
Cherry Hill, New Jersey Office: 1820 Chapel Avenue West, Suite 380.
Telephone: 609-662-8444.
Telecopier: 609-662-6203.
New York, New York Office: Suite 2247, One World Trade Center.
Telephone: 212-466-9018.
Telecopier: 212-432-6568.
Boca Raton, Florida Office: 2255 Glades Road, Suite 319-A.
Telephone: 561-994-6262.
Telecopier: 561-241-0798.
Wilmington, Delaware Office: Mellon Bank Center, 919 Market Street.
Telephone: 302-654-8010.
Telecopier: 302-654-0795.
Philadelphia, Pennsylvania Office: One Commerce Square, 2005 Market Street, Suite 3600.
Telephone: 215-557-7700.
Telecopier: 215-557-6544.

MEMBER OF FIRM
Richard M. Eittreim
OF COUNSEL
Thomas F. Daly

For Complete List of Firm Personnel, See General Section

For full biographical listings, see the Martindale-Hubbell Law Directory

MEYNER AND LANDIS (AV)

One Gateway Center, Suite 2500, 07102-5311
Telephone: 973-624-2800
Fax: 973-624-0356
Email: attys@meyner.com *URL:* http://www.meyner.com

Robert B. Meyner (1908-1990)
Edwin C. Landis, Jr.
John N. Malyska
William J. Fiore
Anthony F. Siliato
Francis R. Perkins
Howard O. Thompson
Scott T. McCleary
Linda Townley Snyder
William H. Schmidt, Jr.
David B. Grantz

For full biographical listings, see the Martindale-Hubbell Law Directory

SILLS CUMMIS RADIN TISCHMAN EPSTEIN & GROSS, A PROFESSIONAL CORPORATION (AV)

One Riverfront Plaza, 07102-5400
Telephone: 973-643-7000
Fax: 973-643-6500
Telex: 820630 Sillsbeck Nwk
Email: sillsmail@sillscummis.com *URL:* http://www.sillscummis.com
Atlantic City, New Jersey Office: 17 Gordon's Alley.
Telephone: 609-344-2800.
New York, N.Y. Office: 712 Fifth Avenue.
Telephone: 212-643-7000.

(See Next Column)

Washington, D.C. Office: 1800 K Street, N.W.
Telephone: 202-296-4750.

MEMBERS OF FIRM

Steven S. Radin
Ira A. Rosenberg
Philip R. Sellinger
Thomas S. Novak
James M. Hirschhorn

OF COUNSEL
Mitchel E. Ostrer

Noel D. Humphreys

Representative Clients: GTE Sprint Communications; MCI Communications Corp.; Corporate Satellite Communications; Gannett Outdoor Company of New Jersey; Bellcore, Inc.; WWOR-TV.

For Complete List of Firm Personnel, See General Section

For full biographical listings, see the Martindale-Hubbell Law Directory

SOMERSET, Somerset Co.

McGIMPSEY & CAFFERTY (AV)

285 Davidson Avenue, Suite 404, 08873
Telephone: 732-560-1900
Fax: 732-560-1904
Email: mcgcaff@earthlink.net

Alexander F. McGimpsey, Jr.
Thomas J. Cafferty

Arlene M. Turinchak

LEGAL SUPPORT PERSONNEL
Susan Rusnock (Office Manager)

Representative Clients: New Jersey Press Assn.; Home News Tribune; North Jersey Herald & News; NJN Publishing Co.; Hunterdon County Democrat, Inc.; McGraw-Hill; Morristown Daily Record; Suburban News; Shopper News; The Bergen Record Corp.

For full biographical listings, see the Martindale-Hubbell Law Directory

WESTFIELD, Union Co.

THE ROTHFELDER LAW OFFICES (AV)

625 Central Avenue, 07090
Telephone: 908-301-1211
Fax: 908-301-1212
URL: http://www.lawyers.com/rothfelder,law
Email: mail@rlo-law.com *URL:* http://www.rlo-law.com

Martin C. Rothfelder
Maureen Rothfelder
Nathan T. Foose (Not admitted in NJ)

For full biographical listings, see the Martindale-Hubbell Law Directory

WEST ORANGE, Essex Co.

ALPERT, BUTLER & SANDERS, P.C. (AV)

The Alpert Professional Building, 449 Mount Pleasant Avenue, 07052
Telephone: 973-325-1188
Fax: 973-325-3399
Email: mailbox@abslaw.com *URL:* http://www.abslaw.com
New York, New York Office: 509 Madison Avenue.
Telephone: 212-758-6958.
Fax: 212-758-2817.

Clark E. Alpert
David N. Butler
William D. Sanders

OF COUNSEL

Martin L. Bearg
Ted M. Rosen (Not admitted in NJ)

Elliot L. Lewis
Matthew J. Rice

LEGAL SUPPORT PERSONNEL
PARALEGAL
Robin S. Karpel

For full biographical listings, see the Martindale-Hubbell Law Directory

NEW MEXICO

*ALBUQUERQUE,** Bernalillo Co.

DINES, GROSS & ESQUIVEL, P.C. (AV)

6301 Indian School Road, N.E., Suite 900, 87110
Telephone: 505-889-4050
Fax: 505-889-4049
Email: law@dge.psemail.com *URL:* http://www.lawyers.com/dgelaw

(See Next Column)

DINES, GROSS & ESQUIVEL P.C., *Albuquerque—Continued*

James M. Dines | Michael A. Gross
Martin R. Esquivel

For full biographical listings, see the Martindale-Hubbell Law Directory

NEW YORK

*BUFFALO,** Erie Co.

ROLLS KOHN & ASSOCIATES, LLP (AV)

Twenty Court Street, 14202-3201
Telephone: 716-856-2700
Fax: 716-856-2777

MEMBERS OF FIRM

James E. Rolls | Gerald L. Kohn
Robert M. Goldstein

For full biographical listings, see the Martindale-Hubbell Law Directory

*NEW YORK,** New York Co.

RIDLEY M. WHITAKER (AV)

One Rockefeller Plaza, 10020
Telephone: 212-218-5656
Telecopier: 212-218-5665
Email: 74051.3574@compuserve.com

For full biographical listings, see the Martindale-Hubbell Law Directory

*POUGHKEEPSIE,** Dutchess Co.

VAN DEWATER & VAN DEWATER (AV)

40 Garden Street, P.O. Box 112, 12602
Telephone: 914-452-5900
Fax: 914-452-5848
Pawling, New York Office: 243 Route 22, P.O. Box 668.
Telephone: 914-855-5900.
Fax: 914-855-5945.

MEMBERS OF FIRM

John B. Van DeWater (1892-1968)
Robert B. Van DeWater (1920-1990)
David D. Hagstrom
John K. Gifford
James E. Nelson
Craig T. Digilio
Gerard J. Comatos
Ronald C. Blass, Jr.

OF COUNSEL

Noel deCordova, Jr. | James D. Benson
Edward VK. Cunningham, Jr. | Susanna E. Bedell

ASSOCIATES

Rebecca Supple Mensch | Michael G. Hayes

Counsel for: J. D. Johnson Co., Inc.; The Fishkill National Bank; The Bank of the Hudson; Vassar Brothers Hospital.
Local Counsel for: Vassar College; Chemprene Div. of Witco Chemical Corp.; Gannett Satellite Information Network, Inc.

For full biographical listings, see the Martindale-Hubbell Law Directory

NORTH CAROLINA

*RALEIGH,** Wake Co.

CRISP PAGE & CURRIN, L.L.P. (AV)

1305 Navaho Drive, Suite 302, 27609-7444
Telephone: 919-876-8282
Fax: 919-876-8285

MEMBERS OF FIRM

William T. Crisp (1924-1992) | Robert F. Page
Cynthia M. Currin

For full biographical listings, see the Martindale-Hubbell Law Directory

TWIGGS, ABRAMS, STRICKLAND & TREHY, P.A. (AV)

First Union Capitol Center, 150 Fayetteville Street Mall, Suite 1100, P.O. Drawer 30, 27602
Telephone: 919-828-4357
Fax: 919-833-7924
Email: tastlaw@tast.com

(See Next Column)

Howard F. Twiggs | Donald R. Strickland
Douglas B. Abrams | Jerome P. Trehy, Jr.
Karen M. Rabenau

OF COUNSEL

Donald H. Beskind | Margaret Smith Abrams
Jeff Erick Essen

For full biographical listings, see the Martindale-Hubbell Law Directory

*WINSTON-SALEM,** Forsyth Co.

WOMBLE CARLYLE SANDRIDGE & RICE (AV)

A Professional Limited Liability Company
200 West Second Street, P.O. Drawer 84, 27102
Telephone: 336-721-3600
Fax: 336-721-3660
Email: lawyers@wcsr.com *URL:* http://www.wcsr.com
Charlotte, North Carolina Office: 3300 One First Union Center, 301 South College Street.
Telephone: 704-331-4900.
Fax: 704-331-4955.
Raleigh, North Carolina Office: 2100 First Union Capitol Center, 150 Fayetteville Street Mall, P.O. Box 831.
Telephone: 919-755-2100.
Fax: 919-755-2150.
Research Triangle Park, North Carolina Office: 2505 Meridian Parkway, Suite 300 (Durham), 27713.
Telephone: 919-484-2300.
Fax: 919-484-2340.
Atlanta, Georgia Office: One Atlantic Center, 1201 West Peachtree Street, Suite 3500.
Telephone: 404-872-7000.
Fax: 404-888-7490.
Other Atlanta, Georgia Office: Suite 404, 2296 Henderson Mill Road, N.E.
Telephone: 770-492-9030.
Fax: 770-492-9609.
Washington, D.C. Office: 1120 Nineteenth Street, N.W., Eighth Floor.
Telephone: 202-857-4400.
Fax: 202-467-6910.
Greenville, South Carolina Office: 15 South Main Street, Suite 601, P.O. Box 10208.
Telephone: 864-255-5400.
Fax: 864-255-5440.

RESIDENT MEMBER

John L. W. Garrou

Representative Clients: Brad Ragan, Inc.; Brenner Companies; Food Lion, Inc.; Hanes Companies, Inc.; North Carolina Baptist Hospitals, Inc.; R.J. Reynolds Tobacco Co.; Thomasville Furniture Industries, Inc.; Wachovia Corp.; Wake Forest University.

For Complete List of Firm Personnel, See General Section

For full biographical listings, see the Martindale-Hubbell Law Directory

NORTH DAKOTA

*BISMARCK,** Burleigh Co.

PEARCE AND DURICK, PLLP (AV)

314 East Thayer Avenue, P.O. Box 400, 58502
Telephone: 701-223-2890
Fax: 701-223-7865
Email: law.office@pearce-durick.com *URL:* http://www.pearce-durick.com

MEMBERS OF FIRM

Patrick W. Durick | Jerome C. Kettleson
Gary R. Thune | Larry L. Boschee

ASSOCIATE

Jonathan P. Sanstead

Representative Clients: Meyer Broadcasting Co.; Telecommunications, Inc.

For Complete List of Firm Personnel, See General Section

For full biographical listings, see the Martindale-Hubbell Law Directory

OHIO

*CINCINNATI,** Hamilton Co.

FROST & JACOBS LLP (AV)

2500 PNC Center, 201 East Fifth Street, 45202
Telephone: 513-651-6800
Telecopier: 513-651-6981
URL: http://www.frojac.com
Columbus, Ohio Office: One Columbus, 10 West Broad Street, 43215.
Telephone: 614-464-1211.
Telecopier: 614-464-1737.
Lexington, Kentucky Office: 1100 Vine Center Tower, 333 West Vine Street, 40507.
Telephone: 606-254-1100.
Telecopier: 606-253-2990.
Middletown, Ohio Office: 400 First National Bank Building, 2 North Main Street, 45042.
Telephone: 513-422-2001.
Telecopier: 513-422-3010.
Frankfort, Kentucky Office: 201 W. Main Street, 40601.
Telephone: 502-223-1400.
Telecopier: 502-223-1410.

MEMBERS OF FIRM

Susan Grogan Faller
Richard M. Goehler
Scott D. Phillips

ASSOCIATES

Jill Meyer Vollman
Jeffrey S. Rosenstiel

Representative Clients: Hearst/Argyle Communications; Gannett Co.; Raycom Media, Inc.; Brown Publishing Company; National Underwriter Company; Thomson Newspapers; Sinclair Communications; Media-Professional Insurance Company; Employers Reinsurance Co.; The McGraw-Hill Companies; Cincinnati Business Courier.

For Complete List of Firm Personnel, See General Section

For full biographical listings, see the Martindale-Hubbell Law Directory

*CLEVELAND,** Cuyahoga Co.

BAKER & HOSTETLER LLP (AV)

3200 National City Center, 1900 East Ninth Street, 44114-3485
Telephone: 216-621-0200
Telecopier: 216-696-0740
TWX: 810 421 8375
RCA Telex: 215032
To contact an attorney on the Internet use first initial and surname followed by @baker-hostetler.com
URL: http://www.bakerlaw.com
In Cincinnati, Ohio: 312 Walnut Street, Suite 2650.
Telephone: 513-929-3400.
In Columbus, Ohio: Capitol Square, Suite 2100, 65 East State Street.
Telephone: 614-228-1541.
In Denver, Colorado: 303 East 17th Avenue, Suite 1100.
Telephone: 303-861-0600.
In Houston, Texas: 1000 Louisiana, Suite 2000.
Telephone: 713-751-1600.
In Beverly Hills, California: 9150 Wilshire Boulevard, Suite 205.
Telephone: 310-385-7500.
In Long Beach, California: 300 Oceangate, Suite 620.
Telephone: 562-432-2827.
In Los Angeles, California: 600 Wilshire Boulevard.
Telephone: 213-624-2400.
In Orlando, Florida: SunBank Center, Suite 2300, 200 South Orange Avenue.
Telephone: 407-649-4000.
In Washington, D.C.: Washington Square, Suite 1100, 1050 Connecticut Avenue, N.W.
Telephone: 202-861-1500.

PARTNERS

Louis A. Colombo
David L. Marburger

For Complete List of Firm Personnel, See General Section

For full biographical listings, see the Martindale-Hubbell Law Directory

WALTER & HAVERFIELD, P.L.L. (AV)

1300 Terminal Tower, 44113-2253
Telephone: 216-781-1212
Telecopier: 216-575-0911
Email: law@walterhav.com *URL:* http://www.walterhav.com
Columbus, Ohio Office: 88 East Broad Street.
Telephone: 614-898-1096.

MANAGING PARTNER

Michael T. McMenamin

MEMBERS OF FIRM

Christopher L. Gibbon
Nancy A. Noall
Frederick W. Whatley
Kenneth A. Zirm

(See Next Column)

ASSOCIATES

Randal G. Ammons
Darrell A. Clay

Representative Clients: The Associated Press; The Cleveland Free Times; Media/Professional Insurance, Inc.; The Readers Digest Association; WJW-TV; Fox Television Stations, Inc.; Random House Publishers, Inc.; Stern Publishing.

For Complete List of Firm Personnel, See General Section

For full biographical listings, see the Martindale-Hubbell Law Directory

*COLUMBUS,** Franklin Co.

ZEIGER & CARPENTER (AV)

1600 Huntington Center, 41 South High Street, 43215
Telephone: 614-365-4100
Facsimile: 614-365-9145

MEMBERS OF FIRM

John W. Zeiger
Michael H. Carpenter
Jeffrey A. Lipps
Steven W. Tigges
David A. Wallace
Marion H. Little, Jr.
Michael Romanello

ASSOCIATES

Timothy R. Bricker
Daniel R. Mordarski
Joseph T. Olecki
Michael N. Beekhuizen
Ronald E. Laymon
Angela Paul
Craig Calcaterra
John J. Todor

OF COUNSEL

Daniel R. Freytag
Mary R. True
Douglas R. Cole (Not admitted in OH)
Stuart G. Parsell

For full biographical listings, see the Martindale-Hubbell Law Directory

*TOLEDO,** Lucas Co.

FRITZ BYERS (AV)

Suite 824 The Spitzer Building, 43604
Telephone: 419-241-8013
Telecopier: 419-241-4215
Email: fbyers@accesstoledo.com

General Counsel for: Blade Communications, Inc.; Toledo Blade Co.; Buckeye Cablevision, Inc.; Pittsburgh Post Gazette.
Reference: Capital Bank N.A.

For full biographical listings, see the Martindale-Hubbell Law Directory

PENNSYLVANIA

*ALLENTOWN,** Lehigh Co.

GROSS, MCGINLEY, LABARRE & EATON, LLP (AV)

33 South Seventh Street, P.O. Box 4060, 18105-4060
Telephone: 610-820-5450
Fax: 610-820-6006
Email: attorney@gmle.com

MEMBERS OF FIRM

Malcolm J. Gross
Paul A. McGinley
Donald L. LaBarre, Jr.
J. Jackson Eaton, III
Michael A. Henry
Patrick J. Reilly
William J. Fries
Anne K. Manley
Susan Ellis Wild

ASSOCIATES

Elizabeth M. Racht
Allen I. Tullar
Sara J. Hogan
John F. Gross
Kimberly Gobla Krupka

For full biographical listings, see the Martindale-Hubbell Law Directory

RHODE ISLAND

*PROVIDENCE,** Providence Co.

EDWARDS & ANGELL, LLP (AV)

A Partnership including Professional Corporations
2800 BankBoston Plaza, 02903
Telephone: 401-274-9200
Telecopier: 401-276-6611
Cable Address: "Edwangle Providence"
Telex: 952001 "E A PVD"
Email: postmaster@ealaw.com *URL:* http://www.ealaw.com
Boston, Massachusetts Office: 101 Federal Street, 02110-1800.
Telephone: 617-439-4444.
Telecopier: 617-439-4170.
New York, New York Office: 750 Lexington Avenue, 10022-1200.
Telephone: 212-308-4411.
Telecopier: 212-308-4844.
Palm Beach, Florida Office: 250 Royal Palm Way, Suite 300, 33480-4356.
Telephone: 561-833-7700.
Telecopier: 561-655-8719.
Short Hills, New Jersey Office: 51 John F. Kennedy Parkway, 07078.
Telephone: 973-376-7700.
Telecopier: 973-376-3380.
Hartford, Connecticut Office: 90 State House Square, 06103-2715.
Telephone: 860-525-5065.
Telecopier: 860-527-4198.
Newport, Rhode Island Office: 130 Bellevue Avenue, 02840.
Telephone: 401-849-7800.
Telecopier: 401-849-7887.

MEMBERS OF FIRM

David K. Duffell
Terrence M. Finn (Resident Boston, Massachusetts Office)
Christopher D. Graham
Benjamin P. Harris III
Mary P. Heffner
John G. Igoe (Resident Palm Beach, Florida Office)
Jonathan M. Lourie (Not admitted in RI; Resident, Boston, Massachusetts Office)
Christine M. Marx (Resident, Short Hills, New Jersey Office; Partner-in-Charge, New Jersey Office)
Stephen O. Meredith (Resident Boston, Massachusetts Office)
Elizabeth H. Munnell (Not admitted in RI; Resident Boston, Massachusetts Office)
Walter G. D. Reed
Susan E. Siebert (Not admitted in RI; Resident Boston, Massachusetts Office)
Leonard Q. Slap (Resident Boston, Massachusetts Office)

OF COUNSEL

George Michaels (Not admitted in RI; Resident Boston, Massachusetts Office)

For Complete List of Firm Personnel, See General Section

For full biographical listings, see the Martindale-Hubbell Law Directory

SOUTH CAROLINA

*COLUMBIA,** Richland Co.

WILLOUGHBY & HOEFER, P.A. (AV)

1022 Calhoun Street, Suite 302, P.O. Box 8416, 29202-8416
Telephone: 803-252-3300
Telecopier: 803-256-8062
Email: willhoef@sc-online.net

Mitchell M. Willoughby
John M. S. Hoefer
Alvis J. Bynum, Jr.
B. Craig Collins

Elizabeth Zeck

Representative Clients: Bell Atlantic Mobile; National Educational Communications Association; SCANA Communications, Inc.; Northland Communications; ITC DeltaCommunications, Inc.

For full biographical listings, see the Martindale-Hubbell Law Directory

TENNESSEE

*KNOXVILLE,** Knox Co.

WATSON, HOLLOW & REEVES, P.L.C. (AV)

1700 First Tennessee Plaza, 800 South Gay Street, P.O. Box 131, 37901-0131
Telephone: 423-637-1700
Telecopier: 423-525-2514

(See Next Column)

MEMBERS OF FIRM

Robert Harmon Watson, Jr.
Richard L. Hollow
Pamela L. Reeves
Jon Gilbert Roach
John Chapman Duffy
John T. Batson, Jr.
Earl Jerome Melson

ASSOCIATES

Nathan D. Rowell
Laura C. Webb
Beverley S. Cornett
Jenny Coques Rogers

Representative Clients: The Knoxville News Sentinel; The Greenville Sun; The Tennessee Press Association; Media Services Group; WKXT-TV.

For full biographical listings, see the Martindale-Hubbell Law Directory

*MEMPHIS,** Shelby Co.

ARMSTRONG ALLEN PREWITT GENTRY JOHNSTON & HOLMES, PLLC (AV)

Brinkley Plaza, Suite 700, 80 Monroe Avenue, 38103-2467
Telephone: 901-523-8211
Facsimile: 901-524-4936
Little Rock, Arkansas Office: Suite 100, 100 Morgan Keegan Drive, 72202.
Telephone: 501-280-0100.
Facsimile: 501-280-0166.
Jackson, Mississippi Office: 2525 Lakeward Drive, Suite 200, 39216.
Telephone: 601-713-1192.
Facsimile: 601-713-2049.
Jackson, Tennessee Office: 464 North Parkway, Suite A, 38305.
Telephone: 901-660-2332.
Facsimile: 901-664-1109.

MEMBER OF FIRM

Lucian T. Pera

Kathy Laughter Laizure

For Complete List of Firm Personnel, See General Section

For full biographical listings, see the Martindale-Hubbell Law Directory

FARRIS, MATHEWS, BRANAN & HELLEN, P.L.C. (AV)

One Commerce Square, Suite 2000, 38103
Telephone: 901-259-7100
Fax: 901-259-7150
Email: firm@farris-law.com
East Memphis, Tennessee Office: Suite 400. First Commercial Bank Building. 5384 Poplar Avenue.
Telephone: 901-763-4000.
Fax: 901-763-4095.
Nashville, Tennessee Office: Nashville City Center, 511 Union Street, Suite 2400.
Telephone: 615-726-1200.
Fax: 615-726-1776.

MEMBERS OF FIRM

Charles B. Welch, Jr. (Resident, Nashville Office)
John M. Farris

ASSOCIATE

Harold W. Fonville, II

For Complete List of Firm Personnel, See General Section

For full biographical listings, see the Martindale-Hubbell Law Directory

HALE HEADRICK DEWEY & WOLF, PLLC (AV)

One Memphis Place, 200 Jefferson Avenue Suite 1450, 38103
Telephone: 901-523-1123
Fax: 901-523-7472
Nashville, Tennessee Office: Suntrust Bank Building, 201 Fourth Avenue North, Suite 1450, 37219.
Telephone: 615-843-5160.
Fax: 615-843-5165

Stephen P. Hale
S. Russell Headrick
H. Tucker Dewey
Herbert B. Wolf, Jr.
John S. Golwen

OF COUNSEL

Steven L. Gill

Jennifer Ziegenhorn
Wendy A. Geurin
John W. Campbell
Joseph M. Koury
Holly N. Knight
Charles S. Blatteis
Jennifer S. Kiesewetter
J. William Williams

For full biographical listings, see the Martindale-Hubbell Law Directory

*NASHVILLE,** Davidson Co.

KING & BALLOW (AV)

Union Street Plaza, 315 Union Street, Suite 1100, 37201
Telephone: 615-259-3456
Fax: 615-254-7907
Email: lawfirm@king-ballow.com *URL:* http://www.king-ballow.com
San Diego, California Office: 2700 Symphony Towers, 750 B Street, 92101.
Telephone: 619-236-9401.
Fax: 619-236-9437.

MEMBERS OF FIRM

Frank S. King, Jr.
Robert L. Ballow
Richard C. Lowe
R. Eddie Wayland
Larry D. Crabtree
Alan L. Marx
Paul H. Duvall (Resident, San Diego, California Office)
Steven C. Douse
Douglas R. Pierce
Howard M. Kastrinsky
Mark E. Hunt
R. Brent Ballow
Michael D. Oesterle

ASSOCIATES

James P. Thompson
Patrick M. Thomas
D'Lesli M. Davis
Nels Jacobson

Representative Clients: Denver Post, Denver, Colorado; Gaylord Entertainment Co., Nashville, TN; Knight-Ridder, Inc., Miami, Florida; Opryland USA, Inc., Nashville, Tennessee; Parade Magazine, Inc.; Tribune Company, Chicago, Illinois; Union Tribune Publishing Co., San Diego, California.

For Complete List of Firm Personnel, See General Section

For full biographical listings, see the Martindale-Hubbell Law Directory

WYATT, TARRANT & COMBS (AV)

1500 Nashville City Center, 511 Union Street, 37219-1750
Telephone: 615-244-0020
Telecopier: 615-256-1726
URL: http://www.wyattfirm.com
Music Row Office: 29 Music Square East, Nashville, 37203.
Telephone: 615-255-6161.
Telecopier: 615-254-4490.
Hendersonville, Tennessee Office: 313 E. Main Street, Suite 1, Hendersonville, 37075.
Telephone: 615-822-8822.
Telecopier: 615-824-4684.
Memphis, Tennessee Office: Crescent Center, Suite 650, 6075 Poplar Avenue, Memphis, 38119.
Telephone: 901-537-1000.
Telecopier: 901-537-1010.
Tri-Cities, Tennessee Office: Northeast Tennessee Business Park, 10368 Wallace Alley Street, Suite 6, Kingsport, Tennessee, 37663.
Telephone: 423-279-1825.
Telecopier: 423-279-9357.
Louisville, Kentucky Office: Citizens Plaza.
Telephone: 502-589-5235.
Telecopier: 502-589-0309.
Lexington, Kentucky Office: 1700 Lexington Financial Center.
Telephone: 606-233-2012.
Telecopier: 606-259-0649.
Frankfort, Kentucky Office: The Taylor-Scott Building, 311 West Main Street.
Telephone: 502-223-2104.
Telecopier: 502-227-7681.
New Albany, Indiana Office: The Elsby Building, 117 East Spring Street,
Telephone: 812-945-3561.
Telecopier: 812-949-2524.

MEMBERS OF FIRM

W. Michael Milom (Resident, Music Row Office)
Christian A. Horsnell (Resident, Music Row Office)

ASSOCIATE

Grace H. Awh (Resident, Music Row Office)

COUNSEL

Robin Mitchell Joyce (Resident, Music Row Office)

Representative Clients: Country Radio Broadcasters, Inc.; Gospel Music Assn.; Media Services Group; Shop at Home, Inc.; Thomas Nelson, Inc.; Wireless Group Inc.; Word, Inc.

For Complete List of Firm Personnel, See General Section

For full biographical listings, see the Martindale-Hubbell Law Directory

TEXAS

*AUSTIN,** Travis Co.

CASEY, GENTZ & SIFUENTES, L.L.P. (AV)

919 Congress Avenue, Suite 1060, 78701
Telephone: 512-480-9900
Facsimile: 512-480-9200
Email: rcasey@phonelaw.com

MEMBERS OF FIRM

Robin A. Casey
Susan C. Gentz
Jesús Sifuentes
Diane M. Barlow
Eric H. Drummond
Valerie P. Kirk

ASSOCIATES

Miguel A. Huerta
Bradford W. Bayliff

LEGISLATIVE CONSULTANT

Kathryn L. Grant

Representative Clients: Air Touch Paging; Birch Telecom of Texas, L.P.; Cable Plus; Excel Telecommunications, Inc.; GST Telecom, Inc.; ICG Communications, Intermedia Communications, Inc.; Metromedia Fiber Network Comapny; Time Warner Telecom, L.P.; Teligent, Inc.

For full biographical listings, see the Martindale-Hubbell Law Directory

JACKSON WALKER L.L.P. (AV)

100 Congress Avenue, Suite 1100, 78701-4099
Telephone: 512-236-2000
Fax: 512-236-2002
Email: hloftin@jw.com *URL:* http://www.jw.com
Dallas, Texas Office: 901 Main Street, Suite 6000.
Telephone: 214-953-6000.
Fax: 214-953-5822.
Fort Worth, Texas Office: 301 Commerce Street, Suite 2400.
Telephone: 817-334-7200.
Fax: 817-334-7290.
Houston, Texas Office: 1100 Louisiana, Suite 4200.
Telephone: 713-752-4200.
Fax: 713-752-4221.
Richardson, Texas Office: 2435 North Central Expressway, Suite 600.
Telephone: 972-671-2560.
Fax: 972-671-2566.
San Angelo, Texas Office: 225 West Beauregard Avenue.
Telephone: 915-481-2550.
Fax: 915-481-2552.
San Antonio, Texas Office: 112 E. Pecan Street, Suite 2100.
Telephone: 210-978-7700.
Fax: 210-978-7790.

MEMBERS OF FIRM

Laura Lee Stapleton
Lawrence A. Waks

For Complete List of Firm Personnel, See General Section

For full biographical listings, see the Martindale-Hubbell Law Directory

McCOLLOUGH & ASSOCIATES, P.C. (AV)

1801 North Lamar, Suite 104, 78701
Telephone: 512-485-7920
Fax: 512-485-7921
Email: wsmc@smccollough.com *URL:* http://www.smccollough.com

W. Scott McCollough

David Bolduc

LEGAL SUPPORT PERSONNEL

Carrie L. Keese (Paralegal)
Debbie Vera (Paralegal)

For full biographical listings, see the Martindale-Hubbell Law Directory

*DALLAS,** Dallas Co.

CALHOUN & STACY (AV)

Suite 5700 - Bank of America Plaza, 901 Main Street, 75202-3713
Telephone: 214-748-5000
Facsimile: 214-748-1421
Email: info@calhounstacy.com *URL:* http://www.calhounstacy.com

MEMBERS OF FIRM

Mark Alan Calhoun
David W. Elrod

For Complete List of Firm Personnel, See General Section

For full biographical listings, see the Martindale-Hubbell Law Directory

Dallas—Continued

JACKSON WALKER L.L.P. (AV)

901 Main Street, Suite 6000, 75202-3797
Telephone: 214-953-6000
Fax: 214-953-5822
URL: http://www.jw.com
Austin, Texas Office: 100 Congress Avenue, Suite 1100.
Telephone: 512-236-2000.
Fax: 512-236-2002.
Fort Worth, Texas Office: 301 Commerce Street, Suite 2400.
Telephone: 817-334-7200.
Fax: 817-334-7290.
Houston, Texas Office: 1100 Louisiana, Suite 4200.
Telephone: 713-752-4200.
Fax: 713-752-4221.
Richardson, Texas Office: 2435 North Central Expressway, Suite 600.
Telephone: 972-671-2560.
Fax: 972-671-2566.
San Angelo, Texas Office: 225 West Beauregard Avenue.
Telephone: 915-481-2550.
Fax: 915-481-2552.
San Antonio, Texas Office: 112 E. Pecan Street, Suite 2100.
Telephone: 210-978-7700.
Fax: 210-978-7790.

MEMBERS OF FIRM

Charles L. Babcock
Carl C. Butzer
E. Leon Carter
Alan N. Greenspan
Robert P. Latham
David T. Moran
David C. Myers
Frank C. Vecella

Representative Clients Furnished Upon Request.

For Complete List of Firm Personnel, See General Section

For full biographical listings, see the Martindale-Hubbell Law Directory

*HOUSTON,** Harris Co.

JACKSON WALKER L.L.P. (AV)

1100 Louisiana, Suite 4200, P.O. Box 4771, 77002
Telephone: 713-752-4200
Fax: 713-752-4221
URL: http://www.jw.com
Austin, Texas Office: 100 Congress Avenue, Suite 1100.
Telephone: 512-236-2000.
Fax: 512-236-2002.
Dallas, Texas Office: 901 Main Street, Suite 6000.
Telephone: 214-953-6000.
Fax: 214-953-5822.
Fort Worth, Texas Office: 301 Commerce Street, Suite 2400.
Telephone: 817-334-7200.
Fax: 817-334-7290.
Richardson, Texas Office: 2435 North Central Expressway, Suite 600.
Telephone: 972-671-2560.
Fax: 972-671-2566.
San Angelo, Texas Office: 225 West Beauregard Avenue.
Telephone: 915-481-2550.
Fax: 915-481-2552.
San Antonio, Texas Office: 112 E. Pecan Street, Suite 2100.
Telephone: 210-978-7700.
Fax: 210-978-7790.

MEMBERS OF FIRM

Charles L. Babcock
Nancy Wells Hamilton

For Complete List of Firm Personnel, See General Section

For full biographical listings, see the Martindale-Hubbell Law Directory

UTAH

*SALT LAKE CITY,** Salt Lake Co.

VAN COTT, BAGLEY, CORNWALL & MCCARTHY, A PROFESSIONAL CORPORATION (AV)

50 South Main Street, Suite 1600, P.O. Box 45340, 84145-0340
Telephone: 801-532-3333
Telecopier: 801-534-0058
Email: info@vancott.com *URL:* http://www.vancott.com
Ogden, Utah Office: 2404 Washington Boulevard, Suite 900.
Telephone: 801-394-5783.
Park City, Utah Office: 2200 Park Avenue, Suite C200-A.
Telephone: 435-649-3889.

Robert M. Anderson (President of Firm)

(See Next Column)

Jennifer K. Anderson
Bradley M. Strassberg
Evan S. Strassberg

For Complete List of Firm Personnel, See General Section

For full biographical listings, see the Martindale-Hubbell Law Directory

VIRGINIA

*ARLINGTON,** Arlington Co.

HALEY BADER & POTTS P.L.C. (AV)

4350 North Fairfax Drive, Suite 900, 22203-1633
Telephone: 703-841-0606
Fax: 703-841-2345
Email: haleybp@haleybp.com *URL:* http://www.haleybp.com

MEMBERS OF FIRM

Andrew G. Haley (1904-1966)
Michael H. Bader
Henry A. Solomon
John Wells King
John M. Pelkey
John Crigler
Melodie A. Virtue
James E. Dunstan
Benjamin J. Lambiotte

Paul Ferguson
Lisa M. Patera
Julie M. Kearney
Adam R. Brownstein

OF COUNSEL

Theodore D. Kramer

For full biographical listings, see the Martindale-Hubbell Law Directory

MCLEAN, Fairfax Co.

HELEIN & ASSOCIATES, P.C. (AV)

8180 Greensboro Drive Suite 700, 22102
Telephone: 703-714-1300
Facsimile: 703-714-1330
Email: mail@helein.com *URL:* http://www.helein.com

Charles H. Helein

Harisha J. Bastiampillai (Not admitted in VA)
Rogena Harris
Brian A. Cute (Not admitted in VA)
Jonathan S. Marashlian (Not admitted in VA)

For full biographical listings, see the Martindale-Hubbell Law Directory

RICHMOND, (Independent City)

WILLIAMS, MULLEN, CLARK & DOBBINS, A PROFESSIONAL CORPORATION (AV)

Two James Center, 1021 East Cary Street, P.O. Box 1320, 23218-1320
Telephone: 804-643-1991
Fax: 804-783-6507
URL: http://www.wmcd.com
Newport News Office: Harbor Bank Center, Suite 210, One Old Oyster Point Road, 23602-7119.
Telephone: 757-249-5100.
Fax: 757-249-5109.
Virginia Beach Office: One Columbus Center, 23462-6763.
Telephone: 757-499-8800.
Fax: 757-473-0395.
Vienna Office: 1593 Spring Hill Road, Suite 510, 22182.
Telephone: 703-760-5200.
Fax: 703-748-0244.
Washington, D.C. Office: The Farragut Building, 900 17th Street, N.W., Suite 700, 20006.
Telephone: 202-293-0213.
Fax: 804-783-6507. Fax Within D.C.: 202-293-5939.
London, England Office: Blake Lodge, Bridge Lane, SW11 3AD.
Telephone: (011-44-71) 223-2756.
Fax: (011-44-71) 350-0156.
Riyadh, Saudi Arabia Affiliate Office: Saudi-American Legal Consultants Commercial Building #2, Diplomatic Quarter, P.O. Box 57270, 11574.
Telephone: (011-966-1) 488-1563.
Fax: (011-966-1) 488-0542.

Calvin W. Fowler, Jr.
Reginald N. Jones

David H. Hallock, Jr.

For Complete List of Firm Personnel, See General Section

For full biographical listings, see the Martindale-Hubbell Law Directory

WASHINGTON

*SPOKANE,** Spokane Co.

WITHERSPOON, KELLEY, DAVENPORT & TOOLE, P.S. (AV)

1100 U.S. Bank Building, 422 West Riverside, 99201
Telephone: 509-624-5265
Fax: 509-458-2728
Coeur d'Alene, Idaho Office: 608 Northwest Boulevard, Suite 401.
Telephone: 208-667-4000.
Fax: 208-667-8470.

Robert L. Magnuson
Ned M. Barnes
William D. Symmes
Robert H. Lamp
K. Thomas Connolly
Thomas D. Cochran
Duane M. Swinton
Joseph H. Wessman
Jeffrey L. Supinger
Donald J. Lukes
Leslie R. Weatherhead
Michael D. Currin
Brian T. Rekofke
R. Max Etter, Jr.
Stanley R. Schultz
Michael F. Nienstedt
John M. Riley, III
F. J. Dullanty, Jr.
Daniel E Finney
Mary R. Giannini

Timothy M. Lawlor
William M. Symmes
Robert S. Magnuson
David M. Knutson
Jody M. McCormick
Paul C. Swainston
Eric J. Roth
Shelley N. Swanson

Representative Clients: KHQ TV; Media Professional Insuranc Co.; The Spokesman-Review; Unicom Broadcasting, Inc.; United Broadcasting, Inc.

For Complete List of Firm Personnel, See General Section

For full biographical listings, see the Martindale-Hubbell Law Directory

CANADA
ONTARIO

*TORONTO,** Regional Munic. of Toronto

BORDEN & ELLIOT (AV)

Barristers & Solicitors
Scotia Plaza, 40 King Street West, M5H 3Y4
Telephone: 416-367-6000
Telecopier: 416-367-6749
Email: info@borden.com *URL:* http://www.borden.com
Ottawa, Ontario Office: Borden Elliot Scott & Aylen, 1000-60 Rue Queen Street.
Telephone: 613-237-5160; 800-661-4237. General
Facsimile: 613-230-8842. IP Dept.
Facsimile: 613-787-3558. Email: ottinfo@scottaylen.com. URL: http://www.borden.com.

John D. Hylton, Q.C.

For Complete List of Firm Personnel, See General Section

For full biographical listings, see the Martindale-Hubbell Law Directory

COMPUTER LAW

NEBRASKA

*OMAHA,** Douglas Co.

DWYER, SMITH, GARDNER, LAZER, POHREN, ROGERS & FORREST (AV)

Suite 400, 8712 West Dodge Road, 68114
Telephone: 402-392-0101
Telefax: 402-392-1011
Email: dwyerlaw@dwyer-smith.com *URL:* http://www.dwyer-smith.com

MEMBERS OF FIRM

H. Daniel Smith
Bruce J. Goracke

Representative Clients: Nebraska Health System; Clarkson College; Turner & Associates; Bellevue Data Communications; Sirius Retail, L.L.C.

For Complete List of Firm Personnel, See General Section

For full biographical listings, see the Martindale-Hubbell Law Directory

NEW JERSEY

MOORESTOWN, Burlington Co.

ESTELLA S. GOLD (AV)

Blason II, 505 South Lenola Road, 08057
Telephone: 609-234-1004
Telecopier: 609-234-7836
Email: esglaw@aol.com

Representative Clients: South Jersey Processing, Inc.; OM Assn., Inc.

For full biographical listings, see the Martindale-Hubbell Law Directory

*NEWARK,** Essex Co.

McCARTER & ENGLISH, LLP (AV)

Four Gateway Center, 100 Mulberry Street, P.O. Box 652, 07101-0652
Telephone: 973-622-4444
Telecopier: 973-624-7070
URL: http://www.mccarter.com
Cherry Hill, New Jersey Office: 1820 Chapel Avenue West, Suite 380.
Telephone: 609-662-8444.
Telecopier: 609-662-6203.
New York, New York Office: Suite 2247, One World Trade Center.
Telephone: 212-466-9018.
Telecopier: 212-432-6568.
Boca Raton, Florida Office: 2255 Glades Road, Suite 319-A.
Telephone: 561-994-6262.
Telecopier: 561-241-0798.
Wilmington, Delaware Office: Mellon Bank Center, 919 Market Street.
Telephone: 302-654-8010.
Telecopier: 302-654-0795.
Philadelphia, Pennsylvania Office: One Commerce Square, 2005 Market Street, Suite 3600.
Telephone: 215-557-7700.
Telecopier: 215-557-6544.

MEMBERS OF FIRM

Charles R. Merrill
William J. Heller
Myrna L. Wigod

SPECIAL COUNSEL

Allen N. Friedman

ASSOCIATES

David W. Opderbeck
Robert J. Burger

For Complete List of Firm Personnel, See General Section

For full biographical listings, see the Martindale-Hubbell Law Directory

SILLS CUMMIS RADIN TISCHMAN EPSTEIN & GROSS, A PROFESSIONAL CORPORATION (AV)

One Riverfront Plaza, 07102-5400
Telephone: 973-643-7000
Fax: 973-643-6500
Telex: 820630 Sillsbeck Nwk
Email: sillsmail@sillscummis.com *URL:* http://www.sillscummis.com
Atlantic City, New Jersey Office: 17 Gordon's Alley.
Telephone: 609-344-2800.
New York, N.Y. Office: 712 Fifth Avenue.
Telephone: 212-643-7000.
Washington, D.C. Office: 1800 K Street, N.W.
Telephone: 202-296-4750.

(See Next Column)

MEMBERS OF FIRM

Ira A. Rosenberg
Joseph L. Buckley
Philip R. Sellinger
Victor H. Boyajian
Frederic M. Tudor

Noel D. Humphreys
Eric W. Sleeper
Robert I. Siegel

Representative Clients: BellCore; K2 Design; Cybershop; Hitachi Data Systems Corp.; Creative Guidance, Inc.; Data Kinetics, Inc.; Trecom Business Systems, Inc.

For Complete List of Firm Personnel, See General Section

For full biographical listings, see the Martindale-Hubbell Law Directory

NEW YORK

MELVILLE, Suffolk Co.

LAMB & BARNOSKY, LLP (AV)

534 Broadhollow Road-CS 9034, 11747-9034
Telephone: 631-694-2300
Telecopier: 631-694-2309
Email: thefirm@lambbarnosky.com *URL:* http://www.lambbarnosky.com

PARTNERS

Eugene R. Barnosky
Robert H. Cohen
Marcia Lyn Finkelstein
Michael J. Heller
Gary Holman
Scott M. Karson
P. L. Lamb
Arthur A. Lane
Joel M. Markowitz
Gerald P. Rosenberg
Patrice Dowd Shenn

OF COUNSEL

Louis E. Black
James F. Gesualdi
Howard W. Newman
Joseph J. Salvatore
Joseph H. Wishod

COUNSEL

Lloyd K. Chanin
Scott P. McBride

ASSOCIATES

Cathleen D. Allen
Catherine Healy Kanzler
Rita Fishman Sheena
Shari Lee Sugarman

For full biographical listings, see the Martindale-Hubbell Law Directory

*NEW YORK,** New York Co.

COBRIN & GITTES (AV)

750 Lexington Avenue, 10022
Telephone: 212-486-4000
Telecopier: 212-486-4007
Email: cgpats@ix.netcom.com

Peter T. Cobrin
Marvin S. Gittes
Richard M. Lehrer
David W. Denenberg

Robert J. Hess
Michael A. Adler
Gerald J. Cechony (Not admitted in NY)
Oren J. Warshavsky
Clyde Alvin Shuman
Lawrence E. Russ

For full biographical listings, see the Martindale-Hubbell Law Directory

GRAHAM, CAMPAIGN P.C. (AV)

The Bar Building, 36 West 44th Street, 10036-8178
Telephone: 212-354-5650
Cable Address: "Forbland"
Telex: 6502048313 MCI UW
MCI Mail: 204-8313
Telecopier: 212-354-6354
Email: gracam@aol.com *URL:* http://www.lawyers.com/trademarks

Andrew J. Graham (1911-1986)
William L. McGuire, Sr. (1926-1992)
H. John Campaign
John M. Keene
Charles H. Knull
Gail E. Nickols
William C. Wright

OF COUNSEL

Gerard H. Davis

For full biographical listings, see the Martindale-Hubbell Law Directory

PILIERO GOLDSTEIN JENKINS & SULLIVAN, LLP (AV)

292 Madison Avenue, 10017
Telephone: 212-213-8200
Fax: 212-685-2028
Email: lawyers@pgjhlaw.com *URL:* http://www.pgjhlaw.com
Carlstadt, New Jersey Office: One Palmer Terrace.
Telephone: 201-507-5157.
FAX: 201-507-5221.

(See Next Column)

PILIERO GOLDSTEIN JENKINS & SULLIVAN LLP, *New York—Continued*

Washington, D.C. Office: 888 17th Street, N.W., Suite 1100.
Telephone: 202-467-6991.
FAX: 202-467-6703.
San Francisco, California Office: 507 Howard Street, Suite 200.
Telephone: 415-281-3631.
Fax: 415-281-3630.

MEMBERS OF FIRM

Kimberlee S. Bogen
Edward J. Goldstein
Jon Mark Jenkins
Marc A. Lebowitz
Robert D. Piliero
George O. Richardson, III
Michael T. Sullivan

ASSOCIATES

Craig Avedisian
Rosemary G. Feit
Eric M. Kogan
Mariano Schwed

OF COUNSEL

Kenneth D. Arbeeny
Christopher P. Hall

For full biographical listings, see the Martindale-Hubbell Law Directory

SCHILLER & ASSOCIATES, P.C. (AV)

598 Madison Avenue, 15th Floor, 10022
Telephone: 212-688-4100
Telecopier: 212-753-8940

Craig Schiller

OF COUNSEL

Paul K. Landau
Richard J. Weiss

For full biographical listings, see the Martindale-Hubbell Law Directory

NORTH CAROLINA

*RALEIGH,** Wake Co.

WOMBLE CARLYLE SANDRIDGE & RICE (AV)

A Professional Limited Liability Company
2100 First Union Capitol Center, 150 Fayetteville Street Mall, P.O. Box 831, 27602
Telephone: 919-755-2100
Fax: 919-755-2150
Email: lawyers@wcsr.com *URL:* http://www.wcsr.com
Charlotte, North Carolina Office: 3300 One First Union Center, 301 South College Street.
Telephone: 704-331-4900.
Fax: 704-331-4955.
Winston-Salem, North Carolina Office: 200 West Second Street, P.O. Drawer 84.
Telephone: 336-721-3600.
Fax: 336-721-3660.
Research Triangle Park, North Carolina Office: 2505 Meridian Parkway, Suite 300 (Durham), 27713.
Telephone: 919-484-2300.
Fax: 919-484-2340.
Atlanta, Georgia Office: One Atlantic Center, 1201 West Peachtree Street, Suite 3500.
Telephone: 404-872-7000.
Fax: 404-888-7490.
Other Atlanta, Georgia Office: Suite 404, 2296 Henderson Mill Road, N.E.
Telephone: 770-492-9030.
Fax: 770-492-9609.
Washington, D.C. Office: 1120 Nineteenth Street, N.W., Eighth Floor.
Telephone: 202-857-4400.
Fax: 202-467-6910.
Greenville, South Carolina Office: 15 South Main Street, Suite 601, P.O. Box 10208.
Telephone: 864-255-5400.
Fax: 864-255-5440.

RESIDENT MEMBERS

M. Christopher Bolen
Charles A. Edwards

RESIDENT ASSOCIATE

Jennifer Long Collins

Representative Clients: Aetna Casualty and Surety Co., Inc.; ALSCO/AmeriMark Building Products, Inc.; Aoki Corporation America, Inc.; Hackney Brothers, Inc.; Lawyers Mutual Liability Insurance Company of North Carolina; Meredith College; Regency Park Corp.; Wachovia Bank, N.A.

For Complete List of Firm Personnel, See General Section

For full biographical listings, see the Martindale-Hubbell Law Directory

*WINSTON-SALEM,** Forsyth Co.

WOMBLE CARLYLE SANDRIDGE & RICE (AV)

A Professional Limited Liability Company
200 West Second Street, P.O. Drawer 84, 27102
Telephone: 336-721-3600
Fax: 336-721-3660
Email: lawyers@wcsr.com *URL:* http://www.wcsr.com
Charlotte, North Carolina Office: 3300 One First Union Center, 301 South College Street.
Telephone: 704-331-4900.
Fax: 704-331-4955.
Raleigh, North Carolina Office: 2100 First Union Capitol Center, 150 Fayetteville Street Mall, P.O. Box 831.
Telephone: 919-755-2100.
Fax: 919-755-2150.
Research Triangle Park, North Carolina Office: 2505 Meridian Parkway, Suite 300 (Durham), 27713.
Telephone: 919-484-2300.
Fax: 919-484-2340.
Atlanta, Georgia Office: One Atlantic Center, 1201 West Peachtree Street, Suite 3500.
Telephone: 404-872-7000.
Fax: 404-888-7490.
Other Atlanta, Georgia Office: Suite 404, 2296 Henderson Mill Road, N.E.
Telephone: 770-492-9030.
Fax: 770-492-9609.
Washington, D.C. Office: 1120 Nineteenth Street, N.W., Eighth Floor.
Telephone: 202-857-4400.
Fax: 202-467-6910.
Greenville, South Carolina Office: 15 South Main Street, Suite 601, P.O. Box 10208.
Telephone: 864-255-5400.
Fax: 864-255-5440.

RESIDENT MEMBERS

Charles A. Burke
Michael E. Ray

RESIDENT ASSOCIATES

Christopher G. Daniel
John F. Morrow, Jr.
David H. Read
Sharon A. Riegel
Randel S. Springer

Representative Clients: Brad Ragan, Inc.; Brenner Companies; Food Lion, Inc.; Hanes Companies, Inc.; North Carolina Baptist Hospitals, Inc.; R.J. Reynolds Tobacco Co.; Thomasville Furniture Industries, Inc.; Wachovia Corp.; Wake Forest University.

For Complete List of Firm Personnel, See General Section

For full biographical listings, see the Martindale-Hubbell Law Directory

OHIO

*COLUMBUS,** Franklin Co.

BRICKER & ECKLER LLP (AV)

100 South Third Street, 43215-4291
Telephone: 614-227-2300
Telecopy: 614-227-2390
Email: info@be.bricker.com *URL:* http://www.bricker.com

Michael S. Holman
Randolph C. Wiseman
John W. Cook, III
Michael E. Flowers
Mark A. Engel
Richard S. Lovering
Diane M. Signoracci
Joyce B. Link
Mark C. Pomeroy
James F. Flynn
Harry Wright, IV
Drew H. Campbell

Wendi R. Huntley
Stephen C. Gray
T. Earl LeVere
Hope M. Goings

OF COUNSEL

Anne Marie Sferra

Representative Clients: The Ohio Manufacturers Association; Horizons Video and Film, Inc.; Copper Net, Inc.; Lan Soft USA, Inc.; Micro Gallery, Inc.

For Complete List of Firm Personnel, See General Section

For full biographical listings, see the Martindale-Hubbell Law Directory

MUELLER AND SMITH A LEGAL PROFESSIONAL ASSOCIATION (AV)

Mueller-Smith Building, 7700 Rivers Edge Drive, 43235-1131
Telephone: 614-436-0600
Telecopier: 614-436-0057
Email: patents@infinet.com *URL:* http://www.lawyers.com/muellerandsmith

(See Next Column)

MUELLER AND SMITH A LEGAL PROFESSIONAL ASSOCIATION—*Continued*

Jerry K. Mueller, Jr. Gerald L. Smith

Representative Clients: Ashland Chemical Co.; Battelle Columbus Laboratories; General Electric Co.; Liebert Corp.; OCLC Online Computer Library Center, Inc.; Neoprobe Corporation; The Edward Orton, Jr. Ceramic Foundation; The Ohio State University Research Foundation.

For full biographical listings, see the Martindale-Hubbell Law Directory

PENNSYLVANIA

*PHILADELPHIA,** Philadelphia Co.

CAESAR, RIVISE, BERNSTEIN, COHEN & POKOTILOW, LTD. (AV)

12th Floor, 1635 Market Street, 19103-2212
Telephone: 215-567-2010
Telecopier: 215-751-1142
Email: gatekeeper@Caesarrivise.com

Alan H. Bernstein
Stanley H. Cohen
Manny D. Pokotilow
Barry A. Stein
Martin L. Faigus
Eric S. Marzluf
Robert S. Silver
Michael J. Berkowitz
Scott M. Slomowitz
Mona Gupta
David M. Tener
James J. Kozuch
Salvatore Guerriero (Not admitted in PA)
William J. Castillo (Not admitted in PA)
Francis M. Linguiti

OF COUNSEL

Max Goldman

For full biographical listings, see the Martindale-Hubbell Law Directory

DANN, DORFMAN, HERRELL AND SKILLMAN, A PROFESSIONAL CORPORATION (AV)

Suite 720, 1601 Market Street, 19103-2307
Telephone: 215-563-4100
Fax: 215-563-4044
Email: internet:email@ddhs.com

John C. Dorfman
Henry H. Skillman
Roger W. Herrell
Patrick J. Hagan
Donald R. Piper, Jr.
Vincent T. Pace
Janet E. Reed
Stephen H. Eland
Craig M. Bell
Clement A. Berard (Not admitted in PA)
Alfred W. Zaher

OF COUNSEL

C. Marshall Dann
John S. Child, Jr.
Charles N. Quinn

LEGAL SUPPORT PERSONNEL

PATENT AGENTS

John B. Berryhill
Kathleen D. Rigaut

TECHNICAL ADVISOR

Ellen Klann
Niels Haun (Technical Advisor)

For full biographical listings, see the Martindale-Hubbell Law Directory

F. EMMETT FITZPATRICK, P.C. (AV)

926 Public Ledger Building, 19106
Telephone: 215-925-5200
Fax: 215-925-5991
Email: info@toplaw.com *URL:* http://www.toplaw.com

F. Emmett Fitzpatrick
F. Emmett Fitzpatrick, III
NiaLena Caravasos

LEGAL SUPPORT PERSONNEL

Doreen Howley (Paralegal)

For full biographical listings, see the Martindale-Hubbell Law Directory

SYNNESTVEDT & LECHNER LLP (AV)

2600 Aramark Tower, 1101 Market Street, 19107-2950
Telephone: 215-923-4466
Facsimile: 215-923-2189
Email: synnlech@synnlech.com *URL:* http://www.synnlech.com

Paul Synnestvedt (1870-1950)
Harvey L. Lechner (1885-1954)
Raymond H. Synnestvedt (1902-1986)
Andrew R. Klein (1928-1987)
Albert L. Free (1922-1996)
William H. Elliott, Jr. (1918-1997)

MEMBERS OF FIRM

John T. Synnestvedt
Charles H. Lindrooth
Alexis Barron
Joseph F. Posillico
Bryna S. Silver
Gary A. Hecht
Theodore Naccarella

(See Next Column)

SENIOR COUNSEL

Irving Newman (Not admitted in PA)

ASSOCIATES

Lisa B. Lane
Stephen J. Driscoll
Joshua R. Slavitt
Mark D. Simpson
Patrick John Kelly
John A. Chionchio
Gregory S. Bernabeo
Stephen James Weed (Not admitted in PA)
Peter J. Butch III (Not admitted in PA)

OF COUNSEL

Richard D. Weber

LEGAL SUPPORT PERSONNEL

SCIENTIFIC ADVISORS

Brett T. Freeman
Gene J. Yao

For full biographical listings, see the Martindale-Hubbell Law Directory

RHODE ISLAND

*PROVIDENCE,** Providence Co.

HINCKLEY, ALLEN & SNYDER LLP (AV)

1500 Fleet Center, 02903-2393
Telephone: 401-274-2000
Fax: 401-277-9600
Email: firm@haslaw.com *URL:* http://www.haslaw.com
Boston, Massachusetts Office: 28 State Street, 30th Floor.
Telephone: 617-345-9000.
Fax: 617-345-9020. URL: http://www.haslaw.com.

MEMBERS OF FIRM

Paula K. Andrews (Not admitted in RI)
David D. Barricelli
Jonathan Bell
Paul Bork (Not admitted in RI)
Stephen J. Carlotti
Joseph P. Curran
Michael P. DeFanti
Eric F. Eisenberg (Not admitted in RI)
Malcolm Farmer, III
Hugh J. Gorman, III (Not admitted in RI)
William R. Grimm
Richard L. E. Jocelyn
Elizabeth Murdock Myers
Paul F. O'Donnell, III (Not admitted in RI)
H. Peter Olsen
John J. Pendergast, III
Gerald J. Petros
Herman Snyder (Not admitted in RI)
David R. Sullivan (Not admitted in RI)
Robert F. Sylvia (Not admitted in RI)
Howard E. Walker
Richard D. Wayne (Not admitted in RI)

ASSOCIATES

Mark Bianchi
Andrew D. Cummings (Not admitted in RI)
June E. Daniel
Kelley Jordan-Price
Catherine S. Kim (Not admitted in RI)
Christopher W. Morog (Not admitted in RI)
Elena B. Olson (Not admitted in RI)
Joseph D. Whelan

For Complete List of Firm Personnel, See General Section

For full biographical listings, see the Martindale-Hubbell Law Directory

TENNESSEE

*KNOXVILLE,** Knox Co.

LUEDEKA, NEELY & GRAHAM, P.C. (AV)

Suite 1871, Riverview Tower, 900 South Gay Street, P.O. Box 1871, 37901-1871
Telephone: 423-546-4305
Fax: 423-523-4478
Email: firm@lng-patent.com *URL:* http://www.LNG-patent.com

Edwin M. Luedeka (1920-1999)
Andrew S. Neely
Mark S. Graham
Robert O. Fox
David E. LaRose
Michael E. Sellers
Richard W. Barnes, Jr.

Jason L. Hornkohl
Mark P. Crockett

OF COUNSEL

J. Frederick Thomsen

For full biographical listings, see the Martindale-Hubbell Law Directory

*MEMPHIS,** Shelby Co.

ARMSTRONG ALLEN PREWITT GENTRY JOHNSTON & HOLMES, PLLC (AV)

Brinkley Plaza, Suite 700, 80 Monroe Avenue, 38103-2467
Telephone: 901-523-8211
Facsimile: 901-524-4936
Little Rock, Arkansas Office: Suite 100, 100 Morgan Keegan Drive, 72202.
Telephone: 501-280-0100.
Facsimile: 501-280-0166.
Jackson, Mississippi Office: 2525 Lakeward Drive, Suite 200, 39216.
Telephone: 601-713-1192.
Facsimile: 601-713-2049.
Jackson, Tennessee Office: 464 North Parkway, Suite A, 38305.
Telephone: 901-660-2332.
Facsimile: 901-664-1109.

MEMBERS OF FIRM

Joseph Brent Walker
Paul A. Matthews
Lucian T. Pera

For Complete List of Firm Personnel, See General Section

For full biographical listings, see the Martindale-Hubbell Law Directory

TEXAS

*AUSTIN,** Travis Co.

KARL BAYER (AV)

900 Norwood Tower, 114 West Seventh Street, 78701
Telephone: 512-476-1226
Fax: 512-476-1280
Email: karl@karlbayer.com

Karl Bayer

For full biographical listings, see the Martindale-Hubbell Law Directory

*DALLAS,** Dallas Co.

JACKSON WALKER L.L.P. (AV)

901 Main Street, Suite 6000, 75202-3797
Telephone: 214-953-6000
Fax: 214-953-5822
URL: http://www.jw.com
Austin, Texas Office: 100 Congress Avenue, Suite 1100.
Telephone: 512-236-2000.
Fax: 512-236-2002.
Fort Worth, Texas Office: 301 Commerce Street, Suite 2400.
Telephone: 817-334-7200.
Fax: 817-334-7290.
Houston, Texas Office: 1100 Louisiana, Suite 4200.
Telephone: 713-752-4200.
Fax: 713-752-4221.
Richardson, Texas Office: 2435 North Central Expressway, Suite 600.
Telephone: 972-671-2560.
Fax: 972-671-2566.
San Angelo, Texas Office: 225 West Beauregard Avenue.
Telephone: 915-481-2550.
Fax: 915-481-2552.
San Antonio, Texas Office: 112 E. Pecan Street, Suite 2100.
Telephone: 210-978-7700.
Fax: 210-978-7790.

MEMBERS OF FIRM

Larry L. Bean
Carl C. Butzer
Emily Stacy Donahue
Alan N. Greenspan
Michael L. Knapek
John A. Koepke
John L. Lancaster, III
Robert P. Latham
Frank C. Vecella

Representative Clients Furnished Upon Request.

For Complete List of Firm Personnel, See General Section

For full biographical listings, see the Martindale-Hubbell Law Directory

THOMPSON & KNIGHT L.L.P. (AV)

(Attorneys and Counselors)
1700 Pacific Avenue Suite 3300, 75201
Telephone: 214-969-1700
Telecopy: 214-969-1751
Telex: 732 298
URL: http://www.tklaw.com
Austin, Texas Office: 1200 San Jacinto Center, 98 San Jacinto Boulevard, 78701.
Telephone: 512-469-6100.
Telecopy: 512-469-6180.

(See Next Column)

Fort Worth, Texas Office: 801 Cherry Street, Suite 1600, 76102.
Telephone: 817-347-1700.
Telecopy: 817-347-1799.
Houston, Texas Office: Thompson Knight Brown Parker & Leahy L.L.P., 1200 Smith Street, Suite 3600, 77002-4595.
Telephone: 713-654-8111.
Telecopier: 713-654-1871.
San Pedro Garza Garcia, Nuevo León, Mexico Office: Edificio Losoles PD-4, Av. Lázaro Cárdenas No. 2400 Pte., C.P. 66220.
Telephone: (52-8) 363-0096.
Telecopy: (52-8) 363-3067.

PARTNER

Herbert J. Hammond

For Complete List of Firm Personnel, See General Section

For full biographical listings, see the Martindale-Hubbell Law Directory

*SAN ANTONIO,** Bexar Co.

COX & SMITH INCORPORATED (AV)

112 East Pecan Street, Suite 1800, 78205-1521
Telephone: 210-554-5500
Fax: 210-226-8395
Email: info@coxsmith.com *URL:* http://www.coxsmith.com

Dan G. Webster, III
Gale R. Peterson
J. Daniel Harkins
Brett W. Schouest
Elizabeth Johnson Keig
Courtenay B. Allen

Representative Clients: ATX Technologies, Inc.; Clarke American Checks, Inc.; Computer Solutions, Inc.; Critical Path Strategies, Inc.; Cyberlog International Inc.; Eye Care Centers of America; Karta Technologies; TPS Systems, Inc.; San Antonio Federal Credit Union; Trinity University.

For Complete List of Firm Personnel, See General Section

For full biographical listings, see the Martindale-Hubbell Law Directory

UTAH

SANDY, Salt Lake Co.

CLAYTON, HOWARTH & CANNON, P.C. (AV)

10150 South Centennial Parkway, Suite 400, P.O. Box 1909, 84091
Telephone: 801-255-5335
Fax: 801-256-2043
Email: patlaw@chcpat.com

Grant R. Clayton
Alan J. Howarth
Karl R. Cannon

For full biographical listings, see the Martindale-Hubbell Law Directory

THORPE, NORTH & WESTERN, L.L.P. (AV)

A Partnership including a Professional Corporation
8180 South 700 East, Suite 200, 84070
Telephone: 801-566-6633
Fax: 801-566-0750
Mailing Address: P.O. Box 1219, Sandy, Utah, 84091
Email: patlaw@tnw.com *URL:* http://www.tnw.com
Las Vegas, Nevada Office: 2345 Red Rock Street, Suite 310. Telephone 702-368-7767.

Calvin E. Thorpe (1938-1999)
Vaughn W. North
M. Wayne Western

ASSOCIATES

Michael W. Starkweather (Not admitted in UT)
Clifton W. Thompson (Not admitted in UT)
Garron M. Hobson
Peter M. deJonge
Weili Cheng, PhD.
David R. McKinney
Steve M. Perry
Gary P. Oakeson
David W. Osborne

TECHNICAL CONSULTANT

Loren Hulse

OF COUNSEL

Neil J. Beller (Resident, Las Vegas, Nevada Office)

For full biographical listings, see the Martindale-Hubbell Law Directory

VIRGINIA

*FAIRFAX,** (Ind. City; Seat of Fairfax Co.)

McCandlish & Lillard, A Professional Corporation (AV)

Fair Oaks Plaza, 11350 Random Hills Road, Suite 500, 22030-7429
Telephone: 703-273-2288
Fax: 703-352-4300
Email: mccand@patriot.net *URL:* http://www.mccandlaw.com
Leesburg, Virginia Office: 305 Harrison Street, S.E., Third Floor.
Telephone: 703-737-0200.
Fax: 703-737-0165.

Robert J. McCandlish, Jr. (1909-1996)
Rothwell J. Lillard (1910-1989)
Jesse B. Wilson, III
Peter A. Arntson
Gary W. Brown
Randolph A. Sutliff
Robert H. J. Loftus
William McCauley Arnold
Stephen C. Price
Stephen K. Fox
Douglas J. Sanderson
R. Peyton Mahaffey
William L. Carey
John W. Farrell
Eric J. Berghold
Ralph M. Tener
Vicki L. Layman
Adam W. Smith

Daniel P. Lyon
Lawrence J. McClafferty
Brian R. Sanderson

For full biographical listings, see the Martindale-Hubbell Law Directory

CANADA NEWFOUNDLAND

*ST. JOHN'S,**

McInnes Cooper (AV)

Barristers, Solicitors & Trade Mark Agents
Baine Johnston Centre, 5th Floor, 10 Fort William Place, P.O. Box 5939, A1C 5X4
Telephone: 709-722-8735
Telecopier: 709-722-1763
Email: mcrsj@mcrlaw.com *URL:* http://www.mcrlaw.com
Halifax, Nova Scotia Office: Summit Place, 1601 Lower Water Street, P.O. Box 730, B3J 2V1.
Telephone: 902-425-6500.
Fax: 902-425-6350. Email: mcrhfx@mcrlaw.com.
Moncton, New Brunswick Office: Place Moncton Place, 655 Main Street, P.O. Box 1368, E1C 8T6.
Telephone: 506-857-8970.
Fax: 506-857-4095. Email: mcrmctn@mcrlaw.com.
Charlottetown, Prince Edward Island Office: BDC Place, Suite 620, 119 Kent Street, C1A 1N3.
Telephone: 902-368-8473.
Fax: 902-368-8346. Email: mcrpei@mcrlaw.com.
Fredericton, New Brunswick Office: Suite 600, 570 Queen Street, P.O. Box 610.
Telephone: 506-458-8572.
Fax: 506-458-9903. Email: mcrfton@mcrlaw.com.

ASSOCIATE

Jacqueline S. Bartlett

For Complete List of Firm Personnel, See General Section

For full biographical listings, see the Martindale-Hubbell Law Directory

CANADA NOVA SCOTIA

*HALIFAX,** Regional Munic. of Halifax

McInnes Cooper (AV)

Barristers, Solicitors & Trade Mark Agents
Summit Place, 1601 Lower Water Street, P.O. Box 730, B3J 2V1
Telephone: 902-425-6500
Fax: 902-425-6350
Email: mcrhfx@mcrlaw.com *URL:* http://www.mcrlaw.com
St. John's, Newfoundland Office: Baine Johnston Centre, 5th Floor, 10 Fort William Place, P.O. Box 5939, A1C 5X4.
Telephone: 709-722-8735.
Telecopier: 709-722-1763. Email: mcrsj@mcrlaw.com.

(See Next Column)

Moncton, New Brunswick Office: Place Moncton Place, 655 Main Street, P.O. Box 1368, E1C 8T6.
Telephone: 506-857-8970.
Fax: 506-857-4095. Email: mcrmctn@mcrlaw.com.
Charlottetown, Prince Edward Island Office: BDC Place, Suite 620, 119 Kent Street, C1A 1N3.
Telephone: 902-368-8473.
Fax: 902-368-8346. Email: mcrpei@mcrlaw.com.
Fredericton, New Brunswick Office: Suite 600, 570 Queen Street, P.O. Box 610.
Telephone: 506-458-8572.
Fax: 506-458-9903. Email: mcrfton@mcrlaw.com.

PARTNER

F. Van W. Penick

For Complete List of Firm Personnel, See General Section

For full biographical listings, see the Martindale-Hubbell Law Directory

CANADA ONTARIO

*TORONTO,** Regional Munic. of Toronto

Davies, Ward & Beck (AV)

1 First Canadian Place, M5X 1B1
Telephone: 416-863-0900
Fax: 416-863-0871
Email: info@dwb.com *URL:* http://www.dwb.com

PARTNERS AND ASSOCIATES

David W. Smith, Q.C.
Edward C. Hannah
Neal H. Armstrong
Mark S. Hayes
Cameron M. Rusaw
Timothy H. Moran
Geoffrey S. Turner
Gillian R. Stacey
Brian A. Facey
Ronald S. Wilson
Jeffrey O. Palmer
Duncan C. Card
Joel T. Kissack
Matthew P. Gottlieb
Richard F. D. Corley
Christine J. Prudham
Lori A. Cornwall
Terrance J. Ritchie
Paul W. Golding

For Complete List of Firm Personnel, See General Section

For full biographical listings, see the Martindale-Hubbell Law Directory

Deeth Williams Wall, LLP (AV)

National Bank Building, 150 York Street, Suite 400, M5H 3S5
Telephone: 416-941-9440
Facsimile: 416-941-9443
Email: info@dww.com *URL:* http://www.dww.com

MEMBERS OF FIRM

Douglas N. Deeth
Amy-Lynne Williams
Gervas W. Wall
A. Marijo Coates
Victor V. Butsky
Michael Erdle

ASSOCIATES

Gordon S. Jepson
Diane M. LaCalamita
Noel A. Courage
Shereen Hamdy
Ailbe C. Flynn

For full biographical listings, see the Martindale-Hubbell Law Directory

Dimock Stratton Clarizio (AV)

20 Queen Street West, Suite 3202, P.O. Box 102, M5H 3R3
Telephone: 416-971-7202
Fax: 416-971-6638
Email: firm@dimock.com *URL:* http://www.dimock.com

PARTNERS

Ronald E. Dimock
Bruce W. Stratton
Dino P. Clarizio
Michelle L. Wassenaar
Mark B. Eisen
David M. Reive
Henry Lue

ASSOCIATES

Cynthia J. Ledgley
Andrew Mark Shaughnessy
C. Michelle Nelles
Angela Furlanetto

For full biographical listings, see the Martindale-Hubbell Law Directory

Sim, Hughes, Ashton & McKay (AV)

Sixth Floor, 330 University Avenue, M5G 1R7
Telephone: 416-595-1155
Cable Address: "Simbas" Toronto
Telex: 065-24567
Telecopier: 416-595-1163
Email: mailsim@sim-mcburney.com *URL:* http://www.sim-mcburney.com

(See Next Column)

SIM, HUGHES, ASHTON & MCKAY, *Toronto—Continued*

Donald F. Sim, Q.C. (1927-1986)	Timothy M. Lowman
Roger T. Hughes, Q.C.	Stephen M. Lane
Toni B. Polson Ashton	Arthur B. Renaud
Kenneth D. McKay	Patricia A. Rae
	Barbara J. Murchie

ASSOCIATES

John N. Allport	Kamleh J. Nicola
Steven L. Nemetz	Gillian M. Smith
Robert C. T. Liang	L. E. Trent Horne

PATENT AND TRADEMARK AGENTS

Peter W. McBurney	David A. Ruston
Michael I. Stewart	Thomas T. Rieder
John H. Woodley	Warren J. Galloway
Brenda L. Boardman	Lola A. Bartoszewicz
Stephen J. Perry	Jeffrey W. Wong

TECHNICAL ASSISTANTS

Ursula M. McGuinness	Kimberly A. McManus

For full biographical listings, see the Martindale-Hubbell Law Directory

CANADA
QUEBEC

*MONTREAL,** Montreal Dist.

MCMASTER GERVAIS (AV)

A General Partnership
1000 de La Gauchetière Street West, Suite 900, H3B 5H4
Telephone: 514-879-1212
Fax: 514-954-1905
Email: info@mcmastergervais.com *URL:* http://www.mcmastergervais.com

MEMBERS OF FIRM

Raymond Picard	Michael Patry
H. John Godber	Michael Bantey
Patrice Martin	Geneviève Bergeron
Grégoire Baillargeon	

For Complete List of Firm Personnel, See General Section

For full biographical listings, see the Martindale-Hubbell Law Directory

CONSTITUTIONAL LAW

MISSISSIPPI

*OXFORD,** Lafayette Co.

FREELAND & FREELAND (AV)

1013 Jackson Avenue, P.O. Box 269, 38655
Telephone: 662-234-3414
Telecopier: 662-234-0604
Email: thf4@watervalley.net

MEMBERS OF FIRM

T. H. Freeland, III — T. H. Freeland, IV

Representative Clients: The Ohio Casualty Group; Crum & Forester.

For full biographical listings, see the Martindale-Hubbell Law Directory

MISSOURI

ST. LOUIS, (Independent City)

OTTSEN, MAUZÉ, LEGGAT & BELZ, L.C. (AV)

The Midvale Building, 112 South Hanley Road, 63105-3418
Telephone: 314-726-2800
Telecopier: 314-863-3821

Timothy Belz

For full biographical listings, see the Martindale-Hubbell Law Directory

NEVADA

*LAS VEGAS,** Clark Co.

GOODMAN CHESNOFF & KEACH, A PROFESSIONAL CORPORATION (AV)

520 South Fourth Street, 89101-6593
Telephone: 702-384-5563
Fax: 702-598-1425

Oscar B. Goodman — David Z. Chesnoff
Eckley M. Keach

For full biographical listings, see the Martindale-Hubbell Law Directory

NEW YORK

*BUFFALO,** Erie Co.

STENGER & FINNERTY (AV)

1800 Main Place Tower, 14202
Telephone: 716-849-1700
Fax: 716-849-1717
Email: stenfinn@stenfinn.com *URL:* http://www.stenfinn.com

John H. Stenger — Joseph M. Finnerty

ASSOCIATES

Mitchell M. Stenger — David E. Gutowski

For full biographical listings, see the Martindale-Hubbell Law Directory

*NEW YORK,** New York Co.

EMERY CUTI BRINCKERHOFF & ABADY PC (AV)

545 Madison Avenue, 3rd Floor, 10022-4219
Telephone: 212-763-5000
Facsimile: 212-763-5001
Email: mail@ecbalaw.com *URL:* http://www.ecbalaw.com

Richard D. Emery — Jonathan S. Abady
Matthew D. Brinckerhoff — John R. Cuti

Ilann M. Maazel — Alexandra D. Lahav (Not admitted in NY)
David H. Gans

For full biographical listings, see the Martindale-Hubbell Law Directory

OHIO

*CINCINNATI,** Hamilton Co.

SIRKIN PINALES MEZIBOV & SCHWARTZ (AV)

920 Fourth & Race Tower, 105 West Fourth Street, 45202-2776
Telephone: 513-721-4876
Telecopier: 513-721-0876
Email: spms@fuse.net

MEMBERS OF FIRM

H. Louis Sirkin — Marc D. Mezibov
Martin S. Pinales — Howard M. Schwartz

Reference: The Huntington National Bank.

For full biographical listings, see the Martindale-Hubbell Law Directory

PENNSYLVANIA

*PHILADELPHIA,** Philadelphia Co.

RALPH D. SAMUEL & CO. A PROFESSIONAL CORPORATION (AV)

225 South 15th Street, Suite 1776, 19102
Telephone: 215-893-9992
Fax: 215-893-9996
Email: RalphSamuel@lawmine.com *URL:* http://www.lawyers.com/ralphdsamuellaw

Ralph David Samuel — Lynn Malmgren

For full biographical listings, see the Martindale-Hubbell Law Directory

TEXAS

*DALLAS,** Dallas Co.

TOOLEY & VOSS (AV)

8214 Westchester Drive, Suite 420, 75225
Telephone: 214-368-2224
Fax: 214-368-8307
Email: JCToutfit@aol.com

Joe C. Tooley — Edwin P. Voss Jr.

For full biographical listings, see the Martindale-Hubbell Law Directory

UTAH

*SALT LAKE CITY,** Salt Lake Co.

VAN COTT, BAGLEY, CORNWALL & MCCARTHY, A PROFESSIONAL CORPORATION (AV)

50 South Main Street, Suite 1600, P.O. Box 45340, 84145-0340
Telephone: 801-532-3333
Telecopier: 801-534-0058
Email: info@vancott.com *URL:* http://www.vancott.com
Ogden, Utah Office: 2404 Washington Boulevard, Suite 900.
Telephone: 801-394-5783.
Park City, Utah Office: 2200 Park Avenue, Suite C200-A.
Telephone: 435-649-3889.

Robert M. Anderson (President of Firm) — David A. Greenwood
Kenneth W. Yeates

Jennifer K. Anderson — Evan S. Strassberg

For Complete List of Firm Personnel, See General Section

For full biographical listings, see the Martindale-Hubbell Law Directory

VIRGINIA

ROANOKE, Roanoke City Co.

WOOTEN & HART, A PROFESSIONAL CORPORATION (AV)

707 Building, Suite 300, P.O. Box 12247, 24024-2247
Telephone: 540-343-2451; 540-342-9672
Telecopier: 540-345-6417
URL: http://www.wootenhart.com

George W. Wooten
David B. Hart
L. Thompson Hanes
Susan A. Waddell
Bradley D. McGraw
John L. Cooley
Thomas W. Farrell
Paul C. Kuhnel
Peter D. Vieth

David W. Hearn
John Mark Cooley
Christopher W. Stevens
Elizabeth D. Guilbert
Eunice Park Austin

OF COUNSEL
M. Lanier Woodrum

Representative Clients: Wachovia Bank; St. Paul Insurance Cos.
Approved Attorneys for: Lawyers Title Insurance Corp.
Reference: First Union National Bank.

For full biographical listings, see the Martindale-Hubbell Law Directory

WISCONSIN

*MILWAUKEE,** Milwaukee Co.

GUNTA & REAK, S.C. (AV)

219 North Milwaukee Street, 53202
Telephone: 414-291-7979
Facsimile: 414-291-7960
Email: gntareak@execpc.com *URL:* http://www.lawyers.com/gntareak

Gregg J. Gunta
Kevin P. Reak
Joseph A. McCarthy

Ann C. Wirth

OF COUNSEL
Gary A. Gerlach

For full biographical listings, see the Martindale-Hubbell Law Directory

CANADA ALBERTA

*EDMONTON,** Edmonton Jud. Dist.

PARLEE MCLAWS (AV)

15th Floor Manulife Place, 10180 101st Street, T5J 4K1
Telephone: 403-423-8500
Telecopier: 403-423-2870
Email: lawyers@parlee.com *URL:* http://www.parlee.com
Calgary, Alberta Office: 3400 Petro-Canada Centre, 150 - 6th Avenue, SW.
Telephone: 403-294-7000.
Telecopier: 403-265-8263.

ASSOCIATES

Priscilla E. S. J. Kennedy
Diana W. Kwan

For Complete List of Firm Personnel, See General Section

For full biographical listings, see the Martindale-Hubbell Law Directory

CANADA NOVA SCOTIA

*HALIFAX,** Regional Munic. of Halifax

MCINNES COOPER (AV)

Barristers, Solicitors & Trade Mark Agents
Summit Place, 1601 Lower Water Street, P.O. Box 730, B3J 2V1
Telephone: 902-425-6500
Fax: 902-425-6350
Email: mcrhfx@mcrlaw.com *URL:* http://www.mcrlaw.com
St. John's, Newfoundland Office: Baine Johnston Centre, 5th Floor, 10 Fort William Place, P.O. Box 5939, A1C 5X4.
Telephone: 709-722-8735.
Telecopier: 709-722-1763. Email: mcrsj@mcrlaw.com.
Moncton, New Brunswick Office: Place Moncton Place, 655 Main Street, P.O. Box 1368, E1C 8T6.
Telephone: 506-857-8970.
Fax: 506-857-4095. Email: mcrmctn@mcrlaw.com.
Charlottetown, Prince Edward Island Office: BDC Place, Suite 620, 119 Kent Street, C1A 1N3.
Telephone: 902-368-8473.
Fax: 902-368-8346. Email: mcrpei@mcrlaw.com.
Fredericton, New Brunswick Office: Suite 600, 570 Queen Street, P.O. Box 610.
Telephone: 506-458-8572.
Fax: 506-458-9903. Email: mcrfton@mcrlaw.com.

PARTNER
F. Van W. Penick

For Complete List of Firm Personnel, See General Section

For full biographical listings, see the Martindale-Hubbell Law Directory

CONSTRUCTION LAW

MINNESOTA

*MINNEAPOLIS,** Hennepin Co.

COLEMAN, HULL & VAN VLIET, P.L.L.P. (AV)
8500 Normandale Lake Boulevard Suite 2110, 55437
Telephone: 612-841-0001
Fax: 612-841-0041
URL: http://www.chvv.com

Willem F. van Vliet (1924-1996)
Katherine M. Bergenthal
Michael P. Coaty
Jeffrey W. Coleman
Timothy R. Duncan
William D. Hull
Marcia B. Haffmans
Eric R. Heiberg

Reference: Richfield Bank & Trust Co.

For full biographical listings, see the Martindale-Hubbell Law Directory

*ST. PAUL,** Ramsey Co.

GERAGHTY, O'LOUGHLIN & KENNEY, PROFESSIONAL ASSOCIATION (AV)
1400 Ecolab University Center, 386 North Wabasha Street, 55102-1308
Telephone: 651-291-1177
Fax: 651-291-9477
Email: gok@pclink.com

Terence J. O'Loughlin
Robert M. Mahoney
David C. Hutchinson
William H. Leary, III
Mary H. Alcorn
Matthew J. Hanzel
Ann D. Bray
Jean B. Hoppe
Kyle M. Thomas

OF COUNSEL

James H. Geraghty (Retired)
James W. Kenney (Retired)

Representative Clients: Hammel, Green and Abrahamson, Inc.; St. Paul Cos.; Midwest Medical Insurance Co.; Minnesota Lawyers Mutual Insurance Co.; University of Minnesota Hospital & Clinic; HealthPartners; Allina Health System; HealthEast; MMI Cos.

For full biographical listings, see the Martindale-Hubbell Law Directory

MISSISSIPPI

*GULFPORT,** Harrison Co.

DUKES, DUKES, KEATING AND FANECA, P.A. (AV)
2909 13th Street, 6th Floor, P.O. Drawer W, 39501
Telephone: 228-868-1111
Fax: 228-863-2886
Email: ddkf@ddkf.com

Hugh D. Keating
Cy Faneca
William W. Abbott, Jr.

For Complete List of Firm Personnel, See General Section

For full biographical listings, see the Martindale-Hubbell Law Directory

*JACKSON,** Hinds Co.

MOCKBEE HALL & DRAKE, A PROFESSIONAL ASSOCIATION (AV)
The Plaza Building, Suite 900, 120 North Congress Street, 39201
Telephone: 601-353-0035
Facsimile: 601-353-0045

David W. Mockbee
Mary Elizabeth Hall
Danny A. Drake
Julie Sneed Muller
William F. Selph, III

For full biographical listings, see the Martindale-Hubbell Law Directory

SULLIVAN AND SULLIVAN (AV)
Suite 200, 5448 I-55 North, 39211
Telephone: 601-952-0799
Facsimile: 601-952-0599;
Cable Address: "Sullaw"

MEMBERS OF FIRM

John C. Sullivan, Sr. (1910-1993)
John C. Sullivan, Jr.

(See Next Column)

ASSOCIATE

Patricia Alexander Killgore

For full biographical listings, see the Martindale-Hubbell Law Directory

MISSOURI

KANSAS CITY, Jackson, Clay, Platte & Cass Cos.

MILLER LAW FIRM, A PROFESSIONAL CORPORATION (AV)
4310 Madison Avenue, 64111
Telephone: 816-531-0755
Telefax: 816-561-6361
Email: MLFIRM@aol.com

Richard W. Miller
Stephen R. Miller
Weston A. Sechtem
Andrew C. Gately
Danne W. Webb
Michael T. Metcalf

Jennifer V. Ballengee
Scott H. Murphy
David R. Vandeginste

For full biographical listings, see the Martindale-Hubbell Law Directory

MONTANA

*BOZEMAN,** Gallatin Co.

KIRWAN & BARRETT, P.C. (AV)
215 West Mendenhall, P.O. Box 1348, 59771-1348
Telephone: 406-586-1553
Fax: 406-586-8971

Peter M. Kirwan
Stephen M. Barrett

Representative Clients: Kenyon Noble Lumber Company; McLees Incorporated; Concrete Specialties, Inc.

For full biographical listings, see the Martindale-Hubbell Law Directory

NEVADA

HENDERSON, Clark Co.

ROOKER & GIBSON (AV)
Suite 105, 701 North Green Valley Parkway, 89014
Telephone: 702-990-8100
Telecopier: 702-932-5266

C. Keith Rooker
James B. Gibson

Reference: BankWest of Nevada.

For full biographical listings, see the Martindale-Hubbell Law Directory

*LAS VEGAS,** Clark Co.

ALBRIGHT, STODDARD, WARNICK & ALBRIGHT, A PROFESSIONAL CORPORATION (AV)
Quail Park I, Building D-4, 801 South Rancho Drive, 89106
Telephone: 702-384-7111
Fax: 702-384-0605
URL: http://www.aswalaw.com

G. Vern Albright
William H. Stoddard
Whitney B. Warnick
G. Mark Albright

D. Chris Albright
Tami C. Budo
Corey D. Randall (Not admitted in NV)

Representative Clients: Tokio Marine and Fire Insurance Co.; INAPRO, a CIGNA Co.; Nevada Ready Mix; North American Health Care, Inc. (Nursing Home); Royal Insurance; First Security Bank of Utah; Nevada Community Bank; Nationwide Insurance Co.; Liberty Mutual Insurance; CB Commercial.

For full biographical listings, see the Martindale-Hubbell Law Directory

Las Vegas—Continued

ALVERSON, TAYLOR, MORTENSEN, NELSON & SANDERS (AV)

7401 West Charleston Boulevard, 89117
Telephone: 702-384-7000
FAX: 702-385-7000
Email: alverson@intermind.net
Reno, Nevada Office: 245 East Liberty, Suite 520, 89505.
Telephone: 775-329-0473.
Fax: 775-329-3303.

MEMBERS OF FIRM

J. Bruce Alverson
Eric K. Taylor
David J. Mortensen
Erven T. Nelson
LeAnn Sanders

OF COUNSEL

Jack C. Cherry
Kurt D. Anderson
Philip C. Van Alstyne

ASSOCIATES

Rebecca Hopkins Miller
Sandra Smagac
Victoria L. Nelson
Aaron D. Lovaas
Diane Obritsch
Michael A. Olsen
Randal D. Shimon
Catherine A. Olendorff
Monica L. Pierce
Gabriel D. Lither
Kurt R. Bonds
Darius F. Rafie
Mark J. King, IV
Shell L. Mercer
Carrie S. Bourdeau
Jason Lane Earnest
Nathan R. Reinmiller
Donn C. Alexander
Afshin Tadayon
Eric O. Freeman
Lindsay L. Stadtlander
Julie M. Sueoka

Representative Clients: Trophy Homes; FFC Consulting Engineers; Petacore Engineering, Inc.; The Machinery Center, Inc.; Frontier Bonding and Surety Group; Citibank Corporation; First Interstate Bank; RMJ Development, Inc.

For full biographical listings, see the Martindale-Hubbell Law Directory

LELAND EUGENE BACKUS & ASSOCIATES LTD. (AV)

2810 West Charleston Boulevard, Suite H-74, P.O. Box 28700, 89126-2700
Telephone: 702-872-5555
Facsimile: 702-872-5545
Email: backuslaw@earthlink.net *URL:* http://www.backuslaw.com

Leland Eugene Backus

John S. Delikanakis
Edgar Carranza
Robert Earl Werbicky
John L. Krieger
Megan Mahoney

For full biographical listings, see the Martindale-Hubbell Law Directory

CURRAN & PARRY (AV)

Quail Park II, Suite C-23, 601 South Rancho Drive, 89106
Telephone: 702-471-7000
Fax: 702-471-7070

MEMBERS OF FIRM

William P. Curran
Stanley W. Parry
Lynn Kirsch
John W. Burge
J. Lynn Johnson
Joshua H. Reisman (Not admitted in NV)

LEGAL SUPPORT PERSONNEL

Diane Loew (Paralegal)
Samara Johnston (Not admitted in NV; Law Clerk)

For full biographical listings, see the Martindale-Hubbell Law Directory

EDWARDS, SOOY & BYRON, A PROFESSIONAL CORPORATION (AV®)

3960 Howard Hughes Parkway Fifth Floor, 89109
Telephone: 702-474-0861
Fax: 702-474-4538
Email: esb-legal.com *URL:* http://www.esb-legal.com
San Diego, California Office: 101 West Broadway, Ninth Floor, 92101.
Telephone: 619-231-1500.
Fax: 619-231-1588.

Michael M. Edwards (Not admitted in NV)
Richard R. Sooy
Thomas W. Byron

Alfred Paul Centofanti, III
Bart M. Blechschmidt
Michael M. Edwards, Jr.

For full biographical listings, see the Martindale-Hubbell Law Directory

FOLEY & JONES (AV)

850 East Bonneville Avenue, 89101
Telephone: 702-383-9852
Fax: 702-383-8154
Email: FoleyJones@worldnet.att.net *URL:* http://www.lawyers.com/f&jlaw

(See Next Column)

Joseph M. Foley
Daniel T. Foley
Diana J. Foley
Mark M. Jones

For full biographical listings, see the Martindale-Hubbell Law Directory

JOLLEY, URGA, WIRTH & WOODBURY (AV)

3800 Howard Hughes Parkway Suite 1600, 89109
Telephone: 702-699-7500
Facsimile: 702-699-7555
URL: http://www.juww.com
Boulder City, Nevada Office: Suite 105, 1000 Nevada Highway, 89005.
Telephone: 702-293-3674.

MEMBER OF FIRM

Roger A. Wirth

ASSOCIATE

Scott Day Freeman

Representative Clients: Melvin Simon & Associates, Inc.; Champion Home Builders Co.; Carl's Air Conditioning; Dean Roofing Co.; Dynalectric Company of Nevada, Inc.; Emerson Electric Co.; Western Pipeline Construction Corp.

For Complete List of Firm Personnel, See General Section

For full biographical listings, see the Martindale-Hubbell Law Directory

LEFEBVRE, BARRON & VIVONE, CHTD. (AV)

1404 South Jones Boulevard, 89146-1231
Telephone: 702-383-8668
Facsimile: 702-383-6828
Email: lb@coam.net

Alan J. Lefebvre
David L. Barron
Thomas J. Vivone
Raymond W. Holland
Michelle O. Tobler
William Howard Pruitt
Bradley V. Gibbons
Jared Casper (Not admitted in NV)
Kevin S. Smith

LEGAL SUPPORT PERSONNEL

Jennifer L. Hageman

For full biographical listings, see the Martindale-Hubbell Law Directory

MAINOR & HARRIS (AV)

A Partnership of Professional Corporations
530 South Sixth Street, 89101
Telephone: 702-385-1400
Fax: 702-385-9408
Email: admin@mainorandharris.com *URL:* http://www.lawyers.com/mainorandharris

W. Randall Mainor (A Professional Corporation)
Richard A. Harris (A Professional Corporation)
Clark Seegmiller
Robert M. Adams
Nancy Quon
Robert W. Cottle

Reference: First Security Bank of Nevada, Las Vegas, Nevada.

For full biographical listings, see the Martindale-Hubbell Law Directory

MCDONALD CARANO WILSON MCCUNE BERGIN FRANKOVICH & HICKS LLP (AV)

Suite 1000, 2300 West Sahara Avenue, 89102
Telephone: 702-873-4100
Telecopier: 702-873-9966
URL: http://www.mcdonaldcarano.com
Reno, Nevada Office: 241 Ridge Street.
Telephone: 775-788-2000.
Telecopier: 775-788-2020.

MEMBERS OF FIRM

George F. Ogilvie III
Andrew P. Gordon
Bryan R. Clark

ASSOCIATE

Jeffrey A. Silvestri

Representative Clients: Scott Company of California; Tacoma Electric Supply; Kiewit Construction Company; D.C. Vient; K & N Plumbing; SDB of Nevada; Ash Grove Cement Company; Sun West Homes; Madera Component Systems.

For Complete List of Firm Personnel, See General Section

For full biographical listings, see the Martindale-Hubbell Law Directory

MORSE & MOWBRAY, A PROFESSIONAL CORPORATION (AV)

Suite 1400 Bank of America Plaza, 300 South Fourth Street, 89101
Telephone: 702-384-6340
Telecopier: 702-384-4596
London, England Office: Lamb Building, Temple.
Telephone: 071-353-6701.

(See Next Column)

MORSE & MOWBRAY A PROFESSIONAL CORPORATION—*Continued*

William R. Morse | John H. Mowbray
Harold M. Morse | Christopher H. Byrd
Kimberly A. Buchanan

For full biographical listings, see the Martindale-Hubbell Law Directory

PICO & MITCHELL (AV)

2000 South Eastern Avenue, 89104
Telephone: 702-457-9099
FAX: 702-457-8451
Email: lawyers@picomitchell.com

MEMBERS OF FIRM

James F. Pico | Christy Brad Escobar
Bert O. Mitchell | James R. Rosenberger
E. Breen Arntz

ASSOCIATES

Michelle Schwarz | Jill M. Chase
Rebecca L. Mastrangelo | Daniel E. Carvalho
Stephen H. Rogers

Representative Clients: Home Insurance Co.; State Farm Mutual Insurance Co.; Industrial Indemnity Insurance Co.; Great American Insurance Co.; Argonaut Insurance Cos.; Clark County Medical Society; Rose de Lima Hospital; Fairway Chevrolet; American States Insurance Co.; The Hartford Insurance Co.

For full biographical listings, see the Martindale-Hubbell Law Directory

RYAN MARKS JOHNSON TODD & BRODER (AV Ⓣ)

1160 Town Center Drive, Suite 300, 89134
Telephone: 702-341-7870
Facsimile: 702-341-8049
San Diego, California Office: Wingert Grebing Brubaker & Ryan LLP, One America Plaza, Seventh Floor, 600 West Broadway, 92101-3370.
Telephone: 619-232-8151.
Facsimile: 619-232-4665.

MEMBERS OF FIRM

Norman A. Ryan | Robert L. Johnson
Eileen Mulligan Marks | Christopher W. Todd
James P. Broder

ASSOCIATES

Stephen C. Grebing | Jay A. Kenyon

For full biographical listings, see the Martindale-Hubbell Law Directory

SCHOFIELD & ASSOCIATES (AV)

2675 South Jones Boulevard, Suite 211, 89146
Telephone: 702-474-4444
Fax: 702-474-4449
Email: phslaw@wizard.com *URL:* http://www.lawyers.com/schofield&associates

MEMBER OF FIRM

Paul H. Schofield

For full biographical listings, see the Martindale-Hubbell Law Directory

SHIRINIAN & ROITMAN (AV)

333 North Rancho Drive, Suite 520, 89106
Telephone: 702-631-5650
Fax: 702-631-5603
Email: ashirinian@aol.com *URL:* http://www.lawyers.com/shirinian&roitman
San Francisco, California Office: 44 Montgomery Street, Suite 1500, 94104.
Telephone: 415-788-1771.
Fax: 415-788-1744.

Ara H. Shirinian | Howard Roitman

For full biographical listings, see the Martindale-Hubbell Law Directory

LAW OFFICE OF GARY P. SINKELDAM (AV)

4270 South Decatur Blvd.. Suite B6-106, 89103
Telephone: 702-968-8037
Fax: 702-968-8069
San Diego, California Office: 550 West C Street, Suite 530.
Telephone: 619-515-1155.
Fax: 619-515-1159.
Los Angeles, California Office: 555 South Flower Street, Suite 4640.
Telephone: 213-236-9878.
Fax: 213-489-7559.
Newport Beach, California Office: 110 Newport Center Drive, Suite 200.
Telephone: 714-644-8136.
Fax: 714-644-7526.
Sacramento, California Office: 400 Capital Mall, Suite 235.
Telephone: 916-444-5566.
Fax: 916-444-5494.
(Not admitted in NV)

For full biographical listings, see the Martindale-Hubbell Law Directory

SMITH LARSEN & WIXOM, CHARTERED (AV)

3360 West Sahara Avenue, Suite 175, 89102
Telephone: 702-252-5002
Fax: 702-252-5006
Email: slwlaw@slwlaw.com

Jay Earl Smith | Kent F. Larsen
Michael B. Wixom

Stewart C. Fitts

Representative Clients: Norwest Bank Nevada, N.A.; Wells Fargo Bank; Chicago Title Comapny; General Star Management Company; Northwestern National Casualty Co.; Luxor Hotel & Casino; Excalibur Hotel & Casino; New-Com, Inc.; MMC, Inc.; AMRESCO Capital Corporation.

For full biographical listings, see the Martindale-Hubbell Law Directory

VANNAH COSTELLO CANEPA RIEDY & RUBINO (AV)

A Partnership including a Professional Corporation
Greystone, 1850 East Flamingo, Suite 236, 89119
Telephone: 702-369-4161
Fax: 702-369-0104
Email: vannahnet@vannahnet.com

MEMBERS OF FIRM

Robert D. Vannah (Chartered) | Scott K. Canepa
Nathan M. Costello | Terry W. Riedy
Michael C. Rubino

ASSOCIATES

Connie J. Forsythe | Matthew Vannah
Shawn D. Dorman | Ronald J. Flinders
Adam Ganz | Russell M. Rowe
Denise M. Cooper | Jonathan G. Lattie
Jeffrey Ferguson | (Not admitted in NV)

Representative Clients: Prudential Property and Casualty Insurance Co.; Continental Insurance Health Care; Chubb Group of Insurance; Reliance Insurance Co.; Transamerica Insurance Group; Foremost Insurance Co.; CNA Insurance Co.; Scottsdale Insurance Co.; The Maryland Insurance Group; Insurance Company of the West.

For full biographical listings, see the Martindale-Hubbell Law Directory

*RENO,** Washoe Co.

BIBLE, HOY & TRACHOK, A PROFESSIONAL CORPORATION (AV)

201 West Liberty Street, Third Floor, 89501
Telephone: 775-786-8000
Fax: 775-786-7426
Email: firm@nevadalaw.com *URL:* http://www.nevadalaw.com

Paul A. Bible | Michael D. Hoy
David R. Hoy | Mark S. Sertic
Richard M. Trachok, II | Jon M. Ludwig

Mark F. Bruce | Andrew Alan List
Mark J. Lenz | Ralph A. Fellows (Not admitted in NV)

For full biographical listings, see the Martindale-Hubbell Law Directory

ERICKSON, THORPE & SWAINSTON, LTD. (AV)

99 West Arroyo Street, P.O. Box 3559, 89505
Telephone: 702-786-3930
Fax: 702-786-4160
Email: etsreno@aol.com

Roger L. Erickson | Thomas Peter Beko
Donald A. Thorpe | John A. Aberasturi
George W. Swainston | Paul M. Bertone
William G. Cobb | Lisa E. Bruce
Gary A. Cardinal | John C. Boyden

Representative Clients: Airport Authority of Washoe County; Reno-Sparks Convention and Visitors Authority; Nevada Public Agency Insurance Pool; Bailey & McGah Developers; Summit Engineering; Dolven Simpson Associates.

For full biographical listings, see the Martindale-Hubbell Law Directory

MCDONALD CARANO WILSON MCCUNE BERGIN FRANKOVICH & HICKS LLP (AV)

241 Ridge Street, 89501
Telephone: 775-788-2000
Telecopier: 775-788-2020
URL: http://www.mcdonaldcarano.com
Las Vegas, Nevada Office: Suite 1000, 2300 West Sahara Avenue.
Telephone: 702-873-4100.
Telecopier: 702-873-9966.

(See Next Column)

McDONALD CARANO WILSON McCUNE BERGIN FRANKOVICH & HICKS LLP, *Reno—Continued*

MEMBERS OF FIRM

John J. McCune
Thomas R. C. Wilson
Larry R. Hicks
William A. S. Magrath, II
Timothy E. Rowe
James W. Bradshaw
George F. Ogilvie III
James C. Giudici
Andrew P. Gordon
Matthew C. Addison
Bryan R. Clark

ASSOCIATES

Paul J. Georgeson
Anthony D. Guenther

Representative Clients: Associated General Contractors of America; Clark & Sullivan Constructors, Inc.; Harker & Harker, Inc.; Monterrey Mechanical, Inc.; Shaver Construction; Sierra Builders of Nevada; Q & D Construction, Inc.

For Complete List of Firm Personnel, See General Section

For full biographical listings, see the Martindale-Hubbell Law Directory

WALTHER, KEY, MAUPIN, OATS, COX & LEGOY, A PROFESSIONAL CORPORATION (AV)

Lakeside Professional Plaza, 3500 Lakeside Court, 89509
Telephone: 775-827-2000
Facsimile: 775-827-2185
Mailing Address: P.O. Box 30000, Reno, Nevada, 89520

Steven T. Walther
Jon J. Key
Ernest J. Maupin
C. Robert Cox
L. Robert LeGoy, Jr.
Michael E. Malloy
W. Douglass Maupin
G. Barton Mowry
Kim G. Rowe
Procter J. Hug
Donald A. Lattin
Gustave J. Rossi
Robert A. Winkel
Kurt O. Hunsberger
Michael A. Nivinskus
Christopher D. Jaime

Rick R. Hsu
Michaelle D. Rafferty
Debra O. Waggoner

Representative Clients: Bank America of Nevada (Trust Dept.); Bechtel Corporations; Bill Pearce Olds, BMW, Volvo; The Ralph M. Parsons Corporation, Parsons Corporation; Washoe Health System; Washoe County School District.

For full biographical listings, see the Martindale-Hubbell Law Directory

NEW JERSEY

CEDAR KNOLLS, Morris Co.

LEARY, BRIDE, TINKER & MORAN, A PROFESSIONAL CORPORATION (AV)

7 Ridgedale Avenue, 07927
Telephone: 973-539-2090
Fax: 973-539-0806

W. Stephen Leary
James D. Bride
John G. Tinker, Jr.
Glenn R. Moran
James T. Gill
William H. Mergner, Jr.
Mark Bongiovanni

Tracey L. VanWiemokly
James P. McHugh III
Brian Peoples
Marguerite Anne Leary
Mark J. Brancato
Wendy Allyson Reek
David J. Dering
Peter M. Bouton
Christopher H. Frick
Mark A. Trudeau

For full biographical listings, see the Martindale-Hubbell Law Directory

*HACKENSACK,** Bergen Co.

THURBER CAPPELL, L.L.C. (AV)

235 Main Street, Suite 300, 07601
Telephone: 201-488-0594
Telecopier: 201-488-5283
Email: thurblaw@aol.com *URL:* http://www.lawyers.com/thurber,cappell,law

Mary F. Thurber
Cynthia A. Cappell

ASSOCIATES

Allison Turley Madden
Anne Marie Fox

OF COUNSEL

Frank Huttle, III

For full biographical listings, see the Martindale-Hubbell Law Directory

*MORRISTOWN,** Morris Co.

McELROY, DEUTSCH AND MULVANEY (AV)

1300 Mount Kemble Avenue, P.O. Box 2075, 07962-2075
Telephone: 973-993-8100
Fax: 973-425-0161
URL: http://www.MDMlaw.com
Denver, Colorado Office: 1099 18th Street, Suite 3120.
Telephone: 303-293-8800.
Fax: 303-293-3116.
New York, New York Office: Wall Street Plaza, 88 Pine Street.
Telephone: 212-766-1807.
Fax: 212-483-9129.
Ridgewood, New Jersey Office: 40 West Ridgewood Avenue.
Telephone: 201-445-6722.
Fax: 201-445-8075.

MEMBERS OF FIRM

Lorraine M. Armenti (Resident Partner, Denver Colorado Office)
Grace C. Bertone
John P. Beyel
William C. Carey
Stephen H. Cohen (1938-1992)
Kevin T. Coughlin
John F. Darcy (Resident, Ridgewood Office)
Edward B. Deutsch
Timothy I. Duffy
Kevin P. Galvin
Robert J. Kelly
Joseph P. La Sala
James P. Lisovicz
Paul A. Lisovicz
Fred A. Manley, Jr.
Michael J. Marone
Nancy McDonald
William T. McElroy
Laurence M. McHeffey (Resident Partner, Denver, Colorado Office)
Robert W. Muilenburg
James M. Mulvaney
Alfred S. Nugent, Jr. (1925-1989)
Octavius A. Orbe (Resident, Ridgewood Office)
Loren L. Pierce
Warren K. Racusin
Mark A. Rosen
Thomas P. Scrivo
John H. Suminski
Walter F. Timpone
Kevin E. Wolff

COUNSEL TO THE FIRM

Robert L. Clifford

OF COUNSEL

John K. Bradley
John F. Whitteaker

ASSOCIATES

Susan Freeman Anthony
H. George Avery
Elizabeth Addison Barrow
Joseph F. Bermudez
Thomas Richard Calcagni
Patrick J. Casey (Resident Associate, Denver, Colorado Office)
Lisbeth W. Cload (Resident, Ridgewood Office)
Daniel J. Cohen
Craig J. Compoli, Jr.
John P. Cookson (Resident Associate, New York, NY Office)
John Thomas Coyne
Andrew J. D'Arcy
Andrew M. Csaszar
Michael B. Devins
John W. DiNicola, II
Robin A. Donato
Rebecca Ward Donohue
Steven F. Dorry
Julienne S. Duncan
Brian F. Fowler (Resident, Ridgewood Office)
Aaron C. Foy (Not admitted in NJ; Resident, Denver, Colorado Office)
Christopher S. Frangeš
Lorna A. Friel
Kevin P. Harkins (Resident, Ridgewood Office)
Sarah C. Herzog
Eric J. Hughes
George A. Kelman
Justin N. Kinney
Linda F. Kitz
John P. Leonard
Joseph J. McGlone
Robert McGuire
Kaneez Fatema Madraswalla
Nadine Maleski
Faith Martin
Suzanne Cocco Midlige
Heidi S. Minuskin
Louis A. Modugno
Florina A. Moldovan
John W. Morris
Francis C. Porada (Resident Associate, Denver, Colorado Office)
Robert J. Re
Vincent E. Reilly
Jay R. Ruble
Craig T. Sashihara
Adam R. Schwartz
Peter W. Smith
Timothy P. Smith
Ronnie H. Spring
Michael J. Sullivan
Catharine Acker Vaughan
Meredith A. Walling
Richard J. Williams, Jr.

Representative Clients: ADT Security Systems, Inc.; Chubb Insurance Cos.; Crum & Forster Insurance Co.; Eaton Corp.; Fireman's Fund Insurance Cos.; New Jersey Manufacturers Insurance Co.; The Home Indemnity Co.; The Pittston Company; Security Pacific Finance Corporation; American Honda Motor Co., Inc.

For full biographical listings, see the Martindale-Hubbell Law Directory

RAND, ALGEIER, TOSTI & WOODRUFF, A PROFESSIONAL CORPORATION (AV)

60 Washington Street, 07960
Telephone: 973-539-2600
Telecopier: 973-984-0430
Email: randlaw@bellatlantic.net

(See Next Column)

RAND, ALGEIER, TOSTI & WOODRUFF A PROFESSIONAL CORPORATION—*Continued*

Gary C. Algeier
David B. Rand
Robert M. Tosti
Robert B. Woodruff
John F. McDonnell
John E. Croot, Jr.

Kathryn J. Kingree
Deborah A. White

OF COUNSEL

Ronald M. Pflug
Ellen S. Bass
Tamara Krikorian

For full biographical listings, see the Martindale-Hubbell Law Directory

*NEWARK,** Essex Co.

SILLS CUMMIS RADIN TISCHMAN EPSTEIN & GROSS, A PROFESSIONAL CORPORATION (AV)

One Riverfront Plaza, 07102-5400
Telephone: 973-643-7000
Fax: 973-643-6500
Telex: 820630 Sillsbeck Nwk
Email: sillsmail@sillscummis.com *URL:* http://www.sillscummis.com
Atlantic City, New Jersey Office: 17 Gordon's Alley.
Telephone: 609-344-2800.
New York, N.Y. Office: 712 Fifth Avenue.
Telephone: 212-643-7000.
Washington, D.C. Office: 1800 K Street, N.W.
Telephone: 202-296-4750.

MEMBERS OF FIRM

Morton S. Bunis
Thomas J. Demski
Philip R. White

Steven S. Katz

Representative Clients: Horizon House; The International Group; O'Brien Environmental Energy, Inc.; International Fidelity Insurance Company; Bally's Park Place, Inc.; City of Woodbridge; Fluor Daniel, Inc.; The O'Brien & Gere Companies.

For Complete List of Firm Personnel, See General Section

For full biographical listings, see the Martindale-Hubbell Law Directory

*NEW BRUNSWICK,** Middlesex Co.

HOAGLAND, LONGO, MORAN, DUNST & DOUKAS (AV)

40 Paterson Street, P.O. Box 480, 08903
Telephone: 732-545-4717
Fax: 732-545-4579
Email: info@hlmdd.com

MEMBERS OF FIRM

Bartholomew A. Longo
James B. Moran
Alan I. Dunst
Kenneth J. Doukas, Jr.
Michael John Stone
Donald D. Davidson
Thaddeus J. Hubert, III
Joan Alster Weisblatt
Karen M. Buerle
Robert G. Kenny
Michael J. Baker
Andrew J. Carlowicz, Jr.
Gary J. Hoagland
Jeffrey S. Intravatola
Jamie D. Happas
Thomas J. Walsh, Jr.
Robert S. Helwig
Michael F. Dolan
Douglas M. Fasciale
Marc S. Gaffrey
John Charles Simons
Susan K. O'Connor
Stephen G. Perrella
Jacquelyn L. Poland
Douglas Susan
Patrick J. McDonald

OF COUNSEL

John J. Hoagland
Herman L. Breitkopf
Richard S. Cohen

ASSOCIATES

Andrew N. Kessler
John P. Barnes
Christopher M. Longo
Nancy A. Freedman
Tiffany C. Chong
Michael Dermody
Diane Hoagland
Michael T. Kearns
Keith C. Northridge
Andrew J. DiMarsico
Edward J. Rebenack
Paul N. Harris
Denis A. Gooding
Kevin J. Musiakiewicz
Michael N. Porter
Kenneth Sisco
M. Stephanie Beaty

Representative Clients: CNA/Continental Casualty; National Indemnity Company; Providence Washington Insurance Company; The Mutual Fire, Marine & Inland Insurance Company; INAPRO/CIGNA; Allstate Insurance Company; Home Depot; American Reliance Insurance Company; Shand, Morahan & Company; CPC International.

For full biographical listings, see the Martindale-Hubbell Law Directory

RIVER EDGE, Bergen Co.

PECKAR & ABRAMSON, A PROFESSIONAL CORPORATION (AV)

70 Grand Avenue, 07661
Telephone: 201-343-3434
Fax: 201-343-6306
Email: mail@pecklaw.com *URL:* http://www.pecklaw.com
New York, N.Y. Office: Peckar & Abramson, P.C., 1185 Avenue of the Americas.
Telephone: 212-382-0909.
Fax: 212-382-3456.
San Francisco, California Office: Peckar & Abramson, P.C., 601 Montgomery Street, Suite 325.
Telephone: 415-837-1968.
Fax: 415-837-1320.

Robert S. Peckar
Richard L. Abramson
Bruce D. Meller
Robert A. Drucker
Charles F. Kenny
Charles E. Williams, III (Not admitted in NJ)
Steven M. Charney
Howard M. Rosen (Not admitted in NJ)
Priscilla J. Triolo
Patrick J. Greene, Jr.
Raymond M. Buddie (Not admitted in NJ)
Roger S. Markowitz (Not admitted in NJ)
Gerard J. Onorata

Carlo J. Camporeale
Gregory H. Chertoff
Frank A. Hess (Not admitted in NJ)
Joseph J. Hocking
Craig B. Johnson
Jason A. Lazar
Lisa H. Lesser
Eugene J. McTague, Jr.
Marc A. Raso (Also at New York, N.Y. Office)
Lynn Daly Shavelson
Steven D. Sladkus
Linda A. Turteltaub
Alan Winkler
Orna Wolfzahn (Resident, New York, N.Y. Office)

OF COUNSEL

Laura S. Kirsch
Stephen R. Bosin

For full biographical listings, see the Martindale-Hubbell Law Directory

ROSELAND, Essex Co.

BRACH, EICHLER, ROSENBERG, SILVER, BERNSTEIN, HAMMER & GLADSTONE, A PROFESSIONAL CORPORATION (AV)

101 Eisenhower Parkway, 07068
Telephone: 973-228-5700
Telecopier: 973-228-7852
Email: law@bracheichler.com *URL:* http://www.bracheichler.com

Alan H. Bernstein
William L. Brach
Richard J. Driver
Burton L. Eichler
Alan S. Pralgever

Representative Clients: Bridgewater/Raritan Regional School District; Coastal Group, Inc.; Danella Contractors, Inc.; Davidoff of Geneva, Inc.; I. Heller Construction Co. Inc.; Kushner Companies; Sparta Steel Corporation; Glass Gardens ShopRite, Inc.; North Jersey District Water Supply Commission; Protameen Chemicals, Inc.

For Complete List of Firm Personnel, See General Section

For full biographical listings, see the Martindale-Hubbell Law Directory

SPRINGFIELD, Union Co.

HARDIN, KUNDLA, McKEON, POLETTO & POLIFRONI, P.A., A PROFESSIONAL CORPORATION (AV)

673 Morris Avenue, P.O. Box 730, 07081
Telephone: 973-912-5222
Fax: 973-912-9212
Email: info@HKMPP.com
New York, New York Office: 55 John Street, 10038.
Telephone: 212-571-0111.
Fax: 212-571-1117.

George R. Hardin
Robert L. Polifroni
Janet L. Poletto
Mark S. Kundla
John F. McKeon
James R. Greene
Nicea J. D'Annunzio
John Samuel Favate
Patrick J. Clare
Anna Marie Strand

Jeffrey A. Oshin
Joseph R. Lowicky
Tracy C. Forsyth
Joseph A. DeFuria
John G. Kilbride
Jeffrey H. Goldsmith
Jeffrey Roth
Nora J. Grimbergen
William C. Sullivan, Jr.
Paul Daly
V. Christopher Hirsch
Richard S. Reig
Sam A. Dotro
Brian K. Kaiser
David M. Steiner
Lani M. D'Agostino
Sheila A. Glackin
Michael S. Schwartz
Kirsten L. McCaw
Sanjoy Mukherjee
Louisa B. Sargent
Michael A. Cifelli
James J. A. Mulhall
Kevin M. Regan

(See Next Column)

HARDIN, KUNDLA, MCKEON, POLETTO & POLIFRONI, P.A. A PROFESSIONAL CORPORATION, *Springfield—Continued*

Lisa D. Chanel
Maria-Milagros Herrero
Brian A. King
Christina Fichera Dente
Andrea L. Strack
Roger J. Imhof
John P. Monaghan
Stephen J. Donahue
Cindy L. Thompson
Lisa A. Ganzhorn

Representative Clients: Crum & Forster Insurance; St. Paul Fire and Marine Insurance; Wausau Insurance Cos.; CNA Insurance; McDonald's Corp.; SSVK; Tarmac America.

For full biographical listings, see the Martindale-Hubbell Law Directory

*TRENTON,** Mercer Co.

NEEDELL, SIEKERKA & CASTELLANI, A PROFESSIONAL CORPORATION (AV)

Quakerbridge Commons, 2681 Quakerbridge Road, 08619-1625
Telephone: 609-584-7700
Fax: 609-584-0123
Email: nsclaw@aol.com

Stanley H. Needell
Michele N. Siekerka
Anthony P. Castellani

John M. Cinti
Dean C. Gresek

LEGAL SUPPORT PERSONNEL

PARALEGALS

Marlene Griesbach
Carolyn D. Shaw
Veronica A. Mitchell

For full biographical listings, see the Martindale-Hubbell Law Directory

WESTFIELD, Union Co.

LINDABURY, MCCORMICK & ESTABROOK, P.A. (AV)

53 Cardinal Drive, P.O. Box 2369, 07091
Telephone: 908-233-6800
Fax: 908-233-5078
New York, N.Y. Office: 26 Broadway, Suite 2300.
Telephone: 212-742-3390.
Fax: 212-269-5016.

Richard R. Width
Edward J. Frisch
Donald F. Nicolai
Bruce P. Ogden
Barry J. Donohue
Richard J. Cino

OF COUNSEL

Kenneth L. Estabrook

Representative Clients: Air Con, Inc.; American Subcontractors Association - New Jersey; Clinton Township Board of Education; DPIC Companies; Donald C. Rodner, Inc.; Elling Brothers; Great American Insurance Companies; Mechanical Contractors Association of America, Inc.; Mechanical Contractors Association of New Jersey; Thomas H. Barham Co., Inc.

For Complete List of Firm Personnel, See General Section

For full biographical listings, see the Martindale-Hubbell Law Directory

WOODBRIDGE, Middlesex Co.

DEUTCH & FALK, A PROFESSIONAL CORPORATION (AV)

843 Rahway Avenue, 07095-3699
Telephone: 732-636-4200
Fax: 732-636-3575
URL: http://www.deutchfalk.com
URL: http://www.lawyers.com/dflaw
Linden, New Jersey Office: 924 North Wood Avenue, Second Floor, 07036.
Telephone: 908-486-2422.
New York, N.Y. Office: 2 Pennsylvania Plaza, Suite 1910, 10121.
Telephone: 212-319-7332.

Victor A. Deutch
Kenneth B. Falk

John F. Kwasnik
Monica Kowalski

OF COUNSEL

Kenneth A. Wallach

Representative Clients: Electrical Design & Construction, Inc.; General Trading Company, Inc.; Hamilton & Co., Inc.; LRW Development Corporation; Parkview Villiage Condominium Owners'Association, Inc.; Ronson Corporation; Securitek International Corporation; Whitesville Business Park, Inc.; Woodbridge Investment Corp.

For full biographical listings, see the Martindale-Hubbell Law Directory

NEW MEXICO

*ALBUQUERQUE,** Bernalillo Co.

RODEY, DICKASON, SLOAN, AKIN & ROBB, P.A. (AV)

Albuquerque Plaza, Suite 2200, 201 Third Street, N.W., P.O. Box 1888, 87103-1888
Telephone: 505-765-5900
Fax: 505-768-7395
Email: info@rodey.com *URL:* http://www.rodey.com
Santa Fe, New Mexico Office: Suite 101 Marcy Plaza, 123 East Marcy Street, P.O. Box 1357, 87504-1357.
Telephone: 505-984-0100.
Fax: 505-989-9542.

John P. Burton (Resident, Santa Fe Office)
Jonathan W. Hewes
Travis R. Collier
Henry M. Bohnhoff
David W. Bunting

For Complete List of Firm Personnel, See General Section

For full biographical listings, see the Martindale-Hubbell Law Directory

NEW YORK

*ALBANY,** Albany Co.

COUCH WHITE, LLP (AV)

540 Broadway, P.O. Box 22222, 12201
Telephone: 518-426-4600
Telecopier: 518-426-0376
Email: CouchWhiteBrenn@Global2000.net *URL:* http://www.couchwhite.com
Washington, D.C. Office: 700 Thirteenth Street, N.W., Suite 950.
Telephone: 202-434-4503.
Fax: 202-434-4562.

MEMBERS OF FIRM

Leslie F. Couch
Algird F. White, Jr.
Barbara S. Brenner
Joel M. Howard, III
Paul A. Feigenbaum
Robert M. Loughney
Harold N. Iselin
Leonard H. Singer
Keith B. Rose
Christopher A. Cernik
Michael B. Mager
Mark F. Glaser
Pamela A. Madeiros
James J. Barriere
Doreen Unis Saia

SENIOR COUNSEL

Lawrence H. Cooke

ASSOCIATES

David G. Anderson
Tricia A. Asaro
James S. King
Marc A. Madia

For full biographical listings, see the Martindale-Hubbell Law Directory

ISEMAN, CUNNINGHAM, RIESTER & HYDE, LLP (AV)

9 Thurlow Terrace, 12203
Telephone: 518-462-3000
Telecopier: 518-462-4199
Email: lawfirm@icrh.com *URL:* http://www.icrh.com
Canandaigua, New York Office: 37 East Gibson Street, P.O. Box 179, 14424.
Telephone: 716-394-1450.
Fax: 716-394-5121.

MEMBERS OF FIRM

Frederick C. Riester
Michael J. Cunningham
Robert Hall Iseman
Carol Ann Hyde
Linda J. Clark

Brian M. Culnan
Kihyun S. Kim
Richard A. Frankel
Stephanie E. Moriarty
Valerie R. Lape Handy
Marcia B. Smith
Ellen Gillerman Cox
Jennifer A. Grego
Cara E. Johnson

OF COUNSEL

Michael J. McNeil
Deborah A. Kirby

For full biographical listings, see the Martindale-Hubbell Law Directory

ROCHE CORRIGAN MCCOY & BUSH (AV)

The Wilem Van Zandt Building, 36 South Pearl Street, 12207
Telephone: 518-436-9370
Fax: 518-436-8233

(See Next Column)

ROCHE CORRIGAN MCCOY & BUSH—*Continued*

MEMBERS OF FIRM

Robert P. Roche
Joseph M. McCoy
Peter J. Corrigan
Scott W. Bush

For full biographical listings, see the Martindale-Hubbell Law Directory

*BINGHAMTON,** Broome Co.

O'CONNOR, GACIOCH, POPE & TAIT, L.L.P. (AV)

One Marine Midland Plaza, East Tower-Seventh Floor, P.O. Box 1964, 13902
Telephone: 607-772-9262
Fax: 607-724-6002
Email: ogplaw@compuserve.com

Thomas F. O'Connor
Robert N. Nielsen, Jr.
James C. Gacioch
Stephen B. Atkinson
Alan J. Pope
Kurt D. Schrader
Jeffrey A. Tait
Richard M. Hill
Hugh B. Leonard
Patricia A. Cummings
Robert C. Murphy

OF COUNSEL

Walter T. Gorman
Cheryl Insinga

For full biographical listings, see the Martindale-Hubbell Law Directory

*BUFFALO,** Erie Co.

GRESENS & GILLEN LLP (AV)

510 Fleet Building, 12 Fountain Plaza, 14202-2292
Telephone: 716-842-1600
Fax: 716-842-6161
Email: greslaw@pcom.net *URL:* http://www.greslaw.com

James W. Gresens
Patricia Gillen

Andrew B. Isenberg
Peter L. Powers

For full biographical listings, see the Martindale-Hubbell Law Directory

ZDARSKY, SAWICKI & AGOSTINELLI (AV)

404 Cathedral Place, 298 Main Street, 14202
Telephone: 716-855-3200
Telecopier: 716-855-3101
Email: zsagtw@buffnet.net

MEMBERS OF FIRM

Joseph E. Zdarsky
Guy J. Agostinelli
K. Michael Sawicki
Gerald T. Walsh
Mark J. Schlant

ASSOCIATES

Patrick A. Dudley
John A. Moscati, Jr.

Reference: Marine Midland Bank, N.A.

For full biographical listings, see the Martindale-Hubbell Law Directory

GARDEN CITY, Nassau Co.

TRYON & ASSOCIATES, P.C. (AV)

1325 Franklin Avenue, Suite 325, P.O. Box 8022, 11530
Telephone: 516-746-3400
Fax: 516-746-5756
URL: http://www.lawyers.com/tryon&associates

Michael D. Tryon

Susan Marie Pascale

For full biographical listings, see the Martindale-Hubbell Law Directory

WESTERMANN HAMILTON & SHEEHY (AV)

Garden City Center, 100 Quentin Roosevelt Boulevard, Suite 205, 11530
Telephone: 516-794-7500
Telecopier: 516-794-1277
Saddle River, New Jersey Office: The Commons, Suite 6, 82 East Allendale Road, 07458.
Telephone: 201-995-0890.
Telecopier: 201-934-8681.

MEMBERS OF FIRM

David Westermann, Jr.
Christopher J. Sheehy
John F. Hamilton
George F. Mackey

ASSOCIATE

Christine A. Gormsen
Stacey M. Fleming

OF COUNSEL

Jeffrey B. Mulhall
Leonard M. Ridini, Jr.

For full biographical listings, see the Martindale-Hubbell Law Directory

*GOSHEN,** Orange Co.

NORTON & CHRISTENSEN (AV)

Goshen Executive Building, 60 Erie Street, P.O. Box 308, 10924
Telephone: 914-294-7949
Fax: 914-294-7791
Email: norchris@frontiernet.net
Rochelle Park, New Jersey Office: 151 West Passaic Street.
Telephone: 201-909-3735.
Fax: 201-368-2102.

MEMBERS OF FIRM

Stanley J. Norton (1916-1998)
Harold M. Pressberg
Henry N. Christensen, Jr.
Kenneth J. Frank

OF COUNSEL

John T. Mayo

For full biographical listings, see the Martindale-Hubbell Law Directory

*NEW YORK,** New York Co.

BERMAN, PALEY, GOLDSTEIN & KANNRY, LLP (AV)

500 Fifth Avenue, 10110
Telephone: 212-354-9600
Fax: 212-354-9873

Murray Tim Berman (1901-1991)

MEMBERS OF FIRM

Tony Berman
Robert G. Benisch
Alvin Goldstein
Howard Burger
Jack S. Kannry
Robert A. Banner

COUNSEL

David R. Paley

ASSOCIATES

Paul G. Monte
Darshan V. Patel
Saranjit S. Bindra

For full biographical listings, see the Martindale-Hubbell Law Directory

FISHER, FISHER & BERGER (AV)

A Partnership including a Professional Corporation
One Whitehall Street, 10004
Telephone: 212-514-8888
Fax: 212-514-9016
Email: fisherberger@earthlink.net

Andrew S. Fisher, P.C.
Henry T. Berger

ASSOCIATES

Melinda H. Vollmer
Eric L. Cooper
Diane C. Lorenc

OF COUNSEL

Harold L. Fisher
Robert A. Straniere
Judith E. Held
Stanley Kalmon Schlein
Gerald A. Resnick
Laurence J. Kaiser

Reference: The Chase Manhattan Bank, N.A.

For full biographical listings, see the Martindale-Hubbell Law Directory

INGRAM YUZEK GAINEN CARROLL & BERTOLOTTI, LLP (AV)

250 Park Avenue, 10177
Telephone: 212-907-9600
Facsimile: 212-907-9681

MEMBERS OF FIRM

Ernest J. Bertolotti (1942-1999)
Samuel W. Ingram, Jr.
Daniel L. Carroll
Paulette Kendler
Roger Cukras
Steven Mastbaum
David G. Ebert
Shane O'Neill
Larry F. Gainen
Dean G. Yuzek

ASSOCIATES

Warren E. Barrows
Jeanne F. Pucci
Amy Bertolotti
Leigh A. Roveda
Patricia Hewitt
Jennifer E. Schwartz
Theodore M. Kakoyiannis
Paul H. Slaney

OF COUNSEL

Karin J. Barkhorn
Mark E. Klein
Beverly L. Deickler
Paulette Lemay Peters
Cory L. Weiss

For full biographical listings, see the Martindale-Hubbell Law Directory

LEAHEY & JOHNSON, P.C. (AV)

Suite 2220, 120 Wall Street, 10005
Telephone: 212-269-7308
Facsimile: 212-422-4751
Email: Leaheylaw@Aol.com

(See Next Column)

LEAHEY & JOHNSON P.C., *New York—Continued*

Peter James Johnson
Peter James Johnson, Jr.
William G. Murphy
Kevin Brian Lynch

James P. Tenney
Steven Martin
William J. Gordon
Christopher Delamere Clarke
Vincent L. Gallo, Jr.
Joseph Francis Ferrette
Gregory Wilson
Michael Cannella
James Gerard Mcgovern
Nadine M. Duhamel
Sharon A. Toussaint
Melissa Ann Weinberg
Edward J. White
Daniel Michael Sullivan
Lennon C. Edwards
Carmen M. Vasquez
Eric L. Horn
Sean T. O'Leary (Not admitted in NY)

For full biographical listings, see the Martindale-Hubbell Law Directory

LONDON FISCHER LLP (AV)

59 Maiden Lane, 10038
Telephone: 212-972-1000
Facsimile: 212-972-1030
Email: Law@LondonFischer.com

MEMBERS OF FIRM

Bernard London
James L. Fischer
Daniel Zemann, Jr.
John E. Sparling
Richard S. Endres
Leah Campbell
Marvin B. Segal
James Walsh
Anthony F. Tagliagambe

For full biographical listings, see the Martindale-Hubbell Law Directory

MAZUR, CARP & RUBIN, P.C. (AV)

2 Park Avenue, 10016
Telephone: 212-686-7700
Telecopier: 212-532-1425
Email: mcrlaw@sprynet.com

Gerald I. Carp
Sayward Mazur
Gary L. Rubin
Ira M. Schulman

OF COUNSEL

Charles H. Weinberg

Thomas G. Draper, Jr.
Richard Raab
Frank L. Wagner

For full biographical listings, see the Martindale-Hubbell Law Directory

OTTERBOURG, STEINDLER, HOUSTON & ROSEN, P.C. (AV)

230 Park Avenue, 29th Floor, 10169
Telephone: 212-661-9100
Telecopier: 212-682-6104

Donald N. Gellert
Daniel Wallen
Anthony M. Piccione
Richard G. Haddad

GENERAL COUNSEL

Kurt J. Wolff

Lloyd M. Green

For Complete List of Firm Personnel, See General Section

For full biographical listings, see the Martindale-Hubbell Law Directory

PLUNKETT & JAFFE, P.C. (AV)

230 Park Avenue, Suite 1847, 10169
Telephone: 212-922-1800
Facsimile: 212-922-1819
Email: plunkettjaffe.com
White Plains, New York Office: 1 North Broadway.
Telephone: 914-948-7722.
Facsimile: 914-948-7603.
Albany, New York Office: 111 Washington Avenue.
Telephone: 518-462-1800.
Facsimile: 518-462-4875.

Kevin J. Plunkett
Justin E. Driscoll, III

For Complete List of Firm Personnel, See General Section

For full biographical listings, see the Martindale-Hubbell Law Directory

POSTNER & RUBIN (AV)

17 Battery Place, 10004
Telephone: 212-269-2510
Fax: 212-425-0968
Email: postner@aol.com
Holmdel, New Jersey Office: 42 West Main Street,
Telephone: 732-946-9001.
Fax: 732-946-9005.

(See Next Column)

Robert A. Rubin
William J. Postner
Robert J. MacPherson
Jeffrey R. Cruz

ASSOCIATES

Patricia M. Caplicki
Dana Wordes
Michael W. Bautz

NEW JERSEY RESIDENT COUNSEL

Sarah B. Biser

For full biographical listings, see the Martindale-Hubbell Law Directory

ROSS & COHEN, LLP (AV)

711 Third Avenue, 10017
Telephone: 212-370-1200
Telecopier: 212-370-0334
Email: law@rosscohen.com

MEMBERS OF FIRM

Allen Ross
Frederick S. Cohen
Dennis A. Konner
Charles Fastenberg
Michael A. Mulqueen
Mark Canizio
Michael L. Chartan
John S. Wojak, Jr.
Gerard J. Romski

ASSOCIATES

Midge J. Nutman
Andrew L. Richards
Lawrence Chiarelli
Jose A. Aquino
Frank X. Acocella
David A. Etkind
Lori Marks
Gregory J. Colao (Not admitted in NY)

OF COUNSEL

Irwin M. Echtman
Kenneth H. Lazaruk

For full biographical listings, see the Martindale-Hubbell Law Directory

SACKS MONTGOMERY, P.C. (AV)

800 Third Avenue, 10022
Telephone: 212-355-4660
Telecopier: 212-593-7257
Email: sm@sacksmontgomery.com
Westport, Connecticut Office: Sacks, Montgomery, Pastore & Levine, P.C., 1071 Post Road East, Suite 3.
Telephone: 203-291-6844.

Harry P. Sacks
David E. Montgomery
Stuart M. Levine (Resident, Westport, Connecticut Office)
Jeffrey A. Aronson
Frederick R. Rohn
Scott D. St. Marie
Stephen A. Stallings

Thomas F. Giordano
Amy S. Cohen
Kathleen M. Fay

OF COUNSEL

Steven J. Brill

For full biographical listings, see the Martindale-Hubbell Law Directory

WAGNER, DAVIS & GOLD, P.C. (AV)

99 Madison Avenue, 10016
Telephone: 212-481-9600
Telefax: 212-481-8245

Steven R. Wagner
Ronald Jay Gold
John R. Wagner
Bonnie Reid Berkow
William R. Fried

OF COUNSEL

Deborah Lynn Davis

Adam D. Finkelstein
Keith L. Woodside
Robert J. Patchen
Glen C. Rosenberg
Mikelle V. Lipsius (Not admitted in NY)

LEGAL SUPPORT PERSONNEL

Nicole J. Ottley (Paralegal)
Steven Henderson (Paralegal)
Tracey A. Lewis (Paralegal)
Karen Chin (Paralegal)
Daniel E. Glatter (Law Clerk)

For full biographical listings, see the Martindale-Hubbell Law Directory

WHITE, FLEISCHNER & FINO (AV)

140 Broadway, 10005
Telephone: 212-487-9700
Telecopier: 212-487-9777
Email: infor@wff-law.com
Red Bank, New Jersey Office: 272 Broad Street.
Telephone: 732-530-7787.
Telecopier: 732-530-8552.

(See Next Column)

WHITE, FLEISCHNER & FINO—*Continued*

MEMBERS OF FIRM

Patti F. Potash | Wendy K. Carrano

Representative Clients: Wausau Insurance Companies; Island Construction Company; Kemper Insurance Company; CNA Insurance Company; Interstate Insurance Company; Gerling Insurance Company; Lloyd's Syndicates; Fireman's Fund Insurance Company.

For Complete List of Firm Personnel, See General Section

For full biographical listings, see the Martindale-Hubbell Law Directory

*POUGHKEEPSIE,** Dutchess Co.

LEWIS & GREER, P.C. (AV)

11 Raymond Avenue, P.O. Box 2990, 12603
Telephone: 914-454-1200
Telecopier: 914-454-3315
Email: info@lewisgreer.com *URL:* http://www.lewisgreer.com

Lou Lewis
J. Scott Greer
Michael J. Englert

Daniel P. Adams
Veronica A. McMillan

For full biographical listings, see the Martindale-Hubbell Law Directory

*ROCHESTER,** Monroe Co.

ERNSTROM & DRESTE, LLP (AV)

Crossbridge Office Park, 2000 Winton Road South Building One, Suite 300, 14618-3922
Telephone: 716-473-3100
Fax: 716-473-3113
URL: http://www.ernstromdreste.com
New York, N.Y. Office: 317 Madison Avenue, Suite 703, 10017-5201.
Telephone: 212-687-0303.
Fax: 212-687-1597.

MEMBERS OF FIRM

J. William Ernstrom
John W. Dreste
Theodore M. B. Baum
Todd R. Braggins

ASSOCIATES

Martha A. Connolly
Kevin F. Peartree
Michael F. Dehmler

COUNSEL

William E. Brueckner, III
Michael E. O'Neill

For full biographical listings, see the Martindale-Hubbell Law Directory

ROCKVILLE CENTRE, Nassau Co.

GOLDBERG & CONNOLLY (AV)

66 North Village Avenue, 11570
Telephone: 516-764-2800; 718-343-6340
Telecopier: 516-764-2827
Email: email@goldbergconnolly.com

MEMBERS OF FIRM

David Goldberg (1914-1988)
Henry L. Goldberg
Janet M. Connolly
David E. Wolff

ASSOCIATES

Robert C. Buff
Robert J. Fryman
Debra J. Hopke
Michael F. Kuzow
Ralph Pernick
C. Allan Reeve
Carl A. Haberbusch
Robert L. Underberg

OF COUNSEL

Michael J. Hogan
Norman A. Steiger
Eugene Drexler

For full biographical listings, see the Martindale-Hubbell Law Directory

*SYRACUSE,** Onondaga Co.

SUGARMAN, WALLACE, MANHEIM & SCHOENWALD (AV)

HSBC Center, Fifth Floor, 360 South Warren Street, 13202-2680
Telephone: 315-474-2943
Fax: 315-474-0235
URL: http://www.sugarmanlaw.com
Buffalo Office: 1720 Rand Building, 14 Lafayette Square, 14203.
Telephone: 716-847-2523.
Fax: 716-847-2589.

MEMBERS OF FIRM

George E. DeMore
James G. Stevens, Jr.
Samuel Vulcano

Representative Clients: Allstate Insurance Co.; CNA Insurance Companies; Chubb & Son; Liberty Mutual Insurance Co.; Carpenter Manufacturing Co., Inc.; General Accident Group; Hartford Accident & Indemnity Co.; Firemans Fund; New York Central Mutual; Progressive Insurance Co.
Reference: HSBC.

For full biographical listings, see the Martindale-Hubbell Law Directory

*WHITE PLAINS,** Westchester Co.

BOEGGEMAN, GEORGE, HODGES & CORDE, P.C. (AV)

11 Martine Avenue, 10606
Telephone: 914-761-2252
Telecopier: 914-761-5211
Email: boeggeman@bghc-law.com *URL:* http://www.bghc-law.com
Albany, New York Office: 46 Columbia Street, 12207-2716.
Telephone: 518-465-1100.
Fax: 518-465-1800.

George S. Hodges
Richard G. Corde
John J. Walsh, II
Harold L. Moroknek
Robert S. Ondrovic
Thomas A. Sica (Resident Managing Attorney, Albany Office)

Karen A.D. Jockimo
William M. Wingertzahn
Elizabeth C. Mirisola
Cynthia Dolan
Marcella M. Green
Paul A. Hurley
Leslie K. Arfine
John T. Holden
James J. Lofrese
Jeanne M. Hurley
Ira H. Lapp
Matt Randolph Belkin
Cynthia K. Messemer

OF COUNSEL

Joseph H. George
John E. Boeggeman (1919-1993)

Representative Clients: American Telephone & Telegraph; Anheuser-Busch Companies, Inc.; Lowe's Home Centers; Great Atlantic & Pacific Tea Company; Reliance National Insurance Company; Metropolitan Property & Casualty Insurance Company; Fisher Price, Inc.; CGU Insurance Company; United Services Automobile Association; New York Central Mutual Fire Insurance Company.

For full biographical listings, see the Martindale-Hubbell Law Directory

NORTH CAROLINA

*CHARLOTTE,** Mecklenburg Co.

BLAIR CONAWAY BOGRAD & MARTIN, P.A.

(See Shumaker, Loop & Kendrick, LLP)

JOHNSTON, ALLISON & HORD, P.A. (AV)

610 East Morehead Street, P.O. Box 36469, 28236
Telephone: 704-332-1181
Fax: 704-376-1628
Email: jahlaw.com *URL:* http://www.jahlaw.com

James W. Allison
Robert L. Burchette
Greg C. Ahlum
Alice Keith Moore
Gary J. Welch

Brian K. Fielden
Michael L. Wilson
Kenneth T. Lautenschlager
Alicia Almeida Bowers
Russell D. Babb

Representative Clients: F.N. Thompson Co.; Carolinas Associated General Contractors; Crowder Construction Co.; Rodgers Builders, Inc; Gilbane Building Company; Geupel DeMars, Inc.; Hepaco, Inc.; S.C. Hondros & Associates, Inc.; David M. Sidbury, Inc.; Hickory Construction Co.

For Complete List of Firm Personnel, See General Section

For full biographical listings, see the Martindale-Hubbell Law Directory

WOMBLE CARLYLE SANDRIDGE & RICE (AV)

A Professional Limited Liability Company
3300 One First Union Center, 301 South College Street, 28202-6025
Telephone: 704-331-4900
Fax: 704-331-4955
Email: lawyers@wcsr.com *URL:* http://www.wcsr.com
Winston-Salem, North Carolina Office: 200 West Second Street, P.O. Drawer 84.
Telephone: 336-721-3600.
Fax: 336-721-3660.
Raleigh, North Carolina Office: 2100 First Union Capitol Center, 150 Fayetteville Street Mall, P.O. Box 831.
Telephone: 919-755-2100.
Fax: 919-755-2150.
Research Triangle Park, North Carolina Office: 2505 Meridian Parkway, Suite 300 (Durham), 27713.
Telephone: 919-484-2300.
Fax: 919-484-2340.
Atlanta, Georgia Office: One Atlantic Center, 1201 West Peachtree Street, Suite 3500.
Telephone: 404-872-7000.
Fax: 404-888-7490.

(See Next Column)

WOMBLE CARLYLE SANDRIDGE & RICE, *Charlotte—Continued*

Other Atlanta, Georgia Office: Suite 404, 2296 Henderson Mill Road, N.E.
Telephone: 770-492-9030.
Fax: 770-492-9609.
Washington, D.C. Office: 1120 Nineteenth Street, N.W., Eighth Floor.
Telephone: 202-857-4400.
Fax: 202-467-6910.
Greenville, South Carolina Office: 15 South Main Street, Suite 601, P.O. Box 10208.
Telephone: 864-255-5400.
Fax: 864-255-5440.

RESIDENT MEMBERS

Timothy G. Barber
Jim D. Cooley
Mark P. Henriques

Representative Clients: Childress Klein Properties, Inc.; Food Lion, Inc.; J.A. Jones Construction Co.; Parkdale Mills, Inc.; Pillowtex; Duke Power Co.; Bowles Hollowell Conner & Co.; ALLTEL Carolina, Inc.; Belk Store Services, Inc.; Philip Holzmann A.G.

For Complete List of Firm Personnel, See General Section

For full biographical listings, see the Martindale-Hubbell Law Directory

*DURHAM,** Durham Co.

DAILEY J. DERR, P.A. (AV)

3622 Lyckan Parkway, Suite 4005, P.O. Box 51266, 27717
Telephone: 919-493-5500
Fax: 919-493-5054

Dailey J. Derr

Representative Clients: Briggs Acoustical & Flooring, Inc.; Brown Brothers Plumbing and Heating Co., Inc.; Century Guild (The), Inc.; Duane K. Stewart & Associates, Inc.; Ellerbe Becket, Inc.; Outdoor Lighting, Inc.; Right-Way Construction Co., Inc.; Tai and Associates; Tar Heel Inspection Services, Inc.; Tops Petroleum Corp.; Triangle Surveyors, Inc.

For full biographical listings, see the Martindale-Hubbell Law Directory

HAYES HOFLER & ASSOCIATES, P.A. (AV)

1007 Vickers Avenue, 27707-1355
Telephone: 919-682-9663
Fax: 919-682-2016

R. Hayes Hofler

OF COUNSEL

Daniel B. Hill

For full biographical listings, see the Martindale-Hubbell Law Directory

*RALEIGH,** Wake Co.

JORDAN PRICE WALL GRAY JONES & CARLTON (AV)

A Professional Limited Liability Company
225 Hillsborough Street, 200 Hillsborough Place, P.O. Box 2021, 27602
Telephone: 919-828-2501; 919-831-4462
Telecopier: 919-834-8447
Email: law@jordanprice.com

MEMBERS OF FIRM

Robert R. Price
Joseph E. Wall
R. Frank Gray
Henry W. Jones, Jr.
Paul T. Flick
Terry J. Carlton
Hope Derby Carmichael

ASSOCIATES

Stephen R. Dolan
Shawna Y. Staton
Jonathan P. Carr
C. Marshall Lindsay
Christopher G. Lewis
Emily W. Eisele
Chad R. Clapp

OF COUNSEL

John R. Jordan, Jr.
Karen Kelly Carlton

Representative Clients: Carolinas Electrical Contractors Association; North Carolina Association of Plumbing-Heating-Cooling Contractors; Carolinas Chapter, American Fire Sprinkler Contractors Association; WATCO Corporation; Triangle Mechanical Contractor, Inc.; Brown Brothers Plumbing and Heating Co.; Climate Control, Inc.; J.M. Thompson, Inc.
Reference: First Citizens Bank & Trust Co., Raleigh, North Carolina.

For full biographical listings, see the Martindale-Hubbell Law Directory

LEWIS & ROBERTS, P.L.L.C. (AV)

1305 Navaho Drive, Suite 400, 27609-7482
Telephone: 919-981-0191
888-981-0939
Facsimile: 919-981-0199
Mailing Address: P.O. Box 17529, Raleigh, N.C., 27619-7529
Rock Hill, South Carolina Office: 448 Lakeshore Parkway, Suite 200.
Telephone: 803-324-8118.
Facsimile: 803-324-2093.

(See Next Column)

Richard M. Lewis
James A. Roberts, III
Steven M. Rudisill (Resident, Rock Hill, South Carolina Office)
Winston L. Page, Jr.
Timothy S. Riordan
Jack Spain Holmes
Daniel K. Bryson
John D. Elvers
A. Graham Shirley
Brian D. Lake
John H. Ruocchio
Robert L. Pratt
Garth Hinsdale White (Resident, Rock Hill, South Carolina Office)
Devin Ferree Thomas
James T. Johnson
Daniel T. Tower

For full biographical listings, see the Martindale-Hubbell Law Directory

WOMBLE CARLYLE SANDRIDGE & RICE (AV)

A Professional Limited Liability Company
2100 First Union Capitol Center, 150 Fayetteville Street Mall, P.O. Box 831, 27602
Telephone: 919-755-2100
Fax: 919-755-2150
Email: lawyers@wcsr.com *URL:* http://www.wcsr.com
Charlotte, North Carolina Office: 3300 One First Union Center, 301 South College Street.
Telephone: 704-331-4900.
Fax: 704-331-4955.
Winston-Salem, North Carolina Office: 200 West Second Street, P.O. Drawer 84.
Telephone: 336-721-3600.
Fax: 336-721-3660.
Research Triangle Park, North Carolina Office: 2505 Meridian Parkway, Suite 300 (Durham), 27713.
Telephone: 919-484-2300.
Fax: 919-484-2340.
Atlanta, Georgia Office: One Atlantic Center, 1201 West Peachtree Street, Suite 3500.
Telephone: 404-872-7000.
Fax: 404-888-7490.
Other Atlanta, Georgia Office: Suite 404, 2296 Henderson Mill Road, N.E.
Telephone: 770-492-9030.
Fax: 770-492-9609.
Washington, D.C. Office: 1120 Nineteenth Street, N.W., Eighth Floor.
Telephone: 202-857-4400.
Fax: 202-467-6910.
Greenville, South Carolina Office: 15 South Main Street, Suite 601, P.O. Box 10208.
Telephone: 864-255-5400.
Fax: 864-255-5440.

RESIDENT MEMBERS

Donald A. Donadio
Robert H. Sasser, III

Representative Clients: Aetna Casualty and Surety Co., Inc.; ALSCO/AmeriMark Building Products, Inc.; Aoki Corporation America, Inc.; Hackney Brothers, Inc.; Lawyers Mutual Liability Insurance Company of North Carolina; Meredith College; Regency Park Corp.; Wachovia Bank, N.A.

For Complete List of Firm Personnel, See General Section

For full biographical listings, see the Martindale-Hubbell Law Directory

*WILMINGTON,** New Hanover Co.

SHIPMAN & ASSOCIATES, L.L.P. (AV)

11 South Fifth Avenue, 28401
Telephone: 910-762-1990
Fax: 910-762-6752
Email: shipman-associates@orotech.com

MEMBER OF FIRM

Gary K. Shipman

ASSOCIATES

Carl W. Thurman, III
C. Wes Hodges, II
Jennifer Jernigan Slusser

For full biographical listings, see the Martindale-Hubbell Law Directory

*WINSTON-SALEM,** Forsyth Co.

BENNETT & GUTHRIE, P.L.L.C. (AV)

3334 Healy Drive, Suite 203, 27103-1476
Telephone: 336-765-3121
Fax: 336-765-8622

Richard V. Bennett
Rodney A. Guthrie
Stanley P. Dean

Kevin J. Williams

Representative Clients: American Continental Insurance Company; Commercial Union Insurance Company; Integon Insurance; Kentucky Medical Insurance Company; Medtronic, Inc.; Montgomery Mutual Insurance Company; Novant Health, Inc.; Pennsylvania Lumberman's Mutual Insurance Company; St. Paul Fire & Marine Insurance Company; Zurich Insurance Company.

(See Next Column)

BENNETT & GUTHRIE P.L.L.C.—*Continued*

For full biographical listings, see the Martindale-Hubbell Law Directory

WOMBLE CARLYLE SANDRIDGE & RICE (AV)

A Professional Limited Liability Company
200 West Second Street, P.O. Drawer 84, 27102
Telephone: 336-721-3600
Fax: 336-721-3660
Email: lawyers@wcsr.com *URL:* http://www.wcsr.com
Charlotte, North Carolina Office: 3300 One First Union Center, 301 South College Street.
Telephone: 704-331-4900.
Fax: 704-331-4955.
Raleigh, North Carolina Office: 2100 First Union Capitol Center, 150 Fayetteville Street Mall, P.O. Box 831.
Telephone: 919-755-2100.
Fax: 919-755-2150.
Research Triangle Park, North Carolina Office: 2505 Meridian Parkway, Suite 300 (Durham), 27713.
Telephone: 919-484-2300.
Fax: 919-484-2340.
Atlanta, Georgia Office: One Atlantic Center, 1201 West Peachtree Street, Suite 3500.
Telephone: 404-872-7000.
Fax: 404-888-7490.
Other Atlanta, Georgia Office: Suite 404, 2296 Henderson Mill Road, N.E.
Telephone: 770-492-9030.
Fax: 770-492-9609.
Washington, D.C. Office: 1120 Nineteenth Street, N.W., Eighth Floor.
Telephone: 202-857-4400.
Fax: 202-467-6910.
Greenville, South Carolina Office: 15 South Main Street, Suite 601, P.O. Box 10208.
Telephone: 864-255-5400.
Fax: 864-255-5440.

RESIDENT MEMBERS

Conrad C. Baldwin, Jr. — Karen Estelle Carey
Keith A. Clinard

RESIDENT ASSOCIATE

Kenneth R. Michael

Representative Clients: Brad Ragan, Inc.; Brenner Companies; Food Lion, Inc.; Hanes Companies, Inc.; North Carolina Baptist Hospitals, Inc.; R.J. Reynolds Tobacco Co.; Thomasville Furniture Industries, Inc.; Wachovia Corp.; Wake Forest University.

For Complete List of Firm Personnel, See General Section

For full biographical listings, see the Martindale-Hubbell Law Directory

OHIO

*AKRON,** Summit Co.

FORTNEY & KLINGSHIRN (AV)

100 Commonwealth Square, 300 North Cleveland-Massillon Road, 44333-2484
Telephone: 330-665-5445
Telefax: 330-665-5446
URL: http://www.fklaborlaw.com

Michael L. Fortney — Neil E. Klingshirn

For full biographical listings, see the Martindale-Hubbell Law Directory

*CLEVELAND,** Cuyahoga Co.

BAKER & HOSTETLER LLP (AV)

3200 National City Center, 1900 East Ninth Street, 44114-3485
Telephone: 216-621-0200
Telecopier: 216-696-0740
TWX: 810 421 8375
RCA Telex: 215032
To contact an attorney on the Internet use first initial and surname followed by @baker-hostetler.com
URL: http://www.bakerlaw.com
In Cincinnati, Ohio: 312 Walnut Street, Suite 2650.
Telephone: 513-929-3400.
In Columbus, Ohio: Capitol Square, Suite 2100, 65 East State Street.
Telephone: 614-228-1541.
In Denver, Colorado: 303 East 17th Avenue, Suite 1100.
Telephone: 303-861-0600.
In Houston, Texas: 1000 Louisiana, Suite 2000.
Telephone: 713-751-1600.
In Beverly Hills, California: 9150 Wilshire Boulevard, Suite 205.
Telephone: 310-385-7500.
In Long Beach, California: 300 Oceangate, Suite 620.
Telephone: 562-432-2827.

(See Next Column)

In Los Angeles, California: 600 Wilshire Boulevard.
Telephone: 213-624-2400.
In Orlando, Florida: SunBank Center, Suite 2300, 200 South Orange Avenue.
Telephone: 407-649-4000.
In Washington, D.C.: Washington Square, Suite 1100, 1050 Connecticut Avenue, N.W.
Telephone: 202-861-1500.

PARTNERS

Elliot Stephen Azoff — Lawrence V. Lindberg
Diane P. Chapman — Thomas R. Lucchesi
José C. Feliciano — Thomas H. Shunk
Randall L. Solomon

For Complete List of Firm Personnel, See General Section

For full biographical listings, see the Martindale-Hubbell Law Directory

JANIK & FORBES (AV)

Building Two, 8223 Brecksville Road, 44141-1371
Telephone: 440-838-7600
Fax: 440-838-7601

MEMBER OF FIRM

Steven G. Janik

For Complete List of Firm Personnel, See General Section

For full biographical listings, see the Martindale-Hubbell Law Directory

RODGERS AND CO., L.P.A. (AV)

1750 Guildhall, Landmark Office Towers, 45 Prospect Avenue, West, 44115
Telephone: 216-861-6191
Fax: 216-861-4699
Email: attys@rodgers-lpa.com

Walter A. Rodgers

Jeffrey M. Elzeer — Shawn A. Cormier

For full biographical listings, see the Martindale-Hubbell Law Directory

*COLUMBUS,** Franklin Co.

BRICKER & ECKLER LLP (AV)

100 South Third Street, 43215-4291
Telephone: 614-227-2300
Telecopy: 614-227-2390
Email: info@be.bricker.com *URL:* http://www.bricker.com

Elbert J. Kram — Luther L. Liggett, Jr.
Michael S. Holman — Jack R. Rosati

Sylvia Lynn Gillis — Warren I. Grody
Kimberly J. Brown — Maureen P. Taylor

Representative Clients: NECA, Ohio Conference; Turner Construction Co.; Consulting Engineers Council of Ohio; NBBJ; Lakota Local School District; Ohio Roofing Contractors Assn.; Complete General Construction Company; Indiana Kentucky Ohio Concrete Pipe Association; Julian Speer Companies; Hanlin Rainaldi Construction Co.

For Complete List of Firm Personnel, See General Section

For full biographical listings, see the Martindale-Hubbell Law Directory

KEGLER, BROWN, HILL & RITTER (AV)

Capitol Square Suite 1800, 65 East State Street, 43215-4294
Telephone: 614-462-5400
Telecopier: 614-464-2634
Cable Address: "Law KBHR"
Telex: 246671
Email: info@kbhr.com *URL:* http://www.kbhr.com
Marion, Ohio Office: 250 Executive Drive, Suite B, P.O. Box 919.
Telephone: 614-387-3501.
Facsimile: 614-387-3630.

Stephen E. Chappelear — Gene W. Holliker
Donald W. Gregory — Ronald L. Mason
Richard W. Schuermann, Jr.

Patrick M. O'Neill — Christopher J. Weber
Anthony C. White

Representative Clients: American Subcontractors Association; Associated Builders and Contractors; Danis Industries, Inc.; George J. Igel Co.; Lincoln Construction, Inc.; Presidential Construction, Inc.; S.G. Loewendick & Sons, Inc.; The Ohio State University.

For Complete List of Firm Personnel, See General Section

For full biographical listings, see the Martindale-Hubbell Law Directory

Columbus—Continued

McNamara and McNamara (AV)

Suite 1250, 88 East Broad Street, 43215-3558
Telephone: 614-228-6131
FAX: 614-228-6126

MEMBERS OF FIRM

J. Paul McNamara (1908-1994)
John J. Petro
John L. Miller
William H. Woods
Lisa Weekley Coulter

ASSOCIATE

Jonathan M. Bryan

OF COUNSEL

Dennis D. Liston
Keith McNamara

References: BancOhio National Bank; The City National Bank & Trust Co.; Huntington National Bank.

For full biographical listings, see the Martindale-Hubbell Law Directory

Postlewaite & Jordan (AV)

3040 Riverside Drive, Suite 122, 43221
Telephone: 614-486-2111
Fax: 614-486-8943

Charles C. Postlewaite
Jeffrey H. Jordan

ASSOCIATE

Holly N. Wolf

For full biographical listings, see the Martindale-Hubbell Law Directory

Schottenstein, Zox & Dunn A Legal Professional Association (AV)

The Huntington Center, 41 South High Street, 43215
Telephone: 614-462-2700
Telecopier: 614-462-5135
Telex: 650 24 444 365
URL: http://www.szd.com
Cincinnati, Ohio Office: Bank One Towers, 8044 Montgomery Road, Suite 700, 45236-2926.
Telephone: 513-792-2730.
Cleveland, Ohio Office: One Cleveland Center, 1375 East 9th Street, Suite 950.
Telephone: 216-621-6501.
Fax: 216-621-6502.

John P. Gilligan
Roger L. Sabo
Michael D. Tarullo
Corey V. Crognale
Patrick A. Devine
Joanne I. Goldhand

Stephen R. Kleinman
Mary Frances Geswein
Stephen Withee

OF COUNSEL

Kristopher M. Huelsman

Reference: Bank One of Columbus, N.A.

For Complete List of Firm Personnel, See General Section

For full biographical listings, see the Martindale-Hubbell Law Directory

*DAYTON,** Montgomery Co.

Freund, Freeze & Arnold A Legal Professional Association (AV)

Suite 1800 One Dayton Centre, One South Main Street, 45402-2017
Telephone: 937-222-2424
Telecopier: 937-222-5369
Email: ffalawda@ffalaw.com *URL:* http://www.ffalaw.com
Cincinnati, Ohio Office: 8805 Governor's Hill Drive, Suite 300, 45249-3313.
Telephone: 513-583-3700.
FAX: 513-583-3703. Email: ffalawci@ffalaw.com.

Stephen V. Freeze
Gordon D. Arnold
Stephen C. Findley
Scott F. McDaniel
John G. Witherspoon, Jr.
Shawn M. Blatt
Kevin C. Connell

Local Counsel for: Auto-Owners Insurance Co.; CNA Insurance Co.; Crum and Foster Underwriters; Employers Reinsurance Corp.; Farmers Insurance Group; Midwestern Group; Motorists Mutual Ins.; State Farm Mutual Automobile Insurance Co.

For full biographical listings, see the Martindale-Hubbell Law Directory

*TOLEDO,** Lucas Co.

Shumaker, Loop & Kendrick, LLP (AV)

North Courthouse Square, 1000 Jackson, 43624-1573
Telephone: 419-241-9000
Fax: 419-241-6894
Tampa, Florida Office: Barnett Plaza, Suite 2800, 101 East Kennedy Boulevard, 33602-5151,
Telephone: 813-229-7600.
Fax: 813-229-1660.
Charlotte, North Carolina Office: 128 South Tryon Street, Suite 1800, 28202.
Telephone: 704-375-0057.
Fax: 704-332-1197.
Columbus, Ohio Office: Huntington Center, 41 South High Street, Suite 2210, 43215.
Telephone: 614-463-9441.
Fax: 614-463-1108.

MEMBERS OF FIRM

John C. Barron
Larry A. Becker
Edward Bograd (Resident, Charlotte, North Carolina Office)
Aleta M. Bonini
Michael E. Born (Resident, Columbus, Ohio Office)
Michael M. Briley
Eric D. Britton
John H. Burson
C. Philip Campbell, Jr. (Resident, Tampa, Florida Office)
Philip S. Chubb (Resident, Charlotte, North Carolina Office)
David Harris Conaway (Resident, Charlotte, North Carolina Office)
Thomas A. Cotter (Resident, Tampa, Florida Office)
Marlene (Neema) M. Cottrill-Bell
David J. Coyle
Jeffrey S. Creamer
William E. Curphey (Resident, Tampa, Florida Office)
Joseph A. D'Amico (Resident, Charlotte, North Carolina Office)
Diane Vulich Davis
Terrance K. Davis
Scott G. Deller
Gary R. Diesing
Thomas P. Dillon
Victoria J. Elliot (Resident, Tampa, Florida Office)
Edwin G. Emerson
William G. Fischer
Vivian C. Folk
Jeffrey E. Fort
Jack G. Fynes
Marc Gertner
Bruce H. Gordon (Resident, Tampa, Florida Office)
William H. Gosline
Kevin H. Graham (Resident, Tampa, Florida Office)
David M. Grogan (Resident, Charlotte, North Carolina Office)
Douglas G. Haynam
John F. Hayward
William H. Heywood, III
John W. Hilbert, II
Charles W. Hiller
John S. Inglis (Resident, Tampa, Florida Office)
Regina M. Joseph
Robert A. Koenig
Kathleen A. Kress
Gregory T. Lodge
Oksana M. Ludd
Moses Luski (Resident, Charlotte, North Carolina Office)
Paul R. Lynch (Resident, Tampa, Florida Office)
John N. MacKay
Maria Maistrellis (Resident, Tampa, Florida Office)
Bentford E. Martin (Resident, Charlotte, North Carolina Office)
Timothy C. McCarthy
Susan D. McClay
Michael S. McGowan
Brian N. McMahon
William H. McNair (Resident, Charlotte, North Carolina Office)
Donald M. Mewhort, Jr.
Jeffrey H. Miller
Richard A. Mitchell
Michael J. O'Callaghan (Resident, Columbus, Ohio Office)
Barbara R. Pankau (Resident, Tampa, Florida Office)
William L. Patberg
Mary Ellen Pisanelli
Thomas G. Pletz
David J. Rectenwald
Cynthia L. Rerucha
Edward J. Richardson (Resident, Tampa, Florida Office)
Joseph A. Rideout
Stephen A. Rothschild
Michael G. Sanderson
Rolf H. Scheidel
Steven G. Schember (Resident, Tampa, Florida Office)
Gregory S. Shumaker
John J. Siciliano
Peter R. Silverman
Joseph S. Simpson
Darrell C. Smith (Resident, Tampa, Florida Office)
Lyman F. Spitzer
Harry J. Stathopoulos (Resident, Charlotte, North Carolina Office)
Mark C. Stewart
John L. Straub
William H. Sturges (Resident, Charlotte, North Carolina Office)
John B. Taylor (Resident, Charlotte, North Carolina Office)
W. Thompson Thorn, III (Resident, Tampa, Florida Office)
Louis E. Tosi
Michael T. Trocke (Resident, Tampa, Florida Office)
Barton L. Wagenman
David F. Waterman
Thomas I. Webb, Jr.
David W. Wicklund
Dennis P. Witherell
Thomas M. Wood (Resident, Tampa, Florida Office)
Kathryn J. Woodward
Gregory C. Yadley (Resident, Tampa, Florida Office)

(See Next Column)

SHUMAKER, LOOP & KENDRICK LLP—*Continued*

ASSOCIATES

M. Scott Aubry
Stacy Solochek Beckman (Resident, Columbus, Ohio Office)
Jenifer A. Belt
Stefanie E. Berk
Eileen M. Best
Kathleen M. Bickelhaupt (Resident, Tampa, Florida Office)
C. Graham Carothers, Jr. (Resident, Tampa, Florida Office)
Mark A. Catchur (Resident, Tampa, Florida Office)
Emily K. Cooper
Julio C. Esquivel (Resident, Tampa, Florida Office)
Sharon M. Fulop
Tammy N. Giroux (Resident, Tampa, Florida Office)
Daniel R. Hansen (Resident, Charlotte, North Carolina Office)
D. Scott Harves
W. Reed Hauptman
Lynn M. Hoover
John V. Ivsan
Ernest J. Marquart (Resident, Tampa, Florida Office)
Darrick M Mix
Daniel G. Musca (Resident, Tampa, Florida Office)
Christian A. Petersen (Resident, Tampa, Florida Office)
Christopher J. Pooley
Joseph A. Porrello (Resident, Tampa, Florida Office)
Brian Wayne Prewitt (Resident, Charlotte, North Carolina Office)
Eugene F. Rash (Resident, Charlotte, North Carolina Office)
Brenda A. Ray
Michael H. Robbins (Resident, Tampa, Florida Office)
James I. Rothschild
Joseph J. Santaniello (Resident, Charlotte, North Carolina Office)
Gregory L. Shelton (Resident, Tampa, Florida Office)
Angelina M. Stayton (Resident, Tampa, Florida Office)
Karen M. Steffens (Resident, Charlotte, North Carolina Office)
Frederick M. Thurman, Jr. (Resident, Charlotte, North Carolina Office)
J. Todd Timmerman (Resident, Tampa, Florida Office)
Mark D. Wagoner, Jr.

COUNSEL

James F. White, Jr.

OF COUNSEL

Gregory G. Alexander
Mary Li Creasy (Resident, Tampa, Florida Office)
Robert R. Warchola (Resident, Tampa, Florida Office)
George O. Wilson, III (Resident, Tampa, Florida Office)

For full biographical listings, see the Martindale-Hubbell Law Directory

OKLAHOMA

*OKLAHOMA CITY,** Oklahoma Co.

DAY, EDWARDS, FEDERMAN, PROPESTER & CHRISTENSEN, P.C. (AV)

Suite 2900 Oklahoma Tower, 210 Park Avenue, 73102-5605
Telephone: 405-239-2121
Telecopier: 405-236-1012
URL: http://lawlinks.com/attys/ok/defpc.html

Joe E. Edwards
Richard P. Propester
Kent A. Gilliland

Joel Warren Harmon

Representative Clients: BancFirst; Bank One, Oklahoma City; Bank of America, N.A.; First Community Bank, Binger; First National Bank and Trust Company of Weatherford; First State Bank & Trust Co., Hollis; Harris Developments, Inc.; Local Oklahoma Bank.

For Complete List of Firm Personnel, See General Section

For full biographical listings, see the Martindale-Hubbell Law Directory

OREGON

*PORTLAND,** Multnomah Co.

JAMES L. KNOLL (AV)

1500 S.W. Taylor Street, 97205
Telephone: 503-222-9000
Fax: 503-226-2801
Email: knolljl@aol.com

For full biographical listings, see the Martindale-Hubbell Law Directory

PENNSYLVANIA

CAMP HILL, Cumberland Co.

REAGER & ADLER, P.C. (AV)

2331 Market Street, 17011
Telephone: 717-763-1383
Fax: 717-730-7366
Email: reagerpc@epix.net *URL:* http://www.ReagerAdlerPC.com

Theodore A. Adler
David W. Reager
Linus E. Fenicle

Thomas O. Williams

Representative Clients: General Contractors: Miller-Norford; The Shane Group; H.W. Nauman & Sons, Inc.; Eichelberger Construction, Inc.; G.M. McCrossin, Inc. Mechanical Contractors: McClure Company; G.R. Sponaugle & Sons. Plumbing Contractors: Jay R. Reynolds, Inc. Electrical Contractors: The Farfield Co.; Lombardo & Lipe.

For full biographical listings, see the Martindale-Hubbell Law Directory

FORT WASHINGTON, Montgomery Co.

DALLER GREENBERG & DIETRICH, LLP (AV)

Valley Green Corporate Center, 7111 Valley Green Road, 19034
Telephone: 215-836-1100
Facsimile: 215-836-2845
URL: http://www.dallergreenberg.com
Haddon Heights, New Jersey Office: 2 White Horse Pike.
Telephone: 856-547-9068.
Facsimile: 856-547-2391.

PARTNERS

Morton F. Daller
Edward A. Greenberg
Gerhard P. Dietrich
Eileen M. Johnson
Dennis R. Callahan

ASSOCIATES

Tracy Canuso Nugent (Resident, Haddon Heights, New Jersey Office)
Catherine N. Walto
Mark S. Kirby
Marie Handrich Kramer
Alison R. Rohmer

For full biographical listings, see the Martindale-Hubbell Law Directory

*HARRISBURG,** Dauphin Co.

BECKLEY & MADDEN (AV)

Cranberry Court, 212 North Third Street, P.O. Box 11998, 17108
Telephone: 717-233-7691
Fax: 717-233-3740
Email: becks@pa.net

MEMBERS OF FIRM

Thomas A. Beckley
John G. Milakovic

ASSOCIATES

Charles O. Beckley, II
Elizabeth S. Beckley
Thomas S. Beckley

For Complete List of Firm Personnel, See General Section

For full biographical listings, see the Martindale-Hubbell Law Directory

MCNEES, WALLACE & NURICK (AV)

100 Pine Street, P.O. Box 1166, 17108-1166
Telephone: 717-232-8000
Fax: 717-237-5300
Email: info@mwn.com *URL:* http://www.mwn.com
Columbus, Ohio Office: 21 East State Street, Suite 1700, 43215.
Telephone: 614-469-8000.
Fax: 614-469-4653.
Washington, D.C. Office: 1200 G Street, N.W., 20005.
Telephone: 202-434-8991.
Fax: 202-434-8707.
Hazleton, Pennsylvania Office: 1 South Church Street, Suite 302, 18201.
Telephone: 570-455-8300.
Fax: 570-455-8390.

MEMBERS OF THE FIRM

James W. Kutz
Stephen A. Moore
Nedric L. Nissly
Diane M. Tokarsky

OF COUNSEL

Jonathan H. Rudd

ASSOCIATE

Brian F. Jackson

For Complete List of Firm Personnel, See General Section

For full biographical listings, see the Martindale-Hubbell Law Directory

Harrisburg—Continued

METTE, EVANS & WOODSIDE, A PROFESSIONAL CORPORATION (AV)

3401 North Front Street, P.O. Box 5950, 17110-0950
Telephone: 717-232-5000
Fax: 717-236-1816
Email: MEW@Mette.com *URL:* HTTP://WWW.METTE.COM

Craig A. Stone
Christopher C. Conner
Daniel L. Sullivan
Michael D. Reed
David A. Fitzsimons

Elizabeth J. Goldstein
John M. Hartzell

For Complete List of Firm Personnel, See General Section

For full biographical listings, see the Martindale-Hubbell Law Directory

LATROBE, Westmoreland Co.

ROBERT P. LIGHTCAP (AV)

757 Lloyd Avenue Extension, P.O. Box 364, 15650
Telephone: 412-539-3007
Fax: 412-537-7562
Email: rlightcap@juno.com

For full biographical listings, see the Martindale-Hubbell Law Directory

*PHILADELPHIA,** Philadelphia Co.

VENZIE, PHILLIPS & WARSHAWER, A PROFESSIONAL CORPORATION (AV)

2032 Chancellor Street, 19103
Telephone: 215-567-3322; 647-5121
Telecopier: 215-864-9292
Email: hvenzie@venzie.com *URL:* http://www.venzie.com

Howard D. Venzie, Jr.
Sam L. Warshawer, Jr.
Bruce L. Phillips
K. Gerard Amadio

Jeffrey C. Venzie

Representative Clients: Wausau Insurance Cos.; Turner Construction Company; The Hartford Accident & Indemnity Co.

For full biographical listings, see the Martindale-Hubbell Law Directory

*PITTSBURGH,** Allegheny Co.

BABST, CALLAND, CLEMENTS AND ZOMNIR, A PROFESSIONAL CORPORATION (AV)

Two Gateway Center, 15222
Telephone: 412-394-5400
Fax: 412-394-6576
Email: BCCZ@BCCZ.com
Philadelphia, Pennsylvania Office: The Widener Building, Suite 1700, One South Penn Square.
Telephone: 215-567-1020.
Fax: 215-751-1425.

Tarek F. Abdalla
Edward B. Gentilcore
Albert Bates, Jr. IV
Robert A. King
Kenneth R. Bruce
J. Frank McKenna, III
Bruce E. Stanley

Virgil E. Alexander
Amy L. Ronallo
David A. Hudock
Lisa G. Silverman
Laura Schleich Irwin
Jennifer A. Smokelin
D. Matthew Jameson III
John M. Tedder
Timothy C. Wolfson

For full biographical listings, see the Martindale-Hubbell Law Directory

MOLLICA & MURRAY (AV)

450 Trimont Plaza, 1305 Grandview Avenue, 15211
Telephone: 412-381-7000
Fax: 412-381-7111
Email: firm@mollicamurray.com *URL:* http://www.mollicamurray.com

MEMBERS OF FIRM

James A. Mollica, Jr.
Cathy Ann Chromulak
Dr. John E. Murray, Jr.
Timothy Murray
William J. Moorhead, Jr.

Michael E. Flaherty
Michelle D. Smith

For full biographical listings, see the Martindale-Hubbell Law Directory

PLOWMAN, SPIEGEL & LEWIS, P.C. (AV)

Second Floor, The Grant Building, 310 Grant Street, 15219-2201
Telephone: 412-471-8521
Fax: 412-471-4481

(See Next Column)

Jack W. Plowman
John L. Spiegel

Kurt F. Fernsler
Frank J. Kernan
Kenneth W. Lee

Reference: Pittsburgh National Bank.

For Complete List of Firm Personnel, See General Section

For full biographical listings, see the Martindale-Hubbell Law Directory

PLYMOUTH MEETING, Montgomery Co.

KORN & COHN, PROFESSIONAL CORPORATION (AV)

Suite 450, Plymouth Meeting Executive Campus, 620 West Germantown Pike, 19462
Telephone: 610-825-7070
Telecopier: 610-825-7957
URL: http://www.lawyers.com/korn&cohn
Philadelphia, Pennsylvania Office: Two Penn Center Plaza, Suite 200. 19102-1706.
Telephone: 610-825-7070.
Telecopier: 610-825-7957.
Marlton, New Jersey Office: Sagemore Corporate Center, 8000 Sagemore Drive, Suite 8303.
Telephone: 609-988-0786.
Telecopier: 609-988-0194.

Robert A. Korn
Robert P. Ewing
Andrew B. Cohn
Travis L. Kreiser

LEGAL SUPPORT PERSONNEL

A. Lynne Scott

For full biographical listings, see the Martindale-Hubbell Law Directory

RHODE ISLAND

*PROVIDENCE,** Providence Co.

BLISH & CAVANAGH (AV)

Commerce Center, 30 Exchange Terrace, 02903
Telephone: 401-831-8900
Telecopier: 401-751-7542
Email: BLISHCAV@AOL.COM

MEMBERS OF FIRM

Joseph V. Cavanagh, Jr.
Stephen J. Reid, Jr.
William R. Landry
Karen A. Pelczarski
Edmund L. Alves, Jr.
Scott T. Spear
Raymond A. Marcaccio

Michael W. Carroll
Staci L. Sawyer
Kristin Rodgers Sullivan

OF COUNSEL

John H. Blish

Representative Clients: Providence Journal Co.; Rhode Island Hospital Trust National Bank; Fleet Bank; Metropolitan Insurance Co.; Allstate Insurance Co.; Delta Dental of Rhode Island; Colony Communications; Providence Housing Authority; Textron; A.T. Cross.

For full biographical listings, see the Martindale-Hubbell Law Directory

HINCKLEY, ALLEN & SNYDER LLP (AV)

1500 Fleet Center, 02903-2393
Telephone: 401-274-2000
Fax: 401-277-9600
Email: firm@haslaw.com *URL:* http://www.haslaw.com
Boston, Massachusetts Office: 28 State Street, 30th Floor.
Telephone: 617-345-9000.
Fax: 617-345-9020. URL: http://www.haslaw.com.

MEMBERS OF FIRM

David D. Barricelli
E. Jerome Batty
Paul Bork (Not admitted in RI)
Stephen J. Carlotti
David Barry Connolly (Not admitted in RI)
Eric F. Eisenberg (Not admitted in RI)
Malcolm Farmer, III
Hugh J. Gorman, III (Not admitted in RI)
Alan P. Gottlieb (Not admitted in RI)
William R. Grimm
Paul A. Hedstrom (Not admitted in RI)
Richard L. E. Jocelyn
Joel Lewin (Not admitted in RI)
Matthew T. Marcello, III
Frederick P. McClure
Paul F. O'Donnell, III (Not admitted in RI)
H. Peter Olsen
John J. Pendergast, III
Gerald J. Petros
Jeremy Ritzenberg (Not admitted in RI)
David J. Rubin
Charles E. Schaub, Jr. (Not admitted in RI)
Douglas F. Seaver (Not admitted in RI)
Herman Snyder (Not admitted in RI)
David R. Sullivan (Not admitted in RI)

(See Next Column)

HINCKLEY, ALLEN & SNYDER LLP—*Continued*

MEMBERS OF FIRM (Continued)

Robert F. Sylvia (Not admitted in RI)
Howard E. Walker
Richard D. Wayne (Not admitted in RI)

ASSOCIATES

Mark Bianchi
Alexandra K. Callam
Jane E. Cohen (Not admitted in RI)
Andrew D. Cummings (Not admitted in RI)
June E. Daniel
Kim Herman Goslant (Not admitted in RI)
Gloria Maria Gutierrez (Not admitted in RI)
Christopher P. Hamilton (Not admitted in RI)
Kelley Jordan-Price
Catherine S. Kim (Not admitted in RI)
Christopher W. Morog (Not admitted in RI)
Elena B. Olson (Not admitted in RI)
Michael T. Renaud (Not admitted in RI)
Joseph D. Whelan

OF COUNSEL

Willard Krasnow (Not admitted in RI)
Willard R. Pope (Not admitted in RI)

For Complete List of Firm Personnel, See General Section

For full biographical listings, see the Martindale-Hubbell Law Directory

SOUTH CAROLINA

*CHARLESTON,** Charleston Co.

BARNWELL WHALEY PATTERSON & HELMS, LLC (AV)

134 Meeting Street, Suite 300, P.O. Drawer H, 29402
Telephone: 843-577-7700
Telecopier: 843-577-7708
Email: bwph@barnwell-whaley.com *URL:* http://barnwell-whaley.com

MEMBERS OF FIRM

William C. Helms, III
Bruce E. Miller
Frank E. Grimball
James E. Reeves

ASSOCIATES

J. Matthew Dillon
James H. Elliott, Jr.

Representative Clients: Brown & Root, Inc.; The Cannon Corp.; Design Professionals Ins. Co.; Nielson Construction, Inc.; Reliance Ins. Co.; Ryland Group, Inc.

For full biographical listings, see the Martindale-Hubbell Law Directory

BUIST, MOORE, SMYTHE & MCGEE, P.A. (AV)

Successors to Buist, Buist, Smythe and Smythe and Moore, Mouzon and McGee.
Five Exchange Street, P.O. Box 999, 29402
Telephone: 843-722-3400
Cable Address: "Conferees"
Telex: 57-6488
Telecopier: 843-723-7398
Email: bmsm@lawyer-sc.com *URL:* http://www.lawyer-sc.com

C. Allen Gibson, Jr.
Elizabeth Henry Warner

David S. Cox
Jonathan D. Crumly, Sr.

OF COUNSEL

Charles J. Baker, III

Representative Clients: Barton Malow Company; Beers Construction Company; Frederick R. Harris, Inc.; Frontier Insurance Company; McKellar & Associates Architects; Mitchell, Small & Donahue Architects; Phillips & Jordan, Inc.; Pizzagalli Construction Company; Reliance Surety Company; Star Insurance Company.

For Complete List of Firm Personnel, See General Section

For full biographical listings, see the Martindale-Hubbell Law Directory

LEATH, BOUCH & CRAWFORD, L.L.P. (AV)

134 Meeting Street, P.O. Box 59, 29402-0059
Telephone: 843-937-8811
Fax: 843-937-0606
Columbia, South Carolina Office: 221 Pickens Street (29205), P.O. Box 5066, 29250.
Telephone: 803-254-0048.
Facsimile: 803-254-0063.

MEMBERS OF FIRM

W. Jefferson Leath, Jr.
Timothy W. Bouch
B. Lindsay Crawford, III

(See Next Column)

Linda J. Amason
Elizabeth Rice Polk (Resident, Columbia Office)

For full biographical listings, see the Martindale-Hubbell Law Directory

ROBERTSON & ASSOCIATES (AV)

First Union Center, 177 Meeting Street, Suite 300, 29401
Telephone: 843-723-6470
Fax: 843-853-9045
Email: roblaw@internetx.net *URL:* http://www.roblaw.net
Columbia, South Carolina Office: 1517 Gregg Street, 29201.
Telephone: 803-771-9850.
Fax: 803-771-9851. Email: SKAmes@gte.net.

MEMBERS OF FIRM

Claron A. Robertson, III
Dunn D. Hollingsworth
R. Patrick Flynn

ASSOCIATES

Theodore L. Manos
Paul R. Rahn

OF COUNSEL

Scott K. Ames (Not admitted in SC; Resident, Columbia Office)

For full biographical listings, see the Martindale-Hubbell Law Directory

*COLUMBIA,** Richland Co.

BARNES, ALFORD, STORK & JOHNSON, L.L.P. (AV)

1613 Main Street, P.O. Box 8448, 29202
Telephone: 803-799-1111
Telefax: 803-254-1335
Email: basj@basjlaw.com

Weldon R. Johnson
Thomas C. Cofield
Robert Thomas Strickland

Representative Clients: M.B. Kahn Construction Co., Inc.; Kline Iron & Steel Co.

For Complete List of Firm Personnel, See General Section

For full biographical listings, see the Martindale-Hubbell Law Directory

FINKEL & ALTMAN, L.L.C. (AV)

Suite 1800, 1201 Main Street, P.O. Box 1799, 29202
Telephone: 803-765-2935
Fax: 803-252-0786
Email: webmaster@finkellaw.com *URL:* http://www.finkellaw.com
Charleston, South Carolina Office: 12 Exchange Street, P.O. Box 225.
Telephone: 843-577-5460.
Fax: 843-577-5135.

Gerald M. Finkel
Charles S. Altman (Resident, Charleston South Carolina Office)
Harry L. Goldberg
Howard S. Sheftman
Elizabeth Henderson McCullough
Beverly J. Finkel
Richard R. Gleissner

Janet B. Haigler
Michael M. Shetterly
Joseph Alton Bivens
Kelley Y. Woody
Laurie Pineau Davidson
Robert E. Culver

COUNSEL

Ralph C. McCullough, II
Elizabeth Rhodes

Representative Clients: Hewitt-Robins; 1st Union National Bank; Banc One Mortgage Co.; Motorola Communications & Electronics Corp.

For full biographical listings, see the Martindale-Hubbell Law Directory

NEXSEN PRUET JACOBS & POLLARD, LLP (AV)

1441 Main Street, 15th Floor, P.O. Drawer 2426, 29202
Telephone: 803-771-8900
Facsimile: 803-253-8277
Email: NPJP@NPJP.COM *URL:* HTTP://WWW.NPJP.COM
Charleston, South Carolina Office: 200 Meeting Street, Suite 301. P.O. Box 486.
Telephone: 803-577-9440.
Facsimile: 803-720-1777.
Greenville, South Carolina Office: 201 West McBee Avenue, Fourth Floor, P.O. Box 10648.
Telephone: 864-370-2211.
Facsimile: 864-282-1177.
Myrtle Beach, South Carolina Office: 2411 Oak Street, Suite 105.
Telephone: 843-445-9688.
Facsimile: 843-445-9949.
Charlotte, North Carolina Office: 212 South Tryon Street, Suite 1700.
Telephone: 704-339-0304.
Facsimile: 704-338-5377.

MEMBERS OF FIRM

Henry W. Brown
Robert W. Hassold, Jr. (Resident, Greenville, SC Office)
Richard W. Wilson (Resident, Charlotte, NC Office)

(See Next Column)

NEXSEN PRUET JACOBS & POLLARD LLP, *Columbia—Continued*

ASSOCIATES

William G. Lyles III (Resident, Charleston, SC Office)

For Complete List of Firm Personnel, See General Section

For full biographical listings, see the Martindale-Hubbell Law Directory

RICHARDSON, PLOWDEN, CARPENTER & ROBINSON, P.A. (AV)

1600 Marion Street, P.O. Drawer 7788, 29202
Telephone: 803-771-4400
Telecopy: 803-779-0016
Email: atty@rpcrlaw.com *URL:* http://www.rpcrlaw.com
Myrtle Beach, South Carolina Office: 2103 B Farlow Street, P.O. Box 3646, 29578.
Telephone: 843-448-1008.
FAX: 843-448-1533.

Francis M. Mack
Franklin Jennings Smith, Jr.
Douglas C. Baxter

OF COUNSEL

Donald V. Richardson, III
Michael A. Pulliam

Representative Clients: S.C. Department of Public Transportation; Richland County School District No. 1; Northlake Construction Co., Inc.; Boozer Lumber Co.; Osmose Wood Preserving Inc.; Ralph Whitehead & Assoc.; School District Five of Lexington and Richland Counties.

For Complete List of Firm Personnel, See General Section

For full biographical listings, see the Martindale-Hubbell Law Directory

WILLIAM DIXON ROBERTSON III (AV)

1122 Lady Street, Suite 620, P.O. Box 11401, 29211-1401
Telephone: 803-988-0040
Fax: 803-988-0041
Email: wdrlaw@msn.com

For full biographical listings, see the Martindale-Hubbell Law Directory

ROGERS TOWNSEND & THOMAS, PC (AV)

1441 Main Street, 10th Floor, P.O. Box 100200, 29202-3200
Telephone: 803-771-7900
Fax: 803-254-6305; 343-7017; 343-7019
URL: http://www.rtt-law.com

Robert Bryan Barnes
Stacey Lynch Hewson
Kendall R. Walker

For Complete List of Firm Personnel, See General Section

For full biographical listings, see the Martindale-Hubbell Law Directory

TURNER, PADGET, GRAHAM & LANEY, P.A. (AV)

Seventeenth Floor, 1901 Main Street, P.O. Box 1473, 29202
Telephone: 803-254-2200
Telecopy: 803-799-3957
Florence, South Carolina Office: Fourth Floor, 1831 West Evans Street, P.O. Box 5478, 29502.
Telephone: 843-662-9008.
Fax: 843-667-0828.
Charleston, South Carolina Office: 21 Broad Street, 1st Floor, P.O. Box 836, 29402.
Telephone: 843-723-1622.
Fax: 843-577-3369.

W. Duvall Spruill
Steven W. Ouzts
John E. Cuttino
Arthur E. Justice, Jr. (Resident, Florence, SC, Office)
Hugh M. Claytor (Resident, Florence, SC, Office)
O. Carlisle Edwards, Jr.

For Complete List of Firm Personnel, See General Section

For full biographical listings, see the Martindale-Hubbell Law Directory

TYLER, CASSELL, JACKSON, PEACE & SILVER, L.L.P. (AV)

1331 Elmwood Avenue, Suite 300, P.O. Box 11656, 29211-1656
Telephone: 803-779-4997
Telecopier: 803-765-2468

MEMBERS OF FIRM

Donald W. Tyler
Herbert C. Cassell, Jr.
Thomas B. Jackson, III
M. Alan Peace
Jeffrey L. Silver

OF COUNSEL

Eugene L. Brantley

References: Republic Contracting Corporation; Martin Engineering, Inc.; Horizon Steel Erectors, Inc.; BE&K Engineering Co.; Hercules Contractors and Engineers, Inc.; Contract Constructors, Inc.; McMahan Brothers Pipeline, Inc.; New South Supply, In.c; Len Hazen Painters, Inc.

For full biographical listings, see the Martindale-Hubbell Law Directory

WOODWARD COTHRAN & HERNDON (AV)

1200 Main Street, Suite 600, 29201
Telephone: 803-799-9772
Fax: 803-799-3256
Mailing Address: P.O. Box 12399, Columbia, South Carolina, 29211
Email: wch1@usit.net

MEMBERS OF FIRM

Edward M. Woodward, Jr.
Darra Williamson Cothran
Warren R. Herndon, Jr.

ASSOCIATE

Janet T. Butcher

OF COUNSEL

Edward M. Woodward, Sr.

General Counsel for: The Columbia College; Sandhills Bank; Heater Utilities.

For full biographical listings, see the Martindale-Hubbell Law Directory

*CONWAY,** Horry Co.

THE THOMPSON LAW FIRM, P.A. (AV)

1318 Third Avenue, P.O. Box 1533, 29528
Telephone: 843-248-5741
Fax: 843-248-5112
Myrtle Beach, South Carolina Office: 1314 Professional Drive, P.O. Box 1290.
Telephone: 843-692-2628.
Fax: 843-692-0918.

John C. Thompson
John P. Henry
Linda Weeks Gangi
Emma Ruth Brittain
Lynn Gatlin Stevens
Philip C. Thompson
Catherine M. Hedgepath

Representative Clients: NationsBank; Burroughs & Chapin Co., Inc.; Canal Industries, Inc.; State Farm Mutual Automobile Insurance Co.; State Farm Fire and Casualty Insurance Co.; Horry County; Nationwide Insurance Co.; United Carolina Bank; First Union National Bank.
Reference: NationsBank.

For full biographical listings, see the Martindale-Hubbell Law Directory

*GREENVILLE,** Greenville Co.

CLARKSON, FORTSON, WALSH & RHENEY, P.A. (AV)

117 Manly Street, P.O. Box 6186, 29606
Telephone: 864-232-4400
Fax: 864-235-4399
Email: cfwr@cfwr.com

N. Heyward Clarkson, III
H. Brent Fortson
James P. Walsh
T. David Rheney
Sarah Jennings Johnstone
Elizabeth J. Smith

For full biographical listings, see the Martindale-Hubbell Law Directory

THE HARPER LAW FIRM, P.A. (AV)

Old Chamber Building, 6th Floor, 135 South Main Street, P.O. Box 908, 29602
Telephone: 864-235-5535
Fax: 864-235-6866
Email: HARPERFIRM@aol.com

Donald A. Harper
Norman Ward Lambert
Cynthia Buck Brown

For full biographical listings, see the Martindale-Hubbell Law Directory

HAYNSWORTH, MARION, MCKAY & GUÉRARD, L.L.P. (AV)

75 Beattie Place, Eleventh Floor, P.O. Box 2048, 29602
Telephone: 864-240-3200
Facsimile: 864-240-3300
Columbia, South Carolina Office: Suite 2400 Affinity Building, 1201 Main Street, P.O. Drawer 7157, 29202
Telephone: 803-765-1818.
Facsimile: 803-765-2399.
Charleston, South Carolina Office: 134 Meeting Street, P.O. Box 1119, 29402.
Telephone: 843-722-7606.
Facsimile: 843-724-8016.

MEMBERS OF FIRM

Jesse C. Belcher
H. Donald Sellers
Thomas H. Coker, Jr.
Bryan Francis Hickey
Moffatt Grier McDonald

ASSOCIATE

Boyd B. Nicholson, Jr.

OF COUNSEL

Maye R. Johnson, Jr.

Representative Clients: Fluor-Daniel, Inc.; Yeargin Enterprises, Inc.; American Equipment Co., Inc.; Raytheon Engineering and Constructors; Modern Continental South Construction Co.; Westinghouse Savannah River Co.; University of South Carolina; Watkins Engineers and Constructors, Inc.

(See Next Column)

HAYNSWORTH, MARION, MCKAY & GUÉRARD L.L.P.—*Continued*

For Complete List of Firm Personnel, See General Section

For full biographical listings, see the Martindale-Hubbell Law Directory

LEATHERWOOD WALKER TODD & MANN, P.C. (AV)

100 East Coffee Street, P.O. Box 87, 29602
Telephone: 864-242-6440
FAX: 864-240-2477
Email: leatherwood@lwtm.com *URL:* http://www.lwtm.com
Spartanburg, South Carolina Office: 1451 East Main Street, P.O. Box 3188.
Telephone: 864-582-4365.
Telefax: 864-583-8961.

J. Richard Kelly
Robert A. deHoll

Daniel C. Patterson

Representative Clients: Beers/York Construction Company; Builder Marts of America; M.L. Garrett Construction Company; O'Neal Engineering Incorporated; Shelco Construction Company; Suitt Construction Company; Triangle Construction Company, Incorporated; Vulcan Materials Company.

For Complete List of Firm Personnel, See General Section

For full biographical listings, see the Martindale-Hubbell Law Directory

HILTON HEAD ISLAND, Beaufort Co.

LAUGHLIN AND BOWEN (AV)

20 Palmetto Parkway, Suites A & B, Drawer 21119, 29925-1119
Telephone: 843-689-5700
Fax: 843-689-9300
Email: Jazzlaw@Hargray.com

MEMBERS OF FIRM

Drew A. Laughlin
John R. C. Bowen

For full biographical listings, see the Martindale-Hubbell Law Directory

MYRTLE BEACH, Horry Co.

THE THOMPSON LAW FIRM, P.A. (AV)

1314 Professional Drive, P.O. Box 1290, 29578-1290
Telephone: 843-692-2628
Fax: 843-692-0918
Conway, South Carolina Office: 1318 Third Avenue, P.O. Box 1533.
Telephone: 843-248-5741.
Fax: 843-248-5112.

J. Jackson Thomas
Clay D. Brittain, III
G. Michael Smith

Russell V. Traw
Thomas C. Stanley
Stacy L. Stanley

Representative Clients: The Citizens and Southern National Bank of South Carolina; Burroughs & Collins Co.; Canal Industries, Inc.; Nationwide Mutual Insurance Co.; State Farm Mutual Automobile Insurance Co.; State Farm Fire and Casualty Insurance Co.; Horry County; United Carolina Bank; First Union National Bank; First Financial Savings Bank, Inc.

For full biographical listings, see the Martindale-Hubbell Law Directory

SOUTH DAKOTA

*ABERDEEN,** Brown Co.

MALONEY & MALONEY (AV)

722 South Highway 281, P.O. Box 755, 57402-0755
Telephone: 605-229-2752
Fax: 605-226-0276
Email: maloney@nvc.net

MEMBERS OF FIRM

Dennis Maloney
Marilyn Marshall Maloney

For full biographical listings, see the Martindale-Hubbell Law Directory

TENNESSEE

*CHATTANOOGA,** Hamilton Co.

FOSTER, FOSTER, ALLEN & DURRENCE, P.C. (AV)

Formerly Hall, Haynes, Lusk & Foster
801 Broad Street - Suite 515, 37402
Telephone: 423-266-1141
Telecopier: 423-266-4618
Email: dward@ffadlaw.com

George Lane Foster
William M. Foster
Craig R. Allen
Phillip M. Durrence, Jr.
David J. Ward
Clayton M. Whittaker
John M. Hull

LEGAL SUPPORT PERSONNEL

Peggy Sue Bates

Division Counsel For: Norfolk Southern Railway Co.
Attorneys For: CNA/Insurance; United States Fidelity & Guaranty Co. (USF&G); Bridgestone-Firestone, Inc.; Exxon Corp.; Murphy Oil Corp.; Chicago Title Insurance Co.; Jim Walter Homes; Mid-State Homes, Inc.

For full biographical listings, see the Martindale-Hubbell Law Directory

*CLEVELAND,** Bradley Co.

JENNE, SCOTT & JENNE (AV)

260 Ocoee Street, P.O. Box 161, 37364-0161
Telephone: 423-476-5506
Fax: 423-476-5058
Email: MichaelJenne@mindspring.com

MEMBERS OF FIRM

Roger E. Jenne
Robert A. Scott (1940-1984)
Michael E. Jenne

For full biographical listings, see the Martindale-Hubbell Law Directory

*DYERSBURG,** Dyer Co.

ASHLEY, ASHLEY & ARNOLD (AV)

322 Church Avenue, P.O. Box H, 38024
Telephone: 901-285-5074
Telecopier: 901-285-5089
Email: aaafirm@usit.net *URL:* http://www.lawyers.com/ashleylaw

MEMBERS OF FIRM

Barret Ashley
Randolph A. Ashley, Jr.
S. Leo Arnold
Marianna Williams
Anthony Lee Winchester
Jason G. Yarbro

OF COUNSEL

Joree G. Brownlow

Representative Clients: Illinois Central Gulf Railroad; Bekeart Steel Wire Corp.; Fidelity and Deposit Company of Maryland; St. Paul Fire and Marine Insurance Co.
Construction Company Clients: Chancellor & Sons, Inc.; Davco Corp; Dumey Excavation, Inc.; Folk Construction Co.; Ford Construction Co.; Fordice Construction Co.

For full biographical listings, see the Martindale-Hubbell Law Directory

JOHNSON CITY, Washington Co.

LAW OFFICE OF EPPS AND EPPS (AV)

115 East Unaka Avenue, P.O. Drawer 2288, 37605-2288
Telephone: 423-928-7256
Fax: 423-928-0207

James H. Epps, III

For full biographical listings, see the Martindale-Hubbell Law Directory

*KNOXVILLE,** Knox Co.

BERNSTEIN, STAIR & MCADAMS LLP (AV)

Suite 600, 530 South Gay Street, 37902
Telephone: 423-546-8030
Telecopier: 423-522-8879
Effective October 1, 1999 Area Code will change to 865.

MEMBERS OF FIRM

Bernard E. Bernstein
L. Caesar Stair III
Thomas N. McAdams
Doris C. Allen
Celeste H. Herbert
James W. Parris

ASSOCIATES

W. Tyler Chastain
Lauren G. Strange-Boston
Margo J. Maxwell

Representative Clients: ABB Flakt, Inc.; Clayton Homes, Inc.; Modern Supply Co.; Nova, Inc.; Plasti-Line, Inc.; Public Building Authority of County of Knox and City of Knoxville; Rafferty's Restaurants; Richardson Turner Construction Co., Inc.; Vanderbilt Mortgage and Finance, Inc.; West Town Mall.

(See Next Column)

BERNSTEIN, STAIR & MCADAMS LLP, *Knoxville—Continued*

For full biographical listings, see the Martindale-Hubbell Law Directory

LEIBOWITZ & COHEN (AV)

608 Gay Street, S.W., 37902
Telephone: 423-637-1809
FAX: 423-637-9276

MEMBERS OF FIRM

Arnold G. Cohen
Lawrence P. Leibowitz

ASSOCIATE

Melissa A. Ashburn

OF COUNSEL

Russell T. Greene

For full biographical listings, see the Martindale-Hubbell Law Directory

SOBIESKI, MESSER & ASSOCIATES (AV)

900 South Gay Street, Suite 1801, 37902
Telephone: 423-546-7770
Fax: 423-546-7969
Email: sobilaw@aol.com

Wanda G. Sobieski
Diane M. Messer

ASSOCIATE

R. Richard Carl, II

For full biographical listings, see the Martindale-Hubbell Law Directory

*MEMPHIS,** Shelby Co.

GLASSMAN, JETER, EDWARDS & WADE, P.C. (AV)

26 North Second Street Building, 38103
Telephone: 901-527-4673
Telecopier: 901-521-0940
Email: GJEWW@Memphisonline.com

William M. Jeter
Carl K. Wyatt, Jr.
B. J. Wade
Dale H. Tuttle
Lori J. Keen

For full biographical listings, see the Martindale-Hubbell Law Directory

HALE HEADRICK DEWEY & WOLF, PLLC (AV)

One Memphis Place, 200 Jefferson Avenue Suite 1450, 38103
Telephone: 901-523-1123
Fax: 901-523-7472
Nashville, Tennessee Office: Suntrust Bank Building, 201 Fourth Avenue North, Suite 1450, 37219.
Telephone: 615-843-5160.
Fax: 615-843-5165

Stephen P. Hale
H. Tucker Dewey
S. Russell Headrick
Herbert B. Wolf, Jr.
John S. Golwen

OF COUNSEL

Steven L. Gill

Jennifer Ziegenhorn
Holly N. Knight
Wendy A. Geurin
Charles S. Blatteis
John W. Campbell
Jennifer S. Kiesewetter
Joseph M. Koury
J. William Williams

For full biographical listings, see the Martindale-Hubbell Law Directory

LESS, GETZ & LIPMAN (AV)

100 Peabody Place, Suite 1000, 38103
Telephone: 901-525-8700
Telecopier: 901-525-3569
URL: http://www.lgllaw.com

MEMBERS OF FIRM

Michael I. Less
Clifton M. Lipman
Joseph Thaddeus Getz
Ted M. Hayden
Elizabeth B. Stengel

ASSOCIATES

Michael D. Herrin
Christopher M. Caputo (Not admitted in TN)
Michele R. Fosco Salazar

For full biographical listings, see the Martindale-Hubbell Law Directory

*NASHVILLE,** Davidson Co.

SMITH & CASHION, PLC (AV)

Suite 1200, Suntrust Center, 424 Church Street, 37219-2306
Telephone: 615-742-8555
Telecopier: 615-742-8556
Email: sclaw@bellsouth.net

(See Next Column)

Don L. Smith
Jefferson C. Orr
Gregory L. Cashion
Lawrence B. Hammet II
Richard McCallister Smith
O. Wade Nelson
Kenneth S. Schrupp

Carol Rose Dunn
H. Brent Patrick
Vic L. McConnell

For full biographical listings, see the Martindale-Hubbell Law Directory

TEXAS

*AUSTIN,** Travis Co.

BASKIN, BENNETT & KOMKOV, L.L.P. (AV)

919 Congress Avenue, Suite 1000, 78701
Telephone: 512-322-9250
Fax: 512-322-9280
URL: http://www.baskin.com

James D. Baskin, III
J. Bruce Bennett
Leon V. Komkov

For full biographical listings, see the Martindale-Hubbell Law Directory

*BROWNSVILLE,** Cameron Co.

RANSOME AND RAY, P.C. (AV)

550 East Levee Street, 78520-5343
Telephone: 956-542-3642
Telecopier: 956-542-3698
Email: ransomeray@aol.com

Marshall R. Ray
Mary Lou Ryan Ray

Cecilia De La Garza De Garcia

OF COUNSEL

C. Fount Ray

For full biographical listings, see the Martindale-Hubbell Law Directory

*DALLAS,** Dallas Co.

CALHOUN & STACY (AV)

Suite 5700 - Bank of America Plaza, 901 Main Street, 75202-3713
Telephone: 214-748-5000
Facsimile: 214-748-1421
Email: info@calhounstacy.com *URL:* http://www.calhounstacy.com

MEMBERS OF FIRM

Mark Alan Calhoun
Parker Nelson
David W. Elrod
Thomas E. Rosen
Roy L. Stacy

For Complete List of Firm Personnel, See General Section

For full biographical listings, see the Martindale-Hubbell Law Directory

GOINS, UNDERKOFLER, CRAWFORD & LANGDON, L.L.P. (AV)

3300 Thanksgiving Tower, 1601 Elm Street, 75201
Telephone: 214-969-5454
Fax: 214-969-5902 ABA Net 17432

MEMBERS OF FIRM

Hance W. Burrow, III
Neil J. Orleans
Durwood D. Crawford
John D. Rosenberg
E. Eldridge Goins, Jr.
Richard E. Schellhammer
John O. Langdon
John J. Sheedy, Jr.
Ira F. Levy
Paul B. Underkofler
Paul A. Mohtares
Frank L. Broyles
James W. Morris, Jr.
David L. Paschall

ASSOCIATE

Jeffrey S. Wigder

For full biographical listings, see the Martindale-Hubbell Law Directory

GRIFFITH & NIXON, P.C. (AV)

One Lincoln Center, 5400 LBJ Freeway, Suite 1025, 75240
Telephone: 972-386-8988
Fax: 972-386-8985
Email: griffnix@flash.net

Scott Griffith
Michael S. Nixon

Kimberly A. Davison
Anthony P. Jach
Benjamin D. Halpern
Jeffery Harold Rusthoven
L. Christopher Harris
Scott V. Siddons

For full biographical listings, see the Martindale-Hubbell Law Directory

Dallas—Continued

SMITH, UNDERWOOD & PERKINS, A PROFESSIONAL CORPORATION (AV)

600 Two Lincoln Centre, 5420 LBJ Freeway, 75240
Telephone: 972-661-5114
Telecopier: 972-661-5691
Email: firm@suandp.com *URL:* http://www.suplaw.com

Timothy S. Perkins
G. Lynn Smith
David W. Ralston
William J. Underwood, Jr.

Christine A. McGuire
Ellen P. Stewart
Amy K. Ratzlaff
Todd W. Shadle
P. Theodore Stoinoff, II
Ruth C. Logan
Val C. Cronin
Christina L. Betanzos
Kent D. Williamson

For full biographical listings, see the Martindale-Hubbell Law Directory

SOPUCH NOUHAN HIGGINS & ARNETT, L.L.P. (AV)

400 North St. Paul Street Suite 840, 75201
Telephone: 214-760-0900
Fax: 214-760-0905
Email: SNHADALLAS@aol.com *URL:* http://www.SNHA.com
Chicago, Illinois Office: 311 South Wacker Drive, Suite 5600.
Telephone: 312-922-0900.
Fax: 312-922-2255. Email: SNHACHGO@aol.com

James Robert Arnett, II
Michael L. Gaubert
Jamil N. Alibhai

For full biographical listings, see the Martindale-Hubbell Law Directory

THOMAS, FELDMAN & WILSHUSEN, L.L.P. (AV)

9400 NCX Tower, 9400 North Central Expressway, Suite 900, 75231
Telephone: 214-369-3008
Facsimile: 214-369-8393

MEMBERS OF FIRM

Richard Gary Thomas
Robert L. Feldman
Fred D. Wilshusen

ASSOCIATES

Regan Gayle O'Steen
Trice Ragon Richey
Edward (Ted) J. Laperouse, II

OF COUNSEL

Joseph M. Stuhl

Representative Clients: Baker Drywall Co., Inc.; CMC Steel Group; Dallas Door and Supply Company; Dallas Fire Insurance Company; Fischbach & Moore, Inc.; Mills Electrical Contractors, Inc.; SGB Construction Services, Inc.; TD Mechanical; Spaw Glass General Contractors, Inc.; TAS Construction, Inc.

For full biographical listings, see the Martindale-Hubbell Law Directory

THOMPSON & KNIGHT L.L.P. (AV)

(Attorneys and Counselors)
1700 Pacific Avenue Suite 3300, 75201
Telephone: 214-969-1700
Telecopy: 214-969-1751
Telex: 732 298
URL: http://www.tklaw.com
Austin, Texas Office: 1200 San Jacinto Center, 98 San Jacinto Boulevard, 78701.
Telephone: 512-469-6100.
Telecopy: 512-469-6180.
Fort Worth, Texas Office: 801 Cherry Street, Suite 1600, 76102.
Telephone: 817-347-1700.
Telecopy: 817-347-1799.
Houston, Texas Office: Thompson Knight Brown Parker & Leahy L.L.P., 1200 Smith Street, Suite 3600, 77002-4595.
Telephone: 713-654-8111.
Telecopier: 713-654-1871.
San Pedro Garza Garcia, Nuevo León, Mexico Office: Edificio Losoles PD-4, Av. Lázaro Cárdenas No. 2400 Pte., C.P. 66220.
Telephone: (52-8) 363-0096.
Telecopy: (52-8) 363-3067.

PARTNERS

Steven R. Baggett
Joseph S. Pevsner
F. Barrett Davis
Stephen C. Schoettmer
Stephen S. Livingston
Molly Steele

For Complete List of Firm Personnel, See General Section

For full biographical listings, see the Martindale-Hubbell Law Directory

*EL PASO,** El Paso Co.

AINSA PARTNERS, LLP (AV)

5809 Acacia Circle, 79912
Telephone: 915-845-5300
Fax: 915-845-7800
Email: fain@acaciapark.com *URL:* http://www.ainsa.com

Francis S. Ainsa, Jr.
Michael F. Ainsa
David M. Driscoll

For full biographical listings, see the Martindale-Hubbell Law Directory

*FORT WORTH,** Tarrant Co.

MCMULLEN LAW FIRM (AV)

6300 Ridglea Place Suite 509, 76116-5731
Telephone: 817-731-4163
Fax: 817-731-4340
Email: wademcmullen@msn.com

Wade H. McMullen

For full biographical listings, see the Martindale-Hubbell Law Directory

THOMPSON & KNIGHT L.L.P. (AV)

(Attorneys and Counselors)
801 Cherry Street, Suite 1600, 76102
Telephone: 817-347-1700
Telecopy: 817-347-1799
URL: http://www.tklaw.com
Dallas, Texas Office: 1700 Pacific Avenue, Suite 3300, 75201.
Telephone: 214-969-1700.
Telecopy: 214-969-1751.
Telex: 732298.
Austin, Texas Office: 1200 San Jacinto Center, 98 San Jacinto Boulevard, 78701.
Telephone: 512-469-6100.
Telecopy: 512-469-6180.
Houston, Texas Office: Thompson Knight Brown Parker & Leahy L.L.P., 1200 Smith Street, Suite 3600, 77002-4595.
Telephone: 713-654-8111.
Telecopier: 713-654-1871.
San Pedro Garza Garcia, Nuevo León, Mexico Office: Edificio Losoles PD-4, Av. Lázaro Cárdenas No. 2400 Pte., C.P. 66220.
Telephone: (52-8) 363-0096.
Telecopy: (52-8) 363-3067.

PARTNER

Lonnie J. Copps

For Complete List of Firm Personnel, See General Section

For full biographical listings, see the Martindale-Hubbell Law Directory

*HOUSTON,** Harris Co.

BREWER & PRITCHARD, A PROFESSIONAL CORPORATION (AV)

24th Floor, Heritage Plaza, 1111 Bagby, 77002
Telephone: 713-209-2950
Facsimile: 713-659-5302
Email: info@bplaw.com *URL:* http://www.bplaw.com

J. Mark Brewer
Patrick E. Gaas

For full biographical listings, see the Martindale-Hubbell Law Directory

PATRICIA KAY DUBE, P.C. (AV)

4140 Bank of America Center, 700 Louisiana Street, 77002
Telephone: 713-225-2297
Facsimile: 713-225-2298
Email: pkdube@wt.net *URL:* http://www.lawyers.com/dubelaw

Patricia Kay Dube
Clare I. Vetters
Lee Broze

OF COUNSEL

Alan J. Winters
Harold J. Eisenman

For full biographical listings, see the Martindale-Hubbell Law Directory

GILPIN, PAXSON & BERSCH (AV)

A Registered Limited Liability Partnership
Attorney at Law
1900 West Loop South, Suite 2000, 77027-3259
Telephone: 713-623-8800
Telecopier: 713-993-8451
Email: gpb@gpblaw.com *URL:* http://www.texinslaw.com

PARTNERS

Gary M. Alletag
Darryl W. Malone
Timothy R. Bersch
Michael J. Pappert
John D. Gilpin
Stephen Paxson
Kevin F. Risley

(See Next Column)

GILPIN, PAXSON & BERSCH, *Houston—Continued*

OF COUNSEL

Harless R. Benthul
David F. Webb

ASSOCIATES

Joseph D. Batson
Jeri Pharis Wechsler

Representative Clients: BMW of North America, Inc.; Federal Deposit Insurance Corporation; Greater Houston Builders Association; Owens Corning Fiberglas Corporation; Shaw Industries, Inc.; Southwest Guaranty Trust Company, N.A.; Sprint Communications Company L.P.; Volkswagen of America, Inc.; Volvo North America Corporation; Wells Fargo Bank (Texas), N.A.

For full biographical listings, see the Martindale-Hubbell Law Directory

SCHWARTZ JUNELL CAMPBELL & OATHOUT, L.L.P. (AV)

Two Houston Center, 909 Fannin, Suite 2000, 77010
Telephone: 713-752-0017
Telecopier: 713-752-0327
Email: dschwartz@schwartz-junell.com

Richard A. Schwartz
Marshall S. Campbell
William Edward Junell, Jr.
Monica F. Oathout
Steven R. Rech

Phillip W. Bechter
J. Parker Fauntleroy, Jr.

OF COUNSEL

Joe H. Reynolds
A. R. Schwartz

LEGAL SUPPORT PERSONNEL

PARALEGALS

Nannette Koger
Maria Woods
Shelly A. Savage, CLA

For full biographical listings, see the Martindale-Hubbell Law Directory

THOMPSON KNIGHT BROWN PARKER & LEAHY L.L.P. (AV)

A Registered Limited Liability Partnership including Professional Corporations
(Attorneys and Counselors)
1200 Smith Street, Suite 3600, 77002-4595
Telephone: 713-654-8111
Telecopier: 713-654-1871
URL: http://www.tklaw.com
Dallas, Texas Office: Thompson & Knight L.L.P., 1700 Pacific Avenue, Suite 3300, 75201.
Telephone: 214-969-1700.
Telecopy: 214-969-1751.
Telex: 732298.
Austin, Texas Office: Thompson & Knight L.L.P., 1200 San Jacinto Center, 98 San Jacinto Boulevard, 78701.
Telephone: 512-469-6100.
Telecopy: 512-469-6180.
Fort Worth, Texas Office: Thompson & Knight L.L.P., 801 Cherry Street, Suite 1600, 76102.
Telephone: 817-347-1700.
Telecopy: 817-347-1799.
San Pedro Garza Garcia, Nuevo León, Mexico Office: Thompson & Knight L.L.P., Edificio Losoles PD-4, Av. Lázaro Cárdenas No. 2400 PTE., C.P. 66220.
Telephone: (52-8) 363-0096.
Telecopy: (52-8) 363-3067.

PARTNERS

E.F. Mano DeAyala
Boris A. Hidalgo
Regina Giovannini
Jon L. Tankersley

For Complete List of Firm Personnel, See General Section

For full biographical listings, see the Martindale-Hubbell Law Directory

*SAN ANTONIO,** Bexar Co.

O'CONNELL, BENJAMIN & COGHLAN, L.L.P. (AV)

153 Treeline Park, Suite 200, 78209
Telephone: 210-824-0009
Fax: 210-824-9429
Email: obcllp@oconben.com

Keith B. O'Connell
Ernest F. Avery
David P. Benjamin
Les Katona, Jr.
G. Thomas Coghlan
Dan Vana

Gayla S. Corley
Cathrin J. Martinez

For full biographical listings, see the Martindale-Hubbell Law Directory

*WICHITA FALLS,** Wichita Co.

GIBSON, HOTCHKISS, ROACH & DAVENPORT (AV)

807 8th Street, 8th Floor, 76301
Telephone: 940-322-7856
Fax: 940-322-1204
Email: ed@ghrdlaw.com *URL:* http://www.lawyers.com/ghrdlaw

MEMBER OF FIRM

Robert K. Roach

ASSOCIATE

John D. Rosentreter

Representative Clients: American National Bank, Wichita Falls; First National Bank of Bowie; Wichita Falls PCA; Bennett Production Co.; Red River Authority of Texas; Burcamp Steel Co.

For Complete List of Firm Personnel, See General Section

For full biographical listings, see the Martindale-Hubbell Law Directory

UTAH

*SALT LAKE CITY,** Salt Lake Co.

DART ADAMSON DONOVAN & HANSON (AV)

A Partnership of Professional Corporations
370 E. South Temple, Suite 400, 84111
Telephone: 801-521-6383
Telefax: 801-355-2513

Craig G. Adamson (P.C.)

ASSOCIATES

Eric P. Lee (P.C.)
Cameron S. Denning

A list of References will be furnished upon request.

For full biographical listings, see the Martindale-Hubbell Law Directory

MORGAN, MEYER & RICE, L.C. (AV)

Kearns Building, Eighth Floor, 136 South Main Street, 84101
Telephone: 801-531-7888
Telefax: 801-531-9732
Email: morgan@inquo.net

MEMBERS OF FIRM

Stephen G. Morgan
Mitchel T. Rice
Cynthia K.C. Meyer
Joseph E. Minnock
Jeffrey C. Miner

For full biographical listings, see the Martindale-Hubbell Law Directory

PARR WADDOUPS BROWN GEE & LOVELESS, A PROFESSIONAL CORPORATION (AV)

Suite 1300, 185 South State Street, 84111-1537
Telephone: 801-532-7840
Fax: 801-532-7750
URL: http://www.pwlaw.com

Clark Waddoups
Stephen E. W. Hale
Ronald G. Russell
Gregory M. Hess
Roger D. Henriksen
Terry E. Welch
Brian J. Romriell
Mark A. Wagner
Brett J. Swanson

For Complete List of Firm Personnel, See General Section

For full biographical listings, see the Martindale-Hubbell Law Directory

VAN COTT, BAGLEY, CORNWALL & MCCARTHY, A PROFESSIONAL CORPORATION (AV)

50 South Main Street, Suite 1600, P.O. Box 45340, 84145-0340
Telephone: 801-532-3333
Telecopier: 801-534-0058
Email: info@vancott.com *URL:* http://www.vancott.com
Ogden, Utah Office: 2404 Washington Boulevard, Suite 900.
Telephone: 801-394-5783.
Park City, Utah Office: 2200 Park Avenue, Suite C200-A.
Telephone: 435-649-3889.

Robert M. Anderson (President of Firm)
David A. Greenwood
Jeremy M. Hoffman
John L. Young

Kevin L. Jones
Bradley M. Strassberg

(See Next Column)

VAN COTT, BAGLEY, CORNWALL & MCCARTHY A PROFESSIONAL CORPORATION—*Continued*

OF COUNSEL

Franklin N. Smith

For Complete List of Firm Personnel, See General Section

For full biographical listings, see the Martindale-Hubbell Law Directory

VIRGINIA

ALEXANDRIA, (Independent City)

THOMPSON & WALDRON (AV)

1055 North Fairfax Street, 4th Floor, 22314
Telephone: 703-684-3340
Facsimile: 703-684-6225
Email: TW@Contractlaw.com

William W. Thompson, Jr.
Paul L. Waldron
Martin Healy
Jeffrey B. Krashin (Not admitted in VA)
Michael A. Branca
Scott W. Barber (Not admitted in VA)
Michael E. Pardi (Not admitted in VA)
Susan M. Swafford

For full biographical listings, see the Martindale-Hubbell Law Directory

*FAIRFAX,** (Ind. City; Seat of Fairfax Co.)

HART & HORAN, P.C. (AV)

3905 Railroad Avenue, Suite 202 South, 22030
Telephone: 703-352-7330
Fax: 703-352-6940
Email: jhart@tidalwave.net *URL:* http://www.lawyers.com/hart&horanlaw

James R. Hart

For full biographical listings, see the Martindale-Hubbell Law Directory

MCLEAN, Fairfax Co.

VENABLE ATTORNEYS AT LAW VENABLE, BAETJER AND HOWARD, LLP (AV)

A Partnership including Professional Corporations
Suite 400, 2010 Corporate Ridge, 22102
Telephone: 703-760-1600
Fax: 703-821-8949
URL: http://www.venable.com
Baltimore, Maryland Office: 1800 Mercantile Bank & Trust Building, 2 Hopkins Plaza.
Telephone: 410-244-7400.
Fax: 410-244-7742.
Washington, D.C. Office: Venable, Baetjer, Howard & Civiletti LLP, Suite 1000, 1201 New York Avenue, N.W.
Telephone: 202-962-4800.
Fax: 202-962-8300.
Rockville, Maryland Office: Suite 500, One Church Street, P.O. Box 1906.
Telephone: 301-217-5600.
Fax: 301-217-5617.
Towson, Maryland Office: 210 Allegheny Avenue, P. O. Box 5517.
Telephone: 410-494-6200.
Fax: 410-821-0147.

MEMBERS OF FIRM

A. Wayne Lalle, Jr.
David G. Lane
David C. Mancini
Christine M. McAnney
Michael W. Robinson

ASSOCIATE

Charles W. Durant

For Complete List of Firm Personnel, See General Section

For full biographical listings, see the Martindale-Hubbell Law Directory

WATT, TIEDER, HOFFAR & FITZGERALD, L.L.P. (AV)

7929 Westpark Drive, Suite 400, 22102
Telephone: 703-749-1000
Telecopier: 703-893-8029
Email: contactus@wthf.com *URL:* http://www.wthf.com
Washington, D.C. Office: 601 Pennsylvania Ave, N.W., Suite 900.
Telephone: 703-749-1000.
Irvine, California Office: 3 Park Plaza, Suite 1500.
Telephone: 949-852-6700.

MEMBERS OF FIRM

John B. Tieder, Jr.
Robert G. Watt
Julian F. Hoffar
Robert M. Fitzgerald
Robert K. Cox
Charles E. Raley
Lewis J. Baker
Benjamin T. Riddles, II

(See Next Column)

MEMBERS OF FIRM (Continued)

Wayne G. Tatusko
Richard G. Mann, Jr.
Henry D. Danforth
Carter B. Reid
Mark A. Sgarlata
Michael G. Long (Resident, Irvine, California Office)
Thomas J. Powell
Edward Parrott
Steven J. Weber
Paul A. Varela
Vivian Katsantonis
Kathleen Olden Barnes
Christopher P. Pappas (Resident, Irvine, California Office)
Shelly L. Ewald
Christopher J. Brasco
John G. Lavoie
Robert C. Niesley (Resident, Irvine, California Office)
Colin J. Smith
Fred A. Mendicino
Timothy E. Heffernan (Not admitted in VA)

OF COUNSEL

Avv. Roberto Tassi

ASSOCIATES

Robert G. Barbour
Keith C. Phillips
Marybeth Z. Gaul
William Drew Mallender
Joseph W. Rasnic
Heidi B. Hering
James M. Donahue
Bennett J. Lee (Not admitted in VA)
Todd R. Metz (Not admitted in VA)
Joseph S. Guarino
Lewis I. Askew, Jr.
Erica S. Beardsley
Robert James Lloyd, III
Harish C. Mirchandani (Not admitted in VA)
William Kennedy
Michael J. Kirwin (Not admitted in VA)
Peter L. Vanderloo
Scott W. Kowalski
Carol Kelly Skrabak
J. Brian Cashmere
Michele Mintz
David A. Leib (Not admitted in VA)
Denis W. Kohl
Elizabeth A. Hall

For full biographical listings, see the Martindale-Hubbell Law Directory

NORFOLK, (Independent City)

PAYNE, GATES, FARTHING & RADD, P.C. (AV)

15th Floor, Dominion Tower, 999 Waterside Drive, Suite 1515, 23510-3309
Telephone: 757-640-1500
Facsimile: 757-627-6583
URL: http://www.paynegates.com

Ronald M. Gates
Philip R. Farthing
Anthony F. Radd
Glen M. Robertson
Brian R. Dinning
Todd J. Preti
Marshall A. Winslow, Jr.

C. Arthur Robinson, II
Stephen E. Heretick
Raymond L. Hogge, Jr.

OF COUNSEL

Charles E. Payne

For full biographical listings, see the Martindale-Hubbell Law Directory

RICHMOND, (Independent City)

MALONEY, HUENNEKENS, PARKS, GECKER & PARSONS, A PROFESSIONAL CORPORATION (AV)

Bank of America Center, 1111 East Main Street, Suite 800, 23219-3103
Telephone: 804-644-0313
Telecopier: 804-783-6192

Daniel A. Gecker

Reference: First Union National Bank.

For Complete List of Firm Personnel, See General Section

For full biographical listings, see the Martindale-Hubbell Law Directory

WILLIAMS, MULLEN, CLARK & DOBBINS, A PROFESSIONAL CORPORATION (AV)

Two James Center, 1021 East Cary Street, P.O. Box 1320, 23218-1320
Telephone: 804-643-1991
Fax: 804-783-6507
URL: http://www.wmcd.com
Newport News Office: Harbor Bank Center, Suite 210, One Old Oyster Point Road, 23602-7119.
Telephone: 757-249-5100.
Fax: 757-249-5109.
Virginia Beach Office: One Columbus Center, 23462-6763.
Telephone: 757-499-8800.
Fax: 757-473-0395.
Vienna Office: 1593 Spring Hill Road, Suite 510, 22182.
Telephone: 703-760-5200.
Fax: 703-748-0244.
Washington, D.C. Office: The Farragut Building, 900 17th Street, N.W., Suite 700, 20006.
Telephone: 202-293-0213.
Fax: 804-783-6507. Fax Within D.C.: 202-293-5939.

(See Next Column)

WILLIAMS, MULLEN, CLARK & DOBBINS A PROFESSIONAL CORPORATION, *Richmond—Continued*

London, England Office: Blake Lodge, Bridge Lane, SW11 3AD.
Telephone: (011-44-71) 223-2756.
Fax: (011-44-71) 350-0156.
Riyadh, Saudi Arabia Affiliate Office: Saudi-American Legal Consultants Commercial Building #2, Diplomatic Quarter, P.O. Box 57270, 11574.
Telephone: (011-966-1) 488-1563.
Fax: (011-966-1) 488-0542.

William D. Bayliss
Charles L. Cabell
Robert E. Eicher
Samuel W. Hixon, III
A. Brooks Hock
William R. Mauck, Jr.
Walter H. Ryland
Andrea Rowse Stiles

Andrew M. Condlin

For Complete List of Firm Personnel, See General Section

For full biographical listings, see the Martindale-Hubbell Law Directory

WASHINGTON

*SEATTLE,** King Co.

BAROKAS, MARTIN, AHLERS & TOMLINSON (AV)

1422 Bellevue Avenue, 98122-3634
Telephone: 206-621-1871
Fax: 206-621-9907
Email: bmlf@aol.com
Anchorage, Alaska Office: 1029 W. Third Avenue, Suite 100.
Telephone: 907-276-8010.
Fax: 907-276-5334.

MEMBERS OF FIRM

Larry L. Barokas
Dale R. Martin
John P. Ahlers
John R. Tomlinson, Jr.
Joseph J. Straus

OF COUNSEL

Rex M. Walker

ASSOCIATES

Scott R. Sleight
John J. Limb
Amanda E. Vedrich
Craig A. Robertson

Reference: Western Bank.

For full biographical listings, see the Martindale-Hubbell Law Directory

DANIELSON HARRIGAN & TOLLEFSON, LLP (AV)

A Limited Liability Partnership including a Professional Service Corporation
999 Third Avenue, 44th Floor, 98104
Telephone: 206-623-1700
Facsimile: 206-623-8717
Email: lawfirm@dh-t.com

David Danielson (P.S.)
Arthur W. Harrigan, Jr.
G. Val Tollefson
Timothy G. Leyh
Michelle Buhler
Karl F. Oles
Charles Jordan

COUNSEL

Richard H. Holmquist
Katherine See Kennedy
Matthew R. Kenney
Terence K. McGee

ASSOCIATES

Randall Thomsen
Michael M.K. Hemphill

For full biographical listings, see the Martindale-Hubbell Law Directory

OLES, MORRISON, RINKER & BAKER L.L.P. (AV)

3300 Columbia Center, 701 Fifth Avenue, 98104-7082
Telephone: 206-623-3427
Telecopier: 206-682-6234
Email: omr@oles.com *URL:* http://www.omr@oles.com
Anchorage, Alaska Office: 745 West 4th Avenue, Suite 502.
Telephone: 907-258-0106.
Fax: 907-277-8002.

MEMBERS OF FIRM

Stuart G. Oles (Retired)
Seth W. Morrison
David C. Stewart
Sam E. Baker, Jr.
Arthur D. McGarry
B. Michael Schestopol
Robert J. Burke
Bradley L. Powell
Douglas S. Oles
Peter N. Ralston
John Lukjanowicz
James F. Nagle
Glenn R. Nelson
J. Craig Rusk
Traeger Machetanz
David R. Chappel

(See Next Column)

ASSOCIATES

Emmanuel P. Tangas
William K. Renno (Resident, Anchorage Office)
Catherine C. Clark
Mark D. Walters
W. Gregory Guedel
Cynthia Dale Turner
C. Russell Lewis (Not admitted in WA; Resident, Anchorage, Alaska Office)
Michael R. Beyer
Laura Kleisle
Xiaoqiu Wang
Kelly Blazy
Eileen I. McKillop
Kevin G. Brady (Not admitted in WA)

For full biographical listings, see the Martindale-Hubbell Law Directory

SCHIFFRIN OLSON SCHLEMLEIN & HOPKINS, P.L.L.C. (AV)

First and Cedar Building Suite 300, 2701 First Avenue, 98121
Telephone: 206-448-8100
Telecopier: 206-448-8514
URL: http://www.soslaw.com

David W. Schiffrin
James T. Hopkins
Robert L. Olson
Garth A. Schlemlein
Theresa A. Goetz

Representative Clients: Fluor Daniel; Coogan Construction Co.; Cree Construction Co.; The Evans Company; Ketchikan Drywall, Inc.; Layfield Plastics; Leo Finnegan Construction Co.; Lundeen's; Reliance Insurance; R.W. Rhine Inc.

For full biographical listings, see the Martindale-Hubbell Law Directory

STANISLAW ASHBAUGH, LLP (AV)

4400 Columbia Center, 701 Fifth Avenue, 98104-7012
Telephone: 206-386-5900
Fax: 206-344-7400
Email: info@stanislaw.com *URL:* http://www.stanislaw.com

MEMBERS OF FIRM

R. Miles Stanislaw
David L. Ashbaugh
John S. Riper
Richard T. Beal, Jr.
Robert S. Marconi
Richard H. Skalbania
Robert P. Majerus
Michael T. Zoretic
Joseph Michael Campos

ASSOCIATES

Todd C. Hayes
J. Robert Smith
Christopher A. Wright
John R. Welch
Michael R. Fields
Jennifer L. Mentor

LEGAL SUPPORT PERSONNEL

Carl William LaFraugh (Construction Consultant)
Diane C. Grauer (Construction Consultant)
Richard Lee (Construction Consultant)
Kyle R. Braget (Construction Consultant)

Reference: Security Pacific.

For full biographical listings, see the Martindale-Hubbell Law Directory

WEST VIRGINIA

*CHARLESTON,** Kanawha Co.

JACKSON & KELLY (AV)

1600 Laidley Tower, P.O. Box 553, 25322
Telephone: 304-340-1000
Fax: 304-340-1130
Email: info@jacksonkelly.com *URL:* http://www.jacksonkelly.com
Martinsburg, West Virginia Office: 300 Foxcroft Avenue, P.O. Box 1068.
Telephone: 304-263-8800.
Fax: 304-263-7110.
Morgantown, West Virginia Office: 6000 Hampton Center, P.O. Box 619.
Telephone: 304-599-3000.
Fax: 304-285-2040.
New Martinsville, West Virginia Office: 256 Russell Avenue, P.O. Box 68.
Telephone: 304-455-1751.
Fax: 304-455-6314.
Parkersburg, West Virginia Office: 412 Market Street, Suite 202, P.O. Box 1144.
Telephone: 304-424-3490.
Fax: 304-424-3499.
Fairmont, West Virginia Office: 1000 Technology Drive, Suite 1310.
Telephone: 304-368-2000.
Fax: 304-368-2020.
Lexington, Kentucky Office: 175 East Main Street, Suite 500, P.O. Box 2150.
Telephone: 606-255-9500.
Fax: 606-281-6478.
Washington, D. C. Office: 2401 Pennsylvania Avenue, N.W., Suite 400.
Telephone: 202-973-0200.
Fax: 202-973-0232.

(See Next Column)

JACKSON & KELLY—*Continued*

Denver, Colorado Office: Suite 2710, 1660 Lincoln Street.
Telephone: 303-390-0003.
Fax: 303-390-0040.
Wheeling, West Virginia Office: 1144 Market Street.
Telephone: 304-233-4000.
Fax: 304-233-4077.

MEMBERS OF FIRM

Thomas E. Potter
John R. Lukens
Stephen R. Crislip
James R. Snyder
Mary Clare Eros (Administrative Manager, Martinsburg and Charles Town, West Virginia Offices)
John Philip Melick
William Prentice Young (Martinsburg and Charles Town, West Virginia Offices)

For Complete List of Firm Personnel, See General Section

For full biographical listings, see the Martindale-Hubbell Law Directory

SHUMAN ANNAND BAILEY WYANT & EARLES (AV)

Suite 1007, 405 Capitol Street, P.O. Box 3953, 25339
Telephone: 304-345-1400
Telecopier: 304-343-1826
Email: shuman@newwave.net
Wheeling, West Virginia Office: Suite 3002, 1233 Main Street, 26003.
Telephone: 304-233-3100.
Telecopier: 304-233-0201.

MEMBERS OF FIRM

David L. Shuman
Stephen Darley Annand
Charles R. Bailey
Richard L. Earles
David L. Wyant (Resident, Wheeling, West Virginia Office)
Mark William Browning
William R. Slicer
George J. Joseph
Thomas E. Buck (Resident at Wheeling, West Virginia Office)

ASSOCIATES

DesireéHalkias Divita
Roberta F. Green
Paul Kipling Reese
Heidi A. Kossuth (Resident, Wheeling, West Virginia Office)
Lou Ann S. Cassell
Dwayne E. Cyrus
Eric W. Santos (Not admitted in WV; Resident, Wheeling, West Virginia Office)
John T. Molleur
Mark A. Kepple (Resident, Wheeling, West Virginia Office)
David J. Mincer
Karen M. Tracy
Virginia Ann Grottendieck
Arden J. Cogar
Melissa A. Morris
Stacie L. Price (Resident, Wheeling, West Virginia Office)
J. Parker Bazzle
Lisa Bray
Darin C. James
Brian D. Morrison

OF COUNSEL

John F. McCuskey

Representative Clients: American International/Companies (AIG); CNA Insurance Companies; Insurance Corporation of America; Metropolitan Property & Liability Insurance Co.; MMI Companies, Inc.; Motorists Insurance Cos.; Travelers Insurance Cos.; Westfield Companies.
Reference: One Valley Bank.

For full biographical listings, see the Martindale-Hubbell Law Directory

*CLARKSBURG,** Harrison Co.

JOHNSON, SIMMERMAN & BROUGHTON, L.C. (AV)

Ogden Building, 203 West Main Street, 26301
Telephone: 304-624-6555; 304-623-4900
Telecopier: 304-623-4933
Mailing Address: P.O. Box 150, Clarksburg, West Virginia, 26302-0150

Charles G. Johnson
Frank E. Simmerman, Jr.
Marcia Allen Broughton
Bridget D. Furbee
Robin Queen Triplett

For full biographical listings, see the Martindale-Hubbell Law Directory

MCNEER, HIGHLAND, MCMUNN AND VARNER, L.C. (AV)

One Valley Bank Building, P.O. Drawer 2040, 26302-2040
Telephone: 304-626-1100
Facsimile: 304-623-3035
Martinsburg Office: 2520 Aikens Center, P.O. Box 2509.
Telephone: 304-264-4621.
Fax: 304-264-8623.
Parkersburg Office: 404 Market Street, Suite 204, P.O. Box 1507.
Telephone: 304-422-7193.
Facsimile: 304-422-7196.

(See Next Column)

C. David McMunn
J. Cecil Jarvis
James A. Varner
Robert W. Trumble (Resident, Martinsburg Office)
Catherine D. Munster
James N. Riley
Steven R. Bratke (Resident, Parkersburg Office)
Michael J. Novotny (Resident, Martinsburg Office)
Dennis M. Shreve
Geraldine S. Roberts
William F. Rohrbaugh (Resident, Martinsburg Office)
Gregory H. Schillace
Judy L. Shanholtz
Tiffany R. Durst
Gene W. Bailey, II

OF COUNSEL

James E. McNeer
Cecil B. Highland, Jr.
William L. Fury

Representative Clients: One Valley Bank of Clarksburg, National Assn.; Bruceton Bank; Harrison County Bank; Nationwide Mutual Insurance Cos.; Clarksburg Publishing Co.; C.I.T. Financial Services; State Automobile Mutual Insurance Co.; United Hospital Center, Inc.; West Virginia Coals, Inc.; Swanson Plating Co.

For full biographical listings, see the Martindale-Hubbell Law Directory

WISCONSIN

*MADISON,** Dane Co.

KAY & ANDERSEN, S.C. (AV)

One Point Place, Suite 201, 53719
Telephone: 608-833-0077
Fax: 608-833-3901
Email: KandA@execpc.com

Robert J. Kay
Randall J. Andersen

James N. Graham
Robert A. Mich, Jr.

For full biographical listings, see the Martindale-Hubbell Law Directory

LAWTON & CATES, S.C. (AV)

10 East Doty Street Suite 400, P.O. Box 2965, 53701-2965
Telephone: 608-282-6200
Fax: 608-282-6252
Email: lawcat@madison.tds.net *URL:* http://www.lawtoncates.com

John C. Carlson
Kent I. Carnell

Reference: Bank One, Madison.

For full biographical listings, see the Martindale-Hubbell Law Directory

QUARLES & BRADY LLP (AV)

Firstar Plaza, One South Pinckney Street, P.O. Box 2113, 53701-2113
Telephone: 608-251-5000
Fax: 608-251-9166
URL: http://www.quarles.com
Milwaukee, Wisconsin Office: 411 East Wisconsin Avenue, 53202-4497.
Telephone: 414-277-5000.
Fax: 414-271-3552.
West Palm Beach, Florida Office: 222 Lakeview Avenue, 4th Floor, 33401.
Telephone: 561-653-5000.
Fax: 561-653-5333.
Naples, Florida Office: Barnett Center, 4501 Tamiami Trail North, Suite 300, 34103-3060.
Telephone: 941-262-5959.
Fax: 941-434-4999.
Phoenix, Arizona Office: One Camelback Building, One East Camelback Road, Suite 400, 85012-1649.
Telephone: 602-230-5500.
Fax: 602-230-5598.
Chicago, Illinois Office: Quarles & Brady LLC, Citicorp Center, 500 West Madison Street, Suite 3700.
Telephone: 312-715-5000.
Fax: 312-715-5155.

PARTNERS

Jeremy C. Shea
James R. Cole
Roy L. Prange, Jr.
Kevin A. Delorey

ASSOCIATE

Valerie L. Bailey-Rihn

For Complete List of Firm Personnel, See General Section

For full biographical listings, see the Martindale-Hubbell Law Directory

*MILWAUKEE,** Milwaukee Co.

GUNTA & REAK, S.C. (AV)

219 North Milwaukee Street, 53202
Telephone: 414-291-7979
Facsimile: 414-291-7960
Email: gntareak@execpc.com *URL:* http://www.lawyers.com/gntareak

(See Next Column)

GUNTA & REAK S.C., *Milwaukee—Continued*

Gregg J. Gunta | Kevin P. Reak
Joseph A. McCarthy

Ann C. Wirth

OF COUNSEL

Gary A. Gerlach

For full biographical listings, see the Martindale-Hubbell Law Directory

JAMES L. KIRSCHNIK, S.C. (AV)

12845 West Burleigh Road, 53005
Telephone: 262-786-0200
Facsimile: 262-786-3527
Email: JLKSC@EXECPC.COM *URL:* http://www.lawyers.com/kirschniklaw

James L. Kirschnik

Daniel P. Kirschnik

Representative Clients: DPIC Cos.; Ruekert & Mielke, Inc.; The Stubenrauch Architects, Inc.; Tractor Loader Sales, Inc.; Cadwell-Burg Associates, Inc.; Ray Prell & Associates, Inc.; Rawson Contractors.

For full biographical listings, see the Martindale-Hubbell Law Directory

KOHNER, MANN & KAILAS, S.C. (AV)

1572 East Capitol Drive, P.O. Box 11982, 53211-0982
Telephone: 414-962-5110
Fax: 414-962-8725
Email: kmksc@execpc.com

Marvin L. Kohner (1908-1975)

OF COUNSEL

Robert L. Mann

MEMBERS OF FIRM

Steve Kailas
Mark R. Wolters
Jordan B. Reich
David S. Chartier
Roy Paul Roth
Gary P. Lantzy
Christopher C. Kailas
Matthew P. Gerdisch

Robert E. Nailen
Darrell R. Zall
Daniel J. Flynn
Timothy L. Zuberbier
David M. Henry
Lorinne J Cunningham
Palma M. Forte
Daniel J. Emma

Representative Clients: Ecolab, Inc.; Manpower, Inc.; Abbott Laboratories; Norwest Bank Wisconsin, N.A.; Firstar Bank Corporation; Sysco Food Services; Johnson Controls, Inc.; Worth Inc.; Rayovac, Inc.; York International Corporation.

For full biographical listings, see the Martindale-Hubbell Law Directory

QUARLES & BRADY LLP (AV)

411 East Wisconsin Avenue, 53202-4497
Telephone: 414-277-5000
Fax: 414-271-3552
URL: http://www.quarles.com
Madison, Wisconsin Office: Firstar Plaza, One South Pinckney Street, P.O. Box 2113, 53701-2113.
Telephone: 608-251-5000.
Fax: 608-251-9166.
West Palm Beach, Florida Office: 222 Lakeview Avenue, 4th Floor, 33401.
Telephone: 561-653-5000.
Fax: 561-653-5333.
Naples, Florida Office: Barnett Center, 4501 Tamiami Trail North, Suite 300, 34103-3060.
Telephone: 941-262-5959.
Fax: 941-434-4999.
Phoenix, Arizona Office: One Camelback Building, One East Camelback Road, Suite 400, 85012-1649.
Telephone: 602-230-5500.
Fax: 602-230-5598.
Chicago, Illinois Office: Quarles & Brady LLC, Citicorp Center, 500 West Madison Street, Suite 3700.
Telephone: 312-715-5000.
Fax: 312-715-5155.

MEMBERS OF FIRM

(ALPHABETICALLY BY YEAR OF ADMISSION TO BAR)

Jeremy C. Shea (Resident, Madison Office)
David L. Petersen (Resident, Naples, Florida Office)
Lawrence J. Jost
Ronald L. Wallenfang
Anthony H. Driessen
James D. Friedman
John R. Maynard
F. Joseph McMackin, III (Resident, Naples, Florida Office)
Robert T. Bailes (Resident, Phoenix, Arizona Office)
Leonard S. Shifflett (Resident, Chicago, Illinois Office)
Robert E. Doyle, Jr. (Resident, Naples, Florida Office)

(See Next Column)

MEMBERS OF FIRM

(ALPHABETICALLY BY YEAR OF ADMISSION TO BAR) (Continued)

Roy L. Prange, Jr. (Resident, Madison Office)
Roger K. Spencer (Resident, Phoenix, Arizona Office)
Peter C. Christianson
John A. Rothstein
Charles H. McMullen
Mary N. Fertl
Kevin A. Delorey (Resident, Madison Office)
John D. Humphreville (Resident, Naples, Florida Office)
Scott L. Langlois
Joseph E. Puchner
Michael J. Ostermeyer

ASSOCIATES

Patrick J. Schoen
Susan A. Cerbins
Valerie L. Bailey-Rihn (Resident, Madison Office)
Mark Hubert Muller (Resident, Naples, Florida Office)
Kevin M. Long
James T. Demarest (Resident, Naples, Florida Office)

For Complete List of Firm Personnel, See General Section

For full biographical listings, see the Martindale-Hubbell Law Directory

WYOMING

*CASPER,** Natrona Co.

BROWN, DREW & MASSEY, LLP (AV)

Casper Business Center, Suite 800, 123 West First Street, 82601-2486
Telephone: 307-234-1000
800-877-6755
Telefax: 307-265-8025
Email: brwndrew@coffey.com

MEMBERS OF FIRM

Morris R. Massey
Harry B. Durham, III
Donn J. McCall
Thomas F. Reese
Courtney Robert Kepler

ASSOCIATE

Timothy M. Stubson

OF COUNSEL

B. J. Baker

For Complete List of Firm Personnel, See General Section

For full biographical listings, see the Martindale-Hubbell Law Directory

PUERTO RICO

SAN JUAN, San Juan Dist.

INDIANO, WILLIAMS & WEINSTEIN-BACAL

Hato Rey Tower, 21st Floor, 268 Muñoz Rivera Avenue (Hato Rey), 00918
Telephone: 787-754-2323; 763-0485
Fax: 787-766-3366
Email: iww@microjuris.com

MEMBERS OF FIRM

Stuart A. Weinstein-Bacal
David C. Indiano
Jeffrey M. Williams

ASSOCIATES

Peter W. Miller
Edgar A. Lee-Navas
Edward W. Hill Tollinche
Alexander H. Bopp (Not admitted in PR)

For full biographical listings, see the Martindale-Hubbell Law Directory

JIMÉNEZ, GRAFFAM & LAUSELL

Suite 505, Midtown Building, 421 Muñoz Rivera Avenue, Hato Rey, P.O. Box 366104, 00936-6104
Telephone: 787-767-1030; 767-1000; 767-1061; 767-1064
Telefax: 787-751-4068;
Cable: "Nezte"
RCA Telex: 325-2730
Email: manager@jgl.com *URL:* http://www.jgl.com

OF COUNSEL

Nicolás Jiménez

MEMBERS OF FIRM

William A. Graffam
Steven C. Lausell
José Juan Torres-Escalera
Manolo T. Rodríguez-Bird

(See Next Column)

JIMÉNEZ, GRAFFAM & LAUSELL—*Continued*

ASSOCIATES

Patricia A. Garrity
Isabel J. Vélez-Serrano
Edgardo A. Vega-López
Rafael A. Rosado-Marrero

Representative Clients: Sea-Land Service, Inc.; McAllister Brothers, Inc.; Crowley Maritime Corp.; General Motors Overseas Distribution Corp.; HIH Casualty & General Insurance Ltd.

For Complete List of Firm Personnel, See General Section

For full biographical listings, see the Martindale-Hubbell Law Directory

CANADA ALBERTA

*EDMONTON,** Edmonton Jud. Dist.

PARLEE MCLAWS (AV)

15th Floor Manulife Place, 10180 101st Street, T5J 4K1
Telephone: 403-423-8500
Telecopier: 403-423-2870
Email: lawyers@parlee.com *URL:* http://www.parlee.com
Calgary, Alberta Office: 3400 Petro-Canada Centre, 150 - 6th Avenue, SW.
Telephone: 403-294-7000.
Telecopier: 403-265-8263.

MEMBERS OF FIRM

Kenneth F. Bailey, Q.C.
H. Douglas Montemurro
James K. McFadyen

For Complete List of Firm Personnel, See General Section

For full biographical listings, see the Martindale-Hubbell Law Directory

CANADA BRITISH COLUMBIA

*VANCOUVER,** Vancouver Co.

JENKINS MARZBAN LOGAN (AV)

A Partnership of Law Corporations
Suite 1414, Nelson Square, 808 Nelson Street, P.O. Box 12144, V6Z 2H2
Telephone: 604-681-6564
Facsimile: 604-681-0766
URL: http://www.JML.CA

Dinyar Marzban
Robert W. Jenkins
John S. Logan

William S. McLean
Donald A. Thompson
Brent D. Jordan
Scott Booth

For full biographical listings, see the Martindale-Hubbell Law Directory

SINGLETON URQUHART (AV)

1200 - 1125 Howe Street, V6Z 2K8
Telephone: 604-682-7474
Fax: 604-682-1283
Email: reception@singleton.com *URL:* http://www.singleton.com

John R. Singleton, Q.C.
Derek A. Brindle
Dale B. Pope
Jeffery A. Hand

ASSOCIATE COUNSEL

Glenn A. Urquhart, Q.C.
Bonita J. Thompson, Q.C.

Representative Clients: Agra Industries Ltd.; Architecture; B.H. Levelton & Associates; Baker McGarva Hart Inc.; Golder Associates Ltd.; IBI Group; N.D. Lea International Ltd.; Patkau Architects Inc.; Poon Gardner Garrett; SNC-Kilborn Engineering Ltd.

For Complete List of Firm Personnel, See General Section

For full biographical listings, see the Martindale-Hubbell Law Directory

CANADA NEW BRUNSWICK

*FREDERICTON,** York Co.

COX HANSON O'REILLY MATHESON (AV)

(Formerly Hanson Hashey)
Suite 400, Phoenix Square, P.O. Box 310, E3B 4Y9
Telephone: 506-453-7771
Fax: 506-453-9600
Email: fredericton@coxhanson.ca *URL:* http://www.coxhanson.ca
Halifax, Nova Scotia Office: Suite 1100, Purdy's Wharf Tower 1, P.O. Box 2380 Station Central RPO, B3J 3E5.
Telephone: 902-421-6262.
Fax: 902-421-3130. E-Mail: halifax@coxhanson.ca
Saint John, New Brunswick Office: 1212-One Brunswick Square, 1 Germain St. E2L 4V1.
Telephone: 506-652-7771.
Fax: 506-632-9600.
St. John's, Newfoundland Office: Scotia Centre, 401-235 Water Street, A1C 1B6.
Telephone: 709-726-3321.
Fax: 709-726-2992. E-Mail: stjohns@coxhanson.ca
Charlottetown, Prince Edward Island Office: Queen Square, Suite 202, 119 Queen Street, P.O. Box 875, Station Central, C1A 7L9.
Telephone: 902-894-7051.
Fax: 902-368-3762. E-Mail: charlottetown@coxhanson.ca

MEMBERS OF FIRM

H. A. Hanson, Q.C. (1909-1985)
David T. Hashey, Q.C.
David M. Norman, Q.C.
J. Ian M. Whitcomb, Q.C.
John M. Hanson, Q.C.
Walter D. Vail, Q.C.
Michael E. Bowlin
John D. Larlee, Q.C.
Bruce D. Hatfield, Q.C.
Julian A. G. Dickson, Q.C.
Anne D. Wooder
Terrence J. Morrison
Lucie Richard
Catherine M. Bowlen
J. Marc Richard

ASSOCIATES

Amanda J. Frenette
Monika M. L. Zauhar
Jade A. Spalding
William E. Gould
Christopher R. DeLong
Deborah M. Power
Corinne A. Godbout
Marc-Antoine Chiasson

For full biographical listings, see the Martindale-Hubbell Law Directory

MCINNES COOPER (AV)

Suite 600, 570 Queen Street, P.O. Box 610, E3B 5A6
Telephone: 506-458-8572
Fax: 506-458-9903
Email: mcrfton@mcrlaw.com *URL:* http://www.mcrlaw.com
Halifax, Nova Scotia Office: Summit Place, 1601 Lower Water Street, P.O. Box 730, B3J 2V1.
Telephone: 902-425-6500.
Fax: 902-425-6350. Email: mcrhfx@mcrlaw.com.
St. John's, Newfoundland Office: Baine Johnston Centre, 5th Floor, 10 Fort William Place, P.O. Box 5939, A1C 5X4.
Telephone: 709-722-8735.
Telecopier: 709-722-1763. Email: mcrsj@mcrlaw.com.
Moncton, New Brunswick Office: Place Moncton Place, 655 Main Street, P.O. Box 1368, E1C 8T6.
Telephone: 506-857-8970.
Fax: 506-857-4095. Email: mcrmctn@mcrlaw.com.
Charlottetown, Prince Edward Island Office: BDC Place, Suite 620, 119 Kent Street, C1A 1N3.
Telephone: 902-368-8473.
Fax: 902-368-8346. Email: mcrpei@mcrlaw.com.

PARTNER

David Duncan Young

For Complete List of Firm Personnel, See General Section

For full biographical listings, see the Martindale-Hubbell Law Directory

*MONCTON,** Westmorland Co.

MCINNES COOPER (AV)

Barristers, Solicitors & Trade Mark Agents
Place Moncton Place, 655 Main Street, P.O. Box 1368, E1C 8T6
Telephone: 506-857-8970
Fax: 506-857-4095
Email: mcrmctn@mcrlaw.com *URL:* http://www.mcrlaw.com
Halifax, Nova Scotia Office: Summit Place, 1601 Lower Water Street, P.O. Box 730, B3J 2V1.
Telephone: 902-425-6500.
Fax: 902-425-6350. Email: mcrhfx@mcrlaw.com.
St. John's, Newfoundland Office: Baine Johnston Centre, 5th Floor, 10 Fort William Place, P.O. Box 5939, A1C 5X4.
Telephone: 709-722-8735.
Telecopier: 709-722-1763. Email: mcrsj@mcrlaw.com.

(See Next Column)

McINNES COOPER, *Moncton—Continued*

Charlottetown, Prince Edward Island Office: BDC Place, Suite 620, 119 Kent Street, C1A 1N3.
Telephone: 902-368-8473.
Fax: 902-368-8346. Email: mcrpei@mcrlaw.com.
Fredericton, New Brunswick Office: Suite 600, 570 Queen Street, P.O. Box 610.
Telephone: 506-458-8572.
Fax: 506-458-9903. Email: mcrfton@mcrlaw.com.

PARTNER

Eric LeDrew

For Complete List of Firm Personnel, See General Section

For full biographical listings, see the Martindale-Hubbell Law Directory

CANADA NEWFOUNDLAND

*ST. JOHN'S,**

McINNES COOPER (AV)

Barristers, Solicitors & Trade Mark Agents
Baine Johnston Centre, 5th Floor, 10 Fort William Place, P.O. Box 5939, A1C 5X4
Telephone: 709-722-8735
Telecopier: 709-722-1763
Email: mcrsj@mcrlaw.com *URL:* http://www.mcrlaw.com
Halifax, Nova Scotia Office: Summit Place, 1601 Lower Water Street, P.O. Box 730, B3J 2V1.
Telephone: 902-425-6500.
Fax: 902-425-6350. Email: mcrhfx@mcrlaw.com.
Moncton, New Brunswick Office: Place Moncton Place, 655 Main Street, P.O. Box 1368, E1C 8T6.
Telephone: 506-857-8970.
Fax: 506-857-4095. Email: mcrmctn@mcrlaw.com.
Charlottetown, Prince Edward Island Office: BDC Place, Suite 620, 119 Kent Street, C1A 1N3.
Telephone: 902-368-8473.
Fax: 902-368-8346. Email: mcrpei@mcrlaw.com.
Fredericton, New Brunswick Office: Suite 600, 570 Queen Street, P.O. Box 610.
Telephone: 506-458-8572.
Fax: 506-458-9903. Email: mcrfton@mcrlaw.com.

PARTNERS

James R. Chalker, Q.C.
Thomas R. Kendell
Michael J. Crosbie

ASSOCIATE

Genevieve M. Dawson

For Complete List of Firm Personnel, See General Section

For full biographical listings, see the Martindale-Hubbell Law Directory

CANADA NOVA SCOTIA

*HALIFAX,** Regional Munic. of Halifax

McINNES COOPER (AV)

Barristers, Solicitors & Trade Mark Agents
Summit Place, 1601 Lower Water Street, P.O. Box 730, B3J 2V1
Telephone: 902-425-6500
Fax: 902-425-6350
Email: mcrhfx@mcrlaw.com *URL:* http://www.mcrlaw.com
St. John's, Newfoundland Office: Baine Johnston Centre, 5th Floor, 10 Fort William Place, P.O. Box 5939, A1C 5X4.
Telephone: 709-722-8735.
Telecopier: 709-722-1763. Email: mcrsj@mcrlaw.com.
Moncton, New Brunswick Office: Place Moncton Place, 655 Main Street, P.O. Box 1368, E1C 8T6.
Telephone: 506-857-8970.
Fax: 506-857-4095. Email: mcrmctn@mcrlaw.com.
Charlottetown, Prince Edward Island Office: BDC Place, Suite 620, 119 Kent Street, C1A 1N3.
Telephone: 902-368-8473.
Fax: 902-368-8346. Email: mcrpei@mcrlaw.com.
Fredericton, New Brunswick Office: Suite 600, 570 Queen Street, P.O. Box 610.
Telephone: 506-458-8572.
Fax: 506-458-9903. Email: mcrfton@mcrlaw.com.

(See Next Column)

PARTNERS

Reginald A. Cluney, Q.C.
Stewart McInnes, P.C., Q.C.
George W. MacDonald, Q.C.
Christopher C. Robinson, Q.C.
Harvey L. Morrison
David A. Graves
Malcolm D. Boyle
John Kulik
Michelle C. Awad

For Complete List of Firm Personnel, See General Section

For full biographical listings, see the Martindale-Hubbell Law Directory

CANADA ONTARIO

*TORONTO,** Regional Munic. of Toronto

BORDEN & ELLIOT (AV)

Barristers & Solicitors
Scotia Plaza, 40 King Street West, M5H 3Y4
Telephone: 416-367-6000
Telecopier: 416-367-6749
Email: info@borden.com *URL:* http://www.borden.com
Ottawa, Ontario Office: Borden Elliot Scott & Aylen, 1000-60 Rue Queen Street.
Telephone: 613-237-5160; 800-661-4237. General
Facsimile: 613-230-8842. IP Dept.
Facsimile: 613-787-3558. Email: ottinfo@scottaylen.com. URL: http://www.borden.com.

Kenneth W. Scott, Q.C.

For Complete List of Firm Personnel, See General Section

For full biographical listings, see the Martindale-Hubbell Law Directory

KELLY AFFLECK GREENE (AV)

One First Canadian Place, Suite 840, P.O. Box 489, M5X 1E5
Telephone: 416-360-2800
Fax: 416-360-5960
Email: info@kag.net *URL:* http://www.kag.net

MEMBERS OF FIRM

W. Anthony Kelly, Q.C.
James C. Orr
Donald S. Affleck, Q.C.
Peter C. Wardle
Peter R. Greene
Helen A. Daley
Donald B. Houston
Melissa J. Kennedy

ASSOCIATES

Kenneth A. Dekker
Jason C. Markwell
W. Michael G. Osborne
Patrice F. Band

For full biographical listings, see the Martindale-Hubbell Law Directory

CANADA PRINCE EDWARD ISLAND

*CHARLOTTETOWN,** Queen's Co.

McINNES COOPER (AV㊦)

Barristers, Solicitors & Trade Mark Agents
BDC Place, Suite 620, 119 Kent Street, C1A 1N3
Telephone: 902-368-8473
Fax: 902-368-8346
Email: mcrpei@mcrlaw.com *URL:* http://www.mcrlaw.com
Halifax, Nova Scotia Office: Summit Place, 1601 Lower Water Street, P.O. Box 730, B3J 2V1.
Telephone: 902-425-6500.
Fax: 902-425-6350. Email: mcrhfx@mcrlaw.com.
St. John's, Newfoundland Office: Baine Johnston Centre, 5th Floor, 10 Fort William Place, P.O. Box 5939, A1C 5X4.
Telephone: 709-722-8735.
Telecopier: 709-722-1763. Email: mcrsj@mcrlaw.com.
Moncton, New Brunswick Office: Place Moncton Place, 655 Main Street, P.O. Box 1368, E1C 8T6.
Telephone: 506-857-8970.
Fax: 506-857-4095. Email: mcrmctn@mcrlaw.com.
Fredericton, New Brunswick Office: Suite 600, 570 Queen Street, P.O. Box 610.
Telephone: 506-458-8572.
Fax: 506-458-9903. Email: mcrfton@mcrlaw.com.

ASSOCIATE

Kevin J. Kiley

For Complete List of Firm Personnel, See General Section

For full biographical listings, see the Martindale-Hubbell Law Directory

CANADA
QUEBEC

*MONTREAL,** Montreal Dist.

de Grandpré Chait (AV)

1000, De La Gauchetière Street West, Suite 2900, H3B 4W5
Telephone: 514-878-4311
Fax: 514-878-4333
Email: info@degrandpre-chait.com

PARTNER OF FIRM

Founding Partner Samuel Chait, Q.C. (1904-1982)

Christiane Alary
Normand Amyot
Jacques L. Archambault
André P. Asselin
François Beauchamp
Marc Beauchemin
Jean Benoît
Jacques Bourque
Arthur I. Bronstein
Pierre Brossoit
J. Brian Cornish
Louis Demers
Jean-Pierre Desmarais
Gilles Fafard
Jean-Jacques Gagnon
Guy Gilain
Jean François Giroux
Gilles Godin, Q.C.
Andrée Gosselin
Frederica Jacobs
David H. Kauffman
Sandor J. Klein
Gabriel Kordovi
Pierre Labelle
Diane Lajeunesse
Eric Lalanne
Virginia K. H. Lam
Benoît Larose
Philippe Leclercq
Daniel Lessard
Ronald H. Levy
C. Ralph Lipper
Jean-François Ménard
Pierre Mercille
Benoît Pelchat
Yves Poirier
Olivier Prat, Q.C.
Alain Robichaud
Marc J. Rubin
Louis Samuel
Ronald L. Stein
Mark E. Turcot

For full biographical listings, see the Martindale-Hubbell Law Directory

McMaster Gervais (AV)

A General Partnership
1000 de La Gauchetière Street West, Suite 900, H3B 5H4
Telephone: 514-879-1212
Fax: 514-954-1905
Email: info@mcmastergervais.com *URL:* http://www.mcmastergervais.com

MEMBERS OF FIRM

Daniel Ayotte
John G. Murphy
Patrice Morin
Yvan Houle
Marie Audren
Robert Fosco

COUNSEL

Jacques Brien

For Complete List of Firm Personnel, See General Section

For full biographical listings, see the Martindale-Hubbell Law Directory

Woods & Partners (AV)

2000 McGill College Avenue, Suite 1100, H3A 3H3
Telephone: 514-982-4545
Telecopier: 514-284-2046
Email: general@woods.qc.ca

MEMBERS OF FIRM

James A. Woods
Christian Immer
Julien Cools-Lartigue
Nathalie Chalifour
Christopher Lund Richter
Annie Galarneau
Sébastien Richemont
Kathleen Beaugé
Marjorie Delagrave

For full biographical listings, see the Martindale-Hubbell Law Directory

CANADA
SASKATCHEWAN

*REGINA,** Regina Jud. Centre

MacPherson Leslie & Tyerman (AV)

1500-1874 Scarth Street, S4P 4E9
Telephone: 306-347-8000
Telecopier: 306-352-5250
Email: mltreg@mlt.com
Saskatoon, Saskatchewan Office: 1500-410 22nd Street East, S7K 5T6.
Telephone: 306-975-7100.
Telecopier: 306-975-7145.

MEMBERS OF FIRM

Maurice O. Laprairie, Q.C.
Douglas C. Hodson
Leonard D. Andrychuk
Robert W. Leurer

For Complete List of Firm Personnel, See General Section

For full biographical listings, see the Martindale-Hubbell Law Directory

CORPORATE LAW

MINNESOTA

*MINNEAPOLIS,** Hennepin Co.

PARSINEN KAPLAN LEVY ROSBERG & GOTLIEB P.A. (AV)

100 South 5th Street Suite 1100, 55402-1298
Telephone: 612-333-2111
Fax: 612-333-6798

John Parsinen
Robert A. Levy
Sidney Kaplan
Jack A. Rosberg
David Gotlieb
Karen A. Ciegler Hansen
Joseph M. Sokolowski
Howard J. Rubin
David A. Orenstein
John C. Levy
Steven R. Katz
Kathleen Doar
Brian R. Martens
Rebecca J. McDaniel
Stephen M. Hickok
Ann Marks Sanford
Jude Anne Carluccio
Pamela A. Curran
David B. Gollin

Theresa M. Kowalski
Joan P. Kurlander
Bryan D. Biesterfeld
Daniel W. Eck
Nels E. Carlson
John Scott De Lanoy
Ann S. Grayson
Kimberley Ste. Marie Becker
Heidi E. Pergament

For full biographical listings, see the Martindale-Hubbell Law Directory

MISSISSIPPI

BILOXI, Harrison Co.

BROWN, WATT & BUCHANAN, P.A. (AV)

115 Main Street, P.O. Box 1377, 39533-1377
Telephone: 228-374-2999
Telecopier: 228-435-7090
Email: mail@bwblaw.com *URL:* http://www.bwblaw.com
Pascagoula, Mississippi Office: 3112 Canty Street, P.O. Box 2220.
Telephone: 228-762-0035.
Fax: 228-762-0299.

Raymond L. Brown
W. Lee Watt
Patrick R. Buchanan
W. Mark Edwards
A. Kelly Sessoms, III
Alan K. Sudduth

General Counsel for: Mississippi Export Railroad Co.; Pascagoula Municipal Separate School District.
Representative Clients: United States Fidelity & Guaranty Co.; The Travelers Companies; The Home Insurance Co.; CSX Transportation, Inc.; Blue Cross-Blue Shield of Mississippi; Burlington Insurance Co.; Continental Insurance; Deere & Co.

For full biographical listings, see the Martindale-Hubbell Law Directory

*CLEVELAND,** Bolivar Co.

LEVINGSTON & LEVINGSTON (AV)

201 South Pearman Avenue, P.O. Box 1327, 38732-3247
Telephone: 601-843-2791
Fax: 601-843-2797
Email: jleving@tecinfo.com

MEMBERS OF FIRM

Alfred A. Levingston (1917-1997)
Jeffrey A. Levingston

General Counsel for: Bolivar County Drainage Commissioners; Bolivar County Hospital; City of Shelby.
Local Counsel for: Commercial Union; Maryland Casualty Co.; Federated Mutual Implement & Hardware Insurance Co.; Baxter-Travenol Laboratories, Inc.

For full biographical listings, see the Martindale-Hubbell Law Directory

*GULFPORT,** Harrison Co.

ALLEN, VAUGHN, COBB & HOOD, P.A. (AV)

One Hancock Plaza, Suite 1209, P.O. Drawer 4108, 39502-4108
Telephone: 601-864-4011
Fax: 601-864-4852
Email: avchlaw@sunherald.infinet.com

(See Next Column)

Harry R. Allen
Thomas E. Vaughn
David L. Cobb
Billy W. Hood
Joy Lambert Phillips
Robert W. Atkinson
Benjamin U. Bowden
Richard B. Tubertini
Rodney Douglas Robinson
E. Colette Towles
David W. Crane
John A. Foxworth, Jr.

J. Adrian Smith
Michael J. Casano

OF COUNSEL
D. Knox White

LEGAL SUPPORT PERSONNEL
Kevin C. Stachowski (Paralegal)

For full biographical listings, see the Martindale-Hubbell Law Directory

BLACKWELL & WHITE (AV)

1613 Twenty-Third Avenue, 39501
Telephone: 228-864-1484
FAX: 228-868-6484
Mailing Address: P.O. Box 430, 39502-0430,

MEMBERS OF FIRM

Leonard A. Blackwell, II
Gary White

ASSOCIATES

James B. Wright, Jr.
Patricia S. Tisdale

References: Merchants Bank & Trust Co.; Hancock Bank.

For full biographical listings, see the Martindale-Hubbell Law Directory

DUKES, DUKES, KEATING AND FANECA, P.A. (AV)

2909 13th Street, 6th Floor, P.O. Drawer W, 39501
Telephone: 228-868-1111
Fax: 228-863-2886
Email: ddkf@ddkf.com

William F. Dukes
Walter W. Dukes
Hugh D. Keating
Cy Faneca
Phillip W. Jarrell

Joan E. Lund
W. Edward Hatten, Jr.
Thomas William Busby
William W. Abbott, Jr.
Trace D. McRaney
Stephen M. Cozart
Derek R. Cusick

For full biographical listings, see the Martindale-Hubbell Law Directory

BOYCE HOLLEMAN A PROFESSIONAL CORPORATION (AV)

1913 15th Street, P.O. Drawer 1030, 39502
Telephone: 228-863-3142; 1-800-863-3140
Telecopier: 228-863-9829
Email: boyce1913@aol.com

Boyce Holleman

Timothy C. Holleman
Leslie Dean Holleman
David J. "Jeff" White

References: Hancock Bank, Gulfport; Merchants Bank & Trust Co., Gulfport; Bank of Wiggins, Wiggins, Mississippi.

For full biographical listings, see the Martindale-Hubbell Law Directory

MEADOWS RILEY LAW FIRM (AV)

1720 23rd Avenue, P.O. Box 550, 39502
Telephone: 601-864-4511
Telecopier: 601-868-2178

Joseph R. Meadows
Donnie D. Riley
Jerry D. Riley
Karen J. Young

Representative Clients: Bubba Oustalat Lincoln Mercury, Inc.; Lee Tractor Co. of Mississippi.
Reference: Hancock Bank.

For full biographical listings, see the Martindale-Hubbell Law Directory

NEWTON AND HOFF, L.L.P. (AV)

2019 23rd Avenue, P.O. Box 910, 39502-0910
Telephone: 228-863-8827
Fax: 228-868-6007
Email: newtonhoff@aol.com *URL:* http://www.newtonhoff.com

Paul M. Newton (Resident)
Frederick T. Hoff, Jr. (Resident)
Paul M. Newton, Jr. (Resident)

For full biographical listings, see the Martindale-Hubbell Law Directory

*PASCAGOULA,** Jackson Co.

BROWN, WATT & BUCHANAN, P.A. (AV)

3112 Canty Street, P.O. Box 2220, 39569-2220
Telephone: 228-762-0035
Telecopier: 228-762-0299
Email: mail@bwblaw.com *URL:* http://www.bwblaw.com
Biloxi, Mississippi Office: 115 Main Street, P.O. Box 1377.
Telephone: 228-374-2999.
Fax: 228-435-7090.

Raymond L. Brown
W. Lee Watt
Patrick R. Buchanan
W. Mark Edwards
A. Kelly Sessoms, III
Alan K. Sudduth

General Counsel for: Mississippi Export Railroad Co.; Pascagoula Municipal Separate School District.
Representative Clients: United States Fidelity & Guaranty Co.; The Travelers Companies; The Home Insurance Co.; CSX Transportation, Inc.; Blue Cross-Blue Shield of Mississippi; Burlington Insurance Co.; Continental Insurance; Deere & Co.

For full biographical listings, see the Martindale-Hubbell Law Directory

BRYAN, NELSON, SCHROEDER, CASTIGLIOLA & BANAHAN (AV)

1103 Jackson Avenue, P.O. Drawer 1529, 39568-1529
Telephone: 228-762-6631
Fax: 228-769-6392
Email: bns@datasync.com

MEMBERS OF FIRM

E. S. Ned Nelson (1928-1985)
John F. Bryan, III (1915-1994)
Ernest R. Schroeder
Vincent J. Castigliola, Jr.
John A. Banahan
H. Benjamin Mullen

ASSOCIATES

Melinda O. Johnson
Scott Corlew

For full biographical listings, see the Martindale-Hubbell Law Directory

MISSOURI

KANSAS CITY, Jackson, Clay, Platte & Cass Cos.

KURLBAUM STOLL SEAMAN & MUSTOE, P.C. (AV)

City Center Square, 1100 Main Street, Suite 2001, 64105
Telephone: 816-221-5444
Telecopy: 816-474-6822
Email: kssrsm@micro.com

Scuyler M. P. Kurlbaum
Steven H. Mustoe
James M. Seaman
Thomas G. Stoll
Roger K. McCrummen
Jeffrey M. Rinne

Theodore M. Meierotto
Eric C. Carter (Not admitted in MO)

For full biographical listings, see the Martindale-Hubbell Law Directory

ST. LOUIS, (Independent City)

BELZ & JONES P.C. (AV)

7777 Bonhomme, Suite 1710, 63105-1911
Telephone: 314-863-0200
Fax: 314-863-4247

Mark Belz
Terry L. Jones
D. Allen Calhoun

Matthew Hill Hearne

OF COUNSEL

Robert Hickel

For full biographical listings, see the Martindale-Hubbell Law Directory

THE LOWENBAUM PARTNERSHIP, L.L.C. (AV)

222 South Central Avenue, Suite 901 (Clayton), 63105
Telephone: 314-863-0092
Facsimile: 314-746-4848
Email: rml@lowenbaumlaw.com

Timothy L. Elliott
J. Timothy Gorman

Representative Clients: Sinclair Broadcast Group; Unity Health; LaserSight Incorporated; Nesco Container Corporation.

For full biographical listings, see the Martindale-Hubbell Law Directory

PAULE, CAMAZINE & BLUMENTHAL, A PROFESSIONAL CORPORATION (AV)

Sixth Floor, 165 North Meramec Avenue (Clayton), 63105
Telephone: 314-727-2266
Telecopier: 314-727-2101
Email: pcblaw@stlnet.com

Donald W. Paule
Daniel P. Card, II
Thomas M. Blumenthal
Stanley H. Chorlins
Joann N. Lynch Dyroff
D. Keith Henson
Susan A. McNary
Bernard W. Gerdelman
Stefanie L. London

OF COUNSEL

James L. McHugh

For full biographical listings, see the Martindale-Hubbell Law Directory

ROSENBLUM, GOLDENHERSH, SILVERSTEIN & ZAFFT, P.C. (AV)

Fourth Floor, 7733 Forsyth Boulevard, 63105
Telephone: 314-726-6868
Telecopier: 314-726-6786
Belleville, Illinois Office: 2 Park Place Professional Centre, 62221.
Telephone: 618-234-9900.
Columbia, Missouri Office: 3201 South Providence, Suite 101, 65205-4000.
Telephone: 573-441-8686.

Stanley M. Rosenblum
Robert S. Goldenhersh
Merle L. Silverstein
Gene M. Zafft
Carl C. Lang
Richard S. Bender
Michael A. Markenson
David V. Capes
Mark E. Goodman
Jay A. Nathanson
Richard Greenberg
Bennett S. Keller
Leonard D. Vines
Roger M. Herman
Thomas A. Duda
Paul G. Klug
Ira L. Blank
Ellen Levy Siwak
Joshua M. Schindler
Sanford J. Boxerman
Carl R. Desenberg
Scott H. Malin

Jeffrey Alan Cohen
Kristen L. Maly
Todd C. Brockmann
Marilyn Eichler Nathanson
Shelley H. Koren
Jared M. Minkoff

For full biographical listings, see the Martindale-Hubbell Law Directory

NEBRASKA

*LINCOLN,** Lancaster Co.

WOLFE, SNOWDEN, HURD, LUERS & AHL (AV)

Suite 830, NBC Center, 68508-1424
Telephone: 402-474-1507
Fax: 402-474-3170

MEMBERS OF FIRM

Jack G. Wolfe
James A. Snowden
John C. Hurd
James B. Luers
Stephen L. Ahl
Dean J. Sitzmann

ASSOCIATES

Douglas L. Kluender
Thomas B. Wood

For full biographical listings, see the Martindale-Hubbell Law Directory

*OMAHA,** Douglas Co.

DWYER, SMITH, GARDNER, LAZER, POHREN, ROGERS & FORREST (AV)

Suite 400, 8712 West Dodge Road, 68114
Telephone: 402-392-0101
Telefax: 402-392-1011
Email: dwyerlaw@dwyer-smith.com *URL:* http://www.dwyer-smith.com

MEMBERS OF FIRM

Michael L. Lazer
Robert V. Dwyer, Jr.
Charles O. Forrest
Clay M. Rogers
Bruce H. Abrahamson
Paul J. Gardner
H. Daniel Smith
Edward F. Pohren
John L. Apker
Christopher D. Curzon
Bruce J. Goracke

ASSOCIATES

John A. Kinney
Patrick Edward Griffin, Jr.

Representative Clients: Nebraska Health System; Ford Motor Credit Company, Dearborn, Michigan; Nebraska Hospital Association subsidiary Bio Electronics, Lincoln, Oak Bancorporation; Lynn Roberts International; Elliot Equipment Co.; Design Plastics, Inc.

For full biographical listings, see the Martindale-Hubbell Law Directory

Omaha—Continued

RASMUSSEN & MITCHELL (AV)

11605 Miracle Hills Drive, Suite 205, 68154
Telephone: 402-493-3300
Fax: 402-496-0766
Email: lawman000@aol.com *URL:*
http://www.lawyers.com/rasmussen&mitchell

MEMBERS OF FIRM

Wayne S. Rasmussen
James S. Mitchell
Kathryn J. Derr
Shane M. Niebergall

For full biographical listings, see the Martindale-Hubbell Law Directory

NEVADA

*CARSON CITY,** (Independent City)

HALE LANE PEEK DENNISON HOWARD AND ANDERSON (AV)

777 East William Street, Suite 200, P.O. Box 2620, 89702
Telephone: 775-684-6000
Telefax: 775-684-6001
Email: info@halelane.com
Reno, Nevada Office: 100 West Liberty Street, Tenth Floor, P.O. Box 3237.
Telephone: 775-327-3000.
Fax: 775-786-6179.
Las Vegas, Nevada Office: Nevada Financial Center, 2300 West Sahara Avenue, Eighth Floor, Box 8.
Telephone: 702-222-2500.
Fax: 702-365-6940.

MEMBERS OF FIRM

Robert C. Anderson
Richard Bennett (Resident, Reno, Nevada)
James L. Kelly (Resident, Reno, Nevada)
David A. Garcia

ASSOCIATE

James Newman (Resident, Reno, Nevada)

OF COUNSEL

Roy L. Farrow

Representative Clients: Pan Pacific Retail Properties, Inc.; Northwest Funding, Inc.

For Complete List of Firm Personnel, See General Section

For full biographical listings, see the Martindale-Hubbell Law Directory

HENDERSON, Clark Co.

ROOKER & GIBSON (AV)

Suite 105, 701 North Green Valley Parkway, 89014
Telephone: 702-990-8100
Telecopier: 702-932-5266

C. Keith Rooker
James B. Gibson

Reference: BankWest of Nevada.

For full biographical listings, see the Martindale-Hubbell Law Directory

*LAS VEGAS,** Clark Co.

EDWARDS & WINTERTON, CHTD. (AV)

401 North Buffalo Drive, Suite 200, 89128
Telephone: 702-363-0317
Telecopier: 702-363-1630
Email: EOWW.LAW@worldnet.att.net

George T. Morse, III (1945-1996)
Douglas M. Edwards
David J. Winterton

Nazario J. Jureidini
Robert B. Gerard
Thomas E. Trojan
Chris A. Beecroft, Jr.

OF COUNSEL

Nicholas A. Boylan (Not admitted in NV)

For full biographical listings, see the Martindale-Hubbell Law Directory

HALE LANE PEEK DENNISON HOWARD AND ANDERSON (AV)

Nevada Financial Center, 2300 West Sahara Avenue, Eighth Floor, Box 8, 89102
Telephone: 702-222-2500
Fax: 702-365-6940
Email: info@halelane.com
Reno, Nevada Office: 100 West Liberty Street, Tenth Floor, P.O. Box 3237.
Telephone: 775-327-3000.
Telefax: 775-786-6179.

(See Next Column)

Carson City, Nevada Office: 777 East William Street, Suite 200, P.O. Box 2620.
Telephone: 775-684-6000.
Telefax: 775-684-6001.

MEMBERS OF FIRM

Robert C. Anderson (Resident, Reno, Nevada)
Patricia J. Curtis

Representative Clients: Sunterra Corporation; Pan Pacific Retail Properties, Inc.

For Complete List of Firm Personnel, See General Section

For full biographical listings, see the Martindale-Hubbell Law Directory

BILL C. HAMMER & ASSOCIATES (AV)

BankWest Building, 4270 South Decatur Boulevard, Suite B-10, 89103
Telephone: 702-387-0530
Fax: 702-387-0928
Email: bchlawoff@aol.com *URL:* http://www.lawyers.com/billchammer

Bill C. Hammer

For full biographical listings, see the Martindale-Hubbell Law Directory

SHIRINIAN & ROITMAN (AV)

333 North Rancho Drive, Suite 520, 89106
Telephone: 702-631-5650
Fax: 702-631-5603
Email: ashirinian@aol.com *URL:*
http://www.lawyers.com/shirinian&roitman
San Francisco, California Office: 44 Montgomery Street, Suite 1500, 94104.
Telephone: 415-788-1771.
Fax: 415-788-1744.

Ara H. Shirinian
Howard Roitman

For full biographical listings, see the Martindale-Hubbell Law Directory

*RENO,** Washoe Co.

ERWIN THOMPSON & HASCHEFF (AV)

A Partnership including Professional Corporations
Suite 424, One East Liberty Street, P.O. Box 40817, 89501-2123
Telephone: 775-786-9494
Facsimile: 775-786-1180
Email: erwin@renolaw.com *URL:* http://www.renolaw.com

Pierre A. Hascheff
Frank W. Thompson
Thomas P. Erwin

Reference: U.S. Bank (Reno, Nevada, Main Office).

For full biographical listings, see the Martindale-Hubbell Law Directory

GUILD, RUSSELL, GALLAGHER & FULLER, LTD. (AV)

100 West Liberty, Suite 800, P.O. Box 2838, 89505
Telephone: 775-786-2366
Telecopier: 775-322-9105
Email: attorneys@grgflaw.com

Clark J. Guild (1887-1971)
Clark J. Guild, Jr.
C. David Russell
John K. Gallagher
Gary M. Fuller

Jason J. Freelin

Representative Clients: Caithness Resources, Inc.; Chevron USA, Inc.; Dickson Realty; DRGM Advertising Agency; Federal Deposit Insurance Corp.; Intermountain Power Project; Land Rover North America; Porsche Cars North America; Jones-West Ford; City of Los Angeles, Department of Water & Power; Metropolitan Water District of Southern California; Microsoft Corporation; 100 W. Liberty Ltd. Partnership.

For full biographical listings, see the Martindale-Hubbell Law Directory

HALE LANE PEEK DENNISON HOWARD AND ANDERSON (AV)

100 West Liberty Street, Tenth Floor, P.O. Box 3237, 89505
Telephone: 775-327-3000
Telefax: 775-786-6179
Email: info@halelane.com
Las Vegas, Nevada Office: Nevada Financial Center, 2300 West Sahara Avenue, Eighth Floor, Box 8.
Telephone: 702-222-2500.
Fax: 702-365-6940.
Carson City, Nevada Office: 777 East William Street, Suite 200, P.O. Box 2620.
Telephone: 775-684-6000.
Telefax: 775-684-6001.

MEMBERS OF FIRM

Robert C. Anderson
Richard Bennett
James L. Kelly
David A. Garcia

ASSOCIATE

James Newman

(See Next Column)

HALE LANE PEEK DENNISON HOWARD AND ANDERSON, *Reno—Continued*

OF COUNSEL

Roy L. Farrow (Resident, Carson City, Nevada)

Representative Clients: Northwest Funding, Inc.; Pan Pacific Retail Properties, Inc.

For Complete List of Firm Personnel, See General Section

For full biographical listings, see the Martindale-Hubbell Law Directory

MARSHALL HILL CASSAS & DE LIPKAU (AV)

Suite 300 Holcomb Professional Building, 333 Holcomb Avenue, P.O. Box 2790, 89505-2790
Telephone: 775-323-1601
Telecopier: 775-348-7250
Email: general@MHCL-law.com

MEMBERS OF FIRM

Robert W. Marshall
Earl M. Hill
Frank Cassas
Ross E. de Lipkau
John P. Fowler
Rew R. Goodenow
Michael R. Kealy
A. Stanyan Peck

For full biographical listings, see the Martindale-Hubbell Law Directory

WALTHER, KEY, MAUPIN, OATS, COX & LEGOY, A PROFESSIONAL CORPORATION (AV)

Lakeside Professional Plaza, 3500 Lakeside Court, 89509
Telephone: 775-827-2000
Facsimile: 775-827-2185
Mailing Address: P.O. Box 30000, Reno, Nevada, 89520

Steven T. Walther
Jon J. Key
Ernest J. Maupin
C. Robert Cox
L. Robert LeGoy, Jr.
Michael E. Malloy
W. Douglass Maupin
G. Barton Mowry
Kim G. Rowe
Procter J. Hug
Donald A. Lattin
Gustave J. Rossi
Robert A. Winkel
Kurt O. Hunsberger
Michael A. Nivinskus
Christopher D. Jaime

Rick R. Hsu
Michaelle D. Rafferty

Representative Clients: Bank America of Nevada (Trust Dept.); Bechtel Corporations; Bill Pearce Olds, BMW, Volvo; Wells Fargo, N.A. (Trust Dept.); General Motors Acceptance Corp.; Nevada Realtors; Radiation Oncology Associates; The Ralph M. Parsons Corporation; Parsons Corporation; Reno Air, Inc.

For full biographical listings, see the Martindale-Hubbell Law Directory

NEW HAMPSHIRE

HAMPTON, Rockingham Co.

CASASSA AND RYAN (AV)

459 Lafayette Road, 03842
Telephone: 603-926-6336
Fax: 603-926-4127
Email: casassa@concentric.net

MEMBERS OF FIRM

H. Alfred Casassa
John J. Ryan
Peter J. Saari
Robert A. Casassa
Faye R. Goldberg

ASSOCIATE

Daniel R. Hartley

General Counsel: Foss Manufacturing Company.
Representative Clients: Town of Hampton Falls; Town of North Hampton; Rye Beach Village District; Hampton School District; Susan Conway Enterprises; Wal-Mart Inc.

For full biographical listings, see the Martindale-Hubbell Law Directory

*LACONIA,** Belknap Co.

NORMANDIN, CHENEY & O'NEIL (AV)

Normandin Square, 213 Union Avenue, P.O. Box 575, 03247-0575
Telephone: 603-524-4380
Fax: 603-528-6831
Email: nco@lr.net

MEMBERS OF FIRM

Paul L. Normandin
Robert A. Dietz

(See Next Column)

OF COUNSEL

Duncan J. Farmer

Counsel for: Laconia Savings Bank; Lakes Region Mental Health Center; Laconia Airport Authority; Central New Hampshire Realty, Inc.; All Metals Industries, Inc.; Lakes Region Anesthesiology, P.A.; Cormier Corp.; Scotia Technology; Vemaline Products.

For Complete List of Firm Personnel, See General Section

For full biographical listings, see the Martindale-Hubbell Law Directory

NEW JERSEY

ASBURY PARK, Monmouth Co.

CARTON, WITT, ARVANITIS & BARISCILLO, L.L.C. (AV)

(Formerly Durand, Ivins & Carton)
4001 Route 66 At Garden State Parkway, P.O. Box 1229, 07712
Telephone: 732-922-9500
Telecopier: 732-922-1625
Manasquan, New Jersey Office: 40 Union Avenue, P.O. Box 367.
Telephones: 908-223-1800; 449-5311.

MEMBERS OF FIRM

George N. Arvanitis
James D. Carton, III (Manasquan Office)
John C. Carton (Manasquan Office)
Stephen C. Carton
H. Frank Carpentier
Dana C. Argeris
Martin J. McGreevy
Albert A. Zager
Mark R. Aikins
K. Edward Jacobi
Joseph J. Colao, Jr.
James D. Carton (1868-1943)
Forman T. Bailey (1887-1964)
J. Victor Carton (1900-1982)
Thomas D. Nary (1904-1985)
Robert R. Witt (1921-1988)

ASSOCIATES

Thomas F. Heaney, Jr.
Peter V. Koenig
Susan J. F. Weiss
James D. Carton, IV
Aaron J. Rosenfeld
Russell J. Malta
Janice B. Venables
Marc J. Comer

OF COUNSEL

Francis X. Crahay
Henry E. Kordes
George A. Bariscillo, Jr.
Robert V. Carton

Attorneys for: New Jersey Bell Telephone Co.; Garden State Indemnity Co.; Jersey Shore Medical Center, Inc.
Local Attorneys for: Travelers Insurance Co.; Aetna Casualty & Surety Co.; New Jersey Manufacturers Insurance Co.; Liberty Mutual; Prudential Insurance Co.; Chubb & Son.

For full biographical listings, see the Martindale-Hubbell Law Directory

BEDMINSTER, Somerset Co.

PURCELL, RIES, SHANNON, MULCAHY & O'NEILL (AV)

One Pluckemin Way, P.O. Box 754, 07921
Telephone: 908-658-3800
Fax: 908-658-4659
Email: general@prsmo.com *URL:* http://www.prsmo.com
Philadelphia, Pennsylvania Office: 12th Floor, East Tower, Centre Square, 1500 Market Square.
Telephone: 215-665-5602.
Fax: 215-569-8228.

MEMBERS OF FIRM

Eugene M. Purcell
William P. Ries
John J. Shannon
Thomas M. Mulcahy
Michael F. O'Neill
David M. Hawkins
Joseph R. Purcell
Kevin R. Brotz
John M. Bowens
Kevin Kovacs
Kenneth D. Merin
Valerie K. Bollheimer
Andrew L. Indeck
Joseph M. Donegan
Mark Mattia

ASSOCIATES

Rita F. Barone
Kathleen J. Devlin
Paul L. Gallagher
Gary Grabas
John R. Haggerty
William T. Hilliard
Eric J. Konecke
Susan Lawless
Michael J. McCaffrey
Kathleen M. Quinn
Thomas Charles Savoth
Donna M. Stephan-Nolan
Barbara C. Zimmerman

OF COUNSEL

David D. Furman
C. Judson Hamlin

LEGAL SUPPORT PERSONNEL

Gary Molloy

Reference: Somerset Trust Co.

For full biographical listings, see the Martindale-Hubbell Law Directory

BERNARDSVILLE, Somerset Co.

SHAIN, SCHAFFER & RAFANELLO, A PROFESSIONAL CORPORATION (AV)

Plaza 202, 150 Morristown Road, Suite 105, 07924
Telephone: 908-953-9300
Fax: 908-953-2969
Email: ssrpc@aol.com

Joel L. Shain
Marguerite M. Schaffer
Richard A. Rafanello
Gary L. Maher
Robert A. Pinel
Phedra R. Rudell (Not admitted in NJ)

OF COUNSEL

Elliott L. Katz

LEGAL SUPPORT PERSONNEL

Tracy DeWitt (Legal Researcher)

For full biographical listings, see the Martindale-Hubbell Law Directory

FLORHAM PARK, Morris Co.

DRINKER BIDDLE & SHANLEY LLP (AV)

A Pennsylvania Limited Liability Partnership
500 Campus Drive, 07932-1047
Telephone: 973-360-1100
Fax: 973-285-1625; 360-9831
URL: http://www.dbr.com
Philadelphia, Pennsylvania Office: Drinker Biddle & Reath LLP, One Logan Square, 18th & Cherry Streets.
Telephone: 215-988-2700.
Telefax: 215-988-2757.
Cable Address: "Debemac."
Washington, D.C. Office: Drinker Biddle & Reath LLP, 1500 K Street, N.W., Suite 1100.
Telephone: 202-842-8800.
Telefax: 202-842-8465.
Princeton, New Jersey Office: Suite 300, 105 College Road East.
Telephone: 609-716-6500.
Telefax: 609-799-7000.
Berwyn, Pennsylvania Office: Drinker Biddle & Reath LLP, Suite 300, 1000 Westlakes Drive.
Telephone: 610-993-2200.
Telefax: 610-993-8585.
New York, New York Office: Drinker Biddle & Reath LLP, 89th Floor, One World Trade Center.
Telephone: 212-321-1812.
Telecopier: 1-212-466-0569.

John Kandravy
James H. Freis
Stewart E. Lavey
Lydia C. Stefanowicz
Ieva Miesnieks Rogers
Michael E. Helmer

COUNSEL

Michael J. Nita

Romney L. Grippo

For Complete List of Firm Personnel, See General Section

For full biographical listings, see the Martindale-Hubbell Law Directory

*HACKENSACK,** Bergen Co.

NICOLETTE & PERKINS, P.A. (AV)

3 University Plaza, Fifth Floor, 07601
Telephone: 201-488-9080
Telecopier: 201-488-5580
Email: nicoletteperkins@juno.com *URL:* http://www.lawyers.com/nicolette&perkins

David A. Nicolette, Jr.
Eric R. Perkins

Jeanette A. Odynski
Laura N. Keenan
Toni Marie McPhillips

For full biographical listings, see the Martindale-Hubbell Law Directory

SHAPIRO & CROLAND (AV)

A Partnership including Professional Corporations
Continental Plaza II, 411 Hackensack Avenue, 07601
Telephone: 201-488-3900
Fax: 201-488-9481

Barry I. Croland, P.C.
Robert P. Shapiro, P.C.
Barry L. Baime
Jay Rubenstein
Kenneth S. Apfel
Kenneth S. Goldrich, P.C.
Bruce J. Ackerman
Stuart Reiser, P.C.
Meridith J. Bronson
John P. Di Iorio
David O. Marcus
Robert F. Green
Lizabeth Sarakin
David Torchin
Robin C. Bogan
Craig D. Spector

OF COUNSEL

Harvey R. Sorkow

(See Next Column)

Donald R. Sorkow (1930-1985)

Reference: Bank of New York-National Community Division.

For full biographical listings, see the Martindale-Hubbell Law Directory

MANASQUAN, Monmouth Co.

CARTON, WITT, ARVANITIS & BARISCILLO, L.L.C. (AV)

(Formerly Durand, Ivins & Carton)
40 Union Avenue, P.O. Box 367, 08736
Telephone: 908-223-1800
Asbury Park, New Jersey Office: 4001 Route 66 at Garden State Parkway, P.O. Box 1229.
Telephone: 732-922-9500.
Telecopier: 732-922-1625.

RESIDENT PARTNERS

James D. Carton, III
John C. Carton

Attorneys for: New Jersey Bell Telephone Co.; Jersey Shore Medical Center, Inc.
Local Attorneys for: Travelers Insurance Co.; Aetna Casualty & Surety Co.; New Jersey Manufacturers Insurance Co.; Liberty Mutual; Prudential Insurance Co.; Chubb & Son.; Princeton Insurance Co.; Garden State Indemnity Co.

For full biographical listings, see the Martindale-Hubbell Law Directory

*NEWARK,** Essex Co.

MCMANIMON & SCOTLAND, L.L.C. (AV)

One Riverfront Plaza, 4th Floor, 07102-5311
Telephone: 973-622-1800
Fax: 973-622-7333; 973-622-3744

MEMBERS OF FIRM

Joseph P. Baumann, Jr.
John V. Cavaliere
John B. Hall
Glenn F. Scotland
Ronald J. Ianoale
Andrea L. Kahn
Jeffrey G. Kramer
Leslie G. London
Edward J. McManimon, III

OF COUNSEL

Norman M. Robertson
Carla J. Brundage

ASSOCIATES

Peter S. Crisafi
Sheila Newsome Maddox
M. Frances Ciesla
Kristin Dwyer Ganley
Joseph C. Jasaitis
Stephen N. Severud
Thomas J. Hastie, Jr.

LEGAL SUPPORT PERSONNEL

Helen Lysaght

PARALEGALS

Sandra Simoes

For full biographical listings, see the Martindale-Hubbell Law Directory

MEYNER AND LANDIS (AV)

One Gateway Center, Suite 2500, 07102-5311
Telephone: 973-624-2800
Fax: 973-624-0356
Email: attys@meyner.com *URL:* http://www.meyner.com

Robert B. Meyner (1908-1990)
Edwin C. Landis, Jr.
John N. Malyska
William J. Fiore
Anthony F. Siliato
Francis R. Perkins
Howard O. Thompson
Scott T. McCleary
Linda Townley Snyder
William H. Schmidt, Jr.
David B. Grantz

For full biographical listings, see the Martindale-Hubbell Law Directory

OCEAN TOWNSHIP, Monmouth Co.

EVANS, OSBORNE & KREIZMAN (AV)

CN 7808 1500 Lawrence Avenue, 07712-7808
Telephone: 732-643-0300
Fax: 732-643-0340
New York, New York Office: Suite 7967, One World Trade Center.
Telephone: 212-466-1207.

MEMBERS OF FIRM

Harry S. Evans
Harry V. Osborne, II
Joel N. Kreizman
Mary O'Keefe Massey
Kevin E. Hoffman

ASSOCIATES

Marie A. Accardi
James F. McDonough
Kenneth P. Skibinski

Representative Clients: United Kingdom P&I Club (Thomas R. Miller Insurance Services); American Marine Underwriters, Inc.; Continental Insurance Cos.; Hartford Insurance Cos.; CIGNA Cos.; Jersey Central Power & Light Co.; First Union Bank; CNA Insurance Cos.; General Public Utilities, Inc.

For full biographical listings, see the Martindale-Hubbell Law Directory

PARSIPPANY, Morris Co.

CUYLER BURK (AV)

Parsippany Corporate Center, Four Century Drive, 07054-4663
Telephone: 973-734-3200
Telex: 429071
Telecopier: 973-734-3201
Email: Main@Cuyler.com *URL:* http://www.cuyler.com
New York, New York Office: 350 Fifth Avenue, Suite 3304. 10018.
Telephone: 212-645-4039.

MEMBERS OF FIRM

Stephen D. Cuyler
Jo Ann Burk
Stefano Calogero
David L. Menzel
Peter Petrou
Richard A. Crooker
Michael J. Jones

COUNSEL

Anne M. Mohan
Frank J. Miele

ASSOCIATES

Jan C. Walker
Kathleen Jane Olear
Claudia L. Marchese
Mark G. Eliades
Kimberly A. Joel
Christy A. Ramunno
Catherine E. Youngman
Andrew K. Craig
Mark S. Winter
Thomas J. Castano
Hugo A. Hilgendorff, IV

LEGAL SUPPORT PERSONNEL

Frederick M. H. Currie, Jr.

For full biographical listings, see the Martindale-Hubbell Law Directory

SADDLE BROOK, Bergen Co.

COHN LIFLAND PEARLMAN HERRMANN & KNOPF LLP (AV)

Park 80 Plaza West-One, 07663
Telephone: 201-845-9600
Telecopier: 201-845-9423
Email: info@njlawfirm.com *URL:* http://www.njlawfirm.com

MEMBERS OF FIRM

Albert L. Cohn
Peter S. Pearlman
Barry A. Knopf
Daniel Crystal (Retired)
Jeffrey W. Herrmann
Robert D. Zatorski
Allen Susser
Mary Ann T. Stokes
Brian D. Zinn
Joshua P. Cohn

ASSOCIATES

Virginia A. Harper
Leonard Z. Kaufmann
Audra DePaolo
Robert Ricci, Jr.
Maurice W. McLaughlin
Andrew C. Abrams
Jessica V. Henry

OF COUNSEL

Sylvia J. Cohn
Jodi B. Scherl

For full biographical listings, see the Martindale-Hubbell Law Directory

KRUGMAN & KAILES LLP (AV)

Park 80 West-Plaza Two, 07663-5835
Telephone: 201-845-3434; 212-695-3262
Telecopier: 201-845-9627
Email: counsel@krugmankailes.com
New York, New York Office: 99 Park Avenue, Suite 2200.
Telephone: 212-599-1060.
Telecopier: 212-599-6282.
London, England Office: 90 Fetter Lane, London EC4A-1PT.
Telephone: 011 (44) 171-421-7918.
Telecopier: 011 (44) 171-831-6407.

MEMBERS OF FIRM

Martin Krugman (1916-1994)
Howard Kailes
Thomas J. Goodwin
Ward C. Laracy
Robert I. Wexler
Alan H. Fox
Joy M. Mercer
Kerry B. Flowers

OF COUNSEL

James D. Krugman

COUNSEL

Judith S. Musicant

ASSOCIATES

Anne M. Wallace (Not admitted in NJ)
April A. Savoye
Lisa Ann Miller
Patrizia E. DeBari
David J. Hanley, Jr.
Anjana D. Patel
W. Mark O'Brien

For full biographical listings, see the Martindale-Hubbell Law Directory

SKILLMAN, Somerset Co.

GERALD P. SEID (AV)

144 Tamarack Circle, Montgomery Knoll, U.S. Highway 206 North, 08558
Telephone: 609-921-3747
Fax: 609-921-3936
Email: 72624.2715@compuserve.com

For full biographical listings, see the Martindale-Hubbell Law Directory

*SOMERVILLE,** Somerset Co.

SCHACHTER, TROMBADORE, OFFEN, STANTON & PAVICS, A PROFESSIONAL CORPORATION (AV)

45 East High Street, P.O. Box 520, 08876-0520
Telephone: 908-722-5700
Fax: 908-722-8853

Richard J. Schachter
John J. Trombadore
Stephen M. Offen
Michael J. Stanton
Thomas A. Pavics

Timothy P. McKeown
Jerry S. D'Aniello

For full biographical listings, see the Martindale-Hubbell Law Directory

RAYMOND R. & DAVID W. TROMBADORE, P.C. A PROFESSIONAL CORPORATION (AV)

33 East High Street, 08876
Telephone: 908-722-7555
Fax: 908-722-6269
URL: http://www.trombadorelaw.com

Raymond R. Trombadore
David W. Trombadore

OF COUNSEL

Ann W. Trombadore

References: Summit Bank; Somerset Savings & Loan Assn.

For full biographical listings, see the Martindale-Hubbell Law Directory

NEW MEXICO

*ALBUQUERQUE,** Bernalillo Co.

KENNETH C. LEACH, P.C. (AV)

1110 Pennsylvania N.E., Suite A, 87110
Telephone: 505-243-3322
Fax: 505-242-1268
URL: http://www.lawyers.com/leachlaw

Kenneth C. Leach

Jonathan Reid Mowrer

LEGAL SUPPORT PERSONNEL

Wayne C. Edwards (CEO)
Marilyn Alires Marsh (Paralegal)
Virginia Bosworth (Paralegal)

For full biographical listings, see the Martindale-Hubbell Law Directory

NEW YORK

*ALBANY,** Albany Co.

FEATHERSTONHAUGH, CONWAY, WILEY & CLYNE, L.L.P. (AV)

99 Pine Street, Suite 207, 12207
Telephone: 518-436-0786
Fax: 518-427-0452
URL: http://www.fcwc-law.com

MEMBERS OF FIRM

James D. Featherstonhaugh
Thomas A. Conway
Stephen J. Wiley
Elizabeth K. Clyne

ASSOCIATES

Nadine Feiden Shadlock
Denis R. Hurley, Jr.
Andrew W. Kirby
William F. Conway, IV
Gerard L. Conway, Jr.
Steven M. Connolly

OF COUNSEL

William F. Conway
Jeffrey J. Conklin
David Weinraub
Randall J. Ezick

(See Next Column)

FEATHERSTONHAUGH, CONWAY, WILEY & CLYNE L.L.P.—*Continued*

LEGAL SUPPORT PERSONNEL
GOVERNMENTAL RELATIONS

John L. Hardy
Daniel G. Plummer
John P. Griffin
David F. Fleming

For full biographical listings, see the Martindale-Hubbell Law Directory

ISEMAN, CUNNINGHAM, RIESTER & HYDE, LLP (AV)

9 Thurlow Terrace, 12203
Telephone: 518-462-3000
Telecopier: 518-462-4199
Email: lawfirm@icrh.com *URL:* http://www.icrh.com
Canandaigua, New York Office: 37 East Gibson Street, P.O. Box 179, 14424.
Telephone: 716-394-1450.
Fax: 716-394-5121.

MEMBERS OF FIRM

Frederick C. Riester
Michael J. Cunningham
Robert Hall Iseman
Carol Ann Hyde
Linda J. Clark

Brian M. Culnan
Kihyun S. Kim
Richard A. Frankel
Stephanie E. Moriarty
Valerie R. Lape Handy
Marcia B. Smith
Ellen Gillerman Cox
Jennifer A. Grego
Cara E. Johnson

OF COUNSEL

Michael J. McNeil
Deborah A. Kirby

For full biographical listings, see the Martindale-Hubbell Law Directory

SHANLEY, SWEENEY, REILLY & ALLEN, P.C. (AV)

The Castle at Ten Thurlow Terrace, 12203
Telephone: 518-463-1415
Fax: 518-463-3210
Email: lawyers@shanleysweeney.com *URL:* http://www.shanleysweeney.com

Michael P. Shanley, Jr.
Robert L. Sweeney
J. Stephen Reilly
John L. Allen
Gregory D. Faucher
J. Michael Naughton
Steven S. Heyman
Scott P. Olson
David C. Kuracina
Thomas A. Shepardson
Melissa M. Beskid
Mark T. Sweeney

Christopher E. Buckey
Stacey Weisenfeld

For full biographical listings, see the Martindale-Hubbell Law Directory

ARDSLEY, Westchester Co.

KOO, LARRABEE & LAU-KEE, LLP (AV)

Ardsley Park Science & Technology Center, 410 Saw Mill River Road, 10502
Telephone: 914-674-8000
Fax: 914-674-8244
URL: http://www.KOOLAW.com

Richard Koo
Susan B. Larrabee
Glenn Lau-Kee

OF COUNSEL

Norman Lau-Kee
Paul M. Bochner

For full biographical listings, see the Martindale-Hubbell Law Directory

*BINGHAMTON,** Broome Co.

HINMAN, HOWARD & KATTELL, LLP (AV)

700 Security Mutual Building, 80 Exchange Street, P.O. Box 5250, 13902-5250
Telephone: 607-723-5341
Fax: 607-723-6605
Email: jworband@hhk.com *URL:* http://www.hhk.com
Norwich, New York Office: 48 Hale Street, 13815-2039.
Telephone: 607-334-5896.
Fax: 607-336-1628.
Oneonta, New York Office: 12 South Main Street, 13820-2542.
Telephone: 607-432-5331.
Fax: 607-432-2683.
New York, N.Y. Office: 500 5th Avenue, Suite 1725, 10110.
Telephone: 212-840-3017.
Fax: 212-840-2345.

MEMBERS OF FIRM

James W. Orband
Lawrence C. Anderson
Clayton M. Axtell, Jr.
Keith E. Osber
Colin T. Naylor, III
Richard H. Pille
Eugene E. Peckham
James M. Hayes
Peter J. Vivona
Clayton M. Axtell, III
John G. Dowd
Katherine A. Fitzgerald

(See Next Column)

MEMBERS OF FIRM (Continued)

James R. Franz
Lillian L. Levy
Kenneth F. Tomko
Allen J. Hall
Thomas A. Conlon, Jr.

COUNSEL

A. Edward Hill
Darwin R. Wales

SPECIAL COUNSEL

Brian R. Wright
Robert H. Wedlake
Frederick A. Griffen
Scott J. Clippinger (Resident, Norwich Office)
Richard C. Lewis

ASSOCIATES

Michael S. Sinicki
Eric D. Farrell
Dianne Oakes
Ronald Louis Greene
Erik T. Koons
Jeffrey LaBarge
Stacey M. Gates

Representative Clients: The Chase Manhattan Bank; BSB Bank & Trust Co.; International Business Machines Corp.; Universal Instruments Corp.; Security Mutual Life Insurance Company of New York; Bell Atlantic; Preferred Mutual Insurance Company; New York State Electric & Gas Corp.; Exxon Corp.

For Complete List of Firm Personnel, See General Section

For full biographical listings, see the Martindale-Hubbell Law Directory

BRONXVILLE, Westchester Co.

GRIFFIN, COOGAN & VENERUSO, P.C. (AV)

51 Pondfield Road, 10708
Telephone: 914-961-1300
Telecopier: 914-961-1476; 914-961-9385

William E. Griffin
James M. Coogan
James J. Veneruso

Daniel J. Griffin
Paul R. Herrick
Thomas G. Marzullo
William E. Sulzer (Not admitted in NY)

Approved Closing Attorneys: Hudson Valley Bank.

For full biographical listings, see the Martindale-Hubbell Law Directory

*BUFFALO,** Erie Co.

BLOCK & COLUCCI, P.C. (AV)

1250 Statler Towers, 14202-3695
Telephone: 716-854-4080; 1-800-388-2595
Fax: 716-854-0059
Litigation Telephone: 716-853-4080
Jupiter, Florida Office: 1001 N. U.S. Highway One, Suite 400.
Telephone: 561-747-0110.
Fax: 561-743-0046.
Clifton Park, New York Office: 9 Executive Park Drive, P.O. Box 5018.
Telephone: 518-348-1000.
Fax: 518-348-2000.
Rochester, New York Office: 311 Alexander Street, Suite 415.
Telephone: 716-454-1660.
Fax: 716-454-7461.

Lester H. Block (1906-1997)
Ernest L. Colucci (1909-1989)
Anthony J. Colucci, Jr.

Elpiniki M. Bechakas
Brandi Burns (Resident, Clifton Park Office)
Heather A. Corey-Mongue (Resident, Clifton Park Office)
Dennis M. Hyatt
Scott J. Leitten (Not admitted in NY)
Mark J. Longo
Melanie C. Marotto
Joel P. Peller
Michael W. Schafer
Debra A. Spellman
Jennifer L. Stoeckl (Resident, Rochester Office)
Kevin P. Wheatley (Resident, Clifton Park Office)

References: Manufacturers & Traders Trust Co.; Palm Beach National Bank & Trust Co.

For full biographical listings, see the Martindale-Hubbell Law Directory

RAICHLE, BANNING, WEISS & STEPHENS (AV)

410 Main Street, 14202
Telephone: 716-852-7587
Telecopier: 716-852-7599
Email: RBWS@MSN.COM

MEMBERS OF FIRM

Frank G. Raichle (1898-1986)
Derrick C. Banning (1916-1995)
Arnold Weiss
R. William Stephens

ASSOCIATES

Lisa Parlato Neff
R. Hugh Stephens

Representative Clients: General Motors Corp.; Cliffstar Corp.; Blue Cross & Blue Shield of Michigan; Sony Picture Releasing Inc.; Superior Jamestown Corp., Adanlock Office Environments Division; Permclip Products Corp.; Living Monuments Inc.

(See Next Column)

RAICHLE, BANNING, WEISS & STEPHENS, *Buffalo—Continued*

For full biographical listings, see the Martindale-Hubbell Law Directory

ROLLS KOHN & ASSOCIATES, LLP (AV)

Twenty Court Street, 14202-3201
Telephone: 716-856-2700
Fax: 716-856-2777

MEMBERS OF FIRM

James E. Rolls
Gerald L. Kohn

Robert M. Goldstein

For full biographical listings, see the Martindale-Hubbell Law Directory

*ELMIRA,** Chemung Co.

SAYLES & EVANS (AV)

One West Church Street, 14901
Telephone: 607-734-2271
Fax: 607-734-1754
Email: saylesev@aol.com

Halsey Sayles (1876-1958)
Pierre W. Evans (1895-1982)

COUNSEL

Harry Treinin
Alan Parsons
William C. Ughetta

MEMBERS OF FIRM

Lewis W. Morse, Jr.
J. Philip Hunter
James F. Young
John R. Alexander
Lawrence LeClair
Clover M. Drinkwater
Cynthia S. Hutchinson
Steven E. Agan
Donna M. Hutchison
James D. Young

ASSOCIATES

Jonathan Edward McKeon
Curt N. Meeder
Conrad R. Wolan
Alan R. Hamilton

For full biographical listings, see the Martindale-Hubbell Law Directory

HUNTINGTON, Suffolk Co.

SMYTH & LACK (AV)

143 Main Street, 11743
Telephone: 516-271-7500
Telecopier: 516-271-7504
URL: http://www.lawyers.com/smyth&lacklaw

MEMBERS OF FIRM

Vincent A. Smyth
James J. Lack

ASSOCIATES

Dana M. Barberis
Edmund J.M. Smyth
Karen E. Nora

Reference: Chemical Bank.

For full biographical listings, see the Martindale-Hubbell Law Directory

JAMESTOWN, Chautauqua Co.

ERICKSON, WEBB & SCOLTON (AV)

111 West Second Street, 14701
Telephone: 716-488-1178
Fax: 716-488-1448
Email: ews@netsync.net

MEMBERS OF FIRM

Alton R. Erickson (1904-1968)
Philip A. Erickson
Paul V. Webb, Jr.
Bruce S. Scolton
Lyle T. Hajdu

References: Marine Midland Bank, N.A.; Chase Manhattan Bank.

For full biographical listings, see the Martindale-Hubbell Law Directory

JERICHO, Nassau Co.

BLAU, KRAMER, WACTLAR & LIEBERMAN, P.C. (AV)

100 Jericho Quadrangle, 11753
Telephone: 516-822-4820
Telecopier: 516-822-4824
Email: BKWLLAW@aol.com

Harvey R. Blau
Edward I. Kramer
David H. Lieberman, P.C.
Edward S. Wactlar
Lonnie Coleman
Nancy D. Lieberman

Reference: Fleet Bank.

For full biographical listings, see the Martindale-Hubbell Law Directory

LATHAM, Albany Co.

GORDON, SIEGEL, MASTRO, MULLANEY, GORDON & GALVIN, P.C. (AV)

9 Cornell Road, Airport Park, 12110
Telephone: 518-690-7000
Telefax: 518-690-7010
Email: firm@gordonsiegel.com *URL:* http://www.gordonsiegel.com

Harold A. Gordon (1889-1956)
Robert Siegel (1916-1992)
Arnold M. Gordon
Michael P. Mullaney
Harold D. Gordon
Arkley L. Mastro, Jr.
Christine M. Galvin

Barbara J. King
Jeffrey T. Culkin
Marc H. Goldberg
Gillian A. Hirsch

OF COUNSEL

N. Robert Hayes, Jr.

References: Key Bank, N.A.; Fleet Bank.

For full biographical listings, see the Martindale-Hubbell Law Directory

*LOCKPORT,** Niagara Co.

SACCA AND SACCA (AV)

102 East Avenue, 14094
Telephone: 716-434-5518
Fax: 716-434-8050
Email: gssacca@aol.com *URL:* http://www.lawyers.com/gsacca

MEMBERS OF FIRM

Stephen A. Sacca
Gerald Stephen Sacca

LEGAL SUPPORT PERSONNEL

Anna Marie Holman (Paralegal)
Lauree E. Chase (Paralegal)

Representative Clients: Lawyers Title Insurance Corp. (Virginia); Village of Wilson.
References: Manufacturers & Traders Trust Co.; Marine Midland Bank; Lockport Savings Bank.

For full biographical listings, see the Martindale-Hubbell Law Directory

MELVILLE, Suffolk Co.

CAHN WISHOD & KNAUER, LLP (AV)

425 Broadhollow Road Suite 315, 11747
Telephone: 631-752-1600
Fax: 631-752-1555
URL: http://www.cahnwishod.com
URL: http://www.lawyers.com/cahnwishod&knauer

MEMBERS OF FIRM

Richard C. Cahn
Eugene L. Wishod
Todd A. Knauer

ASSOCIATES

Brian T. Egan
Patricia A. Rooney

LEGAL SUPPORT PERSONNEL

Susan M. Stonelli (Paralegal)

For full biographical listings, see the Martindale-Hubbell Law Directory

LAMB & BARNOSKY, LLP (AV)

534 Broadhollow Road-CS 9034, 11747-9034
Telephone: 631-694-2300
Telecopier: 631-694-2309
Email: thefirm@lambbarnosky.com *URL:* http://www.lambbarnosky.com

PARTNERS

Eugene R. Barnosky
Robert H. Cohen
Marcia Lyn Finkelstein
Michael J. Heller
Gary Holman
Scott M. Karson
P. L. Lamb
Arthur A. Lane
Joel M. Markowitz
Gerald P. Rosenberg
Patrice Dowd Shenn

OF COUNSEL

Louis E. Black
James F. Gesualdi
Howard W. Newman
Joseph J. Salvatore
Joseph H. Wishod

COUNSEL

Lloyd K. Chanin
Scott P. McBride

ASSOCIATES

Cathleen D. Allen
Catherine Healy Kanzler
Rita Fishman Sheena
Shari Lee Sugarman

For full biographical listings, see the Martindale-Hubbell Law Directory

*NEW YORK,** New York Co.

CARDILLO & CORBETT (AV)

29 Broadway, 10006
Telephone: 212-344-0464
Telex: 421757
Cable Address: "Avocard, N.Y."
Telecopier: 212-797-1212

MEMBERS OF FIRM

Joseph Cardillo, Jr. (1913-1980)
Robert V. Corbett
Christophil B. Costas
Tulio R. Prieto
James P. Rau
Peter G. Drakos

OF COUNSEL

Francis H. McNamara
Donald Burke

For full biographical listings, see the Martindale-Hubbell Law Directory

CHIMEL DORADO (AV)

1180 Avenue of the Americas, Suite 1459, 10036
Telephone: 212-899-5454
Fax: 212-899-5459
Email: cd@cdlawfirm.com *URL:* http://www.lawyers.com/cdlawfirm

Rita A. Chimel
Marianne Gaertner Dorado

OF COUNSEL

Samuel M. Hung

For full biographical listings, see the Martindale-Hubbell Law Directory

COOPERMAN LEVITT WINIKOFF LESTER & NEWMAN, P.C. (AV)

800 Third Avenue, 10022-7601
Telephone: 212-688-7000
Fax: 212-755-2839
URL: http://www.clwln.com
Long Island, New York Office: 1129 Northern Boulevard, Manhasset, 11030.
Telephone: 516-365-1400.
Fax: 516-365-1404.

Robert N. Cooperman
Jack B. Levitt
Robert L. Winikoff
David S. Lester
David B. Newman
Asher H. Miller
H. Frances Kleiner
Harry J. Petchesky
Elliot E. Brecher
Ira I. Roxland
Harris S. Jaffe
Mark L. Lubin
Allen G. Reiter

OF COUNSEL

Vivian L. Dubin

Edward J. Reich
Barry A. Cassell
Gary S. Sastow
Susan Denburg Yellin
Joseph H. Schmitt
Stephen Brodsky
Stephen E. Fox
Jill L. Schechterman (Not admitted in NY)
Carol B. Koch
Stephen W. Semian
Helise Harrington

For full biographical listings, see the Martindale-Hubbell Law Directory

CORBIN SILVERMAN & SANSEVERINO LLP (AV)

805 Third Avenue, 10022-7513
Telephone: 212-308-5000
Telecopier: 212-308-7189

MEMBERS OF FIRM

Stephen B. Silverman
Raymond A. Sanseverino
Joseph W. Muccia
Richard A. Nardi
Kenneth W. Sold
Marc J. Gottridge
John J. Gallagher, Jr.
James T. Sandnes
Garry C. Berman
Adam H. Schuman
Mary B. Templeton

SENIOR COUNSEL

Sol Neil Corbin

OF COUNSEL

Joseph L. Broadwin

ASSOCIATES

Mark A. Shapiro
Joseph J. Macchiarola
Theodora L. Hunter

For full biographical listings, see the Martindale-Hubbell Law Directory

FISHER, FISHER & BERGER (AV)

A Partnership including a Professional Corporation
One Whitehall Street, 10004
Telephone: 212-514-8888
Fax: 212-514-9016
Email: fisherberger@earthlink.net

Andrew S. Fisher, P.C.
Henry T. Berger

(See Next Column)

ASSOCIATES

Melinda H. Vollmer
Eric L. Cooper
Diane C. Lorenc

OF COUNSEL

Harold L. Fisher
Judith E. Held
Gerald A. Resnick
Robert A. Straniere
Stanley Kalmon Schlein
Laurence J. Kaiser

Reference: The Chase Manhattan Bank, N.A.

For full biographical listings, see the Martindale-Hubbell Law Directory

FORD MARRIN ESPOSITO WITMEYER & GLESER, L.L.P. (AV)

Wall Street Plaza, 10005-1875
Telephone: 212-269-4900
Facsimile: 212-344-4294
Cable Address: "Formarew-New York"
Email: postmaster@fmew.com *URL:* http://www.fmew.com
Montclair, New Jersey Office: 49 Park Street.
Telephone: 973-744-3700.
Facsimile: 973-509-1565.

MEMBERS OF FIRM

James M. Adrian
Michael L. Anania
Charles A. Booth
Cushing O'Malley Condon
Elizabeth M. De Cristofaro
Thomas R. Esposito
William P. Ford
Victor G. Gleser (1948-1992)
Stuart C. Levene
Richard B. Marrin
Edward M. Pinter
Philip S. Plexico (1931-1983)
John J. Witmeyer III

COUNSEL

James F. X. Hiler

ASSOCIATES

Jay R. Alicandri
Jody M. Barringer
David A. Beke
Christopher J. Carney
Todd S. Corey
Joseph D'Ambrosio
Serena C. Hunn
Matthew J. Lasky
Paul V. Majkowski
Michael A. Rowe
Michael J. Tricarico

For full biographical listings, see the Martindale-Hubbell Law Directory

FRIEDMAN, WITTENSTEIN & HOCHMAN, A PROFESSIONAL CORPORATION (AV)

101 East 52nd Street, 10022
Telephone: 212-750-8700
Telecopier: 212-223-8391
Email: friedwitt@aol.com

Stuart I. Friedman
Andrew A. Wittenstein

COUNSEL

Stephen A. Hochman
John T. McLoughlin (Not admitted in NY)

Mary Hillyer Dontzin
Paul S. Grossman
David O. Lloyd
Gianna M. McCarthy
Allison D. Powell

For full biographical listings, see the Martindale-Hubbell Law Directory

FROMME SCHWARTZ NEWMAN & CORNICELLO, LLP (AV)

The Woolworth Building, 233 Broadway, Suite 2702, 10279-2799
Telephone: 212-267-8100
Fax: 212-406-2222
Email: attorneys@fsnc.com *URL:* http://www.fsnc.com

Martin D. Newman
Peter A. Schwartz
Anthony J. Cornicello
Eric F. Fromme
Paul F. Peragine

ASSOCIATES

Robert David Werth
David Tendler
Charlotte G. Anderson-Bedford
John Pizzano

COUNSEL

Michael B. Rosenblatt

For full biographical listings, see the Martindale-Hubbell Law Directory

GOLENBOCK, EISEMAN, ASSOR & BELL (AV)

437 Madison Avenue, 10022
Telephone: 212-907-7300
Telecopier: 212-754-0330
Email: postmaster@golenbock.com

MEMBERS OF FIRM

Nathan E. Assor
Lawrence M. Bell
David J. Eiseman
Jeffrey T. Golenbock
Andrew C. Peskoe
Richard S. Taffet
Robert B. Goebel
Leonard Eisenberg
Martin S. Hyman
Steven G. Chill
Donald A. Hamburg
Charles D. Schmerler

(See Next Column)

GOLENBOCK, EISEMAN, ASSOR & BELL, *New York—Continued*

MEMBERS OF FIRM (Continued)

Jeffrey S. Berger
Lawrence R. Haut
Andrew M. Singer
Janice B. Grubin
Jacqueline G. Veit

OF COUNSEL

William G. Pearlstein
Jonathan S. Hacker

ASSOCIATES

Debra S. Schachtel
Charles B. Rich
Thomas J. Wilson
Elizabeth A. Jaffe
Adam C. Silverstein
Alvin R. Chin
Joel S. Tennenberg
Ruth G. Hirshfeld
Leslie J. Sherman
Hilda B. Gilfillan
David A. Collins
David K. Leitner
Richard S. Kaplan
Aielleen P. Fajardo
(Not admitted in NY)
Gioia M. Ligos
(Not admitted in NY)
Elaine S. Moshe

For full biographical listings, see the Martindale-Hubbell Law Directory

GRATCH JACOBS & BROZMAN, P.C. (AV)

950 Third Avenue, 10022
Telephone: 212-935-2560
Telecopier: (212) 319-0856

Ariel Gratch
Alan S. Jacobs
Andrew P. Brozman
Stephen Wagner
Andrew D. Feiner
Jennifer C. DeMarco

Holly S. Falkowitz
Nicholas H. Laduzinski
Robert J. McDermott, Jr.
Thomas M. Rao
Mitchell B. Reiter

For full biographical listings, see the Martindale-Hubbell Law Directory

HOFFINGER FRIEDLAND DOBRISH & STERN, P.C. (AV)

A Professional Corporation including Professional Corporations
110 East 59th Street, 10022-1392
Telephone: 212-421-4000
Telecopier: 212-223-3857

Jack S. Hoffinger
Lawrence N. Friedland
Robert Z. Dobrish (P.C.)
Stephen R. Stern (P.C.)
Samuel P. Ross
Warren R. Gleicher
Philip S. Ross

Michael J. Sherman
Fran Hoffinger
John H. Friedland
Lydia A. Milone
Devorah S. Weinschneider
Eric I. Wrubel
Nina S. Gross
Scott Lawrence D'Aloise

For full biographical listings, see the Martindale-Hubbell Law Directory

LOVELL & STEWART, LLP (AV)

A Limited Liability Partnership including a Professional Corporation
500 Fifth Avenue, 10110
Telephone: 212-608-1900
Telefax: 212-719-4677
Email: sklovell@aol.com

Christopher Lovell, P.C.
Victor E. Stewart
Gary S. Jacobson

Peggy J. Wedgworth
Geoffrey M. Horn
William W. Foshay, III
Ian T. Stoll

For full biographical listings, see the Martindale-Hubbell Law Directory

RICHARDS SPEARS KIBBE & ORBE (AV)

One Chase Manhattan Plaza 57th Floor, 10005-3102
Telephone: 212-530-1800
Fax: 212-530-1801
Email: info@rsko.com
Washington, D.C. Office: 1775 Eye Street, N.W., 20006-2401.
Telephone: 202-261-2960.
Fax: 202-291-2999.

MEMBERS OF FIRM

MaryJeanette Dee
Donna I. Dennis
Brian S. Fraser
Arthur S. Greenspan
Larry G. Halperin
Paul B. Haskel
Linda Imes
Jonathan Kibbe
Michael D. Mann
Adam D. Mitzner
William Q. Orbe
Lee S. Richards III
David Spears
James Q. Walker
Andrew M. Weinfeld

(See Next Column)

ASSOCIATES

James M. Aquilina
Eva Marie Carney
(Not admitted in NY)
Lauren E. Fischer
Michael Friedman
Shanah D. Glick
(Not admitted in NY)
Kenneth P. Held
James J. Ohlig
Eric M. O'Meara
Jahan Sharifi
Susan J. Steinthal
Kimberly M. Versace
Daniel C. Zinman

OF COUNSEL

Paul A. Leder
(Not admitted in NY)
Lucinda O. McConathy
(Not admitted in NY)

For full biographical listings, see the Martindale-Hubbell Law Directory

RICK, STEINER, P.C. (AV)

Three New York Plaza, 10004
Telephone: 212-422-0488
Facsimile: 212-422-0158

Jay H. Rick
Jacob Steiner
Jack Segal
Alan Fell

Ariane C. Economon

OF COUNSEL

Joel A. Drucker

For full biographical listings, see the Martindale-Hubbell Law Directory

SOLOVAY, EDLIN & EISEMAN (AV)

845 Third Avenue, Eighth Floor, 10022
Telephone: 212-752-1000
Facsimile: 212-355-4608

Richard A. Edlin
Norman Solovay
Michael B. Solovay
Jonathan Eiseman
Wayne R. Lehrhaupt
Eric R. Levine

OF COUNSEL

Daniel James Cooper
Joseph M. Harary
Stephen L. Weinstein
Peter Kakoyiannis
Sam Schwartz

ASSOCIATES

Murray D. Schneier
Howard S. Roitman

For full biographical listings, see the Martindale-Hubbell Law Directory

SPITZER & FELDMAN, P.C. (AV)

405 Park Avenue, 10022
Telephone: 212-888-6680
Cable Address: "Chastra"
Telecopier: 212-838-7472

M. James Spitzer
Ronald J. Offenkrantz
Leonard Lichter
M. James Spitzer, Jr.
Kenneth Gliedman
Edwin W. Weinberg
Thomas R. Westle

Rita C. Dattola
Michael H. Smith
Charles B. Baron
Lawrence Y. Vincent
Orit Kadosh

For full biographical listings, see the Martindale-Hubbell Law Directory

WACHTEL & MASYR, LLP (AV)

110 East 59th Street, 10022
Telephone: 212-909-9500
Telecopier: (212) 371-0320

MEMBERS OF FIRM

Robert W. Berend
Steven J. Cohen
William F. Dowling
Scott J. Lesser
Marvin J. Levine
Jesse Masyr
John H. Reichman
I. Frederick Shotkin
Jeffrey T. Strauss
William B. Wachtel
Morris Missry
Evan S. Weintraub
John W. McConnell
Brian G. Lustbader
Howard J. Goldman

OF COUNSEL

Walter Castore (Legal Consultant on the Laws of Italy)
Walter P. Stasiuk
Robert Stone
Vladimir Zlobinsky
Rosemary Ginty
Francesco Penta (Not admitted in United States)
Maurizio Ulrich-Bansa (Not admitted in United States)
Karen Binder

ASSOCIATES

Aimee Cain
Michele D'Avolio
Howard I. Elman
Aaron D. Greenberg
Avram E. Posner
Allan Joseph Weiss
Anne F. McCaughey

For full biographical listings, see the Martindale-Hubbell Law Directory

New York—Continued

WALLMAN, GREENBERG, GASMAN & MCKNIGHT, LLP (AV)

350 Fifth Avenue, Suite 3000, 10118
Telephone: 212-695-6000
Fax: 212-695-6007

MEMBERS OF FIRM

Lester Wallman
Philip A. Greenberg
Gerald B. Gasman
Elaine McKnight
Donald R. Wall

OF COUNSEL

Clement Segal
Daniel E. Clement
Roy L. Jacobs
Frank J. Hariton

LEGAL SUPPORT PERSONNEL

Lisa Chiodi (Office Administrator)

For full biographical listings, see the Martindale-Hubbell Law Directory

*PLATTSBURGH,** Clinton Co.

LEWIS, ROGERS & KUDRLE, P.C. (AV)

53 Court Street, 12901-2834
Telephone: 518-561-3700
Fax: 518-561-2080
Email: lrk@westelcom.com *URL:* http://www.lawyers.com/lrklaw

Clyde A. Lewis
Mark J. Rogers
Larry A. Kudrle
Harold A. Jerry (1893-1990)
Robert A. Lyon (1924-1982)

Attorneys for: Graystone Materials, Inc.; Plattsburgh Motor Service Inc.; The Development Corporation, Clinton County, New York.

For full biographical listings, see the Martindale-Hubbell Law Directory

ROSLYN HEIGHTS, Nassau Co.

NATISS, NATISS & GORDON, P.C. (AV)

277 Willis Avenue, 11577
Telephone: 516-621-0900
Telecopier: 516-621-1304
Email: MNatisslaw@aol.com

Marvin Natiss
Gary M. Natiss
Stacey Natiss Gordon

Sharon G. Haut

For full biographical listings, see the Martindale-Hubbell Law Directory

SALAMANCA, Cattaraugus Co.

BRADY, BROOKS & O'CONNELL, LLP (AV)

41 Main Street, P.O. Box 227, 14779
Telephone: 716-945-2000
Telecopier: 716-945-3566
Email: bbolaw@aol.com *URL:* http://www.lawyers.com/bbolaw
Randolph, New York Office: 165 Main Street.
Telephone: 716-358-6800.
Ellicottville, New York Office: 1887 Building, 1 Washington Street, P.O. Box 550.
Telephone: 716-699-8010.

MEMBERS OF FIRM

Thomas C. Brady
Kameron K. G. Brooks
Brian E. O'Connell, Jr.

Lori Pettit Rieman

For full biographical listings, see the Martindale-Hubbell Law Directory

SCARSDALE, Westchester Co.

BERTINE, HUFNAGEL, HEADLEY, ZELTNER, DRUMMOND & DOHN, LLP (AV)

700 White Plains Road, 10583
Telephone: 914-472-7700
Telecopier: 914-472-1946
Bronxville, New York Office: 44 Pondfield Road.
Telephone: 914-337-4600.
Telecopier: 914-337-4864.

Edwin K. Bertine (1929-1960)
Frederick F. Hufnagel (1934-1996)
Peter K. Bertine
Frank M. Headley, Jr.
John E. Hufnagel
Peter P. Zeltner
William H. Drummond
Robert P. Dohn

Susan Feder Gibralter

(See Next Column)

OF COUNSEL

Stephen Hochhauser
Stephen J. Jones
Peter T. Gahagan
Elizabeth C. Liscio
Richard M. Gardella

Counsel for: The Bank of New York; Chase Manhattan Bank, N.A.; North Fork Bank; Riverside Cemetery Assn.
Reference: The Bank of New York.

For full biographical listings, see the Martindale-Hubbell Law Directory

*SYRACUSE,** Onondaga Co.

COSTELLO COONEY & FEARON, LLP (AV)

Salina Place, 205 South Salina Street, 13202
Telephone: 315-422-1152
Fax: 315-422-1139
Email: ccf-law.com *URL:* http://www.ccf-law.com

MEMBERS OF FIRM

David F. Costello (1872-1934)
Charles E. Cooney (1873-1958)
George R. Fearon (1883-1976)
Donald L. Nicholas
Warren W. Bader
Robert D. Essig
Kevin M. Gilligan
Robert J. Smith
Michael A. Tremont
Alicia S. Calagiovanni
James J. Gascon
Paul G. Ferrara
Maureen G. Fatcheric
Timothy J. Conan
John R. Langey
Daniel Fletcher

ASSOCIATES

Robert W. Connolly
W. Scott Gambee
David S. Grasso
Edmund J. Gegan
Louis J. Viviani
Michael P. McCarthy
Joseph N. Bulko
Edward G. Melvin
Lauren M. Mumford
Samuel C. Young

OF COUNSEL

Vincent A. O'Neil
Richard D. Hillman

General Counsel for: Auburn Memorial Hospital; Crouse Hospital; Health Services Association of Central New York; St. Joseph's Hospital Health Center.
Local Counsel for: Deere & Co.; New York Telephone Co.; Crum & Forster Insurance Co.; The Travelers Insurance Companies; Caterpillar, Inc.; Otis Elevator.

For full biographical listings, see the Martindale-Hubbell Law Directory

*TROY,** Rensselaer Co.

MARTIN, SHUDT, WALLACE, DILORENZO & JOHNSON (AV)

The Dauchy Building, 279 River Street, P.O. Box 1530, 12181
Telephone: 518-272-6565
Fax: 518-272-5573
URL: http://www.estateplanning.com/martinlawfirm

Carl E. Martin (1902-1988)
Edwyn L. Shudt
Richard P. Wallace
Kirby W. DiLorenzo
Robert Wm. Johnson, III
James E. Prout
Frank C. Sarratori
Paul M. Macari

ASSOCIATES

Jennifer A. Cusack
Jaime B. Thomas
Matthew L. Hosford
Ronald J. Moss

OF COUNSEL

Thomas B. Hunt (Not admitted in NY)

For full biographical listings, see the Martindale-Hubbell Law Directory

*WHITE PLAINS,** Westchester Co.

BOEGGEMAN, GEORGE, HODGES & CORDE, P.C. (AV)

11 Martine Avenue, 10606
Telephone: 914-761-2252
Telecopier: 914-761-5211
Email: boeggeman@bghc-law.com *URL:* http://www.bghc-law.com
Albany, New York Office: 46 Columbia Street, 12207-2716.
Telephone: 518-465-1100.
Fax: 518-465-1800.

George S. Hodges
Richard G. Corde
John J. Walsh, II
Harold L. Moroknek
Robert S. Ondrovic
Thomas A. Sica (Resident Managing Attorney, Albany Office)

Karen A.D. Jockimo
William M. Wingertzahn
Elizabeth C. Mirisola
Cynthia Dolan
Marcella M. Green
Paul A. Hurley
Leslie K. Arfine
John T. Holden
James J. Lofrese
Jeanne M. Hurley
Ira H. Lapp
Matt Randolph Belkin
Cynthia K. Messemer

(See Next Column)

BOEGGEMAN, GEORGE, HODGES & CORDE P.C., *White Plains—Continued*

OF COUNSEL

Joseph H. George
John E. Boeggeman (1919-1993)

Representative Clients: American Telephone & Telegraph; Anheuser-Busch Companies, Inc.; Lowe's Home Centers; Great Atlantic & Pacific Tea Company; Reliance National Insurance Company; Metropolitan Property & Casualty Insurance Company; Fisher Price, Inc.; CGU Insurance Company; United Services Automobile Association; New York Central Mutual Fire Insurance Company.

For full biographical listings, see the Martindale-Hubbell Law Directory

GREENE & ZINNER, P.C. (AV)

202 Mamaroneck Avenue, 10601
Telephone: 914-948-4800
FAX: 914-948-4936

Andrew Greene
Stanley S. Zinner
Arthur M. Neiss
Jarrod S. Schlesinger

For full biographical listings, see the Martindale-Hubbell Law Directory

KENT, HAZZARD, JAEGER, GREER, WILSON & FAY (AV)

50 Main Street, 10606
Telephone: 914-948-4700
Telecopier: 914-948-4721
Email: KentHazz@aol.com

MEMBERS OF FIRM

Ralph S. Kent (1878-1949)
Lawrence S. Hazzard (1900-1958)
William J. Greer (1920-1994)
Mizell Wilson, Jr. (1927-1995)
Lawrence F. Fay
Robert D. Hazzard
Katharine Wilson Conroy

ASSOCIATE

John A. Verni

OF COUNSEL

Malcolm Wilson
Otto C. Jaeger
John R. Dinin
Harold L. Wood

Representative Client: The Bank of New York.
References: Bank of New York.

For full biographical listings, see the Martindale-Hubbell Law Directory

ROGAN GUIDA & ORENSTEIN (AV)

235 Mamaroneck Avenue, 10605
Telephone: 1-888-WIN-WITH-US; 914-328-4480
Fax: 914-328-4479
URL: http://www.NYlawyers.com
Email: RoganGO@aol.com *URL:* http://www.lawyers.com/personalinjury

Jeffrey P. Rogan
Toni M. Guida
David L. Orenstein

Representative Clients: Recore One Mortgage Corp.; LEASCO; Pappas Enterprises Inc.; Steelcase, Inc.; Printing Center of Westchester Inc.; Corporate Imaging, Inc.; King Jolo's Flowers, Inc.; Systems Exchange, Inc.; Domus Realty.
Reference: Fleet Bank.

For full biographical listings, see the Martindale-Hubbell Law Directory

SERCHUK & ZELERMYER, LLP (AV)

81 Main Street, 10601
Telephone: 914-761-2100
Telecopier: 914-761-2299
Email: sz@cloud9.net
New York, New York Office: 641 Lexington Avenue.
Telephone: 212-751-7100.

MEMBERS OF FIRM

Ivan Serchuk
Benjamin Zelermyer
Jay L. Hack
Peter A. Meisels
Clifford S. Weber
Wesley Chen

ASSOCIATES

Jaine Elkind Eney
Veronica E. Rendón
Kevin P. Sweeny
Jacqueline J. Warner (Not admitted in NY)

OF COUNSEL

David M. Pollack

For full biographical listings, see the Martindale-Hubbell Law Directory

SMITH, RANSCHT, CONNORS, MUTINO, NORDELL & SIRIGNANO, P.C. (AV)

235 Main Street, 10601
Telephone: 914-946-8800
Telecopier: 914-946-8861
Cable Address: "Smiran" White Plains, New York

(See Next Column)

James P. Connors, Jr.
Peter J. Mutino
Michael Nordell
George A. Sirignano, Jr.

Counsel for: Universal Builders Supply, Inc.; The Walter Karl Cos.; Hartsdale Canine Cemetery; Wise Components, Inc.; Facsimile Communications Industries, Inc.; Carlcraft Knit Sales, Inc.
Closing Attorney for: First Union Mortgage Corp.
Representative Client: United Airlines, Corporate Express, Inc.

For full biographical listings, see the Martindale-Hubbell Law Directory

STEPHENS, BARONI, REILLY & LEWIS LLP (AV)

Northcourt Building, 175 Main Street, 10601
Telephone: 914-761-0300; 683-5185
Telecopier: 914-761-0995; 683-1323
URL: http://www.lawyers.com/sbrl
Cross River, New York Office: Northern Westchester Office, Old Post Road Professional Building, 10518.
Telephone: 914-763-3232.

MEMBERS OF FIRM

Gerald D. Reilly
Roland A. Baroni, Jr.
Stephen R. Lewis

ASSOCIATE

Roland T. Koke

OF COUNSEL

James R. Caruso (1906-1994)

For full biographical listings, see the Martindale-Hubbell Law Directory

JOHN E. WATKINS, JR. (AV)

175 Main Street, 10601
Telephone: 914-428-1292
Telecopier: 914-428-4104
Local 800 Service: 1-800-33WATKINS
Email: wat2kins@netcom.com *URL:* http://www.lawyers.com/johnewatkinsjr
New York, New York Office: 29 Broadway.
Telephone: 212-968-1500.

ASSOCIATE

Ira S. Levy

For full biographical listings, see the Martindale-Hubbell Law Directory

YONKERS, Westchester Co.

ECKER, LOEHR, ECKER & ECKER, L.L.P. (AV)

One Executive Boulevard, 10701
Telephone: 914-968-0500; 914-965-4288
FAX: 914-968-0918
Email: eleellp@aol.com
New York, New York Office: 521 Fifth Avenue, 27th Floor, 10175.
Telephone: 914-965-4288;
Fax: 914-968-0918.

MEMBERS OF FIRM

Gerald E. Loehr
Louis A. Ecker
Lawrence H. Ecker
Robert L. Ecker

OF COUNSEL

Jock Thornton
Iris J. Iler
Tammi L. Blank-Ecker

LEGAL SUPPORT PERSONNEL

Carolyn Caruso

Reference: Hudson Valley National Bank.

For full biographical listings, see the Martindale-Hubbell Law Directory

NORTH CAROLINA

*GREENSBORO,** Guilford Co.

ALEXANDER RALSTON, SPECKHARD & SPECKHARD, L.L.P. (AV)

218 West Friendly Avenue, 27401
Telephone: 336-379-9302
Fax: 336-370-1232
URL: http://www.lawyers.com/aralston,speckhard

Donald K. Speckhard
Stanley E. Speckhard

Representative Clients: Preferred Furniture Components, Inc.; Spring Financial Services, Inc.; Blazer Financial Services; Omega Sports, Inc.; Power & Heat Systems, Inc.; Branch & Company, P.A.; Acme Florist Supply, Inc.

For full biographical listings, see the Martindale-Hubbell Law Directory

*WINSTON-SALEM,** Forsyth Co.

McCall, Doughton & Blancato, P.L.L.C. (AV)

Suite 150, 633 West Fourth Street, 27101
Telephone: 336-725-7531
Fax: 336-725-5129
Email: mcbd@netunlimited.net

G. Emmett McCall
Thomas J. Doughton
William A. Blancato

ASSOCIATE

Andrew D. Hart

References: Wachovia Bank & Trust Co., N.A.; NCNB National Bank of North Carolina; Chicago Title Insurance Co.; Lawyers Title Insurance Corp.

For full biographical listings, see the Martindale-Hubbell Law Directory

OHIO

*AKRON,** Summit Co.

Stark & Knoll Co., L.P.A. (AV)

76 South Main Street, Suite 1512, 44308-1824
Telephone: 330-376-3300
Telecopier: 330-376-6237
URL: http://www.stark-knoll.com

Michael L. Stark
Thomas G. Knoll
James L. Rench
Richard W. Burke
John K. Krajewski
John P. Susany
Jeffrey T. Knoll

Benjamin B. de Forest
Michael P. Morley
Ronald K. Starkey
Ralph R. Waszak, Jr.
Catherine Kemp Erisey
Aaron G. Lepp
Robert W. Spencer, Jr.
Mary Jo Lockshin

LEGAL SUPPORT PERSONNEL

Melissa L. Shinaberry
Diane Petrella
Teresa A. Corall

References: Bank One Akron; Society Bank of Akron.

For full biographical listings, see the Martindale-Hubbell Law Directory

*CLEVELAND,** Cuyahoga Co.

Chattman, Gaines & Stern (AV)

1400 Renaissance Center, 1350 Euclid Avenue, 44115-1817
Telephone: 216-781-1700; 800-321-1700
Telecopier: 216-781-1972
Lorain, Ohio Office: 5300 Baumhart Road.
Telephone: 216-282-4598.
Fax: 216-960-1298.

Harold S. Stern
John J. Sutula
Roger W. Van Deusen
James M. Mackey
Douglas J. Paul
John V. Scharon, Jr.
Ronald F. Wayne
Thomas C. Wagner

Dale A. Nowak
John Patrick

OF COUNSEL

Albert Krill
Paul B. Madow
Jane B. Marciniszyn

For full biographical listings, see the Martindale-Hubbell Law Directory

Keller and Curtin Co., L.P.A. (AV)

Suite 330 The Hanna Building, 44115-1901
Telephone: 216-566-7100
Fax: 216-566-5430
Email: keller@en.com
Akron, Ohio Office: 920 Key Building, 159 South Main Street, 44308-1318.
Telephone: 330-376-7245.
Fax: 330-376-8128. Email: kcakron@en.com.
Elyria, Ohio Office: 120 East Avenue, 44035-5228.
Telephone: 440-323-8662.
Fax: 440-323-6610.

Stanley S. Keller
G. Michael Curtin
Walter H. Krohngold
James M. Johnson
Joseph G. Ritzler
Thomas M. Coughlin, Jr.
John Swansinger
Camille D. Kuri
Franklin C. Malemud
Brian D. Spitz
Deena Charisse Miller

Reference: Bank One, Cleveland.

For full biographical listings, see the Martindale-Hubbell Law Directory

*PAINESVILLE,** Lake Co.

Dworken & Bernstein Co., L.P.A. A Professional Corporation (AV)

153 East Erie, 44077
Telephone: 440-946-7656
Fax: 440-352-3469
Mailing Address: 55 Public Square, Suite 950, Cleveland, Ohio, 44113

Howard W. Bernstein
Marvin P. Dworken
Melvyn E. Resnick
David J. Richards, Jr.
Patrick J. Perotti
Irving Rosner
Alec Berezin
Howard S. Rabb

Patrick T. Murphy
Gary S. Okin
Dean M. Rooney
Geoffrey H. Turoff
Lisa M. Spano-Harting

SENIOR COUNSEL

David M. Dworken (Retired)

For full biographical listings, see the Martindale-Hubbell Law Directory

*TOLEDO,** Lucas Co.

Doyle, Lewis & Warner (AV)

202 North Erie Street, P.O. Box 2168, 43603
Telephone: 419-248-1500
Fax: 419-248-2002
Email: dlw1@primenet.com

MEMBERS OF FIRM

Steven Timonere
Richard F. Ellenberger
Michael E. Hyrne
Michael A. Bruno
David W. Doerner

ASSOCIATES

Kevin A. Pituch
Maureen O. Atkins

Counsel for: Consolidated Rail Corp.; The Lakefront Dock & Railroad Terminal Co.; Prudential Insurance Co. of America; Equitable Life Assurance Society of the U.S.; Metropolitan Life Insurance Co.; Greyhound Lines; Fireman's Fund Insurance Cos.

For Complete List of Firm Personnel, See General Section

For full biographical listings, see the Martindale-Hubbell Law Directory

Ritter, Robinson, McCready & James (AV)

1850 National City Bank Building, 405 Madison Avenue, 43624
Telephone: 419-241-3213
FAX: 419-241-4925

MEMBER OF FIRM

William S. McCready

Counsel for: Chrysler Corp.; Rubini Motors, Inc.; Ohio Casualty Insurance Co.; National Mutual Insurance Co.; Celina Mutual Insurance Co.; Westfield Insurance Co.; Northwestern National Insurance Co.; Midwestern Insurance Co.; United Ohio Insurance Co.; Toledo Auto Electric Co.

For Complete List of Firm Personnel, See General Section

For full biographical listings, see the Martindale-Hubbell Law Directory

Schnorf & Schnorf Co., L.P.A. A Professional Corporation (AV)

1400 National City Bank Building, 405 Madison Avenue, 43604
Telephone: 419-248-2646
Facsimile: 419-248-2889

Brandon G. Schnorf, Sr. (1904-1977)
David M. Schnorf
Christopher F. Parker
Johna M. Bella
Barry F. Hudgin

Local Counsel for: Universal Underwriters Group; Charter One Bank; Medical Mutual of Ohio; Bankers Multiple Line Insurance Company; National City Bank, Northwest; Charter One Bank.
Representative Clients: American Federation of Teachers, AFL-CIO; Ohio Federation of Teachers, AFL-CIO; Toledo Federation of Teachers, AFL-CIO; Hart Associates, Inc.

For full biographical listings, see the Martindale-Hubbell Law Directory

OKLAHOMA

*NORMAN,** Cleveland Co.

Crowe & Dunlevy (AV)

A Professional Corporation
2500 South McGee, Suite 140, 73072-6705
Telephone: 405-321-7317
Fax: 405-360-4002
Email: marketing@crowedunlevy.com *URL:* http://www.crowedunlevy.com
Oklahoma City, Oklahoma Office: Crowe & Dunlevy, A Professional Corporation, 1800 Mid-America Tower, 20 North Broadway, 73102-8273.
Telephone: 405-235-7700.
Fax: 405-239-6651.
Tulsa, Oklahoma Office: Crowe & Dunlevy, A Professional Corporation, 500 Kennedy Building, 321 South Boston Avenue, 74103-3313.
Telephone: 918-592-9800.
Fax: 918-592-9801.

Gary C. Rawlinson

Christopher R. Graves

For Complete List of Firm Personnel, See General Section

For full biographical listings, see the Martindale-Hubbell Law Directory

*OKLAHOMA CITY,** Oklahoma Co.

Crowe & Dunlevy, A Professional Corporation (AV)

1800 Mid-America Tower, 20 North Broadway, 73102-8273
Telephone: 405-235-7700
Fax: 405-239-6651
Email: marketing@crowedunlevy.com *URL:* http://www.crowedunlevy.com
Tulsa, Oklahoma Office: 500 Kennedy Building, 321 South Boston Avenue, 74103-3313.
Telephone: 918-592-9800.
Fax: 918-592-9801.
Norman, Oklahoma Office: Crowe & Dunlevy, 2500 South McGee, Suite 140, 73072-6705.
Telephone: 405-321-7317.
Fax: 405-360-4002.

J. Lawrence Blankenship
Earl A. Skarky
James H. Holloman, Jr.
Michael M. Stewart
Kenni B. Merritt
Karen S. Rieger
Reeder E. Ratliff
Todd Taylor
Roger A. Stong

Cynthia L. Andrews
J. Robert Kalsu
Eric S. Fisher
Lynne Faith Saunders

OF COUNSEL

James C. Gibbens

For Complete List of Firm Personnel, See General Section

For full biographical listings, see the Martindale-Hubbell Law Directory

Day, Edwards, Federman, Propester & Christensen, P.C. (AV)

Suite 2900 Oklahoma Tower, 210 Park Avenue, 73102-5605
Telephone: 405-239-2121
Telecopier: 405-236-1012
URL: http://lawlinks.com/attys/ok/defpc.html

Bruce W. Day
Kent A. Gilliland
Joe E. Edwards
Jeanette Cook Timmons

Lawn B. Gardner
Edgar G. McQueen, Jr.

Representative Clients: Applied Thermal Systems, Inc.; Aztec Specialty Co., Inc.; Aztec Rig Equipment Company; BancFirst Corporation; Bobby Joe Cudd Company; CD Warehouse, Inc.; Harris Developments, Inc.; Peripheral Enhancements Corporation; Wild Well Control, Inc.; Worldwide Well, Inc.

For Complete List of Firm Personnel, See General Section

For full biographical listings, see the Martindale-Hubbell Law Directory

Kerr, Irvine, Rhodes & Ables, A Professional Corporation (AV)

201 Robert S. Kerr Avenue, Suite 600, 73102-4267
Telephone: 405-272-9221
Fax: 405-236-3121
Email: kira201@aol.com

(See Next Column)

Robert S. Kerr, Jr.
Horace G. Rhodes
J. Angela Ables
James W. Rhodes
James R. Barnett
R. Thomas Lay

Kevin R. Wisner

OF COUNSEL

Henry B. Taliaferro, Jr.

Representative Clients: Financial Security Assurance Co.; Harbor Insuran ce Co.; Midlands Management Corp.; Pegasus Insurance Co.; Wellington Insurance Co.; Pre-Paid Legal Casualty, Inc.; 66 Federal Credit Union; Honor Co., Inc.

For full biographical listings, see the Martindale-Hubbell Law Directory

*TULSA,** Tulsa Co.

Crowe & Dunlevy, A Professional Corporation (AV)

500 Kennedy Building, 321 South Boston Avenue, 74103-3313
Telephone: 918-592-9800
Fax: 918-592-9801
Email: marketing@crowedunlevy.com *URL:* http://www.crowedunlevy.com
Oklahoma City, Oklahoma Office: 1800 Mid-America Tower, 20 North Broadway, 73102-8273.
Telephone: 405-235-7700.
Fax: 405-239-6651.
Norman, Oklahoma Office: Crowe & Dunlevy, 2500 South McGee, Suite 140, 73072-6705.
Telephone: 405-321-7317.
Fax: 405-360-4002.

Lon Foster, III
Gary L. Betow
J. Bradford Hammond
W. Kyle Tresch

Nancy Lynn Roberts
Elizabeth Moseley Guse
David G. Harris
J. Ryan Sacra

For Complete List of Firm Personnel, See General Section

For full biographical listings, see the Martindale-Hubbell Law Directory

OREGON

*PORTLAND,** Multnomah Co.

Kell, Alterman & Runstein, LLP (AV)

1001 S.W. Fifth Avenue, Suite 1800, 97204
Telephone: 503-222-3531
Telecopier: 503-227-2980
Email: kell@teleport.com

MEMBERS OF FIRM

Raymond M. Kell (1911-1991)
Clifford B. Alterman (1925-1995)
Ted E. Runstein
Lee Davis Kell
Wayne D. Palmer
Lloyd R. Summers
William D. Dickas
Gary P. Compa
Charles R. Williamson
Mary Ellen Page Farr
Eric Sogge
Thomas J. Matsuda
Thomas R. Rask, III
Nicholas S. Fish

Dana L. Barnes
Cory Larvik
Robert E. Kabacy
Robin M. Runstein

References: Union Bank of California, N.A. (Portland Branch); The Bank of Tokyo-Mitsubishi, Ltd. (Portland Branch); Bank of America (5th S. Main Branch).

For full biographical listings, see the Martindale-Hubbell Law Directory

PENNSYLVANIA

BALA CYNWYD, Montgomery Co.

Kania, Lindner, Lasak and Feeney (AV)

Suite 525, Two Bala Plaza, 19004
Telephone: 610-667-3240
Fax: 610-668-9676
Email: kllf@aol.com

Arthur J. Kania
Albert A. Lindner
John Lasak
Thomas J. Feeney, III
Robert A. Griffiths

A list of Representative Clients for which the firm serves as General Counsel or Local Counsel will be supplied upon request.

(See Next Column)

KANIA, LINDNER, LASAK AND FEENEY—*Continued*

For full biographical listings, see the Martindale-Hubbell Law Directory

BLUE BELL, Montgomery Co.

KELLEY & MURPHY (AV)

Union Meeting Corporate Center V, Suite 160 925 Harvest Drive, 19422
Telephone: 215-643-6500
Fax: 215-643-8356
Cable Address: "BIGTIME"
Email: kmlaw@counsel.com

Joseph T. Kelley, Jr. Patrick G. Murphy
Joseph T. Kelley, III

LEGAL SUPPORT PERSONNEL

Marianne Rowen Tanja M.Z. Barron

For full biographical listings, see the Martindale-Hubbell Law Directory

*MEDIA,** Delaware Co.

BEATTY, CRAMP, KAUFFMAN & LINCKE (AV)

215 North Olive Street, P.O. Box 901, 19063
Telephone: 610-565-8800
Fax: 610-565-8127
Email: BCKLLaw@aol.com

MEMBERS OF FIRM

Lewis B. Beatty, Jr.
Joseph W. Kauffman
David J. Otis
David G. Blake
William P. Lincke
Natalie M. Habert
Peter W. Dicce

ASSOCIATES

Regina M. MacKenzie
Bereth K. Graeff
Daniel J. McCusker
Kelly A. Barnes

OF COUNSEL

John F. Cramp Ralph B. D'Iorio
Robert C. Grasberger

Joseph R. Young (1921-1993)

For full biographical listings, see the Martindale-Hubbell Law Directory

*PHILADELPHIA,** Philadelphia Co.

ADELMAN LAVINE GOLD AND LEVIN, A PROFESSIONAL CORPORATION (AV)

Suite 1900, Two Penn Center Plaza, 19102-1799
Telephone: 215-568-7515
Facsimile: 215-557-7922
Wayne Office: 1101 West DeKalb Pike, 2nd Floor, 19087.
Telephone: 610-992-0400.
Facsimile: 610-992-1005.

Lewis H. Gold
Robert H. Levin
Gary M. Schildhorn
Barry D. Kleban
Gary D. Bressler
Steven D. Usdin
Kevin W. Walsh
Raymond H. Lemisch

Leon R. Barson
Matthew J. Swett
Robert J. Lenahan
Bradford J. Sandler
William R. Hinchman
Victoria M. Endriss
Sebastian Ferrer

LEGAL SUPPORT PERSONNEL

Jacqueline Parsio (Paralegal) Diana J. Papalini (Paralegal)
Wendy A. Raskas (Paralegal)

For full biographical listings, see the Martindale-Hubbell Law Directory

DONOHUE AND DONOHUE (AV)

232 South Fourth Street, 19106
Telephone: 215-574-1080
Fax: 215-574-1255
URL: http://www.lawyers.com/donohuelaw
New York, N.Y. Office: 26 Broadway.
Telephone: 212-269-2330.
Telecopier: 212-269-5016.

John P. Donohue (Resident)

Patrick J. Egan Melissa G. Pinheiro

For full biographical listings, see the Martindale-Hubbell Law Directory

KLEINBARD, BELL & BRECKER LLP (AV)

Suite 700, 1900 Market Street, 19103
Telephone: 215-568-2000
Facsimile: 215-568-0140
Montclair, New Jersey Office: 240 Claremont Avenue, 07042.
Telephone: 973-233-0600.
Facsimile: 973-233-9390.

Joseph S. Kleinbard (1905-1994) Robert John Brecker (1916-1996)

COUNSEL TO THE FIRM

Arthur S. Keyser

MEMBERS OF FIRM

Paul E. Bomze
Murray I. Blackman
Howard J. Davis
Steven R. Waxman
Steven J. Engelmyer (Resident, Montclair Office)
David L. Hyman (Resident, Montclair Office)
Imogene E. Hughes
John P. Hickey
Jay R. Goldstein
Ralph J. Mauro
Thomas H. Speranza
Lisa E. Brody

ASSOCIATES

Mary Beth H. Gray
Eric J. Rothschild
Mary Vassallo Slinkard
Michael A. Frattone
Benjamin C. Graff (Not admitted in PA)
Ralph F. Salgado

COUNSEL

Joseph Bell

For full biographical listings, see the Martindale-Hubbell Law Directory

ROTAN E. LEE (AV)

6333 Woodbine Avenue, 19151
Telephone: 215-790-2450

For full biographical listings, see the Martindale-Hubbell Law Directory

SCHUBERT, BELLWOAR, CAHILL & QUINN, A PROFESSIONAL CORPORATION (AV)

Two Penn Center, Suite 1400, 1500 John F. Kennedy Boulevard, 19102-1890
Telephone: 215-569-3535
Fax: 215-557-7426
Email: attorneys@sbcq.com
Haddon Township, New Jersey Office: 311 West Cuthbert Boulevard, 08108.
Telephone: 856-854-5757.

Thomas M. Schubert (1924-1989)
William E. Schubert, Jr. (1921-1998)
Harry J. J. Bellwoar, III
John P. Quinn
John J. Cahill, Jr.
Robert T. Lynch
Robert G. Bellwoar
John P. Gallagher
James O. Hausch
Deborah E. Kolodner
Richard T. Mulcahey, Jr.
James M. Tyler
Jan M. Ritchie

Joseph W. Cunningham
Michael S. Piotrowicz
Patricia Farrell Kerelo
Christopher B. Hogan
Kathleen M. O'Connell
Mark Pfeiffer
Eric A. Feldhake

OF COUNSEL

John D. Lucey, Jr. Robert F. Blanck

For full biographical listings, see the Martindale-Hubbell Law Directory

*PITTSBURGH,** Allegheny Co.

MARCUS & SHAPIRA LLP (AV)

35th Floor, One Oxford Centre, 301 Grant Street, 15219-6401
Telephone: 412-471-3490
Telecopier: 412-391-8758
Email: info@marcus-shapira.com *URL:* http://www.marcus-shapira.com

MEMBERS OF FIRM

Robert L. Allman, II
Joseph J. Barnes
Robert M. Barnes
Estelle F. Comay
Elly Heller-Toig
Charles G. Knox
Carrie Kochenbach
James S. Larrimer
Scott D. Livingston
Bernard D. Marcus
Darlene M. Nowak
Daniel H. Shapira
Stephen S. Zubrow

ASSOCIATES

Henry G. Barr Moira E. Cain
Traci L. McDonald

For Complete List of Firm Personnel, See General Section

For full biographical listings, see the Martindale-Hubbell Law Directory

Pittsburgh—Continued

YUKEVICH, MARCHETTI, LIEKAR & ZANGRILLI, P.C. (AV)

Sixth Floor, One Gateway Center, 15222-1424
Telephone: 412-261-6777
Fax: 412-261-6789
URL: http://www.ymlz.com

Michael Yukevich, Jr.
Christopher J. Marchetti
John P. Liekar, Jr.
Albert J. Zangrilli, Jr.
Mark Fischer
Michael I. Frachioni
Lori Nolan Lindey
Keith J. Rothfus

For full biographical listings, see the Martindale-Hubbell Law Directory

RHODE ISLAND

SMITHFIELD, Providence Co.

CHARLES S. SOKOLOFF INCORPORATED (AV)

Eleven Thurber Boulevard, 02917-1859
Telephone: 401-233-2800; Toll Free: 888-SOKOLAW
Fax: 401-233-2890
URL: http://www.sokolawyer.com
Email: sokolaw@sokolawyer.com *URL:* http://www.lawyers.com/sokolaw

Charles S. Sokoloff

Anne-Marie Krollman

For full biographical listings, see the Martindale-Hubbell Law Directory

SOUTH CAROLINA

*BEAUFORT,** Beaufort Co.

DAVIS, TUPPER & GRIMSLEY, L.L.P. (AV)

611 Bay Street, P.O. Box 2055, 29901-2055
Telephone: 843-524-1116
Facsimile: 843-524-1463
Email: DTGS@Hargray.com

MEMBERS OF FIRM

Ralph E. Tupper
James A. Grimsley, III

For full biographical listings, see the Martindale-Hubbell Law Directory

*COLUMBIA,** Richland Co.

WHITENER & WHARTON, P.A. (AV)

2001 Park Street Park at Calhoun, 29201-2006
Telephone: 803-779-7830
Facsimile: 803-765-4649
Email: wwlaw@bellsouth.net

H. Dave Whitener, Jr.
L. Patricia Wharton

Representative Clients: Mortgage Lenders Network; D.R. Horton, Inc.; Torrey Homes; Investors Title Insurance Company of South Carolina; Better Business Bureau of South Carolina; Coastal Federal Savings Bank; Newberry Federal Savings Bank; SouthTrust Bank, N.A., Boyd & Company; Boyd Management Company.
References: NationsBank, N.A., (Carolina); Wachovia Bank.

For full biographical listings, see the Martindale-Hubbell Law Directory

*GREENVILLE,** Greenville Co.

LOVE, THORNTON, ARNOLD & THOMASON, P.A. (AV)

410 East Washington Street, P.O. Box 10045, 29603
Telephone: 864-242-6360
Telefax: 864-271-7972
Email: lovelaw@globalvision.net *URL:* http://www.ltatlaw.com
Greer, South Carolina Office: 1115 West Poinsett Street, P.O. Box 449, 29652-0449.
Telephone: 864-879-0144.
Telefax: 864-879-0149.

Mason A. Goldsmith
Jennings L. Graves, Jr.
James A. Blair, III

OF COUNSEL

Edward J. Hamilton, Jr.

Counsel for: Avado Brands, Inc.; Greenville Association of Realtors, Inc.

For Complete List of Firm Personnel, See General Section

For full biographical listings, see the Martindale-Hubbell Law Directory

HILTON HEAD ISLAND, Beaufort Co.

RUTH & MACNEILLE, PROFESSIONAL ASSOCIATION (AV)

40 Pope Avenue, 29928
Telephone: 843-785-4251
Telex: 988944
Telecopier: 843-686-5404
Mailing Address: P.O. Box 5706, Hilton Head Island, SC, 29938
Bluffton, South Carolina Office: 7 Simmonsville Road, Suite 200.
Telephone: 803-815-5353.
Fax: 803-815-5354.

William A. Ruth
Douglas W. MacNeille
Michael G. Olivetti

References: NationsBank of South Carolina, N.A.; Anchor Bank; Wachovia Bank, N.A.; Chicago Title Insurance Corp.; First American Title Insurance Co.

For full biographical listings, see the Martindale-Hubbell Law Directory

SOUTH DAKOTA

LEAD, Lawrence Co.

FULLER, TELLINGHUISEN, GORDON & PERCY, P.C. (AV)

203 West Main Street, P.O. Box 898, 57754
Telephone: 605-584-2440
Fax: 605-584-1979
Email: leadlaw@mato.com
Spearfish, South Dakota Office: 132 East Illinois, 57783.
Telephone: 605-642-8080.
Fax: 605-642-1756. E-mail: spflaw@mato.com

A. P. Fuller
Roger A. Tellinghuisen
Bradley P. Gordon
Michelle Palmer Percy

Representative Clients: Homestake Mining Co.; Hotel Franklin & Gaming; Black Hills Novelty/Automatic Vending, Inc.; Northern Hills General Hospital; Lantis Enterprises, Inc.; Norwest Bank South Dakota N.A.; Lead-Deadwood Independent School District # 40-1; City of Lead.

For full biographical listings, see the Martindale-Hubbell Law Directory

*RAPID CITY,** Pennington Co.

BANGS, MCCULLEN, BUTLER, FOYE & SIMMONS, L.L.P. (AV)

818 St. Joseph Street, P.O. Box 2670, 57709
Telephone: 605-343-1040
Telecopier: 605-343-1503
URL: http://www.bangsmccullen.com

MEMBERS OF FIRM

Thomas H. Foye
Charles L. Riter
John H. Raforth

Representative Clients: Norwest Bank South Dakota, N.A., Rapid City, S.D.; Pete Lien & Sons; The Travelers Insurance Co.; Rapid City Regional Hospital; Dakota Steel & Supply Co.; Great American Insurance Co.; Fireman's Fund Insurance; United States Automobile Association; Moyle Petroleum; Rapid City Area School District 51-4.

For Complete List of Firm Personnel, See General Section

For full biographical listings, see the Martindale-Hubbell Law Directory

TENNESSEE

*MEMPHIS,** Shelby Co.

THE BUHLER LAW FIRM (AV)

Morgan Keegan Tower, 50 North Front Street, Suite 610, 38103
Telephone: 901-527-9007
Fax: 901-527-9067
Email: lbuhler@worldnet.att.net

Lynn Buhler

For full biographical listings, see the Martindale-Hubbell Law Directory

HALE HEADRICK DEWEY & WOLF, PLLC (AV)

One Memphis Place, 200 Jefferson Avenue Suite 1450, 38103
Telephone: 901-523-1123
Fax: 901-523-7472
Nashville, Tennessee Office: Suntrust Bank Building, 201 Fourth Avenue North, Suite 1450, 37219.
Telephone: 615-843-5160.
Fax: 615-843-5165

(See Next Column)

HALE HEADRICK DEWEY & WOLF PLLC—*Continued*

Stephen P. Hale
S. Russell Headrick
H. Tucker Dewey
Herbert B. Wolf, Jr.
John S. Golwen

OF COUNSEL

Steven L. Gill

Jennifer Ziegenhorn
Wendy A. Geurin
John W. Campbell
Joseph M. Koury
Holly N. Knight
Charles S. Blatteis
Jennifer S. Kiesewetter
J. William Williams

For full biographical listings, see the Martindale-Hubbell Law Directory

*NASHVILLE,** Davidson Co.

BAKER, DONELSON, BEARMAN & CALDWELL (AV)

1700 Nashville City Center, 511 Union Street, 37219
Telephone: 615-726-5600
Telecopier: 615-726-0464
Email: info@bdbc.com *URL:* http://www.bakerdonelson.com
Memphis, Tennessee Office: 20th Floor, First Tennessee Building, 165 Madison, 38103.
Telephone: 901-526-2000.
Telecopier: 901-577-2303.
Chattanooga, Tennessee Office: 1800 Republic Centre, 633 Chestnut Street, 37450-1800.
Telephone: 423-756-2010.
Telecopier: 423-756-3447.
Knoxville, Tennessee Office: 2200 Riverview Tower, 900 South Gay Street, 37901.
Telephone: 423-549-7000.
Telecopier: 423-525-8569.
Johnson City, Tennessee Office: SunTrust Bank Building, 207 Mockingbird Lane, P.O. Box 3038, 37602.
Telephone: 423-928-0181.
Telecopier: 423-928-5694; 423-928-3654; Kingsport: 423-246-6191.
Huntsville, Tennessee Office: 3 Courthouse Square, 37756.
Telephone: 423-663-2321.
Telecopier: 423-663-2111.
Washington, D.C. Office: Market Square, 801 Pennsylvania Avenue, N.W., 20004.
Telephone: 202-508-3400.
Telecopier: 202-508-3402.
Jackson, Mississippi Office: Suite 500, 700 North State Street, 39202.
Telephone: 601-351-2400.
Telecopier: 601-351-2424.

SHAREHOLDERS

Steven J. Eisen
Philip Stuart McSween

ASSOCIATE

J. Adin Lara

For Complete List of Firm Personnel, See General Section

For full biographical listings, see the Martindale-Hubbell Law Directory

RANDOLPH B. JONES (AV)

3200 West End Avenue, Suite 500, 37203
Telephone: 615-783-1705
Facsimile: 615-783-1606

TEXAS

ADDISON, Dallas Co.

BARRETT BURKE WILSON CASTLE DAFFIN & FRAPPIER, L.L.P. (AV)

A Limited Liability Partnership including Professional Corporations
15000 Surveyor Boulevard, Suite 100, 75001
Telephone: 972-386-5040
Fax: 972-386-7673
Houston, Texas Office: 24 Greenway Plaza, Suite 2001.
Telephone: 713-621-8673.
Denver, Colorado Affiliated Office: Castle Barrett Daffin & Frappier, 1099 Eighteenth Street, Suite 2200.
Telephone: 303-299-1800.
Fax: 303-299-1808.
Little Rock, Arkansas Affiliated Office: Wilson & Associates, P.A. 1521 Merrill Drive, Suite D220.
Telephone: 501-219-9388.

(See Next Column)

Michael C. Barrett
Robert M. Wilson, Jr.
Lawrence E. Castle (Not admitted in TX)
Robert F. Frappier (Manager, Houston Office)
Mary A. Daffin (P.C.)
Stephen C. Porter
G. Tommy Bastian
Caren Jacobs Castle (P.C.) (Not admitted in TX)
Clay A. Cornett (Resident, Dallas, Texas Office)

Rosa Jean Bryant
James C. Frappier
Cristina Camarata
Anthony J Flores
Steve M. Cone
Cheryl Hughes Cannon
James L. DeLoach
Erin Archer Rush
Michael Wayne Zientz
David Seybold
Yvonne Renee Knesek
Jennifer Poe Umphress
William "Marty" Ferguson

For full biographical listings, see the Martindale-Hubbell Law Directory

*AUSTIN,** Travis Co.

THOMPSON & KNIGHT L.L.P. (AV)

(Attorneys and Counselors)
1200 San Jacinto Center, 98 San Jacinto Boulevard, 78701
Telephone: 512-469-6100
Telecopy: 512-469-6180
URL: http://www.tklaw.com
Dallas, Texas Office: 1700 Pacific Avenue, Suite 3300, 75201.
Telephone: 214-969-1700.
Telecopy: 512-969-1751.
Telex: 732298.
Fort Worth, Texas Office: 801 Cherry Street, Suite 1600, 76102.
Telephone: 817-347-1700.
Telecopy: 817-347-1799.
Houston, Texas Office: Thompson Knight Brown Parker & Leahy L.L.P., 1200 Smith Street, Suite 3600, 77002-4595.
Telephone: 713-654-8111.
Telecopier: 713-654-1871.
San Pedro Garza Garcia, Nuevo León, Mexico Office: Edificio Losoles PD-4, Av. Lázaro Cárdenas No. 2400 Pte., C.P. 66220.
Telephone: (52-8) 363-0096.
Telecopy: (52-8) 363-3067.

PARTNER

Michael L. Bengtson

ASSOCIATE

Kari Lavelle Arneil

For Complete List of Firm Personnel, See General Section

For full biographical listings, see the Martindale-Hubbell Law Directory

*DALLAS,** Dallas Co.

CALHOUN & STACY (AV)

Suite 5700 - Bank of America Plaza, 901 Main Street, 75202-3713
Telephone: 214-748-5000
Facsimile: 214-748-1421
Email: info@calhounstacy.com *URL:* http://www.calhounstacy.com

MEMBERS OF FIRM

Rees T. Bowen, III
Mark Alan Calhoun
LeAnn Wainscott Cross
David W. Elrod
Parker Nelson
Thomas E. Rosen
Shannon B. Schuster
Roy L. Stacy
Pamela J. Touchstone
Michael C. Wright

ASSOCIATES

David G. Allen
Joseph G. Barkate, Jr.
Scott S. Crocker
Sean P. Fitzgerald
Elizabeth Reding Gambrell
Leanne Capps Medford
Jonathan G. Polak
Joel W. Reese
Barbara L. Wohlrabe

For Complete List of Firm Personnel, See General Section

For full biographical listings, see the Martindale-Hubbell Law Directory

CLARK, WEST, KELLER, BUTLER & ELLIS, L.L.P. (AV)

4800 Renaissance Tower, 1201 Elm Street, 75270-2146
Telephone: 214-741-1001
Telecopier: 214-760-9812

MEMBERS OF FIRM

William H. Clark (1861-1931)
William H. Clark, Jr. (1895-1943)
Robert L. Clark (1903-1963)
William L. Keller
Allen Butler
David M. Ellis
Melvyn L. Douglas
Mike M. Tabor
Mark A. Shank
Michael P. Maslanka
Kervyn B. Altaffer, Jr.
Kelly Gaffney McClure

(See Next Column)

CLARK, WEST, KELLER, BUTLER & ELLIS L.L.P., *Dallas—Continued*

ASSOCIATES

Veronica Cuadra
Melinda L. Eitzen
Wade A. Forsman
Theresa M. Gegen
M. Brenk Johnson
Christie A. Newkirk
Robert J. Wood, Jr.
John Peter Hagan
Sonja J. McGill

For full biographical listings, see the Martindale-Hubbell Law Directory

ERHARD, RUEBEL & JENNINGS, A PROFESSIONAL CORPORATION (AV)

1600 Pacific Avenue, 75201-3509
Telephone: 214-720-4001, 741-6201
Fax: 214-871-1655
Email: erjennings@compuserve.com *URL:* http://www.lawyers.com/erruje

John A. Erhard (1893-1979)
Alfred L. Ruebel
James Albert Jennings
W. Christopher W. Haynes

OF COUNSEL

Susan Jane Stedman Jennings

Representative Client: Halliburton Co./Halliburton Energy Services.

For full biographical listings, see the Martindale-Hubbell Law Directory

FERNANDEZ & KNEBEL, A PROFESSIONAL CORPORATION (AV)

Bank One Center, 1717 Main Street, Suite 2100, 75201
Telephone: 214-747-2100
Fax: 214-747-2144

Bennett I. Abramowitz
Clint A. Corrie
Raymond R. Fernandez, Jr.
Delbert L. Gibbs
Robert L. Knebel, Jr.
Mary Jo Vida

Barbara F. Blaylock
Herbert J. Gilles
Maria Isabel Roman
Jon M. Payne
Joseph L. Mira

For full biographical listings, see the Martindale-Hubbell Law Directory

KRAGE & JANVEY, L.L.P. (AV)

2001 Bryan Tower, Suite 2700, 75201-3059
Telephone: 214-969-7500
Telecopier: 214-220-0230

Ralph Janvey
Kristie L. Garrison

Representative Client: Regal Capital Co.

For full biographical listings, see the Martindale-Hubbell Law Directory

MEADOWS, OWENS, COLLIER, REED, COUSINS & BLAU, L.L.P. (AV)

901 Main Street, Suite 3700, 75202-3725
Telephone: 214-744-3700; 800-451-0093
Fax: 214-747-3732
URL: http://www.meadowsowens.com

MEMBERS OF FIRM

Charles M. Meadows, Jr.
Rodney J. Owens
Robert Don Collier
David N. Reed
Thomas G. Hineman
William R. Cousins, III
Charles W. Blau
George R. Bedell
Michael E. McCue
Fielder F. Nelms
Joel N. Crouch
Alan K. Davis
Charles D. Pulman

ASSOCIATES

Patricia King Dorey
Robert M. Bolton
M. Todd Welty
Josh O. Ungerman
Robyn A. Frohlin
Gregory A. Cardenas
Sara E. Lankford
Sarah Q. Qureshi
Bradley G. Korell
Todd A. Kraft
Alan L. Stroud
Matthew D. Richards

For full biographical listings, see the Martindale-Hubbell Law Directory

SAYLES & LIDJI, A PROFESSIONAL CORPORATION (AV)

4400 Renaissance Tower, 1201 Elm Street, 75270
Telephone: 214-939-8700
Fax: 214-939-8787
Email: admin@saylid.com

Richard A. Sayles
Brian M. Lidji
Mark S. Werbner
Michael R. Dorey
Eric D. Pearson
William S. Snyder
Kyle C. Hooper
Anne R. Myers
J. Craig Falls

For full biographical listings, see the Martindale-Hubbell Law Directory

THOMPSON & KNIGHT L.L.P. (AV)

(Attorneys and Counselors)
1700 Pacific Avenue Suite 3300, 75201
Telephone: 214-969-1700
Telecopy: 214-969-1751
Telex: 732 298
URL: http://www.tklaw.com
Austin, Texas Office: 1200 San Jacinto Center, 98 San Jacinto Boulevard, 78701.
Telephone: 512-469-6100.
Telecopy: 512-469-6180.
Fort Worth, Texas Office: 801 Cherry Street, Suite 1600, 76102.
Telephone: 817-347-1700.
Telecopy: 817-347-1799.
Houston, Texas Office: Thompson Knight Brown Parker & Leahy L.L.P., 1200 Smith Street, Suite 3600, 77002-4595.
Telephone: 713-654-8111.
Telecopier: 713-654-1871.
San Pedro Garza Garcia, Nuevo León, Mexico Office: Edificio Losoles PD-4, Av. Lázaro Cárdenas No. 2400 Pte., C.P. 66220.
Telephone: (52-8) 363-0096.
Telecopy: (52-8) 363-3067.

PARTNERS

Craig N. Adams
Sam P. Burford, Jr.
Steven K. Cochran
O. Paul Corley, Jr.
Joe Dannenmaier
David L. Emmons
Fred W. Fulton
James L. Irish, III
Paul M. Johnston
Harold F. Kleinman
C. Neel Lemon III
Jack M. Little
Peter A. Lodwick
Susan Monaco
David E. Morrison
James R. Peacock III
William J. Schuerger
Clint Shouse
Stephen E. Stein
Michael C. Titens
Kenn W. Webb
Jeffrey A. Zlotky

ASSOCIATES

Amy Cleek
Ann Marie Cowdrey
Amy Ray Curtis
Paul A. Jorge
D. Thomas Keltner
Grant Clayton Lightle
Jane E. Rast
Kirsten Ellen Richesson

For Complete List of Firm Personnel, See General Section

For full biographical listings, see the Martindale-Hubbell Law Directory

*EL PASO,** El Paso Co.

AINSA PARTNERS, LLP (AV)

5809 Acacia Circle, 79912
Telephone: 915-845-5300
Fax: 915-845-7800
Email: fain@acaciapark.com *URL:* http://www.ainsa.com

Francis S. Ainsa, Jr.
Michael F. Ainsa
David M. Driscoll

For full biographical listings, see the Martindale-Hubbell Law Directory

*FORT WORTH,** Tarrant Co.

DECKER, JONES, MCMACKIN, MCCLANE, HALL & BATES, A PROFESSIONAL CORPORATION (AV)

2500 Bank One Tower, 500 Throckmorton Street, 76102-3812
Telephone: 817-336-2400; Metro: 817-429-5260
Fax: 817-332-3043; 336-2181
Email: email@deckerjones.com *URL:* http://www.deckerjones.com

Daniel L. Bates
Robert W. Decker
Mark S. Dugan
Janet L. Hahn
Randy J. Hall
Raymond B. Kelly, III
John B. McClane
John W. McMackin
Charles B. Milliken
Gary M. Moates
Bradley H. Rice
Jeffrey W. Storie
James L. Stripling
Brian K. Yost
Tamera H. Bennett
Arthur F. Zobal
Geoffrey A. Mantooth

Representative Clients: Martin-Sprocket and Gear, Inc.; Williamson-Dickie Manufacturing Co.; MICA Corp.; Ibertech, Inc.; Harbison-Fischer Manufacturing Co.; Employers Insurance of Texas; American International Group; Medical Protective Co.; Redman Homes, Inc.; Liberty Mutual Insurance.

For full biographical listings, see the Martindale-Hubbell Law Directory

FRISCO, Collin & Denton Cos.

WINIKATES & WINIKATES (AV)

Prosper State Bank Building, 7700 Main Street, P.O. Box 249, 75034-0249
Telephone: 972-335-1122
Fax: 972-335-1125

(See Next Column)

WINIKATES & WINIKATES—*Continued*

MEMBERS OF FIRM

Charles J. Winikates
Charles J. Winikates, Jr.
Regina W. Mentesana
Frances A. Fazio

For full biographical listings, see the Martindale-Hubbell Law Directory

*HOUSTON,** Harris Co.

MOERER & BURTON, L.L.P. (AV)

440 Louisiana, Suite 350, 77002
Telephone: 713-222-6262
Fax: 713-222-6811
Email: moerer_burton@msn.com

MEMBER OF FIRM

Randy Burton

For full biographical listings, see the Martindale-Hubbell Law Directory

THOMPSON KNIGHT BROWN PARKER & LEAHY L.L.P. (AV)

A Registered Limited Liability Partnership including Professional Corporations
(Attorneys and Counselors)
1200 Smith Street, Suite 3600, 77002-4595
Telephone: 713-654-8111
Telecopier: 713-654-1871
URL: http://www.tklaw.com
Dallas, Texas Office: Thompson & Knight L.L.P., 1700 Pacific Avenue, Suite 3300, 75201.
Telephone: 214-969-1700.
Telecopy: 214-969-1751.
Telex: 732298.
Austin, Texas Office: Thompson & Knight L.L.P., 1200 San Jacinto Center, 98 San Jacinto Boulevard, 78701.
Telephone: 512-469-6100.
Telecopy: 512-469-6180.
Fort Worth, Texas Office: Thompson & Knight L.L.P., 801 Cherry Street, Suite 1600, 76102.
Telephone: 817-347-1700.
Telecopy: 817-347-1799.
San Pedro Garza Garcia, Nuevo León, Mexico Office: Thompson & Knight L.L.P., Edificio Losoles PD-4, Av. Lázaro Cárdenas No. 2400 PTE., C.P. 66220.
Telephone: (52-8) 363-0096.
Telecopy: (52-8) 363-3067.

PARTNER

Michael K. Pierce

ASSOCIATE

Christopher R. Hernandez

For Complete List of Firm Personnel, See General Section

For full biographical listings, see the Martindale-Hubbell Law Directory

*SAN ANTONIO,** Bexar Co.

BENTON CLARK & TAYLOR, P.C. (AV)

105 South St. Marys Street, Suite 905, 78205
Telephone: 210-472-1800
Fax: 210-472-1872

Barry G. Benton
R. Christopher Clark
Richard M. Taylor, III

Phillip R. Hall

For full biographical listings, see the Martindale-Hubbell Law Directory

GRESHAM, DAVIS, GREGORY, WORTHY & MOORE, A PROFESSIONAL CORPORATION (AV)

Formerly Boyle, Wheeler, Gresham, Davis & Gregory
112 East Pecan Street, Ninth Floor, 78205-1542
Telephone: 210-226-4157
Telecopier: 210-226-5154

Rupert Neely Gresham (1892-1973)
Richard T. Davis (1911-1991)
Albert W. Worthy (1922-1998)
Claiborne B. Gregory
Richard B. Moore
Claiborne B. Gregory, Jr.
Moulton S. Dowler, Jr.
Marshall B. Miller, Jr.
John Wallis Harris
Nancy A. Norman
Peter E. Hosey
Brad S. Akin
Matthew D. Bradley

OF COUNSEL

Ben J. Chilcutt
Samuel H. Bayless
Ann M. Leafstedt
James E. McCutcheon, III
Raul M. Calderon

(See Next Column)

Justin G. Rice
Bart W. Huffman

For full biographical listings, see the Martindale-Hubbell Law Directory

UTAH

*SALT LAKE CITY,** Salt Lake Co.

CALLISTER NEBEKER & McCULLOUGH, A PROFESSIONAL CORPORATION (AV)

Gateway Tower East, Suite 900, 10 East South Temple, 84133
Telephone: 801-530-7300
Telecopier: 801-364-9127
Email: mjeaston@cnmlaw.com *URL:* http://www.cnmlaw.com

Leland S. McCullough
Craig F. McCullough
George E. Harris, Jr.
Damon E. Coombs
Laurie S. Hart
Douglas K. Cummings

David R. York
Lee S. McCullough, III

Representative Clients: Zions First National Bank; Sears Roebuck & Company; Utah Automobile Dealers Association; Sinclair Oil Corporation (Little America); Keystone Communications; Central Valley Water Reclamation Facility Board; Citicorp; Intermountain Health Care, Inc.; Children's Miracle Network (Osmond Foundation); Nu Skin International, Inc.

For Complete List of Firm Personnel, See General Section

For full biographical listings, see the Martindale-Hubbell Law Directory

VAN COTT, BAGLEY, CORNWALL & McCARTHY, A PROFESSIONAL CORPORATION (AV)

50 South Main Street, Suite 1600, P.O. Box 45340, 84145-0340
Telephone: 801-532-3333
Telecopier: 801-534-0058
Email: info@vancott.com *URL:* http://www.vancott.com
Ogden, Utah Office: 2404 Washington Boulevard, Suite 900.
Telephone: 801-394-5783.
Park City, Utah Office: 2200 Park Avenue, Suite C200-A.
Telephone: 435-649-3889.

Rand L. Cook
Arthur B. Ralph
David E. Sloan
David J. Smith
Stephen D. Swindle

Kim S Colton
Tacy A. Hartman
Kevin M. Sheff

OF COUNSEL

M. Scott Woodland

For Complete List of Firm Personnel, See General Section

For full biographical listings, see the Martindale-Hubbell Law Directory

VIRGINIA

MCLEAN, Fairfax Co.

THOMAS M. DAVIDSON (AV Ⓣ)

1750 Tysons Boulevard Suite 240, 22102
Telephone: 703-556-8887
Email: TMD@DAVIDSONCAPITAL.com *URL:* http://www.lawyers.com/davidsonlaw
(Not admitted in VA)

ASSOCIATE

Amy Davidson Bryant (Not admitted in VA)

For full biographical listings, see the Martindale-Hubbell Law Directory

ROEDER AND ASSOCIATES, P.C. (AV)

8280 Greensboro Drive, Suite 601, 22102
Telephone: 703-749-6050
Fax: 703-749-6027
Email: wfroeder@erols.com

William F. Roeder, Jr.

Brian J. Lubkeman

For full biographical listings, see the Martindale-Hubbell Law Directory

McLean—Continued

TALBOTT AND GALLAGHER, A PROFESSIONAL CORPORATION (AV)

6824 Elm Street, Suite 350, 22101
Telephone: 703-893-6361
Facsimile: 703-893-6825
Email: jct@talbottgallagher.com *URL:* http://www.lawyers.com/talbottgallagher

John C. Talbott
Kathleen G. Gallagher

For full biographical listings, see the Martindale-Hubbell Law Directory

ROANOKE, Roanoke City Co.

WOOTEN & HART, A PROFESSIONAL CORPORATION (AV)

707 Building, Suite 300, P.O. Box 12247, 24024-2247
Telephone: 540-343-2451; 540-342-9672
Telecopier: 540-345-6417
URL: http://www.wootenhart.com

George W. Wooten
David B. Hart
L. Thompson Hanes
Susan A. Waddell
Bradley D. McGraw
John L. Cooley
Thomas W. Farrell
Paul C. Kuhnel
Peter D. Vieth

David W. Hearn
John Mark Cooley
Christopher W. Stevens
Elizabeth D. Guilbert
Eunice Park Austin

OF COUNSEL

M. Lanier Woodrum

Representative Clients: Wachovia Bank; St. Paul Insurance Cos.
Approved Attorneys for: Lawyers Title Insurance Corp.
Reference: First Union National Bank.

For full biographical listings, see the Martindale-Hubbell Law Directory

VIENNA, Fairfax Co.

GARY & GOODMAN LIMITED (AV)

8500 Leesburg Pike, Suite 7000 (Tysons Corner), 22182
Telephone: 703-848-2828
Facsimile: 703-893-9276
Email: garygoodman@ggllaw.com

Bernard E. Goodman
Stuart H. Gary

OF COUNSEL

George B. Delta

For full biographical listings, see the Martindale-Hubbell Law Directory

WASHINGTON

*SEATTLE,** King Co.

SUMMIT LAW GROUP, PLLC (AV)

1505 Westlake Avenue North, Suite 300, 98109
Telephone: 206-281-9881
Fax: 206-281-9882
Email: info@summitlaw.com *URL:* http://www.summitlaw.com

Karen A. Andersen
Kristin D. Anger
Laura A. Bertin
Lynn M. Engel
Michael J. Erickson
Matthew R. Harris
David M. Heineck
Elizabeth Butler Kennar
Otto G. Klein, III
Lawrence C. Locker
Philip S. McCune
Polly L. McNeill
Ralph H. Palumbo
Bruce L. Schroeder
William R. Squires III
Monika Vasil
Mark F. Worthington
Rodney B. Younker

For full biographical listings, see the Martindale-Hubbell Law Directory

WEST VIRGINIA

*CHARLESTON,** Kanawha Co.

GOODWIN & GOODWIN (AV)

1500 One Valley Square, 25301
Telephone: 304-346-7000
Fax: 304-344-9692
Email: g&glaw@goodwin.goodwin.com *URL:* http://www.goodwingoodwin.com
Ripley, West Virginia Office: 500 Church Street, P.O. Box 349.
Telephone: 304-372-2651.

(See Next Column)

Parkersburg, West Virginia Office: 201 Third Street, Town Square.
Telephone: 304-485-2345.
Fax: 304-485-3459.

Robert B. Goodwin (1909-1955)

OF COUNSEL

C. E. Goodwin

MEMBERS OF FIRM

Thomas R. Goodwin
Stephen P. Goodwin
Michael I. Spiker
Steven F. White
Richard E. Rowe
Leonard S. Coleman
Susan C. Wittemeier
Robert W. Full (Resident at Parkersburg Office)
Richard D. Owen
Tammy J. Owen
J. David Fenwick
Alexander Macia

ASSOCIATES

Suzanne Jett Trowbridge
William K. Bragg, Jr.
George M. Smith
John N. Ellem (Resident, Parkersburg Office)
Lisa A. Tackett
Robert (Booth) Goodwin, II
Carrie Goodwin Fenwick
Tiffany E. Davis

Representative Clients: Bucyrus-Erie Co.; CSX Corp.; Eastern American Energy Corp.; The Eureka Pipe Line Co.

For full biographical listings, see the Martindale-Hubbell Law Directory

WISCONSIN

*MILWAUKEE,** Milwaukee Co.

BECK, CHAET, MOLONY & BAMBERGER, S.C. (AV)

Two Plaza East, 330 East Kilbourn Avenue, Suite 1085, 53202
Telephone: 414-273-4200
Fax: 414-273-7786
Email: bcmb@execpc.com *URL:* http://www.bcmblaw.com
Madison, Wisconsin Office: 44 East Mifflin Street, Suite 304.
Telephone: 608-255-1140.
Fax: 608-255-0160.

Arthur E. Beck
Barry L. Chaet
Maureen A. Molony (Resident, Madison, Wisconsin Office)
Michael Bamberger
E. Vanessa Jones
Katherine L. Williams
Christopher J. Johnson
Kevin L. Keeler
Joshua B. Levy
LouAnn Koval
Daniel M. Lowndes
Edward B. Matkom

Drew J. Cochrane

OF COUNSEL

Robert P. Mandel

For full biographical listings, see the Martindale-Hubbell Law Directory

CHERNOV, STERN & KRINGS, S.C. (AV)

Suite 1275, Two Plaza East, 330 East Kilbourn Avenue, 53202
Telephone: 414-276-4080
Fax: 414-276-4152
Email: mail@chernovlaw.com *URL:* http://www.lawyers.com/chernovlaw

Benjamin S. Stern
Jerome D. Krings

OF COUNSEL

Ben L. Chernov

For full biographical listings, see the Martindale-Hubbell Law Directory

DEMET & DEMET, S.C. (AV)

815 North Cass Street, 53202
Telephone: 414-291-0800
Fax: 414-291-9560
URL: http://www.lawyers.com/demetdemet

Francis Joseph Demet (1923-1993)
Margadette Moffatt Demet
Donal Moffatt Demet
Kevin J. Demet

Reference: Marshall & Ilsley Bank of Milwaukee.

For full biographical listings, see the Martindale-Hubbell Law Directory

DRINKA, LEVINE & MASSON, S.C. (AV)

2000 Milwaukee Center, 111 East Kilbourn Avenue, 53202-6618
Telephone: 414-291-6080
Fax: 414-291-6090
URL: http://www.lawyers.com/drinkalevine&masson

(See Next Column)

DRINKA, LEVINE & MASSON S.C.—*Continued*

Judith A. Drinka
Micaela H. Levine
Grace M. Masson

For full biographical listings, see the Martindale-Hubbell Law Directory

RICHARD H. HART, JR. LAW OFFICES (AV)

Suite 601, 1100 West Wells Street, 53233
Telephone: 414-271-1225
Fax: 414-271-0457
Email: rhart@execpc.com *URL:* http://www.rhart.com

For full biographical listings, see the Martindale-Hubbell Law Directory

D. WINTHROP HASS, S.C. (AV)

205 East Wisconsin Avenue, Suite 405, 53202
Telephone: 414-276-1776
Fax: 414-276-4850
Email: david@imericana.com *URL:* http://www.lawyers.com/dhass

D. Winthrop Hass

OF COUNSEL

Hal Harlowe

For full biographical listings, see the Martindale-Hubbell Law Directory

WALSH & KEATING, S.C. (AV)

1505 Wawatosa Avenue, 53213
Telephone: 414-257-9929
Fax: 414-257-9959
URL: http://www.lawyers.com/walshandkeating

Gerald S. Walsh
David C. Keating

ASSOCIATE

Peter J. Walsh

OF COUNSEL

Lloyd W. Herrold

Representative Clients: Immtech International, Inc.; Howard Precision Metals Inc.; James L. Callan Inc.; Milwaukee Chaplet & Mfg. Co., Inc.; Milwaukee Envelope, Inc.; Stearns Foundation, Inc.; Wausau Tile, Inc.; August Urbanek Investments, Inc.; Germantown Market Place, Inc.; Precision Metrology, Inc.

For full biographical listings, see the Martindale-Hubbell Law Directory

PUERTO RICO

SAN JUAN, San Juan Dist.

BARRY A. WOODS

Capital Center Building, 239 Arterial Hostos, Suite 706, 00918-1476
Telephone: 787-759-8181
Fax: 787-751-3115
Email: baw@canibe.net/bawbat@cs.com

For full biographical listings, see the Martindale-Hubbell Law Directory

CANADA ALBERTA

*CALGARY,** Calgary Jud. Dist.

PARLEE MCLAWS (AV)

3400 Petro-Canada Centre, 150 - 6th Avenue, SW, T2P 3Y7
Telephone: 403-294-7000
Telecopier: 403-265-8263
Email: lawyers@parlee.com *URL:* http://www.parlee.com
Edmonton, Alberta Office: 15th Floor Manulife Place, 10180 101st Street.
Telephone: 403-423-8500.
Telecopier: 403-423-2870.

MEMBERS OF FIRM

William R. Pieschel, Q.C.
Lindsay J. Holmes
Richard B. Mask
Nancy M. Penner
Gordon M. Adams
Dale R. Spackman, Q.C.
Bruce A. Lawrence
Andrew P. Bedford

ASSOCIATES

Dennis J. Pelkie
Alec N. Silenzi
Ariane E. Young
Angela M. Tripathy
Seema S. Johal

For Complete List of Firm Personnel, See General Section

For full biographical listings, see the Martindale-Hubbell Law Directory

*EDMONTON,** Edmonton Jud. Dist.

PARLEE MCLAWS (AV)

15th Floor Manulife Place, 10180 101st Street, T5J 4K1
Telephone: 403-423-8500
Telecopier: 403-423-2870
Email: lawyers@parlee.com *URL:* http://www.parlee.com
Calgary, Alberta Office: 3400 Petro-Canada Centre, 150 - 6th Avenue, SW.
Telephone: 403-294-7000.
Telecopier: 403-265-8263.

MEMBERS OF FIRM

Terence A. Cockrall, Q.C.
F. Richard Haldane, Q.C.
David G. Finlay
Brian J. Curial
John W. McClure
H. Douglas Montemurro
Bruce D. Hirsche, Q.C.
Ian L. MacLachlan
Kevin L. Lynch
David S. Tam

ASSOCIATES

Lorne J. Ruzicka
George E. Flemming
Gregory P. Nakonechny

For Complete List of Firm Personnel, See General Section

For full biographical listings, see the Martindale-Hubbell Law Directory

CANADA NEW BRUNSWICK

*FREDERICTON,** York Co.

MCINNES COOPER (AV)

Suite 600, 570 Queen Street, P.O. Box 610, E3B 5A6
Telephone: 506-458-8572
Fax: 506-458-9903
Email: mcrfton@mcrlaw.com *URL:* http://www.mcrlaw.com
Halifax, Nova Scotia Office: Summit Place, 1601 Lower Water Street, P.O. Box 730, B3J 2V1.
Telephone: 902-425-6500.
Fax: 902-425-6350. Email: mcrhfx@mcrlaw.com.
St. John's, Newfoundland Office: Baine Johnston Centre, 5th Floor, 10 Fort William Place, P.O. Box 5939, A1C 5X4.
Telephone: 709-722-8735.
Telecopier: 709-722-1763. Email: mcrsj@mcrlaw.com.
Moncton, New Brunswick Office: Place Moncton Place, 655 Main Street, P.O. Box 1368, E1C 8T6.
Telephone: 506-857-8970.
Fax: 506-857-4095. Email: mcrmctn@mcrlaw.com.
Charlottetown, Prince Edward Island Office: BDC Place, Suite 620, 119 Kent Street, C1A 1N3.
Telephone: 902-368-8473.
Fax: 902-368-8346. Email: mcrpei@mcrlaw.com.

PARTNERS

R. Bruce Eddy, Q.C.
Leonard T. Hoyt
Carol J. Downs

ASSOCIATES

Alan Rockwell
Steven D. Christie

For Complete List of Firm Personnel, See General Section

For full biographical listings, see the Martindale-Hubbell Law Directory

*MONCTON,** Westmorland Co.

MCINNES COOPER (AV)

Barristers, Solicitors & Trade Mark Agents
Place Moncton Place, 655 Main Street, P.O. Box 1368, E1C 8T6
Telephone: 506-857-8970
Fax: 506-857-4095
Email: mcrmctn@mcrlaw.com *URL:* http://www.mcrlaw.com
Halifax, Nova Scotia Office: Summit Place, 1601 Lower Water Street, P.O. Box 730, B3J 2V1.
Telephone: 902-425-6500.
Fax: 902-425-6350. Email: mcrhfx@mcrlaw.com.
St. John's, Newfoundland Office: Baine Johnston Centre, 5th Floor, 10 Fort William Place, P.O. Box 5939, A1C 5X4.
Telephone: 709-722-8735.
Telecopier: 709-722-1763. Email: mcrsj@mcrlaw.com.
Charlottetown, Prince Edward Island Office: BDC Place, Suite 620, 119 Kent Street, C1A 1N3.
Telephone: 902-368-8473.
Fax: 902-368-8346. Email: mcrpei@mcrlaw.com.
Fredericton, New Brunswick Office: Suite 600, 570 Queen Street, P.O. Box 610.
Telephone: 506-458-8572.
Fax: 506-458-9903. Email: mcrfton@mcrlaw.com.

(See Next Column)

McINNES COOPER, *Moncton—Continued*

ASSOCIATE

Christopher A. Borden

For Complete List of Firm Personnel, See General Section

For full biographical listings, see the Martindale-Hubbell Law Directory

CANADA NEWFOUNDLAND

*ST. JOHN'S,**

McINNES COOPER (AV)

Barristers, Solicitors & Trade Mark Agents
Baine Johnston Centre, 5th Floor, 10 Fort William Place, P.O. Box 5939, A1C 5X4
Telephone: 709-722-8735
Telecopier: 709-722-1763
Email: mcrsj@mcrlaw.com *URL:* http://www.mcrlaw.com
Halifax, Nova Scotia Office: Summit Place, 1601 Lower Water Street, P.O. Box 730, B3J 2V1.
Telephone: 902-425-6500.
Fax: 902-425-6350. Email: mcrhfx@mcrlaw.com.
Moncton, New Brunswick Office: Place Moncton Place, 655 Main Street, P.O. Box 1368, E1C 8T6.
Telephone: 506-857-8970.
Fax: 506-857-4095. Email: mcrmctn@mcrlaw.com.
Charlottetown, Prince Edward Island Office: BDC Place, Suite 620, 119 Kent Street, C1A 1N3.
Telephone: 902-368-8473.
Fax: 902-368-8346. Email: mcrpei@mcrlaw.com.
Fredericton, New Brunswick Office: Suite 600, 570 Queen Street, P.O. Box 610.
Telephone: 506-458-8572.
Fax: 506-458-9903. Email: mcrfton@mcrlaw.com.

PARTNERS

John M. Green, Q.C.
W. Gary Rowe, Q.C.
Thomas R. Kendell
Michael J. Crosbie
Deborah L. J. Hutchings
Caroline C. Watton

ASSOCIATES

Dennis N. Clarke
Jacqueline S. Bartlett

For Complete List of Firm Personnel, See General Section

For full biographical listings, see the Martindale-Hubbell Law Directory

CANADA NOVA SCOTIA

*HALIFAX,** Regional Munic. of Halifax

McINNES COOPER (AV)

Barristers, Solicitors & Trade Mark Agents
Summit Place, 1601 Lower Water Street, P.O. Box 730, B3J 2V1
Telephone: 902-425-6500
Fax: 902-425-6350
Email: mcrhfx@mcrlaw.com *URL:* http://www.mcrlaw.com
St. John's, Newfoundland Office: Baine Johnston Centre, 5th Floor, 10 Fort William Place, P.O. Box 5939, A1C 5X4.
Telephone: 709-722-8735.
Telecopier: 709-722-1763. Email: mcrsj@mcrlaw.com.
Moncton, New Brunswick Office: Place Moncton Place, 655 Main Street, P.O. Box 1368, E1C 8T6.
Telephone: 506-857-8970.
Fax: 506-857-4095. Email: mcrmctn@mcrlaw.com.
Charlottetown, Prince Edward Island Office: BDC Place, Suite 620, 119 Kent Street, C1A 1N3.
Telephone: 902-368-8473.
Fax: 902-368-8346. Email: mcrpei@mcrlaw.com.
Fredericton, New Brunswick Office: Suite 600, 570 Queen Street, P.O. Box 610.
Telephone: 506-458-8572.
Fax: 506-458-9903. Email: mcrfton@mcrlaw.com.

PARTNERS

Lawrence J. Hayes, Q.C.
Joseph A. F. Macdonald, Q.C.
George T. H. Cooper, Q.C.
David H. Reardon, Q.C.
Lawrence A. Freeman
F. Van W. Penick
Marcia L. Brennan
Fae J. Shaw

ASSOCIATES

Frank E. Hughes
Jeffrey R. Blucher
Jennifer A. Healy
Kristi Sebalj

For Complete List of Firm Personnel, See General Section

For full biographical listings, see the Martindale-Hubbell Law Directory

CANADA PRINCE EDWARD ISLAND

*CHARLOTTETOWN,** Queen's Co.

McINNES COOPER (AV®)

Barristers, Solicitors & Trade Mark Agents
BDC Place, Suite 620, 119 Kent Street, C1A 1N3
Telephone: 902-368-8473
Fax: 902-368-8346
Email: mcrpei@mcrlaw.com *URL:* http://www.mcrlaw.com
Halifax, Nova Scotia Office: Summit Place, 1601 Lower Water Street, P.O. Box 730, B3J 2V1.
Telephone: 902-425-6500.
Fax: 902-425-6350. Email: mcrhfx@mcrlaw.com.
St. John's, Newfoundland Office: Baine Johnston Centre, 5th Floor, 10 Fort William Place, P.O. Box 5939, A1C 5X4.
Telephone: 709-722-8735.
Telecopier: 709-722-1763. Email: mcrsj@mcrlaw.com.
Moncton, New Brunswick Office: Place Moncton Place, 655 Main Street, P.O. Box 1368, E1C 8T6.
Telephone: 506-857-8970.
Fax: 506-857-4095. Email: mcrmctn@mcrlaw.com.
Fredericton, New Brunswick Office: Suite 600, 570 Queen Street, P.O. Box 610.
Telephone: 506-458-8572.
Fax: 506-458-9903. Email: mcrfton@mcrlaw.com.

PARTNERS

Horace B. Carver, Q.C.
Michele M. Murphy

ASSOCIATES

L. Charles Keizer
Kevin J. Kiley
Paul Kiley
Kim Petrie

For Complete List of Firm Personnel, See General Section

For full biographical listings, see the Martindale-Hubbell Law Directory

CANADA QUEBEC

*MONTREAL,** Montreal Dist.

McMASTER GERVAIS (AV)

A General Partnership
1000 de La Gauchetière Street West, Suite 900, H3B 5H4
Telephone: 514-879-1212
Fax: 514-954-1905
Email: info@mcmastergervais.com *URL:* http://www.mcmastergervais.com

MEMBERS OF FIRM

Lionel J. Blanshay
Peter C. Casey
Paul R. Marchand
Brian M. Schneiderman
Luc LaRochelle
Charles P. Marquette
André Dufour
Pierre B. Côté
François Morin
Patrice Martin
Marc-Antoine La Rochelle
Sophia Tolias

COUNSEL

Tass G. Grivakes, Q.C.

For Complete List of Firm Personnel, See General Section

For full biographical listings, see the Martindale-Hubbell Law Directory

CREDITORS RIGHTS

MISSOURI

ST. LOUIS, (Independent City)

DAVIS & WEISMAN, P.C. (AV)

2025 South Brentwood Boulevard, Suite 204, 63144
Telephone: 314-962-1115; Toll Free: 1-888-673-9136
Fax: 314-962-7728
URL: http://www.lawyers.com/davis&weisman

Katharyn B. Davis
Jeffrey T. Weisman

Representative Clients: Household Finance Co.; Bank of America; MorEquity, Inc.; Lindell Trust Co.; FDIC; Educational Employees Credit Union; Apartment Exchange, Inc.

For full biographical listings, see the Martindale-Hubbell Law Directory

KRAMER & FRANK, P.C. (AV)

9666 Olive Boulevard, Suite 450, 63132
Telephone: 314-991-1177; 800-288-5437
Telecopier: 314-991-0485
Email: george@lawusa.com *URL:* http://www.lawusa.com
Kansas City, Missouri Office: 1101 Walnut, Suite 1202, 64106.
Telephone: 816-471-0030.
Fax: 816-472-0963.

Donald B. Kramer
I. James Frankel
George J. Skupnik, Jr.
David J. Kozeny
Timothy M. Bosslet
Jay B. Umansky
David L. Smith
Bradley D. Pierce

Pamela P. Floro
Tammy F. Wool
D. Jay Cohen
Diane W. Ortlip
Janice Valdez

For full biographical listings, see the Martindale-Hubbell Law Directory

THE STOLAR PARTNERSHIP (AV)

7th Floor, 911 Washington Avenue, 63101
Telephone: 314-231-2800
Telex: 880984
Telecopier: 314-436-8400
Belleville, Illinois Office: 7 North High Street.
Telephone: 618-277-1030.

MEMBERS OF FIRM

Kathryn J. Giddings
Myron A. Hanna (Not admitted in MO)
Jay L. Levitch
Henry F. Luepke III
Cherie K. MacDonald
Randall A. Martin

ASSOCIATE

Deborah J. Volmert ***

***Admitted Illinois and Missouri

For full biographical listings, see the Martindale-Hubbell Law Directory

NEBRASKA

*OMAHA,** Douglas Co.

MCGILL, GOTSDINER, WORKMAN & LEPP, P.C. (AV)

Suite 500 - First National Plaza, 11404 West Dodge Road, 68154
Telephone - 402-492-9200
Telecopier: 402-492-9222
Email: mgwl@mgwl.com

Alan E. Pedersen
Julie A. Engelhardt

OF COUNSEL

Richard D. Myers

Representative Clients: First National Bank of Omaha; Norwest Bank Nebraska N.A.; Fremont National Bank; Behlen Mfg. Co.; Baxter Chrysler-Plymouth; Metz Baking Co.; Bethesda Living Centers; Mutual of Omaha; Vetter Health Services; Woolworth Corp.

For Complete List of Firm Personnel, See General Section

For full biographical listings, see the Martindale-Hubbell Law Directory

RASMUSSEN & MITCHELL (AV)

11605 Miracle Hills Drive, Suite 205, 68154
Telephone: 402-493-3300
Fax: 402-496-0766
Email: lawman000@aol.com *URL:* http://www.lawyers.com/rasmussen&mitchell

MEMBERS OF FIRM

Wayne S. Rasmussen
James S. Mitchell
Kathryn J. Derr
Shane M. Niebergall

For full biographical listings, see the Martindale-Hubbell Law Directory

NEW JERSEY

*NEWARK,** Essex Co.

MEYNER AND LANDIS (AV)

One Gateway Center, Suite 2500, 07102-5311
Telephone: 973-624-2800
Fax: 973-624-0356
Email: attys@meyner.com *URL:* http://www.meyner.com

Robert B. Meyner (1908-1990)
Edwin C. Landis, Jr.
John N. Malyska
William J. Fiore
Anthony F. Siliato
Francis R. Perkins
Howard O. Thompson
Scott T. McCleary
Linda Townley Snyder
William H. Schmidt, Jr.
David B. Grantz

For full biographical listings, see the Martindale-Hubbell Law Directory

PRINCETON, Mercer Co.

MCCARTHY AND SCHATZMAN, P.A. (AV)

228 Alexander Street, P.O. Box 2329, 08543-2329
Telephone: 609-924-1199
Fax: 609-683-5251

John F. McCarthy, Jr.
Richard Schatzman
G. Christopher Baker
John F. McCarthy, III
Michael A. Spero
Barbara Strapp Nelson
W. Scott Stoner
James J. Britt, Jr.

Charly Gayden

Representative Clients: Trustees of Princeton University; Carnegie Center Associates; Merrill Lynch Pierce Fenner & Smith, Inc.; Calton Homes, Inc.

For full biographical listings, see the Martindale-Hubbell Law Directory

WEST ORANGE, Essex Co.

RABINOWITZ, TRENK, LUBETKIN & TULLY, P.C. (AV)

200 Executive Drive Suite 225, 07052-3303
Telephone: 973-243-8600
Facsimile: 973-243-8677
URL: http://www.Rabinowitztrenk.com

Jonathan I. Rabinowitz
Richard D. Trenk
Jay L. Lubetkin
Mary Ellen Tully

Joseph J. DiPasquale
Joshua H. Raymond
Henry M. Karwowski
Shoshana Schiff

For full biographical listings, see the Martindale-Hubbell Law Directory

NEW MEXICO

*ALBUQUERQUE,** Bernalillo Co.

MARTIN E. THREET & ASSOCIATES (AV)

6400 Uptown Boulevard N.E. Suite 500 West Tower, 87110
Telephone: 505-881-5155
Fax: 505-881-5356
Email: threetlaw@aol.com

MEMBER OF FIRM

Martin E. Threet

ASSOCIATES

Joseph L. Romero
Joey B. Wright

For Complete List of Firm Personnel, See General Section

For full biographical listings, see the Martindale-Hubbell Law Directory

NEW YORK

*MINEOLA,** Nassau Co.

GUTMAN & GUTMAN LLP (AV)

Gutman Building, 19 Roslyn Road, 11501-4521
Telephone: 516-248-0470
Telecopier: 516-746-6997
Email: aegutman@aol.com *URL:*
http://www.lawyers.com/gutman,gutman&gutman

MEMBERS OF FIRM

Lawrence C. Gutman
Elizabeth A. Gutman
Andrew E. Gutman

Reference: United Mercantile Agencies, Inc.

For full biographical listings, see the Martindale-Hubbell Law Directory

*NEW YORK,** New York Co.

FINKEL GOLDSTEIN BERZOW ROSENBLOOM & NASH, LLP (AV)

26 Broadway, 10004
Telephone: 212-344-2929
Telecopier: 212-422-6836
Email: finkgold@aol.com

MEMBERS OF FIRM

Benjamin Finkel (1905-1986)
Harvey L. Goldstein
Harold S. Berzow
Neal M. Rosenbloom
Kevin J. Nash

ASSOCIATES

Arthur A. Hirschler
Charles Fischer
David J. Ciminesi

For full biographical listings, see the Martindale-Hubbell Law Directory

PILIERO GOLDSTEIN JENKINS & SULLIVAN, LLP (AV)

292 Madison Avenue, 10017
Telephone: 212-213-8200
Fax: 212-685-2028
Email: lawyers@pgjhlaw.com *URL:* http://www.pgjhlaw.com
Carlstadt, New Jersey Office: One Palmer Terrace.
Telephone: 201-507-5157.
FAX: 201-507-5221.
Washington, D.C. Office: 888 17th Street, N.W., Suite 1100.
Telephone: 202-467-6991.
FAX: 202-467-6703.
San Francisco, California Office: 507 Howard Street, Suite 200.
Telephone: 415-281-3631.
Fax: 415-281-3630.

MEMBERS OF FIRM

Kimberlee S. Bogen
Edward J. Goldstein
Jon Mark Jenkins
Marc A. Lebowitz
Robert D. Piliero
George O. Richardson, III
Michael T. Sullivan

ASSOCIATES

Craig Avedisian
Rosemary G. Feit
Eric M. Kogan
Mariano Schwed

OF COUNSEL

Kenneth D. Arbeeny
Christopher P. Hall

For full biographical listings, see the Martindale-Hubbell Law Directory

*ROCHESTER,** Monroe Co.

FORSYTH, HOWE, O'DWYER, KALB & MURPHY, P.C. (AV)

Suite 1600, Midtown Tower, 14604
Telephone: 716-325-7515
Fax: 716-325-6407
URL: http://www.forsythhowe.com

Charles B. Forsyth (1890-1968)
C. Benn Forsyth
Gordon A. Howe, II
Duncan W. O'Dwyer
Robert J. Kalb
Gerald N. Murphy

Nancy A. Pappal

OF COUNSEL

John F. Forsyth (Retired)
Allan Wolk
Hoffman Stone
Debra A. Martin
Janice M. Iati
Cathleen W. Smith
Thad F. Sondej

References: The Chase Manhattan Bank; Fleet Bank.

For full biographical listings, see the Martindale-Hubbell Law Directory

LAWRENCE, WERNER, KESSELRING, SWARTOUT & BROWN, LLP (AV)

Formerly Suter Doyle Kesselring Lawrence & Werner
700 First Federal Plaza, 14614-1909
Telephone: 716-325-6446
Fax: 716-262-5185
Email: rochester@lwksb.com *URL:* http://www.lwksb.com
Canandaigua, New York Office: 23 Sly Street, 14424.
Telephone: 716-396-4000.
Fax: 716-396-1210. Email: canandaigua@lwksb.com.
Clifton Springs, New York: 26 East Main Street, P.O. Box 604, 14432.
Telephone: 315-462-3010.
Fax: 315-462-5039. Email: clifton_springs@lwksb.com

Paul J. Suter (1918-1989)

MEMBERS OF FIRM

Leo J. Kesselring
C. Bruce Lawrence
Christopher K. Werner
Colleen A. Brown
Steven H. Swartout
Mary Jo S. Korona

OF COUNSEL

James B. Doyle
Craig J. Doran
John F. Riley

ASSOCIATE

Jeffrey D. Graff

Representative Clients: Canandaigua National Bank; Hadlock Paint Company, Inc.; F.F. Thompson Health Systems, Inc.; Keuka College; Towns of Farmington and Gorham, NY; Toyota Motor Credit Corp.
References: Canandaigua National Bank; Fleet Bank, Rochester; National Association of Credit Manager, Rochester.

For full biographical listings, see the Martindale-Hubbell Law Directory

RELIN, GOLDSTEIN AND CRANE, LLP (AV)

1800 First Federal Plaza, 14614-1909
Telephone: 716-325-6202
Fax: 716-325-6201
Email: RGCattys@aol.com

MEMBERS OF FIRM

Lloyd H. Relin (1939-1986)
Paul L. Goldstein
Howard R. Crane
Mark K. Broyles

ASSOCIATE

Joseph M. Shur

Reference: Marine Midland Bank.

For full biographical listings, see the Martindale-Hubbell Law Directory

*SYRACUSE,** Onondaga Co.

ALI, PAPPAS & COX, P.C. (AV)

Syracuse Building, 224 Harrison Street, 13202
Telephone: 315-472-4481
FAX: 315-472-8299
Email: alpaco@dreamscape.com

Lucien Ali
C. Andrew Pappas
Robert B. Cox
Thomas P. Givas
P. Douglas Dodd
David P. Doherty

OF COUNSEL

Edward F. Gerber

LEGAL SUPPORT PERSONNEL

Brenda M. Barch

Representative Clients: Agway, Inc.; Agway Petroleum Corp.; Arcom Labs; Countryside Federal Credit Union; PineCone Federal Credit Union; Oswego City Savings Bank; Telmark, Inc.; Syracuse Executive Air Services, Inc.; Fairbanks Capital Corp.
References: M&T Bank; 1st National Bank of Rochester.

For full biographical listings, see the Martindale-Hubbell Law Directory

NORTH CAROLINA

*WILMINGTON,** New Hanover Co.

KAUFMAN & GREEN, L.L.P. (AV)

Landfall Park North, 1985 Eastwood Road, Suite 200, 28403
Telephone: 910-256-5135
Fax: 910-256-6451

James J. Kaufman
Michael A. Green

Owen D. Lewis, Jr.

Representative Clients: T.F.S.I.; First State Bank of Austin; Eastern Acceptance Corp.; SRS Development, Inc.

For full biographical listings, see the Martindale-Hubbell Law Directory

OHIO

*CINCINNATI,** Hamilton Co.

MASON, SLOVIN & SCHILLING CO., L.P.A. (AV)

11340 Montgomery Road, Suite 210, 45249-2313
Telephone: 513-489-0829
800-840-3514
Fax: 513-489-0834
Email: msscolpa@worldnet.att.net
Covington, Kentucky Office: Heritage International, Suite 203, P.O. Box 2158.
Telephone: 513-489-0829.
Fax: 513-489-0834.
Columbus Office: 10 West Broad Street, Suite 2400 One Columbus.
Telephone: 513-489-0829.
Fax: 513-489-0834.
Dayton Office: 319 Liberty Tower.
Telephone: 513-489-0829.
Fax: 513-489-0834.
Lima Office: 809 West Vine Street, P.O. Box 937.
Telephone: 513-489-0829.
Fax: 513-489-0834.

Jonathan A. Mason
Randy T. Slovin
Richard D. Schilling

David C. Nalley
Joseph Ruwe

OF COUNSEL

Fred H. Summe (Not admitted in OH; Resident, Covington, KY Office)
Richard L. Levine

LEGAL SUPPORT PERSONNEL

Brenda L. Norton (Office Manager and Executive Legal Secretary)
Lisa K. Spencer (Sr. Case Manager; Accounting Manager)
Amy J. Luipold (Sr. Case Manager; Recovery Manager)
William M. Luipold (Manager, Court Administration)
Marilyn E. Mason (Sr. Legal Assistant-Accounting)
Jeremy R. Mason (Sr. Law Clerk)
Rachel J. Mason (Law Clerk)
Sarah Hopkins (Legal Assistant-Recovery)
Becky Grandstaff (Legal Assistant-Claims & Billing)
Connie Shutt (Legal Assistant-Litigation)

For full biographical listings, see the Martindale-Hubbell Law Directory

*CLEVELAND,** Cuyahoga Co.

CHARLES J. PALMERI CO., L.P.A. (AV)

Suite 250, Corporate Circle, 30100 Chagrin Boulevard, 44124-5705
Telephone: 216-831-7338
Facsimile: 216-765-1258
Email: cjpalmeri@lawyers.com *URL:* http://www.lawyers.com/cjpalmeri

Charles J. Palmeri

For full biographical listings, see the Martindale-Hubbell Law Directory

*COLUMBUS,** Franklin Co.

CHEEK & ZEEHANDELAR, LLP (AV)

471 East Broad Street, 18th Floor, P.O. Box 15069, 43215-3872
Telephone: 614-229-3888; 1-800-689-6677
Fax: 614-241-5865
Email: candz@iwaynet.net

MEMBERS OF FIRM

Emerson Cheek, III
Steven J. Zeehandelar

ASSOCIATES

Alessandro Sabatino
James C. Zury

Representative Clients: State Farm Insurance Co.; AT&T Universal Card; Huntington National Bank; Grange Mutual Casualty Co.; Citicorp Mortgage, Inc.; National City Bank; Motorists Insurance Co.; Fidelity Financial Services; Central Ohio Credit Corp.; Elsea Mobile Homes.

For full biographical listings, see the Martindale-Hubbell Law Directory

OKLAHOMA

*OKLAHOMA CITY,** Oklahoma Co.

DAY, EDWARDS, FEDERMAN, PROPESTER & CHRISTENSEN, P.C. (AV)

Suite 2900 Oklahoma Tower, 210 Park Avenue, 73102-5605
Telephone: 405-239-2121
Telecopier: 405-236-1012
URL: http://lawlinks.com/attys/ok/defpc.html

Joe E. Edwards
J. Clay Christensen
Richard P. Propester
Kent A. Gilliland

Ricki Valerie Sonders
Thomas Pitchlynn Howell, IV
Joel Warren Harmon

Representative Clients: BancFirst; Bank One, Oklahoma City; Bank of America, N.A.; Federal Deposit Insurance Corp.; First Community Bank, Binger; First National Bank and Trust Company of Weatherford; First State Bank & Trust Co., Hollis; Local Oklahoma Bank.

For Complete List of Firm Personnel, See General Section

For full biographical listings, see the Martindale-Hubbell Law Directory

*TULSA,** Tulsa Co.

MAC D. FINLAYSON, P.C. (AV)

115 West 3rd Street, Suite 480, 74103-3410
Telephone: 918-583-2900
Facsimile: 918-583-6811
Email: mdfinlayson@abanet.org

Mac D. Finlayson

For full biographical listings, see the Martindale-Hubbell Law Directory

OREGON

*EUGENE,** Lane Co.

MUHLHEIM PALMER & WADE, A PROFESSIONAL CORPORATION (AV)

U.S. Bank Center, 800 Willamette Street, Suite 700, 97401-2933
Telephone: 541-687-4757
Facsimile: 541-687-4780
Email: mpw-law.com *URL:* http://www.lawyers.com/muhleimpalmer&wade

Wilson C. Muhlheim
R. Scott Palmer
Carolyn G. Wade

Pamela Egan Singer
Stephen C.P. Carroll
Heidi Von Ravensberg
Edward C Singer

LEGAL SUPPORT PERSONNEL

Dawnne L. Linenbrink, CLAS
Fern Puls
Richard Rickson

Representative Clients: Harvest Ford Lincoln Mercury; Georgia Pacific Employees Federal Credit Union; Valley of The Rogue Bank; Bank of Southern Oregon; The Boulders on the River, Inc.; Trans Union Corporation; Heritage Mall, Ltd.; Sandpines Golf Resort; Ariki Co., Ltd.; Water Sports, Inc.; Lowther Assets.

For full biographical listings, see the Martindale-Hubbell Law Directory

*PORTLAND,** Multnomah Co.

KELL, ALTERMAN & RUNSTEIN, LLP (AV)

1001 S.W. Fifth Avenue, Suite 1800, 97204
Telephone: 503-222-3531
Telecopier: 503-227-2980
Email: kell@teleport.com

MEMBERS OF FIRM

Raymond M. Kell (1911-1991)
Clifford B. Alterman (1925-1995)
Ted E. Runstein
Lee Davis Kell
Wayne D. Palmer
Lloyd R. Summers
William D. Dickas
Gary P. Compa
Charles R. Williamson
Mary Ellen Page Farr
Eric Sogge
Thomas J. Matsuda
Thomas R. Rask, III
Nicholas S. Fish

(See Next Column)

KELL, ALTERMAN & RUNSTEIN LLP, *Portland—Continued*

Dana L. Barnes
Cory Larvik
Robert E. Kabacy
Robin M. Runstein

References: Union Bank of California, N.A. (Portland Branch); The Bank of Tokyo-Mitsubishi, Ltd. (Portland Branch); Bank of America (5th S. Main Branch).

For full biographical listings, see the Martindale-Hubbell Law Directory

PENNSYLVANIA

*PHILADELPHIA,** Philadelphia Co.

CIARDI, MASCHMEYER & KARALIS, P.C. (AV)

1900 Spruce Street, 19103
Telephone: 215-546-4500
Fax: 215-985-4175
Cherry Hill, New Jersey Office: 413 Route 70 East, Suite 300, 08034.
Telephone: 609-428-8400.
Telecopier: 609-428-8571.

Albert A. Ciardi, Jr.
Paul Brinton Maschmeyer
Aris J. Karalis
Albert A. Ciardi, III
Camille Spinale
Thomas J. Maiorino
Andrew Henry

Davis A. Schultz

LEGAL SUPPORT PERSONNEL

PARALEGALS

Janice Lazar

For full biographical listings, see the Martindale-Hubbell Law Directory

DIDONATO & WINTERHALTER, P.C. (AV)

1818 Market Street, Suite 3520, 19103-3629
Telephone: 215-564-5050
Telecopier: 215-564-5597
URL: http://www.lawyers.com/didonato
Marlton, New Jersey Office: One Greentree Centre, Route 73 & Greenfield Road, Suite 201, 08053.
Telephone: 609-263-2700.
Telecopier: 609-263-9192.

Edward J. DiDonato
Paul J. Winterhalter
Eugene Camposano

For full biographical listings, see the Martindale-Hubbell Law Directory

KLEINBARD, BELL & BRECKER LLP (AV)

Suite 700, 1900 Market Street, 19103
Telephone: 215-568-2000
Facsimile: 215-568-0140
Montclair, New Jersey Office: 240 Claremont Avenue, 07042.
Telephone: 973-233-0600.
Facsimile: 973-233-9390.

Joseph S. Kleinbard (1905-1994)
Robert John Brecker (1916-1996)

COUNSEL TO THE FIRM

Arthur S. Keyser

MEMBERS OF FIRM

Paul E. Bomze
Murray I. Blackman
Howard J. Davis
Steven R. Waxman
Steven J. Engelmyer (Resident, Montclair Office)
David L. Hyman (Resident, Montclair Office)
Imogene E. Hughes
John P. Hickey
Jay R. Goldstein
Ralph J. Mauro
Thomas H. Speranza
Lisa E. Brody

ASSOCIATES

Mary Beth H. Gray
Eric J. Rothschild
Mary Vassallo Slinkard
Michael A. Frattone
Benjamin C. Graff (Not admitted in PA)
Ralph F. Salgado

COUNSEL

Joseph Bell

For full biographical listings, see the Martindale-Hubbell Law Directory

LAW OFFICES OF PETER E. MELTZER & ASSOCIATES, P.C. (AV)

1600 Locust Street Suite 200, 19103
Telephone: 215-545-3300
Fax: 215-545-0666
Email: pmeltzer@lawyers.com *URL:* http://www.lawyers.com/meltzerlaw

(See Next Column)

Peter E. Meltzer

For full biographical listings, see the Martindale-Hubbell Law Directory

WEIR & PARTNERS LLP (AV)

A Pennsylvania Limited Liability Partnership
Suite 500, The Widener Building, 1339 Chestnut Street, 19107
Telephone: 215-665-8181
Telefax: 215-665-8464
Email: info@weirpartners.com
Turnersville, New Jersey Office: 215 Fries Mill Road, 08012.
Telephone: 609-740-1490.
Telefax: 609-740-1491.

MEMBERS OF FIRM

Walter Weir, Jr.
Leonard S. Goodman
Susan Verbonitz
Jeffrey L. Rudnick
Robert D. Sayre
Stephen M. Giroux
Richard P. Coe, Jr.
Brett A. Datto
John B. York
Joseph C. Hare

ASSOCIATES

Bonnie R. Golub
Debra N. Nathanson
Tina L. Colman
Andrew K. Stutzman
Jeffrey A. Guth
Jason M Reiser
Madeline Flanagan

For full biographical listings, see the Martindale-Hubbell Law Directory

*PITTSBURGH,** Allegheny Co.

APPLE AND APPLE, A PROFESSIONAL CORPORATION (AV)

4650 Baum Boulevard, 15213
Telephone: 412-682-1466; 800-477-APPLE
Fax: 412-682-3138
Email: applelaw@aol.com

Marvin J. Apple
James R. Apple

Charles F. Bennett
Joel E. Hausman
Marylouise Wagner

LEGAL SUPPORT PERSONNEL

Michelle A. Bernard-Danielson (Office Manager)

Representative Clients: Citibank; Bank of America; Providian Financial; PNC Bank; National City Bank; BP Oil; N.A.C.M.; Associates Commercial Corp.; Kemper Insurance; Conrail.

For full biographical listings, see the Martindale-Hubbell Law Directory

GLOSSER & SHREVE (AV)

Suite 200, 213 Smithfield Street, 15222-2224
Telephone: 412-281-6555
FAX: 412-281-6597
Email: mark.glosser@commersel.com *URL:* http://www.lawyers.com/debtorcreditlaw

Mark L. Glosser
Steven T. Shreve

Representative Clients: Crawford Construction Company, Inc.; Franklin & Locust Realty, Inc.; Digital Equipment Corporation, Inc.; Household Financial Corporation; First Union Bank; C.J. Betters Co.

For full biographical listings, see the Martindale-Hubbell Law Directory

VOLLMER RULONG & KEATING, P.C. (AV)

Suite 1212 Grant Building, 310 Grant Street, 15219
Telephone: 412-391-2121
Telecopier: 412-391-3578
Email: vollmer@vollmerlaw.com *URL:* http://www.vollmerlaw.com

Charles J. Vollmer
Roger G. Rulong, Jr.
John R. Keating

Pamela J. Royesky

For full biographical listings, see the Martindale-Hubbell Law Directory

*READING,** Berks Co.

BINGAMAN, HESS, COBLENTZ & BELL, A PROFESSIONAL CORPORATION (AV)

Suite 660, 601 Penn Street, P.O. Box 61, 19603-0061
Telephone: 610-374-8377
Fax: 610-376-3105
URL: http://www.bhcb.com
Cherry Hill, New Jersey Office: Shawn J. Lau, P.C., Building Q, Suite 14B, 1930 East Marlton Pike, 08003-4222.
Telephone: 609-751-4158.
Fax: 609-424-7112.

Llewellyn R. Bingaman (1907-1996)
James F. Bell (1921-1988)
Ralph J. Althouse, Jr. (Retired)

(See Next Column)

BINGAMAN, HESS, COBLENTZ & BELL A PROFESSIONAL CORPORATION—*Continued*

OF COUNSEL

Raymond K. Hess
J. Wendell Coblentz

David E. Turner
Mark G. Yoder
Carl D. Cronrath, Jr.
Kurt Althouse
Harry D. McMunigal
Patrick T. Barrett
Karen Feryo Longenecker
Shawn J. Lau

Lynne K. Beust
Elizabethanne D. McMunigal
Kevin W. Rethore
Eric J. Fabrizio
Elizabeth A. Magovern

General Counsel for: First Union National Bank; Berks Products Corp.; Utilities Employees Credit Union.
Local Counsel for: Erie Insurance Exchange; Liberty Mutual Insurance Co.; Old Guard Mutual Insurance Co.

For full biographical listings, see the Martindale-Hubbell Law Directory

RHODE ISLAND

*PROVIDENCE,** Providence Co.

HINCKLEY, ALLEN & SNYDER LLP (AV)

1500 Fleet Center, 02903-2393
Telephone: 401-274-2000
Fax: 401-277-9600
Email: firm@haslaw.com *URL:* http://www.haslaw.com
Boston, Massachusetts Office: 28 State Street, 30th Floor.
Telephone: 617-345-9000.
Fax: 617-345-9020. URL: http://www.haslaw.com.

MEMBERS OF FIRM

Paula K. Andrews (Not admitted in RI)
David D. Barricelli
E. Jerome Batty
Jonathan Bell
Paul Bork (Not admitted in RI)
Stephen J. Carlotti
David Barry Connolly (Not admitted in RI)
Joseph P. Curran
Michael P. DeFanti
Eric F. Eisenberg (Not admitted in RI)
Malcolm Farmer, III
Margaret D. Farrell
Hugh J. Gorman, III (Not admitted in RI)
Alan P. Gottlieb (Not admitted in RI)
William R. Grimm
Paul A. Hedstrom (Not admitted in RI)
Joel Lewin (Not admitted in RI)
Matthew T. Marcello, III
Frederick P. McClure
Elizabeth Murdock Myers
Paul F. O'Donnell, III (Not admitted in RI)
H. Peter Olsen
Gerald J. Petros
James O. Reavis
Jeremy Ritzenberg (Not admitted in RI)
Ralph J. Rivkind (Not admitted in RI)
David J. Rubin
Douglas F. Seaver (Not admitted in RI)
Herman Snyder (Not admitted in RI)
David R. Sullivan (Not admitted in RI)
Robert F. Sylvia (Not admitted in RI)
Howard E. Walker

ASSOCIATES

Mark Bianchi
Andrew D. Cummings (Not admitted in RI)
June E. Daniel
Kim Herman Goslant (Not admitted in RI)
Gloria Maria Gutierrez (Not admitted in RI)
Kelley Jordan-Price
Catherine S. Kim (Not admitted in RI)
Christopher W. Morog (Not admitted in RI)
Joseph D. Whelan

OF COUNSEL

Bentley Tobin

For Complete List of Firm Personnel, See General Section

For full biographical listings, see the Martindale-Hubbell Law Directory

SOUTH CAROLINA

*CHARLESTON,** Charleston Co.

LEATH, BOUCH & CRAWFORD, L.L.P. (AV)

134 Meeting Street, P.O. Box 59, 29402-0059
Telephone: 843-937-8811
Fax: 843-937-0606
Columbia, South Carolina Office: 221 Pickens Street (29205), P.O. Box 5066, 29250.
Telephone: 803-254-0048.
Facsimile: 803-254-0063.

MEMBERS OF FIRM

W. Jefferson Leath, Jr.
Timothy W. Bouch
B. Lindsay Crawford, III

Linda J. Amason
Elizabeth Rice Polk (Resident, Columbia Office)

For full biographical listings, see the Martindale-Hubbell Law Directory

*COLUMBIA,** Richland Co.

NEXSEN PRUET JACOBS & POLLARD, LLP (AV)

1441 Main Street, 15th Floor, P.O. Drawer 2426, 29202
Telephone: 803-771-8900
Facsimile: 803-253-8277
Email: NPJP@NPJP.COM *URL:* HTTP://WWW.NPJP.COM
Charleston, South Carolina Office: 200 Meeting Street, Suite 301. P.O. Box 486.
Telephone: 803-577-9440.
Facsimile: 803-720-1777.
Greenville, South Carolina Office: 201 West McBee Avenue, Fourth Floor, P.O. Box 10648.
Telephone: 864-370-2211.
Facsimile: 864-282-1177.
Myrtle Beach, South Carolina Office: 2411 Oak Street, Suite 105.
Telephone: 843-445-9688.
Facsimile: 843-445-9949.
Charlotte, North Carolina Office: 212 South Tryon Street, Suite 1700.
Telephone: 704-339-0304.
Facsimile: 704-338-5377.

MEMBERS OF FIRM

T. Eugene Allen, III
Julio E. Mendoza, Jr.

SPECIAL COUNSEL

Helen Elizabeth Burris (Resident, Greenville, SC Office)
Rose Duggan Manos

For Complete List of Firm Personnel, See General Section

For full biographical listings, see the Martindale-Hubbell Law Directory

TURNER, PADGET, GRAHAM & LANEY, P.A. (AV)

Seventeenth Floor, 1901 Main Street, P.O. Box 1473, 29202
Telephone: 803-254-2200
Telecopy: 803-799-3957
Florence, South Carolina Office: Fourth Floor, 1831 West Evans Street, P.O. Box 5478, 29502.
Telephone: 843-662-9008.
Fax: 843-667-0828.
Charleston, South Carolina Office: 21 Broad Street, 1st Floor, P.O. Box 836, 29402.
Telephone: 843-723-1622.
Fax: 843-577-3369.

OF COUNSEL

Stephen A. Husman

For Complete List of Firm Personnel, See General Section

For full biographical listings, see the Martindale-Hubbell Law Directory

TENNESSEE

*KNOXVILLE,** Knox Co.

BERNSTEIN, STAIR & McADAMS LLP (AV)

Suite 600, 530 South Gay Street, 37902
Telephone: 423-546-8030
Telecopier: 423-522-8879
Effective October 1, 1999 Area Code will change to 865.

MEMBERS OF FIRM

Bernard E. Bernstein
L. Caesar Stair III
Thomas N. McAdams
Doris C. Allen
Celeste H. Herbert
James W. Parris

(See Next Column)

BERNSTEIN, STAIR & MCADAMS LLP, *Knoxville—Continued*

ASSOCIATES

W. Tyler Chastain
Lauren G. Strange-Boston
Margo J. Maxwell

Representative Clients: ABB Flakt, Inc.; Camel Manufacturing Company; Clayton Homes, Inc.; Modern Supply Co.; Plasti-Line, Inc.; Rafferty's Restaurants; Saks, Inc.; Vanderbilt Mortgage and Finance, Inc.; West Town Mall.

For full biographical listings, see the Martindale-Hubbell Law Directory

WALKER & WALKER, P.C. (AV)

910 First American Center, P.O. Box 2774, 37901
Telephone: 423-523-0700
Telecopier: 423-523-4990
Email: jwalkerjr@aol.com

John A. Walker, Jr.
Kathryn D. Higginbotham

For full biographical listings, see the Martindale-Hubbell Law Directory

*MEMPHIS,** Shelby Co.

HALE HEADRICK DEWEY & WOLF, PLLC (AV)

One Memphis Place, 200 Jefferson Avenue Suite 1450, 38103
Telephone: 901-523-1123
Fax: 901-523-7472
Nashville, Tennessee Office: Suntrust Bank Building, 201 Fourth Avenue North, Suite 1450, 37219.
Telephone: 615-843-5160.
Fax: 615-843-5165

Stephen P. Hale
H. Tucker Dewey
S. Russell Headrick
Herbert B. Wolf, Jr.
John S. Golwen

OF COUNSEL

Steven L. Gill

Jennifer Ziegenhorn
Holly N. Knight
Wendy A. Geurin
Charles S. Blatteis
John W. Campbell
Jennifer S. Kiesewetter
Joseph M. Koury
J. William Williams

For full biographical listings, see the Martindale-Hubbell Law Directory

*NASHVILLE,** Davidson Co.

CHEADLE & CHEADLE (AV)

An Association of Attorneys
129 Second Avenue, North, 37201-1998
Telephone: 615-254-1009
Facsimile: 615-242-7378
Email: cheadle@edgenet.com
Knoxville, Tennessee Office: One Centre Square, 620 Market Street, Suite 260. 37902.
Telephone: 423-522-8440.
Facsimile: 423-522-8102.

John R. Cheadle, Sr. (1930-1997)
John R. Cheadle, Jr.
Evalina C. Cheadle

LEGAL SUPPORT PERSONNEL

Gail A. Dodd (Office Manager)
Joy Westerbeck (Paralegal)
Wendy H. Williams (Paralegal)
Michelle Primm (Paralegal)

References: First American National Bank of Nashville, Nashville, Tennessee; NationsBank, Nashville, Tennessee.

For full biographical listings, see the Martindale-Hubbell Law Directory

TEXAS

*DALLAS,** Dallas Co.

CAVAZOS, HENDRICKS, POIROT & DEWEY, P.C. (AV)

Suite 570, Founders Square, 900 Jackson Street, 75202-4425
Telephone: 214-748-8171
Facsimile: 214-748-6750
Email: Firm@chfirm.com *URL:* http://www.chfirm.com

Arnaldo N. Cavazos, Jr.
Rod L. Poirot
Charles B. Hendricks
Alicia M. Dewey

Craig H. Smitham

(See Next Column)

OF COUNSEL

Frank E. Sheeder, III
Ron Edmondson
R. Matt Dawson
Terry L. Jacobson
Glenn A. Sodd
John Clayton Beard

For full biographical listings, see the Martindale-Hubbell Law Directory

KRAGE & JANVEY, L.L.P. (AV)

2001 Bryan Tower, Suite 2700, 75201-3059
Telephone: 214-969-7500
Telecopier: 214-220-0230

Cyril David Kasmir (1944-1997)
Ralph Janvey
Ben L. Krage
C. Clinton Davis, Jr.
Kristie L. Garrison

Representative Client: Regal Capital Co.

For full biographical listings, see the Martindale-Hubbell Law Directory

THE SEIB LAW FIRM A PROFESSIONAL CORPORATION (AV)

350 Founders Square, 900 Jackson Street, 75202
Telephone: 214-752-1234
Fax: 214-752-1212

John A. Seib, Jr. (P.C.)

Gregory T. Pratt

For full biographical listings, see the Martindale-Hubbell Law Directory

*EL PASO,** El Paso Co.

CROWSON & INGRAM (AV)

Suite 706, The Cortez, 310 North Mesa, P.O. Box 862, 79945
Telephone: 915-533-7717
Telefax: 915-533-1495
Email: crowsing@huntleigh.net

MEMBERS OF FIRM

Harold E. Crowson, Jr.
Temple B. Ingram, Jr.

Reference: Bank of America, N.A.; Norwest Bank, El Paso, N.A.; Bank of the West, El Paso, Texas.

For full biographical listings, see the Martindale-Hubbell Law Directory

*HOUSTON,** Harris Co.

BAYLESS & STOKES (AV)

2931 Ferndale Street, 77098
Telephone: 713-522-2224
Fax: 713-522-2218
Email: bayless@baylessstokes.com

MEMBER OF FIRM

Bobbie G. Bayless

ASSOCIATE

Spencer W. Creed

For full biographical listings, see the Martindale-Hubbell Law Directory

PLANO, Collin Co.

GOLD & GOLD (AV)

Harrington Place, Suite 300, 1700 Alma Drive, 75075-6936
Telephone: 972-578-1050
Fax: 972-578-1555
Email: goldlaw@flash.net

Jacob M. Gold

For full biographical listings, see the Martindale-Hubbell Law Directory

*SAN ANTONIO,** Bexar Co.

JOEL KLEIN & ASSOCIATES (AV)

6800 Park Ten Boulevard, Suite 264S, 78213-4204
Telephone: 210-734-4488
Fax: 210-734-4482
Email: joel@joelklein.com *URL:* http://www.joelklein.com

Joel H. Klein

OF COUNSEL

Lester L. Klein

For full biographical listings, see the Martindale-Hubbell Law Directory

*SHERMAN,** Grayson Co.

NIX & WINEGEART, P.C. (AV)

717 North Crockett Street, 75090
Telephone: 903-870-0212
Fax: 903-870-0109
Email: rnix@gte.net

(See Next Column)

NIX & WINEGEART P.C.—*Continued*

William Riley Nix
Graham C. Winegeart

Representative Clients: American Bank of Texas; Bonham State Bank; BVAC Federal Credit Union; First Bank of Farmersville; First Bank Howe; First National Bank of Durant; First United Bank and Trust Co.; First National Bank of Whitewright; Lamesa National Bank; Security Bank of Whitesboro.

For full biographical listings, see the Martindale-Hubbell Law Directory

UTAH

*SALT LAKE CITY,** Salt Lake Co.

PARSONS, DAVIES, KINGHORN & PETERS, P.C. (AV)

185 South State Street, Suite 700, 84111
Telephone: 801-363-4300
Facsimile: 801-363-4378
Email: Attorneys@pdkplaw.com

John M. Parsons
Glen E. Davies
Gerald H. Kinghorn
Bill Thomas Peters
Langdon T. Owen, Jr.
R. Kimball Mosier
John N. Brems
Ken P. Jones
David W. Scofield
Stuart W. Hinckley
John S. Bradley
Harold L. Reiser
Wm. Shane Topham
J. Scott Brown
Katherine S. Gregory
Paige Bigelow

For full biographical listings, see the Martindale-Hubbell Law Directory

VAN COTT, BAGLEY, CORNWALL & MCCARTHY, A PROFESSIONAL CORPORATION (AV)

50 South Main Street, Suite 1600, P.O. Box 45340, 84145-0340
Telephone: 801-532-3333
Telecopier: 801-534-0058
Email: info@vancott.com *URL:* http://www.vancott.com
Ogden, Utah Office: 2404 Washington Boulevard, Suite 900.
Telephone: 801-394-5783.
Park City, Utah Office: 2200 Park Avenue, Suite C200-A.
Telephone: 435-649-3889.

Timothy W. Blackburn (Resident, Ogden, Utah Office)
Gerald H. Suniville

Mara A. Brown

OF COUNSEL

William G. Fowler

For Complete List of Firm Personnel, See General Section

For full biographical listings, see the Martindale-Hubbell Law Directory

VIRGINIA

ALEXANDRIA, (Independent City)

PETER C. WILLIAMS (AV)

510 King Street, Suite 416, 22314
Telephone: 703-684-8813
Fax: 703-548-4742
Email: pcwlaw@erols.com

For full biographical listings, see the Martindale-Hubbell Law Directory

YOUNG, GOLDMAN & VAN BEEK, A PROFESSIONAL CORPORATION (AV)

510 King Street, Suite 416, 22314
Telephone: 703-684-3260
Facsimile: 703-548-4742
Email: YGVB@Erols.com
Washington, D.C. Office: 2000 L Street, N.W. Suite 800.
Telephone: 703-684-3260.

H. Alan Young
Neil D. Goldman
John P. Van Beek

OF COUNSEL

Garrett C. Burke

For full biographical listings, see the Martindale-Hubbell Law Directory

*ARLINGTON,** Arlington Co.

WOODROW W. WALKER (AV)

2055 North 15th Street Suite 202-203, 22201
Telephone: 703-524-7860; 524-7861
Fax: 703-528-8472

Representative Clients: Sears Roebuck & Co.; Bob Peck Chevrolet.

For full biographical listings, see the Martindale-Hubbell Law Directory

ROANOKE, Roanoke City Co.

WOOTEN & HART, A PROFESSIONAL CORPORATION (AV)

707 Building, Suite 300, P.O. Box 12247, 24024-2247
Telephone: 540-343-2451; 540-342-9672
Telecopier: 540-345-6417
URL: http://www.wootenhart.com

George W. Wooten
David B. Hart
L. Thompson Hanes
Susan A. Waddell
Bradley D. McGraw
John L. Cooley
Thomas W. Farrell
Paul C. Kuhnel
Peter D. Vieth

David W. Hearn
John Mark Cooley
Christopher W. Stevens
Elizabeth D. Guilbert
Eunice Park Austin

OF COUNSEL

M. Lanier Woodrum

Representative Clients: Wachovia Bank; St. Paul Insurance Cos.
Approved Attorneys for: Lawyers Title Insurance Corp.
Reference: First Union National Bank.

For full biographical listings, see the Martindale-Hubbell Law Directory

WEST VIRGINIA

HUNTINGTON, Cabell & Wayne Cos.

BAKER, LANCIANESE, CAMPBELL & CONATY (AV)

The River Tower, 1108 Third Avenue, Suite 300, 25701-1578
Telephone: 304-522-6906
Facsimile: 304-522-6910
Email: BLCC@BLCCLAW.COM *URL:* http://www.BLCCLAW.COM
Washington, D.C. Office: 1090 Vermont Avenue, N.W. Suite 800.
Telephone: 202-966-1500.
Fax: 202-966-7075. E-Mail: BLCC@BLCCLAW.COM.
Lexington, Kentucky Office: 2265 Harrodsburg Road, Suite 200, 40504-3517.
Telephone: 606-278-0297.
Fax: 206-278-0334. E-Mail: BLCC@BLCCLAW.COM.

Roy D. Baker, Jr.
Richard L. Lancianese
David L. Campbell
Brian P. Conaty
Janice P. Epperly

OF COUNSEL

Margaret M. Brizzolara (Not admitted in WV)

For full biographical listings, see the Martindale-Hubbell Law Directory

WISCONSIN

*MILWAUKEE,** Milwaukee Co.

CHERNOV, STERN & KRINGS, S.C. (AV)

Suite 1275, Two Plaza East, 330 East Kilbourn Avenue, 53202
Telephone: 414-276-4080
Fax: 414-276-4152
Email: mail@chernovlaw.com *URL:* http://www.lawyers.com/chernovlaw

Jerome D. Krings

For full biographical listings, see the Martindale-Hubbell Law Directory

KOHNER, MANN & KAILAS, S.C. (AV)

1572 East Capitol Drive, P.O. Box 11982, 53211-0982
Telephone: 414-962-5110
Fax: 414-962-8725
Email: kmksc@execpc.com

Marvin L. Kohner (1908-1975)

OF COUNSEL

Robert L. Mann

(See Next Column)

KOHNER, MANN & KAILAS S.C., *Milwaukee—Continued*

MEMBERS OF FIRM

Steve Kailas
Mark R. Wolters
Jordan B. Reich
David S. Chartier
Roy Paul Roth
Gary P. Lantzy
Christopher C. Kailas
Matthew P. Gerdisch

Robert E. Nailen
Darrell R. Zall
Daniel J. Flynn
Timothy L. Zuberbier
David M. Henry
Lorinne J Cunningham
Palma M. Forte
Daniel J. Emma

Representative Clients: Ecolab, Inc.; Manpower, Inc.; Abbott Laboratories; Norwest Bank Wisconsin, N.A.; Firstar Bank Corporation; Sysco Food Services; Johnson Controls, Inc.; Worth Inc.; Rayovac, Inc.; York International Corporation.

For full biographical listings, see the Martindale-Hubbell Law Directory

WYOMING

*CASPER,** Natrona Co.

BROWN, DREW & MASSEY, LLP (AV)

Casper Business Center, Suite 800, 123 West First Street, 82601-2486
Telephone: 307-234-1000
800-877-6755
Telefax: 307-265-8025
Email: brwndrew@coffey.com

MEMBERS OF FIRM

Morris R. Massey
Harry B. Durham, III
Donn J. McCall
Thomas F. Reese
J. Kenneth Barbe
P. Jaye Rippley
Courtney Robert Kepler

ASSOCIATE

Timothy M. Stubson

OF COUNSEL

Hampton K. O'Neill

Attorneys for: Norwest Bank Wyoming, N.A.; Wells Fargo Bank, N.A.; The CIT Group/Equpment Financing; Norwest Mortgage, Inc.

For Complete List of Firm Personnel, See General Section

For full biographical listings, see the Martindale-Hubbell Law Directory

CANADA
NEW BRUNSWICK

*FREDERICTON,** York Co.

MCINNES COOPER (AV)

Suite 600, 570 Queen Street, P.O. Box 610, E3B 5A6
Telephone: 506-458-8572
Fax: 506-458-9903
Email: mcrfton@mcrlaw.com *URL:* http://www.mcrlaw.com
Halifax, Nova Scotia Office: Summit Place, 1601 Lower Water Street, P.O. Box 730, B3J 2V1.
Telephone: 902-425-6500.
Fax: 902-425-6350. Email: mcrhfx@mcrlaw.com.
St. John's, Newfoundland Office: Baine Johnston Centre, 5th Floor, 10 Fort William Place, P.O. Box 5939, A1C 5X4.
Telephone: 709-722-8735.
Telecopier: 709-722-1763. Email: mcrsj@mcrlaw.com.
Moncton, New Brunswick Office: Place Moncton Place, 655 Main Street, P.O. Box 1368, E1C 8T6.
Telephone: 506-857-8970.
Fax: 506-857-4095. Email: mcrmctn@mcrlaw.com.
Charlottetown, Prince Edward Island Office: BDC Place, Suite 620, 119 Kent Street, C1A 1N3.
Telephone: 902-368-8473.
Fax: 902-368-8346. Email: mcrpei@mcrlaw.com.

PARTNER

David Duncan Young

ASSOCIATE

Patrick V. Windle

For Complete List of Firm Personnel, See General Section

For full biographical listings, see the Martindale-Hubbell Law Directory

*MONCTON,** Westmorland Co.

MCINNES COOPER (AV)

Barristers, Solicitors & Trade Mark Agents
Place Moncton Place, 655 Main Street, P.O. Box 1368, E1C 8T6
Telephone: 506-857-8970
Fax: 506-857-4095
Email: mcrmctn@mcrlaw.com *URL:* http://www.mcrlaw.com
Halifax, Nova Scotia Office: Summit Place, 1601 Lower Water Street, P.O. Box 730, B3J 2V1.
Telephone: 902-425-6500.
Fax: 902-425-6350. Email: mcrhfx@mcrlaw.com.
St. John's, Newfoundland Office: Baine Johnston Centre, 5th Floor, 10 Fort William Place, P.O. Box 5939, A1C 5X4.
Telephone: 709-722-8735.
Telecopier: 709-722-1763. Email: mcrsj@mcrlaw.com.
Charlottetown, Prince Edward Island Office: BDC Place, Suite 620, 119 Kent Street, C1A 1N3.
Telephone: 902-368-8473.
Fax: 902-368-8346. Email: mcrpei@mcrlaw.com.
Fredericton, New Brunswick Office: Suite 600, 570 Queen Street, P.O. Box 610.
Telephone: 506-458-8572.
Fax: 506-458-9903. Email: mcrfton@mcrlaw.com.

ASSOCIATE

Christopher A. Borden

For Complete List of Firm Personnel, See General Section

For full biographical listings, see the Martindale-Hubbell Law Directory

CANADA
NEWFOUNDLAND

*ST. JOHN'S,**

MCINNES COOPER (AV)

Barristers, Solicitors & Trade Mark Agents
Baine Johnston Centre, 5th Floor, 10 Fort William Place, P.O. Box 5939, A1C 5X4
Telephone: 709-722-8735
Telecopier: 709-722-1763
Email: mcrsj@mcrlaw.com *URL:* http://www.mcrlaw.com
Halifax, Nova Scotia Office: Summit Place, 1601 Lower Water Street, P.O. Box 730, B3J 2V1.
Telephone: 902-425-6500.
Fax: 902-425-6350. Email: mcrhfx@mcrlaw.com.
Moncton, New Brunswick Office: Place Moncton Place, 655 Main Street, P.O. Box 1368, E1C 8T6.
Telephone: 506-857-8970.
Fax: 506-857-4095. Email: mcrmctn@mcrlaw.com.
Charlottetown, Prince Edward Island Office: BDC Place, Suite 620, 119 Kent Street, C1A 1N3.
Telephone: 902-368-8473.
Fax: 902-368-8346. Email: mcrpei@mcrlaw.com.
Fredericton, New Brunswick Office: Suite 600, 570 Queen Street, P.O. Box 610.
Telephone: 506-458-8572.
Fax: 506-458-9903. Email: mcrfton@mcrlaw.com.

PARTNER

Deborah L. J. Hutchings

For Complete List of Firm Personnel, See General Section

For full biographical listings, see the Martindale-Hubbell Law Directory

CANADA
NOVA SCOTIA

*HALIFAX,** Regional Munic. of Halifax

MCINNES COOPER (AV)

Barristers, Solicitors & Trade Mark Agents
Summit Place, 1601 Lower Water Street, P.O. Box 730, B3J 2V1
Telephone: 902-425-6500
Fax: 902-425-6350
Email: mcrhfx@mcrlaw.com *URL:* http://www.mcrlaw.com
St. John's, Newfoundland Office: Baine Johnston Centre, 5th Floor, 10 Fort William Place, P.O. Box 5939, A1C 5X4.
Telephone: 709-722-8735.
Telecopier: 709-722-1763. Email: mcrsj@mcrlaw.com.

(See Next Column)

McINNES COOPER—*Continued*

Moncton, New Brunswick Office: Place Moncton Place, 655 Main Street, P.O. Box 1368, E1C 8T6.
Telephone: 506-857-8970.
Fax: 506-857-4095. Email: mcrmctn@mcrlaw.com.
Charlottetown, Prince Edward Island Office: BDC Place, Suite 620, 119 Kent Street, C1A 1N3.
Telephone: 902-368-8473.
Fax: 902-368-8346. Email: mcrpei@mcrlaw.com.
Fredericton, New Brunswick Office: Suite 600, 570 Queen Street, P.O. Box 610.
Telephone: 506-458-8572.
Fax: 506-458-9903. Email: mcrfton@mcrlaw.com.

PARTNERS

David H. Reardon, Q.C.
John D. Stringer, Q.C.
F. Van W. Penick
John Kulik

ASSOCIATE

Frank E. Hughes

For Complete List of Firm Personnel, See General Section

For full biographical listings, see the Martindale-Hubbell Law Directory

CANADA
PRINCE EDWARD ISLAND

*CHARLOTTETOWN,** Queen's Co.

McINNES COOPER (AV㉷)

Barristers, Solicitors & Trade Mark Agents
BDC Place, Suite 620, 119 Kent Street, C1A 1N3
Telephone: 902-368-8473
Fax: 902-368-8346
Email: mcrpei@mcrlaw.com *URL:* http://www.mcrlaw.com
Halifax, Nova Scotia Office: Summit Place, 1601 Lower Water Street, P.O. Box 730, B3J 2V1.
Telephone: 902-425-6500.
Fax: 902-425-6350. Email: mcrhfx@mcrlaw.com.
St. John's, Newfoundland Office: Baine Johnston Centre, 5th Floor, 10 Fort William Place, P.O. Box 5939, A1C 5X4.
Telephone: 709-722-8735.
Telecopier: 709-722-1763. Email: mcrsj@mcrlaw.com.
Moncton, New Brunswick Office: Place Moncton Place, 655 Main Street, P.O. Box 1368, E1C 8T6.
Telephone: 506-857-8970.
Fax: 506-857-4095. Email: mcrmctn@mcrlaw.com.
Fredericton, New Brunswick Office: Suite 600, 570 Queen Street, P.O. Box 610.
Telephone: 506-458-8572.
Fax: 506-458-9903. Email: mcrfton@mcrlaw.com.

PARTNER

Michele M. Murphy

ASSOCIATE

Kevin J. Kiley

For Complete List of Firm Personnel, See General Section

For full biographical listings, see the Martindale-Hubbell Law Directory

CRIMINAL TRIAL PRACTICE

MINNESOTA

*MINNEAPOLIS,** Hennepin Co.

FREDERIC BRUNO & ASSOCIATES (AV)

The Colonnade, 5500 Wayzata Boulevard, Suite 730, 55416
Telephone: 612-545-7900
Fax: 612-545-0834
Email: bruno@brunolaw.com

ASSOCIATE

Timothy R. Anderson

For full biographical listings, see the Martindale-Hubbell Law Directory

JOSEPH S. FRIEDBERG CHARTERED (AV)

Suite 205, Commerce At The Crossings, 250 Second Avenue, South, 55401
Telephone: 612-339-8626

Joseph S. Friedberg

For full biographical listings, see the Martindale-Hubbell Law Directory

HANLEY & DEJORAS, P.A. (AV)

2520 Park Avenue South, 55404
Telephone: 612-872-9616
Fax: 612-872-9780
Email: HANLEY@VISI.COM

Bruce H. Hanley   Lisa D. Dejoras

For full biographical listings, see the Martindale-Hubbell Law Directory

MAUZY LAW FIRM (AV)

510 First Avenue North Suite 610, 55403
Telephone: 612-340-9108
Fax: 612-340-1628

William J. Mauzy

Douglas H.R. Olson   Matthew D. Forsgren

For full biographical listings, see the Martindale-Hubbell Law Directory

MESHBESHER & SPENCE (AV)

1616 Park Avenue, 55404
Telephone: 612-339-9121
Fax: 612-339-9188
URL: http://www.meshbesher.com
Woodbury, Minnesota Office: 8360 City Centre Drive, 55125.
Telephone: 651-578-8055.
St. Cloud, Minnesota Office: 510 Zapp Bank Plaza, 56301.
Telephone: 320-656-0484.
Rochester, Minnesota Office: 21 SW 2nd Street, 55902.
Telephone: 507-280-8090.
Maplewood, Minnesota Office: 2603 White Bear Avenue, 55109.
Telephone: 651-777-5858.
St. Louis Park, Minnesota Office: 9950 Wayzata Boulevard, 55426.
Telephone: 612-544-5959.

MEMBERS OF FIRM

Kenneth Meshbesher   John P. Sheehy
Ronald I. Meshbesher   Howard I. Bass
Daniel C. Guerrero

For full biographical listings, see the Martindale-Hubbell Law Directory

JAMES E. OSTGARD, II (AV)

2415 Foshay Tower, 821 Marquette Avenue, 55402
Telephone: 612-825-1092
Fax: 612-332-8870
URL: http://www.ostgard-law.com

For full biographical listings, see the Martindale-Hubbell Law Directory

KEVIN J. SHORT (AV)

2890 Metropolitan Centre, 333 South Seventh Street, 55402
Telephone: 612-333-9006
Fax: 612-333-5015

For full biographical listings, see the Martindale-Hubbell Law Directory

*ROCHESTER,** Olmsted Co.

GEORGE F. RESTOVICH & ASSOCIATES (AV)

117 East Center Street, 55904
Telephone: 507-288-4840
Fax: 507-288-4908
Email: gfrlaw@infonet.isl.net

ASSOCIATES

Bruce K. Piotrowski   Richard W. Kimlinger
Gary A. Gittus

For full biographical listings, see the Martindale-Hubbell Law Directory

MISSISSIPPI

*GULFPORT,** Harrison Co.

BOYCE HOLLEMAN A PROFESSIONAL CORPORATION (AV)

1913 15th Street, P.O. Drawer 1030, 39502
Telephone: 228-863-3142; 1-800-863-3140
Telecopier: 228-863-9829
Email: boyce1913@aol.com

Boyce Holleman

Timothy C. Holleman   Leslie Dean Holleman
David J. "Jeff" White

References: Hancock Bank, Gulfport; Merchants Bank & Trust Co., Gulfport; Bank of Wiggins, Wiggins, Mississippi.

For full biographical listings, see the Martindale-Hubbell Law Directory

*JACKSON,** Hinds Co.

THOMAS E. ROYALS (AV)

The Plaza Building, Suite 1100, 120 North Congress Street, P.O. Box 22909, 39225-2909
Telephone: 601-948-7777
Telecopier: 601-948-7780
Email: royalslaw@aol.com

For full biographical listings, see the Martindale-Hubbell Law Directory

MISSOURI

*CLAYTON,** St. Louis Co.

LAW OFFICES OF WOLFF AND D'AGROSA (AV)

8019 Forsyth (St. Louis), 63105
Telephone: 314-725-8019
Fax: 314-725-8443

Donald L. Wolff   Paul J. D'Agrosa

ASSOCIATE

William J. Ekiss

For full biographical listings, see the Martindale-Hubbell Law Directory

KANSAS CITY, Jackson, Clay, Platte & Cass Cos.

SIMON AND SIMON (AV)

600 Gumbel Building, 801 Walnut Street, 64106
Telephone: 816-471-3430
Fax: 816-471-0408
Email: simonlaw@postoffice.swbell.net

MEMBERS OF FIRM

Kenneth K. Simon (1916-1977)   Bruce W. Simon

LEGAL SUPPORT PERSONNEL

Stacey Villegas

Reference: Mercantile Bank & Trust, Kansas City.

For full biographical listings, see the Martindale-Hubbell Law Directory

WYRSCH HOBBS MIRAKIAN & LEE, P.C. (AV)

1300 Mercantile Tower 1101 Walnut, 64106-2122
Telephone: 816-221-0080
Fax: 816-221-3280
Email: whml@sprintmail.com

(See Next Column)

WYRSCH HOBBS MIRAKIAN & LEE P.C., *Kansas City—Continued*

James R. Wyrsch
Stephen G. Mirakian
Ronald D. Lee
James R. Hobbs
Keith E. Drill
Jacqueline A. Cook
Charles M. Rogers
Marilyn B. Keller
Cheryl A. Pilate
W. Brian Gaddy

OF COUNSEL

James W. Fletcher

David Andrew Kelly

LEGAL SUPPORT PERSONNEL

Darlene Wyrsch (Paralegal)
Dru A. Colhour (Paralegal)
Katherine Vetsch (Paralegal)
Leslie R. Elkins (Paralegal)
William J. Baltrusaitis, II (Investigator)

For full biographical listings, see the Martindale-Hubbell Law Directory

RAYMORE, Cass Co.

HENSLEY & HENSLEY (AV)

401 West 58 Highway, P.O. Box 620, 64083
Telephone: 816-322-4466
Email: hensley8.@worldnet.att.net

MEMBERS OF FIRM

Kenneth C. Hensley
Teresa Hensley

Representative Clients: Farmers Bank of Northern Missouri; Corporate Dental Care, Inc.; Cole & Myers Oil Co.

For full biographical listings, see the Martindale-Hubbell Law Directory

ST. LOUIS, (Independent City)

GREENBERG & PLEBAN (AV)

100 South Fourth Street, Suite 600, 63102
Telephone: 314-241-4141
Telecopier: 314-241-1038

Burton M. Greenberg
C. John Pleban

ASSOCIATES

Karen A. Greenberg
Michael J. Schaller
Richard P. Hereford

OF COUNSEL

Sarah Shelledy Pleban

Reference: Boatmen's National Bank.

For full biographical listings, see the Martindale-Hubbell Law Directory

HELFREY, SIMON & JONES, P.C. (AV)

120 South Central Avenue Suite 1500, 63105
Telephone: 314-725-9100
Facsimile: 314-725-5754

David B. B. Helfrey
Michael H. Musich
Paul Simon, Jr.

Mark W. Hagemeister

For full biographical listings, see the Martindale-Hubbell Law Directory

JENKINS & KLING, P.C. (AV)

10 South Brentwood, Suite 200, 63105
Telephone: 314-721-2525
Telecopier: 314-721-5525
Email: jklaw@swbell.net

Ronald E. Jenkins

Roger W. Pecha

For full biographical listings, see the Martindale-Hubbell Law Directory

MARGULIS GRANT & MARGULIS, P.C. (AV)

11 South Meramec Avenue Suite 1330, 63105-1716
Telephone: 314-721-6677
Fax: 314-721-1710

Arthur S. Margulis
William P. Grant
William S. Margulis

Linda Hogan
Diane M. Monahan

OF COUNSEL

Dorothy Duncan Danforth
Eugene P. Walsh

Reference: First National Bank, Clayton, Mo.

For full biographical listings, see the Martindale-Hubbell Law Directory

THE O'MALLEY LAW FIRM, P.C. (AV)

Suite 102, Ten South Brentwood Boulevard, 63105
Telephone: 314-721-8001
Telecopier: 314-721-3754
Email: omalfirm@stlnet.com

Kevin F. O'Malley
John F. Cooney
Mary L. Reitz
Debra Stachowski Pierce
Linda Cary Hinshaw
Weldon N. Johnson

For full biographical listings, see the Martindale-Hubbell Law Directory

ROSENBLUM, SCHWARTZ & ROGERS, L.L.C. (AV)

Bonhomme Place, 7700 Bonhomme, Suite 400 (Clayton), 63105
Telephone: 314-862-4332
Facsimile: 314-862-8050
Email: rsrcrimlaw@aol.com *URL:* http://www.lawyers.com/rosenblumschwartz&rogers

MEMBERS OF FIRM

N. Scott Rosenblum
Joel J. Schwartz
John P. Rogers

ASSOCIATES

Susan M. Pavlow
Jenna K. Glass

For full biographical listings, see the Martindale-Hubbell Law Directory

SINDEL & SINDEL, P.C. (AV)

Suite 301, 8008 Carondelet, 63105
Telephone: 314-721-6040
Telecopier: 314-721-8545
Email: CSindel@sindellaw.cnchost.com *URL:* http://www.sindellaw.com

Richard H. Sindel

For full biographical listings, see the Martindale-Hubbell Law Directory

MONTANA

*BILLINGS,** Yellowstone Co.

CROWLEY, HAUGHEY, HANSON, TOOLE & DIETRICH, P.L.L.P. (AV)

500 Transwestern II, 490 North 31st Street, P.O. Box 2529, 59103
Telephone: 406-252-3441
Fax: 406-259-4159
Email: crowley@crowleylaw.com
Helena, Montana Office: IBM Building, 100 North Park Avenue, Suite 300, 59601.
Telephone: 406-449-4165.
Fax: 406-449-5149.
Kalispell, Montana Office: 431 1st Avenue West, 59901.
Telephone: 406-752-6644.
Fax: 406-752-5108.
Williston, North Dakota Office: 113 East Broadway, 58801.
Telephone: 701-572-2200.
Fax: 701-572-7072.

MEMBERS OF FIRM

Donald L. Harris
Steven Robert Milch
Michael S. Lahr (Resident, Helena, Montana Office)

Representative Clients: Montana Power Co.; First Interstate Bank of Commerce; MDU Resources Group, Inc.; Chevron U.S.A., Inc.; Noranda Minerals Corp.; United Parcel Service.
Insurance Clients: Farmers Insurance Group; New York Life Insurance Co.

For Complete List of Firm Personnel, See General Section

For full biographical listings, see the Martindale-Hubbell Law Directory

NEBRASKA

*LINCOLN,** Lancaster Co.

BERRY, KELLEY & HANSEN (AV)

2650 North 48th Street, P.O. Box 4554, 68504
Telephone: 402-466-8444
Fax: 402-466-1793
URL: http://www.JSBerrylaw.com

MEMBERS OF FIRM

John Stevens Berry
James M. Kelley
Michael J. Hansen

For full biographical listings, see the Martindale-Hubbell Law Directory

Lincoln—Continued

CLINE, WILLIAMS, WRIGHT, JOHNSON & OLDFATHER (AV)

1900 U.S. Bank Building, 233 South 13th Street, 68508
Telephone: 402-474-6900
Fax: 402-474-5393
Email: postmaster@cline-law.com *URL:* http://www.cline-law.com
Omaha, Nebraska Office: Suite 720, One Pacific Place, 1125 South 103rd Street, 68124.
Telephone: 402-397-1700.
Fax: 402-397-1806.

ATTORNEYS

Allen L. Graves
Charles M. Pallesen, Jr.
Fredric H. Kauffman
Donald F. Burt
Alan E. Peterson
Stephen E. Gehring
Robert J. Routh
Kevin Colleran
L. Bruce Wright
James M. Bausch
Larry A. Holle
David R. Buntain
Stephen H. Nelsen
Michael C. Mueller
Lauren W. Wismer
Daniel R. Stogsdill
Scott D. Kelly
Terry R. Wittler
Pamela Hastings Carrier
Mark A. Christensen
Richard P. Garden, Jr.
Shawn D. Renner
John C. Miles
Mary Kay Frank
Thomas C. Huston
Sonya S. Ekart
Don R. Janssen
Susan Kubert Sapp
Kevin J. Schneider
Andrew D. Strotman
Jill Gossin Jensen
Rochelle A. Mullen
John L. Horan
Bryan S. Hatch
Steven C. Likes
Tracy A. Oldemeyer
Jolene M. Papa
Timothy G. Aschoff
Eric N. Bergquist
Janis J. Winterhof
Andrea Dylan Snowden

OF COUNSEL

Charles E. Wright
Richard P. Jeffries
Mary M. Campbell

RETIRED PARTNERS

Flavel A. Wright (Retired)
Warren C. Johnson (Retired)
Charles E. Oldfather (1927-1998)

Representative Clients: U.S. Bank National Association; University of Nebraska; Nebraska Medical Assn.; Saint Elizabeth Regional Medical Center; Media of Nebraska; Cargill Inc.; State Farm Insurance Cos.; Wal-Mart Stores, Inc.; Textron/Cushman; Isco, Inc.

For full biographical listings, see the Martindale-Hubbell Law Directory

*OMAHA,** Douglas Co.

JAMES MARTIN DAVIS (AV)

Suite 500, Farnam Plaza, 1623 Farnam Street, 68102
Telephone: 402-341-9900
Fax: 402-341-8144

For full biographical listings, see the Martindale-Hubbell Law Directory

DOMINA LAW PC (AV)

1065 North 115th Street, 68154-4423
Telephone: 402-493-4100
Fax: 402-493-9782
Email: law@dominalaw.com

David A. Domina
Cletus W. Blakeman
Jerold V. Fennell

W. Craig Howell
Pamela J. Dahlquist
Nora M. Kane
James F. Cann

For full biographical listings, see the Martindale-Hubbell Law Directory

NEVADA

*LAS VEGAS,** Clark Co.

THOMAS D. BEATTY (AV)

601 East Bridger Avenue, 89101
Telephone: 702-382-5111
Facsimile: 702-382-2892

ASSOCIATE

Rena G. Hughes

Reference: Wells Fargo Bank.

For full biographical listings, see the Martindale-Hubbell Law Directory

KENNETH C. CORY A PROFESSIONAL CORPORATION (AV)

626 South Third Street, 89101
Telephone: 702-384-0111
Fax: 702-384-0763
Email: kcory@accessnv.com *URL:* http://www.lawyers.com/kennethcory

Kenneth C. Cory

For full biographical listings, see the Martindale-Hubbell Law Directory

FRANK J. CREMEN (AV)

Suite 1004, 302 East Carson, 89101
Telephone: 702-385-7475
Fax: 702-385-9703
Email: cremenlaw@aol.com

ASSOCIATE

Daryl E. Martin

Reference: Wells Fargo Bank.

For full biographical listings, see the Martindale-Hubbell Law Directory

GOODMAN CHESNOFF & KEACH, A PROFESSIONAL CORPORATION (AV)

520 South Fourth Street, 89101-6593
Telephone: 702-384-5563
Fax: 702-598-1425

Oscar B. Goodman
David Z. Chesnoff
Eckley M. Keach

For full biographical listings, see the Martindale-Hubbell Law Directory

STEPHEN STEIN CHARTERED (AV)

520 South Fourth Street, 89101-6593
Telephone: 702-384-5563
Fax: 702-598-1425

Stephen Stein

OF COUNSEL

Oscar B. Goodman

For full biographical listings, see the Martindale-Hubbell Law Directory

WILLIAM B. TERRY CHARTERED (AV)

530 South Seventh Street, 89101
Telephone: 702-385-0799
Fax: 702-385-9788

William B. Terry

For full biographical listings, see the Martindale-Hubbell Law Directory

WRIGHT, JUDD & WINCKLER (AV)

302 East Carson Avenue, 3rd Floor, 89101
Telephone: 702-382-4004
FAX: 702-382-4800
Email: wjw@netxs.net

MEMBERS OF FIRM

Richard A. Wright
Bruce M. Judd
Karen C. Winckler

For full biographical listings, see the Martindale-Hubbell Law Directory

*RENO,** Washoe Co.

LAW OFFICES OF RICHARD W. YOUNG A PROFESSIONAL CORPORATION (AV)

327 Marsh Avenue, 89509
Telephone: 702-322-9477
Facsimile: 702-322-3758

Richard W. Young

Reference: Pioneer Citizens Bank (Reno Main Branch).

For full biographical listings, see the Martindale-Hubbell Law Directory

NEW JERSEY

*BRIDGETON,** Cumberland Co.

JOHN P. MORRIS (AV)

200 West Commerce Street, P.O. Box 299, 08302
Telephone: 609-453-1000
Fax: 609-453-0200
URL: http://www.lawyers.com/johnpmorris

(See Next Column)

JOHN P. MORRIS, *Bridgeton—Continued*

LEGAL SUPPORT PERSONNEL

Tara Dickson (Paralegal)

For full biographical listings, see the Martindale-Hubbell Law Directory

CHATHAM, Morris Co.

ARSENEAULT & FASSETT (AV)

560 Main Street, 07928-2119
Telephone: 973-635-3366
Fax: 973-635-0855
Email: www.aklaw.com *URL:* http://www.lawyers.com/arsenaultkrovatinattys

MEMBERS OF FIRM

Jack Arseneault | David W. Fassett

ASSOCIATE

Steven G. Sanders (Not admitted in NJ)

For full biographical listings, see the Martindale-Hubbell Law Directory

ALAN L. ZEGAS (AV)

552 Main Street, 07928
Telephone: 973-701-7080
Fax: 973-701-7081
Email: alanatLaw@aol.com *URL:* http://www.lawyers.com/zegas

Gina L. Mendola | Patricia A. Lee
Sharon B. Kean | Aimee Blakeslee

For full biographical listings, see the Martindale-Hubbell Law Directory

*HACKENSACK,** Bergen Co.

BRIAN J. NEARY (AV)

190 Moore Street, 07601
Telephone: 201-488-0544
Fax: 201-488-0240
Email: brianneary@erols.com *URL:* http://www.lawyers.com/brianneary criminaldefense
New York, N.Y. Office: 475 Park Avenue, South, Suite 3300.
Telephone: 212-683-8000.

Judith A. Eisenberg

For full biographical listings, see the Martindale-Hubbell Law Directory

JOHN L. WEICHSEL (AV)

79 Main Street, 07601
Telephone: 201-488-1400
Fax: 201-488-3970
URL: http://www.weichlaw.baweb.com
Email: weichlaw@idt.net *URL:* http://www.lawyers.com/weichselatty

Reference: First Union National Bank.

For full biographical listings, see the Martindale-Hubbell Law Directory

HADDONFIELD, Camden Co.

WILBRAHAM, LAWLER & BUBA, A PROFESSIONAL CORPORATION (AV(T))

24 Kings Highway West, 08033-2122
Telephone: 856-795-4422
Fax: 856-795-4699
Philadelphia, Pennsylvania Office: 1818 Market Street, Suite 3100.
Telephone: 215-564-4141.
Fax: 215-564-4385.
Wilmington, Delaware Office: Stoney Batter Office Building, 5301 Limestone Road, Suite 221.
Telephone: 302-234-8217.
Fax: 302-234-8218.

Edward J. Wilbraham | Michael J. Block
Mary S. Cook

For full biographical listings, see the Martindale-Hubbell Law Directory

*MORRISTOWN,** Morris Co.

PITNEY, HARDIN, KIPP & SZUCH LLP (AV)

P.O. Box 1945, 07962-1945
Telephone: 973-966-6300
New York City: 212-687-6000
Telex: 642014
Telecopier: 973-966-1550
URL: http://www.phks.com
New York, New York Office: 711 Third Avenue, 10017-4014.
Telephone: 212-687-6000.
Fax: 212-682-3485.

(See Next Column)

MEMBERS OF FIRM

J. Michael Nolan, Jr. | Dennis T. Kearney

COUNSEL

John J. O'Reilly

Representative Clients: Blue Cross & Blue Shield; Base Ten Systems, Inc.; PNC Bank, N.A.

For Complete List of Firm Personnel, See General Section

For full biographical listings, see the Martindale-Hubbell Law Directory

STEPHEN S. WEINSTEIN A PROFESSIONAL CORPORATION (AV)

20 Park Place, Suite 301, 07960
Telephone: 973-267-5200
Fax: 973-538-1779
Email: skippy@sswpa.com *URL:* http://www.sswpa.com

Stephen S. Weinstein

Gail S. Boertzel | William G. Johnson
Melissa H. Luce

For full biographical listings, see the Martindale-Hubbell Law Directory

*NEWARK,** Essex Co.

ALAN DEXTER BOWMAN, P.A. (AV)

One Gateway Center, Suite 105, 07102
Telephone: 973-622-2225
Fax: 973-242-6768

Alan Dexter Bowman

For full biographical listings, see the Martindale-Hubbell Law Directory

FITZSIMMONS RINGLE & JACOBS, P.C. (AV)

50 Park Place, 07102
Telephone: 973-623-5350
Fax: 973-623-5927
New York, New York: 130 E. 35th Street, 10016.
Telephone: 212-343-0677.

Frank J. Fitzsimmons | Richard Ringle
Andrew R. Jacobs

COUNSEL

Ronald Leibman

Michael E. Coslit | Lisa M. Papp
Martin Trevor Hughes Lyons

For full biographical listings, see the Martindale-Hubbell Law Directory

GREENBERG DAUBER EPSTEIN & TUCKER, A PROFESSIONAL CORPORATION (AV)

Suite 600, One Gateway Center, 07102-5311
Telephone: 973-643-3700
Facsimile: 973-643-1218
URL: http://www.greenbergdauber.com

Melvin Greenberg | Edward J. Dauber

For Complete List of Firm Personnel, See General Section

For full biographical listings, see the Martindale-Hubbell Law Directory

HELLRING LINDEMAN GOLDSTEIN & SIEGAL LLP (AV)

One Gateway Center, 07102-5386
Telephone: 973-621-9020
Fax: 973-621-7406
Englewood, New Jersey Office: 32-40 North Dean Street.
Telephone: 201-871-3060.

Joel D. Siegal | Ronny Jo Greenwald Siegal
Jonathan L. Goldstein | Stephen L. Dreyfuss
Richard D. Shapiro | Rachel N. Davidson

For Complete List of Firm Personnel, See General Section

For full biographical listings, see the Martindale-Hubbell Law Directory

LITE, DE PALMA, GREENBERG & RIVAS, LLC (AV)

Two Gateway Center, 12th Floor, 07102-5003
Telephone: 973-623-3000
Fax: 973-623-0858

MEMBERS OF FIRM

Allyn Z. Lite | Bruce D. Greenberg
Joseph J. De Palma | Alberto Rivas

ASSOCIATE

Michele Soto

For full biographical listings, see the Martindale-Hubbell Law Directory

Newark—Continued

SILLS CUMMIS RADIN TISCHMAN EPSTEIN & GROSS, A PROFESSIONAL CORPORATION (AV)

One Riverfront Plaza, 07102-5400
Telephone: 973-643-7000
Fax: 973-643-6500
Telex: 820630 Sillsbeck Nwk
Email: sillsmail@sillscummis.com *URL:* http://www.sillscummis.com
Atlantic City, New Jersey Office: 17 Gordon's Alley.
Telephone: 609-344-2800.
New York, N.Y. Office: 712 Fifth Avenue.
Telephone: 212-643-7000.
Washington, D.C. Office: 1800 K Street, N.W.
Telephone: 202-296-4750.

MEMBERS OF FIRM

Barry M. Epstein
Lawrence S. Horn
Robert J. Alter
Philip R. Sellinger
Mark S. Olinsky
Richard J. Sapinski
Jack Wenik
A. Ross Pearlson

SENIOR COUNSEL

Herbert L. Zuckerman

For Complete List of Firm Personnel, See General Section

For full biographical listings, see the Martindale-Hubbell Law Directory

TOMPKINS, MCGUIRE, WACHENFELD & BARRY (AV)

A New Jersey Limited Liability Partnership including a Professional Association
Four Gateway Center, 100 Mulberry Street, 07102-4070
Telephone: 973-622-3000
Telecopier: 973-623-7780
Email: attorneys@tompkinsmcguire.com
New York, New York Office: 1 Bankers Trust Plaza. 130 Liberty Street, Suite 2707. 10006.
Telephone: 212-714-1720.

MEMBERS OF FIRM

James F. Flanagan, III
Patrick M. Callahan

Representative Clients: Corbo Jewelers, Inc.; General Electric Co.; Hartford Insurance Group; Marriott Corp.; Underwriters at Lloyd's, London.

For Complete List of Firm Personnel, See General Section

For full biographical listings, see the Martindale-Hubbell Law Directory

*NEW BRUNSWICK,** Middlesex Co.

BENEDICT AND ALTMAN (AV)

247 Livingston Avenue, 08901
Telephone: 732-745-9000
Fax: 732-214-1897

MEMBERS OF FIRM

Joseph J. Benedict
Steven D. Altman

ASSOCIATE

Doris E. McNeil

For full biographical listings, see the Martindale-Hubbell Law Directory

NORTH BRUNSWICK, Middlesex Co.

BORRUS, GOLDIN, FOLEY, VIGNUOLO, HYMAN, STAHL & CLARKIN, A PROFESSIONAL CORPORATION (AV)

2875 U.S. Highway 1, Route 1 & Finnigans Lane, P.O. Box 7463, 08902
Telephone: 732-422-1000
Fax: 732-422-1016
Email: attys@borrus.com *URL:* http://www.borrus.com

Jack Borrus
Martin S. Goldin
David M. Foley
Anthony B. Vignuolo
Jeffrey M. Hyman
James E. Stahl
James F. Clarkin III
Eileen Mary Foley

Robert C. Nisenson
Rosalind Westlake
Lisa M. Vignuolo
Steven L. Fox
Peter A. Vignuolo
Gerald T. Foley (1903-1976)

Representative Clients: Summit Bank; R. J. Reynolds Tobacco Co.; K. Hovnanian Enterprises, Inc.; Johnson and Johnson; Foster Wheeler, Inc.; Hartz Mountain Industries; Middlesex County Vocational Services Commission; Borough of South Plainfield Board of Adjustment; U-Haul of Northern NJ.

For full biographical listings, see the Martindale-Hubbell Law Directory

RED BANK, Monmouth Co.

PHILIP G. AUERBACH A PROFESSIONAL CORPORATION (AV)

231 Maple Avenue, P.O. Box Y, 07701
Telephone: 732-842-6660
Fax: 732-530-7925

(See Next Column)

Philip G. Auerbach

Edward A. Genz
John J. Ryan
John F. McLaughlin

For full biographical listings, see the Martindale-Hubbell Law Directory

ROSELAND, Essex Co.

WALDER, SONDAK & BROGAN, A PROFESSIONAL CORPORATION (AV)

5 Becker Farm Road, P.O. Box 901, 07068
Telephone: 973-992-5300
Telecopier: 973-992-1505; 992-1006
Email: general@wsbesqs.com *URL:* http://www.wsbesqs.com

Justin P. Walder
John A. Brogan
Barry A. Kozyra
James A. Plaisted
Jeffrey A. Walder

John S. Redden
Shalom D. Stone
Christopher M. Farella

For Complete List of Firm Personnel, See General Section

For full biographical listings, see the Martindale-Hubbell Law Directory

SHORT HILLS, Essex Co.

PETER W. TILL (AV)

820 Morris Turnpike, Suite 201, 07078
Telephone: 973-467-0300
Fax: 973-467-4628
Email: peterwtill@aol.com *URL:* http://www.lawyers.com/peterwtilllaw
(Also Of Counsel, Wilf & Silverman)

For full biographical listings, see the Martindale-Hubbell Law Directory

*SOMERVILLE,** Somerset Co.

SCHACHTER, TROMBADORE, OFFEN, STANTON & PAVICS, A PROFESSIONAL CORPORATION (AV)

45 East High Street, P.O. Box 520, 08876-0520
Telephone: 908-722-5700
Fax: 908-722-8853

Thomas A. Pavics

For full biographical listings, see the Martindale-Hubbell Law Directory

RAYMOND R. & DAVID W. TROMBADORE, P.C. A PROFESSIONAL CORPORATION (AV)

33 East High Street, 08876
Telephone: 908-722-7555
Fax: 908-722-6269
URL: http://www.trombadorelaw.com

Raymond R. Trombadore
David W. Trombadore

OF COUNSEL

Ann W. Trombadore

References: Summit Bank; Somerset Savings & Loan Assn.

For full biographical listings, see the Martindale-Hubbell Law Directory

SPRINGFIELD, Union Co.

MCDONOUGH, KORN & EICHHORN, A PROFESSIONAL CORPORATION (AV)

Park Place Legal Center, 959 South Springfield Avenue, P.O. Box 712, 07081-0712
Telephone: 973-912-9099
Fax: 973-912-8604

Peter L. Korn
R. Scott Eichhorn
James R. Korn
William S. Mezzomo
Timothy J. Jaeger
Wilfred P. Coronato

Julia A. Klubenspies
Matthew S. Schorr
Danielle M. Verrastro
Jeffrey John Berezny

OF COUNSEL

Robert P. McDonough

Reference: First Union, Summit, N.J.

For full biographical listings, see the Martindale-Hubbell Law Directory

*TOMS RIVER,** Ocean Co.

NOVINS, YORK & PENTONY, A PROFESSIONAL CORPORATION (AV)

202 Main Street, 08753
Telephone: 732-349-7100
Email: info@nyplaw.com

Robert F. Novins

Counsel for: Allstate Insurance Co.; Motor Club of America.

For Complete List of Firm Personnel, See General Section

For full biographical listings, see the Martindale-Hubbell Law Directory

*TRENTON,** Mercer Co.

SCHRAGGER, LAVINE & NAGY (AV)

Mountainview Office Park, 840 Bear Tavern Road, Suite 307, 08628
Telephone: 609-771-0700
Fax: 609-771-9535

Bruce M. Schragger

LEGAL SUPPORT PERSONNEL

Annemarie Saccani (Office Administrator)

Representative Clients: New Jersey Manufacturers Insurance Co.; Mercer County Community College; Mercer Mutual Insurance Co.; New Jersey Optometric Association; Allentown Caging; Dick Greenfield Dodge.

For Complete List of Firm Personnel, See General Section

For full biographical listings, see the Martindale-Hubbell Law Directory

VINELAND, Cumberland Co.

JOSEPH D. O'NEILL A PROFESSIONAL CORPORATION (AV)

30 West Chestnut Avenue, P.O. Box 847, 08360
Telephone: 856-692-2400
Telecopier: 856-696-9036
URL: http://www.lawyers.com/josephoneill

Joseph D. O'Neill

Charles I. Coant
James T. Dugan
Amber Sharp Pallante

For full biographical listings, see the Martindale-Hubbell Law Directory

WOODBRIDGE, Middlesex Co.

WILENTZ, GOLDMAN & SPITZER, A PROFESSIONAL CORPORATION (AV)

90 Woodbridge Center Drive Suite 900, Box 10, 07095
Telephone: 732-636-8000
Telecopier: 732-855-6117
URL: http://www.newjerseylaw.com
Eatontown, New Jersey Office: Meridian Center I, Two Industrial Way West, 07724.
Telephone: 732-542-4500.
Telecopier: 732-493-8387.
New York, New York Office: Wall Street Plaza, 88 Pine Street, 9th Floor, 10005.
Telephone: 212-267-3091.
Telecopier: 212-267-3828.

Warren W. Wilentz
James E. Trabilsy
Barry T. Albin
Eric J. Marcy

Isabel McGinty
Darren M. Gelber
John E. Hogan

Representative Firm Clients: Amerada Hess Corp.; Chevron, U.S.A.; Cumberland Farms, Inc.; Middlesex County Utilities Authority; New Jersey Automobile Dealers Assn.; Co-Steel Raritan; The Rouse Co.

For Complete List of Firm Personnel, See General Section

For full biographical listings, see the Martindale-Hubbell Law Directory

NEW MEXICO

*ALBUQUERQUE,** Bernalillo Co.

FREEDMAN BOYD DANIELS HOLLANDER GOLDBERG & CLINE P.A. (AV)

20 First Plaza, Suite 700, 87102
Telephone: 505-842-9960
Fax: 505-842-0761

(See Next Column)

David A. Freedman
Nancy Hollander
Charles W. Daniels
John D. Cline

Eric J. Knapp
K.C. Maxwell

For full biographical listings, see the Martindale-Hubbell Law Directory

RON KOCH, P.A. (AV)

503 Slate Avenue, N.W., 87102
Telephone: 505-247-2972
Fax: 505-243-3669
URL: http://www.ronkoch.com
Email: kingkoch@aol.com *URL:* http://www.lawyers.com/ronkoch

Ron Koch

For full biographical listings, see the Martindale-Hubbell Law Directory

RODEY, DICKASON, SLOAN, AKIN & ROBB, P.A. (AV)

Albuquerque Plaza, Suite 2200, 201 Third Street, N.W., P.O. Box 1888, 87103-1888
Telephone: 505-765-5900
Fax: 505-768-7395
Email: info@rodey.com *URL:* http://www.rodey.com
Santa Fe, New Mexico Office: Suite 101 Marcy Plaza, 123 East Marcy Street, P.O. Box 1357, 87504-1357.
Telephone: 505-984-0100.
Fax: 505-989-9542.

William S. Dixon
R. Nelson Franse

Thomas A. Outler

For Complete List of Firm Personnel, See General Section

For full biographical listings, see the Martindale-Hubbell Law Directory

SÍLVA, RIEDER & MAESTAS, P.C. (AV)

Albuquerque Plaza, Suite 1700, 201 3rd Street, N.W., P.O. Box 1670, 87103-1670
Telephone: 505-767-9800
Facsimile: 505-767-9807
Email: srmlaw@srmlaw.com *URL:* http://www.lawyers.com/srmlaw

Benjamin Sílva, Jr.
Geoffrey D. Rieder
Paul Maestas

Wayne R. Suggett
Christopher A. Riehl
Richard A. Allen

For full biographical listings, see the Martindale-Hubbell Law Directory

RAY TWOHIG, P.C. (AV)

8998 Rio Grande Boulevard N.W., 87114
Telephone: 505-898-0400
Fax: 505-898-0004
Email: rambaud@flash.net

Ray Twohig

*ROSWELL,** Chaves Co.

LAW OFFICES OF MICHAEL L. STOUT (AV)

215 West 6th Street, 88201
Telephone: 505-624-1471
Fax: 505-622-1086
Email: mlstout@nm.net

For full biographical listings, see the Martindale-Hubbell Law Directory

*SANTA FE,** Santa Fe Co.

AARONS LAW FIRM, P.C. (AV)

300 Catron Street, P.O. Box 1027, 87504-1027
Telephone: 505-984-1100
Fax: 505-984-1110
Toll Free: 888-984-1120
Email: mail@aarons.org *URL:* http://www.aarons.org

Stephen D. Aarons

For full biographical listings, see the Martindale-Hubbell Law Directory

STEVEN G. FARBER (AV)

306 Catron Street, P.O. Box 2473, 87504-2473
Telephone: 505-988-9725
Fax: 505-988-9250
Email: sgfsaf@aol.com

For full biographical listings, see the Martindale-Hubbell Law Directory

Santa Fe—Continued

ROTHSTEIN, DONATELLI, HUGHES, DAHLSTROM & SCHOENBURG, LLP (AV)

P.O. Box 8180, 87504-8180
Telephone: 505-988-8004
Fax: 505-982-0307
Email: manager@rothsteinlaw.com
Albuquerque Office: 320 Central S.W., Suite 30.
Telephone: 505-243-1443.
Fax: 505-242-7845. Email: ROTHLAWABQ@aol.com.
Phoenix, Arizona Office: 234 North Central, Suite 722.
Telephone: 602-252-3226.
Fax: 602-253-3088. Email: RLAWFPHX@aol.com.

MEMBERS OF FIRM

Robert R. Rothstein
Mark H. Donatelli
Richard W. Hughes
Eric N. Dahlstrom (Not admitted in NM; Resident, Phoenix, AZ Office)
Peter Schoenburg (Resident, Albuquerque Office)

ASSOCIATES

Michael C. Shiel (Not admitted in NM; Resident, Phoenix, AZ Office)
John L. Sullivan

OF COUNSEL

Sarah E. Bennett

For full biographical listings, see the Martindale-Hubbell Law Directory

WHITE, KOCH, KELLY & McCARTHY, A PROFESSIONAL ASSOCIATION (AV)

433 Paseo De Peralta, P.O. Box 787, 87504-0787
Telephone: 505-982-4374
ABA/NET: 1154
Fax: 505-982-0350; 984-8631
Email: WKKM@NM.NET

David F. Cunningham
Janet Clow
Aaron J. Wolf

For Complete List of Firm Personnel, See General Section

For full biographical listings, see the Martindale-Hubbell Law Directory

NEW YORK

*ALBANY,** Albany Co.

O'CONNELL AND ARONOWITZ, P.C. (AV)

100 State Street, 12207-1885
Telephone: 518-462-5601
Telecopier: 518-462-2670
Email: info@oalaw.com
Plattsburgh, New York Office: 206 West Bay Plaza.
Telephone: 518-562-0600.
Fax: 518-562-0657.
Saratoga Springs, New York Office: Suite 204, 358 Broadway.
Telephone: 518-587-0425.

Stephen R. Coffey
Gloria Herron Arthur

Michael L. Koenig
Joseph Muia, Jr.

For full biographical listings, see the Martindale-Hubbell Law Directory

BAY SHORE, Suffolk Co.

LONG, TUMINELLO, BESSO, SELIGMAN, QUINLAN & WERNER (AV)

120 Fourth Avenue, P.O. Box 591 P, 11706
Telephone: 516-666-5766; 516-666-2500
Fax: 516-666-8401
Email: bob_quinlan_ltbsqw@msn.com
Naples, Florida Office: 1300 Third Street South, Suite 302 B.
Telephone: 813-262-3377.
Fax: 813-262-0313.

MEMBERS OF FIRM

John E. Long, Jr. (Resident, Naples, Florida Office)
Barry M. Tuminello
David H. Besso
Harold Seligman
Robert F. Quinlan
Kevin J. Werner

ASSOCIATE

Kevin R. Johnston

(See Next Column)

OF COUNSEL

Hon. Arthur M. Cromarty
Thomas J. Lavallee

For full biographical listings, see the Martindale-Hubbell Law Directory

*BINGHAMTON,** Broome Co.

ASWAD & INGRAHAM (AV)

46 Front Street, 13905
Telephone: 607-722-3495
Fax: 607-722-2566; 607-722-7269
Email: office@AILAW.COM

MEMBERS OF FIRM

Richard N. Aswad
Charles O. Ingraham
Thomas A. Saitta
James F. Haley, Jr.
Angelina C. Cutrona
William M. Thomas

SPECIAL COUNSEL

James F. Moran

ASSOCIATE

Jeffrey Husisian

Reference: Charter One Bank.

For full biographical listings, see the Martindale-Hubbell Law Directory

*BUFFALO,** Erie Co.

BROWN & KELLY, L.L.P. (AV)

1500 Liberty Building, 14202-3663
Telephone: 716-854-2620
Fax: 716-854-0082
Email: mail@brownkelly.com *URL:* http://www.brownkelly.com

MEMBERS OF FIRM

Thomas J. Kelly
Rodney O. Personius
Frederick D. Turner
Paul Michael Hassett
Peter E. Klaasesz
Donald B. Eppers
Andrew D. Merrick
William P. Wiles
William D. Harrington
Joseph M. Schnitter
Paula L. Feroleto
Daniel J. Marren
Lisa T. Sofferin

OF COUNSEL

Ogden R. Brown
Charles F. Harrington
James T. Duggan
Karen Cook Serotte
Roland R. Benzow
Philip B. Abramowitz
Elizabeth R. O'Connor
Catherine E. Marra

ASSOCIATES

David S. Zygaj
Olney H. Clowe
Brian M. Melber
David O. Teach
Patricia S. Ciccarelli
Susan J. Schmidt

For full biographical listings, see the Martindale-Hubbell Law Directory

CONNORS & VILARDO, LLP (AV)

1020 Liberty Building, 420 Main Street, 14202
Telephone: 716-852-5533
Fax: 716-852-5649
Email: c-v@connors-vilardo.com

MEMBERS OF FIRM

Joseph J. Ricotta (1921-1993)
Terrence M. Connors
Lawrence J. Vilardo
Kevin A. Ricotta
Randall D. White
John T. Loss
Vincent E. Doyle III

ASSOCIATES

Michael J. Roach
Mark R. Uba
Margaret L. Phillips
Henry J. Nowak
Lawlor F. Quinlan III
James W. Grable, Jr.

For full biographical listings, see the Martindale-Hubbell Law Directory

CENTRAL ISLIP, Suffolk Co.

EFMAN & OBEDIN (AV)

83 Carleton Avenue, 11722-3019
Telephone: 516-232-3400
Fax: 516-232-5343
Email: eoattorney@aol.com

Martin I. Efman
Glenn A. Obedin

For full biographical listings, see the Martindale-Hubbell Law Directory

*ITHACA,** Tompkins Co.

WIGGINS AND MASSON, LLP (AV)

308 North Tioga Street, P.O. Box 399, 14851
Telephone: 607-272-0479
Telecopier: 607-273-0502
Email: law@wigginsandmasson.com *URL:* http://www.wigginsandmasson.com

(See Next Column)

WIGGINS AND MASSON LLP, *Ithaca—Continued*

MEMBER OF FIRM

Walter J. Wiggins

Approved Attorneys for: Ticor Title Guaranty Corp.
References: Tompkins County Trust Co.

For Complete List of Firm Personnel, See General Section

For full biographical listings, see the Martindale-Hubbell Law Directory

JACKSON HEIGHTS, Queens Co.

LAWRENCE M. HERRMANN (AV)

37-51 76th Street, 11372-6533
Telephone: 718-779-6630
Fax: 718-565-7278

For full biographical listings, see the Martindale-Hubbell Law Directory

LAKE SUCCESS, Nassau Co.

DIKMAN AND DIKMAN (AV)

5 Dakota Drive, Suite 208, 11042
Telephone: 516-354-2526
Fax: 516-354-2528
Jamaica, New York Office: 161-10 Jamaica Avenue,
Telephone: 718-739-4830.

MEMBER OF FIRM

David S. Dikman

Reference: Chase Manhattan Bank.

For full biographical listings, see the Martindale-Hubbell Law Directory

MILLBROOK, Dutchess Co.

WILLIAM E. STANTON (AV)

Merritt Avenue and Elm Drive, P.O. Box 1252, 12545
Telephone: 914-677-9060
FAX: 914-677-9392
Stanfordville, New York Office: Bulls Head Road, 12581.
Telephone: 914-868-7514.
Fax: 914-868-7761.

Representative Clients: Dupont de Nemours & Co.; Millbrook School; New York Telephone Co.
Reference: Pawling Savings Bank.

For full biographical listings, see the Martindale-Hubbell Law Directory

*MINEOLA,** Nassau Co.

ROBERT L. CLAREY (AV)

96 Willis Avenue, 11501
Telephone: 516-747-6660
Voice Mail: 516-742-9116
Fax: 516-742-5278
URL: http://www.lawyers.com/clareylaw

For full biographical listings, see the Martindale-Hubbell Law Directory

HESSION & BEKOFF (AV)

29 Roslyn Road, 11501
Telephone: 516-746-2900
Telecopier: 516-877-0789

MEMBERS OF FIRM

Ronald Jay Bekoff
Thomas R. Hession

ASSOCIATE

William Scott Petrillo

For full biographical listings, see the Martindale-Hubbell Law Directory

*NEW YORK,** New York Co.

ARKIN SCHAFFER & KAPLAN LLP (AV)

590 Madison Avenue, 10022
Telephone: 212-333-0200
Fax: 212-333-2350
Email: info@ARKIN-LAW.com

Stanley S. Arkin
Hyman L. Schaffer
Jeffrey M. Kaplan
Mark S. Cohen
Howard J. Kaplan

ASSOCIATES

Harry B. Feder
Sean R. O'Brien
Robert Pfeffer

OF COUNSEL

Michelle A. Rice

For full biographical listings, see the Martindale-Hubbell Law Directory

BARRETT GRAVANTE CARPINELLO & STERN LLP (AV)

570 Lexington Avenue, 10022
Telephone: 212-446-2300
Telecopier: 212-446-2350
Albany, New York Office: 100 State Street, 12207.
Telephone: 518-434-0600.
Telecopier: 518-434-0665.
Fort Lauderdale, Florida Office: Barnett Bank Plaza, One East Broward Boulevard, 33301.
Telephone: 954-356-0011.
Telecopier: 954-356-0022.

David A. Barrett
Nicholas A. Gravante, Jr.
George F. Carpinello
Jack G. Stern
Michael I. Endler
Harlan A. Levy
Kathleen M. Franklin
Roland G. Riopelle
Steven I. Froot
Andrew B. Peretz, P.A.
Carla E. Hogan

OF COUNSEL

Michael Straus
Howard A. Wintner
Norman P. Fivel
Karen Martino Valle
Philippa Bainbridge

Jeffrey S. Shelly
Kenneth G. Walsh
Philip J. Iovieno
Evan Glassman
Bradley J. Gross (Resident, Fort Lauderdale, Florida Office)
Jessica M. Tourk
Magda M. Jimenez
Kahlia E. Fisher
Elizabeth Ann Butler
Ryan K. Higgins

For full biographical listings, see the Martindale-Hubbell Law Directory

BELDOCK LEVINE & HOFFMAN LLP (AV)

99 Park Avenue, 10016-1503
Telephone: 212-490-0400
Cable Address: "Telhofflaw, N.Y."
Telecopier: 212-557-0565
URL: http://www.blhny.com

MEMBERS OF FIRM

Myron Beldock
Brian E. Maas

For full biographical listings, see the Martindale-Hubbell Law Directory

BRAFMAN & ROSS, P.C. (AV)

26th Floor, 767 Third Avenue, 10017
Telephone: 212-750-7800
Telecopier: 212-750-3906
URL: http://www.lawyers.com/brafman&rosspc

Benjamin Brafman
Charles A. Ross

Melissa M Beck

OF COUNSEL

Mark M. Baker

For full biographical listings, see the Martindale-Hubbell Law Directory

CALLAN, REGENSTREICH, KOSTER & BRADY (AV)

One Whitehall Street 10th Floor, 10004
Telephone: 212-248-8800
Fax: 212-248-6815
Shrewsbury, New Jersey Office: 740 Broad Street.
Telephone: 732-345-9333.
Fax: 732-345-9444.
Garden City, New York Office: 1205 Franklin Avenue.
Telephone: 516-294-4383.
Fax: 516-294-4386.

MEMBERS OF FIRM

Paul F. Callan
Bruce N. Regenstreich
Warren S. Koster
Bruce M. Brady
William L. Brennan
Vincent A. Nagler
Scott W. Bermack

ASSOCIATES

Kenneth S. Merber
Michael P. Kandler
Vincent D. Finnegan
Stephanie Palermo
Walter Paterson Burrell
Beth S. Block
Meredith B. Borg
Pamela Patton Fynes
Mara J. Sibley
Eric A. Wasserfall
Amie Catherine Kalac (Resident, Shrewsbury, New Jersey Office)
Lisa B. Katz

For full biographical listings, see the Martindale-Hubbell Law Directory

CAPLIN & DRYSDALE, CHARTERED (AV)

399 Park Avenue 36th Floor, 10022
Telephone: 212-319-7125
Fax: 212-644-6755
Washington, D.C. Office: One Thomas Circle, N.W.
Telephone: 202-862-5000.
Fax: 202-429-3301.

(See Next Column)

CAPLIN & DRYSDALE CHARTERED—*Continued*

Elihu Inselbuch

Rita C. Tobin

For full biographical listings, see the Martindale-Hubbell Law Directory

LAW OFFICES OF CHRISTOPHER E. CHANG (AV)

140 Broadway, 46th Floor, 10005
Telephone: 212-208-1470
Fax: 212-208-1468
Email: cechang@juno.com

For full biographical listings, see the Martindale-Hubbell Law Directory

FREDERICK H. COHN (AV)

500 Fifth Avenue, 33rd Floor, 10110
Telephone: 212-768-1110
Fax: 212-764-3701
Email: fcohn@interport.net *URL:* http://www.lawyers.com/frederickcohn

For full biographical listings, see the Martindale-Hubbell Law Directory

CURTIS, MALLET-PREVOST, COLT & MOSLE LLP (AV)

101 Park Avenue, 10178-0061
Telephone: 212-696-6000
Telecopier: 212-697-1559
Email: info@cm-p.com *URL:* http://www.cm-p.com
Washington, D.C. Office: Suite 1205L, 1801 K Street, N.W.
Telephone: 202-452-7373.
Telecopier: 202-452-7333.
Newark, New Jersey Office: One Gateway Center, Suite 403.
Telephone: 973-622-0605.
Telecopier: 973-622-5646.
Houston, Texas Office: 2 Houston Center, 909 Fannin Street, Suite 3725.
Telephone: 713-759-9555.
Telecopier: 713-759-0712.
Stamford, Connecticut Office: One Canterbury Green.
Telephone: 203-359-6200.
Telecopier: 203-328-2617.
Mexico City, D.F., Mexico Office: Curtis, Mallet-Prevost, Colt & Mosle, Ruben Dario 281, Piso 9, Col. Bosque de Chapultepec, 11530 Mexico, D.F.
Telephone: 525-282-0444.
Telecopier: 525-282-0637.
Paris, France Office: 15 rue d'Astorg, 75008.
Telephone: +33-1 42-66-39-10.
Telecopier: +33-1 42-66-39-62.
London, England Office: Two Throgmorton Avenue, EC2N 2DL.
Telephone: 0207-638-7957.
Telecopier: 0207-638-5512.
Frankfurt am Main 1, Germany Office: Staufenstrasse 42.
Telephone: +49-69-971-4420.
Telecopier: +49-69-17 33 99.
Muscat, Sultanate of Oman Office: Jewel Beach-134.
Telephone: 968-607-725.
Telecopier: 968-607-724.
Milan, Italy Office: Curtis, Mallet-Prevost & Gilioli, Piazzale Principessa Clotilde 8, 20121.
Telephone: +(39) 02 29 00 29 32.
Telefax: +(39) 02 65 75 969.

MEMBERS OF FIRM

Peter E. Fleming Jr.
T. Barry Kingham
Eliot Lauer
Jacques Semmelman

For full biographical listings, see the Martindale-Hubbell Law Directory

EMERY CUTI BRINCKERHOFF & ABADY PC (AV)

545 Madison Avenue, 3rd Floor, 10022-4219
Telephone: 212-763-5000
Facsimile: 212-763-5001
Email: mail@ecbalaw.com *URL:* http://www.ecbalaw.com

Richard D. Emery
Matthew D. Brinckerhoff
Jonathan S. Abady
John R. Cuti

Ilann M. Maazel
David H. Gans
Alexandra D. Lahav (Not admitted in NY)

For full biographical listings, see the Martindale-Hubbell Law Directory

LAW OFFICES OF ALAN S. FUTERFAS (AV)

260 Madison Avenue, 22nd Floor, 10016
Telephone: 212-684-8400
Telefax: 212-679-1844
Email: asfuterfas@aol.com

Ellen Beth Resnick

For full biographical listings, see the Martindale-Hubbell Law Directory

GETNICK & GETNICK (AV)

Tower 49, 12 East 49th Street, 31st Floor, 10017-1028
Telephone: 212-376-5666
Telefax: 212-292-3942
Email: info@getnicklaw.com *URL:* http://www.lawyers.com/getnick&getnick

MEMBERS OF FIRM

Irving M. Getnick
Neil V. Getnick
Lesley Ann Skillen
Margaret J. Finerty

OF COUNSEL

David A. Koenigsberg
Michael E. Getnick

ASSOCIATE

Richard J. Dircks

For full biographical listings, see the Martindale-Hubbell Law Directory

JAY GOLDBERG, P.C. (AV)

Twentieth Floor, 250 Park Avenue, 10177-2099
Telephone: 212-983-6000
Telecopier: 212-983-6008
Telex: 5101008171

Jay Goldberg

Debra A. Karlstein
Steven D. Isser

OF COUNSEL

Seth Ginsberg

Representative Clients: Donald Trump; Carl Icahn; Willie Nelson; Kris Kristofferson; Riddick Bowe.

For full biographical listings, see the Martindale-Hubbell Law Directory

GOLDBERGER AND DUBIN, P.C. (AV)

401 Broadway, 10013
Telephone: 212-431-9380
Fax: 212-966-0588
Email: GND401@aol.com *URL:* http://www.ny-attorney.com

Paul A. Goldberger
Lawrence Dubin

Robert A. Horne

For full biographical listings, see the Martindale-Hubbell Law Directory

GOLDMAN & HAFETZ (AV)

500 Fifth Avenue 29th Floor, 10110
Telephone: 212-997-7400
Fax: 212-997-7597
Email: info@goldman-hafetz.com

MEMBERS OF FIRM

Lawrence S. Goldman
Frederick P. Hafetz
Susan R. Necheles

ASSOCIATES

Elizabeth M. Johnson
William H. Devaney
Jill R. Shellow-Lavine (Not admitted in NY)

For full biographical listings, see the Martindale-Hubbell Law Directory

HOFFINGER FRIEDLAND DOBRISH & STERN, P.C. (AV)

A Professional Corporation including Professional Corporations
110 East 59th Street, 10022-1392
Telephone: 212-421-4000
Telecopier: 212-223-3857

Jack S. Hoffinger
Lawrence N. Friedland
Robert Z. Dobrish (P.C.)
Stephen R. Stern (P.C.)
Samuel P. Ross
Warren R. Gleicher
Philip S. Ross

Michael J. Sherman
Fran Hoffinger
John H. Friedland
Lydia A. Milone
Devorah S. Weinschneider
Eric I. Wrubel
Nina S. Gross
Scott Lawrence D'Aloise

For full biographical listings, see the Martindale-Hubbell Law Directory

HOFFMAN POLLOK & PICKHOLZ LLP (AV)

260 Madison Avenue, 10016
Telephone: 212-679-2900
FAX: 212-679-1844
Email: hppdefen@WEBSPAN.NET

MEMBERS OF FIRM

Jeffrey C. Hoffman
John L. Pollok
Marvin G. Pickholz
Susan C. Wolfe

ASSOCIATE

Francine Miller

(See Next Column)

HOFFMAN POLLOK & PICKHOLZ LLP, *New York—Continued*

OF COUNSEL

Michael S. Pollok

For full biographical listings, see the Martindale-Hubbell Law Directory

JONES, DAY, REAVIS & POGUE (AV)

599 Lexington Avenue, 10022
Telephone: 212-326-3939
Telecopier: 212-755-7306
Email: counsel@jonesday.com *URL:* http://www.jonesday.com
In Atlanta, Georgia: 3500 SunTrust Plaza, 303 Peachtree Street.
Telephone: 404-521-3939.
Telecopier: 404-581-8330.
In Brussels, Belgium: Avenue Louise 480, 7th Floor, B-1050 Brussels.
Telephone: 32-2-645-14-11.
Telecopier: 32-2-645-14-45.
In Chicago, Illinois: 77 West Wacker.
Telephone: 312-782-3939.
Telecopier: 312-782-8585.
In Cleveland, Ohio: North Point, 901 Lakeside Avenue.
Telephone: 216-586-3939.
Telecopier: 216-579-0212.
In Columbus, Ohio: 1900 Huntington Center.
Telephone: 614-469-3939.
Telecopier: 614-461-4198.
In Dallas, Texas: 2727 North Harwood Street.
Telephone: 214-220-3939.
Telecopier: 214-969-5100.
In Frankfurt, Germany: Hochhaus am Park, Grüneburgweg 102, 60323 Frankfurt am Main.
Telephone: 49-69-9726-3939.
Telecopier: 49-69-9726-3993.
In Geneva, Switzerland: 20, rue de Candolle.
Telephone: 41-22-320-2339.
Telecopier: 41-22-320-1232.
In Hong Kong: 29th Floor, Entertainment Building, 30 Queen's Road Central.
Telephone: 852-2526-6895.
Telecopier: 852-2868-5871.
In Irvine, California: 5 Park Plaza, Suite 1100.
Telephone: 949-851-3939.
Telecopier: 949-553-7539.
In London, England: Bucklersbury House, 3 Queen Victoria Street.
Telephone: 44-20-7236-3939
Telecopier: 44-20-7236-1113.
In Los Angeles, California: 555 West Fifth Street, Suite 4600.
Telephone: 213-489-3939.
Telecopier: 213-243-2539.
In Paris, France: 120, rue du Faubourg Saint-Honoré.
Telephone: 33-1-56-59-39-39.
Telecopier: 33-1-56-59-39-38
In Pittsburgh, Pennsylvania: 500 Grant Street, 31st Floor.
Telephone: 412-391-3939.
Telecopier: 412-394-7959.
In Riyadh, Saudi Arabia: The International Law Firm (In Association with Jones, Day, Reavis & Pogue), Sulaymaniyah, Prince Mishari IBN, Abdulaziz Street, P.O. Box 22166.
Telephone: (966-1) 462-8866.
Telecopier: (966-1) 462-9001.
In Shanghai, China: 2805 Kerry Centre, 1515 Nanjing Road West.
Telephone: 86-21-5298-6568.
Telecopier: 86-21-5298-6569.
In Sydney, Australia: Governor Phillip Tower, Level 38, 1 Farrer Place.
Telephone: 61-2-9210-6921.
Telecopier: 61-2-9210-6926.
In Taipei, Taiwan: 8th Floor, 2 Tun Hwa South Road, Section 2.
Telephone: (886-2) 2704-6808.
Telecopier: (886-2) 2704-6791.
In Tokyo, Japan: Toranomon 45 Mori Building, 3rd Floor, 1-5, Toranomon 5-Chome, Minato-Ku, Tokyo 105, Japan.
Telephone: 81-3-3433-3939.
Telecopier: 81-3-5401-2725.
In Washington, D.C.: 51 Louisiana Avenue, N.W.
Telephone: 202-879-3939.
Telecopier: 202-626-1700.

MEMBER OF FIRM IN NEW YORK

Charles M. Carberry

For Complete List of Firm Personnel, See General Section

For full biographical listings, see the Martindale-Hubbell Law Directory

KOSTELANETZ & FINK, LLP (AV)

530 Fifth Avenue, 22nd Floor, 10036
Telephone: 212-808-8100
Fax: 212-808-8108
Email: mail@kostelanetzfink.com

SENIOR COUNSEL

Boris Kostelanetz

(See Next Column)

MEMBERS OF FIRM

Robert S. Fink
Kevin M. Flynn
Bryan C. Skarlatos

COUNSEL

Norman Sinrich
Theodore F. Dickson
Caroline Rule
Brian C. Wille
William F. Cuozzi, III
Dawn Ngo

For full biographical listings, see the Martindale-Hubbell Law Directory

LANKLER SIFFERT & WOHL LLP (AV)

33rd Floor, 500 Fifth Avenue, 10110-3398
Telephone: 212-921-8399
Telefax: 212-764-3701
Telex: 4939413 LSWU1
URL: http://www.LSWLAW.com

MEMBERS OF FIRM

Jess Fardella
Helen Gredd
Roderick C. Lankler
John Sand Siffert
Charles T. Spada
Frank H. Wohl

OF COUNSEL

Susan L. Sommer
Peter Herbert

Lisa A. Baroni
Brett S. Deutsch
Brian Fleischer (Not admitted in NY)
Rebecca E. Hollander-Blumoff
Sara Lesch
Ghillaine A Reid
Daniel E. Reynolds
Laura H. Stasior

For full biographical listings, see the Martindale-Hubbell Law Directory

LA ROSSA & ROSS (AV)

41 Madison Avenue, 10010-2202
Telephone: 212-696-9700
Fax: 212-686-3013
URL: http://www.lawyers.com/larossa&ross

MEMBERS OF FIRM

James M. La Rossa
Michael S. Ross

ASSOCIATE

Melissa B. Ringel

For full biographical listings, see the Martindale-Hubbell Law Directory

ANDREW M. LAWLER, P.C. (AV)

220 East 42nd Street, 10017
Telephone: 212-687-8850
Telecopier: 212-972-6387

Andrew M. Lawler
Sharon D. Feldman

For full biographical listings, see the Martindale-Hubbell Law Directory

LITMAN, ASCHE & GIOIELLA, LLP (AV)

45 Broadway Atrium, 10006
Telephone: 212-809-4500
Telecopier: GP II, III (212) 509-8403

MEMBERS OF FIRM

Richard M. Asche
Jack T. Litman
Russell M. Gioiella

ASSOCIATES

Thomas H. Burt
Howard Weiner

OF COUNSEL

Stephen Hogan

For full biographical listings, see the Martindale-Hubbell Law Directory

LOVELL & STEWART, LLP (AV)

A Limited Liability Partnership including a Professional Corporation
500 Fifth Avenue, 10110
Telephone: 212-608-1900
Telefax: 212-719-4677
Email: sklovell@aol.com

Christopher Lovell, P.C.
Victor E. Stewart
Gary S. Jacobson

Peggy J. Wedgworth
Geoffrey M. Horn
William W. Foshay, III
Ian T. Stoll

For full biographical listings, see the Martindale-Hubbell Law Directory

New York—Continued

Morganroth & Morganroth (AV)

156 W. 56th Street, Suite 1101, 10019
Telephone: 212-586-5905
URL: http://www.lawyers.com/morganroth&morganrothlaw
Southfield, Michigan Office: 3000 Town Center, Suite 1500, 48075.
Telephone: 248-355-3084.
Fax: 248-355-3017.

Mayer Morganroth
Jeffrey B. Morganroth

For full biographical listings, see the Martindale-Hubbell Law Directory

Morvillo, Abramowitz, Grand, Iason & Silberberg, P.C. (AV)

565 Fifth Avenue, 10017
Telephone: 212-856-9600
Fax: 212-856-9494
Cable Address: "Litigator, New York"

Robert G. Morvillo
Elkan Abramowitz
Paul R. Grand
Lawrence Iason
Michael C. Silberberg
John J. Tigue, Jr.
Richard D. Weinberg
Barry A. Bohrer
Lawrence S. Bader
Edward M. Spiro
Robert J. Anello
Catherine M. Foti
Jeremy H. Temkin

OF COUNSEL

Robert J. McGuire
Michael W. Mitchell
Diana D. Parker

David Axinn
Anirudh Bansal
Neil M. Barofsky
Steven Harley Breslow
Jennifer Arbittier Bromley (Not admitted in NY)
Jamie Alter Deutsch (Not admitted in NY)
James C. Dugan
Mary P. Etheridge
Rebecca Glaser
Daniel B. Kosove (Not admitted in NY)
Tracy Lehman
Mary Margulis-Ohnuma
Michael R. Marra
Sara Mogulescu
Helen L. Monaco
Gretchan R. Ohlig
Jodi Misher Peikin
Elizabeth Small
Peter M. Spett

For full biographical listings, see the Martindale-Hubbell Law Directory

Newman Schwartz & Greenberg (AV)

950 Third Avenue, 10022
Telephone: 212-308-7900
Telecopier: 212-826-3273

MEMBERS OF FIRM

Gustave H. Newman
Robert Hill Schwartz
Richard A. Greenberg

ASSOCIATES

Karl E. Pflanz
Annemarie Hassett
Steven Y. Yurowitz

For full biographical listings, see the Martindale-Hubbell Law Directory

Martin L. Schmukler, P.C. (AV)

Forty-One Madison Avenue Fifth Floor, 10010-2202
Telephone: 212-213-9400
Fax: 212-684-0620
Email: MartinS@mlspclaw.com

Martin L. Schmukler

For full biographical listings, see the Martindale-Hubbell Law Directory

Schulte Roth & Zabel LLP (AV)

900 Third Avenue, 10022
Telephone: 212-756-2000; 800-346-9644
Cable Address: "Olympus NewYork"
Telex: 426775
Email: wwwmail@srz.com *URL:* http://www.srz.com

MEMBERS OF FIRM

Michael S. Feldberg
Daniel J. Kramer
Martin L. Perschetz
Frederick P. Schaffer

For Complete List of Firm Personnel, See General Section

For full biographical listings, see the Martindale-Hubbell Law Directory

Seidman, Silverman & Seidman, P.C. (AV)

600 Third Avenue 33rd Floor, 10016-2001
Telephone: 212-922-1900

Irving P. Seidman
Lawrence H. Silverman
Brian William Seidman

(See Next Column)

Joseph M. Fein

For full biographical listings, see the Martindale-Hubbell Law Directory

Skadden, Arps, Slate, Meagher & Flom LLP (AV)

Four Times Square, 10036
Telephone: 212-735-3000
Fax: 212-735-2000
URL: http://www.sasmf.com
Firm/Affiliate Offices:
Boston, Massachusetts: One Beacon Street, 02108.
Telephone: 617-573-4800.
Fax: 617-573-4822.
Washington, D.C.: 1440 New York Avenue, N.W., 20005.
Telephone: 202-371-7000.
Fax: 202-393-5760.
Wilmington, Delaware: One Rodney Square, P.O. Box 636, 19899.
Telephone: 302-651-3000.
Fax: 302-651-3001.
Los Angeles, California: 300 South Grand Avenue, 90071.
Telephone: 213-687-5000.
Fax: 213-687-5600.
Chicago, Illinois: Skadden, Arps, Slate, Meagher & Flom (Illinois), 333 West Wacker Drive, 60606.
Telephone: 312-407-0700.
Fax: 312-407-0411.
San Francisco, California: Four Embarcadero Center, 94111.
Telephone: 415-984-6400.
Fax: 415-984-2698.
Houston, Texas: 1600 Smith Street, Suite 4460, 77002.
Telephone: 713-655-5100.
Fax: 713-655-5181.
Newark, New Jersey: One Newark Center, 07102.
Telephone: 973-639-6800.
Fax: 973-639-6858.
Palo Alto, California: 525 University Avenue, Suite 220, 94301.
Telephone: 650-470-4500.
Fax: 650-470-4570.
Tokyo, Japan: ATT Main Tower 12F, 2-17-22, Akasaka, Minato-ku, 107-0052.
Telephone: 011-813-3568-2600.
Fax: 011-813-3568-2626.
London, England: One Canada Square, Canary Wharf, E14 5DS.
Telephone: 011-44-207-519-7000.
Fax: 011-44-207-519-7070.
Hong Kong, China: 30/F Tower Two, Lippo Centre, 89 Queensway, Central.
Telephone: 011-852-2820-0700.
Fax: 011-852-2820-0727.
Sydney, New South Wales 2000, Australia: Skadden, Arps, Slate, Meagher & Flom (International), Level 13, 131 Macquarie Street.
Telephone: 011-61-2-9253-6000.
Fax: 011-61-2-9253-6044.
Toronto, Ontario, Canada: Suite 1820, North Tower, P.O. Box 189, Royal Bank Plaza, M5J 2J4.
Telephone: 416-777-4700.
Fax: 416-777-4747.
Brussels, Belgium: 523 avenue Louise, Box 30, 1050.
Telephone: 011-32-2-639-0300.
Fax: 011-32-2-639-0339.
Frankfurt am Main, Germany: MesseTurm, 27th Floor, 60308.
Telephone: 011-49-69-742200.
Fax: 011-49-69-74220300.
Paris, France: 68, rue du Faubourg Saint-Honoré, 75008.
Telephone: 011-331-55-27-11-00.
Fax: 011-331-55-27-11-99.
Beijing, China: East Wing Office, Level 4, China World Trade Center, No. 1 Jian Guo Men Wai Avenue, 100004.
Telephone: 011-86-10-6505-5511.
Fax: 011-86-10-6505-5522.
Moscow, Russia: Degtyarniy Pereulok 4, Building 1, 103009.
Telephone: 011-7-501-797-4600.
Fax: 011-7-501-797-4601.
Singapore, Singapore: Skadden, Arps, Slate, Meagher & Flom (International), 9 Temasek Boulevard, Suite 29-01, Suntec Tower Two, 038989.
Telephone: 011-65-434-2900.
Fax: 011-65-434-2988.

MEMBERS OF FIRM/AFFILIATES

William P. Frank
Jeffrey Glekel
David M. Zornow
Robert J. Del Tufo
Keith D. Krakaur

FIRM/AFFILIATE OFFICES:

BOSTON, MASSACHUSETTS

PARTNERS

Thomas J. Dougherty
George J. Skelly

CHICAGO, ILLINOIS

PARTNER

Susan Getzendanner

(See Next Column)

SKADDEN, ARPS, SLATE, MEAGHER & FLOM LLP, *New York—Continued*

LOS ANGELES, CALIFORNIA

PARTNERS

Frank Rothman | Eric S. Waxman
Harriet S. Posner

WASHINGTON, D.C.

PARTNERS

Richard L. Brusca | Albert H. Turkus
Robert S. Bennett | Mitchell S. Ettinger
Alan Kriegel | Andrew L. Sandler
Carl S. Rauh | Edward J. Meehan
Saul M. Pilchen

COUNSEL

Amy R. Sabrin

SPECIAL COUNSEL

Edward D. Ross, Jr.

WILMINGTON, DELAWARE

PARTNER

Marc B. Tucker

NEWARK, NEW JERSEY

PARTNER

Robert J. Del Tufo

NEW YORK, NEW YORK

ASSOCIATES

Eric R. Komitee | Lawrence S. Spiegel

WASHINGTON, D.C.

ASSOCIATES

Bonnie J. Austin | Martin T. Moe
Catharine A. Hartzenbusch | Anand S. Raman
Stephen P. Vaughn

For Complete List of Firm Personnel, See General Section

For full biographical listings, see the Martindale-Hubbell Law Directory

SLADE & ASSOCIATES, P.C. (AV)

11 Vestry Street, 5th Floor, 10013
Telephone: 212-226-8787
Fax: 212-226-3619
URL: http://www.lawyers.com/slade&associatespc

Jeffrey C. Slade

Marianne Yen | Bridget Connolly

OF COUNSEL

Douglas E. Grover | Norman A. Bloch

For full biographical listings, see the Martindale-Hubbell Law Directory

STEIN RISO MANTEL HASPEL & JACOBS LLP (AV)

405 Lexington Avenue, 42nd Floor, 10174
Telephone: 212-599-1515
Fax: 212-599-6155
Email: email@srmhj.com
New City, New York Office: 254 South Main Street, 10956.
Telephone: 914-634-1010.
Fax: 914-634-8317.

Dennis L. Stein | Allan D. Mantel
Gerard A. Riso | Joseph J. Haspel
Neil I. Jacobs

Beth E. Spickler | Kevin M. McDonough

COUNSEL

Mark Ira Chinitz

For full biographical listings, see the Martindale-Hubbell Law Directory

STILLMAN & FRIEDMAN, P.C. (AV)

425 Park Avenue, 10022
Telephone: 212-223-0200
Telecopier: 212-223-1942

Charles A. Stillman | Scott M. Himes
Julian W. Friedman | Marjorie J. Peerce
Paul Shechtman | John B. Harris
Peter A. Chavkin | James A. Mitchell
Michael J. Grudberg

Peter E. Dolotta | Nathaniel Z. Marmur
Sara Beth Savage | Sean T. Haran
Lauren Goldberg | Jody L. King
Samantha J. Leventhal

For full biographical listings, see the Martindale-Hubbell Law Directory

STANLEY A. TEITLER, P.C. (AV)

299 Broadway, Suite 1500, 10007
Telephone: 212-233-8031
Fax: 212-233-8864

Stanley A. Teitler

For full biographical listings, see the Martindale-Hubbell Law Directory

WHITE & CASE (AV)

Limited Liability Partnership
1155 Avenue of the Americas, 10036-2787
Telephone: 212-819-8200
Telex: 233188 WHCA UR
Facsimile: 212-354-8113
URL: http://www.whitecase.com
New York, New York: 1140 Avenue of the Americas, New York, NY 10036-6700.
Telephone: 212-819-8900.
New York, New York: Litigation Support Center, 1120 Avenue of the Americas, New York, NY 10036-6700.
Telephone: 212-819-7977.
Facsimile: 212-7970/71.
Los Angeles, California:
Telephone: 213-620-7700.
Facsimile: 213-687-0758; 213-452-2330; 213-452-2331.
Palo Alto, California:
Telephone: 650-213-0300.
Facsimile: 650-213-8158.
San Francisco, California:
Telephone: 415-544-1100.
Facsimile: 415-544-0202.
Miami, Florida:
Telephone: 305-371-2700.
Telephone: 305-358-5744.
Facsimile: 305-358-5766.
Washington, D.C.:
Telephone: 202-626-3600.
Facsimile: 202-639-9355.
Bratislava, Slovak Republic:
Telephone: (421-7) 5441-5100.
Facsimile: (421-7) 5441-6100.
Brussels, Belgium:
Telephone: (32-2) 219-16-20.
Facsimile: (32-2) 219-16-26.
Budapest, Hungary: Réczicza Law Firm White & Case.
Telephone: (36-1) 488-5200.
Facsimile: (36-1) 488-5299.
Frankfurt, Germany: White & Case (Rechtsanwälte).
Telephone: (49-69) 713-77-(0).
Facsimile: (49-69) 713-77-100.
Helsinki, Finland: Asianajotoimisto White & Case Oy.
Telephone: (358-9) 228-641.
Facsimile: (358-9) 228-64228.
Istanbul, Turkey:
Telephone: (90-212) 275-75-33.
Facsimile: (90-212) 275-75-43.
London, England:
Telephone: (44-20) 7600-7300.
Facsimile: (44-20) 7600-7030.
Moscow, Russia:
Telephone: (7-095) 787-3000.
Facsimile: (7-095) 787-3001.
Paris, France:
Telephone: (33-1) 55-04-15-15.
Facsimile: (33-1) 55-04-15-16.
Prague, Czech Republic:
Telephone: (420-2) 2481-0808; 2481-1796.
Facsimile: (420-2) 2481-0330; 2481-0252.
Stockholm, Sweden: White & Case Advokat AB.
Telephone: (46-8) 506-323-00.
Facsimile: (46-8) 611-21-22.
Warsaw, Poland: White & Case (Poland) Sp. z o.o.
Telephone: (48-22) 625-33-33; (48-22) 622-67-67; (48-39) 12-19-06.
Facsimile: (48-22) 628-22-28.
Johannesburg, Republic of South Africa:
Telephone: 27 (11) 884-7689.
Facsimile: 27 (11) 884-7229.
Almaty, Kazakhstan:
Telephone: (7-3272) 50-74-91.
Facsimile: (7-3272) 50-74-93.
Ankara, Turkey:
Telephone: (90-312) 442-5680.
Facsimile: (90-312) 442-5691/4.
Bangkok, Thailand: White & Case (Thailand) Limited.
Telephone: (662) 656-1721 to 32.
Facsimile: (662) 656-1733/34.
Bombay/Mumbai, India: Liaison Office, (91-22) 282-6300/01/02/03.
Facsimile: (91-22) 282-6305.
Hanoi, Vietnam:
Telephone: (84-4) 934-5355.
Facsimile: (84-4) 934-5356.

(See Next Column)

WHITE & CASE—Continued

Ho Chi Minh City, Vietnam:
Telephone: (84-8) 821-0888.
Facsimile: (84-8) 823-6902.
Hong Kong:
Telephone: White & Case, Solicitors. (852) 2822-8700.
Facsimile: (852) 2845-9070.
Singapore, Republic of Singapore:
Telephone: (65) 225-6000.
Facsimile: (65) 225-6009.
Tokyo, Japan: White & Case Kandabashi Law Offices.
Telephone: (81-3) 3259-0200.
Facsimile: (81-3) 3259-0150.
Jeddah, Saudi Arabia: Law Office of Hassan Mahassni,
Telephone: (966-2) 665-4353.
Facsimile: (966-2) 669-2996.
Riyadh, Saudi Arabia: Law Office of Hassan Mahassni,
Telephone: (966-1) 464-4006.
Facsimile: (966-1) 465-1348.
Mexico City, Mexico: White & Case, S.C.
Telephone: (52) 5-540-9600.
Facsimile: (52) 5-540-9699.
São Paulo, SP, Brazil:
Telephone: (55-11) 3171-0011.
Facsimile: (55-11) 3171-0041.
Bombay/Mumbai, India: Associated Law Firm; India Law Services (ILS).
Telephones: (91-22) 284-1995; (91-22) 284-1847.
Facsimile: (91-22) 285-0824.
New Delhi, India: Associated Law Firm; India Law Services (ILS).
Telephone: (91-11) 697-1602/3/4.
Facsimile: (91-11) 698-8860.

MEMBERS OF FIRM

Richard J. Holwell
Marcos D. Jiménez (Miami, Florida Office)
Carolyn B. Lamm (Washington, D.C. Office)
Thomas McGanney
James J. McGuire
Philip H. Schaeffer

For Complete List of Firm Personnel, See General Section

For full biographical listings, see the Martindale-Hubbell Law Directory

*ROCHESTER,** Monroe Co.

TREVETT, LENWEAVER & SALZER, P.C. (AV)

700 Reynolds Arcade, 16 East Main Street, 14614
Telephone: 716-454-2181
Telecopier: 716-454-4026

Oscar J. Brown (1884-1958)
Melvin H. Zurett (1905-1967)
Eric P. Smith (1900-1967)
Thomas W. Sullivan (1916-1981)
William V. Gough (1922-1985)
Walter C. Eves (Retired)
Robert T. Skipworth (Retired)
Ronald James Summers (Retired)
Thomas N. Trevett
Bohdan Wenglowskyj
Thomas E. Lenweaver
Kenneth Bersani
Richard M. Doyle
James A. Valenti
Karl F. Salzer
Peter A. Jacobson
Louis B. Cristo
Cynthia A. Constantino
Henry L. Jesserer, III
Lawrence J. Andolina
James C. Gocker

John C. Palermo
Jon Paul Getz
Nicole L. Black

Representative Clients: American Motorists Insurance Co.; Lumbermens Mutual Casualty Co.; Nationwide Mutual Insurance Co.; Interboro Mutual Indemnity Insurance Co.; Michigan Mutual Liability Insurance Co.; Virginia Surety Co.; Allstate Insurance Co.; American Hardware Insurance Co.; Pearl Assurance Co., Ltd.

For full biographical listings, see the Martindale-Hubbell Law Directory

*SYRACUSE,** Onondaga Co.

LYNN LAW OFFICE (AV)

802 M & T Bank Building, 101 S. Salina Street, 13202
Telephone: 315-474-1267
Fax: 315-474-4514
Skaneateles, New York Office: 88 East Genesee Street.
Telephone: 315-685-1207.
Fax: 315-685-1047.

MEMBERS OF FIRM

William F. Lynn
Patricia A. Lynn-Ford
Thomas F. Shannon

For full biographical listings, see the Martindale-Hubbell Law Directory

SANFORD MELTZER (AV)

712 Empire Building, 472 South Salina Street, 13202-2493
Telephone: 315-474-4205; 1-800-875-2493
Fax: 315-474-3199
Email: smeltzer@Dreamscape.com
DeWitt, New York Office: 120 Clearview Road.
Telephone: 315-474-4205.
Fax: 315-474-3199.

John P. Wallace

References: Merchants National Bank & Trust Co.; Bank of New York-Central Region.

For full biographical listings, see the Martindale-Hubbell Law Directory

*TROY,** Rensselaer Co.

E. STEWART JONES (AV)

28 Second Street, 12181
Telephone: 518-274-5820
Fax: 518-274-5875
Email: info@esjlaw.com

E. Stewart Jones, Jr.
W. Farley Jones
Jeffrey K. Anderson
David J. Taffany
Peter J. Moschetti, Jr.

OF COUNSEL

E. Stewart Jones
Arthur L. Rosen
Abbott H. Jones (1873-1939)
Charles W. Marshall (1882-1945)

References: Key Bank and On Bank; Troy Savings Bank.

For full biographical listings, see the Martindale-Hubbell Law Directory

*WHITE PLAINS,** Westchester Co.

JAMES F. DONOHUE (AV)

81 Main Street, Suite 505, 10601
Telephone: 914-949-7766
Fax: 914-949-0324

ASSOCIATE

Thomas M. Roach, Jr.

Representative Clients: Nova Casualty Co.
Reference: Chase Bank/NBW Division, White Plains Branch.

For full biographical listings, see the Martindale-Hubbell Law Directory

GREENSPAN & GREENSPAN (AV)

34 South Broadway, Suite 605, 10601-4400
Telephone: 914-946-2500
Cable Address: "Gadlex"
Telecopier: 914-946-1432
Email: GandGEsqs@aol.com
Boca Raton, Florida Office: Greenspan & Kane, 301 Yamato Road, Suite 3160.
Telephone: 561-995-8140.
Oradell, New Jersey Office: 690 Kinderkamack Rd., 07649.
Telephone: 201-599-2849; 800-553-6009.

MEMBERS OF FIRM

Leon J. Greenspan
Michael E. Greenspan

For full biographical listings, see the Martindale-Hubbell Law Directory

STEPHENS, BARONI, REILLY & LEWIS LLP (AV)

Northcourt Building, 175 Main Street, 10601
Telephone: 914-761-0300; 683-5185
Telecopier: 914-761-0995; 683-1323
URL: http://www.lawyers.com/sbrl
Cross River, New York Office: Northern Westchester Office, Old Post Road Professional Building, 10518.
Telephone: 914-763-3232.

MEMBERS OF FIRM

Gerald D. Reilly
Roland A. Baroni, Jr.
Stephen R. Lewis

ASSOCIATE

Roland T. Koke

OF COUNSEL

James R. Caruso (1906-1994)

For full biographical listings, see the Martindale-Hubbell Law Directory

NORTH CAROLINA

*ALBEMARLE,** Stanly Co.

FRED STOKES (AV)

237 North Second Street, P.O. Box 637, 28001
Telephone: 704-986-2200
Fax: 704-986-2210

For full biographical listings, see the Martindale-Hubbell Law Directory

*ASHEVILLE,** Buncombe Co.

ELMORE, ELMORE & WILLIAMS, P.A. (AV)

53 North Market Street, 28801
Telephone: 828-253-1492
Fax: 828-253-9648
Email: eewlaw@wnc.com *URL:* http://www.lawyers.com/elmore-elmore-williams

Bruce A. Elmore
Bruce A. Elmore, Jr.
Reed G. Williams

For full biographical listings, see the Martindale-Hubbell Law Directory

LONG, PARKER, WARREN & JONES, P.A. (AV)

Suite 600, 14 South Pack Square, P.O. Box 7216, 28801
Telephone: 828-258-2296
Fax: 828-253-1073

Robert B. Long, Jr.
William A. Parker
Steve Ray Warren
W. Scott Jones

Kimberly A. Lyda
Philip Scott Anderson

For full biographical listings, see the Martindale-Hubbell Law Directory

CHAPEL HILL, Orange Co.

J. KIRK OSBORN (AV)

100 Europa Drive, Suite 421, 27514
Telephone: 919-929-0987
Fax: 919-942-1822
Email: kirkosborn@aol.com

For full biographical listings, see the Martindale-Hubbell Law Directory

RUDOLF & MAHER, P.A. (AV)

312 West Franklin Street, 27516
Telephone: 919-967-4900
Fax: 919-967-4953

David S. Rudolf
Thomas K. Maher

For full biographical listings, see the Martindale-Hubbell Law Directory

BARRY T. WINSTON (AV)

The Center, Suite 300, 1506 East Franklin Street, 27514
Telephone: 919-967-8553
Fax: 919-968-4698

Reference: Village Bank.

For full biographical listings, see the Martindale-Hubbell Law Directory

*CHARLOTTE,** Mecklenburg Co.

BAILEY, PATTERSON, CADDELL, HART, MILLIKEN & BAILEY, P.A. (AV)

Suite 502, Cameron Brown Building, 301 South McDowell Street, 28204
Telephone: 704-333-8612
FAX: 704-333-5279
Email: BaileyPA8@aol.com

Allen A. Bailey
Michael A. Bailey
William J. Patterson
H. Morris Caddell, Jr.
Walter L. Hart, IV
Emery E. Milliken
Martha L. Ramsay
Helen Ruth Harwell

For full biographical listings, see the Martindale-Hubbell Law Directory

HAROLD J. BENDER (AV)

The John Price Carr House, 200 North McDowell Street, 28204
Telephone: 704-333-2169
Fax: 704-333-0837
Email: benderlaw@aol.com *URL:* http://www.lawyers.com/haroldbender

ASSOCIATES

Kevin L. Barnett
Richard Deke Falls

Reference: First Union National Bank.

For full biographical listings, see the Martindale-Hubbell Law Directory

DOZIER, MILLER, POLLARD & MURPHY (AV)

Cameron Brown Building, 301 South McDowell Street, Suite 700, 28204
Telephone: 704-372-6373
Fax: 704-347-0674
URL: http://www.dmpm.com

MEMBERS OF FIRM

W. Joseph Dozier, Jr.
R. Craig Miller, Jr.
Scott T. Pollard
Gary L. Murphy
William Patrick Hobson
Timothy H. Graham
George N. Miller
Richard S. Gordon
Thomas J. Falish
Kristin L. Smith

For full biographical listings, see the Martindale-Hubbell Law Directory

FERGUSON, STEIN, WALLAS, ADKINS, GRESHAM & SUMTER, P.A. (AV)

741 Kenilworth Avenue, Suite 300, 28204-2828
Telephone: 704-375-8461
Fax: 704-334-5654
Mailing Address: P.O. Box 36486, 28236-6486
Email: FSWAGS@aol.com
Chapel Hill, North Carolina Office: Suite 2, 312 West Franklin Street.
Telephone: 919-933-5300.
Fax: 919-967-4953.

James E. Ferguson, II
Adam Stein
(Resident, Chapel Hill Office)
Jonathan Wallas
Karl Adkins
John W. Gresham
Geraldine Sumter
Henderson Hill
Thomas M. Stern
(Resident, Chapel Hill Office)
C. Margaret Errington
Stephen Luke Largess

Rebecca Ann Thorne
James E. Ferguson, III
Corie Diane Pauling
Ann C. Todd

For full biographical listings, see the Martindale-Hubbell Law Directory

RAWLS & DICKINSON, P.A. (AV)

The Carillon Building, 227 West Trade Street Suite 2140, 28202
Telephone: 704-376-3200
Facsimile: 704-332-2716
URL: http://www.lawyers.com/rawls&dickinson

Eben T. Rawls III

Anthony G. Scheer

References: NationsBank of North Carolina; First Union National Bank of North Carolina.

For full biographical listings, see the Martindale-Hubbell Law Directory

LAW OFFICES OF JAMES F. WYATT III (AV)

435 East Morehead Street, 28202-2609
Telephone: 704-331-0767
Fax: 704-331-0773
Email: jfwlaw@charlotte.infi.net *URL:* http://www.lawyers.com/jamesfwyatt

ASSOCIATE

Robert A. Blake, Jr.

For full biographical listings, see the Martindale-Hubbell Law Directory

YURKO & OWENS, P.A. (AV)

402 West Trade Street, Suite 101, 28202
Telephone: 704-347-0407
Fax: 704-347-0441
URL: http://www.lawyers.com/yurkoandowens

Lyle J. Yurko
N. Todd Owens

For full biographical listings, see the Martindale-Hubbell Law Directory

*GREENSBORO,** Guilford Co.

CLIFFORD CLENDENIN O'HALE & JONES, L.L.P. (AV)

415 West Friendly Avenue, 27401
Telephone: 336-378-1212
Fax: 336-333-9820
Email: ccojcd@nr.infi.net

MEMBERS OF FIRM

Locke T. Clifford
Robert O'Hale
Walter L. Jones

For full biographical listings, see the Martindale-Hubbell Law Directory

*MORGANTON,** Burke Co.

BYRD, BYRD, ERVIN, WHISNANT, MCMAHON & ERVIN, P.A. (AV)

One Northsquare, Post Office Drawer 1269, 28680
Telephone: 828-437-4220
Fax: 828-438-4517
Email: info@byrdlaw.com

Joe K. Byrd (Retired)
Robert B. Byrd
John W. Ervin, Jr.
C. Scott Whisnant
Lawrence D. McMahon, Jr.
Robert C. Ervin
Peggy McDaniel Saunders

Michelle C. Pritchard

For full biographical listings, see the Martindale-Hubbell Law Directory

*RALEIGH,** Wake Co.

MANNING & CROUCH (AV)

133 Fayetteville Street Mall, Suite 210, P.O. Box 350, 27602
Telephone: 919-828-5778
Fax: 919-828-5045
Email: manninglaw@worldnet.att.net

Thomas C. Manning
James A. Crouch

LEGAL SUPPORT PERSONNEL
Janie Riggan (Paralegal)

For full biographical listings, see the Martindale-Hubbell Law Directory

*WILMINGTON,** New Hanover Co.

STEPHEN E. CULBRETH (AV)

514 Chestnut Street, P.O. Box 446, 28402
Telephone: 910-763-3416
Facsimile: 910-763-9975
Email: culbreth@wilmington.net *URL:* http://www.lawyers.com/culbrethlaw

For full biographical listings, see the Martindale-Hubbell Law Directory

HALL, CASHWELL & SULLIVAN, L.L.P. (AV)

718 Market Street, 28401
Telephone: 910-343-8433
Fax: 910-343-8165
Email: alex@hcslaw.com

Alexander M. Hall
Roseanna C. Cashwell
Dennis H. Sullivan, Jr.
John Green, II

For full biographical listings, see the Martindale-Hubbell Law Directory

HEWLETT, COLLINS AND ALLARD (AV)

515 Princess Street, P.O. Box 121, 28402
Telephone: 910-763-0156
Fax: 910-763-9998

MEMBERS OF FIRM

Addison Hewlett, Jr. (1912-1989)
John C. Collins
James L. Allard, Jr.

References: Centura Bank; North Carolina Troopers Assn. Inc.; North Carolina Police Benevolent Assn. Inc.

For full biographical listings, see the Martindale-Hubbell Law Directory

JOHNSON & LAMBETH (AV)

232 Princess Street, P.O. Box 660, 28402
Telephone: 910-763-0481
Fax: 910-251-1276
Email: johnlam@wilmington.net

MEMBERS OF FIRM

Robert White Johnson
Carter Tate Lambeth
Maynard M. Brown
Beth M. Bryant
John Gregory Tillery, III

References: BB & T; NationsBank.

For full biographical listings, see the Martindale-Hubbell Law Directory

ZIMMER AND ZIMMER, L.L.P. (AV)

111 Princess Street, P.O. Box 2628, 28402
Telephone: 910-763-4669
Telecopier: 910-762-1999

MEMBERS OF FIRM

Herbert J. Zimmer
Jeffrey Lee Zimmer

(See Next Column)

Miriam M. Thompson
Susan E. Sutton
Jay S. Neisen

Reference: Wachovia Bank of North Carolina, N.A.; Centura Bank.

For full biographical listings, see the Martindale-Hubbell Law Directory

*WINSTON-SALEM,** Forsyth Co.

WILLIAM L. COFER, P.A. (AV)

NationsBank Building, Suite 550, 380 Knollwood Street, 27103
Telephone: 336-722-2323
FAX: 336-724-6956

William L. Cofer

References: Wachovia Bank & Trust Co., N.A.; BB&T; CC&B.

For full biographical listings, see the Martindale-Hubbell Law Directory

EDDIE C. MITCHELL, P.A. (AV)

Suite 550 380 Knollwood Street, 27103
Telephone: 336-725-9597
Fax: 336-725-6662

Eddie C. Mitchell

References: Wachovia Bank & Trust Co., N.A.; First Citizens Bank and Trust Company.

For full biographical listings, see the Martindale-Hubbell Law Directory

WHITE AND CRUMPLER (AV)

11 West Fourth Street, 27101
Telephone: 336-725-1304
Fax: 336-761-8845

MEMBERS OF FIRM

James G. White (1924-1974)
Frank M. Armstrong (1900-1979)
Clyde C. Randolph, Jr. (1928-1995)
Fred G. Crumpler, Jr.
G. Edgar Parker
David B. Freedman
Dudley A. Witt

ASSOCIATES

Laurie A. Schlossberg
F. Kevin Mauney

OF COUNSEL

Barbara C. Westmoreland
Fred S. Hutchins, Jr.

Reference: Wachovia Bank and Trust Co., N.A., Winston-Salem, North Carolina.

For full biographical listings, see the Martindale-Hubbell Law Directory

NORTH DAKOTA

*FARGO,** Cass Co.

OHNSTAD TWICHELL, P.C. (AV)

15 Broadway, Suite 206, 58102
Telephone: 701-280-5801
Fax: 701-280-5803
West Fargo, North Dakota Office: 901 13th Avenue East, P.O. Box 458. Telephone 701-282-3249.
Fax: 701-282-0825.
Hillsboro, North Dakota Office: West Caledonia Avenue, P.O. Box 220. Telephone 701-436-5700.
Fax: 701-436-4025.
Mayville, North Dakota Office: 12 Third Street S.E., P.O. Box 547.
Telephone: 701-786-3251.
Fax: 701-786-4243.

Duane R. Breitling
Robert G. Hoy (Resident, West Fargo Office)

Representative Clients: First National Bank North Dakota; Bank of North Dakota; Quality Boneless Beef; City of West Fargo; Bond Counsel for Cities of Fargo, Jamestown, West Fargo and Valley City; Industrial Indemnity Co.; Integrity Insurance Co.; Westchester Fire Insurance Co.

For Complete List of Firm Personnel, See General Section

For full biographical listings, see the Martindale-Hubbell Law Directory

VOGEL, WEIR, BYE, HUNKE & MCCORMICK, LTD. (AV)

502 First Avenue North, P.O. Box 1389, 58107
Telephone: 701-237-6983
Facsimile: 701-237-0847
Email: vogellaw@vogellaw.com *URL:* http://www.vogellaw.com

(See Next Column)

VOGEL, WEIR, BYE, HUNKE & MCCORMICK LTD., *Fargo—Continued*

Mart Daniel Vogel | Bruce Douglas Quick

For Complete List of Firm Personnel, See General Section

For full biographical listings, see the Martindale-Hubbell Law Directory

OHIO

*AKRON,** Summit Co.

MENTZER, VUILLEMIN AND MYGRANT LTD. (AV)

1 Cascade Plaza, 20th Floor, 44308-1114
Telephone: 330-376-7500
Telecopier: 330-376-8018
Email: mvmlaw@juno.com

Lawrence W. Vuillemin | Donald J. Malarcik, Jr.

Reference: National City Bank, Akron, Ohio.

For full biographical listings, see the Martindale-Hubbell Law Directory

*CINCINNATI,** Hamilton Co.

CATHY R. COOK (AV)

250 Pendleton Square, 430 Reading Road, 45202-1103
Telephone: 513-241-4029
Fax: 513-723-8634
Email: CCook98767@aol.com *URL:* http://www.lawyers.com/cathycooklaw

For full biographical listings, see the Martindale-Hubbell Law Directory

SIRKIN PINALES MEZIBOV & SCHWARTZ (AV)

920 Fourth & Race Tower, 105 West Fourth Street, 45202-2776
Telephone: 513-721-4876
Telecopier: 513-721-0876
Email: spms@fuse.net

MEMBERS OF FIRM

H. Louis Sirkin | Marc D. Mezibov
Martin S. Pinales | Howard M. Schwartz

Reference: The Huntington National Bank.

For full biographical listings, see the Martindale-Hubbell Law Directory

*CLEVELAND,** Cuyahoga Co.

BERNARD, HAFFEY & BOHNERT CO., L.P.A. (AV)

Jefferson Centre, 5001 Mayfield Road #301, P.O. Box 24005, 44124-0005
Telephone: 216-291-3600
FAX: 216-291-0159
URL: http://www.lawyers.com/bernardhaffey&bohnert

Clifford H. Bernard (1907-1985) | Edward G. Bohnert
J. Ross Haffey, Jr. | Timothy P. Haffey

Reference: KeyBank.

For full biographical listings, see the Martindale-Hubbell Law Directory

JOHN B. GIBBONS (AV)

2000 Standard Building, 1370 Ontario Street, 44113
Telephone: 216-363-6048
Fax: 216-363-6013; 216-363-6075
Voice Mail: 216-363-6086
URL: http://www.lawyers.com/jbgibbonslaw

For full biographical listings, see the Martindale-Hubbell Law Directory

HENNENBERG & ASSOCIATES (AV)

30100 Chagrin Boulevard, Suite 301, 44124-5704
Telephone: 216-765-9600
Fax: 216-765-8292
Email: Hennenberg@aol.com

Michael C. Hennenberg

ASSOCIATE

John A. Fatica

For full biographical listings, see the Martindale-Hubbell Law Directory

JONES, DAY, REAVIS & POGUE (AV)

North Point, 901 Lakeside Avenue, 44114
Telephone: 216-586-3939
Telecopier: 216-579-0212
Email: counsel@jonesday.com *URL:* http://www.jonesday.com
In Columbus, Ohio: 1900 Huntington Center.
Telephone: 614-469-3939.
Telecopier: 614-461-4198.

(See Next Column)

In Atlanta, Georgia: 3500 SunTrust Plaza, 303 Peachtree Street.
Telephone: 404-521-3939.
Telecopier: 404-581-8330.
In Brussels, Belgium: Avenue Louise 480, 7th Floor. B-1050 Brussels.
Telephone: 32-2-645-14-11.
Telecopier: 32-2-645-14-45.
In Chicago, Illinois: 77 West Wacker.
Telephone: 312-782-3939.
Telecopier: 312-782-8585.
In Dallas, Texas: 2727 North Harwood Street.
Telephone: 214-220-3939.
Telecopier: 214-969-5100.
In Frankfurt, Germany: Hochhaus am Park, Grüneburgweg 102, 60323 Frankfurt am Main.
Telephone: 49-69-9726-3939.
Telecopier: 49-69-9726-3993.
In Geneva, Switzerland: 20, rue de Candolle.
Telephone: 41-22-320-2339.
Telecopier: 41-22-320-1232.
In Hong Kong, China: 29th Floor, Entertainment Building, 30 Queen's Road Central.
Telephone: 852-2526-6895.
Telecopier: 852-2868-5871 or 852-2868-5699.
In Irvine, California: 5 Park Plaza, Suite 1100.
Telephone: 949-851-3939.
Telecopier: 949-553-7539.
In London, England: Bucklersbury House, 3 Queen Victoria Street.
Telephone: 44-171-236-3939.
Telecopier: 44-171-236-1113.
In Los Angeles, California: 555 West Fifth Street, Suite 4600.
Telephone: 213-489-3939.
Telecopier: 213-243-2539.
In New Delhi, India (Associate Office): Pathak & Associates (an associate firm of Jones, Day, Reavis & Pogue), 1st Floor, Dr. Gopal Das Bhaven, 28 Barakhamba Road.
Telephone: 91-11-373-8793; 91-11-335-7345.
Telecopier: 91-11-335-3761.
In New York, N.Y.: 599 Lexington Avenue.
Telephone: 212-326-3939.
Telecopier: 212-755-7306.
In Paris, France: 120, rue du Faubourg Saint-Honoré.
Telephone: 33-1-56-59-39-39.
Telecopier: 33-1-56-59-39-38
In Pittsburgh, Pennsylvania: 500 Grant Street, 31st Floor.
Telephone: 412-391-3939.
Telecopier: 412-394-7959.
In Riyadh, Saudi Arabia: The International Law Firm (In Association with Jones, Day, Reavis & Pogue), Sulaymaniyah, Prince Mishari IBN, Abdulaziz Street, P.O. Box 22166.
Telephone: (966-1) 462-8866.
Telecopier: (966-1) 462-9001.
In Shanghai, China: 2805 Kerry Centre, 1515 Nanjing Road West.
Telephone: 86-21-5298-6568.
Telecopier: 86-21-5298-6569.
In Sydney, Australia: Governor Phillip Tower, Level 38, 1 Farrer Place.
Telephone: 61-2-9210-6921.
Telecopier: 61-2-9210-6926.
In Taipei, Taiwan: 8th Floor, Tun Hwa South Road, Section 2.
Telephone: (886-2) 2704-6808.
Telecopier: (886-2) 2704-6791.
In Tokyo, Japan: Toranomon MT Building, 4th Floor, 10-3, Toranomon 3-Chome, Minato-ku, Tokyo 105, Japan.
Telephone: 81-3-3433-3939.
Telecopier: 81-3-5401-2725.
In Washington, D.C.: 51 Louisiana Avenue, N.W.
Telephone: 202-879-3939.
Telecopier: 202-626-1700.

MEMBER OF FIRM IN CLEVELAND

George J. Moscarino

For Complete List of Firm Personnel, See General Section

For full biographical listings, see the Martindale-Hubbell Law Directory

KOBLENTZ & KOBLENTZ (AV)

55 Public Square, Suite 1170, 44113
Telephone: 216-621-3012
Fax: 216-621-6567
URL: http://www.lawyers.com/koblentz&koblentz

Richard S. Koblentz

For full biographical listings, see the Martindale-Hubbell Law Directory

*COLUMBUS,** Franklin Co.

GERTNER & GERTNER (AV)

Suite 1780, 88 East Broad Street, 43215
Telephone: 614-463-9393
Fax: 614-463-9669
URL: http://www.lawyers.com/gertner&gertner

(See Next Column)

GERTNER & GERTNER—*Continued*

MEMBERS OF FIRM

Abraham Gertner (1909-1996) Michael H. Gertner

For full biographical listings, see the Martindale-Hubbell Law Directory

KETCHAM & KETCHAM (AV)

Suite 1416, 50 West Broad Street, 43215
Telephone: 614-224-2176

MEMBERS OF FIRM

Victor A. Ketcham Richard S. Ketcham

Reference: Key Bank.

For full biographical listings, see the Martindale-Hubbell Law Directory

SAMUEL B. WEINER CO., L.P.A. (AV)

743 South Front Street, 43206
Telephone: 614-443-6581
Fax: 614-443-9978

Samuel Weiner

For full biographical listings, see the Martindale-Hubbell Law Directory

WINTERS & MERKLE (AV)

500 South Front Street, Suite 900, 43215
Telephone: 614-228-0068
FAX: 614-228-1660

David C. Winters H. Tim Merkle

Reference: National City Bank.

For full biographical listings, see the Martindale-Hubbell Law Directory

*DAYTON,** Montgomery Co.

RION, RION & RION, L.P.A. INC. (AV)

Suite 1630, One First National Plaza, 130 West Second Street, P.O. Box 1262, 45402
Telephone: 937-223-9133
Fax: 937-223-7540
Email: info@rionlaw.com

John H. Rion Kevin L. Lennen
Jon Paul Rion Steven T. Pierson
David P. Mesaros

OF COUNSEL

Matthew H. Wilson

For full biographical listings, see the Martindale-Hubbell Law Directory

*EATON,** Preble Co.

BENNETT & BENNETT (AV)

Bennett Law Building, 200 West Main Street, 45320
Telephone: 937-456-5100; 456-4100
Fax: 937-456-4300; 456-7278

MEMBERS OF FIRM

Lloyd B. Bennett (1909-1983) Herd L. Bennett
Gray W. Bennett

Representative Clients: The National Hummel Foundation and Museum; Star Bank NA, Eaton, Ohio; Eaton National Bank & Trust Co.; First National Bank of Southwestern Ohio; Brookville National Bank; Farm Credit Services of Mid-America, ACA; Miller's Super Markets, Inc.; Northedge Shopping Center, Inc.; Herman M. Brubaker Registered Holstein Cattle; The Eaton Foundation.

For Complete List of Firm Personnel, See General Section

For full biographical listings, see the Martindale-Hubbell Law Directory

ROCKY RIVER, Cuyahoga Co.

LAW OFFICES OF JAY MILANO (AV)

2639 Wooster Road, 44116
Telephone: 440-356-2828
Fax: 440-356-2873
Email: milanolaw@aol.com *URL:* http://www.lawyers.com/jmilanolaw
Cleveland Heights, Ohio Office: 3820 Monticello Boulevard, 44121.
Telephone: 216-382-1500.
Fax: 216-382-6843.

ASSOCIATES

Michael P. Mayer Kathryn Gonser Eloff
Rachel M. Weiser

For full biographical listings, see the Martindale-Hubbell Law Directory

OKLAHOMA

*ENID,** Garfield Co.

JONES & WYATT (AV)

Suite 1100 Broadway Tower, 114 East Broadway, P.O. Box 472, 73702
Telephone: 580-242-5500
Fax: 580-242-4556

MEMBERS OF FIRM

Stephen Jones Robert L. Wyatt, IV

ASSOCIATES

April McCurdy Davis Leah Fillbach Lenzendorf

Representative Clients: Timothy McVeigh (OKC bombing); City of Enid, Oklahoma; Bert M. Avery, M.D.; John H. Migliaccio, M.D.; Father Phillip Berrigan; Abbie Hoffman; Sid Laughlin, D.O.; Col. Thomas Hill; Cummins Construction Co.; Independent Postal System of America (IPSA).

For full biographical listings, see the Martindale-Hubbell Law Directory

*OKLAHOMA CITY,** Oklahoma Co.

ADAMS & ASSOCIATES (AV)

City Place Building, 204 North Robinson Twenty-Fifth Floor, 73102
Telephone: 405-232-9100
Fax: 405-232-9114
Email: Adams1@IAmerica.net

R. Scott Adams

ASSOCIATES

Josh T. Welch Joe Brett Reynolds

OF COUNSEL

O. Clifton Gooding

For full biographical listings, see the Martindale-Hubbell Law Directory

FRANCIS COURBOIS (AV)

2000 Citizens Tower, 2200 Classen Boulevard, 73106
Telephone: 405-524-7507
Telecopier: 405-524-7505

For full biographical listings, see the Martindale-Hubbell Law Directory

GARY J. JAMES (AV)

3700 North Classen Boulevard, Suite 210, P.O. Box 26684, 73126
Telephone: 405-521-9900
Fax: 405-525-6004

For full biographical listings, see the Martindale-Hubbell Law Directory

MARTIN LAW OFFICE (AV)

Suite 360, 119 North Robinson Avenue, 73102
Telephone: 405-236-8888
Fax: 405-236-8844

Mack K. Martin Laurel Susan Darrow
J. David Ogle

For full biographical listings, see the Martindale-Hubbell Law Directory

JOSEPH LUIS RUFFIN, P.C. (AV)

City Place Building, 204 North Robinson, Suite 2300, 73102
Telephone: 405-232-6006
Fax: 405-232-9114
Email: ruflaw@aol.com

Joseph Luis Ruffin

For full biographical listings, see the Martindale-Hubbell Law Directory

WHITE LAW FIRM (AV)

900 N.E. 63rd Street, P.O. Box 18427, 73154
Telephone: 405-858-8899
Fax: 405-858-8844
Email: whitelawok@aol.com

Joe E. White, Jr.

ASSOCIATES

Greg S. Wilson Derek B. Smith

For full biographical listings, see the Martindale-Hubbell Law Directory

*TULSA,** Tulsa Co.

SNEED LANG, P.C. (AV)

2300 Williams Center Tower II, Two West Second Street, 74103
Telephone: 918-583-3145
Telecopier: 918-582-0410

(See Next Column)

SNEED LANG P.C., *Tulsa—Continued*

James C. Lang
D. Faith Orlowski
Brian S. Gaskill
G. Steven Stidham
Stephen R. McNamara
Thomas E. Black, Jr.
Robbie Emery Burke
Patrick O. Waddel
Randolph P. Stainer
Steven K. Balman
Brian T. Inbody
D. Michael McBride III

OF COUNSEL

James L. Sneed

Representative Clients: Amoco Production Co.; Bank One, Texas; Enron Corp.; Halliburton Energy Services; Helmerich & Payne, Inc.; Shell Oil Co.; State Farm Mutual Automobile Insurance Co.; The Williams Companies.

For full biographical listings, see the Martindale-Hubbell Law Directory

PENNSYLVANIA

*ALLENTOWN,** Lehigh Co.

HUBER AND WALDRON (AV)

535 Hamilton Mall, Suite 301, 18101
Telephone: 610-435-9790
FAX: 610-435-1238

MEMBERS OF FIRM

James T. Huber
John J. Waldron

For full biographical listings, see the Martindale-Hubbell Law Directory

BETHLEHEM, Northampton Co.

O'HARE & HEITCZMAN (AV)

18 East Market Street, P.O. Box 1446, 18018
Telephone: 610-691-5500
Fax: 610-691-7866
Email: heitczman@nni.com *URL:* http://www.heitczman.com

MEMBERS OF FIRM

Bernard V. O'Hare, Jr. (1923-1990)
George A. Heitczman

References: Summit Bank; CoreStates Bank.

For full biographical listings, see the Martindale-Hubbell Law Directory

BLUE BELL, Montgomery Co.

GERBER & GERBER (AV)

790 Penllyn-Blue Bell Pike, Suite 100, 19422
Telephone: 610-279-6700; 215-540-9100
Fax: 215-540-9424
Email: grbrlaw@dynanet.com *URL:* http://www.lawyers.com/gerber&gerber

Morris Gerber (1908-1995)

MEMBER OF FIRM

A. Richard Gerber

For full biographical listings, see the Martindale-Hubbell Law Directory

SHINGLES & CAPPELLI (AV)

794 Penllyn Blue Bell Pike, Suite 101, 19422
Telephone: 610-941-4444
Fax: 610-941-9880
800-974-9444
URL: http://www.lawyers.com/shingles&cappelli

MEMBERS OF FIRM

Stanley M. Shingles
Joseph J. Cappelli

ASSOCIATES

Elizabeth L. Schmidt
Shawn M. Sassaman

OF COUNSEL

Robert J. F. Brobyn

SPECIAL COUNSEL

Joseph S. Ziccardi

For full biographical listings, see the Martindale-Hubbell Law Directory

*EASTON,** Northampton Co.

PHILIP D. LAUER, P.C. (AV)

704 Washington Street, 18042
Telephone: 610-258-5329
Fax: 610-258-0155
Email: laueresq@enter.net *URL:* http://www.lawyers.com/laueresq

Philip D. Lauer

(See Next Column)

Robert Einar Sletvold

Reference: Nazareth National Bank.

For full biographical listings, see the Martindale-Hubbell Law Directory

*GREENSBURG,** Westmoreland Co.

BELDEN, BELDEN, PERSIN & JOHNSTON (AV)

Belden Building, 117 North Main Street, 15601
Telephone: 724-834-0300
Fax: 724-834-1307

MEMBERS OF FIRM

H. Reginald Belden (1907-1993)
H. Reginald Belden, Jr.
Dennis N. Persin
Robert I. Johnston

ASSOCIATES

John K. Greiner
Jeffrey D. Monzo

Represent: GenCorp.; Moore & Morford, Inc.; Standard Steel; Equipment Finance Co.; The Home Insurance Co.; Westmoreland Museum of Art; Grange Mutual Insurance Co.; Bell Telephone of Pennsylvania; Coregil Group; Westmoreland-Fayette Municipal Sewage Authority.

For full biographical listings, see the Martindale-Hubbell Law Directory

*HARRISBURG,** Dauphin Co.

GOLDBERG, KATZMAN & SHIPMAN, P.C. (AV)

320 Market Street - Strawberry Square, P.O. Box 1268, 17108-1268
Telephone: 717-234-4161
Telecopier: 717-234-6808; 717-234-6810
Email: gks@gkslaw.com

Ronald M. Katzman
Paul J. Esposito
Jerry J. Russo

Diana Woodside

OF COUNSEL

Arthur L. Goldberg
Joshua D. Lock

Reference: Fulton Bank.

For Complete List of Firm Personnel, See General Section

For full biographical listings, see the Martindale-Hubbell Law Directory

KILLIAN & GEPHART, LLP (AV)

218 Pine Street, P.O. Box 886, 17108
Telephone: 717-232-1851
Telecopier: 717-238-0592
Email: kg@killiangephart.com *URL:* http://www.killiangephart.com

MEMBERS OF FIRM

Smith B. Gephart
Terrence J. McGowan

ASSOCIATE

Bradley A. Schutjer

Reference: Fulton Bank.

For full biographical listings, see the Martindale-Hubbell Law Directory

THE LAW OFFICES OF SPERO T. LAPPAS (AV)

205 State Street, P.O. Box 808, 17108-0808
Telephone: 717-238-4286
Fax: 717-238-4826
Email: Lawyers@Lawyers1.com *URL:* http://www.Lawyer1.com

ASSOCIATE

Ann Economou Ariano

For full biographical listings, see the Martindale-Hubbell Law Directory

MANCKE, WAGNER, HERSHEY AND TULLY (AV)

2233 North Front Street, 17110
Telephone: 717-234-7051

MEMBERS OF FIRM

John B. Mancke
P. Richard Wagner
David E. Hershey
William T. Tully

For full biographical listings, see the Martindale-Hubbell Law Directory

*MEDIA,** Delaware Co.

MICHAEL G. DEFINO (AV)

200 East State Street, Suite 108, 19063-3434
Telephone: 610-566-3131
Fax: 610-566-3232
Email: mgdlaw@dca.net *URL:* http://www.definolaw.com

OF COUNSEL

Dorothy S. Langton
Henry J. Lunardi
Jody T. Curcillo

For full biographical listings, see the Martindale-Hubbell Law Directory

Media—Continued

HUGHEY, FLICK & CATANIA (AV)

Monroe Professional Building, 117 North Monroe Street, P.O. Box 87, 19063-0087
Telephone: 610-565-9050; 565-9060
Fax: 610-891-7960
Email: hfcesq@erols.com *URL:* http://www.lawyers.com/hfcesq

Richard L. Hughey
James R. Flick
Joseph V. Catania
Stephen J. Schukraft

For full biographical listings, see the Martindale-Hubbell Law Directory

*PHILADELPHIA,** Philadelphia Co.

BRUCE G. CASSIDY & ASSOCIATES, P.A. (AV)

Suite 1040, 21 South 12th Street, 19107
Telephone: 215-568-6700
Fax: 215-568-4077
Email: bgclaw@aol.com
Princeton, New Jersey Office: 345 Witherspoon Street, 08542.
Telephone: 609-252-9800.
Fax: 609-252-9111.

Bruce G. Cassidy

David E. Breslau

OF COUNSEL

Dr. Peter H. Feuerstein (Not admitted United States)
Halina Pilarska (Not Admitted in United States)

For full biographical listings, see the Martindale-Hubbell Law Directory

CONRAD O'BRIEN GELLMAN & ROHN, P.C. (AV)

Sixteenth Floor, 1515 Market Street, 19102-1916
Telephone: 215-864-9600
Fax: 215-864-9620; 864-9621; 864-9622
Email: lawyers@cogr.com *URL:* http://www.COGR.COM
Cherry Hill, New Jersey Office: Woodland Falls Corporate Park, 200 Lake Drive East, Suite 206.
Telephone: 856-665-0888.
Fax: 856-665-5888.
West Chester, Pennsylvania Office: 17 West Gay Street, Suite 100.
Telephone: 610-701-9100.
Fax: 610-701-9195.

K. Robert Conrad
William J. O'Brien
Nancy J. Gellman
James J. Rohn
John (Jack) A. Guernsey
John H. McKeon, Jr.
Howard M. Klein
Robert N. Feltoon
Deborah J. Krabbendam
Patricia M. Hamill
Nicholas M. Centrella

OF COUNSEL

Alan Paul Novak
Robert A. Klein
Stephen Weaver
Clare Keefe Foster

Lisa B. Wershaw
Helen J. Esbenshade
Debra C. Swartz
Thomas W. Blair
Gabriel H. Holdsman
Jonathan K.M. Crawford (Not admitted in PA)
Andrew C. Hanan
Frank R. Emmerich Jr.
Jacquelyn J. Ager
Andrew R. Duffy
Kelly G. Huller
Steven Pachman
Susan L. Bucknum

For full biographical listings, see the Martindale-Hubbell Law Directory

DONOHUE AND DONOHUE (AV)

232 South Fourth Street, 19106
Telephone: 215-574-1080
Fax: 215-574-1255
URL: http://www.lawyers.com/donohuelaw
New York, N.Y. Office: 26 Broadway.
Telephone: 212-269-2330.
Telecopier: 212-269-5016.

John P. Donohue (Resident)

Patrick J. Egan
Melissa G. Pinheiro

For full biographical listings, see the Martindale-Hubbell Law Directory

F. EMMETT FITZPATRICK, P.C. (AV)

926 Public Ledger Building, 19106
Telephone: 215-925-5200
Fax: 215-925-5991
Email: info@toplaw.com *URL:* http://www.toplaw.com

F. Emmett Fitzpatrick
F. Emmett Fitzpatrick, III

NiaLena Caravasos

(See Next Column)

LEGAL SUPPORT PERSONNEL

Doreen Howley (Paralegal)

For full biographical listings, see the Martindale-Hubbell Law Directory

KIRK T. KARASZKIEWICZ & ASSOCIATES, P.C. (AV)

Suite 2230 100 South Broad Street, 19110
Telephone: 215-563-1900
Fax: 215-563-8330

Kirk T. Karaszkiewicz

For full biographical listings, see the Martindale-Hubbell Law Directory

EARL G. KAUFFMAN (AV)

The Bourse Building, Suite 585, 111 S. Independence Mall East, 19106
Telephone: 215-625-2708
Fax: 215-625-3998
Email: theatty@bellatlantic.net *URL:* http://www.lawyers.com/militarylawyer

For full biographical listings, see the Martindale-Hubbell Law Directory

LAW OFFICES OF HOWARD BRUCE KLEIN (AV)

(Previously with Blank, Rome, Comisky & McCauley)
1700 Market Street Suite 2632, 19103
Telephone: 215-972-1411
Fax: 215-972-0277
URL: http://www.howbrklein@aol.com

For full biographical listings, see the Martindale-Hubbell Law Directory

MARK JAY KRUM (AV)

1515 Market Street, Suite 1100, 19102
Telephone: 215-569-2650
Facsimile: 215-564-3066
Email: markjaykrum@attymail.com

For full biographical listings, see the Martindale-Hubbell Law Directory

NICHOLAS J. NASTASI A PROFESSIONAL CORPORATION (AV)

241 South 7th Street, 19106
Telephone: 215-625-2991
Fax: 215-923-7151
URL: http://www.njnlaw.com
URL: http://www.lawyers.com/njnlaw

Nicholas J. Nastasi

For full biographical listings, see the Martindale-Hubbell Law Directory

DANIEL M. PREMINGER, P.C. (AV)

Suite 1050, Robinson Building, 42 South 15th Street, 19102
Telephone: 215-564-1227
Fax: 215-564-0396
Cape May, New Jersey Office: 811 Columbia Avenue, P.O. Box 908, 08204.
Telephone: 609-463-9091.
Fax: 609-465-4061.

Daniel M. Preminger

For full biographical listings, see the Martindale-Hubbell Law Directory

ROSENTHAL AND WEISBERG, P.C. (AV)

Two Logan Square Suite 1565, 18th & Arch Streets, 19103
Telephone: 215-656-4100
Fax: 215-656-4119

Brian D. Rosenthal
Michael Stuart Weisberg

Neil T. Murray
Margaret M. Foley

LEGAL SUPPORT PERSONNEL

Wendy Frost (Paralegal)
Lynn Gibbs (Paralegal)

For full biographical listings, see the Martindale-Hubbell Law Directory

JAMES C. SCHWARTZMAN & ASSOCIATES, P.C. (AV)

1760 Market Street, 12th Floor, 19103
Telephone: 215-563-2233
Fax: 215-563-2134

James C. Schwartzman

Gary Tilles
Dana Pirone Garrity

For full biographical listings, see the Martindale-Hubbell Law Directory

Philadelphia—Continued

WILBRAHAM, LAWLER & BUBA, A PROFESSIONAL CORPORATION (AV)

1818 Market Street, Suite 3100, 19103-3631
Telephone: 215-564-4141
Fax: 215-564-4385
Email: @wlbdeflaw.com
Haddonfield, New Jersey Office: 24 Kings Highway West.
Telephone: 856-795-4422.
Fax: 856-795-4699.
Wilmington, Delaware Office: Stoney Batter Office Building, 5301 Limestone Road, Suite 221.
Telephone: 302-234-8217.
Fax: 302-234-8218.

Edward J. Wilbraham — Barbara J. Buba
Robert B. Lawler — Michael J. Block

R. Erick Chizmar — John S. Howarth
Kevin J. Maginnis — David M. Maselli
InSook Kim — Renee E. Berger
Sandra D. Terry-Crawford — Edward T. Finch
Sean P. Buggy

OF COUNSEL

Walter J. Timby, Jr. — Daniel J. Allan

Representative Clients: GAF Corporation; Armstrong World Industries, Inc.; U.S. Gypsum Company; Georgia-Pacific Corporation; ARCO; Shell; Royal; AIG; Chubb; Keystone.

For full biographical listings, see the Martindale-Hubbell Law Directory

*PITTSBURGH,** Allegheny Co.

GREENFIELD, BREWER, BAILOR & KAY (AV)

Greenfield Court, 1035-37 Fifth Avenue, 15219
Telephone: 412-261-4466
Fax: 412-261-4408
Email: galaw@nauticom.net *URL:* http://www.lawyers.com/gbbk

Stanley W. Greenfield — Martha E. Bailor
Graydon R. Brewer — Paul G. Kay

For full biographical listings, see the Martindale-Hubbell Law Directory

SWENSEN PERER & KONTOS (AV)

Two PNC Plaza, Suite 2710, 15222
Telephone: 412-281-1970
Fax: 412-281-2808
Email: general2@swensenperer.com
Erie, Pennsylvania Office: Swensen Perer & McCandless. 209 Court House Commons.
Telephone: 814-456-0489. Email: erie@swensenperer.com.

MEMBERS OF FIRM

Jan C. Swensen — John W. McCandless (Resident Partner, Erie Office)
Alan H. Perer
George M. Kontos

ASSOCIATES

Anthony C. Mengine — Daniel J. Sinclair

OF COUNSEL

Diane W. Perer — David A. Schroeder
Anthony J. Sciarrino

For full biographical listings, see the Martindale-Hubbell Law Directory

*POTTSVILLE,** Schuylkill Co.

EMMANUEL H. DIMITRIOU, P.C.

(See Reading)

*READING,** Berks Co.

EMMANUEL H. DIMITRIOU, P.C. (AV)

522-24 Court Street, P.O. Box 677, 19603
Telephone: 610-376-7466
Fax: 610-376-1259
Email: ehdpc@aol.com

Emmanuel H. Dimitriou — Eleni Dimitriou Geishauser

For full biographical listings, see the Martindale-Hubbell Law Directory

*SCRANTON,** Lackawanna Co.

MUNLEY, MUNLEY & CARTWRIGHT, P.C. (AV)

205 Madison Avenue, 18503
Telephone: 570-346-7401
Fax: 570-346-3452
URL: http://www.lawyers.com/mmclaw
Email: lawyers@munley.com *URL:* http://www.munley.com

(See Next Column)

Robert W. Munley

Reference: First National Bank of Jermyn.

For full biographical listings, see the Martindale-Hubbell Law Directory

*WEST CHESTER,** Chester Co.

DUFFY & GREEN (AV)

10 North Church Street, Suite 307, 19380
Telephone: 610-692-0500
Fax: 610-430-6668

MEMBERS OF FIRM

John J. Duffy — Joseph P. Green, Jr.

ASSOCIATE

P.J. Redmond

For full biographical listings, see the Martindale-Hubbell Law Directory

RHODE ISLAND

*PROVIDENCE,** Providence Co.

MANN & MITCHELL (AV)

Suite 501 Turks Head Place, 02903
Telephone: 401-351-5770
Telecopier: 401-521-4305
Email: rmann29@idt.net *URL:* http://www.lawyers.com/mannlaw

MEMBERS OF FIRM

Robert B. Mann — Suzanna J. Mitchell

For full biographical listings, see the Martindale-Hubbell Law Directory

WILLIAM T. MURPHY LAW OFFICES, INC. (AV)

The Calart Tower, 400 Reservoir Avenue, Suite 3L, 02907
Telephone: 401-461-7740
Telecopier: 401-461-7753

William T. Murphy

Charles A. Pisaturo, Jr. — Steven T. Hayes

Reference: Citizens Bank.

For full biographical listings, see the Martindale-Hubbell Law Directory

WESTERLY, Washington Co.

ADAMO AND NEWMAN (AV)

42 Granite Street, 02891
Telephone: 401-596-7795
Telecopier: 401-596-9000
URL: http://www.lawyers.com/adamonewmanlaw

MEMBERS OF FIRM

John Joseph Adamo — Edward H. Newman

For full biographical listings, see the Martindale-Hubbell Law Directory

SOUTH CAROLINA

*ANDERSON,** Anderson Co.

CHAPMAN, BYRHOLDT & YON (AV)

117 West Benson Street, P.O. Box 2506, 29622
Telephone: 864-225-1411
Fax: 864-231-9131

MEMBER OF FIRM

Bruce A. Byrholdt

For full biographical listings, see the Martindale-Hubbell Law Directory

*CHARLESTON,** Charleston Co.

BARR, UNGER AND MCINTOSH, L.L.C. (AV)

11 Broad Street, P.O. Box 1037, 29401
Telephone: 843-577-5083
Fax: 843-723-9039
Walterboro, South Carolina Office: 111A East Washington Street, 29488-3915.
Telephone: 843-549-9406.
Fax: 843-549-1058.
Edisto Island, South Carolina Office: 806 Oyster Park, 29438.
Telephone: 843-869-2389.
Fax: 843-869-0110.

(See Next Column)

BARR, UNGER AND MCINTOSH L.L.C.—*Continued*

MEMBERS OF FIRM

Capers G. Barr, III
William S. Barr
H. Wayne Unger, Jr.
H. Thomas McIntosh, Jr.
Capers G. Barr, IV

Adam E. Barr

Approved Attorneys for: Lawyers Title Insurance Corp.; Old Republic National Title Insurance Company.
References: NationsBank; Bank of South Carolina.

For full biographical listings, see the Martindale-Hubbell Law Directory

GEDNEY M. HOWE, III, P.A. (AV)
8 Chalmers Street, P.O. Box 1034, 29402
Telephone: 843-722-8048
FAX: 843-722-2140

Gedney M. Howe, Jr. (1914-1981)
Gedney M. Howe, III
Alvin J. Hammer

Caroline M.W. Dillon

For full biographical listings, see the Martindale-Hubbell Law Directory

LIONEL S. LOFTON (AV)
174 East Bay Street, Suite 302, P.O. Box 449, 29402-0449
Telephone: 803-722-6319
FAX: 803-722-6372

ASSOCIATE

Frances Cain-Lofton

For full biographical listings, see the Martindale-Hubbell Law Directory

SAVAGE & SAVAGE, P.A. (AV)
15 Prioleau Street, P.O. Box 1002, 29402-1002
Telephone: 843-720-7470
Fax: 843-720-7478
Email: savage@savlaw.com *URL:* http://savlaw.com

Andrew J. Savage, III
David L. Savage

For full biographical listings, see the Martindale-Hubbell Law Directory

URICCHIO, HOWE, KRELL, JACOBSON, TOPOREK & THEOS, P.A. (AV)
17 1/2 Broad Street, 29401
Telephone: 803-723-7491
1-800-899-1683
Fax: 803-577-4179
Mailing Address: P.O. Box 399, Charleston, S.C., 29402-0399
Email: uricchio@ix.netcom.com

Paul N. Uricchio, Jr.
Carl H. Jacobson
Arthur G. Howe
Alan David Toporek
Barry Krell
Jerry N. Theos
Gregory Daulton Keith

For full biographical listings, see the Martindale-Hubbell Law Directory

*COLUMBIA,** Richland Co.

FINKEL & ALTMAN, L.L.C. (AV)
Suite 1800, 1201 Main Street, P.O. Box 1799, 29202
Telephone: 803-765-2935
Fax: 803-252-0786
Email: webmaster@finkellaw.com *URL:* http://www.finkellaw.com
Charleston, South Carolina Office: 12 Exchange Street, P.O. Box 225.
Telephone: 843-577-5460.
Fax: 843-577-5135.

Gerald M. Finkel
Howard S. Sheftman
Charles S. Altman (Resident, Charleston South Carolina Office)
Elizabeth Henderson McCullough
Beverly J. Finkel
Harry L. Goldberg
Richard R. Gleissner

Janet B. Haigler
Kelley Y. Woody
Michael M. Shetterly
Laurie Pineau Davidson
Joseph Alton Bivens
Robert E. Culver

COUNSEL

Ralph C. McCullough, II
Elizabeth Rhodes

Representative Clients: Hewitt-Robins; 1st Union National Bank; Banc One Mortgage Co.; Motorola Communications & Electronics Corp.

For full biographical listings, see the Martindale-Hubbell Law Directory

GLENN MURPHY GRAY & STEPP, L.L.P. (AV)
B B & T Bank Building, Suite 390, 1901 Assembly Street, P.O. Box 1550, 29202-1550
Telephone: 803-765-1100
Telecopy: 803-765-0755

Terrell L. Glenn (1930-1993)

MEMBERS OF FIRM

Peter L. Murphy
Robert E. Stepp
Elizabeth Van Doren Gray
Elizabeth G. Howard

Robert C. Rhodes
Roland M. Franklin
Laura W. Robinson
C. Shawn Dryer

Reference: BB&T.

For full biographical listings, see the Martindale-Hubbell Law Directory

KING & VERNON, P.A. (AV)
1426 Richland Street, P.O. Box 7667, 29202
Telephone: 803-779-3090
Fax: 803-779-3396
Email: TVernon@usit.net *URL:* http://www.usit.net/users/lawyer/

Kermit S. King
W. Thomas Vernon

For Complete List of Firm Personnel, See General Section

For full biographical listings, see the Martindale-Hubbell Law Directory

JAN S. STRIFLING, P.A. (AV)
1116 Blanding Street, 29201
Telephone: 803-799-9650
Fax: 803-799-1625

Jan S. Strifling

For full biographical listings, see the Martindale-Hubbell Law Directory

JACK B. SWERLING (AV)
1720 Main Street, Suite 301, 29201
Telephone: 803-765-2626
Fax: 803-799-4059
Email: jacklaw@aol.com

For full biographical listings, see the Martindale-Hubbell Law Directory

TOMPKINS AND MCMASTER (AV)
Palmetto Building, Fourth Floor, 1400 Main Street, P.O. Box 7337, 29202
Telephone: 803-799-4499
Telefax: 803-252-2240

MEMBERS OF FIRM

Frank G. Tompkins (1874-1956)
John Gregg McMaster
Frank G. Tompkins, Jr. (1908-1973)
Henry Dargan McMaster
George Hunter McMaster
Elizabeth Eldridge (1895-1976)
Frank Barnwell McMaster

ASSOCIATE

Bryan P. Stirling
Karl S. Bowers

OF COUNSEL

Joseph D. McMaster

LEGAL SUPPORT PERSONNEL

Martin J. McClellan (Office Manager)

For full biographical listings, see the Martindale-Hubbell Law Directory

TURNER, PADGET, GRAHAM & LANEY, P.A. (AV)
Seventeenth Floor, 1901 Main Street, P.O. Box 1473, 29202
Telephone: 803-254-2200
Telecopy: 803-799-3957
Florence, South Carolina Office: Fourth Floor, 1831 West Evans Street, P.O. Box 5478, 29502.
Telephone: 843-662-9008.
Fax: 843-667-0828.
Charleston, South Carolina Office: 21 Broad Street, 1st Floor, P.O. Box 836, 29402.
Telephone: 843-723-1622.
Fax: 843-577-3369.

David W. Keller, Jr. (Resident, Florence, SC Office)

For Complete List of Firm Personnel, See General Section

For full biographical listings, see the Martindale-Hubbell Law Directory

*CONWAY,** Horry Co.

HEARN, BRITTAIN & MARTIN, P.A. (AV)

1206 Third Avenue, 29526
Telephone: 843-248-3172
Fax: 843-248-4911
Myrtle Beach, South Carolina Office: 4614 Oleander Drive.
Telephone: 843-449-8562.
Fax: 843-497-6124.

George M. Hearn, Jr.
L. Morgan Martin
Thomas C. Brittain
Scott B. Umstead
G. Scott Bellamy

Peter Lee Hearn, Sr.

For full biographical listings, see the Martindale-Hubbell Law Directory

*GREENVILLE,** Greenville Co.

LOVE, THORNTON, ARNOLD & THOMASON, P.A. (AV)

410 East Washington Street, P.O. Box 10045, 29603
Telephone: 864-242-6360
Telefax: 864-271-7972
Email: lovelaw@globalvision.net *URL:* http://www.ltatlaw.com
Greer, South Carolina Office: 1115 West Poinsett Street, P.O. Box 449, 29652-0449.
Telephone: 864-879-0144.
Telefax: 864-879-0149.

William A. Coates

For Complete List of Firm Personnel, See General Section

For full biographical listings, see the Martindale-Hubbell Law Directory

*SUMTER,** Sumter Co.

LEE, ERTER, WILSON, HOLLER & SMITH, L.L.C. (AV)

126 North Main Street, P.O. Box 580, 29150
Telephone: 803-778-2471
Telecopier: 803-778-1643

MEMBERS OF FIRM

John Dozier Lee, Jr. (1921-1999)
Harry C. Wilson, Jr.
Jack W. Erter, Jr.
David Cornwell Holler
G. Murrell Smith, Jr.

Representative Clients: South Carolina National Bank; Carolina Power and Light Co.; Peoples Natural Gas Company of South Carolina; BB&T; Allstate Insurance Co.; American Surety Co.; Prudential Insurance Company of America; General Telephone; Korn Industries, Inc.; V-B William Furniture Co., Inc.

For full biographical listings, see the Martindale-Hubbell Law Directory

SOUTH DAKOTA

LEAD, Lawrence Co.

FULLER, TELLINGHUISEN, GORDON & PERCY, P.C. (AV)

203 West Main Street, P.O. Box 898, 57754
Telephone: 605-584-2440
Fax: 605-584-1979
Email: leadlaw@mato.com
Spearfish, South Dakota Office: 132 East Illinois, 57783.
Telephone: 605-642-8080.
Fax: 605-642-1756. E-mail: spflaw@mato.com

A. P. Fuller
Bradley P. Gordon
Roger A. Tellinghuisen
Michelle Palmer Percy

Representative Clients: Homestake Mining Co.; Hotel Franklin & Gaming; Black Hills Novelty/Automatic Vending, Inc.; Northern Hills General Hospital; Lantis Enterprises, Inc.; Norwest Bank South Dakota N.A.; Lead-Deadwood Independent School District # 40-1; City of Lead.

For full biographical listings, see the Martindale-Hubbell Law Directory

TENNESSEE

*CHATTANOOGA,** Hamilton Co.

SUMMERS & WYATT, P.C. (AV)

500 Lindsay Street, 37402
Telephone: 423-265-2385
Fax: 423-266-5211
Email: summers@voy.net

(See Next Column)

Jerry H. Summers
Thomas L. Wyatt
Jeffrey W. Rufolo

For Complete List of Firm Personnel, See General Section

For full biographical listings, see the Martindale-Hubbell Law Directory

*KNOXVILLE,** Knox Co.

DANIEL & OBERMAN (AV)

An Association including a Professional Corporation
550 West Main Street, Suite 950, 37902
Telephone: 423-546-4292
Fax: 423-546-4294
URL: http://www.daolaw.com
URL: http://www.lawyers.com/daolaw

W. Zane Daniel (P.C.)
Steven Oberman

Jeffrey Zane Daniel
Jonathan D. Cooper
William Todd Daniel

Reference: NationsBank.

For full biographical listings, see the Martindale-Hubbell Law Directory

LEIBOWITZ & COHEN (AV)

608 Gay Street, S.W., 37902
Telephone: 423-637-1809
FAX: 423-637-9276

MEMBERS OF FIRM

Arnold G. Cohen
Lawrence P. Leibowitz

ASSOCIATE

Melissa A. Ashburn

OF COUNSEL

Russell T. Greene

For full biographical listings, see the Martindale-Hubbell Law Directory

PRYOR, FLYNN, PRIEST & HARBER (AV)

Suite 600 Two Centre Square, 625 Gay Street, P.O. Box 870, 37901
Telephone: 423-522-4191
Telecopier: 423-522-0910

Robert E. Pryor
Timothy A. Priest
Frank L. Flynn, Jr.
John K. Harber

ASSOCIATES

Mark E. Floyd
M. Christopher Coffey
Donald R. Coffey
Robert E. Pryor, Jr.

References: First Vantage Bank; Sun Trust Bank.

For full biographical listings, see the Martindale-Hubbell Law Directory

*MEMPHIS,** Shelby Co.

CAUSEY, CAYWOOD, TAYLOR, MCMANUS & BAILEY (AV)

A Professional Association, Not a Partnership
Suite 2400, 100 North Main Building, 38103
Telephone: 901-526-0206
Telecopier: 901-525-1540

James D. Causey

Jean E. Markowitz
David Shepherd Walker

For Complete List of Firm Personnel, See General Section

For full biographical listings, see the Martindale-Hubbell Law Directory

EVANS & PETREE (AV)

81 Monroe Avenue, 38103
Telephone: 901-525-6781
Telecopier: 901-527-7756

MEMBERS OF FIRM

Marion G. Evans (1877-1957)
Jack Petree (1921-1973)
Charles Pittman Cobb (Retired)
Elwood L. Edwards (Retired)
W. Lytle Nichol IV
John W. McQuiston II
Ernest G. Kelly, Jr.
Michael C. Williams
Joseph W. Barnwell, Jr.
David C. Scruggs
Leonard C. Dunavant, Jr.
E. Woods Weathersby
C. Bradford Foster III
Andrew H. Raines
Frank N. Stockdale Carney
Paul F. T. Edwards
Percy H. Harvey
Katharine A. Jungkind
Scott A. Frick
Michael R. Marshall
Richard E.M. Nichol, Jr.

Karen Baim Reagler

For full biographical listings, see the Martindale-Hubbell Law Directory

Memphis—Continued

HALE HEADRICK DEWEY & WOLF, PLLC (AV)

One Memphis Place, 200 Jefferson Avenue Suite 1450, 38103
Telephone: 901-523-1123
Fax: 901-523-7472
Nashville, Tennessee Office: Suntrust Bank Building, 201 Fourth Avenue North, Suite 1450, 37219.
Telephone: 615-843-5160.
Fax: 615-843-5165

Stephen P. Hale
S. Russell Headrick
H. Tucker Dewey
Herbert B. Wolf, Jr.
John S. Golwen

OF COUNSEL

Steven L. Gill

Jennifer Ziegenhorn
Wendy A. Geurin
John W. Campbell
Joseph M. Koury
Holly N. Knight
Charles S. Blatteis
Jennifer S. Kiesewetter
J. William Williams

For full biographical listings, see the Martindale-Hubbell Law Directory

HARRIS, SHELTON, DUNLAP AND COBB, P.L.L.C. (AV)

Suite 2700, One Commerce Square, 38103-2555
Telephone: 901-525-1455
Telecopier: 901-526-4084
Email: hsdclaw@hsdclaw.com
Other Memphis Office: 6363 Poplar, Suite 430.
Telephone: 901-682-1455.
Fax: 901-682-4446.
Oxford, Mississippi Office: 428 North Lamar Boulevard, Suite 2.
Telephone: 662-238-2855.
Fax: 662-238-2895.

MEMBERS OF FIRM

Walter Chandler (1887-1967)
John H. Harris, Jr.
Max Shelton
William W. Dunlap, Jr.
M. Anderson Cobb, Jr.
James L. Kirby
James R. Garts, Jr.
George T. Wheeler, Jr.
James D. Wilson
Charles C. Drennon, III (Resident, Poplar Avenue Office)
Michael F. Rafferty
A. Neal Graham
G. Rice Byars, Jr.
Jonathan E. Scharff

ASSOCIATES

Tabitha Francisco McNabb
Brett A. Hughes
Chesney Falk McAfee
Christopher S. Campbell
Estelle C. Gaerig
Donrua Barnes-Hulsey
Shawn L. Verner

For full biographical listings, see the Martindale-Hubbell Law Directory

*NASHVILLE,** Davidson Co.

HOLLINS, WAGSTER & YARBROUGH, P.C. (AV)

22nd Floor SunTrust Center, 424 Church Street, 37219
Telephone: 615-256-6666
Telecopier: 615-254-4254

John J. Hollins
John W. Wagster
Edward M. Yarbrough
John L. Norris
David L. Raybin
James L. Weatherly, Jr.
John J. Hollins, Jr.
Patrick T. McNally

Jacqueline B. Dixon

References: First American National Bank; Sun Trust Bank.

For full biographical listings, see the Martindale-Hubbell Law Directory

CHARLES R. RAY (AV)

211 Third Avenue, North, 37201
Telephone: 615-256-2111
Email: lawdog@worldnet.att.net

ASSOCIATE

Jeffrey S. Frensley

For full biographical listings, see the Martindale-Hubbell Law Directory

*TRENTON,** Gibson Co.

HARRELL AND HARRELL (AV)

110 NW Court Square, 38382
Telephone: 901-855-1351; 855-1352
Fax: 901-855-1212
Email: harrell@usit.net

MEMBER OF FIRM

Limmie Lee Harrell, Jr.

(See Next Column)

ASSOCIATE

Jerald M. Campbell, Jr.

Representative Clients: Trenton Gin Co., Trenton, Tenn.; Bank of Commerce, Trenton, Tenn.; Toshiba America; Chuck Graves Chevrolet, Olsmobile, Cadillac, GMC Trucks; Donnie Hatcher Chevrolet, Buick, Oldsmobile; Wade Electric Co.; Tecumseh, Inc., New Pacific Machinery, Inc.; Kellwood.
Reference: The Bank of Commerce, Trenton.

For full biographical listings, see the Martindale-Hubbell Law Directory

TEXAS

*AUSTIN,** Travis Co.

ALLISON & BASSETT, L.L.P. (AV)

2414 Exposition Boulevard Suite D-200, 78703
Telephone: 512-472-0144
Facsimile: 512-472-8418
URL: http://www.lawyers.com/ayblaw

William P. Allison
Samuel E. Bassett

For full biographical listings, see the Martindale-Hubbell Law Directory

MINTON, BURTON, FOSTER & COLLINS, A PROFESSIONAL CORPORATION (AV)

1100 Guadalupe Street, 78701-2198
Telephone: 512-476-4873
Fax: 512-479-8315

Perry L. Jones (1908-1969)
J. Travis Blakeslee (1919-1990)
Paul T. Holt (1906-1995)
Roy Q. Minton
Charles R. Burton
John L. Foster
Warren L. (Rip) Collins, Jr.
Randy T. Leavitt
Martha S. Dickie
Scott A. Young
John C. Carsey
David F. Minton
Jennifer Ramsey
Michael L.R. Burnett
Jeffrey David Miller

Representative Clients: South Texas Nuclear Operating Project; Reliant Energy; Stratus Properties; City of Cedar Park; Eco Resources, Inc.; International Game Technology; Texas Department of Public Safety; Texas Instruments; Intel, Inc.; Southern Union Gas Company.

For full biographical listings, see the Martindale-Hubbell Law Directory

MORRIS & FLOREY, L.L.P. (AV)

704 West 9th Street, 78701
Telephone: 512-479-8600

E. Gerry Morris
Ben Florey

References: Texas Commerce Bank; NationsBank.

For full biographical listings, see the Martindale-Hubbell Law Directory

THE LAW OFFICE OF WILLIAM A. WHITE (AV)

608 West 12th Street, Suite B, 78701
Telephone: 512-476-1494
Facsimile: 512-476-8050

For full biographical listings, see the Martindale-Hubbell Law Directory

CARROLLTON, Dallas & Denton Cos.

LAW OFFICES OF FRANK SHOR (AV)

Herald Hall, 1620 East Belt Line Road, 75006
Telephone: 972-242-8887
Fax: 972-446-7976

Representative Clients: Dallas Police Patrolman's Union; Lake Point Medical Center; Rudy's Tortillas; The Gas Pipe.
References: Fuller & Parker Court Reporters; Professional Civil Process.

For full biographical listings, see the Martindale-Hubbell Law Directory

*CORPUS CHRISTI,** Nueces Co.

CANALES & SIMONSON, P.C. (AV)

2601 Morgan Avenue, P.O. Box 5624, 78465-5624
Telephone: 512-883-0601
Telecopier: 512-884-7023
Email: tonycanales@canalessimonson.com

J. A. "Tony" Canales
Nancy M. Simonson

Barbara Canales Black
Jo Ellen Hewins
Patricia N. Canales

For full biographical listings, see the Martindale-Hubbell Law Directory

Corpus Christi—Continued

LAW OFFICES OF PAUL G. KRATZIG (AV)

600 Leopard Street, Suite 2100, 78473
Telephone: 361-883-3563
Telecopier: 361-883-0210
Email: kratzig@flash.net

For full biographical listings, see the Martindale-Hubbell Law Directory

*DALLAS,** Dallas Co.

BRUCE ANTON (AV)

705 Ross Avenue, 75202
Telephone: 214-741-9027
Telecopier: 214-748-7676
Email: BANTON28@aol.com *URL:* http://www.antonattorney.com

For full biographical listings, see the Martindale-Hubbell Law Directory

WILLIAM A. BRATTON, III (AV)

One Quadrangle Tower, 2828 Routh Street, Suite 850-LB10, 75201
Telephone: 214-871-1133
Telecopier: 214-871-0620
Email: wabatty@aol.com *URL:* http://www.lawyers.com/wmbratton

For full biographical listings, see the Martindale-Hubbell Law Directory

ELLISTON & ORMESHER, L.L.P. (AV)

1401 Elm Street, Suite 4585, 75202-2953
Telephone: 214-752-0400
Fax: 214-752-0404
URL: http://www.lawyers.com/elliston&ormesher

PARTNERS

D. Mark Elliston J. Russell Ormesher

OF COUNSEL

Susan R. Patterson

For full biographical listings, see the Martindale-Hubbell Law Directory

HUGHES & LUCE, L.L.P. (AV)

A Registered Limited Liability Partnership including Professional Corporations
1717 Main Street, Suite 2800, 75201
Telephone: 214-939-5500
Fax: 214-939-6100; 214-939-5849
Email: H&L@hugheslucecom *URL:* http://www.hughesluce.com
Austin, Texas Office: 111 Congress, Suite 900.
Telephone: 512-482-6800.
Fax: 512-482-6859.
Houston, Texas Office: 1600 Smith Street, Suite 3550.
Telephone: 713-754-5200.
Fax: 713-754-5270.

MEMBERS OF FIRM

Robert Edwin Davis Weston C. Loegering

ASSOCIATE

Marion Turner (Van) Van Bebber

For Complete List of Firm Personnel, See General Section

For full biographical listings, see the Martindale-Hubbell Law Directory

MILLS PRESBY AND ASSOCIATES, L.L.P. (AV)

5910 North Central Expressway Premier Place Suite 900, 75206-5141
Telephone: 214-265-9265
Fax: 214-363-3167
URL: http://www.millspresby.com

Thomas W. Mills, Jr. John M. Frick
Ellen A. Presby Lisa A. Schumacher

David S. Weber Jonathan Mark Spigel
Joseph D. Cohen

For full biographical listings, see the Martindale-Hubbell Law Directory

MILNER, LOBEL, GORANSON, SORRELS, UDASHEN & WELLS (AV)

Chateau Plaza, Suite 1500, 2515 McKinney Avenue, 75201
Telephone: 214-651-1121
Fax: 214-953-1366
URL: http://www.lawyers.com/mlgs-law

George R. Milner, Jr. Robert N. Udashen
Shirley Baccus-Lobel Gary A. Udashen
Ronald L. Goranson Ronald D. Wells
Barry Sorrels George R. Milner, III
J. Michael Price, II

(See Next Column)

LEGAL SUPPORT PERSONNEL

Janine Hargraves (Office Manager)

For full biographical listings, see the Martindale-Hubbell Law Directory

PROSPERE & RUSSELL (AV)

8111 Preston Road, Suite 500, 75225
Telephone: 214-750-8555; 888-892-7465
FAX: 214-750-8001
Email: texcrimlaw@aol.com *URL:* http://www.texcrimlaw.com

Reed W. Prospere Frederick M. Russell

LEGAL SUPPORT PERSONNEL

PARALEGALS

Leticia Sims Stan Smith

For full biographical listings, see the Martindale-Hubbell Law Directory

*DENTON,** Denton Co.

PHILIPS, HOPKINS, EAMES & COBB, P.C. (AV)

525 North Locust, P.O. Box 2027, 76202-2027
Telephone: 940-566-7010; Metro 940-243-0946
Facsimile: 940-898-0502
Email: dentonlaw.com

Gerald W. Cobb

OF COUNSEL

George Hopkins

Representative Clients: First Federal Bank of North Texas; First State Bank of Texas, Denton, Texas; Sanger Bank, Sanger, Texas; BankOne, Texas, N.A.; Provident Bank, Denton, Texas; Dentex Title Co., Denton, Texas.

For full biographical listings, see the Martindale-Hubbell Law Directory

*FORT WORTH,** Tarrant Co.

BATES & CASEY (AV)

201 Sundance Court, 115 West Second Street, 76102
Telephone: 817-332-6614
Fax: 817-332-2838

Earl E. "Ernie" Bates, Jr. Ward P. Casey

For full biographical listings, see the Martindale-Hubbell Law Directory

EVANS, GANDY, DANIEL & MOORE (AV)

An Association of Attorneys, Not a Partnership
Sundance Square, 115 West Second Street, Suite 202, 76102
Telephone: 817-332-3822
Metro: 817-429-4194

Tim Evans Mark G. Daniel
Donald S. Gandy Tim Moore
Lance Evans

For full biographical listings, see the Martindale-Hubbell Law Directory

KEARNEY & WESTFALL (AV)

1801 Bank One Tower, 500 Throckmorton Street, 76102-7414
Telephone: 817-336-5600
FAX: 817-336-5610
Email: kwilliams@kearneywestfall.com *URL:* http://www.kearneywestfall.com

Jeffrey A. Kearney Gregory B. Westfall

ASSOCIATE

Wm. Reagan Wynn

OF COUNSEL

Byron Matthews

For full biographical listings, see the Martindale-Hubbell Law Directory

MICHAEL L. WARE (AV)

111 North Houston, Suite 210, 76102
Telephone: 817-338-4100
Telecopier: 817-332-2416
URL: http://www.lawyers.com/michaelware

For full biographical listings, see the Martindale-Hubbell Law Directory

*HOUSTON,** Harris Co.

BERG & ANDROPHY (AV)

3704 Travis, 77002-9550
Telephone: 713-529-5622
Fax: 713-529-3785
URL: http://www.lawyers.com/b&alaw
Email: mail@bahou.com *URL:* http://www.bafirm.com
New York, New York Office: 230 Park Avenue, Suite 1000, 10169-1099.
Telephone: 212-808-6580.
Fax: 212-808-3020.

David H. Berg (P.C.) Joel M. Androphy

Wade T. Howard
Geoffrey A. Berg
Gabriel A. Berg (Not admitted in TX)

For full biographical listings, see the Martindale-Hubbell Law Directory

CARPENTER & ASSOCIATES (AV)

Suite 604, River Oaks Bank Building, 2001 Kirby Drive, 77019
Telephone: 713-528-3118
Facsimile: 713-528-3198
Email: wscarpenter@juno.com

W. Scott Carpenter

For full biographical listings, see the Martindale-Hubbell Law Directory

J. GORDON DEES A PROFESSIONAL CORPORATION (AV)

440 Louisiana Street, Suite 1950, 77002-1636
Telephone: 713-236-1551
Fax: 713-236-1738
Email: Gordondees@msn.com *URL:* http://www.lawyers.com/deeslaw

J. Gordon Dees

For full biographical listings, see the Martindale-Hubbell Law Directory

DEGUERIN & DICKSON (AV)

Seventh Floor, The Republic Building, 1018 Preston Avenue, 77002-1818
Telephone: 713-223-5959
Fax: 713-223-9231
Email: DDeGuerin@aol.com

MEMBER OF FIRM
Dick DeGuerin
OF COUNSEL
Lewis Dickson
ASSOCIATES

Matt Hennessy
Robert R. Luke
Neal Davis
John Parras

For full biographical listings, see the Martindale-Hubbell Law Directory

PHILIP H. HILDER & ASSOCIATES, P.C. (AV)

Two Houston Center, 909 Fannin Street, Suite 2020, 77010
Telephone: 713-655-9111
Fax: 713-655-9112
Email: hilderlaw@counsel.com *URL:* http://www.lawyers.com/hilderlaw

Philip H. Hilder

John Guidroz
OF COUNSEL
James A. Cerks

For full biographical listings, see the Martindale-Hubbell Law Directory

MITCHELL BAYLOR LANSDEN (AV)

700 Louisiana, Suite 4200, 77002
Telephone: 713-220-2224
Fax: 713-230-0016
Email: mlansden@kir.com *URL:* http://www.lawyers.com/fedstatecriminallaw

For full biographical listings, see the Martindale-Hubbell Law Directory

DOUGLAS C. MCNABB (AV)

6200 Chase Tower, 600 Travis Street, 77002
Telephone: 800-870-0828
Fax: 800-679-0679
URL: http://www.lawyers.com/federalcrimes
Email: dmcnabb@mciworld.com *URL:* http://www.federalcrimes.com

For full biographical listings, see the Martindale-Hubbell Law Directory

MOEN, CAIN & O'BRIEN (AV)

1800 Chase Bank Building, 707 Travis, 77002
Telephone: 713-222-9955
Fax: 713-222-6515

(See Next Column)

Robert A. Moen Dennis Cain
Douglas M. O'Brien

For full biographical listings, see the Martindale-Hubbell Law Directory

THOMAS L. ROYCE, JR. (AV)

614 River Oaks Bank Building, 2001 Kirby Drive, 77019
Telephone: 713-528-0055
Fax: 713-528-0199
Email: troycejr@aol.com *URL:* http://www.lawyers.com/thomaslroycejr

For full biographical listings, see the Martindale-Hubbell Law Directory

GEORGE H. TYSON, JR. (AV)

2120 Welch, 77019
Telephone: 713-523-7878
Fax: 713-523-7887
Email: TYSOR@aol.com

For full biographical listings, see the Martindale-Hubbell Law Directory

RONALD J. WASKA A PROFESSIONAL CORPORATION (AV)

952 Echo Lane, Suite 180, 77024-2783
Telephone: 713-461-8181
Fax: 713-461-8186
Email: rjwaska@worldnet.att.net

Ronald J. Waska

For full biographical listings, see the Martindale-Hubbell Law Directory

RONALD G. WOODS (AV)

5300 Memorial, Suite 1000, 77007
Telephone: 713-862-9600
Fax: 713-864-8738

For full biographical listings, see the Martindale-Hubbell Law Directory

*SAN ANTONIO,** Bexar Co.

EDERER & PRICE, L.L.C. (AV)

7800 IH 10 West Suite 135, 78230
Telephone: 210-341-4070
Fax: 210-892-5510 or 210-341-4459
Email: rone@edererprice.com

Ronald F. Ederer Steven P. Price

Randall A. Parker

For full biographical listings, see the Martindale-Hubbell Law Directory

GOLDSTEIN, GOLDSTEIN AND HILLEY (AV)

29th Floor, Tower Life Building, 310 S. St. Mary's Street, 78205
Telephone: 210-226-1463
Fax: 210-226-8367

MEMBERS OF FIRM

Eli Goldstein (1910-1998) Gerald H. Goldstein
Van G. Hilley

Patrick T. Peranteau Cynthia Hujar Orr
Anne More Burnham

For full biographical listings, see the Martindale-Hubbell Law Directory

HEARD LINEBARGER GRAHAM GOGGAN BLAIR PEÑA & SAMPSON, LLP (AV)

Tenth Floor, Tower Life Building, 310 South St. Mary's, 78205
Telephone: 210-225-6763
Facsimile: 210-225-6410
URL: http://www.publicans.com
Austin, Texas Office: 1949 South IH 35, 78741.
Telephone: 512-447-6675.
Fax: 512-443-3494.
Beaumont, Texas Office: 1148 Park, 77701.
Telephone: 409-832-9483.
Fax: 409-833-2638.
Brownsville, Texas Office: 3302 Boca Chica, Suite 105, 78521.
Telephone: 956-546-1216.
Fax: 956-546-4624.
Conroe, Texas Office: 103 W. Phillips, 77301.
Telephone: 409-760-1410.
Fax: 409-760-1285.
Corpus Christi, Texas Office: 500 N. Shoreline, Suite 1111, 78471.
Telephone: 512-888-6898.
Fax: 512-888-4405.
Corsicana, Texas Office: 1501 Northwood Boulevard, 75110.
Telephone: 903-872-3096.
Fax: 903-874-5007.

(See Next Column)

HEARD LINEBARGER GRAHAM GOGGAN BLAIR PEÑA & SAMPSON LLP, *San Antonio—Continued*

Dallas, Texas Office: 1720 Allianz Financial Centre, 2323 Bryan Street, 75201.
Telephone: 214-880-0089.
Fax: 214-754-7167.
Denton, Texas Office: 326-G East McKinney, 76201.
Telephone: 940-383-4460.
Fax: 940-382-2829.
Edinburg, Texas Office: 110 S. 12th Street, 78539.
Telephone: 956-383-4500.
Fax: 956-383-7820.
El Paso, Texas Office: 215 N. Stanton Street, 79901.
Telephone: 915-533-6637.
Fax: 915-532-7085.
Fort Worth, Texas Office: Oil & Gas Building, Suite 1414, 309 W. 7th Street, 76102.
Telephone: 817-877-4589.
Fax: 817-877-0601.
Houston, Texas Office: 1021 Main Street, Suite 1500, 77002.
Telephone: 713- 844-3400.
Fax: 713-844-3501.
Laredo, Texas Office: 1102 Scott, Suite 2B, 78041.
Telephone: 956-723-1303.
Fax: 956-723-1327.
Longview, Texas Office: 1127 Judson Road, Suite 111, 75601.
Telephone: 903-757-5448.
Fax: 903-758-3331.
Odessa, Texas Office: 1301 E. 8th Street, Suite 200, 79761.
Telephone: 915-332-9047.
Fax: 915-333-7012.
Richmond, Texas Office: 301 S. 9th Street, Suite 222, 77469.
Telephone: 281-342-9636.
Fax: 281-341-7808.
Sherman, Texas Office: 115 E. Lamar, 75091.
Telephone: 903-893-4941.
Fax: 903-868-0688.
Tyler, Texas Office: 1517 W. Front Street, Suite 202, 75702.
Telephone: 903-597-2897.
Fax: 903-597-2402.
The Woodlands, Texas Office: 10077 Grogan's Mill Road, Suite 535,v 77380-2924.
Telephone: 713-363-3632.
Fax: 281-363-3998.
New Orleans, Louisiana Office: 1515 Poydras Street, Suite 1840, 70112.
Telephone: 504-522-9100.
Fax: 504-522-9145.
Philadelphia, Pennsylvania Office: 123 S. Broad Street, Suite 1830, 19109.
Telephone: 215-790-1117.
Fax: 215-790-1197.

MEMBERS OF FIRM

Oliver S. Heard, Sr. (1915-1977)
Oliver S. Heard, Jr.
Dale Linebarger (Resident, Austin Office)
Russell R. Graham (Resident, Austin Office)
Thomas S. Goggan, III (Resident, Austin Office)
Stephen S. Blair (Resident, Austin Office)
Jim Blair (Resident, The Woodlands Office)
Juan M. Peña (Resident, Edinburg Office)
DeMetris Aquilla Sampson (Resident, Dallas Office)
David G. Aelvoet
Drew Aldinger (Resident, Philadelphia, Pennsylvania Office)
Bruce W. Anderson (Resident, Austin Office)
Kaye Applewhite (Resident, Conroe Office)
Thelma Banduch (Resident, Brownsville Office)
Gary B. Bennett (At Denton, Fort Worth and Sherman Offices)
Douglas S. Bird (Resident, Austin Office)
John R. Bolster (Resident, Tyler Office)
Phillipa L. Bowers (Resident, New Orleans, Louisiana Office)
Brian E. Brown (Resident, Austin Office)
Jeffrey K. Brown (Resident, Austin Office)
James H. Burshtyn (Resident, Austin Office)
Rebecca Bustamante
Olivero E. Canales (Resident, Laredo Office)
Paul D. Chapa (Resident, Corpus Christi Office)
Kevin D. Chester (Resident, Corsicana Office)
Cormac P. Creaven (Houston and Richmond Offices)
L. W. "Rusty" Dean (Resident, Tyler Office)
Michael W. Deeds (Resident, Houston Office)
Mary Belan Doggett
Clifton F. Douglass, III
James R. Evans, Jr. (Resident, Austin Office)
F. Duane Force (Resident, Austin Office)
Cynthia Y. Garza (Resident, Edinburg Office)
Jay T. Garrett (Resident, Austin Office)
Lucy Gonzàlez-Canales (Resident, Edinburg Office)
Lee Gordon (Resident, Austin Office)
Sandra Griffin (Resident, Austin Office)
Eloise A. Guzman (Resident, Houston Office)
Judith A. Hargrove (Resident, Austin Office)
Edward Hernández (Resident, El Paso Office)
Sharon N. Humble
Pamela Pope Johnson (Resident, Dallas Office)
William E. King (Resident, Houston Office)
Glenn Lewis (Resident, Fort Worth Office)

(See Next Column)

MEMBERS OF FIRM (Continued)

Edward Lopez, Jr. (Resident, Dallas Office)
Clayton E. Mayfield (Resident, Beaumont Office)
Russell N. McInturff (Resident, Odessa Office)
Stephen T. Meeks (Resident, Fort Worth Office)
Beverly Meltontree (Resident, Houston Office)
Kathleen D. Morrison (Resident, Corpus Christi Office)
Harry L. Munsinger
Norman J. Nelson (Resident, Houston Office)
J. Scott Novy (Resident, Longview Office)
Pankaj R. Parmar (Resident, Houston Office)
Carmen I. Perez (Resident, El Paso Office)
Monica McCoy Purdy (Resident, Dallas Office)
Harold D. Putman, Jr.
Kent M. Rider (Resident, Austin Office)
Lori Gruver Robertson (Resident, Austin Office)
Craig Schumacher (Resident, Tyler Office)
Michael J. Siwierka (Resident, Houston Office)
Glenn E. Smith (Resident, Fort Worth Office)
Leah L. Stolar (Resident, Houston Office)
Charles A. Sutton (Resident, Corpus Christi Office)
Michael T. Vallandingham (Resident, Austin Office)
Nancy Vasquez-Perez (Resident, Corpus Christi Office)
H. Elizabeth "Beth" Weller (Resident, Dallas Office)
Barbara M. Williams (Resident, Fort Worth Office)
Donald Lee Wolf (Resident, Tyler Office)
Scott D. Wylie (Resident, Corsicana Office)
Craig Young (Resident, Austin Office)
Lupe Zamarripa (Resident, Austin Office)

OF COUNSEL

Debra Danburg (Resident, Houston Office)
Richard R. Orsinger
Humberto Hernandez-Haddad (Not admitted in United States)
Vince Ryan (Resident, Houston Office)

For full biographical listings, see the Martindale-Hubbell Law Directory

LEON, AMBERSON & CARROLL, L.L.P. (AV)

500 Lexington, 78215
Telephone: 210-223-4254
Fax: 210-227-7721

Jack Paul Leon
Jon Christian Amberson

OF COUNSEL

Gilbert Lang Mathews

For full biographical listings, see the Martindale-Hubbell Law Directory

WEIR & ALVARADO, P.C. (AV)

115 Camaron Street, Suite 100, 78205
Telephone: 210-223-2685
Fax: 210-223-9464

Warren Weir
Leo Alvarado, Jr.

For full biographical listings, see the Martindale-Hubbell Law Directory

TEXARKANA, Bowie Co.

YOUNG & PICKETT (AV)

4122 Texas Boulevard, P.O. Box 1897, 75504
Telephone: 870-774-3206; 903-794-1303
Facsimile: 903-792-5098; 903-794-5098
Email: YP1303@aol.com

Damon Young
John M. Pickett

ASSOCIATE

Lance Lee

Representative Clients: AT&T Corporation; AmeriSource Corporation; Bridgestone/Firestone, Inc.; Exxon Chemical Americas; Century Bank of New Boston, Texas; International Paper Company, Inc.; Lucent Technologies, Inc.; Medtronic, Inc.; Michelin North America; SmithKline Beecham Corporation.

For full biographical listings, see the Martindale-Hubbell I aw Directory

*WACO,** McLennan Co.

DUNNAM & DUNNAM, L.L.P. (AV)

4125 West Waco Drive, P.O. Box 8418, 76714-8418
Telephone: 254-753-6437
Fax: 254-753-7434

MEMBERS OF FIRM

W. V. Dunnam (1891-1974)
W. V. Dunnam, Jr.
Vance Dunnam
Vance Dunnam, Jr.
James R. Dunnam

(See Next Column)

DUNNAM & DUNNAM L.L.P.—*Continued*

ASSOCIATES

Alan Stucky
John Porter Mabry, Jr.
James Robert Angel

For full biographical listings, see the Martindale-Hubbell Law Directory

RUSSELL DAVID HUNT (AV)

ALICO Building 1202, 425 Austin Avenue, P.O. Box 726, 76701
Telephone: 254-753-3738
FAX: 254-753-8118
Mailing Address: P.O. Box 726, Waco, TX, 76703-0726
URL: http://www.rhuntlaw.com

ASSOCIATE

Russell D. Hunt, Jr.

For full biographical listings, see the Martindale-Hubbell Law Directory

UTAH

*SALT LAKE CITY,** Salt Lake Co.

McCAUGHEY & METOS (AV)

10 West Broadway Suite 650, 84101
Telephone: 801-364-6474
Fax: 801-364-5014

Stephen R. McCaughey
G. Fred Metos

For full biographical listings, see the Martindale-Hubbell Law Directory

WEISS BERRETT PETTY, L.C. (AV)

Key Bank Tower, 50 South Main Street, Suite 530, 84144
Telephone: 801-531-7733
Facsimile: 801-531-7711

Loren E. Weiss
Barbara K. Berrett
Ralph C. Petty

Bret M. Hanna

OF COUNSEL

Charles F. Loyd

For full biographical listings, see the Martindale-Hubbell Law Directory

YENGICH, RICH & XAIZ (AV)

175 East 400 South, Suite 400, 84111
Telephone: 801-355-0320
Fax: 801-364-6026

MEMBERS OF FIRM

Ronald J. Yengich
Bradley P. Rich
Earl Xaiz

ASSOCIATE

Vanessa M. Ramos-Smith

For full biographical listings, see the Martindale-Hubbell Law Directory

VERMONT

*BURLINGTON,** Chittenden Co.

GRAVEL AND SHEA, A PROFESSIONAL CORPORATION (AV)

Corporate Plaza, 76 St. Paul Street, P.O. Box 369, 05402-0369
Telephone: 802-658-0220
Fax: 802-658-1456

Robert F. O'Neill

For Complete List of Firm Personnel, See General Section

For full biographical listings, see the Martindale-Hubbell Law Directory

O'NEILL CRAWFORD & GREEN, P.C. (AV)

159 Bank Street, P.O. Box 5359, 05402-5359
Telephone: 802-865-4700
Fax: 802-865-4778

Jerome F. O'Neill

For full biographical listings, see the Martindale-Hubbell Law Directory

VIRGINIA

*ACCOMAC,** Accomack Co.

JON C. POULSON (AV)

23349 Cross Street, P.O. Box 478, 23301-0478
Telephone: 757-787-2620
Facsimile: 757-787-2749

For full biographical listings, see the Martindale-Hubbell Law Directory

ALEXANDRIA, (Independent City)

LAW OFFICES OF PLATO CACHERIS (AV)

120 North Alfred Street, 22314
Telephone: 703-549-8181
Email: cacheris@erols.com *URL:* http://www.cacheris.com
Washington, D.C. Office: 1100 Connecticut Avenue, North West, Suite 730.
Telephone: 202-775-8700.
Fax: 202-775-8702; 202-775-8722.

Plato Cacheris
Preston Burton
John F. Hundley

OF COUNSEL

Sydney J. Hoffmann

For full biographical listings, see the Martindale-Hubbell Law Directory

*ARLINGTON,** Arlington Co.

COHEN, GETTINGS & DUNHAM, P.C. (AV)

2200 Wilson Boulevard, Suite 800, 22201
Telephone: 703-525-2260
Fax: 703-525-2489
Email: info@cohengettings.com *URL:* http://www.cohengettings.com
Alexandria, Virginia Office: 211 North Union Street, Suite 350.
Telephone: 703-525-2260.
Washington, D.C. Office: 1225 19th Street, N.W., 7th Floor.
Silver Spring, Maryland Office: Suite 700, 8701 Georgia Avenue.
Telephone: 301-589-6072.

Harvey B. Cohen
Brian P. Gettings (1933-1995)
Frank W. Dunham, Jr.
R. Scott Caulkins
Joel L. Dahnke
John E. Gagliano
Manuel A. Capsalis
John C. Pasierb

Carole H. Capsalis
Michael S. Nachmanoff
Kristen L. Loesch

OF COUNSEL

Carroll E. Dubuc
Joseph A. Fisher, III
Nancy Lee Feldman

References: First Virginia Bank; Virginia Commerce Bank; Crestar Bank; United Bank.

For full biographical listings, see the Martindale-Hubbell Law Directory

*CHARLOTTESVILLE,** Charlottesville City Co.

HAUGH & HAUGH, P.C. (AV)

435 Park Street, 22901
Telephone: 804-296-0185
Fax: 804-296-1146

Charles R. Haugh
Lair Dayton Haugh

For full biographical listings, see the Martindale-Hubbell Law Directory

*EASTVILLE,** Northampton Co.

TANKARD AND GORDON (AV)

Court Green, P.O. Box 5, 23347-0005
Telephone: 757-678-5117
Fax: 757-678-7664
Email: lawyer@esva.net

MEMBERS OF FIRM

Baxley T. Tankard
Croxton Gordon

Representative Clients: Chesapeake Bay Bridge and Tunnel District; A & N Electric Cooperative; First Virginia Bank-Tidewater, Exmore, Virginia.
Approved Attorneys for: Lawyers Title Insurance Corp.; Ticor Title Insurance Co.

For full biographical listings, see the Martindale-Hubbell Law Directory

*FAIRFAX,** (Ind. City; Seat of Fairfax Co.)

PETER D. GREENSPUN & ASSOCIATES, P.C. (AV)

Building A-5, 10605 Judicial Drive, 22030-5167
Telephone: 703-352-0100
Fax: 703-591-7268
Email: G&A@Greenspunlaw.com

(See Next Column)

PETER D. GREENSPUN & ASSOCIATES, P.C., *Fairfax—Continued*

Peter D. Greenspun

Thomas Peter Mann
Cynthia Ann Bailey
Vladimir I. Arezina

Representative Client: Moore Cadillac Co.

For full biographical listings, see the Martindale-Hubbell Law Directory

LEFFLER, HYLAND & THOMPSON, A PROFESSIONAL CORPORATION (AV)

Inns of Court, 4163 Chain Bridge Road, 22030-4102
Telephone: 703-293-9300
Facsimile: 703-293-9301
Email: mail@lefflerhyland.com *URL:* http://www.lefflerhyland.com

Rodney G. Leffler
Sharon E. Thompson

For full biographical listings, see the Martindale-Hubbell Law Directory

PHILLIPS, BECKWITH & HALL (AV)

10513 Judicial Drive Suite 100, 22030
Telephone: 703-691-4100
Facsimile: 703-385-2745
Email: jpandfirm@aol.com

MEMBERS OF FIRM

Jerry M. Phillips
Gregory Beckwith
David M. Hall
Bradley Chase

Representative Clients: Saturn of Sterling, Inc.; Saturn of Fairfax, Inc.; Saturn of Manassas, Inc.; Sterling-Chevrolet-Geo, Inc.; Fairfax County Deputy Sheriffs Association; Broyhill Homes, Inc.; Mama's Restaurants; Town of Vienna (Criminal Prosecutions).

For full biographical listings, see the Martindale-Hubbell Law Directory

NORFOLK, (Independent City)

SACKS & SACKS, A PROFESSIONAL CORPORATION (AV)

Suite 501 Town Point Center, 150 Boush Street, 23510-1615
Telephone: 757-623-2753
FAX: 757-640-7170
Email: sacks@series2000.com *URL:* http://www.lawyers.com/sacks&sacks-com

Herman A. Sacks (1886-1983)
Stanley E. Sacks
Andrew M. Sacks

LEGAL SUPPORT PERSONNEL

James S. McMahan (Litigation Manager)
Virginia S. McCann (Paralegal)
Maryjane Evans (Paralegal)
Thomas L. Gilchrist (Legal Assistant)
Marshall T. Walker, Jr. (Investigator)

For full biographical listings, see the Martindale-Hubbell Law Directory

*ORANGE,** Orange Co.

SHACKELFORD, HONENBERGER, THOMAS, WILLIS & GREGG, P.L.C. (AV)

149 West Main Street, P.O. Box 871, 22960
Telephone: 540-672-2711
Fax: 540-672-2714
Email: shtwg1@ns.gemlink.com
Culpeper, Virginia Office: 147 West Davis Street, P.O. Box 1002.
Telephone: 540-825-0305.

OF COUNSEL

Virginius R. Shackelford, Jr.

MEMBERS OF FIRM

Virginius R. Shackelford, III
Christopher J. Honenberger
Frank A. Thomas, III
Jere M. H. Willis, III (Resident, Culpeper, Virginia Office)
Sarah Collins Honenberger
Sean D. Gregg

For full biographical listings, see the Martindale-Hubbell Law Directory

RESTON, Fairfax Co.

GARVER LAW OFFICES, P.C. (AV)

11702 Bowman Green Drive, P.O. Box 2430, 20195
Telephone: 703-471-1090; 800-440-8605
Fax: 703-471-1095
Email: GLAW@Erols.com *URL:* http://www.lawyers.com/stevengarver

Steven M. Garver
Cheryl Gilley Rice

For full biographical listings, see the Martindale-Hubbell Law Directory

RICHMOND, (Independent City)

BOONE, BEALE, COSBY & LONG (AV)

A Partnership including Professional Law Corporations
27 North 17th Street, 23219
Telephone: 804-780-1729
Fax: 804-648-6211
Woodbridge, Virginia Office: 4391 Ridgewood Center Drive, Suite H.
Telephone: 703-690-1222.
Fax: 703-680-0559.

David E. Boone
J. Burkhardt Beale (Resident, Woodbridge Office)
Charles C. Cosby, Jr.
Andrea C. Long
Stacy F. Garrett, III
W. Edward Riley, IV

Reference: Nations Bank, Richmond, Virginia.

For full biographical listings, see the Martindale-Hubbell Law Directory

BRENNER, DOHNAL, EVANS & YOFFY, P.C. (AV)

411 East Franklin Street, Suite 200, P.O. Box 470, 23218-0470
Telephone: 804-644-1300
Facsimile: 804-644-1354
Email: bdeyp@erols.com

Theodore I. Brenner
Dennis W. Dohnal
Ronald S. Evans
James S. Yoffy

Jay O. Millman
Gregory S. Hooe
Kathryn Spruill Lingle
Mary J. Bennett
Thomas D. Stokes, III

For full biographical listings, see the Martindale-Hubbell Law Directory

ROBERT CABELL & ASSOCIATES (AV)

2800 Patterson Avenue, Suite 101, 23221-1700
Telephone: 804-643-9066
Fax: 804-358-5290
Email: rcabell@erols.com
Powhatan, Virginia Office: Powhatan Courthouse, Powhatan, Virginia, 23139.
Telephone: 804-794-4300.

ASSOCIATE

H. Pratt Cook, III

For full biographical listings, see the Martindale-Hubbell Law Directory

MORCHOWER, LUXTON AND WHALEY (AV)

An Affiliation of Attorneys
9 East Franklin Street, 23219
Telephone: 804-643-0147
FAX: 804-648-5514

Michael Morchower
John W. Luxton
C. David Whaley

ASSOCIATES

S. Michael Glass
Sharon Gregory Jacobs
Joseph J. Pecoraro
Lauren A. Caudill
Anthony G. Spencer
Lee White Kilduff
Sherry L. Gill

For full biographical listings, see the Martindale-Hubbell Law Directory

SPRINGFIELD, Fairfax Co.

BECKER, HICKS, IRVING & HADEED, P.C. (AV)

5501 Backlick Road, Suite 220, 22151
Telephone: 703-256-1300
Fax: 703-256-3467
Email: mail@bhihlaw.com *URL:* http://www.bhihlaw.com

Larry E. Becker
B. R. Hicks
James V. Irving
Michael Mitry Hadeed, Jr.
Mark E. Kellogg, P.C.
Lynn E. Berry
Scott R. Sexauer

May Shallal Kheder
Alix L. Mattingly
Ashraf W. Nubani

For full biographical listings, see the Martindale-Hubbell Law Directory

*TAZEWELL,** Tazewell Co.

DUDLEY, GALUMBECK & NECESSARY (AV)

104 West Main Street, P.O. Box 626, 24651
Telephone: 540-988-9436; 988-6561
Telecopier: 540-988-2921
Bluefield, Virginia Office: 728 Virginia Avenue, P.O. Box 468, 24605.
Telephone: 540-322-3454; 540-988-6590; 1-800-580-6590.
Telecopier: 540-322-4420.

(See Next Column)

DUDLEY, GALUMBECK & NECESSARY—*Continued*

Wytheville, Virginia Office: 100 West Main Street, Suite 201, 24382.
Telephone: 540-228-6060.
Fax: 540-228-7573.

MEMBERS OF FIRM

James W. Dudley (Resident, Bluefield Office)
Charles A. Stacy (Resident, Bluefield Office)
Robert M. Galumbeck (Resident)
Clinton Sherwood Kegley (Resident, Wytheville Office)
Kelly Combs Necessary (Resident)

References: Lawyers Title Insurance; Bank of Tazewell County.

For full biographical listings, see the Martindale-Hubbell Law Directory

VIRGINIA BEACH, (Independent City)

BRYDGES, MAHAN, O'BRIEN & FRUCCI, P.C. (AV)

Professional Building, 1369 Laskin Road, 23451
Telephone: 757-428-6021
Fax: 757-491-7634

Richard G. Brydges
Stephen C. Mahan
William R. "Buster" O'Brien
Steven C. Frucci

Approved Mediators/Arbitrators for: United States Arbitration and Mediation, Inc.; Arbitration Associates, Inc.- Jams/Endispute.
Reference: The Bank of Tidewater.

For full biographical listings, see the Martindale-Hubbell Law Directory

SHUTTLEWORTH RULOFF & GIORDANO, P.C. (AV)

4525 South Boulevard, Suite 300, 23452
Telephone: 757-671-6000
Fax: 757-671-6004
Email: srg@visi.net *URL:* http://www.srgpclaw.com
Newport News, Virginia Office: Historic Hilton Village, 10234 Warwick Boulevard, 23605.
Telephone: 757-873-9999.
Facsimile: 757-873-8758.

Robert J. Haddad
Robert G. Morecock
Lisa Palmer O'Donnell
Thomas B. Shuttleworth, II
Lawrence H. Woodward, Jr.

For full biographical listings, see the Martindale-Hubbell Law Directory

WASHINGTON

*SEATTLE,** King Co.

WILLIAM H. FLIGELTAUB (AV)

4100 First Interstate Center, 999 Third Avenue, 98104
Telephone: 206-343-9490
Fax: 206-464-9559

For full biographical listings, see the Martindale-Hubbell Law Directory

JOHN W. LUNDIN, P.S. (AV)

710 Cherry Street, 98104
Telephone: 206-623-8346
Fax: 206-623-5951
Email: jwlundin@nwnexus.com

John W. Lundin

Reference: Key Bank (Main Branch).

For full biographical listings, see the Martindale-Hubbell Law Directory

SCHROETER, GOLDMARK & BENDER, P.S. (AV)

500 Central Building, 810 Third Avenue, 98104
Telephone: 206-622-8000; 1-800-809-2234
FAX: 206-682-2305
Email: lastname@schroeter-goldmark.com

Croil J. Anderson
Adam J. Berger
James D. Hailey
Kristin Houser
Amanda E. Lee
Mark Leemon
Douglas D. McBroom
Janet L. Rice
Jeffery P. Robinson
Rebecca J. Roe
Sidney Stillerman Royer
William Rutzick
Sandra E. Widlan
Corrie Johnson Yackulic
John Goldmark (1917-1979)
Dean Bender (1933-1988)

OF COUNSEL

Jenny A. Durkan

For full biographical listings, see the Martindale-Hubbell Law Directory

*VANCOUVER,** Clark Co.

STEVEN W. THAYER, P.S. (AV)

900 Washington Street, Suite 820, 98660
Telephone: 360-694-8290
FAX: 360-694-7921

Steven W. Thayer

Jon J. McMullen

For full biographical listings, see the Martindale-Hubbell Law Directory

WEST VIRGINIA

*CHARLESTON,** Kanawha Co.

ALLEN GUTHRIE & MCHUGH (AV)

1300 Bank One Center, P.O. Box 3394, 25333
Telephone: 304-345-7250
Telecopier: 304-345-9941
Email: kagwv@kagww.com

Robert B. Allen
Thomas E. McHugh
S. Benjamin Bryant
Wm. Scott Wickline
Pamela Lynn Kandzari
James P. McHugh

Michelle M. Price
John K. McHugh
Nicholas P. Mooney II
Teresa K. Thompson
Charles W. Pace, Jr.

For full biographical listings, see the Martindale-Hubbell Law Directory

JACKSON & KELLY (AV)

1600 Laidley Tower, P.O. Box 553, 25322
Telephone: 304-340-1000
Fax: 304-340-1130
Email: info@jacksonkelly.com *URL:* http://www.jacksonkelly.com
Martinsburg, West Virginia Office: 300 Foxcroft Avenue, P.O. Box 1068.
Telephone: 304-263-8800.
Fax: 304-263-7110.
Morgantown, West Virginia Office: 6000 Hampton Center, P.O. Box 619.
Telephone: 304-599-3000.
Fax: 304-285-2040.
New Martinsville, West Virginia Office: 256 Russell Avenue, P.O. Box 68.
Telephone: 304-455-1751.
Fax: 304-455-6314.
Parkersburg, West Virginia Office: 412 Market Street, Suite 202, P.O. Box 1144.
Telephone: 304-424-3490.
Fax: 304-424-3499.
Fairmont, West Virginia Office: 1000 Technology Drive, Suite 1310.
Telephone: 304-368-2000.
Fax: 304-368-2020.
Lexington, Kentucky Office: 175 East Main Street, Suite 500, P.O. Box 2150.
Telephone: 606-255-9500.
Fax: 606-281-6478.
Washington, D. C. Office: 2401 Pennsylvania Avenue, N.W., Suite 400.
Telephone: 202-973-0200.
Fax: 202-973-0232.
Denver, Colorado Office: Suite 2710, 1660 Lincoln Street.
Telephone: 303-390-0003.
Fax: 303-390-0040.
Wheeling, West Virginia Office: 1144 Market Street.
Telephone: 304-233-4000.
Fax: 304-233-4077.

MEMBERS OF FIRM

W. Warren Upton
William J. Powell

For Complete List of Firm Personnel, See General Section

For full biographical listings, see the Martindale-Hubbell Law Directory

SALSBERY & DRUCKMAN (AV)

606 Virginia Street East, Suite 100, 25305
Telephone: 304-343-0075
Fax: 304-343-0099
Email: salsdruck@citynet.net

H. F. Salsbery
William S. Druckman
Madonna C. Estep

OF COUNSEL

Anne E. Shaffer

For full biographical listings, see the Martindale-Hubbell Law Directory

*PRINCETON,** Mercer Co.

GIBSON, LEFLER & ASSOCIATES (AV)

1345 Mercer Street, 24740
Telephone: 304-425-8276
800-742-3545

MEMBERS OF FIRM

Michael F. Gibson
Derrick W. Lefler

LEGAL SUPPORT PERSONNEL

NURSE PARALEGAL

Melody Lambert, RN-RLNC

SOCIAL SECURITY PARALEGAL

Nancy Belcher

PERSONAL INJURY PARALEGAL

Kathy Richards

WORKERS COMPENSATION PARALEGAL

Carol Hylton

MEDICAL NEGLIGENCE PARALEGAL

Deborah Frye

For full biographical listings, see the Martindale-Hubbell Law Directory

*WHEELING,** Ohio Co.

SCHRADER BYRD & COMPANION, PLLC (AV)

(A Professional Limited Liability Company)
The Maxwell Centre, 32-20th Street, Suite 500, P.O. Box 6336, 26003
Telephone: 304-233-3390
Fax: 304-233-2769
URL: http://www.schraderlaw.com
Martins Ferry, Ohio Office: 205 North Fifth Street, P.O. Box 309, 43935.
Telephone: 740-633-9976.
Fax: 740-633-0400.
Weirton, West Virginia Office: 3205 Pennsylvania Avenue, Suite 103, Penn Place, P.O. Box 2785, 26062.
Telephone: 304-723-2674.
Fax: 304-723-2876.

MEMBERS

Ray A. Byrd
James F. Companion
Frank X. Duff
Teresa Rieman-Camilletti
Yolonda G. Lambert
Daniel P. Fry (Resident Partner, Martins Ferry, Ohio Office)
James P. Mazzone (Resident Member, Weirton, West Virginia Office)
Sandra K. Law
D. Kevin Coleman

SPECIAL COUNSEL

Thomas B. Miller

ASSOCIATES

Denise D. Klug
Michael A. Adams
John Porco
Aimee Morgan Stern
Kimberly R. Wilson
Christopher J. Adams

OF COUNSEL

James A. Byrum, Jr.

General Counsel: Reynolds Memorial Hospital; WesBanco Bank-Elm Grove.
Representative Clients: American Cyanamid Company; Bank One; Matlack Systems, Inc.; Moutaineer Gas Co.; Ohio County Board of Education; PHICO Insurance Co.; Wheeling Hospital; Wheeling-Pittsburg Steel Corp.

For full biographical listings, see the Martindale-Hubbell Law Directory

WISCONSIN

*KENOSHA,** Kenosha Co.

ROSE & ROSE (AV)

5529 Sixth Avenue, 53140
Telephone: 262-658-8550, 657-7556
Fax: 262-658-1313

MEMBERS OF FIRM

William S. Rose (1914-1994)
Terry W. Rose
Christopher W. Rose

For full biographical listings, see the Martindale-Hubbell Law Directory

*MADISON,** Dane Co.

LAWTON & CATES, S.C. (AV)

10 East Doty Street Suite 400, P.O. Box 2965, 53701-2965
Telephone: 608-282-6200
Fax: 608-282-6252
Email: lawcat@madison.tds.net *URL:* http://www.lawtoncates.com

(See Next Column)

Bruce M. Davey
P. Scott Hassett
Victor M. Arellano
Dixon R. Gahnz

OF COUNSEL

Richard L. Cates

Reference: Bank One, Madison.

For full biographical listings, see the Martindale-Hubbell Law Directory

*MILWAUKEE,** Milwaukee Co.

KOHLER & HART (AV)

First National Bank Building, 735 North Water Street, Suite 1212, 53202
Telephone: 414-271-9595
Facsimile: 414-271-3701
Email: khlaw@netstream.net *URL:* http://www.lawyers.com/khlaw

MEMBERS OF FIRM

Martin E. Kohler
Michael F. Hart
John C. Thomure, Jr.

For full biographical listings, see the Martindale-Hubbell Law Directory

SHELLOW, SHELLOW & GLYNN, S.C. (AV)

222 East Mason Street, 53202
Telephone: 414-271-8535
Fax: 414-272-5441
Email: shellowglynn@compuserve.com

James M. Shellow
Gilda B. Shellow
Stephen M. Glynn
Robert R. Henak
Carol S. Josten
Craig W. Albee

Representative Clients: Aladdin Hotel Corporation; Capitol News Agency; Cargill, Incorporated; Case Corporation; Criticare Systems, Inc.; Ladish Malting Co.; Miller Brands-Milwaukee, Inc.; Milliman & Robertson, Inc.; S.C. Johnson and Son, Inc.

For full biographical listings, see the Martindale-Hubbell Law Directory

WYOMING

*CHEYENNE,** Laramie Co.

HICKEY, MACKEY, EVANS & WALKER (AV)

1800 Carey Avenue, Suite 700, P.O. Drawer 467, 82003
Telephone: 307-634-1525
Telecopier: 307-638-7335
URL: http://www.hickeymackey.com

MEMBERS OF FIRM

Paul J. Hickey
Terry W. Mackey
David F. Evans
John M. Walker
Roger C. Fransen
Richard D. Tim Bush
Mary A. Throne

A List of Representative Clients will be furnished upon request.
Reference: Norwest Bank, Cheyenne, N.A.

For full biographical listings, see the Martindale-Hubbell Law Directory

WOLF & TIEDEKEN (AV)

Suite 300 Equality State Bank Building, P.O. Box 491, 82001
Telephone: 307-635-2876
Fax: 307-632-4902
Email: lawyers@cheyenneweb.com

MEMBERS OF FIRM

Richard C. Wolf
Robert W. Tiedeken

For full biographical listings, see the Martindale-Hubbell Law Directory

*JACKSON,** Teton Co.

W. KEITH GOODY (AV)

155 E. Pearl, P.O. Box 2488, 83001
Telephone: 307-733-4446
Fax: 307-733-2774
Email: goodylaw@blissnet.com

LEGAL SUPPORT PERSONNEL

Mary C. Goody

For full biographical listings, see the Martindale-Hubbell Law Directory

SPENCE, MORIARITY & SCHUSTER, LLC (AV)

15 South Jackson Street, P.O. Box 548, 83001
Telephone: 307-733-7290
Fax: 307-733-5248
Salt Lake City, Utah Office: 39 Exchange Place, Suite 101, 84111.
Telephone: 801-521-0811.
Fax: 801-521-0437.

(See Next Column)

SPENCE, MORIARITY & SCHUSTER LLC—*Continued*

MEMBERS OF FIRM

Gerry L. Spence, P.C.
Edward P. Moriarity
Robert P. Schuster
Gary L. Shockey
J. Douglas McCalla
Roy A. Jacobson, Jr.
Kent W. Spence
Robert A. Krause

ASSOCIATES

Glen G. Debroder
R. Daniel Fleck
G. Bryan Ulmer, III
Laura N. MacPherson
(Not admitted in WY)
David M. Gosar
Gerard R. Bosch
Jeffrey Gooch

Reference: First Interstate Bank, Casper, Wyoming.

For full biographical listings, see the Martindale-Hubbell Law Directory

CANADA NEWFOUNDLAND

*ST. JOHN'S,**

MCINNES COOPER (AV)

Barristers, Solicitors & Trade Mark Agents
Baine Johnston Centre, 5th Floor, 10 Fort William Place, P.O. Box 5939, A1C 5X4
Telephone: 709-722-8735
Telecopier: 709-722-1763
Email: mcrsj@mcrlaw.com *URL:* http://www.mcrlaw.com
Halifax, Nova Scotia Office: Summit Place, 1601 Lower Water Street, P.O. Box 730, B3J 2V1.
Telephone: 902-425-6500.
Fax: 902-425-6350. Email: mcrhfx@mcrlaw.com.
Moncton, New Brunswick Office: Place Moncton Place, 655 Main Street, P.O. Box 1368, E1C 8T6.
Telephone: 506-857-8970.
Fax: 506-857-4095. Email: mcrmctn@mcrlaw.com.
Charlottetown, Prince Edward Island Office: BDC Place, Suite 620, 119 Kent Street, C1A 1N3.
Telephone: 902-368-8473.
Fax: 902-368-8346. Email: mcrpei@mcrlaw.com.
Fredericton, New Brunswick Office: Suite 600, 570 Queen Street, P.O. Box 610.
Telephone: 506-458-8572.
Fax: 506-458-9903. Email: mcrfton@mcrlaw.com.

PARTNER

J. David B. Eaton

For Complete List of Firm Personnel, See General Section

For full biographical listings, see the Martindale-Hubbell Law Directory

CANADA ONTARIO

*WINDSOR,** Essex Co.

SUTTS, STROSBERG LLP (AV)

600 Westcourt Place, 251 Goyeau Street, P.O. Box 670, N9A 6V4
Telephone: 519-258-9333
Detroit Michigan: 313-962-0137
Facsimile: Windsor 519-258-9527
Detroit 313-962-0139

MEMBERS OF FIRM

Achille F. Gignac, Q.C. (1902-1984)
Robert E. Barnes, Q.C.
Clifford N. Sutts, Q.C.
Harvey T. Strosberg, Q.C.
Gary V. Wortley
James K. Ball
John C. Holland
Mary M. S. Fox
William C. Chapman
Donald M. Gordon
Paul C. Nesseth
Heather Rumble Peterson
Patricia A. Speight
Edward W. Ducharme
Michelle A. Gagnon
Craig J. Allen
Werner H. Keller
Francine A. Herlehy
Paul Simard
Jasminka Kalajdzic

COUNSEL FOR CRIMINAL MATTERS

Patrick J. Ducharme

For full biographical listings, see the Martindale-Hubbell Law Directory

CANADA SASKATCHEWAN

*REGINA,** Regina Jud. Centre

MACPHERSON LESLIE & TYERMAN (AV)

1500-1874 Scarth Street, S4P 4E9
Telephone: 306-347-8000
Telecopier: 306-352-5250
Email: mltreg@mlt.com
Saskatoon, Saskatchewan Office: 1500-410 22nd Street East, S7K 5T6.
Telephone: 306-975-7100.
Telecopier: 306-975-7145.

MEMBERS OF FIRM

Douglas C. Hodson
(Resident, Saskatoon Office)

ASSOCIATES

Michael D. Tochor
Dana D.J. Schindelka

For Complete List of Firm Personnel, See General Section

For full biographical listings, see the Martindale-Hubbell Law Directory

EDUCATION LAW

MISSOURI

KANSAS CITY, Jackson, Clay, Platte & Cass Cos.

SWANSON MIDGLEY, LLC (AV)
Crown Center, 2420 Pershing Road, Suite 400, 64108
Telephone: 816-842-6100
Fax: 816-842-0013
Email: mail@swansonmidgley.com *URL:* http://www.swansonmidgley.com
Overland Park, Kansas Office: Commerce Plaza I, 7th Floor, 7300 W. 110th Street.
Telephone: 913-317-2717.
FAX: 913-317-1505.

James A. Durbin
Craig T. Kenworthy

Counsel For: Unified School District No. 231.

For Complete List of Firm Personnel, See General Section

For full biographical listings, see the Martindale-Hubbell Law Directory

NEW JERSEY

*MORRISTOWN,** Morris Co.

RAND, ALGEIER, TOSTI & WOODRUFF, A PROFESSIONAL CORPORATION (AV)
60 Washington Street, 07960
Telephone: 973-539-2600
Telecopier: 973-984-0430
Email: randlaw@bellatlantic.net

Gary C. Algeier
David B. Rand
Robert M. Tosti
Robert B. Woodruff
John F. McDonnell
John E. Croot, Jr.

Kathryn J. Kingree
Deborah A. White

OF COUNSEL

Ronald M. Pflug
Ellen S. Bass
Tamara Krikorian

For full biographical listings, see the Martindale-Hubbell Law Directory

NEW YORK

*ALBANY,** Albany Co.

RUBERTI, GIRVIN & FERLAZZO, P.C. (AV)
120 State Street, 2nd Floor, 12207-2829
Telephone: 518-462-0300
Fax: 518-462-5037
Email: attorneys@rgflaw.com

PARTNERS

E. Michael Ruberti
James E. Girvin
Salvatore D. Ferlazzo
Kristine Amodeo Lanchantin
Jeffrey D. Honeywell
M. Cornelia Cahill
Gregg Tyler Johnson

ASSOCIATES

Patrick J. McKenna
Kathy Ann Wolverton
Christopher P. Langlois
Bruce I. Kopf
Maureen Finnegan Harris

SPECIAL COUNSEL

Mary Helen Moses
James A. P. McCarthy
Elaine M. Pers
Karen S. Norlander

For full biographical listings, see the Martindale-Hubbell Law Directory

*BINGHAMTON,** Broome Co.

HOGAN & SARZYNSKI, L.L.P. (AV)
20 Hawley Street, P.O. Box 660, 13902-0660
Telephone: 607-723-7413
Fax: 607-723-0129
Email: hsatty@pronetisp.net

(See Next Column)

MEMBERS OF FIRM

John B. Hogan
Edward J. Sarzynski
John P. Lynch
Michael G. Surowka

Wendy K. DeWind

For full biographical listings, see the Martindale-Hubbell Law Directory

*NEW YORK,** New York Co.

McGUIRE, KEHL & NEALON, LLP (AV)
230 Park Avenue, Suite 2830, 10169
Telephone: 212-557-0040
Telecopier: 212-953-0768

MEMBER OF FIRM

Jeffrey A. Kehl

OF COUNSEL

Marion C. Katzive
Shelley Sanders Kehl

For full biographical listings, see the Martindale-Hubbell Law Directory

*SYRACUSE,** Onondaga Co.

FERRARA, FIORENZA, LARRISON, BARRETT & REITZ, P.C. (AV)
5010 Campuswood Drive, 13057
Telephone: 315-437-7600
Fax: 315-437-7744

Benjamin J. Ferrara
Nicholas J. Fiorenza
David W. Larrison
Dennis T. Barrett
Marc H. Reitz
Henry F. Sobota
Susan T. Johns
Frank W. Miller
Craig M. Atlas

Norman H. Gross
Miles G. Lawlor
Michael L. Dodd
Marina L.C. Bottone
Jennifer G. Speller
Perri Karen Rosenfeld Guido

For full biographical listings, see the Martindale-Hubbell Law Directory

NORTH CAROLINA

*CHARLOTTE,** Mecklenburg Co.

FERGUSON, STEIN, WALLAS, ADKINS, GRESHAM & SUMTER, P.A. (AV)
741 Kenilworth Avenue, Suite 300, 28204-2828
Telephone: 704-375-8461
Fax: 704-334-5654
Mailing Address: P.O. Box 36486, 28236-6486
Email: FSWAGS@aol.com
Chapel Hill, North Carolina Office: Suite 2, 312 West Franklin Street.
Telephone: 919-933-5300.
Fax: 919-967-4953.

James E. Ferguson, II
Adam Stein (Resident, Chapel Hill Office)
Jonathan Wallas
Karl Adkins
John W. Gresham
Geraldine Sumter
Henderson Hill
Thomas M. Stern (Resident, Chapel Hill Office)
C. Margaret Errington
Stephen Luke Largess

Rebecca Ann Thorne
James E. Ferguson, III
Corie Diane Pauling
Ann C. Todd

For full biographical listings, see the Martindale-Hubbell Law Directory

TEXAS

*FORT WORTH,** Tarrant Co.

CHAPPELL, PARMELEE, JOHNSON & HILL, P.C. (AV)
1800 City Center Tower II, 301 Commerce Street, 76102-4118
Telephone: 817-332-1800
Metro: 817-654-2140
Telecopy: 817-332-1956
Email: cpjh@cmlaw.com *URL:* http://www.cmlaw.com

David F. Chappell
Robert A. Parmelee
Robert S. Johnson
Cynthia L. Hill

Suzanne K. Rosen
William F. Peters, Jr.

(See Next Column)

CHAPPELL, PARMELEE, JOHNSON & HILL P.C., *Fort Worth—Continued*

OF COUNSEL

James L. Williams, Jr.
Carolyn Mitchell
Christopher Cooke
C.C. "Kit" Cooke, III

For full biographical listings, see the Martindale-Hubbell Law Directory

ELDER LAW

MINNESOTA

*FERGUS FALLS,** Otter Tail Co.

DAVID F. LUNDEEN (AV)

107 Court Street, 56537
Telephone: 218-736-4866
FAX: 218-736-7747
Email: dlundlaw@prtel.com

For full biographical listings, see the Martindale-Hubbell Law Directory

MISSOURI

ST. LOUIS, (Independent City)

DAVID G. LUPO, P.C. (AV)

13610 Barrett Office Drive, 63021
Telephone: 314-822-3580
Telecopier: 314-822-0361
Email: DGLUPO@aol.com

David G. Lupo

Reference: Nations Bank.

NEVADA

*LAS VEGAS,** Clark Co.

BRYAN A LOWE & ASSOCIATES A PROFESSIONAL LAW CORPORATION (AV)

4011 Meadows Lane, Suite 102, 89107
Telephone: 702-259-0002
Fax: 702-259-7774
Email: LoweAssoc@aol.com *URL:* http://www.lawyers.com/lowelaw
Boulder City, Nevada Office: 916 Nevada highway, Suite 6, 89005.
Telephone: 702-293-6888.

Bryan A. Lowe

Robert Winn
S. Craig Stone, II

Representative Client: Clark County Housing Authority.
References: Wells Fargo Bank, Trust Department; Bank of America, Trust Department; Clark County, Nevada, Public Administrator.

For full biographical listings, see the Martindale-Hubbell Law Directory

NEW JERSEY

CRANBURY, Middlesex Co.

HUFF, MORAN & ORRON (AV)

1246 South River Road, 08512
Telephone: 609-655-3600
Fax: 609-655-5825
URL: http://www.lawyers.com/hm&olaw

MEMBERS OF FIRM

William C. Moran, Jr.
David E. Orron

OF COUNSEL

Donald Katz
J. Schuyler Huff (Retired)

Counsel For: Township of Cranbury; East Windsor Township; Monroe Township Municipal Utilities Authority; Trustees, I.B.E.W. Local #456 Pension and Annuity Fund; Trustees, New Jersey I.B.E.W. Joint Welfare Fund; Better Community Housing of Trenton, Inc.
Representative Clients: John C. Dolph Co.; Consolidated Models, Inc.; I.E. Shaffer Co.; ERX Trucking, Inc.

For full biographical listings, see the Martindale-Hubbell Law Directory

NEW YORK

*ITHACA,** Tompkins Co.

WIGGINS AND MASSON, LLP (AV)

308 North Tioga Street, P.O. Box 399, 14851
Telephone: 607-272-0479
Telecopier: 607-273-0502
Email: law@wigginsandmasson.com *URL:* http://www.wigginsandmasson.com

MEMBERS OF FIRM

Walter J. Wiggins
Robin Abrahamson Masson
Erin E. McKinley
Lorraine Moynihan

Approved Attorneys for: Ticor Title Guaranty Corp.
References: Tompkins County Trust Co.

For full biographical listings, see the Martindale-Hubbell Law Directory

*NEW YORK,** New York Co.

FREEDMAN AND FISH (AV)

260 Madison Avenue, 10016
Telephone: 212-481-0810
Fax: 212-213-0924
Email: fandf1985@aol.com *URL:* http://www.lawyers.com/freedmanandfish

MEMBERS OF FIRM

Robert M. Freedman
Daniel G. Fish
Barry I. Lutzky

ASSOCIATES

Allison Jill Busch
Sheryl R. Frishman
Lawrence I. Garbuz
Marcie G. Roth

For full biographical listings, see the Martindale-Hubbell Law Directory

JAY J. SANGERMAN & ASSOCIATES (AV)

60 East 42nd Street Suite 650, 10165
Telephone: 212-922-0711
Telephone: Florida 561-989-9095
Fax: 212-922-0709
Email: law@sangerman.com *URL:* http://www.sangerman.com
Boca Raton, Florida Office: 4115 N.W. 60th Circle, 33496.
Telephone: 561-989-9095.
Fax: 561-989-9096.
Clifton, New Jersey Office: 4 Brighton Road, Suite 200, 07015.
Telephone: 973-778-3422.

For full biographical listings, see the Martindale-Hubbell Law Directory

*SYRACUSE,** Onondaga Co.

DELANEY AND O'CONNOR LLP (AV)

Suite 275, Lincoln Center, 13202
Telephone: 315-476-8450
Telecopier: 315-476-8730
Email: deloco@dreamscape.com *URL:* http://www.dreamscape.com/deloco

MEMBERS OF FIRM

John M. DeLaney
Michael E. O'Connor
Denise P. Cambs

ASSOCIATES

Carol Currie Olech
Karin Sloan

For full biographical listings, see the Martindale-Hubbell Law Directory

PENNSYLVANIA

*EASTON,** Northampton Co.

FOX, OLDT & BROWN (AV)

Suite 508, First Union Bank Building, Six South Third Street, Center Square, 18042
Telephone: 610-258-6111
Fax: 610-253-4532
URL: http://www.lawyers.com/foxoldt&brown

MEMBERS OF FIRM

Charles L. Oldt
Robert C. Brown, Jr.

Counsel for: First Union National Bank; Easton Cemetery; Travelers Insurance Co.

For full biographical listings, see the Martindale-Hubbell Law Directory

*NORRISTOWN,** Montgomery Co.

MURPHY, OLIVER, CAIOLA & GOWEN, A PROFESSIONAL LAW CORPORATION (AV)

43 East Marshall Street, 19401-4828
Telephone: 610-272-4222; 610-279-3838
Fax: 610-272-2549; 610-275-0140
Email: molaw@injury-law.com *URL:* http://www.injury-law.com
Spring City, Pennsylvania Office: 500 S. Main Street, 19475.
Telephone: 610-948-3770.
Pottstown, Pennsylvania Office: 5 Sunnybrook Road, 19464.
Telephone: 610-323-3480.
West Chester, Pennsylvania Office: 1534 McDaniel Drive, Westtown Business Center, 19250.
Telephone: 610-272-4222.

James J. Oliver — Thomas L. Gowen, Jr.
Frank P. Murphy — Carla E. Connor
Frank L. Caiola — Barbara A. Barnes

John F. Haskins, Jr. — Cynthia Love Dengler
Carol A. Crisci

LEGAL SUPPORT PERSONNEL

Patricia A. Talese (Paralegal) — Kathleen Nicholson

For full biographical listings, see the Martindale-Hubbell Law Directory

SOUTH CAROLINA

*BEAUFORT,** Beaufort Co.

HARVEY & BATTEY, P.A. (AV)

1001 Craven Street, P.O. Drawer 1107, 29902
Telephone: 843-524-3109
Telefax: 843-524-6973

W. Brantley Harvey (1893-1981) — Thomas C. Davis
W. Brantley Harvey, Jr. — H. Grady Brown, III
Colden R. Battey, Jr. — E. Carew Rice, III
William B. Harvey, III — Thomas A. Holloway
John M. Tatum, III — Derek C. Gilbert

OF COUNSEL

Noel M. Seeburg, Jr.

Approved Attorneys for: Lawyers Title Insurance Corp.; Chicago Title Insurance Corp.
Representative Clients: Nations Bank; First Bank, F.S.B.; Pleasant Point Plantation Associates; Century 21-Carolina Realty, Inc.; Lobeco Products, Inc.; Beaufort County Association of Realtors; The Fripp Company.

For full biographical listings, see the Martindale-Hubbell Law Directory

*COLUMBIA,** Richland Co.

SHERRILL & ROOF, L.L.P. (AV)

1122 Lady Street, Suite 1100, P.O. Box 11497, 29211-1497
Telephone: 803-733-3433
Fax: 803-733-2990
Email: info@sherrillandroof.com

Franchelle Cole Millender

For full biographical listings, see the Martindale-Hubbell Law Directory

HILTON HEAD ISLAND, Beaufort Co.

RUTH & MACNEILLE, PROFESSIONAL ASSOCIATION (AV)

40 Pope Avenue, 29928
Telephone: 843-785-4251
Telex: 988944
Telecopier: 843-686-5404
Mailing Address: P.O. Box 5706, Hilton Head Island, SC, 29938
Bluffton, South Carolina Office: 7 Simmonsville Road, Suite 200.
Telephone: 803-815-5353.
Fax: 803-815-5354.

William A. Ruth

References: NationsBank of South Carolina, N.A.; Anchor Bank; Wachovia Bank, N.A.; Chicago Title Insurance Corp.; First American Title Insurance Co.

For full biographical listings, see the Martindale-Hubbell Law Directory

TENNESSEE

*MARYVILLE,** Blount Co.

NICHOLSON, GARNER & DUGGAN (AV)

250 High Street, P.O. Box 5059, 37802-5059
Telephone: 423-984-1460
Knoxville: 423-637-1970
Telecopier: 423-982-2595
Real Estate Fax: 423-982-2595
Litigation Fax: 423-984-9275
Email: jnicholson@earthlink.net *URL:* http://www.lawyers.com/ngdlaw

MEMBERS OF FIRM

Joe Nicholson — J. Michael Garner
David R. Duggan

ASSOCIATES

Angelia D. Morie — Daphne H. Cornwell

Representative Clients: Will be furnished upon request.

For full biographical listings, see the Martindale-Hubbell Law Directory

WASHINGTON

*SPOKANE,** Spokane Co.

SAYRE & SAYRE, P.S. (AV)

111 West Cataldo, Suite 210, 99201-3203
Telephone: 509-325-7330
FAX: 509-325-7334
URL: http://www.lawyers.com/sayrelaw

Richard L. Sayre — Karen L. Sayre

For full biographical listings, see the Martindale-Hubbell Law Directory

WISCONSIN

*MILWAUKEE,** Milwaukee Co.

MEISSNER TIERNEY FISHER & NICHOLS S.C. (AV)

The Milwaukee Center, 111 East Kilbourn Avenue, 19th Floor, 53202-6622
Telephone: 414-273-1300
Facsimile: 414-273-5840
URL: http://www.mtfn.com

Joseph E. Tierney III — Thomas J. Nichols
Dennis L. Fisher — Randal J. Brotherhood
Michael J. Cohen

Michael A. Kallas — William T. Stuart
Christopher L. Rexroat — Jeffrey A. Ellis
Justin B. Nelsen — Adam J. Tutaj

OF COUNSEL

Paul F. Meissner

For full biographical listings, see the Martindale-Hubbell Law Directory

EMINENT DOMAIN

MISSISSIPPI

*GULFPORT,** Harrison Co.

BLACKWELL & WHITE (AV)

1613 Twenty-Third Avenue, 39501
Telephone: 228-864-1484
FAX: 228-868-6484
Mailing Address: P.O. Box 430, 39502-0430,

MEMBERS OF FIRM

Leonard A. Blackwell, II
Gary White

ASSOCIATES

James B. Wright, Jr.
Patricia S. Tisdale

References: Merchants Bank & Trust Co.; Hancock Bank.

For full biographical listings, see the Martindale-Hubbell Law Directory

NEVADA

*LAS VEGAS,** Clark Co.

LAURA WIGHTMAN FITZSIMMONS (AV)

704 South Ninth Street, 89101
Telephone: 702-733-8877
Fax: 702-731-1964
Email: outlawyer@prodigy.com

For full biographical listings, see the Martindale-Hubbell Law Directory

SCHOFIELD & ASSOCIATES (AV)

2675 South Jones Boulevard, Suite 211, 89146
Telephone: 702-474-4444
Fax: 702-474-4449
Email: phslaw@wizard.com *URL:* http://www.lawyers.com/schofield&associates

MEMBER OF FIRM

Paul H. Schofield

For full biographical listings, see the Martindale-Hubbell Law Directory

NEW JERSEY

*MORRISTOWN,** Morris Co.

MCKIRDY AND RISKIN, A PROFESSIONAL CORPORATION (AV)

136 South Street, 07962-2379
Telephone: 973-539-8900
Fax: 973-984-5529
URL: http://www.lawyers.com/m&rlaw

Edward D. McKirdy
Harry J. Riskin
John H. Buonocore, Jr.
Thomas M. Olson
Anthony F. Della Pelle

Debra L. Kudriavetz

For full biographical listings, see the Martindale-Hubbell Law Directory

NEW YORK

*ROCHESTER,** Monroe Co.

FORSYTH, HOWE, O'DWYER, KALB & MURPHY, P.C. (AV)

Suite 1600, Midtown Tower, 14604
Telephone: 716-325-7515
Fax: 716-325-6407
URL: http://www.forsythhowe.com

Charles B. Forsyth (1890-1968)
C. Benn Forsyth
Gordon A. Howe, II
Duncan W. O'Dwyer
Robert J. Kalb
Gerald N. Murphy

Nancy A. Pappal

(See Next Column)

OF COUNSEL

John F. Forsyth (Retired)
Allan Wolk
Hoffman Stone
Debra A. Martin
Janice M. Iati
Cathleen W. Smith
Thad F. Sondej

References: The Chase Manhattan Bank; Fleet Bank.

For full biographical listings, see the Martindale-Hubbell Law Directory

OKLAHOMA

*TULSA,** Tulsa Co.

RHODES, HIERONYMUS, JONES, TUCKER & GABLE, P.L.L.C. (AV)

Oneok Plaza, 100 West 5th Street, Suite 400, P.O. Box 21100, 74121-1100
Telephone: 918-582-1173
Fax: 918-592-3390
URL: http://www.rhodesokla.com

MEMBERS OF FIRM

Chris L. Rhodes, III
John H. Tucker

OF COUNSEL

Larry J. Fulton

Representative Clients: American International Companies; Bechtel; Chubb Group of Insurance Companies; General Motors Corporation; Merrill, Lynch; Nissan Motor Corporation in U.S.A.; Pfizer, Inc.; Volkswagen of America, Volkswagen, A.G.; Zurich U.S.

For full biographical listings, see the Martindale-Hubbell Law Directory

PENNSYLVANIA

BLUE BELL, Montgomery Co.

GERBER & GERBER (AV)

790 Penllyn-Blue Bell Pike, Suite 100, 19422
Telephone: 610-279-6700; 215-540-9100
Fax: 215-540-9424
Email: grbrlaw@dynanet.com *URL:* http://www.lawyers.com/gerber&gerber

Morris Gerber (1908-1995)

MEMBER OF FIRM

A. Richard Gerber

For full biographical listings, see the Martindale-Hubbell Law Directory

SOUTH CAROLINA

LORIS, Horry Co.

STEVENS LAW FIRM, P.C. (AV)

3341 Broad Street P.O. Drawer 127, 29569-0127
Telephone: 843-756-7652
Fax: 843-756-3785
E-Mail: RUMMPOLE@AOL.COM
Email: JPKLAW@AOL.COM

James P. Stevens, Jr.
Jonathan P. Kresken

For full biographical listings, see the Martindale-Hubbell Law Directory

TENNESSEE

*MEMPHIS,** Shelby Co.

HALE HEADRICK DEWEY & WOLF, PLLC (AV)

One Memphis Place, 200 Jefferson Avenue Suite 1450, 38103
Telephone: 901-523-1123
Fax: 901-523-7472
Nashville, Tennessee Office: Suntrust Bank Building, 201 Fourth Avenue North, Suite 1450, 37219.
Telephone: 615-843-5160.
Fax: 615-843-5165

(See Next Column)

HALE HEADRICK DEWEY & WOLF PLLC, *Memphis—Continued*

Stephen P. Hale
S. Russell Headrick
H. Tucker Dewey
Herbert B. Wolf, Jr.
John S. Golwen

OF COUNSEL

Steven L. Gill

Jennifer Ziegenhorn
Wendy A. Geurin
John W. Campbell
Joseph M. Koury
Holly N. Knight
Charles S. Blatteis
Jennifer S. Kiesewetter
J. William Williams

For full biographical listings, see the Martindale-Hubbell Law Directory

TEXAS

*AUSTIN,** Travis Co.

WOMACK, MCCLISH & WALL, P.C. (AV)

1801 Lavaca, Suite 120, 78701-1398
Telephone: 512-474-9875
Fax: 512-474-9894
Email: wmc@womackmcclish.com

Danny M. Womack
John N. McClish
Sue Domingue Wall
Dan Foster

For full biographical listings, see the Martindale-Hubbell Law Directory

*DALLAS,** Dallas Co.

GEARY, PORTER & DONOVAN, P.C. (AV)

One Bent Tree Tower, 16475 Dallas Parkway, Suite 500, 75001-6837
Telephone: 972-931-9901
Facsimile: 972-931-9208
Mailing Address: P.O. Box 700248, Dallas, Texas, 75370-0248
Email: firm@gpd.com *URL:* http://www.gpd.com

Emmett W. Berryman
Paul K. Braswell
Bruce W. Claycombe
Nancy L. DeLeon
Daniel P. Donovan
Jeffrey L. Fisher
Joseph W. Geary
Michael P. Geary
Troy S. Gilreath
Ronald D. Gray
David J. Kaplan
Catherine C. Kays
Laura M. Keith
Nicole T. LeBoeuf
Jeffrey T. Libby
Larry L. Martin
Gregory L. Miller
James T. Porter
Amy D. Reilly
Theodore J. Riney
Kim Alan Roberts
Bradley T. Sharpe
Thomas L. Staley
David M. Tatum

OF COUNSEL

Jerry L. Arnold
Susan Land Finnell
Henry M. Wade
Roger O. West

For full biographical listings, see the Martindale-Hubbell Law Directory

LAW OFFICES OF EDDIE VASSALLO, P.C. (AV)

Regency Plaza, 3710 Rawlins, Suite 1200, 75219-4217
Telephone: 214-559-7200
Fax: 214-559-7209
Email: mikkiwes@aol.com *URL:* http://www.lawyers.com/vassallolaw

Edward DiMare Vassallo, Jr.

Charles A. Salazar
Christene Jones
Scott T. Doggett

For full biographical listings, see the Martindale-Hubbell Law Directory

*EL PASO,** El Paso Co.

AINSA PARTNERS, LLP (AV)

5809 Acacia Circle, 79912
Telephone: 915-845-5300
Fax: 915-845-7800
Email: fain@acaciapark.com *URL:* http://www.ainsa.com

Francis S. Ainsa, Jr.
Michael F. Ainsa
David M. Driscoll

For full biographical listings, see the Martindale-Hubbell Law Directory

UTAH

*SALT LAKE CITY,** Salt Lake Co.

VAN COTT, BAGLEY, CORNWALL & MCCARTHY, A PROFESSIONAL CORPORATION (AV)

50 South Main Street, Suite 1600, P.O. Box 45340, 84145-0340
Telephone: 801-532-3333
Telecopier: 801-534-0058
Email: info@vancott.com *URL:* http://www.vancott.com
Ogden, Utah Office: 2404 Washington Boulevard, Suite 900.
Telephone: 801-394-5783.
Park City, Utah Office: 2200 Park Avenue, Suite C200-A.
Telephone: 435-649-3889.

David A. Greenwood

Stephen K. Christiansen
Bradley M. Strassberg

For Complete List of Firm Personnel, See General Section

For full biographical listings, see the Martindale-Hubbell Law Directory

EMPLOYMENT BENEFITS LAW

MINNESOTA

*FERGUS FALLS,** Otter Tail Co.

David F. Lundeen (AV)

107 Court Street, 56537
Telephone: 218-736-4866
FAX: 218-736-7747
Email: dlundlaw@prtel.com

For full biographical listings, see the Martindale-Hubbell Law Directory

PLYMOUTH, Hennepin Co.

Frank Madden & Associates (AV)

505 North Highway 169, 55441-6448
Telephone: 612-545-2525
Facsimile: 612-545-2866

Frank J. Madden

Pamela R. Galanter
Susan K. Hansen

For full biographical listings, see the Martindale-Hubbell Law Directory

MISSISSIPPI

*PASCAGOULA,** Jackson Co.

Colingo, Williams, Heidelberg, Steinberger & McElhaney, P.A. (AV)

711 Delmas Avenue, P.O. Box 1407, 39568-1407
Telephone: 228-762-8021
FAX: 228-762-7589
Email: info@colingowilliams.com *URL:* http://www.ColingoWilliams.com

Karl R. Steinberger
Michael J. McElhaney, Jr.

Gina Bardwell Thompkins

Representative Clients: International Paper Co.; R.J. Reynolds; CBS Corp.; Kemper Group; Singing River Hospital System; Mississippi Gulf Coast Regional Wastewater Authority; Medical Assurance Company of Mississippi; Mutual Assurance of Alabama; Dole Food Co.

For full biographical listings, see the Martindale-Hubbell Law Directory

MISSOURI

ST. LOUIS, (Independent City)

Weinhaus and Dobson (AV)

Suite 900, 906 Olive Street, 63101
Telephone: 314-621-8363
Telecopier: 314-621-8366
Email: weidob@nela.org

MEMBERS OF FIRM

S. Sheldon Weinhaus
Michael Craig Goldberg
Jerome J. Dobson
Mark E. Moreland

ASSOCIATES

Jonathan Charles Berns
Gregory Alan Rich
Scott P. Holwitt

Reference: The Boatmen's National Bank of St. Louis.

For full biographical listings, see the Martindale-Hubbell Law Directory

MONTANA

*BILLINGS,** Yellowstone Co.

Crowley, Haughey, Hanson, Toole & Dietrich, P.L.L.P. (AV)

500 Transwestern II, 490 North 31st Street, P.O. Box 2529, 59103
Telephone: 406-252-3441
Fax: 406-259-4159
Email: crowley@crowleylaw.com
Helena, Montana Office: IBM Building, 100 North Park Avenue, Suite 300, 59601.
Telephone: 406-449-4165.
Fax: 406-449-5149.
Kalispell, Montana Office: 431 1st Avenue West, 59901.
Telephone: 406-752-6644.
Fax: 406-752-5108.
Williston, North Dakota Office: 113 East Broadway, 58801.
Telephone: 701-572-2200.
Fax: 701-572-7072.

OF COUNSEL

Gareld F. Krieg

MEMBERS OF FIRM

Terry B. Cosgrove (Resident, Helena, Montana Office)
Steven J. Lehman
John R. Alexander
William J. Mattix
Joe C. Maynard, Jr.

Representative Clients: Xerox Corporation; Valley Motor Supply; Montana Power Company; Armstrong World Industries; Peabody Coal Co.; United Parcel Service; Billings Clinic; Yellowstone County; MDU Resources Group, Inc.; General Electric Co.

For Complete List of Firm Personnel, See General Section

For full biographical listings, see the Martindale-Hubbell Law Directory

NEBRASKA

*LINCOLN,** Lancaster Co.

Cline, Williams, Wright, Johnson & Oldfather (AV)

1900 U.S. Bank Building, 233 South 13th Street, 68508
Telephone: 402-474-6900
Fax: 402-474-5393
Email: postmaster@cline-law.com *URL:* http://www.cline-law.com
Omaha, Nebraska Office: Suite 720, One Pacific Place, 1125 South 103rd Street, 68124.
Telephone: 402-397-1700.
Fax: 402-397-1806.

ATTORNEYS

Allen L. Graves
Charles M. Pallesen, Jr.
Fredric H. Kauffman
Donald F. Burt
Alan E. Peterson
Stephen E. Gehring
Robert J. Routh
Kevin Colleran
L. Bruce Wright
James M. Bausch
Larry A. Holle
David R. Buntain
Stephen H. Nelsen
Michael C. Mueller
Lauren W. Wismer
Daniel R. Stogsdill
Scott D. Kelly
Terry R. Wittler
Pamela Hastings Carrier
Mark A. Christensen
Richard P. Garden, Jr.
Shawn D. Renner
John C. Miles
Mary Kay Frank
Thomas C. Huston
Sonya S. Ekart
Don R. Janssen
Susan Kubert Sapp
Kevin J. Schneider
Andrew D. Strotman
Jill Gossin Jensen
Rochelle A. Mullen
John L. Horan
Bryan S. Hatch
Steven C. Likes
Tracy A. Oldemeyer
Jolene M. Papa
Timothy G. Aschoff
Eric N. Bergquist
Janis J. Winterhof
Andrea Dylan Snowden

OF COUNSEL

Charles E. Wright
Richard P. Jeffries
Mary M. Campbell

RETIRED PARTNERS

Flavel A. Wright (Retired)
Warren C. Johnson (Retired)
Charles E. Oldfather (1927-1998)

Representative Clients: U.S. Bank National Association; University of Nebraska; Nebraska Medical Assn.; Saint Elizabeth Regional Medical Center; Media of Nebraska; Cargill Inc.; State Farm Insurance Cos.; Wal-Mart Stores, Inc.; Textron/Cushman; Isco, Inc.

For full biographical listings, see the Martindale-Hubbell Law Directory

*OMAHA,** Douglas Co.

BERENS & TATE, P.C. (AV)

Suite 400, 10050 Regency Circle, 68114
Telephone: 402-391-1991
Fax: 402-391-7363
Email: Berems@Berenstate.com

Kelvin C. Berens
Joseph Dreesen
Timothy D. Loudon
Christopher E. Hoyme
Mark E. McQueen
Donna S. Colley
Jerylyn R. Bridgeford
Timothy M. Welsh
William M. Muth, Jr.
Nancy A. Wood
David D. Gale

Michaelle L. Behrns

OF COUNSEL

John E. Tate
Donald E. Leonard (1933-1994)

For full biographical listings, see the Martindale-Hubbell Law Directory

CLINE, WILLIAMS, WRIGHT, JOHNSON & OLDFATHER (AV)

One Pacific Place, 1125 South 103rd Street, Suite 720, 68124
Telephone: 402-397-1700
Fax: 402-397-1806
Email: postmaster@cline-law.com *URL:* http://www.cline-law.com
Lincoln, Nebraska Office: 1900 U.S. Bank Building, 233 South 13th Street, 68508.
Telephone: 402-474-6900.
Fax: 402-474-5393.

ATTORNEYS

Donald F. Burt
Stephen E. Gehring
James M. Bausch
Michael C. Mueller
Daniel R. Stogsdill
Scott D. Kelly
John C. Miles
Mary Kay Frank
Andrew D. Strotman
Rochelle A. Mullen
Steven C. Likes
Tracy A. Oldemeyer
Timothy G. Aschoff

OF COUNSEL

Richard P. Jeffries

Representative Clients: U.S. Bank National Association; University of Nebraska; Nebraska Medical Assn.; Saint Elizabeth Regional Medical Center; Media of Nebraska; Cargill Inc.; State Farm Insurance Cos.; Wal-Mart Stores, Inc.; Textron/Cushman; ISCO, Inc.

For full biographical listings, see the Martindale-Hubbell Law Directory

NEVADA

*RENO,** Washoe Co.

McDONALD CARANO WILSON McCUNE BERGIN FRANKOVICH & HICKS LLP (AV)

241 Ridge Street, 89501
Telephone: 775-788-2000
Telecopier: 775-788-2020
URL: http://www.mcdonaldcarano.com
Las Vegas, Nevada Office: Suite 1000, 2300 West Sahara Avenue.
Telephone: 702-873-4100.
Telecopier: 702-873-9966.

MEMBERS OF FIRM

John J. McCune
John J. Frankovich
Timothy E. Rowe
James W. Bradshaw
Pat Lundvall
Andrew P. Gordon
Bryan R. Clark

ASSOCIATES

Miranda M. Du
Bonnie Fleischer Drinkwater
Jeffrey A. Silvestri
Judy P. Osgood

Representative Clients: CDS of Nevada, Inc.; Eldorado Hotel & Casino; Jackpot Enterprises, Inc.; Q & D Construction Company; Scolari's Warehouse Markets, Inc.; Sierra Nevada Production Credit Association; The Gibbons Company.

For Complete List of Firm Personnel, See General Section

For full biographical listings, see the Martindale-Hubbell Law Directory

WALTHER, KEY, MAUPIN, OATS, COX & LEGOY, A PROFESSIONAL CORPORATION (AV)

Lakeside Professional Plaza, 3500 Lakeside Court, 89509
Telephone: 775-827-2000
Facsimile: 775-827-2185
Mailing Address: P.O. Box 30000, Reno, Nevada, 89520

(See Next Column)

L. Robert LeGoy, Jr.
Michael E. Malloy
Kim G. Rowe
Donald A. Lattin
Gustave J. Rossi
Kurt O. Hunsberger

Representative Clients: Associated Anesthesiologists of Reno; Bi-State Petroleum; Model Dairy, Inc.; Radiation Oncology; Regional Ambulance Services; Reno Radiological; Sierra Anesthesiologists; Sparks Nugget, Inc.; Washoe Health System; Western Nevada Supply Co.

For full biographical listings, see the Martindale-Hubbell Law Directory

NEW JERSEY

*HACKENSACK,** Bergen Co.

HEIN, SMITH, BEREZIN, MALOOF & JACOBS, L.L.C. (AV)

Court Plaza East, 19 Main Street, 07601-7023
Telephone: 201-487-7400
Telecopier: 201-487-4228
Email: counsel@heinsmith.com

OF COUNSEL

Seymour A. Smith

For Complete List of Firm Personnel, See General Section

For full biographical listings, see the Martindale-Hubbell Law Directory

STOLDT, HORAN AND KOWAL, A PROFESSIONAL CORPORATION (AV)

Continental Plaza I, 401 Hackensack Avenue, 07601
Telephone: 201-646-9200
Telecopier: 201-646-0167
Email: shlaw@bellatlantic.net *URL:* http://www.lawyers.com/stoldthoran&kowal

Sydney V. Stoldt, Jr.
John D. Horan
Dorothy A. Kowal
Heather A. Gallagher
Brian O'Reilly

OF COUNSEL

Judith R. Levinson

For full biographical listings, see the Martindale-Hubbell Law Directory

*MORRISTOWN,** Morris Co.

PITNEY, HARDIN, KIPP & SZUCH LLP (AV)

P.O. Box 1945, 07962-1945
Telephone: 973-966-6300
New York City: 212-687-6000
Telex: 642014
Telecopier: 973-966-1550
URL: http://www.phks.com
New York, New York Office: 711 Third Avenue, 10017-4014.
Telephone: 212-687-6000.
Fax: 212-682-3485.

MEMBERS OF FIRM

S. Joseph Fortunato
Kevin J. O'Donnell
Kathy A. Lawler
Theresa Donahue Egler
David P. Doyle

COUNSEL

Michael J. Duane (Not admitted in NJ)

ASSOCIATES

Amanda Berlowe Jaffe
Glenn Eric Butash (Not admitted in NJ)
Marjorie F. Sheron

Representative Clients: American Home Products Corporation; Base ten Systems, Inc.; Lucent Technologies.

For Complete List of Firm Personnel, See General Section

For full biographical listings, see the Martindale-Hubbell Law Directory

*NEWARK,** Essex Co.

CARPENTER, BENNETT & MORRISSEY (AV)

Three Gateway Center, 17th Floor, 100 Mulberry Street, 07102-4079
Telephone: 973-622-7711
New York City: 212-943-6530
Telex: 139405
Telecopier: 973-622-5314
Email: cbm@carpben.com

MEMBERS OF FIRM

Laurence Reich
James J. Crowley, Jr.
Donald A. Romano
Francis X. Dee
Irving L. Hurwitz
Rosemary J. Bruno
Patrick G. Brady
Stephen F. Payerle
Kevin C. Donovan
James Peter Lidon
David J. Reilly
Vincent P. Browne

(See Next Column)

CARPENTER, BENNETT & MORRISSEY—*Continued*

OF COUNSEL

Edward F. Day, Jr.

ASSOCIATES

Hans G. Polak
Michael P. Einbinder (Not admitted in NJ)

Representative Clients: General Motors Corp.; Johnson & Johnson; Litton Industries; AT&T; International Specialty Products; South Jersey Hospital; Schindler Elevator Corp.; MAN Capital Corp.; International Flavors & Fragrances Inc.; Chubb & Son, Inc.

For Complete List of Firm Personnel, See General Section

For full biographical listings, see the Martindale-Hubbell Law Directory

---

McCARTER & ENGLISH, LLP (AV)

Four Gateway Center, 100 Mulberry Street, P.O. Box 652, 07101-0652
Telephone: 973-622-4444
Telecopier: 973-624-7070
URL: http://www.mccarter.com
Cherry Hill, New Jersey Office: 1820 Chapel Avenue West, Suite 380.
Telephone: 609-662-8444.
Telecopier: 609-662-6203.
New York, New York Office: Suite 2247, One World Trade Center.
Telephone: 212-466-9018.
Telecopier: 212-432-6568.
Boca Raton, Florida Office: 2255 Glades Road, Suite 319-A.
Telephone: 561-994-6262.
Telecopier: 561-241-0798.
Wilmington, Delaware Office: Mellon Bank Center, 919 Market Street.
Telephone: 302-654-8010.
Telecopier: 302-654-0795.
Philadelphia, Pennsylvania Office: One Commerce Square, 2005 Market Street, Suite 3600.
Telephone: 215-557-7700.
Telecopier: 215-557-6544.

MEMBERS OF FIRM

Richard C. Cooper
William S. Greenberg
John E. Flaherty
John B. Brescher, Jr.
Rosemary Alito
Theodore D. Moskowitz
Mark A. Daniele
B. John Pendleton, Jr.
John C. McGuire

For Complete List of Firm Personnel, See General Section

For full biographical listings, see the Martindale-Hubbell Law Directory

---

SILLS CUMMIS RADIN TISCHMAN EPSTEIN & GROSS, A PROFESSIONAL CORPORATION (AV)

One Riverfront Plaza, 07102-5400
Telephone: 973-643-7000
Fax: 973-643-6500
Telex: 820630 Sillsbeck Nwk
Email: sillsmail@sillscummis.com *URL:* http://www.sillscummis.com
Atlantic City, New Jersey Office: 17 Gordon's Alley.
Telephone: 609-344-2800.
New York, N.Y. Office: 712 Fifth Avenue.
Telephone: 212-643-7000.
Washington, D.C. Office: 1800 K Street, N.W.
Telephone: 202-296-4750.

MEMBERS OF FIRM

Barry M. Epstein
Jeffrey J. Greenbaum
Lester Aron
Stuart M. Feinblatt
David W. Garland
Alan J. Cohen (Resident at Atlantic City, N.J. Office)

OF COUNSEL

Cherie L. Maxwell

Paul P. Josephson

Representative Clients: Becton Dickinson & Company; Allied Signal; Bally Manufacturing Corp.; Rutgers University; McKinsey & Co.; Melvin Simon; N.J.. Nets; P.S.E.& G.; Syms; WWOR-TV.

For Complete List of Firm Personnel, See General Section

For full biographical listings, see the Martindale-Hubbell Law Directory

---

*TRENTON,** Mercer Co.

NEEDELL, SIEKERKA & CASTELLANI, A PROFESSIONAL CORPORATION (AV)

Quakerbridge Commons, 2681 Quakerbridge Road, 08619-1625
Telephone: 609-584-7700
Fax: 609-584-0123
Email: nsclaw@aol.com

Stanley H. Needell
Michele N. Siekerka
Anthony P. Castellani

John M. Cinti
Dean C. Gresek

(See Next Column)

LEGAL SUPPORT PERSONNEL

PARALEGALS

Marlene Griesbach
Carolyn D. Shaw
Veronica A. Mitchell

For full biographical listings, see the Martindale-Hubbell Law Directory

---

NEW MEXICO

*ALBUQUERQUE,** Bernalillo Co.

EAVES, BARDACKE, BAUGH KIERST & KIERNAN, P.A. (AV)

6400 Uptown Boulevard, N.E., Suite 110-W, P.O. Box 35670, 87176
Telephone: 505-888-4300
Facsimile: 505-883-4406
Email: LGLEAVES@EB-B.com

John M. Eaves
Paul Bardacke
John G. Baugh
Peter S. Kierst
Kerry Kiernan

Derek V. Larson
Karen S. Mendenhall
C. Shannon Bacon

OF COUNSEL

Jennifer J. Pruett

For full biographical listings, see the Martindale-Hubbell Law Directory

---

NEW YORK

*ALBANY,** Albany Co.

ROBERT S. CATAPANO-FRIEDMAN, P.C. (AV)

744 Broadway, 12207
Telephone: 518-463-7501; 518-463-7502
Fax: 518-463-1948
Email: catapan@worldnet.att.net

Robert S. Catapano-Friedman

For full biographical listings, see the Martindale-Hubbell Law Directory

---

GARDEN CITY, Nassau Co.

GALLAGHER GOSSEEN FALLER KAPLAN & CROWLEY (AV)

1010 Franklin Avenue, Suite 400, 11530-2927
Telephone: 516-742-2500
Fax: 516-742-2516
Email: GGFKC_Postmaster@GGFKC.com
New York, New York Office: 350 Fifth Avenue, Suite 603.
Telephone: 212-947-5800.
Fax: 212-967-4965.

MEMBERS OF FIRM

James A. Gallagher, Jr.
Robert I. Gosseen (Resident, New York City Office)
Robert A. Faller
Alan D. Kaplan
Michael J. Crowley
William E. Vita
Brian P. Morrissey

ASSOCIATES

David H. Arntsen
Joseph A. Latasso
Amy L. Ruina
Gerald A. Corallo, Jr.

OF COUNSEL

John P. Coogan
Peter F. Vetro
William A. Bales, Jr.

For full biographical listings, see the Martindale-Hubbell Law Directory

---

JERICHO, Nassau Co.

KAUFMAN, SCHNEIDER & BIANCO, LLP (AV)

390 North Broadway, 11753
Telephone: 516-681-1100
Fax: 516-681-1101
Email: ksb@managementattyorney.com

Arthur R. Kaufman
Peter A. Schneider
Thomas J. Bianco
Carmelo Grimaldi
Michael A. Kaufman

Richard M. Howard
Christina Bennett
Jill S. Ellner
David Greenhaus

For full biographical listings, see the Martindale-Hubbell Law Directory

*NEW YORK,** New York Co.

BERLACK, ISRAELS & LIBERMAN LLP (AV)

120 West 45th Street, 10036
Telephone: 212-704-0100
Cable Address: "Berilib"
Telecopier: 212-704-0196
Email: info@berlack.com
Morristown, New Jersey Office: 65 Madison Avenue.
Telephone: 201-644-3400.
Telecopier: 201-644-3159.

MEMBERS OF FIRM

Harris Berlack (1946-1968)
Carlos L. Israels (1946-1969)
Kenneth R. Asher
Claude A. Baum
Scott M. Berman
Wade M. Boswell
Douglas E. Davidson
Alan N. Forman
Steven E. Greenbaum
Harvey M. Katz
James B. Liberman
Stuart Neuhauser
Robert D. Schmicker
Martin S. Siegel
Steven F. Wasserman
Edward S. Weisfelner

SENIOR ATTORNEYS

Andrew S. Dash
Erica M. Ryland

ASSOCIATES

John P. Biedermann
Anne M. Cunningham
Pauline Foley (Resident, Morristown, New Jersey Office)
Julie L. Friedberg (Resident, Morristown, New Jersey Office)
Emilio A. Galván
Linda B. Goebel
Louis Lombardo
Rachel F. Mayerson (Not admitted in NY)
Amy P. K. Motzenbecker (Resident, Morristown, New Jersey Office)
Antonio Peguero, Jr.
Elizabeth Quirk (Resident, Morristown, New Jersey Office)
Marcela M. Sanchez
Melissa Sarubbi

OF COUNSEL

Gerald W. Conway (Not admitted in NY; Resident, Morristown, New Jersey Office)
Marc B. Lasky (Resident, Morristown, New Jersey Office)

For full biographical listings, see the Martindale-Hubbell Law Directory

O'DONNELL, SCHWARTZ, GLANSTEIN, ROSEN, DI PRETA & GOLDSTEIN, L.L.P. (AV)

Suite 1022, 60 East 42nd Street, 10165
Telephone: 212-370-5100
Fax: 212-697-6299
Email: odsgr@worldnet.att.net
Washington, D.C. Offices: O'Donnell, Schwartz & Anderson, Suite 1200, 1300 L Street, N.W.
Telephone: 202-898-1707.
Telex: 202-429-8928 and Suite 707, 1900 L Street, N.W.
Telephone: 202-898-1824.

RESIDENT MEMBERS

John F. O'Donnell (1907-1993)
Asher W. Schwartz
Joel C. Glanstein
David B. Rosen
Malcolm A. Goldstein
Manlio Di Preta

RESIDENT ASSOCIATES

Edmond V. Pendleton
David M. Glanstein

OF COUNSEL

Suzanne McCarthy

For full biographical listings, see the Martindale-Hubbell Law Directory

OTTERBOURG, STEINDLER, HOUSTON & ROSEN, P.C. (AV)

230 Park Avenue, 29th Floor, 10169
Telephone: 212-661-9100
Telecopier: 212-682-6104

Donald N. Gellert

Lloyd M. Green

For Complete List of Firm Personnel, See General Section

For full biographical listings, see the Martindale-Hubbell Law Directory

REED SMITH SHAW & MCCLAY LLP (AV®)

375 Park Avenue, 17th Floor, 10152
Telephone: 212-521-5400
FAX: 212-521-5450
Email: rssm@rssm.com *URL:* http://www.rssm.com
Pittsburgh, Pennsylvania Office: 435 Sixth Avenue, 15219-1886.
Telephone: 412-288-3131.
FAX: 412-288-3063.

(See Next Column)

Washington, D.C. Office: Suite 1100 - East Tower, 1301 K Street, N.W., 20005-3317.
Telephone: 202-414-9200.
FAX: 202-414-9299.
Philadelphia, Pennsylvania Office: 2500 One Liberty Place, 19103-7301.
Telephone: 215-851-8100.
FAX: 215-851-1420.
Harrisburg, Pennsylvania Office: 213 Market Street, 17101-2132.
Telephone: 717-234-5988.
FAX: 717-236-3777.
Princeton, New Jersey Office: 136 Main Street, Suite 250, 08540-5799.
Telephone: 609-987-0050.
FAX: 609-951-0824.
Newark, New Jersey Office: The Legal Center, One Riverfront Plaza, First Floor, 07102-5400.
Telephone: 973-621-3200.
FAX: 973-621-3199.
McLean, Virginia Office: Reed Smith Hazel & Thomas LLP, Suite 1100, 8251 Greensboro Drive, 22102-3844.
Telephone: 703-734-4600.
FAX: 703-734-4699.
Falls Church, Virginia Office: Reed Smith Hazel & Thomas, Suite 1400, 3110 Fairview Park Drive, P.O. Box 12001.
Telephone: 703-641-4200.
Fax: 703-641-4340.
Leesburg, Virginia Office: Reed Smith Hazel & Thomas LLP, 44084 Riverside Parkway, Suite 300.
Telephone: 703-729-8500. Metro: 703-478-1992.
Fax: 703-478-8003.
Richmond, Virginia Office: Reed Smith Hazel & Thomas LLP, Suite 600, 411 East Franklin Street, P.O. Box 788.
Telephone: 804-344-3400.
Fax: 804-344-3410.

MEMBERS OF FIRM

Alan A. D'Ambrosio
Ruth S. Perfido (Not admitted in NY; Also at Pittsburgh, Pennsylvania)
David L. Weissman
Jonathan Young

COUNSEL

Adria De Landri
Andrew B. Messite
Marlene A. Zarfes

ASSOCIATES

Werner S. Achatz
Feini Ardelean
Ellen McPhillips Baumann
John F. Curran, Jr.
Annmarie D'Amour
Joseph M. Marger
Scott S. McKessy
Andre T. Nobles
Kipling Oren
Darren M. Sharlach
William R. Wright

For full biographical listings, see the Martindale-Hubbell Law Directory

RIDLEY M. WHITAKER (AV)

One Rockefeller Plaza, 10020
Telephone: 212-218-5656
Telecopier: 212-218-5665
Email: 74051.3574@compuserve.com

For full biographical listings, see the Martindale-Hubbell Law Directory

NORTH CAROLINA

*CHARLOTTE,** Mecklenburg Co.

WOMBLE CARLYLE SANDRIDGE & RICE (AV)

A Professional Limited Liability Company
3300 One First Union Center, 301 South College Street, 28202-6025
Telephone: 704-331-4900
Fax: 704-331-4955
Email: lawyers@wcsr.com *URL:* http://www.wcsr.com
Winston-Salem, North Carolina Office: 200 West Second Street, P.O. Drawer 84.
Telephone: 336-721-3600.
Fax: 336-721-3660.
Raleigh, North Carolina Office: 2100 First Union Capitol Center, 150 Fayetteville Street Mall, P.O. Box 831.
Telephone: 919-755-2100.
Fax: 919-755-2150.
Research Triangle Park, North Carolina Office: 2505 Meridian Parkway, Suite 300 (Durham), 27713.
Telephone: 919-484-2300.
Fax: 919-484-2340.
Atlanta, Georgia Office: One Atlantic Center, 1201 West Peachtree Street, Suite 3500.
Telephone: 404-872-7000.
Fax: 404-888-7490.
Other Atlanta, Georgia Office: Suite 404, 2296 Henderson Mill Road, N.E.
Telephone: 770-492-9030.
Fax: 770-492-9609.

(See Next Column)

WOMBLE CARLYLE SANDRIDGE & RICE—*Continued*

Washington, D.C. Office: 1120 Nineteenth Street, N.W., Eighth Floor.
Telephone: 202-857-4400.
Fax: 202-467-6910.
Greenville, South Carolina Office: 15 South Main Street, Suite 601, P.O. Box 10208.
Telephone: 864-255-5400.
Fax: 864-255-5440.

RESIDENT MEMBER

James E. Daniel

RESIDENT OF COUNSEL

Jane Jeffries Jones

Representative Clients: Childress Klein Properties, Inc.; Food Lion, Inc.; J.A. Jones Construction Co.; Parkdale Mills, Inc.; Pillowtex; Duke Power Co.; Bowles Hollowell Conner & Co.; ALLTEL Carolina, Inc.; Belk Store Services, Inc.; Philip Holzmann A.G.

For Complete List of Firm Personnel, See General Section

For full biographical listings, see the Martindale-Hubbell Law Directory

*RALEIGH,** Wake Co.

WOMBLE CARLYLE SANDRIDGE & RICE (AV)

A Professional Limited Liability Company
2100 First Union Capitol Center, 150 Fayetteville Street Mall, P.O. Box 831, 27602
Telephone: 919-755-2100
Fax: 919-755-2150
Email: lawyers@wcsr.com *URL:* http://www.wcsr.com
Charlotte, North Carolina Office: 3300 One First Union Center, 301 South College Street.
Telephone: 704-331-4900.
Fax: 704-331-4955.
Winston-Salem, North Carolina Office: 200 West Second Street, P.O. Drawer 84.
Telephone: 336-721-3600.
Fax: 336-721-3660.
Research Triangle Park, North Carolina Office: 2505 Meridian Parkway, Suite 300 (Durham), 27713.
Telephone: 919-484-2300.
Fax: 919-484-2340.
Atlanta, Georgia Office: One Atlantic Center, 1201 West Peachtree Street, Suite 3500.
Telephone: 404-872-7000.
Fax: 404-888-7490.
Other Atlanta, Georgia Office: Suite 404, 2296 Henderson Mill Road, N.E.
Telephone: 770-492-9030.
Fax: 770-492-9609.
Washington, D.C. Office: 1120 Nineteenth Street, N.W., Eighth Floor.
Telephone: 202-857-4400.
Fax: 202-467-6910.
Greenville, South Carolina Office: 15 South Main Street, Suite 601, P.O. Box 10208.
Telephone: 864-255-5400.
Fax: 864-255-5440.

RESIDENT MEMBER

Charles A. Edwards

RESIDENT ASSOCIATES

Richard M. Feathers
Jeffrey M. Hahn
M. Todd Sullivan

Representative Clients: Aetna Casualty and Surety Co., Inc.; ALSCO/AmeriMark Building Products, Inc.; Aoki Corporation America, Inc.; Hackney Brothers, Inc.; Lawyers Mutual Liability Insurance Company of North Carolina; Meredith College; Regency Park Corp.; Wachovia Bank, N.A.

For Complete List of Firm Personnel, See General Section

For full biographical listings, see the Martindale-Hubbell Law Directory

*WINSTON-SALEM,** Forsyth Co.

WOMBLE CARLYLE SANDRIDGE & RICE (AV)

A Professional Limited Liability Company
200 West Second Street, P.O. Drawer 84, 27102
Telephone: 336-721-3600
Fax: 336-721-3660
Email: lawyers@wcsr.com *URL:* http://www.wcsr.com
Charlotte, North Carolina Office: 3300 One First Union Center, 301 South College Street.
Telephone: 704-331-4900.
Fax: 704-331-4955.
Raleigh, North Carolina Office: 2100 First Union Capitol Center, 150 Fayetteville Street Mall, P.O. Box 831.
Telephone: 919-755-2100.
Fax: 919-755-2150.
Research Triangle Park, North Carolina Office: 2505 Meridian Parkway, Suite 300 (Durham), 27713.
Telephone: 919-484-2300.
Fax: 919-484-2340.

(See Next Column)

Atlanta, Georgia Office: One Atlantic Center, 1201 West Peachtree Street, Suite 3500.
Telephone: 404-872-7000.
Fax: 404-888-7490.
Other Atlanta, Georgia Office: Suite 404, 2296 Henderson Mill Road, N.E.
Telephone: 770-492-9030.
Fax: 770-492-9609.
Washington, D.C. Office: 1120 Nineteenth Street, N.W., Eighth Floor.
Telephone: 202-857-4400.
Fax: 202-467-6910.
Greenville, South Carolina Office: 15 South Main Street, Suite 601, P.O. Box 10208.
Telephone: 864-255-5400.
Fax: 864-255-5440.

RESIDENT MEMBERS

Janice C. Baldwin
Michael D. Gunter
William R. Whitehurst

RESIDENT ASSOCIATE

Patrick M. Allen

Representative Clients: Brad Ragan, Inc.; Brenner Companies; Food Lion, Inc.; Hanes Companies, Inc.; North Carolina Baptist Hospitals, Inc.; R.J. Reynolds Tobacco Co.; Thomasville Furniture Industries, Inc.; Wachovia Corp.; Wake Forest University.

For Complete List of Firm Personnel, See General Section

For full biographical listings, see the Martindale-Hubbell Law Directory

OHIO

*CINCINNATI,** Hamilton Co.

KATZ, TELLER, BRANT & HILD A LEGAL PROFESSIONAL ASSOCIATION (AV)

2400 Chemed Center, 255 East Fifth Street, 45202-4724
Telephone: 513-721-4532
Telecopier: 513-721-7120
Email: corp@ktbh.com

Robert E. Brant
Stephen C. Kisling
Suzanne Prieur Land

Joel S. Brant

For Complete List of Firm Personnel, See General Section

For full biographical listings, see the Martindale-Hubbell Law Directory

STRAUSS & TROY A LEGAL PROFESSIONAL ASSOCIATION (AV)

The Federal Reserve Building, 150 East Fourth Street, 45202-4018
Telephone: 513-621-2120
Telecopier: 513-241-8259
URL: http://www.strauss-troy.com
Northern Kentucky Office: Suite 1400, 50 East Rivercenter Boulevard, Covington, Kentucky, 41011.
Telephone: 513-621-8900; 513-621-2120.
Telecopier: 513-629-9444.

Larry A. Neuman
Claudia G. Allen

Representative Clients: PNC Bank, N.A. (Ohio and Kentucky); Corporex Companies, Inc.; Mercantile Stores Co., Inc.; Star Bank, N.A. (Ohio and Kentucky).

For Complete List of Firm Personnel, See General Section

For full biographical listings, see the Martindale-Hubbell Law Directory

*CLEVELAND,** Cuyahoga Co.

BAKER & HOSTETLER LLP (AV)

3200 National City Center, 1900 East Ninth Street, 44114-3485
Telephone: 216-621-0200
Telecopier: 216-696-0740
TWX: 810 421 8375
RCA Telex: 215032
To contact an attorney on the Internet use first initial and surname followed by @baker-hostetler.com
URL: http://www.bakerlaw.com
In Cincinnati, Ohio: 312 Walnut Street, Suite 2650.
Telephone: 513-929-3400.
In Columbus, Ohio: Capitol Square, Suite 2100, 65 East State Street.
Telephone: 614-228-1541.
In Denver, Colorado: 303 East 17th Avenue, Suite 1100.
Telephone: 303-861-0600.
In Houston, Texas: 1000 Louisiana, Suite 2000.
Telephone: 713-751-1600.
In Beverly Hills, California: 9150 Wilshire Boulevard, Suite 205.
Telephone: 310-385-7500.
In Long Beach, California: 300 Oceangate, Suite 620.
Telephone: 562-432-2827.

(See Next Column)

BAKER & HOSTETLER LLP, *Cleveland—Continued*

In Los Angeles, California: 600 Wilshire Boulevard.
Telephone: 213-624-2400.
In Orlando, Florida: SunBank Center, Suite 2300, 200 South Orange Avenue.
Telephone: 407-649-4000.
In Washington, D.C.: Washington Square, Suite 1100, 1050 Connecticut Avenue, N.W.
Telephone: 202-861-1500.

PARTNERS

Richard H. Bamberger
Raymond M. Malone
John J. McGowan, Jr.
W. James Ollinger
R. Byron Wallace

For Complete List of Firm Personnel, See General Section

For full biographical listings, see the Martindale-Hubbell Law Directory

DUVIN, CAHN & HUTTON A LEGAL PROFESSIONAL ASSOCIATION (AV)

Erieview Tower, 20th Floor, 1301 East Ninth Street, 44114
Telephone: 216-696-7600
Facsimile: 216-696-2038
Email: attorneys@duvin.com *URL:* http://www.duvinlaw.com
Southfield, Michigan Office: 26211 Central Park Boulevard, Suite 500, 48076.
Telephone: 248-945-1977.
Fax: 248-945-1162.

Robert P. Duvin
Stephen J. Cahn
Lee J. Hutton
Marc J. Bloch
Andrew C. Meyer
Martin S. List
Craig M. Brown
Frank W. Buck
Neal B. Wainblat
Kenneth B. Stark
Martin T. Wymer
Robert M. Wolff
Steven W. Albert
Stephen J. Sferra
Christine C. Covey
Richard C. Hubbard, III
Jon M. Dileno
Suellen Oswald
David A. Posner
Janette McCarthy Louard

Lisa Froimson Mann
David W. Neel
Kathleen M. Kordeleski
Michael T. Pearson
Kenneth D. Schwartz
Brett S. Krantz
Barry Y. Freeman
Bradley A. Sherman
Jonathan S. Forman
Mark F. Humenik
Robert C. Pivonka
Fredrick W Englehart
Jonathan T. Hyman
Latha M. Srinivasan
Shannon K. Patton

OF COUNSEL

Mark V. Webber

Representative Clients: Ameritech; Lincoln Electric; Cleveland-Akron-Canton Supermarket Industry; The Scott Fetzer Co.; Electronic Data Systems Corporation; Cleveland Clinic Foundation; Steris; Praxair.

For full biographical listings, see the Martindale-Hubbell Law Directory

MCDONALD, HOPKINS, BURKE & HABER CO., L.P.A. (AV)

2100 Bank One Center, 600 Superior Avenue, E., 44114-2653
Telephone: 216-348-5400
Telecopier: 216-348-5474
Email: attorney@mhbh.com *URL:* http://www.mhbh.com

Patrick J. Berry
Jeffrey P. Consolo
Jerome W. Cook
Richard S. Cooper
Anthony J. DiVenere
Paul N. Edwards
Theodore J. Esborn
Steven L. Gardner
Carl J. Grassi
James A. Griffith
Jeffrey R. Huntsberger
Brian J. Jereb
Bernard L. Karr
Thomas W. Keen
Roger L. Kleinman
Joseph J. LoPresti, Jr.
Dan L. Makee
George L. McGaughey, Jr.
John T. Mulligan
Brian M. O'Neill
William J. O'Neill
Stephen T. Parisi
R. Jeffrey Pollock
Michael G. Riley
Shawn M. Riley
Albert N. Salvatore
Thomas C. Schrader
Roger L. Shumaker
Barbara J. Smith
James M. Stone
Dale R. Vlasek
Kenneth J. Walsh
John M. Wirtshafter
Jane Marie Pine Wood
Charles B. Zellmer

OF COUNSEL

John J. Monroe

Julie A. Callsen
Anne T. Corrigan
Steven A. Eisenberg
G. Andrew Gardner
Anuj Goswami
Donald E. Kacmar
David M. Kall
Jeffrey B. Keiper
Kevin J. Kessinger
Mark D. Klimek
Alan M. Koschik
Deviani M. Kuhar

(See Next Column)

Paul W. Linehan
Tyler L. Mathews
Jennifer A. Mills
Antoinette K. Palmer
Ketan K. Patel
Sharon Szolosi Regas
Douglas B. Schnee
Michele Smolin
Glenn D. Southworth
Michael R. Spreng

For full biographical listings, see the Martindale-Hubbell Law Directory

WALTER & HAVERFIELD, P.L.L. (AV)

1300 Terminal Tower, 44113-2253
Telephone: 216-781-1212
Telecopier: 216-575-0911
Email: law@walterhav.com *URL:* http://www.walterhav.com
Columbus, Ohio Office: 88 East Broad Street.
Telephone: 614-898-1096.

MEMBER OF FIRM

Russell C. Shaw

OF COUNSEL

Sheldon M. Young
Ricky Lee Bertram

LEGAL SUPPORT PERSONNEL

John B. Eldred

Representative Clients: AGA Gas, Inc.; Andrews Moving & Storage Company1 Bellevue Manufacturing; Louis Berkman Company; Braden Sutphin, Inc.; Flair Corporation; International Metal Hose Co.; Key Trust Company of Ohio, N.A.; Sea-Land Chemical Company.

For Complete List of Firm Personnel, See General Section

For full biographical listings, see the Martindale-Hubbell Law Directory

*COLUMBUS,** Franklin Co.

BAKER & HOSTETLER LLP (AV)

Capitol Square, Suite 2100, 65 East State Street, 43215-4260
Telephone: 614-228-1541
Telecopier: 614-462-2616
To contact an attorney on the Internet use first initial and surname followed by @baker-hostetler.com
URL: http://www.bakerlaw.com
In Cleveland, Ohio: 3200 National City Center, 1900 East Ninth Street.
Telephone: 216-621-0200.
In Cincinnati, Ohio: 312 Walnut Street, Suite 2650.
Telephone: 513-929-3400.
In Denver, Colorado: 303 East 17th Avenue, Suite 1100.
Telephone: 303-861-0600.
In Houston, Texas: 1000 Louisiana, Suite 2000.
Telephone: 713-751-1600.
In Beverly Hills, California: 9150 Wilshire Boulevard, Suite 205.
Telephone: 310-385-7500.
In Long Beach, California: 300 Oceangate, Suite 620.
Telephone: 562-432-2827.
In Los Angeles, California: 600 Wilshire Boulevard.
Telephone: 213-624-2400.
In Orlando, Florida: SunBank Center, Suite 2300, 200 South Orange Avenue.
Telephone: 407-649-4000.
In Washington, D. C.: Washington Square, Suite 1100, 1050 Connecticut Avenue, N.W.
Telephone: 202-861-1500.

PARTNER

Georgeann G. Peters

For Complete List of Firm Personnel, See General Section

For full biographical listings, see the Martindale-Hubbell Law Directory

BRENNER, BROWN, GOLIAN & MCCAFFREY CO., L.P.A. (AV)

1654 East Broad Street, 43203-2079
Telephone: 614-258-6000
Telecopier: 614-258-6006
Email: bbgm@netwalk.com

Philip F. Brown
Joseph J. Golian
Todd Austin Brenner
Patrick McCaffrey, Jr.

For full biographical listings, see the Martindale-Hubbell Law Directory

KEGLER, BROWN, HILL & RITTER (AV)

Capitol Square Suite 1800, 65 East State Street, 43215-4294
Telephone: 614-462-5400
Telecopier: 614-464-2634
Cable Address: "Law KBHR"
Telex: 246671
Email: info@kbhr.com *URL:* http://www.kbhr.com
Marion, Ohio Office: 250 Executive Drive, Suite B, P.O. Box 919.
Telephone: 614-387-3501.
Facsimile: 614-387-3630.

Paul D. Ritter, Jr.

Representative Clients: The Benatty Corp.; Diocese of Columbus; Drug Emporium, Inc.

(See Next Column)

KEGLER, BROWN, HILL & RITTER—*Continued*

For Complete List of Firm Personnel, See General Section

For full biographical listings, see the Martindale-Hubbell Law Directory

SCHOTTENSTEIN, ZOX & DUNN A LEGAL PROFESSIONAL ASSOCIATION (AV)

The Huntington Center, 41 South High Street, 43215
Telephone: 614-462-2700
Telecopier: 614-462-5135
Telex: 650 24 444 365
URL: http://www.szd.com
Cincinnati, Ohio Office: Bank One Towers, 8044 Montgomery Road, Suite 700, 45236-2926.
Telephone: 513-792-2730.
Cleveland, Ohio Office: One Cleveland Center, 1375 East 9th Street, Suite 950.
Telephone: 216-621-6501.
Fax: 216-621-6502.

John Terakedis, Jr.
Martin S. Rosenthal
Thomas J. Sigmund

J. Troy Terakedis

Reference: Bank One of Columbus, N.A.

For Complete List of Firm Personnel, See General Section

For full biographical listings, see the Martindale-Hubbell Law Directory

OKLAHOMA

*OKLAHOMA CITY,** Oklahoma Co.

MCAFEE & TAFT, A PROFESSIONAL CORPORATION (AV)

Tenth Floor, Two Leadership Square, 73102
Telephone: 405-235-9621
Facsimile: (405) 235-0439 (405) 232-2404
Email: mcafee@ionet.net *URL:* http://www.mcafee-taft.com

James Dudley Hyde
Richard D. Nix
John A. Papahronis

Representative Clients: Bank of Oklahoma, N.A.; Fleming Companies, Inc.; Paine Webber Group, Inc.; Arthur Andersen & Co.; Exxon Corp.; St. Paul Fire & Marine Insurance Co.; Columbia/HCA Healthcare Corp.

For Complete List of Firm Personnel, See General Section

For full biographical listings, see the Martindale-Hubbell Law Directory

*TULSA,** Tulsa Co.

BOESCHE, MCDERMOTT & ESKRIDGE (AV)

Suite 800 Oneok Plaza, 100 West Fifth Street, 74103
Telephone: 918-583-1777
Fax: 918-592-5809
Email: bme@intellex.com
Muskogee, Oklahoma Office: 1111 West Broadway, P.O. Box 2669, 74402.
Telephone: 918-683-6100.
Fax: 918-683-2303.

MEMBERS OF FIRM

R. Casey Cooper
David A. Johnson
David B. McKinney
R. Kevin Layton
Sheila M. Powers

ASSOCIATE

Byron E. (Rusty) Brown

OF COUNSEL

Clifford K. Cate, Jr. (Resident at Muskogee)

Representative Clients: University of Tulsa; Phillips Petroleum; Springer Clinic; Vinson Supply; Phoenix Home Life Mutual Insurance.

For Complete List of Firm Personnel, See General Section

For full biographical listings, see the Martindale-Hubbell Law Directory

CONNER & WINTERS, A PROFESSIONAL CORPORATION (AV)

3700 First Place Tower, 15 East 5th Street, 74103-4344
Telephone: 918-586-5711
Fax: 918-586-8982
Email: postmaster@cwlaw.com
Oklahoma City, Oklahoma Office: One Leadership Square, 211 North Robinson, Suite 1700, 73102-7101.
Telephone: 405-272-5711.
Facsimile: 405-232-2695.
Fayetteville, Arkansas Office: Conner & Winters, P.L.L.C., 100 West Center Street, Suite 200, 72701-6081.
Telephone: 501-582-5711.
Facsimile: 501-587-1426.

(See Next Column)

Washington, D.C. Office: 1050 Seventeenth Street, N.W., Suite 810, 20036-5503.
Telephone: 202-783-5711.
Facsimile: 202-783-5720.

Steven W. McGrath
Paul E. Braden
Martin R. Wing
Gregory D. Renberg

Anne B. Sublett

OF COUNSEL

Debbie L. Blackwell

For Complete List of Firm Personnel, See General Section

For full biographical listings, see the Martindale-Hubbell Law Directory

EAGLETON, EAGLETON AND HARRISON, INC. (AV)

Suite 1700, 320 South Boston Avenue, 74103-4706
Telephone: 918-584-0462
Fax: 918-584-3724
Email: eagleton@worldnet.att.net

E. John Eagleton
James R. Eagleton
Charles D. Harrison

OF COUNSEL

Norma Eagleton

For full biographical listings, see the Martindale-Hubbell Law Directory

PENNSYLVANIA

*HARRISBURG,** Dauphin Co.

JOHNSTON, ARONSON & DIAMOND, A PROFESSIONAL CORPORATION (AV)

150 Corporate Center Drive, Suite 100 (Camp Hill), 17011
Telephone: 717-975-5500
Telecopier: 717-975-5511

Charles W. Johnston
James A. Diamond
Irwin W. Aronson
John T. Kupchinsky

For full biographical listings, see the Martindale-Hubbell Law Directory

*PHILADELPHIA,** Philadelphia Co.

BALLARD SPAHR ANDREWS & INGERSOLL, LLP (AV)

1735 Market Street, 51st Floor, 19103-7599
Telephone: 215-665-8500
Fax: 215-864-8999
URL: http://www.ballardspahr.com
Baltimore, Maryland Office: 300 East Lombard Street. 19th Floor.
Telephone: 410-528-5600.
Fax: 410-528-5650.
Camden, New Jersey Office: 800 Hudson Square, 5th Floor.
Telephone: 856-541-5577.
Fax: 856-541-8272.
Denver, Colorado Office: Seventeenth Street Plaza Building, Suite 2300, 1225 17th Street.
Telephone: 303-292-2400.
Fax: 303-296-3956.
Salt Lake City, Utah Office: One Utah Center, Suite 1200, 201 South Main Street.
Telephone: 801-531-3000.
Fax: 801-531-3001.
Voorhees, New Jersey Office: Suite 100, 1101 Laurel Oak Drive.
Telephone: 856-627-8555.
Fax: 856-627-1153.
Washington, D.C. Office: Suite 1000 South, 601 13th Street, N.W.
Telephone: 202-661-2200.
Fax: 202-661-2299.

John M. Bernard
Rhonda Resnick Cohen
Paul J. Schneider

OF COUNSEL

Kurt R. Anderson
Jean C. Hemphill

COUNSEL

Edward Ira Leeds

Michele Berman Golkow
Brian Michael Pinheiro
Sharmon Priaulx
Pedro A. Ramos
Kathleen M. Ranalli
Marla G. Roshkoff
Esther L. von Laue

For Complete List of Firm Personnel, See General Section

For full biographical listings, see the Martindale-Hubbell Law Directory

Philadelphia—Continued

CHRISTIE, PABARUE, MORTENSEN AND YOUNG, A PROFESSIONAL CORPORATION (AV)

1880 JFK Boulevard - Tenth Floor, 19103
Telephone: 215-587-1600
Fax: 215-587-1699
Email: cpmy@cpmy.com *URL:* http://www.cpmy.com
Cherry Hill, New Jersey Office: Woodland Falls Corporate Park, 200 Lake Drive East.
Telephone: 609-482-7887.
Fax: 609-482-7438.
New York, N.Y. Office: 20 Exchange Place, 31st Floor.
Telephone: 212-366-1310.
Fax: 212-797-3545.
Boston, Massachusetts, Office: One State Street, Fifteenth Floor.
Telephone: 617-854-8315.
Fax: 617-854-8311.
Radnor, Pennsylvania Office: Radnor Station Building No. 2, Suite 222, 290 King of Prussia Road.
Telephone: 610-688-5778.
Fax: 610-688-5788.

James W. Christie
Bradley J. Mortensen
James A. A. Pabarue, Jr.
James A. Young
Jerome E. Bogutz
Marc L. Bogutz
John D. Frumer (Resident, Boston, Massachusetts Office)
Ralph J. Luongo
Peter J. Lynch
Stella M. Tsai
Brian C. Vance

Anthony J. Arena
Carolyn Bates
Rex F. Brien
K. Tia Burke
Michael J. Burns
Michael E. DiFebbo, Jr.
John C. Falls (Resident, Cherry Hill, New Jersey Office)
Christie L. Gamble
Nadine M. Hunt
Elaine Whiteman Klinger
Randy J. Maniloff
Richard S. Margulies
Christopher M. Martin
Etienne C. Maumus
William F. McDevitt
Catherine O. Raymond
Heather A. Salko
Marie T. Sarkees
Barbara L. Schmuck
Paul V. Shehadi
Randee Lynn Strair
June A. Taima
Christina G. Tershakovec
Thaddeus J. Weaver
Marybeth Smith Werb
Lisa B. Zucker

For full biographical listings, see the Martindale-Hubbell Law Directory

REED SMITH SHAW & MCCLAY LLP (AV)

2500 One Liberty Place, 19103-7301
Telephone: 215-851-8100
FAX: 215-851-1420
Email: rssm@rssm.com *URL:* http://www.rssm.com
Pittsburgh, Pennsylvania Office: 435 Sixth Avenue, 15219-1886.
Telephone: 412-288-3131.
FAX: 412-288-3063.
Washington, D.C. Office: Suite 1100 - East Tower, 1301 K Street, N.W., 20005-3317.
Telephone: 202-414-9200.
FAX: 202-414-9299.
Harrisburg, Pennsylvania Office: 213 Market Street, 17101-2132.
Telephone: 717-234-5988.
FAX: 717-236-3777.
Princeton, New Jersey Office: 136 Main Street, Suite 250, 08540-5799.
Telephone: 609-987-0050.
FAX: 609-951-0824.
New York, N.Y. Office: 375 Park Avenue, 17th Floor, 10152.
Telephone: 212-521-5400.
FAX: 212-521-5450.
Newark, New Jersey Office: The Legal Center, One Riverfront Plaza, First Floor, 07102-5400.
Telephone: 973-621-3200.
FAX: 973-621-3199.
Falls Church, Virginia Office: Reed Smith Hazel & Thomas, Suite 1400, 3110 Fairview Park Drive, P.O. Box 12001.
Telephone: 703-641-4200.
Fax: 703-641-4340.
Leesburg, Virginia Office: Reed Smith Hazel & Thomas LLP, 44084 Riverside Parkway, Suite 300.
Telephone: 703-729-8500. Metro: 703-478-1992.
Fax: 703-478-8003.
McLean, Virginia Office: Reed Smith Hazel & Thomas LLP, Suite 1100, 8251 Greensboro Drive, 22102-3844.
Telephone: 703-734-4600.
FAX: 703-734-4699.
Richmond, Virginia Office: Reed Smith Hazel & Thomas LLP, Suite 600, 411 East Franklin Street, P.O. Box 788.
Telephone: 804-344-3400.
Fax: 804-344-3410.

MEMBERS OF FIRM

David C. Auten
Sara A. Begley
Leonard A. Bernstein
Lloyd C. Birnbaum
Michael L. Browne
Douglas Y. Christian
Carl E. Esser
Solomon Fisher

(See Next Column)

MEMBERS OF FIRM (Continued)

Robert P. Frank
Karl A. Fritton
Richard H. Glanton
John W. Goldschmidt, Jr.
Daniel H. Golub
Curt L. Heffler
Marilyn Heffley
Louis M. Heidelberger
Selwyn A. Horvitz
Ben Burke Howell
Robert A. Kauffman
Kenneth M. Kolaski
Wendi L. Kotzen
Bari Susan Krein
Lori Leigh Lasher
Ira S. Lefton
Stephen M. Lyons, III
David W. Marston
Thomas J. McGarrigle
William J. McNichol, Jr.
Barbara S. Mishkin
Robert A. Nicholas
Michael B. Pollack
John E. Quinn
Henry F. Reichner
S. William Richter
Joseph C. Rudolf
Michael T. Scott
Joseph M. Sedlack
Carolyn P. Short
John F. Smith, III
Karl A. Thallner, Jr.
Andrew J. Trevelise
Peter J. Tucci
Christopher K. Walters
Bradford F. Whitman

COUNSEL

Lawrence F. Gilberti (Not admitted in PA)
Jonathan L. Levin
Michael P. Meehan
Margery K. Miller
Carol Ann Mueller
Bradley D. O'Brien

ASSOCIATES

Deirdre J. Attea
Linda M. Barone
Jonathan E. Becker (Not admitted in PA)
Barbara R. Binis
Vijay V. Bondada
Ryan J. Cassidy
Ethan D. Civan
Michael S. Cohen
David J. Croft
Tobey M. Daluz
Reetu Dandora
R. Anthony Diehl
John A. Di Nome
J. Christopher Erb
Darlene Marchesani Fasic
Mark Featherman
Maryellen Feehery
Tracy Z. Frisch
Jennifer A. Furman
Jo-Anne R. Garrido
Peter F. Giamporcaro
Kelley A. Grady
Sean M. Halpin
Catherine A. Hewett
Justin Tze-Chieh Huang
Andrea M. Kahn-Kothmann
Martin H. Karo
Jeanine M. Kasulis
Theodore Marasciulo, Jr.
David L. Marcus
Renee H. Martin
John J. McCullough, Jr.
Sean E. Mitchell
James F. Mogan III
Christine Mullen
Erin D. Murray
Elaine T. Petrossian
Joseph M. Profy
Steven C. Robbins
Louis W. Schack
Lisa A. Schworm (Not admitted in PA)
Robin Sheldon
Manisha Singh
Michael S. Smith
Rebecca Rosenberger Smolen
Andrew J. Soven
Wayne C. Stansfield
Michael P. Walsh
Alison Bennett Weisberg
Tracy Gilstrap Weiss

For full biographical listings, see the Martindale-Hubbell Law Directory

SANDALS, LANGER & TAYLOR, LLP (AV)

One Liberty Place 50th Floor, 1650 Market Street, 19103-7301
Telephone: 215-419-6500
Fax: 215-419-6501
Email: Main@SLT-LAW.COM *URL:* http://www.slt-law.com

Howard I. Langer
Alan M. Sandals
John R. Taylor

Scott M. Lempert
Kay E. Sickles

For full biographical listings, see the Martindale-Hubbell Law Directory

SCHUBERT, BELLWOAR, CAHILL & QUINN, A PROFESSIONAL CORPORATION (AV)

Two Penn Center, Suite 1400, 1500 John F. Kennedy Boulevard, 19102-1890
Telephone: 215-569-3535
Fax: 215-557-7426
Email: attorneys@sbcq.com
Haddon Township, New Jersey Office: 311 West Cuthbert Boulevard, 08108.
Telephone: 856-854-5757.

Thomas M. Schubert (1924-1989)
William E. Schubert, Jr. (1921-1998)
Harry J. J. Bellwoar, III
John P. Quinn
John J. Cahill, Jr.
Robert T. Lynch
Robert G. Bellwoar
John P. Gallagher
James O. Hausch
Deborah E. Kolodner
Richard T. Mulcahey, Jr.
James M. Tyler
Jan M. Ritchie

Joseph W. Cunningham
Michael S. Piotrowicz
Patricia Farrell Kerelo
Christopher B. Hogan
Kathleen M. O'Connell
Mark Pfeiffer
Eric A. Feldhake

(See Next Column)

SCHUBERT, BELLWOAR, CAHILL & QUINN A PROFESSIONAL CORPORATION—*Continued*

OF COUNSEL

John D. Lucey, Jr.
Robert F. Blanck

For full biographical listings, see the Martindale-Hubbell Law Directory

*PITTSBURGH,** Allegheny Co.

FELDSTEIN GRINBERG STEIN & MCKEE, A PROFESSIONAL CORPORATION (AV)

428 Boulevard of the Allies, 15219
Telephone: 412-471-0677
Fax: 412-263-6129
URL: http://www.fgsmlaw.com
Elizabeth, Pennsylvania Office: 400 Second Street.
Telephone: 412-384-6111.

Edwin I. Grinberg
Stanley M. Stein
Robert E. McKee, Jr.

For full biographical listings, see the Martindale-Hubbell Law Directory

GABLER & ASSOCIATES, P.C. (AV)

2543 Washington Road, Suite 910, Summerfield Commons, 15241
Telephone: 412-854-3838
Fax: 412-854-3842
Email: gablerpc@aol.com *URL:* http://www.benefit-law.com
Other Pittsburgh, Pennsylvania Office: 1000 Oliver Building, 535 Smithfield Street.
Telephone: 412-854-3838.
Fax: 412-854-3842.

Bruce G. Gabler

OF COUNSEL

Donald E. Hawkins (Not admitted in PA)

For full biographical listings, see the Martindale-Hubbell Law Directory

REED SMITH SHAW & MCCLAY LLP (AV)

435 Sixth Avenue, 15219-1886
Telephone: 412-288-3131
FAX: 412-288-3063
Mailing Address: P.O. Box 2009, 15230-2009
Email: rssm@rssm.com *URL:* http://www.rssm.com
Washington, D.C. Office: Suite 1100 - East Tower, 1301 K Street, N.W., 20005-3317.
Telephone: 202-414-9200.
FAX: 202-414-9299.
Philadelphia, Pennsylvania Office: 2500 One Liberty Place, 19103-7301.
Telephone: 215-851-8100.
FAX: 215-851-1420.
Harrisburg, Pennsylvania Office: 213 Market Street, 17101-2132.
Telephone: 717-234-5988.
FAX: 717-236-3777.
Princeton, New Jersey Office: 136 Main Street, Suite 250, 08540-5799.
Telephone: 609-987-0050.
FAX: 609-951-0824.
New York, N.Y. Office: 375 Park Avenue, 17th Floor, 10152.
Telephone: 212-521-5400.
FAX: 212-521-5450.
Newark, New Jersey Office: The Legal Center, One Riverfront Plaza, First Floor, 07102-5400.
Telephone: 973-621-3200.
FAX: 973-621-3199.
Falls Church, Virginia Office: Reed Smith Hazel & Thomas, Suite 1400, 3110 Fairview Park Drive, P.O. Box 12001.
Telephone: 703-641-4200.
Fax: 703-641-4340.
Leesburg, Virginia Office: Reed Smith Hazel & Thomas LLP, 44084 Riverside Parkway, Suite 300.
Telephone: 703-729-8500. Metro: 703-478-1992.
Fax: 703-478-8003.
McLean, Virginia Office: Reed Smith Hazel & Thomas LLP, Suite 1100, 8251 Greensboro Drive, 22102-3844.
Telephone: 703-734-4600.
FAX: 703-734-4699.
Richmond, Virginia Office: Reed Smith Hazel & Thomas LLP, Suite 600, 411 East Franklin Street, P.O. Box 788.
Telephone: 804-344-3400.
Fax: 804-344-3410.

MEMBERS OF FIRM

Joel P. Aaronson
Thomas L. Allen
Jeffrey G. Aromatorio
Anthony J. Basinski
James W. Bentz
William Bevan, III
Peter C. Blasier
Russell J. Boehner
Dennis R. Bonessa
Daniel I. Booker
Mark Bookman
Douglas E. Cameron
Jack B. Cobetto
Frederick H. Colen
Kathy K. Condo
Eugene K. Connors
Robert B. Cottington
Lawrence A. Demase
David L. DeNinno
Debra H. Dermody

(See Next Column)

MEMBERS OF FIRM (Continued)

Thomas J. Duman
Carolyn D. Duronio
Lawrence E. Flatley
Daniel P. Gallagher, Jr.
Pasquale D. Gentile, Jr.
G. Donald Gerlach
Dodi Walker Gross
Frank T. Guadagnino
James R. Haggerty
Thomas M. Hardiman
John C. Harmon
Robert W. Hartland
Ronald G. Hartman
Leo N. Hitt
Edward Hoopes
Craig W. Jones
Gregory B. Jordan
Gary L. Kaplan (Not admitted in PA)
Carole S. Katz
Kerry A. Kearney
Cynthia E. Kernick
Kenneth C. Kettering
Joseph W. Klein
Thomas P. Lawton III
John F. LeBlond
Frederick C. Leech
H. Kennedy Linge
Alan E. London
Robert G. Lovett
Michael E. Lowenstein
Glenn R. Mahone
E. David Margolis
Jan A. Marks
David J. McAllister
W. Thomas McGough, Jr.
J. Sherman McLaughlin
Joseph T. Moran
Robert K. Morris
Martha Hartle Munsch
Philip H. Myers (Not admitted in PA)
Perry A. Napolitano
Louis A. Naugle
Arlie R. Nogay
Ruth S. Perfido (Aldo at New York, N.Y.)
Peter D. Post
Robert F. Prorok
W. Franklin Reed
James J. Restivo, Jr.
Patrick W. Ritchey
William M. Robinson
Kimberly L. Sachse
Eric A. Schaffer
Edward W. Seifert
Nancy J. Shurlow
Paul M. Singer
William J. Smith
Arland T. Stein
George L. Stewart, II
Leonard L. Stewart
Edward N. Stoner, II
Arthur H. Stroyd
Patrick E. Sweeney
Gene A. Tabachnick
Thomas Todd
Harley N. Trice, II
John C. Unkovic
John L. Vitsas
Arnd N. von Waldow
Richard T. Wentley
Daniel E. Wille
Nelson W. Winter
Thomas R. Wright
David Ziegler
Scott F. Zimmerman

COUNSEL

Elizabeth S. Athol
Paul D. Bangor, Jr.
Rosemary Carroll
Linda Rhone Enion
J. Tomlinson Fort
James H. Hardie
Henry M. Ingram
Ronald S. Krasnow
Barbara L. Krause
Blair S. McMillin
Thomas C. Reed
Carl R. Reisacher
Wayne W. Ringeisen
Leonard L. Scheinholtz
David S. Smith
Guy L. Warman
Harry H. Weil
John H. White

OF COUNSEL

Davis C. Burroughs, Jr.
John P. Davis, Jr.
John H. Demmler
Henry P. Hoffstot, Jr.
Edward W. Marsh
Regis D. Murrin
John H. Scott, Jr.
Edmund K. Trent
Joseph Van Buskirk
Charles Holmes Wolfe, Jr.

ASSOCIATES

Roy W. Arnold
Lisa A. Balestrini
Cathy Bissoon
Jay T. Blount
Lauren A. Bradbury (Not admitted in PA)
Brian J. Burt
Ann P. Cahouet
John A. Camp
Patrick K. Cavanaugh
Anthony T. Cicchino
Michael G. Connelly
Barry J. Coyne
Karen A. Craig
Daniel McN. Cramer
Joseph E. Culleiton
Stephen J. Del Sole
Monica B. Deoras
Donna M. Doblick
James M. Doerfler
Ronald L. Francis, Jr.
David P. Franklin
Jennifer Otto Giotto
Efrem M. Grail
Angela D. Haney (Not admitted in PA)
Brian T. Himmel
Courtney C.T. Horrigan
Daniel C. Hudock
Stacy L. Kelly (Not admitted in PA)
Maxine S. Kisilinsky
Paul S. Kline
Kimberly J. Koerner
Joni L. Landy
Gregory M. Luyt
Colleen K. Lynch
Daniel P. Lynch
Lisa D. McAnany
Joseph P. McHugh
George F. Magera
Dara L. Mancini
Daniel M. Miller
Raymond A. Miller (Not admitted in PA)
James W. Mizgala
Natalie Chetlin Moritz
Stacey C. Palmer
Stephen P. Paschall
Kimberly J. Pierson
Traci S. Rea
Jennifer M. Reinke
Joseph F. Rodkey, Jr.
Thomas L. Roland
Maria N. Rullo
Catherine S. Ryan
Kirsten R. Rydstrom
Amy E. Sable
Sarah K. Schano
Susan P. Schupansky
David J. Shrager
Christopher J. Soller
Hannah L. Thompson
James L. Weinberg
Kevin L. Welsh
Travis E. Williams

(See Next Column)

REED SMITH SHAW & MCCLAY LLP, *Pittsburgh—Continued*

ASSOCIATES (Continued)

Cher E. Wynkoop (Not admitted in PA)
Dianna Calaboyias Wyrick
Colleen A. Zak

For full biographical listings, see the Martindale-Hubbell Law Directory

RHODE ISLAND

*PROVIDENCE,** Providence Co.

HINCKLEY, ALLEN & SNYDER LLP (AV)

1500 Fleet Center, 02903-2393
Telephone: 401-274-2000
Fax: 401-277-9600
Email: firm@haslaw.com *URL:* http://www.haslaw.com
Boston, Massachusetts Office: 28 State Street, 30th Floor.
Telephone: 617-345-9000.
Fax: 617-345-9020. URL: http://www.haslaw.com.

MEMBERS OF FIRM

David D. Barricelli
Jonathan Bell
Paul Bork (Not admitted in RI)
Stephen J. Carlotti
Eric F. Eisenberg (Not admitted in RI)
Malcolm Farmer, III
Margaret D. Farrell
William R. Grimm
Richard L. E. Jocelyn
Michael J. Kelly (Not admitted in RI)
Frederick P. McClure
Elizabeth Murdock Myers
H. Peter Olsen
Julianne Palumbo (Not admitted in RI)
John J. Pendergast, III
Charles E. Schaub, Jr. (Not admitted in RI)
Douglas F. Seaver (Not admitted in RI)
David R. Sullivan (Not admitted in RI)
Robert F. Sylvia (Not admitted in RI)
Howard E. Walker
Richard D. Wayne (Not admitted in RI)

ASSOCIATES

Mark Bianchi
Kelley Jordan-Price
Catherine S. Kim (Not admitted in RI)
Christopher W. Morog (Not admitted in RI)
Elena B. Olson (Not admitted in RI)
Joseph D. Whelan

OF COUNSEL

Willard Krasnow (Not admitted in RI)

For Complete List of Firm Personnel, See General Section

For full biographical listings, see the Martindale-Hubbell Law Directory

VETTER & WHITE, INCORPORATED (AV)

20 Washington Place, 02903
Telephone: 401-421-3060
Telecopier: 401-272-6803
Email: vetlit@aol.com

Benjamin V. White, III
Gordon P. Cleary
Howard A. Merten, Jr.
Brooks R. Magratten

OF COUNSEL

George Vetter

Kimberly A. Simpson
Michael W. Long

For full biographical listings, see the Martindale-Hubbell Law Directory

SOUTH CAROLINA

*CHARLESTON,** Charleston Co.

HAYNSWORTH, MARION, MCKAY & GUÉRARD, L.L.P. (AV)

134 Meeting Street, P.O. Box 1119, 29402
Telephone: 843-722-7606
Facsimile: 843-724-8016
Columbia, South Carolina Office: Suite 2400 Affinity Building, 1201 Main Street, P.O. Drawer 7157, 29202.
Telephone: 803-765-1818. Facsimile 803-765-2399.
Greenville, South Carolina Office: 75 Beattie Place, Eleventh Floor, P.O. Box 2048, 29602.
Telephone: 864-240-3200.
Facsimile: 864-240-3300.

MEMBERS OF FIRM

James J. Hinchey, Jr.
Thomas S. White

Counsel for: Baker Hospital; Healthsource of South Carolina; Allstate Insurance Co.; CSX Corporation; Lloyd's Underwriters; Coward-Hund Construction Co.; South Carolina Public Service Authority.

(See Next Column)

For Complete List of Firm Personnel, See General Section

For full biographical listings, see the Martindale-Hubbell Law Directory

*COLUMBIA,** Richland Co.

GIGNILLIAT, SAVITZ & BETTIS (AV)

900 Elmwood Avenue Suite 100, 29201
Telephone: 803-799-9311
Fax: 803-254-6951

MEMBERS OF FIRM

Julian H. Gignilliat
Stephen T. Savitz
Vance J. Bettis
Linda Pearce Edwards
M. Richbourg Roberson
Kathryn Thomas
Caroline Wrenn Cleveland
D. L. (Dirk) Aydlette, III

Reference: National Bank of South Carolina.

For full biographical listings, see the Martindale-Hubbell Law Directory

HAYNSWORTH, MARION, MCKAY & GUÉRARD, L.L.P. (AV)

Suite 2400 Affinity Building, 1201 Main Street, P.O. Drawer 7157, 29202
Telephone: 803-765-1818
Facsimile: 803-765-2399
Greenville, South Carolina Office: 75 Beattie Place, Eleventh Floor, P.O. Box 2048, 29602.
Telephone: 864-240-3200.
Facsimile: 864-240-3300.
Charleston, South Carolina Office: 134 Meeting Street, P.O. Box 1119, 29402.
Telephone: 843-722-7606.
Facsimile: 843-724-8016.

MEMBERS OF FIRM

Steven Todd Moon
Stephen F. McKinney

For Complete List of Firm Personnel, See General Section

For full biographical listings, see the Martindale-Hubbell Law Directory

*GREENVILLE,** Greenville Co.

HAYNSWORTH, MARION, MCKAY & GUÉRARD, L.L.P. (AV)

75 Beattie Place, Eleventh Floor, P.O. Box 2048, 29602
Telephone: 864-240-3200
Facsimile: 864-240-3300
Columbia, South Carolina Office: Suite 2400 Affinity Building, 1201 Main Street, P.O. Drawer 7157, 29202
Telephone: 803-765-1818.
Facsimile: 803-765-2399.
Charleston, South Carolina Office: 134 Meeting Street, P.O. Box 1119, 29402.
Telephone: 843-722-7606.
Facsimile: 843-724-8016.

MEMBERS OF FIRM

Jesse C. Belcher
John B. McLeod
H. Sam Mabry, III
Arthur Frazier McLean, III
J. Derrick Quattlebaum

Counsel for: Duke Power Co.; Liberty Mutual Insurance Co.; Equitable Life Assurance Society of the United States; St. Paul Insurance Group; Allstate Insurance Co.; Fluor-Daniel Corp.; Synalloy Corp.; Greenville Hospital System; TNS Mills, Inc.

For Complete List of Firm Personnel, See General Section

For full biographical listings, see the Martindale-Hubbell Law Directory

*SPARTANBURG,** Spartanburg Co.

EDWARDS, BALLARD, BISHOP, STURM, CLARK & KEIM, P.A. (AV)

International Center, Suite 400, 101 North Pine Street, P.O. Box 5398, 29304-5398
Telephone: 864-542-8612
Fax: 864-542-8712
Email: lawfirm@ebbsck.com
Winston-Salem, North Carolina Office: Edwards, Ballard, Clark, Barrett and Carlson, P.A., 380 Knollwood, Suite 730, P.O. Box 1708. 27102-1708.
Telephone: 336-750-0707.
Fax: 336-750-0711.

James F. Edwards, Jr.
Wade E. Ballard
Michael W. Bishop
Kevin W. Sturm
Terry A. Clark (Resident Partner, Edwards, Ballard, Clark, Barrett and Carlson, P.A., Winston-Salem, North Carolina)
Thomas H. Keim, Jr.
Karen M. Tyner
Roger G. Chandler
Patrick L. Cont

(See Next Column)

EDWARDS, BALLARD, BISHOP, STURM, CLARK & KEIM P.A.—*Continued*

S. Clay Keim | W. Allen Myrick, Jr.
Krishna Y. McVey | Penny Correll Wofford

Representative Clients: Texfi Industries, Inc.; Coca-Cola Bottling Co. Consolidated; Kobe Copper Products, Inc.; Van Waters & Rogers, Inc.; Spartanburg Steel Products, Inc.; Century Furniture Co.; Grimes Aerospace Corp.; Sulzer Ruti, Inc.; Comm/Scope, Inc.; South Carolina Insurance Reserve Fund.

For full biographical listings, see the Martindale-Hubbell Law Directory

SOUTH DAKOTA

*ABERDEEN,** Brown Co.

MALONEY & MALONEY (AV)

722 South Highway 281, P.O. Box 755, 57402-0755
Telephone: 605-229-2752
Fax: 605-226-0276
Email: maloney@nvc.net

MEMBERS OF FIRM

Dennis Maloney | Marilyn Marshall Maloney

For full biographical listings, see the Martindale-Hubbell Law Directory

TENNESSEE

*CHATTANOOGA,** Hamilton Co.

WITT, GAITHER & WHITAKER, P.C. (AV)

1100 SunTrust Bank Building, 37402-2608
Telephone: 423-265-8881
Telefax: 423-266-4138; 423-756-5612

Harold Alan Schwartz, Jr. | Douglas E. Peck
Jane K. Ricci

Representative Clients: American Consumers, Inc.; Carriage Industries, Inc.; Coca-Cola Bottling Co. Consolidated; Crescent Hosiery Mills, Inc.; The Dixie Group, Inc.; Masland Carpets, Inc.; River Associates, Inc.; Signal Apparel Company, Inc.; Top Flight, Inc.; Suntrust Bank, Chattanooga, N.A.

For Complete List of Firm Personnel, See General Section

For full biographical listings, see the Martindale-Hubbell Law Directory

*MEMPHIS,** Shelby Co.

ARMSTRONG ALLEN PREWITT GENTRY JOHNSTON & HOLMES, PLLC (AV)

Brinkley Plaza, Suite 700, 80 Monroe Avenue, 38103-2467
Telephone: 901-523-8211
Facsimile: 901-524-4936
Little Rock, Arkansas Office: Suite 100, 100 Morgan Keegan Drive, 72202.
Telephone: 501-280-0100.
Facsimile: 501-280-0166.
Jackson, Mississippi Office: 2525 Lakeward Drive, Suite 200, 39216.
Telephone: 601-713-1192.
Facsimile: 601-713-2049.
Jackson, Tennessee Office: 464 North Parkway, Suite A, 38305.
Telephone: 901-660-2332.
Facsimile: 901-664-1109.

MEMBERS OF FIRM

Elmore Holmes, III | David A. Thornton

For Complete List of Firm Personnel, See General Section

For full biographical listings, see the Martindale-Hubbell Law Directory

TEXAS

*BEAUMONT,** Jefferson Co.

MEHAFFY & WEBER, A PROFESSIONAL CORPORATION (AV)

2615 Calder Avenue, Suite 800, P.O. Box 16, 77704
Telephone: 409-835-5011
Fax: 409-835-5729; 835-5177
Email: MehaffyWeber.com
Orange, Texas Office: 1006 Green Avenue, P.O. Drawer 189.
Telephone: 409-886-7766.

(See Next Column)

Houston, Texas Office: One Allen Center, 500 Dallas, Suite 1200.
Telephone: 713-655-1200.

James W. Mehaffy (1914-1985) | Elizabeth Brandes Pratt

E. Wade Carpenter

OF COUNSEL

Dewey J. Gonsoulin | John J. Durkay

Representative Clients: E.I. du Pont de Nemours and Co.; Eli Lilly & Co.; Merrell Dow; Jefferson County Tax Appraisal District; W.R. Grace & Co.-Conn.; Bank of America; Christus Health; Christus St. Elizabeth; Christus St. Mary; Burlington Northern Santa Fe Railway.
Approved Attorneys for: Stewart Title Guaranty Co.

For Complete List of Firm Personnel, See General Section

For full biographical listings, see the Martindale-Hubbell Law Directory

*DALLAS,** Dallas Co.

HUGHES & LUCE, L.L.P. (AV)

A Registered Limited Liability Partnership including Professional Corporations
1717 Main Street, Suite 2800, 75201
Telephone: 214-939-5500
Fax: 214-939-6100; 214-939-5849
Email: H&L@hughesluce.com *URL:* http://www.hughesluce.com
Austin, Texas Office: 111 Congress, Suite 900.
Telephone: 512-482-6800.
Fax: 512-482-6859.
Houston, Texas Office: 1600 Smith Street, Suite 3550.
Telephone: 713-754-5200.
Fax: 713-754-5270.

MEMBERS OF FIRM

Jeff W. Dorrill | Vester T. Hughes, Jr.
Karen K. Suhre

ASSOCIATE

Paul J. Kardish

For Complete List of Firm Personnel, See General Section

For full biographical listings, see the Martindale-Hubbell Law Directory

SMITH, UNDERWOOD & PERKINS, A PROFESSIONAL CORPORATION (AV)

600 Two Lincoln Centre, 5420 LBJ Freeway, 75240
Telephone: 972-661-5114
Telecopier: 972-661-5691
Email: firm@suandp.com *URL:* http://www.suplaw.com

Timothy S. Perkins | G. Lynn Smith
David W. Ralston | William J. Underwood, Jr.

Christine A. McGuire | Ellen P. Stewart
Amy K. Ratzlaff | Todd W. Shadle
P. Theodore Stoinoff, II | Ruth C. Logan
Val C. Cronin | Christina L. Betanzos
Kent D. Williamson

For full biographical listings, see the Martindale-Hubbell Law Directory

THOMPSON & KNIGHT L.L.P. (AV)

(Attorneys and Counselors)
1700 Pacific Avenue Suite 3300, 75201
Telephone: 214-969-1700
Telecopy: 214-969-1751
Telex: 732 298
URL: http://www.tklaw.com
Austin, Texas Office: 1200 San Jacinto Center, 98 San Jacinto Boulevard, 78701.
Telephone: 512-469-6100.
Telecopy: 512-469-6180.
Fort Worth, Texas Office: 801 Cherry Street, Suite 1600, 76102.
Telephone: 817-347-1700.
Telecopy: 817-347-1799.
Houston, Texas Office: Thompson Knight Brown Parker & Leahy L.L.P., 1200 Smith Street, Suite 3600, 77002-4595.
Telephone: 713-654-8111.
Telecopier: 713-654-1871.
San Pedro Garza Garcia, Nuevo León, Mexico Office: Edificio Losoles PD-4, Av. Lázaro Cárdenas No. 2400 Pte., C.P. 66220.
Telephone: (52-8) 363-0096.
Telecopy: (52-8) 363-3067.

PARTNERS

Sharon M. Fountain | J. Mike Holt
Russell G. Gully | Shelly A. Youree

(See Next Column)

THOMPSON & KNIGHT L.L.P., *Dallas—Continued*

STAFF ATTORNEY

Tracy B. Liden

For Complete List of Firm Personnel, See General Section

For full biographical listings, see the Martindale-Hubbell Law Directory

*SAN ANTONIO,** Bexar Co.

SCHOENBAUM, CURPHY & SCANLAN, P.C. (AV)

NationsBank Plaza, Suite 1775, 300 Convent Street, 78205-3744
Telephone: 210-224-4491
Fax: 210-224-7983

Stanley Schoenbaum
R. James Curphy
William Scanlan, Jr.
Alfred G. Holcomb
Banks M. Smith
Darin N. Digby
Patricia Flora Sitchler
Emily Harrison Liljenwall

Stacey Alison Warnix

For full biographical listings, see the Martindale-Hubbell Law Directory

TEXARKANA, Bowie Co.

PATTON, TIDWELL & SANDEFUR, L.L.P. (AV)

4605 Texas Boulevard, P.O. Box 5398, 75505-5398
Telephone: 903-792-7080; 903-792-5859
Fax: 903-792-8233
Email: KTIDW87157@aol.com

Nicholas H. Patton
Kelly B. Tidwell
Gregory C. Sandefur

For Complete List of Firm Personnel, See General Section

For full biographical listings, see the Martindale-Hubbell Law Directory

UTAH

*SALT LAKE CITY,** Salt Lake Co.

CALLISTER NEBEKER & McCULLOUGH, A PROFESSIONAL CORPORATION (AV)

Gateway Tower East, Suite 900, 10 East South Temple, 84133
Telephone: 801-530-7300
Telecopier: 801-364-9127
Email: mjeaston@cnmlaw.com *URL:* http://www.cnmlaw.com

Leland S. McCullough
Jeffrey N. Clayton
W. Waldan Lloyd
Lynda Cook

Representative Clients: Zions Bancorporation; Intermountain Health Care; Novell, Inc.; Sinclair Oil Corporation (Little America); Flying J Inc.; Nu Skin International, Inc.; Dyno Nobel, Inc.; Wal-Mart, Inc.

For Complete List of Firm Personnel, See General Section

For full biographical listings, see the Martindale-Hubbell Law Directory

PARR WADDOUPS BROWN GEE & LOVELESS, A PROFESSIONAL CORPORATION (AV)

Suite 1300, 185 South State Street, 84111-1537
Telephone: 801-532-7840
Fax: 801-532-7750
URL: http://www.pwlaw.com

Bentley J. Tolk

For Complete List of Firm Personnel, See General Section

For full biographical listings, see the Martindale-Hubbell Law Directory

VAN COTT, BAGLEY, CORNWALL & McCARTHY, A PROFESSIONAL CORPORATION (AV)

50 South Main Street, Suite 1600, P.O. Box 45340, 84145-0340
Telephone: 801-532-3333
Telecopier: 801-534-0058
Email: info@vancott.com *URL:* http://www.vancott.com
Ogden, Utah Office: 2404 Washington Boulevard, Suite 900.
Telephone: 801-394-5783.
Park City, Utah Office: 2200 Park Avenue, Suite C200-A.
Telephone: 435-649-3889.

Arthur B. Ralph
David E. Sloan
Stephen D. Swindle

Stephen R. Sloan

(See Next Column)

OF COUNSEL

David E. Salisbury

For Complete List of Firm Personnel, See General Section

For full biographical listings, see the Martindale-Hubbell Law Directory

VIRGINIA

ALEXANDRIA, (Independent City)

CARTER & COLEMAN (AV)

602 Cameron Street, 22314
Telephone: 703-739-4200
Fax: 703-739-4210
Email: rcarter@cartercoleman.com *URL:* http://www.lawyers.com/carter&coleman
Washington, D.C. Office: 900 Seventeenth Street, N.W., Suite 900, 20006.
Telephone: 202-326-8600.
Fax: 202-289-0184.

Richard D. Carter
Douglas M. Coleman
David C. Simmons
(Not admitted in VA)
James M. Loots
(Not admitted in VA)

ASSOCIATES

Juliane C. Miller
Mercedes Madole
(Not admitted in VA)
Paul A. Daniels

For full biographical listings, see the Martindale-Hubbell Law Directory

MCLEAN, Fairfax Co.

REED SMITH HAZEL & THOMAS LLP (AV)

Suite 1100, 8251 Greensboro Drive, 22102-3844
Telephone: 703-734-4600
FAX: 703-734-4699
Email: rssm@rssm.com *URL:* http://www.rssm.com
Fairfax County (Falls Church), Virginia Office: Suite 1400, 3110 Fairview Park Drive.
Telephone: 703-641-4200.
Fax: 703-641-4340.
Leesburg, Virginia Office: 44084 Riverside Parkway, Suite 300.
Telephone: 703-729-8500. Metro: 703-478-1992.
Fax: 703-478-8003.
Richmond, Virginia Office: 901 East Byrd Street, Suite 1700, 23219.
Telephone: 804-344-3400.
Fax: 804-344-3410.
Pittsburgh, Pennsylvania Office: Reed Smith Shaw & McClay LLP, 435 Sixth Avenue, 15219-1886.
Telephone: 412-288-3131.
FAX: 412-288-3063.
Philadelphia, Pennsylvania Office: Reed Smith Shaw & McClay LLP, 2500 One Liberty Place, 19103-7301.
Telephone: 215-851-8100.
FAX: 215-851-1420.
Harrisburg, Pennsylvania Office: Reed Smith Shaw & McClay LLP 213 Market Street, 17101-2132.
Telephone: 717-234-5988.
FAX: 717-236-3777.
Washington, D.C. Office: Reed Smith Shaw & McClay LLP, Suite 1100 - East Tower, 1301 K Street, N.W., 20005-3317.
Telephone: 202-414-9200.
FAX: 202-414-9299.
Princeton, New Jersey Office: Reed Smith Shaw & McClay LLP, 136 Main Street, Suite 250, 08540-5799.
Telephone: 609-987-0050.
FAX: 609-951-0824.
New York, N.Y. Office: 375 Park Avenue, 17th Floor, 10152.
Telephone: 212-521-5400.
FAX: 212-521-5450.
Newark, New Jersey Office: Reed Smith Shaw & McClay LLP, The Legal Center, One Riverfront Plaza, First Floor, 07102-5400.
Telephone: 973-621-3200.
FAX: 973-621-3199.

MEMBERS OF FIRM

Kirk D. Beckhorn
Giovanna M. Cinelli
John R. Erickson
Robert E. Gregg
John P. Holman
W. Scott Railton
Merrell B. Renaud
John J. Sabourin, Jr.
Robert B. Webb, III

COUNSEL

L. James D'Agostino
Kenneth J. Nunnenkamp
William M. Weisberg
(Not admitted in VA)

(See Next Column)

REED SMITH HAZEL & THOMAS LLP—*Continued*

ASSOCIATES

LeeAnne DiFilippo
Heather L. Garrow
Leigh T. Hansson (Not admitted in VA)
Jeff S. Robinette
Matthew R. Sheldon
Alexander Y. Thomas

For full biographical listings, see the Martindale-Hubbell Law Directory

RICHMOND, (Independent City)

WILLIAMS, MULLEN, CLARK & DOBBINS, A PROFESSIONAL CORPORATION (AV)

Two James Center, 1021 East Cary Street, P.O. Box 1320, 23218-1320
Telephone: 804-643-1991
Fax: 804-783-6507
URL: http://www.wmcd.com
Newport News Office: Harbor Bank Center, Suite 210, One Old Oyster Point Road, 23602-7119.
Telephone: 757-249-5100.
Fax: 757-249-5109.
Virginia Beach Office: One Columbus Center, 23462-6763.
Telephone: 757-499-8800.
Fax: 757-473-0395.
Vienna Office: 1593 Spring Hill Road, Suite 510, 22182.
Telephone: 703-760-5200.
Fax: 703-748-0244.
Washington, D.C. Office: The Farragut Building, 900 17th Street, N.W., Suite 700, 20006.
Telephone: 202-293-0213.
Fax: 804-783-6507. Fax Within D.C.: 202-293-5939.
London, England Office: Blake Lodge, Bridge Lane, SW11 3AD.
Telephone: (011-44-71) 223-2756.
Fax: (011-44-71) 350-0156.
Riyadh, Saudi Arabia Affiliate Office: Saudi-American Legal Consultants Commercial Building #2, Diplomatic Quarter, P.O. Box 57270, 11574.
Telephone: (011-966-1) 488-1563.
Fax: (011-966-1) 488-0542.

C. Richard Davis
Calvin W. Fowler, Jr.
Lynn F. Jacob
Robert L. Musick, Jr.
B. Randolph Wellford, Jr.

OF COUNSEL

David George Ball (Resident, Washington, D.C. Office)

William D. Perun, Jr.
King F. Tower

For Complete List of Firm Personnel, See General Section
For full biographical listings, see the Martindale-Hubbell Law Directory

VIENNA, Fairfax Co.

BORING & PILGER, P.C. (AV)

307 Maple Avenue West, Suite D, 22180-4307
Telephone: 703-281-2161
Fax: 703-281-9464
URL: http://www.boringandpilger.com

James L. Boring

Sharon C. Williams (Not admitted in VA)

Representative Clients: Balmar, Inc.; Toshiba America Information Systems, Inc.; King Wholesale, Inc.; Northern Virginia Surgical Associates, P.C.

For full biographical listings, see the Martindale-Hubbell Law Directory

WASHINGTON

*SEATTLE,** King Co.

SCHROETER, GOLDMARK & BENDER, P.S. (AV)

500 Central Building, 810 Third Avenue, 98104
Telephone: 206-622-8000; 1-800-809-2234
FAX: 206-682-2305
Email: lastname@schroeter-goldmark.com

Croil J. Anderson
Adam J. Berger
James D. Hailey
Kristin Houser
Amanda E. Lee
Mark Leemon
Douglas D. McBroom
Janet L. Rice
Jeffery P. Robinson
Rebecca J. Roe
Sidney Stillerman Royer
William Rutzick
Sandra E. Widlan
Corrie Johnson Yackulic
John Goldmark (1917-1979)
Dean Bender (1933-1988)

OF COUNSEL

Jenny A. Durkan

For full biographical listings, see the Martindale-Hubbell Law Directory

WEST VIRGINIA

*CHARLESTON,** Kanawha Co.

JACKSON & KELLY (AV)

1600 Laidley Tower, P.O. Box 553, 25322
Telephone: 304-340-1000
Fax: 304-340-1130
Email: info@jacksonkelly.com *URL:* http://www.jacksonkelly.com
Martinsburg, West Virginia Office: 300 Foxcroft Avenue, P.O. Box 1068.
Telephone: 304-263-8800.
Fax: 304-263-7110.
Morgantown, West Virginia Office: 6000 Hampton Center, P.O. Box 619.
Telephone: 304-599-3000.
Fax: 304-285-2040.
New Martinsville, West Virginia Office: 256 Russell Avenue, P.O. Box 68.
Telephone: 304-455-1751.
Fax: 304-455-6314.
Parkersburg, West Virginia Office: 412 Market Street, Suite 202, P.O. Box 1144.
Telephone: 304-424-3490.
Fax: 304-424-3499.
Fairmont, West Virginia Office: 1000 Technology Drive, Suite 1310.
Telephone: 304-368-2000.
Fax: 304-368-2020.
Lexington, Kentucky Office: 175 East Main Street, Suite 500, P.O. Box 2150.
Telephone: 606-255-9500.
Fax: 606-281-6478.
Washington, D. C. Office: 2401 Pennsylvania Avenue, N.W., Suite 400.
Telephone: 202-973-0200.
Fax: 202-973-0232.
Denver, Colorado Office: Suite 2710, 1660 Lincoln Street.
Telephone: 303-390-0003.
Fax: 303-390-0040.
Wheeling, West Virginia Office: 1144 Market Street.
Telephone: 304-233-4000.
Fax: 304-233-4077.

MEMBERS OF FIRM

Louis S. Southworth, II
Michael D. Foster

Representative Clients: Camcare, Inc.; West Virginia Bankers Association; Shawnee Hills, Inc.; United Bankshares, Inc.; Huntington National Bank West Virginia; Go-Mart, Inc.; Associated Radiologists, Inc.; CONSOL Inc.

For Complete List of Firm Personnel, See General Section

For full biographical listings, see the Martindale-Hubbell Law Directory

*WHEELING,** Ohio Co.

SCHRADER BYRD & COMPANION, PLLC (AV)

(A Professional Limited Liability Company)
The Maxwell Centre, 32-20th Street, Suite 500, P.O. Box 6336, 26003
Telephone: 304-233-3390
Fax: 304-233-2769
URL: http://www.schraderlaw.com
Martins Ferry, Ohio Office: 205 North Fifth Street, P.O. Box 309, 43935.
Telephone: 740-633-9976.
Fax: 740-633-0400.
Weirton, West Virginia Office: 3205 Pennsylvania Avenue, Suite 103, Penn Place, P.O. Box 2785, 26062.
Telephone: 304-723-2674.
Fax: 304-723-2876.

MEMBERS

Ray A. Byrd
James F. Companion
Frank X. Duff
Teresa Rieman-Camilletti
Yolonda G. Lambert
Daniel P. Fry (Resident Partner, Martins Ferry, Ohio Office)
James P. Mazzone (Resident Member, Weirton, West Virginia Office)
Sandra K. Law
D. Kevin Coleman

SPECIAL COUNSEL

Thomas B. Miller

ASSOCIATES

Denise D. Klug
Michael A. Adams
John Porco
Aimee Morgan Stern
Kimberly R. Wilson
Christopher J. Adams

OF COUNSEL

James A. Byrum, Jr.

General Counsel: Reynolds Memorial Hospital; WesBanco Bank-Elm Grove.
Representative Clients: American Cyanamid Company; Bank One; Matlack Systems, Inc.; Moutaineer Gas Co.; Ohio County Board of Education; PHICO Insurance Co.; Wheeling Hospital; Wheeling-Pittsburg Steel Corp.

For full biographical listings, see the Martindale-Hubbell Law Directory

WISCONSIN

*MILWAUKEE,** Milwaukee Co.

MEISSNER TIERNEY FISHER & NICHOLS S.C. (AV)

The Milwaukee Center, 111 East Kilbourn Avenue, 19th Floor, 53202-6622
Telephone: 414-273-1300
Facsimile: 414-273-5840
URL: http://www.mtfn.com

Joseph E. Tierney III
Dennis L. Fisher
Thomas J. Nichols

Michael A. Kallas

For full biographical listings, see the Martindale-Hubbell Law Directory

QUARLES & BRADY LLP (AV)

411 East Wisconsin Avenue, 53202-4497
Telephone: 414-277-5000
Fax: 414-271-3552
URL: http://www.quarles.com
Madison, Wisconsin Office: Firstar Plaza, One South Pinckney Street, P.O. Box 2113, 53701-2113.
Telephone: 608-251-5000.
Fax: 608-251-9166.
West Palm Beach, Florida Office: 222 Lakeview Avenue, 4th Floor, 33401.
Telephone: 561-653-5000.
Fax: 561-653-5333.
Naples, Florida Office: Barnett Center, 4501 Tamiami Trail North, Suite 300, 34103-3060.
Telephone: 941-262-5959.
Fax: 941-434-4999.
Phoenix, Arizona Office: One Camelback Building, One East Camelback Road, Suite 400, 85012-1649.
Telephone: 602-230-5500.
Fax: 602-230-5598.
Chicago, Illinois Office: Quarles & Brady LLC, Citicorp Center, 500 West Madison Street, Suite 3700.
Telephone: 312-715-5000.
Fax: 312-715-5155.

MEMBERS OF FIRM
(ALPHABETICALLY BY YEAR OF ADMISSION TO BAR)

Arthur B. Harris
J. Paul Jacobson
John T. Bannen
Kimberly Leach Johnson (Resident, Naples, Florida Office)
Sarah M. Linsley (Resident, Chicago, Illinois Office)
Dana L. O'Brien
David P. Olson

For Complete List of Firm Personnel, See General Section

For full biographical listings, see the Martindale-Hubbell Law Directory

CANADA ALBERTA

*CALGARY,** Calgary Jud. Dist.

BENNETT JONES (AV)

4500 Bankers Hall East, 855-2nd Street S.W., T2P 4K7
Telephone: 403-298-3100
Facsimile: 403-265-7219
Email: firmwatch@bennettjones.ca *URL:* http://www.bennettjones.ca
Edmonton, Alberta Office: 1000, 10035-105 Street.
Telephone: 780-421-8133.
Facsimile: 780-421-7951.
Toronto, Ontario Office: 3400 1 First Canadian Place, P.O. Box 130.
Telephone: 416-863-1200.
Facsimile: 416-863-1716.

MEMBER OF FIRM
Douglas A. Ast

For Complete List of Firm Personnel, See General Section

For full biographical listings, see the Martindale-Hubbell Law Directory

CANADA NEW BRUNSWICK

*FREDERICTON,** York Co.

McINNES COOPER (AV)

Suite 600, 570 Queen Street, P.O. Box 610, E3B 5A6
Telephone: 506-458-8572
Fax: 506-458-9903
Email: mcrfton@mcrlaw.com *URL:* http://www.mcrlaw.com
Halifax, Nova Scotia Office: Summit Place, 1601 Lower Water Street, P.O. Box 730, B3J 2V1.
Telephone: 902-425-6500.
Fax: 902-425-6350. Email: mcrhfx@mcrlaw.com.
St. John's, Newfoundland Office: Baine Johnston Centre, 5th Floor, 10 Fort William Place, P.O. Box 5939, A1C 5X4.
Telephone: 709-722-8735.
Telecopier: 709-722-1763. Email: mcrsj@mcrlaw.com.
Moncton, New Brunswick Office: Place Moncton Place, 655 Main Street, P.O. Box 1368, E1C 8T6.
Telephone: 506-857-8970.
Fax: 506-857-4095. Email: mcrmctn@mcrlaw.com.
Charlottetown, Prince Edward Island Office: BDC Place, Suite 620, 119 Kent Street, C1A 1N3.
Telephone: 902-368-8473.
Fax: 902-368-8346. Email: mcrpei@mcrlaw.com.

PARTNER
David Duncan Young

For Complete List of Firm Personnel, See General Section

For full biographical listings, see the Martindale-Hubbell Law Directory

*MONCTON,** Westmorland Co.

McINNES COOPER (AV)

Barristers, Solicitors & Trade Mark Agents
Place Moncton Place, 655 Main Street, P.O. Box 1368, E1C 8T6
Telephone: 506-857-8970
Fax: 506-857-4095
Email: mcrmctn@mcrlaw.com *URL:* http://www.mcrlaw.com
Halifax, Nova Scotia Office: Summit Place, 1601 Lower Water Street, P.O. Box 730, B3J 2V1.
Telephone: 902-425-6500.
Fax: 902-425-6350. Email: mcrhfx@mcrlaw.com.
St. John's, Newfoundland Office: Baine Johnston Centre, 5th Floor, 10 Fort William Place, P.O. Box 5939, A1C 5X4.
Telephone: 709-722-8735.
Telecopier: 709-722-1763. Email: mcrsj@mcrlaw.com.
Charlottetown, Prince Edward Island Office: BDC Place, Suite 620, 119 Kent Street, C1A 1N3.
Telephone: 902-368-8473.
Fax: 902-368-8346. Email: mcrpei@mcrlaw.com.
Fredericton, New Brunswick Office: Suite 600, 570 Queen Street, P.O. Box 610.
Telephone: 506-458-8572.
Fax: 506-458-9903. Email: mcrfton@mcrlaw.com.

ASSOCIATE
John C. Friel, Q.C.

For Complete List of Firm Personnel, See General Section

For full biographical listings, see the Martindale-Hubbell Law Directory

CANADA NEWFOUNDLAND

*ST. JOHN'S,**

McINNES COOPER (AV)

Barristers, Solicitors & Trade Mark Agents
Baine Johnston Centre, 5th Floor, 10 Fort William Place, P.O. Box 5939, A1C 5X4
Telephone: 709-722-8735
Telecopier: 709-722-1763
Email: mcrsj@mcrlaw.com *URL:* http://www.mcrlaw.com
Halifax, Nova Scotia Office: Summit Place, 1601 Lower Water Street, P.O. Box 730, B3J 2V1.
Telephone: 902-425-6500.
Fax: 902-425-6350. Email: mcrhfx@mcrlaw.com.
Moncton, New Brunswick Office: Place Moncton Place, 655 Main Street, P.O. Box 1368, E1C 8T6.
Telephone: 506-857-8970.
Fax: 506-857-4095. Email: mcrmctn@mcrlaw.com.

(See Next Column)

McInnes Cooper—*Continued*

Charlottetown, Prince Edward Island Office: BDC Place, Suite 620, 119 Kent Street, C1A 1N3.
Telephone: 902-368-8473.
Fax: 902-368-8346. Email: mcrpei@mcrlaw.com.
Fredericton, New Brunswick Office: Suite 600, 570 Queen Street, P.O. Box 610.
Telephone: 506-458-8572.
Fax: 506-458-9903. Email: mcrfton@mcrlaw.com.

PARTNERS

Christine A. Fagan, Q.C.
Denis J. Mahoney

For Complete List of Firm Personnel, See General Section

For full biographical listings, see the Martindale-Hubbell Law Directory

CANADA
NOVA SCOTIA

*HALIFAX,** Regional Munic. of Halifax

McInnes Cooper (AV)

Barristers, Solicitors & Trade Mark Agents
Summit Place, 1601 Lower Water Street, P.O. Box 730, B3J 2V1
Telephone: 902-425-6500
Fax: 902-425-6350
Email: mcrhfx@mcrlaw.com *URL:* http://www.mcrlaw.com
St. John's, Newfoundland Office: Baine Johnston Centre, 5th Floor, 10 Fort William Place, P.O. Box 5939, A1C 5X4.
Telephone: 709-722-8735.
Telecopier: 709-722-1763. Email: mcrsj@mcrlaw.com.
Moncton, New Brunswick Office: Place Moncton Place, 655 Main Street, P.O. Box 1368, E1C 8T6.
Telephone: 506-857-8970.
Fax: 506-857-4095. Email: mcrmctn@mcrlaw.com.
Charlottetown, Prince Edward Island Office: BDC Place, Suite 620, 119 Kent Street, C1A 1N3.
Telephone: 902-368-8473.
Fax: 902-368-8346. Email: mcrpei@mcrlaw.com.
Fredericton, New Brunswick Office: Suite 600, 570 Queen Street, P.O. Box 610.
Telephone: 506-458-8572.
Fax: 506-458-9903. Email: mcrfton@mcrlaw.com.

PARTNERS

Eric Durnford, Q.C.
Malcolm D. Boyle
Peter McLellan, Q.C.
John H. (Jack) Graham

For Complete List of Firm Personnel, See General Section

For full biographical listings, see the Martindale-Hubbell Law Directory

CANADA
ONTARIO

*TORONTO,** Regional Munic. of Toronto

Borden & Elliot (AV)

Barristers & Solicitors
Scotia Plaza, 40 King Street West, M5H 3Y4
Telephone: 416-367-6000
Telecopier: 416-367-6749
Email: info@borden.com *URL:* http://www.borden.com
Ottawa, Ontario Office: Borden Elliot Scott & Aylen, 1000-60 Rue Queen Street.
Telephone: 613-237-5160; 800-661-4237. General
Facsimile: 613-230-8842. IP Dept.
Facsimile: 613-787-3558. Email: ottinfo@scottaylen.com. URL: http://www.borden.com.

Randall Scott Echlin

For Complete List of Firm Personnel, See General Section

For full biographical listings, see the Martindale-Hubbell Law Directory

CANADA
SASKATCHEWAN

*REGINA,** Regina Jud. Centre

MacPherson Leslie & Tyerman (AV)

1500-1874 Scarth Street, S4P 4E9
Telephone: 306-347-8000
Telecopier: 306-352-5250
Email: mltreg@mlt.com
Saskatoon, Saskatchewan Office: 1500-410 22nd Street East, S7K 5T6.
Telephone: 306-975-7100.
Telecopier: 306-975-7145.

MEMBERS OF FIRM

Dennis P. Ball, Q.C.
Larry B. LeBlanc, Q.C.
Melissa A. Brunsdon (Resident, Saskatoon Office)
A. Robson Garden, Q.C. (Resident, Saskatoon Office)
Brian J. Kenny
Eileen V. Libby

ASSOCIATES

M. Jean Torrens (Resident, Saskatoon Office)
Kurt G. Wintermute (Resident, Saskatoon Office)
Heather D. Heavin

For Complete List of Firm Personnel, See General Section

For full biographical listings, see the Martindale-Hubbell Law Directory

ENERGY LAW

MISSISSIPPI

*NATCHEZ,** Adams Co.

TRULY, SMITH & LATHAM (AV)

100 South Pearl Street, P.O. Box 1307, 39121-1307
Telephone: 601-442-6495
Telecopier: 601-442-8874
URL: http://www.lawyers.com/trulysmith&latham

George Lawrence Adams (1913-1994)
R. Brent Forman (1917-1994)
E. C. Ward (1928-1994)

MEMBERS OF FIRM

William Marion Smith
Robert C. Latham

OF COUNSEL

Everette Truly

Representative Clients: Deposit Guaranty National Bank; Exxon U.S.A.; Mississippi Power & Light Co.; Southwest Mississippi Electric Power Assn.; South Central Bell Telephone Co.; Sears, Roebuck & Co.; American International Group; Kemper Insurance Co.

For full biographical listings, see the Martindale-Hubbell Law Directory

NEVADA

*CARSON CITY,** (Independent City)

THE LAW OFFICE OF DANIEL R. WALSH (AV)

Westwinds Professional Complex, 307 West Winnie Lane, Suite 3, 89703
Telephone: 775-882-8080
Fax: 775-882-6161

Daniel R. Walsh

ASSOCIATE

Kevin P. Walsh

For full biographical listings, see the Martindale-Hubbell Law Directory

NEW JERSEY

*NEWARK,** Essex Co.

SILLS CUMMIS RADIN TISCHMAN EPSTEIN & GROSS, A PROFESSIONAL CORPORATION (AV)

One Riverfront Plaza, 07102-5400
Telephone: 973-643-7000
Fax: 973-643-6500
Telex: 820630 Sillsbeck Nwk
Email: sillsmail@sillscummis.com *URL:* http://www.sillscummis.com
Atlantic City, New Jersey Office: 17 Gordon's Alley.
Telephone: 609-344-2800.
New York, N.Y. Office: 712 Fifth Avenue.
Telephone: 212-643-7000.
Washington, D.C. Office: 1800 K Street, N.W.
Telephone: 202-296-4750.

MEMBERS OF FIRM

Clive S. Cummis
Robert Max Crane
Brian S. Coven
James M. Hirschhorn

For Complete List of Firm Personnel, See General Section

For full biographical listings, see the Martindale-Hubbell Law Directory

WESTFIELD, Union Co.

THE ROTHFELDER LAW OFFICES (AV)

625 Central Avenue, 07090
Telephone: 908-301-1211
Fax: 908-301-1212
URL: http://www.lawyers.com/rothfelder,law
Email: mail@rlo-law.com *URL:* http://www.rlo-law.com

Martin C. Rothfelder
Maureen Rothfelder
Nathan T. Foose (Not admitted in NJ)

For full biographical listings, see the Martindale-Hubbell Law Directory

NEW YORK

*ALBANY,** Albany Co.

COUCH WHITE, LLP (AV)

540 Broadway, P.O. Box 22222, 12201
Telephone: 518-426-4600
Telecopier: 518-426-0376
Email: CouchWhiteBrenn@Global2000.net *URL:* http://www.couchwhite.com
Washington, D.C. Office: 700 Thirteenth Street, N.W., Suite 950.
Telephone: 202-434-4503.
Fax: 202-434-4562.

MEMBERS OF FIRM

Leslie F. Couch
Algird F. White, Jr.
Barbara S. Brenner
Joel M. Howard, III
Paul A. Feigenbaum
Robert M. Loughney
Harold N. Iselin
Leonard H. Singer
Keith B. Rose
Christopher A. Cernik
Michael B. Mager
Mark F. Glaser
Pamela A. Madeiros
James J. Barriere
Doreen Unis Saia

SENIOR COUNSEL

Lawrence H. Cooke

ASSOCIATES

David G. Anderson
Tricia A. Asaro
James S. King
Marc A. Madia

For full biographical listings, see the Martindale-Hubbell Law Directory

*NEW YORK,** New York Co.

BERLACK, ISRAELS & LIBERMAN LLP (AV)

120 West 45th Street, 10036
Telephone: 212-704-0100
Cable Address: "Berilib"
Telecopier: 212-704-0196
Email: info@berlack.com
Morristown, New Jersey Office: 65 Madison Avenue.
Telephone: 201-644-3400.
Telecopier: 201-644-3159.

MEMBERS OF FIRM

Harris Berlack (1946-1968)
Carlos L. Israels (1946-1969)
Kenneth R. Asher
Claude A. Baum
Scott M. Berman
Wade M. Boswell
Douglas E. Davidson
Alan N. Forman
Steven E. Greenbaum
Harvey M. Katz
James B. Liberman
Stuart Neuhauser
Robert D. Schmicker
Martin S. Siegel
Steven F. Wasserman
Edward S. Weisfelner

SENIOR ATTORNEYS

Andrew S. Dash
Erica M. Ryland

ASSOCIATES

John P. Biedermann
Anne M. Cunningham
Pauline Foley (Resident, Morristown, New Jersey Office)
Julie L. Friedberg (Resident, Morristown, New Jersey Office)
Emilio A. Galván
Linda B. Goebel
Louis Lombardo
Rachel F. Mayerson (Not admitted in NY)
Amy P. K. Motzenbecker (Resident, Morristown, New Jersey Office)
Antonio Peguero, Jr.
Elizabeth Quirk (Resident, Morristown, New Jersey Office)
Marcela M. Sanchez
Melissa Sarubbi

OF COUNSEL

Gerald W. Conway (Not admitted in NY; Resident, Morristown, New Jersey Office)
Marc B. Lasky (Resident, Morristown, New Jersey Office)

For full biographical listings, see the Martindale-Hubbell Law Directory

OHIO

*COLUMBUS,** Franklin Co.

MCNEES, WALLACE & NURICK (AV)

21 East State Street, Suite 1700, 43215
Telephone: 614-469-8000
Fax: 614-469-4653
Email: info@mwn.com *URL:* http://www.mwn.com
Harrisburg, Pennsylvania Office: 100 Pine Street, P.O. Box 1166, 17108.
Telephone: 717-232-8000.
Fax: 717-237-5300.

(See Next Column)

McNees, Wallace & Nurick, *Columbus—Continued*

Washington, D.C. Office: 1200 G Street, N.W., Suite 800, 20005.
Telephone: 202-434-8991.
Fax: 202-434-8707.
Hazleton, Pennsylvania Office: 1 South Church Street, Suite 302, 18201.
Telephone: 570-455-8300.
Fax: 570-455-8390.

MEMBERS OF THE FIRM

Samuel C. Randazzo
James P. Dougherty (Harrisburg, Pennsylvania Office)
David M. Kleppinger (Harrisburg, Pennsylvania Office)
Robert A. Mills (Harrisburg, Pennsylvania Office)

ASSOCIATES

Samuel W. Grossmann
Kimberly J. Wile
Susan E. Bruce (Harrisburg, Pennsylvania Office)
Charis M. Burak (Harrisburg, Pennsylvania Office)
Pamela C. Polacek (Harrisburg, Pennsylvania Office)
Robert A. Weishaar, Jr. (Harrisburg, Pennsylvania Office)
Derrick P. Williamson (Washington, D.C. Office)

For full biographical listings, see the Martindale-Hubbell Law Directory

OKLAHOMA

*OKLAHOMA CITY,** Oklahoma Co.

Day, Edwards, Federman, Propester & Christensen, P.C. (AV)

Suite 2900 Oklahoma Tower, 210 Park Avenue, 73102-5605
Telephone: 405-239-2121
Telecopier: 405-236-1012
URL: http://lawlinks.com/attys/ok/defpc.html

Joe E. Edwards
J. Clay Christensen
William B. Federman
Kent A. Gilliland

Ricki Valerie Sonders

Representative Clients: Applied Thermal Systems, Inc.; Aztec Specialty Co., Inc.; Aztec Rig Equipment Company; Bobby Joe Cudd Company; Delta Western Drilling Funds; Fluid Technologies; Scientific Drilling International, Inc.; Wild Well Control, Inc.

For Complete List of Firm Personnel, See General Section

For full biographical listings, see the Martindale-Hubbell Law Directory

*TULSA,** Tulsa Co.

Boesche, McDermott & Eskridge (AV)

Suite 800 Oneok Plaza, 100 West Fifth Street, 74103
Telephone: 918-583-1777
Fax: 918-592-5809
Email: bme@intellex.com
Muskogee, Oklahoma Office: 1111 West Broadway, P.O. Box 2669, 74402.
Telephone: 918-683-6100.
Fax: 918-683-2303.

MEMBERS OF FIRM

Fenelon Boesche (1910-1993)
Richard B. McDermott (1905-1977)
R. Casey Cooper
David B. McKinney
Bradley K. Beasley
David A. Johnson
Nik Jones
R. Kevin Layton
Sheila M. Powers

ASSOCIATES

Byron E. (Rusty) Brown
Christopher K. Woosley
Eric Morrow (Resident, Muskogee Office)

OF COUNSEL

T. Hillis Eskridge
Clifford K. Cate, Jr. (Resident at Muskogee)
Linda McQuillen Kulp

Representative Clients: Apache Corporation; Helmerich & Payne; Shell Oil Company; Williford Energy.

For full biographical listings, see the Martindale-Hubbell Law Directory

Sneed Lang, P.C. (AV)

2300 Williams Center Tower II, Two West Second Street, 74103
Telephone: 918-583-3145
Telecopier: 918-582-0410

(See Next Column)

James C. Lang
D. Faith Orlowski
Brian S. Gaskill
G. Steven Stidham
Stephen R. McNamara
Thomas E. Black, Jr.
Robbie Emery Burke
Patrick O. Waddel
Randolph P. Stainer
Steven K. Balman
Brian T. Inbody
D. Michael McBride III

OF COUNSEL

James L. Sneed

Representative Clients: Amoco Production Co.; Bank One, Texas; Enron Corp.; Halliburton Energy Services; Helmerich & Payne, Inc.; Shell Oil Co.; State Farm Mutual Automobile Insurance Co.; The Williams Companies.

For full biographical listings, see the Martindale-Hubbell Law Directory

PENNSYLVANIA

*HARRISBURG,** Dauphin Co.

McNees, Wallace & Nurick (AV)

100 Pine Street, P.O. Box 1166, 17108-1166
Telephone: 717-232-8000
Fax: 717-237-5300
Email: info@mwn.com *URL:* http://www.mwn.com
Columbus, Ohio Office: 21 East State Street, Suite 1700, 43215.
Telephone: 614-469-8000.
Fax: 614-469-4653.
Washington, D.C. Office: 1200 G Street, N.W., 20005.
Telephone: 202-434-8991.
Fax: 202-434-8707.
Hazleton, Pennsylvania Office: 1 South Church Street, Suite 302, 18201.
Telephone: 570-455-8300.
Fax: 570-455-8390.

MEMBERS OF THE FIRM

James P. Dougherty
David M. Kleppinger
Robert A. Mills
Samuel C. Randazzo (Resident, Columbus, Ohio Office)

ASSOCIATES

Susan E. Bruce
Charis M. Burak
Samuel W. Grossmann (Resident, Columbus, Ohio Office)
Pamela C. Polacek
Robert A. Weishaar, Jr.
Kimberly J. Wile (Resident, Columbus, Ohio Office)
Derrick P. Williamson

For Complete List of Firm Personnel, See General Section

For full biographical listings, see the Martindale-Hubbell Law Directory

RHODE ISLAND

*PROVIDENCE,** Providence Co.

Hinckley, Allen & Snyder LLP (AV)

1500 Fleet Center, 02903-2393
Telephone: 401-274-2000
Fax: 401-277-9600
Email: firm@haslaw.com *URL:* http://www.haslaw.com
Boston, Massachusetts Office: 28 State Street, 30th Floor.
Telephone: 617-345-9000.
Fax: 617-345-9020. URL: http://www.haslaw.com.

MEMBERS OF FIRM

David D. Barricelli
E. Jerome Batty
Jonathan Bell
Paul Bork (Not admitted in RI)
Stephen J. Carlotti
David Barry Connolly (Not admitted in RI)
Eric F. Eisenberg (Not admitted in RI)
Malcolm Farmer, III
Margaret D. Farrell
William R. Grimm
Paul A. Hedstrom (Not admitted in RI)
Joel Lewin (Not admitted in RI)
Sandra Matrone Mack
H. Peter Olsen
John J. Pendergast, III
Gerald J. Petros
Charles E. Schaub, Jr. (Not admitted in RI)
Douglas F. Seaver (Not admitted in RI)
Scott E. Sheridan (Not admitted in RI)
David R. Sullivan (Not admitted in RI)
Robert F. Sylvia (Not admitted in RI)
Howard E. Walker
Richard D. Wayne (Not admitted in RI)

ASSOCIATES

Alexandra K. Callam
Kelley Jordan-Price

OF COUNSEL

Willard R. Pope (Not admitted in RI)

For Complete List of Firm Personnel, See General Section

For full biographical listings, see the Martindale-Hubbell Law Directory

TEXAS

*AUSTIN,** Travis Co.

THOMPSON & KNIGHT L.L.P. (AV)

(Attorneys and Counselors)
1200 San Jacinto Center, 98 San Jacinto Boulevard, 78701
Telephone: 512-469-6100
Telecopy: 512-469-6180
URL: http://www.tklaw.com
Dallas, Texas Office: 1700 Pacific Avenue, Suite 3300, 75201.
Telephone: 214-969-1700.
Telecopy: 512-969-1751.
Telex: 732298.
Fort Worth, Texas Office: 801 Cherry Street, Suite 1600, 76102.
Telephone: 817-347-1700.
Telecopy: 817-347-1799.
Houston, Texas Office: Thompson Knight Brown Parker & Leahy L.L.P., 1200 Smith Street, Suite 3600, 77002-4595.
Telephone: 713-654-8111.
Telecopier: 713-654-1871.
San Pedro Garza Garcia, Nuevo León, Mexico Office: Edificio Losoles PD-4, Av. Lázaro Cárdenas No. 2400 Pte., C.P. 66220.
Telephone: (52-8) 363-0096.
Telecopy: (52-8) 363-3067.

PARTNER

James E. Cousar

For Complete List of Firm Personnel, See General Section

For full biographical listings, see the Martindale-Hubbell Law Directory

*DALLAS,** Dallas Co.

HUGHES & LUCE, L.L.P. (AV)

A Registered Limited Liability Partnership including Professional Corporations
1717 Main Street, Suite 2800, 75201
Telephone: 214-939-5500
Fax: 214-939-6100; 214-939-5849
Email: H&L@hughesluce.com *URL:* http://www.hughesluce.com
Austin, Texas Office: 111 Congress, Suite 900.
Telephone: 512-482-6800.
Fax: 512-482-6859.
Houston, Texas Office: 1600 Smith Street, Suite 3550.
Telephone: 713-754-5200.
Fax: 713-754-5270.

MEMBERS OF FIRM

Bert Black
John B. Holden, Jr., (P.C.)
Clifton T. Hutchinson
MaryAnn Joerres
Jeffrey C. King
Mark K. Sales

For Complete List of Firm Personnel, See General Section

For full biographical listings, see the Martindale-Hubbell Law Directory

THOMPSON & KNIGHT L.L.P. (AV)

(Attorneys and Counselors)
1700 Pacific Avenue Suite 3300, 75201
Telephone: 214-969-1700
Telecopy: 214-969-1751
Telex: 732 298
URL: http://www.tklaw.com
Austin, Texas Office: 1200 San Jacinto Center, 98 San Jacinto Boulevard, 78701.
Telephone: 512-469-6100.
Telecopy: 512-469-6180.
Fort Worth, Texas Office: 801 Cherry Street, Suite 1600, 76102.
Telephone: 817-347-1700.
Telecopy: 817-347-1799.
Houston, Texas Office: Thompson Knight Brown Parker & Leahy L.L.P., 1200 Smith Street, Suite 3600, 77002-4595.
Telephone: 713-654-8111.
Telecopier: 713-654-1871.
San Pedro Garza Garcia, Nuevo León, Mexico Office: Edificio Losoles PD-4, Av. Lázaro Cárdenas No. 2400 Pte., C.P. 66220.
Telephone: (52-8) 363-0096.
Telecopy: (52-8) 363-3067.

PARTNERS

P. Jefferson Ballew
Michael R. Berry
Jane Politz Brandt
Greg W. Curry
Lori L. Dalton
Craig A. Haynes

(See Next Column)

OF COUNSEL

Jerry P. Jones

For Complete List of Firm Personnel, See General Section

For full biographical listings, see the Martindale-Hubbell Law Directory

*HOUSTON,** Harris Co.

JACKSON WALKER L.L.P. (AV)

1100 Louisiana, Suite 4200, P.O. Box 4771, 77002
Telephone: 713-752-4200
Fax: 713-752-4221
URL: http://www.jw.com
Austin, Texas Office: 100 Congress Avenue, Suite 1100.
Telephone: 512-236-2000.
Fax: 512-236-2002.
Dallas, Texas Office: 901 Main Street, Suite 6000.
Telephone: 214-953-6000.
Fax: 214-953-5822.
Fort Worth, Texas Office: 301 Commerce Street, Suite 2400.
Telephone: 817-334-7200.
Fax: 817-334-7290.
Richardson, Texas Office: 2435 North Central Expressway, Suite 600.
Telephone: 972-671-2560.
Fax: 972-671-2566.
San Angelo, Texas Office: 225 West Beauregard Avenue.
Telephone: 915-481-2550.
Fax: 915-481-2552.
San Antonio, Texas Office: 112 E. Pecan Street, Suite 2100.
Telephone: 210-978-7700.
Fax: 210-978-7790.

MEMBERS OF FIRM

Janet Douvas Chafin
Wayne G. Dotson
David G. Dunlap
Michael P. Pearson

OF COUNSEL

Frank L. Cascio, Jr.
Robert H. Walls

For Complete List of Firm Personnel, See General Section

For full biographical listings, see the Martindale-Hubbell Law Directory

KILLEEN & FIERRO (AV)

1717 St. James Place, Suite 620, 77056
Telephone: 713-626-5100
Facsimile: 713-626-4545

Robert Joseph Killeen, Jr.
John M. Longoria
L. Byron Wilson

Candace A. Ourso

OF COUNSEL

Gerald M. Johnson, III

For full biographical listings, see the Martindale-Hubbell Law Directory

SCHWARTZ JUNELL CAMPBELL & OATHOUT, L.L.P. (AV)

Two Houston Center, 909 Fannin, Suite 2000, 77010
Telephone: 713-752-0017
Telecopier: 713-752-0327
Email: dschwartz@schwartz-junell.com

Richard A. Schwartz
William Edward Junell, Jr.
Marshall S. Campbell
Monica F. Oathout
Steven R. Rech

Phillip W. Bechter
J. Parker Fauntleroy, Jr.

OF COUNSEL

Joe H. Reynolds
A. R. Schwartz

LEGAL SUPPORT PERSONNEL

PARALEGALS

Nannette Koger
Maria Woods
Shelly A. Savage, CLA

For full biographical listings, see the Martindale-Hubbell Law Directory

THOMPSON KNIGHT BROWN PARKER & LEAHY L.L.P. (AV)

A Registered Limited Liability Partnership including Professional Corporations
(Attorneys and Counselors)
1200 Smith Street, Suite 3600, 77002-4595
Telephone: 713-654-8111
Telecopier: 713-654-1871
URL: http://www.tklaw.com
Dallas, Texas Office: Thompson & Knight L.L.P., 1700 Pacific Avenue, Suite 3300, 75201.
Telephone: 214-969-1700.
Telecopy: 214-969-1751.
Telex: 732298.

(See Next Column)

THOMPSON KNIGHT BROWN PARKER & LEAHY L.L.P., *Houston—Continued*

Austin, Texas Office: Thompson & Knight L.L.P., 1200 San Jacinto Center, 98 San Jacinto Boulevard, 78701.
Telephone: 512-469-6100.
Telecopy: 512-469-6180.
Fort Worth, Texas Office: Thompson & Knight L.L.P., 801 Cherry Street, Suite 1600, 76102.
Telephone: 817-347-1700.
Telecopy: 817-347-1799.
San Pedro Garza Garcia, Nuevo León, Mexico Office: Thompson & Knight L.L.P., Edificio Losoles PD-4, Av. Lázaro Cárdenas No. 2400 PTE., C.P. 66220.
Telephone: (52-8) 363-0096.
Telecopy: (52-8) 363-3067.

PARTNERS

E.F. Mano DeAyala
Diana M. Woodman

ASSOCIATE

Christopher P. Hanslik

For Complete List of Firm Personnel, See General Section

For full biographical listings, see the Martindale-Hubbell Law Directory

VINSON & ELKINS L.L.P. (AV)

2300 First City Tower, 1001 Fannin, 77002-6760
Telephone: 713-758-2222
Fax: 713-758-2346
Email: info@velaw.com *URL:* http://www.velaw.com
Austin, Texas Office: One American Center Suite 2700, 600 Congress Avenue, Austin, Texas, 78701-3200.
Telephone: 512-495-8400.
Fax: 512-495-8612.
Beijing, China Office: 20/F, Beijing Silver Tower, No. 2, Dong San Huan Bei Lu, Chaoyang District, 100027.
Telephone: +86-10-6410-6300.
Fax: +86-10-6410-6360.
Dallas, Texas Office: 3700 Trammell Crow Center, 2001 Ross Avenue, Dallas, Texas, 75201-2975.
Telephone: 214-220-7700.
Fax: 214-220-7716.
London, England Office: Regis House, 8th Floor, 45 King William Street, London, EC4R 9AN, England.
Telephone: (44-171) 618-6000.
Fax: (44-171) 618-6001.
Moscow, Russia Office: 16 Ulitsa Spiridonovka, Second Floor, 103001 Moscow, Russia.
Telephone: (7-095) 956-1995. Local
Fax: (7-095) 956-1996. U.S. Satellite
Fax: (212) 803-0142.
New York, N.Y. Office: 1325 Avenue of the Americas, 17th Floor, New York, N.Y., 10019.
Telephone: 917-206-8000.
Fax: 917-206-8100.
Singapore Office: 6 Battery Road, #39-01, Singapore, 049909.
Telephone: (65) 536-8300.
Fax: (65) 536-8311.
Washington, D.C. Office: The Willard Office Building, 1455 Pennsylvania Avenue, N.W., Washington, D.C., 20004-1008.
Telephone: 202-639-6500.
Fax: 202-639-6604.

MEMBERS OF FIRM

David T. Andril (Resident, Washington, D.C. Office)
Marcia E. Backus
Larry G. Barbour
John H. Barquin (Not admitted in TX)
Robert F. Barrett
Bruce R. Bilger
Douglas S. Bland
James Mark Brazzil (Resident, Beijing, China Office)
Charles F. Caldwell
Fielding B. Cochran, III
David B. Cohen (Resident, Washington, D.C. Office)
Thomas Crichton, IV (Resident, Dallas, Texas Office)
James L. Cuclis
Platt W. Davis, III
John C. Dawson, Jr.
Paul C. Deemer (Resident, London, England Office)
Joseph C. Dilg
Kenneth B. Fenelon
Robin S. Fredrickson
Douglas B. Glass (Resident, London, England Office)
Michael J. Henke (Resident, Washington, D.C. Office)
Bruce C. Herzog
Judith M. Johnson
Theodore W. Kassinger (Resident, Washington, D.C. Office)
John E. Kennedy
Gary M. Kotara (Resident, Washington, D.C. Office)
Kathleen C. Lake
John C. LaMaster (Resident, London, England Office)
Handel C.H. Lee (Resident, Beijing, China Office)
Kevin P. Lewis
Henry S. May, Jr.
Elizabeth Anne Moler (Resident, Washington, D.C. Office)
Craig W. Murray
Benjamin H. Powell, III
Robert René Rabalais
Mark R. Spivak (Resident, Washington, D.C. Office)
Albert S. Tabor, Jr.
Charles D. Tetrault (Resident, Washington, D.C. Office)
Patrick Ford Thompson (Resident, Austin, Texas Office)
James "Rell" Tipton, Jr.
William H. Weiland
Sanford A. Weiner

(See Next Column)

MEMBERS OF FIRM (Continued)

Adam Wenner (Resident, Washington, D.C. Office)
Anita Rutkowski Wilson (Resident, Washington, D.C. Office)

HOUSTON OF COUNSEL

Philip M. Kinkaid
Catherine O'Harra

WASHINGTON, D.C. OF COUNSEL

Becky M. Bruner

ASSOCIATES

Rasmani Bhattacharya
Jeffery M. Cooper
John S. Decker (Resident, Washington, D.C. Office)
Shelby Scott Gaille
Mark Reid Klupt (Resident, Washington, D.C. Office)
Dean H. Lefler
Jeffrey Scott Mũnoz
Clifton S. Rankin
James D. Seegers
Dirk P. Walker

For Complete List of Firm Personnel, See General Section

For full biographical listings, see the Martindale-Hubbell Law Directory

UTAH

*SALT LAKE CITY,** Salt Lake Co.

PARSONS, DAVIES, KINGHORN & PETERS, P.C. (AV)

185 South State Street, Suite 700, 84111
Telephone: 801-363-4300
Facsimile: 801-363-4378
Email: Attorneys@pdkplaw.com

Glen E. Davies
Gerald H. Kinghorn

For Complete List of Firm Personnel, See General Section

For full biographical listings, see the Martindale-Hubbell Law Directory

VAN COTT, BAGLEY, CORNWALL & MCCARTHY, A PROFESSIONAL CORPORATION (AV)

50 South Main Street, Suite 1600, P.O. Box 45340, 84145-0340
Telephone: 801-532-3333
Telecopier: 801-534-0058
Email: info@vancott.com *URL:* http://www.vancott.com
Ogden, Utah Office: 2404 Washington Boulevard, Suite 900.
Telephone: 801-394-5783.
Park City, Utah Office: 2200 Park Avenue, Suite C200-A.
Telephone: 435-649-3889.

Thomas W. Clawson
H. Michael Keller
Matthew F. McNulty, III
Gregory P. Williams

Mara A. Brown
Mary E. Westby (On Leave)

OF COUNSEL

Franklin N. Smith

For Complete List of Firm Personnel, See General Section

For full biographical listings, see the Martindale-Hubbell Law Directory

CANADA
NEW BRUNSWICK

*FREDERICTON,** York Co.

MCINNES COOPER (AV)

Suite 600, 570 Queen Street, P.O. Box 610, E3B 5A6
Telephone: 506-458-8572
Fax: 506-458-9903
Email: mcrfton@mcrlaw.com *URL:* http://www.mcrlaw.com
Halifax, Nova Scotia Office: Summit Place, 1601 Lower Water Street, P.O. Box 730, B3J 2V1.
Telephone: 902-425-6500.
Fax: 902-425-6350. Email: mcrhfx@mcrlaw.com.
St. John's, Newfoundland Office: Baine Johnston Centre, 5th Floor, 10 Fort William Place, P.O. Box 5939, A1C 5X4.
Telephone: 709-722-8735.
Telecopier: 709-722-1763. Email: mcrsj@mcrlaw.com.
Moncton, New Brunswick Office: Place Moncton Place, 655 Main Street, P.O. Box 1368, E1C 8T6.
Telephone: 506-857-8970.
Fax: 506-857-4095. Email: mcrmctn@mcrlaw.com.
Charlottetown, Prince Edward Island Office: BDC Place, Suite 620, 119 Kent Street, C1A 1N3.
Telephone: 902-368-8473.
Fax: 902-368-8346. Email: mcrpei@mcrlaw.com.

(See Next Column)

McInnes Cooper—*Continued*

PARTNER

Leonard T. Hoyt

For Complete List of Firm Personnel, See General Section

For full biographical listings, see the Martindale-Hubbell Law Directory

CANADA NEWFOUNDLAND

*ST. JOHN'S,**

McInnes Cooper (AV)

Barristers, Solicitors & Trade Mark Agents
Baine Johnston Centre, 5th Floor, 10 Fort William Place, P.O. Box 5939, A1C 5X4
Telephone: 709-722-8735
Telecopier: 709-722-1763
Email: mcrsj@mcrlaw.com *URL:* http://www.mcrlaw.com
Halifax, Nova Scotia Office: Summit Place, 1601 Lower Water Street, P.O. Box 730, B3J 2V1.
Telephone: 902-425-6500.
Fax: 902-425-6350. Email: mcrhfx@mcrlaw.com.
Moncton, New Brunswick Office: Place Moncton Place, 655 Main Street, P.O. Box 1368, E1C 8T6.
Telephone: 506-857-8970.
Fax: 506-857-4095. Email: mcrmctn@mcrlaw.com.
Charlottetown, Prince Edward Island Office: BDC Place, Suite 620, 119 Kent Street, C1A 1N3.
Telephone: 902-368-8473.
Fax: 902-368-8346. Email: mcrpei@mcrlaw.com.
Fredericton, New Brunswick Office: Suite 600, 570 Queen Street, P.O. Box 610.
Telephone: 506-458-8572.
Fax: 506-458-9903. Email: mcrfton@mcrlaw.com.

PARTNERS

James R. Chalker, Q.C. Thomas R. Kendell
Christine A. Fagan, Q.C.

For Complete List of Firm Personnel, See General Section

For full biographical listings, see the Martindale-Hubbell Law Directory

CANADA NOVA SCOTIA

*HALIFAX,** Regional Munic. of Halifax

McInnes Cooper (AV)

Barristers, Solicitors & Trade Mark Agents
Summit Place, 1601 Lower Water Street, P.O. Box 730, B3J 2V1
Telephone: 902-425-6500
Fax: 902-425-6350
Email: mcrhfx@mcrlaw.com *URL:* http://www.mcrlaw.com
St. John's, Newfoundland Office: Baine Johnston Centre, 5th Floor, 10 Fort William Place, P.O. Box 5939, A1C 5X4.
Telephone: 709-722-8735.
Telecopier: 709-722-1763. Email: mcrsj@mcrlaw.com.
Moncton, New Brunswick Office: Place Moncton Place, 655 Main Street, P.O. Box 1368, E1C 8T6.
Telephone: 506-857-8970.
Fax: 506-857-4095. Email: mcrmctn@mcrlaw.com.
Charlottetown, Prince Edward Island Office: BDC Place, Suite 620, 119 Kent Street, C1A 1N3.
Telephone: 902-368-8473.
Fax: 902-368-8346. Email: mcrpei@mcrlaw.com.
Fredericton, New Brunswick Office: Suite 600, 570 Queen Street, P.O. Box 610.
Telephone: 506-458-8572.
Fax: 506-458-9903. Email: mcrfton@mcrlaw.com.

PARTNERS

George T. H. Cooper, Q.C. F. Van W. Penick
Aidan J. Meade

ASSOCIATE

Kristi Sebalj

For Complete List of Firm Personnel, See General Section

For full biographical listings, see the Martindale-Hubbell Law Directory

CANADA PRINCE EDWARD ISLAND

*CHARLOTTETOWN,** Queen's Co.

McInnes Cooper (AV Ⓣ)

Barristers, Solicitors & Trade Mark Agents
BDC Place, Suite 620, 119 Kent Street, C1A 1N3
Telephone: 902-368-8473
Fax: 902-368-8346
Email: mcrpei@mcrlaw.com *URL:* http://www.mcrlaw.com
Halifax, Nova Scotia Office: Summit Place, 1601 Lower Water Street, P.O. Box 730, B3J 2V1.
Telephone: 902-425-6500.
Fax: 902-425-6350. Email: mcrhfx@mcrlaw.com.
St. John's, Newfoundland Office: Baine Johnston Centre, 5th Floor, 10 Fort William Place, P.O. Box 5939, A1C 5X4.
Telephone: 709-722-8735.
Telecopier: 709-722-1763. Email: mcrsj@mcrlaw.com.
Moncton, New Brunswick Office: Place Moncton Place, 655 Main Street, P.O. Box 1368, E1C 8T6.
Telephone: 506-857-8970.
Fax: 506-857-4095. Email: mcrmctn@mcrlaw.com.
Fredericton, New Brunswick Office: Suite 600, 570 Queen Street, P.O. Box 610.
Telephone: 506-458-8572.
Fax: 506-458-9903. Email: mcrfton@mcrlaw.com.

PARTNER

Mark Ledwell

ASSOCIATE

L. Charles Keizer

For Complete List of Firm Personnel, See General Section

For full biographical listings, see the Martindale-Hubbell Law Directory

ENVIRONMENTAL LAW

MINNESOTA

*MINNEAPOLIS,** Hennepin Co.

ABDO AND ABDO, P.A. (AV)

710 Northstar West 625 Marquette Avenue, 55402
Telephone: 612-333-1526
Fax: 612-342-2608
Email: abdoabdo@aol.com *URL:* http://www.abdo.com.br

E. John Abdo (1912-1993)
Robert P. Abdo
Steven R. Hedges
Keith J. Broady
Timothy C. Matson

Representative Client: Gopher Oil Co.; Barrel Reconditioner, Inc.

For Complete List of Firm Personnel, See General Section

For full biographical listings, see the Martindale-Hubbell Law Directory

BASSFORD, LOCKHART, TRUESDELL & BRIGGS, P.A. (AV)

(Formerly Richards, Montgomery, Cobb & Bassford, P.A.)
3550 Multifoods Tower, 55402-3787
Telephone: 612-333-3000
Telecopier: 612-333-8829

Greer E. Lockhart
Frederick E. Finch
John M. Degnan
Lewis A. Remele, Jr.
Kevin P. Keenan
James O. Redman
Rebecca Egge Moos
John M. Anderson
Charles E. Lundberg
Gregory P. Bulinski
Dale M. Wagner
Louis J. Speltz
Laura J. McKnight
Mark P. Hodkinson
Thomas J. Niemiec
Andrew L. Marshall
Michael A. Klutho
Gregory W. Deckert
Kevin P. Hickey
Stanford P. Hill
Mark R. Whitmore
Fred B. Snyder (1859-1951)
Edward C. Gale (1862-1943)
Frank A. Janes (1908-1959)
Nathan A. Cobb, Sr. (1905-1976)
Bergmann Richards (1888-1978)
Edmund T. Montgomery (1904-1987)
Charles A. Bassford (1914-1990)
Jerome C. Briggs (Retired)
Lynn G. Truesdell (Retired)

Dani M. Shimon
Christopher R. Morris
Kelly A. Putney
Jennifer L. Hill
Robin Ann Williams
Michael A. Switzer
Shalanda Denise Ballard

Representative Clients: Chubb/Pacific Indemnity Group; John Hancock Mutual Life Insurance Co.; The Travelers Insurance Cos.; Commercial Union Insurance Co.; American States Insurance Co.

For full biographical listings, see the Martindale-Hubbell Law Directory

HENSON & EFRON, P.A. (AV)

400 Second Avenue South, Suite 1200, 55401-2496
Telephone: 612-339-2500
Fax: 612-339-6364
Email: firm@hensonefron.com

Joseph T. Dixon, Jr.
Stuart T. Williams

Representative Clients: Edward Kraemer & Sons, Inc.; Hawkins Chemical, Inc.; Pentair, Inc.

For Complete List of Firm Personnel, See General Section

For full biographical listings, see the Martindale-Hubbell Law Directory

OPPENHEIMER WOLFF & DONNELLY LLP (AV)

3400 Plaza VII, 45 South Seventh Street, 55402
Telephone: 612-607-7000
FAX: 612-607-7100
URL: http://www.owdlaw.com
Amsterdam, The Netherlands Office: Keizergracht 241.
Telephone: 31-20-423-4555.
FAX: 31-20-423-4545.
Brussels, Belgium Office: Avenue Louise 240, Box 5, 1050.
Telephone: 32-2-626-0500.
FAX: 32-2-626-0510.
Geneva, Switzerland Office: Rue Gabriel Eynard, 6, 1205.
Telephone: (41/22) 311-7410.
FAX: (41/22) 311-7407.
New York, N.Y. Office: Citicorp Center, 153 East 53rd Street, 10022.
Telephone: 212-826-5000.
FAX: 212-486-0708.

(See Next Column)

Newport Beach, California Office: 500 Newport Center Drive, Suite 700, 92660.
Telephone: 949-719-6000.
FAX: 949-719-6020.
Paris, France Office: 53 Avenue Montaigne, 75008.
Telephone: (33/1) 44 95 03 50.
FAX: (33/1) 44 95 03 40.
St. Paul, Minnesota Office: 1700 First National Bank Building, 55101.
Telephone: 651-605-2000.
FAX: 651-605-2100.
Washington, D.C. Office: Oppenheimer Wolff Donnelly & Bayh LLP, 1350 Eye Street, N.W., Suite 200, 20005.
Telephone: 202-312-8000.
FAX: 202-312-8100.
Los Angeles, California Office: 2029 Century Park East, 38th Floor, 90067
Telephone: 310-788-5000.
FAX: 310-277-1297.
San Jose, California Office: 101 Park Center Plaza, Suite 300, 95113.
Telephone: 408-795-3000.
FAX: 408-795-3100.
Chicago, Illinois Office: Oppenheimer Wolff & Donnelly (Illinois), Two Prudential Plaza, 45th Floor, 180 North Stetson Avenue, 60601.
Telephone: 312-616-1800.
Fax: 312-616-5800.

RESIDENT PARTNERS

G. Robert Johnson
W. C. Blanton
James A. Payne
Gary P. Gengel II
Jonathon H. Bloomberg
Thaddeus R. Lightfoot
Kenneth A. Podpeskar
James A. Mennell

RESIDENT ASSOCIATES

Rachel A. Igel
Lowell M. Rothschild
Vanessa L. Parvin
Ranelle A. Leier

For Complete List of Firm Personnel, See General Section

For full biographical listings, see the Martindale-Hubbell Law Directory

MISSISSIPPI

BILOXI, Harrison Co.

BROWN, WATT & BUCHANAN, P.A. (AV)

115 Main Street, P.O. Box 1377, 39533-1377
Telephone: 228-374-2999
Telecopier: 228-435-7090
Email: mail@bwblaw.com *URL:* http://www.bwblaw.com
Pascagoula, Mississippi Office: 3112 Canty Street, P.O. Box 2220.
Telephone: 228-762-0035.
Fax: 228-762-0299.

Raymond L. Brown
W. Lee Watt
Patrick R. Buchanan
W. Mark Edwards
A. Kelly Sessoms, III
Alan K. Sudduth

Representative Clients: Chevron USA, Inc.; CSX Transportation, Inc.; First Chemical Corp.; Georgia Pacific Corp.; Mississippi Phosphates Corp.; Morton International; White Consolidated Industries.

For full biographical listings, see the Martindale-Hubbell Law Directory

*COLUMBIA,** Marion Co.

AULTMAN, TYNER, RUFFIN & YARBOROUGH, LTD., A PROFESSIONAL LAW CORPORATION (AV)

329 Church Street, P.O. Drawer 707, 39429
Telephone: 601-736-2222
FAX: 601-736-9884
Email: rfyjr@cblink.com
Hattiesburg, Mississippi Office: 315 Hemphill Street, P.O. Drawer 750.
Telephone: 601-583-2671.
FAX: 601-583-2677.
Gulfport, Mississippi Office: 1201 25th Avenue, Suite 300, P.O. Box 607.
Telephone: 228-863-6913.
FAX: 228-868-8505. Email: atmr@digiscape.com.
New Orleans, Louisiana Office: The Texaco Center, 400 Poydras Street, Suite 2250.
Telephone: 504-528-9616.
FAX: 504-528-9640.

Richard F. Yarborough, Jr.

OF COUNSEL

Ernest Ray Duff

Representative Clients: Hercules, Inc.; United States Steel Corp.; Ford Motor Co.; International Paper Co.; Phillips Petroleum Co.; Aetna Casualty & Surety Co.; CNA Group; Liberty Mutual Insurance Co.; St. Paul Fire & Marine Insurance Co.; Fireman's Fund.

For full biographical listings, see the Martindale-Hubbell Law Directory

*GREENWOOD,** Leflore Co.

UPSHAW, WILLIAMS, BIGGERS, BECKHAM & RIDDICK, LLP (AV)

309 Fulton Street, 38930
Telephone: 662-455-1613
Facsimile: 662-453-9245
Mailing Address: P.O. Drawer 8230, Greenwood, Mississippi, 38935-8230
Email: lexgwd@uwbbr.com
Jackson, Mississippi Office: Suite 300 Plaza One, 715 South Pear Orchard Road, P.O. Box 9147, 39286-9147.
Telephone: 601-978-1996.
Facsimile: 601-978-1949. Email: lexjax@uwbbr.com.

MEMBERS OF FIRM

James E. Upshaw
Tommie G. Williams
Marc A. Biggers
Glenn F. Beckham
Roger C. Riddick (Resident, Jackson Office)
F. Ewin Henson III
Lonnie D. Bailey
Robert S. Upshaw
Clinton M. Guenther
Richard C. Williams, Jr. (Resident, Jackson Office)
Richard L. Kimmel
Mark C. Carroll (Resident, Jackson Office)
W. Hugh Gillon IV (Resident, Jackson Office)
Paul L. Goodman
Walter C. Morrison IV (Resident, Jackson Office)

ASSOCIATES

Steven H. Funderburg (Resident, Jackson Office)
Bonnie Bridgers Smith (Resident, Jackson Office)

OF COUNSEL

Ben L. Riddick (Resident, Jackson Office)
John R. Countiss III (Resident, Jackson Office)

Representative Clients: United States Fidelity & Guaranty Co.; State Farm Mutual Automobile Insurance Co.; CNA Insurance Cos.; St. Paul Fire & Marine Insurance Co.; Travelers/Aetna Property and Casualty Corp.; Kemper Insurance Co.; Zurich-American Insurance Group; Risk Enterprise Management, Ltd.; Allstate Insurance Co.

For Complete List of Firm Personnel, See General Section

For full biographical listings, see the Martindale-Hubbell Law Directory

*GULFPORT,** Harrison Co.

AULTMAN, TYNER, RUFFIN & YARBOROUGH, LTD., A PROFESSIONAL LAW CORPORATION (AV)

1201 25th Avenue, Suite 300, P.O. Box 607, 39502
Telephone: 228-863-6913
FAX: 228-868-8505
Email: atmr@digiscape.com
Hattiesburg, Mississippi Office: 315 Hemphill Street, P.O. Drawer 750.
Telephone: 601-583-2671.
FAX: 601-583-2677.
Columbia, Mississippi Office: 329 Church Street, P.O. Drawer 707.
Telephone: 601-736-2222.
FAX: 601-736-9884. Email: rfyjr@cblink.com.
New Orleans, Louisiana Office: The Texaco Center, 400 Poydras Street, Suite 2250.
Telephone: 504-528-9616.
FAX: 504-528-9640.

Ben E. Sheely
Dorrance (Dee) Aultman, Jr.

For Complete List of Firm Personnel, See General Section

For full biographical listings, see the Martindale-Hubbell Law Directory

DUKES, DUKES, KEATING AND FANECA, P.A. (AV)

2909 13th Street, 6th Floor, P.O. Drawer W, 39501
Telephone: 228-868-1111
Fax: 228-863-2886
Email: ddkf@ddkf.com

Walter W. Dukes
Hugh D. Keating

Thomas William Busby

For Complete List of Firm Personnel, See General Section

For full biographical listings, see the Martindale-Hubbell Law Directory

FRANKE, RAINEY & SALLOUM, PLLC (AV)

2605 14th Street, P.O. Drawer 460, 39502
Telephone: 228-868-7070
Telecopier: 228-868-7090
Email: frs@diversicomm.com

Paul M. Franke, Jr.
William M. Rainey
Richard P. Salloum
Paul B. Howell
Fredrick B. Feeney, II
Traci M. Castille
Donald P. Moore

(See Next Column)

Kaleel G. Salloum, Jr.
Brandi C. Schwartz
James C. Simpson, Jr.

For full biographical listings, see the Martindale-Hubbell Law Directory

HOPKINS, CRAWLEY, BAGWELL & UPSHAW, P.L.L.C. (AV)

2701 24th Avenue, P.O. Box 1510, 39501-4941
Telephone: 228-864-2200
Mississippi and USA Wats: 1-800-421-3629
Fax: 228-868-9358; 228-863-4227
Email: Hopkins@MSLawyer.com
Jackson, Mississippi Office: 499 South President Street, Second Floor, Suite 1.
Telephone: 601-355-6510.
Fax: 601-355-6503. Email: TCrawley@MSLawyer.com.

MEMBERS OF FIRM

Alben N. Hopkins
Timothy D. Crawley
Douglas Bagwell
Jessica Sibley Upshaw
Thomas Alan Waller

ASSOCIATES

Raymond D. Carter
Kenneth S. Womack
Mary Benton-Shaw
Pat Sharkey Burke, Jr.
David E. Wilson
Laura Faye Paulk
Ronald C. Small (Not admitted in MS)

Representative Clients: Coregis Group; General Cable Corp.; Insurance Company of North America; Liberty Mutual Insurance Group; Reliance Insurance Co.; USX Corp.; Employers Insurance of Wausau; American International Group (AIG); Quaker Chemical Corp.

For full biographical listings, see the Martindale-Hubbell Law Directory

MEADOWS RILEY LAW FIRM (AV)

1720 23rd Avenue, P.O. Box 550, 39502
Telephone: 601-864-4511
Telecopier: 601-868-2178

Joseph R. Meadows
Donnie D. Riley
Jerry D. Riley
Karen J. Young

Representative Clients: Bubba Oustalat Lincoln Mercury, Inc.; Lee Tractor Co. of Mississippi.
Reference: Hancock Bank.

For full biographical listings, see the Martindale-Hubbell Law Directory

*HATTIESBURG,** Forrest Co.

AULTMAN, TYNER, RUFFIN & YARBOROUGH, LTD., A PROFESSIONAL LAW CORPORATION (AV)

315 Hemphill Street, P.O. Drawer 750, 39403-0750
Telephone: 601-583-2671
FAX: 601-583-2677
Email: aultyn@c-gate.net
Columbia, Mississippi Office: 329 Church Street, P.O. Drawer 707.
Telephone: 601-736-2222.
FAX: 601-736-9884. Email: rfyjr@cblink.com.
Gulfport, Mississippi Office: 1201 25th Avenue, Suite 300, P.O. Box 607.
Telephone: 228-863-6913.
FAX: 228-868-8505. Email: atmr@digiscape.com.
New Orleans, Louisiana Office: The Texaco Center, 400 Poydras Street, Suite 2250.
Telephone: 504-528-9616.
FAX: 504-528-9640.

Dorrance Aultman
Thomas W. Tyner
Louie F. Ruffin
Richard F. Yarborough, Jr. (Resident, Columbia Office)
Ben E. Sheely (Resident, Gulfport Office)
R. Curtis Smith, II
Dorrance (Dee) Aultman, Jr. (Resident, Gulfport Office)
William Nelson Graham

Victor A. DuBose

OF COUNSEL

Ernest Ray Duff (Resident, Columbia Office)

Representative Clients: Hercules, Inc.; U.S. Steel Corp.; Ford Motor Co.; Phillips Petroleum Co.; Aetna Casualty & Surety Co.; CNA Group; Liberty Mutual Insurance Co.; St. Paul Fire & Marine Insurance Co.; Fireman's Fund; L & A Contracting Co.

For Complete List of Firm Personnel, See General Section

For full biographical listings, see the Martindale-Hubbell Law Directory

*JACKSON,** Hinds Co.

BAKER, DONELSON, BEARMAN & CALDWELL (AV)

Suite 500, 700 North State Street, 39202
Telephone: 601-351-2400
Telecopier: 601-351-2424
Email: info@bdbc.com *URL:* http://www.bakerdonelson.com
Memphis, Tennessee Office: 20th Floor, First Tennessee Building, 165 Madison, 38103.
Telephone: 901-526-2000.
Telecopier: 901-577-2303.
Nashville, Tennessee Office: 1700 Nashville City Center, 511 Union Street, 37219.
Telephone: 615-726-5600.
Telecopier: 615-726-0464.
Chattanooga, Tennessee Office: 1800 Republic Centre, 633 Chestnut Street, 37450-1800.
Telephone: 423-756-2010.
Telecopier: 423-756-3447.
Knoxville, Tennessee Office: 2200 Riverview Tower, 900 South Gay Street, 37901.
Telephone: 423-549-7000.
Telecopier: 423-525-8569.
Johnson City, Tennessee Office: SunTrust Bank Building, 207 Mockingbird Lane, P.O. Box 3038, 37602.
Telephone: 423-928-0181.
Telecopier: 423-928-5694; 423-928-3654; Kingsport: 423-246-6191.
Huntsville, Tennessee Office: 3 Courthouse Square, 37756.
Telephone: 423-663-2321.
Telecopier: 423-663-2111.
Washington, D.C. Office: Market Square, 801 Pennsylvania Avenue, N.W., 20004.
Telephone: 202-508-3400.
Telecopier: 202-508-3402.

PARTNER

Michael T. Dawkins

For Complete List of Firm Personnel, See General Section

For full biographical listings, see the Martindale-Hubbell Law Directory

BENNETT LOTTERHOS SULSER & WILSON, P.A. (AV)

One Jackson Place Suite 1400, 188 East Capitol Street, P.O. Box 98, 39205-0098
Telephone: 601-944-0466
Telecopier: 601-944-0467

Richard T. Bennett
Joseph E. Lotterhos
Marcus M. Wilson
Edward E. Lawler, Jr.
Mary E. McAlister
J. Mark Franklin, III
Ronald Keith Foreman
John L. Pannier

OF COUNSEL

Floyd M. Sulser, Jr.

Representative Clients: Agristor Leasing; Chubb Group of Insurance Companies; 84 Lumber Company; European American Bank; FSLIC; Great Southern Federal Savings; Hibernia National Bank; Holiday Inns, Inc; Masonite Corp.

For full biographical listings, see the Martindale-Hubbell Law Directory

MARKOW, WALKER & REEVES, P.A. (AV)

Atrium North Building, 805 South Wheatley, Suite 400, P.O. Box 13669, 39236-3669
Telephone: 601-956-8500
Telecopier: 601-956-8423
Oxford, Mississippi Office: 1006 Van Buren Avenue, 38655.
Telephone: 601-234-9899.
Telecopier: 601-234-9762.

Peter J. Markow, Jr.
Christopher J. Walker
William C. Reeves
Terry B. Germany
Richard C. Coker
Gilson Davis (Dave) Peterson
Alfonso Nuzzo
Richard M. Edmonson, Jr.
Hubert Wesley Williams, III
L. Pepper Cossar
J. Hale Freeland (Resident, Oxford Office)

Delia R. Owens
T.G. Bolen, Jr.
Holly Bridges Wiggs
Michael D. Young
S. Deann Thomas
Robert Niles Hooper
L. Abraham Rowe, Jr.
Andrew D. Shull (Resident, Oxford Office)

Reference: Trustmark National Bank, Jackson, Miss.

For full biographical listings, see the Martindale-Hubbell Law Directory

WATKINS & EAGER (AV)

A Professional Limited Liability Company
Suite 300 The Emporium Building, 400 East Capitol Street, P.O. Box 650, 39205
Telephone: 601-948-6470
Facsimile: 601-354-3623

(See Next Column)

MEMBERS OF FIRM

Charles Clark
P. Nicholas Harkins, III
John G. Corlew
William F. Goodman, III
Virginia T. Munford

Representative Clients: Ashland, Inc.; Chevron U.S.A. Inc.; International Paper Co.; Shell Oil Co.; Trustmark National Bank; Laidlaw Environmental Services, Inc.; McDermott Inc.

For Complete List of Firm Personnel, See General Section

For full biographical listings, see the Martindale-Hubbell Law Directory

*LAUREL,** Jones Co.

GIBBES GRAVES MULLINS HORTMAN HARLOW MARTINDALE & JONES, PLLC (AV)

414 West Oak Street, P.O. Drawer 1409, 39441-1409
Telephone: 601-649-8611
FAX: 601-649-6062

MEMBERS OF FIRM

William S. Mullins, III
Norman Gene Hortman, Jr.
Eugene M. Harlow
David L. Martindale
Deidra D. Jones

ASSOCIATES

Brett W. Robinson
Leslie P. Barry

Representative Clients: Texaco Inc.; Masonite Corp., a Division of International Paper Co.; St. Paul Insurance; Chevron U.S.A., Inc.; BellSouth; Shell Oil; Exxon Corp.; Amoco Prod. Co.; Oryx Energy Co.; Mobil Exploration & Production N.A., Inc.

For full biographical listings, see the Martindale-Hubbell Law Directory

*PASCAGOULA,** Jackson Co.

BROWN, WATT & BUCHANAN, P.A. (AV)

3112 Canty Street, P.O. Box 2220, 39569-2220
Telephone: 228-762-0035
Telecopier: 228-762-0299
Email: mail@bwblaw.com *URL:* http://www.bwblaw.com
Biloxi, Mississippi Office: 115 Main Street, P.O. Box 1377.
Telephone: 228-374-2999.
Fax: 228-435-7090.

Raymond L. Brown
W. Lee Watt
Patrick R. Buchanan
W. Mark Edwards
A. Kelly Sessoms, III
Alan K. Sudduth

Representative Clients: Chevron, USA, Inc.; CSX Transportation, Inc.; First Chemical Corp.; Georgia Pacific Corp.; Mississippi Phosphates Corp.; Morton International; White Consolidated Industries.

For full biographical listings, see the Martindale-Hubbell Law Directory

COLINGO, WILLIAMS, HEIDELBERG, STEINBERGER & McELHANEY, P.A. (AV)

711 Delmas Avenue, P.O. Box 1407, 39568-1407
Telephone: 228-762-8021
FAX: 228-762-7589
Email: info@colingowilliams.com *URL:* http://www.ColingoWilliams.com

Joe R. Colingo
James H. Heidelberg
Karl R. Steinberger
Brett K. Williams

Representative Clients: International Paper Co.; R.J. Reynolds; CBS Corp.; Kemper Group; Singing River Hospital System; Mississippi Gulf Coast Regional Wastewater Authority; Medical Assurance Company of Mississippi; Mutual Assurance of Alabama; Dole Food Co.

For full biographical listings, see the Martindale-Hubbell Law Directory

MISSOURI

KANSAS CITY, Jackson, Clay, Platte & Cass Cos.

SPENCER FANE BRITT & BROWNE LLP (AV)

1000 Walnut Street, Suite 1400, 64106-2140
Telephone: 816-474-8100
URL: http://www.spencerfane.com
Overland Park, Kansas Office: Suite 700, 40 Corporate Woods, 9401 Indian Creek Parkway.
Telephone: 913-345-8100.

MEMBERS OF FIRM

James H. Andreasen
J. Nick Badgerow (Resident, Overland Park, Kansas Office)
Russell W. Baker, Jr.
Bruce E. Cavitt
Scott J. Goldstein
Carl H. Helmstetter
Michael D. Hockley
James W. Kapp, Jr.
Michael C. Kirk
Elaine Drodge Koch
James R. McKown
Barry L. Pickens
James T. Price

(See Next Column)

SPENCER FANE BRITT & BROWNE LLP, *Kansas City—Continued*

Richard W. Scarritt
Terry W. Schackmann
Lowell L. Smithson
Mark A. Thornhill
Teresa A. Woody

OF COUNSEL

Alan R. Clever (Resident, Overland Park, Kansas Office)

ASSOCIATES

Jennifer Downs O'Shaughnessy
Evan L. Randall
Elizabeth Brand Six
Eric J. Voogt

Representative Clients: Allied Waste Systems; AT&T, Inc.; Exide Corp.; Farmland Industries; W. R. Grace Co.; Kansas City Power and Light Co.; Lucent Technologies; Philips Electronics North America Corp.; Sequa Corporation.

For full biographical listings, see the Martindale-Hubbell Law Directory

ST. LOUIS, (Independent City)

ARMSTRONG TEASDALE LLP (AV)

A Partnership including Professional Corporations
One Metropolitan Square, 63102-2740
Telephone: 314-621-5070
Facsimile: 314-621-5065
Twx: 910 761-2246
Cable: ATKV LAW
Email: armstrongteasdale@armstrongteasdale.com *URL:* http://www.armstrongteasdale.com
Kansas City, Missouri Office: 2345 Grand Boulevard, Suite 2000, 64108.
Telephone: 816-221-3420.
Facsimile: 816-221-0786.
Jefferson City, Missouri Office: 3405 W. Truman Blvd., Suite 210, 65109.
Telephone: 573-636-8394.
Washington, D.C. Office: 1747 Pennsylvania Avenue, N.W., Suite 300, 20006.
Telephone: 202-347-0259.
Belleville, Illinois Office: 23 South First Street, 62220.
Telephone: 618-397-4411.
Olathe, Kansas Office: 100 East Park, 66061.
Telephone: 913-345-0706.
Shanghai, China Office: A-T International Consultants, LLC, Suite 310, No. 12 Zhongshan Road (E1), Shanghai 200002 P.R.C.
Telephone: 86-21-6326-7001.
Facsimile: 86-21-6326-0626.

MEMBERS OF FIRM

John R. Barsanti, Jr., (P.C.)
John F. Cowling
Byron E. Francis (P.C.)
Edwin L. Noel (P.C.)
George M. von Stamwitz
Richard L. Waters
Thomas B. Weaver (P.C.)

ASSOCIATES

Jennifer E. Cook
Norella V. Huggins
Lisa A. Larkin
Jeffery T. McPherson

Representative Clients: Anheuser-Busch Companies, Inc.; Chemetco, Inc.; ICI Explosives U.S.A. and its subsidiary, ICI Explosives Environmental; Anschutz Corporation; Owens-Corning Fiberglas Corporation; Clark Refining and Marketing Company; Syntex Corporation and its Subsidiary Syntex Agribusiness, Inc.; AmerenUE; DeSoto, Inc.; GSX Corporation.

For Complete List of Firm Personnel, See General Section

For full biographical listings, see the Martindale-Hubbell Law Directory

ROBERTS, PERRYMAN, BOMKAMP & MEIVES, P.C. (AV)

Suite 2300, One Mercantile Center, 63101
Telephone: 314-421-1850
Cable Address: "Henrogo"
Telecopier: 314-421-4346
Email: rpbm@istnet.net
Belleville, Illinois Office: 23 Public Square, Suite 402.
Telephone: 618-277-9955.

Ted L. Perryman
Gary W. Bomkamp
John L. Walker
Thomas J. Kernell

Reference: Boatmen's National Bank.

For full biographical listings, see the Martindale-Hubbell Law Directory

THE STOLAR PARTNERSHIP (AV)

7th Floor, 911 Washington Avenue, 63101
Telephone: 314-231-2800
Telex: 880984
Telecopier: 314-436-8400
Belleville, Illinois Office: 7 North High Street.
Telephone: 618-277-1030.

MEMBERS OF FIRM

Dale E. Hermeling
William J. Kuehling
Jay L. Levitch
William R. Werner

(See Next Column)

ASSOCIATE

Musette H. Vogel ***

***Admitted Illinois and Missouri

For full biographical listings, see the Martindale-Hubbell Law Directory

MONTANA

*BILLINGS,** Yellowstone Co.

CROWLEY, HAUGHEY, HANSON, TOOLE & DIETRICH, P.L.L.P. (AV)

500 Transwestern II, 490 North 31st Street, P.O. Box 2529, 59103
Telephone: 406-252-3441
Fax: 406-259-4159
Email: crowley@crowleylaw.com
Helena, Montana Office: IBM Building, 100 North Park Avenue, Suite 300, 59601.
Telephone: 406-449-4165.
Fax: 406-449-5149.
Kalispell, Montana Office: 431 1st Avenue West, 59901.
Telephone: 406-752-6644.
Fax: 406-752-5108.
Williston, North Dakota Office: 113 East Broadway, 58801.
Telephone: 701-572-2200.
Fax: 701-572-7072.

OF COUNSEL

Bruce R. Toole

MEMBERS OF FIRM

Arthur F. Lamey, Jr.
Steven P. Ruffatto
Allan L. Karell
Carolyn S. Ostby
Mary Scrim Dyre (Resident, Kalispell, Montana Office)
Jon T. Dyre (Resident, Kalispell, Montana Office)
Renee L. Coppock
Janice L. Rehberg
John R. Lee (Resident, Williston, North Dakota Office)

Representative Clients: The Western Sugar Company; Natural Gas Processing; Peabody Coal; Grace Petroleum Corporation; Federated Insurance Company; Conoco; Inter-City Gas Corporation; First Interstate Bank of Commerce.

For Complete List of Firm Personnel, See General Section

For full biographical listings, see the Martindale-Hubbell Law Directory

*HELENA,** Lewis and Clark Co.

BROWNING, KALECZYC, BERRY & HOVEN, P.C. (AV)

139 North Last Chance Gulch, P.O. Box 1697, 59624
Telephone: 406-443-6820
Telefax: 406-443-6882
Email: BKBH@BKBH.COM *URL:* http://www.BKBH.com

R. Stephen Browning
Leo Berry
J. Daniel Hoven
Catherine A. Laughner
Mark D. Etchart

Steven T. Wade
Mark R. Taylor
G. Andy Adamek

Representative Clients: The Burlington Northern and Santa Fe Railway Co.; Columbia Falls Aluminum Company; Crane Company; RIBI ImmunoChem Research, Inc.; Watkins and Shepard Trucking, Inc.; Pacific Steel and Recycling; Rhone-Poulene; CNA Surety.

For full biographical listings, see the Martindale-Hubbell Law Directory

NEBRASKA

*LINCOLN,** Lancaster Co.

CLINE, WILLIAMS, WRIGHT, JOHNSON & OLDFATHER (AV)

1900 U.S. Bank Building, 233 South 13th Street, 68508
Telephone: 402-474-6900
Fax: 402-474-5393
Email: postmaster@cline-law.com *URL:* http://www.cline-law.com
Omaha, Nebraska Office: Suite 720, One Pacific Place, 1125 South 103rd Street, 68124.
Telephone: 402-397-1700.
Fax: 402-397-1806.

ATTORNEYS

Allen L. Graves
Charles M. Pallesen, Jr.
Fredric H. Kauffman
Donald F. Burt
Alan E. Peterson
Stephen E. Gehring
Robert J. Routh
Kevin Colleran

(See Next Column)

CLINE, WILLIAMS, WRIGHT, JOHNSON & OLDFATHER—*Continued*

ATTORNEYS (Continued)

L. Bruce Wright
James M. Bausch
Larry A. Holle
David R. Buntain
Stephen H. Nelsen
Michael C. Mueller
Lauren W. Wismer
Daniel R. Stogsdill
Scott D. Kelly
Terry R. Wittler
Pamela Hastings Carrier
Mark A. Christensen
Richard P. Garden, Jr.
Shawn D. Renner
John C. Miles
Mary Kay Frank
Thomas C. Huston
Sonya S. Ekart
Don R. Janssen
Susan Kubert Sapp
Kevin J. Schneider
Andrew D. Strotman
Jill Gossin Jensen
Rochelle A. Mullen
John L. Horan
Bryan S. Hatch
Steven C. Likes
Tracy A. Oldemeyer
Jolene M. Papa
Timothy G. Aschoff
Eric N. Bergquist
Janis J. Winterhof
Andrea Dylan Snowden

OF COUNSEL

Charles E. Wright
Richard P. Jeffries
Mary M. Campbell

RETIRED PARTNERS

Flavel A. Wright (Retired)
Warren C. Johnson (Retired)
Charles E. Oldfather (1927-1998)

Representative Clients: U.S. Bank National Association; University of Nebraska; Nebraska Medical Assn.; Saint Elizabeth Regional Medical Center; Media of Nebraska; Cargill Inc.; State Farm Insurance Cos.; Wal-Mart Stores, Inc.; Textron/Cushman; Isco, Inc.

For full biographical listings, see the Martindale-Hubbell Law Directory

*OMAHA,** Douglas Co.

ERICKSON & SEDERSTROM, P.C. (AV)

Regency Westpointe, 10330 Regency Parkway Drive, Suite 100, 68114-3761
Telephone: 402-397-2200
Fax: 402-390-7137
Lincoln, Nebraska Office: Suite 400, Cornhusker Plaza, 301 South 13th Street, 68508-2571.
Telephone: 402-476-1000.
Fax: 402-476-6167.

Donald H. Erickson
Gary L. Hoffman

Representative Clients: Nebraska State Bank of Omaha; Berkshire Hathaway, Inc.; Bozell, Inc.; IBP, Inc. Quaker Oats Co.; United A-G Cooperative, Inc.; Immanuel Medical Center; Cornhusker Casualty Co.; Hartford Accident & Indemnity Co.; Mortgage Guaranty Insurance Corp. (MGIC).

For Complete List of Firm Personnel, See General Section

For full biographical listings, see the Martindale-Hubbell Law Directory

FRASER, STRYKER, VAUGHN, MEUSEY, OLSON, BOYER & BLOCH, P.C. (AV)

500 Energy Plaza, 409 South 17th Street, 68102
Telephone: 402-341-6000
Telecopier: 402-341-8290
Email: fraserstryker.com

Joseph K. Meusey
Wayne J. Mark
Robert W. Rieke
Stephen M. Bruckner
Rex A. Rezac
Lon A. Licata

Representative Clients: Omaha Public Power District; ASARCO; Arcadian Corp.; Gould, Inc.; Ashgrove Cement Co.

For Complete List of Firm Personnel, See General Section

For full biographical listings, see the Martindale-Hubbell Law Directory

NEVADA

*CARSON CITY,** (Independent City)

THE LAW OFFICE OF DANIEL R. WALSH (AV)

Westwinds Professional Complex, 307 West Winnie Lane, Suite 3, 89703
Telephone: 775-882-8080
Fax: 775-882-6161

Daniel R. Walsh

ASSOCIATE

Kevin P. Walsh

For full biographical listings, see the Martindale-Hubbell Law Directory

HENDERSON, Clark Co.

ROOKER & GIBSON (AV)

Suite 105, 701 North Green Valley Parkway, 89014
Telephone: 702-990-8100
Telecopier: 702-932-5266

C. Keith Rooker
James B. Gibson

Reference: BankWest of Nevada.

For full biographical listings, see the Martindale-Hubbell Law Directory

*LAS VEGAS,** Clark Co.

JOLLEY, URGA, WIRTH & WOODBURY (AV)

3800 Howard Hughes Parkway Suite 1600, 89109
Telephone: 702-699-7500
Facsimile: 702-699-7555
URL: http://www.juww.com
Boulder City, Nevada Office: Suite 105, 1000 Nevada Highway, 89005.
Telephone: 702-293-3674.

MEMBERS OF FIRM

R. Gardner Jolley
Allen D. Emmel

Representative Clients: Wells Fargo Bank and its predecessor, First Interstate Bank of Nevada; Nevada State Bank; Melvin Simon & Associates, Inc.; Nevada Mobilehome Park Owners Association; First Nationwide Bank; Wells Cargo, Inc.; Dean Roofing Co.; Lincoln Property Co.; First Security Bank of Nevada.

For Complete List of Firm Personnel, See General Section

For full biographical listings, see the Martindale-Hubbell Law Directory

*RENO,** Washoe Co.

HARRIS, TRIMMER & THOMPSON (AV)

An Association of Attorneys
6121 Lakeside Drive, Suite 260, P.O. Box 70250, 89570-0250
Telephone: 702-825-4300
Fax: 702-825-4829

Richard W. Harris
Kathleen S. Trimmer
Richard Kent Thompson

For full biographical listings, see the Martindale-Hubbell Law Directory

McDONALD CARANO WILSON McCUNE BERGIN FRANKOVICH & HICKS LLP (AV)

241 Ridge Street, 89501
Telephone: 775-788-2000
Telecopier: 775-788-2020
URL: http://www.mcdonaldcarano.com
Las Vegas, Nevada Office: Suite 1000, 2300 West Sahara Avenue.
Telephone: 702-873-4100.
Telecopier: 702-873-9966.

MEMBERS OF FIRM

Thomas R. C. Wilson
Sylvia L. Harrison
James C. Giudici
Andrew P. Gordon
Matthew C. Addison

ASSOCIATES

Miranda M. Du
Jane M. Long (Not admitted in NV)

Representative Clients: Scolari's Warehouse Market's, Inc.; Shaver Construction; Time Oil Co. (Nevada Counsel); Q & D Construction, Inc.

For Complete List of Firm Personnel, See General Section

For full biographical listings, see the Martindale-Hubbell Law Directory

WALTHER, KEY, MAUPIN, OATS, COX & LeGOY, A PROFESSIONAL CORPORATION (AV)

Lakeside Professional Plaza, 3500 Lakeside Court, 89509
Telephone: 775-827-2000
Facsimile: 775-827-2185
Mailing Address: P.O. Box 30000, Reno, Nevada, 89520

Steven T. Walther
Jon J. Key
Ernest J. Maupin
C. Robert Cox
L. Robert LeGoy, Jr.
Michael E. Malloy
W. Douglass Maupin
G. Barton Mowry
Kim G. Rowe
Procter J. Hug
Donald A. Lattin
Gustave J. Rossi
Robert A. Winkel
Kurt O. Hunsberger
Michael A. Nivinskus
Christopher D. Jaime

Rick R. Hsu
Michaelle D. Rafferty

Representative Clients: Bank America of Nevada (Trust Dept.); Bechtel Corporations; Bill Pearce Olds, BMW, Volvo; Wells Fargo, N.A. (Trust Dept.); General Motors Acceptance Corp.; Nevada Realtors; Radiation Oncology

(See Next Column)

WALTHER, KEY, MAUPIN, OATS, COX & LEGOY A PROFESSIONAL CORPORATION, *Reno—Continued*

Associates; The Ralph M. Parsons Corporation; Parsons Corporation; Reno Air, Inc.

For full biographical listings, see the Martindale-Hubbell Law Directory

NEW HAMPSHIRE

*CONCORD,** Merrimack Co.

RATH, YOUNG AND PIGNATELLI, PROFESSIONAL ASSOCIATION (AV)

One Capital Plaza, P.O. Box 1500, 03302-1500
Telephone: 603-226-2600
Telecopier: 603-226-2700; 228-2294; 225-9774
Email: ryp@rathlaw.com *URL:* http://www.rathlaw.com
Nashua, New Hampshire Office: The Glass Tower, 20 Trafalgar Square.
Telephone: 603-889-9952.
Telecopier: 603-595-7489.

Thomas D. Rath
Sherilyn Burnett Young
Michael A. Pignatelli
Andrew W. Serell
Charles G. Willing, Jr.

For Complete List of Firm Personnel, See General Section

For full biographical listings, see the Martindale-Hubbell Law Directory

*LACONIA,** Belknap Co.

NORMANDIN, CHENEY & O'NEIL (AV)

Normandin Square, 213 Union Avenue, P.O. Box 575, 03247-0575
Telephone: 603-524-4380
Fax: 603-528-6831
Email: nco@lr.net

MEMBERS OF FIRM

Paul L. Normandin
Robert A. Dietz

ASSOCIATE

Regina A. Nadeau

Counsel for: Laconia Savings Bank; Lakes Region Mental Health Center; Laconia Airport Authority; Central New Hampshire Realty, Inc.; All Metals Industries, Inc.; Lakes Region Anesthesiology, P.A.; Cormier Corp.; Scotia Technology; Vemaline Products.

For Complete List of Firm Personnel, See General Section

For full biographical listings, see the Martindale-Hubbell Law Directory

*MANCHESTER,** Hillsborough Co.

SHEEHAN PHINNEY BASS + GREEN, PROFESSIONAL ASSOCIATION (AV)

Hampshire Plaza, 1000 Elm Street, P.O. Box 3701, 03105-3701
Telephone: 603-668-0300
800-625-SPBG
Fax: 603-627-8121
Email: postmaster@sheehan.com *URL:* http://www.sheehan.com
Portsmouth, New Hampshire Office: Old City Hall, 126 Daniel Street.
Telephone: 603-433-2111.
Fax: 603-433-3126.
Concord, New Hampshire Office: 143 North Main Street.
Telephone: 603-223-2020.
Fax: 603-224-8899.

James Q. Shirley
John E. Peltonen
Katherine M. Hanna
Robert P. Cheney, Jr.
Thomas S. Burack

Representative Clients: Anheuser-Busch, Inc.; Bank of New Hampshire Corp.; The Elliot Hospital of Manchester; Granite State Packing Co.; Moore Business Forms, Inc.; New Hampshire College; New Hampshire Dental Service Corp.; New Hampshire Yankee Electric Corp.; Numerica Financial Corp.

For Complete List of Firm Personnel, See General Section

For full biographical listings, see the Martindale-Hubbell Law Directory

NEW JERSEY

BEDMINSTER, Somerset Co.

PURCELL, RIES, SHANNON, MULCAHY & O'NEILL (AV)

One Pluckemin Way, P.O. Box 754, 07921
Telephone: 908-658-3800
Fax: 908-658-4659
Email: general@prsmo.com *URL:* http://www.prsmo.com
Philadelphia, Pennsylvania Office: 12th Floor, East Tower, Centre Square, 1500 Market Square.
Telephone: 215-665-5602.
Fax: 215-569-8228.

MEMBERS OF FIRM

Eugene M. Purcell
William P. Ries
John J. Shannon
Thomas M. Mulcahy
Michael F. O'Neill
David M. Hawkins
Joseph R. Purcell
Kevin R. Brotz
John M. Bowens
Kevin Kovacs
Kenneth D. Merin
Valerie K. Bollheimer
Andrew L. Indeck
Joseph M. Donegan
Mark Mattia

ASSOCIATES

Rita F. Barone
Kathleen J. Devlin
Paul L. Gallagher
Gary Grabas
John R. Haggerty
William T. Hilliard
Eric J. Konecke
Susan Lawless
Michael J. McCaffrey
Kathleen M. Quinn
Thomas Charles Savoth
Donna M. Stephan-Nolan
Barbara C. Zimmerman

OF COUNSEL

David D. Furman
C. Judson Hamlin

LEGAL SUPPORT PERSONNEL

Gary Molloy

Reference: Somerset Trust Co.

For full biographical listings, see the Martindale-Hubbell Law Directory

CEDAR KNOLLS, Morris Co.

LEARY, BRIDE, TINKER & MORAN, A PROFESSIONAL CORPORATION (AV)

7 Ridgedale Avenue, 07927
Telephone: 973-539-2090
Fax: 973-539-0806

W. Stephen Leary
James D. Bride
John G. Tinker, Jr.
Glenn R. Moran
James T. Gill
William H. Mergner, Jr.
Mark Bongiovanni

Tracey L. VanWiemokly
James P. McHugh III
Brian Peoples
Marguerite Anne Leary
Mark J. Brancato
Wendy Allyson Reek
David J. Dering
Peter M. Bouton
Christopher H. Frick
Mark A. Trudeau

For full biographical listings, see the Martindale-Hubbell Law Directory

CHERRY HILL, Camden Co.

KENNEY & KEARNEY LLP (AV)

Woodland Falls Corporate Park, Suite 210, 220 Lake Drive East, P.O. Box 5034, 08034-0421
Telephone: 856-779-7000
Telecopier: 856-779-1342

Joseph H. Kenney
John B. Kearney
John A. Miller, Jr.
Allen A. Etish
Michele Mareschi Fox
Thomas J. Hagner
William J. DeSantis
Charles J. Connery
John A. Zohlman, III

ASSOCIATES

John J. Bannan
David A. Haworth
Paul F. Jenkins
Margaret J. Quinn
Laura D. Ruccolo

OF COUNSEL

Jane A. Kenney
Joel B. Korin

For full biographical listings, see the Martindale-Hubbell Law Directory

JAMES L. MCKENNA, P.C. (AV)

Woodcrest Pavilion, Ten Melrose Avenue, Suite 450, 08003
Telephone: 856-429-6662
Telecopier: 856-429-0064
Email: jlmpcnj@erols.com
Wynnewood, Pennsylvania Office: 30-31 Hampstead Circle.
Telephone: 610-642-5768.
Fax: 610-642-1130.

(See Next Column)

JAMES L. MCKENNA, P.C.—*Continued*

James L. McKenna

Joanne M. Walker
Arnold E. Capriotti, Jr.
Mary L. Russell

OF COUNSEL

Deborah M. Wilson

For full biographical listings, see the Martindale-Hubbell Law Directory

FLORHAM PARK, Morris Co.

CARLIN, MADDOCK, FAY & CERBONE, P.C. (AV)

25 Vreeland Road, P.O. Box 751, 07932
Telephone: 201-377-3350
Fax: 201-377-5626
URL: http://www.lawyers.com/cmfclaw

John J. Carlin, Jr.
Laurence R. Maddock
Donald J. Fay
Richard R. Cerbone

Arthur G. Warden, III

For full biographical listings, see the Martindale-Hubbell Law Directory

DRINKER BIDDLE & SHANLEY LLP (AV)

A Pennsylvania Limited Liability Partnership
500 Campus Drive, 07932-1047
Telephone: 973-360-1100
Fax: 973-285-1625; 360-9831
URL: http://www.dbr.com
Philadelphia, Pennsylvania Office: Drinker Biddle & Reath LLP, One Logan Square, 18th & Cherry Streets.
Telephone: 215-988-2700.
Telefax: 215-988-2757.
Cable Address: "Debemac."
Washington, D.C. Office: Drinker Biddle & Reath LLP, 1500 K Street, N.W., Suite 1100.
Telephone: 202-842-8800.
Telefax: 202-842-8465.
Princeton, New Jersey Office: Suite 300, 105 College Road East.
Telephone: 609-716-6500.
Telefax: 609-799-7000.
Berwyn, Pennsylvania Office: Drinker Biddle & Reath LLP, Suite 300, 1000 Westlakes Drive.
Telephone: 610-993-2200.
Telefax: 610-993-8585.
New York, New York Office: Drinker Biddle & Reath LLP, 89th Floor, One World Trade Center.
Telephone: 212-321-1812.
Telecopier: 1-212-466-0569.

Richard A. Levao
Nan Bernardo
Michael O. Adelman
Sean Monaghan

Joan E. Pearson
John M. O'Reilly
James A. Kozachek
Robert C. Ciolek

For Complete List of Firm Personnel, See General Section

For full biographical listings, see the Martindale-Hubbell Law Directory

HACK, PIRO, O'DAY, MERKLINGER, WALLACE & MCKENNA, P.A. (AV)

30 Columbia Turnpike, P.O. Box 941, 07932-0941
Telephone: 973-301-6500
Fax: 973-301-0094
Email: hpom@ix.netcom.com

M. Richard Merklinger
Robert G. Alencewicz

Representative Clients: The H.B. Smith Company, Inc.; The Johansen Company; Tishman Realty & Construction Co., Inc.; Plasco Safety Products; American Biltrite, Inc.; Hawley Industrial Supplies, Inc.; Unisul, Inc.; The Travelers Insurance Company; Special Liability Group.

For Complete List of Firm Personnel, See General Section

For full biographical listings, see the Martindale-Hubbell Law Directory

SCHWARTZ SIMON EDELSTEIN CELSO & KESSLER (AV)

A Partnership including a Professional Corporation
Ten James Street, 07932
Telephone: 973-301-0001
Fax: 973-301-0203
Email: sseck1@aol.com

Stephen J. Edelstein
Nathanya Guritzky Simon
Donald A. Kessler
John B. Mariano, Jr.
Raymond W. Fisher
Burton Zitomer

Stefani C Schwartz
Denis G. Murphy

(See Next Column)

OF COUNSEL

Glenn C. Guritzky
Miguel A. Maza
Scott A. Elk (P.A.)
(Not admitted in NJ)

For full biographical listings, see the Martindale-Hubbell Law Directory

*HACKENSACK,** Bergen Co.

NOWELL AMOROSO KLEIN BIERMAN, P.A. (AV)

155 Polifly Road, 07601
Telephone: 201-343-5001
Facsimile: 201-343-5181
Email: nakb@erols.com
New York, New York Office: 140 Broadway.
Telephone: 212-858-7710.
Facsimile: 212-858-7750.

Daniel C. Nowell
Henry J. Amoroso
Herbert C. Klein
William D. Bierman
Jeanne M. Damgen
Linda Dunne
William R. DeLorenzo, Jr.
Richard J. Kapner
David Edelberg

Craig E. Parles
Andrew A. Elman
Christopher M. McGarry
William T. Curran
Lisa M. Parles
Daniel S. Eichhorn
Brian M. Doyno
Samer E. Khalaf

OF COUNSEL

John J. Cariddi
Barbara L. de Mare
Karen A. Passaro

For full biographical listings, see the Martindale-Hubbell Law Directory

SOKOL, BEHOT AND FIORENZO (AV)

433 Hackensack Avenue, 07601
Telephone: 201-488-1300
Fax: 201-488-6541

MEMBERS OF FIRM

Leon J. Sokol
Joseph F. Behot, Jr.
Joseph B. Fiorenzo
Jeffrey A. Zenn
Arthur Bergman
Michael P. Feltman

ASSOCIATES

Siobhan Spillane Bailey
Mitchell B. Levine
Steven Seigel
Andrew S. Bosin

COUNSEL

Alan Prigal

For full biographical listings, see the Martindale-Hubbell Law Directory

STOLDT, HORAN AND KOWAL, A PROFESSIONAL CORPORATION (AV)

Continental Plaza I, 401 Hackensack Avenue, 07601
Telephone: 201-646-9200
Telecopier: 201-646-0167
Email: shlaw@bellatlantic.net *URL:* http://www.lawyers.com/stoldthoran&kowal

Sydney V. Stoldt, Jr.
John D. Horan
Dorothy A. Kowal
Heather A. Gallagher
Brian O'Reilly

OF COUNSEL

Judith R. Levinson

For full biographical listings, see the Martindale-Hubbell Law Directory

HADDONFIELD, Camden Co.

WILBRAHAM, LAWLER & BUBA, A PROFESSIONAL CORPORATION (AV⊤)

24 Kings Highway West, 08033-2122
Telephone: 856-795-4422
Fax: 856-795-4699
Philadelphia, Pennsylvania Office: 1818 Market Street, Suite 3100.
Telephone: 215-564-4141.
Fax: 215-564-4385.
Wilmington, Delaware Office: Stoney Batter Office Building, 5301 Limestone Road, Suite 221.
Telephone: 302-234-8217.
Fax: 302-234-8218.

Edward J. Wilbraham
Michael J. Block
Mary S. Cook

For full biographical listings, see the Martindale-Hubbell Law Directory

LAKEWOOD, Ocean Co.

BATHGATE, WEGENER & WOLF, P.C. (AV)

One Airport Road, P.O. Box 2043, 08701
Telephone: 732-363-0666
Telecopier: 732-363-9864
Email: bathweg@idt.net

Lawrence E. Bathgate, II
Peter H. Wegener
William J. Wolf
Jan L. Wouters
Ross D. Gertner
Edward B. Kasselman
Dominic J. Aprile
Nancy G. Wright
Michael M. DiCicco

COUNSEL

Neil Brodsky
Peter A. Valenti

Jonathan S. Fabricant
Robert J. Gillispie, Jr.
Peter G. Licata
Steven E Robertson

For full biographical listings, see the Martindale-Hubbell Law Directory

LAWRENCEVILLE, Mercer Co.

SZAFERMAN, LAKIND, BLUMSTEIN, WATTER & BLADER, P.C. (AV)

Suite 104 Quakerbridge Executive Center, 101 Grovers Mill Road, 08648
Telephone: 609-275-0400
Telefax: 609-275-4511

Arnold C. Lakind
Barry D. Szaferman
Jeffrey P. Blumstein
Paul N. Watter
Steven Blader
Sidney H. Lehmann
Gerald B. Schenkman
David B. Beckett
Scott P. Borsack
Mary Lou Delahanty

Jennifer Weisberg Millner
Cathyanne A. Pisciotta
Jason N. Fruhschein
Demery J. Roberts
Stuart A. Tucker
Brian G. Paul
Victoria Rivera-Cruz
Thomas J. Burns III

LEGAL SUPPORT PERSONNEL

Paula M. Rossi (Office Administrator)
Patricia Hallstrum (Controller)

Representative Clients: Sun National Bank; First Washington Bank; Gilmore Securities & Co.; Communication Workers of America; The Eagle Group; Water's Edge Convalescent Center; Ronson Aviation, Inc.; Holmdel Township Board of Adjustment; Public Service Managers Association; Chemical Leaman Tank Lines.

For full biographical listings, see the Martindale-Hubbell Law Directory

LIVINGSTON, Essex Co.

GENOVA, BURNS & VERNOIA (AV)

Eisenhower Plaza II, 354 Eisenhower Parkway, 07039
Telephone: 973-533-0777
Facsimile: 973-533-1112
URL: http://www.gbvlaw.com
Trenton, New Jersey Office: The Princeton House, 160 West State Street.
Telephone: 609-393-1131.

MEMBERS OF FIRM

Angelo J. Genova
James M. Burns
Francis J. Vernoia
John C. Petrella
James J. McGovern, III
Carmel Joy Decker

ASSOCIATES

Sandro Polledri
Celia S. Bosco
Lynn S. Degen
Elizabeth A. Daly
Brian O. Lipman
J. Frank Vespa-Papaleo
Susan B. Burns
Bruno Genova
Robert C. Gifford, Jr.
Courtney Gaccione

For full biographical listings, see the Martindale-Hubbell Law Directory

*MORRISTOWN,** Morris Co.

BAUMEISTER & SAMUELS, P.C. (AV Ⓣ)

1776 On The Green, P.O. Box 1116, 07962-1116
Telephone: 973-267-6666
Telecopier: 973-605-1812
Email: BAUMSAM@AOL.COM
New York, N.Y. Office: One Exchange Plaza, 10006-3008.
Telephone: 212-363-1200.
Telecopier: 212-363-1346.

Michel F. Baumeister
Douglas A. Latto (Not admitted in NJ)
Dorothea M. Capone

(See Next Column)

OF COUNSEL

Lynn F. Samuels
Robert S. Franklin (Not admitted in NJ)
Marc Z. Edell

For full biographical listings, see the Martindale-Hubbell Law Directory

McELROY, DEUTSCH AND MULVANEY (AV)

1300 Mount Kemble Avenue, P.O. Box 2075, 07962-2075
Telephone: 973-993-8100
Fax: 973-425-0161
URL: http://www.MDMlaw.com
Denver, Colorado Office: 1099 18th Street, Suite 3120.
Telephone: 303-293-8800.
Fax: 303-293-3116.
New York, New York Office: Wall Street Plaza, 88 Pine Street.
Telephone: 212-766-1807.
Fax: 212-483-9129.
Ridgewood, New Jersey Office: 40 West Ridgewood Avenue.
Telephone: 201-445-6722.
Fax: 201-445-8075.

MEMBERS OF FIRM

Lorraine M. Armenti (Resident Partner, Denver Colorado Office)
Grace C. Bertone
John P. Beyel
William C. Carey
Stephen H. Cohen (1938-1992)
Kevin T. Coughlin
John F. Darcy (Resident, Ridgewood Office)
Edward B. Deutsch
Timothy I. Duffy
Kevin P. Galvin
Robert J. Kelly
Joseph P. La Sala
James P. Lisovicz
Paul A. Lisovicz
Fred A. Manley, Jr.
Michael J. Marone
Nancy McDonald
William T. McElroy
Laurence M. McHeffey (Resident Partner, Denver, Colorado Office)
Robert W. Muilenburg
James M. Mulvaney
Alfred S. Nugent, Jr. (1925-1989)
Octavius A. Orbe (Resident, Ridgewood Office)
Loren L. Pierce
Warren K. Racusin
Mark A. Rosen
Thomas P. Scrivo
John H. Suminski
Walter F. Timpone
Kevin E. Wolff

COUNSEL TO THE FIRM

Robert L. Clifford

OF COUNSEL

John K. Bradley
John F. Whitteaker

ASSOCIATES

Susan Freeman Anthony
H. George Avery
Elizabeth Addison Barrow
Joseph F. Bermudez
Thomas Richard Calcagni
Patrick J. Casey (Resident Associate, Denver, Colorado Office)
Lisbeth W. Cload (Resident, Ridgewood Office)
Daniel J. Cohen
Craig J. Compoli, Jr.
John P. Cookson (Resident Associate, New York, NY Office)
John Thomas Coyne
Andrew J. D'Arcy
Andrew M. Csaszar
Michael B. Devins
John W. DiNicola, II
Robin A. Donato
Rebecca Ward Donohue
Steven F. Dorry
Julienne S. Duncan
Brian F. Fowler (Resident, Ridgewood Office)
Aaron C. Foy (Not admitted in NJ; Resident, Denver, Colorado Office)
Christopher S. Frangeš
Lorna A. Friel
Kevin P. Harkins (Resident, Ridgewood Office)
Sarah C. Herzog
Eric J. Hughes
George A. Kelman
Justin N. Kinney
Linda F. Kitz
John P. Leonard
Joseph J. McGlone
Robert McGuire
Kaneez Fatema Madraswalla
Nadine Maleski
Faith Martin
Suzanne Cocco Midlige
Heidi S. Minuskin
Louis A. Modugno
Florina A. Moldovan
John W. Morris
Francis C. Porada (Resident Associate, Denver, Colorado Office)
Robert J. Re
Vincent E. Reilly
Jay R. Ruble
Craig T. Sashihara
Adam R. Schwartz
Peter W. Smith
Timothy P. Smith
Ronnie H. Spring
Michael J. Sullivan
Catharine Acker Vaughan
Meredith A. Walling
Richard J. Williams, Jr.

Representative Clients: ADT Security Systems, Inc.; Admiral Insurance Company; Crum & Forster Insurance Co.; Eaton Corp.; Fireman's Fund Insurance Cos.; New Jersey Manufacturers Insurance Co.; The Home Indemnity Co.; The Pittston Company; Security Pacific Finance Corporation; American Honda Motor Co., Inc.

For full biographical listings, see the Martindale-Hubbell Law Directory

Morristown—Continued

PITNEY, HARDIN, KIPP & SZUCH LLP (AV)

P.O. Box 1945, 07962-1945
Telephone: 973-966-6300
New York City: 212-687-6000
Telex: 642014
Telecopier: 973-966-1550
URL: http://www.phks.com
New York, New York Office: 711 Third Avenue, 10017-4014.
Telephone: 212-687-6000.
Fax: 212-682-3485.

MEMBERS OF FIRM

William H. Hyatt, Jr.
Robert G. Rose
Peter J. Herzberg
Gail H. Allyn
Donald W. Kiel
Colleen R. Donovan
David W. Payne
Brian S. Montag

COUNSEL

Kathy Dutton Helmer

ASSOCIATES

Bruce D. Taterka
William S. Hatfield
Emily L. Won
Gail Howie Conenello
Laurie Droughton Matthews
Catherine A. Trinkle
Alison T. Saling

Representative Clients: American Home Products Corporation; E.I. DuPont de Nemours & Co.; Rohm and Haas Company; W.R. Grace & Co.

For Complete List of Firm Personnel, See General Section

For full biographical listings, see the Martindale-Hubbell Law Directory

PORZIO, BROMBERG & NEWMAN, A PROFESSIONAL CORPORATION (AV)

163 Madison Avenue, 07962-1997
Telephone: 973-538-4006
Facsimile: 973-538-5146
URL: http://www.pbnlaw.com
New York, New York Office: 156 West 56th Street, 10019.
Telephone: 212-265-6888.
Fax: 212-957-3983.
Brick, New Jersey Office: 263 Drum Point Road, 08723.
Telephone: 732-262-9248.
Fax: 732-262-9673.

Lisa Murtha Bromberg
Edward A. Hogan
John M. Newman
Thomas Spiesman

Jeffry H. Koenig

Representative Clients: Allied Signal, Inc.; Black and Decker Corporation; CITGO Petroleum Corporation; Legget and Platt, Inc.; Masco Corporation; Octagon Process Inc.; Trace International Holdings, Inc.

For Complete List of Firm Personnel, See General Section

For full biographical listings, see the Martindale-Hubbell Law Directory

*NEWARK,** Essex Co.

CARPENTER, BENNETT & MORRISSEY (AV)

Three Gateway Center, 17th Floor, 100 Mulberry Street, 07102-4079
Telephone: 973-622-7711
New York City: 212-943-6530
Telex: 139405
Telecopier: 973-622-5314
Email: cbm@carpben.com

MEMBERS OF FIRM

John F. Lynch, Jr.
Francis X. O'Brien
John D. Goldsmith
Louis M. DeStefano
Lois H. Goodman

OF COUNSEL

Edward F. Day, Jr.

ASSOCIATES

Jennifer L. Kapell
Steven J. Santarsiero
Kerry A. O'Shea

Representative Clients: General Motors Corp.; Texaco Inc.; Allied Signal; E.I. du Pont de Nemours and Co.; Curtiss-Wright Corp.; American Home Products Corp.; BASF Corp.; Lucent Technologies Inc.; Dow Chemical Co.; Witco Corp..

For Complete List of Firm Personnel, See General Section

For full biographical listings, see the Martindale-Hubbell Law Directory

HELLRING LINDEMAN GOLDSTEIN & SIEGAL LLP (AV)

One Gateway Center, 07102-5386
Telephone: 973-621-9020
Fax: 973-621-7406
Englewood, New Jersey Office: 32-40 North Dean Street.
Telephone: 201-871-3060.

(See Next Column)

Jonathan L. Goldstein
Richard D. Shapiro
Charles Oransky
Robert S. Raymar
John A. Adler
Ronnie F. Liebowitz

For Complete List of Firm Personnel, See General Section

For full biographical listings, see the Martindale-Hubbell Law Directory

LITE, DE PALMA, GREENBERG & RIVAS, LLC (AV)

Two Gateway Center, 12th Floor, 07102-5003
Telephone: 973-623-3000
Fax: 973-623-0858

MEMBERS OF FIRM

Allyn Z. Lite
Joseph J. De Palma
Bruce D. Greenberg
Alberto Rivas

ASSOCIATES

Michele Soto
Mary Jean Pizza
Stephanie Kay Austin

For full biographical listings, see the Martindale-Hubbell Law Directory

McMANIMON & SCOTLAND, L.L.C. (AV)

One Riverfront Plaza, 4th Floor, 07102-5311
Telephone: 973-622-1800
Fax: 973-622-7333; 973-622-3744

MEMBERS OF FIRM

Joseph P. Baumann, Jr.
John V. Cavaliere
John B. Hall
Glenn F. Scotland
Ronald J. Ianoale
Andrea L. Kahn
Jeffrey G. Kramer
Leslie G. London
Edward J. McManimon, III

OF COUNSEL

Norman M. Robertson
Carla J. Brundage

ASSOCIATES

Peter S. Crisafi
Sheila Newsome Maddox
M. Frances Ciesla
Kristin Dwyer Ganley
Joseph C. Jasaitis
Stephen N. Severud
Thomas J. Hastie, Jr.

LEGAL SUPPORT PERSONNEL

Helen Lysaght

PARALEGALS

Sandra Simoes

For full biographical listings, see the Martindale-Hubbell Law Directory

ST. JOHN & WAYNE, L.L.C. (AV)

Two Penn Plaza East, 07105-2249
Telephone: 973-491-3600
Fax: 973-491-3555
Email: firm@nwk.stjohn-law.com *URL:* http://www.stjohn-law.com
Rochester, New York Office: St. John & Curtin, L.L.C., First Federal Plaza.
Telephone: 716-262-6780.
Fax: 716-262-6755.
New York, New York Office: Heron Tower, 70 East 55th. Street.
Telephone: 212-446-5000.
Fax: 212-446-5055.

Joseph F. Lagrotteria
Karol Corbin Walker
Vincent S. Ziccolella

Gregory S. Thomas
Gregory G. Tole

For Complete List of Firm Personnel, See General Section

For full biographical listings, see the Martindale-Hubbell Law Directory

SILLS CUMMIS RADIN TISCHMAN EPSTEIN & GROSS, A PROFESSIONAL CORPORATION (AV)

One Riverfront Plaza, 07102-5400
Telephone: 973-643-7000
Fax: 973-643-6500
Telex: 820630 Sillsbeck Nwk
Email: sillsmail@sillscummis.com *URL:* http://www.sillscummis.com
Atlantic City, New Jersey Office: 17 Gordon's Alley.
Telephone: 609-344-2800.
New York, N.Y. Office: 712 Fifth Avenue.
Telephone: 212-643-7000.
Washington, D.C. Office: 1800 K Street, N.W.
Telephone: 202-296-4750.

MEMBERS OF FIRM

Barry M. Epstein
Philip R. Sellinger
Lori G. Singer
Jeffrey M. Pollock

James E. Brandt (Not admitted in NJ)
Ross N. Herman
Helen E. Kleiner
David Jay
Elbert F. Nasis
Kristen Skog Buerstetta
Steven M. Mager

(See Next Column)

SILLS CUMMIS RADIN TISCHMAN EPSTEIN & GROSS A PROFESSIONAL CORPORATION, *Newark—Continued*

Representative Clients: Sterling Winthrop Inc.; O'Brien Environmental Energy, Inc.; Schering AG Berlex Laboratories; Solid Waste Transfer & Recycling; Sorin Biomedical, Inc.; Bristol-Myers Squibb Corp.; First Fidelity Bank; Continental Bank, N.A.; Nabisco Brands, Inc.; Kodak, Inc.

For Complete List of Firm Personnel, See General Section

For full biographical listings, see the Martindale-Hubbell Law Directory

*NEW BRUNSWICK,** Middlesex Co.

HOAGLAND, LONGO, MORAN, DUNST & DOUKAS (AV)

40 Paterson Street, P.O. Box 480, 08903
Telephone: 732-545-4717
Fax: 732-545-4579
Email: info@hlmdd.com

MEMBERS OF FIRM

Bartholomew A. Longo
James B. Moran
Alan I. Dunst
Kenneth J. Doukas, Jr.
Michael John Stone
Donald D. Davidson
Thaddeus J. Hubert, III
Joan Alster Weisblatt
Karen M. Buerle
Robert G. Kenny
Michael J. Baker
Andrew J. Carlowicz, Jr.
Gary J. Hoagland
Jeffrey S. Intravatola
Jamie D. Happas
Thomas J. Walsh, Jr.
Robert S. Helwig
Michael F. Dolan
Douglas M. Fasciale
Marc S. Gaffrey
John Charles Simons
Susan K. O'Connor
Stephen G. Perrella
Jacquelyn L. Poland
Douglas Susan
Patrick J. McDonald

OF COUNSEL

John J. Hoagland
Herman L. Breitkopf
Richard S. Cohen

ASSOCIATES

Andrew N. Kessler
John P. Barnes
Christopher M. Longo
Nancy A. Freedman
Tiffany C. Chong
Michael Dermody
Diane Hoagland
Michael T. Kearns
Keith C. Northridge
Andrew J. DiMarsico
Edward J. Rebenack
Paul N. Harris
Denis A. Gooding
Kevin J. Musiakiewicz
Michael N. Porter
Kenneth Sisco
M. Stephanie Beaty

Representative Clients: CNA/Continental Casualty; National Indemnity Company; Providence Washington Insurance Company; The Mutual Fire, Marine & Inland Insurance Company; INAPRO/CIGNA; Allstate Insurance Company; Home Depot; American Reliance Insurance Company; Shand, Morahan & Company; CPC International.

For full biographical listings, see the Martindale-Hubbell Law Directory

NORTHFIELD, Atlantic Co.

TOMAR, SIMONOFF, ADOURIAN, O'BRIEN, KAPLAN, JACOBY & GRAZIANO, A PROFESSIONAL CORPORATION (AV)

The Executive Plaza, Suite 101, 2111 New Road, 08225
Telephone: 609-485-0800
Telecopier: 609-484-9388
Cherry Hill, New Jersey Office: 20 Brace Road.
Telephone: 609-429-1100.
Telecopier: 609-429-8164.
Atlantic City, New Jersey Office: Commerce Building, Suite 220, 1200 Atlantic Avenue.
Telephone: 609-348-5900.
Camden, New Jersey Office: 200 North Fifth Street.
Telephone: 609-338-0553.
Wilmington, Delaware Office: Tomar, Simonoff, Adourian, O'Brien, Kaplan, Jacoby & Graziano, The Mellon Bank Center, Suite 1701, 919 Market Street.
Telephone: 302-655-0500.
Telecopier: 302-428-0963.
Media, Pennsylvania Office: 334 West Front Street.
Telephone: 215-574-0635.

William Tomar
David Jacoby
Alan H. Sklarsky
Joshua M. Spielberg

For full biographical listings, see the Martindale-Hubbell Law Directory

PARSIPPANY, Morris Co.

CUYLER BURK (AV)

Parsippany Corporate Center, Four Century Drive, 07054-4663
Telephone: 973-734-3200
Telex: 429071
Telecopier: 973-734-3201
Email: Main@Cuyler.com *URL:* http://www.cuyler.com
New York, New York Office: 350 Fifth Avenue, Suite 3304. 10018.
Telephone: 212-645-4039.

(See Next Column)

MEMBERS OF FIRM

Stephen D. Cuyler
Jo Ann Burk
Stefano Calogero
David L. Menzel
Peter Petrou
Richard A. Crooker
Michael J. Jones

COUNSEL

Anne M. Mohan
Frank J. Miele

ASSOCIATES

Jan C. Walker
Kathleen Jane Olear
Claudia L. Marchese
Mark G. Eliades
Kimberly A. Joel
Christy A. Ramunno
Catherine E. Youngman
Andrew K. Craig
Mark S. Winter
Thomas J. Castano
Hugo A. Hilgendorff, IV

LEGAL SUPPORT PERSONNEL

Frederick M. H. Currie, Jr.

For full biographical listings, see the Martindale-Hubbell Law Directory

PLAINSBORO, Middlesex Co.

GOLDSHORE & WOLF, P.C. (AV)

501 Plainsboro Road, 08536
Telephone: 609-514-1400
Telecopier: 609-514-0033
URL: http://www.members.aol.com/njenvlaw/index.html
URL: http://www.lawyers.com/goldshore&wolf

Lewis P. Goldshore
Robert J. Cash
Stuart J. Lieberman

OF COUNSEL

Marsha Wolf

For full biographical listings, see the Martindale-Hubbell Law Directory

ROSELAND, Essex Co.

BRACH, EICHLER, ROSENBERG, SILVER, BERNSTEIN, HAMMER & GLADSTONE, A PROFESSIONAL CORPORATION (AV)

101 Eisenhower Parkway, 07068
Telephone: 973-228-5700
Telecopier: 973-228-7852
Email: law@bracheichler.com *URL:* http://www.bracheichler.com

Richard J. Driver
William J. Friedman

John P. Wyciskala, III
Christopher A. Erd

Representive Clients: The Asbury Graphite Mills, Inc.; Gist-brocades, Inc.; I. Heller Construction Co. Inc.; Kushner Companies; Saint Barnabas Health Care System; Valley National Bank.

For Complete List of Firm Personnel, See General Section

For full biographical listings, see the Martindale-Hubbell Law Directory

WALDER, SONDAK & BROGAN, A PROFESSIONAL CORPORATION (AV)

5 Becker Farm Road, P.O. Box 901, 07068
Telephone: 973-992-5300
Telecopier: 973-992-1505; 992-1006
Email: general@wsbesqs.com *URL:* http://www.wsbesqs.com

Justin P. Walder
Barry A. Kozyra
James A. Plaisted
Jeffrey A. Walder

Representative Client: Ronson Corporation.

For Complete List of Firm Personnel, See General Section

For full biographical listings, see the Martindale-Hubbell Law Directory

SADDLE BROOK, Bergen Co.

KRUGMAN & KAILES LLP (AV)

Park 80 West-Plaza Two, 07663-5835
Telephone: 201-845-3434; 212-695-3262
Telecopier: 201-845-9627
Email: counsel@krugmankailes.com
New York, New York Office: 99 Park Avenue, Suite 2200.
Telephone: 212-599-1060.
Telecopier: 212-599-6282.
London, England Office: 90 Fetter Lane, London EC4A-1PT.
Telephone: 011 (44) 171-421-7918.
Telecopier: 011 (44) 171-831-6407.

MEMBERS OF FIRM

Martin Krugman (1916-1994)
Howard Kailes
Thomas J. Goodwin
Ward C. Laracy
Robert I. Wexler
Alan H. Fox
Joy M. Mercer
Kerry B. Flowers

OF COUNSEL

James D. Krugman

(See Next Column)

KRUGMAN & KAILES LLP—*Continued*

COUNSEL

Judith S. Musicant

ASSOCIATES

Anne M. Wallace (Not admitted in NJ)
April A. Savoye
Lisa Ann Miller
Patrizia E. DeBari
David J. Hanley, Jr.
Anjana D. Patel
W. Mark O'Brien

For full biographical listings, see the Martindale-Hubbell Law Directory

SHORT HILLS, Essex Co.

EDWIN R. MATTHEWS, P.C. (AV)

150 John F. Kennedy Parkway CN 5008, 07078-2707
Telephone: 973-912-9500
Telecopier: 973-912-9411
Email: mwgf@mail.att.net

Edwin R. Matthews

Robert J. Pansulla
Daniel J. Bonner
Drew D. Krause
Lisa A. Grattan

For full biographical listings, see the Martindale-Hubbell Law Directory

SPRINGFIELD, Union Co.

HARDIN, KUNDLA, MCKEON, POLETTO & POLIFRONI, P.A., A PROFESSIONAL CORPORATION (AV)

673 Morris Avenue, P.O. Box 730, 07081
Telephone: 973-912-5222
Fax: 973-912-9212
Email: info@HKMPP.com
New York, New York Office: 55 John Street, 10038.
Telephone: 212-571-0111.
Fax: 212-571-1117.

George R. Hardin
Robert L. Polifroni
Janet L. Poletto
Mark S. Kundla
John F. McKeon
James R. Greene
Nicea J. D'Annunzio
John Samuel Favate
Patrick J. Clare
Anna Marie Strand

Jeffrey A. Oshin
Joseph R. Lowicky
Tracy C. Forsyth
Joseph A. DeFuria
John G. Kilbride
Jeffrey H. Goldsmith
Jeffrey Roth
Nora J. Grimbergen
William C. Sullivan, Jr.
Paul Daly
V. Christopher Hirsch
Richard S. Reig
Sam A. Dotro
Brian K. Kaiser
David M. Steiner
Lani M. D'Agostino
Sheila A. Glackin
Michael S. Schwartz
Kirsten L. McCaw
Sanjoy Mukherjee
Louisa B. Sargent
Michael A. Cifelli
James J. A. Mulhall
Kevin M. Regan
Lisa D. Chanel
Maria-Milagros Herrero
Brian A. King
Christina Fichera Dente
Andrea L. Strack
Roger J. Imhof
John P. Monaghan
Stephen J. Donahue
Cindy L. Thompson
Lisa A. Ganzhorn

Representative Clients: Envision Claims Mgmt.; U.S.F.&G.; Royal Insurance Co.; Prudential Property & Casualty; CNA Insurance; Xerxes Corp.

For full biographical listings, see the Martindale-Hubbell Law Directory

*TOMS RIVER,** Ocean Co.

LOMELL, MUCCIFORI, ADLER, RAVASCHIERE, AMABILE & PEHLIVANIAN, A PROFESSIONAL CORPORATION (AV)

250 Washington Street, P.O. Box 787, 08754
Telephone: 732-349-2443
Fax: 732-349-6917
Email: thefirm@lomell.com *URL:* http://www.lomell.com

Herman A. Adler
Dominic Ravaschiere
John S. Pehlivanian
Ronald E. Prusek
Jeffrey R. Surenian
James M. McKenna
Teresa K. Gierla
Arthur F. Leyden, III

Marc S. Galella
Robyn A. Belluardo
Janet Zaorski Kalapos
James S. Braaten
Regina M. Butler
Paul J Capotorto

Representative Clients: Ingersoll-Rand Company; Cigna Insurance Company; Fireman's Fund Insurance Company; Seico; Commercial Union Insurance Company; Allstate Insurance Company; Liberty Mutual Insurance Company; Home Insurance Company; Cooper Industries; Georgia Pacific Corp.

For Complete List of Firm Personnel, See General Section

For full biographical listings, see the Martindale-Hubbell Law Directory

VINELAND, Cumberland Co.

RIESENBURGER & KIZNER, P.C. (AV)

190 South Main Road, P.O. Box 640, 08362-0640
Telephone: 856-691-6200
Telecopier: 856-696-8150
Email: rieskizn@eticomm.net *URL:* http://www.rklawyers.com
Cherry Hill Office: 413 Route 70 East.
Telephone: 609-354-7500.

Franklin J. Riesenburger
Mitchell H. Kizner

Vivian R. Salmon
Robert P. Merenich

For full biographical listings, see the Martindale-Hubbell Law Directory

WAYNE, Passaic Co.

DEYOE HEISSENBUTTEL, L.L.C. (AV)

401 Hamburg Turnpike, P.O. Box 2449, 07474-2449
Telephone: 973-595-6300
Fax: 973-595-0146
Email: deyoelaw@ix.netcom.com *URL:* http://www.deyoe.com

MEMBERS OF FIRM

Charles P. DeYoe (1923-1973)
Wood M. DeYoe
Frederick C. Heissenbuttel
Scott B. Piekarsky

ASSOCIATES

Raymond F. Shenekji
Anne Hutton
Albert C. Buglione
Laureen A. Moloney

LEGAL SUPPORT PERSONNEL

Marilyn Moore (Office Manager)

Representative Clients: Hanover Insurance Inc.; Maryland Casualty Co.; Ohio Casualty Insurance Co.; Motor Club of America; Selective Insurance Co.; Prudential Property & Casualty; Reliance Ins. Co.

For full biographical listings, see the Martindale-Hubbell Law Directory

WEST ORANGE, Essex Co.

SACHS, MAITLIN, FLEMING, GREENE, WILSON & MAROTTE (AV)

80 Main Street, 3rd Floor, 07052
Telephone: 973-731-3400
Fax: 973-731-2896

Harold D. Feuerstein (1933-1967)
Marvin A. Sachs
Allan Maitlin
Raymond J. Fleming
Peter A. Greene
Bradley M. Wilson
Michael Marotte

ASSOCIATES

Steven L. Albertson
Philip B. Harrison
David Eric Maitlin
Theresa Mullen
Rosa Marques
Laura L. Milcsik

Reference: Fidelity Union Trust Co.

For full biographical listings, see the Martindale-Hubbell Law Directory

WOODBRIDGE, Middlesex Co.

WILENTZ, GOLDMAN & SPITZER, A PROFESSIONAL CORPORATION (AV)

90 Woodbridge Center Drive Suite 900, Box 10, 07095
Telephone: 732-636-8000
Telecopier: 732-855-6117
URL: http://www.newjerseylaw.com
Eatontown, New Jersey Office: Meridian Center I, Two Industrial Way West, 07724.
Telephone: 732-542-4500.
Telecopier: 732-493-8387.
New York, New York Office: Wall Street Plaza, 88 Pine Street, 9th Floor, 10005.
Telephone: 212-267-3091.
Telecopier: 212-267-3828.

Matthias D. Dileo
Stephen E. Barcan
Robert J. Cirafesi
Brian J. Molloy
Steven J. Tripp
Leslie Jeddis Lang
Francis X. Journick, Jr.

Richard A. Catalina, Jr.
Donna M. Jennings
John Michael August

Representative Clients: Amerada Hess Corporation; Chevron, U.S.A., Inc.; Wakefern Food Corp.

For Complete List of Firm Personnel, See General Section

For full biographical listings, see the Martindale-Hubbell Law Directory

NEW MEXICO

*ALBUQUERQUE,** Bernalillo Co.

EAVES, BARDACKE, BAUGH KIERST & KIERNAN, P.A. (AV)
6400 Uptown Boulevard, N.E., Suite 110-W, P.O. Box 35670, 87176
Telephone: 505-888-4300
Facsimile: 505-883-4406
Email: LGLEAVES@EB-B.com

John M. Eaves
John G. Baugh
Paul Bardacke
Peter S. Kierst
Kerry Kiernan

Derek V. Larson
Karen S. Mendenhall
C. Shannon Bacon

OF COUNSEL

Jennifer J. Pruett

For full biographical listings, see the Martindale-Hubbell Law Directory

*SANTA FE,** Santa Fe Co.

HUFFAKER & CONWAY, A PROFESSIONAL CORPORATION (AV)
155 Grant Avenue, P.O. Box 1868, 87504-1868
Telephone: 505-988-8921
Fax: 505-983-3927
Email: sfstaff@sisna.com
Albuquerque, New Mexico Office: 201 Third Street, N.W., Suite 1910.
Telephone: 505-244-0021.
Facsimile: 505-244-1372.

Gregory D. Huffaker, Jr.
Lisa A. Joynes
Ann Maloney Conway
Seth L. Sparks
Edward C. Bagley

Representative Clients: Chevron Products Co.; Southwest Water Disposal Inc.

For full biographical listings, see the Martindale-Hubbell Law Directory

MONTGOMERY & ANDREWS, PROFESSIONAL ASSOCIATION (AV)
325 Paseo de Peralta, P.O. Box 2307, 87504-2307
Telephone: 505-982-3873
Fax: 505-982-4289
Email: montand@montand.com

John B. Draper
Edmund H. Kendrick
Louis W. Rose

Representative Clients: Cobisa Corp.; Conoco, Inc.; Copar Pumice Company; El Paso Corp.; General Electric Co.; Giant Industries Arizona, Inc.; Huntsman Plymers Corporation; INTEL Corporation; LAC Minerals (USA) Inc.; Marathon Oil Company; Public Service Co. of NM.

For Complete List of Firm Personnel, See General Section

For full biographical listings, see the Martindale-Hubbell Law Directory

SCHEUER, YOST & PATTERSON, A PROFESSIONAL CORPORATION (AV)
125 Lincoln Avenue, Suite 223, P.O. Drawer 9570, 87504
Telephone: 505-982-9911
505-989-7500
Fax: 505-982-1621
Email: firm@santafelawyers.com

Melvin T. Yost (Retired)
Byron L. Treaster
Ralph H. Scheuer
Donald A. Walcott
Mel E. Yost
Christopher M. Grimmer
John N. Patterson
Daniel J. Monte

OF COUNSEL

Reverdy Johnson

Representative Clients: Cyprus-AMAX, Inc.; Century Bank, FSB; Chicago Title Insurance Co.; St. John's College; Espanola Mercantile Co., Inc.; Sun Loan Companies; Territorial Abstract & Title Co.

For full biographical listings, see the Martindale-Hubbell Law Directory

NEW YORK

*ALBANY,** Albany Co.

SHANLEY, SWEENEY, REILLY & ALLEN, P.C. (AV)
The Castle at Ten Thurlow Terrace, 12203
Telephone: 518-463-1415
Fax: 518-463-3210
Email: lawyers@shanleysweeney.com *URL:* http://www.shanleysweeney.com

(See Next Column)

Michael P. Shanley, Jr.
Steven S. Heyman
Robert L. Sweeney
Scott P. Olson
J. Stephen Reilly
David C. Kuracina
John L. Allen
Thomas A. Shepardson
Gregory D. Faucher
Melissa M. Beskid
J. Michael Naughton
Mark T. Sweeney

Christopher E. Buckey
Stacey Weisenfeld

For full biographical listings, see the Martindale-Hubbell Law Directory

*BINGHAMTON,** Broome Co.

O'CONNOR, GACIOCH, POPE & TAIT, L.L.P. (AV)
One Marine Midland Plaza, East Tower-Seventh Floor, P.O. Box 1964, 13902
Telephone: 607-772-9262
Fax: 607-724-6002
Email: ogplaw@compuserve.com

Thomas F. O'Connor
Robert N. Nielsen, Jr.
James C. Gacioch
Stephen B. Atkinson
Alan J. Pope
Kurt D. Schrader
Jeffrey A. Tait
Richard M. Hill
Hugh B. Leonard
Patricia A. Cummings
Robert C. Murphy

OF COUNSEL

Walter T. Gorman
Cheryl Insinga

For full biographical listings, see the Martindale-Hubbell Law Directory

*BUFFALO,** Erie Co.

FELDMAN, KIEFFER & HERMAN, LLP (AV)
110 Pearl Street, Suite 400, 14202
Telephone: 716-852-5875
Fax: 716-852-4253
Email: info@fkhattys.com *URL:* http://www.fkhattys.com

PRINCIPALS OF THE FIRM

Andrew Feldman
Mark F. Scarcello
James M. Kieffer
Gordon D. Tresch
Ann W. Herman
Mary Jo Herrscher

For full biographical listings, see the Martindale-Hubbell Law Directory

RAICHLE, BANNING, WEISS & STEPHENS (AV)
410 Main Street, 14202
Telephone: 716-852-7587
Telecopier: 716-852-7599
Email: RBWS@MSN.COM

MEMBER OF FIRM

R. William Stephens

ASSOCIATES

Lisa Parlato Neff
R. Hugh Stephens

Representative Client: General Motors Corp.

For Complete List of Firm Personnel, See General Section

For full biographical listings, see the Martindale-Hubbell Law Directory

STENGER & FINNERTY (AV)
1800 Main Place Tower, 14202
Telephone: 716-849-1700
Fax: 716-849-1717
Email: stenfinn@stenfinn.com *URL:* http://www.stenfinn.com

John H. Stenger
Joseph M. Finnerty

ASSOCIATES

Mitchell M. Stenger
David E. Gutowski

For full biographical listings, see the Martindale-Hubbell Law Directory

GARDEN CITY, Nassau Co.

MONTFORT, HEALY, MCGUIRE & SALLEY (AV)
1140 Franklin Avenue, 11530
Telephone: 516-747-4082
Telecopier: 516-746-0748

MEMBERS OF FIRM

E. Richard Rimmels, Jr. (1930-1999)
Fredric C. Montfort
Donald S. Neumann, Jr.
Frank J. Cafaro
James J. Keefe, Jr.
Philip J. Catapano
Michael A. Baranowicz
James Michael Murphy

OF COUNSEL

Fredric H. Montfort
David J. Fleming
Edward M. Salley, Jr.
Robert J. Mettalia

(See Next Column)

MONTFORT, HEALY, MCGUIRE & SALLEY—*Continued*

ASSOCIATES

Claudia C. Glacken
Marcie K. Glasser
Bruce A. Cook
Jeffrey D. Present
Joan E. Resnik
Susan H. Dempsey
Camille L. Hansen
Christopher T. Cafaro
Kathleen Dumont
Jeffrey B. Siler
Michael G. Kruzynski
Karen J. Cooper

For full biographical listings, see the Martindale-Hubbell Law Directory

*GOSHEN,** Orange Co.

NORTON & CHRISTENSEN (AV)

Goshen Executive Building, 60 Erie Street, P.O. Box 308, 10924
Telephone: 914-294-7949
Fax: 914-294-7791
Email: norchris@frontiernet.net
Rochelle Park, New Jersey Office: 151 West Passaic Street.
Telephone: 201-909-3735.
Fax: 201-368-2102.

MEMBERS OF FIRM

Stanley J. Norton (1916-1998)
Henry N. Christensen, Jr.
Harold M. Pressberg
Kenneth J. Frank

OF COUNSEL

John T. Mayo

For full biographical listings, see the Martindale-Hubbell Law Directory

HAUPPAUGE, Suffolk Co.

FREDERICK EISENBUD (AV)

700 Veterans Memorial Highway Third Floor, 11788-2131
Telephone: 516-265-4411
Fax: 516-724-1096
Email: feisenbud@trial.com *URL:* http://www.lawyers.com/eisenbudlaw

For full biographical listings, see the Martindale-Hubbell Law Directory

ERIC H. HOLTZMAN (AV)

330 Vanderbilt Motor Parkway, P.O. Box 11005, 11788-0903
Telephone: 631-435-8800
Fax: 631-435-8832

Richard E. Trachtenberg
David H. Eisenberg

Reference: European-American Bank & Trust Co.

For full biographical listings, see the Martindale-Hubbell Law Directory

MELVILLE, Suffolk Co.

CAHN WISHOD & KNAUER, LLP (AV)

425 Broadhollow Road Suite 315, 11747
Telephone: 631-752-1600
Fax: 631-752-1555
URL: http://www.cahnwishod.com
URL: http://www.lawyers.com/cahnwishod&knauer

MEMBERS OF FIRM

Richard C. Cahn
Eugene L. Wishod
Todd A. Knauer

ASSOCIATES

Brian T. Egan
Patricia A. Rooney

LEGAL SUPPORT PERSONNEL

Susan M. Stonelli (Paralegal)

For full biographical listings, see the Martindale-Hubbell Law Directory

LAMB & BARNOSKY, LLP (AV)

534 Broadhollow Road-CS 9034, 11747-9034
Telephone: 631-694-2300
Telecopier: 631-694-2309
Email: thefirm@lambbarnosky.com *URL:* http://www.lambbarnosky.com

PARTNERS

Eugene R. Barnosky
Robert H. Cohen
Marcia Lyn Finkelstein
Michael J. Heller
Gary Holman
Scott M. Karson
P. L. Lamb
Arthur A. Lane
Joel M. Markowitz
Gerald P. Rosenberg
Patrice Dowd Shenn

OF COUNSEL

Louis E. Black
James F. Gesualdi
Howard W. Newman
Joseph J. Salvatore
Joseph H. Wishod

COUNSEL

Lloyd K. Chanin
Scott P. McBride

(See Next Column)

ASSOCIATES

Cathleen D. Allen
Catherine Healy Kanzler
Rita Fishman Sheena
Shari Lee Sugarman

For full biographical listings, see the Martindale-Hubbell Law Directory

MOUNT KISCO, Westchester Co.

SHAMBERG MARWELL HOCHERMAN DAVIS & HOLLIS, P.C. (AV)

55 Smith Avenue, 10549
Telephone: 914-666-5600
Telecopier: 914-666-6267
Email: smhdh@ix.netcom.com

Stuart R. Shamberg
John S. Marwell
Henry M. Hocherman
Robert F. Davis
P. Daniel Hollis, III
Adam L. Wekstein
Geraldine N. Tortorella
Frederick J. Koelsch
Catherine B. Andreycak

Donald W. Macaulay
Anne A. Colucci

OF COUNSEL

Stanley E. Anderson, Jr.

For full biographical listings, see the Martindale-Hubbell Law Directory

*NEW YORK,** New York Co.

BAUMEISTER & SAMUELS, P.C. (AV)

One Exchange Plaza, 10006-3008
Telephone: 212-363-1200
Telecopier: 212-363-1346
Email: BAUMSAM@AOL.COM
Morristown, New Jersey Office: 1776 On The Green, P.O. Box 1116, 07962-1116.
Telephone: 973-267-6666.
Telecopier: 973-605-1812.

Michel F. Baumeister
Douglas A. Latto
Dorothea M. Capone

OF COUNSEL

Lynn F. Samuels
Robert S. Franklin
Marc Z. Edell

For full biographical listings, see the Martindale-Hubbell Law Directory

BEATIE AND OSBORN LLP (AV)

599 Lexington Avenue, 42nd Floor, 10022
Telephone: 212-888-9000
Fax: 212-888-9664
Email: bandolaw@aol.com *URL:* http://www.bandolaw@aol.com

Russel H. Beatie, Jr.
Daniel A. Osborn

ASSOCIATES

Curt D. Marshall
Eduard Korsinsky

OF COUNSEL

Richard M. Cummings

For full biographical listings, see the Martindale-Hubbell Law Directory

BERMAN, PALEY, GOLDSTEIN & KANNRY, LLP (AV)

500 Fifth Avenue, 10110
Telephone: 212-354-9600
Fax: 212-354-9873

Murray Tim Berman (1901-1991)

MEMBERS OF FIRM

Tony Berman
Alvin Goldstein
Jack S. Kannry
Robert G. Benisch
Howard Burger
Robert A. Banner

COUNSEL

David R. Paley

ASSOCIATES

Paul G. Monte
Darshan V. Patel
Saranjit S. Bindra

For full biographical listings, see the Martindale-Hubbell Law Directory

COBRIN & GITTES (AV)

750 Lexington Avenue, 10022
Telephone: 212-486-4000
Telecopier: 212-486-4007
Email: cgpats@ix.netcom.com

Peter T. Cobrin
Marvin S. Gittes
Richard M. Lehrer
David W. Denenberg

(See Next Column)

COBRIN & GITTES, *New York—Continued*

Robert J. Hess
Michael A. Adler
Gerald J. Cechony
(Not admitted in NY)
Oren J. Warshavsky
Clyde Alvin Shuman
Lawrence E. Russ

Representative Clients: Northern Telecom, Inc.; DataPoint Corporation; Magnivision, Inc.; Atico; Global Direct Mail Corporation; MW.; Oxigene, Inc.; Horphag Research, LTD.

For full biographical listings, see the Martindale-Hubbell Law Directory

NEUFELD & O'LEARY (AV)

Suite 527, 230 Park Avenue, 10169
Telephone: 212-986-0999
Telecopier: 212-986-6341
Long Island Office: Melville Law Center, 225 Old Country Road, Melville, New York, 11747.
Telephone: 516-549-1717.

MEMBERS OF FIRM

David S. J. Neufeld
Denis P. O'Leary

ASSOCIATES

Lisa Mendelson Hecht
Donald M. Spector
Peter J. Schancupp

OF COUNSEL

Edwin T. Broderick

For full biographical listings, see the Martindale-Hubbell Law Directory

OPPENHEIMER WOLFF & DONNELLY LLP (AV)

The Chrysler East Building 19th Floor, 666 Third Avenue, 10017
Telephone: 212-826-5000
FAX: 212-486-0708
URL: http://www.oppenheimer.com
Minneapolis, Minnesota Office: 3300 Plaza VII, 45 South Seventh Street. 55402.
Telephone: 612-607-7000.
FAX: 612-607-7100.
Amsterdam, The Netherlands Office: Keizergracht 241.
Telephone: 31-20-423-4555.
FAX: 312-20-423-4545.
Brussels, Belgium Office: Avenue Louise 240, Box 5, 1050.
Telephone: 32-2-626-0500.
FAX: 32-2-626-0510.
Geneva, Switzerland Office: Rue Gabriel Eynard, 6, 1205.
Telephone: (41/22) 311-7410.
FAX: (41/22) 311-4707.
Newport Beach, California Office: 500 Newport Center Drive, Suite 700, 92660.
Telephone: 949-823-6000.
FAX: 949-823-6100.
Paris, France Office: 35 Boulevard des Capucines, 75002.
Telephone: (33/1) 53 45 40 00.
FAX: (33/1) 53 45 40 10.
St. Paul, Minnesota Office: 1700 First National Bank Building, 55101.
Telephone: 651-605-2000.
FAX: 651-605-2100.
Washington, D.C. Office: Oppenheimer Wolff Donnelly & Bayh LLP, 1350 Eye Street, N.W., Suite 200, 20005.
Telephone: 202-312-8000.
FAX: 202-312-8100.
Los Angeles, California Office: 2029 Century Park East, 38th Floor, 90067.
Telephone: 310-788-5000.
FAX: 310-277-1297.
Palo Alto, California Office: 3373 Hillview Avenue, Suite 200, 94304.
Telephone: 650-320-4000.
FAX: 650-320-4100.
Chicago, Illinois Office: Oppenheimer Wolff & Donnelly (Illinois), Two Prudential Plaza, 45th Floor, 180 North Stetson Avenue, 60601.
Telephone: 312-616-1800.
Fax: 312-616-5800.

RESIDENT PARTNER

Thomas M. Gandolfo

For full biographical listings, see the Martindale-Hubbell Law Directory

POSTNER & RUBIN (AV)

17 Battery Place, 10004
Telephone: 212-269-2510
Fax: 212-425-0968
Email: postner@aol.com
Holmdel, New Jersey Office: 42 West Main Street,
Telephone: 732-946-9001.
Fax: 732-946-9005.

Robert A. Rubin
William J. Postner
Robert J. MacPherson
Jeffrey R. Cruz

ASSOCIATES

Patricia M. Caplicki
Dana Wordes
Michael W. Bautz

(See Next Column)

NEW JERSEY RESIDENT COUNSEL

Sarah B. Biser

For full biographical listings, see the Martindale-Hubbell Law Directory

WHITE, FLEISCHNER & FINO (AV)

140 Broadway, 10005
Telephone: 212-487-9700
Telecopier: 212-487-9777
Email: infor@wff-law.com
Red Bank, New Jersey Office: 272 Broad Street.
Telephone: 732-530-7787.
Telecopier: 732-530-8552.

MEMBER OF FIRM

James A. Robbins

For Complete List of Firm Personnel, See General Section

For full biographical listings, see the Martindale-Hubbell Law Directory

*ROCHESTER,** Monroe Co.

UNDERBERG & KESSLER LLP (AV)

1800 Chase Square, 14604
Telephone: 716-258-2800
Fax: 716-258-2821
Email: INFO@UNDERBERG-KESSLER.COM
Buffalo, New York Office: 1100 Main Place Tower. 14202.
Telephone: 716-848-9000.
Fax: 716-847-6004.

MEMBERS OF FIRM

Alan J. Underberg (1929-1998)
Irving L. Kessler
Michael J. Beyma
James A. Coniglio
Frank T. Crego
Robert W. Croessmann
John W. Crowe
Patrick L. Cusato
Michael C. Dwyer
Bernard A. Frank
Steven R. Gersz
Katherine Howk Karl
Lawrence P. Keller
Gordon J. Lipson
Anna E. Lynch
Robert F. Mechur
Paul V. Nunes
Terry M. Richman
J. David Sampson
(Resident, Buffalo Office)
Sharon P. Stiller
Stephen H. Waite
Russell I. Zuckerman

OF COUNSEL

Andrew M. Greenstein

SENIOR ATTORNEYS

Duncan R. Farney
Ronald G. Hull

ASSOCIATES

James F. Armstrong
(Resident, Buffalo Office)
Karen A. DiNardo
Lise C. Hamilton
Jeffrey D. Hummel
Paul F. Keneally
Ella L. Krzanowicz
Maureen E. Mulholland
Suzanne D. Nott
Kelly L. Odorisi
Thomas A. Rall

For full biographical listings, see the Martindale-Hubbell Law Directory

*SYRACUSE,** Onondaga Co.

DEVORSETZ STINZIANO GILBERTI HEINTZ & SMITH, P.C. (AV)

555 East Genesee Street, 13202-2159
Telephone: 315-442-0100
Telecopier: 315-442-0106
Email: law@dsghs.com *URL:* http://www.devorsetzlaw.com
Albany, New York Office: 146 State Street.
Telephone: 518-476-2001.
Telecopier: 518-476-9646.
Harrisburg, Pennsylvania Office: 105 North Front Street, Suite 400.
Telephone: 717-232-5555.
Telecopier: 717-232-5515.

Tarky Lombardi, Jr.
Sidney Devorsetz
Francis D. Stinziano
William J. Gilberti, Jr.
Lynn H. Smith
Joshua H. Heintz

Reference: Fleet Bank.

For full biographical listings, see the Martindale-Hubbell Law Directory

*UTICA,** Oneida Co.

PETRONE & PETRONE, P.C. (AV)

1624 Genesee Street, 13502
Telephone: 315-735-7566
Fax: 315-735-5368
Email: pnp@borg.com *URL:* http://www.lawyers.com/petrone
Rochester, New York Office: 929 Times Square Building, 45 Exchange Street.
Telephone: 800-521-1260.
FAX: 716-232-7788.
Syracuse, New York Office: 314 East Fayette Street, 13202.
Telephone: 800-521-1260.
Fax: 315-735-5368.

(See Next Column)

PETRONE & PETRONE P.C.—*Continued*

Buffalo, New York Office: 1606 Liberty Building.
Telephone: 800-521-1260.
FAX: 716-852-6216.

Marcus M. Curry (1924-1996)
Louis S. Petrone
John R. Petrone, II
Lori E. Petrone

Reynolds E. Hahn (Resident, Rochester Office)
Edward J. Taublieb (Resident, Buffalo Office)
Mark J. Halpin
James P. Godemann
Frank Leonard Madia

For full biographical listings, see the Martindale-Hubbell Law Directory

*WHITE PLAINS,** Westchester Co.

DELBELLO DONNELLAN WEINGARTEN & TARTAGLIA, LLP (AV)

One North Lexington Avenue, 10601
Telephone: 914-681-0200
Telecopier: 914-684-0288
Email: general@ddwt.com

Alfred B. DelBello
Alfred E. Donnellan (Managing Partner)
Mark P. Weingarten
Daniel D. Tartaglia
Peter J. Wise
Lee S. Wiederkehr
Patrick M. Reilly
Robert A. Korren

ASSOCIATES

William E. Dumke
Christine Moccia
Suzanne Bogdanoff
Allyse B. Dunefsky
Jerry F. Kebrdle, II
Bradley D. Wank
Ann Farrissey Carlson
Janet J. Giris

OF COUNSEL

J. David Jutkowitz
Andrew J. Balint
Robert C. Epstein

For full biographical listings, see the Martindale-Hubbell Law Directory

KEANE & BEANE, P.C. (AV)

One North Broadway, 10601
Telephone: 914-946-4777
Telecopier: 914-946-6868
Rye, New York Office: 15 Elm Place.
Telephone: 914-967-3936.

Thomas F. Keane, Jr. (1932-1991)
Edward F. Beane
Donna E. Frosco
David Glasser
Lance H. Klein
Ronald A. Longo
Richard L. O'Rourke
Lawrence Praga
Joel H. Sachs
Steven A. Schurkman
Judson K. Siebert

Stephanie L. Burns
Eric L. Gordon
Jonathan Kornblatt
Stephanie M. Orefice
Patrick J. O'Sullivan
Frances M. Pantaleo
Nicholas M. Ward-Willis

OF COUNSEL

Peter A. Borrok
John F. Burkhardt
Eric F. Jensen

LEGAL SUPPORT PERSONNEL

Lenny Amodeo (Legal Assistant)
Barbara S. Durkin (Office Manager)
Sylvia J. Zuckerman (Legal Assistant)

For full biographical listings, see the Martindale-Hubbell Law Directory

POSNER, POSNER & ASSOCIATES, PC (AV)

399 Knollwood Road, 10603
Telephone: 914-948-6620
Telecopier: 914-948-0864
Email: relawyer@aol.com *URL:* http://www.lawyers.com/posner_posner&assoc

Henry A. Greenburg
Martin Louis Posner
Jane Y. Posner

Peter J. McCarthy
Karen Olson

References: Chemical Bank; Citibank.

For full biographical listings, see the Martindale-Hubbell Law Directory

NORTH CAROLINA

*CHARLOTTE,** Mecklenburg Co.

CAUDLE & SPEARS, P.A. (AV)

2600 Interstate Tower, 121 West Trade Street, 28202
Telephone: 704-377-1200
Telecopier: 704-338-5858
Email: caudlespears@caudlespears.com

Lloyd C. Caudle
L. Cameron Caudle, Jr.
Jeffrey L. Helms
Christopher J. Loebsack

Counsel for: Bituminous Casualty Corp; Bauman Springs A.G.; The A.G. Boone Co.; Capitol Funds, Inc.; Consolidated Freightways; Employers Mutual Casualty Co.; Mark Oil Company, Inc.; Metromont Materials; Otis Elevator Co.; N.C. Farm Bureau Mutual Insurance Co.

For Complete List of Firm Personnel, See General Section

For full biographical listings, see the Martindale-Hubbell Law Directory

WOMBLE CARLYLE SANDRIDGE & RICE (AV)

A Professional Limited Liability Company
3300 One First Union Center, 301 South College Street, 28202-6025
Telephone: 704-331-4900
Fax: 704-331-4955
Email: lawyers@wcsr.com *URL:* http://www.wcsr.com
Winston-Salem, North Carolina Office: 200 West Second Street, P.O. Drawer 84.
Telephone: 336-721-3600.
Fax: 336-721-3660.
Raleigh, North Carolina Office: 2100 First Union Capitol Center, 150 Fayetteville Street Mall, P.O. Box 831.
Telephone: 919-755-2100.
Fax: 919-755-2150.
Research Triangle Park, North Carolina Office: 2505 Meridian Parkway, Suite 300 (Durham), 27713.
Telephone: 919-484-2300.
Fax: 919-484-2340.
Atlanta, Georgia Office: One Atlantic Center, 1201 West Peachtree Street, Suite 3500.
Telephone: 404-872-7000.
Fax: 404-888-7490.
Other Atlanta, Georgia Office: Suite 404, 2296 Henderson Mill Road, N.E.
Telephone: 770-492-9030.
Fax: 770-492-9609.
Washington, D.C. Office: 1120 Nineteenth Street, N.W., Eighth Floor.
Telephone: 202-857-4400.
Fax: 202-467-6910.
Greenville, South Carolina Office: 15 South Main Street, Suite 601, P.O. Box 10208.
Telephone: 864-255-5400.
Fax: 864-255-5440.

RESIDENT MEMBER

Bradford A. DeVore

RESIDENT ASSOCIATE

Brian E. Heim

Representative Clients: Childress Klein Properties, Inc.; Food Lion, Inc.; J.A. Jones Construction Co.; Parkdale Mills, Inc.; Pillowtex; Duke Power Co.; Bowles Hollowell Conner & Co.; ALLTEL Carolina, Inc.; Belk Store Services, Inc.; Philip Holzmann A.G.

For Complete List of Firm Personnel, See General Section

For full biographical listings, see the Martindale-Hubbell Law Directory

*RALEIGH,** Wake Co.

MARVIN SCHILLER (AV)

Two Hannover Square, Suite 1250, 434 Fayetteville Street Mall, 27601
Telephone: 919-836-8800
Fax: 919-836-8838
URL: http://www.lawyers.com/marvinschiller

For full biographical listings, see the Martindale-Hubbell Law Directory

WOMBLE CARLYLE SANDRIDGE & RICE (AV)

A Professional Limited Liability Company
2100 First Union Capitol Center, 150 Fayetteville Street Mall, P.O. Box 831, 27602
Telephone: 919-755-2100
Fax: 919-755-2150
Email: lawyers@wcsr.com *URL:* http://www.wcsr.com
Charlotte, North Carolina Office: 3300 One First Union Center, 301 South College Street.
Telephone: 704-331-4900.
Fax: 704-331-4955.

(See Next Column)

WOMBLE CARLYLE SANDRIDGE & RICE, *Raleigh—Continued*

Winston-Salem, North Carolina Office: 200 West Second Street, P.O. Drawer 84.
Telephone: 336-721-3600.
Fax: 336-721-3660.
Research Triangle Park, North Carolina Office: 2505 Meridian Parkway, Suite 300 (Durham), 27713.
Telephone: 919-484-2300.
Fax: 919-484-2340.
Atlanta, Georgia Office: One Atlantic Center, 1201 West Peachtree Street, Suite 3500.
Telephone: 404-872-7000.
Fax: 404-888-7490.
Other Atlanta, Georgia Office: Suite 404, 2296 Henderson Mill Road, N.E.
Telephone: 770-492-9030.
Fax: 770-492-9609.
Washington, D.C. Office: 1120 Nineteenth Street, N.W., Eighth Floor.
Telephone: 202-857-4400.
Fax: 202-467-6910.
Greenville, South Carolina Office: 15 South Main Street, Suite 601, P.O. Box 10208.
Telephone: 864-255-5400.
Fax: 864-255-5440.

RESIDENT MEMBER

Marilyn R. Forbes

RESIDENT OF COUNSEL

Kurt D. Weaver (Not admitted in NC)

Representative Clients: Aetna Casualty and Surety Co., Inc.; ALSCO/AmeriMark Building Products, Inc.; Aoki Corporation America, Inc.; Hackney Brothers, Inc.; Lawyers Mutual Liability Insurance Company of North Carolina; Meredith College; Regency Park Corp.; Wachovia Bank, N.A.

For Complete List of Firm Personnel, See General Section

For full biographical listings, see the Martindale-Hubbell Law Directory

*WINSTON-SALEM,** Forsyth Co.

BENNETT & GUTHRIE, P.L.L.C. (AV)

3334 Healy Drive, Suite 203, 27103-1476
Telephone: 336-765-3121
Fax: 336-765-8622

Richard V. Bennett
Rodney A. Guthrie
Stanley P. Dean

Kevin J. Williams

Representative Clients: American Continental Insurance Company; Commercial Union Insurance Company; Integon Insurance; Kentucky Medical Insurance Company; Medtronic, Inc.; Montgomery Mutual Insurance Company; Novant Health, Inc.; Pennsylvania Lumberman's Mutual Insurance Company; St. Paul Fire & Marine Insurance Company; Zurich Insurance Company.

For full biographical listings, see the Martindale-Hubbell Law Directory

WOMBLE CARLYLE SANDRIDGE & RICE (AV)

A Professional Limited Liability Company
200 West Second Street, P.O. Drawer 84, 27102
Telephone: 336-721-3600
Fax: 336-721-3660
Email: lawyers@wcsr.com *URL:* http://www.wcsr.com
Charlotte, North Carolina Office: 3300 One First Union Center, 301 South College Street.
Telephone: 704-331-4900.
Fax: 704-331-4955.
Raleigh, North Carolina Office: 2100 First Union Capitol Center, 150 Fayetteville Street Mall, P.O. Box 831.
Telephone: 919-755-2100.
Fax: 919-755-2150.
Research Triangle Park, North Carolina Office: 2505 Meridian Parkway, Suite 300 (Durham), 27713.
Telephone: 919-484-2300.
Fax: 919-484-2340.
Atlanta, Georgia Office: One Atlantic Center, 1201 West Peachtree Street, Suite 3500.
Telephone: 404-872-7000.
Fax: 404-888-7490.
Other Atlanta, Georgia Office: Suite 404, 2296 Henderson Mill Road, N.E.
Telephone: 770-492-9030.
Fax: 770-492-9609.
Washington, D.C. Office: 1120 Nineteenth Street, N.W., Eighth Floor.
Telephone: 202-857-4400.
Fax: 202-467-6910.
Greenville, South Carolina Office: 15 South Main Street, Suite 601, P.O. Box 10208.
Telephone: 864-255-5400.
Fax: 864-255-5440.

(See Next Column)

RESIDENT MEMBERS

Jeffrey L. Furr
Ellen M. Gregg
R. Howard Grubbs
Lori Privette Hinnant
Martin L. Holton, III
Keith W. Vaughan
G. Criston Windham

RESIDENT ASSOCIATES

Amy L. Bircher
Brandy K. Gillenwater
Murray C. Greason (Not admitted in NC)
Stanley B. Green
Ursula M. Henninger
Neil D. Kodsi
Christopher A. Kreiner
William E. Latham II
G. Wriston Marshburn, Jr
Stephanie U. Roberts
Patricia G. Scales
Lawrence B. Somers
Theresa M. Sprain
John R. Still
Allison L. Thompson (Not admitted in NC)

MEMBER OF COUNSEL

W. David Edwards

STAFF ATTORNEY

Daniel Patrick Foley (Not admitted in NC)

Representative Clients: Brad Ragan, Inc.; Brenner Companies; Food Lion, Inc.; Hanes Companies, Inc.; North Carolina Baptist Hospitals, Inc.; R.J. Reynolds Tobacco Co.; Thomasville Furniture Industries, Inc.; Wachovia Corp.; Wake Forest University.

For Complete List of Firm Personnel, See General Section

For full biographical listings, see the Martindale-Hubbell Law Directory

NORTH DAKOTA

*MANDAN,** Morton Co.

KELSCH KELSCH RUFF & KRANDA (AV)

103 Collins Avenue, P.O. Box 1266, 58554-7266
Telephone: 701-663-9818
Fax: 701-663-9810
Email: kelsch@corpcomm.net

MEMBERS OF FIRM

C. F. Kelsch (1890-1987)
William C. Kelsch
Thomas F. Kelsch
Arlen M. Ruff
Thomas D. Kelsch
Todd D. Kranda

ASSOCIATES

Timothy J. Wahlin
Rob Forward
William J. Delmore

Representative Clients: Seven Seas Motor Inn; L & H Manufacturing Co.; Cloverdale Foods Co.; Microage Computer Store; Logan Hill Realty, Bismarck.

For full biographical listings, see the Martindale-Hubbell Law Directory

OHIO

*CINCINNATI,** Hamilton Co.

D. DAVID ALTMAN CO. A LEGAL PROFESSIONAL ASSOCIATION (AV)

15 East Eighth Street, Suite 200W, 45202
Telephone: 513-721-2180
Fax: 513-721-2299
Email: daltman@one.net *URL:* http://www.environlaw.com

D. David Altman

Amy J. Leonard

For full biographical listings, see the Martindale-Hubbell Law Directory

FROST & JACOBS LLP (AV)

2500 PNC Center, 201 East Fifth Street, 45202
Telephone: 513-651-6800
Telecopier: 513-651-6981
URL: http://www.frojac.com
Columbus, Ohio Office: One Columbus, 10 West Broad Street, 43215.
Telephone: 614-464-1211.
Telecopier: 614-464-1737.
Lexington, Kentucky Office: 1100 Vine Center Tower, 333 West Vine Street, 40507.
Telephone: 606-254-1100.
Telecopier: 606-253-2990.
Middletown, Ohio Office: 400 First National Bank Building, 2 North Main Street, 45042.
Telephone: 513-422-2001.
Telecopier: 513-422-3010.

(See Next Column)

FROST & JACOBS LLP—*Continued*

Frankfort, Kentucky Office: 201 W. Main Street, 40601.
Telephone: 502-223-1400.
Telecopier: 502-223-1410.

MEMBERS OF FIRM

William H. Hawkins II
Stephen N. Haughey
Paul W. Casper, Jr.
Kevin N. McMurray

SENIOR ATTORNEY

Stephen J. Axtell

ASSOCIATES

Christopher S. Habel
Steven M. Wesloh
Kellye J. Bowers

COLUMBUS, OHIO OFFICE
MEMBER OF FIRM

Michael K. Yarbrough

COLUMBUS, OHIO OFFICE
OF COUNSEL

Robert E. Leininger

Representative Clients: AK Steel; Aurora Casket; B.F. Goodrich-Hilton Davis; Butler County; Cincinnati Bell; Harvard Industries; Hohman Plating; LensCrafters; Lucas Sumitomo Brakes; Norfolk Southern; Smurfit-Stone Container; Waste Management.

For Complete List of Firm Personnel, See General Section

For full biographical listings, see the Martindale-Hubbell Law Directory

KATZ, TELLER, BRANT & HILD A LEGAL PROFESSIONAL ASSOCIATION (AV)

2400 Chemed Center, 255 East Fifth Street, 45202-4724
Telephone: 513-721-4532
Telecopier: 513-721-7120
Email: corp@ktbh.com

Ronald J. Goret
Daniel P. Utt

Wijdan Jreisat

For Complete List of Firm Personnel, See General Section

For full biographical listings, see the Martindale-Hubbell Law Directory

KEATING, MUETHING & KLEKAMP, P.L.L. (AV)

1400 Provident Tower, One East Fourth Street, 45202
Telephone: 513-579-6400
Facsimile: 513-579-6457
URL: http://www.kmklaw.com

MEMBERS OF FIRM

Jerome C. Randolph
Brian M. Babb

ASSOCIATES

Douglas L. Hensley
Lisa Kim (Not admitted in OH)

Representative Clients: American Financial Group; BP America Inc.; Chiquita Brands International, Inc.; Cintas Corporation; Comair Holdings, Inc.; Duke Realty Limited Partnership; LSI Industries Inc.; Mosler Inc.; Provident Financial Group Inc.

For Complete List of Firm Personnel, See General Section

For full biographical listings, see the Martindale-Hubbell Law Directory

*CLEVELAND,** Cuyahoga Co.

BAKER & HOSTETLER LLP (AV)

3200 National City Center, 1900 East Ninth Street, 44114-3485
Telephone: 216-621-0200
Telecopier: 216-696-0740
TWX: 810 421 8375
RCA Telex: 215032
To contact an attorney on the Internet use first initial and surname followed by @baker-hostetler.com
URL: http://www.bakerlaw.com
In Cincinnati, Ohio: 312 Walnut Street, Suite 2650.
Telephone: 513-929-3400.
In Columbus, Ohio: Capitol Square, Suite 2100, 65 East State Street.
Telephone: 614-228-1541.
In Denver, Colorado: 303 East 17th Avenue, Suite 1100.
Telephone: 303-861-0600.
In Houston, Texas: 1000 Louisiana, Suite 2000.
Telephone: 713-751-1600.
In Beverly Hills, California: 9150 Wilshire Boulevard, Suite 205.
Telephone: 310-385-7500.
In Long Beach, California: 300 Oceangate, Suite 620.
Telephone: 562-432-2827.
In Los Angeles, California: 600 Wilshire Boulevard.
Telephone: 213-624-2400.
In Orlando, Florida: SunBank Center, Suite 2300, 200 South Orange Avenue.
Telephone: 407-649-4000.

(See Next Column)

In Washington, D.C.: Washington Square, Suite 1100, 1050 Connecticut Avenue, N.W.
Telephone: 202-861-1500.

PARTNERS

Mary M. Bittence
William W. Falsgraf
Maureen A. Brennan
John E. Sullivan

RETIRED PARTNER

George Downing

For Complete List of Firm Personnel, See General Section

For full biographical listings, see the Martindale-Hubbell Law Directory

GALLAGHER, SHARP, FULTON & NORMAN (AV)

(Formerly Hauxhurst, Sharp, Mollison & Gallagher)
Bulkley Building, Seventh Floor, 1501 Euclid Avenue, 44115
Telephone: 216-241-5310
Telecopier: 216-241-1608
Email: gsfn.com *URL:* http://www.gsfn.com

MEMBERS OF FIRM

H. Austin Hauxhurst (1881-1962)
Frank X. Cull (1887-1965)
I. Walter Sharp (1884-1966)
Clarence L. Mollison (1906-1981)
Robert C. Horrigan (1916-1993)
Forrest A. Norman
Edward J. Cass
John B. Robertson
Thomas E. Betz
Alan M. Petrov
Alton L. Stephens, Jr.
Virginia L. Heidloff
Jay Clinton Rice
Joseph W. Pappalardo
Thomas E. Dover
James F. Koehler
Robert H. Eddy
Thomas J. Kaiser
D John Travis
Paul J. Schumacher, Jr.
William F. Gibson
Gary L. Nicholson
Lynn L. Moore
Ernest W. Auciello, Jr.
Patrick M. Foy
Kevin C. Alexandersen
Stanley M. Dub
Timothy T. Brick
Sheila A. McKeon
Thomas J. Cabral
Timothy J. Fitzgerald
Mark A. Greer

OF COUNSEL

Michael R. Gallagher
Robert W. Sharp
George W. Stuhldreher
Burt J. Fulton
James F. Sweeney
James G. Gowan
James L. Ryhal, Jr.

Edward G. Kagels
John T. Murphy
M. Terence Cawley
Todd M. Haemmerle
Brian R. McGraw
Timothy P. Whitford
Daniel J. Michalec
Alexander E. Goetsch
Joseph J. Santoro
Monica A. Sansalone
John A. Simon
Dennis G. Rehor
Beth A. Nagel
Timothy Patrick Roth
Gregory K. Boop
Janice Aitken
Gary F. Werner
Mark Joseph Savage
Catherine A. Davis
Charles Allston Bowers
Pamela S. Schremp
James T. Tyminski, Jr.
Matthew J. Hatchadorian

STAFF ATTORNEY

Daniel L. Herak

Counsel for: Associated Aviation Underwriters; Conrail; The Continental Insurance Cos.; Continental National American Group; Fireman's Fund Insurance Cos.; The Home Insurance Co.; Motorist Ins. Co.; Norfolk Southern Corp.; Royal Insurance Co.; United States Aviation Underwriters.

For full biographical listings, see the Martindale-Hubbell Law Directory

JANIK & FORBES (AV)

Building Two, 8223 Brecksville Road, 44141-1371
Telephone: 440-838-7600
Fax: 440-838-7601

MEMBER OF FIRM

Steven G. Janik

For Complete List of Firm Personnel, See General Section

For full biographical listings, see the Martindale-Hubbell Law Directory

JOHNSON AND ANGELO (AV)

1001 Lakeside Avenue, Suite 1700, 44114
Telephone: 216-696-5222
Fax: 216-696-5288

MEMBERS OF FIRM

Gary C. Johnson
Michael J. Angelo

ASSOCIATES

James A. Budzik
Thomas L. Colaluca
Jack P. DeSario
Jack L. Petronelli
Gina A. Kuhlman
William F. Schmitz
Jeffrey C. Miller
Amy L. Phillips

For full biographical listings, see the Martindale-Hubbell Law Directory

Cleveland—Continued

KELLER AND CURTIN CO., L.P.A. (AV)

Suite 330 The Hanna Building, 44115-1901
Telephone: 216-566-7100
Fax: 216-566-5430
Email: keller@en.com
Akron, Ohio Office: 920 Key Building, 159 South Main Street, 44308-1318.
Telephone: 330-376-7245.
Fax: 330-376-8128. Email: kcakron@en.com.
Elyria, Ohio Office: 120 East Avenue, 44035-5228.
Telephone: 440-323-8662.
Fax: 440-323-6610.

Stanley S. Keller
G. Michael Curtin
Walter H. Krohngold
James M. Johnson
Joseph G. Ritzler
Thomas M. Coughlin, Jr.
John Swansinger
Camille D. Kuri
Franklin C. Malemud
Brian D. Spitz
Deena Charisse Miller

Reference: Bank One, Cleveland.

For full biographical listings, see the Martindale-Hubbell Law Directory

KELLEY, McCANN & LIVINGSTONE, LLP (AV)

3500 BP Tower, 200 Public Square, 44114-2302
Telephone: 216-241-3141
Fax: 216-241-3707
Email: Attorneys@kmlegal.com

MEMBERS OF FIRM

Stephen M. O'Bryan
John D. Brown
Mary Grace Balazs
Bruce L. Waterhouse, Jr.
Robert A. Brindza II
Peter M. Poulos

ASSOCIATE

Timothy J. Duff

For Complete List of Firm Personnel, See General Section

For full biographical listings, see the Martindale-Hubbell Law Directory

WALTER & HAVERFIELD, P.L.L. (AV)

1300 Terminal Tower, 44113-2253
Telephone: 216-781-1212
Telecopier: 216-575-0911
Email: law@walterhav.com *URL:* http://www.walterhav.com
Columbus, Ohio Office: 88 East Broad Street.
Telephone: 614-898-1096.

MEMBER OF FIRM

Ralph E. Cascarilla

ASSOCIATE

Debora S. Lasch

Representative Clients: Liberty Mutual Insurance Company; The Sherwin Williams Company; Fields Group Ohio PRP Group.

For Complete List of Firm Personnel, See General Section

For full biographical listings, see the Martindale-Hubbell Law Directory

WESTON HURD FALLON PAISLEY & HOWLEY L.L.P. (AV)

2500 Terminal Tower, 50 Public Square, 44113-2241
Telephone: 216-241-6602;
Ohio Toll Free: 800-336-4952
FAX: 216-621-8369
Email: Hurd2500@westonhurd.com

MEMBERS OF FIRM

Ronald A. Rispo
Carolyn M. Cappel
Deirdre G. Henry
Dana A. Rose

For Complete List of Firm Personnel, See General Section

For full biographical listings, see the Martindale-Hubbell Law Directory

*COLUMBUS,** Franklin Co.

BRICKER & ECKLER LLP (AV)

100 South Third Street, 43215-4291
Telephone: 614-227-2300
Telecopy: 614-227-2390
Email: info@be.bricker.com *URL:* http://www.bricker.com

James J. Hughes
Charles H. Waterman III
Frank L. Merrill

Martha E. Horvitz

Representative Clients: PPG Industries, Inc.; Von Roll America/Waste Technologies Industries; Mineral Processing, Inc.; Ohio Cast Products, Inc.; City of Columbus; Dayton Power & Light Co.; Southdown, Inc.

For Complete List of Firm Personnel, See General Section

For full biographical listings, see the Martindale-Hubbell Law Directory

KEGLER, BROWN, HILL & RITTER (AV)

Capitol Square Suite 1800, 65 East State Street, 43215-4294
Telephone: 614-462-5400
Telecopier: 614-464-2634
Cable Address: "Law KBHR"
Telex: 246671
Email: info@kbhr.com *URL:* http://www.kbhr.com
Marion, Ohio Office: 250 Executive Drive, Suite B, P.O. Box 919.
Telephone: 614-387-3501.
Facsimile: 614-387-3630.

William J. Brown

Representative Clients: Artic Express, Inc.; AT&T Wireless; The Benatty Corp.; Butler County Transportation District; Time Warner Communications.

For Complete List of Firm Personnel, See General Section

For full biographical listings, see the Martindale-Hubbell Law Directory

PORTER WRIGHT MORRIS & ARTHUR LLP (AV)

41 South High Street, 43215-6194
Telephone: 614-227-2000; (800-533-2794)
Fax: 614-227-2100
Email: cmh@porterwright.com *URL:* http://www.porterwright.com
Cincinnati, Ohio Office: 250 E. Fifth Street, Suite 2200, 45202-4199.
Telephones: 513-381-4700; (800-582-5813).
Fax: 513-421-0991. Internet: cvg@porterwright.com.
Cleveland, Ohio Office: 925 Euclid Avenue, Suite 1700, 44115-1483.
Telephones: 216-443-9000; (800-824-1980).
Fax: 216-443-9011. Internet: cle@porterwright.com.
Dayton, Ohio Office: One Dayton Centre, One South Main Street, Suite 1600, 45402-2028.
Telephones: 937-449-6810; (800-533-4434).
Fax: 937-449-6820. Internet: day@porterwright.com.
Naples, Florida Office: 5801 Pelican Bay Boulevard, Suite 300, 34108-2709.
Telephones: 941-593-2900; (800-876-7962).
Fax: 941-593-2990. Internet: apf@porterwright.com.
Washington, D.C. Office: 1667 K Street, N.W., Suite 1100, 20006-1605.
Telephones: 202-778-3000; (800-456-7962).
Fax: 202-778-3063. Internet: dca@porterwright.com.

MEMBERS OF FIRM
COLUMBUS, OHIO OFFICE

Robert L. Brubaker
Daniel R. Conway
Janet J. Henry
Daniel J. Massey
J. Jeffrey McNealey
Samuel H. Porter
Christopher R. Schraff
Martin S. Seltzer

ASSOCIATES
COLUMBUS, OHIO OFFICE

Matthew J. Burkhart
Katerina M. Eftimoff

OF COUNSEL
COLUMBUS, OHIO OFFICE

Scott E. Baughman
Mary Ryan Fenlon

CLEVELAND, OHIO OFFICE
RESIDENT MEMBER

Alan D. Wright

For Complete List of Firm Personnel, See General Section

For full biographical listings, see the Martindale-Hubbell Law Directory

SCHOTTENSTEIN, ZOX & DUNN A LEGAL PROFESSIONAL ASSOCIATION (AV)

The Huntington Center, 41 South High Street, 43215
Telephone: 614-462-2700
Telecopier: 614-462-5135
Telex: 650 24 444 365
URL: http://www.szd.com
Cincinnati, Ohio Office: Bank One Towers, 8044 Montgomery Road, Suite 700, 45236-2926.
Telephone: 513-792-2730.
Cleveland, Ohio Office: One Cleveland Center, 1375 East 9th Street, Suite 950.
Telephone: 216-621-6501.
Fax: 216-621-6502.

John D. Robinett
John C. McDonald
Victoria E. Powers
Robert M. Robenalt
Joanne I. Goldhand

Susan K. Cliffel
Marcus D. Dunn
Darrel R. Davison
Kevin R. Fease
(Not admitted in OH)

OF COUNSEL

Kristopher M. Huelsman

Reference: Bank One of Columbus, N.A.

For Complete List of Firm Personnel, See General Section

For full biographical listings, see the Martindale-Hubbell Law Directory

Columbus—Continued

Shumaker, Loop & Kendrick, LLP (AV)

Huntington Center, 41 South High Street, Suite 2210, 43215
Telephone: 614-463-9441
Fax: 614-463-1108
Toledo, Ohio Office: North Courthouse Square, 1000 Jackson, 43624-1573.
Telephone: 419-241-9000.
Fax: 419-241-6894.
Tampa, Florida Office: Barnett Plaza, Suite 2800, 101 East Kennedy Boulevard, 33602-5151.
Telephone: 813-229-7600.
Fax: 813-229-1660.
Charlotte, North Carolina Office: 128 South Tryon Street, Suite 1800, 28202.
Telephone: 704-375-0057.
Fax: 704-332-1197.

RESIDENT PARTNERS

Michael E. Born
Michael J. O'Callaghan

RESIDENT ASSOCIATE

Stacy Solochek Beckman

For full biographical listings, see the Martindale-Hubbell Law Directory

*DAYTON,** Montgomery Co.

Sebaly, Shillito & Dyer A Legal Professional Association (AV)

1300 Courthouse Plaza, NE, P.O. Box 220, 45402-0220
Telephone: 937-222-2500
Telefax: 937-222-6554; 222-8279
URL: http://www.ssdlaw.com

Martin A. Beyer
Daniel A. Brown
James A. Dyer
Gale S. Finley
John R. Glankler
Deborah D. Hunt
Michael P. Moloney
Jon M. Sebaly
Beverly F. Shillito
Jeffrey B. Shulman
Karl R. Ulrich
Lawrence S. Walter
Nita S. Yates

OF COUNSEL

William W. Lambert

Michael A. Booth
Robert E. Goff, Jr.
Leslie Blair Graden
Joseph V. Hatala
J. David Ruffner, II
Kendra F. Thompson

For full biographical listings, see the Martindale-Hubbell Law Directory

DUBLIN, Franklin Co.

Blaugrund, Herbert & Martin, Incorporated (AV)

5455 Rings Road, Suite 500, 43017-7517
Telephone: 614-764-0681
Fax: 614-764-0774
Email: bhm@bhmlaw.net

Michael C. Mentel

For full biographical listings, see the Martindale-Hubbell Law Directory

*TOLEDO,** Lucas Co.

Eastman & Smith Ltd. (AV)

One Seagate, Twenty-Fourth Floor, P.O. Box 10032, 43699-0032
Telephone: 419-241-6000
Telecopier: 419-247-1777
Columbus, Ohio Office: 65 East State Street, Suite 1000, 43215.
Telephone: 614-460-3556.
Telecopier: 614-228-5371.

MEMBERS OF FIRM

Richard T. Sargeant
Robert J. Gilmer, Jr.
Joseph A. Gregg
Dirk P. Plessner
David W. Nunn

ASSOCIATES

Albin Bauer, II
Barbara A. McGinn

Representative Clients: Envirosafe Services of Ohio, Inc.; 21 International Holdings, Inc.; United Technologies Corporation; Toledo-Lucas County Port Authority; Kelsey-Hayes Company; BEC Laboratories; Marathon Oil Company; OmniSource Corporation; Ameritech Services, Inc.; Master Chemical.

For Complete List of Firm Personnel, See General Section

For full biographical listings, see the Martindale-Hubbell Law Directory

Rohrbachers, Light, Cron, Zmuda & Trimble Co., L.P.A. (AV)

National City Bank Building 8th Floor, 405 Madison Avenue, 43604-1243
Telephone: 419-248-2600
Telecopier: 419-248-2614
URL: http://www.rlczt.com
URL: http://www.lawyers.com/rlcztcom

Vernon E. Rohrbacher (1920-1978)
David J. Rohrbacher
Matthew J. Rohrbacher
C. Randolph Light
Nicholas J. Cron
Gene A. Zmuda
J. Mark Trimble

Beverly J. St. Clair
Diane J. Knoblauch
Todd M. Zimmerman

OF COUNSEL

Brent B. Nicholson

LEGAL SUPPORT PERSONNEL

PARALEGAL

Anne E. Scott

For full biographical listings, see the Martindale-Hubbell Law Directory

Shumaker, Loop & Kendrick, LLP (AV)

North Courthouse Square, 1000 Jackson, 43624-1573
Telephone: 419-241-9000
Fax: 419-241-6894
Tampa, Florida Office: Barnett Plaza, Suite 2800, 101 East Kennedy Boulevard, 33602-5151,
Telephone: 813-229-7600.
Fax: 813-229-1660.
Charlotte, North Carolina Office: 128 South Tryon Street, Suite 1800, 28202.
Telephone: 704-375-0057.
Fax: 704-332-1197.
Columbus, Ohio Office: Huntington Center, 41 South High Street, Suite 2210, 43215.
Telephone: 614-463-9441.
Fax: 614-463-1108.

MEMBERS OF FIRM

Michael E. Born (Resident, Columbus, Ohio Office)
Jeffrey S. Creamer
Scott G. Deller
Jeffrey E. Fort
Douglas G. Haynam
Michael J. O'Callaghan (Resident, Columbus, Ohio Office)
William L. Patberg
John J. Siciliano
Joseph S. Simpson
Louis E. Tosi

ASSOCIATE

Stacy Solochek Beckman (Resident, Columbus, Ohio Office)

For full biographical listings, see the Martindale-Hubbell Law Directory

OKLAHOMA

*OKLAHOMA CITY,** Oklahoma Co.

Day, Edwards, Federman, Propester & Christensen, P.C. (AV)

Suite 2900 Oklahoma Tower, 210 Park Avenue, 73102-5605
Telephone: 405-239-2121
Telecopier: 405-236-1012
URL: http://lawlinks.com/attys/ok/defpc.html

Joe E. Edwards
Kent A. Gilliland
William B. Federman
Rodney J. Heggy

Stuart W. Emmons
Bill Powell Guest

Representative Clients: BancFirst; Bank One, Oklahoma City; Bank of America, N.A.; Bobby Joe Cudd Company; Delta Western Drilling Funds; Fluid Technologies; Federal Deposit Insurance Corp.; Community Bank, Binger; First National Bank and Trust Company of Weatherford; First State Bank & Trust Co., Hollis.

For Complete List of Firm Personnel, See General Section

For full biographical listings, see the Martindale-Hubbell Law Directory

Kerr, Irvine, Rhodes & Ables, A Professional Corporation (AV)

201 Robert S. Kerr Avenue, Suite 600, 73102-4267
Telephone: 405-272-9221
Fax: 405-236-3121
Email: kira201@aol.com

James R. Barnett
R. Thomas Lay

(See Next Column)

KERR, IRVINE, RHODES & ABLES A PROFESSIONAL CORPORATION, *Oklahoma City—Continued*

Kevin R. Wisner

Representative Clients: Groundwater Technology; Oklahoma Gas and Electric Co.; Pig Improvement Co.; Seaboard Farms; Sequoyah Fuels; City of Ada; City of Crescent; City of Ponca City; Hanor Co., Inc; Land O Lakes.

For Complete List of Firm Personnel, See General Section

For full biographical listings, see the Martindale-Hubbell Law Directory

JAYNE JARNIGAN ROBERTSON, P.C. (AV)

119 North Robinson, Suite 825, 73102
Telephone: 405-319-0400
Fax: 405-319-0404
Email: jaynerobertson@compuserve.com

Jayne J. Robertson

For full biographical listings, see the Martindale-Hubbell Law Directory

*TULSA,** Tulsa Co.

ATKINSON, HASKINS, NELLIS, BOUDREAUX, HOLEMAN, PHIPPS & BRITTINGHAM, A PROFESSIONAL CORPORATION (AV)

1500 ParkCentre, 525 South Main Street, 74103
Telephone: 918-582-8877
Fax: 918-585-8096
Email: ahnmail@ahn-law.com

Michael P. Atkinson, P.C.
Walter D. Haskins, P.C.
Gregory D. Nellis, P.C.

Representative Clients: Allstate Insurance Co.; Bayer Corp.; Crum & Forster Insurance Co.; Hartford Insurance Company; National American Insurance Co.; Federated Insurance Co.; Liberty Mutual Insurance Co.; Physicians Liability Insurance Co.; State Farm Mutual Automobile Insurance Co.; United States Aviation Underwriters.

For full biographical listings, see the Martindale-Hubbell Law Directory

CRUMP, TOLSON & PAGE LLP (AV)

1516 South Boston Avenue, Suite 310, 74119-4019
Telephone: 918-583-2393
Fax: 918-583-2394
Email: kcrump@crumptolson.com *URL:* http://www.lawyers.com/crumplaw

MEMBERS OF FIRM

Kenneth E. Crump Jr.
Michael B. Tolson
David P. Page (Resident)

ASSOCIATE

Rodney H. Dusinberre

For full biographical listings, see the Martindale-Hubbell Law Directory

RHODES, HIERONYMUS, JONES, TUCKER & GABLE, P.L.L.C. (AV)

Oneok Plaza, 100 West 5th Street, Suite 400, P.O. Box 21100, 74121-1100
Telephone: 918-582-1173
Fax: 918-592-3390
URL: http://www.rhodesokla.com

MEMBERS OF FIRM

Kevin D. Berry
Jo Anne Deaton
Richard M. Eldridge
E. D. Hieronymus (1908 -1994)
Bert M. Jones
William S. Leach
Michael W. McGivern
William D. Perrine
Mary Quinn-Cooper
Robert P. Redemann
David P. Reid
Chris L. Rhodes, III
Thomas E. Steichen
Catherine C. Taylor
John H. Tucker
Wilson T. White
Harold C. Zuckerman

Ann E. Allison
Steven K. Bunting
Robert P. Coffey, Jr.
J. Christopher Davis
Andrew D. Downing
Dana L. Gish
Kerry R. Lewis
Andrew L. Richardson
Michael F. Smith
Leslie J. Southerland
Kimberly E. West
Keith A. Wilkes

OF COUNSEL

George W. Gable (Retired Partner)
Larry J. Fulton
Kelly M. Greenough

Representative Clients: American International Companies; Bechtel; Chubb Group of Insurance Companies; General Motors Corporation; Merrill, Lynch; Nissan Motor Corporation in U.S.A.; Pfizer, Inc.; Volkswagen of America, Volkswagen, A.G.; Zurich U.S.

For full biographical listings, see the Martindale-Hubbell Law Directory

SHIPLEY, JENNINGS & CHAMPLIN, P.C. (AV)

201 West Fifth Street, Suite 400, 74103-4230
Telephone: 918-582-1720
Fax: 918-584-7681
Email: sjclaw@ionet.net
Oklahoma City, Oklahoma Office: Two Leadership Square, 211 North Robinson, Suite 1300, 73102-7114.
Telephone: 405-235-0808.
Facsimile: 405-232-3746. Email: sjcokc@ionet.net.

Charles W. Shipley
Mark B. Jennings
Blake K. Champlin

Jamie Taylor Boyd

OF COUNSEL

Dee E. Dismukes
Robert D. Kellogg (Resident, Oklahoma City Office)

Reference: Nations Bank.

For full biographical listings, see the Martindale-Hubbell Law Directory

OREGON

*PORTLAND,** Multnomah Co.

BLACK HELTERLINE LLP (AV)

1200 Union Bank of California Tower, 707 S.W. Washington Street, 97205
Telephone: 503-224-5560
Telecopier: 503-224-6148
URL: http://www.bhlaw.com

MEMBERS OF FIRM

Stark Ackerman
Ronald T. Adams
Paul R. Hribernick
Steven R. Schell

ASSOCIATE

Eric J. TenBrook

Representative Clients: Columbia Corridor Association; Columbia Edgewater Country Club; Gull Industries, Inc.; Home Builders Association of Metropolitan Portland; K-4, Inc.; NACCO Materials Handling Group, Inc.; Morse Bros.; The Sivers Companies; The Statesman Journal; Windsor Rock Products, Inc.

For Complete List of Firm Personnel, See General Section

For full biographical listings, see the Martindale-Hubbell Law Directory

COPELAND, LANDYE, BENNETT AND WOLF, LLP (AV)

1300 S.W. 5th Avenue, Suite 3500, 97201
Telephone: 503-224-4100
Facsimile: 503-224-4133
Anchorage, Alaska Office: 701 West Eighth Avenue, Suite 1200, 99501.
Telephone: 907-276-5152.
Facsimile: 907-276-8433.

MEMBERS OF FIRM

J. David Bennett
David L. Blount
David S. Case (Resident, Anchorage, Alaska Office)
Mitchel R. Cohen
Stuart K. Cohen
Mark G. Copeland (Resident, Anchorage, Alaska Office)
James S. Crane
David N. Goulder
Robert B. Hopkins
Robert H. Hume, Jr. (Resident, Anchorage, Alaska Office)
Thomas M. Landye
Jeffrey S. Mutnick
P. Stephen Russell, III
Richard L. Sadler
Thane W. Tienson

ASSOCIATES

Robert P. Owens (Resident, Anchorage, Alaska Office)
Patrick S. Galvin (Resident, Anchorage, Alaska Office)
Karna R. Gustafson
Alison S. Browdie
Katherine A. Dreyfus
David Voluck (Resident, Anchorage, Alaska Office)

For full biographical listings, see the Martindale-Hubbell Law Directory

PENNSYLVANIA

*ALLENTOWN,** Lehigh Co.

RICHARD W. SHAFFER (AV)

740 Hamilton Mall, 18101
Telephone: 610-439-0800
Fax: 610-439-8852
Email: Rwspalaw@aol.com

(See Next Column)

RICHARD W. SHAFFER—*Continued*

LEGAL SUPPORT PERSONNEL

Barbara J. Nemes (Paralegal)

For full biographical listings, see the Martindale-Hubbell Law Directory

BERWYN, Chester Co.

LEGROS LAW PARTNERS, P.C. (AV)

Five Westlakes, Suite 275, 1000 Westlakes Drive, 19312
Telephone: 610-640-7350
Fax: 610-640-7359
Email: LeGrosLaw@AOL.COM *URL:* http://www.legroslaw.com
Princeton, New Jersey Office: 229 Nassau Street,
Telephone: 609-497-2356,
Fax: 609-497-2377.

Susan P. LeGros
Frances K. Davis

For full biographical listings, see the Martindale-Hubbell Law Directory

FORT WASHINGTON, Montgomery Co.

DALLER GREENBERG & DIETRICH, LLP (AV)

Valley Green Corporate Center, 7111 Valley Green Road, 19034
Telephone: 215-836-1100
Facsimile: 215-836-2845
URL: http://www.dallergreenberg.com
Haddon Heights, New Jersey Office: 2 White Horse Pike.
Telephone: 856-547-9068.
Facsimile: 856-547-2391.

PARTNERS

Morton F. Daller
Edward A. Greenberg
Gerhard P. Dietrich
Eileen M. Johnson
Dennis R. Callahan

ASSOCIATES

Tracy Canuso Nugent (Resident, Haddon Heights, New Jersey Office)
Catherine N. Walto
Mark S. Kirby
Marie Handrich Kramer
Alison R. Rohmer

For full biographical listings, see the Martindale-Hubbell Law Directory

*HARRISBURG,** Dauphin Co.

KILLIAN & GEPHART, LLP (AV)

218 Pine Street, P.O. Box 886, 17108
Telephone: 717-232-1851
Telecopier: 717-238-0592
Email: kg@killiangephart.com *URL:* http://www.killiangephart.com

MEMBERS OF FIRM

John D. Killian
Smith B. Gephart
Thomas W. Scott
Jane Gowen Penny
Paula J. McDermott

Reference: Fulton Bank.

For full biographical listings, see the Martindale-Hubbell Law Directory

METTE, EVANS & WOODSIDE, A PROFESSIONAL CORPORATION (AV)

3401 North Front Street, P.O. Box 5950, 17110-0950
Telephone: 717-232-5000
Fax: 717-236-1816
Email: MEW@Mette.com *URL:* HTTP://WWW.METTE.COM

Charles B. Zwally
Daniel L. Sullivan
P. Daniel Altland
Michael D. Reed
Paula J. Leicht
Michael D. Pipa
Guy P. Beneventano

Robyn Katzman Bowman
Bryan Scott Megary

For Complete List of Firm Personnel, See General Section

For full biographical listings, see the Martindale-Hubbell Law Directory

RHOADS & SINON LLP (AV)

One South Market Square, 12th Floor, P.O. Box 1146, 17108-1146
Telephone: 717-233-5731
Fax: 717-232-1459
Boca Raton, Florida Affiliated Office: Charles L. Sieck, 1700 South Dixie Highway, Suite 2-C.
Telephone: 561-395-5595.
Fax: 561-395-9497.
York, Pennsylvania Office: 15 North Cherry Lane, Suite 21.
Telephone: 717-843-1718.
Fax: 717-232-1459.

OF COUNSEL

R. Stephen Shibla

(See Next Column)

MEMBERS OF FIRM

Sherill T. Moyer
Jan P. Paden
Charles E. Gutshall

ASSOCIATE

Kenneth L. Joel

For Complete List of Firm Personnel, See General Section

For full biographical listings, see the Martindale-Hubbell Law Directory

*PHILADELPHIA,** Philadelphia Co.

ANAPOL, SCHWARTZ, WEISS, COHAN, FELDMAN AND SMALLEY, P.C. (AV)

1900 Delancey Place, 19103
Telephone: 215-735-1130
Fax: 215-735-2024
URL: http://www.aswc.net
Other Philadelphia, Pennsylvania Office: 1710 Spruce Street.
Fax: 215-735-2211.
Cherry Hill, New Jersey Office: 402 Park Boulevard, 08002.
Telephone: 1-609-427-9229.
Fax: 609-488-1396.
Fairless Hills, Pennsylvania Office: 920 Trenton Road.
Telephone: 215-945-6799.
Reading, Pennsylvania Office: 146 North 6th Street.
Telephone: 610-375-7488.
Media, Pennsylvania Office: 334 W. Front Street, 19063.
Telephone: 610-892-3714.

Alan Schwartz
Sol H. Weiss
Lawrence R. Cohan
Joel D. Feldman
Howard J. Levin
Bernard W. Smalley
Stanton Dubin
Margaret A. Barry
Stephen J. Pokiniewski, Jr.
Sidney M. Grobman
Nelson Levin

Nathaniel E.P. Ehrlich
Thomas R. Anapol
Miriam Benton Barish
Patrice A. Gillotti
Michele Lee Reed
Heather J. Lipson
Michelle L. Altenpohl
Lisa R. Schwartz
Kevin R. Marciano
Brian J. Taylor
Tobias L. Millrood
Tracy A. Finken

OF COUNSEL

Paul R. Anapol
Richard B. Schwartz (Resident, Other Philadelphia Office)
Mark F. Seltzer

Reference: Meridian Bank, Philadelphia, Pennsylvania.

For full biographical listings, see the Martindale-Hubbell Law Directory

BALLARD SPAHR ANDREWS & INGERSOLL, LLP (AV)

1735 Market Street, 51st Floor, 19103-7599
Telephone: 215-665-8500
Fax: 215-864-8999
URL: http://www.ballardspahr.com
Baltimore, Maryland Office: 300 East Lombard Street. 19th Floor.
Telephone: 410-528-5600.
Fax: 410-528-5650.
Camden, New Jersey Office: 800 Hudson Square, 5th Floor.
Telephone: 856-541-5577.
Fax: 856-541-8272.
Denver, Colorado Office: Seventeenth Street Plaza Building, Suite 2300, 1225 17th Street.
Telephone: 303-292-2400.
Fax: 303-296-3956.
Salt Lake City, Utah Office: One Utah Center, Suite 1200, 201 South Main Street.
Telephone: 801-531-3000.
Fax: 801-531-3001.
Voorhees, New Jersey Office: Suite 100, 1101 Laurel Oak Drive.
Telephone: 856-627-8555.
Fax: 856-627-1153.
Washington, D.C. Office: Suite 1000 South, 601 13th Street, N.W.
Telephone: 202-661-2200.
Fax: 202-661-2299.

Brendan K. Collins
Robert B. McKinstry, Jr.
Glenn L. Unterberger
David G. Mandelbaum
Ronald A. Sarachan
Harry Weiss

OF COUNSEL

J. Joseph Cullen

Samantha R. Corson
Jeanne J. Dworetzky
Marc Davies
William H. Gelles, III
Leslie W. Ledogar

For Complete List of Firm Personnel, See General Section

For full biographical listings, see the Martindale-Hubbell Law Directory

Philadelphia—Continued

JOHN GERARD DEVLIN & ASSOCIATES, P.C. (AV)

1515 Market Street Suite 2010, 19102
Telephone: 215-564-6740
Telefax: 215-564-6732
Email: devlinlaw@aol.com
Allentown, Pennsylvania Office: The Sovereign Building, Executive Suite 103, 609 Hamilton Mall.
Telephone: 215-820-6422.
Westmont, New Jersey Office: 216 Haddon Avenue, Suite 103.
Telephone: 609-858-1690.
Fax: 609-858-8998.
East Brunswick, New Jersey Office: 190 Route 18, Suite 3000.
Telephone: 908-214-2621.
Fax: 908-246-2917.
Wilkes-Barre, Pennsylvania Office: Cross Creek Pointe, 1065 Hwy 315, Suite H.
Telephone: 610-820-6422.

John Gerard Devlin
James B. Corrigan, Jr.
Joseph T. Murphy, Jr.
Thomas Paschos
Michael Malarick
Suzanne Curran Murphy
Arthur F. Wheeler
Paul A. Lawless, Jr.

Representative Clients: Lloyds of London; Commercial Union; John Hancock Property and Casualty Insurance Co.; Wausau Insurance Co.; Hanseco Insurance Co.; American Family Insurance Co.; Liberty Mutual Insurance Co.; Linberg Adjustment Co.

For full biographical listings, see the Martindale-Hubbell Law Directory

KITTREDGE, DONLEY, ELSON, FULLEM & EMBICK, LLP (AV)

Fifth Floor, The Bank Building, 421 Chestnut Street, 19106-2416
Telephone: 215-829-9900
Fax: 215-829-9888
Email: lawoffice@kdefe.com *URL:* http://www.kdefe.com

MEMBERS OF FIRM

Patrick W. Kittredge
Joseph M. Donley
Barry R. Elson
Joseph W. Fullem, Jr.
John R. Embick
Keith E. Johnston

ASSOCIATES

Glenn E. Davis
Michael S. Soule
Patricia Powers
Brendan P. McGlynn
Lisa G. Miller
Edward Bigham
Michael K. Smith (1963-1995)

OF COUNSEL

Richard B. Pearl

For full biographical listings, see the Martindale-Hubbell Law Directory

KLEINBARD, BELL & BRECKER LLP (AV)

Suite 700, 1900 Market Street, 19103
Telephone: 215-568-2000
Facsimile: 215-568-0140
Montclair, New Jersey Office: 240 Claremont Avenue, 07042.
Telephone: 973-233-0600.
Facsimile: 973-233-9390.

Joseph S. Kleinbard (1905-1994)
Robert John Brecker (1916-1996)

COUNSEL TO THE FIRM

Arthur S. Keyser

MEMBERS OF FIRM

Paul E. Bomze
Murray I. Blackman
Howard J. Davis
Steven R. Waxman
Steven J. Engelmyer (Resident, Montclair Office)
David L. Hyman (Resident, Montclair Office)
Imogene E. Hughes
John P. Hickey
Jay R. Goldstein
Ralph J. Mauro
Thomas H. Speranza
Lisa E. Brody

ASSOCIATES

Mary Beth H. Gray
Eric J. Rothschild
Mary Vassallo Slinkard
Michael A. Frattone
Benjamin C. Graff (Not admitted in PA)
Ralph F. Salgado

COUNSEL

Joseph Bell

For full biographical listings, see the Martindale-Hubbell Law Directory

LEVIN, FISHBEIN, SEDRAN & BERMAN (AV)

Suite 500, 510 Walnut Street, 19106-3697
Telephone: 215-592-1500
Fax: 215-592-4663
Email: lfsb@psinet.com

MEMBERS OF FIRM

Arnold Levin
Michael D. Fishbein
Howard J. Sedran
Laurence S. Berman
Frederick S. Longer

(See Next Column)

Craig D. Ginsburg
Cheryl R. Brown Hill
Donald E. Haviland, Jr.
Daniel C. Levin
Terrianne Benedetto
Charles E. Schaffer
Austin B. Cohen

LEGAL SUPPORT PERSONNEL

Lee Ann Fitzpatrick
Cheryl Hesson

For full biographical listings, see the Martindale-Hubbell Law Directory

MANTA AND WELGE, A PROFESSIONAL CORPORATION (AV)

2000 Market Street, 6th Floor, 19103
Telephone: 215-851-6600
Telecopy: 215-851-6644
URL: http://www.mantalaw.com
Allentown, Pennsylvania Office: Suite 204, 5000 Tilghman Street.
Telephone: 610-395-7499.
Fax: 610-366-5096.
Harrisburg, Pennsylvania Office: Governors Row, 27 North Front Street.
Telephone: 717-236-8420.
West Trenton, New Jersey Office: 810 Bear Tavern Road, Suite 301.
Telephone: 609-883-6990.
Fax: 609-883-7730.
Wilmington, Delaware Office: Suite 1400, Mellon Bank Center, 919 Market Street.
Telephone: 302-655-7460.
Fax: 302-655-7004.

MEMBERS OF FIRM

Stephen W. Miller
Kathleen Misturak-Gingrich
Thomas B. O'Brien, Jr.
Kim Hollaender

Jennifer M. Welding
Robert S. Stickley

For full biographical listings, see the Martindale-Hubbell Law Directory

MARKS, O'NEILL, REILLY, O'BRIEN & COURTNEY, P.C. (AV)

1880 John F. Kennedy Boulevard Suite 1200, 19103
Telephone: 215-564-6688
Fax: 215-564-2526
Email: moro1@morocpa.com
Norristown, Pennsylvania Office: 411 Cherry Street.
Telephone: 215-277-7601.
Pittsburgh, Pennsylvania Office: 707 Grant Street, Gulf Tower, Suite 3200.
Telephone: 412-391-6171.
Fax: 412-391-8804.
Westmont, New Jersey Office: 216 Haddon Avenue, Suite 500.
Telephone: 856-858-6110.
Fax: 856-858-3687. E-Mail: moro1@morocnj.com
Wilmington, Delaware Office: 2004 Foulk Road, Suite 7.
Telephone: 302-475-5500.
Fax: 302-475-5584.

Jerome E. Marks
Joseph M. O'Neill
Vincent F. Reilly
Kevin J. O'Brien
Dawn R. Courtney
Sean Xavier Kelly
Gino P. Mecoli
John J. Repcheck (Resident, Pittsburgh Office)

David P. Helwig (Resident, Pittsburgh Office)
Maureen Murray-O'Toole
Patrick C. Lamb
Christine G. Boyle
Nancy E. Mancheski
Michael T. Hamilton
Kelly L. Bracken
Tracey Marie McDevitt
Sharon A. Connors (Resident, Westmont, New Jersey Office)
Malissa A. Richetti
Patricia M. Henrich
Judith H. Ring
Gary Weinberg (Resident, Westmont, New Jersey Office)
Lee J. Janiczek
Wendy D. Testa (Resident, Westmont, New Jersey Office)
Gary F. Sharlock (Resident, Pittsburgh Office)
Robert Dale Leidigh (Resident, Pittsburgh Office)
Joseph L. Orszulak, II (Resident, Pittsburgh Office)
Diane Beckman Carvell
Karen J. Stanzione
Michael A. Kosar
Susan D. Grant (Resident, Westmont, New Jersey Office)
Frances Wang-Deveney (Resident, Westmont, New Jersey)
Courtney E. Passin
Stephanie Victoria Shreibman
Megan Kochell D'Iorio (Resident, Wilmington, Delaware Office)
Megan Trocki Mantzavinos (Resident, Wilmington, Delaware Office)
Toni Anderson Moore
Natalie M. Nugent
Frank Gattuso
Michael A. Ring (Resident, Westmont, New Jersey Office)
Ann M. Madden (Not admitted in PA)
Matthew J. Zamites
Salvatore A. Clemente

LEGAL SUPPORT PERSONNEL

PARALEGALS

Gregory P. Sabo
Elisa LaRosa
Frances P. Rossi
Heather Feenan
Jerry Ezekiel
Steven Randisi
Sharon Williams
Melanie Gaskins

For full biographical listings, see the Martindale-Hubbell Law Directory

Philadelphia—Continued

MATTIONI, LTD. (AV)

399 Market Street, 2nd Floor, 19106
Telephone: 215-629-1600
Cable Address: "Mattioni"
Fax: 215-923-2227
Email: firmmail@mattioni.com *URL:* http://www.mattioni.com
Westmont, New Jersey Office: Mattioni, LLP, Suite 100, Sentry Office Plaza, 216 Haddon Avenue, 08108.
Telephone: 856-854-6200.
Fax: 856-854-3338.
Montgomery County Office: Suite 200, 1101 Fayette Street, Conshohocken, Pennsylvania, 19428.
Telephone: 610-941-9530.
Fax: 610-940-4489.

John Mattioni
Robert W. Weidner, Jr.
Scott J. Schwarz
Itzchak E. Kornfeld
Bridget C. Sciamanna

Kristi L. Treadway **

**Of Counsel

For Complete List of Firm Personnel, See General Section

For full biographical listings, see the Martindale-Hubbell Law Directory

MCCORMICK & PRIORE, P.C. (AV)

One Penn Square West, 30 S. 15th Street, Suite 1500, 19102
Telephone: 215-972-0161
Fax: 215-972-5580
Email: mccormick5@aol.com
Marlton, New Jersey Office: One Greentree Centre, Suite 201, 08053.
Telephone: 609-988-5452.
Fax: 609-596-8359.

David M. McCormick
Philip D. Priore
Stephen M. McManus

OF COUNSEL

Harry A. Short, Jr.

Wendy L. Schmidt-Levin
H. Joseph Byron
Michelle Nick Rossi
Christina A. Toriello
Jill Schneider
John P. Lock

LEGAL SUPPORT PERSONNEL

Deborah Stefan
Jane Coley

For full biographical listings, see the Martindale-Hubbell Law Directory

CLAYTON H. THOMAS, JR. (AV)

37th Floor, Bell Atlantic Tower Building, 1717 Arch Street, 19103-2793
Telephone: 215-994-5290
Fax: 215-994-5296

Benjamin Rose

For full biographical listings, see the Martindale-Hubbell Law Directory

WILBRAHAM, LAWLER & BUBA, A PROFESSIONAL CORPORATION (AV)

1818 Market Street, Suite 3100, 19103-3631
Telephone: 215-564-4141
Fax: 215-564-4385
Email: @wlbdeflaw.com
Haddonfield, New Jersey Office: 24 Kings Highway West.
Telephone: 856-795-4422.
Fax: 856-795-4699.
Wilmington, Delaware Office: Stoney Batter Office Building, 5301 Limestone Road, Suite 221.
Telephone: 302-234-8217.
Fax: 302-234-8218.

Edward J. Wilbraham
Robert B. Lawler
Barbara J. Buba
Michael J. Block

R. Erick Chizmar
Kevin J. Maginnis
InSook Kim
Sandra D. Terry-Crawford
John S. Howarth
David M. Maselli
Renee E. Berger
Edward T. Finch
Sean P. Buggy

OF COUNSEL

Walter J. Timby, Jr.
Daniel J. Allan

Representative Clients: GAF Corporation; Armstrong World Industries, Inc.; U.S. Gypsum Company; Georgia-Pacific Corporation; ARCO; Shell; Royal; AIG; Chubb; Keystone.

For full biographical listings, see the Martindale-Hubbell Law Directory

ROBERT H. ZIMMERMAN (AV)

The Ninth Floor, 1608 Walnut Street, 19103
Telephone: 215-546-8825
Fax: 215-735-1858
Email: RHZIM@AOL.COM

For full biographical listings, see the Martindale-Hubbell Law Directory

*PITTSBURGH,** Allegheny Co.

BABST, CALLAND, CLEMENTS AND ZOMNIR, A PROFESSIONAL CORPORATION (AV)

Two Gateway Center, 15222
Telephone: 412-394-5400
Fax: 412-394-6576
Email: BCCZ@BCCZ.com
Philadelphia, Pennsylvania Office: The Widener Building, Suite 1700, One South Penn Square.
Telephone: 215-567-1020.
Fax: 215-751-1425.

Chester R. Babst III
Dean A. Calland
Donald C. Bluedorn II
Colleen Grace Donofrio (Resident, Philadelphia, Pennsylvania Office)
Monica Gambino
Kevin J. Garber
Michele M. Gutman
Lindsay P. Howard
Joseph K. Reinhart

Stacia A. Christman
Joseph P. Pohl, III
Gregory D. Timmons
Christine L. Wettach
Michael H. Winek

For full biographical listings, see the Martindale-Hubbell Law Directory

PLOWMAN, SPIEGEL & LEWIS, P.C. (AV)

Second Floor, The Grant Building, 310 Grant Street, 15219-2201
Telephone: 412-471-8521
Fax: 412-471-4481

Jack W. Plowman
John L. Spiegel

Frank J. Kernan
Kenneth W. Lee

Reference: Pittsburgh National Bank.

For Complete List of Firm Personnel, See General Section

For full biographical listings, see the Martindale-Hubbell Law Directory

WILLMAN & ARNOLD, LLP (AV)

Suite 705-708, 700 McKnight Park Drive, 15237
Telephone: 412-366-3333
Fax: 412-366-3462
Email: RANTINON@IX.NETCOM.COM *URL:* http://www.wilandarn.com

MEMBERS OF FIRM

Gene E. Arnold
R. Kenneth Willman
James W. Young, Jr.
Ruth A. Antinone
Concetta A. Silvaggio

ASSOCIATES

Glenn A. Huetter, Jr.
Lola M. James
Joseph D. Silvaggio
Thomas A. Smolinski
Steven G. Blackmer
Maureen A. Shannon
Robert Anthony Conroy
Jeffrey Thomas Strittmatter

For full biographical listings, see the Martindale-Hubbell Law Directory

*SCRANTON,** Lackawanna Co.

O'MALLEY & HARRIS, P.C. (AV)

345 Wyoming Avenue, 18503
Telephone: 570-348-3711
Fax: 570-348-4092
Email: ohpc@epix.net *URL:* http://www.ohpclaw.com
Stroudsburg, Pennsylvania Office: 111 North Seventh Street.
Telephone: 570-421-2252; 570-422-1280.
FAX: 570-422-1281. Email: cerato@ptdprolog.net.
Wilkes-Barre, Pennsylvania Office: 61 North Washington Street.
Telephone: 570-829-3232.
FAX: 570-829-4418. Email: ohpcwb@epix.net.
Williamsport, Pennsylvania Office: 321 Pine Street, Suite 308.
Telephone: 570-323-4380.

Eugene Nogi (1905-1975)
Henry Nogi (1900-1976)
Russell J. O'Malley, Sr. (1904-1993)
Norman Harris (1907-1998)
William H. Amesbury (Resident, Wilkes-Barre Office)
Paul A. Barrett
Matthew P. Barrett
J. Scott Brady (Resident, Wilkes-Barre Office)
Lori J. Cerato (Resident, Stroudsburg Office)
Bruce L. Coyer
John Q. Durkin
Gerald J. Hanchulak
Richard K. Hodges

(See Next Column)

O'MALLEY & HARRIS P.C., *Scranton—Continued*

Timothy J. Holland (Resident, Wilkes-Barre Office)
John F. Kennedy (Resident, Wilkes-Barre Office)
Daniel Morgan
Michael Perry
James M. Tressler
Joseph Timothy Healey
A. Ruth Whalen (Resident, Wilkes-Barre Office)

Representative Clients: Pennsylvania Hospital Insurance Co.; MMI Systems Agency, Inc.; State Farm Insurance Company; ITT Specialty Risk Services; St. Paul Fire & Marine Insurance Co.; Chubb Group of Insurance Companies; Geisingen System Services; Princeton Insurance Company; Northeastern Pennsylvania Physicians Organization; Catholic Healthcare Partners.

For full biographical listings, see the Martindale-Hubbell Law Directory

RHODE ISLAND

*PROVIDENCE,** Providence Co.

BLISH & CAVANAGH (AV)

Commerce Center, 30 Exchange Terrace, 02903
Telephone: 401-831-8900
Telecopier: 401-751-7542
Email: BLISHCAV@AOL.COM

MEMBERS OF FIRM

Joseph V. Cavanagh, Jr.
William R. Landry
Edmund L. Alves, Jr.
Stephen J. Reid, Jr.
Karen A. Pelczarski
Scott T. Spear
Raymond A. Marcaccio

Michael W. Carroll
Staci L. Sawyer
Kristin Rodgers Sullivan

OF COUNSEL

John H. Blish

Representative Clients: Providence Journal Co.; Rhode Island Hospital Trust National Bank; Fleet Bank; Metropolitan Insurance Co.; Allstate Insurance Co.; Delta Dental of Rhode Island; Colony Communications; Providence Housing Authority; Textron; A.T. Cross.

For full biographical listings, see the Martindale-Hubbell Law Directory

EDWARDS & ANGELL, LLP (AV)

A Partnership including Professional Corporations
2800 BankBoston Plaza, 02903
Telephone: 401-274-9200
Telecopier: 401-276-6611
Cable Address: "Edwangle Providence"
Telex: 952001 "E A PVD"
Email: postmaster@ealaw.com *URL:* http://www.ealaw.com
Boston, Massachusetts Office: 101 Federal Street, 02110-1800.
Telephone: 617-439-4444.
Telecopier: 617-439-4170.
New York, New York Office: 750 Lexington Avenue, 10022-1200.
Telephone: 212-308-4411.
Telecopier: 212-308-4844.
Palm Beach, Florida Office: 250 Royal Palm Way, Suite 300, 33480-4356.
Telephone: 561-833-7700.
Telecopier: 561-655-8719.
Short Hills, New Jersey Office: 51 John F. Kennedy Parkway, 07078.
Telephone: 973-376-7700.
Telecopier: 973-376-3380.
Hartford, Connecticut Office: 90 State House Square, 06103-2715.
Telephone: 860-525-5065.
Telecopier: 860-527-4198.
Newport, Rhode Island Office: 130 Bellevue Avenue, 02840.
Telephone: 401-849-7800.
Telecopier: 401-849-7887.

MEMBERS OF FIRM

Gail E. McCann
Lorne W. McDougall
Mark A. Pogue
Deming E. Sherman
Lynn Wright (Not admitted in RI; New York, New York and Newark, New Jersey Office)

For Complete List of Firm Personnel, See General Section

For full biographical listings, see the Martindale-Hubbell Law Directory

HANSON, CURRAN, PARKS & WHITMAN (AV)

146 Westminster Street, 02903-2218
Telephone: 401-421-2154
Telecopier: 401-521-7040
URL: http://www.hcpw.com

Kirk Hanson (1948-1991)

(See Next Column)

MEMBERS OF FIRM

A. Lauriston Parks
David P. Whitman
Michael T. F. Wallor
Dennis J. McCarten
James T. Murphy
Seth E. Bowerman
Thomas R. Bender
Mark W. Dana

ASSOCIATES

Richard H. Burrows
Christopher J. Zangari (Resident)
Wendy J. Taylor

OF COUNSEL

William A. Curran

General Counsel for: Medical Malpractice Joint Underwriting Association of Rhode Island.
Rhode Island Counsel for: Amica Mutual Insurance Co.; CIGNA; St. Paul Insurance Cos.; Occidental Life Insurance Co.; Exchange Mutual Insurance Co.; Aetna Casualty & Surety Co.

For full biographical listings, see the Martindale-Hubbell Law Directory

SOUTH CAROLINA

*BEAUFORT,** Beaufort Co.

HARVEY & BATTEY, P.A. (AV)

1001 Craven Street, P.O. Drawer 1107, 29902
Telephone: 843-524-3109
Telefax: 843-524-6973

W. Brantley Harvey, Jr.
Thomas A. Holloway

Approved Attorneys for: Lawyers Title Insurance Corp.; Chicago Title Insurance Corp.
Representative Clients: Nations Bank; First Bank, F.S.B.; Pleasant Point Plantation Associates; Century 21-Carolina Realty, Inc.; Lobeco Products, Inc.; Beaufort County Association of Realtors; The Fripp Company.

For Complete List of Firm Personnel, See General Section

For full biographical listings, see the Martindale-Hubbell Law Directory

*CHARLESTON,** Charleston Co.

BUIST, MOORE, SMYTHE & MCGEE, P.A. (AV)

Successors to Buist, Buist, Smythe and Smythe and Moore, Mouzon and McGee.
Five Exchange Street, P.O. Box 999, 29402
Telephone: 843-722-3400
Cable Address: "Conferees"
Telex: 57-6488
Telecopier: 843-723-7398
Email: bmsm@lawyer-sc.com *URL:* http://www.lawyer-sc.com

Gordon D. Schreck
W. Foster Gaillard
James D. Myrick
Elizabeth Henry Warner
David H. Crawford

Margaret O. Dullanty

Representative Clients: NationsBank; Beazer East, Inc.; Daniel Island Co.; The Harry Frank Guggenheim Foundation; Lowcountry Open Land Trust; Provident; Otis Elevator Co.; Mediterranean Shipping Co., S.A.

For Complete List of Firm Personnel, See General Section

For full biographical listings, see the Martindale-Hubbell Law Directory

LEATH, BOUCH & CRAWFORD, L.L.P. (AV)

134 Meeting Street, P.O. Box 59, 29402-0059
Telephone: 843-937-8811
Fax: 843-937-0606
Columbia, South Carolina Office: 221 Pickens Street (29205), P.O. Box 5066, 29250.
Telephone: 803-254-0048.
Facsimile: 803-254-0063.

MEMBERS OF FIRM

W. Jefferson Leath, Jr.
Timothy W. Bouch
B. Lindsay Crawford, III

Linda J. Amason
Elizabeth Rice Polk (Resident, Columbia Office)

For full biographical listings, see the Martindale-Hubbell Law Directory

*COLUMBIA,** Richland Co.

HAYNSWORTH, MARION, MCKAY & GUÉRARD, L.L.P. (AV)

Suite 2400 Affinity Building, 1201 Main Street, P.O. Drawer 7157, 29202
Telephone: 803-765-1818
Facsimile: 803-765-2399
Greenville, South Carolina Office: 75 Beattie Place, Eleventh Floor, P.O. Box 2048, 29602.
Telephone: 864-240-3200.
Facsimile: 864-240-3300.
Charleston, South Carolina Office: 134 Meeting Street, P.O. Box 1119, 29402.
Telephone: 843-722-7606.
Facsimile: 843-724-8016.

MEMBERS OF FIRM

Michael R. Daniel
Russell B. Shetterly

SPECIAL COUNSEL

John Adams Hodge

For Complete List of Firm Personnel, See General Section

For full biographical listings, see the Martindale-Hubbell Law Directory

NEXSEN PRUET JACOBS & POLLARD, LLP (AV)

1441 Main Street, 15th Floor, P.O. Drawer 2426, 29202
Telephone: 803-771-8900
Facsimile: 803-253-8277
Email: NPJP@NPJP.COM *URL:* HTTP://WWW.NPJP.COM
Charleston, South Carolina Office: 200 Meeting Street, Suite 301. P.O. Box 486.
Telephone: 803-577-9440.
Facsimile: 803-720-1777.
Greenville, South Carolina Office: 201 West McBee Avenue, Fourth Floor, P.O. Box 10648.
Telephone: 864-370-2211.
Facsimile: 864-282-1177.
Myrtle Beach, South Carolina Office: 2411 Oak Street, Suite 105.
Telephone: 843-445-9688.
Facsimile: 843-445-9949.
Charlotte, North Carolina Office: 212 South Tryon Street, Suite 1700.
Telephone: 704-339-0304.
Facsimile: 704-338-5377.

MEMBERS OF FIRM

Leon C. Harmon (Resident, Greenville, SC Office)
W. Thomas Lavender, Jr.
James W. Potter

ASSOCIATES

Daniel James Brown
John W. Davidson

For Complete List of Firm Personnel, See General Section

For full biographical listings, see the Martindale-Hubbell Law Directory

RICHARDSON, PLOWDEN, CARPENTER & ROBINSON, P.A. (AV)

1600 Marion Street, P.O. Drawer 7788, 29202
Telephone: 803-771-4400
Telecopy: 803-779-0016
Email: atty@rpcrlaw.com *URL:* http://www.rpcrlaw.com
Myrtle Beach, South Carolina Office: 2103 B Farlow Street, P.O. Box 3646, 29578.
Telephone: 843-448-1008.
FAX: 843-448-1533.

Francis M. Mack
Franklin Jennings Smith, Jr.
Leslie A. Cotter, Jr.

OF COUNSEL

Michael A. Pulliam

Representative Clients: W. R. Grace; Conwed Corp.; Amphenol Corp.; Toledo Scale, Inc.; S.C. Insurance Reserve Fund; Empire Ace Manufacturing; CIGNA; Osmose Wood Preserving Inc.

For Complete List of Firm Personnel, See General Section

For full biographical listings, see the Martindale-Hubbell Law Directory

SIMMONS, GRIFFIN & LYDON, L.L.P. (AV)

1711 Pickens Street, P.O. Box Five, 29202
Telephone: 803-779-4600
Facsimile: 803-254-8874
URL: http://www.lawyers.com/simmonsgriffinlydonlaw

John S. Simmons
James Mixon Griffin
Thomas E. Lydon

Representative Clients: First Union National Bank; First Financial Mortgage Services; Fleet Mortgage Group.

For full biographical listings, see the Martindale-Hubbell Law Directory

TURNER, PADGET, GRAHAM & LANEY, P.A. (AV)

Seventeenth Floor, 1901 Main Street, P.O. Box 1473, 29202
Telephone: 803-254-2200
Telecopy: 803-799-3957
Florence, South Carolina Office: Fourth Floor, 1831 West Evans Street, P.O. Box 5478, 29502.
Telephone: 843-662-9008.
Fax: 843-667-0828.
Charleston, South Carolina Office: 21 Broad Street, 1st Floor, P.O. Box 836, 29402.
Telephone: 843-723-1622.
Fax: 843-577-3369.

Thomas C. Salane
Steven W. Ouzts

For Complete List of Firm Personnel, See General Section

For full biographical listings, see the Martindale-Hubbell Law Directory

*GREENVILLE,** Greenville Co.

GRANT, LEATHERWOOD & PITTS, P.A. (AV)

Palmetto Bank Building, 306 East North Street, 2nd Floor, P.O. Box 10367, 29603-0367
Telephone: 864-242-2300
Facsimile: 864-242-2280
Email: attorneys@grantleatherwood.com

William M. Grant, Jr.
Judith A. Leatherwood
Michael S. Pitts

Langdon Cheves, III
Paul C. Rathke

LEGAL SUPPORT PERSONNEL

Jackie L. Carver (Litigation Paralegal)
Sarah A. Carmichael (Paralegal)
Mary A. Fuller (Paralegal)

For full biographical listings, see the Martindale-Hubbell Law Directory

HAYNSWORTH, MARION, MCKAY & GUÉRARD, L.L.P. (AV)

75 Beattie Place, Eleventh Floor, P.O. Box 2048, 29602
Telephone: 864-240-3200
Facsimile: 864-240-3300
Columbia, South Carolina Office: Suite 2400 Affinity Building, 1201 Main Street, P.O. Drawer 7157, 29202
Telephone: 803-765-1818.
Facsimile: 803-765-2399.
Charleston, South Carolina Office: 134 Meeting Street, P.O. Box 1119, 29402.
Telephone: 843-722-7606.
Facsimile: 843-724-8016.

MEMBERS OF FIRM

James B. Pressly, Jr.
John B. McLeod
Moffatt Grier McDonald

SPECIAL COUNSEL

John Adams Hodge

Representative Clients: Fluor Daniel, Inc.; Eagle-Picher Industries; Rockwool Manufacturing Co., Inc.; Morton International.

For Complete List of Firm Personnel, See General Section

For full biographical listings, see the Martindale-Hubbell Law Directory

LEATHERWOOD WALKER TODD & MANN, P.C. (AV)

100 East Coffee Street, P.O. Box 87, 29602
Telephone: 864-242-6440
FAX: 864-240-2477
Email: leatherwood@lwtm.com *URL:* http://www.lwtm.com
Spartanburg, South Carolina Office: 1451 East Main Street, P.O. Box 3188.
Telephone: 864-582-4365.
Telefax: 864-583-8961.

J. Richard Kelly
Robert A. deHoll
Eugene C. McCall, Jr.

Counsel for: NationsBank; John D. Hollingsworth on Wheels, Inc.; Canal Insurance Co.; Hollingsworth Saco Lowell Inc.
Representative Clients: Springs Industries, Inc.; General Motors Acceptance Corp.; Suitt Construction Co.

For Complete List of Firm Personnel, See General Section

For full biographical listings, see the Martindale-Hubbell Law Directory

LOVE, THORNTON, ARNOLD & THOMASON, P.A. (AV)

410 East Washington Street, P.O. Box 10045, 29603
Telephone: 864-242-6360
Telefax: 864-271-7972
Email: lovelaw@globalvision.net *URL:* http://www.ltatlaw.com
Greer, South Carolina Office: 1115 West Poinsett Street, P.O. Box 449, 29652-0449.
Telephone: 864-879-0144.
Telefax: 864-879-0149.

(See Next Column)

LOVE, THORNTON, ARNOLD & THOMASON P.A., *Greenville—Continued*

William A. Coates

Counsel for: Owens-Corning; Exide Corp.; Minnesota Mining and Manufacturing Corp.

For Complete List of Firm Personnel, See General Section

For full biographical listings, see the Martindale-Hubbell Law Directory

OGLETREE, DEAKINS, NASH, SMOAK & STEWART, P.C. (AV)

The Ogletree Building, 300 North Main Street, P.O. Box 2757, 29602
Telephone: 864-271-1300
Facsimile: 864-235-8806
Email: Greenville@odnss.com *URL:* http://www.Ogletreedeakins.com
Atlanta, Georgia Office: 600 Peachtree Street, N.E., Suite 2100.
Telephone: 404-881-1300.
Washington, D.C. Office: Fifth Floor, 2400 N Street, N.W.
Telephone: 202-887-0855.
Houston, Texas Office: One Allen Center, 500 Dallas Street, Suite 3000.
Telephone: 713-655-0855.
Chicago, Illinois Office: Twenty-Fifth Floor, Two First National Plaza, 20 South Clark Street.
Telephone: 312-558-1220.
Nashville, Tennessee Office: SunTrust Center, Suite 800, 424 Church Street.
Telephone: 615-254-1900.
Birmingham, Alabama Office: 1900 SouthTrust Tower, 420 North 20th Street.
Telephone: 205-328-1900.
Charleston, South Carolina Office: 134 Meeting Street, Suite 500, P.O. Box 1808.
Telephone: 843-853-1300.
Columbia, South Carolina Office: 1501 Main Street, Suite 600, P.O. Box 11206.
Telephone: 803-252-1300.
Raleigh, North Carolina Office: 4101 Lake Boone Trail, Suite 511, P.O. Box 31608.
Telephone: 919-787-9700.
Winston-Salem, North Carolina Office: 150 South Stratford Road, Suite 350.
Telephone: 336-725-2110.

Ralph M. Mellom
Eric C. Schweitzer
Ronald E. Cardwell
Phillip Lee Conner
Nancy Walker Monts
Elizabeth B. Partlow

Representative Clients: ATMI; Ethyl Corporation; General Electric Company; W.R. Grace; Hoechst Celanese Corporation; Laidlaw Environmental Services; Ravenswood Aluminum Corporation; Schlumberger Limited; Shell Oil; Westinghouse Electric.

For full biographical listings, see the Martindale-Hubbell Law Directory

*SPARTANBURG,** Spartanburg Co.

EDWARDS, BALLARD, BISHOP, STURM, CLARK & KEIM, P.A. (AV)

International Center, Suite 400, 101 North Pine Street, P.O. Box 5398, 29304-5398
Telephone: 864-542-8612
Fax: 864-542-8712
Email: lawfirm@ebbsck.com
Winston-Salem, North Carolina Office: Edwards, Ballard, Clark, Barrett and Carlson, P.A., 380 Knollwood, Suite 730, P.O. Box 1708. 27102-1708.
Telephone: 336-750-0707.
Fax: 336-750-0711.

James F. Edwards, Jr.
Wade E. Ballard
Michael W. Bishop
Kevin W. Sturm
Terry A. Clark (Resident Partner, Edwards, Ballard, Clark, Barrett and Carlson, P.A., Winston-Salem, North Carolina)
Thomas H. Keim, Jr.
Karen M. Tyner
Roger G. Chandler
Patrick L. Cont

S. Clay Keim
Krishna Y. McVey
W. Allen Myrick, Jr.
Penny Correll Wofford

Representative Clients: Texfi Industries, Inc.; Coca-Cola Bottling Co. Consolidated; Kobe Copper Products, Inc.; Van Waters & Rogers, Inc.; Spartanburg Steel Products, Inc.; Century Furniture Co.; Grimes Aerospace Corp.; Sulzer Ruti, Inc.; Comm/Scope, Inc.; South Carolina Insurance Reserve Fund.

For full biographical listings, see the Martindale-Hubbell Law Directory

TENNESSEE

*CHATTANOOGA,** Hamilton Co.

PHILLIP A. FLEISSNER, PLLC (AV)

600 Georgia Avenue, 37402
Telephone: 423-756-3591
Telecopier: 423-266-5455

Phillip A. Fleissner
David C. Nagle
Christopher Price Butler

For full biographical listings, see the Martindale-Hubbell Law Directory

FOSTER, FOSTER, ALLEN & DURRENCE, P.C. (AV)

Formerly Hall, Haynes, Lusk & Foster
801 Broad Street - Suite 515, 37402
Telephone: 423-266-1141
Telecopier: 423-266-4618
Email: dward@ffadlaw.com

George Lane Foster
William M. Foster
Craig R. Allen
Phillip M. Durrence, Jr.
David J. Ward
Clayton M. Whittaker
John M. Hull

LEGAL SUPPORT PERSONNEL

Peggy Sue Bates

Division Counsel For: Norfolk Southern Railway Co.
Attorneys For: CNA/Insurance; United States Fidelity & Guaranty Co. (USF&G); Bridgestone-Firestone, Inc.; Exxon Corp.; Murphy Oil Corp.; Chicago Title Insurance Co.; Jim Walter Homnes; Mid-State Homes, Inc.

For full biographical listings, see the Martindale-Hubbell Law Directory

NELSON, MCMAHAN & NOBLETT (AV)

(An Association of Attorneys)
400 Pioneer Bank Building, 37402
Telephone: 423-756-2291
Fax: 423-756-0737

Randall L. Nelson
Michael A. McMahan
Phillip A. Noblett
Douglas M. Cox
Kenneth O. Fritz
Lawrence W. Kelly

For full biographical listings, see the Martindale-Hubbell Law Directory

WITT, GAITHER & WHITAKER, P.C. (AV)

1100 SunTrust Bank Building, 37402-2608
Telephone: 423-265-8881
Telefax: 423-266-4138; 423-756-5612

Hugh J. Moore, Jr.
Douglas E. Peck

Representative Clients: Carriage Industries, Inc.; Chattanooga Metropolitan Airport Authority; Coca-Cola Bottling Co. Consolidated; Detrex Corporation; The Dixie Group, Inc.; Signal Apparel Company, Inc.; Tecumseh Products Company; U.S. Xpress Enterprises, Inc.

For Complete List of Firm Personnel, See General Section

For full biographical listings, see the Martindale-Hubbell Law Directory

KINGSPORT, Sullivan Co.

HUNTER, SMITH & DAVIS, LLP (AV)

1212 North Eastman Road, P.O. Box 3740, 37664
Telephone: 423-378-8800
Telecopier: 423-378-8801
Email: info@hsdlaw.com *URL:* http://www.hsdlaw.com
Johnson City, Tennessee Office: Suite 500 First American Center, 208 Sunset Drive, 37604.
Telephone: 423-283-6300.
Telecopier: 423-283-6301.

MEMBERS OF FIRM

William T. Wray, Jr.
William C. Argabrite
Gregory K. Haden
Michael L. Forrester
Cynthia S. Kessler

COUNSEL

Edwin L. Treadway

Representative Clients: WMX Technologies (formerly Waste Management of North America); Chemical Waste Management; The Mead Corp.; The Budd Co.; American Greetings Corp.; Birmingham Steel Corp.; Spatco Inc.

For Complete List of Firm Personnel, See General Section

For full biographical listings, see the Martindale-Hubbell Law Directory

*KNOXVILLE,** Knox Co.

BAKER, DONELSON, BEARMAN & CALDWELL (AV)

2200 Riverview Tower, 900 South Gay Street, 37901
Telephone: 423-549-7000
Telecopier: 423-525-8569
Email: info@bdbc.com *URL:* http://www.bakerdonelson.com
Memphis, Tennessee Office: 20th Floor, First Tennessee Building, 165 Madison, 38103.
Telephone: 901-526-2000.
Telecopier: 901-577-2303.
Nashville, Tennessee Office: 1700 Nashville City Center, 511 Union Street, 37219.
Telephone: 615-726-5600.
Telecopier: 615-726-0464.
Chattanooga, Tennessee Office: 1800 Republic Centre, 633 Chestnut Street, 37450-1800.
Telephone: 423-756-2010.
Telecopier: 423-756-3447.
Johnson City, Tennessee Office: SunTrust Bank Building, 207 Mockingbird Lane, P.O. Box 3038, 37602.
Telephone: 423-928-0181.
Telecopier: 423-928-5694; 423-928-3654; Kingsport: 423-246-6191.
Huntsville, Tennessee Office: 3 Courthouse Square, 37756.
Telephone: 423-663-2321.
Telecopier: 423-663-2111.
Washington, D.C. Office: Market Square, 801 Pennsylvania Avenue, N.W., 20004.
Telephone: 202-508-3400.
Telecopier: 202-508-3402.
Jackson, Mississippi Office: Suite 500, 700 North State Street, 39202.
Telephone: 601-351-2400.
Telecopier: 601-351-2424.

MANAGING PARTNER

Stephen E. Roth

PARTNERS

Lewis R. Donelson, III
Howard H. Baker, Jr.
Robert F. Worthington, Jr.
Robert G. McCullough
Richard B. Gossett
James A. McIntosh
Stephen G. Anderson
David E. Fielder
P. Edward Pratt
Mary Dillard Miller
Nelwyn W. Inman
Bruce C. Doeg
Kelli L. Thompson

ASSOCIATES

Wm. Gregory Hall, Jr.
Mary LeAnn Mynatt
Andrew L. Colocotronis
Clarence Risin
Richard D. Plumley
Jason I. Epstein
Suzanne Hefner Bauknight
David L. Morehous (Not admitted in TN)
H. Susanne Bales

For full biographical listings, see the Martindale-Hubbell Law Directory

GILREATH & ASSOCIATES (AV)

550 Main Avenue, Suite 600, P.O. Box 1270, 37901-1270
Telephone: 423-637-2442
Fax: 423-971-4116
Email: gilknox@sidgilreath.com *URL:* http://www.sidgilreath.com
Nashville, Tennessee Office: 2828 Renaissance Tower, 611 Commerce Street.
Telephone: 615-256-3388.
Memphis, Tennessee Office: 44 North Second Street, Suite 200.
Telephone: 901-527-8288.

MEMBER OF FIRM

Sidney W. Gilreath

ASSOCIATES

Meridith C. Bond
Paul Kaufman
Richard L. Duncan
Dianne E. Lashmit
R. Christopher Gilreath
Patricia Taylor Bruner (Not admitted in TN)

LEGAL SUPPORT PERSONNEL

Tammy Ailshie (Legal Assistant to Senior Partner)
Janie Howerton (Legal Assistant)
Darla R. Johnson (Legal Assistant)
Janet L. Tucker (Legal Assistant to Senior Partner)
Pamela Smith Wise (Senior Legal Assistant)
Susan Stogner (Legal Assistant to Senior Partner)
Bryan L. Capps (Legal Administrator)
Danielle E. Barto (Firm Administrator)

Representative Client: Transportation Communications International Union; Brotherhood of Locomotive Engineers Union.
Reference: Suntrust Bank.

For full biographical listings, see the Martindale-Hubbell Law Directory

*MEMPHIS,** Shelby Co.

ARMSTRONG ALLEN PREWITT GENTRY JOHNSTON & HOLMES, PLLC (AV)

Brinkley Plaza, Suite 700, 80 Monroe Avenue, 38103-2467
Telephone: 901-523-8211
Facsimile: 901-524-4936
Little Rock, Arkansas Office: Suite 100, 100 Morgan Keegan Drive, 72202.
Telephone: 501-280-0100.
Facsimile: 501-280-0166.
Jackson, Mississippi Office: 2525 Lakeward Drive, Suite 200, 39216.
Telephone: 601-713-1192.
Facsimile: 601-713-2049.
Jackson, Tennessee Office: 464 North Parkway, Suite A, 38305.
Telephone: 901-660-2332.
Facsimile: 901-664-1109.

MEMBERS OF FIRM

Paul A. Matthews
Randall D. Noel
Mark S. Norris
Sidney W. Farnsworth, III

For Complete List of Firm Personnel, See General Section

For full biographical listings, see the Martindale-Hubbell Law Directory

BAKER, DONELSON, BEARMAN & CALDWELL (AV)

20th Floor, First Tennessee Building, 165 Madison, 38103
Telephone: 901-526-2000
Telecopier: 901-577-2303
Email: info@bdbc.com *URL:* http://www.bakerdonelson.com
Nashville, Tennessee Office: 1700 Nashville City Center, 511 Union Street, 37219.
Telephone: 615-726-5600.
Telecopier: 615-726-0464.
Chattanooga, Tennessee Office: 1800 Republic Centre, 633 Chestnut Street, 37450-1800.
Telephone: 423-756-2010.
Telecopier: 423-756-3447.
Knoxville, Tennessee Office: 2200 Riverview Tower, 900 South Gay Street, 37901.
Telephone: 423-549-7000.
Telecopier: 423-525-8569.
Johnson City, Tennessee Office: SunTrust Bank Building, 207 Mockingbird Lane, P.O. Box 3038, 37602.
Telephone: 423-928-0181.
Telecopier: 423-928-5694; 423-928-3654; Kingsport: 423-246-6191.
Huntsville, Tennessee Office: 3 Courthouse Square, 37756.
Telephone: 423-663-2321.
Telecopier: 423-663-2111.
Washington, D.C. Office: Market Square, 801 Pennsylvania Avenue, N.W., 20004.
Telephone: 202-508-3400.
Telecopier: 202-508-3402.
Jackson, Mississippi Office: Suite 500, 700 North State Street, 39202.
Telephone: 601-351-2400.
Telecopier: 601-351-2424.

MANAGING PARTNER

Robert Mark Glover

SHAREHOLDERS

Lewis R. Donelson, III
Roy Keathley
David G. Williams
Leo Bearman, Jr.
Maurice Wexler
Frank L. Watson, Jr.
Robert Walker
Boyd L. Rhodes, Jr.
W. Michael Richards
John C. Speer
Charles T. Tuggle, Jr.
Larry E. Killebrew
Jerry Stauffer
Robert C. Liddon
William H.D. Fones, Jr.
William P. Kenworthy
Allan J. Wade
Gregory G. Fletcher
Charles C. Harrell
Stephen D. Goodwin
George T. Lewis, III
Ben C. Adams, Jr.
Eugene J. Podesta, Jr.
Sam B. Blair, Jr.
Carla Peacher-Ryan
Mary Aronov
Jill M. Steinberg
Matthew S. Heiter
Michael C. Patton
Janis Wild Kesser
Stephen William Ragland
Monique A. Nassar
Bradley E. Trammell
M. Clay Bethell
Desiree M. Franklin
R. Alan Pritchard, Jr.
Peter H. Kesser

OF COUNSEL

Frierson M. Graves, Jr.
Donald A. Malmo
Lynn Ackerman Landau
Paul E. Risner (Not admitted in TN)

ASSOCIATES

Paul R. O'Rourke
Anne B. Mathes
Elizabeth Einstman Chance
Frank L. Watson, III
W. Douglas Sweet
Wm. Scott Young
Mary Ann Jackson
Angela R. Merideth
Jackie G. Prester
David L. Bearman
Clarissa M. Cissell
Robert C. McConkey, III

(See Next Column)

BAKER, DONELSON, BEARMAN & CALDWELL, *Memphis—Continued*

ASSOCIATES (Continued)

Jennifer R. Keown
Brett T. Parks
Cedric C.Y. Tan
Lang Wiseman
Diane Schratz Holitik
D. Benjamin Bullen
Shannon M. Hernandez
Sylvia Monique Reed
Christopher G. Boling
Louise P. Gaerig
Lori Hackleman Patterson
Lea Hall Speed

For full biographical listings, see the Martindale-Hubbell Law Directory

HARKAVY, SHAINBERG, KOSTEN, KAPLAN & DUNSTAN, PC (AV)

100 Peabody Place, Suite 1300, 38103
Telephone: 901-761-1263
Telecopier: 901-763-3340
Downtown Telecopier: 901-843-0864
Downtown Office: Memphis, Tennessee, 6060 Poplar Avenue, Suite 140, 38119.

MEMBERS AND ASSOCIATES

Ronald M. Harkavy
Raymond M. Shainberg
Alan L. Kosten
Michael D. Kaplan
Allen C. Dunstan
Neil Harkavy
Jerome A. Broadhurst
Alan M. Harkavy

OF COUNSEL

Ira D. Pruitt, Jr.
Laurie A. Cooper
G. Thomas McPherson

For full biographical listings, see the Martindale-Hubbell Law Directory

HARRIS, SHELTON, DUNLAP AND COBB, P.L.L.C. (AV)

Suite 2700, One Commerce Square, 38103-2555
Telephone: 901-525-1455
Telecopier: 901-526-4084
Email: hsdclaw@hsdclaw.com
Other Memphis Office: 6363 Poplar, Suite 430.
Telephone: 901-682-1455.
Fax: 901-682-4446.
Oxford, Mississippi Office: 428 North Lamar Boulevard, Suite 2.
Telephone: 662-238-2855.
Fax: 662-238-2895.

MEMBERS OF FIRM

Walter Chandler (1887-1967)
John H. Harris, Jr.
Max Shelton
William W. Dunlap, Jr.
M. Anderson Cobb, Jr.
James L. Kirby
James R. Garts, Jr.
George T. Wheeler, Jr.
James D. Wilson
Charles C. Drennon, III (Resident, Poplar Avenue Office)
Michael F. Rafferty
A. Neal Graham
G. Rice Byars, Jr.
Jonathan E. Scharff

ASSOCIATES

Tabitha Francisco McNabb
Brett A. Hughes
Chesney Falk McAfee
Christopher S. Campbell
Estelle C. Gaerig
Donrua Barnes-Hulsey
Shawn L. Verner

For full biographical listings, see the Martindale-Hubbell Law Directory

*NASHVILLE,** Davidson Co.

BAKER, DONELSON, BEARMAN & CALDWELL (AV)

1700 Nashville City Center, 511 Union Street, 37219
Telephone: 615-726-5600
Telecopier: 615-726-0464
Email: info@bdbc.com *URL:* http://www.bakerdonelson.com
Memphis, Tennessee Office: 20th Floor, First Tennessee Building, 165 Madison, 38103.
Telephone: 901-526-2000.
Telecopier: 901-577-2303.
Chattanooga, Tennessee Office: 1800 Republic Centre, 633 Chestnut Street, 37450-1800.
Telephone: 423-756-2010.
Telecopier: 423-756-3447.
Knoxville, Tennessee Office: 2200 Riverview Tower, 900 South Gay Street, 37901.
Telephone: 423-549-7000.
Telecopier: 423-525-8569.
Johnson City, Tennessee Office: SunTrust Bank Building, 207 Mockingbird Lane, P.O. Box 3038, 37602.
Telephone: 423-928-0181.
Telecopier: 423-928-5694; 423-928-3654; Kingsport: 423-246-6191.
Huntsville, Tennessee Office: 3 Courthouse Square, 37756.
Telephone: 423-663-2321.
Telecopier: 423-663-2111.
Washington, D.C. Office: Market Square, 801 Pennsylvania Avenue, N.W., 20004.
Telephone: 202-508-3400.
Telecopier: 202-508-3402.
Jackson, Mississippi Office: Suite 500, 700 North State Street, 39202.
Telephone: 601-351-2400.
Telecopier: 601-351-2424.

(See Next Column)

SHAREHOLDERS

Robert M. Steele
Gary C. Shockley

For Complete List of Firm Personnel, See General Section

For full biographical listings, see the Martindale-Hubbell Law Directory

BASS, BERRY & SIMS PLC (AV)

2700 First American Center, 37238-2700
Telephone: 615-742-6200
Telecopy: 615-742-6293
URL: http://www.bassberry.com
Knoxville, Tennessee Office: 1700 Riverview Tower, 900 S. Gay Street, 37902 and P.O. Box 1509, 37901-1509.
Telephone: 423-521-6200.
Telecopy: 423-521-6234.
Memphis, Tennessee Office: 119 S. Main Street, Suite 500, 38103.
Telephone: 901-312-9100.
Fax: 901-312-9101.

MEMBERS OF FIRM

L. Wearen Hughes
J. Andrew Goddard
G. Scott Thomas

ASSOCIATE

Jessalyn Hershinger

Representative Clients: American Water Heater Company; AmeriSteel; Bowater Inc.; General Electric Co.; Goodyear Tire & Rubber Co. Inc.; ITT Corporation; PACCAR, Inc.; Quebecor Printing, Inc.; Santek, Inc.; Smithkline Beecham.

For full biographical listings, see the Martindale-Hubbell Law Directory

TEXAS

*AUSTIN,** Travis Co.

BAKER BOTTS L.L.P. (AV)

1600 San Jacinto Center, 98 San Jacinto Boulevard, 78701
Telephone: 512-322-2500
Fax: 512-322-2501
Email: postmaster@bakerbotts.com *URL:* http://www.bakerbotts.com
Houston, Texas Office: One Shell Plaza, 910 Louisiana.
Telephone: 713-229-1234.
Dallas, Texas Office: 2001 Ross Avenue.
Telephone: 214-953-6500.
Washington, D.C. Office: The Warner, 1299 Pennsylvania Avenue, N.W.
Telephone: 202-639-7700.
New York, New York Office: 599 Lexington Avenue.
Telephone: 212-705-5000.
Moscow, Russia Office: 10 ul. Bolshaya Dimitrovka (formerly Pushkinskaya), 103031.
Telephone: 7095/921-5300 (Local); 7501/929-7070 (International).
London, England Office: 45 Ludgate Hill.
Telephone: 0171-778-1400 (Local); 011-44-171-778-1400 (International).
Baku, Azerbaijan Office: 6-10 Vagif Mustafa-zadeh Street, Third Floor, Icheri Sheher, 370004.
Telephone: 994-12-97-63-88 (Local); 011-994-12-97-63-88 (International).
Fax: 994-12-97-63-61 (Local); 011-994-12-97-63-91 (International).

MEMBERS OF FIRM

Pamela M. Giblin
Aileen M. Hooks
Jennifer Keane
Kevin M. Sadler
Robert T. Stewart
Mark J. White
Larry F. York

SPECIAL COUNSEL

Cynthia C. Smiley

ASSOCIATES

Derek R. McDonald
David A. Savage
Whitney L. Swift

For Complete List of Firm Personnel, See General Section

For full biographical listings, see the Martindale-Hubbell Law Directory

JACKSON WALKER L.L.P. (AV)

100 Congress Avenue, Suite 1100, 78701-4099
Telephone: 512-236-2000
Fax: 512-236-2002
Email: hloftin@jw.com *URL:* http://www.jw.com
Dallas, Texas Office: 901 Main Street, Suite 6000.
Telephone: 214-953-6000.
Fax: 214-953-5822.
Fort Worth, Texas Office: 301 Commerce Street, Suite 2400.
Telephone: 817-334-7200.
Fax: 817-334-7290.
Houston, Texas Office: 1100 Louisiana, Suite 4200.
Telephone: 713-752-4200.
Fax: 713-752-4221.

(See Next Column)

JACKSON WALKER L.L.P.—*Continued*

Richardson, Texas Office: 2435 North Central Expressway, Suite 600.
Telephone: 972-671-2560.
Fax: 972-671-2566.
San Angelo, Texas Office: 225 West Beauregard Avenue.
Telephone: 915-481-2550.
Fax: 915-481-2552.
San Antonio, Texas Office: 112 E. Pecan Street, Suite 2100.
Telephone: 210-978-7700.
Fax: 210-978-7790.

MEMBERS OF FIRM

Leonard H. Dougal
Thomas F. Sedberry
Edward C. Small
Lawrence A. Waks

SENIOR COUNSEL

John A. Riley

For Complete List of Firm Personnel, See General Section

For full biographical listings, see the Martindale-Hubbell Law Directory

LLOYD, GOSSELINK, BLEVINS, ROCHELLE, BALDWIN & TOWNSEND, P.C. (AV)

111 Congress Avenue, Suite 1800, 78701
Telephone: 512-322-5800
Fax: 512-472-0532
Georgetown, Texas Office: 807 South Austin Avenue, 78626.
Telephone: 512-930-1317.
Fax: 512-930-1625.

Robert H. Lloyd
Paul G. Gosselink
Chesley N. Blevins
Martin C. Rochelle
George C. Baldwin
R. Lambeth Townsend
Kerry E. Russell
Georgia N. Crump

Richard L. Hamala
Paula Fisher Baldwin
Erich M. Birch
Michael J. Nasi
Lauren J. Kalisek
Cindy L. Becker
Angela K. Moorman
Judith I. McGeary
Brian L. Sledge
Steven A. Porter
Geoffrey M. Gay

GOVERNMENT RELATIONS

Marc A. Rodriguez (Government Relations Consultant)

For full biographical listings, see the Martindale-Hubbell Law Directory

THOMPSON & KNIGHT L.L.P. (AV)

(Attorneys and Counselors)
1200 San Jacinto Center, 98 San Jacinto Boulevard, 78701
Telephone: 512-469-6100
Telecopy: 512-469-6180
URL: http://www.tklaw.com
Dallas, Texas Office: 1700 Pacific Avenue, Suite 3300, 75201.
Telephone: 214-969-1700.
Telecopy: 512-969-1751.
Telex: 732298.
Fort Worth, Texas Office: 801 Cherry Street, Suite 1600, 76102.
Telephone: 817-347-1700.
Telecopy: 817-347-1799.
Houston, Texas Office: Thompson Knight Brown Parker & Leahy L.L.P., 1200 Smith Street, Suite 3600, 77002-4595.
Telephone: 713-654-8111.
Telecopier: 713-654-1871.
San Pedro Garza Garcia, Nuevo León, Mexico Office: Edificio Losoles PD-4, Av. Lázaro Cárdenas No. 2400 Pte., C.P. 66220.
Telephone: (52-8) 363-0096.
Telecopy: (52-8) 363-3067.

PARTNERS

Becky L. Jolin
James C. Morriss III

ASSOCIATE

Matthew J. Knifton

SENIOR ATTORNEY

Elizabeth A. Webb

OF COUNSEL

Mark L. Murdock

For Complete List of Firm Personnel, See General Section

For full biographical listings, see the Martindale-Hubbell Law Directory

*BEAUMONT,** Jefferson Co.

BENCKENSTEIN & OXFORD, L.L.P. (AV)

Community Bank Building, P.O. Box 150, 77704
Telephone: 409-833-9182
Cable Address: "Bmor"
Telex: 779485
Telefax: 409-833-8819
Email: lawfirm@benoxford.com
Houston, Texas Office: Two Post Oak Central, 1980 Post Oak Boulevard, Suite 1600, 77056.
Telephone: 713-629-0345.
Fax: 713-629-0614.

MEMBERS OF FIRM

L. J. Benckenstein (1894-1966)
F. L. Benckenstein (1918-1987)
Hubert Oxford, III
Alan G. Sampson
Frank D. Calvert
Dana Timaeus
Frances Blair Bethea
Robert J. Rose, Sr.

ASSOCIATES

F. Blair Clarke
Michael K. Eaves
Alex J. Stelly, Jr.
Robert W. Craft
Lauren Miller Robbins (Resident, Houston Office)

Representative Clients: Marine Office of American Corp. (MOAC); Moran Towing and Transportation Co., Inc.

For full biographical listings, see the Martindale-Hubbell Law Directory

MEHAFFY & WEBER, A PROFESSIONAL CORPORATION (AV)

2615 Calder Avenue, Suite 800, P.O. Box 16, 77704
Telephone: 409-835-5011
Fax: 409-835-5729; 835-5177
Email: MehaffyWeber.com
Orange, Texas Office: 1006 Green Avenue, P.O. Drawer 189.
Telephone: 409-886-7766.
Houston, Texas Office: One Allen Center, 500 Dallas, Suite 1200.
Telephone: 713-655-1200.

James W. Mehaffy (1914-1985)
Jim I. Graves
John Cash Smith
Arthur R. Almquist
Gene M. Williams
David B. Gaultney
Sandra F. Clark
M. C. Carrington
Barbara J. Barron
Keith W. Foley
Charles Stanton Perry
Ernest W. Boyd
Michele Y. Smith

Vickie R. Thompson
Paul R. Heyburn
Debra N. Bigler
Charles W. Goehringer, Jr.
Peter T. Gregg
Nikkee E. Rutherford
Maryalyce W. Cox
Timothy A. Gasaway
Elna Nguyen Griggs
Sean Stotsky

OF COUNSEL

Otto J. Weber, Jr.

Representative Clients: E.I. du Pont de Nemours and Co.; Eli Lilly & Co.; Merrell Dow; Jefferson County Tax Appraisal District; W.R. Grace & Co.-Conn.; Bank of America; Christus Health; Christus St. Elizabeth; Christus St. Mary; Burlington Northern Santa Fe Railway.
Approved Attorneys for: Stewart Title Guaranty Co.

For Complete List of Firm Personnel, See General Section

For full biographical listings, see the Martindale-Hubbell Law Directory

*BROWNSVILLE,** Cameron Co.

RODRIGUEZ, COLVIN & CHANEY, L.L.P. (AV)

1201 East Van Buren, P.O. Box 2155, 78520
Telephone: 956-542-7441
Fax: 956-541-2170
McAllen, Texas Office: 4900 North 10th.
Telephone: 956-686-1287.
Telecopier: 956-686-6197.
Harlingen, Texas Office: 402 East Van Buren.
Telephone: 956-423-0216.
Telecopier: 956-423-2035.

MEMBERS OF FIRM

Eduardo R. Rodriguez
Norton A. Colvin, Jr.
Mitchell C. Chaney
Marjory Colvin Batsell
Jaime A. Saenz
Joseph A. (Tony) Rodriguez
Alison D. Kennamer

ASSOCIATES

Laura J. Urbis
Lecia L. Chaney
Daniel D. Herink
Robert Patrick Rodriguez
Rosa Maria Villagomez
Vanessa Garza
Teri L. Danish

(See Next Column)

RODRIGUEZ, COLVIN & CHANEY L.L.P., *Brownsville—Continued*

OF COUNSEL

Orrin W. Johnson (Resident, Harlingen Office)
Benjamin S. Hardy (1912-1993)
Neil E. Norquest (Resident, McAllen Office)
Chris A. Brisack (Resident, McAllen Office)
Raymond A. Cowley

Division Attorneys for: Union Pacific Railroad.
Counsel for: Texas Commerce Bank-Rio Grande Valley, N.A.; Texas Commerce Bancshares, Inc.

For full biographical listings, see the Martindale-Hubbell Law Directory

*DALLAS,** Dallas Co.

CALHOUN & STACY (AV)

Suite 5700 - Bank of America Plaza, 901 Main Street, 75202-3713
Telephone: 214-748-5000
Facsimile: 214-748-1421
Email: info@calhounstacy.com *URL:* http://www.calhounstacy.com

MEMBERS OF FIRM

Mark Alan Calhoun
Dennis D. Conder
LeAnn Wainscott Cross
David W. Elrod
Roy L. Stacy
Michael C. Wright

ASSOCIATES

Scott S. Crocker
Sean P. Fitzgerald
Elizabeth Reding Gambrell
Joel W. Reese
Barbara L. Wohlrabe

For Complete List of Firm Personnel, See General Section

For full biographical listings, see the Martindale-Hubbell Law Directory

THOMPSON & KNIGHT L.L.P. (AV)

(Attorneys and Counselors)
1700 Pacific Avenue Suite 3300, 75201
Telephone: 214-969-1700
Telecopy: 214-969-1751
Telex: 732 298
URL: http://www.tklaw.com
Austin, Texas Office: 1200 San Jacinto Center, 98 San Jacinto Boulevard, 78701.
Telephone: 512-469-6100.
Telecopy: 512-469-6180.
Fort Worth, Texas Office: 801 Cherry Street, Suite 1600, 76102.
Telephone: 817-347-1700.
Telecopy: 817-347-1799.
Houston, Texas Office: Thompson Knight Brown Parker & Leahy L.L.P., 1200 Smith Street, Suite 3600, 77002-4595.
Telephone: 713-654-8111.
Telecopier: 713-654-1871.
San Pedro Garza Garcia, Nuevo León, Mexico Office: Edificio Losoles PD-4, Av. Lázaro Cárdenas No. 2400 Pte., C.P. 66220.
Telephone: (52-8) 363-0096.
Telecopy: (52-8) 363-3067.

PARTNERS

Gregg C. Davis
Scott D. Deatherage
Howard L. Gilberg
James B. Harris
A. Kay Roska

ASSOCIATE

Scott F. Wendorf

For Complete List of Firm Personnel, See General Section

For full biographical listings, see the Martindale-Hubbell Law Directory

*HOUSTON,** Harris Co.

BAKER BOTTS L.L.P. (AV)

One Shell Plaza, 910 Louisiana, 77002
Telephone: 713-229-1234
Cable Address: "Boterlove"
Fax: 713-229-1522
Email: postmaster@bakerbotts.com *URL:* http://www.bakerbotts.com
Washington, D.C. Office: The Warner, 1299 Pennsylvania Avenue, N.W.
Telephone: 202-639-7700.
New York, New York Office: 599 Lexington Avenue.
Telephone: 212-705-5000.
Austin, Texas Office: 1600 San Jacinto Center, 98 San Jacinto Boulevard.
Telephone: 512-322-2500.
Dallas, Texas Office: 2001 Ross Avenue.
Telephone: 214-953-6500.
Moscow, Russia Office: 10 ul. Bolshaya Dimitrovka (formerly Pushkinskaya), 103031.
Telephone: 7095/921-5300 (Local); 7095/929-7070 (International).
London, England Office: 45 Ludgate Hill.
Telephone: 0171-778-1400 (Local); 011-44-171-778-1400 (International).
Baku, Azerbaijan Office: 6-10 Vagif Mustafa-zadeh Street, Third Floor, Icheri Sheher, 370004.
Telephone: 994-12-97-63-88 (Local); 011-994-12-97-63-88 (International).
Fax: 994-12-97-63-91 (Local); 011-994-12-97-63-91 (International)

(See Next Column)

MEMBERS OF FIRM

David F. Asmus
F. Walter Conrad, Jr.
Larry B. Feldcamp
Frank W. R. Hubert, Jr.
Matthew L. Kuryla
Karen Kay Maston
Bradley I. Raffle
George T. Shipley
Stephen Gillham Tipps
Hugh Tucker
Robert P. Wright

ASSOCIATES

Jed P. Anderson
Pamela Roger Laborde

For Complete List of Firm Personnel, See General Section

For full biographical listings, see the Martindale-Hubbell Law Directory

FLEMING & ASSOCIATES, L.L.P. (AV)

1330 Post Oak Boulevard, Suite 3030, 77056
Telephone: 713-621-7944
Fax: 713-621-9638
URL: http://www.fleming-law.com

George M. Fleming
Robert R. Herring, Jr.
Sylvia Davidow
Bruce B. Kemp
Jim Doyle
Russell T. Abney
D'Lisa R. Simmons
Katrina Von Hedemann
Rand P. Nolen
Christopher A. Kesler
Andres C. Pereira
G. Sean Jez
Anthony E. Farah

For full biographical listings, see the Martindale-Hubbell Law Directory

GALLAGHER, YOUNG, LEWIS, HAMPTON & DOWNEY, L.L.P. (AV)

NationsBank Building, 700 Louisiana, 40th Floor, 77002
Telephone: 713-222-8080
Fax: 713-222-0066

Michael T. Gallagher
William H. Young
Craig Lewis
Hartley Hampton
Daniel M. Downey

Martin John de la Torre
Andrew Sher
Candace Kaiser Eindorf
Scott H. Mclemore
John J. Klevenhagen, III
Araceli E. Flores

OF COUNSEL

Rosemary Conlon McCarthy

For full biographical listings, see the Martindale-Hubbell Law Directory

GILPIN, PAXSON & BERSCH (AV)

A Registered Limited Liability Partnership
Attorney at Law
1900 West Loop South, Suite 2000, 77027-3259
Telephone: 713-623-8800
Telecopier: 713-993-8451
Email: gpb@gpblaw.com *URL:* http://www.texinslaw.com

PARTNERS

Gary M. Alletag
Timothy R. Bersch
John D. Gilpin
Darryl W. Malone
Michael J. Pappert
Stephen Paxson
Kevin F. Risley

OF COUNSEL

Harless R. Benthul
David F. Webb

ASSOCIATES

Joseph D. Batson
Jeri Pharis Wechsler

Representative Clients: BMW of North America, Inc.; Federal Deposit Insurance Corporation; Greater Houston Builders Association; Owens Corning Fiberglas Corporation; Shaw Industries, Inc.; Southwest Guaranty Trust Company, N.A.; Sprint Communications Company L.P.; Volkswagen of America, Inc.; Volvo North America Corporation; Wells Fargo Bank (Texas), N.A.

For full biographical listings, see the Martindale-Hubbell Law Directory

JACKSON WALKER L.L.P. (AV)

1100 Louisiana, Suite 4200, P.O. Box 4771, 77002
Telephone: 713-752-4200
Fax: 713-752-4221
URL: http://www.jw.com
Austin, Texas Office: 100 Congress Avenue, Suite 1100.
Telephone: 512-236-2000.
Fax: 512-236-2002.
Dallas, Texas Office: 901 Main Street, Suite 6000.
Telephone: 214-953-6000.
Fax: 214-953-5822.
Fort Worth, Texas Office: 301 Commerce Street, Suite 2400.
Telephone: 817-334-7200.
Fax: 817-334-7290.

(See Next Column)

JACKSON WALKER L.L.P.—*Continued*

Richardson, Texas Office: 2435 North Central Expressway, Suite 600.
Telephone: 972-671-2560.
Fax: 972-671-2566.
San Angelo, Texas Office: 225 West Beauregard Avenue.
Telephone: 915-481-2550.
Fax: 915-481-2552.
San Antonio, Texas Office: 112 E. Pecan Street, Suite 2100.
Telephone: 210-978-7700.
Fax: 210-978-7790.

MEMBERS OF FIRM

John R. Clayton
Tracey Smith Lindeen
Charles G. Miller

For Complete List of Firm Personnel, See General Section

For full biographical listings, see the Martindale-Hubbell Law Directory

MEHAFFY & WEBER, A PROFESSIONAL CORPORATION (AV)

One Allen Center, 500 Dallas, Suite 1200, 77002
Telephone: 713-655-1200
Fax: 713-655-0222
Email: MehaffyWeber.com
Beaumont, Texas Office: 2615 Calder Avenue, Suite 800, P.O. Box 16.
Telephone: 409-835-5011.
Orange, Texas Office: 1006 Green Avenue, P.O. Drawer 189.
Telephone: 409-886-7766.

Jim I. Graves
Arthur R. Almquist
Charles Stanton Perry

Paul R. Heyburn
Debra N. Bigler
James G. Martingano
Peter T. Gregg
Elna Nguyen Griggs

Representative Clients: E.I. duPont de Nemours and Co.; W.R. Grace & Co.-Conn.; Merrill Dow; Eli Lilly & Company; Burlington, Northen, Santa Fe Railway Company; Christus Health.

For full biographical listings, see the Martindale-Hubbell Law Directory

RAMSEY & MURRAY, A PROFESSIONAL CORPORATION (AV)

10000 Memorial Drive, Suite 700, 77024-3412
Telephone: 713-613-5400
Fax: 713-613-5414

Ben Ramsey
Mark Ramsey
John A. Murray, Jr.
Curtis D. Collette
Russell J. Ramsey
Michael Stout Wright
Rick McRory

Joseph W. Gagnon
Adrian V. Villacorta
R. Russell Hollenbeck
Brenda Renee Ferguson

Representative Clients: Great Central Insurance Co.; Republic Insurance Co.

For full biographical listings, see the Martindale-Hubbell Law Directory

MCALLEN, Hidalgo Co.

RODRIGUEZ, COLVIN & CHANEY, L.L.P. (AV)

4900 North 10th Street, 78504
Telephone: 956-686-1287
Telecopier: 956-686-6197
Brownsville, Texas Office: 1201 East Van Buren Street.
Telephone: 956-542-7441.
Telecopier: 956-541-2170.
Harlingen, Texas Office: 402 East Van Buren.
Telephone: 956-423-0216.
Telecopier: 956-423-2035.

OF COUNSEL

Neil E. Norquest
Chris A. Brisack
Raymond A. Cowley

Division Attorneys for: Union Pacific Railroad.
Counsel for: Texas Commerce Bank-Rio Grande Valley, N.A.; Texas Commerce Bancshares, Inc.

For full biographical listings, see the Martindale-Hubbell Law Directory

*ORANGE,** Orange Co.

MEHAFFY & WEBER, A PROFESSIONAL CORPORATION (AV)

1006 Green Avenue, P.O. Drawer 189, 77630
Telephone: 409-886-7766
Fax: 409-886-7790
Email: MehaffyWeber.com
Beaumont, Texas Office: 2615 Calder Avenue, Suite 800, P.O. Box 16.
Telephone: 409-835-5011.
Houston, Texas Office: One Allen Center, 500 Dallas, Suite 1200.
Telephone: 713-655-1200.

(See Next Column)

John Cash Smith

Representative Clients: Sabine River Authority of Texas; Equitable Bag Co., Southern Division; Texas Farm Bureau; City of Orange; CNA Insurance, Maryland Casualty/Zurich Insurance Co.

For full biographical listings, see the Martindale-Hubbell Law Directory

*VICTORIA,** Victoria Co.

WALKER, KEELING & CARROLL, L.L.P. (AV)

210 East Constitution, P.O. Box 108, 77902
Telephone: 361-576-6800
Fax: 361-576-6196
Email: wkc@wkcfirm.com

Ronald B. Walker
W. Lee Keeling
Terry M. Carroll, Jr.
Patricia L. Hayden
Donna K. Grafe

LEGAL SUPPORT PERSONNEL

Sue A. Comstock (Legal Assistant)

For full biographical listings, see the Martindale-Hubbell Law Directory

UTAH

*SALT LAKE CITY,** Salt Lake Co.

CALLISTER NEBEKER & MCCULLOUGH, A PROFESSIONAL CORPORATION (AV)

Gateway Tower East, Suite 900, 10 East South Temple, 84133
Telephone: 801-530-7300
Telecopier: 801-364-9127
Email: mjeaston@cnmlaw.com *URL:* http://www.cnmlaw.com

Fred W. Finlinson
Brian W. Burnett
James R. Holbrook
Jan M. Bergeson
John B. Lindsay

Representative Clients: Central Valley Water Reclamation Facility Board; Washington County Conservancy District; Sinclair Oil (Little America).

For Complete List of Firm Personnel, See General Section

For full biographical listings, see the Martindale-Hubbell Law Directory

PARR WADDOUPS BROWN GEE & LOVELESS, A PROFESSIONAL CORPORATION (AV)

Suite 1300, 185 South State Street, 84111-1537
Telephone: 801-532-7840
Fax: 801-532-7750
URL: http://www.pwlaw.com

Clark Waddoups
Steven J. Christiansen
Carolyn B. McHugh
John M. Burke
Mark A. Wagner

For Complete List of Firm Personnel, See General Section

For full biographical listings, see the Martindale-Hubbell Law Directory

PARSONS BEHLE & LATIMER, A PROFESSIONAL CORPORATION (AV)

One Utah Center, 201 South Main Street, Suite 1800, P.O. Box 45898, 84145-0898
Telephone: 801-532-1234
Telecopy: 801-536-6111
Email: pbl@pblutah.com *URL:* http://www.pblutah.com

James B. Lee
Jim Butler
Gordon L. Roberts
Craig D. Galli
Lawrence E. Stevens
James E. Karkut
Daniel M. Allred
Michael J. Malmquist
Dallin W. Jensen
H. Douglas Owens
David R. Bird
Alan K. Flake Jr.
David W. Tundermann
Lisa A. Kirschner
Neil Orloff
Michael A. Zody
Lee Kapaloski
Michael J. Tomko
Lucy B. Jenkins
Edward B. Grandy
David L. Deisley
Richard J. Angell
Hal J. Pos
Anne E. Rice
J. Michael Bailey
Vicki M. Baldwin
M. Lindsay Ford
Jared G. Parkinson (Not admitted in UT)

OF COUNSEL

Keith E. Taylor

Representative Clients: Barrick Gold Corp.; Kennecott Corp.; Questar Corp.; EG&G Defense Materials, Inc.

(See Next Column)

PARSONS BEHLE & LATIMER A PROFESSIONAL CORPORATION, *Salt Lake City—Continued*

For Complete List of Firm Personnel, See General Section

For full biographical listings, see the Martindale-Hubbell Law Directory

PARSONS, DAVIES, KINGHORN & PETERS, P.C. (AV)

185 South State Street, Suite 700, 84111
Telephone: 801-363-4300
Facsimile: 801-363-4378
Email: Attorneys@pdkplaw.com

Glen E. Davies
Gerald H. Kinghorn

For Complete List of Firm Personnel, See General Section

For full biographical listings, see the Martindale-Hubbell Law Directory

SCALLEY & READING, A PROFESSIONAL CORPORATION (AV)

261 East 300 South, Second Floor, 84111
Telephone: 801-531-7870
Fax: 801-531-7968
Email: law@scalleyreading.com

Ford G. Scalley
J. Bruce Reading
Marlon L. Bates
John Edward Hansen
Scott N. Rasmussen
Steven B. Smith

Wesley D. Hutchins
Kami L. Peterson
Amy D. Kraus
Darwin H. Bingham
Lisa A. Jones

For full biographical listings, see the Martindale-Hubbell Law Directory

SNELL & WILMER L.L.P. (AV)

111 East Broadway, Suite 900, 84111-1004
Telephone: 801-237-1900
Fax: 801-237-1950
URL: http://www.swlaw.com
Phoenix, Arizona Office: One Arizona Center, 85004-2202.
Telephone: 602-382-6000.
Fax: 602-382-6070.
Tucson, Arizona Office: One South Church Avenue, Suite 1500, 85701-1612.
Telephone: 520-882-1200.
Fax: 520-884-1294.
Orange County Office: 1920 Main Street, Suite 1200, Irvine, California 92614-7230.
Telephone: 949-253-2700.
Fax: 949-955-2507.

MEMBERS OF FIRM

Phillip Wm. Lear
Denise A. Dragoo

ASSOCIATES

Erik G. Davis
Chris D. Jones

Representative Clients: For list of Representative Clients, see end of biographical listings in the Martindale-Hubbell Law Directory.

For Complete List of Firm Personnel, See General Section

For full biographical listings, see the Martindale-Hubbell Law Directory

VAN COTT, BAGLEY, CORNWALL & MCCARTHY, A PROFESSIONAL CORPORATION (AV)

50 South Main Street, Suite 1600, P.O. Box 45340, 84145-0340
Telephone: 801-532-3333
Telecopier: 801-534-0058
Email: info@vancott.com *URL:* http://www.vancott.com
Ogden, Utah Office: 2404 Washington Boulevard, Suite 900.
Telephone: 801-394-5783.
Park City, Utah Office: 2200 Park Avenue, Suite C200-A.
Telephone: 435-649-3889.

Thomas W. Clawson
H. Michael Keller
Matthew F. McNulty, III
Gregory P. Williams

Mara A. Brown

For Complete List of Firm Personnel, See General Section

For full biographical listings, see the Martindale-Hubbell Law Directory

VERMONT

*BURLINGTON,** Chittenden Co.

GRAVEL AND SHEA, A PROFESSIONAL CORPORATION (AV)

Corporate Plaza, 76 St. Paul Street, P.O. Box 369, 05402-0369
Telephone: 802-658-0220
Fax: 802-658-1456

Stephen R. Crampton
John R. Ponsetto
Dennis R. Pearson
Robert F. O'Neill
Robert H. Rushford

For Complete List of Firm Personnel, See General Section

For full biographical listings, see the Martindale-Hubbell Law Directory

MANCHESTER LAW OFFICES, PROFESSIONAL CORPORATION (AV)

One Lawson Lane, P.O. Box 1459, 05402-1459
Telephone: 802-658-7444
Fax: 802-658-2078
Email: mlo@together.net *URL:* http://www.lawyers.com/manchesterlaw

Robert E. Manchester

Tina L. Shoup
George N. Collias

LEGAL SUPPORT PERSONNEL

Maureen P. Neacy (Legal Nurse Consultant)

For full biographical listings, see the Martindale-Hubbell Law Directory

VIRGINIA

NORFOLK, (Independent City)

VANDEVENTER BLACK LLP (AV)

500 World Trade Center, 23510-1699
Telephone: 757-446-8600
Cable Address: "Hughsvan"
Telecopier: 757-446-8670
URL: http://www.vanblk.com
Kitty Hawk, North Carolina Office: 6 Juniper Trail.
Telephone: 252-261-5055.
Fax: 252-261-8444. E-Mail: nshearin@pinn.net.
London, England Office: Mitre House, 4th Floor, 12-14 Mitre Street.
Telephone: (0171) 623-2081.
Facsimile: (0171) 929-0043.

PARTNERS OF FIRM

Carter T. Gunn
Michael L. Sterling
Patrick A. Genzler
Neil S. Lowenstein

For Complete List of Firm Personnel, See General Section

For full biographical listings, see the Martindale-Hubbell Law Directory

PORTSMOUTH, (Independent City)

COOPER, SPONG & DAVIS, P.C. (AV)

Wachovia Bank Building, 200 High Street Suite 500, P.O. Box 1475, 23705-1475
Telephone: 757-397-3481
Fax: 757-397-8167
Email: csdlaw@pop.erols.com

Clyde W. Cooper (1893-1980)
William B. Spong, Jr. (1920-1997)
Richard J. Davis (1921-1999)
Vincent L. Parker (1920-1989)
H. Thomas Fennell, Jr. (1937-1981)
James H. Flippen, III (1957-1996)
Robert C. Barclay, III
Albert J. Taylor, Jr.
Ralph W. Buxton
David R. Tynch
Gregory M. Pomije
Susan Taylor Hansen
Robert C. Barclay IV

Christopher S. Boynton
Branch H. Daniels, Jr.
Stephen A. Leon
Jeffrey S. Miller
C. Gerard Thompson
Paul L. Warren

OF COUNSEL

Arnold H. Leon

General Counsel: Portsmouth Redevelopment and Housing Authority; Maryview Hospital; Virga Pizza Crust of Virginia, Inc.; Tidewater Area Central Hospital Laundry, Inc.; Action Oldsmobile-Cadillac-GMC Trucks, Inc.; Don Comer Ford.
Local Counsel: Wachovia Bank; Bell Atlantic.

For full biographical listings, see the Martindale-Hubbell Law Directory

RICHMOND, (Independent City)

LITTLE, PARSLEY & CLUVERIUS, P.C. (AV)

1300 Federal Reserve Bank Building, P.O. Box 555, 23218
Telephone: 804-644-4100
Facsimile: 804-644-0800
Email: admin@lpc-va.com

George B. Little
J. Terry Parsley
James K. Cluverius

Nathan McAdams Lord
Andrew M. Lohmann

Reference: Crestar Bank.

For full biographical listings, see the Martindale-Hubbell Law Directory

WILLIAMS, MULLEN, CLARK & DOBBINS, A PROFESSIONAL CORPORATION (AV)

Two James Center, 1021 East Cary Street, P.O. Box 1320, 23218-1320
Telephone: 804-643-1991
Fax: 804-783-6507
URL: http://www.wmcd.com
Newport News Office: Harbor Bank Center, Suite 210, One Old Oyster Point Road, 23602-7119.
Telephone: 757-249-5100.
Fax: 757-249-5109.
Virginia Beach Office: One Columbus Center, 23462-6763.
Telephone: 757-499-8800.
Fax: 757-473-0395.
Vienna Office: 1593 Spring Hill Road, Suite 510, 22182.
Telephone: 703-760-5200.
Fax: 703-748-0244.
Washington, D.C. Office: The Farragut Building, 900 17th Street, N.W., Suite 700, 20006.
Telephone: 202-293-0213.
Fax: 804-783-6507. Fax Within D.C.: 202-293-5939.
London, England Office: Blake Lodge, Bridge Lane, SW11 3AD.
Telephone: (011-44-71) 223-2756.
Fax: (011-44-71) 350-0156.
Riyadh, Saudi Arabia Affiliate Office: Saudi-American Legal Consultants Commercial Building #2, Diplomatic Quarter, P.O. Box 57270, 11574.
Telephone: (011-966-1) 488-1563.
Fax: (011-966-1) 488-0542.

Thomas E. Knauer
William R. Mauck, Jr.
Channing J. Martin
Clayton L. Walton

For Complete List of Firm Personnel, See General Section

For full biographical listings, see the Martindale-Hubbell Law Directory

ROANOKE, Roanoke City Co.

WOOTEN & HART, A PROFESSIONAL CORPORATION (AV)

707 Building, Suite 300, P.O. Box 12247, 24024-2247
Telephone: 540-343-2451; 540-342-9672
Telecopier: 540-345-6417
URL: http://www.wootenhart.com

George W. Wooten
Bradley D. McGraw
David B. Hart
John L. Cooley
L. Thompson Hanes
Thomas W. Farrell
Susan A. Waddell
Paul C. Kuhnel
Peter D. Vieth

David W. Hearn
Christopher W. Stevens
John Mark Cooley
Elizabeth D. Guilbert
Eunice Park Austin

OF COUNSEL

M. Lanier Woodrum

Representative Clients: Wachovia Bank; St. Paul Insurance Cos.
Approved Attorneys for: Lawyers Title Insurance Corp.
Reference: First Union National Bank.

For full biographical listings, see the Martindale-Hubbell Law Directory

WASHINGTON

*SEATTLE,** King Co.

BARRETT GILMAN & ZIKER (AV)

A Partnership including Professional Service Corporations
1000 Second Avenue, Suite 3500, 98104-1063
Telephone: 206-464-1900
Fax: 206-667-9087
Email: bgz@bgz.com *URL:* http://www.bgz.com

(See Next Column)

MEMBERS OF FIRM

Paul A. Barrett (P.S.)
Barry G. Ziker (P.S.)
Thomas L. Gilman (P.S.)
Thomas A. Carr (P.S.)

ASSOCIATE

Amy C. Hevly

OF COUNSEL

David A. Shaw

Reference: U.S. Bank, Seattle, Washington.

For full biographical listings, see the Martindale-Hubbell Law Directory

BUCK & GORDON LLP (AV)

902 Waterfront Place, 1011 Western Avenue, 98104-1097
Telephone: 206-382-9540
Telecopier: 206-626-0675
Email: BG@buckgordon.com

Alison D. Birmingham
Jay P. Derr
William H. Block
Joel M. Gordon
Peter L. Buck
Amy L. Kosterlitz
Brent Carson
Keith E. Moxon
Samuel W. Plauché, IV

Susan M. Ridgley

OF COUNSEL

Aliza C. Allen
Kitteridge Oldham

LEGAL SUPPORT PERSONNEL

PROJECT MANAGER

Bradley J. S. Liljequist

COMMUNITY RELATIONS

Margaret E. Potter

PARALEGAL

Patricia J. Wolfson

Reference: Seafirst Bank, Seattle, Washington (Metropolitan Branch).

For full biographical listings, see the Martindale-Hubbell Law Directory

LANE POWELL SPEARS LUBERSKY LLP (AV)

Limited Liability Partnership composed of Individuals and Professional Service Corporations
1420 Fifth Avenue, Suite 4100, 98101-2338
Telephone: 206-223-7000
Facsimile: 206-223-7107
Email: information@lanepowell.com *URL:* http://www.lanepowell.com
Other Offices at: Portland, Oregon; Anchorage, Alaska; Olympia and Mount Vernon, Washington; London, England.

MEMBERS OF FIRM

Glenn J. Amster
Dale E. Kremer
Robert R. Davis, Jr.
Michael A. Nesteroff
Grant S. Degginger
Douglas E. Wheeler

Representative Clients: Battle Mountain Gold Company; Exxon Corp.; Fort James Corp.; Georgia-Pacific Corp.; Home Depot USA, Inc.; Les Schwab Tire Centers, Inc.; Nucor Corp.; Texaco Inc.; Union pacific Railroad Company; Wells Fargo Bank.

For Complete List of Firm Personnel, See General Section

For full biographical listings, see the Martindale-Hubbell Law Directory

JOHN W. LUNDIN, P.S. (AV)

710 Cherry Street, 98104
Telephone: 206-623-8346
Fax: 206-623-5951
Email: jwlundin@nwnexus.com

John W. Lundin

Reference: Key Bank (Main Branch).

For full biographical listings, see the Martindale-Hubbell Law Directory

MARTEN & BROWN LLP (AV)

1191 Second Avenue, Suite 2200, 98101
Telephone: 206-292-6300
Fax: 206-292-6301
Email: lawyers@martenbrown.com
Olympia, Washington Office: 421 South Capital Way, Suite 303, 98501.
Telephone: 360-786-5057.
Fax: 360-786-1835.

MEMBERS OF FIRM

Rodney L. Brown, Jr.
Jay J. Manning
Bradley M. Marten
Stephen T. Parkinson
Gillis E. Reavis
Gregory T. Costello

ASSOCIATES

Joshua M. Lipsky
Kurt B. Peterson
Lorna Luebbe
Alexandra K. Smith

(See Next Column)

MARTEN & BROWN LLP, *Seattle—Continued*

OF COUNSEL

Tanya Barnett
Stimson Bullitt
Robin Kix Rock

LEGAL SUPPORT PERSONNEL

J. Daniel Ballbach (Chief Executive Officer)
Larry D. Christian (Chief Administrative Officer)

For full biographical listings, see the Martindale-Hubbell Law Directory

SUMMIT LAW GROUP, PLLC (AV)

1505 Westlake Avenue North, Suite 300, 98109
Telephone: 206-281-9881
Fax: 206-281-9882
Email: info@summitlaw.com *URL:* http://www.summitlaw.com

Karen A. Andersen
Kristin D. Anger
Laura A. Bertin
Lynn M. Engel
Michael J. Erickson
Matthew R. Harris
David M. Heineck
Elizabeth Butler Kennar
Otto G. Klein, III
Lawrence C. Locker
Philip S. McCune
Polly L. McNeill
Ralph H. Palumbo
Bruce L. Schroeder
William R. Squires III
Monika Vasil
Mark F. Worthington
Rodney B. Younker

For full biographical listings, see the Martindale-Hubbell Law Directory

WEST VIRGINIA

*CHARLESTON,** Kanawha Co.

JACKSON & KELLY (AV)

1600 Laidley Tower, P.O. Box 553, 25322
Telephone: 304-340-1000
Fax: 304-340-1130
Email: info@jacksonkelly.com *URL:* http://www.jacksonkelly.com
Martinsburg, West Virginia Office: 300 Foxcroft Avenue, P.O. Box 1068.
Telephone: 304-263-8800.
Fax: 304-263-7110.
Morgantown, West Virginia Office: 6000 Hampton Center, P.O. Box 619.
Telephone: 304-599-3000.
Fax: 304-285-2040.
New Martinsville, West Virginia Office: 256 Russell Avenue, P.O. Box 68.
Telephone: 304-455-1751.
Fax: 304-455-6314.
Parkersburg, West Virginia Office: 412 Market Street, Suite 202, P.O. Box 1144.
Telephone: 304-424-3490.
Fax: 304-424-3499.
Fairmont, West Virginia Office: 1000 Technology Drive, Suite 1310.
Telephone: 304-368-2000.
Fax: 304-368-2020.
Lexington, Kentucky Office: 175 East Main Street, Suite 500, P.O. Box 2150.
Telephone: 606-255-9500.
Fax: 606-281-6478.
Washington, D. C. Office: 2401 Pennsylvania Avenue, N.W., Suite 400.
Telephone: 202-973-0200.
Fax: 202-973-0232.
Denver, Colorado Office: Suite 2710, 1660 Lincoln Street.
Telephone: 303-390-0003.
Fax: 303-390-0040.
Wheeling, West Virginia Office: 1144 Market Street.
Telephone: 304-233-4000.
Fax: 304-233-4077.

MEMBERS OF FIRM

Charles Q. Gage
A. L. Emch
James R. Snyder
Barbara D. Little
Dennis C. Sauter
Robert G. McLusky
Daniel L. Stickler (Administrative Manager)
Thomas J. Hurney, Jr.
Lynn Oliver Frye
Thad S. Huffman (Administrative Manager, Washington, D.C. Office)
Kevin M. McGuire (Resident, Lexington, Kentucky Office)
David M. Flannery
Kathy G. Beckett

Representative Clients: Union Carbide Corp.; Rhone-Poulenc Ag Co.; FMC Corp. ; Elkem Metals Co.; West Virginia Coal Assn.; CONSOL Inc.; Pittston Coal Management Company; Arch Coal, Inc.; S&S Grading, Inc.; Westvaco Corp.

For Complete List of Firm Personnel, See General Section

For full biographical listings, see the Martindale-Hubbell Law Directory

*CLARKSBURG,** Harrison Co.

JOHNSON, SIMMERMAN & BROUGHTON, L.C. (AV)

Ogden Building, 203 West Main Street, 26301
Telephone: 304-624-6555; 304-623-4900
Telecopier: 304-623-4933
Mailing Address: P.O. Box 150, Clarksburg, West Virginia, 26302-0150

Charles G. Johnson
Frank E. Simmerman, Jr.
Marcia Allen Broughton
Bridget D. Furbee
Robin Queen Triplett

For full biographical listings, see the Martindale-Hubbell Law Directory

MCNEER, HIGHLAND, MCMUNN AND VARNER, L.C. (AV)

One Valley Bank Building, P.O. Drawer 2040, 26302-2040
Telephone: 304-626-1100
Facsimile: 304-623-3035
Martinsburg Office: 2520 Aikens Center, P.O. Box 2509.
Telephone: 304-264-4621.
Fax: 304-264-8623.
Parkersburg Office: 404 Market Street, Suite 204, P.O. Box 1507.
Telephone: 304-422-7193.
Facsimile: 304-422-7196.

C. David McMunn
J. Cecil Jarvis
James A. Varner
Robert W. Trumble (Resident, Martinsburg Office)
Catherine D. Munster
James N. Riley
Steven R. Bratke (Resident, Parkersburg Office)
Michael J. Novotny (Resident, Martinsburg Office)
Dennis M. Shreve
Geraldine S. Roberts
William F. Rohrbaugh (Resident, Martinsburg Office)
Gregory H. Schillace
Judy L. Shanholtz
Tiffany R. Durst
Gene W. Bailey, II

OF COUNSEL

James E. McNeer
Cecil B. Highland, Jr.
William L. Fury

Representative Clients: One Valley Bank of Clarksburg, National Assn.; Bruceton Bank; Harrison County Bank; Nationwide Mutual Insurance Cos.; Clarksburg Publishing Co.; C.I.T. Financial Services; State Automobile Mutual Insurance Co.; United Hospital Center, Inc.; West Virginia Coals, Inc.; Swanson Plating Co.

For full biographical listings, see the Martindale-Hubbell Law Directory

WISCONSIN

*MADISON,** Dane Co.

AXLEY BRYNELSON, LLP (AV)

(Formerly Brynelson, Herrick, Bucaida, Dorschel & Armstrong Including the former Easton & Assoc., S.C.)
2 East Mifflin Street, P.O. Box 1767, 53701-1767
Telephone: 608-257-5661
Fax: 608-257-5444
Email: law@axley.com *URL:* http://www.axley.com

MEMBER OF FIRM

Steven M. Streck

ASSOCIATES

Andrew J. Clarkowski
Lori M. Lubinsky

For Complete List of Firm Personnel, See General Section

For full biographical listings, see the Martindale-Hubbell Law Directory

KAY & ANDERSEN, S.C. (AV)

One Point Place, Suite 201, 53719
Telephone: 608-833-0077
Fax: 608-833-3901
Email: KandA@execpc.com

Robert J. Kay
Randall J. Andersen

James N. Graham
Robert A. Mich, Jr.

For full biographical listings, see the Martindale-Hubbell Law Directory

QUARLES & BRADY LLP (AV)

Firstar Plaza, One South Pinckney Street, P.O. Box 2113, 53701-2113
Telephone: 608-251-5000
Fax: 608-251-9166
URL: http://www.quarles.com
Milwaukee, Wisconsin Office: 411 East Wisconsin Avenue, 53202-4497.
Telephone: 414-277-5000.
Fax: 414-271-3552.

(See Next Column)

QUARLES & BRADY LLP—*Continued*

West Palm Beach, Florida Office: 222 Lakeview Avenue, 4th Floor, 33401.
Telephone: 561-653-5000.
Fax: 561-653-5333.
Naples, Florida Office: Barnett Center, 4501 Tamiami Trail North, Suite 300, 34103-3060.
Telephone: 941-262-5959.
Fax: 941-434-4999.
Phoenix, Arizona Office: One Camelback Building, One East Camelback Road, Suite 400, 85012-1649.
Telephone: 602-230-5500.
Fax: 602-230-5598.
Chicago, Illinois Office: Quarles & Brady LLC, Citicorp Center, 500 West Madison Street, Suite 3700.
Telephone: 312-715-5000.
Fax: 312-715-5155.

PARTNERS

Anthony S. Earl, Michael L. Zaleski, Anthony H. Driessen, Roy L. Prange, Jr., Waltraud A. Arts, Ralph V. Topinka, Jane F. Clokey

ASSOCIATE

Elizabeth A. Hartman

For Complete List of Firm Personnel, See General Section

For full biographical listings, see the Martindale-Hubbell Law Directory

*MILWAUKEE,** Milwaukee Co.

DAVIS & KUELTHAU, S.C. (AV)

111 East Kilbourn Avenue, Suite 1400, 53202-6613
Telephone: 414-276-0200
Facsimile: 414-276-9369
Cable Address: "Shiplaw"
Email: info@daviskuelthau.com *URL:* http://www.daviskuelthau.com
Madison, Wisconsin Office: Ten East Doty Street, Suite 600, P.O. Box 1068, 53703.
Telephone: 608-280-8235.
Fax: 608-280-8231.
Sheboygan, Wisconsin Office: 605 North Eighth, Suite 610, P.O. Box 1287.
Telephone: 920-451-1461.
Fax: 920-451-1465.
Green Bay, Wisconsin Office: 414 East Walnut Street, Suite 240.
Telephone: 920-435-9378.
Fax: 920-435-9391.

James E. Culhane, Richard J. Delacenserie (Resident at Madison Office), Paul G. Kent (Resident at Madison Office), William J. Mulligan, David W. Neeb, William S. Roush, Jr.

Walter Scott Leedom

For full biographical listings, see the Martindale-Hubbell Law Directory

FRAZER SCHAPIRO & RICH, S.C. (AV)

1110 N. Old World Third Street, Suite 218, 53203
Telephone: 414-347-9500
Fax: 414-347-9455
URL: http://www.fsrlaw.net

Douglas H. Frazer, Karen M. Schapiro, Elizabeth G. Rich

For full biographical listings, see the Martindale-Hubbell Law Directory

MEISSNER TIERNEY FISHER & NICHOLS S.C. (AV)

The Milwaukee Center, 111 East Kilbourn Avenue, 19th Floor, 53202-6622
Telephone: 414-273-1300
Facsimile: 414-273-5840
URL: http://www.mtfn.com

Dennis L. Fisher, Michael J. Cohen

Christopher L. Rexroat, William T. Stuart

For full biographical listings, see the Martindale-Hubbell Law Directory

QUARLES & BRADY LLP (AV)

411 East Wisconsin Avenue, 53202-4497
Telephone: 414-277-5000
Fax: 414-271-3552
URL: http://www.quarles.com
Madison, Wisconsin Office: Firstar Plaza, One South Pinckney Street, P.O. Box 2113, 53701-2113.
Telephone: 608-251-5000.
Fax: 608-251-9166.

(See Next Column)

West Palm Beach, Florida Office: 222 Lakeview Avenue, 4th Floor, 33401.
Telephone: 561-653-5000.
Fax: 561-653-5333.
Naples, Florida Office: Barnett Center, 4501 Tamiami Trail North, Suite 300, 34103-3060.
Telephone: 941-262-5959.
Fax: 941-434-4999.
Phoenix, Arizona Office: One Camelback Building, One East Camelback Road, Suite 400, 85012-1649.
Telephone: 602-230-5500.
Fax: 602-230-5598.
Chicago, Illinois Office: Quarles & Brady LLC, Citicorp Center, 500 West Madison Street, Suite 3700.
Telephone: 312-715-5000.
Fax: 312-715-5155.

MEMBERS OF FIRM
(ALPHABETICALLY BY YEAR OF ADMISSION TO BAR)

Charles Q. Kamps, Anthony S. Earl (Resident, Madison Office), Michael L. Zaleski (Resident, Madison Office), Frank J. Daily, Anthony H. Driessen, James H. Baxter III, James D. Vieregg (Resident, Phoenix, Arizona Office), Peter A. Sarasek (Resident, Chicago, Illinois Office), Roy L. Prange, Jr. (Resident, Madison Office), Michael S. McCauley, Waltraud A. Arts (Resident, Madison Office), Jeffrey Morris, John A. Rothstein, Arthur A. Vogel, Jr., William H. Harbeck, Donald K. Schott (Resident, Madison Office), Ralph V. Topinka (Resident, Madison Office), David B. Bartel, David G. Beauchamp (Resident, Phoenix, Arizona Office), Daniel L. Muchow (Resident, Phoenix, Arizona Office), Dennis P. Reis, Thomas P. McElligott, Nancy K. Peterson, Jane F. Clokey (Resident, Madison Office), Richard P. Blessen (Resident, Chicago, Illinois Office), George J. Marek

OF COUNSEL

Richard W. Cutler

ASSOCIATES

Michael A. Hatfield, Jr., Rachel A. Schneider, William B. Gaschler, Elizabeth A. Hartman (Resident, Madison, Wisconsin Office)

For Complete List of Firm Personnel, See General Section

For full biographical listings, see the Martindale-Hubbell Law Directory

*RACINE,** Racine Co.

JEFFREY LEAVELL, S.C. (AV)

723 South Main Street, 53403
Telephone: 414-633-7322
Fax: 414-633-7323
Email: 102661.3312@compuserve.com

Jeffrey L. Leavell

ASSOCIATES

Michael R. Vescio, Christine M. Genthner

For full biographical listings, see the Martindale-Hubbell Law Directory

WYOMING

*CASPER,** Natrona Co.

BROWN, DREW & MASSEY, LLP (AV)

Casper Business Center, Suite 800, 123 West First Street, 82601-2486
Telephone: 307-234-1000
800-877-6755
Telefax: 307-265-8025
Email: brwndrew@coffey.com

MEMBERS OF FIRM

Morris R. Massey, Harry B. Durham, III, Donn J. McCall, Thomas F. Reese, Jeffrey C. Brinkerhoff, P. Jaye Rippley, Courtney Robert Kepler

ASSOCIATE

Timothy M. Stubson

For Complete List of Firm Personnel, See General Section

For full biographical listings, see the Martindale-Hubbell Law Directory

WILLIAMS, PORTER, DAY & NEVILLE, P.C. (AV)

159 North Wolcott Street Suite 400, P.O. Box 10700, 82602
Telephone: 307-265-0700
Fax: 307-266-2306
Email: wpdn@trib.com

(See Next Column)

WILLIAMS, PORTER, DAY & NEVILLE P.C., *Casper—Continued*

Richard E. Day
Frank D. Neville
Stuart R. Day
Ann M. Rochelle
Margo Harlan Sabec
Scott W. Skavdahl
Kevin D. Huber

Representative Clients: Sinclair Oil Company; Union Oil Company of California, Inc.; PNC Exploration (U.S.A.) Inc.; Amoco Corp.; True Industries; Texaco, Inc.; Conoco, Inc.; Phillips Petroleum Co.; Marathon Oil Co.; PacifiCorp.

For Complete List of Firm Personnel, See General Section

For full biographical listings, see the Martindale-Hubbell Law Directory

PUERTO RICO

SAN JUAN, San Juan Dist.

FIDDLER GONZÁLEZ & RODRÍGUEZ, LLP

254 Muñoz Rivera Avenue (Hato Rey), P.O. Box 363507, 00936-3507
Telephone: 787-753-3113
Telecopier: 787-759-3123
Email: fiddler@fgrlaw.com *URL:* http://www.fgrlaw.com

MEMBERS OF FIRM

Eduardo M. Negrón-Navas
Juan Carlos Gómez Escarce
María Luisa González-Hernández
Pedro J. Reyes-Bibiloni

Representative Clients: Browning Ferris; Metcalf & Eddy; The Eastman Kodak Co.; Bacardi Corp.; AES Corp.

For Complete List of Firm Personnel, See General Section

For full biographical listings, see the Martindale-Hubbell Law Directory

GOLDMAN ANTONETTI & CÓRDOVA

American International Plaza Fourteenth & Fifteenth Floors, 250 Muñoz Rivera Avenue (Hato Rey), P.O. Box 70364, 00936-0364
Telephone: 787-759-8000
Telecopiers: 787-767-9333 (Main)
787-767-9177 (Litigation Department)
787-767-8660 (Labor & Corporate Law Departments)
787-767-9325 (Tax & Environmental Law Departments)
URL: http://www.gaclaw.com

MEMBERS OF FIRM

Francis Torres-Fernández
Braulio García Jiménez
Karín G. Díaz-Toro

ASSOCIATES

Gretchen M. Mendez-Villela
Mayra Del C. Doble-Ruiz
Raul Negron Casasnovas
Guillermo J. Silva-Wiscovich
Alicia Lamboy

Representative Clients: Baxter Health Care Corp.; Chevron U.S.A.; Owen-Illinois; Puerto Rico Manufacturers Association; Britol Myers Squibb.

For Complete List of Firm Personnel, See General Section

For full biographical listings, see the Martindale-Hubbell Law Directory

JIMÉNEZ, GRAFFAM & LAUSELL

Suite 505, Midtown Building, 421 Muñoz Rivera Avenue, Hato Rey, P.O. Box 366104, 00936-6104
Telephone: 787-767-1030; 767-1000; 767-1061; 767-1064
Telefax: 787-751-4068;
Cable: "Nezte"
RCA Telex: 325-2730
Email: manager@jgl.com *URL:* http://www.jgl.com

MEMBERS OF FIRM

William A. Graffam
J. Ramón Rivera-Morales
Manolo T. Rodríguez-Bird

ASSOCIATES

Patricia A. Garrity
Isabel J. Vélez-Serrano
Edgardo A. Vega-López
Jorge F. Blasini
Rafael A. Rosado-Marrero

Representative Clients: Crowley Environmental Services; Bristol Myers Squibb Co.; Smithkline Beecham Pharmaceuticals Co.; Monsanto Agricultural Co.; Water Quality Insurance Syndicate.

For Complete List of Firm Personnel, See General Section

For full biographical listings, see the Martindale-Hubbell Law Directory

MARTÍNEZ ODELL & CALABRIA

Banco Popular Center, 209 Muñoz Rivera Avenue, Suite 1600 (Hato Rey), P.O. Box 190998, 00919-0998
Telephone: 787-753-8914
Facsimile: 787-753-8402; 787-759-9075; 787-764-5664
Email: postmaster@mocpr.com

MEMBERS OF FIRM

Juan Carlos Fierres
Jorge J. Garcia-Diaz

Representative Clients: Banco Popular de Puerto Rico; Daewoo Motor Corporation; Eckerd Corporation; Empresas Fonalledas; Hilton International; L'Aire Liquide, S.A.; Loctile Corporation; Lucent Technologies; Lutron Electronics Co., Inc.; Waste Management, Inc.

For Complete List of Firm Personnel, See General Section

For full biographical listings, see the Martindale-Hubbell Law Directory

VIRGIN ISLANDS

*CHRISTIANSTED, ST. CROIX,** St. Croix

LAW OFFICES OF JOHN K. DEMA, P.C. (AV)

1236 Strand Street, Suite 103, 00820-5008
Telephone: 340-773-6142
Fax: 340-773-3944
Email: 76656.2073@COMPUSERVE.COM *URL:* http://www.lawyers.com/demalaw

John K. Dema

For full biographical listings, see the Martindale-Hubbell Law Directory

*CHARLOTTE AMALIE, ST. THOMAS,** St. Thomas

CAMPBELL, ARELLANO & RICH

No. 4 A & B Kongens Gade, P.O. Box 11899, 00801
Telephone: 340-774-4858
Telecopier: 340-776-8442
Email: carvilaw@viaccess.net *URL:* http://www.lawyers.com/lisvilaw
Cruz Bay, St. John, Virgin Islands Office: Scandic Executive Offices, Mongoose Junction, 00831.
Telephone: 304-693-8655.
Telecopier: 304-776-8442.

MEMBERS OF FIRM

Joseph Bruce Wm. Arellano
Carol Ann Rich

ASSOCIATE

W. Mark Hillsman

OF COUNSEL

Roger L. Campbell

Representative Clients: Citibank, N.A.; Cigna Property and Casualty Companies; Royal Insurance.

For full biographical listings, see the Martindale-Hubbell Law Directory

CANADA
ALBERTA

*CALGARY,** Calgary Jud. Dist.

BENNETT JONES (AV)

4500 Bankers Hall East, 855-2nd Street S.W., T2P 4K7
Telephone: 403-298-3100
Facsimile: 403-265-7219
Email: firmwatch@bennettjones.ca *URL:* http://www.bennettjones.ca
Edmonton, Alberta Office: 1000, 10035-105 Street.
Telephone: 780-421-8133.
Facsimile: 780-421-7951.
Toronto, Ontario Office: 3400 1 First Canadian Place, P.O. Box 130.
Telephone: 416-863-1200.
Facsimile: 416-863-1716.

MEMBER OF FIRM

Lawrence E. Smith

For Complete List of Firm Personnel, See General Section

For full biographical listings, see the Martindale-Hubbell Law Directory

Calgary—Continued

PARLEE McLAWS (AV)

3400 Petro-Canada Centre, 150 - 6th Avenue, SW, T2P 3Y7
Telephone: 403-294-7000
Telecopier: 403-265-8263
Email: lawyers@parlee.com *URL:* http://www.parlee.com
Edmonton, Alberta Office: 15th Floor Manulife Place, 10180 101st Street.
Telephone: 403-423-8500.
Telecopier: 403-423-2870.

MEMBER OF FIRM

Terry R. Davis

ASSOCIATE

Tasha D. Backus

For Complete List of Firm Personnel, See General Section

For full biographical listings, see the Martindale-Hubbell Law Directory

*EDMONTON,** Edmonton Jud. Dist.

LUCAS BOWKER & WHITE (AV)

Scotia 2 Tower - Scotia Place, 1201-10060 Jasper Avenue, T5J 4E5
Telephone: 780-426-5330
Fax: 780-428-1066
Email: Lucas@lbw.ab.ca *URL:* http://www.lbw.ab.ca
Calgary, Alberta Office: Suite 3800, Bankers Hall, 855 2nd Street S.W., T2P 4J8.
Telephone: 403-218-1795.
Fax: 403-264-2993. Email: Lucas@lbw.ab.ca. URL: http://www.lbw.ab.ca

MEMBERS OF FIRM

Gerald A. I. Lucas, Q.C.
George E. Bowker, Q.C.
Robert B. White, Q.C.
David J. Stratton, Q.C.
John Reginald Day, Q.C.
Norman J. Pollock, Q.C.
Robert C. Dunseith
Douglas H. Shell
Kent H. Davidson
Alan R. Gray
Robert A. Seidel, Q.C.
Robert P. Bruce
David J. Stam
Donald J. Wilson
Kevin J. Smith
Gordon V. Garside
Debbie L. Hughes
Douglas A. Bodner

COUNSEL

Joseph J. Stratton, Q.C.

Reference: Canadian Imperial Bank of Commerce.

For full biographical listings, see the Martindale-Hubbell Law Directory

PARLEE McLAWS (AV)

15th Floor Manulife Place, 10180 101st Street, T5J 4K1
Telephone: 403-423-8500
Telecopier: 403-423-2870
Email: lawyers@parlee.com *URL:* http://www.parlee.com
Calgary, Alberta Office: 3400 Petro-Canada Centre, 150 - 6th Avenue, SW.
Telephone: 403-294-7000.
Telecopier: 403-265-8263.

MEMBER OF FIRM

Michael D. MacDonald

For Complete List of Firm Personnel, See General Section

For full biographical listings, see the Martindale-Hubbell Law Directory

CANADA
BRITISH COLUMBIA

*VANCOUVER,** Vancouver Co.

SINGLETON URQUHART (AV)

1200 - 1125 Howe Street, V6Z 2K8
Telephone: 604-682-7474
Fax: 604-682-1283
Email: reception@singleton.com *URL:* http://www.singleton.com

John R. Singleton, Q.C.

Representative Clients: Canadian National Railway; B.C. Hydro & Power Authority.

For Complete List of Firm Personnel, See General Section

For full biographical listings, see the Martindale-Hubbell Law Directory

CANADA
NEW BRUNSWICK

*FREDERICTON,** York Co.

COX HANSON O'REILLY MATHESON (AV)

(Formerly Hanson Hashey)
Suite 400, Phoenix Square, P.O. Box 310, E3B 4Y9
Telephone: 506-453-7771
Fax: 506-453-9600
Email: fredericton@coxhanson.ca *URL:* http://www.coxhanson.ca
Halifax, Nova Scotia Office: Suite 1100, Purdy's Wharf Tower 1, P.O. Box 2380 Station Central RPO, B3J 3E5.
Telephone: 902-421-6262.
Fax: 902-421-3130. E-Mail: halifax@coxhanson.ca
Saint John, New Brunswick Office: 1212-One Brunswick Square, 1 Germain St. E2L 4V1.
Telephone: 506-652-7771.
Fax: 506-632-9600.
St. John's, Newfoundland Office: Scotia Centre, 401-235 Water Street, A1C 1B6.
Telephone: 709-726-3321.
Fax: 709-726-2992. E-Mail: stjohns@coxhanson.ca
Charlottetown, Prince Edward Island Office: Queen Square, Suite 202, 119 Queen Street, P.O. Box 875, Station Central, C1A 7L9.
Telephone: 902-894-7051.
Fax: 902-368-3762. E-Mail: charlottetown@coxhanson.ca

MEMBERS OF FIRM

H. A. Hanson, Q.C. (1909-1985)
David T. Hashey, Q.C.
David M. Norman, Q.C.
J. Ian M. Whitcomb, Q.C.
John M. Hanson, Q.C.
Walter D. Vail, Q.C.
Michael E. Bowlin
John D. Larlee, Q.C.
Bruce D. Hatfield, Q.C.
Julian A. G. Dickson, Q.C.
Anne D. Wooder
Terrence J. Morrison
Lucie Richard
Catherine M. Bowlen
J. Marc Richard

ASSOCIATES

Amanda J. Frenette
Monika M. L. Zauhar
Jade A. Spalding
William E. Gould
Christopher R. DeLong
Deborah M. Power
Corinne A. Godbout
Marc-Antoine Chiasson

For full biographical listings, see the Martindale-Hubbell Law Directory

*MONCTON,** Westmorland Co.

McINNES COOPER (AV)

Barristers, Solicitors & Trade Mark Agents
Place Moncton Place, 655 Main Street, P.O. Box 1368, E1C 8T6
Telephone: 506-857-8970
Fax: 506-857-4095
Email: mcrmctn@mcrlaw.com *URL:* http://www.mcrlaw.com
Halifax, Nova Scotia Office: Summit Place, 1601 Lower Water Street, P.O. Box 730, B3J 2V1.
Telephone: 902-425-6500.
Fax: 902-425-6350. Email: mcrhfx@mcrlaw.com.
St. John's, Newfoundland Office: Baine Johnston Centre, 5th Floor, 10 Fort William Place, P.O. Box 5939, A1C 5X4.
Telephone: 709-722-8735.
Telecopier: 709-722-1763. Email: mcrsj@mcrlaw.com.
Charlottetown, Prince Edward Island Office: BDC Place, Suite 620, 119 Kent Street, C1A 1N3.
Telephone: 902-368-8473.
Fax: 902-368-8346. Email: mcrpei@mcrlaw.com.
Fredericton, New Brunswick Office: Suite 600, 570 Queen Street, P.O. Box 610.
Telephone: 506-458-8572.
Fax: 506-458-9903. Email: mcrfton@mcrlaw.com.

PARTNER

Bernard F. Miller

ASSOCIATE

Sylvie C. Roussel

For Complete List of Firm Personnel, See General Section

For full biographical listings, see the Martindale-Hubbell Law Directory

*SAINT JOHN,** Saint John Co.

CLARK DRUMMIE (AV)

40 Wellington Row, P.O. Box 6850, E2L 4S3
Telephone: 506-633-3800
Telecopier (Automatic): 506-633-3811
Email: cd@nbnet.nb.ca

MEMBERS OF FIRM

Barry R. Morrison, Q.C.
Terrence W. Hutchinson
William B. Richards

Reference: Royal Bank of Canada.

(See Next Column)

CLARK DRUMMIE, *Saint John—Continued*

For Complete List of Firm Personnel, See General Section

For full biographical listings, see the Martindale-Hubbell Law Directory

CANADA NEWFOUNDLAND

*ST. JOHN'S,**

MCINNES COOPER (AV)

Barristers, Solicitors & Trade Mark Agents
Baine Johnston Centre, 5th Floor, 10 Fort William Place, P.O. Box 5939, A1C 5X4
Telephone: 709-722-8735
Telecopier: 709-722-1763
Email: mcrsj@mcrlaw.com *URL:* http://www.mcrlaw.com
Halifax, Nova Scotia Office: Summit Place, 1601 Lower Water Street, P.O. Box 730, B3J 2V1.
Telephone: 902-425-6500.
Fax: 902-425-6350. Email: mcrhfx@mcrlaw.com.
Moncton, New Brunswick Office: Place Moncton Place, 655 Main Street, P.O. Box 1368, E1C 8T6.
Telephone: 506-857-8970.
Fax: 506-857-4095. Email: mcrmctn@mcrlaw.com.
Charlottetown, Prince Edward Island Office: BDC Place, Suite 620, 119 Kent Street, C1A 1N3.
Telephone: 902-368-8473.
Fax: 902-368-8346. Email: mcrpei@mcrlaw.com.
Fredericton, New Brunswick Office: Suite 600, 570 Queen Street, P.O. Box 610.
Telephone: 506-458-8572.
Fax: 506-458-9903. Email: mcrfton@mcrlaw.com.

PARTNERS

Deborah L. J. Hutchings
Caroline C. Watton

ASSOCIATE

Dennis N. Clarke

For Complete List of Firm Personnel, See General Section

For full biographical listings, see the Martindale-Hubbell Law Directory

CANADA NOVA SCOTIA

*HALIFAX,** Regional Munic. of Halifax

MCINNES COOPER (AV)

Barristers, Solicitors & Trade Mark Agents
Summit Place, 1601 Lower Water Street, P.O. Box 730, B3J 2V1
Telephone: 902-425-6500
Fax: 902-425-6350
Email: mcrhfx@mcrlaw.com *URL:* http://www.mcrlaw.com
St. John's, Newfoundland Office: Baine Johnston Centre, 5th Floor, 10 Fort William Place, P.O. Box 5939, A1C 5X4.
Telephone: 709-722-8735.
Telecopier: 709-722-1763. Email: mcrsj@mcrlaw.com.
Moncton, New Brunswick Office: Place Moncton Place, 655 Main Street, P.O. Box 1368, E1C 8T6.
Telephone: 506-857-8970.
Fax: 506-857-4095. Email: mcrmctn@mcrlaw.com.
Charlottetown, Prince Edward Island Office: BDC Place, Suite 620, 119 Kent Street, C1A 1N3.
Telephone: 902-368-8473.
Fax: 902-368-8346. Email: mcrpei@mcrlaw.com.
Fredericton, New Brunswick Office: Suite 600, 570 Queen Street, P.O. Box 610.
Telephone: 506-458-8572.
Fax: 506-458-9903. Email: mcrfton@mcrlaw.com.

PARTNERS

George T. H. Cooper, Q.C.
James E. Gould, Q.C.
Harvey L. Morrison

ASSOCIATE

Kristi Sebalj

For Complete List of Firm Personnel, See General Section

For full biographical listings, see the Martindale-Hubbell Law Directory

CANADA ONTARIO

*TORONTO,** Regional Munic. of Toronto

BORDEN & ELLIOT (AV)

Barristers & Solicitors
Scotia Plaza, 40 King Street West, M5H 3Y4
Telephone: 416-367-6000
Telecopier: 416-367-6749
Email: info@borden.com *URL:* http://www.borden.com
Ottawa, Ontario Office: Borden Elliot Scott & Aylen, 1000-60 Rue Queen Street.
Telephone: 613-237-5160; 800-661-4237. General
Facsimile: 613-230-8842. IP Dept.
Facsimile: 613-787-3558. Email: ottinfo@scottaylen.com. URL: http://www.borden.com.

Stephen F. Waqué

For Complete List of Firm Personnel, See General Section

For full biographical listings, see the Martindale-Hubbell Law Directory

DAVIES, WARD & BECK (AV)

1 First Canadian Place, M5X 1B1
Telephone: 416-863-0900
Fax: 416-863-0871
Email: info@dwb.com *URL:* http://www.dwb.com

PARTNERS AND ASSOCIATES

Gray E. Taylor
Catherine G. Ross
Sarah V. Powell

For Complete List of Firm Personnel, See General Section

For full biographical listings, see the Martindale-Hubbell Law Directory

KELLY AFFLECK GREENE (AV)

One First Canadian Place, Suite 840, P.O. Box 489, M5X 1E5
Telephone: 416-360-2800
Fax: 416-360-5960
Email: info@kag.net *URL:* http://www.kag.net

MEMBERS OF FIRM

W. Anthony Kelly, Q.C.
Donald S. Affleck, Q.C.
Peter R. Greene
Donald B. Houston
James C. Orr
Peter C. Wardle
Helen A. Daley
Melissa J. Kennedy

ASSOCIATES

Kenneth A. Dekker
W. Michael G. Osborne
Jason C. Markwell
Patrice F. Band

For full biographical listings, see the Martindale-Hubbell Law Directory

CANADA QUEBEC

*MONTREAL,** Montreal Dist.

MCMASTER GERVAIS (AV)

A General Partnership
1000 de La Gauchetière Street West, Suite 900, H3B 5H4
Telephone: 514-879-1212
Fax: 514-954-1905
Email: info@mcmastergervais.com *URL:* http://www.mcmastergervais.com

MEMBERS OF FIRM

Robert E. Charbonneau
Christine Duchaine
Yves A. Dubois
Sébastien Lormeau

For Complete List of Firm Personnel, See General Section

For full biographical listings, see the Martindale-Hubbell Law Directory

POULIOT, MERCURE (AV)

CIBC Tower, 31st Floor, 1155 René-Lévesque Boulevard, West, H3B 3S6
Telephone: 514-875-5210
Telecopier: 514-875-4308
Email: POUMER@CEDEP.COM
Genève, Suisse Office: 8, Rue de la Rôtisserie, 1204 Geneva, Switzerland.
Telephone: +41 22-28 79 40.
Telecopier: +41 22-21 23 67.

(See Next Column)

POULIOT, MERCURE—*Continued*

MEMBERS OF FIRM

Georges A. Pouliot, Q.C.	Gilles Bertrand
Gilles Brunelle	Jean Larivière
Luc Gratton	Louis-Michel Tremblay
Brian Riordan	David I. Johnston
Pierre Paquet	Stéphane Hébert
Anne-Marie Gauthier	Jacques LeBel, Q.C.
Yvon Brizard	Joel A. Silcoff
Robert Tessier	Ronald M. Auclair
Daniel Gagné	Philippe Roy
Lilia Pouliot	Maxime B. Rhéaume
Marco Veilleux	Serge Desrochers
Alain Nadon	C. Keenan LaPierre
Jean H. Gagnon	Alain Bond
Richard Fontaine	Louis Coallier
Normand Royal	Nicole Chouinard

Stéphane Teasdale

ASSOCIATES

Micheline Perrault	Brent J. Muir
Caroline Lemoine	Louise Tremblay
Béatrice Arronis	Chantal Joubert
Yvan Nantel	Normand D'Amour
Sylvie Boulanger	Pascale Cloutier
Vincent Frenette	Eric Couture
Robert Cardin	Frédéric Chatel
Alexandre Henri	Mary-Lynn Breton

Alexandre Ajami

For full biographical listings, see the Martindale-Hubbell Law Directory

CANADA
SASKATCHEWAN

*REGINA,** Regina Jud. Centre

MACPHERSON LESLIE & TYERMAN (AV)

1500-1874 Scarth Street, S4P 4E9
Telephone: 306-347-8000
Telecopier: 306-352-5250
Email: mltreg@mlt.com
Saskatoon, Saskatchewan Office: 1500-410 22nd Street East, S7K 5T6.
Telephone: 306-975-7100.
Telecopier: 306-975-7145.

MEMBERS OF FIRM

Harold H. MacKay, Q.C.	Larry B. LeBlanc, Q.C.
Leonard D. Andrychuk	Robert G. Richards, Q.C.
Danny R. Anderson (Resident, Saskatoon Office)	

ASSOCIATE

Michele T. Klebuc-Simes

For Complete List of Firm Personnel, See General Section

For full biographical listings, see the Martindale-Hubbell Law Directory

BELGIUM

*BRUSSELS,**

American Lawyers In Brussels

OPPENHEIMER WOLFF & DONNELLY LLP

Avenue Louise 240, Box 5, 1050 Brussels
Telephone: +32-2-626-0500
FAX: +32-2-626-0510
Email: info@oppenheimer.com *URL:* http://www.oppenheimer.com
Minneapolis, Minnesota Office: 3300 Plaza VII, 45 South Seventh Street. 55402.
Telephone: 612-607-7000.
FAX: 612-607-7100.
Amsterdam, The Netherlands Office: Keizergracht 241.
Telephone: 31-20-423-4555.
FAX: 312-20-423-4545.
Geneva, Switzerland Office: Rue Gabriel Eynard, 6, 1205.
Telephone: (41/22) 311-7410.
FAX: (41/22) 311-4707.
Newport Beach, California Office: 500 Newport Center Drive, Suite 700, 92660.
Telephone: 949-823-6000.
FAX: 949-823-6100.
New York, N.Y. Office: The Chrysler East Building, 19th Floor, 666 Third Avenue, 10017.
Telephone: 212-826-5000.
FAX: 212-486-0708.
Paris, France Office: 35 Boulevard des Capucines, 75002.
Telephone: (33/1) 53 45 40 00.
FAX: (33/1) 53 45 40 10.
St. Paul, Minnesota Office: 1700 First National Bank Building, 55101.
Telephone: 651-605-2000.
FAX: 651-605-2100.
Washington, D.C. Office: 1350 Eye Street, N.W., Suite 200, 20005.
Telephone: 202-312-8000.
FAX: 202-312-8100.
Los Angeles, California Office: 2029 Century Park East, 38th Floor, 90067.
Telephone: 310-788-5000.
FAX: 310-277-1297.
Palo Alto, California Office: 3373 Hillview Avenue, Suite 200, 94304.
Telephone: 650-320-4000.
FAX: 650-320-4100.
Chicago, Illinois Office: Oppenheimer Wolff & Donnelly (Illinois), Two Prudential Plaza, 45th Floor, 180 North Stetson Avenue, 60601.
Telephone: 312-616-1800.
Fax: 312-616-5800.

PARTNERS

James H. Searles	Ursula Schliessner

ASSOCIATES

Brian D. Sheridan	Goli-Schabnam Akbarian

(Not admitted to practice in Belgian courts)

For full biographical listings, see the Martindale-Hubbell Law Directory

FAMILY LAW

MINNESOTA

EDINA, Hennepin Co.

KISSOON, CLUGG, LINDER & DITTBERNER, LTD. (AV)
3205 West 76th Street, 55435-5244
Telephone: 612-896-1099
Fax: 612-896-1132
Email: kcld@uswest.net

K. Worner Kissoon
Lorraine S. Clugg
Karen I. Linder
Michael D. Dittberner
Gerald O. Williams, Jr.

For full biographical listings, see the Martindale-Hubbell Law Directory

SWADEN LAW OFFICES (AV)
7301 Ohms Lane, Suite 550, 55439
Telephone: 612-832-5990
Fax: 612-832-0984

Martin L. Swaden

Tsippi Wray
LEGAL SUPPORT PERSONNEL
Alice W. Hoak
Debra S. Kember

For full biographical listings, see the Martindale-Hubbell Law Directory

*MINNEAPOLIS,** Hennepin Co.

ARNOLD, ANDERSON & DOVE, P.L.L.P. (AV)
5881 Cedar Lake Road, 55416-1492
Telephone: 612-545-9000
Wats Line: 800-343-4545
Fax: 612-545-1793; 612-542-9210
Email: aad@aadlaw.com
Princeton, Minnesota Office: 501 South Fourth Street.
Telephone: 612-389-2214.
Hutchinson, Minnesota Office: 101 Park Place.
Telephone: 320-587-7575.
Red Wing, Minnesota Office: 481 Fridell Crescent, 55066.
Telephone: 651-388-3454.

MEMBERS OF FIRM
David B. Arnold
Laura K. Fretland
Jane Van Valkenburg

For Complete List of Firm Personnel, See General Section

For full biographical listings, see the Martindale-Hubbell Law Directory

HENSON & EFRON, P.A. (AV)
400 Second Avenue South, Suite 1200, 55401-2496
Telephone: 612-339-2500
Fax: 612-339-6364
Email: firm@hensonefron.com

Robert F. Henson
Alan C. Eidsness
William F. Forsyth

Kristi L. Skordahl

For Complete List of Firm Personnel, See General Section

For full biographical listings, see the Martindale-Hubbell Law Directory

KATZ & MANKA, LTD. (AV)
4150 First Bank Place, 601 2nd Avenue South, 55402
Telephone: 612-333-1671
Fax: 612-333-1608
Email: km@katzandmanka.com

A. Larry Katz
Gary L. Manka
Brian L. Sobol
Scott A. Teplinsky
Robert W. Due

Kathryn A. Graves
Elizabeth B. Bowling
Cameron M. Parkhurst
Catherine A. Krisik

For full biographical listings, see the Martindale-Hubbell Law Directory

OLUP & ASSOCIATES (AV)
7300 Metro Boulevard (Edina), 55439
Telephone: 612-835-4070
Fax: 612-835-3107
Email: oluplaw@worldnet.att.net

(See Next Column)

Linda A. Olup
ASSOCIATE
Brion L. Hybertson

For full biographical listings, see the Martindale-Hubbell Law Directory

ZALK & WOOD, P.A. (AV)
5861 Cedar Lake Road, 55416
Telephone: 612-545-3392
Fax: 612-545-2399
Email: zalkwood@winternet.com

Robert H. Zalk
Jennifer L. Wood

For full biographical listings, see the Martindale-Hubbell Law Directory

*ROCHESTER,** Olmsted Co.

GEORGE F. RESTOVICH & ASSOCIATES (AV)
117 East Center Street, 55904
Telephone: 507-288-4840
Fax: 507-288-4908
Email: gfrlaw@infonet.isl.net

ASSOCIATES
Bruce K. Piotrowski
Richard W. Kimlinger
Gary A. Gittus

For full biographical listings, see the Martindale-Hubbell Law Directory

*ST. PAUL,** Ramsey Co.

COLLINS, BUCKLEY, SAUNTRY AND HAUGH, P.L.L.P. (AV)
West 1100 First National Bank Building, 332 Minnesota Street, 55101
Telephone: 651-227-0611
Telecopier: 651-227-0758
Email: info@cbsh.net *URL:* http://www.cbsh.net

MEMBERS OF FIRM
William E. Haugh, Jr.
John R. Schulz
Thomas R. O'Connell
Dan C. O'Connell
Christine L. Stroemer
ASSOCIATES
Matthew A. Slaven
Michael D. Wentzell
OF COUNSEL
Theodore J. Collins

For Complete List of Firm Personnel, See General Section

For full biographical listings, see the Martindale-Hubbell Law Directory

McCULLOUGH, SMITH, WRIGHT & KEMPE, P.A. (AV)
Maple Hills Office Center, 905 Parkway Drive, 55106
Telephone: 612-772-3446
Fax: 612-772-2177

D. Patrick McCullough
Dianne Wright
John R. Kempe

Cary E. Miller-Dolan

For full biographical listings, see the Martindale-Hubbell Law Directory

MISSISSIPPI

*BROOKHAVEN,** Lincoln Co.

ALLEN, ALLEN, BOERNER & BREELAND (AV)
214 Justice Street, P.O. Box 751, 39602-0751
Telephone: 601-833-4361
Fax: 601-833-6647
Email: aabblaw@tislink.com

Emmette P. Allen (1915-1999)
Robert O. Allen
William D. Boerner
Durwood J. Breeland
ASSOCIATE
Sally Burchfield Doty

For full biographical listings, see the Martindale-Hubbell Law Directory

*GULFPORT,** Harrison Co.

BOYCE HOLLEMAN A PROFESSIONAL CORPORATION (AV)
1913 15th Street, P.O. Drawer 1030, 39502
Telephone: 228-863-3142; 1-800-863-3140
Telecopier: 228-863-9829
Email: boyce1913@aol.com

Boyce Holleman

(See Next Column)

BOYCE HOLLEMAN A PROFESSIONAL CORPORATION, *Gulfport—Continued*

Timothy C. Holleman
Leslie Dean Holleman
David J. "Jeff" White

References: Hancock Bank, Gulfport; Merchants Bank & Trust Co., Gulfport; Bank of Wiggins, Wiggins, Mississippi.

For full biographical listings, see the Martindale-Hubbell Law Directory

MEADOWS RILEY LAW FIRM (AV)

1720 23rd Avenue, P.O. Box 550, 39502
Telephone: 601-864-4511
Telecopier: 601-868-2178

Joseph R. Meadows
Jerry D. Riley
Donnie D. Riley
Karen J. Young

Representative Clients: Bubba Oustalat Lincoln Mercury, Inc.; Lee Tractor Co. of Mississippi.
Reference: Hancock Bank.

For full biographical listings, see the Martindale-Hubbell Law Directory

*JACKSON,** Hinds Co.

CHINN & ASSOCIATES, PLLC (AV)

4316 Old Canton Road, P.O. Box 13483, 39211
Telephone: 601-366-4410
Facsimile: 601-366-4010
Toll Free: 888-477-4410
URL: http://www.lawyers.com/chinnandassociates
Email: divorce@meta3.net *URL:* http://www.chinnandassoc.com

Mark A. Chinn

ASSOCIATES

Rex B. Foster
W. David Ross

For full biographical listings, see the Martindale-Hubbell Law Directory

MADISON, Madison Co.

BELL & ASSOCIATES, P.A. (AV)

967 Madison Avenue, 39110
Telephone: 601-898-1111
Toll Free: 1-888-898-1600
Fax: 601-898-1102
Mailing Address: P.O. Box 890, Madison, Mississippi, 39130-0890
Email: JamesDBell@aol.com *URL:* http://www.lawyers.com/bell&associates

James D. Bell

Eduardo Alberto Flechas

For full biographical listings, see the Martindale-Hubbell Law Directory

MISSOURI

*JEFFERSON CITY,** Cole Co.

CARSON & COIL, P.C. (AV)

515 East High, P.O. Box 28, 65102
Telephone: 573-636-2177
Telecopier: 573-636-7119
Email: general@carsoncoil.com

Michael P. Riley
Edward C. Clausen
James W. Gallaher
Carla G. Holste
Lori J. Levine
Paul T. Graham

Jack C. Hauser, Jr.

General Counsel for: Capital Reserve Life Insurance Co.; Missouri Farm Bureau; Healthcare Services Group.
Reference: Central Trust Bank.

For full biographical listings, see the Martindale-Hubbell Law Directory

KANSAS CITY, Jackson, Clay, Platte & Cass Cos.

LAW OFFICES OF BLOND & ALLISON, P.C. (AV)

One Ward Parkway, Suite 118, 64112
Telephone: 816-756-0080
Fax: 816-756-1121

Barton S. Blond
Jill C. Allison

For full biographical listings, see the Martindale-Hubbell Law Directory

THAYER, BERNSTEIN & BASS, P.C. (AV)

8900 Ward Parkway, Suite 210, 64114
Telephone: 816-444-8030
Fax: 816-523-2158

Charlotte P. Thayer
Regina Keelan Bass
Sheldon Bernstein
Anita I. Rodarte
Tamara S. Hatheway

OF COUNSEL

Daniel H. Bowers
Steven John Braun

For full biographical listings, see the Martindale-Hubbell Law Directory

*KIRKSVILLE,** Adair Co.

OSWALD, COTTEY & TEMPLETON, A PROFESSIONAL CORPORATION (AV)

Suite A, 210 North Elson, P.O. Box K, 63501
Telephone: 660-665-5628
Fax: 660-665-6035
Email: oswaldcotteytempleton@yahoo.com

Louis F. Cottey (1931-1999)
Thomas R. Oswald
Scott L. Templeton

Brenda Wall-Swedberg
Susan R. Barrow
Theresa L. Kenney
David Briggs

For full biographical listings, see the Martindale-Hubbell Law Directory

RAYMORE, Cass Co.

HENSLEY & HENSLEY (AV)

401 West 58 Highway, P.O. Box 620, 64083
Telephone: 816-322-4466
Email: hensley8.@worldnet.att.net

MEMBERS OF FIRM

Kenneth C. Hensley
Teresa Hensley

Representative Clients: Farmers Bank of Northern Missouri; Corporate Dental Care, Inc.; Cole & Myers Oil Co.

For full biographical listings, see the Martindale-Hubbell Law Directory

ST. LOUIS, (Independent City)

ALAN E. DEWOSKIN, P.C. (AV)

Suite 426 T, 225 South Meramec Avenue, 63105
Telephone: 314-727-6330
Telecopier: 314-727-5297
URL: http://www.lawyers.com/dewoskinlaw

Alan E. DeWoskin
Henry M. DeWoskin

For full biographical listings, see the Martindale-Hubbell Law Directory

GREEN CORDONNIER & HOUSE LLP (AV)

8000 Maryland Avenue, Suite 400, 63105
Telephone: 314-726-0455
Fax: 314-726-0840

PRINCIPALS

Margo L. Green
Michelle S. House
Justin C. Cordonnier
Elliott I. Goldberger

Barbara L. Graham

For full biographical listings, see the Martindale-Hubbell Law Directory

NEWMAN, FREYMAN, KLEIN & GAMACHE, P.C. (AV)

7777 Bonhomme, 24th Floor, 63105
Telephone: 314-727-0220
Telecopier: 314-727-9246
URL: http://www.nfk-law.com

Morton R. Newman

For full biographical listings, see the Martindale-Hubbell Law Directory

PAULE, CAMAZINE & BLUMENTHAL, A PROFESSIONAL CORPORATION (AV)

Sixth Floor, 165 North Meramec Avenue (Clayton), 63105
Telephone: 314-727-2266
Telecopier: 314-727-2101
Email: pcblaw@stlnet.com

Alisse C. Camazine
Alan E. Freed
Bruce E. Friedman
Kathryn L. Dudley
Lisa G. Moore

For full biographical listings, see the Martindale-Hubbell Law Directory

St. Louis—Continued

THE SCHECHTER LAW FIRM, P.C. (AV)

Suite 950, 8000 Maryland Avenue, 63105-3752
Telephone: 314-727-7289
Fax: 314-727-2230
URL: http://www.lawyers.com/schechterlawfirm

Theodore S. Schechter
Jeffrey S. Schechter
Michael L. Schechter

Joseph M. Taylor
Theresa Ann Malone

Reference: First National Bank of Clayton.

For full biographical listings, see the Martindale-Hubbell Law Directory

SCHRAMM & PINES, L.L.C. (AV)

Suite 950 The Bemiston Tower, 231 South Bemiston Avenue, 63105
Telephone: 314-721-5321
Telecopier: 314-721-0790

MEMBERS OF FIRM

Paul H. Schramm
M. Harvey Pines
Daniel R. Schramm

Timothy I. Nicholson
Dean A. Schramm

Reference: Magna Bank.

For full biographical listings, see the Martindale-Hubbell Law Directory

THE TODT LAW FIRM P.C. (AV)

212 South Meramec, 63105
Telephone: 314-862-5520
Fax: 314-862-1516

Charles P. Todt

Kathleen Evelyn Shaul
Kenneth V. Byrne

For full biographical listings, see the Martindale-Hubbell Law Directory

ZERMAN & MOGERMAN, L.L.C. (AV)

100 South Brentwood, Suite 325, 63105
Telephone: 314-862-4444
Fax: 314-727-4440
Email: zermog@aol.com *URL:* http://www.zermanmogerman.com

Allan H. Zerman
Susan L. Ward
Cary J. Mogerman
Anne Kanela Yannakakis
Mary E. Niemira

For full biographical listings, see the Martindale-Hubbell Law Directory

MONTANA

*BILLINGS,** Yellowstone Co.

CROWLEY, HAUGHEY, HANSON, TOOLE & DIETRICH, P.L.L.P. (AV)

500 Transwestern II, 490 North 31st Street, P.O. Box 2529, 59103
Telephone: 406-252-3441
Fax: 406-259-4159
Email: crowley@crowleylaw.com
Helena, Montana Office: IBM Building, 100 North Park Avenue, Suite 300, 59601.
Telephone: 406-449-4165.
Fax: 406-449-5149.
Kalispell, Montana Office: 431 1st Avenue West, 59901.
Telephone: 406-752-6644.
Fax: 406-752-5108.
Williston, North Dakota Office: 113 East Broadway, 58801.
Telephone: 701-572-2200.
Fax: 701-572-7072.

MEMBERS OF FIRM

Donald L. Harris
Michael S. Lahr (Resident, Helena, Montana Office)

Representative Clients: Montana Power Co.; First Interstate Bank of Commerce; MDU Resources Group, Inc.; Chevron U.S.A., Inc.; Noranda Minerals Corp.; United Parcel Service.
Insurance Clients: Farmers Insurance Group; New York Life Insurance Co.

For Complete List of Firm Personnel, See General Section

For full biographical listings, see the Martindale-Hubbell Law Directory

WRIGHT, TOLLIVER AND GUTHALS A PROFESSIONAL SERVICE CORPORATION (AV)

Windsor Court, 10 North 27th Street, P.O. Box 1977, 59103-1977
Telephone: 406-245-3071
Telecopier: 406-245-3074
Email: lawfirm@mcn.net

Ralph S. Wright (1939-1985)
Kenneth D. Tolliver
Joel E. Guthals
Virginia A. Bryan
Susan Fisher Stevens
J. Reuss
Jeffery A. Hunnes
James W. Thompson

David Paul Wilkins

For full biographical listings, see the Martindale-Hubbell Law Directory

NEBRASKA

*LINCOLN,** Lancaster Co.

JOHNSON, FLODMAN, GUENZEL, ESKE & WIDGER (AV)

1227 Lincoln Mall, P.O. Box 81686, 68501-1686
Telephone: 402-475-4240
Fax: 402-475-0329
URL: http://www.linclaw.com

MEMBERS OF FIRM

Steven J. Flodman
Abbie J. Widger

Special Counsel: Nebraska Public Power District.
Representative Clients: Atlanta Casualty; Chubb/Pacific Indemnity Group; Citizens State Bank, Polk, Nebraska; Crum & Foster; Federated Rural Electric Insurance Corp.; Runza Drive-Inns of America; State Farm Insurance Cos.; Viking Insurance Company of Wisconsin.

For full biographical listings, see the Martindale-Hubbell Law Directory

NEVADA

*LAS VEGAS,** Clark Co.

ALBRIGHT, STODDARD, WARNICK & ALBRIGHT, A PROFESSIONAL CORPORATION (AV)

Quail Park I, Building D-4, 801 South Rancho Drive, 89106
Telephone: 702-384-7111
Fax: 702-384-0605
URL: http://www.aswalaw.com

G. Vern Albright
William H. Stoddard
Whitney B. Warnick
G. Mark Albright

D. Chris Albright
Tami C. Budo
Corey D. Randall (Not admitted in NV)

Representative Clients: Tokio Marine and Fire Insurance Co.; INAPRO, a CIGNA Co.; Nevada Ready Mix; North American Health Care, Inc. (Nursing Home); Royal Insurance; First Security Bank of Utah; Nevada Community Bank; Nationwide Insurance Co.; Liberty Mutual Insurance; CB Commercial.

For full biographical listings, see the Martindale-Hubbell Law Directory

DICKERSON, DICKERSON, CONSUL & POCKER (AV)

Suite 1130, 330 South Third Street, 89101
Telephone: 702-388-8600
Fax: 702-388-0210

MEMBERS OF FIRM

George M. Dickerson
Robert P. Dickerson
Vincent A. Consul
Richard J. Pocker
Douglass A. Mitchell
Paul J. Lal
Bryce C. Duckworth

ASSOCIATES

Stacie L. Brown
Shann D. Winesett
David F. Sampson

Reference: Citibank.

For full biographical listings, see the Martindale-Hubbell Law Directory

ECKER & STANDISH, CHARTERED (AV)

Bank of America-Nevada Plaza, Suite 611, 300 South Fourth Street, 89101
Telephone: 702-384-1700
Fax: 702-384-8150

Howard Ecker
Thomas Standish

(See Next Column)

ECKER & STANDISH CHARTERED, *Las Vegas—Continued*

Edward L. Kainen

LEGAL SUPPORT PERSONNEL

Patricia J. Coyne

For full biographical listings, see the Martindale-Hubbell Law Directory

JOLLEY, URGA, WIRTH & WOODBURY (AV)

3800 Howard Hughes Parkway Suite 1600, 89109
Telephone: 702-699-7500
Facsimile: 702-699-7555
URL: http://www.juww.com
Boulder City, Nevada Office: Suite 105, 1000 Nevada Highway, 89005.
Telephone: 702-293-3674.

MEMBERS OF FIRM

Roger A. Wirth
Kathryn Stryker Wirth

ASSOCIATE

Gregory G. Gordon

For Complete List of Firm Personnel, See General Section

For full biographical listings, see the Martindale-Hubbell Law Directory

PICO & MITCHELL (AV)

2000 South Eastern Avenue, 89104
Telephone: 702-457-9099
FAX: 702-457-8451
Email: lawyers@picomitchell.com

MEMBERS OF FIRM

James F. Pico
Bert O. Mitchell
Christy Brad Escobar
James R. Rosenberger
E. Breen Arntz

ASSOCIATES

Michelle Schwarz
Rebecca L. Mastrangelo
Jill M. Chase
Daniel E. Carvalho
Stephen H. Rogers

Representative Clients: Home Insurance Co.; State Farm Mutual Insurance Co.; Industrial Indemnity Insurance Co.; Great American Insurance Co.; Argonaut Insurance Cos.; Clark County Medical Society; Rose de Lima Hospital; Fairway Chevrolet; American States Insurance Co.; The Hartford Insurance Co.

For full biographical listings, see the Martindale-Hubbell Law Directory

*RENO,** Washoe Co.

SILVERMAN & DECARIA, CHARTERED (AV)

290 South Arlington Avenue, Suite 100, 89501
Telephone: 775-322-3223
Facsimile: 775-322-3649
Email: SandD@intercomm.com

Gary R. Silverman
Mary Anne Decaria
Michael V. Kattelman

LEGAL SUPPORT PERSONNEL

Merrilyn Marsh

Representative Client: Western Nevada Supply Co.

For full biographical listings, see the Martindale-Hubbell Law Directory

LAW OFFICES OF RICHARD W. YOUNG A PROFESSIONAL CORPORATION (AV)

327 Marsh Avenue, 89509
Telephone: 702-322-9477
Facsimile: 702-322-3758

Richard W. Young

Reference: Pioneer Citizens Bank (Reno Main Branch).

For full biographical listings, see the Martindale-Hubbell Law Directory

NEW HAMPSHIRE

*CONCORD,** Merrimack Co.

DOUGLAS, ROBINSON, LEONARD & GARVEY, P.C. (AV)

6 Loudon Road Suite 502, 03301
Telephone: 603-224-1988
Fax: 603-229-1988
Email: drlg@grolen.com *URL:* http://www.lawyers.com/drl&glaw

(See Next Column)

Charles G. Douglas, III
Timothy I. Robinson
C. Kevin Leonard
Carolyn S. Garvey
Susanna G. Robinson

For full biographical listings, see the Martindale-Hubbell Law Directory

NEW JERSEY

FLORHAM PARK, Morris Co.

SCHWARTZ SIMON EDELSTEIN CELSO & KESSLER (AV)

A Partnership including a Professional Corporation
Ten James Street, 07932
Telephone: 973-301-0001
Fax: 973-301-0203
Email: sseck1@aol.com

Burton Zitomer

OF COUNSEL

Glenn C. Guritzky

For full biographical listings, see the Martindale-Hubbell Law Directory

*HACKENSACK,** Bergen Co.

ARONSOHN WEINER, A PROFESSIONAL CORPORATION (AV)

263 Main Street, 07601
Telephone: 201-487-4747
Telecopier: 201-487-7601

Richard F. Aronsohn (1938-1996)
Richard H. Weiner
John E. Selser, III
Gerald R. Salerno

Patrick W. Harrington
Gaiana S. Flynn

For full biographical listings, see the Martindale-Hubbell Law Directory

ROBERT T. CORCORAN, P.C. (AV)

401 Hackensack Avenue, 07601
Telephone: 201-342-5151
Facsimile: 201-342-7190
URL: http://www.lawyers.com/robertcorcoran
Email: law@robertcorcoran.com *URL:* http://www.robertcorcoran.com

Robert T. Corcoran
Jason J. Miller
Karen M. Venice
Christopher R. Cavalli

OF COUNSEL

Michael J. Powers

For full biographical listings, see the Martindale-Hubbell Law Directory

PASHMAN STEIN, A PROFESSIONAL CORPORATION (AV)

45 Essex Street, 07601-5415
Telephone: 201-488-8200
Fax: 201-488-5556
Email: info@pashmanstein.com *URL:* http://www.lawyers.com/pashmanstein

Louis Pashman
Samuel J. Samaro
Dennis T. Smith
Michael S. Stein

Amy E. Whitteaker
John T. Whipple

SPECIAL COUNSEL

Morris Pashman

For full biographical listings, see the Martindale-Hubbell Law Directory

STEPHEN H. ROTH (AV)

62 Summit Avenue, 07601
Telephone: 201-489-3737
Fax: 201-489-0557

ASSOCIATE

Michele M. De Santis

For full biographical listings, see the Martindale-Hubbell Law Directory

SHAPIRO & CROLAND (AV)

A Partnership including Professional Corporations
Continental Plaza II, 411 Hackensack Avenue, 07601
Telephone: 201-488-3900
Fax: 201-488-9481

(See Next Column)

SHAPIRO & CROLAND—*Continued*

Barry I. Croland, P.C.
Robert P. Shapiro, P.C.
Barry L. Baime
Jay Rubenstein
Kenneth S. Apfel
Kenneth S. Goldrich, P.C.
Bruce J. Ackerman
Stuart Reiser, P.C.
Meridith J. Bronson
John P. Di Iorio
David O. Marcus
Robert F. Green
Lizabeth Sarakin
David Torchin
Robin C. Bogan
Craig D. Spector

OF COUNSEL

Harvey R. Sorkow

Donald R. Sorkow (1930-1985)

Reference: Bank of New York-National Community Division.

For full biographical listings, see the Martindale-Hubbell Law Directory

THURBER CAPPELL, L.L.C. (AV)

235 Main Street, Suite 300, 07601
Telephone: 201-488-0594
Telecopier: 201-488-5283
Email: thurblaw@aol.com *URL:* http://www.lawyers.com/thurber,cappell,law

Mary F. Thurber
Cynthia A. Cappell

ASSOCIATES

Allison Turley Madden
Anne Marie Fox

OF COUNSEL

Frank Huttle, III

For full biographical listings, see the Martindale-Hubbell Law Directory

HADDONFIELD, Camden Co.

WEINBERG, MCCORMICK, CHATZINOFF AND PAUL, A PROFESSIONAL ASSOCIATION (AV)

109 Haddon Avenue, 08033
Telephone: 609-795-1600
Telecopier: 609-795-9469

Joseph M. Weinberg
Joseph A. McCormick, Jr.
Barry Chatzinoff
Edward L. Paul
Donafaye Wilson Zoll
Michael A. Weinberg

Representative Clients: Emtec Corp.; John Dere; Aurora Financial Group, Inc.; Case Credit Corp.
Local Counsel for: John Deere Credit Services, Inc.; John Deere Co.; John Deere Industrial Equipment Co.
Solicitor for: Berlin Township Planning Board.
Reference: Summit Bank

For full biographical listings, see the Martindale-Hubbell Law Directory

LAWRENCEVILLE, Mercer Co.

SZAFERMAN, LAKIND, BLUMSTEIN, WATTER & BLADER, P.C. (AV)

Suite 104 Quakerbridge Executive Center, 101 Grovers Mill Road, 08648
Telephone: 609-275-0400
Telefax: 609-275-4511

Arnold C. Lakind
Barry D. Szaferman
Jeffrey P. Blumstein
Paul N. Watter
Steven Blader
Sidney H. Lehmann
Gerald B. Schenkman
David B. Beckett
Scott P. Borsack
Mary Lou Delahanty

Jennifer Weisberg Millner
Cathyanne A. Pisciotta
Jason N. Fruhschein
Demery J. Roberts
Stuart A. Tucker
Brian G. Paul
Victoria Rivera-Cruz
Thomas J. Burns III

LEGAL SUPPORT PERSONNEL

Paula M. Rossi (Office Administrator)
Patricia Hallstrum (Controller)

Representative Clients: Sun National Bank; First Washington Bank; Gilmore Securities & Co.; Communication Workers of America; The Eagle Group; Water's Edge Convalescent Center; Ronson Aviation, Inc.; Holmdel Township Board of Adjustment; Public Service Managers Association; Chemical Leaman Tank Lines.

For full biographical listings, see the Martindale-Hubbell Law Directory

LIVINGSTON, Essex Co.

SKOLOFF & WOLFE, P.C. (AV)

293 Eisenhower Parkway, 07039
Telephone: 973-992-0900
Fax: 973-992-0301
Morristown, New Jersey Office: 10 Park Place.
Telephone: 973-267-3511.

(See Next Column)

Gary N. Skoloff
Richard H. Singer, Jr. (Resident at Morristown Office)
Stephen P. Haller
Edward J. O'Donnell
Beatrice E. Kandell

OF COUNSEL

Bertram Polow

For Complete List of Firm Personnel, See General Section

For full biographical listings, see the Martindale-Hubbell Law Directory

MILLBURN, Essex Co.

GROSMAN & GROSMAN (AV)

75 Main Street Suite 205, 07041
Telephone: 973-467-9520
FAX: 973-467-0322
Email: agrosman@bellatlantic.net

Charles M. Grosman (1921-1970)
Alan M. Grosman

References: The Bank of New York; National Community Bank Division.

For full biographical listings, see the Martindale-Hubbell Law Directory

*MORRISTOWN,** Morris Co.

CELLI, SCHLOSSBERG & DIAMOND, L.L.C. (AV)

10 Park Place, Suite 305, 07960
Telephone: 973-292-7500
Fax: 973-539-3359
Email: csdcounsel@aol.com. *URL:* http://www.lawyers.com/csdlaw

Vincent P. Celli
Michael J. Schlossberg
Howard S. Diamond

ASSOCIATES

Shivaun M. McConnell
Hope E. Tuber
Antonietta L. Milelli
Gregory Paul Day

OF COUNSEL

William H. Claxton
Albert B. Jeffers
Joseph A. Molinaro

LEGAL SUPPORT PERSONNEL

Renée Orrico
Debra A. Gerhold

For full biographical listings, see the Martindale-Hubbell Law Directory

LAURENCE J. CUTLER (AV)

60 Washington Street, 07960
Telephone: 201-539-0075
Telecopier: 201-539-4151
URL: http://www.lawyers.com/cutlerlaw
Email: ljc@cutlaw.com *URL:* http://www.cutlaw.com

ASSOCIATES

Salvatore A. Simeone
Deanna V. Delplato

For full biographical listings, see the Martindale-Hubbell Law Directory

*NEWARK,** Essex Co.

HELLRING LINDEMAN GOLDSTEIN & SIEGAL LLP (AV)

One Gateway Center, 07102-5386
Telephone: 973-621-9020
Fax: 973-621-7406
Englewood, New Jersey Office: 32-40 North Dean Street.
Telephone: 201-871-3060.

Joel D. Siegal
Margaret Dee Hellring
Charles Oransky
Richard K. Coplon
Robert S. Raymar
Ronny Jo Greenwald Siegal
Bruce S. Etterman
Ronnie F. Liebowitz
Sheryl E. Koomer

Lisa P. Parker
Catherine J. Bick

For Complete List of Firm Personnel, See General Section

For full biographical listings, see the Martindale-Hubbell Law Directory

MCCARTER & ENGLISH, LLP (AV)

Four Gateway Center, 100 Mulberry Street, P.O. Box 652, 07101-0652
Telephone: 973-622-4444
Telecopier: 973-624-7070
URL: http://www.mccarter.com
Cherry Hill, New Jersey Office: 1820 Chapel Avenue West, Suite 380.
Telephone: 609-662-8444.
Telecopier: 609-662-6203.
New York, New York Office: Suite 2247, One World Trade Center.
Telephone: 212-466-9018.
Telecopier: 212-432-6568.
Boca Raton, Florida Office: 2255 Glades Road, Suite 319-A.
Telephone: 561-994-6262.
Telecopier: 561-241-0798.

(See Next Column)

McCARTER & ENGLISH LLP, *Newark—Continued*

Wilmington, Delaware Office: Mellon Bank Center, 919 Market Street.
Telephone: 302-654-8010.
Telecopier: 302-654-0795.
Philadelphia, Pennsylvania Office: One Commerce Square, 2005 Market Street, Suite 3600.
Telephone: 215-557-7700.
Telecopier: 215-557-6544.

MEMBERS OF FIRM

Alfred L. Ferguson — Myrna L. Wigod

ASSOCIATES

Cynthia Spera Neff — Kimberly J. Hines

For Complete List of Firm Personnel, See General Section

For full biographical listings, see the Martindale-Hubbell Law Directory

SILLS CUMMIS RADIN TISCHMAN EPSTEIN & GROSS, A PROFESSIONAL CORPORATION (AV)

One Riverfront Plaza, 07102-5400
Telephone: 973-643-7000
Fax: 973-643-6500
Telex: 820630 Sillsbeck Nwk
Email: sillsmail@sillscummis.com *URL:* http://www.sillscummis.com
Atlantic City, New Jersey Office: 17 Gordon's Alley.
Telephone: 609-344-2800.
New York, N.Y. Office: 712 Fifth Avenue.
Telephone: 212-643-7000.
Washington, D.C. Office: 1800 K Street, N.W.
Telephone: 202-296-4750.

MEMBER OF FIRM

Morton S. Bunis

For Complete List of Firm Personnel, See General Section

For full biographical listings, see the Martindale-Hubbell Law Directory

NORTH BRUNSWICK, Middlesex Co.

BORRUS, GOLDIN, FOLEY, VIGNUOLO, HYMAN, STAHL & CLARKIN, A PROFESSIONAL CORPORATION (AV)

2875 U.S. Highway 1, Route 1 & Finnigans Lane, P.O. Box 7463, 08902
Telephone: 732-422-1000
Fax: 732-422-1016
Email: attys@borrus.com *URL:* http://www.borrus.com

Jack Borrus — Jeffrey M. Hyman
Martin S. Goldin — James E. Stahl
David M. Foley — James F. Clarkin III
Anthony B. Vignuolo — Eileen Mary Foley

Robert C. Nisenson — Steven L. Fox
Rosalind Westlake — Peter A. Vignuolo
Lisa M. Vignuolo — Gerald T. Foley (1903-1976)

Representative Clients: Summit Bank; R. J. Reynolds Tobacco Co.; K. Hovnanian Enterprises, Inc.; Johnson and Johnson; Foster Wheeler, Inc.; Hartz Mountain Industries; Middlesex County Vocational Services Commission; Borough of South Plainfield Board of Adjustment; U-Haul of Northern NJ.

For full biographical listings, see the Martindale-Hubbell Law Directory

BUSCH AND BUSCH, LLP (AV)

215 North Center Drive, Commerce Center - U.S. #1 South, P.O. Box 7448, 08902-7448
Telephone: 732-821-2300
Telecopier: 732-821-5588
Email: busch@ifu.net

MEMBERS OF FIRM

Lewis D. Busch (1901-1986) — Bertram E. Busch
Henry Busch (Retired) — Mark N. Busch
Malcolm R. Busch — Leonard R. Busch
Ronald J. Busch — Steven F. Satz
Donald J. Sears

ASSOCIATE

Paul Alan VanBuskirk

Representative Clients: Utica Mutual Insurance Co.; New Brunswick Tomorrow; Township of South Brunswick; Township of Monroe, Board of Education; Township of East Brunswick; Minnesota Mutual Life Insurance Co.

For full biographical listings, see the Martindale-Hubbell Law Directory

NORTHFIELD, Atlantic Co.

THE LAW OFFICES OF CHARLES A. MATISON (AV)

1640 Tilton Road, P.O. Box 669, 08225
Telephone: 609-407-1100
Fax: 609-407-1030
Email: cmatisonesquire@worldnet.att.net *URL:* http://www.matison.baweb.comm

(See Next Column)

Charles A. Matison

Elizabeth Logan

For full biographical listings, see the Martindale-Hubbell Law Directory

OAKHURST, Monmouth Co.

JACOBOWITZ, GRABELLE, DEFINO, MCGOUGHRAN & LATIMER (AV)

257 Monmouth Road, P.O. Box 609, 07755-0609
Telephone: 732-517-0900
Email: Tfmlaw@aol.com

Philip E. Jacobowitz — Timothy F. McGoughran
Toby Grabelle — Brian P. Latimer
Joseph F. Defino — Edward P. Fradkin

For full biographical listings, see the Martindale-Hubbell Law Directory

OCEAN CITY, Cape May Co.

RICHARD A. RUSSELL A PROFESSIONAL CORPORATION (AV)

117 Atlantic Avenue, P.O. Box 30, 08226
Telephone: 609-398-1900
Fax: 609-398-7292

Richard A. Russell

Janiffer E. Loder

For full biographical listings, see the Martindale-Hubbell Law Directory

PARAMUS, Bergen Co.

FINNERTY & LAROCCA, P.C. (AV)

Country Club Plaza, W 115 Century Road, 07652
Telephone: 201-845-4000
Facsimile: 201-845-6799
URL: http://finnertylarocca
URL: http://www.familylaw-nj.com

John E. Finnerty — Frank J. LaRocca

Erin K. Burke — Gina R. Pacinella

OF COUNSEL

Eugenie F. Temmler

For full biographical listings, see the Martindale-Hubbell Law Directory

PRINCETON, Mercer Co.

BERGMAN & BARRETT (AV)

9 Tamarack Circle, Montgomery Knoll, U.S. Highway 206 North, P.O. Box 1273, 08542
Telephone: 609-921-1502
Fax: 609-683-0288

Edward J. Bergman — Michael T. Barrett

LEGAL SUPPORT PERSONNEL

Kelli E. Murphy (Paralegal)

For full biographical listings, see the Martindale-Hubbell Law Directory

McCARTHY AND SCHATZMAN, P.A. (AV)

228 Alexander Street, P.O. Box 2329, 08543-2329
Telephone: 609-924-1199
Fax: 609-683-5251

John F. McCarthy, Jr. — Michael A. Spero
Richard Schatzman — Barbara Strapp Nelson
G. Christopher Baker — W. Scott Stoner
John F. McCarthy, III — James J. Britt, Jr.

Charly Gayden

Representative Clients: Trustees of Princeton University; Carnegie Center Associates; Merrill Lynch Pierce Fenner & Smith, Inc.; Calton Homes, Inc.

For full biographical listings, see the Martindale-Hubbell Law Directory

STARK & STARK, A PROFESSIONAL CORPORATION (AV)

Princeton Pike Corporate Center, P.O. Box 5315, 08543-5315
Telephone: 609-896-9060
Fax: 609-896-0629
Email: info@stark-stark.com *URL:* http://www.stark-stark.com

Robert J. Durst, II

OF COUNSEL

Maria P. Imbalzano — Frances M. Merritt

(See Next Column)

STARK & STARK A PROFESSIONAL CORPORATION—*Continued*

Sudha Tiwari Kantor

For full biographical listings, see the Martindale-Hubbell Law Directory

ROSELAND, Essex Co.

BRACH, EICHLER, ROSENBERG, SILVER, BERNSTEIN, HAMMER & GLADSTONE, A PROFESSIONAL CORPORATION (AV)

101 Eisenhower Parkway, 07068
Telephone: 973-228-5700
Telecopier: 973-228-7852
Email: law@bracheichler.com *URL:* http://www.bracheichler.com

Kristine Bogardus Purcell

OF COUNSEL

Harris R. Silver

Representative Clients: Advance Realty Goup; ARC Properties, Inc.; I. Heller Industrial Parks; The Kushner Companies; Mercer Medical Center; Ohio Casualty Insurance Group; Perlmart Shop-Rites; Saint Barnabas Health Care System; Silverline Building Products Corp.

For Complete List of Firm Personnel, See General Section

For full biographical listings, see the Martindale-Hubbell Law Directory

POST, POLAK, GOODSELL & MACNEILL, P.A. (AV)

75 Livingston Avenue, 07068-3701
Telephone: 973-994-1100
Telecopier: 973-994-1705
Email: administrator@ppgm.com
New York, New York Office: 575 Madison Avenue, Suite 1006.
Telephone: 212-486-1455.

John N. Post
Mary H. Post

Loretta B. Critchley
Joseph Tripodi

For Complete List of Firm Personnel, See General Section

For full biographical listings, see the Martindale-Hubbell Law Directory

WEINSTEIN SNYDER, A PROFESSIONAL CORPORATION (AV)

103 Eisenhower Parkway, 07068
Telephone: 973-403-6000
Fax: 973-403-7872

Jeffrey P. Weinstein
Edward S. Snyder
Cynthia Borsella Lindemann
Laura Marie D'Orsi
Rachel Zakarin
Angelo Sarno
Stephanie Sonzogni

For full biographical listings, see the Martindale-Hubbell Law Directory

SADDLE BROOK, Bergen Co.

COHN LIFLAND PEARLMAN HERRMANN & KNOPF LLP (AV)

Park 80 Plaza West-One, 07663
Telephone: 201-845-9600
Telecopier: 201-845-9423
Email: info@njlawfirm.com *URL:* http://www.njlawfirm.com

MEMBERS OF FIRM

Albert L. Cohn
Peter S. Pearlman
Barry A. Knopf
Daniel Crystal (Retired)
Jeffrey W. Herrmann
Robert D. Zatorski
Allen Susser
Mary Ann T. Stokes
Brian D. Zinn
Joshua P. Cohn

ASSOCIATES

Virginia A. Harper
Leonard Z. Kaufmann
Audra DePaolo
Robert Ricci, Jr.
Maurice W. McLaughlin
Andrew C. Abrams
Jessica V. Henry

OF COUNSEL

Sylvia J. Cohn
Jodi B. Scherl

For full biographical listings, see the Martindale-Hubbell Law Directory

*SOMERVILLE,** Somerset Co.

SCHACHTER, TROMBADORE, OFFEN, STANTON & PAVICS, A PROFESSIONAL CORPORATION (AV)

45 East High Street, P.O. Box 520, 08876-0520
Telephone: 908-722-5700
Fax: 908-722-8853

John J. Trombadore
Michael J. Stanton

Jerry S. D'Aniello

For full biographical listings, see the Martindale-Hubbell Law Directory

SPRINGFIELD, Union Co.

ELLIOT H. GOURVITZ, P.A. (AV)

150 Morris Avenue, P.O. Box 476, 07081-1315
Telephone: 973-467-3200
Fax: 973-912-0432
Email: ehg@gourvitz.com *URL:* http://www.ehg@gourvitz.com

Elliot H. Gourvitz

Richard A. Outhwaite

For full biographical listings, see the Martindale-Hubbell Law Directory

JAMES P. YUDES A PROFESSIONAL CORPORATION (AV)

80 Morris Avenue, 07081
Telephone: 973-467-3700
Fax: 973-467-9303
Email: jyudes@yudesfamilylaw.com *URL:* http://www.lawyers.com/yudesjames

James P. Yudes
Kevin M. Mazza

Elizabeth Bedell
Holly M. Friedland
John W. Callinan
Karen Tichenor Willitts
Nicole C. Solvibile

For full biographical listings, see the Martindale-Hubbell Law Directory

TENAFLY, Bergen Co.

ROBERT A. VORT (AV)

45 Central Avenue, P.O. Box 142, 07670-0142
Telephone: 201-816-9444
Fax: 201-894-1718
Email: r.vort@vortlaw.com *URL:* http://www.vortlaw.com

ASSOCIATE

Avrin Slatkin

OF COUNSEL

Anne M. Ronan

For full biographical listings, see the Martindale-Hubbell Law Directory

*TRENTON,** Mercer Co.

NEEDELL, SIEKERKA & CASTELLANI, A PROFESSIONAL CORPORATION (AV)

Quakerbridge Commons, 2681 Quakerbridge Road, 08619-1625
Telephone: 609-584-7700
Fax: 609-584-0123
Email: nsclaw@aol.com

Stanley H. Needell
Michele N. Siekerka
Anthony P. Castellani

John M. Cinti
Dean C. Gresek

LEGAL SUPPORT PERSONNEL

PARALEGALS

Marlene Griesbach
Carolyn D. Shaw
Veronica A. Mitchell

For full biographical listings, see the Martindale-Hubbell Law Directory

TEICH, GROH AND FROST (AV)

691 State Highway 33, 08619-4492
Telephone: 609-890-1500
Fax: 609-890-6961
Email: teich1g2f3@aol.com
Lawrenceville, New Jersey Office: 109 Franklin Corner Road.
Telephone: 609-844-0488.
Fax: 609-844-0784.

MEMBERS OF FIRM

Arthur Teich (1915-1997)
William C. Groh
Barry W. Frost
Carol Oswald (Also at Lawrenceville Office)
Carol L. Knowlton
Allen I. Gorski
Arthur R. Sypek, Jr.
Dean S. Nalbone

ASSOCIATES

Jill M. Wittenborn (Also at Lawrenceville Office)
Michael W. Krutman
David A. Martin
Kimberley M. Lake

References: CoreStates/New Jersey National Bank; United National Bank.

For full biographical listings, see the Martindale-Hubbell Law Directory

WARREN, Somerset Co.

FREDERICK J. SIKORA, P.A. (AV)

51 Mt. Bethel Road, P.O. Box 4623, 07059-0623
Telephone: 908-755-8700
Fax: 908-755-8706

Frederick J. Sikora

James J. Moloughney

Approved Attorneys for: Chelsea Title and Guaranty Co.; Chicago Title Insurance Co.; Commonwealth Land Title Insurance Co.; Inter-County Title and Abstract Co.; Lawyers Title Insurance Corporation of Richmond, Va.; New Jersey Realty Title Insurance Co.
Reference: United National Bank, Plainfield, New Jersey.

For full biographical listings, see the Martindale-Hubbell Law Directory

WAYNE, Passaic Co.

DEYOE HEISSENBUTTEL, L.L.C. (AV)

401 Hamburg Turnpike, P.O. Box 2449, 07474-2449
Telephone: 973-595-6300
Fax: 973-595-0146
Email: deyoelaw@ix.netcom.com *URL:* http://www.deyoe.com

MEMBERS OF FIRM

Charles P. DeYoe (1923-1973)
Wood M. DeYoe
Frederick C. Heissenbuttel
Scott B. Piekarsky

ASSOCIATES

Raymond F. Shenekji
Anne Hutton
Albert C. Buglione
Laureen A. Moloney

LEGAL SUPPORT PERSONNEL

Marilyn Moore (Office Manager)

Representative Clients: Hanover Insurance Inc.; Maryland Casualty Co.; Ohio Casualty Insurance Co.; Motor Club of America; Selective Insurance Co.; Prudential Property & Casualty; Reliance Ins. Co.

For full biographical listings, see the Martindale-Hubbell Law Directory

FELDMAN & FIORELLO (AV)

65 Willowbrook Boulevard, 4th Floor, 07470
Telephone: 973-890-9222
Fax: 973-890-7068
Email: wfeldmanesq@worldnet.att.net

William A. Feldman
John Fiorello

ASSOCIATES

Linda Couso Puccio
Melissa Feldman Michalsky
Jeffrey Fiorello
Frank R. Butterfield

References: First Union Bank, N.A.; Valley National Bank (Willowbrook Branch).

For full biographical listings, see the Martindale-Hubbell Law Directory

WOODBRIDGE, Middlesex Co.

WILENTZ, GOLDMAN & SPITZER, A PROFESSIONAL CORPORATION (AV)

90 Woodbridge Center Drive Suite 900, Box 10, 07095
Telephone: 732-636-8000
Telecopier: 732-855-6117
URL: http://www.newjerseylaw.com
Eatontown, New Jersey Office: Meridian Center I, Two Industrial Way West, 07724.
Telephone: 732-542-4500.
Telecopier: 732-493-8387.
New York, New York Office: Wall Street Plaza, 88 Pine Street, 9th Floor, 10005.
Telephone: 212-267-3091.
Telecopier: 212-267-3828.

David M. Wildstein
Jay J. Ziznewski
Noel S. Tonneman (Resident, Eatontown Office)
Jeffrey K. Epstein

Charles F. Vuotto, Jr.
Risa A. Kleiner
Lee Ann McCabe
Andrea White O'Brien (Resident, Eatontown, New Jersey Office)
Steven R. Enis

Representative Firm Clients: Amerada Hess Corp.; Chevron, U.S.A.; Cumberland Farms, Inc.; Middlesex County Utilities Authority; New Jersey Automobile Dealers Assn.; Co-Steel Raritan; The Rouse Co.

For Complete List of Firm Personnel, See General Section

For full biographical listings, see the Martindale-Hubbell Law Directory

NEW MEXICO

*ALBUQUERQUE,** Bernalillo Co.

ATKINSON & KELSEY, P.A. (AV)

2155 Louisiana Boulevard, NE Suite 2000, P.O. Box 3070, 87110
Telephone: 505-883-3070
Fax: 505-889-3111
Email: ak@atkinsonkelsey.com

David H. Kelsey
Jon A. Feder
Thomas C. Montoya
Stephen J. E. Sprague
Claire E. Sanderson Hanna
Gretchen M. Walther
Fred C. Martinez
Virginia Ruth Dugan
Linda André-Wells

PARALEGALS

Keith Eckrich
Jennifer L. Schouman, CLA (Legal Assistant)

Reference: Norwest Bank New Mexico, N.A.

For full biographical listings, see the Martindale-Hubbell Law Directory

CARMODY LAW OFFICES (AV)

1200 Pennsylvania Street, N.E., 87110
Telephone: 505-232-2800
Fax: 505-268-7027
Email: carmlaw@aol.com

John J. Carmody, Jr.

For full biographical listings, see the Martindale-Hubbell Law Directory

LITTLE, GILMAN & VELASQUEZ, P.A. (AV)

500 Marquette NW Suite 770, P.O. Box 26717, 87125
Telephone: 505-246-0500
Facsimile: 505-246-9953
URL: http://www.lawyers.com/l&gfirm

Sandra Morgan Little
Jan B. Gilman
Gregg G. Velasquez

LEGAL SUPPORT PERSONNEL

M. Esther Lopez (Paralegal)
Shilott G. Napier, CLA (Paralegal)

For full biographical listings, see the Martindale-Hubbell Law Directory

WALTHER ASSOCIATES (AV)

4316 Carlisle Boulevard, N.E., Suite D, 87107
Telephone: 505-889-8240
Fax: 505-889-8242
Email: walther@swcp.com
Santa Fe, New Mexico Office: 141 E. Palace Avenue, 87501.
Telephone: 505-984-0097.
Fax: 505-983-2467.

David L. Walther

ASSOCIATES

Jami B. Hotsinpiller
Twila B. Larkin
Constance T. Fuqua (Resident, Santa Fe, New Mexico Office)

For full biographical listings, see the Martindale-Hubbell Law Directory

*SANTA FE,** Santa Fe Co.

GERBER & BATEMAN, A PROFESSIONAL ASSOCIATION (AV)

417 East Palace Avenue, P.O. Box 2325, 87501
Telephone: 505-988-9646
Facsimile: 505-989-7335
Email: gb@swcp.com

Paul D. Gerber
Kenneth Bateman

Peter Burman

References: The First National Bank of Santa Fe; Century Bank.

For full biographical listings, see the Martindale-Hubbell Law Directory

WALTHER ASSOCIATES (AV)

141 E. Palace Avenue, 87501
Telephone: 505-984-0097
Fax: 505-983-2467
Email: walther@swcp.com
Albuquerque, New Mexico Office: 4316 Carlisle Boulevard, N.E., Suite D. 87107.
Telephone: 505-889-8240.
Fax: 505-889-8242.

David L. Walther

(See Next Column)

WALTHER ASSOCIATES—*Continued*

ASSOCIATES

Jami B. Hotsinpiller | Twila B. Larkin
Constance T. Fuqua (Resident)

For full biographical listings, see the Martindale-Hubbell Law Directory

WHITE, KOCH, KELLY & MCCARTHY, A PROFESSIONAL ASSOCIATION (AV)

433 Paseo De Peralta, P.O. Box 787, 87504-0787
Telephone: 505-982-4374
ABA/NET: 1154
Fax: 505-982-0350; 984-8631
Email: WKKM@NM.NET

Janet Clow | Aaron J. Wolf

Julie A. Wittenberger

For Complete List of Firm Personnel, See General Section

For full biographical listings, see the Martindale-Hubbell Law Directory

NEW YORK

*BUFFALO,** Erie Co.

BORINS, SETEL, SNITZER & BROWNSTEIN (AV)

710 Statler Towers, 14202-2907
Telephone: 716-854-5200
Fax: 716-854-5204

MEMBERS OF FIRM

Louis Borins (1908-1979) | Eugene M. Setel
Isadore Snitzer | Joel Brownstein

Reference: HSBC.

For full biographical listings, see the Martindale-Hubbell Law Directory

SULLIVAN & OLIVERIO (AV)

600 Main Place Tower, 14202-3706
Telephone: 716-854-5300
Telecopier: 716-854-5299
Email: sulliolaw@aol.com

MEMBERS OF FIRM

Richard T. Sullivan | B. P. Oliverio
Bruce W. Hoover

Thomas M. Moll | Michael E. Appelbaum
Kevin M. Carter

OF COUNSEL

Paul D. Pearson

For full biographical listings, see the Martindale-Hubbell Law Directory

COMMACK, Suffolk Co.

KRAMER, FEINGOLD & CASTROVINCI, PLLC (AV)

Formerly Law Offices of Lynne Adair Kramer
6165 Jericho Turnpike, 11725
Telephone: 516-462-5850
Telecopier: 516-462-5862

Lynne Adair Kramer | Jennifer Feingold
Philip John Castrovinci

Stacy J. Evans

OF COUNSEL

Ruth Sovronsky

For full biographical listings, see the Martindale-Hubbell Law Directory

GARDEN CITY, Nassau Co.

DASILVA, HILOWITZ & MCEVILY LLP (AV)

585 Stewart Avenue, 11530
Telephone: 516-222-0700
Fax: 516-222-0743

Willard H. DaSilva | Lynne S. Hilowitz
Charles J. McEvily

OF COUNSEL

Frank G. D'Angelo, Jr.

For full biographical listings, see the Martindale-Hubbell Law Directory

THE LAW OFFICES OF JOHN P. DIMASCIO (AV)

300 Garden City Plaza, Suite 306, 11530-3331
Telephone: 516-747-4343
Telefax: 516-747-0204
Email: JDimas9249@aol.com *URL:* http://www.lawyers.com/jpdlaw

ASSOCIATES

Jeffrey S. Chang | John P. DiMascio, Jr.

For full biographical listings, see the Martindale-Hubbell Law Directory

LAW OFFICES OF STEPHEN GASSMAN (AV)

666 Old Country Road, 11530
Telephone: 516-228-9181
Telecopier: 516-745-6712

MEMBER OF FIRM

Stephen Gassman

Charlotte Betts | Rosalia Baiamonte

OF COUNSEL

Richard J. Keidel | Cynthia J. Cornaire
Timothy M. Tippins | Mary Sullivan Calabrese

For full biographical listings, see the Martindale-Hubbell Law Directory

OSTROW AND TAUB, LLP (AV)

300 Garden City Plaza, 11530
Telephone: 516-877-1800
Telecopier: 516-294-0227
Email: ostrowtaub@aol.com *URL:* http://www.lawyers.com/ostrowtaub

MEMBERS OF FIRM

Michael J. Ostrow | Stephen R. Taub

ASSOCIATES

Barbara Brown | A. James Temsamani

For full biographical listings, see the Martindale-Hubbell Law Directory

SAMUELSON RIEGER & YOVINO, LLP (AV)

300 Garden City Plaza, 11530
Telephone: 516-294-6666
Telecopier: 516-294-6622
Email: saillex@aol.com

Elliot D. Samuelson | Richard L. Hause
Kieth I. Rieger | Wendy B. Samuelson
Anthony Yovino | Edward A. Andrews

For full biographical listings, see the Martindale-Hubbell Law Directory

ISLIP, Suffolk Co.

SHLIMBAUM, SHLIMBAUM AND JABLONSKI (AV)

265 Main Street, P.O. Box 8, 11751-0008
Telephone: 516-277-4300
Telecopier: 516-277-4350

MEMBERS OF FIRM

C. Donald Shlimbaum | Lark J. Shlimbaum
Edward C. Jablonski

ASSOCIATES

Laura Mc Kenna | Joseph R. Mercurio

For full biographical listings, see the Martindale-Hubbell Law Directory

*ITHACA,** Tompkins Co.

WIGGINS AND MASSON, LLP (AV)

308 North Tioga Street, P.O. Box 399, 14851
Telephone: 607-272-0479
Telecopier: 607-273-0502
Email: law@wigginsandmasson.com *URL:* http://www.wigginsandmasson.com

MEMBERS OF FIRM

Walter J. Wiggins | Robin Abrahamson Masson
Erin E. McKinley

Approved Attorneys for: Ticor Title Guaranty Corp.
References: Tompkins County Trust Co.

For Complete List of Firm Personnel, See General Section

For full biographical listings, see the Martindale-Hubbell Law Directory

JAMESTOWN, Chautauqua Co.

BURGETT & ROBBINS (AV)

15 East Fifth Street, P.O. Box 3090, 14702-3090
Telephone: 716-488-3090
Fax: 716-483-3765
1-800-832-6582
Email: help@burgettandrobbins.com *URL:* http://www.burgettandrobbins.com

(See Next Column)

BURGETT & ROBBINS, *Jamestown—Continued*

Dalton J. Burgett
Mary Speedy Hajdu
Dale C. Robbins
Robert A. Liebers
Kenneth M. Lasker
Andrew T. Radack

References: Fleet Bank, Jamestown, New York; Marine Midland Bank, Jamestown, New York; Lake Shore Savings and Loan Association, Jamestown, New York.

For full biographical listings, see the Martindale-Hubbell Law Directory

LAKE SUCCESS, Nassau Co.

DIKMAN AND DIKMAN (AV)

5 Dakota Drive, Suite 208, 11042
Telephone: 516-354-2526
Fax: 516-354-2528
Jamaica, New York Office: 161-10 Jamaica Avenue,
Telephone: 718-739-4830.

MEMBERS OF FIRM

Leo Dikman
Michael Dikman
David S. Dikman

ASSOCIATE

Donna Dikman Dubinsky

Reference: Chase Manhattan Bank.

For full biographical listings, see the Martindale-Hubbell Law Directory

KOOPERSMITH & BROWN, LLP (AV)

3000 Marcus Avenue, Suite 3W7, 11042
Telephone: 516-354-0800
Telecopier: 516-488-4387

MEMBERS OF FIRM

Kenneth Koopersmith
Debra L. Rubin
Amy Lesserson Brown
Charles Margett (1907-1997)

LEGAL SUPPORT PERSONNEL

Eileen Rajecki (Office Manager)

For full biographical listings, see the Martindale-Hubbell Law Directory

*NEW YORK,** New York Co.

BELDOCK LEVINE & HOFFMAN LLP (AV)

99 Park Avenue, 10016-1503
Telephone: 212-490-0400
Cable Address: "Telhofflaw, N.Y."
Telecopier: 212-557-0565
URL: http://www.blhny.com

MEMBER OF FIRM

Katherine G. Thompson

For full biographical listings, see the Martindale-Hubbell Law Directory

BRONSTEIN, VAN VEEN & BRONSTEIN, P.C. (AV)

Carnegie Hall Tower, 152 West 57th Street, 10019
Telephone: 212-956-8300
Telefax: 212-956-1452

Peter E. Bronstein

Ann Cynthia Diamond
Leigh Baseheart Kahn

OF COUNSEL

Donald Lockhart Schuck
Eli H. Bronstein (1903-1979)
Donna S. Levin
Henry G. Van Veen (1904-1992)

For full biographical listings, see the Martindale-Hubbell Law Directory

BUTTERMAN KAHN & GARDNER, LLP (AV)

425 Park Avenue, 26th Floor, 10022
Telephone: 212-308-7697
Fax: 212-223-4209

MEMBERS OF FIRM

Jay R. Butterman
Deborah Beth Kahn
Howard A. Gardner

For full biographical listings, see the Martindale-Hubbell Law Directory

COHEN, HENNESSEY & BIENSTOCK, P.C. (AV)

605 Third Avenue - 25th Floor, 10158-0125
Telephone: 212-843-6230
Fax: 212-949-7052
URL: http://www.chblaw.com

Harriet Newman Cohen
Peter Bienstock
Patricia Hennessey
Martha Cohen Stine
Bonnie Rabin

For full biographical listings, see the Martindale-Hubbell Law Directory

ELLENBOGEN & GOLDSTEIN, P.C. (AV)

Metropolitan Tower, 142 West 57th Street, 10019
Telephone: 212-245-3260

Joan L. Ellenbogen
Kenneth Ludman
Marcia C. Goldstein
Raimonde Schwarz
Joseph R. Donohue

For full biographical listings, see the Martindale-Hubbell Law Directory

HOFFINGER FRIEDLAND DOBRISH & STERN, P.C. (AV)

A Professional Corporation including Professional Corporations
110 East 59th Street, 10022-1392
Telephone: 212-421-4000
Telecopier: 212-223-3857

Jack S. Hoffinger
Stephen R. Stern (P.C.)
Lawrence N. Friedland
Samuel P. Ross
Robert Z. Dobrish (P.C.)
Warren R. Gleicher
Philip S. Ross

Michael J. Sherman
Devorah S. Weinschneider
Fran Hoffinger
Eric I. Wrubel
John H. Friedland
Nina S. Gross
Lydia A. Milone
Scott Lawrence D'Aloise

For full biographical listings, see the Martindale-Hubbell Law Directory

LIDDLE & ROBINSON, L.L.P. (AV)

685 Third Avenue, 10017
Telephone: 212-687-8500
Telecopier: 212-687-1505

MEMBERS OF FIRM

Samuel Finkelstein (1906-1996)
W. Dan Boone
Jeffrey L. Liddle
Ethan A. Brecher
Miriam M. Robinson
James A. Batson
Laurence S. Moy
Blaine H. Bortnick
Susan Potter Ellis

ASSOCIATES

Marc A. Susswein
Richard B. Palmer, Jr.
Allan S. Bloom
Christine A. Palmieri
Michael E. Grenert
Keith A. Markel

For full biographical listings, see the Martindale-Hubbell Law Directory

SHERESKY ARONSON & MAYEFSKY, LLP (AV)

750 Lexington Avenue, 19th Floor, 10022
Telephone: 212-521-3500
Fax: 212-838-5505

Norman M. Sheresky
Allan E. Mayefsky
David Aronson
Alton L. Abramowitz

OF COUNSEL

Lawrence B. Trachtenberg

ASSOCIATES

Diane B. Steiner
Patricia A. Kindregan
Heidi Harris
Dana M. Sherins
Michael A. Mosberg

For full biographical listings, see the Martindale-Hubbell Law Directory

STEIN RISO MANTEL HASPEL & JACOBS LLP (AV)

405 Lexington Avenue, 42nd Floor, 10174
Telephone: 212-599-1515
Fax: 212-599-6155
Email: email@srmhj.com
New City, New York Office: 254 South Main Street, 10956.
Telephone: 914-634-1010.
Fax: 914-634-8317.

Dennis L. Stein
Allan D. Mantel
Gerard A. Riso
Joseph J. Haspel
Neil I. Jacobs

Beth E. Spickler
Kevin M. McDonough

COUNSEL

Mark Ira Chinitz

For full biographical listings, see the Martindale-Hubbell Law Directory

HERMAN H. TARNOW (AV)

488 Madison Avenue, 8th Floor, 10022
Telephone: 212-371-9915
Fax: 212-752-0097
Email: tarnow@worldnet.att.net
Southport, Connecticut Office: 2425 Post Road, Suite 203.
Telephone: 203-256-8648.
Facsimile: 203-256-8746

For full biographical listings, see the Martindale-Hubbell Law Directory

New York—Continued

WALLMAN, GREENBERG, GASMAN & McKNIGHT, LLP (AV)

350 Fifth Avenue, Suite 3000, 10118
Telephone: 212-695-6000
Fax: 212-695-6007

MEMBERS OF FIRM

Lester Wallman
Philip A. Greenberg
Gerald B. Gasman
Elaine McKnight
Donald R. Wall

OF COUNSEL

Clement Segal
Daniel E. Clement
Roy L. Jacobs
Frank J. Hariton

LEGAL SUPPORT PERSONNEL

Lisa Chiodi (Office Administrator)

For full biographical listings, see the Martindale-Hubbell Law Directory

PEARL RIVER, Rockland Co.

DRANOFF & GOLDSCHMIDT, L.L.P. (AV)

Suite 800, One Blue Hill Plaza, P.O. Box 1629, 10965-8629
Telephone: 914-735-6200
Fax: 735-7585
Elmsford, New York Office: 570 Taxter Road, 10523.
Telephone: 914-345-5800.
New York, New York Office: 331 Madison Avenue, 10017.
Telephone: 212-643-5351.

PARTNERS

Sanford S. Dranoff
Sylvia Goldschmidt
Donna M. Genovese

ASSOCIATES

Katherine M. Knight
Lisa Colin
Geraldine Helen Dransite
Stamatia Kampitsis
David Warren
Sheri Ann Yodowitz
K. Jody Cucolo

OF COUNSEL

Daniel J. Block

For full biographical listings, see the Martindale-Hubbell Law Directory

*POUGHKEEPSIE,** Dutchess Co.

SATZ & KIRSHON, P.C. (AV)

309 Mill Street, 12601
Telephone: 914-454-4040
Fax: 914-454-2938
URL: http://www.lawyers.com/satz&kirshon

Perry Satz

Juliana Muyot Lobiondo

Reference: Premier National Bank.

For full biographical listings, see the Martindale-Hubbell Law Directory

STEWART T. SCHANTZ (AV)

Riverside Office Park, 404 South Road, Suite 230, 12601
Telephone: 914-473-3171
Fax: 914-473-3194

Betty J. Potenza

For full biographical listings, see the Martindale-Hubbell Law Directory

VAN DEWATER & VAN DEWATER (AV)

40 Garden Street, P.O. Box 112, 12602
Telephone: 914-452-5900
Fax: 914-452-5848
Pawling, New York Office: 243 Route 22, P.O. Box 668.
Telephone: 914-855-5900.
Fax: 914-855-5945.

MEMBERS OF FIRM

John B. Van DeWater (1892-1968)
Robert B. Van DeWater (1920-1990)
David D. Hagstrom
John K. Gifford
James E. Nelson
Craig T. Digilio
Gerard J. Comatos
Ronald C. Blass, Jr.

OF COUNSEL

Noel deCordova, Jr.
Edward VK. Cunningham, Jr.
James D. Benson
Susanna E. Bedell

ASSOCIATES

Rebecca Supple Mensch
Michael G. Hayes

Counsel for: J. D. Johnson Co., Inc.; The Fishkill National Bank; The Bank of the Hudson; Vassar Brothers Hospital.
Local Counsel for: Vassar College; Chemprene Div. of Witco Chemical Corp.; Gannett Satellite Information Network, Inc.

(See Next Column)

For full biographical listings, see the Martindale-Hubbell Law Directory

*ROCHESTER,** Monroe Co.

BECKERMAN & BECKERMAN, LLP (AV)

1 West Main Street Four Corners Building, Suite 300, 14614
Telephone: 716-546-6010
Facsimile: 716-546-7035

MEMBERS OF FIRM

David S. Beckerman (1958-1997)
Gerald Beckerman
Steven M. Beckerman

ASSOCIATE

Elizabeth J. Jewett-Owen

Reference: Marine Midland Bank, Rochester.

For full biographical listings, see the Martindale-Hubbell Law Directory

LACY, KATZEN, RYEN & MITTLEMAN, LLP (AV)

The Granite Building, 130 East Main Street, 14604
Telephone: 716-454-5650
FAX: 716-454-6525
Email: MSS@Frontiernet.net
Charlotte, New York Office: 4292 Lake Avenue.
Telephone: 716-663-4543.
Hilton, New York Office: 20 Main Street.
Telephone: 716-392-2990.
Canandaigua, New York Office: 23 North Main Street.
Telephone: 716-394-5220.
Greece, New York Office: County Village Center, 110 Long Pond Road, Suite 214.
Telephone: 716-225-2470.
Fax: 716-225-5620.
Bergen, New York Office: 16 North Lake Street.
Telephone: 716-494-1382.
Ontario, New York Office: 1276 Ridge Road.
Telephone: 315-524-5000.
Roseland, New Jersey Office: 103 Eisenhower Parkway.
Telephone: 201-403-8001.
Penn Yan, New York Office: 116 Main Street, 2nd Floor, P.O. Box 439.
Telephone: 315-536-6281.

MEMBERS OF FIRM

Louis A. Ryen
Ronald A. Mittleman
Michael S. Schnittman
Peter T. Rodgers
Sally A. Smith
Karen Schaefer
Richard G. Curtis
Lawrence J. Schwind
David H. Walsh IV
David E. Anderson
Craig R. Welch
Christopher B. Mumford
Leslie W. Kernan, Jr.

COUNSEL

Leon Katzen
George F. Frey, Jr.
John J. Keigher
Paul A. Sandars, III

ASSOCIATES

David D. MacKnight
Nia J. Nichols
Terrance W. Emmens
Mark H. Stein
Denine K. Carr
Jacqueline M. Thomas
Stephen M. O'Neill
Jennifer Lynn Chadwick
William H. Drumm
Matthew A. Ryen
Roxanne A. Marvasti
Julie E. Meyer

General Counsel for: Village of Bergen, Bergen, New York; Village of Hilton, Hilton, New York; Byron-Bergen Central School District No. 1, Bergen, New York; Ferris Industries, Inc.; L. Woerner, Inc.d/b/a HCR.
Reference: The Chase Manhattan Bank, Rochester, N.Y.

For full biographical listings, see the Martindale-Hubbell Law Directory

ROME, Oneida Co.

PAUL L. PILECKAS (AV)

Professional Building, 217 North Washington Street, 13440
Telephone: 315-339-3020
Utica: 315-724-6381
Fax: 315-337-3876

Representative Clients: Don Davidson Motors, Inc.; Rome Rental, Inc.; West Electric, Inc.

For full biographical listings, see the Martindale-Hubbell Law Directory

ROSLYN HEIGHTS, Nassau Co.

NATISS, NATISS & GORDON, P.C. (AV)

277 Willis Avenue, 11577
Telephone: 516-621-0900
Telecopier: 516-621-1304
Email: MNatisslaw@aol.com

Marvin Natiss
Gary M. Natiss
Stacey Natiss Gordon

(See Next Column)

NATISS, NATISS & GORDON P.C., *Roslyn Heights—Continued*

Sharon G. Haut

For full biographical listings, see the Martindale-Hubbell Law Directory

*SYRACUSE,** Onondaga Co.

ALDERMAN AND ALDERMAN (AV)

Suite 555 Empire Building, 472 South Salina Street, 13202
Telephone: 315-422-8131
Fax: 315-474-7507
Email: aldermanoffice@worldnet.att.net *URL:* http://www.lawyers.com/aldermanlaw

MEMBERS OF FIRM

Saul H. Alderman (1901-1985)
Bernard Samuels (1907-1985)
Edward B. Alderman
Richard B. Alderman

ASSOCIATE

Janet Jule Dougherty

LEGAL SUPPORT PERSONNEL

Judy M. Conger
Leticia A. Wicks
Tracy A. Esposito

Reference: First National of Rochester.

For full biographical listings, see the Martindale-Hubbell Law Directory

SANFORD MELTZER (AV)

712 Empire Building, 472 South Salina Street, 13202-2493
Telephone: 315-474-4205; 1-800-875-2493
Fax: 315-474-3199
Email: smeltzer@Dreamscape.com
DeWitt, New York Office: 120 Clearview Road.
Telephone: 315-474-4205.
Fax: 315-474-3199.

John P. Wallace

References: Merchants National Bank & Trust Co.; Bank of New York-Central Region.

For full biographical listings, see the Martindale-Hubbell Law Directory

*WARSAW,** Wyoming Co.

SMALLWOOD-COOK & SCHMIEDER (AV)

140 North Main Street, 14569-1103
Telephone: 716-786-2274
FAX: 716-786-2138
Email: smallwood@wycol.com

MEMBERS OF FIRM

Charlotte Smallwood-Cook
Jane A.C. Schmieder

Reference: Wyoming County Bank.

For full biographical listings, see the Martindale-Hubbell Law Directory

*WHITE PLAINS,** Westchester Co.

JOSEPH P. GOVERNALI (AV)

Inns of Court, North Suite, 99 Court Street, 10601
Telephone: 914-946-5300
Telecopier: 914-946-1058

For full biographical listings, see the Martindale-Hubbell Law Directory

ROGAN GUIDA & ORENSTEIN (AV)

235 Mamaroneck Avenue, 10605
Telephone: 1-888-WIN-WITH-US; 914-328-4480
Fax: 914-328-4479
URL: http://www.NYlawyers.com
Email: RoganGO@aol.com *URL:* http://www.lawyers.com/personalinjury

Jeffrey P. Rogan
Toni M. Guida
David L. Orenstein

Representative Clients: Recore One Mortgage Corp.; LEASCO; Pappas Enterprises Inc.; Steelcase, Inc.; Printing Center of Westchester Inc.; Corporate Imaging, Inc.; King Jolo's Flowers, Inc.; Systems Exchange, Inc.; Domus Realty.
Reference: Fleet Bank.

For full biographical listings, see the Martindale-Hubbell Law Directory

YONKERS, Westchester Co.

ECKER, LOEHR, ECKER & ECKER, L.L.P. (AV)

One Executive Boulevard, 10701
Telephone: 914-968-0500; 914-965-4288
FAX: 914-968-0918
Email: eleellp@aol.com
New York, New York Office: 521 Fifth Avenue, 27th Floor, 10175.
Telephone: 914-965-4288;
Fax: 914-968-0918.

(See Next Column)

MEMBERS OF FIRM

Gerald E. Loehr
Louis A. Ecker
Lawrence H. Ecker
Robert L. Ecker

OF COUNSEL

Jock Thornton
Iris J. Iler
Tammi L. Blank-Ecker

LEGAL SUPPORT PERSONNEL

Carolyn Caruso

Reference: Hudson Valley National Bank.

For full biographical listings, see the Martindale-Hubbell Law Directory

NORTH CAROLINA

*ASHEVILLE,** Buncombe Co.

GUM & HILLIER, P.A. (AV)

47 N. Market Street, P.O. Box 3235, 28801
Telephone: 704-258-3368
Fax: 704-252-6721
Email: hgum@interpath.com

Howard L. Gum

Representative Client: Shoney's Restaurants.
References: Asheville Savings Bank; Wachovia Bank and Trust Co.

For full biographical listings, see the Martindale-Hubbell Law Directory

CHAPEL HILL, Orange Co.

EPTING & HACKNEY (AV)

410 Airport Road, P.O. Box 1329, 27514
Telephone: 919-929-0323
Fax: 919-929-3960

MEMBERS OF FIRM

Robert Epting
Joe Hackney
Elizabeth Lackey Jacobs
Karen P. Davidson
Steve Lackey

For full biographical listings, see the Martindale-Hubbell Law Directory

LONG & LONG (AV)

127 TimberHill Place, 27514
Telephone: 919-929-0408
Fax: 919-929-6819

MEMBERS OF FIRM

Lunsford Long
Florence J. Long

For full biographical listings, see the Martindale-Hubbell Law Directory

J. KIRK OSBORN (AV)

100 Europa Drive, Suite 421, 27514
Telephone: 919-929-0987
Fax: 919-942-1822
Email: kirkosborn@aol.com

For full biographical listings, see the Martindale-Hubbell Law Directory

*CHARLOTTE,** Mecklenburg Co.

DOZIER, MILLER, POLLARD & MURPHY (AV)

Cameron Brown Building, 301 South McDowell Street, Suite 700, 28204
Telephone: 704-372-6373
Fax: 704-347-0674
URL: http://www.dmpm.com

MEMBERS OF FIRM

W. Joseph Dozier, Jr.
R. Craig Miller, Jr.
Scott T. Pollard
Gary L. Murphy
William Patrick Hobson
Timothy H. Graham
George N. Miller
Richard S. Gordon
Thomas J. Falish
Kristin L. Smith

For full biographical listings, see the Martindale-Hubbell Law Directory

*CLINTON,** Sampson Co.

BENJAMIN R. WARRICK (AV)

609 College Street, P.O. Box 1416, 28328
Telephone: 910-590-2900
Fax: 910-590-2555

For full biographical listings, see the Martindale-Hubbell Law Directory

*GREENSBORO,** Guilford Co.

SCHOCH & WOODRUFF, L.L.P. (AV)

420 West Market Street, 27401
Telephone: 336-272-9122
Fax: 336-272-7991
Email: swlawgbo@bellsouth.net
High Point, North Carolina Office: 500 East Green Drive, P.O. Box 1893, 27261.
Telephone: 336-884-4151.
Telecopier: 336-883-7151.

Carolyn J. Woodruff

Anna E. Worley — Dwight G. Rodgers, Jr.

For full biographical listings, see the Martindale-Hubbell Law Directory

HIGH POINT, Guilford Co.

SCHOCH & WOODRUFF, L.L.P. (AV)

500 East Green Drive, P.O. Box 1893, 27261
Telephone: 336-884-4151
Telecopier: 336-883-7151
Email: swlawgbo@bellsouth.net
Greensboro, North Carolina Office: 420 West Market Street, 27401.
Telephone: 336-272-9122.
Telecopier: 336-272-7991.

MEMBERS OF FIRM

Arch K. Schoch (1909-1980) — Arch K. Schoch IV
Louise Rodes Schoch (1909-1995)

ASSOCIATE

Arch K. Schoch V

Representative Clients: Archdale Oil Co.; Classic Gallery, Inc.; Cramer Wood Products, Inc.; The High Point Enterprise, Inc.; Jones & Peacock Insurance, Inc.; Phillips Industries, Inc.; Piedmont Chemical Industries, Inc.

For full biographical listings, see the Martindale-Hubbell Law Directory

*RALEIGH,** Wake Co.

GAILOR & ASSOCIATES, P.L.L.C. (AV)

One Hundred Eighteen St. Mary's Street, 27605
Telephone: 919-832-8488
Facsimile: 919-832-8283
Email: cgailor@gailor.com

Carole S. Gailor

Alice L. McNeer — Kimberly Ann Wallis
Sarah Dalonzo-Baker

OF COUNSEL

Frank R. Gailor

LEGAL SUPPORT PERSONNEL

Nancy Burek — Elizabeth Morgan
Lisa A. Seaward

For full biographical listings, see the Martindale-Hubbell Law Directory

HOWARD, GREEN & McDARRIS, L.L.P. (AV)

4000 Westchase Boulevard Suite 200, P.O. Box 10305, 27605
Telephone: 919-833-2422
Fax: 919-833-2430
Email: HGMCD@mindspring.com

Robert E. Howard — Charles P. Green, Jr.
Dori Casey McDarris

ASSOCIATE

Katherine R. Sumrall

References: NationsBank; First Citizens Bank & Trust, Wachovia Bank.

For full biographical listings, see the Martindale-Hubbell Law Directory

*SMITHFIELD,** Johnston Co.

ARMSTRONG & ARMSTRONG, P.A. (AV)

602 South Third Street, P.O. Box 27, 27577
Telephone: 919-934-1575
Fax: 919-934-1846

Marcia H. Armstrong

For full biographical listings, see the Martindale-Hubbell Law Directory

*WINSTON-SALEM,** Forsyth Co.

WHITE AND CRUMPLER (AV)

11 West Fourth Street, 27101
Telephone: 336-725-1304
Fax: 336-761-8845

(See Next Column)

MEMBERS OF FIRM

James G. White (1924-1974) — Fred G. Crumpler, Jr.
Frank M. Armstrong (1900-1979) — G. Edgar Parker
Clyde C. Randolph, Jr. (1928-1995) — David B. Freedman
Dudley A. Witt

ASSOCIATES

Laurie A. Schlossberg — F. Kevin Mauney

OF COUNSEL

Barbara C. Westmoreland — Fred S. Hutchins, Jr.

Reference: Wachovia Bank and Trust Co., N.A., Winston-Salem, North Carolina.

For full biographical listings, see the Martindale-Hubbell Law Directory

WOMBLE CARLYLE SANDRIDGE & RICE (AV)

A Professional Limited Liability Company
200 West Second Street, P.O. Drawer 84, 27102
Telephone: 336-721-3600
Fax: 336-721-3660
Email: lawyers@wcsr.com *URL:* http://www.wcsr.com
Charlotte, North Carolina Office: 3300 One First Union Center, 301 South College Street.
Telephone: 704-331-4900.
Fax: 704-331-4955.
Raleigh, North Carolina Office: 2100 First Union Capitol Center, 150 Fayetteville Street Mall, P.O. Box 831.
Telephone: 919-755-2100.
Fax: 919-755-2150.
Research Triangle Park, North Carolina Office: 2505 Meridian Parkway, Suite 300 (Durham), 27713.
Telephone: 919-484-2300.
Fax: 919-484-2340.
Atlanta, Georgia Office: One Atlantic Center, 1201 West Peachtree Street, Suite 3500.
Telephone: 404-872-7000.
Fax: 404-888-7490.
Other Atlanta, Georgia Office: Suite 404, 2296 Henderson Mill Road, N.E.
Telephone: 770-492-9030.
Fax: 770-492-9609.
Washington, D.C. Office: 1120 Nineteenth Street, N.W., Eighth Floor.
Telephone: 202-857-4400.
Fax: 202-467-6910.
Greenville, South Carolina Office: 15 South Main Street, Suite 601, P.O. Box 10208.
Telephone: 864-255-5400.
Fax: 864-255-5440.

RESIDENT MEMBER

Jimmy H. Barnhill

RESIDENT ASSOCIATE

Mary Nell Craven

Representative Clients: Brad Ragan, Inc.; Brenner Companies; Food Lion, Inc.; Hanes Companies, Inc.; North Carolina Baptist Hospitals, Inc.; R.J. Reynolds Tobacco Co.; Thomasville Furniture Industries, Inc.; Wachovia Corp.; Wake Forest University.

For Complete List of Firm Personnel, See General Section

For full biographical listings, see the Martindale-Hubbell Law Directory

OHIO

*AKRON,** Summit Co.

GOLDMAN & ROSEN, LTD. (AV)

12th Floor, One Cascade Plaza, 44308-1196
Telephone: 330-376-8336
Telecopier: 330-376-2522
Email: Goldman@Raex.com

Samuel Goldman — Michael B. Hendler
Bernard I. Rosen — Marc P. Gertz
George P. Tsarnas — Gary M. Rosen
Irving B. Sugerman

Thomas K. Seeker — Stacey Tsarnas Hackenberg

OF COUNSEL

Frank E. Steel, Jr. — Joseph F. Gorman

References: First National Bank of Ohio; National City Bank, Akron.

For full biographical listings, see the Martindale-Hubbell Law Directory

*CINCINNATI,** Hamilton Co.

PHYLLIS G. BOSSIN CO., L.P.A. (AV)

Suite 1210, 36 East Fourth Street, 45202
Telephone: 513-421-4420
Fax: 513-421-0691
Email: PGB201@aol.com

Phyllis G. Bossin

Adrienne J. Roach

For full biographical listings, see the Martindale-Hubbell Law Directory

CATHY R. COOK (AV)

250 Pendleton Square, 430 Reading Road, 45202-1103
Telephone: 513-241-4029
Fax: 513-723-8634
Email: CCook98767@aol.com *URL:* http://www.lawyers.com/cathycooklaw

For full biographical listings, see the Martindale-Hubbell Law Directory

GOODMAN & GOODMAN A LEGAL PROFESSIONAL ASSOCIATION (AV)

123 East Fourth Street, 45202
Telephone: 513-621-1505; 1-800-494-4529
Fax: 513-621-6900
URL: http://www.goodlaw.com

Reneé S. Frankel — Jeffrey S. Goodman

For full biographical listings, see the Martindale-Hubbell Law Directory

KATZ, TELLER, BRANT & HILD A LEGAL PROFESSIONAL ASSOCIATION (AV)

2400 Chemed Center, 255 East Fifth Street, 45202-4724
Telephone: 513-721-4532
Telecopier: 513-721-7120
Email: corp@ktbh.com

Jerome S. Teller — Guy M. Hild
Bruce A. Hunter

For Complete List of Firm Personnel, See General Section

For full biographical listings, see the Martindale-Hubbell Law Directory

MOSKOWITZ & MOSKOWITZ (AV)

4300 Carew Tower, 441 Vine Street, 45202
Telephone: 513-721-3111
Fax: 513-721-3077

MEMBERS OF FIRM

Joel S. Moskowitz — Michael A. Moskowitz
James H. Moskowitz

Representative Clients: H.R.B., Inc. (Heavy Machinery Sales, Service & Repair); AVC-ACE Exterminating Co.; Three Rivers Convalescent Center, Inc.

For full biographical listings, see the Martindale-Hubbell Law Directory

*CLEVELAND,** Cuyahoga Co.

HERMANN, CAHN & SCHNEIDER (AV)

Suite 500, 1301 East Ninth Street, 44114
Telephone: 216-781-5515
Facsimile: 216-781-1030
Email: hcs@en.com

MEMBER OF FIRM

James S. Cahn

For full biographical listings, see the Martindale-Hubbell Law Directory

KELLEY, McCANN & LIVINGSTONE, LLP (AV)

3500 BP Tower, 200 Public Square, 44114-2302
Telephone: 216-241-3141
Fax: 216-241-3707
Email: Attorneys@kmlegal.com

MEMBERS OF FIRM

John D. Brown — Carl A. Murway
Joel A. Makee — Peter M. Poulos

ASSOCIATES

Renee B. Weiss — Michelle R. Arendt

For Complete List of Firm Personnel, See General Section

For full biographical listings, see the Martindale-Hubbell Law Directory

KOBLENTZ & KOBLENTZ (AV)

55 Public Square, Suite 1170, 44113
Telephone: 216-621-3012
Fax: 216-621-6567
URL: http://www.lawyers.com/koblentz&koblentz

Richard S. Koblentz

Peter A. Russell — Craig J. Morice
Marvin A. Koblentz (1922-1995)

For full biographical listings, see the Martindale-Hubbell Law Directory

LAZZARO AND KRAUS (AV)

940 Leader Building, 526 Superior Avenue, 44114
Telephone: 216-621-8771
Fax: 216-861-6565

Michele M. Lazzaro — Alan H. Kraus

For full biographical listings, see the Martindale-Hubbell Law Directory

MORGANSTERN, MACADAMS & DEVITO CO., L.P.A. (AV)

Burgess Building, Suite 400, 1406 West Sixth Street, 44113
Telephone: 216-621-4244; 216-687-1212
Fax: 216-621-2951
Email: smorgan153@aol.com

Stanley Morganstern — Pamela J. MacAdams
Christopher Michael DeVito

Michael A. Partlow — Cheryl Lukacs
Patrice R. T. Yarham

For full biographical listings, see the Martindale-Hubbell Law Directory

NISCHWITZ, PEMBRIDGE & CHRISZT CO., L.P.A. (AV)

1220 Bond Court Office Building, 1300 East Ninth Street, 44114-1503
Telephone: 216-861-8100
Telecopier: 216-861-8180
Email: dnpc@dnpc.com *URL:* http://www.dnpc.com

OF COUNSEL

Maureen Fiorilli Zito

For full biographical listings, see the Martindale-Hubbell Law Directory

HERBERT PALKOVITZ (AV)

1600 Standard Building, 44113
Telephone: 216-771-3777
FAX: 216-771-1950
Email: palkovlaw@aol.com *URL:* http://www.lawyers.com/palkovlaw

ASSOCIATE

Adam J. Thurman

LEGAL SUPPORT PERSONNEL

Sherri A. Lanzilotta (Legal Assistant)

References: National City Bank; Society National Bank.

For full biographical listings, see the Martindale-Hubbell Law Directory

RANDALL M. PERLA (AV)

19443 Lorain Road, 44126
Telephone: 440-333-2503
Fax: 440-333-9650
URL: http://www.lawyers.com/perlalaw

For full biographical listings, see the Martindale-Hubbell Law Directory

JOHN F. SEELIE (AV)

55 Public Square, Suite 1310, 44113
Telephone: 216-363-1313
Fax: 216-363-1433
Email: jseelie@aol.com

For full biographical listings, see the Martindale-Hubbell Law Directory

WILSMAN & SCHOONOVER (AV)

1920 Bond Court Building, 1300 East 9th Street, 44114-1804
Telephone: 216-589-9600
Fax: 216-589-9800
Email: wslegal@worldnet.att.net *URL:* http://www.att.net/~wslegal

James M. Wilsman — John E. Schoonover

ASSOCIATES

Joseph S Simms — Scott S. Rosenthal

For full biographical listings, see the Martindale-Hubbell Law Directory

Cleveland—Continued

WOLF AND AKERS A LEGAL PROFESSIONAL ASSOCIATION (AV)

1515 The East Ohio Building, 1717 East Ninth Street, 44114
Telephone: 216-623-9999
Fax: 216-623-0629

Marshall J. Wolf — Deborah R. Akers

For full biographical listings, see the Martindale-Hubbell Law Directory

*COLUMBUS,** Franklin Co.

FRIEDMAN & BABBITT CO., L.P.A. (AV)

503 South Front Street Suite 250, 43215-5666
Telephone: 614-221-0090
Fax: 614-221-7213
Email: fbco@ee.net *URL:* http://www.lawyers.com/friedmanbabbittlaw

William S. Friedman — Gerald J. Babbitt

Gary S. Wellbaum — Amy J Weis
Scott N. Friedman

For full biographical listings, see the Martindale-Hubbell Law Directory

WILLIAM L. GEARY (AV)

Suite 101 Waterford Tower, 155 West Main Street, 43215-5000
Telephone: 614-228-1968
Fax: 614-228-7630
URL: http://www.pageomatic.com/williamlgearylawoffice/
Email: williamgeary@martindalemail.com *URL:* http://www.lawyers.com/gearylaw

Gaither Brettell Deluca

For full biographical listings, see the Martindale-Hubbell Law Directory

GERRITY AND BURRIER (AV)

50 West Broad Street, 43215
Telephone: 614-464-2211
Fax: 614-464-0110
URL: http://www.lawyers.com/gerrity&associates

Timothy D. Gerrity — Brian C. Burrier

For full biographical listings, see the Martindale-Hubbell Law Directory

GROSSMAN LAW OFFICES (AV)

32 West Hoster Street, 43215
Telephone: 614-221-7711
Fax: 614-221-7145
Email: lawyers@grossman-law.com *URL:* http://www.lawyers.com/grossmanlaw-divorce

Jeffrey A. Grossman

Thomas J. Jedinak — Anthony R. Auten
Andrew Scott Grossman

For full biographical listings, see the Martindale-Hubbell Law Directory

R. CHRIS HARBOLD AND ASSOCIATES (AV)

32 West Hoster Street, Suite 100, 43215-5632
Telephone: 614-221-7711
Fax: 614-221-7145
URL: http://www.lawyers.com/rcharboldlaw

ASSOCIATE
Amy M. McKinlay

Reference: Bank One.

For full biographical listings, see the Martindale-Hubbell Law Directory

JOSEPH & JOSEPH (AV)

931 South Front Street, 43206
Telephone: 614-449-8282
FAX: 614-449-8287
Email: jandjoseph@aol.com *URL:* http://www.lawyers.com/joseph&joseph

MEMBERS OF FIRM
John J. Joseph — Jennifer J. Joseph

For full biographical listings, see the Martindale-Hubbell Law Directory

HARVEY M. SAMUELS (AV)

529 South Third Street, 43215
Telephone: 614-221-2580
Fax: 614-221-2575

Representative Client: Preferred Risk Mutual Insurance Co.

For full biographical listings, see the Martindale-Hubbell Law Directory

WHITE & FISH, L.P.A., INC. (AV)

1335 Dublin Road Suite 201 (C), 43215
Telephone: 614-485-9300
Fax: 614-485-9462
Email: WFLPA@AOL.COM *URL:* http://www.lawyers.com/white&fish

Arnold S. White — Jeffrey D. Fish

For full biographical listings, see the Martindale-Hubbell Law Directory

*DAYTON,** Montgomery Co.

ROGERS & GREENBERG (AV)

2160 Kettering Tower, 45423
Telephone: 937-223-8171
Fax: 937-223-1649
Email: rgattys@aol.com

MEMBERS OF FIRM
Stanley Z. Greenberg — Keith R. Kearney

L. Anthony Lush

For Complete List of Firm Personnel, See General Section

For full biographical listings, see the Martindale-Hubbell Law Directory

DUBLIN, Franklin Co.

BLAUGRUND, HERBERT & MARTIN, INCORPORATED (AV)

5455 Rings Road, Suite 500, 43017-7517
Telephone: 614-764-0681
Fax: 614-764-0774
Email: bhm@bhmlaw.net

Christopher T. Cline — Beverly J. Farlow

Steven E. Hillman

For full biographical listings, see the Martindale-Hubbell Law Directory

*TOLEDO,** Lucas Co.

LACKEY, NUSBAUM, HARRIS, RENY & TORZEWSKI A LEGAL PROFESSIONAL ASSOCIATION (AV)

Two Maritime Plaza Third Floor, 43604
Telephone: 419-243-1105
Fax: 419-243-8953

Melvin G. Nusbaum

Kenneth E. Boyd

References: Fifth Third Bank; Society Bank.

For full biographical listings, see the Martindale-Hubbell Law Directory

MORAN & MORAN (AV)

626 Madison Avenue, Suite 300, 43604
Telephone: 419-241-8171
Fax: Available Upon Request

Peter L. Moran — Mary Beth Moran

Representative Clients: The Exchange Bank; Payak Insurance Agency; Monroe Pharmacy, Inc.
References: Society Bank; The Fifth Third Bank, Toledo, Ohio.

For Complete List of Firm Personnel, See General Section

For full biographical listings, see the Martindale-Hubbell Law Directory

OKLAHOMA

*ENID,** Garfield Co.

JON R. FORD (AV)

1625 W. Owen K. Garriott, Suite G, 73703-5653
Telephone: 580-234-0253
Fax: 580-234-0256
Email: fordjon@10net.net

LEGAL SUPPORT PERSONNEL
Sue Qualls — Lori Runser

For full biographical listings, see the Martindale-Hubbell Law Directory

*OKLAHOMA CITY,** Oklahoma Co.

JON L. HESTER, P.C. A PROFESSIONAL CORPORATION (AV)

Suite 265, 5400 N. Grand Boulevard, 73112
Telephone: 405-947-8866
Fax: 405-947-1140
Email: HESTERPC@IONET.NET

Jon L. Hester

Reference: BancFirst, Oklahoma City.

For full biographical listings, see the Martindale-Hubbell Law Directory

*TULSA,** Tulsa Co.

BARBARA ANN BARTLETT (AV)

406 South Boulder, Suite 400, 74103
Telephone: 918-584-1894
Fax: 918-584-1891
Email: bab@morelaw.com

For full biographical listings, see the Martindale-Hubbell Law Directory

CLARK & WILLIAMS (AV)

Suite 600 Fox Plaza Office Center, 5416 South Yale Avenue, 74135
Telephone: 918-496-9200
Fax: 918-496-3851
Email: CLAWIL96@aol.com

MEMBERS OF FIRM

Wendell W. Clark
Darrell E. Williams

ASSOCIATES

Mark R. Reents
Michael DeCarlo
Kathryn A. Herwig

References: Bank of Oklahoma; Peoples State Bank.

For full biographical listings, see the Martindale-Hubbell Law Directory

CORBITT & JOHNSON, P.C. (AV)

2900 NationsBank Center, 15 West Sixth Street, 74119
Telephone: 918-583-1818
Fax: 918-587-8537

Sharon L. Corbitt
N. Scott Johnson

For full biographical listings, see the Martindale-Hubbell Law Directory

EAGLETON, EAGLETON AND HARRISON, INC. (AV)

Suite 1700, 320 South Boston Avenue, 74103-4706
Telephone: 918-584-0462
Fax: 918-584-3724
Email: eagleton@worldnet.att.net

E. John Eagleton
James R. Eagleton
Charles D. Harrison

OF COUNSEL

Norma Eagleton

For full biographical listings, see the Martindale-Hubbell Law Directory

HOOD & RAYNOLDS, P.C. (AV)

1914 South Boston, 74119
Telephone: 918-583-5825
Fax: 918-583-8740

William W. Hood
William F. Raynolds, II

For full biographical listings, see the Martindale-Hubbell Law Directory

RONALD MAIN, P.C. (AV)

Center 2800, Suite 821, 2815 East Skelly Drive, 74105-6251
Telephone: 918-742-1990
Fax: 918-742-2004
Email: rmainbtl@aol.com

Ronald Main

Representative Clients: Brumbaugh & Fulton, Co.; Miles Shipping Co.; H.S. Boyd, Co.; Kemco Fuels, Inc.; McDonnell-Douglas Corp.; Oklahoma Bar Professional Liability Insurance Co.; Sawyer Manufacturing Co.
Approved Attorneys For: Columbia Title Insurance Co.
References: Bank IV of Tulsa; Bank of Oklahoma, N.A.

For full biographical listings, see the Martindale-Hubbell Law Directory

LAW OFFICES OF MAYNARD I. UNGERMAN (AV)

Riverbridge Office Park, 1323 East 71st Street, Suite 300, 74136-5043
Telephone: 918-495-0550
Fax: 918-495-0561
Mailing Address: P.O. Box 701917, Tulsa, Oklahoma, 74170-1917

MEMBERS OF FIRM

Irvine E. Ungerman (1908-1980)
Maynard I. Ungerman

(See Next Column)

Stephen J. Greubel

Representative Clients: Tulsa Paint; Norvell-Marcum Company; Tulsa Classroom Teachers Association; Oklahoma Education Association; Born Inc.

For full biographical listings, see the Martindale-Hubbell Law Directory

WAGNER AND GRUNDY (AV)

Suite 1100, 525 Main Mall, 74103
Telephone: 918-587-2547
Fax: 918-587-2886

MEMBERS OF FIRM

Richard A. Wagner, II
Bradley A. Grundy

ASSOCIATE

Tiffany N. Arend

LEGAL SUPPORT PERSONNEL

Sharon Lemonds
Kathy Wagner

For full biographical listings, see the Martindale-Hubbell Law Directory

OREGON

*PORTLAND,** Multnomah Co.

KELL, ALTERMAN & RUNSTEIN, LLP (AV)

1001 S.W. Fifth Avenue, Suite 1800, 97204
Telephone: 503-222-3531
Telecopier: 503-227-2980
Email: kell@teleport.com

MEMBERS OF FIRM

Raymond M. Kell (1911-1991)
Clifford B. Alterman (1925-1995)
Ted E. Runstein
Lee Davis Kell
Wayne D. Palmer
Lloyd R. Summers
William D. Dickas
Gary P. Compa
Charles R. Williamson
Mary Ellen Page Farr
Eric Sogge
Thomas J. Matsuda
Thomas R. Rask, III
Nicholas S. Fish

Dana L. Barnes
Cory Larvik
Robert E. Kabacy
Robin M. Runstein

References: Union Bank of California, N.A. (Portland Branch); The Bank of Tokyo-Mitsubishi, Ltd. (Portland Branch); Bank of America (5th S. Main Branch).

For full biographical listings, see the Martindale-Hubbell Law Directory

STAHANCYK, GEARING & RACKNER, P.C. (AV)

200 Jackson Tower, 806 S.W. Broadway, 97205-3304
Telephone: 503-222-9115
Facsimile: 503-222-4037
URL: http://www.stahancyk.com
Bend, Oregon Office: 141 N.W. Greenwood Avenue, Suite 100.
Telephone: 541-318-9115.
Fax: 541-318-9116.
Astoria, Oregon Office: 52 Commercial Street, 97103.
Telephone: 503-325-9117.

Jody L. Stahancyk
David C. Gearing
Laura E. Rackner

Joel J. Kent (Resident, Bend Office)
Brett E. Engel
Elizabeth M. Cline
Pierre L. Robert

For full biographical listings, see the Martindale-Hubbell Law Directory

PENNSYLVANIA

*ALLENTOWN,** Lehigh Co.

MONDSCHEIN ASSOCIATES (AV)

1809 W. Allen Street, 18104
Telephone: 610-437-7850
Fax: 610-437-7122
URL: http://www.lawyers.com/mondschein

John R. Mondschein

ASSOCIATES

Elizabeth A. Drey
Meredith R. Levin

(See Next Column)

MONDSCHEIN ASSOCIATES—*Continued*

LEGAL SUPPORT PERSONNEL

Helen L. Jones (Paralegal)

For full biographical listings, see the Martindale-Hubbell Law Directory

WIENER AND WIENER LLP (AV)

Suite 400 Commonwealth Building, 512 Hamilton Street, 18101-1505
Telephone: 610-821-8600
Fax: 610-821-8635
West Palm Beach, Florida Office: Suite 900, 1655 Palm Beach Lakes Boulevard.
Telephone: 561-689-6660.
Fax: 561-683-1559.

MEMBERS OF FIRM

Howard A. Wiener
Joel B. Wiener
Stephen W. Wiener
C. Steven Miller
David C. Schattenstein
John H. McKeever

Representative Clients Available Upon Request.

For full biographical listings, see the Martindale-Hubbell Law Directory

BETHLEHEM, Northampton Co.

O'HARE & HEITCZMAN (AV)

18 East Market Street, P.O. Box 1446, 18018
Telephone: 610-691-5500
Fax: 610-691-7866
Email: heitczman@nni.com *URL:* http://www.heitczman.com

MEMBERS OF FIRM

Bernard V. O'Hare, Jr. (1923-1990)
George A. Heitczman

References: Summit Bank; CoreStates Bank.

For full biographical listings, see the Martindale-Hubbell Law Directory

*EASTON,** Northampton Co.

GUS MILIDES (AV)

654 Wolf Avenue, 18042
Telephone: 610-258-0433
Fax: 610-258-4875

For full biographical listings, see the Martindale-Hubbell Law Directory

*HARRISBURG,** Dauphin Co.

GOLDBERG, KATZMAN & SHIPMAN, P.C. (AV)

320 Market Street - Strawberry Square, P.O. Box 1268, 17108-1268
Telephone: 717-234-4161
Telecopier: 717-234-6808; 717-234-6810
Email: gks@gkslaw.com

Ronald M. Katzman
Paul J. Esposito

Diana Woodside

Representative Client: Fulton Bank.

For Complete List of Firm Personnel, See General Section

For full biographical listings, see the Martindale-Hubbell Law Directory

HOWETT, KISSINGER & MILES, P.C. (AV)

130 Walnut Street, P.O. Box 810, 17108
Telephone: 717-234-2616
Fax: 717-234-5402

John C. Howett, Jr.
Donald T. Kissinger
Cindy Sebastian Conley

For full biographical listings, see the Martindale-Hubbell Law Directory

*MEDIA,** Delaware Co.

DIORIO & SERENI, LLP (AV)

Front and Plum Streets, P.O. Box 1789, 19063
Telephone: 610-565-5700
Fax: 610-891-0652
Email: info@dioriosereni.com

Robert M. DiOrio
Mark A. Sereni

ASSOCIATES

Kenneth J. D. Boyden
Christopher R. Mattox

For full biographical listings, see the Martindale-Hubbell Law Directory

*NORRISTOWN,** Montgomery Co.

MURPHY, OLIVER, CAIOLA & GOWEN, A PROFESSIONAL LAW CORPORATION (AV)

43 East Marshall Street, 19401-4828
Telephone: 610-272-4222; 610-279-3838
Fax: 610-272-2549; 610-275-0140
Email: molaw@injury-law.com *URL:* http://www.injury-law.com
Spring City, Pennsylvania Office: 500 S. Main Street, 19475.
Telephone: 610-948-3770.
Pottstown, Pennsylvania Office: 5 Sunnybrook Road, 19464.
Telephone: 610-323-3480.
West Chester, Pennsylvania Office: 1534 McDaniel Drive, Westtown Business Center, 19250.
Telephone: 610-272-4222.

James J. Oliver
Frank P. Murphy
Frank L. Caiola
Thomas L. Gowen, Jr.
Carla E. Connor
Barbara A. Barnes

John F. Haskins, Jr.
Cynthia Love Dengler
Carol A. Crisci

LEGAL SUPPORT PERSONNEL

Patricia A. Talese (Paralegal)
Kathleen Nicholson

For full biographical listings, see the Martindale-Hubbell Law Directory

*PHILADELPHIA,** Philadelphia Co.

ASTOR WEISS KAPLAN & ROSENBLUM, LLP (AV)

The Bellevue, 6th Floor, 200 South Broad Street, 19102
Telephone: 215-790-0100
Fax: 215-790-0509
Email: lawyers@astorweiss.com
Bala Cynwyd, Pennsylvania Office: 401 City Avenue, Suite 500.
Telephone: 610-667-8660.
Fax: 610-667-2783.

MEMBERS OF FIRM

Alvin M. Weiss (1936-1976)
Paul C. Astor
G. David Rosenblum
Arthur H. Kaplan
Barbara Oaks Silver
David S. Workman
David Gutin
David S. Mandel
Gerald J. Schorr

ASSOCIATES

Christopher P. Flannery
Janet G. Felgoise
Elizabeth F. Warner
Daniel A. Shabel
Frances F. Freedman

SPECIAL COUNSEL

Neil Hurowitz
Jerrold V. Moss
Robert P. Style

OF COUNSEL

Edward W. Silver

For full biographical listings, see the Martindale-Hubbell Law Directory

MICHAEL D. FIORETTI (AV)

The Bourse Building, Suite 790, 111 South Independence Mall East, 19106
Telephone: 215-440-7612
Fax: 215-440-0328
Email: fioretti@aol.com *URL:* http://www.lawyers.com/michaelfioretti
Cherry Hill, New Jersey Office: 1765 Springdale Road, Suite B-1, 08003-2177.
Telephone: 609-482-2488.
Fax: 609-424-3690.

ASSOCIATE

Philip A. Charamella

For full biographical listings, see the Martindale-Hubbell Law Directory

DOROTHY K. PHILLIPS (AV)

121 South Broad Street 21st Floor, 19107
Telephone: 215-568-7757
Fax: 215-568-1711
Email: Dkphil@aol.com *URL:* http://www.mydivorceattorney.com
Wynnewood, Pennsylvania Office: P.O. Box 527, 19096.
Telephone: 610-645-5722.
Fax: 215-568-1711.
Cherry Hill, New Jersey office: 220 Lake Drive, Suite 220, 08002.
Telephone: 609-755-9393.
Fax: 609-779-2526.

For full biographical listings, see the Martindale-Hubbell Law Directory

*PITTSBURGH,** Allegheny Co.

Feldstein Grinberg Stein & McKee, A Professional Corporation (AV)

428 Boulevard of the Allies, 15219
Telephone: 412-471-0677
Fax: 412-263-6129
URL: http://www.fgsmlaw.com
Elizabeth, Pennsylvania Office: 400 Second Street.
Telephone: 412-384-6111.

Christine Gale

Natalie M. Garland

For full biographical listings, see the Martindale-Hubbell Law Directory

Gillotti, Capristo & Beck, P.C. (AV)

Suite 215 Grant Building, 15219
Telephone: 412-391-4242
Fax: 412-391-7693
URL: http://www.lawyers.com/gcblaw

Chris F. Gillotti
Robert C. Capristo
James L. Beck
Samantha R. LeComte
Lori A. Kornfeld

Alexis Gursky

For full biographical listings, see the Martindale-Hubbell Law Directory

Goldberg, Gruener, Gentile, Horoho & Avalli, P.C. (AV)

Suite 1320 Grant Building, 15219
Telephone: 412-261-9900
Fax: 412-261-7100

Mark J. Goldberg
Harry J. Gruener
Gary G. Gentile
Kenneth J. Horoho, Jr.
Charles J. Avalli

Velma B. Hirsch
Kerri Lee Cappella
Serena M. Williams
Mark R. Alberts

For full biographical listings, see the Martindale-Hubbell Law Directory

Pillar • Mulroy & Ferber, Professional Corporation (AV)

1106 Frick Building, 15219-6101
Telephone: 412-471-3300
Fax: 412-471-6068
URL: http://www.lawyers.com/pmf__law

Thomas M. Mulroy
Peggy Lynn Ferber

Anthony A. Seethaler, Jr.
Lorraine W. Mervan
Paula Hopkins

Reference: Pittsburgh National Bank.

For full biographical listings, see the Martindale-Hubbell Law Directory

*READING,** Berks Co.

Mogel, Speidel, Bobb & Kershner, A Professional Corporation (AV)

520 Walnut Street, P.O. Box 8581, 19603-8581
Telephone: 610-376-1515
Telecopier: 610-372-8710

George B. Balmer (1902-1969)
George A. Kershner (1907-1969)
Carl F. Mogel (1919-1994)
Edwin H. Kershner
Frederick R. Mogel
Michael L. Mixell
George M. Lutz
Paul M. Yatron
Stephen H. Price
Kathryn K. Harenza

Sean J. O'Brien
Matthew Earl Glinn

OF COUNSEL

Harry W. Speidel
Donald K. Bobb
Henry A. Gass

Representative Clients: Great Valley Bank; Union Township, Berks County, Pennsylvania.

For full biographical listings, see the Martindale-Hubbell Law Directory

*SCRANTON,** Lackawanna Co.

O'Malley & Harris, P.C. (AV)

345 Wyoming Avenue, 18503
Telephone: 570-348-3711
Fax: 570-348-4092
Email: ohpc@epix.net *URL:* http://www.ohpclaw.com
Stroudsburg, Pennsylvania Office: 111 North Seventh Street.
Telephone: 570-421-2252; 570-422-1280.
FAX: 570-422-1281. Email: cerato@ptdprolog.net.
Wilkes-Barre, Pennsylvania Office: 61 North Washington Street.
Telephone: 570-829-3232.
FAX: 570-829-4418. Email: ohpcwb@epix.net.
Williamsport, Pennsylvania Office: 321 Pine Street, Suite 308.
Telephone: 570-323-4380.

Eugene Nogi (1905-1975)
Henry Nogi (1900-1976)
Russell J. O'Malley, Sr. (1904-1993)
Norman Harris (1907-1998)
William H. Amesbury (Resident, Wilkes-Barre Office)
Paul A. Barrett
Matthew P. Barrett
J. Scott Brady (Resident, Wilkes-Barre Office)
Lori J. Cerato (Resident, Stroudsburg Office)
Bruce L. Coyer
John Q. Durkin
Gerald J. Hanchulak
Richard K. Hodges
Timothy J. Holland (Resident, Wilkes-Barre Office)
John F. Kennedy (Resident, Wilkes-Barre Office)
Daniel Morgan
Michael Perry
James M. Tressler
Joseph Timothy Healey
A. Ruth Whalen (Resident, Wilkes-Barre Office)

Representative Clients: Pennsylvania Hospital Insurance Co.; MMI Systems Agency, Inc.; State Farm Insurance Company; ITT Specialty Risk Services; St. Paul Fire & Marine Insurance Co.; Chubb Group of Insurance Companies; Geisingen System Services; Princeton Insurance Company; Northeastern Pennsylvania Physicians Organization; Catholic Healthcare Partners.

For full biographical listings, see the Martindale-Hubbell Law Directory

STATE COLLEGE, Centre Co.

Law Offices I.B. Sinclair (AV)

7 College Court 1535 North Atherton Street, 16803-3043
Telephone: 814-861-3794
Fax: 814-231-1477
Media, Pennsylvania Office; 200 North Jackson Street. Telephone: 610-892-7500.
Fax: 610-892-7504.

LEGAL SUPPORT PERSONNEL

Bonnie Yocom

For full biographical listings, see the Martindale-Hubbell Law Directory

RHODE ISLAND

WARWICK, Kent Co.

Kirshenbaum Law Associates (AV)

67 Jefferson Boulevard, 02888-1053
Telephone: 401-467-5300
Fax: 401-461-4464

MEMBERS OF FIRM

Allen M. Kirshenbaum
Carolyn R. Barone

Lauri Medwin Fine
Evan M. Kirshenbaum

For full biographical listings, see the Martindale-Hubbell Law Directory

WESTERLY, Washington Co.

Adamo and Newman (AV)

42 Granite Street, 02891
Telephone: 401-596-7795
Telecopier: 401-596-9000
URL: http://www.lawyers.com/adamonewmanlaw

MEMBERS OF FIRM

John Joseph Adamo
Edward H. Newman

For full biographical listings, see the Martindale-Hubbell Law Directory

SOUTH CAROLINA

*BEAUFORT,** Beaufort Co.

Davis, Tupper & Grimsley, L.L.P. (AV)

611 Bay Street, P.O. Box 2055, 29901-2055
Telephone: 843-524-1116
Facsimile: 843-524-1463
Email: DTGS@Hargray.com

MEMBERS OF FIRM

Ralph E. Tupper
Erin D. Dean
R. Gerald Chambers, Jr.

For full biographical listings, see the Martindale-Hubbell Law Directory

Harvey & Battey, P.A. (AV)

1001 Craven Street, P.O. Drawer 1107, 29902
Telephone: 843-524-3109
Telefax: 843-524-6973

W. Brantley Harvey, Jr.
H. Grady Brown, III

Approved Attorneys for: Lawyers Title Insurance Corp.; Chicago Title Insurance Corp.
Representative Clients: Nations Bank; First Bank, F.S.B.; Pleasant Point Plantation Associates; Century 21-Carolina Realty, Inc.; Lobeco Products, Inc.; Beaufort County Association of Realtors; The Fripp Company.

For Complete List of Firm Personnel, See General Section

For full biographical listings, see the Martindale-Hubbell Law Directory

*CHARLESTON,** Charleston Co.

Oberman & Oberman (AV)

38 Broad Street, 29401
Telephone: 843-577-7010
Fax: 843-722-7359

MEMBERS OF FIRM

Marvin I. Oberman
Harold A. Oberman

For full biographical listings, see the Martindale-Hubbell Law Directory

Solomon, Budman, Stricker & Schwartz, L.L.P. (AV)

Parkshore Centre, 1 Poston Road, Suite 395, P.O. Box 30280, 29417-0280
Telephone: 843-763-1118
Telecopier: 843-763-7518

A. Bernard Solomon
Donald J. Budman
Michael A. Stricker
Lester S. Schwartz

Local Counsel for: Lawyers Title Insurance Corp.

For full biographical listings, see the Martindale-Hubbell Law Directory

Uricchio, Howe, Krell, Jacobson, Toporek & Theos, P.A. (AV)

17 1/2 Broad Street, 29401
Telephone: 803-723-7491
1-800-899-1683
Fax: 803-577-4179
Mailing Address: P.O. Box 399, Charleston, S.C., 29402-0399
Email: uricchio@ix.netcom.com

Paul N. Uricchio, Jr.
Arthur G. Howe
Barry Krell
Carl H. Jacobson
Alan David Toporek
Jerry N. Theos
Gregory Daulton Keith

For full biographical listings, see the Martindale-Hubbell Law Directory

*COLUMBIA,** Richland Co.

Golden, Taylor & Potterfield (AV)

A Law Partnership between a Professional Association & Attorneys
1712-1714 Main Street, 29201
Telephone: 803-779-3700
Telefax: 803-779-3422
Email: goldenlaw@worldnett.att.net

Harvey L. Golden
J. Michael Taylor
Ashlin Blanchard Potterfield

ASSOCIATE

Almand James Barron

For full biographical listings, see the Martindale-Hubbell Law Directory

King & Vernon, P.A. (AV)

1426 Richland Street, P.O. Box 7667, 29202
Telephone: 803-779-3090
Fax: 803-779-3396
Email: TVernon@usit.net *URL:* http://www.usit.net/users/lawyer/

(See Next Column)

Kermit S. King
W. Thomas Vernon

For Complete List of Firm Personnel, See General Section

For full biographical listings, see the Martindale-Hubbell Law Directory

Rogers Townsend & Thomas, PC (AV)

1441 Main Street, 10th Floor, P.O. Box 100200, 29202-3200
Telephone: 803-771-7900
Fax: 803-254-6305; 343-7017; 343-7019
URL: http://www.rtt-law.com

Robert Bryan Barnes
B. Michael Brackett
Sherwood M. Cleveland
Harry B. Gregory, Jr.
Clifford O. Koon, Jr.
Albert L. Moses
Eugene F. Rogers
Robert J. Thomas
Joe W. Underwood
Samuel C. Waters
W. Alex Weatherly, Jr.
Robert P. Wood
James C. Leventis
Richard M. Unger
Cheryl H. Fisher
D. Randolph Whitt
Stacey Lynch Hewson
Kendall R. Walker
Wm. Bert Brannon

Glen Paul Caulk
Thomas McRoy Shelley, III
Denis A. Brosnan, Jr.
Paul D. de Holczer

OF COUNSEL

James S. Guignard
Gwendelyn Geidel

LEGAL SUPPORT PERSONNEL

Carol A. Cummings

For full biographical listings, see the Martindale-Hubbell Law Directory

*CONWAY,** Horry Co.

Hearn, Brittain & Martin, P.A. (AV)

1206 Third Avenue, 29526
Telephone: 843-248-3172
Fax: 843-248-4911
Myrtle Beach, South Carolina Office: 4614 Oleander Drive.
Telephone: 843-449-8562.
Fax: 843-497-6124.

George M. Hearn, Jr.
Thomas C. Brittain
L. Morgan Martin
Scott B. Umstead
G. Scott Bellamy

Peter Lee Hearn, Sr.

For full biographical listings, see the Martindale-Hubbell Law Directory

*GREENVILLE,** Greenville Co.

Wilkins & Madden, P.A. (AV)

408 East North Street, 29601-3042
Telephone: 864-232-5629
Fax: 864-233-6943

David H. Wilkins
Timothy E. Madden

Rochelle Y. Williamson
Joseph M. Ramseur, Jr.

References: Carolina First Bank; The Palmetto Bank.

For full biographical listings, see the Martindale-Hubbell Law Directory

*SUMTER,** Sumter Co.

Lee, Erter, Wilson, Holler & Smith, L.L.C. (AV)

126 North Main Street, P.O. Box 580, 29150
Telephone: 803-778-2471
Telecopier: 803-778-1643

MEMBERS OF FIRM

John Dozier Lee, Jr. (1921-1999)
Jack W. Erter, Jr.
Harry C. Wilson, Jr.
David Cornwell Holler
G. Murrell Smith, Jr.

Representative Clients: South Carolina National Bank; Carolina Power and Light Co.; Peoples Natural Gas Company of South Carolina; BB&T; Allstate Insurance Co.; American Surety Co.; Prudential Insurance Company of America; General Telephone; Korn Industries, Inc.; V-B William Furniture Co., Inc.

For full biographical listings, see the Martindale-Hubbell Law Directory

McDougall & Self, L.L.P. (AV)

21 East Calhoun Street, P.O. Box 2197, 29151-2197
Telephone: 803-778-5062
Telecopier: 803-778-6908
Columbia, South Carolina Office: 791 Greenlawn Drive, Suite 4, 29209.
Telephone: 803-776-3130.
Telecopier: 803-776-7748.

(See Next Column)

McDougall & Self L.L.P., *Sumter—Continued*

MEMBERS OF FIRM

John O. McDougall
Patricia L. Forbis
Michael W. Self
Peter G. Currence

For full biographical listings, see the Martindale-Hubbell Law Directory

SOUTH DAKOTA

LEAD, Lawrence Co.

Fuller, Tellinghuisen, Gordon & Percy, P.C. (AV)

203 West Main Street, P.O. Box 898, 57754
Telephone: 605-584-2440
Fax: 605-584-1979
Email: leadlaw@mato.com
Spearfish, South Dakota Office: 132 East Illinois, 57783.
Telephone: 605-642-8080.
Fax: 605-642-1756. E-mail: spflaw@mato.com

A. P. Fuller
Bradley P. Gordon
Roger A. Tellinghuisen
Michelle Palmer Percy

Representative Clients: Homestake Mining Co.; Hotel Franklin & Gaming; Black Hills Novelty/Automatic Vending, Inc.; Northern Hills General Hospital; Lantis Enterprises, Inc.; Norwest Bank South Dakota N.A.; Lead-Deadwood Independent School District # 40-1; City of Lead.

For full biographical listings, see the Martindale-Hubbell Law Directory

*RAPID CITY,** Pennington Co.

Delaney & Sumner (AV)

623 Quincy Street Suite 103, 57701
Telephone: 605-388-3153
Fax: 605-388-3155
Mailing Address: P.O. Box 8305, Rapid City, SD, 57709-8305
Email: toogoodoo1@aol.com

MEMBERS OF FIRM

John J. Delaney
Scott Sumner

For full biographical listings, see the Martindale-Hubbell Law Directory

TENNESSEE

BRISTOL, Sullivan Co.

Paul R. Wohlford (AV)

Legal Arts Building, 900 Anderson Street, Suite C, 37620
Telephone: 423-968-7081
Fax: 423-968-4800
Mailing Address: P.O. Box 667, Bristol, TN, 37621
Email: Prwolf2161@aol.com

For full biographical listings, see the Martindale-Hubbell Law Directory

*CLARKSVILLE,** Montgomery Co.

Runyon and Runyon, PLLC (AV)

301 Main Street, P.O. Box 1023, 37041-1023
Telephone: 931-647-3377
Fax: 931-551-3561
URL: http://www.lawyers.com/runyonandrunyon
Erin Office: 143 East Main.
Telephone: 931-289-5900.

MEMBERS OF FIRM

Charles V. Runyon (1886-1973)
Markley Runyon Gill
Frank J. Runyon
Frank J. Runyon, III
Raymond F. Runyon

Representative Clients: Clarksville Department of Electricity; St. Paul Insurance Co.; The Trane Co.; Aetna Life & Casualty Co.; Houston County; Union Planters Bank, National Association; Prudential Professional Realty.
Reference: First Union Bank, Clarksville.

For full biographical listings, see the Martindale-Hubbell Law Directory

*GREENEVILLE,** Greene Co.

King & King (AV)

125 South Main Street, 37743
Telephone: 423-639-6881
Facsimile: 423-639-3629
Email: kking2@aol.com

(See Next Column)

MEMBERS OF FIRM

Kyle K. King
K. Kidwell King, Jr.
C. Todd Chapman

For full biographical listings, see the Martindale-Hubbell Law Directory

*KNOXVILLE,** Knox Co.

Bernstein, Stair & McAdams LLP (AV)

Suite 600, 530 South Gay Street, 37902
Telephone: 423-546-8030
Telecopier: 423-522-8879
Effective October 1, 1999 Area Code will change to 865.

MEMBERS OF FIRM

Bernard E. Bernstein
Doris C. Allen
L. Caesar Stair III
Celeste H. Herbert
Thomas N. McAdams
James W. Parris

ASSOCIATES

W. Tyler Chastain
Lauren G. Strange-Boston
Margo J. Maxwell

Representative Clients: ABB Flakt, Inc.; Camel Manufacturing Company; Clayton Homes, Inc.; Modern Supply Co.; Plasti-Line, Inc.; Rafferty's Restaurants; Saks, Inc.; Vanderbilt Mortgage and Finance, Inc.; West Town Mall.

For full biographical listings, see the Martindale-Hubbell Law Directory

Sobieski, Messer & Associates (AV)

900 South Gay Street, Suite 1801, 37902
Telephone: 423-546-7770
Fax: 423-546-7969
Email: sobilaw@aol.com

Wanda G. Sobieski
Diane M. Messer

ASSOCIATE

R. Richard Carl, II

For full biographical listings, see the Martindale-Hubbell Law Directory

*MEMPHIS,** Shelby Co.

Armstrong Allen Prewitt Gentry Johnston & Holmes, PLLC (AV)

Brinkley Plaza, Suite 700, 80 Monroe Avenue, 38103-2467
Telephone: 901-523-8211
Facsimile: 901-524-4936
Little Rock, Arkansas Office: Suite 100, 100 Morgan Keegan Drive, 72202.
Telephone: 501-280-0100.
Facsimile: 501-280-0166.
Jackson, Mississippi Office: 2525 Lakeward Drive, Suite 200, 39216.
Telephone: 601-713-1192.
Facsimile: 601-713-2049.
Jackson, Tennessee Office: 464 North Parkway, Suite A, 38305.
Telephone: 901-660-2332.
Facsimile: 901-664-1109.

MEMBER OF FIRM

Carl H. Langschmidt, Jr.

Kathy Laughter Laizure

For Complete List of Firm Personnel, See General Section

For full biographical listings, see the Martindale-Hubbell Law Directory

Causey, Caywood, Taylor, McManus & Bailey (AV)

A Professional Association, Not a Partnership
Suite 2400, 100 North Main Building, 38103
Telephone: 901-526-0206
Telecopier: 901-525-1540

James D. Causey
Daniel Loyd Taylor
David E. Caywood
John E. McManus

Craig B. Flood, II
John N. Bean
Jean E. Markowitz
Susan A. Shubert
Amy R. Fulton
Stacy Armstrong Ingle
David Shepherd Walker
Glenn Keith Vines, Jr.

For Complete List of Firm Personnel, See General Section

For full biographical listings, see the Martindale-Hubbell Law Directory

Krivcher Magids PLC (AV)

International Place II, 6410 Poplar Avenue, Suite 300, 38119-4839
Telephone: 901-682-6431
Facsimile: 901-682-6453
Email: lawfirm@kmplc.com

James F. Arthur, III

(See Next Column)

KRIVCHER MAGIDS PLC—*Continued*

ASSOCIATE

Aubrey Lee Brown, Jr.

For Complete List of Firm Personnel, See General Section

For full biographical listings, see the Martindale-Hubbell Law Directory

SEVIER LAW FIRM, P.C. (AV)

One Memphis Place, 200 Jefferson Avenue, Suite 975, 38103-2390
Telephone: 901-529-8888
Fax: 901-529-1234

Charles A. Sevier

Gail R. Sevier
Bruce A. Ralston

For full biographical listings, see the Martindale-Hubbell Law Directory

*NASHVILLE,** Davidson Co.

MICHAEL W. BINKLEY, P.C. (AV)

150 Second Avenue North, Suite 300, 37201
Telephone: 615-244-8630
Fax: 615-244-8644
Email: Mwbpc@aol.com *URL:* http://www.lawyers.com/binkleylaw

Michael W. Binkley

For full biographical listings, see the Martindale-Hubbell Law Directory

TEXAS

*ABILENE,** Taylor Co.

CELIA TRIMBLE BOONE (AV)

104 Pine Street, Suite 705, P.O. Box 2797, 79604
Telephone: 915-695-6800
Fax: 915-677-0073
Email: mail@celia.net

For full biographical listings, see the Martindale-Hubbell Law Directory

WHITTEN & YOUNG, P.C. (AV)

500 Chestnut, Suite 1402, P.O. Box 208, 79602
Telephone: 915-672-7824
Fax: 915-672-2158
Email: wypc@camalott.com

O. Henry (Mike) Young
Gary L. Hacker
C. Terry Hagin
Donald L. Anderson, Jr.
Cynthia Rucker Allen
Charles C. Self, III

Paul R. Rotenberry

OF COUNSEL

C. G. Whitten

For full biographical listings, see the Martindale-Hubbell Law Directory

*ALICE,** Jim Wells Co.

WARBURTON, ADAMI, MCNEILL, PAISLEY & APPELL, P.C. (AV)

Norwest Bank Building, Fourth Floor, 601 East Main Street, P.O. Box 331, 78333-0331
Telephone: 361-668-8101
Fax: 361-668-8106
Beeville Office: 107 North Washington Street, P.O. Box 278, 78104-0278.
Telephone: 361-358-2525.
Fax: 361-358-2532.

Lawrence H. Warburton, Jr.
Wallis D. McNeill, Jr.
Mark R. Paisley
R. Michael Appell

Representative Clients: Norwest Bank, Alice; Bowden Ford Lincoln Mercury Co.; Brooks County Independent School District; Jim Wells County; Lundells, Inc.; Brush County Bank; Mildred Talbert Estate; Ruth Moos Estate; John G. Kenedy Charitable Trust; San Diego Independent School District.

For Complete List of Firm Personnel, See General Section

For full biographical listings, see the Martindale-Hubbell Law Directory

ARLINGTON, Tarrant Co.

GOODMAN & CLARK (AV)

1600 East Lamar Boulevard, Suite 250, 76011
Telephone: 817-460-8171
Metro: 817-265-9195
Fax: 817-861-2125

MEMBERS OF FIRM

Toby R. Goodman
John A. Clark

For full biographical listings, see the Martindale-Hubbell Law Directory

*AUSTIN,** Travis Co.

AUSLEY & ALGERT, L.L.P. (AV)

3307 Northland Drive Mopac at Northland, Suite 420, 78731
Telephone: 512-454-8791
Fax: 512-454-9091
Email: tausley@iamerica.net

Thomas L. Ausley
Kristen A. Algert
Eric Robertson
Kelly Ausley-Flores

LEGAL SUPPORT PERSONNEL

Charlyne Ragsdale
Ann G. Young
Sherry McMillin
Martha L. Jones

Reference: NationsBank of Austin.

For full biographical listings, see the Martindale-Hubbell Law Directory

KAREN L. KRETSCHMAN (AV)

Barton Oaks Plaza Two, 901 South Mopac Expressway, Suite 315, 78746
Telephone: 512-328-4162
Fax: 512-328-3549
Email: kkretsch@ix.netcom.com

LEGAL SUPPORT PERSONNEL

Karen Werner

For full biographical listings, see the Martindale-Hubbell Law Directory

LAW OFFICES OF JO BETSY LEWALLEN (AV)

3307 Northland Drive, Suite 420, 78731
Telephone: 512-454-8791
Telefax: 512-454-9091

For full biographical listings, see the Martindale-Hubbell Law Directory

LAW OFFICES OF SARA E. SALTMARSH (AV)

812 San Antonio Street, Suite 511, 78701
Telephone: 512-472-3391
Facsimile: 512-472-2832

For full biographical listings, see the Martindale-Hubbell Law Directory

LAW OFFICES OF EDWIN J. (TED) TERRY, JR. (AV)

805 West 10th Street, Suite 300, 78701
Telephone: 512-476-9597
Fax: 512-476-6106
Email: tterry@tx-law.com

ASSOCIATES

James A. Vaught
Karl E. Hays

LEGAL SUPPORT PERSONNEL

LEGAL ASSISTANTS

Maria Ruiz Sandford
Betty R. Dye
Claudia R. Mann
Julie L. Hill, CLA

For full biographical listings, see the Martindale-Hubbell Law Directory

LAW OFFICE OF WILLIAM R. TRAVIS (AV)

507 West 10th Street, 78701
Telephone: 512-476-9002
Fax: 512-327-3818
URL: http://www.lawyers.com/williamrtravis

For full biographical listings, see the Martindale-Hubbell Law Directory

*CORPUS CHRISTI,** Nueces Co.

COOVER & COOVER (AV)

921 North Chaparral, Suite 102, 78401
Telephone: 361-882-2100
Fax: 361-882-9542

(See Next Column)

COOVER & COOVER, *Corpus Christi—Continued*

Ann E. Coover David M. Coover, Jr.

Reference: American Bank.

*DALLAS,** Dallas Co.

ANNE TURNER BELETIC (AV)

2929 Carlisle Street, Suite 170, 75204
Telephone: 214-953-0017
Fax: 214-953-1312
Email: ATBLAW@SWbell.net

For full biographical listings, see the Martindale-Hubbell Law Directory

DAVID CARLOCK, P.C. (AV)

8111 Preston Road, Suite 550, 75225-6326
Telephone: 214-346-0306
Facsimile: 214-346-0353
Email: dcarlock@swbell.net *URL:* http://www.lawyers.com/davidcarlocklaw

G. David Carlock

Judy M. Spalding Blaise M. Gormley

For full biographical listings, see the Martindale-Hubbell Law Directory

CLARK, WEST, KELLER, BUTLER & ELLIS, L.L.P. (AV)

4800 Renaissance Tower, 1201 Elm Street, 75270-2146
Telephone: 214-741-1001
Telecopier: 214-760-9812

MEMBERS OF FIRM

William H. Clark (1861-1931)
William H. Clark, Jr. (1895-1943)
Robert L. Clark (1903-1963)
William L. Keller
Allen Butler
David M. Ellis
Melvyn L. Douglas
Mike M. Tabor
Mark A. Shank
Michael P. Maslanka
Kervyn B. Altaffer, Jr.
Kelly Gaffney McClure

ASSOCIATES

Veronica Cuadra
Melinda L. Eitzen
Wade A. Forsman
Theresa M. Gegen
M. Brenk Johnson
Christie A. Newkirk
Robert J. Wood, Jr.
John Peter Hagan
Sonja J. McGill

For full biographical listings, see the Martindale-Hubbell Law Directory

GEARY, PORTER & DONOVAN, P.C. (AV)

One Bent Tree Tower, 16475 Dallas Parkway, Suite 500, 75001-6837
Telephone: 972-931-9901
Facsimile: 972-931-9208
Mailing Address: P.O. Box 700248, Dallas, Texas, 75370-0248
Email: firm@gpd.com *URL:* http://www.gpd.com

Joseph W. Geary Michael P. Geary
Larry L. Martin

For full biographical listings, see the Martindale-Hubbell Law Directory

GORANSON, BAIN & LARSEN, L.C. (AV)

8150 North Central Expressway, Suite 1850, 75206
Telephone: 214-373-7676
Facsimile: 214-373-9959
Email: gbl@gbl-law.com

Thomas P. Goranson
Angeline Lindley Bain
Paula Kurko Larsen
Thomas A. Greenwald

K. Dennise Garcia Lynn D. Ward

For full biographical listings, see the Martindale-Hubbell Law Directory

CHARLES R. HODGES, P.C. (AV)

3838 Oak Lawn Avenue Suite 1800, 75219-4575
Telephone: 214-528-5000
Fax: 214-528-3315
Email: chodges@hodges-law.com

Charles R. Hodges

For full biographical listings, see the Martindale-Hubbell Law Directory

HOLMES, WOODS & GARZA (AV)

Highland Park Place, Suite 550, 4514 Cole Avenue, L.B. 32, 75205
Telephone: 214-520-8100
Facsimile: 214-520-6565
Email: familylaw@texfamlaw.com *URL:* http://www.texasfamilylawyers.com
McKinney, Texas Office: 1700 Redbud Boulevard, Suite 190, 75070.
Telephone: 972-569-3166.
Facsimile: 972-569-3167. Email: familylaw@texfamlaw.com.
Houston, Texas Office: 2550 North Loop West, Suite 860, 77092.
Telephone: 713-812-1113.
Facsimile: 713-812-7819. Email: familylaw@texfamlaw.com.

MEMBERS OF FIRM

Robert E. Holmes Jr. D. Kay Woods
Lisa G. Garza

ASSOCIATES

Brad M. LaMorgese
Troy A. Reimer
Gregory T. Brewer
Cynthia Thomson Diggs

For full biographical listings, see the Martindale-Hubbell Law Directory

KOONS, FULLER, VANDEN EYKEL & ROBERTSON, A PROFESSIONAL CORPORATION (AV)

2311 Cedar Springs Road, Suite 300, 75201
Telephone: 214-871-2727
Fax: 214-871-0196
Email: email@kfvr-law.com
Plano Office: 5700 West Plano Parkway, Suite 2200.
Telephone: 972-769-2727.

William C. Koons
Kenneth D. Fuller
Ike Vanden Eykel
Richard L. Robertson
Kevin R. Fuller
Michael R. DeBruin

Joseph H. Amberson, III
Karen Blakely Turner
Kathryn J. Murphy
Amy McElroy
Allen Griffin

For full biographical listings, see the Martindale-Hubbell Law Directory

MCCURLEY, KINSER, MCCURLEY & NELSON, L.L.P. (AV)

5950 Sherry Lane, Suite 800, 75225
Telephone: 214-273-2400
Facsimile: 214-273-2470

PARTNERS

Mike McCurley
Katherine A. Kinser
Mary Johanna McCurley
Keith M. Nelson
Diana S. Friedman
Kim W. Mercier

ASSOCIATE

Randall Scott Downing

For full biographical listings, see the Martindale-Hubbell Law Directory

MCSHANE, DAVIS & HANCE, L.L.P. (AV)

The Rolex Building, Suite 550, 2651 North Harwood Street, 75201
Telephone: 214-969-7300
Fax: 214-969-7531

John V. McShane Edwin W. Davis
Larry Hance

ASSOCIATES

George R. Bienfang Shannon B. Sill

For full biographical listings, see the Martindale-Hubbell Law Directory

RAGGIO AND RAGGIO, P.L.L.C. (AV)

3316 Oak Grove, Suite 100, 75204
Telephone: 214-880-7500
Telecopier: 214-880-7506
Email: raggio@raggiolaw.com *URL:* http://www.raggiolaw.com

Grier H. Raggio (1913-1988)
Louise B. Raggio
Thomas L. Raggio
Kenneth G. Raggio
Grier H. Raggio, Jr.
Patricia DeJonge Keane
Dawn E. Fowler

ASSOCIATE

Cindy H. Williams

For full biographical listings, see the Martindale-Hubbell Law Directory

VERNER & BRUMLEY, A PROFESSIONAL CORPORATION (AV)

3131 Turtle Creek Boulevard Suite 1020, 75219
Telephone: 214-526-5234
Fax: 214-526-0957
Email: info@vernerbrumley.com *URL:* http://www.vernerbrumley.com

Jimmy L. Verner, Jr. Janet Phillips Brumley
Paul Brumley

(See Next Column)

VERNER & BRUMLEY A PROFESSIONAL CORPORATION—*Continued*

Diana E. Meier

For full biographical listings, see the Martindale-Hubbell Law Directory

WEBB & TIHOLIZ, LLP (AV)

2730 Maxus Energy Tower, 717 North Harwood, 75201
Telephone: 214-871-2730
Fax: 214-871-9339
URL: http://www.lawyers.com/webb&tiholiz

PARTNERS

Brian L. Webb — John C. Tiholiz

Miriam L. Ackels

For full biographical listings, see the Martindale-Hubbell Law Directory

*DENTON,** Denton Co.

CURTIS M. LOVELESS (AV)

218 North Elm, 76201
Telephone: 817-387-3776; D/FW Metro: 214-434-3844
Fax: 817-898-0196

For full biographical listings, see the Martindale-Hubbell Law Directory

PHILIPS, HOPKINS, EAMES & COBB, P.C. (AV)

525 North Locust, P.O. Box 2027, 76202-2027
Telephone: 940-566-7010; Metro 940-243-0946
Facsimile: 940-898-0502
Email: dentonlaw.com

Robert N. Eames

Representative Clients: First Federal Bank of North Texas; First State Bank of Texas, Denton, Texas; Sanger Bank, Sanger, Texas; BankOne, Texas, N.A.; Provident Bank, Denton, Texas; Dentex Title Co., Denton, Texas.

For full biographical listings, see the Martindale-Hubbell Law Directory

WOOD, THACKER & WEATHERLY, P.C. (AV)

513 West Oak Street, 76201
Telephone: 817-565-6565
Fax: 817-566-6673

C. Jane Thacker

For full biographical listings, see the Martindale-Hubbell Law Directory

*FORT WORTH,** Tarrant Co.

LOE, WARREN, ROSENFIELD, KAITCER & HIBBS, A PROFESSIONAL CORPORATION (AV)

4420 West Vickery Boulevard, P.O. Box 100609, 76185-0609
Telephone: 817-377-0060
Fax: 817-377-1120

H. Joe Loe (1911-1987) — Jeffrey N. Kaitcer
William M. Warren — Kelcie A. Hibbs
Mark J. Rosenfield — M. A. "Mike" Windsor
David E. Kelley, II

General Counsel for: United States Crystal Corp.

For full biographical listings, see the Martindale-Hubbell Law Directory

*GREENVILLE,** Hunt Co.

MORGAN AND GOTCHER (AV)

2610-A Stonewall Street, P.O. Box 556, 75403-0556
Telephone: 903-455-3183
Metro Tel: 903-450-8800
Fax: 903-454-4654
Email: jhmorgan@koyote.com

J. Harris Morgan — Holly H. Gotcher

Representative Clients: Huffines Enterprises; Greenville Independent School District; International Cassettes, Inc.; Universal Health Services, Inc.; Hunt County Appraisal District; Bank One Greenville; Citizens Bank of Royce City.

For full biographical listings, see the Martindale-Hubbell Law Directory

*HOUSTON,** Harris Co.

TOM ALEXANDER & ASSOCIATES (AV)

Bank of America Center, 37th Floor, 700 Louisiana, 77002
Telephone: 713-439-0000
Telecopy: 713-963-8478

(See Next Column)

Tom Alexander

References: American Bank; Chasewood Bank; Southwest Bank of Texas.

For full biographical listings, see the Martindale-Hubbell Law Directory

JOHN GORDON BOCK (AV)

The Lyric Centre, 440 Louisiana, Suite 850, 77002
Telephone: 713-739-0902
Fax: 713-650-3816
Email: Bocklaw@aol.com

For full biographical listings, see the Martindale-Hubbell Law Directory

BILL DE LA GARZA & ASSOCIATES, P.C. (AV)

17050 El Camino Real, 77058-2610
Telephone: 281-486-7007
Fax: 281-486-0229
Email: bdlg@priorityx.net

Bill De La Garza

For full biographical listings, see the Martindale-Hubbell Law Directory

JACK H. EMMOTT III & ASSOCIATES, P.C. (AV)

5120 Woodway Suite 10002, 77056
Telephone: 713-840-1300
Fax: 713-840-1303
Email: jemmott@net1.net *URL:* http://www.j-emmott.com

Jack H. Emmott III

For full biographical listings, see the Martindale-Hubbell Law Directory

FULLENWEIDER & ASSOCIATES (AV)

4265 San Felipe, Suite 1400, 77027
Telephone: 713-624-4100
Telecopy: 713-624-4141
Email: fulnwdr@ix.netcom.com

Donn C. Fullenweider

Linda A. Hinds — Jane Joseph
Steven H. Schweitzer — Michael C. Childs

For full biographical listings, see the Martindale-Hubbell Law Directory

LIPSTET & HIRSCH, L.L.P. (AV)

A Partnership including a Professional Corporation
Suite 1780, Two Post Oak Central, 1980 Post Oak Boulevard, 77056
Telephone: 713-961-7800
Fax: 713-961-3453

MEMBERS OF FIRM

Robert Leighton Lipstet (P.C.) — Reginald A. Hirsch

For full biographical listings, see the Martindale-Hubbell Law Directory

PLUMMER & FARMER (AV)

Formerly: Bradshaw & Plummer, 1979-1990
Brown, Bradshaw & Plummer, 1974-1979
Brown & Bradshaw, 1963-1974
3000 Smith, 77006
Telephone: 713-524-2400
Fax: 713-524-6371

MEMBERS OF FIRM

Hugh J. Plummer — Michael D. Farmer

For full biographical listings, see the Martindale-Hubbell Law Directory

BRENDA KEEN SCHWARTZ, P.C. (AV)

1800 Bering Drive, Suite 690, 77057-3158
Telephone: 713-972-1320
Telecopier: 713-972-1064
URL: http://www.bkeenschwartz.com
Email: bks@bkeenschwartz.com *URL:* http://www.lawyers.com/bkeenschwartz

Brenda Keen Schwartz

For full biographical listings, see the Martindale-Hubbell Law Directory

SHORT & JENKINS A PROFESSIONAL LEGAL CORPORATION (AV)

1 Greenway Plaza, Suite 700, 77046
Telephone: 713-626-0208
Telefax: 713-877-1658

J. Lindsey Short, Jr. — Joan F. Jenkins

(See Next Column)

SHORT & JENKINS A PROFESSIONAL LEGAL CORPORATION, *Houston—Continued*

Lynn Kamin
Sharon D. Cammack
Elva Cockrell Godwin
Sherri A. Evans
Sallee S. Smyth

For full biographical listings, see the Martindale-Hubbell Law Directory

TINDALL & FOSTER, P.C. (AV)
600 Travis, Suite 2800, 77002-3094
Telephone: 713-229-8733
Fax: 713-228-1303
Email: info@tindallfoster.com *URL:* http://www.tindallfoster.com

Harry L. Tindall

Angela G. Pence

Reference: Texas Commerce Bank, N.A., Houston, Texas.

For full biographical listings, see the Martindale-Hubbell Law Directory

*LUBBOCK,** Lubbock Co.

CARR, HUNT & JOY L.L.P. (AV)
1001 Texas Avenue, P.O. Box 2585, 79408
Telephone: 806-765-7491
Fax: 806-765-0553
Email: info@chjlaw.com
Amarillo, Texas Office: Amarillo National Plaza II, Ste. 509, 500 S. Taylor Street, P.O. Box 989, Amarillo, Texas. 79105.
Telephone: 806-342-3055.
Fax: 806-342-9907.

MEMBERS OF FIRM

Marvin Warlick Carr
Latrelle Bright Joy

Representative Clients: Bank of America; Brown-McKee, Inc.; Burk Royalty Co.; Colorado Interstate Gas Co.; Cooper Industries, Inc.; Int'l Bank of Commerce; Motorola, Inc.; Smithlawn Maternity Home & Adoption Agency.

For Complete List of Firm Personnel, See General Section

For full biographical listings, see the Martindale-Hubbell Law Directory

MCALLEN, Hidalgo Co.

WILLIAM E. CORCORAN (AV)
100 South Bicentennial, 78501-7050
Telephone: 956-631-3381
Telecopier: 956-687-5542
Email: wecorcoran@aol.com

Representative Client: Valley Lease Services, Inc.

For full biographical listings, see the Martindale-Hubbell Law Directory

DALE & KLEIN, L.L.P. (AV)
A Partnership including Professional Corporations
6301 North Tenth Street, 78504
Telephone: 956-687-8700
FAX: 956-687-2416
Brownsville Office: 815 Ridgewood.
Telephone: 956-546-5100.

Roy S. Dale (P.C.)
Martin E. Morris
Katie Pearson Klein (P.C.)
William D. Mount, Jr.

A. Peter Thaddeus, Jr.
Catherine Anderson Garcia
Kathryn M. Flagg
Marina Garcia

For full biographical listings, see the Martindale-Hubbell Law Directory

*MOUNT PLEASANT,** Titus Co.

LAW OFFICES OF DANNY WOODSON (AV)
806 North Jefferson, P.O. Box 399, 75456-0399
Telephone: 903-572-6675
Fax: 903-572-7348

For full biographical listings, see the Martindale-Hubbell Law Directory

PLANO, Collin Co.

KOONS, FULLER, VANDEN EYKEL & ROBERTSON, A PROFESSIONAL CORPORATION (AV)
5700 West Plano Parkway, Suite 2200, 75093
Telephone: 972-769-2727
Email: email@kfvr-law.com
Dallas Office: 2311 Cedar Springs Road, Suite 300.
Telephone: 214-871-2727.
Fax: 214-871-0196.

(See Next Column)

Ike Vanden Eykel
Richard L. Robertson

Kathryn J. Murphy
Allen Griffin
Christopher M. Lake

For full biographical listings, see the Martindale-Hubbell Law Directory

*SAN ANTONIO,** Bexar Co.

LAW OFFICES OF JAMES R. BASS, INC. (AV)
9002 Wurzbach Road, 78240
Telephone: 210-614-4444
Fax: 210-614-7737
Email: JBASSLAW@AOL.COM *URL:* http://www.lawyers.com/basslaw

James R. Bass

Michele Kay Jura

Reference: Frost National Bank.

For full biographical listings, see the Martindale-Hubbell Law Directory

HEARD LINEBARGER GRAHAM GOGGAN BLAIR PEÑA & SAMPSON, LLP (AV)
Tenth Floor, Tower Life Building, 310 South St. Mary's, 78205
Telephone: 210-225-6763
Facsimile: 210-225-6410
URL: http://www.publicans.com
Austin, Texas Office: 1949 South IH 35, 78741.
Telephone: 512-447-6675.
Fax: 512-443-3494.
Beaumont, Texas Office: 1148 Park, 77701.
Telephone: 409-832-9483.
Fax: 409-833-2638.
Brownsville, Texas Office: 3302 Boca Chica, Suite 105, 78521.
Telephone: 956-546-1216.
Fax: 956-546-4624.
Conroe, Texas Office: 103 W. Phillips, 77301.
Telephone: 409-760-1410.
Fax: 409-760-1285.
Corpus Christi, Texas Office: 500 N. Shoreline, Suite 1111, 78471.
Telephone: 512-888-6898.
Fax: 512-888-4405.
Corsicana, Texas Office: 1501 Northwood Boulevard, 75110.
Telephone: 903-872-3096.
Fax: 903-874-5007.
Dallas, Texas Office: 1720 Allianz Financial Centre, 2323 Bryan Street, 75201.
Telephone: 214-880-0089.
Fax: 214-754-7167.
Denton, Texas Office: 326-G East McKinney, 76201.
Telephone: 940-383-4460.
Fax: 940-382-2829.
Edinburg, Texas Office: 110 S. 12th Street, 78539.
Telephone: 956-383-4500.
Fax: 956-383-7820.
El Paso, Texas Office: 215 N. Stanton Street, 79901.
Telephone: 915-533-6637.
Fax: 915-532-7085.
Fort Worth, Texas Office: Oil & Gas Building, Suite 1414, 309 W. 7th Street, 76102.
Telephone: 817-877-4589.
Fax: 817-877-0601.
Houston, Texas Office: 1021 Main Street, Suite 1500, 77002.
Telephone: 713- 844-3400.
Fax: 713-844-3501.
Laredo, Texas Office: 1102 Scott, Suite 2B, 78041.
Telephone: 956-723-1303.
Fax: 956-723-1327.
Longview, Texas Office: 1127 Judson Road, Suite 111, 75601.
Telephone: 903-757-5448.
Fax: 903-758-3331.
Odessa, Texas Office: 1301 E. 8th Street, Suite 200, 79761.
Telephone: 915-332-9047.
Fax: 915-333-7012.
Richmond, Texas Office: 301 S. 9th Street, Suite 222, 77469.
Telephone: 281-342-9636.
Fax: 281-341-7808.
Sherman, Texas Office: 115 E. Lamar, 75091.
Telephone: 903-893-4941.
Fax: 903-868-0688.
Tyler, Texas Office: 1517 W. Front Street, Suite 202, 75702.
Telephone: 903-597-2897.
Fax: 903-597-2402.
The Woodlands, Texas Office: 10077 Grogan's Mill Road, Suite 535,v 77380-2924.
Telephone: 713-363-3632.
Fax: 281-363-3998.
New Orleans, Louisiana Office: 1515 Poydras Street, Suite 1840, 70112.
Telephone: 504-522-9100.
Fax: 504-522-9145.

(See Next Column)

HEARD LINEBARGER GRAHAM GOGGAN BLAIR PEÑA & SAMPSON LLP—*Continued*

Philadelphia, Pennsylvania Office: 123 S. Broad Street, Suite 1830, 19109.
Telephone: 215-790-1117.
Fax: 215-790-1197.

MEMBERS OF FIRM

Oliver S. Heard, Sr. (1915-1977)
Oliver S. Heard, Jr.
Dale Linebarger (Resident, Austin Office)
Russell R. Graham (Resident, Austin Office)
Thomas S. Goggan, III (Resident, Austin Office)
Stephen S. Blair (Resident, Austin Office)
Jim Blair (Resident, The Woodlands Office)
Juan M. Peña (Resident, Edinburg Office)
DeMetris Aquilla Sampson (Resident, Dallas Office)
David G. Aelvoet
Drew Aldinger (Resident, Philadelphia, Pennsylvania Office)
Bruce W. Anderson (Resident, Austin Office)
Kaye Applewhite (Resident, Conroe Office)
Thelma Banduch (Resident, Brownsville Office)
Gary B. Bennett (At Denton, Fort Worth and Sherman Offices)
Douglas S. Bird (Resident, Austin Office)
John R. Bolster (Resident, Tyler Office)
Phillipa L. Bowers (Resident, New Orleans, Louisiana Office)
Brian E. Brown (Resident, Austin Office)
Jeffrey K. Brown (Resident, Austin Office)
James H. Burshtyn (Resident, Austin Office)
Rebecca Bustamante
Olivero E. Canales (Resident, Laredo Office)
Paul D. Chapa (Resident, Corpus Christi Office)
Kevin D. Chester (Resident, Corsicana Office)
Cormac P. Creaven (Houston and Richmond Offices)
L. W. "Rusty" Dean (Resident, Tyler Office)
Michael W. Deeds (Resident, Houston Office)
Mary Belan Doggett
Clifton F. Douglass, III
James R. Evans, Jr. (Resident, Austin Office)
F. Duane Force (Resident, Austin Office)
Cynthia Y. Garza (Resident, Edinburg Office)
Jay T. Garrett (Resident, Austin Office)
Lucy Gonzàlez-Canales (Resident, Edinburg Office)
Lee Gordon (Resident, Austin Office)
Sandra Griffin (Resident, Austin Office)
Eloise A. Guzman (Resident, Houston Office)
Judith A. Hargrove (Resident, Austin Office)
Edward Hernández (Resident, El Paso Office)
Sharon N. Humble
Pamela Pope Johnson (Resident, Dallas Office)
William E. King (Resident, Houston Office)
Glenn Lewis (Resident, Fort Worth Office)
Edward Lopez, Jr. (Resident, Dallas Office)
Clayton E. Mayfield (Resident, Beaumont Office)
Russell N. McInturff (Resident, Odessa Office)
Stephen T. Meeks (Resident, Fort Worth Office)
Beverly Meltontree (Resident, Houston Office)
Kathleen D. Morrison (Resident, Corpus Christi Office)
Harry L. Munsinger
Norman J. Nelson (Resident, Houston Office)
J. Scott Novy (Resident, Longview Office)
Pankaj R. Parmar (Resident, Houston Office)
Carmen I. Perez (Resident, El Paso Office)
Monica McCoy Purdy (Resident, Dallas Office)
Harold D. Putman, Jr.
Kent M. Rider (Resident, Austin Office)
Lori Gruver Robertson (Resident, Austin Office)
Craig Schumacher (Resident, Tyler Office)
Michael J. Siwierka (Resident, Houston Office)
Glenn E. Smith (Resident, Fort Worth Office)
Leah L. Stolar (Resident, Houston Office)
Charles A. Sutton (Resident, Corpus Christi Office)
Michael T. Vallandingham (Resident, Austin Office)
Nancy Vasquez-Perez (Resident, Corpus Christi Office)
H. Elizabeth "Beth" Weller (Resident, Dallas Office)
Barbara M. Williams (Resident, Fort Worth Office)
Donald Lee Wolf (Resident, Tyler Office)
Scott D. Wylie (Resident, Corsicana Office)
Craig Young (Resident, Austin Office)
Lupe Zamarripa (Resident, Austin Office)

OF COUNSEL

Debra Danburg (Resident, Houston Office)
Richard R. Orsinger
Humberto Hernandez-Haddad (Not admitted in United States)
Vince Ryan (Resident, Houston Office)

For full biographical listings, see the Martindale-Hubbell Law Directory

JAMES D. STEWART AND ASSOCIATES, INC. (AV)

115 East Travis Street, Suite 1900, 78205
Telephone: 210-225-4321
Fax: 210-225-2019

(See Next Column)

James D. Stewart
Robert L. Graul, Jr.
Christopher H. Negem

For full biographical listings, see the Martindale-Hubbell Law Directory

*WACO,** McLennan Co.

DUNNAM & DUNNAM, L.L.P. (AV)

4125 West Waco Drive, P.O. Box 8418, 76714-8418
Telephone: 254-753-6437
Fax: 254-753-7434

MEMBERS OF FIRM

W. V. Dunnam (1891-1974)
W. V. Dunnam, Jr.
Vance Dunnam
Vance Dunnam, Jr.
James R. Dunnam

ASSOCIATES

Alan Stucky
John Porter Mabry, Jr.
James Robert Angel

For full biographical listings, see the Martindale-Hubbell Law Directory

JIM MEYER & ASSOCIATES, P.C. (AV)

4734 West Waco Drive, P.O. Box 21957, 76710
Telephone: 817-772-9255
Fax: 817-776-9110
Email: jmeyer@calpha.com

Jim Meyer

For full biographical listings, see the Martindale-Hubbell Law Directory

*WICHITA FALLS,** Wichita Co.

RICHARD T. SUTHERLAND (AV)

The Wichita Tower, 705 8th Street, Suite 620, 76301
Telephone: 940-322-1747
Facsimile: 940-767-4570

LEGAL SUPPORT PERSONNEL

Amy C. Neal

For full biographical listings, see the Martindale-Hubbell Law Directory

UTAH

*SALT LAKE CITY,** Salt Lake Co.

DART ADAMSON DONOVAN & HANSON (AV)

A Partnership of Professional Corporations
370 E. South Temple, Suite 400, 84111
Telephone: 801-521-6383
Telefax: 801-355-2513

B. L. Dart (P.C.)
Sharon A. Donovan (P.C.)
John D. Sheaffer, Jr. (P.C.)

ASSOCIATES

Lori W. Nelson
Cameron S. Denning

A list of References will be furnished upon request.

For full biographical listings, see the Martindale-Hubbell Law Directory

VAN COTT, BAGLEY, CORNWALL & McCARTHY, A PROFESSIONAL CORPORATION (AV)

50 South Main Street, Suite 1600, P.O. Box 45340, 84145-0340
Telephone: 801-532-3333
Telecopier: 801-534-0058
Email: info@vancott.com *URL:* http://www.vancott.com
Ogden, Utah Office: 2404 Washington Boulevard, Suite 900.
Telephone: 801-394-5783.
Park City, Utah Office: 2200 Park Avenue, Suite C200-A.
Telephone: 435-649-3889.

Timothy W. Blackburn (Resident, Ogden, Utah Office)
Matthew F. McNulty, III

L. Kelly Lowrey

For Complete List of Firm Personnel, See General Section

For full biographical listings, see the Martindale-Hubbell Law Directory

VIRGINIA

ALEXANDRIA, (Independent City)

Gwendolyn Jo M. Carlberg (AV)

420 South Washington Street, 22314
Telephone: 703-549-5551
Fax: 703-549-5558
Email: divorce@erols.com *URL:* http://www.lawyers.com/divorcelaw

ASSOCIATES

Timothy Bryan Beason Donald E. Anderson, III

For full biographical listings, see the Martindale-Hubbell Law Directory

Gannon, Cottrell & Ward, P.C. (AV)

411 North Washington Street, P.O. Box 1286, 22313
Telephone: 703-836-2770
FAX: 703-836-9086
Fairfax, Virginia Office: Suite 203, The Equity Building, 4085 Chain Bridge Road, Fairfax, Virginia, 20030.
Telephone: 703-591-7700.

Martin A. Gannon James Ray Cottrell
Michael A. Ward

David H. Fletcher Kyle F. Bartol
Christopher W. Schinstock

LEGAL SUPPORT PERSONNEL

Laurie Lee Sheldon Carla A. Drew

General Counsel For: Virginia Military Institute, Research Laboratories.
Approved Attorneys For: Columbia Real Estate Title Insurance Co; Lawyers Title Insurance Co.; American Title Insurance Co.; Commonwealth Land Title Insurance Co.; Chicago Title Insurance Co.

For full biographical listings, see the Martindale-Hubbell Law Directory

Grenadier, Simpson & Duffett, P.C. (AV)

649 South Washington Street, 22314
Telephone: 703-683-9000
Fax: 703-549-3087
URL: http://www.lawyers.com/vadivorcelaw

Ilona Ely Freedman Grenadier Stephen K. Simpson
Benton S. Duffett, III

Dawn Titus-Rogan Elaine M. Vadas
Sheryl Joy Schwartz

For full biographical listings, see the Martindale-Hubbell Law Directory

*ARLINGTON,** Arlington Co.

Bean, Kinney & Korman, A Professional Corporation (AV)

2000 North 14th Street, Suite 100, 22201
Telephone: 703-525-4000
Facsimile: 703-525-2207
Email: bkk@beankinney.com

L. Lee Bean (1916-1989) James Bruce Davis
David B. Kinney (Emeritus) James R. Schroll
James W. Korman Carol Schrier-Polak
Jonathan C. Kinney Joseph P. Corish
Frederick R. Taylor Jennifer A. Brust
Leo S. Fisher David C. Canfield
C. Erik Gustafson

OF COUNSEL

John Morland

Marbeth M. Spreyer Timothy J. McEvoy
Thomas W. Repczynski William E. Buchanan
Daryl S. Taylor Jennifer C. Bier
Christie L. Dowling Leslie J. Long
Lisa J. Tomasseti

Counsel for: First Union National Banks of Virginia; Bank of America.

For full biographical listings, see the Martindale-Hubbell Law Directory

Schwartz and Ellis, Ltd. (AV)

6950 North Fairfax Drive, 22213
Telephone: 703-532-9300
Telex: 892320
Facsimile: 703-534-0329
Email: schwellis@aol.com *URL:* http://www.lawyers.com/schwartzandellis

Philip Schwartz

(See Next Column)

John S. Petrillo

References: First Virginia Bank; Bank of America; First Union National Bank.

For full biographical listings, see the Martindale-Hubbell Law Directory

Betty A. Thompson, Ltd. (AV)

Suite 1001, Plaza East, 1800 North Kent Street, 22209
Telephone: 703-522-8100
FAX: 703-522-3770

Betty A. Thompson

References: Central Fidelity Bank of Northern Virginia; First American Bank of Virginia.

For full biographical listings, see the Martindale-Hubbell Law Directory

*FAIRFAX,** (Ind. City; Seat of Fairfax Co.)

Byrd, Mische, Bevis, Bowen, Joseph & O'Connor, P.C. (AV)

Suite 120, 10521 Judicial Drive, 22030
Telephone: 703-273-0500
Fax: 703-691-7690
Leesburg, Virginia Office: 205 Edwards Ferry Rd. N.W.,
Telephone: 703-777-7740.
FAX: 703-777-7741.

Richard J. Byrd Lawrence H. Bowen
Ann Wood Mische Nan M. Joseph
John W. Bevis Edward V. O'Connor, Jr.

Paula Winchester Rank

References: Community Bank; NationsBank.

For full biographical listings, see the Martindale-Hubbell Law Directory

Gannon, Cottrell & Ward, P.C. (AV)

Suite 203, The Equity Building, 4085 Chain Bridge Road, 22030
Telephone: 703-591-7700
Alexandria, Virginia Office: 411 North Washington Street. 22313.
Telephone: 703-836-2770.

Martin A. Gannon James Ray Cottrell
Michael A. Ward

David H. Fletcher Kyle F. Bartol
Christopher W. Schinstock

General Counsel For: Virginia Military Institute, Research Laboratories.
Approved Attorneys For: Columbia Real Estate Title Insurance Co; Lawyers Title Insurance Co.; American Title Insurance Co.; Commonwealth Land Title Insurance Co.; Chicago Title Insurance Co.

For full biographical listings, see the Martindale-Hubbell Law Directory

Dennis M. Hottell & Associates (AV)

10680 Main Street, Suite 200, 22030
Telephone: 703-352-5666
FAX: 703-352-5669

ASSOCIATES

David Lawrence Ginsberg Pamela M. Pacetti

For full biographical listings, see the Martindale-Hubbell Law Directory

Odin, Feldman & Pittleman, P.C. (AV)

9302 Lee Highway, Suite 1100, 22031
Telephone: 703-218-2100
Facsimile: 703-218-2160
Email: OFP@OFPLAW.COM

David E. Feldman Leslye S. Fenton
J. Patrick McConnell Elizabeth L. Salans

Timothy S. Bird

For Complete List of Firm Personnel, See General Section

For full biographical listings, see the Martindale-Hubbell Law Directory

Shoun & Bach, P.C. (AV)

12700 Fair Lakes Circle, Suite 300, 22033
Telephone: 703-222-3330
Fax: 703-222-3340
Email: jmacleod@shoun.com *URL:* http://www.shoun.com

Robert E. Shoun Gerald R. Curran
Beverly J. Bach Heather A. Cooper
Edward J. Walinsky Carolyn T. Hogans
Marc A. Astore Richard Brent Orsino

(See Next Column)

SHOUN & BACH P.C.—*Continued*

LEGAL SUPPORT PERSONNEL

Joan W. Macleod

For full biographical listings, see the Martindale-Hubbell Law Directory

SUROVELL, JACKSON, COLTEN & DUGAN, P.C. (AV)

4010 University Drive Second Floor, 22030
Telephone: 703-591-1300
Facsimile: 703-591-1579
Email: attys@surovelljackson.com

Robert J. Surovell
Richard J. Colten
Thomas P. Dugan
John P. J. Cummins III
James A. Watson II
Kenneth W. Curtis
Arlene T. Starace
David M. Levy
G. Donald Markle
Dorothy M. Isaacs

OF COUNSEL

David J. Fudala

Elizabeth D. Teare
John E. Arnett
Howard R. Philips
Edna Ruth Vincent
Margaret B. Craig
Scott Anthony Surovell
Lucy C. Chiu
Colleen C. Sweeney
Anita Van McFadden

For full biographical listings, see the Martindale-Hubbell Law Directory

*HARRISONBURG,** (Ind. City; Seat of Rockingham Co.)

LAW OFFICES OF FRANKLIN R. BLATT (AV)

71 East Market Street, P.O. Box 1449, 22801
Telephone: 540-433-0202
Facsimile: 540-433-0210
Email: BlattLaw@rica.net

ASSOCIATE

Laura A. Thornton

Representative Clients: Alpha Computing & Electronics; Joe Bowman Chevrolet, Inc.; HI-REV Enterprises, Ltd.; D & J Auto Sales, Inc.; Dave Hunter's Rent-A-Ride; Turkeywood Farms; Lock & Load Distributors, Inc.

For full biographical listings, see the Martindale-Hubbell Law Directory

*LEESBURG,** Loudoun Co.

SEVILA, SAUNDERS, HUDDLESTON & WHITE, A PROFESSIONAL CORPORATION (AV)

30 North King Street, 20176
Telephone: 703-777-5700
Metro: 471-9800; Fax: 703-771-4161

Robert E. Sevila
Richard R. Saunders, Jr.
Jon D. Huddleston
Craig E. White

Jeffrey A. Tuten
Jeanine M. Irving

LEGAL SUPPORT PERSONNEL

Joan Rust

For full biographical listings, see the Martindale-Hubbell Law Directory

MCLEAN, Fairfax Co.

FITE & O'BRIEN, LTD. (AV)

Suite 300, 6824 Elm Street, 22101
Telephone: 703-821-8575
Telecopier: 703-442-9472
Email: fiteobrien@fiteobrien.com

Frances Fite
Kathleen O'Brien

Suzanne Gilbert Scheer

OF COUNSEL

Anne E. Goodwin

For full biographical listings, see the Martindale-Hubbell Law Directory

NORFOLK, (Independent City)

GOLDBLATT, LIPKIN & COHEN, P.C. (AV)

Suite 300, 415 St. Paul's Boulevard, P.O. Box 3505, 23514
Telephone: 757-627-6225
Telefax: 757-622-3698

Paul M. Lipkin
Mary G. Commander

For full biographical listings, see the Martindale-Hubbell Law Directory

RICHMOND, (Independent City)

BRENNER, DOHNAL, EVANS & YOFFY, P.C. (AV)

411 East Franklin Street, Suite 200, P.O. Box 470, 23218-0470
Telephone: 804-644-1300
Facsimile: 804-644-1354
Email: bdeyp@erols.com

Theodore I. Brenner
Dennis W. Dohnal
Ronald S. Evans
James S. Yoffy

Jay O. Millman
Gregory S. Hooe
Kathryn Spruill Lingle
Mary J. Bennett
Thomas D. Stokes, III

For full biographical listings, see the Martindale-Hubbell Law Directory

ROANOKE, Roanoke City Co.

MUNDY, ROGERS & FRITH, LLP (AV)

Third Street and Woods Avenue, S.W., P.O. Box 2240, 24009
Telephone: 540-982-2900
FAX: 540-982-1362
Email: info@mrf-law.com *URL:* http://www.mrf-law.com

MEMBERS OF FIRM

G. Marshall Mundy
Frank W. Rogers, III
T. Daniel Frith, III
Cheryl Watson Smith
Edward B. Walker

Reference: First Union.

For full biographical listings, see the Martindale-Hubbell Law Directory

WOOTEN & HART, A PROFESSIONAL CORPORATION (AV)

707 Building, Suite 300, P.O. Box 12247, 24024-2247
Telephone: 540-343-2451; 540-342-9672
Telecopier: 540-345-6417
URL: http://www.wootenhart.com

George W. Wooten
David B. Hart
L. Thompson Hanes
Susan A. Waddell
Bradley D. McGraw
John L. Cooley
Thomas W. Farrell
Paul C. Kuhnel
Peter D. Vieth

David W. Hearn
John Mark Cooley
Christopher W. Stevens
Elizabeth D. Guilbert
Eunice Park Austin

OF COUNSEL

M. Lanier Woodrum

Representative Clients: Wachovia Bank; St. Paul Insurance Cos.
Approved Attorneys for: Lawyers Title Insurance Corp.
Reference: First Union National Bank.

For full biographical listings, see the Martindale-Hubbell Law Directory

SPRINGFIELD, Fairfax Co.

BECKER, HICKS, IRVING & HADEED, P.C. (AV)

5501 Backlick Road, Suite 220, 22151
Telephone: 703-256-1300
Fax: 703-256-3467
Email: mail@bhihlaw.com *URL:* http://www.bhihlaw.com

Larry E. Becker
B. R. Hicks
James V. Irving
Michael Mitry Hadeed, Jr.
Mark E. Kellogg, P.C.
Lynn E. Berry
Scott R. Sexauer

May Shallal Kheder
Alix L. Mattingly
Ashraf W. Nubani

For full biographical listings, see the Martindale-Hubbell Law Directory

VIENNA, Fairfax Co.

CONDO & MASTERMAN, P.C. (AV)

Suite 830, 1921 Gallows Road Tysons Corner, 22182
Telephone: 703-442-0888
Facsimile: 703-442-0294
Leesburg, Virginia Office: 105 East Market Street SE, 20175.
Telephone: 703-777-8891.
Fax: 703-777-6820.

Joseph A. Condo
David D. Masterman

Evelyn H. Sandground
David E. Roop, Jr.
Sean P. Kelly
Cheryl K. Graham
John E. Byrnes

For full biographical listings, see the Martindale-Hubbell Law Directory

Vienna—Continued

SMOLEN & PLEVY P.C. (AV)

Seventh Floor 8045 Leesburg Pike, 22182
Telephone: 703-790-1900
Telecopier: 703-790-1754
Email: smolenplevy@smolenplevy.com

Jason D. Smolen
Alan B. Plevy
Daniel H. Ruttenberg

For full biographical listings, see the Martindale-Hubbell Law Directory

VIRGINIA BEACH, (Independent City)

BRYDGES, MAHAN, O'BRIEN & FRUCCI, P.C. (AV)

Professional Building, 1369 Laskin Road, 23451
Telephone: 757-428-6021
Fax: 757-491-7634

Richard G. Brydges
William R. "Buster" O'Brien
Stephen C. Mahan
Steven C. Frucci

Approved Mediators/Arbitrators for: United States Arbitration and Mediation, Inc.; Arbitration Associates, Inc.- Jams/Endispute.
Reference: The Bank of Tidewater.

For full biographical listings, see the Martindale-Hubbell Law Directory

WOLCOTT, RIVERS, WHEARY, BASNIGHT & KELLY, P.C. (AV)

One Columbus Center, Suite 1100, 23462-6765
Telephone: 757-497-6633
FAX: 757-497-7267
Email: wolriv@series2000.com

Wilson L. Rivers
Barry Dorans
William A. Wheary, III
Leslie R. Watson
W. Brantley Basnight, III
David N. Reda
Monroe Kelly, III
Richard E. Biemiller
Carl A. Eason
Cheshire I'Anson Eveleigh
Joseph R. Mayes
M. Powell Peters
Samuel W. Meekins, Jr.
Neil L. Rose
Edward W. Wolcott, Jr.
Robert D. Marotta

David M. Bastiaans
Deborah Kirkpatrick

Counsel for: Metropolitan Life Insurance Co.; Ford Motor Co.
Approved Attorneys for: Lawyers Title Insurance Corp.

For full biographical listings, see the Martindale-Hubbell Law Directory

WASHINGTON

*SEATTLE,** King Co.

GORDON W. WILCOX, INC. P.S. (AV)

1201 Third Avenue, Suite 5160, 98101-3810
Telephone: 206-233-9300
Fax: 206-233-9194

Gordon W. Wilcox

Carl T. Edwards
Susan J. Shulenberger

For full biographical listings, see the Martindale-Hubbell Law Directory

WEST VIRGINIA

*WHEELING,** Ohio Co.

SCHRADER BYRD & COMPANION, PLLC (AV)

(A Professional Limited Liability Company)
The Maxwell Centre, 32-20th Street, Suite 500, P.O. Box 6336, 26003
Telephone: 304-233-3390
Fax: 304-233-2769
URL: http://www.schraderlaw.com
Martins Ferry, Ohio Office: 205 North Fifth Street, P.O. Box 309, 43935.
Telephone: 740-633-9976.
Fax: 740-633-0400.
Weirton, West Virginia Office: 3205 Pennsylvania Avenue, Suite 103, Penn Place, P.O. Box 2785, 26062.
Telephone: 304-723-2674.
Fax: 304-723-2876.

(See Next Column)

MEMBERS

Ray A. Byrd
James P. Mazzone (Resident Member, Weirton, West Virginia Office)
James F. Companion
Frank X. Duff
Sandra K. Law
Teresa Rieman-Camilletti
D. Kevin Coleman
Yolonda G. Lambert
Daniel P. Fry (Resident Partner, Martins Ferry, Ohio Office)

SPECIAL COUNSEL

Thomas B. Miller

ASSOCIATES

Denise D. Klug
Aimee Morgan Stern
Michael A. Adams
Kimberly R. Wilson
John Porco
Christopher J. Adams

OF COUNSEL

James A. Byrum, Jr.

General Counsel: Reynolds Memorial Hospital; WesBanco Bank-Elm Grove.
Representative Clients: American Cyanamid Company; Bank One; Matlack Systems, Inc.; Moutaineer Gas Co.; Ohio County Board of Education; PHICO Insurance Co.; Wheeling Hospital; Wheeling-Pittsburg Steel Corp.

For full biographical listings, see the Martindale-Hubbell Law Directory

WISCONSIN

*MADISON,** Dane Co.

BALISLE & ROBERSON, S.C. (AV)

217 South Hamilton, Suite 302, P.O. Box 870, 53701-0870
Telephone: 608-259-8702
Fax: 608-259-0807
Email: office@mail.b-rlaw.com

Linda S. Balisle
Linda Roberson
Jane Dragisic Clark

ASSOCIATE

Sarah A. Davies

LEGAL SUPPORT PERSONNEL

Diana K. Fleming
Anne C. Harrington (Paralegal)
Laura M. Roenning (Paralegal)

For full biographical listings, see the Martindale-Hubbell Law Directory

*MILWAUKEE,** Milwaukee Co.

DRINKA, LEVINE & MASSON, S.C. (AV)

2000 Milwaukee Center, 111 East Kilbourn Avenue, 53202-6618
Telephone: 414-291-6080
Fax: 414-291-6090
URL: http://www.lawyers.com/drinkalevine&masson

Judith A. Drinka
Micaela H. Levine
Grace M. Masson

For full biographical listings, see the Martindale-Hubbell Law Directory

MARGOLIS & CASSIDY (AV)

324 East Wisconsin Avenue Suite 700, 53202-4304
Telephone: 414-272-5333
Fax: 414-272-5338
Email: mclaw@execpc.com

Marvin A. Margolis
F. Brian McElligott
Julie A. O'Halloran

Reference: First Bank (N.A.)

For full biographical listings, see the Martindale-Hubbell Law Directory

KATHLEEN ORTMAN MILLER, S.C. (AV)

100 East Wisconsin Avenue, Suite 1010, 53202-4107
Telephone: 414-272-7227
Email: komiller@execpc.com *URL:* http://www.lawyers.com/komiller

Kathleen Ortman Miller

For full biographical listings, see the Martindale-Hubbell Law Directory

PODELL & PODELL (AV)

Suite 204, 250 West Coventry Court, 53217-3963
Telephone: 414-228-5800
Fax: 414-228-5815

MEMBERS OF FIRM

James J. Podell
Peggy L. Podell
Gregory S. Mager

For full biographical listings, see the Martindale-Hubbell Law Directory

Milwaukee—Continued

QUARLES & BRADY LLP (AV)

411 East Wisconsin Avenue, 53202-4497
Telephone: 414-277-5000
Fax: 414-271-3552
URL: http://www.quarles.com
Madison, Wisconsin Office: Firstar Plaza, One South Pinckney Street, P.O. Box 2113, 53701-2113.
Telephone: 608-251-5000.
Fax: 608-251-9166.
West Palm Beach, Florida Office: 222 Lakeview Avenue, 4th Floor, 33401.
Telephone: 561-653-5000.
Fax: 561-653-5333.
Naples, Florida Office: Barnett Center, 4501 Tamiami Trail North, Suite 300, 34103-3060.
Telephone: 941-262-5959.
Fax: 941-434-4999.
Phoenix, Arizona Office: One Camelback Building, One East Camelback Road, Suite 400, 85012-1649.
Telephone: 602-230-5500.
Fax: 602-230-5598.
Chicago, Illinois Office: Quarles & Brady LLC, Citicorp Center, 500 West Madison Street, Suite 3700.
Telephone: 312-715-5000.
Fax: 312-715-5155.

MEMBERS OF FIRM
(ALPHABETICALLY BY YEAR OF ADMISSION TO BAR)

David E. Jarvis
Patricia K. Ballman

For Complete List of Firm Personnel, See General Section

For full biographical listings, see the Martindale-Hubbell Law Directory

WYOMING

*CASPER,** Natrona Co.

BROWN, DREW & MASSEY, LLP (AV)

Casper Business Center, Suite 800, 123 West First Street, 82601-2486
Telephone: 307-234-1000
800-877-6755
Telefax: 307-265-8025
Email: brwndrew@coffey.com

MEMBER OF FIRM

P. Jaye Rippley

For Complete List of Firm Personnel, See General Section

For full biographical listings, see the Martindale-Hubbell Law Directory

*JACKSON,** Teton Co.

W. KEITH GOODY (AV)

155 E. Pearl, P.O. Box 2488, 83001
Telephone: 307-733-4446
Fax: 307-733-2774
Email: goodylaw@blissnet.com

LEGAL SUPPORT PERSONNEL

Mary C. Goody

For full biographical listings, see the Martindale-Hubbell Law Directory

CANADA BRITISH COLUMBIA

*VANCOUVER,** Vancouver Co.

JENKINS MARZBAN LOGAN (AV)

A Partnership of Law Corporations
Suite 1414, Nelson Square, 808 Nelson Street, P.O. Box 12144, V6Z 2H2
Telephone: 604-681-6564
Facsimile: 604-681-0766
URL: http://www.JML.CA

Dinyar Marzban

Scott Booth

For full biographical listings, see the Martindale-Hubbell Law Directory

CANADA NEW BRUNSWICK

*FREDERICTON,** York Co.

COX HANSON O'REILLY MATHESON (AV)

(Formerly Hanson Hashey)
Suite 400, Phoenix Square, P.O. Box 310, E3B 4Y9
Telephone: 506-453-7771
Fax: 506-453-9600
Email: fredericton@coxhanson.ca *URL:* http://www.coxhanson.ca
Halifax, Nova Scotia Office: Suite 1100, Purdy's Wharf Tower 1, P.O. Box 2380 Station Central RPO, B3J 3E5.
Telephone: 902-421-6262.
Fax: 902-421-3130. E-Mail: halifax@coxhanson.ca
Saint John, New Brunswick Office: 1212-One Brunswick Square, 1 Germain St. E2L 4V1.
Telephone: 506-652-7771.
Fax: 506-632-9600.
St. John's, Newfoundland Office: Scotia Centre, 401-235 Water Street, A1C 1B6.
Telephone: 709-726-3321.
Fax: 709-726-2992. E-Mail: stjohns@coxhanson.ca
Charlottetown, Prince Edward Island Office: Queen Square, Suite 202, 119 Queen Street, P.O. Box 875, Station Central, C1A 7L9.
Telephone: 902-894-7051.
Fax: 902-368-3762. E-Mail: charlottetown@coxhanson.ca

MEMBERS OF FIRM

H. A. Hanson, Q.C. (1909-1985)
David T. Hashey, Q.C.
David M. Norman, Q.C.
J. Ian M. Whitcomb, Q.C.
John M. Hanson, Q.C.
Walter D. Vail, Q.C.
Michael E. Bowlin
John D. Larlee, Q.C.
Bruce D. Hatfield, Q.C.
Julian A. G. Dickson, Q.C.
Anne D. Wooder
Terrence J. Morrison
Lucie Richard
Catherine M. Bowlen
J. Marc Richard

ASSOCIATES

Amanda J. Frenette
Monika M. L. Zauhar
Jade A. Spalding
William E. Gould
Christopher R. DeLong
Deborah M. Power
Corinne A. Godbout
Marc-Antoine Chiasson

For full biographical listings, see the Martindale-Hubbell Law Directory

CANADA ONTARIO

KITCHENER, Regional Munic. of Waterloo

GIFFEN LEE (AV)

50 Queen Street North, P.O. Box 2396, N2H 6M3
Telephone: 519-578-4150
Fax: 519-578-8740
Email: info@GiffenLeeLaw.com *URL:* http://www.GiffenLeeLaw.com

MEMBERS OF FIRM

J. Peter Giffen, Q.C.
Bruce L. Lee
J. Scott Morley
Brian R. Wagner
Philip A. Garbutt
Daniel J. Fife

ASSOCIATES

(Ms.) Milena Protich
Cindy L. Dickinson
Edward J. Vanderkloet
Graham M. Bennett
Mitra Golnaraghi
Donald C. Olson

For full biographical listings, see the Martindale-Hubbell Law Directory

*TORONTO,** Regional Munic. of Toronto

BASTEDO STEWART SMITH (AV)

180 Dundas Street West, Suite 1800, M5G 1Z8
Telephone: 416-595-1916
Facsimile: 416-596-7538

MEMBERS OF FIRM

Thomas G. Bastedo, Q.C.
Joanne H. Stewart
Bryan R. G. Smith

ASSOCIATE

C. Samantha Kennedy

For full biographical listings, see the Martindale-Hubbell Law Directory

Toronto—Continued

BORDEN & ELLIOT (AV)

Barristers & Solicitors
Scotia Plaza, 40 King Street West, M5H 3Y4
Telephone: 416-367-6000
Telecopier: 416-367-6749
Email: info@borden.com *URL:* http://www.borden.com
Ottawa, Ontario Office: Borden Elliot Scott & Aylen, 1000-60 Rue Queen Street.
Telephone: 613-237-5160; 800-661-4237. General
Facsimile: 613-230-8842. IP Dept.
Facsimile: 613-787-3558. Email: ottinfo@scottaylen.com. URL: http://www.borden.com.

W. Douglas R. Beamish

For Complete List of Firm Personnel, See General Section

For full biographical listings, see the Martindale-Hubbell Law Directory

McDONALD & HAYDEN (AV)

One Queen Street East Suite 1500, M5C 2Y3
Telephone: 416-364-3100
Telecopier: 416-601-4100
Email: ddouglas@mchayden.on.ca *URL:* http://www.mchayden.on.ca

MEMBERS OF FIRM

John G. McDonald, Q.C. (1922-1993)
Peter Reginald Hayden, Q.C.
David C. Nathanson, Q.C.
Marvin D. Demone
D. H. Jack
David R. Street
Clifford M. Goldlist
Wendy C. Posluns
Warren S. Rapoport
David H. Goldman
A. Richard Rodier
Mark Adilman
John D. Brunt
Kevin Cai
Jane Southren
Shea T. Small

ASSOCIATE

Bram J. Green

For full biographical listings, see the Martindale-Hubbell Law Directory

*WINDSOR,** Essex Co.

SUTTS, STROSBERG LLP (AV)

600 Westcourt Place, 251 Goyeau Street, P.O. Box 670, N9A 6V4
Telephone: 519-258-9333
Detroit Michigan: 313-962-0137
Facsimile: Windsor 519-258-9527
Detroit 313-962-0139

MEMBERS OF FIRM

Achille F. Gignac, Q.C. (1902-1984)
Robert E. Barnes, Q.C.
Clifford N. Sutts, Q.C.
Harvey T. Strosberg, Q.C.
Gary V. Wortley
James K. Ball
John C. Holland
Mary M. S. Fox
William C. Chapman
Donald M. Gordon
Paul C. Nesseth
Heather Rumble Peterson
Patricia A. Speight
Edward W. Ducharme
Michelle A. Gagnon
Craig J. Allen
Werner H. Keller
Francine A. Herlehy
Paul Simard
Jasminka Kalajdzic

COUNSEL FOR CRIMINAL MATTERS

Patrick J. Ducharme

For full biographical listings, see the Martindale-Hubbell Law Directory

CANADA
SASKATCHEWAN

*REGINA,** Regina Jud. Centre

MacPHERSON LESLIE & TYERMAN (AV)

1500-1874 Scarth Street, S4P 4E9
Telephone: 306-347-8000
Telecopier: 306-352-5250
Email: mltreg@mlt.com
Saskatoon, Saskatchewan Office: 1500-410 22nd Street East, S7K 5T6.
Telephone: 306-975-7100.
Telecopier: 306-975-7145.

ASSOCIATES

R. M. Louise Simard, Q.C.
Linda A. Christensen
Wendy Y. Martin White (Resident, Saskatoon Office)
F. Neil Turcotte (Resident, Saskatoon Office)

For Complete List of Firm Personnel, See General Section

For full biographical listings, see the Martindale-Hubbell Law Directory

FRANCHISE LAW

MISSOURI

KANSAS CITY, Jackson, Clay, Platte & Cass Cos.

SWANSON MIDGLEY, LLC (AV)

Crown Center, 2420 Pershing Road, Suite 400, 64108
Telephone: 816-842-6100
Fax: 816-842-0013
Email: mail@swansonmidgley.com *URL:* http://www.swansonmidgley.com
Overland Park, Kansas Office: Commerce Plaza I, 7th Floor, 7300 W. 110th Street.
Telephone: 913-317-2717.
FAX: 913-317-1505.

Wm. Bruce Day
Edward M. Dolson
Charles F. Zarter

Counsel For: First Horizon Corp. (United Country Real Estate); Mr. Goodcents Franchise Systems, Inc.; CarStar Franchise Systems; Lamar Donuts Franchising, Inc.; AFC Enterprises (Chucks/Popeye's Fried Chicken); Metromedia Steak Houses; Master Protection Corp. (Firemaster).

For Complete List of Firm Personnel, See General Section

For full biographical listings, see the Martindale-Hubbell Law Directory

NEW JERSEY

SADDLE BROOK, Bergen Co.

COHN LIFLAND PEARLMAN HERRMANN & KNOPF LLP (AV)

Park 80 Plaza West-One, 07663
Telephone: 201-845-9600
Telecopier: 201-845-9423
Email: info@njlawfirm.com *URL:* http://www.njlawfirm.com

MEMBERS OF FIRM

Albert L. Cohn
Peter S. Pearlman
Barry A. Knopf
Daniel Crystal (Retired)
Jeffrey W. Herrmann
Robert D. Zatorski
Allen Susser
Mary Ann T. Stokes
Brian D. Zinn
Joshua P. Cohn

ASSOCIATES

Virginia A. Harper
Leonard Z. Kaufmann
Audra DePaolo
Robert Ricci, Jr.
Maurice W. McLaughlin
Andrew C. Abrams
Jessica V. Henry

OF COUNSEL

Sylvia J. Cohn
Jodi B. Scherl

For full biographical listings, see the Martindale-Hubbell Law Directory

NEW YORK

GARDEN CITY, Nassau Co.

HAROLD L. KESTENBAUM, P.C. (AV)

585 Stewart Avenue, Suite 700, 11530
Telephone: 516-745-0099
Fax: 516-745-0293
Email: hkesten@worldnet.att.net *URL:* http://www.lawyers.com/kestenbaumfranchiselaw

Harold L. Kestenbaum

For full biographical listings, see the Martindale-Hubbell Law Directory

*NEW YORK,** New York Co.

PILIERO GOLDSTEIN JENKINS & SULLIVAN, LLP (AV)

292 Madison Avenue, 10017
Telephone: 212-213-8200
Fax: 212-685-2028
Email: lawyers@pgjhlaw.com *URL:* http://www.pgjhlaw.com
Carlstadt, New Jersey Office: One Palmer Terrace.
Telephone: 201-507-5157.
FAX: 201-507-5221.
Washington, D.C. Office: 888 17th Street, N.W., Suite 1100.
Telephone: 202-467-6991.
FAX: 202-467-6703.

(See Next Column)

San Francisco, California Office: 507 Howard Street, Suite 200.
Telephone: 415-281-3631.
Fax: 415-281-3630.

MEMBERS OF FIRM

Kimberlee S. Bogen
Edward J. Goldstein
Jon Mark Jenkins
Marc A. Lebowitz
Robert D. Piliero
George O. Richardson, III
Michael T. Sullivan

ASSOCIATES

Craig Avedisian
Rosemary G. Feit
Eric M. Kogan
Mariano Schwed

OF COUNSEL

Kenneth D. Arbeeny
Christopher P. Hall

For full biographical listings, see the Martindale-Hubbell Law Directory

OHIO

*COLUMBUS,** Franklin Co.

ZEIGER & CARPENTER (AV)

1600 Huntington Center, 41 South High Street, 43215
Telephone: 614-365-4100
Facsimile: 614-365-9145

MEMBERS OF FIRM

John W. Zeiger
Michael H. Carpenter
Jeffrey A. Lipps
Steven W. Tigges
David A. Wallace
Marion H. Little, Jr.
Michael Romanello

ASSOCIATES

Timothy R. Bricker
Daniel R. Mordarski
Joseph T. Olecki
Michael N. Beekhuizen
Ronald E. Laymon
Angela Paul
Craig Calcaterra
John J. Todor

OF COUNSEL

Daniel R. Freytag
Mary R. True
Douglas R. Cole (Not admitted in OH)
Stuart G. Parsell

For full biographical listings, see the Martindale-Hubbell Law Directory

RHODE ISLAND

SMITHFIELD, Providence Co.

CHARLES S. SOKOLOFF INCORPORATED (AV)

Eleven Thurber Boulevard, 02917-1859
Telephone: 401-233-2800; Toll Free: 888-SOKOLAW
Fax: 401-233-2890
URL: http://www.sokolawyer.com
Email: sokolaw@sokolawyer.com *URL:* http://www.lawyers.com/sokolaw

Charles S. Sokoloff

Anne-Marie Krollman

For full biographical listings, see the Martindale-Hubbell Law Directory

TEXAS

*DALLAS,** Dallas Co.

THOMPSON & KNIGHT L.L.P. (AV)

(Attorneys and Counselors)
1700 Pacific Avenue Suite 3300, 75201
Telephone: 214-969-1700
Telecopy: 214-969-1751
Telex: 732 298
URL: http://www.tklaw.com
Austin, Texas Office: 1200 San Jacinto Center, 98 San Jacinto Boulevard, 78701.
Telephone: 512-469-6100.
Telecopy: 512-469-6180.
Fort Worth, Texas Office: 801 Cherry Street, Suite 1600, 76102.
Telephone: 817-347-1700.
Telecopy: 817-347-1799.
Houston, Texas Office: Thompson Knight Brown Parker & Leahy L.L.P., 1200 Smith Street, Suite 3600, 77002-4595.
Telephone: 713-654-8111.
Telecopier: 713-654-1871.

(See Next Column)

THOMPSON & KNIGHT L.L.P., *Dallas—Continued*

San Pedro Garza Garcia, Nuevo León, Mexico Office: Edificio Losoles PD-4, Av. Lázaro Cárdenas No. 2400 Pte., C.P. 66220.
Telephone: (52-8) 363-0096.
Telecopy: (52-8) 363-3067.

OF COUNSEL

Gayle E. Cannon

For Complete List of Firm Personnel, See General Section

For full biographical listings, see the Martindale-Hubbell Law Directory

GENERAL PRACTICE

MINNESOTA

*AITKIN,** Aitkin Co.

RYAN & RYAN (AV)

201 Minnesota Avenue, N., P.O. Box 388, 56431
Telephone: 218-927-2136

MEMBERS OF FIRM

Michael F. Ryan
Heinrich A. Brucker

Representative Clients: Woodland Container Corp.; The First National Bank of Aitkin; First National Bank of Deerwood; State Bank of McGregor; Mille Lacs Electric Cooperative; City of Aitkin; City of Deerwood; City of Emily.

For full biographical listings, see the Martindale-Hubbell Law Directory

*ALEXANDRIA,** Douglas Co.

THORNTON, HEGG, REIF, DOLAN & BOWEN, P.A. (AV)

1017 Broadway, P.O. Box 819, 56308
Telephone: 320-762-2361
FAX: 320-762-1638
Email: thrjd@rea-alp.com

R. S. Thornton (1892-1960)
Joseph G. Thornton (1923-1996)
Robert M. Hegg
Thomas J. Reif
Michael J. Dolan
Lisa J. Bowen

Representative Clients: National Farmers Union Property & Casualty Co.; Austin Mutual Insurance Co.; North Star Mutual Insurance Co.; American Family; Western National Insurance Co.; Milwaukee Mutual; Grinnell Mutual.
General Counsel for: Nodland Construction Co.; Buttweiler Do-All, Inc.; Pope/Douglas Solid Waste Board.

For full biographical listings, see the Martindale-Hubbell Law Directory

*AUSTIN,** Mower Co.

BAUDLER, BAUDLER, MAUS & BLAHNIK (AV)

108 North Main Street, 55912
Telephone: 507-433-2393
Fax: 507-433-9530
Email: bbmb@smig.net *URL:* http://www.baudlerlaw.com
Spring Valley, Minnesota Office: 304 So. Broadway.
Telephone: 507-346-7301.
FAX: 507-346-2537.

MEMBERS OF FIRM

Carl Baudler (1879-1954)
Otto Baudler (1881-1970)
William J. Baudler (1914-1992)
Richard C. Baudler (Retired)
Bryan J. Baudler
Lawrence E. Maus
Robert M. Maus
Robert E. Blahnik (Resident at Spring Valley Office)
Thomas C. Baudler
David L. Forman
Lee A. Bjorndal

Representative Clients: Farmers Insurance Group; Grinnell Mutual Insurance Co.; Northbrook Property & Casualty Ins. Co.; Mower County Farmers Fire & Lightning Ins. Co.; Spring Valley Mutual Ins. Co.; Terra Industries; Austin Packaging Co.; Norwest Bank; US Bank; Home Federal Savings Bank.

For full biographical listings, see the Martindale-Hubbell Law Directory

*DULUTH,** St. Louis Co.

BOYD AGNEW DRYER & STORAASLI, LTD. (AV)

200 Sellwood Building, 202 West Superior Street, 55802-1960
Telephone: 218-727-8451
Fax: 218-727-6081
Email: pbdx08a@prodigy.com

Richard L. Bye (Retired)
Robert W. Boyd
Jerome P. Agnew
R. Craft Dryer
Elizabeth A. Storaasli
Mark L. Knutson
Gerald A. Pommerville
Lisa D. Wilson

Rebekah R. Syck

General Counsel: Independent School District 709, Duluth.
Representative Clients: Western National Bank of Duluth; Duluth Steel Fabricators; Mielke Electric Works, Inc.; Lutheran Social Services of Minnesota; Inter City Oil Co.; Benna Ford, Inc.
Reference: Norwest Bank Minnesota North, N.A.

For full biographical listings, see the Martindale-Hubbell Law Directory

HALVERSON, WATTERS, DOWNS, REYELTS & BATEMAN, LTD. (AV)

700 Providence Building, 55802
Telephone: 218-727-6833
Fax: 218-727-4632
Email: hwdrb@computerpro.com

W. D. Watters (1926-1995)
Anthony S. Downs
Steven L. Reyelts
Charles B. Bateman
Steven W. Schneider
Eric L. D. Hylden
Sonia M. Sturdevant

Richard J. Leighton
Aaron Bransky
Diana B. Dodge
Anne L. Roeser

OF COUNSEL

G. W. Halverson

Representative Clients: Duluth Teachers Retirement Fund; Duluth Teachers Credit Union; Duluth Clinic, Ltd.; CIGNA Cos.; CNA Group; Farm Bureau Mutual Ins. Co.

For full biographical listings, see the Martindale-Hubbell Law Directory

HANFT, FRIDE, O'BRIEN, HARRIES, SWELBAR & BURNS, P.A. (AV)

1000 U.S. Bank Place, 130 West Superior Street, 55802-2094
Telephone: 218-722-4766
Fax: 218-529-2401
Email: firm@hanftlaw.com

Gilbert W. Harries
William M. Burns
Richard R. Burns
John D. Kelly
Frederick A. Dudderar, Jr.
John R. Baumgarth
Tim A. Strom
R. Thomas Torgerson
Cheryl M. Prince
Robin C. Merritt
Jennifer L. Carey
Kathleen S. Bray

OF COUNSEL

Gaylord W. Swelbar

Mark D. Pilon
Melanie S. Ford

Counsel for: Canadian National Railways; First Bank National Association; Great American Insurance Companies; Johnson-Wilson Constructors, Inc.; Minnesota Power; Murphy McGinnis Media, Inc.; Northern Minnesota Utilities; Oglebay Norton Company; United States Fidelity and Guaranty Company; U.S. Insurance Group.

For full biographical listings, see the Martindale-Hubbell Law Directory

MAGIE, ANDRESEN, HAAG, PACIOTTI, BUTTERWORTH & MCCARTHY, P.A. (AV)

1000 Alworth Building, P.O. Box 745, 55801
Telephone: 218-722-1411
Telecopier: 218-720-6817
Email: lawduluth@aol.com

Robert H. Magie, III
Charles H. Andresen
Michael W. Haag
James P. Paciotti
Sandra E. Butterworth
Brian R. McCarthy
Bryan N. Anderson
Robert C. Barnes
Steven J. Sheridan
Robert K. McCarthy (1915-1986)

Representative Clients: North Country Equipment; Upper Lakes Foods, Inc.; AMSOIL, Inc.; Housing and Redevelopment Authority of Duluth, Minnesota; USX Corporation; Arrowhead Redevelopment Commission; Lakehead Pipe Line Company; Inland Steel Company; Great Lakes Gas Transmission Company; Oneida Realty; Murphy Oil Co.; Duluth Plumbing Supplies; LTV Steel Mining Company.

For full biographical listings, see the Martindale-Hubbell Law Directory

*FERGUS FALLS,** Otter Tail Co.

DAVID F. LUNDEEN (AV)

107 Court Street, 56537
Telephone: 218-736-4866
FAX: 218-736-7747
Email: dlundlaw@prtel.com

For full biographical listings, see the Martindale-Hubbell Law Directory

*HALLOCK,** Kittson Co.

BRINK, SOBOLIK, SEVERSON, MALM & ALBRECHT, P.A. (AV)

217 South Birch Avenue, P.O. Box 790, 56728
Telephone: 218-843-3686
FAX: 218-843-2724
Email: brink@rural-access.com

(See Next Column)

BRINK, SOBOLIK, SEVERSON, MALM & ALBRECHT P.A., *Hallock—Continued*

Lyman A. Brink (1909-1972)
Roger C. Malm
Dennis M. Sobolik
Robert M. Albrecht
Robert K. Severson
Blake S. Sobolik
Jeffrey W. Hane

Representative Clients: Northwestern State Bank, Hallock, Minn.; Prime Security Bank, Karlstad, Minn.; Argyle State Bank, Argyle, Minn.; City of Hallock; American Federal Savings & Loan Assn.; State Farm Insurance Co.; Minnesota Rice Growers, Inc.

For full biographical listings, see the Martindale-Hubbell Law Directory

*LE CENTER,** Le Sueur Co.

CHRISTIAN, SPARTZ, KEOGH & CHRISTIAN (AV)

65 South Park Avenue, P.O. Box 156, 56057
Telephone: 507-357-2278
Fax: 507-357-2270
Email: cskc@frontiernet.net

MEMBERS OF FIRM

Douglas J. Christian
Michael T. Keogh
Donald H. Spartz
Brent Christian

OF COUNSEL

Harry F. Christian

Representative Clients: First National Bank, Le Center, Minnesota; Elysian State Bank, Elysian, Minnesota; First State Bank, Le Center, Minnesota.
Reference: First National Bank, Le Center, Minnesota.

For full biographical listings, see the Martindale-Hubbell Law Directory

*MANKATO,** Blue Earth Co.

FARRISH, JOHNSON & MASCHKA, P.L.L.P. (AV)

Union Square Business Center, 201 North Broad Street, P.O. Box 550, 56002-0550
Telephone: 507-387-3002
Telecopier: 507-625-4002
Mailing Address: P.O. Box 550, 56002-0550
Email: farrish@mctcnet.net *URL:* http://www.fjm-law.com

MEMBERS OF FIRM

Gerald L. Maschka
Scott V. Kelly
Howard F. Haugh
William S. Partridge
John M. Riedy
Kenneth R. White
David A. Salsbery
Mary Anne Wray
Charles W. Ries
John C. Peterson

ASSOCIATES

Steven H. Fink
Paul J. Simonett
Renee C. Rubish

OF COUNSEL

Robert G. Johnson

Representative Clients: Travelers Insurance Co.; CNA Insurance Co.; Hartford Accident and Indemnity Co.; St. Paul Insurance Cos.; Employers Mutual Companies; State Farm Co.; Federated Insurance Co.; Fireman's Fund Insurance Co.; Maryland Casualty Co.; American Family Insurance Group.

For full biographical listings, see the Martindale-Hubbell Law Directory

*MINNEAPOLIS,** Hennepin Co.

ABDO AND ABDO, P.A. (AV)

710 Northstar West 625 Marquette Avenue, 55402
Telephone: 612-333-1526
Fax: 612-342-2608
Email: abdoabdo@aol.com *URL:* http://www.abdo.com.br

E. John Abdo (1912-1993)
Keith J. Broady
Robert P. Abdo
Kenneth J. Abdo
Steven R. Hedges
Daniel M. Satorius
Timothy C. Matson

Representative Client: ADT Security Services, Inc.

For full biographical listings, see the Martindale-Hubbell Law Directory

ARNOLD, ANDERSON & DOVE, P.L.L.P. (AV)

5881 Cedar Lake Road, 55416-1492
Telephone: 612-545-9000
Wats Line: 800-343-4545
Fax: 612-545-1793; 612-542-9210
Email: aad@aadlaw.com
Princeton, Minnesota Office: 501 South Fourth Street.
Telephone: 612-389-2214.
Hutchinson, Minnesota Office: 101 Park Place.
Telephone: 320-587-7575.
Red Wing, Minnesota Office: 481 Fridell Crescent, 55066.
Telephone: 651-388-3454.

(See Next Column)

MEMBERS OF FIRM

David B. Arnold
Paul D. Dove
Steven A. Anderson
Laura K. Fretland
Jane Van Valkenburg

ASSOCIATES

Richard G. McGee
James Utley
Walter P. Michels, III (Resident, Red Wing Office)
Marc A. Sebora

OF COUNSEL

Richard J. Schieffer
Robert M. Gardner

For full biographical listings, see the Martindale-Hubbell Law Directory

BASSFORD, LOCKHART, TRUESDELL & BRIGGS, P.A. (AV)

(Formerly Richards, Montgomery, Cobb & Bassford, P.A.)
3550 Multifoods Tower, 55402-3787
Telephone: 612-333-3000
Telecopier: 612-333-8829

Greer E. Lockhart
Michael A. Klutho
Frederick E. Finch
Gregory W. Deckert
John M. Degnan
Kevin P. Hickey
Lewis A. Remele, Jr.
Stanford P. Hill
Kevin P. Keenan
Mark R. Whitmore
James O. Redman
Fred B. Snyder (1859-1951)
Rebecca Egge Moos
Edward C. Gale (1862-1943)
John M. Anderson
Frank A. Janes (1908-1959)
Charles E. Lundberg
Nathan A. Cobb, Sr. (1905-1976)
Gregory P. Bulinski
Dale M. Wagner
Bergmann Richards (1888-1978)
Louis J. Speltz
Edmund T. Montgomery (1904-1987)
Laura J. McKnight
Mark P. Hodkinson
Charles A. Bassford (1914-1990)
Thomas J. Niemiec
Jerome C. Briggs (Retired)
Andrew L. Marshall
Lynn G. Truesdell (Retired)

Dani M. Shimon
Jennifer L. Hill
Christopher R. Morris
Robin Ann Williams
Kelly A. Putney
Michael A. Switzer
Shalanda Denise Ballard

Representative Clients: Chubb/Pacific Indemnity Group; John Hancock Mutual Life Insurance Co.; Medical Protective Co.; Metropolitan Life Insurance Co.; The Travelers Insurance Cos.

For full biographical listings, see the Martindale-Hubbell Law Directory

BURSTEIN, HERTOGS & McFARLAND, P.A. (AV)

Suite 610, 510 First Avenue North, 55402
Telephone: 612-339-6561
Fax: 612-337-5572
Hastings, Minnesota Office: 1350 South Frontage Road.
Telephone: 612-437-1818.

Fred Burstein
Dylan J. McFarland
Samuel H. Hertogs (Resident, Hastings Office)
Steven M. Burstein

OF COUNSEL

Robert J. Sevenich
Melvin L. Burstein

Reference: Firstar Bank of Minnesota, N.A.

For full biographical listings, see the Martindale-Hubbell Law Directory

DORSEY & WHITNEY LLP (AV)

220 South 6th Street, 55402
Telephone: 612-340-2600
Facsimile: 612-340-2868
Email: postmaster@dorseylaw.com *URL:* http://www.dorseylaw.com
Rochester, Minnesota Office: 201 First Avenue, S.W., Suite 340, 55902.
Telephone: 507-288-3156.
Des Moines, Iowa Office: 801 Grand, Suite 3900, 50309.
Telephone: 515-283-1000.
New York, New York Office: 250 Park Avenue, 10177.
Telephone: 212-415-9200.
Washington, D.C. Office: 1001 Pennsylvania Avenue, N.W., Suite 300 South, 20004.
Telephone: 202-824-8800.
Brussels, Belgium Office: 35 Square De Meeûs 1000.
Telephone: 011-32-2-504-4611.
London, England Office: Veritas House, 125 Finsbury Pavement, EC2A 1NQ.
Telephone: 011-44-171-588-0800.
Billings, Montana Office: 1200 First Interstate Center, 401 North 31st Street, P.O. Box 7188, 59103.
Telephone: 406-252-3800.
Great Falls, Montana Office: 507 Davidson Building, 8 Third Street North, P.O. Box 1566, 59401.
Telephone: 406-727-3632.
Missoula, Montana Office: 127 East Front Street, Suite 310, 59802.
Telephone: 406-721-6025.

(See Next Column)

DORSEY & WHITNEY LLP—*Continued*

Denver, Colorado Office: 370 Seventeenth Street, Republic Plaza Building, Suite 4400, 80202-5644.
Telephone: 303-629-3400.
Salt Lake City, Utah Office: Wells Fargo Plaza, 170 South Main Street, Suite 925, 84101.
Telephone: 801-350-3581.
Orange County, California Office: Center Tower, 650 Town Center Drive, Suite 1850, P.O. Box 5066, Costa Mesa, 92626.
Telephone: 714-662-7300.
Fargo, North Dakota Office: Dakota Center, 51 North Broadway, Suite 402, P.O. Box 1344, 58107-1344.
Telephone: 701-235-6000.
Seattle, Washington Office: U.S. Bank Building Centre, 1420 Fifth Avenue, Suite 4200, 98101.
Telephone: 206-903-8800.
Hong Kong Office: Suite 801, Citic Tower, 1 Tim Mei Avenue, Central Hong Kong.
Telephone: 011-852-252-65000.
Fax: 011-852-252-43000.
Paramus, New Jersey Office: East 80, Route 4, 07652.
Telephone: 201-291-8904.
Fax: 201-712-9444.
Anchorage, Alaska Office: 1031 West 4th Avenue, Suite 600, 99501.
Telephone: 907-276-4557.
Vancouver, British Columbia Office: Suite 1300 Park Place, 666 Burrard Street, V6C 3J8.
Telephone: 604-687-5151.

MEMBERS OF FIRM

Jonathan B. Abram
Michael J. Ahern
James D. Alt
Kim A. Anderson
Leslie J. Anderson
Rodney D. Anderson
Amy E. Ayotte
Jeffrey R. Benson
William J. Berens
Philip F. Boelter
Timothy E. Branson
B. Andrew Brown
Ronald J. Brown
Elizabeth C. Buckingham
Forrest G. Burke
Robert A. Burns
Don D. Carlson
Steven E. Carlson
Peter W. Carter
Robert E. Cattanach, Jr.
Steven K. Champlin
Douglas R. Christensen
Rebecca A. Comstock
Katherine A. Constantine
Jay F. Cook
John A. Cooney
Patrick F. Courtemanche
Craig A. Currie
Kenneth L. Cutler
Craig D. Diviney
Nelson G. Dong
Vernle C. (Skip) Durocher, Jr.
J. Marquis Eastwood
George G. Eck
Verlane L. Endorf
Gregory A. Fontaine
David N. Fronek
L. Joseph Genereux
Jerome P. Gilligan
Mark Ginder
Roy A. Ginsburg
Catherine A. Gnatek
Joseph C. Gonnella
Elizabeth A. Goodman
Stephen E. Gottschalk
G. Larry Griffith (P.A.)
John W. Haine
Mark E. Hamel
Joseph W. Hammell
Raymond A. Hayward (Resident, Rochester, Minnesota Office)
Timothy S. Hearn
Robert A. Heiberg
Richard A. Helde
Stuart R. Hemphill
Peter S. Hendrixson
Robert G. Hensley
John S. Hibbs (P.A.)
William R. Hibbs
Frederic F. Hillier
Elizabeth Cardle Hinck
William H. Hippee, Jr.
Robert L. Hobbins
Jean F. Holloway
Virginia Anne Housum (Not admitted in MN)
Alison C. Humphrey
J. David Jackson
Mark A. Jarboe
Gary M. Johnson
William A. Johnstone
William A. Jonason (Resident, Rochester, Minnesota Office)
Mark R. Kaster
Karin A. Keitel
Thomas O. Kelly III
John D. Kirby
Paul B. Klaas
Loren R. Knott
John T. Kramer
James D. Kremer
Peter M. Lancaster
James K. Langdon II
W. Charles Lantz (Resident, Rochester, Minnesota Office)
David J. Lauth
Michael A. Lindsay
Bridget A. Logstrom
Stephen P. Lucke
James B. Lynch
Edward B. Magarian
Creighton R. Magid
Roger J. Magnuson
Diane D. Malfeld
Thomas R. Manthey
Phillip H. Martin (P.A.)
Thomas O. Martin
David L. McCuskey
Michael J. McDonnell
Patrick J. McLaughlin
Bruce J. McNeil
David R. Melloh
Thomas O. Moe (P.A.)
Walter F. Mondale
Cornell L. Moore
Ralph K. Morris
Steven C. Nelson
Brian E. Palmer
William B. Payne
James F. Pedersen
Edward J. Pluimer
Charles L. Potuznik
Kathleen L. Prudhomme
Michael J. Radmer
David A. Ranheim
Melissa Raphan
Julia L. Rau
Michael E. Reeslund
Stanley M. Rein
Robert R. Reinhart, Jr.
Leonard S. Rice
Paula S. Rindels
Robert A. Rosenbaum
Charles F. Sawyer
Paul J. Scheerer
Robert A. Schwartzbauer
Robert A. Seng

(See Next Column)

MEMBERS OF FIRM (Continued)

Christopher T. Shaheen
Bruce J. Shnider
Robert J. Silverman
Peter W. Sipkins
Richard B. Solum
William R. Soth (P.A.)
William R. Stoeri
Mary J. Streitz
Robert J. Struyk
Jay L. Swanson
David P. Swanson
Janice M. Symchych
John C. Thomas
Thomas W. Tinkham
Paul M. Torgerson
James E. Townsend
Michael Trucano
Jon F. Tuttle
Gary L. Tygesson
Kenneth T. Tyra
Suzanne B. Van Dyk
Thomas D. Vander Molen
J. Thomas Vitt
Frank H. Voigt
Michael J. Wahoske
Steven J. Wells
William J. Wernz
John R. Wicks (Resident, Rochester, Minnesota Office)
Perry M. Wilson, III

SENIOR ATTORNEYS

Ross S. Antonson
David E. Bruhn
Paul R. Dieseth
William R. Goetz
Melinda K. Greer
Peter L. Harris
Gordon P. Heinson
Bricker L. Lavik
Gerald H. Sullivan, Jr.
David Y. Trevor
Doris K. Tuura

ASSOCIATES

A. Minnie Alexander
Clifford S. Anderson
Timothy B. Arends
John T. Arnason
Scott L. Barrington
Philip E. Bauer
Peter C. Beckerman
Lisagaye A. Biersay
Kevin C. Braley
Bethany S. Brand
Raquel A. Briskin
Michael J. Broich
LaFleur C. Browne
Joshua J. Burke
Theodore C. Cadwell, Jr.
Mark J. Chasteen
Monica L. Clark
Richard K. Cozine
Melanie J. Dahlberg
Lucy A. Dalglish
Ross D'Emanuele
Dharminder S. Devgun
Jeffrey S. Dillen
William A. Dossett
Michael R. Drysdale
Holly S.A. Eng
Dean C. Eyler
Michael R. Fehner
Orlando A. Flores
James M. Frommelt
Randall Frykberg
Gordon I. Gendler
Sara E. Gross Methner
Joseph F. Haag
Andre T. Hanson
Theodore D. Herzog
Mary E. Honess
Roseanne M. Hope
Sara E. Hopper
Patrick A. Hrbacek
Jonathan V. Hulse
Michael Iwan
Grant A. Johnson
Marie-Flore V. Johnson
Thad C. Johnson
Thomas M. Johnston
Heather J. Klaas
Alexandra B. Klass
Matthew Klein
Jeryn A. Konezny
Stephen K. Kozachok
Robert A. Kuhns
Robert A. Kukuljan
Sonja G. Lemmer-Martens
Kenneth E. Levitt
Diana E. Lugo
Thomas P. Lynch
Niall A. MacLeod
A. Melinda Maher
Liza L.S. Mark (Not admitted in MN)
David W. McElroy
Francis J. McAnulty (Resident, Rochester, Minnesota Office)
Tracy L. McGuire
Saiko Y. McIvor
Julie G. Meany
Sonny F. Miller
Kathleen A. Moccio
Kristyn M.W. Mullin
Richard W. Murphy
Aaron J. Mysliwiec
Jamie N. Nafziger
James A. Neal
Katherine McConahay Nealon
Barry J. Newman
Scott A. Nicholas
Thomas L. Nuss
Steven B. Nyquist
Tonya A. Olsen
Robert J. Olson
David J. Overstreet
Devan V. Padmanabhan
Laura A. Pagano
Alexandra M. Peters
Jon L. Peterson
Neal N. Peterson
Patricia L. Peterson
Christine L. Peterson-Stromgren
Elizabeth Catherine Porter
Benjamin C. Randall
Amy Hallman Rice
Julie A. Rich
Paul Robbennolt
Daniel P. Rogan
Amy Katz Rotenberg
John G. Ruckdaschel
Claudia I. Saavedra
Michael P. Sampson
Lenor A. Scheffler
Kent J. Schmidt (Not admitted in MN)
Todd W. Schnell
Sharon M. Scott
Sandra M. Sedo
Jennifer A. Service
Kim A. Severson
Dannette L. Smith
D. Christopher Smith
Elizabeth A. Soderberg
John O. Somers
Melissa N. Starkey
David M. Steglich
Jonathan A. Strauss
Sara A. Strothman
Thomas P. Swigert
Eric R. Tausner (Not admitted in MN)
Sarah M. Thier
Mary B. Thomas
Julie A. Tilton
Jodi L. Topel
Claire H. Topp
Beth W. Van Hecke
Lance L. Vietzke
A. Marie Villafaña
Nicholas A.J. Vlietstra
Michael J. Voves
Kristin S. Westgard
Judith Williams-Killackey
Elizabeth S. Wright
Christopher A. Young
James M. Zappa
Bianca Zick
Margaret M. Zverinova

(See Next Column)

DORSEY & WHITNEY LLP, *Minneapolis—Continued*

OF COUNSEL

David R. Abrams
Eugene L. Johnson (P.A.)
Larry W. Johnson
John D. Levine
Carolyn M. Sandberg
James D. Southwick
Bryn R. Vaaler
James B. Vessey (P.A.)
John W. Windhorst, Jr.

RETIRED PARTNERS

Craig A. Beck (Resident, Rochester, Minnesota Office)
Michael E. Bress (P.A.)
David R. Brink
Thomas M. Brown
Peter Dorsey
Thomas S. Erickson (P.A.)
John F. Finn
George P. Flannery
Robert O. Flotten (P.A.)
Thomas S. Hay
Charles J. Hauenstein
Horace Hitch
Duane E. Joseph (P.A.)
Russell W. Lindquist
Jerry C. D. Mahoney (P.A.)
Waldo F. Marquart
Michael Prichard
Raymond A. Reister
Curtis L. Roy
Warren R. Spannaus
Richard G. Swanson
John J. Taylor
Arthur E. Weisberg (P.A.)
William A. Whitlock
John C. Zwakman

For full biographical listings, see the Martindale-Hubbell Law Directory

FAEGRE & BENSON LLP (AV)

2200 Norwest Center, 90 South Seventh Street, 55402-3901
Telephone: 612-336-3000
Facsimile: 612-336-3026
Email: postmaster@faegre.com *URL:* http://www.faegre.com
Denver, Colorado: 2500 Republic Plaza, 370 Seventeenth Street.
Telephone: 303-592-9000.
Facsimile: 303-820-0600.
Des Moines, Iowa: 400 Capital Square, 400 Locust Street.
Telephone: 515-248-9000.
Facsimile: 515-248-9010.
London, England: Faegre Benson Hobson Audley, 7 Pilgrim Street, EC4V 6DR.
Telephone: 0171-450-4510.
Facsimile: 0171-450-4544.
Frankfurt, Germany: Wiesenau 1, 60323 Frankfurt am Main.
Telephone: 011-49-69-971-227-0.
Facsimile: 011-49-69-971-227-70.

MEMBERS OF FIRM

MINNEAPOLIS, MINNESOTA

John D. French
Martin N. Burke
John E. Harris
David R. Brennan
Richard C. Schmoker
Thomas M. Crosby, Jr.
Philip L. Bruner
Duane W. Krohnke
James A. Dueholm
Hubert V. Forcier
James M. Samples
Richard M. Berman
Gale R. Mellum
Jerry W. Snider
Timothy M. O'Brien
Stephen Rosholt
Frank B. Butler
Gordon B. Conn, Jr.
Bruce A. Ackerman
John H. Herman (P.A.)
Michael H. Harper, Jr.
Thomas L. Kimer
Joseph M. Price
W. Smith Sharpe, Jr.
Philip S. Garon
John F. Beukema
Walter J. Duffy, Jr.
James P. Stephenson
Reid Carron
John K. Steffen
John B. Gordon
Thomas M. Mayerle
Thomas G. Morgan
Kent E. Richey
John H. Hinderaker
Robert L. Schnell, Jr.
Richard A. Nelson
Brian B. O'Neill
Gary L. Gandrud
Michael E. Murphy
William R. Busch, Jr.
Bonnie M. Fleming
Winthrop A. Rockwell
Jack M. Fribley
John P. Borger
Steven R. Anderson
Jay D. Christiansen
Charles S. Ferrell
David B. Miller
James E. Nicholson
Rebecca L. Rom
Richard A. Forschler
Robert C. Hentges
James A. O'Neal
Walter H. Rockenstein, II
Robert L. Collins
Bruce M. Engler
Susan L. Jacobson
Walter A. Pickhardt
Donald C. Shepard
Wendy J. Wildung
James L. Volling
Kenneth A. Liebman
Gerard M. Nolting
Michael R. Stewart
David M. Vander Haar
Peter J. Withoff
Marianne T. Remedios
Daniel G. Wilczek
Charles T. Parks, Jr.
Mary E. Stumo
Peter C. Halls
Patrick J. O'Connor, Jr.
Daniel J. Amen
Jeff H. Eckland
Douglas J. Heffernan
Jennifer R. Mewaldt
John M. Haurykiewicz
Lyle G. Ward
Delmar R. Ehrich
James M. Pfau
Steven L. Severson
Calvin L. Litsey
Diana Young Morrissey
D. Charles Macdonald
John R. Wheaton
Douglas M. Rutherford
Douglas P. Long
Dennis M. Ryan
John W. Polley
J. Hazen Graves
William R. Joyce
Bruce Jones
Daniel C. Gerhan

(See Next Column)

MEMBERS OF FIRM

MINNEAPOLIS, MINNESOTA (Continued)

Steven C. Kennedy
Matthew L. Thompson
David J. Goldstein
Paul S. Moe
Mark D. Savin
Linda S. Svitak
Lori Ann Wagner
Andrew G. Humphrey
Jeffrey D. Hedlund
Paul W. Heiring
Felicia J. Boyd
Laura S. Carlson
Kathlyn E. Noecker
Daniel J. Connolly
Michael T. McCormick
Thomas J. Vollbrecht
Walter C. Linder
Ronald J. Lee
Richard A. Duncan
Ann Marie Hanrahan
David J. Shannon
Sonia A. Shewchuk
Michael F. Kelly, Jr.
Kathleen H. Sanberg
Randy L. Gegelman
John P. Mandler
Scott A. Anderegg
Michael A. Ponto
James R. Steffen
Mary Cullen Yeager
Matthew R. Bogart
Randall E. Kahnke
Michael J. Macaluso
Mark W. Binder
George D. Martin (Not admitted in MN)
Andrea M. Fike
David B. Clark
Stephen M. Mertz
Charles F. Webber
William L. Roberts
Richard Yoshiharu Sako
James E. Bowlus
Bridget M. Ahmann
Peggy Steif Abram
Eric E. Jorstad
Charles F. Knapp
Brian Melendez
Thomas S. Schroeder
P. Graham van der Leeuw
David J.F. Gross
David B. Kagan

DENVER, COLORADO

John D. Shively
Bruce W. Sattler
Dirk W. De Roos
William J. Campbell
Thomas B. Kelley
Michael S. McCarthy
Michael J. Cook
Gerald A. Niederman
James R. Spaanstra
Leslie A. Fields
Catherine A. Lemon
Elizabeth A. MacDonald
Russell O. Stewart
Linda L. Rockwood
Diane B. Davies
Charlotte Wiessner
J. William Callison
Natalie Hanlon-Leh
Michael J. Pankow
Jeanne M. Coleman

DES MOINES, IOWA

Michael A. Giudicessi
Kimberly J Walker
Kasey W. Kincaid
Terri L. Combs
John W. Blyth

LONDON, ENGLAND

Scott M. James

FRANKFURT, GERMANY

Philip B. Haleen
Ralph W. Hummel

MINNEAPOLIS, MINNESOTA

SPECIAL COUNSEL

Richard A. Hassel
Elizabeth L. Taylor
Stefanie N. Galey
R. Carl Moy
Scott W. Wright
Karl G. Schwappach

MINNEAPOLIS, MINNESOTA

CHINA COUNSEL

Andrew Wenhui Zeng

MINNEAPOLIS, MINNESOTA

STAFF ATTORNEYS

Heather B. Thayer
Kristin A. Jameson
Beth E. Carlson
Keri N. Swanson
Cindy J. Unkenholt (Not admitted in MN)

DENVER, COLORADO

OF COUNSEL

Frederic K. Conover, II

DENVER, COLORADO

SPECIAL COUNSEL

Charles D. Calvin
J. David Arkell
Richard F. Busch II
Jo Frances Walsh
Gail D. Zirkelbach
Ann C. McCullough
Julie L. Bernard

DENVER, COLORADO

STAFF ATTORNEY

Jeffrey H. Desautels

DES MOINES, IOWA

EASTERN EUROPEAN COUNSEL

Iliana Haleen
Hinrich A. Mummenthey

J. B. Faegre (1887-1986)
John C. Benson (1890-1986)
Paul Christopherson (1902-1987)
Robert J. Christianson (1908-1981)
George D. McClintock (Retired)
Rodger L. Nordbye (Retired)
George E. Harding (Retired)
John S. Holten (Retired)
Robert W. Oelke (Retired)
James A. Halls (Retired)
Gerald T. Flom (Retired)
Charles L. Horn (Retired)
Jack D. Gage (Retired)
James Fitzmaurice (1931-1994)
Ronald B. Hemstad (Retired)
Henry F. Frisch (1947-1995)
G. Alan Cunningham (Retired)
Paul T. Birkeland (Retired)
David M. Beadie (Retired)

(See Next Column)

FAEGRE & BENSON LLP—*Continued*

Norman R. Carpenter (Retired)
Gordon G. Busdicker (Retired)
Lawrence C. Brown (Retired)
Joseph M. Montano

ASSOCIATES

MINNEAPOLIS, MINNESOTA

Jacqueline R. Rolfs
Marit Westman Zosel
Christin Eaton Garcia
Jane Elizabeth Kiker
Jason D. Topp
John Edward Connelly
Elizabeth H. Schmiesing
Andrew J. Ritten
Julianne J. Knox-Chosy
Keyna Pidcock Skeffington
Karen Wilson
James J. Hartnett, IV
Gary S. Weinstein
Samuel Rosenstein
Maureen M. Maly
Eleasalo V. Ale
Mark J. Carpenter
Jennifer L. Haskin Will
Kara L. Benson
Laura F. Bednarski
Ann M. Kraemer
Peter A. Yost (Not admitted in MN)
Vanya S. Hogen-Kind
Ramona L. Baskerville
Jacques T. Cowan
Eunice P. de Carvalho
Jonathan W. Dettmann
Stephen C. Lee
Deborah J. MacKay
Lisa A. Misher
Keith P. Radtke
Michael A. Stanchfield
Deborah A. Ellingboe
Peter J. Ekberg
Terri J. Keeley
Anne M. Wilson
W. Morgan Burns
Eric J. Buss
Michael K. Coddington
Richard G. Erstad
Peter J. Goss
Matthew S. Luxton
Dara D. Mann
Elizabeth M. Misiaveg-Patel
Ahna M. Thoresen
Kimberly S. Jordahl
Wendy B. Mahling
Pamela Zhulkie Santer
Sachin Jay Darji
Andrea M. Carruthers
Kelly L. Tickle
R. Stanton Farmer
C. David Flower (Not admitted in MN)
Sandra K. Radeke (Not admitted in MN)
Bradley J. Hennen
Chris E. Hofstad
Caryn A. Kauffman
Sonia Miller-Van Oort
William L. Underwood
Andrew T. Vedder
Jeremy E. White
Holly M. Robbins
Bridget A. Hust
Michael D. Beach
Kristin R. Eads
Stephanie J. Hill
Christina A. Smith
Susanne E. Starr
Marklan M. Strefling
Nan A. Remus
Gordon S. Weber
Jonathan M. Asner
Lynn C. Cameron
Amy R. Freestone
Michael B. Lapicola
Kristen M. Ludgate
Lisa R. Pugh
J. Brendan Regan
Alan B. Schafer
Amy C. Seidel
Angela M. Crandall
Jennifer L. Cumming (Not admitted in MN)
Corina L. Leske
Tina L. Lorleberg
Chris A. Rauschl
Seema R. Shah
Jonathon G. Soler (Not admitted in MN)

Raymond B. Eby

DENVER, COLORADO

Adrienne O'Connell McNamara
Jack R. Sperber
Colin C. Deihl
Laury E. Bowman
Bret R. Gunnell
Steven D. Zansberg
Benjamin M. Chin
K. Megan Doberneck
Carol A. Deck
Janet L. McDaniel
Luis M. Agosto
Jennifer Bradfield
Christopher P. Beall
Jessica F. Toll
Catherine A. Traugott
Kristi B. Tyler

Peggy Pei-Ru Chiu

DES MOINES, IOWA

Melissa Shafter
William J. Hunnicutt

Benjamin W. Hopkins

FRANKFURT, GERMANY

Jörg Rehder

For complete list of firms clients see Professional Biographies at Minneapolis, Minnesota.

For full biographical listings, see the Martindale-Hubbell Law Directory

---

FELHABER, LARSON, FENLON & VOGT, PROFESSIONAL ASSOCIATION (AV)

601 2nd Avenue South, Suite 4200, 55402-4302
Telephone: 612-339-6321
800-989-6321
Facsimile: 612-338-0535
St. Paul, Minnesota Office: 30 East Seventh Street, 2100 Minnesota World Trade Center.
Telephone: 651-222-6321; 800-229-6321.
Facsimile: 651-222-8905.

Robert L. Bach
Richard A. Beens
James A. Blomquist
Edward J. Bohrer
John G. Brian, III
Stephen J. Burton
Edward Q. Cassidy
Karen M. Charlson
David M. Cremons
James J. Cronin
Steven E. Culbert
Terrance M. Cullen

(See Next Column)

James M. Dawson
Gerald G. Dederick
Thomas J. Doyle
Stanley J. Duran
William K. Ecklund
David B. Eide
Robert J. Fenlon
Roger H. Frommelt
Jan Douglas Halverson
David L. Hashmall
Catharine F. Haukedahl
Christopher S. Hayhoe
David R. Hols
Jon M. Hopeman
Katherine A. Jones
Ronald R. Kirchoff
Fredrick R. Krietzman
Lee A. Lastovich
Ruth Silseth Marcott
Sara Gullickson McGrane
Dennis J. Merley
Brad J. Miller
Janet A. Newberg
Byron D. Olsen
Penelope J. Phillips
Mark S. Radke
Steven L. Ross
James W. Rude
Karen G. Schanfield
Randy J. Sparling
Thomas R. Trachsel
Russell J. Sudeith, Jr.
Frederick W. Vogt
Thomas M. Vogt
Honnen S. Weiss
Paul H. Yoo

Paul J. Zech

OF COUNSEL

Kareen R. Ecklund

For full biographical listings, see the Martindale-Hubbell Law Directory

---

HEAD, SEIFERT & VANDER WEIDE, A PROFESSIONAL ASSOCIATION (AV)

One Financial Plaza, Suite 2400, 120 South Sixth Street, 55402
Telephone: 612-339-1601
Fax: 612-339-3372
Email: hsvw@wavefront.com

Jerome Truhn (1940-1982)
Douglas M. Head
Thomas V. Seifert
Vernon J. Vander Weide
Howard J. Kauffman
Kenneth A. Larson
Marianne E. Durkin
Charles H. Clay

Aaron F. Biber

For full biographical listings, see the Martindale-Hubbell Law Directory

---

HENSON & EFRON, P.A. (AV)

400 Second Avenue South, Suite 1200, 55401-2496
Telephone: 612-339-2500
Fax: 612-339-6364
Email: firm@hensonefron.com

Robert F. Henson
Stanley Efron
Wellington W. Tully, Jr.
Joseph T. Dixon, Jr.
Alan C. Eidsness
William F. Forsyth
Stuart T. Williams
Bruce C. Recher
Stephen L. Hopkins
Susan E. Vandenberg
Clark D. Opdahl
David Bradley Olsen
Karen S. Johnston
Jennie A. Clarke

Charles W. DuFresne
Scott A. Neilson
Angela D. Lageson
Kristi L. Skordahl
Brigitt M. Orfield
Neil M. Kliebenstein

Representative Clients: Pentair, Inc., Fraser Papers Inc. and Minnesota Freezer Warehouse Co.

For full biographical listings, see the Martindale-Hubbell Law Directory

---

KAPLAN, STRANGIS AND KAPLAN, P.A. (AV)

5500 Norwest Center, 90 South Seventh Street, 55402
Telephone: 612-375-1138
Fax: 612-375-1143
Email: ksk@kskpa.com

Sheldon Kaplan
Samuel L. Kaplan
Ralph Strangis
Harvey F. Kaplan
Andris A. Baltins
David Karan
Bruce J. Parker
Catherine A. Bartlett
Robert T. York
Nancy S. Bender-Kelner
Karlin S. Symons
James C. Melville

Mary S. Giesler

OF COUNSEL

Phillips & Potach, P.A., Minneapolis, Minnesota
John H. Matheson

Representative Clients: Affinity Group, Inc.; Allianz Life Insurance Company of North America; Ceridian Corporation; Dain Rauscher, Incorporated; Damark International, Inc.; LifeUSA Insurance Company; Piper Jaffray, Inc.; Polaris Industries Inc.; TCF Financial Corporation; US Airways, Inc.

For full biographical listings, see the Martindale-Hubbell Law Directory

Minneapolis—Continued

LEONARD, STREET AND DEINARD, PROFESSIONAL ASSOCIATION (AV)

Suite 2300, 150 South Fifth Street, 55402
Telephone: 612-335-1500
Telecopier: 612-335-1657
Email: lsd1500@leonard.com *URL:* http://www.leonard.com
St. Paul, Minnesota Office: World Trade Center, 30 East Seventh Street, Suite 2270.
Telephone: 651-222-7455.
Fax: 651-222-7644.
Mankato, Minnesota Office: 121 East Walnut Street, P. O. Box 967.
Telephone: 507-345-1179.
Fax: 507-345-1182.

George B. Leonard (1872-1956)
Arthur L. H. Street (1877-1961)
Benedict S. Deinard (1899-1969)
Amos S. Deinard (1898-1985)
Sidney Barrows (1918-1998)
Allen I. Saeks (P.A.)
Thomas D. Feinberg
Morris M. Sherman
Charles K. Dayton
Stephen R. Pflaum
Charles A. Mays
Lowell J. Noteboom
George F. McGunnigle
Richard G. Pepin, Jr.
John E. Regan (Resident, Mankato Office)
Byron E. Starns, Jr. (Resident, St. Paul Office)
Steven M. Rubin
Steven D. DeRuyter
James R. Dorsey
Stephen J. Davidson
Stephen R. Litman (P.A.)
Edward M. Moersfelder (Resident, Mankato Office)
Robert L. Barrows
Mark E. Jacobson
Daniel J. McInerney, Jr.
Hugh M. Maynard
Frederick W. Morris
John C. Kuehn (P.A.)
John M. Sheran
Bradley J. Gillan
Janie S. Mayeron
Michael A. Nekich
David N. Haynes
Richard H. Martin (Resident, St. Paul Office)
Robyn Hansen (Resident, St. Paul Office)
Thomas F. Nelson
Robert L. DeMay
Angela M. Bohmann
Timothy J. Pabst
Robert P. Thavis
James G. Bullard
Joseph M. Finley
Lawrence J. Field
David W. Kelley
Mark S. Weitz
David L. Lillehaug
Robert J. Huber
Barbara L. Portwood
Paul J. Linstroth
David Kantor
Angela Mulkerin Christy
Mark A. Lindgren
Jeffrey P. Cairns
Douglas R. Peterson (Resident, Mankato Office)
Lowell V. Stortz
Douglas B. Greenswag
Ellen G. Sampson
Scott R. Erickson
Rosanne Nathanson
Michael G. Taylor
John W. Getsinger
Thomas P. Sanders
Robert Zeglovitch
Timothy Welch
Susan M. Robiner
Bradley J. Gunn
Blake Shepard, Jr.
Nancy A. Wiltgen
Marc D. Simpson
Shaun C. McElhatton
James J. Bertrand
Carolyn V. Wolski
Steven R. Lindemann
Ronald J. Schultz
Jerry S. Podkopacz
Debra G. Strehlow
William H. Gotlieb
Wendy C. Skjerven
Robert H. Torgerson
Timothy A. Johnson
Thomas J. Conley
Joshua J. Kanassatega
Jann M. Eichlersmith
Andrew P. Lee
I. Daniel Colton
Nicole A. Engisch
Jeffrey E. Grell
Keith S. Moheban (Resident, St. Paul Office)
Alan W. Van Dellen
Dominic J. Cecere
Jane F. Godfrey
Eric H. Galatz
Daniel L. Palmquist
Catherine A. McEnroe
Mariana R. Shulstad
John T. Roberts
Craig M. Ayers
Michael J. Dioguardi
Carolyn M. McCann

Eric D. Paulsrud
Susan S. Fauver
Stephen M. Quinlivan
Daniel Oberdorfer
Jeffrey A. Eyres
Bradley J. Swenson
Steven P. Zabel
David R. Crosby
Elizabeth A. Cumming
Todd A. Noteboom
David H. Sampsell
Robert L. Striker
Susan M. Humiston
Susan J. Thompson
Brendan W. Randall
Joel E. Abrahamson
Tracey L. Baubie
Daniel P. Tschida
Jill Hutchinson Bollettieri
Jeffrey L. Cotter
Paula K. Beck
Lynn Bebeau
Rachel Spector
Paul C. Rachie
Jennifer R. Junker (Not admitted in MN)
James L. Heine
Keri Barney
Thomas C. Snook
Robert F. Devolve
Mary E. Schwind
Samuel R. Bloom
Scott R. Goings
Christopher M. McGlincey
Eric J. Skytte
Lisa Marie Buck
Jerry D. Perron (Resident, St. Paul Office)
Daniel M. Bryant, Jr. (Resident, Mankato Office)
James J. Sticha
Laurie J. Dechery
Mee Moua (Resident, St. Paul Office)
Lynn M. Burley
Marna J. Johnson
Nicholas W. Chase
Richard W. Pins

(See Next Column)

Doris E. Yock
Michael R. Phelps
Melanie Heitzenroder
Scott J. Bergs
Jewelie A. Grape

OF COUNSEL

Sidney Lorber
Harold D. Field, Jr., (P.A.)
George F. Reilly
David G. Baratti
John J. McGirl, Jr.
Barry McGrath

Representative Clients: Hubbard Broadcasting, Inc.; Midcontinent Media, Inc.

For full biographical listings, see the Martindale-Hubbell Law Directory

---

THOMAS G. LOVETT, JR. (AV)

100 South Fifth Street, Suite 2250, 55402
Telephone: 612-339-4567
Voice Mail: 612-573-4685
Fax: 612-349-6210
Email: LOVET001@tc.UMN.EDU

For full biographical listings, see the Martindale-Hubbell Law Directory

---

MACKALL, CROUNSE & MOORE, PLC (AV)

1400 AT&T Tower, 901 Marquette Avenue, 55402-2859
Telephone: 612-305-1400
Fax: 612-305-1414
URL: http://www.mcmlaw.com

Henry C. Mackall (1885-1979)
Robert M. Crounse (1893-1974)
Perry R. Moore (1894-1969)

MEMBERS OF FIRM

G. Thomas MacIntosh, II
Lawrence R. Commers
Leslie H. Novak
Timothy D. Moratzka
Denis E. Grande
Martin V. Aydelott
Shane H. Anderson
Glenn R. Drury
Robert F. Strauss
Robert S. Lee
Allen E. Christy, Jr.
Elizabeth H. Cobb
Timothy J. Grande
David M. Morehouse
Gerald E. Helget
James A. Wahl
Sheila Engelmeier
Michael R. Gray
William J. O'Brien
Tim A. Staum
Lynn M. Starkovich
Bradley J. Halberstadt
Scott S. Payzant
Nelson R. Capes
Joanne H. Turner

ASSOCIATES

Mark R. Geier
Tina A. Syring-Petrocchi
Jon M. Tynjala
Jonathan J. Hegre

OF COUNSEL

Frederick L. Thorson
Winston E. Munson
Clay R. Moore
Stephen P. Kelley
Lavon Emerson-Henry

For full biographical listings, see the Martindale-Hubbell Law Directory

---

OPPENHEIMER WOLFF & DONNELLY LLP (AV)

3400 Plaza VII, 45 South Seventh Street, 55402
Telephone: 612-607-7000
FAX: 612-607-7100
URL: http://www.owdlaw.com
Amsterdam, The Netherlands Office: Keizersgracht 241.
Telephone: 31-20-423-4555.
FAX: 31-20-423-4545.
Brussels, Belgium Office: Avenue Louise 240, Box 5, 1050.
Telephone: 32-2-626-0500.
FAX: 32-2-626-0510.
Geneva, Switzerland Office: Rue Gabriel Eynard, 6, 1205.
Telephone: (41/22) 311-7410.
FAX: (41/22) 311-7407.
New York, N.Y. Office: Citicorp Center, 153 East 53rd Street, 10022.
Telephone: 212-826-5000.
FAX: 212-486-0708.
Newport Beach, California Office: 500 Newport Center Drive, Suite 700, 92660.
Telephone: 949-719-6000.
FAX: 949-719-6020.
Paris, France Office: 53 Avenue Montaigne, 75008.
Telephone: (33/1) 44 95 03 50.
FAX: (33/1) 44 95 03 40.
St. Paul, Minnesota Office: 1700 First National Bank Building, 55101.
Telephone: 651-605-2000.
FAX: 651-605-2100.
Washington, D.C. Office: Oppenheimer Wolff Donnelly & Bayh LLP, 1350 Eye Street, N.W., Suite 200, 20005.
Telephone: 202-312-8000.
FAX: 202-312-8100.
Los Angeles, California Office: 2029 Century Park East, 38th Floor, 90067.
Telephone: 310-788-5000.
FAX: 310-277-1297.
San Jose, California Office: 101 Park Center Plaza, Suite 300, 95113.
Telephone: 408-795-3000.
FAX: 408-795-3100.

(See Next Column)

OPPENHEIMER WOLFF & DONNELLY LLP—*Continued*

Chicago, Illinois Office: Oppenheimer Wolff & Donnelly (Illinois), Two Prudential Plaza, 45th Floor, 180 North Stetson Avenue, 60601.
Telephone: 312-616-1800.
Fax: 312-616-5800.

RESIDENT PARTNERS

William H. Oppenheimer (1883-1975)
Richard G. Lareau
Bruce W. Blackburn
Harold D. Jastram
Bruce E. Hanson
Donald P. Norwich
Craig W. Gagnon
G. Robert Johnson
Richard M. Bisanz
Duane L. Paulson
William P. Studer
Edward J. Hayward
Richard H. Massopust, Jr.
James E. Schatz
Steven A. Wellvang
C. Robert Beattie, III
Richard J. Wegener
Gary Hansen
Edward M. Laine
William L. Sippel
W. C. Blanton
Michael J. Bleck
James M. Christenson
Bradley G. Clary
Lloyd G. Kepple, II
Timothy R. Quinn
D. William Kaufman
Jeffrey B. Oberman
Mark S. Olson
James A. Payne
Margo S. Struthers
Dennis P. Whelpley
Barbara J. Grahn
Paula D. Osborn
Brian G. Belisle
Edward F. Fox
Sue Ann Nelson
Christopher M. Scotti
Bruce A. Machmeier
Jerome A. Miranowski
David B. Potter
Robert C. Castle
Shannon M. O'Toole
Michael D. Zalk
Cynthia J. Atsatt
Mary E. Senkus
Edward T. Wahl
Bradley S. Keil
Mark J. Kalla
Thomas R. Marek
Steven W. Meyer
Gary P. Gengel II
Timothy J. Scallen
Martin A. Culhane III
Kenneth C. Rowe
Julie A. Wrase
Jeffrey J. Bouslog
Michael B. Fisco
Daniel C. Mott
James J. Schwert
Kevin M. Klemz
Thomas A. Letscher
Cary B. Johnson
David P. Graham
Jonathon H. Bloomberg
Michael E. Keyes
Thaddeus R. Lightfoot
Robert J. McGillivray
Jake M. Holdreith
Kenneth A. Podpeskar
Mark G. Rabogliatti
Craig J. Lervick
James A. Mennell

RESIDENT ASSOCIATES

Alan D. Kamrath
Marc L. Kruger
Jacqueline Casey Olson
Linda M. Pallarino
Daniel R. Sundell
Chad A. Klingbeil
Wilma L Zippel
Meredith A. Forgosh
James C. Zacharski
Elliott M. Fliés
Meg G. Newell
Dawn R. Koestner
Kathryn L. Boyne
Erika S. Koster
Michael C. Zender
Rikke A. Dierssen-Morice
Carol Ann Eiden
Rachel A. Igel
James M. Jorissen
Anne F. Larsen
Jacqueline M. Moen
Bradley C. Olson
Leonard B. Segal
Rachel E. Soffer
J. Aron Allen
Amy L. DuMond
Jennifer K. Eggers
Jason S. Kilene
Michael J. Kolar
Timothy C. Krsul
JoAnn H. Maloney
Thomas E. Ring
Lowell M. Rothschild
Mark J. Sexton
Elizabeth A. Wefel
Amy E. Culbert
Ernest W. Grumbles, III
Marcus A. Mollison
Anne Marie Solberg
Pamela A. Thein
Bradley F. Williams
Patrice H. Kloss
Kerri L. Klover
Connie A. Lunceford-Hedtke
Vanessa L. Parvin
Stacy S. Ramdas
Seth J. Sergent-Leventhal
Carey Sirota Meyer
Bridget A. Sullivan
Bliss A. Baldwin
Kristin L. Boetticher
Michael F. Cockson
Ranelle A. Leier
Jonathan W. Lips
Chad D. Striker
David E. Runck
Raymond L. Veldman
Kari L. Wraspir
Daniel G. Chapik
Stacey L. Drentlaw
Andrew S. Hansen
Frederick H. Lee
Kimberly A. Lowe
Juli A. Lund
Phillip B. Martin
Cyrus A. Morton
Susan C. Snyder
Aaron G. Gunderson

OF COUNSEL

Donald E. Engle
John F. Stone

Kimberley K. Adams (New York, New York)
M. Peter Adler (Washington, D.C.)
Goli-Schabnam Akbarian (Brussels, Belgium)
J. Aron Allen (Minneapolis, Minnesota)
Cynthia J. Atsatt (Minneapolis, Minnesota)
Thomas C. Bacon (Newport Beach, California)
Bliss A. Baldwin (Minneapolis, Minnesota)
Birch E. Bayh (Washington, D.C.)

(See Next Column)

Ronald S. Beacher (New York, New York)
C. Robert Beattie, III (Minneapolis, Minnesota)
Brian G. Belisle (Minneapolis, Minnesota)
Barry M. Benjamin (New York, New York)
Charles Berman (Los Angeles, California)
Alan E. Bernick (St. Paul, Minnesota)
Richard M. Bisanz (Minneapolis, Minnesota)
Bruce W. Blackburn (Minneapolis, Minnesota)
W. C. Blanton (Minneapolis, Minnesota)
Michael J. Bleck (Minneapolis, Minnesota)
Alan P. Block (Los Angeles, California)
Jonathon H. Bloomberg (Minneapolis, Minnesota)
Kristin L. Boetticher (Minneapolis, Minnesota)
David C. Bohrer
Hannes C. Boner (Brussels, Belgium)
Jeffrey F. Boothe (Washington, D.C.)
William S. Borchers (Minneapolis, Minnesota)
Michael K. Bosworth (San Jose, California)
Jeffrey J. Bouslog (Minneapolis, Minnesota)
Louis J. Bovasso (Los Angeles, California)
Justin F. Boyce (San Jose, California)
Kathryn L. Boyne (Brussels, Belgium)
Lisa C. Breen (Chicago, Illinois)
Marc E. Brown (Los Angeles, California)
Richard H. Bruck (Newport Beach, California)
Lynn A. Bulan (Washington, D.C.)
Jenny Ann Carles (New York, New York)
Fiona M. Carlin (Brussels, Belgium)
Robert C. Castle (Minneapolis, Minnesota)
Michael A. Chabraja
Daniel G. Chapik (Minneapolis, Minnesota)
Chien (Chris) W. Chou (San Jose, California)
James M. Christenson (Minneapolis, Minnesota)
Harry W. Cladouhos (Washington, D.C.)
Bradley G. Clary (Minneapolis, Minnesota)
Michael F. Cockson (Minneapolis, Minnesota)
Mattie Cohan Condray (Washington, D.C.)
Thomas A. Connaughton (Washington, D.C.)
Amy E. Culbert (Minneapolis, Minnesota)
Martin A. Culhane, III (Minneapolis, Minnesota)
Bethany K. Culp (St. Paul, Minnesota)
Christopher Darrow (Los Angeles, California)
Manjari M. Datta (New York, New York)
Peter A. Davidson (Los Angeles, California)
Stefaan G. De Boeck (Brussels, Belgium)
Erwin De Deyn (Brussels, Belgium)
Didier De Vliegher (Brussels, Belgium)
Denis Debost (Paris, France)

(See Next Column)

Jeffrey P. Diebel (St. Paul, Minnesota)
Rikke A. Dierssen-Morice (Minneapolis, Minnesota)
Daniel K. Donahue (Newport Beach, California)
Stacey L. Drentlaw (Minneapolis, Minnesota)
Amy L. DuMond (Minneapolis, Minnesota)
Jennifer K. Eggers (Minneapolis, Minnesota)
Carol Ann Eiden (Minneapolis, Minnesota)
Courtenay Ellis (Washington, D.C.)
Donald E. Engle (Minneapolis, Minnesota)
Kevin O. Faley (Washington, D.C.)
Michael B. Farber (Los Angeles, California)
Paul J. Fegelson (Washington, D.C.)
Michel Ferrand (Paris, France)
Teresa T. Fineman (Newport Beach, California)
Michael B. Fisco (Minneapolis, Minnesota)
Edward J. Fishman (Washington, D.C.)
James A. Fletcher (Chicago, Illinois)
Elliott M. Fliés (Minneapolis, Minnesota)
Steven R. Foletta (San Jose, California)
Meredith A. Forgosh (Minneapolis, Minnesota)
George L. Fountain (Los Angeles, California)
Edward F. Fox (Minneapolis, Minnesota)
Michael M. Gaba (Washington, D.C.)
Craig W. Gagnon (Minneapolis, Minnesota)
Thomas M. Gandolfo (New York, New York)
Lynn M. Geerdes
Gary P. Gengel II (Minneapolis, Minnesota)
Leon R. Goodrich (St. Paul, Minnesota)
Vineet Gosain (Chicago, Illinois)
Lance Gotthoffer (New York, New York)
David P. Graham (Minneapolis, Minnesota)
Barbara J. Grahn (Minneapolis, Minnesota)
Ernest W. Grumbles, III (Minneapolis, Minnesota)
Robert O. Guillot (San Jose, California)
Aaron G. Gunderson (Minneapolis, Minnesota)
Rebecca R. Haller
Claude A. S. Hamrick (San Jose, California)
Andrew S. Hansen (Minneapolis, Minnesota)
Gary Hansen (Minneapolis, Minnesota)
Karen M. Hansen (Minneapolis, Minnesota)
Scott R. Hansen (Los Angeles, California)
Bruce E. Hanson
Michael D. Harris (Los Angeles, California)
Sheldon J. Harris (Washington, D.C.)
Edward J. Hayward (Minneapolis, Minnesota)
Donald G. Heeman (St. Paul, Minnesota)
James D. Helenhouse
Jake M. Holdreith (Minneapolis, Minnesota)
Grace Horoupian (Los Angeles, California)

(See Next Column)

OPPENHEIMER WOLFF & DONNELLY LLP, *Minneapolis—Continued*

Marcel A. J. Houben (Brussels, Belgium)
Laurie Paulsen Huusko (St. Paul, Minnesota)
Marisa B. Iasenza (Newport Beach, California)
Rachel A. Igel (Minneapolis, Minnesota)
Lauren M. Ilvento (Brussels, Belgium)
Marc A. Indeglia (Newport Beach, California)
James W. Inskeep (Los Angeles, California)
Marie-Helene Jacquemin (Brussels, Belgium)
Harold D. Jastram (Minneapolis, Minnesota)
Jonathan D. Jay (St. Paul, Minnesota)
Cary B. Johnson (Minneapolis, Minnesota)
G. Robert Johnson (Minneapolis, Minnesota)
Christopher W. Jones (New York, New York)
David L. Jordan-Huffman (St. Paul, Minnesota)
James M. Jorissen (Minneapolis, Minnesota)
Mark L. Jubelt (Los Angeles, California)
Mark J. Kalla (Minneapolis, Minnesota)
Alan D. Kamrath (Minneapolis, Minnesota)
Thomas P. Kane (St. Paul, Minnesota)
D. William Kaufman (Minneapolis, Minnesota)
Bradley S. Keil (Minneapolis, Minnesota)
Lloyd G. Kepple, II (Minneapolis, Minnesota)
Bert S. Kerkman (Amsterdam, The Netherlands)
Michael E. Keyes (Minneapolis, Minnesota)
Jason S. Kilene
Kevin W. Kirsch (Newport Beach, California)
Kevin M. Klemz (Minneapolis, Minnesota)
Chad A. Klingbeil (Minneapolis, Minnesota)
Patrice H. Kloss (Minneapolis, Minnesota)
Kerri L. Klover (Minneapolis, Minnesota)
Dawn R. Koestner (Minneapolis, Minnesota)
Michael J. Kolar (Minneapolis, Minnesota)
Michael A. Kondzella (Newport Beach, California)
John H. Korns (Washington, D.C.)
Efthymia C. Korodima (Brussels, Belgium)
Erika S. Koster (Minneapolis, Minnesota)
Colleen Young Kraus (Chicago, Illinois)
Timothy C. Krsul
Marc L. Kruger (Minneapolis, Minnesota)
Edward M. Laine (Minneapolis, Minnesota)
Gary E. Lande (Los Angeles, California)
Martin K. LaPointe
Richard G. Lareau (Minneapolis, Minnesota)
Anne F. Larsen (Minneapolis, Minnesota)
Douglas N. Larson (Los Angeles, California)
Paul M. Laurenza (Washington, D.C.)
Thomas Lawrence, III (Washington, D.C.)
Frederick H. Lee (Minneapolis, Minnesota)
John Y. E. Lee
Ranelle A. Leier (Minneapolis, Minnesota)
Edward K. Lenci (New York, New York)
Craig J. Lervick (Minneapolis, Minnesota)
Thomas A. Letscher (Minneapolis, Minnesota)
Charles M. Levenberg (St. Paul, Minnesota)
Lizbeth R. Levinson (Washington, D.C.)
W. Mark Levinson (Los Angeles, California)
Thaddeus R. Lightfoot (Minneapolis, Minnesota)
Jonathan W. Lips
Thomas J. Litwiler
Cynthia A. Lock (Los Angeles, California)
Philippe Logelain (Brussels, Belgium)
Kimberly A. Lowe
Winston I. Lowe (Chicago, Illinois)
Irina M. Lucidi (Paris, France)
Frederick L. Lukoff (Brussels, Belgium)
Connie A. Lunceford-Hedtke (Minneapolis, Minnesota)
Juli A. Lund (Minneapolis, Minnesota)
Thomas E. Lund (St. Paul, Minnesota)
Bruce A. Machmeier (Minneapolis, Minnesota)
Kurt A. MacLean (Newport Beach, California)
Kathleen M. Mahoney (St. Paul, Minnesota)
JoAnn H. Maloney (Minneapolis, Minnesota)
Barry S. Maram
Thomas R. Marek (Minneapolis, Minnesota)
Phillip B. Martin (Minneapolis, Minnesota)
Richard H. Massopust, Jr. (Minneapolis, Minnesota)
Robert J. McGillivray (Minneapolis, Minnesota)
James A. Mennell (Minneapolis, Minnesota)
Kirk D. Messmer (Brussels, Belgium; Amsterdam, The Netherlands)
Steven W. Meyer (Minneapolis, Minnesota)
Jerome A. Miranowski (Minneapolis, Minnesota)
Jacqueline M. Moen (Minneapolis, Minnesota)
Byron Z. Moldo (Los Angeles, California)
Marcus A. Mollison (Minneapolis, Minnesota)
Cyrus A. Morton (Minneapolis, Minnesota)
Daniel C. Mott
Abraham Mouritz (Amsterdam, The Netherlands)
Nicolas Narbel (Geneva, Switzerland)
Sue Ann Nelson
Yvette Nelson (Minneapolis, Minnesota)
Terrance C. Newby (St. Paul, Minnesota)
Meg G. Newell (Minneapolis, Minnesota)
Gregory S. Norrod
Donald P. Norwich (Minneapolis, Minnesota)

(See Next Column)

Paul C. Nyquist (Newport Beach, California)
Edward F. O'Connor (Newport Beach, California)
Shannon M. O'Toole (Minneapolis, Minnesota)
Jeffrey B. Oberman
David J. Oldenkamp (Los Angeles, California)
Bradley C. Olson (Minneapolis, Minnesota)
Jacqueline Casey Olson (Minneapolis, Minnesota)
Mark S. Olson (Minneapolis, Minnesota)
Teresa J. Olson (New York, New York)
James R. Oppenheimer (St. Paul, Minnesota)
Paula D. Osborn (Minneapolis, Minnesota)
Eric Osterweil (Brussels, Belgium)
Linda M. Pallarino (Minneapolis, Minnesota)
Jee Hi Park (Newport Beach, California)
Sandra M. Parker (Los Angeles, California)
Vanessa L. Parvin (Minneapolis, Minnesota)
Duane L. Paulson (Minneapolis, Minnesota)
James A. Payne (Minneapolis, Minnesota)
Russell M. Pelton (Chicago, Illinois)
David J. Perry (Newport Beach, California)
Joseph E. Petersen (New York, New York)
Kenneth A. Podpeskar (Minneapolis, Minnesota)
William Poms (Los Angeles, California)
David B. Potter (Minneapolis, Minnesota)
Christopher E.V. Quinn
Timothy R. Quinn
Mark G. Rabogliatti (Minneapolis, Minnesota)
Stacy Suby Ramdas (Minneapolis, Minnesota)
Boynton M. Rawlings (Paris, France)
Thomas E. Ring (Minneapolis, Minnesota)
Nicholas A. Ritrivi (New York, New York)
Ranfi R. Rivera (New York, New York)
Alan C. Rose (Los Angeles, California)
Charles Rosenberg (Los Angeles, California)
Herbert C. Ross, Jr. (New York, New York)
Allan Rothenberg (Newport Beach, California)
Lowell M. Rothschild (Minneapolis, Minnesota)
Kenneth C. Rowe (Minneapolis, Minnesota)
David E. Runck (Minneapolis, Minnesota)
Jean Russotto
Lehan J. Ryan (St. Paul, Minnesota)
Michael G. Ryan
Timothy J. Scallen (Minneapolis, Minnesota)
James E. Schatz (Minneapolis, Minnesota)
Ursula Schliessner (Brussels, Belgium)
Lawrence H. Schwartz (Washington, D.C.)
James J. Schwert (Minneapolis, Minnesota)
Christopher M. Scotti (Minneapolis, Minnesota)
James H. Searles (Brussels, Belgium)
Leonard B. Segal
Ted G. Semaya (New York, New York)
Mary E. Senkus (Minneapolis, Minnesota)
Seth J. Sergent-Leventhal (Minneapolis, Minnesota)
Mark J. Sexton (Minneapolis, Minnesota)
Gordon Shepard (St. Paul, Minnesota)
Brian D. Sheridan (Brussels, Belgium)
Kevin M. Sheys (Washington, D.C.)
Jeffrey A. Siderius
William L. Sippel
Carey L. Sirota (Minneapolis, Minnesota)
Craig A. Slavin (Los Angeles, California)
Guy Porter Smith (Los Angeles, California)
Jennifer R. Snyder (New York, New York)
Susan C. Snyder (Minneapolis, Minnesota)
Rachel E. Soffer
Anne Marie Solberg (Minneapolis, Minnesota)
Tracie D. Spear (Washington, D.C.)
John F. Stone (Minneapolis, Minnesota)
Margaret N. Strand (Washington, D.C.)
Chad D. Striker (Minneapolis, Minnesota)
Margo S. Struthers (Minneapolis, Minnesota)
William P. Studer (Minneapolis, Minnesota)
Bridget Ann Sullivan (Minneapolis, Minnesota)
Daniel R. Sundell (Minneapolis, Minnesota)
Ronald S. Tamura (Los Angeles, California)
Jake A. Taylor (Los Angeles, California)
Benoît M. Taymans (Brussels, Belgium)
Pamela A. Thein (Minneapolis, Minnesota)
Kathryn C. Thomas
Thomas C. Thomas (San Jose, California)
Anne Tilleux (Brussels, Belgium)
Randolph L. Tom (San Jose, California)
Robert J. Tracy (New York, New York)
Elmer B. Trousdale (Minneapolis, Minnesota)
Amédée Edward Turner, Q.C. (Brussels, Belgium)
Pieter van der Meer (Brussels, Belgium)
Raymond L. Veldman (Minneapolis, Minnesota)
Joseph J. Vicinanza (New York, New York)
Joel D. Voelzke (Los Angeles, California)
Alessandra von Planta (Geneva, Switzerland)
Edward T. Wahl (Minneapolis, Minnesota)
Jane Shay Wald (Los Angeles, California)
Elizabeth A. Wefel (Minneapolis, Minnesota)
Richard J. Wegener (Minneapolis, Minnesota)
Frank L. Weidema (Amsterdam, The Netherlands)
J. Patrick Weir (Los Angeles, California)
Steven A. Wellvang (Minneapolis, Minnesota)
Robert H. Wheeler
Dennis P. Whelpley (Minneapolis, Minnesota)

(See Next Column)

OPPENHEIMER WOLFF & DONNELLY LLP—*Continued*

Jennifer K. Wichelman (St. Paul, Minnesota)
David M. Wilk (St. Paul, Minnesota)
P. Jay Wilker (New York, New York)
Bradley F. Williams (Minneapolis, Minnesota)
Robin A. Williams (Not admitted in MN; Washington, D.C.)
Stephanie E. P. Wilms (Brussels, Belgium)
Mark P. Wine (Los Angeles, California)
Karen Nicolai Winnett (Newport Beach, California)
Alix Debost Witter (Paris, France)
Benno F. Wolff (St. Paul, Minnesota)
Aimee Y. Wong (Los Angeles, California)
Gregory B. Wood (Los Angeles, California)
Philip Woolfson (Brussels, Belgium)
Julie A. Wrase (Minneapolis, Minnesota)
Kari L. Wraspir (Minneapolis, Minnesota)
James C. Zacharski (Minneapolis, Minnesota)
Michael D. Zalk (Minneapolis, Minnesota)
Michael C. Zender (Minneapolis, Minnesota)
Wilma L Zippel (Minneapolis, Minnesota)

For full biographical listings, see the Martindale-Hubbell Law Directory

PHILLIPS & POTACH, P.A. (AV)

5420 Norwest Center, 90 South Seventh Street, 55402
Telephone: 612-349-6786
Telecopier: 612-349-2824
Email: pppa@visi.com

Felix M. Phillips
Steven G. Potach

OF COUNSEL

Kaplan, Strangis and Kaplan, P.C. , Minneapolis, Minnesota
Bert M. Gross

Representative Clients: Regis Corporation; Johnson Brothers Liquor Co.; United States Distilled Products Co.; Lieberman Companies, Inc.; A & W Restaurants, Inc.; Shea Architects, Inc.; Rosenbloom Insurance; Kurt Manufacturing Co.; Midwest Management, Inc.
Reference: Bank Windsor.

ROBINS, KAPLAN, MILLER & CIRESI L.L.P. (AV)

2800 LaSalle Plaza, 800 LaSalle Avenue, 55402-2015
Telephone: 612-349-8500
Telecopier: 612-339-4181
TWX: 910-576-2737
Fax: 612-339-4181
URL: http://www.rkmc.com
Atlanta, Georgia Office: 2600 One Atlanta Plaza, 950 East Paces Ferry Road NE.
Telephone: 404-233-1114.
Fax: 404-233-1267.
Boston, Massachusetts Office: Suite 2200, 222 Berkeley Street.
Telephone: 617-267-2300.
Fax: 617-267-8288.
Chicago, Illinois Office: Suite 1400, 55 West Wacker Drive.
Telephone: 312-782-9200.
Fax: 312-782-7756.
Costa Mesa, California Office: 600 Anton Boulevard, Suite 1600.
Telephone: 714-540-6200.
Fax: 714-545-6915.
Los Angeles, California Office: 2049 Century Park East, Suite 3700.
Telephone: 310-552-0130.
Fax: 310-229-5800.
Washington, D.C. Office: Suite 1200, 1801 K Street, N.W.
Telephone: 202-775-0725.
Fax: 202-223-8604.

PARTNERS

Richard B. Allyn
David W. Beehler
David E. Bland
Steve A. Brand
Tyrone P. Bujold
Michael V. Ciresi
Jan M. Conlin
Thomas J. Conlin
Kevin D. Conneely
Kevin L. Crudden
Annamarie A. Daley
Rita Coyle DeMeules
Mel I. Dickstein
John F. Eisberg
Brad P. Engdahl
David A. Engen
Janet C. Evans
David S. Evinger
Leo F. Feeney
Bruce A. Finzen
Linda S. Foreman
John F. Gibbs
Robert J. Gilbertson
Richard L. Gill
Corey L. Gordon
Thomas L. Hamlin
Thomas B. Hatch
Andrew W. Horstman
Terrence R. Joy
Elliot S. Kaplan
Thomas C. Kayser
Robert T. Kugler
William A. LeMire
Charles O. Lentz
Martin R. Lueck
Eric O. Madson
William H. Manning
Kathleen A. Marron
Richard M. Martinez
John R. McDonald
Emmett J. McMahon
Chris A. Messerly
David L. Mitchell
Vincent J. Moccio
Robert T. Montague
Susan Richard Nelson
Daniel A. O'Fallon
Howard R. Orenstein

(See Next Column)

PARTNERS (Continued)

David E. Oslund
Deborah J. Palmer
Kathleen Flynn Peterson
Philip A. Pfaffly
Sara A. Poulos
Brent L. Reichert
Anne M. Rosenberg
James R. Safley
Peter A. Schmit
Steven A. Schumeister
Ronald J. Schutz
James D. Steiner
Robert J. Tansey, Jr.
Randall Tietjen
Thomas J. Undlin
Terry L. Wade
William A. Webster
Gary L. Wilson
Martha K. Wivell
Matthew L. Woods

ASSOCIATES

John C. Adkisson
Richard W. Bale
M. Michael Baxter
Douglas R. Boettge
Jane S. Borden
Courtney Candalino
Ann N. Cathcart
Marilyn J. Conklin
Cole M. Fauver
Celeste Pulju Grant
Barbara J. Haley
Ken R. Hall
Todd G. Hartman
Amy J. Hasbargen
Andrew R.K. Johnson
Frederick R. Juckniess
Gregory J. Klint
Stephanie J. Kravetz
Sonja A. Larson
Katie Crosby Lehmann
William M. Lutz
Thomas C. Mahlum
Nauni Jo Manty
William A. Mayson
Michael P. McNamee
Joel A. Mintzer
Abigail R. Nesbitt
Stacie E. Oberts
Steven K. Orloff
Timothy J. Pramas
Peter M. Reyes, Jr.
Adam M. Samaha
Darren Schwiebert
Philip Sieff
Diane L. Simerson
J. Sebastian Stewart
Scott R. Strand
Keiko L. Sugisaka
Tara D. Sutton
David S. Toepfer
David J. Wallace-Jackson
Mark D. Wisser
Heidi E. Viesturs
Wendy J. Zeller

STAFF ATTORNEYS

Anne E. Workman
Patricia Yoedicke

OF COUNSEL

Roberta B. Walburn

For full biographical listings, see the Martindale-Hubbell Law Directory

ROBERT MERRILL ROSENBERG, P.A. (AV)

520 Marquette Avenue South, Suite 900, 55402-1105
Telephone: 612-349-5290
Facsimile: 612-349-9962
Email: RMR@Rosenberg-Law.com

Robert Merrill Rosenberg

For full biographical listings, see the Martindale-Hubbell Law Directory

SALITERMAN & SIEFFERMAN, P.C. (AV)

Suite 1000 Northstar Center East, 608 Second Avenue South, 55402
Telephone: 612-339-1400
Fax: 612-349-2908
URL: http://www.saliterman.com

Richard A. Saliterman
Floyd E. Siefferman, Jr.
Nicholas M. Wenner
Thomas J. Seymour
Paul A. Ledford

For full biographical listings, see the Martindale-Hubbell Law Directory

SIEGEL, BRILL, GREUPNER, DUFFY & FOSTER, P.A. (AV)

1300 Washington Square, 100 Washington Avenue South, 55401
Telephone: 612-339-7131
Telecopier: 612-339-6591

Josiah E. Brill, Jr.
James R. Greupner
Gerald S. Duffy
Wood R. Foster, Jr.
Thomas H. Goodman
John S. Watson
Wm. Christopher Penwell
Susan M. Voigt
Anthony J. Gleekel
Joel H. Jensen
Sherri L. Rohlf
Jordan M. Lewis
Brian E. Weisberg

Michelle R. Klegon
James A. Yarosh
Steven Weintraut
Troy J. Seibert

OF COUNSEL

Richard Siegel

Representative Clients: Champion Auto Stores, Inc.; Holiday Companies, Inc.; Ron-Vik, Inc.; Super America Stations, Inc.; Ashland Oil, Inc.; Aveda Corporation; Richard Manufacturing Co.; Mann Theaters; AVR, Inc; The McNeilus Companies.

For full biographical listings, see the Martindale-Hubbell Law Directory

Minneapolis—Continued

ZELLE, HOFMANN, VOELBEL & GETTE, LLP (AV)

33 South Sixth Street, City Center, Suite 4400, 55402
Telephone: 612-339-2020
Telecopier: 612-336-9100
Waltham, Massachusetts Office: 3 University Office Park, 95 Sawyer Road, Suite 500.
Telephone: 781-891-7020.
Dallas, Texas Office: Zelle, Hofmann, Voelbel & Gette, L.L.P., 1201 Main Street, Suite 3000.
Telephone: 214-742-3000.
San Francisco, California Office: 500 Sansome Street, Suite 400.
Telephone: 415-693-0700.
Los Angeles, California Office: 11601 Wilshire Boulevard, Sixth Floor.
Telephone: 310-478-7877.

MEMBERS OF FIRM

Steven J. Badger (Resident, Dallas, Texas Office)
Eric Berg (Resident, Los Angeles, California Office)
Michelle R. Bernard Bitter (Resident, San Francisco, California Office)
Kerry K. Brown (Resident, Dallas, Texas Office)
Michael R. Cashman
Thomas B. Caswell, III
Christopher J. Clifford (Resident, San Francisco, California Office)
Catherine M. Colinvaux (Resident, Waltham, Massachusetts Office)
Thomas M. Darden
Michelle Kathleen Enright
Mark J. Feinberg
H. Jerome Gette (Resident, Dallas, Texas Office)
Rolf E. Gilbertson
Paul L. Gingras
John C. Goodnow
Richard M. Hagstrom
Lawrence T. Hofmann
Ronald S. Kravitz (Resident, San Francisco, California Office)
David S. Markun (Resident, Los Angeles, California Office)
John Buck Massopust
William Gerald McElroy, Jr. (Resident, Waltham, Massachusetts Office)
Terrence C. McRea (Resident, Dallas, Texas Office)
Steven D. Meier (Resident, San Francisco, California Office)
Devera L. Petak (Resident, Los Angeles, California Office)
James S. Reece
Timothy W. Regan
Jeff Ross
Patricia St. Peter
Karl S. Vasiloff (Resident, Waltham, Massachusetts Office)
Richard L. Voelbel
Stephen A. Watson (Resident, Los Angeles, California Office)
Robert M. Wattson
Edward S. Zusman (Resident, San Francisco, California Office)

OF COUNSEL

Lawrence Zelle

ASSOCIATES

Brad E. Brewer (Resident, Dallas, Texas Office)
Desiree Brutocao (Resident, Los Angeles, California Office)
David M. Cogliano (Resident, Waltham, Massachusetts Office)
Jeffrey K. Compton (Resident, Los Angeles, California Office)
Thomas H. Cook, Jr. (Resident, Dallas, Texas Office)
Paula R. Domanski (Resident, Waltham, Massachusetts Office)
René I. Gamboa, IV (Resident, San Francisco, California Office)
Shenne J. Hahn (Resident, Los Angeles, California Office)
Lowell H. Haky (Resident, San Francisco, California Office)
Ingrid Hallett
Craig M. Hughes (Resident, San Francisco, California Office)
Dennis J. Kelly (Resident, San Francisco, California Office)
Jonathan H. Koenig (Resident, Waltham, Massachusetts Office)
Aaron B. Latto
Jonathan F. Mack
Dawn Midkiff (Not admitted in MN)
Daniel J. Millea
Jonathan D. Mutch (Resident, Waltham, Massachusetts Office)
Sarah A. Olivier (Resident, Waltham, Massachusetts Office)
M. Anthony Parsons II (Resident, Dallas, Texas Office)
Adam Pollack (Resident, Los Angeles, California Office)
Kendra L. Rubbright (Not admitted in MN)
Jennifer L. Shea
Eugene Sheih
Lee H. Shidlofsky (Resident, Dallas, Texas Office)
Marc J. Shrake
Chad A. Snyder
Richard G. Urquhart (Resident, Dallas, Texas Office)
Daniel S. Weiss
Tricia M. Whitehill

For full biographical listings, see the Martindale-Hubbell Law Directory

MONTEVIDEO, * Chippewa Co.

NELSON OYEN TORVIK (AV)

A Professional Limited Liability Partnership
221 North First Street, P.O. Box 656, 56265
Telephone: 320-269-6461
Fax: 320-269-8024
Clarkfield, Minnesota Office:
Telephone: 320-669-4447.

(See Next Column)

Appleton, Minnesota Office:
Telephone: 320-289-2022.

MEMBERS OF FIRM

John P. Nelson (1917-1997)
Sigvald B. Oyen (Retired)
Stephen S. Torvik
David M. Gilbertson
Janice M. Nelson

ASSOCIATES

Geoffrey J. Hathaway
Ann E. Gabrielson

Representative Clients: Minnwest Bank Montevideo; Minnesota Valley Cooperative Light & Power Assn.; Co-op Credit Union.
References: Minnwest Bank Montevideo; General Adjustment Bureau, Inc.

For full biographical listings, see the Martindale-Hubbell Law Directory

PRINDLE, MALAND, SELLNER, STENNES AND KNUTSEN, CHARTERED (AV)

102 Parkway Drive, P.O. Box 591, 56265
Telephone: 320-269-6491
Fax: 320-269-5433
URL: http://www.montelaw.com
Clara City, Minnesota Office: 16 First Avenue NW.
Telephone: 612-847-2418.
Fax: 612-367-2373.

W. D. Prindle (Retired)
Donald L. Maland
John P. Sellner
Stephen L. Stennes
Dwayne N. Knutsen
J. Richard Stermer

General Counsel for: First National Bank in Montevideo, Minn.
Representative Clients: Citizens State Bank, Clara City, Minn.; Mutual Service Casualty Insurance Co., St. Paul, Minn.; Milbank Mutual Insurance Co., Milbank, S. Dakota; National Farmers Union Property & Casualty Co., Denver, Colo.

For full biographical listings, see the Martindale-Hubbell Law Directory

MOORHEAD, * Clay Co.

CAHILL & MARQUART, P.A. (AV)

Second Floor, F-M Center, 403 Center Avenue, P.O. Box 1238, 56561
Telephone: 218-236-4900
Facsimile: 218-236-4909
Email: cahill_marquart@uswest.net

James D. Cahill (1924-1994)
Steven J. Cahill
Steven L. Marquart
Barton J. Cahill

Representative Clients: American Family Insurance Co.; Farm Bureau Mutual; Farmers Insurance Group; National Farmers Union Insurance Co.; New England Insurance Co.; St. Paul Insurance Cos.; State Farm Insurance Cos.; U. S. Fidelity & Guaranty Co.; Westfield Insurance Co.

For full biographical listings, see the Martindale-Hubbell Law Directory

GUNHUS, GRINNELL, KLINGER, SWENSON & GUY, LTD. (AV)

215 North 30th Street, P.O. Box 1077, 56561-1077
Telephone: 218-236-6462
Telecopier: 218-236-9873
Email: GUNHUSLAW@LINKUP.NET *URL:* http://www.fm-law.com
Fargo, North Dakota Office: 514 Gate City Building, P.O. Box 2783.
Telephone: 701-235-2506.
Telecopier: 701-235-9862.

ATTORNEYS

Gunder Gunhus (1928-1997)
Paul E. Grinnell
Edward F. Klinger
Robert H. Swenson
William L. Guy, III
Craig R. Campbell
Bernard E. Reynolds
Eric K. Fosaaen
Gregory P. Hammes
Steven E. Noack
Michelle Caduff Winkis
Susan E. Johnson-Drenth
Deenelle Ruud Stephenson

Insurance Clients: Aetna Life and Casualty Co.; Crum & Forster; Home Insurance Co.; Sentry Insurance Company; St. Paul Cos.; United States Fidelity and Guaranty Co.
Representative Clients: Certainteed Corp.; Farm Credit Services; Dakota Heartland Health System; U.S. West Communications.

For full biographical listings, see the Martindale-Hubbell Law Directory

JEFFRIES, OLSON, FLOM & BULLIS, P.A. (AV)

403 Center Avenue, P.O. Box 9, 56561-0009
Telephone: 218-233-3222
Fax: 218-233-7065
Fargo, North Dakota Office: 1325 23rd Street SW, 58103.
Telephone: 701-280-2300.
Fax: 701-280-1880.

Richard N. Jeffries
Thomas R. Olson
Joel A. Flom
James R. Bullis
Ronald J. Knoll
Michael S. Montgomery
Michelle M. Donarski

(See Next Column)

JEFFRIES, OLSON, FLOM & BULLIS P.A.—*Continued*

John T. Goff

Representative Clients: American International Adjustment Co.; American States/Western Insurance Co.; Farmers Insurance Group; Federated Mutual Insurance Co.; Hartford Insurance Co.; Midwest Medical Insurance Co.; Nodak Mutual Insurance Co.; St. Paul Fire & Marine Insurance Co.

For full biographical listings, see the Martindale-Hubbell Law Directory

*NEW ULM,** Brown Co.

GISLASON & HUNTER LLP (AV)

2700 South Broadway, P.O. Box 458, 56073-0458
Telephone: 507-354-3111
Facsimile: 507-354-8447
Email: mail@gislason.com *URL:* http://www.gislason.com
Minneapolis, Minnesota Office: Opus Center, Suite 215E, 9900 Bren Road East, P.O. Box 5297.
Telephone: 612-933-9900.
Facsimile: 612-933-0242.
Mankato, Minnesota Office: 424 North Riverfront Drive, Suite 250.
Telephone: 507-387-1115.
Facsimile: 507-387-4413.

MEMBERS OF FIRM

Sidney P. Gislason (1908-1985)
Robert M. Halvorson (1945-1993)
C. Allen Dosland
Daniel A. Gislason
C. Thomas Wilson
Ruth Ann Webster
Gary W. Koch
William A. Moeller
Kurt D. Johnson
David W. Sturges (Not admitted in MN)
Mark S. Ullery
Jeffry C. Braegelmann
Reed H. Glawe
Noel L. Phifer
Michael S. Dove
Dustan J. Cross
Richard F. Prim

Counsel for: Associated Milk Producers, Inc.
Representative Clients: St. Paul Companies; Farmers Insurance Group; Auto-Owners Insurance Co.; AgriBank, FCB and Farm Credit Services; Wirtz Corporation; Wal-Mart Stores, Inc.; Midwest Medical Insurance Co.; The Travelers Indemnity Co.; Minnesota Lawyers Mutual Insurance Co.

For full biographical listings, see the Martindale-Hubbell Law Directory

*OWATONNA,** Steele Co.

DOW, EINHAUS & MATTISON, P.A. (AV)

Parrott Building, 202 North Cedar Street, P.O. Box 545, 55060
Telephone: 507-451-3580
Fax: 507-451-3532

Harold S. Nelson (1890-1972)
Otto J. Nelson (1894-1947)
George E. Dow, Jr.
David L. Einhaus
Eric J. Mattison
Byron J. Casey (Retired)
Wallace M. Tripp (Retired)
Mark R. Carver

Representative Clients: U.S. Bank of Owatonna; Owatonna School District; Central Co-op Oil Assn.; Gopher Sport; Owatonna Clinic, P.A.

*ROCHESTER,** Olmsted Co.

DUNLAP & SEEGER, P.A. (AV)

Marquette Bank Building, 206 South Broadway, Suite 505, P.O. Box 549, 55903-0549
Telephone: 507-288-9111
Fax: 507-288-9342

Robert R. Dunlap (1915-1992)
Ronald L. Seeger
Milton A. Rosenblad
Paul A. Finseth
Daniel E. Berndt
John B. Arnold
Peter C. Sandberg
Tina L. Mohr
Jeffrey A. Hanson
Kenneth R. Moen
William J. Ryan
Paul W. Bucher
Douglas A. Boese
Thomas W. Jacobson
Mary H. Dunlap
William P. Volkmar
Mark E. Fosse
Ken D. Schueler
Gregory J. Griffiths
Michael S. Dietz
Eric D. Larson

OF COUNSEL

Franklin Michaels
Alexander M. (Sandy) Keith

Representative Clients: Norwest Bank Minnesota South N.A.; Marquette Bank Rochester; Farm Credit Services of Southern Minnesota, ACA; Minnesota Lawyers Mutual Insurance Co.; Allied Mutual Insurance Co.; State Farm Mutual Automobile Insurance Co.; Auto-Owners Insurance Co.; Farmers Insurance Group; County of Olmsted.

For full biographical listings, see the Martindale-Hubbell Law Directory

O'BRIEN, EHRICK, WOLF, DEANER & MAUS, L.L.P. (AV)

206 South Broadway, Suite 611, P.O. Box 968, 55903-0968
Telephone: 507-289-4041
Fax: 507-281-4778

(See Next Column)

MEMBERS OF FIRM

F. J. O'Brien (1904-1992)
Richard V. Ehrick (Retired)
Thomas Wolf
Ted E. Deaner
Terence L. Maus
Joseph F. Chase
Jill I. Frieders

OF COUNSEL

Allan R. DeBoer

Representative Clients: City of Rochester; County of Olmsted; Mayo Clinic; AgSTAR Farm Credit Services; U.S. Bank National Association; F & M Community Bank.

For full biographical listings, see the Martindale-Hubbell Law Directory

*ST. PAUL,** Ramsey Co.

COLLINS, BUCKLEY, SAUNTRY AND HAUGH, P.L.L.P. (AV)

West 1100 First National Bank Building, 332 Minnesota Street, 55101
Telephone: 651-227-0611
Telecopier: 651-227-0758
Email: info@cbsh.net *URL:* http://www.cbsh.net

MEMBERS OF FIRM

Eugene D. Buckley (Retired)
Michael J. Sauntry
William E. Haugh, Jr.
Mark W. Gehan, Jr.
Patrick T. Tierney
Thomas J. Germscheid
John R. Schulz
Thomas R. O'Connell
Dan C. O'Connell
Christine L. Stroemer
Thomas E. McEllistrem

ASSOCIATES

Matthew A. Slaven
Michael D. Wentzell

OF COUNSEL

Theodore J. Collins

For full biographical listings, see the Martindale-Hubbell Law Directory

FELHABER, LARSON, FENLON & VOGT, PROFESSIONAL ASSOCIATION (AV)

30 East Seventh Street, 2100 Minnesota World Trade Center, 55101
Telephone: 651-222-6321
800-229-6321
Facsimile: 651-222-8905
Minneapolis, Minnesota Office: 601 2nd Avenue South, Suite 4200.
Telephones: 612-339-6321; 800-989-6321.
Facsimile: 612-338-0535.

Robert L. Bach
Richard A. Beens
James A. Blomquist
Edward J. Bohrer
John G. Brian, III
Stephen J. Burton
Edward Q. Cassidy
Karen M. Charlson
David M. Cremons
James J. Cronin
Steven E. Culbert
Terrance M. Cullen
James M. Dawson
Gerald G. Dederick
Thomas J. Doyle
Stanley J. Duran
William K. Ecklund
David B. Eide
Robert J. Fenlon
Roger H. Frommelt
Jan Douglas Halverson
David L. Hashmall
Timothy J. Hassett
Catharine F. Haukedahl
Christopher S. Hayhoe
David R. Hols
Jon M. Hopeman
Katherine A. Jones
Ronald R. Kirchoff
Fredrick R. Krietzman
Lee A. Lastovich
Ruth Silseth Marcott
Sara Gullickson McGrane
Dennis J. Merley
Brad J. Miller
Janet A. Newberg
Byron D. Olsen
Penelope J. Phillips
Mark S. Radke
Steven L. Ross
James W. Rude
Karen G. Schanfield
Randy J. Sparling
Russell J. Sudeith, Jr.
Frederick W. Vogt
Thomas M. Vogt
Honnen S. Weiss
Paul H. Yoo
Paul J. Zech

OF COUNSEL

Kareen R. Ecklund

For full biographical listings, see the Martindale-Hubbell Law Directory

MURNANE, CONLIN, WHITE & BRANDT, PROFESSIONAL ASSOCIATION (AV)

1800 Piper Jaffray Plaza, 444 Cedar Street, 55101
Telephone: 612-227-9411
Fax: 612-223-5199
URL: http://www.murnane.com

E. Willard Murnane (1907-1976)
Charles R. Murnane (1913-1982)
Robert T. White (Retired)
Thomas M. Conlin
Robert W. Murnane
John E. Brandt
John D. Hirte
Steven J. Kirsch
Andrew T. Shern
Michael S. Ryan
James F. Baldwin
C. Todd Koebele

(See Next Column)

MURNANE, CONLIN, WHITE & BRANDT PROFESSIONAL ASSOCIATION, *St. Paul—Continued*

Michael P. Tierney
Daniel A. Haws
William L. Moran
Thomas A. Gilligan, Jr.
Daniel J. Young

Thomas J. Norby
Kammey M.K. Mahowald
Peter B. Tiede
Mark D. Covin
H. Le Phan
Nancy A. Proffitt
Stacy Elizabeth Cudd
Todd J. Klemmensen
Joseph H. Bollettieri
Shelly B. Martin

Representative Clients: Aetna Life & Casualty Co.; Amoco; BIC Corp.; Combustion Engineering; Dresser Industries; Northland Companies; State Farm Mutual Insurance Co.; Travelers Insurance Co.; Wausau Insurance Co.

For full biographical listings, see the Martindale-Hubbell Law Directory

WINTHROP & WEINSTINE, A PROFESSIONAL ASSOCIATION (AV)

3200 Minnesota World Trade Center, 30 East Seventh Street, 55101
Telephone: 651-290-8400
FAX: 651-292-9347
Email: hkuller@winthrop.com *URL:* http://www.winthrop.com/
Minneapolis Office: 3000 Dain Rauscher Plaza, 60 South Sixth Street.
Telephone: 612-347-0700.
Fax: 612-347-0600.

Sherman Winthrop
Robert R. Weinstine
Richard A. Hoel
Roger D. Gordon
Steven C. Tourek
Stephen J. Snyder
Marvin C. Ingber
Hart Kuller
David P. Pearson
Thomas M. Hart, IV
Darron C. Knutson
John A. Knapp
K. Craig Wildfang
Michele D. Vaillancourt
David E. Moran, Jr.
Donald J. Brown
Jon J. Hoganson
Sandra J. Martin
Todd B. Urness
Timothy M. Barnett
Scott J. Dongoske
Peter J. Gleekel
Edward J. Drenttel
Jeffrey R. Ansel
Laurie A. Knocke
Lloyd W. Grooms, Jr.
Mark T. Johnson
Brooks F. Poley
Thomas H. Boyd
Daniel C. Beck
Eric J. Nystrom
Joanne L. Matzen
Patrick W. Weber
Paul W. Markwardt
Craig A. Brandt
James W. Dierking
Therese Marie Marso
Melissa A. Grant
Christopher W. Madel
Jeffrey L. Leclerc

Thomas A. Walker
Suzanne M. Spellacy
Trevor V. Gunderson
John C. Holper
M. Catherine Powell
Steven E. Uhr
Tiffany A. Blofield
Andrew D. Pugh
Ryan K. Crayne (Not admitted in MN)
Beth Gerstein Timm
Julie A. Silverman
Laura A. Pfeiffer
Craig S. Krummen
Celeste J. Taylor
Ann Dunn Wessberg
Richard W. Black
Mark R. Privratsky
Philip R. Mahowald
Norman Lyle Jones, III
Karl Edward Robinson
Jonathan W. J. Armour
John C. Ekman
Daniel G. Currell
Charles J. Schoenwetter
Ingrid Neill Nyberg
Darrell Elijah Graham
Ann E. Walters

OF COUNSEL

Joseph S. Friedberg

Representative Clients: Aero Systems Engineering, Inc.; American National Bank and Trust Co.; Bremer Financial Corp.; Otto Bremer Foundation; Juran & Moody, Inc.; St. Paul Progress Corp.; Wick Building Systems, Inc.

For full biographical listings, see the Martindale-Hubbell Law Directory

SPRING VALLEY, Fillmore Co.

BAUDLER, BAUDLER, MAUS & BLAHNIK (AV)

304 South Broadway, 55975
Telephone: 507-346-7301
Fax: 507-346-2537
Email: bbmb@smig.net
Austin, Minnesota Office: 108 North Main Street.
Telephone: 507-433-2393.
Fax: 507-433-9530.

Lawrence E. Maus
Robert E. Blahnik
Thomas C. Baudler

Representative Clients: First National Bank of Spring Valley; Home Federal Savings Bank; First State Bank-Spring Valley; First Farmers & Merchants State Bank; Security State Bank; TCF National Bank; Norwest Bank MN; Farmers Insurance Group; Grinnell Mutual Ins. Co.; Northbrook Property & Casulaty Ins. Co.

*THIEF RIVER FALLS,** Pennington Co.

CHARLSON, MARBEN & JORGENSON, P.A. (AV)

119 West Second Street, P.O. Box 506, 56701
Telephone: 218-681-4002
Fax: 218-681-4004

Kurt J. Marben
Michael L. Jorgenson

Representative Clients: Northern State Bank of Thief River Falls; American Hardware Mutual Insurance Co.; American Family Insurance Co.; Employers Mutual of Wausau; Milbank Mutual Insurance Co.; National Family Insurance Co.; Wikstrom Telephone Co.; Dairyland Mutual Insurance Co.; Preferred Risk Mutual Insurance Co.; North Star Mutual Insurance Co.

For full biographical listings, see the Martindale-Hubbell Law Directory

VIRGINIA, St. Louis Co.

TRENTI LAW FIRM (AV)

225 1st Street North, Suite 1000, P.O. Box 958, 55792
Telephone: 218-749-1962
Fax: 218-749-4308
Edina, Minnesota Office: 6600 France Avenue, Suite 465.
Telephone: 612-929-7512.
Fax: 612-929-2464.
Cook, Minnesota Office: 219 South River St., Box 1177, 55723.
Telephone: 218-666-5781.
Fax: 218-666-5782.

John A. Trenti
Patrick J. Roche
Robert H. Stephenson
Carver Richards
Sam A. Aluni
Joseph Lyons-Leoni
Scott C. Neff
Paul D. Cerkvenik

Representative Clients: St. Paul Cos.; Queen City Federal Savings Bank; Cliffs Mining Co.; Eveleth Fee Office (Mineral Interests).

For full biographical listings, see the Martindale-Hubbell Law Directory

*WADENA,** Wadena Co.

KENNEDY, NERVIG & CARLISLE, LLP (AV)

503 Jefferson Street South, P.O. Box 647, 56482-0647
Telephone: 218-631-2505
Fax: 218-631-9078
Email: knc@wcta.net

MEMBERS OF FIRM

Charles R. Kennedy
Luther P. Nervig
Daniel T. Carlisle

Brent Eliot Walz

OF COUNSEL

Charles W. Kennedy

Representative Clients: Wadena State Bank; First National Bank of Menahga; First National Bank of Bertha-Verndale; Security State Bank of Sebeka; Todd-Wadena Electric Co-op (REA); West Central Telephone Co.; Wadena-Deer Creek Public Schools; Dorn & Co., Inc.; Mason Brothers Company; Federated Rural Electric Insurance Corporation.

For full biographical listings, see the Martindale-Hubbell Law Directory

*WINONA,** Winona Co.

STREATER & MURPHY, P.A. (AV)

64 East Fourth Street, 55987-0310
Telephone: 507-454-2925
Fax: 507-454-2929
Email: kentg@luminet.net

Leo F. Murphy, Jr. (1922-1995)
Kent A. Gernander
James R. Forsythe
Cindy K. Telstad
Lee Ann Riehle
John Borman

OF COUNSEL

Harold S. Streater

Representative Clients: Winona Banc Holding Co.; Winona National and Savings Bank; Town & Country State Bank; Winona Daily News; Winona School District; Badger Construction Equipment Co.; Winona General Hospital Assn.; EMD Associates, Inc.; Fastenal Co.; Hiawatha Education Foundation.

For full biographical listings, see the Martindale-Hubbell Law Directory

*WORTHINGTON,** Nobles Co.

HEDEEN, HUGHES, WETERING & KNESS (AV)

1206 Oxford Street, P.O. Box 9, 56187
Telephone: 507-376-3181
Telecopier: 507-376-9404
Adrian, Minnesota Office: Adrian State Bank Building.
Telephone: 507-483-2033.

(See Next Column)

HEDEEN, HUGHES, WETERING & KNESS—*Continued*

MEMBERS OF FIRM

Arnold W. Brecht (Deceased)
William T. Hedeen
Laurence B. Hughes
William J. Wetering
Bruce N. Kness

Representative Clients: Norwest Bank, Worthington; First State Bank of Rushmore; Adrian State Bank; Worthington Federal Savings and Loan Assn.; Farm Bureau Mutual Insurance Co.; United Co-ops, Bigelow, MN; Norwest Mortage Inc.; Johnson Builders and Realtors; Coldwell Bankers, Worthington.
Approved Agent For: Chicago Title Insurance Co.

For full biographical listings, see the Martindale-Hubbell Law Directory

MISSISSIPPI

*ABERDEEN,** Monroe Co.

PATTERSON & PATTERSON (AV)

304 East Jefferson Street, P.O. Box 663, 39730
Telephone: 662-369-2476
Fax: 662-369-9806
Email: JPP@ebicom.net

MEMBERS OF FIRM

Robert D. Patterson
Jan P. Patterson
Peter T. Martin

Local Counsel for: National Bank of Commerce of Mississippi; American Colloid Company; Condea Vista Company; Pruet Production Co.; Arco Oil & Gas Co.; Chemical Corporation; Unimin Corporation; Hughes Eastern Corp.; Legget & Platt.
Approved Title Attorneys for: First American Title Insurance Co.

For full biographical listings, see the Martindale-Hubbell Law Directory

BILOXI, Harrison Co.

CORBAN & GUNN (AV)

770 Water Street, P.O. Drawer 1916, 39533-1916
Telephone: 228-432-7826
Telecopier: 228-435-5702

MEMBERS OF FIRM

Lawrence C. Corban, Jr.
Clyde H. Gunn, III

Representative Clients: Dees Chevrolet Co.; First Federal Savings & Loan Association of Pascagoula-Moss Point; Frank P. Corso & Co., Inc.; Munro Petroleum & Terminal Corp.; Ship Services Corp.

For full biographical listings, see the Martindale-Hubbell Law Directory

MINOR AND ASSOCIATES (AV)

A Partnership including a Professional Association
160 Main Street, Drawer 1388, 39533-1388
Telephone: 228-374-5151
Fax: 228-374-6630
Email: pminoratty@aol.com

Paul S. Minor (P.A.)

Mark D. Lumpkin
James R. Reeves, Jr.
Christopher C. VanCleave

For full biographical listings, see the Martindale-Hubbell Law Directory

PAGE, MANNINO, PERESICH & MCDERMOTT (AV)

A Professional Limited Liability Company
759 Vieux Marché Mall, P.O. Drawer 289, 39533
Telephone: 228-374-2100
Facsimile: 228-432-5539
Email: pmp@pmp.org

MEMBERS OF FIRM

Lyle M. Page (Resident)
Frederick J. Mannino (Resident)
Ronald G. Peresich (Resident)
Stephen G. Peresich (Resident)
Michael B. McDermott (Resident)
Tere Richardson Steel (Resident)
Michael E. Whitehead (Resident)
Mary Alexander Nichols (Resident)
David M. Allen (Resident)

ASSOCIATES

Henry N. Dick, III
Les W. Smith (Resident)
Emilie Whitehead
Kaara L. Liskow
Joel L. Blackledge

Representative Clients: United States Fidelity & Guaranty Co.; St. Paul Fire & Marine Insurance Co.; Crawford & Co.; Anheuser-Busch Corp.
General Counsel for: Peoples Bank of Biloxi, Mississippi; Biloxi Regional Medical Center; Bank of Mississippi (Gulf Coast Division).

(See Next Column)

For full biographical listings, see the Martindale-Hubbell Law Directory

*BROOKHAVEN,** Lincoln Co.

ALLEN, ALLEN, BOERNER & BREELAND (AV)

214 Justice Street, P.O. Box 751, 39602-0751
Telephone: 601-833-4361
Fax: 601-833-6647
Email: aabblaw@tislink.com

Emmette P. Allen (1915-1999)
Robert O. Allen
William D. Boerner
Durwood J. Breeland

ASSOCIATE

Sally Burchfield Doty

For full biographical listings, see the Martindale-Hubbell Law Directory

*CLARKSDALE,** Coahoma Co.

CHAPMAN, LEWIS & SWAN (AV)

501 First Street, P.O. Box 428, 38614
Telephone: 601-627-4105
FAX: 601-627-4171
Email: cls@gminet *URL:* http://www.lawyers.com/clslaw

Ralph E. Chapman
Richard B. Lewis
Dana J. Swan

ASSOCIATE

Sherry S. Fernandez

For full biographical listings, see the Martindale-Hubbell Law Directory

HOLCOMB DUNBAR, A PROFESSIONAL ASSOCIATION (AV)

152 Delta Avenue, P.O. Box 368, 38614
Telephone: 601-627-2241
Facsimile: 601-627-9788
Email: mchaffin@clarksdale.com *URL:* http://www.holcombdunbar.com
Oxford, Mississippi Office: 1217 Jackson Avenue, P.O. Drawer 707, 38655.
Telephone: 601-234-8775.
Facsimile: 601-238-7552.
Southaven, Mississippi Office: Suite 1, 728 Goodman Road East, P.O. Box 190, 38671.
Telephone: 601-349-0664.
Facsimile: 601-349-2432.

Pat D. Holcomb (1909-1996)
William M. Chaffin
Michael K. Graves
Edward (Ted) P. Connell, Jr.
Daniel M. Czamanske, Jr.

OF COUNSEL

Chester H. Curtis

Representative Clients: Union Planters Bank, National Association; Deposit Guaranty National Bank; Trustmark National Bank; Mississippi Power & Light Co.; Southern Farm Bureau Casualty Insurance Co.; Bituminous Insurance Co.; State Farm Fire & Casualty Insurance Co.; Fireman's Fund Insurance Cos.; Atlanta Casualty Insurance Cos.; Drexel Chemical Co.

For full biographical listings, see the Martindale-Hubbell Law Directory

HUNT & ROSS, A PROFESSIONAL ASSOCIATION (AV)

123 Court Street, P.O. Box 1196, 38614
Telephone: 601-627-5251
Telecopier No.: 601-627-5254
Email: huntross@clarksdale.com *URL:* http://www.lawyers.com/h&rlaw

Tom T. Ross (1903-1993)
David R. Hunt
Tom T. Ross, Jr.

Thomas W. Allen
Katherine Blackwell Parker

Representative Clients: Talbot Pool & Patio, Inc.; Temperature Control, Inc., Clarksdale, Mississippi.

For full biographical listings, see the Martindale-Hubbell Law Directory

LUCKETT LAW FIRM, A PROFESSIONAL ASSOCIATION (AV)

143 Yazoo Avenue, P.O. Drawer 1000, 38614-1000
Telephone: 601-624-2591
Telecopier: 601-627-5403
Email: llf@gmi.net

William O. Luckett (1922-1996)
William O. Luckett, Jr.

John B. Gillis
Rivers H. Humber
Robert M. Tyner, Jr.
Jonathan S. Masters

District and Local Counsel for: Liberty Mutual Insurance Co.; CNA Group; Deere & Co.; Indiana Lumbermens Insurance Co.; Texas Gas Transmission Corp.; American Interstate Insurance Company of Georgia; Elliston, Inc.; Graward General Insurance; Wal-Mart Stores, Inc.; Grand Casinos, Inc.

For full biographical listings, see the Martindale-Hubbell Law Directory

*CLEVELAND,** Bolivar Co.

JACKS, ADAMS & WESTERFIELD, P.A. (AV)

106 South Pearman Avenue, P.O. Box 1209, 38732
Telephone: 662-843-6171
FAX: 662-843-6176
Email: jaws@tecinfo.com

Gerald H. Jacks
William S. Adams, Jr.
Andrew M. W. Westerfield
S. David Norquist
Thomas B. Janoush

General Counsel for: The Valley Bank; Cleveland School District 4; Commonwealth National Life Insurance Co.
Area Counsel for: Commercial Union; United States Fidelity & Guaranty Co.; Baxter International, Inc.; New Hampshire Insurance Co.; American International Adjustment Co.; Imperial Casualty Co.; Self Insurers Service, Inc.

For full biographical listings, see the Martindale-Hubbell Law Directory

*COLUMBIA,** Marion Co.

AULTMAN, TYNER, RUFFIN & YARBOROUGH, LTD., A PROFESSIONAL LAW CORPORATION (AV)

329 Church Street, P.O. Drawer 707, 39429
Telephone: 601-736-2222
FAX: 601-736-9884
Email: rfyjr@cblink.com
Hattiesburg, Mississippi Office: 315 Hemphill Street, P.O. Drawer 750.
Telephone: 601-583-2671.
FAX: 601-583-2677.
Gulfport, Mississippi Office: 1201 25th Avenue, Suite 300, P.O. Box 607.
Telephone: 228-863-6913.
FAX: 228-868-8505. Email: atmr@digiscape.com.
New Orleans, Louisiana Office: The Texaco Center, 400 Poydras Street, Suite 2250.
Telephone: 504-528-9616.
FAX: 504-528-9640.

Richard F. Yarborough, Jr.

OF COUNSEL

Ernest Ray Duff

Representative Clients: Hercules, Inc.; United States Steel Corp.; Ford Motor Co.; International Paper Co.; Phillips Petroleum Co.; Aetna Casualty & Surety Co.; CNA Group; Liberty Mutual Insurance Co.; St. Paul Fire & Marine Insurance Co.; Fireman's Fund.

For full biographical listings, see the Martindale-Hubbell Law Directory

*COLUMBUS,** Lowndes Co.

GHOLSON, HICKS & NICHOLS, A PROFESSIONAL ASSOCIATION (AV)

Deposit Guaranty National Bank, 710 Main Street, Third Floor, P.O. Box 1111, 39703-1111
Telephone: 662-243-7300
Fax: 662-327-6217
Email: ghnlaw@ghnlaw.com *URL:* http://www.ghnlaw.com

Hunter M. Gholson
Dewitt T. Hicks, Jr.
Aubrey E. Nichols
Ralph E. Rood
John W. Crowell
J. Gordon Flowers
Katherine S. Kerby
David B. Jolly
William F. Gillis
P. Nelson Smith, Jr.
William T. Cooper
Marc D. Amos
M. Jay Nichols
Jarret P. Nichols

Counsel for: National Bank of Commerce of Mississippi; Trustmark National Bank; The St. Paul Insurance Co.; Fireman's Fund American Insurance Cos.; Coregis; Mississippi Municipal Service Co.; Cargill, Inc.; Kerr-McGee Chemical, L.L.C.; Airline Manufacturing Co.; Lowndes County Port Authority.

For full biographical listings, see the Martindale-Hubbell Law Directory

MITCHELL, MCNUTT, THREADGILL, SMITH & SAMS, P.A. (AV)

215 Fifth Street North, P.O. Box 1366, 39703-1366
Telephone: 662-328-2316
Facsimile: 662-328-8035
Email: MMTSSCOL@EBICOM.NET
Tupelo, Mississippi Office: 105 South Front Street, P.O. Box 7120.
Telephone: 662-842-3871.
Facsimile: 662-842-8450.
Corinth, Mississippi Office: 508 Waldron Street, P.O. Box 1200.
Telephone: 662-286-9931.
Facsimile: 662-286-8984.
Oxford, Mississippi Office: 1216 Van Buren, P.O. Box 947.
Telephone: 662-234-4845.
Facsimile: 662-234-9071.
Jackson, Mississippi Office: Skytel Centre, 200 S. Lamar, Suite 900, P.O. Box 1005.
Telephone: 662-948-8508.
Facsimile: 662-948-8537.

(See Next Column)

Memphis, Tennessee Office: 1255 Lynnfield Road, Building A, Suite 123.
Telephone: 901-767-5185.
Facsimile: 901-767-5918.

L. F. Sams, Jr.
Taylor B. Smith
Guy W. Mitchell, III
William C. Spencer
David L. Sanders
Claude F. Clayton, Jr.
William C. Murphree
Ronald L. Roberts
John S. Hill
Michael D. Ferris
Richard H. Spann (Resident)
W. Scott Collins
Otis R. Tims
Martha Bost Stegall
J. Douglas Ford (Resident)
Jeffrey J. Turnage (Resident)
Berkley N. Huskison (Resident)
James P. Wilson, Jr. (Also at Memphis and Tupelo Offices)

OF COUNSEL

William J. Threadgill
W. H. (Hank) Jolly, Jr. (Resident)

Representative Clients: Ceco Buildings Division, Robertson-Ceco Corporation; First Columbus National Bank; The General Tire & Rubber Co.; Weyerhaeuser Co.; The Commercial Dispatch Publishing Co.; St. Paul Insurance Cos.; Imes Communication Group; Sanderson Plumbing Products Corp.; Federated Mutual Insurance Co.; Southern Farm Bureau Casualty Insurance Co.

For full biographical listings, see the Martindale-Hubbell Law Directory

*GREENVILLE,** Washington Co.

LAKE TINDALL, LLP (AV)

127 South Poplar Street, P.O. Box 918, 38701
Telephone: 601-378-2121
Facsimile: 601-378-2183
Jackson, Mississippi Office: One Jackson Place, 188 East Capitol Street, Suite 450, P.O. Box 1789.
Telephone: 601-948-2121.
Facsimile: 601-948-0603.

William T. Wynn (1890-1959)
Jerome S. Hafter (1895-1969)
J. A. Lake (1905-1997)
Franklin S. Thackston, Jr. (Resident, Greenville)
Charles S. Tindall, III (Resident, Greenville)
Jerome C. Hafter (Resident, Greenville)
Stephen L. Thomas (Resident, Greenville)
Edwin W. Tindall (Resident, Greenville)
W. Wayne Drinkwater, Jr. (Resident, Jackson, Mississippi Office)
David W. Clark (Resident, Jackson, Mississippi Office)
Andrew N. Alexander, III (Resident, Greenville)
Clinton W. Walker, III (Resident, Greenville)
Marian S. Alexander (Resident, Greenville)
Jenny M. Virden (Resident, Greenville)
Paul Mathis, Jr. (Resident, Greenville)
Shawn Neill Sullivan (Resident, Jackson, Mississippi Office)
Laura Limerick Gibbes (Resident, Jackson, Mississippi Office)
Margaret Stewart Oertling (Resident, Jackson, Mississippi Office)
O. Stephen Montagnet, III (Resident, Jackson, Mississippi Office)
Bradley Truett Golmon (Resident, Greenville)
Susan E. Wright (Resident, Greenville)
Jeffrey R. Blackwood (Resident, Jackson, Mississippi Office)

Neely C. Carlton (Resident, Greenville)
Seale Pylate (Resident, Greenville)

OF COUNSEL

Charles S. Tindall, Jr.

General Counsel for: Greenville Bank (Branch of Deposit Guaranty National Bank of Jackson); Bunge Towing, Inc.; SUPERVALU INC., Lewis Grocer Division; Greenville Port Commission; Stein Mart Inc.; Delta and Pine Land Co.
Local Counsel for: Insurance: Aetna Casualty & Surety Co.; Cigna-Aetna Insurance Co.; Allstate Insurance Co.; Shelter Insurance Co.

For full biographical listings, see the Martindale-Hubbell Law Directory

*GREENWOOD,** Leflore Co.

LOTT, FRANKLIN, FONDA & FLANAGAN (AV)

202 West Market, P.O. Box 1176, 38935
Telephone: 601-453-6576
Telecopier: 601-453-2777
Email: tmf@mircosped.com

MEMBERS OF FIRM

Hardy Lott (1908-1995)
Stanny Sanders (1918-1972)
Webb Franklin
Sam N. Fonda
Thomas M. Flanagan, Jr.

Attorneys for: Deposit Guaranty National Bank; Delta Electric Power Assn.; Zurich American Insurance Co.; Coca-Cola Bottling Works of Greenwood; J.J. Ferguson Enterprises; Greenwood Utilities; The Travelers Insurance Group; Ranger Insurance Co.; Bally's Olympia Limited Partnership; State of Mississippi (State Bond Attorney).

For full biographical listings, see the Martindale-Hubbell Law Directory

Greenwood—Continued

UPSHAW, WILLIAMS, BIGGERS, BECKHAM & RIDDICK, LLP (AV)

309 Fulton Street, 38930
Telephone: 662-455-1613
Facsimile: 662-453-9245
Mailing Address: P.O. Drawer 8230, Greenwood, Mississippi, 38935-8230
Email: lexgwd@uwbbr.com
Jackson, Mississippi Office: Suite 300 Plaza One, 715 South Pear Orchard Road, P.O. Box 9147, 39286-9147.
Telephone: 601-978-1996.
Facsimile: 601-978-1949. Email: lexjax@uwbbr.com.

MEMBERS OF FIRM

James E. Upshaw
Tommie G. Williams
Marc A. Biggers
Glenn F. Beckham
Roger C. Riddick (Resident, Jackson Office)
F. Ewin Henson III
Lonnie D. Bailey
Robert S. Upshaw
Clinton M. Guenther
Richard C. Williams, Jr. (Resident, Jackson Office)
Richard L. Kimmel
Mark C. Carroll (Resident, Jackson Office)
W. Hugh Gillon IV (Resident, Jackson Office)
Paul L. Goodman
Walter C. Morrison IV (Resident, Jackson Office)

ASSOCIATES

Steven H. Funderburg (Resident, Jackson Office)
Bonnie Bridgers Smith (Resident, Jackson Office)
Patrick M. Tatum (Resident, Jackson Office)
Craig R. Sessums (Resident, Jackson Office)
James K. Warrington
Tammra O. Cascio
Cecil D. McClellan, III (Resident, Jackson Office)
Christopher W. Winter
J. L. Wilson, IV
Steven C. Cookston
Adrienne D. Cox (Resident, Jackson Office)

OF COUNSEL

Ben L. Riddick (Resident, Jackson Office)
John R. Countiss III (Resident, Jackson Office)

Representative Clients: United States Fidelity & Guaranty Co.; State Farm Mutual Automobile Insurance Co.; CNA Insurance Cos.; St. Paul Fire & Marine Insurance Co.; Travelers/Aetna Property and Casualty Corp.; Kemper Insurance Co.; Zurich-American Insurance Group; Risk Enterprise Management, Ltd.; Allstate Insurance Co.

For full biographical listings, see the Martindale-Hubbell Law Directory

---

GRENADA, * Grenada Co.

LISTON/LANCASTER

(See Winona)

GULFPORT, * Harrison Co.

ALLEN, VAUGHN, COBB & HOOD, P.A. (AV)

One Hancock Plaza, Suite 1209, P.O. Drawer 4108, 39502-4108
Telephone: 601-864-4011
Fax: 601-864-4852
Email: avchlaw@sunherald.infinet.com

Harry R. Allen
Thomas E. Vaughn
David L. Cobb
Billy W. Hood
Joy Lambert Phillips
Robert W. Atkinson
Benjamin U. Bowden
Richard B. Tubertini
Rodney Douglas Robinson
E. Colette Towles
David W. Crane
John A. Foxworth, Jr.

J. Adrian Smith
Michael J. Casano

OF COUNSEL

D. Knox White

LEGAL SUPPORT PERSONNEL

Kevin C. Stachowski (Paralegal)

For full biographical listings, see the Martindale-Hubbell Law Directory

AULTMAN, TYNER, RUFFIN & YARBOROUGH, LTD., A PROFESSIONAL LAW CORPORATION (AV)

1201 25th Avenue, Suite 300, P.O. Box 607, 39502
Telephone: 228-863-6913
FAX: 228-868-8505
Email: atmr@digiscape.com
Hattiesburg, Mississippi Office: 315 Hemphill Street, P.O. Drawer 750.
Telephone: 601-583-2671.
FAX: 601-583-2677.
Columbia, Mississippi Office: 329 Church Street, P.O. Drawer 707.
Telephone: 601-736-2222.
FAX: 601-736-9884. Email: rfyjr@cblink.com.

(See Next Column)

New Orleans, Louisiana Office: The Texaco Center, 400 Poydras Street, Suite 2250.
Telephone: 504-528-9616.
FAX: 504-528-9640.

Ben E. Sheely
Dorrance (Dee) Aultman, Jr.

Kyle Stuart Moran

For full biographical listings, see the Martindale-Hubbell Law Directory

BLACKWELL & WHITE (AV)

1613 Twenty-Third Avenue, 39501
Telephone: 228-864-1484
FAX: 228-868-6484
Mailing Address: P.O. Box 430, 39502-0430,

MEMBERS OF FIRM

Leonard A. Blackwell, II
Gary White

ASSOCIATES

James B. Wright, Jr.
Patricia S. Tisdale

References: Merchants Bank & Trust Co.; Hancock Bank.

For full biographical listings, see the Martindale-Hubbell Law Directory

DUKES, DUKES, KEATING AND FANECA, P.A. (AV)

2909 13th Street, 6th Floor, P.O. Drawer W, 39501
Telephone: 228-868-1111
Fax: 228-863-2886
Email: ddkf@ddkf.com

William F. Dukes
Walter W. Dukes
Hugh D. Keating
Cy Faneca
Phillip W. Jarrell

Joan E. Lund
W. Edward Hatten, Jr.
Thomas William Busby
William W. Abbott, Jr.
Trace D. McRaney
Stephen M. Cozart
Derek R. Cusick

For full biographical listings, see the Martindale-Hubbell Law Directory

FRANKE, RAINEY & SALLOUM, PLLC (AV)

2605 14th Street, P.O. Drawer 460, 39502
Telephone: 228-868-7070
Telecopier: 228-868-7090
Email: frs@diversicomm.com

Paul M. Franke, Jr.
William M. Rainey
Richard P. Salloum
Paul B. Howell
Fredrick B. Feeney, II
Traci M. Castille
Donald P. Moore

Kaleel G. Salloum, Jr.
Brandi C. Schwartz
James C. Simpson, Jr.

For full biographical listings, see the Martindale-Hubbell Law Directory

BOYCE HOLLEMAN A PROFESSIONAL CORPORATION (AV)

1913 15th Street, P.O. Drawer 1030, 39502
Telephone: 228-863-3142; 1-800-863-3140
Telecopier: 228-863-9829
Email: boyce1913@aol.com

Boyce Holleman

Timothy C. Holleman
Leslie Dean Holleman
David J. "Jeff" White

References: Hancock Bank, Gulfport; Merchants Bank & Trust Co., Gulfport; Bank of Wiggins, Wiggins, Mississippi.

For full biographical listings, see the Martindale-Hubbell Law Directory

---

HATTIESBURG, * Forrest Co.

AULTMAN, TYNER, RUFFIN & YARBOROUGH, LTD., A PROFESSIONAL LAW CORPORATION (AV)

315 Hemphill Street, P.O. Drawer 750, 39403-0750
Telephone: 601-583-2671
FAX: 601-583-2677
Email: aultyn@c-gate.net
Columbia, Mississippi Office: 329 Church Street, P.O. Drawer 707.
Telephone: 601-736-2222.
FAX: 601-736-9884. Email: rfyjr@cblink.com.
Gulfport, Mississippi Office: 1201 25th Avenue, Suite 300, P.O. Box 607.
Telephone: 228-863-6913.
FAX: 228-868-8505. Email: atmr@digiscape.com.
New Orleans, Louisiana Office: The Texaco Center, 400 Poydras Street, Suite 2250.
Telephone: 504-528-9616.
FAX: 504-528-9640.

(See Next Column)

AULTMAN, TYNER, RUFFIN & YARBOROUGH, LTD. A PROFESSIONAL LAW CORPORATION, *Hattiesburg—Continued*

Dorrance Aultman
Thomas W. Tyner
Louie F. Ruffin
Richard F. Yarborough, Jr. (Resident, Columbia Office)
Ben E. Sheely (Resident, Gulfport Office)
R. Curtis Smith, II
Dorrance (Dee) Aultman, Jr. (Resident, Gulfport Office)
William Nelson Graham
Glenn L. M. Swetman (Resident, New Orleans, Louisiana Office)
Troy Nathan Bell (Resident, New Orleans, Louisiana Office)

Victor A. DuBose
Daphne M. Lancaster
Jennifer J. Selby
Kyle Stuart Moran (Resident, Gulfport Office)
Jennifer Walley Mozingo
Robert P. Vining (Resident, New Orleans, Louisiana Office)

OF COUNSEL

Ernest Ray Duff (Resident, Columbia Office)

Representative Clients: Hercules, Inc.; U.S. Steel Corp.; Ford Motor Co.; Phillips Petroleum Co.; Aetna Casualty & Surety Co.; CNA Group; Liberty Mutual Insurance Co.; St. Paul Fire & Marine Insurance Co.; Fireman's Fund; L & A Contracting Co.

For full biographical listings, see the Martindale-Hubbell Law Directory

*HERNANDO,** De Soto Co.

CHATHAM LAW FIRM (AV)

291 Losher Street, 38632
Telephone: 662-429-9871
Telecopier: 662-429-0242
Email: gchatham@desotoonline.com

Gerald W. Chatham, Sr.

References: Bank of Mississippi; Senatobia Bank.

For full biographical listings, see the Martindale-Hubbell Law Directory

*JACKSON,** Hinds Co.

ALSTON & JONES (AV)

A Professional Limited Liability Company
121 North State Street, P.O. Drawer 1532, 39215-1532
Telephone: 601-948-6882
Fax: 601-948-6902
Email: ARVS@Teclink.net

MEMBERS OF FIRM

Alex A. Alston, Jr.
Richard L. Jones
Sheldon G. Alston

OF COUNSEL

Beth C. Clay
Rowan H. Taylor

Counsel for: Anheuser-Busch Companies, Inc.; Motion Picture Association of America, Inc.; E. I. du Pont de Nemours & Co.; The Dow Chemical Co.; Dean Witter Reynolds Inc.; Ford Motor Co.; Yellow Freight System, Inc.; Xerox Corp.; Gannett Co. Inc.; Mississippi Baptist Foundation.

For full biographical listings, see the Martindale-Hubbell Law Directory

BAKER, DONELSON, BEARMAN & CALDWELL (AV)

Suite 500, 700 North State Street, 39202
Telephone: 601-351-2400
Telecopier: 601-351-2424
Email: info@bdbc.com *URL:* http://www.bakerdonelson.com
Memphis, Tennessee Office: 20th Floor, First Tennessee Building, 165 Madison, 38103.
Telephone: 901-526-2000.
Telecopier: 901-577-2303.
Nashville, Tennessee Office: 1700 Nashville City Center, 511 Union Street, 37219.
Telephone: 615-726-5600.
Telecopier: 615-726-0464.
Chattanooga, Tennessee Office: 1800 Republic Centre, 633 Chestnut Street, 37450-1800.
Telephone: 423-756-2010.
Telecopier: 423-756-3447.
Knoxville, Tennessee Office: 2200 Riverview Tower, 900 South Gay Street, 37901.
Telephone: 423-549-7000.
Telecopier: 423-525-8569.
Johnson City, Tennessee Office: SunTrust Bank Building, 207 Mockingbird Lane, P.O. Box 3038, 37602.
Telephone: 423-928-0181.
Telecopier: 423-928-5694; 423-928-3654; Kingsport: 423-246-6191.
Huntsville, Tennessee Office: 3 Courthouse Square, 37756.
Telephone: 423-663-2321.
Telecopier: 423-663-2111.

(See Next Column)

Washington, D.C. Office: Market Square, 801 Pennsylvania Avenue, N.W., 20004.
Telephone: 202-508-3400.
Telecopier: 202-508-3402.

MANAGING PARTNER

James K. Dossett, Jr.

PARTNERS

Robert Engelbrecht Hauberg, Jr.
Walker W. (Bill) Jones, III
William S. Painter
James L. Jones
William N. Reed
Richard G. Cowart
Barry K. Cockrell
Leonard C. Martin
Jonell B. Williamson
William B. Grete
Michael T. Dawkins

ASSOCIATES

Sheryl Bey
J. Randall Patterson
Stacy E. Thomas
Philip W. Thomas
Jody Brian Martin
Bradley W. Smith
Charles W. Ferguson
Charles R. Galloway
Scott W. Pedigo
Tiffanee N. Wade
Michael R. Hess
Michelle Dawn Alexander (Not admitted in MS)
Scott W. Bates

OF COUNSEL

John B. Beard
Raymond E. Mabus, Jr.
Karen H. Spencer

For full biographical listings, see the Martindale-Hubbell Law Directory

BUTLER, SNOW, O'MARA, STEVENS & CANNADA, PLLC (AV)

17th Floor, Deposit Guaranty Plaza, 210 East Capitol Street, P.O. Box 22567, 39225-2567
Telephone: 601-948-5711
Telecopier: 601-949-4555
Email: first.last@butlersnow.com *URL:* http://www.butlersnow.com
Gulfport, Mississippi Office: Suite 204, Whitney National Bank Building, 1300 Twenty Fifth Avenue, P.O. Drawer 4248, 39502.
Telephone: 228-864-1170.
Telecopier: 228-868-1531.
Memphis, Tennessee Office: Suite 330, The Colonnade, 1661 International Place Drive, P.O. Box 171443, 38187-1443.
Telephone: 901-766-2100.
Telecopier: 901-766-2199.

Geo. Butler (1877-1948)
J. Morgan Stevens (1876-1951)
Chas. B. Snow (1894-1960)
Junior O'Mara (1914-1986)
Geo. Butler, Jr. (1917-1998)

MEMBERS, ASSOCIATES AND SPECIAL COUNSEL OF FIRM

Phil B. Abernethy
Paula Graves Ardelean
Tammy L. Barham
Kenneth W. Barton
Leslie Joyner Bobo
Bernard H. Booth
Lucien L. Bourgeois
Ann Bowden-Hollis (Gulfport, Mississippi Office)
Charles L. Brocato
Brooks R. Buchanan
Denise D. Burke (Memphis, Tennessee Office)
Don B. Cannada
Tommie S. Cardin
Donald Clark, Jr.
Ann Fortenberry Corso
John A. Crawford
John A. Crawford, Jr.
Paul N. Davis
Richard M. Dye
Herbert C. Ehrhardt
John F. England
Mike Espy
Robert M. Frey
William Massie Gage
James B. Galloway (Gulfport, Mississippi Office)
John L. Galloway (Gulfport, Mississippi Office)
Robert C. Galloway (Gulfport, Mississippi Office)
J. Clifford Harrison
John J. Healy III
C. Maison Heidelberg
John C. Henegan
Daniel G. Hise
Frank L. Holbrook
Paul A. Hurst
Selby Allen Ireland
Donna Brown Jacobs
Charles F. Johnson, III
Christy D. Jones
Daniel P. Jordan III
Samuel Keyes, Jr.
Clifton L. Kling
Thomas C. Lacey, Jr.
Karen E. Livingston-Wilson
Ronald I. Loeb
William Eugene Magee
Jamie Planck Martin
Brandon Galloway McManus (Gulfport, Mississippi Office)
Michael E. McWilliams
Harold D. Miller, Jr.
Robert A. Miller
Meade W. Mitchell
Anita Modak-Truran
O. Kendall Moore
Paige L. Purvis
J. Stevenson Ray
Stephanie M. Rippee
Benjamin W. Roberson
E. Barney Robinson III
Stephen W. Rosenblatt
Donna E. Sharpe (Memphis, Tennessee Office)
Arthur Dennis Spratlin, Jr.
R. Andrew Taggart
Ronald G. Taylor
Lee Davis Thames
J. Carter Thompson, Jr.
Timothy M. Threadgill
Jay A. Travis, III
John E. Travis
Gilbert C. Van Loon
J. Paul Varner
Thad W. Varner
J. Wilbourn Vise
Vangela M. Wade
Jeffrey A. Walker
Louis H. Watson, Jr.
W. Scott Welch, III
Thomas E. Williams
Edward A. Wilmesherr
J. Collins Wohner Jr.

(See Next Column)

UPSHAW, WILLIAMS, BIGGERS, BECKHAM & RIDDICK LLP, *Jackson—Continued*

OF COUNSEL

Ben L. Riddick
John R. Countiss III

Representative Clients: United States Fidelity & Guaranty Co.; State Farm Mutual Automobile Insurance Co.; CNA Insurance Cos.; St. Paul Fire & Marine Insurance Co.; Travelers/Aetna Property and Casualty Corp.; Kemper Insurance Co.; Zurich-America Insurance Group; Risk Enterprise Management, Ltd.; Allstate Insurance Co.

For full biographical listings, see the Martindale-Hubbell Law Directory

WATKINS & EAGER (AV)

A Professional Limited Liability Company
Suite 300 The Emporium Building, 400 East Capitol Street, P.O. Box 650, 39205
Telephone: 601-948-6470
Facsimile: 601-354-3623

William H. Watkins (1895-1959)
Pat H. Eager, Jr. (1916-1970)
Elizabeth Watkins Hulen (1934-1977)
Hassell H. Whitworth (1964-1991)
Thomas H. Watkins (1933-1994)
Vardaman S. Dunn (1935-1997)

OF COUNSEL

William E. Suddath, Jr.

MEMBERS OF FIRM

William F. Goodman, Jr.
Charles Clark
James A. Becker, Jr.
William H. Cox, Jr.
Thomas R. Crews
P. Nicholas Harkins, III
John G. Corlew
George R. Fair
Kenneth E. Milam
John L. Low, IV
Michael W. Ulmer
Paul H. Stephenson, III
William F. Goodman, III
Clifford B. Ammons
Jamie G. Houston, III
Frank J. Hammond, III
Richard T. Lawrence
Robert H. Pedersen
James E. Higginbotham
Virginia T. Munford
Steven D. Orlansky
Douglas J. Gunn
David L. Ayers
Frank A. Wood, Jr.
Mildred M. Morris
Rebecca Lee Wiggs
William F. Ray
Michael O. Gwin
M. Binford Williams, Jr.
Lewis W. Bell
J. Fred Spencer, Jr.
Walter J. Brand
Louis B. Lanoux
J. Grant Sellers
Walter T. Johnson
Susan Latham Steffey
Mark D. Jicka
Kathleen P. Morgan
Lynn Plimpton Risley

ASSOCIATES

Leah Draayer McDowell
W. Thomas McCraney, III
Joe D. Nosef, III
Katherine A. Smith
Jimmy B. Wilkins
Martin E. Willoughby, Jr.
Gordon Urban "Sandy" Sanford, III
Jesse M. Harrington

Representative Clients: Ashland, Inc.; Bayer Corp.; Chevron U.S.A. Inc.; CIGNA Property and Casualty Companies; Mazda (North America), Inc.; R.J. Reynolds Tobacco Co.; Shell Oil Co.; Trustmark National Bank.

For full biographical listings, see the Martindale-Hubbell Law Directory

*LAUREL,** Jones Co.

GIBBES GRAVES MULLINS HORTMAN HARLOW MARTINDALE & JONES, PLLC (AV)

414 West Oak Street, P.O. Drawer 1409, 39441-1409
Telephone: 601-649-8611
FAX: 601-649-6062

MEMBERS OF FIRM

William S. Mullins, III
Norman Gene Hortman, Jr.
Eugene M. Harlow
David L. Martindale
Deidra D. Jones

ASSOCIATES

Brett W. Robinson
Leslie P. Barry

Representative Clients: Texaco Inc.; Masonite Corp., a Division of International Paper Co.; St. Paul Insurance; The Virginia Insurance Reciprocal; Chevron U.S.A., Inc.; BellSouth; Shell Oil; Sanderson Farms, Inc.; Denbury Management, Inc.; Utica Mutual Insurance Co.

For full biographical listings, see the Martindale-Hubbell Law Directory

MC COMB, Pike Co.

NORMAN B. GILLIS, JR. (AV)

Professional Building, 109 21st Street, P.O. Box 1907, 39648-5111
Telephone: 601-684-1341
Fax: 601-684-4119

Representative Clients: Trustmark National Bank; Day Motors (G.M.); Trademark Motors; Kellwood Co.; Peterbilt of Mississippi and Louisiana; Mississippi Power and Light Co.; Paccar Financial Corp.; Shell Western E & P; Home Insurance Co.

(See Next Column)

Approved Attorney for: Lawyers Title Insurance Co.

*MERIDIAN,** Lauderdale Co.

GLOVER, YOUNG, WALTON, PHILLIPS & TUCKER, PLLC (AV)

Jefferson Square Office Plaza, 1724-A 23rd Avenue, P.O. Box 5514, 39302-5514
Telephone: 601-693-1301
Telecopy: 601-693-1363
Email: gywptpsp@hotmail.com

H. Wingfield Glover, Jr.
Ralph E. Young, Jr.
Ronnie L. Walton
P. Scott Phillips
H. Wingfield Glover, III
Judson T. Tucker

Representative Clients: Alfa Insurance Companies; American States Insurance Co.; Deposit Guaranty National Bank; General Agents Insurance Company of America, Inc.; Great River Insurance; Jeff Anderson Regional Medical Center; Liberty National Life Insurance Co.; Mississippi Power Co.; State Auto Insurance Companies; Universal Underwriters.

For full biographical listings, see the Martindale-Hubbell Law Directory

HAMILTON & LINDER (AV)

2713 Seventh Street, P.O. Box 1511, 39302-1511
Telephone: 601-693-5548
Fax: 601-693-2949
URL: http://www.lawyers.com/handllaw

MEMBERS OF FIRM

Joe Clay Hamilton
David H. Linder

ASSOCIATES

Will Parker
G. Richard Baker

For full biographical listings, see the Martindale-Hubbell Law Directory

*NATCHEZ,** Adams Co.

GWIN, LEWIS & PUNCHES, LLP (AV)

319 Market Street, P.O. Box 1344, 39120-3465
Telephone: 601-446-6621
FAX: 601-442-6175
Email: gwin1p@bkbank.com
Woodville, Mississippi Office: 457 Main Street.
Telephone: 601-446-6621.

MEMBERS OF FIRM

Lucien C. Gwin, Jr.
W. Bruce Lewis
Robert R. Punches
Lucien C. Gwin, III
Christopher E. Kelley

Mississippi Counsel for: International Paper Company.
Representative Clients: Sammons Communications, Inc.; Britton & Koontz First National Bank; Mississippi Farm Bureau Insurance Co.

For full biographical listings, see the Martindale-Hubbell Law Directory

MULHEARN & MULHEARN (AV)

202 South Wall Street, P.O. Box 967, 39120
Telephone: 601-442-4808
Fax: 601-446-6224
Email: woodland@bkbank.com *URL:* http://www.lawyers.com/mulhearnlaw

MEMBERS OF FIRM

John E. Mulhearn (1910-1981)
John E. Mulhearn, Jr.

LEGAL SUPPORT PERSONNEL

Eva Ruth Seale
Judith A. Strickland

Representative Clients: Ashland Plantation; Exxon Corporation; Belle Oil, Inc.; Supermarket Operations, Inc.; Petron, Inc.; Concordia Bank & Trust Co.; Dunleith; J.M. Jones Lumber Co., Inc.; Southwest Mississippi Anesthesia P.A.; Paradise Foods, Inc.

For full biographical listings, see the Martindale-Hubbell Law Directory

*OXFORD,** Lafayette Co.

HOLCOMB DUNBAR, A PROFESSIONAL ASSOCIATION (AV)

1217 Jackson Avenue P.O. Drawer 707, 38655
Telephone: 601-234-8775
Facsimile: 601-238-7552
Email: hdccw@holcombdunbar.com *URL:* http://www.holcombdunbar.com
Clarksdale, Mississippi Office: 152 Delta Avenue, P.O. Box 368, 38614.
Telephone: 601-627-2241.
Facsimile: 601-627-9788.
Southaven, Mississippi Office: Suite 1, 728 Goodman Road East, P.O. Box 190, 38671.
Telephone: 601-349-0664.
Facsimile: 601-349-2432.

(See Next Column)

BUTLER, SNOW, O'MARA, STEVENS & CANNADA PLLC—*Continued*

SENIOR ATTORNEYS

Walter J. Eades (Gulfport, Mississippi Office)	Camille Henick Evans
	Thomas A. Webb

STAFF ATTORNEYS

Dorsey R. Carson, Jr.	LeAnn Mercer
Debora L. Horn	Edward W. Mizell

OF COUNSEL

Robert G. Barnett	R. Barry Cannada

Frank O. Crosthwait

COUNSEL

D. Carl Black, Jr.	Lauch M. Magruder, Jr.
Robert C. Cannada	Dan McCullen
Lawrence J. Franck	C. Eugene McRoberts, Jr.
Charles R. Galloway, Jr. (Gulfport, Mississippi Office)	Hugh C. Montgomery, Jr.
	Phineas Stevens

Counsel for: American Cyanamid Co.; Beneficial Corp.; Deposit Guaranty National Bank; Eli Lilly & Co.; Ergon, Inc.; Gulf Guaranty Life Insurance Co.; Miller Transporters, Inc.; Reliance National Insurance Co.; South Central Bell Telephone Co.

For full biographical listings, see the Martindale-Hubbell Law Directory

CURRIE JOHNSON GRIFFIN GAINES & MYERS, PLLC (AV)

Mississippi Valley Title Building, 315 Tombigbee Street, P.O. Box 750, 39205-0750
Telephone: 601-969-1010
Telecopier: 601-969-5120
URL: http://www.curriejohnson.com

MEMBERS OF FIRM

Edward J. Currie, Jr.	Philip W. Gaines
Whitman B. Johnson, III	Michael F. Myers
William C. Griffin	Frances R. Shields

William H. Creel, Jr.

Lisa L. Williams	Robert B. Ogletree
James F. Noble, III	James M. Priest, Jr.
William W. McKinley, Jr.	Shelly G. Burns
Timothy D. Moore	Yumeka C. Burt
Trent L. Walker	Kristi A. Duncan

For full biographical listings, see the Martindale-Hubbell Law Directory

LISTON/LANCASTER (AV)

304 North Congress Street, P.O. Box 22983, 39225
Telephone: 601-944-0820
Fax: 601-355-2175
Winona, Mississippi Office: P.O. Box 645, 126 North Quitman Avenue.
Telephone: 662-283-2132.
Fax: 662-283-3742.

William H. Liston	William Liston, III
Alan D. Lancaster	W. Joseph Reid

For full biographical listings, see the Martindale-Hubbell Law Directory

PHELPS DUNBAR, L.L.P. (AV)

Suite 500, SkyTel Centre, 200 South Lamar Street, P.O. Box 23066, 39225-3066
Telephone: 601-352-2300
Telecopier: 601-360-9777
Email: info@phelps.com
New Orleans, Louisiana Office: Texaco Center, 400 Poydras Street.
Telephone: 504-566-1311.
Telecopier: 504-568-9130; 504-568-9007.
Cable Address: "Howspencer."
Telex: 584125 WU.
Telex: 6821155 WUI.
Baton Rouge, Louisiana Office: Suite 701, 445 North Boulevard, P.O. Box 4412.
Telephone: 225-346-0285.
Telecopier: 225-381-9197.
Tupelo, Mississippi Office: Seventh Floor, One Mississippi Plaza, P.O. Box 1220.
Telephone: 662-842-7907.
Telecopier: 662-842-3873.
Houston, Texas Office: Suite 900, 3040 Post Oak Boulevard.
Telephone: 713-626-1386.
Telecopier: 713-626-1388.
London, England Office: Suite 731, Level 7, Lloyd's, 1 Lime Street, London EC3M 7DQ England.
Telephone: 011-44-207-929-4765.
Telecopier: 011-44-207-929-0046.
Telex: 987321.

RESIDENT PARTNERS

Reuben V. Anderson	R. Pepper Crutcher, Jr.
Ross F. Bass, Jr.	Deborah Shelby Dees
William C. Brabec	Gary E. Friedman
James W. Craig	E. Clifton Hodge, Jr.

(See Next Column)

RESIDENT PARTNERS (Continued)

C. Delbert Hosemann, Jr.	Glover A. Russell, Jr.
Stephen H. Leech, Jr.	W. Thomas Siler, Jr.
Dan M. McDaniel, Jr.	John P. Sneed
Paul O. Miller, III	David M. Thomas, II
Armin J. Moeller, Jr.	Frank W. Trapp
Luther T. Munford	Michael B. Wallace
James W. O'Mara	David P. Webb
John W. Robinson, III	Stephen M. Wilson

COUNSEL

Linda Bounds Sherman

RESIDENT ASSOCIATES

Joseph Lee Adams	Rebecca Hawkins
Debra M. Brown	R. Hayes Johnson, Jr.
Stratton Bull	Amanda Jones
Heather J. Camp	J. Douglas Minor, Jr.
Ken Fairly	Wendy Russell Mullins
Mark Fijman	Douglas C. Noble
Kari L. Foster	A. Matt Pesnell
Christopher R. Green (Not admitted in MS)	Chelye E. Prichard
	James W. Shelson
Eric T. Hamer	E. Russell Turner

Representative Clients: Bank of Mississippi; Blue Cross & Blue Shield of Mississippi; Deposit Guaranty National Bank; General Motors Corporation; The Kroger Co.; Mississippi Municipal Liability Plan; Philip Morris Incorporated; Underwriters at Lloyd's, London; Westinghouse Electric Corporation.

For full biographical listings, see the Martindale-Hubbell Law Directory

THOMAS E. ROYALS (AV)

The Plaza Building, Suite 1100, 120 North Congress Street, P.O. Box 22909, 39225-2909
Telephone: 601-948-7777
Telecopier: 601-948-7780
Email: royalslaw@aol.com

For full biographical listings, see the Martindale-Hubbell Law Directory

SULLIVAN AND SULLIVAN (AV)

Suite 200, 5448 I-55 North, 39211
Telephone: 601-952-0799
Facsimile: 601-952-0599;
Cable Address: "Sullaw"

MEMBERS OF FIRM

John C. Sullivan, Sr. (1910-1993)	John C. Sullivan, Jr.

ASSOCIATE

Patricia Alexander Killgore

For full biographical listings, see the Martindale-Hubbell Law Directory

UPSHAW, WILLIAMS, BIGGERS, BECKHAM & RIDDICK, LLP (AV)

Suite 300 Plaza One, 715 South Pear Orchard Road (Ridgeland), 39147
Telephone: 601-978-1996
Facsimile: 601-978-1949
Mailing Address: P.O. Box 9147, Jackson, Mississippi, 39286-9147
Email: lexjax@uwbbr.com
Greenwood, Mississippi Office: 309 Fulton Street, P.O. Drawer 8230, 38935-8230.
Telephone: 662-455-1613.
Facsimile: 662-453-9245. Email: lexgwd@uwbbr.com.

MEMBERS OF FIRM

James E. Upshaw (Resident, Greenwood Office)	Robert S. Upshaw (Resident, Greenwood Office)
Tommie G. Williams (Resident, Greenwood Office)	Clinton M. Guenther (Resident, Greenwood Office)
Marc A. Biggers (Resident, Greenwood Office)	Richard C. Williams, Jr.
Glenn F. Beckham (Resident, Greenwood Office)	Richard L. Kimmel (Resident, Greenwood Office)
Roger C. Riddick	Mark C. Carroll
F. Ewin Henson III (Resident, Greenwood Office)	W. Hugh Gillon IV
Lonnie D. Bailey (Resident, Greenwood Office)	Paul L. Goodman (Resident, Greenwood Office)
	Walter C. Morrison IV

ASSOCIATES

Steven H. Funderburg	Cecil D. McClellan, III
Bonnie Bridgers Smith	Christopher W. Winter (Resident, Greenwood Office)
Patrick M. Tatum	
Craig R. Sessums	J. L. Wilson, IV (Resident, Greenwood Office)
James K. Warrington (Resident, Greenwood Office)	Steven C. Cookston (Resident, Greenwood Office)
Tammra O. Cascio (Resident, Greenwood Office)	Adrienne D. Cox

(See Next Column)

HOLCOMB DUNBAR A PROFESSIONAL ASSOCIATION—*Continued*

Pat D. Holcomb (1909-1996)
Jack F. Dunbar
Edward A. Moss
Thomas J. Suszek
Michael N. Watts
Marjorie T. O'Donnell
David D. O'Donnell
T. Swayze Alford
R. Bradley Best
Angela M. Spivey
Walter Alan Davis
Mark R. Smith

OF COUNSEL

Chester H. Curtis

Representative Clients: Union Planters Bank, National Association; Deposit Guaranty National Bank; Trustmark National Bank; Mississippi Power & Light Co.; Southern Farm Bureau Casualty Insurance Co.; Bituminous Insurance Co.; State Farm Fire & Casualty Insurance Co.; Fireman's Fund Insurance Cos.; Atlanta Casualty Insurance Cos.; Drexel Chemical Co.

For full biographical listings, see the Martindale-Hubbell Law Directory

*POPLARVILLE,** Pearl River Co.

WILLIAMS, WILLIAMS AND MONTGOMERY, P.A. (AV)

109 Erlanger Street, P.O. Box 113, 39470
Telephone: 601-795-4572
Fax: 601-795-8382

E. B. Williams (1890-1976)
E. B. Williams, Jr. (1917-1990)
Lampton O'Neal Williams
Joseph H. Montgomery
E. Bragg Williams, III
L. O'Neal Williams, Jr.

Michael E. Patten
Anne M. Parker

Representative Clients: Hancock Bank, Bank of Commerce Branch; Lumberton Linne School District; Garrett Industries, Inc.; Bass Pecan Co., Lumberton, Miss.; Joe N. Miles & Sons Lumber Co., Inc., Lumberton and Silver Creek, Miss. and Bogalusa, La.
Reference: Hancock Bank, Bank of Commerce Branch, Poplarville, Mississippi.

For full biographical listings, see the Martindale-Hubbell Law Directory

SOUTHAVEN, De Soto Co.

HOLCOMB DUNBAR, A PROFESSIONAL ASSOCIATION (AV)

Suite 1, 728 Goodman Road East, P.O. Box 190, 38671
Telephone: 601-349-0664
Facsimile: 601-349-2432
Email: hdccw@holcombdunbar.com *URL:* http://www.holcombdunbar.com
Clarksdale, Mississippi Office: 152 Delta Avenue, P.O. Box 368, 38614.
Telephone: 601-627-2241.
Facsimile: 601-627-9788.
Oxford, Mississippi Office: 1217 Jackson Avenue, P.O. Drawer 707, 38655.
Telephone: 601-234-8775.
Facsimile: 601-238-7552.

Pat D. Holcomb (1909-1996)
William A. Baskin
John Ramsey McCarroll, III
Michael K. Graves
Billy C. Campbell, Jr.
Mary Launa Gray
Jeffrey S. McCaskill

OF COUNSEL

Chester H. Curtis

Representative Clients: Union Planters Bank, National Association; BanCorp South; Trustmark National Bank; Mississippi Power & Light Co.; Southern Farm Bureau Casualty Insurance Co.; Bituminous Insurance Co.; State Farm Fire & Casualty Insurance Co.; Fireman's Fund Insurance Cos.; Atlanta Casualty Insurance Cos.; Drexel Chemical Co.

For full biographical listings, see the Martindale-Hubbell Law Directory

*TUPELO,** Lee Co.

MITCHELL, MCNUTT, THREADGILL, SMITH & SAMS, P.A. (AV)

105 South Front Street, P.O. Box 7120, 38802
Telephone: 662-842-3871
Facsimile: 662-842-8450
Email: MMTSS@EBICOM.NET
Columbus, Mississippi Office: 215 Fifth Street North, P.O. Box 1366.
Telephone: 662-328-2316.
Facsimile: 662-328-8035.
Corinth, Mississippi Office: 508 Waldron Street, P.O. Box 1200.
Telephone: 662-286-9931.
Facsimile: 662-286-8984.
Oxford, Mississippi Office: 1216 Van Buren, P.O. Box 947.
Telephone: 662-234-4845.
Facsimile: 662-234-9071.
Jackson, Mississippi Office: Skytel Centre, 200 S. Lamar, Suite 900, P.O. Box 1005.
Telephone: 662-948-8508.
Facsimile: 662-948-8537.
Memphis, Tennessee Office: 1255 Lynnfield Road, Building A, Suite 123.
Telephone: 901-767-5185.
Facsimile: 901-767-5918,

(See Next Column)

Guy W. Mitchell, Sr. (1881-1969)
Guy W. Mitchell, Jr. (1912-1986)
L. F. Sams, Jr.
Taylor B. Smith
Guy W. Mitchell, III
William C. Spencer
David L. Sanders (Resident at Columbus Office)
James L. Carroll
Claude F. Clayton, Jr.
Wendell H. Trapp, Jr. (Resident at Corinth Office)
William C. Murphree
Ronald L. Roberts
Albert G. Delgadillo
John S. Hill
Michael D. Ferris
Richard H. Spann (Resident, Columbus Office)
W. Scott Collins
James A. Barnett, Jr.
Timothy W. Lindsay
Otis R. Tims
Donna M. Barnes
Michael D. Chase
James L Warren, III (Resident, Jackson Office)
Martha Bost Stegall
John G. Wheeler
Tacey Clark Clayton
D. Andrew Phillips (Resident, Oxford Office)
Gregg A. Caraway
Myles A. Parker
D. Bradley Walsh
J. Douglas Ford (Resident at Columbus Office)
Jeffrey J. Turnage (Resident at Columbus Office)
Berkley N. Huskison (Resident at Columbus Office)
William G. Armistead
Pope S. Mallette (Resident at Oxford Office)
L. Bradley Dillard
Don L. Fruge', Jr. (Resident at Oxford Office)
William Collins Spencer, Jr. (Resident)
William H. Davis, Jr. (Resident at Corinth Office)
David K. Pharr (Resident at Jackson Office)
Bradley R. Peacock (Also at Jackson Office)
Elizabeth S. Mitchell (Resident at Jackson Office)
James P. Wilson, Jr. (Also at Columbus and Memphis Offices)
Charles E. Winfield (Resident at Jackson Office)
J. Chadwick Mask (Also at Jackson Office)

COUNSEL

Sonja A. Jenkins

OF COUNSEL

Robert N. McNutt
William J. Threadgill
Wade H. Lagrone
W. H. (Hank) Jolly, Jr. (Resident at Columbus Office)

Representative Clients: See Clients under Professional Biographies.

For full biographical listings, see the Martindale-Hubbell Law Directory

MITCHELL, VOGE, CORBAN AND MORRIS (AV)

108 North Broadway Street, P.O. Box 29, 38802-0029
Telephone: 601-842-4231
Telecopier: 601-842-2689
Email: mvcm1@ebicom.net

W. P. Mitchell
Jess B. Rogers (1924-1975)
Dennis W. Voge
Stephen M. Corban
Stephen H. Morris

ASSOCIATE

Scott R. Hendrix

For full biographical listings, see the Martindale-Hubbell Law Directory

PHELPS DUNBAR, L.L.P. (AV)

Seventh Floor, One Mississippi Plaza, P.O. Box 1220, 38802-1220
Telephone: 662-842-7907
Telecopier: 662-842-3873
Email: info@phelps.com
New Orleans, Louisiana Office: Texaco Center, 400 Poydras Street.
Telephone: 504-566-1311.
Telecopier: 504-568-9130; 504-568-9007.
Cable Address: "Howspencer."
Telex: 584125 WU.
Telex: 6821155 WUI.
Baton Rouge, Louisiana Office: Suite 701, 445 North Boulevard, P.O. Box 4412.
Telephone: 225-346-0285.
Telecopier: 225-381-9197.
Jackson, Mississippi Office: Suite 500, SkyTel Centre, 200 South Lamar Street, P.O. Box 23066.
Telephone: 601-352-2300.
Telecopier: 601-360-9777.
Houston, Texas Office: Suite 900, 3040 Post Oak Boulevard.
Telephone: 713-626-1386.
Telecopier: 713-626-1388.
London, England Office: Suite 731, Level 7, Lloyd's, 1 Lime Street, London EC3M 7DQ England.
Telephone: 011-44-207-929-4765.
Telecopier: 011-44-207-929-0046.
Telex: 987321.

OF COUNSEL

Fred M. Bush, Jr.

(See Next Column)

PHELPS DUNBAR L.L.P., *Tupelo—Continued*

RESIDENT PARTNERS

William M. Beasley
F. M. Bush, III
Jean Magee Hogan
Dinetia M. Newman
Gregory D. Pirkle

COUNSEL

Jeffrey S. Moore
G. Kay L. Trapp

RESIDENT ASSOCIATES

Scott Ellzey
Gregory M. Hunsucker
Mark Stewart Johnson
Mark C. Lewis
Barry L. McGraw
(Not admitted in MS)
Elizabeth E. Thomas

Representative Clients: Bank of Mississippi; CBI Equifax; General Motors Corporation; JESCO, Inc.; The Kroger Co.; Lee County, Mississippi; Mississippi Municipal Liability Plan; North Mississippi Health Services, Inc. (and affiliated entities); Philip Morris Incorporated; Underwriters at Lloyd's, London.

For full biographical listings, see the Martindale-Hubbell Law Directory

*TYLERTOWN,** Walthall Co.

JOSEPH M. STINSON (AV)

1108 Beulah Avenue, 39667
Telephone: 601-876-5121; 876-5122
Fax: 601-876-5882

Representative Clients: Stringer Industries, Inc.; Jones Lumber Co., Inc.
Approved Attorney for: Mississippi Valley Title Insurance Co.; Farm Credit Bank of Texas.

For full biographical listings, see the Martindale-Hubbell Law Directory

*VICKSBURG,** Warren Co.

TELLER, CHANEY, HASSELL & HOPSON, LLP (AV)

Suite 500 Bancorpsouth Bank, 820 South Street, P.O. Box 789, 39181
Telephone: 601-636-6565
Fax: 601-631-0114
Email: attorneys@tellerlaw.com

Landman Teller, Jr.
M. James Chaney, Jr.
Douglas E. Hassell
Frank J. Campbell
B. Blake Teller
W. Briggs Hopson, III

Representative Clients: International Paper Co.; U.S. Rubber Reclaiming, Inc.; Bancorp South Bank; Anderson-Tully Co.; Vicksburg Warren School District; River Region Medical Corp.
Approved Attorneys for: Mississippi Valley Title Insurance Co.; First American Title Insurance Co.; Lawyers Title Insurance Corp; Stewart Title Insurance Co.

For full biographical listings, see the Martindale-Hubbell Law Directory

*WINONA,** Montgomery Co.

LISTON/LANCASTER (AV)

126 North Quitman Avenue, P.O. Box 645, 38967
Telephone: 662-283-2132
Fax: 662-283-3742
Email: lislan@aol.com
Jackson, Mississippi Office: 304 North Congress Street, P.O. Box 22983, 39225.
Telephone: 601-944-0820.
Fax: 601-355-2175.

William H. Liston
Alan D. Lancaster
William Liston, III
W. Joseph Reid

For full biographical listings, see the Martindale-Hubbell Law Directory

*WOODVILLE,** Wilkinson Co.

GWIN, LEWIS & PUNCHES, LLP (AV)

457 Main Street, 39669
Telephone: 601-446-6621
Natchez, Mississippi Office: 319 Market Street.
Telephone: 601-446-6621.
FAX: 601-442-6175.

W. Bruce Lewis
Lucien C. Gwin, III

Mississippi Counsel for: International Paper Company.
Representative Clients: Sammons Communications, Inc.; Britton & Koontz First National Bank; Mississippi Farm Bureau Insurance Co.

MISSOURI

CAPE GIRARDEAU, Cape Girardeau Co.

BRADSHAW, STEELE, COCHRANE & BERENS, L.C. (AV)

3113 Independence, P.O. Box 1300, 63702-1300
Telephone: 573-334-0555
Fax: 573-334-2947
Email: info@bradshawsteele.com

Stephen E. Strom (Retired)
John P. Bradshaw
Richard G. Steele
James A. Cochrane, III
Paul H. Berens
Dale E. Gerecke
Craig M. Billmeyer
Matthew M. Mocherman
Stephen C. Christiansen
James E. Laramore
Michael Deimund

Representative Clients: Royal-Globe Insurance Co; United States Fidelity & Guaranty Co.; John Deere Co.; Associates Commercial Corp.; KFVS-TV; Liberty Mutual Insurance Co.; Southern Illinois Stone Co.; St. Francis Medical Center; Mercantile Banks of Southeast Missouri; Southeast Missouri Hospital.

For full biographical listings, see the Martindale-Hubbell Law Directory

OLIVER, OLIVER & WALTZ, P.C. (AV)

400 Broadway, P.O. Box 559, 63702-0559
Telephone: 573-335-8278
Fax: 573-334-6375
Email: oliver@ldd.net

R. B. Oliver (1850-1934)
R. B. Oliver, Jr. (1880-1971)
Allen Laws Oliver (1886-1970)
John (Jack) L. Oliver (1916-1978)
John L. Oliver, Jr.
James Frederick Waltz

Jason Glennon Crowell

OF COUNSEL

A. J. Seier

Representative Clients: Mercantile Bank of Southern Missouri; Union Electric Co.; Southwestern Bell Corp.; Ford Motor Co.; Consolidated Drainage District; MOMEDICO; The Travelers; The Hartford; The Kemper Group; AAA of Missouri.

For full biographical listings, see the Martindale-Hubbell Law Directory

*COLUMBIA,** Boone Co.

KNIGHT, FORD, ATWILL, PARSHALL & BAKER (AV)

609 East Walnut Street, P.O. Box 1097, 65205
Telephone: 573-449-2613
Telecopier: 573-875-8154
Email: kfwapb@computerland.com

MEMBERS OF FIRM

David L. Knight
Hamp Ford
Daniel K. Atwill
Jeffrey O. Parshall
Michael R. Baker
Susan Ford Robertson
Jeffrey H. Blaylock
David W. Walker
Mariam W. Decker
Edward L. Guinn
Richard L. Montgomery, Jr.

ASSOCIATES

Justin R. Davis
Elizabeth Hodge Weber
Daniel E. Himmelberg
Robert J. Buckley
Jordan M. Humphreys

OF COUNSEL

James R. Green

General Counsel for: Commerce Bank; Boone Hospital Center and Boone Clinic.
Representative Clients: Hartford Insurance Group; State Farm Mutual Automobile Ins. Co.; Automobile Club Inter-Insurance Exchange; Medical Protective Co.; Stephens College; Boone County Fire Protection District; Columbia College.

For full biographical listings, see the Martindale-Hubbell Law Directory

SMITH, LEWIS, BECKETT, POWELL, ROARK & DURLEY, L.L.P. (AV)

Haden Building, 901 East Broadway, Suite 100, 65201-4857
Telephone: 573-443-3141
Fax: 573-442-6686

MEMBERS OF FIRM

Robert C. Smith (Retired)
Raymond C. Lewis, Jr.
Bruce H. Beckett
William Jay Powell
John L. Roark
Colly J. Durley

(See Next Column)

SMITH, LEWIS, BECKETT, POWELL, ROARK & DURLEY L.L.P.—*Continued*

ASSOCIATES

James B. Lowery
Sandra J. Colhour
Raymond E. Williams
Michael R. Tripp

Representative Clients: Allied Group Insurance; AmerenUE; Boone National Savings & Loan Assn.; CNA HealthPro; Central Electric Power Cooperative; First National Bank and Trust Co.; LeMone-Smith Development Co.; Medical Defense Associates, Ltd.; The Medical Protective Co. of Fort Wayne; University of Missouri.

For full biographical listings, see the Martindale-Hubbell Law Directory

HANNIBAL, Marion Co.

CARY, WELCH & HICKMAN, L.L.P. (AV)

1000 Center Street, P.O. Box 710, 63401
Telephone: 573-221-0080
Fax: 573-221-3856
URL: http://www.lawyers.com/cwhlaw

MEMBERS OF FIRM

James E. Cary
Joseph D. Welch
Charles L. Hickman

Ross Walden

Representative Clients: American Family Insurance Group; American General Finance, Inc.; Automobile Club Inter-Insurance Exchange; Bank of Kirksville; City of Palmyra, Community State Bank of Shelbina; Continental Cement Co.; Farmers and Merchants Bank; Federated Insurance Co.; Goodhart Realty, Inc.; Hannibal Housing Authority.

For full biographical listings, see the Martindale-Hubbell Law Directory

THE RENDLEN LAW FIRM, P.C. (AV)

800 Broadway, P.O. Box 1255, 63401
Telephone: 573-221-4060
Fax: 573-221-2371
Email: renlaw@nemonet.com *URL:* http://www.lawyers.com/rendlenlawfirm

Charles E. Rendlen, Sr. (1878-1957)
Branham Rendlen (1906-1985)
Charles E. Rendlen, Jr.
Charles E. Rendlen, III

C. Todd Ahrens
Debora L. Hale

General Counsel for: Commerce Bank of Hannibal; Wells Abstract Co.; American Loan & Savings Assn.; Wendy's of Hannibal; Country Kitchen of Hannibal.

For full biographical listings, see the Martindale-Hubbell Law Directory

*HILLSBORO,** Jefferson Co.

THURMAN, HOWALD, WEBER, SENKEL & NORRICK, L.L.C. (AV)

One Thurman Court, 63050
Telephone: 314-789-2601, 797-2601
Telecopier: 314-797-2904
Email: thurmanlaw@theriver.net

MEMBERS OF FIRM

J. W. Thurman (1902-1986)
John W. Howald
Louis J. Weber
David P. Senkel
Floyd T. Norrick

Julianne Platz Hand

For full biographical listings, see the Martindale-Hubbell Law Directory

WEGMANN, GASAWAY, STEWART, SCHNEIDER, DIEFFENBACH, TESREAU & SHERMAN, P.C. (AV)

Court House Square, P.O. Box 740, 63050
Telephone: 636-797-2665
Direct Dial, St. Louis: 636-296-5769
Telecopier: 636-797-3505
Email: mail@wegmannlaw.com

Will B. Dearing (1902-1975)
Samuel Richeson (1904-1976)
J. Richard Roberts (1928-1975)
John A. Schneider (1942-1992)
Roland A. (Ray) Wegmann
Nicholas G. Gasaway, Jr.
Jack C. Stewart
Albert W. Dieffenbach, Jr.
Dennis H. Tesreau
Randall D. Sherman

Darrell E. Missey
Todd M. Siegel
Christine Stahlman

For full biographical listings, see the Martindale-Hubbell Law Directory

*INDEPENDENCE,** Jackson Co.

STEWART, COOK, CONSTANCE, STEWART & MINTON, L.L.C. (AV)

501 West Lexington Avenue, 64050
Telephone: 816-833-1800
FAX: 816-833-1805

MEMBERS OF FIRM

Byron A. Stewart, Jr.
David H. Cook
Bradley A. Constance
Byron G. Stewart
Kent Minton

OF COUNSEL

Byron Constance

Representative Clients: Branch Banking & Trust; Jackson County Board of Election Commissioners.
Approved Attorneys for: Rural Development (U.S.D.A.); First American Title Insurance Co.; Commonwealth Land Title Insurance Co.; Manufacturers Hanover Agent Bank Services.

For full biographical listings, see the Martindale-Hubbell Law Directory

*JEFFERSON CITY,** Cole Co.

BRYDON, SWEARENGEN & ENGLAND, PROFESSIONAL CORPORATION (AV)

The Hammond Building, 312 East Capitol Avenue, P.O. Box 456, 65102-0456
Telephone: 573-635-7166
Facsimile: 573-635-0427
Email: bsepc@aol.com

David V. G. Brydon
James C. Swearengen
William R. England, III
Johnny K. Richardson
Gary W. Duffy
Paul A. Boudreau
Sondra B. Morgan
Charles E. Smarr
Mark G. Anderson
Dean L. Cooper
Timothy T. Stewart
Gregory C. Mitchell
Rachel M. Craig
Brian T. McCartney

Dale Smith

OF COUNSEL

Richard T. Ciottone

Representative Clients: The Empire District Electric Co.; St. Joseph Light & Power Co.; UtiliCorp United Inc.; Southern Union Company; Missouri Gas Energy; Missouri-American Water Co.; ALLTEL Missouri, Inc.; Citizens Telephone Company of Higginsville, Missouri; Missouri Automobile Dealers Assn.; Jefferson City Medical Group, P.C.

For full biographical listings, see the Martindale-Hubbell Law Directory

HENDREN AND ANDRAE (AV)

Riverview Office Center, 221 Bolivar Street, Suite 300, P.O. Box 1069, 65102
Telephone: 573-636-8135
Telecopier: 573-636-5226
Email: henand@socket.net

OF COUNSEL

Henry Andrae

MEMBERS OF FIRM

Charles H. Howard (1925-1970)
John E. Burruss, Jr. (1933-1985)
John H. Hendren (1907-1988)
Gerald E. Roark (1956-1995)
Richard S. Brownlee, III
Michael A. Dallmeyer
Duane E. Schreimann
Douglas L. Van Camp
Michael G. Berry
John W. Kuebler
Susan M. Turner
Christopher P. Rackers

ASSOCIATES

Sara C. Michael
Patricia D. Perkins
Brian K. Francka

Representative Clients: Westinghouse; Chesebrough-Pond's, Inc.; Union Pacific Railroad; Purina Mills, Inc.; American Cancer Society; Cargill, Inc.; Jefferson Bank & Exchange Bank.

For full biographical listings, see the Martindale-Hubbell Law Directory

INGLISH & MONACO, P.C. (AV)

Monroe House Law Center, 237 East High Street, P.O. Box 67, 65102
Telephone: 573-634-2522
Telecopier: 573-634-4526
Email: inglishmonaco-jc@socket.net
California, Missouri Office: 329 South Oak.
Telephone: 573-796-4333.
Lake Ozark, Missouri Office: Cliffside Office Center, 2140 Bagnell Dam Boulevard, 65049.
Telephone: 573-964-6211.
Telecopier: 573-964-6787.

(See Next Column)

INGLISH & MONACO P.C., *Jefferson City—Continued*

John W. Inglish
Nicholas M. Monaco
Ann Monaco Warren
Mark G. R. Warren
Lewis Z. Bridges
Timothy R. Cisar
David G. Bandré
Daniel E. Hunt
Daniel C. Mizell
Stephen W. Richey
William Barton
Charles P. Dribben (1929-1991)

OF COUNSEL

Andrew Jackson Higgins

References: Central Trust Bank; Jefferson Bank.

For full biographical listings, see the Martindale-Hubbell Law Directory

WESNER, KEMPTON, RUSSELL AND DOMINIQUE (AV)

621 East McCarty Street, Suite C, P.O. Box 1108, 65102-1108
Telephone: 573-635-7241
Fax: 573-635-2631
Sedalia Office: 114 East 5th Street, P.O. Box 815.
Telephone: 660-827-0314.
Fax: 660-827-1200.

P. Pierre Dominique
Mark T. Kempton (Resident, Sedalia Office)
Robert G. Russell (Resident, Sedalia Office)
J. Christopher Spangler (Resident, Sedalia Office)
Robert W. Russell (Resident, Sedalia Office)

Representative Clients: Home Savings Bank; St. Paul Title Insurance Corp.; State Farm Mutual Insurance Co.; Kemper Insurance Co.; Great American Insurance Co.

For full biographical listings, see the Martindale-Hubbell Law Directory

JOPLIN, Jasper Co.

BLANCHARD, ROBERTSON, MITCHELL & CARTER, P.C. (AV)

320 West Fourth Street, P.O. Box 1626, 64802
Telephone: 417-623-1515
Facsimile: 417-623-6865

Karl W. Blanchard
John R. Martin (1922-1982)
Malcolm L. Robertson
Karl W. Blanchard, Jr.
Ronald E. Mitchell
Greg B. Carter

OF COUNSEL

Herbert Van Fleet

Ronald G. Sparlin
John Anthony Nicholas
Tondra J. Phillips
Heather A. Prendergast
Phillip D. Greathouse

Representative Clients: Chubb Group; First National Bank of Sarcoxie; First State Bank; Liberty Mutual Insurance Co.; Missouri Southern State College; St. Paul Insurance Co.; State Farm Insurance Co.; Southwestern Bell Telephone Co.; Tamko Asphalt Products; United States Fidelity & Guaranty Co..

For full biographical listings, see the Martindale-Hubbell Law Directory

KANSAS CITY, Jackson, Clay, Platte & Cass Cos.

ARMSTRONG TEASDALE LLP (AV)

A Partnership including Professional Corporations
2345 Grand Boulevard, Suite 2000, 64108
Telephone: 816-221-3420
Facsimile: 816-221-0786
Email: armstrongteasdale@armstrongteasdale.com *URL:* http://www.armstrongteasdale.com
St. Louis, Missouri Office: One Metropolitan Square.
Telephone: 314-621-5070.
Facsimile: 314-621-5065.
Twx: 910-761-2246.
Cable: ATKV LAW.
Jefferson City, Missouri Office: 3405 W. Truman Blvd., Suite 210, 65109.
Telephone: 573-636-8394.
Washington, D.C. Office: 1747 Pennsylvania Avenue, N.W., Suite 300, 20006
Telephone: 202-347-0259.
Belleville, Illinois Office: 23 South First Street, 62220.
Telephone: 618-397-4411.
Olathe, Kansas Office: 100 East Park, 66061.
Telephone: 913-345-0706.
Shanghai, China Office: A-T International Consultants, LLC, Suite 310, No. 12 Zhongshan Road (E1), Shanghai 200002 P.R.C.
Telephone: 86-21-6326-7001.
Facsimile: 86-21-6326-0626.

MEMBERS OF FIRM

Christopher J. Anderson
Thomas M. Bradshaw (P.C.)
Stephen A. Crystal
Roy R. Darke
James F. Duncan
Truman K. Eldridge, Jr.
Gary V. Fulghum
Daniel Owen Herrington
Lynn W. Hursh
David J. Kornelis
Jennifer Putman Kyner
Randal J. Leimer

(See Next Column)

MEMBERS OF FIRM (Continued)

Ford R. Nelson, Jr.
Douglas R. Richmond
Marc A. Salle
Edward E. Schmitt
Donald G. Scott
William J. Shapiro
Edward R. Spalty
Charles F. Speer
Thomas H. Stahl (P.C.)
Laurence R. Tucker
John A. Vering, III

ASSOCIATES

Renana B. Abrams
David R. Barnard
Mark F. Brady
S. Matthew Burgess
Brian E. Engel
Derek E. Feagans
Casey O. Housley
Gianni M. Hughes
Gerald A. King
Phyllis G. Leach
Michael L. Matula
Jill A. Morris
Deborah A. Polk
Elizabeth Dross Reefer
Martin L. Rosemann
William E. Scanlan
Stuart Kent Shaw
Eugene J. Twellman
Amy E. Vickery
Tanya L. Wilson

OF COUNSEL

Philip A. Klawuhn
Kevin F. Warren (Not admitted in MO)

Representative Clients: American International Group; Century 21 Real Estate Corp.; Dow Corning Corp.; Faultless Starch/Bon Ami Co.; General Mills, Inc.; Kansas City Southern Industries; Sprint International, Inc.; State Farm Fire and Casualty Company; The Kansas City, Missouri Employment Retirement System.

For full biographical listings, see the Martindale-Hubbell Law Directory

SHOOK, HARDY & BACON L.L.P. (AV)

One Kansas City Place, 1200 Main Street, 64105-2118
Telephone: 816-474-6550
Facsimile: 816-421-5547
URL: http://www.shb.com
Other Kansas City, Missouri Office: UMB Bank Building, 1010 Grand Boulevard, Fifth Floor, 64106-0607.
Telephone: 816-474-6550.
Facsimile: 816-842-3190.
Overland Park, Kansas Office: Suite 1000, 10801 Mastin, 66210-1669.
Telephone: 913-451-6060.
Facsimile: 913-451-8879.
Houston, Texas Office: Chase Tower, Suite 1600, 600 Travis Street, 77002-2911.
Telephone: 713-227-8008.
Facsimile: 713-227-9508.
Washington, D.C. Office: Hamilton Square, 600 14th Street, N.W., Suite 800, 20005-2004.
Telephone: 202-783-8400.
Facsimile: 202-783-4211.
Miami, Florida Office: Miami Center, Suite 2400, 201 South Biscayne Boulevard, 33131-4332.
Telephone: 305-358-5171.
Facsimile: 305-358-7470.
San Francisco, California Office: One Market, Steuart Tower, Ninth Floor, 94105-1310.
Telephone: 415-904-6300.
Facsimile: 415-904-6303.
Buenos Aires, Argentina Office: Pte. Roque Saenz Pena 832, 4 Piso, 1388.
Telephone: 011-54-11-4320-4500.
Facsimile: 011-54-11-4328-7900.
London, England Office: Manning House, 22 Carlisle Place, SW1P 1JA.
Telephone: 011-44-171-821-5595.
Facsimile: 011-44-171-834-5918.
Melbourne, Australia Office: Level 50, 101 Collins Street, Victoria 3000.
Telephone: 011-61-3-9653-9287.
Facsimile: 011-61-3-9653-9494.
Zurich, Switzerland Office: Gerechtig Keitsgasse 23, 8002 Zurich.
Telephone: 011-41-1280-2505.
Facsimile: 011-41-1280-2507.
Geneva, Switzerland Office: 118, rue du Rhône, 1204.
Telephone: 011-41-22-787-2000.
Facsimile: 011-41-22-786-5008.

Frank P. Sebree (1854-1940)
Sam B. Sebree (1886-1958)
Edgar Shook (1894-1970)
David R. Hardy (1917-1976)
Charles L. Bacon (1909-1989)

PARTNERS

Robert T. Adams
Stephen D. Aliber
William L. Allinder
Anthony J. Andrade
James M. Beck
Joseph B. Bowman
David W. Brooks
Jeffrey A. Burns
Jamie M. Clark
Walter L. Cofer
William J. Crampton
M. James Daley
Stanley D. Davis
Leanne Deshong
John C. Dods
Dennis R. Dow
Leo P. Dreyer
James R. Eiszner, Jr.
Gregory L. Fowler
Joseph S. Gall
Roger C. Geary
J. Richard Golub
Kirk J. Goza
Michael J. Gross
Craig E. Gustafson
Lisa W. Hardwick
David K. Hardy
Mark Hargrave
Sandra T. Hawley
Mark C. Hegarty

(See Next Column)

SHOOK, HARDY & BACON L.L.P.—*Continued*

PARTNERS (Continued)

Bradley D. Honnold
Michael B. Hurd
Robert J. Janowitz
Richard R. Johnson
John S. Johnston
Harvey L. Kaplan
Matthew D. Keenan
Donald J. Kemna
William B. Kircher
Robert K. Kirkland
Michael L. Koon
(Not admitted in MO)
Margaret D. Lineberry
Gary R. Long
Michelle R. Mangrum
J. Scott McCandless
Christopher M. McDonald
Madeleine M. McDonough
Lori C. McGroder
Patrick McLarney
Mark Moedritzer
John C. Monica
James P. Muehlberger
(Not admitted in MO)
John F. Murphy
James O. Neet, Jr.
Jeffrey S. Nelson
James T. Newsom
Robert E. Northrip
Larry R. O'Neal
Bernard V. O'Neill, Jr.
Mark D. Ovington
Eugene S. Peck
Randall E. Pratt
Timothy A. Pratt
Billy R. Randles
Joseph M. Rebein
Todd W. Ruskamp
Scott W. Sayler
Larry M. Schumaker
Kelley D. Sears
Andrew See
Edward Sheppard
John K. Sherk, III
Daniel W. Shinn
Sylvan Siegler
John W. Simpson
Michael P. Socarras
Neil E. Sprague
Kevin R. Sweeney
Gay L. Tedder
Gene E. Voigts
Martha S. Warren
Stanley P. Weiner
Victoria R. Westerhaus
J. David Wharton
Gary L. Whittier
George E. Wolf, III
Marie S. Woodbury
Richard D. Woods
William G. Zimmerman

OF COUNSEL

Michael E. Baker
Ron D. Beal
(Not admitted in MO)
Susan A. Berson
Michael B. Buser
Deborah A. Calton
Catherine Castelluccio
Niles S. Corson
Mark W. Cowing
Daniel B. Dorsch
Scott E. Dupree
Larry C. Frarey
Joan Optican Herman
John A. Holtmann
Karen I. Johnson
(Not admitted in MO)
Donnamarie Landsberg
James H. Marsh, Jr.
Dyanna Nye
Staci J. Pratt
Stacey L. Rainey
Devon A. Rolf
Michael A. Scearce
Stephen P. Schuster
Thomas A. Sheehan
Michael L. Short
Annette G. Siebert
David W. Smith
Mareta J. Smith
Tina A. Smith
Lee E. Stanford
Wanda M. Temm
Dale Elizabeth Walker
John A. Weresh
Sharon M. Williams

Phillip R. Anderson
Paula L. Andres
Eric M. Anielak
James R. Arnold
John Baroni
Jane J. Bartley
Linda K. Beck
James E. Berger
Timothy C. Bickham
Michael L. Blumenthal
Karen A. Brady
Curtis J. Braukmann
Jennifer L. Brown
Noel C. Capps
Andrew D. Carpenter
Patricia J. Castellano
Tammy Grubb Coker
Lorianne G. Conklin
Christopher J. Cullen
(Not admitted in MO)
James H. Davis, Jr.
Daniel P. Devers
Carole K. DeWald
Mark A. Dover
Thomas A. Duncan
Jennifer Clifton Ferguson
Laura Clark Fey
Diego M. Gandolfo
Richard L. Gray
Patrick T. Hanrahan
Tina L. Harris
(Not admitted in MO)
Nicola R. Heskett
Micah L. Hobbs
Cynthia Hughes-Coons
Timothy M. Huskey
Brian A. Jackson
Jolie L. Justus
Kamran Q. Khan
Barbara A. Knops
Jeffrey A. Kruse
Joseph A. Lanahan
Benjamin H. Lane III
Shana J. Long
Patrick A. Lujin
Lisa A. Lukaszewski
Ann Marie MacPherson
Joseph G. Matye
Christine L. McDaniel
Andrew D. Mendez
Eric T. Mikkelson
Brandon D. Mizner
Deborah A. Moeller
Michael D. Moeller
Matthew J. Moore
Catherine H. Murphy
Dylan L. Murray
Clinton G. Newton
Laurie A. Novion
Curtis L. Perry
(Not admitted in MO)
Arvids V. Petersons
Craig E. Proctor
Paige A. Queen
Paul M. Quin
Karen A. Read
Michael A. Riley
Douglas W. Robinson
Lisa A. Sapcoe
Paula R. H. Schaefer
Angela M. Seaton
Frank P. Sebree, III
Veronica M. Sellers
Terrence J. Sexton
Jennifer D. Sherrill
Deborah A. Smith
Steven D. Soden
Gail Spotts-Cantwell

(See Next Column)

Edward S. Stevens
M. Jan Stout
Anthony J. Strait
Scott B. Strohm
J. Patrick Sullivan
Roberta J. Sullivan
Mark C. Tatum
Bruce R. Tepikian
Steven M. Thomas
David B. Thorne
J. Margaret Tretbar
Matthew E. Turner
M. Kevin Underhill
Mauricio A. Uribe
Samuel R. Watkins
B. Trent Webb
Susan J. Wharton
Paul A. Williams
L. Christopher Wittman
Susan Dumay Wolfe
David M. Woods
Jennifer L. Yevoli

STAFF ATTORNEYS

Dawn E. Akin
Carol J. Athey
Heather L. Baroni
Jonathan D. Beeker
Claudette Bienvenu
Valerie J. Blevins
Diane C. Brown
Randall W. Brown
Loretta Burns-Bucklew
Johnnye L. Dennis
(Not admitted in MO)
Tammy R. Dodson
Jack W. Green, Jr.
Susan D. Green
Jennifer Groover
Michelle E. Groth
Steven H. Hann
Kristen F. Heidenreich
Carrie A. Holcomb
Judith A. Hollinger
(Not admitted in MO)
Christophe A. Johnson
Constance M. Jordan
Jerami D. Kemnitz
(Not admitted in MO)
Melissa D. Krepps
Kerry J. Manning
Lindsay K. McFerrin
Heather Petznick
Sheryl Reynolds
M. Kristina Roberts
Erick J. Roeder
Rebecca A. Ryan
James A. Rynard, Jr.
Stephen M. Schutter
Kimberly Houser Seten

For full biographical listings, see the Martindale-Hubbell Law Directory

SHUGHART THOMSON & KILROY, A PROFESSIONAL CORPORATION (AV)

Twelve Wyandotte Plaza, 120 West 12th Street, 64105
Telephone: 816-421-3355
Email: Solutions@KC.STKLAW.COM *URL:* http://www.STKLAW.COM
Overland Park, Kansas Office: Suite 1100, 32 Corporate Woods, 9225 Indian Creek Parkway 66210.
Telephone: 913-451-3355.
Springfield, Missouri Office: Suite 1200, Hammons Tower, 901 St. Louis, 65806.
Telephone: 417-869-3353.
Denver, Colorado Office: 1050 17th Street, Suite 2350. 80265.
Telephone: 303-572-9300.
Fax: 303-572-7883.

Henry M. Shughart (1897-1962)
Harry P. Thomson (1917-1988)
William P. Eckels (1946-1987)
Ralph G. Trogdon (1910-1993)
R. Lawrence Ward
J. Harlan Stamper
George E. Leonard
William B. Prugh
Perry M. Toll
Thomas F. Fisher
Thomas G. Kokoruda
Jack L. Campbell
John M. Kilroy, Jr.
Timothy D. O'Leary
Roy Bash
Steven H. Goodman
Dennis D. Palmer
William E. Quirk
Jennifer Gille Bacon
W. Terrence Kilroy
William L. Yocum
Steven D. Ruse
Robert A. Henderson
John S. Conner
Robert E. Fitzgerald, Jr.
P. John Brady
Jacob W. Bayer, Jr.
Russell S. Jones, Jr.
Bradley J. Baumgart
G. Stephen Long
John D. Phillips, Jr.
(Not admitted in MO)
Robert T. Schendel
Norris E. Greer
James P. O'Hara
David L. McMurray
Daniel T. Murphy
Joel R. Mosher
Gregory M. Bentz
Philip W. Bledsoe
Anthony F. Rupp
Judith S. Heeter
John S. Black
Randal L. Schultz
Tommy W. Taylor
Gregory L. Musil
Roger P. Wright
Mark A. Olthoff
David B. Pursell
Lawrence A. Swain
Thomas J. O'Neal
John R. Cleary
Karen J. Halbrook
G. William Quatman
James C. Sullivan
Andrew L. McMullen
Michael B. Shteamer
Sheryl Feutz-Harter
Scott E. Vincent
David E. Shay
Greg J. Mermis
Christopher F. Pickering

Lynn Deal Cockle
Thomas W. Gray
Roland J. Cole
Richard E. Lenza
Kurt D. Tilton
Cyprienne Simchowitz
Leah M. Gagne
Ricardo E. Fontg
Christopher J. Molzen
Brian D. Malkmus
Linda J. Sheppard
Theodore M. Green
Christine M. Graham
Andrew M. DeMarea
Douglas S. Neville
Amy Jurevic Sokol
Heather A. Suve
Leslie A. Greathouse
Susan L. Stockdale
(Not admitted in MO)
Lance V. Baughman
Richard M. Paul III

(See Next Column)

SHUGHART THOMSON & KILROY A PROFESSIONAL CORPORATION, *Kansas City—Continued*

J. Calvin Downing, III
Daniel D. Owen
Julie B. Tincknell
Karen M. Gleason
Kelly Anne Kolars
Anne E. Popper
Jamee Maurer Klein
Jeffrey S. Brenner
Maureen A. Mannion
Donald E. Maxwell
Jennifer E. Alexander
Michael J. Mohlman
Tom Rottinghaus
Heather R. Hamilton
Anne E. Gusewelle
Eric F. Broucek (Not admitted in MO)
Cindy L. Neagle
Jonathan H. Gregor
G. Edgar James
Amy E. Patton (Not admitted in MO)
Kristin N. Costa
Jace Kentner
Autumn L. Fox (Not admitted in MO)

OF COUNSEL

John M. Kilroy
Donald L. Shughart
Thomas J. Leittem
Ben L. Guenther
Claudia J. York
William V. North
Robert R. Raymond

For full biographical listings, see the Martindale-Hubbell Law Directory

SONNENSCHEIN NATH & ROSENTHAL (AV)

Suite 1100, 4520 Main Street, 64111
Telephone: 816-932-4400
Facsimile: 816-531-7545
URL: http://www.sonnenschein.com
Chicago, Illinois Office: Suite 8000 Sears Tower, 233 South Wacker Drive.
Telephone: 312-876-8000.
Cable Address: "Sonberk".
Telex: 25-3526.
Facsimile: 312-876-7934.
New York, N.Y. Office: 1221 Avenue of the Americas, 24th Floor.
Telephone: 212-768-6700.
Facsimile: 212-391-1247.
Washington, D.C. Office: 1301 K Street, N.W., Suite 600 East Tower.
Telephone: 202-408-6400.
Fax: 202-408-6399.
San Francisco, California Office: 685 Market Street, 6th Floor.
Telephone: 415-882-5000.
Facsimile: 415-543-5472.
Los Angeles, California Office: 601 South Figueroa Street, Suite 1500.
Telephone: 213-623-9300.
Facsimile: 213-623-9924.
St. Louis, Missouri Office: One Metropolitan Square, Suite 3000.
Telephone: 314-241-1800.
Facsimile: 314-259-5959.
London, England Office: Sonnenscheins, Royex House, Aldermanbury Square, EC2V 7HR.
Telephone: 0171-600-2222.
Facsimile: 0171-600-2221.

G. Robert Fisher
Mark G. Flaherty
James A. Heeter
Jan P. Helder, Jr.
Mark P. Johnson
Michelle Stark Kaufman
J. Bradley Leitch
William G. Levi
John F. Marvin
Martin J. Moderson
James L. Moeller
Steven L. Rist
Jerome T. Wolf
Curtis E. Woods

OF COUNSEL

David D. Gatchell
Brian N. Kaufman
Wendy Byers Marvin

ASSOCIATES

Mitchell Edward Albert
S. Todd Barfield
Amy E. Bauman
Katharina E. Beal
Diane M. Bono
Stacey A. Campbell
Lisa C. Creighton
Timothy A. Davis
Gretchen M. Fleischut
Tamara L. Frantzen (Not admitted in MO)
Jennifer A. Hammond
Leonard W. Jurden
Shaun M. Klein
Lana M. Knedlik
Timothy J. Kuester
David S. Ladwig
James D. McMullen
Rowdy B. Meeks
Dean A. Newton
Alicia A. Prather
Amy E. Rush
Arjun S. Sanga
Tamara Seyler-James
Norman E. Siegel
Angelina McGehee Stayton (Not admitted in MO)

For full biographical listings, see the Martindale-Hubbell Law Directory

SWANSON MIDGLEY, LLC (AV)

Crown Center, 2420 Pershing Road, Suite 400, 64108
Telephone: 816-842-6100
Fax: 816-842-0013
Email: mail@swansonmidgley.com *URL:* http://www.swansonmidgley.com
Overland Park, Kansas Office: Commerce Plaza I, 7th Floor, 7300 W. 110th Street.
Telephone: 913-317-2717.
FAX: 913-317-1505.

(See Next Column)

Roy P. Swanson (1896-1985)
Kenneth E. Midgley (1903-1990)
Henry G. Eager (1923-1972)
Richard K. Andrews (1936-1993)

Robert R. Bartunek
Douglas M. Beck
Stanley M. Burnstein
Henry R. Cox
Wm. Bruce Day
Edward M. Dolson
James A. Durbin
George H. Gangwere, Jr.
W. Ann Hansbrough
Daniel V. Hiatt
Rodney V. Hipp
Craig T. Kenworthy
John J. Kitchin
Don R. Lolli
James H. McLarney
G. David Porter
Lindsay L. Wood
Charles F. Zarter

Rebecca S. Bihr
Richard E. Gier
Valerie Rose Yaffe Lawrence

OF COUNSEL

Ronald E. Sandhaus

Counsel for: National Collegiate Athletic Assoc.; Pizza Hut; Veterans of Foreign Wars of the U.S.; Danka Business Systems; Physicians Reference Laboratory; National Compressed Steel; Equitable Life Assurance; Mr. Dell Foods, Inc.; Healthcare Medical Solutions, Inc.; Prudential Insurance Co. of America.

For full biographical listings, see the Martindale-Hubbell Law Directory

WYRSCH HOBBS MIRAKIAN & LEE, P.C. (AV)

1300 Mercantile Tower 1101 Walnut, 64106-2122
Telephone: 816-221-0080
Fax: 816-221-3280
Email: whml@sprintmail.com

James R. Wyrsch
Stephen G. Mirakian
Ronald D. Lee
James R. Hobbs
Keith E. Drill
Jacqueline A. Cook
Charles M. Rogers
Marilyn B. Keller
Cheryl A. Pilate
W. Brian Gaddy

OF COUNSEL

James W. Fletcher

David Andrew Kelly

LEGAL SUPPORT PERSONNEL

Darlene Wyrsch (Paralegal)
Dru A. Colhour (Paralegal)
Katherine Vetsch (Paralegal)
Leslie R. Elkins (Paralegal)
William J. Baltrusaitis, II (Investigator)

For full biographical listings, see the Martindale-Hubbell Law Directory

*KENNETT,** Dunklin Co.

DALTON, TREASURE & MOWRER (AV)

203 College Street, P.O. Box 529, 63857
Telephone: 573-888-4631
Facsimile: 573-888-2127
Email: dtmlaw@jrwent.com

MEMBERS OF FIRM

John Hall Dalton
Harold B. Treasure
J. Michael Mowrer
John Hall Dalton, Jr.
Phillip M. Britt

General Counsel: Kennett National Bank; Riggs Wholesale Co. John Prohnce Co.
Representative Clients: The Equitable Life Assurance Society; Aetna Insurance Group; John Hancock Mutual Life Insurance Co.; The Travelers; International Association of Aviation Underwriters; Shelter Insurance Cos.; Liberty Mutual Insurance Cos.; Hanover Insurance Co.

For full biographical listings, see the Martindale-Hubbell Law Directory

*KIRKSVILLE,** Adair Co.

OSWALD, COTTEY & TEMPLETON, A PROFESSIONAL CORPORATION (AV)

Suite A, 210 North Elson, P.O. Box K, 63501
Telephone: 660-665-5628
Fax: 660-665-6035
Email: oswaldcotteytempleton@yahoo.com

Louis F. Cottey (1931-1999)
Thomas R. Oswald
Scott L. Templeton

Brenda Wall-Swedberg
Theresa L. Kenney
Susan R. Barrow
David Briggs

For full biographical listings, see the Martindale-Hubbell Law Directory

*LIBERTY,** Clay Co.

HALE, KINCAID & SKINNER, P.C. (AV)

17 West Kansas Street, 64068
Telephone: 816-781-4757
1-800-456-5722
Fax: 816-781-1953
Email: www.halelaw@aol.com

Martin E. Lawson (1867-1957)
Francis G. Hale (1889-1977)
Robert E. Coleberd (1896-1971)
William B. Waters (1916-1985)
Thomas E. Allen (1938-1991)
Arthur R. Kincaid (Retired)
Leary G. Skinner

Joe Van Ackeren

For full biographical listings, see the Martindale-Hubbell Law Directory

WITHERS, BRANT, IGOE & MULLENNIX, P.C. (AV)

Two South Main Street, 64068
Telephone: 816-781-4788
Fax: 816-792-2807
Email: wbimlaw@aol.com

Conn Withers (1907-1993)
Jerome E. Brant
Vincent F. Igoe, Jr.
Ronald C. Mullennix
Steven D. Wolcott
John M. Crossett
Thomas C. Capps
Alison K. Blessing
Mark E. Kelly

Michael S. Shipley
Susan E. Long
Leigh A. Goucher
Joseph F. O'Hara
Duane A. Martin

OF COUNSEL

Nancy A. Norton

For full biographical listings, see the Martindale-Hubbell Law Directory

*NEVADA,** Vernon Co.

EWING & HOBEROCK (AV)

123 North Main Street, P.O. Box 287, 64772-0287
Telephone: 417-667-3318; 1-800-572-1271
Fax: 417-667-9503
Email: ewinglaw@ipa.net

MEMBERS OF FIRM

Lynn M. Ewing, Jr.
Christopher Hoberock
Lynn M. Ewing, III

General Counsel for: Sac Osage Electric Cooperative; Joseph L. Phol, Inc.; Cottey College; Miltenberger Oil Co., Inc.; Jump Oil & Propane.
Attorneys for: Community Bank of El Dorado Springs; Missouri League of Savings Institution; Mercantile Mortgage Bank; Farm Bureau Insurance Co.; Garton Equipment Co.

For full biographical listings, see the Martindale-Hubbell Law Directory

RUSSELL, BROWN, BICKEL & BRECKENRIDGE (AV)

108 West Walnut Street, P.O. Drawer J, 64772
Telephone: 417-667-5076
Fax: 417-667-3013

MEMBERS OF FIRM

Donald B. Russell
Keith Brown
James R. Bickel
Bryan C. Breckenridge

ASSOCIATE

Anita Donaldson Conboy

For full biographical listings, see the Martindale-Hubbell Law Directory

*ROLLA,** Phelps Co.

THOMAS, BIRDSONG & BECKER, P.C. (AV)

1100 North Elm Street, 65401
Telephone: 573-364-4097;
573-774-5252 (direct from Waynesville)
Telecopier: 573-364-0664
Mailing Address: P.O. Box 248, Rolla, Missouri, 65402-0248
Email: rollalaw@fidnet.com

Dewey A. Routh (1898-1981)
W. H. (Tom) Thomas, Jr.
Dan L. Birdsong
Howard Benson Becker

David L. Mills

Representative Clients: Phelps County Regional Medical Center; Mercantile Bank; Ozark Equipment Co.; Sellers-Sexton Motors.
Representative Insurance Clients: U.S.F. & G.; Medical Protective Co.; Safeco Insurance Co.; Aetna Life & Casualty.
References: Mercantile Bank; Phelps County Bank.

For full biographical listings, see the Martindale-Hubbell Law Directory

*ST. JOSEPH,** Buchanan Co.

UTZ, LITVAK, SUMMERS, POWERS & MANRING (AV)

Suite 500 Frederick Towers, 2400 Frederick Avenue, 64506
Telephone: 816-233-0257
Fax: 816-233-9411

W. H. Utz, Jr. (1907-1995).

MEMBERS OF FIRM

Thomas R. Summers
G. Brent Powers
John Manring
David R. Schmitt

OF COUNSEL

Milton Litvak

Representative Clients: Travelers Insurance Co.; KQTV; Boehringer-Ingelheim Animal Health, Inc.; Citizens Bank of Oregon, Mo.; Mercantile Bank of St. Joseph; Heaton-Bowman-Smith Funeral Home, Inc.; Prime Tanning Corp.; Farmers Bank of Northern Missouri; Jari, Inc.; Clark & Thomas Construction, Inc.

For full biographical listings, see the Martindale-Hubbell Law Directory

WATKINS, BOULWARE, LUCAS, MINER, MURPHY & TAYLOR (AV)

3101 Frederick Avenue, 64506
Telephone: 816-364-2117
Telecopier: 816-279-3977
URL: http://www.wblmmt.com
Kansas City, Missouri Office: Suite 600, North Pointe Tower, 10220 N. Executive Hills Blvd, 64153.
Telephone: 816-880-0600.
Telecopier: 816-880-0601.

MEMBERS OF FIRM

Thomas D. Watkins
R. Dan Boulware
Gregory C. Lucas
Robert B. Miner
R. Edward Murphy
Michael L. Taylor
Joseph W. Elliott
Mark R. Woodbury
Carol C. Barnett
Craig D. Ritchie
Kenneth E. Siemens

ASSOCIATES

William W. Bird
Erin A. Webber
Todd H. Bartels

OF COUNSEL

Grace S. Day

For full biographical listings, see the Martindale-Hubbell Law Directory

ST. LOUIS, (Independent City)

ANDERSON & GILBERT (AV)

200 S. Hanley, Suite 710, 63105
Telephone: 314-721-2777
Telecopier: 314-721-3515
Email: aglawfirm@brick.net

MEMBERS OF FIRM

Roscoe Anderson (1884-1951)
William R. Gilbert (1886-1963)
Jesse A. Wolfort (1882-1967)
Norman Bierman (1907-1987)
Norris H. Allen (1904-1991)
Robert G. Burridge
Francis X. Duda
Stuart M. Haw
Fortis M. Lawder
Joel D. Monson
D. Paul Myre

Representative Clients: Foremost Insurance Co.; Medical Defense Associates; Schneider Nat'l, Inc.; Intermed Insurance Co.; INS Insurance, Inc.; American Specialty Claims Service; OUM Group; Fireman's Fund Insurance Co.; Wausaw Insurance Cos.; ITT Hartford.

For full biographical listings, see the Martindale-Hubbell Law Directory

ARMSTRONG TEASDALE LLP (AV)

A Partnership including Professional Corporations
One Metropolitan Square, 63102-2740
Telephone: 314-621-5070
Facsimile: 314-621-5065
Twx: 910 761-2246
Cable: ATKV LAW
Email: armstrongteasdale@armstrongteasdale.com *URL:* http://www.armstrongteasdale.com
Kansas City, Missouri Office: 2345 Grand Boulevard, Suite 2000, 64108.
Telephone: 816-221-3420.
Facsimile: 816-221-0786.
Jefferson City, Missouri Office: 3405 W. Truman Blvd., Suite 210, 65109.
Telephone: 573-636-8394.
Washington, D.C. Office: 1747 Pennsylvania Avenue, N.W., Suite 300, 20006.
Telephone: 202-347-0259.
Belleville, Illinois Office: 23 South First Street, 62220.
Telephone: 618-397-4411.
Olathe, Kansas Office: 100 East Park, 66061.
Telephone: 913-345-0706.

(See Next Column)

ARMSTRONG TEASDALE LLP, *St. Louis—Continued*

Shanghai, China Office: A-T International Consultants, LLC, Suite 310, No. 12 Zhongshan Road (E1), Shanghai 200002 P.R.C.
Telephone: 86-21-6326-7001.
Facsimile: 86-21-6326-0626.

MEMBERS OF FIRM

John R. Barsanti, Jr., (P.C.)	Paul E. Kovacs (P.C.)
Karen A. Baudendistel	Peter J. Krane
John S. Beulick	Fred Leicht, Jr., (P.C.)
Thomas H. Bottini	David G. Loseman
Ann E. Buckley	Philip G. Louis, Jr.
Susan Bradley Buse	Andrew B. Mayfield
Michael A. Chivell	Timothy R. McFadden
A. J. Chivetta	James E. Mello
Peter L. Clark (P.C.)	Vance D. Miller
Joan Z. Cohen	Edwin L. Noel (P.C.)
Clark H. Cole	Daniel K. O'Toole
O. Kirby Colson, III	Thomas L. Orris
William M. Corrigan, Jr.	David G. Ott (P.C.)
Steven N. Cousins	John H. Quinn, III, (P.C.)
John F. Cowling	Keith A. Rabenberg
Thomas Cummings (P.C.)	Mark J. Rubinelli
Glenn E. Davis (Assistant Chair, Litigation Department. Chair, Antitrust Trade Regulation and Distribution Law Practice Group)	Steven P. Sanders
	John Talbot Sant, Jr. (P.C)
	Richard B. Scherrer (P.C.) (Managing Partner)
	Kathleen S. Schoene
Richard W. Engel, Jr.	Robert G. Schwendinger
Diane E. Felix	Larry M. Sewell (P.C.)
Raymond R. Fournie	Mark D. Sophir (P.C.)
Byron E. Francis (P.C.)	James L. Stockberger
Deirdre C. Gallagher	John L. Sullivan
John L. Gillis, Jr., (P.C.)	Jay A. Summerville
Daniel J. Godar	Kenneth F. Teasdale (P.C.)
David L. Going	Wilbur L. Tomlinson (P.C.)
Robert C. Graham, III	Therese Rolufs Trelz
Frank N. Gundlach (P.C.)	Timothy J. Tryniecki
Theodore H. Hellmuth (P.C.)	Paul N. Venker
Andrew T. Hoyne	James J. Virtel
Scott Hunt	Joseph S. von Kaenel (P.C.)
Jonathan W. Igoe	George M. von Stamwitz
John J. Inkley, Jr.	Richard L. Waters
Robert Lewis Jackson (P.C.)	Thomas B. Weaver (P.C.)
Stephen C. Jones	David W. Welch
Robert A. Kaiser	Theodore J. Williams, Jr. (Chair, Transportation Department)
Mary C. Kickham	

Lisa M. Wood

ASSOCIATES

Jennifer Lee Arendes	Yiqiang Li (Not admitted in MO)
Bruce T. Atkins	
Scott A. Bailey	Connie McFarland-Butler
Kristi L. Boardman	Jeffery T. McPherson
Mark A. Boatman	Daniel C. Nelson
David W. Braswell	John J. O'Brien
Alan L. Cassel	Elizabeth D. Odell
Jennifer E. Cook	M. Kathleen Padfield
C. Wayne Davis	Jill M. Palmquist
Milton M. Frazier	Mary Carol Parker
Timothy J. Gearin	Steven E. Pozaric
Pamela L. Giss	Countess W. Price
Stephen C. Hartnett	Patrick W. Rasche
Joseph F. Hipskind, Jr.	Robert B. Reeser, III
Marshall R. Hoekel	Heather L. Reinsch
Virginia H. Howell	Cynthia A. Sciuto
Norella V. Huggins	Amit B. Shah
Michael B. Hunter	Mark L. Stoneman
Michael S. Jefferies	David W. Terry
David B. Jennings	Michael Tersillo
Patrick J. Kenny	Benjamin A. Trujillo
Anita M. Kidd	Ann E. Verrett
Christine M. Kocot	Steven S. Wasserman
Lisa A. Larkin	Michael A. Wazlawek

OF COUNSEL

Edwin S. Baldwin (P.C.)	John P. Emde (P.C.)
Bourne Bean (P.C.)	Carl R. Gaertner
Donald U. Beimdiek (P.C.)	August L. Griesedieck
Ralph J. Capio (Not admitted in MO)	Frederick O. Hanser (P.C.)
	Frederick H. Mayer (P.C.)
John J. Cole (P.C.)	Robert F. Schlafly
Charles E. Dapron	Kevin F. Warren (Not admitted in MO)
Lilian Castellani De Fernandez	

Bruce E. Woodruff (P.C.)

PATENT AGENT

Tara A. Nealey

Representative Clients: AmerenUE; Anheuser-Busch, Inc.; BJC Health System; General Electric Company; Procter & Gamble, Inc.; Southwestern Bell Telephone; St. Louis Cardinals, L.P.; Sprint Communications Company, L.P.; United Parcel Service of America, Inc.

For full biographical listings, see the Martindale-Hubbell Law Directory

BRYAN CAVE LLP (AV)

A Partnership including a Professional Corporation
One Metropolitan Square, 211 N. Broadway, 63102-2750
Telephone: (314) 259-2000
Facsimile: (314) 259-2020
For attorney e-mails use: First initials of first and middle names, last name, firm name, e.g., rmsmith@bryancave.com
URL: http://www.bryancave.com
Washington, D.C. Office: 700 Thirteenth Street, N.W., 20005-3960.
Telephone: (202) 508-6000.
Facsimile: (202) 508-6200.
New York, N.Y. Office: 245 Park Avenue, 10167-0034.
Telephone: (212) 692-1800.
Facsimile: (212) 692-1900.
Kansas City, Missouri Office: 3500 One Kansas City Place, 1200 Main Street, 64105-2100.
Telephone: (816) 374-3200.
Facsimile: (816) 374-3300.
Overland Park, Kansas Office: 7500 College Boulevard, Suite 1100, 66210-4035.
Telephone: (913) 338-7700.
Facsimile: (913) 338-7777.
Jefferson City, Missouri Office: 221 Bolivar Street, 65102-1670.
Telephone: (573) 556-6620.
Facsimile: (573) 556-6630.
Phoenix, Arizona Office: Two North Central Avenue, Suite 2200, 85004-4406.
Telephone: (602) 364-7000.
Facsimile: (602) 364-7070.
Santa Monica, California Office: 120 Broadway, Suite 300, 90401-2305.
Telephone: (310) 576-2100.
Facsimile: (310) 576-2200.
Irvine, California Office: 18881 Von Karman, Suite 1500, 92612-1582.
Telephone: (949) 223-7000.
Facsimile: (949) 223-7100.
London, England Office: 29 Queen Anne's Gate, SW1H 9BU.
Telephone: 171-896-1900.
Facsimile: 171-896-1919.
Riyadh 11465 Saudi Arabia Office: In Cooperation with Kadasah Law Firm, P.O. Box 20883.
Telephone: 966-1-474-0888.
Facsimile: 966-1-476-2881.
Kuwait City, Kuwait Office: Mashora Advocates & Legal Consultants, Sheraton Towers, Second Floor, P.O. Box 5902 Safat, 13060.
Telephone: 965-240-4470.
Facsimile: 965-242-4047.
Dubai, U.A.E. Office: Al-Mehairi Legal Consultants - Bryan Cave LLP, Holiday Centre, Suite 1103, P.O. Box 13677.
Telephone: 971-4-314-123.
Facsimile: 971-4-318-287.
Abu Dhabi, U.A.E. Office: Al-Mehairi Legal Consultants - Bryan Cave LLP, Dhabi Tower, Suite 304, P.O. Box 47645.
Telephone: 971-2-260-335.
Facsimile: 971-2-260-332.
Hong Kong Office: Suite 2106, Lippo Centre, 89 Queensway.
Telephone: 852-2522-2821.
Facsimile: 852-2522-3830.
Shanghai 200040, People's Republic of China Office: Suite 448, Shanghai Centre, 1376 Nanjing Road West.
Telephone: 8621-6279-8166.
Facsimile: 8621-6279-8165.

PARTNERS

Kevin M. Abel	Mark H. Goran
John I. Alber	Dale A. Guariglia
J. Thomas Archer	Peter W. Herzog III
Leo J. Asaro	Mark B. Hillis
Hollye Stolz Atwood	John W. Hoffman IV
Ketrina G. Bakewell	Zachary A. Hummel
Frederick W. Bartelsmeyer	Jerry M. Hunter
Brian Berglund	Rebecca R. Jackson
Harold G. Blatt	E. Perry Johnson
Ellen E. Bonacorsi	James A. Kearns, III
Louis F. Bonacorsi	Juan D. Keller
John G. Boyle	Douglas W. King
Lawrence Brody	J. Mark Klamer
James G. Buell	Kenneth A. Kleban
Michael P. Burke	Steven D. Korenblat
Harold R. Burroughs	Mark B. Leadlove
Gerard T. Carmody	Ned O. Lemkemeier
Gary T. Carr	Eric V. Lemon
Elizabeth C. Carver	Don G. Lents
John Michael Clear	John V. Lonsberg
Joseph A. Colagiovanni, Jr.	Kenneth J. Mallin
Jonathan F. Dalton	James P. Mannion, Jr.
John C. Danforth	Lisa Demet Martin
Steven L. Davis	Linda M. Martínez
Mark S. Deiermann	David J. Massa
Alan J. Dixon	Denis P. McCusker
Dennis C. Donnelly	Michael B. McKinnis
Robert T. Ebert, Jr.	George V. Meisel
James H. Erlinger III	Walter L. Metcalfe, Jr.
Karen W. Fries	John Strauch Meyer, Jr.
Edwin S. Fryer	Joseph F. Mueller

(See Next Column)

BRYAN CAVE LLP—*Continued*

PARTNERS (Continued)

George E. Murray
Charles A. Newman
James L. Nouss, Jr.
Dennis E. O'Connell
Bruce C. Oetter
Daniel R. O'Neill
Terrence J. O'Toole
Lloyd A. Palans
Steven J. Poplawski
Edward W. Rataj
Mary Gassmann Reichert
Douglas D. Ritterskamp
David A. Roodman
Jeffrey S. Russell
Llewellyn Sale III
John D. Schaperkotter
Frederick W. Scherrer
Thomas A. Schweich
William F. Seabaugh
Kathleen R. Sherby
David S. Slavkin
Carl J. Spector
Peter D. Van Cleve
William M. Van Cleve
Lisa A. Van Fleet
Nick H. Varsam
Thomas E. Wack
Franklin F. Wallis
Thomas C. Walsh
R. Randall Wang
Paul P. Weil
Charles A. Weiss
Gregory D. Willard
Kathy A. Wisniewski
Frank P. Wolff, Jr.
James J. Wotruba
Philip B. Wright

SENIOR COUNSEL

John J. Goebel
Veryl L. Riddle

OF COUNSEL

John P. Denneen
Timothy A. Garnett
Charles Hansen
George S. Hecker
I. Jack Lerner
Jerome M. Rubenstein
John T. Sant
Robert L. Sweney

COUNSEL

Lucinda A. Althauser
Janice C. Forsyth
Helen Paulin Gab
Troy W. Gordon
Robert G. Lancaster
Hal B. Morgan
Lloyd R. Schneider
Stephen R. Snodgrass
Cheryl D.S. Walker

ASSOCIATES

James Robert Arnold, Jr.
Jane E. Arnold
Jennifer M. Arthur
Barbara S. Barrett
Steven M. Baumer
James F. Bennett
Rebecca L. (Berkeley) Brown
Jeffrey S. Buschmann
Jane Byers
Eric C. Chung
William L. Cole
Daniel A. Crowe
Bradford J. Cytron
Stephen B. Daiker
Carol J. Dick
Karen A. Dill
Deryl L. Earsom
Robert J. Endicott
Robert F. Epperson, Jr.
Christopher E. Erker
Kelley Field Farrell
David M. Fedder
James H. Ferrick, III
Patricia M. Ferrick
Nathan Lewis Garroway
Veronica A. Gioia
Victoria I. Goldson
Geoffrey F. Green
Kathleen L. Hammock
John Robert Haug
Christopher J. Hayes
Jarrod Henshaw
Polly D. Heseman
Gregory A. Hewett
Diane M. Hoelzl
Mark G. Holden
Joy L. Holley
Lisa Anne Houdyshell
Charles B. Jellinek
Xueqing (Linda) Ji
(Not admitted in MO)
Julie R. Jones
Jay Lee Kanzler, Jr.
Carol M. Keith
Alice Ann Kelly
Barbara Krause
Dana A. Lasley
Mark Stephen LaVigne
John W. Lemkemeier
Gregg M. Lemley
Dan M. Lesicko
James R. Levey
Stacie L. Liening
Donald A. Lohman
Kathryn Elliott Love
Bruce E. Lowry, Je.
Paula Finlay Luepke
Robert G. Malkin
Jeanne M. Martin
(Not admitted in MO)
Jason Edward Maschmann
Abby M. Mendillo
Jeanne M. Miller
Melissa L. Mitchell
Timothy C. Mooney
Michele R. Namm
Rebecca A.D. Nelson
Daniel C. Nester
Michael I. Oberlander
Carolyn M. Ohlsen
Daniel M. O'Keefe
Jennifer Auer O'Keefe
Megan Phillips
Kathleen C. Reardon
John W. Rogers
B. Derek Rose
Shannon J. Ryser
Lawrence J. Samuelson
Erika Z. Schenk
Diana M. Schmidt
David P. Scott
Dean J. Scoular
Jeremy D. Shook
Michael J. Silver
Sarah Roe Sise
Amy J. Thompson
David Malcolm Unseth
Thomas D. Veltz
Bart D. Wall
Vivian H. Waters
John M. Welge
William F. Werries
Daniel Chiel White
Jennifer L. Winn
Roxana Wizorek
Jennifer L. Woods

Representative Clients: Financial & Insurance: Commerce Banks (St. Louis area); Edward D. Jones & Co.; Stifel, Nicolaus & Company, Incorporated; Industrial: Anheuser-Busch Companies, Inc.; Brown Group, Inc.; Emerson Electric Co.; McDonnell Douglas Corp. Others: The Pulitzer Publishing Co. (St. Louis Post-Dispatch).

For full biographical listings, see the Martindale-Hubbell Law Directory

GALLOP, JOHNSON & NEUMAN, L.C. (AV)

Interco Corporate Tower, 101 S. Hanley, 63105
Telephone: 314-862-1200
Facsimile: 314-862-1219
Email: www.gjn.com *URL:* http://www.gjn.com

Donald P. Gallop
Sanford S. Neuman
Stuart Symington, Jr.
Marvin O. Young
William E. Buckley
Stephen W. Skrainka
Edwin D. Akers, Jr.
Michael N. Newmark
Harold S. Goodman
Robert H. Wexler
David W. Harlan
Lawrence P. Kaplan
Richard A. Stockenberg
Thomas G. Lewin
John P. Walsh
Mark W. Weisman
Ronald L. Pallmann
Patrick M. Sanders
Thomas H. Mug
Edward F. Reilly
Randy S. Gerber
Bradley G. Kafka
James R. Strong
Ronald L. Hack
Peter D. Kerth
Cawood K. Bebout
Barbara J. Hartung
Linda C. Shubow
Richard A. Yawitz
Donald G. Mueller, Jr.
Craig J. Hoefer
Thomas P. Hohenstein
John T. "Jack" Walsh
Douglas J. Bates
Thomas J. Campbell
Nancy J. Dilley
Rosalie Wacker O'Brien
Mary S. McMath
Alan S. Breckenridge
Rebecca Epstein Walsh

Cynthia C. Bottini
Bruce A. Tannahill
Abigail T. Kelman
Melanie R. King
John D. Harkins
Linda K. Baxter
George A. Kiser
David J. Harris
Douglas J. Stanley
Mary M. Bannister
Michael G. Re
Michelle M. Gaffney
E.W. Gentry Sayad
Joshua Avigad
Nicole M. Chaput
Robert L. Newmark
Ruben K. Chuquimia
Barbara M. Dite
Sandra L. Freeman
Christopher W. Byron
Joy M. Harris
Nicole L. Morris
Daniel J. Weber
Matthew D. Wohl
Jon A. Bierman
Andrew L. Krueger
Stephen C. Jones

OF COUNSEL

Charles M. Tureen
Barbara L. Behrens
Kay R. Sherman
Suzanne L. Zatlin

Representative Clients: Bass Pro, L.P.; Blue Cross and Blue Shield of Missouri; Crane Co.; Data Research Associates, Inc.; Dial Corporation; Deutsche Financial Services Corp.; Falcon Products, Inc.; Jackson Products, Inc.; KV Pharmaceutical Co.; Magna Group, Inc. and subsidiary banks.

For full biographical listings, see the Martindale-Hubbell Law Directory

LEWIS, RICE & FINGERSH (AV)

A Limited Liability Company
500 North Broadway, Suite 2000, 63102-2147
Telephone: 314-444-7600
Telecopier: 314-241-6056
URL: http://www.lrf.com
Belleville, Illinois Office: 325 South High Street.
Telephone: 618-234-8636.
Leawood, Kansas Office: Suite 375, 8900 State Line Road.
Telephone: 913-381-8898.
Creve Coeur, Missouri Office: 700 Office Parkway, Suite 15.
Telephone: 314-569-2262.
Kansas City, Missouri Office: 1010 Walnut, Suite 500.
Telephone: 816-421-2500.
Washington, Missouri Office: 216 West Main, P.O. Box 1040.
Telephone: 636-239-7747.

RESIDENT MEMBERS

Fred M. Reichman
Eugene J. Gabianelli
Henry F. Luepke, Jr.
Robert B. Hoemeke
John Torrey Berger, Jr.
Henry H. Stern, Jr.
James W. Herron
John K. Pruellage
Bernard N. Frank
Colleen H. Nemanick
Joseph H. Weyhrich
Lawrence H. Weltman
Michael P. Casey
Allen S. Boston
Barry A. Short
Michael R. Turley
Jacob W. Reby
Michael D. Mulligan
Mark T. Keaney
Andrew Rothschild
John J. Gazzoli, Jr.
Richard A. Ahrens
Kimball R. McMullin
Larry L. Deskins
John J. Moellering
John M. Hessel
Robert N. Kahn
John D. Valentine
Thomas C. Erb
Richard A. Wunderlich
Douglas D. Hommert
Steven H. Akre
James V. O'Brien
Marian V. Mehan
Joseph J. Trad
John J. Riffle
Joseph E. Martineau
Tracy Mathis
Frank B. Janoski
Curtis C. Calloway
Lori W. Jones
Rosemarie M. Karcher
Richard B. Walsh, Jr.
Jeffrey B. Hunt
David L. Coffman
John E. Hall

(See Next Column)

LEWIS, RICE & FINGERSH, *St. Louis—Continued*

RESIDENT MEMBERS (Continued)

Duane L. Coleman
Brian D. Bouquet
Steven C. Drapekin
Daniel E. Claggett
Thomas L. Caradonna
Robert J. Golterman
Catherine R. Phillips
Robert J. Will
Ronald A. Norwood
Beverly A. Marcin
Lawrence E. Parres
Kimberly N. Springer
Tom W. Zook
Timothy E. Kastner
Leonard J. Essig
Theodore H. Lucas
Jon A. Santangelo
Lynn Ann Hinrichs
Gary M. Smith
Kristine K. Kraft
Richard J. Behr
Benjamin A. Lipman
Jeana D. McFerron
Robert S. Moore
Neal F. Perryman

OF COUNSEL

Charles C. Allen, Jr.
Robert Smith Allen
Speros B. Boudoures
John M. Drescher, Jr.
Charles F. Teschner, Jr.

RETIRED

Edmonstone F. Thompson
Daniel J. Sullivan
F. Wm. McCalpin
Walter J. Taylor

ASSOCIATES

Keith J. Grady
Thomas P. Berra, Jr.
Ann M. Salamon
Anna A. Shabsin
John J. Hall
Scott A. Heitland
Mark C. Winings
Winthrop B. Reed, III
Paul J. Schulte
Paul J. Berra III
Thad N. Leach
Ari M. Bai
Gregory R. Beekman
David W. Brown
Shevon L. Harris
Mark N. Light
C. David Goerisch
Keith C. Ott
Jeffrey G. Morrison
John C. Bodnar
Erin E. Fuller
Jaime R. Mendez
Christopher C. Swenson
Kristie Ann Rooney
David B. Helms
Brian C. Humphrey
Maureen C. Beekley
Jeffery N. Brooks
Marisa Byram
Julie Stenger
Jennifer R. Lynn
Jennifer A. Coke
Nathan C. Collins
Erin M. Driscoll
Dirk R. Gardner
Christopher M. Hinsley
Kristen Howell
Susan Elizabeth Jones
James P. Martin
Timothy A. Nathan (Not admitted in MO)
Douglas M. Nieder
Alexander P. Paul
Stephanie L. Tueth
Martin M. Clay, Jr.

For full biographical listings, see the Martindale-Hubbell Law Directory

LOWENHAUPT & CHASNOFF, L.L.C. (AV)

10 South Broadway, Suite 600, 63102-1733
Telephone: 314-241-5950
Facsimile: 314-436-2667

Abraham Lowenhaupt (1878-1958)
Jacob Chasnoff (1883-1977)
Henry C. Lowenhaupt (1913-1990)
Bernard Mellitz (1912-1993)
Jules Chasnoff
Hugh R. Law
Charles A. Lowenhaupt
Douglas M. Baron
Peter A. Smith

ASSOCIATES

Harvard W. Muhm
Daniel J Skomal
Jeffrey K. Elnicki
Douglas R. Thornburg (Not admitted in MO)
Jeffrey H. Kass

OF COUNSEL

Jack M. Chasnoff

RETIRED

Owen T. Armstrong

For full biographical listings, see the Martindale-Hubbell Law Directory

SONNENSCHEIN NATH & ROSENTHAL (AV)

One Metropolitan Square, Suite 3000, 63102
Telephone: 314-241-1800
Telecopier: 314-259-5959
URL: http://www.sonnenschein.com
Chicago, Illinois Office: Suite 8000 Sears Tower, 233 South Wacker Drive.
Telephone: 312-876-8000.
Cable Address: "Sonberk".
Telex: 25-3526.
Facsimile: 312-876-7934.
New York, N.Y. Office: 1221 Avenue of the Americas, 24th Floor.
Telephone: 212-768-6700.
Facsimile: 212-391-1247.
Washington, D.C. Office: 1301 K Street, N.W., Suite 600, East Tower.
Telephone: 202-408-6400.
Facsimile: 202-408-6399.
Los Angeles, California Office: Suite 1500, 601 South Figueroa Street.
Telephone: 213-623-9300.
Facsimile: 213-623-9924.

(See Next Column)

San Francisco, California Office: 685 Market Street, 6th Floor.
Telephone: 415-882-5000.
Facsimile: 415-543-5472.
Kansas City, Missouri Office: Suite 1100, 4520 Main Street, 64111.
Telephone: 816-932-4400.
Facsimile: 816-531-7545.
London, England Office: Sonnenscheins, Royex House, Aldermanbury Square.
Telephone: 0171-600-2222.
Facsimile: 0171-600-2221.

Alan B. Bornstein
Edward J. Buchholz
Lori L. Bockman
Frank H. Hackmann
Roger K. Heidenreich
Carl B. Hillemann III
Stacey L. Murphy
Charles A. Redd
Kurtis B. Reeg
Stephen H. Rovak
Jane Snoddy Smith
Leslie Chambers Strohm
Thomas K. Vandiver
James G. Wiehl
Daniel R. Wofsey

ASSOCIATES

Christine Comer Alfaro
Kimberly L. Cofman
Gary A. Francesconi
K. Scott Gronowski
Kevin D. Gunn
Robert J. Jakubeck
Katherine Jough
Steven R. Karl
Tamara A. Kenny
Nancy S. McCahan
Robert M. Motes
Stephen J. O'Brien
Gregory M. Otto
Timothy J. Prosser
Teresa Dale Pupillo
David T. Rankin
Edward H. Rice
Sarah W. Rubenstein
Brian R. St. James
David P. Stoeberl

For full biographical listings, see the Martindale-Hubbell Law Directory

THOMPSON COBURN LLP (AV)

One Mercantile Center, 63101
Telephone: 314-552-6000
Telecopier: 314-552-7000
Email: info@thompsoncoburn.com *URL:* http://www.thompsoncoburn.com
Belleville, Illinois Office: 525 West Main Street.
Telephone: 618-277-4700.
Telecopier: 618-236-3434.
Washington, D.C. Office: 700 14th Street, N.W., Suite 900.
Telephone: 202-508-1000.
Telecopier: 202-508-1010.
Billings, Montana Office: Norwest Center, 175 North 27th Street, Suite 903, 59101.
Telephone: 406-896-4100.
Fax: 406-896-4199.

MEMBERS OF FIRM

William G. Guerri
Joseph P. Logan
Charles B. Baron
David F. Ulmer
Thomas F. Eagleton
Lewis R. Mills
William J. McNamara
Rollin J. Moerschel
W. Stanley Walch
Millard Backerman
Michael D. O'Keefe
Fred E. Arnold
Gary S. Heifetz
David Wells
James F. Gunn
Kenneth R. Heineman
Gerard K. Sandweg, Jr.
J. William Newbold
John R. Musgrave
Richard E. Jaudes
David A. Lander
David F. Yates
Thomas R. Corbett
Guy A. Schmitz
Joan M. Newman
Lawrence P. Katzenstein
Michael F. Lause
Thomas E. Douglass
Gordon L. Ankney
Rhonda C. Thomas
Donald B. Dorwart
Raymond L. Massey
Gary Mayes
Joseph G. Nassif
Paul G. Griesemer
James L. Fogle
Peter A. Fanchi
Richard S. Cornfeld
Allan McD. Goodloe, Jr.
Michael Lazaroff
Robert H. Brownlee
James W. Erwin
Thomas R. Jayne
Richard A. Mueller
Dale R. Joerling
Stephen B. Higgins
Gregory E. Upchurch
Mary M. Bonacorsi
Allen D. Allred
William J. Falk
Dan H. Ball
Kenton E. Knickmeyer
William R. Bay
Michael B. Minton
Timothy F. Noelker
Stephen D. Smith
Bruce D. Ryder
Thomas J. Minogue
Paul M. Brown
Mark Sableman
Henry A. Bettendorf
Stephen E. Cupples
Charles M. Poplstein
Robert M. LaRose
Daniel T. Engle
Richard J. Pautler
Eric Kendall Banks
Harry W. Wellford, Jr.
Bradley A. Winters
Stephen G. Jeffery
Jordan B. Cherrick
Jan Robey Alonzo
Edwin G. Harvey
Mark A. Bayles
Michael J. Morris
Liza S. Forshaw
Thomas A. Litz
Edward A. Cohen
John B. Kinsella
Charles R. Saulsberry
Paul M. Macon
Richard M. Greenhall
Dean L. Franklin
Mark L. Kaltenrieder
Nicholas J. Lamb
Cathryn A. Conrad

(See Next Column)

THOMPSON COBURN LLP—*Continued*

MEMBERS OF FIRM (Continued)

Linda L. Shapiro
Gordon F. Sieckmann
Francis X. Buckley, Jr.
Lawrence C. Friedman
Craig A. Olschansky
Ronald E. Haglof
Richard L. Lawton
Harris A. Maynord
Anne-Marie Kienker
Dudley W. Von Holt
James J. Murphy
Peter S. Strassner
Clifford A. Godiner
Carl L. Rowley
Linda W. Tape
Steven D. Graham
David A. Stratmann
Roman P. Wuller
Charles H. Binger
Timothy J. Sarsfield
James M. Cox
Mark V. Bossi
Sara E. Kotthoff
William D. Hakes
Raymond W. Gruender
Joseph C. Orlet
Crystal M. Kennedy
Benjamin H. Hulsey
Robert F. Wilkinson
Mike W. Bartolacci
Charles H. Fendell
J. Powell Carman
David S. Corwin
Steven E. Garlock
Richard P. Jacobs
Ellen F. Cruickshank
Steven C. Schwendemann
Carl J. Pesce
Halpin J. Burke
Cheryl A. Kelly
Ruthanne C. Hammett
Joseph M. Kellmeyer
Adam E. Miller

OF COUNSEL

Robert T. Berendt
Ronald L. Cupples
Edwin J. Putzell, Jr.

ASSOCIATES

Hope K. Abramov
Jennifer Anderson Baetje
Denise H. Bloch
Kelly M. Brown
Mark L. Brown
Stacy V. Brown
William E. Burris
Charles E. Callier Jr.
Paul D. Chesterton
Philip J. Christofferson
Laurence G. Christopher
Richard P. Cassetta
Eugene W. Chianelli, Jr.
Tracy J. Cowan
Daniel C. Cox
Matthew S. Darrough
David A. Dick
Laura M. Duncan
Matthew J. Fairless
John S. Farmer
David D. Farrell
Jeffrey R. Fink
Anthony L. Franks
Suzanne J. Gau
Michael M. Godsy
Evan R. Goldfarb
Steven B. Gorin
Thomas J. Green
Leigh Svetanics Gutting
Kelly A. Hardin
Reginald L. Harris
Christopher M. Hohn
Kara Leigh Horton
Bettina L. Joist
Christopher S. Jones
Grant D. Kang
Andrew J. Klinghammer
Scott C. Linden
Krissa P. Lubben
Jennifer A. Marler
Steven B. Mitchell
David F. Morris
Lisa Kramer Mueller
Valerie J. Pacer
Robert W. Phillips
Christopher B. Reid
Rebecca S. Robeson
Elizabeth J. Romines
Deborah K. Rush
Jennifer L. Ruyle
Tara Simmons
Dee Anne Sjögren
Ruth A. Streit
Kevin A. Sullivan
Carol L. Tate
Jason P. Thein
Elizabeth K. Thorp
Janet M. Varley
Frans Joseph Von Kaenel
Tiffany Slack Wachter
Robert J. Wagner
Steven R. Wild
Jennifer A. Willingham
Margaret Hart-Mahon
Rodney A. Harrison
Patricia A. Hart
Brett M. Hastings
Charles R. Hobbs II
L. Bryan Hopkins
J. Eric Berry
Regina C. Ashley
Stephen Gerard Strauss
Nicholas A. Mirkay, III
Meredith E. Wolfarth
Daniel R. Woodruff
Steven E. Kellogg
Thomas E. Proost
Fernando Bermudez
Daniel J. Carpenter
Nicholas B. Clifford, Jr.
Carrie L. Schierer
Timm W. Schowalter
Michael T. Marrah
Jennifer M. Martin (Not admitted in MO)
Pamela J. Meanes
Colleen E. Michuda
Catherine A. Schroeder
Jennifer Sharp
Steven M. Sherman

BELLEVILLE, ILLINOIS OFFICE

RESIDENT MEMBERS OF FIRM

Joseph R. Lowery
W. Thomas Coghill, Jr.
Thomas W. Alvey, Jr.
Karl D. Dexheimer
Garrett C. Reuter
Thomas F. Hennessy, III
William A. Schmitt
Edward S. Bott, Jr.
Kurt E. Reitz
Kurt S. Schroeder
Joseph C. Orlet

OF COUNSEL

Robert L. Broderick
James R. Parham

ASSOCIATES

Ann C. Barron
Aaron A. Buckley
Eric R. Riess
Kaori Horikawa Smith
Erick E. VanDorn

BILLINGS, MONTANA OFFICE

PARTNERS

Jeff Hedger
Jon M. Moyers

(See Next Column)

ASSOCIATES

Dennis Nettiksimmons
Triel Dustin Culver
Michael J. Hynes

WASHINGTON, D.C. OFFICE

MEMBERS OF FIRM

Murray J. Belman
Milton D. Andrews
Michael A. Greenspan
John V. Austin
Barbara B. Powell
Edward J. Sheppard, IV
Patricia N. Snyder
David R. Straus
Gerald D. Stoltz
Marcela B. Stras
Bonnie S. Blair
Warren L. Dean, Jr.
Andrew A. Jaxa-Debicki
Marjorie F. Krumholz

ASSOCIATES

Mercia Elayne Arnold
Eileen P. Brown
Jacqueline T. Colclough
Judith "Jan" Elston
Matthew H. Kaiser
Heather Leigh Miller
David M. Schwartz

Representative Clients: American Commercial Lines, Inc.; Emerson Electric Company; The Earthgrains Company; Enterprise Rent-A-Car; Mallinckrodt, Inc.; Mercantile Bank; Peabody Holding Co.; Union Pacific Railroad Company.

For full biographical listings, see the Martindale-Hubbell Law Directory

SEDALIA, * Pettis Co.

WESNER, KEMPTON, RUSSELL AND DOMINIQUE (AV)

114 East 5th Street, P.O. Box 815, 65302-0815
Telephone: 660-827-0314
Fax: 660-827-1200
Jefferson City Office: 621 East McCarty Street, Suite C, P.O. Box 1108.
Telephone: 573-635-7241.
Fax: 573-635-2631.

Fred F. Wesner (1898-1974)
Robert L. Wesner (1924-1988)
Mark T. Kempton
Robert G. Russell
J. Christopher Spangler
Robert W. Russell
P. Pierre Dominique (Resident, Jefferson City Office)

Representative Clients: State Farm Mutual Automobile Insurance Co.; Shelter Insurance Co.;
Reference: Third National Bank, Sedalia.

For full biographical listings, see the Martindale-Hubbell Law Directory

SIKESTON, Scott Co.

DRUMM & THORNTON (AV)

113 West North Street, P.O. Box 40, 63801
Telephone: 573-471-1207
Fax: 573-471-1050

MEMBERS OF FIRM

Manuel Drumm
Fred Howell Thornton, III

Representative Clients: Aetna Casualty & Surety Co.; Cameron Mutual Insurance Co.; Boyer Construction Co.

For full biographical listings, see the Martindale-Hubbell Law Directory

SPRINGFIELD, * Greene Co.

WILLIAM H. MCDONALD & ASSOCIATES, P.C. (AV)

300 South Jefferson, Suite 600, P.O. Box 1245, 65801
Telephone: 417-869-0581
Facsimile: 417-831-7852
Email: mcdassoc@dialnet.net *URL:* http://www.mcdonaldassoc.com

William H. McDonald

William Craig Hosmer
Stuart H. King
James Richard Royce
James A. Endicott
David Andrew Collins
Dana A. Chamblee
Joseph S. Dressner
Eric O. Nau
Venus V. Harry

For full biographical listings, see the Martindale-Hubbell Law Directory

REYNOLDS & CONWAY, P.C. (AV)

406 McDaniel Building, 318 Park Central East, 65806
Telephone: 417-869-0768
Fax: 417-869-6007
Email: rclaw@cland.net

Jerry L. Reynolds
Ronald A. Conway

Reference: NationsBank.

For full biographical listings, see the Martindale-Hubbell Law Directory

MONTANA

*BILLINGS,** Yellowstone Co.

BROWN LAW FIRM, P.C. (AV)

315 North 24th Street, P.O. Drawer 849, 59103-0849
Telephone: 406-248-2611
FAX: 406-248-3128
URL: http://www.brownfirm.com
Bozeman, Montana Office: 510 South 23rd Street.
Telephone: 406-587-8486.
Fax: 406-587-4524.

Rockwood Brown
Claude J. Gerbase, Jr.
Angus B. Fulton
Steven J. Harman
John J. Russell
Timothy A. Filz
Michael P. Heringer
Guy W. Rogers
Scott G. Gratton
Don M. Hayes
Lisa A. Rodeghiero
James E. Roberts
Margy Bonner
William A. D'Alton

OF COUNSEL

John Walker Ross

For full biographical listings, see the Martindale-Hubbell Law Directory

CROWLEY, HAUGHEY, HANSON, TOOLE & DIETRICH, P.L.L.P. (AV)

500 Transwestern II, 490 North 31st Street, P.O. Box 2529, 59103
Telephone: 406-252-3441
Fax: 406-259-4159
Email: crowley@crowleylaw.com
Helena, Montana Office: IBM Building, 100 North Park Avenue, Suite 300, 59601.
Telephone: 406-449-4165.
Fax: 406-449-5149.
Kalispell, Montana Office: 431 1st Avenue West, 59901.
Telephone: 406-752-6644.
Fax: 406-752-5108.
Williston, North Dakota Office: 113 East Broadway, 58801.
Telephone: 701-572-2200.
Fax: 701-572-7072.

RETIRED

Stuart W. Conner
James M. Haughey

OF COUNSEL

Norman Hanson
Bruce R. Toole
John M. Dietrich
Louis R. Moore
Neil S. Keefer
Gareld F. Krieg
Myles J. Thomas
George C. Dalthorp
Fred E. Whisenand (Resident, Williston, North Dakota Office)
Calvin S. Robinson (Resident, Kalispell, Montana Office)

MEMBERS OF FIRM

Henry J. Coleman (1885-1961)
Arthur F. Lamey (1892-1963)
James H. Kilbourne (1912-1974)
Frank A. Gallagher (1907-1976)
Cale J. Crowley (1912-1997)
Arthur F. Lamey, Jr.
I. James Heckathorn (Resident, Kalispell, Montana Office)
David L. Johnson
Kemp J. Wilson
Herbert I. Pierce, III
Terry B. Cosgrove (Resident, Helena, Montana Office)
Ronald R. Lodders
John B. Dudis, Jr. (Resident, Kalispell, Montana Office)
Lawrence B. Cozzens
Steven P. Ruffatto
Allan L. Karell
James P. Sites
Daniel D. Johns (Resident, Kalispell, Montana Office)
Carolyn S. Ostby
Steven J. Lehman
Christopher Mangen, Jr.
Michael E. Webster
Daniel N. McLean (Resident, Helena, Montana Office)
Robert G. Michelotti, Jr.
Donald R. Murray, Jr. (Resident, Kalispell, Montana Office)
John R. Alexander
Donald L. Harris
William D. Lamdin, III
William J. Mattix
Peter F. Habein
Michael S. Dockery
Debra D. Parker (Resident, Kalispell, Montana Office)
Malcolm H. Goodrich
Mary Scrim Dyre (Resident, Kalispell, Montana Office)
Jon T. Dyre (Resident, Kalispell, Montana Office)
Eric K. Anderson
Bruce A. Fredrickson
Renee L. Coppock
Janice L. Rehberg
Joe C. Maynard, Jr.
John R. Lee (Resident, Williston, North Dakota Office)
Steven Robert Milch
Scott M. Heard
Leonard H. Smith
Neil G. Westesen
Antoinette Marie Tease
Jill B. Keller
Michael S. Lahr (Resident, Helena, Montana Office)

(See Next Column)

ASSOCIATES

Marcia J. Davenport (Resident, Helena, Montana Office)
Fred C. Rathert (Resident, Williston, North Dakota Office)
John H. Maynard (Resident, Helena, Montana Office)
Patrick O. Sogard (Resident, Williston, North Dakota Office)
Kurt G. Alme
Michael E. Frank (Resident, Helena, Montana Office)
Robert C. Griffin
David M. Wagner
Alice J. Hinshaw (Resident, Helena, Montana Office)
Shane Douglas Peterson (Resident, Williston, North Dakota Office)
Matthew F. McLean
Joel L. Kaleva (Resident, Helena, Montana Office)
William L. Davies
Vincent G. Rieger (Resident, Kalispell, Montana Office)
Allison Fontenot
Colette Baumgardner Davies
Jeffrey A Coop
Kenneth A Kalvig (Resident, Kalispell, Montana Office)
Ian C McIntosh

STAFF ATTORNEYS

Gary M. Connelley
Kristin L. Omvig

LEGAL SUPPORT PERSONNEL

Jolyn Beringer (Litigation Legal Assistant)
Marilyn J. Bennett (Commercial Paralegal)
Donna Meehan (Legal Assistant/Certified Public Accountant)
Holly C. Carter (Commercial Paralegal)
Margaret Webster (Librarian)
Barbara Kautz (Legal Assistant)
Denise S. Williams (Paralegal)
Darcey D. Pipinich (Paralegal)
Stacey Rowcliffe (Paralegal)

Representative Clients: Montana Power Co.; First Interstate Bank of Commerce; MDU Resources Group, Inc.; Chevron U.S.A., Inc.; Noranda Minerals Corp.; United Parcel Service.
Insurance Clients: Farmers Insurance Group; New York Life Insurance Co.

For full biographical listings, see the Martindale-Hubbell Law Directory

MOULTON, BELLINGHAM, LONGO & MATHER, P.C. (AV)

Suite 1900 Sheraton Plaza, 27 North 27th Street, P.O. Box 2559, 59103
Telephone: 406-248-7731
Fax: 406-248-7889
Email: Moulton@wtp.Net *URL:* http://www.moultonlawfirm.com

Brent R. Cromley
Gerald B. Murphy
Konrad Kent Koolen
Gregory G. Murphy
William A. Forsythe
Doug James
Brad H. Anderson
Thomas E. Smith
John T. Jones
T. Thomas Singer
Harlan B. Krogh

OF COUNSEL

Bernard E. Longo
William H. Bellingham

Duncan Albert Peete
Nancy Bennett
Christopher Flann
Jeffrey A. Weldon
William J. Speare
Gerry P. Fagan
Vicki L. Nelson

Counsel for: First Bank-Montana; Lee Enterprises, Inc. (Billings Gazette); Fireman's Fund Insurance Cos.; Kampgrounds of America, Inc.; State Farm Insurance Companies; Mutual Automobile Insurance Co.; General Motors Corp.; MDU Resources Group, Inc.; Saint Vincent Hospital and Health Center, Inc.

For full biographical listings, see the Martindale-Hubbell Law Directory

STACEY & WALEN (AV)

The Grand, 100 North 27th Street, Suite 700, 59103
Telephone: 406-259-4545
Fax: 406-259-4540

MEMBERS OF FIRM

Calvin J. Stacey
James D. Walen

ASSOCIATE

Kevin M. Funyak

References: First Bank, Billings, Montana; Norwest Bank, Billings, Montana.

For full biographical listings, see the Martindale-Hubbell Law Directory

*BOZEMAN,** Gallatin Co.

LANDOE, BROWN, PLANALP, BRAAKSMA & REIDA, P.C. (AV)

27 North Tracy, P.O. Box One, 59771-0001
Telephone: 406-586-4351
Fax: 406-586-7877

Hjalmar B. Landoe (1907-1990)
Gene I. Brown
J. Robert Planalp
Calvin L. Braaksma
Steven W. Reida
Mark E. Miller
Sheldon J. Hauck, Jr.

(See Next Column)

LANDOE, BROWN, PLANALP, BRAAKSMA & REIDA P.C.—*Continued*

OF COUNSEL

Joseph B. Gary

Representative Clients: Fireman's Fund Insurance Co.; Mountain West Farm Bureau Insurance Co.; USAA Insurance Co.; Safeco Insurance Co.; Allstate Insurance Co.; National Chiropractic Mutual Insurance Company; First Security Bank of Bozeman; First Security Bank of West Yellowstone; Montana Bank of Bozeman; Metropolitan Mortgage and Securities Company, Inc.

For full biographical listings, see the Martindale-Hubbell Law Directory

SEDIVY, WHITE AND WHITE, P.C. PROFESSIONAL CORPORATION (AV)

P.O. Box 1906, 59771-1906
Telephone: 406-586-4311
Fax: 406-586-8681
Email: white@montana.campuscwix.net

J. H. Morrow (1908-1992)
Edmund P. Sedivy, Jr.
Thomas M. White
Lynda S. White
Larry W. Moran

Representative Clients furnished upon request.
Reference: First Security Bank of Bozeman.

For full biographical listings, see the Martindale-Hubbell Law Directory

*BUTTE,** Silver Bow Co.

CORETTE POHLMAN & KEBE, A PROFESSIONAL CORPORATION (AV)

Mayer Building, 129 West Park Street, P.O. Box 509, 59703
Telephone: 406-782-5800
FAX: 406-723-8919
Email: corette@montana.com

R. D. Corette
Dolphy O. Pohlman
William M. Kebe, Jr.
Gregory C. Black
Robert M. Carlson
Marshal L. Mickelson
John T. Johnston
William M. O'Leary
C. Kathleen McBride
Helen Waldbillig McCarthy
Daniel D. Manson
Jesse B. Beaudette

OF COUNSEL

Keith P. Johnson

State Counsel for: Union Pacific Railroad Co.
Representative Clients: CNA; Dow Elanco; Allstate Insurance Co.; Kemper Insurance Group; Ford Motor Company; Safeway Stores; Eli Lily Co.; Wyeth Laboratories, Inc.

For full biographical listings, see the Martindale-Hubbell Law Directory

*HELENA,** Lewis and Clark Co.

GOUGH, SHANAHAN, JOHNSON & WATERMAN (AV)

33 South Last Chance Gulch, P.O. Box 1715, 59601-1715
Telephone: 406-442-8560
Telecopier: 406-442-8783
Email: gsjw@gsjw.com *URL:* http://www.gsjw.com

T. B. Weir (1883-1962)
Edwin S. Booth (1907-1976)
Newell Gough, Jr. (Retired)
Cordell Johnson (Retired)

PARTNERS

William H. Coldiron
Ward A. Shanahan
Ronald F. Waterman
Jock O. Anderson
Alan L. Joscelyn
William P. Driscoll
Thomas E. Hattersley, III
Sarah M. Power
Holly J. Franz
Catherine M. Swift
Rebecca W. Watson
William L. MacBride, Jr.
David C. Dalthorp
Jeffrey M. Hindoien
Jon Metropoulos

ASSOCIATES

James B. Lippert
Teri A. Walter
Joseph P. Beckman
Christopher M. Herriges

Representative Clients: Ash Grove Cement; Borden, Inc.; Case Corp.; Chevron Companies; Farmers Insurance Group; Golden Sunlight Mines; Montana Power Co.; Noranda Minerals Corp.

For full biographical listings, see the Martindale-Hubbell Law Directory

LUXAN & MURFITT (AV)

Fourth Floor, Montana Club Building, 24 West Sixth Avenue, P.O. Box 1144, 59624
Telephone: 406-442-7450
Fax: 406-442-7361
Email: manager@luxanmurfitt.com *URL:* http://www.luxanmurfitt.com

H. J. Luxan (1918-1984)

MEMBERS OF FIRM

Gary L. Davis
Dale E. Reagor
Patrick E. Melby
Kristi Blazer

(See Next Column)

OF COUNSEL

Walter S. Murfitt

ASSOCIATES

Michael J. Mulroney
Patrick F. Hooks
Candace Torgerson Payne
Gregory G. Gould
Benjamin W. Reed

LEGAL SUPPORT PERSONNEL

Viola J. Zindell
Lori J. Idland

Representative Clients: Norwest Bank, Montana, N.A.; Norwest Investment Management and Trust; Nicholson Cos.; St. Peter's Hospital; First Montana Title Co.; Lee Enterprises, Inc.
References: Norwest Bank; First Montana Title Co.; Old Republic National Title Insurance Company.

For full biographical listings, see the Martindale-Hubbell Law Directory

*KALISPELL,** Flathead Co.

HASH & O'BRIEN, PLLP (AV)

Plaza West, 136 First Avenue, West, P.O. Box 1178, 59901
Telephone: 406-755-6919
Fax: 406-755-6911
Email: cmhash@digisys.net

MEMBERS OF FIRM

Charles L. Hash
Kenneth E. O'Brien
C. Mark Hash

General Counsel for: Glacier Bancorp, Inc; Glacier Bank, Eureka and Whitefish; First National Bank of Eureka; Vortex Fishing Systems.
Representative Clients: Western Surety Co.; Liberty Mutual Insurance Co.; Allstate Insurance Co.; Lincoln Electric Cooperative; Read Enterprises.
Reference: Glacier Bancorp, Inc.

For full biographical listings, see the Martindale-Hubbell Law Directory

*LIVINGSTON,** Park Co.

HUPPERT & SWINDLEHURST, P.C. (AV)

420 South Second Street, P.O. Box 523, 59047
Telephone: 406-222-2023
Fax: 406-222-7944

Arnold Huppert, Jr. (Retired)
Joseph T. Swindlehurst

Counsel for: Empire Federal Savings Bank; First Interstate Bank of Commerce; Park Electric Co-operative, Inc.; Park Clinic; Dime Insurance.
References: First Interstate Bank of Commerce; Empire Federal Savings Bank.

For full biographical listings, see the Martindale-Hubbell Law Directory

*MILES CITY,** Custer Co.

LUCAS & TONN, P.C. (AV)

513 Main Street, P.O. Box 728, 59301
Telephone: 406-232-4070
Fax: 406-232-4093

James P. Lucas
A. Lance Tonn

For full biographical listings, see the Martindale-Hubbell Law Directory

*MISSOULA,** Missoula Co.

BOONE, KARLBERG AND HADDON P.C. (AV)

201 West Main Street, Suite 300, P.O. Box 9199, 59807-9199
Telephone: 406-543-6646
FAX: 406-549-6804
Email: bkh@bkhlaw.com *URL:* http://www.bkhlaw.com

Jack W. Rimel (1916-1958)
William T. Boone (1910-1984)
Karl R. Karlberg (1923-1988)
James J. Benn (1944-1992)
Thomas H. Boone
Sam E. Haddon
William L. Crowley
Randy J. Cox
Robert J. Sullivan
David B. Cotner
Dean A. Stensland

Steven C. Haddon
Cynthia K. Thiel
Paul J. Lopach
James A. Bowditch
Ross D. Tillman

Insurance Clients: St. Paul Fire & Marine Insurance Co.; Fireman's Fund; Commerce Mortgage Co.; Industrial Indemnity Co.; United States Fidelity & Guaranty Co.; Montana Municipal Insurance Authority.
Counsel for: First Interstate Bank, Missoula.

For full biographical listings, see the Martindale-Hubbell Law Directory

GARLINGTON, LOHN & ROBINSON, PLLP (AV)

199 West Pine Street, P.O. Box 7909, 59807
Telephone: 406-523-2500
Telefax: 406-523-2595
Email: information@garlington.com

(See Next Column)

GARLINGTON, LOHN & ROBINSON PLLP, *Missoula—Continued*

J. C. Garlington (1908-1995)

OF COUNSEL

R. H. Robinson

PARTNERS

Sherman V. Lohn
William Evan Jones
George D. Goodrich
Larry E. Riley
Robert E. Sheridan
Lawrence F. Daly
Gary L. Graham
Gregory L. Hanson
Gary B. Chumrau
Bradley J. Luck
Candace C. Fetscher
John O. Mudd
W. Dennis Starkel
William T. Wagner
Charles E. McNeil
Dean A. Hoistad
Susan P. Roy
Kelly M. Wills
Terry J. MacDonald
Maureen L. Hall
Anita Harper Poe
Stephen Ross Brown

ASSOCIATES

Lucy T. France
Peter J. Stokstad
Shane N. Reely
Robert C. Lukes
David C. Berkoff

LEGAL SUPPORT PERSONNEL

Bonnie L. March (Administrator/Controller)

Counsel for: U.S. Bancorp Montana; Columbia Falls Aluminum Co.
Local Attorneys for: Stone Container Co.; Western Montana Clinic; Montana Power Co.; The Daily Missoulian; Community Medical Center; Amtrak; Allstate Insurance Co.; State Farm Mutual Insurance Co.

For full biographical listings, see the Martindale-Hubbell Law Directory

MILODRAGOVICH, DALE, STEINBRENNER & BINNEY, P.C. (AV)

620 High Park Way, P.O. Box 4947, 59806-4947
Telephone: 406-728-1455
Fax: 406-549-7077
Email: bigskylaw@montana.com *URL:* http://www.bigskylawyers.com

Michael J. Milodragovich
Lon J. Dale
Jon R. Binney
Gerald W. Steinbrenner
Christian T. Nygren
J. Tiffin Hall
G. Patrick HagEstad

OF COUNSEL

Brian J. Smith

Representative Clients: First Security Bank; Ford Motor Credit Co.; GMAC; Chrysler Financial Corp.; Intermountain Administrators; Long Machinery; Norwest Bank.

For full biographical listings, see the Martindale-Hubbell Law Directory

WORDEN, THANE & HAINES, P.C. (AV)

Suite 600, 111 N. Higgins, P.O. Box 4747, 59806
Telephone: 406-721-3400
Fax: 406-721-6985
Email: wth@bigsky.net

Donovan Worden (1893-1968)
Jeremy G. Thane
Harry A. Haines
Ronald A. Bender
Molly R. Shepherd
Patrick G. Frank
Ralph B. Kirscher
Martin S. King
Patrick D. Dougherty
W. Carl Mendenhall
Peter S. Dayton

Gail M. Haviland
Shane A. Vannatta
Bradley D. Dantic
Matthew J. Cuffe
Sean Michael Morris
Mark Phares

OF COUNSEL

Donovan Worden, Jr.
Robert W. Minto, Jr.

Counsel for: Employers Association of Western Montana; Western Federal Savings Bank; Chrysler Credit Corporation; General Motors Corp.
Insurance Clients: Allstate Insurance; Farmers Insurance Group; Millers Insurance Group; The St. Paul Companies; Royal Insurance.

For full biographical listings, see the Martindale-Hubbell Law Directory

*SIDNEY,** Richland Co.

HABEDANK, CUMMING, BEST & SAVAGE (AV)

302 West Main Street, P.O. Box 1250, 59270
Telephone: 406-482-1802
Fax: 406-482-6411

MEMBERS OF FIRM

Jacque W. Best
Robert J. Savage

ASSOCIATE

Diane Savage

OF COUNSEL

Otto T. Habedank
Wayne K. Cumming

Counsel for: Holly Sugar Corp.; Community Memorial Hospital; Richland National Bank; Lower Yellowstone R.E.A.; Montana-Dakota Utility.

(See Next Column)

Insurance Clients: Royal-Milbank Insurance Co.; Milbank Mutual Insurance Co.; Farmer's Union Insurance Co.; State Farm Insurance Co.; Phico Insurance Co.

For full biographical listings, see the Martindale-Hubbell Law Directory

NEBRASKA

*BROKEN BOW,** Custer Co.

CARLOS E. SCHAPER LAW OFFICE (AV)

345 South 10th Avenue, P.O. Box 586, 68822
Telephone: 308-872-6481
Fax: 308-872-6385

William C. Schaper (1890-1977)

General Counsel for: Custer Federal Savings & Loan Assn., Broken Bow; United Nebraska Bank, Broken Bow, Nebraska; Jennie Malham Memorial Medical Center.
Local Counsel for: Federated Mutual Implement and Hardware Insurance Co.; Shield of Shelter Insurance Co.; John Hancock Mutual Life Insurance Co.; Prudential Life Insurance Co.; Massey-Ferguson, Inc.; F.D.I.C.; Resolution Trust Corporation.

For full biographical listings, see the Martindale-Hubbell Law Directory

CAMBRIDGE, Furnas Co.

EISENHART & EISENHART (AV)

Eisenhart Building, P.O. Box 250, 69022
Telephone: 308-697-3737
Fax: 308-697-3225
Email: eisenlaw@swebr.net

Hugh W. Eisenhart (1916-1995)
Eric B. Eisenhart

Representative Clients: First National Bank; Cambridge Telephone Co.

*CHADRON,** Dawes Co.

BUMP AND BUMP (AV)

P.O. Box 1140, 69337-1140
Telephone: 308-432-4411
Fax: 308-432-4412
Email: bumplaw@bbc.net *URL:* http://www.lawyers.com/bumplaw

MEMBERS OF FIRM

Leo Bump (1900-1958)
Bevin B. Bump

General Counsel for: City of Chadron; Chadron State College; Chadron Medical Clinic, P.C.; Chamberlain Chapel, Inc.; Eitemiller Oil Co.; Manning OO Ranches, Inc.; Metal Products Company; Pine Springs Ranch, Inc.; Service Drug, Inc.; Vrtatko, Inc.

For full biographical listings, see the Martindale-Hubbell Law Directory

*GERING,** Scotts Bluff Co.

HOLTORF, KOVARIK, ELLISON & MATHIS, P.C. (AV)

1715 11th Street, P.O. Box 340, 69341-0340
Telephone: 308-436-5297
Fax: 308-436-2297
Email: hkem@prairieweb.com *URL:* http://www.prairieweb.com/hkem

Hans J. Holtorf, Jr. (1914-1992)
Leland K. Kovarik
James W. Ellison
James M. Mathis

Representative Clients: Travelers Insurance Co.; State Farm Mutual Auto Insurance Co.; Allied Group; Hawkeye Security Insurance Co.; Aetna Life & Casualty Co.; Casualty Underwriters.; John Deere Ins. Co.; Coast West Casualty Co.; Wausau Insurance Co.; Federated Mutual Insurance Co.
Counsel: North Platte Natural Resources District.
References: First State Bank of Gering; Gering State Bank.

For full biographical listings, see the Martindale-Hubbell Law Directory

*GRAND ISLAND,** Hall Co.

CUNNINGHAM, BLACKBURN, FRANCIS, BROCK & CUNNINGHAM (AV)

222 North Cedar Street, P.O. Box 2280, 68802-2280
Telephone: 308-384-2636
Fax: 308-384-6556

MEMBERS OF FIRM

B. J. Cunningham (1888-1977)
B. J. Cunningham, Jr.
William G. Blackburn
William A. Francis
Patrick A. Brock
John M. Cunningham

Representative Clients: Five Points Bank; Skag-Way Discount Dept. Stores, Inc.; Johnson Cashway Lumber Company of Grand Island; Spelts-Schultz Lumber Co.; City of Wood River Nebraska; Norwest Financial Services; Platte River Whooping Crane Maintenance Trust, Inc.; Catholic Diocese of Grand Island, Nebraska; Toner's Inc. of Grand Island; Ord Equipment, Inc.

(See Next Column)

CUNNINGHAM, BLACKBURN, FRANCIS, BROCK & CUNNINGHAM—*Continued*

For full biographical listings, see the Martindale-Hubbell Law Directory

SHAMBERG, WOLF, MCDERMOTT & DEPUÉ (AV)

Norwest Bank Building, P.O. Box 460, 68802
Telephone: 308-384-1635; 308-384-0770
Fax: 308-384-1759

MEMBERS OF FIRM

James I. Shamberg
John A. Wolf
John B. McDermott
Ronald S. Depué
C.E. Cronin (1908-1977)

Attorneys for: Northwestern Public Service; Norwest Bank Nebraska, N.A.; Central Platte Natural Resources District; Hall County Airport Authority.
Representative Clients: Royal Globe Group; The Equitable Life Assurance Society; Federated Mutual Insurance Cos.; Iowa Mutual Insurance Co.; Allstate Insurance Co.; Universal Underwriters Insurance Co.

For full biographical listings, see the Martindale-Hubbell Law Directory

*LINCOLN,** Lancaster Co.

BAYLOR, EVNEN, CURTISS, GRIMIT & WITT (AV)

Suite 1200, 206 South 13th Street, 68508
Telephone: 402-475-1075
Telecopier: 402-475-9515
Email: Lnklaw@baylorevnen.com

MEMBERS OF FIRM

F. B. Baylor (1884-1967)
H. B. Evnen (1905-1988)
Robert T. Grimit
Donald R. Witt
M. Douglas Deitchler
Walter E. Zink, II
Randall L. Goyette
Stephen S. Gealy
Gail S. Perry
Dallas D. Jones
Jill Gradwohl Schroeder
David A. Dudley
Brenda S. Spilker
David D. Zwart
Stephanie F. Stacy

ASSOCIATES

Kelly Dean Brende
Christopher M. Ferdico
Darin J. Lang
Jarrod S. Boitnott
Darla S. Ideus
Timothy E. Clarke

OF COUNSEL

J. Arthur Curtiss
John R. Baylor

Representative Clients: Allstate Insurance Co.; Employers Mutual of Wausau; CNA; Farmers Insurance Group; Farmland Insurance; J.S. Kemper Group; State Farm; Aliant Employee's Credit Union; General Excavating Co.

For full biographical listings, see the Martindale-Hubbell Law Directory

CLINE, WILLIAMS, WRIGHT, JOHNSON & OLDFATHER (AV)

1900 U.S. Bank Building, 233 South 13th Street, 68508
Telephone: 402-474-6900
Fax: 402-474-5393
Email: postmaster@cline-law.com *URL:* http://www.cline-law.com
Omaha, Nebraska Office: Suite 720, One Pacific Place, 1125 South 103rd Street, 68124.
Telephone: 402-397-1700.
Fax: 402-397-1806.

ATTORNEYS

Allen L. Graves
Charles M. Pallesen, Jr.
Fredric H. Kauffman
Donald F. Burt
Alan E. Peterson
Stephen E. Gehring
Robert J. Routh
Kevin Colleran
L. Bruce Wright
James M. Bausch
Larry A. Holle
David R. Buntain
Stephen H. Nelsen
Michael C. Mueller
Lauren W. Wismer
Daniel R. Stogsdill
Scott D. Kelly
Terry R. Wittler
Pamela Hastings Carrier
Mark A. Christensen
Richard P. Garden, Jr.
Shawn D. Renner
John C. Miles
Mary Kay Frank
Thomas C. Huston
Sonya S. Ekart
Don R. Janssen
Susan Kubert Sapp
Kevin J. Schneider
Andrew D. Strotman
Jill Gossin Jensen
Rochelle A. Mullen
John L. Horan
Bryan S. Hatch
Steven C. Likes
Tracy A. Oldemeyer
Jolene M. Papa
Timothy G. Aschoff
Eric N. Bergquist
Janis J. Winterhof
Andrea Dylan Snowden

OF COUNSEL

Charles E. Wright
Richard P. Jeffries
Mary M. Campbell

(See Next Column)

RETIRED PARTNERS

Flavel A. Wright (Retired)
Warren C. Johnson (Retired)
Charles E. Oldfather (1927-1998)

Representative Clients: U.S. Bank National Association; University of Nebraska; Nebraska Medical Assn.; Saint Elizabeth Regional Medical Center; Media of Nebraska; Cargill Inc.; State Farm Insurance Cos.; Wal-Mart Stores, Inc.; Textron/Cushman; Isco, Inc.

For full biographical listings, see the Martindale-Hubbell Law Directory

ERICKSON & SEDERSTROM, P.C. (AV)

Suite 400, Cornhusker Plaza, 301 South 13th Street, 68508
Telephone: 402-476-1000
Fax: 402-476-6167
Omaha, Nebraska Office: Regency Westpointe, 10330 Regency Parkway Drive, Suite 100, 68114-3761.
Telephone: 402-397-2200.
Fax: 402-390-7137.

Charles Thone
Charles D. Humble
Alan M. Wood
William F. Austin
Mark M. Schorr
Linda W. Rohman
David C. Mussman

Travis A. Ginest

Representative Clients: Lincoln Electric System; Lincoln General Hospital; Nash Finch Co.; LinWeld, Inc.; Bryant Air Conditioning & Heating; Osco Drug; Citadel Communication; Douglas Theatres; Sioux City Foundry; American Honda.

For full biographical listings, see the Martindale-Hubbell Law Directory

JAMES W. HEWITT (AV)

1815 Y Street, P.O. Box 80268, 68501
Telephone: 402-434-1212
Fax: 402-434-1799

Representative Clients: Universal Surety Co.; Inland Insurance Co.; Ready Mixed Concrete Co.; Kerford Limestone Co.; Western Sand and Gravel Co.

For full biographical listings, see the Martindale-Hubbell Law Directory

KNUDSEN, BERKHEIMER, RICHARDSON & ENDACOTT (AV)

1248 "O" Street, 1000 NBC Center, 68508
Telephone: 402-475-7011
Facsimile: 402-475-8912
URL: http://www.knudsenlaw.com

MEMBERS OF FIRM

Wallace A. Richardson
Richard R. Endacott
Rodney M. Confer
Richard C. Reier
Robert A. Cannon
Paula J. Metcalf
John R. Hoffert
Trev E. Peterson
William L. Tannehill
Shirley K. Williams
Cheryl R. Zwart
Douglas J. Peterson
Thomas C. Sattler

ASSOCIATES

Jeanelle R. Robson
Corey L. Stull

OF COUNSEL

Richard A. Knudsen

Representative Clients: The Burlington Northern and Santa Fe Railroad Company; National Bank of Commerce Trust and Savings Association; Stuart Enterprises; Cooper Foundation; Dain Rauscher Corp.
Insurance Clients: Travelers Indemnity Co.; General Casualty Company of Wisconsin; St. Paul Insurance Co.; United States Fidelity & Guaranty Co.; Conseco, Inc.

For full biographical listings, see the Martindale-Hubbell Law Directory

MATTSON, RICKETTS, DAVIES, STEWART & CALKINS (AV)

US Bank Building, 233 South 13th Street, Suite 1401, 68508
Telephone: 402-475-8433
Fax: 402-475-0105
Email: mattsor@navix.net
Hickman, Nebraska Office: 103 Locust.
Telephone: 402-792-2905.
Waverly, Nebraska Office: 10440 North 140th Street, Suite 3.
Telephone: 402-786-2905.
Adams, Nebraska Office: 601 Main Street.
Telephone: 402-988-2112.

MEMBERS OF FIRM

C. Russell Mattson (1905-1988)
Lewis R. Ricketts (1910-1990)
Thomas M. Davies
Daniel E. Wherry
Lawayne L. Feit
Randall V. Petersen
Jacqueline M Schaneman
J. L. Spray
Reginald S. Kuhn
Stephen D. Mossman

ASSOCIATES

G. Roderic Anderson

(See Next Column)

MATTSON, RICKETTS, DAVIES, STEWART & CALKINS, *Lincoln—Continued*

OF COUNSEL

John W. Stewart

RETIRED PARTNER

Raymond K. Calkins

LEGAL SUPPORT PERSONNEL

Joan M. Carpenter

General Counsel: Management Recruiters of Lincoln; Iowa Foundation for Medical Care; The Sunderbruch Corp., Nebraska; City of Hickman; Nebraska Masonic Eastern Star Home for Children; Lincoln Stars Hockey.
Representative Clients: Texaco, Inc.; Nebraska Farm Bureau Federation; Old Republic Surety Co.; Commercial State Bank, Clay Center, Nebraska.

For full biographical listings, see the Martindale-Hubbell Law Directory

*MCCOOK,** Red Willow Co.

COLFER, WOOD, LYONS & WOOD (AV)

124 West C Street, P.O. Box 100, 69001
Telephone: 308-345-5063
Fax: 308-345-2426

MEMBERS OF FIRM

Joseph D. Wood, Jr.
Philip P. Lyons
Paul M. Wood

RETIRED

Thomas F. Colfer

For full biographical listings, see the Martindale-Hubbell Law Directory

HANSON & HANSON (AV)

316 Norris Avenue, P.O. Box 338, 69001
Telephone: 308-345-5120
Fax: 308-345-3812

Fred T. Hanson (1902-1990)
John F. Hanson

Representative Clients: Bank of Indianola; AMFirst Bank of Hayes Center.
References: Bank of Indianola; Mc Cook National Bank.

For full biographical listings, see the Martindale-Hubbell Law Directory

NORFOLK, Madison Co.

JEWELL, COLLINS & DELAY (AV)

105 South 2nd Street, P.O. Box 1367, 68701
Telephone: 402-371-4844
Fax: 402-371-5673
Email: jcdpc@ncfcomm.com

MEMBERS OF FIRM

Daniel D. Jewell
Dennis W. Collins
Thomas H. DeLay

ASSOCIATE

Scott A. Gray

Insurance Company Clients: Allied Group; Allstate Insurance Co.; Employers Mutual of Wausau; Farm Bureau of Nebraska; Farmers Mutual of Nebraska; State Farm Insurance Companies.
Local Counsel for: Nucor Corp.; Minnesota Mining and Manufacturing Co.; Federal Land Bank of Omaha; Norwest Bank Nebraska, N.A., Norfolk, Nebraska (Member, Norwest Bancorporation, Minneapolis, Minnesota).

For full biographical listings, see the Martindale-Hubbell Law Directory

*OGALLALA,** Keith Co.

MCGINLEY, O'DONNELL, REYNOLDS & EDWARDS, P.C. (AV)

711 East First Street, P.O. Box 119, 69153
Telephone: 308-284-4001
Fax: 308-284-8319
Email: morepc@megavision.com
Benkelman, Nebraska Office: 507 Chief Street, P.O. Box 607, 69021.
Telephone: 308-423-2611.
Fax: 308-423-2628.

Gerald J. McGinley (1904-1981)
R. Kevin O'Donnell
Robert B. Reynolds
J. Blake Edwards

Robert S. Harvoy
Charles J. Stolz

Representative Clients: Employers-Commercial Union Cos.; State Farm Mutual Insurance Co.; John Hancock Mutual Life Insurance Co.; Hawkeye-Security Insurance Co.; Maryland Casualty Co.; Hartford Insurance Group; Stromberg Carlson Corp.; Adams Bank & Trust, Ogallala, Nebr.

For full biographical listings, see the Martindale-Hubbell Law Directory

*OMAHA,** Douglas Co.

ABRAHAMS KASLOW & CASSMAN (AV)

8712 West Dodge Road, Suite 300, 68114-3419
Telephone: 402-392-1250
Telecopier: 402-392-0816
Email: attorneys@akclaw.com

MEMBERS OF FIRM

Ben E. Kaslow (1907-1993)
Frederick S. Cassman
Howard J. Kaslow
Frank F. Pospishil
Ronald K. Parsonage
William H. Coates
John W. Herdzina
Harvey B. Cooper
Randall C. Hanson
R. Craig Fry
Timothy M. Kenny
Teresa A. Beaufait
Terrence P. Maher
Eric H. Lindquist
Sandra L. Maass
Thomas J. Malicki
Aaron D. Weiner

ASSOCIATES

James M. Pfeffer
Jeffrey J. Blumel
Kim M. Argo
Mark A. Williams
Sean M. Gillen

OF COUNSEL

Milton R. Abrahams

Representative Clients: American National Bank; Data Transmission Network Corp.; Lozier Corp. (store fixture manufacturer); Omaha Steaks International, Inc.; PDM, Inc. (shopping center development and management); Pamida, Inc. (discount stores); SITEL (telemarketing services); Tenaska, Inc. (cogeneration and independent power plants).

For full biographical listings, see the Martindale-Hubbell Law Directory

ANDERSEN, BERKSHIRE, LAURITSEN & BROWER (AV)

A Partnership including a Professional Corporation
Suite 200, 8805 Indian Hills Drive, 68114-4070
Telephone: 402-397-0666
Facsimile: 402-397-4633

Robert K. Andersen (1921-1988)
Robert H. Berkshire
Thomas C. Lauritsen
Sam R. Brower (P.C.)
Richard N. Berkshire
John C. Hewitt
Robert J. Kirby
Thomas M. Houston
Christian R. Blunk
Laurie B. Meyers
Angela L. Burmeister

Representative Clients: The Chicago Lumber Company of Omaha; Hunt Transportation, Inc.; Great Plains Natural Gas Co.; Durham Resources, Inc.; Johnson Hardware Co.; Bekins Van & Storage Co.; The Swanson Corp.; Paxton & Vierling Steel Co.; Owen Industries, Inc.

For full biographical listings, see the Martindale-Hubbell Law Directory

BERENS & TATE, P.C. (AV)

Suite 400, 10050 Regency Circle, 68114
Telephone: 402-391-1991
Fax: 402-391-7363
Email: Berems@Berenstate.com

Kelvin C. Berens
Joseph Dreesen
Timothy D. Loudon
Christopher E. Hoyme
Mark E. McQueen
Donna S. Colley
Jerylyn R. Bridgeford
Timothy M. Welsh
William M. Muth, Jr.
Nancy A. Wood
David D. Gale

Michaelle L. Behrns

OF COUNSEL

John E. Tate
Donald E. Leonard (1933-1994)

For full biographical listings, see the Martindale-Hubbell Law Directory

BRADFORD, COENEN & WELSH (AV)

1800 First National Center, 1620 Dodge Street, 68102-1500
Telephone: 402-342-4200
Fax: 402-342-4202
URL: http://www.bcwlaw.com

MEMBERS OF FIRM

D.C. "Woody" Bradford
James R. Welsh
Richard J. Coenen

ASSOCIATE

James Polack

Reference: First National Bank of Omaha.

For full biographical listings, see the Martindale-Hubbell Law Directory

Omaha—Continued

CLINE, WILLIAMS, WRIGHT, JOHNSON & OLDFATHER (AV)

One Pacific Place, 1125 South 103rd Street, Suite 720, 68124
Telephone: 402-397-1700
Fax: 402-397-1806
Email: postmaster@cline-law.com *URL:* http://www.cline-law.com
Lincoln, Nebraska Office: 1900 U.S. Bank Building, 233 South 13th Street, 68508.
Telephone: 402-474-6900.
Fax: 402-474-5393.

ATTORNEYS

Donald F. Burt
Stephen E. Gehring
James M. Bausch
Michael C. Mueller
Daniel R. Stogsdill
Scott D. Kelly
John C. Miles
Mary Kay Frank
Andrew D. Strotman
Rochelle A. Mullen
Steven C. Likes
Tracy A. Oldemeyer
Timothy G. Aschoff

OF COUNSEL

Richard P. Jeffries

Representative Clients: U.S. Bank National Association; University of Nebraska; Nebraska Medical Assn.; Saint Elizabeth Regional Medical Center; Media of Nebraska; Cargill Inc.; State Farm Insurance Cos.; Wal-Mart Stores, Inc.; Textron/Cushman; ISCO, Inc.

For full biographical listings, see the Martindale-Hubbell Law Directory

DWYER, SMITH, GARDNER, LAZER, POHREN, ROGERS & FORREST (AV)

Suite 400, 8712 West Dodge Road, 68114
Telephone: 402-392-0101
Telefax: 402-392-1011
Email: dwyerlaw@dwyer-smith.com *URL:* http://www.dwyer-smith.com

MEMBERS OF FIRM

Michael L. Lazer
Robert V. Dwyer, Jr.
Charles O. Forrest
Clay M. Rogers
Bruce H. Abrahamson
Paul J. Gardner
H. Daniel Smith
Edward F. Pohren
John L. Apker
Christopher D. Curzon
Bruce J. Goracke

ASSOCIATES

John A. Kinney
Patrick Edward Griffin, Jr.

Representative Clients: Nebraska Health System; Ford Motor Credit Company, Dearborn, Michigan; Nebraska Hospital Association subsidiary Bio Electronics, Lincoln, Oak Bancorporation; Lynn Roberts International; Elliot Equipment Co.; Design Plastics, Inc.

For full biographical listings, see the Martindale-Hubbell Law Directory

ERICKSON & SEDERSTROM, P.C. (AV)

Regency Westpointe, 10330 Regency Parkway Drive, Suite 100, 68114-3761
Telephone: 402-397-2200
Fax: 402-390-7137
Lincoln, Nebraska Office: Suite 400, Cornhusker Plaza, 301 South 13th Street, 68508-2571.
Telephone: 402-476-1000.
Fax: 402-476-6167.

Donald H. Erickson
Daniel D. Koukol
Wm. E. Morrow, Jr.
Soren S. Jensen
Daniel B. Kinnamon
Thomas J. Guilfoyle
Virgil K. Johnson
Charles V. Sederstrom, Jr.
Michael C. Washburn
John C. Brownrigg
Thomas J. Culhane
Richard J. Gilloon
Samuel Earle Clark
Gary L. Hoffman
J Russell Derr
Jerald L. Rauterkus
William T. Foley
David C. Mussman

Andrea M. Jahn
Kevin R. McManaman
Michelle B. Miller

OF COUNSEL

Lewis R. Leigh
Leo Eisenstatt
Roland J. Santoni

Representative Clients: Nebraska State Bank of Omaha; Berkshire Hathaway, Inc.; Bozell, Inc.; IBP, Inc. Quaker Oats Co.; United A-G Cooperative, Inc.; Immanuel Medical Center; Cornhusker Casualty Co.; Hartford Accident & Indemnity Co.; Mortgage Guaranty Insurance Corp. (MGIC).

For full biographical listings, see the Martindale-Hubbell Law Directory

FRASER, STRYKER, VAUGHN, MEUSEY, OLSON, BOYER & BLOCH, P.C. (AV)

500 Energy Plaza, 409 South 17th Street, 68102
Telephone: 402-341-6000
Telecopier: 402-341-8290
Email: fraserstryker.com

(See Next Column)

Peter J. Vaughn
Joseph K. Meusey
Stephen G. Olson
John K. Boyer
Steven Bloch
Wayne J. Mark
George C. Rozmarin
James L. Quinlan
Michael L. Schleich
Thomas F. Flaherty
George F. Heiden
Kenneth W. Sharp
Joseph E. Jones
Robert L. Freeman
Robert W. Rieke
Robert F. Rossiter, Jr.
Stephen M. Bruckner
Michael F. Coyle
Rex A. Rezac
John M. Ryan
Dwight E. Steiner
Lon A. Licata
Roger L. Shiffermiller
Mark C. Laughlin
Sue E. Weiske (Not admitted in NE)

Eric A. Anderson
Michael J. Mooney
John J. McCarthy
Mark L. Brasee
Paul R. Dietsch
Danene J. Tushar
Travis S. Tyler
Julia Plucker Schwartz
John R. Freeman, Jr.
Mary M. Carnazzo
Samantha B. Trimble
Jason David Abboud
Jason C. Reed (Not admitted in NE)
David J. Stubstad
Patrick J. Duffy
Tracy J. Edgerton
John D. Belkin (Not admitted in NE)
Matthew N. Cavarra (Not admitted in NE)
Jason T. Moilanen (Not admitted in NE)
Torry Garland

OF COUNSEL

Robert G. Fraser
Hird Stryker
Robert R. Veach
Terrence J. Ferguson

For full biographical listings, see the Martindale-Hubbell Law Directory

HILLMAN, FORMAN, NELSEN CHILDERS, LINGO & McCORMACK (AV)

Suite 650, 7171 Mercy Road, 68106
Telephone: 402-397-8051
Fax: 402-397-2868
Email: hfnclm@radiks.net

MEMBERS OF FIRM

Robert E. McCormack (1906-1984)
Patrick L. Cooney (1930-1984)
Eugene L. Hillman
Larry R. Forman
Michael A. Nelsen
Emmett D. Childers
John S. Lingo
Patricia McCormack

OF COUNSEL

John R. McCormack
William J. Elder

Representative Clients: American Family Insurance Group; Great West Casualty Co.; Horace Mann Insurance Co.; Bargstadt Properties, L.L.C. (Summer Kitchen Cafes); Upper Missouri Trading Co.; American National Bank; First National Bank; Sanitary and Improvement Districts No. 23, 127, 138, 155 and 206.
Reference: Norwest Bank, Omaha, Nebraska.

For full biographical listings, see the Martindale-Hubbell Law Directory

KATSKEE, HENATSCH & SUING (AV)

10404 Essex Court, Suite 100, 68114
Telephone: 402-391-1697
Fax: 402-391-8932
Email: katskee@uswest.net

MEMBERS OF FIRM

Milton A. Katskee
Dean F. Suing
Jerry W. Katskee

ASSOCIATES

Francis T. Belsky
David A. Castello
John B. Henley
Todd W. Weidemann

OF COUNSEL

Harry R. Henatsch

Reference: Mid-City Bank.

For full biographical listings, see the Martindale-Hubbell Law Directory

KOLEY, JESSEN, DAUBMAN & RUPIPER, PROFESSIONAL CORPORATION (AV)

One Pacific Place, Suite 800, 1125 South 103 Street, 68124
Telephone: 402-390-9500
Telecopier: 402-390-9005

James L. Koley
Paul C. Jessen
Allen E. Daubman
Arden J. Rupiper (1951-1991)
Mara L. Rasure
Michael M. Hupp
Donald L. Swanson
M. Shaun McGaughey
Michael C. Cox
Jay A. Vankat
Kurt F. Tjaden
Karen M. Shuler
Gregory C. Scaglione
Margaret Coyle Hershiser
Mark D. Frederiksen
Mark Peterson
Michael J. King
Roberta J. Christensen

(See Next Column)

KOLEY, JESSEN, DAUBMAN & RUPIPER PROFESSIONAL CORPORATION, *Omaha—Continued*

David M. Dvorak
Rana A. Scarlett-Johnson
Matthew D. Maser
Joseph M. Colaiano
Daniel C. Muffly

Max J. Burbach
Thomas F. Ackley

For full biographical listings, see the Martindale-Hubbell Law Directory

KUTAK ROCK (AV)

The Omaha Building, 1650 Farnam Street, 68102-2186
Telephone: 402-346-6000
Fax: 402-346-1148
URL: http://www.kutakrock.com
Atlanta, Georgia Office: Suite 2100, 225 Peachtree Street, NE, 30303-1731.
Telephone: 404-222-4600.
Facsimile: 404-222-4654.
Denver, Colorado Office: Suite 2900, 717 Seventeenth Street, 80202-3329.
Telephone: 303-297-2400.
Facsimile: 303-292-7799.
Kansas City, Missouri Office: One Main Plaza, Suite 810, 4435 Main Street, 64111-7727.
Telephone: 816-960-0090.
Telefax: 816-960-0041.
Little Rock, Arkansas Office: Suite 1100, 425 West Capitol Avenue, 72201-3409.
Telephone: 501-975-3000.
Facsimile: 501-975-3001.
New York, New York Office: 650 Fifth Avenue, 10019-6108.
Telephone: 212-713-6480.
Facsimile: 212-713-6481.
Oklahoma City, Oklahoma Office: Suite 475, 6305 Waterford Boulevard, 73118-1116.
Telephone: 405-848-2475.
Facsimile: 405-842-5748.
Phoenix, Arizona Office: 16th Floor, 3300 North Central Avenue, 85012-2516.
Telephone: 602-285-1700.
Facsimile: 602-285-1868.
Pittsburgh, Pennsylvania Office: 1214 Frick Building, 437 Grant Street, 15219-6002.
Telephone: 412-261-6720.
Facsimile: 412-261-6717.
Washington, D.C. Office: Suite 1000, 1101 Connecticut Avenue, NW, 20036-4374.
Telephone: 202-828-2400.
Facsimile: 202-828-2488.
Newport Beach, California Office: Suite 450, 620 Newport Center Drive, 92660-8019.
Telephone: 949-718-6700.
Facsimile: 949-718-6708.

MEMBERS OF FIRM

Robert J. Kutak (1932-1983)
John J. Wagner
Joe E. Armstrong
David A. Jacobson
Michael L. Curry
Katherine A. Carey
Walter L. Griffiths
Robert L. Cohen
Lauren M. Ronald
Michael G. Connery
Patrick W. Kennison, Jr.
Wayne B. Henry
Jo Bass
Patricia Schuett Peterson
Patricia A. Burdyny
Kenneth R. Dodds (1949-1986)
Curtis L. Christensen
Judith A. Schweikart
Gregg S. Yeutter
Richard K. Bonness
Bartholomew L. McLeay
John L. Petr
Bradley J. Nielsen
Steven S. Huff
Raymond J. Fehringer
Denis P. Burke
Steven P. Amen
Jeffrey T. Wegner
Robert M. Slovek
Bryan G. Handlos
Bruce A. Wilson
John E. Musselman
Karilyn E. Kober
Tracy T. Bridges
Alissa G. Sandin
Tory M. Bishop
Jane Erdenberger
Patrick B. Griffin
Christopher D. Phillips
Mark A. Ellis
Jeff A. Anderson
David H. Dahl
Dennis L. Holsapple
John Detisch
Thomas J. Kenny
J. Toger Swanson
Michelle S. Mapes
Margaret A. Nelson
Joel W. VanderVeen
Michael J. Mills
Dianne E. Pierson
Randal S. Putnam
Kevin M. Saltzman
Kristine M. Thomas
Paul J. Halbur
Matthew J. Effken

OF COUNSEL

Harold L. Rock
George H. Krauss
David K. Karnes
Jerre A. Tritsch
Brenda J. Council
Don Blankenau
Jeanette M. Smith
Fred Bunker Davis
Nancy A. Roberts
Kimberly A. Dunovan
Steven W. Seline
Sheila Phillips Hawes
Debbie Sinclair Ruskin
Allan Jay Garfinkle

(See Next Column)

OF COUNSEL (Continued)

Allan L. Grauer
Roman L. Hruska (1904-1999)
William Grodinsky (1894-1985)
Frank L. Burbridge (1903-1988)
Gail E. Burbridge (1909-1993)

ASSOCIATES

Bernadette A. Tate
David A. Weill
Richard P. Jeffries
Robin E. Clark
John E. Schembari (Not admitted in NE)
Jill H. Goldstein
Jeffrey P. McGinnis
Kevin M. Keating
Jonathan Nash, Jr.
Margot Wickman-Bennett
David L. Heim
David L. Bracht
Richard J. Rosenblatt
David A. Stage
Kevin D. Hartzell
Lyneth A. Rhoten
Gregory C. Schaecher
Andrew P. Romshek
Marcia A. Rezac
Steven M. Virgil (Not admitted in NE)
Theresa Bima-Reeves
Mercedes A. Anderson
Brent C. Burmood
Robert D. Coon
Kimberly A. Lammers
Jill Vinjamuri
Brian L. Harr
Eric Likins Preston
Carrie A. Hoppe
Courtney E. Koziol
Suzanne M. Shehan
Timothy Dunning
Clara Juwon Ohr
Patricia C. Ryan-Westpfahl
Garrett Spear-Smith
John P. Glode
Debra Fiala Breen
Julie M. Cornwell (Not admitted in NE)

For full biographical listings, see the Martindale-Hubbell Law Directory

LAUGHLIN, PETERSON & LANG (AV)

11306 Davenport Street, 68154
Telephone: 402-330-1900
Fax: 402-330-0936
Email: mlaugh43@aol.com

MEMBERS OF FIRM

Mark L. Laughlin
Robert F. Peterson
James E. Lang

Representative Clients: General Electric Capital Corp.; Dodge Land Co.; Security Mutual Life Insurance Co. of Lincoln, NE; Century Development Co.

For full biographical listings, see the Martindale-Hubbell Law Directory

McGILL, GOTSDINER, WORKMAN & LEPP, P.C. (AV)

Suite 500 - First National Plaza, 11404 West Dodge Road, 68154
Telephone: 402-492-9200
Telecopier: 402-492-9222
Email: mgwl@mgwl.com

Stephen T. McGill (1932-1997)
R. Thomas Workman
Gary M. Gotsdiner
Robert L. Lepp
Michael S. Mostek
Paul R. Elofson
Robert J. Kmiecik
Keith A. Green
Mark A. Pieper
Mary L. Hewitt
Alan E. Pedersen
Nancy L. Crawford
Julie A. Engelhardt
Robyn N. Davis

OF COUNSEL

Richard D. Myers
William E. Mooney, Jr.
Ronald R. Volkmer
G. Michael Fenner

Representative Clients: Norwest Bank Nebraska N.A.; First National Bank of Omaha; Mutual of Omaha; Nebraska Health Care Assn.; Bethesda Living Centers; Behlen Mfg. Co.; Metz Baking Co.; Lozier Corporation; Service Data Corporation; Slosburg Co.

For full biographical listings, see the Martindale-Hubbell Law Directory

McGRATH, NORTH, MULLIN & KRATZ, P.C. (AV)

Suite 1400, One Central Park Plaza, 68102
Telephone: 402-341-3070
Fax: 402-341-0216

George B. Boland (1897-1975)
Raymond E. McGrath (1905-1986)
Thomas A. Walsh (1920-1972)
John A. O'Malley (1914-1990)
John E. North
Dean G. Kratz
Robert D. Mullin, Sr.
David L. Hefflinger
James P. Fitzgerald
Leo A. Knowles
Terrence D. O'Hare
John F. Thomas
Jeffrey J. Pirruccello
John P. Passarelli
Lee H. Hamann
Randal M. Limbeck
Mark F. Enenbach
Roger J. Miller
Timothy J. Pugh
Robert D. Mullin, Jr.
James D. Wegner
Thomas C. McGowan
John E. North, Jr.
A. Stevenson Bogue
William F. Hargens
Roger W. Wells
Robert J. Bothe
Edward G. Warin
J. Terry Macnamara
Michael G. Mullin
Nicholas K. Niemann
Pamela K. Black
Patrick J. Barrett
Steven P. Case
James G. Powers
Ronald L. Comes
Gary F. Wence
David G. Anderson
David H. Roe

(See Next Column)

McGRATH, NORTH, MULLIN & KRATZ P.C.—*Continued*

Robert G. Dailey
Douglas E. Quinn
J. Scott Paul
James J. Frost
Guy Lawson
John A. Andreasen
Martel J. Bundy
Sandra D. Morar
David C. Nelson
James J. Niemeier
Keith P. Larsen
Patrick C. Stephenson
Patrick E. Brookhouser, Jr.
Daniel C. Pape
Michael J. Weaver, Jr.
James M. Sulentic
Thomas J. Kelley
Terry Bauman White
William J. Birkel
John J. Schirger
Patrick J. Straka
Aaron A. Clark
Patrick R. McGill
Jean E. Connolly
Christopher M. Bikus
Meredith M. Wilkes
Jennifer J. Sellers
Kristopher J. Covi
Jeffrey S. Penne
Dimiter V. Todorov
Amy E. Wallace
Vicki L. Colwell

OF COUNSEL

Donald B. da Parma
Rodney Shkolnick

General Counsel for: ConAgra, Inc.; InaCom Corp.; Omaha Airport Authority; Physicians Mutual Insurance Co.; Supertel Hospitality, Inc.; Valmont Industries, Inc.
Representative Clients: Clarkson Hospital; Omaha Chamber of Commerce.
Insurance Clients: American Family Insurance Group; Blue Cross-Blue Shield of Nebraska.

For full biographical listings, see the Martindale-Hubbell Law Directory

SCOTTSBLUFF, Scotts Bluff Co.

SIMMONS, OLSEN, EDIGER, SELZER, FERGUSON & CARNEY, P.C. (AV)

Professional and Business Center, 1502 Second Avenue, 69361
Telephone: 308-632-3811
Fax: 308-635-0907
Email: soesfc@ricochet.net
Bridgeport, Nebraska Office: 1003 Main Street, 69336.
Telephone: 308-262-1070.
Fax: 308-635-0907.

Howard P. Olsen, Jr.
John F. Simmons
Rick L. Ediger
John A. Selzer
Steven W. Olsen
James M. Carney
Jeffrey L. Hansen
Kent A. Hadenfeldt

Representative Clients: First State Bank; Continental Western Insurance Co.; Allied Insurance Group; Farm Credit Services; Security Pacific Finance Corp.; City of Scottsbluff; The Travelers Companies.

For full biographical listings, see the Martindale-Hubbell Law Directory

*VALENTINE,** Cherry Co.

QUIGLEY, DILL & QUIGLEY (AV)

229 North Main Street, P.O. Box 748, 69201-0748
Telephone: 402-376-3001; 376-3002
Fax: 402-376-1422

MEMBERS OF FIRM

William B. Quigley (1899-1995)
William S. Dill
William Byron Quigley

Reference: Community First State Bank, Valentine, Nebraska.

For full biographical listings, see the Martindale-Hubbell Law Directory

*WEST POINT,** Cuming Co.

MOODIE, MOODIE & WORTMAN (AV)

Moodie Building, P.O. Box 15, 68788
Telephone: 402-372-5436
Fax: 402-372-5437

MEMBERS OF FIRM

P. M. Moodie (Retired)
Robert D. Moodie
Michael R. Wortman

Representative Clients: Farmers & Merchants National Bank; First National Bank; Cuming County Public Power District; United States Fidelity and Guaranty Co.; State Farm Mutual Insurance Cos.; General Insurance Co. of America; The Prudential Insurance Co. of America; Charter West National Bank, West Point, Nebr.

For full biographical listings, see the Martindale-Hubbell Law Directory

*YORK,** York Co.

ANGLE, MURPHY, VALENTINO & CAMPBELL, P.C. (AV)

617 Grant Avenue, P.O. Box 584, 68467
Telephone: 402-362-7725
Fax: 402-362-3875
Email: amvc@navix.net

(See Next Column)

Wallace W. Angle
Michael J. Murphy
Vincent Valentino
Charles William Campbell

Representative Clients: State Troopers Association of Nebraska; E & O Professionals Underwriting Administrators; Nebraska Association of County Officials; Nebraska Intergovernmental Risk Management Association; State Enforcement Bargaining Council.

For full biographical listings, see the Martindale-Hubbell Law Directory

NEVADA

*CARSON CITY,** (Independent City)

ALLISON, MACKENZIE, HARTMAN, SOUMBENIOTIS & RUSSELL, LTD. (AV)

402 North Division Street, P.O. Box 646, 89702
Telephone: 775-687-0202
Fax: 775-882-7918
Email: law@amhsr.com

George V. Allison
Andrew MacKenzie
Mike Soumbeniotis (1932-1997)
James T. Russell
Mike Pavlakis
Joan C. Wright
Patrick V. Fagan
Karen A. Peterson
Mark E. Amodei
Michael A. Pintar
James R. Cavilia
Audrey P. Damonte

Christopher MacKenzie
James W. Puzey
John W. Griffin

OF COUNSEL

Stephen D. Hartman

Representative Clients: Boeing North America, Inc. (Rocketdyne Division); Carson Station Hotel Casino; Carson City School District; Carson-Tahoe Hospital; Frontier Travel & Tours; GTE of Nevada; Conrad N. Hilton Foundation; Nevada State Board of Accounting; Nevada Geothermal Council, Inc.; Quintus Resorts.

For full biographical listings, see the Martindale-Hubbell Law Directory

HALE LANE PEEK DENNISON HOWARD AND ANDERSON (AV)

777 East William Street, Suite 200, P.O. Box 2620, 89702
Telephone: 775-684-6000
Telefax: 775-684-6001
Email: info@halelane.com
Reno, Nevada Office: 100 West Liberty Street, Tenth Floor, P.O. Box 3237.
Telephone: 775-327-3000.
Fax: 775-786-6179.
Las Vegas, Nevada Office: Nevada Financial Center, 2300 West Sahara Avenue, Eighth Floor, Box 8.
Telephone: 702-222-2500.
Fax: 702-365-6940.

MEMBERS OF FIRM

R. Craig Howard (Resident, Reno, Nevada)
Robert C. Anderson
Richard Bennett (Resident, Reno, Nevada)
Alex J. Flangas (Resident, Reno, Nevada)
William C. Davis, Jr.
James L. Kelly (Resident, Reno, Nevada)
David A. Garcia

ASSOCIATES

Richard P. Schulze, III
James Newman (Resident, Reno, Nevada)

OF COUNSEL

Roy L. Farrow
Linda E. Johnson

For full biographical listings, see the Martindale-Hubbell Law Directory

SCARPELLO & ALLING, LTD. A PROFESSIONAL CORPORATION (AV)

Formerly Manoukian, Scarpello & Alling, Ltd., A Professional Corporation
Bank of America Center Suite 300, 600 East William Street, 89701-4048
Telephone: 775-882-4577
Fax: 775-882-0810
Stateline (Lake Tahoe), Nevada Office: Kingsbury Square, Suite 2000. P.O. Box 3390, 89449-3390.
Telephone: 702-588-6676.
Fax: 702-588-4970.

Fred V. Scarpello (Resident)
Ronald D. Alling (Resident, Stateline-Lake Tahoe Office)
W. F. "Bill" Huss (Resident)
Richard Glasson (Resident, Stateline-Lake Tahoe Office)
Richard A. Oshinski (Resident)

(See Next Column)

SCARPELLO & ALLING LTD. A PROFESSIONAL CORPORATION, *Carson City—Continued*

Susan N. Wasko (Resident)
James A. Kalicki (Resident)
Kenneth R. Jillson, Jr. (Stateline-Lake Tahoe Office)
Michael K. Johnson (Resident, Stateline-Lake Tahoe Office)
Steven D. Mond (Resident)

Representative Clients: Harveys Casino Resorts; Caesars Tahoe Resort; Embassy Suites (Lake Tahoe); Western Title Company, Inc. (formerly Lawyer's Title Insurance Corp.); Coldwell-Banker-Itildo Realty Co.; El Dorado Savings Bank; Heavenly Ski Area; Yantrak, LLC (People Mover Systems); Nevada Occupational Safety and Health Review Board (OSHA); Aetna Surety Co.; Pacific Coast Building Products.

For full biographical listings, see the Martindale-Hubbell Law Directory

*ELKO,** Elko Co.

LAW OFFICES GOICOECHEA & DI GRAZIA, LTD. A PROFESSIONAL CORPORATION (AV)

In Association with
Vaughan & Hull, Ltd.
A Professional Corporation
200, Blohm Building, P.O. Box 1358, 89803
Telephone: 775-738-8091
Fax: 775-738-4220
Email: gdclaws@cyberhighway.net

Robert B. Goicoechea
Gary E. Di Grazia
Thomas J. Coyle, Jr.

David M. Stanton

Representative Clients: Independence Minning Co., Inc.; Alpark Petroleum, Inc.; Nevada Bank & Trust; Metropolitan Life Insurance.

For full biographical listings, see the Martindale-Hubbell Law Directory

PUCCINELLI & PUCCINELLI (AV)

700 Idaho Street, 89801-0130
Telephone: 775-738-7293
FAX: 775-738-0454
Mailing Address: P.O. Box 130, 89803

MEMBERS OF FIRM

Leo J. Puccinelli
Andrew J. Puccinelli

Michael Shurtz

Representative Clients: Credit Bureau of Elko County; Wells Fargo Bank of Nevada; Elko Sanitation Co.; Beehive Telephone Co.; A & E Enterprises, Inc.; Elko Television District.
References: Wells Fargo Bank of Nevada, N.A.; Bank of America.

For full biographical listings, see the Martindale-Hubbell Law Directory

LAW OFFICES VAUGHAN & HULL, LTD. A PROFESSIONAL CORPORATION (AV)

In Association with
Goicoechea & Di Grazia, Ltd.
A Professional Corporation
530 Idaho Street, P.O. Box 1420, 89803
Telephone: 775-738-4031
Fax: 775-738-4036
Email: rvaughan@cyberhighway.com

Robert O. Vaughan

OF COUNSEL

Jack E. Hull

Representative Clients: Ellison Ranching Co.; George Gund III; Metropolitan Life Insurance Co.; Wells Rural Electric Co.; Elko Veterinary Clinic.
Reference: Wells Fargo Bank, N.A., (Elko Main Branch).

For full biographical listings, see the Martindale-Hubbell Law Directory

WILSON AND BARROWS, LTD. (AV)

442 Court Street, 89801
Telephone: 775-738-7271
Fax: 775-738-5041
Email: R.Barrows@WilsonandBarrows.com *URL:* http://www.WilsonandBarrows.com

Stewart R. Wilson
Richard G. Barrows

Robert M. Salyer

For full biographical listings, see the Martindale-Hubbell Law Directory

*LAS VEGAS,** Clark Co.

ALBRIGHT, STODDARD, WARNICK & ALBRIGHT, A PROFESSIONAL CORPORATION (AV)

Quail Park I, Building D-4, 801 South Rancho Drive, 89106
Telephone: 702-384-7111
Fax: 702-384-0605
URL: http://www.aswalaw.com

G. Vern Albright
Whitney B. Warnick
William H. Stoddard
G. Mark Albright

D. Chris Albright
Corey D. Randall (Not admitted in NV)
Tami C. Budo

Representative Clients: Tokio Marine and Fire Insurance Co.; INAPRO, a CIGNA Co.; Nevada Ready Mix; North American Health Care, Inc. (Nursing Home); Royal Insurance; First Security Bank of Utah; Nevada Community Bank; Nationwide Insurance Co.; Liberty Mutual Insurance; CB Commercial.

For full biographical listings, see the Martindale-Hubbell Law Directory

DEANER, DEANER, SCANN, MALAN & LARSEN (AV)

720 South Fourth Street, Suite 300, 89101
Telephone: 702-382-6911
Fax: 702-386-6048
Email: CDeaner@ix.netcom.com *URL:* http://www.lawyers.com/ddsm&lfirm

MEMBERS OF FIRM

Charles W. Deaner
Susan Williams Scann
J. Douglas Deaner (1944-1990)
Douglas R. Malan
Brent A. Larsen

ASSOCIATE

Anthony Ciulla

Representative Clients: California Federal Bank; White Concrete, Inc. Silver State Schools Federal Credit Union.
Reference: First Security Bank.

For full biographical listings, see the Martindale-Hubbell Law Directory

DENTON & LOPEZ (AV)

626 South Seventh Street, 89101
Telephone: 702-384-1723
Fax: 702-384-8019

Ralph L. Denton
Joseph A. Lopez, IV

Representative Clients: Shetakis Wholesalers, Inc.; TRW, Inc.; Leprechaun Mining & Chemical, Inc.; USA Hosts, Ltd; Experian Information Solutions, Inc.
Reference: Bank of America.

For full biographical listings, see the Martindale-Hubbell Law Directory

GOOLD PATTERSON DEVORE ALES & ROADHOUSE (AV)

4496 South Pecos Road, 89121
Telephone: 702-436-2600
Telecopier: 702-436-2650
URL: http://www.gooldpatterson.com

Barry Stephen Goold
Thomas J. DeVore
Jeffrey D. Patterson
Barney C. Ales
Wilbur M. Roadhouse

ASSOCIATES

Bryan K. Day
E. Bruce Jorgensen
James A. Kohl

Representative Clients: Adams Management; The Allen Group; Archon Financial, L.P.; Desert Oak Development; Lockheed Martin Corporation; Newcourt Financial Corporation; Olympic Land Corporation; Presley Homes; Red Rock Land, LLC; Sunrise Company.

For full biographical listings, see the Martindale-Hubbell Law Directory

HALE LANE PEEK DENNISON HOWARD AND ANDERSON (AV)

Nevada Financial Center, 2300 West Sahara Avenue, Eighth Floor, Box 8, 89102
Telephone: 702-222-2500
Fax: 702-365-6940
Email: info@halelane.com
Reno, Nevada Office: 100 West Liberty Street, Tenth Floor, P.O. Box 3237.
Telephone: 775-327-3000.
Telefax: 775-786-6179.
Carson City, Nevada Office: 777 East William Street, Suite 200, P.O. Box 2620.
Telephone: 775-684-6000.
Telefax: 775-684-6001.

(See Next Column)

HALE LANE PEEK DENNISON HOWARD AND ANDERSON—*Continued*

MEMBERS OF FIRM

Edward Everett Hale (1929-1993)
Steve Lane
J. Stephen Peek
Karen D. Dennison (Resident, Reno, Nevada)
R. Craig Howard (Resident, Reno, Nevada)
Stephen V. Novacek (Resident, Reno, Nevada)
Richard L. Elmore (Resident, Reno, Nevada)
Marilyn L. Skender (Resident, Reno, Nevada)
Lenard E. Schwartzer
Robert C. Anderson (Resident, Reno, Nevada)
Richard Bennett (Resident, Reno, Nevada)
Alex J. Flangas (Resident, Reno, Nevada)
William C. Davis, Jr.
Robert D. Martin
Patricia J. Curtis
Kristin B. McMillan
James L. Kelly (Resident, Reno, Nevada)
James M. Walsh (Resident, Reno, Nevada)
Kelly Testolin
Norman Patrick Flanagan (Resident, Reno, Nevada)
Matthew E. Woodhead
Michelle D. Mullins
Roger W. Jeppson (Resident, Reno, Nevada)
Lance C. Earl
Jeremy J. Nork (Resident, Reno, Nevada)
David A. Garcia (Resident, Reno, Nevada)
Fred D. Gibson, III

ASSOCIATES

Robert C. Vohl (Resident, Reno, Nevada)
Elissa F. Cadish
Pauline Ng Lee
Timothy A. Lukas (Resident, Reno, Nevada)
Jeanette E. McPherson
Michele Eber
Richard P. Schulze, III (Resident, Reno, Nevada)
Julia S. Gold (Resident, Reno, Nevada)
James Newman (Resident, Reno, Nevada)
W. West Allen
Dania M. Severson (Resident, Reno, Nevada)
Torry R. Somers
Kevin M. Crosby (Resident, Reno, Nevada)
Patrick J. Reilly
Noah G. Allison
Michael C. Mathis (Not admitted in NV)
Christopher T. Byrd

OF COUNSEL

Andrew Pearl (Resident, Reno, Nevada)
Roy L. Farrow (Resident, Carson City, Nevada)
Linda E. Johnson (Resident, Carson City, Nevada)

Representative Clients: Lenders: Bank of America, N.A.; U.S. Bank National Association; Wells Fargo Bank. Title Companies: Chicago Title Insurance Co. General: Lake at Las Vegas Joint Venture; United Coin Machine Co.; Alliance Gaming.

For full biographical listings, see the Martindale-Hubbell Law Directory

HILBRECHT & ASSOCIATES, CHARTERED (AV)

723 South Casino Center Boulevard, 89101-6716
Telephone: 702-384-1036
Facsimile: 702-384-2LAW
URL: http://www.lawyers.com/hilbrecht&associates
Email: hilbrcht@skylink.net *URL:* http://1stpage.sharednet.com/1/hilbrecht

Norman Ty Hilbrecht

Representative Clients: Bristol-Myers Squibb; Calzona Tankways; City Wide Enterprises; Coldwell Banker; Desert Chrysler-Plymouth; Enstrom Helicopter Co.; Las Vegas Congeneration; New England Life; Paul Revere Insurance;
Reference: First Security Bank of Nevada.

For full biographical listings, see the Martindale-Hubbell Law Directory

JOLLEY, URGA, WIRTH & WOODBURY (AV)

3800 Howard Hughes Parkway Suite 1600, 89109
Telephone: 702-699-7500
Facsimile: 702-699-7555
URL: http://www.juww.com
Boulder City, Nevada Office: Suite 105, 1000 Nevada Highway, 89005.
Telephone: 702-293-3674.

MEMBERS OF FIRM

R. Gardner Jolley
William R. Urga
Roger A. Wirth
Bruce L. Woodbury
Kathryn Stryker Wirth
Brian E. Holthus
Allen D. Emmel

OF COUNSEL

Stephanie M. Smith

ASSOCIATES

Gregory G. Gordon
Scott Day Freeman
Mark Rosencrantz
Kelly J. Brinkman
Derek J. Pfaff
Stefany Tewell Miley

Representative Clients: Wells Fargo Bank and its predecessor, First Interstate Bank of Nevada; Nevada State Bank; Chicago Title Insurance Co.; Melvin Simon & Associates, Inc.; General Motors Acceptance Corp.; Toyota Motor Credit Corporation; Champion Home Builders Co.; Circus Circus Casinos, Inc.

(See Next Column)

For full biographical listings, see the Martindale-Hubbell Law Directory

JOHN PETER LEE, LTD. (AV)

830 Las Vegas Boulevard South, 89101
Telephone: 702-382-4044
Telecopier: 702-383-9950

John Peter Lee

Nancy L. Allf
Paul C. Ray
Timothy P. Thomas

LEGAL SUPPORT PERSONNEL

Lori Grove Kivatisky

For full biographical listings, see the Martindale-Hubbell Law Directory

LIONEL SAWYER & COLLINS (AV)

1700 Bank of America Plaza, 300 South Fourth Street, 89101
Telephone: 702-383-8888
Fax: 702-383-8845
Email: first initial last@lionelsawyer.com
Reno, Nevada Office: Suite 1100, Bank of America Plaza, 50 West Liberty Street.
Telephone: 702-788-8666.
Fax: 702-788-8682.

MEMBERS OF FIRM

Samuel S. Lionel
Jeffrey P. Zucker
Paul Hejmanowski (Managing Partner)
Robert D. Faiss
David N. Frederick
Dennis L. Kennedy
Richard W. Horton (Resident, Reno Office)
Dan C. Bowen (Resident, Reno Office)
Mark A. Solomon
Rodney M. Jean
Harvey Whittemore (Resident, Reno Office)
Todd M. Touton
David C. Whittemore
Cam Ferenbach
Lynda Sue Mabry
Mark H. Goldstein
Anthony N. Cabot
Kirby J. Smith
Colleen A. Dolan (Resident, Reno Office)
Jennifer A. Smith (Resident, Reno Office)
John R. Bailey
Gary Wayne Duhon (Resident, Reno Office)
Laurel Elizabeth Davis
Dan R. Reaser (Resident, Reno Office)
Carl D. Savely (Resident, Reno Office)
Layne J. Butt
Mark Lemmons
Howard E. Cole
Paul E. Larsen
Christopher R. Hooper (Resident, Reno Office)
Suvinder S. Ahluwalia
P. Gregory Giordano

OF COUNSEL

Robert M. Buckalew
Brian McKay (Resident, Reno Office)
Ellen F. Whittemore

ASSOCIATES

Jeffrey D. Menicucci (Resident, Reno Office)
Madelene C. Amendola (Resident, Reno Office)
Mark A. McIntire
Stephen R. Hackett
Robert P. Spretnak
Allen Jay Wilt (Resident, Reno Office)
Lynn S. Fulstone
Michael D. Rawlins
Etta L. Walker (Resident, Reno Office)
Kevin D. Doty
Daniel Clay McGuire
Christopher R. Coley (Resident, Reno Office)
Nathalie Huynh (Resident, Reno Office)
Leslie Bryan Hart (Resident, Reno Office)
David J. Merrill
Craig E. Etem (Resident, Reno Office)
Todd E. Kennedy
Deidre J. Call
Steven A. Gibson
Laura J. Thalacker
Abbie Green Friedman
Elizabeth Brickfield
Shawn M. Elicegui (Resident, Reno Office)
Broady R. Hodder
Kenneth Robert Myers
James M. Sarnecky
Hector J. Carbajal, II
Emilia K. Cargill
Janet Sue Bessemer
G. Lance Coburn
Scott A. Eaton
Joshua M. Dickey
Christopher M. Strongosky
Shawn A. Mangano
Dean Alexis Zerbe (Not admitted in NV; Resident, Reno Office)
Joanna L. Blake (Not admitted in NV)
Brian Harris (Resident, Reno Office)
Kirk Douglas Johnson (Not admitted in NV)
Lisa S. Koenig (Not admitted in NV)
Matthew E. Watson
John M. Naylor

Representative Clients: Aztar Corporation; Caesars Palace; Citicorp; General Motors Corporation; Humana Inc.; Kerr McGee Corporation; Lewis Homes of Nevada; Sunrise Hospital and Medical Center.

For full biographical listings, see the Martindale-Hubbell Law Directory

Las Vegas—Continued

McDONALD CARANO WILSON McCUNE BERGIN FRANKOVICH & HICKS LLP (AV)

Suite 1000, 2300 West Sahara Avenue, 89102
Telephone: 702-873-4100
Telecopier: 702-873-9966
URL: http://www.mcdonaldcarano.com
Reno, Nevada Office: 241 Ridge Street.
Telephone: 775-788-2000.
Telecopier: 775-788-2020.

MEMBERS OF FIRM

Robert L. McDonald
Thomas R. C. Wilson
Alvin J. (Bud) Hicks
Robert E. Armstrong
James W. Bradshaw
David W. Huston
George F. Ogilvie III
Sylvia L. Harrison
Pat Lundvall
Scott A. Swain
Andrew P. Gordon
Bryan R. Clark

ASSOCIATES

Andrew S. Gabriel
Anthony D. Guenther
Jeffrey A. Silvestri
David S. Jennings
Donald G. Martin

OF COUNSEL

William S. Boyd
Charles E. Huff

Representative Clients: AT&T Communications of Nevada; Boyd Gaming Corp.; Jackpot Enterprises, Inc.; Nevada State Bank; Shaver Construction.

For full biographical listings, see the Martindale-Hubbell Law Directory

OSHINS & ASSOCIATES, P.C. (AV)

Suite 170, 1645 Village Center Circle, 89134
Telephone: 702-341-6000
Fax: 702-341-6001
Email: Steveo@wizard.com
Email: Dickoshins@aol.com *URL:* http://firms.findlaw.com/oshins

Richard A. Oshins
Steven J. Oshins

For full biographical listings, see the Martindale-Hubbell Law Directory

PICO & MITCHELL (AV)

2000 South Eastern Avenue, 89104
Telephone: 702-457-9099
FAX: 702-457-8451
Email: lawyers@picomitchell.com

MEMBERS OF FIRM

James F. Pico
Bert O. Mitchell
Christy Brad Escobar
James R. Rosenberger
E. Breen Arntz

ASSOCIATES

Michelle Schwarz
Rebecca L. Mastrangelo
Jill M. Chase
Daniel E. Carvalho
Stephen H. Rogers

Representative Clients: Home Insurance Co.; State Farm Mutual Insurance Co.; Industrial Indemnity Insurance Co.; Great American Insurance Co.; Argonaut Insurance Cos.; Clark County Medical Society; Rose de Lima Hospital; Fairway Chevrolet; American States Insurance Co.; The Hartford Insurance Co.

For full biographical listings, see the Martindale-Hubbell Law Directory

LOVELOCK, * Pershing Co.

BELANGER & PLIMPTON (AV)

1135 Central Avenue, P.O. Box 59, 89419
Telephone: 702-273-2631
Fax: 702-273-2649
Email: todd@todd.lovelock.nv.us

MEMBERS OF FIRM

Roland W. Belanger
Todd A. Plimpton

Representative Clients: Sturgeon's Log Cabin, Inc.; Burns Bros., Inc.; Humboldt River Ranch Homeowner's Association.
Reference: Burns Bros., Inc.

For full biographical listings, see the Martindale-Hubbell Law Directory

RENO, * Washoe Co.

ERICKSON, THORPE & SWAINSTON, LTD. (AV)

99 West Arroyo Street, P.O. Box 3559, 89505
Telephone: 702-786-3930
Fax: 702-786-4160
Email: etsreno@aol.com

(See Next Column)

Roger L. Erickson
Donald A. Thorpe
George W. Swainston
William G. Cobb
Gary A. Cardinal
Thomas Peter Beko
John A. Aberasturi
Paul M. Bertone
Lisa E. Bruce
John C. Boyden

Representative Clients: Albertson's, Inc.; Avis Rent-A-Car System; Airport Authority of Washoe County; Peppermill Casinos, Inc.; Bank of America NT & SA; Reno Sparks Convention & Visitors Authority; Reno Toyota/Lexus; Bailey & McGah, Inc.; Sears Roebuck & Co.

For full biographical listings, see the Martindale-Hubbell Law Directory

GUILD, RUSSELL, GALLAGHER & FULLER, LTD. (AV)

100 West Liberty, Suite 800, P.O. Box 2838, 89505
Telephone: 775-786-2366
Telecopier: 775-322-9105
Email: attorneys@grgflaw.com

Clark J. Guild (1887-1971)
Clark J. Guild, Jr.
C. David Russell
John K. Gallagher
Gary M. Fuller

Jason J. Freelin

Representative Clients: Caithness Resources, Inc.; Chevron USA, Inc.; Dickson Realty; DRGM Advertising Agency; Federal Deposit Insurance Corp.; Intermountain Power Project; Land Rover North America; Porsche Cars North America; Jones-West Ford; City of Los Angeles, Department of Water & Power; Metropolitan Water District of Southern California; Microsoft Corporation; 100 W. Liberty Ltd. Partnership.

For full biographical listings, see the Martindale-Hubbell Law Directory

HALE LANE PEEK DENNISON HOWARD AND ANDERSON (AV)

100 West Liberty Street, Tenth Floor, P.O. Box 3237, 89505
Telephone: 775-327-3000
Telefax: 775-786-6179
Email: info@halelane.com
Las Vegas, Nevada Office: Nevada Financial Center, 2300 West Sahara Avenue, Eighth Floor, Box 8.
Telephone: 702-222-2500.
Fax: 702-365-6940.
Carson City, Nevada Office: 777 East William Street, Suite 200, P.O. Box 2620.
Telephone: 775-684-6000.
Telefax: 775-684-6001.

MEMBERS OF FIRM

Edward Everett Hale (1929-1993)
Steve Lane (Resident, Las Vegas, Nevada)
J. Stephen Peek
Karen D. Dennison
R. Craig Howard
Stephen V. Novacek
Richard L. Elmore
Marilyn L. Skender
Lenard E. Schwartzer (Resident, Las Vegas, Nevada)
Robert C. Anderson
Richard Bennett
Alex J. Flangas
William C. Davis, Jr.
Robert D. Martin (Resident, Las Vegas, Nevada)
Patricia J. Curtis (Resident, Las Vegas, Nevada)
Kristin B. McMillan (Resident, Las Vegas, Nevada)
James L. Kelly
James M. Walsh
Kelly Testolin
Norman Patrick Flanagan
Matthew E. Woodhead
Michelle D. Mullins (Resident, Las Vegas, Nevada)
Roger W. Jeppson
Lance C. Earl (Resident, Las Vegas, Nevada)
Jeremy J. Nork
David A. Garcia
Fred D. Gibson, III (Resident, Las Vegas, Nevada)

ASSOCIATES

Robert C. Vohl
Elissa F. Cadish (Resident, Las Vegas, Nevada)
Pauline Ng Lee (Resident, Las Vegas, Nevada)
Timothy A. Lukas
Jeanette E. McPherson (Resident, Las Vegas, Nevada)
Michele Eber (Resident, Las Vegas, Nevada)
Richard P. Schulze, III
Julia S. Gold (Not admitted in NV)
James Newman
W. West Allen (Resident, Las Vegas, Nevada)
Dania M. Severson
Torry R. Somers (Resident, Las Vegas, Nevada)
Kevin M. Crosby
Patrick J. Reilly (Resident, Las Vegas, Nevada)
Noah G. Allison (Resident, Las Vegas, Nevada)
Michael C. Mathis (Resident, Las Vegas, Nevada)
Christopher T. Byrd (Resident, Las Vegas, Nevada)

OF COUNSEL

Andrew Pearl
Roy L. Farrow (Resident, Carson City, Nevada)
Linda E. Johnson (Resident, Carson City, Nevada)

Representative Clients: Lenders: Bank of America, N.A.; U.S. Bank National Association. Title Companies: Stewart Title Co. of Northern Nevada; Chicago Title Insurance Co. Construction and Development: Centex Homes; Caughlin Ranch.

For full biographical listings, see the Martindale-Hubbell Law Directory

Reno—Continued

LIONEL SAWYER & COLLINS (AV)

Suite 1100, Bank of America Plaza, 50 West Liberty Street, 89501
Telephone: 702-788-8666
Fax: 702-788-8682
Email: first initial last@lionelsawyer.com
Las Vegas, Nevada Office: 1700 Bank of America Plaza, 300 South Fourth Street.
Telephone: 702-383-8888.
Fax: 702-383-8845.

MEMBERS OF FIRM

Samuel S. Lionel
Richard W. Horton (Resident)
Dan C. Bowen (Resident)
Harvey Whittemore (Resident)
Colleen A. Dolan (Resident)
Jennifer A. Smith (Resident)
Gary Wayne Duhon (Resident)
Dan R. Reaser (Resident)
Carl D. Savely (Resident)
Christopher R. Hooper (Resident)

OF COUNSEL

Brian McKay (Resident)

ASSOCIATES

Jeffrey D. Menicucci (Resident)
Madelene C. Amendola (Resident)
Allen Jay Wilt (Resident)
Etta L. Walker (Resident)
Christopher R. Coley (Resident)
Nathalie Huynh (Resident)
Leslie Bryan Hart (Resident)
Craig E. Etem (Resident)
Shawn M. Elicegui (Resident)
Dean Alexis Zerbe (Not admitted in NV; Resident)
Brian Harris (Resident)

Representative Clients: Aztar Corporation; Caesars Palace; Citicorp; General Motors Corporation; Humana, Inc.; Kerr McGee Corporation; Lewis Homes of Nevada; Sunrise Hospital and Medical Center.

For full biographical listings, see the Martindale-Hubbell Law Directory

McDONALD CARANO WILSON McCUNE BERGIN FRANKOVICH & HICKS LLP (AV)

241 Ridge Street, 89501
Telephone: 775-788-2000
Telecopier: 775-788-2020
URL: http://www.mcdonaldcarano.com
Las Vegas, Nevada Office: Suite 1000, 2300 West Sahara Avenue.
Telephone: 702-873-4100.
Telecopier: 702-873-9966.

MEMBERS OF FIRM

Robert L. McDonald
John J. McCune
Thomas R. C. Wilson
Leo P. Bergin, III
John J. Frankovich
Larry R. Hicks
Alvin J. (Bud) Hicks
Robert E. Armstrong
William A. S. Magrath, II
Timothy E. Rowe
James W. Bradshaw
David W. Huston
John B. Galvin
Sylvia L. Harrison
George F. Ogilvie III
James C. Giudici
Pat Lundvall
Scott A. Swain
Andrew P. Gordon
Valerie P. Cooke
Matthew C. Addison
Bryan R. Clark

ASSOCIATES

David F. Grove
Paul J. Georgeson
Miranda M. Du
Bonnie Fleischer Drinkwater
Andrew S. Gabriel
Anthony D. Guenther
Jeffrey A. Silvestri
Jane M. Long (Not admitted in NV)
Judy P. Osgood
David S. Jennings
Donald Gregory Martin

OF COUNSEL

Donald L. Carano
William S. Boyd
Charles E. Huff
James J. Guinan

Representative Clients: AT&T Communications of Nevada; Associated General Contractors of America; Scolari's Warehouse Markets; Time Oil Co. (Nevada Counsel); Nevada State Bank; GE Capital Small Business Finance Corp.; Silver Legacy Resort Hotel and Casino; Boyd Gaming Corp.

For full biographical listings, see the Martindale-Hubbell Law Directory

MORTIMER SOURWINE & SLOANE, LTD. (AV)

Sierrawest Bank Building, 4950 Kietzke Lane, Suite 302, P.O. Box 460, 89504-0460
Telephone: 775-828-0200
Facsimile: 775-828-0211

Wayne L. Mortimer
Julien G. Sourwine
Douglas A. Sloane

Representative Clients: American International Group; California Casualty; Capital Ford; General Motors Corp.; Martin Iron Works, Inc.; United States Fidelity and Guaranty Co.; Reliance Insurance Co.; Dean Witter Reynolds, Inc.
Reference: Bank of America, Nevada.

For full biographical listings, see the Martindale-Hubbell Law Directory

ROBISON, BELAUSTEGUI, ROBB AND SHARP, A PROFESSIONAL CORPORATION (AV)

71 Washington Street, 89503
Telephone: 775-329-3151
FAX: 775-329-7941
Email: RBRS@rbrslaw.com
Las Vegas, Nevada Office: 3800 Howard Hughes Parkway, Sixteenth Floor, Wells Fargo Tower, 89109.

Kent R. Robison
Thomas L. Belaustegui
Walter Bruce Robb
F. DeArmond Sharp
Keegan Graham Low
Barry L. Breslow
Michelle Marie Erlach
Mark G. Simons

LEGAL SUPPORT PERSONNEL

PARALEGALS

James Stewart
V. Jayne Ferretto

Representative Clients: Great Western Bank; Young Electric Sign Co.; Allstate Life Insurance Co.; Pacific Mutual Life Insurance Co.; The Equitable Life Assurance Society of the U.S.; John Alden Life Insurance Co.; Circus Circus Enterprises, Inc.; General Star Management Co.; State of Nevada Board of Registered Professional Engineers and Land Surveyors; Red Lion Inns.

For full biographical listings, see the Martindale-Hubbell Law Directory

STATELINE, Douglas Co.

SCARPELLO & ALLING, LTD. A PROFESSIONAL CORPORATION (AV)

Formerly Manoukian, Scarpello & Alling, Ltd., A Professional Corporation
Kingsbury Square Suite 2000, P.O. Box 3390 (Lake Tahoe), 89449-3390
Telephone: 702-588-6676
Fax: 702-588-4970
Carson City, Nevada Office: Bank of America Center, Suite 300, 600 East William Street, 89701.
Telephone: 702-882-4577.
Fax: 702-882-0810.

Ronald D. Alling
Richard Glasson

Kenneth R. Jillson, Jr.
Michael K. Johnson

Representative Clients: Harveys Casino Resorts; Caesars Tahoe Resort; Embassy Suites (Lake Tahoe); Western Title Company, Inc. (formerly Lawyers Title Insurance Corp.); El Dorado Savings Bank; Heavenly Ski Area; Yantrak, LLC (People Mover Systems); Nevada Occupational Safety and Health Review Board (OSHA); Aetna Surety Co.; Hartford Casualty Insurance Company; Zurich-American Insurance Co.

For full biographical listings, see the Martindale-Hubbell Law Directory

NEW HAMPSHIRE

CLAREMONT, Sullivan Co.

LEAHY & DENAULT, LLP (AV)

178 Broad Street, P.O. Box 829, 03743
Telephone: 603-543-3185
Fax: 603-543-1514
URL: http://www.lawyers.com/leahydenaultlaw

Raymond V. Denault (1908-1983)
Albert D. Leahy (1903-1994)

MEMBERS OF FIRM

Albert D. Leahy, Jr.
Thomas P. Connair
James G. Feleen

Counsel for: Claremont Savings Bank.
Approved Attorneys for: American Title Insurance Co.; Chicago Title Insurance Co.; Lawyers Title Insurance Corp.; USLIFE Title Insurance Co.; Stewart Title Guaranty Co.
Representative Client: First Vermont Bank & Trust Co.

For full biographical listings, see the Martindale-Hubbell Law Directory

*CONCORD,** Merrimack Co.

RATH, YOUNG AND PIGNATELLI, PROFESSIONAL ASSOCIATION (AV)

One Capital Plaza, P.O. Box 1500, 03302-1500
Telephone: 603-226-2600
Telecopier: 603-226-2700; 228-2294; 225-9774
Email: ryp@rathlaw.com *URL:* http://www.rathlaw.com
Nashua, New Hampshire Office: The Glass Tower, 20 Trafalgar Square.
Telephone: 603-889-9952.
Telecopier: 603-595-7489.

(See Next Column)

RATH, YOUNG AND PIGNATELLI PROFESSIONAL ASSOCIATION, *Concord—Continued*

Thomas D. Rath
Sherilyn Burnett Young
Michael A. Pignatelli
Ann McLane Kuster
David M. Howe
William F. J. Ardinger
M. Curtis Whittaker
Andrew W. Serell
Brian T. Tucker
David L. Dubrow
Charles G. Willing, Jr.
Raquel S. Colby

Lucy C. Hodder
Claire W. Rouillard
Maura M. Weston
Christopher J. Sullivan
Kenneth C. Bartholomew
Christine Fillmore

OF COUNSEL

Irvin A. Mermelstein (Not admitted in NH)

For full biographical listings, see the Martindale-Hubbell Law Directory

SULLOWAY & HOLLIS, P.L.L.C. (AV)

9 Capitol Street, P.O. Box 1256, 03302-1256
Telephone: 603-224-2341
Fax: 603-224-2557; 226-2404; 226-2405; 228-0787
Email: info@sulloway.com *URL:* http://www.sulloway.com

MEMBERS OF FIRM

Frank J. Sulloway (1883-1981)
Franklin Hollis (1904-1980)
Irving H. Soden (1919-1989)
Charles F. Sheridan, Jr.
Martin L. Gross
Michael M. Lonergan
Edward M. Kaplan
Irvin D. Gordon
Michael P. Lehman
Michel A. LaFond
Fred L. Potter
Peter F. Imse
R. Carl Anderson
Robert M. Larsen
Margaret H. Nelson
David F. Conley
Eleanor Holmes MacLellan
John M. Sullivan
John B. Garvey
James O. Barney
James E. Owers
Robert J. Lanney
Peter Alexander Meyer
John Ray Harrington
Daniel P. Luker
William D. Pandolph
Jeanine L. Poole
Gregory A. Moffett
Kimberlee G. Burgess
W. Kirk Abbott, Jr.

ASSOCIATES

Richard P. McCaffrey
Elise H. Salek
Sarah S. Murdough
Gregory R. Kirsch
Timothy A. Gudas
Richard G. Korman
Daphne Lessard
Philip G. Lake
Carolyn A. Koegler

OF COUNSEL

Guy A. Swenson, Jr.

Representative Clients: Public Service of N.H.; AMICA Mutual Ins. Co.; Bank of N.H.; Jefferson-Pilot Corp.; CIGNA Corp.; Universal Packaging Corp.; American Ins. Assocociation; American Honda Motor Corp.; N.H. Medical Malpractice Joint Underwriting Association; Aavid Thermal Technologies, Inc.

For full biographical listings, see the Martindale-Hubbell Law Directory

HAMPTON, Rockingham Co.

CASASSA AND RYAN (AV)

459 Lafayette Road, 03842
Telephone: 603-926-6336
Fax: 603-926-4127
Email: casassa@concentric.net

MEMBERS OF FIRM

H. Alfred Casassa
John J. Ryan
Peter J. Saari
Robert A. Casassa
Faye R. Goldberg

ASSOCIATE

Daniel R. Hartley

General Counsel: Foss Manufacturing Company.
Representative Clients: Town of Hampton Falls; Town of North Hampton; Rye Beach Village District; Hampton School District; Susan Conway Enterprises; Wal-Mart Inc.

For full biographical listings, see the Martindale-Hubbell Law Directory

*LACONIA,** Belknap Co.

NORMANDIN, CHENEY & O'NEIL (AV)

Normandin Square, 213 Union Avenue, P.O. Box 575, 03247-0575
Telephone: 603-524-4380
Fax: 603-528-6831
Email: nco@lr.net

MEMBERS OF FIRM

Fortunat Ernest Normandin (1890-1967)
Fortunat A. Normandin (1909-1967)
Thomas Perkins Cheney (1918-1970)
A. Gerard O'Neil
Paul L. Normandin
John D. O'Shea, Jr.
A.G. O'Neil, Jr.
Robert A. Dietz
James F. LaFrance

(See Next Column)

ASSOCIATES

Philip P. Bonafide
Susanne M. Weldon
Regina A. Nadeau
Anne Marshall Rice

OF COUNSEL

Duncan J. Farmer

Counsel for: Laconia Savings Bank; Lakes Region Mental Health Center; Laconia Airport Authority; Central New Hampshire Realty, Inc.; All Metals Industries, Inc.; Lakes Region Anesthesiology, P.A.; Cormier Corp.; Scotia Technology; Vemaline Products.

For full biographical listings, see the Martindale-Hubbell Law Directory

*LANCASTER,** Coos Co.

PAUL F. DONOVAN PROFESSIONAL CORPORATION (AV)

133 Main Street, P.O. Box 438, 03584
Telephone: 603-788-2525
Fax: 603-788-3942

Paul F. Donovan

Representative Clients: Portland Pipeline Corp.; Lancaster National Bank; Merchants Mutual Casualty Co.; Metropolitan Life Insurance Co.; Town of Northumberland; Groveton Paper Board, Inc.

For full biographical listings, see the Martindale-Hubbell Law Directory

LEBANON, Grafton Co.

DASCHBACH, COOPER, HOTCHKISS & CSATARI, PROFESSIONAL ASSOCIATION (AV)

8 South Park Street, P.O. Box 191, 03766
Telephone: 603-448-2211
Fax: 603-448-9967
URL: http://www.lawyers.com/daschbachcooper&hotchkiss

Charles F. Tesreau (1916-1978)
Joseph F. Daschbach
Deborah Jones Cooper
Darrell A. Hotchkiss
Thomas C. Csatari

Local Counsel for: Dartmouth College.
Approved Attorneys for: Chicago Title Insurance Co.; First American Title Insurance Co.
References: Ledyard National Bank, Hanover, N.H.; First N H Bank.

For full biographical listings, see the Martindale-Hubbell Law Directory

*MANCHESTER,** Hillsborough Co.

DEVINE, MILLIMET & BRANCH, PROFESSIONAL ASSOCIATION (AV)

111 Amherst Street, P.O. Box 719, 03105
Telephone: 603-669-1000
Fax: 603-669-8547
Email: firm-info@dmb.com *URL:* http://www.dmb.com
Andover, Massachusetts Office: 12 Essex Street, P.O. Box 39, 01810.
Telephone: 978-475-9100; 781-942-0932.
Fax: 978-470-0618.
North Hampton, New Hampshire Office: 216 Lafayette Road, P.O. Box 974, 03862.
Telephone: 603-964-4990.
Fax: 603-964-4997.

Joseph A. Millimet (Retired)
Joseph M. McDonough, III
Paul C. Remus
Andrew D. Dunn
David H. Barnes
George R. Moore
Susan V. Duprey
Donald E. Gardner
Daniel J. Callaghan
Frederick J. Coolbroth
Steven Cohen
Robert C. Dewhirst
Richard E. Mills
Newton H. Kershaw, Jr.
Karen Solomon McGinley
Donald A. Burns
Steven E. Grill
Ovide M. Lamontagne
Thomas Quarles, Jr.
Paul L. Salafia
Mark T. Broth
Debra Weiss Ford (Resident, North Hampton Office)
Peter G. Beeson
Eric G. Falkenham
Nelson A. Raust
Charles T. Giacopelli
Camille Holton Di Croce
Jon B. Sparkman
Anu R. Mullikin
Ronald D. Ciotti

Diane Murphy Quinlan
Melinda S. Gehris
Alexander J. Walker, Jr.
David S. Phillips
Cindy Robertson
Margaret A. O'Brien
Patrick C. McHugh
John P. Sherman
David P. Eby
Scott W. Ellison
Bret D. Gifford
Jennifer Shea Moeckel
Charles R. Powell, III
Kevin G. Collimore
John E. Friberg
Daniel E. Will
Donna M. Head
Kristin Kohler
Christopher J. Poulin
Joelle G. Collins
Matthew R. Johnson
Patricia M. McGrath
Paul R. Kfoury, Jr.
Linda M. Foulsham (Not admitted in NH)
Giuseppe E. Bellavita

(See Next Column)

DEVINE, MILLIMET & BRANCH PROFESSIONAL ASSOCIATION—*Continued*

ANDOVER, MASSACHUSETTS OFFICE

Richard G. Asoian
Mark E. Tully
Aaron A. Gilman
Nicholas Forgione
Robert W. Lavoie
Mark J. Sampson

Michael Dana Rosen
Michael E. Kushnir
Kathleen Lawler Bodmer
Eileen O'Connor Bernal

For full biographical listings, see the Martindale-Hubbell Law Directory

JOSEPH F. McDOWELL, III, P.A. (AV)

282 River Road, P.O. Box 3360, 03105
Telephone: 603-623-9300
Telecopier: 603-623-5390

Joseph F. McDowell, III

Edward C. Dial, Jr.
Richard J. Walsh
David C. Dunn
Mark D. Morrissette

For full biographical listings, see the Martindale-Hubbell Law Directory

SHEEHAN PHINNEY BASS + GREEN, PROFESSIONAL ASSOCIATION (AV)

Hampshire Plaza, 1000 Elm Street, P.O. Box 3701, 03105-3701
Telephone: 603-668-0300
800-625-SPBG
Fax: 603-627-8121
Email: postmaster@sheehan.com *URL:* http://www.sheehan.com
Portsmouth, New Hampshire Office: Old City Hall, 126 Daniel Street.
Telephone: 603-433-2111.
Fax: 603-433-3126.
Concord, New Hampshire Office: 143 North Main Street.
Telephone: 603-223-2020.
Fax: 603-224-8899.

John J. Sheehan (1899-1993)
William L. Phinney (1909-1977)
William S. Green
Kimon S. Zachos
Robert E. Dastin
Alan L. Reische
James E. Higgins
W. Michael Dunn
Peter F. Kearns
James Q. Shirley
John E. Peltonen
Robert B. Field, Jr.
William J. Donovan
Bradford E. Cook
John D. Colliander
Alan P. Cleveland
Claudia Cords Damon
Edward A. Haffer
Michael C. Harvell
Stephen E. Weyl
Susan A. Manchester
Peter S. Cowan
David S. Brown
Katherine M. Hanna
Daniel N. Gregoire
Daniel S. Coolidge
Bruce A. Harwood
James T. Cain
Robert P. Cheney, Jr.
Denise A. Poulos (Resident, Portsmouth, New Hampshire Office)
Douglas G. Verge
Peter W. Leberman
Colleen Lyons
Kenneth A. Viscarello
Ann Meissner Flood
Michael Jeffrey Drooff
Joseph A. DiBrigida, Jr.
Christopher Cole
Thomas S. Burack
James P. Reidy
Joel T. Brighton
Robert R. Lucic
Peter T. Beach
Matthew J. Lapointe
Kenneth F. Kozik
David W. McGrath
James F. Ogorchock
Priscilla E. Kimball
Kerry T. Scarlott
Michael Jay Kasten
Elizabeth A. Bailey
Michael J. Lambert
Raymond E. Nichols
William F. Dee
Von E. Sanborn (Not admitted in NH)
Richard P. O'Neil
Jennifer P. Hopkins

OF COUNSEL

Perkins Bass
Joseph F. Devan
Raymond S. Perry, Jr.

LEGAL SUPPORT PERSONNEL

Ann McArdle (Administrator)

Representative Clients: Anheuser-Busch, Inc.; Bank of New Hampshire Corp.; The Elliot Hospital of Manchester; Granite State Packing Co.; Moore Business Forms, Inc.; New Hampshire College; New Hampshire Dental Service Corp.; New Hampshire Yankee Electric Corp.; Numerica Financial Corp.

For full biographical listings, see the Martindale-Hubbell Law Directory

WADLEIGH, STARR & PETERS, P.L.L.C. (AV)

Formerly Wadleigh, Langdell, Starr, Peters & Dunn
95 Market Street, 03101
Telephone: 603-669-4140
Telecopy: 603-669-6018

(See Next Column)

MEMBERS OF FIRM

Philip G. Peters
Theodore Wadleigh
William C. Tucker
Eugene M. Van Loan, III
John E. Friberg
James C. Wheat
William S. Gannon
John A. Lassey
Ronald J. Lajoie
Kathleen N. Sullivan
Jeffrey H. Karlin
Donald J. Perrault
Marc R. Scheer
Gregory G. Peters
Robert E. Murphy, Jr.
Dean B. Eggert
Michael R. Mortimer
Kathleen C. Peahl
Richard Thorner
Charles F. Cleary

ASSOCIATES

Christine Desmarais-Gordon
Jennifer L. Murphy
Paul L. Apple
Alan R. Gutzmer
Todd J. Hathaway

Representative Clients: Aetna Life Insurance Co.; American Motors Corp.; First Deposit National Bank; Hartford Insurance Co.; John Hancock Mutual Life Insurance Co.; Liberty Mutual Insurance Co.; Metropolitan Life Insurance Co.; St. Paul Insurance Co.; Travelers Insurance Co.

For full biographical listings, see the Martindale-Hubbell Law Directory

WIGGIN & NOURIE, P.A. (AV)

20 Market Street, P.O. Box 808, 03105
Telephone: 603-669-2211
Facsimile: 603-623-8442
Email: attys@wiggin-nourie.com *URL:* http://www.wiggin-nourie.com

J. Walker Wiggin (1901-1995)
Paul E. Nourie (1908-1978)
T. William Bigelow (Retired)
Dort S. Bigg
William S. Orcutt
W. Wright Danenbarger
L. Jonathan Ross
John R. Monson
Jeffrey B. Osburn
Benjamin F. Gayman
Gordon A. Rehnborg, Jr.
Douglas R. Chamberlain
Wilfred J. Desmarais
Richard B. McNamara
Gregory A. Holmes
Gary Ellis Hicks
Andrew A. Merrill
Thomas John Pappas
Dennis T. Ducharme
Gary M. Burt
Doreen F. Connor
Scott Ames Ewing
Stephanie A. Bray
Shari M. Jankowski
Ellen M. Joseph
Andrea Grilli Chatfield
David W. Johnston

Stephen A. Gould
Jean M. Long
James V. Ferro, Jr.
Daniel Duckett
Elizabeth Maher Leonard
Gail E. Bakis
Douglas J. Wenners
Meredith P. Cook
Ralph Suozzo
Brian G. Vaughan
Erik T. Barstow
Jodi L. Nourse
Carol L. Kunz

LEGAL SUPPORT PERSONNEL

Richard D. M. Strawbridge

Representative Clients: Associated Anesthesiologists of Manchester, PA; Atomic Ski USA; Eckman Construction, Inc.; Fleet Financial Group; Keane, Inc.; New Hampshire Automobile Dealers Association; State Farm; Wausau; Zurich-American.

For full biographical listings, see the Martindale-Hubbell Law Directory

NASHUA, Hillsborough Co.

RATH, YOUNG AND PIGNATELLI, PROFESSIONAL ASSOCIATION (AV)

The Glass Tower, 20 Trafalgar Square, 03063
Telephone: 603-889-9952
Telecopier: 603-595-7489
Email: ryp@rathlaw.com *URL:* http://www.rathlaw.com
Concord, New Hampshire Office: One Capital Plaza, P.O. Box 1500.
Telephone: 603-226-2600.
Telecopier: 603-226-2700.

Thomas D. Rath
Michael A. Pignatelli

For full biographical listings, see the Martindale-Hubbell Law Directory

ROCHESTER, Strafford Co.

COOPER, HALL, WHITTUM AND SHILLABER, P.C. (AV)

76 Wakefield Street, P.O. Box 1200, 03867
Telephone: 603-332-1234; 1-800-339-2958
Fax: 603-332-5797
Email: cooper.hall@rscs.net

Burt R. Cooper (1888-1959)
Richard F. Cooper (1915-1985)
Donald F. Whittum
C. Russell Shillaber
Daniel J. Harkinson

SENIOR COUNSEL

Fred W. Hall, Jr.

Representative Clients: Fiduciary Trust Company of New Hampshire; Town of Farmington.

(See Next Column)

COOPER, HALL, WHITTUM AND SHILLABER P.C., *Rochester—Continued*

For full biographical listings, see the Martindale-Hubbell Law Directory

NEW JERSEY

ASBURY PARK, Monmouth Co.

CARTON, WITT, ARVANITIS & BARISCILLO, L.L.C. (AV)

(Formerly Durand, Ivins & Carton)
4001 Route 66 At Garden State Parkway, P.O. Box 1229, 07712
Telephone: 732-922-9500
Telecopier: 732-922-1625
Manasquan, New Jersey Office: 40 Union Avenue, P.O. Box 367.
Telephones: 908-223-1800; 449-5311.

MEMBERS OF FIRM

George N. Arvanitis
James D. Carton, III (Manasquan Office)
John C. Carton (Manasquan Office)
Stephen C. Carton
H. Frank Carpentier
Dana C. Argeris
Martin J. McGreevy
Albert A. Zager
Mark R. Aikins
K. Edward Jacobi
Joseph J. Colao, Jr.
James D. Carton (1868-1943)
Forman T. Bailey (1887-1964)
J. Victor Carton (1900-1982)
Thomas D. Nary (1904-1985)
Robert R. Witt (1921-1988)

ASSOCIATES

Thomas F. Heaney, Jr.
Peter V. Koenig
Susan J. F. Weiss
James D. Carton, IV
Aaron J. Rosenfeld
Russell J. Malta
Janice B. Venables
Marc J. Comer

OF COUNSEL

Francis X. Crahay
Henry E. Kordes
George A. Bariscillo, Jr.
Robert V. Carton

Attorneys for: New Jersey Bell Telephone Co.; Garden State Indemnity Co.; Jersey Shore Medical Center, Inc.
Local Attorneys for: Travelers Insurance Co.; Aetna Casualty & Surety Co.; New Jersey Manufacturers Insurance Co.; Liberty Mutual; Prudential Insurance Co.; Chubb & Son.

For full biographical listings, see the Martindale-Hubbell Law Directory

ATLANTIC CITY, Atlantic Co.

MCGAHN, FRISS, FRANKS & TRIPICIAN (AV)

26 South Pennsylvania Avenue, P.O. Box 1137, 08404-1137
Telephone: 609-345-3261
Telefax: 609-347-7983
Longport, New Jersey Office: P.O. Box 566, 1600 Atlantic Avenue.
Telephone: 609-823-2635.
Northfield, New Jersey Office: 2300 New Road, Suite 102.
Telephone: 609-487-9500.

MEMBER OF FIRM

Patrick T. McGahn, Jr.
Solomon Friss
Harry E. Franks, Jr.
Carl N. Tripician

OF COUNSEL

Solomon Forman (1911-1994)

For full biographical listings, see the Martindale-Hubbell Law Directory

SILLS CUMMIS RADIN TISCHMAN EPSTEIN & GROSS, A PROFESSIONAL CORPORATION (AV)

17 Gordon's Alley, 08401-7406
Telephone: 609-344-2800
Fax: 609-344-7035
Telex: 820630 Sillsbeck Nwk
Email: sillsmail@sillscummis.com *URL:* http://www.sillscummis.com
Newark, New Jersey Office: One Riverfront Plaza.
Telephone: 973-643-7000.
New York, N.Y. Office: 712 Fifth Avenue.
Telephone: 212-643-7000.
Washington, D.C. Office: 1800 K Street, N.W.
Telephone: 202-296-4750.

MEMBERS OF FIRM

Clive S. Cummis
Michael B. Tischman
Gerald Span
Noah Bronkesh
Kenneth F. Oettle
Philip R. Sellinger
James D. Toll (Resident)
Alan J. Cohen (Resident)

Eric D. Mann (Resident)

Representative Clients: Bally's Park Place Hotel & Casino; The Claridge at Park Place, Inc.; Resorts International Hotel, Inc.; Arawak Paving Co.; Cumberland Mutual Fire Insurance Co.; The Press & Sunday Press; Ameritelephone, Inc.; Crestmont Federal Savings.

For full biographical listings, see the Martindale-Hubbell Law Directory

STERNS & WEINROTH, A PROFESSIONAL CORPORATION (AV)

2901 Atlantic Avenue, 08401
Telephone: 609-340-8300
Fax: 609-340-8722
Email: admin@sternslaw.com
Trenton, New Jersey Office: 50 West State Street, Suite 1400, P.O. Box 1298.
Telephone: 609-392-2100.
Fax: 609-392-7956.

Nicholas Casiello, Jr.
William J. Downey, III
Nicholas F. Talvacchia

Marie J. Jones
Nancy A. Natello

For full biographical listings, see the Martindale-Hubbell Law Directory

BAYONNE, Hudson Co.

FITZPATRICK & WATERMAN (AV)

90 West 40th Street, P.O. Box 1227, 07002
Telephone: 201-339-4000
800 BOND LAW
Secaucus, New Jersey Office: 400 Plaza Drive, P.O. Box 3159, 07096-3159.
Telephone: 201-865-9100.
Facsimile: 201-865-4805.

Harold F. Fitzpatrick

For full biographical listings, see the Martindale-Hubbell Law Directory

BEDMINSTER, Somerset Co.

PURCELL, RIES, SHANNON, MULCAHY & O'NEILL (AV)

One Pluckemin Way, P.O. Box 754, 07921
Telephone: 908-658-3800
Fax: 908-658-4659
Email: general@prsmo.com *URL:* http://www.prsmo.com
Philadelphia, Pennsylvania Office: 12th Floor, East Tower, Centre Square, 1500 Market Square.
Telephone: 215-665-5602.
Fax: 215-569-8228.

MEMBERS OF FIRM

Eugene M. Purcell
William P. Ries
John J. Shannon
Thomas M. Mulcahy
Michael F. O'Neill
David M. Hawkins
Joseph R. Purcell
Kevin R. Brotz
John M. Bowens
Kevin Kovacs
Kenneth D. Merin
Valerie K. Bollheimer
Andrew L. Indeck
Joseph M. Donegan
Mark Mattia

ASSOCIATES

Rita F. Barone
Kathleen J. Devlin
Paul L. Gallagher
Gary Grabas
John R. Haggerty
William T. Hilliard
Eric J. Konecke
Susan Lawless
Michael J. McCaffrey
Kathleen M. Quinn
Thomas Charles Savoth
Donna M. Stephan-Nolan
Barbara C. Zimmerman

OF COUNSEL

David D. Furman
C. Judson Hamlin

LEGAL SUPPORT PERSONNEL

Gary Molloy

Reference: Somerset Trust Co.

For full biographical listings, see the Martindale-Hubbell Law Directory

BERNARDSVILLE, Somerset Co.

SHAIN, SCHAFFER & RAFANELLO, A PROFESSIONAL CORPORATION (AV)

Plaza 202, 150 Morristown Road, Suite 105, 07924
Telephone: 908-953-9300
Fax: 908-953-2969
Email: ssrpc@aol.com

Joel L. Shain
Marguerite M. Schaffer
Richard A. Rafanello
Gary L. Maher
Robert A. Pinel
Phedra R. Rudell (Not admitted in NJ)

OF COUNSEL

Elliott L. Katz

LEGAL SUPPORT PERSONNEL

Tracy DeWitt (Legal Researcher)

For full biographical listings, see the Martindale-Hubbell Law Directory

*BRIDGETON,** Cumberland Co.

RITTER AND JESPERSON (AV)

55 Fayette Street, P.O. Box 320, 08302
Telephone: 856-451-3030
Fax: 856-453-0911

MEMBERS OF FIRM

Theodore Henry Ritter | John E. Jesperson

ASSOCIATE

Susan E. Iacovone

OF COUNSEL

Isabella A. Garofola

References: Farmers & Merchants National Bank of Bridgeton; Bridgeton Onized Federal Credit Union.

For full biographical listings, see the Martindale-Hubbell Law Directory

BURLINGTON, Burlington Co.

SMITH, GOLDSTEIN, MAGRAM & BERENATO, A PROFESSIONAL CORPORATION (AV)

415 High Street, P.O. Box 603, 08016-0603
Telephone: 609-386-2633
Fax: 609-386-8674

Louis A. Smith | Edward J. Magram
Jeffrey N. Goldstein | Elizabeth D. Berenato

David C. Michaud

Reference: First Union Bank, Burlington, New Jersey.

For full biographical listings, see the Martindale-Hubbell Law Directory

*CAMDEN,** Camden Co.

BROWN & CONNERY, LLP (AV)

518 Market Street, P.O. Box 1449, 08101
Telephone: 609-365-5100
Facsimile: 609-858-4967
Westmont, New Jersey Office: 360 Haddon Avenue, P.O. Box 539.
Telephone: 609-854-8900.

MEMBERS OF FIRM

Horace G. Brown (1902-1990)
Edward T. Curry (1890-1972)
George Purnell (1896-1979)
J. Lawrence Finlayson (1908-1986)
Howard G. Kulp, Jr. (1906-1987)
Thomas F. Connery, Jr.
Warren W. Faulk
Steven G. Wolschina
Paul Mainardi
Michael J. Vassalotti
Dennis P. Blake
William M. Tambussi
Mark P. Asselta
Stephen J. DeFeo
Joseph M Nardi, III

ASSOCIATES

Joseph A. Zechman
Karen A. McGuinness
Jeffrey E. Ugoretz
Christine O'Hearn
Christine A. Campbell
Joseph T. Carney
Richard C. Belli, Jr.
Stephanie E. Nolan
Shawn C. Huber
Susan M. Leming
Beth L. Marlin
Louis R. Lessig
Kevin C. Heil
Patrick J. Holston

Representative Clients: Camden County Health Services Center; Delaware River Port Authority; Federal Deposit Insurance Corp.; Mercedes-Benz Credit Corp.; Philadelphia Newspaper, Inc.; Philip Morris Inc.; Pollution Control Financing Authority of Camden County; Underwood-Memorial Hospital.

For full biographical listings, see the Martindale-Hubbell Law Directory

CHATHAM, Morris Co.

ALAN L. ZEGAS (AV)

552 Main Street, 07928
Telephone: 973-701-7080
Fax: 973-701-7081
Email: alanatLaw@aol.com *URL:* http://www.lawyers.com/zegas

Gina L. Mendola | Patricia A. Lee
Sharon B. Kean | Aimee Blakeslee

For full biographical listings, see the Martindale-Hubbell Law Directory

CHERRY HILL, Camden Co.

DUANE, MORRIS & HECKSCHER LLP (AV)

A Pennsylvania Limited Liability Partnership
51 Haddonfield Road, Suite 340, 08002-4180
Telephone: 856-488-7300
Fax: 609-856-7021
URL: http://www.duanemorris.com
Philadelphia, Pennsylvania Office: Suite 4200, One Liberty Place.
Telephone: 215-979-1000.
Fax: 215-979-1020.
New York, New York Office: 380 Lexington Avenue.
Telephone: 212-692-1000.
Fax: 212-692-1020.
Chicago, Illinois Office: 227 West Monroe Street, Suite 3400.
Telephone: 312-499-6700.
Fax: 312-499-6701.
Washington, D.C. Office: 1667 K Street, N.W., Suite 700.
Telephone: 202-776-7800.
Fax: 202-776-7801.
San Francisco, California Office: 100 Spear Street.
Telephone: 415-371-2200.
Fax: 415-371-2201.
Boston, Massachusetts Office: One International Place, 14th Floor.
Telephone: 617-598-3100.
Fax: 617-598-3101.
Miami, Florida Office: 200 South Biscayne Boulevard, Suite 3410.
Telephone: 305-960-2200.
Fax: 305-960-2201.
Wilmington, Delaware Office: 1201 Market Street, Suite 1500.
Telephone: 302-571-5550.
Fax: 302-571-5560.
Harrisburg, Pennsylvania Office: 305 North Front Street, 5th Floor, P.O. Box 1003.
Telephone: 717-237-5500.
Fax: 717-232-4015.
Wayne, Pennsylvania Office: 735 Chesterbrook Boulevard, Suite 300.
Telephone: 610-647-3555.
Fax: 610-640-2619.
Newark, New Jersey Office: One Riverfront Plaza.
Telephone: 973-424-2000.
Fax: 973-424-2001.
Palm Beach, Florida Office: 249 Royal Palm Way, Suite 403.
Telephone: 561-366-5400.
Fax: 561-366-5401.
Allentown, Pennsylvania Office: 968 Postal Road, Suite 200, P.O. Box 90400.
Telephone: 610-266-3650.
Fax: 610-266-3651.
Houston, Texas Office: One Greenway Plaza, Suite 500.
Telephone: 713-552-9900.
Fax: 713-552-0109.
Dover, Delaware Office: 314 S. State Street.
Telephone: 302-736-0156.
Fax: 302-736-0336.
Bangor, Maine Office: 15 Columbia Street, 4th Floor.
Telephone: 207-990-4800.
Fax: 207-990-4804.
Princeton, New Jersey Office: Princeton Forrestal Village, 116 Village Boulevard, Suite 200.
Telephone: 609-734-4323.
Fax: 609-734-4387.

PARTNERS

Peter J. Cronk
Kenneth M. Denti (Resident)
James J. Ferrelli (Resident)
David I. Haas
Steven M. Janove
Frank A. Luchak, Partner-in-Charge, Cherry Hill Office, Duane, Morris & Heckscher LLP (Resident)
Arthur J. Momjian
Diane E. Vuocolo

ASSOCIATES

John J. Coughlin (Resident)
Suzanne Hasson dePillis (Resident)
Christian Johnson
Michael W. O'Hara (Resident)
Kathleen A. O'Malley (Resident)
Christopher J. Stanchina

For full biographical listings, see the Martindale-Hubbell Law Directory

GARRIGLE, PALM AND THOMASSON (AV)

Suite 204, 1415 State Highway 70 East, 08034
Telephone: 609-427-9300
Fax: 609-427-9590
Email: garrigle@aol.com *URL:* http://www.lawyers.com/garriglepalm&thomasson

MEMBERS OF FIRM

William A. Garrigle | John M. Palm
Harold H. Thomasson

(See Next Column)

GARRIGLE, PALM AND THOMASSON, *Cherry Hill—Continued*

ASSOCIATES

Paul F. Kulinski
Eleanore A. Rogalski

Representative Clients: Crum & Forster Group; Kemper Insurance Group; Atlantic Mutual Group; American Hardware Mutual; National General Insurance Co.; Transamerica Group; State Farm Fire Insurance Co.; Progressive Insurance Co.; United Southern Insurance Co.; New Jersey Market Transition Facility and Joint Underwriting Association.

For full biographical listings, see the Martindale-Hubbell Law Directory

GREEN, LUNDGREN & RYAN, A PROFESSIONAL CORPORATION (AV)

1010 Kings Highway South, Building Two, 08034
Telephone: 609-428-5800
Telecopier: 609-428-9802
Mailing Address: P.O. Box 70, Haddonfield, NJ, 08033-0085

Peter P. Green
William L. Lundgren, III
Francis X. Ryan
Daniel J. DiStasi
Charles F. Blumenstein, II
James E. Mulroy

Laurence Todd Bennett
Matthew K. Mitchell
Karen L. Eisele
Frank P. Brennan
Mark A. Leonetti
Michele A. Naipawer
Jennifer Hiller
Jeffrey R. Owens
Pina M. Vricella
Thomas L. Wilkinson
David A. Grabowski
Patrick W. Conner
Danielle J. Skypala
Janet Law
Gregory S. Soffian
Tobin A. Butler
Robert Fraser Miller

Representative Clients: Allstate Insurance Company; Amtrack; Bell Atlantic Corporation; Boruogh of Haddonfield; Coolidge Mortgage Service; CNA Insurance Companies; Gloucester, Salem, Cumberland Counties Municipal Joint Insurance Fund; Pettinaro Enterprises, Inc.; Prudential Insurance Company; Modern Plastics Techniques, Inc.; Market Transition Facility; New Jersey Citizens Reciprocal Exchange Insurance Company (NJ Cure); The Travelers Insurance Company.
Counsel for: Penn Central Co.; Allstate Insurance Co.; New Jersey Bell Telephone Co.; Hartford Accident & Indemnity Co.; Continental Casualty Co.; Sentry Insurance Co.; The Travelers Insurance Co.; Coldwell Banker Real Estate Corp.; Amtrak Conrail.

For full biographical listings, see the Martindale-Hubbell Law Directory

McCARTER & ENGLISH, LLP (AV)

1820 Chapel Avenue West, Suite 380, 08002
Telephone: 609-662-8444
Telecopier: 609-662-6203
URL: http://www.mccarter.com
Newark, New Jersey Office: Four Gateway Center, 100 Mulberry Street. P.O. Box 652.
Telephone: 973-622-4444.
Telecopier: 973-624-7070.
New York, New York Office: Suite 2247, One World Trade Center.
Telephone: 212-466-9018.
Telecopier: 212-432-6568.
Boca Raton, Florida Office: 2255 Glades Road, Suite 319-A.
Telephone: 561-994-6262.
Telecopier: 561-241-0798.
Wilmington, Delaware Office: Mellon Bank Center, 919 Market Street.
Telephone: 302-654-8010
Telecopier: 302-654-0795
Philadelphia, Pennsylvania Office: One Commerce Square, 2005 Market Street, Suite 3600.
Telephone: 215-557-7700.
Telecopier: 215-557-6544.

MEMBERS OF FIRM

James F. Hammill
Glenn P. Callahan
Therese M. Keeley
Nathan A. Schachtman

RESIDENT ASSOCIATES

Evolea C. Watson
Carol A. Hucks
Barbara K. Gotthelf
Anthony J. Di Marino, III
A. Nicole Friant

For full biographical listings, see the Martindale-Hubbell Law Directory

PARKER, McCAY & CRISCUOLO, P.A. (AV)

Commerce Atrium, Suite 500, 1701 Route 70 East, P.O. Box 1806, 08034
Telephone: 856-424-4300
Telecopier: 856-424-1006
Email: pmc@pmclaw.com *URL:* http://www.pmclaw.com
Marlton, New Jersey Office: Suite 401 Three Greentree Center, Route 73 & Greentree Road.
Telephone: 856-596-8900.
Telecopier: 856-596-9631.
Lawrenceville, New Jersey Office: Princeton Pike Office Park, 3131 Princeton Pike, Building 4, Room 200.
Telephone: 609-219-0699.
Fax: 609-219-0708.

(See Next Column)

Robert C. Beck
Richard M. Berman
Emmanuel J. Argentieri

John S. Kennedy

Local Counsel for: Aetna Casualty & Surety Co.; U.S. Fidelity & Guaranty Co.; Keystone Insurance Co.; Zurich-American Insurance Co.; Commerce Bank, N.A.; First Fidelity Bank; Midlantic Bank.

For full biographical listings, see the Martindale-Hubbell Law Directory

PEPPER HAMILTON LLP (AV)

A Pennsylvania Limited Liability Partnership
LibertyView Building, Suite 420, 457 Haddonfield Road, 08002-2220
Telephone: 856-910-7200
Telecopy: 856-665-7743
Email: phinfo@pepperlaw.com *URL:* http://www.pepperlaw.com
Philadelphia, Pennsylvania Office: 3000 Two Logan Square, Eighteenth and Arch Streets, 19103-2799.
Telephone: 215-981-4000.
Fax: 215-981-4750.
Washington, D.C. Office: Hamilton Square, 600 Fourteenth Street, N.W. 20005-2004.
Telephone: 202-220-1200.
Fax: 202-220-1665.
Detroit, Michigan Office: 100 Renaissance Center, 36th Floor, 48243-1157.
Telephone: 313-259-7110.
Fax: 313-259-7926.
New York, New York Office: 750 Lexington Avenue, Suite 600, 10022-1200.
Telephone: 212-813-9668.
Fax: 212-813-9802.
Wilmington, Delaware Office: 1201 Market Street, Suite 1600, P.O. Box 1709, 19899-1709.
Telephone: 302-777-6500.
Fax: 302-656-8865.
Pittsburgh, Pennsylvania Office: 500 Grant Street, 50th Floor, 15219-2502.
Telephone: 412-454-5000.
Fax: 412-281-0717.
Harrisburg, Pennsylvania Office: 200 One Keystone Plaza, North Front and Market Streets, P.O. Box 1181, 17108-1181.
Telephone: 717-255-1155.
Fax: 717-238-0575.
Berwyn, Pennsylvania Office: 1235 Westlakes Drive, Suite 400, 19312-2401.
Telephone: 610-640-7800.
Fax: 610-640-7835.

PARTNERS

Nicholas M. Kouletsis (Managing Partner, Cherry Hill Office)
Matthew H. Adler
Jonathan D. Bennett
Mitchell R. Cohen
Robert L. Hickok
Joel E. Horowitz
James D. Rosener
Patricia A. Smith

OF COUNSEL

Susan Bass Levin

ASSOCIATES

Julie R. Battista
Scott J. Ciocco
Cynthia Newsome Graham
Steven R. Klammer
Constance Petroni Lahoda
Ralph R. Smith, 3rd

For full biographical listings, see the Martindale-Hubbell Law Directory

CLINTON, Hunterdon Co.

GEBHARDT & KIEFER, P.C. (AV)

1318 Route 31 CN 4001, 08809
Telephone: 908-735-5161
Telecopier: 908-735-9351
Email: GKLegal@Worldnet.ATT.NET
Bridgewater, New Jersey Office: 1170 Route 22 East.
Telephone: 908-725-5157.

William C. Gebhardt (1884-1929)
W. Reading Gebhardt (1919-1980)
Philip R. Gebhardt (1924-1986)
E. Herbert Kiefer (1933-1988)
Richard Dieterly
James H. Knox
Richard P. Cushing
Mark H. Chazin
William W. Goodwin, Jr.
Sharon H. Moore
Robert C. Ward
Jacob A. Papay, Jr.
Joseph F. Trinity

Judith A. Kopen
Lori Kopf MacWilliam
Steven P. Gruenberg
Deborah B. Rosenthal
William J. Rudnik
Arthur D. Fialk
Robert G. Wilson
David M. Snyder

Representative Clients: Summit Bank; Meridian Bank; United National Bank; American Telephone & Telegraph Co; Atlantic Development and Management Corp.; Republic Steel Corp.; Spectrum Technology Group, Inc.; The Henderson Corp.; Adcock Air Drilling; Republic Financial Services.

For full biographical listings, see the Martindale-Hubbell Law Directory

EATONTOWN, Monmouth Co.

WILENTZ, GOLDMAN & SPITZER, A PROFESSIONAL CORPORATION (AV)

Meridian Center I, Two Industrial Way West, 07724
Telephone: 732-542-4500
Telecopier: 732-493-8387
URL: http://www.newjerseylaw.com
Woodbridge, New Jersey Office: 90 Woodbridge Center Drive, Suite 900, Box 10, 07095.
Telephone: 732-636-8000.
Telecopier: 732-855-6117.
New York, New York Office: Wall Street Plaza, 88 Pine Street, 9th Floor, 10005.
Telephone: 212-267-3091.
Telecopier: 212-267-3828.

Francis V. Bonello
Noel S. Tonneman

Andrea White O'Brien (Resident)

For full biographical listings, see the Martindale-Hubbell Law Directory

EDISON, Middlesex Co.

WONG FLEMING, P.C. (AV)

Edison Square West, Suite 1050, 2035 Lincoln Highway, 08817
Telephone: 732-248-4111
Fax: 732-248-8665
Mailing Address: P.O. Box 985, 08818-0985
Email: info@wongfleming.com *URL:* http://www.wongfleming.com
Philadelphia, Pennsylvania Office: 230 South Broad Street, Suite 601, 19102.
Telephone: 215-546-2776.
Fax: 215-546-3206.
New York, New York Office: The Empire State Building, 350 Fifth Avenue, Suite 5411, 10118.
Telephone: 212-643-9668.
Fax: 212-643-9640.

Linda Wong
Daniel C. Fleming
Katherine C. Lee

Andrew J. Bayne
Stephen Tsai
Theresa Homisak
Paul J. Young
Wenjun Zhang (Not admitted in NJ)
Tanya E. Lawrence
Fei F. Lam

For full biographical listings, see the Martindale-Hubbell Law Directory

FLORHAM PARK, Morris Co.

CARLIN, MADDOCK, FAY & CERBONE, P.C. (AV)

25 Vreeland Road, P.O. Box 751, 07932
Telephone: 201-377-3350
Fax: 201-377-5626
URL: http://www.lawyers.com/cmfclaw

John J. Carlin, Jr.
Laurence R. Maddock
Donald J. Fay
Richard R. Cerbone

Arthur G. Warden, III

For full biographical listings, see the Martindale-Hubbell Law Directory

D'ALESSANDRO, JACOVINO & GERSON (AV)

147 Columbia Turnpike, 07932
Telephone: 201-966-1910
Fax: 201-966-6774
URL: http://www.lawyers.com/djgattys
New York, N.Y. Office: 321 Broadway, 4th Floor.
Telephone: 212-608-7500.

MEMBERS OF FIRM

Edward G. D'Alessandro
Amedeo C. Jacovino
Frederick E. Gerson

ASSOCIATES

Edward G. D'Alessandro, Jr.
Anthony J. Bianciella

Reference: Midatlantic Bank.

For full biographical listings, see the Martindale-Hubbell Law Directory

DRINKER BIDDLE & SHANLEY LLP (AV)

A Pennsylvania Limited Liability Partnership
500 Campus Drive, 07932-1047
Telephone: 973-360-1100
Fax: 973-285-1625; 360-9831
URL: http://www.dbr.com
Philadelphia, Pennsylvania Office: Drinker Biddle & Reath LLP, One Logan Square, 18th & Cherry Streets.
Telephone: 215-988-2700.
Telefax: 215-988-2757.
Cable Address: "Debemac."
Washington, D.C. Office: Drinker Biddle & Reath LLP, 1500 K Street, N.W., Suite 1100.
Telephone: 202-842-8800.
Telefax: 202-842-8465.
Princeton, New Jersey Office: Suite 300, 105 College Road East.
Telephone: 609-716-6500.
Telefax: 609-799-7000.
Berwyn, Pennsylvania Office: Drinker Biddle & Reath LLP, Suite 300, 1000 Westlakes Drive.
Telephone: 610-993-2200.
Telefax: 610-993-8585.
New York, New York Office: Drinker Biddle & Reath LLP, 89th Floor, One World Trade Center.
Telephone: 212-321-1812.
Telecopier: 1-212-466-0569.

John Kandravy
Raymond M. Tierney, Jr.
Arthur R. Schmauder
Thomas F. Campion
John J. Francis, Jr.
Gerald W. Hull, Jr.
A. Dennis Terrell
Richard E. Brennan
Thomas J. Alworth
Jeffrey A. Peck
James H. Freis
Matthew Farley
Daniel F. O'Connell
Richard A. Levao
Charles A. Reid, III
Stewart E. Lavey
Paul G. Nittoly
Glenn S. Pantel
Walter J. Fleischer, Jr.
Lydia C. Stefanowicz
Susan M. Sharko
Kevin M. Kilcullen
Stephen R. Long (Chairman, Litigation Department, 1995—)
Brian F. McDonough
James M. Altieri
Richard D. Prentice
Robert M. Leonard
Robert A. Gladstone
Nan Bernardo
Theodore S. Smith
Michael O. Adelman
Robert K. Malone
Neil S. Cartusciello
Kenneth J. Wilbur
Ieva Miesnieks Rogers
Robert A. Klausner
William T. Corbett, Jr.
Sean Monaghan
Michael E. Helmer
Kathleen H. Dooley
Edward A. Gramigna, Jr.
Kathleen B. Harden
Michael R. Clarke

OF COUNSEL

Alvin C. Martin
Michael J. Faigen

COUNSEL

Jodi Sydell Rosenzweig
Bruce L. Shapiro
Joan M. Neri
Michael J. Nita
Lynn Ciolino Boyajian
Robert A. Del Vecchio
Stephen A. Urban

Maureen Nesbitt Warshaw
Joan E. Pearson
Jeffrey S. Lipkin
Stephanie Mergel Hadley
Michael E. Rothpletz, Jr.
William J. Mendrzycki
John M. O'Reilly
James A. Kozachek
William J. Metcalf
H. Lockwood Miller, III
Laura A. Brady
Robert M. Vinci
Pasquale J. Rufolo
Ethan D. Stein
Gregory B. Pasquale
Daniel B. Carroll
Christopher C. Loeber
Stacey P. Rappaport
Andrew B. Joseph
Melissa L. Klipp
John M. Blumers
Robert C. Ciolek
Diane M. Flynn
Christina Butler Murphy
Dean J. Donatelli
Charles J. Falletta
Michael P. Pompeo
Cheryl Whitney
Lisa Ann DeMarzo
Paul C. Pawlowski
Decanda M. Faulk
Thomas P. Rohan, III
Rachelle H. Milstein
Joseph G. Dolan
Romney L. Grippo
Douglas J. McGill
Michelle M. Bufano
Dana J. Scancarella
Amy E. Watkins
Scott C. Carroll
Jennifer La Mont
David K. Richter
Brenda Eady Stafford
Christena A. Lambrianakos
Marianne Calabrese
Benjamin L. Siegel
Mark C. Errico
Gary J. Hacker
Jeffrey S. Mandel

For full biographical listings, see the Martindale-Hubbell Law Directory

(See Next Column)

GEDNEY, SEAMAN & HILGENDORFF (AV)
248 Columbia Turnpike, P.O. Box 166, 07932-0166
Telephone: 973-377-9120
Fax: 973-377-9126
Morristown, New Jersey Office: 15 James Street.
Telephone: 973-539-3088.
Fax: 973-539-0163

MEMBERS OF FIRM

Stanley L. Gedney, Jr. (1889-1977)
Bradford C. Seaman (1898-1986)
Hugo A. Hilgendorff, Jr. (1914-1991)
Hugo A. Hilgendorff, III

ASSOCIATES

Peter B. Hilgendorff
George B. Wright

For full biographical listings, see the Martindale-Hubbell Law Directory

HACK, PIRO, O'DAY, MERKLINGER, WALLACE & MCKENNA, P.A. (AV)
30 Columbia Turnpike, P.O. Box 941, 07932-0941
Telephone: 973-301-6500
Fax: 973-301-0094
Email: hpom@ix.netcom.com

Peter A. Piro
William J. O'Day
M. Richard Merklinger
Joseph V. Wallace
John M. McKenna
Peter T. Melnyk
Patrick M. Sages
Bonny G. Rafel
Robert G. Alencewicz
John T. West
Thomas M. Madden

Robert P. Morgan
Angela J. Mendelsohn
Michael J. Leegan
Stephen DeNaro
Joanne Vos
Peter Nastasi
Carol A. Rankin

OF COUNSEL

David L. Hack
William D. Dougherty
George A. West

For full biographical listings, see the Martindale-Hubbell Law Directory

*FREEHOLD,** Monmouth Co.

CERRATO, DAWES, COLLINS, SAKER & BROWN, A PROFESSIONAL CORPORATION (AV)
Wemrock Professional Mall, 509 Stillwells Corner Road, P.O. Box 6009, 07728
Telephone: 732-431-5000; 462-0480
Fax: 732-462-0483

Dominick A. Cerrato
John I. Dawes
James E. Collins
Mark F. Saker
Sanford D. Brown

Helen M. Wilder

OF COUNSEL

Barry William Messinger (Not admitted in NJ)

Representative Clients: Nat West; Freehold Regional High School; New Jersey Conservation Foundation; United Methodist Homes of New Jersey; Southern New Jersey Conference, United Methodist Church; Presbytery of Monmouth; Monmouth Council, Boy Scouts of America; Bayliner Marine Corp.

For full biographical listings, see the Martindale-Hubbell Law Directory

MEHR & LAFRANCE (AV)
10 East Main Street, P.O. Box 680, 07728
Telephone: 732-431-4100
Real Estate Dept.: 732-431-4208
Telefax: 732-431-2232
Email: MLBLAW@WORLDNET.ATT.NET *URL:* http://www.lawyers.com/mehr&lafrance

MEMBERS OF FIRM

William J. Mehr
Peter R. LaFrance
Scott J. Basen

Representative Clients: Freehold Raceway Mall; Norkus Enterprises, Inc. (Foodtown); Wal-Mart Stores, Inc.; Welsh Farms, Inc.; Sears Roebuck & Co.; Sony Theatres; Windsor Industrial Park; Nestle Beverage Co., Inc.; Community Bank of New Jersey; Harley-Davidson Motor Credit.

For full biographical listings, see the Martindale-Hubbell Law Directory

*HACKENSACK,** Bergen Co.

CONTANT, SCHERBY & ATKINS (AV)
33 Hudson Street, 07601
Telephone: 201-342-1070
Fax: 201-342-5213
Email: LawfirmCSA@aol.com *URL:* http://www.lawyers.com/csalaw

MEMBERS OF THE FIRM

John M. Contant (1907-1988)
Richard J. Contant
Matthew S. Rogers
Andrew T. Fede
Michael L. Scherby
Bruce L. Atkins
Brian T. Keane
Robert B. Hille

ASSOCIATES

Geraldine E. Beers
Suzanne J. Ryderman
Lisa R. Aljian
Christina A. Stoneburner
Sheila O'Shea

OF COUNSEL

Fenster & Weiss, New City, New York

For full biographical listings, see the Martindale-Hubbell Law Directory

CUCCIO AND CUCCIO (AV)
45 Essex Street, 07601
Telephone: 201-487-7411
Fax: 201-487-6574
Mailing Address: P.O. Box 2223, South Hackensack, New Jersey, 07606
URL: http://www.lawyers.com/cucciolaw

MEMBERS OF FIRM

Frank J. Cuccio
Emil S. Cuccio

ASSOCIATE

Jonathan M. Remshak

Representative Clients: Tele-Communications, Inc.; Cablevision of Oakland, Inc.; Vanderbilt Home Furnishings, Inc.; Huffman Koos, Inc.; Blue Circle-Raia, Inc.; Napp Technologies, Inc.; River Terrace Gardens Assoc.; Reliable-Miller Casket Co.; Borough of Paramus; Borough of Fort Lee.

For full biographical listings, see the Martindale-Hubbell Law Directory

DEENER, FEINGOLD & STERN, A PROFESSIONAL CORPORATION (AV)
2 University Plaza, Suite 503, 07601
Telephone: 201-343-8788
Fax: 201-343-4640
Email: JeromeDeener@DeenerFeingold.com *URL:* http://www.lawyers.com/deenerfeingold&stern

Jerome A. Deener
Cal R. Feingold
Robert A. Stern
David M. Edelblum
Anthony M. Vizzoni

Debra T. Hirsch
Andrew M. Grumet
Ronen Gabbay

References: Hudson United Bank; Commerce Bank.

For full biographical listings, see the Martindale-Hubbell Law Directory

HEIN, SMITH, BEREZIN, MALOOF & JACOBS, L.L.C. (AV)
Court Plaza East, 19 Main Street, 07601-7023
Telephone: 201-487-7400
Telecopier: 201-487-4228
Email: counsel@heinsmith.com

MEMBERS OF FIRM

Robert J. Maloof
Sidney Berezin
Robert L. Baum
Lawrence H. Jacobs
Ellen W. Smith
Carla H. Madnick

ASSOCIATES

John L. Shanahan
Douglas V. Sanchez
Robert J. Logan
Eileen P. Mulroy

OF COUNSEL

Seymour A. Smith

Representative Clients: Bergen County Joint Municipal Insurance Fund; Commercial General Union Insurance Cos. of New York; Crawford & Co.; Health Care Insurance Co.; Princeton Insurance Co.; St. Paul Fire & Marine Insurance Co.; Pro Mutual Insurance Company; NJ Cure.
Reference: Summit Bank.

For full biographical listings, see the Martindale-Hubbell Law Directory

NICOLETTE & PERKINS, P.A. (AV)
3 University Plaza, Fifth Floor, 07601
Telephone: 201-488-9080
Telecopier: 201-488-5580
Email: nicoletteperkins@juno.com *URL:* http://www.lawyers.com/nicolette&perkins

David A. Nicolette, Jr.
Eric R. Perkins

Jeanette A. Odynski
Laura N. Keenan
Toni Marie McPhillips

For full biographical listings, see the Martindale-Hubbell Law Directory

PASHMAN STEIN, A PROFESSIONAL CORPORATION (AV)
45 Essex Street, 07601-5415
Telephone: 201-488-8200
Fax: 201-488-5556
Email: info@pashmanstein.com *URL:* http://www.lawyers.com/pashmanstein

(See Next Column)

PASHMAN STEIN A PROFESSIONAL CORPORATION—*Continued*

Louis Pashman
Samuel J. Samaro
Dennis T. Smith
Michael S. Stein

Amy E. Whitteaker
John T. Whipple

SPECIAL COUNSEL

Morris Pashman

For full biographical listings, see the Martindale-Hubbell Law Directory

SHAPIRO & CROLAND (AV)

A Partnership including Professional Corporations
Continental Plaza II, 411 Hackensack Avenue, 07601
Telephone: 201-488-3900
Fax: 201-488-9481

Barry I. Croland, P.C.
Robert P. Shapiro, P.C.
Barry L. Baime
Jay Rubenstein
Kenneth S. Apfel
Kenneth S. Goldrich, P.C.
Bruce J. Ackerman
Stuart Reiser, P.C.
Meridith J. Bronson
John P. Di Iorio
David O. Marcus
Robert F. Green
Lizabeth Sarakin
David Torchin
Robin C. Bogan
Craig D. Spector

OF COUNSEL

Harvey R. Sorkow

Donald R. Sorkow (1930-1985)

Reference: Bank of New York-National Community Division.

For full biographical listings, see the Martindale-Hubbell Law Directory

SOKOL, BEHOT AND FIORENZO (AV)

433 Hackensack Avenue, 07601
Telephone: 201-488-1300
Fax: 201-488-6541

MEMBERS OF FIRM

Leon J. Sokol
Joseph F. Behot, Jr.
Joseph B. Fiorenzo
Jeffrey A. Zenn
Arthur Bergman
Michael P. Feltman

ASSOCIATES

Siobhan Spillane Bailey
Mitchell B. Levine
Steven Seigel
Andrew S. Bosin

COUNSEL

Alan Prigal

For full biographical listings, see the Martindale-Hubbell Law Directory

HADDONFIELD, Camden Co.

GERSTEIN GRAYSON, LLP (AV)

Twenty Kings Highway West, 08033
Telephone: 856-795-6700
Fax: 856-354-0020
Email: gcglaw@aol.com

Samuel Gerstein
Mitchell T. Grayson
Andrew B. Cohen

Deena L. Betze
Rebecca Brandt Condit
Karen R. Scheiner
Bruce P. Matez
Meredith Siegel Cohen

OF COUNSEL

Manya L. Kamerling

For full biographical listings, see the Martindale-Hubbell Law Directory

MADDEN, MADDEN AND DEL DUCA, P.A. (AV)

108 Kings Highway East, P.O. Box 210, 08033
Telephone: 609-428-9520
Telecopier: 609-428-7335
Email: mmd108@aol.com

James J. Madden
Michael P. Madden
Joseph A. Del Duca
Anthony M. Pugliese
Damien O. Del Duca

Patrick Joseph Madden
Mara Wexler-Wuebker

For full biographical listings, see the Martindale-Hubbell Law Directory

HAWTHORNE, Passaic Co.

JEFFER, HOPKINSON & VOGEL (AV)

(Formerly Jeffer, Walter, Tierney, DeKorte, Hopkinson & Vogel)
Law Building, 1600 Route 208N, P.O. Box 507, 07507
Telephone: 973-423-0100
Fax: 973-423-5614
Tequesta, Florida Office: Jeffer, Cioffi & Cicalese. 250 Tequesta Drive, 33469.
Telephone: 561-747-6000.
Fax: 561-575-9167.

MEMBERS OF FIRM

Herman M. Jeffer
Reginald F. Hopkinson
Jerome A. Vogel
Peter Hofstra (1886-1961)
George Tierney (1895-1976)
Joseph V. Fumagalli (1901-1965)
Richard W. DeKorte (1936-1975)
Robert Walter (1908-1990)

ASSOCIATES

Melinda B. Maidens
E. David Becker
David H. Altman

LEGAL SUPPORT PERSONNEL

Janet Faber (Office Administrator)

Counsel for: Brioschi, Inc.; Opici Wine Co.; Gas Pumpers of America Corp.; The Paterson Market Growers Assn.; Dowling Fuel Oil Co.; Becton, Dickinson; JFC International, Inc.; Loews Theaters; Christian Health Care Center.

For full biographical listings, see the Martindale-Hubbell Law Directory

LAKEWOOD, Ocean Co.

BATHGATE, WEGENER & WOLF, P.C. (AV)

One Airport Road, P.O. Box 2043, 08701
Telephone: 732-363-0666
Telecopier: 732-363-9864
Email: bathweg@idt.net

Lawrence E. Bathgate, II
Peter H. Wegener
William J. Wolf
Jan L. Wouters
Ross D. Gertner
Edward B. Kasselman
Dominic J. Aprile
Nancy G. Wright
Michael M. DiCicco

COUNSEL

Neil Brodsky
Peter A. Valenti

Jonathan S. Fabricant
Robert J. Gillispie, Jr.
Peter G. Licata
Steven E Robertson

For full biographical listings, see the Martindale-Hubbell Law Directory

LINDEN, Union Co.

WINETSKY AND WINETSKY (AV)

401 North Wood Avenue, P.O. Box 1053, 07036
Telephone: 908-486-2761; 908-486-2762
Fax: 908-486-2661

MEMBERS OF FIRM

Lewis Winetsky (1929-1986)
Charles N. Winetsky

Reference: First Union Bank, Linden, New Jersey.

For full biographical listings, see the Martindale-Hubbell Law Directory

LIVINGSTON, Essex Co.

SKOLOFF & WOLFE, P.C. (AV)

293 Eisenhower Parkway, 07039
Telephone: 973-992-0900
Fax: 973-992-0301
Morristown, New Jersey Office: 10 Park Place.
Telephone: 973-267-3511.

Saul A. Wolfe
Gary N. Skoloff
Richard H. Singer, Jr. (Resident at Morristown Office)
Stephen P. Haller
Robert F. Giancaterino
Edward J. O'Donnell
Beatrice E. Kandell
Heather A. Turnbull

Garry J. Roettger
Nancy C. Richmond
Gigi Hanna

OF COUNSEL

Bertram Polow

For full biographical listings, see the Martindale-Hubbell Law Directory

MANASQUAN, Monmouth Co.

CARTON, WITT, ARVANITIS & BARISCILLO, L.L.C. (AV)

(Formerly Durand, Ivins & Carton)
40 Union Avenue, P.O. Box 367, 08736
Telephone: 908-223-1800
Asbury Park, New Jersey Office: 4001 Route 66 at Garden State Parkway, P.O. Box 1229.
Telephone: 732-922-9500.
Telecopier: 732-922-1625.

RESIDENT PARTNERS

James D. Carton, III
John C. Carton

Attorneys for: New Jersey Bell Telephone Co.; Jersey Shore Medical Center, Inc.
Local Attorneys for: Travelers Insurance Co.; Aetna Casualty & Surety Co.; New Jersey Manufacturers Insurance Co.; Liberty Mutual; Prudential Insurance Co.; Chubb & Son.; Princeton Insurance Co.; Garden State Indemnity Co.

For full biographical listings, see the Martindale-Hubbell Law Directory

MARLTON, Burlington Co.

PARKER, MCCAY & CRISCUOLO, P.A. (AV)

Suite 401 Three Greentree Centre, Route 73 & Greentree Road, P.O. Box 974, 08053
Telephone: 856-596-8900
Telecopier: 856-596-9631
Email: pmc@pmclaw.com *URL:* http://www.pmclaw.com
Cherry Hill, New Jersey Office: Commerce Atrium, Suite 500, 1701 Route 70 East, P.O. Box 1806.
Telephone: 856-424-4300.
Telecopier: 856-424-1006.
Lawrenceville, New Jersey Office: Princeton Pike Office Park, 3131 Princeton Pike, Building 4, Room 200.
Telephone: 609-219-0699.
Fax: 609-219-0708.

Robert C. Beck (Resident at Cherry Hill, New Jersey Office)
David A. Parker
Robert J. Partlow
Carl J. Gregorio
John Michael Devlin
Yves C. Veenstra
Thomas M. Masick
Marc M. Baldwin
Thomas M. Barron
Stephen J. Mushinski
Ronald C. Morgan
Stacy L. Moore, Jr.
John C. Gillespie
Drew J. Parker
Thomas M. Walsh
Gary F. Piserchia
Philip A. Norcross
Carolyn Reinhard Sleeper
Richard M. Berman (Resident at Cherry Hill, New Jersey Office)
Richard W. Hunt
Emmanuel J. Argentieri (Resident at Cherry Hill, New Jersey Office)
Nola R. Bencze
Jeanne M. Stiefel
Susan E. Bacso

COUNSEL

Frank P. Cavallo, Jr.

Irving G. Finkel
Victoria C. Fannon
Lynn S. Besancon
Joseph A. Carita
Lisa B. Baughman
Francine M. Cracker
J. Brooks DiDonato
Laurence D. Granite
Anthony Young
Steven Antinoff
Elena B. Zuares
Mary Kay Wysocki
Lora M. Giovacchini
Brad A. Parker
Brooke D. Schmoll
Diana R. Seuer
Douglas L. Heinold
Gene R. Mariano
Diane Tungol
Debra S. Hantman
John S. Kennedy (Resident at Cherry Hill, New Jersey Office)
Richard J. Nocella
Scott N. Wilson
Sujal D. Mehta
Dean J. Buono
Sandra G. Zeidman
Rhonda K. Dohanick

OF COUNSEL

Barry T. Parker
William V. Webster, Jr.
Richard J. Dill

Representative Clients: Banking: Commerce Bank; Insurance: Aetna Casualty & Surety; Continental Insurance Company; USF&G; Zurich-American Insurance Company; Rider Insurance Company.

For full biographical listings, see the Martindale-Hubbell Law Directory

MIDDLETOWN, Monmouth Co.

GIORDANO, HALLERAN & CIESLA, A PROFESSIONAL CORPORATION (AV)

125 Half Mile Road, P.O. Box 190, 07748
Telephone: 732-741-3900
Fax: 732-224-6599
Email: info@ghclaw.com
Trenton, New Jersey Office: 441 East State Street.
Telephone: 609-695-3900.

(See Next Column)

Toms River, New Jersey Office: 500 Hooper Avenue.
Telephone: 732-341-9600.

John C. Giordano, Jr.
John R. Halleran
Frank R. Ciesla
Bernard J. Berry, Jr.
Thomas A. Pliskin
John A. Aiello
Michael J. Gross
Richard L. Friedman
George J. Tyler
John A. Giunco, Jr.
Norman M. Hobbie
Edward S. Radzely
Sharlene A. Hunt
Philip D. Forlenza
Michael J. Canning
Paul H. Schneider
M. Scott Tashjy
Michele A. Querques
David P. Corrigan
Edward C. Bertucio, Jr.
Andrew B. Robins
Michael A. Bruno
Margaret B. Carmeli
Kurt E. Anderson
Paul T. Colella
Steven J. Brodman
Gerald Patrick Lally
Paul V. Fernicola
Sean E. Regan
Debra J. Rubenstein

Laura Nigris Anderson
Jay Seth Becker
Timothy D. Lyons
Michael R. Hobbie
Michael A. Pane, Jr.
J. Scott Anderson
Craig S. Virgil
Charles A. Cerussi
Patrick S. Convery
Jacqueline DeCarlo
Steven M. Dalton
Nicole Devaney
Edward C. Normandin
Michele E. Hart
Jeffrey M. Thomen
Thomas D. Atkinson
Leann E. Foster
Monica J. Ceres

COUNSEL

Elizabeth Hellmers Christian
Joanne S. Gray

OF COUNSEL

S. Thomas Gagliano

Representative Clients: Bayshore Community Hospital; South Jersey Hospital; Roberts Pharmaceutical Corp.; Utica Mutual Insurance Co.

For full biographical listings, see the Martindale-Hubbell Law Directory

MILLBURN, Essex Co.

MCDERMOTT & MCGEE (AV)

75 Main Street, P.O. Box 192, 07041-0192
Telephone: 973-467-8080
Fax: 973-376-8669

MEMBERS OF FIRM

John L. McDermott
John P. McGee
Richard P. Maggi
Thomas A. Wester
Richard M. Tango
Frank P. Leanza
John L. McDermott, Jr.
David J. Dickinson
A. Charles Lorenzo
Robert A. McDermott
Kevin John McGee

ASSOCIATES

Anthony John Verardi
Lindsay K. O'Shaughnessy
Andre L. McGuire

OF COUNSEL

Daniel K. Van Dorn

Representative Clients: Affiliated Building Service, Inc.; Allstate Insurance Co.; General Agents Insurance Company of America; Greater New York Mutual; General Accident Group; ISS International Service System, Inc.; Zurich-American Insurance Co.; Penn National Insurance Co.; Tokio Marine & Fire Insurance Co.; Medical Inter-Insurance Exchange of New Jersey.

For full biographical listings, see the Martindale-Hubbell Law Directory

MONTVALE, Bergen Co.

BEATTIE PADOVANO, LLC (AV)

50 Chestnut Ridge Road, P.O. Box 244, 07645
Telephone: 201-573-1810
Fax: 201-573-9736
Email: beattie-padovano@worldnet.att.net

MEMBERS OF FIRM

James R. Beattie
Ralph J. Padovano
Roger W. Breslin, Jr.
Thomas W. Dunn
Martin W. Kafafian
Adolph A. Romei
Brian R. Martinotti
John J. Lamb
John R. Holsinger
Antimo A. Del Vecchio

SENIOR ASSOCIATES

Emery C. Duell
Brenda J. Stewart
Kathleen S. Cook
Dana B. Cobb
Steven A. Weisfeld
Robert A. Blass
Alan G. White

ASSOCIATES

Gregg A. Padovano
James V. Zarrillo
Andrew D. Hopp
Jennifer Bretz
Matthew T. Rose
Renata A. Helstoski
Maria V. Martin

(See Next Column)

BEATTIE PADOVANO LLC—*Continued*

OF COUNSEL

Ira J. Kaltman
Francis B. Sheehan

For full biographical listings, see the Martindale-Hubbell Law Directory

MOORESTOWN, Burlington Co.

CHIERICI, CHIERICI & SMITH, A PROFESSIONAL CORPORATION (AV)

Blason Campus - III, 509 South Lenola Road Building Six, 08057-1561
Telephone: 856-234-6300
Fax: 856-234-9490

Donald R. Chierici, Jr.
Elizabeth Coleman Chierici
Julie C. Smith

Carolyn J. Kornas
Mark G. Esposito
Richard D. DiTomaso
Melvin McDowell
David J. Karbasian
Peter P. Sanchez
Donald R. Chierici, III

For full biographical listings, see the Martindale-Hubbell Law Directory

*MORRISTOWN,** Morris Co.

GRAHAM, CURTIN & SHERIDAN, A PROFESSIONAL ASSOCIATION (AV)

Four Headquarters Plaza, P.O. Box 1991, 07962-1991
Telephone: 973-292-1700
Fax: 973-292-1767
URL: http://www.gcslaw.com
Trenton, New Jersey Office: Suite 1008, 50 West State Street, 08608.
Telephone: 609-695-0098.
Fax: 609-695-1298.
Washington, D.C. Office: Suite 400, 1825 I Street, N.W., 20006.
Telephone: 202-775-6937.
Fax: 202-857-8054.

MEMBERS OF FIRM

Jerome J. Graham, Jr.
Thomas R. Curtin
Peter G. Sheridan (Resident, Trenton, New Jersey Office)
Stephen V. Gimigliano
George C. Jones
Peter M. Laughlin
Edward P. McKenzie
James J. O'Hara
Frederick W. Peters (Resident, Washington, D.C. Office)
Robert P. Regimbal
Thomas D. Shea, Jr.
Kenneth W. Vest
Janyce M. Wilson
Paul L. Zelenty

OF COUNSEL

Jerard F. Maher
Joseph M. Lamastra
Richard T. Laughlin
Francis P. Crotty
James R. Lacey
William A. Fox

ASSOCIATES

Kathleen Noonan Fennelly
Dorothy A. Harbeck (Resident, Trenton, New Jersey Office)
Laura Ann Kelly
Dennis P. Monaghan
Robert W. Mauriello, Jr.
Peter T. Donnelly
Lynn B. Kegelman (Resident, Trenton, New Jersey Office)
Kent L. Schwarz
David J. Pascrell (Resident, Trenton, New Jersey Office)
Michael D. Witt (Not admitted in NJ)
Christopher J. Keale (Resident, Trenton, New Jersey Office)
Christopher Viceconte
Sandra Lee Gonzalez
Stephanie M. Bushell

For full biographical listings, see the Martindale-Hubbell Law Directory

MCELROY, DEUTSCH AND MULVANEY (AV)

1300 Mount Kemble Avenue, P.O. Box 2075, 07962-2075
Telephone: 973-993-8100
Fax: 973-425-0161
URL: http://www.MDMlaw.com
Denver, Colorado Office: 1099 18th Street, Suite 3120.
Telephone: 303-293-8800.
Fax: 303-293-3116.
New York, New York Office: Wall Street Plaza, 88 Pine Street.
Telephone: 212-766-1807.
Fax: 212-483-9129.
Ridgewood, New Jersey Office: 40 West Ridgewood Avenue.
Telephone: 201-445-6722.
Fax: 201-445-8075.

MEMBERS OF FIRM

Lorraine M. Armenti (Resident Partner, Denver Colorado Office)
Grace C. Bertone
John P. Beyel
William C. Carey
Stephen H. Cohen (1938-1992)
Kevin T. Coughlin
John F. Darcy (Resident, Ridgewood Office)
Edward B. Deutsch
Timothy I. Duffy
Kevin P. Galvin
Robert J. Kelly
Joseph P. La Sala
James P. Lisovicz
Paul A. Lisovicz
Fred A. Manley, Jr.
Michael J. Marone
Nancy McDonald

(See Next Column)

MEMBERS OF FIRM (Continued)

William T. McElroy
Laurence M. McHeffey (Resident Partner, Denver, Colorado Office)
Robert W. Muilenburg
James M. Mulvaney
Alfred S. Nugent, Jr. (1925-1989)
Octavius A. Orbe (Resident, Ridgewood Office)
Loren L. Pierce
Warren K. Racusin
Mark A. Rosen
Thomas P. Scrivo
John H. Suminski
Walter F. Timpone
Kevin E. Wolff

COUNSEL TO THE FIRM

Robert L. Clifford

OF COUNSEL

John K. Bradley
John F. Whitteaker

ASSOCIATES

Susan Freeman Anthony
H. George Avery
Elizabeth Addison Barrow
Joseph F. Bermudez
Thomas Richard Calcagni
Patrick J. Casey (Resident Associate, Denver, Colorado Office)
Lisbeth W. Cload (Resident, Ridgewood Office)
Daniel J. Cohen
Craig J. Compoli, Jr.
John P. Cookson (Resident Associate, New York, NY Office)
John Thomas Coyne
Andrew J. D'Arcy
Andrew M. Csaszar
Michael B. Devins
John W. DiNicola, II
Robin A. Donato
Rebecca Ward Donohue
Steven F. Dorry
Julienne S. Duncan
Brian F. Fowler (Resident, Ridgewood Office)
Aaron C. Foy (Not admitted in NJ; Resident, Denver, Colorado Office)
Christopher S. Frangeš
Lorna A. Friel
Kevin P. Harkins (Resident, Ridgewood Office)
Sarah C. Herzog
Eric J. Hughes
George A. Kelman
Justin N. Kinney
Linda F. Kitz
John P. Leonard
Joseph J. McGlone
Robert McGuire
Kaneez Fatema Madraswalla
Nadine Maleski
Faith Martin
Suzanne Cocco Midlige
Heidi S. Minuskin
Louis A. Modugno
Florina A. Moldovan
John W. Morris
Francis C. Porada (Resident Associate, Denver, Colorado Office)
Robert J. Re
Vincent E. Reilly
Jay R. Ruble
Craig T. Sashihara
Adam R. Schwartz
Peter W. Smith
Timothy P. Smith
Ronnie H. Spring
Michael J. Sullivan
Catharine Acker Vaughan
Meredith A. Walling
Richard J. Williams, Jr.

Representative Clients: ADT Security Systems, Inc.; Crum & Forster Insurance Co.; Eaton Corp.; The Pittston Co.; Security Pacific Finance Corp.; American Hondo Motor Co., Inc.; UpRight, Inc.; Porsche Cars North America, Inc.

For full biographical listings, see the Martindale-Hubbell Law Directory

PITNEY, HARDIN, KIPP & SZUCH LLP (AV)

P.O. Box 1945, 07962-1945
Telephone: 973-966-6300
New York City: 212-687-6000
Telex: 642014
Telecopier: 973-966-1550
URL: http://www.phks.com
New York, New York Office: 711 Third Avenue, 10017-4014.
Telephone: 212-687-6000.
Fax: 212-682-3485.

MEMBERS OF FIRM

Clyde A. Szuch
S. Joseph Fortunato
David J. Connolly, Jr.
William H. Hyatt, Jr.
Lawrence F. Reilly
Murray J. Laulicht
Robert C. Neff
Richard Kahn
Edward P. Lynch
Gerald Levy (Not admitted in NJ)
Joseph Lunin
Peter A. Forgosh
Richard L. Plotkin
Robert L. Hollingshead
Frederick L. Whitmer
Gregory C. Parliman
Robert G. Rose
Patrick J. McCarthy
Roger R. Gottilla
Anthony J. Marchetta
Mary Lou Parker
J. Michael Nolan, Jr.
Warren J. Casey
Kevin J. O'Donnell
Peter J. Herzberg
Ronald H. Janis
Glenn C. Geiger
Dennis R. LaFiura
Gail H. Allyn
Henry Nelson Massey
Dennis T. Kearney
Kenneth J. Norcross
Donald W. Kiel
Joel M. Rosen
Kathy A. Lawler
Elizabeth J. Sher
Theresa Donahue Egler
Michael J. Dunne
Hope S. Cone
John C. Maloney, Jr.
Lori J. Braender
Thomas J. Malman
David P. Doyle
Colleen R. Donovan
David W. Payne
Michael W. Zelenty
Benjamin E. Haglund
Joy Harmon Sperling
Christopher John Stracco

(See Next Column)

PITNEY, HARDIN, KIPP & SZUCH LLP, *Morristown—Continued*

MEMBERS OF FIRM (Continued)

Brian S. Montag
Deirdre E. Moore
Michael P. Turner
Michael E. Waller
Michael T. Bissinger
David S. Sager

OF COUNSEL

George A. Aguilar
Joseph C. Sullivan (Not admitted in NJ)

COUNSEL

Jane H. Hardin
Ronald R. Santucci (Not admitted in NJ)
L. Allison Garde
Paul E. Flanagan
Kathy Dutton Helmer
Theresa A. Kelly
Jonathan E. Hill
John P. Scordo
Kathryn M. Decker
Linda K. Connolly
Jonathan S. Bristol
Michael J. Duane (Not admitted in NJ)
John J. O'Reilly
Mary B. Rogers
Stephen H. Skoller
Marjorie F. Chertok
Heidi Jan Sorvino
Charles P. Abraham
James F. Baxley
Paul J. Halasz
Charles Allen Yuen
Scott A. Zuber

ASSOCIATES

Debra H. Sweetwood
Ronald T. Nagle
Rosemarie DaSilva
Maureen C. Pavely
Rosalie J. Shoeman
Richard D. Ballot
Maritza Berdote Byrne
Ronald D. Coleman
Amanda Berlowe Jaffe
Christopher W. Nanos
Bruce D. Taterka
Richard H. Brown III
William S. Hatfield
Wendy Johnson Lario
Karen Raihofer
Michael V. Simio
Emily L. Won
Debra K. Bampton
Lisa A. Breen
Vanessa M. Brill
Shari L. Chertoff
Gail Howie Conenello
Michael T. Lavigne
Helen A. Nau
Alissa Pyrich
Zachary D. Rosenbaum
Grace J. Shin
Susan Yeu
Melinda Fellner Bramwit
John B. Buckman IV
Glenn Eric Butash (Not admitted in NJ)
Alashia Chan
Joseph W. Chouinard
Mark J. Farinella
Kristine J. Feher
Wendy B. Green
Gregory J. Kerr
Sonya A. Lecount-McClanahan (Not admitted in NJ)
Laurie Droughton Matthews
Brian Edward Moffitt
Anna L. Musacchio
Michael J. Rave
Thomas C. Regan
Keith E. Riley
Rhonda L. Rivera
Gail E. Slaughter
George A. Sorial
Mia Lidde Stuart
Joseph M. Boyan
Ronald E. Brown (Not admitted in NJ)
Marc D. Crowley
Richard J. Danyko, Jr. (Not admitted in NJ)
John F. Gulbin
Jonathan J. Harper
Robert P. Schreiber
Marjorie F. Sheron
Catherine A. Trinkle
Michael J. Vitiello
Ellen A. Feeney
Erin S. Hennessy (Not admitted in NJ)
Elliot D. Ostrove
Jill Petroro
Alison T. Saling
Daniel H. Solomon
Clifford A. Ulrich (Not admitted in NJ)
Meghan A. Bennett
April Mary Gilmore
Scott W. Goodman
Jerry Y. Hirschkorn
Kara Kantor Lewis
Melanie L. Mecka
Steven A. Muhlstock
Maureen B. O'Neill
Kara McCarthy Perry
Lisa Ness Seidman
Cindy L. Szabo
David M. Waizer

Representative Clients: Air & Water Technologies Corporation; AGFA Division, Bayer Corporation; AlliedSignal Inc.; American Home Products Corporation; Alfa Laval, Inc.; Arthur Andersen & Co.; Atlantic States Cast Iron Pipe; AT&T Corporation; Base Ten Systems, Inc.; BASF Corporation.

For full biographical listings, see the Martindale-Hubbell Law Directory

PORZIO, BROMBERG & NEWMAN, A PROFESSIONAL CORPORATION (AV)

163 Madison Avenue, 07962-1997
Telephone: 973-538-4006
Facsimile: 973-538-5146
URL: http://www.pbnlaw.com
New York, New York Office: 156 West 56th Street, 10019.
Telephone: 212-265-6888.
Fax: 212-957-3983.
Brick, New Jersey Office: 263 Drum Point Road, 08723.
Telephone: 732-262-9248.
Fax: 732-262-9673.

Steven P. Benenson
Robert J. Brennan
Lisa Murtha Bromberg
Myron J. Bromberg
D. Jeffrey Campbell
Thomas R. Chesson
Roy Alan Cohen
Robert C. Epstein
Frank Fazio
Lauren E. Handler
Edward A. Hogan
Anita Hotchkiss
William A. Krais
Connie A. Matteo
Jay R. McDaniel
Kenneth R. Meyer
John M. Newman
Howard J. Schwartz
Thomas Spiesman
Charles J. Stoia

COUNSEL

Craig B. Bleifer
Gordon L. DeMario
Christopher P. DePhillips
Cynthia J. Dreeman
Charles E. Erway, III
Morna L. Sweeney
Alvin Weiss
Allan I. Young

Mary-Alice Barrett
Joseph G. Calella
Lynette J. Carhart
John T. Chester
Laura C. Conway
Garineh S. Dovletian
Richard P. Earley
Vanessa R. Elliott
Elisabeth W. Gehringer
Jacqueline Greenberg
Amy C. Grossman
Jay S. Karp
Jeffry H. Koenig
Jonathan R. Kuhlman
Barbara Lawrence
Lauren Blair McRae (Not admitted in NJ)
Lisa J. Morelli (Not admitted in NJ)
Tara A. Murphy
Linda Pissott Reig
Jennifer A. Romanski
Stephen W. Smithson
Ronald E. Steinvarzel
William J. VonDerHeide
Christina H. Wang
Jennifer Fisher Weiss
Michael C. Weiss
Daniel K. Winters

Representative Clients: AlliedSignal, Inc.; American Home Products; ASARCO Incorporated; Black and Decker Corporation; Ingersoll-Rand Company; Johnson & Johnson; Minnesota Mining and Manufacturing Company; Smith Kline Beecham Corporation; Unisys Corporation; Warner Lambert Company.

For full biographical listings, see the Martindale-Hubbell Law Directory

RAND, ALGEIER, TOSTI & WOODRUFF, A PROFESSIONAL CORPORATION (AV)

60 Washington Street, 07960
Telephone: 973-539-2600
Telecopier: 973-984-0430
Email: randlaw@bellatlantic.net

Gary C. Algeier
David B. Rand
Robert M. Tosti
Robert B. Woodruff
John F. McDonnell
John E. Croot, Jr.

Kathryn J. Kingree
Deborah A. White

OF COUNSEL

Ronald M. Pflug
Ellen S. Bass
Tamara Krikorian

For full biographical listings, see the Martindale-Hubbell Law Directory

RIKER, DANZIG, SCHERER, HYLAND & PERRETTI LLP (AV)

Headquarters Plaza, One Speedwell Avenue, 07962-1981
Telephone: 973-538-0800
Fax: 973-538-1984
Email: info@riker.com *URL:* http://www.riker.com
Trenton, New Jersey Office: 50 West State Street, Suite 1010.
Telephone: 609-396-2121.
Fax: 609-396-4578.

MEMBERS OF FIRM

Irving Riker (1921-1969)
William I. Riker (1951-1973)
Charles Danzig (1934-1992)
Benjamin P. Michel
Gerald A. Liloia
John P. Sheridan, Jr.
James S. Rothschild, Jr.
Vincent J. Sharkey, Jr.
Dennis J. O'Grady
Michael K. Furey
Gary E. Walsh
Robert D. Borteck
Edward K. DeHope
Shawn L. Kelly
Mark S. Rattner
Dennis J. Krumholz
Alan E. Kraus
Glenn A. Clark
Robert J. Schoenberg
Maryann Dougherty Kicenuik
Samuel P. Moulthrop
Victoria A. Morrison
Andrew J. Stamelman
Kenneth M. Van Deventer
Jan L. Bernstein
Sigrid S. Franzblau
Anne M. Patterson
John M. Pellecchia (Trenton Office)
Anthony J. Sylvester
Peter C. Harvey
Glenn D. Curving
Robert J. Gilson
Jeffrey B. Wagenbach
Warren J. Martin Jr.
Sandra Brown Sherman
Nicholas Racioppi, Jr.
Robert C. Daleo
James C. Meyer
Julian W. Wells
Brian E. O'Donnell
Stuart M. Lederman
Marilynn R. Greenberg
Michael R. O'Donnell
Anthony J. Zarillo, Jr.

OF COUNSEL

Everett M. Scherer
William F. Hyland
Peter N. Perretti, Jr.
Peter L. Berkley
William C. Connelly
Edward A. Zunz, Jr.
Sidney M. Schreiber
Stewart G. Pollock
Peter F. Eld

(See Next Column)

RIKER, DANZIG, SCHERER, HYLAND & PERRETTI LLP—*Continued*

COUNSEL

Ernest D. Buff
Charles F. Waskevich, Jr.
Linda H. Prentiss
Richard D. Sanders
James A. Harkness (Trenton Office)
Rafael Perez

ASSOCIATES

Nancy Stewart
Judith J. Sullivan
James A. Raborn
Lynn A. Lurie
J. Alex Kress
Stephanie D. Edelson
Nancy C. Eberhardt
Harold L. Kofman
Scott A. Ohnegian
William G. Connolly
Harold S. Atlas
Mary Kathryn Roberts (Trenton Office)
Joseph L. Schwartz
Evan A. Showell
Cathleen H. Giuliana
Bruce A. Harris
Craig L. Steinfeld
James L. Lott Jr.
Keith J. Weingold
Thomas J. Perry
Larisa V. K. Gjivoje
Steven K. Parness
Edwin F. Chociey, Jr.
Kelly Strange Crawford
Jacqueline F. McGowan
Leslie Gladstone Restaino
David L. Isabel
Ronald D. Puhala
Mary Ellen Burke
Francine Halushka Katz
John S. Mairo
Marcia Ann Miller
Lisa Santapietro
Jeffrey J. Brookner (Not admitted in NJ)
Katherine H. Wigness
Marc D'Angiolillo
Jack Sheridan
Andrea J. Giannetta
Michael J. Loesberg
Alfred J. Sargente
Alexa Richman La-Londe
Brett M. Reina
Craig H. Feldman
Deborah S. Gadek
Sarah L. Kambour
Rodney N. Tendai Richards
Carol Cespedes
Steven T. Senior
Christopher C. Ash
Jennifer L. Smiles
Anthony Fernandez
Michael H. Wilck
Noah Franzblau
Beth Ann Stemmler
James P. Gianakis
Cathy K. Brown
Karen M. Kozlowski
Debra D. Tedesco
Nina G. Holbrook
Curt M. Hapward
David R. Hausmann
Richard S. Kohn
Sandra Hall Mulrain
Richard E. Hamilton
Keena M. Mackay
Matthew H. Lewis
Craig Demareski
Eric W. Landy
Marcella M. Bodner
Andrew M. Contreras
Geoffrey G. Gussis
Todd Julian
Maha F. Munayyer
Ayesha C. Blackwell
Dorit T. Robbins
Michael A. Schmerling
Eric Blumenfeld
Keith D. Barrack
Kris Ann E. Cappelluti (Trenton Office)

Representative Clients: American Telephone & Telegraph Co.; AlliedSignal; First Union National Bank; International Business Machines Corp.; New Jersey Health Care Facilities Financing Authority; New Jersey Turnpike Authority; Summit Bank.

For full biographical listings, see the Martindale-Hubbell Law Directory

---

SCHENCK, PRICE, SMITH & KING, LLP (AV)

10 Washington Street, P.O. Box 905, 07963-0905
Telephone: 973-539-1000
Telecopier: 973-540-7300
Email: SCHENCK@SPSK.COM
New York, New York Office: 261 Madison Avenue, Suite 800.
Telephone: 212-986-6482.

MEMBERS OF FIRM

Clinton J. Curtis
James E. Davidson
Julius J. Denzler
Charles D. LaFiura
William C. Dodd
Willard Bergman, Jr.
Edward W. Ahart
Thomas C. C. Humick
Thomas F. Craig, II
Sidney A. Sayovitz
Douglas S. Brierley
Edward John Trawinski
Roy J. Evans
Howard P. Shaw
Gilbert S. Leeds
Monica E. Peck
Anita Joy Siegel
Lisa K. Pantel
James P. Wyse
Michael K. Mullen
M. Sheilah O'Halloran
Anne E. Aronovitch
John M. DeMarco
Michael A. Moroney
James B. Garland
Joanne L. Butler
Basil F. O'Connor
Patti S. Liberman
Kurt G. Senesky
Gary Mazart
Shirley Berger Whitenack
Richard J. Conway, Jr.

ASSOCIATES

Mary Elizabeth Warner
Barbara W. Stoller
Jeffrey T. LaRosa
Eric A. Inglis
Peter A. Marra
Wynne A. Whitman
Meredith L. Grocott
Karin S. Riecker
Maria A. Volarich
Jason E. Marx

OF COUNSEL

Kenneth J. Quinn
Patrick W. Turner
Douglas S. Zucker
Joseph E. Krakora

For full biographical listings, see the Martindale-Hubbell Law Directory

*NEWARK,** Essex Co.

BALK, OXFELD, MANDELL & COHEN, A PROFESSIONAL CORPORATION (AV)

50 Commerce Street, 07102-4003
Telephone: 973-623-0353
Fax: 973-802-1055
Elizabeth, New Jersey Office: 27 Prince Street, 07208.
Telephone: 908-353-0500.
Fax: 908-353-1495.

Louis David Balk
Sanford R. Oxfeld
Jack Mandell
Arnold Shep Cohen
Nancy Iris Oxfeld
Denzil R. Dunkley
Daniel Geddes

Randi Doner April
Gail Oxfeld Kanef
Sherri Litt Goldman
Henry J. Cistrelli

OF COUNSEL

Jacob L. Balk
Dora P. Rothschild

For full biographical listings, see the Martindale-Hubbell Law Directory

---

CARPENTER, BENNETT & MORRISSEY (AV)

Three Gateway Center, 17th Floor, 100 Mulberry Street, 07102-4079
Telephone: 973-622-7711
New York City: 212-943-6530
Telex: 139405
Telecopier: 973-622-5314
Email: cbm@carpben.com

MEMBERS OF FIRM

James D. Carpenter (1885-1972)
Elmer J. Bennett (1909-1996)
Laurence Reich
John E. Keale
James J. Crowley, Jr.
John P. Dwyer
Michael S. Waters
Anthony C. Famulari
James G. Gardner
John F. Lynch, Jr.
Francis X. O'Brien
Donald A. Romano
Francis X. Dee
Irving L. Hurwitz
Rosemary J. Bruno
William A. Carpenter, Jr.
John J. Peirano
Linda B. Celauro
John D. Goldsmith
Patrick G. Brady
Louis M. DeStefano
Michael J. Greenwood
Thomas F. McGuane
Joseph D. Rasnek
Robert J. Stickles
Robert M. Goodman
Thomas M. Moore
Stephen F. Payerle
Kevin C. Donovan
Lois H. Goodman
James Peter Lidon
David J. Reilly
Jane A. Rigby
Vincent P. Browne

OF COUNSEL

Thomas L. Morrissey
Warren Lloyd Lewis
Edward F. Ryan
John C. Heavey
Edward F. Day, Jr.

ASSOCIATES

Glenn F. Corbett
Jennifer L. Kapell
Hans G. Polak
Michelle S. Hydrusko
Jeffrey Bernstein
Joseph Gerard Lee
Daniel J. O'Hern, Jr.
Steven J. Santarsiero
Marc E. Wolin
C. Brian Kornbrek
John M. O'Connor
David A. Cohen
Vimal K. Shah
Linda Pope Torres
David B. Beal
Thomas C. Bigosinski
Melissa B. Popkin
Gary S. Prish
Mary B. Goldhirsch
Robert P. McGovern
Claire C. Cecchi
Kenneth B. Rotter
Yvette M. Gordon
Kerry A. O'Shea
Paula M. Castaldo
Robert L. Ghelli
Mason C. Miller
Marny Lundy Solazzo
Stephanie J. Hart
Ivanyla D. Vargas (Not admitted in NJ)
George M. Macchia
Elizabeth A. Kenny
Catherine Brennan Rinaldi
Deborah A. Young
Seth Ptasiewicz
George P. Barbatsuly
Lisa E. Stern
Michael D. Thompson (Not admitted in NJ)
Cindy E. Switzer (Not admitted in the United States)
Michael P. Einbinder (Not admitted in NJ)

Representative Clients: General Motors Corp.; E. I. du Pont de Nemours and Co.; Texaco Inc.; AT&T; Litton Industries; ITT Industries, Inc.; Johnson & Johnson; International Flavors & Fragrances Inc.; Prudential Insurance Company of America; Hartford Insurance Co.

For full biographical listings, see the Martindale-Hubbell Law Directory

Newark—Continued

CURTIS, MALLET-PREVOST, COLT & MOSLE LLP (AV⓪)

One Gateway Center, Suite 403, 07102-5311
Telephone: 973-622-0605
Telecopier: 973-622-5646
Email: info@cm-p.com *URL:* http://www.cm-p.com
New York, N.Y. Office: 101 Park Avenue.
Telephone: 212-696-6000.
Telecopier: 212-697-1559.
Washington, D.C. Office: Suite 1205L, 1801 K Street, N.W.
Telephone: 202-452-7373.
Telecopier: 202-452-7333.
Houston, Texas Office: 2 Houston, Center, 909 Fannin Street, Suite 3725.
Telephone: 713-759-9555.
Telecopier: 713-759-0712.
Stamford, Connecticut Office: One Canterbury Green.
Telephone: 203-359-6200.
Telecopier: 203-328-2617.
Mexico City, D.F., Mexico Office: Curtis, Mallet-Prevost, Colt & Mosle, Ruben Dario 281, Piso 9, Col. Bosque de Chapultepec, 11580 Mexico, D.F.
Telephone: 525-282-0444.
Telecopier: 525-282-0637.
Paris, France Office: 15 rue d'Astorg, 75008.
Telephone: 42-66-39-10.
Telecopier: 42-66-39-62.
London, England Office: Two Throgmorton Avenue, EC2N 2DL.
Telephone: 0207-638-7957.
Telecopier: 0207-638-5512.
Frankfurt am Main 1, Germany Office: Staufenstrasse 42.
Telephone: 69-971-4420.
Telecopier: 69-17 33 99.
Muscat, Sultanate of Oman Office: P.O. Box 200, Jewel Beach-134.
Telephone: 968-607-725.
Telecopier: 968-607-724.
Milan, Italy Office: Curtis, Mallet-Prevost, Colt & Mosle, Piazzale Principessa Clotilde 8, 20121.
Telephone: (39) 02-2900-2932.
Telecopier: (39) 02-657-5969.

RESIDENT PARTNERS

Anthony W. Fitzgerald
Martin Wendel

ASSOCIATE

Pamela J. Labaj

For full biographical listings, see the Martindale-Hubbell Law Directory

DUANE, MORRIS & HECKSCHER LLP (AV)

A Pennsylvania Limited Liability Partnership
One Riverfront Plaza, 07102
Telephone: 973-424-2000
Fax: 973-424-2001
URL: http://www.duanemorris.com
Philadelphia, Pennsylvania Office: Suite 4200, One Liberty Place.
Telephone: 215-979-1000.
Fax: 215-979-1020.
New York, New York Office: 380 Lexington Avenue.
Telephone: 212-692-1000.
Fax: 212-692-1020.
Chicago, Illinois Office: 227 West Monroe Street, Suite 3400.
Telephone: 312-499-6700.
Fax: 312-499-6701.
Washington, D.C. Office: 1667 K Street, N.W., Suite 700.
Telephone: 202-776-7800.
Fax: 202-776-7801.
San Francisco, California Office: 100 Spear Street.
Telephone: 415-371-2200.
Fax: 415-371-2201.
Boston, Massachusetts Office: One International Place, 14th Floor.
Telephone: 617-598-3100.
Fax: 617-598-3101.
Miami, Florida Office: 200 South Biscayne Boulevard, Suite 3410.
Telephone: 305-960-2200.
Fax: 305-960-2201.
Wilmington, Delaware Office: 1201 Market Street, Suite 1500.
Telephone: 302-571-5550.
Fax: 302-571-5560.
Harrisburg, Pennsylvania Office: 305 North Front Street, 5th Floor, P.O. Box 1003.
Telephone: 717-237-5500.
Fax: 717-232-4015.
Wayne, Pennsylvania Office: 735 Chesterbrook Boulevard, Suite 300.
Telephone: 610-647-3555.
Fax: 610-640-2619.
Cherry Hill, New Jersey Office: 51 Haddonfield Road, Suite 340.
Telephone: 856-488-7300.
Fax: 856-488-7021.
Palm Beach, Florida Office: 249 Royal Palm Way, Suite 403.
Telephone: 561-366-5400.
Fax: 561-366-5401.

(See Next Column)

Allentown, Pennsylvania Office: 968 Postal Road, Suite 200, P.O. Box 90400.
Telephone: 610-266-3650.
Fax: 610-266-3651.
Houston, Texas Office: One Greenway Plaza, Suite 500.
Telephone: 713-552-9900.
Fax: 713-552-0109.
Dover, Delaware Office: 314 S. State Street.
Telephone: 302-736-0156.
Fax: 302-736-0336.
Bangor, Maine Office: 15 Columbia Street, 4th Floor.
Telephone: 207-990-4800.
Fax: 207-990-4804.
Princeton, New Jersey Office: Princeton Forrestal Village, 116 Village Boulevard, Suite 200.
Telephone: 609-734-4323.
Fax: 609-734-4387.

PARTNERS

Lawrence W. Diamond
Walter J. Greenhalgh (Partner-in-Charge, Newark, NJ Office)
Gregory R. Haworth

ASSOCIATES

David J. DiSabato
Marco A. Gonzalez, Jr.

SPECIAL COUNSEL

David H. Stein

For full biographical listings, see the Martindale-Hubbell Law Directory

GREENBERG DAUBER EPSTEIN & TUCKER, A PROFESSIONAL CORPORATION (AV)

Suite 600, One Gateway Center, 07102-5311
Telephone: 973-643-3700
Facsimile: 973-643-1218
URL: http://www.greenbergdauber.com

Melvin Greenberg
Edward J. Dauber
Stanley A. Epstein
H. Glenn Tucker
Linda G. Harvey
Russell S. Burnside

Sumeeta A. Gawande
Richard H. Schwartz
Michael H. Freeman
Charles J. Hayden
Scott W. Miller

For full biographical listings, see the Martindale-Hubbell Law Directory

HELLRING LINDEMAN GOLDSTEIN & SIEGAL LLP (AV)

One Gateway Center, 07102-5386
Telephone: 973-621-9020
Fax: 973-621-7406
Englewood, New Jersey Office: 32-40 North Dean Street.
Telephone: 201-871-3060.

Bernard Hellring (1916-1991)
Philip Lindeman, II
Joel D. Siegal
Jonathan L. Goldstein
Barry H. Evenchick
James A. Scarpone
Michael Edelson
Margaret Dee Hellring
Richard D. Shapiro
Charles Oransky
Richard B. Honig
Richard K. Coplon
Robert S. Raymar
Ronny Jo Greenwald Siegal
Stephen L. Dreyfuss
John A. Adler
Judah I. Elstein
Bruce S. Etterman
Matthew E. Moloshok
Rachel N. Davidson
David N. Narciso
Ronnie F. Liebowitz
Robert B. Rosen
Sheryl E. Koomer

David Wolff
Lisa P. Parker
Jonathan Wayne
Catherine J. Bick
Joanne M. Frasca

For full biographical listings, see the Martindale-Hubbell Law Directory

LEVY, EHRLICH & PETRIELLO, A PROFESSIONAL CORPORATION (AV)

60 Park Place Suite 1016, 07102
Telephone: 973-643-0040
Telecopier: 973-596-1781
URL: http://www.lep-lawyers.com

Ira A. Levy
Alan Ehrlich
John J. Petriello
Bruce E. Gudin

Janet Edelman
Jeffrey William Plaza
Stephen F. Cea

Representative Clients: Transamerica; General Electric; U.S. Department of HUD.
Reference: First Union Bank.

For full biographical listings, see the Martindale-Hubbell Law Directory

Newark—Continued

McCarter & English, LLP (AV)

Four Gateway Center, 100 Mulberry Street, P.O. Box 652, 07101-0652
Telephone: 973-622-4444
Telecopier: 973-624-7070
URL: http://www.mccarter.com
Cherry Hill, New Jersey Office: 1820 Chapel Avenue West, Suite 380.
Telephone: 609-662-8444.
Telecopier: 609-662-6203.
New York, New York Office: Suite 2247, One World Trade Center.
Telephone: 212-466-9018.
Telecopier: 212-432-6568.
Boca Raton, Florida Office: 2255 Glades Road, Suite 319-A.
Telephone: 561-994-6262.
Telecopier: 561-241-0798.
Wilmington, Delaware Office: Mellon Bank Center, 919 Market Street.
Telephone: 302-654-8010.
Telecopier: 302-654-0795.
Philadelphia, Pennsylvania Office: One Commerce Square, 2005 Market Street, Suite 3600.
Telephone: 215-557-7700.
Telecopier: 215-557-6544.

MEMBERS OF FIRM

Thomas N. McCarter (1845-1901)
Robert H. McCarter (1882-1941)
Conover English (1902-1963)
Francis E. P. McCarter (1947-1988)
Woodruff J. English (1947-1981)
Steven Barrett Hoskins
Rodney N. Houghton
Alfred L. Ferguson
Charles R. Merrill
Andrew T. Berry
Richard C. Cooper
Michael M. Horn
Richard W. Hill
William H. Horton
James F. Hammill (Resident Partner, Cherry Hill, New Jersey Office)
William J. O'Shaughnessy
William S. Greenberg
Frederick B. Lehlbach
Bart J. Colli
Richard M. Eittreim
John E. Flaherty
John A. McKinney, Jr.
William T. Reilly
Hayden Smith, Jr.
John B. Brescher, Jr.
Todd M. Poland
John J. Scally, Jr.
Roslyn S. Harrison
Gita F. Rothschild
David R. Kott
Lois M. Van Deusen
Glenn P. Callahan (Cherry Hill, New Jersey and Philadelphia, Pennsylvania Offices)
Michael A. Guariglia
Lanny S. Kurzweil
David A. Ludgin
Richard J. Webb
Rosemary Alito
William J. Heller
John F. Brenner
Frank E. Ferruggia
Keith E. Lynott
Michael A. Tanenbaum
Richard P. O'Leary
Theodore D. Moskowitz
Scott A. Kobler
Therese M. Keeley (Cherry Hill, New Jersey and Philadelphia, Pennsylvania Offices)
Nathan A. Schachtman (Resident, Cherry Hill, New Jersey Office)
Seth T. Taube
Robert B. Anderson (Resident, Wilmington, Delaware Office)
Stephen M. Vajtay, Jr.
Myrna L. Wigod
Joseph Lubertazzi, Jr.
Mark A. Daniele
Carol C. Stern
Peter S. Twombly
David F. Broderick
James H. Keale
B. John Pendleton, Jr.
Stephen B. Pearlman
Lisa M. Goldman
Martin F. Dowd
Frederick T. Smith
Paul A. Bradley (Resident Partner, Wilmington, Delaware Office)
George H. Kendall
Jacqueline P. Shanes
Charles F. Rysavy
John C. Garde
Anthony Bartell
David C. Apy
William D. Wallach
Penelope M. Taylor
Susan A. Feeney
Thomas W. Ladd
Kenneth E. Thompson
John C. McGuire
Patrick J. Perrone
Richard A. Beran
Lisa W.S. Bonsall
David S. Osterman
Gerard G. Brew
Sherilyn Pastor
David J. Cooner
Harvey C. Kaish
Gary Duescher
Thomas D. Robertson
Arnold L. Natali, Jr.
Edward J. Butler, Jr.
Katie A. Gummer

OF COUNSEL

Eugene M. Haring
George C. Witte, Jr.
Jeffrey H. Aminoff (Not admitted in NJ)
Peter C. Aslanides
Julius B. Poppinga
Arthur C. Hensler, Jr.
Nicholas Conover English
Thomas F. Daly

COUNSEL

Joseph F. Falgiani
Steven A. Beckelman
Beth Yingling
Gary T. Hall
Jerry P. Sattin
J. Forrest Jones
Curtis A. Johnson
Robert W. Smith
Phyllis Gutto
Paul C. Dritsas
Debra M. Perry

(See Next Column)

SPECIAL COUNSEL

Allen N. Friedman
Michael J. Glasheen (Resident, Philadelphia, Pennsylvania Office)
Samuel J. Abate, Jr. (Resident, New York, New York Office)
Robert A. Mintz
Charles M. Costenbader
Jeannette M. Bond
W. Wade W. Scott (Resident, Wilmington, Delaware Office)

ASSOCIATES

Charles J. Benjamin, Jr.
Brenda C. Liss
Kathleen O'Connell Keating
Kevin J. Connell
Teresa L. Moore
Evolea C. Watson (Resident, Cherry Hill, New Jersey Office)
Eric J. Kadish (Resident, Philadelphia, Pennsylvania Office)
Vito A. Pinto
Andrew O. Bunn
Debra S. Groisser
Anthony Palmisano Jr.
Deborah S. Verderame
David J. Adler
Mary E. Whiteman
David W. Opderbeck
Sheila E. Calello
Gregory M. Dyer
Anthony J. Del Piano
Richard T. Nolan, Jr.
Joseph T. Boccassini
Nancy A. Washington
Cynthia Spera Neff
J. Wylie Donald
Susan M. Mello
Audrey A. Hale
Cynthia C. Beagles
John Carl Mills
Patricia A. Celano
Brian J. Leddin
Edward J. Fanning, Jr.
Gregory H. Horowitz
Clement J. Farley
Nancy K. Foley
William L. Turok
Nicholas A. Concilio, III
Norby L. Foss
Margaret C. Wilson
Jeffrey A. Petit
Joseph R. Scholz
Kimberly A. Leegan
Carol A. Hucks (Resident, Cherry Hill, New Jersey Office)
Diane M. Pompei
James M. Sullivan
Christopher R. Carton
Joseph F. LaSala
Michael A. Alfano (Resident, Philadelphia, Pennsylvania Office)
Eduardo J. Glas
Kevin J. Quinn
Kristin L. Wynne
Ann Marie Collins
Barbara K. Gotthelf (Resident, Cherry Hill, New Jersey Office)
Robert J. Burger
Anthony J. Di Marino, III (Cherry Hill, New Jersey and Philadelphia, Pennsylvania Offices)
Michael N. Feder (Resident, Philadelphia, Pennsylvania Office)
E. Johanna Gibbon
Hugh C. Welsh
Kimberly J. Hines
Michael R. Von Ohlen
Geraldine S. Bowen
Mark E. Hopkins
Vincent N. Avallone
Sidney G. Wigfall (Not admitted in NJ)
Gregory J. Hindy
Theresa G. Fisher
Laura L. Kravantka
Ronald B. Weisenberg
Paul Bertoni
Lisa M. DeRose
Joseph R. DiSalvo
James C. Jacobus
Laura A. Leacy
Edward R. Schreiber
R. Andrew Richards
Eric D. Sherman
Dennis P. Powers
David A. Thomas
Tracey A. Ballard
Evan M. Turtz
Eliot S. Choy (Not admitted in NJ)
Lisa M. Slocum
William G. Barrett
Eric Owen Costello
Michael J. Caccavelli
Alison G. Greenberg
Francis A. Kirk
Meredith L. Bryant
Paul L. Kattas
Whitney A. Klein
Robert F. Ripley
Jonathan E. Sachs
Christian E. Samay
Ilan E. Simon
Ronald J. Wronko, Jr.
Louis A. Chiafullo
Rachel L. Diehl
Christine Kerper Kraft
Nicholas Albano III
Eric R. Fish
Marc E. Fishman
Kerri A. Holt
Patricia Mullon Zohn
Kimberly A. Arndt
Daniel J. Malooly
Dawn Marmo
Christina M. Thomas
Carol Ann Von Urff
Adam B. Cantor
Lino DiCuollo
Donald M. Rohan
Elizabeth A. Saurman (Resident, Wilmington, Delaware Office)
Jane S. Kimball
John E. Olsson (Not admitted in NJ)
Lynn L. Owens (Resident, Philadelphia, Pennsylvania Office)
EllaCortland Goodyear (Not admitted in NJ)
Rachel B. Adler
Paul E. DelloRusso
Meredith Walsh
Paul A. Sangillo
Rui M. Santos
Shelia D. Diggs
Jennifer R. Schuster (Not admitted in NJ)
A. Nicole Friant

STAFF ATTORNEYS

Laura S. Mello (Not admitted in NJ)
Alexander Barbarisi
Meera S. Coilparampil
Robert D. Grauer (Not admitted in NJ)
Janice P. Holness (Not admitted in NJ)
Maliza J.A. Lynch (Not admitted in NJ)
Stephanie J. Cohen
Linda Dobbins
Andrew N. Musicus (Not admitted in NJ)
Thomas C. Cahalan (Not admitted in NJ)

For full biographical listings, see the Martindale-Hubbell Law Directory

Newark—Continued

McManimon & Scotland, L.L.C. (AV)

One Riverfront Plaza, 4th Floor, 07102-5311
Telephone: 973-622-1800
Fax: 973-622-7333; 973-622-3744

MEMBERS OF FIRM

Joseph P. Baumann, Jr.
John V. Cavaliere
John B. Hall
Glenn F. Scotland
Ronald J. Ianoale
Andrea L. Kahn
Jeffrey G. Kramer
Leslie G. London
Edward J. McManimon, III

OF COUNSEL

Norman M. Robertson
Carla J. Brundage

ASSOCIATES

Peter S. Crisafi
Sheila Newsome Maddox
M. Frances Ciesla
Kristin Dwyer Ganley
Joseph C. Jasaitis
Stephen N. Severud
Thomas J. Hastie, Jr.

LEGAL SUPPORT PERSONNEL

Helen Lysaght

PARALEGALS

Sandra Simoes

For full biographical listings, see the Martindale-Hubbell Law Directory

Meyner and Landis (AV)

One Gateway Center, Suite 2500, 07102-5311
Telephone: 973-624-2800
Fax: 973-624-0356
Email: attys@meyner.com *URL:* http://www.meyner.com

Robert B. Meyner (1908-1990)
Edwin C. Landis, Jr.
John N. Malyska
William J. Fiore
Anthony F. Siliato
Francis R. Perkins
Howard O. Thompson
Scott T. McCleary
Linda Townley Snyder
William H. Schmidt, Jr.
David B. Grantz

For full biographical listings, see the Martindale-Hubbell Law Directory

St. John & Wayne, L.L.C. (AV)

Two Penn Plaza East, 07105-2249
Telephone: 973-491-3600
Fax: 973-491-3555
Email: firm@nwk.stjohn-law.com *URL:* http://www.stjohn-law.com
Rochester, New York Office: St. John & Curtin, L.L.C., First Federal Plaza.
Telephone: 716-262-6780.
Fax: 716-262-6755.
New York, New York Office: Heron Tower, 70 East 55th. Street.
Telephone: 212-446-5000.
Fax: 212-446-5055.

Lee A. Albanese
James P. Anelli
Richard I. Bier
Timothy R. Curtin (Resident at Rochester, New York Office)
Bernard S. Davis
Nicholas J. DeFabrizio
William A. Despo
Paul D. Drobbin
Bruce S. Edington
David C. Freinberg
Todd Mark Galante
David T. Harmon (Resident, New York, New York Office)
Rocco F. Iossa
Joseph F. Lagrotteria
Timothy R. McGill (Resident at Rochester, New York Office)
John J. Oberdorf
William P. Oberdorf
Bryan G. Petkanics (Resident at New York, New York Office)
David W. Phillips
John Patrick Reilly
Thomas D. Ruane (Resident, New York, New York Office)
Jerome M. St. John (Resident, New York, New York Office)
Peter G. Seiden (Resident, New York, New York Office)
Lisa Deitsch Taylor
Peter B. Van Deventer, Jr.
Karol Corbin Walker
Robert A. Wayne
E. Kenneth Williams, Jr.
Vincent S. Ziccolella

Bryant Kenneth Aaron
Douglas H. Amster
Robyn M. Gnudi
Anthony S. McCaskey
Jonathan S. Park
Brian L. Petrequin
Timothy E. Shanley
Gregory S. Thomas
Gregory G. Tole
Harshad R. Vaidya
Christopher R. Welgos

OF COUNSEL

James I. Wyer

For full biographical listings, see the Martindale-Hubbell Law Directory

Sills Cummis Radin Tischman Epstein & Gross, A Professional Corporation (AV)

One Riverfront Plaza, 07102-5400
Telephone: 973-643-7000
Fax: 973-643-6500
Telex: 820630 Sillsbeck Nwk
Email: sillsmail@sillscummis.com *URL:* http://www.sillscummis.com
Atlantic City, New Jersey Office: 17 Gordon's Alley.
Telephone: 609-344-2800.
New York, N.Y. Office: 712 Fifth Avenue.
Telephone: 212-643-7000.
Washington, D.C. Office: 1800 K Street, N.W.
Telephone: 202-296-4750.

MEMBERS OF FIRM

Arthur J. Sills (1917-1982)
Clive S. Cummis
Steven S. Radin
Michael B. Tischman
Morton S. Bunis
Barry M. Epstein
Steven E. Gross
Thomas J. Demski
Jeffrey Hugh Newman
Lawrence S. Horn
Jeffrey J. Greenbaum
Simon Levin
Stephen J. Moses
Morris Yamner
Gerald Span
Andrew P. Napolitano
William J. Martini
Jeffrey Barton Cahn
Noah Bronkesh
Lester Aron
Steven M. Goldman
Kenneth F. Oettle
Alan E. Sherman
Robert J. Alter
Ira A. Rosenberg
Robert Max Crane
Philip R. Sellinger
Jack M. Zackin
Arlene Elgart Mirsky
Thomas S. Novak
Jerry Genberg
Stuart M. Feinblatt
Margaret F. Black
Brian S. Coven
Trent S. Dickey
Joseph L. Buckley
Kathleen Gengaro
David J. Rabinowitz
Thomas Jay Hall
Stanley U. North, III
James D. Toll (Resident at Atlantic City, N.J. Office)
James M. Hirschhorn
Allan C. Bell
Ronald C. Rak
David W. Garland
Mark S. Olinsky
Richard J. Sapinski
Victor H. Boyajian
Philip R. White
Stuart J. Glick
Alan J. Cohen (Resident at Atlantic City, N.J. Office)
Lori G. Singer
Mark E. Duckstein
Beth S. Rose
Jack Wenik
Frederic M. Tudor
Jeffrey M. Pollock
Ted Zangari
Steven R. Kamen
Nathan E. Arnell
Robert R. DiVita
A. Ross Pearlson
Linda Badash Katz
Michael I. Chakansky (Resident, New York, N.Y. Office)

SENIOR COUNSEL

David Beck
Herbert L. Zuckerman

OF COUNSEL

Mitchel E. Ostrer
Kenneth R. Weiner (Not admitted in NJ)
Diane M. Lavenda
Cherie L. Maxwell
Steven R. Rowland
Eric S. Aronson

Noel D. Humphreys
Katherine Sloss (Not admitted in NJ)
Harry B. Noretsky
Julia L. Bonsal (Not admitted in NJ)
Laurence W. Futterman (Not admitted in NJ)
Cynthia P. Liebling
James E. Brandt (Not admitted in NJ)
Eric D. Mann (Resident at Atlantic City, N.J. Office)
Eric W. Sleeper
Bennet Susser
Steven S. Katz
Ross N. Herman
Brenda J. Rediess-Hoosein
Barbara Quackenbos
Loryn P. Riggiola
Lynne Anne Anderson
David J. Papier
Karen Levine
Gary W. Herschman
Richard H. Epstein
Philip Edward Stern
Paul P. Josephson
Paul F. Doda
Helen E. Kleiner
Rhonda Sobral O'Toole
Andrew H. Sherman
A. Thomas Southwick
Ivan J. Kaplan
Adam J. Kaiser
William J. Tinsley, Jr.
William R. Stuart III
Robert I. Siegel
Andrew W. Schwartz
Jennifer L. Borofsky
Robert R. Hempstead
Gwen L. Coleman
Susanne Kaufmann Rosenzweig
Lori M. Waldron
Daniel A. Schlein
Amy M. Belger
Ben-Tzion H. Zur
Christian Peter Johnson (Not admitted in NJ)
Carolyn M. Stockdale
David Jay
Eric I. Abraham
Derrick R. Freijomil
Jacqueline Valouch
Kelly Ann Guariglia
Elbert F. Nasis
Jodie F. Bouer
Kristen Skog Buerstetta
Jonathan N. Marcus
Elnardo J. Webster, II
Marguerita B. Dolatly
James E. Jasaitis
Michael S. Mirone
Joseph A. Becht, Jr.
Robert J. Farkas
Richard T. Cadigan
Kathleen A. Crocco
Kenneth Hayes
Naomi I. Cohen
Vincent R. Lodato
Steven M. Mager

(See Next Column)

SILLS CUMMIS RADIN TISCHMAN EPSTEIN & GROSS A PROFESSIONAL CORPORATION—*Continued*

Brigette N. Shrank
William Louis Hurlock
William R. Horwitz
Emilia M. De Meo
Albert D. Pailet (Not admitted in NJ)
Steven D. Gorelick
Jason L. Jurkevich
Anne Buckley
Brett M. Popolow
Michele K. Thomas
Joshua M. Sachs
Debra M. Lightner
Paul Meier
Matthew J. Henderson (Not admitted in NJ)
Laura Lencses McLester

LEGAL SUPPORT PERSONNEL

William P. Rebarick (Executive Director)
John A. White (Chief Financial Officer)
Marcia Jeffers (Director of Marketing)
Kerry Jean Moore (Director of Professional Personnel)
Katherine Morningstar (Director of Human Resources)
Bruce Reinhart (Director of Office Operations)
Jeffrey Hutchinson (Director of Information Services)
Paul M. Sutton (Director of Training and Staff Development)
Dina Cappuccio (Recruiting Manager)
Melissa Manzanares (Paralegal Manager)
Matthew Larkin (Records Manager)

Representative Clients: Blue Cross/Blue Shield of New Jersey; Bristol-Myers Squibb Co.; Circuit City Stores; Eastman Kodak; New Jersey Performing Arts Center; Six Flags Corporation; WWOR-TV, Inc.; PNC Bank Corp.

For full biographical listings, see the Martindale-Hubbell Law Directory

STRYKER, TAMS & DILL LLP (AV)

Two Penn Plaza East, 07105
Telephone: 973-491-9500
Fax: 973-491-9692
URL: http://www.stryker.com
New York, N.Y. Office: One World Trade Center, Suite 7967.
Telephone: 212-432-9180.

MEMBERS OF FIRM

Harold Friedman
Charles H. Friedrich, III
Martin G. Gilbert
Dennis C. Linken
Edward N. Lippincott
Robert A. Marsico
John J. Rizzo
Alan D. Wiener

COUNSEL

Jeffrey A. Donner
John R. Kettle, III
Janice Manganello
Susan G. Rosmarin
Bruce R. Volpe

OF COUNSEL

Burtis W. Horner

ASSOCIATES

Claudia A. Costa
Anthony DiMaggio
Tracee A. Graubart

Counsel for: ACF Industries; Comcast Corporation; Concord Camera Corp.; First Union National Bank; Household International; Mita Copystar America; Morgan Guaranty Trust Company of New York; The Newark Museum; The Prudential Insurance Company of America.

For full biographical listings, see the Martindale-Hubbell Law Directory

TOMPKINS, MCGUIRE, WACHENFELD & BARRY (AV)

A New Jersey Limited Liability Partnership including a Professional Association
Four Gateway Center, 100 Mulberry Street, 07102-4070
Telephone: 973-622-3000
Telecopier: 973-623-7780
Email: attorneys@tompkinsmcguire.com
New York, New York Office: 1 Bankers Trust Plaza. 130 Liberty Street, Suite 2707. 10006.
Telephone: 212-714-1720.

MEMBERS OF FIRM

William F. Tompkins (1913-1989)
William J. Prout, Jr. (1947-1996)
William B. McGuire (P.A.)
Howard G. Wachenfeld
Theodore L. Abeles
John J. Barry
Rex K. Harriott
James F. Flanagan, III
Marianne Espinosa Murphy
Eugene J. Sullivan
Frederic S. Kessler
Michael F. Nestor
Marianne M. DeMarco
Patrick M. Callahan
Paul S. Werther
Mark Falk
Michael S. Miller
Douglas E. Motzenbecker
Evelyn R. Storch
Ellen Nunno Corbo
William H. Trousdale
George G. Campion
Joseph K. Cobuzio
Richard F. Connors, Jr.
Richard A. Ulsamer
Madeline E. Cox
Nadia Walker Brunetto
Angelo R. Giacchi
Adam N. Saravay

OF COUNSEL

Michael F. DeCapua
Frances S. Margolis
Paul B. Thompson
Raymond W. Troy (1911-1992)
William T. Wachenfeld

(See Next Column)

COUNSEL

Peter A. Bogaard
Brian M. English
Leonore C. Lewis

ASSOCIATES

Christopher A. Barbarisi
Thomas A. Callahan, Jr.
Joann K. Dobransky
Thomas F. Doherty
Robert Leonardo
Stephen C. Matthews
Grant W. McGuire
Matthew P. O'Malley
Michael P. Pasquale
Colleen Duffy Shiarella

Representative Clients: Corbo Jewelers, Inc.; General Electric Co.; Hartford Insurance Group; Marriott Corp.; National Union Fire Insurance Co.; Underwriters at Lloyd's, London.

For full biographical listings, see the Martindale-Hubbell Law Directory

*NEW BRUNSWICK,** Middlesex Co.

BORRUS, GOLDIN & FOLEY, A PROFESSIONAL CORPORATION

(See Borrus, Goldin, Foley, Vignuolo, Hyman, Stahl & Clarkin, A Professional Corporation, North Brunswick)

*NEWTON,** Sussex Co.

DOLAN AND DOLAN, P.A. A PROFESSIONAL CORPORATION (AV)

One Legal Lane at Fifty-Three Spring Street, P.O. Box D, 07860-0605
Telephone: 973-383-1600
Fax: 973-383-7823
Email: dolanlaw@warwick.net *URL:* http://www.dolanlaw.com
Blairstown, New Jersey Office: 18 Bank Street, P.O. Box 647.
Telephone: 908-362-5600.
Fax: 973-383-7823.

William A. Dolan (1883-1952)
Lewis P. Dolan (1898-1974)
William M. Cox
Richard V. Hollyer
Robert T. Morgenstern
Roger W. Thomas
William T. Haggerty
Donald M. Ross
Mark J. Hontz

Eileen McCarthy Born
John P. Morgenstern

OF COUNSEL

Francis E. Bright
Charles J. Brand
Glenn T. Gavan

Counsel for: PNC National Bank; National Bank of Sussex County; Sussex Rural Electric Cooperative; Warwick Valley Telephone Co.
Local Counsel for: Selective Insurance Company of America.

For full biographical listings, see the Martindale-Hubbell Law Directory

NORTH BRUNSWICK, Middlesex Co.

BORRUS, GOLDIN, FOLEY, VIGNUOLO, HYMAN, STAHL & CLARKIN, A PROFESSIONAL CORPORATION (AV)

2875 U.S. Highway 1, Route 1 & Finnigans Lane, P.O. Box 7463, 08902
Telephone: 732-422-1000
Fax: 732-422-1016
Email: attys@borrus.com *URL:* http://www.borrus.com

Jack Borrus
Martin S. Goldin
David M. Foley
Anthony B. Vignuolo
Jeffrey M. Hyman
James E. Stahl
James F. Clarkin III
Eileen Mary Foley

Robert C. Nisenson
Rosalind Westlake
Lisa M. Vignuolo
Steven L. Fox
Peter A. Vignuolo
Gerald T. Foley (1903-1976)

Representative Clients: Summit Bank; R. J. Reynolds Tobacco Co.; K. Hovnanian Enterprises, Inc.; Johnson and Johnson; Foster Wheeler, Inc.; Hartz Mountain Industries; Middlesex County Vocational Services Commission; Borough of South Plainfield Board of Adjustment; U-Haul of Northern NJ.

For full biographical listings, see the Martindale-Hubbell Law Directory

BUSCH AND BUSCH, LLP (AV)

215 North Center Drive, Commerce Center - U.S. #1 South, P.O. Box 7448, 08902-7448
Telephone: 732-821-2300
Telecopier: 732-821-5588
Email: busch@ifu.net

MEMBERS OF FIRM

Lewis D. Busch (1901-1986)
Henry Busch (Retired)
Malcolm R. Busch
Ronald J. Busch
Bertram E. Busch
Mark N. Busch
Leonard R. Busch
Steven F. Satz
Donald J. Sears

ASSOCIATE

Paul Alan VanBuskirk

Representative Clients: Utica Mutual Insurance Co.; New Brunswick Tomorrow; Township of South Brunswick; Township of Monroe, Board of Education; Township of East Brunswick; Minnesota Mutual Life Insurance Co.

(See Next Column)

BUSCH AND BUSCH LLP, *North Brunswick—Continued*

For full biographical listings, see the Martindale-Hubbell Law Directory

LYNCH, MARTIN, KANE, KUPER, KEEFE & BARTELS, LLC (AV)

1368 How Lane, P.O. Box 6022, 08902-6022
Telephone: 732-545-0745
Fax: 732-545-4780
Email: LYNCHMRTN@aol.com

John A. Lynch, Sr. (1908-1978)
John A. Lynch
James D. Martin, Jr.
John J. Kane
Eric Kuper
John E. Keefe, Jr.
Patrick J. Bartels
Carl W. Swanson
James Den Uyl
John W. Harding
Lori A. Dvorak
Bernard P. Hvozdovic, Jr.
Joseph J. LaCosta
Timothy E. Annin

Laura M. Shea
Robyn M. Mitchell
Christine Klimczuk

OF COUNSEL

Robert T. Quackenboss (Retired Superior Court Judge)

LEGAL SUPPORT PERSONNEL

Sharon Stewart (Administrator)

For full biographical listings, see the Martindale-Hubbell Law Directory

OCEAN TOWNSHIP, Monmouth Co.

EVANS, OSBORNE & KREIZMAN (AV)

CN 7808 1500 Lawrence Avenue, 07712-7808
Telephone: 732-643-0300
Fax: 732-643-0340
New York, New York Office: Suite 7967, One World Trade Center.
Telephone: 212-466-1207.

MEMBERS OF FIRM

Harry S. Evans
Harry V. Osborne, II
Joel N. Kreizman
Mary O'Keefe Massey
Kevin E. Hoffman

ASSOCIATES

Marie A. Accardi
James F. McDonough
Kenneth P. Skibinski

Representative Clients: United Kingdom P&I Club (Thomas R. Miller Insurance Services); American Marine Underwriters, Inc.; Continental Insurance Cos.; Hartford Insurance Cos.; CIGNA Cos.; Jersey Central Power & Light Co.; First Union Bank; CNA Insurance Cos.; General Public Utilities, Inc.

For full biographical listings, see the Martindale-Hubbell Law Directory

PARAMUS, Bergen Co.

STRASSER & ASSOCIATES, A PROFESSIONAL CORPORATION (AV)

Paramus Plaza I, 140 Route 17 North, Suite 265, 07652-2816
Telephone: 201-262-7177
Fax: 201-262-3113

William I. Strasser

Conrad M. Olear
Constantinos J. Ballas

Representative Clients: Consumer Value Stores (CVS); Melville Corp.; Melville Realty Corp.; Linens 'N Things, Inc.; This End Up Furniture Co., Inc.; Universal Foods Corp.; Essex Computers, Inc.; Polevoy Associates; Footstar, Inc.; Bob's Stores.

For full biographical listings, see the Martindale-Hubbell Law Directory

PARSIPPANY, Morris Co.

CUYLER BURK (AV)

Parsippany Corporate Center, Four Century Drive, 07054-4663
Telephone: 973-734-3200
Telex: 429071
Telecopier: 973-734-3201
Email: Main@Cuyler.com *URL:* http://www.cuyler.com
New York, New York Office: 350 Fifth Avenue, Suite 3304. 10018.
Telephone: 212-645-4039.

MEMBERS OF FIRM

Stephen D. Cuyler
Jo Ann Burk
Stefano Calogero
David L. Menzel
Peter Petrou
Richard A. Crooker
Michael J. Jones

COUNSEL

Anne M. Mohan
Frank J. Miele

(See Next Column)

ASSOCIATES

Jan C. Walker
Kathleen Jane Olear
Claudia L. Marchese
Mark G. Eliades
Kimberly A. Joel
Christy A. Ramunno
Catherine E. Youngman
Andrew K. Craig
Mark S. Winter
Thomas J. Castano
Hugo A. Hilgendorff, IV

LEGAL SUPPORT PERSONNEL

Frederick M. H. Currie, Jr.

For full biographical listings, see the Martindale-Hubbell Law Directory

PENNSAUKEN, Camden Co.

SHERMAN, SILVERSTEIN, KOHL, ROSE & PODOLSKY, A PROFESSIONAL CORPORATION (AV)

Fairway Corporate Center, 4300 Haddonfield Road, Suite 311, 08109
Telephone: 856-662-0700
Fax: 856-662-0165
URL: http://www.sskrplaw.com
Bala Cynwyd, Pennsylvania Office: 11 Bala Avenue.
Telephone: 215-923-2513.

Lee S. Sherman
Lee Silverstein
John W. Kohl
M. Zev Rose
Steven M. Podolsky
Alan C. Milstein
Andrew J. Karcich
Nan S. Famular
John R. Lolio, Jr.
Robert W. Lynch
Phyllis Z. Sherman
Daniel J. Barrison
Thomas J. Tamburelli
Rhonda R. Feld
Leon H. Rose
Leonard R. Rossetti
Robert E. Schwartz
Charles Bender
Harris L. Pogust
Nancy L. Wasch (Not admitted in NJ)
John M. Hanamirian
David C. Silverman
Matthew Podolnick
Jeffrey Resnick
Derek T. Braslow

OF COUNSEL

Robert M. Washburn

For full biographical listings, see the Martindale-Hubbell Law Directory

PERTH AMBOY, Middlesex Co.

WILENTZ, GOLDMAN & SPITZER, A PROFESSIONAL CORPORATION

(See Woodbridge)

PRINCETON, Mercer Co.

DECHERT PRICE & RHOADS (AV)

Princeton Pike Corporate Center, P.O. Box 5218, 08543-5218
Telephone: 609-620-3200
Telefax: 609-620-3259
URL: http://www.dechert.com
Philadelphia, Pennsylvania: 4000 Bell Atlantic Tower, 1717 Arch Street, 19103-2793.
Telephone: 215-994-4000.
Harrisburg, Pennsylvania: Thirty North Third Street, 17101-1603.
Telephone: 717-237-2000.
New York, New York: 30 Rockefeller Plaza, 10112.
Telephone: 212-698-3500.
Washington, D.C.: 1775 Eye Street, N.W., 20006.
Telephone: 202-261-3300.
Boston, Massachusetts: Ten Post Office Square South, 02109-4603.
Telephone: 617-728-7100.
Hartford, Connecticut: 90 State House Square, 06103-3702.
Telephone: 860-524-3999.
London, England: 2 Serjeants' Inn, EC4Y 1LT.
Telephone: (0171) 583-5353. (Also see Titmuss Sainer Dechert).
Brussels, Belgium: 65 Avenue Louise, 1050.
Telephone: (02) 535-5411.
Paris, France: 55, Avenue Kléber, 76116.
Telephone: 33-(0) 1-53 65 05 00.

PARTNERS

Robert A. Baime
Allen Bloom
Raffaella De Trizio
Matthew V. DelDuca
Susan M. Hendrickson
Todd D. Johnston
James J. Marino
Ezra D. Rosenberg
Gil C. Tily

RESIDENT COUNSEL

Bruce W. Clark
Richard A. Zimmer

(See Next Column)

DECHERT PRICE & RHOADS—*Continued*

RESIDENT ASSOCIATES

Laura L. Decker
Thomas Deibert
(Not admitted in NJ)
Arthur E. Jackson
Luis Wolff Kono
(Not admitted in NJ)
David A. Kotler
Christopher J. Michie
Robert D. Rhoad
David J. Shipley
Valerie Tamburo
David Waksman
Debra M. Wallin
David Zatuchni

For full biographical listings, see the Martindale-Hubbell Law Directory

JAMIESON, MOORE, PESKIN & SPICER, A PROFESSIONAL CORPORATION (AV)

300 Alexander Park CN 5276, 08543-5276
Telephone: 609-452-0808
Fax: 609-452-1147; 452-0943; 951-0096
Email: JMPS@JMPS.Com *URL:* http://www.jamiesonmoore.com
Morristown, New Jersey Office: 177 Madison Avenue.
Telephone: 973-984-1616.
Fax: 973-984-9549.

Dennis R. Casale
Samuel G. Destito
Thomas Crawford Jamieson, Jr.
Edwin S. Leavitt-Gruberger
Thomas M. Letizia
Ross A. Lewin
Michael J. Mann
John D. McQuarrie, Jr.
Kevin J. Moore
Timothy J. O'Neill
Jonathan M. Preziosi
Jay Samuels
Robert A. Schwartz
Mark A. Solomon
Michael F. Spicer
Thomas P. Weidner
Audrey D. Wisotsky

OF COUNSEL

Herbert F. Moore

Alma Lutjen Abrams
Michael J. Canavan
Charles M. Fisher
Claudine M. Leone
Daniel G. Murray
Michael G. Petrone
Donald R. Readlinger
Steven J. Robinson
Angelo A. Stio
David F. Swerdlow
Julie Riley Tattoni
Nancy J. Truesdale
John W. Verlaque
Jared M. Witt
Sheila Woolson

Representative Clients: Berlitz International; Bristol-Myers Squibb; Educational Testing Service; Institute for Advanced Study; Johnson & Johnson; Merrill Lynch; New Jersey Bankers Association; PaineWebber Trust Co.; State Farm Insurance Companies; and Summit Bank.

For full biographical listings, see the Martindale-Hubbell Law Directory

MCCARTHY AND SCHATZMAN, P.A. (AV)

228 Alexander Street, P.O. Box 2329, 08543-2329
Telephone: 609-924-1199
Fax: 609-683-5251

John F. McCarthy, Jr.
Richard Schatzman
G. Christopher Baker
John F. McCarthy, III
Michael A. Spero
Barbara Strapp Nelson
W. Scott Stoner
James J. Britt, Jr.

Charly Gayden

Representative Clients: Trustees of Princeton University; Carnegie Center Associates; Merrill Lynch Pierce Fenner & Smith, Inc.; Calton Homes, Inc.

For full biographical listings, see the Martindale-Hubbell Law Directory

MILLER, PORTER & MULLER, P.C. (AV)

One Palmer Square, Suite 540, 08542
Telephone: 609-921-6077
Fax: 609-497-1439
Email: mpmlaw@aol.com *URL:* http://www.lawyers.com/mpmlaw

William Miller (1913-1977)
Allen D. Porter
Gerald J. Muller

Reference: PNC Bank; Summit Bank.

For full biographical listings, see the Martindale-Hubbell Law Directory

SMITH, STRATTON, WISE, HEHER & BRENNAN (AV)

600 College Road East, 08540
Telephone: 609-924-6000
FAX: 609-987-6651
Email: SSWHB@SSWHB.COM *URL:* http://www.sswhb.com

MEMBERS OF FIRM

John Robert Heher
William J. Brennan, III
Christopher S. Tarr
Ann Reichelderfer
Wendy L. Mager
Richard J. Pinto
Brian P. Sullivan
Suzanne M. McSorley
Marsha E. Novick
Robert C. Johnston
Peter R. Freed
Thomas E. Hastings

(See Next Column)

MEMBERS OF FIRM (Continued)

Diane M. Frenier
Paul H. Shur
Jay A. Ganzman
William E. McGrath, Jr.
Thomas E. Schorr
Yale H. Bohn
Gerald D. Wixted
Megan E. Thomas

ASSOCIATES

Edward P. Bromley III
Bradley L. Mitchell
Stephanie Monique Bosworth
Christopher P. Morrison
Miyuki Kaneko
Douglas S. Cohen
Scott C. Pyfer
Richard J. Orr
William A. Haumann
Grayson H. Heberley III
Susan L. Olgiati
Christine M. Carpenter
James N. Welsh, III
Ephraim Z. Zinkin
Stephanie N. Bland
Lisa Dorio Ruch
Christine L. Nici
Christine A. Beyer-Savoca
David Glogoff
Michael P. Lynch
Tracie H. Kaminin
Nancy S. Hearne
James B. MacDonald
Theodora McCormick
Carol B. Novinson

OF COUNSEL

Hugh D. Wise, Jr.
James Scott Hill

COUNSEL

Robert D. Frawley

Representative Clients: Alteon Inc.; Atlantic Mutual Insurance Cos.; Bristol-Myers Squibb Co.; The Home Insurance Co.; Liberty Mutual Insurance Co.; The Medical Center at Princeton; PNC Bank; Princeton Theological Seminary; Summit Bank.

For full biographical listings, see the Martindale-Hubbell Law Directory

RAMSEY, Bergen Co.

DONALD C. OHNEGIAN (AV)

88 West Main Street, P.O. Box 360, 07446
Telephone: 201-327-7000
Telefax: 201-327-6651
URL: http://www.lawyers.com/donaldcohnegianlaw

ASSOCIATE

Diane K. Gaylinn

Representative Clients: Available Upon Request.

For full biographical listings, see the Martindale-Hubbell Law Directory

RED BANK, Monmouth Co.

PHILIP G. AUERBACH A PROFESSIONAL CORPORATION (AV)

231 Maple Avenue, P.O. Box Y, 07701
Telephone: 732-842-6660
Fax: 732-530-7925

Philip G. Auerbach

Edward A. Genz
John J. Ryan
John F. McLaughlin

For full biographical listings, see the Martindale-Hubbell Law Directory

ROSELAND, Essex Co.

BRACH, EICHLER, ROSENBERG, SILVER, BERNSTEIN, HAMMER & GLADSTONE, A PROFESSIONAL CORPORATION (AV)

101 Eisenhower Parkway, 07068
Telephone: 973-228-5700
Telecopier: 973-228-7852
Email: law@bracheichler.com *URL:* http://www.bracheichler.com

Alan H. Bernstein
William L. Brach
Todd C. Brower
Thomas E. Cohn
Richard J. Driver
Burton L. Eichler
John D. Fanburg
William J. Friedman
Stuart M. Gladstone
Charles X. Gormally
Joseph M. Gorrell
Alan R. Hammer
Bruce Kleinman
Brian R. Lenker
Susan Y. Leonard
Robert C. Mignella
Stuart L. Pachman
Alan S. Pralgever
David J. Ritter
Paul F. Rosenberg
Michael I. Schneck

Ann D. Stevens
Jeffrey H. Itzkowitz
Carol Grelecki
Richard B. Robins
Joseph M. Davis
Brian Kalver
John P. Inglesino
Stuart Jeffrey Polkowitz
Jed S. Freeman
John P. Wyciskala, III
Susan K. Dromsky-Reed
Matthew M. Collins
Carl J. Soranno
Simone E. Handler Hutchinson
Gary L. Koenigsberg
Kristine Bogardus Purcell
Christopher A. Erd
Allen J. Popowitz
Jonathan E. Levitt
Lisa S. Paye
Terri R. Soaries
Mark E. Manigan
Evan S. Glanz
Dahesh D. Patel

(See Next Column)

BRACH, EICHLER, ROSENBERG, SILVER, BERNSTEIN, HAMMER & GLADSTONE A PROFESSIONAL CORPORATION, *Roseland—Continued*

Alexis Goldberger
Douglas J. Sitar
Mark Sblendorio
Jill H. Blumberg

OF COUNSEL

Harris R. Silver
Lance A. Posner
George Y. Sodowick
Henry N. Portner

COUNSEL

Alois V. Habjan
David J. Klein
David S. Bernstein
Dorothy G. Black (1927-1996)

Representative Clients: Advance Realty Goup; ARC Properties, Inc.; I. Heller Industrial Parks; The Kushner Companies; Mercer Medical Center; Ohio Casualty Insurance Group; Perlmart Shop-Rites; Saint Barnabas Health Care System; Silverline Building Products Corp.

For full biographical listings, see the Martindale-Hubbell Law Directory

---

CARELLA, BYRNE, BAIN, GILFILLAN, CECCHI, STEWART & OLSTEIN, A PROFESSIONAL CORPORATION (AV)

Six Becker Farm Road, 07068-1739
Telephone: 973-994-1700
Telecopier: 973-994-1744

Charles C. Carella
Brendan T. Byrne
John N. Bain
John G. Gilfillan, III
Peter G. Stewart
Elliot M. Olstein
Arthur T. Vanderbilt, II
Jan Alan Brody
John M. Agnello
James T. Byers
Donald F. Miceli
A. Richard Ross
Kenneth L. Winters
Jeffrey A. Cooper
Carl R. Woodward, III
Walter G. Luger
Charles M. Carella
James E. Cecchi
David G. White

Raymond J. Lillie
William Squire
Dennis F. Gleason
David G. Gilfillan
Brian H. Fenlon
Melissa E. Flax
Nabil N. Kassem
Jo Anne C. Gerber
Mark D. Miller
Justine A. Niccollai
Jason S. Klein
Robert P. Donovan
Alan J. Grant
(Not admitted in NJ)
Nicola R.J. Hadziosmanovic
Joseph N. Minish

OF COUNSEL

Richard K. Matanle, II
Donald S. Brooks
Herbert M. Rinaldi
Raymond R. Siberine
Michael A. Gallo, Jr.

Representative Clients: American Funding Limited, Montvale, N.J.; Archdiocese of Newark, Newark, N.J.; Carter-Wallace, Inc., New York, N.Y.; Ingersoll-Rand; Johnson Controls, Milwaukee, Wi.; Nichols Markets, North Haledon, N.J.; Werner and Pfeiderer Corp., Ramsey, N.J.; Witco Corporation, New York, N.Y.; Trustee/Receiver Assets of "Crazy Eddie" Antar.

For full biographical listings, see the Martindale-Hubbell Law Directory

---

CONNELL, FOLEY & GEISER LLP (AV)

85 Livingston Avenue, 07068
Telephone: 973-535-0500
Telefax: 973-535-9217
Email: info@cfglaw.com *URL:* http://www.cfglaw.com

MEMBERS OF FIRM

John A. Pindar (1948-1969)
George W. Connell
Adrian M. Foley, Jr.
Theodore W. Geiser
John B. La Vecchia
George J. Kenny
Kenneth F. Kunzman
Samuel Darrow Lord
Richard D. Catenacci
Richard J. Badolato
Peter D. Manahan
John B. Murray
Mark L. Fleder
Kevin J. Coakley
Linda A. Palazzolo
John F. Neary
Thomas S. Cosma
Kathleen S. Murphy
Keith A. Krauss
Patrick J. McAuley
Peter J. Pizzi
Kevin R. Gardner
Robert Emmett Ryan
Michael X. McBride
Jeffrey W. Moryan
John K. Bennett
Donald S. MacLachlan
Patricia J. Pindar
Peter J. Smith
Brian G. Steller
Judith A. Wahrenberger
Philip F. McGovern, Jr.
Karen Munster Cassidy
Karen Painter Randall
Liza M. Walsh
John P. Lacey
Timothy E. Corriston
Ernest W. Schoellkopff
Heidi Willis Currier
Patrick J. Hughes
John D. Cromie
Guy T. Lytle
Angela A. Iuso
John H. Denton
George H. Parsells, III
Paul T. Fader
Glenn T. Dyer
William T. McGloin
Brendan Judge
Daren S. McNally

COUNSEL

Edward Delesky

(See Next Column)

ASSOCIATES

Pamela M. Kapsimalis
James P. McBarron
Stephen V. Falanga
Jeffrey L. O'Hara
Tricia Bevelock O'Reilly
Thomas A. Sparno
Maureen McLoughlin
Richard T. Bayer
Marc D. Haefner
Mollie K. O'Brien
Steve Barnett
Kevin L. Leahy
Karen L. Mayer
Christine M. Crutchlow
Angelica S. Liem
Jonathan P. McHenry
Kathleen Huntley-Robertson
John C. Lenzen
James P. Rhatican
Leslie A. Cascone
Stuart J. Wells
Lisa M. Fontoura
Maureen T. Bartoli
Walter R. Krzastek, Jr.
Lynne A. Aretsky
Richard A. Jagen
W. Nevins McCann
Stephen L. Petrillo
Mitchell W. Taraschi
Jennifer Choe

OF COUNSEL

Anthony F. Vitiello

Representative Clients: Bethlehem Steel Corp.; Borden Inc.; Chase Manhattan Bank; CNA Insurance; Conrail; Hilton Hotels Corp.; Merrill Lynch; Microsoft; New Jersey Manufacturers Insurance.

For full biographical listings, see the Martindale-Hubbell Law Directory

---

POST, POLAK, GOODSELL & MACNEILL, P.A. (AV)

75 Livingston Avenue, 07068-3701
Telephone: 973-994-1100
Telecopier: 973-994-1705
Email: administrator@ppgm.com
New York, New York Office: 575 Madison Avenue, Suite 1006.
Telephone: 212-486-1455.

John N. Post
Frederick B. Polak
Robert A. Goodsell
Jay Scott MacNeill
Paul D. Strauchler
Mary H. Post
David L. Epstein
Lauren Koffler O'Neill

Loretta B. Critchley
Franca D. Maiorano
Nilufer O. DeScherer
Joseph Tripodi
Thomas J. Pyle, Jr.
Christopher O. Eriksen
Kelly Mack Carey

LEGAL SUPPORT PERSONNEL

Charles A. Tamasaukas (Firm Administrator)

PARALEGALS

Nancy Mendelsohn
Glenn A. Harris
Susan B. Cobb
Nancy G. Barrett

For full biographical listings, see the Martindale-Hubbell Law Directory

---

CHARLES A. ROSEN (AV)

280 Corporate Center, 5 Becker Farm Road, 07068
Telephone: 973-535-2800
Telecopier: 973-535-9777
New York, New York Office: 60 East 42nd Street, Suite 1217.
Telephone: 212-921-2236.

ASSOCIATE

Cecilia M.E. Lindenfelser

Reference: Summit Bank.

For full biographical listings, see the Martindale-Hubbell Law Directory

---

WALDER, SONDAK & BROGAN, A PROFESSIONAL CORPORATION (AV)

5 Becker Farm Road, P.O. Box 901, 07068
Telephone: 973-992-5300
Telecopier: 973-992-1505; 992-1006
Email: general@wsbesqs.com *URL:* http://www.wsbesqs.com

Joel Sondak (1932-1995)
Justin P. Walder
John A. Brogan
Melvyn H. Bergstein
Thomas J. Spies
Barry A. Kozyra
James A. Plaisted
Heather Grasz Suarez
Michael J. Faul, Jr.
Jeffrey A. Walder
Patricia M. Talbert

John S. Redden
Shalom D. Stone
Judith A. Hartz
Christopher M. Farella
Barbara F. Buchta
Steven D. Grossman
K. Roger Plawker

OF COUNSEL

John H. Skarbnik
Robert C. Shelton, Jr.

For full biographical listings, see the Martindale-Hubbell Law Directory

Roseland—Continued

Wolff & Samson, A Professional Corporation (AV)

280 Corporate Center, 5 Becker Farm Road, 07068-1776
Telephone: 973-740-0500
Fax: 973-740-1407
Email: info@wolffsamson.com *URL:* http://www.wolffsamson.com
New York, New York Office: 140 Broadway, Forty-Sixth Floor.
Telephone: 212-973-0572.
Fax: 212-858-7524.
Hackensack, New Jersey Office: 58-60 Main Street, P.O. Box 157.
Telephone: 201-488-3338.
Fax: 201-488-4164.

David Samson
Ronald E. Wiss
Arthur S. Goldstein
Armen Shahinian
Martin L. Wiener
Gage Andretta
Daniel A. Schwartz
Karen L. Gilman
Kenneth N. Laptook
David L. Schlossberg
Paul M. Colwell
Robert E. Nies
Morris Bienenfeld
Dennis M. Toft
Jeffrey M. Gussoff
Joseph A. Ferriero
M. Jeremy Ostow
Jeffrey M. Davis
John F. Casey
James D. Ferrucci
John M. Simon
Laurence M. Smith
William E. Goydan
Darryl Weissman
Michael R. Friscia
Peter E. Nussbaum
Michelle A. Schaap

OF COUNSEL

Joel A. Wolff
Roger J. Breene
Carl B. Levy
Daniel C. Becker
Howard J. Menaker
Angelo A. Mastrangelo

SENIOR ATTORNEYS

Aaron D. Bassan
Roxanna Epling Hammett
Lauren M. O'Sullivan
Robert Tchack
Joseph Zawila
Stephen H. Bier
Mary Jane Dobbs
James J. Ross

Robert M. Silverstein
Howard K. Uniman
Lori E. Grifa
Thomas W. Sabino
Catherine P. Wells
Myrna Blume
Mark R. Micucci
Frank J. Kontely, III
Adam P. Friedman
Jonathan S. Bondy
Arnold F. Mascali
Adam K. Derman
Martin L. Borosko
Andrew S. Kent
Eric J. Levine
Douglas M. Cohen
Andrew Samson
Jordan S. Solomon
Mitchell L. Pascual
Scott D. Baron
David J. Sprong
Sharon L. Weiner
Vanessa Jachzel
Dorit F. Kressel
Jeffrey B. Ulin
Arthur M. Nalbandian
Susan G. Greenwald
Junie Hahn
Michele S. Kayne
Stacy B. Krieger
John O. Lukanski
Marci DiFrancesco
Noreen M. Giblin

Representative Clients: International Fidelity Insurance Co.; Celentano Brothers, Inc.; Chicago Title Insurance Co.; Hartz Mountain Industries; The Hillier Group; Foster Wheeler Corp.; Ernst & Co.; Prudential Securities, Inc.; Independence Community Bank; Cogen Technologies, Inc.; The Hiller Group, Inc.

For full biographical listings, see the Martindale-Hubbell Law Directory

SADDLE BROOK, Bergen Co.

Krugman & Kailes LLP (AV)

Park 80 West-Plaza Two, 07663-5835
Telephone: 201-845-3434; 212-695-3262
Telecopier: 201-845-9627
Email: counsel@krugmankailes.com
New York, New York Office: 99 Park Avenue, Suite 2200.
Telephone: 212-599-1060.
Telecopier: 212-599-6282.
London, England Office: 90 Fetter Lane, London EC4A-1PT.
Telephone: 011 (44) 171-421-7918.
Telecopier: 011 (44) 171-831-6407.

MEMBERS OF FIRM

Martin Krugman (1916-1994)
Howard Kailes
Thomas J. Goodwin
Ward C. Laracy
Robert I. Wexler
Alan H. Fox
Joy M. Mercer
Kerry B. Flowers

OF COUNSEL

James D. Krugman

COUNSEL

Judith S. Musicant

(See Next Column)

ASSOCIATES

Anne M. Wallace
(Not admitted in NJ)
April A. Savoye
Lisa Ann Miller
Patrizia E. DeBari
David J. Hanley, Jr.
Anjana D. Patel
W. Mark O'Brien

For full biographical listings, see the Martindale-Hubbell Law Directory

SECAUCUS, Hudson Co.

Fitzpatrick & Waterman (AV)

400 Plaza Drive, P.O. Box 3159, 07096-3159
Telephone: 201-865-9100
800 BOND LAW
Facsimile: 201-865-4805
Bayonne, New Jersey Office: 90 West 40th Street, P.O. Box 1227, 07002.
Telephone: 201-339-4000; 1-800 BOND LAW.

Harold F. Fitzpatrick
Stephen P. Waterman

ASSOCIATES

Glenn C. Merritt
Jeanette M. Samra

OF COUNSEL

Michael J. Israels
Andre Shramenko

For full biographical listings, see the Martindale-Hubbell Law Directory

Waters, McPherson, McNeill, P.C. (AV)

300 Lighting Way, 7th Floor, 07096
Telephone: 201-863-4400
Telecopy: 201-863-2866
Email: managingpartner@lawwmm.com *URL:* www.lawwmm.com
Trenton, New Jersey Office: 172 West State Street.
Telephone: 609-599-1000.
New York, N.Y. Office: The Woolworth Building, 233 Broadway, Suite 970.
Telephone: 212-227-7878.

David A. Waters
(Member of Firm: 1962-1998)
Kenneth D. McPherson
John H. McNeill
John J. Kot
Daniel E. Horgan
William J. Ward
Gregory J. Castano
Frank G. Capece
Steven R. Gray
Lawrence Z. Kotler
E. Neal Zimmermann
Nicholas I. Filocco
Kenneth D. McPherson, Jr.
Thomas J. O'Connor
Joseph G. Ragno
James P. Bruno
Charles J. Harriman
Patrick J. Arre
David A. McPherson
Perry Florio
Giovanni Regina
Paul A. Conciatori
Marc S. Faecher
Robert M. Marshall
Mark J. McPherson
Daniel J. Pollak
Salvatore A. Giampiccolo
Paul K. Hennessy
Lucille Jane Karp
Barbara Packer-Rosen
Howard A. Kantrowitz

COUNSEL TO THE FIRM

Blake S. Davis
Mark J. Ingber

Neil J. Carroll
Gregory J. Castano, Jr.
Benjamin B. Choi
Joanne Clark
Shari T. Competiello
Anthony Coppola
Jane Fontana
Patricia M. Forsyth
Joan H. Langer
Brian D. Lieberman
Renee A. Rubino
James J. Seaman
Nancy A. Skidmore

OF COUNSEL

James P. Dugan
Morton Goldfein
Bernard M. Jaffe
(Not admitted in NJ)
Joseph Lesser
(Not admitted in NJ)
David J. Mahoney, Jr.
(Not admitted in NJ)
Michael J. Mehr
Herbert I. Olarsch
John B. Wefing

Representative Clients: American Institute of Certified Public Accountants; Crown, Cork & Seal Co., Inc.; Hartz Mountain Industries, Inc.; Liberty Mutual Insurance Co.; Tropicana Products, Inc.

For full biographical listings, see the Martindale-Hubbell Law Directory

SHIP BOTTOM, Ocean Co.

Shackleton, Hazeltine and Bishop (AV)

22nd Street and Long Beach Boulevard, P.O. Box 410, 08008
Telephone: 609-494-2136
Telefax: 609-494-0870
Fairfield, New Jersey Office: One Passaic Avenue.
Telephone: 201-882-4646.
Telefax: 201-882-4620.

MEMBERS OF FIRM

Richard J. Shackleton
Colin R. Hazeltine
James E. Bishop

(See Next Column)

SHACKLETON, HAZELTINE AND BISHOP, *Ship Bottom—Continued*

ASSOCIATES

Laura M. O'Regan
Marc Baden Powell
Robert Emmet Rue

OF COUNSEL

Kenneth L. Leiby, Jr. (Resident, Fairfield Office)

References: Commerce Bank / Shore N / A; Summit Bank Corp.

For full biographical listings, see the Martindale-Hubbell Law Directory

SKILLMAN, Somerset Co.

GERALD P. SEID (AV)

144 Tamarack Circle, Montgomery Knoll, U.S. Highway 206 North, 08558
Telephone: 609-921-3747
Fax: 609-921-3936
Email: 72624.2715@compuserve.com

For full biographical listings, see the Martindale-Hubbell Law Directory

SOMERSET, Somerset Co.

McGIMPSEY & CAFFERTY (AV)

285 Davidson Avenue, Suite 404, 08873
Telephone: 732-560-1900
Fax: 732-560-1904
Email: mcgcaff@earthlink.net

Alexander F. McGimpsey, Jr.
Thomas J. Cafferty

Arlene M. Turinchak

LEGAL SUPPORT PERSONNEL

Susan Rusnock (Office Manager)

Representative Clients: New Jersey Press Assn.; Home News Tribune; North Jersey Herald & News; NJN Publishing Co.; Hunterdon County Democrat, Inc.; McGraw-Hill; Morristown Daily Record; Suburban News; Shopper News; The Bergen Record Corp.

For full biographical listings, see the Martindale-Hubbell Law Directory

*SOMERVILLE,** Somerset Co.

RAYMOND R. & DAVID W. TROMBADORE, P.C. A PROFESSIONAL CORPORATION (AV)

33 East High Street, 08876
Telephone: 908-722-7555
Fax: 908-722-6269
URL: http://www.trombadorelaw.com

Raymond R. Trombadore
David W. Trombadore

OF COUNSEL

Ann W. Trombadore

References: Summit Bank; Somerset Savings & Loan Assn.

For full biographical listings, see the Martindale-Hubbell Law Directory

FRANK N. YURASKO (AV)

139 West End Avenue, P.O. Box 1041, 08876
Telephone: 908-231-0220
Telefax: 908-231-8967
Email: fyurasko@compuserve.com *URL:* http://www.lawyers.com/yuraskolaw

Representative Clients: Ethicon, Inc.; Crown Oil Corp.; Johnson & Johnson; Searle Drug; Devro Corp.; ComVideo Systems, Inc.; Northbrook Insurance Co.; Selected Risks Insurance Co.; National Casualty Co.; Scottsdale Insuarnce Co.

For full biographical listings, see the Martindale-Hubbell Law Directory

SOUTH ORANGE, Essex Co.

LAW OFFICE OF CHARLES B. TURNER (AV)

76 South Orange Avenue, P.O. Box 526, 07079
Telephone: 973-763-5000
Fax: 973-763-0568

ASSOCIATES

Marcia Klosk Graydon
Andrew R. Turner

For full biographical listings, see the Martindale-Hubbell Law Directory

SPRINGFIELD, Union Co.

McDONOUGH, KORN & EICHHORN, A PROFESSIONAL CORPORATION (AV)

Park Place Legal Center, 959 South Springfield Avenue, P.O. Box 712, 07081-0712
Telephone: 973-912-9099
Fax: 973-912-8604

Peter L. Korn
R. Scott Eichhorn
James R. Korn
William S. Mezzomo
Timothy J. Jaeger
Wilfred P. Coronato

Julia A. Klubenspies
Matthew S. Schorr
Danielle M. Verrastro
Jeffrey John Berezny

OF COUNSEL

Robert P. McDonough

Representative Client: Meeker Sharkey & MacBean.
Reference: First Union, Summit, N.J.

For full biographical listings, see the Martindale-Hubbell Law Directory

SUMMIT, Union Co.

BOURNE, NOLL & KENYON, A PROFESSIONAL CORPORATION (AV)

382 Springfield Avenue, P.O. Box 690, 07902-0690
Telephone: 908-277-2200
Facsimile: 908-277-6808

Cary R. Hardy
Charles R. Berman
Martin Rubashkin
Roger Mehner
James R. Ottobre
Lawrence A. Rudnick
John F. Kuntz

OF COUNSEL

Edward T. Kenyon
Robert B. Bourne

COUNSEL

Ellyn A. Draikiwicz

Jaime A. O'Brien
Timothy A. Kalas
Alan F. Schwarz
Ross W. Smith

For full biographical listings, see the Martindale-Hubbell Law Directory

*TOMS RIVER,** Ocean Co.

HIERING, DUPIGNAC & STANZIONE, A PROFESSIONAL CORPORATION (AV)

64 Washington Street, CN 2015, 08754-2015
Telephone: 732-349-1212
Telefax: 732-349-1217
Email: hds@americom.net

William T. Hiering
Frank J. Dupignac, Jr.
Richard D. Stanzione

Lynne A. Dunn

OF COUNSEL

Richard H. Woods

Representative Clients: Ocean County Utilities Authority; Sambol Construction Co.; Venice Amusement Corporation and Subsidiaries; Crestwood Village, Inc.; Union Valley, Inc.; Bell Atlantic Mobile Systems, Inc.; U.S. Homes Corp.; Nextel Communications; Omnipoint Communications; Ocean County Joint Insurance Fund.

For full biographical listings, see the Martindale-Hubbell Law Directory

LOMELL, MUCCIFORI, ADLER, RAVASCHIERE, AMABILE & PEHLIVANIAN, A PROFESSIONAL CORPORATION (AV)

250 Washington Street, P.O. Box 787, 08754
Telephone: 732-349-2443
Fax: 732-349-6917
Email: thefirm@lomell.com *URL:* http://www.lomell.com

A. Thomas Amabile (1936-1993)
Herman A. Adler
Dominic Ravaschiere
John S. Pehlivanian
Ronald E. Prusek
Jeffrey R. Surenian
James M. McKenna
Teresa K. Gierla
Arthur F. Leyden, III

Marc S. Galella
Robyn A. Belluardo
Janet Zaorski Kalapos
James S. Braaten
Regina M. Butler
Paul J Capotorto

OF COUNSEL

Leonard G. Lomell
Thomas J. Muccifori

For full biographical listings, see the Martindale-Hubbell Law Directory

Toms River—Continued

NOVINS, YORK & PENTONY, A PROFESSIONAL CORPORATION (AV)

202 Main Street, 08753
Telephone: 732-349-7100
Email: info@nyplaw.com

Robert J. Novins (1910-1973)
Robert F. Novins
Harvey L. York
Kenneth R. Pentony
Ann K. Haskell
Robert M. McKeon

W. Mark Bayles
Robert J. Roth
Gregory S. Heizler
Anthony M. Pagano
Danziger Patricia Christoff
Michael A. Jacobus

OF COUNSEL

William E. O'Connor
Lorna S. Scanlon

Counsel for: Allstate Insurance Co.; Motor Club of America.

For full biographical listings, see the Martindale-Hubbell Law Directory

STARKEY, KELLY, BLANEY & WHITE (AV)

2 Hooper Avenue, 08753
Telephone: 732-240-3600
Fax: 732-240-3777
Brick, New Jersey Office: 459 Jack Martin Boulevard, 08724.
Telephone: 732-840-5900.
Fax: 732-840-5901.
Manasquan, New Jersey Office: 23 Route 71, 08736.
Telephone: 732-223-7328.
Fax: 732-240-3777.

MEMBERS OF FIRM

Charles E. Starkey
William V. Kelly
James M. Blaney

ASSOCIATES

Natalie Pouch
Anthony Mancuso
Robert A. Bauer
Scott W. Kenneally
Susan K. White
Brent D. Miller

Representative Clients: Hartford Insurance Co.; New Jersey Education Assn.; New Jersey Psychiatric Assn.; Ocean County Utilities Authority; Brick Township Municipal Utilities Authority; Manasquan River Regional Sewerage Authority; Hanover Insurance Co.; John Hancock Insurance Co.; Rider Inc. Co.

For full biographical listings, see the Martindale-Hubbell Law Directory

*TRENTON,** Mercer Co.

BACKES & HILL (AV)

(Originally Backes & Backes)
15 West Front Street, 08608-2098
Telephone: 609-396-8257
Telefax: 609-989-7323

Peter Backes (1858-1941)
Herbert W. Backes (1891-1970)
William Wright Backes (1904-1980)
Michael J. Nizolek (1950-1994)

OF COUNSEL

Robert Maddock Backes

PARTNERS

Harry R. Hill, Jr.
Robert C. Billmeier
Brenda Farr Engel

ASSOCIATES

Robert Carlson Leventhal
Michael B. Roth

LEGAL SUPPORT PERSONNEL

Patricia R. O'Brien (Office Manager)

Representative Clients: New Jersey Manufacturers Insurance Co.; United Services Automobile Association; Mercer Medical Center; Catholic Diocese of Trenton; St. Francis Medical Center; Trenton Savings Bank, FSB; Richie & Page Distributing Co., Inc.; General Sullivan Group, Inc.; Trenton Orthopedic Group; City Beef, Inc..

For full biographical listings, see the Martindale-Hubbell Law Directory

FOX, ROTHSCHILD, O'BRIEN & FRANKEL, LLP (AV)

Princeton Pike Corporate Center, 997 Lenox Drive, Building 3 (Lawrenceville), 08648-2311
Telephone: 609-896-3600
Fax: 609-896-1469
Email: frof@frof.com *URL:* http://www.frof.com
Philadelphia, Pennsylvania Office: 2000 Market Street, Tenth Floor, 19103-3291.
Telephone: 215-299-2000.
Cable Address: FROF.
Fax: 215-299-2150. 215-299-2150.

(See Next Column)

Atlantic City, New Jersey Office: CitiCenter Building, Suite 500, 1300 Atlantic Avenue, 08401.
Telephone: 609-348-4515.
Fax: 609-348-6834.
Doylestown, Pennsylvania Office: 102 North Main Street, P.O. Box 1589, 18901-0700.
Telephone: 215-345-7500.
Fax: 215-345-7507.
Exton, Pennsylvania Office: Eagleview Corporate Center, 760 Constitution Drive, Suite 104, P.O. Box 673, 19341-0673.
Telephone: 610-458-7500.
Fax: 610-458-7337.
Lansdale, Pennsylvania Office: 1250 South Broad Street, Suite 1000, P.O. Box 431, 19446.
Telephone: 215-699-6000.
Fax: 215-699-0231.
Sellersville, Pennsylvania Office: 64 North Main Street, 18960-0580.
Telephone: 215-257-3661.
Fax: 215-257-7999.
Voorhees, New Jersey Office: Laurelwood, Suite 103, 1103 Laurel Oak Road, 08043.
Telephone: 856-782-6000.
Fax: 856-346-9866.

Richard M. Kohn
Victor Walcoff
Mark Z. Segal
Michael J. Kline
Jonathan D. Weiner
Steven C. Levitt
Kenneth H. Mack
Phillip E. Griffin
James F. X. Rudy
Linda Mack
Jeffrey H. Nicholas
Matthew H. Lubart
Jon C. Martin
Martin L. Monaco, Jr.
June H. Millington
Jack L. Kolpen
Thomas J. Heitzman
R. James Kravitz
Ian D. Meklinsky
Douglas J. Zeltt

ASSOCIATES

William L. Weiner
Susan D. Bonfield
Holly Lichtenstein Goldberg
Philip S. Rosenzweig
Lynn B. McDougall
Magdalena Schardt
Madeleine H. Cozine
Richard E. Wegryn Jr.
Maureen E. Kerns
Christina Almanzor
Michael B. Dahl
Thomas R. Hower
Mark R. Kossow
Gregory A. Petroff
Alicia A. Zonetti
Anthony Argiropoulos
Tess Brennan
Neil M. Day
Wan-Mo Kang

SPECIAL COUNSEL

Elaine C. Britt

For full biographical listings, see the Martindale-Hubbell Law Directory

RIKER, DANZIG, SCHERER, HYLAND & PERRETTI LLP (AV)

50 West State Street, Suite 1010, 08608-1220
Telephone: 609-396-2121
Fax: 609-396-4578
Email: info@riker.com *URL:* http://www.riker.com
Morristown, New Jersey Office: Headquarters Plaza, One Speedwell Avenue.
Telephone: 973-538-0800.
Fax: 973-538-1984.

John P. Sheridan, Jr.
John M. Pellecchia

OF COUNSEL

William F. Hyland

COUNSEL

James A. Harkness

ASSOCIATES

Kris Ann E. Cappelluti
Mary Kathryn Roberts

For full biographical listings, see the Martindale-Hubbell Law Directory

SCHRAGGER, LAVINE & NAGY (AV)

Mountainview Office Park, 840 Bear Tavern Road, Suite 307, 08628
Telephone: 609-771-0700
Fax: 609-771-9535

Bruce M. Schragger
Raymond L. Nagy
James A. Schragger
Jonathan S. Robinson
Michael E. Sullivan

OF COUNSEL

Henry C. Schragger
Alan S. Lavine
Frank P. Reiche
A. Jerome Moore

LEGAL SUPPORT PERSONNEL

Annemarie Saccani (Office Administrator)

Representative Clients: New Jersey Manufacturers Insurance Co.; Mercer County Community College; Mercer Mutual Insurance Co.; New Jersey Optometric Association; Allentown Caging; Dick Greenfield Dodge.

For full biographical listings, see the Martindale-Hubbell Law Directory

Trenton—Continued

Sterns & Weinroth, A Professional Corporation (AV)

50 West State Street, P.O. Box 1298, 08607-1298
Telephone: 609-392-2100
Fax: 609-392-7956
Email: admin@sternslaw.com
Atlantic City, New Jersey Office: 2901 Atlantic Avenue.
Telephone: 609-340-8300.
Fax: 609-340-8722.

William J. Bigham
Marshall D. Bilder
Nicholas Casiello, Jr. (Resident, Atlantic City Office)
Karen A. Confoy
Bernadette Fallows Davidson
William J. Downey, III (Resident, Atlantic City Office)
Simon Kimmelman
Mitchell A. Livingston
Brian J. Mulligan
Paul M. O'Gara
Vincent J. Paluzzi
Frank J. Petrino
Michael L. Rosenberg
David M. Roskos
Mark D. Schorr
John F. Semple
Joel H. Sterns
Susan Stryker
Nicholas F. Talvacchia (Resident, Atlantic City Office)
Richard J. Van Wagner
Richard K. Weinroth
Robert Paul Zoller

COUNSEL

Jeffrey S. Posta

OF COUNSEL

Stephen F. Lichtenstein
Elmer M. Matthews

Edgar Alden Dunham, IV
Anthony E. Bush
Andrea Dobin
Kathleen Meehan DalCortivo
Bart Q Hollander
Jason S. Feinstein
Marie J. Jones (Resident, Atlantic City Office)
Valerie A. Hamilton
Christopher E. Torkelson
Nancy A. Natello (Resident, Atlantic City Office)

For full biographical listings, see the Martindale-Hubbell Law Directory

---

Teich, Groh and Frost (AV)

691 State Highway 33, 08619-4492
Telephone: 609-890-1500
Fax: 609-890-6961
Email: teich1g2f3@aol.com
Lawrenceville, New Jersey Office: 109 Franklin Corner Road.
Telephone: 609-844-0488.
Fax: 609-844-0784.

MEMBERS OF FIRM

Arthur Teich (1915-1997)
William C. Groh
Barry W. Frost
Carol Oswald (Also at Lawrenceville Office)
Carol L. Knowlton
Allen I. Gorski
Arthur R. Sypek, Jr.
Dean S. Nalbone

ASSOCIATES

Jill M. Wittenborn (Also at Lawrenceville Office)
Michael W. Krutman
David A. Martin
Kimberley M. Lake

References: CoreStates/New Jersey National Bank; United National Bank.

For full biographical listings, see the Martindale-Hubbell Law Directory

---

VINELAND, Cumberland Co.

Basile & Testa, A Professional Corporation (AV)

424 Landis Avenue, P.O. Box 460, 08360
Telephone: 609-691-2300
Telefax: 609-691-5655
Email: LAW424@AOL.COM

Francis G. Basile
Michael L. Testa
Todd W. Heck
Michelle J. Douglass

Michael J. Gruccio
Walter A. Schultz, Jr.
Renee E. Scrocca
Eve-Marie Niskey
Jeffrey A. DiLazzero

OF COUNSEL

Frank J. Testa

Representative Client: U.S. Insurance Group.

For full biographical listings, see the Martindale-Hubbell Law Directory

---

Eisenstat, Gabage, Berman & Furman, A Professional Corporation (AV)

1179 East Landis Avenue, 08360
Telephone: 856-691-1200
Telecopier: 856-691-0414
Mailing Address: P.O. Box 420, Vineland, NJ, 08360-4278

(See Next Column)

Gerald (Jere) M. Eisenstat
Charles W. Gabage
Mitchell S. Berman
Harry Furman

Patricia Powell

For full biographical listings, see the Martindale-Hubbell Law Directory

---

Jay H. Greenblatt & Associates A Professional Corporation (AV)

200 North Eighth Street, P.O. Box 883, 08360-0883
Telephone: 609-691-0424
Facsimile: 609-696-1010
Email: jhg@algorithms.com *URL:* http://home.earthlink.net/~greenblatt/

M. Joseph Greenblatt (1896-1992)
Jay H. Greenblatt

Bonnie L. Laube
Nicholas Kiernesky

For full biographical listings, see the Martindale-Hubbell Law Directory

---

Gruccio, Pepper Giovinazzi, DeSanto & Farnoly, P.A. (AV)

817 Landis Avenue, P.O. Box 1501, 08362
Telephone: 856-691-0100
Fax: 856-692-4095
Email: Gruccio1@eticomm.net
Woodbury, New Jersey Office: 21 Delaware Street.
Telephone: 856-848-5558.
Fax: 856-384-1181.
Bridgeton, New Jersey Office: 120 West Broad Street.
Telephone: 856-459-3334.
Fax: 856-692-4095.

James J. Gruccio, Sr.
Lawrence Pepper, Jr.
Cosmo A. Giovinazzi, III
Robert A. DeSanto
Thomas P. Farnoly
E. Edward Bowman

Walter F. Gavigan
Gerald R. Spall
Stephen D. Barse
Joseph E. Ruth
Judith C. Arnold
James J. Gruccio, Jr.
Gregory S. Martinelli

OF COUNSEL

Richard M. Milstead

Representative Clients: State Farm Mutual Automobile Insurance Cos.; United States Fidelity & Guaranty Co.; South Jersey Transportation Authority; County of Salem; County of Cape May; Cumberland Mutual Fire Insurance Co.; Farmers and Merchants National Bank of Bridgeton; Vineland Board of Education; Southern Intercounty Medical Association; Sun National Bank of N.J.

For full biographical listings, see the Martindale-Hubbell Law Directory

---

Lipman, Antonelli, Batt, Dunlap, Wodlinger & Gilson, A Professional Corporation (AV)

110 North Sixth Street, P.O. Box 280, 08360-3703
Telephone: 856-692-8000
Telecopier: 856-692-7580
Email: lipmanlaw@aol.com
Millville, New Jersey Office: 117 Smith Street.
Telephone: 856-825-8800.
Fax: 856-825-3283.

Philip L. Lipman
Gerald J. Batt
Gary D. Wodlinger
William M. Gilson
Robert G. Malestein
Steven L. Rothman
Edward A. Lopez

OF COUNSEL

Marvin M. Wodlinger (Resident, Millville, New Jersey Office)

For full biographical listings, see the Martindale-Hubbell Law Directory

---

WALL TOWNSHIP, Monmouth Co.

Magee and Isherwood, L.L.P. (AV)

Mirne & Simmill
Mirne, Nowels, Fundler Magee & Kirschner
1937 Route 35 at Allaire Road, P.O. Box 1200, 07719
Telephone: 732-449-2500
Telecopier: 732-449-4005

MEMBERS OF FIRM

Granville D. Magee
Thomas Isherwood

ASSOCIATE

Granville M. Magee

(See Next Column)

MAGEE AND ISHERWOOD L.L.P.—*Continued*

OF COUNSEL

Michael B. Kirschner

Representative Clients: Royal Insurance Cos.; Township of Upper Freehold.
References: Central Jersey Bank & Trust Co.; Commerce Bank Shore N.A.

For full biographical listings, see the Martindale-Hubbell Law Directory

WARREN, Somerset Co.

HEROLD AND HAINES, PROFESSIONAL ASSOCIATION (AV)

25 Independence Boulevard, 07059-6747
Telephone: 908-647-1022
Telecopier: 908-647-7721
Email: firm@heroldhaines.com

Richard H. Herold
Gordon A. Millspaugh, Jr.
Robert B. Haines
John W. McGowan III
Anthony J. Reitano, Jr.
Gary E. Walker
Patricia Kelley Fleetwood
Howard G. Katz
Craig S. Provorny
Michael Osterman
Glenn R. Gordon
Sheryl M. Schwartz

Joseph M. Lemond
Brian F. Curley
John W. Hersperger
John Kenyon Fetterly
Linda Nash Engleby
(Not admitted in NJ)
Cynthia Terzakis Gakos

Representative Clients: ADESA Corporation; Agway Petroleum Corp.; E.I. duPont de Nemours; Fleet Bank, N.A.; Hatco Corporation; Hoechst-Celanese Corp.; Ingersol-Rand, Inc.; United Way of Somerset County, Inc.

For full biographical listings, see the Martindale-Hubbell Law Directory

WAYNE, Passaic Co.

DEYOE HEISSENBUTTEL, L.L.C. (AV)

401 Hamburg Turnpike, P.O. Box 2449, 07474-2449
Telephone: 973-595-6300
Fax: 973-595-0146
Email: deyoelaw@ix.netcom.com *URL:* http://www.deyoe.com

MEMBERS OF FIRM

Charles P. DeYoe (1923-1973)
Wood M. DeYoe
Frederick C. Heissenbuttel
Scott B. Piekarsky

ASSOCIATES

Raymond F. Shenekji
Anne Hutton
Albert C. Buglione
Laureen A. Moloney

LEGAL SUPPORT PERSONNEL

Marilyn Moore (Office Manager)

Representative Clients: Hanover Insurance Inc.; Maryland Casualty Co.; Ohio Casualty Insurance Co.; Motor Club of America; Selective Insurance Co.; Prudential Property & Casualty; Reliance Ins. Co.

For full biographical listings, see the Martindale-Hubbell Law Directory

WESTFIELD, Union Co.

LINDABURY, MCCORMICK & ESTABROOK, P.A. (AV)

53 Cardinal Drive, P.O. Box 2369, 07091
Telephone: 908-233-6800
Fax: 908-233-5078
New York, N.Y. Office: 26 Broadway, Suite 2300.
Telephone: 212-742-3390.
Fax: 212-269-5016.

Joseph S. Lindabury (1898-1984)
Richard R. Width
Anthony J. La Russo
Peter A. Somers
William R. Watkins
Edward J. Frisch
John R. Blasi
John H. Schmidt, Jr.
Donald F. Nicolai
Bruce P. Ogden
James K. Estabrook
James D. DeRose
Barry J. Donohue
Robert S. Burney
David R. Pierce
Jay Lavroff
Anthony P. Sciarrillo
Robert W. Anderson
Robert S. Schwartz
Richard J. Cino
Stephen A. Santola

COUNSEL

James McGlew, II

Kathleen M. Connelly
Daniel F. Crowe
Kelly A. Briganti
Jennifer F. Barry
Jany Sabins
Eric B. Levine
Athina Lekas Cornell
Elizabeth Engert Manzo
Greg K. Vitali
Bruce W. McCoy, Jr.
Isabel Machado

(See Next Column)

OF COUNSEL

Kenneth L. Estabrook
Francis X. McCormick

Representative Clients: Elizabeth General Medical Center; Great American Insurance Co.; Kessler Institute for Rehabilitation; Kuehne Chemical Co., Inc.; Mechanical Contractors Association of New Jersey, Inc.; New Jersey Industrial Energy Users; Summit Bank; Western Industries, Inc.

For full biographical listings, see the Martindale-Hubbell Law Directory

WESTMONT, Camden Co.

BROWN & CONNERY, LLP (AV)

360 Haddon Avenue, P.O. Box 539, 08108
Telephone: 609-854-8900
Facsimile: 609-858-4967
Camden, New Jersey Office: 518 Market Street, P.O. Box 1449.
Telephone: 609-365-5100.
Telecopier: 609-858-4967.

MEMBERS OF FIRM

Thomas F. Connery, Jr.
Warren W. Faulk
Steven G. Wolschina
Paul Mainardi
Michael J. Vassalotti
Dennis P. Blake
William M. Tambussi
Mark P. Asselta
Stephen J. DeFeo
Joseph M Nardi, III

ASSOCIATES

Joseph A. Zechman
Karen A. McGuinness
Jeffrey E. Ugoretz
Christine O'Hearn
Christine A. Campbell
Joseph T. Carney
Richard C. Belli, Jr.
Stephanie E. Nolan
Shawn C. Huber
Susan M. Leming
Beth L. Marlin
Louis R. Lessig
Kevin C. Heil
Patrick J. Holston

Representative Clients: Camden County Health Services Center; Delaware River Port Authority; Federal Deposit Insurance Corp.; Mercedes-Benz Credit Corp.; Philadelphia Newspaper, Inc.; Philip Morris Inc.; Pollution Control Financing Authority of Camden County; Underwood-Memorial Hospital.

For full biographical listings, see the Martindale-Hubbell Law Directory

WEST ORANGE, Essex Co.

HOWARD M. DAVIS, P.C. (AV)

743 Northfield Avenue, 07052
Telephone: 201-325-8383
Telefax: 201-325-1159
Email: HMDPC@AOL.COM *URL:* http://www.lawyers.com/davislaw

Howard M. Davis

Howard J. Ehrlich

Reference: PNC Bank, West Orange.

For full biographical listings, see the Martindale-Hubbell Law Directory

MANDELBAUM, SALSBURG, GOLD, LAZRIS, DISCENZA & STEINBERG, P.A. (AV)

155 Prospect Avenue, 07052
Telephone: 973-736-4600
Fax: 973-325-7467
Email: msgldslaw@aol.com
Elizabeth, New Jersey Office: 75 Elizabeth Avenue, 07206.
Telephone: 908-353-6764.

Irving Mandelbaum (1907-1993)

Barry R. Mandelbaum
Richard M. Salsburg
Avrom J. Gold
Yale I. Lazris
Richard H. Steinberg
John R. Dusinberre
Joseph J. Discenza
Barry M. Packin
Joseph A. Vena
Lynne Strober
Owen T. Hughes
Robert W. Gluck
Gary S. Young
Richard L. Slavitt
Richard I. Simon

OF COUNSEL

Linda S. Leparulo

Ronald S. Kaplan
Lisa R. Guller
Manuel R. Grova, Jr.
Craig W. Alexander
Gary T. Lesser
Daniel M. Serviss
Deborah L. Greene
Lawrence C. Weiner
Pamela Brown-Jones
William S. Barrett

For full biographical listings, see the Martindale-Hubbell Law Directory

WOODBRIDGE, Middlesex Co.

Greenbaum, Rowe, Smith, Ravin, Davis and Himmel LLP (AV)

Metro Corporate Campus I, P.O. Box 5600, 07095-0988
Telephone: 732-549-5600
Fax: 732-549-1881 529
Email: info@greenbaumlaw.com *URL:* http://www.greenbaumlaw.com
Roseland, New Jersey Office: 6 Becker Farm Road.
Telephone: 973-535-1600.
Fax: 973-535-1698.

MEMBERS OF FIRM

Wm. L. Greenbaum (1914-1983)
Allen Ravin (1957-1997)
Robert S. Greenbaum
Arthur M. Greenbaum
Paul A. Rowe
Wendell A. Smith
Alan E. Davis
David L. Bruck
Michael B. Himmel
Michael A. Backer
Dean A. Gaver
Robert C. Schachter
Martin L. Lepelstat
Dennis A. Estis
William D. Grand
Benjamin D. Lambert, Jr.
Alan S. Naar
Mark H. Sobel (Resident, Roseland Office)
Hal W. Mandel
Barry S. Goodman
Peter A. Buchsbaum
Lawrence P. Maher
Thomas J. Denitzio, Jr.
Robert S. Goldsmith
John D. North
Kenneth T. Bills
Thomas C. Senter
Margaret Goodzeit
Robert J. Kipnees
W. Raymond Felton
Christine F. Li
Meryl Ann Greenhause Gonchar
Michael K. Feinberg
Carlton T. Spiller
Joseph M. Oriolo
Lloyd H. Tubman
Aron M. Schwartz
Sabrina A. Kogel
Jacqueline M. Printz (Resident, Roseland Office)
Lawrence H. Wertheim
David Himelman
Gary Keith Wolinetz
Kevin T. McNamara
Richard L. Hertzberg
Ellen Ann Silver
Andrea J. Sullivan

ASSOCIATES

Stephen R. Geller
Allen V. Brown
Robert S. Underhill
Steven Firkser
James A. Mohoney
Jessica R. Mayer
Christine F. Marks
Marc D. Policastro
Diane V. Garrity
Jonathan W. Philipp
Marc Jonathan Gross (Resident, Roseland Office)
Luke J. Kealy
Christopher S. Porrino
Jeffrey M. Shapiro
Michele Gibson
Jodi L. Rosenberg
Richard L. Elbert
Aaron R. Easley
Jessica L. Kyle
Keita A. Young
Cipora Winters
Marcus A. Banks
Dilip B. Patel
Jodi S. Eligberg
Victoria A. Karlson
Rosemary Culcasi
William D. Brick
Rachel M. Coe
Kelly Michele Brown
Emily A. Kaller
Deirdre Marie Naughton
Mark T. Wuillamey
Brian J. Waters
Arren S. Goldman
Darren C. Barreiro
Olivier Salvagno
Claudia L. Guglielmo

OF COUNSEL

Daniel L. Golden
Steven S. Goldenberg
Susan Okin Goldsmith
Lora L. Fong
Sherryl W. Kaufman

For full biographical listings, see the Martindale-Hubbell Law Directory

Wilentz, Goldman & Spitzer, A Professional Corporation (AV)

90 Woodbridge Center Drive Suite 900, Box 10, 07095
Telephone: 732-636-8000
Telecopier: 732-855-6117
URL: http://www.newjerseylaw.com
Eatontown, New Jersey Office: Meridian Center I, Two Industrial Way West, 07724.
Telephone: 732-542-4500.
Telecopier: 732-493-8387.
New York, New York Office: Wall Street Plaza, 88 Pine Street, 9th Floor, 10005.
Telephone: 212-267-3091.
Telecopier: 212-267-3828.

David T. Wilentz (1894-1988)
G. George Goldman (1900-1959)
Henry M. Spitzer (1903-1988)
Warren W. Wilentz
Matthias D. Dileo
Robert A. Petito
Morris Brown
Frederic K. Becker
Nicholas L. Santowasso
Richard F. Lert
John A. Hoffman
Stephen E. Barcan
Robert J. Cirafesi
Francis V. Bonello
Vincent P. Maltese
David M. Wildstein
Alan M. Darnell
Gordon J. Golum
Frank M. Ciuffani
Marvin J. Brauth
Stuart A. Hoberman
Stephen A. Spitzer
Richard R. Bonamo
Anne S. Babineau

(See Next Column)

Christine D. Petruzzell
Roger B. Kaplan
Philip A. Pahigian
Brian J. Molloy
Randall J. Richards
Barry T. Albin
Sheldon E. Jaffe
Stuart T. Cox, Jr.
Joseph J. Jankowski
Frederick J. Dennehy
Roy H. Tanzman
Steven J. Tripp
Christopher M. Placitella
Jay J. Ziznewski
James E. Trabilsy
Maureen S. Binetti
Anthony J. Pannella, Jr.
Michael J. Barrett
Jeffrey R. Rich
Michael F. Schaff
Angelo J. Cifaldi
Leslie Jeddis Lang
Francis X. Journick, Jr.
Kevin M. Berry (Resident, New York, N.Y. Office)
Louis T. DeLucia
Noel S. Tonneman (Resident, Eatontown Office)
Frank M. Ortiz (Resident, New York, N.Y. Office)
John T. Kelly
C. Kenneth Shank
Jon G. Kupilik
Peter R. Herman
Edward T. Kole
Hesser G. McBride, Jr.
Eric J. Marcy
Robert C. Kautz
Viola S. Lordi
Jeffrey K. Epstein
Lynne M. Kizis
Myron Rosner
Steven P. Marshall
Douglas Watson Lubic
Cheryl J. Oberdorf
Lisa A. Gorab
Russell J. Fishkind

OF COUNSEL

Harold G. Smith
Alfred J. Hill
Clay Constantinou
Alan B. Handler

Linda Lashbrook
Betsy Ann Rosenbloom
Yvonne Marcuse
Susanne Salzer O'Donohue
Elizabeth Connolly Dell
Charles F. Vuotto, Jr.
Isabel McGinty
Risa A. Kleiner
Ruth D. Marcus (Not admitted in NJ)
Mitchell Rait
Richard J. Byrnes
Jonathan P. Falk
Richard A. Catalina, Jr.
Robert T. Haefele
Richard S. Panitch
Donald E. Taylor
Fred Hopke
David P. Pepe
Steven P. Knowlton (Resident, New York, N.Y. Office)
Barry R. Sugarman
Lisa Martinez Wolmart
Brett R. Harris
Roberto Benites
Alan J. Brody
Matthew M. Weissman
Alfred M. Anthony
Lee Ann McCabe
Darren M. Gelber
Helen C. Lee
Anthony Cowell
Elizabeth Farley Murphy
James L. Petsche
Nancy A. Slowe
Timothy J. Dengler
Christopher W. Hager
James E. Tonrey, Jr.
Andrea White O'Brien (Resident, Eatontown, New Jersey Office)
Elizabeth Micheletti
Lori Ann Buza
Kirsten Scheurer
Joseph M. Accardi
Donna M. Jennings
Elizabeth Siso Bair
Paul Levinsohn
Giovanni Anzalone
O. Glen Pottinger
Steven R. Enis
Jessica L. Stein
M. Matthew Mannion
John Michael August
Elizabeth W. Eaton
Flavio L. Komuves
William Matsikoudis
Nicole Huberfeld
Valerie A. Jackson
Valerie L. Meyers (Resident, New York, N.Y. Office)
Gregory B. Noble
Donna A. Sisco
John E. Hogan
Daniel W. Zappo
Kaileen T. Alston (Not admitted in NJ)
Daniel A. Hagan

Representative Clients: Amerada Hess Corp.; Chevron, U.S.A.; Co-Steel Raritan; Cumberland Farms, Inc.; Middlesex County Utilities Authority; New Jersey Automobile Dealers Assn.; The Rouse Co.

For full biographical listings, see the Martindale-Hubbell Law Directory

NEW MEXICO

*ALAMOGORDO,** Otero Co.

Wayne A. Jordon (AV)

1200 B New York Avenue, P.O. Box 509, 88310
Telephone: 505-434-2700
Fax: 505-434-5510
Email: alaw@wazoo.com

Representative Clients: NorWest Bank; First Savings Bank; Texas-New Mexico Power Co.; Alamogordo Abstract & Title Co.; United Services Automobile Assn.; Sudderth Nelson, Inc.
Reference: NorWest Bank.

For full biographical listings, see the Martindale-Hubbell Law Directory

*ALBUQUERQUE,** Bernalillo Co.

CIVEROLO, GRALOW & HILL, A PROFESSIONAL ASSOCIATION (AV)

500 Marquette, N.W., Suite 1400, P.O. Drawer 887, 87103
Telephone: 505-842-8255
Telecopier: 505-764-6099

Richard C. Civerolo
William P. Gralow
Lawrence H. Hill
W. R. Logan
Roberto C. Armijo
Robert J. Curtis
Judith M. Oliva
Lisa Entress Pullen

M. Clea Gutterson
Sandy Henderson Knight
David A. Streubel
Gregory W. MacKenzie
Victor Patrick Montoya
Kerri L. Sanchez
Timothy R. Mortimer

Representative Clients: KPMG Peat Marwick, LLP; M.M.I. Companies, Inc.; Volvo North America Corp.; Western Bank of Albuquerque.

For full biographical listings, see the Martindale-Hubbell Law Directory

MILLER, STRATVERT & TORGERSON, P.A. (AV)

500 Marquette Avenue, N.W., Suite 1100, P.O. Box 25687, 87102
Telephone: 505-842-1950
Facsimile: 505-243-4408
Email: info@mstLAW.com *URL:* http://www.mstLAW.com
Farmington, New Mexico Office: 300 West Arrington, Suite 300, P.O. Box 869.
Telephone: 505-326-4521.
Facsimile: 505-325-5474.
Las Cruces, New Mexico Office: 500 South Main, Suite 800, P.O. Box 1209.
Telephone: 505-523-2481.
Facsimile: 505-526-2215.
Santa Fe, New Mexico Office: 150 Washington Avenue, Suite 300, P.O. Box 1986.
Telephone: 505-989-9614.
Facsimile: 505-989-9857.

Ranne B. Miller
Alan C. Torgerson
Alice Tomlinson Lorenz
Gregory W. Chase
Lyman G. Sandy
Stephen M. Williams
Stephan M. Vidmar
Robert C. Gutierrez
Seth V. Bingham (Resident at Farmington Office)
James B. Collins (Resident at Farmington Office)
Timothy Ray Briggs
Rudolph A. Lucero
Deborah A. Solove
Gary L. Gordon
Lawrence R. White (Resident at Las Cruces Office)
Sharon P. Gross
Virginia Anderman
Marte D. Lightstone
J. Scott Hall (Resident at Santa Fe Office)
Thomas R. Mack
Terri L. Sauer
Joel T. Newton (Resident at Las Cruces Office)
Thomas M. Domme
Ruth O. Pregenzer
Jeffrey E. Jones (Resident at Santa Fe Office)
Manuel I. Arrieta (Resident at Las Cruces Office)
Robin A. Goble
James R. Wood
Dana M. Kyle (Resident at Las Cruces Office)
Kirk R. Allen
Ruth M. Fuess
Kyle M. Finch (Resident at Farmington Office)
Henry Brook Laskey
Katherine Weeks Hall (Resident at Santa Fe Office)
Fred Schiller (Resident at Las Cruces Office)
Lara L. White (Resident at Las Cruces Office)
Paula G. Maynes (Resident at Santa Fe Office)
Dean B. Cross (Resident at Las Cruces Office)
Michael C. Ross
Carla Prando (Resident at Santa Fe Office)
Katherine N. Blackett
Jennifer L. Stone
Andrew M. Sanchez
M. Dylan O'Reilly
Amina Quargnali-Linsley
Beate Boudro

COUNSEL

William K. Stratvert
Paul W. Robinson
Ralph Wm. Richards (Resident at Las Cruces Office)
Ross B. Perkal
James J. Widland
Bradley D. Tepper

Representative Clients: Bank 1st; BASF Corp.; BP Amoco Corp.; Massachusetts Mutual Life Insurance; Medical Protective Co.; Mutual Insurance Corp. of America; St. Paul Insurance Cos.; State Farm Mutual Automobile Insurance Co.; Texaco, Inc.; Ultramar Diamond Shamrock.

For full biographical listings, see the Martindale-Hubbell Law Directory

MODRALL, SPERLING, ROEHL, HARRIS & SISK, P.A. (AV)

500 Fourth Street, N.W., Bank of America Centre, Suite 1000, P.O. Box 2168, 87103-2168
Telephone: 505-848-1800
Fax: 505-848-1889
Email: modrall@swcp.com
Santa Fe, New Mexico Office: 123 East Marcy, Suite 201, P.O. Box 9318.
Telephone: 505-983-2020.
Fax: 505-988-8996.
Las Cruces, New Mexico Office: 277 East Amador Avenue, Suite 304 Matrix Capital Building, P.O. Box 578.
Telephone: 505-526-6655.
Fax: 505-526-6656.
Roswell, New Mexico Office: 400 Penn Plaza, Suite 900, P.O. Box 2564.
Telephone: 505-625-8868.
Fax: 505-625-9535.

Allen C. Dewey, Jr.
John R. Cooney
Kenneth L. Harrigan
James M. Parker
Dennis J. Falk
Arthur D. Melendres
James P. Houghton
Judy A. Fry
Paul M. Fish
R. E. Thompson
Curtis W. Schwartz (Resident, Santa Fe Office)
Ruth M. Schifani
Lynn H. Slade
Douglas A. Baker
Larry P. Ausherman
Douglas R. Vadnais
Walter E. Stern, III
Patrick J. Rogers
John A. Darden, III (Resident, Las Cruces Office)
Duane E. Brown
Martha G. Brown
Kevin T. Riedel (Resident, Las Cruces Office)
Eleanor Katherine Bratton
William C. Scott
Tim L. Fields
Douglas G. Schneebeck
Kyle H. Moberly (Resident, Las Cruces Office)
Charles A. Armgardt
Timothy R. Van Valen
Earl E. DeBrine, Jr.
Timothy C. Holm
George R. McFall
Bonnie J. Paisley
Roberta Cooper Ramo
Suzanne M. Barker
William R. Keleher
Lisa F. Mann
Russell D. Mann (Resident, Roswell Office)
Stuart R. Butzier
Donald A. DeCandia
R. Alfred Walker
Timothy J. De Young
Margaret L. Meister

Michael L. Carrico
Angelo J. Artuso
Daniel W. Long
Max J. Madrid
Jennifer A. Noya
Katherine M. Creagan
Christopher P. Muirhead
Mary T. Torres (Resident, Las Cruces Office)
Stan N. Harris
Wade L. Woodard
Diane Harrison Ogawa
Megan A. C. Tourek Muirhead
Maria O'Brien
Deena L. Beard
Elizabeth A. Garcia
Marco E. Gonzales
Patrick A. Hoffman
Matthew R. Hoyt
Kirtan K. Khalsa
Michelle A. Martinez
David Matthew Overstreet (Resident, Las Cruces Office)
Thomas Smidt, III
Valerie V. Vigil

OF COUNSEL

Daniel A. Sisk

COUNSEL

Joe C. Diaz

Representative Clients: Albuquerque Public Schools; The Atchison, Topeka & Santa Fe Railway Co,; Commercial Union Insurance Cos.; Meridian Oil Inc.; Mountain States Mutual Casualty Co.

For full biographical listings, see the Martindale-Hubbell Law Directory

RODEY, DICKASON, SLOAN, AKIN & ROBB, P.A. (AV)

Albuquerque Plaza, Suite 2200, 201 Third Street, N.W., P.O. Box 1888, 87103-1888
Telephone: 505-765-5900
Fax: 505-768-7395
Email: info@rodey.com *URL:* http://www.rodey.com
Santa Fe, New Mexico Office: Suite 101 Marcy Plaza, 123 East Marcy Street, P.O. Box 1357, 87504-1357.
Telephone: 505-984-0100.
Fax: 505-989-9542.

Pearce C. Rodey (1889-1958)
William A. Sloan (1910-1993)
James C. Ritchie
Robert M. St. John
Joseph J. Mullins
Mark K. Adams
Robert G. McCorkle
Bruce Hall
John P. Salazar
William S. Dixon
John P. Burton (Resident, Santa Fe Office)
Rex D. Throckmorton
Jonathan W. Hewes
W. Robert Lasater, Jr.
Mark C. Meiering
Catherine T. Goldberg
Travis R. Collier
Jo Saxton Brayer
Edward Ricco
W. Mark Mowery (Resident, Santa Fe Office)
Patrick M. Shay
Nancy J. Appleby
David C. Davenport, Jr. (Resident, Santa Fe Office)
Ellen T. Skrak
Tracy McGee Jenks

(See Next Column)

RODEY, DICKASON, SLOAN, AKIN & ROBB P.A., *Albuquerque—Continued*

Henry M. Bohnhoff
Charles K. Purcell
Andrew G. Schultz
John M. Brant
Joseph B. Rochelle
Scott D. Gordon
Susan S. Throckmorton
DeWitt Michael Morgan
Mark A. Smith
R. Nelson Franse
Theresa W. Parrish
Paul R. Koller
James P. Bieg (Resident, Santa Fe Office)
Jay D. Hill
Charles J. Vigil
Mary Keleher Castle
Thomas L. Stahl
David W. Bunting
Benjamin C. Roybal
Gary D. Eisenberg
Leslie McCarthy Apodaca
Susan K. Barger
MacDonnell Gordon (Resident, Santa Fe Office)

Paul C. Collins
Kevin Lynn Wildenstein
Jeffrey M. Croasdell
Jeffrey L. Lowry
Deborah E. Mann
Alice Nystel Page
Amy E. Badger
Thomas A. Outler
Glenn A. Beard
Lisa A. Chavez
Jocelyn C. Drennan

COUNSEL

Jeffrey W. Loubet
Richard C. Minzner
Thomas P. Gulley
S. I. Betzer, Jr.

OF COUNSEL

Jackson G. Akin
Ray H. Rodey
John D. Robb
Debra Romero Thal

Representative Clients: Albuquerque Publishing Co.; ASCAP; Associated Aviation Underwriters Co.; Automobile Club Insurance Co.; Avonite, Inc.; Canal Insurance Co.; KOAT-TV; Liberty Mutual Insurance Co.

For full biographical listings, see the Martindale-Hubbell Law Directory

THE ROWE LAW FIRM, P.C. (AV(T))

1200 Pennsylvania N.E., Suite 2B, 87110
Telephone: 505-232-2800
Fax: 505-266-1030
South Fork, Colorado Office: Gordon H. Rowe, Jr. and Charles C. Powers, 0020 West Lodge Drive, 81154. P.O. Box 1273.
Telephone: 719-873-1740.
Fax: 719-873-1742.

Gordon H. Rowe, III

OF COUNSEL

Gordon H. Rowe, Jr. (Not admitted in NM)
Charles C. Powers (Resident, South Fork, Colorado with firm of Gordon H. Rowe, Jr. and Charles C. Powers)

For full biographical listings, see the Martindale-Hubbell Law Directory

MARTIN E. THREET & ASSOCIATES (AV)

6400 Uptown Boulevard N.E. Suite 500 West Tower, 87110
Telephone: 505-881-5155
Fax: 505-881-5356
Email: threetlaw@aol.com

MEMBERS OF FIRM

Martin A. Threet (1892-1963)
Martin E. Threet

ASSOCIATES

Joseph L. Romero
Joey B. Wright

LEGAL SUPPORT STAFF

(Administrator) Laura E. Threet
Cheri F. Melkus (Paralegal)
Laura M. Threet (Technology and Commercial Collections)
Paula M. Beldon (Certified Legal Assistant)
Daniel R. Olsen (Law Clerk)

For full biographical listings, see the Martindale-Hubbell Law Directory

*CLOVIS,** Curry Co.

ROWLEY LAW FIRM, P.C. (AV)

305 Pile, P.O. Box 790, 88101
Telephone: 505-763-4457
Fax: 505-763-4450
Email: rowleylaw@3lefties.com

Richard F. Rowley (1908-1980)
Richard F. Rowley, II

Jill Henson

LEGAL SUPPORT PERSONNEL

Antoinette Linder

Representative Clients: Northwestern Mutual Life Insurance Co.; Prudential Insurance Company of America; Equitable Life Assurance Society; Farm Credit Services; Cigna Capitol Advisors, Inc.; New Mexico American Water Co.; Feed Bag, Inc.; Production Credit Association of Eastern New Mexico; Muleshoe State Bank.

(See Next Column)

For full biographical listings, see the Martindale-Hubbell Law Directory

TATUM & MCDOWELL (AV)

Suite E, Sagebrush Professional Office Complex, 921 East 21st Street, P.O. Drawer 1270, 88101
Telephone: 505-762-7756
Fax: 505-769-1606

MEMBERS OF FIRM

Edwin B. Tatum
James F. McDowell, III

Representative Clients: High Plains Federal Credit Union; Valley Rendering Co.; Citizens Bank of Clovis; Clovis Feedyard, Inc.; Mc Daniel's, Inc.; Clovis Feedyard, Inc.; Retirement Ranch, Inc.

For full biographical listings, see the Martindale-Hubbell Law Directory

*LAS CRUCES,** Dona Ana Co.

MODRALL, SPERLING, ROEHL, HARRIS & SISK, P.A. (AV)

277 East Amador Avenue, Suite 304 Matrix Capital Building, P.O. Box 578, 88004
Telephone: 505-526-6655
Fax: 505-526-6656
URL: http://www.HUNTEL.com/modrall
Albuquerque, New Mexico Office: 500 Fourth Street, N.W., Bank of America Centre, Suite 1000, P.O. Box 2168.
Telephone: 505-848-1800.
Fax: 505-848-1889.
Santa Fe, New Mexico Office: 123 East Marcy, Suite 201, P.O. Box 9318.
Telephone: 505-983-2020.
Fax: 505-988-8996.
Roswell, New Mexico Office: 400 Penn Plaza, Suite 900, P.O. Box 2564.
Telephone: 505-625-8868.
Fax: 505-625-9535.

John A. Darden, III
Kevin T. Riedel
Kyle H. Moberly

Mary T. Torres
David Matthew Overstreet

Representative Clients: El Paso Bell Federal Credit Union; L & P Building Supply, Inc.; L & P Building Supply of Las Cruces, Inc.; Las Cruces Abstract & Title Company; Las Cruces Builders Supply; Las Cruces Sun News; New Mexico Department of Agriculture; Sunwest Bank of Las Cruces, N.A.; Wallace Westwind Chevrolet-Oldsmobile-Cadillac-Geo.

For full biographical listings, see the Martindale-Hubbell Law Directory

*SANTA FE,** Santa Fe Co.

CATRON, CATRON & SAWTELL, A PROFESSIONAL ASSOCIATION (AV)

2006 Botulph Road, P.O. Box 788, 87504-0788
Telephone: 505-982-1947
Telecopier: 505-986-1013
Email: catronlaw@aol.com

Thomas B. Catron (1840-1921)
Charles C. Catron (1879-1951)
Fletcher A. Catron (1890-1964)
Thomas B. Catron III
John S. Catron
William A. Sawtell, Jr.
Fletcher R. Catron
W. Anthony Sawtell
Forrest S. Smith
Michael T. Pottow
Bryan P. Biedscheid

LEGAL SUPPORT PERSONNEL

Peggy L. Feldt (Certified Public Accountant)

For full biographical listings, see the Martindale-Hubbell Law Directory

COMEAU, MALDEGEN, TEMPLEMAN & INDALL, L.L.P. (AV)

Coronado Building, 141 East Palace Avenue, P.O. Box 669, 87504-0669
Telephone: 505-982-4611
Telecopier: 505-988-2987
Email: cmtilaw@earthlink.net

MEMBERS OF FIRM

Michael R. Comeau
Larry D. Maldegen
William P. Templeman
Jon J. Indall
Stephen J. Lauer
Paula Ann Cook
Grey Handy
Joseph E. Manges

Michael C. Smith
Christian A. Hatfield

OF COUNSEL

Jeffrey R. Brannen

Representative Clients: AirTouch Cellular; GTE; Homestake Mining Co.; N.M. Banquest Investors Corp.; United Nuclear Corp.; First National Bank of Santa Fe; Uranium Producers of America; United Van Lines; Mayflower Transit; State of New Mexico.

For full biographical listings, see the Martindale-Hubbell Law Directory

Santa Fe—Continued

MODRALL, SPERLING, ROEHL, HARRIS & SISK, P.A. (AV)

123 East Marcy, Suite 201, P.O. Box 9318, 87504-9318
Telephone: 505-983-2020
Fax: 505-988-8996
Email: cws@modrall.com
Albuquerque, New Mexico Office: 500 Fourth Street, N.W., Bank of America Centre, Suite 1000, P.O. Box 2168.
Telephone: 505-848-1800.
Fax: 505-848-1889.
Las Cruces, New Mexico Office: 277 East Amador Avenue, Suite 304 Matrix Capital Building, P.O. Box 578.
Telephone: 505-526-6655.
Fax: 505-526-6656.
Roswell, New Mexico Office: 400 Penn Plaza, Suite 900, P.O. Box 2564.
Telephone: 505-625-8868.
Fax: 505-625-9535.

Curtis W. Schwartz

Peter Franklin

Representative Clients: Jackalope, Inc,; Martin Marietta; NCR Corp.; Sierra Telcom Services, Inc; Thornburg Management Co., Inc.

For full biographical listings, see the Martindale-Hubbell Law Directory

MONTGOMERY & ANDREWS, PROFESSIONAL ASSOCIATION (AV)

325 Paseo de Peralta, P.O. Box 2307, 87504-2307
Telephone: 505-982-3873
Fax: 505-982-4289
Email: montand@montand.com

Victor R. Ortega
Gary Kilpatric
Thomas W. Olson
Walter J. Melendres
Bruce Herr
John B. Draper
Nancy M. Anderson King
Sarah Michael Singleton
Stephen S. Hamilton
Galen M. Buller
Edmund H. Kendrick
Louis W. Rose
Carolyn Wolf
Andrew S. Montgomery
Grace Philips
Jennifer Lynn Weed
Brett J. Olsen

OF COUNSEL
William R. Federici

Representative Clients: Community Bank of Santa Fe; El Paso Energy Corp.; Mobil Exploration and Producing, U.S. Inc.; New Mexico Utilities, Inc.; St. John's College; St. Vincent Hospital; Travelers Insurance Co.; U S West Communications, Inc.; United States Fidelity & Guaranty Co.; University of California/Los Alamos National Laboratory.

For full biographical listings, see the Martindale-Hubbell Law Directory

RODEY, DICKASON, SLOAN, AKIN & ROBB, P.A. (AV)

Suite 101 Marcy Plaza, 123 East Marcy Street, 87501
Telephone: 505-984-0100
Fax: 505-989-9542
Mailing Address: P.O. Box 1357, Santa Fe, New Mexico, 87504-1357
URL: http://www.rodey.com
Albuquerque, New Mexico Office: Albuquerque Plaza, Suite 2200, 201 Third Street, N.W.
Telephone: 505-765-5900.
Fax: 505-768-7395.

John P. Burton (Resident)
W. Mark Mowery (Resident)
David C. Davenport, Jr. (Resident)
James P. Bieg (Resident)
MacDonnell Gordon (Resident)

OF COUNSEL
Ray H. Rodey

For full biographical listings, see the Martindale-Hubbell Law Directory

SCHEUER, YOST & PATTERSON, A PROFESSIONAL CORPORATION (AV)

125 Lincoln Avenue, Suite 223, P.O. Drawer 9570, 87504
Telephone: 505-982-9911
505-989-7500
Fax: 505-982-1621
Email: firm@santafelawyers.com

Melvin T. Yost (Retired)
Ralph H. Scheuer
Mel E. Yost
John N. Patterson
Byron L. Treaster
Donald A. Walcott
Christopher M. Grimmer
Daniel J. Monte

OF COUNSEL
Reverdy Johnson

Representative Clients: Cyprus-AMAX, Inc.; Century Bank, FSB; Chicago Title Insurance Co.; County of Los Alamos; Davis Selected Venture Advisors; GEICO; St. John's College; Stewart Title Guaranty Co.; Sun Loan Companies; Territorial Abstract & Title Co.

(See Next Column)

For full biographical listings, see the Martindale-Hubbell Law Directory

VIRTUE NAJJAR BARTELL MATTHEWS & BROWN P.C. (AV)

300 Paseo de Peralta, Suite 200, P.O. Box 4265, 87502-4265
Telephone: 505-983-6101; 505-986-5850
Fax: 505-983-8304
Email: firm@virtuelaw.com
Albuquerque, New Mexico Office: 2929 Coors Boulevard Northwest, Suite 306, 87120.
Telephone: 505-352-1614.
Fax: 505-836-5656.

Richard L. C. Virtue
Daniel A. Najjar
Randy S. Bartell
Pamela Lord Matthews

ASSOCIATE
Laura A. Ward

OF COUNSEL
Bob D. Barberousse

For full biographical listings, see the Martindale-Hubbell Law Directory

WHITE, KOCH, KELLY & McCARTHY, A PROFESSIONAL ASSOCIATION (AV)

433 Paseo De Peralta, P.O. Box 787, 87504-0787
Telephone: 505-982-4374
ABA/NET: 1154
Fax: 505-982-0350; 984-8631
Email: WKKM@NM.NET

John F. McCarthy, Jr.
Benjamin J. Phillips
David F. Cunningham
Albert V. Gonzales
Janet Clow
Kevin V. Reilly
Charles W. N. Thompson, Jr.
M. Karen Kilgore
Sandra J. Brinck
Aaron J. Wolf
Mary E. Walta
Rebecca A. Dempsey

OF COUNSEL
John M. Hickey

SPECIAL COUNSEL
Paul L. Bloom

Julie A. Wittenberger
Suzanne C. Odom (Not admitted in NM)

Representative Clients: City of Albuquerque, New Mexico; City of Santa Fe, New Mexico; Pueblo of Zuni; El Paso Electric, Co.; Santa Fe Community College; Rio Grande School.

For full biographical listings, see the Martindale-Hubbell Law Directory

*SILVER CITY,** Grant Co.

J. WAYNE WOODBURY (AV)

214 North Bullard, P.O. Box 857, 88062
Telephone: 505-538-3729
Fax: 505-538-3956

Representative Clients: Pacific Western Land Co.; Phelps Dodge Corp.; Wells Fargo Bank, Silver City, New Mexico.
Reference: Wells Fargo Bank, Silver City, New Mexico.

NEW YORK

*ALBANY,** Albany Co.

AINSWORTH, SULLIVAN, TRACY, KNAUF, WARNER & RUSLANDER, P.C. (AV)

Brandon Place, 403 New Karner Road, P.O. Box 12849, 12212-2849
Telephone: 518-464-0600
Fax: 518-464-0679
Email: foc@brokerlaw.com *URL:* http://www.brokerlaw.com

Danforth E. Ainsworth (1908-1927)
Charles B. Sullivan (1881-1975)
Thomas F. Tracy (1914-1994)
John E. Knauf (1914-1996)
Frank J. Warner, Jr.
Robert K. Ruslander
James E. McHenry
John W. Bailey
Frank M. Pell
Elizabeth M. Dumas
Margaret Comard Lynch
Michael J. Murphy
Timothy J. O'Connor
Dennis W. Habel
Maria C. Tebano

Colleen M. O'Connell
Anthony V. Cardona, Jr.
Rebecca A. Slezak
Scott R. Almas

(See Next Column)

AINSWORTH, SULLIVAN, TRACY, KNAUF, WARNER & RUSLANDER P.C., *Albany—Continued*

OF COUNSEL

Bruce R. Sullivan

Local Counsel for: Liberty Insurance Co.; United Service Auto Assn.; Continental Insurance Cos.; American International Insurance Co.; Aetna Insurance Co.; Kemper Insurance Co.; Sears Roebuck & Co.; Yamaha Motor Corp.; Chubb & Sons, Inc.; Grand Union Co.

For full biographical listings, see the Martindale-Hubbell Law Directory

BRENNAN, REHFUSS AND LIGUORI, P.C. (AV)

50 Chapel Street, 12207
Telephone: 518-434-2690
Fax: 518-434-5671
URL: http://www.lawyers.com/brllaw

Joseph M. Brennan
Stephen J. Rehfuss
John W. Liguori

OF COUNSEL

John W. Rehfuss

Representative Clients: Interboro Mutual Indemnity Insurance Co.; Michigan Mutual Insurance Co.
Reference: Norstar Bank, Upstate N.Y.

For full biographical listings, see the Martindale-Hubbell Law Directory

COUCH WHITE, LLP (AV)

540 Broadway, P.O. Box 22222, 12201
Telephone: 518-426-4600
Telecopier: 518-426-0376
Email: CouchWhiteBrenn@Global2000.net *URL:* http://www.couchwhite.com
Washington, D.C. Office: 700 Thirteenth Street, N.W., Suite 950.
Telephone: 202-434-4503.
Fax: 202-434-4562.

MEMBERS OF FIRM

Leslie F. Couch
Algird F. White, Jr.
Barbara S. Brenner
Joel M. Howard, III
Paul A. Feigenbaum
Robert M. Loughney
Harold N. Iselin
Leonard H. Singer
Keith B. Rose
Christopher A. Cernik
Michael B. Mager
Mark F. Glaser
Pamela A. Madeiros
James J. Barriere
Doreen Unis Saia

SENIOR COUNSEL

Lawrence H. Cooke

ASSOCIATES

David G. Anderson
Tricia A. Asaro
James S. King
Marc A. Madia

For full biographical listings, see the Martindale-Hubbell Law Directory

D'AGOSTINO, KRACKELER, BAYNES & MAGUIRE, P.C. (AV)

The Sage Mansion, 16 Sage Estate, 12204
Telephone: 518-434-9807
Fax: 518-434-9826
Email: dkbm@albany.net

Mae A. D'Agostino
Christine Kirwin Krackeler
Brendan F. Baynes
Richard R. Maguire
Arete Sprio

Wendy Mia Pardew

For full biographical listings, see the Martindale-Hubbell Law Directory

HARVEY AND MUMFORD (AV)

20 Corporate Woods Boulevard, 12211-2396
Telephone: 518-463-4491
Telecopier: 518-463-5665
Email: thefirm@harveyandmumford.com

Arthur J. Harvey (1903-1986)

MEMBERS OF FIRM

Jonathan P. Harvey
Brian F. Mumford

ASSOCIATES

Eva Lynn M. Hayko
Karen Hendricks
Peter Baird Joslin, Jr.
Trudy L. Boulia
Keith J. Starlin

OF COUNSEL

Jack D. Harvey

For full biographical listings, see the Martindale-Hubbell Law Directory

HODGSON, RUSS, ANDREWS, WOODS & GOODYEAR, LLP (AV)

A Registered Limited Liability Partnership including Professional Associations
Three City Square, 12207
Telephone: 518-465-2333
Fax: 518-465-1567
Email: info@hodgsonruss.com *URL:* www.hodgsonruss.com
Buffalo, New York Office: One M & T Plaza, Suite 2000, 14203.
Telephone: 716-856-4000.
Fax: 716-849-0349.
Boca Raton, Florida Office: Suite 400, 2000 Glades Road, 33431.
Telephone: 561-394-0500.
Fax: 561-394-3862.
Toronto, Ontario, Canada Office: 150 King Street West, Suite 2309, P.O. Box 30, M5H 1J9.
Telephone: 416-595-5100.
Fax: 416-595-5021.
New York, New York Office: 65 East 55th Street, 10th Floor, 10022.
Telephone: 212-751-4300.
Fax: 212-751-0928.
Gloversville, New York Office: 6 Fremont Street, 12078.
Telephone: 518-725-6347.
Fax: 518-773-7350.
Newark, New Jersey Office: One Gateway Center, Suite 2600, 07102.
Telephone: 973-645-0577.
Fax: 973-645-0551.

MEMBERS OF FIRM

(ALPHABETICALLY BY YEAR OF ADMISSION TO BAR)

Richard L. Weisz
A. Joseph Scott, III
Deborah L. Kelly
George W. Cregg, Jr.
Paul Groenwegen

SPECIAL COUNSEL

David A. Pratt

Barbara Rusin Scheuermann
Annette M. Tambasco
Nadene E. Carbery
Michael J Kotin
Peter R. Keane

For full biographical listings, see the Martindale-Hubbell Law Directory

McCLUNG, PETERS AND SIMON (AV)

41 State Street, Suite 700, 12207
Telephone: 518-462-7481 Toll Free 1-800-777-7481
Telecopier: 518-462-0112
Email: McClunglaw@aol.com

MEMBERS OF FIRM

Benjamin McClung (1867-1940)
George M. Simon (1909-1981)
Homer E. Peters (1905-1992)
Joseph B. Carr
John W. Scott
Stephen M. Kerwin
Lynda S. Battiste

ASSOCIATES

Marshall A. Courtney
Patrick H. Cartwright

OF COUNSEL

Stephen J. Arlington
Lawrence E. Becker
David N. Goldin

Representative Clients: Aetna Casualty & Surety Co.; Chemical Bank; Continental Insurance Cos.; Firemen's Insurance Co.; Hartford Insurance Co.; Underwriter's Adjusting Co.

For full biographical listings, see the Martindale-Hubbell Law Directory

ROCHE CORRIGAN McCOY & BUSH (AV)

The Wilem Van Zandt Building, 36 South Pearl Street, 12207
Telephone: 518-436-9370
Fax: 518-436-8233

MEMBERS OF FIRM

Robert P. Roche
Peter J. Corrigan
Joseph M. McCoy
Scott W. Bush

For full biographical listings, see the Martindale-Hubbell Law Directory

RUBERTI, GIRVIN & FERLAZZO, P.C. (AV)

120 State Street, 2nd Floor, 12207-2829
Telephone: 518-462-0300
Fax: 518-462-5037
Email: attorneys@rgflaw.com

PARTNERS

E. Michael Ruberti
James E. Girvin
Salvatore D. Ferlazzo
Kristine Amodeo Lanchantin
Jeffrey D. Honeywell
M. Cornelia Cahill
Gregg Tyler Johnson

ASSOCIATES

Patrick J. McKenna
Kathy Ann Wolverton
Christopher P. Langlois
Bruce I. Kopf
Maureen Finnegan Harris

(See Next Column)

RUBERTI, GIRVIN & FERLAZZO P.C.—*Continued*

SPECIAL COUNSEL

Mary Helen Moses — Elaine M. Pers
James A. P. McCarthy — Karen S. Norlander

For full biographical listings, see the Martindale-Hubbell Law Directory

SHANLEY, SWEENEY, REILLY & ALLEN, P.C. (AV)

The Castle at Ten Thurlow Terrace, 12203
Telephone: 518-463-1415
Fax: 518-463-3210
Email: lawyers@shanleysweeney.com *URL:* http://www.shanleysweeney.com

Michael P. Shanley, Jr. — Steven S. Heyman
Robert L. Sweeney — Scott P. Olson
J. Stephen Reilly — David C. Kuracina
John L. Allen — Thomas A. Shepardson
Gregory D. Faucher — Melissa M. Beskid
J. Michael Naughton — Mark T. Sweeney

Christopher E. Buckey — Stacey Weisenfeld

For full biographical listings, see the Martindale-Hubbell Law Directory

TABNER, RYAN AND KENIRY (AV)

26 Computer Drive West, P.O. Box 12605, 12212-2605
Telephone: 518-459-9000
Telecopier: 518-459-9165
Email: trk@tabnerryanandkeniry.com

MEMBERS OF FIRM

John W. Tabner — William F. Ryan, Jr.
William J. Keniry

OF COUNSEL

C. Theodore Carlson

ASSOCIATES

Eric N. Dratler — Jennifer K. Corona
Donald W. Biggs

Special Counsel for: Water and Sewer District for Towns of Colonie, Coxsackie, Guilderland, Johnstown, Queensbury, Rotterdam and Village Castleton.
References: FleetBank; Trustco Bank.

For full biographical listings, see the Martindale-Hubbell Law Directory

*AUBURN,** Cayuga Co.

CONTIGUGLIA & GIACONA (AV)

The Federal House, 7 William Street, 13021
Telephone: 315-253-9746
Fax: 315-253-0880

MEMBERS OF FIRM

Anthony J. Contiguglia (1897-1986) — Louis P. Contiguglia
Samuel P. Giacona

David A. Contiguglia

Representative Clients: Cayuga Bank; Cayuga Homesite Development Corp.; Homested Funding Corp.; Statewide Funding Corp.; American Residential Mortgage Corp.; GE Capital Home Equity Services; Commonwealth Mortgage Co., Inc.
References: Marine Midland Bank (Auburn Office); Cayuga Savings Bank; The Key Bank of Central New York.

For full biographical listings, see the Martindale-Hubbell Law Directory

*BATH,** Steuben Co.

COLE LAW OFFICES, P.C. (AV)

7 East Steuben Street, P.O. Box 232, 14810
Telephone: 607-776-3306
Fax: 607-776-4189
Email: RCole@LinkNY.Com
Hammondsport, New York Office: Railroad Station Depot, Water Street, P.O. Box 396, 14840.
Telephone: 607-569-2213.
Fax: 607-569-2214,

Robert H. Cole

Christine Valkenburgh — James H. Burns
William H. Reed

General Counsel for: Bath National Bank; Mercury Aircraft, Inc.
Local Counsel for: Equitable Life Assurance Society of the United States.
Reference: Bath National Bank.

For full biographical listings, see the Martindale-Hubbell Law Directory

*BINGHAMTON,** Broome Co.

CHERNIN & GOLD, LLP (AV)

Bache Building, 71 State Street, P.O. Box 1563, 13902
Telephone: 607-723-9581
Fax: 607-723-0634
URL: http://www.binghamtonlaw.com
Hallstead, Pennsylvania Office: P.O. Box 885, 18822.
Telephone: 717-879-4824.

MEMBERS OF FIRM

Sanford P. Tanenhaus — John F. Artman
Donald M. Flanagan — Robert G. Bullis
Bruno Colapietro — Dorian D. Ames
Richard N. Matties — Sam P. Monachino
John P. Rittinger — Margaret J. Fowler

ASSOCIATES

Christopher A. Pogson — Michael T. Baker

SPECIAL COUNSEL

Jon S. Blechman — Daniel L. Gorman

OF COUNSEL

Herbert M. Matties — James B. Gitlitz

Representative Clients: Continental National-American Group; Atlantic Mutual Insurance Co.; Triple Cities Construction Co.; Travelers Insurance Co.
Approved Attorneys for: Lawyers Title Insurance Corp., New York; Monroe title Insurance Corp., New York.

For full biographical listings, see the Martindale-Hubbell Law Directory

COUGHLIN & GERHART, L.L.P. (AV)

20 Hawley Street, P.O. Box 2039, 13902-2039
Telephone: 607-723-9511
Fax: 607-723-1530; 722-6073
Email: info@cglawllp.com
Afton, New York Office: 190 Main Street, 13730.
Telephone: 607-639-2222.
Unadilla, New York Office: 71-73 Main Street, 13849.
Telephone: 607-369-3811.
Owego, New York Office: 32-34 Lake Street, 13827.
Telephone: 607-687-1831.
Deposit, New York Office: 105 Front Street, 13754.
Telephone: 607-467-4010.

MEMBERS OF FIRM

Richard B. Long — Carl A. Kieper
Robert J. Smith — Joseph J. Steflik, Jr.
Henry J. Rode, II — Jeffrey A. Brown
Peter H. Bouman — David H. Guy
Gordon E. Thompson — Beth E. Westfall
Mark S. Gorgos — Gary B. Kline
James P. O'Brien (Coughlin & Gerhart, L.L.P., Group Manager, Litigation Group) — Susan L. English
Todd D. Kilpatrick
Robert R. Jones
Richard W. Mertens — Paul J. Sweeney
Susan A. Inneo

SPECIAL COUNSEL

Brian C. Madigan — Scott B. Anglehart

ASSOCIATES

Keith A. O'Hara — Oliver N. Blaise, III
Ann M. Sharpe — Jennifer C. Ruppel
Noelle M. Long

OF COUNSEL

Eugene C. Gerhart — Loren W. Guy
Edward S. Dermody — Carl R. Gitlitz
George L. Ingalls — Rollin L. Twining
Frank A. Nemia

General Counsel for: Crowley Foods, Inc.; McIntosh Laboratory, Inc.; Azon Corp.; Binghamton City School District; Dover Technologies International, Inc.; Universal Instruments Corp.
Representative Clients: HSBC Bank; NBT Bank, NA; Time Warner Cable; M & T Bank.

For full biographical listings, see the Martindale-Hubbell Law Directory

HINMAN, HOWARD & KATTELL, LLP (AV)

700 Security Mutual Building, 80 Exchange Street, P.O. Box 5250, 13902-5250
Telephone: 607-723-5341
Fax: 607-723-6605
Email: jworband@hhk.com *URL:* http://www.hhk.com
Norwich, New York Office: 48 Hale Street, 13815-2039.
Telephone: 607-334-5896.
Fax: 607-336-1628.
Oneonta, New York Office: 12 South Main Street, 13820-2542.
Telephone: 607-432-5331.
Fax: 607-432-2683.
New York, N.Y. Office: 500 5th Avenue, Suite 1725, 10110.
Telephone: 212-840-3017.
Fax: 212-840-2345.

(See Next Column)

HINMAN, HOWARD & KATTELL LLP, *Binghamton—Continued*

MEMBERS OF FIRM

Harvey D. Hinman (1864-1954)
Archibald Howard (1872-1962)
Thomas B. Kattell (1875-1947)
Dana B. Hinman (1874-1970)
Roger P. Clark (1869-1934)
C. Addison Keeler (1897-1979)
Thomas H. Fogarty (1902-1966)
Prescott D. Perkins (1902-1969)
Morris Gitlitz (1902-1984)
Charles F. Fish (1910-1987)
William L. Ransom, Jr. (1918-1967)
Edward L. Tirrell, Jr. (1917-1993)
John M. Keane (1914-1994)
A. Lawrence Abrams (1906-1996)
George Lyon Hinman (1905-1997)
Lee R. Cirba (1954-1999)
James W. Orband
Lawrence C. Anderson
James S. Gleason
Clayton M. Axtell, Jr.
Warren M. Anderson
Keith E. Osber
Colin T. Naylor, III
Richard H. Pille
N. Theodore Sommer
Eugene E. Peckham
John C. Fish
James L. Chivers
James M. Hayes
Peter J. Vivona
Clayton M. Axtell, III
James F. Lee
John G. Dowd
Katherine A. Fitzgerald
James R. Franz
Albert J. Millus, Jr.
Lillian L. Levy
Wilbur D. Dahlgren
Kenneth F. Tomko
Paul T. Sheppard
Harvey D. Mervis
Leslie Prechtl Guy
Thomas W. Cusimano, Jr.
John E. Jones
Eugene D. Faughnan
Allen J. Hall
Thomas A. Conlon, Jr.
John M. Keeler
C. Addison Keeler, Jr.

COUNSEL

A. Edward Hill
Joseph P. Minnich, Jr.
Darwin R. Wales
Erik Edward Joh
Paul J. Sternberg

RESIDENT COUNSEL

Bernard I. Flateman (Resident, New York Office)

SPECIAL COUNSEL

Donald R. Campbell
Richard S. Ringwood
Brian R. Wright
Robert H. Wedlake
Catherine M. Berthel (Resident, Oneonta Office)
Kurt D. Schulte (Resident, Oneonta Office)
Amy Shapiro
Frederick A. Griffen
Scott J. Clippinger (Resident, Norwich Office)
Lori Grumet Schapiro
Martin J. Kane
Richard C. Lewis
William C. Burtis, Jr.

ASSOCIATES

Michael S. Sinicki
John D. Denmon
Alyssa M. Barreiro
Alex C. Dell
Eric D. Farrell
Dianne Oakes
Ronald Louis Greene
Anne Hillis
Kathleen S. Campbell
Laurie M. Ceparano
Dominic S. DePersis
Erik T. Koons
Jeffrey LaBarge
Anthony J. D'Elia
Stacey M. Gates

Representative Clients: The Chase Manhattan Bank; BSB Bank & Trust Co.; International Business Machines Corp.; Universal Instruments Corp.; Security Mutual Life Insurance Company of New York; Bell Atlantic; Preferred Mutual Insurance Company; New York State Electric & Gas Corp.; Exxon Corp.

For full biographical listings, see the Martindale-Hubbell Law Directory

BRIDGEHAMPTON, Suffolk Co.

PAYNE, WOOD & LITTLEJOHN (AV)

1936 Montauk Highway, P.O. Box 1980, 11932-1980
Telephone: 516-537-3100
Telefax: 516-537-0560
Email: mail@paynewood.com
Melville, New York Office: 290 Broad Hollow Road.
Telephone: 516-547-8400.
Telefax: 516-547-0501.
Locust Valley, New York Office: 83 Birch Hill Road.
Telephone: 516-676-0700.
Telefax: 516-676-0703.

MEMBER OF FIRM

Alan C. Polacek (Managing Partner)

For full biographical listings, see the Martindale-Hubbell Law Directory

*BRONX,** Bronx Co.

MAXWELL S. PFEIFER (AV)

714 East 241st Street, 10470
Telephone: 718-325-5000
Fax: 718-324-0333
Email: mspfeifer@aol.com
New York, New York Office: 18 East 50th Street, 7th Floor, 10022.
Telephone: 212-980-0777.
Fax: 718-324-0333.

(See Next Column)

Hallandale, Florida Office: 1920 East Hallandale Beach Boulevard, Suite 606.
Telephone: 954-454-1550.

ASSOCIATES

Steven E. Millon
Robert S. Summer

OF COUNSEL

Sandra Krevitsky Janin
Anthony J. Hatab
Hon. Alexander A. Delle Cese (1919-1997)

For full biographical listings, see the Martindale-Hubbell Law Directory

*BUFFALO,** Erie Co.

BORINS, SETEL, SNITZER & BROWNSTEIN (AV)

710 Statler Towers, 14202-2907
Telephone: 716-854-5200
Fax: 716-854-5204

MEMBERS OF FIRM

Louis Borins (1908-1979)
Isadore Snitzer
Eugene M. Setel
Joel Brownstein

Reference: HSBC.

For full biographical listings, see the Martindale-Hubbell Law Directory

COHEN & LOMBARDO, P.C. (AV)

343 Elmwood Avenue, P.O. Box 5204, 14213-5204
Telephone: 716-881-3010
Fax: 716-881-2755
Email: law@cohenlombardo.com *URL:* http://www.cohenlombardo.com

Joseph Cohen (1909-1966)
Ernest Lombardo (1913-1993)
Richard N. Blewett
Donald A. Fisher
Robert N. Convissar
Rocco Lucente, II
Stuart Brian Shapiro
Neil R. Sherwood
Douglas S. Cream

Robert R. Goods
Katherine J. Bestine
Mark S. Nemeth
Daniel M. Caro
Maria T. Buchanan-Sidorski
Thomas J. Navarro, Jr.
Jennifer D. Bowen
Christopher A. Zampogna

OF COUNSEL

Maryann Saccomando Freedman
Anthony M. Nosek
Dean C. Stathacos
Norman J. Pecora
David R. Koepsell

For full biographical listings, see the Martindale-Hubbell Law Directory

FALK & SIEMER, LLP (AV)

Suite 2600 Main Place Tower, 14202-3785
Telephone: 716-852-6670
Fax: 716-852-6881
Email: falksiemer@aol.com
Amherst, New York Office: 3980 Sheridan Drive, Suite 310, 14226.
Telephone: 716-929-2000.
Fax: 716-929-2005.

MEMBERS OF FIRM

Donald G. McGrath
Kevin P. Maloney
Edward J. Carland (Resident, Amherst Office)
Robert E. Lipp (Resident, Amherst Office)
Carol D. Collard
J. Joseph Wilder (Managing Partner, 1995-1998)
Dennis P. Cleary
Gary M. Kanaley
Stephen F. Szymoniak
Robert L. Bencini

OF COUNSEL

Alvin M. Glick

ASSOCIATES

Christopher A. Cardillo
Laura Ann Linneball
Andrea R. Polvino
Theresa A. Smyth
David J. Luzon

Representative Clients: Blue Cross and Blue Shield of Western New York; Millard Fillmore Hospital; New York State Electric & Gas Corp.

For full biographical listings, see the Martindale-Hubbell Law Directory

GROSS SHUMAN BRIZDLE & GILFILLAN, P.C. (AV)

600 Lafayette Court, 465 Main Street, 14203
Telephone: 716-854-4300
Telecopier: 716-854-2787
Email: office@gross-shuman.com

Gordon R. Gross
Irving M. Shuman
Leonard J. Brizdle (1905-1987)
Peter S. Gilfillan
David H. Alexander
Robert J. Feldman
Leslie M. Greenbaum
Jeffrey A. Human
Hugh C. Carlin
Howard B. Cohen
Cindy Algase Gradl

(See Next Column)

GROSS SHUMAN BRIZDLE & GILFILLAN P.C.—*Continued*

John K. Rottaris
John F. Leone
Jonathan D. Schechter
Christine Ghislaine LaBarre
John C. Jacobs
David H. Elibol
Marjorie A. Bialy

SPECIAL COUNSEL

George A. Rusk

Representative Clients: American Penn Energy, Inc.; American Bureal of Collections, Inc.; Burgess-Manning, Inc.; Ecology and Environment, Inc.; Midland Asphalt Corp.; Nitram Energy, Inc.; Nova Casualty Company; Stetron International, Inc.; Anchor Savings Bank; FSB.
Reference: Key Bank of Western New York, N.A.

For full biographical listings, see the Martindale-Hubbell Law Directory

HODGSON, RUSS, ANDREWS, WOODS & GOODYEAR, LLP (AV)

A Registered Limited Liability Partnership including Professional Associations
One M & T Plaza, Suite 2000, 14203
Telephone: 716-856-4000
Fax: 716-849-0349
Email: info@hodgsonruss.com *URL:* www.hodgsonruss.com
Albany, New York Office: Three City Square, 12207.
Telephone: 518-465-2333.
Fax: 518-465-1567.
Boca Raton, Florida Office: Suite 400, 2000 Glades Road, 33431.
Telephone: 561-394-0500.
Fax: 561-394-3862.
Toronto, Ontario, Canada Office: 150 King Street West, Suite 2309, M5H 1J9, P.O. Box 30.
Telephone: 416-595-5100.
Fax: 416-595-5021.
New York, New York Office: 65 East 55th Street, 10th Floor, 10022.
Telephone: 212-751-4300.
Fax: 212-751-0928.
Gloversville, New York Office: 6 Fremont Street, 12078.
Telephone: 518-725-6347.
Fax: 518-773-7350.
Newark, New Jersey Office: One Gateway Center, Suite 2600, 07102.
Telephone: 973-645-0577.
Fax: 973-645-0551.

MEMBERS OF FIRM

(ALPHABETICALLY BY YEAR OF ADMISSION TO BAR)

Richard E. Heath (Boca Raton, Florida Office)
Edwin T. Bean, Jr.
Richard B. Dopkins
William H. Gardner
Charles J. Hahn
H. Kenneth Schroeder, Jr.
Anthony L. Dutton (P.A.) (Boca Raton, Florida Office)
Michael H. Gora (P.A.)
David E. Hall
James M. Wadsworth (Chairman)
Robert W. Keller
Robert B. Conklin
Richard A. Goetz (P.A.) (Boca Raton, Florida Office)
Karl W. Kristoff
Thomas E. Sliney (P.A.) (Boca Raton, Florida Office)
Martin G. Linihan
Stephen M. Newman
F. William Gray, III
Joseph V. Sedita
Harry G. Meyer
Mario J. Papa (Gloversville Office)
James M. Hankins (Boca Raton, Florida Office)
Christian G. Koelbl, III
Jerome D. Schad
Lance J. Madden
Paul R. Comeau
Lawrence R. Bailey, Jr. (New York, N.Y. Office)
Todd M. Joseph
Tricia Thomas Semmelhack
Dianne Bennett (President)
Richard F. Campbell
Pamela Davis Heilman
Ward B. Hinkle
Daniel R. Sharpe
John P. Amershadian
Ellen V. Weissman
Anne Smith Simet
Kenneth F. Barone
David A. Farmelo
Robert B. Fleming, Jr.
Garry M. Graber
Richard L. Weisz (Albany Office)
Jerrold S. Brown
Kenneth P. Friedman
Paul I. Perlman
Gary M. Schober
Richard W. Kaiser
Edward C. Northwood
Larry Corman (P.A.) (Boca Raton, Florida Office)
Rick W. Kennedy
Mark S. Klein
Daniel C. Oliverio
Lawrence F. Beyer (Boca Raton, Florida Office)
Alice Accola Joseffer
Robert J. Lane, Jr.
A. Joseph Scott, III
David M. Stark
Jeffrey W. Stone
Kathleen A. Wall
Benjamin M. Zuffranieri, Jr.
Joseph L. Braccio
Elizabeth G. Clark
Thomas W. Nelson
Bonnie A. Redder
John J. Zak
Carol Anne Fitzsimmons (Newark, New Jersey & New York, N.Y. Offices)
Kevin M. Kearney (Newark, New Jersey and New York, N.Y. Offices)
Michael P. Murphy
Cheryl R. Storie
John J. Christopher
Christopher L. Doyle
Deborah L. Kelly (Albany Office)
Hugh M. Russ, III
Terrence M. Gilbride
Michael E. Maxwell
Paul D. Meosky

(See Next Column)

MEMBERS OF FIRM
(ALPHABETICALLY BY YEAR OF ADMISSION TO BAR) (Continued)

Michel Pierre Cassier
Lisa A. Coppola
Patrick M. Tomovic
Leecia Roberta Eve
George F. deClaire (Boca Raton, Florida Office)
Dudley M. Ferguson (Gloversville Office)
George W. Cregg, Jr. (Albany Office)
Alvan L. Bobrow (New York, N.Y. Office)
Susan K. Baumel (Boca Raton, Florida Office)
Paul E. Roman (Boca Raton, Florida Office)
Peter A. Muth
Paul Groenwegen (Albany Office)
Peter K. Bradley
Deborah A. Waldbillig (Boca Raton, Florida Office)

SENIOR COUNSEL

James G. Meagley
Anna L. Case
Sharon M. Kelly

COUNSEL

John E. Dickinson
Edwin O. Tilton
Arnold T. Olena
James A. Porter (P.A.) (Boca Raton, Florida Office)

ASSOCIATES

(ALPHABETICALLY BY YEAR OF ADMISSION TO BAR)

Gerard M. Meehan
Barbara Rusin Scheuermann (Albany Office)
Alice F. Jacobs
Michael F. Scalise
Mary Catherine Malley
Tim Sawers
Annette M. Tambasco (Albany Office)
Amy J. Vigneron
Stephen A. Aschettino (New York, N.Y. Office)
Nadene E. Carbery (Albany Office)
Edward Cooper
John M. Flannery
Diane Nowak Kent (Boca Raton, Florida Office)
Sally B. Logan
James R. Maloney
Aidan M. McCormack (New York, N.Y. Office)
Margot L. Watt
Thomas R. Hyde
R. Anthony Rupp III
Sujata Yalamanchili (Not admitted in NY)
Samantha A. Fong (New York, N.Y. Office)
Elizabeth Q. Boehmcke
David L. Principe
R. Kent Roberts (Not admitted in NY)
Daniel A. Spitzer
Jeffrey F. Swiatek
Stephen L. Yonaty
Jeffrey F. Baase
Julia S. Kreher
Michael V. McLaughlin
Kevin D. McCarthy
James P. Milbrand
Adam W. Perry
Andrew B. Sabol
Elana K. Scoler (Boca Raton, Florida Office)
Lynda M. Tarantino
Paul J. Vallone
Christine A. Bonaguide
Jeffrey S. Geller (Boca Raton, Florida Office)
Leslie R. Kellogg
Mirna E. Martinez (New York, N.Y. Office)
Kevin D. Szczepanski
John W. Crowe, Jr.
George J. Eydt
Peter C. Godfrey
Dartaganan L. Jackson
Ranjana Kadle
Jason E. Markel
Melissa O. Heimerl
Scott K. Rohring
Lorrie Turner-Proulx
Amy J. Fitch
Brad A. Birmingham
Jason A. Yots
Arthur K. Bartlett
Anita Coles Costello
Peter R. Keane (Albany Office)
Michael J. Kotin (Albany Office)
David R. Pfalzgraf, Jr.
James T. Ritzel
Kimberly M. Sebastian
Kathleen M. Sellers
Jonathan P. Taber (Not admitted in NY)
Rosanna Berardi (Not admitted in NY)
Jodyann Galvin
Tracie L. Lopardi

For full biographical listings, see the Martindale-Hubbell Law Directory

JAECKLE FLEISCHMANN & MUGEL, LLP (AV)

Fleet Bank Building, Twelve Fountain Plaza, 14202-2292
Telephone: 716-856-0600
Telecopier: 716-856-0432
Email: office@jaeckle.com *URL:* http://www.jaeckle.com
Rochester, New York Office: Ellwanger and Barry Building, 39 State Street.
Telephone: 716-262-3640.
Fax: 716-262-4133.

Joseph W. Allen
Mitchell J. Banas, Jr.
Paul A. Battaglia
George F. Bellows
David G. Brock
Thomas E. Brydges
Anne Fox Downey
Gayle L. Vaillancourt Eagan
Mary C. Fitzgerald
Manly Fleischmann (1908-1987)
William L. Giroux
Robert D. Gunderman
Ralph L. Halpern
Vincent O. Hanley
Dennis P. Harkawik
Michele O. Heffernan
Thomas J. Hurley
Edwin F. Jaeckle (1894-1992)
Brenda J. Joyce
Peter G. Klein
John T. Kolaga
Joseph P. Kubarek
Anthony J. Latona
Tim C. Loftis
Philip H. McIntyre
John M. Montfort (1929-1990)
Albert R. Mugel
Randall M. Odza
Samuel J. Palisano
Thomas A. Palmer

(See Next Column)

JAECKLE FLEISCHMANN & MUGEL LLP, *Buffalo—Continued*

Michael A. Piette
Edward G. Piwowarczyk
Jean C. Powers
John G. Putnam, Jr.
Raymond P. Reichert
Steven J. Ricca
Howard S. Rosenhoch
William I. Schapiro
Charles C. Swanekamp
James J. Tanous
Lawrence H. Wagner
Paul C. Weaver

Sean P. Beiter
Bridget Cawley Bidonde
Janet G. Burhyte
Min Chan
Jennifer M. Demert
Lawrence C. DiGiulio
Elizabeth J. Dobosiewicz
Christopher J. Dow
A. Nicholas Falkides
Daniel W. Gerber
Charles D. Grieco
Kayla E. (Sandway) Klos
Robert A. Klump
Anne K. Kyzmir
Richard L. Mugel
Heidi K. Brauer Ruchala
Randy C. Rucinski
Mary C. Tanner
Robert C. Weissflach
Kelly V. Zarcone

OF COUNSEL

Thomas F. Disare
Adelbert Fleischmann
Brian J. Troy

For full biographical listings, see the Martindale-Hubbell Law Directory

MCGEE & GELMAN (AV)

200 Summer Street, 14222-2271
Telephone: 716-883-7272
Fax: 716-883-7084
Email: counsel@mcgee-gelman.com

MEMBERS OF FIRM

Michael R. McGee
Warren B. Gelman
F. Brendan Burke, Jr.
Laura A. Colca
Jennifer L. Friedman

David S. Widenor

For full biographical listings, see the Martindale-Hubbell Law Directory

PHILLIPS, LYTLE, HITCHCOCK, BLAINE & HUBER LLP (AV)

(Formerly Kenefick, Letchworth, Baldy, Phillips & Emblidge)
3400 HSBC Center, 14203
Telephone: 716-847-8400
Telecopier: 716-852-6100
Email: info@phillipslytle.com *URL:* http://www.phillipslytle.com
Jamestown, New York Office: 307 Chase Bank Building, 8 E. Third Street.
Telephone: 716-664-3906.
Telecopier: 716-664-4230.
Rochester, New York Office: 1400 First Federal Plaza.
Telephone: 716-238-2000.
Telecopier: 716-232-3141.
New York, New York Office: 437 Madison Avenue.
Telephone: 212-759-4888.
Telecopier: 212-308-9079.
Fredonia, New York Office: 11 East Main Street.
Telephone: 716-672-2164.
FAX: 716-672-7979.

John F. Huber, Jr. (1906-1969)
George F. Phillips (1892-1971)
Robert M. Hitchcock (1904-1981)
William E. Lytle (1905-1989)

OF COUNSEL

William A. Bain, Jr.
Thomas M. Barney
Richard G. Birmingham
Charles G. Blaine
Irving D. Brott, Jr.
Alexander C. Cordes
John F. Donovan
David K. Floyd
Gerard R. Haas
John K. McCormick
William L. Rieth
Edward L. Robinson
Arthur M. Sherwood
Robert M. Spaulding

PARTNERS

Frederick G. Attea
Cindy Kaplan Bennes
Allen R. Bivens
Edward S. Bloomberg
Mark E. Brand
Peter D. Braun
William J. Brennan
William J. Brown
Caroline Hassett Buerk
William D. Christ
David A. Clemens
James J. Contino
Douglas W. Dimitroff
James D. Donathen
Deborah A. Doxey
John B. Drenning
Kevin J. English
David P. Flynn
Robert E. Glanville
Morgan G. Graham
George R. Grasser
James R. Grasso
Robert M. Greene
Richard F. Griffin
Edward M. Griffith, Jr.
Tamar P. Halpern
Waldron S. Hayes, Jr.
Kevin M. Hogan
Annabelle V. Irey
Paul F. Jones
David H. Kernan
Gary F. Kotaska
James A. Locke
Kenneth A. Manning
Jeremiah J. McCarthy
Lisa McDougall
David J. McNamara
Michael R. Moravec
Paul Morrison-Taylor
David J. Murray
John A. Pappano
Michael B. Powers

(See Next Column)

PARTNERS (Continued)

Joseph Ritzert
Martha L. Salzman
Victoria J. Saxon
Raymond H. Seitz
Ronald S. Shubert
Lisa L. Smith
James W. Smyton
Peter K. Sommer
John C. Spitzmiller
Paul K. Stecker
James H. Watz
James W. Whitcomb
Sharon L. Wick
Alan M. Wishnoff
Thomas S. Wiswall
Paul B. Zuydhoek

SPECIAL COUNSEL

Mary B. Ferguson
Donna M. Lanham
Paul K. Wustrack, Jr.

ASSOCIATES

Gretchen P. Aylward
Michael J. Berchou
Alafair S. Burke
(Not admitted in NY)
Joseph P. DiVincenzo
Alan Donatelli
Victoria Lyn Grady
Maria K. Hadley
(Not admitted in NY)
Donald J. Held
P. Stephen Kim
Giovanna Macri
Ellen J. Malone
Amy Church Marinovic
M. Rogan Morton
Christopher S. Nickson
Rowland Richards
Karen E. Richardson
Joseph R. Saab
John G. Schmidt, Jr.
Tracy M. Sendor
Kedra L. Small
Scott L. Sroka
Michelle L. Struble
Sharon A. Swift
W. Clark Trow
Jennifer A. Tumminelli
(Not admitted in NY)
Roberta A. Vallone
Adam S. Walters
Brian Richard Yoshida
Preston L. Zarlock
Daniel E. Zea
Angela M. Zwirecki

General Counsel for: Astronics Corp.; Bryant & Stratton Business Institute; Canisius College; Chase Manhattan Bank, N.A.; Columbus McKinnon Corp.
Local Counsel for: A.O. Smith Corp.; Allied Signal; Bethlehem Steel Corp.; Chrysler Motor Corp.; E.I. DuPont deNemours Co., Inc.

For full biographical listings, see the Martindale-Hubbell Law Directory

RAICHLE, BANNING, WEISS & STEPHENS (AV)

410 Main Street, 14202
Telephone: 716-852-7587
Telecopier: 716-852-7599
Email: RBWS@MSN.COM

MEMBERS OF FIRM

Frank G. Raichle (1898-1986)
Derrick C. Banning (1916-1995)
Arnold Weiss
R. William Stephens

ASSOCIATES

Lisa Parlato Neff
R. Hugh Stephens

Representative Clients: General Motors Corp.; Cliffstar Corp.; Blue Cross & Blue Shield of Michigan; Sony Picture Releasing Inc.; Superior Jamestown Corp., Adanlock Office Environments Division; Permclip Products Corp.; Living Monuments Inc.

For full biographical listings, see the Martindale-Hubbell Law Directory

ROACH, BROWN, MCCARTHY & GRUBER, P.C. (AV)

1620 Liberty Building, 420 Main Street, 14202-3511
Telephone: 716-852-0400
Fax: 716-852-2535
Email: roachbrown@roachbrown.com

Daniel T. Roach
Edmund S. Brown, Jr.
T. Alan Brown
Joseph V. McCarthy
J. Mark Gruber
Mary J. Murray
John P. Danieu
Elizabeth G. Redmond
Gregory T. Miller
Teresa C. Brophy Bair
Jason A. Botticelli
Jennifer L. Noah
Joel J. Java, Jr.

OF COUNSEL

Arthur J. Maloney
John Y. Gallup

Local Attorneys for: American International Group; Chubb Group of Insurance Co.; Healthcare Underwriters Mutual Insurance Co.; Peter J. McBreen and Associates; Frontier Insurance Co.; Medical Liability Mutual Insurance Co.; Medical Malpractice Insurance Assn.; Merrill Dow; Reliance Insurance Group; Travelers Group.

For full biographical listings, see the Martindale-Hubbell Law Directory

ROLLS KOHN & ASSOCIATES, LLP (AV)

Twenty Court Street, 14202-3201
Telephone: 716-856-2700
Fax: 716-856-2777

MEMBERS OF FIRM

James E. Rolls
Gerald L. Kohn

Robert M. Goldstein

For full biographical listings, see the Martindale-Hubbell Law Directory

Buffalo—Continued

SULLIVAN & OLIVERIO (AV)

600 Main Place Tower, 14202-3706
Telephone: 716-854-5300
Telecopier: 716-854-5299
Email: sulliolaw@aol.com

MEMBERS OF FIRM

Richard T. Sullivan
B. P. Oliverio
Bruce W. Hoover

Thomas M. Moll
Michael E. Appelbaum
Kevin M. Carter

OF COUNSEL

Paul D. Pearson

For full biographical listings, see the Martindale-Hubbell Law Directory

CARLE PLACE, Nassau Co.

DOLLINGER, GONSKI & GROSSMAN (AV)

One Old Country Road, 11514
Telephone: 516-747-1010
Telecopier: 516-747-2494
Fairfield, New Jersey Office: 710 Route 46 East, Suite 212, 07004.
Telephone: 973-276-0530.
Fax: 973-276-0533.

MEMBERS OF FIRM

Matthew Dollinger
Dennis M. Gonski
Floyd G. Grossman

ASSOCIATES

Leslie Ann Foodim
Michael J. Spithogiannis
Jessica M. Seidman
Bruce N. Roberts
Alicia B. Devins
Mindy Anne Wallach
Joshua N. Krellen

OF COUNSEL

Joseph Goldstein

Reference: Marine Midland National Bank, Carle Place, New York.

For full biographical listings, see the Martindale-Hubbell Law Directory

CARTHAGE, Jefferson Co.

CONBOY, MCKAY, BACHMAN & KENDALL, LLP (AV)

307 State Street, 13619
Telephone: 315-493-0030
Fax: 315-493-7549
Email: conboy@imcnet.net *URL:* http://www.gisco.net/conboy
Watertown, New York Office: 407 Sherman Street.
Telephone: 315-788-5100.
Fax: 315-788-3463.
Canton, New York Office: 2 Judson Street.
Telephone: 315-386-8544.
Fax: 315-379-0126.

RESIDENT PARTNER

Lawrence D. Hasseler

For full biographical listings, see the Martindale-Hubbell Law Directory

CAZENOVIA, Madison Co.

O'HARA & HANLON, LLP (AV)

9 Albany Street, 13035
Telephone: 315-655-9061
Telecopier: 315-655-2960

MEMBERS OF FIRM

David Patrick O'Hara
Kerry J. Hanlon (1941-1996)

OF COUNSEL

Robert G. Ritz

For full biographical listings, see the Martindale-Hubbell Law Directory

*COOPERSTOWN,** Otsego Co.

GOZIGIAN, WASHBURN & CLINTON (AV)

Orange L. Van Horne (1907-1946)
Van Horne & Feury (1946-1970)
Van Horne, Feury & Gozigian (1970-1979)
Feury, Gozigian & Washburn (1979-1992)
201-204 Key Bank Building, P.O. Box 431, 13326
Telephone: 607-547-2522
Fax: 607-547-2845
Email: GozigianWC@aol.com

MEMBERS OF FIRM

Edward Gozigian
Philip L. Washburn
David J. Clinton

(See Next Column)

ASSOCIATE

E.W. Garo Gozigan

Counsel for: New York Central Mutual Insurance Co.
Local Counsel for: Key Bank, N.A.; Empire Farm Credit ACA.

For full biographical listings, see the Martindale-Hubbell Law Directory

EAST MEADOW, Nassau Co.

CERTILMAN BALIN ADLER & HYMAN, LLP (AV)

90 Merrick Avenue, 11554
Telephone: 516-296-7000
Telecopier: 516-296-7111
URL: http://www.cbah.com

MEMBERS OF FIRM

Ira J. Adler
Dale Allinson
Michael C. Axelrod
Herbert M. Balin
Bruce J. Bergman
Eileen O'Boyle Bitetto
Michael D. Brofman
Lewis J. Campanella
Morton L. Certilman
Robert J. Ciovacco
Brian J. Davis
Wayne G. Edwards
Joseph P. Famighetti
Howard R. Gladston
Murray Greenberg
Gavin C. Grusd
David Z. Herman
Richard Herzbach
M. Allan Hyman
Bernard Hyman
Donna-Marie Korth
Steven J. Kuperschmid
Jeffrey S. Lisabeth
Jaspreet S. Mayall
Richard J. McCord
Thomas J. McNamara
Michael F. O'Shea
Marilyn Price
Fred S. Skolnik
Louis Soloway
Harold Somer
Howard M. Stein
Brian K. Ziegler

OF COUNSEL

Daniel S. Cohan
Joseph N. Mondello

ASSOCIATES

Lawrence A. Altholtz
Meredith W. Ayres
Daniel J. Baker
Kimberly I. Berson
Scott B. Black
Brendan J. DeRiggi
Thomas M. Farrell
Mary C. Florentz
Candace Reid Gladston
Harry P. Greenbaum
David E. Herold
Jodi S. Hoffman
James G. Kapralos
Linda P. Manfredi
Edward G. McCabe
Patrick McCormick
Susan L. McWalters
Jothy Narendran
James A. Rose
Wayne J. Schaefer
Leslie H. Scharf
Afsheen Ashley Shah
Victor Spinnelli
Russell H. Stern
Robert G. Wilk

For full biographical listings, see the Martindale-Hubbell Law Directory

ROSENTHAL & CURRY (AV)

1600 Front Street, 11554
Telephone: 516-485-5577
Telecopier: 516-485-5285
Email: rcesqs@aol.com

MEMBERS OF FIRM

John E. Curry
Jerrold P. Rosenthal
Edward M. Rosenthal
Patrick W. Curry

Reference: Fleet Bank.

For full biographical listings, see the Martindale-Hubbell Law Directory

FREDONIA, Chautauqua Co.

PHILLIPS, LYTLE, HITCHCOCK, BLAINE & HUBER LLP (AV)

11 East Main Street, P.O. Box 149, 14063-0149
Telephone: 716-672-2164
FAX: 716-672-7979
URL: http://www.phillipslytle.com
Buffalo, New York Office: 3400 HSBC Center.
Telephone: 716-847-8400.
Telecopier: 716-852-6100.
Jamestown, New York Office: 307 Chase Bank Building, 8 E. Third Street.
Telephone: 716-664-3906.
Telecopier: 716-664-4230.
Rochester, New York Office: 1400 First Federal Plaza.
Telephone: 716-238-2000.
Telecopier: 716-232-3141.
New York, New York Office: 437 Madison Avenue.
Telephone: 212-759-4888.
Telecopier: 212-308-9079.

OF COUNSEL

Sherwood S. Cadwell

MEMBERS OF FIRM

Caroline Hassett Buerk
Michael C. Foley
Martin F. Idzik (Also at Jamestown Office)
Gregory L. Peterson

(See Next Column)

PHILLIPS, LYTLE, HITCHCOCK, BLAINE & HUBER LLP, *Fredonia—Continued*

SPECIAL COUNSEL

James A. Sommer

ASSOCIATES

R. Timothy Eades
Nancy Lighthart Young

Of Counsel for: HSBC Bank USA; National Fuel Gas Co.; Dunlop Tire & Rubber Co.
Local Counsel for: Bethlehem Steel Corp.; Mobil Oil Corp.; New York Telephone Co.

For full biographical listings, see the Martindale-Hubbell Law Directory

GARDEN CITY, Nassau Co.

COLLERAN, O'HARA & MILLS (AV)

1225 Franklin Avenue, Suite 450, 11530
Telephone: 516-248-5757; 212-614-9119
Telecopier: 516-742-1765

Walter M. Colleran (1912-1998)
Richard L. O'Hara
John F. Mills
Edward J. Groarke
Christopher P. O'Hara
Carol L. O'Rourke

ASSOCIATES

Scott P. Shelkin
Jennifer Berlingieri
Denis A. Engel
Michael D. Jew
Stephanie Suarez
Robin A. Young

COUNSEL

Glenn A. Krebs
Elizabeth Pollina Donlon
Patricia Ann Harold

LEGAL SUPPORT PERSONNEL

Ann Carolan
Laura Harrington
Jack Groarke
Madeleine B. Solarchik

For full biographical listings, see the Martindale-Hubbell Law Directory

GALLAGHER GOSSEEN FALLER KAPLAN & CROWLEY (AV)

1010 Franklin Avenue, Suite 400, 11530-2927
Telephone: 516-742-2500
Fax: 516-742-2516
Email: GGFKC__Postmaster@GGFKC.com
New York, New York Office: 350 Fifth Avenue, Suite 603.
Telephone: 212-947-5800.
Fax: 212-967-4965.

MEMBERS OF FIRM

James A. Gallagher, Jr.
Robert I. Gosseen (Resident, New York City Office)
Robert A. Faller
Alan D. Kaplan
Michael J. Crowley
William E. Vita
Brian P. Morrissey

ASSOCIATES

David H. Arntsen
Joseph A. Latasso
Amy L. Ruina
Gerald A. Corallo, Jr.

OF COUNSEL

John P. Coogan
Peter F. Vetro
William A. Bales, Jr.

For full biographical listings, see the Martindale-Hubbell Law Directory

GOLDEN, WEXLER & SARNESE, P.C. (AV)

377 Oak Street, 11530-9998
Telephone: 516-745-6830
Telecopier: 516-745-6844
Email: goldwexlaw@mail.idt.net *URL:* http://www.goldwexlaw.com
Elmsford, New York Office: 570 Taxter Road.
Telephone: 914-347-8060.

Christopher A. Golden
Joel G. Wexler
Regina M. Sarnese
Maryanne Buatti
William P. Tucker
Paul J. Patacca

Kevin M. McDermott
Randi E. Taub
Jill B. Garfinkel
George Paidoussis
Carolyn Austin
Russell W. Shepherd, Jr.
Denise L. Wagner

For full biographical listings, see the Martindale-Hubbell Law Directory

JONES & JONES (AV)

1000 Franklin Avenue Suite 302, 11530
Telephone: 516-747-1141
Fax: 516-741-5842
URL: http://www.lawyers.com/jones&joneslaw

MEMBERS OF FIRM

C. H. Tunnicliffe Jones (1900-1991)
Lawrence T. Jones

(See Next Column)

OF COUNSEL

Howard L. DeMott

Reference: Bank of New York, Long Island Region.

For full biographical listings, see the Martindale-Hubbell Law Directory

JOEL S. KAPLAN (AV)

585 Stewart Avenue, 11530
Telephone: 516-745-1100
Telecopier: 516-745-6912

For full biographical listings, see the Martindale-Hubbell Law Directory

L'ABBATE, BALKAN, COLAVITA & CONTINI, L.L.P. (AV)

1050 Franklin Avenue, 11530
Telephone: 516-294-8844
Telecopier: 516-294-8202; 742-6563
Email: law@labbatebalkan.com *URL:* http://www.labbatebalkan.com
Livingston, New Jersey Office: 7 Regent Street, Suite 711, 07039.
Telephone: 973-422-0422.
Telecopier: 973-422-0420.

MEMBERS OF FIRM

Donald R. L'Abbate
Anthony P. Colavita
Peter L. Contini
Monte E. Sokol
Douglas L. Pintauro
Richard P. Byrne
Jane M. Myers
Paula M. Gart
Anna M. DiLonardo
David B. Kosakoff
Lewis A. Bartell
Marian C. Rice
Ralph A. Catalano
Douglas R. Halstrom
Steven R. Goldstein
Gary Petropoulos
Domingo R. Gallardo
Mercedes Colwin

COUNSEL TO THE FIRM

Kenneth J. Balkan

SPECIAL COUNSEL

Arthur D. Bromberg (Resident, Livingston, New Jersey Office)
Jonathan M. Kuller (Resident, Livingston, New Jersey Office)

OF COUNSEL

Marianne S. Conklin
Joanne C. Watson
Marie Ann Hoenings

ASSOCIATES

Colleen M. Cronin
Wendy S. Van Dorn
Nicholas Toumbekis
Andrew Marc Warshauer
Michelle J. Simon
Annalee J. Cataldo-Barile
Martin A. Schwartzberg
Louis M. Goldberg
Scott Evan Kossove
Peter D. Rigelhaupt
Orin J. Ketyer
Anthony T. Battaglia
Christopher B. Block (Resident, Livingston, New Jersey Office)
James S. Montano (Resident, Livingston, New Jersey Office)
Maureen E. Scott
John D. McKenna
Michael B. Curan
Jeffrey E. Edelman (Resident, Livingston, New Jersey Office)
Matthew K. Flanagan
Claudia M. Kessler

A list of References and Representative Clients will be furnished upon request.

For full biographical listings, see the Martindale-Hubbell Law Directory

MONTFORT, HEALY, MCGUIRE & SALLEY (AV)

1140 Franklin Avenue, 11530
Telephone: 516-747-4082
Telecopier: 516-746-0748

MEMBERS OF FIRM

E. Richard Rimmels, Jr. (1930-1999)
Frank J. Cafaro
Philip J. Catapano
Fredric C. Montfort
Donald S. Neumann, Jr.
James J. Keefe, Jr.
Michael A. Baranowicz
James Michael Murphy

OF COUNSEL

Fredric H. Montfort
Edward M. Salley, Jr.
David J. Fleming
Robert J. Mettalia

ASSOCIATES

Claudia C. Glacken
Marcie K. Glasser
Bruce A. Cook
Jeffrey D. Present
Joan E. Resnik
Susan H. Dempsey
Camille L. Hansen
Christopher T. Cafaro
Kathleen Dumont
Jeffrey B. Siler
Michael G. Kruzynski
Karen J. Cooper

For full biographical listings, see the Martindale-Hubbell Law Directory

SHAW, LICITRA, BOHNER, ESERNIO & SCHWARTZ, P.C. (AV)

1010 Franklin Avenue, 11530
Telephone: 516-742-0610
Telecopier: 516-742-2670
Email: shaw0610@aol.com

(See Next Column)

SHAW, LICITRA, BOHNER, ESERNIO & SCHWARTZ P.C.—*Continued*

Joseph Licitra (1930-1987)
J. Stanley Shaw
Robert J. Bohner
George P. Esernio
Jeffrey L. Schwartz
Anton J. Borovina
Edward M. Flint
Stuart I. Gordon
John H. Hall, Jr.
Sarah M. Keenan
Frank J. Livoti
Alan E. Marder
Peter Marullo
Roberta L. McManus

David P. Gesser
Steven H. Blatt
Michael Clark

COUNSEL

Victor G. Beaudet (1919-1993)
Alan M. Parente

For full biographical listings, see the Martindale-Hubbell Law Directory

*GOSHEN,** Orange Co.

NORTON & CHRISTENSEN (AV)

Goshen Executive Building, 60 Erie Street, P.O. Box 308, 10924
Telephone: 914-294-7949
Fax: 914-294-7791
Email: norchris@frontiernet.net
Rochelle Park, New Jersey Office: 151 West Passaic Street.
Telephone: 201-909-3735.
Fax: 201-368-2102.

MEMBERS OF FIRM

Stanley J. Norton (1916-1998)
Henry N. Christensen, Jr.
Harold M. Pressberg
Kenneth J. Frank

OF COUNSEL

John T. Mayo

For full biographical listings, see the Martindale-Hubbell Law Directory

HAUPPAUGE, Suffolk Co.

ERIC H. HOLTZMAN (AV)

330 Vanderbilt Motor Parkway, P.O. Box 11005, 11788-0903
Telephone: 631-435-8800
Fax: 631-435-8832

Richard E. Trachtenberg
David H. Eisenberg

Reference: European-American Bank & Trust Co.

For full biographical listings, see the Martindale-Hubbell Law Directory

HEMPSTEAD, Nassau Co.

DEEGAN & DEEGAN, L.L.P. (AV)

550 Front Street, 11550
Telephone: 516-486-9400
Telecopier: 516-486-8680
Email: deegan550@aol.com

MEMBERS OF FIRM

Donald E. Deegan
James V. Deegan

ASSOCIATES

Michael A. Wolf
James M. Hayes
Robert H. Doud
Mary E. Hayes
Gregg M. McGrath

OF COUNSEL

Diane Klaum Farrell
Thomas G. Nolan
John S. White
George Planos
Donald F. McCarthy
Gregory M. Maurer
George A. Boehling
Theresa Rho

For full biographical listings, see the Martindale-Hubbell Law Directory

*HUDSON,** Columbia Co.

RAPPORT, MEYERS, WHITBECK, SHAW & RODENHAUSEN, LLP (AV)

436 Union Street, 12534
Telephone: 518-828-9444
Telecopier: 518-828-9719
Email: tslemp@rapportmeyers.com
Poughkeepsie, New York Office: 110 Main Street. 12601.
Telephone: 914-473-7766.
Telecopier: 914-473-7790.

Carmi Rapport
Victor M. Meyers
Carl G. Whitbeck, Jr.
Jason L. Shaw
George A. Rodenhausen
Christine M. Chale

Shannon Martin LaFrance
Elisabeth S. Straus
Lisa M. Orrantia

(See Next Column)

OF COUNSEL

John J. Faso
Stephen M. Saland

References: Key Bank of New York; Hudson River Bank & Trust; Trustco Bank; Fleet Bank of New York.

For full biographical listings, see the Martindale-Hubbell Law Directory

HUNTINGTON, Suffolk Co.

SMYTH & LACK (AV)

143 Main Street, 11743
Telephone: 516-271-7500
Telecopier: 516-271-7504
URL: http://www.lawyers.com/smyth&lacklaw

MEMBERS OF FIRM

Vincent A. Smyth
James J. Lack

ASSOCIATES

Dana M. Barberis
Edmund J.M. Smyth
Karen E. Nora

Reference: Chemical Bank.

For full biographical listings, see the Martindale-Hubbell Law Directory

ISLANDIA, Suffolk Co.

BRACKEN & MARGOLIN, LLP (AV)

One Suffolk Square, Suite 300, 11722
Telephone: 516-234-8585
Telecopier: 516-234-8702
URL: http://www.bracken-margolin.com

MEMBERS OF FIRM

John P. Bracken
Linda U. Margolin

ASSOCIATES

Olympia Gouvis
William J. Graham
Patricia M. Meisenheimer
Ralph J. Reissman
Peter L. Verdon

Representative Clients: Rason Asphalt, Inc.; S & H Building Materials Corp.
Reference: Marine Midland Bank, N.A.

For full biographical listings, see the Martindale-Hubbell Law Directory

*ITHACA,** Tompkins Co.

BARNEY, GROSSMAN, DUBOW & MARCUS (AV)

Seneca Building West, Suite 400, 119 East Seneca Street, 14850
Telephone: 607-273-6841
Facsimile: 607-272-8806 (Not for service of papers)

MEMBERS OF FIRM

John C. Barney
Peter G. Grossman
David A. Dubow
Randall B. Marcus
William J. Troy, III
Jonathan A. Orkin

Attorneys for: Elmira Savings & Loan FA; Pace Funding Company; Town of Ithaca; Town of Caroline; Town of Danby; Village of Groton; Village of Lansing; Paolangeli Contractor.

For full biographical listings, see the Martindale-Hubbell Law Directory

WIGGINS AND MASSON, LLP (AV)

308 North Tioga Street, P.O. Box 399, 14851
Telephone: 607-272-0479
Telecopier: 607-273-0502
Email: law@wigginsandmasson.com *URL:* http://www.wigginsandmasson.com

MEMBERS OF FIRM

Walter J. Wiggins
Robin Abrahamson Masson
Erin E. McKinley
Lorraine Moynihan

Approved Attorneys for: Ticor Title Guaranty Corp.
References: Tompkins County Trust Co.

For full biographical listings, see the Martindale-Hubbell Law Directory

JAMESTOWN, Chautauqua Co.

BURGETT & ROBBINS (AV)

15 East Fifth Street, P.O. Box 3090, 14702-3090
Telephone: 716-488-3090
Fax: 716-483-3765
1-800-832-6582
Email: help@burgettandrobbins.com *URL:* http://www.burgettandrobbins.com

Dalton J. Burgett
Dale C. Robbins
Kenneth M. Lasker
Mary Speedy Hajdu
Robert A. Liebers
Andrew T. Radack

References: Fleet Bank, Jamestown, New York; Marine Midland Bank, Jamestown, New York; Lake Shore Savings and Loan Association, Jamestown, New York.

For full biographical listings, see the Martindale-Hubbell Law Directory

Jamestown—Continued

ERICKSON, WEBB & SCOLTON (AV)

111 West Second Street, 14701
Telephone: 716-488-1178
Fax: 716-488-1448
Email: ews@netsync.net

MEMBERS OF FIRM

Alton R. Erickson (1904-1968)
Philip A. Erickson
Paul V. Webb, Jr.
Bruce S. Scolton
Lyle T. Hajdu

References: Marine Midland Bank, N.A.; Chase Manhattan Bank.

For full biographical listings, see the Martindale-Hubbell Law Directory

PHILLIPS, LYTLE, HITCHCOCK, BLAINE & HUBER LLP (AV)

307 Chase Bank Building, 8 E. Third Street, 14702-1279
Telephone: 716-664-3906
Telecopier: 716-664-4230
URL: http://www.phillipslytle.com
Buffalo, New York Office: 3400 HSBC Center.
Telephone: 716-847-8400.
Telecopier: 716-852-6100.
Rochester, New York Office: 1400 First Federal Plaza.
Telephone: 716-238-2000.
Telecopier: 716-232-3141.
New York, New York Office: 437 Madison Avenue.
Telephone: 212-759-4888.
Telecopier: 212-308-9079.
Fredonia, New York Office: 11 East Main Street.
Telephone: 716-672-2164.
FAX: 716-672-7979.

OF COUNSEL

Sherwood S. Cadwell

PARTNERS

Michael C. Foley
Martin F. Idzik (Also at Fredonia Office)
Gregory L. Peterson

For full biographical listings, see the Martindale-Hubbell Law Directory

*KINGSTON,** Ulster Co.

COOK, TUCKER, NETTER & CLOONAN, P.C. (AV)

85 Main Street, P.O. Box 3939, 12401
Telephone: 914-331-0702
Fax: 914-331-1003
Email: ctnc@prodigy.net

Andrew J. Cook (1884-1958)
Francis X. Tucker (1923-1987)
Andrew J. Cook, Jr. (1918-1997)
Robert E. Netter
William N. Cloonan
Robert D. Cook
Eric M. Kurtz
Thomas A. Murphy
Michael T. Cook

Counsel for: Town of Rochester.
Representative Clients: Central Hudson Gas & Electric Corp.; CNA Insurance Co.; Covenant Group; Hanover Insurance Co.; Metropolitan Property & Liability Insurance Co.; Norstar Bank; USF&G; Allstate Insurance Co.; AIA Insurance Group; Universal Underwriters.

For full biographical listings, see the Martindale-Hubbell Law Directory

HOWARD C. ST. JOHN AND ASSOCIATES (AV)

P.O. Box 4380, 12402
Telephone: 914-338-4500
Fax: 914-338-0638

ASSOCIATES

Richard A. Anthony
Joseph L. Canino
John J. Cook
Michael Francis Jordan
J. Michael Bruhn, Jr.

General Counsel for: Ulster Savings Bank.
Representative Clients: Government Employees Insurance Co.; National Grange Insurance Co.; New York Central Mutual Fire Insurance Co.; AT&T (local counsel); Volkswagen of America, Inc. (local counsel); Inland Steel (local counsel).

For full biographical listings, see the Martindale-Hubbell Law Directory

LARCHMONT, Westchester Co.

MCMILLAN CONSTABILE, LLP (AV)

2180 Boston Post Road, P.O. Box 300, 10538
Telephone: 914-834-3500
FAX: 914-834-0620

(See Next Column)

MEMBERS OF FIRM

Thomas R. Constabile, Jr.
Stewart J. McMillan
Keith J. McMillan
William Maker, Jr.
Kevin J. Keelan
Robert Neill
Gary M. Rikoon

COUNSEL

Rita J. Miller
William G. Halby
Katherine A. Bialo
Pamela A. Banks
Amy Siegel Mauser

Gary P. Kyme

For full biographical listings, see the Martindale-Hubbell Law Directory

*LOCKPORT,** Niagara Co.

SACCA AND SACCA (AV)

102 East Avenue, 14094
Telephone: 716-434-5518
Fax: 716-434-8050
Email: gssacca@aol.com *URL:* http://www.lawyers.com/gsacca

MEMBERS OF FIRM

Stephen A. Sacca
Gerald Stephen Sacca

LEGAL SUPPORT PERSONNEL

Anna Marie Holman (Paralegal)
Lauree E. Chase (Paralegal)

Representative Clients: Lawyers Title Insurance Corp. (Virginia); Village of Wilson.
References: Manufacturers & Traders Trust Co.; Marine Midland Bank; Lockport Savings Bank.

For full biographical listings, see the Martindale-Hubbell Law Directory

MANHASSET, Nassau Co.

FLETCHER, SIBELL & MIGATZ, P.C. (AV)

Molloy Building, 22 Bayview Avenue, P.O. Box N, 11030
Telephone: 516-627-6600
Facsimile: 516-627-5241

James H. Fletcher
Stanley J. Sibell
Bruce W. Migatz
Kenneth D. Molloy (1919-1999)

Representative Clients: Joseph Eletlo Transfer Co., Inc.; Micro Contacts, Inc.; Centerbank Mortgage Company; Home Mortgage Corporation; North Shore University Hospital; Smith Barney; Shearson Lehman Hutton; Mall Properties; Chase Manhattan Bank, N.A.; New England Development.
References: European-American Bank; Fleet Bank; First American Title Insurance Co.; Chicago Title Insurance Co.; Statewide Abstract Co.; The Bank of New York; Chase Manhattan Bank.

For full biographical listings, see the Martindale-Hubbell Law Directory

MELVILLE, Suffolk Co.

PAYNE, WOOD & LITTLEJOHN (AV)

290 Broad Hollow Road, 11747-4805
Telephone: 516-547-8400
Telefax: 516-547-0501
Email: mail@paynewood.com
Bridgehampton, New York Office: 1936 Montauk Highway. P.O. Box 1980, 11932.
Telephone: 516-537-3100.
Telefax: 516-537-0560.
Locust Valley, New York Office: 83 Birch Hill Road, 11560.
Telephone: 516-676-0700.
Fax: 516-676-0703.

MEMBERS OF FIRM

Philip C. Kilian
Beverly J. Bell
Alan C. Polacek (Managing Partner)
Jed C. Albert
Peter B. Colgrove
Theresa K. Quigley
Janet Ganio
John P. McEntee

OF COUNSEL

Daren A. Rathkopf
Victor C. McCuaig, Jr.
Warren I. Titus, Jr.
Edwin F. Hendrickson
James A. Eisenman

COUNSEL

Kevin J. Barry
Mark A. Cuthbertson

ASSOCIATES

Susan H. Jannace
Ilene S. Kreitzer
Joseph L. Hunsberger
Carol King
Kevin M. Knab
Walter J. Johnson

For full biographical listings, see the Martindale-Hubbell Law Directory

MIDDLETOWN, Orange Co.

MacVean, Lewis, Sherwin & McDermott, P.C. (AV)

34 Grove Street, P.O. Box 310, 10940
Telephone: 914-343-3000
Fax: 914-343-3866

Kenneth A. MacVean (1926-1999)
Kermit W. Lewis
Louis H. Sherwin
Paul T. McDermott
Jeffrey D. Sherwin
Thomas P. Clarke, Jr.
John M. Clancy

SENIOR TRIAL COUNSEL

George F. Roesch, III

Kevin F. Preston
Ferol Reed McDermott
Anthony R. LoBiondo
James V. Galvin

OF COUNSEL

Samuel W. Eager, Jr.

Counsel for: Orange County Trust Co.; Middletown Savings Bank; First Federal Savings & Loan Association of Middletown; Goshen Savings Bank; Advest Bank.

For full biographical listings, see the Martindale-Hubbell Law Directory

MOUNT KISCO, Westchester Co.

Singleton & Singleton (AV)

50 Main Street, 10549
Telephone: 914-666-4400
Telecopier: 914-666-6442

Thomas J. Singleton
Whitney Singleton

For full biographical listings, see the Martindale-Hubbell Law Directory

NEWBURGH, Orange Co.

Drake, Sommers, Loeb, Tarshis & Catania, PLLC (AV)

One Corwin Court, P.O. Box 1479, 12550
Telephone: 914-565-1100
Telecopier: 914-565-1999
Email: dsltc@dsltc.com *URL:* http://www.dsltc.com

Bernard J. Sommers
James R. Loeb
Richard J. Drake
Steven L. Tarshis
Joseph A. Catania, Jr.
Richard F. Liberth
Glen L. Heller
Kevin T. Dowd
Richard M. Mahon, II
Steven I. Milligram
Stephen J. Gaba
Marianna R. Kennedy

Adam L. Rodd
Karen Collins
Denis E. McGuinness
Gary J. Gogerty
Randall V. Coffill
Edward C. Bruno
Charles T. Bazydlo
Ralph L. Puglielle, Jr.

OF COUNSEL

Ellen Villamil
Kathleen A. Mishkin

Representative Clients: M&T Bank; Tri-Seal International, Inc.; Town of Cornwall; Town of Newburgh; Sterling Forest Corporation; Woodbury Common/Chelsea GCA; Elizabeth Arden; Coregis Insurance Co.; A.C. Moore Incorporated; St. Luke's Hospital.

For full biographical listings, see the Martindale-Hubbell Law Directory

*NEW YORK,** New York Co.

Andrews & Kurth L.L.P. (AV)

A Registered Limited Liability Partnership
805 Third Avenue, 10022
Telephone: 212-850-2800
Telecopier: 212-850-2929
Telex: 960534 AKLAW NYC
Email: webmaster@andrews-kurth.com *URL:* http://www.andrews-kurth.com
Houston, Texas Office: Suite 4200, 600 Travis, 77002.
Telephone: 713-220-4200.
Telecopier: 713-220-4285. E-Mail: webmaster@andrews-kurth.com.
Washington, D.C. Office: Suite 300, 1701 Pennsylvania Avenue, N.W.
Telephone: 202-662-2700.
Telecopier: 202-662-2739.
Dallas, Texas Office: Suite 3700, 1717 Main Street.
Telephone: 214-659-4400.
Telecopier: 214-659-4401.
The Woodlands, Texas Office: Suite 150, 2170 Buckthorne Place, 77380.
Telephone: 713-220-4801.
Telecopier: 713-220-4815.
Los Angeles, California Office: Suite 4200, 601 S. Figueroa Street.
Telephone: 213-896-3100.
Telecopier: 213-986-3137.
London, England Office: 2 Creed Court, 5-11 Ludgate Hill, EC4M 7AA.
Telephone: 0171-236-3456.
Telecopier: 0171-236-4276.

(See Next Column)

MEMBERS OF FIRM

Arthur D. Felsenfeld
Peter S. Goodman
Hugh M. Ray
Allan D. Reiss
Mike Rosenwasser
Paul N. Silverstein
Michael J. Swidler
Lynne Fischman Uniman

OF COUNSEL

Walter L. Stratton

ASSOCIATES

Melissa Baal
Richard Baumfield
Charles E. Carpenter (Not admitted in NY)
David J. Hoyt
Geoffrey R. Krouse
Lara K. Pitaro
Emilia A. Simonelli
Jennifer Lee Sulzberger
Aaron J. Tehan
Jonathan D. Wallach
Daniel N. Zinman

SENIOR ATTORNEY

Karen Beth Pettigrew (Not admitted in NY)

For full biographical listings, see the Martindale-Hubbell Law Directory

Badiak Will & Ruddy (AV)

Suite 1040, 120 Broadway, 10271
Telephone: 212-376-6767
Telecopier: 212-376-6777
Telex: 6716686 BANDW
Email: admiralaw@aol.com
North Miami Beach, Florida Office: Badiak, Will & Kallen, 17071 West Dixie Highway, P.O. Box 600550.
Telephone: 305-945-1851.

MEMBERS OF FIRM

Roman Badiak
Alfred J. Will
James J. Ruddy
John D. Kallen (Resident, North Miami, Florida Office)
David L. Maloof (1924-1992)

ASSOCIATES

Stephen A. Frank
Nicholas Kalfa
James P. Krauzlis
Martin L. Lindahl
Lisa A. Scognamillo
Deborah R. Reid

OF COUNSEL

Charles C. Goodenough

For full biographical listings, see the Martindale-Hubbell Law Directory

Baer Marks & Upham LLP (AV)

A Partnership including a Professional Corporation
805 Third Avenue, 10022
Telephone: 212-702-5700
Fax: 212-702-5941

Jill Cobert-Alvarez
Mary Jane Augustine
Neal S. Barlia
Donald J. Bezahler
Stanley E. Bloch
Michael V. Blumenthal
Kenneth S. Brown
Barbara E. Champoux
Jeffrey M. Cole
Ella W. Dodson
Ivan W. Dreyer
William B. Duff
Edward S. Feig
Bernard A. Feuerstein
James E. Frankel
Steven M. Goldman
Jay L. Gottlieb
Howard Graff
Joel M. Handel
Larry D. Henin
Christopher J. Lagno
Leslie J. Levinson
Eric D. Martins
David L. Mathus
William B. Norden
Samuel F. Ottensoser
Anne E. Pitter
Steven S. Pretsfelder
Charles S. Rich
Jonathan J. Russo
Eugene R. Scheiman
Deborah A. Skakel
Donald S. Snider
Gerald L. Sobol
Morris A. Wirth

ASSOCIATES

Debra E. Altschuler
Constance Elaine Arabatzis
Daniel Baldwin
Brian D. Bauman
Mark A. Bloom
Gerard S. Catalanello
Stephen J. Czarnik
Aimee B. Davis
Jeannine R. Feneran
Daniel J. Friedman
Catherine V. Greco
Brian E. Greer
Karen J. Krause
Victoria A. Kummer
Jeanette Luoh
Stephanie E. Paulos
Shari L. Pine
Stewart D. Pollak
Roger M. Quinland
Laurence P. Rabinowitz
Richard M. Rosier
Andrew Ross
Susan Sawyer
Veronica T. Stork
Louise I. Tudor
Carl Van Demark
Alexander D. Widell

OF COUNSEL

Stuart W. Berg
Andrew M. Crisses
Aaron L. Danzig
Milton B. Eulau
Walter Feldesman (P.C.)
Arnold Forster
Joseph Korff
Lawrence W. Milas
Robert M. Miller
Herman Sassower
Stephen F. Selig

For full biographical listings, see the Martindale-Hubbell Law Directory

New York—Continued

BAKER BOTTS L.L.P. (AV)

599 Lexington Avenue, 10022-6030 and 30 Rockefeller Plaza, 10112-0228
Telephone: 212-705-5000
Fax: 212-705-5125 (599 Lexington Ave.)
Fax: 212-705-5020 (30 Rockeffeller Plaza)
Email: postmaster@bakerbotts.com *URL:* http://www.bakerbotts.com
Washington, D.C. Office: The Warner, 1299 Pennsylvania Avenue, N.W.
Telephone: 202-639-7700.
Austin, Texas Office: 1600 San Jacinto Center, 98 San Jacinto Boulevard.
Telephone: 512-322-2500.
Dallas, Texas Office: 2001 Ross Avenue.
Telephone: 214-953-6500.
Houston, Texas Office: One Shell Plaza, 910 Louisiana.
Telephone: 713-229-1234.
Moscow, Russia Office: 10 ul. Bolshaya Dimitrovka (formerly ul. Pushkinskaya), 103031.
Telephone: 7095/921-5300 (Local); 7095/929-7070 (International).
London, England Office: 45 Ludgate Hill.
Telephone: 0171-778-1400 (Local); 011-44-171-778-1400.
Baku, Azerbaijan Office: 6-10 Vagif Mustafa-zadeh Street, Third Floor, Icheri Sheher, 370004.
Telephone: 994-12-97-63-88 (Local); 011-994-12-97-63-88 (International).
Fax: 994-12-97-63-91 (Local); 011-994-12-97-63-61 (International).

MEMBERS OF FIRM

Richard G. Berkley
Kenneth M. Bialo
Gary M. Butter
Lee D. Charles
Richard S. Clark
Doreen Leavens Costa
Marta E. Delsignore
Russell H. Falconer
John A. Fogarty, Jr.
Jonathan Gordon
Bradley B. Geist
John M. Huggins (Not admitted in NY)
Lisa B. Kole
Marc A. Leaf
Michael A. Lippert
Elizabeth M. Markowski
James J. Maune
Frederick H. McGrath
John D. Murnane
Robert W. Murray Jr.
Thomas R. Nesbitt, Jr.
Robert Neuner
Robert C. Scheinfeld
Rochelle K. Seide
Louis S. Sorell
Henry Tang

RETIRED FIRM MEMBERS

Frederick C. Carver
Dana M. Raymond
Arthur S. Tenser

SPECIAL COUNSEL

Thomas V. D'Ambrosio
William Nix
Thomas R. Trowbridge, III

OF COUNSEL

Joseph D. Garon
Ronald B. Hildreth
Francis J. Hone
Robert S. Langley, Jr.
Bertram Perkel

ASSOCIATES

Paul D. Ackerman
Lindsay S. Adams
Richard L. Blaylock
Adam Dick
Brayton Dresser
Igor Ermilin
Kristin G. Francis (Not admitted in NY)
Anthony Giaccio
Robert L. Greenfeld
Steven R. Gustavson
Jeanne M. Hamburg
Samuel SungMok Lee (Not admitted in NY)
Dr. Janet M. MacLeod
Matthew K. McCoy
Thomas R. Pappas
Paul A. Ragusa
Paul J. Reilly
Glen W. Roberts II
Anne W. Salisbury
Michael L. Shore
Neil P. Sirota
Carmella L. Stephens
Robert A. Stewart (Not admitted in NY)
Jeffrey D. Sullivan
Craig Troyer (Not admitted in NY)
Robert M. Wasnofski, Jr.
David W. Whealan
Karen Wuertz
Douglas Charles Wyatt

For full biographical listings, see the Martindale-Hubbell Law Directory

BAKER & MCKENZIE (AV)

805 Third Avenue, 10022
Telephone: (212) 751-5700
Intn'l. Dialing: (1-212) 751-5700
Cable Address: ABOGADO
Telex: 62572
Answer Back: ABOGADO
Facsimile: (1-212) 759-9133
URL: http://www.bakerinfo.com
Associated Offices of Baker & McKenzie in: Almaty, Amsterdam, Bahrain, Baku, Bangkok, Barcelona, Beijing, Berlin, Bogotá, Brasília, Brussels, Budapest, Buenos Aires, Cairo, Caracas, Chicago, Dallas, Düsseldorf, Frankfurt, Geneva, Hanoi, Ho Chi Minh City, Hong Kong, Houston, Hsinchu, Juárez, Kiev, London, Madrid, Manila, Melbourne, México City, Miami, Milan, Monterrey, Moscow, Münich, Palo Alto, Paris, Prague, Rio de Janeiro, Riyadh, Rome, St. Petersburg, San Diego, San Francisco, Santiago, São Paulo, Singapore, Stockholm, Sydney, Taipei, Tijuana, Tokyo, Toronto, Valencia, Warsaw, Washington, D.C. and Zürich.
Correspondent Law Firm: Hadiputranto, Hadinoto & Partners, Jakarta.

(See Next Column)

MEMBERS OF FIRM

Janna H. J. Bellwin
Howard M. Berkower
James R. Cameron
Robert B. Cartwright
Charles J. Conroy
Robert B. Davidson
Gerald J. Hayes
James David Jacobs
Marc M. Levey
Thomas R. May (Not admitted in NY)
Richard L. Nevins
Lawrence Walker Newman
William D. Outman, II
Malcolm I. Ross
Arthur W. Rovine
Xavier Ruiz
Joseph Samet
Thomas W. Studwell
David Zaslowsky

NATIONAL PARTNERS

Peter J. Connors
Maria G. Gutierrez
Klas S. D. Holm
Howard L. Margulis
Michael S. Novins
F. Roy Sedore
David R. Tillinghast

OF COUNSEL

Peter D. Lederer
Anthony G. Petrello

SENIOR ATTORNEY

Charles B. Cummings

COUNSEL

Peter J. Norton

ASSOCIATES

Harry K. Ahn (Not admitted in NY)
David M. Balaban
Sandra G. Blundetto
Scott L. Brandman
William L. Clydesdale
Walda M. Decreus
Victor DeVito
Robin L. Filion (Not admitted in NY)
Colleen A. Finnegan
Frank M. Gasparo
David A. Grech
George A. Greenslade
Renuka Gupta
Bonnie L. Guth
Amy B. Jones
Susan R. Knox
Robert P. Lewis
Lalit K. Loomba
Allan K. A. Marson
Corinne E. Mathez (Not admitted in United States)
Deidre E. Michael
Donna Mitchell
Mary Ann B. Nessel
Euhnee Park
Valerie C. Picard
Christopher S. Roehrs
Rachel Anne Rotstein (Not admitted in NY)
H. David Schwartz
Geoffrey E. Secol
Laszlo Serester
Lawrence W. Shapiro
Glenn H. J. Woll (Not admitted in NY)
Natasha G. Ziabkina

For full biographical listings, see the Martindale-Hubbell Law Directory

BALLON STOLL BADER & NADLER, P.C. (AV)

1450 Broadway 14th Floor, 10018-2268
Telephone: 212-575-7900
Telecopier: 212-764-5060
Email: mail@ballonstoll.com *URL:* http://www.ballonstoll.com
Hackensack, New Jersey Office: 505 Main Street, 07601.
Telephone: 201-342-7808.
Fax: 201-488-5788.

Howard D. Bader
David Nadler
Barry M. Karson
Marshall B. Bellovin
Arthur E. Lasker
Richard Weinberger
Robert M. Shepard
Harry Levinson
Dwight Yellen
Robert M. Jaffe
Will Levins (Resident, Hackensack, New Jersey Office)
Richard Turyn
Stephen P. Long

COUNSEL EMERITUS

Arthur L. Stoll (1911-1993)
Frederick E. M. Ballon (1908-1997)

OF COUNSEL

Mitchell D. Kessler
Warren E. Stoller

Maren Coburn
Chris Muladaradelis
Susan Schneiderman
Mark Berenson
Benzion Frankel
Jay Sung Lee
Nancy Zecca
Kevin D. Shafton

For full biographical listings, see the Martindale-Hubbell Law Directory

BATTLE FOWLER LLP (AV)

A Limited Liability Partnership
Park Avenue Tower, 75 East 55th Street, 10022
Telephone: 212-856-7000
Cable Address: "Counsellor"
Telex: 127053
Telecopier: (212) 339-9150
Email: info@battlefowler.com *URL:* http://www.battlefowler.com
Los Angeles, California Office: 2049 Century Park East, Suite 2300, 90067.
Telephone: 310-788-3000.

(See Next Column)

BATTLE FOWLER LLP—*Continued*

MEMBERS OF FIRM

George Gordon Battle (1897-1949)
Ludlow S. Fowler (1924-1961)
Charles H. Baker
Charles Burton
John A. Cahill
Steven B. Carlin
Richard F. Davis (Resident, Los Angeles Office)
Robert J. DeAngelis
Carl A. de Brito
Howard S. Denburg
David E. Eagan
Peter M. Fass
Gerald J. Fields
Steven A. Fishman
David Fleischer
David J. Freeman
Douglas L. Furth
Sharyn Gibau-Heyman
Thomas V. Glynn
Charles J. Hamilton, Jr.
Luke P. Iovine, III
Les Jacobowitz
John L. Kelly
Taro J. Kawamura
Steven Koch
Thomas E. Kruger
Eric R. Landau
Jonathan M. Lehr
Harold Levine
Steven L. Lichtenfeld
Leslie H. Loffman
Michael J. P. Malone, III
Mark W. Masters
Colleen M. McIntosh
Mary McKenna
William J. McSherry, Jr.
Gregg Miller
Michael A. Mishaan
Lawrence Mittman
Peter Conrad Olsen
Richard L. O'Toole
Edward L. Peck
Sanford C. Presant (Resident, Los Angeles Office)
Madlyn Gleich Primoff
Douglas A. Raelson
Patrick J. Rohan
Michael R. Rosella
Michael J. Saltser
Walter F. Schleimer
Mark Schonberger
Paul D. Selver
Eric W. Shaw
Ann Shipley
Dean A. Stiffle
John N. Turitzin
Mary Ann Villari
Louis Vitali
David M. Warburg
Robert J. Wertheimer
Gregory M. Weston
Michael L. Zuppone

OF COUNSEL

Hyman L. Battle, Jr.
Martin L. Edelman
Robert W. Gelfman
David D. Griffin
Charles L. Jaffin
Theodore W. Kheel

SPECIAL COUNSEL

Ralph E. Arpajian
Janet Beck
Robert A. Boresta
Thomas More Griffin
Lori B. Katz
Margaret Elias Lehman
Michael J. Lendino
Donna H. Lieberman
Lois Nitti-Verlen
Gary D. Rawitz
Raymond J. Soffientini
Elise Wagner

ASSOCIATES

Gregory R. Belcamino
David M. Brooks
Richard S. Brown
Robert R. Buzard
Jeremiah H. Candreva
Frank T. Cannone
Benjamin Dean
Ann Marie McGrath Denning
Carolene S. Eaddy
Lydia E. Fadool
Edward C. Fargis
Julie A. Fergang
Brian J. Fisher
Robin M. Freundlich
Scott E. Goldsmith
Thomas C. Humbert, Jr.
John A. Jadhon
David J. Kaplan
Michael H. Kessel
Moon Yung Kim
Nina H. Kim
Jodi A. Kleinick
Jon W. Knipe
Ilan A. Lerman
David P. Luci
Michael J. Maratea
James M. McCarrick
James M. McKnight
John E. McLean
Valerie A. Molinaro
Glenn E. Motelson
Hedwig O'Hara
Judith A. Pacitti
Jeffrey J. Pellegrino
Salvatore Rappa
Igor Roitburg
Jeffrey E. Romanow
Lawrence A. Rosenbloom
Rachel N. Schatten
Trudi A. Seery
Marilyn B. Selig
Paul Allan Straus
Carolyn Sullivan
Ralph S. Toussie
John C. Tracy
Peter D. Tremblay
Vasilia H.A. Tsismenakis
Carla P.S. Vogel
Jill A. Weinstock-Ames

For full biographical listings, see the Martindale-Hubbell Law Directory

---

BECKER, GLYNN, MELAMED & MUFFLY LLP (AV)

299 Park Avenue, 10171
Telephone: 212-888-3033
Facsimile: 212-888-0255
URL: http://www.beckerglynn.com

David J. Melamed (1930-1990)

MEMBERS OF FIRM

Robert C. Muffly
Richard S. Bashner
Richard N. Chassin
Kenneth L. Everett
Peter M. Hosinski
Bruce A. Rich
Peter Van Nuys
Rachel Korn Wasserman

OF COUNSEL

Joseph D. Becker
Robert B. Glynn

(See Next Column)

ASSOCIATES

Roland E. Bluemle
Curt D. Buyum
Karin P. E. Gustafson
Stephen B. Kaplitt
Carin V. Khatchikian
M. Zeb Landsman
Imke Ratschko

For full biographical listings, see the Martindale-Hubbell Law Directory

---

BEVERIDGE & DIAMOND, P.C. (AV)

15th Floor, 477 Madison Avenue, 10022-5802
Telephone: 212-702-5400
Telecopier: 212-702-5450
URL: http://www.beveridgediamond.com
Washington, D.C. Office: 1350 I Street, N.W., Suite 700, 20005-3311.
Telephone: 202-789-6000.
Telecopier: 202-789-6190.
Saddle Brook, New Jersey Office: Beveridge & Diamond, Park 80 West, Plaza II Suite 200, 07663-5836.
Telephone: 201-585-8162.
Telecopier: 201-368-1944.
San Francisco, California Office: Beveridge & Diamond LLP, One Sansome Street, Suite 3400, 94204-4438.
Telephone: 415-397-0100.
Telecopier: 415-397-4238.
Sacramento, California Office: Beveridge & Diamond LLP, Suite 1860, 400 Capitol Mall, 95814-4407.
Telephone: 916-553-4533.
Telecopier: 916-553-4539.
Baltimore, Maryland Office: Suite 2210, 201 North Charles Street, 21201-4150.
Telephone: 410-230-3850.
Telecopier: 410-230-3868.

Stephen L. Gordon
John S. Guttmann, Jr.
John H. Kazanjian

OF COUNSEL

Sy Gruza

Kathleen Lennon
Christopher J. McKenzie
Ward M. Miller, III
Michael G. Murphy

For full biographical listings, see the Martindale-Hubbell Law Directory

---

WILLIAM N. BINDERMAN (AV)

685 Third Avenue, Suite 2700, 10017-4024
Telephone: 212-297-0011
URL: http://www.lawyers.com/binderman
Philadelphia, Pennsylvania Office: 1919 Walnut Street, 19103-4605.
Telephone: 215-496-0500.

For full biographical listings, see the Martindale-Hubbell Law Directory

---

BROBECK, PHLEGER & HARRISON LLP (AV)

A Limited Liability Partnership
1633 Broadway, 47th Floor, 10019
Telephone: 212-581-1600
Facsimile: 212-586-7878
Email: info@brobeck.com *URL:* http://www.brobeck.com/
San Francisco, California Office: Spear Street Tower, One Market.
Telephone: 415-442-0900.
Facsimile: 415-442-1010.
Los Angeles, California Office: 550 South Hope Street.
Telephone: 213-489-4060.
Facsimile: 213-745-3345.
Palo Alto, California Office: Two Embarcadero Place, 2200 Geng Road.
Telephone: 650-424-0160.
Facsimile: 650-496-2885.
San Diego, California Office: 550 West C Street, Suite 1300.
Telephone: 619-234-1966.
Facsimile: 619-236-1403.
Irvine, California Office: 38 Technology Drive.
Telephone: 949-790-6300.
Facsimile: 949-790-6301.
Austin, Texas Office: 301 Congress Avenue, Suite 1200.
Telephone: 512-477-5495.
Facsimile: 512-477-5813.
Denver, Colorado Office: 370 Interlocken Bld., Suite 500.
Telephone: 303-410-2000.
Facsimile: 303-410-2199.
Washington, D.C. Office: 701 Pennsylvania Avenue, NW, Suite 220.
Telephone: 202-220-6000.
Facsimile: 202-824-0949.
London, England Office: Brobeck Hale and Dorr International, Hasilwood House, 60 Bishopsgate, London EC2N 4AJ.
Telephone: 011 44 171 638 6688.
Facsimile: 011 44 171 638 5888.

OFFICE LEADER

Gregory A. Markel

(See Next Column)

BROBECK, PHLEGER & HARRISON LLP, *New York—Continued*

PARTNERS

Luci Staller Altman
Gerard R. Boyce
Ellen B. Corenswet
Lawrence E. Fenster
Nigel L. Howard
Beth D. Jacob
Christopher P. Johnson
Kenneth J. King
Alexander D. Lynch
Eric Simonson

OF COUNSEL

Gail J. Berritt
Joy F. Forster
Charna L. Gerstenhaber
Kenneth R. McVay (Not admitted in NY)
Kelly L. Morron
Nancy I. Ruskin

ASSOCIATES

Francis S. Chlapowski
Lawrence H. Cooke II
Adam M. Dinow
Daryn A. Grossman
Arthur L. Hoag
Mark J. Horowitz
Nicole M. Hunn
Kenneth L. Johnson
Scott L. Kaufman
Jzaneen Lalani
Diane E. Lifton
Brian B. Margolis
Caryn Mazin
Barbara A. Milnamow (Not admitted in NY)
David J. Pashman
Erin Peyton
Nanci I. Prado
Michael Racanelli
Poojitha G. Rao
Ronit Setton
Alan N. Shapiro
John J. Sivolella
Karen Solimando
Laurie J. Sternberg
Ann D. Thompson
Lisa Tsou
Rishi A. Varma
Daniel Weisberg (Not admitted in NY)
Jeremy S. Westin
Nicole L. Woo
Babak Yaghmaie (Not admitted in NY)

For full biographical listings, see the Martindale-Hubbell Law Directory

BROWN RAYSMAN MILLSTEIN FELDER & STEINER LLP (AV)

120 West Forty-Fifth Street, 10036
Telephone: 212-944-1515
Fax: 212-840-2429
URL: http://www.brownraysman.com
Los Angeles, California Office: 1880 Century Park East, Suite 711.
Telephone: 310-712-8300.
Fax: 310-712-8383.
Hartford, Connecticut Office: City Place II, 185 Asylum Street, 10th Floor.
Telephone: 860-275-6400.
Fax: 860-275-6410.
Morristown, New Jersey Office: 55 Madison Avenue, Suite 70.
Telephone: 973-285-3222.
Fax: 973-538-0503.
Uniondale, New York Office: EAB Plaza, West Tower, 6th Floor, 11556-0615 (Long Island).
Telephone: 516-522-2520.
Fax: 516-522-2731.

MEMBERS OF FIRM

Richard Raysman
Peter Brown
Julian S. Millstein
Barry G. Felder
Jeffrey B. Steiner
Robert M. Unger
Edward A. Pisacreta
Catherine M. McGrath
Kenneth M. Block
Henry J. Silberberg
Kenneth A. Adler
Rand G. Boyers
Jeffrey D. Neuburger
Norman H. Roos (Resident, Hartford, Connecticut Office)
Benzion J. Westreich (Resident, Los Angeles, California Office)
Monte E. Wetzler (Resident, Hartford, Connecticut Office)
Sarah Hewitt
R. Kenneth MacCallum
Andrew L. Kramer
Jeffrey P. Weingart
J. Christopher Giancarlo
Maureen Massa
Scott A. Weinberg
Seth H. Ostrow
Harold A. Flegelman
Carla E. Craig
William E. Bandon, III
Beverly W. Garofalo (Resident, Hartford, Connecticut Office)
Russell V. D'Italia (Resident, Morristown, New Jersey Office)
Frank J. De Rosa
Stuart Bressman
Robert D. Gilbert (Resident, Hartford, Connecticut Office)
Fredric M. Sanders

COUNSEL

Michael A. Gerber
Yukio Kashiba
H. David Leventhal (Resident, Hartford, Connecticut Office)
Edward P. Tolley, Jr.
Jonathan T. Kaplan

ASSOCIATES

Samuel L. Molinari (Resident, Hartford, Connecticut Office)
Shoshana B. Botnick (Resident, Los Angeles, California Office)
James R. Kinyon (Resident, Hartford, Connecticut Office)
M. Lauren McGill
Candace M. Cunningham (Resident, Hartford, Connecticut Office)
Melanie Finkel
Nancy J. Mertzel
Timothy J. Martin (Resident, Los Angeles, California Office)
Louis Greco
Lauren E. McCollester
Frank A. Pugliese
Anthony J. Natoli
Marc S. Roth
Brooks Sandeman Clark

(See Next Column)

ASSOCIATES (Continued)

Susan L. Loring Crane
John A. Gliedman
Diane Duhaime (Resident, Hartford, Connecticut Office)
John C. Ohman
Mitchell L. Fishberg (Resident, Hartford, Connecticut Office)
Robert S. Mower
Jeremy Pomeroy
Kevin C. Taylor
Randy Ilene Monkarsh
Jill Amanda Westmoreland
Michael D. Maline
Larry Liberchuk (Not admitted in NY)
Matthew D. Moren
Marc Seewald Brodsky
Jenevra Georgini
Ira Wurcel
John M. Mrsich
Leo K. Chen
Rebecca A. Tapie
Andrew E. Miller
Robert Siedlecki, Jr. (Resident, Hartford, Connecticut Office)
Laura Land Sigal
Irene E. Bassock (Resident, Hartford, Connecticut Office)
Edward J. Leen
Steve A. Semerdjian
Karen D. Nemeth
John M. Strong
Jason R. Goldstein
Jason S. Stevens
Herbert H. Detrick II
Ronald M. Leshnower
Toni S. Jordan
Richard L. Green (Resident, Hartford, Connecticut Office)
Lindsay Mara Schoen
Wayne R. Kaufman
Viktoria Makarevich
John D. Gigante
Vincent Laspisa III
Kristen J. Mathews
Dax Scharfstein
John F. Greco

For full biographical listings, see the Martindale-Hubbell Law Directory

BROWN & WOOD LLP (AV)

One World Trade Center, 10048-0557
Telephone: 212-839-5300
Cable Address: "Browoodlaw"
Telex: 127324.
Telecopier: 212-839-5599
URL: http://www.brownwoodlaw.com
San Francisco, California Office: 555 California Street, 94104-1715.
Telephone: 415-772-1200.
Washington, D.C. Office: 1666 K Street, N.W., Suite 700, 20006-1208.
Telephone: 202-533-1300.
Los Angeles, California Office: 10877 Wilshire Boulevard, 90024.
Telephone: 310-443-0200.
London, England Office: Brown & Wood, Princes Court, 7 Princes Street, EC2R 8AQ.
Telephone: 011-44-171-778-1800.
Hong Kong Office: Brown & Wood, Bank of China Tower, 1 Garden Road, Central.
Telephone: 011-852-2509-7888.
Beijing, China Office: 3527, China World Tower, China World Trade Center 1, Jian Guo Men Wai Avenue.
Telephone: 011-8610-6505-5359; 011-8610-6505-1807.

MEMBERS OF FIRM

Thomas J. Amico
Joseph W. Armbrust, Jr.
John Arnholz (Resident at Washington, D.C. Office)
Peter D. Arnold
Lawrence A. Bauer
I. Scott Bieler
Margaret E. Boswell (Resident at London, England Office)
Michael P. Braun
Nicholas R. Brown
Frank P. Bruno
Regina L. Bryant-Fields (Resident at San Francisco Office)
Scott P.F. Cameron (Resident at London, England Office)
Neil Campbell (Resident at Hong Kong Office)
Craig E. Chapman
Jay Gordon Cohen (Resident at Washington, D.C. Office)
John M. Costello, Jr.
Kenneth T. Cote (Resident at Hong Kong Office)
Christina Nelson Crosby (Resident at San Francisco Office)
J. Gerard Cummins
Lori Anne Czepiel (Not admitted in NY)
Bennett I. Deutsch
Robert J. Donatucci
Michael P. Doran (Resident at London, England Office)
James Kevin Dougherty
R. Michael Durrer (Resident at London, England Office)
Cecilia P. Dyba (Resident at Los Angeles Office)
Stephen B. Esko
Jeff Feigelson
Edward J. Fine
Michael L. Fitzgerald
Connie M. Friesen
Edward E. Gainor (Resident at Washington D.C. Office)
A. J. Alexis Gelinas
Clifford M. Gerber (Resident at San Francisco Office)
Howard G. Godwin, Jr.
Martin E. Gold
William M. Goldman
Frank R. Goldstein (Resident at Washington, D.C. Office)
James A. Gouwar
Joshua G. Grunat
Robert P. Hardy
Susan D. Harrington
Eric S. Haueter (Resident at San Francisco Office)
Roger J. Hawke
Robert M. Huber (Resident at Washington, D.C. Office)
John K. Hughes (Resident at Washington, D.C. Office)
Thomas A. Humphreys
Alan L. Jakimo
Jack I. Kantrowitz
Cathy M. Kaplan
Brian M. Kaplowitz
Michael A. King
Henry S. Klaiman
Laurin Blumenthal Kleiman
Howard M. Kleinman
Sharon A. Knight
Siegfried P. Knopf
Michael T. Kohler
Mark J. Kowal
Robert M. Kreitman
Allan Neil Krinsman
David R. Kuney (Resident at Washington, D.C. Office)
Susan D. Lewis

(See Next Column)

Brown & Wood LLP—*Continued*

MEMBERS OF FIRM (Continued)

F. Lee Liebolt, Jr.
Dale W. Lum (Resident at San Francisco Office)
Thomas J. Lyden (Resident at Washington, D.C. Office)
John A. MacKinnon
Renwick D. Martin
William R. Massey
Gerald J. McGovern (Resident at San Francisco Office)
Joseph McLaughlin
Christopher B. Mead (Resident at London, England Office)
Peter J. Michel
Jonathan B. Miller
Henry F. Minnerop
William D. Morrison (Resident at London, England Office)
Patricia A. Murphy
John H. Newman
Jaemin Park (Resident at Washington, D.C. Office)
Michael P. Peck
Edward F. Petrosky, Jr.
A. Robert Pietrzak
Paul C. Pringle (Los Angeles and San Francisco Offices)
A. Francis Robinson, Jr.
Carlos A. Rodriguez
Daniel M. Rossner
R. J. Ruble
John Russell (Resident at London, England Office)
James J. Sabella
Lee S. Saltzman
Charles J. Sanders
Homer D. Schaaf
Michael J. Schiavone
Eileen Caulfield Schwab
Yoshiki Shimada
Marc L. Silverman
Peter T. Simor
R. Nicholas Singh (Resident at Washington, D.C. Office)
Norman D. Slonaker
Thomas R. Smith, Jr.
Thomas McCarthy Souther
H. John Steele (Resident at Washington, D.C. Office)
Andrew W. Stern
Elizabeth Storch
William E. Sudow (Resident at Washington, D.C. Office)
Eric D. Tashman (Resident at San Francisco Office)
Michael F. Taylor
Lawrence C. Tondel
Peter J. Toren
Max Von Hollweg
E. Mark Walsh (Resident at London, England Office)
Gail G. Watson
David J. Weinberger
Judith Welcom
Jonathan P. Williams
L. Markus Wiltshire
Michael G. Wolfson
Patti T. Wu
James D. Zirin

OF COUNSEL

Charles J. Johnson, Jr.
Robert L. Mitchell
John A. Quisenberry
Karel Westerling

COUNSEL

James L. Copeland (Resident at San Francisco Office)
Louis A. Evans
Karen M. Feher
Ellen W. Harris
Dennis C. Hensley (Not admitted in NY)
Joseph V. Jest (Resident at Washington, D.C. Office)
Neil J. Kaplan
Darcy M. Katris
John F. P. Lamb
Steven A. Malsin
Jeanne M. Quinn Marks
Taisa Markus
Gisele C. Rainer (Resident at San Francisco Office)
Tuuli-Ann Ristkok
Robert J. Robinson
Michael S. Sackheim
Timothy Sadler (Resident at Washington, D.C. Office)
Sarah M. Starkweather
Brenda F. Szydlo
David Toren
Charles W. Tricomi

ASSOCIATES

Tara Harkins Adams
Michael P. Ashkar
Anjali G. Asnanee
Glenn F. Baity (Resident at San Francisco Office)
David S. Bakst (Resident at Hong Kong Office)
Cristina Basso (Resident at London, England Office)
William H. Boericke
Angela Borreggine
Robert J. Borzone, Jr.
Kimberly H. Bothner (Not admitted in NY)
Jonathan J. Brennan
Robert A. Briedis
Michael Burke
Peter J. Carbone
Lucia A. Cardone
Theresa Mary Cetina
Aileen Chang
Cynthia Cheung (Resident at London, England Office)
Anna H. Choe
Jennifer Coates
Susan Comparato
Amanda Lydia Cook
Michael Cummings
Diane Daltner
Susan M. Davies
Nicholas H. De Baun
Stacy R. Dees (Resident at Washington, D.C. Office)
Jennifer A. DeMarrais
Stephen P. Diamond, Jr.
Henry Haihua Ding (Resident at Beijing, China Office)
Elaine Donato
Madeleine J. Dowling
Kevin P. Downes
Lita Mercedes Dwight
Jamie R. Eisner
Hays Ellisen (Not admitted in NY)
Jason S. Elphick (Not admitted in the United States) (Legal Consultant on the laws of Australia)
Barbara Jean Endres (Resident at Washington, D.C. Office)
Nancy Lynn Epstein
Amy H. Farris (Not admitted in NY)
John C. Feldkamp (Not admitted in NY)
Bradley S. Fenner (Resident at San Francisco Office)
Scott J. Ferretti
David R. Fishkin
Matthew J. Fitzgerald (Resident at Washington, D.C. Office)
Barbara Fortson
Andrew F. Fowler
Hugh V. Frame (Resident at London, England Office)
Julie Freeman (Resident at London, England Office)
Christine R. Fryer
Kenji Fujimoto
Samir A. Gandhi

(See Next Column)

ASSOCIATES (Continued)

Jennifer M. Gaylord
Patricia Gelfond
Susanne Gennusa
Brenda L. Gill
Daniel J. Glusker
Michael D. Golden
David B. Gordon
Kimberly W. Gordon (Resident at Washington, D.C. Office)
David S. Gronsman
Robert J. Gross (Resident at Washington, D.C. Office)
Robyn L. Helmlinger (Not admitted in NY)
Nick A. Henderson (Resident at Washington, D.C. Office)
Steven Z. Hodaszy
Nick G. Holcombe
David E. Howe (Resident at London, England Office)
James Y. Huang
Kimberly A. Johns
Jeffrey R. Johnson (Resident at Washington, D.C. Office)
Peter Kambeseles
Phillip John Kardis (Resident at Washington, D.C. Office)
Elizabeth Keeley
Peter J. Kenny
William Kilgallen
Heather H. Kim
Helen Kim (Resident at London, England Office)
Taehun Kim
Edward A. King
Darius R. Kingsley (Resident at Washington, D.C. Office)
Cormac Kissane (Resident at London, England Office)
Myongsu Kong
Tan-Yuan Kueh (Not admitted in NY)
Jason Tzu-Cheng Kuo (Resident at Hong Kong Office)
Stephan R. Kuppenheimer
Cynthia Lai
Lisa B. Lai (Resident at San Francisco Office)
Q. Gwynn Lam
Hyeon Lee
James Y. Lee
Jennifer W. Lewis (Resident at Washington, D.C. Office)
Huanting "Tim" Li (Resident at Hong Kong Office)
Julianne M. Linder
Edward B. Locke
Christine K. Loo
Adam Nicolas Lyle (Resident at Hong Kong Office)
Elizabeth B. Lynch
Drew Malakoff
Shifra Malina
Robert Mandell
Michael Markson (Not admitted in NY)
Christina M. Marshall
Jorge Martin (Resident at San Francisco Office)
Paul Matthews (Resident at London, England Office)
Susan Mattisinko
Jean Marie McConney
Colleen Heather McDonald (Resident at San Francisco Office)
Stephen H. McElhennon (Resident at Washington, D.C. Office)
Christopher W. McGovern (Resident at San Francisco Office)
Daniel A. McLaughlin
Matthew C. McMurdo
María De Los Angeles Meléndez
Stephanie K. Meth
Byung Joon Min (Resident at Washington, D.C. Office)
Ellen R. Moring
Peter C. Morreale (Resident at Washington, D.C. Office)
Kalinka H. Moudrova
H. L. Scott Nearing (Not admitted in NY)
Vincent A. Nicoletta
Mark O. Norell
Coleman A. Nutter
James O'Connor
Alastair Onglingswan
Christina M. Pan-Marshall
Steven J. Pappas
Jamie A. Patinelli
David A. Perl
Kevin Andrew Pollack
Mark Allan Poole
Ann Marie Prévost
Arthur Isom Prostick
Lucy Purkiss (Resident at London, England Office)
Erik F. Remmler
Edward D. Ricchiuto
James G. Richards
Andrew Robertson (Not admitted in NY)
Dorothy M. Robins (Resident at San Francisco Office)
Albert M. Rodriguez
Steven Rosenthal
Laurence J. Salva
Elena E. Salzman
Emily E. Sanderson
Trina Sandoval
James P. Sawicz
Edward Scharfenberg
John Schwartz
Bartholomew A. Sheehan III
Francis M. Sheehan
Elissa Jill Shendalman
Benjamin E. Sherwin
Kimberly K. Short
Randall Eron Shy (Resident at Hong Kong Office)
Nizam M. Siddiq
Marian Staton Singer (Not admitted in NY)
Steven Sirotic
Trisha L. Smith (Not admitted in NY)
Zafar Sobhan
Laurel J. Southworth
Laurence C. Stein
Jeffrey W. Stewart
Y. Ping Sun
Amy Sunshine
Marina C. Szteinbok
David S. Tan (Resident at San Francisco Office)
Michelle Taylor (Resident at Hong Kong Office)
Hanna Tedla Teshome (Resident at Washington, D.C. Office)
Michael J. Toke (Resident at San Francisco Office)
Kirk Tong
Robert Charles Torch (Resident at London, England Office)
Paul S. Tufaro (Not admitted in NY)
Mark H. Vacha
Nancy S. Vann
Jason C. Vargelis
Milton A. Vescovacci (Not admitted in NY)
John R. Vetterli
Christina Voulgarelis
Scott B. Waldman
Mark G. Walsh
Cheng Wang (Not admitted in NY)
Craig Harrison Weise (Resident at Washington, D.C. Office)
Carolyn D. Wember
Michael Read Whipple
Jeffrey S. Wiseman
Thomas W. Yang
Thomas Yih
James Z. Zhang (Resident at Washington, D.C. Office)
Marianne K. Zychal

For full biographical listings, see the Martindale-Hubbell Law Directory

New York—Continued

CADWALADER, WICKERSHAM & TAFT (AV)

100 Maiden Lane, 10038
Telephone: 212-504-6000
Fax: 212-504-6666
Email: cwtinfo@cwt.com *URL:* http://www.cadwalader.com
New York Conference Center: 350 Park Avenue, 10022.
Telephone: 212-415-8300.
Fax: 212-415-8350.
Charlotte, North Carolina Office: Suite 2400, 227 West Trade Street, 28202.
Telephone: 704-348-5100.
Fax: 704-348-5200.
Washington, D.C. Office: 1333 New Hampshire Avenue, N.W., 20036.
Telephone: 202-862-2200.
Fax: 202-862-2400.
London, England Office: Gracechurch House, First Floor, 55 Gracechurch Street, EC3V OEE. Telephone 0171-456-8500.
Fax: 0171-456-8600.

MEMBERS OF FIRM

Richard A. Aborn
Charles M. Adelman
Fredric L. Altschuler
Maurine R. Bartlett
Peter G. Bergmann
Louis J. Bevilacqua
Dennis J. Block
Steven G. Brody
John J. Busillo
Derrick D. Cephas
Kathy Hirata Chin
Steven N. Cohen
Kenneth P. Coleman
Barry J. Dichter
Michael G. Dolan
Scott E. Eckas
Gerald A. Eppner
David W. Feeney
David C. L. Frauman
John F. Fritts
Michael S. Gambro
Karen B. Gelernt
Karsten P. Giesecke
Terence F. Gilheany
Donald G. Glascoff, Jr.
Anna H. Glick
Michael M. Gordon
Bronislaw E. Grala
Edmund W. Granski, Jr.
H. Peter Haveles, Jr.
Howard R. Hawkins, Jr.
Jonathan M. Hoff
Brian Hoffmann
Jennifer B. Jordan
Denice Rassas Krez
Lawrence A. Larose
Robert C. Lawrence, III
Robert O. Link, Jr.
Robert F. McDonough
Jay H. McDowell
William P. McInerney
David S. Miller
David S. Mitchell
Paul W. Mourning
Gregory M. Petrick
Jonathan D. Polkes
Patrick T. Quinn
Edwin David Robertson
Roger W. Rosendahl
Michael C. Ryan
Michael J. Sage
Ira J. Schacter
Richard M. Schetman
Edmund R. Schroeder
Jordan M. Schwartz
Francis J. Serbaroli
Ray I. Shirazi
Jeffrey Q. Smith
Mitchell I. Sonkin
Debra Brown Steinberg
Lary Stromfeld
Linda Z. Swartz
Robert L. Vitale
Jonathan M. Wainwright
Malcolm P. Wattman
W. Christopher White
Bruce R. Zirinsky
John M. Zizzo

SENIOR COUNSEL

Grant B. Hering
Arnold J. Zurcher, Jr.

COUNSEL

Jack Adelman
Jeffrey S. Ashendorf
Jeanne P. Bolger
Harvey P. Dale
Allen Curtis Greer, II
William Jordan, Jr.
Steven Lenkowsky
William J. Moss
William J. Natbony
John J. O'Grady, III
Albert P. Pacelli
Alan M. Parness
Renata C. Pompa
William Schwartz
Jerome Shelby
Cynthia A. Smith
Harvey M. Spear
Burton Spivak
Joan A. Stumpf
Susan Knapp Szoke

SPECIAL COUNSEL

Andrea Paretts Ascher
John H. Bae
Barbara T. Barrantes
Michael R. Barz
Susan R. Chalfin
Mary Louise Guttmann
Lawrence D. Fruchtman
Jason M. Halper
Michael S. Himmel
Richard C. Hoffman (Not admitted in NY)
Lech R. Kalembka
David H. Kanefsky
Susan Jacobs Lobel
Peter C. Manbeck
Brian T. McGovern
Shimon A. Rosenfeld
Mary Lou Schwemle
Christine A. Spletzer
Toula Stroumbakis
Soo Kyong Yi

CONSULTING

Genevieve Lam Fraiman
Richard L. Lavoie

ASSOCIATES

Athena E. Alexander
R. Colby Allsbrook
Richard M. Andrade
Rick B. Antonoff
Michael B. Arouh
Robert Arroyo
Mabél Arteaga
Ingrid M. Bagby
Christina M. Baltz
Vincent Basulto
Kyle C. Bisceglie
Joshua M. Bloomstein
Melissa M. Bradley
Colin M. Breeze
Eric Burner
William S. Busch

(See Next Column)

ASSOCIATES (Continued)

George Caballero
Mary Ann Campo
Nadine Cancell
Lawrence A. Ceriello
Elizabeth C. Cheng
Andrew E. Cherrick (Not admitted in NY)
Jason A. Cohen
Elizabeth A. Cooney
Thomas M. Cosenza
Michael J. Damast
Patricia L. Demaras
Harry C. Demiris Jr.
James F. De Varso
Susan Felice DiCicco
Matthew M. Donaher
Stephen Doody
Virginia L. Dyer
Marsena M. Farris
Dino Fazlibegu
Matthew S. Fenster
Robert C. Fermann
Tom M. Fini
Maureen A. Flanigan
Jason Dwight Fraser
Douglas L. Friedman
Martín Alejandro Furlong (A Legal Consultant on the Laws of the Country)
Julienne K. Goldfine
Stuart N. Goldstein
Laura C. Gonzalez
Garry Gordon
Peter Gottlieb
Karen A. Gray
Susan Sieger Grimm
Jonathan R. Gross
Jack I. Habert
Vincent M. Haley
Christopher Hart-Zafra
Stephen G. Hauck
Robert N. Hay, Jr.
Lawrence Holzman
Joon P. Hong
Faith T. Hudnell
Jennifer L. Hurley
Charles M. Hurr
Christine P. Jackson
David J. Janow
Edwin C. Jean (Not admitted in NY)
Richard C. Jensen, Jr.
Mitchell Kahn (Not admitted in NY)
Dina Kapur
Robin J. Katz
Gerard C. Keegan, Jr.
Paul A. Keenan
Aaron H. Kim
Mary Jane Kimmeth
Michael P. King (Not admitted in NY)
Matthew I. Kliegman
Douglas I. Koff
Todd R. Kornfeld
Nikolai Krylov
Pamela Landman
Ronald N. Lanning, Jr.
Robin L. Larmer
C. Mark Laskay
Werner R. Lehfellner
Deirdre A. Long
Elena G. Madariaga (Not Admitted in United States) (Legal Consultant)
Gary Malhotra
Deborah Lichtenstein Marcus
Ian S. Marx
Reese Mason
Nikiforos Mathews
John Maithya Mbiti (Not Admitted in United States)
Michael A. McCormack
Hugh M. McDonald
Patrick M. McGuirk
Marlene Y. McLarty
Todd F. McTavish
Keith W. Miller
William P. Mills, III
Paula Mott
Gwendolyn Moy
William Timothy Moy
Jacqueline C. Maduneme
Negar Nabavinejad
Jeanne Naughton-Carr
Lars R. Norell
Warner D. Norton
Loren Mark Osher
Bernard Park
Lisa J. Pauquette
Melissa M. Pearsall
Colin Pennycooke
Maria J. Petti
Drew C. Phillips
Kevin T. Pigott
Eric W. Plotkin
Gary D. Pogeler
Frank Polverino
Keren Porter
Lisa S. Post
Poppy B. Quattlebaum
Mark F. Radom
Niloufar Rafi-Kian (Not Admitted in United States) (Legal Consultant)
Felix B. Reznick
Charles G. Roberts
Suzanne J. Romajas
Simon C. Roosevelt
Rivkah Rothschild
Beth J. Rosen
Jeffrey Y. Rotblat
Michelle L. Roth
Jason S. Rozes
Andrew Ruskin
Cindy D. Salvo
Barbara Sands
Frank J. Scaturro
Andrew P Schriever
James E. Schwartz
Gregory A. Segal
Timothy P. Selby
Viqar M. Shariff
James P. Sheesley, II
Eric James Sheridan
Elisa Shevlin-Rizzo
Anna K. Sils
Amit Singh
Adam D. Solowsky
C. Becket Sorce
Lee J. Stoller
Joseph P. Sverchek
Mary Elizabeth Taylor
Sharif Touray
Winnie Tsang
Anthony J. Tuths
Robert L. Ughetta
Joseph P. Vidulich
Ron William Walden
Lance A. Warrick
Neil J. Weidner
J. Christopher Winckler
Pasha Zargarof
Karyn B. Zeldman

CHARLOTTE, NORTH CAROLINA PARTNERS

James P. Carroll
Steven N. Cohen
Richard Madden, Jr.
Christopher M. McDermott

CHARLOTTE, NORTH CAROLINA COUNSEL

Robinson O. Everett

CHARLOTTE, NORTH CAROLINA SPECIAL COUNSEL

Henry A. LaBrun

CHARLOTTE, NORTH CAROLINA ASSOCIATES

Anderson Drew Caperton
Marvin S. Cash
Julie Circio
David A. Doughty
Paul C. Hurdle, III
Andrew Martin Johnson
Bradley H. Johnson
Heather R. Kushner
Francisco J. Linares
Patrick M. McNeely
Geoffrey R. Maibohm
Holly S. Marcille

(See Next Column)

CADWALADER, WICKERSHAM & TAFT—*Continued*

CHARLOTTE, NORTH CAROLINA ASSOCIATES (Continued)

Evan R. Morrison
Eric James Ourada
Michael J. Schepis
Wendy L. Spanbauer
Thomas M. Tracy
Robert W. Watson, Jr.
Phillip A. Wertz
Evan N. Wolkofsky

WASHINGTON, D.C. PARTNERS

Frederick R. Anderson
Raymond Banoun
Charles E. Bryan
James P. Carroll
Diana R. de Brito
Mark C. Ellenberg
Mark P. Howe
Laurence S. Kirsch
Kenneth Klein
Edwin L. Lyon
Daniel J. Mulcahy
David F. Williams

WASHINGTON, D.C. SENIOR COUNSEL

Wendell B. Alcorn, Jr.
Daniel T. Brooks
Robert T. Lasky
James W. Moorman
James A. Rossi

WASHINGTON, D.C. COUNSEL

Peter M. Dodson
Julius Kaplan
Marvin M. Solomon

WASHINGTON, D.C. SPECIAL COUNSEL

Joyce J. Gorman
Thomas R. Petty

WASHINGTON, D.C. ASSOCIATES

Cheryl D. Barnes
Karen Brown-McAfee
Robert A. Davis, Jr.
Geraldine E. Edens
Steven J. Heim
Carol Ann Johnson
Gregg S. Jubin
Earl Allan Lariscy
Stephanie J. Meltzer
Stephen P. Mullery, III
Helen C. Rogers
Kathleen Seungsun Kim
Seth B. Shapiro
Jonathan R. Stone
Elizabeth T. Van Horn

LONDON, ENGLAND PARTNERS

James J. Croke, Jr.
Paul J. Griffin
Russell L. Jacobs
James H.D. Roome
James T. Starky
John S. Walker
Andrew J.O. Wilkinson

LONDON, ENGLAND SPECIAL COUNSEL

Alan W. Lawrence

LONDON, ENGLAND ASSOCIATES

Jeanette Best
Nena Bhandari
Yvette Croucher
Nicholas Dunstone
Richard C. East
Vinay B. Ganga
Vicki C. Hazelden
Vincent T. Keaveny
Sean MacGloin
Ian McKim
Abigail Milburn
Lyndon E. Norley
Sarah J. Squires
Richard Streat
James Mark Warbey
Matthew Williams

For full biographical listings, see the Martindale-Hubbell Law Directory

CAHILL GORDON & REINDEL (AV)

A Partnership including a Professional Corporation
80 Pine Street, 10005-1702
Telephone: 212-701-3000
Facsimile: 212-269-5420
Confirmation: 212-701-3557
European Office: 19 rue Francois 1er, 75008, Paris, France.
Telephone: 33.1-47.20.10.50.
Facsimile: 33.1-47.23.06.38.
District of Columbia Office: 1990 K Street, N.W., Washington, D.C., 20006-1103.
Telephone: 202-862-8900.
Facsimile: 202-862-8958.

MEMBERS OF FIRM

Floyd Abrams
L. Howard Adams
Robert A. Alessi
Roger Andrus
Helene R. Banks
Michael A. Becker
Susan Buckley
Kevin J. Burke
P. Kevin Castel
James J. Clark
Walter C. Cliff (P.C.)
Benjamin J. Cohen
W. Leslie Duffy
Patricia Farren
Joan Murtagh Frankel
Bart Friedman
Ciro A. Gamboni
William B. Gannett
Charles A. Gilman
Stephen A. Greene
Robert M. Hallman
William M. Hartnett
Craig M. Horowitz
David G. Januszewski
Thomas J. Kavaler
Lawrence A. Kobrin
Immanuel Kohn
Edward P. Krugman
Geoffrey E. Liebmann
William T. Lifland
Michael Macris
Jonathan I. Mark
Gerard M. Meistrell
Roger Meltzer
Clifford L. Michel
Michael E. Michetti
John P. Mitchell
Athy A. Mobilia
Mathias E. Mone
Donald J. Mulvihill (Resident Partner, Washington, D.C. Office)
Kenneth W. Orce
Roy L. Regozin
Dean Ringel
James C. Robinson
Thorn Rosenthal
Jonathan A. Schaffzin

(See Next Column)

MEMBERS OF FIRM (Continued)

John J. Schuster
Howard G. Sloane
Laurence T. Sorkin
Leonard A. Spivak
Gerald S. Tanenbaum
Jonathan D. Thier
John A. Tripodoro
Robert Usadi
George Wailand
Glenn J. Waldrip, Jr.
Gary W. Wolf
John R. Young
Daniel J. Zubkoff

SENIOR COUNSEL

Joseph P. Conway
David R. Hyde
Denis McInerney
Irwin Schneiderman
John R. Vaughan
Ralph O. Winger

COUNSEL

Corydon B. Dunham
Philip A. Heimowitz

EUROPEAN COUNSEL

Freddy Dressen (Paris, France Office)

SENIOR ATTORNEYS

John H. de Boisblanc
Kirsten Emigholz
Joanne M. Hawkins
Mary A. Stokinger

For full biographical listings, see the Martindale-Hubbell Law Directory

CHADBOURNE & PARKE LLP (AV)

30 Rockefeller Plaza, 10112
Telephone: 212-408-5100
Facsimile: 212-541-5369
Washington, D.C. Office: 1200 New Hampshire Avenue, N.W., 20036.
Telephone: 202-974-5600.
Facsimile: 202-974-5602.
Los Angeles, California Office: 601 South Figueroa Street, 90017.
Telephone: 213-892-1000.
Facsimile: 213-622-9865.
London, England Affiliate Office: Chadbourne & Parke, a multinational partnership of Registered Foreign Lawyers and Solicitors, Regis House, 45 King William Street, London, EC4R 9AN.
Telephone: 44-171-337-8000.
Facsimile: 44-171-337-8001.
Moscow, Russia Office: 52/5 Kosmodamianskaya Naberezhnaya, 113054.
Telephone: 7095-974-2424.
Facsimile: 7095-974-2425. International satellite lines via U.S.:
Telephone: 212-408-1190.
Facsimile: 212-408-1199.
Hong Kong, China Office: 1701A The Hong Kong Club Building, 3A Chater Road, Central, Hong Kong.
Telephone: 852-2842-5400.
Facsimile: 852-2521-7527.

MEMBERS OF FIRM

Marc A. Alpert
John T. Baecher
Stuart D. Baker
Barbara L. Becker
Thomas E. Bezanson
Laura M. Brank
Mary Rose Brusewitz
William G. Cavanagh
Peter R. Chaffetz
A. Robert Colby
Andrew C. Coronios
William S. D'Amico (Resident in Washington, DC)
Barry A. Dinaburg
Vincent Dunn
Peter F. Fitzgerald (Resident in Washington, DC)
Douglas M. Fried
Dennis J. Friedman
Lynne E. Gedanken (Resident in London)
Whitney I. Gerard
Andrew A. Giaccia (Resident in Washington, DC)
Charles F. Gibbs
Robert J. Gillispie
Marjorie M. Glover
Cornelius J. Golden, Jr. (Resident in Washington, DC)
William Greason (Resident in London)
Morton E. Grosz
Deborah L. Guider
Thomas J. Hall
Kenneth W. Hansen (Resident in Washington, DC)
Jay R. Henneberry (Resident in Los Angeles, CA)
Peter N. Hillman
Charles E. Hord, III
Peter K. Ingerman
Dean L. Jarmel
Emily F. Johnson
Jerome C. Katz
Peter R. Kolyer
Kenneth J. Langan (Resident in Los Angeles, CA)
Tracey W. Laws (Resident in Washington, DC)
Richard M. Leder
Eric J. Lobenfeld
Gregory M. Loss
Keith Martin (Resident in Washington, DC)
Malcolm E. Martin
Bernard W. McCarthy
Thomas J. McCormack
Roy K. Meilman
Thomas C. Meriam
J. Allen Miller
Garyowen P. Morrisroe
Richard J. Ney (Resident in Los Angeles, CA)
John Nyhan (Not admitted in NY)
Charles K. O'Neill
Daniel J. O'Neill
John B. O'Sullivan (Resident in Washington, DC)
Henry J. Oechler, Jr.
William K. Perry (Resident in Washington, DC)
Nancy W. Pierce
Bruce J. Rader
David M. Raim (Resident in Washington, DC)
Thomas E. Riley
Anthony M. Roncalli
Lawrence Rosenberg
Mikhail A. Rozenberg (Resident in Moscow)
Andrea N. Satty
Ira J. Schaefer
Donald Schapiro
Leslie John Schreyer
David K. Schumacher (Resident in Washington, DC)
David M. Schwartzbaum

(See Next Column)

CHADBOURNE & PARKE LLP, *New York—Continued*

MEMBERS OF FIRM (Continued)

Robert A. Schwinger
Howard Seife
Claude S. Serfilippi
Robert F. Shapiro (Resident in Washington, DC)
Bruce G. Sheffler
Karina Siegel
Edward P. Smith
Richard Sonkin
Donald I Strauber
Eugene R. Sullivan, Jr.
Chaim Wachsberger
David L. Wallace
Paul L. Weber (Resident in London)
David M. Wilf
Drew M. Wintringham
Ellen H. Woodbury (Resident in Washington, DC)
Mary T. Yelenick
Nancy A. Zajac
George E. Zeitlin
N. Theodore Zink, Jr.

COUNSEL

Noam Ayali
Peter N. Bassano
Alberto L. Calafell
Peter K. Eck
Lynn N. Hargis (Resident in Washington, DC)
William J. Kelley, III (Resident in Los Angeles, CA)
Lauren D. Kelly
James C. La Forge
Susan C. Maxson (Resident in Washington, DC)
Wm. Colm McKeveny
Don J. Mros (Resident in Washington, DC)
Talbert I. Navia
Jeffrey A. Robins
Lawrence E. Savell
Steven C. Schwartz
H. Hedley Stothers, Jr.
Carl Thomas (Resident in Los Angeles, CA)

OF COUNSEL

William M. Bradner, Jr.
David D. Brown, III
Stephen J. Buchman
Donald L. Deming
William J. Geen
Edmund E. Harvey (Resident in Washington, DC)
Charles B. Lauren
William H. Mathers
Edward C. McLean, Jr.
Paul G. Pennoyer, Jr.
Paul A. Randour
Zachary Shimer
Frank B. Stone
Peter M. Ward
Harold L. Warner, Jr.
John Wilcox

NEW YORK ASSOCIATES

Jerome B. Abelman
Ariel Acevedo
Allison M. Alcasabas
David S. Allinson
Lauren J. Aste (Not admitted in NY)
Marian E. Baldwin
Amy B. Beller
Thane Benedict IV
Romy E. Berk
Melissa J. Bernstein
Scott D. Berson
Jeffrey N. Blair
Nicholas S. Booke
Richard B. Brosnick
Thomas E. Butler
Aruna Chandra
Marjorie L. Cohen
Michelle R. Conde
Ana Elizabeth Cruz (Not admitted in NY)
Eyal Dagan
Russell DeClerck
Beth D. Diamond
Angela B. Dinger
Roland A. Diniz
Barry S. Eisler
Daniel J. Endick
Daniel E. Estrin
Arthur C. Fahlbusch, Jr.
Joseph G. Falcone
Jaime Fernandez de Zubiria
Lawrence Ferreira
Thomas T. Freedman, Jr.
Cecilia C. Froelich
Adriana Gardella (Not admitted in NY)
Kathleen E. Gardner
Eryn P. Gittleman
Jeffrey W. Gladstone
Robert S. Goldberg
Lauren S. Goodstein
Shari Leigh Gordon
Michael R. Graif
Véronique Gubser
Steven John Hawes
Aime L. Hendricks
Barbara E. Hoecklin
Timothy M. Hughes
Karen A. Iafe
Jennifer E. Johnson
Meera Dodeja Karwal
Scott A. Kislin
Evan M. Koster (Not admitted in NY)
Clara Krivoy
Charles F. Lacina
Danielle J. Pareja Langhoff
Mary Elizabeth LaRuffa
Joaquina Lazaro
Christian G. Le Brun (Not admitted in NY)
Sey-Hyo Lee
Michael S. Lemley
Emily W. S. Leong
Jennifer L. M. Levin
Jeff Lifur
Susan A. Littell
Stanley B. Lutz
Stephen J. Manetta
Frank L. McPhillips, Jr.
Brian A. Miller
Francis G. Montgomery
Nancy L. Montmarquet
Rita Anne O'Keeffe
Olusola Oyebolu
Julie Pape
Robert S. Pruyne
Kyle A. Reed
Sarah C. Richards (Not admitted in NY)
Andrew Rosenblatt
Zachary E. Samton
Alejandro R. San Miguel
Christine Pamela Searl
Anne-Marie Shelley
Kevin C. Smith
Jonathan M. Sobel
Lauren Solomon
Caroline Sorokoff
Tami Scarola Stark
Runa S. Stephen
Gregory Woo Hin Tan (Not admitted in the United States) (Legal Consultant on the Laws of England)
Alexander José Trías
Maura K. Tully
Shelby K. Ulan
Chryssa Valletta
Francisco Vazquez
Frank S. Vellucci
Patrick W. Vogel (Not admitted in the United States) (Legal Consultant on the Laws of Switzerland)

(*See Next Column*)

NEW YORK ASSOCIATES (Continued)

Danielle N. Voogt
Tina L. Waltke
Cindy L. Wenig
Daniel T. Whichard
Austin T. Wilkie
Phoebe A. Wilkinson

STAFF ATTORNEY

Linda Anne Sanislo

LEGAL SUPPORT PERSONNEL

Laura M. Schachter

For full biographical listings, see the Martindale-Hubbell Law Directory

---

CLEARY, GOTTLIEB, STEEN & HAMILTON (AV)

One Liberty Plaza, 10006
Telephone: 212-225-2000
Cable Address: "Clearglaw New York"
Telex:
WUI 62985
Facsimile: 212-225-3999
Washington, D.C. Office: 2000 Pennsylvania Avenue, N.W., Suite 9000, Washington, D.C. 20006-1801.
Telephone: 202-974-1500.
Paris, France Office: 41, Avenue de Friedland, 75008 Paris, France.
Telephone: 33-1-40-74-68-00.
Brussels, Belgium Office: Rue de la Loi 23, 1040 Brussels, Belgium.
Telephone: 32-2-287-2000.
London, England Office: City Place House, 55 Basinghall Street, London EC2V 5EH England.
Telephone: 44-71-614-2200.
Hong Kong Office: 39th Floor, Bank of China Tower, One Garden Road, Hong Kong.
Telephone: 852-2521-4122.
Tokyo, Japan Office: Cleary, Gottlieb, Steen & Hamilton Gaikokuho Jimubengoshi Jimusho, 20th Floor, Shin Kasumigaseki Building, 3-2, Kasumigaseki 3-Chome, Chiyoda-Ku, Tokyo 100-0013, Japan.
Telephone: 81-3-3595-3911.
Frankfurt, Germany Office: Main Tower, Neue Mainzer Strasse 52, 60311 Frankfurt am Main, Germany.
Telephone: 49-69-971-03-0.
Rome, Italy Office: Piazza di Spagna 15, 00187 Rome, Italy.
Telephone: 39-06-69-52-22-1.

George E. Cleary (1890-1981)
Leo Gottlieb (1896-1989)
Melvin C. Steen (1907-1992)
Fowler Hamilton (1911-1984)

COUNSEL

James G. Johnson, Jr.
Jerome E. Hyman
Mark W. Frawley, Jr.
George DeSipio
Walter S. Rothschild
Richard W. Hulbert
Thomas H. Hagoort
Sydney M. Cone, III
Richard Crawford Pugh
Alan Appelbaum
J. Speed Carroll
Peter S. Paine, Jr.
George J. Grumbach, Jr.
Louis Kahn
J. Webb Moniz

MEMBERS OF FIRM

George Weisz
Ned B. Stiles
Edwin B. Mishkin
Anthony C. Gooch
Roger W. Thomas
Peter Karasz
Mark A. Walker
Leslie B. Samuels
Allan G. Sperling
Peter H. Darrow
James F. Munsell
Sandra S. Weiksner
Evan A. Davis
Robert T. Greig
Laurent Alpert
Barry M. Fox
Victor I. Lewkow
Leslie N. Silverman
Robert L. Tortoriello
A. Richard Susko
Stephen H. Shalen
Richard F. Ziegler
Lee C. Buchheit
James M. Peaslee
Alan L. Beller
Thomas J. Moloney
David G. Sabel
Edward D. Kleinbard
Jonathan I. Blackman
William F. Gorin
Michael L. Ryan
Robert P. Davis
Yaron Z. Reich
Jaime A. El Koury
Steven G. Horowitz
Andrea G. Podolsky
Russell H. Pollack
Steven M. Loeb
Daniel S. Sternberg
Donald A. Stern
Craig B. Brod
Sheldon H. Alster
Wanda J. Olson
Tsunemasa Terai
Mitchell A. Lowenthal
Deborah M. Buell
Edward J. Rosen
James E. Millstein
Lawrence B. Friedman
Nicolas Grabar
Christopher E. Austin
Seth Grosshandler
William A. Groll
Janet L. Fisher
David L. Sugerman
Howard Zelbo
David E. Brodsky
Arthur H. Kohn
Ana Demel
Raymond B. Check
Richard J. Cooper
Jeffrey S. Lewis
Filip Moerman
Paul J. Shim
Yvette P. Teofan
Steven L. Wilner
Erika W. Nijenhuis
Lindsee P. Granfield
Andrés De la Cruz
David C. Lopez
Carmen Amalia Corrales
James L. Bromley
John D. Brinitzer
Paul E. Glotzer
Yong G. Lee
Michael A. Gerstenzang

(*See Next Column*)

CLEARY, GOTTLIEB, STEEN & HAMILTON—*Continued*

MEMBERS OF FIRM (Continued)

Jorge U. Juantorena
David Leinwand
Michael D. Weinberger
Neil Q. Whoriskey

SPECIAL COUNSEL

Sandra M. Rocks
Ellen M. Creede
S. Douglas Borisky
Judith Kassel
Dana G. Fleischman
David E. Webb
Joshua H. Rawson
Scott C. Senecal
Christopher J. Walton
Penelope L. Christophorou
Deborah E. Kurtzberg

NEW YORK OFFICE
ASSOCIATES

Gesine Albrecht
Mary E. Alcock
Justin S. Anand
Linda M. Beale
Jennifer C. Bender
David S. Berg
Vera Bergelson
Patricia Blanchini
Carmine D. Boccuzzi, Jr.
Catherine A. Borneo
Lawrence N. Bowlus
Ward Breeze
Peter F. Buettner
Brian E. Burns
William A. Candelaria
Trecia M. Canty
Arturo Carrillo
Vanessa Chien
David H. Chung
Laura Gonzalez Ciabarra (Not admitted in NY)
Richard V. Conza
Thomas W. Cox (Not admitted in the United States; Legal Consultant on the Laws of South Australia)
James A. Crowe
A. Taylor Custis
Elena L. Daly
Michael D. Dayan
Bieke K. G. P. Debruyne
Susan Devenyi
Daniel D. Dex
Joseph T. Dixon, III
Curtis A. Doty
Juliet A. Drake
Joshua P. Eaton
Daniel J. Epstein
Jason Factor
Afsar Farman-Farmaian
Barthelemy Faye
Janet Ford
Sandra J. Galvis
Abbey Gans
John R. Garry
Jonathan J. Gass
Stephen W. Gauster
Beata Gocyk-Farber
Geoffrey B. Goldman
Maria Gonzalez-Mañes
David I. Gottlieb
Gary S. Greenstein
Melanie F. Griffith
Erik S. Groothuis
Cheryl L. Haas-Goldstein
Sang Jin Han
Jonathan L. Hatch
Allyson W. Haynes
Michelle L. Healy
Adam C. Henry
Alexa A. Holmes
Wenchi Hu
David S. Huntington
Heide H. Ilgenfritz
Dawn L. Jasiak
Clare M. Johnson
Brad M. Johnston
Kierith Anne Jones
Shannon C. Jones
Jacqueline Jones-Peace
Michele H. Kalstein
Jeffrey D. Karpf
Tal Kastner
Ayano Kato
Anne S. Kim (Not admitted in NY)
Anne-Marie C. Kim
Ji-Hyun Kim
Joon H. Kim
Daniel P. Klein
Ethan Klingsberg
Raymond P. Ko
Chantal E. Kordula
Jennifer L. Kroman
Eric D. Kuhn
Marco A. Lau
Francesca Lavin
Michele K. Leibson
Michelle T. Lin
Doron Lipshitz
Yuliya Lyubovnaya
Kira Malyarov
Duane McLaughlin
William McRae
David M. Meisels
Gabriel J. Mesa
Joel W. L. Millar
Boaz S. Morag
John W. B. Morrow
Elisabeth J. Mueller
Peter M. Mundheim
Timothy H. Murphy
Alexandra M. Noble
Van Luong Nguyen
B. Shea Owens
David Parish
Franklin M. Parlamis
Albert Gustav Pastore
Breon S. Peace
Seth Pinsky
Ruth Z. Plave
Karyn S. Polak
Mitchell Raab
Steven W. Rabitz
Robert J. Raymond
Martha M. Redding
Julia Reytblat
Jeffrey A. Rosenthal
Eric Rosof
Stefanie H. Roth
Gregory J. St. Clair
David H. Saltzman
Beth M. Sasfai
Katherine Ann Sawyer
Lisa M. Schweitzer
Ethan A. Skerry
Deborah R. Skolnik
Dylan D. Smith
John E. Sorkin
Andrea L. Spalla
Tad Stahnke
Johan A. Steele
Margaret E. Stowers
Carlin H. Stratton
Seth A. Stuhl
Michael J. Volkovitsch
Karl Wachter
Kathleen A. Walsh
Mary P. Watson
Jessica Weiner
Niping Wu
Anna Xanthos
Herbert Yeh

WASHINGTON, D.C. OFFICE

COUNSEL

Robert C. Barnard
Fred D. Turnage
Douglas E. Kliever
Daniel B. Silver

(See Next Column)

PARTNERS

Donald L. Morgan
J. Eugene Marans
Kenneth L. Bachman, Jr.
Charles F. Lettow
Richard deC. Hinds
Sara D. Schotland
John S. Magney
Mark Leddy
John C. Murphy, Jr.
George S. Cary
Janet L. Weller
Mitchell S. Dupler
Linda J. Soldo
Giovanni P. Prezioso
John T. Byam
Matthew D. Slater
Steven N. Robinson
Michael R. Lazerwitz
David I. Gelfand
Ricardo A. Anzaldúa-Montoya

SPECIAL COUNSEL

Scott N. Benedict
W. Richard Bidstrup
Linda S. Matlack
Kevin A. Griffin

ASSOCIATES

Robin M. Bergen
Barbara W. Bernstein
Brent E. Binge
Marcilynn A. Burke
Derek M. Bush
Brian Byrne
Kimble C. Cannon
Natalie G. Coburn
Robert W. Cook
L. Burton Davis
Onnig H. Dombalagian
John L. Farry
James Filippatos
William S. Fultz
Erik F. Gerding
Scott R. Goodwin
Kristofer W. Hess
Richard B. Holbrook, Jr.
Steven J. Kaiser
Elizabeth L. Katkin
Karen A. Kerr
Elke M. Krauland
James D. Livingstone
Michael A. Mazzuchi
Joyce E. McCarty
Dipali B. Mehta
Paolo Morante
Andrew K. Niebler
Mark W. Nelson
Eruch P. Nowrojee
Henry Kwasi Prempeh
Mitchell L. Rabinowitz
Emily Ryo
David S. Snyder
Michael L. Travers
Timothy A. Vogel
Michael W. Waldron

RESIDENT SPECIAL COUNSEL

Jan Van Gysegem
Till Müller-Ibold
Annette Luise Schild

For full biographical listings, see the Martindale-Hubbell Law Directory

---

CLIFFORD CHANCE ROGERS & WELLS LLP (AV)

Two Hundred Park Avenue, 10166-0153
Telephone: 212-878-8000
Facsimile: 212-878-8375
Telex: 234493 RKWUR
URL: http://www.cliffordchance.com
Washington, D.C. Office: 607 Fourteenth Street, N.W., Washington, D.C. 20005-2018.
Telephone: 202-434-0700.
Facsimile: 202-434-0800.
Other Offices: Amsterdam, Bangkok, Barcelona, Berlin, Brussels, Budapest, Dubai, Dusseldorf, Frankfurt, Hanoi, Ho Chi Minh City, Hong Kong, Leipzig, London, Madrid, Milan, Moscow, Munich, Padua, Paris, Prague, Rome, Sao Paulo, Shanghai, Singapore, Tokyo, Warsaw.

SENIOR PARTNER

William P. Rogers

REGIONAL MANAGING PARTNER

Laurence E. Cranch

PARTNERS

Kevin J. Arquit
Bonnie A. Barsamian
Brad R. Becker
Leora Ben-Ami
James N. Benedict
David W. Bernstein
Jay L. Bernstein
David J. H. Billington
G. David Brinton
Alejandro E. Camacho
John K. Carroll
Richard S. Catalano
Alan M. Christenfeld
John M. Christian
Lewis Rinaudo Cohen
John D. Dadakis
Dennis J. Drebsky
Samuel M. Feder (Not admitted in NY)
Joanne Feil
David Felsenthal
Joseph Ferraro
Robert S. Finley (Registered Foreign Lawyer, Law Society of England and Wales)
Johannes K. Gäbel
L. Martin Gibbs
Aimee H. Goldstein
Alan L. Gosule (Not admitted in NY)
Jan Ter Haar (Not admitted in the United States; Licensed Foreign Legal Consultant, New York, 1998)
John A. Healy
Steven A. Hobbs
Mark Holland
Paul M. Hopkins
Nancy Jacklin
Klaus H. Jander
Dr. Andreas Junius
Kevin Kelley
John E. Kidd
Robert E. King, Jr.
Mark A. Kirsch
Steven T. Kolyer
Richard M. Kosnik
C. Joseph Laughon, II
David B. Levinson
Donald F. Luke
John T. Lutz
Leonard B. Mackey, Jr.
Jerry R. Marlatt
Richard T. McDermott
Thomas A. McGavin, Jr.
Craig S. Medwick
David Meister
Shephard W. Melzer
Paul C. Meyer
David T. Moldenhauer

(See Next Column)

CLIFFORD CHANCE ROGERS & WELLS LLP, *New York—Continued*

PARTNERS (Continued)

James F. Moyle
Raymond O'Connor (Not admitted in the United States)
Anthony Oldfield (Not admitted in United States)
Andrew L. Oringer
James W. Paul
Robert Penchina
Stephen E. Poltrack
Mark F. Pomerantz
Keila D. Ravelo
James M. Ringer
Philip E. Roux
Ronald M. Sanders
Jutta Schneider
Thomas K. Schulte
David A. Schulz
Robert K. Sharp
Victor Siber
Margaret Blair Soyster
David H. Spencer
David L. Taub
Frederick B. Utley, III
Craig M. Walker
Herbert S. Washer
Eli S. Weber
James B. Weidner
Jeffrey H. Weitzman
Kathleen L. Werner
Peter Whitridge Williams
Richard N. Winfield
David J. Yeres
Alice F. Yurke
Jonathan Zonis

COUNSEL

Helayne L. Baron
Gary R. Carney, Jr.
David C. Djaha
Warren L. Feldman
Thomas F. Fleming
David L. Glass
Barbara M. Goodstein
Margaret B. Kelley
Jeffrey A. Lieberman
Carlos E. Martínez
Michael J. Pantuliano
Guy C. Quinlan
Robert D. Schaffer
Melvin L. Schweitzer
Walter G. Van Dorn, Jr.
Norman J. Wachtel

ASSOCIATES

Navaid Alam
Amy H. Albert
Kimberly A. Altschul
Edgard Alvarez
Mary T. Ambron
Mark R. Anderson
Keith M. Andruschak
Matthew J. Antonelli
Michael F. Beckert
Mark Warren Bennett
Michael I. W. Benster (Not admitted in United States)
Pablo Berckholtz
Laura M. Bergamini
Michelle N. Lewis Blash
Joel N. Bock
Angelyn M. Bohland
Carolynn R. Bonner (Not admitted in United States)
Michael E. Breede
Brian V. Breheny
Pierre C. Brochet (Not admitted in United States)
Scott S. Broock (Not admitted in NY)
Geoffrey G. B. Brow
Kirsty Brown (Not admitted in United States)
Roderick A. Bryce (Not admitted in United States)
Walter A. Buchanan
Charlotte Byers
Theodore V. Cacioppi
John M. Cafiero
Patrick D. Canavan
Bari B. Cariello
Thomas T. Carroll
Dr. Patricia A. Carson
Bradford L. Caswell
Douglas Chia
Kenneth J. Choi
Kiwon Choi
Ellen H. Clark
Gail Patrick Cleary
Ness M. Cohen
John K. Collins
Jill Conway (Not admitted in United States)
David L. Cook
Erica Coope
Tia A. Counts
Robert E. Creese
Dennis J. Crilly
Nicholas P. Crowell
Kevin M. Curran
Pamela Czewska
Jason A. D'Angelo
Richard J. Davis
Edward C. Delk
Karen L. DeMeo
Teresa A. De Turris
Rashi Dhir
Ella Dlin
Carlos Döring (Not admitted in United States)
Jeffrey H. Drichta
Vladimir V. Drozdoff
Rachel L. Dubow
Lisl J. Dunlop
Ana L. Dutra (Not admitted in United States)
Anne E. K. Emmert
Benjamin S. Encarnacion
Andrew S. Epstein
Lara S. Fetsco
Michael A. Fleischer
Abigail K. Foster (Not admitted in NY)
Robert E. Freeman
Roland F. Fürst
Anthony J. Galioto
Susan M. Garcia
Robert J. Gavigan
Paula S. Gibbs
Jeffrey Gimpel
Dawn E. Goldberg
Scott J. Gordon
Penelope A. Graboys
Sharon Graham
Rosalind Gray
Steven S. Grieco
Carlos A. Guidotti (Not admitted in United States)
Neer Gupta
Nancy E. Hay
Todd E. Heller
Brian W. Henry
John J. Herbst
Robert G. Houck
Farah Hussain
Inna Idelchik
Jake Jackaman
Nada Jain
Miles D. Jessup
John T. Johnson
Christopher M. Joralemon
Srinandan R. Kasi
Ani H. Kasparian
John A. Kehoe
Lainie L. Kernis
Dov Kesselman
Judy J. Kim
Joseph P. Kincart
Laura Kohn
Polly Kolotas
Timothy W. Korth
Timothy E. Ladin
Hilary Lane
Nicole A. Laskin
Michelle B. Lee
Heidi W. Leonard
Joseph E. Levi
Marc W. Levy
Sara B. Lewis (Not admitted in NY)
Rachel J. Littman

(See Next Column)

ASSOCIATES (Continued)

Tina Locatelli (Not admitted in NY)
M. Sharmini Mahendran
James V. Mahon
Victoria Manthas
James P. Masterson
Joan B. Mazur
Kathryn A. McCarthy
David E. McCraw
John T. McManus
Briar L. McNutt
Michael E. McTiernan
Larry P. Medvinsky
John M. Megara
Michael H. Meissner (Not admitted in United States)
Gildardo Michel-Garcia
James D. Miller
Daniel Miranda
Hans D. Montag
Gianluca Morello
E. Scott Morvillo
Elizabeth Sanders Munsell
Sean M. Murphy
John A. Nathanson
Michael C. Naughton
Dr. Gerard P. Norton
Frank J. Nuzzi
Brian E. O'Keefe
Christopher J. O'Rourke
Regina O'Shea
Sheila O'Shea
David K. Park
Tina Passalaris
Joshua L. Peirez
Michelle M. Pfeiffenberger
Sara K. Pinto
David A. Poureshagh (Not admitted in United States)
Wesley R. Powell
Danielle A. Prill
Stephen J. Quine
Gregory J. Radke
M. Amr I. Razzak
Alyson Leigh Redman (Not admitted in NY)
Judith M. Reilly
Nicole A. Reninger
Scott W. Reynolds
Sean Rheuben
Pedro Lanna Ribeiro (Not admitted in United States)
Kirstie A. Rickett
David F. Ries (Not admitted in NY)
Dineen A. Riviezzo
Cosmo Roe (Not admitted in United States)
Karl A. Roessner
Kurt M. Rogers
Kirstin Romann
Darren Rosenblum
Maurice N. Ross
Luis M. Roth
Lenford A. Rowe
Pierre-Georges Roy
Brian H. Rubenstein (Not admitted in NY)
Maureen Ryan
Keeto H. Sabharwal
Joanne M. Scalard
Teresa B. Schiller
Marc J. Schneider
Charles J. Scibetta, Jr.
Alison Scott (Not admitted in NY)
Scott D. Segal
Martin L. Seidel
Christopher Serbagi
Vincent Serpico
Gregory D. Shanklin
Thomas G. Sharpe
Steven T. Shelton
Michael W. Shepherd
Benjamin K. Sibbett
Roger D. Singer
Sigurd Ansgar Sorenson
Rita McCloy Stephanz
Robert A. Stone
Howard S. Suh
Joseph E. Suh
Susan M. Sullivan-Bisceglia
Jeffrey M. Sulman
Stephen W. Swanson
Sasha Thomas-Nuruddin
John E. Tobin-de la Puente
Jeffrey P. Travers
Dennis J. Uhlir
Francisco E. Ulloa
Jacqueline M. Vernon
William R. Wagner
Craig A. Waldman
Mark A. Weissman
Jennifer L. Wendy
Robert T. White, Jr.
John (Ian) McN. Wilkie, Jr.
Tina Woo (Not admitted in NY)
Joel D. Wright
Oda Wypior
Keum A. Yoon
Douglas I. Youngman
Earl S. Zimmerman

STAFF ATTORNEYS

Marisol Cardona
Leslie C. Cernava
Alicia R. DiBacco
Victoria Winter Dienst
Mary K. Dulka
Theodore G. Lindsay
Laurie C. Nelson
Joseph Rotella
Heather M. Ryan (Not admitted in NY)
Adrian H. von Hassell
Richard H. Wolfram

WASHINGTON, D.C. OFFICE

SENIOR PARTNER

William P. Rogers

PARTNERS

Kevin J. Arquit
Jeremy A. Connick (Not admitted in United States)
Anthony F. Essaye
David J. Evans
Kenneth A. Gallo
Ira D. Hammerman
Sara P. Hanks
John Paul Ketels
Steven A. Newborn
Michael A. O'Shea
Anthony J. Renzi, Jr.
Rodney N.T. Short (Not admitted in United States)
William Silverman
Joseph J. Simons
Ryan Trainer
Dale C. Turza

COUNSEL

Leiv H. Blad, Jr.
David D. DiBari
James C. Egan, Jr.
Douglas J. Heffner
Jon Randall Roellke
Carrie A. Simon
John M. Sipple, Jr.
Laura A. Wilkinson

CONSULTANTS

Jon McCormick
Virginia L. Snider

For full biographical listings, see the Martindale-Hubbell Law Directory

New York—Continued

COOPER & DUNHAM LLP (AV)

1185 Avenue of the Americas, 10036
Telephone: 212-278-0400
Fax: 212-391-0525
Email: counsel@cooperdunham.com *URL:* http://www.cooperdunham.com

MEMBERS OF FIRM

Christopher C. Dunham
Norman H. Zivin
John P. White
William E. Pelton
Robert D. Katz
Peter J. Phillips
Wendy E. Miller
Ivan S. Kavrukov
Peter D. Murray
Jay H. Maioli
Robert B. G. Horowitz
Donald S. Dowden
Donna A. Tobin
Richard S. Milner
Albert Wai-Kit Chan

ASSOCIATES

Robert T. Maldonado
Elizabeth M. Wieckowski
Pedro C. Fernandez
Todd W. Evans
Michael F. Morano
Spencer H. Schneider
Paul Teng
Richard F. Jaworski
Gary J. Gershik
William Y. Lee (Not admitted in NY)
Raymond A. DiPerna

OF COUNSEL

Gerald W. Griffin
John R. Garber

LEGAL SUPPORT PERSONNEL

SCIENTIFIC ADVISORS

Jane M. Love
Alan D. Miller

For full biographical listings, see the Martindale-Hubbell Law Directory

COOPERMAN LEVITT WINIKOFF LESTER & NEWMAN, P.C. (AV)

800 Third Avenue, 10022-7601
Telephone: 212-688-7000
Fax: 212-755-2839
URL: http://www.clwln.com
Long Island, New York Office: 1129 Northern Boulevard, Manhasset, 11030.
Telephone: 516-365-1400.
Fax: 516-365-1404.

Robert N. Cooperman
Jack B. Levitt
Robert L. Winikoff
David S. Lester
David B. Newman
Asher H. Miller
H. Frances Kleiner
Harry J. Petchesky
Elliot E. Brecher
Ira I. Roxland
Harris S. Jaffe
Mark L. Lubin
Allen G. Reiter

OF COUNSEL

Vivian L. Dubin

Edward J. Reich
Barry A. Cassell
Gary S. Sastow
Susan Denburg Yellin
Joseph H. Schmitt
Stephen Brodsky
Stephen E. Fox
Jill L. Schechterman (Not admitted in NY)
Carol B. Koch
Stephen W. Semian
Helise Harrington

For full biographical listings, see the Martindale-Hubbell Law Directory

COX PADMORE SKOLNIK & SHAKARCHY (AV)

630 Third Avenue, 10017
Telephone: 212-953-6633
Fax: 212-949-6943
Email: babshak@aol.com
Palo Alto, California Office: 755 Page Mill Road, Suite A280.
Telephone: 650-424-0608.
Fax: 650-493-9408.
Denver, Colorado Office: Suite 2550, 1775 Sherman Street.
Telephone: 303-839-9191.
Fax: 303-839-9318.

Jacob S. Shakarchy
Steven D. Skolnik
Jonathan C. S. Cox (Resident, Palo Alto California Office)
Gerald Padmore (Not admitted in NY)

ASSOCIATE

Eric J. Gruber

OF COUNSEL

Lawrence Greenapple
Mitchell R. Mass
Eric M. Bates

For full biographical listings, see the Martindale-Hubbell Law Directory

CRAVATH, SWAINE & MOORE (AV)

Worldwide Plaza, 825 Eighth Avenue, 10019
Telephone: 212-474-1000
Facsimile: 212-474-3700
URL: http://www.cravath.com
London, England Office: 33 King William Street, London, EC4R 9DU.
Telephone: 171-453-1000.
Facsimile: 171-860-1150.
Hong Kong, China Office: Suite 2609, Asia Pacific Finance Tower, 3 Garden Road, Central, Hong Kong, China.
Telephone: 852-2509-7200.
Facsimile: 852-2509-7272.

Paul Drennan Cravath (1861-1940)
Robert Taylor Swaine (1886-1949)
Hoyt Augustus Moore (1870-1958)

MEMBERS OF FIRM

Samuel C. Butler
George J. Gillespie, III
Thomas D. Barr
Melvin L. Bedrick
George T. Lowy
Robert Rosenman
Alan J. Hruska
James M. Edwards
Frederick A.O. Schwarz, Jr.
Christine Beshar
Robert S. Rifkind
David O. Brownwood (Resident Partner, London Office)
Paul M. Dodyk
Thomas R. Brome
Robert D. Joffe
Allen Finkelson
Ronald S. Rolfe
Paul C. Saunders
Martin L. Senzel
Douglas D. Broadwater
Alan C. Stephenson
Max R. Shulman
Stuart W. Gold
John W. White
John E. Beerbower
Evan R. Chesler
Patricia Geoghegan
D. Collier Kirkham
Michael L. Schler
Daniel P. Cunningham
Kris F. Heinzelman
B. Robbins Kiessling
Roger D. Turner
Philip A. Gelston
Rory O. Millson
Neil P. Westreich
Francis P. Barron
Richard W. Clary
William P. Rogers, Jr.
James D. Cooper
Stephen L. Gordon
Robert A. Kindler
Daniel L. Mosley
Gregory M. Shaw
Peter S. Wilson
James C. Vardell, III
Robert H. Baron
Kevin J. Grehan
W. Clayton Johnson (Resident Partner, Hong Kong, China Office)
Stephen S. Madsen
C. Allen Parker
Marc S. Rosenberg
William B. Brannan
Lewis R. Steinberg
Susan Webster
William H. Widen
Timothy G. Massad (Resident Partner, Hong Kong, China Office)
David Mercado
Rowan D. Wilson
John T. Gaffney
Peter T. Barbur
Sandra C. Goldstein
Paul Michalski (Resident Partner, London Office)
Thomas G. Rafferty
Michael S. Goldman
George W. Bilicic, Jr.
Richard Hall
Elizabeth L. Grayer
Julie A. North
Stephen L. Burns
Katherine B. Forrest
Keith R. Hummel
Daniel Slifkin
Jeffrey A. Smith
Robert I. Townsend, III
William J. Whelan, III
Scott A. Barshay
Philip J. Boeckman
Roger G. Brooks
William V. Fogg
Faiza J. Saeed
Richard J. Stark
Thomas E. Dunn
Julie T. Spellman

RETIRED PARTNERS

Albert R. Connelly
John H. Morse
Allen H. Merrill
William J. Schrenk, Jr.
Henry P. Riordan
James H. Duffy
Steward R. Bross, Jr.
Benjamin F. Crane
Allen F. Maulsby
John R. Hupper
John F. Hunt
John E. Young
David G. Ormsby
Richard J. Hiegel
Richard M. Allen
Herbert L. Camp

DERIVATIVES COUNSEL

Joshua D. Cohn

SENIOR ATTORNEYS

Constance M. Ayars
Peter M. Crevi
Ralph B. Currey, III
Gerald A. Ford
Joanne M. Gentile
John Gerhard
Jody A. Healy
G. Douglas Johnson
Richard S. Lasker
Martin R. Levine
Mark R. Malina
Henry I. Morgenbesser
Patrick J. Moriarty
Paul D. Siniawer
Kimberley S. Drexler
Gabriel Saltarelli

For full biographical listings, see the Martindale-Hubbell Law Directory

New York—Continued

DAVIS POLK & WARDWELL (AV)

450 Lexington Avenue, 10017
Telephone: 212-450-4000
Fax: 212-450-4800
URL: http://www.dpw.com
Washington, D.C. Office: 1300 I Street, N.W., Washington, D.C., 20005.
Telephone: 202-962-7000.
Fax: 202-962-7111.
Menlo Park, California Office: 1600 El Camino Real, Menlo Park, California, 94025.
Telephone: 650-752-2000.
Fax: 650-752-2195.
Paris, France Office: 15, avenue Matignon, 75008 Paris, France.
Telephone: 33-01-56-59-36-00.
Fax: 33-01-56-59-36-90.
London, England Office: 99 Gresham Street, London EC2V 7NG, England.
Telephone: 44-171-418-1300.
Fax: 44-171-418-1400.
Tokyo, Japan Office: Akasaka Twin Tower East, 11th Floor, 17-22, Akasaka 2-Chome, Minato-ku, Tokyo 107-0052, Japan.
Telephone: 81-3-5561-4421.
Fax: 81-3-5561-4425.
Frankfurt, Germany Office: MesseTurm, 60308 Frankfurt am Main, Germany.
Telephone: 49-69-97-57-03-0.
Fax: 49-69-74-77-44.
Hong Kong, China Office: The Hong Kong Club Building, 3A Chater Road, Hong Kong.
Telephone: 852-2533-3300.
Fax: 852-2533-3388.

SENIOR COUNSEL

D. Nelson Adams
John P. Carroll, Jr.
Joseph Chubb **
Jonathan M. Clark
John A. Corry
Christopher Crowley
James F. Dolan
William C. Gifford
S. Hazard Gillespie
Charles S. Hoppin
Henry L. King
Edwin Deane Leonard
Herbert M. Lobl
Bartlett H. McGuire
Richard E. Nolan
David C. Oxman
Philip C. Potter, Jr.
Samuel F. Pryor III
Edward S. Reid
Andrew Y. Rogers
Richard B. Smith
Peter O. A. Solbert
Richard D. Spizzirri
William D. Tucker, Jr.

RETIRED PARTNERS

William A. Kaynor
William F. Kroener, III
James P. Lawton
Troland S. Link
Richard Moe
Donaldson C. Pillsbury
Lawrence E. Walsh

MEMBERS OF FIRM

Robert B. Fiske, Jr.
M. Carr Ferguson, Jr.
Lydia E. Kess
James W. B. Benkard
Colin E. Harley
Daniel F. Kolb
David J. Strupp
Guy Miller Struve
James Woodman Lloyd
Stephen H. Case ***
Francis J. Morison
Frank S. Moseley
Jeffrey Small
William Parsons, Jr.
Charles S. Whitman, III
Lewis B. Kaden
Arthur F. Golden
Dennis S. Hersch
Winthrop B. Conrad, Jr.
Lowell Gordon Harriss
Richard Jay Sandler
Robert F. Wise, Jr.
John P. Cooney, Jr.
Robert L. Heckart
Ogden N. Lewis
Bradley Y. Smith
Marlene Alva
Peter R. Douglas
John Fouhey
Christopher Mayer
Francis S. Currie
(Not admitted in NY)
Pierre de Saint Phalle
Robert J. Levine *******
Gary G. Lynch
John J. McCarthy, Jr. **
Jerome G. Snider
William E. Wurtz
Howard A. Ellins
Patrick S. Kenadjian *********
William H. Weigel
Beverly Fanger Chase
Keith L. Kearney **
Scott W. Muller ***
George R. Bason, Jr.
Donald S. Bernstein
Alan Dean
John R. Ettinger
(Managing Partner)
Daniel G. Kelly, Jr.
James Duncan Phyfe ******
E. Waide Warner, Jr.
Thomas Patrick Dore, Jr.
David W. Ferguson
Avishai Shachar
Linda A. Simpson
David M. Wells **
D. Scott Wise
Paul W. Bartel, II
Richard A. Drucker
Dennis E. Glazer
Paul E. Kumleben **
Karen E. Wagner
Laureen F. Bedell
John M. Brandow
Michael P. Carroll
Diane G. Kerr
Peter S. W. Levin
Andrés V. Gil
Paul R. Kingsley
Joseph Rinaldi
Dana L. Trier ***
John A. Bick
Thomas P. Ogden
Barbara Nims
Lawrence E. Wieman
Samuel Dimon
Carey R. Dunne
Phillip R. Mills
Richard D. Truesdell, Jr.
Sarah Jones Beshar
John W. Buttrick

(See Next Column)

MEMBERS OF FIRM (Continued)

David L. Caplan
Bruce K. Dallas
James A. Florack
Ronan P. Harty
Yukako Kawata
Susan L. Merrill
Randal K. Quarles
Danforth Townley
William F. Barron ******
Jeffrey D. Berman **
Juliet Cain
Karin S. Day
Nora M. Jordan
Thomas J. Reid **
Po Y. Sit
William L. Taylor
Joel M. Cohen
Gail A. Flesher
Eugene C. Gregor ******
Joseph P. Hadley
Lawrence J. Portnoy
James P. Rouhandeh
Carole Schiffman
Kathleen L. Ferrell
(Not admitted in NY)
Louis L. Goldberg
Sharon Katz
Deanna L. Kirkpatrick
John K. Knight
Denis J. McInerney
Michael T. Mollerus
(Not admitted in NY)
John D. Paton **
Margaret Tahyar
(Not admitted in NY)
Mario J. Verdolini, Jr.
James H.R. Windels
Patrick A. Bradford
Julia K. Cowles
Steven David Lofchie
Jordan Luke
***(Not admitted in NY)
Jeffrey M. Oakes **
Andrew W. Stumpff
Harry Ballan
John W. Banes
Ulrika Ekman
Joseph A. Hall
Leonard Kreynin
Nicholas A. Kronfeld
James T. Rothwell
Nancy L. Sanborn
Tiziana M. Tabucchi
Raul F. Yanes

COUNSEL

Leslie J. Altus
Margaret M. Ayres
***(Not admitted in NY)
Laura M. Barzilai
Sally A. Brammell
Daniel N. Budofsky
Lynn Earl Busath
Vincent T. Chang
Loyti Cheng
John J. Clarke, Jr.
Mary B. Conway
Sue Ann G. Dillport
Theodore A. Doremus, Jr.
***(Not admitted in NY)
Thomas J. Gallagher, Jr.
Marcie A. Goldstein
Gary L. Granik
George R. Ince, Jr.
Susan D. Kennedy
James L. Kerr
Nancy L. Lazar
James D. Liss
Nancy J. Marchand *
Robin J. H. Maxwell
James P. McIntyre
Warren Motley
Theodore A. Paradise *******
Susan F. Reibstein
Kiye M. Sakai
Joseph J. Sperber
Irene A. Steiner
Mark G. Strauch *****
Robert W. Weaver ***
John T. Wright

MANAGING ATTORNEY

Lawrence Evan Jacobs

ASSOCIATES

NEW YORK OFFICE

William H. Aaronson
Erika J. Adkins
Woodrow Ahn
Carsten Albers
Meenakshi Ambardar
C. Ian Anderson
Pamela Arnsten
Witold Balaban
Gregory G. Ballard
Stuart A. Barr
Todd M. Baskin
Suzanne A. Beddoe
Angela Bellizzi
Peter P. Bevacqua
Norwood P. Beveridge, III
Prabha Sipi Bhandari
Frances E. Bivens
Jason Block
Susan M. Boccardi
Edward P. Boyle
William A. Braverman
Lawrence J. Burian
Arthur J. Burke
John H. Butler
James M. Cahillane
Max Calne
Gina Caruso
Marina Martino Casani
Anna Caspersen
Marc A.R. Chambers
Lily Changchien
Kenneth H. Chase
Show-Mao Chen
Harry A. Chernoff
Elaine P. Chiew
Helen H. Chin
Ning Chiu
Erin K. Cho
Lawrence M. Chu
John D. Ciorciari
Jeffrey C. Cohen
Joseph S. Cohn
Lisa G. Connor
Jane E. Hewett Cooney
Alexander M. Cooper
Christopher Cooper
Alexei J. Cowett
Jennifer A. Crossett
John G. Crowley
Clive Davis
Daryl E. Davis
Henry P. Davis
Shane de Burca
Mary Lyn DeNiro
Dorothy D. DeWitt
Barbara D. Diggs
W. Scott Dove
Charles S. Duggan
Nicole Duncan
Michael S. Farber
Lucy W. Farr
Edith Fassberg
Luciana Fato
Renata J. Ferrari
Kelly A. Finley
Lisa F. Firenze
Edmond T. FitzGerald
Michael S. Flynn
Marianne Fogarty
Manuel Garciadiaz
Brian J. Gavsie
Stephanie S. Gold
Jonathan E. Goldberg
Ricardo M. Gonzalez
Christina Gross
Eric F. Grossman
Rajiv Gupta
Rebecca G. Haile
(Not admitted in NY)
Darrell C. Hall
Melanie R. Hallums
Timothy P. Harkness
Thomas E. Haroldson
Kimberley D. Harris
Laurel R. Henneman
Joy Henry Hinton

(See Next Column)

DAVIS POLK & WARDWELL—*Continued*

ASSOCIATES
NEW YORK OFFICE (Continued)

Sheldon V. Hirt
Hilary E. Hoover
Anne Berry Howe
Marshall S. Huebner
Matthew H. Hurlock
David E. Izhakoff
Ethan T. James
Xiao-Hong Jing
Nicole S. Jones
Benjamin S. Kaminetzky
Edward C. Kang
Michael P. Kaplan
Diane Kelleher
Copely T. Kelly
Steven Ted Kern
Suzanne E. Kerrigan
Jinsoo H. Kim
Susan S. Kim
Tracy Kimmel
Deborah K. Klein
Matthew Kline
Scott B. Klugman
Anne Mori Kobayashi (Not admitted in NY)
William C. Komaroff
Christian W. Kopfli
Maxim S. Kulikov
Angelica Kwan
Alexander B. Kwit
Leor S. Landa
Serge A. Learsy
Jeffrey M. Leavitt
Joshua A. Levine
Arthur S. Long
Laura A. Lopez
Marjorie B. Lotfi
Nancy B. Ludmerer
Kevin M. Lyman
Christopher A. Maher
Patricia M. Maribona
Marina Martino-Casani
David B. Massey
Charlita Mays
Linda Mc Mahon
T.A. McKinney
Jean M. McLoughlin
K. Heather McRay
William F. Megevick, Jr.
Marlane Melican
Mark Mermelstein
Mark W. Messenbaugh
Patrick Michel
Matthew L. Moore
Betty Moy
James E. Murray
Courtenay U. Myers
Jeffrey N. Neuman
Jonathan B. New
Jennifer G. Newstead
Diem-Suong T. Nguyen
Christine Kelly Nichols (Not admitted in NY)
Alison F. Nicoll
Patricia T. Northrop
Cindy J. O'Hagan
Terrance O'Malley
Patrick C. O'Reilly
Michael F. Osborne
Michael M. Paese
Alice Palmer (Not admitted in the United States) (Legal Consultant on the Laws of Australia)
Sally E. Park
Mona J. Patel
Robert E. Phay, Jr.
Jonathan Philips
Devorah I. Pomerantz
Michael M. Purpura
Alex Raskolnikov
Jennifer H. Rearden
Ola N. Rech
Jeanette Redmond
Lisa D. Reifenberg
Paul M. Rodel
Amy Rossabi (Not admitted in NY)
Diego Rotsztain
Kirsten E. Rutnik
Paula Aileen Ryan
Joy Sayour
Kimberly A. Schmidt
Robin F. Schuh
Jeffrey N. Schwartz
Michael R. Schwenk
Karen Sculli
Scott L. Semer
Terri A. Sewell
Saurabh K. Shah
Lin Jun Shaw
Connie Shoemaker
Adreme M. Shubrick
Michele Siano
Leslie A. Simon
Alexander G. Simpson
Heather Stack
Amelia T. R. Starr
Christian M. Steiner
James Steinthal
Katharine Strobos
Patti Stuckler
Pimkaeo Sundaravej
Kyoko Takahashi
C. Siri Thomas
Matteo Tonello
David B. Toscano
Tobias Trautner
D. Scott Tucker
Elisha Kidane Tuku
Philip R. Wagman
Gretchen A. Wagner
Ian K. O. Walker
Joseph F. Warganz, Jr.
Brian S. Weinstein
Elizabeth Schutz Weinstein
Elizabeth Weiss
Philip S. Welt
Erika Diane White
Shelley R. White
Anne M. Wildhaber
Rebecca Winters
Roger S. Wise
Manish Yadav
Shirley Yeung
David L. Zimmerman

PARIS, FRANCE OFFICE

Kathleen de Carbuccia
Pippa F. Tubman

LONDON, ENGLAND OFFICE

John D. Amorosi
Alexander A. Bafi
Richard M. Baumann
Dina T. Brewer
Donna M. Chambers
Eric R. Dann
Chinedu Reginald Ezetah
Avrohom C. Gelber
Brian J. Gill
Sonia K. Han
Marcelle R. Joseph
Mira Kothari
Joyce McCarthy
Catherine Moroz
Ebelechukwu A. Okobi
David W. Parento
Ryan F. Pearson
Daniel Rabinowitz
Simona Spazzini
Jennifer A. Spiegel
Eva H. Studenny
Anna Torstensson
Amy L. Valley
Michael J. Willisch

TOKYO, JAPAN OFFICE

Lisa Ono
Edwin W. Paxson, III
Akiko Yamahara

FRANKFURT, GERMANY OFFICE

Ann M. Bradley
Constantin Schoelkopf

(See Next Column)

HONG KONG OFFICE

Suzin Ahn
Janet J. Anderson
Sandip C. Bhattacharji
Show-Mao Chen
Veronica W. Gibb
Charles Hsieh
Christopher M. Ing
Sarah E. Kim
Mark J. Lehmkuhler
Kim H. Liou
James C. Lin
Paul Robinson
K. Christopher Shen
Timothy A. Steinert

MENLO PARK, CALIFORNIA OFFICE

D. Barnaby Gibson
Ashraf R. Ibrahim
Michelle K. Lynd
Sarah K. Solum

*Resident Paris Office
**Resident London Office
***Resident Washington, D.C. Office
*****Resident Frankfurt Office
******Resident Hong Kong Office
*******Resident Tokyo Office
*********Frankfurt and Paris Offices

For full biographical listings, see the Martindale-Hubbell Law Directory

DEBEVOISE & PLIMPTON (AV)

875 Third Avenue, 10022
Telephone: 212-909-6000
Domestic Telex: 148377 DEBSTEVE NYK
Telecopier: (212) 909-6836
Washington, D.C. Office: 555 13th Street, N.W., 20004.
Telephone: 202-383-8000.
Telecopier: (202) 383-8118.
Paris, France Office: 21 Avenue George V 75008.
Telephone: (33-1) 40 73 12 12.
Telecopier: (33-1) 47 20 50 82.
Telex: 648141F DPPAR.
London, England Office: Old Broad Street, EC2N 1HQ.
Telephone: (44-171) 786-9000.
Telex: 88 4569 DPLON G.
Telecopier: (44-171) 588-4180.
Hong Kong Office: 13/F Entertainment Building, 30 Queen's Road Central.
Telephone: (852) 2160-9800.
Fax: (852) 2810-9828.
Moscow, Russia Representative Office: Debevoise & Plimpton, LLC, Bolshoi Palashevsky Pereulok 13/2, 4th Floor, 103104.
Telephone: 7 (095 or 503) 956-3858.
Fax: 7 (095 or 503) 956-3868.

Eli Whitney Debevoise (1899-1990)
Francis T. P. Plimpton (1900-1983)

MEMBERS OF FIRM

Louis Begley
Judah Best (Washington, D.C. Office)
Robert L. King
Stephen J. Friedman
Meredith M. Brown
Bruce D. Haims
Edward A. Perell
Theodore A. Kurz
Hugh Rowland, Jr.
Robert J. Gibbons
Barbara Paul Robinson
Paul H. Wilson, Jr.
Wolcott B. Dunham, Jr.
Jeffrey S. Wood (Resident, Hong Kong Office)
Steven M. Alden
John H. Hall
Ralph C. Ferrara (Washington, D.C. Office)
James A. Kiernan III (Resident, London and Paris Offices)
Robert R. Bruce (Resident, London Office)
Arthur L. Marriott, QC (London Office)
Hans Bertram-Nothnagel
Martin Frederic Evans
Steven R. Gross
Roger E. Podesta
Woodrow W. Campbell, Jr.
Marcus H. Strock
Ralph Arditi
David A. Duff
Loren Kieve (Washington, D.C. Office)
Bruce G. Merritt
Alan H. Paley
Robert J. Cubitto
Robert N. Shwartz
Robert J. Staffaroni
Darius Tencza
John M. Allen, Jr.
Franci J. Blassberg
Steven Klugman
Richard D. Bohm
Peter L. Borowitz
Barry Mills
Deborah F. Stiles
Andrew N. Berg
Marcia L. MacHarg (Washington, D.C. Office)
Steven M. Ostner
Robert F. Quaintance, Jr.
Michael E. Wiles
Daniel M. Abuhoff
Bruce P. Keller
John S. Kiernan
David W. Rivkin
Burt Rosen
Christopher Smeall
William B. Beekman
Michael W. Blair
Jeffrey P. Cunard (Washington, D.C. Office)
John T. Curry, III
Seth L. Rosen
Edwin G. Schallert
Lawrence K. Cagney
Joseph P. Moodhe
Donald Francis Donovan
Gary M. Friedman
Richard F. Hahn
Lorna G. Schofield
Andrew L. Sommer
David A. Brittenham
John M. Vasily
Anne E. Cohen
Thomas M. Kelly
Ivan E. Mattei
George E. B. Maguire
Peter R. Schwartz
Bruce E. Yannett
Paul S. Bird
Margaret Andrews Davenport
Michael J. Gillespie

(See Next Column)

DEBEVOISE & PLIMPTON, *New York—Continued*

MEMBERS OF FIRM (Continued)

David F. Hickok (Budapest and Paris Offices)
Gary W. Kubek
Elizabeth Pagel Serebransky
Katherine Ashton (Resident, London, England Office)
Gregory V. Gooding
Michael P. Harrell
Antoine F. Kirry (Paris Office)
Lorin L. Reisner
James C. Scoville
Colby A. Smith (Resident, Washington, D.C. Office)
Mark P. Goodman
David H. Bernstein
Peter J. Loughran
David P. Mason
Christopher K. Tahbaz
Sara A. W. Fitts
Mark W. Friedman
Mary Beth Hogan
Byungkwon Lim
Andrew M. Ostrognai (Hong Kong Office)

OF COUNSEL

George B. Adams
John B. Brady, Jr.
Barry R. Bryan
Bevis Longstreth
Roswell B. Perkins
Jonathan A. Small

INTERNATIONAL COUNSEL AND COUNSEL

Ann M. Ashton (Not admitted in NY)
Ann G. Baker (Paris Office)
Colin William Bogie (Not admitted in United States) (Legal Consultant on the Laws of Scotland, England and Wales)
Sherri G. Caplan
John Dembeck
Antoine d'Ornano (Paris Office)
Barbara W. Friedman
Stephen R. Hertz
Jonathan H. Hines
Adele M. Karig
Barton Legum
Ellen Lieberman
Dmitri V. Nikiforov (Not admitted in the United States) (Legal Consultant on the Laws of Russia)
Paul C. Palmer (Washington, D.C. Office)
Phillip D. Parker (Washington, D.C. Office)
Nicholas F. Potter
A. David Reynolds
Jonathan E. Richman
Jonathan J. Rikoon
David J. Schwartz
Michael A. Solomon
James Cecil Swank (Paris, France Office)
Herbert C. Thomas (Not admitted in NY)
Raymond G. Wells

RETIRED PARTNERS

Stephen Benjamin
Chester Billings, Jr.
D. Bret Carlson
William Everdell
Robert J. Geniesse (Washington, D.C. Office)
Michael Harper Goff
James C. Goodale
Andrew C. Hartzell, Jr.
Harold H. Healy, Jr.
John F. Johnston, 2nd
Richard D. Kahn
William B. Matteson
Guy Paschal
Stanley R. Resor
Asa Rountree
Oscar M. Ruebhausen
David V. Smalley
Vincent M. Smith
Robert B. von Mehren
Philip S. Winterer
Cecil Wray

ASSOCIATES

V. Mary Abraham
Jacqueline Glassman Africk
Innokenty Y. Alekseev (Moscow Office)
Khadija Amsrouy
Juliette Antoine
David M. Appel
Justin G. Askew
Chad Atkins
Scott N. Auby (Washington, D.C. Office)
Andrew L. Bab
Manoj Bhargava
D. Benjamin Barros
Timothy S.T. Bass
Stephen Baum
John Beaglehole
Timothy K. Beeken
Michael Ben-Jacob
Joshua J.G. Berick
Merril R. Bernstein
E. Raman Bet-Mansour
Lisa B. Bialkin
Pascal Bine (Paris Office)
Craig Bloom
Jeannette K. Boot
Andrew S. Borodach
Ezra B. Borut
Craig A. Bowman
Jonathan Boyarin
Nicholas James Boyle (London Office)
Laura R. Bradford
Julie Brandfield
Kyra K. Bromley
David Irving Brown
Paul D. Brusiloff
Brandon S. Bryant
Scott C. Budlong (London Office)
Geoffrey P. Burgess (London Office)
Jennifer J. Burleigh
Elizabeth G. Bynum (Hong Kong Office)
Erin Callahan (London Office)
Thomas C. Canfield
Marc Castagnède (Paris Office)
Sarah R. Cebik
Ch'iu Lien Chang
Lech Choroszucha
Judith L. Church
Karin M. Ciano
Ada Clapp
Barton B. Clark
Shannon Conaty
Sandra Cobden
Beth Ann Collier
Jennifer B. Coplan
Jennifer R. Cowan
Danielle Wrobel Davies
R. Townsend Davis, Jr.
Ashima A. Dayal
Sylvie DeParis-Maze (Paris Office)
Faune Devlin
Andrew C. DeVore
Russell G. D'Oench, III
Robert M. Dickson
George Djurasovic

(See Next Column)

ASSOCIATES (Continued)

Michael D. Dorum
Gérard Dufrêne (Paris Office)
Robert J. Driscoll
John M. Driscoll, III
Edward Drew Dutton
Mariela Markelis Dybner
Bettina R. Eckerle
Monique C. Carkum Edwards
Roy Engel
Jane Engelhardt
Gregg S. Farano (Washington, D.C. Office)
Molly S. Farrell
Jeremy Feigelson
Sally Fitzgerald (London Office)
Olga Frolova (Moscow Office)
Peter A. Furci
Peter G. Furniss
Adam D. Gale
Michelle Helene Gluskin
Tzechien Goh (London Office)
Susan M. Goldbaum
Martin M. Goldberg
Matthew T. Golden
Mariana Gonatas (France Office)
Robert D. Goodman
Xavier P. Grappotte
Carlos G. Gonzalez
Susan J. Greene
Kara L. Gross
Stuart Hammer
Haider Ala Hamoudi
Giselle P. Hantz (London Office)
Richard C. Harmon
Michael A. Hartman
Russell Hartman
Junhua Melody He
Felicia A. Henderson
Peter R. Herman
Diane Hester
Wolfgang Hohensee (Paris Office)
Sean K. Hornbeck (Washington, D.C. Office)
Dennis H. Hranitzky
Abraham B. Hsuan
Emilie Hsu
Suzanne J. Irving
Jeffrey S. Jacobson
Stacey R. Jessiman
Melanie Johnson (Paris Office)
Peter C. Johnson
Elizabeth N. Kaplan (Washington, D.C. Office)
Matthew E. Kaplan (London Office)
Christopher G. Karagheuzoff
Alan V. Kartashkin (Not admitted in the United States)
Frances L. Kellner
Philip S. Khinda (Washington, D.C. Office)
Alice J. Kim (Century City, CA Office)
Geoffrey Kittredge
Lothar A. Kneifel (Washington, D.C. Office)
Jamin R. Koslowe
Prabha Kotiswaran
Jeffrey I. Lang
Kevin R. Learned
Eugene Y. Lee
Huey-Fun Lee
Young Lee
Maurizio Levi-Minzi (Hong Kong Office)
Alan M. Levine
Thomas R. Levy
Kirk D. Lipsey
Vera Losonci (London Office)
Karen C. Lu
Rory Macmillan (London Office)
Charles E. Malone (Paris Office)
Mark Marmer
Jean-Louis Martin (Paris Office)
Pierre Maugüé (Hong Kong Office)
Gregory M. McAndrew
Sandra C. McCallion
Alicia C. McCarthy
Mark Adrian McComiskey
Deena R. Merlen
Carl J. Micarelli
Steven S. Michaels
Charles R.A. Morse
Mary Beth Navin
Cheryl Nelson
Harold A. Neu
Carl W. Oberdier
P. Bradley O'Neill
Daniela Ortega
Nicole A. Ortsman-Dauer
Michael M. Ostrove (Paris Office)
Ellen Paltiel
Julie Perchenet (France Office)
Jonathan A. Popolow
Jeffrey Kenneth Powell
Thomas H. Prochnow
Etienne Pujol (Paris Office)
Sheri Lynn Rabiner
Philippe Raybaud (Paris Office)
William D. Regner
David M. Reilly (France Office)
Emily S. Reisbaum
Nadia Y. Rendak (Moscow Office)
Jonathan E. Richmond
Carl Riehl
G. Enrique Rivera
Julie Rosaz (Paris Office)
Joshua P. Rubin
David W. Runtz
Cristine M. Sapers
Matthew D. Saronson
Kristen K. Sauer
Leigh R. Schachter
Carolyn K. Schindel
Kevin M. Schmidt
David H. Schnabel
Kelly J. Schnabel
Kenneth Schneider (Moscow Office)
Peter F.G. Schuur
Inbar Schwartz
Karin S. Schwartz
David N. Sharpe
Paul F. Sheridan, Jr. (Washington, D.C. Office)
Wendy A. Semel (London Office)
Elana W. Sigall
Rebecca F. Silberstein
Steven J. Slutzky
Catherine W. H. So
Jaeyong So
Melissa P. Sobel
Nicole E. Soffin
Dana Stangel-Plowe
Ariadne Staples
Toby Starr (London Office)
David A. Stein
Joan M. Stout
Eileen E. Sullivan
Heidi M.V. Sullivan
Kathryn E. Sun (Hong Kong Office)
Michael J.D. Sweeney
Judith Taft
Joshua L. Targoff
Rita Tendolkar
Richard Gordon Thorpe
Antoine Tinnion
My Chi To
Debra Todres
Jo Anne P. Tsung
Jonathan R. Tuttle (Washington, D.C. Office)
Natalie Williams Umlauf
Steve W. Vaccaro
Gerald Von Thomas II
Claude E. Vuillieme
Randee J. Waldman
Kathleen D. Warner
Euphemia B. Warren
Steven Wayland
David A. Weinstein
Harriet J. Whiting
Katherine Birmingham Wilmore
Jan S. Wimpfheimer
Eric S. Wittstein
Naomi Wolfensohn
Richard Yun Xu (Hong Kong Office)
Alexander A. Yanos
Issa Yesufu

(See Next Column)

DEBEVOISE & PLIMPTON—*Continued*

ASSOCIATES (Continued)

Abigail B. Young
Ayse Yuksel
Alicia R. Zalesin
Martin Ziessler
Harry Zirlin
Perry V. Zizzi

For full biographical listings, see the Martindale-Hubbell Law Directory

DECHERT PRICE & RHOADS (AV)

30 Rockefeller Plaza, 10112
Telephone: 212-698-3500
Telefax: 212-698-3599
URL: http://www.dechert.com
Philadelphia, Pennsylvania: 4000 Bell Atlantic Tower, 1717 Arch Street, 19103-2793.
Telephone: 215-994-4000.
Washington, D.C.: 1775 Eye Street, N.W., 20006.
Telephone: 202-261-3300.
Harrisburg, Pennsylvania: Thirty North Third Street, 17101-1603.
Telephone: 717-237-2000.
Princeton, New Jersey: Princeton Pike Corporate Center, P.O. Box 5218, 08543-5218.
Telephone: 609-620-3200.
Boston, Massachusetts: Ten Post Office Square South, 02109-4603.
Telephone: 617-728-7100.
Hartford, Connecticut: 90 State House Square, 06103-3702.
Telephone: 860-524-3999.
London, England: 2 Serjeants' Inn, EC4Y 1LT.
Telephone: (0171) 583-5353. (Also see Titmuss Sainer Dechert).
Brussels, Belgium: 65 Avenue Louise, 1050.
Telephone: (02) 535-5411.
Paris, France: 55, avenue Kléber, 76116.
Telephone: 33-(0) 1-53 65 05 00.
Fax: 33-(0) 1-53 65 05 05.

PARTNERS IN NEW YORK

Robert A. Baime
Margaret A. Bancroft
Robert A. Cohen
Leonard J. Connolly
William K. Dodds
Patrick D. Dolan
Malcolm S. Dorris
G. Monique Escudero
Paul Gluck
Nina P. Grayson
Richard M. Hervey
Michael Hirschfeld
Ronald R. Jewell
Barbara J. Kelly
Fredric J. Klink
Joel H. Levitin
Glyndwr P. Lobo
Roger Mulvihill
Thomas F. Munno
Harriet Orol
Abbe G. Shapiro
Richard M. Sharfman
Timothy A. Stafford
James E. Tolan
Bruce B. Wood

OF COUNSEL

William F. Downey

COUNSEL IN NEW YORK

Naomi Friedland-Wechsler
Bruce J. Lieber
Anna E. Panayotou
Charles I. Poret
Daniel A. Ross

ASSOCIATES IN NEW YORK

Peter L. Critchell
Troy W. Doll
Christopher Eliopulos (Not admitted in NY)
Tara A. Farrelly
Sheryl Cohen Fine (Not admitted in NY)
Karen Fiorentino
Martin Gorham
Holly Johnsen Hoehner
Gregory S. Konzal
Stephenie L. Larsen
Daniel Malone
Jeffrey F. Manzella
William L. Neilson
Debra DuBritz O'Gorman
Sean K. O'Neill
Simona S. Papazian
Sang Hyuk Park
Valerie A. Potenza
Nancy Prahofer
Paul A. Sherrington
Jonathan Edward Silverblatt
Amianna Stovall
Richard Torres
Maureen Weiss
Paul M. Weisenfeld
Scott Welkis
Mireet S. Wolf
Rodney M. Zerbe

For full biographical listings, see the Martindale-Hubbell Law Directory

DEWEY BALLANTINE LLP (AV)

1301 Avenue of the Americas, 10019-6092
Telephone: 212-259-8000
Cable Address: "Dewbalaw"
Telex: 12-6825
Facsimile: 212-259-6333
URL: http://www.deweyballantine.com
Washington, D.C. Office: 1775 Pennsylvania Avenue, N.W., 20006-4605.
Telephone: 202-862-1000.
Fax: 202-862-1093.
Los Angeles, California Office: 333 South Hope Street, 90071-1406.
Telephone: 213-626-3399.
Fax: 213-625-0562.
London, England Office: Dewey Ballantine, 1 Undershaft, London EC3A 8LP, England.
Telephone: 011 44 171 456-6000.
Fax: 011 44 171 456-6001.

(See Next Column)

Hong Kong Office: Asia Pacific Finance Tower, Suite 3907, Citibank Plaza, 3 Garden Road, Central, Hong Kong.
Telephone: 011-852-2509-7000.
Fax: 011-852-2509-7088.
Budapest, Hungary Office: Dewey Ballantine, Andrássy út 60, H-1062 Budapest, Hungary.
Telephone: 36 1 374-2660.
Fax: 36 1 374-2661.
Prague, Czech Republic Office: Dewey Ballantine, Adria Palace, Jungmannova 31, 5th Floor, 110 00 Prague 1, Czech Republic.
Telephone: 420 2 2494-9005.
Fax: 420 2 2494-9010.
Warsaw, Poland Office: Dewey Ballantine Sp. z.o.o., Warsaw Towers, ul. Sienna 39, 00-121 Warsaw, Poland.
Telephone: 48-22-526-9999.
Fax: 48-22-526-9988.

MEMBERS OF FIRM

Camille Abousleiman (Resident Partner, London Office)
Alan M. Albright (Resident Partner, Los Angeles, California Office)
Timothy J. Alvino
Joseph Angland
J. Bradford Anwyll (Resident Partner, Washington, D.C. Office)
Emil Arca
Donna M. Attanasio (Resident Partner, Washington, D.C. Office)
Aldo A. Badini
Bradford J. Badke
Eileen Bannon
Fredric K. Bass
Keith W. Berglund (Resident Partner, Los Angeles, California Office)
Louise Roman Bernstein
James F. Bowe, Jr. (Resident Partner, Washington, D.C. Office)
Paul J. Bschorr
Richard J. Burdge, Jr. (Resident Partner, Los Angeles, California Office)
Denise A. Cerasani
Betty Cerini
John C. Chappell
Junaid H. Chida
John F. Collins
Douglas John Colliver (Resident Partner, London, England Office)
Wayne A. Cross
Ronald W. Davis
Christopher J. DiAngelo
Eliza A. Dolin
Joseph K. Dowley (Resident Partner, Washington, D.C. Office)
Lee Smalley Edmon (Resident Partner, Los Angeles, California Office)
E.N. Ellis, IV
Kathryn C. Ellsworth
Zori G. Ferkin (Resident Partner, Washington, D.C. Office)
Robert W. Fischer, Jr. (Resident Partner, Los Angeles, California Office)
James A. FitzPatrick, Jr.
Vincent R. FitzPatrick, Jr.
John P. Flynn (Resident Partner, Los Angeles, California Office)
Bruce W. Fraser (Resident Partner, Los Angeles, California Office)
Jonathan L. Freedman
John G. Fritzinger, Jr.
Leo V. Gagion
Fred R. Gander (Resident Partner, London Office)
Douglas L. Getter
Thomas W. Giegerich
E. Ann Gill
Eileen B. Gordon
Linda Grant Williams
Charles R. Hager
Russel T. Hamilton
Anne K. Hilker
Stuart Hirshfield
Benjamin Hoch
Graham R. Hone
Thomas R. Howell (Resident Partner, Washington, D.C. Office)
Peter S. Humphreys
David M. Irwin
Carol W. Trencher Ivanick
Everett L. Jassy
Stephen M. Jones (Resident Partner, London Office)
Joseph M. Juhas
Kevin A. Juran
Gerald A. Kafka (Resident, Washington, D.C. Office)
Frederick W. Kanner
Jack Kaufmann
Andrew W. Kentz (Resident Partner, Washington, D.C. Office)
Linda B. Klein
Bernard E. Kury
Harvey Kurzweil
Felix B. Laughlin (Resident Partner, Washington, D.C. Office)
Jeff S. Liebmann
Steven R. Loeshelle
Stanton J. Lovenworth
Steven P. Lund
Myles V. Lynk (Resident Partner, Washington, D.C. Office)
Stephen R. MacDonald
Cecily P. Maguire
Moni Mannings (Resident Partner, London, England Office)
Thomas C. Mazza
A. Grant McCrea
Robert J. McDermott
W. Clark McFadden II (Resident Partner, Washington, D.C. Office)
David S. McLeod (Resident Partner, Los Angeles, California Office)
Aileen C. Meehan
Janis M. Meyer
Jonathan W. Miller
Richard S. Miller
Robert A. Milne
Sean Moran
Frank E. Morgan II
Saul P. Morgenstern
Sanford W. Morhouse
Brian J. Morris
Donald J. Murray
Robert C. Myers
Paul L. Nash
Stuart I. Odell (Resident Partner, London Office)
Earle H. O'Donnell (Resident Partner, Washington, D.C.)
John A. Otoshi (Resident Partner, Hong Kong Office)
Marc R. Packer
Ira M. Palgon
Joseph M. Pari (Resident Partner, Washington, D.C. Office)
William J. Phillips
Morton A. Pierce
Richard D. Pritz
John A. Ragosta (Resident, Washington, D.C. Office)
Linda E. Ransom
Richard W. Reinthaler

(See Next Column)

DEWEY BALLANTINE LLP, *New York—Continued*

MEMBERS OF FIRM (Continued)

Richard B. Romney
William W. Rosenblatt
Howard J. Rosenstock (Resident Partner, Washington, D.C. Office)
David A. Rosinus
Michelle B. Rutta
John J. Salmon (Resident Partner, Washington, D.C. Office)
Drew D. Salvest (Resident Partner, London Office)
Mark Bradley Saunders (Resident Partner, London, England Office)
Betty M. Shumener (Resident Partner, Los Angeles, California Office)
Richard Shutran
James D. Simpson, Jr. (Resident Partner, London Office)
Joseph A. Smith
Karen A. Smith
Robert M. Smith (Resident Partner, Los Angeles, California Office)
Val A. Soupios
John P. Spuches
Michael H. Stein (Resident Partner, Washington, D.C. Office)
Richard A. Stenberg
Donald W. Stever, Jr.
Joanna R. Swomley
Richard B. Sypher
Martha J. Talley (Resident Partner, Washington, D.C. Office)
Roslyn Tom
Elizabeth W. Walker (Resident Partner, Los Angeles, California Office)
Paul R. Walker (Resident Partner, Los Angeles, California Office)
Clark E. Walter
Gordon E. Warnke
William B. Warren
Alan Wayte (Resident Partner, Los Angeles, California Office)
Hershel Wein
George C. Weiss
Paul J. Wessel
Robert H.C. Wilkerson (Resident Partner, Washington, D.C. Office)
Joe W. Williams
Jeffrey R. Witham (Resident Partner, Los Angeles, California Office)
Alan Wm. Wolff (Resident and Managing Partner, Washington, D.C. Office)
Donald F. Woods, Jr. (Resident Partner, Los Angeles, California Office)

COUNSEL

Lawrence Brocchini
Harry Lewis Clark (Resident Counsel, Washington, D.C. Office)
Dianne F. Coffino
Daisy Hilse Dwyer
Ellen S. Friedman
Ronald K. Giller (Resident Counsel, Los Angeles, California Office)
Andras I. Hanak (Resident Counsel, Budapest, Hungary Office)
Anna-Liza B. Harris (Resident Counsel, Washington, D.C. Office)
Maureen R. Healy
Lynnette Hotchkiss
Joel I. Krasnow
Gayle P. Levy
Michael S. Marx (Resident Counsel, Los Angeles, California Office)
Robert J. Morrow
Gregory M. Owens
Sandor E. Schick

OF COUNSEL

Frank W. Crabill
Julia Dryden English (Resident Of Counsel, Washington, D.C. Office)
L. Robert Fullem
Laurel W. Glassman (Resident Of Counsel, Washington, D.C. Office)
Robert H. Haggerty
Leonard Joseph
Michael J. Kunz
Kenneth R. La Voy, Jr.
Scotta E. McFarland (Resident Of Counsel, Washington, D.C. Office)
C. Gorham Phillips
Horace B. B. Robinson
Keith M. Schwartz (Resident Of Counsel, Washington, D.C. Office)
E. Deane Turner
John K. Van De Kamp (Resident, Los Angeles, California Office)
Bradford L. Ward (Resident Of Counsel, Washington, D.C. Office)
David E. Watts
William Wemple
John H. Whitworth, Jr.
Everett I. Willis

For full biographical listings, see the Martindale-Hubbell Law Directory

DUANE, MORRIS & HECKSCHER LLP (AV)

380 Lexington Avenue, 10168
Telephone: 212-692-1000
Fax: 212-692-1020
URL: http://www.duanemorris.com
Philadelphia, Pennsylvania Office: Suite 4200, One Liberty Place.
Telephone: 215-979-1000.
Fax: 215-979-1020.
Chicago, Illinois Office: 227 West Monroe Street, Suite 3400.
Telephone: 312-499-6700.
Fax: 312-499-6701.
Washington, D.C. Office: 1667 K Street, N.W., Suite 700.
Telephone: 202-776-7800.
Fax: 202-776-7801.
San Francisco, California Office: 100 Spear Street.
Telephone: 415-371-2200.
Fax: 415-371-2201.
Boston, Massachusetts Office: One International Place, 14th Floor.
Telephone: 617-598-3100.
Fax: 617-598-3101.
Miami, Florida Office: 200 South Biscayne Boulevard, Suite 3410.
Telephone: 305-960-2200.
Fax: 305-960-2201.

(See Next Column)

Wilmington, Delaware Office: 1201 Market Street, Suite 1500.
Telephone: 302-571-5550.
Fax: 302-571-5560.
Harrisburg, Pennsylvania Office: 305 North Front Street, 5th Floor, P.O. Box 1003.
Telephone: 717-237-5500.
Fax: 717-232-4015.
Wayne, Pennsylvania Office: 735 Chesterbrook Boulevard, Suite 300.
Telephone: 610-647-3555.
Fax: 610-640-2619.
Cherry Hill, New Jersey Office: 51 Haddonfield Road, Suite 340.
Telephone: 856-488-7300.
Fax: 856-488-7021.
Newark, New Jersey Office: One Riverfront Plaza.
Telephone: 973-424-2000.
Fax: 973-424-2001.
Palm Beach, Florida Office: 249 Royal Palm Way, Suite 403.
Telephone: 561-366-5400.
Fax: 561-366-5401.
Allentown, Pennsylvania Office: 968 Postal Road, Suite 200, P.O. Box 90400.
Telephone: 610-266-3650.
Fax: 610-266-3651.
Houston, Texas Office: One Greenway Plaza, Suite 500.
Telephone: 713-552-9900.
Fax: 713-552-0109.
Dover, Delaware Office: 314 S. State Street.
Telephone: 302-736-0156.
Fax: 302-736-0336.
Bangor, Maine Office: 15 Columbia Street, 4th Floor.
Telephone: 207-990-4800.
Fax: 207-990-4804.
Princeton, New Jersey Office: Princeton Forrestal Village, 116 Village Boulevard, Suite 200.
Telephone: 609-734-4323.
Fax: 609-734-4387.

RESIDENT PARTNERS

Nathan Abramowitz
Anthony J. Costantini
Michael D. Grohman
Grant Hanessian
T. Steven Har
Robert J. Hasday (Partner-in-Charge, New York Office)
Fran M. Jacobs
Eve I. Klein
Owen D. Kurtin
Michael H. Margulis
Curtis E. Pew
David H. Relkin
Barbara J. Scheiner
David S. Tannenbaum

ASSOCIATES

Jordan M. Anger
Maria Cilenti
Lynn P. Consentino
Charles M. Davidson
Rosemary Halligan
Beth Simone Noveck
Patrick N.Z. Róna

SPECIAL COUNSEL

Karen S. Frieman
Rona E. Senior

OF COUNSEL

Donald B. Relkin

For full biographical listings, see the Martindale-Hubbell Law Directory

EPSTEIN BECKER & GREEN, P.C. (AV)

250 Park Avenue, 10177
Telephone: 212-351-4500
Facsimile: 212-661-0989
Email: mail@ebglaw.com *URL:* http://www.ebglaw.com
Washington, D.C. Office: 1227 25th Street, N.W., Suite 700. 20037.
Telephone: 202-861-0900.
San Francisco, California Office: Epstein Becker & Green, Two Embarcadero Center, Suite 1650. 94111.
Telephone: 415-398-3500.
Los Angeles, California Office: Epstein Becker & Green, Suite 500, 1875 Century Park East. 90067.
Telephone: 310-556-8861.
Dallas, Texas Office: Park Central VII, 12750 Merit Drive, Suite 1320. 75251.
Telephone: 972-628-2450.
Stamford, Connecticut Office: One Landmark Square, Suite 1800. 06901.
Telephone: 203-348-3737.
Newark, New Jersey Office: Seventh Floor, The Legal Center, One Riverfront Plaza. 07102.
Telephone: 973-642-1900.
Miami, Florida Office: Epstein Becker & Green, 2400 South Dixie Highway, Suite 100. 33133.
Telephone: 305-856-1100.
Alexandria, Virginia Office: 510 King Street, Suite 301. 22314.
Telephone: 703-684-1204.
Boston, Massachusetts Office: 75 State Street. 02109.
Telephone: 617-342-4000.
Baltimore, Maryland Office: 111 South Calvert Street, Suite 2700. 21202.
Telephone: 410-385-5275.
Chicago, Illinois Office: Epstein Becker & Green, 55 East Monroe Street, 29th Floor. 60603.
Telephone: 312-845-1999.

(See Next Column)

EPSTEIN BECKER & GREEN P.C.—*Continued*

MEMBERS OF THE FIRM

Peter L. Altieri
Eric L. Altman
Gordon C. Andrews
Edwin H. Baker
Jeffrey H. Becker
Amy J. Beech
David C. Denowitz
Kenneth W. DiGia
Philip M. Gassel
Stuart M. Gerson (Washington, D.C. Office)
Jay E. Gerzog
Robert D. Goldstein
Ronald M. Green
Robert S. Groban, Jr.
Joseph L. Hutner
Michael A. Kalish
Paul M. Kaplan
Stanley L. Kay
Kenneth J. Kelly
Lowell S. Lifschultz
Margaret M. Madden
Frances Mary Maloney
Elliot J. Mandel
Mary Anne Mayo
Matthew T. Miklave
William J. Milani
Philip D. Mitchell
Patricia A. Murphy
Christopher S. Panczner
Peter M. Panken
Lawrence Peikes
Howard Pianko
Brian J. Platton
Dorothy Rosensweig
Dean L. Silverberg
Joseph A. Smith
Evan J. Spelfogel
Paul D. Squire
Peter D. Stergios
Peter J. Strauss
Steven M. Swirsky
Sidney Todres
Seamus M. Tuohey
Michael R. Zeller

SENIOR ATTORNEYS

Stacey B. Babson
Jerrold I. Ehrlich
Randell Montellaro
James G. Murphy
Richard G. Schwartz
Judith F. Stempler

OF COUNSEL

Robert E. DeRight, Jr.

SPECIAL COUNSEL

Fritz W. Alexander, II
Richard L. Campbell

ASSOCIATES

Russell N. Adler
Stacey L. Baker
Erik J. Belanoff
Hany S. Brollesy
Darryll A. Buford
Cathleen G. Cachero
Erin M. Carney
Kevin G. Casey
Mary Elizabeth C. Cisneros
Patrick M. Collins
Denise J. D'Ambrosio
Scott M. Dubowsky
L. Melissa Fleischer
Stefanie Gatti
Julie K. Gershman
Mark Jay Goldberg
Wendy C. Goldstein
Sean T. Granahan (Not admitted in NY)
Mark K. Hsu
Richard O. Hughes
Alesia J. Kantor
Traycee E. Klein
Stewart J. Kong
Jeffrey M. Landes
Jessica M. Lermond
Lauren A. Malanga
Elana S. Marcus
Deborah S. Markowitz
Ann L. Moscow
Robert J. Muchnick
Cesar Alexander Perez
Mark A. Polemeni
Theodore L. Polin
Lauri Faith Rasnick
Laurie Nicole Robinson
Clare M. Sproule
A. Jonathan Trafimow
David A. Turetsky
Jeannette M. Welsh
James D. Williams, Jr.
Jeffery D. Williams
Brian M. Wyatt (Not admitted in NY)

For full biographical listings, see the Martindale-Hubbell Law Directory

FISHER, FISHER & BERGER (AV)

A Partnership including a Professional Corporation
One Whitehall Street, 10004
Telephone: 212-514-8888
Fax: 212-514-9016
Email: fisherberger@earthlink.net

Andrew S. Fisher, P.C.
Henry T. Berger

ASSOCIATES

Melinda H. Vollmer
Eric L. Cooper
Diane C. Lorenc

OF COUNSEL

Harold L. Fisher
Judith E. Held
Gerald A. Resnick
Robert A. Straniere
Stanley Kalmon Schlein
Laurence J. Kaiser

Reference: The Chase Manhattan Bank, N.A.

For full biographical listings, see the Martindale-Hubbell Law Directory

FORD MARRIN ESPOSITO WITMEYER & GLESER, L.L.P. (AV)

Wall Street Plaza, 10005-1875
Telephone: 212-269-4900
Facsimile: 212-344-4294
Cable Address: "Formarew-New York"
Email: postmaster@fmew.com *URL:* http://www.fmew.com
Montclair, New Jersey Office: 49 Park Street.
Telephone: 973-744-3700.
Facsimile: 973-509-1565.

(See Next Column)

MEMBERS OF FIRM

James M. Adrian
Michael L. Anania
Charles A. Booth
Cushing O'Malley Condon
Elizabeth M. De Cristofaro
Thomas R. Esposito
William P. Ford
Victor G. Gleser (1948-1992)
Stuart C. Levene
Richard B. Marrin
Edward M. Pinter
Philip S. Plexico (1931-1983)
John J. Witmeyer III

COUNSEL

James F. X. Hiler

ASSOCIATES

Jay R. Alicandri
Jody M. Barringer
David A. Beke
Christopher J. Carney
Todd S. Corey
Joseph D'Ambrosio
Serena C. Hunn
Matthew J. Lasky
Paul V. Majkowski
Michael A. Rowe
Michael J. Tricarico

For full biographical listings, see the Martindale-Hubbell Law Directory

FRIED, FRANK, HARRIS, SHRIVER & JACOBSON (AV)

A Partnership including Professional Corporations
One New York Plaza, 10004
Telephone: 212-859-8000
Cable Address: "Steric New York" W.U. Int.
Telex: 662119 W.U. Domestic: 128173
Telecopier: 212-859-4000 (Dex 6200).
Email: info@ffhsj.com *URL:* http://www.ffhsj.com
Washington, D.C. Office: Suite 800, 1001 Pennsylvania Avenue.
Telephone: 202-639-7000.
Los Angeles, California Office: 350 South Grand Avenue, 32nd Floor.
Telephone: 213-473-2000.
London, England Office: 4 Chiswell Street, London EC1Y 4UP.
Telephone: 011-44-171-972-9600.
Fax: 011-44-171-972-9602.
Other London, England Office: International Securities Unit, 21 Wilson Street, London EC2M 2TX.
Telephone: 011-44-171-825-3093.
Paris, France Office: 7, Rue Royale, 75008.
Telephone: (011 331) 40 17 04 04.
Fax: (011 331) 40-17-08-30.

MEMBERS OF FIRM

Charles A. Riegelman (1879-1950)
Arthur L. Strasser (1880-1967)
Hermann E. Simon (1900-1990)
George A. Spiegelberg (1897-1979)
Sam Harris (1912-1980)
William I. Riegelman (1913-1984)
Arnold Hoffman (1921-1993)
Steven M. Abramowitz
Howard B. Adler
T. J. Anthony, Jr.
Rachel L. Arfa
Jeffrey Bagner
Lawrence N. Barshay
Barry S. Berger
John M. Bibona
Kenneth R. Blackman
Linda R. Blumkin
Michael R. Bromwich (Not admitted in NY)
Richard A. Brown (Not admitted in NY)
Donald P. Carleen
Robert Cassanos
Marc P. Cherno
Thomas W. Christopher
Peter V. Z. Cobb
Gary P. Cooperstein
Andrew J. Dady
Warren S. de Wied
Aviva F. Diamant
Lawrence A. First
Douglas H. Flaum
Arthur Fleischer, Jr. (P.C.)
Frederick H. Fogel
Jessica Forbes
Michele E. Foster (Not admitted in NY)
Stephen Fraidin (P.C.)
Victor S. Friedman (P.C.)
Stuart H. Gelfond
Robert E. Gerber
Matthew Gluck
David C. Golay
Peter S. Golden
Howard W. Goldstein
Franklin L. Green
Jean E. Hanson
Lois F. Herzeca
Allen I. Isaacson (P.C.)
Laurence Bryan Isaacson
Valerie Ford Jacob
Jack L. Jacobson
Gregory P. Joseph
Robert E. Juceam
Stuart Z. Katz
Arthur S. Kaufman
Allen Kezsbom
Sanford Krieger
Meyer Last
Ann Berger Lesk
Lisa A. Levy
Richard O. Loengard, Jr. (P.C.)
Janice MacAvoy
William G. McGuinness
Jonathan L. Mechanic
Joshua Mermelstein
Craig F. Miller
David M. Morris
Charles M. Nathan
Lee S. Parks
Eric J. Peterman
Harvey L. Pitt
Sheldon Raab (P.C.)
Michael H. Rauch
F. William Reindel
Paul M. Reinstein
Kenneth I. Rosh
Laraine S. Rothenberg
Ira S. Sacks
Anthony E. Satula, Jr.
Joel Scharfstein
Daniel P. Schechter
Steven G. Scheinfeld
Brad Eric Scheler
Richard M. Schwartz
Robert C. Schwenkel
Barry G. Sher
David N. Shine
Ross Z. Silver
Peter L. Simmons
Robert J. Sorin
George B. South III
Mark J. Stein
Bonnie Kayatta Steingart
Richard A. Steinwurtzel

(See Next Column)

FRIED, FRANK, HARRIS, SHRIVER & JACOBSON, *New York—Continued*

MEMBERS OF FIRM (Continued)

Joseph A. Stern
Lewis A. Stern (P.C.)
Audrey Strauss
John C. Sullivan
Alexander R. Sussman
Debra M. Torres
Gregg L. Weiner
Gail L. Weinstein
Richard A. Wolfe
(Not admitted in NY)

OF COUNSEL

Marvin V. Ausubel
Franklin L. Bass (P.C.)
Mitchell B. Birner
Diane E. Burkley
(Not admitted in NY)
Hans J. Frank
Walter J. Fried
Herbert L. Galant (P.C.)
Barbara S. Gillers
Herbert Hirsch
Leslie A. Jacobson
William Josephson
Stanley I. Katz
Charlie King
Frederick Lubcher (P.C.)
Benjamin Nassau
Robert H. Preiskel (P.C.)
Alan N. Resnick
Leon Silverman (P.C.)

SPECIAL COUNSEL

Edward M. Alterman
Gerald C. Bender
John A. Borek
Lily Chang
Elia Fischer
Bryan H. Hall
Joelle L. Halperin
Lynne A. Johnson
Kim J. Kirk
Ronald A. Lehmann
Joel L. London
John P. MacDonald
Eric H. Queen
Frances P. Schreiber
Paul I. Steinberg
Jedd H. Wider

RETIRED PARTNERS

Milton R. Ackman (P.C.)
Edwin Heller (P.C.)
Lee S. Parker
Harold E. Rosen
Howard D. Westrich

ASSOCIATES

Jonathan S. Adler
M. Kamal Ahmad
Emma M. Bailey
Kenneth Robert Barish
Matthew S. Barr
Fernando R. Bertoni
Christopher V. Blum
John W. Brewer
Adam Brodsky
William P. Burt
Joseph T. Calto
Ipek N. Candan
Alan T. Chan
Kit Wan Chiu
Jeffrey E. Clarke
Ellen M. Collins
Jennifer L. Colyer
Tom Combs
Abbott Cooper
Valerie F. Cursio
Joseph D. D'Angelo
George P. Danenhauer
(Not admitted in NY)
Israel O. David
Valerie P. Debler
Michael Birney de Leeuw
John Dellaportas
Rana Dershowitz
Terrence Dougherty
Sharon Schwartz Dove
Arthur T. Doyle
Philip C. Dublin
Hal M. Edelman
Alexandra E. Ekpiken
Jacques Erdos
Marcus A. Ernst
Margret Jonnson Evangelista
Christopher Ewan (Not admitted in the United States) (Legal Consultant)
Craig R. Farber
Brian M. Feldman
Eric M. Feuerstein
Catherine E. Finnerty
Rachel S. Fleishman
Michael P. Fox
Carey Gabay
Andrew T. Gardner
Ophir Gazit
Alyssa E. Gelper
Gregory C. Gibson
Janine Gilbert
Joshua C. Gillette
Natalie Glazer
Beth F. Goldstein
Stephanie J. Goldstein
Yekaterina A. Gordon
Jonathan Gray
Jason Ross Grebin
Jill Greenwald
Angela L. Grinstead
(Not admitted in NY)
Samuel A. Gunsburg
Nir Harel
Matthew Hawkins
David B. Hennes
Eric A. Hirsch
Monica Hsiao
Brett D. Jaffe
Peter R. Jerdee
(Not admitted in NY)
Mark Brent Joachim
J. Stuart Kagen
Bina Kalola
Gary L. Kaplan
Kristen I. Klass
Christopher J. Kopka
(Not admitted in NY)
Andrew Kwok
Gregory B. Lare
Corynne A. Lebetkin
Mark D. Lehrman
Maria E. Leibholtz
Andrew S. Lerner
Mara Leventhal
Michael A. Levitt
Jonathan F. Lewis
Deborah Lifshey
Jonathan F. Linker
Sandra M. Lipsman
Chiu-Ti Liu
Chelsea R. Lyford (not admitted in the United States)
Michael Marchant
Catherine Marten
Jeffrey I. Martin
Debra M. May
Michael S. McGarry
Vivek Melwani
Robert Meyer
Albert S. Mishaan
Eugene E. Mueller
Jonathan Muskat
Donna F. Mussio
Janai S. Nelson
Marcus Neupert
Tram N. Nguyen
Kevin J. O'Connor
Kalman Ochs
Carla Oliveira
Lori A. Palumbo
Kirsa Phillips
Peter R. Piazza
Louis Ramos
Gil A. Raviv
Brigette H. Renaud
Philip Richter
Neil C. Rifkind

(See Next Column)

ASSOCIATES (Continued)

Carl J. Rohling
Dan Ronnen
Marcy C. Rosenbaum
Andrea R. Rosenblum
Kenneth A. Rosenblum
Marian J. Rothman
Randall S. Rothschild
Arthur Rublin
Alan D. Sacks
James R. Savin
Steven Scheichet
Jesse Brian Schneider
Katie J. Schoultz (not admitted in the United States)
Barbara A. Schwartz
David Schwartz
David I. Shapiro
Michelle J. Shapiro
Zvia A. Shapiro
David L. Shaw
Matthew Sheehan (not admitted in the United States)
Sean Shields
Mark L. Shwartz
Andrew Silberstein
Hillel R. Silvera
Lauren J. Simmons
Peter Song
Tanya M. Stanich
Steven J. Steinman
Alberta Stewart
John Stewart
Vincent Sum
David M. Susswein
Virginia M. Tam
Alan S. Trager
Jane C. W. Tse
Joseph A. Tuchman
Kathleen K. Veteri
Robert R. Viducich
William G. Vreeland, III
Alan Nathan Walkow
Joshua Wechsler
Aliza F. Wein
Ian Weinstock
Pamela Weinstock
Pauline L. Wen
Cassandra D. Williams
Thea Ann Winarsky
Jason Wolkove
Judy C. Wong
Guy Yonay
Oscar A. Zamora
Oren L. Zeve
David A. Zilberberg

LOS ANGELES, CALIFORNIA SPECIAL COUNSEL

William A. Molinski

For full biographical listings, see the Martindale-Hubbell Law Directory

FRIEDMAN, WITTENSTEIN & HOCHMAN, A PROFESSIONAL CORPORATION (AV)

101 East 52nd Street, 10022
Telephone: 212-750-8700
Telecopier: 212-223-8391
Email: friedwitt@aol.com

Stuart I. Friedman
Andrew A. Wittenstein

COUNSEL

Stephen A. Hochman
John T. McLoughlin
(Not admitted in NY)

Mary Hillyer Dontzin
Paul S. Grossman
David O. Lloyd
Gianna M. McCarthy
Allison D. Powell

For full biographical listings, see the Martindale-Hubbell Law Directory

GAIR, GAIR, CONASON, STEIGMAN & MACKAUF (AV)

80 Pine Street, 10005
Telephone: 212-943-1090
Fax: 212-425-7513
Email: mail@gairgair.com *URL:* http://www.gairgair.com

MEMBERS OF FIRM

Harry A. Gair (1894-1975)
Robert L. Conason
Seymour Boyers
Ernest R. Steigman
Stephen H. Mackauf
Jerome I. Katz
David G. Miller
Candice Singer Ram
Jeffrey B. Bloom
Anthony H. Gair
Ben B. Rubinowitz
Howard S. Hershenhorn
Mary Nicholls
Rhonda E. Kay

APPELLATE COUNSEL

Herman Schmertz

ASSOCIATES

Herbert H. Hirschhorn
Warren J. Willinger
Ronald Berson
Vincent F. Maher
Daniel A. Gair
Richard M. Steigman
Diana M.A. Carnemolla

COUNSEL

Harriet E. Gair

For full biographical listings, see the Martindale-Hubbell Law Directory

GIBNEY, ANTHONY & FLAHERTY, LLP (AV)

A Limited Liability Partnership including a Professional Corporation
665 Fifth Avenue, 10022
Telephone: 212-688-5151
Telecopier: 212-688-8315
URL: http://www.gibney.com

MEMBERS OF FIRM

Wilson J. Gibney (1917-1987)
Ralph F. Anthony (1917-1996)
John F. Flaherty
Barry Zalaznick
James H. McGivney
Frederick W. Anthony
Robert V. Okulski
Stephen F. Ruffino
Gerald J. Dunworth
Stephen J. O. Maltby

(See Next Column)

GIBNEY, ANTHONY & FLAHERTY LLP—*Continued*

MEMBERS OF FIRM (Continued)

Kenneth N. Sacks
Brian W. Brokate
Pierre Cournot
Wm. Lee Kinnally, Jr.
Peter Cousins
Melville Southard, Jr.
Robert J. Costello
Heather J. McDonald
Joseph Di Cesare
Paul G. Kelly
Alan M. Weintraub
Melvyn H. Halper
Angelo E. P. Mazza
Beth M. Frenchman
John Macaluso
Marc Ragovin

ASSOCIATES

Pierre G. Bonnefil
Robert G. Kinnally
Kenneth D. Suzan
Ebonette Bates
Thao P. Nguyen

COUNSEL

Donald J. Williamson
Christopher Magrath
Richard L. Fisch
Stuart H. Brody
Paolo S. Grassi

For full biographical listings, see the Martindale-Hubbell Law Directory

GOLENBOCK, EISEMAN, ASSOR & BELL (AV)

437 Madison Avenue, 10022
Telephone: 212-907-7300
Telecopier: 212-754-0330
Email: postmaster@golenbock.com

MEMBERS OF FIRM

Nathan E. Assor
Lawrence M. Bell
David J. Eiseman
Jeffrey T. Golenbock
Andrew C. Peskoe
Richard S. Taffet
Robert B. Goebel
Leonard Eisenberg
Martin S. Hyman
Steven G. Chill
Donald A. Hamburg
Charles D. Schmerler
Jeffrey S. Berger
Lawrence R. Haut
Andrew M. Singer
Janice B. Grubin
Jacqueline G. Veit

OF COUNSEL

William G. Pearlstein
Jonathan S. Hacker

ASSOCIATES

Debra S. Schachtel
Charles B. Rich
Thomas J. Wilson
Elizabeth A. Jaffe
Adam C. Silverstein
Alvin R. Chin
Joel S. Tennenberg
Ruth G. Hirshfeld
Leslie J. Sherman
Hilda B. Gilfillan
David A. Collins
David K. Leitner
Richard S. Kaplan
Aielleen P. Fajardo (Not admitted in NY)
Gioia M. Ligos (Not admitted in NY)
Elaine S. Moshe

For full biographical listings, see the Martindale-Hubbell Law Directory

HAIGHT GARDNER HOLLAND & KNIGHT (AV)

A Law office of Holland & Knight, LLP
195 Broadway, 24th Floor, 10007
Telephone: 212-513-3200
Fax: 212-385-9010
Email: hklaw.com *URL:* http://www.hklaw.com
Atlanta, Georgia Office: 1201 West Peachtree Street, N.E., Suite 2000.
Telephone: 404-817-8500.
Fax: 404-881-0470.
Boston, Massachusetts Office: One Beacon Street.
Telephone: 617-523-2700.
Fax: 617-523-6850.
Bradenton, Florida Office: 1001 3rd Avenue West, Suite 600.
Telephone: 941-748-7076.
Fax: 941-747-9774.
Falls Church, Virginia Office: 3110 Fairview Park Drive, Suite 900.
Telephone: 703-645-8600.
Fax: 703-645-8610.
Fort Lauderdale, Florida Office: One East Broward Boulevard, Suite 1300.
Telephone: 954-525-1000.
Fax: 954-463-2030.
Jacksonville, Florida Office: 50 North Laura Street, Suite 3900.
Telephone: 904-353-2000.
Fax: 904-358-1872.
Lakeland, Florida Office: 92 Lake Wire Drive.
Telephone: 941-682-1161.
Fax: 941-688-1186.
Melbourne, Florida Office: 1499 South Harbor City Boulevard, Suite 201.
Telephone: 407-951-1776.
Fax: 407-951-1849.
Miami, Florida Office: 701 Brickell Avenue, Suite 3000.
Telephone: 305-374-8500.
Fax: 305-789-7799.
Orlando, Florida Office: 200 South Orange Avenue, Suite 2600.
Telephone: 407-425-8500.
Fax: 407-244-5288.

(See Next Column)

Providence, Rhode Island Office: 50 Exchange Terrace, Suite 300, Union Station Plaza.
Telephone: 401-751-8500.
Fax: 401-553-6850.
San Francisco, California Office: 44 Montgomery Street, Suite 4050.
Telephone: 415-743-6900.
Fax: 415-743-6910.
St. Petersburg, Florida Office: 200 Central Avenue, Suite 1600.
Telephone: 727-896-7171.
Fax: 727-822-8048.
Tallahassee, Florida Office: 315 South Calhoun Street, Suite 600.
Telephone: 850-224-7000.
Fax: 850-224-8832.
Tampa, Florida Office: 400 North Ashley Drive, Suite 2300.
Telephone: 813-227-8500.
Fax: 813-229-0134.
Washington, D.C. Office: 2100 Pennsylvania Avenue, N.W., Suite 400.
Telephone: 202-955-3000.
Fax: 202-955-5564.
West Palm Beach, Florida Office: 625 North Flagler Drive, Suite 700.
Telephone: 561-833-2000.
Fax: 561-650-8399.
Mexico City, Mexico Office: HOLLAND & KNIGHT-GALLÁSTEGUI Y LOZANO, S.C. (Joint Venture Office) Avenida Paseo de los Tamarindos No. 400, Torre "B" - 2° Piso, Col. Bosques de las Lomas, C.P. 05120 Mexico, D.F.
Telephone: 011-525-261-1866.
Fax: 011-525-261-1867.
Tel Aviv, Israel Office: Holland & Knight LTD, 23 Derech Petach-Tikva, 18th Floor.
Telephone: +011-972-3-566-7666.
Fax: +011-972-3-566-7667.
Buenos Aires, Argentina Office: San Martin 323--Piso 18, 1004.
Telephone: +54-11 4324-7600.
Fax: +54-11 4324-7601.

NEW YORK MEMBERS AND ASSOCIATES

Michael Alexander
Frederick P. Alimonti
Juan A. Anduiza
Jon Yard Arnason
Robert Bergen
Jerry D. Bernstein
William C. Brown, III
Randal R. Craft, Jr.
Richard A. Crowley
Randolph A. DelFranco
Oliver Edwards
Grant Gardner
David Goren
Alan Heblack
Nancy L. Hengen
James H. Hohenstein
William J. Honan III
Chester D. Hooper
Christopher G. Kelly
Bonny L. Y. Kwoh
Marisa Marinelli
Sandra E. Mayerson
Richard A. Menchini
Michael J. Mitchell
Mary Lynn Nicholas
John F. Pritchard
P. Michael Puleo
Lennard K. Rambusch
John J. Reilly
Alan D. Reitzfeld
Ludwig A. Saskor
Mark A. Saunders
James T. Shirley, Jr.
Brian D. Starer
Jovi Tenev
John M. Toriello
John K. Weir
Edward G. Williams
Glenn J. Winuk
D. Farrington Yates

SENIOR COUNSEL

Lars Forsberg
Barbara S. Friedman
George L. Selden
Frank G. Sinatra

Joshua J. Albert
Anne-Mette Elkjaer Andersen
Ann S. Beddingfield
Cristina M. Brennan
Douglas R. Burnett
Mary Lynne Calkins
Kari E. Chachkes
Brandon S. Collier
Michael N. Donofrio
Janet Epp-Rosenthal
Elizabeth Flavin
Vincent J. Foley
Hugh A. Forde
Peter A. Frazier
Michael Joseph Frevola
Marjorie Northrop Friedman
Nicholas S. Gatto
Jennifer A. Goodrich
David G. Harris
James V. Marks
Kenneth W. Marvet
Raymer W. McQuiston
Camille Nicodemus
Hilary Semel
Lisa Simone
M.J. Spelliscy
Fazl Syed
Eva Helen Wang
Kenneth K. Yoon

For full biographical listings, see the Martindale-Hubbell Law Directory

HEALY & BAILLIE, LLP (AV)

29 Broadway, 10006-3293
Telephone: 212-943-3980
Telecopier: 212-425-0131
Cable Address: "Mainbrace New York"
Telex: 422089
Email: reception@healy.com *URL:* http://www.healy.com
Hong Kong Office: Healy & Baillie, Suite 1303, Dina House, Ruttonjee Centre, 11 Duddell Street, Central.
Telephone: 852-2537-8628.
Telecopier: 852-2521-9072. Email: gryu@healy.com.hk.

(See Next Column)

HEALY & BAILLIE LLP, *New York—Continued*

Stamford, Connecticut Office: Stamford Harbor Park, 333 Ludlow Street, 06902-6987.
Telephone: 203-961-7250.
Telecopier: 203-357-7909. Email: reception@healy.com.

MEMBERS OF FIRM

Allan A. Baillie (1911-1983)
W. Cameron Beard
Nigel J. Binnersley (Resident Partner, Hong Kong Office)
Andrew V. Buchsbaum
Sharon S.H. Chen (Resident Partner, Hong Kong Office)
William N. France, II
Jack A. Greenbaum
Karen I. Hansen
Simon Harter
Jeremy J. Harwood
Nicholas J. Healy
John G. Ingram
John D. Kimball
John C. Koster
Andrew N. Krinsky
LeRoy Lambert
Philip S. LaPenta
Matthew A. Marion
Howard M. McCormack
Michael J. Murphy
Glen T. Oxton
Robert G. Shaw
Richard V. Singleton, II
John W. Wall (Resident Partner, Stamford, Connecticut Office)
Robert E. Wilder
Genrong Yu (Resident Partner, Hong Kong Office)

OF COUNSEL

Gordon W. Paulsen

ASSOCIATES

Avisheh Avini
Gregory J. Batista (Not admitted in NY)
Thomas H. Belknap, Jr.
Daniel Carr
Richard S. Ciacci
Brian P. Devine
Sarah B. Herlihy
Ari Staiman
Julie Pateman Ward
Arthur Zagorsky

For full biographical listings, see the Martindale-Hubbell Law Directory

HERZFELD & RUBIN, P.C. (AV)

40 Wall Street, 10005
Telephone: 212-344-5500
Telefax: 212-344-3333
Email: Herzfeld-Rubin.com
Affiliated Offices:
Los Angeles, California: Herzfeld & Rubin LLP, 1925 Century Park East.
Telephone: 310-553-0451.
Telefax: 310-553-0648.
Orange County, California: Herzfeld & Rubin LLP, 625 The City Drive, Orange.
Telephone: 714-750-0901.
Telefax: 714-750-4708.
Miami, Florida: Herzfeld & Rubin, 801 Brickell Avenue.
Telephone: 305-381-7999.
Telefax: 305-381-8203.
Winter Park, Florida: DeCiccio, Johnson, Herzfeld & Rubin, 652 W. Morse Boulevard.
Telephone: 407-740-4111.
Telefax: 407-740-4011.
Tampa, Florida: Barr, Murman, Tonelli, Herzfeld & Rubin, 201 East Kennedy Boulevard.
Telephone: 813-223-3951.
Telefax: 813-229-2254.
Jacksonville, Florida: Bullock, Childs, Pendley, Reed, Herzfeld & Rubin, 233 East Bay Street.
Telephone: 904-354-0286.
Telefax: 904-354-2778.
West Palm Beach, Florida: Koeppel, Gottlieb, Mesches, Herzfeld & Rubin, Suite 260, Esperante Building, 222 Lakeview Avenue.
Telephone: 561-659-4020.
Fax: 561-659-5399.
Newark, New Jersey: Chase Kurshan Suhr Weidenfeld Herzfeld & Rubin, LLC, P.O. Box 200057, The Legal Center, Suite 500, One Riverfront Plaza,
Telephone: 973-596-9484.
Telefax: 973-596-0762.
Bucharest, Romania: Herzfeld & Rubin (Romania) S.R.L., 62, Strada Dionisie Lupu, Sector 1.
Telephone: 40-1-22.333.58.
Telefax: 40-1-22.333.77.
Representative Office: Düsseldorf, Germany: Convenstrasse 2, 40211.
Telephone: (49) 211 36 35 35.
Telefax: (49) 211 36 35 37.

Walter Herzfeld (1907-1968)
Herbert Rubin
Bernard J. Wald
Michael Hoenig
Edward L. Birnbaum
Ian Ceresney
Fred W. Rauskolb, III
Leonard M. Polisar
Daniel V. Gsovski
Jeffrey L. Chase
Terry Myers
Harry P. Braunstein
Roger Arentzen
David B. Hamm
John M. Schwartz
C. Thomas Schweizer
Howard L. Wexler
Harold J. McKay
Cary Stewart Sklaren
Eugene P. Feit
William C. Guida
Carl T. Grasso
Peter J. Kurshan
Isaac D. Szpilzinger
Mark A. Meyer
J. Nicholas Suhr

(See Next Column)

Harold M. Weidenfeld
Gisella Levi Caroti
Miriam Skolnik
Michael B. Gallub
Clifford B. Aaron
Maureen Doerner Fogel
Andrew J. Levinson
James S. Kaplan
Janet O'Connor Cornell
Noreen M. Giusti
Victor E. Smukler
Wendy L. Prince
Joseph E. Donat

RESIDENT PARTNERS, LOS ANGELES, CALIFORNIA OFFICE

Richard L. Ackerman
Craig L. Winterman
Michael A. Zuk

RESIDENT MEMBERS, NEW JERSEY OFFICE

Peter J. Kurshan
J. Nicholas Suhr

RESIDENT PARTNERS, MIAMI, FLORIDA OFFICE

Myron Shapiro
Jeffrey B. Shapiro
Michael D. Lozoff
Alfredo Marquez-Sterling
David M. Krause
Bruce M. Boiko
Daniel L. Koch
Felicia M. Gordon
Kenn W. Goff

Howard S. Edinburgh
Leslie T. Williams (Not admitted in NY)
Donna S. Friedman
Linda Genero Sklaren
Linda Marie Brown
Jeannine LaPlace
Herbert L. Lazar
Anthony V. Raftopol
Joseph A. Churgin
Anja Wiesenberg
Homer B. Ramsey
Joseph Fishman
April Z. Dunleavy
Alisa Silverstein
Sacks David Olarsch
Natalie M. Drutz
Gail K. McCallion
Cynthia Dionne Watson
Christopher Albanese
Michael V. Reddy, Jr.
Christopher P. Nesterczuk
Edward T. Paulis, III
Albertina Webb (Not admitted in NY)

OF COUNSEL

Martin A. Roeder
Kevin J. Vernick
Arthur M. Strauss
Mortimer N. Felsinger
Martin Evans
Lawrence Kalik
Christian Hammerl
Paul P. E. Bookson
Ronald G. Russo
Charles A. Crum
David Cohen

SPECIAL COUNSEL

Aaron D. Twerski

For full biographical listings, see the Martindale-Hubbell Law Directory

INGRAM YUZEK GAINEN CARROLL & BERTOLOTTI, LLP (AV)

250 Park Avenue, 10177
Telephone: 212-907-9600
Facsimile: 212-907-9681

MEMBERS OF FIRM

Ernest J. Bertolotti (1942-1999)
Daniel L. Carroll
Roger Cukras
David G. Ebert
Larry F. Gainen
Samuel W. Ingram, Jr.
Paulette Kendler
Steven Mastbaum
Shane O'Neill
Dean G. Yuzek

ASSOCIATES

Warren E. Barrows
Amy Bertolotti
Patricia Hewitt
Theodore M. Kakoyiannis
Jeanne F. Pucci
Leigh A. Roveda
Jennifer E. Schwartz
Paul H. Slaney

OF COUNSEL

Karin J. Barkhorn
Beverly L. Deickler
Mark E. Klein
Paulette Lemay Peters
Cory L. Weiss

For full biographical listings, see the Martindale-Hubbell Law Directory

JONES, DAY, REAVIS & POGUE (AV)

599 Lexington Avenue, 10022
Telephone: 212-326-3939
Telecopier: 212-755-7306
Email: counsel@jonesday.com *URL:* http://www.jonesday.com
In Atlanta, Georgia: 3500 SunTrust Plaza, 303 Peachtree Street.
Telephone: 404-521-3939.
Telecopier: 404-581-8330.
In Brussels, Belgium: Avenue Louise 480, 7th Floor, B-1050 Brussels.
Telephone: 32-2-645-14-11.
Telecopier: 32-2-645-14-45.
In Chicago, Illinois: 77 West Wacker.
Telephone: 312-782-3939.
Telecopier: 312-782-8585.
In Cleveland, Ohio: North Point, 901 Lakeside Avenue.
Telephone: 216-586-3939.
Telecopier: 216-579-0212.
In Columbus, Ohio: 1900 Huntington Center.
Telephone: 614-469-3939.
Telecopier: 614-461-4198.
In Dallas, Texas: 2727 North Harwood Street.
Telephone: 214-220-3939.
Telecopier: 214-969-5100.

(See Next Column)

JONES, DAY, REAVIS & POGUE—*Continued*

In Frankfurt, Germany: Hochhaus am Park, Grüneburgweg 102, 60323 Frankfurt am Main.
Telephone: 49-69-9726-3939.
Telecopier: 49-69-9726-3993.
In Geneva, Switzerland: 20, rue de Candolle.
Telephone: 41-22-320-2339.
Telecopier: 41-22-320-1232.
In Hong Kong: 29th Floor, Entertainment Building, 30 Queen's Road Central.
Telephone: 852-2526-6895.
Telecopier: 852-2868-5871.
In Irvine, California: 5 Park Plaza, Suite 1100.
Telephone: 949-851-3939.
Telecopier: 949-553-7539.
In London, England: Bucklersbury House, 3 Queen Victoria Street.
Telephone: 44-20-7236-3939
Telecopier: 44-20-7236-1113.
In Los Angeles, California: 555 West Fifth Street, Suite 4600.
Telephone: 213-489-3939.
Telecopier: 213-243-2539.
In Paris, France: 120, rue du Faubourg Saint-Honoré.
Telephone: 33-1-56-59-39-39.
Telecopier: 33-1-56-59-39-38
In Pittsburgh, Pennsylvania: 500 Grant Street, 31st Floor.
Telephone: 412-391-3939.
Telecopier: 412-394-7959.
In Riyadh, Saudi Arabia: The International Law Firm (In Association with Jones, Day, Reavis & Pogue), Sulaymaniyah, Prince Mishari IBN, Abdulaziz Street, P.O. Box 22166.
Telephone: (966-1) 462-8866.
Telecopier: (966-1) 462-9001.
In Shanghai, China: 2805 Kerry Centre, 1515 Nanjing Road West.
Telephone: 86-21-5298-6568.
Telecopier: 86-21-5298-6569.
In Sydney, Australia: Governor Phillip Tower, Level 38, 1 Farrer Place.
Telephone: 61-2-9210-6921.
Telecopier: 61-2-9210-6926.
In Taipei, Taiwan: 8th Floor, 2 Tun Hwa South Road, Section 2.
Telephone: (886-2) 2704-6808.
Telecopier: (886-2) 2704-6791.
In Tokyo, Japan: Toranomon 45 Mori Building, 3rd Floor, 1-5, Toranomon 5-Chome, Minato-Ku, Tokyo 105, Japan.
Telephone: 81-3-3433-3939.
Telecopier: 81-3-5401-2725.
In Washington, D.C.: 51 Louisiana Avenue, N.W.
Telephone: 202-879-3939.
Telecopier: 202-626-1700.

MEMBERS OF FIRM IN NEW YORK

Thomas V. Heyman
Robert W. Sparks
E. Michael Bradley
David F. Clossey
(Not admitted in NY)
Marc S. Kirschner
Dennis W. LaBarre
(Not admitted in NY)
David M. Mahle
Fredrick E. Sherman
Jere Rogers Thomson
(Not admitted in NY)
Leonard C. Pojednic
Donald F. Devine
Susanna S. Fodor
Karl G. Herold
Robert J. Shansky
Robert L. Cunningham, Jr.
Thomas H. Sear
William F. Henze, II
Theresa M. Gillis
Robert A. Profusek
Barry R. Satine
Charles M. Carberry
Andrew J. Green
John J. Hyland
Stephan J. Mallenbaum
Michael J. Templeton
Steven D. Guynn
(Not admitted in NY)
Richard E. Andersen
Wanda N. Goodloe
Valerie P. Roberts
Cindy E. Tzerman
Dan A. Kusnetz
Steven C. Bennett
Jane Rue Wittstein
Glenn S. Arden
Ronald S. Gross
Conrad E. J. Everhard
J. Eric Maki
Olga V. Seixas
Randi L. Strudler
Michael R. Bassett
Harold K. Gordon
Mark A. Haddad
Sanford B. Kaynor, Jr.
Mark S. Mandel
Thomas W. Bark
Emad H. Khalil

OF COUNSEL

Thomas E. Albright
Ann F. Vinci

COUNSEL

Robert Iscaro
Lynne M. Figman
Marla S. K. Gale

ASSOCIATES

Diane L. Rose
Robert K. Smits
Flavia N. DeZotti
John K. Kane
(Not admitted in NY)
Micheleen C. Karnacewicz
Cara E. Mitnick
A. Michael Covino
James P. Jeffry
Darren B. Pocsik
Sharyl A. Reisman
David A. Rubin
Eileen M. Scanlon
Mark R. Seiden
John F. Simon
(Not admitted in NY)
Jayant W. Tambe
Lee A. Armstrong

(See Next Column)

ASSOCIATES (Continued)

Patricia M. Carroll
Shirin Johri (Not Admitted in the United States) Legal Consultant
Stacey N. Lefont
James J. Salerno
Marilyn W. Sonnie
(Not admitted in NY)
Allen S. Gage
Nathalie M. Legendre
Kristi L. Midboe Miller
Daniel L. Russo, Jr.
Thomas J. Speechley (Not admitted in United States)
Michael S. Chernis
Noreen M. English
Meredith S. Goldberg
Megyn M. Kelly
Kimberly Clark Roosevelt
Edward J. Zabrocki III
(Not admitted in NY)
Penny Zagalis
Marcell S. Clark
Bettina de Catalogne
Daniel de Miranda Faco
Monica Ferrer
Marc F. Holzapfel
Gerald S. Janoff
Kalyn J. Johnson
(Not admitted in NY)
Catherine B. Stevens
(Not admitted in NY)
Patricia B. Wong
Karen B. Elizaga
Bonnie L. Hemenway
Barbra S. Levy
Christopher J. Lopata
Gian-Michele a Marca
Steven M. Rosefsky
Osama Siddique
Byron G. Stier
Patrick G. Broderick
Joseph T. McKernan
Lubna A. Mian
Karen A. Ramos
Sheila Saegh
Tanya Singh
(Not admitted in NY)
Kavita Verma
Gwen A. Ashton
Randi C. Berger
Lance M. Breiland
Dickson Chin
Meredith L. Deutsch
Andrew M. Levine
Hallie G. Ludsin
Thomas E. Lynch
Durré Nabi

For full biographical listings, see the Martindale-Hubbell Law Directory

KAYE, SCHOLER, FIERMAN, HAYS & HANDLER, LLP (AV)

A New York Limited Liability Partnership
425 Park Avenue, 10022-3598
Telephone: 212-836-8000
Telex: 234860 KAY UR.
Facsimile: 212-836-8689
URL: http://www.kayescholer.com
Washington, D.C.: McPherson Building, 901 Fifteenth Street, N.W., Suite 1100, 20005-2327.
Telephone: 202-682-3500.
Facsimile: 202-682-3580.
Los Angeles, California: 1999 Avenue of the Stars, Suite 1600, 90067-6048.
Telephone: 310-788-1000.
Facsimile: 310-788-1200.
West Palm Beach, Florida Office: Phillips Point, West Tower 1002, 777 South Flagler Drive, 33401.
Telephone: 561-802-3230.
Facsimile: 561-802-3217.
Hong Kong: No. 1 Harbor View Street, Central.
Telephone: 852-28458989.
Facsimile: 852-28452389.
Shanghai, China: Suite 405 Shanghai Centre, 1376 Nanjing Xi Lu, 200040.
Telephone: 86-21-62797356.
Facsimile: 86-21-62797351.

MEMBERS OF FIRM

Benj. M. Kaye (1883-1970)
Harold L. Fierman (1898-1978)
Jacob Scholer (1887-1983)
James S. Hays (1901-1989)
Milton Handler (1903-1998)
David K. Barr
Julius Berman
Gary B. Bernstein
Warren J. Bernstein
Alfred J. Bianco
Michael D. Blechman
Michael D. Braff
Steven G. Canner
Emanuel S. Cherney
Andrea S. Christensen
David S. Copeland
Michael J. Crames
Thomas L. Creel
Lawrence A. Darby, III
Daniel P. DiNapoli
Bea Krain Drechsler
Herbert S. Edelman
Edmund M. Emrich
Jeffrey M. Epstein
Albert M. Fenster
Peter M. Fishbein
Lynn Toby Fisher
Kenneth A. Freeling
Nancy E. Fuchs
Edmond Gabbay
Thomas P. Gannon, Jr.
John D. Geelan
Phillip A. Geraci
Steven J. Glassman
Stephen Gliatta
Steven J. Glickstein
Adam H. Golden
Alan Franklin Gootit
Richard G. Greco
Joel I. Greenberg
Rory A. Greiss
Louis J. Hait
Joseph D. Hansen
Pamela Jones Harbour
Robert C. Helander
James D. Herschlein
John J. P. Howley
Ellen R. Joseph
Joel Katcoff
Karen E. Katzman
Mark S. Kingsley
Myron Kirschbaum
Lester M. Kirshenbaum
David Klingsberg
Stephen C. Koval
Andrew A. Kress
Ruthanne Kurtyka
Andrew Macdonald
Michael Malina
Eric P. Marcus
Fred H. Marcusa
Jay P. Mayesh
Henry G. Morriello
Terry D. Novetsky
Edward J. O'Connell
Jane W. Parver
Allan M. Pepper
Mitchel H. Perkiel

(See Next Column)

KAYE, SCHOLER, FIERMAN, HAYS & HANDLER LLP, *New York—Continued*

MEMBERS OF FIRM (Continued)

Michael Peskowitz
Thomas C. Ragan
Susan Berkman Rahm
Michael A. Rogoff
Aaron Rubinstein
Sanford J. Schlesinger
Willys H. Schneider
Mark Selinger
Richard C. Seltzer
Milton Sherman
Randolph S. Sherman
Thomas A. Smart
Gerald Sobel
Arthur J. Steinberg
Richard M. Steuer
Aaron Stiefel
Jay G. Strum
William A. Tanenbaum
Louis Tuchman
Sydney E. Unger
Jay W. Waks
William E. Wallace, Jr.
Gregory J. Wallance
Barry A. Willner
Arthur F. Woodard
Fredric W. Yerman
Alice Young
William C. Zifchak

SPECIAL COUNSEL

Seymour H. Chalif
Paul J. Curran
Donald J. Currie
Peter J. De Luca
Stanley H. Fuld
Walter G. Gans
Sheldon Oliensis
Milton J. Schubin
Peter H. Weil

RETIRED PARTNERS

Gerald Feller
Fred N. Fishman
Fred A. Freund
Donen Gleick
Joshua F. Greenberg
Stuart Marks
Melvin Michaelson
Bernard William Nimkin
Stanley D. Robinson
Stanley Rosenberg
Martin S. Saiman
Sidney J. Silberman
Henry K. Uman
Ronald L. Unger

NEW YORK COUNSEL

Laurie Abramowitz
Sharon H. Anson
Howard A. Becker
Simon D. Cices
Steven H. Cohen
Roger Du Broff
Howard J. Finkelstein
Wallace L. Ford II
Sheryl M. Gittlitz
Mark D. Godler
Anita Jones-Lee
Vera O. Kachnykewych
Michael A. Lynn
Steven T. Marom
(Not admitted in NY)
Glenn J. Pogust
Marc D. Rosenberg
Steven D. Roth
Stuart D. Sender
Spencer Weber Waller

OF COUNSEL

Robert B. Bernstein
Richard A. De Sevo
Kathleen M. Faccini
M.E. Freeman
Arlene Harris
John M. Johnson
Robert A. Kandel
Bert L. Slonim
Maris Veidemanis
Rhonda Yacker

NEW YORK ASSOCIATES

Eric L. Aaronson
Sara R. Adler
David Albalah
Ana M. Alfonso
Dina Leshetz Bakst
Jennifer Ross Bassett
(Not admitted in NY)
Elizabeth A. Beil
Kathryn Beller
(Not admitted in NY)
Lauren M. Bernstein
Michael S. Bertisch
Daniel Besser
Jeanette Bionda
Sheila S. Boston
Kimberly Dee Branch
Jon W. Brayshaw
Nichelle Bussey
Roderick W. Chin
Wing K. Chiu
David L. Cohen
David Cotta
Peter G. Danias
Scott I. Davidson
Arturo Diaz
Lois F. Dix
Joseph M. Drayton
Denis A. Dufresne
Sharyn Faye Feinbloom
Martin Feinstein
Greg R. Fidlon
Jennifer C. Foster
Jeffrey A. Fuisz
William Gardner
Karin E. Garvey
Jana Gerken
Mercer A. Givhan, III
(Not admitted in NY)
Alan Glantz
Scott B. Goldberg
Jonathan M. Gottsegen
(Not admitted in NY)
Robert Grass
Richard J. Halloran
Danielle Heimann
Lawrence Hersh
Douglas T. Hirai
Cary S. Hoffman
Todd A. Holmbo
Benjamin C. Hsing
Brenda M. Janowitz
Daniel Javitch
Martin J. Jones
Andrew Kanter
Allan A. Kassenoff
Jeffrey H. Kapner
Liza Ilona Karsai
(Not admitted in NY)
Cherise M. Wolas
Jeffrey Kirshner
Howard Kleinhendler
Bruce J. Koch
Lianne Lazetera
Aaron Y. Lehrfield
Lori B. Leskin
Eli Levine
Ian Seth Linker
Paul C. Llewellyn
Susan Marie Luciano
Leslie A. Lynn
Richard R. Mammon
Jeffrey S. Mann
Dana L. Mark
Deborah A. Marrone
Salvatore J. Mastrosimone
Manvin S. Mayell
Thomas J. McGahren
Alison McKinnell
Thomas J. McNiff
Benjamin Mintz
Lisa Hope Nicholson
Karen L. Nielsen
Melissa A. Noah
(Not admitted in NY)

(See Next Column)

NEW YORK ASSOCIATES (Continued)

Jonathan G. Offenkrantz
June A. O'Hea
Kathleen M. O'Keefe
Craig Allen Opp
Thomas P. Orfanos
Frederick H. Paulmann, IV
Michael M. Pomerantz
Frank A. Pozzuoli
Gary N. Rawlins
Agigail M. Rehm
(Not admitted in NY)
Daniel Reisner
John Roberti
Jonathan Rochwarger
Antonino B. Roman, III
Mollie D. Roth
Alan E. Rothman
Marlo Deborah Salz
Jesse L. Sands
Michael Sapienza
Debra Schaumberger
Rina Scheiner
Efrem T. Schwalb
Marci Guttentag Settle
Gregory P. Silberman
(Not admitted in NY)
Julie A. Simms
Kurt Skonberg
Lori A. Smeal
Andrew K. Solow
Sara Jane Steinberg
Tamara Stephen
Derek Michael Stoldt
Jonnie Strong
Robin A. Tauber
Joshua S. Teitelbaum
Rina Elizabeth Teran
Michelle Tong
Sandra L. Tsang
Emily Rebecca Waldman
Sapna C. Walter
(Not admitted in NY)
Veronica Julia Wiles
(Not admitted in NY)
Rachel Yarkon

WASHINGTON, D.C. OFFICE
RESIDENT PARTNERS

Sylvia M. Becker
David O. Bickart
Donald B. Cameron, Jr.
G. Christopher Griner
Ronald K. Henry
Michael P. House
Julie C. Mendoza
Mark S. Popofsky
Kerry Alan Scanlon
Jason L. Shrinsky
Randall L. Speck

WASHINGTON, D.C. SPECIAL COUNSEL

William S. Eberle (P.A.)
Steven L. Schwarcz

WASHINGTON, D.C. COUNSEL

Christopher R. Brewster
Bruce Alan Eisen
Farhad Jalinous
Raymond Paretzky
R. Will Planert
John P. Rynkiewicz
John W. Schryber
James M. Weitzman

WASHINGTON, D.C. ASSOCIATES

Todd B. Elmer
Dean C. Garfield
Larry J. Gusman
Craig Guthery
John R. Miles
Brady W. Mills
Allan Gary Moskowitz
Randi S. Turner
Deborah L. Wengel

HONG KONG OFFICE
PARTNERS

Franklin D. Chu
Kenneth G. M. Mason
David T. Zhang

HONG KONG ASSOCIATES

Maurice L. Hoo
Shuang Hu
Victor Wang

SHANGHAI OFFICE
PARTNERS

Franklin D. Chu
Yingxi Fu-Tomlinson

SHANGHAI ASSOCIATE

Amanda Chi

LOS ANGELES, CALIFORNIA OFFICE
PARTNERS

Aton Arbisser
Robert Barnes
Russ Alan Cashdan
T. Brent Costello
Barry L. Dastin
Michael D. Fernhoff
Jeffrey S. Gordon
Peter L. Haviland
Sheri Jeffrey
Barry H. Lawrence
Ronald L. Leibow
Joseph M. Malinowski
Michael A. Santoro
Regina T. Shanney-Saborsky

LOS ANGELES, CALIFORNIA OFFICE
SPECIAL COUNSEL

Cruz Reynoso

LOS ANGELES, CALIFORNIA OFFICE
COUNSEL

Michael J. Eliasberg
Carole E. Handler
Ronald E. Levinson
B.J. Yankowitz

LOS ANGELES, CALIFORNIA ASSOCIATES

Andrew W. Ash
Lawrence B. Behrendt
Gordon M. Bobb
Reid Hunter Breitman
Julian Brew
Ashleigh A. Danker
Jon E. Gelb
Stephanie Granato
Gina Guerra
James R. Hoskinson, Jr.
Asher Isaacs
Jason E. Miller
Quimby Pierce
Sergey Trakhtenberg
Rhonda Renee Trotter
Jeremy M. Weitz

WEST PALM BEACH, FLORIDA OFFICE
PARTNERS

Donald J. Currie
Abraham M. Mora

(See Next Column)

KAYE, SCHOLER, FIERMAN, HAYS & HANDLER LLP—*Continued*

WEST PALM BEACH, FLORIDA ASSOCIATES

Jodi R. Lustgarten

For full biographical listings, see the Martindale-Hubbell Law Directory

KELLEY DRYE & WARREN LLP (AV)

101 Park Avenue, 10178
Telephone: 212-808-7800
Fax: (212) 808-7897
Email: info@kelleydrye.com *URL:* http://www.kelleydrye.com
Los Angeles, California Office: 777 South Figueroa Street, Suite 2700.
Telephone: 213-689-1300.
Fax: (213) 688-8150.
Stamford, Connecticut Office: Two Stamford Plaza, 281 Tresser Boulevard.
Telephone: 203-324-1400.
Fax: (203) 327-2669; (203) 964-3188.
Washington, D.C. Office: 1200 19th Street, N.W., Suite 500.
Telephone: 202-955-9600.
Fax: (202) 955-9792.
Parsippany, New Jersey Office: 5 Sylvan Way.
Telephone: 973-539-0099.
Fax: (973) 539-3167.
Chicago, Illinois Office: 303 West Madison Street, Suite 1400.
Telephone: 312-346-6350.
Fax: (312) 346-8982.
Brussels, Belgium Office: 106 Avenue Louise, 1050.
Telephone: (011) (32-2) 646-1110.
Fax: (011) (32-2) 640-0589.
Hong Kong Office: Suite 1602, Fairmont House, 8 Cotton Tree Drive.
Telephone: (011) (85-2) 2869-0821.
Fax: (011) (85-2) 2869-0049.
Affiliated Offices:
Jakarta, Indonesia: Soebagjo, Roosdiono, Jatim & Djarot, Plaza Mashill, 17th Floor, Jalan Jend. Sudirman Kav. 25, Jakarta 12920, Indonesia.
Telephone: (011) (62-21) 5229765.
Fax: (011) (62-21) 5229752.
Tokyo, Japan: Yumoto & Ota, Kioi Royal Heights, 3-29, Kioi-Cho, Chiyoda-Ku, Tokyo 102, Japan.
Telephone: (011) (81-3) 3234-2441.
Fax: (011) (81-3) 3262-2729.
Manila, Philippines: Oporto Law, 2111 BSA Suites, 103 C. Palanca Street, Legaspi Village, Makati City, Metro Manila.
Telephone: (011) (63-2) 888-6951; 888-6953.
Fax: (011) (63-2) 724-1642. E-Mail: joporto@kelleydrye.com.
Bangkok, Thailand: Dej-Udom & Associates, Charn Issara Tower, 9th Floor, 942/142-3 Rama IV Road, Bangkok 10500 Thailand.
Telephone: (011) (66-2) 233-0055.
Fax: (011) (66-2) 236-6681. E-Mail: dejudom@loxinfo.co.th.

MEMBERS OF FIRM

Robert J. Aamoth (Washington Office)
Danny E. Adams (Washington Office)
Robert B. Adams
Talat M. Ansari
James L. Armstrong, III, (P.A.) (Not admitted in NY)
Mark I. Bane
M. Ridgway Barker (Stamford Office)
David E. Barry
Robert M. Berson
Robert D. Bickford, Jr. (Parsippany and New York Offices)
Joseph A. Boyle
Richard W. Brady
Paul L. Bressan (Los Angeles Office)
Richard G. Brodrick (Stamford Office)
Steven P. Caley
John M. Callagy (New York and Stamford Offices)
Brian J. Calvey
Jonathan E. Canis (Washington Office)
John T. Capetta (Stamford Office)
James S. Carr
Carolyn R. Caufield
Richard S. Chargar (Stamford Office)
Justine M. Clark
Richard J. Concannon
Jonathan K. Cooperman
John J. Costello
Robert E. Crotty
Eugene T. D'Ablemont
John Dames (Chicago Office)
Patrick Del Duca (Los Angeles Office)
Richard E. Donovan (Parsippany and New York Offices)
Paul F. Doyle
W. Christian Drewes
Robert Ehrenbard
Alan M. Epstein
William A. Escobar
Anne M. Falvey
Walter T. Faulkner
B. Harrison Frankel
John A. Garraty, Jr.
John F. Gibbons
William R. Golden, Jr.
Benjamin H. Green (Stamford Office)
Mark S. Gregory (Stamford Office)
Paul C. Guth
Robert L. Haig
James R. Hays
William C. Heck
Barbara E. Hoey
Joseph B. Hoffman (Washington Office)
Bud G. Holman
Ronald D. Husdon (Los Angeles Office)
John G. Immer (Not admitted in NY)
Michael S. Insel
Jane E. Jablons
Thomas C. Jackson (Washington Office)
Michael P. Kaelin (Stamford Office)
Sherman E. Katz (Washington Office)

(See Next Column)

MEMBERS OF FIRM (Continued)

William H. Kiekhofer, III (Los Angeles Office)
John E. Kiley
Thomas B. Kinzler
James J. Kirk (Parsippany and New York Offices)
Kenneth Kirschner
Jay R. Kolmar (Parsippany Office)
Theresa A. Kristovich (Los Angeles Office)
William A. Krohley
Alan J. Laska
Patricia M. Lee
Evelyn J. Lehman
Douglas P. Lobel (Washington Office)
Michael Lublinski (Los Angeles Office)
Richard R. Lury
John J. Lynagh
Paul G. Madison (Washington Office)
George J. Marchese
Paul F. McCurdy (Stamford Office)
Neil Merkl
Yves Miedzianogora
Jacob J. Miles
Talbott Miller (Parsippany, Stamford and New York Offices)
Jun Mori (Los Angeles Office)
Brad E. Mutschelknaus (Washington Office)
Frederic S. Nathan
James V. O'Gara
Susan J. Onuma
Christopher C. Palermo
Mary K. Periolat (Chicago Office)
Philip V. Permut (Washington Office)
Aileen A. Pisciotta (Washington Office)
Eric F. Quandt (Chicago Office)
Sarah L. Reid
David E. Retter
Ronald B. Risdon
Theodore J. Roper (Los Angeles Office)
Audrey M. Roth
Frederic A. Rubinstein
Joel S. Rublin
Judith St. Ledger-Roty (Washington Office)
Jay R. Schifferli (Stamford Office)
Francis Y. Sogi
Julian Solotorovsky (Chicago Office)
Stuart T. Solsky
Michael W. Stamm
Stephen W. Stein
Daniel M. Steinway (Washington Office)
Marshall C. Stoddard, Jr. (Not admitted in NY)
Merrill B. Stone (Parsippany and New York Offices)
Elisheva S. Teitz
André Van Landuyt (Brussels Office)
David L. Vaughan (Washington Office)
Salvatore J. Vitiello
Shabbir S. Wakhariya
Kevin J. Walsh
Shigeru Watanabe (Los Angeles Office)
William A. Wilson III (Hong Kong Office)
Peter Wolfram
Edward A. Yorkgitis, Jr. (Washington Office)
Kyuhong Yuh
Harvey Folks Zimand

OF COUNSEL

James J. Freeman (Washington Office)
Roberta S. Karmel
Eugene E. Mulhern (Stamford Office)
Francis T. Murphy
Alfred P. O'Hara

SPECIAL COUNSEL

Joan M. Griffin (Washington Office)
Rochelle M. Lindsey (Los Angeles Office)
Charles M. Oliver (Washington Office)
M. Jasmine S. Oporto (Hong Kong Office)
Karen Ostad

DIRECTOR

Theodore R. Voss (Director of Marketing)

NEW YORK ASSOCIATES

Jennifer L. Adams
Bryan J. Alter
David O. Amendola
John F. Beggs
Jason K. Brown
Gary M. Buechler
Andrea L. Calvaruso
Aaron M. Cohen
Karyn E. Corlett
Jennifer R. Danzo
Mayleen E. Devonish
Ata Dinlenc
Frank C. DiPrisco
Jeffrey C. Dodson
Barbara Kreinik Ehudin
Margaret Ferguson
Robert S. Friedman
Joseph N. Froehlich
Paul W. Garrity
Joseph E. Geoghan III
Alan J. Gerson
Antonia F. Giuliana
Stephen P. Goulet
Michelle M. Graham
Kathleen E. Groom
Steven A. Hantz
Satyanarayan S. Hegde
Jay N. Heinrich (Not admitted in NY)
David J. Hubbard
Scott A. Jalowayski
Pamela D. Kaplan
Jeffrey A. Katz
Stacey A. Kinnamon
Martin A. Krolewski
Bruce P. Levine
Elizabeth Luciano
John P. Maloney
Scott H. Mandel
Christina M. Mason
James P. McCabe
Monique A. Mc Clure
Gregory M. McKenzie
Timothy M. Meehan
Fern R. Mehler
Martin B. Miller
Sara Dodman Miller
Neil J. O'Halloran
I. Russell Oken (Not admitted in NY)
Juliana O'Niell
Richard C. Paice
Nicholas J. Panarella
Jean Y. Park
Shari L. Prussin
John A. Reade, Jr.
Allison Reich
Carolyn D. Richmond
Philip D. Robben
Dana M. Roth (Not admitted in NY)
Salvatore G. Siino
Gurpreet M. Singh
Jeanne R. Solomon
Mark R. Somerstein
Joseph J. Sperber, IV

(See Next Column)

KELLEY DRYE & WARREN LLP, *New York—Continued*

NEW YORK ASSOCIATES (Continued)

Bennet Steinberg
Eric Steinberg
Robert I. Steiner
Loren R. Taub
Thomas E. Tether
Lisa A. Thompson
Kathy M. Togni
Christine E. Tormey
Bertrand J. Tzeng
Christopher Walcott
Kevin C. Walker
Robin S. Weinberg
Marion B. Worth
Sue C. Yi (Not admitted in NY)

Karen E. Abrams (Parsippany Office)
Allison-Claire Acker (Los Angeles Office)
Francisco Javier Aparicio (Los Angeles Office)
Myrna E. Arroyo (Stamford Office)
Steven A. Augustino (Washington Office)
Leila M. Baheri (Washington Office)
Peter A. Batacan (Washington Office)
Michael K. Beran (Stamford Office)
Winafred R. Brantl (Washington Office)
Gabrielle M. Buckley (Chicago Office)
Ross A. Buntrock (Washington Office)
James A. Cordone (Stamford Office)
Peter E. Carlson (Chicago Office)
Geoffrey W. Castello (Parsippany Office)
Elaine D. Critides (Washington Office)
William M. Dailey (Stamford Office)
Todd D. Daubert (Washington Office)
Lloyd D. Daughtry (Stamford Office)
James W. Deacon II (Washington Office)
K. DeAnne Dixson (Los Angeles Office)
Wesley D. Dupont (Stamford Office)
Michael Don Olsen (Washington Office)
William V. Essig (Chicago Office)
Muna A. Farid (Hong Kong Office)
Michael J. Francesconi (Washington Office)
John I. Gordon (Hong Kong Office)
Tracey Hammer (Stamford Office)
Randi-Jean G. Hedin (Stamford Office)
John J. Heitmann (Washington Office)
Marianne Hoffman (Stamford Office)
Andrew R. Hough (Washington Office)
Xuhua Huang (Hong Kong Office)
Steven L. Humphreys (Washington Office)
Edward J. Hunter (Parsippany Office)
Rebekah J. Kinnett (Washington Office)
Michelle M. La Mar (Los Angeles Office)
John M. Lambros (Washington Office)
Brian J. MacDonald (Stamford Office)
Paul V. May (Stamford Office)
Nichelle Maynard-Elliott (Stamford Office)
Edward Meyers
Michael P. McGovern (Washington Office)
Duccio Mortillaro (Los Angeles Office)
Hamid R. Namazie (Los Angeles Office)
James E. Nealon (Stamford Office)
Cynthia S. Papsdorf (Los Angeles Office)
Joseph M. Pastore III (Stamford Office)
W. Joseph Price (Washington Office)
Andrea D. Pruitt (Washington Office)
Steven E. Rich (Los Angeles Office)
Karlene J. Rogers (Stamford Office)
Daniel A. Rowin (Chicago Office)
Pamela A. Russell (Parsippany Office)
Sheri M. Schwartz (Los Angeles Office)
J. Barton Seitz (Washington Office)
Christopher T. Sheean (Chicago Office)
Carol Weiss Sherman (Stamford Office)
Melissa M. Smith (Washington Office)
Enrico C. Soriano (Washington Office)
David B. Sudzus (Chicago Office)
Erin R. Swansiger (Washington Office)
Alyson T. Todd (Chicago Office)
Steven M. Torkelsen (Stamford Office)
Rebecca Landon Tzou (Washington Office)
Kelly C. H. Warrick (Stamford Office)
Rebecca J. Winthrop (Los Angeles Office)
Stephen A. Wood (Chicago Office)
Akiko Nakatani Yoong (Los Angeles Office)

For full biographical listings, see the Martindale-Hubbell Law Directory

KIRKLAND & ELLIS (AV)

A Partnership including Professional Corporations
Citicorp Center, 153 East 53rd Street, 10022-4675
Telephone: 212-446-4800
Facsimile: 212-446-4900
URL: http://www.kirkland.com
Chicago, Illinois Office: 200 East Randolph Drive.
Telephone: 312-861-2000.
Facsimile: 312-861-2200.
Telex: 25-4361.

(See Next Column)

Los Angeles, California Office: 777 South Figueroa Street.
Telephone: 213-680-8400.
Facsimile: 213-680-8500.
Washington, D.C. Office: 655 Fifteenth Street, N.W.
Telephone: 202-879-5000.
Facsimile: (202) 879-5200.
London, England Office: International Financial Centre, Old Broad Street.
Telephone: 171-816-8700; New Telephone Effective April 1, 2000: 207-816-8700.
Facsimile: 171-816-8800.

MEMBERS OF FIRM

Roy M. Adams
Debra B. Arenare
Gregory S. Arovas
Lance C. Balk
Peter A. Bellacosa
Sandra A. Bresnick
Brian E. Cameron (Not admitted in NY)
Eunu Chun
John M. Desmarais
Jack M. Feder (Not admitted in NY)
Theodore L. Freedman
James H. Gale
Patrick C. Gallagher
Jean Reed Haynes
Glen E. Hess (P.C.)
Francis M. Holozubiec
Paul F. Jock, II (P.C.)
Stephen P. H. Johnson
Joshua N. Korff
John L. Kuehn
Glenn Kurlander
Eric F. Leon
Geoffrey W. Levin
Marjorie Press Lindblom
Karl E. Lutz (P.C.)
Ellen M. Moskowitz
Michael Movsovich
Andrew E. Nagel
John C. Novogrod
William H. Pratt
Jonathan F. Putnam
Mark A. Racanelli
Kirk A. Radke
Yosef J. Riemer
Lisa A. Samenfeld
Joseph Serino, Jr.
Sarah Slover
Kenneth W. Starr (Not admitted in NY)
Frederick Tanne
Kimberly Paap Taylor
Kevin W. Treesh
Adrian van Schie
Victor D. Xistris

ASSOCIATES

Jai Agrawal
Lee E. Allison
Lisa M. Anastos
Marion Annau
Robert A. Appleby
Peter J. Armenio
Emily Bab
James T. Bailey
Natasha Balendra (Not admitted in the United States) (Legal Consultant)
Javier Bleichmar
Markus P. Bolsinger
Adrian Boutel
David S. Brafman
Michael A. Brosse
Naim Dutch Bulbulia
Micah Burch
Christopher D. Catalano
RoseAnn Younghee Cho
Steven E. Clemens
Edwin M. Collins (Not admitted in NY)
Jennifer L. Danis
Erica C.Y. Dao
Michael N. Delgass (Not admitted in NY)
Armand A. Della Monica
Peter D. Doyle
Carolyn A. Edgar
Daniel J. Eisner (Not admitted in NY)
Michael Brett Flaschen
Robert J. Frances
Joseph C. Gioconda
Drew N. Grabel
Maxine Yvette Graham
Adam M. Grenker (Not admitted in NY)
Jeff A. Hess
Mia Higgins
Paul S. Hong
Pamela A. Huelster
Hessam Kalantar
Michael G. Kalish (Not admitted in NY)
Stephen Mark Lebowitz
Mary Jane Lee (Not admitted in NY)
John Leone
J. Andrew Lindholm
John Lynn
David MacDonald
Lena Mandel
Kimberly Marlar
Heidi C. Matterfis
Kathleen M. McCarthy
Adam Mikkelsen (Not admitted in the United States) (Legal Consultant)
Andrew N. Moers (Not admitted in NY)
Gregory P. Nero
Howard Neuthaler
Kimberly Ziev Niehaus
Thomas D. Pease
Christopher Jon Peters
Duncan Quinn-Smith
W. Brian Raftery
Eileen A. Reardon
Ezra J. Reinstein
William F. Rowley III
Scott R. Samay
Henry G. Sawtelle
Todd S. Schulman
Jennifer M. H. Selendy
Shiva A. Sooudi
Lee Ann Stevenson
Ariel B. Taitz
Martin A. Voelker
Clifford E. Wilkins Jr.

For full biographical listings, see the Martindale-Hubbell Law Directory

KRAMER LEVIN NAFTALIS & FRANKEL LLP (AV)

919 Third Avenue, 10022
Telephone: 212-715-9100
Cable Address: "Nickral"
TWX: 710 581-5340
Telex: 645041
Telecopier: 212-715-8000
URL: http://www.kramerlevin.com
Paris, France Office: 47, Avenue Hoche, 75008.
Telephone: +33-1 44 09 46 00.
Telecopier: +33-1 44 09 46 01.

(See Next Column)

KRAMER LEVIN NAFTALIS & FRANKEL LLP—*Continued*

MEMBERS OF FIRM

Arthur H. Aufses III
Thomas D. Balliett
Jay G. Baris
Philip Bentley
Barry H. Berke
Saul Eliot Burian
Nicholas L. Coch
Thomas E. Constance
John E. Daniel
Michael J. Dell
Abbe L. Dienstag
Kenneth H. Eckstein
Charlotte Moses Fischman
David S. Frankel
Marvin E. Frankel
Alan R. Friedman
Carl Frischling
Mark J. Headley
Robert M. Heller
Gregory Aaron Horowitz
Philip S. Kaufman
Peter S. Kolevzon
Kenneth P. Kopelman
Michael Paul Korotkin
Shari Kahn Krouner
Kevin B. Leblang
Philippe X. Ledoux (Resident, Paris, France Office)
David P. Levin
Ezra G. Levin
Randy Lipsitz
Larry M. Loeb
Monica C. Lord
Cynthia D. Mann
Richard Marlin
Alexander Marquardt (Resident, Paris, France Office)
Thomas Moers Mayer
Thomas E. Molner
Thomas H. Moreland
Ellen R. Nadler
Gary P. Naftalis
Michael J. Nassau
Michael S. Nelson
Jay A. Neveloff
Michael S. Oberman
Christian Orengo (Resident, Paris, France Office)
Peter J. O'Rourke
Antoine Paszkiewicz (Resident, Paris, France Office)
Paul S. Pearlman
Susan J. Penry-Williams
Bruce Rabb
Allan E. Reznick
Donald L. Rhoads
Scott S. Rosenblum (Managing Partner)
Michele D. Ross
Howard J. Rothman
Judith Singer
Peter G. Smith
Howard A. Sobel
John A. Stevenson (Resident, Paris, France Office)
Jeffrey S. Trachtman
Neil R. Tucker
Jonathan M. Wagner
Harold P. Weinberger
E. Lisk Wyckoff, Jr.

COUNSEL

Peter A. Abruzzese (Not admitted in NY)
Martin Balsam
Joshua M. Berman
Jules Buchwald
S. Elliott Cohan
Rudolph de Winter
Arthur D. Emil
Maria T. Jones
Sherwin Kamin
Andrew J. Maloney
George M. Murphy
Maxwell M. Rabb

SPECIAL COUNSEL

M. Frances Buchinsky
Jeffrey W. Davis
Marilyn Feuer
Ronald S. Greenberg
Brad J. Richter
Robert T. Schmidt
Helayne Oberman Stoopack

ASSOCIATES

Kenneth A. Adams
Ronald W. Adelman
Rachel Ahn
Alexandra Kambouris Alberstadt
Robert E. Alderson, Jr.
Beth H. Alter
Dana Anagnostou (Resident, Paris, France Office)
Natacha Ankri (Resident, Paris, France Office)
George P. Attisano
Helaine B. Batoff
Mary Jo Brady
Vivian Lee Brady
Alice M. Bray
Avram J. Cahn
Kimon Cambouroglou
Jonathan H. Canter
Jonathan S. Caplan
Pamela M. Capps
Mark Irwin Chass
Albert B. Chen
Jonathan K. Cohn
Karen D. Coombs (Not admitted in NY)
Kathryn Cooperman
Vito J. DeBari
Patricia A. De Meyere
Dinh Q. Doan
Garrett J. Dowd
Frank W. Dunham, III
Justine J. Eisenstein
Richard K. Elbaum
Joel Patrick Erb
Paul M. Fakler
David M. Feldman
Patrick C. Finnegan
Daniel A. Fiore
David C. Flatto
Marie-Christine Fournier-Gille (Resident, Paris, France Office)
Jonathan L. Fried
Isabelle Garcin (Resident, Paris, France Office)
Andrea Geiger (Resident, Paris, France Office)
Philip A. Gilman
Melanie C. Girton
Gabrielle L. Gould
Douglas C. Gray
James A. Grayer
Aviva L. Grossman
Alexandra S. H. Guest
Sylvie Guillou-Halle (Resident, Paris, France Office)
Justine A. Harris
Susan D. Hawkins
Timothy J. Helwick
Barry Herzog
Robert N. Holtzman
Daniel S. Holzman
Susan Jacquemot
Thomas T. Janover
Edward L. Jewett
A. David Joran
Susan Kantor
Stephen P. Katz
Steven Knecht
Susan R. Kohn
Chris Kolefas
Thomas J. Kratochvil
Karen Y. Kusko
Claire Lavergne (Resident, Paris, France Office)
Kerri Ann Law
Ellen M. Leigh
David J. Leviss
Yehudis S. Lewis

(See Next Column)

ASSOCIATES (Continued)

Alexander T. Lin
Sharon H. Makower
Benjamin Marks
Géraldine Maspetiol-Lunven (Resident, Paris, France Office)
J. Michael Mayerfeld
Henry E. Mazurek, Jr.
Izabel Pasagian McDonald
Marc D. Merriweather
Richard Kolb Milin
Ann Marie P. Mitchell
Anna C. Moody (Not admitted in NY)
Kevin Michael Moss
Richard L. Moss
Randal D. Murdock
Christian O. Nagler
Delbridge E. Narron
Christian E. O'Connell (Resident, Paris, France Office)
Elizabeth A. O'Connor (Legal Consultant on the Laws of Ireland and England and Wales)
Stefanie P. Olshan
Patricia G. Paul
Dominique Penin (Resident, Paris, France Office)
Caleb Pollack
Wena Poon
Geoffrey Potter
Carrie Printz
William J. Quintavalle
Anatoly Rabinovich
Mary W. Richardson
Leonard H. Ritz
Gina M. J. Rosenberg
Jennifer G. Ross
Margaret Rowe
Wadie K. Sanbar (Resident, Paris, France Office)
Dawn Schauder
Arielle N. Schiffman
Douglas J. Schneller
Francesca M. Sena
James B. Shapiro (Not admitted in NY)
Marjorie E. Sheldon
Ian Silver
Norman Christopher Simon
Stephen M. Sinaiko
Howard T. Spilko
Lisa Stanger
Marlene Stulbach
Howard E. Sullivan III
Alan D. Surchin
Daphne Tchao
Ely D. Tendler
Marika Tourres (Resident, Paris, France Office)
Laurent Trastour (Resident, Paris, France Office)
Catherine Verhoff
Muriel Vernier (Resident, Paris, France Office)
David Weber (Resident, Paris, France Office)
David J. Weisz
Robin M. Wilcox
Matthew J. Williams
Elizabeth Wolstein
David M. Zlotchew

Michael C. Nicholson (Managing Attorney)

For full biographical listings, see the Martindale-Hubbell Law Directory

---

KROLL, RUBIN & FIORELLA LLP (AV)

520 Madison Avenue, 10022-4235
Telephone: 212-223-9400
Telecopier: 212-750-4467 or 212-750-4469
Los Angeles, California Office: Biltmore Court & Tower, 520 South Grand Avenue, 8th Floor.
Telephone: 213-629-1600.
Telex: 181723.
Telecopier: 213-629-1660.
Garden City, New York Office: 1205 Franklin Avenue, Suite 390.
Telephone: 516-747-7333.
Telecopier: 516-747-3540.
White Plains, New York Office: 11 Martine Avenue.
Telephone: 914-946-0773.
Telecopier: 914-946-2216.
Newark, New Jersey Office: One Gateway Center, 2nd Floor.
Telephone: 201-622-3955.
Telecopier: 201-622-1112.
London England Office: Asia House, 31/33 Lime Street, London EC3M 7HR, England.
Telephone: +44-171-621-1142.
Telecopier: +44-171-283-6391.

MEMBERS OF FIRM

John P. Dearie, Jr.
Kenneth S. Fiorella
Mark S. Fragner
Bruce M. Friedman
Elliott M. Kroll
Patrick J. Moynihan
Charles T. Rubin
Franklin Ciaccio
Maureen Rothschild DiTata
H. Douglas Galt (Resident, Los Angeles, California Office)
Harvey A. Feintuch
Paul Kovner
James E. Mercante
Lori M. Meyers
Steven Jay Monn (Resident, White Plains Office)
James D. Otto (Resident, Los Angeles, California Office)
John E. Peer (Resident, Los Angeles, California Office)
Richard D. Picini (Resident, Newark, New Jersey Office)
Jeffrey N. Rejan
Julius A. Rousseau, III

Dena S. Aghabeg (Resident, Los Angeles, California Office)
Marissa F. Bloom (Resident, Los Angeles, California Office)
John K. Bosee, 4th
Brian J. Convery (Resident, Newark, New Jersey Office)
Heather Golin (Resident, Garden City Office)
Stewart B. Greenspan
Edward F. Kenny, III
Jonathan Kline
Adam G.L. Kominsky
James T. Liell (Resident, White Plains, New York Office)
Alan R. Lyons
Grant M. Meisels
Jo Ann Montoya (Los Angeles, California Office)
Susan A. O'Neal (Resident, Los Angeles, California Office)

(See Next Column)

KROLL, RUBIN & FIORELLA LLP, *New York—Continued*

Christine A. Roney (Resident, Los Angeles, California Office)
Gregory B. Scher (Resident, Los Angeles, California Office)
Sarah Scofield
Nadeem A. Waeen

OF COUNSEL

Morton Greenspan

For full biographical listings, see the Martindale-Hubbell Law Directory

LA ROSSA & ROSS (AV)

41 Madison Avenue, 10010-2202
Telephone: 212-696-9700
Fax: 212-686-3013
URL: http://www.lawyers.com/larossa&ross

MEMBERS OF FIRM

James M. La Rossa
Michael S. Ross

ASSOCIATE

Melissa B. Ringel

For full biographical listings, see the Martindale-Hubbell Law Directory

LOEB & LOEB LLP (AV)

A Limited Liability Partnership including Professional Corporations
345 Park Avenue, 10154-0037
Telephone: 212-407-4000
Facsimile: 212-407-4990
Email: info@loeb.com *URL:* http://www.loeb.com
Los Angeles, California Office: Suite 1800, 1000 Wilshire Boulevard, 90017-2475.
Telephone: 213-688-3400.
Facsimile: 213-688-3460.
Century City (Los Angeles), California Office: Suite 2200, 10100 Santa Monica Boulevard, Los Angeles, 90067-4164.
Telephone: 310-282-2000.
Facsimile: 310-282-2192.
Nashville, Tennessee Office: 45 Music Square West, 37203-3205.
Telephone: 615-749-8300.
Facsimile: 615-749-8308.
Rome, Italy Office: Piazza Digione 1, 00197.
Telephone: 011-3906-808-8456.
Facsimile: 011-3906-808-8288.

MEMBERS OF FIRM

Mortimer H. Hess (1889-1968)
Christopher K. Aidun
Kenneth B. Anderson
Roger M. Arar
Donald L. B. Baraf
Michael D. Beck (A.P.C.)
David H. Carlin
Marc Chamlin
David B. Eizenman
Jay Fenster
David C. Fischer
Kenneth D. Freeman
Helen Gavaris
Seth D. Gelblum
Stanley M. Johnson
Michael Bryce Kinney
John F. Lang
Jerome L. Levine
Andrew E. Lippmann
William J. Marlow
Charles H. Miller
Robert L. Pelz
Martin R. Pollner
Robert S. Reich
Andrew M. Ross
David M. Satnick
David S. Schaefer
Scott I. Schneider
P. Gregory Schwed
Terri J. Seligman
Brian R. Socolow
Lee N. Steiner
Richard P. Streicher
Alan J. Tarr
James D. Taylor
Bruce J. Wexler
Michael P. Zweig

OF COUNSEL

Frank E. Feder (A P.C.)
Harold I. Kahen

SENIOR COUNSEL

Richard E. Garmise
Harry S. Prawer
Laurie S. Ruckel

ASSOCIATES

Christian D. Carbone
Paula K. Colbath
Kenneth R. Florin
Barbara D. Griff
James R. Guerette
Ronald L. Israel
Roni A. Jacobson
Robert B. Lachenauer
Michael J. Linowes
Lynda C. Loigman
Nina B. Luban
Samuel Mark Mizrahi
Deborah L. Saltzman
Philippa J. Smith
Maria L. Zanfini
Robin Zeidel

For full biographical listings, see the Martindale-Hubbell Law Directory

MAYER, BROWN & PLATT (AV)

1675 Broadway, 10019-5820
Telephone: (212) 506-2500
Facsimile: (212) 262-1910
Telex: 701842
Cable: LEMAYEN
URL: http://www.mayerbrown.com
Chicago, Illinois Office: 190 South LaSalle Street, 60603-3441.
Telephone: (312) 782-0600.
Facsimile: (312) 701-7711.
Telex: 190404.
Cable: LEMAY.
Berlin, Germany Office: Breite Strasse 29, Muehlendamm, 10178.
Telephone: 011-49-30-2060-7710.
Facsimile: 011-49-30-2060-7744.
Charlotte, North Carolina Office: 100 North Tryon Street, Suite 2400.
Telephone: (704) 444-3500.
Fax: (704) 377-2033.
Cologne, Germany Office: Kaiser-Wilhelm-Ring 27-29, 50672.
Telephone: 011-49-221-5771-100.
Facsimile: 011-49-221-5771-199.
Houston, Texas Office: 700 Louisiana Street, Suite 3600, 77002-2730.
Telephone: (713) 221-1651.
Facsimile: (713) 224-6410.
Telex: 775809.
Cable: LEMAYHOU.
London, England Office: Bucklersbury House, 3 Queen Victoria Street, London, EC4N 8EL, England.
Telephone: 011-44-171-246-6200.
Facsimile: 011-44-171-329-4465.
Telex: 8811095.
Cable: LEMAYLDN.
Los Angeles, California Office: 350 South Grand Avenue, 25th Floor, 90071-1503.
Telephone: (213) 229-9500.
Facsimile: (213) 625-0248.
Telex: 188089.
Cable: LEMAYLA.
New York, New York Office: 1675 Broadway, 10019-5820.
Telephone: (212) 506-2500.
Facsimile: (212) 262-1910.
Telex: 701842.
Cable: LEMAYEN.
Washington, D.C. Office: 1909 K Street, N.W., 20006-1101.
Telephone: (202) 263-3000.
Facsimile: (202) 263-3300.
Telex: 892603.
Cable: LEMAYDC.
Representative Offices:
Ashgabat, Turkmenistan: 28 Gogol Street, 744000.
Telephone: 011-99-312-355247.
Facsimile: 011-99-312-510074.
Bishkek, Kyrgyz Republic: 66 Kalyka Akieva Str. 720010.
Telephone: 011-996-312-65-02-56.
Facsimile: 011-996-312-65-09-80.
Tashkent, Republic of Uzbekistan: 3rd Floor, 1 Turab Tula Street, 700003.
Telephone: 011-998 71-1206-627.
Facsimile: 011-998-71-1206-329.
Mexico City, Mexico, D.F., Independent Mexico Correspondent: Jáuregui, Navarrete, Nader y Rojas, S.C., Torre Arcos, Paseo de los Tamarindos No. 400-B. Col. Bosques de las Lomas, 05120.
Telephone: 011-525-267-45-00.
Facsimile: 011-525-267-45-99.
Paris, France, Independent Paris Correspondent: Lambert & Lee, 13 Avenue Hoche, 75008.
Telephone: 011-33-1-53-53-43-43.
Facsimile: 011-33-1-53-96-03-83.

PARTNERS

Jean-Marie L. Atamian
Nicole V.F. Bergman Fong
Barry P. Biggar
Robert I. Bressman
Ronald S. Brody
James B. Carlson
Jean S. Chin
Diane Citron (Not admitted in NY)
Peter V. Darrow
John J. Dedyo
Laura A. DeFelice
David K. Duffee
Andrew L. Frey
Gary D. Friedman
Salvatore Guerrera
Thomas R. Hood
Philip Allen Lacovara
Andrew Mattei
Jay Parry Monge
Dennis P. Orr
Michael P. Richman
Michael N. Sloyer
Richard A. Spehr
Ellyn Steuer-Miller
Thomas M. Vitale
Kathleen Anne Walsh
Robert J. Ward
Douglas L. Wisner
Mark S. Wojciechowski
Steven Wolowitz
Michael I. Zinder

SENIOR COUNSEL

Albert I. Edelman

(See Next Column)

MAYER, BROWN & PLATT—*Continued*

COUNSEL

Raniero D'Aversa, Jr.
Andrea Lodahl Henneman
John R. Hewitt (Not admitted in NY)
Warren L. Jervey
Beth R. Kramer
Allen D. Moreland
Thomas M. Mueller
Werner M. Nikowitz
Stephen Van Dolsen
Craig A. Wolson
Scott M. Zemser

ASSOCIATES

M. John Andrade (Not admitted in United States)
Stephen J. Angelson
Lesa A. Barkowsky-Starkins
Audrey I. Bender
Joanne E. Benisch
Andrew J. Bettwy
Howard Alan Blaustein
Philip O. Brandes
Vaughn J. Buffalo
Shant H. Chalian
Leslie Chebli
Eric N. Cohen
Martin J. Collins
John M. Conlon
Robert L. Cordell, II
Edward A. Davis
Anthony J. Diana
Courtney A. Dinsmore
Sean O. Dougherty (Not admitted in NY)
Grant J. Esposito
Ryan P. Farley
Ron D. Franklin
Karen P. Fredericks
Kristin Frey
Francis A. Fuselier
Thomas N. Glushko
Jennifer B. Gold
David M. Goldman
Carolyn Greenwald
Thomas P. Hallinan
George R. Hatzmann
Catherine J. Hertzig
Mark F. Herzinger
David M. Hillman
Natalie M. Hiott-Levine
Matthew D. Ingber
Jason Kanner
Joshua P. Kaufman
Carl Richard Kolbet
Karen L. Kupetz
Nicholas A. Laveris
Jennifer May
Douglas E. McCormack
Scott Mortman
Donna Mulvihill
Scott T. Nonaka
Melanie L. Oxhorn
Trupti S. Patel (Not admitted in NY)
Michael C. Petronio
Antonio N. Piccirillo
Christopher M. Read
Mark J. Robertson
Christina Saber
Andrew H. Schapiro
Andrea J. Schwartzman
Gilda M. Smart
S. Hayes Smith
Kenneth Suh
David A. Trapani (Not admitted in NY)
Christopher N. Travers
Oliver Ott Trumbo, II
Aditi Viswanathan
Barbara S. Wang
Norman R. Williams, II
John Yatchisin, Jr.
Alexander Zolfaghari
Margarita Zubkus

For full biographical listings, see the Martindale-Hubbell Law Directory

HENRY S. MIDDENDORF, JR. (AV)

175 West 12th Street, Suite 15E, 10011
Telephone: 212-575-0350

For full biographical listings, see the Martindale-Hubbell Law Directory

MILBANK, TWEED, HADLEY & McCLOY LLP (AV)

1 Chase Manhattan Plaza, 10005-1413
Telephone: 212-530-5000
Fax: 212-530-5219
Email: postmaster@milbank.com *URL:* http://www.milbank.com
Midtown Office: 375 Park Avenue, Suite 3601, 10152.
Telephone: 212-530-5800.
Fax: 212-530-0158.
Los Angeles, California Office: 601 South Figueroa Street, 30th Floor, 90017.
Telephone: 213-892-4000.
Fax: 213-629-5063.
Washington, D.C. Office: International Square Building, Suite 1100, 1825 Eye Street, N.W., 20006.
Telephone: 202-835-7500.
Fax: 202-835-7586.
Tokyo, Japan Office: Fukoku Seimei Building, 2-2, Uchisaiwai-cho 2-Chome, Chiyoda-ku, Tokyo 100-0011, Japan.
Telephone: 011-81-3-3504-1050.
Fax: 011-81-3-3595-2790, 011-81-3-3595-2840.
London, England Office: Dashwood House, 69 Old Broad Street, London EC2M 1QS.
Telephone: 011-44-207-448-3000.
Fax: 011-44-207-448-3029.
Hong Kong Office: 3007 Alexandra House, 16 Chater Road.
Telephone: 011-852-2971-4888.
Fax: 011-852-2840-0792; 011-852-2845-9046.
Singapore Office: 14-00 Caltex House, 30 Raffles Place, 048622.
Telephone: 011-65-428-2400.
Fax: 011-65-428-2500.
Moscow, Russia Office: 24/27 Sadovaya-Samotyochnya, Moscow, 103051.
Telephone: 011-7-501-258-5015.
Fax: 011-7-501-258-5014.

(See Next Column)

MEMBERS OF FIRM

Caroline G. Angoorly (Resident Hong Kong Office)
Paul S. Aronzon (Resident, Los Angeles, California Office)
Oren B. Azar (Resident, Singapore Office)
Parker H. Bagley
John Cooley Baity
Michael C. Banks
Jeffrey Barist
Kenneth J. Baronsky (Resident, Los Angeles, California Office)
Deborah Baumgart (Resident, Los Angeles, California Office)
Devan D. Beck (Resident, Los Angeles, California Office)
W. Rogers Benson, Jr.
Elizabeth Besio
Jonathan G. Blattmachr
Richard S. Brach
Donald B. Brant, Jr.
Barbara J. Briggs
Russell E. Brooks
Christopher E. Chalsen
Carolyn C. Clark
Warren F. Cooke
Linda Dakin-Grimm (Resident, Los Angeles, California Office)
Trayton M. Davis
Luc A. Despins
John Dewar (Resident, London, England Office)
M. Douglas Dunn
Dennis F. Dunne
Scott A. Edelman
Edwin F. Feo (Resident, Los Angeles, California Office)
Drew S. Fine
Raymond J. Fisher
Phillip D. Fletcher (Resident, London, England Office)
Wilbur F. Foster, Jr.
Mark Frewin (Resident, London, England Office)
Simon Friedman (Resident, Los Angeles, California Office)
Joy K. Gallup
Guilford W. Gaylord
David R. Gelfand
Joseph S. Genova
Glenn S. Gerstell (Resident, Washington, D.C. Office)
Elliot Gewirtz
Michael W. Goroff (Resident, London, England Office)
Richard M. Gray (Resident, Singapore Office)
Jonathan J. Green
Jay D. Grushkin
L. Douglas Harris
Peter Windley Herman
Michael L. Hirschfeld
Roland Hlawaty
Joris M. Hogan
C. Stephen Howard (Resident, Los Angeles, California Office)
David Michael Hudanish
Mel M. Immergut
Robert A. Jacobs
Douglas W. Jones
Mark A. Kantor (Resident, Washington, D.C. Office)
Bruce E. Kayle
Howard S. Kelberg
Young Joon Kim (Resident, Tokyo, Japan Office)
Frederick C. Kneip
David A. Lamb (Resident, Los Angeles, California Office)
Robert F. Lawrence (Resident, Washington, D.C. Office)
Lawrence Lederman
Toni C. Lichstein
William J. Mahoney
Jonathan A. Maizel (Resident, Tokyo, Japan Office)
Robert Jay Moore (Resident, Los Angeles, California Office)
Peter M. Mortimer
Eric K. Moser
Marcelo A. Mottesi
Robert W. Mullen, Jr.
Daniel R. Mummery
Peter D. Nesgos
Holly A. Nielsen (Resident, Moscow, Russia Office)
Michael D. Nolan
Ted Obrzut (Resident, Los Angeles, California Office)
John T. O'Connor
Robert S. O'Hara, Jr.
Arnold B. Peinado, III
Dale L. Ponikvar
Frank C. Puleo
Robert S. Reder
Mark L. Regante
Elihu F. Robertson
Anthony Root (Resident, Hong Kong Office)
Eric H. Schunk (Resident, Los Angeles, California Office)
Helfried J. Schwarz
John E. Shockey (Resident, Washington, D.C. Office)
Thomas B. Siebens (Resident, London, England Office)
Eric F. Silverman
Georgiana J. Slade
James S. Sligar
Robert E. Spring
David A. Stagliano
Douglas A. Tanner (Resident, Hong Kong Office)
Jane Templeton-Knight (Partner in an Affiliated Partnership); (Resident, London, England Office)
Andrew E. Tomback
Richard C. Tufaro (Resident, Washington, D.C. Office)
Tsugumichi D. Watanabe
William H. Webster (Resident, Washington, D.C. Office)
Mark L. Weissler
Neil J Wertlieb (Resident, Los Angeles, California Office)
Harry E. White, Jr.
Richard J. Wight
Gary S. Wigmore (Resident, Singapore Office)
Robert B. Williams
Karen B. Wong (Resident, Los Angeles, California Office)

CONSULTING PARTNERS

Squire N. Bozorth
William E. Jackson
Roger B. Oresman
Carroll L. Wainwright, Jr.

SPECIAL COUNSEL

Alexander D. Forger

OF COUNSEL

Stephen J. Blauner
Robert R. Douglass
Michael J. Edelman
Alan M. Fenning (Resident, Los Angeles, California Office)
John A. Funk (Resident, Los Angeles, California Office)
Bruce T. Gardner
Jane L. Hanson
Joseph M. Persinger
Samuel S. Polk
Fred W. Reinke (Resident, Washington, D.C. Office)

SENIOR ATTORNEYS

Charles W. Westland

(See Next Column)

MILBANK, TWEED, HADLEY & MCCLOY LLP, *New York—Continued*

ASSOCIATES

Steven J. Abrams
Sally Agel (Resident, Los Angeles, California Office)
Ross D. Agre
Taline A. Aharonian (Resident, Los Angeles, California Office)
Lawrence J. Alfieri
Suzanne V. Alwan
Loren P. Ambinder
Nimish Amin
Peter M. Anderson (Resident, Washington, D.C. Office)
Jennifer M. Anglim
Thomas A. Arena
John C. Ashby (Resident, Los Angeles, California Office)
Katherine Aydin (Resident, Washington, D.C. Office)
Roya Lin Babanoury
James H. Ball, Jr.
Dino Barajas (Resident, Los Angeles, California Office)
Daniel D. Bartfeld
Elizabeth E. Bauza (Resident, London, England Office)
Scott V. Beechert
Christopher L. Beers
Steven Anthony Behar (Not admitted in NY)
Crayton L. Bell
Michael J. Bellucci
Aaron J. Benjamin (Not admitted in NY; Not admitted in United States) (Legal Consultant)
Charles D. Bethill
Sabina Bhalla (Resident, Los Angeles, California Office)
William B. Bice (Resident, Tokyo, Japan Office)
Michael C. Bisignano (Resident, Washington, D.C. Office)
Leigh Kim Borrello (Resident, Singapore Office)
Lisa Brabant
Thomas F. Brenner
Barry P. Burland
Richard M. Campo
Mitchell I. Carlin
Christine Luba Carver
Steven L. Chan
Doris P. Chang
Shelli M. Ching (Resident, Singapore Office)
Keri A. Christ
David Clayton (Not admitted in NY; Not admitted in United States) (Legal Consultant)
David S. Cohen (Resident, Washington, D.C. Office)
Douglas N. Cohen
Henry J. Cort (Resident, London, England Office)
Gabriel Kristopher Coy (Resident, Los Angeles, California Office)
Bridget Crawford
Kenneth E. Crowell
Jeanette B. Cruz (Resident, Los Angeles, California Office)
Michael Dayen (Resident, Los Angeles, California Office)
Nicholas DeCarlo (Resident, Washington, D.C. Office)
Hillary S. DeNigro (Resident, Washington, D.C. Office)
Anne K. DeSimone
Uttam Dhillon (Resident, Los Angeles, California Office)
Craig P. Druehl
Michael B. Dunn
Mitchell E. Epner
Joseph K. Falzon
Michael Farrar
Troy Ficarra
Alisa Nicole Fiddes
Robert M. Finkel
Marc F. Flusche
Miriam F. Foley
Michael R. Fordham Jr.
John D. Franchini
Robert Freedman
Seth D. Garland (Resident, Washington, D.C. Office)
R. Lee Garner III (Resident, Los Angeles, California Office)
Francesca Godi (Resident, Los Angeles, California Office)
Brett D. Goldblatt (Resident, Los Angeles, California Office)
Teresa A. Gonsalves
Chandra L. Gooding (Resident, Los Angeles, California Office)
Michael Gottfried
Federico Goudie
John M. Griem, Jr.
John Joseph Griggs (Resident, Los Angeles, California Office0
Daniel J. Guyder
Quang J. Ha
Brian D. Hail
L. Timothy Halleron
Caroline Sang-Un Han (Resident, Hong Kong Office)
Roberto Tomas Helguera
Douglas W. Henkin
Elliot D. Hinds (Resident, Los Angeles, California Office)
James G. Hnat II
Kathryn E. Hoff-Patrinos (Resident, Washington, D.C. Office)
Joon-Yeung Huh
Vanessa Wai Shan Hui (Resident, Singapore Office0
David H. Hwang
David J. Impastato (Resident, Los Angeles, California Office)
Sharon E. Jackson (Resident, Los Angeles, California Office)
Julie M. Jacobs (Resident, Washington, D.C. Office)
Michael H. Jacobs (Resident, Washington, D.C. Office)
Linda E. Jolly
Sital Kalantry
Hilary R. Kao (Resident, Washington, D.C. Office)
Alexander Kaye
Edward V. Kayukov (Resident, Los Angeles, California Office)
Joseph J. Kelleher
Kelly S. Kibbie
Charlotte J. Kim
Edward K. Kim (Resident, Los Angeles, California Office)
Robert S. Kim
Young Il Kim
Susheel Kirpalani
James R. Klaiber
Agnieszka Klich (Resident, London, England Office)
Jonathan M. Kohl
Nicholas L. Kondoleon (Resident, Los Angeles, California Office)
Isaac Koyfman
Christian D. Kraus
Thomas R. Kreller (Resident, Los Angeles, California Office)
Ariel Z. Kronman
Deborah P. Kubiak
Elena A. Kuryatnikova (Resident, Moscow, Russia Office)
Indrani Lall
Suzanne S. Lee
Thomas C. Lee (Resident, Tokyo, Japan Office)
Alex G. Lempiner
Alvin K. Leong
Jacqueline Leung (Resident, Hong Kong Office)
Evelyn Lim
Tobin D. Lippert (Resident, Los Angeles, California Office)
Duncan J. Logan
Melainie K. Mansfield (Resident, Los Angeles, California Office)

ASSOCIATES (Continued)

(See Next Column)

Dean A. Manson (Resident, Washington, D.C. Office)
Allan T. Marks (Resident, Los Angeles, California Office)
Bredt D. Martin (Resident, Los Angeles, California Office)
Richard A. Mathurin (Resident, Los Angeles, California Office)
William Jackson Matney, Jr. (Resident, Washington, D.C. Office)
Aline Matta
Matthew E. McDonald (Resident, Los Angeles, California Office)
Kevin R. McSpadden (Resident, Los Angeles, California Office)
Barbara J. Melby (Resident, Washington, D.C. Office)
Thomas Christopher Mellor
Scott P. Miller
Gail Miranda-Schmidt
Cross K. Moceri (Resident, Los Angeles, California Office)
Alison Naidech
Yasufumi Nakamori (Resident, Tokyo, Japan Office)
Jonathan W. Nash (Resident, London, England Office)
Fred Neufeld (Resident, Los Angeles, California Office)
Michael C. Newman (Resident, Los Angeles, California Office)
Stephen D. Nordahl
Elizabeth Noyes
Yeshim O'Donnell
Brian J. O'Donoghue
Dara A. Panahy (Resident, Washington, D.C. Office)
Steven C. Papkin (Resident, Los Angeles, California Office)
Sujay Parikh
Swati Patel (Resident, London, England Office)
Janice Payne
David A. Pawlak
Edward Pearson (Resident, Singapore Office)
Geoffrey Peck
Albert A. Pisa
Delia Poon (Resident, London, England Office)
Lara M. Posner
Clifton Prabhu (Not admitted in United States) (Legal Consultant)
Stacey J. Rappaport
Stanford Renas
Raymond R. Richards
Kathleen M. Riester
Steven A. Rivers (Resident, Los Angeles, California Office)
Madeline J. Rivlin
Anne E. Robinson
Felice Roggen (Resident, Washington, D.C. Office)
Richard E. Rosberger
Dayan R. Rosen
Robert Lawrence Rosen
Jennifer R. Rossi
Kendrick F. Royer (Resident, Los Angeles, California Office)
Matthew D. Royko
Eric Sanford
Denyse J. Santoro
John P. Sare
Tracey L. Schell (Resident, Hong Kong Office)
Cary B. Schmelzer (Resident, Singapore Office)
Franceska O. Schroeder (Resident, Washington, D.C. Office)
Kathy Schumacher
Zarrar Sehgal
Gayle O. Sered
Hiral H. Shah
Robert C. Shenfeld
Harry Sherman
Greg Short (Resident, Los Angeles, California Office)
Anat Sideman (Resident, Los Angeles, California Office)
Stephen Simoni
Lalenya W. Siegel
Nicholas Smithberg
Bing Song (Resident, Hong Kong Office)
William R. Spiegelberger
Theodore J. Stachtiaris
Allana F. Stark
Robin C. Stephan
Ian W. Sterling
Robert Sternthal
Juliet L. Stone (Resident, Los Angeles, California Office)
Walter L. Stone (Resident, Washington, D.C. Office)
Ronald D. Stuber (Resident, London, England Office)
Tiziana Sucharitkul (Resident, Los Angeles, California Office)
Doreen A. Sullivan
Mary M. Sullivan
Jacqueline M. Sutton (Resident, Los Angeles, California Office)
Jay W. Swanson
Megan Siau Feng Tang (Resident, Singapore Office)
Roland K. Tellis (Resident, Los Angeles, California Office)
Nancy Toross (Resident, Los Angeles, California Office)
Lee-ford Tritt
Edward S. Tsai
Susan E. Turner (Resident, Singapore Office)
Blair M. Tyson
J. Andrew Underwood
Carla J. Urquhart (Resident, Washington, D.C. Office)
M. Benjamin Valerio (Resident, Los Angeles, California Office)
Tedd W. VanBuskirk
Langdon Van Norden
Scott Vick (Resident, Los Angeles, California Office)
Adam E. Vital
Frank Vivero
Andrew R. Walker (Resident, Washington, D.C. Office)
Caroline V. Walther-Meade
A. Joseph Warburton (Resident, Washington, D.C. Office)
David J. Webb
Timothy P. Wei
Andrew Welbourn (Resident, London, England Office)
Mathew B. West
Melanie J. Wilson (Resident, London, England Office)
Anne C. Winston (Resident, Los Angeles, California Office)
Thomas R. Wise, III
David J. Wolfson
Desiree Woo (Resident, Hong Kong Office)
Eugena Yasnogorodsky (Resident, Los Angeles, California Office)
Susan A. Young (Resident, Tokyo, Japan Office)
Martha S. Zawacki
Elizabeth A. Zelinka (Resident, Washington, D.C. Office)
David H. Zemans (Resident, Singapore Office)
David B. Zolkin (Resident, Los Angeles, California Office)
Jay S. Zwerling

For full biographical listings, see the Martindale-Hubbell Law Directory

New York—Continued

MILLER, CANFIELD, PADDOCK AND STONE, P.L.C. (AV⊤)

A Professional Limited Liability Company
Founded in 1852 by Sidney Davy Miller
1450 Broadway, 41st Floor, 10018
Telephone: 212-704-4400
Fax: 212-704-4410
URL: http://www.millercanfield.com
Detroit, Michigan Office: 150 West Jefferson, Suite 2500, 48226-4415.
Telephone: 313-963-6420.
Fax: 313-496-7500.
Cable Address: "Stem Detroit."
Ann Arbor, Michigan Office: 101 North Main Street, 7th Floor, 48104-1400.
Telephone: 734-663-2445.
Fax: 734-747-7147.
Troy, Michigan Office: 840 West Long Lake Road, Suite 200, 48098.
Telephone: 248-879-2000.
Fax: 248-879-2001.
Grand Rapids, Michigan Office: 99 Monroe, N.W., Suite 1200, 49503-2639.
Telephone: 616-454-8656.
Fax: 616-776-6322.
Howell, Michigan Office: 121 South Barnard Street, Suite 4, 48843-2305.
Telephone: 517-546-7600.
Telecopier: 517-546-6974.
Kalamazoo, Michigan Office: 444 West Michigan Avenue, 49007-3752.
Telephone: 616-381-7030.
Fax: 616-382-0244.
Lansing, Michigan Office: One Michigan Avenue, Suite 900, 48933-1609.
Telephone: 517-487-2070.
Fax: 517-374-6304.
Monroe, Michigan Office: 214 East Elm Avenue, Suite 100, 48162-2682.
Telephone: 734-243-2000.
Fax: 734-243-0901.
Washington, D.C. Office: 1900 K Street, N.W., Suite 1150. 20006.
Telephone: 202-429-5575; 785-0600.
Fax: 202-331-1118; 785-1234.
Pensacola, Florida Office: 25 West Cedar, 32501.
Telephone: 850-469-1088.
Fax: 850-432-0677.
Gdynia, Poland Office: UL. Slaska 21, 81-319.
Telephone: 011-485-831-2808.
Fax: 011-48-58-628 6411.
Warsaw, Poland Office: UL. Nowogrodzkall, 5th Floor, 00-513.
Telephone: 011-4822 529 0200.
Fax: 011-4822 529 0201.
Katowice, Poland Office: UL. Francuska 35/37, 40-027.
Telephone: 011 (48-32) 757-2414.
Fax: 011 (48-32) 757-2483.

RESIDENT PRINCIPAL

Gregory L. Curtner (Not admitted in NY)

OF COUNSEL/SENIOR COUNSEL

Geoffrey M. Chinn

RESIDENT ASSOCIATE

Susan I. Robbins

Representative Firm Clients: Chrysler Corp.; Comerica, Inc.; City of Detroit, Mich.; Detroit Tigers, Inc.; First of Michigan; Fretter, Inc.; Ford Motor Co.; Ford Motor Credit Co.; Great Lakes Bancorp; Henry Ford Hospital.

For full biographical listings, see the Martindale-Hubbell Law Directory

MORRISON COHEN SINGER & WEINSTEIN, LLP (AV)

750 Lexington Avenue, 10022
Telephone: 212-735-8600
Facsimile: 212-735-8708
URL: http://www.mcsw.com

MEMBERS OF FIRM

Peter H. Morrison (1935-1988)
Andrew M. Arsiotis
Bradley Bernstein
Stephen I. Budow
Thomas R. Califano
Donald H. Chase
Arthur J. Ciampi
Alan S. Cohen
Robert H. Cohen
Robert Stephan Cohen
Stephen A. Cohen
Michael Connolly
Jeffrey P. Englander
Joel A. Feldman
Mary E. Flynn
C. Lawrence Grubman
G. William Haas
Lisa E. Kadin
Michele A. Katz
Deborah E. Lans
David Lerner
Shira Nadich Levin
Jack Levy
Malcolm I. Lewin
Sarah C. Lichtenstein
Robert Londin
Jonathan W. Lubell
Theodore L. Marks
Fred H. Perkins
Michael R. Reiner
Lawrence B. Rodman
Steven B. Ruchefsky
Salomon R. Sassoon
David A. Scherl
Andrew M. Schreier
Jay W. Seeman
Henry A. Singer
Brian B. Snarr
Jerome Tarnoff
Mara T. Thorpe
Peter D. Weinstein

(See Next Column)

SENIOR COUNSEL

Laurie F. Golub
Michael B. Guss
Amelia A. Nickles

Kieran X. Bastible
Jonathan K. Bender
Susan K. Bloom
Frances B. Carlisle
Susanne Marie Connolly
Juliet M. DeMasi
Catherine F. Duggan
Stephen J. Fitzgerald
Pia Flanagan
Edward P. Gilbert
Terry J. Gushner
David Ismailer
Sally Klemperer
Jonathan A. Kulish
Robert D. Lah
Danielle C. Lesser
John P. McNicholas
Jenny K. Needelman
Wesley J. Paul
David A. Piedra
Jonathan M. Plissner
Julie L. Rosen
Robert Louis Savino
Henry A. Zangara

OF COUNSEL

Martin J. Hertz
Martin N. Leaf
Leroy E. Rodman

For full biographical listings, see the Martindale-Hubbell Law Directory

MORVILLO, ABRAMOWITZ, GRAND, IASON & SILBERBERG, P.C. (AV)

565 Fifth Avenue, 10017
Telephone: 212-856-9600
Fax: 212-856-9494
Cable Address: "Litigator, New York"

Robert G. Morvillo
Elkan Abramowitz
Paul R. Grand
Lawrence Iason
Michael C. Silberberg
John J. Tigue, Jr.
Richard D. Weinberg
Barry A. Bohrer
Lawrence S. Bader
Edward M. Spiro
Robert J. Anello
Catherine M. Foti
Jeremy H. Temkin

OF COUNSEL

Robert J. McGuire
Michael W. Mitchell
Diana D. Parker

David Axinn
Anirudh Bansal
Neil M. Barofsky
Steven Harley Breslow
Jennifer Arbittier Bromley (Not admitted in NY)
Jamie Alter Deutsch (Not admitted in NY)
James C. Dugan
Mary P. Etheridge
Rebecca Glaser
Daniel B. Kosove (Not admitted in NY)
Tracy Lehman
Mary Margulis-Ohnuma
Michael R. Marra
Sara Mogulescu
Helen L. Monaco
Gretchan R. Ohlig
Jodi Misher Peikin
Elizabeth Small
Peter M. Spett

For full biographical listings, see the Martindale-Hubbell Law Directory

MOUND, COTTON & WOLLAN (AV)

One Battery Park Plaza, 10004
Telephone: 212-804-4200
Facsimile: 212-344-8066
San Francisco, California Office: 1700 California Street, Suite 470.
Telephone: 415-434-4301.
Telecopier: 415-434-4303.
London, England Office: Longbow House, 14-20 Chiswell Street.
Telephone: 0071-638-3688.
Newark, New Jersey Office: The Legal Center, One Riverfront Plaza, 8th Floor, 07102-5497.
Telephone: 973-242-2050.
Telecopier: 973-242-4244.

Arthur N. Brook (1933-1997)
Bert Cotton (1911-1981)
Maurice Mound (1907-1994)
Ernest E. Rosenberg (1924-1983)

MEMBERS OF FIRM

Stuart Cotton
Jeffrey C. Crawford
Leonard S. Dome
Wayne R. Glaubinger
Michael H. Goldstein
Lawrence S. Greengrass
Lloyd A. Gura
Bruce R. Kaliner
Michael R. Koblenz
Ellen G. Margolis
Daniel Markewich
John C. Mezzacappa
Frederic R. Mindlin
Francis A. Montbach
David A. Silva
Philip C. Silverberg
Costantino P. Suriano
James D. Veach
Jeffrey S. Weinstein

COUNSEL

Eugene A. Leiman
Eugene Wollan

RESIDENT OF COUNSEL
SAN FRANCISCO, CALIFORNIA OFFICE

Anna Maria Martin (Not admitted in NY)
Joseph M. Rimac, Jr. (Not admitted in NY)

RESIDENT MEMBER
NEWARK, NEW JERSEY OFFICE

William D. Wilson

(See Next Column)

MOUND, COTTON & WOLLAN, *New York—Continued*

ASSOCIATES

Michael Altman
Emilie L. Bakal
Todd A. Bakal
Kevin F. Buckley
Doreen A. Cronin
Frank J. DeAngelis
Alyssa DeSimone
Lauren G. Dome
Douglas K. Eisenstein
Maria Fazzolari
Joseph W. Ferraro
Aaron F. Fishbein
Elisa T. Gilbert
Diana E. Goldberg
Hilary M. Henkind
Mark S. Katz
David W. Kenna
David S. Mahaffey
Mark D. Marino
Catherine F. Megret
Mitchell D. Otto
Albert J. Pinzon
Renee M. Plessner
Jon Quint
Ronnie A. Rifkin
Mark J. Weber
Christina M. Wood

RESIDENT OF COUNSEL
LONDON, ENGLAND OFFICE

David M. MacLoughlin

For full biographical listings, see the Martindale-Hubbell Law Directory

NIXON PEABODY LLP (AV)

437 Madison Avenue, 10022
Telephone: 212-940-3000
Fax: 212-940-3111
Email: nixonpeabody@nixonpeabody.com *URL:* http://www.nixonpeabody.com
Rochester, New York Office: Clinton Square.
Telephone: 716-263-1000.
Fax: 716-263-1600.
Washington, D.C. Office: 1255 23rd Street, N.W.
Telephone: 202-973-7700.
Fax: 202-97307750.
Other Washington, D.C. Office: Suite 700, One Thomas Circle.
Telephone: 202-457-5300.
Fax: 202-457-5355.
Albany, New York Office: Omni Plaza, 30 South Pearl Street.
Telephone: 518-427-2650.
Fax: 518-427-2666.
Garden City, New York Office: 990 Stewart Avenue.
Telephone: 516-832-7500.
Fax: 516-832-7555.
Buffalo, New York Office: 1600 Main Place Tower.
Telephone: 716-853-8100.
Fax: 716-853-8109.
Hartford, Connecticut Office: City Place, 185 Asylum Street.
Telephone: 860-275-6820.
Fax: 860-275-6821.
Boston, Massachusetts Office: 101 Federal Street.
Telephone: 617-345-1000.
Fax: 617-345-1300.
Manchester, New Hampshire Office: 889 Elm Street.
Telephone: 603-628-4000.
Fax: 603-628-4040.
Providence, Rhode Island Office: One Citizens Plaza.
Telephone: 401-454-1000.
Fax: 401-454-1030.

PARTNERS

William S. Andrews
Michael S. Anglin
Roger E. Berg
Constance M. Boland
Stefan R. Boshkov
John G. Bove
John D. Canoni
Mats G. Carlston
Jerome P. Coleman
Michael J. Cooney (Resident at Rochester, N.Y. Office)
Christopher A. D'Angelo
Thomas S. D'Antonio
Thomas J. Dee
Henry J. DePippo (Resident at Rochester, N.Y. Office)
William B. Deyo, Jr.
Gordon L. Elicker
John T. Fitzgerald, Jr. (Also at Garden City, N.Y. Office and Resident at Rochester, N.Y. Office)
Marc L. Fried
Lyell G. Galbraith (Resident at Rochester, N.Y. Office)
Edward R. Hughes
D. Bruce Kratz
David P. Land
Richard F. Langan, Jr.
B. G. Staffan Lundback (Resident at Rochester, N.Y. Office)
Arthur F. McMahon, Jr.
Elizabeth D. Moore
Christopher M. Paparella
Frank H. Penski
David M. Portal
Susan S. Robfogel
Richard M. Rosenbaum
Arthur J. Rosner
Robert C. Sentner
Lisa P. Soeder
Alphonso E. Tindall, Jr.
Harry P. Trueheart III
Michael A. Vaccari
William F. Weir
Lauren E. Wiesenberg

COUNSEL

Robert N. H. Christmas
Grant E. Pollack
Bruce E. Rosenthal
Peter W. Rothberg
Louis R. Satriale, Jr.
Andrew W. Sheldrick
Marc S. Silverstein

(See Next Column)

ASSOCIATES

Elizabeth Antonakakis
Isabel Arista (Not admitted in NY)
Elizabeth Mihalyak Columbo
Molly S. Cusson
Rafael A. Declet, Jr.
David A. Feldman
Allison P. Gioia
Laura M. Guadagno
Isabel Guerra
Donna M. Hart
Nancy P. Hill
Robert C. Illig
Karyn D. Jefferson
Michael D. Kestan
Terri C. Matthews
Toni Anne Nichels
Virginia M. O'Connell
Bart Pisella
Francis W. Ryan IV
Deborah A. Shapiro
Alice L. Shih
Stacey B. Slater
Abigail-Mary Sterling
Tab Timothy Stewart
Joyce J. Sun
Sani Ahmadu Williams (Not admitted in NY)

For full biographical listings, see the Martindale-Hubbell Law Directory

ORANS, ELSEN & LUPERT LLP (AV)

33rd Floor, One Rockefeller Plaza, 10020
Telephone: 212-586-2211
Telecopier: 212-765-3662
Email: oel@oellaw.com

MEMBERS OF FIRM

Sheldon H. Elsen
Leslie A. Lupert
Gary H. Greenberg
Robert L. Plotz

ASSOCIATES

Thomas A. Brown II
Peter E. Seidman
Bonnie Melissa Baker
Peter Adelman
Steven David Feldman

For full biographical listings, see the Martindale-Hubbell Law Directory

OTTERBOURG, STEINDLER, HOUSTON & ROSEN, P.C. (AV)

230 Park Avenue, 29th Floor, 10169
Telephone: 212-661-9100
Telecopier: 212-682-6104

Donald N. Gellert
William M. Silverman
Peter H. Stolzar
Alan R. Weiskopf
Jonathan N. Helfat
Daniel Wallen
Scott L. Hazan
Glenn B. Rice
Albert F. Reisman
Anthony M. Piccione
Steven B. Soll
Alan Kardon
Mitchell M. Brand
Stanley L. Lane, Jr.
David W. Morse
Peter L. Feldman
Richard G. Haddad
Andrew M. Kramer
Valerie S. Mason

GENERAL COUNSEL

Kurt J. Wolff

COUNSEL

Bernard Beitel
Morton L. Gitter

Lloyd M. Green
Enid Nagler Stuart
Craig D. Zlotnick
Stephen H. Alpert
Jenette A. Barrow-Bosshart
Brett H. Miller
Matthew J. Miller
John J. Kenny
Richard L. Stehl
Susan A. Joyce
Rosanne A. Finkel
Lorenzo Marinuzzi
Frederick M. Klein
Jennifer S. Feeney
Daniel F. Fiorillo
Lon M. Singer
Allen Cremer
Frederick A. Avila
Daniel P. Greenstein
Patricia L. Murrell
Remy J. Ferrario
Michael A. Samuels

For full biographical listings, see the Martindale-Hubbell Law Directory

PARKER CHAPIN LLP (AV)

Chrysler Building, 405 Lexington Avenue, 10017
Telephone: 212-704-6000
Telecopier: 212-704-6288
URL: http://www.parkerchapin.com
Great Neck, New York Office: 175 Great Neck Road.
Telephone: 516-482-4422.
Telecopier: 516-482-4469.
Hackensack, New Jersey: 190 Morre Street, Suite 307.
Telephone: 210-883-6400.
Telecopier: 210-883-6404.
Beverly Hills, California: 9454 Wilshire Boulevard.
Telephone: 310-288-8367.
Telecopier: 310-288-8365.

MEMBERS OF FIRM

Mark Abramowitz
James Alterbaum
Christopher Stewart Auguste
Miles M. Borden
Barry J. Brett
Carol F. Burger
Robert M. Carmen
Aurora Cassirer
Elliot Cohen
Lloyd Frank
William D. Freedman
Michael D. Friedman
Brian R. Gallagher
James D. Garbus
Scott A. Goldfarb
Charles P. Greenman

(See Next Column)

PARKER CHAPIN LLP—*Continued*

MEMBERS OF FIRM (Continued)

Stephen F. Harmon
Mark S. Hirsch
Jordan A. Horvath
Timothy I. Kahler
Karen F. Lederer
Michael A. Leichtling
Joel Lewittes
Mark A. Limardo
Edward R. Mandell
Mitchell P. Portnoy
Stephen G. Rinehart
Henry I. Rothman
Richard A. Rubin
Will Burt Sandler
Michael J. Shef
Gary J. Simon
Alvin M. Stein
Lee W. Stremba
Lawrence David Swift
Angela D. Vitali
Melvin Weinberg
Michael Weinsier
Martin Eric Weisberg

SENIOR COUNSEL

Seymour Levine
Irving Rosenzweig

OF COUNSEL

Katherine Cooney Ash
Harvey M. Boneparth
Richard G. Cushing
Raymond W. Dusch
Linda R. Giannattasio
Allan Grauberd
Daniel S. Greenfeld
Lee Henig-Elona
Philip J. Hoblin, Jr.
Norman Alexander Jenkins, III
M. Jane Kronenberger
Herbert L. Rosedale
Mark I. Schlesinger
Flora Schnall
Richard E. Schneyer
Patricia Lynne Truscelli
Karl M. Zielaznicki

ASSOCIATES

Amos Alter
Mary Amendola
Ayelet Amrani
Brett R. Baker
J. Russell Bulkeley
JeanMarie Campbell
John Carlson
Yvette Y. Chang
Leslie W. Chervokas
Betty L. Ciacchi
Elaine Cook
Stephen G. Cordaro
Jennifer Bancroft DaSilva
Bruce S. De Paola
Paul A. Deutsch
Evelyn Finster
Jens Fischer
Kenneth B. Furry
Sheri L. Gitlin
John G. Gleacher
Heath H. Grayson
Eliezer Hecht
Aureon Herron-Hinds
Mitchel A. Hill
Gilbert C. Hoover, IV
David B. Horn
Paul C. Hughes
Thomas G. Huszar
Marisa Joss
Erica S. Katz
David Levine
R. Frederick Linfesty
Suzanne Liptack
Peter C. Noyes
Mitchell S. Nussbaum
Damian Pietanza
Michael J. Rimon
Charles Samuelson
Edward M. Slezak
Sharon H. Stern
Anne Taback
Eitan Tabak
Jennifer T. Teu
Jaime L. Weiss
Elizabeth Wubneh

For full biographical listings, see the Martindale-Hubbell Law Directory

PATTERSON, BELKNAP, WEBB & TYLER LLP (AV)

1133 Avenue of the Americas, 10036-6710
Telephone: 212-336-2000
Fax: 212-336-2222
Email: info@pbwt.com *URL:* http://www.pbwt.com

MEMBERS OF FIRM

Christopher C. Angell
Douglas E. Barzelay
Susan Frank Bloom
Henry P. Bubel
William F. Cavanaugh, Jr.
Lisa E. Cleary
Edward F. Cox
John Delli Venneri
John M. DiMatteo
Gregory L. Diskant
David F. Dobbins
David W. Dykhouse
Robert J. Egan
Philip R. Forlenza
Eugene M. Gelernter
Alan Gettner
David M. Glaser
Antonia M. Grumbach
Dana W. Hiscock
Scott Horton
Rochelle Korman
Robin Krause
Jeffrey E. LaGueux
Kim J. Landsman
Robert W. Lehrburger
Jeffrey I. D. Lewis
Robert P. LoBue
Ellen M. Martin
Maureen W. McCarthy
Thomas C. Morrison
Bernard F. O'Hare
Peter J. Pettibone
Thomas W. Pippert
Andrew D. Schau
John Emile Schmeltzer, III
John P. Schmitt
Stephen W. Schwarz
Arthur D. Sederbaum
Karl E. Seib, Jr.
Saul B. Shapiro
Richard R. Upton
Frederick B. Warder III
William W. Weisner
John D. Winter
Stephen P. Younger
Steven A. Zalesin

OF COUNSEL

Harold R. Tyler, Jr.
Robert H. M. Ferguson
George S. Frazza
Robert M. Pennoyer
Robert B. Shea
Ira T. Wender

(See Next Column)

COUNSEL

Blair Axel
Janet L. Blakeman
Karen C. Hunter
Cecilia Loving
Christine H. Miller
Gloria C. Phares
Herman H. Raspé
Stephen J. Schreiber
Gail F. Stone
Robert D. Wilson, Jr.
Bruce L. Wolff

ASSOCIATES

Daniel L. Abrams
Natasha Alexeeva
Dahlia A. Balsam
Andrew P. Beame
Andrew J. Beckler
Karen Renée Berry
Joshua Burstein
Laura E. Butzel
Deborah Ann Buyer
Jessica Schaetzl Carter
Eugene L. Chang
Noah H. Charlson
Alexis S. Coll
Kieran M. Corcoran
Richard P. Davies
Jeannette Dayan
Russell W. Faegenburg
Scott Fenstermaker
Catherine M. Flanders
Kimberly A. Frye
William F. Gaske
Stephanie Bunting Glaser
Joshua A. Goldberg
Steven D. Gordon
Erik Haas
Jeb Harben
Scott B. Howard
Erika M. Heise (Not admitted in NY)
David G. Jacoby
Alla Kazakina (Not admitted in the United States)
James L. Kronenberg
Raquiba N. LaBrie
Megan A. Lawless (Not admitted in NY)
Benjamin Levi
Alexander Lewis
Ole W. Lyngklip, III
Carrie A. Mandel
Karen M. McCarthy
Mary E. McDonald
John R. Middleton Jr.
Diane L. Millar (Not admitted in NY)
Diane R. Moriarty
Adrienne R. Moss
Melissa E. Moss
Veronica Mullally
Roosevelt N. Nesmith
Rebecca Lee Noonan
Jennifer L. Pariser
Graeme Philp
Wayne W. Plasha
Jamie J. Reiffel
Marc S. Reiner
Amy J. Roberts
Dawn P. Robertson
Christopher A. Rose
Susanne E. Rosenberg
Allison Rutledge-Parisi
Karla G. Sanchez
Clare F. Saperstein
Peter J. Schaeffer
Catherine Grevers Schmidt
Naomi J. Schrag
Alexander Shapiro
Willard C. Shih
Elizabeth H. Shofner
Rosa E. Son
Margaret R. Sparks
Michael J. Stacchini (Not admitted in NY)
J. Andrew Stephenson
Sheryl A. Stoessel
Michael J. Timmons
Peter W. Tomlinson
Steven L. Vollins
Douglas L. Whitaker
Douglas J. Widmann
Inga-Kerstin Wilder
Sarah E. Zgliniec

For full biographical listings, see the Martindale-Hubbell Law Directory

PAUL, HASTINGS, JANOFSKY & WALKER LLP (AV)

A Limited Liability Partnership including Professional Corporations
Firm Established in 1951; Office in 1986
399 Park Avenue, 10022-4697
Telephone: 212-318-6000
Facsimile: 212-319-4090
URL: http://www.phjw.com
Atlanta, Georgia Office: 24th Floor, 600 Peachtree Street, N.E.
Telephone: 404-815-2400.
Los Angeles, California Office: 555 South Flower Street.
Telephone: 213-683-6000.
Orange County, California Office: 695 Town Center Drive, Costa Mesa.
Telephone: 714-668-6200.
San Francisco, California Office: 345 California Street.
Telephone: 415-835-1600.
Stamford, Connecticut Office: 1055 Washington Boulevard.
Telephone: 203-961-7400.
Washington, D.C. Office: 1299 Pennsylvania Avenue, N.W.
Telephone: 202-508-9500.
Tokyo, Japan Office: Ark Mori Building, 12-32 Akasaka, P.O. Box 577, 1-Chome, Minato-Ku.
Telephone: (03) 3586-4711.
London, England Office: The International Financial Centre, 25 Old Broad Street.
Telephone: (011) 44-171-562-4000.
ATTORNEY E-MAIL ADDRESSES: first initial middle initial last name @phjw.com (e.g. rmasbill@phjw.com)

MEMBERS OF FIRM

Daniel G. Bergstein
Barry A. Brooks
Victoria A. Cundiff
Mark J. Eagan
George L. Graff
Lawrence J. Hass
John P. Howitt
Euclid A. Irving
Marguerite R. Kahn
James W. Kennedy
Ronald K. Kreismann
Kevin C. Logue
Roger M. Milgrim
Joseph P. Opich
Kevin J. O'Shea
Thomas R. Pollock
Samuel D. Rosen
Leigh P. Ryan
Cheryl R. Saban
William F. Schwitter, Jr.

(See Next Column)

PAUL, HASTINGS, JANOFSKY & WALKER LLP, *New York—Continued*

MEMBERS OF FIRM (Continued)

Robert L. Sherman
Andrew M. Short
Neil A. Torpey
Scott M. Wornow
Seth M. Zachary

OF COUNSEL

Anthony A. Dreyspool
Stephen M. Fields
Alexander G. Fraser
Richard C. Hamlin
Steven D. Johnson
Peter W. LaVigne
Andrew M. Mayer
Lucy Prashker
Knute J. Salhus
Harvey A. Strickon
Steven L. Wasserman

ASSOCIATES

Claudia A. Barria
David S. Benyacar
James E. Berger
Jonathan A. Bloom
Marco J. Caggiano
Patricia M. Carroll
Marie Censoplano
Sarka Cerna-Fagan
Katherine S. Chang
Michael K. Chernick
TanYee Cheung
Jennifer A. Cotton
Jeremiah A. DeBerry
Alan M. Feld
Scott D. Fischer
Margaret A. Gilleran
David M Greenberg
Scott N. Hudson
Christine A. Huebner
David C. Katz
Michael B. Kaufman
Judy H. Kim
Shulammite Kim (Not admitted in NY)
Young Lee
Brigitte P. Lippmann
Katherine B. Lipton
Valencia N. Macon
Sean Harris McGrady
Anne P. Merchant
David Meredith
Ingrid M. Mesa
John S. Miller
Deborah E. Morningstar
Mark G. Pedretti
Peter A. Businger (Not admitted in NY)
Karen M. Petrosino
Philip J. Ragona
William C. Rand
Michael J. Reinhardt
Nancy M. Ruzich
Jennifer B. Sack
Joseph A. Satto
Susan R. Schick
Sheryl J. Seiden
Eric M. Sherbet
Juliet Yoo Shin
Jason A. Shrensky
Janine E. Sisak
Robert A. Stevenson
Iowna Stryjnik
Jonathan C. Tyras
Ivan J. Wolpert
Lily L. Wong
Jessica Yoo

For full biographical listings, see the Martindale-Hubbell Law Directory

PAUL, WEISS, RIFKIND, WHARTON & GARRISON (AV)

1285 Avenue of the Americas, 10019-6064
Telephone: 212-373-3000
TDD 212-373-2000
Facsimile: 212-757-3990
Email: mailbox@paulweiss.com *URL:* http://www.paulweiss.com
Washington, D.C. Office: 1615 L Street, NW, Suite 1300, 20036-5694.
Telephones: 202-223-7300, TDD 202-223-7490.
Facsimile: 202-223-7420.
Paris, France Office: 62, rue du Faubourg Saint-Honoré, 75008.
Telephone: (33-1) 53.43.14.14.
Facsimile: (33-1) 53.43.00.23.
Tokyo, Japan Office: Fukoku Seimei Building, 2-2 Uchisaiwaicho 2-chome, Chiyoda-ku, Tokyo 100-0011, Japan.
Telephone: (81-3) 3597-8101.
Facsimile: (81-3) 3597-8120.
Beijing, China Office: 2918 China World Tower II, No. 1 Jianguomenwai Dajie, 100004.
Telephone: (86-10) 6505-6822.
Facsimile: (86-10) 6505-6830.
Hong Kong, China Office: 12th Floor, Hong Kong Club Building, 3A Chater Road, (Central) Hong Kong.
Telephone: (852) 2536-9933.
Facsimile: (852) 2536-9622.

Lloyd K. Garrison (1946-1991)
Randolph E. Paul (1946-1956)
Simon H. Rifkind (1950-1995)
Louis S. Weiss (1927-1950)
John F. Wharton (1927-1977)

MEMBERS OF FIRM

Neale M. Albert
Mark H. Alcott
Allan J. Arffa
Robert A. Atkins
Jonathan R. Bell
Daniel J. Beller
Mitchell L. Berg
Mark S. Bergman
Bruce Birenboim
Richard S. Borisoff
John F. Breglio
Richard J. Bronstein
Jeanette K. Chan (Resident, Hong Kong Office)
Douglas A. Cifu
Lewis R. Clayton
Jay Cohen
Jerome Alan Cohen
Russell E. Colwell (Resident at Tokyo, Japan Office)
Douglas R. Davis
Robert D. Drain
James M. Dubin
Leslie Gordon Fagen
Dominique Fargue (Resident at Paris, France Office)
Peter L. Felcher
Peter E. Fisch
Robert C. Fleder
Martin Flumenbaum
Terence J. Fortune (Resident at Washington, D.C. Office)
Harris B. Freidus
Michael E. Gertzman
Paul D. Ginsberg
Eric S. Goldstein

(See Next Column)

MEMBERS OF FIRM (Continued)

Charles H. Googe, Jr.
Bruce A. Gutenplan
Gaines Gwathmey, III
Cheryl E. Hader
Claudia Hammerman
Albert P. Hand
Gerard E. Harper
Robert M. Hirsh
Steven R. Howard
Nicholas C. Howson (Resident at Beijing, China Office)
Annaliese S. Kambour
Meredith J. Kane
Roberta A. Kaplan
Brad S. Karp
John C. Kennedy
G. Frederick Kinmonth
Alan W. Kornberg
Ruben Kraiem
David K. Lakhdhir
Steven E. Landers (Resident at Paris, France Office)
John E. Lange (Resident at Hong Kong, China Office)
Daniel J. Leffell
Walter F. Leinhardt
Martin London
Edwin S. Maynard
John P. McEnroe
Robert E. Montgomery, Jr. (Resident at Washington, D.C. Office)
Toby S. Myerson
Matthew Nimetz
Kevin J. O'Brien
John J. O'Neil
Lionel H. Olmer
Robert P. Parker (Resident, Washington, D.C. Office)
Marc E. Perlmutter
James L. Purcell
Leonard V. Quigley
Valerie E. Radwaner
Carey R. Ramos
Carl L. Reisner
Walter Rieman
Sidney S. Rosdeitcher
Richard A. Rosen
Steven B. Rosenfeld
Peter J. Rothenberg
Warren B. Rudman (Not admitted in NY; Resident at Washington, D.C. Office)
Jeffrey D. Saferstein
Jeffrey B. Samuels
Dale M. Sarro (Resident, Washington, D.C. Office)
Terry E. Schimek
Kenneth M. Schneider
Robert B. Schumer
Michael J. Segal
Stephen J. Shimshak
David R. Sicular
Moses Silverman
Steven Simkin
Robert S. Smith
Marilyn Sobel
Phillip L. Spector (Not admitted in NY; Resident, Washington, D.C. Office)
Stuart G. Steingold (Resident, Washington, D.C. Office)
Judith Reinhardt Thoyer
Maria T. Vullo
Steven L. Wolfram (Resident, Paris, France Office)
Jordan E. Yarett
Alfred D. Youngwood

SENIOR COUNSEL

Samuel J. Silverman
Theodore C. Sorensen

OF COUNSEL

Morris B. Abram
Allan Blumstein
David C. Brodhead
Joseph E. Browdy
Edward N. Costikyan
Adrian W. DeWind
Bernard Finkelstein
Bernard H. Greene
Jay Greenfield
Seymour Hertz
Joseph S. Iseman (Resident at Paris, France Office)
Arthur Kalish
Anthony B. Kuklin
Robert L. Laufer
Robert H. Montgomery, Jr.
Donald F. Moore
Stuart Robinowitz
Mordecai Rochlin
Ernest Rubenstein
John C. Taylor, 3rd
Jay Topkis
David T. Washburn
Norman Zelenko

COUNSEL

Martha Gray Billman
Gordon G. Chang (Resident, Beijing, PRC Office)
Colleen M. Codey
Livia M. Corredor
Carole S. Davie
Richard S. Elliott (Resident at Washington, D.C. Office)
Saul H. Finkelstein
Michael D. Gertler (Resident, Hong Kong Office)
Barry D. Goldberg
Stephen G. Gorell
Scott P. Grader
Bruce Gruder
Robert Hajdu
Susan L. Harris
Deborah Hartnett
Steven C. Herzog
Jay L. Himes
Darrel J. Holstein
Jonathan H. Hurwitz
Michèle R. Jenkinson
Miriam S. Klepner
Robert N. Kravitz
Edwin C. Laurenson
Diane Meyers
William J. O'Brien
Jeffrey H. Olson (Resident at Washington, D.C. Office)
Aidan Synnott
Laura B. Sherman (Resident, Washington, D.C. Office)
Mark A. Underberg
Allen M. Wieder

ASSOCIATES

Matthew Abbott
Kamala Acero
Debo P. Adegbile
Cass Gunther Adelman
Swati Agrawal (Resident, Washington, D.C. Office)
Sajid Ajmeri
Tracy Anbinder Baron
Amy L. Barton
Christopher M. Basile
John F. Baughman
Lynn B. Bayard
S. Ashlie Beringer
Marnie Berk
H. Christopher Boehning
Angelo Bonvino
Cécile Boyer
Amy C. Brown
Pamela J. Campbell
Patrick S. Campbell (Resident at Washington, D.C. Office)
Sheree L. Carter-Galvan
Maria J. Carthy
Christina M. Cerrito
Diane Chan
Yvonne Y. Chan
Lydia Chang (Resident, Beijing, China Office)
Jacqueline C. Charlesworth

(See Next Column)

PAUL, WEISS, RIFKIND, WHARTON & GARRISON—*Continued*

ASSOCIATES (Continued)

Matthew Chavez (Resident, Washington, D.C. Office)
Theodore K. Cheng
Katia Chéron (Resident, Paris, France Office)
Sandra M. Christie
Paul H. Cohen
Peter M. Cohen
S. H. Spencer Compton
John Connon
Danielle R. Cooper
Daniel A. Crane (Not admitted in NY)
Jeremy Creelan
Matthew L. Daniel
Angela Hendricks Davis (Resident, Beijing, China Office)
Ariel J. Deckelbaum
Thomas V. de la Bastide III
Valerie Demont
Sarah Dion
Sarah C. Dodds
Scott C. Dorey (Not admitted in the United States)
Shari E.B. Dreier
Tracy Dreispuc
Jay L. Dubiner
Jennifer L. Dumas
Linda L. Dunn
Matthew R. Elkin
Marcia L. Ellis (Resident, Hong Kong, China Office)
Brian V. Ellner
Marc Falcone
Lewis E. Farberman
Andrew M. Felner
Todd A. Finger
Andrew A. Fink
Lori J. Forlano
Andrew G. Frank
Jonathan J. Freedman
Shelly Friedland
Lesley Szanto Friedman
Andrew D. Froberg
Jacob Frohman
Erin L. Fuller
Kevin Fung (Resident, Hong Kong, China Office)
Diane C. Gaylor (Resident, Washington, D.C. Office)
Gaela K. Gehring-Flores (Resident, Washington, D.C. Office)
Rachel Geman
Thomas Gentile
Manjula Gill
D. Ryan Gledhill
Tania Glowinski (Resident, Paris, France Office)
Adam W. Glucksman
Sara A. Goldberg
Joanna Goldenstein
Robert C. Goldman
Charles F. Goldsmith (Resident, Beijing, China Office)
Bart S. Goldstein
Eric Goodison
Andrea Goodman (Resident, Beijing, China Office)
Marci I. Gordon
Jill M. Graziano (Not admitted in NY)
Joshua Groban (Not admitted in NY)
Barbara A. Gross
Peter J. Guy
Carl Hampe (Resident, Washington, D.C. Office)
Keyes C. Hardin
Donald W. Hawthorne
Jeffrey S. Hellman
Brian Steven Hermann
Lisa S. Herz
Aubrey Holder
Joyce S. Huang
Karen J. Hughes
Gayle M. Hyman (Resident, Hong Kong, China Office)
Holly D. Jarmul
Hakeem S. Jeffries
Deborah K. Johns (Resident, Hong Kong, China Office)
Jennifer L. Johnson
Paul Richard Joklik
Mark S. Kaduboski
Jeannie S. Kang
Gregory A. Kasper
Maria H. Keane
Thomas M. Keane
Michael C. Keats
Heather Keele (Resident, Washington, D.C. Office)
Sherri Lee Keene
Karen S. Kennedy
Hans E. Kim (Resident, Tokyo Office)
Hih Song Kim
Jonathan G.L. King
Diane Knox
Stephen K. Koo
Paul J. Lanzon
Helen H. Lasersohn
Jean Lau (Resident, Hong Kong, China Office)
Stephanie Leclaire (Resident, Paris, France Office)
Sophia Lee
Daniel H. Levi
Hallie B. Levin
Michael D. Levin
Andrea E. Levine
Loren F. Levine
Shawn Lewis
Laurence L. Li
Philip Lipman
Dalia Litay
Mina "Titi" Liu (Resident, Hong Kong, China Office)
W. Andrew P. Logan, III
Kristina Louey
Ji Lu
Erik C. Luchs (Resident, Washington, D.C. Office)
Thomas M. Majewski
Didier Malaquin
Peter Man (Resident, Hong Kong, China Office)
Esteban A. Mancuso
Ronald M. Mandler
Joseph Mann
Jeffrey D. Marell
Marco Masotti
Lisa Mather (Resident, Hong Kong, China Office)
Joel Maxman
Petria May
Heather D. McArn
Melissa Rose McClammy
Timothy J. McCourt
Kimberly E. McCreight
Heather M. McMaster
Lissette P. McPhillips
Douglas C. Melcher (Resident, Washington, D.C. Office)
Laura Anne Menninger
John M. Mercury
Kira A. Merski (Resident, Washington, D.C. Office)
James H. Millar (Not admitted in NY)
Dan Miller
Philip Millward (Resident, Hong Kong, China Office)
Richard S. Mitchell
Roya Moadel-Obedian
Joanne Monteavaro
Sarah Narvaez
Sandra Y. Nay
Christian Neira
Edward D. Nelson
Jesse A. Nicol (Resident, Washington, D.C. Office)
Nkiruka R. Nwokoye
Lauren C. Panora
Kelley D. Parker
Jillian Perlberger
Danya E. Perry
Jason Pickholz
Valeria I. Plastino

ASSOCIATES (Continued)

(*See Next Column*)

Matthew Press
Katherine I. Puzone
Gangliang Qiao (Resident, Beijing, China Office)
Patrick B. Quill
Aseel M. Rabie (Resident, Washington, D.C. Office)
Anthony B. Radin
Ellen Rapoport
Steven G. Rawlings
Natosha Reid-Robinson
Mary Reidy
David J. Reiss
Deborah A. Reiss
Ronald P. Replogle
Keren Rimon
J. Michael Roebuck
Tanya L. Rolle
Kate V. Romain (Resident, Paris, France Office)
Jennifer L. Romer
Dana Rosen
Andrew N. Rosenberg
Lester Ross (Resident in Beijing Office)
Paul Henry Rothenberg
Raphael M. Russo
Regina P. Ryu
Ted Sabety
Dana S. Safran
Wendy J. Schechter
Mark Anthony Schichtel
Pamela Schoenfeld
Rachael A. Schuldiner
Elizabeth J. Schwartz
Stacey Shortall (Not admitted in the United States) (A Legal Consultant on the Laws of New Zealand)
Catherine Sinturel
John W. Smagula (Not admitted in NY)
Hillary B. Smith
J. Ryan Smith (Not admitted in NY)
Robyn Minter Smyers
Natalia T. Sorgente
Robyn Sorid
Julie Stark
Melanie H. Stein
Tarun M. Stewart
Eric Alan Stone
Olivier Sultan
Sandra Tafuri
Robyn F. Tarnofsky
Julia L. Tarver
Ian Tattenbaum
Leza S. Tellam (Resident, Tokyo Office)
Daniel J. Toal
Miriam Tong (Resident, Hong Kong, China Office)
Robert W. Trenchard
Julie Turaj
Eric Twiste
Liza M. Velazquez
Amy Vernick
Helen C. Wan
Linda J. Wank
Lawrence G. Wee
David J. Weiler (Resident, Washington, D.C. Office)
Wendy R. Weiser
Robyn L. Weiss
Robert C. Weisz
Peter D. Weitzner
Susan E. Welber
Matthew H. Wheelock (Resident, Washington, D.C. Office)
Kelly P. Wilson
Tobias Barrington Wolff
Jia Yan (Not admitted in the United States)
Arlene R. Yang
Kaye N. Yoshino
Corinna Yu (Resident, Hong Kong, China Office)
Tong Yu
Rolf Zaiss
David C. Zeiden
Libin Zhang (Resident, Beijing, China Office)
Jon Ziefert
Naïma Zitouni (Resident, Paris, France Office)

For full biographical listings, see the Martindale-Hubbell Law Directory

---

PHILLIPS, LYTLE, HITCHCOCK, BLAINE & HUBER LLP (AV)

437 Madison Avenue, 10022
Telephone: 212-759-4888
Telecopier: 212-308-9079
URL: http://www.phillipslytle.com
Buffalo, New York Office: 3400 HSBC Center.
Telephone: 716-847-8400.
Telecopier: 716-852-6100.
Jamestown, New York Office: 307 Chase Bank Building, 8 E. Third Street.
Telephone: 716-664-3906.
Telecopier: 716-664-4230.
Rochester, New York Office: 1400 First Federal Plaza.
Telephone: 716-238-2000.
Telecopier: 716-232-3141.
Fredonia, New York Office: 11 East Main Street.
Telephone: 716-672-2164.
FAX: 716-672-7979.

PARTNERS

William J. Brown
Robert J. Chanis
Chester L. Cobb
Kenneth R. Crystal
Leon C. Marcus
Claude D. Montgomery
Milan K. Tyler
Lee Papachristou Whidden

SPECIAL COUNSEL

Michael G. Shannon
R. Peyton Gibson

ASSOCIATES

Alan Blattberg
Michael J. DiLeo
Christopher G. Dorman
Raymond R. Granger
Linda C. Jamieson
Paul V. O'Brien
William M. Rossi-Hawkins
Mindi I. Schwartz
John S. Stewart

For full biographical listings, see the Martindale-Hubbell Law Directory

---

PILIERO GOLDSTEIN JENKINS & SULLIVAN, LLP (AV)

292 Madison Avenue, 10017
Telephone: 212-213-8200
Fax: 212-685-2028
Email: lawyers@pgjhlaw.com *URL:* http://www.pgjhlaw.com
Carlstadt, New Jersey Office: One Palmer Terrace.
Telephone: 201-507-5157.
FAX: 201-507-5221.

(*See Next Column*)

PILIERO GOLDSTEIN JENKINS & SULLIVAN LLP, *New York—Continued*

Washington, D.C. Office: 888 17th Street, N.W., Suite 1100.
Telephone: 202-467-6991.
FAX: 202-467-6703.
San Francisco, California Office: 507 Howard Street, Suite 200.
Telephone: 415-281-3631.
Fax: 415-281-3630.

MEMBERS OF FIRM

Kimberlee S. Bogen
Edward J. Goldstein
Jon Mark Jenkins
Marc A. Lebowitz
Robert D. Piliero
George O. Richardson, III
Michael T. Sullivan

ASSOCIATES

Craig Avedisian
Rosemary G. Feit
Eric M. Kogan
Mariano Schwed

OF COUNSEL

Kenneth D. Arbeeny
Christopher P. Hall

For full biographical listings, see the Martindale-Hubbell Law Directory

PLUNKETT & JAFFE, P.C. (AV)

230 Park Avenue, Suite 1847, 10169
Telephone: 212-922-1800
Facsimile: 212-922-1819
Email: plunkettjaffe.com
White Plains, New York Office: 1 North Broadway.
Telephone: 914-948-7722.
Facsimile: 914-948-7603.
Albany, New York Office: 111 Washington Avenue.
Telephone: 518-462-1800.
Facsimile: 518-462-4875.

William F. Plunkett, Jr.
Phyllis S. Jaffe
Kevin J. Plunkett
Patrick E. Brown
Marc E. Sharff
Justin E. Driscoll, III
Robert H. Hermann
Kerry A. Lawrence
John S. Harris
Alan D. Fox
Michael R. Ambrecht
Robert L. Byrne
Gary I. Selinger
Josephine Trovini
Ralph C. DeMarco
Kelly M. Lamendola
Lino J. Sciarretta
Susannah Cahill
Francis J. Earley
Kathleen P. O'Connor

OF COUNSEL

John C. Marbach
Andrew S. Roffe
Stuart Troy
Susan Litwer
Jean Smiertka Huff
David P. Geis
George L. Ryan
Howard G. Seitz
Gregory J. Raphael

For full biographical listings, see the Martindale-Hubbell Law Directory

PROSKAUER ROSE LLP (AV)

1585 Broadway, 10036-8299
Telephone: 212-969-3000
Fax: 212-969-2900
Telex: TRT 175719 ROPUT NY
URL: http://www.proskauer.com
Washington, D.C. Office: 1233 Twentieth Street, N.W., Suite 800.
Telephone: 202-416-6800.
Fax: 202-416-6899.
Los Angeles, California Office: 2049 Century Park East, Suite 3200.
Telephone: 310-557-2900.
Fax: 310-557-2193.
Boca Raton, Florida Office: One Boca Place, Suite 340 West, 2255 Glades Road.
Telephone: 561-241-7400.
Fax: 561-241-7145.
Newark, New Jersey Office: One Newark Center.
Telephone: 973-274-3200.
Fax: 973-274-3299.
Paris, France Office: Proskauer Rose, 68, rue du Faubourg Saint-Honoré.
Telephone: +33-1-53-05-60-00.
Fax: +33-1-53-05-60-05.

MEMBERS OF FIRM

Joseph M. Proskauer (1877-1971)
Alfred L. Rose (1886-1981)
Bertram A. Abrams
Neil H. Abramson
Ira Akselrad
Rory Judd Albert
Julie M. Allen
Alfred Appel
Mark Barnes
L. Robert Batterman
Joseph Baumgarten
Franklin S. Bonem
Edward A. Brill
Edward Brodsky
Lawrence H. Budish
Elana R. Butler
Perry A. Cacace
Robert A. Cantone
Michael A. Cardozo
Alan S. Cohen
Saul S. Cohen
Stuart M. Cohen
Peter D. Conrad
Sandra A. Crawshaw
David H. Diamond
Charles E. Dropkin
Klaus Eppler
Paul H. Epstein
Joseph Erdman
Bruce E. Fader
Allen I. Fagin
Glenn M. Feit
Michael E. Feldman

(See Next Column)

MEMBERS OF FIRM (Continued)

Michael E. Foreman
Jacob I. Friedman
Wilbur H. Friedman
James J. Fuld
Howard L. Ganz
Murray Gartner
Leon Phillip Gold
Sarah S. Gold
Richard L. Goldberg
Herman L. Goldsmith
Richard M. Goldstein
Ira M. Golub
John H. Gross
Claire P. Gutekunst
Charles Guttman
Daniel R. Halem
William M. Hart
Andrew D. Heineman
Kenneth S. Hilton
Sheldon I. Hirshon
Jeffrey A. Horwitz
Alan B. Hyman
Jack P. Jackson
Arnold S. Jacobs
Jerold D. Jacobson
Alan S. Jaffe
Robert J. Kafin
Wayne D. Katz
Robert M. Kaufman
Stephen R. Kaye
Steven M. Kayman
Edward W. Kerson
Nancy A. Kilson
Steven L. Kirshenbaum
Stanley Komaroff
Edward S. Kornreich
Steven C. Krane
Larry M. Lavinsky
Joseph M. Leccese
David M. Lederkramer
Howard N. Lefkowitz
Arnold J. Levine
Robert J. Levinsohn
Jeffrey W. Levitan
Bruce L. Lieb
Lawrence J. Lipson
Charles Looker
Gregg M. Mashberg
Kathleen M. McKenna
James D. Meade
Thomas C. Moore
Carole O'Blenes
Steven E. Obus
Martin J. Oppenheimer
Brendan J. O'Rourke
Charles B. Ortner
Ronald R. Papa
Alan P. Parnes
Bettina B. Plevan
Bernard M. Plum
Andrea S. Rattner
Ronald S. Rauchberg
Stuart L. Rosow
Lawrence J. Rothenberg
Kenneth Rubenstein
Stephen W. Rubin
Myron D. Rumeld
Bradley I. Ruskin
Paul Salvatore
Peter G. Samuels
Gail Sanger
Donald W. Savelson
Neal S. Schelberg
Aaron J. Schindel
Dale A. Schreiber
Wendy J. Schriber
Ronald D. Sernau
Charles S. Sims
Michael S. Sirkin
David W. Sloan
Ronald F. Storette
Philip M. Susswein
James M. Waddington
Solomon L. Warhaftig
Jay D. Waxenberg
Lawrence I. Weinstein
Allan R. Williams
M. David Zurndorfer

RETIRED PARTNERS

Marvin Dicker
Robert Dillof
George G. Gallantz
Bernard Gold
David I. Goldblatt
Philip J. Hirsch
Jacob Imberman
Saul G. Kramer
Morton M. Maneker
Sara S. Portnoy
Alan S. Rosenberg
Ronald S. Schacht
Minna Schrag
Howard A. Shapiro
Edward Silver
Bernard Tannenbaum
Jerold Zieselman

SENIOR COUNSEL

Lee A. Barkan
Ira G. Bogner
Roberta K. Chevlowe
Mark E. Davidson
Jeffrey N. Fink
Martha E. Gifford
Marc J. Goldstein
Abraham Gutwein
Kevin J. Healy
Jeffrey M. Lampiasi
Francis D. Landrey
Fredric C. Leffler
Richard A. Levin
Michael T. Mervis
Donald M. Nisonoff
Gail S. Port
David A. Picon
John W. Ritchie
Bonnie J. Roe
Michael H. Roffer
Scott K. Rutsky
Seth B. Schafler
Henry O. Smith, III
Richard L. Spinogatti
Steven D. Weinstein
Lowell D. Willinger

CONSULTANT

Carole Simon

ASSOCIATES

Daniel L. Ages
Anne T. Amann
Bela P. Amladi
Michael W. Arseneault
Coleen A. Barry
James M. Beach
Steven A. Beede
Charlotte L. Behrendt
Neil S. Belloff
Charles A. Bennett
Lisa A. Berkowitz
Craig A. Bitman
Simon Block
Lauren K. Boglivi
Bruce E. Boyden
John R. Braatz
David M. Brioso
Michelle Capezza
Mark S. Caren
Jeffrey A. Carpenter
Andre G. Castaybert
Lisa A. Chiappetta
Lloyd B. Chinn
Ricky Chung
Aliza R. Cinamon
Denise M. Clark (Not admitted in NY)
Karen E. Clarke
Robert A. Cohen
Anthony C. Coles
Christopher J. Collins
Richard J. Costa
John E. Daly
Douglas J. Davidson
J. D. Davis
Stephen A. Devaney
Dana L. Dorgan
Jennifer Adams Draffen
Mitchell A. Drossman
Scott A. Eggers

(See Next Column)

PROSKAUER ROSE LLP—*Continued*

ASSOCIATES (Continued)

Stacey O'Haire Fahey
Michael S. Fein
Jeremy R. Feinberg
Matthew E. Feiner
Allison B. Feld
Helaine S. Fine
Rachel B. Fine
Ariel A. Fox
Jo-Ann W. Fox-Weingarten
James Scott Frazier (Not admitted in NY)
Tammy D. Fried
David C. Friedman
John F. Fullerton, III
Maria F. Gandarez
Jennifer Rosar Gefsky
Eric J. German
Loren M. Gesinsky
Sheri L. Gilbert
Jonathan M. Glassman
Ilise S. Goldberg
Herschel Goldfield
Gregg I. Goldman
Jeffrey A. Goldstein
Andrew K. Gonsalves
Andrew S. Goodstadt
Kammie M. Gormezano
Deidre A. Grossman
Andrew M. Gutterman
Michael F. Hahn
Marjorie Han
Christine Harman
Leslie J. Harris
Amanda D. Haverstick
Matthew S. Hirshfield
Alan M. Hoffman
Gregory H. Hoffman
Arlene S. Hong
Stacy R. Horth-Neubert
Mark E. Jaffe
Lubna Jafri
Christopher M. Jaskiewicz
Evan L. Kahn
Ruth Kalbitzer
Robert K. Kane
Adam J. Kansler
Michael A. Katz
Daryl I. Kessler
Chang-Joo Kim
S. Jean Kim
Nicholas Kontizas
Stefanie S. Kraus
Sara Krauss
Mark A. Kreitman
David S. Krulwich
Stephen B. Kuhn
Naoko Kumada-Lawrence
Kevin M. Lastorino (Not admitted in NY)
Adam Leaventon
Michael J. Lebowich
Andrew L. Lee
Susan Lee
Henry J. Leibowitz
Laurie S. Leonard
Gary I. Lerner
Kelly B. Levi
Ian L. Levin
Jeffrey Levitin
Tracey I. Levy
Oliverio Lew
Elise G. Liebowitz
Laura A. LoBianco
Gwen J. Lourie
Diane M. Lowenberger
Marc A. Mandelman
John P. Margiotta
Frank F. Martinez
Craig A. Masheb
Nina Massen
Axel Mayo (Not admitted in the United States) (Legal Consultant)
Deidre H. Meehan (Not admitted in NY)
Francine E. Menaker
Paul V. Mifsud, Jr.
Michelle R. Migdon
Adam M. Miller (Not admitted in NY)
Carla M. Miller
Isaac Montal
Ellen H. Moskowitz
Eric D. Most
Ravi B. Motwani
Michael R. Neidell
Manuel C. Nelson
Andrea B. Neuman
Amanda H. Nussbaum
Tandy Meghan O'Donoghue
Vera M. Ovadia
Michele M. Ovesey
Jenifer De Wolf Paine
F. Joseph Paldino
Amy S. Park
Katharine H. Parker
Charles H. Parsons
Melissa Pedone
Christopher L. Pennington
Thomas M. Perone
Kevin J. Perra
Marc A. Persily
Pamela L. Polevoy
Joshua J. Pollack
Rhonda Edwards Powell
A. Cheryl Prince
Robert M. Projansky
Darlene Andrea Quashie
Erik D. Ramanathan
Xan Raskin
Gregg Reed
Howard Z. Robbins
Alyce Rogers-Goodstein
Spencer J. Romoff
Martin J. Rosenburgh
Eric D. Roth
Betty A. Ryberg
Matthew B. Sabloff
Amy Sandgrund
Edward W. Scheuermann
Daniel F. Schiff
Sally L. Schneider
Frank P. Scibilia
Clifford R. Scott
David T. Seiden
Regina E. Shannahan
Peter J. W. Sherwin
Yoon J. Shin
Scott N. Shorr
John Siegal
Joey Silberfein
Deirdre P. Silver
Jennifer Silver
John D. Singer
Ori Solomon
Karen Stefflre
John C. Stellabotte
Joshua H. Sternoff
Priscilla Steward
Patricia M. Suh
Michael Dean Sword
Mark Szubiak
Ivan Taback
Mara L. Taylor
Rossie E. Turman, III
Glenn S. Walter
Ido Warshavski (Not Admitted in the United States) (Legal Consultant)
M. Chloe Wasserman
Elizabeth Weiner
Melissa L. Westbrook
Isabella I. Wezdecki
Susan L. Wiener
Amy J. Williams
Susie S. Wu
Elise A. Yablonski
Karen S. Zemble
Heather Martínez Zona
Joshua Zuckerberg
Jason A. Zweig

(See Next Column)

WASHINGTON, D.C. MEMBERS OF FIRM

Jon A. Baumgarten
Mark J. Biros
Joseph E. Casson
Warren L. Dennis
Malcolm J. Harkins, III
Richard H. Rowe
Christopher Wolf

WASHINGTON, D.C. SENIOR COUNSEL

Thomas H. Brock
Alec W. Farr
James P. Holloway
Lionel E. Pashkoff
Stephen D. Solomon

WASHINGTON, D.C. ASSOCIATES

Mary Ellen Allen
Margaret J. Babb
Christine D. Bachman
Anita M. Bahauddin
Susan Brinkerhoff
William R. Cowden
Timothy E. Delahunt
Brian Elsbernd
Amybeth Garcia-Bokor
Michael C. Hochman
Brian E. Kamoie
Julia McMillen
Richard E. Ramsay
Cheralyn E. Schessler
Pamela B. Small
Megan H. Tinker
Susan A. Turner

LOS ANGELES, CALIFORNIA MEMBERS OF FIRM

Howard D. Behar
Harold M. Brody
Scott P. Cooper
Thomas W. Dollinger
Mitchell M. Gaswirth
Bernard D. Gold
Barry C. Groveman
Paul D. Rubenstein
David R. Scheidemantle
Marvin Sears
Arthur F. Silbergeld
Lois D. Thompson
Scott J. Witlin
Martin S. Zohn

LOS ANGELES, CALIFORNIA ASSOCIATES

Aaron P. Allan
William M. Brockschmidt
Jennifer M. Crome
Steven J. Elkins
Tanya L. Forsheit
Christopher E. Harding
Jeff Garcia Hilger
Gloria C. Jan
Gregory J. Patterson
Michael A. Ramos
Mark R. Rehe
Mary H. Rose
Deborah J. Sager
Stephanie T. Sasaki
Scott Silver
Tracy L. Turner
Donald S. Urrabazo
Rachelle S. Visconte
James M. Wakefield
Carolyn R. Young

BOCA RATON, FLORIDA MEMBERS OF FIRM

Jay S. Blumenkopf
Howard K. Coates, Jr.
Joseph Erdman
Albert W. Gortz
Allan H. Weitzman
Christopher C. Wheeler

BOCA RATON, FLORIDA SENIOR COUNSEL

Kristina B. Pett
George A. Pincus
Donald E. Thompson, II
Matthew H. Triggs

BOCA RATON, FLORIDA ASSOCIATES

Mary F. April
Gayle Coleman
Jonathan M. Fordin
John M. Fox-Snider
Joshua B. Frank
Brenda A. Friedman
Wendy L. Furman
David J. George
Marcy Hahn-Saperstein
Walter J. Harvey
Robert Jacobowitz
Jeannine Cline Jacobson
Stuart T. Kapp
George D. Karibjanian
Andrew D. Levy
Daniel L. Leyton
Michael S. Metta
Julie M. Mihelich
Mara Lerner Robbins
Justin Michael Senior
Susan H. Stern
Michael R. Tricarico
David Todd Zieper

PARIS, FRANCE MEMBERS OF FIRM

Jean-Philippe Berthet
William Krisel
Delia B. Spitzer

PARIS, FRANCE ASSOCIATE

Marie D. Percevault

NEWARK, NEW JERSEY MEMBERS OF FIRM

Marvin M. Goldstein
Kathleen M. McKenna

NEWARK, NEW JERSEY SENIOR COUNSEL

Joseph C. O'Keefe
Donald B. Shanin

NEWARK, NEW JERSEY ASSOCIATES

Jeremy M. Brown
Jennifer Morris Cohen
John Joseph Dabney
Wanda L. Ellert
Elana Gilaad
Gregg S. Kahn
Devora L. Lindeman
David W. MacGregor
Michael MacManus
Anne N. Smith
Steven Yarusinsky

For full biographical listings, see the Martindale-Hubbell Law Directory

New York—Continued

ROSS & HARDIES (AV)

65 East 55th Street, 10022
Telephone: 212-421-5555
Telecopier: 212-421-5682
URL: http://rosshardies.com
Chicago, Illinois Office: Suite 2500, 150 North Michigan Avenue.
Telephone: 312-558-1000.
Telecopier: 312-750-8600.
Washington, D.C. Office: 888 - 16th Street, N.W.
Telephone: 202-296-8600.
Telecopier: 202-296-8791.

RESIDENT PARTNERS

Joseph S. Kaplan
John B. Pellegrini
Yvette Harmon
Richard A. Wilsker
Michael J. Di Mattia
Marshall Beil
Robert S. Blaustein
Seth Goodchild
Hollis A. Bart
Stephen J. Di Cioccio
Philip Goldstein

OF COUNSEL

Leonard Rovins

ASSOCIATES

Jose Anibal Baez
Carol A. Dunning
Donald S. Krueger
Joyce E. Levowitz
Catherine A. Rogers
Allen M. Rose
Kenneth J. Rubinstein

For full biographical listings, see the Martindale-Hubbell Law Directory

RUBINBAUM LLP (AV)

A Partnership including Professional Corporations
30 Rockefeller Plaza, 10112
Telephone: 212-698-7700
Fax: 212-698-7825
Email: info@rubinbaum.com *URL:* http://www.rubinbaum.com
Iselin, New Jersey Office: Woodbridge Towers, 555 Route 1 South.
Telephone: 732-855-2220.
Fax: 732-855-2221.
Short Hills, New Jersey Office: 820 Morris Turnpike, Suite 104.
Telephone: 973-564-6480.
Fax: 973-564-6493.

MEMBERS OF FIRM

Max J. Rubin (1906-1996)
Frederick Baum (1909-1985)
Abraham G. Levin (1919-1995)
Jack G. Friedman (1923-1996)
Ronald Greenberg
Michael J. Weinberger
Martin R. Gold
Stephen A. Marshall
Edward Klimerman
Allan M. Rosenbloom
Thomas G. Barrett
David A. Mandel (P.C.)
Alvin J. Goldman
Stephen L. Solomon
Matthew L. Lifflander
Raymond J. Heslin
Martin J. Schwartz
Michael J. Emont
Martin P. Michael
Paul A. Gajer
Paul V. LiCalsi
Jane G. Stevens
Ivan W. Moskowitz
Brit L. Geiger
Denise M. Tormey
Robert W. Cockren
Arlene G. Dubin
Robert J. Benowitz
Robert B. Zimmerman
Paul H. Aloe
Christine Lepera
Marina Rabinovich
Richard G. Primoff
Mark S. Lafayette
Norman Alpert
Christine A. McGuinness

COUNSEL

Irving Constant (P.C.)
Leonard M. Marks
Burton R. Rubin (P.C.)
Carl R. Aron
Paul Katcher
Daniel A. Besdin
Richard M. Zuckerman
Richard I. Reich

SPECIAL COUNSEL

David M. Goldberg

ASSOCIATES

N Todd Angkatavanich
Christopher T. Bavitz
Darin S. Billig
Howard S. Bonfield
Jeannie Costello
Agatha N. Dzikiewicz (Iselin and Short Hills, New Jersey Offices)
Lisa Marie Emelo
Suzanne M. Finkelstein
Stacey Robin Gilchick
Janet M. Harvilchuck
Andrew R. Haskell
Michele H. Hong
Jacob Inwald
Christopher P. Kohn
Joshua S. Lichtenstein (Iselin and Short Hills, New Jersey Offices)
Amy J. Lippman
Michael Der Manuelian
Jane A. Meyer
Dean M. Monti
Robert P. Mulvey
Barbara Lynn Pedersen
Anita L. Pomerance
Matthew E. Przywozny (Iselin and Short Hills, New Jersey Offices)
Karen Jill Rebish
Jonathan Evan Samnick
Richard Adam Senzer

(See Next Column)

ASSOCIATES (Continued)

Ron B. Sitton
Joel Slawotsky
William J. Smith
Michael David Strugatz (Iselin and Short Hills, New Jersey Offices)
Carol Ellen Thurer
Howard H. Weller
Linda Yassky

For full biographical listings, see the Martindale-Hubbell Law Directory

SACKS MONTGOMERY, P.C. (AV)

800 Third Avenue, 10022
Telephone: 212-355-4660
Telecopier: 212-593-7257
Email: sm@sacksmontgomery.com
Westport, Connecticut Office: Sacks, Montgomery, Pastore & Levine, P.C., 1071 Post Road East, Suite 3.
Telephone: 203-291-6844.

Harry P. Sacks
David E. Montgomery
Stuart M. Levine (Resident, Westport, Connecticut Office)
Jeffrey A. Aronson
Frederick R. Rohn
Scott D. St. Marie
Stephen A. Stallings

Thomas F. Giordano
Amy S. Cohen
Kathleen M. Fay

OF COUNSEL

Steven J. Brill

For full biographical listings, see the Martindale-Hubbell Law Directory

JEFFREY SAMEL & PARTNERS (AV)

150 Broadway, 20th Floor, 10038
Telephone: 212-587-9690
Fax: 212-587-9673

Jeffrey Samel
David S. Gary
Dorothy Samel

ASSOCIATES

Robert G. Spevack
David M. Samel
Stacey L. Schwartz

OF COUNSEL

Richard A. Soberman

Representative Clients: New York City Transit Authority; New York City Housing Authority; Empire Insurance Co.; National General Insurance Co.; Federal Express Corp.; Shell Oil Corp.; American Building Maintenance Corp; United Fidelity & Guaranty Corp.; Little Caesar Enterprises, Inc.; Showbiz Pizza Time, Inc.

For full biographical listings, see the Martindale-Hubbell Law Directory

SAUL, EWING, REMICK & SAUL LLP (AV)

Twenty-First Floor, 237 Park Avenue, 10017
Telephone: 212-551-3502
TWX: 425170
Telecopier: 697-8486
Email: lawyers@saul.com *URL:* http://www.saul.com
Philadelphia, Pennsylvania Office: Centre Square West, 1500 Market Street, 38th Floor, 19102-2186.
Telephone: 215-972-7777.
Cable Address: "Bidsal".
TWX: 83-4798.
Telecopier: XEROX 7020 215-972-7725.
Wilmington, Delaware Office: 222 Delaware Avenue, P.O. Box 1266, 19899-1266. For Courier Delivery: 222 Delaware Avenue, Suite 1200, 19801.
Telephone: 302-421-6800.
Cable Address: "Bidsal".
TWX: 83-4798.
Telecopier: XEROX 7020 302-421-6813.
Berwyn, Pennsylvania Office: 1055 Westlakes Drive, Suite 150.
Telephone: 610-251-5050.
Cable Address: "BIDSAL".
TWX: 83-4798.
Telecopier: 610-651-5930.
Harrisburg, Pennsylvania Office: Penn National Insurance Tower, 2 North Second Street, 7th Floor, 17101.
Telephone: 717-257-7500.
Telecopier: 717-238-4622, 717-257-7516.
Princeton, New Jersey Office: 214 Carnegie Center, Suite 202. Telephone: 609-452-3100.
Fax: 609-452-3122.
Baltimore, Maryland Office: Saul, Ewing, Weinberg & Green, 100 South Charles Street, Suite 1500.
Telephone: 410-332-8600.
Fax: 410-332-8862.

(See Next Column)

SAUL, EWING, REMICK & SAUL LLP—*Continued*

MEMBERS OF FIRM

Marc A. Citron
Nancy S. Cleveland
Spencer W. Franck, Jr.
Pamela S. Goodwin (Managing Partner, Princeton, New Jersey Office)
Michael A. Lampert
Maurice D. Lee, III
Robert N. Sandler
Miles H. Shore
Anthony F. Walsh

For full biographical listings, see the Martindale-Hubbell Law Directory

SCHULTE ROTH & ZABEL LLP (AV)

900 Third Avenue, 10022
Telephone: 212-756-2000; 800-346-9644
Cable Address: "Olympus NewYork"
Telex: 426775
Email: wwwmail@srz.com *URL:* http://www.srz.com

MEMBERS OF FIRM

Robert M. Abrahams
Kim E. Baptiste
Stephanie R. Breslow
Mark E. Brossman
Mark Allen Broude
Brooks R. Burdette
Bruce S. Cybul
Harry S. Davis
Bonnie Lynn Dixon
Edward G. Eisert
Howard B. Epstein
Michael J. Feinman
Michael S. Feldberg
Nancy R. Finkelstein
Steven J. Fredman
Stuart D. Freedman
Susan C. Frunzi
Kenneth S. Gerstein
Alan R. Glickman
Howard O. Godnick
Lawrence S. Goldberg
Fred R. Green
Marcy Ressler Harris
Daniel J. Kramer
Burton Lehman
Jeffrey A. Lenobel
Michael R. Littenberg
Isaac B. Lustgarten
Michael C. Mulitz
Robert S. Nash
Peter A. Nussbaum
James M. Peck
Martin L. Perschetz
Gregory P. Pressman
Frederic L. Ragucci
Ronald E. Richman
Kurt F. Rosell
Robert Rosenberg
Paul N. Roth
Jeffrey S. Sabin
Betty Santangelo
Frederick P. Schaffer
Stephen J. Schulte
Daniel S. Shapiro
Howard F. Sharfstein
Irwin J. Sugarman
Shlomo C. Twerski
Alan S. Waldenberg
Paul N. Watterson, Jr.
Paul E. Weber
Marc Weingarten
André Weiss
William D. Zabel

OF COUNSEL

Robert I. Kleinberg
Joseph R. Simone

SPECIAL COUNSEL

Debra R. Anisman
Eric Asmundsson
Conrad G. Bahlke
Stephen C. Corriss
Mark K. Dowd
Susan R. Galligan
Peter J. Halasz
Lisa Holstein
Jesse R. Rubin
Susan S. Wallach

ASSOCIATES

Steven R. Abrams
Regina M. Alter
Jeremy B. Ament
Vincent P. Andrews
Caryn E. Angelson (Not admitted in NY)
Jessica L. Atkins (Not admitted in NY)
Dana Auslander
Phillip J. Azzollini
Perry Balagur
Philippe Benedict
Suzanne Berman
Susan E. Bernstein
Joshua R. Bressler
Grant E. Buerstetta
Laurel Anne Burk
Vincent Marc Cali
Jane H. Carmody
Yunhui Chae-Banks
Yaffa R. Cheslow
Kirby Chin
Jae Won Chung
Andrew B. Cohen
Mark S. Cohen
Brenda A. Cooper
Matthew L. Craner
Stephen P. Davidson
Jessy Dejoie
Jacqueline M. Didier (Not admitted in NY)
Brett S. Director
Ildiko Duckor
Brian Dunefsky
Fonda Duvanel
Lawrence T. Eckert (Not admitted in NY)
David J. Efron
Marc E. Elovitz
Michelle L. English
Adam J. Epstein
Adam Faber
Paul S. Farber
Steven M. Felsenthal
Todd S. Fishman
Brian H. Fortune
Adam L. Frank
Adam Freedman
Romas Garbaliauskas (Not admitted in NY)
Sara Geelan
Noah D. Genel
Elizabeth C. Go
Scott A. Gold
Ilana Hoschander Goldberg
Matthew Goldfarb
Andrew N. Goldman
Robert Goldstein (Not admitted in NY)
Evelyn S. Grant (Not admitted in NY)
Daniel A. Greenstone
Sami B. Groff
Marnie S. Grossman
Scott E. Grummon
William H. Gussman, Jr.
Ana M. Guzman
Adam J. Heft
A. Michael Henry
Robert Hochstein

(See Next Column)

ASSOCIATES (Continued)

Ross A. Honig
Amy S. Huang
Aimée P. Jalazo
Susan S. Kang
Lynn Stofan Kaplan
Mitchell L. Katz
Deborah L. Kefer
Theodore A. Keyes
Robert R. Kiesel
Paul Jaykun Kim
Eleazer Klein
Lauren M. Kreuter
Marilyn C. Kunstler
Yasho Lahiri
S. Dov Lando
Frank J. LaSalle (Not admitted in NY)
Shulamit Leviant
Audrey Hope Levine
Carol Weiner Levy
Caroline Krass Levy
Yulan Li (Not admitted in NY)
Karen J. Loga (Not admitted in NY)
Robert B. Loper
Tim O'Neal Lorah
Shawn Luther
Gabriel S. Mairzadeh
Jai Maitra
Laurie Claire Malkin (Not admitted in NY)
Farid R. Maluf
Santo Manna
Mary K. (Mulvaney) Marks
D. Lenore Mason
Todd E. Mason (Not admitted in NY)
Kate Marietta McGuire
Michael M. Mezzacappa
Kelli L. Moll
David K. Momborquette
Kimberly M. Monroe
Lindsay H. Myers
Janet M. Nadile
Mari Nakamichi
David Nissenbaum
Dennis C. O'Donnell
Kevin P. O'Donnell
Riyad Omar
Daniel V. Oshinsky
Nathan A. Paul
Steven W. Perlstein
Alix S. Pustilnik
F. Barbara Gluck Reid
Eliot L. Relles
Jeffrey M. Rose
Kristen Gaven Russell
Bret R. Salzer
Lanier Saperstein
Jennifer Ellen Schantz
Lorna J. Scharlacken
Edward H. Schauder
Michael L. Schein
Joel Schmidt
Joseph P. Sciacca
Susan Shanklin
Eliav Sharvit
Jessica Sklute
Steven J. Spencer
Craig Stein
Sung-Hee Suh
Michael E. Swartz
Lynn S. Tanner
Jesse Taran
Molly Jennifer Tatman
Lewis D. Thompson
Susan Blackman Tilson
Jennifer Trahan
Peter C. Trimarchi
Michelle R. Vago
Jess A. Velona
Gary Von Stange
Albert H. Wang
Matthew M. Weber
Aron Egan Weiss
Holly Hexter Weiss
David R. Werbel
Matthew B. White
Herbert J. Willcox
Julian M. Wise
Alexander D. Wolfman
Kyle Wombolt
Heath B. Zarin
Sheila R. Zablow
Martin Zerwitz

For full biographical listings, see the Martindale-Hubbell Law Directory

SEWARD & KISSEL LLP (AV)

(Smith & Martin 1890)
One Battery Park Plaza, 10004
Telephone: 212-574-1200
Cable Address: "Sewkis New York"
Telex: 23-9046; 62-0982
Facsimile: 212-480-8421
Email: sknyc@sewkis.com *URL:* http://www.sewkis.com
Washington, D.C. Office: 1200 G Street, N.W., Suite 350.
Telephone: 202-737-8833.
Facsimile: 202-737-5184.

MEMBERS OF FIRM

Eugene P. Souther
Albert A. Walsh
Arrial S. Cogan
Bruce D. Senzel
James H. Hancock
Anthony R. Mansfield
Anthony C. J. Nuland (Resident, Washington, D.C.)
M. William Munno
Peter E. Pront
Dale C. Christensen, Jr.
David L. Fobes
Hadley S. Roe
Russell C. Prince
Craig T. Hickernell
Robert A. Walder
John E. Tavss
William F. Kuntz, II
Gary J. Wolfe
Lawrence Rutkowski
Ronald L. Cohen
Hume R. Steyer
Mark J. Hyland
Paul T. Clark (Resident, Washington, D.C.)
Jonathan Berger
Thomas G. MacDonald
Mark A. Brody
John J. Cleary
Michael J. McNamara
Kalyan Das
John F. Rigney
Patricia A. Poglinco
Greg B. Cioffi
Margaret R. Smith
Andrew Silverstein
D. Edwin Schmelzer (Resident, Washington, DC)

SENIOR COUNSEL

George C. Seward

COUNSEL

Derick W. Betts, Jr.
Kevin M. Broadwater (Resident, Washington, D.C.)
Kathleen K. Clarke (Resident, Washington, D.C. Office)
Samayla D. Deutch
Lester Kissel
Richard H. Metsch
Bruce G. Paulsen
Richard H. Valentine
Robert B. Van Grover

(See Next Column)

SEWARD & KISSEL LLP, *New York—Continued*

SENIOR ATTORNEYS

Susan J. Leong
John J. Galban

ASSOCIATES

Arlene R. Alves
Svein-Erik M. Christoffersen
Billie Cook
Daniela V. Crispi
Carol M. Degener
Dorothy Derrickson
Meredith S. Elliott (Not admitted in NY)
Laura M. Franco
Michelle H. Frank
Esther Fried
Robert J. Gorzelany (Not admitted in NY)
Harriet Habert
Michael Hession
Jacob Horowitz
Maureen Hurley
Jonathan E. Katz
Laura E. Korfmann
Mark D. Kotwick
Adam D. Lesnick
Susan J. Lorin
Robert E. Lustrin
Samuel L. Martin
Charles M. Miller
William G. Mulligan
Daniel C. Murphy
Steven B. Nadel
Rocky Pan
Elena Paraskevas-Thadani
Anne M. Patin
Dana C. Pawlicki
Sarah Beth Richelew
S. John Ryan
Philip W. Sbaratta
Kevin P. Scanlan
Allison Scher-Bernbach
Susan Seo
Robin M. Shifrin
Gregory D. Shufro
Jeffrey D. Silverstein
Craig A. Sklar
Joseph M. Stefano
Amelia Sweetland
Grant A. Toch
Trevor J. Welch
Jack Yoskowitz
Sandy K. Yu

DIRECTOR OF RECRUITING

Royce L. Wain

For full biographical listings, see the Martindale-Hubbell Law Directory

SHEARMAN & STERLING (AV)

599 Lexington Avenue, 10022-6069
Telephone: (212) 848-4000
Telex: 667290 Num Law
Fax: (212) 848-7179
URL: http://www.shearman.com
Abu Dhabi, United Arab Emirates Office: Butti Al Otaiba Building, 13th Floor, Suite 1302, Sheikh Khalifa Street, P.O. Box 2948.
Telephone: (971-2) 6274477.
Fax: (971-2) 6268933.
Beijing, People's Republic of China Office: Suite #2205, Capital Mansion, No. 6, Xin Yuan Nan Road. Chao Yang District, Beijing, 100004.
Telephone: (86-10) 6465-2299.
Fax: (86-10) 6465-4578.
Düsseldorf, Federal Republic of Germany Office: Couvenstrasse 8 40211 Düsseldorf.
Telephone: (49 211) 178 88-0.
Fax: (49 211) 178 88-88.
Frankfurt, Federal Republic of Germany Office: Trianon Building, Mainzer Landstrasse 16, 60325 Frankfurt am Main.
Telephone: (49-69) 9711-1000.
Fax: (49-69) 9711-1100.
Hong Kong Office: Standard Chartered Bank Building, 4 Des Voeux Road, Central.
Telephone: (852) 2978-8000.
Fax: (852) 2978-8099.
London, England Office: Broadgate West, 9 Appold Street, London EC2A 2AP.
Telephone: (44-020) 7655-5000.
Fax: (44-020) 7655-5500.
Menlo Park, California Office: 1550 El Camino Real, 94025-4100.
Telephone: (650) 330-2200.
Fax: (650) 330-2299.
Paris, France Office: 114, avenue des Champs-Elysées, 75008.
Telephone: (33-1) 53-89-7000.
Fax: (33-1) 53-89-7070.
San Francisco, California Office: 555 California Street, 94104-1522.
Telephone: (415) 616-1100.
Fax: (415) 616-1199.
Singapore Office: 6 Battery Road #25-03. Singapore 049909.
Telephone: (65) 230-3800.
Fax: (65) 230-3899.
Tokyo, Japan Office: Fukoku Seimei Building, 5th Fl. 2-2-2, Uchisaiwaicho, Chiyoda-ku, Tokyo 100-0011. Japan.
Telephone: (81 3) 5251-1601.
Fax: (81 3) 5251-1602.
Toronto, Ontario, Canada Office: Commerce Court West, Suite 4405, P.O. Box 247, M5L 1E8.
Telephone: (416) 360-8484.
Fax: (416) 360-2958.
Washington, D.C. Office: 801 Pennsylvania Avenue, N.W., 20004-2604.
Telephone: (202) 508-8000.
Fax: (202) 508-8100.

MEMBERS OF FIRM

Stephen R. Volk (Senior Partner)
Whitney D. Pidot (Managing Partner)
Cornelius J. Dwyer, Jr.
Jeremy G. Epstein
Mark Kessel
John J. Madden

(See Next Column)

MEMBERS OF FIRM (Continued)

Linda E. Rappaport
Jaculin Aaron
Richard S. Aldrich, Jr.
Clifford Atkins (London)
Laurence M. Bambino
Alexander C. Bancroft
Roger J. Baneman
Gary Barnett
Barry P. Barbash (Washington, D.C.)
Douglas P. Bartner
James M. Bartos (London)
Stuart J. Baskin
Ronald M. Bayer (Not admitted in NY)
Dr. Hanno Berger (Frankfurt)
Robert A. Bergquist (Washington, D.C.)
Emily Berlin
Matthew D. Bersani (Hong Kong)
David J. Beveridge (London)
Henry C. Blackiston, III
David L. Bleich
Peter H. Blessing
Pamela Borgeson
Nicholas Buckworth (London)
William M. Burke (Not admitted in NY)
John J. Cannon, III
Danielle Carbone
Bernard Carrez (Paris)
Sheri P. Chromow
Wayne Dale Collins
Kathleen M. Comfrey
Creighton O'M. Condon
Jeffrey P. Crandall
Laurence E. Crouch (Menlo Park and San Francisco)
Bruce Czachor (Toronto)
Frederick T. Davis
David D. Deck (Managing Partner, Tokyo)
Alan F. Denenberg (Menlo Park and San Francisco)
Dr. Hans Diekmann (Düsseldorf)
Christopher D. Dillon (San Francisco and Menlo Park)
Robert E. Dineen, Jr.
Christophe Dugué (Paris)
Philip B. Dundas, Jr. (Managing Partner, Abu Dhabi)
Jacques-Henri Epstein (Paris)
Robert Evans, III
Jeffrey S. Facter (San Francisco)
Arthur Norman Field
Stephen Fishbein
Stuart K. Fleischmann
William E. Flowers
Jerome S. Fortinsky
Emmanuel Gaillard (Managing Partner, Paris)
Pamela M. Gibson (Managing Partner, London)
Stephen T. Giove
William R. Giusti
Iain M. Goalen (London)
Donald A. Goldsmith
Alan S. Goudiss
Denise M. Grant
Bonnie Greaves
Jonathan L. Greenblatt
Alfred C. Groff (Washington. D.C.)
Faith D. Grossnickle
Kevin R. Hackett
David W. Heleniak
John S. Herbert
William H. Hinman (Managing Partner, San Francisco and Menlo Park)
William E. Hirschberg
Ji Hoon Hong
Dr. Stephan Hutter (Frankfurt)
Phillip L. Jackson
Andrew B. Jánszky
Jonathan Jewett
Salem M. Katsh
Kevin P. Kennedy (Menlo Park and San Francisco)
Joel S. Klaperman
Spencer D. Klein
Dr. Anton Klösters (Düsseldorf)
Adrian Knight (London)
Dr. Thomas N. König (Frankfurt)
Dr. Alfred L. Kossmann (Düsseldorf)
John N. Kramer, Jr.
Kenneth M. Kramer
Dean S. Krystowski (San Francisco)
Lee A. Kuntz
Kenneth J. Laverriere
W. Jeffrey Lawrence (London)
Michael A. Leppert (Frankfurt)
Hervé Letréguilly (Paris)
Hsiao-chiung Li (Hong Kong)
Timothy G. Little
Alberto Luzarraga, Jr.
Peter D. Lyons
Robert H. MacKinnon
Kenneth MacRitchie (London)
Thomas S. Martin (Managing Partner, Washington, D.C.)
Stephen James Marzen (Washington, D.C.)
John A. Marzulli, Jr.
Debra D. McCullough
Douglas R. Mcfadyen
Dr. Hans Jürgen Meyer-Lindemann (Düsseldorf)
John A. Millard
Calvert C. Miller (Singapore)
John D. Morrison, Jr.
Stephen Mostyn-Williams (London)
Susan S. Muck (San Francisco)
Johann Georg Mühlmann (Frankfurt)
Margaret Murphy
Danforth Newcomb
Cyrille Niedzielski (Paris)
Clare O'Brien
Maura E. O'Sullivan
Jeanne C. Olivier
Clarence W. Olmstead, Jr.
John L. Opar, Jr.
Manuel A. Orillac (Paris)
Stephen Peppiatt (London)
C. Jones Perry, Jr.
Christopher J. Pittinger
Werner L. Polak
Richard J. B. Price (Singapore)
Kenneth S. Prince
Linda C. Quinn
Clark T. Randt, Jr. (Hong Kong)
Andrew W. Regan
Gerald Rokoff
William J. F. Roll, III
Alfred J. Ross, Jr.
Marc M. Rossell
Vladimir R. Rossman
Robert A. Rudnick (Washington, D.C.)
Reade H. Ryan, Jr.
Bradley Kent Sabel
Robert H. Saunders
Andrew R. Schleider
Paul S. Schreiber
James S. Scott, Sr. (Counsel)
Mark J. Shapiro
Steven E. Sherman (San Francisco)
Mason C. Sleeper
Chris M. Smith
Justin J. Stevenson III
Antonia E. Stolper
Frank R. Strong (Washington, D.C.)
Hubertus V. Sulkowski (Paris)
Steven C. Sunshine (Washington, D.C.)
John M. Sykes, III
James P. Tallon
Arbie R. Thalacker
Georg F. Thoma (Managing Partner, Europe; Managing Partner, Düsseldorf and Frankfurt)
Wolfgang Tischbirek (Frankfurt)
Sami L. Toutounji (Paris)

(See Next Column)

SHEARMAN & STERLING—*Continued*

MEMBERS OF FIRM (Continued)

Robert C. Treuhold (Deputy Managing Partner, Paris)
Edward L. Turner III (Managing Partner, Beijing and Hong Kong)
Cynthia E. Urda Kassis
Richard B. Vilsoet (Not admitted in NY)
Brice T. Voran (Managing Partner, Toronto)
George J. Wade
Rupert D.E. Walker (London)
Jacques Wantz (Paris)
Anthony Ward (London)
James R. Warnot, Jr.
Rohan S. Weerasinghe
Henry Weisburg
Jonathan M. Weld
M. Holland West
R. Paul Wickes
William J. Wiegmann (London)
Thomas B. Wilner (Washington, D.C.)
John D. Wilson (London)
Mark R. Wingerson
Jeffrey M. Winton (Washington, D.C.)
Mary Kate Wold
William Yaro
T. Robert Zochowski, Jr.

OF COUNSEL

Hans H. Angermueller
Edward Bransilver (Washington, D.C.)
Paul M. Butler, Jr.
Robert Carswell
Robert L. Clare, Jr.
Thomas A. Dieterich
Robert M. Feely
Dr. Michael Gruson
Henry Harfield
Steven M. Herman (San Francisco)
C. Bedford Johnson
Lucian C. Jones
Gilbert Kerlin
Robert H. Knight
Robert A. MacCrindle (Paris)
David T. McGovern (Paris)
Franklin H. Moore, Jr.
Robert H. Mundheim
Stanley I. Rubenfeld
Edward Hallam Tuck

COUNSEL

Wendy E. Ackerman (Washington, D.C.)
Abigail Arms (Washington, D.C.)
Jeanne M. Campanelli
Isabelle Chauvet (French Counsel, Paris)
Juliette F. Denkin
Helen Doo
Chieko Eda (Tokyo)
Robert W. Fagiola (Real Estate Counsel)
Constance A. Fratianni (Counsel)
Kenneth A. Gerasimovich (Counsel)
Fern S. Ginsberg
Charles S. Gittleman (Counsel)
Jack D. Gunther, Jr.
Mark J. Harty (Asian Counsel, Hong Kong)
Joyce E. Heinzerling (Counsel)
Susan L. Hobart
Priscilla C. Hughes
Benjamin B. Iselin
Lisa L. Jacobs
Lynette C. Kelly
Alvin D. Knott (Counsel)
Chu Liu (Senior Asia Counsel, Hong Kong)
Michael S. McBride
Karen Hess McMillan (Washington, D.C.)
Wanda S. McNeil
Lee D. Neumann (Paris)
Tai H. Park
Bernie J. Pistillo, Jr. (London)
Paul G. Prince (Hong Kong)
Joanna Shally (Litigation Counsel)
George T. Spera, Jr. (Compensation and Benefits Counsel)
Howard M. Steinberg
Eric Teynier (French Counsel, Paris)
Sharon L. Trulock
James F. Warren (Washington, D.C.)

For full biographical listings, see the Martindale-Hubbell Law Directory

---

SILLS CUMMIS RADIN TISCHMAN EPSTEIN & GROSS, A PROFESSIONAL CORPORATION (AV)

712 Fifth Avenue, 10019
Telephone: 212-643-7000
Fax: 212-319-6550
Email: sillsmail@sillscummis.com *URL:* http://www.sillscummis.com
Atlantic City, New Jersey Office: 17 Gordon's Alley.
Telephone: 609-344-2800.
Newark, New Jersey Office: One Riverfront Plaza.
Telephone: 973-643-7000.
Washington, D.C. Office: 1800 K Street, N.W.
Telephone: 202-296-4750.

MEMBERS OF FIRM

Clive S. Cummis
Steven S. Radin
Michael B. Tischman
Morton S. Bunis
Barry M. Epstein
Steven E. Gross
Thomas J. Demski
Jeffrey Hugh Newman
Lawrence S. Horn
Jeffrey J. Greenbaum
Simon Levin
Stephen J. Moses
Morris Yamner
Gerald Span
Jeffrey Barton Cahn
Noah Bronkesh
Steven M. Goldman
Alan E. Sherman
Robert J. Alter
Ira A. Rosenberg
Robert Max Crane
Philip R. Sellinger
Jack M. Zackin (Not admitted in NY)
Stuart M. Feinblatt
Margaret F. Black
Trent S. Dickey
Joseph L. Buckley
Stanley U. North, III
Michael I. Chakansky
James M. Hirschhorn
Mark S. Olinsky
Philip R. White
Beth S. Rose
Jack Wenik
Frederic M. Tudor

(See Next Column)

MEMBERS OF FIRM (Continued)

Jeffrey M. Pollock
Steven R. Kamen
Nathan E. Arnell
A. Ross Pearlson
Linda Badash Katz

SENIOR COUNSEL

David Beck
Herbert L. Zuckerman

OF COUNSEL

Mitchel E. Ostrer
Kenneth R. Weiner

Noel D. Humphreys
Eric W. Sleeper
Bennet Susser
Steven S. Katz
Paul F. Doda
Rhonda Sobral O'Toole
Andrew H. Sherman
Adam J. Kaiser
William J. Tinsley, Jr.
Jennifer L. Borofsky
Gwen L. Coleman
Susanne Kaufmann Rosenzweig
Christian Peter Johnson

Representative Clients: Bally Manufacturing Corp.; Becton Dickinson & Co., Inc.; BMW of North America; Bristol-Myers Squibb Co.; Citibank, N.A.; FIAT USA, Inc.; WWOR-TV, Inc.; Rotschild Realty, Inc.; Short Line Bus Co.; PNC Bank Corp.

For full biographical listings, see the Martindale-Hubbell Law Directory

---

SIMPSON THACHER & BARTLETT (AV)

425 Lexington Avenue, 10017-3954
Telephone: 212-455-2000
Cable Address: "Xydsink"
Telex: 129158 (SIMPTHBAR NYK) 232622 (S TBBP UR)
Telecopier: 212-455-2502
URL: http://www.simpsonthacher.com
Columbus, Ohio Office: One Riverside Plaza, 43215.
Telephone: 614-461-7799.
Telecopier: 614-461-0040.
Los Angeles, California Office: 10 Universal City Plaza, Suite 1850, Universal City, CA, 91608.
Telephone: 818-755-7000.
Fax: 818-755-7009.
Palo Alto, California Office: 3373 Hillview Avenue, 94304.
Telephone: 650-251-5000.
Telecopier: 650-251-5002.
London Office: 99 Bishopsgate, London EC2M 3YH, England.
Telephone: 207 422-4000.
Telecopier: 207 422-4022.
Tokyo Office: Ark Mori Building, 30th Floor, 12-32 Akasaka 1-Chome, Minato-Ku, Tokyo 107, Japan.
Telephone: 81-3-5562-8601.
Telecopier: 81-3-5562-8606. ESL 62765846.
Hong Kong Office: Asia Pacific Finance Tower - 7th Floor, 3 Garden Road, Central, Hong Kong.
Telephone: 852-2514-7600.
Telecopier: 852-2869-7694.
Singapore Office: Suntec Tower One, 33rd Floor, 7 Temasek Boulevard, Singapore 038987.
Telephone: 65-430-5100.
Telecopier: 65-430-5151.

MEMBERS OF FIRM

Andrew S. Amer
Bruce D. Angiolillo
Richard I. Beattie
Thomas H. Bell
Victoria B. Bjorklund
Robert A. Bourque
D. Rhett Brandon
Alan G. Brenner (Resident Partner, Singapore Office)
William B. Brentani
Alvin H. Brown
Dickson G. Brown
James C. Buresh
Richard Capelouto (Resident Partner, Palo Alto, California Office)
John W. Carr
Charles F. Carroll
David B. Chapnick
Michael J. Chepiga
Daniel Clivner (Resident Partner, Los Angeles, California Office and Partner, Palo Alto Office)
Cynthia G. Cobden
Sarah E. Cogan
Charles I. Cogut
Gregory W. Conway (Resident Partner, London, England Office)
Michael V. Corrigan
James M. Cotter
John J. Creed
James D. Cross
Mark G. Cunha
William E. Curbow
Paul C. Curnin
Robert F. Cusumano
William R. Dougherty (Resident Partner, London, England Office)
Kenneth C. Edgar Jr.
David M. Eisenberg
Stephan J. Feder
John G. Finley
Paul B. Ford Jr.
John M. Forelle
Mary Beth Forshaw
Andrew T. Frankel
Steven M. Fuhrman
Richard A. Garvey
Peter J. Gordon
I. Scott Gottdiener
Caroline B. Gottschalk
Michael P. Graney (Resident Partner, Columbus, Ohio Office)
Henry B. Gutman
Conrad K. Harper
John C. Hart
Gary I. Horowitz
L. Francis Huck
G. Hartwell Hylton
David W. Ichel
Martin D. Jacobson
Mildred Kalik
Andrew R. Keller
John J. Kenney
John J. Kerr Jr.
Glenn D. Kesselhaut

(See Next Column)

SIMPSON THACHER & BARTLETT, *New York—Continued*

MEMBERS OF FIRM (Continued)

Alan M. Klein
James T. Knight
Kerry L. Konrad
Charles E. Koob (Partner, New York and Palo Alto, California Offices)
James G. Kreissman (Resident Partner, Palo Alto, California Office)
George R. Krouse, Jr.
Marni J. Lerner
David Lieberman
John D. Lobrano
Kenneth R. Logan
Walter A. Looney Jr. (Resident Partner, London, England Office)
David E. Massengill
Mary Elizabeth McGarry
Joseph M. McLaughlin
Lee Meyerson
George Keith Miller
Richard Allen Miller
Gary F. Mottola
Michael D. Nathan
Wilson S. Neely
George M. Newcombe (Resident Partner, Palo Alto, California Office)
Michael J. Nooney (Resident Partner, Palo Alto, California Office)
Risë B. Norman
Barry R. Ostrager (Partner, New York and Palo Alto, California Offices)
Vincent Pagano Jr.
Laura Palma
Mario Ponce
Charles O. Rappaport
Roy L. Reardon (P.C.)
Glenn M. Reiter
Gregory J. Ressa
Gary Rice
Thomas C. Rice
John E. Riley (Resident Partner, Hong Kong, China Office)
Brian D. Robbins
Arthur D. Robinson
Pamela L. Rollins
C. Tanner Rose Jr.
Philip T. Ruegger III
William T. Russell Jr.
Patrick J. Ryan
Alan D. Schnitzer
Alan G. Schwartz
Gary L. Sellers
(Mike) Myer O. Sigal Jr.
Robert H. Smit
David A. Sneider (Resident Partner, Tokyo, Japan Office)
David J. Sorkin
Robert E. Spatt
Brian M. Stadler
John B. Tehan
Jeremiah L. Thomas III
Peter C. Thomas
Mark Thompson
Steven C. Todrys
Edward P. Tolley III
Joseph F. Tringali
David E. Vann Jr.
Mary Kay Vyskocil
Raymond W. Wagner
John L. Walker
Joseph F. Wayland
Gregory A. Weiss
Marissa C. Wesely
David L. Williams
Michael O. Wolfson (Resident Partner, London, England Office)
Michael W. Wolitzer
David J. Woll
Kenneth S. Wyman
Kenneth S. Ziman

SENIOR COUNSEL

Blake A. Bell
J. Scott Dyer
Timothy J. Malin
Seth A. Ribner (Resident Senior Counsel, Los Angeles, California Office)
Margaret L. Riess
Peter F. Riley
Moshe Schwerd

COUNSEL

Steven R. DeLott
Terrence L. Dugan
Adeeb R. Fadil
Tonianne Florentino
Michael Isby
Mark T. Lab
Francis C. Marinelli
Kathrine A. McLendon
Mardi Merjian
Jayma M. Meyer
Helen Pak (Resident Counsel, Hong Kong, China Office)
Robert Y. Pelgrift Jr.
Brynn D. Peltz
Karen Mieko Sakanashi (Resident Counsel, Hong Kong, China Office)
Steven C. Stickler
Kaoru Takada (Resident, Counsel, Palo Alto, California Office)
Mark S. Tibberts (Resident Counsel, Columbus, Ohio Office)

For full biographical listings, see the Martindale-Hubbell Law Directory

SKADDEN, ARPS, SLATE, MEAGHER & FLOM LLP (AV)

Four Times Square, 10036
Telephone: 212-735-3000
Fax: 212-735-2000
URL: http://www.sasmf.com
Firm/Affiliate Offices:
Boston, Massachusetts: One Beacon Street, 02108.
Telephone: 617-573-4800.
Fax: 617-573-4822.
Washington, D.C.: 1440 New York Avenue, N.W., 20005.
Telephone: 202-371-7000.
Fax: 202-393-5760.
Wilmington, Delaware: One Rodney Square, P.O. Box 636, 19899.
Telephone: 302-651-3000.
Fax: 302-651-3001.
Los Angeles, California: 300 South Grand Avenue, 90071.
Telephone: 213-687-5000.
Fax: 213-687-5600.
Chicago, Illinois: Skadden, Arps, Slate, Meagher & Flom (Illinois), 333 West Wacker Drive, 60606.
Telephone: 312-407-0700.
Fax: 312-407-0411.

(See Next Column)

San Francisco, California: Four Embarcadero Center, 94111.
Telephone: 415-984-6400.
Fax: 415-984-2698.
Houston, Texas: 1600 Smith Street, Suite 4460, 77002.
Telephone: 713-655-5100.
Fax: 713-655-5181.
Newark, New Jersey: One Newark Center, 07102.
Telephone: 973-639-6800.
Fax: 973-639-6858.
Palo Alto, California: 525 University Avenue, Suite 220, 94301.
Telephone: 650-470-4500.
Fax: 650-470-4570.
Tokyo, Japan: ATT Main Tower 12F, 2-17-22, Akasaka, Minato-ku, 107-0052.
Telephone: 011-813-3568-2600.
Fax: 011-813-3568-2626.
London, England: One Canada Square, Canary Wharf, E14 5DS.
Telephone: 011-44-207-519-7000.
Fax: 011-44-207-519-7070.
Hong Kong, China: 30/F Tower Two, Lippo Centre, 89 Queensway, Central.
Telephone: 011-852-2820-0700.
Fax: 011-852-2820-0727.
Sydney, New South Wales 2000, Australia: Skadden, Arps, Slate, Meagher & Flom (International), Level 13, 131 Macquarie Street.
Telephone: 011-61-2-9253-6000.
Fax: 011-61-2-9253-6044.
Toronto, Ontario, Canada: Suite 1820, North Tower, P.O. Box 189, Royal Bank Plaza, M5J 2J4.
Telephone: 416-777-4700.
Fax: 416-777-4747.
Brussels, Belgium: 523 avenue Louise, Box 30, 1050.
Telephone: 011-32-2-639-0300.
Fax: 011-32-2-639-0339.
Frankfurt am Main, Germany: MesseTurm, 27th Floor, 60308.
Telephone: 011-49-69-742200.
Fax: 011-49-69-74220300.
Paris, France: 68, rue du Faubourg Saint-Honoré, 75008.
Telephone: 011-331-55-27-11-00.
Fax: 011-331-55-27-11-99.
Beijing, China: East Wing Office, Level 4, China World Trade Center, No. 1 Jian Guo Men Wai Avenue, 100004.
Telephone: 011-86-10-6505-5511.
Fax: 011-86-10-6505-5522.
Moscow, Russia: Degtyarniy Pereulok 4, Building 1, 103009.
Telephone: 011-7-501-797-4600.
Fax: 011-7-501-797-4601.
Singapore, Singapore: Skadden, Arps, Slate, Meagher & Flom (International), 9 Temasek Boulevard, Suite 29-01, Suntec Tower Two, 038989.
Telephone: 011-65-434-2900.
Fax: 011-65-434-2988.

MEMBERS OF FIRM/AFFILIATES

Marshall K. Skadden (1907-1958)
John H. Slate (1913-1967)
William R. Meagher (1903-1981)
Leslie H. Arps (1907-1987)
Joseph H. Flom
Barry H. Garfinkel
Blaine V. Fogg
Robert C. Vincent, Jr.
James F. O'Rorke, Jr.
Roger S. Aaron
Peter Allan Atkins
William P. Frank
Morris J. Kramer
Henry P. Wasserstein
Theodore J. Kozloff
Thomas J. Schwarz
William C. Pelster
Milton G. Strom
Daniel E. Stoller
Robert C. Sheehan
Edward J. Yodowitz
Edmund C. Duffy
Kenneth A. Plevan
Vaughn C. Williams
Jeffrey Glekel
Michael L. Cook
Franklin M. Gittes
Douglas M. Kraus
Jonathan J. Lerner
Barnet Phillips, IV
Neal R. Stoll
Benjamin F. Needell
Peter E. Greene
Jerome S. Hirsch
Irene A. Sullivan
Jeffrey W. Tindell
Robert E. Zimet
Matthew J. Mallow
Michael M. Connery
Richard L. Easton
Shepard Goldfein
J. Gregory Milmoe
Alan C. Myers
Stuart N. Alperin
Richard R. Kalikow
Christopher J. Kell
Matthew A. Rosen
J. Michael Schell
Sheila L. Birnbaum
Stephen M. Banker
Samuel Kadet
Lou R. Kling
Martha E. McGarry
Richard T. Prins
Alesia Ranney-Marinelli
Wallace L. Schwartz
Joseph W. Halliday
Michael E. Gizang
Charles Morgan
Vincent J. Pisano
Isaac Shapiro
Fred B. White, III
C. Thomas Kunz
Robert M. Chilstrom
David J. Friedman
Edward E. Gonzalez
Nancy A. Lieberman
Kayalyn A. Marafioti
Peter J. Neckles
Mitchell J. Solomon
Harvey R. Uris
Margaret L. Wolff
George A. Zimmerman
Kenneth J. Bialkin
Sheldon S. Adler
Katherine M. Bristor
Randall H. Doud
Jay B. Kasner
James M. Schell
Eileen T. Nugent
Alan G. Straus

(See Next Column)

SKADDEN, ARPS, SLATE, MEAGHER & FLOM LLP—*Continued*

MEMBERS OF FIRM/AFFILIATES (Continued)

Barbara Wrubel
Clifford H. Aronson
Susan M. Curtis
James M. Douglas
F. Eugene Hiigel
Constance S. Huttner
Thomas H. Kennedy
William S. Rubenstein
Paul T. Schnell
David M. Zornow
Joseph A. Coco
Martha Feltenstein
David Fox
Richard F. Kadlick
Phyllis G. Korff
Diana M. Lopo
Harold F. Moore
Marco E. Schnabl
Mark C. Smith
Michael L. Weiner
Charles M. Fox
Barry E. Hawk
Sally McDonald Henry
Peter J. McKenna
Seth M. Schwartz
Bertil Lundqvist
John P. Furfaro
Linda C. Hayman
Timothy G. Reynolds
Jonathan L. Koslow
Stuart M. Finkelstein
Richard S. Fortunato
Philip H. Harris
Stacy J. Kanter
Robert J. Sullivan
Robert J. Del Tufo
Eric L. Cochran
Andrew M. Faulkner
Gregory A. Fernicola
Dana H. Freyer
Neil M. Leff
Jeffrey S. Lichtman
Sally A. Thurston
Sarah M. Ward
Mary Sue Butch
John L. Gardiner
James A. Keyte
David M. Rievman
John W. Osborn
Stephen F. Arcano
Neil L. Rock
James S. Stringfellow
Susan J. Sutherland
Jay M. Goffman
Stuart D. Levi
Howard L. Ellin
Eric J. Friedman
Lawrence D. Frishman
Angela G. Garcia
David J. Goldschmidt
Keith D. Krakaur
W. Kirk Wallace
Robert A. Copen
Richard J. Grossman
Lea Haber Kuck
Regina Olshan
Ronald J. Weiss
Marc P. Hanrahan
Daniel A. DeVito
J. Phillip Adams
Jay S. Berke
Anastasia T. Rockas
Susan L. Saltzstein
Allison R. Schneirov
Dean S. Shulman
Audrey L. Sokoloff
Kenneth A. Wright, Jr.
Edward V. Filardi
Jeffrey A. Mishkin

OF COUNSEL

Henry P. Baer
James C. Freund
Helene L. Kaplan
Mark N. Kaplan
James A. Levitan
Peter P. Mullen
Edwin Robbins
Robert B. Smith
Evelyn M. Sommer
Melvin A. Yellin

COUNSEL

Carole V. Aciman
Katherine A. Armstrong
Richard T. Bernardo
Robert P. Blank
Lisa S. Dorushkin
Douglas W. Dunham
Arthur F. Fama, Jr.
Joyce Penn Farnsworth
Wendy R. Fleishman
Thomas E. Fox
Kathleen A. Frederick
Carlene J. Gatting
Ralph A. Gerra, Jr.
Christopher R. Gette
Gerhard Gnaedig
Rita W. Gordon
Paula S. Greenman
Dan Hastings
Michael K. Hoffman (Not admitted in NY)
John P. Hooper
Peter S. Julian
Stephanie J. Kamerow
Bentley Kassal
Matthew J. Knopf (Not admitted in NY)
Diana V. Lopez
Michael Madigan
Christy L. McElhaney
Peter T. McKeon
David H. Midvidy
Joseph P. Nisa
Richard J. Ressler
Carl J. Riley
Lawrence Safran
Eric S. Sarner
Stephanie R. Schwartz
S. Kinnie Smith, Jr. (Not admitted in NY)
Rosa A. Testani
Bert L. Wolff
Elaine D. Ziff

SPECIAL COUNSEL

Jeremy A. Berman
Erskine D. Henderson
Gail Kendall
Steven J. Kolleeny
Ronald J. Tabak

FIRM/AFFILIATE OFFICES:

BOSTON, MASSACHUSETTS

PARTNERS

Louis A. Goodman
Thomas R. Bateman
Thomas J. Dougherty
Margaret A. Brown
David T. Brewster
Kent A. Coit
George J. Skelly
Thomas A. De Capo
Dennis M. Kelleher
James R. Carroll

COUNSEL

John E. Besser
Joan M. Heminway

CHICAGO, ILLINOIS

PARTNERS

Wayne W. Whalen
Charles W. Mulaney, Jr.
Timothy A. Nelsen
Marian P. Wexler
Warren G. Lavey
Susan Getzendanner
N. Lynn Hiestand
Andrew S. Kenoe

(See Next Column)

CHICAGO, ILLINOIS

PARTNERS (Continued)

William R. Kunkel
John D. Rayis
David E. Springer
John Wm. Butler, Jr.
Edward M. Crane
Thomas A. Hale
Randall J. Rademaker
Christina M. Tchen
Gary P. Cullen
John André LeDuc
Ann H. Pollock
Peter C. Krupp
Brian W. Duwe
J. Eric Ivester
Charles F. Smith
Seth E. Jacobson
Maxwell M. Miller
Rodd M. Schreiber
Louis S. Freeman
David S. Kurtz
Matthew R. Kipp
Lynn M. McGovern

OF COUNSEL

Arthur S. Rollin

COUNSEL

Kathleen M. Cronin
Susan J. Levine
Jeffrey W. Linstrom
John K. Lyons
Mark E. Rakoczy
R. Ryan Stoll

LOS ANGELES, CALIFORNIA

PARTNERS

Jerome L. Coben
Rand S. April
Joseph J. Giunta
John A. Donovan
Frank Rothman
Douglas B. Adler
Brian J. McCarthy
Nicholas P. Saggese
Rodrigo A. Guerra, Jr.
Darrel J. Hieber
Michael V. Gisser
Gregg A. Noel
Eric S. Waxman
Jeffrey B. Valle
Jeffrey H. Dasteel
Harriet S. Posner
Peter Simshauser
Michael A. Woronoff
Michael A. Lawson
Jeffrey H. Cohen
Karen L. Corman
Allan G. Mutchnik
John E. Mendez
Richard B. Levin
Joseph M. Doloboff
Jonathan L. Friedman
Moshe J. Kushman
David C. Reamer

OF COUNSEL

Harold M. Williams

COUNSEL

Peter W. Clapp
Garrison G. DeLee
George M. Eshaghian
Ronald P. Givner
David M. Hickey
Carl A. Roth
Daniel J. Weiser

PALO ALTO, CALIFORNIA

PARTNERS

James E. Lyons
Thomas H. Kennedy
Kenton J. King
Garrett J. Waltzer
Ronald S. Laurie
David W. Hansen
Gregory C. Smith

SAN FRANCISCO, CALIFORNIA

PARTNERS

Theodore J. Kozloff
James E. Lyons
José R. Allen
Kenton J. King
Raoul D. Kennedy

COUNSEL

Jane B. Kroesche

WASHINGTON, D.C.

PARTNERS

Lynn R. Coleman
Leslie J. Goldman
Douglas G. Robinson
C. Benjamin Crisman, Jr.
Michael P. Rogan
Thomas R. Graham
Robert E. Lighthizer
Fred T. Goldberg, Jr
Ronald C. Barusch
Stephen W. Hamilton
William J. Sweet, Jr.
Enid L. Veron
Erica A. Ward
Glenn J. Berger
Clifford M. Naeve
Martin Klepper
Paul W. Oosterhuis
Richard L. Brusca
Marcia R. Nirenstein
Robert S. Bennett
Janet L. Goetz
Alan Kriegel
Jeanine L. Matte
Pamela F. Olson
Carl S. Rauh
John J. Mangan
William S. Scherman
Antoinette Cook Bush
Albert H. Turkus
Kenneth Berlin
Mitchell S. Ettinger
Kenneth A. Gross
James V. Alpi
C. Kevin Barnette
Jay L. Birnbaum
Andrew L. Sandler
Mary Lou Steptoe
John C. Quale
John N. Estes, III
Clifford R. Gross
Edward J. Meehan
Pankaj K. Sinha
Colleen P. Mahoney
Lance T. Brasher
James A. Losey
Gary A. MacDonald
Stacie E. McGinn
John S. Moot
Saul M. Pilchen

OF COUNSEL

Martin Hoffmann
Philip McBride Johnson
Neal S. McCoy

(See Next Column)

SKADDEN, ARPS, SLATE, MEAGHER & FLOM LLP, *New York—Continued*

COUNSEL

John A. Amodeo
Jody J. Brewster
June Broadstone
Arthur A. Cohen
Roseann M. Cutrone
Mark C. Del Bianco
Mona E. Ehlenberger
Henry C. Eisenberg
Matthew W. S. Estes
James A. Frazer
Don Joaquin Frost, Jr.
Richard A. Hindman
Jerry L. Jackson
Benjamin B. Klubes
Nancy J. McGlynn
Brian C. Mohr
Stephen J. Narkin
Maureen Nelson
Leonard Rawicz
Catherine Kane Ronis
Nancy G. Rubin
Peter B. Saba
Amy R. Sabrin
Ellen J. Schneider
Frank C. Shaw
Donald L. Toker, Jr.
Charles F. Walker
Troy S. Watkinson

SPECIAL COUNSEL

Kenneth Kraus
Edward D. Ross, Jr.

WILMINGTON, DELAWARE

PARTNERS

Rodman Ward, Jr.
Steven J. Rothschild
Richard L. Easton
Edward P. Welch
Thomas J. Allingham, II
Anthony W. Clark
Robert B. Pincus
Marc B. Tucker
Patricia Moran Chuff
Karen L. Valihura
Gregg M. Galardi

OF COUNSEL

Irving S. Shapiro

COUNSEL

Kevin F. Brady
Mark S. Chehi

SPECIAL COUNSEL

Randolph K. Herndon
Andrew J. Turezyn

HOUSTON, TEXAS

PARTNERS

Lyndon C. Taylor
Thomas E. Weil, Jr.
Frank E. Bayouth

COUNSEL

Dahl C. Thompson
Mark J. Thurber

NEWARK, NEW JERSEY

PARTNER

Robert J. Del Tufo

COUNSEL

Stephen D. Kinnard
Mark L. Manewitz
Andrew Muscato

TOKYO, JAPAN

COUNSEL

Kenju Watanabe

LONDON, ENGLAND

PARTNERS

Bruce M. Buck
Douglas E. Nordlinger
Scott V. Simpson
Richard L. Muglia
Michael E. Hatchard
Hilary S. Foulkes
Hunter S. Baker
James P.L. Healy
Richard A. Ely

COUNSEL

Thomas D. Logan
Wayne J. Rapozo

SPECIAL COUNSEL

Michael V. McKay

SYDNEY, AUSTRALIA

PARTNER

Robert C. Hinkley

HONG KONG

PARTNERS

Jonathan F. Pedersen
Gregory G.H. Miao
Alan G. Schiffman

COUNSEL

Vicki L. Behrend

TORONTO, ONTARIO, CANADA

PARTNER

Milton G. Strom

COUNSEL

Christopher W. Morgan

BRUSSELS, BELGIUM

PARTNERS

Barry E. Hawk
Henry L. Huser

FRANKFURT, GERMANY

PARTNERS

Hilary S. Foulkes
Rainer K. Wachter

(See Next Column)

PARIS, FRANCE

PARTNERS

Isaac Shapiro
Christopher L. Baker

COUNSEL

Laurence Mitrovic

BEIJING, CHINA

PARTNERS

Jon L. Christianson

MOSCOW, RUSSIA

COUNSEL

André De Cort

SINGAPORE, SINGAPORE

PARTNER

Jeffrey S. Christie

NEW YORK, NEW YORK

ASSOCIATES

David J. Abrams
Nancy G. Abudu
Atiba D. Adams
Richard B. Aftanas
Lauren E. Aguiar
Arthur H. Aizley
David D. Almroth
Timothy W. Amata
Bruce Anderson
Joseph M. Asher
(Not admitted in NY)
Shoshanah V. Asnis
Chris T. Athanasia
Lawrence S. Atinsky
Madeline Baer
Michael J. Balch
Michael J. Barker
Matthew S. Barnett
Michael B. Barry
Anne Beckman
Michal Berkner
William E. Bernarduci
Michelle Berninger
Darren E. Bernstein
Caroline E. Berry
Ann Bickford
Veronica A. Bisek
Alexander B. Blades
Carolyn H. Blankenship
Lonny R. Block
Attila I. Bodi
Giorgio Bovenzi
John P. Boyle
Jonathan A. Brenner
Darrell M. Bridgers
Jennifer du Quant Bridges
Jeffrey A. Brill
Mark C. Brooks
Jonathan P. Brose
Darren C. Broughton
(Not admitted in NY)
James W. Brown
Jerome J. Brown
Scott D. Brown
Susan A. Brown
Douglas L. Bryan
(Not admitted in NY)
Gopal M. Burgher
Marco P. Caffuzzi
Jason A. Camhi
John Carey
Julie B. Carlin-Sasaki
Alan J. Carr
Alec Y. Chang
J. Laurence Chang
Linda M. Chang
Mark S. Cheffo
Owen Chen
Stanley A. Chinitz
Linda Chung
Angelo Ciavarella
Leonard P. Ciriello
Thomas E. Claps
Jennifer E.D. Clarke
Harlan L. Cohen
Hayden A. Coleman
Abel R. Coombs
Donna E. Correll
(Not admitted in NY)
Daniel F. Coughlin
(Not admitted in NY)
Christopher D. Cox
Heather S. Cruz
Bal G. Das
John L. Dauer, Jr.
Bernadette H. Davida
Lisa R. D'Avolio
Errol C. Deans, Jr.
Craig M. Deitelzweig
Adrian J.S. Deitz
Joseph DeSimone
Thorsten H. Dietz
Sean C. Doyle
Anthony J. Dreyer
David D. Dueno
(Not admitted in NY)
Natasha Dupont
Kenneth A. Durrsht
Scott R. Ehrlich
Steven B. Eichel
Sylvia Einhorn
Jana Eisinger
Michael S. Emanuel
Adam Endick
Pamela Lawrence Endreny
Jose A. Esteves
Roland O. Ewubare
Thomas R. Fallati
Peter Feist
Marina Feldman
Jennifer A. Ferrante
Howard A. Fine
Patrick J. Flanagan
Douglas E. Fleming, III
Edward Flis
Erika A. Forcione
Jonathan L. Frank
Todd E. Freed
Francis M. Fryscak
Daniel H. Galpern
Avinash V. Ganatra
Sharon Garb
Jason B. Garmise
Michele D. Gartland
Patricia M. Gasaway
Lawrence V. Gelber
James Gelman
Marie L. Gibson
Barry J. Gilman
David Goldberg
Jonathan R. Goldblatt
Jed Goldfarb
Michael Goldman
Bruce J. Goldner
Andrew M. Goldner
Tara J. Goldsmith
Heidi B. Goldstein
Joshua B. Goldstein
Mitchell H. Gordon
Stephen J. Gordon
Sarah C. Gorham
Thomas W. Gowan
Claudia N. Green
Paul Greenan
Thomas Greenberg
Julie A. Grossman
Y. Shukie Grossman
Michael H. Grueneglas
Carl G. Guida
Ragini Gupta
Tasha M. Hailey
Pattie L. Hand
Carolyn B. Handler
Christopher W. Healy
Laura A. Heiman
Susan A. Helfrick
Brian S. Higgins
Christian G. Hildenbrand

(See Next Column)

SKADDEN, ARPS, SLATE, MEAGHER & FLOM LLP—*Continued*

NEW YORK, NEW YORK
ASSOCIATES (Continued)

William J. Hine
Susan Hitzig
Karen M. Hoffman
Victor Hollender
Jacob Hollinger
Christopher S. Hooper
John Horowitz
Gustavo Andres Hoyos
James C. Hsu
Michael A. Humphreys
Adam F. Ingber
David C. Ingles
Neal R. Jacobson
Scott R. Jaffe
Barbara P. Jakubowicz
Jonathan G. James (Not admitted in United States)
Joseph D. Jean
Ian G. John
Alexander B. Johnson
Jong-Hyun Kah
Sean P. Kanuck
Brian S. Kaplan
Jonathan M. Kaplan
E. Michael Karol
Diane J. Kasselman
Honora M. Keane (Not admitted in NY)
Adam J. Katz
Barbara Krasa Kelly
Andrew S. Kessler
Jay J. Kim
Nam Hee Kim
Craig K. Kinosian
William D. Kitay
Matthew H. Kluger
Michael Kofsky
Eric R. Komitee
Paul S. Kraske
Gary M. Kravetz
Kevin Krieger
Bernadette Lajoie
Peter C. Lampasona
Jeffery H. Laska
Jerome J. Lawton
Hae-Joon Joseph Lee
Jaeho Lee
Todd R. Lee
Craig P. Lehner
Loren R. Lembo
Georges Leopold
Nicole S. Levin
Ileana Aguinis Levine
Evan R. Levy
W.H. Ramsay Lewis
Uri Litvak
Jennifer M. Loss
Caroline S. Lovelace
Joy E. Maddox
Thomas G. Maira
Christopher P. Malloy
Michael G. Manasse
Alexandra Margolis
James J. Mastriani
James Mathieu
William A. McBride
Elizabeth L. McGinley
Donna E. McGraw
Jeanine L. McHugh
Sean McKenna
John M. McLeod
Patricia A. McNulty
Anthony P. Mechcatie
James A. Meschewski
Steven M. Messina
Jennifer A. Meyer
Barbara R. Mirza
Joel M. Mitnick
Maureen Moran
Andrew W. Morgan
James C. Munsell
Scott D. Musoff
Bernhardt M. Nadell
David L. Nagler
Jeonghyan S. Nam
Russell E. Nance (Not admitted in NY)
Steven F. Napolitano
Shawn P. Naunton (Not admitted in NY)
Daniel S. Needleman (Not admitted in NY)
Timothy F. Nelson
Douglas R. Nemec
Quoc A. Nguyen
Hope Ni
Stefanie Niebisch
William J. O'Brien, III
Olutoyin Olakanpo
Brooks A. Olbrys
Ruth E. Olson
Thomas Pak
Philip T. Pallone
Richard L. Parker
Brad Parish
Seth L. Pearlstein
Patricia M. Perez
Daniel H. Pine
Debra A. Post
Katherine M. Pratt
David A. Proshan
Ellen P. Quakenbos
Vered Rabia
Anthony Ragozino
Robert C. Rahbari
Shyami U. Rajalingam
Anthony M. Ranieri
Gil A. Raveh
Mark C. Redman
Rose May Registre (Not admitted in NY)
William M. Reichard
Susan B. Reuben
Patrick F. Rice
Paul C. Roberts
Rita A. Rodin
Marian Rosenberg
Steven M. Rosenthal
Jeffrey M. Rosin (Not admitted in NY)
Lissa S. Roth
Elliot Rothstein
Kenneth A. Rubenstein
Audrey P. Rubin
Melissa A. Rule (Not admitted in NY)
Joseph N. Sacca
Hiroshi Sarumida
John W. Scannell
Kimberly Schanzer
Jeffrey L. Schaub
Solan Schwab
David E. Schwartz
Eric I. Schwartz (Not admitted in NY)
Theodore Seltzer
Michael Sessine
Rona G. Shamoon
Mark T. Shehan
Gregory D. Shelton
Katharine Shergalis
Todd H. Siegel
Sharon E. Silver
Rita D. Sinkfield
Steven Snyder (Not admitted in NY)
Jay Sobel
David A. Soloshatz
Linda SooHoo
Lawrence S. Spiegel
Renee L. Stasio (Not admitted in NY)
Neal A. Stern
Evan D. Stone
David A. Straite (Not admitted in NY)
Andrew F. Strobert
Neil P. Stronski
Aparna P. Sulé
William J. Sushon
Andrea W. Taetle
James S. Talbot
James R. Tandler
Julia A. Tchernysh
Stephanie L. Teicher
Luciana Santos Teixeira

NEW YORK, NEW YORK

(See Next Column)

ASSOCIATES (Continued)

Keeva L. Terry (Not admitted in NY)
Joseph K. Todd
Lucyna M. Tokarczyk
Sina Toussi
Esther S. Trakinski
Tiffany T. Tran
Michael P. Trolman
Deborah S. Tuchman
Clem Turner
Eva N. Valik
David Z. Vance
Shmuel Vasser
Joseph Vebman
Brian K. Victor
Adam G. Waitman
Valerie J. Wald
Anne T. Warde
Eric J. Watson
Sarah Watson
Scott E. Way
Romina Weiss
William J. Weiss
Nicholas A. Whitney
Ronan M. Wicks
Robert H. Williams
Gregg J. Winiarski
Andrew S. Wisch
Judith Wise
Daniel E. Wolf
Wendy J. Wolff
Beth R. Wolmer
Linda Wai Mun Wong
Winnie Wing-See Wong
Robert G. Wray
Russell M. Yankwitt
Samuel S. Yoo
Sooryun Youn
Michael G. Zarocostas
Darren Zeidel
Sam M. Zietz
Jason S. Zoto

BOSTON, MASSACHUSETTS
ASSOCIATES

Michael D. Blanchard
Vance R. Brown
David S. Clancy
Margaret A. Crouse
June Duchesne
Kara E. Fay
Paul-Johan Jean
Mark L. Keene
Kenneth M. Lehman
William J. Lundregan
Mary Beth Madarasz
Matthew J. Matule
Jason A. Tucker
Anne Turley

CHICAGO, ILLINOIS
ASSOCIATES

Robert A. Allison
Tracy Staidl Beauchamp
Keith L. Belknap, Jr.
Patrick S. Belville
Kenneth J. Betts
Amarjeet S. Bhachu
Victoria A. Birov
Arthur W. Bresnahan
Stephanie L. Burch
Lisa Butler
Caitlin J. Cameron
Linda F. DiCostanzo
Nancy Eisenhauer
George E. Ellis
Steven H. Forbes
Benjamin R. Foster
Chris Ammerman Gerke
Seth J. Gerson
Brooks T. Giles
Eric J. Gorman
Jeffrey A. Greenblatt
Shilpi Gupta
Matthew R. Hartley
Susan S. Hassan
Pamela R. Henry
Roger J. Higgins
Albert L. Hogan, III
Catherine N. Hoyle
Paul J. Huff, Jr.
Michael D. Ilagan
Eric W. Kaup
Karen M. Lee
David F. Levy
Ronald J. Lieberman
Dietrich A. Loos
Susan J. Macaulay
Matthew J. Maletta
Donna L. McDevitt
Ron Elon Meisler
Joseph E. Miller, III
Steven P. Miriani
Sherri Morissette
Mindy E. Nagorsky
Lily R. Nazerian
Nancy M. Olson
Timothy P. Olson
George N. Panagakis
Nicole M. Pappas
Farhad K. Patel
Nicholas Pavlidis
Felicia Gerber Perlman
Timothy A. Scott
Kirk L. Peterson
Neil E. Petty
Timothy R. Pohl
David Polster
Ian D. Roffman
Erynne A. Ross
David S. Royal
Keith Adam Simon
Steven G. Simon
Janet K. Smith
Deborah G. Solmor
J. Gregory St. Clair
Paula M. Stannard
Charles B. Taylor
Michael S. Terrien
Janet E. Byrne Thabit
Alphonse Valbrune
L. Byron Vance III
Lisa K. Wakida
Douglas D. Weinberg
Stephen D. Williamson
Richard C. Witzel, Jr.
Paul T. Wrycha

HOUSTON, TEXAS
ASSOCIATES

Brian A. Bradshaw
Christian P. Callens
David E. Gohlke
Ann Ainsworth Hawkins
Douglas J. May
Charles H. Still, Jr.
William H. Sultemeier, IV
Vanessa R. Wilson

LOS ANGELES, CALIFORNIA
ASSOCIATES

Aisha H. Abdur-Rahman
Lisa Arakaki
Joshua Armstrong
Karen E. Bedore
Jennifer A. Bensch
Rhonda Bethea
Sheila M. Bradley
Michele Buse
Meryl K. Chae
Connie Chang
Williana Chang
Richard S. Chernicoff
Jodie L. Chusid
Joshua E. Clorfeine
Sharon L. Cohen
Gary Daniel Dean
Shari Del Carlo
Kai Dhaliwal
Janet L. Dhillon
Jamie L. Edmonson
Paul M. Eckles
Ilene R. Eskenazi
Elizabeth S. Farhat
Vlad J. Fayngold

(See Next Column)

SKADDEN, ARPS, SLATE, MEAGHER & FLOM LLP, *New York—Continued*

LOS ANGELES, CALIFORNIA
ASSOCIATES (Continued)

Damon R. Fisher
Matthew Foster
Stacey L. Friedlander
Paul A. Fuhrman
Andrew D. Garelick
Gary S. Glickman
Adam P. Gold
Melissa R. Gray
Amy C. Hagen
Brenda E. Hansen
Henry Havre
Joshua D. Helderman
Stephen J. Helwig
Leonard W. Hersh
Belle H. Hsu
Richard Hynes
Rachel E. Iverson
Thomas J. Ivey
Paul V. Konovalov
Nelson N. Lee
Elayne Levkowitz
Howard S. Liberson
Brian R. Linnekens
Sandra L. Livingston
Kristina S. Lockwood
Rick C. Madden
John A. Makarewich
Shahzad A. Malik
Robyn C. Manos
Chad Mills
Duncan E. Montgomery
Allan R. Mouw
Mona Y. Oh
Anthony Patel
Davidson M. Pattiz
Anthony J. Pearl
Robert P. Pongetti
Martin Alexander Price
Steven M. Ragona
M. Shakil Rahman
Jason S. Reichenthal
Christopher J. Roman
Timothy J. Roth
Jason D. Russell
Ray Sandona
Parker A. Schweich
Geoffrey D. Semro
David H. Seo
Monica Shilling
Tanja K. Shipman
Peter Siembab
Paul E. Simos
Melanie E. Sims
Mark A. Snyder
Barbara C. Sousa
Sandra D. Strassner
Mark Streams
Steven J. Sweeney
Gia C. Twine
Steven A. Velkei
Troy Vigil
Varina W. Whitener
Wallace M. Wong
Susan Yoon

PALO ALTO, CALIFORNIA
ASSOCIATES

Anne D. Clarke
Jason P. Fiorillo
Frederick F. Hadidi
Thomas C. Mavrakakis
Timothy T. O'Donnell
Benjamin R. Ostapuk
Christopher A. Rose
Devang Shah
Calvin Siemer
Melanie D. Vinson
Joseph Yang
Melinda D. Zachar

NEWARK, NEW JERSEY
ASSOCIATES

Aney K. Chandy
Katherine H. Creenan
Frank E. Derby
Cynthia V. Fitzgerald
Diana M. Hendry
Michael T. Heyrich
Mark D. Hoerrner
Ellen O'Connell
Gary J. Ruckelshaus
James J. Savage
Michael A. Shipp

SAN FRANCISCO, CALIFORNIA
ASSOCIATES

Stephen I. Berkman
Todd S. Brecher
Karen Cacace
David Y. Chen
Thomas V. Christopher
Michael J. Cordero
David L. Covington
Celeste E. Greene
Alan D. Hamilton
Elizabeth A. Harlan
Marie Hurabiell
Stacy E. Kray
Edward C. Lyons
Gregory N. Mandel
Sheryl C. Medeiros
Timothy A. Miller
Sidaya Moore
John A. Neu
Spencer G. Park
Carita T. Shanklin
Thomas E. Stevens

WASHINGTON, D.C.
ASSOCIATES

Eric S. Adams
Worth S. Anderson
Katherine D. Ashley
Bonnie J. Austin
Joseph L. Barloon
Kathleen L. Barron
Kurt W. Bilas
Michael Bloise
Sherri L. Booye
Jamie L. Boucher
Jennifer P. Brovey
Raina E. Brubaker
Lily A. Camet
Judith A. Center
Gerard A. Clark
Steven J. Cleveland
Linda G. Coffin
Jodi B. Cohen
Todd R. Coles
Victor A. Contract
Gary DiBianco
Mary Margaret Farren
Cristina M. L. Ferreira
Kathleen A. Foudy
George F. Fraley, III
Brian Geoghegan
Marc S. Gerber
Marc J. Gerson
Thomas A. Gilson
Holly A. Gimbel
Armando Gomez
Catharine A. Hartzenbusch
Babak Hoghooghi
Ki P. Hong
Jessica A. Hough
Cheryl L. Hudson
Chad S. Johnson
Julia M. Kazaks
Mohab T. Khattab
Leif B. King
Stephen M. Klein
Heather Russell Koenig
Joseph A. Laroski, Jr
Rebecca J. Levenson
Melissa F. Levine
Jeremy D. London
Ellen L. Lyons
John H. Lyons

(See Next Column)

WASHINGTON, D.C.
ASSOCIATES (Continued)

Joan M. Macaulay
David S. Maltz
Rachel A. Mariner
August J. Matteis, Jr.
Christine L. McLean
Antone M. Meaux
Molly A. Meegan
Garrett D. Melby
Martin T. Moe
Timothy J. Moran
Linda G. Morrison
Joshua B. Nickerson
Sharon L. Niles-Spencer
Andrew J. O'Connell
David H. Pawlik
Brian Pomper
Kristin L. Pruitt
Phillip A. Pucillo
Robyn C. Quattrone
Anand S. Raman
Harold S. Reeves
Laura P. Regan
Steven M. Reiness
Genae M. Richardson
Caprice L. Roberts
Daniel Schneiderman
Lara Hope Schwartz
Peter M. Seka
Sue Bak Sheehan
Sean M. Shimamoto
Kenneth K. Shiu
Denise A. Simmonds
Ralph L. Stengren
Matthew A. Stevens
Jamison B. Taylor
Sara M. Turner
Stephen P. Vaughn
Jennifer K. Walter
Robert W. Warnement
Brian D. Weimer
Heide M. Werntz
Paul Franklin Wight
Donna L. Wilson
Delroy C. Wright, Jr.

WILMINGTON, DELAWARE
ASSOCIATES

Allison L. Amorison
Martina Bernstein
Laura S. Clare
Anne E. Connolly
James A. Corrodi
Steven J. Daniels
Stephen D. Dargitz
Eric M. Davis
Van C. Durrier, II
Ronald J. Fisher
Rosemary Goodier
Matthew M. Greenberg
Paul J. Lockwood
Thomas G. Macauley
Kevin M. Maloy
Parth S. Munshi
Robert S. Saunders
Cheryl E. Siskin
Leonard P. Stark
James A. Stoltzfus
Julie Tostrup
Kara Renee Yancey

For full biographical listings, see the Martindale-Hubbell Law Directory

SMITH MAZURE DIRECTOR WILKINS YOUNG YAGERMAN & TARALLO, P.C. (AV)

111 John Street, 10038
Telephone: 212-964-7400
Fax: 212-374-1935 (Not for Legal Service)

Gerald Director
David E. Mazure
Stanley Wilkins
Nicholas Tarallo
Jacob J. Young
Mark S. Yagerman

Irwin D. Miller
Marc H. Pillinger
Michael K. Berman
John Kevin Reilly
Cary Maynard
Robert P. Siegel
John Colucci
Haydn J. Brill
Jeffrey T. Miller
Corey A. Tavel
Mark D. Levi
Howard S. Shafer
Peter H. Graber
Irwin Bloom
Michael S. Livow
Steven I. Brizel
Joel M. Simon
Frank J. Keenan
Melissa S. Romano
Paul L. LaClair
Constantine Vlavianos
Joseph A. Schwarzenberg
Stephanie Morfesis
Stacy I. Oberman
Dawn McNamara
David A. Glazer
Lara Jill Miller
Andrew J. Funk
Angela Lurie Milch
Seth M. Katz
Michael G. Brown
Christopher M. FitzPatrick
Neil Thomas Veilleux
Doris M. Carrasquillo
Alan C. Kelhoffer
Howard J. Snyder

For full biographical listings, see the Martindale-Hubbell Law Directory

SOLOVAY, EDLIN & EISEMAN (AV)

845 Third Avenue, Eighth Floor, 10022
Telephone: 212-752-1000
Facsimile: 212-355-4608

Richard A. Edlin
Norman Solovay
Michael B. Solovay
Jonathan Eiseman
Wayne R. Lehrhaupt
Eric R. Levine

OF COUNSEL

Daniel James Cooper
Joseph M. Harary
Stephen L. Weinstein
Peter Kakoyiannis
Sam Schwartz

ASSOCIATES

Murray D. Schneier
Howard S. Roitman

For full biographical listings, see the Martindale-Hubbell Law Directory

New York—Continued

SONNENSCHEIN NATH & ROSENTHAL (AV)

1221 Avenue of the Americas 24th Floor, 10020
Telephone: 212-768-6700
Facsimile: 212-391-1247
URL: http://www.sonnenschein.com
Chicago, Illinois Office: Suite 8000 Sears Tower, 233 South Wacker Drive.
Telephone: 312-876-8000.
Cable Address: "Sonberk".
Telex: 25-3526.
Facsimile: 312-876-7934.
Washington, D.C. Office: 1301 K Street, N.W., Suite 600, East Tower.
Telephone: 202-408-6400.
Facsimile: 202-408-6399.
San Francisco, California Office: 685 Market Street, 6th Floor.
Telephone: 415-882-5000.
Facsimile: 415-543-5472.
Los Angeles, California Office: Suite 1500, 601 South Figueroa Street.
Telephone: 213-623-9300.
Facsimile: 213-623-9924.
St. Louis, Missouri Office: One Metropolitan Square, Suite 3000.
Telephone: 314-241-1800.
Facsimile: 314-259-5959.
Kansas City, Missouri Office: Suite 1100, 4520 Main Street, 64111.
Telephone: 816-932-4400.
Facsimile: 816-531-7545.
London, England Office: Sonnenscheins, Royex House, Aldermanbury Square, EC2V 7HR.
Telephone: 0207-600-2222.
Facsimile: 0207-600- 2221.

RESIDENT PARTNERS

David Albenda
Reid L. Ashinoff
Michael A. Bamberger
Michael H. Barr
Dennis N. Berman
Amy H. Fisher
Linda E. Friedman
David M. Greenbaum
Philip A. Haber
Marc B. Heller
Gregory S. Karawan
Arthur S. Katz
Mark R. Lehrer
Dennis W. Russo
Lawrence R. Sandak
Barry N. Seidel
Joseph H. Smolinsky
Marc D. Teitelbaum
Scott M. Tayne
Michael S. Wien

OF COUNSEL

Andrew L. DaSilva
Charles M. Yablon

RESIDENT ASSOCIATES

Kimberlee C. Abraham
Rachel G. Balaban
Steven K. Barentzen
Vicki D.C. Colca
Richard J. Cunningham
Gregory E. Danenberg
Jacqueline A. Frome
Daniel A. Goldberger
David A. Goldstein
Michael S. Gugig
Sandra D. Hauser
Aliza F. Herzberg
Paul J. Housey
Margaret A. Jacobs
Steven M. Kahaner
Sandra Leibow
Rachel Gordon Lichten
Gary Meyerhoff
Susannah Moy
Nathan C. Nudelman
Deborah Renner
Hilary A. Sokolowski
Kathryn C. Spann
Wendy S. Weingart

For full biographical listings, see the Martindale-Hubbell Law Directory

SQUIRE, SANDERS & DEMPSEY L.L.P. (AV)

350 Park Avenue, 15th Floor, 10022-6002
Telephone: 212-872-9800
Fax: 212-872-9815
URL: http://www.ssd.com
Cincinnati, Ohio Office: PNC Center, 201 East Fifth Street, Suite 1700, Cincinnati, Ohio 45202.
Telephone: 513-361-1200.
Fax: 513-361-1201.
Cleveland, Ohio Office: 4900 Key Tower, 127 Public Square, Cleveland, Ohio 44114-1304.
Telephone: 216-479-8500.
Fax: 216-479-8780.
Columbus, Ohio Office: 1300 Huntington Center, 41 South High Street, Columbus, Ohio 43215-6150.
Telephone: 614-365-2700.
Fax: 614-365-2499.
Houston, Texas Office: 6250 Chase Tower, 600 Travis Street, Houston, Texas 77002-3007.
Telephone: 713-546-5850.
Fax: 713-546-5830.
Jacksonville, Florida Office: One Enterprise Center, Suite 2100, 225 Water Street, Jacksonville, Florida 32202-4424.
Telephone: 904-366-2420.
Fax: 904-356-2986.
Miami, Florida Office: 201 South Biscayne Boulevard, 2900 Miami Center, Miami, Florida 33131-4330.
Telephone: 305-577-8700.
Fax: 305-358-1425.

(See Next Column)

Phoenix, Arizona Office: Two Renaissance Square, 40 North Central Avenue, Suite 2700, Phoenix, Arizona 85004-4498.
Telephone: 602-528-4000.
Fax: 602-253-8129.
Washington, D.C. Office: 1201 Pennsylvania Avenue, N.W., Suite 500, Washington, D.C. 20004-2491.
Telephone: 202-626-6600.
Fax: 202-626-6780.
Almaty, Kazakhstan Office: 141 Ablay Khan Avenue, Second Floor, Almaty, Kazakhstan 480091.
Telephone: +73-27-50-11-25.
Fax: +73-27-50-11-25.
Bratislava, Slovak Republic Office: Zochova 5, 811 03 Bratislava, Slov k Republic.
Telephone: 421-7-5441-7611.
Fax: 42-1-7-6280-2212.
Brussels, Belgium Office: Avenue Louise, 165-Box 15, 1050 Brussels, Belgium.
Telephone: 32-2-627-1111.
Fax: 32-2-627-1100.
Budapest, Hungary Office: H-1062 Budapest, Andrassy ut. 64, Budapest, Hungary.
Telephone: 36-1-428-7111.
Fax: 36-1-428-7100.
Kyiv, Ukraine Office: 14A Yaroslaviv Val, Kyiv 252034, Ukraine.
Telephone: 38-044-228-8687.
Fax: 38-044-228-4938.
London, England Office: Royex House, Aldermanbury Square, London EC2V 7HR.
Telephone: 44-171-776-5200.
Fax: 44-171-776-5233.
Madrid, Spain Office: Calle Velazquez 108-110, 28006 Madrid, Spain.
Telephone: 34-91-590-2420.
Fax: 34-91-590-2421.
Moscow, Russian Federation Office: Paveletskaya Square II, 1 Valovaya Street, 5th Floor, Moscow 113054, Russian Federation.
Telephone: 7-503-956-3750.
Fax: 7-503-956-3635.
Prague, Czech Republic Office: Václavské námēst 1 57/813, 110 00 Praha 1, Czech Republic.
Telephone: 420-2-2166-2111.
Fax: 420-2-2166-2222.
Hong Kong Office: Rooms 1101-2 St. George's Building, 2 Ice House Street, Central, Hong Kong.
Telephone: 852-2509-9732.
Fax: 852-2509-9772.
Taipei, Taiwan Office: 14F, 116 Nanking East Road, Sec. 2, Taipei, Taiwan, Republic of China.
Telephone: 886-2-2531-2888.
Fax: 886-2-2571-6199.

PARTNERS

Kenneth W. Bond
Jackson B. Browning, Jr.
Richard L. Goard
Eugene W. Harper, Jr.
Blaise G. A. Pasztory
Jeffrey L. Piemont
Edward S. Sinick
R. Thomas Stanton
Alan N. Waxman

OF COUNSEL

Charles A. Goldstein
Andrew L. Jagoda
Arnold S. Lehman
David W. Thompson
Deborah L. Wiacek

ASSOCIATES

Allison L. Downing (Not admitted in NY)
Michael Y. Fruchler
Nina Lopez Gordian (Not admitted in NY)
Todd M. Kleinman
Christine H. Kwon
Alexandre-Cyril Manz
Benjamin Mittman
Timothy K. Saunders, Jr.
Jeffrey E. Storch (Not admitted in NY)

For full biographical listings, see the Martindale-Hubbell Law Directory

STROOCK & STROOCK & LAVAN LLP (AV)

180 Maiden Lane, 10038-4982
Telephone: 212-806-5400
Telecopier: 212-806-6006
Telexes: Stroock, UT 177693 and Plastroock NYK 177077 (International)
Email: info@stroock.com *URL:* http://www.stroock.com
New York Conference Center: 767 Third Avenue, New York, N.Y., 10017-2023.
Telephones: 212-806-5767; 5768; 5769; 5770.
Telecopier: 212-421-6234. Email: info@stroock.com
Boston, Massachusetts Office: 100 Federal Street, Boston, MA., 02110-1813 .
Telephone: 617-482-6800.
Fax: 617-330-5111. Email: infoboston@stroock.com
Los Angeles, California Office: 2029 Century Park East, Suite 1800, Los Angeles, CA., 90067-3086.
Telephone: 310-556-5800.
Telecopier: 310-556-5959. Email: infola@stroock.com
Miami, Florida Office: First Union Financial Center, 200 South Biscayne Boulevard, Suite 3300, Miami, FL., 33131-2385.
Telephone: 305-358-9900.
Telecopier: 305-789-9302. Email: infomiami@stroock.com

(See Next Column)

STROOCK & STROOCK & LAVAN LLP, *New York—Continued*

Washington, D.C. Office: 1150 Seventeenth Street, N.W., Suite 600, Washington, D.C., 20036-4652.
Telephone: 202-452-9250.
Telecopier: 202-293-2293. Email: infodc@stroock.com

MEMBERS OF FIRM

Robert Abrams
Wendell H. Adair, Jr. (Not admitted in NY)
Albert M. Appel
Reed D. Auerbach
Martin S. Baker
Jacob Bart
Hillel M. Bennett
Micah W. Bloomfield
Stanley B. Blumberg
Leonard Boxer
Melvin A. Brosterman
William Campbell
Brian M. Cogan
Joel Cohen
Lewis G. Cole
Stuart H. Coleman
Brian Diamond
James F. Downey
Jeffrey L. Dunetz
Melvin Epstein
Michel S. Evanusa
David L. Finkelman
Joseph L. Forstadt
Richard L. Fried
Donald D. Gabay
Howard M. Gitten
Laura E. Goldbard
Marvin J. Goldstein
Mayer Greenberg
Laurence Greenwald
Alan S. Halperin
Lawrence M. Handelsman
Thomas E. Heftler
David H. Kaufman
Robin E. Keller
Alan M. Klinger
Barbara D. Klippert
Richard H. Kronthal
Lewis Kruger
Bradley G. Kulman
Jonathan S. Kusko
William D. Latza
Howard S. Lavin
Mark A. Levy
Robert Lewin
Jeffrey S. Lowenthal
Theodore S. Lynn
Jerome A. Manning
Curtis C. Mechling
Peter A. Miller
Martin Minkowitz
Charles G. Moerdler
Ross F. Moskowitz
Martin H. Neidell
Sharon Parella
Kenneth Pasquale
Steven B. Pokotilow (P.C.)
Susan O. Posen
Mark N. Rae
David A. Rahm
Robert A. Raskin
Mark A. Rosenbaum
Anita S. Rosenbloom
Lawrence Rosenthal
Norman K. Samnick
Bruce H. Schneider
Michael S. Shenberg
George R. Shockey, Jr.
Richard Siegler
Kevin L. Smith
Mark A. Speiser
Ronald J. Stein
David Stephens
Eva Coben Talel
James R. Tanenbaum
Jeffrey D. Uffner
Lois L. Weinroth
Mark S. Wintner
Robert C. Wipperman

SPECIAL COUNSEL

Madelaine R. Berg
Etta Brandman
Charles C. Dorego
David Goldstein
Richard Horowitz
Steven Horowitz
Michele L. Jacobson
David M. Kaston
Abbey L. Keppler
Arlene G. Krieger
David W. Lowden
John R. Murphy
Jeffrey H. Roth
Laurel S. Rotker
Michele P. Schwartz
Matthew W. Siegal

COUNSEL

Thomas Field
William A. Perlmuth

OF COUNSEL

William J. vanden Heuvel

RETIRED PARTNERS

Wallace E. Cowan
Martin D. Eile
Franklin Feldman
Jack Gross
Norman Hammer
Rita E. Hauser
Alvin K. Hellerstein
Charles B. Hochman
Gilbert Lazerus
Erwin Millimet
Vivienne W. Nearing
Julius H. Sherman

Frank A. Alerte
Roger Anscher
Matthew R. Asman
Heidi Balk
Ayesha Mazhar Barnett
James L. Bernard
Paul Bertoni (Not admitted in NY)
Frank E. Bisk
Jonathan D. Blum
Kristian J. Bornemann
Michele Murray Brasch
Ludomir A. Budzyn
James L. Burns
Denis Butkovic
Adam J. Chill
Jessica B. Cooper
James T. Cunningham
Kevin J. Curnin
Sahra Dalfen
Heather L. Danzig
Paul T. Darcy
Eric B. Davis
Matthew Jacob Day
James J. DeCarlo
Nicole S. Deller
Eleni M. Demetriou
Christine M. DeSanze
Ian G. DiBernardo
Christopher R. Donoho, III
Christopher J. Doyle
Evan Michael Drutman
Mark Eichler
Scott R. Emery
David M. Fortunato
Susan R. Friedman
Frederic Mark Garsson
Melissa Garza
Robert W. Geiger
Michael Gellert
Victoria Gerber
Evelyn D. Giaccio
Harris C. Goldblat
Deborah L. Goldstein
Adam S. Grace

(See Next Column)

Michael Grandis (Not admitted in NY)
Joan D. Gray
Robert W. Guazzo
Kristopher M. Hansen
Tareq A. Hassan
Marcia S. Helbling
Joseph Z. Hellerstein
Christine M. Hilla
David A. Hillman
Alison R. Hirsch
Renata B. Holt
Steven B. Horowitz
Lisa A. Jakob
David A. Javdan
Matthew P. Joseph
Faith A. Kaminsky
Rashida A. Karmali
Sigal Kaspi (Not admitted in the United States)
Gretchen Mullins Kim
Dean Kloner
Stephen D. Kong
Jennifer Z. Korff
Todd E. Lenson
Penny Levine
Steve Levitan
Donald Liebman
Burton N. Lipshie
Elizabeth R. Lorton
Michael E. Lubin
Richard G. Madris
Anne Maltz
David A. Markowitz
Edward J. Martin, III
James M. McGovern
Michele McQuillan
A. Paul Melendres
Amy A. Mellon (Not admitted in NY)
Bruce P. Meyerson
Sherry J. Millman
Irving E. Minkin
Michelle D. Monticciolo
Steven P. Moskowitz
Tessa L. Mungen
Katherine Neville
Carole W. Nimaroff
Lawrence D. Norden
Harold A. Olsen
Michele L. Pahmer
Melissa Papke
Keaton S. Parekh
Hersh P. Patel
Jennifer A. Petrilli
Anna T. Pinedo
Christian Porwoll
Meile Rockefeller
Brian D. Rosenstein
Mark Daniel Salzberg
J. Scott Sanpietro
Moshe Sasson
Karen Scanna
Steven L. Schultz
Andrew H. Shapiro
Laura R. Shaw
James A. Shifren
Regan A. Shulman
Jonathan A. Siegel
David A. Sifre
Seth D. Slotkin
Robert Steinman
Joseph E. Strauss
Claude G. Szyfer
Lisa C. Takoudes
Kenneth H. Theil
Charles E. Torres
Michelle L. Turco
Lawrence Wagenberg
Gail B. Wallach
Beth K. Webber
Jason P. Wiesenfeld
Denise K. Wildes
Marci Wilson-Moschetti

BOSTON, MASSACHUSETTS
PARTNERS

Peter J. Antoszyk
Siri F. Boreske
Paul D. Broude
Howard M. Gitten
Jeffrey S. Lowenthal
Stephen M. Richmond
Peter Wittenborg

OF COUNSEL

Stephen M. Sheehy

ASSOCIATES

Bruce H. Bagdasarian
Joel G. Beckman
Ann C. Bonis
Kyle S. Chase
John R. Condon
Christine R. Fitzgerald
Leslie Anne Hawes
David Kantaros

LOS ANGELES
PARTNERS

Gregory A. Bray
Richard S. Forman
Barry B. Langberg
Schuyler M. Moore
Michael F. Perlis
Glenn D. Smith
Julia B. Strickland
Chauncey M. Swalwell

OF COUNSEL

Gerald J. Mehlman
Robert M. Shafton
Michael M. Umansky

SPECIAL COUNSEL

Deborah Drooz
D. Wayne Jeffries
Alan Z. Yudkowsky

RETIRED PARTNER

Merrill E. Jenkins

ASSOCIATES

Mark Y. Abdou
Judith L. Anderson
Wrenn E. Chais
Mary C. Costa
Stephanie E. Deaner
James W. Denison
Karen R. Dinino
John L. Filippone
Lynn T. Galuppo
Jennifer L. Gentin
Seth M. Gerber
Mark D. Grossman
Adam L. Gubner
Jody M. Heitner
Gary S. Hiller
Richard R. Johnson
Stuart Johnson
JiAe Kim
Susan D. Koot
Pamela L. Kunath
Mitchell J. Langberg
Mary D. Manesis
Robert C. Maysey
Heather A. McConnell
David W. Moon
Andrew W. Moritz
Randy J. Myricks
Michael J. Niborski
Scott M. Pearson
Christina M. Rhee
Daniel A. Rozansky
Lisa M. Simonetti
Carol M.L. Smithson
James J. Thompson
Matthew C. Thompson
Robyn B. Tuerk
Mark A. Vega

(See Next Column)

STROOCK & STROOCK & LAVAN LLP—*Continued*

MIAMI
PARTNERS

Scott L. Baena
Michael Basile
Manuel A. Fernandez
Mindy A. Mora
Carey A. Stiss
Robert W. Turken

OF COUNSEL

Richard S. Savitt

SPECIAL COUNSEL

Robert M. Siegel

ASSOCIATES

Marcello A. Benedetto
Richard J. Bernard
Brandon A. Block
Sean M. Cleary
Monica Cunill-Fals
Brent A. Friedman
Daniel R. Green
Karen S. Harkness
Jason Z. Jones
Marina Kievsky
Elena Marquez
Mary E. Moulton
Kevin S. Neiman
Jay M. Sakalo
George S. Savage
Richard B. Simring
Marchèlle A. Wiley

RETIRED PARTNER

Walter Pozen

For full biographical listings, see the Martindale-Hubbell Law Directory

SULLIVAN & CROMWELL (AV)

125 Broad Street, 10004-2498
Telephone: 212-558-4000
Telex: 62694
Telecopier: 212-558-3588
URL: http://www.sullcrom.com
Washington, D.C. Office: 1701 Pennsylvania Avenue, N.W., 20006-5805.
Telephone: 202-956-7500.
Telecopier: 202-293-6330.
Los Angeles, California Office: 1888 Century Park East, 90067-1725.
Telephone: 310-712-6600.
Telecopier: 310-712-8800.
Paris Office: 8, Place Vendôme, 75001 Paris, France.
Telephone: (011)(331) 44 50 60 00.
Telex: 240654.
Telecopier: (011)(331) 44 50 60 60 or (011)(331) 42 60 56 36.
London Office: St. Olave's House, 9a Ironmonger Lane, London EC2V 8EY, England.
Telephone: (011)(44207) 710 6500.
Telecopier: (011)(44207) 710 6565.
Melbourne Office: 101 Collins Street, Melbourne, Victoria 3000, Australia.
Telephone: (011)(613) 9635-1500.
Telecopier: (011)(613) 9654-2422.
Tokyo Office: Sullivan & Cromwell, Gaikokuho Jimu Bengoshi Jimusho, Akai Law Offices (Registered Associated Offices), Otemachi First Square East Tower 16F, 5-1, Otemachi 1-chome, Chiyoda-ku, Tokyo 100-0004, Japan.
Telephone: (011)(813) 3213-6140.
Telecopier: (011)(813) 3213-6470 or (011)(813) 3213-6477.
Hong Kong Office: 28th Floor, Nine Queen's Road, Central, Hong Kong.
Telephone: (011)(852) 2826-8688.
Telecopier: (011)(852) 2522-2280.
Frankfurt Office: Neue Mainzer Strasse 52, 60322 Frankfurt, Germany.
Telephone: (011)(4969) 7191 26-0.
Telecopier: (011)(4969) 7191 26-10.
Beijing Office: The Beijing Representative Office of Sullivan & Cromwell, Suite 501, China World Trade Center, No. 1 Jianguo Menwai Avenue, Beijing 100004, P.R.C.
Telephone: (011)(86) 10 6505 6120.
Telecopier: (011)(86) 10 6505 6136.

MEMBERS OF FIRM

Frederick A. Terry, Jr.
Michael A. Cooper
Ricardo A. Mestres, Jr.
William J. Williams, Jr.
Irvine D. Flinn
Michael M. Maney
Edwin D. Williamson
* (Washington, D.C. Office)
Stephen A. Grant
David M. Huggin
Willard B. Taylor
John L. Warden
Richard R. Howe
William R. Norfolk
Michael W. Weir
Robert M. Thomas, Jr.
Stanley F. Farrar
** (Los Angeles Office)
William F. Indoe
David M. Kies
Robert M. Osgood
(London Office)
Earl D. Weiner
James H. Carter, Jr.
Henry Christensen III
H. Rodgin Cohen (Also at Washington, D.C. Office)
Robert H. Craft, Jr.
* (Washington, D.C. Office)
Philip L. Graham, Jr.
Benjamin F. Stapleton
Neil T. Anderson
Daniel Dunson
Richard G. Asthalter
(Paris Office)
Bruce E. Clark
Richard J. Urowsky
Donald C. Walkovik
William M. Dallas, Jr.
Margaret K. Pfeiffer
* (Washington, D.C. Office)
David B. Tulchin
John E. Baumgardner, Jr.
Jeffrey F. Browne
(Melbourne, Australia Office)
D. Stuart Meiklejohn
Mark J. Welshimer
James I. Black III

(See Next Column)

MEMBERS OF FIRM (Continued)

Ann Bailen Fisher
John P. Mead
Yvonne S. Quinn
Kenneth M. Raisler *
Gandolfo V. DiBlasi
Frank H. Golay, Jr.
** (Los Angeles Office)
Robinson B. Lacy
Michael M. Wiseman
John T. Bostelman
James C. Morphy
David F. Morrison ** (Paris and Frankfurt Offices)
William A. Plapinger
(London Office)
Joseph C. Shenker
Andrew D. Soussloff **
Garrard R. Beeney
Robert E. Buckholz, Jr.
Eliyahu David Jacobson
Richard H. Klapper
Theodore O. Rogers, Jr. *
Andrew S. Rowen
Erik D. Lindauer
Andrew S. Mason
Frederic C. Rich
Alan J. Sinsheimer
George H. White III (London and Frankfurt Offices)
Arthur S. Adler
John L. Hardiman
Robert A. Sacks
** (Los Angeles Office)
Donald J. Toumey *
Theodore Edelman
Sergio J. Galvis
Steven L. Holley
Alison S. Ressler
** (Los Angeles Office)
Francis J. Aquila
Donald R. Crawshaw
Robert G. DeLaMater (Hong Kong and Tokyo Offices)
David B. Harms
Duncan C. McCurrach
Richard C. Morrissey
(London Office)
Joseph E. Neuhaus
Robert Samuel Risoleo
William J. Snipes
Andrew P. Solomon
David H. Braff
Robert W. Reeder III
Mark F. Rosenberg
John Evangelakos
Joseph B. Frumkin
David P. Hariton
Alexandra D. Korry
Daryl A. Libow
* (Washington, D.C. Office)
Mark J. Menting
Scott D. Miller (Not admitted in NY; London Office)
Samuel W. Seymour
Basil P. Zirinis III
Michael H. Steinberg (Not admitted in NY; Los Angeles Office)
William D. Torchiana
Mitchell S. Eitel
David J. Gilberg *
Gary Israel **
Stewart M. Robertson
Kathryn Ann Campbell
(London Office)
Anthony J. Colletta
Michael Lacovara
Emily S. McMahon
Richard A. Pollack
John L. Savva (Not admitted in NY; Los Angeles Office)
Dennis C. Sullivan
* (Washington, D.C. Office)
Chun Wei (Hong Kong and Beijing Offices)
Robin D. Fessel
Robert J. Giuffra, Jr. *
Christopher L. Mann
Pierre Servan-Schreiber
(Paris Office)
Michael T. Tomaino, Jr.
John D. Young, Jr.
(Hong Kong Office)
Steven B. Stokdyk (Not admitted in NY; Los Angeles Office)
Max J. Schwartz
Ronald E. Creamer
Robert Wilson Downes
Matthew G. Hurd
Stephen M. Kotran
Richard C. Pepperman II
David B. Rockwell
(Frankfurt Office)
George J. Sampas
Karen Patton Seymour
Penny Shane
Rebecca J. Simmons
Benjamin R. Weber
Diana L. Wollman **

OF COUNSEL

Patricia A. Ceruzzi
Donald C. Christ
Janet S. Thiele
* (Washington, D.C. Office)
Robert B. Hiden, Jr.
Douglas Mark McCall
* (Washington, D.C. Office)
Chiahua Pan
Charles F. Rechlin
** (Los Angeles Office)

SPECIAL COUNSEL

Richard L. Alpern
Matthew J. Brennan *
William J. Brown
* (Washington, D.C. Office)
Carol I. Buckmann
Shlomo Cohen
Dorothy E. Cumby
Douglas Hayward Evans
William L. Farris
Burr Henly
(Melbourne, Australia Office)
Waldo D. Jones, Jr.
(Melbourne, Australia Office)
Thomas R. Leuba
* (Washington, D.C. Office)
Paul J. McElroy
* (Washington, D.C. Office)
Michael B. Miller
(London Office)
Keith A. Pagnani
William E. Schroeder
Dev R. Sen
Gerald D. Shepherd
Gerald T. Slevin
Michael P. Walutes
Frederick W. Wertheim
James T. Williams

EUROPEAN COUNSEL

Stephen C. Connor
(London Office)
Richard A. Kahn (Paris Office)
John O'Connor (London Office)

SENIOR COUNSEL

M. Bernard Aidinoff *
Mitchell Brock
John F. Cannon
Norris Darrell, Jr.
John W. Dickey
Henry N. Ess III
David S. Henkel
Garfield H. Horn
John C. Jaqua
Edward W. Keane
George C. Kern, Jr.
William J. Kirby
W. Loeber Landau
Robert MacCrate *
Robert J. McDonald
John E. Merow
Kendyl K. Monroe
Donald R. Osborn
William C. Pierce
Richard G. Powell

(See Next Column)

SULLIVAN & CROMWELL, *New York—Continued*

SENIOR COUNSEL (Continued)

Vincent A. Rodriguez
Marvin Schwartz *
Stephen K. West *
William E. Willis

AFFILIATED FIRM LAWYERS

Izumi Akai (Tokyo Office)
Takashi Shimokado (Tokyo Office)

RETIRED AND FORMER MEMBERS OF THE FIRM

Walter J. Coakley *
Robert J. Katz
Randall K.C. Kau *
Gregory K. Palm *
Esta Eiger Stecher
William A. Ziegler

ASSOCIATES

Adel B. Al-Ali (Not admitted in United States) (Washington, D.C. Office)
Francisco D. Almaguer
William S. Anderson
Nikolaos G. Andronikos
Maite Aquino
Andrei A. Baev (Not admitted in NY)
Yael Sima Balsam
Myrna A. Barakat
Erwan Barre (Paris Office)
Matthew S. Bartus
Jean-Christophe Beaury (Paris Office)
James A. Ben (Not admitted in NY)
Christopher B. Bernard (London Office)
Zsolt K. Besskó
Darin A. Bifani (Tokyo Office)
Andrew G. Bleau
Nicolas Bourtin
Michael J. Bowe
Jennifer E. Brady (London Office)
Garth W. Bray
Selene Brett (London Office)
Patrick S. Brown (Not admitted in NY; Los Angeles Office)
Marcia Ann Bruggeman
Roberto Bruno (London Office)
Jacqueline E. Bryks
Jason M. Butler
Toryah S. Cameron (Washington, D.C. Office)
Anthony M. Candido
John E. Capps *(Melbourne, Australia Office)
Tina M. Carew
Elizabeth Hughes Carroll (Not admitted in NY; Washington, D.C. Office)
William F. Cassin
Jennifer A. Cattier
Jeffrey J. Chapman
Jack J. Chen (Melbourne, Australia Office)
Yunfei Chen (Hong Kong Office)
Rosita Cheung
Samir D. Chokshi
William Y. Chua (Hong Kong Office)
Catherine M. Clarkin
Walter J. Clayton III *
Audra D. Cohen
Sandra Wieder Cohen
Philip Leonard Colbran
Eric D. Colchamiro
Ronald J. Colombo
Hugh C. Conroy, Jr.
Richard E. Constable, III
John Francis Cooke
Daniel A. Cord (Paris Office)
Todd G. Cosenza
Mark E. Coyne
T. Addison Crawford
Brendan P. Cullen (Los Angeles Office)
Krystian Marek Czerniecki (Paris Office)
Eleonore Dailly
David Danon
Kristen J. Dayley (Not admitted in NY; Los Angeles Office)
Marc De Leeuw
Dominick P. DeChiara
Michael G. DeSombre (Hong Kong Office)
Ivan D. Deutsch
Andrew G. Dietderich
John C. L. Dixon
Charles T. Dowling
Christian Droop
Daniel G. Dufner, Jr. (London Office)
David A. Ellis
Colleen Enache Brown
Michael T. Escue
John E. Estes
Nina R. Evison (London Office)
William G. Farrar
Richard J. Fine
Judith Rose Fiorini
Dorothee M. Fischer-Appelt
Mark P. Fisher
Michael L. Fleischer
C. Barr Flinn
Brian T. Frawley
Berit R. Freeman-Fisher
Stacey R. Friedman
Matthew M. Friestedt (London Office)
Jingwei Lu Fu
David Gaukrodger
Tuvia J. Geffen
Jonathan A. Gluck *
Jeffrey Benjamin Golden
Alphonzo A. Grant, Jr.
Jeanne E. Greeley
Leslie Sturtevant Grimaldi
Jeffrey M. Grybowski
Peter C. Gyr
Brian E. Hamilton
Adina B. Heino
Benjamin J. Herman
Marcy D. Hirschfeld
Jeffrey D. Hochberg
Neil P. Horne
Mark D. Hunsaker (Tokyo Office)
Fraser L. Hunter, Jr.
Walid Iqbal
Robert J. Jackman
Stanley G. Jacobs, Jr.
Tanya M. Jaeger
Ondraus Jenkins (Los Angeles Office)
Nelle P. Jennings
Craig Joffe (London Office)
Fleur Elizabeth Johns
Craig Jones (London Office)
Peter Lyon Juhas
Aaron J. Katzel
Elana P. Kermaier (Hong Kong Office)
Briana King
Christopher S. Kippes
Eric M. Krautheimer
Amy I. Kroe
Adam M. Kupitz
Calvin C. Lai (Hong Kong Office)
Helene M. Landau
Thomas W. Laryea (London Office)
Kurt M. Lebakken (Paris Office)
Alisa F. Lefkowitz
Stuart B. Leichenko (Hong Kong Office)
Naftali T. Leshkowitz
Robert W. Leung
Dawn L. Levy
Rebecca J. Li (Hong Kong Office)
Soren Lindstrom (Not admitted in the United States)

(See Next Column)

ASSOCIATES (Continued)

Albert Yun-Quan Liu (Not admitted in NY; Los Angeles Office)
George Y. Liu ** (Hong Kong Office)
Xiaoyu Greg Liu (Hong Kong Office)
Leslie Lowenbraun
Beverly W. Lubit
Pierre Magnan
Edouard S. Markson
Elizabeth Palmer Martin
James V. Masella III
Elise C. Masiée (Paris Office)
Joseph James Matelis, II (Washington, D.C. Office)
Arvind N. Mathur
Lee Ann Anderson McCall * (Washington, D.C. Office)
Carl B. McCarthy (London Office)
Keith McKenna
Graceann McKeon
Marianne McKeon
Samuel Neal McKnight (London Office)
Sara M. McLeod *
Oliver Metzger
William P. Meyerhofer
John R. Miller
Dolly Mirchandani (Hong Kong Office)
Christine C. Monterosso
Charles C. Moore (Washington, D.C. Office)
Christine M. Motta
M. Kamal Nasrollah (Not admitted in United States)
Sharon L. Nelles
Daniel A. Nemo
Joseph S. Nussbaum
John J. O'Brien
Frank Ochsenfeld
James R. Oehler (Los Angeles Office)
Chidi J. Ogene (Washington, D.C. Office)
Antony G. Page (London Office)
Jennifer H. Painter (Los Angeles Office)
Wenseng Pan
Andrew Y. Pau
Marina Pearlman
Christoph A. Pereira
Giuseppe Pezzulli
Brian J. Pierce (Paris Office)
Jay L. Pomerantz
Ivan J. Presant (London Office)
Michael J. Purvis
Alan S. Rabinowitz
Glen Alexander Rae
Alessandra Ravetti Jaeger
David M. J. Rein
Sven O. Riethmueller (Frankfurt Office)
David A. Rivera (Los Angeles Office)
John K. Robinson
Kathryn E. Rorer * (Washington, D.C. Office)
Dianne L. Rosky
Samantha Evans Ross * (Washington, D.C. Office)
Wilma S. Rowell
Laurent A. Sacharoff
Ivan A. Sacks
Jonathan A. Schechter
Robert M. Schlein (London Office)
Glen T. Schleyer
Boaz M. Schnitzer
Lynn-Anne M. Schow
Benjamin H. Schwartz (London Office)
Jeffrey I. Schwartz
Lisa B. Schwartz
Jeffrey T. Scott
Evelyn H. Seidman
Megan J. Shafritz
Timothy E. Sheil * (Washington, D.C. Office)
Terrence L. Shen (Hong Kong Office)
Vincent P. Sherman
Ilana M. Shulman
Eric C. Sibbitt (London Office)
Philip M. Sivin
Bradley P. Smith
D. Andrew C. Smith
Daniel E. Sobelsohn (Not admitted in NY; Los Angeles Office)
Scott Ian Sonnenblick
Michael K. Sopchick (Washington, D.C. Office)
Christine A. Spillane (London Office)
Carlos J. Spinelli-Noseda
David C. Spitzer
Eric B. Steiglitz
Rosslyn Coldwell Stevens (Los Angeles Office)
Andrew P. Stone
Lowell A. Strug
Giorgio Giovanni Subiotto
John J. Sullivan
Timothy P. Sullivan
Avi I. Szenberg
Brian Wha-Li Tang
Yoichiro Taniguchi * (Tokyo Office)
Lauren A. Teigland
Jonathan E.A. Ten Oever
Faith T. Teo
Steven W. Thomas ** (Not admitted in NY; Los Angeles Office)
Scott D. Thomson
Martin John Travers
Marc R. Trevino
Theresa Trzaskoma
Kate Usdrowski
Carlos Viana
James J. Vieceli III (Los Angeles Office)
Darren C. Wallis (Not admitted in NY)
Allen C. Wang
Sheri M. Watts (Los Angeles Office)
Joshua B. Waxman
Cory T. Way
Kandance S. Weems
Jeffrey R. Whyte
Catherine A. Wible
Eric Wigginton
Bruce R. Wilde
Joy Marzilli Willing (Washington D.C. Office)
Dawn M. Wilson
Mark V. Wilson
Andrew W. Winden (Washington, D.C. Office)
Joel D. Wine
Mark D. Wiseman (Paris Office)
William J. Yoo
Julie Yoon
Yigal Zemah
Christopher M. Zochowski (Washington, D.C. Office)

David Liebov (Managing Clerk)

*Attorneys also admitted to the District of Columbia Bar
**Attorneys also admitted to the California Bar

For full biographical listings, see the Martindale-Hubbell Law Directory

New York—Continued

THELEN REID & PRIEST LLP (AV)

40 West 57th Street, 10019-4097
Telephone: 212-603-2000
Fax: 212-603-2001
URL: http://www.thelenreid.com
San Francisco, California Office: 101 Second Street, Suite 1800.
Telephone: 415-371-1200.
Fax: 415-371-1211.
Los Angeles, California Office: 34th Floor, 333 South Grand Avenue.
Telephone: 213-621-9800.
Fax: 213-623-4742.
San Jose, California Office: 17th Floor, 333 West San Carlos Street.
Telephone: 408-292-5800.
Fax: 408-287-8040.
Washington, D.C. Office: Market Square, 701 Pennsylvania Avenue, N.W.
Telephone: 202-508-4000.
Fax: 202-508-4321.

MEMBERS OF FIRM

Gerald Aksen
Elizabeth A. Alcorn
Anthony Amaral, Jr.
Peter K. Anglum
William T. Baker, Jr.
Kathleen M. Balderston
Joseph J. Blecher
Lawrence B. Brownridge
Martin G. Bunin
Christopher Connolly
Ezra J. Doner
Richard P. Dyer
Michael S. Elkin
Richard M. Farmer
Michael F. Fitzpatrick, Jr.
Frederick R. Fucci
Marvin G. Goldman
Michael R. Gordon
David P. Graybeal
Richard S. Green
Jesse B. Grove III
Burton K. Haimes
David R. Hardy
Harry G. Heching
Lawrence S. Hirsh
Catherine C. Hood
John T. Hood
Thomas J. Igoe, Jr.
Richard J. Kane
Charles H. Kaplan
James N. Karas, Jr.
Stephen H. Kinney, Jr.
Laura E. Longobardi
Jeffrey A. Lowin
Sean S. Macpherson
Barry G. Magidoff
Eli R. Mattioli
H. Joseph Mello
William F. O'Brien, Jr.
Judith D. O'Neill (Not admitted in NY)
J. Michael Parish
Jonathan E. Polonsky
Robert J. Reger, Jr.
Bruce A. Rich
Marc E. Richards
Jonathan D. Siegfried
Arthur C. Silverman
Garrett K. Smith
Alice B. Stock
Paul J. Sutton
Richard P. Swanson
J. Anthony Terrell
Ronald G. Todd
Robert M. Vilter
Alan R. Vogeler, Jr.
George H. Wang
Michael C. Weinstein
David J. Weisenfeld
Evan S. Widlitz
Peter C. Williams
Paul A. Winick
Timothy S. Wright
Charles Myungsik Yoon

OF COUNSEL

Douglas F. Allen, Jr.
Mark T. Basseches
Daniel Guetta
Michele R. Jawin
K. William Kolbe
Mary M. Popper
David Teschner (Not admitted in NY)
Robert B. Viner
Hongye Zhao

ASSOCIATES

Susan L. Bedford
Michael V. Bonacorsa
Laura R. Brandt
Henry C. Brasch (Not admitted in NY)
Daniel S. Braverman
Daniel J. Buzzetta
Charles Caldarola
Nicole H. Chase
Yolanda Childress
Johanna E. Copeland
Greg Csaszar
Russell A. Divak
Jeffrey E. Dupler
Mareza I. Estevez
Jill R. Franco
Craig E. Freeman
Daniel J. Gallagher (Not admitted in NY)
Thomas P. Giblin, Jr
Jenna R. Glazer
Walter J. Godlewski, III
Marc A. Greendorfer
Thomas P. Hanley, Jr.
Sandra Honegan-Pounder
Jason Horowitz
Barbara J. Jacobs
Safal K. Joshi
Charles P. Juster
Teena Heejung Kim
Andrew P. Kransdorf
Jodi F. Krieger
Thomas P. Lane
Patrick A. MacMurray
Laurie S. Marsh
Sandhya Mehta
Jorge Moros-Nahim (Not admitted in NY)
Philip F. O'Reilly
Carolyn S. Parlato (Not admitted in NY)
Paul L. Porretta
Bradley P. Rolston
Gregory A. Romero
Jeffrey P. Rosenstein
Maria Ross
Andrés Scaminaci
Craig Sloane
Sharon Carlstedt Soto
David A. Stampley
Erik M. Sternberg
Lewis Bart Stone
Janna Honig Torelli
Consuelo A. Vasquez
Lisa S. Vogel
Craig Weiner
Jeffrey S. Weintraub
Allison Wertheim Weiss
Gerard M. Wissing
Karen Young
Lily Shang Yu

For full biographical listings, see the Martindale-Hubbell Law Directory

WAGNER, DAVIS & GOLD, P.C. (AV)

99 Madison Avenue, 10016
Telephone: 212-481-9600
Telefax: 212-481-8245

Steven R. Wagner
Ronald Jay Gold
John R. Wagner
Bonnie Reid Berkow
William R. Fried

OF COUNSEL

Deborah Lynn Davis

Adam D. Finkelstein
Keith L. Woodside
Robert J. Patchen
Glen C. Rosenberg
Mikelle V. Lipsius (Not admitted in NY)

LEGAL SUPPORT PERSONNEL

Nicole J. Ottley (Paralegal)
Steven Henderson (Paralegal)
Tracey A. Lewis (Paralegal)
Karen Chin (Paralegal)
Daniel E. Glatter (Law Clerk)

For full biographical listings, see the Martindale-Hubbell Law Directory

WATSON, FARLEY & WILLIAMS (AV)

380 Madison Avenue, 10017
Telephone: 212-922-2200
Telex: 6790626 WFWNY
Fax: 212-922-1512
Email: josborne@wfw.com *URL:* http://www.wfw.com
London, England Office: 15 Appold Street, London EC2A 2HB.
Telephone: (44 171) 814 8000.
Telex: 8955707 WFWLON G.
Fax: (44 171) 814 8141.
Paris, France Office: 47, rue de Monceau, 75008 Paris.
Telephone: (33 1) 53 83 12 12.
Telex: WFWPAR 651096 F.
Fax: (33 1) 45 61 09 01.
Athens, Greece Office: 5th Floor, Alassia Building, Defteras Merarchias 13, 185-35 Piraeus.
Telephone: (30 1) 422 3660.
Telex: 24 1311 WFWGR.
Fax: (30 1) 422 3664.
Singapore Office: 16 Collyer Quay, #12-02 Hitachi Tower, Singapore 049318.
Telephone: (65) 532-5335.
Fax: (65) 532-5454.
Moscow, Russia Office: 16/2 Tverskaya Ulitsa, Business Centre Bldg. 3, The Actor Gallery, Moscow 103009.
Telephone: 7502 237 7770 (international only); 7095 935 7770.
Fax: 7502 237 7771 (international only); 7095 935 7771.
Copenhagen, Denmark Office: Lille Kongensgade 20 DK-1074 Copenhagen K.
Telephone: (45 33) 91 33 03.
Fax: (45 33) 91 49 12.
Associated Office: Abbas F. Ghazzawi Law Firm, Saudi Arabia.

MEMBERS OF FIRM

Leo Chang
John S. Osborne, Jr.
Alfred E. Yudes, Jr.
Philip H. Spector
Richard L. Jarashow
William S. Haft
Christopher P. Belisle
Caryn Hemsworth
Raymond J. Simon

ASSOCIATES

J. Jorge Barrieu
David Brill
Jane M. Freeberg
John G. Kissane
Craig M. Kline
Rhanda Moussa
Laura Savage Parker
Daniel C. Rodgers (Not admitted in NY)
Craig E. Stearns
Siu Yun Kong (Not admitted in the United States)
Peter E. Van Son
Joydeep Mitra
Kathryn E. Ng

LONDON, ENGLAND
RESIDENT PARTNERS

A. H. Farley
M. A. Watson
D. J. Warder
C. A. L. Preston
C. St. C. Smallwood
F. Dunne
D. N. Osborne
C. M. H. Walford
O. A. Whitty
M. M. Llewellyn
A. H. Wettern
M. J. Lawson
J. A. D. Watters
P. J. Flint
M. L. Vernell
J. D. Wardle
M. G.S. Greville
M. A. Kenny
F. M. Murphy
J. A. Mellmann
J. F. Wilkinson
A. Baird
E. Buchan
J. Kellett
W. H. Jenney
T. Rooth
S. Rigg
S. Kavanagh

PARIS, FRANCE
RESIDENT PARTNERS

N. R. D. Moss
D. I. Syed
S. P. Salou
A. Creelman
A. Gautron
R. Drion
S. Alamowitch
V. Roualet

(See Next Column)

WATSON, FARLEY & WILLIAMS, *New York—Continued*

ATHENS, GREECE
RESIDENT PARTNERS

R. A. Rice
R. Parry

SINGAPORE
RESIDENT PARTNERS

N. A. D. Thomas
I. S. McAlpine

MOSCOW, RUSSIA
RESIDENT PARTNERS

A. J. W. Muriel

COPENHAGEN, DENMARK
PARTNER

C. C. Lowe

For full biographical listings, see the Martindale-Hubbell Law Directory

WEIL, GOTSHAL & MANGES LLP (AV)

A Limited Liability Partnership including Professional Corporations
767 Fifth Avenue, 10153
Telephone: 212-310-8000
Cable Address: "Wegoma"
Telex: 424281; 423144
Telecopier: 212-310-8007
URL: http://www.weil.com
Dallas, Texas Office: 100 Crescent Court, Suite 1300.
Telephone: 214-746-7700.
Fax: 214-746-7777.
Houston, Texas Office: 700 Louisiana Street, Suite 1600.
Telephone: 713-546-5000.
Telecopier: 713-224-9511.
Menlo Park, California Silicon Valley Office: 2882 Sand Hill Road, Suite 280.
Telephone: 650-926-6200.
Telecopier: 650-854-3713.
Miami, Florida Office: 701 Brickell Avenue, Suite 2100.
Telephone: 305-577-3100.
Telecopier: 305-374-7159.
Washington, D.C. Office: 1615 L Street, N.W., Suite 700.
Telephone: 202-682-7000.
Telecopier: 202-857-0939; 857-0940.
Telex: 440045.
Brussels, Belgium Office: 81 avenue Louise, Box 9-10, 1050 Brussels.
Telephone: 011-32-2-543-7460.
Telecopier: 011-32-2-543-7489.
Budapest, Hungary Office: Bank Center, Granite Tower, H-1944, Budapest.
Telephone: 011-36-1-302-9100.
Fax: 011-36-1-302-9110.
London, England Office: The Helicon, One South Place, London EC2M 2WG.
Telephone: 011-44-171-903-1000.
Telecopier: 011-44-171-903-0990.
Prague, Czechoslovakia Office: Charles Bridge Center, Krizovnicke nam. 1, 110 00 Prague 1, Czech Republic.
Telephone: 011-420-2-2409-7300.
Telecopier: 011-420-2-2409-7310.
Warsaw, Poland Office: Warsaw Financial Center, ul.Emilii Plater 53 00-113 Warsaw.
Telephone: 011-48-22-520-4000.
Telecopier: 011-48-22-520-4001.

MEMBERS OF FIRM

Frank L. Weil (1894-1957)
Sylvan Gotshal (1897-1968)
Horace S. Manges (1898-1986)
Robert Abelow (1902-1978)
Gabriel Kaslow (1904-1979)
Arthur M. Kreidmann (1908-1988)
John M. Lewis (1906-1994)
Joseph S. Allerhand
Martin B. Amdur
Gerald S. Backman (P.C.)
Corinne Ball
Staci B. Barber
Carl D. Bellows
Andrea Altman Bernstein
Stephen M. Besen
Martin J. Bienenstock
David M. Blittner
Matthew D. Bloch
Warren T. Buhle
Howard Chatzinoff
Robert N. Chipperfield, Jr.
Norman D. Chirite
Paul T. Cohn
Bruce A. Colbath
Howard B. Comet
Stephen H. Cooper
Ronald F. Daitz
Greg A. Danilow
Stephen J. Dannhauser
Richard J. Davis
Jeremy W. Dickens (Not admitted in NY; Also at Dallas, Texas Office)
Howard B. Dicker
Daniel S. Dokos
Sylvie A. Durham
Michael A. Epstein
Jay N. Fastow
Lori R. Fife
Joseph W. Gelb
Larry J. Gelbfish
Raymond O. Gietz
Steven D. Glazer
George Gluck
Simeon Gold
Stuart J. Goldring
Helyn S. Goldstein
Marcia Landweber Goldstein
Frederick S. Green
Holly J. Gregory
Peter Gruenberger
William M. Gutowitz
Kenneth H. Heitner
Mark Hoenig
Gary T. Holtzer
Kevin P. Hughes
Elliot L. Hurwitz
Marvin E. Jacob
Stephen E. Jacobs (P.C.)

(See Next Column)

MEMBERS OF FIRM (Continued)

Mark A. Jacoby
Helene D. Jaffe
Stephen D. Kahn
Michael K. Kam
Stephen Karotkin
Jeffrey L. Kessler
Jeffrey S. Klein
Richard P. Krasnow
Robert Todd Lang (P.C.)
Alan A. Lascher
Paul D. Leake
David S. Lefkowitz
Richard L. Levine
Judy G. Z. Liu
Carl D. Lobell (P.C.)
Paul R. Lovejoy
Michael E. Lubowitz
Arvin Maskin
Carlyn S. McCaffrey
Jane McDonald
Kevin McMahon
Walter G. McNeill
Robert L. Messineo
Daniel J. Mette
Bruce S. Meyer
Alan B. Miller
Harvey R. Miller (P.C.)
Ira M. Millstein (P.C.)
Michael Nissan
Frank P. Nocco
Otto G. Obermaier
Ellen J. Odoner
Eric Ordway
Deryck A. Palmer
Debra J. Pearlstein
Martin D. Pollack
Alan J. Pomerantz
Mary Jean M. Potenzone
James W. Quinn
Stephen A. Radin
John J. Rapisardi
Steven Alan Reiss
R. Bruce Rich
Thomas A. Roberts
Adam C. Rogoff
Brian S. Rosen
J. Philip Rosen
Stuart M. Rosen
Richard A. Rothman
Lois C. Rubin
Irving Scher (P.C.)
Miranda S. Schiller
Marc L. Silberberg
Marsha E. Simms
Richard W. Slack
Mindy J. Spector
Peter D. Standish
Michael K. Stanton
Kenneth L. Steinthal
David P. Stone
Robert G. Sugarman
Jeffrey E. Tabak
Jeffrey L. Tanenbaum
A. Paul Victor (P.C.)
Mark A. Vogel
Ted S. Waksman
Michael F. Walsh
Irwin Howard Warren
Jeffrey J. Weinberg
Alan J. Weinschel
Jonathan T. Weiss
John R. Wing
Susan Peckett Witkin
Barry M. Wolf
David E. Zeltner
Samuel M. Zylberberg

COUNSEL

Peter A. Antonucci
Lawrence J. Baer
Steve M. Bederman
Konrad L. Cailteux
Peter N. Cubita
David G. Feher
Mitchell D. Haddad
Alan H. Hirschfeld
Gordon D. Henderson (P.C.)
Timothy E. Hoeffner
Jacqueline Marcus
Steven M. Margolis
Allan S. Metrick
Leo L. Schmolka
David G. Schwartz
Jacqueline B. Stuart
John P. Steines, Jr.
Jesse D. Wolff
Harris J. Yale

ASSOCIATES

L. Vanessa Abrahams
Jonathan A. Ain
Anthony J. Albanese
Ashley R. Altschuler (Not admitted in NY)
Mitchell S. Ames
Stephen Wade Angus
Sharon B. Applegate
Violetta V. Argueta
Lori F. Aronstein
Antonios C. Backos
Marita Alina Baker
Morgan Bale (Not admitted in NY; Not admitted in the United States)
Dennis Barsky
Gregory D. Bassuk
Paul M. Basta
Jodi Lynne Bayrd
Curt Peter Beck
Stuart S. Beraha
Robert S. Berezin
Alexander S. Berman
Seth C. Berman
Ilyssa Birnbach
Jonathan Bloom
Mitchell S. Bompey
Philippa Bond
Lynda M. Braun
Michael J. Bresnick
Theresa V. Brown (Not admitted in NY)
Helene Bryks
Eric M. Burt
Robert F. Carangelo, Jr.
Brian D. Carlson
Rex Chen
Andrew J. Clark (Not admitted in NY)
Adam S. Cohen
Tricia R. Cohen
Michael Crosby (Not Admitted in the United States)
Gardenia P. Cucci
Michael Dojlidko
Randi S. Eisenstein
Elyssa K. Eneman
Paul Fasciano
Timothy S. Feltham
Benjamin Ferrucci
David R. Fertig
Jill G. Fieldstein
Kerry C. Foley
Elizabeth R. Forminard
Samson M. Frankel
Joshua M. Fried (Not admitted in NY)
Michael H. Fruchter
Robert D. Gage, Jr.
Terence J. Gallagher III
Daniel S. Gewirtz
Melissa Glasband
Joseph P. Glynn
Steven F. Goldman
Heather R. Goldstein
Naomi Jane Gray
Reginald A. Greene
Timothy A. Greensfelder
Jeffrey M. Greilsheimer
Michael Gribin
Yoav M. Griver
Jacqueline N. Haberfeld
Benjamin M. Hain
Ira R. Halperin
Diane Harvey
Brian A. Haskel
Moshe Heching
Jonathan S. Henes
Wayne G. Hess
Stuart C. Hirsch

(See Next Column)

WEIL, GOTSHAL & MANGES LLP—*Continued*

ASSOCIATES (Continued)

Laura W. Hirschfeld
Anna J. Hong
August T. Horvath
Esther Kinneret Ilan
Michele A. Jacobsen
Beth J. Jacobwitz
Kerri Ann Kazak
Brian William Kemper
Donna L. Killmon
Elyse Garmise Kirschner
Mark N. Klein
Gregory S. Kolton
Brian S. Korn (Not admitted in NY)
Kristin Ann Kreuder
Alan R. Kusinitz
Malcolm E. Landau
David M. Lange (Not admitted in NY)
Benjamin S. Lee
Doreen Lee (Not admitted in NY)
Laura B. Lehman
David Lender
James F. Lerner
Nhadine Leung
Andrew Liebhafsky
Jason R. Lilien
Deborah J. Lotstein
Kenneth K. Lowenstein
Paula Lowitt
Nancy E. Lynch
William R. MacDonald
Michelle Maniccia
Jonathan D. Margolis
Benjamin Ely Marks
Alexandra L. Marshall
Scott A. Martin
David M. Maryles
John P. Mastando III
Bernadette McCann Ezring
Ginger McKnight-Chavers
Alissa A. Meade
Myron J. Meadow
Tasbeen Datoo Meghji (Not admitted in NY)
Michele J. Meises
Wayne A. Melbourne
Silvana M. Merlino
Margaret A. Micallef
Lawrence R. Miller
Rod D. Miller (Not admitted in NY)
Ross Morrison
Celeste M. Murphy
Georgia L. Murray
Jeffrey Nadler
Ariella Nasuti
John A. Neuwirth
Johnson C. Ng
Dale G. Nissenbaum
Jeremy E. Novak
Beth A. Oliak
Jeffrey D. Osterman
Michael P. Overn
Nicholas J. Pappas
Christopher M. Parker
Andrew M. Peken (Not Admitted in the United States)
Lori L. Pines
Stuart E. Pollack
Corinne Pryzanski
Marc D. Puntus
Gene Rachmansky
David C. Radulescu
Richard J. Reilly, Jr.
Jason R. Riesel
Steven Jay Rizzi
Juan B. Roman
Salvatore Romanello
Michael Rona
Andrew E. Roth
Ronald R. Rossi
Lilli Siegel Roth
Sidney M. Ruthenberg
Scott R. Saks
Anne Marie Salan
Amanda Cynthia Samuel
Olga Sandler
Allison R. Scharin
Michael H. Scher
Michael Schor
Stephanie F. Schulman
Arthur L. Scinta
Jennifer Sclar
Amy L. Shane
Jonathan S. Shapiro
Sharon C.K. Sherman
Piotr D. Siemion
Alexander Simon
Daniel G. Simpson
Randi Wolkenbreit Singer
Craig A. Sloane
Craig D. Solar
Scott M. Sontag
Jayne L. South
Gerald A. Stein
Sharyn R. Stein
Jordan Stern
Christopher B. Storey
Elliott Sussman
David G. Tanenbaum
Paul M. Tarr
Mark A. Tashkovich
Kristin L. Tess
Michael M. Tingoli
Nancy Yi-Pei Tong
Michele Traeger
Theodore E. Tsekerides
Peter Tu (Not admitted in NY)
Thierry Valat
Joseph T. Verdesca, Jr.
Lynda R. Vescio
John C. Vetter
Nita S. Vyas
Shai Y. Waisman
Erika Weinberg
Margery N. Weinstein
Elizabeth Stotland Weiswasser
Lynn B. Werner
Pami Wexelman
Christian Wickwire
John Eric Wise (Not admitted in NY)
Dena L. Wolf
Deborah Wolff
Richard C. Wong
Anne-Marie Wood
David L. Yohai
Sharon J. Youdelman
Ross L. Yustein
Todd Bennett Zarin

For full biographical listings, see the Martindale-Hubbell Law Directory

---

WHITE & CASE (AV)

Limited Liability Partnership
1155 Avenue of the Americas, 10036-2787
Telephone: 212-819-8200
Telex: 233188 WHCA UR
Facsimile: 212-354-8113
URL: http://www.whitecase.com
New York, New York: 1140 Avenue of the Americas, New York, NY 10036-6700.
Telephone: 212-819-8900.
New York, New York: Litigation Support Center, 1120 Avenue of the Americas, New York, NY 10036-6700.
Telephone: 212-819-7977.
Facsimile: 212-7970/71.

(See Next Column)

Los Angeles, California:
Telephone: 213-620-7700.
Facsimile: 213-687-0758; 213-452-2330; 213-452-2331.
Palo Alto, California:
Telephone: 650-213-0300.
Facsimile: 650-213-8158.
San Francisco, California:
Telephone: 415-544-1100.
Facsimile: 415-544-0202.
Miami, Florida:
Telephone: 305-371-2700.
Telephone: 305-358-5744.
Facsimile: 305-358-5766.
Washington, D.C.:
Telephone: 202-626-3600.
Facsimile: 202-639-9355.
Bratislava, Slovak Republic:
Telephone: (421-7) 5441-5100.
Facsimile: (421-7) 5441-6100.
Brussels, Belgium:
Telephone: (32-2) 219-16-20.
Facsimile: (32-2) 219-16-26.
Budapest, Hungary: Réczicza Law Firm White & Case.
Telephone: (36-1) 488-5200.
Facsimile: (36-1) 488-5299.
Frankfurt, Germany: White & Case (Rechtsanwälte).
Telephone: (49-69) 713-77-(0).
Facsimile: (49-69) 713-77-100.
Helsinki, Finland: Asianajotoimisto White & Case Oy.
Telephone: (358-9) 228-641.
Facsimile: (358-9) 228-64228.
Istanbul, Turkey:
Telephone: (90-212) 275-75-33.
Facsimile: (90-212) 275-75-43.
London, England:
Telephone: (44-20) 7600-7300.
Facsimile: (44-20) 7600-7030.
Moscow, Russia:
Telephone: (7-095) 787-3000.
Facsimile: (7-095) 787-3001.
Paris, France:
Telephone: (33-1) 55-04-15-15.
Facsimile: (33-1) 55-04-15-16.
Prague, Czech Republic:
Telephone: (420-2) 2481-0808; 2481-1796.
Facsimile: (420-2) 2481-0330; 2481-0252.
Stockholm, Sweden: White & Case Advokat AB.
Telephone: (46-8) 506-323-00.
Facsimile: (46-8) 611-21-22.
Warsaw, Poland: White & Case (Poland) Sp. z o.o.
Telephone: (48-22) 625-33-33; (48-22) 622-67-67; (48-39) 12-19-06.
Facsimile: (48-22) 628-22-28.
Johannesburg, Republic of South Africa:
Telephone: 27 (11) 884-7689.
Facsimile: 27 (11) 884-7229.
Almaty, Kazakhstan:
Telephone: (7-3272) 50-74-91.
Facsimile: (7-3272) 50-74-93.
Ankara, Turkey:
Telephone: (90-312) 442-5680.
Facsimile: (90-312) 442-5691/4.
Bangkok, Thailand: White & Case (Thailand) Limited.
Telephone: (662) 656-1721 to 32.
Facsimile: (662) 656-1733/34.
Bombay/Mumbai, India: Liaison Office, (91-22) 282-6300/01/02/03.
Facsimile: (91-22) 282-6305.
Hanoi, Vietnam:
Telephone: (84-4) 934-5355.
Facsimile: (84-4) 934-5356.
Ho Chi Minh City, Vietnam:
Telephone: (84-8) 821-0888.
Facsimile: (84-8) 823-6902.
Hong Kong:
Telephone: White & Case, Solicitors. (852) 2822-8700.
Facsimile: (852) 2845-9070.
Singapore, Republic of Singapore:
Telephone: (65) 225-6000.
Facsimile: (65) 225-6009.
Tokyo, Japan: White & Case Kandabashi Law Offices.
Telephone: (81-3) 3259-0200.
Facsimile: (81-3) 3259-0150.
Jeddah, Saudi Arabia: Law Office of Hassan Mahassni,
Telephone: (966-2) 665-4353.
Facsimile: (966-2) 669-2996.
Riyadh, Saudi Arabia: Law Office of Hassan Mahassni,
Telephone: (966-1) 464-4006.
Facsimile: (966-1) 465-1348.
Mexico City, Mexico: White & Case, S.C.
Telephone: (52) 5-540-9600.
Facsimile: (52) 5-540-9699.
São Paulo, SP, Brazil:
Telephone: (55-11) 3171-0011.
Facsimile: (55-11) 3171-0041.

(See Next Column)

WHITE & CASE, *New York—Continued*

Bombay/Mumbai, India: Associated Law Firm; India Law Services (ILS).
Telephones: (91-22) 284-1995; (91-22) 284-1847.
Facsimile: (91-22) 285-0824.
New Delhi, India: Associated Law Firm; India Law Services (ILS).
Telephone: (91-11) 697-1602/3/4.
Facsimile: (91-11) 698-8860.

MEMBERS OF FIRM

Troy Alexander
Priscilla Almodovar
Pedro A. Alvarez (Miami, Florida Office)
Victor M. Alvarez (Miami, Florida Office)
Emilio J. Alvarez-Farre (Miami, Florida Office)
Carl H. Amon III
S. Ward Atterbury
Andrew S. Auchincloss
Kevin F. Barnard
Roy M. Bartlett, Jr. (Palo Alto, California Office)
Howard S. Beltzer
Cyrus Benson III
Eric L. Berg
Scott A. Berger
Steven M. Betensky
David Bilkis
J. David Black (Palo Alto, California Office)
Jerry R. Bloom (Los Angeles, California Office)
Oliver C. Brahmst
Charles N. Brower (Washington, D.C. Office)
Maureen S. Brundage
James R. Cairns (Los Angeles, California Office)
Linda E. Carlisle (Washington, D.C. Office)
Sylvia Fung Chin
Robert L. Clare, III
William J. Clinton (Washington, D.C. Office)
Christopher F. Corr (Washington, D.C. Office)
Stephen M. Corse (Miami, Florida Office)
Christopher M. Curran (Washington, D.C. Office)
J. William Dantzler, Jr.
Bruce N. Davis (Washington, D.C. Office)
Andrew P. DeNatale
Victor J. DeSantis (Washington, D.C. Office)
John M. Donovan
Maureen D. Donovan
Alison M. Dreizen
Dimitrios T. Drivas
Michael P. Dunworth
John W. Erickson
C. Randolph Fishburn (Los Angeles, California Office)
Burton H. Fohrman (Tokyo, Japan Office)
Christopher P. Frampton
Jorge L. Freeland (Miami, Florida Office)
Paul D. Friedland
Lawrence J. Gannon
Sean J. Geary
J. Mark Gidley (Washington, D.C. Office)
Michael S. Goetz
Timothy B. Goodell
Barbara J. Goodman
Eugene W. Goodwillie, Jr.
K. Lawrence Gragg (Miami, Florida Office)
Neal F. Grenley
James F. Hayden
Warren S. Heit (Palo Alto, California Office)
Thomas P. Higgins
Lawrence M. Hill
Brian L. Holman (Los Angeles, California Office)
Richard J. Holwell
Richard A. Horsch
David P. Houlihan (Washington, D.C. Office)
David L. Huber
David W. Hunt (Washington, D.C. Office)
James B. Hurlock
Marcos D. Jiménez (Miami, Florida Office)
M. Elaine Johnston
David E. Joyce
Anthony F. Kahn
Joseph M. Karp (Los Angeles, California Office)
Michael E. Kavoukjian (Miami, Florida Office)
Kevin Keogh
Charles C. Kline (Miami, Florida Office)
I. Fred Koenigsberg
David N. Koschik
Alexander S. Kritzalis
Glenn M. Kurtz
Carolyn B. Lamm (Washington, D.C. Office)
Thomas E. Lauria (Miami, Florida Office)
Carmen D. Legato (Washington, D.C. Office)
John T. Lillis
Nels T. Lippert
Cecilia O'Brien Lofters
Donald T. MacNaughton
Wendell C. Maddrey
Philip L. Maloney (Los Angeles, California Office)
William P. McClure (Washington, D.C. Office)
Thomas McGanney
James J. McGuire
Mitchell E. Menaker
J. Roger Mentz (Washington, D.C. Office)
Bryan A. Merryman (Los Angeles, California Office)
Neal S. Millard (Los Angeles, California Office)
Elizabeth P. Munson
John Narducci
Edward R. Neaher, Jr. (Washington, D.C. Office)
Roger W. Noble
Thomas J. O'Sullivan
Robert D. Paul (Washington, D.C. Office)
Owen C. Pell
Laurence Pettit
Gregory P. Pryor
Kenneth A. Raskin
Robert L. Raskopf
John M. Reiss
David S. Robbins
Edward F. Rover
Neil W. Rust (Los Angeles, California Office)
Winthrop Rutherfurd, Jr.
Michael I. Saltzman
John J. Sarchio
Edward E. Sawyer (Miami, Florida Office)
Arthur A. Scavone
Philip H. Schaeffer
Michael S. Shuster
Michael W. Smith
Richard K. Smith, Jr. (Los Angeles, California Office)
Abby Cohen Smutny (Washington, D.C. Office)
Gregory J. Spak (Washington, D.C. Office)
Walter J. Spak (Washington, D.C. Office)
John A. Sturgeon (Los Angeles, California Office)
Jefferson C. Taylor (Miami, Florida Office)
Gregory N. Ullman (Miami, Florida Office)

(See Next Column)

MEMBERS OF FIRM (Continued)

Barrye L. Wall (Los Angeles, California Office)
Duane D. Wall
Sandra J. Warren
John S. Willems
Nicholas R. Williams
Carol A. Witschel
Travers D. Wood (Los Angeles, California Office)
Daniel J. Woods (Los Angeles, California Office)
William F. Wynne, Jr.
Abraham L. Zylberberg

LOCAL PARTNERS

BANGKOK, WHITE & CASE (THAILAND) LTD.

Peangpanor Boonklum
Chinnavat Chinsangaram
Manida Zinmerman

FRANKFURT

Oliver Kessler
Thomas Schrell

HONG KONG, WHITE & CASE, SOLICITORS

Sandra P. S. Fan
Philip B. Gilligan
Kim M. Rooney

WARSAW, WHITE & CASE (POLAND) SP. ZO.O

Beata E. Kiedrowicz
Leslaw Z. Kostórkiewicz
Marek Król

PARTNERS OF COUNSEL

Lauriston Castleman, Jr.
Jay H. Grodin (Los Angeles, California Office)
Donald P. Madden
John Paul Reiner

RETIRED PARTNERS

John W. Barnum
Thomas C. Burke
J. D. Clayton
Malcolm J. Edgerton, Jr.
Marion J. Epley, III
Haliburton Fales, 2d
C. Sims Farr
Macdonald Flinn
Philip H. Hedges
Prof. Joseph Hinsey, IV
Thomas A. Hopkins
John M. Johnston
Francis J. MacLaughlin (Not admitted in NY)
Lenard H. Mandel
James J. Marshall, Jr.
John J. McAvoy
Willis McDonald, IV
John J. McNally
Clyde Mitchell
Morton Moskin
Casimir C. Patrick, II
Stephen M. Piga
John C. Provine
Thomas M. Ramseur, Jr.
John G. Reed
Paul C. Rooney
David Sachs
David W. Swanson
Donald M. Wilkinson, Jr.
Edward Wolfe

COUNSEL

David Bender
Alan Blum
Margery A. Colloff
Susan G. Curtis
Frank L. Eaton (Miami, Florida Office)
John M. Genova
Patricia M. Godoy
Dwight A. Healy
Evan C. Hollander
Ellen M. Jakovic (Washington, D.C. Office)
Robert M. Kelly
Ellen McGinty King (Palo Alto, California Office)
Richard G. Liskov
Ann T. MacLeod (Los Angeles, California Office)
Richard A. Miller
Paul K. Milmed
L. Grant ("Jack") Peeples (Miami, Florida Office)
Steven K. Ross
Anne D. Smith (Washington, D.C. Office)
Ellen W. Smith
James M. Stillwaggon
Jeffrey J. Temple
Mara S. Weissmann
Donald B. Zief

ASSOCIATES

Bernard Abdo
Marc E. Ackerman
Geraldine Acuña-Sunshine (Not admitted in NY)
Boulos A. Alfaks
Omar H. Al-Farisi
Nabeel Almansour (Not admitted in NY)
Veronica A. Angulo (Miami, Florida Office)
Jocelyn A. Aqua (Washington, D.C. Office)
Brian G. Arnold (Los Angeles, California Office)
Karen M. Asner
Mark O. Bagnall (Miami, Florida Office)
Jason Ban
Uriel Barak
Francois Bardonnet
Karl S. Barrios
Marc A. Began
Lori B. Begleiter
Peter H. F. Bekker
Christina C. Benson (Washington, D.C. Office)
Andrea G. Berkley
Mark A. Berube
Felicia Beylerian
Darcy S. Binder
Claudia T. Bogdanos
Gigi L. Bonnici
Aron B. Borukhov
Vincent Bowen (Washington, D.C. Office)
Teresa Boyle
Steven L. Bray (Miami, Florida Office)
Joseph H. Brazil
Boyana Bregovic
Keith L. Britton
Patrick J. Browne, Jr. (Washington, D.C. Office)
Karen Burns
Carolyn Campbell (Washington, D.C. Office)
Fernando Campuzano (Miami, Florida Office)
Mehmet I. Canevi
Peter J. Carney (Washington, D.C. Office)
Yuisa Carrillo Rey
David E. Case
Carlos B. Castillo (Miami, Florida Office)
Francisco J. Cerezo (Miami, Florida Office)
Jennifer L. Chapin
Daniel S. Chen (Washington, D.C. Office)
Wan Chen
Elizabeth L. Cheney (Washington D.C. Office)
Adam Chernichaw

(See Next Column)

WHITE & CASE—*Continued*

ASSOCIATES (Continued)

Joyce C. Chiang (Los Angeles, California Office)
Gustav Chiarello (Washington, D.C. Office)
Mark M. Cho (Miami, Florida Office)
Melissa J. Choi
Hallam Chow
Evan Y. Chuck (Los Angeles, California Office)
Lisa Cintron
Kevin C. Clayton (Washington, D.C. Office)
Jordan S. Cohen (Los Angeles, California Office)
Eileen M. Cole
Lisa A. Cottle (Los Angeles, California Office)
Christopher G. Cross
Jaime M. Crowe (Washington D.C. Office)
John K. Cunningham (Miami, Florida Office)
Jennifer M. Curley (Washington, D.C. Office)
Michael A. Davitz
Fernando J. de la Hoz (Miami, Florida Office)
Jonathan Dennis (Los Angeles, California Office)
Edward T. DeSilva
Stephane P. Des Lauriers (Washington, D.C. Office)
Sahra H. Diament
Colin Diamond (Not admitted in the United States) (Legal Consultant on the Laws of Israel)
Denise L. Diaz
Andrew B. Diaz-Matos
Albert Diaz-Silveira (Miami, Florida Office)
Darin A. DiBello (Miami, Florida Office)
Robert J. Dobson
Charles C. Doumar (Not admitted in NY)
Sean Dowd (Palo Alto, California Office)
David H. Dreier
David L. Elmont (Washington, D.C. Office)
Janice M. Elsesser
Richard H. Engman (Miami, Florida Office)
Nicole Erb (Washington, D.C. Office)
Lynn H. Fabrizio (Washington, D.C. Office)
Vincent Filardo, Jr.
Dyan F. Finguerra-DuCharme
John T. Flippen
Carlos E. Fonseca (Los Angeles, California Office)
Dana Foster (Miami, Florida Office)
Paul L. Freedman
Robert B. Friedrich
Adam R. Gahtan
John Giambalvo
Daniel P. Ginsberg
Christopher J. Glancy
Martin Glass
Sharon Robles Glazier (Miami, Florida Office)
Daniel P. Goldberg
Steven R. Goodman
Robert G. Gosselink (Washington, D.C. Office)
Willem H. Gravett
John M. Grimes
Jenny L. Gross (Los Angeles, California Office)
Peter D. Hadrovic
Elena Haliulin
Mark T. Hamilton
Andrew W. Hammond
Jennifer Hampton
Gregg A. Hand
Craig A. Hart (Not admitted in NY)
Richard D. Hayes (Not admitted in the United States) (Legal Consultant on the Laws of Australia and England and Wales)
Paul G. Hegland (Washington, D.C. Office)
Eckhard R. Hellbeck (Washington, D.C. Office)
Thais Hernandez (Miami, Florida Office)
David G. Hille
David B. Hoppe (Not admitted in NY)
Jane A. Houk (Miami, Florida Office)
Mark M. Huang
Shannon M. Hudnall
Susan P. Huffard
Malvina Edwards Iannone
Francis Idehen
Aron Izower
Nicole Janigian (Los Angeles, California Office)
Beth D. Jarrett (Miami, Florida Office)
Douglas M. Jasinski (Washington, D.C. Office)
Sang I. Ji
Pedro A. Jiménez (Miami, Florida Office)
David M. Johansen
Jennifer L. Johnson
Melissa A. Kaftarian
Perry V. Kalajian
Masahiko Kawakami
Christopher W. Kelly (Los Angeles, California Office)
Matthew S. Kelman
Daniel J. Kessler
Richard G. King (Washington, D.C. Office)
Russell L. King (Miami, Florida Office)
Sheron Korpus
Noelle Kowalczyk
Paul C. Lacourciere (Los Angeles, California Office)
Geoffrey B. Lanning (Washington, D.C. Office)
Judd Lawler (Washington, D.C. Office)
Bleu Kuwanyantiwa Lawless (Washington, D.C. Office)
Ruth E. Lazar
Adams C. Lee (Washington, D.C. Office)
Eric F. Leicht
Danielle M. Levy
Micah A. Levy (Washington, D.C. Office)
Alisa D. Lewis (Not admitted in NY)
Matthew P. Lewis (Los Angeles, California Office)
Richard C. Libert
Felix J. Lopez (Miami, Florida Office)
Gustavo I. Lopez (Miami, Florida Office)
David D. H. Mak (Not admitted in the United States) (Legal Consultant on the Laws of Australia and England)
Joseph W. Marx (Not admitted in NY)
Joanna E. McCarthy
Karen G. McCloat
Kevin X. McGann
Patricia L. McKeogh
Maria I. Boyesen McReddie (Miami, Florida Office)
Victor G. Mendoza, III (Miami, Florida Office)
John A. Mitchell (Los Angeles, California Office)
Maxroy K. Mitchell

ASSOCIATES (Continued)

(See Next Column)

Julian F. Montero (Miami, Florida Office)
Marc L. Moore
Leslie Morioka
Agnieszka A. Moskal
Thomas M. Mullaney
Nathalie Münzberg
John L. Murphy (Miami, Florida Office)
Christopher Murray
Nandan S. Nelivigi
Emil Nemec
Richard A. Nessler
Mary Ellen Dooley Nye
Jeffrey J. Oelke (Miami, Florida Office)
Kori Lyttle Ogrosky
Jon C. Ohrn
Michael C. O'Sullivan
John W. Owczarski (Washington, D.C. Office)
J. Hyung Paek
Frank Panopoulos (Washington, D.C. Office)
George L. Paul (Washington, D.C. Office)
Stephen R. Payne (Washington, D.C. Office)
Eric J. Pelofsky
Daniel H. Peters (Los Angeles, California Office)
Rafael L. Petrone
Lisa D. Pfeffer (Los Angeles, California Office)
Tomer Pinkusiewicz
Craig A. Pintoff
Kevin M. Plante
Gregg D. Polsky (Miami, Florida Office)
Suzanne M. Porter
Joshua Protass
Gary M. Rabkin (Palo Alto, California Office)
Leila Rachlin
Andrea B. Radosevich
Lianne S. Reilly (Not Admitted in the United States) (Legal Consultant on the Laws of England and Wales)
Shahin Rezvani (Los Angeles, California Office)
Raphaël Richard (Not admitted in the United States) (Legal Consultant on the Laws of France)
Joseph D. Richards (Miami, Florida Office)
Amy Robinson
Gregory P. Rodgers (Los Angles, California Office)
Scott L. Rogers (Miami, Florida Office)
Chase Romick
John E. Rosenbaum (Palo Alto, California Office)
Margaret A. Rostker (Los Angeles, California Office)
Eric S. Roth (Miami, Florida Office)
Lester Y. Saito
Michael Samway (Miami, Florida Office)
Michael Sansevero, Jr.
Ehud Schaffer (Not Admitted in the United States) (Legal Consultant on the Laws of Israel)
John P. Scheibeler
Joseph B. Schmit
Rachel K. Schneider
Kathleen A. Scott
Mark S. Scott (Miami, Florida Office)
Mark A. Shalaby (Washington, D.C. Office)
Michael D. Shanabrook
Jean E. Shimotake
J. Christopher Shore
Louis S. Silvestri
Laura M. Sizemore
Claudia A. Smith
Sydney R. Smith
Victoria F. Smith
Eric P. Spooner (Washington, D.C. Office)
Mario D. Springer
Lee A. Steven (Washington, D.C. Office)
Catherine A. Stone (Los Angeles, California Office)
Denise H.M.C. Stoot
Hollace S. W. Swanson
Takeshi Takahashi
David W. Thatch
Peter P. Thieman (Washington, D.C. Office)
Steven G. Thompson
Robert E. Tiedemann, III
Mara E. R. Topping (Washington, D.C. Office)
Johanna Toth
Martin M. Toto
Judy-Beth C. Tyler
Osamu Umejima (Washington, D.C. Office)
Steven J. Vainder (Miami, Florida Office)
Lyle B. Vander Schaaf (Washington, D.C. Office)
Francis A. Vasquez, Jr. (Washington, D.C. Office)
Margaret G. Wachenfeld (Washington, D.C. Office)
Kristin D. Wells (Washington, D.C. Office)
Scott Ian Waldbaum
Andrew S. Walker
Katherine T.E. Ward
Marcia Y. Williams
Elizabeth A. Wilson
Laura M. Wilson (Washington, D.C. Office)
J. Christian Word (Washington, D.C. Office)
Margaret Yanney
Hakan Yazici (Not admitted in the United States) (Legal Consultant on the Laws of Turkey)
Louis Zehil
Kristina Zissis (Washington, D.C. Office)

PARTNER
RūCZICZA LAW FIRM
WHITE & CASE
LIMITED LIABILITY PARTNERSHIP
BUDAPEST OFFICE

Peter Finlay

PARTNER
BRATISLAVA OFFICE

Ivan Cestr

RESIDENT PARTNERS
BRUSSELS, BELGIUM OFFICE

Ian S. Forrester, Q.C.
Pontus Lindfelt
Christopher Norall
Mark D. Powell
Guy Schrans
Alastair Sutton

PARTNER
FRANKFURT OFFICE

Dr. Erich Michel

LOCAL PARTNERS

Oliver Kessler
Thomas Schrell

(See Next Column)

WHITE & CASE, *New York—Continued*

RESIDENT PARTNER, HELSINKI OFFICE

Petri Y.J. Haussila

RESIDENT PARTNER, ISTANBUL OFFICE

Asli F. Basgoz

RESIDENT PARTNER ANKARA OFFICE

Gwynne H. Wales

RESIDENT PARTNERS, LONDON OFFICE

Alasdair Bell
John M. H. Bellhouse
Jonathan M. Clark, Jr.
Margaret B. Cole
Margaret R. Cole
David M. Eisenberg
Peter Finlay
Francis Fitzherbert-Brockholes
Gregory J. Hammond
Jon Lang
David Llewelyn
Mats Sacklén
H. Philip T. Stopford

RESIDENT PARTNERS, MOSCOW OFFICE

Douglas Peel
Hugh Verrier

RESIDENT PARTNERS, PARIS OFFICE

Paule Biensan
Stephen R. Bond
Jean-Luc Boussard
Nicholas Budd
Reinhard Dammann
Anthony Giustini
Rayner M. Hamilton
François Leloup
Rosine Lorotte
Norbert Majerholc
Thomas J. McDonald
Philippe Métais
Vincent Morin
Gilles Peigney
John H. Riggs
Christopher R. Seppala

RESIDENT PARTNERS, PRAGUE OFFICE

Ivan Cestr
Michal Dlouhý
Jan Matějček

RESIDENT PARTNERS, STOCKHOLM OFFICE

Göran Åseborn
Ulf Johansson
Rolf S. Olofsson
Clas Romander
Claes Zettermarck

PARTNERS, WARSAW OFFICE

Jacek Czabański
Witold Danilowicz
Janusz Fiszer
Witold Jurcewicz

LOCAL PARTNERS WARSAW OFFICE

Beata E. Kiedrowicz
Leslaw Z. Kostórkiewicz
Marek Król

PARTNER HANOI OFFICE

K. Minh Dang

PARTNER HO CHI MINH CITY

K. Minh Dang

RESIDENT PARTNERS WHITE & CASE (THAILAND) LTD.

Weerawong Chittmittrapap
Nopadol Intralib
Kevin J. Murphy
Khaisri Utaiwan

LOCAL PARTNERS

Peangpanor Boonklum
Chinnavat Chinsangaram
Manida Zinmerman

RESIDENT PARTNERS HONG KONG OFFICE

George K. Crozer, IV
Allan L. Gropper
Sharon E. Hartline
John T. Kuzmik
Eric S. Yoon

LOCAL PARTNERS

Sandra P. S. Fan
Philip B. Gilligan
Kim M. Rooney

PARTNERS, SINGAPORE OFFICE

Haywood Blakemore
K. Minh Dang
Alistair A. Duffield
Kenneth C. Ellis
Bertie M. Mehigan
Brian M. Miller
Raj Pande
Jeffrey A. Washenko

RESIDENT PARTNERS, TOKYO OFFICE

Burton H. Fohrman
Robert F. Grondine
Gregory J. Ossi
Eric N. Roose
Gary M. Thomas
Christopher P. Wells
Michael J. Yoshii

RESIDENT PARTNER JEDDAH OFFICE

Hassan M.S. Mahassni

(See Next Column)

RESIDENT PARTNERS RIYADH OFFICE

Hassan M.S. Mahassni
Robert C. Nicholls

RESIDENT PARTNERS JOHANNESBURG OFFICE

Darryl B. Deaktor
Ronald E. M. Goodman
John S. Janks
Steven G. Raney

RESIDENT PARTNERS MEXICO CITY OFFICE

Rodrigo González-Luna
Kenneth R. Lee
Alexis E. Rovzar
Alberto Sepúlveda Cosío
Alberto Sepúlveda de la Fuente

PARTNERS SŏO PAULO, BRAZIL

Donald E. Baker
Alexis E. Rovzar

PARTNER ALMATY, KAZAKHSTAN OFFICE

Yuriy V. Maltsev

COUNSEL BRUSSELS, BELGIUM OFFICE

Thomas Tindemans

COUNSEL PRAGUE OFFICE

Monika Rutland
Tomáš Zagar

COUNSEL LONDON, ENGLAND OFFICE

Hugh Brett
Gerard N. Cranley
John F. Runeckles

RESIDENT COUNSEL, PARIS OFFICE

Michael T. Hancock

COUNSEL WARSAW OFFICE

Todd J. Peterson

COUNSEL MOSCOW OFFICE

Avgust A. Rubanov

COUNSEL SINGAPORE OFFICE

Anand S. Dayal

COUNSEL HONG KONG OFFICE

James B. Griffiths

JAPANESE COUNSEL TOKYO OFFICE

Hisao Hirose
Kouji Ishikawa
Michihiro Maeda
Tetsuya Morimoto
Koichiro Ohashi
Chiho Saito
Mika Suzuki
Keiko Tashiro
Mizuho Yamada
Yoshiko Yasuda

RESIDENT COUNSEL ANKARA OFFICE

T. Nurkut Inan

RESIDENT COUNSEL, ISTANBUL OFFICE

M. Fadlullah Cerrahoglu
Serap Zuvin

RESIDENT COUNSEL MEXICO OFFICE

Alejandro Fernandez
Emilio Robles
Miguel A. Velázquez

COUNSEL RŭCZICZA LAW FIRM WHITE & CASE LLP BUDAPEST OFFICE

Robert B. Irving
István Réczicza

ASSOCIATE ISTANBUL OFFICE

Leigh J. Hall

ASSOCIATES BRATISLAVA OFFICE

Peter Bollardt
Beatrix Debnárová
Roman Hamala
J. Russell McGranahan
Marek Staroň

ASSOCIATES BRUSSELS OFFICE

Ana Belen Costillas Caño
Sofie Dejonghe
Katrien Depuyot
Laurence Donnay
Andrea F. Gagliardi
Ana Garcia-Bello
Rony P. Gerrits
Thomas Hartnett
Linda Hiljemark
Suzanne Innes-Stubb
James R. Killick
Maria Isabel F. Utges Manley
Fiona Murray
Madelein Perrick
Walter M. Schuster
Ann Stanley
Werner van Lembergen
Elisabethann Wright

(See Next Column)

WHITE & CASE—*Continued*

ASSOCIATES
RŰCZICZA LAW FIRM WHITE & CASE LLP
BUDAPEST OFFICE

Ildikó Csák
Zoltán Farkas
Balázs Fazekas
Zsuzsanna Kovács
Zsuzsanna Nagy
Szabolcs Posta
Judit Sós
Tashia A. Urland
Janos Volkai

ASSOCIATES
FRANKFURT OFFICE

Torsten Koller
Albrecht S. Münch
Dr. Edzard A. Schmidt-Jortzig
Matthias N. Von Oppen

ASSOCIATES
HELSINKI OFFICE

Timo M. Airisto
Colleen M. Grady
Miika J. Heiskanen
Sven E. Krogius
Tanja Rekola

ASSOCIATES
LONDON OFFICE

David G. Baker
Ellis D. Baker
Jane M.Q. Ballantyne
Richard J. Bamforth
Robyn A. Chew
Marcus Collins
Nicholas Collins
Rebecca Cox
Aydin A. Düren
Gilead Halevy
Adrian Horne
Jason Kerr
Joshua G. Kiernan
Thomas Leo Madden
Paul A. Marchand
Richard G. Marlin
Craig R. Nethercott
Christine Poyer
Kaya H. Proudian
Aloke Ray
Diane Mage Roberts
Zurina Saban
Julie Breene Smith
Sirak Solomon
Miles Thomas
Seema Shah Wadhwani
Andrew C. Weiler
Stuart Weir
Anuita Woodhull
Andrew Wright

ASSOCIATES
MOSCOW OFFICE

Igor Blinov
Irina Chernobai
David Godfrey
Victor M. Khvesenya
Mariana V. Marchuk
Lucy J. McCullagh
Maya Melnikas
Eric Michailov
Natalia Nikitina
Igor Ostapets
Alexander G. Shmakov
Maria Vinogradova

ASSOCIATES
PARIS OFFICE

Catherine Andrieux
Thierry Arachtingi
Jacques Bouillon
Isabelle Combes
Edouard De Chavagnac
Christopher Dempsey
Laurent Develle
Suzanne Durdevic
John H. Elovson
François Farmine
Nicolas Huet
Alexandre Ippolito
John R. W. D. Jones
Beatrice Joyaud
Nicole L. Kelsey
Frederic Lafond
Pierre J. Lastenouse
Jean-Francois Le Corre
Serge Levine
Maud Manon
Robert F. Mayo
Virginie Mosse
Mark B. Richards
Lola Schaufuss
Damien Schmitt
Monika Seidel-Moreau
Patrick Sergant
Kirk E. Sheriff
Gilles Veuillot
Anne Vincent
David Wadham
Sophie Waldberg

ASSOCIATES
PRAGUE OFFICE

Ashley Ballard
Ivo Bárta
Aleš Blažek
Jakub Dostál
David Koláček
Tomáš Kopřiva
Květoslav Krejčí
Petr Kruliš
Petr Kuhn
Tomáš Markovič
Michael R. Mullen
Josef Otčenášek
David Plch
Karolína Salamonová
Jiři' Šimečeu
Martina Suchankova
Jan Vild
Sofia Zlatinovová

ASSOCIATES
STOCKHOLM OFFICE

Frida Grundberg
Johan Holgersson
Tomas Jonasson
Fredrik Schultz
Katarina Segerståhl
Rachel Sklar
Anna Sundberg

ASSOCIATES
WARSAW OFFICE

Marta Bykiewicz
Katarzyna Chróścicka-Drzazga
Malgorzata Chruściak
Aneta Duffek
Agnieszka Dzięgielewska
Arkadiusz Grabalski
Dariusz A. Greszta
Magdalena Guzewicz
Jacek Jachowicz
Barbara E. Jaśniewska
Artur Jończyk
Przemyslaw Kalek
Arkadiusz Korzeniewski
Grzegorz Kuderski
Agnieszka B. Moczulo
Malgorzata Mroczkowska
Igor Muszyński
Dorota Olszanowska
Anna Piatkowska
Magdelena Polujkis

(*See Next Column*)

ASSOCIATES
WARSAW OFFICE (Continued)

Agnieszka Raczkowska
Iwona U. Rykaczewska
Michal Stolarek
Andrzej Sutkowski
Michal Zieniewski

ASSOCIATES
ALMATY OFFICE

Kairat E. Baizakov
Joel B. Benjamin
Marat A. Ibragimov
Yerzhan K. Kumarov

ASSOCIATES
WHITE & CASE (THAILAND) LTD.

Phorntip Janjarussakul
Kamol Kaewnonchai
Noparat Kaewsringarm
Suntus Kirdsinsap
Narong Kritchanchai
Kallaya Laohaganniyom
Seree Manduang
Wiyada Ngamsom
Netima Nilpanich
Nantika Ninvoraskul
Passamas Phromsorn
Kasamci Sakunchaisiriwit
Wallop Sripaisal
Kudun Sukhumanonda
Apisith John Sutham
Thanabodhi Swasdisri
Somphob Thamprida
Sombat Thitapanich
Chatri Trakulmanenate
Duc V. Trang
Dhada Vajaranant
Nitat Wattanakul

ASSOCIATE
HANOI OFFICE

John R. Davis

ASSOCIATES
HO CHI MINH CITY

John R. Davis
Duc V. Trang

ASSOCIATES
HONG KONG OFFICE

Juan Andres D. Bautista
Xia Chao
Ying Woo Chung
Victor Ho
Raymund G. Kawasaki
Bernadette Mak Lomas
Douglas B. Miller
Ka Lam Karen Ng
Pan Qi
Dennis G. Soliven
William A. Thomson
Lydia J. Wingrad

ASSOCIATES,
SINGAPORE OFFICE

Guan Feng Chen
Daniel Chung
John W. Creighton, III
Shonu S.K. Das
Clarinda Tjia Dharmadi
Ashok K. Lalwani
Rudy Lim
Sin Teck Lim
Mary Ng
Iwan Nurjadin
Xiao-Shan Peh
Niket Rele
Edmund W. Sim
Nelson L. Y. Suit
Dipa Swaminathan
Su Ann Teoh
Huey Yann Thong
Brian J. Wesol
Yen-Wen Yu

ASSOCIATES
TOKYO OFFICE

Keld O. Conradsen
Gerald M. Fujii
George J. Hibbert
Junko Iijima
Yvette S. Lanneaux
Kenneth J. Lebrun
Todd M. McHenry
Robert E. Melson, Jr.
Sergey J. Milanov
Samantha D. Naik
Jeffrey K. Natori
Linda L. Ng
Brent O'Leary
Dmitri Rezchikov
Glen E. Sugimoto
Ichizo Takayama
Jonathan A. Tyler

ASSOCIATES
RIYADH OFFICE

Abdul Mosen M. Al-Sheikh
Babul Parikh

ASSOCIATES
JEDDAH OFFICE

Brian L. Conway
Imad El-Dine Ghazi
Anas Keilani
Ayman Abdel Khaleq
M. Farouk Kouatli
Abdullah Murad
Gassim Zanoon

ASSOCIATES
JOHANNESBURG OFFICE

Marvin A. Artis
Shamilah Grimwood
Steven Nackan
Kanthimathie Rattay
Villiers Terblanche
Jerome Graham Webb
Philip Webster

ASSOCIATES
MEXICO CITY OFFICE

Iker I. Arriola
Marcial Ascencio
Adolfo Athie
Ricardo Avila
Eugenio Bernal
David E. Bond
Luis-Miguel Briola
James A. Gerard
Juan Manuel González
Susan E. Grisso De Ortega
Mauricio Ibáñez
John C. Leary
Jose Antonio Lorenzo
Alex Mizrahi
Rodrigo Orozco
Maria Teresa Pailles
Ariel Ramos
Juan P. Rico
Rafael Romo
Eugenio Sepúlveda
Tony Shamosh
Adrienne Wallsten
Matthew F. Wilhoit

(*See Next Column*)

WHITE & CASE, *New York—Continued*

ASSOCIATES
SöO PAULO, BRAZIL

Miguel S. Lawson

For full biographical listings, see the Martindale-Hubbell Law Directory

WHITE, FLEISCHNER & FINO (AV)

140 Broadway, 10005
Telephone: 212-487-9700
Telecopier: 212-487-9777
Email: infor@wff-law.com
Red Bank, New Jersey Office: 272 Broad Street.
Telephone: 732-530-7787.
Telecopier: 732-530-8552.

MEMBERS OF FIRM

Allan P. White
Benjamin A. Fleischner
Paul A. Fino, Jr.
Patti F. Potash
Wendy K. Carrano
Stephanie M. Holzback
Sheri E. Holland
James A. Robbins

ASSOCIATES

Mitchell L. Shadowitz
Virginia L. McGrane
Nancy D. Lyness
Deanna E. Hazen
Dionne G. Sinclair
Daniel MacLaren Stewart
Dan Mesterman
Debra A. Mark
Evan Asher Richman
Joanne Carlozzi
Elaine N. Chou
Jared Greisman
Christopher J. Curylo (Not admitted in NY)
Isatu Kanu

OF COUNSEL

Gil M. Coogler

LEGAL SUPPORT PERSONNEL

Joanne Clark (Claims Consultant)

For full biographical listings, see the Martindale-Hubbell Law Directory

WHITMAN BREED ABBOTT & MORGAN LLP (AV)

200 Park Avenue, 10166
Telephone: 212-351-3000
Cable Address: "Whitsom UR"
Telex: 238436 (RCA)
Telecopier: 212-351-3131
Email: wbam@wbam.com *URL:* http://www.wbam.com
Los Angeles, California Office: 633 West Fifth Street.
Telephone: 213-896-2400.
Greenwich, Connecticut Office: 100 Field Point Road.
Telephone: 203-869-3800.
Newark, New Jersey Office: One Gateway Center.
Telephone: 973-621-2230.
Palm Beach, Florida Office: 220 Sunrise Avenue.
Telephone: 407-832-5458.
London, England Office: 11 Waterloo Place.
Telephone: 71-839-3226.
Telex: 917881.
Tokyo, Japan Office: Suite 450, New Otemachi Building, 2-2-1 Otemachi, Chiyoda-Ku, Tokyo 100.
Telephone: 81-3-3242-1289.
Beirut, Lebanon Office: Tyan & Associes, 22, La Sagesse Street-Rmeil, Lebanon.
Telephone: (961) (1) 56 16 73; (961) (1) 56 16 74.
Fax: (961) (1) 56 14 35

MEMBERS OF FIRM

Robert J. Bagdasarian
Thomas Goodall Bailey, Jr.
Tracy A. Caras
Hollace Topol Cohen
Paul D. Connuck
Richard Crystal
Joseph P. Dailey
D.F.X. de La Chapelle
Alexander T. Deland
John H. Denne
Martin J. Dockery
Linda L. D'Onofrio
William F. Dudine, III
Barry Evans
Stephen W. Feingold
Eugene L. Flanagan III
Charles R. Foy
Michael W. Galligan
Judith A. Gelb
James P. Gerkis
Jay Gladis
Adin C. Goldberg
Jon H. I. Grouf
John M. Hadlock
Thomas C. Havens
C. Stephen Heard, Jr.
Alan S. Hoffman
H. Sidney Holmes III
Hans F. Kaeser
Norman N. Kinel
David F. Kroenlein
Richard F. Lawler
William M. Loafman
Michael K. Madden
Patricia Van B. Madsen
Richard F. Markert
Randolph J. Mayer
C. MacNeil Mitchell
Christian H. Mittweg
David E. Morse
Gregor N. Neff
Eric M. Nelson
Scott D. Newman
James S. Normile
David S. Patterson
Howard E. Peskoe
Benjamin M. Polk
Sander B. Ross
Loren F. Selznick
Berge Setrakian
Stephen L. Sheinfeld
George B. Snyder
Alan J. Sorkowitz
William J. Spatz
Brian L. Sullivan
Kerry S. Sullivan

(See Next Column)

MEMBERS OF FIRM (Continued)

John E. Tardera
Eric P. Taylor
Loran T. Thompson
Neil Underberg
John F. Walsh, Jr.
Kevin Walsh
Howard S. Wolfson

RETIRED PARTNERS

J. Sinclair Armstrong
Frederick H. Bruenner
Richard R. Dailey
Paul E. Doherty
Ellis J. Freedman
Carol Lyttle, Jr.
Robert S. Newman
John O'Callahan
John C. Oram, Jr.
John A. Pateracki, Jr.
Herbert P. Polk
Patrick H. Sullivan

OF COUNSEL

Robert A. Bicks
Hugh L. Carey
David Jaffe
Paul C. Lambert
Stephen R. Lang
Ernest H. Lorch
John J. Marchi
F. Herbert Prem, Jr.
William Rubin

COUNSEL

Nathaniel Levin
Josefa Sicard Mirabal
Andrew L. Tiajoloff

SENIOR ATTORNEYS

Jeffrey W. Berkman
Dean J. M. Heitner
Deborah S. K. Jagoda
Noreen M. Lavan
Melissa Zelen Neier

ASSOCIATES

Eduardo N.T. Andrade
John M. Belbusti
David M. Berger
Christopher P. Bilski
Jonathan A. Bird
Sally S. Blinken
Livia Boyadjian
John E. Boyd
Jill I. Braverman
Brian Burns
Julie Min Chayet
Jennifer M. Chow
Margaret Civetta
James J. Cotter
Paul R. Dehmel
Gerard DiConza
Patricia M. Dineen
Anthony Q. Fletcher
Peter Scott Gold
Amalia G. Greco
James W. Harmon, Jr.
Pamela Christine Holly
Jonathan L. Hornik
Randa A. Jaafar
John C. Kelty
Galina A. Kirman
Erica D. Klein
Carole Klinger
Samuel M. Koda
Patricia Anne Kuhn
Brian J. McCarthy
Daniel E. McManus Jr.
Andrew McNeela
Theodore J. Mlynar
Frank E. Morreale
Arlene D. Morris
Ellen M. O'Toole
Edmund M. O'Toole
Richard E. Parke
Trevor H. Peterson
Jane E. Pinzow-Naidoff
Jeffrey P. Rosier
Risa I. Sackmary
Judi LaMountain Silverstein
Philip M. Smith
Ivy B. Stempel
William M. Sunkel
Christopher J. Wallace
Natalie L. Woodruff
Steven J. Young

LOS ANGELES, CALIFORNIA OFFICE
RESIDENT PARTNERS

Francis W. Costello
Richard A. Eastman
Douglas F. Galanter
James C. Hughes
Robert L. Ivey
Gerold W. Libby
Tasha D. Nguyen
Donald G. Norris (Not admitted in NY)
Maita Deal Prout
Shelly Rothschild
Mark S. Shipow
Fernando Villa
Richard T. Williams
Paul C. Workman

SENIOR ATTORNEY

Roger B. Coven

RESIDENT ASSOCIATES

Alex R. Baghdassarian
Bonnie Chavez
Jay J. Chung
Donald M. Clary
Vito A. Costanzo
Adam S. Hanski
J. Michelle Hickey
Jason J. Liberman
Toby Rose Mallen
Paul S. Marks
Ann Bridget McCarthy
Adam Charles Ritter
Jack S. Sholkoff
Douglas K. Simpson
Alan J. Watson

GREENWICH, CONNECTICUT OFFICE
PARTNERS

Charles E. Coates, III
James A. Fulton
Thomas F. Hartch
Richard F. Lawler
Anthony M. Macleod
Richard E. Mancuso
Robert C. O'Brien
Harry E. Peden, Jr.
Harry E. Peden, III
Charles W. Pieterse
James C. Riley
David P. Tuttle
Kevin A. Walsh

COUNSEL

Robert G. Krause (Not admitted in NY)
Michael B. Weir

RETIRED PARTNERS

Jacob R. Lynch

(See Next Column)

WHITMAN BREED ABBOTT & MORGAN LLP—*Continued*

RESIDENT ASSOCIATES

Ann Dudley Belknap
Margaret E. Conboy
Eric T. Kaplan
Margaret Ann Triolo

NEWARK, NEW JERSEY OFFICE
RESIDENT PARTNERS

Kevin F. Kostyn
David A. Roth

RESIDENT ASSOCIATES

Kathleen Pierce Desjourdy
Christina A. Rallo
James S. Richter

LONDON, ENGLAND OFFICE
(A MULTI-NATIONAL PARTNERSHIP)
MEMBERS OF FIRM

Graeme H. Clark
Jon H. I. Grouf
Michael J. McNulty
Berge Setrakian
Elton Shane

COUNSEL

Gordon L. Jaynes

TOKYO, JAPAN
RESIDENT PARTNER

Richard A. Eastman

For full biographical listings, see the Martindale-Hubbell Law Directory

WILLKIE FARR & GALLAGHER (AV)

The Equitable Center, 787 Seventh Avenue, 10019-6099
Telephone: 212-728-8000
Fax: 212-728-8111
Washington, D.C. Office: Three Lafayette Centre, 1155 21st Street, N.W., 20036-3384.
Telephone: 202-328-8000.
Fax: 202-887-8979; 202-331-8187.
Paris, France Office: 21-23 rue de la Ville l'Evêque, 75008.
Telephone: 011-33-1-53-43-45-00.
Fax: 011-33-1-40-06-96-06.
London, England Office: 35 Wilson Street, EC2M 2SJ.
Telephone: 011-44-171-696-9060.
Fax: 011-44-171-417-9191.

MEMBERS OF FIRM

Marc Abrams
Mitchell J. Auslander
Joseph T. Baio
William H. Barringer (Resident Partner, Washington, D.C. Office)
Stephen R. Bell (Resident Partner, Washington, D.C. Office)
Serge Benchetrit
Roger D. Blanc
Sue D. Blumenfeld (Resident Partner, Washington, D.C. Office)
John B. Cairns
Patrick J. Carmody
Thomas M. Cerabino
Kevin B. Clark (Resident Partner, Washington, D.C. Office)
Henry M. Cohn
Dale S. Collinson
Louis A. Craco
Jean-Luc Cuadrado (Resident Partner, Paris, France Office)
Mario M. Cuomo
John S. D'Alimonte
Frank A. Daniele
Monty Davis
John P. Dean (Resident Partner, Washington, D.C. Office)
Richard K. DeScherer
Dennis R. Deveney
Allard De Waal (Resident Partner, Paris, France Office)
Rose F. DiMartino
Christopher A. Dunn (Resident Partner, Washington, D.C. Office)
James P. Durling (Resident Partner, Washington, D.C. Office)
William N. Dye (Resident Partner, London, England Office)
Dwight W. Ellis III
Laurent Faugérolas (Resident Partner, Paris, France Office)
Matthew A. Feldman
David L. Foster
Michel Frieh (Resident Partner, Paris, France Office)
Alexander T. Galloway II
Steven J. Gartner
William J. Grant, Jr.
Stephen W. Greiner
Yaacov M. Gross
Dan S. Grossman
William H. Gump
Michael H. Hammer (Resident Partner, Washington, D.C. Office)
Peter J. Hanlon
William E. Hiller
Kelly M. Hnatt
Tonny K. Ho
Daniel Hurstel (Resident Partner, Paris, France Office)
Peter H. Jakes
Lawrence O. Kamin
Michael J. Kelly
Henry J. Kennedy
Peter J. Kenny
Robert J. Kheel
Christine M. Kim
Richard L. Klein
Steven D. Klein
Martin B. Klotz
Bruce R. Kraus
Jay F. Leary (Resident Partner, Paris, France Office)
Maurice M. Lefkort
Burton M. Leibert
Bernard Le-Pezron (Resident Partner, Paris, France Office)
Stephen T. Lindo
Alan J. Lipkin
Jeanne M. Luboja
Richard Mancino
Christopher E. Manno
Michael G. Marks
Leslie M. Mazza
David J. McCabe
Francis J. Menton, Jr.
Raymond W. Merritt
Bruce M. Montgomerie
David P. Murray (Resident Partner, Washington, D.C. Office)
Andrew W. Needham

(See Next Column)

MEMBERS OF FIRM (Continued)

Roger D. Netzer
Neil Novikoff
Jack H. Nusbaum
Brian E. O'Connor
John R. Oller
Steven M. Oster (Resident Partner, Washington, D.C. Office)
Daniel Payan (Resident Partner, Paris, France Office)
Annette Peron (Resident Partner, Paris, France Office)
Anthony F. Phillips
Kenneth J. Pierce (Resident Partner, Washington, D.C. Office)
Eugene A. Pinover
Richard L. Posen
Jon S. Rand
Richard L. Reinhold
Steven H. Reisberg
Benito Romano
William H. Rooney
Emmanuel Rosenfeld (Resident Partner, Paris, France Office)
Thomas M. Rothman
Daniel D. Rubino
Richard D. Rudder
Philippe M. Salomon
Richard C. Sammis
Anthony D. Schlesinger
Daniel Schloendorn
Peter W. Schmidt
Michael A. Schwartz
Steven A. Seidman
Harvey L. Sperry
Duncan J. Stewart
Elizabeth S. Stong
Myron Trepper
Douglas Ulene
Philip L. Verveer (Resident Partner, Washington, D.C. Office)
Nora Ann Wallace
Laurence D. Weltman
Brent W. White
Theodore C. Whitehouse (Resident Partner, Washington, D.C. Office)
David S. Wolin
Michael R. Young
Emily M. Zeigler

COUNSEL

Armando T. Belly
Walston S. Brown
Brian Conboy (Resident Partner, Washington, D.C. Office)
Noel Hemmendinger (Resident, Washington, D.C. Office)
Robert B. Hodes
Russell L. Smith (Resident, Washington, D.C. Office)

For full biographical listings, see the Martindale-Hubbell Law Directory

WILMER, CUTLER & PICKERING (AV㊉)

520 Madison Avenue, 10022
Telephone: 212-230-8800
Fax: 212-230-8888
Email: Law@Wilmer.Com *URL:* http://www.wilmer.com
Washington, D.C. Office: 2445 M Street, N.W., 20037-1420.
Telephone: 202-663-6000.
Fax: 202-663-6363. Internet: Law@Wilmer.Com.
Baltimore, Maryland Office: 100 Light Street, 21202.
Telephone: 410-986-2800.
Fax: 410-986-2828.
European Offices:
4 Carlton Gardens, London, SW1Y 5AA, England. Telephone: +44 (20) 7 872 1000.
Fax: +44 (20) 7 839 3537.
Rue de la Loi 15# Wetstraat, B-1040 Brussels, Belgium. Telephone: +32 (2)285 49 00.
Fax: +32 (2) 285 49 49.
Friedrichstrasse 95, D-10117 Berlin, Germany. Telephone: +49 (30) 20 22 64 00.
Fax: +49 (30) 20 22 65 00.

PARTNER

Lewis J. Liman

ASSOCIATES

Franca E. Harris
Matthew P. Previn

For full biographical listings, see the Martindale-Hubbell Law Directory

WINDELS, MARX, DAVIES & IVES (AV)

156 West 56th Street, 10019
Telephone: 212-237-1000
Facsimile: 212-262-1215
New Brunswick, New Jersey Office: 120 Albany Street Plaza.
Telephone: 732-846-7600.
Facsimile: 732-846-8877.
Stamford, Connecticut Office: Six Landmark Square.
Telephone: 203-359-5678.
Facsimile: 203-359-5878.

MEMBERS OF FIRM

Thomas A. Banahan
Eric W. Bruenner
Anthony R. Coscia
Anthony A. Dean
Daniel V. Duff, Jr.
Mitchell A. Gilbert
Walter F. X. Healy
Arthur E. Hoffmann, Jr.
Susan F. Jennison
R. Scott Johnston
Keelin Kavanagh
John M. Kriz
Howard P. Lakind
Jeffrey S. Levin
John J. McDermott
Michael M. Moriarty
Thomas J. Mulligan
Craig P. Murphy
Edward P. Nolan
James J. Periconi
Francis J. Quinn
Robert A. Rossi
James M. Shaughnessy
Edward E. Shea
Charles E. Simpson
Mark A. Slama
Robert D. Taisey
James J. Thomas

(See Next Column)

WINDELS, MARX, DAVIES & IVES, *New York—Continued*

COUNSEL

Paul Windels, Jr.
Raymond T. Munsell
James P. Conroy
John Yeatman Taggart

SPECIAL COUNSEL

Deborah H. Bindler
Daniel Pocchiari
Clifford H. Stein

Henry M. Marx (1908-1984)
Julien T. Davies (1895-1978)
Dermod Ives (1904-1992)

ASSOCIATES

Donna M. Alkin
Wendy H. Lee
Michele M. Arbeeny
Matthew T. McLaughlin
Joseph P. Augustine
Ann Ryan
F. Robert Brusco
Amanda F. Shechter
Gary F. Eisenberg
Douglas A. Stevinson
Tina J. Eisman
Catherine Sun
Matthew C. Frost
Kimberly O. Wise (Not admitted in NY)
Leonard A. LaBarbiera

For full biographical listings, see the Martindale-Hubbell Law Directory

WINSTON & STRAWN (AV)

200 Park Avenue, 10166-4193
Telephone: 212-294-6700
Telecopier: 212-294-4700
Cable Address: "Coledeitz, NYK"
Telex: (RCA) 232459
Email: postmaster@winston.com *URL:* http://www.winston.com
Chicago, Illinois Office: 35 West Wacker Drive, 60601.
Telephone: 312-558-5600.
Cable Address: "Winston Chicago".
Facsimile: 312-558-5700.
Washington, D.C. Office: 1400 L Street, N.W., 20005-3502.
Telephone: 202-371-5700.
Telecopier: 202-371-5950.
Telex: 440574 INTLAW UI.
Los Angeles, California Office: 444 South Flower, 10th Floor, 90071-2911.
Telephone: 213-615-1700.
Geneva, Switzerland Office: 43 Rue du Rhone, 1204.
Telephone: +41-22 317 75 75.
Fax: +41-22 317 75 00
Paris, France Office: 21 Avenue Victor Hugo, 75116.
Telephone: 331-5364-8282.
Fax: 331-5364-8220.

MEMBERS OF FIRM

Robert W. Ericson (Resident)
Robert Everett Bostrom (Resident)
Richard B. Teiman (Resident)
Daniel R. Murdock (Resident)
Anthony J. D'Auria (Resident)
Steven H. Epstein (Resident)
Jonathan Goldstein (Resident)
William A. Kapell (Resident)
Joseph A. DiBenedetto (Resident)
Nelson Kyunam Ahn (Resident)
Jeffrey H. Elkin (Resident)
John W. Kaufmann (Resident)
Robert Scott Edmonds (Resident)
Robert M. Buschmann (Resident)
James J. Terry (Resident)
Christoph C. Heisenberg (Resident)
Susan Berkwitt-Malefakis (Resident)
Daniel A. Ninivaggi (Not admitted in NY; Resident)
Robert S. Fischler (Resident)
James P. Corcoran (Resident)
John C. Phelan (Resident)
Louise Rembar Radin (Resident)
Thomas J. Quigley (Resident)
Susan F. Klein (Resident)
Norman Newman (1952-1998)
James A. Beha II (Resident)
Anthony F. LoFrisco (Resident)
Peter E. Calamari (Resident)
William D. Brewer (Resident)
Edward G. H. Chin (Resident)
Andrea L. Flink (Resident)
Jay A. Dorsch (Resident)
Derek G. P. Mackenzie (Resident)
David B. Hertzog (Resident)
Lori J. Van Auken (Resident)
Angelo P. Lopresti (Resident)
Susan Schenkel-Savitt (Resident)
David E. Mollón (Resident)
William A. Carmell (Resident)
Anthony L. Paccione (Resident)
Anthony DiSarro (Resident)
Steven M. Schwartz (Resident)
Robert C. Miller (Resident)
Joseph A. Adams
Alan B. Howard (Resident)
Manes M. Merrit

RESIDENT OF COUNSEL

Robert E. Lesser (Resident)
Morris N. Simkin (Resident)
Ivan O. Kline
Kenneth L. Spangler
Kathleen A. Drapeau

RESIDENT SENIOR ATTORNEYS

Barry L. Salkin
J. David Reich, Jr. (Resident)

RESIDENT ASSOCIATES

Tracey Allison
Lana C. Fleishman
Lauren J. Bernstein
David Florendo
D. Morgan Burkett
Gretchen Fritz
Linda Cavanna-Wilk
Karen Geiss
Kevin J. Cooper
Emily Fisk Giffin
Catriona M. Cullinane (Not admitted in NY)
Nellie Gilligan
Gary B. Glass
Philip K. Davidoff
Robert B. Grotch
Catherine DiFiglia
Andrew T. Hahn

(See Next Column)

RESIDENT ASSOCIATES (Continued)

Ming-Hsiu (Mark) Huang (Not admitted in NY)
Mayer Naiman
Travis N. Jensen
Christopher M. Nolan (Not admitted in NY)
John G. Kalyvas
Louis C. Katsoris
Rachel A. Nuzzo
James J. Killerlane III
Krishna Patel (Not admitted in NY)
Ann Redlich Koppel (Not admitted in NY)
Elyse Pepper
Maria Rabinovich
Peter L. Korn, Jr.
Anne-Marie P. Rae
R. Alexander Lake, Jr.
Harlee A. Richmond
Edwin M. Larkin
Eric M. Robinson (Not admitted in NY)
Jonathan H. Lewis
Kevin D. Lewis
Nathan John Sawaya
Patricia S. Lociciro
Adam J. Schlatner
Stephen J. Malone (Not admitted in NY)
Jane L. Siegel
Gerald D. Silver
James E. Marina
Lina M. Viviano
Jean M. Migdal
Adam M. Walsh
Ana T. Miranda (Not admitted in NY)
Allyson Dee Wenig
Stacy Yakaboski
David A. Zeitlin

STAFF ATTORNEY

Monika V. Szabo (Not admitted in NY)

For full biographical listings, see the Martindale-Hubbell Law Directory

WINTHROP, STIMSON, PUTNAM & ROBERTS (AV)

One Battery Park Plaza, 10004-1490
Telephone: 212-858-1000
Telex: 62854 WINSTIM
Telefax: 212-858-1500
URL: http://www.winstim.com
Stamford, Connecticut Office: Financial Centre, 695 East Main Street, P.O. Box 6760, 06904-6760.
Telephone: 203-348-2300.
Fax: 203-965-8226.
Washington, D.C. Office: 1133 Connecticut Avenue, N.W., 20036.
Telephone: 202-775-9800.
Fax: 202-833-8491.
Palm Beach, Florida Office: 125 Worth Avenue, Suite 310, 33480.
Telephone: 561-655-7297.
Fax: 561-833-6726.
London Office: 54 Lombard Street, London EC3V 9DH, England.
Telephone: 011-44207-648-9200.
Fax: 011-44207-283-1656.
Tokyo, Japan Office: 608 Atagoyama Bengoshi Building 6-7, Atago 1-chome, Minato-ku, Tokyo 105 Japan.
Telephone: 011-813-3437-9740.
Fax: 011-813-3437-9261.
Hong Kong, China Office: 2505 Asia Pacific Finance Tower, Citibank Plaza, 3 Garden Road, Central.
Telephone: 011-852-2530-3400.
Fax: 011-852-2530-3355.
Singapore Office: 6 Battery Road #38-01/B, Singapore 049909.
Telephone: 65-227-4700.
Fax: 65-227-4711.

Bronson Winthrop (1893-1944)
Albert W. Putnam (1904-1955)
Henry L. Stimson (1893-1950)
George Roberts (1914-1968)

NEW YORK OFFICE
MEMBERS OF FIRM

Kenneth E. Adelsberg
Caroline A. Harcourt
Takeo Akiyama
Richard L. Harden
A. Elisabeth André de la Porte-Hooykaas
Mark R. Hellerer
J. Portis Hicks
Andrew J. Bernstein
Lori S. Hoberman
Richard H. Block
Peter J. Hunt
Carol Seabrook Boulanger
Sutton Keany
William C. Bowers
David G. Keyko
L. Crawford Brickley, Jr.
Susan J. Kohlmann
Frederick A. Brodie
William C. F. Kurz
William L. Burke
Stephen Lefkowitz
John H. Byington, Jr.
David M. Lindley
P. Joseph Campisi, Jr.
Daniel J. McSwiggan
James T. Chudy
E. Leo Milonas
Thomas F. Clauss, Jr.
Harold S. Nathan
Richard G. Cohen
Kent S. Nevins
C. Payson Coleman, Jr.
F. Joseph Owens, Jr.
Leo T. Crowley
Jerry P. Peppers
Michael F. Cusick
John F. Pritchard
Hugh M. Dougan
Stephen R. Rusmisel
Philip Le B. Douglas
Michael P. Schumaecker
Todd W. Eckland
Craig M. Scully
Richard L. Epling
Susan P. Serota
David P. Falck
Leslie E. Shigaki
Edward Flanders
Glenn E. Siegel
Ronald A. Fleming, Jr.
James R. Silkenat
Barton D. Ford
Robin L. Spear
Arthur H. Fredston
Jane Wallison Stein
Max Friedman
Michael V. Sterlacci
Elizabeth H. W. Fry
Timothy M. Toy
Robert W. Gray
Charles H. Vejvoda

(See Next Column)

WINTHROP, STIMSON, PUTNAM & ROBERTS—*Continued*

NEW YORK OFFICE
MEMBERS OF FIRM (Continued)

Robert D. Webster
Stephen A. Weiner
Edwin J. Wesely
Jonathan B. Whitney

COUNSEL

Adrienne W. Bernard
Jonathan H. Churchill
Edward S. Cowen
Glen R. Cuccinello
R. Jay Fortin
Thomas D. Lee
Daniel A Lowenthal III
Ujwala Mahatme
Melanie E. Meyers
Sheila AnnMarie Moeller
Peter S. Smedresman

SENIOR COUNSEL

Allison Choate
Merrell E. Clark, Jr.
John S. Russell, Jr.
Robert Anthoine
William W. Karatz
John B. Jessup
Douglas F. Williamson, Jr.
William M. Evarts, Jr.
Philip G. Hull
A. Edward Grashof
Stephen K. Waite
Ruth Joseph Weinstein

STAMFORD OFFICE
MEMBERS OF FIRM

Thomas F. Clauss, Jr.
Frode Jensen
Kent S. Nevins
Robert J. Rawn
G. William Sisley

STAMFORD OFFICE
COUNSEL

Arthur W. Hooper, Jr.

LONDON OFFICE
MEMBERS OF FIRM

Peter S. Brown
John D. White

PALM BEACH OFFICE
MEMBERS OF FIRM

William D. McEachern
Michael V. Sterlacci

PALM BEACH OFFICE
COUNSEL

John C. Dotterrer

SENIOR COUNSEL

Howard J. Falcon, Jr.
Philip G. Hull
Douglas F. Williamson, Jr.

SINGAPORE OFFICE
MEMBER OF FIRM

L. Crawford Brickley, Jr.

WASHINGTON, D.C. OFFICE
MEMBERS OF FIRM

Isaac D. Benkin
Donald A. Carr
John E. Gillick
Gerald D. Morgan, Jr.
Kenneth P. Quinn
Mary Ann Walker
Christopher R. Wall

WASHINGTON, D.C.
COUNSEL

Roy G. Bowman
Marvin T. Griff
Aileen Meyer
C. Christopher Parlin
Peter S. Watson

TOKYO OFFICE
MEMBER OF FIRM

Jeffrey L. Pote

HONG KONG, CHINA OFFICE
MEMBERS OF FIRM

Yeow Ming Choo
Andrew H. Lo

NEW YORK ASSOCIATES

Robert T. Abramson
Shinya Akiyama
Paul W. Ambrosius
Alexei Auld
Robert E. Bailey
John J. Battaglia
Edmund T. Baumgartner
Anne C. Bederka
Kristi Payne Benitez
Lourdes J. Blanco
David M. Boyhan
Kerry Ann Brennan
Donovan W. Burke
Melissa S. Burke
Michael Burnstein
Emily Campbell
James Chung
David A. Crichlow
John E. Davis
Jeffrey J. Delaney
Karen B. Dine
Joseph W. Downs, IV
Bryan R. Dunlap
Mark B. Dunshee
David Early-Hubelbank
Margot Erlich
Eric Fishman
Valerie L. Fitch
John S. Fronduti
Lourdes Gadioma
Jason A. Grossman
Eric W. Hager
Apryl E. Hand
Audrey E. Haroz
Kenneth L. Hatton (Not admitted in the United States) (Legal Consultant on the Laws of Ireland)
George Januzzi
Enid D. Jean-Claude
Randi F. Kassover
Patricia A. Killian
Avery Ben-Zion Kotler
Elisabeth L'Heureux
David R. Lagasse
Barry Langman
Aline M. Laranja (Not admitted in the United States) (Legal Consultant on the Laws of Brazil)
Jennifer A. Larrabee
James R. Levine

(See Next Column)

NEW YORK ASSOCIATES (Continued)

Donna Li
Li Li
Elizabeth G. Livingston
Pierre-Louis Lydie
Thomas D. Lynn
Thomas W. Maddi
Margaret V. Malone
Armando J. Martinez (Not admitted in the United States) (Legal Consultant on the Laws of Mexico)
Laurie E. Meyers
Yoram J. Miller
Daniel Z. Mollin
Hazel A.W. Mukuna
Mark S. Munro
Karen L. Nachbar
Fusae Nara
Veronica O. Ng (Not admitted in the United States) (Legal Consultant on the Laws of England and Wales and Singapore)
Barbara Jean O'Connor
Charlotta Otterbeck
Elizabeth J. Philp
Erin E. Raccah
Douglas J. Ray
Stephanie L. Ray
Sheryl L. Reba
Harsha Reddy
Michael P. Reed (Not admitted in the United States) (Legal Consultant on the Laws of Canada)
Lynn M. Ryan
Stacey Sabo
Michelle Selig
Patricia A. Spraguer
Shirley Staples
Meredith L. Steigman
Eric T. Streck
Jing-Kai Syz
Takemi Ueno
Nancy Stanger Wood
Shaokun S. Xiang
Grace Sing-Fein Yeh
Andrew J. Yonteff
Marie-Anne Zabrocki (Not admitted in NY)

For full biographical listings, see the Martindale-Hubbell Law Directory

---

ZANE AND RUDOFSKY (AV)

A Partnership including Professional Corporations
Carnegie Hall Tower, 152 West 57th Street, 10019
Telephone: 212-245-2222
Fax: (212) 541-5555 and (212) 541-6666
Easylink: 6284-5474
MCI Mail: 258-4388
Telex: 31-7465
Cable Address: "Zanelex"
Voice Mail: 212-541-4444
Email: info@zrlex.com *URL:* http://www.zrlex.com

MEMBERS OF FIRM

James B. Zane (P.C.)
Edward S. Rudofsky (P.C.)
Eric S. Horowitz

COUNSEL

Arlene H. Schechter

For full biographical listings, see the Martindale-Hubbell Law Directory

---

NYACK, Rockland Co.

MACCARTNEY, MACCARTNEY, KERRIGAN & MACCARTNEY (AV)

MacCartney Building, 13 North Broadway, P.O. Box 350, 10960
Telephone: 914-358-0074
Fax: 914-358-0793

MEMBERS OF FIRM

Harold Y. MacCartney (1901-1988)
Harold Y. MacCartney, III (1968-1996)
Harold Y. MacCartney, Jr.
John D. MacCartney
William K. Kerrigan

Representative Clients: Action Auto Rental, Inc.; American Fidelity; American International Adjusting Co.; The Andover Cos.; Associated Mutual Insurance Company; Atlantic Mutual Ins. Co.; Avis Rent a Car; Bay State Insurance; Callicoon Co-operative Insurance Company; Cambridge Mutual Fire Insurance Company.

For full biographical listings, see the Martindale-Hubbell Law Directory

---

OLEAN, Cattaraugus Co.

DICERBO & PALUMBO (AV)

410 Community Bank Building, 201 North Union Street, 14760
Telephone: 716-373-2165
Fax: 716-373-5180
Email: dicepalu@eznet.net

MEMBERS OF FIRM

Nicholas A. DiCerbo
Daniel R. Palumbo

Reference: Community Bank N.A., Olean, New York.

For full biographical listings, see the Martindale-Hubbell Law Directory

---

ONEONTA, Otsego Co.

GETMAN LAW FIRM (AV)

16 Dietz Street, P.O. Box 613, 13820
Telephone: 607-432-3530
Fax: 607-432-3571
Email: getmanlw@wpe.com

(See Next Column)

GETMAN LAW FIRM, *Oneonta—Continued*

Frank W. Getman Michael F. Getman

References: Key Bank of New York; Wilber National Bank Oneonta, N.Y.

For full biographical listings, see the Martindale-Hubbell Law Directory

OSSINING, Westchester Co.

DALY LAVERY & HALL (AV)

73 Croton Avenue, Suite 209, 10562
Telephone: 914-941-7000
Fax: 914-941-0877

MEMBERS OF FIRM

Hugh A. Lavery (1906-1986)
Emanuel Lauterbach (1899-1989)
John E. Babchak Jr. (1925-1992)
William J. Daly
H. Glen Hall

OF COUNSEL

Hugh A. Lavery, Jr.

Reference: The Bank of New York.

For full biographical listings, see the Martindale-Hubbell Law Directory

*PLATTSBURGH,** Clinton Co.

LEWIS, ROGERS & KUDRLE, P.C. (AV)

53 Court Street, 12901-2834
Telephone: 518-561-3700
Fax: 518-561-2080
Email: lrk@westelcom.com *URL:* http://www.lawyers.com/lrklaw

Clyde A. Lewis
Mark J. Rogers
Larry A. Kudrle
Harold A. Jerry (1893-1990)
Robert A. Lyon (1924-1982)

Attorneys for: Graystone Materials, Inc.; Plattsburgh Motor Service Inc.; The Development Corporation, Clinton County, New York.

For full biographical listings, see the Martindale-Hubbell Law Directory

*POUGHKEEPSIE,** Dutchess Co.

HANKIN, HANIG, STALL, CAPLICKI, REDL & CURTIN, LLP (AV)

319 Main Mall Rear, P.O. Box 911, 12602-0911
Telephone: 914-471-7177
FAX: 914-471-0105
Email: hhscrc@aol.com *URL:* http://www.hvlaw.com
Newburgh, New York Office: 6 Jeanne Drive, P.O. Box 7229, 12550.
Telephone: 914-566-8888.
Fax: 914-566-3886.
LaGrangeville, New York Office: Lexington Park, Route 55, P.O. Box 15, LaGrangeville, New York.
Telephone: 914-473-1200.

MEMBERS OF FIRM

Jerard S. Hankin
Joel D. Hanig
Todd S. Stall
Edmund V. Caplicki, Jr.
Frank E. Redl
Daniel F. Curtin

Lynn M. Smookler
David V. Hasin

For full biographical listings, see the Martindale-Hubbell Law Directory

MCCABE & MACK LLP (AV)

63 Washington Street, P.O. Box 509, 12602-0509
Telephone: 914-486-6800
FAX: 914-485-6971
Email: info@mccm.com *URL:* http://www.mccm.com

MEMBERS OF FIRM

John E. Mack (1874-1958)
Joseph A. McCabe (1890-1973)
Joseph C. McCabe (1925-1981)
Edward J. Mack (1910-1998)
J. Joseph McGowan
Michael A. Hayes, Jr.
Harold L. Mangold
Richard A. Mitchell
David L. Posner
Martin P. Rutberg
Ellen L. Baker
Scott D. Bergin
Richard R. DuVall
Lance N. Portman

OF COUNSEL

Phillip Shatz
John Howley
Jay P. Rolison, Jr.

Jessica Lynn Vinall
M. Randolph Belkin
Matthew V. Mirabile
Elizabeth R. Baum
Laura M. Rapacioli
Christina M. Bookless

Representative Clients: Marine Midland Bank; Central Hudson Gas & Electric Corp.; Associates Commercial Corp.; Amica Mutual Insurance Co.; McDonald's Corp.; Hanover Insurance Co.; Liberty Mutual Insurance Co.; Manufacturers and Traders Trust Co.; Vassar College; County of Dutchess.

For full biographical listings, see the Martindale-Hubbell Law Directory

VAN DEWATER & VAN DEWATER (AV)

40 Garden Street, P.O. Box 112, 12602
Telephone: 914-452-5900
Fax: 914-452-5848
Pawling, New York Office: 243 Route 22, P.O. Box 668.
Telephone: 914-855-5900.
Fax: 914-855-5945.

MEMBERS OF FIRM

John B. Van DeWater (1892-1968)
Robert B. Van DeWater (1920-1990)
David D. Hagstrom
John K. Gifford
James E. Nelson
Craig T. Digilio
Gerard J. Comatos
Ronald C. Blass, Jr.

OF COUNSEL

Noel deCordova, Jr.
Edward VK. Cunningham, Jr.
James D. Benson
Susanna E. Bedell

ASSOCIATES

Rebecca Supple Mensch
Michael G. Hayes

Counsel for: J. D. Johnson Co., Inc.; The Fishkill National Bank; The Bank of the Hudson; Vassar Brothers Hospital.
Local Counsel for: Vassar College; Chemprene Div. of Witco Chemical Corp.; Gannett Satellite Information Network, Inc.

For full biographical listings, see the Martindale-Hubbell Law Directory

PURCHASE, Westchester Co.

GIOFFRE & GIOFFRE, PROFESSIONAL CORPORATION (AV)

2900 Westchester Avenue Suite 206, 10577
Telephone: 914-696-3800
Fax: 914-696-3833

Bruno J. Gioffre
Lisa Gioffre Baird

Anthony B. Gioffre, III
Russell A. Giorno

Representative Clients: Sound Federal Savings & Loan Assn.; Port Chester Public Library; Rye Town Hilton Inn; Westchester Business Institute.

For full biographical listings, see the Martindale-Hubbell Law Directory

*RIVERHEAD,** Suffolk Co.

SMITH, FINKELSTEIN, LUNDBERG, ISLER AND YAKABOSKI, LLP (AV)

456 Griffing Avenue, P.O. Box 389, 11901
Telephone: 516-727-4100
Telecopier: 516-727-4130
Email: sfliy@peconic.net

Reginald C. Smith (1897-1983)

MEMBERS OF FIRM

Howard M. Finkelstein
Pierre G. Lundberg
Francis J. Yakaboski
Frank A. Isler
Susan Rogers Grun
Gair G. Betts
Matthew M. Finkelstein

ASSOCIATE

Dawn C. Thomas

General Counsel for: Suffolk County National Bank; Riverhead Central, Remsenburg-Speonk, East Moriches and Southampton Union Free School Districts; East Quoque, Flanders and Jamesport Fire Districts.
Local Counsel for: Village of Ocean Beach; Towns of Southhold and Riverhead; American Pulverizer, Inc.; Chips & Bits, Inc.; Reynolds Aluminum, Inc.

For full biographical listings, see the Martindale-Hubbell Law Directory

*ROCHESTER,** Monroe Co.

BECKERMAN & BECKERMAN, LLP (AV)

1 West Main Street Four Corners Building, Suite 300, 14614
Telephone: 716-546-6010
Facsimile: 716-546-7035

MEMBERS OF FIRM

David S. Beckerman (1958-1997)
Gerald Beckerman
Steven M. Beckerman

ASSOCIATE

Elizabeth J. Jewett-Owen

Reference: Marine Midland Bank, Rochester.

For full biographical listings, see the Martindale-Hubbell Law Directory

CONNORS & CORCORAN, L.L.P. (AV)

Suite 250, 45 Exchange Street, 14614-2002
Telephone: 716-232-5885
Fax: 716-546-3631
Email: buholtz@frontiernet.net *URL:* http://www.connorscorcoran.com

(See Next Column)

CONNORS & CORCORAN L.L.P.—*Continued*

MEMBERS OF FIRM

Herbert J. LePage
Roger W. Avery
Joseph G. Fritsch, Jr.
James E. Maslyn
Eileen E. Buholtz
Cheryl Loria-Dinolfo
Gregory T. Phillips

Attorneys for: Allstate Insurance Co.; Continental National American Group; Criterion Insurance Co.; General Accident Group; Ideal Mutual Insurance Co.; Prudential Property & Casualty Co.; SAFECO; Sentry Insurance; Travelers Property Casualty.
Reference: Marine Midland Bank.

For full biographical listings, see the Martindale-Hubbell Law Directory

LACY, KATZEN, RYEN & MITTLEMAN, LLP (AV)

The Granite Building, 130 East Main Street, 14604
Telephone: 716-454-5650
FAX: 716-454-6525
Email: MSS@Frontiernet.net
Charlotte, New York Office: 4292 Lake Avenue.
Telephone: 716-663-4543.
Hilton, New York Office: 20 Main Street.
Telephone: 716-392-2990.
Canandaigua, New York Office: 23 North Main Street.
Telephone: 716-394-5220.
Greece, New York Office: County Village Center, 110 Long Pond Road, Suite 214.
Telephone: 716-225-2470.
Fax: 716-225-5620.
Bergen, New York Office: 16 North Lake Street.
Telephone: 716-494-1382.
Ontario, New York Office: 1276 Ridge Road.
Telephone: 315-524-5000.
Roseland, New Jersey Office: 103 Eisenhower Parkway.
Telephone: 201-403-8001.
Penn Yan, New York Office: 116 Main Street, 2nd Floor, P.O. Box 439.
Telephone: 315-536-6281.

MEMBERS OF FIRM

Louis A. Ryen
Ronald A. Mittleman
Michael S. Schnittman
Peter T. Rodgers
Sally A. Smith
Karen Schaefer
Richard G. Curtis
Lawrence J. Schwind
David H. Walsh IV
David E. Anderson
Craig R. Welch
Christopher B. Mumford
Leslie W. Kernan, Jr.

COUNSEL

Leon Katzen
George F. Frey, Jr.
John J. Keigher
Paul A. Sandars, III

ASSOCIATES

David D. MacKnight
Nia J. Nichols
Terrance W. Emmens
Mark H. Stein
Denine K. Carr
Jacqueline M. Thomas
Stephen M. O'Neill
Jennifer Lynn Chadwick
William H. Drumm
Matthew A. Ryen
Roxanne A. Marvasti
Julie E. Meyer

General Counsel for: Village of Bergen, Bergen, New York; Village of Hilton, Hilton, New York; Byron-Bergen Central School District No. 1, Bergen, New York; Ferris Industries, Inc.; L. Woerner, Inc.d/b/a HCR.
Reference: The Chase Manhattan Bank, Rochester, N.Y.

For full biographical listings, see the Martindale-Hubbell Law Directory

NIXON PEABODY LLP (AV)

Clinton Square, P.O. Box 1051, 14603
Telephone: 716-263-1000
FAX: 716-263-1600
Email: nixonpeabody@nixonpeabody.com *URL:* http://www.nixonpeabody.com
New York, N.Y. Office: 437 Madison Avenue.
Telephone: 212-940-3000.
Fax: 212-940-3111.
Washington, D.C. Office: 1255 23rd Street, N.W.
Telephone: 716-263-1000.
Fax: 716-263-1600.
Other Washington, D.C. Office: Suite 700, One Thomas Circle.
Telephone: 202-457-5300.
Fax: 202-457-5355.
Albany, New York Office: One Omni Plaza, 30 South Pearl Street.
Telephone: 518-427-2650.
Fax: 518-427-2666.
Garden City, New York Office: 990 Stewart Avenue.
Telephone: 516-832-7500.
Fax: 516-832-7555.
Buffalo, New York Office: 1600 Main Place Tower.
Telephone: 716-853-8100.
Fax: 716-853-8109.
Hartford, Connecticut Office: City Place, 185 Asylum Street.
Telephone: 860-275-6820.
Fax: 860-275-6821.

(See Next Column)

Boston, Massachusetts Office: 101 Federal Street.
Telephone: 617-345-1000.
Fax: 617-345-1300.
Manchester, New Hampshire Office: 889 Elm Street.
Telephone: 603-628-4000.
Fax: 603-628-4040.
Providence, Rhode Island Office: One Citizens Plaza.
Telephone: 401-454-1000.
Fax: 401-454-1030.

T. Carl Nixon (1890-1967)
Thomas J. Hargrave (1891-1962)
Frank E. Devans (1893-1978)
Justin J. Doyle (1904-1990)

RETIRED PARTNERS

Julian W. Atwater
Edward J. Burns
Philip F. Cronin, Jr.
Richard S. Fischer
William T. French
Kenneth I. Greenstein
Alexander D. Hargrave
William B. Lee
John B. McCrory
Ned W. Roman
John R. Tyler, Jr.
Sterling L. Weaver

PARTNERS

Bruce J. Baker
John K. Bouman
William S. Brandt
Robert W. Burgdorf
Andrew M. Burns
Robert Barnes Calihan
Margaret A. Clemens
Thomas E. Clement
Dwight R. Collin
David L. Cook
Michael J. Cooney
Scott F. Cristman
Thomas S. D'Antonio
Henry J. DePippo
Thomas G. Dignan (Resident at Garden City, N.Y. Office)
Justin P. Doyle
Peter H. Durant
John T. Fitzgerald, Jr.
Brian G. Flanagan
Allan E. Floro
Lyell G. Galbraith
John L. Garrett
Richard N. George
Michael L. Goldman
Lori B. Green
Thomas C. Greiner, Jr.
Elliott W. Gumaer, Jr.
Michael A. Hausknecht
David L. Hoffberg
John B. Hood
Ernest J. Ierardi
Cynthia MacBride Kellner
Francis E. Kenny
James D. Kole
Harold A. Kurland
James A. Locke III
B. G. Staffan Lundback
Patrick D. Martin
Jean H. McCreary
John R. McQueen
Patrice B. Morrison
Judith M. Norman
Gail M. Norris
Carolyn G. Nussbaum
John C. Partigan
Deborah McLean Quinn
Kevin V. Recchia
Thomas E. Reidy
Susan S. Robfogel
Richard D. Rochford, Jr.
David M. Schraver
Jill K. Schultz
Jon L. Schumacher
John Stuart Smith
Sue Stern Stewart
David H. Tennant
William S. Thomas, Jr.
Harry P. Trueheart III
Scott M. Turner
Eugene D. Ulterino
G. Joseph Votava, Jr.
Eric J. Ward
William F. Weir
Stanley W. Widger, Jr.
Robert W. Wild
G. Robert Witmer, Jr.
John D. Witmeyer
Jeffrey G. Wright
Richard T. Yarmel

COUNSEL

Marion Blankopf
Roger Wayne Byrd
Nancy T. Holtby

ASSOCIATES

Johanna Viglucci Bartlett
John C. Beisheim
Robert J. Bird, Jr.
D. Eric Black
Valerie Curry Bradley
Tracy L. Brown
Stephanie M. Caffera
Dana K. Campbell
Georgia Caton
Dennis Michael Connolly
Rafael A. Declet, Jr. (Resident at New York Office)
Cressida A. Dixon
Thomas M. Farace
Alycia A. Farley
Jonathan F. Garvin
Elyse Lubin Gilman
Isabel Guerra
Christian Hancey
Michael D. Kestan (Resident at New York Office)
J. Brian Kopp
Anthony T. Lee
Kathryn K. Lee
Gunnar G. Leinberg
David P. Leve
Regina Ciccone MacAdam
Brian P. Madrazo
Nicole M. Marro
Gregory J. Mascitti
Stanley J. Matusz
Kelly A. McCarthy
Richard A. McGuirk
Edwin V. Merkel
Kristen E. Mollnow
Mark A. Molloy (Resident at Buffalo, N.Y. Office)
Jay S. Mumford
Michael Fitzgerald Orman
J. Claire Razzolini
Jeffrey A. Rosenbloom
Christine A. Sackett
Todd R. Shinaman
Elaine M. Spaull
Patrick J. Solomon
Stacey L. Stritzel
Joyce J. Sun (Resident at New York Office)
Christopher D. Thomas
J. Nelson Thomas
Mark D. Whitaker
Andrew P. Zappia

For full biographical listings, see the Martindale-Hubbell Law Directory

Rochester—Continued

PHILLIPS, LYTLE, HITCHCOCK, BLAINE & HUBER LLP (AV)

1400 First Federal Plaza, 14614
Telephone: 716-238-2000
Telecopier: 716-232-3141
URL: http://www.phillipslytle.com
Buffalo, New York Office: 3400 HSBC Center.
Telephone: 716-847-8400.
Telecopier: 716-852-6100.
Jamestown, New York Office: 307 Chase Bank Building, 8 E. Third Street.
Telephone: 716-664-3906.
Telecopier: 716-664-4230.
New York, New York Office: 437 Madison Avenue.
Telephone: 212-759-4888.
Telecopier: 212-308-9079.
Fredonia, New York Office: 11 East Main Street.
Telephone: 716-672-2164.
FAX: 716-672-7979.

RESIDENT PARTNERS

Richard M. Beers, Jr.
Thomas R. Burns
Robert C. Johnson
Michael R. Law
Albert M. Mercury
Mark J. Moretti
Gerald L. Paley
Raymond L. Ruff
John T. Sullivan, Jr.
Paul A. Vick
Robert F. Zogas

SPECIAL COUNSEL

John L. DeMarco
Patricia A. Obstarczyk
Carl A. Steinbrenner

ASSOCIATES

James O. Bourdeau
James B. Doyle, III
Richard J. Evans, Jr.
Amy Levine Fici
Mark S. Gunther
Steven E. Laprade
Richard J. Mooney, III
Mary K. O'Connell
Lisa M. Powers
Linda Prestegaard
Chandy Z. Sweet

For full biographical listings, see the Martindale-Hubbell Law Directory

UNDERBERG & KESSLER LLP (AV)

1800 Chase Square, 14604
Telephone: 716-258-2800
Fax: 716-258-2821
Email: INFO@UNDERBERG-KESSLER.COM
Buffalo, New York Office: 1100 Main Place Tower. 14202.
Telephone: 716-848-9000.
Fax: 716-847-6004.

MEMBERS OF FIRM

Alan J. Underberg (1929-1998)
Irving L. Kessler
Michael J. Beyma
James A. Coniglio
Frank T. Crego
Robert W. Croessmann
John W. Crowe
Patrick L. Cusato
Michael C. Dwyer
Bernard A. Frank
Steven R. Gersz
Katherine Howk Karl
Lawrence P. Keller
Gordon J. Lipson
Anna E. Lynch
Robert F. Mechur
Paul V. Nunes
Terry M. Richman
J. David Sampson (Resident, Buffalo Office)
Sharon P. Stiller
Stephen H. Waite
Russell I. Zuckerman

OF COUNSEL

Andrew M. Greenstein

SENIOR ATTORNEYS

Duncan R. Farney
Ronald G. Hull

ASSOCIATES

James F. Armstrong (Resident, Buffalo Office)
Karen A. DiNardo
Lise C. Hamilton
Jeffrey D. Hummel
Paul F. Keneally
Ella L. Krzanowicz
Maureen E. Mulholland
Suzanne D. Nott
Kelly L. Odorisi
Thomas A. Rall

For full biographical listings, see the Martindale-Hubbell Law Directory

ROME, Oneida Co.

GRIFFITH LAW OFFICES (AV)

225 North Washington Street, 13440
Telephone: 315-336-6500
Fax: 315-336-6628
Email: griffi@aiusa.com *URL:* http://www.lawyers.com/griffith

MEMBER OF FIRM

Emlyn I. Griffith

Representative Clients: Alcan Aluminum Corporation; Camroden Associates, Inc.; C & H Plastics, Inc.; Covewood Mobile Park; D & H Asphalt Co., Inc.; Legendary Corp.; Statewide Funding Corp; Stonehedge Nursing Home.
Approved Attorneys for: The Title Guarantee Co.

For full biographical listings, see the Martindale-Hubbell Law Directory

PAUL L. PILECKAS (AV)

Professional Building, 217 North Washington Street, 13440
Telephone: 315-339-3020
Utica: 315-724-6381
Fax: 315-337-3876

Representative Clients: Don Davidson Motors, Inc.; Rome Rental, Inc.; West Electric, Inc.

For full biographical listings, see the Martindale-Hubbell Law Directory

ROSLYN HEIGHTS, Nassau Co.

NATISS, NATISS & GORDON, P.C. (AV)

277 Willis Avenue, 11577
Telephone: 516-621-0900
Telecopier: 516-621-1304
Email: MNatisslaw@aol.com

Marvin Natiss
Gary M. Natiss
Stacey Natiss Gordon

Sharon G. Haut

For full biographical listings, see the Martindale-Hubbell Law Directory

SCARSDALE, Westchester Co.

GLORIA CROWLEY MARKUSON (AV)

Scarsdale Law Center Building, 185 Summerfield Street, 10583
Telephone: 914-472-5600
Fax: 914-472-5605
Email: rdm8@aol.com *URL:* http://www.lawyers.com/gloriacrowleymarkuson

Reference: Bank of New York, County Trust Region.

For full biographical listings, see the Martindale-Hubbell Law Directory

STONY POINT, Rockland Co.

HURLEY, FOX, SELIG & KELLEHER (AV)

Liberty Building, Route 9 W, 10980
Telephone: 914-942-2222
Fax: 914-942-0378
Email: HFSKlaw@aol.com
New City, New York Office: 60 Pine Street.
Telephone: 614-634-2050.

MEMBERS OF FIRM

Benjamin E. Selig
Glenn W. Kelleher

ASSOCIATES

Steven L. Kahn
Dana Selig Kahn
Bob A. Kramer
Kenneth P. Silver

Representative Clients: Bradlees, Inc.; Stop & Shop Companies; CNA Insurance Cos.; Federal Insurance Co.; Chubb & Son; Commercial Union Group of Insurance Cos.; Empire Insurance Co.; Omaha, N.B.; Excelsior Insurance Co.; Fireman's Insurance Company of Washington, D.C.

For full biographical listings, see the Martindale-Hubbell Law Directory

*SYRACUSE,** Onondaga Co.

ALI, PAPPAS & COX, P.C. (AV)

Syracuse Building, 224 Harrison Street, 13202
Telephone: 315-472-4481
FAX: 315-472-8299
Email: alpaco@dreamscape.com

Lucien Ali
C. Andrew Pappas
Robert B. Cox
Thomas P. Givas
P. Douglas Dodd
David P. Doherty

OF COUNSEL

Edward F. Gerber

LEGAL SUPPORT PERSONNEL

Brenda M. Barch

Representative Clients: Agway, Inc.; Agway Petroleum Corp.; Arcom Labs; Countryside Federal Credit Union; PineCone Federal Credit Union; Oswego City Savings Bank; Telmark, Inc.; Syracuse Executive Air Services, Inc.; Fairbanks Capital Corp.
References: M&T Bank; 1st National Bank of Rochester.

For full biographical listings, see the Martindale-Hubbell Law Directory

CARROLL, CARROLL, DAVIDSON & YOUNG, P.C. (AV)

The Galleries of Syracuse, Second Floor, 441 South Salina Street, 13202-0352
Telephone: 315-474-5356
Fax: 315-474-5451

(See Next Column)

CARROLL, CARROLL, DAVIDSON & YOUNG P.C.—*Continued*

Lee Carroll
John Benjamin Carroll (P.C.)
Eugene B. Young
J. Alexander Davidson

Woodruff L. Carroll
Sarkis L. Harootunian

For full biographical listings, see the Martindale-Hubbell Law Directory

COSTELLO COONEY & FEARON, LLP (AV)

Salina Place, 205 South Salina Street, 13202
Telephone: 315-422-1152
Fax: 315-422-1139
Email: ccf-law.com *URL:* http://www.ccf-law.com

MEMBERS OF FIRM

David F. Costello (1872-1934)
Charles E. Cooney (1873-1958)
George R. Fearon (1883-1976)
Donald L. Nicholas
Warren W. Bader
Robert D. Essig
Kevin M. Gilligan
Robert J. Smith
Michael A. Tremont
Alicia S. Calagiovanni
James J. Gascon
Paul G. Ferrara
Maureen G. Fatcheric
Timothy J. Conan
John R. Langey
Daniel Fletcher

ASSOCIATES

Robert W. Connolly
W. Scott Gambee
David S. Grasso
Edmund J. Gegan
Louis J. Viviani
Michael P. McCarthy
Joseph N. Bulko
Edward G. Melvin
Lauren M. Mumford
Samuel C. Young

OF COUNSEL

Vincent A. O'Neil
Richard D. Hillman

General Counsel for: Auburn Memorial Hospital; Crouse Hospital; Health Services Association of Central New York; St. Joseph's Hospital Health Center.
Local Counsel for: Deere & Co.; New York Telephone Co.; Crum & Forster Insurance Co.; The Travelers Insurance Companies; Caterpillar, Inc.; Otis Elevator.

For full biographical listings, see the Martindale-Hubbell Law Directory

HANCOCK & ESTABROOK, LLP (AV)

MONY Tower 1, P.O. Box 4976, 13221-4976
Telephone: 315-471-3151
Telecopier: 315-471-3167
Email: DBYRNE@HANCOCKLAW.COM
Albany, New York Office: Suite 505, 125 Wolf Road.
Telephone: 518-458-7660.
Telecopier: 518-458-7731.

Stewart F. Hancock (1883-1966)
Theodore M. Hancock (1913-1988)
Lewis C. Ryan (1891-1961)
Charles S. Estabrook (1879-1975)
Benjamin E. Shove (1892-1977)
Morris Berman (1906-1987)
Joseph H. Murphy (1916-1986)
A. Van W. Hancock (1909-1993)
Charles H. Bassett (1915-1994)
Raymond A. Hust (1913-1997)

COUNSEL

W. Carroll Coyne
Stewart F. Hancock, Jr.
Kevin E. McCormack
Charles S. McGuire

MEMBERS OF FIRM

Paul M. Hanrahan
John R. Varney
William L. Allen, Jr.
Charles H. Umbrecht, Jr.
Walter L. Meagher, Jr.
Donald A. Denton
Raymond R. D'Agostino
J. Thomas Bassett
Richard W. Cook
David S. Howe
Gregory R. Thornton
Doreen A. Simmons
David E. Peebles
James J. Canfield
Gerald F. Stack
James E. Hughes
Jeffrey B. Andrus
Janet D. Callahan
Thomas C. Buckel, Jr.
Michael L. Corp
Daniel B. Berman
John T. McCann
Steven R. Shaw
David T. Garvey (Resident, Albany Office)
John L. Murad, Jr.
Stephen A. Donato
Kenneth P. Holden
Mark J. Schulte
Alan J. Pierce
R. John Clark
Renee L. James
David G. Linger
August E. Roehrig, Jr.
Michael A. Oropallo
Camille Wolnik Hill
Patrick M. Connors
Timothy P. Murphy
Marion Hancock Fish
Elizabeth A. Salvagno
Cora A. Alsante
Douglas H. Zamelis
Debra Chini Sullivan
Edward J. Smith III
Catherine A. Diviney
James R. Muldoon
Michael J. Sciotti
Eric C. Nordby
Peter V. White
John F. Corcoran
Cindy A. Granger
George R. McGuire
Charles J. Sullivan

(See Next Column)

ASSOCIATES

Rodney W. Jennings, Jr.
Sonya G. Bonneau
Wendy A. Marsh
J. Jay Guiliano
Lindsey Helmer Hazelton
Joseph T. Mancuso
Nicholas A. Scarfone
Michael J. Allan
Joshua D. Shorr

Representative Clients: HSBC; Crucible Materials Corp.; Mobil Oil Corp.; Syracuse City School District; Metropolitan Development Assoc.; Metropolitan Life Insurance Co.; Amerada Hess Corp.; Cooper Industries, Inc.; Carrier Corp.; LeMoyne College; Conmed; Crouse Hospital; Chrysler Corporation; Ryder Transportation Services, Inc.

For full biographical listings, see the Martindale-Hubbell Law Directory

HISCOCK & BARCLAY, LLP (AV)

Financial Plaza, P.O. Box 4878, 13221
Telephone: 315-422-2131
Fax: 315-472-3059
Email: reachus@hiscockbarclay.com *URL:* http://www.hiscockbarclay.com
Buffalo, New York Office: Suite 301 The Key Bank Towers at Key Center, 50 Fountain Plaza.
Telephone: 716-856-0911.
Fax: 716-856-2567.
Albany, New York Office: 40 Beaver Street.
Telephone: 518-434-2163.
Fax: 518-434-2621.

Frank H. Hiscock (1856-1946)

MEMBERS OF FIRM

H. Douglas Barclay
Taylor H. Obold
David B. Liddell
George S. Deptula
John P. Sindoni
Frederick S. Marty
Richard K. Hughes
J. Eric Charlton
Thomas S. Squire
Clifford H. Wilson
Robert A. Barrer
Christopher J. Bonner
Judith M. Sayles
Peter H. Swartz
John P. Langan
Catherine Keib Johnson
Richard J. Paul
Jon P. Devendorf
Richard R. Capozza

ASSOCIATES

Deborah A. Bentley
Alan R. Peterman
Kathleen M. O'Connor
Jennifer K. Frank
Matthew S. Moses
Christopher J. Centore
Jean K. Sehl
Bonnie Angela Buccina
Joseph P. McRae
Yvonne E. Marciano
Andrew J. Leja
William A. Barclay

OF COUNSEL

Donald M. Mawhinney, Jr.
Roger J. Edinger
Ferdinand L. Picardi
Jan R. Farr

General Counsel for: Syracuse Savings Bank; Key Corp; Key Bank of New York N.A. ; Solvay Bank; Excelsior Insurance Co.; Key Trust Co.; Auburn Steel Co., Inc.
Local Counsel for: Firestone Tire & Rubber Co.; Fidelity & Deposit Company of Maryland.

For full biographical listings, see the Martindale-Hubbell Law Directory

MELVIN & MELVIN, LLP (AV)

217 South Salina Street, Seventh Floor, 13202
Telephone: 315-422-1311
Telefax: 315-479-7612
Email: info@melvinlaw.com *URL:* http://www.melvinlaw.com/mmmenu.html

MEMBERS OF FIRM

Jonathan E. Fox
Roger W. Bradley
Robert S. Scalione
Ronald S. Carr
Louis Levine
Douglas H. Young
Richard M. Storto
Kenneth J. Bobrycki
Howard J. Woronov
Edward J. Sheats, Jr.
Susan E. Otto
Holly Salop Wallace
Mark N. Wladis

ASSOCIATES

Michael R. Vaccaro
Amy M. Bittner
Kelly A. Wales
Elizabeth A. Genung

COUNSEL

Louis Young
Domenic A. Mazza
William C. Fox
Merle D. Melvin
Charles R. Greiner

Special Counsel for: Manufacturers and Traders Trust Co. ; The Equitable Life Assurance Society of the United States; Government Employees Insurance Co.
Reference: Manufacturers and Traders Trust Company.

For full biographical listings, see the Martindale-Hubbell Law Directory

Syracuse—Continued

SMITH, SOVIK, KENDRICK & SUGNET, P.C. (AV)

250 South Clinton Street, Suite 600, 13202-1252
Telephone: 315-474-2911
Fax: 315-474-6015
URL: http://www.smithsovik.com

John Timothy Smith (1902-1964)
Nelson J. Smith (1923-1967)
Martin F. Kendrick (1917-1983)
Laurence Sovik (1904-1998)
Laurence F. Sovik
William E. Sugnet (Retired)
James A. O'Shea
James D. Lantier
Michael P. Ringwood
Peter J. Cambs
Kevin E. Hulslander
Thomas N. Kaufmann
Daniel A. Bronk
Steven W. Williams
Mary Kendrick-Gaffney
James W. Cunningham

Thomas P. Roerden
Robert P Cahalan
Denis J. Bastible
G. John Flemma
Theresa N. C. McCorry

OF COUNSEL

Gary A. Hall

For full biographical listings, see the Martindale-Hubbell Law Directory

---

*TROY,** Rensselaer Co.

E. STEWART JONES (AV)

28 Second Street, 12181
Telephone: 518-274-5820
Fax: 518-274-5875
Email: info@esjlaw.com

E. Stewart Jones, Jr.
W. Farley Jones
Jeffrey K. Anderson
David J. Taffany
Peter J. Moschetti, Jr.

OF COUNSEL

E. Stewart Jones
Arthur L. Rosen
Abbott H. Jones (1873-1939)
Charles W. Marshall (1882-1945)

References: Key Bank and On Bank; Troy Savings Bank.

For full biographical listings, see the Martindale-Hubbell Law Directory

---

UNIONDALE, Nassau Co.

RIVKIN, RADLER & KREMER LLP (AV)

A Partnership including Professional Corporations
EAB Plaza (Long Island), 11556-0111
Telephone: 516-357-3000
Cable Address: "Atlaw"
Telex: 645-074
Telecopier: 516-357-3333
URL: http://www.rivkinradler.com
Chicago, Illinois Office: Suite 4300, 30 North LaSalle Street.
Telephone: 312-782-5680.
Telecopier: 312-782-3112.
New York, New York Office: 275 Madison Avenue.
Telephone: 212-455-9555.
Telecopier: 212-687-9044.
Santa Rosa, California Office: 100 B Street, Suite 300, P.O. Box 14609.
Telephone: 707-525-5400.
Telecopier: 707-576-7955.
Newark, New Jersey Office: One Gateway Center, Suite 1226.
Telephone: 973-622-0900.
Fax: 973-622-7878.

MEMBERS OF FIRM

Arthur J. Kremer
Bruce D. Drucker (P.C.)
William M. Savino
Donald T. McMillan (Resident, Santa Rosa, California Office)
John L. Rivkin
Stephen J. Smirti, Jr. (P.C.)
Richard S. Feldman
Gary D. Centola
Anthony R. Gambardella
Peter C. Contino
Erica B. Garay
Alan S. Rutkin
Jay V. Krafsur (Resident, Chicago Office)
Evan H. Krinick
Alan C. Eagle
Peter P. McNamara
Bruce A. Bendix
Charlotte Biblow
Christopher J. Borders (Resident, Santa Rosa Office)
Steven Brock
Michael E. Buckley
Celeste M. Butera
Thomas F. Byrne (Resident, Santa Rosa Office)
David M. Cassidy
Peter R. Chatzinoff
George K. DeHaven
Janice J. DiGennaro
Scott Eisenmesser (Resident, New York City Office)
Bernard Feigen
Frank J. Giliberti
M. Paul Gorfinkel
Jesse J. Graham, II
Kelsey D. Graham (Resident, New York City Office)
Howard R. Greenwald
José A. Isasi, II (Resident, Chicago Office)
James J. Jennings
George D. Kappus
Cameron "Scott" Kirk, Jr. (Resident, Santa Rosa Office)
Howard B. Kleinberg
Cheryl Korman
Michael A. Kotula
Lawrence A. Levy

(See Next Column)

MEMBERS OF FIRM (Continued)

Shari C. Lewis
Jill Rosen Nikoloff
Kenneth A. Novikoff
Gary Potters (Resident, Newark Office)
James F. Quinn
David E. Richman
Eric L. Routman (Resident, Chicago Office)
D. Douglas Shureen (Resident, Santa Rosa Office)
Michael A. Sirignano
William Slivka (Resident, New York City Office)
Norman L. Tolle
Howard M. Tollin
Linda E. Unger (Resident, Chicago Office)
Stephen B. Weissman
Thomas F. Werring

OF COUNSEL

William J. Candee, III
Peter I. Cavallaro
Warren S. Radler (Resident, Chicago, Illinois Office)
Charles H. Reinhardt, Jr.
Barry R. Shapiro
Jeffrey L. Stadler
George J. Tsunis

ASSOCIATES

Michelle I. Allen
Ginamarie Alvino
Marvin J. Bellovin
Todd M. Belous
Merril C. Biscone
Amy E. Blakeley (Resident, Newark Office)
Stuart M. Bodoff
Lewis Scott Calderon
Michael D. Cassell
Larinzo D. Clayton
Eileen M. Cohan
Leonard B. Cooper
Michael V. DeSantis
Anthony DiPaolo
Anne P. Edelman
Joanne M. Engeldrum
Brian Ross Feinstein
Carrie D. Feldman
Chris J. Fichtl
Geri A. Friedman
Robert G. Frucht
Michael S. Gollub
Theodore F. Goralski, Jr.
James M. Harinski
Jeffrey D. Hayes (Resident, Santa Rosa Office)
Mary A. Jewels
Jack D. Jordan
Lana E. Joslin
George J. Keller (Resident, Santa Rosa Office)
Jay D. Kenigsberg
John E. Knudsen
Yaron J. Kornblum
Scott C. Lascari (Resident, Chicago Office)
Carol Lastorino
Syma Shulman Levine
Richard T. Lunger
Maria Maestranzi Paciullo
Janine N. Marallo
Karin M. McCarthy
David R. McGill
Michael A. Monahan (Resident, Newark Office)
Veena A. Mitchell (Resident, Santa Rosa Office)
John F. Morrison
Anne M. Murray
Frank W. Nagorka (Resident, Chicago Office)
Peter T. Neill
Camille Nieves
Matthew D. Norfolk
Philip D. Nykamp
Yoshimi Ohye
William J. O'Mahony
John J. Panagopoulos
Troy G. Pieper
Dominic M. Pisani
Gregory Gennady Plotko
Frank J. Raia
Pia Elena Riverso
David L. Rudolph (Resident, Chicago Office)
Alan E. Sash
Frank M. Scalera
Lee S. Siegel
Ted A.V. Smith (Resident, Santa Rosa Office)
Eric S. Strober (Resident, New York City Office)
Scott Y. Stuart
Deirdre E. Taber (Resident, Santa Rosa Office)
Douglas G. Tischler
Robert Tugander
Michael P. Versichelli
Steven M. Zuckermann

Representative Clients: Fireman's Fund Insurance Companies; Allstate Insurance Company; Aegis Insurance Services Inc.; Commercial Union Insurance Company; Home Insurance Company; State Farm Insurance Company; Royal Insurance Company; Aetna Property & Casualty; ITT Hartford Insurance Group; Medical Liability Mutual.

For full biographical listings, see the Martindale-Hubbell Law Directory

---

*UTICA,** Oneida Co.

GORMAN, WASZKIEWICZ, GORMAN & SCHMITT (AV)

1508 Genesee Street, 13502-5178
Telephone: 315-724-2147
Fax: 315-724-1183
Email: gwgslaw@borg.com

MEMBERS OF FIRM

Bartle Gorman (1897-1974)
Edwin A. Waszkiewicz (1917-1998)
Bartle J. Gorman
William P. Schmitt

ASSOCIATE

Darryl B. Rahn

General Counsel for: Carton Foundation, Inc.; T. C. Peters Printing Co., Inc.; Insight House Chemical Dependency Services, Inc.; Town of Whitestown; Village of Clinton.
Local Counsel for: Utica Mutual Insurance Co.; Graphic Arts Mutual Insurance Co.; United National Insurance Co.;
References: Key Bank of N.Y.; Marine Midland Bank.

For full biographical listings, see the Martindale-Hubbell Law Directory

Utica—Continued

ROSSI, MURNANE & HUGHES (AV)

209 Elizabeth Street, P.O. Box 209, 13503-0209
Telephone: 315-733-4671
Fax: 315-733-4609

Vincent J. Rossi
Don P. Murnane
Vincent J. Rossi, Jr.
Thomas P. Hughes

ASSOCIATE

Douglas M. DeMarché, Jr.

General Counsel for: Utica First Insurance Co.
Reference: Chase Bank, Utica, New York.

For full biographical listings, see the Martindale-Hubbell Law Directory

VALATIE, Columbia Co.

BURNS F. BARFORD, JR. (AV)

1019 Kinderhook Street, 12184
Telephone: 518-758-7161
Facsimile: 518-758-9885

Counsel for: National Union Bank of Kinderhook.

For full biographical listings, see the Martindale-Hubbell Law Directory

*WARSAW,** Wyoming Co.

SMALLWOOD-COOK & SCHMIEDER (AV)

140 North Main Street, 14569-1103
Telephone: 716-786-2274
FAX: 716-786-2138
Email: smallwood@wycol.com

MEMBERS OF FIRM

Charlotte Smallwood-Cook
Jane A.C. Schmieder

Reference: Wyoming County Bank.

For full biographical listings, see the Martindale-Hubbell Law Directory

*WATERTOWN,** Jefferson Co.

CONBOY, MCKAY, BACHMAN & KENDALL, LLP (AV)

407 Sherman Street, 13601-3998
Telephone: 315-788-5100
Fax: 315-788-3463
Email: conboy@imcnet.net *URL:* http://www.gisco.net/conboy
Carthage, New York Office: 307 State Street.
Telephone: 315-493-0030.
Fax: 315-493-7549.
Canton, New York Office: 2 Judson Street.
Telephone: 315-386-8544.
Fax: 315-379-0126.

OF COUNSEL

Joanne M. Novak (Resident, Canton Office)

MEMBERS OF FIRM

Floyd J. Chandler
Lawrence D. Hasseler (Resident, Carthage Office)
Stephen W. Gebo
Arthur C. Stever, III
Peter L. Walton
David B. Geurtsen
Gerald J. Ducharme (Resident, Canton, New York Office)

ASSOCIATES

Scott B. Goldie
Edward A. Gibson
John V. Hartzell
Kimberly A. Wood

Attorneys for: Travelers Indemnity Co.; Royal Insurance Co.; Niagara Mohawk Power Corp.; Marine Midland Bank, N.A.; Community Bank, N.A.; State Farm Insurance; Hartford; CNA; Utica Mutual Insurance; New York Casualty.

For full biographical listings, see the Martindale-Hubbell Law Directory

*WHITE PLAINS,** Westchester Co.

BARTELS & FEUREISEN, LLP (AV)

925 Westchester Avenue, Suite 304, 10604
Telephone: 914-681-7175
Telecopier: 914-681-0013

MEMBERS OF FIRM

David Feureisen
Michael Fahey

OF COUNSEL

John R. Bartels, Jr.
Hynes, Randazo & Quinn, LLP, White Plains, New York

References: Bank of New York; The Home Insurance Co.; Republic National Bank of New York; Marine Midland Bank.

For full biographical listings, see the Martindale-Hubbell Law Directory

JOSEPH P. GOVERNALI (AV)

Inns of Court, North Suite, 99 Court Street, 10601
Telephone: 914-946-5300
Telecopier: 914-946-1058

For full biographical listings, see the Martindale-Hubbell Law Directory

GREENE & ZINNER, P.C. (AV)

202 Mamaroneck Avenue, 10601
Telephone: 914-948-4800
FAX: 914-948-4936

Andrew Greene
Stanley S. Zinner

Arthur M. Neiss
Jarrod S. Schlesinger

For full biographical listings, see the Martindale-Hubbell Law Directory

HOFFMAN, WACHTELL, KOSTER & MAIER (AV)

399 Knollwood Road, 10603
Telephone: 914-682-8000
FAX: 914-682-1512
URL: http://www.lawyers.com/hwk&mlaw

MEMBERS OF FIRM

Lee A. Hoffman, Jr.
Marc J. Wachtell
Eric D. Koster
Lynn J. Maier

Representative Clients: Mount Hope Mines, Inc.; Eastern Educational Consortium; Westchester Community College; Prime Office Systems, Inc.; Purchase Environmental Protection Association, Inc.; The Jay Coalition; The Town of Greenburgh; The Town of Mamaroneck; The City of Mt. Vernon.
Reference: Citibank, N.A. (White Plains Branch).

For full biographical listings, see the Martindale-Hubbell Law Directory

KATZ & KLEIN (AV)

Suite 601, 200 Mamaroneck Avenue, 10601-5301
Telephone: 914-428-1400
FAX: 914-428-5052
Email: ascher416@aol.com
Croton-on-Hudson, New York Office: 380 Albany Post Road.
Telephone: 914-271-6601.

MEMBERS OF FIRM

Ascher Katz
Gerald M. Klein

References: Bank of New York; Barclays Bank.

For full biographical listings, see the Martindale-Hubbell Law Directory

KEANE & BEANE, P.C. (AV)

One North Broadway, 10601
Telephone: 914-946-4777
Telecopier: 914-946-6868
Rye, New York Office: 15 Elm Place.
Telephone: 914-967-3936.

Thomas F. Keane, Jr. (1932-1991)
Edward F. Beane
Donna E. Frosco
David Glasser
Lance H. Klein
Ronald A. Longo
Richard L. O'Rourke
Lawrence Praga
Joel H. Sachs
Steven A. Schurkman
Judson K. Siebert

Stephanie L. Burns
Eric L. Gordon
Jonathan Kornblatt
Stephanie M. Orefice
Patrick J. O'Sullivan
Frances M. Pantaleo
Nicholas M. Ward-Willis

OF COUNSEL

Peter A. Borrok
John F. Burkhardt
Eric F. Jensen

LEGAL SUPPORT PERSONNEL

Lenny Amodeo (Legal Assistant)
Barbara S. Durkin (Office Manager)
Sylvia J. Zuckerman (Legal Assistant)

For full biographical listings, see the Martindale-Hubbell Law Directory

KENT, HAZZARD, JAEGER, GREER, WILSON & FAY (AV)

50 Main Street, 10606
Telephone: 914-948-4700
Telecopier: 914-948-4721
Email: KentHazz@aol.com

MEMBERS OF FIRM

Ralph S. Kent (1878-1949)
Lawrence S. Hazzard (1900-1958)
William J. Greer (1920-1994)
Mizell Wilson, Jr. (1927-1995)
Lawrence F. Fay
Robert D. Hazzard
Katharine Wilson Conroy

ASSOCIATE

John A. Verni

(See Next Column)

KENT, HAZZARD, JAEGER, GREER, WILSON & FAY, *White Plains—Continued*

OF COUNSEL

Malcolm Wilson
Otto C. Jaeger
John R. Dinin
Harold L. Wood

Representative Client: The Bank of New York.
References: Bank of New York.

For full biographical listings, see the Martindale-Hubbell Law Directory

MEAD, HECHT, CONKLIN & GALLAGHER (AV)

399 Knollwood Road, Suite 100, 10603
Telephone: 914-686-6200
Fax: 914-686-1007

MEMBERS OF FIRM

Donald A. Mead (1922-1996)
Elizabeth M. Hecht
Kevin Thomas Conklin
Eugene G. Gallagher

ASSOCIATES

Ernest S. Buonocore
Marcia O. Andreoli
Daniel D. Cassidy
Michael Patrick Heffernan
Philip J. O'Rourke
John J. Phelan
Sara Luca Salvi

OF COUNSEL

Vincent Gurahian (1927-1999)
Kingdon P. Locker
Sharon A. Scanlan

For full biographical listings, see the Martindale-Hubbell Law Directory

SMITH, RANSCHT, CONNORS, MUTINO, NORDELL & SIRIGNANO, P.C. (AV)

235 Main Street, 10601
Telephone: 914-946-8800
Telecopier: 914-946-8861
Cable Address: "Smiran" White Plains, New York

James P. Connors, Jr.
Peter J. Mutino
Michael Nordell
George A. Sirignano, Jr.

Counsel for: Universal Builders Supply, Inc.; The Walter Karl Cos.; Hartsdale Canine Cemetery; Wise Components, Inc.; Facsimile Communications Industries, Inc.; Carlcraft Knit Sales, Inc.
Closing Attorney for: First Union Mortgage Corp.
Representative Client: United Airlines, Corporate Express, Inc.

For full biographical listings, see the Martindale-Hubbell Law Directory

STEPHENS, BARONI, REILLY & LEWIS LLP (AV)

Northcourt Building, 175 Main Street, 10601
Telephone: 914-761-0300; 683-5185
Telecopier: 914-761-0995; 683-1323
URL: http://www.lawyers.com/sbrl
Cross River, New York Office: Northern Westchester Office, Old Post Road Professional Building, 10518.
Telephone: 914-763-3232.

MEMBERS OF FIRM

Gerald D. Reilly
Roland A. Baroni, Jr.
Stephen R. Lewis

ASSOCIATE

Roland T. Koke

OF COUNSEL

James R. Caruso (1906-1994)

For full biographical listings, see the Martindale-Hubbell Law Directory

VOUTÉ, LOHRFINK, MAGRO & COLLINS, LLP (AV)

170 Hamilton Avenue, 10601-1789
Telephone: 914-946-1400
Facsimile: 914-946-8024

Arthur J. Vouté, Jr.
Richard L. Magro
Charles D. Lohrfink, Jr.
Charles A. Collins, Jr.

Elliot A. Cristantello
Stephen F. Fischer
Ralph F. Schoene
Kevin P. Fitzpatrick
Catherine F. Gale
Hal Roberts
Stephen J. Riebling, Jr.
John A. Howard
Michael A. Sonkin
Kelly E. Cardany

Representative Clients: Aetna Casualty & Surety Co.; Allstate Insurance Co.; Chubb Group; CNA Companies; Medical Liability Mutual Insurance Co.; National Car Rental System, Inc.; Physicians Reciprocal Insurance Co.; Preferred Physicians Medical Insurance Co.; Risk Enterprise Management; St. Josephs Medical Center.

For full biographical listings, see the Martindale-Hubbell Law Directory

WILSON, BAVE, CONBOY, COZZA & COUZENS, P.C. (AV)

Two William Street, 10601
Telephone: 914-686-9010
Telecopier: 914-686-0873
Email: wbcc@aol.com

William H. Bave (1919-1991)
Donald C. Wilson (1917-1994)
R. Kevin Conboy
William H. Bave, Jr.
Michael J. Cozza
John C. Couzens, Jr.
Patricia Bave-Planell
Kevin D. Odell
Leo T. McGrath
Alexandra C. Karamitsos
Joel A. Hirshfield
Megan J. Conboy
Teresa A. Gruber

LEGAL SUPPORT PERSONNEL

PARALEGAL

John R. Pearsall

Representative Clients: State Farm Mutual Automobile Insurance Co.; Continental National American Group; Medical Liability Mutual Insurance Co.; General Accident Insurance Co.; Metropolitan Property and Liability; Royal Insurance; County of Westchester; City of Yonkers.

For full biographical listings, see the Martindale-Hubbell Law Directory

NORTH CAROLINA

*ASHEVILLE,** Buncombe Co.

McGUIRE, WOOD & BISSETTE, P.A. (AV)

Drhumor Building, 48 Patton Avenue, P.O. Box 3180, 28802
Telephone: 828-254-8800
Fax: 828-252-2438
Email: mwb@mwbavl.com

Richard A. Wood, Jr.
W. Louis Bissette, Jr.
Douglas O. Thigpen
Joseph P. McGuire
Doris Phillips Loomis
M. Charles Cloninger
Thomas C. Grella
Grant B. Osborne
T. Douglas Wilson, Jr.
Richard A. Kort
John N. Fleming

Sarah Sparboe Thornburg
Heather Whitaker Goldstein

RETIRED

Walter R. McGuire

Representative Clients: Asheville Citizen-Times Publishing Co.; Dave Steel Co., Inc. (Steel Fabricating); WLOS-TV; The Givens Estates, Inc. (Retirement Community); Hayes & Lunsford Electrical Contractors, Inc.; Wellco Enterprises, Inc.; BASF Corp.; First Union National Bank of North Carolina; St. Joseph's Hospital; Carolina Power & Light Company.

For full biographical listings, see the Martindale-Hubbell Law Directory

PATLA, STRAUS, ROBINSON & MOORE, P.A. (AV)

Suite 300, 29 North Market, P.O. Box 7625, 28802
Telephone: 828-255-7641
Fax: 828-258-9222
Email: PSRM@mindspring.com

Joseph A. Patla (1881-1979)
Robert J. Robinson
William C. Moore (Retired, 1987)
Steven I. Goldstein
Victor W. Buchanan
Robert A. Freeman, III
Richard S. Daniels
Kerry A. Friedman
Virginia P. Litzenberger
Sharon Tracey Barrett
Mark C. Martin
Clifford Paul Parson
Carol Eubank
Eileen M. McMinn
Harris Miller Livingstain
Alan Z. Thornburg

OF COUNSEL

Karl H. Straus

Representative Clients: Asheville City Board of Education; Asheville Regional Airport Authority; Asheville Waste Paper Co.; Giles Chemical Corp.; Matthews Ford, Inc.; Memorial Mission Hospital, Inc.; Pelle Automotive Group, Inc.; Price/McNabb Advertising Agency; H. Putsch & Co., a Division of H. Putsch & Co. (Germany); Royal Crown Cola Bottling Co.

For full biographical listings, see the Martindale-Hubbell Law Directory

VAN WINKLE, BUCK, WALL, STARNES AND DAVIS, P.A. (AV)

11 North Market Street, P.O. Box 7376, 28801
Telephone: 828-258-2991
FAX: 828-255-0255; 257-2767
Hendersonville, North Carolina Office: 422 South Main Street.
Telephone: 828-697-6196.
Fax: 828-693-3999.

(See Next Column)

VAN WINKLE, BUCK, WALL, STARNES AND DAVIS P.A.—*Continued*

Kingsland Van Winkle (1879-1972)
Charles G. Buck (Retired)
Robertson Wall (1913-1996)
O. E. Starnes
Roy W. Davis, Jr.
Brian F. D. Lavelle
Larry S. McDevitt
Philip J. Smith
Barry B. Kempson
Albert L. Sneed, Jr.
Robert H. Haggard (Resident, Hendersonville)
Marla Tugwell Adams
Jones Pharr Byrd
Allan R. Tarleton
Larry C. Harris, Jr.
Michelle Rippon
William Perry Fisher, II
Michael M. Thompson (Resident, Hendersonville, North Carolina Office)
Mark A. Pinkston
Stephen J. Grabenstein
Craig D. Justus
Cynthia W. Eller
Stephen B. Williamson
Adam Langdon Shealy
John G. Kelso
Dale A. Curriden
W. Carleton Metcalf
David G. Redding
W. Kevin McLaughlin, Jr.
Jennifer Wayland Moore
Robert J. Fedder
Juliet M. Sarkessian
Carolyn Lloyd Coward

Western Region General Counsel for: Wachovia Bank & Trust Co.
Attorneys for: Carolina Power & Light Co.; Charles D. Owen Manufacturing Co.; Clyde Savings and Loan Assn.; Continental Telephone Company of N.C.; Gerber Products Co.; Liberty Mutual Insurance Co.; Reliance Insurance Co.; State Farm Mutual Automobile Insurance Co.; United States Fidelity & Guaranty Co.

For full biographical listings, see the Martindale-Hubbell Law Directory

BURLINGTON, Alamance Co.

HOLT, LONGEST, WALL & BLAETZ, P.L.L.C. (AV)

407 South Broad Street, P.O. Drawer 59, 27216
Telephone: 336-227-7461
FAX: 336-227-9716

W. Clary Holt
Frank A. Longest, Jr.
N. Madison Wall, II
Peter T. Blaetz

Counsel for: NationsBank, N.A.; Burlington Industries; AT&T Technologies; Burlington Board of Realtors; Nationwide Mutual Insurance Co.; The Times-News Publishing Co., Inc.; United States Fidelity and Guaranty Co.

For full biographical listings, see the Martindale-Hubbell Law Directory

CHAPEL HILL, Orange Co.

EPTING & HACKNEY (AV)

410 Airport Road, P.O. Box 1329, 27514
Telephone: 919-929-0323
Fax: 919-929-3960

MEMBERS OF FIRM

Robert Epting
Joe Hackney
Elizabeth Lackey Jacobs
Karen P. Davidson
Steve Lackey

For full biographical listings, see the Martindale-Hubbell Law Directory

*CHARLOTTE,** Mecklenburg Co.

BLEDSOE & BLEDSOE, P.L.L.C. (AV)

1057 East Morehead Street, P.O. Box 36779, 28236-6779
Telephone: 704-372-1676
Fax: 704-372-1677
Email: labjrbled@aol.com

Louis A. Bledsoe, Jr.

Margaret M. Bledsoe (1966-1996)

General Counsel for: Milner Airco, Inc.; Grace Christian Center, Inc.; Rasberry Agency, Ltd.; McEwen Indusries, Inc.; The Charlotte Montessori School, Inc.; Charlotte Country Day School; JOAL Realty, LLC; Fabrictex, Inc.

For full biographical listings, see the Martindale-Hubbell Law Directory

CASSTEVENS, HANNER, GUNTER & CONRAD, P.A. (AV)

602 East Morehead Street, P.O. Box 34607, 28234
Telephone: 704-372-2140
Fax: 704-372-1150

Nelson M. Casstevens, Jr.
Robert P. Hanner, II
Dorian H. Gunter
Teresa L. Conrad
Mark D. Riopel

Approved Attorneys for: Lawyers Title Insurance Corp.; Old Republic Title Co.; Fidelity National Title Co.; First American Title Co.; Investors Title Co.; Stewart Title Co.
Reference: Central Carolina Bank.

For full biographical listings, see the Martindale-Hubbell Law Directory

CAUDLE & SPEARS, P.A. (AV)

2600 Interstate Tower, 121 West Trade Street, 28202
Telephone: 704-377-1200
Telecopier: 704-338-5858
Email: caudlespears@caudlespears.com

Lloyd C. Caudle
Harold C. Spears
L. Cameron Caudle, Jr.
Timothy T. Leach
Jeffrey L. Helms
Christopher J. Loebsack
Michael J. Selle

Counsel for: Bituminous Casualty Corp.; Baumann Springs A.G.; The A. G. Boone Co.; Capitol Funds, Inc.; Consolidated Freightways; Employers Mutual Casualty Co.; Mark Oil Company, Inc.; Metromont Materials; Otis Elevator Co.; N.C. Farm Bureau Mutual Insurance Co.

For full biographical listings, see the Martindale-Hubbell Law Directory

THE HAMEL LAW FIRM, P.A. (AV)

Morrison Boulevard, Suite 418, 6525 Morrison Boulevard, 28211
Telephone: 704-365-2552
Telecopier: 704-442-5556

Reginald S. Hamel
William F. Hamel
William B. Hamel, Sr.

For full biographical listings, see the Martindale-Hubbell Law Directory

JOHNSTON, ALLISON & HORD, P.A. (AV)

610 East Morehead Street, P.O. Box 36469, 28236
Telephone: 704-332-1181
Fax: 704-376-1628
Email: jahlaw.com *URL:* http://www.jahlaw.com

Claude A. Cochran (1884-1958)
Frank A. McCleneghan (1901-1970)
F. Thomas Miller, Jr. (1917-1985)
H. Morrison Johnston, Jr.
James W. Allison
Robert C. Hord, Jr.
Robert L. Burchette
Paul A. Kohut
John A. Morrice
J. Darrell Shealy
Greg C. Ahlum
Patrick E. Kelly
Stephen P. Gennett, II
John R. Buben, Jr.
Alice Keith Moore
Paula Jordan Banks
Gary J. Welch

Brian K. Fielden
Brian J. Schoeck
Michael L. Wilson
Kenneth T. Lautenschlager
Alicia Almeida Bowers
Nancy Lucille Siler
Russell D. Babb

OF COUNSEL

Lelia M. Alexander (Miss) (1911-1991)
B. Irvin Boyle

Attorneys for: The Presbyterian Hospital; F.N. Thompson, Co.; Pharr Yarns; SouthTrust; Centura Bank; American Truetzschler, Inc.; Carolinas Associated General Contractors; Eastern Federal Corp.; Novant Health, Inc.; Crowder Construction Co.

For full biographical listings, see the Martindale-Hubbell Law Directory

JONES, HEWSON & WOOLARD (AV)

301 South McDowell Street Suite 320, 28204
Telephone: 704-372-6541
FAX: 704-331-9068

MEMBERS OF FIRM

Hunter M. Jones (1902-1996)
Robert Gilroy Spratt, III
Kenneth H. Boyer
Lawrence J. Goldman

OF COUNSEL

Harry C. Hewson
William L. Woolard

Representative Clients: Norfolk Southern Corp.; Norfolk Southern Railway Co. (Assistant Division Counsel); Cincinnati Insurance Co.; CNA Insurance; Zurich Insurance Co. ; Provident Life & Accident Insurance Co.; St. Paul Insurance Co.; Virginia Mutual Insurance Co.; City of Charlotte.

For full biographical listings, see the Martindale-Hubbell Law Directory

KENNEDY COVINGTON LOBDELL & HICKMAN, L.L.P. (AV)

Bank of America Corporate Center Suite 4200, 100 North Tryon Street, 28202-4006
Telephone: 704-331-7400
Fax: 704-331-7598
URL: http://www.kclh.com
Raleigh, North Carolina Office: Two Hannover Square, 434 Fayetteville Street Mall, P.O. Box 1070, 27602-1070.
Telephone: 919-743-7300.
Fax: 919-743-7358.
Rock Hill, South Carolina Office: First Union Center, 113 E. Main Street, 29730.
Telephone: 803-329-7600.
Fax: 803-329-7677.

(See Next Column)

KENNEDY COVINGTON LOBDELL & HICKMAN L.L.P., *Charlotte—Continued*

MEMBERS OF FIRM

Frank H. Kennedy (1893-1975)
Hugh L. Lobdell (1908-1982)
Clarence W. Walker
Dalbert U. Shefte
Francis M. Pinckney
Henry C. Lomax
Edgar Love III
Charles V. Tompkins, Jr.
Glen B. Hardymon
J. Donnell Lassiter
A. Zachary Smith III
William F. Drew, Jr.
Charles O. DuBose
Raleigh A. Shoemaker
John M. Murchison, Jr.
Richard D. Stephens
F. Fincher Jarrell
Maynard E. Tipps
Wayne P. Huckel
J. Norfleet Pruden III
William C. Livingston
Lee West Movius
Joseph B. C. Kluttz
Jonathan A. Barrett
Eugene C. Pridgen
Stephen K. Rhyne
E. Allen Prichard
Raymond E. Owens, Jr.
Henry W. Flint
David H. Jones
James C. Hardin III (Resident, Rock Hill, South Carolina Office)
Kent F. Christison (Resident, Raleigh, North Carolina Office)
Alan H. Peterson (Resident, Raleigh, North Carolina Office)
Lacy H. Reaves (Resident, Raleigh, North Carolina Office)
John L. Sarratt (Resident, Raleigh, North Carolina Office)
Karl S. Sawyer, Jr.
Robert B. Womble (Resident, Raleigh, North Carolina Office)
Peter McLean III
Kiran H. Mehta
Michael S. Hawley
James P. Cooney III
Brian P. Evans
Jefferson W. Brown
Lynn Oliver Wenige
George C. Covington
Daniel L. Johnson, Jr.
Walter D. Fisher, Jr.
Stephen R. McCrae, Jr. (Resident, Rock Hill, South Carolina Office)
Alice Carmichael Richey
John H. Culver III
Herbert W. Hamilton (Resident, Rock Hill, South Carolina Office)
Dean A. Warren
W. Henry Sipe III (Resident, Rock Hill, South Carolina Office)
Beverly A. Carroll (Resident, Rock Hill, South Carolina Office)
Michael L. Flynn
William N. Harris
Warren P. Kean
A. Lee Hogewood III (Resident Raleigh, North Carolina Office)
Cory Hohnbaum
C. Corley Holt
Felicia A. Washington
James E. Earle
David A. Franchina
Clifford R. Jarrett
Sean M. Jones
Carol A. Jones Van Buren
John D. Allison
A. Bradley Ives

OF COUNSEL

Marcus T. Hickman

SPECIAL COUNSEL

Robert R. Carpenter (Resident, Rock Hill, South Carolina Office)
Leslee K. Daugherty
Nancy Lynne Olah (Resident, Rock Hill, South Carolina Office)

RETIRED

William T. Covington, Jr.
Ross J. Smyth

ASSOCIATES

Kimberly Raymer Robertson
Daniel J. Ballou (Resident, Rock Hill, South Carolina Office)
Jennifer Campbell
Amy Pritchard-Williams
David L. Batty
G. Lee Cory, Jr.
Caroline L. Osborne
Kevin P. Stichter
John Nicholas Suhr, Jr.
David Q. Burgess
J. Patrick Hayden
James T. Hedrick, Jr.
Mickey A. Herrin, Jr. (Resident, Raleigh, North Carolina Office)
Kimberly Short Kirk
Joseph W. Moss, Jr.
Eric S. Rohm
Philip S. Runkel
Skottowe W. Smith, Jr.
Michael R. Thornton (Resident, Raleigh, North Carolina Office)
Chad Dustin Tillman
Nancy Talavera Wood
Benjamin A. Yarbrough
Curtis C. Brewer, IV (Resident, Raleigh, North Carolina Office)
Mark R. Busch
Linde Hodson Carley
W. Keith Martens (Resident, Rock Hill, South Carolina Office)
Robert W. McCleave (Resident, Rock Hill, South Carolina Office)
Michael E. Robbe
Tracy N. Stouse
Russell S. Woodward
Stanford D. Baird
Peter A. Bynum
Selena M. Childress
Christopher L. Ekman
T. Richard Giovannelli
Susan Brown Grady
Sara Wyche Higgins
Diane Scobie Joyce (Resident, Raleigh, North Carolina Office)
G. William Joyner, III (Resident, Raleigh, North Carolina Office)
Lewis S. Morris, III
Jonathan J. Nugent
Anne M. Package
Russell F. Sizemore
Paul A. Steffens
Jack D. Todd
Michael A. Tobin
William J. Walsh
Chad O. Breunig
Erin Lang Breunig

(See Next Column)

ASSOCIATES (Continued)

Eric L. Burk
John S. DuPuy
Wendi Amos Figard
Marie E. Gibbs
Robert Preston Bryan III
Faith S. Bushnaq
Brian C. Cox
Michael F. King (Resident, Raleigh, North Carolina Office)
William B. Macurda
Taryn Gordon Mecia
Valerie Nicole Nichols
Patrick L. Ridinger
R. Alexander Sullivan (Resident, Rock Hill, South Carolina Office)
Julie Konneker Szeker
H. Manning Unger
Margaret Rose Westbrook (Resident, Raleigh, North Carolina Office)
Gail Wheeler
Klaus J. Buchstab
Sara R. Lincoln
Susan Serad Jackson
Michael Zahn
Brandon C. Fernald
Scott Alan Haenni
Debra M. Ingraham
Daniel P. Quesnel
Andre Rose
Kimberley Weber Silver (Resident, Raleigh, North Carolina Office)
Mark V. Thigpen
James M. Tucker

Representative Clients: Bank of America and Subsidiaries; Crescent Resources, Inc.; Duke Energy Corporation; First Union Corporation and Subsidiaries; Fluor Daniel; Guilford Mills, Inc.; Lance, Inc.; The Lundy Packing Company; Piedmont Health Care System; Summit Properties, Inc.

For full biographical listings, see the Martindale-Hubbell Law Directory

MAYER, BROWN & PLATT (AV)

100 North Tryon Street, Suite 2400, 28202
Telephone: (704)-444-3500
Fax: (704)-377-2033
URL: http://www.mayerbrown.com
Chicago, Illinois Office: 190 South LaSalle Street, 60603-3441.
Telephone: (312) 782-0600.
Facsimile: (312) 701-7711.
Telex: 190404.
Cable Address: LEMAY.
Berlin, Germany Office: Spreeufer 5, 10178.
Telephone: 011-49-30-247-3800.
Facsimile: 011-49-30-247-38044.
Cologne, Germany Office: Kaiser-Wilhelm-Ring 27-29, 50672.
Telephone: 011-49-221-5771-100.
Facsimile: 011-49-221-5771-199.
Houston, Texas Office: 700 Louisiana Street, Suite 3600, 77002-2730.
Telephone: (713) 221-1651.
Facsimile: (713) 224-6410.
Telex: 775809.
Cable: LEMAYHOU.
London, England Office: Bucklersbury House, 3 Queen Victoria Street, London, EC4N 8EL, England.
Telephone: 011-44-171-246-6200.
Facsimile: 011-44-171-329-4465.
Telex: 8811095.
Cable: LEMAYLDN.
Los Angeles, California Office: 350 South Grand Avenue, 25th Floor, 90071-1503.
Telephone: (213) 229-9500.
Facsimile: (213) 625-0248.
Telex: 188089.
Cable: LEMAYLA.
Washington, D.C. Office: 1909 K Street, N.W., 20006-1101.
Telephone: (202) 263-3000.
Facsimile: (202) 263-3300.
Telex: 892603.
Cable: LEMAYDC.
Representative Offices:
Ashgabat, Turkmenistan: 28 Gogol Street, 744000.
Telephone: 011-99-312-355247.
Facsimile: 011-99-312-510074.
Bishkek, Kyrgyz Republic: 66 Kalyka Akieva Str. 720001.
Telephone: 011-996-312-65-02-56.
Facsimile: 011-996-312-65-09-80.
Tashkent, Republic of Uzbekistan: 3rd Floor, 1 Turab Tula Street, 700003.
Telephones: 011-998-71-1206-627.
Facsimile: 011-998-71-1206-329.
Mexico City, Mexico, D.F., Independent Mexico Correspondent: Jáuregui, Navarrete, Nader y Rojas, S.C., Torre Arcos, Paseo de los Tamarindos No. 400-B. Col. Bosques de las Lomas, 05120.
Telephone: 011-525-267-45-00.
Facsimile: 011-525-267-45-98.
Paris, France, Independent Paris Correspondent: Lambert & Lee, 13 Avenue Hoche, 75008.
Telephone: 011-33-1-53-53-43-43.
Facsimile: 011-33-1-53-96-03-83.

MEMBERS OF FIRM

Francis J. Blanchfield, Jr.
Hayden D. Brown
Jeffrey P. Cantrell (Not admitted in NC)
Robert B. Cordle
Robert T. Duffy
R. Douglas Harmon
Mary K. Mandeville
Robert L. Mendenhall
Myron L. Moore, III
Eileen McDermott Taylor

(See Next Column)

MAYER, BROWN & PLATT—*Continued*

ASSOCIATES

Kelli Lester Lash
Sean K. Murphy (Not admitted in NC)

For full biographical listings, see the Martindale-Hubbell Law Directory

MOORE & VAN ALLEN, PLLC (AV)

100 North Tryon Street, Floor 47, 28202-4003
Telephone: 704-331-1000
Fax: 704-331-1159
URL: http://www.mvalaw.com
Charleston, South Carolina Office: 40 Calhoun Street, Suite 300.
Telephone: 843-579-7000.
Fax: 843-579-7099.
Durham, North Carolina Office: Suite 800, 2200 West Main Street.
Telephone: 919-286-8000.
Fax: 919-286-8199.
Raleigh, North Carolina Office: One Hannover Square, Suite 1700, P.O. Box 26507.
Telephone: 919-821-6200.
Fax: 919-821-6500.

W. Miller Abernethy, Jr.
A. Mark Adcock
H. Heath Alexander
Robert V. Baker
W. Doak Barnhardt
John E. Beltz
Edward S. Booher, Jr.
Mark E. Carpenter
R. Michael Childs
John S. Chinuntdet (Not admitted in NC)
Bernard B. Clark
Dumont Clarke, IV
Daniel G. Clodfelter
Kenneth S. Coe
Ted E. Corvette
Jeffrey J. Davis
Ernest S. (Mike) DeLaney III
Miriam Ann Dixon
David L. Eades
John T. Gathings, Jr.
Granice Geyer-Smith
Douglas R. Ghidina
Jeffrey W. Glenney
C. Wells Hall, III
George V. Hanna III
W. B. Hawfield, Jr.
Stephen D. Hope
James W. Hovis
Lea Stromire Johnson
Robert I. Kenny
Christopher C. Kupec
Hal A. Levinson
Neill G. McBryde
Kathleen Amalia McGill
Peter J. McGrath, Jr.
John V. McIntosh
James P. McLoughlin, Jr.
William H. Moore, Jr.
Gregory J. Murphy
Paul G. Murphy
Thomas C. O'Bannon
J. Christopher Oates
Edward K. Oden
Bradley E. Pearce
Randel E. Phillips
David J. Quattlebaum
T. Edmund Rast
Ernest W. Reigel
Scott W. Schattenfield
Curtis J. Shipley
Barney Stewart, III
David S. Walls

OF COUNSEL

Jay S. Bilas
Aaron D. Cowell, Jr.
Harry J. Grim
Donald J. Hodgens
William K. Van Allen

COUNSEL

Carol Ewald Bowen
Lynn F. Chandler
Timothy W. Corrigan
Kenneth P. Kerr
Karin M. McGinnis
David L. Ralls
Richard S. Sweet (Not admitted in NC)
John M. Timperio
William A. White
Jodi Pearson Zbinden

ASSOCIATES

James E. Akers (Not admitted in NC)
Timothy W. Arant
Brian Thomas Atkinson
Christopher T. Buchanan
Valerie Y. Busch
Keith D. Butcher
Alan J. Chadd
James E. Dillon
Russel B. Duckworth
Joseph A. Fernandez
Edgar B. Fisher III
William H. Fuller, III
Bernard J. Gallagher (Not admitted in NC)
M. Bryant Gatrell
Eric D. Gazin (Not admitted in NC)
Jeremy H. Godwin
Cynthia A. Gray (Not admitted in NC)
W. Mark Griffith
M. James Grode, Jr.
Hollie H. Hart
Meredith W. Holler
William W. Jetton
Christopher J.C. Jones (Not admitted in NC)
Leah A. Kahl
Sarah J. Kromer
Sandra M. Lazorcheck
Karen S. Marston
Valecia M. McDowell
C. Wayne McKinzie
Brian D. Mesibov
Thomas L. Mitchell
James R. Mortimer, Jr.
Keith A. Mrochek
John W. Nurkin
Andrew S. O'Hara
Carlos L. Pauling
W. Ruffin Pearce, Jr.
M. Matthew Plyler
Alan W. Pope
Stephen G. Porter, Jr.
Deann R. Richardson
Rebecca C. Rogers
Nancy F. Smith
Ryan M. Smith
Sumner N. Smith
Philip D. Song
J. René Toadvine
Beth S. Turner
Scott M. Tyler
David R. Vines
Victoria S. Windell
Michael E. Zeller

(See Next Column)

LEGAL SUPPORT PERSONNEL

C. Edward Burklin, Jr. (Executive Director)
Patti J. Oswald (Director of Human Resources)
Lisa W. McGuire (Controller)
JoAnn A. Roth (Recruiting Administrator, Charlotte)
John W. Chaffin (Director of Records Management)
William L. Ferguson (Director of Information Services)
G. Jean Anglin (Office Administrator, Raleigh)
A. Kay Lancaster (Office Administrator, Durham)
Rhonda B. Little (Benefits Manager)

CHARLESTON, SOUTH CAROLINA OFFICE

MEMBERS

W. E. Applegate, III
Martha Dantzler Ballenger
Cynthia Jordan Lowery
Paul M. Lynch
Donald Bancroft Meyer
Wm. Howell Morrison
Thomas Waring
David B. Wheeler

OF COUNSEL

Coleman M. Legerton

COUNSEL

W. Thomas Rutledge, Jr.
Elizabeth T. Thomas

ASSOCIATES

Christopher T. Cunniffe
Benjamin P. Glass
Patricia L. Quentel
Trudy H. Robertson

DURHAM, NORTH CAROLINA OFFICE

MEMBERS

Brian R. Brown
Loni S. Caudill
Lewis A. Cheek
Dominic J. Chiantera
James H. Clarke
Andrew B. Cohen
Ted E. Corvette
Edward L. Embree, III
Randolph M. Fletcher
William E. Freeman
David A. Harlow
Charles R. Holton
Laura Bernstein Luger
James M. Tatum, Jr.
Reich L. Welborn

OF COUNSEL

William G. Dossé
William L. London, III
E. K. Powe

COUNSEL

Rita M.K. Purut

ASSOCIATES

Kevin M. Capalbo
Arlene D. Hanks
Christopher C. Herbst
Michael G. Johnston
Laura Keohane
Julie A. King
Natalie J. McKinney
Scott W. Reid
Pamela A. Wachter
Mark H. Webbink

RALEIGH, NORTH CAROLINA OFFICE

MEMBERS

Christopher J. Blake
Martin H. Brinkley
Denise Smith Cline
Lisa James Dixon
Joseph W. Eason
David E. Fox
William H. Gammon
Joseph D. Joyner, Jr.
Charles H. Mercer, Jr.
Jonathan D. Sasser
Hayden J. Silver, III
George M. Teague
Joy Heath Thomas

OF COUNSEL

Anthony Gaeta, Jr.
Leon M. Killian, III

ASSOCIATES

Reed J. Hollander
John S. Hughes, IV
Robert A. Meynardie
Sue A. Sprunger
Jeffrey M. Young

For full biographical listings, see the Martindale-Hubbell Law Directory

PARKER, POE, ADAMS & BERNSTEIN L.L.P. (AV)

2500 Charlotte Plaza, 201 South College Street, 28244
Telephone: 704-372-9000
Facsimile: 704-334-4706
Email: info@parkerpoe.com *URL:* http://www.parkerpoe.com
South Park Office: The Rotunda, 4201 Congress Street, Suite 145, Charlotte, 28209.
Telephone: 704-556-9600.
Facsimile: 704-556-9601.
Raleigh, North Carolina Office: First Union Capitol Center, 150 Fayetteville Street Mall, Suite 1400, P.O. Box 389, 27602-0389.
Telephone: 919-828-0564.
Facsimile: 919-834-4564.
Columbia, South Carolina Office: 1201 Main Street, Suite 1450, 29201.
Telephone: 803-255-8000.
Facsimile: 803-255-8017.
Spartanburg, South Carolina Office: 101 W. St. John Street, Suite 203, 29306.
Telephone: 803-591-2030.
Facsimile: 803-591-2050.
Frankfurt, Germany Office: Limes Park, Otto-Volger-Strasse 5B, D-65843.
Telephone: (011)(49)6196-750081.
Telefax: (011)(49)6196-750088.

(See Next Column)

PARKER, POE, ADAMS & BERNSTEIN L.L.P., *Charlotte—Continued*

PARTNERS

Mark R. Bernstein
Gaston H. Gage
James Y. Preston
Ashley L. Hogewood, Jr.
W. Samuel Woodard
Max Edward Justice
William L. Rikard, Jr.
Donald P. Ubell
Fred T. Lowrance
R. Anthony Orsbon
Woodard E. Farmer, Jr.
Edward W. Wellman, Jr.
William P. Farthing, Jr.
Fred C. Thompson, Jr.
Irvin W. Hankins III
E. Thomas Watson
Heloise C. Merrill
J. William Porter
George H. Pretty II
William L. Brown
A. Grant Whitney, Jr.
David Neal Allen
I. Faison Hicks
Roy L. Smart III
Sally Nan Barber
Gary C. Ivey
Debra Lee Foster
Anthony Fox
Thomas N. Griffin III
Charles B. Lee, Jr.
Alan G. Dexter
Richard K. Schell
James N. Brennan IV
Albert E. Guarnieri
Josephine H. Hicks
William L. Hirata
(Not admitted in NC)
Craig T. Lynch
Regina Jay Wheeler
John F. Baron
Stephen M. Hader
Keith M. Weddington
Jonathan M. Crotty
Josiah C. T. Lucas
Peter J. Shea
Eric D. Welsh
(Not admitted in NC)
Michael G. Adams
Ronald R. Stuff
Paul S. Donohue
John R. Hairr III
J. Michael Wilson
Barbara E. Heim
S. Rogers Warner, Jr.
Stacy K. Weinberg
Brent M. Milgrom, Jr.

OF COUNSEL

Francis I. Parker
William E. Poe
Sydnor Thompson

ASSOCIATES

Patrick Fogarty, Jr.
Sam Z. Haviland
(Not admitted in NC)
Cynthia T. Fenninger
John W. Francisco
Steven D. Weber
Stephen K. Coss
Kiah T. Ford, IV
Neil B. Kapadia
Debra E. Kleman
Nicole Lehmann Tharrington
P. Neal Cook
Gates E. Grainger
John E. Grupp
Joy M. Hord
Alison M. Jordan
Michael S. Malloy
John B. Anderson
Rachel E. Berry
S. Walt Coleman IV
James A.L. Daniel, Jr.
William G.C. Mitchell, Jr.
Melissa M. Kemmer
James C. Davis, Jr.
Deborah L. Edney
J. Keith Jones
Scott E. Leo
Brandon K. Lewisohn
Thomas H. O'Donnell, Jr.
John E. Russ, III
Scott D. Syfert
George T. Brady
W. Lewis Glenn, III
Lori R. Keeton
Thomas M. Quirk
Anna F. Schleunes
Amy Flanary-Smith
Kimberly A. Betz
Jonathan W. Dion
Elizabeth D. Gibbes
James N. Greene III
Jami M. Jackson
Stacey T. Kern
Kristi E. Kessler
James F. Mondani

STAFF ATTORNEY

Maria B. Barry

Representative Clients: Advantica Restaurant Group (formerly Flagstar Companies); American City Business Journals; Carolina Power and Light; Duke Energy; First Union National Bank; Georgetown Steel; GS Industries; Hoechst Corporation; Kemper National Insurance Companies; N. Schlumberger (USA), Inc.

For full biographical listings, see the Martindale-Hubbell Law Directory

---

PERRY, PATRICK, FARMER & MICHAUX, P.A. (AV)

2200 The Carillon, 227 West Trade Street, 28202
Telephone: 704-372-1120
Fax: 704-372-9635
Other Charlotte, North Carolina Office: South Park, 1901 Roxborough Road, Suite 100.
Telephone: 704-364-9695.
Fax: 704-364-9698.
Raleigh, North Carolina Office: 3716 National Drive, Suite 100.
Telephone: 919-787-8812.
Fax: 919-787-3312.

Robert E. Perry, Jr.
Bailey Patrick, Jr.
B. D. Farmer, III
Roy H. Michaux, Jr.
James G. Wallace
Carolyn Gilmer Hisley
Bryan W. Pittman
Laura L. Yaeger
Richard W. Moore
(Resident, Raleigh Office)
Leslie Miller Webb
Susan K. Irvin
John H. Carmichael

G. Mark Teague
(Resident, Raleigh Office)
Charles David Cheney
Todd J. Combs
Virginia G. Dockery
Peggy Sue Howard

(See Next Column)

Representative Clients: The Bissell Cos.; Centex Real Estate Corp.; Charlotte Pipe and Foundry Co.; The Crosland Group, Inc.; Crown Life Insurance Co.; C.D. Spangler Construction Co.; International Construction Equipment, Inc.; The Manufacturers Life Insurance Co.; M/I Schottenstein Cos., Inc.; The Ryland Group, Inc.

For full biographical listings, see the Martindale-Hubbell Law Directory

---

RAYBURN, MOON & SMITH, P.A. (AV)

The Carillon, 227 West Trade Street, Suite 1200, 28202-1675
Telephone: 704-334-0891
Fax: 704-377-1897; 704-377-0395
Email: rmslaw@aol.com

Albert F. Durham
Travis W. Moon
C. Richard Rayburn, Jr.
James C. Smith
W. Scott Cooper
Paul R. Baynard
James B. Gatehouse
G. Kirkland Hardymon
James L. Bagwell
Patricia B. Edmondson
Natalie R. Denton
Robert Aubrey Cox, Jr.
Tricia L. Rolewicz

For full biographical listings, see the Martindale-Hubbell Law Directory

---

ROBINSON, BRADSHAW & HINSON, P.A. (AV)

101 North Tryon Street, Suite 1900, 28246-1900
Telephone: 704-377-2536
Fax: 704-378-4000
E-Mail: Attorneys first initial and last name plus "@rbh.com" Example: "rrobinson@rbh.com"
Email: ylevine@rbh.com *URL:* http://www.rbh.com
Rock Hill, South Carolina Office: The Guardian Building, 223 East Main Street, Suite 600, Post Office Drawer 12070.
Telephone: 803-325-2900.
FAX: 803-325-2929.

Russell M. Robinson II
Robert W. Bradshaw, Jr.
Robin L. Hinson
Robert C. Sink
A. Ward McKeithen
Gibson L. Smith, Jr.
Graham D. Holding, Jr.
Carl E. Johnson, Jr.
Richard A. Vinroot
Claude Q. Freeman, Jr.
William T. Graves
John R. Wester
Martin L. Brackett, Jr.
John R. Miller
Peter C. Buck
Robert M. Bryan
Christy Eve Reid
Robert G. Griffin
Edwin F. Lucas III
Robert C. Jones, Jr.
Everett J. Bowman
Haynes P. Lea
Caroline Wannamaker Sink
Henry H. Ralston
Herman Spence III
Brent A. Torstrick
Mark W. Merritt
Garland S. Cassada
Robert W. Fuller
Kent J. McCready
David C. Wright III
Robert W. Simmons
Frank E. Emory, Jr.
Louis A. Bledsoe III
Christopher W. Loeb
Richard W. Gibson, Jr.
Stokely G. Caldwell, Jr.
Stephen M. Lynch
R. Steven DeGeorge
Jane S. Ratteree
Benjamin W. Baldwin
John B. Garver, III
Edward F. Hennessey, IV
Richard L. Mack
Allen K. Robertson
Stuart H. Johnson
Karen A. Gledhill
Allain C. Andry, IV
Patrick S. Bryant
David W. Dabbs
Julie C. Chiu
David M. Schilli
William W. Toole
Sarah Boucher Kemble
Frank H. Lancaster
Robert S. McLean
Robert E. Harrington
S. Graham Robinson
Julian H. Wright, Jr.
Stephan J. Willen
Matthew S. Churchill
Thomas P. Holderness
Susan I. McCrory
John M. Herring
Lawrence C. Moore, III
Patrick C. Heinrich
Douglas M. Jarrell
Amy K. Johnson
Donald R. Esposito, Jr.
Alice Pinckney Adams
Jeffrey C. Hart
Richard S. Starling
W. Alexander Kendall, Jr
Letitia Utley Alfonsi
Jeffrey A. Henson
Krista R. Bowen
Thomas J. Molony
Steven D. Newmark
Daniel F. Basnight
Carl R. Boehm
T. Thomas Gates

OF COUNSEL

John M. Conley
Gundars Aperans
(Not admitted in NC)
Robert W. Allen
Thomas E. McNeill

For full biographical listings, see the Martindale-Hubbell Law Directory

Charlotte—Continued

SMITH HELMS MULLISS & MOORE, L.L.P. (AV)

201 North Tryon Street, P.O. Box 31247, 28231
Telephone: 704-343-2000
Fax: 704-334-8467
Telex: 572460
Email: smith_helms@shmm.com *URL:* http://www.shmm.com
Greensboro, North Carolina Office: Suite 1400, First Union Tower, 300 North Greene Street, P.O. Box 21927.
Telephone: 336-378-5200.
Fax: 336-379-9558.
Raleigh, North Carolina Office: 2800 Two Hannover Square, P.O. Box 27525.
Telephone: 919-755-8700.
Fax: 919-755-8800.
Wilmington, North Carolina Office: 127 Grace Street, P.O. Box 3235.
Telephone: 910-254-3800.
Fax: 910-254-3900.
Atlanta, Georgia Office: 1355 Peachtree Street N.E., Suite 750.
Telephone: 404-962-1000.
Fax: 404-962-1200.

William H. Bobbitt (1926-1968) | William F. Mulliss (1911-1987)
Fred B. Helms (1896-1998)

MEMBERS OF FIRM

E. Osborne Ayscue, Jr.
Brian D. Barger
Irving M. Brenner
Robert G. Brinkley
Herbert H. Browne, Jr.
Jonathan E. Buchan, Jr.
Boyd C. Campbell, Jr.
Rebecca S. Chaffin
Rolly L. Chambers
Saxby M. Chaplin
Stephen L. Cordell
Peter J. Covington
Robert W. Cramer
James H. Culbreth, Jr.
Larry J. Dagenhart
Robert M. Donlon
Douglas W. Ey, Jr.
Elizabeth Whitener Goode
Eugene Steven Griggs
Julie Zydron Griggs
J. Richard Hazlett
Gregory S. Hilderbran
Benne C. Hutson
Wade M. Kennedy
Bradley R. Kutrow
Harrison L. Marshall, Jr.
B. Palmer McArthur, Jr.
E. Graham McGoogan, Jr.
R. Malloy McKeithen
James G. Middlebrooks
Thomas W. Murrell, III
Thomas D. Myrick
Kathy L. Pilkington
William F. Potts, Jr.
Robert H. Pryor
Manley W. Roberts
L. D. Simmons, II
Catherine E. Thompson
Scott P. Vaughn
H. Landis Wade, Jr.
John B. Yorke

ASSOCIATES

T. Jonathan Adams
Stephen David Allred
Corby Cochran Anderson
Craig R. Baldauf
Alice Carlton Bragg
Stephanie K. Briggs
Elizabeth Chase Coale
David B. Fountain
Maurice O. Green
Jill Crawley Griset
Bradley B. Honnold
David Lamothe
Amy Rickner Langdon
Marcus S. Lee
Michael Scott Mansfield
William Kenan Maready, Jr.
William C. Mayberry
John G. Mc Donald
Mark R. McGrath
Paul M. Navarro
Christopher S. M. Nesbit
David F. Paulson, Jr.
Rose Caroline Petroff
Leonard "Holden" Reaves
Babette Maria Reynolds
Elizabeth Baker Scanlan
Lucy Lynch Tate
William DeVane Tidwell
Richard W. Viola

OF COUNSEL

John H. Cobb | James H. Guterman

For full biographical listings, see the Martindale-Hubbell Law Directory

UNDERWOOD KINSEY WARREN & TUCKER, P.A. (AV)

2020 Charlotte Plaza, 201 South College Street, 28244-2020
Telephone: 704-333-1200
Facsimile: 704-377-9630

William E. Underwood, Jr.
C. Ralph Kinsey, Jr.
Joseph Warren, III
Robert B. Tucker, Jr.
John H. Northey III
Shirley J. Linn
Susan L. Sowell
Carlton A. Shannon, Jr.
Richard L. Farley
Russell M. Black
Francis Morris Pinckney, III
Margo F. Evans

Janeen R. Miller

Representative Clients: Arnold Palmer Cadillac; Bojangles' Restaurants Inc.; Charlotte/Douglas International Airport; Decision One Mortgage Co.; Dillard's, Inc.; HLM Design, Inc.; Keffer Company; MJD Communications, Inc.; Sabco Racing; Thor-Lo, Inc.

For full biographical listings, see the Martindale-Hubbell Law Directory

WOMBLE CARLYLE SANDRIDGE & RICE (AV)

A Professional Limited Liability Company
3300 One First Union Center, 301 South College Street, 28202-6025
Telephone: 704-331-4900
Fax: 704-331-4955
Email: lawyers@wcsr.com *URL:* http://www.wcsr.com
Winston-Salem, North Carolina Office: 200 West Second Street, P.O. Drawer 84.
Telephone: 336-721-3600.
Fax: 336-721-3660.
Raleigh, North Carolina Office: 2100 First Union Capitol Center, 150 Fayetteville Street Mall, P.O. Box 831.
Telephone: 919-755-2100.
Fax: 919-755-2150.
Research Triangle Park, North Carolina Office: 2505 Meridian Parkway, Suite 300 (Durham), 27713.
Telephone: 919-484-2300.
Fax: 919-484-2340.
Atlanta, Georgia Office: One Atlantic Center, 1201 West Peachtree Street, Suite 3500.
Telephone: 404-872-7000.
Fax: 404-888-7490.
Other Atlanta, Georgia Office: Suite 404, 2296 Henderson Mill Road, N.E.
Telephone: 770-492-9030.
Fax: 770-492-9609.
Washington, D.C. Office: 1120 Nineteenth Street, N.W., Eighth Floor.
Telephone: 202-857-4400.
Fax: 202-467-6910.
Greenville, South Carolina Office: 15 South Main Street, Suite 601, P.O. Box 10208.
Telephone: 864-255-5400.
Fax: 864-255-5440.

RESIDENT MEMBERS

Timothy G. Barber
G. Michael Barnhill
Gary D. Chamblee
Joe B. Cogdell, Jr.
Cornelius W. Coghill, III
Jim D. Cooley
James E. Daniel
Bradford A. DeVore
J. Carlton Fleming
Debbie Weston Harden
Mark P. Henriques
Bobby D. Hinson
Mark J. Horoschak
Cyrus M. Johnson, Jr.
James E. Johnson, Jr.
Eugene M. Katz (Not admitted in NC)
William P. McMillan
Lesley G. Powell
Richard L. Rainey
William C. Raper
J. Alexander Salisbury
F. Lane Williamson

RESIDENT ASSOCIATES

A. Britten Canady
Donna L. Casto
Andrea Del Duca
Patricia E. Dowds
Steven D. Gardner
Patrick T. Gillen
W. Clark Goodman
Brian E. Heim
Katherine Thompson Lange
Douglas A. Mays
Lynn W. Neumann
Kenneth B. Oettinger, Jr.
Ellen A. Perrin
Joyce E. Plyler
Daniel G. Schmedlen, Jr.
Todd C. Taylor

RESIDENT OF COUNSEL

Elizabeth C. Coss | Jane Jeffries Jones

LEGAL SUPPORT PERSONNEL

Hassel L. Parker (Executive Director)
Marvin E. Chavis (Director of Technology)
Donald H. Adamick (Director of Library Services)
Keith Tedrow (Director of Administration)
John E. Turlington (Office Administrator - Raleigh)
Patricia A. Kight (Human Resources Administrator)
Charles R. Allison (Office Administrator - Charlotte)
Terry Michael Wiley (Director of Finance and Systems)
Paula G. Blanchat (Marketing Administrator)
Beth Keasler (Attorney Recruitment Administrator)

Representative Clients: Childress Klein Properties, Inc.; Food Lion, Inc.; J.A. Jones Construction Co.; Parkdale Mills, Inc.; Pillowtex; Duke Power Co.; Bowles Hollowell Conner & Co.; ALLTEL Carolina, Inc.; Belk Store Services, Inc.; Philip Holzmann A.G.

For full biographical listings, see the Martindale-Hubbell Law Directory

CLAYTON, Johnston Co.

TEW & ATCHISON, P.A. (AV)

202 South Lombard Street, P.O. Box 145, 27520
Telephone: 919-553-6142; 553-2143
Fax: 919-553-8742
Email: atewlaw@mindspring.com

Allen R. Tew | Alexander R. Atchison

For full biographical listings, see the Martindale-Hubbell Law Directory

*DURHAM,** Durham Co.

NEWSOM, GRAHAM, HEDRICK & KENNON, P.A. (AV)

Suite 1200 University Tower, 3100 Tower Boulevard, P.O. Box 51579, 27717-1579
Telephone: 919-490-0500
Telecopier: 919-490-0873
URL: http://www.nghk.com

James T. Hedrick
Josiah S. Murray, III
A. William Kennon
John L. Crill
John E. Markham, Jr.
Katherine McKee Henrichs
William P. Daniell
Evelyn M. Coman
Robert O. Belo
Joel M. Craig
John R. Long
David S. Kennett
G. Rhodes Craver
Lynne Townsend Albert
Dieter Mauch

J. Alan Campbell
Thomas H. Lee, Jr.
James R. Easthom
Alfred Thomas Ripley
William T. Hutchins, Jr.
John C. Rogers, III

OF COUNSEL

James L. Newsom
Alexander H. Graham, Jr.

Representative Clients: Wachovia Bank & Trust Co.; Duke Power Co.; Liggett Group, Inc.; General Telephone Company of the South; Exxon Corp.

For full biographical listings, see the Martindale-Hubbell Law Directory

EDEN, Rockingham Co.

THOMAS S. HARRINGTON (AV)

708 West Washington Street, 27288-6029
Telephone: 910-227-7461
Fax: 910-227-9716
Wentworth Office: 2 Courthouse Square, 27375.
Telephone: 910-349-2943.
Fax: 910-627-4243.

Local Counsel: Duke Power Co.
Approved Attorneys for: Lawyers Title Insurance Corp.; United Title Insurance Co.; Chicago Title Insurance Co.; Jefferson Pilot Title Insurance Co.; First Title Insurance Co.

For full biographical listings, see the Martindale-Hubbell Law Directory

*ELIZABETH CITY,** Pasquotank Co.

HORNTHAL, RILEY, ELLIS & MALAND, L.L.P. (AV)

301 East Main Street, P.O. Box 220, 27909
Telephone: 252-335-0871
Fax: 252-335-4223
URL: http://www.hrem.com
Nags Head, North Carolina Office: 2502 South Croatan Highway, P.O. Box 310, 27959-0310.
Telephone: 252-441-0871.
Telefax: 252-441-8822.

L. P. Hornthal, Jr.
J. Fred Riley
L. Phillip Hornthal III
Thomas L. White, Jr. (Resident, Nags Head Office)
M. H. Hood Ellis
Mark M. Maland
Donald C. Prentiss
Robert B. Hobbs, Jr. (Resident, Nags Head Office)
John D. Leidy
Michael P. Sanders
Lee L. Leidy
David A. Miller

John Charles White

Representative Clients: CIGNA Group; Elizabeth City-Pasquotank County Board of Education; Camden County Board of Education; Kemper Insurance Group; State Farm Mutual; Travelers Insurance Co.; Wachovia Bank of North Carolina, N.A.; Branch Banking & Trust Co.; College of the Albemarle; USF&G.

For full biographical listings, see the Martindale-Hubbell Law Directory

*ELIZABETHTOWN,** Bladen Co.

HESTER, GRADY, HESTER, GREENE & PAYNE (AV)

115 Courthouse Drive, P.O. Drawer 130, 28337
Telephone: 910-862-3191
FAX: 910-862-4802

MEMBERS OF FIRM

Worth H. Hester
Gary A. Grady
H. Clifton Hester
Paula Hobbs Greene
Donna Gooden Payne

OF COUNSEL

Frank T. Grady

For full biographical listings, see the Martindale-Hubbell Law Directory

*FAYETTEVILLE,** Cumberland Co.

MCCOY, WEAVER, WIGGINS, CLEVELAND & RAPER, PLLC (AV)

202 Fairway Drive, P.O. Box 87009, 28304
Telephone: 910-483-8104
FAX: 910-483-0094

MEMBERS OF FIRM

Donald W. McCoy (1919-1995)
Elmo R. Zumwalt (1946-1988)
Jeffrey Neill Surles (1960-1995)
L. Stacy Weaver, Jr.
Richard M. Wiggins
Alfred E. Cleveland
John E. Raper, Jr.
Anne Mayo Evans
Jeff Dunham
Rodney B. Davis
Jim Wade Goodman

General Counsel for: North Carolina Natural Gas Corp.; Branch Banking & Trust Co.; Mid-South Insurance Co.; Putt-Putt Golf Courses of America, Inc.; Fayetteville Technical Community College; Methodist College, Inc.
Representative Clients: St. Paul Companies; Ellis-Walker Builders, Inc.; Time-Warner, Inc.; Riddle Commercial Properties; Lee-Moore Oil Co.

For full biographical listings, see the Martindale-Hubbell Law Directory

THORP AND CLARKE (AV)

1014 Hay Street, P.O. Box 670, 28302
Telephone: 910-323-4111
Fax: 910-483-1247

MEMBERS OF FIRM

Herbert H. Thorp (1932-1996)
F. Stuart Clarke
Matthew R. Plyler
Susan E. Hyatt

Counsel for: W. R. Co.; W.S. Wellons Realty, Inc.; Cape Fear Broadcasting Co.; Cross Creek Mall; Cross Creek Plaza, Inc.; Centura Bank, Inc.; Bass Construction; Dickens Construction.
Reference: Branch Banking & Trust.

For full biographical listings, see the Martindale-Hubbell Law Directory

*FRANKLIN,** Macon Co.

JONES, KEY, MELVIN & PATTON, P.A. (AV)

61 East Main Street, 28734
Telephone: 828-524-4444
Fax: 828-369-7343
Highlands, North Carolina Office: Professional Building, Suite 3, South Street.
Telephone: 828-526-3762.

Richard S. Jones, Jr.
Bobby Joe Key
Richard Melvin
Lawrence M. Patton, Jr.
Gilbert R. Key, II
Fred Howell Jones
Chester M. Jones

Representative Clients: Macon Savings Bank; Wildcat Cliffs Country Club; County of Macon; First Union National Bank; Town of Franklin; Bank of Clayton; County of Graham.
Approved Attorneys for: Fidelity National Title Insurance Co.; Lawyers Title Insurance Corp.; Investors Title Insurance Company.

For full biographical listings, see the Martindale-Hubbell Law Directory

*GOLDSBORO,** Wayne Co.

BADDOUR, PARKER & HINE, PROFESSIONAL CORPORATION (AV)

208 South William Street, Drawer 916, 27530
Telephone: 919-735-7275
Fax: 919-736-3297

Philip A. Baddour, Jr.
E. B. Borden Parker
John C. Hine

William D. Orander, III
Philip A. Baddour, III

Representative Clients: Wayne County; Wayne County Department of Social Services; First Union National Bank; Southern Medical Oncology Center, P.A.; Goldsboro Eye Clinic; Shepherd Electric Supply Co., Inc.; Quality Forest Products, Inc.; Seegars Fence Co.

For full biographical listings, see the Martindale-Hubbell Law Directory

*GREENSBORO,** Guilford Co.

BROOKS, PIERCE, MCLENDON, HUMPHREY & LEONARD, L.L.P. (AV)

2000 Renaissance Plaza, 230 North Elm Street (27401), P.O. Box 26000, 27420-6000
Telephone: 336-373-8850
Facsimile: 336-378-1001
Raleigh, North Carolina Office: 1600 First Union Capitol Center, 150 Fayetteville Street Mall, 27601, P.O. Box 1800, 27602-1800.
Telephone: 919-839-0300.
Facsimile: 919-839-0304.

(See Next Column)

BROOKS, PIERCE, MCLENDON, HUMPHREY & LEONARD L.L.P.—*Continued*

MEMBERS OF FIRM

Aubrey L. Brooks (1872-1958)
William H. Holderness (1904-1965)
Lennox P. McLendon (1890-1968)
Kenneth M. Brim (1898-1974)
C. Theodore Leonard, Jr. (1929-1983)
Claude C. Pierce (1913-1988)
Thornton H. Brooks (1912-1988)
G. Neil Daniels (1911-1997)
Lennox P. McLendon, Jr.
Hubert Humphrey
Edgar B. Fisher, Jr.
W. Erwin Fuller, Jr.
James T. Williams, Jr.
Wade H. Hargrove
M. Daniel McGinn
Michael D. Meeker
William G. McNairy
Edward C. Winslow, III
Howard L. Williams
George W. House
William P. H. Cary
Reid L. Phillips
Robert A. Singer
John H. Small
Randall A. Underwood
S. Leigh Rodenbough, IV
William G. Ross, Jr.
Mark J. Prak
Jill R. Wilson
Marc D. Bishop
Jim W. Phillips, Jr.
Mack Sperling
Jeffrey E. Oleynik
Mark Davidson
James R. Saintsing
John W. Ormand, III
Robert J. King, III
Steven J. Levitas
V. Randall Tinsley
John R. Archambault
S. Kyle Woosley
Daniel M. Sroka
Forrest W. Campbell, Jr.
Marcus W. Trathen
Jean C. Brooks
Ellen P. Hamrick
James C. Adams, II
Allison M. Grimm
Elizabeth S. Brewington

ASSOCIATES

H. Arthur Bolick, II
Natasha Rath Marcus
John M. Cross, Jr.
Jennifer K. Van Zant
Kearns Davis
David W. Sar
Kathleen M. Thornton
Brian J. McMillan
Jennifer L. Bolick
David Kushner
Derek J. Allen
Elizabeth V. LaFollette
Ginger S. Shields
Harold H. Chen
Coe W. Ramsey
Natalie Kay Sanders
Robert W. Saunders
David Shub
Jennifer T. Harrod
Matthew G. Bibbens
Charles E. Coble
John M. DeAngelis
Clinton R. Pinyan
Kathryn V. Purdom
Andrew Kirk Susong

General Counsel for: North Carolina Bankers Association; Trident Securities, Inc.
Division Counsel for: Norfolk Southern Railway Co.
Attorneys for: Burlington Industries, Inc.; Guilford Mills, Inc.; Wachovia Bank, N.A.; PCS Phosphate Company, Inc.; CCB Financial Corporation; Public Service Company of North Carolina.
Labor Counsel for: Lorillard Tobacco Co.

For full biographical listings, see the Martindale-Hubbell Law Directory

CARRUTHERS & ROTH, P.A. (AV)

235 North Edgeworth Street, P.O. Box 540, 27402
Telephone: 336-379-8651
Fax: 336-273-7885

Joseph T. Carruthers, Jr. (1906-1992)
Charles E. Roth (1917-1992)
Walter Rand
Seldon E. Patty
Thomas E. Wagg, III
Kenneth M. Greene
Richard L. Vanore
William L. Tankersley, III
Kenneth R. Keller
L. Worth Holleman, Jr.
Arthur A. Vreeland
Thomas W. Sinks
Jack B. Bayliss, Jr.
Howard L. Borum
J. Scott Dillon
J. Stanley Atwell
Kenneth L. Jones
June L. Basden
Desmond G. Sheridan
Michael J. Allen
Pamela Sarsfield Fox
Gregory S. Williams
John M. Flynn

Keith A. Wood
Christopher J. Vaughn
Norman F. Klick, Jr.
Joe Franklin Teague, Jr.

Representative Clients: AC Corp.; The Bank of New York; First Union Commercial Corp.; Kay Chemical Co.; Kemper Insurance Group; Marine Midland Bank; Metropolitan Life Insurance Co.; Fleet Capital Corp.; Thompson-Arthur Paving Co.

For full biographical listings, see the Martindale-Hubbell Law Directory

CLARK BLOSS & MCIVER, PLLC (AV)

600 Dixie Building, 125 South Elm Street, P.O. Box 1349, 27402
Telephone: 336-275-7275
Fax: 336-275-1401
Email: cbm@cbm-law.com

David M. Clark
John F. Bloss
Robert G. McIver
Jonathan Wall

Representative Clients: The Prudential Insurance Company of America (litigation); Johnson Controls, Inc.

(See Next Column)

Approved Attorneys for: Jefferson-Pilot Insurance Co.

For full biographical listings, see the Martindale-Hubbell Law Directory

COOKE & COOKE (AV)

Suite 301 First Citizens Bank Building, 100 South Elm Street, P.O. Box 187, 27402
Telephone: 336-272-4514
Facsimile: 336-272-4516

MEMBERS OF FIRM

Arthur O. Cooke (1916-1983)
William Owen Cooke
Barden W. Cooke
William O. Cooke, Jr.

Representative Clients: N. C. Grange Mutual Insurance Co.; Piedmont Triad Airport Authority; Brown-Gardiner Drug Co.; Engineered Plastics, Inc.; Strandberg Engineering Laboratories; ICBT, Inc.

For full biographical listings, see the Martindale-Hubbell Law Directory

HILL, EVANS, DUNCAN, JORDAN & DAVIS (AV)

A Professional Limited Liability Company
1400 Renaissance Plaza, 230 North Elm Street, P.O. Box 989, 27402
Telephone: 336-379-1390
Fax: 336-379-1198
Email: hedjd@worldnet.att.net

MEMBERS OF FIRM

Welch Jordan (1912-1976)
William D. Caffrey (1928-1991)
Karl N. Hill, Jr.
Thomas C. Duncan
William Welch Jordan
Lindsay Reeves Davis, Jr.
Joseph R. Beatty
R. Thompson Wright
Everett B. Saslow, Jr.
Richard J. Votta
Polly D. Sizemore
Charles W. Coltrane
George G. Lockhart

ASSOCIATES

Michele G. Smith
Joseph P. Gram
Elaine Hedrick Ashley
Scott B. Murray (Not admitted in NC)
Richard T. Granowsky

OF COUNSEL

G. Marlin Evans

Representative Clients: Ford Motor Credit Co.; Gilbarco, Inc.; Jefferson-Pilot Corp.; Rheem Manufacturing Co.; Overnight Transportation Co.

For full biographical listings, see the Martindale-Hubbell Law Directory

HUNTER, JOHNSTON, ELAM & BENJAMIN, PLLC (AV)

822 North Elm Street, Suite 200, 27401
Telephone: 336-273-1600
Fax: 336-274-4650
Mailing Address: P.O. Box 20570, Greensboro, North Carolina, 27420
Email: hjeb@greensborolaw.com

Robert N. Hunter, Jr.
Robert L. Johnston
John Claibourne Elam

William P. Benjamin
Brian Tomlin

For full biographical listings, see the Martindale-Hubbell Law Directory

ISAACSON & ISAACSON (AV)

Suite 400 Bank of America Building, 101 West Friendly Avenue, P.O. Box 1888, 27402
Telephone: 336-275-7626
Fax: 336-273-7293
Email: ikeandike@aol.com *URL:* http://www.lawyers.com/isaacson

MEMBERS OF FIRM

Henry H. Isaacson
Marc L. Isaacson

ASSOCIATES

Jennifer N. Fountain
Anna Gregory Wagoner

For full biographical listings, see the Martindale-Hubbell Law Directory

IVEY, MCCLELLAN, GATTON & TALCOTT, L.L.P. (AV)

121 South Elm Street, P.O. Box 3324, 27402
Telephone: 336-274-4658
Telefax: 336-274-4540

MEMBERS OF FIRM

Charles M. Ivey, Jr. (1914-1993)
Charles M. Ivey, III
Robert L. McClellan
Edwin R. Gatton
James K. Talcott
Lillian H. Pinto

ASSOCIATES

John M. Blust
Dirk W. Siegmund
Eric A. Richardson
Mary Beth B. Swecker

Representative Clients: First Home Federal Savings and Loan Assn.; First Citizens Bank & Trust Co.; First National Bank of Randolph Co.; Wachovia Bank and Trust; Friendly Rubber & Seal Co.; Mercedes-Benz Credit Corp.; Norwest Financial, North Carolina.
Approved Attorneys for: Jefferson-Pilot Title Insurance Co.; Lawyers Title Insurance Corp.

(See Next Column)

IVEY, MCCLELLAN, GATTON & TALCOTT L.L.P., *Greensboro—Continued*

For full biographical listings, see the Martindale-Hubbell Law Directory

LAWING SHARPLESS & STAVOLA, P.A. (AV)

826 North Elm Street, P.O. Box 22106, 27420
Telephone: 336-333-6400
Facsimile: 336-333-6399
URL: http://www.elsfirm.com

Sally A. Lawing
Pamela A. Robertson
Brenda S. McClearn
Frederick K. Sharpless
Joseph M. Stavola

Joseph P. Booth, III
Eugene E. Lester, III
Marylynn E. Skaggs

Representative Clients: CNA Insurance Group; Jefferson Pilot Corporation; C. Wayne McDonald Contractor, Inc.; Moses H. Cone Memorial Hospital.

For full biographical listings, see the Martindale-Hubbell Law Directory

SMITH HELMS MULLISS & MOORE, L.L.P. (AV)

Suite 1400, First Union Tower, 300 North Greene Street, P.O. Box 21927, 27420
Telephone: 336-378-5200
Fax: 336-379-9558
Email: smith__helms@shmm.com *URL:* http://www.shmm.com
Charlotte, North Carolina Office: 201 North Tryon Street, P.O. Box 31247.
Telephone: 704-343-2000.
Fax: 704-334-8467.
Telex: 572460.
Raleigh, North Carolina Office: 2800 Two Hannover Square, P.O. Box 27525.
Telephone: 919-755-8700.
Fax: 919-755-8800.
Wilmington, North Carolina Office: 127 Grace Street, P.O. Box 3235.
Telephone: 910-254-3800.
Fax: 910-254-3900.
Atlanta, Georgia Office: 1355 Peachtree Street N.E., Suite 750.
Telephone: 404-962-1000.
Fax: 404-962-1200.

Julius C. Smith (1889-1968)
John J. Dortch (1930-1984)

PARTNERS EMERITUS

Beverly C. Moore
Julius C. Smith, III
McNeill Smith

MEMBERS OF FIRM

D. Erik Albright
Bynum M. Hunter
Bruce P. Ashley
Michael E. Kelly
Evan Kent Auberry
Donald C. Lampe
W. Alexander Audilet
Caroline Hudson Lock
Jonathan A. Berkelhammer
Alexander L. Maultsby
Richmond G. Bernhardt, Jr.
James A. Medford
Lyn K. Broom
Charles E. Melvin, Jr.
Carole Watkins Bruce
Stephen Perry Millikin
Harold N. Bynum
David M. Moore II
Andrew S. Chamberlin
Maureen Demarest Murray
J. Donald Cowan, Jr.
Ramona Cunningham O'Bryant
Gerard H. Davidson, Jr.
Timothy Peck
Benjamin F. Davis, Jr.
Barbara C. Ruby
Herbert O. Davis
Allan L. Shackelford
Alan W. Duncan
Larry B. Sitton
Stephen W. Earp
Thomas S. Stukes
Martin N. Erwin
Julianna C. Theall
Marilyn Feuchs-Marker
E. Garrett Walker
Jo Ann T. Harllee
Jeri L. Whitfield
Terrill Johnson Harris
William L. Young

ASSOCIATES

Shannon Joines Adcock
Gregory G. Holland
Laura Deddish Burton
Neale T. Johnson
William E. Burton III
Shannon R. Joseph
Brian W. Byrd
Robert D. Kidwell
Amie Flowers Carmack
Amy H. Kincaid
Robert Bryson Carter
Henry L. Kitchin, Jr.
Manning A. Connors, III
Amy Smith Klass
Christine Nero Coughlin
Stephen E. Klee
Richard A. Coughlin
John J. Korzen
Elizabeth Wood Crossley
David L. Kyger
Lawrence G. DeGraaf
Robert R. Marcus
Susan McNear Fradenburg
Michael C. Mascia
Lisa Frye Garrison
Edward A. Meyer
Eileen King Gillis
Allison K. Overbay
Jonathan Heyl
D. Marsh Prause

OF COUNSEL

John L. Barber
Kathy E. Manning
James G. Exum, Jr.
Davis McDonald

For full biographical listings, see the Martindale-Hubbell Law Directory

*GREENVILLE,** Pitt Co.

GAYLORD, MCNALLY, STRICKLAND & SNYDER, L.L.P. (AV)

498 Red Banks Road, P.O. Drawer 545, 27835-0545
Telephone: 252-321-7111
Fax: 252-321-7112

MEMBERS OF FIRM

Louis W. Gaylord, Jr. (Retired)
D. Michael Strickland
Danny D. McNally
Vernon G. Snyder, III

ASSOCIATE

Emma Stallings Holscher

Representative Clients: Wachovia Bank, N.A.; Nationsbank, N.A.; Garris Evans Lumber Co., Inc.; United States Fidelity and Guaranty Co.; The Daily Reflector, Inc.; Hastings Ford, Inc.; Nationwide Mutual Insurance Co.; U.S. Cellular; Ironwood Development, Inc.

For full biographical listings, see the Martindale-Hubbell Law Directory

*HENDERSON,** Vance Co.

PERRY, KITTRELL, BLACKBURN & BLACKBURN (AV)

109 Young Street, P.O. Box 139, 27536
Telephone: 252-438-8131
Fax: 252-438-8643

Bennett H. Perry (1884-1963)
R. G. Kittrell (1877-1957)

MEMBERS OF FIRM

George T. Blackburn
Charles F. Blackburn

ASSOCIATE

Cameron C. Bush
Bennett H. Perry, Jr.

OF COUNSEL

Robert G. Kittrell, Jr.

Representative Clients: NCNB National Bank of North Carolina; J. W. Jenkins, Inc.; Vance Medical Arts, Inc.; Henderson Mall, Ltd.; Rose's Stores, Inc.
Approved Attorneys for: Lawyers Title Insurance Corp.; Investors Title Insurance Co.

For full biographical listings, see the Martindale-Hubbell Law Directory

*HENDERSONVILLE,** Henderson Co.

HOWE, WATERS & CARPENTER, P.A. (AV)

134 South Main Street, P.O. Box 586, 28793
Telephone: 828-692-9636
Telefax: 828-692-2643

William B. W. Howe
Walter C. Carpenter
R. Charles Waters
Linda A. Moxley

General Counsel for: Hendersonville Housing Authority.
Approved Attorneys for: Lawyers Title Insurance Corp.; Chicago Title Insurance Co.; Investors Title Insurance Co.
References: Wachovia Bank and Trust Co.; First Union National Bank of North Carolina; First Citizens Bank & Trust Co.; Centura Bank.

For full biographical listings, see the Martindale-Hubbell Law Directory

PRINCE, YOUNGBLOOD & MASSAGEE (AV)

240 Third Avenue, West, 28739
Telephone: 828-692-2595
FAX: 828-693-0177

MEMBERS OF FIRM

L. B. Prince (1898-1982)
Sharon B. Alexander
Kenneth R. Youngblood
Peter B. Knight
Boyd B. Massagee, Jr.
James L. Epperson
B. B. Massagee, III
Christopher Page Collie

Representative Clients: Margaret R. Pardee Memorial Hospital; E. I. DuPont DeNemours & Co.; Nations Bank; First Citizens Bank and Trust Co.; Duke Power Co.; Blue Cross & Blue Shield of North Carolina; Blue Ridge Community College; Fletcher Motor Co., Inc.; Hunter Chevrolet-Volvo-Subaru Co., Inc.

For full biographical listings, see the Martindale-Hubbell Law Directory

HICKORY, Catawba Co.

PATRICK, HARPER & DIXON L.L.P. (AV)

Centura Bank Building, 34 Second Street, N.W., P.O. Box 218, 28603
Telephone: 828-322-7741
Fax: 828-322-9340

MEMBERS OF FIRM

Bailey Patrick (1898-1989)
Gary F. Young
James T. Patrick (1936-1990)
Kim Stafford Clarke
F. Gwyn Harper, Jr. (1911-1994)
Eloise DeLaney Bradshaw
Charles D. Dixon
Robert Allen Ingram, Jr.
Stephen Mason Thomas
David Wallace Hood
Donald R. Fuller, Jr.
Robert Oren Eades

(See Next Column)

PATRICK, HARPER & DIXON L.L.P.—*Continued*

ASSOCIATE

Kimberly H. Whitley

General Counsel for: Century Furniture Co.; Shuford Mills, Inc.; Hickory Chair Co.
Special Counsel for: Norfolk-Southern Railway Co.
Local Counsel for: Duke Power Co.; Martin Marietta Corp.; The Lane Co.; Nationwide Insurance Co.

For full biographical listings, see the Martindale-Hubbell Law Directory

SIGMON, CLARK, MACKIE, HUTTON & HANVEY, P.A. (AV)

420 Third Avenue, N.W., P.O. Drawer 1470, 28603
Telephone: 828-328-2596
FAX: 828-328-6876

William R. Sigmon
E. Fielding Clark, II
Jeffrey T. Mackie
Warren A. Hutton
J. Scott Hanvey
Forrest A. Ferrell

Stephen L. Palmer

OF COUNSEL

Marshall V. Yount

Representative Clients: First Union National Bank; Cox Manufacturing Co.; Alba-Waldensian, Inc.; Hancock & Moore, Inc.; J. Royale Furniture, Inc.; Disque Furniture, LLC; Taylor-King Furniture, Inc.
Local Counsel for: The Ohio Casualty Group of Insurance Cos.; United States Fidelity and Guaranty Insurance Co.

For full biographical listings, see the Martindale-Hubbell Law Directory

HIGHLANDS, Macon Co.

MAYER & RISER, PLLC (AV)

Smallwood Avenue & Fifth Street, P.O. Box 750, 28741
Telephone: 828-526-3731
Fax: 828-526-3734
Email: info@mayer-riser.com *URL:* http://www.mayer-riser.com

MEMBERS OF FIRM

John R. Mayer
Elizabeth Mayer Riser
Christopher M. Riser

For full biographical listings, see the Martindale-Hubbell Law Directory

HIGH POINT, Guilford Co.

BAKER & BOYAN, P.L.L.C. (AV)

820 North Elm Street, 27261
Telephone: 336-885-0111
Fax: 336-885-1460
URL: http://www.lawyers.com/baker&boyan

Walter W. Baker, Jr.
Robert S. Boyan
Jeffrey L. Mabe
Dina M. Draeger
Maxine D. Kennedy

For full biographical listings, see the Martindale-Hubbell Law Directory

FISHER CLINARD & CRAIG, PLLC (AV)

Suite 800 First Factors Building, 101 S. Main Street, P.O. Box 1150, 27261
Telephone: 336-883-9156
Fax: 336-886-8593

Louis J. Fisher (1901-1981)
Louis J. Fisher, Jr. (Retired)
Aaron Neal Clinard
John O. Craig III
Alyce E. Hill

Rick Cornwell
Shane T. Stutts

Representative Clients: U.S. Furniture Industries, Inc.; Phillips Interests, Inc.; Branch Banking and Trust Company; Cornerstone Health Care, P.A.; ACW Management Corporation d/b/a/ A Cleaner World; Carolina Process Piping, Inc.; Carolina Cardiology Associates, P.A.; Sharrard McGee and Co., P.A.; Medical Software Specialties, Inc.

For full biographical listings, see the Martindale-Hubbell Law Directory

HAWORTH RIGGS (AV)

Law Building, 212 East Green Drive, Suite 300, P.O. Box 109, 27261
Telephone: 336-883-0191
Telecopier: 336-883-6478
Email: HRKHAttys@aol.com

MEMBERS OF FIRM

John Haworth
John C. Riggs
William B. Haworth

Representative Clients: Davis Furniture Industries, Inc.; Thayer Coggin, Inc.; High Point Medical Center, Inc.; Cloverleaf Super Market, Inc.; Kennedy Oil Co.; Oakhurst Textiles, Inc; Ven-Ply, Inc.; Landon Furniture, Inc.

(See Next Column)

For full biographical listings, see the Martindale-Hubbell Law Directory

KEZIAH, GATES & SAMET, L.L.P. (AV)

Suite 400 High Point Bank & Trust Building, 300 North Main Street, P.O. Box 2608, 27261-2608
Telephone: 336-889-6900
Telecopier: 336-889-7055
Email: kgs@hpe.infi.net

MEMBERS OF FIRM

S. Perry Keziah
Gilbert L. Gates
Jan H. Samet
Charles E. Lynch, Jr.
Maurice S. S. Hull
Andrew S. Lasine
Steven H. Bouldin

Counsel for: Furniture Manufacturers Credit Assn., Inc.; High Point Bank & Trust Co.; International Home Furnishings Center, Inc.; NationsBank, N.A.; Harris Teeter, Inc.; W.F. Mickey Body Co., Inc.; North Pointe Partners, LLC.

For full biographical listings, see the Martindale-Hubbell Law Directory

POST & POST (AV)

516 North Wrenn, P.O. Box 2531, 27261
Telephone: 336-887-7566
Telecopier: 336-887-2133

MEMBERS OF FIRM

Edward N. Post
Alan N. Post

General Counsel for: Housing Authority of City of High Point.
Counsel for: North State Telephone Co.; Nations Bank; Pump & Tank Shop, Inc.; Lighting Creations, Inc.; Lighting & Accessories, Inc; Spencer & Lester of High Point, Inc.; Smith General Contractors.
Local Counsel for: Mortgage Loans: Federal National Mortgage Assn.; Federal Housing Administration.

For full biographical listings, see the Martindale-Hubbell Law Directory

WYATT, EARLY, HARRIS & WHEELER, L.L.P. (AV)

1912 Eastchester Drive, Suite 400, P.O. Drawer 2086, 27261
Telephone: 336-884-4444
Fax: 336-889-5232
Email: wyattlaw@northstate.net

MEMBERS OF FIRM

Frank Burkhead Wyatt
William P. Harris
A. Doyle Early, Jr.
William E. Wheeler
David B. Ashcraft
Kim W. Gallimore
Kim R. Bauman
Calvin B. Bryant
R. Bruce Laney
Charles A. Alt
Frederick G. Sawyer
James R. Hundley
Charles L. Cain
Thomas E. Terrell, Jr.
Lee M. Cecil
Ann E. Hanks
John D. Bryson
Stanley F. Hammer
Scott Fitzgerald Wyatt
Debbi L. Aberman (Retired)

Representative Clients: Allstate Insurance Co.; Davis Furniture Industries; First Union National Bank; Dar-Ran Furniture Industries; First Citizens Bank & Trust Co.; Ohio Casualty Insurance Co.; Mid-State Petroleum; Branch Bank & Trust Co.; British Vita.

For full biographical listings, see the Martindale-Hubbell Law Directory

*JACKSONVILLE,** Onslow Co.

ELLIS, HOOPER, WARLICK & MORGAN, LLP (AV)

313 New Bridge Street, P.O. Drawer 1006, 28541-1006
Telephone: 910-455-3637
Fax: 910-455-4068
Email: ehwmlaw@coastalnet.com

MEMBERS OF FIRM

John D. Warlick, Sr. (1890-1952)
Albert J. Ellis (1913-1969)
Glenn L. Hooper, Jr. (1927-1978)
John D. Warlick, Jr.
William J. Morgan

ASSOCIATES

Victor H.E. Morgan, Jr.
John P. (Jack) Swart
Robert A. Warlick
Deke Slayton Owens

For full biographical listings, see the Martindale-Hubbell Law Directory

WARLICK MILSTED DOTSON & CARTER (AV)

320 New Bridge Street, P.O. Box 766, 28541-0766
Telephone: 910-455-1215
Fax: 910-455-4702

MEMBERS OF FIRM

Alex Warlick, Jr.
Carl S. Milsted
Marshall F. Dotson, Jr.
John T. Carter, Jr.

General Counsel for: Coastal Carolina Community College; City of Jacksonville; Padgett Motors; Major Furniture & Appliance; Hurst Management Associates, Inc.

(See Next Column)

WARLICK MILSTED DOTSON & CARTER, *Jacksonville—Continued*

References: First Citizens Bank & Trust Co.; Centura Bank; Wachovia Bank; Cooperative Bank for Savings.

For full biographical listings, see the Martindale-Hubbell Law Directory

*KINSTON,** Lenoir Co.

WALLACE, MORRIS & BARWICK, P.A. (AV)

131 South Queen Street, P.O. Box 3557, 28502-3557
Telephone: 252-523-2000
Fax: 252-523-0408

Fitzhugh E. Wallace, Jr. (Retired)
Thomas H. Morris
P. C. Barwick, Jr.
Richard F. Landis, II
Paul A. Rodgman
Edwin M. Braswell, Jr.
Elizabeth A. Heath
William E. Manning, Jr.
Stuart L. Stroud

Annette W. Strickland

Regional and Local Clients: Seaboard Coast Line Railroad.
Representative Clients: E.I. du Pont De Nemours & Co., Inc.; First Citizens Bank & Trust Co.; Branch Banking & Trust Co.; City of Kinston; Kinston Daily Free Press Co.
Insurance Clients: Aetna Casualty & Surety Co.; Nationwide Mutual Insurance Co.; State Farm Insurance Cos.; Allstate Insurance Co.

For full biographical listings, see the Martindale-Hubbell Law Directory

*LAURINBURG,** Scotland Co.

ETHERIDGE, MOSER, GARNER AND BRUNER, P.A. (AV)

600 E. South Main Street, P.O. Box 1827, 28353
Telephone: 910-276-2631
Fax: 910-276-0326

Kennieth S. Etheridge (Retired)
William F. Moser
Terry R. Garner
Jerry L. Bruner

Representative Clients: First Union National Bank of North Carolina; Jasper Textiles, Inc.; Laurinburg-Maxton Airport Commission; Scotland Container, Inc.; Wachovia Bank of North Carolina, N.A.

For full biographical listings, see the Martindale-Hubbell Law Directory

WILLIAMSON, DEAN, WILLIAMSON, PURCELL & SOJKA, L.L.P. (AV)

213C East Cronly Street, P.O. Box 1627, 28353
Telephone: 910-276-8082
Fax: 910-276-1011

OF COUNSEL

Andrew G. Williamson

MEMBERS OF FIRM

Daniel B. Dean
Andrew G. Williamson, Jr.
William R. Purcell, II
Nickolas J. Sojka, Jr.
Lisa D. Griswold

Counsel for: Scotland Memorial Hospital; St. Andrews Presbyterian College; Scotland County Board of Education; Charles Craft, Inc.; Waverly Mills, Inc.
Representative Clients: McCarter Electrical Co.; Laurinburg Housing Authority; Cooper Petroleum, Inc.; McArthur Construction Company; Integon Insurance Co.

For full biographical listings, see the Martindale-Hubbell Law Directory

*LENOIR,** Caldwell Co.

TODD, VANDERBLOEMEN AND BRADY, P.A. (AV)

214 Ridge Street, Northwest, P.O. Drawer 1320, 28645-5227
Telephone: 828-758-0044
Fax: 828-758-8467

Folger L. Townsend (1899-1973)
James R. Todd, Jr.
Bruce W. Vanderbloemen
Charles A. Brady, III
Rachael A. LeClair

Representative Clients: NationsBank; Beall Oil Company; Duke Power Company; Southern Bell Telephone & Telegraph Company; Bush Oldsmobile, Inc.; Integon Indemnity Corp.; Nationwide Mutual Insurance Company; Anderson Truck Lines, Inc.; Stevens Furniture Company, Inc.; First Union National Bank.

For full biographical listings, see the Martindale-Hubbell Law Directory

*LILLINGTON,** Harnett Co.

BAIN & MCRAE (AV)

813 Main Street, P.O. Box 99, 27546
Telephone: 910-893-5111
Fax: 910-893-6342
Email: Bain-McRae@mindspring.com

(See Next Column)

MEMBERS OF FIRM

Edgar R. Bain
Alton D. Bain
David F. McRae

Representative Clients: Andrews Company, Inc.; Centura Bank; First Bank; Shaw Construction Co., Inc.; Becker Mineral Co.

For full biographical listings, see the Martindale-Hubbell Law Directory

*LOUISBURG,** Franklin Co.

DAVIS, STURGES & TOMLINSON (AV)

DSS Building, 101 North Church Street, P.O. Drawer 708, 27549
Telephone: 919-496-2137
Telecopier: 919-496-6291

MEMBERS OF FIRM

Charles M. Davis
Conrad B. Sturges, Jr.
Aubrey S. Tomlinson, Jr.
John Wyatt Davis

ASSOCIATE

C. Boyd Sturges, III

General Counsel for: National American Corp.
Representative Clients: Kemper Insurance Co.; Union Camp Corp.
Approved Attorneys for: Lawyers Title Insurance Corp.; Fidelity National Insurance Co.
References: First Citizens Bank & Trust Co.; United Carolina Bank.

For full biographical listings, see the Martindale-Hubbell Law Directory

MOREHEAD CITY, Carteret Co.

TAYLOR & TAYLOR (AV)

610 Arendell Street, P.O. Drawer 3627, 28557
Telephone: 252-726-0001
Fax: 252-726-2438
Email: talrlaw@bmd.clis.com *URL:* http://www.lawyers.com/nccoast-taylor&taylor

Nelson W. Taylor, III
Derek Taylor

Representative Clients: Town of Morehead City; Town of Newport; Carteret Craven Electric Membership Corp.; Down East Togs; Harborview Health Care Center; Chicago Title Insurance Co.
Approved Attorneys for: Lawyers Title Insurance Corp.; Chicago Title Insurance Co.
Reference: Branch Banking & Trust Co.

For full biographical listings, see the Martindale-Hubbell Law Directory

*MORGANTON,** Burke Co.

BYRD, BYRD, ERVIN, WHISNANT, MCMAHON & ERVIN, P.A. (AV)

One Northsquare, Post Office Drawer 1269, 28680
Telephone: 828-437-4220
Fax: 828-438-4517
Email: info@byrdlaw.com

Joe K. Byrd (Retired)
Robert B. Byrd
John W. Ervin, Jr.
C. Scott Whisnant
Lawrence D. McMahon, Jr.
Robert C. Ervin
Peggy McDaniel Saunders

Michelle C. Pritchard

For full biographical listings, see the Martindale-Hubbell Law Directory

SIMPSON AYCOCK, P.A. (AV)

204 East McDowell Street, P.O. Drawer 1329, 28655
Telephone: 828-437-9744
Fax: 828-433-7708

Dan R. Simpson
Samuel E. Aycock
James Reid Simpson, II
Louis E. Vinay, Jr.

Representative Clients: WSMP, Inc.; Town of Glen Alpine; Unigard Insurance Co.; Foothills Harley-Davidson, Inc.

For full biographical listings, see the Martindale-Hubbell Law Directory

MOUNT AIRY, Surry Co.

FAW, FOLGER, JOHNSON & CAMPBELL, L.L.P. (AV)

Branch Banking and Trust Building, 541 North Main Street, P.O. Drawer 512, 27030
Telephone: 336-786-2401
Fax: 336-786-2620
Email: fgjohnson@advi.net
Dobson Office: 220 West Kapp Street, P.O. Box 332.
Telephone: 336-386-8173.
Fax: 336-386-8298.

MEMBERS OF FIRM

Thomas M. Faw
Fredrick G. Johnson (Resident, Dobson Office)
Hugh B. Campbell, III
Charles L. Folger (1970-1998)

(See Next Column)

FAW, FOLGER, JOHNSON & CAMPBELL L.L.P.—*Continued*

Approved Attorneys for: Lawyers Title Insurance Co.

For full biographical listings, see the Martindale-Hubbell Law Directory

MURFREESBORO, Hertford Co.

REVELLE, BURLESON, LEE & REVELLE, L.L.P. (AV)

201 East Main Street, P.O. Box 448, 27855
Telephone: 252-398-4171
Fax: 252-398-4051
Email: revellelawfirm@coastalnet.com

MEMBERS OF FIRM

L. Frank Burleson, Jr.
Robert Edward Lee, Jr.
Charles L. Revelle, III

ASSOCIATE

Terrence N. Evans

OF COUNSEL

J. Guy Revelle, Jr.

General Counsel for: Hertford County; Chowan College; Town of Murfreesboro; Roanoke Chowan Human Services; Hertford County Department of Social Service.
Representative Clients: Severn Peanut Company; United Turf, Inc.
Approved Attorneys for: Rural Economic Development Services; Lawyers Title Insurance Corp.; United Title Insurance Co.

For full biographical listings, see the Martindale-Hubbell Law Directory

*NASHVILLE,** Nash Co.

VALENTINE, ADAMS & LAMAR, L.L.P. (AV)

203 South Barnes Street, P.O. Box 847, 27856
Telephone: 252-459-1111
Fax: 252-459-1112

MEMBERS OF FIRM

Itimous T. Valentine (1887-1970)
Itimous T. Valentine, Jr. (Retired)
Franklin L. Adams, Jr.
L. Wardlaw Lamar

ASSOCIATES

Lewis W. Lamar, Jr.
V. Katherine Wiggins

Approved Attorneys for: Lawyers Title Insurance Corp.; Title Guarantee Co.; Farm Credit Service; Commonwealth Land Title Insurance Co.; Investors Title Insurance Co.
References: Centura Bank; First Citizens Bank and Southern Bank & Trust Co., Nashville, N.C.

For full biographical listings, see the Martindale-Hubbell Law Directory

NORTH WILKESBORO, Wilkes Co.

VANNOY, COLVARD, TRIPLETT & VANNOY, P.L.L.C. (AV)

922 "C" Street, P.O. Box 1388, 28659
Telephone: 336-667-7201
Fax: 336-838-7250
Email: VANNOYLAW@AOL.COM *URL:* HTTP://WWW.VCTMV.COM

MEMBERS OF FIRM

J. Gary Vannoy
Howard C. Colvard, Jr.
Anthony R. Triplett
John G. (Jay) Vannoy, Jr.

Phillip R. Batten
Maitri "Mike" Klinkosum

Representative Clients: Branch Bank & Trust Co.; Carolina Mirror Co.
References: Branch Bank & Trust Co.; 1st Citizens Bank & Trust Co.

For full biographical listings, see the Martindale-Hubbell Law Directory

PINEHURST, Moore Co.

VAN CAMP, HAYES & MEACHAM, A PROFESSIONAL ASSOCIATION (AV)

Two Regional Drive, P.O. Box 1389, 28374
Telephone: 910-295-2525
Fax: 910-295-2001
Carthage, North Carolina Office: The Courthouse Square, P.O. Drawer 429, 28327.
Telephone: 910-947-1711.
Fax: 910-947-3700.

James R. Van Camp
Lu Pendleton Hayes
Eddie H. Meacham
Katharine McLeod
Michael J. Newman
Thomas M. Van Camp
Donnell G. Adams, Jr.

For full biographical listings, see the Martindale-Hubbell Law Directory

*RALEIGH,** Wake Co.

HOWARD, GREEN & McDARRIS, L.L.P. (AV)

4000 Westchase Boulevard Suite 200, P.O. Box 10305, 27605
Telephone: 919-833-2422
Fax: 919-833-2430
Email: HGMCD@mindspring.com

Robert E. Howard
Charles P. Green, Jr.
Dori Casey McDarris

ASSOCIATE

Katherine R. Sumrall

References: NationsBank; First Citizens Bank & Trust, Wachovia Bank.

For full biographical listings, see the Martindale-Hubbell Law Directory

JORDAN PRICE WALL GRAY JONES & CARLTON (AV)

A Professional Limited Liability Company
225 Hillsborough Street, 200 Hillsborough Place, P.O. Box 2021, 27602
Telephone: 919-828-2501; 919-831-4462
Telecopier: 919-834-8447
Email: law@jordanprice.com

MEMBERS OF FIRM

Robert R. Price
Joseph E. Wall
R. Frank Gray
Henry W. Jones, Jr.
Paul T. Flick
Terry J. Carlton
Hope Derby Carmichael

ASSOCIATES

Stephen R. Dolan
Shawna Y. Staton
Jonathan P. Carr
C. Marshall Lindsay
Christopher G. Lewis
Emily W. Eisele
Chad R. Clapp

OF COUNSEL

John R. Jordan, Jr.
Karen Kelly Carlton

Counsel for: Association of North Carolina Life Insurance Cos.; Family Health International; The Prudential Insurance Company of America; Texasgulf, Inc.; American Express; Jefferson-Pilot Life Insurance Co.; North Carolina Manufactured Housing Institute; First Citizens Bank & Trust Co.
Reference: First Citizens Bank & Trust Co., Raleigh, North Carolina.

For full biographical listings, see the Martindale-Hubbell Law Directory

KENNEDY COVINGTON LOBDELL & HICKMAN, L.L.P. (AV)

Two Hannover Square, 434 Fayetteville Street Mall, P.O. Box 1070, 27602-1070
Telephone: 919-743-7300
Fax: 919-743-7358
URL: http://www.kclh.com
Charlotte, North Carolina Office: Bank of America Corporate Center, Suite 4200, 100 North Tryon Street, 28202-4006.
Telephone: 704-331-7400.
Fax: 704-331-7598.
Rock Hill, South Carolina Office: First Union Center, 113 E. Main Street, 29730.
Telephone: 803-329-7600.
Fax: 803-329-7677.

RESIDENT PARTNERS

Lacy H. Reaves
Kent F. Christison
Alan H. Peterson
John L. Sarratt
Robert B. Womble
A. Lee Hogewood III

RESIDENT ASSOCIATES

Mickey A. Herrin, Jr.
Michael R. Thornton
Curtis C. Brewer, IV
Diane Scobie Joyce
G. William Joyner, III
Michael F. King
Margaret Rose Westbrook
Kimberley Weber Silver

Representative Clients: Bank of America and Subsidiaries; Crescent Resources, Inc.; Duke Energy Corporation ; First Union Corporation and Subsidiaries; Fluor Daniel; Guilford Mills, Inc.; Lance, Inc.; The Lundy Packing Company; Piedmont Health Care System; Summit Properties, Inc.

For full biographical listings, see the Martindale-Hubbell Law Directory

MANNING, FULTON & SKINNER, P.A. (AV)

UCB Plaza, Suite 500, 3605 Glenwood Avenue, P.O. Box 20389, 27619-0389
Telephone: 919-787-8880
Telecopier: 919-787-8902 (Litigation); 781-0811 (Real Estate); 571-2504 (Business-Tax)
Email: info@mfslaw.com *URL:* http://www.mfslaw.com

Howard E. Manning
Charles L. Fulton
William P. Skinner, Jr.
John B. McMillan
W. Gerald Thornton
Charles B. Morris, Jr. (1936-1995)
M. Marshall Happer, III
Michael T. Medford
Samuel T. Oliver, Jr.
David D. Dahl
Charles E. Nichols, Jr.
Barry D. Mann
John C. Dorsey

(See Next Column)

MANNING, FULTON & SKINNER P.A., *Raleigh—Continued*

David J. Witheft
William C. Smith, Jr.
Deborah L. Hildebran-Bachofen
Stephen T. Byrd
Michael S. Harrell
Alison R. Cayton

David T. Pryzwansky
Cary Elizabeth Close
Kristen Gardner Lingo
Tanya Denton Van Roekel
Thomas C. Kilpatrick
S. Nicole Taylor
Michael C. Phillips
Judson A. Welborn
Ralph J. DiLeone
Sandra M. Clark
Ritchie W. Taylor

Counsel for: Raleigh Merchants Bureau; Carolantic Realty, Inc.; Troxler Electronic Laboratories, Inc.; General Parts, Inc. (CARQUEST).
Representative Clients: International Business Machines Corp.; Siemens Energy & Authomation, Inc.; Mallinckrodt, Inc.; Employers Reinsurance Corp.

For full biographical listings, see the Martindale-Hubbell Law Directory

MAUPIN TAYLOR & ELLIS, P.A. (AV)

Highwoods Tower One, Suite 500, 3200 Beechleaf Court, P.O. Drawer 19764, 27619
Telephone: 919-981-4000
Telecopier: 919-981-4300
URL: http://www.maupinlaw.com
Research Triangle Park, North Carolina Office: 480 Beta Building, Headquarters Park, Post Office Box 13646, 27709-3646.
Telephone: 919-361-4900.

Armistead J. Maupin
William W. Taylor, Jr. (Retired)
Thomas F. Ellis
Charles B. Neely, Jr.
Thomas Willis Haywood Alexander
Robert A. Valois
John T. Williamson
Frank P. Ward, Jr.
Nancy S. Rendleman
Margie Toy Case
M. Keith Kapp
Mark S. Thomas
David R. Dorton
Thomas A. Farr
Holmes P. Harden
D. Royce Powell
William B. Gwyn, Jr.
James E. Gates
Amos C. Dawson, III
Gilbert C. Laite, III
Ronald R. Rogers
Elizabeth Davenport Scott
Reuben G. Clark, III
Arlene J. Diosegy
Gretchen W. Ewalt
Michael C. Lord
Karon B. Thornton
Theron McK. vanDusen
William P. Barrett
James C. Dever, III
Kurt J. Olson
John W. (Jack) Marin
John I. Mabe, Jr.
Charles L. Steel, IV
David A. Bookhout
Joel H. Katz
Abby T. Nathans
Steven B. Long
Laura A. Edgerton
Kevin W. Benedict
Joshua M. Krasner
Joanne Lambert
Terence D. Friedman
Anthony J. Biller
Robert B. Jones, Jr.
Thomas I. Lyon
Mark H. Shelburne
Roy H. Wyman, Jr.
Alexander W. Parrish (Not admitted in NC)
Mark A. Whitson
Gerald A. Tingen
Brett T. Hanna
Tanisha L. Brown (Not admitted in NC)
Camden R. Webb
Meredith L. Taylor
Richard A. Bynum
Aaron G.B. Spencer
Evan W. Fuguet

OF COUNSEL

Robert B. Broughton
W. Travis Porter
Laura Kay W. Berry

Representative Clients: American International Group; Blue Cross/Blue Shield of North Carolina; CSX Transportation, Inc.; Fluor Daniel Midland, Inc.; E & J Gallo Winery; Glaxo Wellcome; Northern Telecom Inc.; Reichhold Chemical Co. Inc.; Sampson Regional Medical Center; Smithfield Foods, Inc.; SouthTrust Bank, N.A.

For full biographical listings, see the Martindale-Hubbell Law Directory

PARKER, POE, ADAMS & BERNSTEIN L.L.P. (AV)

First Union Capitol Center, 150 Fayetteville Street Mall, Suite 1400, P.O. Box 389, 27602-0389
Telephone: 919-828-0564
Facsimile: 919-834-4564
Email: info@parkerpoe.com *URL:* http://www.parkerpoe.com
Charlotte, North Carolina Offices: 2500 Charlotte Plaza, 201 South College Street, 28244.
Telephone: 704-372-9000.
Facsimile: 704-334-4706 and South Park Office: The Rotunda, 4201 Congress Street, Suite 145, 28209.
Telephone: 704-556-9600.
Facsimile: 704-556-9601.
Columbia, South Carolina Office: 1201 Main Street, Suite 1450, 29201.
Telephone: 803-255-8000.
Facsimile: 803-255-8017.
Spartanburg, South Carolina Office: 101 W. St. John Street, Suite 203, 29306.
Telephone: 803-591-2030.
Facsimile: 803-591-2050.

(See Next Column)

Frankfurt, Germany Office: Limes Park, Otto-Volger-Strasse 5B, D-65843.
Telephone: (011) (49) 6196-750081.
Telefax: (011) (49) 6196-750088.

PARTNERS

J. Allen Adams
William H. McCullough
John F. Graybeal
Robert W. Spearman
Jack L. Cozort
Charles C. Meeker
Mary Carr Tolton
Catharine Biggs Arrowood
William G. Pappas
Stephen D. Coggins
Renee J. Montgomery
Stephen D. Lowry
Terri Toth McGaughey
Cynthia Leigh Wittmer
John J. Butler
Henry C. Campen, Jr.
Isabel Worthy Mattox
James C. Thornton
Robert H. Tiller

ASSOCIATES

John Michael Harlow
Russell B. Killen
Patricia T. Munchel
Amy Campbell Petty
R. Bruce Thompson, II
Brandon G. Bordeaux
Kevin L. Chignell
Melanie L. Black Dubis
Jason J. Kaus
Nancy LeCroy Mohler
Frank E. Silber
William B. Wright, III
Jeffrey A. Bandini
Brian D. Darer
Layth S. Elhassani

Representative Clients: Advantica Restaurant Group (formerly Flagstar Companies); American City Business Journals; Carolina Power and Light; Duke Energy; First Union National Bank; Georgetown Steel; GS Industries; Hoechst Corporation; Kemper National Insurance Companies; N. Schlumberger (USA),Inc.

For full biographical listings, see the Martindale-Hubbell Law Directory

PERRY, PATRICK, FARMER & MICHAUX, P.A. (AV)

3716 National Drive, Suite 100, 27612
Telephone: 919-787-8812
Fax: 919-787-3312
Charlotte, North Carolina Office: 2200 The Carillon, 227 West Trade Street.
Telephone: 704-372-1120.
Fax: 704-372-9635.
Other Charlotte, North Carolina Office: South Park, 1901 Roxborough Road, Suite 100.
Telephone: 704-364-9695.
Fax: 704-364-9698.

Richard W. Moore

G. Mark Teague
Virginia G. Dockery
Katherine M. Lewis

Representative Clients: The Bissell Cos.; Centex Real Estate Corp.; Charlotte Pipe and Foundry Co.; The Crosland Group, Inc.; Crown Life Insurance Co.; C.D. Spangler Construction Co.; International Construction Equipment, Inc.; The Manufacturers Life Insurance Co.; M/I Schottenstein Cos., Inc.; The Ryland Group, Inc.

For full biographical listings, see the Martindale-Hubbell Law Directory

PIPKIN, KNOTT, CLARK & BERGER, L.L.P. (AV)

3101 Glenwood Avenue, Suite 250, 27612-5096
Telephone: 919-783-5900
Telecopier: 919-783-9650

MEMBERS OF FIRM

Ashmead P. Pipkin
Joe Thomas Knott, III
Michael Wood Clark
Bruce W. Berger

For full biographical listings, see the Martindale-Hubbell Law Directory

SINK, POWERS, SINK & POTTER, L.L.P. (AV)

115 South St. Mary's Street, P.O. Box 27602, 27603
Telephone: 919-828-0684
Fax: 919-828-5386

MEMBERS OF FIRM

Henry H. Sink (1918-1989)
Charles F. Powers, III
Henry H. Sink, Jr.
William H. Potter, Jr.

Approved Attorneys: Lawyers Title Insurance Corp.

For full biographical listings, see the Martindale-Hubbell Law Directory

SMITH HELMS MULLISS & MOORE, L.L.P. (AV)

2800 Two Hannover Square, 27601
Telephone: 919-755-8700
Fax: 919-755-8800
Mailing Address: P.O. Box 27525, 27611
Email: smith_helms@shmm.com *URL:* http://www.shmm.com
Charlotte, North Carolina Office: 201 North Tryon Street, P.O. Box 31247.
Telephone: 704-343-2000.
Fax: 704-334-8467.
Telex: 572460.

(See Next Column)

SMITH HELMS MULLISS & MOORE L.L.P.—*Continued*

Greensboro, North Carolina Office: Suite 1400, First Union Tower, 300 North Greene Street, P.O. Box 21927.
Telephone: 336-378-5200.
Fax: 336-379-9558.
Wilmington, North Carolina Office: 127 Grace Street, P.O. Box 3235.
Telephone: 910-254-3800.
Fax: 910-254-3900.
Atlanta, Georgia Office: 1355 Peachtree Street N.E., Suite 750.
Telephone: 404-962-1000.
Fax: 404-962-1200.

MEMBERS OF FIRM

Charles N. Anderson, Jr.
William Sam Byassee
Richard W. Ellis
James L. Gale
Leslie C. O'Toole
George J. Oliver
David V. Otterson
J. Anthony Penry
Bradley M. Risinger
Cathy M. Rudisill
Matthew W. Sawchak
Samuel O. Southern
Paul K. Sun, Jr.
Robert L. Wilson, Jr.
Michael G. Winters

ASSOCIATES

Diana Semel Allen
Thomas D. Blue, Jr.
Donna Kaye Blumberg
Tracy Hamrick Davis
Mary Margaret Dillon
Alex J. Hagan
Michael V. Lee
John William Mann
Patricia Markus Pinkley
Neil A. Riemann
Clayton D. Somers
Sandra D. van der Vaart
Julia Furr Youngman

OF COUNSEL

Hampton Y. Dellinger
Gary R. Govert

For full biographical listings, see the Martindale-Hubbell Law Directory

WOMBLE CARLYLE SANDRIDGE & RICE (AV)

A Professional Limited Liability Company
2100 First Union Capitol Center, 150 Fayetteville Street Mall, P.O. Box 831, 27602
Telephone: 919-755-2100
Fax: 919-755-2150
Email: lawyers@wcsr.com *URL:* http://www.wcsr.com
Charlotte, North Carolina Office: 3300 One First Union Center, 301 South College Street.
Telephone: 704-331-4900.
Fax: 704-331-4955.
Winston-Salem, North Carolina Office: 200 West Second Street, P.O. Drawer 84.
Telephone: 336-721-3600.
Fax: 336-721-3660.
Research Triangle Park, North Carolina Office: 2505 Meridian Parkway, Suite 300 (Durham), 27713.
Telephone: 919-484-2300.
Fax: 919-484-2340.
Atlanta, Georgia Office: One Atlantic Center, 1201 West Peachtree Street, Suite 3500.
Telephone: 404-872-7000.
Fax: 404-888-7490.
Other Atlanta, Georgia Office: Suite 404, 2296 Henderson Mill Road, N.E.
Telephone: 770-492-9030.
Fax: 770-492-9609.
Washington, D.C. Office: 1120 Nineteenth Street, N.W., Eighth Floor.
Telephone: 202-857-4400.
Fax: 202-467-6910.
Greenville, South Carolina Office: 15 South Main Street, Suite 601, P.O. Box 10208.
Telephone: 864-255-5400.
Fax: 864-255-5440.

RESIDENT MEMBERS

Jerry S. Alvis
Thomas B. Anderson, Jr.
M. Christopher Bolen
John C. Cooke
Susan Davis Crooks
Donald A. Donadio
Charles A. Edwards
Robert E. Fields III
Marilyn R. Forbes
Christopher T. Graebe
Johnny M. Loper
Heather K. Mallard
William C. Matthews, Jr.
Pressly M. Millen
Burley B. Mitchell, Jr.
Frederick W. Rom
Alexander P. Sands, III
Robert H. Sasser, III
Stephen A. Yeagy

RESIDENT ASSOCIATES

Sean E. Andrussier
Charles L. Becker
Richard J. Caira, Jr.
Jennifer Long Collins
Angela C. Corenevsky
Coleman M. Cowan
Mark A. Davis
Carol Wooten Exum
Richard M. Feathers
Bryan D. Graham
Jeffrey M. Hahn
Gene A. Jones, Jr.
Scott P. Mebane
Christine Carlisle Odom
G. Christopher Olson
John W. O'Tuel, III
Mary Sheehan Pollard
M. Todd Sullivan
Samuel M. Taylor
Jacqueline Terry
Nellie Shipley Tomlinson

(See Next Column)

RESIDENT OF COUNSEL

Kurt D. Weaver (Not admitted in NC)
E. Lawrence Davis, III
Elizabeth LeVan Riley

LEGAL SUPPORT PERSONNEL

Hassel L. Parker (Executive Director)
Marvin E. Chavis (Director of Technology)
Donald H. Adamick (Director of Library Services)
Keith Tedrow (Director of Administration)
John E. Turlington (Office Administrator - Raleigh)
Patricia A. Kight (Human Resources Administrator)
Charles R. Allison (Office Administrator - Charlotte)
Terry Michael Wiley (Director of Finance and Systems)
Paula G. Blanchat (Marketing Administrator)
Beth Keasler (Recruitment Administrator)

Representative Clients: Aetna Casualty and Surety Co., Inc.; ALSCO/AmeriMark Building Products, Inc.; Aoki Corporation America, Inc.; Hackney Brothers, Inc.; Lawyers Mutual Liability Insurance Company of North Carolina; Meredith College; Regency Park Corp.; Wachovia Bank, N.A.

For full biographical listings, see the Martindale-Hubbell Law Directory

*ROCKINGHAM,** Richmond Co.

KITCHIN, NEAL, WEBB, WEBB & FUTRELL, P.A. (AV)

111 Washington Street, 28379
Telephone: 910-997-2206
Fax: 910-997-3821
Mailing Address: P.O. Box 1657, 28380
Hamlet, North Carolina Office: 54 Main Street, 28345.
Telephone: 910-582-3277.

Henry L. Kitchin
F. Brent Neal
Alden B. Webb
William R. Webb, Jr.
Stephan R. Futrell

Representative Clients: Richmond County, N.C.; Richmond Memorial Hospital, Inc.; State Farm Mutual Insurance Company; L.G. DeWitt Trucking Company, Inc.; Richmond Yarns, Inc.
Approved Attorneys for: Lawyers Title Insurance Corp.

For full biographical listings, see the Martindale-Hubbell Law Directory

*ROXBORO,** Person Co.

HUBBARD, CATES & LONG (AV)

36 Court Street, P.O. Box 679, 27573
Telephone: 336-597-2251; 599-2443
Fax: 336-597-3042

MEMBERS OF FIRM

Charles E. Hubbard
Walter Bradsher Cates
Daniel R. Long, Jr.
Ursula P. Long

LEGAL SUPPORT PERSONNEL

Deborah L. Barker

Representative Clients: Person County Memorial Hospital; Person County Family Medical Center; Carolane Propane Gas, Inc.; Camp Chemical Corp.; Person-Caswell Lake Authority.
Approved Attorneys for: Branch Banking and Trust; First Union National Bank of North Carolina; Central Carolina Bank and Trust Co., N.A.
References: First Union National Bank of North Carolina; Roxboro Savings Bank, SSB.

For full biographical listings, see the Martindale-Hubbell Law Directory

*SALISBURY,** Rowan Co.

KLUTTZ, REAMER, BLANKENSHIP, HAYES & RANDOLPH, L.L.P. (AV)

131 North Main Street, P.O. Drawer 1617, 28145-1617
Telephone: 704-636-7100
Telecopier: 704-636-2284
Email: kluttzlaw@salisbury.net

Wm. Clarence Kluttz (1917-1996)
Lewis P. Hamlin, Jr. (1919-1988)
Richard R. Reamer
Malcolm B. Blankenship, Jr.
William C. Kluttz, Jr.
Glenn S. Hayes
James D.K.F. Randolph

ASSOCIATE

Roman C. Pibl

Representative Clients: Duke Power Co.; General Electric Co.; Cone Mills Corp.; Central Carolina Bank; Nationwide Mutual Insurance Co.; Kemper Insurance Group; North Carolina Farm Bureau Mutual Insurance Co.; The Papco Group, Inc.; Johnson Concrete, Inc.; Rowan Regional Medical Center, Inc.

For full biographical listings, see the Martindale-Hubbell Law Directory

SHUFORD, CADDELL & FRALEY (AV)

205 Wachovia Bank Building, 130 South Main Street, 28144
Telephone: 704-636-8050

(See Next Column)

SHUFORD, CADDELL & FRALEY, *Salisbury—Continued*

MEMBERS OF FIRM

W. T. Shuford (1905-1990) Thomas M. Caddell
Lucinda L. Fraley

Representative Clients: Wachovia Bank, N.A.; Taylor Clay Products; Rowan Corp.; Ironwood Development, Inc.; Rockwell Farms; Gardner Glass Products, Inc; Premtec, Inc.; Home Concrete Co.; J.H. Cook & Sons, Inc.; Central Carolina Insurance Agency, Inc.

For full biographical listings, see the Martindale-Hubbell Law Directory

*SANFORD,** Lee Co.

STATON, PERKINSON, DOSTER, POST, SILVERMAN & ADCOCK, P.A. (AV)

205 Courtland Drive, P.O. Box 1320, 27331
Telephone: 919-775-5616
Fax: 919-774-7148

J. C. Pittman (1900-1975)
Robert L. Gavin (1916-1981)
William Wayne Staton
Ronald L. Perkinson
W. Woods Doster
Norman C. Post, Jr.
Jonathan Silverman
Paul J. Adcock

Representative Clients: Golden Corral Corp.; Federal Spinning Corp.; Virginia-Carolina Tools of Sanford, Inc.; GC Development Corp.; Imperial Freezer Services, L.L.C.
Local Counsel for: Nationwide Insurance Co.; State Farm Mutual Insurance Co.; Aetna Casualty & Surety Co.; Allstate Insurance Co.

For full biographical listings, see the Martindale-Hubbell Law Directory

SHALLOTTE, Brunswick Co.

FRINK, FOY & YOUNT, P.A. (AV)

4646 Main Street, P.O. Box 3207, 28459
Telephone: 910-754-6934
Fax: 910-754-9224
Southport, North Carolina Office: 319 North Howe Street.
Telephone: 910-457-5284.
Fax: 910-457-6335.

Stephen B. Yount

Richard Russell Davis

Local Counsel for: Seaboard Coast Line Railroad Co.
Representative Clients: United Carolina Bank; Pilot Life Insurance Co.; Jefferson Standard Life Insurance Co.; Reeves Telecom Corp.; Nationwide Insurance Co.
Approved Attorneys for: Lawyers Title Insurance Corp.; First Title Insurance Corp.
References: United Carolina Bank; Security Savings Bank S.S.B.

*SMITHFIELD,** Johnston Co.

NARRON, O'HALE & WHITTINGTON, P.A. (AV)

Market & Third Streets, P.O. Box 1567, 27577
Telephone: 919-934-6021
Fax: 919-934-6280
Benson, North Carolina Office: 207 East Main Street, P.O. Box 457.
Telephone: 919-894-8565.

James W. Narron
John P. O'Hale
O. Hampton Whittington, Jr. (Resident, Benson Office)

Jacquelyn L. Lee

Representative Clients: Georgia-Pacific Corp.; Carolina Telephone & Telegraph Co.; Coor Farm Supply Service, Inc.; NationsBank; Etheridge Oil Co.

For full biographical listings, see the Martindale-Hubbell Law Directory

SOUTHPORT, Brunswick Co.

FRINK, FOY & YOUNT, P.A. (AV)

319 North Howe Street, P.O. Box 10485, 28461
Telephone: 910-457-5284
Fax: 910-457-6335
Shallotte, North Carolina Office: 4646 Main Street, P.O. Box 3207.
Telephone: 910-754-6934.
Fax: 910-754-9224.

S. Bunn Frink (1899-1989) Henry G. Foy
Stephen B. Yount

Local Counsel for: Seaboard Coast Line Railroad Co.
Representative Clients: Branch Bank and Trust Co.; Pilot Life Insurance Co.; Jefferson Standard Life Insurance Co.; Reeves Telecom Corp.; Nationwide Insurance Co.
Approved Attorneys for: Lawyers Title Insurance Corp.; First Title Insurance Corp.
References: Branch Bank and Trust Co.; Security Savings Bank S.S.B.

For full biographical listings, see the Martindale-Hubbell Law Directory

*STATESVILLE,** Iredell Co.

POPE, MCMILLAN, KUTTEH, SIMON & BAKER, P.A. (AV)

113 North Center Street, Suite 200, P.O. Drawer 1776, 28687-1776
Telephone: 704-873-2131; 704-664-2254
Fax: 704-872-7629
Mooresville, North Carolina Office: 123 North Main Street.
Telephone: 704-664-2254.

William P. Pope
William H. McMillan
Constantine H. Kutteh, II
Pamela H. Simon
Anthony Joseph Baker (Resident, Mooresville Office)

Anthony S. Privette

Representative Clients: Nationwide Insurance Co.; Aetna Life & Casualty Insurance Co.; NationsBank; Davis Community Hospital; Bank of Iredell; Piedmont Farm Credit Assn.; Allstate Insurance Co.; Travelers Insurance Co.
Approved Attorneys for: Lawyers Title Insurance Corp.; Farmers Home and Federal Land Bank Assn.

For full biographical listings, see the Martindale-Hubbell Law Directory

TABOR CITY, Columbus Co.

MCGOUGAN, WRIGHT, WORLEY AND HARPER, L.L.P. (AV)

200 South Lewis Street, P.O. Box 457, 28463
Telephone: 910-653-3682; 653-2082
FAX: 910-653-5726
Email: tclaw@mailcity.com
Whiteville, North Carolina Office: 130 Jefferson Street.
Telephone: 910-640-1485.
Fax: 910-640-3132.

MEMBERS OF FIRM

Duncan F. McGougan, Jr. (1921-1994)
O. Richard Wright, Jr.
Dennis T. Worley

General Counsel for: The Brunswick Electric Membership Corp.; Town of Tabor City; Frank Horne Construction Co.; Atlantic Publishing & Paper Co.; Town of Bolton; Town of Bordman; Town of Brunswick; Town of Fair Bluff; Town of Cerro Gordo; The Gore Co.

For full biographical listings, see the Martindale-Hubbell Law Directory

*WARRENTON,** Warren Co.

BANZET, BANZET & THOMPSON (AV)

Court House Square, 101 North Front Street, P.O. Box 535, 27589
Telephone: 252-257-3166; 257-2201
Fax: 252-257-2053
Email: banzet@vance.net

MEMBERS OF FIRM

Julius Banzet, III Lewis A. Thompson, III

Representative Clients: Branch Banking & Trust Co.; Town of Norlina; The Peck Manufacturing Company of North Carolina, Inc.; Warren County Board of Education.
Approved Attorneys for: Federal Land Bank of Columbia; Lawyers Title Insurance Corp.; Chicago Title Insurance Co.; Commonwealth Land Title Insurance Co.; AMI Title Insurance Co.

For full biographical listings, see the Martindale-Hubbell Law Directory

WARSAW, Duplin Co.

E.C. THOMPSON, III, P.C. (AV)

114 West Hill Street, P.O. Box 901, 28398-0901
Telephone: 910-293-3124
Facsimile: 910-293-7171
Email: thompson@duplinnet.com

E. C. Thompson, III

Susan Collins Mikitka

For full biographical listings, see the Martindale-Hubbell Law Directory

*WENTWORTH,** Rockingham Co.

THOMAS S. HARRINGTON (AV)

2 Courthouse Square, 27375
Telephone: 910-349-2943
Fax: 910-627-4243
Eden Office: 708 West Washington Street, 27288-6029.
Telephone: 910-227-7461.
Fax: 910-227-9716.

(See Next Column)

THOMAS S. HARRINGTON—*Continued*

Local Counsel: Duke Power Co.
Approved Attorneys for: Lawyers Title Insurance Corp.; United Title Insurance Co.; Chicago Title Insurance Co.; Jefferson Pilot Title Insurance Co.; First Title Insurance Co.

*WHITEVILLE,** Columbus Co.

LEE, LEE & GARNER (AV)

812 Pinckney Street, 28472
Telephone: 910-642-3708
Fax: 910-642-9058
Email: llg@weblnk.net

MEMBERS OF FIRM

Junius B. Lee, Jr. (1919-1989)
Junius B. Lee, III
Hugh Griffith Garner

Representative Clients: Branch Banking & Trust, Whiteville Office; National Spinning Co.; Security Insurance Group; United Carolina Bank Trust Dept.; J. W. Cook & Sons, Inc.; V & M Supply Co., Inc.
Approved Attorneys for: Lawyers Title Insurance Corp.

For full biographical listings, see the Martindale-Hubbell Law Directory

*WILKESBORO,** Wilkes Co.

WILLARDSON & LIPSCOMB, LLP (AV)

206 East Main Street, 28697
Telephone: 336-838-5129
Fax: 336-838-8959

MEMBERS OF FIRM

John S. Willardson
William F. Lipscomb

Representative Clients: Aetna Casualty & Surety Co.; Allstate Insurance Co.; Integon General Insurance Co.; North Carolina Farm Bureau Mutual; Pennsylvania National Mutual Insurance; Pennsylvania Mutual Insurance Co.; Nationwide Insurance Co.; The Travelers Indemnity Co.; Virginia Mutual Ins. Co.; Wausau Insurance Co.

For full biographical listings, see the Martindale-Hubbell Law Directory

*WILMINGTON,** New Hanover Co.

HOGUE, HILL, JONES, NASH AND LYNCH, L.L.P. (AV)

101 S. Third Street, P.O. Drawer 2178, 28402
Telephone: 910-763-4565
Telecopier: 910-762-6687

MEMBERS OF FIRM

Cyrus D. Hogue (1888-1960)
W. Talmage Jones
David A. Nash
William O. J. Lynch
James B. Snow, III
Wayne A. Bullard

OF COUNSEL

Cyrus D. Hogue, Jr.
William L. Hill, II
Roy C. Bain

ASSOCIATE

Stacey L. Fuller

Representative Clients: NationsBank N.A.; International Paper Company; Lower Cape Fear Water & Sewer Authority; New Hanover County Board of Education; Kaiser Aluminum & Chemical Corporation; Wilmington Shipping Company; Clancy & Theys Construction Company; Cooperative Bank for Savings; Independence Mall Associates.

For full biographical listings, see the Martindale-Hubbell Law Directory

MARSHALL, WILLIAMS & GORHAM, L.L.P. (AV)

14 South Fifth Street, P.O. Drawer 2088, 28402-2088
Telephone: 910-763-9891
Telecopier: 910-343-8604
URL: http://www.mwglaw.com

MEMBERS OF FIRM

Alan A. Marshall (1908-1979)
Lonnie B. Williams
A. Dumay Gorham, Jr.
Jerry C. Woodell
William Robert Cherry, Jr.
Ronald H. Woodruff
Lonnie B. Williams, Jr.
John Dearman Martin
Charles D. Meier
John L. Coble

Representative Clients: Miller Building Corp.; Kemper Insurance Cos.; New Hanover Regional Medical Center; Wilmington Health Associates, P.A.; The Housing Authority of the City of Wilmington; Ryan-Walsh, Inc.; CIGNA Cos.; Aetna Casualty & Surety Co.; Bituminous Insurance Co.; Government Employers Insurance Co.

For full biographical listings, see the Martindale-Hubbell Law Directory

*WILSON,** Wilson Co.

CONNOR, BUNN, ROGERSON & WOODARD, P.L.L.C. (AV)

P.O. Box 3299, 27895-3299
Telephone: 252-243-3136
Fax: 252-243-8243; 252-243-2558

(See Next Column)

Henry Groves Connor (1911-1989)
David M. Connor (1935-1994)
Turner B. Bunn, III
James F. Rogerson
David W. Woodard
Elizabeth Blair McKinney
Julie M. Watson
L. Patrick Fleming, Jr.

General Counsel for: The Wilson Daily Times, Inc.; New Hope Development Corp.; Bunn & Co.; Southern Piping Co.; Nash Realty Co.; Williamson Thermo King Dealerships, Inc.; Boone's Antiques, Inc.; Southern Testing & Research Laboratories, Inc.

For full biographical listings, see the Martindale-Hubbell Law Directory

ROSE, RAND, ORCUTT, CAULEY, BLAKE & ELLIS, P.A. (AV)

2500 West Nash Street, Unit C, P.O. Drawer 2367, 27894-2367
Telephone: 252-291-3848
Telecopier: 252-291-9555

William A. Lucas (1881-1967)
Oliver G. Rand (1895-1967)
Naomi E. Morris (1921-1986)
Z. Hardy Rose (1913-1999)
William R. Rand
David S. Orcutt
James P. Cauley, III
Paul N. Blake, III
Susan K. Ellis
William O. Kuhn
Tom Slade Rand, Jr.

Representative Clients: City of Wilson; Wilson County Board of Education; Region L Council of Governments; Barton College; Wilson County Properties, Inc.; Braswell Equipment Company, Inc.; Town of Scotland Neck; Wilson-Greene Mental Health Association; Wilson Landholding Corporation; Global TransPark Development Commission.

For full biographical listings, see the Martindale-Hubbell Law Directory

*WINSTON-SALEM,** Forsyth Co.

ALLMAN SPRY LEGGETT & CRUMPLER, P.A. (AV)

Suite 700, 380 Knollwood Street, Drawer 5129, 27113-5129
Telephone: 336-722-2300
Telecopier: 336-721-0414

C. Edwin Allman (1926-1991)
James E. Humphreys, Jr. (1938-1989)
W. Dennie Spry
R. Bradford Leggett
Donald M. VonCannon
C. Edwin Allman, III
Thomas T. Crumpler
Edward E. Raymer, Jr.
M. Joseph Allman
Walter R. Hinnant
George T. "Ted" Mann
Joseph J. Gatto
Carrie M. Koontz
Denise M. Gold

Representative Clients: Highwoods Properties, Inc.; Pluma, Inc.; Malayan United Industries Behrad; Regent Carolina Corporation; Brendles, Incorporated; Centura Bank; Nationwide Mutual Insurance Company; Mutual of Omaha Insurance Company; Crowder Realty & Investment Co., Inc.; First Carolina Corporate Credit Union.

For full biographical listings, see the Martindale-Hubbell Law Directory

BELL, DAVIS & PITT, P.A. (AV)

635 West Fourth Street, P.O. Box 21029, 27120-1029
Telephone: 336-722-3700
Fax: 336-722-8153
URL: http://www.belldavispitt.com

William D. Harper (1943-1995)
Frank M. Bell, Jr.
William Davis
Walter W. Pitt, Jr.
Joseph T. Carruthers
James R. Fox
Stephen M. Russell
D. Anderson Carmen
John W. Babcock
J. Dennis Bailey
Stephen D. Poe
Amy K. Smith
Charlot F. Wood
Thomas W. Waldrep, Jr.
James D. Wall
Elizabeth M. Repetti
Alan M. Ruley
Mallory M. Oldham
Michelle B. Clifton

Robin J. Stinson
Daniel C. Bruton
Jon L. Spargur, Jr.
Kevin G. Williams
John A. Cocklereece, Jr.
R. Anthony Hartsoe
Galen G. Craun, III

Local Counsel for: Branch Banking and Trust Co.; Builders Transport, Inc.; Chrysler Credit Corp.; Lawyers Mutual Insurance Co.; NationsBank, N.A.; Piedmont Natural Gas Co.; St. Paul Insurance Co.; SmithKline Beecham Corp.;
General Counsel for: Adele Knits, Inc.; Landmark Builders of The Triad, Inc.;

For full biographical listings, see the Martindale-Hubbell Law Directory

CRAIGE, BRAWLEY, LIIPFERT & WALKER, L.L.P. (AV)

500 West Fourth Street, Suite 200, P.O. Box 1666, 27102-1666
Telephone: 336-725-0583
Fax: 336-725-4677

MEMBERS OF FIRM

Cowles Liipfert
William W. Walker
B. Bailey Liipfert, III

(See Next Column)

CRAIGE, BRAWLEY, LIIPFERT & WALKER L.L.P., *Winston-Salem—Continued*

ASSOCIATES

John A. Keiger
J. Laross Ketner
Robert A. Lefkowitz
Brent Wayne Stephens
Robert Martin Addison

Approved Attorneys for: Lawyers Title Insurance Corp.; Chicago Title Insurance Co.; Commonwealth Land Title Insurance Co.; First American Title Insurance Co.; Jefferson-Pilot Title Insurance Co.

For full biographical listings, see the Martindale-Hubbell Law Directory

DAVIS & HAMRICK, L.L.P. (AV)

115 West Third Street, P.O. Drawer 20039, 27120-0039
Telephone: 336-725-8385
Telecopier: 336-723-8838
Email: dhlaw@vnet.net

Fred S. Hutchins, Sr. (1893-1977)
John M. Minor (1917-1974)
Roy L. Deal (1889-1982)

MEMBERS OF FIRM

H. Lee Davis, Jr.
Kent L. Hamrick
Shannon L. Warf

James G. Welsh, Jr.
L. Kathryn Slocumb

Local Counsel for: Travelers Insurance Co.; Maryland Casualty Co.; State Farm Insurance Co.; Liberty Mutual Insurance Co.; Shelby Mutual Insurance Co.; Transport Insurance Co; U.S.F. & G.; Safeco Ins. Co.

For full biographical listings, see the Martindale-Hubbell Law Directory

WOMBLE CARLYLE SANDRIDGE & RICE (AV)

A Professional Limited Liability Company
200 West Second Street, P.O. Drawer 84, 27102
Telephone: 336-721-3600
Fax: 336-721-3660
Email: lawyers@wcsr.com *URL:* http://www.wcsr.com
Charlotte, North Carolina Office: 3300 One First Union Center, 301 South College Street.
Telephone: 704-331-4900.
Fax: 704-331-4955.
Raleigh, North Carolina Office: 2100 First Union Capitol Center, 150 Fayetteville Street Mall, P.O. Box 831.
Telephone: 919-755-2100.
Fax: 919-755-2150.
Research Triangle Park, North Carolina Office: 2505 Meridian Parkway, Suite 300 (Durham), 27713.
Telephone: 919-484-2300.
Fax: 919-484-2340.
Atlanta, Georgia Office: One Atlantic Center, 1201 West Peachtree Street, Suite 3500.
Telephone: 404-872-7000.
Fax: 404-888-7490.
Other Atlanta, Georgia Office: Suite 404, 2296 Henderson Mill Road, N.E.
Telephone: 770-492-9030.
Fax: 770-492-9609.
Washington, D.C. Office: 1120 Nineteenth Street, N.W., Eighth Floor.
Telephone: 202-857-4400.
Fax: 202-467-6910.
Greenville, South Carolina Office: 15 South Main Street, Suite 601, P.O. Box 10208.
Telephone: 864-255-5400.
Fax: 864-255-5440.

RESIDENT MEMBERS

B. S. Womble (1882-1976)
Irving E. Carlyle (1896-1971)
W. Pendleton Sandridge (1904-1982)
Leon L. Rice Jr. (1912-1987)
Jean Taylor Adams
Reid C. Adams, Jr.
Conrad C. Baldwin, Jr.
Janice C. Baldwin
H. Grady Barnhill, Jr.
Jimmy H. Barnhill
S. Fraley Bost
Anthony H. Brett
Leslie E. Browder
Charles A. Burke
Karen Estelle Carey
Keith A. Clinard
W. Andrew Copenhaver
Clayton M. Custer
Tyrus V. Dahl, Jr.
Linwood L. Davis
Ronald R. Davis
William A. Davis, II
Bonnie Kay Donahue
Richard N. Drake
Jonathan M. Engram
Gusti W. Frankel
Jeffrey L. Furr
John L. W. Garrou
Allan R. Gitter
Murray C. Greason, Jr.
Ellen M. Gregg
R. Howard Grubbs
Michael D. Gunter
Hardin G. Halsey
Hada V. Haulsee
Lori Privette Hinnant
Martin L. Holton, III
Jeffrey C. Howland
David A. Irvin
Christopher E. Leon
R. Michael Leonard
Roddey M. Ligon, Jr.
Kim Kelly Mann
Dennis W. McNames
James R. Morgan, Jr.
Kenneth A. Moser
Alexander S. Nicholas
James K. Phillips
Robert S. Pierce
Mark N. Poovey
Elizabeth L. Quick

(See Next Column)

RESIDENT MEMBERS (Continued)

Robert L. Quick
George A. Ragland
Michael E. Ray
Richard T. Rice
W. P. Sandridge, Jr.
Thomas D. Schroeder
David A. Shirlen
Greg L. Smith
William B. Sullivan
J. Keith Tart
Ashley O. Thrift
James E. Vaughan
Keith W. Vaughan
Robert A. West
William R. Whitehurst
C. Mark Wiley
G. Criston Windham
Calder W. Womble
Erna A. P. Womble
William F. Womble
William F. Womble, Jr.

RESIDENT ASSOCIATES

Patrick M. Allen
Kenneth R. Ashford
Amy L. Bircher
Alison R. Bost
John J. Bowers
Andrew C. Buckner
Roger E. Cole
Mary Nell Craven
Christopher G. Daniel
Christina U. Douglas
Lisa M. Drabik (Not admitted in NC)
Elizabeth A. Flagg
C. Lynn Gargis
Brandy K. Gillenwater
Jacqueline M. Goble
Murray C. Greason (Not admitted in NC)
Stanley B. Green
Ursula M. Henninger
Kimberly S. Herring
Adam B. Hirschfeld
D. Christopher Howard (Not admitted in NC)
Neil D. Kodsi
Christopher A. Kreiner
William E. Latham II
Joel M. Leander
Andrew J. Logan
G. Wriston Marshburn, Jr
David J. Mazza (Not admitted in NC)
Kenneth R. Michael
Philip J. Mohr
Michael Montecalvo
John F. Morrow, Jr.
Neil G. O'Rourke
Robert F. Pomper
Patricia F. Poole
David H. Read
Sharon A. Riegel
Stephanie U. Roberts
Donald J. Scales
Patricia G. Scales
Lisa M. Sheppard (Not admitted in NC)
Lawrence B. Somers
Cynthia G. Spivey
Theresa M. Sprain
Randel S. Springer
John R. Still
Stacey M. Stone
Jack M. Strauch
F. Scott Thomas
Brent L. Thompson (Not admitted in NC)
Allison L. Thompson (Not admitted in NC)
Sydney J. Warren
C. Andrew Wattleworth
William G. Winter
Robyn B. Withrow
Laura M. Wolfe
Peter A. Zorn

MEMBER OF COUNSEL

H. Jesse Arnelle (Not admitted in NC)
Ranlet S. Bell
W. David Edwards
Kurt C. Stakeman
Susan P. Strommer
Dewey W. Wells

STAFF ATTORNEY

Daniel Patrick Foley (Not admitted in NC)

LEGAL SUPPORT PERSONNEL

Hassel L. Parker (Executive Director)
Marvin E. Chavis (Director of Technology)
Donald H. Adamick (Director of Library Services)
Susan DeVore (Office Administrator - Atlanta)
Keith Tedrow (Director of Administration)
John E. Turlington (Office Administrator - Raleigh)
Patricia A. Kight (Human Resources Administrator)
Beth Keasler (Attorney Recruitment Administrator)
Charles R. Allison (Office Administrator - Charlotte)
Terry Michael Wiley (Director of Finance and Systems)
Paula G. Blanchat (Marketing Administrator)

Representative Clients: Brad Ragan, Inc.; Brenner Companies; Food Lion, Inc.; Hanes Companies, Inc.; North Carolina Baptist Hospitals, Inc.; R.J. Reynolds Tobacco Co.; Thomasville Furniture Industries, Inc.; Wachovia Corp.; Wake Forest University.

For full biographical listings, see the Martindale-Hubbell Law Directory

*YANCEYVILLE,** Caswell Co.

FARMER & WATLINGTON, L.L.P. (AV)

21 Main Street West, P.O. Drawer B, 27379-0330
Telephone: 336-694-4361; 694-6549
FAX: 336-694-5448

MEMBERS OF FIRM

R. Lee Farmer
Stuart N. Watlington

General Counsel for: Watlington's Inc.; Ronco, Inc.; A. D. Swann Trucking Co., Inc.; Gregory Pallet Co.
Representative Clients: Wachovia Bank of North Carolina, N.A.; Duke Power Co.; First Virginia Bank Piedmont.
Approved Attorneys for: Lawyers Title Insurance Corp.; Farmers Home Administration, U.S.D.A.

For full biographical listings, see the Martindale-Hubbell Law Directory

NORTH DAKOTA

*BISMARCK,** Burleigh Co.

PEARCE AND DURICK, PLLP (AV)

314 East Thayer Avenue, P.O. Box 400, 58502
Telephone: 701-223-2890
Fax: 701-223-7865
Email: law.office@pearce-durick.com *URL:* http://www.pearce-durick.com

MEMBERS OF FIRM

William R. Pearce (1910-1978)
William P. Pearce
Patrick W. Durick
B. Timothy Durick
Gary R. Thune
David E. Reich
Jerome C. Kettleson
Larry L. Boschee
Lawrence Bender

ASSOCIATES

Jonathan P. Sanstead
Jeffrey G. Transtrom

OF COUNSEL

Harry J. Pearce

LEGAL SUPPORT PERSONNEL

Suzanne Cahill (Paralegal)
Tori Vetter (Paralegal)

Representative Clients: American Insurance Assn.; Cigna-INA Insurance Co.; Deere & Co.; Ford Motor Co.; General Motors Corp.; MDU Resources Group, Inc.; Meyer Broadcasting Co.; Royal Insurance Co.; Travelers Insurance Co.

For full biographical listings, see the Martindale-Hubbell Law Directory

ZUGER KIRMIS & SMITH (AV)

A Partnership including Professional Corporations
316 North Fifth Street, P.O. Box 1695, 58502-1695
Telephone: 701-223-2711
Fax: 701-223-7387; 701-223-9619
Email: zkslaw@zkslaw.com *URL:* http://www.zkslaw.com

Lyle W. Kirmis
Thomas O. Smith, P.C.
Lance D. Schreiner, P.C.
James S. Hill, P.C.
Patrick J. Ward
Rebecca S. Thiem, P.C.
Daniel S. Kuntz, P.C.
Brenda L. Blazer, P.C.
Jerry W. Evenson, P.C.
Brent J. Edison, P.C.
Christine A. Hogan
Lawrence A. Dopson
Lawrence E. King

ASSOCIATES

Jodi Billing Bjornson
Tracy Vigness Kolb

OF COUNSEL

John A. Zuger, P.C.

Representative Clients: American Counsel of Life Insurance; Bank of America; Burlington Northern Railroad Co.; Knife River Coal Mining Company; Loewen Group, Inc.; Medcenter One Health Systems; Mor-Gran-Sou Electric Cooperative, Inc.; North Dakota Grain Dealers Assn.; North Dakota Workers Compensation Bureau; US WEST.

For full biographical listings, see the Martindale-Hubbell Law Directory

*DEVILS LAKE,** Ramsey Co.

TRAYNOR, RUTTEN & TRAYNOR (AV)

Traynor Building, 509 Fifth Street, P.O. Box 838, 58301
Telephone: 701-662-4077
Fax: 701-662-7537
URL: http://www.traynor-rutten.com

MEMBERS OF FIRM

John T. Traynor
Thomas E. Rutten
J. Thomas Traynor, Jr.
Daniel M. Traynor

Representative Clients: Dakota Fire Insurance Co.; Nodak Mutual Insurance Co.; Horace Mann Insurance Co.; Federated Insurance Co.; Great West Casualty Co.; Grinnell Mutual Reinsurance Group; City of Devils Lake; Bremer Bank of Devils Lake, N.D.; Ramsey National Bank and Trust Co., Devils Lake, N.D.; Western State Bank, Devils Lake, N.D.

For full biographical listings, see the Martindale-Hubbell Law Directory

*DICKINSON,** Stark Co.

MACKOFF KELLOGG LAW FIRM (AV)

(Mackoff, Kellogg, Kirby & Kloster, P.C.)
46 West Second Street, P.O. Box 1097, 58601
Telephone: 701-227-1841
Fax: 701-227-4739
Email: firm@mackoff.com *URL:* http://www.mackoff.com
Beach, North Dakota Office: 41 Central Avenue, South.
Telephone: 701-872-3731.
FAX: 701-872-4695.
Baker, Montana Office: 15 South Main, P.O. Box 1075. Telephone/
FAX: 406-778-2808.

(See Next Column)

H. A. Mackoff (1888-1963)
Theodore Kellogg (1904-1990)
Ward M. Kirby (1922-1993)
Paul G. Kloster
John L. Sherman
Gordon W. Schnell
Paul F. Ebeltoft, Jr.
Timothy A. Priebe
Charles J. Peterson (Dickinson, Beach, North Dakota and Baker, Montana Offices)
Glen R. Bruhschwein
Michael C. Waller
Randall N. Sickler
Sandra K. Kuntz
Paul R. Emerson

Representative Clients: Norwest Bank, North Dakota, N.A.; St. Paul Companies; State Farm Group; ITT Hartford; North Dakota Stockmen's Assn.; United Power Assn.; Trinity High School of Dickinson; Steffes ETC, Inc.; TMI Systems Design Corp.; WellPro, Inc.

For full biographical listings, see the Martindale-Hubbell Law Directory

*FARGO,** Cass Co.

CAHILL & MARQUART, P.A.

(See Moorhead, Minnesota)

CONMY, FESTE, HUBBARD, CORWIN & BRUST, LTD. (AV)

200 Norwest Center, 406 Main Avenue, 58126
Telephone: 701-293-9911
Fax: 701-293-3133
URL: http://www.conmylaw.com

Charles A. Feste
Paul M. Hubbard
Wickham Corwin
Kim E. Brust
Michael M. Thomas
Robert J. Schultz
Nancy J. Morris

OF COUNSEL

Lauris N. Molbert
E. T. Conmy, Jr.

For full biographical listings, see the Martindale-Hubbell Law Directory

GUNHUS, GRINNELL, KLINGER, SWENSON & GUY, LTD. (AV)

514 Gate City Building, P.O. Box 2783, 58108-2783
Telephone: 701-235-2506
Telecopier: 701-235-9862
Email: GUNHUSLAW@LINKUP.NET *URL:* http://www.fm-law.com
Moorhead, Minnesota Office: 215 North 30th Street, P.O. Box 1072.
Telephone: 218-236-6462.
Telecopier: 218-236-9873.

ATTORNEYS

Gunder Gunhus (1928-1997)
Paul E. Grinnell
Edward F. Klinger
Robert H. Swenson
William L. Guy, III
Craig R. Campbell
Bernard E. Reynolds
Eric K. Fosaaen
Gregory P. Hammes
Steven E. Noack
Michelle Caduff Winkis
Susan E. Johnson-Drenth
Deenelle Rudd Stephenson

Insurance Clients: Aetna Life and Casualty Co.; Crum & Forster Group; Home Insurance Co.; Sentry Insurance Co.; St. Paul Cos.; United States Fidelity and Guaranty Co.
Representative Clients: Certainteed Corp.; Farm Credit Services; Dakota Heartland Health System; U.S. West Communications.

For full biographical listings, see the Martindale-Hubbell Law Directory

JEFFRIES, OLSON, FLOM & BULLIS, P.A. (AV)

1325 23rd Street S.W., 58103
Telephone: 701-280-2300
Fax: 701-280-1880
Moorhead, Minnesota Office: 403 Center Avenue, P.O. Box 9, 56561-0001.
Telephone: 218-233-3222.
Fax: 218-233-7065.

Richard N. Jeffries
Thomas R. Olson
Joel A. Flom
James R. Bullis
Ronald J. Knoll
Michael S. Montgomery
Michelle M. Donarski

John T. Goff

Representative Clients: American International Adjustment Co.; American States Insurance Co.; Farmers Insurance Group; Federated Mutual Insurance Co.; Fireman's Fund Insurance Co.; Hartford Insurance Co.; Midwest Medical Insurance Co.; Nodak Mutual Insurance Co.; St. Paul Fire & Marine Insurance Co.

For full biographical listings, see the Martindale-Hubbell Law Directory

NILLES, HANSEN & DAVIES, LTD. (AV)

1800 Radisson Tower, P.O. Box 2626, 58108
Telephone: 701-237-5544
Facsimile: 701-280-0762
Williston, North Dakota Office: Energy Resource Building, 504 East Broadway, Suite 101, P.O. Box 1525.
Telephone: 701-572-5544.
Fax: 701-572-5561.

(See Next Column)

NILLES, HANSEN & DAVIES LTD., *Fargo—Continued*

Timothy Q. Davies
Duane H. Ilvedson
Robert L. Stroup, II
Russell F. Freeman
E. Thomas Conmy, III
Stephen W. Plambeck
Gregory B. Selbo
Leo F. J. Wilking
Richard Henderson
Daniel J. Crothers
William P. Harrie
Mark R. Hanson
Harry M. Pippin
Douglas W. Gigler
Andrew L. B. Noah
Jacqueline S. Anderson
Virginia G. Carter
Joel M. Fremstad
Fred J. Hofman
LaDonne R. Vik

State Counsel: Burlington Northern, Inc.
General Counsel: U.S. Bank National Association; Blue Cross and Blue Shield of North Dakota; Nodak Mutual Insurance Co.; Pioneer Mutual Life Insurance Co.

For full biographical listings, see the Martindale-Hubbell Law Directory

OHNSTAD TWICHELL, P.C. (AV)

15 Broadway, Suite 206, 58102
Telephone: 701-280-5801
Fax: 701-280-5803
West Fargo, North Dakota Office: 901 13th Avenue East, P.O. Box 458. Telephone 701-282-3249.
Fax: 701-282-0825.
Hillsboro, North Dakota Office: West Caledonia Avenue, P.O. Box 220. Telephone 701-436-5700.
Fax: 701-436-4025.
Mayville, North Dakota Office: 12 Third Street S.E., P.O. Box 547.
Telephone: 701-786-3251.
Fax: 701-786-4243.

Manfred R. Ohnstad (1914-1987)
Daniel R. Twichell (Resident, West Fargo Office)
Duane R. Breitling
Robert E. Rosenvold (Resident, West Fargo Office)
David L. Wanner (Resident, West Fargo Office)
Michael D. Nelson (Resident, West Fargo Office)
Brian D. Neugebauer (Resident, West Fargo Office)
John A. Juelson (Resident, Hillsboro Office)
Dean A. Rindy (Resident, West Fargo Office)
S. Lee Vinje (Resident, Mayville Office)
William J. Brudvik (Resident, Mayville Office)
Steven E. McCullough (Resident, West Fargo Office)
Robert G. Hoy (Resident, West Fargo Office)
Marshall William McCullough (Resident, West Fargo Office)

Ross V. Keller (Resident, Hillsboro Office)
Brenda R. Foyt (Resident, West Fargo Office)
John P. Dosland (Resident, West Fargo Office)

Representative Clients: First National Bank North Dakota; Bank of North Dakota; Quality Boneless Beef; City of West Fargo; Bond Counsel for Cities of Fargo, Jamestown, West Fargo and Valley City; Industrial Indemnity Co.; Integrity Insurance Co.; Westchester Fire Insurance Co.

For full biographical listings, see the Martindale-Hubbell Law Directory

VOGEL, WEIR, BYE, HUNKE & MCCORMICK, LTD. (AV)

502 First Avenue North, P.O. Box 1389, 58107
Telephone: 701-237-6983
Facsimile: 701-237-0847
Email: vogellaw@vogellaw.com *URL:* http://www.vogellaw.com

H. Patrick Weir
Kermit Edward Bye
Carlton J. Hunke
C. Nicholas Vogel
Maurice G. McCormick
Mart Daniel Vogel
William A. Schlossman, Jr.
Jane C. Voglewede
Jon R. Brakke
W. Todd Haggart
Frank G. Gokey
Steven A. Johnson
Bruce Douglas Quick
Wayne W. Carlson
Jerilynn Brantner Adams
Lisa Kay Edison-Smith

Daniel A. Bueide
Angela Elsperger Lord
Sidney J. Spaeth
Tami L. Norgard
Mart R. Vogel (Retired)
Jerry O. Brantner (Retired)

Representative Clients: Associated General Contractors of North Dakota; Blue Shield of North Dakota; Cass County Electric Cooperative, Inc.; Clark Equipment Co.; Forum Communications Company; Merit Care Medical Group; Northern Improvement Co.; Dakota Clinic Ltd.; United Parcel Service; Gateway Chevrolet, Inc.

For full biographical listings, see the Martindale-Hubbell Law Directory

*GRAND FORKS,** Grand Forks Co.

CAMRUD, MADDOCK, OLSON & LARSON, LTD. (AV)

P.O. Box 5849, 58206-5849
Telephone: 701-775-5595
Fax: 701-772-3743
Email: deeolson@camrudlaw.com *URL:* http://www.camrudlaw.com

(See Next Column)

Gerald J. Haga (1940-1999)
Thomas L. Degnan (1909-1997)
Theodore M. Camrud
Patrick J. Maddock
Donald J. Olson
Gordon W. Myerchin
Darrell E. Larson
Scott D. Jensen
Timothy R. Dittus

Randall S. Hanson
Russ J. Melland
Gerad C. Paul
Darin B. Barker

OF COUNSEL

James L. Lamb

RETIRED

Thomas P. McElroy

Representative Clients: Altru Clinic; First National Bank North Dakota; Altru Hospital; Community National Bank of Grand Forks; Peterson Construction Co.; Aetna Insurance Cos.; Hartford Accident and Indemnity Co.; St. Paul Cos.; Phico Insurance Co.

For full biographical listings, see the Martindale-Hubbell Law Directory

FISHER, OLSON, DALEY & BATA, LTD. (AV)

315 First Avenue North, P.O. Box 5788, 58206-5788
Telephone: 701-775-4688
Fax: 701-775-2440
Email: pfisher@grandforks.means.net *URL:* http://www.lawyers.com/fod&blaw
Larimore, North Dakota Office: 200 Towner Avenue.
Telephone: 701-343-2920.

Patrick W. Fisher
Richard W. Olson
Michael F. Daley
Linda E. Bata

Representative Clients: First National Bank North Dakota; Bremer Bank; University of North Dakota; Grand Forks School District; Travelers Insurance Co.; CNA Insurance Cos.; Altru Health System; CENEX; Sears, Roebuck & Co.; Discover Card.

For full biographical listings, see the Martindale-Hubbell Law Directory

VAALER, ZIMNEY, FOSTER & JOHNSON, CHARTERED (AV)

Bremer Financial Center, Suite 200, 3100 South Columbia Road, P.O. Box 13417, 58208-3417
Telephone: 701-772-8111
Fax: 701-772-7328
Email: vaalerlaw@corpcomm.net

Robert Vaaler
Thomas L. Zimney
John S. Foster
Carol E. Johnson
Sandra B. Dittus
Allen J. Flaten
Scott J. Landa

Representative Clients: Bremer Bank, N.A.; Federal Deposit Insurance Co.; U.S. Bank, N.A.; Sioux Manufacturing Co.; The Boeing Co.
Representative Insurance Clients: Fireman's Fund; CIGNA; State Farm Insurance Cos.; Allied Group Insurance Co.; Lawyers Title Insurance Co.

For full biographical listings, see the Martindale-Hubbell Law Directory

*MANDAN,** Morton Co.

KELSCH KELSCH RUFF & KRANDA (AV)

103 Collins Avenue, P.O. Box 1266, 58554-7266
Telephone: 701-663-9818
Fax: 701-663-9810
Email: kelsch@corpcomm.net

MEMBERS OF FIRM

C. F. Kelsch (1890-1987)
William C. Kelsch
Thomas F. Kelsch
Arlen M. Ruff
Thomas D. Kelsch
Todd D. Kranda

ASSOCIATES

Timothy J. Wahlin
Rob Forward
William J. Delmore

Representative Clients: Seven Seas Motor Inn; L & H Manufacturing Co.; Cloverdale Foods Co.; Microage Computer Store; Logan Hill Realty, Bismarck.

For full biographical listings, see the Martindale-Hubbell Law Directory

OHIO

*AKRON,** Summit Co.

PERANTINIDES & NOLAN CO., L.P.A. (AV)

300 Courtyard Square, 80 South Summit Street, 44308-1736
Telephone: 330-253-5454
Telecopier: 330-253-6524
Email: pn@perantinides.com

(See Next Column)

PERANTINIDES & NOLAN CO. L.P.A.—*Continued*

Paul G. Perantinides
Chris T. Nolan

James J. Gutbrod
Christopher L. Parker
Peter D. Janos
Antonios P. Tsarouhas
Christina Simoudis
Sophie Mitsopoulos

References: First National Bank of Akron; National City Bank, Akron; Society Bank; Charter One Bank.

For full biographical listings, see the Martindale-Hubbell Law Directory

ROETZEL & ANDRESS A LEGAL PROFESSIONAL ASSOCIATION (AV)

222 South Main Street, 44308
Telephone: 330-376-2700
Cable Address: "Watand"
Telecopier: 330-376-4577
Email: ramail@ralaw.com *URL:* http://www.ralaw.com
Columbus, Ohio Office: National City Plaza, 155 E. Broad Street, 12th Floor.
Telephone: 614-463-9770.
Telecopier: 614-463-9792.
Naples, Florida Office: 850 Park Shore Drive, Trianon Centre, Suite 300.
Telephones: 941-649-6200; 800-535-7239.
Telecopier: 941-261-3659.
Cleveland, Ohio Office: 10th Floor, One Cleveland Center, 1375 East Ninth Street.
Telephone: 216-623-0150.
Telecopier: 216-623-0134.
Cincinnati, Ohio Office: 250 East Fifth Street, Chiquita Center, Suite 310.
Telephone: 513-361-0200.
Telecopier: 513-361-0335.
Fort Myers, Florida Office: 2320 First Street, Suite 1000.
Telephone: 941-337-3850.
Telecopier: 941-337-0970.
Toledo, Ohio Office: One SeaGate, Suite 999.
Telephone: 419-242-7985.
Facsimile: 419-242-0316.
Bonita Springs, Florida Office: 3461 Bonita Bay Boulevard, Suite 204.
Telephone: 941-649-6200.
Telecopier: 941-948-3613.

Joseph P. Alexander (Resident, Cleveland Office)
J. Timothy Bender (Resident, Cleveland Office)
Aretta K. Bernard
Robert E. Blackham
Susan S. Box
Amie L. Bruggeman
Margaret R. Carmany (Resident, Columbus Office)
Norman S. Carr
Karen A. Carroll (Resident, Cincinnati Office)
Anna Moore Carulas (Resident, Cleveland Office)
Jeffrey J. Casto
John N. Childs
John Clapper, III (Resident, Naples, Florida Office)
Ann Ruley Combs (Resident, Cincinnati Office)
Kenneth B. Cuyler (Resident, Naples, Florida Office)
Elizabeth N. Davis
George A. Dietrich
Thomas A. Dillon (Resident, Columbus Office)
Gerald L. Draper (Resident, Columbus Office)
Steven M. Falk (Resident, Naples, Florida Office)
Shane A. Farolino
Jonathan D. Fishbane (Resident, Naples, Florida Office)
John D. Gast (Resident, Naples, Florida Office)
Amanda E. Gordon
Beverly Grady (Resident, Fort Myers, Florida Office)
C. Neil Gregory (Resident, Naples, Florida Office)
David R. Harbarger (Resident, Cleveland Office)
Frederick R. Hardt (Resident, Naples, Florida Office)
Denise M. Hasbrook (Resident, Toledo Office)
Paul K. Heuerman (Resident, Naples, Florida Office)
Timothy L. Holston (Resident, Columbus Office)
Stuart M. Horwitz
Steven W. Hubbard (Resident, Fort Myers, Florida Office)
Timothy G. Ireland
Duane L. Isham
John V. Jackson, II (Resident, Cleveland Office)
Paul L. Jackson
Kenneth A. Jones (Resident, Fort Myers, Florida Office)
Peter Lawson Jones (Resident, Cleveland Office)
R. Mark Jones (Resident, Cleveland Office)
Stephen D. Jones (Resident, Columbus Office)
Wayne M. Jones
Douglas M. Kennedy (Resident, Columbus Office)
Stephen G. Kolody (Resident, Fort Myers and Bonita Springs, Florida Offices)
Ronald S. Kopp
Peter M. Kostoff
Kenneth M. Lapine (Resident, Cleveland Office)
Joseph L. Lawson
Ronald B. Lee
Michael W. McArdle (Resident, Naples, Florida Office)
G. Carson McEachern (Resident, Naples, Florida Office)
Robert G. Menzies (Resident Managing Partner, Naples, Florida Office)
Russell R. Miller (Resident, Toledo Office)
Brian J. Moore
Randall J. Moore
Timothy J. Ochsenhirt
Kevin J. Osterkamp (Resident, Columbus Office)

(See Next Column)

Thomas M. Parker
Richard A. Plewacki (Resident, Cleveland Office)
David R. Posteraro (Resident, Cleveland Office)
Mark J. Price (Resident, Naples, Florida Office)
George W. Rooney, Jr.
Sue Ellen Salsbury
George R. Sarkis
Donald S. Scherzer (Resident, Cleveland Office)
Bruce R. Schrader, II
Thomas M. Skove
Bradley L. Snyder (Resident, Columbus Office)
Douglas E. Spiker (Resident, Columbus Office)
Gary W. Spring
Mark Steinbeck (Resident, Fort Myers, Florida Office)
Roger J. Stevenson
Richard R. Strong
Stephen E. Thompson (Resident, Naples, Florida Office)
Thomas A. Treadon
June Smith Tyler (Resident, Cincinnati Office)
James R. Vaughn
Wallace W. Walker, Jr.
Bradley Abbott Wright
Michael S. Yashko (Resident, Columbus Office)
Thomas S. Zaremba (Resident, Toledo Office)
Charles E. Zumkehr

Kathleen W. Adams (Resident, Naples, Florida Office)
W. Chad Arfons
John W. Becker
Michael W. Bond (Resident, Fort Myers, Florida Office)
J. Scott Broome (Resident, Cleveland Office)
James L. Cole
Jacqueline S. Cooper
Steven St. Leger Cox
John M. Coyne, III
Thomas O. Crist
Richard DeBoest, II (Resident, Fort Myers, Florida Office)
Anthony J. DeGirolamo
Tiffany N. Del Duca (Resident, Naples, Florida Office)
Breaden M. Douthett (Resident, Cleveland Office)
Dianne D. Einstein (Resident, Columbus Office)
Linda A. Epstein (Resident, Naples, Florida Office)
Laura (Megan) Faust
Amy K. Fehn (Resident, Cleveland Office)
Lisa A. Fike (Resident, Cleveland Office)
Terrence S. Finn
Stephen W. Funk
Jonathan A. Good
Joseph E. Herbert (Resident, Cleveland Office)
Terrence R. Holihen (Resident, Fort Myers, Florida Office)
Suzanne K. Holland
Julianne E. Hood
Kevin J. Hubbart (Resident, Fort Myers, Florida Office)
David J. Hudak
Dawn A. Humphrys
Christian A. Jenkins (Resident, Cincinnati Office)
Geraldine M. Johnson (Resident, Cincinnati Office)
Ingrid A. Kinkopf-Zajac (Resident, Cleveland Office)
Frederick W. Leffler
Monika D. Ludwig (Resident, Naples, Florida Office)
John R. Marconi
Keith R. McMurdy
Juliana S. Moore
Stephen B. Mosier (Resident, Toledo Office)
Douglas S. Musick (Resident, Cleveland Office)
Basil J. Musnuff
Rocco D. Potenza, Jr.
Stacy A. Ragon
Pamela S. Robbins (Resident, Columbus Office)
Britt J. Rossiter (Resident, Toledo Office)
Scott Salsbury
Noel C. Shepard (Resident, Columbus Office)
Erin L. Sherwood
Constance S. Shipley (Resident, Naples, Florida Office)
Constance A. Snyder (Resident, Toledo Office)
Carolann Austin Swanson (Resident, Fort Myers, Florida Office)
Mark C. Terzola
Ruth M. Torok (Resident, Cincinnati Office)
Gregory L. Urbancic (Resident, Naples, Florida Office)
Sanjay K. Varma
Timothy J. Webster
Alisa Labut Wright
Gary G. Yashko (Resident, Columbus Office)
John A. Zervas (Resident, Columbus Office)

Representative Clients: Akron City Hospital; Bank One, Akron, N.A.; Beacon Journal Publishing Co.; Capital University; Chessie Systems Railroads; General Motors Corp.; Pentair, Inc.; Seaman Corp.; State of Ohio; United States Fidelity & Guaranty Co.

For full biographical listings, see the Martindale-Hubbell Law Directory

ARCHBOLD, Fulton Co.

PLASSMAN, RUPP, HENSAL & SHORT (AV)

302 North Defiance Street, P.O. Box 178, 43502-0178
Telephone: 419-445-8815
Fax: 419-445-1080
Email: prhs@bright.net

MEMBERS OF FIRM

Owen Rice (1900-1978)
Harold H. Plassman
David P. Rupp, Jr.
James E. Hensal
Peter D. Short
Mark D. Hagans

Counsel for: The Farmers & Merchants State Bank; Sauder Woodworking Co.; Sauder Manufacturing Co.; Bil-Jax, Inc.; Miller Bros. Const., Inc.; Lugbill Bros., Inc.; Archbold Medical Group, Inc.
Local Counsel for: Michigan Millers; United Ohio Insurance Co.; German Mutual Insurance Co.

For full biographical listings, see the Martindale-Hubbell Law Directory

ASHTABULA, Ashtabula Co.

WARREN AND YOUNG PLL (AV)

134 West 46th Street, P.O. Box 2300, 44005-2300
Telephone: 440-997-6175
Facsimile: 440-992-9114
URL: http://www.warrenyoung.com

Theodore E. Warren (1897-1969)
Myron H. Young (1910-1971)
William E. Riedel
Carl F. Muller
Stuart W. Cordell

Jeffrey L. Coxon
Craig F. Sernik

For full biographical listings, see the Martindale-Hubbell Law Directory

*BUCYRUS,** Crawford Co.

THE NEFF LAW FIRM, LTD. (AV)

840 South Sandusky Avenue, P.O. Box 406, 44820-0406
Telephone: 419-562-1951
Facsimile: 419-562-1660
Email: nefflaw@cybrtown.com *URL:* http://www.lawyers.com/nefflaw

Robert Clark Neff
Robert Clark Neff, Jr.

For full biographical listings, see the Martindale-Hubbell Law Directory

*CANTON,** Stark Co.

BLACK, MCCUSKEY, SOUERS & ARBAUGH A LEGAL PROFESSIONAL ASSOCIATION (AV)

1000 United Bank Plaza, 220 Market Avenue South, 44702
Telephone: 330-456-8341; 877-656-8341
Telecopier: 330-456-5756
Email: info@bmsa.com *URL:* http://www.bmsa.com
Dover Office: 130 West Third Street, P.O. Box 2330, 44622.
Telephone: 330-364-6553; 877-564-6553.
Fax: 330-364-2739.

Ronald K. Bennington
Charles J. Tyburski
Anthony E. Efremoff
Robert I. Friedman
Arnold R. Shifman
Victor R. Marsh
Daniel M. Jonas
Randolph L. Snow (Managing Director)
Stephen D. Thompson
Terrence P. Kessler
James R. Strawn
Joel K. Dayton
Scott P. Sandrock
Gust Callas
Bruce M. Soares
James P. Kamerer
Karen S. Reiland
Richard D. Dodez
Mary E. Randall
John J. Rambacher
Thomas W. Connors
Terrence L. Seeberger
Robert E. Soles, Jr.
Tod T. Morrow
Francis G. Centrone
David M. Hanhart (Resident, Dover Office)
C. Jason Deeds (Resident, Dover Office)
Erick L. Bauer (Resident, Dover Office)

Brenda S. Schwartz
Jane Murphy Timken
Brian C. Cich
Gregory L. Taddonio
Mark E. Owens
Gordon D. Woolbert, II
Edward C. Redder

OF COUNSEL

John D. Jolliffe
Gene Barnhart
Richard M. Hanhart (Resident, Dover Office)

Representative Clients: The Hoover Co.; Diebold, Inc.; Travelers Insurance Co.

For full biographical listings, see the Martindale-Hubbell Law Directory

KRUGLIAK, WILKINS, GRIFFITHS & DOUGHERTY CO., L.P.A. (AV)

4775 Munson Street, N.W., P.O. Box 36963, 44735-6963
Telephone: 330-497-0700
Fax: 330-497-4020
Email: legal@kwgd.com *URL:* http://www.kwgd.com
Alliance, Ohio Office: KeyBank Square Building, 960 West State Street.
Telephone: 330-823-9262.
Additional Canton, Ohio Office: Central Plaza South, 527 FirstMerit Citizens National Building.
Telephone: 330-497-0700.
New Philadelphia, Ohio Office: 158 N. Broadway Street.
Telephone: 330-343-9578.
Salem, Ohio Office: 409 East Second Street.
Telephone: 330-337-6799.

Samuel Krugliak
F. Stuart Wilkins
Raymond E. Griffiths
Ronald W. Dougherty
David L. Simiele
Fred J. Haupt
Daniel A. Pramuk
John Bogniard
Michael A. Thompson
Richard E. Davis

(See Next Column)

Randall C. Hunt
Sam O. Simmerman
Terry A. Moore
Karen Soehnlen McQueen
Jacqueline Bollas Caldwell
David E. Butz
Leslie Iams Kuntz
Charles E. Ringer
Thomas W. Winkhart
Susan Carson Rodgers
Edward D. Murray
James F. Contini II
John M. Tucker
W. Thomas Newell
Adonis A. Caneris
Scott R. Miller
John D. Clark
Brian J. Malone

Representative Clients: FirstMerit Citizens National Bank; Alfred Nickles Bakery, Inc.
Counsel for: National Pro Football Hall of Fame.
References: FirstMerit Citizens National Bank; KeyBank.

For full biographical listings, see the Martindale-Hubbell Law Directory

*CHILLICOTHE,** Ross Co.

CUTRIGHT & CUTRIGHT (AV)

76 West Second Street, 45601
Telephone: 740-772-5595
Fax: 740-773-9261
Email: atlaw@bright.net

MEMBERS OF FIRM

James M. Cutright
James K. Cutright

Representative Clients: Citizens National Bank; Chivaho Federal Credit Union; Rockhold, Brown & Co. Bank; Litter Industries; Scioto Valley Mental Health Center; Paint Valley A.D.A.M.H.S. Board.
Approved Attorneys for: Lawyers Title Insurance Co.; Ohio Bar Title Insurance Co.; Chicago Title Insurance Co., Inc.

For full biographical listings, see the Martindale-Hubbell Law Directory

*CINCINNATI,** Hamilton Co.

FROST & JACOBS LLP (AV)

2500 PNC Center, 201 East Fifth Street, 45202
Telephone: 513-651-6800
Telecopier: 513-651-6981
URL: http://www.frojac.com
Columbus, Ohio Office: One Columbus, 10 West Broad Street, 43215.
Telephone: 614-464-1211.
Telecopier: 614-464-1737.
Lexington, Kentucky Office: 1100 Vine Center Tower, 333 West Vine Street, 40507.
Telephone: 606-254-1100.
Telecopier: 606-253-2990.
Middletown, Ohio Office: 400 First National Bank Building, 2 North Main Street, 45042.
Telephone: 513-422-2001.
Telecopier: 513-422-3010.
Frankfort, Kentucky Office: 201 W. Main Street, 40601.
Telephone: 502-223-1400.
Telecopier: 502-223-1410.

MEMBERS OF FIRM

Henry G. Frost (1875-1951)
Carl M. Jacobs (1886-1967)
James S. Wachs
Ronald E. Heinlen
James R. Adams
John S. Stith
Edmund J. Adams
Albert E. Heekin, III
Lawrence H. Kyte, Jr.
T. Stephen Phillips
James K. L. Lawrence
Robert A. Dimling
Gerald L. Baldwin
Richard J. Erickson
Frederick J. McGavran
Neil Ganulin
John H. Appel
Joseph J. Dehner
Samuel M. Scoggins
Susan Grogan Faller
Jeffery R. Rush
Todd H. Bailey
Mark H. Longenecker, Jr.
Ruth R. Longenecker
George E. Yund
David C. Horn
William H. Hawkins II
Myron L. Dale
E. Richard Oberschmidt
Martin E. Mooney
David C. Olson
P. Reid Lemasters
Walter E. Haggerty
Theodore D. Grosser
David T. Croall
Charles E. Schroer
Paul W. Casper, Jr.
Frederick W. Kindel
Douglas E. Hart
Richard M. Goehler
Beth A. Myers
Deborah S. Adams
Patricia D. Laub
Gregory P. Adams
Stephen N. Haughey
William C. Strangfeld
Grant S. Cowan
Vincent E. Mauer
W. Russell Wilson
Beth Schneider Naylor
William W. Ford, III
Raymond D. Neusch
Douglas D. Thomson
Kevin N. McMurray
John C. Krug
D. Scott Gurney
Ronald E. Gold
Douglas S. Tripp
Adam P. Hall
Hilla M. Zerbst
Scott D. Phillips
Douglas Halpert
David S. Bence

SENIOR ATTORNEYS

Barbara F. Applegarth
Stephen J. Axtell
Daniel W. Scharff
Michael K. Moyers
Christopher DeLuca

(See Next Column)

FROST & JACOBS LLP—*Continued*

ASSOCIATES

J. Paul Allen
Bryan S. Blade
Douglas L. Lutz
David A. Skidmore, Jr.
Elizabeth R. Murray
Jack B. Harrison
Bernard L. McKay
Nancy Leser Smith
Joanne Wissman Glass
Lori A. Landrum
Christopher S. Habel
Sandra L. Nunn
Jeffrey R. Teeters
Laurie K. Ahlers
Michael J. O'Grady
Scott R. Brown
Rachel E. Hansen
Jill Meyer Vollman
Christine M. Strick
Christina M. Sprecher
Rita M. Stolper
Mark J. Chumley
Karen M. Ecker
Daniel R. Wireman
Lorie J. Kravetsky
Robert M.M. Shaffer
Jeffrey S. Rosenstiel
Robert D. Shank
Colleen M. Haas
Jan R. Wenning
Katherine Cook Morgan
Kevin L. Cooney
Kimberly D. Wright (Not admitted in OH)
Caryn Franklin Gleich
Suzanne Wentzel
Bill J. Paliobeis
Douglas Hill Schwartz (Not admitted in OH)
Steven M. Wesloh
Sylvius H. Von Saucken
Robert D. Lewis Jr.
Kellye J. Bowers
Kelly E. Sultzbach
Jarrod B. Pontius
Matthew P. Gunn
Claire Seltz Eichner
Kenton K. Pettit (Not admitted in OH)
Kevin S. Reeve

SENIOR PARTNER

Dennis J. Barron

OF COUNSEL

J. Leland Brewster II
Jerry L. Cowan
James A. Katsanis
Kimberly K. Mauer
Karen M. McLaughlin
Ljubomir Nacev (Not admitted in OH)
Donald McG. Rose
John K. Rose
Carla Haunz Rusconi
Clayton R. Sanders Jr. (Not admitted in OH)
Mary Ann Schenk
Diane S. Shank

PATENT, TRADEMARK AND COPYRIGHT ATTORNEYS
MEMBERS OF FIRM

David E. Schmit
Steven J. Goldstein
Kenneth B. Germain
Edwin R. Acheson, Jr.
Louis K. Ebling

ASSOCIATES

Ann Gallagher Robinson
Kevin S. Sprecher
Sean P. Hodge
Karen E. Kreider
Katherine F. Horvath

OF COUNSEL

Stephen E. Gillen
Gretchen R. Blum
Glenn D. Bellamy

COLUMBUS, OHIO OFFICE
MEMBERS OF FIRM

John I. Cadwallader
Thomas V. Williams
Michael K. Yarbrough
Jeffrey N. Lindemann

COLUMBUS, OHIO OFFICE
ASSOCIATES

Cara E. Gunder
Jeffrey G. Rupert
Jennifer S. Browning

COLUMBUS, OHIO OFFICE
OF COUNSEL

Robert E. Leininger
Susan L. Rhiel

LEXINGTON, KENTUCKY OFFICE
MEMBERS OF FIRM

Denise H. McClelland
Greg E. Mitchell

LEXINGTON, KENTUCKY OFFICE
ASSOCIATES

Shannon Upton Johnson
David L. Kinsella
Andrew W. Green
Douglas J. Hallock
D. Eric Lycan
Thomas G. Grace
Catherine S. Wright

LEXINGTON, KENTUCKY OFFICE
OF COUNSEL

Jackson W. White
Lawrence E. Forgy, Jr.
David C. Trimble
Susan C. Sears

MIDDLETOWN, OHIO OFFICE
MEMBERS OF FIRM

Thomas A. Swope
Donald L. Crain

MIDDLETOWN, OHIO OFFICE
SENIOR ATTORNEY

Daniel J. Picard

MIDDLETOWN, OHIO OFFICE
ASSOCIATE

Thomas B. Allen

(See Next Column)

MIDDLETOWN, OHIO OFFICE
OF COUNSEL

Barry J. Levey

Representative Clients: Anchor Hocking Packaging Company; Armco, Inc.; AK Steel Corporation; Arthur Andersen LLP; Bank One; Bristol-Myers Squibb Co.; Champion International Corporation; Chevron U.S.A., Inc.; Chiquita Brands International; ChoiceCare.

For full biographical listings, see the Martindale-Hubbell Law Directory

---

KATZ, GREENBERGER & NORTON (AV)

105 East Fourth Street 4th Floor, 45202-4011
Telephone: 513-721-5151
Fax: 513-621-9285
Email: kgnlaw.com *URL:* http://www.kgnlaw.com

Leonard H. Freiberg (1885-1954)
Alfred B. Katz
Mark Alan Greenberger
Louis H. Katz
Richard L. Norton
Steven M. Rothstein
Robert Gray Edmiston
Ellen Essig
Scott P. Kadish

ASSOCIATES

Stephen E. Imm
Jeffrey J. Greenberger
Ross M. Evans
Nancy M. Janning
E. Beth Farrell

OF COUNSEL

Charles Weiner

For full biographical listings, see the Martindale-Hubbell Law Directory

---

KATZ, TELLER, BRANT & HILD A LEGAL PROFESSIONAL ASSOCIATION (AV)

2400 Chemed Center, 255 East Fifth Street, 45202-4724
Telephone: 513-721-4532
Telecopier: 513-721-7120
Email: corp@ktbh.com

Reuven J. Katz
Jerome S. Teller
Guy M. Hild
Robert A. Pitcairn, Jr.
Robert E. Brant
Ronald J. Goret
Stephen C. Kisling
James F. McCarthy, III
Andrew R. Berger
Mark J. Jahnke
William F. Russo
John R. Gierl
Bruce A. Hunter
Bradley G. Haas
Daniel P. Utt
Cynthia Loren Gibson
Suzanne Prieur Land

Tedd H. Friedman
Sheila K. Christie
Wijdan Jreisat
Robert S. Fletcher
Joel S. Brant
Jack J. Defevers

OF COUNSEL

Joseph A. Brant

For full biographical listings, see the Martindale-Hubbell Law Directory

---

KEATING, MUETHING & KLEKAMP, P.L.L. (AV)

1400 Provident Tower, One East Fourth Street, 45202
Telephone: 513-579-6400
Facsimile: 513-579-6457
URL: http://www.kmklaw.com

MEMBERS OF FIRM

John L. Muething
Donald P. Klekamp
Timothy A. Garry
Gary P. Kreider
Don R. Gardner
Michael J. Burke
Louis F. Gilligan
Herbert B. Weiss
Joseph P. Rouse
Richard D. Siegel
Joseph L. Trauth, Jr.
James R. Whitaker
J. David Rosenberg
Robert W. Maxwell II
J. Neal Gardner
Richard L. Creighton, Jr.
Paul V. Muething
Jerome C. Randolph
James E. Burke
Kevin E. Irwin
Timothy B. Matthews
William J. Keating, Jr.
William A. Posey
Joseph P. Mellen
Mark J. Weber
Gregory M. Utter
Robert E. Coletti
James M. Jansing
Patrick F. Fischer
David K. Montgomery
James R. Matthews
Michael F. Bigler
Vivian M. Raby
Edward E. Steiner
Stephen M. Goodson
Robert G. Sanker
Lisa Wintersheimer Michel
W. Keith Noel
Daniel J. Donnellon
Brian M. Babb
Laura L. Warren
Daniel E. Izenson
Gail King
Kenneth P. Kreider
Laura S. Petrie
Gail Glassmeyer Pryse
Mary Ellen Malas
Michael L. Scheier
Jody T. Klekamp
Pamela Morgan Hodge
Paul D. Dorger
Mark A. Weiss

(See Next Column)

KEATING, MUETHING & KLEKAMP P.L.L., *Cincinnati—Continued*

ASSOCIATES

Joseph M. Callow Jr.
Douglas L. Hensley
Alan S. Fershtman
Thomas E. Frooman
R. Patrick DeWine
Steven C. Coffaro
Heather L. Thurston
Jennifer Fraley Hieatt
F. Mark Reuter
Michael P. Bacevich
Christopher J. Skufca
Camille Kathleen Kushman
Michael A. Brown
Daniel B. Runk
Stephen M. Sager
Rachael A. Rowe
Joshua D. Goldberg (Not admitted in OH)
Dwight A. Packard, II
Susan Smith Kost
Amy C. Mitchell
Erica L. Strawman
Eric T. Wilkowski
John N. Winstead
Lisa Kim (Not admitted in OH)
Robert G. St. Jacques (Not admitted in OH)
Peter J. Stautberg
Susan J. Moeller

OF COUNSEL

William J. Keating
Gehl P. Babinec
Patricia B. Hogan
James J. McGraw, Jr.

Representative Clients: American Financial Group; BP America Inc.; Chiquita Brands International, Inc.; Cintas Corporation; Comair Holdings, Inc.; Duke Realty Limited Partnership; LSI Industries Inc.; Mosler Inc.; Provident Financial Group Inc.

For full biographical listings, see the Martindale-Hubbell Law Directory

LINDHORST & DREIDAME CO., L.P.A. (AV)

312 Walnut Street, Suite 2300, 45202-4091
Telephone: 513-421-6630
Telecopier: 513-421-0212

Ambrose H. Lindhorst (1913-1997)
Robert F. Dreidame (1914-1978)
William J. Walsh (1919-1996)

SENIOR COUNSEL

Leo J. Breslin
James L. O'Connell
William M. Cussen
Charles J. Kelly
John A. Goldberg
William N. Kirkham
James M. Moore
James H. Smith, III
Jay R. Langenbahn
Thomas E. Martin
James F. Brockman
Michael F. Lyon
Edward S. Dorsey
Harold L. Anness
Dale A. Stalf
Gary F. Franke
James C. Frooman

Peter C. Newberry
Charles G. Skidmore
Barry F. Fagel
Margaret G. Kubicki
Brian M. Kneafsey, Jr.
Michelle L. Clemons
Paul J. Vollman

Representative Clients: CNA; CSX Corp.; Fireman's Fund-American Group; Medical Protective Co.; Norfolk Southern Corp.; Roadway Express, Inc.; Sibcy Cline, Inc.; Jewish Hospital; T.W. Smith Aircraft, Inc.; U.S.F.&G.

For full biographical listings, see the Martindale-Hubbell Law Directory

PORTER WRIGHT MORRIS & ARTHUR LLP (AV)

250 E. Fifth Street, Suite 2200, 45202-4199
Telephone: 513-381-4700; (800-582-5813)
Fax: 513-421-0991
Email: cvg@porterwright.com *URL:* http://www.porterwright.com
Columbus, Ohio Office: 41 South High Street, 43215-6194.
Telephones: 614-227-2000; (800-533-2794).
Fax: 614-227-2100. Internet: cmh@porterwright.com.
Dayton, Ohio Office: One Dayton Centre, One South Main Street, Suite 1600, 45402-2028.
Telephones: 937-449-6810; (800-533-4434).
Fax: 937-449-6820. Internet: day@porterwright.com.
Cleveland, Ohio Office: 925 Euclid Avenue, Suite 1700, 44115-1483.
Telephones: 216-443-9000; (800-824-1980).
Fax: 216-443-9011. Internet: cle@porterwright.com.
Washington, D.C. Office: 1667 K Street, N.W., Suite 1100, 20006-1605.
Telephones: 202-778-3000; (800-456-7962).
Fax: 202-778-3063. Internet: dca@porterwright.com.
Naples, Florida Office: 5801 Pelican Bay Boulevard, Suite 300, 34108-2709.
Telephones: 941-593-2900; (800-876-7962).
Fax: 941-593-2990. Internet: apf@porterwright.com.

RESIDENT MEMBERS

John J. Cruze
Mark E. Elsener
Jerome J. Metz, Jr.
Wm. Cates Rambo
Michael G. Reed
David Reichert
Stephen D. Strauss

RESIDENT ASSOCIATES

Duane A. Boggs
Michael E. McCarty
Darryl Mitchell
Eric J. Plinke

For full biographical listings, see the Martindale-Hubbell Law Directory

STRAUSS & TROY A LEGAL PROFESSIONAL ASSOCIATION (AV)

The Federal Reserve Building, 150 East Fourth Street, 45202-4018
Telephone: 513-621-2120
Telecopier: 513-241-8259
URL: http://www.strauss-troy.com
Northern Kentucky Office: Suite 1400, 50 East Rivercenter Boulevard, Covington, Kentucky, 41011.
Telephone: 513-621-8900; 513-621-2120.
Telecopier: 513-629-9444.

Lucien G. Strauss (1900-1982)
Orville A. Troy (1896-1967)
Kenneth D. Troy (1918-1993)
Mark H. Berliant
William V. Strauss
Larry A. Neuman
William S. Abernethy, Jr.
Alan Comstock Rosser
Thomas C. Rink
Franklin A. Klaine, Jr.
William R. Jacobs
Daniel H. Demmerle, II
James G. Heldman
Charles Jay Postow
Stuart C. Brinn
Martin C. Butler (Resident, Covington, Kentucky Office)
R. Guy Taft
Ann W. Gerwin
Richard S. Wayne
Paul B. Calico
Andrew M. Shott
Claudia G. Allen
Timothy B. Theissen (Resident, Covington, Kentucky Office)
William K. Flynn
Charles C. Ashdown
Marilyn J. Maag
Thomas L. Stachler
Anthony M. Barlow
Marshall K. Dosker (Resident, Covington, Kentucky Office)
Shawn M. Young

Steven F. Stuhlbarg
August T. Janszen
Thomas P. Glass
Daniel J. Whalen (Resident, Covington, Kentucky Office)
Pete A. Smith (Resident, Covington, Kentucky Office)
Michael A. Ruh, Jr.
Joseph J, Braun

OF COUNSEL

Samuel M. Allen (Resident, Covington, Kentucky Office)
Gordon H. Hood (Resident, Covington, Kentucky Office)
Charles G. Atkins
Richard D. Heiser
Leon L. Wolf
Paul J. Theissen (Resident, Covington, Kentucky Office)
Diane Schneiderman
Charles H. Melville
John G. Parnell
Philomena Saldanha Ashdown

Representative Clients: PNC Bank, N.A. (Ohio and Kentucky); Corporex Companies, Inc.; Mercantile Stores Co., Inc.; Star Bank, N.A. (Ohio and Kentucky).

For full biographical listings, see the Martindale-Hubbell Law Directory

TAFT, STETTINIUS & HOLLISTER LLP (AV)

1800 Firstar Tower, 425 Walnut Street, 45202-3957
Telephone: 513-381-2838
Facsimile: 513-381-0205
URL: http://www.taftlaw.com
Columbus, Ohio Office: Twelfth Floor, 21 East State Street.
Telephone: 614-221-2838.
Covington, Kentucky Office: Thomas More Centre, Suite 400, 2670 Chancellor Drive.
Telephone: 606-331-2838; 513-381-2838.
Cleveland, Ohio Office: Sixth Floor, Bond Court Building, 1300 East Ninth Street.
Telephone: 216-241-2838.

MEMBERS OF FIRM

Robert A. Taft (1889-1953)
John B. Hollister (1890-1979)
L. Clifford Craig
William K. Engeman
Thomas D. Heekin
Melvin S. Shotten
Stephen M. Nechemias
R. Joseph Parker
G. Jack Donson Jr.
David L. Johnson (Resident, Columbus, Ohio Office)
Thomas T. Terp
Roger A. Weber
Donald C. Hess
Timothy P. Nagy (Resident, Columbus, Ohio Office)
Timothy J. Quinn
Daniel J. Hoffheimer
John J. McCoy
Timothy P. Reilly
James H. Brun
William K. Smith (Resident, Cleveland, Ohio Office)
Mark J. Stepaniak
Gerald S. Greenberg
Toshio Nakao
Elizabeth A. Galloway
Stephen M. Griffith Jr.
Robert S. Corker
Steven A. Marrer (Resident, Cleveland, Ohio Office)
John L. Stettinius (1882-1924)
Robert G. Stachler
Robert J. Townsend
Jerold A. Fink
J. Alan Lips
Gerald J. Rapien
Robert E. Rich
Timothy E. Hoberg
Richard S. Roberts
Thomas C. Hill
Lawrence J. Barty
Lawrence D. Walker (Resident, Columbus, Ohio Office)
Ross E. Wales
James M. Hall Jr.
William Stuart Dornette
Edward D. Diller
Timothy J. Hurley
Steven W. Weeks
William J. Seitz III
Thomas R. Schuck
Michael J. Zavatsky
Kim K. Burke
Charles Michael Stephan
Margaret Avril Lawson
Robert B. Craig (Resident, Covington, Kentucky Office)
Thomas E. Grossmann
Jeffrey S. Schloemer
Timothy C. Sullivan
Patrick J. Mitchell

(See Next Column)

TAFT, STETTINIUS & HOLLISTER LLP—*Continued*

MEMBERS OF FIRM (Continued)

Philip F. Schultz
Michael A. Byers (Resident, Columbus, Ohio Office)
Mark J. Ruehlmann
Stephen C. Mahon
Mark A. Kobasuk
Marcia Voorhis Andrew
Stephen D. Lerner
Samuel M. Duran
Susan E. Wheatley
Doreen Canton
Gregory Parker Rogers
Ronald C. Christian
Robert A. Bilott
Russell S. Sayre

OF COUNSEL

J. Mack Swigert
Murray S. Monroe
James R. Bridgeland Jr.
Wilbur L. Collins
Cynthia F. Blank
Laura A. Ringenbach
Robert T. Keeler
Charles D. Lindberg
Frank H. Stewart
James J. Ryan
James J. Mayer
J. David Goodman (Resident, Columbus, Ohio Office)

ASSOCIATES

Raymond W. Lembke
Patricia D. Braxton
Earl K. Messer
David Hamilton Peck
Daniel E. Fausz
Howard M. Ullman
Rebecca L. Simpson
Tracey A. Chriske
J. Steven Justice
Julia B. Meister
Curt Carl Hartman
Mary L. Rust
Dawn M. Lampley
Katherine Doggett Goldsmith
David L. Wheeler
Scott A. Kane
Kim D. Seaton
Lori E. Walker
Eric J. Wunsch
Thomas P. Vergamini (Resident, Crestview Hills, Kentucky Office)
Jessica E. Price (Resident, Cleveland, Ohio Office)
Christina E. Hassan
Rachael K. House
Monica L. Olszewski
Douglas A. Schwarz
Ross A. Wright
Janice A. Isakoff (Resident, Cleveland, Ohio Office)
Patricia O. Lowry
Stephen H. Jett
W. Timothy Miller
Keith W. Johnson
Daniel R. Warncke
George D. Molinsky
Ronald A. Bell
John P. Curp (Resident, Columbus, Ohio Office)
Cynthia C. Felson
David V. Allen (Resident, Cleveland, Ohio Office)
Eric K. Combs
Kerry P. Hastings
Jeremy P. Blumenfeld
Linda A. Klimas
Joanna Stern Valdes
Mark J. Sheppard
Brenda M. Breitkreutz
Antonia Mitroussia
Cindy-Ann Thomas
Patricia Anderson Pryor
Lisa M. Brickner
Keith P. Hartzell (Resident, Columbus, Ohio Office)
Terri W. Meldrum (Resident, Columbus, Ohio Office)
David O. Watson
Valerie W. Sinn
Aimee L. Keller
Jeanne Marie Bruns

Counsel for: Cincinnati Bengals; Cincinnati Gas & Electric Co.; CINergy; Gibson Greetings, Inc.; Morton International, Inc.; Sisters of Charity Healthcare Systems, Inc.; Star Banc Corporation; Thiokol Corporation.

For full biographical listings, see the Martindale-Hubbell Law Directory

VORYS, SATER, SEYMOUR AND PEASE LLP (AV)

Suite 2100, 221 East Fourth Street, P.O. Box 0236, 45201-0236
Telephone: 513-723-4000
Telecopier: 513-723-4056
URL: http://www.vssp.com
Columbus, Ohio Office: 52 East Gay Street, P.O. Box 1008, 43216-1008.
Telephone: 614-464-6400.
Telex: 241348.
Telecopier: 614-464-6350.
Cleveland, Ohio Office: 2100 One Cleveland Center, 1375 East Ninth Street, 44114-1724.
Telephone: 216-479-6100.
Telecopier: 216-479-6060.
Washington, D.C. Office: Suite 1111, 1828 L Street, N.W., 20036-5104.
Telephone: 202-467-8800.
Telex: 440693.
Telecopier: 202-467-8900.
Alexandria, Virginia Office: 277 South Washington Street, Suite 310, 22314.
Telephone: 703-549-4282.
Facsimile: 703-549-4492.

RESIDENT MEMBERS

Roger A. Yurchuck
Thomas B. Ridgley
Donald J. Shuller
John C. Vorys
Daniel J. Buckley
Mark A. Norman
Andrew M. Kaplan
Terri Reyering Abare
Charles C. Bissinger, Jr.
Glenn V. Whitaker
W. Breck Weigel
William D. Hayes
Stephen S. Eberly
Thomas L. Gabelman
Melvin A. Bedree

(See Next Column)

RESIDENT ASSOCIATES

Victor A. Walton, Jr.
Nathaniel Lampley, Jr.
Laura H. Martin
Richard L. Moore
Eliot N. Meyers
Phillip J. Smith
Kathleen McAnaney Molinsky
Hani R. Kallas
Scott A. Carroll
Rosemary D. Welsh
Jean R. Crosmun
Mary C. Henkel
Rodney L. Drinnon
David A. Groenke
William D.G. Baldwin
Jeffrey A. Miller
Joshua N. Cash
Eric Richardson
Mel J. Simmons

RESIDENT OF COUNSEL

Jacob E. Davis
Cynthia A. Shafer
Eugene P. Ruehlmann
Kent A. Britt

For full biographical listings, see the Martindale-Hubbell Law Directory

*CLEVELAND,** Cuyahoga Co.

ARTER & HADDEN LLP (AV)

1100 Huntington Building, 925 Euclid Avenue, 44115-1475
Telephone: 216-696-1100
Fax: 216-696-2645
Telex: 98-5384
URL: http://www.arterhadden.com
In Columbus, Ohio: Suite 1200, One Columbus, 10 West Broad Street. 43215-3422.
Telephone: 614-221-3155.
Fax: 614-221-0479.
In Dayton, Ohio: Kettering Tower, Suite 2310, 40 North Main Street. 45423.
Telephone: 937-223-4701.
Fax: 937-223-0170.
In Washington, D.C.: 1801 K Street, N.W., Suite 400K. 20006-3480.
Telephone: 202-775-7100.
Fax: 202-857-0172.
In Dallas, Texas: 1717 Main Street, Suite 4100. 75201-4605.
Telephone: 214-761-2100.
Fax: 214-741-7139.
In Los Angeles, California: 725 South Figueroa Street, Suite 3400. 90017.
Telephone: 213-430-3000.
Fax: 213-617-9255.
In Irvine, California: Five Park Plaza, Suite 1000, Jamboree Center, 92714.
Telephone: 949-252-7500.
Fax: 949-833-9604.
In Austin, Texas: 100 Congress Avenue, Suite 1800.
Telephone: 512-479-6403.
Fax: 512-469-5505.
In San Antonio, Texas: One Riverwalk Place, 700 North Saint Mary's Street, Suite 800, 78205.
Telephone: 210-805-8497.
Fax: 210-805-8519.
In San Francisco, California: Two Embarcadero Center, 5th Floor, 94111.
Telephone: 415-617-2100.
Fax: 415-912-3636.
In Sacramento, California: Wells Fargo Center, 400 Capitol Mall, Suite 900, 95814.
Telephone: 916-449-3917.
Fax: 916-449-8249.
In San Diego, California: 402 West Broadway, Sixth Floor, 92102.
Telephone: 619-238-0001.
Fax: 619-238-8333.
In Woodland Hills, California: 5959 Topanga Canyon Boulevard, Suite 244, 91367.
Telephone: 818-712-0036.
Fax: 818-346-6502.

MEMBERS OF FIRM

Thomas H. Allison
Michael J. Bertsch
Henry E. Billingsley, II
Thomas V. Chema
Lee A. Chilcote
Harry D. Cornett, Jr.
Gary L. Dinner
John T. Doheny
Ed E. Duncan
Michael E. Elliott
Stephen C. Ellis
William H. Falin
Brian W. FitzSimons
John X. Garred
Robert E. Glaser
George Gore
Robert J. Hanna
Michael F. Harris
Irene C. Keyse-Walker
Eugene M. Killeen
Richard M. Knoth
Glenn S. Krassen
James A. Laurenson
John B. Lewis
Mark F. McCarthy
Gregory V. Mersol
Edward F. Meyers, Jr.
Barry J. Miller
Glenn E. Morrical
Thomas J. Onusko
James E. Phillips
Susan E. Raabe
Susan L. Racey
M. Neal Rains
Alan J. Ross
McKinley Hobart Sauer III
James C. Scott
Janet H. Smith
Hugh M. Stanley, Jr.
William J. Stavole
Carter E. Strang
Diana M. Thimmig
Robert B. Tomaro
Robert C. Tucker
Victoria L. Vance
Stanley A. Williams

(See Next Column)

ARTER & HADDEN LLP, *Cleveland—Continued*

RETIRED PARTNERS

Walter A. Bates
Robert S. Burton
Byron D. Fair
David L. Genger
Edwin A. Kennedy
Charles W. Landefeld
Jerome D. Neifach
Robert B. Preston
Joseph A. Rotolo
William W. Taft
James H. Wilkinson

OF COUNSEL

Richard H. Brown
Lisa M. deFilippis
Bourne P. Dempsey
Stanley M. Fisher
R. Patrick (Pat) Kelly
Rita Bartnik Maimbourg
Donald W. Morrison
Frank R. Osborne
Charles J. O'Toole
Thomas A. Quintrell
Lisa Amato Reid
Jacob I. Rosenbaum
Raymond Rundelli
Bernard J. Smith
Ann H. Womer Benjamin
Daniel K. Wright, II

ASSOCIATES

Thomas W. Baker
Terri L. Bowman
Lois J. Cole
Stephen J. Crawford
Debra Csikos
Mary M. Culbertson
Patrick J. Flynn
Jeffrey A. Healy
Joel S. Heiser
Michael A. Jaffe
Jayne L. Jakubaitis
Scott J. Kelly
Timothy M. Kennedy
Alisa Kipnis
Jean Kerr Korman
Lee M. Koury
David S. Lu
Sharon A. Luarde (Not admitted in OH)
Thomas M. Lundin
Timothy E. Manning
Kristen L. Mayer
Rachel McQuade
Nicholas M. Miller
Susan L. Mizer
Joseph J. Morford
Thomas J. Piatak
Keith H. Raker
Christian D. Saine
Michael J. Summerhill
Brooke H. Thayer
Todd R. Tucker
Daniel C. Urban
David S. Winston
Nicholas C. York

For full biographical listings, see the Martindale-Hubbell Law Directory

BAKER & HOSTETLER LLP (AV)

3200 National City Center, 1900 East Ninth Street, 44114-3485
Telephone: 216-621-0200
Telecopier: 216-696-0740
TWX: 810 421 8375
RCA Telex: 215032
To contact an attorney on the Internet use first initial and surname followed by @baker-hostetler.com
URL: http://www.bakerlaw.com
In Cincinnati, Ohio: 312 Walnut Street, Suite 2650.
Telephone: 513-929-3400.
In Columbus, Ohio: Capitol Square, Suite 2100, 65 East State Street.
Telephone: 614-228-1541.
In Denver, Colorado: 303 East 17th Avenue, Suite 1100.
Telephone: 303-861-0600.
In Houston, Texas: 1000 Louisiana, Suite 2000.
Telephone: 713-751-1600.
In Beverly Hills, California: 9150 Wilshire Boulevard, Suite 205.
Telephone: 310-385-7500.
In Long Beach, California: 300 Oceangate, Suite 620.
Telephone: 562-432-2827.
In Los Angeles, California: 600 Wilshire Boulevard.
Telephone: 213-624-2400.
In Orlando, Florida: SunBank Center, Suite 2300, 200 South Orange Avenue.
Telephone: 407-649-4000.
In Washington, D.C.: Washington Square, Suite 1100, 1050 Connecticut Avenue, N.W.
Telephone: 202-861-1500.

Newton D. Baker (1871-1937)
Joseph C. Hostetler (1885-1958)
Thomas L. Sidlo (1888-1955)

EXECUTIVE PARTNER

Gary L. Bryenton (Executive Partner)

OFFICE MANAGING PARTNERS

Kenneth F. Snyder

PARTNERS

Albert T. Adams
Thomas L. Anastos
Frank H. Andorka
Oakley V. Andrews
Elliot Stephen Azoff
Richard H. Bamberger
Brian A. Bash
Bruce O. Baumgartner
Paul E. Bennett
Jordan Berns
Mary M. Bittence
Dale A. Bradford
Maureen A. Brennan
Arthur V.N. Brooks
Robert M. Brucken
David A. Bruscino
John H. Burlingame
Phillip M. Callesen
Diane P. Chapman
Elaine A. Chotlos
Avery S. Cohen
Louis A. Colombo
Wayne C. Dabb, Jr.
John D. Drinko
Paul P. Eyre (Head of Litigation Practice)
William W. Falsgraf
Michael K. Farrell

(See Next Column)

PARTNERS (Continued)

Paul H. Feinberg
José C. Feliciano
John H. M. Fenix
Charles J. French, III
Paula L. Friedman
Robert R. Galloway
John Mills Gherlein
Wendy J. Gibson
Edward S. Ginsburg
Matthew R. Goldman
David B. Graham
James B. Griswold
J. Richard Hamilton
Suzanne K. Hanselman
Jane T. Haylor
Richard R. Hollington, Jr.
Charles E. Jarrett
Norman S. Jeavons
R. Steven Kestner
Catherine M. Kilbane
Tom A. King
Calvin B. Kirchick
Robert K. Lease
Earl M. Leiken
Richard H. Leukart, II
Lawrence V. Lindberg
James A. Loeb
Thomas R. Lucchesi
Raymond M. Malone
Ruth Ann Maloney
David L. Marburger
Robert G. Markey
Gary R. Martz
Daniel P. Mascaro
John J. McGowan, Jr.
Wade A. Mitchell
Karen B. Newborn
Patricia J. O'Donnell
Ronald S. Okada
W. James Ollinger
Gerardo C. Orlando
Jeffrey H. Paravano
John D. Parker
Stephen J. Petras, Jr.
Robert C. Petrulis
Patricia A. Poole
Charles T. Price
Edward G. Ptaszek, Jr.
Jill Sarnoff Riola (Not admitted in OH)
Kevin G. Robertson
Hilary Whipple Rule
Thomas M. Seger
Hewitt B. Shaw, Jr.
Thomas H. Shunk
Randall L. Solomon
Ronald A. Stepanovic
David J. Strauss
Victor Strimbu, Jr.
John E. Sullivan
Christopher J. Swift
Alexander J. Szilvas
William M. Toomajian
Ernest E. Vargo, Jr.
R. Byron Wallace
Robert A. Weible
Charles D. Weller
Deborah A. Schaff Wilcox
John H. Wilharm, Jr.
John A. Zangerle

ASSOCIATES

Lori M. Ambriola
Dana Rountree Andrassy
Barry W. Andrews
Chris Bator
Margaret J. Bieber
Carolyn Broering-Jacobs
R. Timothy Coerdt
Melanie S. Corcoran
Edward M. DeAngelo
Amy M. DeColibus
Donna L. Duffy
Jennifer L. Eschedor
Joy M. Evans
Rhonda S. Ferguson
Michael T. Fishman
Kyle B. Fleming
Kevin P. Gluntz
Heidi L. Goebel
Matthew D. Graban
Fredrick T. Greco
John M. Heffernan
L. Dennis Hoffman Jr.
Scott D. Irwin
Kristin J. Jakiel
Suzanne M. Jambe
Victoria Johnson
Seth M. Jupin
Matthew B. Kall
Amy Elizabeth Kellogg
Amy Klimek
Todd H. Lebowitz
Melissa A. Leonard
Robert M. Loesch
Arthur H. Lundberg
Marcia E. Marsteller
Michael P. McNamara, Jr.
John C. Morrow
James R. Napoli
Edward D. Papp
Gregory S. Patterson
Jack E Peak
Jason P. Perdion
Kathleen A. Pettingill
Melinda L Reynolds
Nichol M. Schoenfield
Laura J. Shaw
Christina N. Smith
James Spallino, Jr.
Stacey S. Staub
Matthew A. Tenerowicz
Halle Fine Terrion
Peter W. Van Euwen, III
Brett A. Wall
Michelle W. Waller
Susan Shaheen Warner
Rose Mary L. Wenstrup
Diane D. Wilcox

OF COUNSEL

William L. Arnold
Theodore W. Jones
Lloyd F. Loux, Jr.

RETIRED PARTNERS

Charles R. Ault
William L. Calfee
Charles H. Cleminshaw
Warren Daane
George Downing
Sherman Dye
William H. Fleming
David R. Fullmer
Donald W. Gruettner
John S. Hopkins, III
Richard Katcher
Charles Klaus
Russell Leasure
H. Stephen Madsen
Robert Joseph Marquard
J. Rita Newton
John F. Novatney, Jr.
Parker M. Orr
Joseph Patchan
Maurice M. Sayre
Richard R. Turney

LEGAL SUPPORT PERSONNEL

Bob Craig (Firmwide Director of Information Services)
Alvin M. Podboy, Jr. (Firmwide Director of Libraries)
Charles B. Thomas (Firmwide Director of Finance)
Michelle C. Vanderlip (Firmwide Director of Human Resources)

For full biographical listings, see the Martindale-Hubbell Law Directory

Cleveland—Continued

Berick, Pearlman & Mills A Legal Professional Association (AV)

1350 Eaton Center, 1111 Superior Avenue, 44114-2569
Telephone: 216-861-4900
Telecopier: 216-861-4929

James H. Berick
Samuel S. Pearlman
Osborne Mills, Jr.
William M. Mills
Paul J. Singerman
Gary S. Desberg
Daniel G. Berick
Edmund G. Kauntz
Laura D. Nemeth

SENIOR COUNSEL

George F. Karch, Jr.

Christine A. Murphy
Ellen K. Meehan
Terence L. Thomas
Raphael J. Omerza
Bryan H. Falk
Alexander G. Burlingame

Representative Clients: Cleveland Browns; The Equitable Life Assurance Society of the United States; The Huntington National Bank; KeyBank National Association; MBNA Corporation; Pressco Technology Inc.; The Provident Bank; A. Schulman, Inc.; The State Teachers Retirement System of Ohio; The Town and Country Trust.

For full biographical listings, see the Martindale-Hubbell Law Directory

Bernard, Haffey & Bohnert Co., L.P.A. (AV)

Jefferson Centre, 5001 Mayfield Road #301, P.O. Box 24005, 44124-0005
Telephone: 216-291-3600
FAX: 216-291-0159
URL: http://www.lawyers.com/bernardhaffey&bohnert

Clifford H. Bernard (1907-1985)
J. Ross Haffey, Jr.
Edward G. Bohnert
Timothy P. Haffey

Reference: KeyBank.

For full biographical listings, see the Martindale-Hubbell Law Directory

Calfee, Halter & Griswold LLP (AV)

1400 McDonald Investment Center, 800 Superior Avenue, 44114-2688
Telephone: 216-622-8200
Telecopier: 216-241-0816
Telex: 980499
URL: http://www.calfee.com
Columbus, Ohio Office: 88 East Broad Street, Suite 1500.
Telephone: 614-321-1500.
Telecopier: 614-621-0010.

MEMBERS OF FIRM

Edwin G. Halter (1906-1975)
Bruce Griswold (1916-1993)
Joseph D. Sullivan
Charles R. Emrick, Jr.
William A. Papenbrock
John D. Wheeler
Michael L. Miller
James F. Streicher
Thomas A. Jorgensen
Dale C. LaPorte
Phillip J. Campanella
Timothy J. Nolan
Brian M. Eisenberg
Frederick W. Assini
David L. Carpenter
Ronald H. Neill
Charles B. Lyon
Philip M. Dawson
Thomas E. Wagner
P. Michael DeAngelo (Resident, Columbus Office)
David E. Bishop
Robert N. Rapp
Harold W. Babbit
William A. Boyd
Thomas A. Cicarella
Walter G. Harper
Kenneth R. Schmeichel
Thomas F. McKee
Mark I. Wallach
Virginia D. Benjamin
Stephen P. Kresnye
James G. Dickinson
Richard J. Hauer, Jr.
Michael D. Phillips
Scott R. Wilson
James M. Lawniczak
Ronald C. Stansbury
Guy F. Guinn
John Paul Batt
Lawrence N. Schultz
Michael E. Brittain
Richard P. Goddard
Bruce J. L. Lowe
Darlene Evans McCoy
Marcia J. Wexberg
John J. Eklund
Thomas W. McCrystal
Marc L. Oberdorff
Mitchell G. Blair
Edward W. Moore
Mary M. Reil
Joseph A. Castrodale
William E. Coughlin
James C. Vanderwist
John T. Wiedemann
Joseph K. Juster
Kathleen Keogh
Brent D. Ballard
Peter J. Comodeca
Jeanne E. Longmuir
JoEllen M. Minchak
John M. Mino
Douglas A. Neary
Robert P. Rink
Robert A. Ross
M. Ann Harlan
Albert J. Lucas (Resident, Columbus Office)
Mary E. Golrick
John R. Cernelich
Kevin P. Hallquist
John J. Jenkins
Anthony J. LaCerva
Robert A. Miller
Lynn M. Gattozzi
William L. S. Ross
Kevin M. Sullivan
Daniel J. McMullen
Shelly G. Dedmon
Martin S. Gates
Thomas I. Michals

(See Next Column)

MEMBERS OF FIRM (Continued)

Leonard L. Lewis
John S. Cipollа
Anthea R. Daniels
Cornelius J. Whitford
Christopher S. Williams

RETIRED PARTNERS

John B. Calfee
John L. Naylor, Jr.
Thomas K. M. Victory
Daniel L. Ekelman
F. Rush McKnight
Richard Cusick
Wm. Tousley Smith
Donald Fredric Woodcock
Richard N. Ogle
William N. Hogg

OF COUNSEL

John E. Gotherman
Thomas M. Hoban

ASSOCIATES

Philip J. Carino
Mara E. Cushwa
Todd F. Palmer
David J. Crandall
Jean M. Cullen
John A. Heer, II
Karl S. Beus
James F. Lang
Gerald A. Monroe
Suzanne K. Saganich
Jason M. Gibbons
Arthur C. Hall III
Maura L. Hughes
Michael F. Marhofer
Sean T. Moorhead
Jay Garrett Volk
Mark L. Belleville
Deborah S. Cousins
Sean P. Dunn (Resident Columbus Office)
Petar Kraguljac
Tracy Scott Johnson
Scott M. Loomis
Sean C. Beckstrom
Murad A. Beg (Not admitted in OH)
S. Paige Christopher
Timothy J. Connors
James A. Dimitrijevs
Karen A. Visocan
Julie A. Harris
Lola L. Johnson
Matthew J. Klaben
Alexandra M. Kowalski
Brian A. McMahon
Howard M. Neuger
Michael R. Peterson
Matthew E. Burke
Henry G. Grendell
Gregory Scot Harvey
Colleen Moran O'Neil
Nenad Pejic
Kenneth G. Saunders
James D. Graham
Richard J. Mattera
Craig L. Moore
June Rickey
Karla M. Rogers
Peter A. Rosato (Resident, Columbus Office)
Tracy Wilson Smirnoff
Wendy E. Stark
Christopher J. Ulery
Deanna L. Brandon
Ronald D. Gutt
Luke F. McConville
James L. Miller
Thomas R. O'Donnell
Michael A. Wahlster
William C. Daroff
Stephen L. McCauley
Brian D. Johnson
Steven R. Malynn
John J. McGuire
Scott C. Matasar (Not admitted in OH)
Sanford E. Watson II
Larry W. Conner, II
Sandra G. Rolitsky

SENIOR ATTORNEYS

Stanley J. Dobrowski (Resident, Columbus Office)
Margaret S. Callesen
Renée Tramble Richard
Pamela A. Docherty
Jean M. Hillman
Tara A. Kastelic
Grace Park Kelly
Cecil Marlowe
Susan R. Strom
James A. Rich (Not admitted in OH)
Barbara-Ann C. Gustaferro
Susan R. Horwitz
Michelle A. Lafferty
Sheryl K. Kelly
Wade Douglass Clark
Eileen T. Mathews
Pauline M. Moorman
Corine Corpora
John E. Miller, Jr.
Kim Moses Oreh
Donald E. Lampert

STAFF ATTORNEYS

Robert J. Bonko
Carol D. Strassman
Mark T. Freeman
Robert A. Gerberry
Scott N. Opincar
Ariel Sudilovsky

For full biographical listings, see the Martindale-Hubbell Law Directory

Davis & Young (AV)

A Legal Professional Association
1700 Midland Building, 44115
Telephone: 216-348-1700
Fax: 216-621-0602
Cable: DANDY CLE
Email: atty@davisyoung.com *URL:* http://www.davisyoung.com
Akron, Ohio Office: 1015 Society Building, 159 South Main Street.
Telephone 216-376-1717.
Fax: 216-376-1797.
Youngstown, Ohio Office: 406 Wick Building, 34 Federal Plaza West, 44503.
Telephone: 330-743-1717.

Rees H. Davis, Sr. (1892-1965)
Fred J. Young (1889-1946)
George W. Lutjen
Martin J. Murphy
C. Richard McDonald
Paul D. Eklund
Jan L. Roller
Thomas W. Wright
David J. Fagnilli
Gregory H. Collins
William Vance
Patrick F. Roche

(See Next Column)

DAVIS & YOUNG, *Cleveland—Continued*

Kevin M. Norchi
David G. Utley
Timothy L. Kerwin
Marc A. Sanchez
Ann Marie O'Brien
Susan L. Fricker
Michele Y. Wharton
Larry D. Wilkes
Timothy G. Welsh

OF COUNSEL

R. Emmett Moran

Counsel for: Westfield Companies; Cincinnati Insurance Company; University Hospitals of Cleveland; Medical Protective Company; Ohio Insurance Guaranty Association; Alliance Insurance Co.; Amerisure Companies; Avis Rent-A-Car Systems Inc.; Black & Decker; Dana Corp.; Central Mutual Insurance Co.; Eagle Picher Industries Inc.; TOPS Friendly Markets; U.S. Fidelity & Guaranty Co.

For full biographical listings, see the Martindale-Hubbell Law Directory

GALLAGHER, SHARP, FULTON & NORMAN (AV)

(Formerly Hauxhurst, Sharp, Mollison & Gallagher)
Bulkley Building, Seventh Floor, 1501 Euclid Avenue, 44115
Telephone: 216-241-5310
Telecopier: 216-241-1608
Email: gsfn.com *URL:* http://www.gsfn.com

MEMBERS OF FIRM

H. Austin Hauxhurst (1881-1962)
Frank X. Cull (1887-1965)
I. Walter Sharp (1884-1966)
Clarence L. Mollison (1906-1981)
Robert C. Horrigan (1916-1993)
Forrest A. Norman
Edward J. Cass
John B. Robertson
Thomas E. Betz
Alan M. Petrov
Alton L. Stephens, Jr.
Virginia L. Heidloff
Jay Clinton Rice
Joseph W. Pappalardo
Thomas E. Dover
James F. Koehler
Robert H. Eddy
Thomas J. Kaiser
D John Travis
Paul J. Schumacher, Jr.
William F. Gibson
Gary L. Nicholson
Lynn L. Moore
Ernest W. Auciello, Jr.
Patrick M. Foy
Kevin C. Alexandersen
Stanley M. Dub
Timothy T. Brick
Sheila A. McKeon
Thomas J. Cabral
Timothy J. Fitzgerald
Mark A. Greer

OF COUNSEL

Michael R. Gallagher
Robert W. Sharp
George W. Stuhldreher
Burt J. Fulton
James F. Sweeney
James G. Gowan
James L. Ryhal, Jr.

Edward G. Kagels
John T. Murphy
M. Terence Cawley
Todd M. Haemmerle
Brian R. McGraw
Timothy P. Whitford
Daniel J. Michalec
Alexander E. Goetsch
Joseph J. Santoro
Monica A. Sansalone
John A. Simon
Dennis G. Rehor
Beth A. Nagel
Timothy Patrick Roth
Gregory K. Boop
Janice Aitken
Gary F. Werner
Mark Joseph Savage
Catherine A. Davis
Charles Allston Bowers
Pamela S. Schremp
James T. Tyminski, Jr.
Matthew J. Hatchadorian

STAFF ATTORNEY

Daniel L. Herak

Counsel for: Associated Aviation Underwriters; Conrail; The Continental Insurance Cos.; Continental National American Group; Fireman's Fund Insurance Cos.; The Home Insurance Co.; Motorist Ins. Co.; Norfolk Southern Corp.; Royal Insurance Co.; United States Aviation Underwriters.

For full biographical listings, see the Martindale-Hubbell Law Directory

JANIK & FORBES (AV)

Building Two, 8223 Brecksville Road, 44141-1371
Telephone: 440-838-7600
Fax: 440-838-7601

MEMBERS OF FIRM

Steven G. Janik
Steven Forbes
Andrew J. Dorman

ASSOCIATES

Sherry A. Croyle
Richard McLain Garner
William J. Muniak
Thomas A. Prislipsky
George W. Schmedlen
Ellyn B. Tamulewicz
Daniel J. White

OF COUNSEL

Thomas D. Lambros
Adrienne L. Deckman
Carrie A. Foliano

For full biographical listings, see the Martindale-Hubbell Law Directory

JONES, DAY, REAVIS & POGUE (AV)

North Point, 901 Lakeside Avenue, 44114
Telephone: 216-586-3939
Telecopier: 216-579-0212
Email: counsel@jonesday.com *URL:* http://www.jonesday.com
In Columbus, Ohio: 1900 Huntington Center.
Telephone: 614-469-3939.
Telecopier: 614-461-4198.
In Atlanta, Georgia: 3500 SunTrust Plaza, 303 Peachtree Street.
Telephone: 404-521-3939.
Telecopier: 404-581-8330.
In Brussels, Belgium: Avenue Louise 480, 7th Floor. B-1050 Brussels.
Telephone: 32-2-645-14-11.
Telecopier: 32-2-645-14-45.
In Chicago, Illinois: 77 West Wacker.
Telephone: 312-782-3939.
Telecopier: 312-782-8585.
In Dallas, Texas: 2727 North Harwood Street.
Telephone: 214-220-3939.
Telecopier: 214-969-5100.
In Frankfurt, Germany: Hochhaus am Park, Grüneburgweg 102, 60323 Frankfurt am Main.
Telephone: 49-69-9726-3939.
Telecopier: 49-69-9726-3993.
In Geneva, Switzerland: 20, rue de Candolle.
Telephone: 41-22-320-2339.
Telecopier: 41-22-320-1232.
In Hong Kong, China: 29th Floor, Entertainment Building, 30 Queen's Road Central.
Telephone: 852-2526-6895.
Telecopier: 852-2868-5871 or 852-2868-5699.
In Irvine, California: 5 Park Plaza, Suite 1100.
Telephone: 949-851-3939.
Telecopier: 949-553-7539.
In London, England: Bucklersbury House, 3 Queen Victoria Street.
Telephone: 44-171-236-3939.
Telecopier: 44-171-236-1113.
In Los Angeles, California: 555 West Fifth Street, Suite 4600.
Telephone: 213-489-3939.
Telecopier: 213-243-2539.
In New Delhi, India (Associate Office): Pathak & Associates (an associate firm of Jones, Day, Reavis & Pogue), 1st Floor, Dr. Gopal Das Bhaven, 28 Barakhamba Road.
Telephone: 91-11-373-8793; 91-11-335-7345.
Telecopier: 91-11-335-3761.
In New York, N.Y.: 599 Lexington Avenue.
Telephone: 212-326-3939.
Telecopier: 212-755-7306.
In Paris, France: 120, rue du Faubourg Saint-Honoré.
Telephone: 33-1-56-59-39-39.
Telecopier: 33-1-56-59-39-38
In Pittsburgh, Pennsylvania: 500 Grant Street, 31st Floor.
Telephone: 412-391-3939.
Telecopier: 412-394-7959.
In Riyadh, Saudi Arabia: The International Law Firm (In Association with Jones, Day, Reavis & Pogue), Sulaymaniyah, Prince Mishari IBN, Abdulaziz Street, P.O. Box 22166.
Telephone: (966-1) 462-8866.
Telecopier: (966-1) 462-9001.
In Shanghai, China: 2805 Kerry Centre, 1515 Nanjing Road West.
Telephone: 86-21-5298-6568.
Telecopier: 86-21-5298-6569.
In Sydney, Australia: Governor Phillip Tower, Level 38, 1 Farrer Place.
Telephone: 61-2-9210-6921.
Telecopier: 61-2-9210-6926.
In Taipei, Taiwan: 8th Floor, Tun Hwa South Road, Section 2.
Telephone: (886-2) 2704-6808.
Telecopier: (886-2) 2704-6791.
In Tokyo, Japan: Toranomon MT Building, 4th Floor, 10-3, Toranomon 3-Chome, Minato-ku, Tokyo 105, Japan.
Telephone: 81-3-3433-3939.
Telecopier: 81-3-5401-2725.
In Washington, D.C.: 51 Louisiana Avenue, N.W.
Telephone: 202-879-3939.
Telecopier: 202-626-1700.

MEMBERS OF FIRM IN CLEVELAND

Patrick F. McCartan
George J. Moscarino
William A. Reale
John L. Strauch
Gary W. Melsher
Irvin A. Leonard
Dennis M. Kelly
Dennis W. LaBarre
Barry L. Springel
John L. Sterling
Brian F. Toohey
John M. Newman, Jr.
Richard H. Sayler
David G. Heiman
Michael A. Nims
William Thomas Plesec
Robert H. Rawson, Jr.
John W. Sager
David W. Sloan
Kenneth E. Updegraft, Jr.
James A. Rydzel
James E. Young
Kathleen B. Burke
Kenneth G. Hochman
Jeffrey S. Leavitt
Zachary T. Paris
Richard B. Whitney
Paul G. Crist
John P. Dunn
John W. Edwards II
Regan J. Fay
Ronald R. Janke
Michael G. Marting
Richard L. Reppert

(See Next Column)

JONES, DAY, REAVIS & POGUE—*Continued*

MEMBERS OF FIRM IN CLEVELAND (Continued)

Hugh R. Whiting
Kenneth R. Adamo
William H. Coquillette
Theodore M. Grossman
Michael J. Horvitz
Robert Conley Kahrl
Barbara J. Leukart
Anthony R. Moore
Louis Rorimer
Steven E. Sigalow
James L. Wamsley, III
Richard G. Stuhan
Robert C. Weber
John D. Currivan
Mary Lynn Durham
Thomas Demitrack
Stephen J. Kaczynski
Janet L. Miller
Stephen J. Squeri
Robert P. Ducatman
Stephen Q. Giblin
Daniel C. Hagen
David A. Kutik
Richard P. Layman
Jeanne M. Rickert
Richard M. Cieri
David P. Porter
Carl M. Jenks
Michael W. Vary
Robert S. Walker
David B. Alden
Mark Herrmann
Lyle G. Ganske
Timothy J. O'Hearn
Joseph D. Pollack
Jeffery D. Ubersax
Richard I. Werder, Jr.
Sanjiv K. Kapur
Mark A. Belasic
Robert L. Canala
Thomas C. Daniels
Paul D. Koethe
John M. Majoras
Stephen C. Mixter
Richard J. Bedell, Jr.
Charles W. Hardin, Jr.
William A. Herzberger
Calvin P. Griffith
Christopher M. Kelly (Not admitted in OH)
John A. Rego
Michelle K. Fischer
Deborah Platt Herman

OF COUNSEL

Katherine Bryan Jenks

COUNSEL

H. Duane Switzer
John C. Duffy, Jr.
Randall A. Cole
Charles M. Steines
Kathleen Hohler
Charles M. Kennedy
Marc Alan Silverstein
Leozino Agozzino
Ted S. Hiser
Timothy M. Opsitnick
Stephen D. Scanlon
Sandra E. Gammie
Ellen E. Halfon
Mary D. Maloney

ASSOCIATES

Benjamin B. Sley
David F. Adler
Cheryl Farine
Lisa B. Gates
Bernadette Mihalic Mast
Lisa A. Roberts-Mamone
Asmita Shirali
Michael L. Snyder
Anne Owings Ford
Anand S. Pathak
Laura R. Anderson
Randal S. Baringer
Elizabeth A. Grove
Maryanne B. Haller
Patrick J. Leddy
Edward Purnell
W. Eric Baisden
J. Joseph Korpics
Dennis L. Murphy
Rachel L. Rawson
Edward J. Sebold
Robert S. Faxon
Laurie F. Humphrey (Not admitted in OH)
Heather Lennox
Sean M. McAvoy
Michael J. Moody
Brian Troyer
Timothy P. Fraelich
Thomas A. Hamilton
Geoffrey J. Ritts
John M. Saada, Jr.
Mark J. Andreini
Susanne H. Deegan
Scott F. Frodyma
Heather Gordon
Lisa K. Kunkle
Robert J. Ringel
Kim M. Rivera-Sanchez
David D. Watson
Stephen E. Baskin
Karen K. Cain (Not admitted in OH)
Denise A. Carkhuff
Floyd Drexel Feeling
Steven N. Geise
Warren M. Haines II (Not admitted in OH)
Elaine J. Herrmann
Christopher J. Hewitt
Walter S. Holzer
Gina M. Killian
Jennifer C. Kogut
Sheryl H. Love
Michelle M. Morgan
Benita Pearson
Ritin Rai, Not admitted in the United States (Not admitted in OH)
Julia Ann Renfro
Paula Batt Wilson
Rebecca J. Bishop
Kevin D. Boyce
David B. Cochran
Thomas R. Goots
Charles T. Haag
Jennifer L. Hanley
Mary Elizabeth Huber
John Q. Lewis
Rachel D. Schmelzer
Deborah B. Uluer
Meredith M. Wilkes (Not admitted in OH)
Gregory A. Bauer
Jennifer W. Berlin
Pearson N. Bownas
Sean P. Costello
Christopher P. Fisher
Jennifer Girard Gehrlein
Paul V. Keller
Arthur P. Licygiewicz
James N. Mastracchio (Not admitted in OH)
Stacey L. McKinley
Eric H. Mosier
Angela Onwuachi-Willig
Jeffrey W. Saks (Not admitted in OH)
Stefan K. Schnopp
John L. Sinatra, Jr.
Juhi Singh
Wendy L. Weiss
Mark A. Whitt
Scott D. Zaret
Charles W. Zepp
Colleen Batcheler
Carl E. Black
Marc D. Browning
John J. Burns
David M. Maiorana (Not admitted in OH)
Melissa Jurecki Nandi
Patrick J. Norton
Theodore C. Parsons

(See Next Column)

ASSOCIATES (Continued)

Jenny L. Sheaffer
Nicole D. Stanger
Tracy K. Stratford
Deborah L. Hamilton
Steven E. Seasly
Wade R. Wagatsuma

SENIOR STAFF ATTORNEYS

Mark B. Farroni
Karen J. Corrigan

INSURANCE COUNSEL

Charles D. Hassell

STAFF ATTORNEYS

Linda H. DeOreo
Michael S. Martis
Noreen DeNuzzo
Kevin P. Roberts
David O. Zimmer
Mary P. McKenna
Thomas P. Alexander
Alison Colwell Snow
John A. Eastwood
Maureen Connolly
William D. Knox, III

For full biographical listings, see the Martindale-Hubbell Law Directory

KAHN, KLEINMAN, YANOWITZ & ARNSON CO., L.P.A. (AV)

The Tower at Erieview, Suite 2600, 44114-1824
Telephone: 216-696-3311
Telecopiers: 216-696-1009; 216-696-1524
URL: http://www.kahnkleinman.com

Kevin D. Barnes
James J. Bartolozzi
Sheldon Berns
Michael H. Diamant
Michael A. Ellis
Robert U. Fein
Bruce E. Gaynor
M. Colette Gibbons
James L. Koewler, Jr.
Neil Kurit
Scott M. Lewis
Gail B. Mayland
Marc H. Morgenstern
Benjamin J. Ockner
William M. Phillips
Richard S. Rivitz
Richard A. Rosner
Morlee A. Rothchild
Lawrence C. Sherman
David R. Tavolier
Robert J. Valerian
Frederick N. Widen

Shira Adler
Douglas V. Bartman (Not admitted in OH)
Joseph S. Chu
Kelly Montgomery Hoy
Mark R. Jacobs
Stuart L. Larsen
Kenneth L. Lohiser
James W. Margulies
Steven M. Moss
Randall S. Newman (Not admitted in OH)
Peter M. Slater
Howard G. Strain
Deborah A. Weisman
Robert A. Zimmerman

SENIOR COUNSEL

Bennett Yanowitz

OF COUNSEL

Matthew S. Friedman

Reference: National City Bank.

For full biographical listings, see the Martindale-Hubbell Law Directory

KELLEY, MCCANN & LIVINGSTONE, LLP (AV)

3500 BP Tower, 200 Public Square, 44114-2302
Telephone: 216-241-3141
Fax: 216-241-3707
Email: Attorneys@kmlegal.com

MEMBERS OF FIRM

Fred J. Livingstone
Stephen M. O'Bryan
John D. Brown
Joel A. Makee
Margaret Anne Cannon
Donna M. Flammang
Mark J. Valponi
Thomas J. Lee
Mary Grace Balazs
Bruce L. Waterhouse, Jr.
Carl A. Murway
David H. Wallace
Robert A. Brindza II
Peter M. Poulos

OF COUNSEL

Walter C. Kelley
George J. Dunn
David E. Burke

ASSOCIATES

Sandra K. Hunter
Timothy J. Duff
Corinne Katz Moore
Colleen G. Treml
Laurie H. Goetz
Gregory J. O'Brien
Andrew Agati
Charles D. Price
Renee B. Weiss
Christine A. Allport
Joshua D. Goldstein
Michelle R. Arendt

For full biographical listings, see the Martindale-Hubbell Law Directory

MCDONALD, HOPKINS, BURKE & HABER CO., L.P.A. (AV)

2100 Bank One Center, 600 Superior Avenue, E., 44114-2653
Telephone: 216-348-5400
Telecopier: 216-348-5474
Email: attorney@mhbh.com *URL:* http://www.mhbh.com

(See Next Column)

McDONALD, HOPKINS, BURKE & HABER CO. L.P.A., *Cleveland—Continued*

Patrick J. Berry
Jeffrey P. Consolo
Jerome W. Cook
Richard S. Cooper
Anthony J. DiVenere
Paul N. Edwards
Theodore J. Esborn
Steven L. Gardner
Carl J. Grassi
James A. Griffith
Jeffrey R. Huntsberger
Brian J. Jereb
Bernard L. Karr
Thomas W. Keen
Roger L. Kleinman
Joseph J. LoPresti, Jr.
Dan L. Makee
George L. McGaughey, Jr.
John T. Mulligan
Brian M. O'Neill
William J. O'Neill
Stephen T. Parisi
R. Jeffrey Pollock
Michael G. Riley
Shawn M. Riley
Albert N. Salvatore
Thomas C. Schrader
Roger L. Shumaker
Barbara J. Smith
James M. Stone
Dale R. Vlasek
Kenneth J. Walsh
John M. Wirtshafter
Jane Marie Pine Wood
Charles B. Zellmer

OF COUNSEL

John J. Monroe

Julie A. Callsen
Anne T. Corrigan
Steven A. Eisenberg
G. Andrew Gardner
Anuj Goswami
Donald E. Kacmar
David M. Kall
Jeffrey B. Keiper
Kevin J. Kessinger
Mark D. Klimek
Alan M. Koschik
Deviani M. Kuhar
Paul W. Linehan
Tyler L. Mathews
Jennifer A. Mills
Antoinette K. Palmer
Ketan K. Patel
Sharon Szolosi Regas
Douglas B. Schnee
Michele Smolin
Glenn D. Southworth
Michael R. Spreng

For full biographical listings, see the Martindale-Hubbell Law Directory

---

MEYERS, HENTEMANN & REA CO., L.P.A. (AV)

21st Floor, Superior Building, 815 Superior Avenue, N.E., 44114
Telephone: 216-241-3435
Telecopier: 216-241-6568
Elyria, Ohio Office: 301 Fifth Street, 44035.
Telephone: 216-323-6920.

Kent H. Meyers (1902-1970)
Richard F. Stevens (1915-1981)
David S. Meyers (1928-1983)
Eugene J. Gilroy (1926-1984)
John S. Rea
Henry A. Hentemann
Gerald L. Jeppe
Lynn A. Lazzaro

J. Michael Creagan
John J. Reagan
Ronald J. Ziehm
Cornelius J. O'Sullivan, Jr.

OF COUNSEL

Richard C. Talbert
Timothy R. Sweeney
Donald E. Worthing

Representative Clients: State Farm Mutual Insurance Co.; Travelers Insurance Co.; Lloyds Underwriters, London, England; Preferred Risk Mutual Insurance Co.; Detroit Automobile Inter-Insurance Exchange; Electrical Mutual.

For full biographical listings, see the Martindale-Hubbell Law Directory

---

PORTER WRIGHT MORRIS & ARTHUR LLP (AV)

925 Euclid Avenue, Suite 1700, 44115-1483
Telephone: 216-443-9000; (800-824-1980)
Fax: 216-443-9011
Email: cle@porterwright.com *URL:* http://www.porterwright.com
Columbus, Ohio Office: 41 South High Street, 43215-6194.
Telephones: 614-227-2000; (800-533-2794).
Fax: 614-227-2100. Internet: cmh@porterwright.com.
Dayton, Ohio Office: One Dayton Centre, One South Main Street, Suite 1600, 45402-2028.
Telephones: 937-449-6810; (800-533-4434).
Fax: 937-449-6820. Internet: day@porterwright.com.
Cincinnati, Ohio Office: 250 E. Fifth Street, Suite 2200, 45202-4199.
Telephones: 513-381-4700; (800-582-5813).
Fax: 513-421-0991. Internet: cvg@porterwright.com.
Washington, D.C. Office: 1667 K Street, N.W., Suite 1100, 20006-1605.
Telephones: 202-778-3000; (800-456-7962).
Fax: 202-778-3063. Internet: dca@porterwright.com.
Naples, Florida Office: 5801 Pelican Bay Boulevard, Suite 300, 34108-2709.
Telephones: 941-593-2900; (800-876-7962).
Fax: 941-593-2990. Internet: apf@porterwright.com.

(See Next Column)

MEMBERS OF FIRM

Robert D. Anderle
Jeffrey Baddeley
David A. Bell
Paul J. Corrado
Donald J. Fisher
Daniel F. Gourash
Margaret M. Koesel
Philip E. Langer
Hugh E. McKay
Patricia A. Screen
Ralph Streza
David C. Tryon
William R. Weir
Alan D. Wright

RESIDENT ASSOCIATES

Mary Kaye Bozza
Ann M. Caresani
Aimee M. Greenfield
Robert M. Higgins
Laura F. Kenney
Natalie L. Peterson
Sandra Becher Sommers
Eric F. Spade
Leo M. Spellacy, Jr.
Tracey L. Turnbull
Jeffrey J. Weber
Alan C. Yarcusko

RESIDENT OF COUNSEL

Robert E. Bingham

For full biographical listings, see the Martindale-Hubbell Law Directory

---

QUANDT, GIFFELS & BUCK CO., L.P.A. (AV)

800 Leader Building, 526 Superior Avenue, E., 44114-1460
Telephone: 216-241-2025
Telecopier: 216-241-2080
Email: attys@qgb.com

Robert G. Quandt (1925-1998)
Walter R. Matchinga
Joseph R. Tira
Beth A. Sebaugh
Laurence F. Buzzelli
Larry C. Greathouse
Hunter S. Havens
Timothy G. Sweeney
Richard A. Hoenigman
Jeffrey A. Schenk
Edward J. Stoll, Jr.
Ernest C. Pisanelli
Richard L. Warren, Jr.
Daniel A. Romaine

OF COUNSEL

Stephen D. Richman

Representative Clients: Physicians Insurance Company of Ohio; Royal Insurance; CNA Insurance Co.; Heritage Mutual Insurance Co.; Reliance Insurance Co.; Safeco Insurance Co.; American International Group.

For full biographical listings, see the Martindale-Hubbell Law Directory

---

RAY, ROBINSON, CARLE & DAVIES P.L.L. (AV)

1650 The East Ohio Building, 1717 East 9th Street, 44114-2898
Telephone: 216-861-4533
Facsimile: 216-861-4568
Email: rayrob@rayrobcle.com

MEMBERS OF FIRM

David G. Davies
Douglas R. Denny
Gene B. George
Julia R. Brouhard
Robert T. Coniam
Sandra Maurer Kelly

ASSOCIATE

Thomas More Wynne

OF COUNSEL

Lucian Y. Ray (1903-1987)
William D. Carle, III (Senior Counsel)
Theodore C. Robinson (Retired)

Representative Clients: The Cleveland-Cliffs Iron Co.; Bethlehem Steel Corp., Great Lakes Steamship Division; Canada Steamship Lines, Ltd.; Canadian Shipowners Assn.; Interlake Steamship Co.; Ispat Inland, Inc.; Amoco Oil Co.; Container Port Group, Inc.; Euclid Universoal Corp.

For full biographical listings, see the Martindale-Hubbell Law Directory

---

SEELEY, SAVIDGE AND EBERT A LEGAL PROFESSIONAL ASSOCIATION (AV)

800 Bank One Center, 600 Superior Avenue, East, 44114-2655
Telephone: 216-566-8200
Fax-Telecopier: 216-566-0213
URL: http://www.sse-law.com

Gregory D. Seeley
Keith A. Savidge
Gary A. Ebert
Jane T. Seelie
William M. Fumich, Jr.

Eric D. Baker
Andrew D. Bemer
Connie S. Carr
Mary Davis
Kathleen S. Grady
Devin J. Oddo
David T. Reed
Glenn J. Seeley
Matthew K. Seeley
Marc N. Silberman
Michael E. Stinn

Reference: KeyBank.

For full biographical listings, see the Martindale-Hubbell Law Directory

Cleveland—Continued

SPANGENBERG, SHIBLEY & LIBER LLP (AV)

2400 National City Center, 1900 East Ninth Street, 44114-3400
Telephone: 216-696-3232
Fax: 216-696-3924
Email: ssl@Spanglaw.com *URL:* http://www.Spanglaw.com

MEMBERS OF FIRM

Craig Spangenberg (1914-1998)
Norman W. Shibley (1921-1992)
Donald P. Traci (Retired)
John D. Liber
Robert A. Marcis
Peter H. Weinberger
William Hawal
Peter J. Brodhead
Dennis R. Lansdowne

ASSOCIATES

Justin F. Madden
Mary A. Cavanaugh
Stuart E. Scott
Rhonda Baker Debevec

For full biographical listings, see the Martindale-Hubbell Law Directory

SPIETH, BELL, McCURDY & NEWELL CO., L.P.A. (AV)

2000 Huntington Building, 925 Euclid Avenue, 44115-1496
Telephone: 216-696-4700
Fax: 216-696-2706
Email: law@spiethbell.com

Clyde E. Williams, Jr.
Glen O. Smith, Jr.
Sterling Newell, Jr.
J. Donald Cairns
Richard T. Watson
Patrick J. Amer
Henry E. Seibert, IV
Frederick I. Taft
James M. Havach
Stanley Dan Pace
Bruce G. Hearey
Dianne Foley Hearey
Rebecca Holloway Dent
James R. Bright
John M. Slivka
Benjamin Calkins
M. Elizabeth Monihan
Kristin L. Ubersax
Wade M. Fricke

Edmund W. Searby
Jennifer Cook Jontz
Timothy G. Warner
Kimberly Y. Smith Buhrow
Jennifer Welfley Nohra
Erica E. McGregor

OF COUNSEL

John J. Whitney

Representative Clients: American Greetings Corp.; Cleveland Cavaliers; Nationwide Advertising Services, Inc.; Independent Steel Co.; Baldwin Wallace College; The Tool-Die Engineering Co.
Representative Labor Relations Clients (Management Only): Parker Hannifin Corp.; Brush Wellman Co.; Elsag Bailey; M.A. Hanna Co.

For full biographical listings, see the Martindale-Hubbell Law Directory

SQUIRE, SANDERS & DEMPSEY L.L.P. (AV)

4900 Key Tower, 127 Public Square, 44114-1304
Telephone: 216-479-8500
Fax: 216-479-8780
URL: http://www.ssd.com
Columbus, Ohio Office: 1300 Huntington Center, 41 South High Street, Columbus, Ohio 43215-6150.
Telephone: 614-365-2700.
Fax: 614-365-2499.
Houston, Texas Office: 6250 Chase Tower, 600 Travis Street, Houston, Texas 77002-3007.
Telephone: 713-546-5850.
Fax: 713-546-5830.
Jacksonville, Florida Office: One Enterprise Center, Suite 2100, 225 Water Street, Jacksonville, Florida 32202-4424.
Telephone: 904-366-2420.
Fax: 904-356-2986.
Miami, Florida Office: 201 South Biscayne Boulevard, 2900 Miami Center, Miami, Florida 33131-4330.
Telephone: 305-577-8700.
Fax: 305-358-1425.
New York, New York Office: 350 Park Avenue, New York, New York 10022-6002.
Telephone: 212-872-9800.
Fax: 212-872-9815.
Phoenix, Arizona Office: Two Renaissance Square, 40 North Central Avenue, Suite 2700, Phoenix, Arizona 85004-4498.
Telephone: 602-528-4000.
Fax: 602-253-8129.
Washington, D.C. Office: 1201 Pennsylvania Avenue, N.W., Suite 500, Washington, D.C. 20004-2491.
Telephone: 202-626-6600.
Fax: 202-626-6780.
Bratislava, Slovak Republic Office: Zochova 5, 811 03 Bratislava, Slovak Republic.
Telephone: 421-7-5441-7611.
Fax: 42-1-7-6280-2212.
Brussels, Belgium Office: Avenue Louise, 165-Box 15, 1050 Brussels, Belgium.
Telephone: 32-2-627-1111.
Fax: 32-2-627-1100.

(See Next Column)

Budapest, Hungary Office: H-1062 Budapest, Andrassy ut. 64, Budapest, Hungary.
Telephone: 36-1-428-7111.
Fax: 36-1-428-7100.
Kyiv, Ukraine Office: 14A Yaroslaviv Val, Kyiv 252034, Ukraine.
Telephone: 38-044-228-8687.
Fax: 38-044-228-4938.
London, England Office: Royex House, Aldermanbury Square, London EC2V 7HR.
Telephone: 44-171-776-5200.
Fax: 44-171-776-5233.
Madrid, Spain Office: Calle Velazquez 108-110, 28006 Madrid, Spain.
Telephone: 34-91-590-2420.
Fax: 34-91-590-2421.
Moscow, Russian Federation Office: 13 Khokhlovskiy Lane, Moscow 109028, Russian Federation.
Telephone: 7-503-956-3750.
Fax: 7-503-956-3635.
Prague, Czech Republic Office: Václavské náměst 1 57/813, 110 00 Praha 1, Czech Republic.
Telephone: 420-2-2166-2111.
Fax: 420-2-2166-2222.
Hong Kong Office: Rooms 1101-2 St. George's Building, 2 Ice House Street, Central, Hong Kong.
Telephone: 852-2509-9732.
Fax: 852-2509-9772.
Taipei, Taiwan Office: 14F, 116 Nanking East Road, Sec. 2, Taipei, Taiwan, Republic of China.
Telephone: 886-2-2531-2888.
Fax: 886-2-2571-6199.

PARTNERS

CLEVELAND OFFICE

Andrew Squire (1850-1934)
William B. Sanders (1854-1929)
James H. Dempsey (1859-1920)
Mara L. Babin
Stacy D. Ballin
Geoffrey K. Barnes
George R. Barry
Dean L. Berry
Daniel L. Brockett
Jonathan F. Buchter
Carolyn J. Buller
David W. Burchmore
Van Carson
Terence J. Clark
Charles F. Clarke
William H. Conner
Mark A. Cusick
Carol F. Dakin
Ernie K. Demanelis
Carl A. Draucker
Robert J. Eidnier
Bebe A. Fairchild
Mark S. Floyd
D. Bruce Gabriel
Frances Floriano Goins
David S. Goodman
Richard Gurbst
W. Michael Hanna
Pamela Iddings Hanover
Susan C. Hastings
Thomas G. Havener
Barbara L. Hawley
Thomas G. Hermann
Laura Kingsley Hong
Ronald J. James
Bruce P. Jones
Mary Ann Jorgenson
Gordon S. Kaiser, Jr.
F. Barry Keefe
Thomas S. Kilbane
Helen Z. Kryshtalowych (Resident Member, Kyiv, Ukraine Office)
John S. Larson
John F. Lewis
Damond R. Mace
Jeffrey J. Margulies
Charles R. McElwee, II
George M. von Mehren
Michael G. Meissner
Cecil R. Mellin
John T. Meredith
G. Christopher Meyer
David J. Millstone
Kenneth C. Moore
Frederick R. Nance
Howard J.C. Nicols
James P. Oliver
M. Patricia Donnelly Oliver
Terrence G. Perris
Walter J. Rekstis, III
Daniel F. Roules
David W. Rowan
Timothy J. Sheeran
John F. Shelley
R. Thomas Stanton
Dale E. Stephenson
Dynda A. Thomas
James D. Troxell
Gregory J. Viviani
Robin G. Weaver
Jeffrey J. Wedel
David A. Zagore

COUNSEL

Joseph R. Cortese
James H. Dempsey Jr.
John C. Dowd
Daniel J. O'Loughlin
Ivan L. Otto

OF COUNSEL

CLEVELAND OFFICE

Timothy J. Cosgrove
Henry T. King Jr.
David Lavey
Jan E. Murray
Jill G. Okun
Katherine G. Petrey
Philip C. Schillawski
Louis Stokes
James D. Thomas
Joseph C. Weinstein

ASSOCIATES

CLEVELAND OFFICE

Alyson Suter Alber
Thomas S. Babel
Mathew B. Beredo
Steven C. Bordenkircher
Elleanor H. Chin
Paula B. Christ
Brian R. Coate
Emanuel J. Cotronakis
William J. Culbertson
Judith G. Deedy
Steven A. Delchin
Harold E. Farling
Adam R. Fox
Steven A. Friedman

(See Next Column)

SQUIRE, SANDERS & DEMPSEY L.L.P., *Cleveland—Continued*

ASSOCIATES
CLEVELAND OFFICE (Continued)

Roger Michael Gold
Rachel J. Grabow
Joseph K. Grant
James D. Gray
Micah D. Green
Valerie M. Hanna
Jarrod Hanson
Karen A. Hauser
Cheryl A. Hipp
James A. Hogan
JuanCarlos M. Hunt
Denise Jackson
Daniel A. Jaffe
Hanna B. Jennings
Robert J. Johnson
Kim I. Kaufman
Joan A. Kavuru
Michael W. Kelly
Robert V. Kelly (Not admitted in OH)
Maureen Sheridan Kenny
Andrew D. Komaromi (Not admitted in OH)
Thomas G. Kovach
Raymond Krncevic
Robert D. Labes
Patricia A. Lantzy
Hans L. Larsen
Lynn Rowe Larsen
Wendlene M. Lavey
Abby Levine
Richard D. Manoloff
Peter T. Massaro
Marcia A. McGratty
Douglas A. McWilliams
Jane S. Messmer
James B. Mooney
Mark C. Neath
Jude J. Nohra
Philip M. Oliss
Elton L. Parker
Thayne L. Peterson
Scott B. Pfahl
Dorothy Regas Richards
David J. Riley
Brian T. Robinson
Joseph P. Rodgers
Laura J. Roman
Richard J. Rudolph
Timothy D. Rudy
Elizabeth M. Sanborn
Margarita D. Santos
James W. Satola
Sanford Schwimmer
Harris A. Senturia
Michael L. Sharb
Archana Sheshadri
Ellen Siebenschuh
Michael T. Sprenger
Martha S. Sullivan
Timothy M. Sullivan
Christina Tait
Catherine Corrigan Tompkins
Ivo J. Travnicek
James A. Vollins
Kristopher Wahlers
Stephen L. Washington (Not admitted in OH)
Kristine M. Wellman
Glenn R. Wilson
Rebecca A. Wistner
Ling Zhu (Not admitted in OH)
Martin J. Zurada

For full biographical listings, see the Martindale-Hubbell Law Directory

---

TAFT, STETTINIUS & HOLLISTER LLP (AV)

Sixth Floor, Bond Court Building, 1300 East Ninth Street, 44114-1503
Telephone: 216-241-2838
Facsimile: 216-241-2837
URL: http://www.taftlaw.com
Cincinnati, Ohio Office: 1800 Firstar Tower, 425 Walnut Street.
Telephone: 513-381-2838.
Columbus, Ohio Office: Twelfth Floor, 21 East State Street.
Telephone: 614-221-2838.
Covington, Kentucky Office: Thomas More Centre, Suite 400, 2670 Chancellor Drive.
Telephone: 606-331-2838; 513-381-2838.

RESIDENT MEMBERS

William K. Smith
Steven A. Marrer

RESIDENT ASSOCIATES

David V. Allen
Jessica E. Price
Janice A. Isakoff

For full biographical listings, see the Martindale-Hubbell Law Directory

---

ULMER & BERNE LLP (AV)

Ninth Floor, Bond Court Building, 1300 East Ninth Street, 44114-1583
Telephone: 216-621-8400
FAX: 216-621-7488
Email: infocleveland@ulmer.com
Email: infocolumbus@ulmer.com *URL:* http://www.ulmer.com/
Columbus, Ohio Office: 88 East Broad Street, Suite 1980.
Telephone: 614-228-8400.
FAX: 614-228-8561.

MEMBERS OF FIRM

Thomas H. Barnard
Lewis T. Barr
Steven D. Bell
Barton A. Bixenstine
Kenneth A. Bravo
Ruth Anna Carlson
Inajo Davis Chappell
Robert E. Chudakoff
Maria Del Monaco
Robert A. Fein
Harold E. Friedman
Bill J. Gagliano
A.B. Glickman
John C. Goheen
James A. Goldsmith
Howard M. Groedel
Neil W. Gurney
Richard G. Hardy
Donald E. Heiser
Ronald H. Isroff
Ronald L. Kahn
Marvin L. Karp
Mark D. Katz
Stuart A. Laven
Murray K. Lenson
David L. Lester
Herbert B. Levine
Bruce P. Mandel
Stephen A. Markus
Craig A. Marvinney
Christopher C. McCracken
Craig S. Miller
Charles R. Olsavsky, Jr.
Brian N. Ramm
Harold (Kip) Reader
Peter A. Rome

(*See Next Column*)

MEMBERS OF FIRM (Continued)

Richard E. Rubinstein
Susan O. Scheutzow
Isaac Schulz
Patricia A. Shlonsky
Alan S. Sims
Richard D. Sweebe
Stephanie E. Trudeau
Michael N. Ungar
Jeffrey W. Van Wagner
F. Thomas Vickers
Richard G. Witkowski

SENIOR ATTORNEYS

Martin W. Elson
Bari E. Goggins

OF COUNSEL

Elliot M. Kaufman

ASSOCIATES

James V. Aveni
Robert B. Baer
Christopher J. Conti
George S. Crisci
Cheryl A. D'Amico
Bernard C. Daley (Not admitted in OH)
Timothy J. Downing
Jeffrey S. Dunlap
Kendra J. Eason
William D. Edwards
Heather E. Ewashinka
Joseph G. Foster
Philip J. Germani
Gregory A. Gordillo
Gary S. Greenlee
Thomas T. Holmes
Elizabeth A. Jerdonek
J. Timothy "jt" Kalnay
James N. Kline
Jennifer R. Lawry
Carrie Menikoff
Stephen C. Merriam
Cash H. Mischka
Andrew A. Paisley
Dean J. Pasalis
Jay W. Pearlman
Bonnie Gust Peskin
Lawrence F. Peskin
Lawrence D. Pollack
Gretchen Rogge
Lynn R. Rogozinski
Michael J. Russo
Jeffrey R. Sadlowski
Eric M. Schreibman
Douglas K. Sesnowitz
Michael J. Shapiro
Edward P. Simms
Michael D. Stovsky
Anne F. Strassfeld
Stephanie E. Straub
Linda Delacourt Summers
Michael S. Tucker
Elin B. Young

RETIRED MEMBERS

Jordan C. Band
William A. Edwards (Retired)
Robert L. Lewis
Morton L. Stone (Retired)

ATTORNEYS IN COLUMBUS, OHIO OFFICE (SEE LISTING)

MEMBERS OF FIRM

Alexander M. Andrews
Timothy M. Fox
Thomas L. Rosenberg

ASSOCIATES

Carl A. Anthony
Margaret C. Bettendorf
David L. Eidelberg
Jeffrey J. Sniderman

For full biographical listings, see the Martindale-Hubbell Law Directory

---

VORYS, SATER, SEYMOUR AND PEASE LLP (AV)

2100 One Cleveland Center, 1375 East Ninth Street, 44114
Telephone: 216-479-6100
Telecopier: 216-479-6060
URL: http://www.vssp.com
Columbus, Ohio Office: 52 East Gay Street, P.O. Box 1008, 43216-1008.
Telephone: 614-464-6400.
Telex: 241348.
Telecopier: 614-464-6350.
Cincinnati, Ohio Office: Suite 2100, 221 East Fourth Street, P.O. Box 0236, 45201-0236.
Telephone: 513-723-4000.
Telecopier: 513-723-4056.
Washington, D.C. Office: Suite 1111, 1828 L Street, N.W., 20036-5104.
Telephone: 202-467-8800.
Telex: 440693.
Telecopier: 202-467-8900.
Alexandria, Virginia Office: 277 South Washington Street, Suite 310, 22314.
Telephone: 703-549-4282.
Facsimile: 703-549-4492.

MEMBERS OF FIRM

F. Daniel Balmert (Resident)
John W. Read
Drew T. Parobek
Anthony J. O'Malley
David J. Tocco

RESIDENT ASSOCIATES

Julie M. Larson
Jerome C. Webbs
K. Ellen Toth
Margaret Dodane Everett
Bruce P. Batista
Amanda Martinsek
Lisa Babish Forbes
Marcel C. Duhamel
Anthony O. Calabrese, III
Kenneth A. Stump

COUNSEL

Karen A. Seawall
John M. Saganich
Joshua S. Berger

For full biographical listings, see the Martindale-Hubbell Law Directory

Cleveland—Continued

WALTER & HAVERFIELD, P.L.L. (AV)

1300 Terminal Tower, 44113-2253
Telephone: 216-781-1212
Telecopier: 216-575-0911
Email: law@walterhav.com *URL:* http://www.walterhav.com
Columbus, Ohio Office: 88 East Broad Street.
Telephone: 614-898-1096.

MANAGING PARTNER

Michael T. McMenamin

MEMBERS OF FIRM

Paul W. Walter (1907-1992)
D. Rusk Haverfield (1907-1993)
Anthony J. Viola
Russell C. Shaw
David D. Noble
Robert J. Crump
Charles R. Schaefer
Robert S. Horbaly
Charles T. Riehl, III
Herbert L. Braverman
John H. Gibbon
James P. Conroy
David W. Welty
Ralph E. Cascarilla
Christopher L. Gibbon
John W. Waldeck, Jr.
Michael J. Jordan
Gary A. Zwick
Carl E. Anderson
Nancy A. Noall
Frederick W. Whatley
Jonathan D. Greenberg
R. Todd Hunt
Kenneth A. Zirm
W. Mowry Connelly
James D. Wilson
David P.N. Silk
Mark P. McGrievy

ASSOCIATES

Barbara Rhodes Marburger
Patricia F. Weisberg
Christopher W. Siemen
Debora S. Lasch
Janet Alter
Patrick J. Rhoa
Randal G. Ammons
Katherine A. Friedell
Susan M. Zidek
Teresa M. Beasley
Vincent L. Cheverine
Amy Leopard Woodhall
Mary E. Zeit
Darrell A. Clay
Mia M. Mounts

OF COUNSEL

William A. Welty
Arthur P. Steinmetz
Sheldon M. Young
J. Robert Malloy
Charles E. Merchant
James E. Betts
Mark D. Weller
Ricky Lee Bertram
Daniel N. Steiger

LEGAL SUPPORT PERSONNEL

John B. Eldred

Representative Clients: AGA Gas, Inc.; A.J. Rose Manufacturing Co.; Applied Medical Technology, Inc.; Arabica Cafes, Inc.; Braden Sutphin Ink Co.; Choice Construction Company; Cooper Tire & Rubber Company; Morse Diesel Internatl; Multi-Care Management; WJW-TV (Cleveland).

For full biographical listings, see the Martindale-Hubbell Law Directory

WESTON HURD FALLON PAISLEY & HOWLEY L.L.P. (AV)

2500 Terminal Tower, 50 Public Square, 44113-2241
Telephone: 216-241-6602;
Ohio Toll Free: 800-336-4952
FAX: 216-621-8369
Email: Hurd2500@westonhurd.com

Joseph Philip Sullivan (1916-1974)
Lee C. Howley (1910-1983)
Harold Fallon (1910-1989)
Frank Seth Hurd (1913-1990)
Lloyd O. Brown (1928-1993)
S. Burns Weston (1904-1994)

MEMBERS OF FIRM

Herbert Buckman
Mark O'Neill
Jason C. Blackford
John W. Jeffers
Robert D. Rosewater
John M. Baker
Ronald A. Rispo
Joseph B. Swartz
David Arnold
Carolyn M. Cappel
Hilary Sheldon Taylor
Kenneth A. Torgerson
John S. Kluznik
Jeffrey D. Fincun
William H. Baughman, Jr.
Robert P. McManus
Stephen D. Walters
William R. Joseph
Gary W. Johnson
Deirdre G. Henry
Harry Sigmier
Warren Rosman
Timothy D. Johnson
Dana A. Rose
Hernan N. Visani
John G. Farnan
Gregory E. O'Brien
Scott C. Smith
Timothy P. Ristau
Kurt Karakul
Todd G. Jackson
Ronald K. Lembright
David C. Lamb
Christopher A. Anselmo

OF COUNSEL

Louis Paisley
John K. Sullivan
Norbert F. Werner

(See Next Column)

ASSOCIATES

Lisa M. Chesler
Maria A. Kortan-Sampson
Daniel A. Richards
John A. Albers
Forrest A. Norman III
Christopher M. Ernst
Marilyn Miller Crisafi
Martin J. Fallon
Mark S. Bennett
Randy L. Taylor
Jeremy R. Sayre
Dennis R. Fogarty
Thomas J. Connick
Jason R. Sussman

For full biographical listings, see the Martindale-Hubbell Law Directory

WULIGER, FADEL & BEYER (AV)

The Brownell Building, 1340 Sumner Court, 44115
Telephone: 216-781-7777
Fax: 216-781-0621

MEMBERS OF FIRM

William I. Fadel
William D. Beyer
Kathleen M. Sasala
Joan E. Pettinelli
Marc D. Wolfe

OF COUNSEL

William T. Wuliger
Mark E. Kremser
Richard G. Lillie, Ph.D.

Reference: National City Bank.

For full biographical listings, see the Martindale-Hubbell Law Directory

*COLUMBUS,** Franklin Co.

ARTER & HADDEN LLP (AV)

Suite 1200, One Columbus, 10 West Broad Street, 43215-3422
Telephone: 614-221-3155
Fax: 614-221-0479
URL: http://www.arterhadden.com
In Cleveland, Ohio: 1100 Huntington Building, 925 Euclid Avenue. 44115-1475.
Telephone: 216-696-1100.
Fax: 216-696-2645.
In Dayton, Ohio: Kettering Tower, Suite 2310, 40 North Main Street, 45423.
Telephone: 937-223-4701.
Fax: 937-223-0170.
In Washington, D.C.: 1801 K Street, N.W., Suite 400K. 20006-3480.
Telephone: 202-775-7100.
Fax: 202-857-0172.
In Dallas, Texas: 1717 Main Street, Suite 4100. 75201-4605.
Telephone: 214-761-2100.
Fax: 214-741-7139.
In Los Angeles, California: 725 South Figueroa Street, Suite 3400, 90017.
Telephone: 213-430-3000.
Fax: 213-617-9255.
In Irvine, California: Five Park Plaza, Suite 1000, Jamboree Center, 92714.
Telephone: 949-252-7500.
Fax: 949-833-9604.
In Austin, Texas: 100 Congress Avenue, Suite 1800.
Telephone: 512-479-6403.
Fax: 512-469-5505.
In San Antonio, Texas: One Riverwalk Place, 700 North Saint Mary's Street, Suite 800, 78205.
Telephone: 210-805-8497.
Fax: 210-805-8519.
In San Francisco, California: Two Embarcadero Center, 5th Floor, 94111.
Telephone: 415-415-2100.
Fax: 415-912-3636.
In Sacramento, California: Wells Fargo Center, 400 Capitol Mall, Suite 900, 95814.
Telephone: 916-449-3917.
Fax: 916-449-8249.
In San Diego, California: 402 West Broadway, Sixth Floor, 92101.
Telephone: 619-238-0001.
Fax: 619-238-8333.
In Woodland Hills, California: 5959 Topanga Canyon Boulevard, Suite 244, 91367.
Telephone: 818-712-0036.
Fax: 818-346-6502.

MEMBERS OF FIRM

William A. Adams
Stephen E. Auch
Russell P. Austin
Dan A. Bailey
Gary S. Batke
Katharine B. Bowman
Douglas M. Bricker
Richard D. Brooks, Jr.
John A. Carnahan
Nick V. Cavalieri
Yvette A. Cox
Michael W. Currie
Danny L. Cvetanovich
Donald A. Davies
Richard P. Fahey
John P. Gartland
R. Cliffton Gibbs
Dennis D. Grant
Daniel R. Hackett
John E. Hoffman, Jr.
R. Stacy Lane
Judith D. Levine
Martin H. Lewis
Michael P. Mahoney
Nancy J. Manougian
Michael L. Maxfield
Thomas E. O'Connor, Jr.
Donald G. Paynter
Ted L. Ramirez
James Gregory Ryan
Peter D. Welin

(See Next Column)

ARTER & HADDEN LLP, *Columbus—Continued*

OF COUNSEL

Jules L. Garel
Sarah E. Lynn
Harley E. Rouda Jr.
Dane Stinson
Debra A. Willet

ASSOCIATES

Rachel A. Adams
Adam J. Biehl
D. David Carroll, II
Shane M. Dawson
Robert R. Dunn
Robert L. Eblin
Daniel F. Edwards
Paula Gluntz
James M. Groner
Laura A. Hauser
Mary Jo Hudson
Darius N. Kandawalla
Robert R. Lech
(Not admitted in OH)
Mark A. Losey
Harlan S. Louis
Timothy A. Riedel

Representative Clients: American Municipal Power-Ohio, Inc.; Bank One, Columbus, N.A.; Basic Inc.; Combustion Engineering; The Federal Home Loan Bank; Health Care & Retirement Corporation of America; Huntington National Bank; Muskingum College; Rockwell International; The W.W. Williams Co.

For full biographical listings, see the Martindale-Hubbell Law Directory

BAKER & HOSTETLER LLP (AV)

Capitol Square, Suite 2100, 65 East State Street, 43215-4260
Telephone: 614-228-1541
Telecopier: 614-462-2616
To contact an attorney on the Internet use first initial and surname followed by @baker-hostetler.com
URL: http://www.bakerlaw.com
In Cleveland, Ohio: 3200 National City Center, 1900 East Ninth Street.
Telephone: 216-621-0200.
In Cincinnati, Ohio: 312 Walnut Street, Suite 2650.
Telephone: 513-929-3400.
In Denver, Colorado: 303 East 17th Avenue, Suite 1100.
Telephone: 303-861-0600.
In Houston, Texas: 1000 Louisiana, Suite 2000.
Telephone: 713-751-1600.
In Beverly Hills, California: 9150 Wilshire Boulevard, Suite 205.
Telephone: 310-385-7500.
In Long Beach, California: 300 Oceangate, Suite 620.
Telephone: 562-432-2827.
In Los Angeles, California: 600 Wilshire Boulevard.
Telephone: 213-624-2400.
In Orlando, Florida: SunBank Center, Suite 2300, 200 South Orange Avenue.
Telephone: 407-649-4000.
In Washington, D. C.: Washington Square, Suite 1100, 1050 Connecticut Avenue, N.W.
Telephone: 202-861-1500.

OFFICE MANAGING PARTNER

George W. Hairston (Managing Partner-Columbus Office)

PARTNERS

M.J. Asensio, III
Edward J. Bernert
Richard L. Bibart
Jack A. Bjerke
Joseph P. Boeckman
John H. Burtch
Pamela A. DeDent
Michael D. Dortch
R. Christopher Doyle
Charles F. Freiburger, IV
Ellen J. Garling
Daniel J. Gunsett
Richard J. Helmreich
Charles H. Hire
James E. Hughes
Kristin Hay Ives
Mark A. Johnson
Robert M. Kincaid, Jr.
Sherri Blank Lazear
David C. Levine
Ronald G. Linville
Thomas L. Long
Robert B. McAlister
Elizabeth A. McNellie
Michael E. Minister
Boyd Moehring
Thomas E. Moloney
Henry P. Montgomery, IV
Georgeann G. Peters
Randall S. Rabe
Nicholas M Ray
Harlan W. Robins
Barry R. Robinson
Robert K. Rupp
David M. Selcer
Mark D. Senff
Amy M. Shepherd
Richard W. Siehl
Robert H. Taylor
A. Charles Tell
J. Stephen Van Heyde
Dale T. Vitale
Gary A. Wadman
Sue A. Watson
Alec Wightman
Jeffrey T. Williams
Barry H. Wolinetz

ASSOCIATES

Otto Beatty, III
Michael D. Bridges
Stephen D. Brown
Timothy C. Brown
Eugene R. Butler
Charmel L. Cross
Brian Timothy Deas
Joseph C. Devine
Nancy Engbers Falk
Christopher D. Fidler
Michele B. Gerroir
Mary Catherine Grillo
Daniel J Guttman
Elizabeth L. Hendershot
Stephen E. Ifeduba
Richard E. Kozlowski
Malesa A. Litteral
Susan Nolan Lubow
Michelle Pepin Metzger
John S. Mulhollan
Sandra K. Parks
Jason D. Seabury

(See Next Column)

ASSOCIATES (Continued)

William B. Shearer
Karen E. Sheffer
Jeffrey L. VanWay
David A. Whitcomb
James G. Vargo

RETIRED PARTNERS

John W. Christensen
Kiehner Johnson
David A. Johnston, Jr.
John P. McMahon
Michael E. Moritz

For full biographical listings, see the Martindale-Hubbell Law Directory

BRICKER & ECKLER LLP (AV)

100 South Third Street, 43215-4291
Telephone: 614-227-2300
Telecopy: 614-227-2390
Email: info@be.bricker.com *URL:* http://www.bricker.com

John W. Bricker (1893-1986)
John Eckler (1913-1994)
James J. Hughes
Elbert J. Kram
Richard D. Rogovin
Edward A. Matto
Michael F. Sullivan
Sally W. Bloomfield
Nicholas A. Pittner
Richard F. Kane
John F. Birath, Jr.
Michael S. Holman
Richard C. Simpson
John P. Beavers
(Managing Partner)
David G. Baker
Jerry E. Nathan
Marshall L. Lerner
Randolph C. Wiseman
Donald R. Keller
Karen Mueller Moore
Steven R. Kerber
Charles H. Walker
Gordon W. Johnston
David A. Rogers
Charles H. Waterman III
Michael K. Gire
James A. Rutledge
David C. Spialter
Randall Edwin Moore
John W. Cook, III
Charles H. McCreary, III
James P. Burnes
Elisabeth A. Squeglia
Kenneth C. Johnson
Michael E. Flowers
Mark A. Engel
David K. Conrad
Richard S. Lovering
Rebecca Coleman Princehorn
Diane M. Signoracci
Percy Squire
Luther L. Liggett, Jr.
Martha Post Baxter
Gretchen A. McBeath
Craig A. Haddox
Charles D. Smith
William T. Conard, II
Robert C. Rafferty
Jerry O. Allen
Quintin F. Lindsmith
Joyce B. Link
H. Randy Bank
Catherine M. Ballard
Gordon F. Litt
L. Brent Miller
Scott W. Taebel
Sue Wyskiver Yount
James J. Hughes, III
Andrew A. Folkerth
Frank L. Merrill
Kurtis A. Tunnell
Mark C. Pomeroy
Betsy A. Swift
Jack R. Rosati
Susan E. Geary
Thomas R. Brownlee, Jr.
James F. Flynn
Price D. Finley
Harry Wright, IV
Drew H. Campbell

Sylvia Lynn Gillis
Wendi R. Huntley
Martha E. Horvitz
Stephen C. Gray
T. Earl LeVere
Susan Beale Greenberger
Faith M. Williams
Stephen Intihar
Laurie A. Briggs
Kimberly J. Brown
Lisa E. Hanger
Mary Leslie Robins
Juliana M. Faris
Matthew J. Arnold
Anne DeVoe
Stephen J. Vamos, III
Julia L. Dorrian
Susan L. Oppenheimer
Amy Straker Bartemes
Katherine Spies Giumenti
Christine A. Bricker
Nelson M. Reid
Lloyd Pierre-Louis
Christine M. Poth
James G. Petrie
Elizabeth H. Watts
Bobbie S. Sprader
Timothy A. Fry
Karen D. Smith
Warren I. Grody
Patrick J. Schmitz
Maureen P. Taylor
Hope M. Goings
Laura Greenberg Anthony
Lauren B. Martin
Bridget Hayward Kahle

OF COUNSEL

John C. Rosenberger
Anne Marie Sferra
Diane Richards Brey
Robert H. Katz

RETIRED

Bruce G. Lynn
Richard C. Pickett
William H. Leighner
Clayton C. Hoskins
James S. Monahan
Charles F. Glander

For full biographical listings, see the Martindale-Hubbell Law Directory

CALFEE, HALTER & GRISWOLD LLP (AV)

88 East Broad Street, Suite 1500, 43215
Telephone: 614-621-1500
Telecopier: 614-621-0010
URL: http://www.calfee.com
Cleveland, Ohio Office: 1400 McDonald Investment Center, 800 Superior Avenue.
Telephone: 216-622-8200.
Telecopier: 216-241-0816.

(See Next Column)

CALFEE, HALTER & GRISWOLD LLP—*Continued*

RESIDENT MEMBERS

P. Michael DeAngelo
Albert J. Lucas

RESIDENT SENIOR ATTORNEY

Stanley J. Dobrowski

RESIDENT ASSOCIATE

Sean P. Dunn
Peter A. Rosato

For full biographical listings, see the Martindale-Hubbell Law Directory

CRABBE, BROWN, JONES, POTTS & SCHMIDT (AV)

500 South Front Street, Suite 1200, 43215
Telephone: 614-228-5511
Telecopier: 614-229-4559
URL: HTTP://WWW.CBJPS.COM
Cincinnati, Ohio Office: 30 Garfield Place, Suite 940, 45202.
Telephone: 513-784-1525.
Telecopier: 513-784-1250. Email: BHurley@Psinet.com
Lancaster, Ohio Office: 111 South Broad Street, Suite 209, 43130.
Telephone: 740-689-1743.
Telecopier: 740-689-1746. Email: sdavis@greenapple.com

MEMBERS OF FIRM

William Page Lewis (1914-1998)
Robert C. Potts (1913-1994)
William T. McCracken (1929-1993)
J. Roth Crabbe (1906-1989)
Charles E. Brown
Theodore D. Sawyer
Vincent J. Lodico
Steven B. Ayers
Keith H. Jung
Jeffrey M. Brown
Larry H. James
Brian E. Hurley (Resident, Cincinnati Office)
Gilbert J. Gradisar
Richard D. Wetzel, Jr.
Jerry A. Eichenberger
James D. Gilbert
Luis M. Alcalde
John C. Albert
George R. McCue, III
Michael R. Henry
Robert C. Buchbinder
Catherine L. Worley
Steven A. Davis (Resident, Lancaster Office)

ASSOCIATES

Francesca Tosi Ward
Todd William Collis
Kristen H. Smith
Daniel J. Hurley
Beth Wayne (Resident, Cincinnati Office)
Heather W. Guthrie
Christina L. Corl
Steven E. Miller
Darlene E. Chavers
Amy M. Fulmer Stevenson
Phillip A. Templeton

OF COUNSEL

William H. Jones
Wilbur W. Jones (1913-1999)
William L. Schmidt

Representative Clients: Allstate Insurance Co.; American States Insurance Co.; General Electric.

For full biographical listings, see the Martindale-Hubbell Law Directory

DENMEAD & MALONEY (AV)

37 West Broad Street, Suite 1150, 43215-4189
Telephone: 614-228-5271
Telecopier: 614-228-7624
Email: cdkmlaw@infinet.com

Craig Denmead
Kevin M. Maloney

Representative Clients: Bode-Finn Co.; Century Surety Co.; COP, Inc.; Inland Products, Inc.; National Head Injury Foundation, Inc., of Washington D.C.; Ohio Head Injury Assn.; Stonhard, Inc.; Sammons Corporate Services, Inc.; Trigg-Hansa Ins. Co., Ltd.; Tuscarawas County, Ohio.

For full biographical listings, see the Martindale-Hubbell Law Directory

JONES, DAY, REAVIS & POGUE (AV)

1900 Huntington Center, 43215
Telephone: 614-469-3939
Telecopier: 614-461-4198
Email: counsel@jonesday.com *URL:* http://www.jonesday.com
In Cleveland, Ohio: North Point, 901 Lakeside Avenue.
Telephone: 216-586-3939.
Telecopier: 216-579-0212.
In Atlanta, Georgia: 3500 SunTrust Plaza, 303 Peachtree Street.
Telephone: 404-521-3939.
Telecopier: 404-581-8330.
In Brussels, Belgium: Avenue Louise 480, 7th Floor, B-1050 Brussels.
Telephone: 32-2-645-14-11.
Telecopier: 32-2-645-14-45.
In Chicago, Illinois: 77 West Wacker.
Telephone: 312-782-3939.
Telecopier: 312-782-8585.
In Dallas, Texas: 2727 North Harwood Street.
Telephone: 214-220-3939.
Telecopier: 214-969-5100.
In Frankfurt, Germany: Hochhaus am Park, Grüneburgweg 102, 60323 Frankfurt am Main.
Telephone: 49-69-9726-3939.
Telecopier: 49-69-9726-3993.

(See Next Column)

In Geneva, Switzerland: 20, rue de Candolle.
Telephone: 41-22-320-2339.
Telecopier: 41-22-320-1232.
In Hong Kong: 29th Floor, Entertainment Building, 30 Queen's Road Central.
Telephone: 852-2526-6895.
Telecopier: 852-2868-5871 or 852-2868-5699.
In Irvine, California: 5 Park Plaza, Suite 1100.
Telephone: 949-851-3939.
Telecopier: 949-553-7539.
In London, England: Bucklersbury House, 3 Queen Victoria Street.
Telephone: 44-171-236-3939.
Telecopier: 44-171-236-1113.
In Los Angeles, California: 555 West Fifth Street, Suite 4600.
Telephone: 213-489-3939.
Telecopier: 213-243-2539.
In New Delhi, India (Associate Office): Pathak & Associates (an associate firm of Jones, Day, Reavis & Pogue), 1st Floor, Dr. Gopal Das Bhaven, 28 Barakhamba Road.
Telephone: 91-11-373-8793; 91-11-335-7345.
Telecopier: 91-11-335-3761.
In New York, New York: 599 Lexington Avenue.
Telephone: 212-326-3939.
Telecopier: 212-755-7306.
In Paris, France: 120, rue du Faubourg Saint-Honoré.
Telephone: 33-1-56-59-39-39.
Telecopier: 33-1-56-59-39-38
In Pittsburgh, Pennsylvania: 500 Grant Street, 31st Floor.
Telephone: 412-391-3939.
Telecopier: 412-394-7959.
In Riyadh, Saudi Arabia: The International Law Firm (In Association with Jones, Day, Reavis & Pogue), Sulaymaniyah, Prince Mishari IBN, Abdulaziz Street, P.O. Box 22166.
Telephone: (966-1) 462-8866.
Telecopier: (966-1) 462-9001.
In Shanghai, China: 2805 Kerry Centre, 1515 Nanjing Road West.
Telephone: 86-21-5298-6568.
Telecopier: 86-21-5298-6569.
In Sydney, Australia: Governor Phillip Tower, Level 38, 1 Farrer Place.
Telephone: 61-2-9210-6921.
Telecopier: 61-2-9210-6926.
In Taipei, Taiwan: 8th Floor, 2 Tun Hwa South Road, Section 2.
Telephone: (886-2) 2704-6808.
Telecopier: (886-2) 2704-6791.
In Tokyo, Japan: Toranomon MT Building, 4th Floor, 10-3, Toranomon 3-Chome, Minato-ku, Tokyo 105, Japan.
Telephone: 81-3-3433-3939.
Telecopier: 81-3-5401-2725.
In Washington, D.C.: 51 Louisiana Avenue, N.W.
Telephone: 202-879-3939.
Telecopier: 202-626-1700.

MEMBERS OF FIRM IN COLUMBUS

John W. Edwards
Maryann Baker Gall
G. Roger King
Roger R. Stinehart
James R. King
J. Kevin Cogan
Fordham E. Huffman
Michael K. Ording
Todd Shawn Swatsler
Marlene P. Frank
Thomas E. Dutton
Gayle E. Parkhill
Robert W. Hamilton
Jeffrey J. Jones
Kevin D. Lyles
Matthew W. Lampe
Shawn J. Organ
Paul E. Harner

OF COUNSEL

Randall M. Walters
Jeffrey S. Sutton

COUNSEL

Helen L. Liebman
Jack A. Van Kley
Margaret L. Gramann

ASSOCIATES

Steven M. McCarty
William E. Nakasian
Jeffrey B. Ellman
Matthew A. Kairis
Charles M. Oellermann
Colleen A. Deep
Gregory A. Gorospe
Kelley M. Griesmer
Jeffrey L. Kapp
Elizabeth P. Kessler
Todd L. Sarver
Jennifer L. Klitch
Douglas M. Mansfield
Ivan C. Smith
Scott C. Walker
Joseph M. Witalec
Andrew M. Ferris
Brian G. Selden
Jonathan K. Stock
Marla D. Clark
Lori A. Clary
Rick J. Gibson
Janice L. Gresko
Rodd B. Lape
Denise L Skingle
Julie M. Vore
Jennifer L. Fate
Brian L. Gifford
J. Todd Kennard
Chad A. Readler
Jeffrey D. Winchester
Kelly A. Bott
Andrea L. Cleland
Katherine L. Murphy
Peter J. Phipps
Kim Potter (Not admitted in OH)
E. Michael Rossman
David S. Torborg

For full biographical listings, see the Martindale-Hubbell Law Directory

Columbus—Continued

KEGLER, BROWN, HILL & RITTER (AV)

Capitol Square Suite 1800, 65 East State Street, 43215-4294
Telephone: 614-462-5400
Telecopier: 614-464-2634
Cable Address: "Law KBHR"
Telex: 246671
Email: info@kbhr.com *URL:* http://www.kbhr.com
Marion, Ohio Office: 250 Executive Drive, Suite B, P.O. Box 919.
Telephone: 614-387-3501.
Facsimile: 614-387-3630.

Donald A. Antrim
John P. Brody
William J. Brown
Stephen E. Chappelear
Robert Garrett Cohen
James R. Eley
Lawrence F. Feheley
Donald W. Gregory
Allen L. Handlan
Edward C. Hertenstein
Paul R. Hess
Thomas W. Hill
Daniel G. Hilson
Gene W. Holliker
Charles J. Kegler
R. Kevin Kerns
Ronald L. Mason
Larry J. McClatchey
Paul D. Ritter, Jr.
O. Judson Scheaf III
Richard W. Schuermann, Jr.
Robert G. Schuler
S. Martijn Steger
Roger P. Sugarman
Kevin L. Sykes
John R. Thomas
Timothy T. Tullis
Melvin D. Weinstein
Shawnell Williams
R. Douglas Wrightsel
Michael E. Zatezalo

COUNSEL

John C. Deal
John L. Gray
Thomas D. Kitch
Robert D. Marotta
Ted M. McKinniss (Resident, Marion Office)
S. Noel Melvin
S. Michael Miller
Joseph M. Millious (Retired)
Leigh Anne Reardon
Geoffrey Stern

Michael F. Copley
Scot C. Crow
Paul V. Danielson
Jeffrey F. DeVoesick
Stephen D. Dunson
Loriann E. Fuhrer
Greg R. Grabovac
Laura L. Gribbin
Erika L. Haupt
Todd M. Kegler
John Lowe, IV
David M. McCarty
Thomas M. L. Metzger
Patrick M. O'Neill
Mark R. Reitz
T.A. Ward, II
Christopher J. Weber
Anthony C. White
Nicholas E. Wilkes

Representative Clients: Columbus Metropolitan Housing Authority; Farmers Insurance Group; National City Bank; The Ohio State University.

For full biographical listings, see the Martindale-Hubbell Law Directory

PORTER WRIGHT MORRIS & ARTHUR LLP (AV)

41 South High Street, 43215-6194
Telephone: 614-227-2000; (800-533-2794)
Fax: 614-227-2100
Email: cmh@porterwright.com *URL:* http://www.porterwright.com
Cincinnati, Ohio Office: 250 E. Fifth Street, Suite 2200, 45202-4199.
Telephones: 513-381-4700; (800-582-5813).
Fax: 513-421-0991. Internet: cvg@porterwright.com.
Cleveland, Ohio Office: 925 Euclid Avenue, Suite 1700, 44115-1483.
Telephones: 216-443-9000; (800-824-1980).
Fax: 216-443-9011. Internet: cle@porterwright.com.
Dayton, Ohio Office: One Dayton Centre, One South Main Street, Suite 1600, 45402-2028.
Telephones: 937-449-6810; (800-533-4434).
Fax: 937-449-6820. Internet: day@porterwright.com.
Naples, Florida Office: 5801 Pelican Bay Boulevard, Suite 300, 34108-2709.
Telephones: 941-593-2900; (800-876-7962).
Fax: 941-593-2990. Internet: apf@porterwright.com.
Washington, D.C. Office: 1667 K Street, N.W., Suite 1100, 20006-1605.
Telephones: 202-778-3000; (800-456-7962).
Fax: 202-778-3063. Internet: dca@porterwright.com.

MEMBERS OF FIRM
COLUMBUS, OHIO OFFICE

Jon M. Anderson
William E. Arthur
Edwin M. Baranowski
Phillip H. Barrett
John C. Beeler
James P. Botti
John E. Brady
Marjorie Crowder Briggs
Robert L. Brubaker
Cornelius Bulman, Jr.
Brian L. Buzby
Thomas C. Coady
Daniel R. Conway
S. Ronald Cook, Jr.
Daniel W. Costello
James D. Curphey
Lloyd G. DePew, Jr.
Joyce D. Edelman
Joseph F. Elliott
Lisa L. Eschleman
Mason Evans, IV
R. Leland Evans
Lloyd E. Fisher, Jr.
Theodore G. Fisher
Robert E. Fultz
Ralph F. Gildehaus
Stuart M. Gordon
Diane K. Goulder
Timothy E. Grady
Kevin E. Griffith
Brian D. Hall
Paul A. Hanke
Polly J. Harris
John C. Hartranft

(See Next Column)

MEMBERS OF FIRM
COLUMBUS, OHIO OFFICE (Continued)

Jeffrey T. Hayes
Harry L. Henning
Janet J. Henry
C. Andrew Ireton, Jr.
Donald W. Jordan
William J. Kelly, Jr.
Robert C. Kiger
Lori-Lou Kimm
James A. King
Amy D. Klaben
Charles J. Kurtz, III
David A. Laing
Wayman C. Lawrence, III
Curtis A. Loveland
John F. Marsh
Daniel J. Massey
James M. Mattimoe
Alvin J. McKenna
J. Jeffrey McNealey
Richard C. McQuown
Mark K. Merkle, Jr.
Dixon F. Miller
Terrance M. Miller
Jennifer T. Mills
Denise M. Mirman
Frank R. Morris, Jr.
Robert J. Nordstrom
Scott E. North
Adele E. O'Conner
James S. Oliphant
Jack R. Pigman
James E. Pohlman
Samuel H. Porter
Fred G. Pressley, Jr.
James H. Prior
W. John Pritchard
Michael T. Radcliffe
Diane C. Reichwein
John B. Rohyans
Donna M. Ruscitti
Christopher C. Russell
Joseph W. Ryan, Jr.
Christopher R. Schraff
Edward M. Segelken
Martin S. Seltzer
Darrell R. Shepard
David P. Shouvlin
Bradd N. Siegel
Patrick J. Smith
Mark S. Stemm
John M. Stephen
H. Grant Stephenson
Karl J. Sutter
Robert J. Tannous
K. Michael Taylor
Richard G. Terapak
Jean Yingling Teteris
Kathleen McManus Trafford
Robert W. Trafford
David A. Tumen
Michael J. Underwood
Charles C. Warner
Deborah S. Winkler
Franck G. Wobst
Nancy B. Young
Thomas A. Young

ASSOCIATES
COLUMBUS, OHIO OFFICE

Douglas L. Anderson
Julie L. Atchison
Carl A. Aveni II
Bradley K. Baker
Daniel A. Bellman
Lisa J. Berger
David S. Bloomfield, Jr.
Matthew J. Burkhart
Craig R. Carlson
Aaron A. Dryer
Mark E. Duell
Robert W. Edmund
Katerina M. Eftimoff
David C. Faure
M. Theresa Finneran
Marc L. Fleischauer
Gregory B. Foliano
Kelly J. Fox
Erin L. Freund
Constance M. Greaney
Mollie K. Grever
James B. Hadden
Karen K. Hammond
Priscilla Hapner
Laurie N. Jacques
William L. Jordan
Kyle A. Knapp
Michael M. Kowsari (Not admitted in OH)
John T. Kranyak
Jeffrey A. Martin
Linda R. Minck
Christine A. Murry
Janice A. Nelson
Barbara A. North
Keith L. O'Korn
M. Melissa Pence-Lavy
John B. Pisaris
Laura S. Profumo
Melissa A. Romig
Robert M. Simmons
Joseph A. Sugar, III
Daniel T. Swanson
Shawn A. Trell
Yvonne Lundwall Twiss
Alexandra B. Urban
Sidney L. Williams
Leslie A. Yovan
Aimee A. Zaleski

OF COUNSEL
COLUMBUS, OHIO OFFICE

John M. Adams
Scott E. Baughman
Robert H. Cohen
Mary Ryan Fenlon
Howard P. Fink
Ralph K. Frasier
Ronald W. Gabriel
Robert D. Hays
William G. Martin
Norman T. Smith

DAYTON, OHIO OFFICE
RESIDENT MEMBERS

William G. Deas
John J. Heron
Jonathan Hollingsworth
Thomas A. Holton
C. Terry Johnson
Charles Y. Kidwell, Jr.
Walter Reynolds
R. Bruce Snyder

DAYTON, OHIO OFFICE
RESIDENT ASSOCIATES

N. Robert Goad, Jr.
Linda S. Holmes
Elizabeth L. Ross

DAYTON, OHIO OFFICE
RESIDENT OF COUNSEL

Barbara A. Duncombe
Roland F. Eichner
Chester E. Finn
Samuel L. Hagans, Jr.
Richard A. Maresca
Jeffrey W. Morris

CINCINNATI, OHIO OFFICE
RESIDENT MEMBERS

John J. Cruze
Mark E. Elsener
Jerome J. Metz, Jr.
Wm. Cates Rambo
Michael G. Reed
David Reichert
Stephen D. Strauss

(See Next Column)

PORTER WRIGHT MORRIS & ARTHUR LLP—*Continued*

CINCINNATI, OHIO OFFICE
RESIDENT ASSOCIATES

Duane A. Boggs
Michael E. McCarty
Darryl Mitchell
Eric J. Plinke

CLEVELAND, OHIO OFFICE
RESIDENT MEMBERS

Robert D. Anderle
Jeffrey Baddeley
David A. Bell
Paul J. Corrado
Donald J. Fisher
Daniel F. Gourash
Margaret M. Koesel
Philip E. Langer
Hugh E. McKay
Patricia A. Screen
Ralph Streza
David C. Tryon
William R. Weir
Alan D. Wright

CLEVELAND, OHIO OFFICE
RESIDENT ASSOCIATES

Mary Kaye Bozza
Ann M. Caresani
Aimee M. Greenfield
Robert M. Higgins
Laura F. Kenney
Natalie L. Peterson
Sandra Becher Sommers
Eric F. Spade
Leo M. Spellacy, Jr.
Tracey L. Turnbull
Jeffrey J. Weber
Alan C. Yarcusko

CLEVELAND, OHIO OFFICE
RESIDENT OF COUNSEL

Robert E. Bingham

WASHINGTON, D.C. OFFICE
MEMBERS

David L. Douglass
Alison MacDonald Duncan
E. Jay Finkel
Leslie Alan Glick
Thomas O. Gorman
Judd L. Kessler
Mark L. Lezell
William P. McGrath, Jr.
James E. Pohlman
W. Scott Simmer
Mitchell A. Stearn

WASHINGTON, D.C. OFFICE
RESIDENT ASSOCIATES

Alfred Campos
Terra E. Castaldi
Kristie G. Haynes
John E. Hedstrom
Claire C. Robinson May
Aisha Q. Murray
Thomas J. Poulin
Virginia E. Richards
Robert T. Rhoad
Heather J. Stewart
Josephine J. Tao
Renata S. Vasconcellos

WASHINGTON, D.C. OFFICE
RESIDENT OF COUNSEL

Bart S. Fisher
James R. Hagerty
Theresa W. Hajost
Alan C. Nessman
Patrice M. Pitts
James C. Stearns

NAPLES, FLORIDA OFFICE
MEMBERS

Robert M. Buckel
W. Jeffrey Cecil
Mary Beth Clary
Robert C. Gebhardt
Harry L. Henning
Jeffrey S. Kannensohn
Dixon F. Miller
Gary K. Wilson

NAPLES, FLORIDA OFFICE
RESIDENT ASSOCIATES

S. Dresden Brunner
Margaret Castellana
Jeanette M. Lombardi

For full biographical listings, see the Martindale-Hubbell Law Directory

SCHOTTENSTEIN, ZOX & DUNN A LEGAL PROFESSIONAL ASSOCIATION (AV)

The Huntington Center, 41 South High Street, 43215
Telephone: 614-462-2700
Telecopier: 614-462-5135
Telex: 650 24 444 365
URL: http://www.szd.com
Cincinnati, Ohio Office: Bank One Towers, 8044 Montgomery Road, Suite 700, 45236-2926.
Telephone: 513-792-2730.
Cleveland, Ohio Office: One Cleveland Center, 1375 East 9th Street, Suite 950.
Telephone: 216-621-6501.
Fax: 216-621-6502.

Melvin L. Schottenstein (1932-1993)
Benjamin L. Zox
Harvey Dunn
Jay R. Dingledy
James M. L. Ferber
Herbert R. Godby
E. James Hopple
John Terakedis, Jr.
Robert D. Weisman
Fredrick L. Fisher
Felix C. Wade
Richard A. Barnhart
Randall S. Arndt
John P. Gilligan
Daniel J. Kayne
William F. Simpson
James E. Davidson
Kevin R. McDermott
John D. Robinett
Peter A. Pavarini
Roger L. Sabo
John C. McDonald
David A. Kadela
Catherine T. Dunlay
Kris M. Dawley
Richard W. Holz
Martin S. Rosenthal
Susan Darnell Rector
Susan Porter

(See Next Column)

Michael D. Tarullo
William J. Barath
Edwin L. Skeens
Victoria E. Powers
Bridgette C. Roman
Corey V. Crognale
John M. Latsko
Robert H. Nichols
Robert M. Robenalt
Daniel R. Swetnam
Michael R. Becker
Terrence A. Grady
Thomas J. Sigmund
Phillip G. Lilly
Patrick A. Devine
Alan G. Starkoff
Stephen J. Smith
Mitchell H. Banchefsky
Gregory J. Dunn
Robert R. Ouellette
Joanne I. Goldhand
Missia H. Vaselaney (Resident, Cleveland Office)

Susan K. Cliffel
William P. Zox
Nancy A. Brigner
Michael A. Womack
Marcus D. Dunn
Denise L. Hanson
Daniel W. Srsic
Daniel M. Anderson
Frank W. Carsonie
J. Troy Terakedis
Russell J. Kutell
Stephen R. Kleinman
Julie E Brigner
Michelle K. Robinson
Josef Keglewitsch
Marcia J. Myers (Resident, Cincinnati Office)
Dennis J. Rasor
Lisa G. Han
Colin A. Mathews
Angelique M. Paul
Ara Mekhjian
Michael S. Jordan
Darrel R. Davison
Nicholas C. Cavalaris
Alison M. Day
Amy Mass
Robert K. Danzinger (Resident, Cleveland Office)
Kyle J. Stroh
Andrew W. Stark
Neil K. Sethi (Not admitted in OH)
Marie A. Malloy
Philip K. Hartmann
Jennifer L. Dutey
Kevin R. Fease (Not admitted in OH)
Christopher L. Miller
Mary Frances Geswein
Michael T. Short
Katrina L. Trimble Coffaro (Resident, Cincinnati Office)
Stephen Withee
William J. Liss

OF COUNSEL

Leigh Ann Wobst
Melissa L. Zox
Kristopher M. Huelsman
Bryan K. Prosek

Reference: Bank One of Columbus, N.A.

For full biographical listings, see the Martindale-Hubbell Law Directory

SIMPSON THACHER & BARTLETT (AV)

One Riverside Plaza, 43215
Telephone: 614-461-7799
Telecopier: 614-461-0040
URL: http://www.simpsonthacher.com
New York, N.Y. Office: 425 Lexington Avenue, 10017-3954.
Telephone: 212-455-2000.
Telecopier: 212-455-2502.
Los Angeles, California Office: 10 Universal City Plaza, Suite 852, Universal City, CA, 91608.
Telephone: 818-755-7000.
Fax: 818-755-7009.
Palo Alto, California Office: 3373 Hillview Avenue, 94304.
Telephone: 650-251-5000.
Telecopier: 650-251-5002.
London Office: 99 Bishopsgate, EC2M 3YH, England.
Telephone: 011-44-207-422-4000.
Telecopier: 011-44-207-422-4022.
Tokyo Office: Ark Mori Building, 30th Floor, 12-32, Akasaka 1-Chome, Minato-Ku, Tokyo 107, Japan.
Telephone: 81-3-5562-8601.
Fax: 81-3-5562-8606. ESL 62765846.
Hong Kong Office: Asia Pacific Finance Tower - 7th Floor, 3 Garden Road, Central, Hong Kong.
Telephone: 852-2514-7600.
Telecopier: 852-2869-7694.
Singapore Office: Suntec Tower One, 33rd Floor, 7 Temasek Boulevard, Singapore 038987.
Telephone: 65-430-5100.
Fax: 65-430-5151.

RESIDENT PARTNER

Michael P. Graney

COUNSEL

Mark S. Tibberts

RESIDENT ASSOCIATES

Brian E. Chisling
Joel C. Fry

For full biographical listings, see the Martindale-Hubbell Law Directory

Columbus—Continued

SQUIRE, SANDERS & DEMPSEY L.L.P. (AV)

1300 Huntington Center, 41 South High Street, 43215-6150
Telephone: 614-365-2700
Fax: 614-365-2499
URL: http://www.ssd.com
Cleveland, Ohio Office: 4900 Key Tower, 127 Public Square, Cleveland, Ohio 44114-1304.
Telephone: 216-479-8500.
Fax: 216-479-8780.
Houston, Texas Office: 6250 Chase Tower, 600 Travis Street, Houston, Texas 77002-3007.
Telephone: 713-546-5850.
Fax: 713-546-5830.
Jacksonville, Florida Office: One Enterprise Center, Suite 2100, 225 Water Street, Jacksonville, Florida 32202-4424.
Telephone: 904-366-2420.
Fax: 904-356-2986.
Miami, Florida Office: 201 South Biscayne Boulevard, 2900 Miami Center, Miami, Florida 33131-4330.
Telephone: 305-577-8700.
Fax: 305-358-1425.
New York, New York Office: 350 Park Avenue, New York, New York 10022-6002.
Telephone: 212-872-9800.
Fax: 212-872-9815.
Phoenix, Arizona Office: Two Renaissance Square, 40 North Central Avenue, Suite 2700, Phoenix, Arizona 85004-4498.
Telephone: 602-528-4000.
Fax: 602-253-8129.
Washington, D.C. Office: 1201 Pennsylvania Avenue, N.W., Suite 500, Washington, D.C. 20004-2491.
Telephone: 202-626-6600.
Fax: 202-626-6780.
Bratislava, Slovak Republic Office: Zochova 5, 811 03 Bratislava, Slovak Republic.
Telephone: 421-7-5441-7611.
Fax: 42-1-7-6280-2212.
Brussels, Belgium Office: Avenue Louise, 165-Box 15, 1050 Brussels, Belgium.
Telephone: 32-2-627-1111.
Fax: 32-2-627-1100.
Budapest, Hungary Office: H-1062 Budapest, Andrassy ut. 64, Budapest, Hungary.
Telephone: 36-1-428-7111.
Fax: 36-1-428-7100.
Kyiv, Ukraine Office: 14A Yaroslaviv Val, Kyiv 252034, Ukraine.
Telephone: 38-044-228-8687.
Fax: 38-044-228-4938.
London, England Office: Royex House, Aldermanbury Square, London EC2V 7HR.
Telephone: 44-171-776-5200.
Fax: 44-171-776-5233.
Madrid, Spain Office: Calle Velazquez 108-110, 28006 Madrid, Spain.
Telephone: 34-91-590-2420.
Fax: 34-91-590-2421.
Moscow, Russian Federation Office: 13 Khokhlovskiy Lane, Moscow 109028, Russian Federation.
Telephone: 7-503-956-3750.
Fax: 7-503-956-3635.
Prague, Czech Republic Office: Václavské náměst 1 57/813, 110 00 Praha 1, Czech Republic.
Telephone: 420-2-2166-2111.
Fax: 420-2-2166-2222.
Hong Kong Office: Rooms 1101-2 St. George's Building, 2 Ice House Street, Central, Hong Kong.
Telephone: 852-2509-9732.
Fax: 852-2509-9772.
Taipei, Taiwan Office: 14F, 116 Nanking East Road, Sec. 2, Taipei, Taiwan, Republic of China.
Telephone: 886-2-2531-2888.
Fax: 886-2-2571-6199.

PARTNERS

Catherine Adams
David W. Alexander
Vincent Atriano
Janice McKimmie Bernard
Ted B. Clevenger
David Cooper Jr.
Philomena M. Dane
Patrick J. Dugan
John R. Gall
Stephen P. Grassbaugh
David Grauer
Steven M. Loewengart
Daniel M. Maher
Steven F. Mount
James P. Mulroy
Richard W. Rubenstein
Michael D. Saad
Paul F. Sefcovic
Alex Shumate
David S. Sidor
Fredric L. Smith
Gregory W. Stype
Kim L. Swanson
William M. Todd
Lee A. Wendel
Karen A. Winters
C. Craig Woods
David J. Young

COUNSEL

Richard R. Murphey Jr.
Fred A. Summer
James M. Tobin
Donald W. Wiper, Jr.

(See Next Column)

OF COUNSEL

Alice K. Blankenship
Timothy J. Cosgrove
H. Cort Doughty, Jr.
David B. Petrel (Resident)
Kim A. Rieck
Bryan J. Venesy

ASSOCIATES

Jill E. Aebker
Todd M. Beutler
Elaine Aten Brown
Kristen J. Brown
John D. Burley
D. Lewis Clark, Jr.
James Comeaux
Patrick Cornelius
Jon T. Davis
Cynthia I. Dawson
Susan M. DiMickele
Christopher J. Franzmann
Thomas J. Grever
Victoria K. Hazemey
Holly Hickman Heer
Donald W. Hughes
Jerome J. Joondeph, Jr.
Marc J. Kessler
Jill Kirila
John M. Kirsner
Scott Cristopher Lehman
Laurie L. McGovern
Michael J. Melliere
William A. Nolan
Michael R. Reed
Erik Rickard
John D. Schuman
Andrea R. Shemberg
Kendra Sherman
Keith Shumate
Michael Soto
Craig A. Sturtz
Anthony J. Sugar
Kristina Sung Kepner
Erin Sutton
Pamela Hackes Thurston
Ezell H. Underdown
Janice K. Van Dyne
Greg Wehrer
Philip R. Westerman
Paul A. Wolfla
Jeffrey Yeager

For full biographical listings, see the Martindale-Hubbell Law Directory

TAFT, STETTINIUS & HOLLISTER LLP (AV)

Twelfth Floor 21 East State Street, 43215-4221
Telephone: 614-221-2838
Facsimile: 614-221-2007
URL: http://www.taftlaw.com
Cincinnati, Ohio Office: 1800 Firstar Tower, 425 Walnut Street.
Telephone: 513-381-2838
Covington, Kentucky Office: Thomas More Centre, Suite 400, 2670 Chancellor Drive.
Telephone: 606-331-2838; 513-381-2838.
Cleveland, Ohio Office: Sixth Floor, Bond Court Building, 1300 East Ninth Street.
Telephone: 216-241-2838.

RESIDENT MEMBERS

David L. Johnson
Timothy P. Nagy
Lawrence D. Walker
Michael A. Byers
J. David Goodman

RESIDENT ASSOCIATES

John P. Curp
Keith P. Hartzell
Terri W. Meldrum

For full biographical listings, see the Martindale-Hubbell Law Directory

VORYS, SATER, SEYMOUR AND PEASE LLP (AV)

52 East Gay Street, P.O. Box 1008, 43216-1008
Telephone: 614-464-6400
Telecopier: 614-464-6350
URL: http://www.vssp.com
Washington, D.C. Office: 1828 L Street, N.W., 20036-5109.
Telephone: 202-467-8800.
Telex: 440693.
Telecopier: 202-467-8900.
Cleveland, Ohio Office: 2100 One Cleveland Center, 1375 East Ninth Street, 44114-1724.
Telephone: 216-479-6100.
Telecopier: 216-479-6060.
Cincinnati, Ohio Office: Suite 2100, 221 East Fourth Street, P.O. Box 0236, 45201-0236.
Telephone: 513-723-4000.
Telecopier: 513-723-4056.
Alexandria, Virginia Office: 277 South Washington St., Suite 310, 22314.
Telephone: 703-549-4282.
Telecopier: 703-549-4492.

Arthur I. Vorys (1856-1933)
Lowry F. Sater (1867-1935)
Augustus T. Seymour (1873-1926)
Edward L. Pease (1873-1924)

MEMBERS OF FIRM

James P. Kennedy
Duke W. Thomas
Sheldon A. Taft
Thomas M. Taggart
Robert W. Werth
George L. Jenkins
James H. Gross
James R. Beatley, Jr.
Lawrence L. Fisher
Thomas B. Ridgley
James P. Friedt
Philip C. Johnston
Michael G. Long
Thomas M. Tarpy
Kenneth M. Royalty
David S. Cupps
Daniel H. Schoedinger
Phillip L. Nunnally
Susan E. Brown
Joseph D. Lonardo (Resident, Washington, D.C. Office)
Michael W. Donaldson
Michael J. Canter
Russell M. Gertmenian
Alan T. Radnor
Mary Ellen Fairfield
C. William O'Neill
Robert E. Tait

(See Next Column)

VORYS, SATER, SEYMOUR AND PEASE LLP—*Continued*

MEMBERS OF FIRM (Continued)

Charles S. DeRousie
George N. Corey
G. Ross Bridgman
W. Jonathan Airey
Philip A. Brown
Stephen R. Buchenroth
James M. Ball
John K. Keller
Robert A. Minor
Ronald L. Rowland
Suzanne K. Richards
Gary E. Davis
Jonathan M. Norman
Robin R. Obetz
Sandra J. Anderson
James A. Yano
Ivery D. Foreman
Bruce L. Ingram
Laura G. Kuykendall
Bruce R. Henke
Raymond D. Anderson
Gerald P. Ferguson
Roger E. Lautzenhiser
J. Scott Jamieson
James E. Phillips
William S. Newcomb, Jr.
Robert J. Sidman
John P. Wellner
Aaron P. Rosenfeld
Chris J. North
John C. Vorys (Resident, Cincinnati, Ohio Office)
Reginald W. Jackson
Carl D. Smallwood
Joseph A. Brunetto
John J. Kulewicz
Terry M. Miller
David W. Hardymon
Robert G. Dykes
Jonathan D. Iten
Anker M. Bell
Michael A. Cline
Douglas L. Rogers
F. James Foley
M. Howard Petricoff
Benita A. Kahn
Elizabeth Turrell Farrar
Thomas E. Szykowny
Jonathan R. Vaughn
Thomas O. Ruby
Robert H. Maynard
Richard D. Schuster
Anthony C. Ciriaco
Carole A. Mitchell
Andrew C. Smith
Shawn M. Flahive
J. Thomas Mason
William G. Porter II
Daniel J. Minor
Robert J. Styduhar
Thomas R. Winters
Dan L. Jaffe
David A. Swift
Elizabeth E. Tulman
Webb I. Vorys
Robert N. Webner
Gail C. Ford
Scott M. Doran
Kenneth A. Golonka, Jr.
James A. Wilson
James E. Arnold
Bradley K. Sinnott
Russell R. Rosler
Mark E. Vannatta
John B. Weimer
Paul J. Coval
Anthony L. Ehler
Randall D. LaTour
Susan A. Cohen
David F. Axelrod
Elizabeth T. Smith
Julia A. Davis
Anthony J. Giuliani
William D. Kloss, Jr.
John L. Landolfi
Douglas R. Matthews
Ronald A. Robins, Jr.
Allen S. Kinzer
Kevin M. Czerwonka
Herbert A. Hedden
Philip F. Downey
David Michael Schira
David W. Cook
Brent C. Taggart
Kristin L. Watt
Susan Barrett Harty
Michael D. Martz

Gregory J. Zelasko
Donald A. Brown
Ajili Hodari
Randall W. Mikes
Theodore P. Mattis
Richard T. Miller
William Evan Price, II
D. Scott Powell
Robert A. Harris
Timothy C. Hall, Jr.
Gregory D. Russell
Lisa Pierce Reisz
Jacklyn J. Ford
Stephen D. Browning
Paula J. Lloyd
Rick J. Shapiro
Melinda R. McAfee
Kristin J. Sabgir
Steven R. Miller
Sheila Nolan Gartland
William J. Pohlman
Christopher J. Yost
Michael F. O'Brien
Jonathan P. Beck
William W. Patmon, III
Nathan C. Hamilton
Gregory E. Sutton
Timothy J. Dobyns
Adam K. Brandt
David A. Campbell, III
David P. Lyons
Julia Falenski White
Gary J. Saalman
J. Allen Rider, III
Craig R. Auge
Joseph C. Blasko
K. William Franken
Mary L. Garceau
Michelle M. Gubola
Cheryl Renee Hankerson
Timothy W. Hoover
Rebecca Beata Swanson
Scott J. Ziance
Suzanne J. Scrutton
Tiffany Strelow Cobb
Mark A. Knueve
Brian James Downey
Patrick M. Lanahan
Andrew Mark Bojko
Anne E. Eckhart
J. Theodore Smith
Joseph R. Miller
Caroline Z. Worley
Jonathan P. Amy
Michael C. Griffaton
Ronald A. Kladder
Allen L. Rutz
Matthew R. Shurte
Barbara U. Nalazek
Travis J. Wahl (Not admitted in OH)
Perry W. Doran II (Not admitted in OH)
Jason J. Kelroy
Kimberly Weber Herlihy
Kelly A. Boggs
Victor J. Ferguson
Sally A. Leach (Not admitted in OH)

OF COUNSEL

Arthur I. Vorys
John C. Elam
Russell P. Herrold, Jr.
Charles D. Minor
Richard G. Ison
Kenneth D. Beck
Robert W. Minor
Michael R. Thomas

(See Next Column)

OF COUNSEL (Continued)

Scott N. Whitlock
Linda R. Mendel
Martyn T. Brodnik
Carol Mahaffey
Joseph R. Dreitler
Edgar A. Strause
Edward A. Schrag, Jr.
Colborn M. Addison
Jacob E. Davis, II
William D. Kloss
Norton R. Webster
Richard Heer Oman
Stephen M. Howard
Theodore A. Boggs
Lester S. Lash
Richard R. Stedman
John W. Hoberg

Representative Client: Honda of America Mfg., Inc.
Local Counsel: Abbott Laboratories; Anheuser-Busch, Inc.; Anthem Insurance Compnies, Inc.; Bob Evans Farms, Inc.; Borden, Inc.; Connecticut General Life Insurance Co.; Coopers & Lybrand; Eaton Corporation; General Motors Corp.

For full biographical listings, see the Martindale-Hubbell Law Directory

---

*DAYTON,** Montgomery Co.

ALTICK & CORWIN CO., L.P.A. (AV)

1700 One Dayton Centre, One South Main Street, 45402
Telephone: 937-223-1201
Fax: 937-223-5100
Email: info@altickcorwin.com *URL:* http://www.altickcorwin.com

Hugh H. Altick (1905-1990)
Robert K. Corwin (1913-1998)
Robert N. Farquhar
Marshall D. Ruchman
Thomas M. Baggott
Dennis J. Adkins
Philip B. Herron
Deborah J. Adler
Stephen M. McHugh
Raymond J. Pikna, Jr.
Scott A. Liberman

Donald K. Scott
Jonathan B. Freeman
Matthew D. Stokely
Peter R. Certo
David E. Larson
Dalma C. Grandjean
Kellie A. Kalbac
David H. Montgomery

OF COUNSEL

David L. Hall

RETIRED

Robert B. Brumbaugh
Ronald H. McDonnell, Jr.

Representative Clients: City of Centerville; The Miami Conservancy District; Miami Valley Cable Council; Woodland Cemetery Assn.

For full biographical listings, see the Martindale-Hubbell Law Directory

---

BIESER, GREER & LANDIS (AV)

400 National City Center, 6 North Main Street, 45402
Telephone: 937-223-3277
Fax: 937-223-6339
Email: bgllaw.com

MEMBERS OF FIRM

Irvin G. Bieser (1902-1989)
Rowan A. Greer, Jr. (1907-1967)
Robert K. Landis (1915-1991)
Charles D. Shook
Edward L. Shank
David C. Greer
Irvin G. Bieser, Jr.
Leo F. Krebs
Howard Penn Krisher, II
Edward H. Siddens
Michael W. Krumholtz
John F. Haviland, Jr.
David P. Williamson
James H. Greer

ASSOCIATES

Charles F. Shane
Joseph C. Oehlers
Carla J. Morman
Nikki Jo Palmer
James P. Fleisher
Sean P. Donovan
Karen T. Dunlevey

Representative Clients: Dayton Power & Light Co.; Miami Valley Regional Transit Authority; Kettering Medical Center; The Dayton Foundation; Greater Dayton Public Television, Inc.; Medical Protective Co.; St. Paul Insurance Co.; Continental Loss Adjusting Services; Motorists Insurance Co.; National City Bank.

For full biographical listings, see the Martindale-Hubbell Law Directory

---

CONWAY & HALL A LEGAL PROFESSIONAL ASSOCIATION (AV)

900 Courthouse Plaza Southwest, 45402
Telephone: 937-228-1111
Facsimile: 937-228-9340
URL: http://www.lawyers.com/conwayhall

Dennis L. Hall
W. Michael Conway

Carolyn L. Mueller

OF COUNSEL

C. Robert Swaninger

For full biographical listings, see the Martindale-Hubbell Law Directory

Dayton—Continued

PORTER WRIGHT MORRIS & ARTHUR LLP (AV)

One Dayton Centre, One South Main Street, Suite 1600, 45402-2028
Telephone: 937-449-6810; (800-533-4434)
Fax: 937-449-6820
Email: day@porterwright.com *URL:* http://www.porterwright.com
Columbus, Ohio Office: 41 South High Street, 43215-6194.
Telephones: 614-227-2000; (800-533-2794).
Fax: 614-227-2100. Internet: cmh@porterwright.com.
Cincinnati, Ohio Office: 250 E. Fifth Street, Suite 2200, 45202-4199.
Telephones: 513-381-4700; (800-582-5813);
Fax: 513-421-0991. Internet: cvg@porterwright.com.
Cleveland, Ohio Office: 925 Euclid Avenue, Suite 1700, 44115-1483.
Telephones: 216-443-9000; (800-824-1980).
Fax: 216-443-9011. Internet: cle@porterwright.com.
Washington, D.C. Office: 1667 K Street, N.W., Suite 1100, 20006-1605.
Telephones: 202-778-3000; (800-456-7962).
Fax: 202-778-3063. Internet: dca@porterwright.com.
Naples, Florida Office: 5801 Pelican Bay Boulevard, Suite 300, 34108-2709.
Telephones: 941-593-2900; (800-876-7962).
Fax: 941-593-2990. Internet: apf@porterwright.com.

RESIDENT MEMBERS

William G. Deas
John J. Heron
Jonathan Hollingsworth
Thomas A. Holton
C. Terry Johnson
Charles Y. Kidwell, Jr.
Walter Reynolds
R. Bruce Snyder

RESIDENT ASSOCIATES

N. Robert Goad, Jr.
Linda S. Holmes
Elizabeth L. Ross

OF COUNSEL

Barbara A. Duncombe (Not admitted in OH)
Roland F. Eichner
Chester E. Finn
Samuel L. Hagans, Jr.
Richard A. Maresca
Jeffrey W. Morris

For full biographical listings, see the Martindale-Hubbell Law Directory

ROGERS & GREENBERG (AV)

2160 Kettering Tower, 45423
Telephone: 937-223-8171
Fax: 937-223-1649
Email: rgattys@aol.com

MEMBERS OF FIRM

William A. Rogers, Jr.
Stanley Z. Greenberg
John M. Cloud
Barry W. Mancz
Keith R. Kearney
James G. Kordik

L. Anthony Lush
Dawn S. Garrett
Michelle S. Vollmar

General Counsel for: Heartland Federal Credit Union; National Management Association; Moraine Materials Co.; Techway Industries, Inc.; Washington Township Park Board.

For full biographical listings, see the Martindale-Hubbell Law Directory

TYE AND TYE (AV)

A Legal Professional Association
5975 Kentshire Drive, 45440
Telephone: 937-291-8646
Telecopier: 937-291-8650
Email: tyelaw@erinet.com

MEMBERS OF FIRM

Rose R. Tye
Timothy N. Tye

References: National City Bank; Bank One, Dayton N.A.

For full biographical listings, see the Martindale-Hubbell Law Directory

*DELAWARE,** Delaware Co.

MANOS, MARTIN, PERGRAM & DIETZ, L.P.A. (AV)

50 North Sandusky Street, 43015
Telephone: 740-363-1313
Telecopier: 740-363-1314
Email: mail@mmpdlaw.com *URL:* http://www.mnpdlaw.com
Columbus, Ohio Office: 69 East Wilson Bridge Road, 43015.
Telephone: 614-436-8000.
Telecopier: 614-846-4691.

SENIOR COUNSEL

Peter J. Manos

Stephen D. Martin
Dennis L. Pergram
James M. Dietz
Maribeth Deavers

OF COUNSEL

Lowell A. Hedlund
Neal H. Magee, II

For full biographical listings, see the Martindale-Hubbell Law Directory

*EATON,** Preble Co.

BENNETT & BENNETT (AV)

Bennett Law Building, 200 West Main Street, 45320
Telephone: 937-456-5100; 456-4100
Fax: 937-456-4300; 456-7278

MEMBERS OF FIRM

Lloyd B. Bennett (1909-1983)
Herd L. Bennett
Gray W. Bennett

LEGAL SUPPORT PERSONNEL

LEGAL ASSISTANTS

Sandra K. Shafer
Laura A. Toschlog
Debbie Bennett
Julie B. Clark
Melissa K. Bear

Representative Clients: The National Hummel Foundation and Museum; Star Bank NA, Eaton, Ohio; Eaton National Bank & Trust Co.; First National Bank of Southwestern Ohio; Brookville National Bank; Farm Credit Services of Mid-America, ACA; Miller's Super Markets, Inc.; Northedge Shopping Center, Inc.; Herman M. Brubaker Registered Holstein Cattle; The Eaton Foundation.

For full biographical listings, see the Martindale-Hubbell Law Directory

*FINDLAY,** Hancock Co.

OXLEY, MALONE, FITZGERALD & HOLLISTER (AV)

301 East Main Cross Street, P.O. Box 1086, 45840
Telephone: 419-422-8713
Fax: 419-422-6495
Email: oxleylaw@bright.net

MEMBERS OF FIRM

Garver Oxley (1919-1997)
Michael J. Malone
Dennis M. Fitzgerald
Robert B. Hollister

ASSOCIATES

Michael E. Gilb
Bradley S. Warren
Bret A. Spaeth

OF COUNSEL

Julie A. Davenport

LEGAL SUPPORT PERSONNEL

PARALEGALS

Amy J. Hancock
Laura L. Nye
Lisa M. Niese

Representative Clients: CNA Insurance Co.; Hancock-Wood Electric Cooperative , Inc.; Buckeye State Mutual Insurance Co.; American States Insurance Co.; Allstate Insurance Co.; Auto-Owners Insurance Co.; Western Reserve Group; Buckeye State Mutual Insurance Co.; Lima Memorial Hospital; Blanchard Valley Regional Health Center.

For full biographical listings, see the Martindale-Hubbell Law Directory

RAKESTRAW & RAKESTRAW (AV)

119 East Crawford Street, 45840-4802
Telephone: 419-422-9455
Fax: 419-422-2482

MEMBERS OF FIRM

Russell E. Rakestraw
Gregory A. Rakestraw

Representative Clients: Budd Co.; Ohio Power Co.

For full biographical listings, see the Martindale-Hubbell Law Directory

*GREENVILLE,** Darke Co.

GOUBEAUX & GOUBEAUX (AV)

100 Washington Avenue, P.O. Box 158, 45331
Telephone: 937-548-2211
Fax: Available Upon Request

MEMBERS OF FIRM

Edward A. Goubeaux, Jr. (1906-1964)
Jerome H. Goubeaux (1908-1978)
James J. Goubeaux
Robert L. Morris
Eric H. Brand
Mark E. Heggie

Representative Clients: Fifth Third Bank; Osgood State Bank; Second National Bank; United Telephone Company of Ohio.
Local Counsel for: Penn Central Co.; Corning Glass Works; The St. Henry Bank, St. Henry, Ohio; New Amsterdam Casualty Co.

For full biographical listings, see the Martindale-Hubbell Law Directory

*LEBANON,** Warren Co.

KAUFMAN & FLORENCE (AV)

144 East Mulberry Street, P.O. Box 280, 45036
Telephone: 513-932-1515; 423-1363; 421-6456
Fax: 513-932-9172
Email: wkaufman@your-net.com

(See Next Column)

KAUFMAN & FLORENCE—*Continued*

MEMBERS OF FIRM

William H. Kaufman | Mark T. Florence

Representative Clients: Farm Credit Services; Lebanon Raceway; Lebanon Citizens National Bank.
Local Counsel for: Cincinnati Gas & Electric Co.; Grange Mutual Casualty Co.; Western Water Company; State Auto Mutual Ins. Co.
Approved Agents and Attorneys for: Ohio Bar Title Insurance Co.; Old Republic National Title Insurance Co.; Farmers Home Administration.

For full biographical listings, see the Martindale-Hubbell Law Directory

*LIMA,** Allen Co.

CORY, MEREDITH, WITTER, ROUSH & CHENEY A LEGAL PROFESSIONAL ASSOCIATION (AV)

101 N. Elizabeth Street Suite 607, P.O. Box 1217, 45802-1217
Telephone: 419-228-6365
Fax: 419-228-5319

Frank B. Cory
James E. Meredith
Donald J. Witter
W. Thomas Roush
David A. Cheney
Michael P. Anderson
Robert J. Meredith
Michael A. Rumer
Victoria U. Maisch

General Counsel for: Northwestern College; Roeder Cortage Company.
Local Counsel for: East Ohio Gas Co.; British Petroleum; State Farm Insurance Company (fire and auto); Auto Owners Insurance Co.; Cincinnati Insurance; Clark.

For full biographical listings, see the Martindale-Hubbell Law Directory

ROBENALT & ROBENALT (AV)

211-215 North Elizabeth Street, 45801-4302
Telephone: 419-229-0054
Telecopier: 419-228-3631
Nokomis, Florida Office: 2440 Tamiami Trail North. P.O. Box 1608. 34275.
Telephone: 941-966-7755.
Fax: 941-966-6678.

MEMBERS OF FIRM

John A. Robenalt (Resident)
John F. Robenalt (Resident, Nokomis, Florida Office)

Representative Clients: National Health Investors, Inc. (listed New York Stock Exchange); National Health Corp. L.P. (listed AMEX); Dot Lines, Inc.; Warehouse Associates, Inc.; The Green and Sawyer Company; Ohio Automobile Club (OAC); Gooding Gallery of Homes; Allen County Regional Transit Authority.
Approved Attorney for: Guardian Title Insurance Co.
Reference: Bank One, Lima, Ohio.

For full biographical listings, see the Martindale-Hubbell Law Directory

LORAIN, Lorain Co.

WICKENS, HERZER & PANZA A LEGAL PROFESSIONAL ASSOCIATION (AV)

1144 West Erie Avenue, P.O. Box 840, 44052-0840
Telephone: 440-246-5268
Facsimile: 440-244-4380
Cleveland Direct Line: 216-447-4418
Cleveland Facsimile: 216-447-0998
Email: pdahm@whplpa.com *URL:* http://www.wickens@whplpa.com

William G. Wickens (Retired, 1996)
David L. Herzer
Richard D. Panza
Robert P. Ellis, Jr.
Thomas Pillari
Richard A. Naegele
Marsha Nicoloff Collett
William F. Kolis, Jr.
Charles J. Pawlukiewicz
Mark P. Altieri
Linda C. Ashar
John D. Rybarczyk
Matthew W. Nakon
William P. Prescott
Russell R. Aukerman
Rachelle Kuznicki Zidar
Mark R. Gross
David Harmon

Representative Clients: The Morning Journal; Norfolk Southern Corp.; Community Health Partners of Ohio; Drs. Russell, Berkebile and Associates, Radiologists; Mike Bass Ford; Ross Environmental Services, Inc.

For full biographical listings, see the Martindale-Hubbell Law Directory

*MANSFIELD,** Richland Co.

BROWN, BEMILLER, MURRAY & MCINTYRE (AV)

70 Park Avenue West, P.O. Box 728, 44901-0728
Telephone: 419-525-1611
FAX: 419-525-3810

(See Next Column)

MEMBERS OF FIRM

John T. Brown
F. Loyal Bemiller
D. Kim Murray
J. Jeffrey Heck
William T. McIntyre
Jeffrey Molyet
Adam Vetter, Jr.
Jason B. Murray
David N. Haring

Local Counsel for: Royal-Globe Group; Westfield Companies; Ohio Edison Co.; Grange Mutual Casualty Co.; Buckeye Union Insurance Co.; Maryland Casualty Co.; Shelby Insurance; Montgomery Ward & Co.; Continental Insurance Group; Artesian Industries, Inc.

For full biographical listings, see the Martindale-Hubbell Law Directory

CALHOUN, KADEMENOS & HEICHEL CO., L.P.A. (AV)

6 West Third Street, Suite 200, P.O. Box 268, 44901-0268
Telephone: 419-524-6011
Fax: 419-526-1431
Sandusky, Ohio Office: 215 W. Washington Row, 44870.
Telephone: 419-625-7770.
Fax: 419-625-8552.

James A. Calhoun (1942-1991)
Robert H. Benzin (1917-1993)
Richard D. Ronk (1957-1991)
William D. Heichel
Victor P. Kademenos
James L. Childress
Anthony P. Trozzolillo

John (Jack) P. Stewart
Janet L. Phillips

General Counsel for: Richland Trust Co.
Special Counsel for: State Automobile Mutual Insurance Co.

For full biographical listings, see the Martindale-Hubbell Law Directory

WELDON, HUSTON & KEYSER (AV)

Eighth and Ninth Floors, Bank One Building, 28 Park Ave W, 44902-1695
Telephone: 419-524-9811
Fax: 419-522-5758

MEMBERS OF FIRM

William McE. Weldon (1868-1952)
C. H. Huston (1871-1957)
Henry P. Huston (1903-1984)
George H. Keyser (Retired)
George Hall
Richard R. Fowler
John H. Siegenthaler
David D. Carto
John S. Hire
Richard H. Otto

ASSOCIATE

John Allen Holmes

Representative Clients: Bank One, Mansfield; Mansfield General Hospital, Corp.; The Medical Protective Co.; Mechanics Bank; Hi-Stat Manufacturing Co., Inc.; Motorists Insurance Companies; Whitey's Auto Mall; United Telephone Long Distance; Milliron Waste Management; Richland Nursing Homes, Inc.

For full biographical listings, see the Martindale-Hubbell Law Directory

*MARYSVILLE,** Union Co.

ALLEN, YURASEK & MERKLIN (AV)

233 West Fifth Street, P.O. Box 391, 43040-0391
Telephone: 937-642-4070
Telecopier: 937-644-4390
Email: aymucta@midohio.net

MEMBERS OF FIRM

Gwynn Sanders (1906-1989)
David F. Allen
Stephen J. Yurasek
Jeffrey A. Merklin

ASSOCIATE

Tina Owens-Ruff

General Counsel for: Ohio Grain Co.; Conklin Dairy Farms, Inc.; Richwood Banking Co.; Community Foundation of Union County; Tuffco Sand & Gravel Co.; Franke's Wood Products, Inc.; Picklesimer Trucking, Inc.
Local Counsel for: John Hancock Mutual Life Insurance Co.; Honda Federal Credit Union; Metropolitan Life Insurance Co.

For full biographical listings, see the Martindale-Hubbell Law Directory

*MEDINA,** Medina Co.

BROWN AND AMODIO A LEGAL PROFESSIONAL ASSOCIATION (AV)

109 West Liberty Street, P.O. Box 1117, 44258
Telephone: 330-725-8816
Fax: 330-723-5448
Email: brownlaw@ohio.net

David N. Brown
James A. Amodio

Representative Clients: FirstMerit Bank, N.A.; Aztec Imports, Inc.

For full biographical listings, see the Martindale-Hubbell Law Directory

MIDDLETOWN, Butler Co.

FROST & JACOBS LLP (AV)

400 First National Bank Building, 2 North Main Street, 45042-1981
Telephone: 513-422-2001
Telecopier: 513-422-3010
Cincinnati, Ohio Office: 2500 PNC Center, 201 East Fifth Street, 45202.
Telephone: 513-651-6800.
Telecopier: 513-651-6981.
Columbus, Ohio Office: One Columbus, 10 West Broad Street, 43215.
Telephone: 614-464-1211.
Telecopier: 614-464-1737.
Lexington, Kentucky Office: 1100 Vine Center Tower, 333 West Vine Street, 40507.
Telephone: 606-524-1100.
Telecopier: 606-253-2990.
Frankfort, Kentucky Office: 201 W. Main Street, 40601.
Telephone: 502-223-1400.
Telecopier: 502-223-1410.

MEMBERS OF FIRM

Thomas A. Swope
Donald L. Crain

SENIOR ATTORNEY

Daniel J. Picard

ASSOCIATE

Thomas B. Allen

OF COUNSEL

Barry J. Levey

Representative Clients: Abilities First Foundation; AK Steel Corporation; Armco Inc.; The Brown-Singer Co.; City of Oxford, Ohio; First Financial Bancorp; First National Bank of Southwestern Ohio; Hamilton Journal News; International Paper Co.; Magnode Corp.; Miami Valley Industrial Park, Inc.; Middletown Journal; Middletown Paperboard Co.; Middletown Board of Education; MTP, Inc.; Picard Paper Processing, Inc.; Union Township, Butler County, Ohio; Voith Suszer Paper Technology.
Labor Relations Counsel For: Butler County, Ohio; Calmar, Inc.; Champion International; City of Cincinnati, Ohio; City of Hamilton, Ohio; City of Middletown, Ohio; Smurfit Stone Packaging Corp.; Middletown Regional Hospital; Southwest Regional Water District; Village of Indian Hill.
Approved Attorneys For: Ohio Bar Title Insurance Co.; The Lawyers Title Insurance Co., Richmond, Va.

For full biographical listings, see the Martindale-Hubbell Law Directory

PERRYSBURG, Wood Co.

LEATHERMAN, WITZLER, DOMBEY & HART (AV)

353 Elm Street, 43551
Telephone: 419-874-3536
Fax: 419-874-3899
Email: OURNET@GLASSCITY.NET *URL:* http://www.lawyers.com/lwdhlaw

MEMBERS OF FIRM

Wayne M. Leatherman
James H. Hart
Philip L. Dombey
T. Hamilton Noll
Kay L. Howard

Representative Clients: Craig Transportation Co.; Ed Schmidt Pontiac, Inc.; Perrysburg Township Trustees; Carlson Travel Co.; Village of Holland; Village of Haskins; Waterville Township Trustees; 577 Foundation.

For full biographical listings, see the Martindale-Hubbell Law Directory

*POMEROY,** Meigs Co.

CROW AND CROW (AV)

110 West Second Street, P.O. Box 668, 45769
Telephone: 740-992-5132; 992-6059 (non-dedicated facsimile line)

MEMBERS OF FIRM

Fred W. Crow, Sr. (1879-1957)
Fred W. Crow, Jr. (1915-1995)
I. Carson Crow

Representative Clients: Midwest Steel; Auto Owners Insurance Co.; State Automobile Insurance Co.; The Farmers Bank & Savings Co.; General Telephone Co.; Orkin Exterminating Company Inc.; Beneficial Ohio Inc.; City Loan Financial Services, Inc.
Approved Attorneys for: Ohio Bar Title Insurance Co. (agent).

*PORTSMOUTH,** Scioto Co.

JOHNSON & OLIVER, A LEGAL PROFESSIONAL ASSOCIATION (AV)

701 Sixth Street, P.O. Box 1505, 45662
Telephone: 740-354-4200
Telecopier: 740-353-2413

C. Clayton Johnson

Stephen L. Oliver

(See Next Column)

OF COUNSEL

Robert Kurt McCurdy

Representative Clients: OSCO Industries, Inc.; Citizens Deposit Bank and Trust; First National Bank of Lewis County, Kentucky; Home Federal Savings and Loan; McDonalds Corp.; National Maintenance & Repair, Inc.; McGinnis, Inc.
Approved Attorney for: Lawyers Title Insurance Co.

For full biographical listings, see the Martindale-Hubbell Law Directory

STEPHEN C. RODEHEFFER (AV)

630 6th Street, 45662
Telephone: 740-354-1300
Fax: 740-354-1301
Email: rody@zoomnet.net

ASSOCIATE

Shane A. Tieman

For full biographical listings, see the Martindale-Hubbell Law Directory

*SANDUSKY,** Erie Co.

BUCKINGHAM, HOLZAPFEL, ZEIHER, WALDOCK & SCHELL CO., L.P.A. (AV)

414 Wayne Street, P.O. Box 929, 44870
Telephone: 419-627-0414
Fax: 419-627-0009
Vermilion, Ohio Office: 678 Main Street.
Telephone: 216-967-6136.
Fax: 216-967-8541.

F. H. Buckingham (1901-1971)
George C. Steinemann (Retired)
Richard D. Holzapfel (Retired)
Arthur W. Zeiher (Retired)
Thomas S. Buckingham
Frederick D. Waldock
Lawrence H. Schell *
Maurice L. McDermond, Jr.
Kevin J. Zeiher
John D. Frankel
W. Zack Dolyk *

Troy Wisehart
John R. Ball
Linda Fritz-Gasteier

Local Counsel: Erie County Cablevision, Inc.
General Counsel: Sandusky Newspapers, Inc.; The Cooke Properties; Firelands Community Hospital.
*Sandusky and Vermilion, Ohio Offices

For full biographical listings, see the Martindale-Hubbell Law Directory

FLYNN, PY & KRUSE A LEGAL PROFESSIONAL ASSOCIATION (AV)

165 East Washington Row, 44870
Telephone: 419-625-8324
Fax: 419-625-9007
Port Clinton, Ohio Office: 115 West Perry Street.
Telephone: 419-734-3174.
Fax: 419-734-3175.

James F. Flynn (1887-1963)
John R. Py (1908-1969)
Richard R. Kruse (1910-1997)
Raymond N. Watts (Retired)
Melvyn J. Stauffer
William C. Steuk
Charles W. Waterfield
John D. Py
John A. Coppeler
John E. Rosino
James W. Hart
Mary Jane Hill
Christopher M. Marinko

Wm. R.S. Steuk

Representative Clients: Allstate Insurance Co.; First National Bank of Bellevue; Nationwide Mutual Insurance Co.; Norfolk and Southern Corp.; Ohio Edison Co.; Westfield Insurance Co.; Dorn Foundation; Firelands Community Hospital; Lutheran Memorial Home; J.H. Routh Packing Co.

For full biographical listings, see the Martindale-Hubbell Law Directory

*SPRINGFIELD,** Clark Co.

MARTIN, BROWNE, HULL & HARPER, P.L.L. (AV)

One South Limestone Street Suite 800, P.O. Box 1488, 45501-1488
Telephone: 937-324-5541
Fax: 937-325-5432
1-800-324-5562
Email: mbhhlaw@martinbrowne.com
London, Ohio Office: 26 East Fourth Street, 43140.
Telephone: 740-852-8383.
Fax: 740-852-1699.

MEMBERS OF THE FIRM

Oscar T. Martin (1848-1913)
Paul C. Martin (1876-1939)
Homer C. Corry (1887-1955)
John C. Durfey (1902-1960)
Anson E. Hull (1915-1983)
Oscar T. Martin (1908-1995)
Robin R. Freeman
Hugh Barnett
Robert E. Harley
Glenn W. Collier
Walter A. Wildman
David A. Weaver

(See Next Column)

MARTIN, BROWNE, HULL & HARPER P.L.L.—*Continued*

MEMBERS OF THE FIRM (Continued)

William R. Groves
Steven J. McCready
Richard F. Heil, Jr.
Austin P. Wildman (Resident, London Office)

OF COUNSEL

John O. Harper

RETIRED PARTNER

Bitner Browne

Regina Watson
Aleita J. Ailes
Michael C. Weaver
Lauren M. Ross
Nikolas P. Mann (Resident, London Office)

Counsel for: Antioch University; Vernay Laboratories; O-Cedar Brands; Rittal Corporation; Morris Bean & Co.
Local Counsel for: Ohio Edison Co.; National City Bank; American States Insurance Co.; Cornerstone Bank.

For full biographical listings, see the Martindale-Hubbell Law Directory

SWANTON, Fulton Co.

THE MCQUADES CO., L.P.A. (AV)

Lincoln at Broadway, P.O. Box 237, 43558
Telephone: 419-826-0055
Fax: 419-825-3871
Email: mcquadelaw@cs.com *URL:* http://www.lawyers.com/mcquadelaw
Archbold, Ohio Office: 200 N. Defiance Street.
Telephone: 419-445-3755.
Whitehouse, Ohio Office: 6632 Providence Street.
Telephone: 419-877-0746.

Richard B. McQuade, Sr. (1912-1996)
Daniel P. McQuade
Colin J. McQuade

Alan J. Lehenbauer

For full biographical listings, see the Martindale-Hubbell Law Directory

*TOLEDO,** Lucas Co.

ANSPACH & SERRAINO (AV)

405 Madison Avenue, Suite 2100, 43604-1236
Telephone: 419-246-5757
Fax: 419-321-6979
Tiffin, Ohio Office: Dell & Anspach, 60 Sycamore Street, 44883.
Telephone: 419-447-6181.
Fax: 419-447-6332.
Buffalo, New York Office: One HSBC Center, Suite 3750.
Telephone: 716-856-5012.

Robert M. Anspach
Stephen R. Serraino
Mark D. Meeks
J. Roy Nunn
Paul F. Burtis
Jane C. Dell
Kent Riesen
Kristin Sacco Sacco
Joshua W. Lanzinger
Elizabeth M. Foley
Garrick O. White
James R. Carnes
Tasha T. Dandridge (Resident, Buffalo, New York Office)

For full biographical listings, see the Martindale-Hubbell Law Directory

DOYLE, LEWIS & WARNER (AV)

202 North Erie Street, P.O. Box 2168, 43603
Telephone: 419-248-1500
Fax: 419-248-2002
Email: dlw1@primenet.com

John H. Doyle (1844-1919)
Charles T. Lewis (1850-1918)
Milo J. Warner (1891-1968)
Harold A. James (1903-1996)
Melvin P. Lewis (1913-1994)

MEMBERS OF FIRM

Steven Timonere
Richard F. Ellenberger
Michael E. Hyrne
Michael A. Bruno
David W. Doerner

ASSOCIATES

Kevin A. Pituch
Maureen O. Atkins

Counsel for: Consolidated Rail Corp.; The Lakefront Dock & Railroad Terminal Co.; Prudential Insurance Co. of America; Equitable Life Assurance Society of the U.S.; Metropolitan Life Insurance Co.; Greyhound Lines; Fireman's Fund Insurance Cos.

For full biographical listings, see the Martindale-Hubbell Law Directory

EASTMAN & SMITH LTD. (AV)

One Seagate, Twenty-Fourth Floor, P.O. Box 10032, 43699-0032
Telephone: 419-241-6000
Telecopier: 419-247-1777
Columbus, Ohio Office: 65 East State Street, Suite 1000, 43215.
Telephone: 614-460-3556.
Telecopier: 614-228-5371.

(See Next Column)

MEMBERS OF FIRM

Frank D. Jacobs
Patrick J. Johnson
James F. Nooney
Bruce L. Smith
Morton Bobowick
David M. Jones
Henry N. Heuerman
John H. Boggs
John T. Landwehr
David L. Kuhl
Richard T. Sargeant
Kenneth C. Baker
Robert J. Gilmer, Jr.
Peter R. Casey, III
David F. Cooper
Rudolph A. Peckinpaugh, Jr.
Ronald J. Tice
Thomas A. Dixon
Gary M. Harden
Barry W. Fissel
John D. Willey, Jr.
Joseph A. Gregg
Roger Paul Klee
Mark C. Abramson
Stuart J. Goldberg
Thomas J. Gibney
Steven D. Reinbolt
Dirk P. Plessner
James L. Rogers
David W. Nunn
David C. Krock

ASSOCIATES

Marcus J. Brubaker
Timothy C. Kuhlman
Albin Bauer, II
David A. Dennis
Michael W. Regnier
Margaret A. Mattimoe
Kevin D. Devaney
Nirakar C. Thakur
M. Charles Collins
Barbara A. McGinn
Mark H. Boss
Erica L. Smith
Michael J. Spisak
Katharine M. Thomas
Lane D. Williamson
Michael P. Henry
Matthew D. Harper
Mary Jo Tarini
Graham A. Bluhm
Scott D. Newsom
Christi S. Bartman
Gary L. Miller
Carrie Lynn Young
Natacha M. Vincent-Kolcun
Kathy L. Zablocki

OF COUNSEL

Jamille G. Jamra
Frank E. Kane
Howard M. Friedman
Gerald P. Moran
Richard E. Antonini
M. Donald Carmin

Counsel for: Chrysler Corp.; Marathon Oil; Envirosafe Service of Ohio, Inc.; Glasstech, Inc.; Toledo-Lucas County Port Authority; Huntington National Bank; Capital Bank, N.A.; Riverside Hospital; The Travelers Group; The Hartford Insurance Group.

For full biographical listings, see the Martindale-Hubbell Law Directory

MORAN & MORAN (AV)

626 Madison Avenue, Suite 300, 43604
Telephone: 419-241-8171
Fax: Available Upon Request

Wayne R. Peppers (1894-1978)
Peter L. Moran
Mary Beth Moran

Representative Clients: The Exchange Bank; Payak Insurance Agency; Monroe Pharmacy, Inc.
References: Society Bank; The Fifth Third Bank, Toledo, Ohio.

For full biographical listings, see the Martindale-Hubbell Law Directory

RITTER, ROBINSON, MCCREADY & JAMES (AV)

1850 National City Bank Building, 405 Madison Avenue, 43624
Telephone: 419-241-3213
FAX: 419-241-4925

MEMBERS OF FIRM

George W. Ritter (1886-1979)
Milton C. Boesel, Sr. (1893-1993)
Ellis F. Robinson (Retired)
Milton C. Boesel, Jr. (Retired)
William S. McCready
Timothy C. James
Mark P. Seitzinger

ASSOCIATE

Raymond H. Pittman, III

Counsel for: Chrysler Corp.; Rubini Motors, Inc.; Ohio Casualty Insurance Co.; National Mutual Insurance Co.; Celina Mutual Insurance Co.; Westfield Insurance Co.; Northwestern National Insurance Co.; Midwestern Insurance Co.; United Ohio Insurance Co.; Toledo Auto Electric Co.

For full biographical listings, see the Martindale-Hubbell Law Directory

SCHNORF & SCHNORF CO., L.P.A. A PROFESSIONAL CORPORATION (AV)

1400 National City Bank Building, 405 Madison Avenue, 43604
Telephone: 419-248-2646
Facsimile: 419-248-2889

Brandon G. Schnorf, Sr. (1904-1977)
David M. Schnorf
Christopher F. Parker
Johna M. Bella
Barry F. Hudgin

Local Counsel for: Universal Underwriters Group; Charter One Bank; Medical Mutual of Ohio; Bankers Multiple Line Insurance Company; National City Bank, Northwest; Charter One Bank.
Representative Clients: American Federation of Teachers, AFL-CIO; Ohio Federation of Teachers, AFL-CIO; Toledo Federation of Teachers, AFL-CIO; Hart Associates, Inc.

For full biographical listings, see the Martindale-Hubbell Law Directory

*TROY,** Miami Co.

FAUST, HARRELSON, FULKER, McCARTHY & SCHLEMMER (AV)

12 South Cherry Street, P.O. Box 8, 45373
Telephone: 937-335-8324
Fax: 937-339-7155
Email: fhfms@erinet.com

MEMBERS OF FIRM

Charles F. Faust (1875-1950)
William M. Harrelson (1921-1985)
J. Andrew Fulker (1953-1989)
Leo H. Faust (1899-1996)
John E. Fulker
Robert A. McCarthy
Robert N. Schlemmer
William J. Fulker
Robert M. Harrelson

OF COUNSEL

Richard J. Fraas

Counsel: Aetna Casualty & Surety Co.; Aetna Life Insurance Co.; Troy Lumber Co.; Fifth-Third Bank of Western Ohio; Westfield Insurance Companies; Star Bank, N.A.; Upper Valley Medical Center; ARC Abrasives, Inc.; Miami Mutual Insurance Co.; Summit Insurance Co.

For full biographical listings, see the Martindale-Hubbell Law Directory

*URBANA,** Champaign Co.

PAULIG AND SINGER (AV)

40 Monument Square Suite 300, 43078
Telephone: 937-653-5257
Facsimile: 937-653-3027

Karl E. Paulig
Brad C. Singer

Representative Clients: Nationwide Mutual Insurance Co.; Ohio Casualty Insurance Co.; Republic Franklin Insurance Co.; Bodey & Sons, Inc. (Building Contractor); Georgia, Inc.; Cincinnati Insurance Co.; Akins Printing, Inc.; The Stephen L. Bodey Co. (Contracting); Urbana City Board of Education; Champaign County Preservation Alliance.

For full biographical listings, see the Martindale-Hubbell Law Directory

*WARREN,** Trumbull Co.

HARRINGTON, HOPPE & MITCHELL, LTD. (AV)

108 Main Avenue, S.W., Suite 500, 44481
Telephone: 330-392-1541
Fax: 330-394-6890
Youngstown, Ohio Office: 1200 Mahoning Bank Building, 44503-1508.
Telephone: 330-744-1111.
Telecopier: 330-744-2029.

William R. Hewitt
Robert S. McGeough
John L. Pogue
Ned C. Gold, Jr.
Michael G. Marando
William L. Hawley
Thomas G. Carey, Jr.
Kevin P. Murphy
Dean E. Nielsen
Patrick K. Wilson
Allen L. Ryan
Henry H. Hoppe (1894-1979)
John Q. T. Ford (1897-1971)
James W. Frey (1922-1985)
John T. Milligan (1929-1994)
John T. Harrington (1873-1932)
Jared P. Huxley (1874-1942)
Charles F. Smith (1877-1949)
Osborne Mitchell (1886-1973)

Representative Clients: Forum Health Hospitals and Medical Centers; Consumers Ohio Water Company (Public Utility); Wilcom Cellular One; SYGNET Communications, Inc.; City of Canfield; The Public Library of Youngstown and Mahoning County; Simon-DeBartolo Group; Office of Attorney General, State of Ohio; Mahoning Valley Economic Development Corporation; National City Bank.

For full biographical listings, see the Martindale-Hubbell Law Directory

*WILMINGTON,** Clinton Co.

BRYANT LAW OFFICES (AV)

21 North South Street, 45177
Telephone: 937-382-7777
Fax: 937-382-2514

J. D. Bryant

ASSOCIATES

Timothy S. Chappars
Mark J. Miars

References: Fifth Third Bank.

For full biographical listings, see the Martindale-Hubbell Law Directory

*YOUNGSTOWN,** Mahoning Co.

HARRINGTON, HOPPE & MITCHELL, LTD. (AV)

1200 Mahoning Bank Building, 44503-1508
Telephone: 330-744-1111
Telecopier: 330-744-2029
Warren, Ohio Office: 108 Main Avenue, S.W., Suite 500, 44481.
Telephone: 330-392-1541.
Telecopier: 330-394-6890.

(See Next Column)

James E. Mitchell
George B. Woodman
Eldon S. Wright
Robert A. Lenga
George James Limbert
Paul M. Dutton
James L. Blomstrom
Frederick S. Coombs, III
Ralph A. Beard
Alan D. Wenger
John T. Dellick
Kelly J. Morrison
Shirley J. Christian
Neil H. Maxwell
Martin J. Boetcher
Mark R. Fortunato
Neil D. Schor
Brad Gessner
Constance E. Pierce
Shawna L. Erb
Lance A. Morrison
John T. Harrington (1873-1932)
Jared P. Huxley (1874-1942)
Charles F. Smith (1877-1949)
Osborne Mitchell (1886-1973)
Henry H. Hoppe (1894-1979)
John Q. T. Ford (1897-1971)
James W. Frey (1922-1985)
John T. Milligan (1929-1994)

Representative Clients: Forum Health Hospitals and Medical Centers; Consumers Ohio Water Company (Public Utility); Wilcom Cellular One; SYGNET Communications, Inc.; City of Canfield; The Public Library of Youngstown and Mahoning County; Simon-DeBartolo Group; Office of Attorney General, State of Ohio; Mahoning Valley Economic Development Corporation; National City Bank.

For full biographical listings, see the Martindale-Hubbell Law Directory

MANCHESTER, BENNETT, POWERS & ULLMAN A LEGAL PROFESSIONAL ASSOCIATION (AV)

Atrium Level Two The Commerce Building, 201 East Commerce Street, 44503-1641
Telephone: 330-743-1171
Fax: 330-743-1190
URL: http://www.mbpu.com

Curtis A. Manchester (1876-1951)
James Eugene Bennett (1889-1964)
Franklin B. Powers (1887-1960)
Myron E. Ullman (1889-1974)
Stephen T. Bolton
John F. Zimmerman, Jr.
James W. Ehrman
Thomas J. Travers, Jr.
Timothy J. Jacob
Charles S. Lanz
Mark A. Beatrice
Joseph R. Young, Jr.
Joseph M. Houser
Jeffrey D. Heintz
Edwin Romero

Martha L. Bushey
Thomas John Lipka

OF COUNSEL

James E. Bennett, Jr.

Local Counsel for: City of Youngstown; Commercial Intertech Corporation; Farmers Insurance Group; The Medical Protective Company; The Vindicator Printing Company; WFMJ Television, Inc.; Youngstown State University.
General Counsel for: Butler Wick & Company; Home Savings and Loan Company; Youngstown Osteopathic Hospital.

For full biographical listings, see the Martindale-Hubbell Law Directory

*ZANESVILLE,** Muskingum Co.

KINCAID, TAYLOR & GEYER (AV)

50 North Fourth Street, P.O. Box 1030, 43702-1030
Telephone: 740-454-2591
Telecopier: 740-454-6975
Email: ktglaw@kincaidlaw.com *URL:* http://www.kincaidlaw.com
Thornville, Ohio Office: 12 West Columbus Street, P.O. Box 609, 43076.
Telephone: 614-246-6700.
Fax: 614-246-6705.

J. Donald Kincaid (Retired)

MEMBERS OF FIRM

R. William Geyer
William J. Taylor
Scott D. Eickelberger

ASSOCIATE

David J. Tarbert

Attorneys for: The Ohio Power Co.; Mutual Federal Savings Bank; Halliburton Services; Bethesda Hospital Assn.; The Oxford Oil Co.; The Buckeye Co.; McDonalds of Zanesville and Cambridge; Nicoff Enterprises; Muskingum College.
Reference: Century National Bank.

For full biographical listings, see the Martindale-Hubbell Law Directory

OKLAHOMA

*ADA,** Pontotoc Co.

DEATON, DAVISON & KESSINGER, A PROFESSIONAL CORPORATION (AV)

300 South Rennie, P.O. Box 1219, 74820
Telephone: 580-332-1752
Fax: 580-332-0827
Email: ddkesq@chickasaw.com

Austin R. Deaton, Jr. | Denver N. Davison | C. Steven Kessinger

For full biographical listings, see the Martindale-Hubbell Law Directory

*ANADARKO,** Caddo Co.

PAIN AND GARLAND (AV)

111 S.W. Second Street, P.O. Box 158, 73005
Telephone: 405-247-3365
Fax: 405-247-7177

MEMBER OF FIRM
John W. Garland
ASSOCIATE
Richard A. Williams
OF COUNSEL
Leslie Pain

Representative Clients: First State Bank, Anadarko, Okla.; Caddo Electric Cooperative, Binger, Okla.; Town of Cement, Okla.; Community Bank; Federal Land Bank of Wichita; City of Anadarko, Okla.

For full biographical listings, see the Martindale-Hubbell Law Directory

*ANTLERS,** Pushmataha Co.

STAMPER, HADLEY & REASOR (AV)

112 North High Street, P.O. Box 100, 74523
Telephone: 580-298-3153; 580-298-3332
Fax: 580-298-3263
Email: joestamper@yahoo.com
Atoka, Oklahoma Office: 209 East Court, P.O. Box 393.
Telephone: 580-889-3343.
Fax: 580-889-9334.

MEMBERS OF FIRM
Joe Stamper
Thomas J. Hadley
Shannon Reasor (Resident, Atoka Office)

Representative Clients: Farmers Exchange Bank, Antlers, Okla.; First National Bank at Antlers, Okla.; Town of Antlers; U. S. F. & G. Co.

For full biographical listings, see the Martindale-Hubbell Law Directory

*ARDMORE,** Carter Co.

HARRY L. BICKFORD LAW OFFICE (AV)

29 B Street, S.W., P.O. Box 1027, 73402
Telephone: 580-223-5566
Fax: 580-226-1893
Email: bickford@brightok.net

Local Counsel: Ultramar Diamond Shamrock Corporation (Total Petroleum, Inc. and Total Pipeline Corporation); The Williams Companies, Inc.; Williams Pipe Line Company.
References: American National Bank of Ardmore; BancFirst; Citizens National Bank & Trust Company.

For full biographical listings, see the Martindale-Hubbell Law Directory

BLACKWELL, Kay Co.

JAMES R. RODGERS (AV)

105 North Main, P.O. Box 514, 74631
Telephone: 580-363-3684
Fax: 580-363-2434
URL: http://www.lawyers.com/rodgerslaw

William W. Rodgers (1907-1979)

For full biographical listings, see the Martindale-Hubbell Law Directory

*DUNCAN,** Stephens Co.

JOHN R. GREEN (AV)

1002 West Main Street, P.O. Box 700, 73534-0700
Telephone: 580-255-7400
Facsimile: 580-255-0800

Representative Clients: Oklahoma National Bank; Duncan Regional Hospital, Inc.; Red River Area Vocational-Technical School District; Wetzel Production Co.; Koch Gathering Systems.

For full biographical listings, see the Martindale-Hubbell Law Directory

LEACH, SULLIVAN, SULLIVAN & WATKINS (AV)

921 Main Street, P.O. Box 160, 73534
Telephone: 580-255-8260
Telecopier: 580-255-5587
URL: http://www.leachsullivan.com

MEMBERS OF FIRM
William O. Leach (1919-1990)
Paul D. Sullivan
Patrick D. Sullivan
Michael P. Sullivan
Kent P. Sullivan
Jay B. Watkins
Scott P. Sullivan

Representative Clients: Citizens' Bank, Velma, Oklahoma; Leffler Construction Co.; Jackson Ranches, Inc.; Jackson Cattle Corp.; Legacy Bank; BancFirst of Marlow; L.A. Edwards Trust; John E. Jackson Trust; Interstate Petroleum Corp.; PaceCo Financial Services, Inc.

For full biographical listings, see the Martindale-Hubbell Law Directory

*EL RENO,** Canadian Co.

HENRICKSEN & HENRICKSEN, INC. (AV)

210 North Choctaw, P.O. Box 1129, 73036-2647
Telephone: 405-262-0983
Fax: 405-262-2049
Oklahoma City, Oklahoma Office: 2224 North West 50th, Suite 265, 73112.
Telephone: 405-848-3977.

Mark Henricksen | Lanita Henricksen

For full biographical listings, see the Martindale-Hubbell Law Directory

*ENID,** Garfield Co.

MITCHELL & DECLERCK, P.L.L.C. (AV)

202 West Broadway, 73701-4018
Telephone: 580-234-5144
Facsimile: 580-234-8890
Satellite Office: 506 Second Street, Pond Creek, Oklahoma, 73766.
Telephone: 580-532-6514

P.C. Simons (1870-1962)
E. B. Mitchell (1895-1976)
Earl B. Mitchell, Jr.
Edward A. DeClerck
Larry D. Lahman
E. W. (Bill) Shaw
Tim E. DeClerck
Matthew Neill Davis

Counsel for: Cleo State Bank; Bank of Drummond; Bank of Garber, Garber, Okla.; Maryland Casualty Co.; Travelers Insurance Co.; Oklahoma Farmers Union Mutual Insurance Co.

For full biographical listings, see the Martindale-Hubbell Law Directory

*GUYMON,** Texas Co.

WRIGHT, DALE, JETT & CARTER (AV)

Dale Building, 114 East 4th Street, P.O. Box 591, 73942
Telephone: 580-338-6591
Fax: 580-338-8244

MEMBERS OF FIRM
F. Hiner Dale (1881-1969)
Vincent Dale (1912-1977)
Bryan L. Wright
Douglas Don Dale
A. Clark Jett
Peggy L. Carter

OF COUNSEL
Don Dale

For full biographical listings, see the Martindale-Hubbell Law Directory

*HUGO,** Choctaw Co.

RABON, WOLF & RABON (AV)

402 East Jackson, P.O. Box 726, 74743
Telephone: 580-326-6427
Fax: 580-326-6032
Email: rawol@1starnet.com

MEMBERS OF FIRM
Lon Kile (1914-1988)
Bob Rabon
J. Frank Wolf, III
Robert L. Rabon

Representative Clients: Lone Star Gas Co.; General Accident Group.
General Counsel for: Security First National Bank, Hugo; Choctaw Nation; Chickasaw Nation; Housing Authority of Choctaw Nation of Oklahoma; Hugo Municipal Authority; Hugo Airport Authority; Hugo Industrial Authority; Red River Farmers Cooperative.

For full biographical listings, see the Martindale-Hubbell Law Directory

*LAWTON,** Comanche Co.

GODLOVE, MAYHALL, DZIALO, DUTCHER & ERWIN, A PROFESSIONAL CORPORATION (AV)

802 "C" Avenue, P.O. Box 29, 73502
Telephone: 580-353-6700
Fax: 580-353-2900
Email: gmdde@sirinet.net

W. W. Godlove (1908-1982)
Ernest F. Godlove
Michael C. Mayhall
Edward W. Dzialo, Jr.
J. Blake Dutcher, Jr.
Shon T. Erwin

Representative Clients: Local Federal Bank; Lawton Teachers Federal Credit Union; Southwest Abstract Company; Comanche County Industrial Development Authority; EZ Go Foods, Inc.; Goodyear Tire & Rubber Company; H.G. Jenkins Construction, Inc.; Jan-L Construction, Inc.; Sears Roebuck and Co.

For full biographical listings, see the Martindale-Hubbell Law Directory

*MADILL,** Marshall Co.

LITTLE, LITTLE, LITTLE, WINDEL & COPPEDGE (AV)

Little Building, 202 West Lillie Boulevard, P.O. Box 618, 73446
Telephone: 580-795-3397
Telefax: 580-795-5072
Tishomingo, Oklahoma Office: 224 West Main Street.
Telephone: 580-371-3655.
Telefax: 580-371-9869

MEMBERS OF FIRM

Reuel W. Little (1901-1993)
Dan Little
Prudence Mae Little
Jerry Lynn Windel
Jack W. Coppedge, II (Resident, Tishomingo Office)

For full biographical listings, see the Martindale-Hubbell Law Directory

*MUSKOGEE,** Muskogee Co.

GAGE & WILLIAMS LAW FIRM (AV)

530 Court Street, P.O. Box 87, 74401
Telephone: 918-687-5424
Fax: 918-687-0761

MEMBERS OF FIRM

Edwin L. Gage
Betty Outhier Williams

Edith M. Gregory
Jonathan Heath Lofton

OF COUNSEL

Julian K. Fite

Representative Clients: Nationwide Insurance Co.; Oklahoma Municipal Assurance Group; Golden Rule Insurance Co.; Electronic Data Systems, Inc.; Trucks-For-You, Inc.; First National Bank and Trust Company, Muskogee.

For full biographical listings, see the Martindale-Hubbell Law Directory

WRIGHT, STOUT, FITE & WILBURN (AV)

300 West Broadway, Suite A, P.O. Box 707, 74402-0707
Telephone: 918-682-0091
Fax: 918-683-6340
Email: weldon@ok.azalea.net

MEMBERS OF FIRM

J. Ron Wright
Weldon W. Stout
C. Bart Fite
Paula A. Ranallo Wilburn

Counsel for: Boatmen's National Bank of Oklahoma, Muskogee; Ft. Howard Paper Co.; Arkhola Sand & Gravel Co.; Equity Mutual Insurance Co.; Home Insurance Co.; United Services Auto Assn.; Equitable Life & Casualty; Universal Underwriters Insurance Co; Oklahoma Turnpike Authority; Oklahoma Department of Transportation.

For full biographical listings, see the Martindale-Hubbell Law Directory

*NORMAN,** Cleveland Co.

CROWE & DUNLEVY (AV)

A Professional Corporation
2500 South McGee, Suite 140, 73072-6705
Telephone: 405-321-7317
Fax: 405-360-4002
Email: marketing@crowedunlevy.com *URL:* http://www.crowedunlevy.com
Oklahoma City, Oklahoma Office: Crowe & Dunlevy, A Professional Corporation, 1800 Mid-America Tower, 20 North Broadway, 73102-8273.
Telephone: 405-235-7700.
Fax: 405-239-6651.
Tulsa, Oklahoma Office: Crowe & Dunlevy, A Professional Corporation, 500 Kennedy Building, 321 South Boston Avenue, 74103-3313.
Telephone: 918-592-9800.
Fax: 918-592-9801.

(See Next Column)

Robert L. Pendarvis
Gary C. Rawlinson
Mary Robertson

Christopher R. Graves

For full biographical listings, see the Martindale-Hubbell Law Directory

*OKLAHOMA CITY,** Oklahoma Co.

ANDREWS DAVIS LEGG BIXLER MILSTEN & PRICE, A PROFESSIONAL CORPORATION (AV)

500 West Main, Suite 500, 73102
Telephone: 405-272-9241
FAX: 405-235-8786
Email: andrewsdavis@andrewsdavis.com *URL:* http://www.andrewsdavis.com

L. Karlton Mosteller (1895-1966)
J. Edward Barth
C. Temple Bixler
John J. Breathwit
Charles C. Callaway, Jr.
Gary S. Chilton
James F. Davis
Timothy D. DeGiusti
Alan C. Durbin
John F. Fischer, II
Lloyd T. Hardin, Jr.
Sally A. Hasenfratz
John D. Hastie
Don G. Holladay
Richard B. Kells, Jr.
Timothy M. Larason
Kieran D. Maye, Jr.
Mark H. Price
D. Joe Rockett
Shelia Darling Tims
R. Brown Wallace
William H. Whitehill, Jr.
Elizabeth Brown
Craig L. Cline
Heidi J. Long
N. Janine Wheeler
Anne E. Zachritz

OF COUNSEL

John C. Andrews
Keith T. Childers
Carolyn Gregg Hill
Lynn O. Holloman
William J. Legg
Robert B. Milsten
Stephen J. Moriarty
Leroy J. Patton
James C. Peck
John P. Roberts
William D. Watts

Representative Clients: Browning-Ferris Industries, Inc.; Marathon Oil Co.; Oklahoma Dental Assn.; Oklahoma State Medical Assn.; Smith Cogeneration, Inc.; Torchmark Development Corp.

For full biographical listings, see the Martindale-Hubbell Law Directory

CONNER & WINTERS, A PROFESSIONAL CORPORATION (AV)

One Leadership Square, 211 North Robinson, Suite 1700, 73102-7101
Telephone: 405-272-5711
Facsimile: 405-232-2695
Email: postmaster@cwlaw.com
Tulsa, Oklahoma Office: 3700 First Place Tower, 15 East 5th Street, 74103-4344.
Telephone: 918-586-5711.
Facsimile: 918-586-8982.
Fayetteville, Arkansas Office: Conner & Winters, P.L.L.C., 100 West Center Street, Suite 200, 72701-6081.
Telephone: 501-582-5711.
Facsimile: 501-587-1426.
Washington, D.C. Office: 1050 Seventeenth Street, N.W., Suite 810, 20036-5503.
Telephone: 202-783-5711.
Facsimile: 202-783-5720.

Peter B. Bradford
Raymond E. Tompkins
Irwin H. Steinhorn
John W. Funk
Kiran A. Phansalkar
Timothy J. Bomhoff
Mitchell D. Blackburn
P. Blake Allen
Mark H. Bennett

L. Don Smitherman
Laura L. McCasland
Cecily H. Murray

OF COUNSEL

S. Paul Hammons

OFFICE PERSONNEL
TULSA, OKLAHOMA

John E. Barry
Henry G. Will
Joseph J. McCain, Jr.
Lynnwood R. Moore, Jr.
Robert A. Curry
Steven W. McGrath
John T. Schmidt
D. Richard Funk
Randolph L. Jones, Jr.
P. David Newsome, Jr.
J. Ronald Petrikin
Larry B. Lipe
James E. Green, Jr.
Martin R. Wing
John W. Ingraham
Andrew R. Turner
Douglas M. Rather
Gentra Abbey Sorem
R. Kevin Redwine
Deirdre O'Neil E. Dexter
Tony W. Haynie
Bruce W. Freeman
David R. Cordell
Paul E. Braden
Robert J. Melgaard
R. Mark Solano
C. Raymond Patton, Jr.
P. Scott Hathaway
John A. Bugg
Lawrence A. Hall

(See Next Column)

CONNER & WINTERS A PROFESSIONAL CORPORATION—*Continued*

OFFICE PERSONNEL
TULSA, OKLAHOMA (Continued)

Timothy T. Trump
Mark E. Dreyer
Nancy E. Vaughn
Gregory D. Renberg
John M. Matheson

Katherine Gallagher Coyle
Anne B. Sublett
Rebecca Sellers Woodward
Beverly K. Smith
Melodie Freeman-Burney
Jacalyn W. Peter
M. Sean Radcliffe
Robert D. James
David H. Herrold
Fern Holland
Elizabeth K. Giddens
Jonathan M. Cinocca
Randie Thompson

OF COUNSEL

Charles C. Killin
James R. Ryan
Russell H. Harbaugh, Jr.
Debbie L. Blackwell
David O. Cordell

RETIRED SHAREHOLDERS

Robert L. McGowen
John S. Athens

OFFICE PERSONNEL
FAYETTEVILLE, ARKANSAS

John R. Elrod
Greg S. Scharlau
Ruth Ann Wisener

Burton E. Stacy, Jr.
Terri Dill Chadick
Vicki S. Bronson

OF COUNSEL

D. Randy Laney
Charles E. Scharlau, Jr.

OFFICE PERSONNEL
WASHINGTON, D.C.

G. Daniel Miller
Carol V. Calhoun

Erica L. Summers

OF COUNSEL

Henry Rose

For full biographical listings, see the Martindale-Hubbell Law Directory

CROWE & DUNLEVY, A PROFESSIONAL CORPORATION (AV)

1800 Mid-America Tower, 20 North Broadway, 73102-8273
Telephone: 405-235-7700
Fax: 405-239-6651
Email: marketing@crowedunlevy.com *URL:* http://www.crowedunlevy.com
Tulsa, Oklahoma Office: 500 Kennedy Building, 321 South Boston Avenue, 74103-3313.
Telephone: 918-592-9800.
Fax: 918-592-9801.
Norman, Oklahoma Office: Crowe & Dunlevy, 2500 South McGee, Suite 140, 73072-6705.
Telephone: 405-321-7317.
Fax: 405-360-4002.

V. P. Crowe (1897-1974)
Fred W. Dunlevy (1914-1994)
L. E. Stringer
Gary W. Davis
Henry Rheinberger
Andrew M. Coats
Allen D. Evans
D. Kent Meyers
Preston G. Gaddis II
Clyde A. Muchmore
Robert M. Johnson
William G. Paul
Arlen E. Fielden
J. Lawrence Blankenship
James F. Hartmann, Jr.
Harry A. Woods, Jr.
Jimmy Goodman
Earl A. Skarky
James H. Holloman, Jr.
Bill D. McCarthy
Richard C. Ford
John J. Griffin, Jr.
Brooke Smith Murphy
Michael M. Stewart
Leonard Court
Cynda C. Ottaway
Judy Hamilton Morse
Kenni B. Merritt
Kelley C. Callahan
Mark D. Christiansen
Michael S. Laird
Mack J. Morgan III
Anton J. Rupert
Karen S. Rieger
Daniel S. Hodgins
Harvey D. Ellis, Jr.
Gayle L. Barrett
L. Mark Walker
Stephen L. DeGiusti
Mark S. Grossman
Kevin D. Gordon
Reeder E. Ratliff
Todd Taylor
Roger A. Stong
Robin D. Jenson
Robert G. McCampbell
LeAnne Burnett
Paul D. Trimble
Timila S. Rother
Timothy E. Foley
Tamela R. Hughlett
Joseph J. Ferretti
Dana M. Tacker

Rustin J. Strubhar
Phillip L. Free, Jr.
Randall K. McCarthy
Mary Hirth Tolbert
Cynthia L. Andrews
C. Robert Stell
Cori Hook Loomis
William H. Hoch
Jeremy Tubb
J. Robert Kalsu
William L. Teague
Eric S. Fisher
Jill F. Padgett
Paige S. Bass

(See Next Column)

Lance W. Cargill
Lynne Faith Saunders
Brian C. Henderson
John M. Thompson
Radha Masilamani
Anthony D. Gould
(Not admitted in OK)
Gregory S. Luster
Courtney K. Warmington

OF COUNSEL

Bruce H. Johnson
Lawrence E. Walsh
Val R. Miller
James C. Gibbens
James A. Peabody
James W. George
Florine G. Crockett
Robert A. Reece
Terry R. Hanna
Ruth Gana Okediji
(Not admitted in OK)

For full biographical listings, see the Martindale-Hubbell Law Directory

DAY, EDWARDS, FEDERMAN, PROPESTER & CHRISTENSEN, P.C. (AV)

Suite 2900 Oklahoma Tower, 210 Park Avenue, 73102-5605
Telephone: 405-239-2121
Telecopier: 405-236-1012
URL: http://lawlinks.com/attys/ok/defpc.html

Bruce W. Day
William B. Federman
D. Wade Christensen
Kent A. Gilliland
Joe E. Edwards
Richard P. Propester
J. Clay Christensen
Rodney J. Heggy
Jeanette Cook Timmons

Ricki Valerie Sonders
Joel Warren Harmon
Stuart W. Emmons
Bill Powell Guest
Edgar G. McQueen, Jr.
Thomas Pitchlynn Howell, IV
Kenneth A. Brokaw
Nick C. Linholm
Lawn B. Gardner
Gary L. Farnum

OF COUNSEL

Robert S. Baker
Herbert F. (Jack) Hewett

Representative Clients: AIG Aviation, Inc.; Applied Thermal Systems, Inc.; Associates in Occupational Medicine, Inc.; Attorney General of the State of Oklahoma; Attorney General of the State of Texas; Aztec Specialty Co., Inc.; Aztec Rig Equipment Company; Banc One Mortgage Corporation; BancFirst Corporation; Bank One, Oklahoma City.

For full biographical listings, see the Martindale-Hubbell Law Directory

FELLERS, SNIDER, BLANKENSHIP, BAILEY & TIPPENS, A PROFESSIONAL CORPORATION (AV)

Bank One Tower, 100 North Broadway, Suite 1700, 73102-8820
Telephone: 405-232-0621
Fax: 405-232-9659
URL: http://www.fellerssnider.com
Tulsa, Oklahoma Office: The Kennedy Building, 321 South Boston, Suite 800.
Telephone: 918-599-0621.
Fax: 918-583-9659.

James D. Fellers (1913-1997)
John Joseph Snider (1928-1997)
Burck Bailey
Terry W. Tippens
K. Nicholas Wilson
Harry H. Selph, II
Warren F. Bickford, IV
John B. Heatly
Michael R. Ford
Eric S. Eissenstat
Stephen R. Stephens
Doneen Douglas Jones
Thomas J. Enis
Barbara G. Bowersox
Joe C. Lewallen, Jr.
Dino E. Viera
Gregory A. Castro
Kevin R. Donelson
Mark K. Stonecipher
Andrew L. Walding
Todd A. Nelson
Tracy A. Poole
Bryan N.B. King
Brent M. Johnson
Amy E. Moore
Sanford C. Coats
Margaret A. Bomhoff

OF COUNSEL

Jap W. Blankenship
Paul W. Dudman

Representative Clients: General Electric Capital Corp.; Halliburton Co.; Hertz Corp.; Chrysler Financial Corp.; Service Corporation Intl.; United Parcel Service; NationsBank; Oklahoma Gas & Electric Corp.; Wexford Capital, LLC.

For full biographical listings, see the Martindale-Hubbell Law Directory

HARTZOG CONGER & CASON, A PROFESSIONAL CORPORATION (AV)

1600 Bank of Oklahoma Plaza 201 Robert S. Kerr, 73102
Telephone: 405-235-7000
Facsimile: 405-235-7329

Larry D. Hartzog
J. William Conger
Len Cason
James C. Prince
Steven C. Davis
Joseph P. Hogsett
John D. Robertson
Kurt M. Rupert
Laura Haag McConnell
Linda G. Scoggins
Susan B. Shields
Ryan S. Wilson

(See Next Column)

HARTZOG CONGER & CASON A PROFESSIONAL CORPORATION, *Oklahoma City—Continued*

Amy J. Sine
Jon H. Trudgeon
Charles E. Geister, III
Phillip G. Whaley
Armand Paliotta

J. Christian Guzzy
Stacey D. Spivey
Melissa Beeson Heindselman
Christin V. Adkins
Byron K. Linkous

OF COUNSEL

Kent F. Frates
Kenneth R. Davis
Alan Newman

For full biographical listings, see the Martindale-Hubbell Law Directory

KERR, IRVINE, RHODES & ABLES, A PROFESSIONAL CORPORATION (AV)

201 Robert S. Kerr Avenue, Suite 600, 73102-4267
Telephone: 405-272-9221
Fax: 405-236-3121
Email: kira201@aol.com

Robert S. Kerr, Jr.
Horace G. Rhodes
J. Angela Ables
James W. Rhodes
James R. Barnett
R. Thomas Lay
Kevin R. Wisner

OF COUNSEL

Henry B. Taliaferro, Jr.

Representative Clients: Bethany-Warr Acres; Public Works Authority; City of Crescent; Fort James Corp.

For full biographical listings, see the Martindale-Hubbell Law Directory

LOONEY, NICHOLS & JOHNSON, PLLC (AV)

528 Northwest 12th, 73103
Telephone: 405-235-7641
Fax: 405-239-2050; 239-2052
Email: firm@lnjlaw.com

Ned Looney (1886-1965)
Clyde J. Watts (1907-1975)
Willard R. Bergstrasser (1922-1993)
Robert Dudley Looney
Henry W. Nichols
Burton J. Johnson
Edwin F. Garrison
Robert D. Looney, Jr.
Tenal S. Cooley, III
Timothy L. Martin
Brigid F. Kennedy
H. Grady Parker, Jr.

Bradley K. Donnell
Christian S. Huckaby
James Leo Gaston, Jr.
Shawn E. Harrell

Representative Clients: U.S. Aviation Insurance Underwriters; CNA Insurance Co.; The Goodyear Tire & Rubber Co.; Home Insurance Co.; MEDMARC; The Maryland Insurance Group; Travelers Property & Casualty Co.; Jefferson Insurance Group; Michelin North America, Inc.; TIG Insurance Co.

For full biographical listings, see the Martindale-Hubbell Law Directory

MCAFEE & TAFT, A PROFESSIONAL CORPORATION (AV)

Tenth Floor, Two Leadership Square, 73102
Telephone: 405-235-9621
Facsimile: (405) 235-0439 (405) 232-2404
Email: mcafee@ionet.net *URL:* http://www.mcafee-taft.com

Kenneth E. McAfee (1903-1986)
Joseph G. Rucks (1913-1988)
Reford Bond (1930-1989)
Stewart W. Mark (1915-1993)
Judson S. Woodruff (1925-1997)
Sheryl N. Barr
Terry R. Barrett
Joseph H. Bocock
Steven W. Bugg
Mark E. Burget
Gary W. Catron
Steven P. Cole
W. Chris Coleman
C. Bruce Crum
Stanley L. Cunningham
Robert W. Dace
C. Clark Dougherty, Jr.
Clifford Clark Dougherty, III
Theodore M. Elam
Sam R. Fulkerson
Gary F. Fuller
Robert L. Garbrecht
E. Harry Gilbert, III
Robert H. Gilliland, Jr.
Lenore Templeton Graham
Philip D. Hart
John N. Hermes
Frank D. Hill
Henry D. Hoss
Laurence M. Huffman
James Dudley Hyde
Michael E. Joseph
John A. Kenney
David J. Ketelsleger
Myrna Schack Latham
Michael F. Lauderdale
Steven T. Ledgerwood
John M. Mee
Sally Mock
John R. Morris
Mark Richard Mullins
Richard D. Nix
John Michael Nordin
John A. Papahronis
Gary C. Pierson
Ross A. Plourde
Frank L. Polk
Louis J. Price
Tony G. Puckett
Anthony L. Rahhal

(See Next Column)

Dee A. Replogle, Jr.
Richard A. Riggs
Reid E. Robison
John E. Sargent, Jr.
John N. Schaefer
Scott W. Sewell
James W. Sharrock
Mark D. Spencer
Joel D. Stafford
C. David Stinson
Elizabeth Dalton Tyrrell
Peter T. Van Dyke
Erin M. Van Laanen
Joseph Walters
Jerry A. Warren
Drew D. Webb
Steven R. Welch
Elizabeth Scott Wood

M. Craig Adkins
T. Michael Blake
Scott A. Briggs
Jennifer H. Callahan
Kymala B. Carrier
Teena P. Dunn
Gregg B. Eichner
Alan G. Holloway
Michael J. LaBrie
Suzanne Mitchell
Jean L. Pinkston
Robert R. Redwine
Stacy L. Smith
John D. Stiner
Kathy Reilly Teel
Jeff L. Todd
Cody L. Towns
Timothy G. Verrall
James R. Webb
Nathan L. Whatley
Jennifer Wheeler

OF COUNSEL

Richard G. Taft
Wendell Ray Guffey (Not admitted in OK)
Neal R. Kennedy
James C. McMillin
John L. Williford

Representative Clients: Bank of Oklahoma, N.A.; Fleming Companies, Inc.; Paine Webber Group, Inc.; Arthur Andersen & Co.; Exxon Corp.; St. Paul Fire & Marine Insurance Co.; Columbia/HCA Healthcare Corp.

For full biographical listings, see the Martindale-Hubbell Law Directory

MONNET, HAYES, BULLIS, THOMPSON & EDWARDS (AV)

Suite 1719 First National Center West, 120 North Robinson, 73102
Telephone: 405-232-5481
Fax: 405-235-9159
Email: MHBullis@AOL.COM

MEMBERS OF FIRM

Claude Monnet (1899-1980)
Lynn J. Bullis, Jr. (1910-1984)
Coleman H. Hayes (1903-1985)
Russell F. Thompson (1920-1985)
John T. Edwards
James M. Peters
James S. Drennan
Randall A. Breshears
Sarah H. Stuhr
Gayle Freeman Cook
Robert C. Smith, Jr.
Steven K. McKinney
Shannon L. Edwards

Christopher James Perry
Michael S. Peters
Phillip A. Dickey
Robert A. French

Representative Clients: Travelers Insurance Co.; Chevron USA, Inc.; Oryx Energy; Toys R Us; Firemen's Fund Insurance Co.; United American Insurance; Globe Life & Accident Insurance Company; Apache Corporation; Chase Manhattan Bank; OXY USA, Inc.

For full biographical listings, see the Martindale-Hubbell Law Directory

PHILLIPS MCFALL MCCAFFREY MCVAY & MURRAH, P.C. (AV)

One Leadership Square, 12th Floor, 211 North Robinson, 73102
Telephone: 405-235-4100
Fax: 405-235-4133
URL: http://www.PhillipsMcFall.com
Other Oklahoma City Office: 1001 N.W. 63rd Street, Suite 200, 73116.
Telephone: 405-840-5240;
Fax: 405-840-2136.
Norman, Oklahoma Office: 232 E. Main, Suite B.
Telephone: 405-364-3346.
Fax: 405-364-4666.

T. Ray Phillips, III
D. Keith McFall
James A. McCaffrey
Melvin R. McVay, Jr.
Robert N. Sheets
J. Mark Lovelace
Terry L. Hawkins
Douglas A. Branch
Thomas G. Wolfe
Joseph K. Heselton, Jr.
Sandra Leah Schovanec
Elizabeth Kemp Brown
Ray E. Zschiesche
Marc Edwards
Robert O. O'Bannon

A. V. Peoples, III
Heather L. Hintz
James W. Bruce, III
B. Kay Carel
Lyndon W. Whitmire
Ellen K. Spiropoulos
Beverly I. Vilardofsky
Thomas P. Manning
Dionna D. Deardorff

OF COUNSEL

Alfred P. Murrah, Jr.
D. Craig Story
Donald A. Pape
Bill Price
Robert D. Allen
E. Carole Barnes
Fred A. Leibrock

Representative Clients: AT&T Communications of Southwest, Inc.; American Home Products Corp.; Chrysler Corporation; Employers Reinsurance Corp.; Federal Employees Credit Union; General Electric Capital Corp.; Local

(See Next Column)

CROWE & DUNLEVY A PROFESSIONAL CORPORATION—*Continued*

Nancy Lynn Roberts
Brad R. Carson
R. Michael Cole
Terry J. Tarwater
Sarah C. Hartmeyer
Gerald L. Jackson
Timothy F. Sterling
Elizabeth Moseley Guse
Alexander F. King
David G. Harris
J. Ryan Sacra
Jennifer A. Golm
Kayci Bair Hughes

For full biographical listings, see the Martindale-Hubbell Law Directory

CRUMP, TOLSON & PAGE LLP (AV)

1516 South Boston Avenue, Suite 310, 74119-4019
Telephone: 918-583-2393
Fax: 918-583-2394
Email: kcrump@crumptolson.com *URL:* http://www.lawyers.com/crumplaw

MEMBERS OF FIRM

Kenneth E. Crump Jr.
Michael B. Tolson
David P. Page (Resident)

ASSOCIATE

Rodney H. Dusinberre

For full biographical listings, see the Martindale-Hubbell Law Directory

DOERNER, SAUNDERS, DANIEL & ANDERSON, L.L.P. (AV)

Suite 500, 320 South Boston Avenue, 74103-3725
Telephone: 918-582-1211
Fax: 918-591-5360
URL: http://www.dsda.com
Oklahoma City, Oklahoma Office: One Leadership Square, Suite 501.
Telephone: 405-319-3500.
Fax: 405-319-3509. URL: http://www.dsda.com.

MEMBERS OF FIRM

Erwin J. Doerner (1897-1980)
Samuel P. Daniel
William C. Anderson
Varley H. Taylor, Jr.
G. Michael Lewis
Lawrence T. Chambers, Jr.
Dallas E. Ferguson
Sam G. Bratton II
Gary M. McDonald
H. Wayne Cooper
Kevin C. Coutant
Richard P. Hix
Lynn Paul Mattson
William F. Riggs
Lewis N. Carter
Linda C. Martin
James Patrick McCann
Richard H. Foster
Charles S. Plumb
Leonard I. Pataki
S. Douglas Dodd
Elise Dunitz Brennan
Jon E. Brightmire
Tom Q. Ferguson
Richard J. Eagleton
Rebecca McCarthy Fowler
Kristen L. Brightmire
Michael C. Redman
Steven K. Metcalf

ASSOCIATES

Shelly L. Dalrymple
Russell W. Kroll
Robert A. Burk
Ronald W. Little
James C. Milton
Harry V. Rouse
Amy L. Osborn
Audra K. Hamilton
Angela M. Knight
James J. Robertson
R. Charles Wilkin

OF COUNSEL

Dickson M. Saunders
William B. Morgan
Kathy R. Neal

ATTORNEYS IN OKLAHOMA CITY, OKLAHOMA

Jacque Brawner Lindsay

Gregory Frogge

Representative Clients: Public Service Company of Oklahoma; Oklahoma Ordnance Works Authority; St. John Medical Center, Inc.

For full biographical listings, see the Martindale-Hubbell Law Directory

FELLERS, SNIDER, BLANKENSHIP, BAILEY & TIPPENS, A PROFESSIONAL CORPORATION (AV)

The Kennedy Building, 321 South Boston, Suite 800, 74103-3318
Telephone: 918-599-0621
Fax: 918-583-9659
URL: http://www.fellerssnider.com
Oklahoma City, Oklahoma Office: Bank One Tower, 100 North Broadway, Suite, 1700.
Telephone: 405-232-0621.
Fax: 405-232-9659.

Roy C. Breedlove
Dennis D. Brown
R. Alan Weeks
R. Daniel Scroggins

(See Next Column)

Terry L. Watt
Scott R. Zingerman

Representative Clients: Bayliner Marine Corporation; Brunswick Corporation; Chalmers-Thornton Companies; Conine Enterprises; Cunningham Lindsey Claims Management; Igloo Corporation; Oklahoma State University; Tyson Foods, Inc.; The Williams Companies; Zebco Corporation.

For full biographical listings, see the Martindale-Hubbell Law Directory

HALL, ESTILL, HARDWICK, GABLE, GOLDEN & NELSON, A PROFESSIONAL CORPORATION (AV)

320 South Boston Avenue, Suite 400, 74103
Telephone: 918-594-0400
Facsimile: 918-594-0505
Email: attorney_name@HallEstill.Com *URL:* http://www.HallEstill.Com
Oklahoma City Office: Bank One Center, Suite 2900, 100 North Broadway, 73102-8805.
Telephone: 405-553-2828.
Facsimile: 405-553-2855.
Washington, D.C. Office: Suite 750, South Building, 1120 20th Street N.W. 20036-3406.
Telephone: 202-822-9100.
Facsimile: 202-293-6492.
Fayetteville, Arkansas Office: One East Center Street, Suite 315, 72701.
Telephone: 501-973-5200.
Facsimile: 501-973-0520.

Walter B. Hall (1923-1986)
Fred S. Nelson (1928-1987)
James C. T. Hardwick
Thomas D. Gable
Thomas F. Golden
Larry W. Sandel
Andrew M. Wolov
Frank M. Hagedorn
J. Patrick Cremin
J. Kevin Hayes
Michael D. Graves
James D. Satrom
Richard A. Groenendyke, Jr.
Graydon D. Luthey, Jr.
Del L. Gustafson
Mark K. Blongewicz
Michael D. Cooke
Kenneth L. Hunt
B. Kenneth Cox, Jr.
Donald L. Kahl
Gerald B. Davenport
D. Kenyon Williams, Jr.
Thomas P. Schroedter
James J. Proszek
James M. Reed
Thomas A. Creekmore, III
Stephen W. Ray (Member, Board of Directors)
Margaret A. Swimmer
Michael T. Keester
Susan L. Gates
Ronald O. Ray, Jr.
Kenneth G. M. Mather
Ronald A. White
Fred M. Buxton
Steven A. Broussard
Steven W. Soulé
Michael L. Nemec
Joseph D. Fincher
R. Mark Petrich
Pamela H. Goldberg
Mark Banner
Robert S. Rizley
Leslie C. Rinn
Robert F. Dougherty
Sarah Jane McKinney
T. Lane Wilson
Heather E. Brown
Betsy Grabel Jackson
Bruce A. Fowler
Marshall J. Wells
William D. Fisher
Heather L. Drake
Heather R. Case
Kyle F. Freeman
T. Gene Monroe II

OF COUNSEL

John S. Estill, Jr.
Raymond B. Kelly
Graydon D. Luthey
Ross O. Swimmer
William W. Pritchard
Jane La Gree Allingham
William J. Sears

OKLAHOMA CITY, OKLAHOMA OFFICE PERSONNEL

H. B. Watson, Jr.
Robert D. Nelon
J. Fred Gist
Donna N. Blakley
Rodney C. Ramsey
Cheryl Plaxico Hunter
Sharon T. Thomas
Daniel J. Glover
Jon A. Epstein
Elaine R. Turner
Janis W. Preslar
Lorinda G. Holloway
Richard D. Olderbak
Kelly R. Becton

OF COUNSEL

Robert D. McCutcheon
Mary Johnson Tidholm

WASHINGTON, D.C. OFFICE PERSONNEL

John B. Rudolph
Joseph R. Membrino, Jr.
Donald R. Dinan
James B. Wilcox, Jr.
Judith A. Taylor
John J. Callahan
Christopher M. Heywood

NORTHWEST ARKANSAS OFFICE PERSONNEL

William E. Bishop
James N. McCord
James L. Harris

Reference: Bank of Oklahoma.

For full biographical listings, see the Martindale-Hubbell Law Directory

Tulsa—Continued

HOLLIMAN LANGHOLZ RUNNELS FORSMAN & SELLERS, A PROFESSIONAL CORPORATION (AV)

Ten East Third Street, Suite 500, 74103-3695
Telephone: 918-584-1471
Fax: 918-587-9652,
Telex: 251773 GRC UR
Email: lawfirm@tulsaokla.com

Robert W. Langholz
Gail R. Runnels
Michael S. Forsman
Keith F. Sellers
James D. Bryant

OF COUNSEL

Joe M. Holliman

Representative Clients: The F & M Bank and Trust Company, Tulsa, Ok.; Transportation Leasing Co., Inc.; Kaiser-Francis Oil Co.

For full biographical listings, see the Martindale-Hubbell Law Directory

JONES, GIVENS, GOTCHER & BOGAN, A PROFESSIONAL CORPORATION (AV)

3800 First National Tower, 74103
Telephone: 918-581-8200
Fax: 918-583-1189 or 918-583-6652
URL: http://www.jonesgivens.com

Neil E. Bogan (1945-1990)
William B. Jones
Jack R. Givens
James E. Weger
Thomas L. Vogt
Jack L. Brown
William G. LaSorsa
C. Michael Copeland
Joseph H. Paulk
Marylinn M. Gravis

Robert R. Peters II
Catherine Parker Bollinger
Paul H. Burgess
Thomas H. Dobbs

OF COUNSEL

Deryl Lee Gotcher
Blake R. Givens

Representative Clients: Local America Bank of Tulsa; Tulsa National Bank; BancOklahoma Mortgage Corporation; Kansas City Life Insurance Company; Liberty Mortgage Company; Liberty National Bank. Professional Services: KPMG, Peat Marwick; Williams Bros. Engineering.

For full biographical listings, see the Martindale-Hubbell Law Directory

RONALD MAIN, P.C. (AV)

Center 2800, Suite 821, 2815 East Skelly Drive, 74105-6251
Telephone: 918-742-1990
Fax: 918-742-2004
Email: rmainbtl@aol.com

Ronald Main

Representative Clients: Brumbaugh & Fulton, Co.; Miles Shipping Co.; H.S. Boyd, Co.; Kemco Fuels, Inc.; McDonnell-Douglas Corp.; Oklahoma Bar Professional Liability Insurance Co.; Sawyer Manufacturing Co.
References: Bank of Oklahoma, N.A.; Tulsa National Bank.

For full biographical listings, see the Martindale-Hubbell Law Directory

MOYERS, MARTIN, SANTEE, IMEL & TETRICK (AV)

Formerly Moyers, Martin, Conway, Santee & Imel
Suite 920, 320 South Boston Building, 74103
Telephone: 918-582-5281
Fax: 918-585-8318
Email: MOYERS@IONET.NET
Bixby, Oklahoma Office: 113 West Dawes, Suite 100, 74408.
Telephone: 918-366-3935.
Fax: 918-366-3936.

MEMBERS OF FIRM

Villard Martin (1889-1965)
Garrett Logan (1901-1975)
Donald P. Moyers (1907-1995)
Jack H. Santee
John M. Imel
Charles B. Tetrick
Ronald G. Raynolds
Steven A. Stecher
James H. Ferris
Robert Scott Savage
D. Stanley Tacker
Patrick D. O'Connor
John E. Rooney, Jr.
Terry M. Kollmorgen
John W. Cannon
James E. Maupin

ASSOCIATES

J. Christopher Darden
Kurston P. McMurray

OF COUNSEL

Villard Martin, Jr.
J. Duff Weddle

For full biographical listings, see the Martindale-Hubbell Law Directory

PRAY, WALKER, JACKMAN, WILLIAMSON & MARLAR, A PROFESSIONAL CORPORATION (AV)

900 ONEOK Plaza, 100 West 5th Street, 74103-4218
Telephone: 918-581-5500
Fax: 918-581-5599
Oklahoma City, Oklahoma Office: One Leadership Square, 211 North Robinson.
Telephone: 405-236-8911.
Fax: 405-236-0011.

J. Warren Jackman
W. Bland Williamson, Jr.
Donald F. Marlar
William D. Toney
Terry R. Doverspike
John F. McCormick, Jr.
Frank D. Spiegelberg
Ira L. Edwards, Jr.
John L. Randolph, Jr.
William L. Eagleton, IV
Donald S. Smith
Randall G. Vaughan
Charles Bretton Crane
Rita J. Gassaway
Kevin Pierce Doyle
Thomas M. Askew
Robert J. Winter
Steven B. Butterfield
Pamela D. Langston
Ryan G. Cole
Harry A. Parrish
David C. Cameron

OF COUNSEL

Donald E. Pray
Floyd L. Walker
Charles A. Kothe
C. Bruce Jones

OKLAHOMA CITY OFFICE

Henry A. Meyer, III
Wm. Gregory James
Gary Peterson
Georgiana T. Peterson
Gregory J. Crawford
Steven J. Goetzinger (Resident, Oklahoma City Office)

For full biographical listings, see the Martindale-Hubbell Law Directory

*WOODWARD,** Woodward Co.

HODGDEN, HALLREN, SMITHTON & HODGDEN, P.L.L.C. (AV)

1002 Ninth Street, P.O. Box 529, 73802
Telephone: 580-256-5517
Fax: 580-256-8459
Email: hhhlaw@nwoknet.net

Bryce Hodgden
Kathleen Lies Hallren
W. Shane Smithton
Cody B. Hodgden

Approved Examining Attorneys for: Chicago Title Co.; Lawyers Title Insurance Co.; American First Title & Trust Co.; Farmers Home Administration.
Attorneys for: First American Bank; John Hancock Mutual Life Insurance Co.
References: Central National Bank of Alva; Stock Exchange Bank; First American Bank, Woodward, Okla.

For full biographical listings, see the Martindale-Hubbell Law Directory

OREGON

*BEND,** Deschutes Co.

BRYANT, LOVLIEN & JARVIS, P.C. (AV)

40 N.W. Greenwood, P.O. Box 1151, 97709-1151
Telephone: 541-382-4331
Fax: 541-389-3386
Email: bljadmin@bryantlovlienjarvis.com *URL:* http://www.bryantlovlienjarvis.com

Neil R. Bryant
Robert S. Lovlien
Lynn F. Jarvis
John A. Berge
Sharon R. Smith
Lisa N. Bertalan

John D. Sorlie
Mark Gregory Reinecke
Melissa P. Lande
Kitri C. Ford

Representative Clients: Arnold Irrigation District; Robberson Ford Sales; Deschutes County Intermediate Education District; Bend-LaPine School District; Bend River Mall; State Farm Insurance Co.; Jack Robinson & Son Construction.

For full biographical listings, see the Martindale-Hubbell Law Directory

HURLEY, LYNCH & RE, P.C. (AV)

747 S.W. Industrial Way, 97702
Telephone: 541-317-5505
Fax: 541-317-5507

James V. Hurley
Gregory P. Lynch
Daniel C. Re
Kevin J. Keillor
Bryan W. Gruetter

Stanley D. Austin
Christopher D. Hatfield
Kelly L. McDole
Milly Whatley
Troy J. Wood

(See Next Column)

HURLEY, LYNCH & RE P.C.—*Continued*

Representative Clients: Eagle Crest Resort; Sunriver Resort; Jeld-Wen, Inc.; AmeriTitle Co.; Bend Research; Deschutes County; Consep, Inc.; Fuqua Homes, Inc.; Scottsdale Insurance; David Evans and Associates.

For full biographical listings, see the Martindale-Hubbell Law Directory

*EUGENE,** Lane Co.

ARNOLD GALLAGHER SAYDACK PERCELL & ROBERTS, P.C. (AV)

800 Willamette Street, Suite 800, P.O. Box 1758, 97440-1758
Telephone: 541-484-0188
Fax: 541-484-0536
Email: admin@agspr.com *URL:* http://www.lawyers.com/arnoldgallagher

John B. Arnold
Donald A. Gallagher, Jr.
Roger M. Saydack
Dennis W. Percell
Rohn M. Roberts
Bradley S. Copeland
Lisa A. Maybee

Bryon L. Land
Rachel A. Kirtner
Joseph G. Schwarte
William E. Flinn
Connie L. Speck

OF COUNSEL

Steven C. Alberty

Reference: Union Bank of California.

For full biographical listings, see the Martindale-Hubbell Law Directory

CALKINS & CALKINS (AV)

1163 Olive Street, 97401
Telephone: 541-345-0371
FAX: 541-342-1220

MEMBERS OF FIRM

Windsor Calkins (1910-1989)
S. M. Calkins (1872-1969)
W. W. Calkins (1860-1945)
Win Calkins
Judy Ann Calkins

Josephine H. Mooney
Eric S. DeFreest

Counsel for: Eugene Water & Electric Board; Sacred Heart Medical Center; Lane County Medical Society; Oregon Automobile Insurance Co.; North Pacific Insurance Co.; St. Paul Insurance Cos.; American States Insurance Co.; Northwest Physicians Mutual Insurance Co.; General Accident Insurance Co.; Farmers Insurance Group.

For full biographical listings, see the Martindale-Hubbell Law Directory

GLEAVES SWEARINGEN LARSEN POTTER SCOTT & SMITH LLP (AV)

8th Floor, 975 Oak Street, 97401
Telephone: 541-686-8833
Fax: 541-345-2034
Email: info@orbuslaw.com *URL:* http://www.orbuslaw.com

MEMBERS OF FIRM

Frederick A. Batson
Jon V. Buerstatte
Michael E. Farthing
Ansel J. Giustina
Thomas P. E. Herrmann
Stephen O. Lane
William H. Martin
Standlee G. Potter
Martha J. Rodman
Douglas R. Schultz
Malcolm H. Scott
Bruce E. Smith
James W. Spickerman

ASSOCIATES

H. Andrew Clark
Joshua A. Clark
Todd R. Johnston
Kristin E. Kernutt
Laura T.Z. Montgomery
Chad G. Potter
Ian T. Richardson
James V. Shepherd
Kurt K. Wanless

SPECIAL COUNSEL TO THE FIRM

Vernon D. Gleaves
Arlen C. Swearingen

Representative Clients: Cascade Title Co.; Giustina Land & Timber Co.; Eugene Association of Realtors; Hamilton Construction Co.; Pacific Western Extruded Plastics Co.; Seneca Sawmill Co.; Sherman Bros. Heavy Trucking; University of Oregon Foundation, Valley River Center.

For full biographical listings, see the Martindale-Hubbell Law Directory

HARRANG LONG GARY RUDNICK P.C. (AV)

400 South Park Building, 101 East Broadway, P.O. Box 11620, 97440-3820
Telephone: 541-485-0220
Fax: 541-686-6564
URL: http://www.harrang.com
Roseburg, Oregon Office: 546 S.E. Jackson Street.
Telephone: 541-672-2525.
Fax: 541-672-3255.

(See Next Column)

Salem, Oregon Office: 333 High Street, N.E., Suite 200.
Telephone: 503-371-3330.
Fax: 503-371-5336.
San Jose, California: One Almaden Boulevard, Eighth Floor.
Telephone: 408-795-1515.
Fax: 408-795-1519.

Bruce A. Bishop (Resident, Salem Office)
David J. Brabender
Patricia Lockary Chapman
William F. Gary
Judith Giers
James P. Harrang
Mary Mertens James (Resident, Salem Office)
Linda J. Kessel
Glenn Klein
Jerome Lidz (Resident, Roseburg Office)
Stanton F. Long
A. Keith Martin
Walter W. Miller
Antoinette Gary Mills (Resident, San Jose, California Office)
James E. Mountain, Jr. (Resident, Salem Office)
Arden J. Olson
Sharon A. Rudnick
Jens Schmidt

Karla H. Alderman
Stephen E. Archer
Maria S. Bellafronto (Resident, San Jose, California Office)
Craig J. Capon
Emily Newton Jerome
Sharon M. Jutila
Alan J. Leiman
E. Bradley Litchfield
Jeffery J. Matthews
Christine Nesbit
Barbara Novak
Joshua P. Stump

OF COUNSEL

William L. Richardson (Resident, Salem Office)

Representative Clients: Schering-Plough Corp.; Mistubishi Silicon America; Hyundai Semi Conductor America; Wal Mart Stores; Travelers Property Casualty; Taco Time International; Foodbrands America, Inc.; Associated Oregon Industries; The City of Eugene; Harvest House Publishers.

For full biographical listings, see the Martindale-Hubbell Law Directory

HERSHNER, HUNTER, ANDREWS, NEILL & SMITH, LLP (AV)

180 East 11th Avenue, P.O. Box 1475, 97440
Telephone: 541-686-8511
Fax: 541-344-2025
Email: info@hershnerhunter.com *URL:* http://www.hershnerhunter.com
Florence, Oregon Office: 1441 7th Street.
Telephone: 541-997-1997.
Fax: 541-997-1817.

MEMBERS OF FIRM

David N. Andrews
Michael C. Arola
William D. Brewer
Nancy K. Cary
Arthur J. Clark
Katherine M. Fritchman
Janice C. Goldberg
Norman J. LeCompte, Jr.
Andrew G. Lewis
Everett R. Moreland
K. Patrick Neill
William R. Potter
Robert S. Quinney
Craig A. Smith
Robert A. Stout
William R. Turnbow
Paul V. Vaughan

OF COUNSEL

Marlin D. Ard
P. Steve Cornacchia
James L. Hershner
Robert E. Moulton

ASSOCIATES

Jeffrey D. Kirtner
Sarah E. Mackey
Sheryl S. McConnell
J. Matthew Patton
Robert E. Quintero
Patrick W. Wade

Representative Clients: Bank of America; Federal Deposit Insurance Corp.; United States National Bank of Oregon; Union Bank of California; Davidson Industries, Inc.; Cascade Title Co.; Delta Sand & Gravel Co.; John Hyland Construction, Inc.; PSC, Inc. and PSC Scanning, Inc. (formerly known as Spectra-Physics Scanning Systems, Inc).

For full biographical listings, see the Martindale-Hubbell Law Directory

WATKINSON LAIRD RUBENSTEIN LASHWAY & BALDWIN, P.C. (AV)

101 East Broadway, Suite 200, P.O. Box 10567, 97440
Telephone: 541-484-2277
Fax: 541-484-2282
Roseburg, Oregon Office: 2750 West Harvard Boulevard.
Telephone: 541-672-2755.
FAX: 541-672-6379.

Steve C. Baldwin
B. Kevin Burgess
Donald R. Laird
J. Lee Lashway
Barry Rubenstein
John C. Watkinson

Leonard A. Hagen
Tami S. P. Carroll
Amanda Tracey Walkup
Daniel J. Drazan

OF COUNSEL

R. Sande Tomlinson

Representative Clients: Lane Individual Practice Association; Whittaker Realty Group; Gateway Mall Shopping Center; Douglas County Independent Practice Association, Inc.; East Earth Herb, Inc.; Far West Fibers, Inc.; Ad-

(See Next Column)

WATKINSON LAIRD RUBENSTEIN LASHWAY & BALDWIN P.C., *Eugene—Continued*

vantage Dental Plan, Inc.; McKenzie Fly Tackle Company, Inc.; Valley River Plaza Shopping Center; Coastwide Laboraties, Inc.

For full biographical listings, see the Martindale-Hubbell Law Directory

*KLAMATH FALLS,** Klamath Co.

J. ANTHONY GIACOMINI PC (AV)

706 Main Street, 97601
Telephone: 541-884-7728
Fax: 541-883-1759

J. Anthony Giacomini

OF COUNSEL

Susan G. Margiloff

Representative Agricultural and Business Clients: Tulelake Cold Storage Co.; LK Produce; Clough Oil Company; Quail Mountain, Inc. (Pepsi-Cola Distributor); Heaton Steel & Supply, Inc.; Orem Land Co.; Lost River Ranch; Baley-Trotman Farms; Novan Auto Parts, Inc.; L & M Produce, Inc.

For full biographical listings, see the Martindale-Hubbell Law Directory

*MEDFORD,** Jackson Co.

BROPHY, MILLS, SCHMOR, GERKING & BROPHY, LLP (AV)

A Limited Liability Partnership including a Professional Corporation
Park Place Building, Fifth Floor, 201 West Main Street, P.O. Box 128, 97501
Telephone: 541-772-7123
Fax: 541-772-7249
Email: bmsgb@mind.net

MEMBERS OF FIRM

Lee A. Mills
Douglass H. Schmor
Timothy C. Gerking
Timothy E. Brophy
David B. Paradis
Todd B. Maddox

ASSOCIATES

Mark R. Weaver
Thaddeus G. Pauck

OF COUNSEL

Carl M. Brophy (P.C.)

General Counsel for: Bear Creek Valley Sanitary Authority; California Oregon Broadcasting, Inc.; KOGAP Enterprises, Inc.; Medford Moulding Co.; Southern Oregon Sales, Inc.
Local Counsel for: Farmers Insurance Group; State Farm Fire & Casualty Co.; Stone Forest Industries; U.S. Forest Industries, Inc.

For full biographical listings, see the Martindale-Hubbell Law Directory

FOSTER, PURDY, ALLAN, PETERSON & DAHLIN, LLP (AV)

201 West Main Street, Suite 400, P.O. Box 1667, 97501
Telephone: 541-770-5466
Facsimile: 541-770-6502

MEMBERS OF FIRM

Donald K. Denman
Stuart E. Foster
Karen C. Allan
Gary C. Peterson
Lewis W. Dahlin
Gerald M. Shean, III

ASSOCIATES

Jason M. Anderson
Timothy L. Jackle

OF COUNSEL

William G. Purdy

Representative Clients: Asante Health System; Eugene F. Burrill Lumber Co.; Cardiology Consultants, P.C.; The Carpenter Foundation; Erickson Air-Crane; LTM Incorporated (construction); Mail Tribune; Oregon Shakespeare Festival Association; Ore-Cal Trade Corp. (import/export); Pulver & Leever Real Estate, Inc.

For full biographical listings, see the Martindale-Hubbell Law Directory

FROHNMAYER, DEATHERAGE, PRATT, JAMIESON, CLARKE & MOORE, P.C. (AV)

Larson Creek Professional Center, 2592 E. Barnett Road, 97504
Telephone: 541-779-2333
Fax: 541-779-6379
Email: fdfirm@internetcds.com

Otto J. Frohnmayer
William V. Deatherage
Steven H. Pratt
Stephen G. Jamieson
Mark D. Clarke
Bernard S. Moore
Thomas F. Armosino, Jr.

Tracy M. McGovern
Frederick H. Lundblade
Christian Oelke

Local Counsel for: Allstate Insurance Company; CNA; Farmers Insurance Group; Northwest Physicians Mutual Insurance Company; Professional Liability Fund.

(See Next Column)

General Counsel for: Lithia Motors, Inc.

For full biographical listings, see the Martindale-Hubbell Law Directory

HORNECKER, COWLING, HASSEN & HEYSELL, L.L.P. (AV)

717 Murphy Road, 97504
Telephone: 541-779-8900
Fax: 541-779-2982

MEMBERS OF FIRM

Gregory T. Hornecker
Robert L. Cowling
John R. Hassen
R. Ray Heysell
H. Scott Plouse
P. David Ingalls
Adam T. Stamper
Joseph E. Kellerman
James A. Wallan
Benjamin M. Bloom

OF COUNSEL

B. Kent Blackhurst
Ervin B. Hogan

ASSOCIATES

William F. Wilson
Charles E. Bolen
Alan Harper
Jason C. Broesder
Ryan J. Vanderhoof

For full biographical listings, see the Martindale-Hubbell Law Directory

MILWAUKIE, Clackamas Co.

JAMES E. REDMAN (AV)

10565 S.E. 23rd Avenue, 97222
Telephone: 503-659-5335
Fax: 503-659-5568

For full biographical listings, see the Martindale-Hubbell Law Directory

*PENDLETON,** Umatilla Co.

MAUTZ BAUM & O'HANLON, LLP (AV)

101 S.E. Byers Avenue, P.O. Box 628, 97801
Telephone: 541-276-2811
Fax: 541-276-0543
Email: mbo@mautzetal.com *URL:* http://www.mautzetal.com
La Grande, Oregon Office: 1902 4th Street, P.O. Box 967. 97850.
Telephone: 541-963-3104.
Fax: 541-963-9254.

MEMBERS OF FIRM

Robert T. Mautz
Timothy J. O'Hanlon
David C. Baum (Resident Partner, La Grande Office)
Raymond S. Baum (Resident Partner, La Grande Office)
Jeffrey D. Capps

For full biographical listings, see the Martindale-Hubbell Law Directory

*PORTLAND,** Multnomah Co.

ATER WYNNE LLP (AV)

Suite 1800, 222 S.W. Columbia Street, 97201-6618
Telephone: 503-226-1191
Telecopier: 503-226-0079
URL: http://www.aterwynne.com
Seattle, Washington Office: Two Union Square, 601 Union Street, Suite 5450, 98101-2327.
Telephone: 206-623-4711.

MEMBERS OF FIRM

William P. Buren (1950-1991)
Carol A. Hewitt (1945-1993)
Jonathan A. Ater
Thomas A. Balmer
Lori Irish Bauman
Steven K. Blackhurst
Arthur A. Butler (Resident Shareholder, Seattle, Washington Office)
William C. Campbell
Fred J. Coccodrilli
Valerie D. Fisher
Kirk H. Gibson
Douglas E. Goe
Stephen M. Going
Peter H. Haller (Resident Shareholder, Seattle, Washington Office)
Gregory R. Harris (Resident Shareholder, Seattle, Washington Office)
Townsend Hyatt
Gregg D. Johnson
Benjamin H. Kaminash
Stephen J. Kennedy (Resident Shareholder, Seattle, Washington Office)
Thomas M. Kilbane, Jr. (Resident Shareholder, Seattle, Washington Office)
Frank V. Langfitt, III
Stacey E. Mark
Brenda L. Meltebeke
Byron W. Milstead
Claudia Kay Powers
Michael J. Sandmire
Ronald L. Saxton (Firm Chairman)
Scott E. Schickli
Jack W. Schifferdecker, Jr.
John M. Schultz
Michael W. Shackelford
Ann L. Sherman
Daniel H. Skerritt
Gregory E. Struxness
Mark A. Turner
Amy M. Wayson

ASSOCIATES

Leslie G. Bottomly
L. David Connell
Michael S. Gadd
Paula Holm Jensen
Daniel P. Larsen
Douglas C. MacCourt
Brenda S. Molner (Resident, Seattle, Washington Office)
Leslie Reade Schenck (Resident, Seattle, Washington Office)

(See Next Column)

ATER WYNNE LLP—*Continued*

ASSOCIATES (Continued)

Michael E. Schrader
Lee K. Shannon
Heather J. Van Meter
Tyler V. Whitehead
Anthonie H. Woller
Angela Wu (Resident, Seattle, Washington Office)
Gregory A. Zafiris

OF COUNSEL

Larry G. Hittle
Joel R. Paisner (Resident, Seattle, Washington Office)
Linda Triplett

LEGAL SUPPORT PERSONNEL

Carol W. Callaway (Public Finance Administrator)

For full biographical listings, see the Martindale-Hubbell Law Directory

BALL JANIK LLP (AV)

One Main Place, 101 S.W. Main Street, Suite 1100, 97204-3219
Telephone: 503-228-2525
Telecopy: 503-295-1058
Email: info@balljanik.com *URL:* http://www.balljanik.com
Washington, D.C. Office: 1455 F Street, N.W., Suite 225, 20005-1004.
Telephone: 202-638-3307.
Telecopy: 202-783-6947.
Salem, Oregon Office: Cascade Pacific Professional Center, 960 Liberty Street, S.E., Suite 200, 97302-4154.
Telephone: 503-581-2845.
Telecopy: 503-399-1029.
Bend, Oregon Office: 15 S.W. Colorado Avenue, Building 2, Suite 260, 97702.
Telephone: 541-617-1309.
Telecopy: 541-617-8824.

MEMBERS OF FIRM

Richard H. Allan
Robert S. Ball
James A. Beall
Gary D. Cole
Nancy Craven
John Joseph Dunbar
Stephen T. Janik
Phillip E. Joseph
Neil D. Kimmelfield
Sally C. Landauer
James T. McDermott
Bradley S. Miller
Jack L. Orchard, Jr.
Barbara W. Radler
Sarah J. Ryan
Leon Simson
Brad T. Summers
Christopher M. Walters

ASSOCIATES

Bruce H. Cahn
Laura M. Craska Cooper
David W. Criswell
Richard M. Fernández
Eghosa D. Omoigui
Timothy M. Parks
Daniel P. Semmens
Justin M. Thorp
Kristin L. Udvari
Christen Carlson White

OF COUNSEL

J. Roger Hamilton
John W. Osburn (P.C.)
William H. Perkins
Richard J. Stone
Jacob B. Tanzer

GOVERNMENT RELATIONS SPECIALIST

Michelle Giguere

Representative Clients: Charles Schwab & Co., Inc.; Crown Pacific Partners, L.P.; Fujitsu Microelectronics; Norris Beggs & Simpson; Spieker Properties, L.P.; Trammell Crow Co.; U.S. Generating Company.

For full biographical listings, see the Martindale-Hubbell Law Directory

BLACK HELTERLINE LLP (AV)

1200 Union Bank of California Tower, 707 S.W. Washington Street, 97205
Telephone: 503-224-5560
Telecopier: 503-224-6148
URL: http://www.bhlaw.com

Borden F. Beck, Jr. (1923-1989)
Harvey N. Black (1895-1986)
Guy J. Rappleyea (1921-1993)
Russell M. Helterline (1921-1995)

MEMBERS OF FIRM

Stark Ackerman
Ronald T. Adams
James M. Baumgartner
Robert W. Donaldson
Clarence H. Greenwood
Paul R. Hribernick
Donald L. Krahmer, Jr.
John M. McGuigan
Michael B. Merchant
Michael O. Moran
David G. Newhall
David P. Roy
Steven R. Schell

ASSOCIATES

Amy P. Alexander
Joshua M. Barrett
James R. George
Christina L. Haring
Steven R. Lastomirsky
Judith Woo Poutasse (Not admitted in OR)
Eric J. TenBrook

OF COUNSEL

Robert E. Glasgow
Frank P. Layton, Q.C. (Canadian Foreign Law Consultant, Oregon, 1995)
Gerald H. Robinson (Retired)

(See Next Column)

For full biographical listings, see the Martindale-Hubbell Law Directory

ROBERT G. BURT, P.C. (AV)

The 1515 Building, Suite 600, 1515 S.W. Fifth Avenue, 97201-5449
Telephone: 503-223-3600
Fax: 503-274-0778

Robert G. Burt

For full biographical listings, see the Martindale-Hubbell Law Directory

COSGRAVE, VERGEER & KESTER, L.L.P. (AV)

Bank of America Financial Center, Suite 1300, 121 S.W. Morrison Street, 97204-3193
Telephone: 503-323-9000
Fax: 503-323-9019
Email: cvk@cvk-law.com

MEMBERS OF FIRM

Duane Vergeer (Retired)
Randall B. Kester
Walter H. Sweek
Frank H. Lagesen
Eugene H. Buckle
David P. Morrison
Thomas W. Brown
David H. Williams
Jeffrey A. Johnson
Robert E. Barton
Charles J. Huber
Timothy J. Coleman
Michael C. Lewton
Norma S. Poitras
Philip R. Bennett
Andrew T. Burns

ASSOCIATES

Kathleen J. Hansa
Wendi K. Weiss
Christine B. Miller
Kenneth J. Abere, Jr
Wendy M. Margolis
William G. Fig
Heather Wright Decker
Sherrill L. Dye
Robert E. Sabido

OF COUNSEL

Walter J. Cosgrave

Counsel for: Boise Cascade Corp.; Farmers Insurance Co. of Oregon; Maryland Casualty Co.; North Pacific Insurance Co.; Professional Liability Fund; State Farm Fire and Casualty Co.; State Farm Mutual Insurance Co.; TIG Insurance Co.; Union Pacific Railroad Co.; Valley Insurance Co.

For full biographical listings, see the Martindale-Hubbell Law Directory

GARVEY, SCHUBERT & BARER (AV)

Eleventh Floor, 121 S.W. Morrison Street, 97204
Telephone: 503-228-3939
Telecopier: 503-226-0259
Seattle, Washington Office: 1191 Second Avenue, 18th Floor, 98101.
Telephone: 206-464-3939.
Cable Address: "Lex, Seattle."
Telecopier: 206-464-0125.
Washington, D.C. Office: 5th Floor, 1000 Potomac Street, N.W., 20007.
Telephone: 202-965-7880.
Telecopier: 202-965-1729.

MEMBERS OF FIRM

Richard Baroway
A. Jeffery Bird
Larry J. Brant
Christine P. Brown
David L. Canary
Stephen J. Connolly
John M. Cowden
Mark E. Friedman
John H. Gadon
Robert R. Griffith
Eric A. Lindenauer
Jennifer L. Palmquist
Robert C. Weaver, Jr.
Kenneth A. Wittenberg

ASSOCIATES

Jeff C. Duncan Brecht
Kathleen C. Bricken
Daniel J. Casey
Michael J. King
John R. San Fellipo
Kenneth L. Schubert, III
Alec J. Shebiel
Lisa M. Umscheid
Lauren E. Winters

OF COUNSEL

Keith S. Dubanevich
Louis D. Savage

CONTRACT ATTORNEY

Susan L. Bigcraft

Representative Clients: Federal Deposit Insurance Corp.; Foss Maritime Company; In Focus Systems, Inc.; NIKE, Inc.; Regence BlueCross BlueShield of Oregon; Regence HMO Oregon; Rentrak Corporation; St. John Medical Center; TriQuint Semiconductor.

For full biographical listings, see the Martindale-Hubbell Law Directory

LANE POWELL SPEARS LUBERSKY LLP (AV)

Limited Liability Partnership composed of Individuals and Professional Service Corporations
601 S.W. Second Avenue, Suite 2100, 97204
Telephone: 503-778-2100
Facsimile: 503-778-2200
Email: information@lanepowell.com *URL:* http://www.lanepowell.com
Other Offices at: Seattle, Washington; Anchorage, Alaska; Olympia and Mount Vernon, Washington; London, England.

(See Next Column)

LANE POWELL SPEARS LUBERSKY LLP, *Portland—Continued*

MEMBERS OF FIRM

Dean N. Alterman
Craig D. Bachman
James H. Clarke
Christopher P. Cline
John H. Durkheimer
John Folawn
Bruce C. Hamlin
Timothy R. Harmon
Lewis M. Horowitz
David Glenn Hosenpud
Charles F. Hudson
Martin W. Jaqua
George L. Kirklin
Peter Livingston
Stanley R. Loeb
Jeffrey S. Love
Robert E. Maloney, Jr.
Christopher J. Marshall
Stephen P. McCarthy
Lee C. Nusich
Paul M. Ostroff
Milo Petranovich
Bryan E. Powell
Charles J. Pruitt
Donald H. Pyle
Vicki L. Smith
Thomas W. Sondag
Leigh D. Stephenson-Kuhn
John C. Stevason
John C. Walsh
Richard H. Williams
O. Meredith Wilson, Jr.
Jeffrey C. Wolfstone

OF COUNSEL

Herbert H. Anderson
John P. Bledsoe
John B. Crowell, Jr.
John Wiley Gould
Wayne Hilliard
William F. Lubersky
Lewis K. Scott
Frank H. Spears
Oglesby H. Young

COUNSEL

Jeffrey W. Knapp

ASSOCIATES

David H. Black, Jr.
Kenneth Ray Davis, II
Pilar Cortwright French
Anne Wheeler Glazer
Robert G. Koury, II
Benjamin G. Lenhart
Vicki Y. Nakahara
Nicholas Phat Nguyen
Melvin D. Oden-Orr
William T. Patton
Claire J. Philpott
(Not admitted in OR)
Dian R. Rubanoff
Carolyn D. Walker

For full biographical listings, see the Martindale-Hubbell Law Directory

MILLER NASH LLP (AV)

A Limited Liability Partnership including Professional Corporations
111 S.W. Fifth Avenue, 97204-3699
Telephone: 503-224-5858
Telex: 364462, Kingmar PTL
Facsimile: 503-224-0155, 503-224-2450
Email: e-mail@millernash.com *URL:* http://www.millernash.com
Seattle, Washington Office: 4400 Two Union Square, 601 Union Street, 98101-2322.
Telephone: 206-622-8484.
Facsimile: 206-622-7485.

PORTLAND, OREGON PARTNERS

Michael E. Arthur, P.C.
Jeffrey D. Austin, P.C.
Joyce M. Bernheim, P.C.
Rece Bly, P.C.
David W. Brown, P.C.
Donald A. Burns, P.C.
John D. Burns
J. Franklin Cable, P.C.
Donna M. Cameron, P.C.
Bruce L. Campbell
Richard A. Canaday, P.C.
D. Gary Christensen
William B. Crow, P.C.
David C. Culpepper, P.C.
Dean D. DeChaine, P.C.
Brian B. Doherty, P.C.
Donald W. Douglas
James F. Dulcich, P.C.
Mary Ann Frantz, P.C.
Jonathon L. Goodling, P.C.
Phillip E. Grillo
M. Christie Helmer, P.C.
David W. Hercher, P.C.
Graham M. Hicks, P.C.
Jerry B. Hodson, P.C.
Suzanne Lacampagne
Laurie Neilson Lee
Louis B. Livingston, P.C.
John A. Lusky, P.C.
Michael W. Meltzer, P.C.
Erich W. Merrill, Jr., P.C.
Jeffrey B. Millner, P.C.
John Casey Mills, P.C.
Conrad L. Moore, P.C.
David M. Munro, P.C.
John F. Neupert, P.C.
G. Todd Norvell, P.C.
John F. Purcell, P.C.
Dennis P. Rawlinson, P.C.
Peter C. Richter, P.C.
Bruce A. Rubin, P.C.
Thomas C. Sand, P.C.
Catherine A. Shaw
Ronald A. Shellan, P.C.
Maureen R. Sloane, P.C.
Jeffrey C. Thede, P.C.
Sharon L. Toncray, P.C.
James N. Westwood, P.C.
R. Alan Wight

SEATTLE, WASHINGTON PARTNERS

James R. Dickens, P.C.
Brooks E. Harlow, P.C.
Peter S. Holmes, P.C.
James H. Jordan Jr., P.C.
Bruce A. Kaser, P.C.
Clyde H. MacIver, P.C.
Paul W. Oden, P.C.
James L. Phillips
Andrew H. Salter, P.C.
D. William Toone, Jr.
Francis L. Van Dusen, Jr., P.C.
John L. West, P.C.

VANCOUVER, WASHINGTON PARTNERS

Stephen W. Horenstein
LeAnne Bremer

PORTLAND, OREGON OF COUNSEL

Harvey C. Barragar
Donald R. Holman

(See Next Column)

PORTLAND, OREGON SPECIAL COUNSEL

Gerald A. Froebe
William R. Knuths
William H. Walters
Robert J. Yanity

PORTLAND, OREGON COUNSEL

Jeffrey G. Condit
Victoria L. MacPherson
Karen Dana Oster

SEATTLE, WASHINGTON COUNSEL

John R. Christiansen
Sarah Weaver

PORTLAND, OREGON RETIRED

Maurice O. Georges
Orval O. Hager
John W. Hill
Frank E. Nash
Norman J. Wiener

PORTLAND, OREGON ASSOCIATES

Craig R. Armstrong
Steven Drew Baker
Stephanie M. Brainerd
David G. Bristol
Brian T. Burton
Steven L. Christensen
Julia A. DeWitt
Steven T. Dyches
Richard L. Fortner
Marilyn K. Frederick
Laura A. Frikert
Jeffrey C. Gardner
Michelle Humberstone
Dustin R. Klinger
(Not admitted in OR)
Caroline E. Kuerschner
Sabrina P. Loiselle
Colleen L. McKellar
Jon J. Napier
Timothy C. Nash
(Not admitted in OR)
Heyke G. Nickerson
Chad E. Paulson
David G. Post
Matthew D. Rabdau
Melissa Lehane Rawlinson
Melissa M. Ryan
Joshua M. F. Sasaki
Amy Silliman
David P. Smith
Matthew M. Werner
James P. Williams
M. Max Williams II

SEATTLE, WASHINGTON ASSOCIATES

Lance W. Bass
Terry F. Berman
Daniel A. Brown
Rosamond J. DeGiacomo
Valerie du Laney
Brian W. Esler
Kevin B. Hansen
Brandon J. Hollis
Elizabeth R. Holohan
Christine A. Marty
Roxanna Nowparast
David L. Rice
Susan K. Stahlfeld
Lance A. Termes
Michelle L. Valier

VANCOUVER, WASHINGTON ASSOCIATES

Cassie N. Crawford
Steven F. Hill
Kim M. Mingo
Meridee E. Pabst

LEGAL SUPPORT PERSONNEL

Leslie M. Meserve (Director of Library Services)

For full biographical listings, see the Martindale-Hubbell Law Directory

STOEL RIVES LLP (AV)

900 S.W. Fifth Avenue, Suite 2600, 97204-1268
Telephone: 503-224-3380
Facsimile: 503-220-2480
Cable Address: "Lawport"
URL: http://www.stoel.com/
Lloyd District Office: Suite 950, 700 N.E. Multnomah Street, Portland, Oregon.
Telephone: 503-294-9100.
Telecopier: 503-230-1907.
Washington, D.C. Office: Suite 810, 1275 K Street, N.W.
Telephone: 202-347-7744.
Seattle, Washington Office: Suite 3600, One Union Square, 600 University.
Telephone: 206-624-0900.
Vancouver, Washington Office: Suite 725, 805 Broadway.
Telephone: 360-699-5900.
Boise, Idaho Office: Suite 1900, 101 S. Capitol Boulevard.
Telephone: 208-389-9000.
Salt Lake City, Utah Office: Suite 1100, One Utah Center, 201 South Main Street.
Telephone: 801-328-3131.

MEMBERS OF FIRM

Steven W. Abel
Gail L. Achterman
John V. Acosta
Charles F. Adams
Richard E. Alexander
Paul S. Angello
Stephen E. Babson
Richard D. Bach
Gary R. Barnum
Todd A. Bauman
Ruth A. Beyer
Alan R. Blank (Resident, Lloyd District Office)
Patrick G. Boylston
Barbara A. Brainard
Henry C. Breithaupt
Paul C. Buchanan
Michael Roame Campbell
Phillip D. Chadsey
Harry S. Chandler
Stuart Chestler
Joseph D. Cohen
D. Jeffrey Courser
Nancy L. Cowgill
Barbara D. Craig
E. Joseph Dean
Eileen Drake
Edward D. Einowski
Barnes H. Ellis
Edward L. Epstein
Mark R. Feichtinger
James F. Fell
Louis A. Ferreira, IV
Howard M. Feuerstein
Jerry R. Fish
David Copley Forman
Randolph C. Foster
Richard A. Franzke
Eugene A. Frassetto
Mark J. Fucile

(See Next Column)

STOEL RIVES LLP—*Continued*

MEMBERS OF FIRM (Continued)

George M. Galloway
Andrew R. Gardner
Richard S. Gleason
Gary W. Glisson
Gersham Goldstein
Eric A. Grasberger
David W. Green
Stephen L. Griffith
Ronald S. Grossmann
John J. Halle
Christopher R. Hermann
Christopher K. Heuer
Henry H. Hewitt
Charles F. Hinkle
William H. Holmes
Pamela L. Jacklin
Peter R. Jarvis
Richard C. Josephson
Scott J. Kaplan
Emily V. Karr
Margaret D. Kirkpatrick
Chris Kitchel
Christine A. Kosydar
Sanjiv N. Kripalani
Margaret Baumgardner Kushner
Charles S. Lewis, III
Dennis Leybold
Steven T. Lovett
Gregory H. Macpherson
Dexter E. Martin (Resident, Lloyd District Office)
Katherine A. McDowell
Charles J. McMurchie
David P. Miller, II
Robert J. Moorman
J. Mark Morford
Gregory Robert Mowe
Annette M. Mulee
Joel A. Mullin
Barbara L. Nay
Thomas R. Nicolai
Mark A. Norby
Margaret Hill Noto
Thomas R. Page
Terrence R. Pancoast
Steven L. Pfeiffer
Per A. Ramfjord
Guy A. Randles
Edward J. Reeves
Campbell Richardson
Michael C. Robinson
Lois Omenn Rosenbaum
Jaime M. W. Sanders
John M. Schweitzer (Resident, Lloyd District Office)
Peter L. Serrurier
Joan P. Snyder
Micah D. Stolowitz
John R. Thomas
Robert H. Thomson
Robert D. Van Brocklin
E. Walter Van Valkenburg
Carolyn M. Vogt
Stephen S. Walters
Jere M. Webb
Marcus Wood
James A. Zehren

OF COUNSEL

Stephen S. Brier
Nancy M. Lashnits
R. Allan Leedy, Jr.
James C. Paine

RETIRED MEMBERS

Ernest Bonyhadi
Thomas P. Deering
John Detjens, III
Gerard K. Drummond
George H. Fraser
David G. Hayhurst
Robert H. Huntington
William M. McAllister
Milo E. Ormseth
George D. Rives
Thomas B. Stoel
Clarence R. Wicks
William W. Wyse

ASSOCIATES

Andrew M. Altschul
Nancie Potter Arellano
Ava E. Bartley
Clarence M. Belnavis
Ralph O. Bloemers
Justin R. Boose
Jason M. Brauser
Jennie L. Bricker
Timothy J. Calderbank
Darin W. Carlson
Christine L. Carr (Not admitted in OR)
Kenneth P. Childs
Scott E. Crawford
Alison W. Daugherty
Andrew I. Davis
Jeffery B. Erb (Resident, Lloyd District Office)
Pedro L. Fernandez, Jr.
Kassim M. Ferris
David E. Filippi
Frank M. Flynn
Scott L. Garland
Bryan S. Geon
Leta E. Gorman
Stephen C. Hall
Sharon Ann Hill
Elaine Malin Hillas
Steven H. Hull
John E. Isselmann, Jr.
LeAnne K. Jabs
Michael E. Jacobs
James M. Kearney
Katherine C. Kellner
Jeffrey M. Krueger
Elizabeth Morley Large
Robert T. Manicke
Steven A. Moore
Peter D. Mostow
John C. Motley
Reginald C. Nettles
Brendan N. O'Scannlain
Kevin T. Pearson
Mary P. Pounds
Joseph A. Pugh
Stephen A. Redshaw
Daniel K. Reising
Jeremy D. Sacks
Penny H. Serrurier
Michael J. Sirtori
Deborah Kathleen Smith
Timothy Daly Smith
Kevin S. Thomas
Richelle M. Tustin
David E. Van't Hof
Christopher G. Winter
Courtney W. Wiswall
James L. Wolfe (Not admitted in OR)
Thomas R. Wood
Kesa L. Yorozu

PATENT AGENTS

Michael L. Levine
Richard B. Preiss

Counsel for: Electro Scientific Industries; Fred Meyer, Inc.; Mentor Graphics Corporation; NIKE, Inc.; Northwest Natural Gas Co.; PacifiCorp; Sequent Computer Systems, Inc.; Tektronix, Inc.; Wells Fargo Bank, N.A.

For full biographical listings, see the Martindale-Hubbell Law Directory

*ROSEBURG,** Douglas Co.

DOLE, COALWELL, CLARK, MOUNTAINSPRING & MORNARICH, P.C. (AV)

810 S.E. Douglas Avenue, P.O. Box 1205, 97470
Telephone: 541-673-5541
Fax: 541-673-1156
Email: dcclaw@rosenet.net

George W. Neuner (1914-1985)
Donald A. Dole
Bruce R. Coalwell
Dan W. Clark
Stephen Mountainspring
Jeffrey A. Mornarich

Ronald W. Aitken

Representative Clients: Douglas County Title Co.; C & D Lumber Co.; Herbert Lumber Co.

For full biographical listings, see the Martindale-Hubbell Law Directory

*SALEM,** Marion Co.

CLARK, LINDAUER, McCLINTON, FETHERSTON, EDMONDS & LIPPOLD (AV)

880 Liberty Street, N.E., P.O. Box 2206, 97308-2206
Telephone: 503-581-1542
Fax: 503-585-3978
Email: clm@cyberis.net

MEMBERS OF FIRM

Eric B. Lindauer
Michael C. McClinton
Ben C. Fetherston, Jr.
James C. Edmonds
Steven M. Lippold

ASSOCIATES

Rebecca Biermann Tom
Sarah Rhoads Troutt

Representative Clients: North Pacific Insurance Co.; State Farm Insurance Co.; Colonial Penn Insurance Co.; Oregon State Bar Professional Liability Fund; Albertson's Inc.; Volkswagen of America, Inc.; Fleetwood Enterprises, Inc.; Portland General Electric Co.; Tillamook County Creamery Association.

For full biographical listings, see the Martindale-Hubbell Law Directory

PENNSYLVANIA

*ALLENTOWN,** Lehigh Co.

DUANE, MORRIS & HECKSCHER LLP (AV)

968 Postal Road, Suite 200, 18109-0400
Telephone: 610-266-3650
Fax: 610-266-3651
URL: http://www.duanemorris.com
Philadelphia, Pennsylvania Office: Suite 4200, One Liberty Place.
Telephone: 215-979-1000.
Fax: 215-979-1020.
New York, New York Office: 380 Lexington Avenue.
Telephone: 212-692-1000.
Fax: 212-692-1020.
Chicago, Illinois Office: 227 West Monroe Street, Suite 3400.
Telephone: 312-499-6700.
Fax: 312-499-6701.
Washington, D.C. Office: 1667 K Street, N.W., Suite 700.
Telephone: 202-776-7800.
Fax: 202-776-7801.
San Francisco, California Office: 100 Spear Street.
Telephone: 415-371-2200.
Fax: 415-371-2201.
Boston, Massachusetts Office: One International Place, 14th Floor.
Telephone: 617-598-3100.
Fax: 617-598-3101.
Miami, Florida Office: 200 South Biscayne Boulevard, Suite 3410
Telephone: 305-960-2200.
Fax: 305-960-2201.
Wilmington, Delaware Office: 1201 Market Street, Suite 1500.
Telephone: 302-571-5550.
Fax: 302-571-5560.
Harrisburg, Pennsylvania Office: 305 North Front Street, 5th Floor, P.O. Box 1003.
Telephone: 717-237-5500.
Fax: 717-232-4015.
Wayne, Pennsylvania Office: 735 Chesterbrook Boulevard, Suite 300.
Telephone: 610-647-3555.
Fax: 610-640-2619.
Cherry Hill, New Jersey Office: 51 Haddonfield Road, Suite 340.
Telephone: 856-488-7300.
Fax: 856-488-7021.
Newark, New Jersey Office: One Riverfront Plaza.
Telephone: 973-424-2000.
Fax: 973-424-2001.

(See Next Column)

DUANE, MORRIS & HECKSCHER LLP, *Allentown—Continued*

Palm Beach, Florida Office: 249 Royal Palm Way, Suite 403.
Telephone: 561-366-5400.
Fax: 561-366-5401.
Houston, Texas Office: One Greenway Plaza, Suite 500.
Telephone: 713-552-9900.
Fax: 713-552-0109.
Dover, Delaware Office: 314 S. State Street.
Telephone: 302-736-0156.
Fax: 302-736-0336.

RESIDENT PARTNER

Maxwell E. Davison

RESIDENT ASSOCIATES

J. Brian Johnson
Dennis M. McCarthy
Richard M. Williams

SPECIAL COUNSEL

Joan R. Sheak

For full biographical listings, see the Martindale-Hubbell Law Directory

FONZONE & ASHLEY (AV)

33 South Seventh Street, P.O. Box 4180, 18105-4180
Telephone: 610-433-0121
Fax: 610-434-8440
Email: fonzlaw@aol.com

MEMBERS OF FIRM

Charles J. Fonzone
John W. Ashley

OF COUNSEL

James L. Weirbach

ASSOCIATES

Christopher W. Gittinger
Brian R. Longenhagen
Frances Ann Fruhwirth
Maryann E. Higgins
Frank G. Procyk

Representative Clients: Erie Insurance Exchange; State Farm Mutual Automobile Insurance Co.; City of Allentown; Cumis Insurance; Mack Trucks; Lehigh-Northampton Airport Authority.

For full biographical listings, see the Martindale-Hubbell Law Directory

LITTNER, DESCHLER & LITTNER

(See Bethlehem)

SCOBLIONKO, SCOBLIONKO, MUIR, BARTHOLOMEW & MELMAN, A PROFESSIONAL CORPORATION (AV)

40 South Fifth Street, P.O. Box 1998, 18105-1998
Telephone: 610-434-7138
Fax: 610-434-6020
Email: mscoblionk@aol.com

E. G. Scoblionko (1909-1975)
Mark H. Scoblionko
Anthony Moyer Muir
James A. Bartholomew
Marla J. Melman
Diana S. Marshall

References: First Union National Bank of Allentown.

For full biographical listings, see the Martindale-Hubbell Law Directory

TALLMAN, HUDDERS & SORRENTINO, P.C. (AV)

Suite 300 The Paragon Centre, 1611 Pond Road, 18104
Telephone: 610-391-1800
Fax: 610-391-1805
Email: info@ths.com *URL:* http://www.thslaw.com

Robert G. Tallman
John R. Hudders (Retired)
Donald H. Lipson
Thomas C. Sadler, Jr.
Donald A. Zamborsky
Oldrich Foucek, III
Matthew R. Sorrentino
Paul McHale, Jr.
Barbara L. Hollenbach
Timothy J. Siegfried
Dolores A. Laputka
Scott B. Allinson

Michael E. Loomis
John K. Baker
Laura J. Herzog
Scott R. Lipson
Theodore J. Zeller, III
Jeffrey A. Durney
Beverly J. Doneker
George C. Hlavac
Douglas G. Cappellini
Ronnie F. Hess
Amy Kohler Howard

OF COUNSEL

Paul J. Schoff

For full biographical listings, see the Martindale-Hubbell Law Directory

*BEAVER,** Beaver Co.

REED, LUCE, TOSH, WOLFORD & DOUGLASS, A PROFESSIONAL CORPORATION (AV)

804 Turnpike Street, 15009
Telephone: 724-774-9220
Fax: 724-774-1363
Email: REEDLUCE@usaor.net

James A. McGregor, Jr. (1924-1994).
Wayne S. Luce (Retired)
Harold F. Reed, Jr.
James C. Tosh
Dennis F. Wolford
Kathryn L. Johnston
Gregory K. Douglass

Counsel for: Jones & Laughlin Steel Corp.; First Western Bank; Century National Bank & Trust Co.; Tuscarora Plastics, Inc.; Beaver Newspaper, Inc.; Pennsylvania Manufacturers Insurance Assn.; Liberty Mutual Insurance Co.; Medical Center of Beaver Co. Inc.; Motorist Insurance Co.

For full biographical listings, see the Martindale-Hubbell Law Directory

*BELLEFONTE,** Centre Co.

LEE, MARTIN, GREEN & REITER, INC. (AV)

115 East High Street, Lock Drawer 179, 16823
Telephone: 814-355-4769
Fax: 814-355-5024
Email: lmgr@csrlink.net
State College, Pennsylvania Office: 101 Innovation Boulevard, Suite 311.
Telephone: 814-237-6291.
Fax: 814-237-5861.

Donald E. Lee
Robert L. Martin
Joseph P. Green
Dennis O. Reiter
Robert A. Mix
William T. Fleming

Representative Clients: Omega Bank, N.A.; State College Borough Water Authority; Jersey Shore State Bank; Erie Insurance Group; Centre Community Hospital; Liberty Mutual Insurance Co.; Centre Area Transportation Authority; Centre County Association of Realtors; Gregg Township; Haines Township; Boggs Township.

For full biographical listings, see the Martindale-Hubbell Law Directory

BERWYN, Chester Co.

PEPPER HAMILTON LLP (AV)

1235 Westlakes Drive, Suite 400, 19312-2401
Telephone: 610-640-7800
Telecopy: 610-640-7835
Email: phinfo@pepperlaw.com *URL:* http://www.pepperlaw.com
Philadelphia, Pennsylvania Office: 3000 Two Logan Square, Eighteenth and Arch Streets, 19103-2799.
Telephone: 215-981-4000.
Fax: 215-981-4750.
Washington, D.C. Office: Hamilton Square, 600 Fourteenth Street, N.W. 20005-2004.
Telephone: 202-220-1200.
Fax: 202-220-1665.
Detroit, Michigan Office: 100 Renaissance Center, 36th Floor, 48243-1157.
Telephone: 313-259-7110.
Fax: 313-259-7926.
New York, New York Office: 750 Lexington Avenue, Suite 600, 10022-1200.
Telephone: 212-813-9668.
Fax: 212-813-9802.
Wilmington, Delaware Office: 1201 Market Street, Suite 1600, P.O. Box 1709, 19899-1709.
Telephone: 302-777-6500.
Fax: 302-656-8865.
Pittsburgh, Pennsylvania Office: 500 Grant Street, 50th Floor, 15219-2502.
Telephone: 412-454-5000.
Fax: 412-281-0717.
Harrisburg, Pennsylvania Office: 200 One Keystone Plaza, North Front and Market Streets, P.O. Box 1181, 17108-1181.
Telephone: 717-255-1155.
Fax: 717-238-0575.
Cherry Hill, New Jersey Office: LibertyView Building, Suite 420, 457 Haddonfield Road, 08002-2220.
Telephone: 856-910-7200.
Fax: 856-665-7743.

PARTNERS

James L. Murray (Firm Executive Partner)
Jeffrey P. Libson (Managing Partner, Berwyn Office)
Gordon R. Downing
Michael P. Gallagher
John B. Huffaker
David H. Huggler
Jonathan Kane
William F. Kershner
James R. Ledwith
Susan K. Lessack
A. John May, III
Paul T. Porrini
James D. Rosener
William A. Scari, Jr.
Ellen Kittredge Scott
Edward M. Watters, III
Kenneth H. Zucker

(See Next Column)

PEPPER HAMILTON LLP—*Continued*

ASSOCIATES

Timothy C. Atkins
Christopher J. Camp
Daniel L. Damstra
Katherine J. Dickinson
Michael S. Hino
Matthew J. Maguire
Robert A. Mascioli
Amy G. McAndrew
Sean P. McDevitt
Christopher S. Miller
Caroline J. Patterson
Christopher A. Rossi
Lynne Sindoni Spangler
Cuyler H. Walker
Arnold W. Winter

For full biographical listings, see the Martindale-Hubbell Law Directory

SAUL, EWING, REMICK & SAUL LLP (AV)

1055 Westlakes Drive Suite 150, 19312
Telephone: 610-251-5050
Cable Address: "BIDSAL"
TWX: 83-4798
Telecopier: XEROX 720 610-651-5930
Email: lawyers@saul.com *URL:* http://www.saul.com
Philadelphia, Pennsylvania Office: Centre Square West, 1500 Market Street, 38th Floor, 19102-2186.
Telephone: 215-972-7777.
Cable Address: "Bidsal".
TWX: 83-4798.
Telecopier: XEROX 7020 215-972-7725.
Wilmington, Delaware Office: 222 Delaware Avenue, P.O. Box 1266, 19899-1266. For Courier Delivery: 222 Delaware Avenue, Suite 1200, 19801.
Telephone: 302-421-6800.
Cable Address: "Bidsal."
TWX: 83-4798.
Telecopier: XEROX 7020 302-421-6813.
New York, New York Office: Twenty-first Floor, 237 Park Avenue.
Telephone: 212-551-3502.
TWX: 425170.
Telecopier: 212-697-8486.
Harrisburg, Pennsylvania Office: Penn National Insurance Tower, 2 North Second Street, 7th Floor, 17101.
Telephone: 717-257-7500.
Telecopier: 717-238-4622, 717-257-7516.
Princeton, New Jersey Office: 214 Carnegie Center, Suite 202.
Telephone: 609-452-3100.
Fax: 609-452-3122.
Baltimore, Maryland Office: Saul, Ewing, Weinberg & Green, 100 South Charles Street, Suite 1500.
Telephone: 410-332-8600.
Fax: 410-332-8862.

MEMBERS OF FIRM

Stephen S. Aichele
David S. Antzis (Resident)
George Asimos, Jr.
Michael S. Burg (Resident)
Richard T. Frazier
Patrick G. Oakes (Resident)
Scott D. Patterson (Resident)
John C. Snyder
John F. Stoviak (Managing Partner)

ASSOCIATES

Dennis H. Bower
Christine S. Kimmel
Francis V. McNamara, III
Deborah Landan Spranger (Not admitted in PA; Resident)
Ivy Barton Wagner
Elizabeth Utz Witmer

SPECIAL COUNSEL

John J. Mahoney (Resident)
Sondra K. Slade

OF COUNSEL

Joseph Neff Ewing, Jr. (Resident)

For full biographical listings, see the Martindale-Hubbell Law Directory

BETHLEHEM, Northampton Co.

LITTNER, DESCHLER & LITTNER (AV)

512 North New Street, P.O. Box 1407, 18016
Telephone: 610-865-6770
Fax: 610-865-6433

MEMBERS OF FIRM

Robert H. Littner
Michael C. Deschler
Robert V. Littner

For full biographical listings, see the Martindale-Hubbell Law Directory

O'HARE & HEITCZMAN (AV)

18 East Market Street, P.O. Box 1446, 18018
Telephone: 610-691-5500
Fax: 610-691-7866
Email: heitczman@nni.com *URL:* http://www.heitczman.com

MEMBERS OF FIRM

Bernard V. O'Hare, Jr. (1923-1990)
George A. Heitczman

References: Summit Bank; CoreStates Bank.

For full biographical listings, see the Martindale-Hubbell Law Directory

BLUE BELL, Montgomery Co.

GERBER & GERBER (AV)

790 Penllyn-Blue Bell Pike, Suite 100, 19422
Telephone: 610-279-6700; 215-540-9100
Fax: 215-540-9424
Email: grbrlaw@dynanet.com *URL:* http://www.lawyers.com/gerber&gerber

Morris Gerber (1908-1995)

MEMBERS OF FIRM

A. Richard Gerber

For full biographical listings, see the Martindale-Hubbell Law Directory

KELLEY & MURPHY (AV)

Union Meeting Corporate Center V, Suite 160 925 Harvest Drive, 19422
Telephone: 215-643-6500
Fax: 215-643-8356
Cable Address: "BIGTIME"
Email: kmlaw@counsel.com

Joseph T. Kelley, Jr.
Patrick G. Murphy
Joseph T. Kelley, III

LEGAL SUPPORT PERSONNEL

Marianne Rowen
Tanja M.Z. Barron

For full biographical listings, see the Martindale-Hubbell Law Directory

BRADFORD, McKean Co.

MCDOWELL, WICK, DALY, GALLUP, HAUSER AND HARTLE (AV)

Forest Oil Building, 78 Main Street, P.O. Box 361, 16701
Telephone: 814-362-5517
Fax: 814-362-5104
Email: mwdlaw@penn.com

MEMBERS OF FIRM

T. L. McDowell (1911-1970)
Daniel W. Daly (1917-1980)
J. J. McDowell (1906-1982)
William J. Kubiak (1952-1991)
Robert H. Wick (1916-1997)
Frederick W. Gallup
Christopher G. Hauser
Daniel J. Hartle

Counsel for: National City Bank of Pennsylvania; Northwest Savings Bank; Bradford City Water Authority; Zippo Manufacturing Co.; Bradford Area School District; University of Pittsburgh, Bradford, Pennsylvania; Werzalit of America, Inc.; McCourt Label Co.; Bradford Forest Products, Inc.

For full biographical listings, see the Martindale-Hubbell Law Directory

BRISTOL, Bucks Co.

BEGLEY, CARLIN & MANDIO (AV)

120 Mill Street, 19007
Telephone: 215-750-0110
Fax: 215-750-0954
Email: bcm@itw.com
Langhorne, Pennsylvania Office: 680 Middletown Boulevard, P.O. Box 308.
Telephone: 215-750-0110.

MEMBERS OF FIRM

William J. Carlin
S. Richard Klinges, III
Thomas J. Profy, III
Richard M. Snyder
Charles F. Sampsel
John P. Koopman
Jeffrey P. Garton
Thomas R. Hecker
James A. Downey, III
Joseph S. Britton
Douglas C. Maloney
Thomas J. Profy, IV

ASSOCIATES

Karen Saraco Burns
Timothy J. Duffy
Randall L. Miller
Jennifer L. McGrath

OF COUNSEL

Anthony A. Mandio

For full biographical listings, see the Martindale-Hubbell Law Directory

*BUTLER,** Butler Co.

DILLON MCCANDLESS KING COULTER & GRAHAM L.L.P. (AV)

128 West Cunningham Street, 16001
Telephone: 724-283-2200
Fax: 724-283-2298
Email: DMKCG@aol.com
Cranberry Township, Pennsylvania Office: Route 19, Cranberry Professional Park, Suite 3, 501 Smith Drive.
Telephone: 724-776-6644.
Fax: 724-776-6608.
Saxonburg, Pennsylvania Office: 333 West Main Street, Dinnerbell Square, Suite 107.
Telephone: 724-352-2500.
Fax: 724-352-2577.

(See Next Column)

DILLON MCCANDLESS KING COULTER & GRAHAM L.L.P., *Butler—Continued*

MEMBERS OF FIRM

Thomas W. King, III
James P. Coulter
Donald P. Graham

ASSOCIATES

Mary Jo Dillon
Thomas E. Breth
Michael D. Hnath
Sandra S. Neuman
Matthew F. Marshall (Resident, Cranberry Township, Pennsylvania Office)
Nicole R. Betters (Resident, Cranberry Township, Pennsylvania Office)
Andrea C. Parenti

OF COUNSEL

Charles E. Dillon
Richard L. McCandless
Charles T. Shaffer

Representative Clients: Pennsylvania Manufacturers Association Insurance Co.; City of Butler; DuCo Ceramics Co.; Carson Industries, Inc.; Butler Area School District; Mellon Bank, N.A.; AG Choice Farm Credit.

For full biographical listings, see the Martindale-Hubbell Law Directory

*CARLISLE,** Cumberland Co.

MARTSON DEARDORFF WILLIAMS & OTTO, A PROFESSIONAL CORPORATION (AV)

Ten East High Street, 17013-3093
Telephone: 717-243-3341
Fax: 717-243-1850
URL: http://www.mdwo.com

William F. Martson
Thomas J. Williams
John B. Fowler, III
Ivo V. Otto, III
Daniel K. Deardorff
Stephen L. Bloom
George B. Faller, Jr.

Carl C. Risch
Benjamin T. Warner

LEGAL SUPPORT PERSONNEL

Corrine L. Myers (Estates Administration)
Nichole L. Myers (Litigation Support)
Lori A. Sullivan (Litigation Support)
Brandi Alleman (Real Estate)
Tricia D. Eckenrood (Litigation Support)
Denise L. Nye (Transactional Support)
Jacqueline A. Decker (Transactional and Litigation Support)

Representative Clients: Aetna Casualty and Surety Co.; Liberty Mutual Insurance Co.; Northland Insurance Co.; Pennsylvania Manufacturers Association Insurance Co.; The Travelers Insurance Group; United States Fidelity & Guarantee; Carlisle Hospital; Keen Leasing, Inc.; TV Cable of Carlisle; Cumberland Crossings Retirement Community.

For full biographical listings, see the Martindale-Hubbell Law Directory

*CHAMBERSBURG,** Franklin Co.

BARLEY, SNYDER, SENFT & COHEN, LLC (AV)

247 Lincoln Way East, 17201
Telephone: 717-264-6494
Fax: 717-264-1662
Email: barley@barley.com *URL:* http://www.barley.com
Harrisburg, Pennsylvania Office: 240 North Third Street.
Telephone: 717-238-8263.
Fax: 717-238-8278.
Lancaster, Pennsylvania Office: 126 East King Street.
Telephone: 717-299-5201.
Fax: 717-291-4660.
York, Pennsylvania Office: 100 East Market Street.
Telephone: 717-846-8888.
Fax: 717-843-8492.
Reading, Pennsylvania Office: 501 Washington Street.
Telephone: 610-376-6651.
Fax: 610-376-5243.
Hanover, Pennsylvania Office: 14 Center Square.
Telephone: 717-637-6239.
Fax: 717-637-5407.
Birdsboro, Pennsylvania Office: 115 E. Main Street.
Telephone: 610-582-2735.
Hamburg, Pennsylvania Office: 239 State Street.
Telephone: 610-562-3721.
Oley, Pennsylvania Office: Route 73 and Main Street.
Telephone: 610-987-6350.
Morgantown, Pennsylvania Office: Route 23.
Telephone: 610-286-5958.

MEMBERS OF FIRM

Martha B. Walker
Carol E. Van Horn
Christopher W. Mattson
Timothy P. Brown
Kathleen Ann Gray
Lynn Y. MacBride
David R. Keller
Michael W. Davis
Melanie A. Zampini

(See Next Column)

ASSOCIATES

Anne S. Johnson
John W. Venskus

For full biographical listings, see the Martindale-Hubbell Law Directory

*DANVILLE,** Montour Co.

JACK C. YOUNKIN (AV)

223 Mill Street, 17821
Telephone: 717-275-7742
Fax: 717-275-7749
Email: jcy1@Postoffice.ptd.net *URL:* http://www.lawyers.com/younkinlaw
Shamokin, Pennsylvania Office: One West Sunbury Street, 17872.
Telephone: 717-648-6821.
Fax: 717-648-4732.

ASSOCIATE

Barbara G. Martin

For full biographical listings, see the Martindale-Hubbell Law Directory

*EASTON,** Northampton Co.

LITTNER, DESCHLER & LITTNER

(See Bethlehem)

GUS MILIDES (AV)

654 Wolf Avenue, 18042
Telephone: 610-258-0433
Fax: 610-258-4875

For full biographical listings, see the Martindale-Hubbell Law Directory

*ERIE,** Erie Co.

KNOX MCLAUGHLIN GORNALL & SENNETT, P.C. (AV)

120 West Tenth Street, 16501-1461
Telephone: 814-459-2800
Fax: 814-453-4530

Conrad A. Pearson (1917-1969)
Donald E. Wright, Jr.
Jackson D. Magenau (1907-1984)
Richard W. Perhacs
Robert G. Dwyer
Mortimer E. Graham (1901-1987)
Mark E. Mioduszewski
Carl N. Moore
John M. McLaughlin (Retired)
David M. Mosier
M. Fletcher Gornall (Retired)
Thomas A. Tupitza
Joseph F. MacKrell (Retired)
Guy C. Fustine
John W. Beatty (Retired)
Richard E. Bordonaro
William C. Sennett
Brian Glowacki
Edwin L. R. McKean
John O. Dodick
Wallace J. Knox, II
Timothy M. Sennett
Richard H. Zamboldi
William C. Wagner
Richard A. Levick
Patricia K. Smith
Jack M. Gornall
Mark T. Wassell
Harry K. Thomas
Richard A. Lanzillo
Michael A. Fetzner
Joanna K. Budde
James T. Marnen
Peter A. Pentz

R. Perrin Baker
Timothy M. Zieziula
Mark G. Claypool
Gregory W. Breski
Thomas C. Hoffman, II
W. John Knox III
Mark J. Kuhar
Jennifer E. Gornall
Christopher J. Sinnott
Vasilios Nacopoulos

For full biographical listings, see the Martindale-Hubbell Law Directory

MACDONALD, ILLIG, JONES & BRITTON LLP (AV)

100 State Street, Suite 700, 16507-1498
Telephone: 814-870-7600
Fax: 814-454-4647
Email: webmaster@macdonaldillig.com

MEMBERS OF FIRM

Henry A. MacDonald (1928-1984)
James M. Antoun
James R. Walczak
William F. Illig (1946-1989)
Russell S. Warner
Frederick F. Jones (1939-1977, retired)
Marcia H. Haller
James E. Spoden
John E. Britton
Dale Huntley
John D. Wilson
John J. Mead
John J. Stroh, Jr.
John W. Draskovic
Norman H. Stark
John J. Mehler
T. Warren Jones
Matthew W. McCullough
Edward W. Goebel, Jr.
Susan Fuhrer Reiter
James D. Cullen
Richard J. Parks
William R. Brown
Mark J. Shaw
Roger H. Taft
John F. Mizner
David E. Holland
Craig R. F. Murphey
Wm. Patrick Delaney
Daniel M. Miller

(See Next Column)

MACDONALD, ILLIG, JONES & BRITTON LLP—*Continued*

ASSOCIATES

Shaun B. Adrian
Kimberly A. Oakes
Eric J. Purchase
Lisa Lynn Smith
Thomas A. Pendleton
Laura Popoff Stefanovski
John A. Lauer
Bruce L. Decker, Jr.
Walter E. Deacon III
Gregory P. Zimmerman
Robert E. Gandley
Catherine M. Moodey

Representative Clients: Erie Insurance Exchange; General Electric Co.; General Motors Corporation; Hamot Health Foundation; International Paper Co.; National City Bank of Pennsylvania.

For full biographical listings, see the Martindale-Hubbell Law Directory

MARSH, SPAEDER, BAUR, SPAEDER & SCHAAF, LLP (AV)

Suite 300, 300 State Street, 16507
Telephone: 814-456-5301
Fax: 814-456-1112
Email: MSBSS@AOL.COM

MEMBERS OF FIRM

James E. Marsh, Sr. (1908-1988)
Ritchie T. Marsh (1870-1947)
John A. Spaeder (1902-1994)
Robert N. Spaeder (1915-1993)
Byron A. Baur (Retired)
Will J. Schaaf
Ritchie T. Marsh
William J. Schaaf
James E. Marsh, Jr.
John P. Eppinger
John C. Brydon
Thomas E. Kuhn
Thomas M. Lent
Francis J. Klemensic
John B. Fessler
Eugene C. Sundberg, Jr.
James R. Fryling
Donald F. Fessler, Jr.
Kurt L. Sundberg

Jeffrey Scibetta

Representative Clients: Borough of Edinboro; Cincinnati Insurance; Donegal Mutual Insurance Co.; Progressive Insurance; Erie Parking Authority; Home Insurance Co.; Marquette Savings Assn.; Motorists Insurance Co.; Northwest Savings Bank; Risk Enterprise and Management, Ltd.

For full biographical listings, see the Martindale-Hubbell Law Directory

THE MCDONALD GROUP, L.L.P. (AV)

Limited Liability Partnership
456 West 6th Street, P.O. Box 1757, 16507-0757
Telephone: 814-456-5318
Fax: 814-456-3840
Email: tmg@tmgattys.com *URL:* http://www.tmgattys.com

James D. McDonald, Jr.
Gary Eiben
Daniel J. Pastore
Thomas J. Buseck

Brian M. McGowan
John J. Estok

OF COUNSEL

John G. Gent

For full biographical listings, see the Martindale-Hubbell Law Directory

EXTON, Chester Co.

MACELREE, HARVEY, GALLAGHER, FEATHERMAN & SEBASTIAN, LTD. (AV)

740 Springdale Drive, Suite 110, 19341
Telephone: 610-524-7575
Fax: 610-524-9857
West Chester, Pennsylvania Office: 17 West Miner Street. P.O. Box 660.
Telephone: 610-435-0100.
Fax: 610-430-7885.
Kennett Square, Pennsylvania Office: 211 E. State Street, P. O. Box 363.
Telephone 610-444-3180.
Fax: 610-444-3270.

Louis N. Teti

References: PNC Bank; Downtown National Bank.

For full biographical listings, see the Martindale-Hubbell Law Directory

*GREENSBURG,** Westmoreland Co.

BELDEN, BELDEN, PERSIN & JOHNSTON (AV)

Belden Building, 117 North Main Street, 15601
Telephone: 724-834-0300
Fax: 724-834-1307

MEMBERS OF FIRM

H. Reginald Belden (1907-1993)
H. Reginald Belden, Jr.
Dennis N. Persin
Robert I. Johnston

(See Next Column)

ASSOCIATES

John K. Greiner
Jeffrey D. Monzo

Representative Clients: GenCorp.; Moore & Morford, Inc.; Standard Steel; Equipment Finance Co.; The Home Insurance Co.; Westmoreland Museum of Art; Grange Mutual Insurance Co.; Bell Telephone of Pennsylvania; Coregil Group; Tara Developers.

For full biographical listings, see the Martindale-Hubbell Law Directory

GROVE CITY, Mercer Co.

MCBRIDE AND MCBRIDE, P.C. (AV)

211 South Center Street, 16127
Telephone: 724-458-6640
Fax: 724-458-5401

Milford L. McBride (1889-1962)
Milford L. McBride, Jr.
Brenda K. McBride
Milford L. McBride, III

Counsel for: Bashlin Industries; George J. Howe Co.; Tri-County Industries, Inc.; Clinch-Tite Corp.; C-B Grove City Federal Credit Union; Liberty and Worth Townships.

For full biographical listings, see the Martindale-Hubbell Law Directory

HANOVER, York Co.

BARLEY, SNYDER, SENFT & COHEN, LLC (AV)

Formerly: Daniel M. Frey & Associates, P.C.
14 Center Square, 17331
Telephone: 717-637-6239
Fax: 717-637-5407
Email: barley@barley.com *URL:* http://www.barley.com
Lancaster, Pennsylvania Office: 126 East King Street.
Telephone: 717-299-5201.
Fax: 717-291-4660.
Harrisburg, Pennsylvania Office: 240 North Third Street.
Telephone: 717-238-8263.
Fax: 717-238-8278.
York, Pennsylvania Office: 100 East Market Street.
Telephone: 717-846-8888.
Fax: 717-843-8492.
Chambersburg, Pennsylvania Office: 247 Lincoln Way East.
Telephone: 717-264-6494.
Fax: 717-264-1662.
Reading, Pennsylvania Office: 501 Washington Street.
Telephone: 610-376-6651.
Fax: 610-376-5243.
Birdsboro, Pennsylvania Office: 115 E. Main Street.
Telephone: 610-582-2735.
Hamburg, Pennsylvania Office: 239 State Street.
Telephone: 610-562-3721.
Oley, Pennsylvania Office: Route 73 and Main Street.
Telephone: 610-987-6350.
Morgantown, Pennsylvania Office: Route 23.
Telephone: 610-286-5958.

MEMBERS OF FIRM

Daniel M. Frey
Rees Griffiths
David R. Keller
Jeffrey D. Lobach
Paul G. Mattaini
Timothy P. Brown
Deborah A. Datte
Michael W. Davis

ASSOCIATES

Craig T. Trebilcock
John L. Senft
Kimberly J. Decker
Andrew T. Kravitz

Representative Clients: Bank of Hanover and Trust Co.; J.A. Myers Building and Development Inc.; Snyders of Hanover; Sheppard Enterprises; D.F. Stauffer Biscuit; Fulton Bank/Fulton Financial Corp.; Summit Health; South Central Community Health.

For full biographical listings, see the Martindale-Hubbell Law Directory

*HARRISBURG,** Dauphin Co.

BARLEY, SNYDER, SENFT & COHEN, LLC (AV)

240 North Third Street, P.O. Box 1129, 17108
Telephone: 717-238-8263
Fax: 717-238-8278
Email: barley@barley.com *URL:* http://www.barley.com
Lancaster, Pennsylvania Office: 126 East King Street.
Telephone: 717-299-5201.
Fax: 717-291-4660.
York, Pennsylvania Office: 100 East Market Street.
Telephone: 717-846-8888.
Fax: 717-843-8492.
Chambersburg, Pennsylvania Office: 247 Lincoln Way East.
Telephone: 717-264-6494.
Fax: 717-264-1662.
Reading, Pennsylvania Office: 501 Washington Street.
Telephone: 610-376-6651.
Fax: 610-376-5243.
Hanover, Pennsylvania Office: 14 Center Square.
Telephone: 717-637-6239.
Fax: 717-637-5407.

(See Next Column)

BARLEY, SNYDER, SENFT & COHEN LLC, *Harrisburg—Continued*

Birdsboro, Pennsylvania Office: 115 E. Main Street.
Telephone: 610-582-2735.
Hamburg, Pennsylvania Office: 239 State Street.
Telephone: 610-562-3721.
Oley, Pennsylvania Office: Route 73 and Main Street.
Telephone: 610-987-6350.
Morgantown, Pennsylvania Office: Route 23.
Telephone: 610-286-5958.

MEMBERS OF FIRM

Harry J. Rubin
David R. Keller
Brian R. Ott
Michael S. Butler
Michael W. Davis

ASSOCIATE

Robert Freedenberg

RETIRED

H. Robert Lasday

Representative State Tax Clients: ABD. Inc.; American Home Products Corporation; Akzo America, Inc.; Combustion Engineering, Inc.; Conoco, Inc.; Dean Witter Reynolds, Inc.; E.I. DuPont de Nemours and Company; Ford Motor Company; General Public Utilities Corporation.

For full biographical listings, see the Martindale-Hubbell Law Directory

BECKLEY & MADDEN (AV)

Cranberry Court, 212 North Third Street, P.O. Box 11998, 17108
Telephone: 717-233-7691
Fax: 717-233-3740
Email: becks@pa.net

MEMBERS OF FIRM

Thomas A. Beckley
William J. Madden, Jr. (1911-1992)
John G. Milakovic

ASSOCIATES

Charles O. Beckley, II
Elizabeth S. Beckley
Thomas S. Beckley

OF COUNSEL

Frances Ruml Beckley

LEGAL SUPPORT PERSONNEL

Mary V. Davis (Administrative Manager)

For full biographical listings, see the Martindale-Hubbell Law Directory

DECHERT PRICE & RHOADS (AV)

Thirty North Third Street, 17101-1603
Telephone: 717-237-2000
Telefax: 717-237-2040
URL: http://www.dechert.com
Philadelphia, Pennsylvania: 4000 Bell Atlantic Tower, 1717 Arch Street, 19103-2793.
Telephone: 215-994-4000.
New York, New York: 30 Rockefeller Plaza, 10112.
Telephone: 212-698-3500.
Washington, D.C.: 1775 Eye Street, N.W., 20006.
Telephone: 202-261-3300.
Princeton, New Jersey: Princeton Pike Corporate Center, P.O. Box 5218, 08543-5218.
Telephone: 609-620-3200.
Boston, Massachusetts: Ten Post Office Square South, 02109-4603.
Telephone: 617-728-7100.
Hartford, Connecticut: 90 State House Square, 06103-3702.
Telephone: 860-524-3999.
London, England: 2 Serjeants' Inn, EC4Y 1LT.
Telephone: (0171) 583-5353. (Also see Titmuss Sainer Dechert).
Brussels, Belgium: 65 Avenue Louise, 1050.
Telephone: (02) 535-5411.
Paris, France: 55, avenue Kléber, 76116.
Telephone: 33-(0) 1-53 65 05 00.

RESIDENT PARTNERS

David R. Kraus

COUNSEL

Robert D. Reber, Jr.

RESIDENT ASSOCIATES

Richard C. Kariss
Debra A. MacPhee
Kevin M. Scott
John E. Van Allen
Aaron M. Young

For full biographical listings, see the Martindale-Hubbell Law Directory

DUANE, MORRIS & HECKSCHER LLP (AV)

305 North Front Street, 5th Floor, P.O. Box 1003, 17108-1003
Telephone: 717-232-4015
Cable-Telegraph Address: TWX 710-670-1164
Fax: 717-232-4015
URL: http://www.duanemorris.com
Philadelphia, Pennsylvania Office: Suite 4200, One Liberty Place.
Telephone: 215-979-1000.
Fax: 215-979-1020.
New York, New York Office: 380 Lexington Avenue.
Telephone: 212-692-1000.
Fax: 212-692-1020.
Chicago, Illinois Office: 227 West Monroe Street, Suite 3400.
Telephone: 312-499-6700.
Fax: 312-499-6701.
Washington, D.C. Office: 1667 K Street, N.W., Suite 700.
Telephone: 202-776-7800.
Fax: 202-776-7801.
San Francisco, California Office: 100 Spear Street.
Telephone: 415-371-2200.
Fax: 415-371-2201.
Boston, Massachusetts Office: One International Place, 14th Floor.
Telephone: 617-598-3100.
Fax: 617-598-3101.
Miami, Florida Office: 200 South Biscayne Boulevard, Suite 3410.
Telephone: 305-571-5550.
Fax: 302-571-5560.
Wilmington, Delaware Office: 1201 Market Street, Suite 1500.
Telephone: 302-571-5550.
Fax: 302-571-5560.
Wayne, Pennsylvania Office: 735 Chesterbrook Boulevard, Suite 300.
Telephone: 610-647-3555.
Fax: 610-640-2619.
Cherry Hill, New Jersey Office: 51 Haddonfield Road, Suite 340.
Telephone: 856-488-7300.
Fax: 856-488-7021.
Newark, New Jersey Office: One Riverfront Plaza.
Telephone: 973-424-2000.
Fax: 973-424-2001.
Palm Beach, Florida Office: 249 Royal Palm Way, Suite 403.
Telephone: 561-366-5400.
Fax: 561-366-5401.
Allentown, Pennsylvania Office: 968 Postal Road, Suite 200, P.O. Box 90400.
Telephone: 610-266-3650.
Fax: 610-266-3651.
Houston, Texas Office: One Greenway Plaza, Suite 500.
Telephone: 713-552-9900.
Fax: 713-552-0109.
Dover, Delaware Office: 314 S. State Street.
Telephone: 302-736-0156.
Fax: 302-736-0336.

RESIDENT PARTNERS

Eric L. Brossman
Matthew Chabal, III
Shaun R. Eisenhauer
Robert J. Goduto
Arthur K. Hoffman
Robert E. Kelly, Jr.
Mary P. Patterson-Lavery
Scott C. Penwell (Partner-in-Charge, Harrisburg)
Gary A. Ritter
Kenneth L. Sable
Catherine E. Walters
Allen C. Warshaw

RESIDENT ASSOCIATES

Robert J. Bein
Brian W. Bisignani
Edward A. McMerty, III
Kirsten C. Miller
Marc A. Moyer
Jennifer L. Murphy
Jeffrey P. Ouellet
Robert A. Quigley
Robin M. Wilder
Douglas M. Wolfberg

COUNSEL

Paul E. Scanlan

For full biographical listings, see the Martindale-Hubbell Law Directory

ECKERT SEAMANS CHERIN & MELLOTT, LLC (AV)

213 Market Street, Eighth Floor, 17101
Telephone: 717-237-6000
Facsimile: 717-237-6019
Email: escm.hsbg@escm.com *URL:* http://www.escm.com
Pittsburgh, Pennsylvania Office: 600 Grant Street, 44th Floor.
Telephone: 412-566-6000.
Facsimile: 412-566-6099.
Philadelphia, Pennsylvania Office: 1515 Market Street, Ninth Floor,
Telephone: 215-851-8400.
Facsimile: 215-851-8383.
Boston, Massachusetts Office: One International Place, 18th Floor.
Telephone: 617-342-6800.
Facsimile: 617-342-6899.
Fort Lauderdale, Florida Office: Las Olas Centre, Suite 800, 450 East Las Olas Boulevard.
Telephone: 954-523-0400.
Facsimile: 954-523-7002.
Haddonfield, New Jersey Office: 36 Tanner Street, Second Floor.
Telephone: 609-427-6240.
Facsimile: 609-427-0611.

(See Next Column)

ECKERT SEAMANS CHERIN & MELLOTT LLC—*Continued*

Washington, D.C. Office: 1250 24th Street, N.W., Suite 700.
Telephone: 202-659-6600.
Facsimile: 202-659-6699.

MEMBERS OF FIRM

LeRoy S. Zimmerman
Loudon L. Campbell
C. Peter Carlucci, Jr.
Christopher M. Cicconi
Carol Porell Cocheres
Mark E. Gebauer
Norman P. Hetrick
John R. Kachur
James J. Kutz
Ronald M. Lucas
Richard D. Michael
Bridget E. Montgomery
Joseph K. Pierce
Charles E. Zaleski
James A. M. Zarrella

RESIDENT SPECIAL COUNSEL

Thomas P. Gacki
Burton D. Morris

RESIDENT OF COUNSEL

Walter W. Shearer

RESIDENT ASSOCIATES

K. Robert Bertram
Mark D. Bradshaw
David L. Bricker
Richard L. Grubb
Thomas L. Isenberg, Jr.
Lauri A. LaFoe
Scott R. Mehok
Joseph D. Shelby
Adam M. Shienvold
Charles M. Suhr
Barbara A. Zemlock

For full biographical listings, see the Martindale-Hubbell Law Directory

GOLDBERG, KATZMAN & SHIPMAN, P.C. (AV)

320 Market Street - Strawberry Square, P.O. Box 1268, 17108-1268
Telephone: 717-234-4161
Telecopier: 717-234-6808; 717-234-6810
Email: gks@gkslaw.com

Ronald M. Katzman
F. Lee Shipman
Paul J. Esposito
Neil Hendershot
Jesse Jay Cooper
Thomas E. Brenner
John A. Statler
April L. Strang-Kutay
Guy H. Brooks
Jefferson J. Shipman
Jerry J. Russo
Michael J. Crocenzi
Thomas J. Weber

Arnold B. Kogan
Evan J. Kline
Steven E. Grubb
John R. Ninosky
John DeLorenzo
Diana Woodside

OF COUNSEL

Arthur L. Goldberg
Joshua D. Lock

Representative Clients: Ameralum, Inc.; Cincinnati Insurance Co.; The Atlantic Mutual Cos.; Erie Insurance Group; Maryland Commercial Insurance Group; State Auto Insurance Co.; Dauphin County General Authority; Flight Systems, Inc.; Tressler Lutheran Services; Merchants & Businessman's Mutual Insurance Co.
Reference: Fulton Bank.

For full biographical listings, see the Martindale-Hubbell Law Directory

KEEFER WOOD ALLEN & RAHAL, LLP (AV)

210 Walnut Street, P.O. Box 11963, 17108-1963
Telephone: 717-255-8000
Telecopier: 717-255-8050
Email: info@keeferwood.com *URL:* http://www.keeferwood.com
Camp Hill, Pennsylvania Office: 415 Fallowfield Road.
Telephone: 717-612-5800.
Telecopier: 717-612-5805.

MEMBERS OF FIRM

Heath L. Allen
N. David Rahal
Charles W. Rubendall II
Robert L. Weldon
Eugene E. Pepinsky, Jr
Thomas E. Wood
John H. Enos, III
Gary E. French
Donna S. Weldon
Bradford Dorrance
Jeffrey S. Stokes
Stephen L. Grose
Robert R. Church
R. Scott Shearer
Wayne M. Pecht

OF COUNSEL

Samuel C. Harry

SENIOR ATTORNEYS

Donald M. Lewis, III
Bridget M. Whitley

ASSOCIATES

Brenda L. Gacki
Allan J. Rossi
John A. Feichtel

Representative Clients: ALCOA; Arnold Industries, Inc.; Bethlehem Steel Co.; Caterpillar, Inc.; Highmark, Inc.; Mellon Bank, N.A.; IBM Corp.

For full biographical listings, see the Martindale-Hubbell Law Directory

MANCKE, WAGNER, HERSHEY AND TULLY (AV)

2233 North Front Street, 17110
Telephone: 717-234-7051

(See Next Column)

MEMBERS OF FIRM

John B. Mancke
P. Richard Wagner
David E. Hershey
William T. Tully

For full biographical listings, see the Martindale-Hubbell Law Directory

MCNEES, WALLACE & NURICK (AV)

100 Pine Street, P.O. Box 1166, 17108-1166
Telephone: 717-232-8000
Fax: 717-237-5300
Email: info@mwn.com *URL:* http://www.mwn.com
Columbus, Ohio Office: 21 East State Street, Suite 1700, 43215.
Telephone: 614-469-8000.
Fax: 614-469-4653.
Washington, D.C. Office: 1200 G Street, N.W., 20005.
Telephone: 202-434-8991.
Fax: 202-434-8707.
Hazleton, Pennsylvania Office: 1 South Church Street, Suite 302, 18201.
Telephone: 570-455-8300.
Fax: 570-455-8390.

Sterling G. McNees (1887-1959)
David M. Wallace (1892-1967)
Gilbert Nurick (1906-1993)

MEMBERS OF THE FIRM

Bruce D. Bagley
Alan R. Boynton, Jr.
Robert M. Cherry
Louis A. Dejoie
David B. Disney
Michael A. Doctrow
James P. Dougherty
Harvey Freedenberg
James L. Fritz
Louise Hutchinson
W. Jeffry Jamouneau
Michael G. Jarman
Donald B. Kaufman
Stephen R. Kern
David M. Kleppinger
James W. Kutz
Delano M. Lantz
David E. Lehman
Elizabeth A. Maguschak (Resident, Hazleton Office)
Franklin A. Miles, Jr.
Robert A. Mills
Stephen A. Moore
Nedric L. Nissly
John S. Oyler
Mark R. Parthemer
Samuel C. Randazzo (Resident, Columbus, Ohio Office)
Carmen Santa Maria
Dana Stevens Scaduto
Richard W. Stevenson
Diane M. Tokarsky
Mark M. Van Blargan
David M. Watts, Jr.
Steven J. Weingarten
Norman I. White
Lawrence R. Wieder
William M. Young, Jr.

OF COUNSEL

Kathleen A. Dunst
Jonathan H. Rudd
Carol A. Steinour

ASSOCIATES

Jennifer LaPorta Baker
James R. Berger
Susan E. Bruce
Charis M. Burak
Jeffrey F. Champagne
Thomas G. Collins
Charles M. Courtney
James P. DeAngelo
Timothy R. Deckert
Marc J. Farrell
Debra P. Fourlas
Helen L. Gemmill
Scott A. Gould
Samuel W. Grossmann (Resident, Columbus, Ohio Office)
Schaun D. Henry
Brian F. Jackson
Michael R. Kelley
Stephanie Kleinfelter
Peter F. Kriete
Jonathan Landesman
Linda J. Laub
Andrew L. Levy
F. Stephenson Matthes
Ellen K. McDonnell (Not admitted in PA)
Sharon R. Paxton
Chad F. Phipps
Pamela C. Polacek
Donald A. Sawyer
Mitchell A. Smolow (Resident, Hazleton Office)
Bruce R. Spicer
Curtis N. Stambaugh
Rhonda Markle Weaver
Robert A. Weishaar, Jr.
Kimberly J. Wile (Resident, Columbus, Ohio Office)
Laura H. Williams
Derrick P. Williamson
Neil W. Yahn
Charles T. Young, Jr.

RETIRED PARTNERS

Francis B. Haas, Jr.
Samuel A. Schreckengaust, Jr.
Richard R. Lefever

For full biographical listings, see the Martindale-Hubbell Law Directory

METTE, EVANS & WOODSIDE, A PROFESSIONAL CORPORATION (AV)

3401 North Front Street, P.O. Box 5950, 17110-0950
Telephone: 717-232-5000
Fax: 717-236-1816
Email: MEW@Mette.com *URL:* HTTP://WWW.METTE.COM

Howell C. Mette
James W. Evans
Robert Moore
Charles B. Zwally
Peter J. Ressler
Lloyd R. Persun
Craig A. Stone
James A. Ulsh
Daniel L. Sullivan
Steven D. Snyder
Christopher C. Conner
Elyse E. Rogers
Jeffrey A. Ernico
Kathryn Lease Simpson

(See Next Column)

METTE, EVANS & WOODSIDE A PROFESSIONAL CORPORATION, *Harrisburg—Continued*

P. Daniel Altland
Andrew H. Dowling
Michael D. Reed
Paula J. Leicht
Gary J. Heim
David A. Fitzsimons
Michael D. Pipa
Guy P. Beneventano
Thomas F. Smida

Robyn Katzman Bowman
John F. Yaninek
Vicky Ann Trimmer
Kathleen Doyle Yaninek
Elizabeth J. Goldstein
Bradley A. Walker
Donna L. Gareis-Smith
James M. Strong, VI
Bryan Scott Megary
John M. Hartzell

For full biographical listings, see the Martindale-Hubbell Law Directory

METZGER, WICKERSHAM, KNAUSS & ERB, P.C. (AV)

3211 North Front Street, P.O. Box 5300, 17110-0300
Telephone: 717-238-8187
Telefax: 717-234-9478
Other Harrisburg, Pennsylvania Office: 4813 Jonestown Road, P.O. Box 5300, 17110-0300.
Telephone: 717-652-7020.

Maurice R. Metzger (1918-1980)
F. Brewster Wickersham (1918-1974)
Edward E. Knauss, III (Retired)
Christian S. Erb, Jr.
Robert E. Yetter
James F. Carl
Edward E. Knauss, IV
Jered L. Hock
Karl R. Hildabrand
Richard B. Druby
Steven P. Miner

Clark DeVere
Carrie L. Carroll

Representative Clients: Allstate Insurance Co.; Chubb Group of Insurance Companies; Fireman's Fund American Insurance Group; Liberty Mutual Insurance Co.; Crum & Forster; CNA Insurance; Prudential Insurance Co.

For full biographical listings, see the Martindale-Hubbell Law Directory

PEPPER HAMILTON LLP (AV)

200 One Keystone Plaza, North Front and Market Streets, P.O. Box 1181, 17108-1181
Telephone: 717-255-1155
Telecopy: 717-238-0575
Email: phinfo@pepperlaw.com *URL:* http://www.pepperlaw.com
Philadelphia, Pennsylvania Office: 3000 Two Logan Square, Eighteenth and Arch Streets, 19103-2799.
Telephone: 215-981-4000.
Fax: 215-981-4750.
Washington, D.C. Office: Hamilton Square, 600 Fourteenth Street, N.W. 20005-2004.
Telephone: 202-220-1200.
Fax: 202-220-1665.
Detroit, Michigan Office: 100 Renaissance Center, 36th Floor, 48243-1157.
Telephone: 313-259-7110.
Fax: 313-259-7926.
New York, New York Office: 750 Lexington Avenue, Suite 600, 10022-1200.
Telephone: 212-813-9668.
Fax: 212-813-9802.
Wilmington, Delaware Office: 1201 Market Street, Suite 1600, P.O. Box 1709, 19899-1709.
Telephone: 302-777-6500.
Fax: 302-656-8865.
Pittsburgh, Pennsylvania Office: 500 Grant Street, 50th Floor, 15219-2502.
Telephone: 412-454-5000.
Fax: 412-281-0717.
Berwyn, Pennsylvania Office: 1235 Westlakes Drive, Suite 400, 19312-2401.
Telephone: 610-640-7800.
Fax: 610-640-7835.
Cherry Hill, New Jersey Office: LibertyView Building, Suite 420, 457 Haddonfield Road, 08002-2220.
Telephone: 856-910-7200.
Fax: 856-665-7743.

PARTNERS

Thomas B. Schmidt, III (Managing Partner, Harrisburg Office)
Timothy B. Anderson
John W. Carroll
Donna L. Fisher
Lois Sherman Hagarty
David W. Sweet

OF COUNSEL

Lewis S. Kunkel, Jr.

ASSOCIATES

Brian P. Downey
Eloise J. Frazier
John A. Greenbaum
Alexandra Makosky
Gregory S. Narsh
Randy L. Varner

For full biographical listings, see the Martindale-Hubbell Law Directory

RHOADS & SINON LLP (AV)

One South Market Square, 12th Floor, P.O. Box 1146, 17108-1146
Telephone: 717-233-5731
Fax: 717-232-1459
Boca Raton, Florida Affiliated Office: Charles L. Sieck, 1700 South Dixie Highway, Suite 2-C.
Telephone: 561-395-5595.
Fax: 561-395-9497.
York, Pennsylvania Office: 15 North Cherry Lane, Suite 21.
Telephone: 717-843-1718.
Fax: 717-232-1459.

OF COUNSEL

Frank A. Sinon
John C. Dowling
R. Stephen Shibla
Nathan H. Waters, Jr.

MEMBERS OF FIRM

Paul H. Rhoads (1907-1984)
John M. Musselman (1919-1980)
Clyle R. Hendershot (1922-1980)
Henry W. Rhoads
Robert H. Long, Jr.
Sherill T. Moyer
Jan P. Paden
Richard B. Wood
Lawrence B. Abrams, III
J. Bruce Walter
John P. Manbeck
Frank J. Leber
Paul A. Lundeen
Jack F. Hurley, Jr.
David B. Dowling
David F. O'Leary
David O. Twaddell
Charles J. Ferry
Stanley A. Smith
Jens H. Damgaard
Drake D. Nicholas
Thomas A. French
Dean H. Dusinberre
Donna M. J. Clark
Charles E. Gutshall
Paul F. Wessell
Shawn D. Lochinger
James H. Cawley
Dean F. Piermattei

ASSOCIATES

Lori J. McElroy
Todd J. Shill
Kenneth L. Joel
Robert F. Frazier
Thomas J. Nehilla
Kevin M. Gold
Carl D. Lundblad
Stephen Moniak
James E. Ellison
Richard E. Artell
Robert J. Tribeck
Timothy J. Nieman
Paul J. Bruder, Jr.
Labros E. Pilalis (Not admitted in PA)
Joanne Book Christine
Susan E. Schwab
Amy J. Mendelsohn

For full biographical listings, see the Martindale-Hubbell Law Directory

*INDIANA,** Indiana Co.

BONYA GAZZA & DEGORY, LLP (AV)

134 South Sixth Street, 15701
Telephone: 724-465-5535
Fax: 724-465-9685

John A. Bonya
Stanley P. DeGory
Beverly A. Gazza
Nicholas J. Mikesic
Michael J. Toretti
David M. Zimmerman

Reference: S & T Bank, of Indiana, Pennsylvania.

For full biographical listings, see the Martindale-Hubbell Law Directory

SIMPSON, KABLACK & BELL (AV)

20 North Seventh Street, 15701
Telephone: 724-465-5559
Fax: 724-465-2046

MEMBERS OF FIRM

John S. Simpson
Wayne A. Kablack
Paul A. Bell, II

ASSOCIATE

Thomas D. Rivosecchi

Attorneys for: S & T Bank, Indiana, PA; Pennsylvania Electric Co.

For full biographical listings, see the Martindale-Hubbell Law Directory

KENNETT SQUARE, Chester Co.

MACELREE, HARVEY, GALLAGHER, FEATHERMAN & SEBASTIAN, LTD. (AV)

211 E. State Street, P.O. Box 363, 19348
Telephone: 610-444-3180
West Chester Office: 17 West Miner Street, P.O. Box 660.
Telephone: 610-436-0100.
Fax: 610-430-7885.
Exton, Pennsylvania Office: 740 Springdale Drive, Suite 110.
Telephone: 610-524-7575.
Fax: 610-524-9857.

William J. Gallagher

For full biographical listings, see the Martindale-Hubbell Law Directory

Kennett Square—Continued

Prickett, Jones & Elliott, P.A. (AV)

217 West State Street, 19348
Telephone: 610-444-1573
Email: attorneys@prickett.com *URL:* http://www.prickett.com
Wilmington, Delaware Office: 1310 King Street.
Telephone: 302-888-6500.
Dover, Delaware Office: 11 North State Street.
Telephone: 302-674-3841.

MEMBERS OF FIRM

Richard I. G. Jones
William J. Martin, III

For full biographical listings, see the Martindale-Hubbell Law Directory

*KITTANNING,** Armstrong Co.

Steiner and Steiner (AV)

160 North McKean Street, P.O. Box 789, 16201-1519
Telephone: 724-543-1469
Fax: 724-545-1611

MEMBERS OF FIRM

Jack J. Steiner
Cindy L. Calarie

ASSOCIATE

Amy R. Smoyer

OF COUNSEL

Edward J. Steiner

General Counsel for: Armstrong County Building and Loan Assn.; PFC Bank; U.S. Energies Expl.
Local Counsel for: Range Resources.
Representative Clients: Commonwealth Land Title Insurance; Mellon Bank NA.

For full biographical listings, see the Martindale-Hubbell Law Directory

*LANCASTER,** Lancaster Co.

Barley, Snyder, Senft & Cohen, LLC (AV)

126 East King Street, 17602-2893
Telephone: 717-299-5201
Fax: 717-291-4660
Email: barley@barley.com *URL:* http://www.barley.com
Reading, Pennsylvania Office: 501 Washington Street.
Telephone: 610-376-6651.
Fax: 610-376-5243.
Harrisburg, Pennsylvania Office: 240 North Third Street.
Telephone: 717-238-8263.
Fax: 717-238-8278.
York, Pennsylvania Office: 100 East Market Street.
Telephone: 717-846-8888.
Fax: 717-843-8492.
Chambersburg, Pennsylvania Office: 247 Lincoln Way East.
Telephone: 717-264-6494.
Fax: 717-264-1662.
Hanover, Pennsylvania Office: 14 Center Square.
Telephone: 717-637-6239.
Fax: 717-637-5407.
Birdsboro, Pennsylvania Office: 115 E. Main Street.
Telephone: 610-582-2735.
Hamburg, Pennsylvania Office: 239 State Street.
Telephone: 610-562-3721.
Oley, Pennsylvania Office: Route 73 and Main Street.
Telephone: 610-987-6350.
Morgantown, Pennsylvania Office: Route 23.
Telephone: 610-286-5958.

MEMBERS OF FIRM

John O. Shirk
James R. Adams
W. Jeffrey Sidebottom
Christopher W. Mattson
Jesse C. Robinson
Paul M. Browning
Kathleen Ann Gray
George C. Werner, Jr.
David R. Keller
Caroline M. Hoffer
Paul G. Mattaini
Elaine Pennington Stanko
Paul D. Clouser
Michael A. Moore
Kendra D. McGuire
Anne E. Doliner
Timothy P. Brown
Deborah A. Datte
Ronald H. Pollock, Jr.
Michael S. Butler
Michael W. Davis
Katherine Betz Kravitz
Bruce J. Wolstoncroft

ASSOCIATES

Nancy Mayer Hughes
Craig T. Trebilcock
Leigh A. J. Ellis
Hanna-Aurelia Dunlap
Barbara M. Boben
Jennifer L. Craighead
Scott F. Landis
Robert A. Evarts
James F. Devine, III
Philip A. Wolgemuth
Theresa M. Melchiorre
John T. Reed
Gene P. Otto
Cynthia A. Otto
Stephanie Carfley
Kurt W. McCabe
Daniel M. Lieberman

(See Next Column)

RETIRED

Paul A. Mueller, Jr.
Charles R. Cooper, Jr.
John T. Barber

Counsel for: Franklin & Marshall College; Fulton Bank/Fulton Financial Corp.; Lancaster Chamber of Commerce and Industry; Lancaster General Hospital; Robert A. Kinsley, Inc.
Local Counsel for: Armstrong World Industries; Susquehanna Pfaltzgraff Co.; Graham Packaging.
Insurance Defense Counsel for: Medical Protective Co.; The PMA Group.

For full biographical listings, see the Martindale-Hubbell Law Directory

Zimmerman, Pfannebecker, Nuffort & Albert, LLP (AV)

22 South Duke Street, 17602
Telephone: 717-299-0711
Fax: 717-299-1092
Columbia, Pennsylvania Office: 342 Walnut Street.
Telephone: 717-684-2665.
Fax: 717-299-1092.
Lititz, Pennsylvania Office: 10 South Broad Street.
Telephone: 717-626-2088.
Quarryville, Pennsylvania Office: 100 East State Street.
Telephone: 717-786-8335.

MEMBERS OF FIRM

S. R. Zimmerman, III
Robert L. Pfannebecker
Richard P. Nuffort
Neil L. Albert
Barry Handwerger

References: First Union Bank, Fulton Bank, Farmers First Bank, all of Lancaster, Pennsylvania.

For full biographical listings, see the Martindale-Hubbell Law Directory

LANGHORNE, Bucks Co.

Begley, Carlin & Mandio (AV)

680 Middletown Boulevard, P.O. Box 308, 19047
Telephone: 215-750-0110
Fax: 215-750-0954
Email: BCM@ITW.COM
Bristol, Pennsylvania Office: 120 Mill Street.
Telephone: 215-750-0110.

MEMBERS OF FIRM

William J. Carlin
S. Richard Klinges, III
Thomas J. Profy, III
Richard M. Snyder
Charles F. Sampsel
John P. Koopman
Jeffrey P. Garton
Thomas R. Hecker
James A. Downey, III
Joseph S. Britton
Douglas C. Maloney
Thomas J. Profy, IV

ASSOCIATES

Karen Saraco Burns
Timothy J. Duffy
Randall L. Miller
Jennifer L. McGrath

OF COUNSEL

Anthony A. Mandio
C. David Krewson

Representative Clients: Borough of Bristol; Bristol Borough School Board; Lower Makefield Township; Waste Management, Inc.

For full biographical listings, see the Martindale-Hubbell Law Directory

*LEBANON,** Lebanon Co.

Henry & Beaver LLP (AV)

937 Willow Street, P.O. Box 1140, 17042-1140
Telephone: 717-274-3644
Facsimile: 717-274-6782
Email: hblaw@redrose.net

MEMBERS OF FIRM

Charles V. Henry, III
R. Hart Beaver
Frederick S. Wolf
Thomas P. Harlan
Wiley P. Parker
John H. Whitmoyer
Christopher J. Coyle
Kevin M. Richards
Marc A. Hess

ASSOCIATE

Ann E. Endres

Representative Clients: Lebanon Valley Farmers Bank; Cornwall Manor; Medical Protective Company of Fort Wayne; Nationwide Insurance Co.; Liberty Mutual Insurance Co.; Utica Mutual Insurance Co.; CIGNA Insurance Co.; Princeton Insurance Company; The Pennsylvania Sports Hall of Fame; Princeton Insurance Co.

For full biographical listings, see the Martindale-Hubbell Law Directory

*MEADVILLE,** Crawford Co.

Shafer, Swick, Bailey, Irwin, Stack & Millin (AV)

360 Chestnut Street, 16335
Telephone: 814-724-4540
Fax: 814-724-4545
URL: http://www.shaferlaw.com

(See Next Column)

SHAFER, SWICK, BAILEY, IRWIN, STACK & MILLIN, *Meadville—Continued*

MEMBERS OF FIRM

Paul E. Thomas (1892-1972) | James R. Irwin
Charles J. Swick | Louis J. Stack
Robert S. Bailey | Jeffrey K. Millin
John C. Swick

OF COUNSEL

Raymond P. Shafer | Paul D. Shafer, Jr.

Local Counsel: Pennsylvania Manufacturers Association Casualty Insurance Co.; Allegheny College; Motorists Mutual Insurance Co.; Mellon Bank, N.A.; Meadville Medical Center; Meadville Area Industrial Commission; Seco-Warwick Corp.; Wesbury United Methodist Community; Ag Choice Farm Credit, ACA; Channellock, Inc.

For full biographical listings, see the Martindale-Hubbell Law Directory

MECHANICSBURG, Cumberland Co.

SNELBAKER, BRENNEMAN & SPARE, P.C. (AV)

44 West Main Street, P.O. Box 318, 17055-6249
Telephone: 717-697-8528
Fax: 717-697-7681

Richard C. Snelbaker | Keith O. Brenneman
Philip H. Spare

Representative Clients: Big Spring School District; Borough of Mount Holly Springs; Cumberland Valley School District; East Pennsboro Area School District; Mechanicsburg Area School District; Middlesex Township Municipal Authority; Silver Spring Township Authority; Township of Hampden; Township of Middlesex; Township of Silver Spring.

For full biographical listings, see the Martindale-Hubbell Law Directory

*MEDIA,** Delaware Co.

BEATTY, CRAMP, KAUFFMAN & LINCKE (AV)

215 North Olive Street, P.O. Box 901, 19063
Telephone: 610-565-8800
Fax: 610-565-8127
Email: BCKLLaw@aol.com

MEMBERS OF FIRM

Lewis B. Beatty, Jr. | David G. Blake
Joseph W. Kauffman | William P. Lincke
David J. Otis | Natalie M. Habert
Peter W. Dicce

ASSOCIATES

Regina M. MacKenzie | Daniel J. McCusker
Bereth K. Graeff | Kelly A. Barnes

OF COUNSEL

John F. Cramp | Ralph B. D'Iorio
Robert C. Grasberger

Joseph R. Young (1921-1993)

For full biographical listings, see the Martindale-Hubbell Law Directory

DIORIO & SERENI, LLP (AV)

Front and Plum Streets, P.O. Box 1789, 19063
Telephone: 610-565-5700
Fax: 610-891-0652
Email: info@diorioserení.com

Robert M. DiOrio | Mark A. Sereni

ASSOCIATES

Kenneth J. D. Boyden | Christopher R. Mattox

For full biographical listings, see the Martindale-Hubbell Law Directory

PETRIKIN, WELLMAN, DAMICO, BROWN & PETROSA, A PROFESSIONAL CORPORATION (AV)

The William Penn Building, 109 Chesley Drive, 19063
Telephone: 610-565-2670
Fax: 610-565-0178

John W. Wellman | Steven A. Cohen
Joseph A. Damico, Jr. | Denis M. Dunn
Steven G. Brown | Mark D. Damico
Donald T. Petrosa | Howard M. Brown

Representative Clients: Sun Oil Co.; Toll Brothers; Wawa Food Markets; Employers Insurance of Wausau; Nationwide Mutual Insurance Co.; American Universal Insurance Co.

For full biographical listings, see the Martindale-Hubbell Law Directory

MILTON, Northumberland Co.

DAVIS, DAVIS & KAAR (AV)

37 Arch Street, P.O. Box 319, 17847
Telephone: 570-742-8777
Fax: 570-742-6155

MEMBERS OF FIRM

Preston B. Davis (1907-1990) | Preston L. Davis
R. Michael Kaar

Representative Clients: Watsontown Bank; Sun Home Health Services, Inc.; Milton Steel, Inc.
Local Counsel for: Pennsylvania Power & Light Co.; PA-American Water Co.; Motorists Insurance Cos.
Counsel for: Delaware Township.
Agents for: Commonwealth Land Title Assurance Co. of Pa.

For full biographical listings, see the Martindale-Hubbell Law Directory

MORRISVILLE, Bucks Co.

CURTIN & HEEFNER, LLP (AV)

250 North Pennsylvania Avenue, P.O. Box 217, 19067
Telephone: 215-736-2521
Telecopier: 215-736-3647
Email: ch@curtinheefner.com

Willard S. Curtin (1932-1996)

MEMBERS OF FIRM

Edward I. Dobin | Maureen Burke Carlton
John W. Donaghy | Dean P. Arthur
Gilbert J. Golding | David J. Truelove
Frank S. Guarrieri | Eileen M. Mitchell
Bonnie S. Stein | John J. Hart
Allan D. Goulding, Jr. | Ernest R. Closser III
Douglas H. Riblet | Yolanda Konopacka DeSipio
Francis X. Stecklair | Joel Steinman
Robert A. Badman, Jr. | Giovanna M. Raffaelli
Robert G. LaBar

OF COUNSEL

William F. Heefner

References: William Penn Savings and Loan Assn.; Bucks County Board of Realtors; Federal Land Bank of Baltimore; Allstate Insurance; First Union National Bank; State Farm Fire & Casualty Insurance Co.

For full biographical listings, see the Martindale-Hubbell Law Directory

NARBERTH, Montgomery Co.

EDWARD M. MEZVINSKY (AV)

815 Woodbine Avenue, 19072
Telephone: 610-664-7115
Fax: 610-664-7225
Email: emmez@aol.com *URL:* http://www.lawyers.com/edwardmmezvinsky

For full biographical listings, see the Martindale-Hubbell Law Directory

*NEW CASTLE,** Lawrence Co.

ROUTMAN, MOORE, GOLDSTONE & VALENTINO (AV)

2656 Wilmington Road, 16105
Telephone: 724-658-6900
Email: lawyers@rmgv.com
Sharon, Pennsylvania Office: 194 East State Street.
Telephone: 724-981-6800.

Joseph Paul Valentino | Richard W. Epstein

For full biographical listings, see the Martindale-Hubbell Law Directory

VERTERANO & MANOLIS (AV)

2622 Wilmington Road, 16105-1530
Telephone: 724-652-0300
Telefax: 724-654-1131

Frank G. Verterano | James W. Manolis

For full biographical listings, see the Martindale-Hubbell Law Directory

NEWTOWN, Bucks Co.

STUCKERT AND YATES (AV)

2 North State Street, P.O. Box 70, 18940
Telephone: 215-968-4700
Fax: 215-968-8875

MEMBERS OF FIRM

Wm. R. Stuckert (1902-1960) | Richard Danese, Jr.
Sidney T. Yates | Don F. Marshall
John J. Kerrigan, Jr. | Steven H. Sailer
D. Keith Brown

(See Next Column)

STUCKERT AND YATES—*Continued*

ASSOCIATES

Stephen L. Needles
Donna J. Wengiel
Thomas J. Walsh III

Representative Clients: First National Bank & Trust Company of Newtown; St. Mary Hospital, Langhorne, Pennsylvania; Newtown Borough; Newtown Bucks County Joint Municipal Authority; Third Federal Savings Bank; Trenton Savings Bank.
Reference: First National Bank & Trust Company of Newtown.

For full biographical listings, see the Martindale-Hubbell Law Directory

*NORRISTOWN,** Montgomery Co.

HIGH, SWARTZ, ROBERTS & SEIDEL LLP (AV)

40 East Airy Street, 19404
Telephone: 610-275-0700
Fax: 610-275-5290
Email: main@hsrs-law.com

MEMBERS OF FIRM

Samuel H. High, Jr. (1931-1978)
Gilbert P. High (1935-1975)
Aaron S. Swartz, 3rd (1940-1982)
Victor J. Roberts (1938-1984)
Marlyn F. Smith (Mr.)
Stephen G. Yusem
Gilbert P. High, Jr.
Paul Baker Bartle
Robert B. Durham, Jr.
D. Barry Pritchard, Jr.
Thomas D. Rees
Mary L. Buckman
Lois A. Nafziger
Mary Cushing Doherty

OF COUNSEL

Raymond M. Seidel
George M. Aman, III
Lindley M. Cowperthwait, Jr.
J. Kenneth Croney
John P. Gregg

ASSOCIATES

Cheri D. Andrews
John A. Gallagher
Craig H. Pizer
Eric B. Smith
Caren E. Morrissey

LEGAL SUPPORT PERSONNEL

Colleen M. O'Brien
Polly M. Stewart
Elaine R. Kimmich (Not admitted in PA)
Susan G. Heine
Faith K. Daley
Chrystyna Savitz
Cynthia Arena Kirkner (Paralegal)

Solicitors for: Bryner Chevrolet, Inc.; Lower Merion Township; Bryn Athyn School District.
Local Counsel for: Nationwide Mutual Insurance Co.; Prudential Insurance Co.; First Valley Bank.

For full biographical listings, see the Martindale-Hubbell Law Directory

McTIGHE, WEISS, O'ROURKE & MILNER, P.C. (AV)

Eleven East Airy Street, P.O. Box 510, 19404
Telephone: 610-275-8800
Telecopier: 610-272-5325
Email: mctighe@montcolawyer.com *URL:* http://www.montcolawyer.com

Desmond J. McTighe (1902-1990)
Philip D. Weiss (Retired)
John R. O'Rourke, Jr.
Kenneth P. Milner
Julia Going Becker
Cynthia Weiss Stein

Philip A. Downey

Representative Clients: Colonial Penn Insurance Cos.; Co.; Penn Mutual Insurance Co.; National Grange Mutual Insurance Co.; Connecticut Specialty Insurance Co.; Celina Group; Penna; Medical Professional Liability Catastrophe Loss Fund; Liberty Mutual Insurance Co.; Zurich-American Insurance Co.; Colony Management Services, Inc.; Executive Risk Insurance Co.

For full biographical listings, see the Martindale-Hubbell Law Directory

*PHILADELPHIA,** Philadelphia Co.

ASTOR WEISS KAPLAN & ROSENBLUM, LLP (AV)

The Bellevue, 6th Floor, 200 South Broad Street, 19102
Telephone: 215-790-0100
Fax: 215-790-0509
Email: lawyers@astorweiss.com
Bala Cynwyd, Pennsylvania Office: 401 City Avenue, Suite 500.
Telephone: 610-667-8660.
Fax: 610-667-2783.

MEMBERS OF FIRM

Alvin M. Weiss (1936-1976)
Paul C. Astor
G. David Rosenblum
Arthur H. Kaplan
Barbara Oaks Silver
David S. Workman
David Gutin
David S. Mandel
Gerald J. Schorr

(See Next Column)

ASSOCIATES

Christopher P. Flannery
Janet G. Felgoise
Elizabeth F. Warner
Daniel A. Shabel
Frances F. Freedman

SPECIAL COUNSEL

Neil Hurowitz
Jerrold V. Moss
Robert P. Style

OF COUNSEL

Edward W. Silver

For full biographical listings, see the Martindale-Hubbell Law Directory

BALLARD SPAHR ANDREWS & INGERSOLL, LLP (AV)

1735 Market Street, 51st Floor, 19103-7599
Telephone: 215-665-8500
Fax: 215-864-8999
URL: http://www.ballardspahr.com
Baltimore, Maryland Office: 300 East Lombard Street. 19th Floor.
Telephone: 410-528-5600.
Fax: 410-528-5650.
Camden, New Jersey Office: 800 Hudson Square, 5th Floor.
Telephone: 856-541-5577.
Fax: 856-541-8272.
Denver, Colorado Office: Seventeenth Street Plaza Building, Suite 2300, 1225 17th Street.
Telephone: 303-292-2400.
Fax: 303-296-3956.
Salt Lake City, Utah Office: One Utah Center, Suite 1200, 201 South Main Street.
Telephone: 801-531-3000.
Fax: 801-531-3001.
Voorhees, New Jersey Office: Suite 100, 1101 Laurel Oak Drive.
Telephone: 856-627-8555.
Fax: 856-627-1153.
Washington, D.C. Office: Suite 1000 South, 601 13th Street, N.W.
Telephone: 202-661-2200.
Fax: 202-661-2299.

Raymond D. Agran
Steven A. Arbittier
Frederic L. Ballard, Jr.
E. Carolan Berkley
John M. Bernard
Richard J. Braemer
C. Baird Brown
Beverly R. Budin
Jeffrey T. Chappelle
Frederic W. Clark
Rhonda Resnick Cohen
Brendan K. Collins
Kevin R. Cunningham
Mark S. DePillis
Walter M. Einhorn, Jr.
Thomas R. Eshelman
David S. Fryman
David B. Gifford
Howard I. Grossman
Martha J. Hays
Cathleen C. Judge
Alan S. Kaplinsky
Philip B. Korb
Mary G. Lawler
Charisse R. Lillie
Arthur Makadon
Vincent J. Marriott, III
Darryl J. May
Robert E. McQuiston
Benjamin R. Neilson
Richard S. Perelman
David H. Pittinsky
H. David Prior
William H. Rheiner
Alan S. Ritterband
Edward D. Rogers
Jeremy T. Rosenblum
Marilyn C. Sanborne
Paul J. Schneider
Eric W. Sitarchuk
William A. Slaughter
Lisa M. Sloan
Mark S. Stewart
Matthew M. Strickler
Regina O'Brien Thomas
Randall J. Towers
Glenn L. Unterberger
William Y. Webb
John N. Ake
Lynn R. Axelroth
Lawrence D. Berger
Steven P. Berman
Robert McLaurin Boote
Jennifer L. Bragg
Martin C. Bryce, Jr.
Bruce L. Castor
Morris Cheston, Jr.
David L. Cohen
James D. Coleman
John L. Culhane, Jr.
Alan J. Davis
Brian D. Doerner
Thomas Jay Ellis
Carl H. Fridy
Robert C. Gerlach
Richard R. Goldberg
Gerald J. Guarcini
Leslie E. John
Geoffrey A. Kahn
Justin P. Klein
John B. Langel
Mark J. Levin
Ann T. Loftus
David G. Mandelbaum
Peter M. Mattoon
Robert B. McKinstry, Jr.
Bart I. Mellits
Brian D. Pedrow
Joanne Phillips
David L. Pollack
Maureen M. Rayborn
Louis W. Ricker
Carl G. Roberts
J. Douglas Rollow, III
Burt M. Rublin
Ronald A. Sarachan
William P. Scott
Michael Sklaroff
Edward D. Slevin
Gary Arlen Smith
Wayne R. Strasbaugh
Richard L. Strouse
Jere G. Thompson
Suzanne E. Turner
J. Brian Walsh
Harry Weiss

SPECIAL COUNSEL

Donald J. Goldberg

(See Next Column)

BALLARD SPAHR ANDREWS & INGERSOLL LLP, *Philadelphia—Continued*

OF COUNSEL

Kurt R. Anderson
Robert R. Batt
Gardner A. Evans
Jean C. Hemphill
Barry L. Klein
Lisa Fair Pliskin
(Not admitted in PA)
Jeffrey S. Rosenblum
Francis Ballard
J. Joseph Cullen
Marcy Newman Hart
H. Ober Hess
Jeffrey Meyers
Thomas B. Roberts
David K. Roscher
Hugh A. A. Sargent
Deborah J. Zateeny

COUNSEL

Barbara R. Beckman
Jamie B. Bischoff
Edward Ira Leeds

Kris Williams Aldridge
John Mark Bacon
Roberta A. Barsotti
Paul William Boltz, Jr.
Stacy L. Broad
Susan Sudick Colton
Samantha R. Corson
Dominic J. De Simone
Austin S. Faberman
Douglas L. Flitter
William H. Gelles, III
David G. Gibson
Shira Goodman
Allan M. Hoffman
Ellen Jerrehian
Rebecca J. Kamp
Ira A. Kauderer
Michael J. Konowal
Albert S. Lee
(Not admitted in PA)
Tina R. Makoulian
Jennifer L. Miller
William L. Morrissey, Jr.
Mary J. Mullany
Katherine L. Paul
Sharmon Priaulx
Pedro A. Ramos
William C. Rhodes
Marta Rose
Yuri Rozenfeld
Mark I. Salvacion
Caroline Mouallem Schultz
Indiya R. Sexton
Michael D. Silbert
Gayle Baumgarten Stein
Elizabeth Farrelly Sur
Joel E. Tasca
Saul D. Treiman
Kelly A. Walenda
Carrie E. Watt
Amanda S. Aronoff
Robert R. Baron, Jr.
Susan R. Becker
Richard F. Booker
Alicia B. Clark
(Not admitted in PA)
Marc Davies
Jeanne J. Dworetzky
Abigail Lee Flitter
Matthew D. Fradin
(Not admitted in PA)
Michele Berman Golkow
Matthew Moesel Gutt
Penny S. Indictor
Daniel V. Johns
Stephen J. Kastenberg
Teresa E. Kibelstis
Leslie W. Ledogar
W. Andrew Macan
John-Paul Madden
Lisa M. Maloney
Monique M. Mooney
Niza Maria Motola
Heidi M. Nicholson
Brian Michael Pinheiro
Raymond Adam Quaglia
Kathleen M. Ranalli
Ann Marie Ritchie
Marla G. Roshkoff
Leslie C. Safran
Kathleen M. Sandone
John K. Semler, Jr.
Kimberly A. Short
Sally A. Steffen
Sharon Suleta
Christian A. Szautner
Scott P. Towers
Esther L. von Laue
Melissa R. Ware
David L. Weinreb
Mara Williams

For full biographical listings, see the Martindale-Hubbell Law Directory

BEASLEY, CASEY & ERBSTEIN (AV)

1125 Walnut Street, 19107-4997
Telephone: 215-592-1000
Telecopier: 215-592-8360
Email: lawyers@tortlaw.com *URL:* http://www.tortlaw.com
Mount Laurel, New Jersey Office: Suite 266, 3000 Atrium Way.
Telephone: 609-273-6966. URL: http://www.tortlaw.com.

MEMBERS OF FIRM

James E. Beasley
Benedict A. Casey
Keith S. Erbstein
Scott A. Bennett
Barbara R. Axelrod
Gershon D. Greenblatt
David C. Federman
Jayne A. Piarulli
Paul A. Lauricella
Andrew J. Stern
Slade H. McLaughlin
Michael A. Smerconish
David A. Yanoff
Marsha F. Santangelo
James J. McHugh, Jr.
James E. Foerstner, Jr.
Andrew B. Bullion
James E. Beasley, Jr.

For full biographical listings, see the Martindale-Hubbell Law Directory

WILLIAM N. BINDERMAN (AV⊤)

1919 Walnut Street, 19103-4605
Telephone: 215-496-0500
URL: http://www.lawyers.com/binderman
New York, New York Office: 685 Third Street, Suite 2700, 10017-4024.
Telephone: 212-297-0011.

For full biographical listings, see the Martindale-Hubbell Law Directory

BLANK ROME COMISKY & MCCAULEY LLP (AV)

One Logan Square, 19103-6998
Telephone: 215-569-5500
Cable Address: "Blarcom"
TWX: 710-670-1073
FAX: 215-569-5555
Media, Pennsylvania Office: 1400 N. Providence Road, Suite 301, 19063.
Telephone: 610-891-7800.
FAX: 610-891-7804.
Cherry Hill, New Jersey Office: 210 Lake Drive East, Suite 200, 08002.
Telephone: 856-779-3600.
FAX: 856-779-7647.
Boca Raton, Florida Office: 1200 North Federal Highway, Suite 417, 33432.
Telephone: 561-417-8100.
FAX: 561-417-8101.
Allentown, Pennsylvania Office: 1620 Pond Road, Suite 200, 18104-2255.
Telephone: 610-706-4300.
FAX: 610-706-4343.
Wilmington, Delaware Office: Chase Manhattan Centre, 1201 Market Street, Suite 2100, 19801-4226.
Telephone: 302-425-6400.
FAX: 302-425-6464.
Washington, D.C. Office: The Farragut Building, 900 17th Street, N.W., 20006.
Telephones: 202-463-7700; 202-785-4100.
FAX: 202-463-6915.
Trenton, New Jersey Office: 200 West State Street, 08608.
Telephone: 609-278-2320.
FAX: 609-278-2323.
Baltimore, Maryland Office: 250 West Pratt Street, Suite 1100, 21201.
Telephone: 410-659-1400.
FAX: 410-659-1414.

CHAIRMAN EMERITUS RETIRED

Marvin Comisky

COUNSEL TO THE FIRM

Leon S. Forman

MEMBERS OF FIRM

Alvin S. Ackerman
(Resident, Media Office)
Arthur Bachman
Lawrence J. Beaser
Samuel H. Becker
Jeffrey I. Bernstein
Jack R Bershad
Barry F. Bevacqua
Thomas E. Biron
Mark Blondman
Fred Blume
Jeffrey Blumenfeld
Alexander D. Bono
Robert M. Broder
Carl M. Buchholz
Edward H. Butz
(Resident, Allentown Office)
Howard M. Camerik (Resident, Boca Raton, Florida Office)
Lawrence S. Chane
Herbert Cohen (Resident, Washington, D.C. Office)
Ian M. Comisky
Matthew James Comisky (Also at Boca Raton, Florida Office)
Scott F. Cooper
Roger F. Cox
Kevin P. Cronin
Francis X. Crowley
(Resident, Media Office)
Morris J. Dean
Francis E. Dehel
James R. Deveney, II (Resident, Baltimore, Maryland Office)
Nelson A. Diaz
Leonard Dubin
Steven Dubow
Karen Du Brul
Bruce A. Eisenberg (Also at Cherry Hill and Trenton, New Jersey Offices)
Edward J. Farrell (Resident, Washington, D.C. Office)
Lawrence Finkelstein
Lawrence F. Flick, II
Harvey I. Forman
Earl M. Forte, III
John W. Fowler, Jr.
Barry Friedman
Robert G. Fryling
Sol B. Genauer
Barry H. Genkin
Alan C. Gershenson
David F. Girard-diCarlo
Bernard Glassman
Howard T. Glassman
Peter A. Gold (Also at Cherry Hill and Trenton, New Jersey Offices)
Gary R. Goldenberg
Michael C. Greenbaum
(Resident, Washington, D.C. Office)
Norman E. Greenspan
Joseph T. Gulant
Arthur W. Hankin
Michael J. Hanlon
Nicholas C. Harbist (Resident, Cherry Hill, New Jersey Office)
Kimon C. Hatza
F. Arnold Heller
Richard K. Herrmann (Resident, Wilmington, Delaware Office)
Jon G. Hillsberg
Alan J. Hoffman (Also at Wilmington, Delaware Office)
Edward J. Hoffman
Regina Stango Kelbon
Peter Foster Kelsen
Kenneth N. Klass
Michael L. Krancer (Also at Cherry Hill, New Jersey Office)
Richard L. Kremnick
George J. Krueger
David M. Kuchinos
Henry M. Kuller
Mark D. Laponsky (Baltimore, Maryland and Washington, D.C. Offices)
Ann Blair Laupheimer
David Lebor
Michael H. Leeds (Resident, Boca Raton, Florida Office)
Bernard M. Lesavoy
(Resident, Allentown Office)
Dale Penneys Levy
Christopher A. Lewis
Alan M. Lieberman
Frederick D. Lipman
G. Craig Lord
Stephen E. Luongo
Harry D. Madonna
Kenneth J. Marino (Resident, Wilmington, Delaware Office)
J. Adam Matlawski
(Resident, Media Office)

(See Next Column)

BLANK ROME COMISKY & MCCAULEY LLP—*Continued*

MEMBERS OF FIRM (Continued)

Mary B. Matterer (Resident, Wilmington, Delaware Office)
Margaret A. McCausland
Kathleen McDermott (Resident, Baltimore, Maryland Office)
Richard P. McElroy
Joseph J. McGovern (Also at Cherry Hill, New Jersey Office)
Richard J. McMahon
Richard S. Meyer
Steven M. Miller
Jeffrey S. Moller
George C. Myers, Jr. (Resident, Washington, D.C. Office)
Jeffrey E. Myers
Leonard P. Nalencz
John A. Nixon
David A. Norcross (Washington, D.C. and Trenton, New Jersey Offices)
D. Christopher Ohly (Resident, Baltimore, Maryland Office)
Harris Ominsky
Grant S. Palmer
Timothy D. Pecsenye
Michael Pollack
Leslie J. Polt (Resident, Baltimore, Maryland Office)
Mark I. Rabinowitz
Samuel N. Rabinowitz
Julian P. Rackow (Also at Wilmington, Delaware Office)
Cathy L. Reese (Resident, Wilmington, Delaware Office)
Jerome R. Richter
William H. Roberts
Morey S. Rosenbloom
Philip R. Rosenfeldt
A. Fred Ruttenberg (Resident, Cherry Hill Office)
Paul H. Schieber
Joel C. Shapiro
Raymond L. Shapiro
Michael D. Shepard
Laurence Shtasel
Matthew J. Siembieda
James T. Smith
Peter J. Soloff
Jeremy A. Spector
Alexander E. Stein
Joan N. Stern
Benjamin G. Stonelake, Jr. (Also at Cherry Hill, New Jersey Office)
Jane K. Storero
Barry E. Sweet
Edward I. Swichar
Seymour Traub (Resident, Allentown Office)
Mary T. Vidas
Kent Walker
Steven D. Weinstein (Resident, Cherry Hill and Trenton, New Jersey Offices)
Victor M. Wigman (Resident, Washington, D.C. Office)
Lawrence R. Wiseman (Also at Wilmington, Delaware Office)
David N. Zeehandelaar (Also at Cherry Hill, New Jersey Office)
Alan L. Zeiger

Robert C. Wert (Firm Executive Director)

SENIOR, SPECIAL AND OF COUNSEL

J. Caleb Boggs, III (Not admitted in PA)
Wendy E. Bookler
Edward N. Cahn (Also at Allentown, Pennsylvania Office)
Bonnie Glantz Fatell
Edward I. Foster
Thomas P. Foy (Resident, Trenton, New Jersey Office)
William E. Gramlich
F. Gillis Green (Resident, Baltimore, Maryland Office)
Donald R. Greene (Resident, Washington, D.C. Office)
Julianne E. Hammond (Resident, Wilmington, Delaware Office)
Michael R. Harris
Lewis J. Hoch
Gregory B. Hook (Resident, Trenton, New Jersey Office)
Harry R. Hughes (Resident, Baltimore, Maryland Office)
Lisa N. Kaufman (Resident, Washington, D.C. Office)
Harry T. Lamb
Denis James Lawler
Peter W. Leibundgut (Resident, Cherry Hill, New Jersey Office)
John J. Maffei (Resident, Media Office)
J. Llewellyn Mathews (Resident, Cherry Hill, New Jersey Office)
Elizabeth D. Sampath
Lisa J. Savitt (Resident, Washington, D.C. Office)
Jane C. Silver
Michael D. White (Resident, Washington, D.C. Office)
James G. Wiles

ASSOCIATES

Nina E. Abraham
Suzanne C. Abt
Stacy L. Asbell (Resident, Cherry Hill, New Jersey Office)
Sheryl L. Axelrod
Lyn Anne Bailey
Kevin J. Baum
Lawrence E. Borska
Rachel Brendzel
Robert A. Burke
William J. Burnett
Steven L. Caponi (Resident, Wilmington, Delaware Office)
Elisa N. Cohen (Resident, Media Office)
Kipp B. Cohen
Jordana Cooper (Resident, Cherry Hill, New Jersey Office)
Roberta Kienast Daghir (Resident, Baltimore, Maryland Office)
Loretta A. Damron
Michael D. DeBaecke (Resident, Wilmington, Delaware Office)
James B. Dilsheimer
David A. Dorey (Resident, Cherry Hill, New Jersey Office)
Kara A. Dougherty
Dale R. Dubé (Resident, Wilmington, Delaware Office)
Thomas P. Dwyer
David J. Edmondson (Resident, Washington, D.C. Office)
Alicia Emery
Beth L. Eskin
Samuel M. First
Scott J. Freedman
Melissa J. Gilstrap
Daphne Goldman
Seth William Goren
Melissa Granovsky
Wilhelm L. Gruszecki
Gregory B. Guarton
Geoffrey M. Hammel
Erin O'Brien Harkiewicz

(See Next Column)

ASSOCIATES (Continued)

Patricia L. Hobbib
James E. Howard (Resident, Washington, D.C. Office)
Jamie Leeson Huber (Resident, Boca Raton, Florida Office)
Cory G. Jacobs
Linda T. Jacobs
Daniel J. Kaliner
Emanuel Kapelsohn (Resident, Allentown Office)
Lisa A. Kaplan
Timothy D. Katsiff
Peter Andrew Keon
William F. Kerr
Ann E. Kim
Don S. Klein (Resident, Allentown Office)
David M. Klieger
Jonathan M. Korn (Resident, Cherry Hill, New Jersey Office)
Denise Catherine Lane (Resident, Washington, D.C. Office)
Steven A. Lessne (Resident, Boca Raton, Florida Office)
Constance R. Lipson
James S. Mackey
Jane S. Markson (Also at Allentown, Pennsylvania Office)
Scott A. Mayer
Joseph E. Mayk
Dennis P. McCooe
William V. McGroarty
Paul D. McNichol (Resident, Media Office)
William C. Mead, Jr. (Resident, Cherry Hill, New Jersey Office)
Michael J. Medveckus
John J. Monsees
Mary Ann Mullaney
Melissa Palat Murawsky
Karl O. Neidert (Resident, Washington, D.C. Office)
Brian S. Paszamant
Raymond M. Patella
Justina L. Pederson
Nancy R. Peterson
Jennifer J. Platzkere
Stuart D. Poppel
Andrew R. Prusky
Louis M. Rappaport
John L. Reed (Resident, Wilmington, Delaware Office)
Suzanne G. Reisman
Adam D. Resnick (Resident, Washington, D.C. Office)
James J. Reynolds, III
Daniel E. Rhynhart
Robert L. Roshkoff
Jerome H. Rosset (Resident, Media Office)
Mathew S. Rotenberg
Michael B. Schaedle
Carl Schaukowitch (Resident, Washington, D.C. Office)
Joseph E. Scocca
Jack M. Seitz (Resident, Allentown Office)
Louis Charles Shapiro
Adam M. Share
Michael J. Shavel
Michael W. Silberman
Michael J. Smith
Elaine D. Solomon
Edward Francis Spaniel, Jr.
Alyson M. Spitalnik (Not admitted in PA)
Laura E. Stegossi
Richard Steven Swartz
Brooke E. Thomas (Washington, D.C. and Baltimore, Maryland Offices)
Anthony Vidovich
Christine L. Viglotti
Rebecca D. Ward
Lisa Washington
Daniel H. Wheeler
Neil R. White (Resident, Baltimore, Maryland Office)
Daniel J. Winters
Randi A. Wolf (Resident, Cherry Hill, New Jersey Office)

For full biographical listings, see the Martindale-Hubbell Law Directory

COZEN AND O'CONNOR, A PROFESSIONAL CORPORATION (AV)

1900 Market Street, 19103
Telephone: 215-665-2000
800-523-2900
Fax: 215-665-2013
Email: postmaster@cozen.com *URL:* http://www.cozen.com
Charlotte, North Carolina Office: One First Union Center, Suite 2100, 301 S. College Street, 28202.
Telephones: 704-376-3400; 800-762-3575.
Fax: 704-334-3351.
Dallas, Texas Office: 2300 BankOne Center, 1717 Main Street, 75201.
Telephones: 214-462-3000; 800-448-1207.
Fax: 214-462-3299.
New York, N.Y. Office: 45 Broadway Atrium, 16th Floor, 10006.
Telephones: 212-509-9400; 800-437-7040.
Fax: 212-509-9492.
West Conshohocken, Pennsylvania Office: 200 Four Falls Corporate Center, Suite 400, P.O. Box 800, 19428.
Telephone: 610-941-5400.
Fax: 610-941-0711.
San Diego, California Office: Suite 1610, 501 West Broadway, 92101.
Telephones: 619-234-1700; 800-782-3366.
Fax: 619-234-7831.
Los Angeles, California Office: 777 Tower, 777 South Figueroa Street, Suite 2850, 90017.
Telephones: 213-892-7900; 800-563-1027.
Fax: 213-892-7999.
Seattle, Washington Office: Suite 5200, Washington Mutual Tower, 1201 Third Avenue, 98101.
Telephones: 206-340-1000; 800-423-1950.
Fax: 206-621-8783.
Westmont, New Jersey Office: 316 Haddon Avenue, 08108.
Telephones: 609-854-4900; 800-523-2900.
Fax: 609-854-1782.
Newark, New Jersey Office: One Newark Center, Suite 1900, 1085 Raymond Boulevard, 07102.
Telephone: 973-286-1200; 888-200-9521.
Fax: 973-242-2121.
Atlanta, Georgia Office: Suite 2200, SunTrust Plaza, 303 Peachtree Street, N.E., 30308.
Telephones: 404-572-2000; 800-890-1393.
Fax: 404-572-2199.

(See Next Column)

COZEN AND O'CONNOR A PROFESSIONAL CORPORATION, *Philadelphia—Continued*

London, England Office: Cozen and O'Connor at Radcliffes, 5 Great College Street, Westminster, SW1P 3SJ.
Telephone: 011-44-207-654-7600.
Fax: 011-44-207-654-7613.
Wilmington, Delaware Office: Chase Manhattan Centre, 1201 North Market Street, Suite 1400, 19801.
Telephone: 302-295-2000; 888-207-2440.
Fax: 302-295-2013.
Mt. Laurel, New Jersey Office: 10,000 Midlantic Drive, Suite 301, 08054.

Sydney C. Orlofsky (1936-1968)
Charles A. Fisher, III (1947-1990)

FIRM MEMBERS IN PHILADELPHIA

Stephen A. Cozen
Marc L. Ackerman
Kevin M. Apollo
A. Richard Bailey
Gaele McLaughlin Barthold (Mrs.)
Paul R. Bartolacci
Joseph J. Bellew
Gerard F. Belz, Jr.
Lillian E. Benedict
Richard C. Bennett
Denise Brinker Bense
Steven L. Biener (Not admitted in PA)
Sandra A. Bloch
Tami L. Bogutz
Jeffrey L. Braff
James E. Brown
John F. Brown, Jr.
Richard J. Busis
Robert M. Caplan
Madeline Caprioli
Elizabeth J. Chambers
William N. Clark, Jr.
Dennis L. Cohen
Neal D. Colton
James P. Cullen, Jr.
Sarah E. Davies
Robert S. Davis
Robert V. Dell'Osa
Martin P. Duffey
John Dwyer
Christopher C. Fallon, Jr.
Dolores F. Faraldo
Elliott R. Feldman
H. Robert Fiebach
Ann Thornton Field
Jim H. Fields, Jr.
William G. Flint
Daniel V. Folt
Douglas B. Fox
Eric D. Freed
Debra S. Friedman
Rhonda M. Fulginiti
Thomas F. Gallagher
Mark H. Gallant
Joseph A. Gerber
Steven K. Gerber
William E. Gericke
June E. Gilson
Henry A. Gladstone
Richard C. Glazer
James D. Golkow
Lewis A. Grafman
Josh M. Greenbaum
David J. Groth
Steven N. Haas
Dexter R. Hamilton
Michael A. Hamilton
Ronald B. Hamilton
Daniel Q. Harrington
Thomas R. Harrington
Robert H. Hawn, Jr.
Patrick J. O'Connor
Robert W. Hayes
James H. Heller
Michael J. Heller
Michael F. Henry
Denise H. Houghton
William H. Howard
Kevin J. Hughes
Michael J. Izzo, Jr.
F. Warren Jacoby
Miles A. Jellinek
Kathie D. King
Barry H. Kitain
John A. Knapp
Katherine M. Layman
Jeffrey A. Leonard
Raymond T. Letulle
Jay M. Levin
Brian L. Lincicome
David S. Lorry
Kathleen Parks Loughhead
Richard M. Mackowsky
W. Scott Magargee
Richard C. Mason
Michael R. McCarty
John K. McDonald
Frances B. McGinley
Vincent R. McGuinness, Jr.
Thomas McKay, III (Not admitted in PA)
Deborah Melamut Minkoff
John Francis Mullen
Mark T. Mullen
Jeffrey L. Nash
Matthew F. Noone
Mark E. Opalisky
Jeffrey Ivan Pasek
Karl L. Prior
Robert R. Reeder
Thomas M. Regan
Joseph H. Riches
E. Gerald Riesenbach
Elaine M. Rinaldi
Peter G. Rossi
John T. Salvucci
William P. Shelley
Steven L. Smith
Cathi Cozen Snyder
Harmon Spolan
William F. Stewart
Jeffrey R. Stoner
John T. Thorn
Scott M. Waldman
Joshua Wall
Donald A. Waltz
Anita B. Weinstein
Thomas G. Wilkinson, Jr.
William J. Winning
Alan F. Wohlstetter, Jr.
Liza Leidner Wolf
Samuel S. Woodhouse, III
Bernard E. Zbrzeznj
Thomas C. Zielinski
Benjamin E. Zuckerman

OF COUNSEL

Judith J. Jamison
Edward N. Polisher
Ronald H. Sherr
Mark C. Stephenson
Herman P. Weinberg

FIRM ASSOCIATES IN PHILADELPHIA

Jennifer Auerbach
Kimberly A. Bane
Joseph C. Bedwick
Patricia Sons Biswanger
Jennifer A. Brandt
Bridget A. Brennan
Scott Evan Brucker
Lisa M. Calvo
Thomas B. Carpenter
Sean Patrick Carter
Andrew B. Clauss
Mitchell A. Cohen
Patrick J. Day
David Maris Doret
Carolann Jackson Dougherty
Frederick J. Fisher

(See Next Column)

FIRM ASSOCIATES IN PHILADELPHIA (Continued)

Wendy Lee Gavin
Saundra J. Godina
Malcolm Stewart Gould
C. Tyler Havey
Lizabeth Huff Henrich
Terry M. Henry
Daniel L. Hessel
Colleen E. Hicks
Christopher D. McDemus
Jennifer M. McHugh
Melanie A. Miller
Peter A. Muhic
Michael Murphy
Julie Negovan
Sean P. O'Donnell
Julie Merritt Pacaro
Elena Park
Jacqueline Promislo
Kevin C. Rakowski
Laura L. Reed
James E. Robinson
John D. Shea
Shahram M. Siddiqui
Matthew J. Siegel
David William Smith
Georgia A. Stanaitis
Nancy C. Thome
Jeffrey M. Vona
Adam B. Weinstein
Kristin Werner
Deborah Winfield
Kathryn L. Zamborsky

Representative Clients: Available upon request.

For full biographical listings, see the Martindale-Hubbell Law Directory

DECHERT PRICE & RHOADS (AV)

4000 Bell Atlantic Tower, 1717 Arch Street, 19103-2793
Telephone: 215-994-4000
Telefax: 215-994-2222
URL: http://www.dechert.com
New York, New York: 30 Rockefeller Plaza, 10112.
Telephone: 212-698-3500.
Washington, D.C.: 1775 Eye Street, N.W., 20006.
Telephone: 202-261-3300.
Harrisburg, Pennsylvania: Thirty North Third Street, 17101-1603.
Telephone: 717-237-2000.
Princeton, New Jersey: Princeton Pike Corporate Center, P.O. Box 5218, 08543-5218.
Telephone: 609-620-3200.
Boston, Massachusetts: Ten Post Office Square South, 02109-4603.
Telephone: 617-728-7100.
Hartford, Connecticut Office: 90 State House Square, 06103-3702.
Telephone: 860-524-3999.
London, England: 2 Serjeants' Inn, EC4Y 1LT.
Telephone: (0171) 583-5353. (Also see Titmuss Sainer Dechert).
Brussels, Belgium: 65 Avenue Louise 1050.
Telephone: (02) 535-5411.
Paris, France: 55, avenue Kléber, 76116.
Telephone: 33-(0) 1-53 65 05 00.

MEMBERS OF FIRM IN PHILADELPHIA

Joseph Patrick Archie
Norbert F. Bergholtz
Richard L. Berkman
Alan D. Berkowitz
Martin J. Black
Glenn D. Blumenfeld
Michael A. Bogdonoff
Stephen D. Brown
Jennifer R. Clarke
Robert C. Clothier III
Abbi L. Cohen
Peter D. Cripps
Diane Siegel Danoff
C. VanLeer Davis III
Ivan S. DeVoren
Norman E. Donoghue II
Thomas E. Doran
Jonathan L. Drake
Robert M. Elwood
Steven B. Feirson
Aaron C. F. Finkbiner III
Linda A. Fisher
John E. Flaherty Jr.
Ethan D. Fogel
Vernon L. Francis
Robert L. Freedman
Hope Seidenberg Freiwald
Marc B. Friedman (Not admitted in PA)
Arthur S. Gabinet
Frederick J. Gerhart
Kevin P. Gilboy
Amy B. Ginensky
Craig L. Godshall
Herbert F. Goodrich Jr.
George G. Gordon
Gregory G. Gosfield
Gary L. Green
Glenn A. Gundersen
Michael F. R. Harris
Robert C. Heim
Frederick G. Herold
Joseph K. Hetrick
Jerome A. Hoffman
David M. Howard
David F. Jones
Richard D. Jones
Christopher G. Karras
Morris C. Kellett
William J. Kennedy
Lois Kimbol
Paul S. Kimbol
H. Ronald Klasko
Samuel E. Klein
Sharon R. Klein
Mark A. Klugheit
John D. LaRocca
James J. Lawless Jr.
William G. Lawlor
James A. Lebovitz
Thomas H. Lee II
Judy L. Leone
Christine C. Levin
Jan P. Levine
Robert A. Limbacher
Wm. Scott Magargee III
Fred T. Magaziner
Francis Mazzola
Mary A. McLaughlin
Thomas B. Morris Jr.
Arthur Newbold
G. Daniel O'Donnell
Paul Wm. Putney
David J. Rachofsky
Arthur H. Rainey
Thomas A. Ralph
Hershel J. Richman
Richard C. Rizzo
Carmen J. Romano
Richard R. Rulon
Stuart T. Saunders Jr.
James J. Spadaro Jr.
Stephen A. Stack Jr.
Joseph A. Tate
Sean P. Wajert
Marshall J. Walthew
Jeffrey G. Weil
Richard P. Wild
Barton J. Winokur
Jay L. Zagoren
Kathleen Ziga
Lee A. Zoeller

(See Next Column)

DECHERT PRICE & RHOADS—*Continued*

OF COUNSEL IN PHILADELPHIA

Wm. Alan Baird
Anthony L. Bartolini
John Bishop VI
William F. Bohlen
Christopher Branda Jr.
John J. Brennan
Matthew J. Broderick
Stanhope S. Browne
John R. Clark
Isaac H. Clothier IV
H. Francis DeLone
Gordon W. Gerber
F. Hastings Griffin Jr.
George J. Hauptfuhrer Jr.
Chester C. Hilinski
William A. Kelley Jr.
Henry Kolowrat
Seymour Kurland
Robert M. Landis
William H. Lowery
Raymond W. Midgett Jr.
George B. Ross
Richard G. Schneider
Robert Deland Williams
Minturn T. Wright III

COUNSEL

M. Joel Bolstein
Nancy J. Bregstein
Donna Ostroff
John T. Subak

ASSOCIATES IN PHILADELPHIA

Michael E. Baughman
James A. Bell, IV
Richard A. Bendit
Sandra G. Berenknopf
Lynne M. Bianco
Michael S. Blume
Adam C. Bonin
Jennifer Caillier Boston
Magdalen Braden
Eli R. Brill
Lisa C.S. Burnett
Kenneth R. Buys
David J. Caputo
Jonathan A. Clark
Everett McCord Clayton
Kathryn L. Connelly
Bradley H.K. Cooper
Christopher J. Culleton
Adam Harris Cutler
Kelly L. Darr
David S. Denious
Philip R. DiGennaro Jr.
Terence A. Dixon
Michael S. Doluisio
Susan J. Dooley
Linda S. Dwoskin
Jeffrey S. Edwards
Maximillian L. Ernst
Michelle Robertson Esser
Aline Fairweather
Carolyn Hazard Feeney
Teresa Fink
Jennifer E. Fitzgerald
Carrie Y. Flaxman
David W. Forti
Joseph B. Freudenberg
Ronni E. Fuchs
Andrew R.C. Gaddes
Frank J. Gallo
Sarah B. Gelb
Howard S. Goldberg
Gary M. Goldstein
Paula F. Goulden
Jay M. Green
John J. Haggerty
Janet V. Hallahan
Andrea G. Hilborn (Not admitted in PA)
Heather A. Hoyt
Solomon Hunter Jr.
Otto W. Immel
Helene S. Jaron
Kevin M. Johnson
Michael L. Kichline
Jacob I. Kobrick
Jill M. Kuntz
Heather J. Lange
Graham R. Laub
R. Jeffrey Legath
Edward Lemanowicz
David A. Levinson
Stephen J. McConnell
John F. McGuiness, Jr.
Andrew S. Miller
Matthew S. Miner
James F. Modzelewski
Martha E. Morse
Louise E. Moyer
Suzanne L. Giegerich Niemeyer
Joseph A. O'Connor
Frank J. O'Hara
Katherine Koenig Olsen
Alan C. Promer
Haleh R. Rabizadeh
Jon S. Robins (Not admitted in PA)
Christopher M. Roe
James F. Rowe, II
Elizabeth Ruddick (Not admitted in PA)
Jill L. Russin
Frances E. Ryan
M. Frances Ryan
Nancy O. Ryan (Not admitted in PA)
Peter M. Ryan
Michael A. Schwartz
Stephanie M. Schwartzberg
Eric M. Schweiker
David G. Shapiro
Marjorie K. Shiekman
Brian D. Short
Daniel W. Simcox
Geraldine A. Sinatra
R. Craig Smith
Kyle O. Sollie
Arthur R.G. Solmssen Jr.
James E. Southworth
Gayle C. Sproul
Stuart T. Steinberg
William A. Stock
Brennan J. Torregrossa
Matthew R. Walker
Darren C. Wallis
Jane M. Ward
Robert Lawrence Wax
Gregory S. Weisman
Heather R. Weiss
Matthew Lee Wiener
Brett E. Wiggins
Phillip E. Wilson, Jr.
Geanne K. Zelkowitz
Michael Zuckerman (Not admitted in PA)

For full biographical listings, see the Martindale-Hubbell Law Directory

DILWORTH PAXSON LLP (AV)

3200 Mellon Bank Center, 1735 Market Street, 19103
Telephone: 215-575-7000
Fax: 215-575-7200
Email: lawyers@dilworthlaw.com *URL:* http://www.dilworthlaw.com
Harrisburg, Pennsylvania Office: 305 N. Front Street, Suite 403.
Telephone: 717-236-4812.
Fax: 717-236-7811.
Cherry Hill, New Jersey Office: Libertyview Suite 700, 457 Haddonfield Road.
Telephone: 856-663-8877.
Fax: 856-663-8855.

(See Next Column)

Media, Pennsylvania Office: One Olive Street.
Telephone: 610-565-4131.
Fax: 610-892-4930.
Turnersville, New Jersey Office: University Executive Campus, Suite 201, 151 Fries Mills Road. P.O. Box 762.
Telephone: 856-227-6100.
Fax: 856-227-7373.
Wilmington, Delaware Office: First Federal Plaza, Suite 500.
Telephone: 302-571-9800.
Fax: 302-571-8875.

MEMBERS OF FIRM

Richardson Dilworth (1898-1974)
Henry D. Paxson (1904-1975)
William J. Henrich, Jr.
Stephen J. Harmelin
Joseph H. Jacovini
Carl H. Hanzelik
Steven L. Friedman
Peter J. Picotte, II
Joel M. Friedman
Ross J. Reese
John R. Latourette, Jr.
Roger F. Wood
Martin J. Sobol
James F. Monteith
James W. Hennessey
Sheryl L. Auerbach
Marc A. Feller
Robert Forrest Stewart, Jr.
Lawrence G. McMichael
John W. Schmehl
Paul W. Baskowsky
James J. Rodgers
John J. Matheussen
Joseph F. Kessler
Virginia Hinrichs McMichael
Victor P. Stabile
Harriet J. Koren
J. Bradford McIlvain
Michael B. Fein
Thomas B. York
Mary T. Tomich
Anne Marie P. Kelley
Robert W. Keyser
Susan E. Pendery
Paul M. Lewis
Sharon L. Sorokin
Barbara Tobin Dubrow
Richard L. Fox
Maura E. Fay
Virginia L. Flick
Martin J. Weis
Gregory F. Cirillo
Linda Carroll Smith
Penny Conly Ellison
Thomas E. Groshens
Francis P. Maneri
Marjorie McMahon Obod
Lynn Rosner Rauch
Steven Roth
Thomas S. Biemer
Peter C. Hughes
Laura Elizabeth Vendzules

COUNSEL

Vincent J. Fumo
Stephen J. Korn
J. Shane Creamer
Milton A. Feldman
J. Roger Williams, Jr.
Ronald Bluestein
John Philip Crampton
Merritt A. Cole
James M. Crowley (Not admitted in PA)
Michael D. Ecker
Dominic S. Liberi
Linda L. Parthemer
John F. Letchford
Mark B. Klein
Nathaniel Budin

ASSOCIATES

Timothy J. Brown
Marianne E. Brown
David P. Perri
David L. Zive
John G. McCormick
C. Lawrence Holmes
Christine DeMichele Consiglio
Rosemary J. Loverdi
Steven B. Goodman
Frank A. Lauletta, III
Patrick M. Northen
Kristen B. Mayhew
Christie M. Callahan
Pierce E. Buller
Sheila E. Dickert
Mark H. Schepps
James E. Elam, IV
John J. Higson
Beth A. Cannon
Kenneth C. Segarnick
David A. Abrams
Dennis J. Brennan
Vijay K. Raju

For full biographical listings, see the Martindale-Hubbell Law Directory

DRINKER BIDDLE & REATH LLP (AV)

A Pennsylvania Limited Liability Partnership
One Logan Square, 18th & Cherry Streets, 19103-6996
Telephone: 215-988-2700
Telefax: 215-988-2757
Cable Address: "Debemac"
URL: http://www.dbr.com
Washington, D.C. Office: 1500 K Street, N.W., Suite 1100.
Telephone: 202-842-8800.
Telefax: 202-842-8465.
Princeton, New Jersey Office: Suite 300, 105 College Road East.
Telephone: 609-716-6500.
Telefax: 609-799-7000.
Berwyn, Pennsylvania Office: Suite 300, 1000 Westlakes Drive.
Telephone: 610-993-2200.
Telefax: 610-993-8585.

MEMBERS OF FIRM

David F. Abernethy
Gary D. Ammon
Bonnie Allyn Barnett
Thomas J. Barton
Marsha W. Beidler (Resident Partner at Princeton, N.J. Office)
John C. Bennett, Jr.
Howard A. Blum
Jill E. Bronson
Michael F. Brown
Peter P. Ackourey (Resident Partner at Princeton, N.J. Office)
Gary R. Battistoni
Thomas A. Belton (Resident Partner at Princeton, N.J. Office)
James Biehl (Resident Partner at Princeton, N.J. Office)
David J. Brooman
Wilson M. Brown, III

(See Next Column)

DRINKER BIDDLE & REATH LLP, *Philadelphia—Continued*

MEMBERS OF FIRM (Continued)

David P. Bruton
William C. Bullitt
John Chesney
Charles B. Congdon
Jeffrey A. Dalke
Seamus C. Duffy
James Eiseman, Jr.
Jonathan I. Epstein (Resident Partner at Princeton, N.J. Office)
Andrew P. Foster
Christopher H. Gadsden (Resident Partner at Berwyn, Pa. Office)
Vincent E. Gentile (Resident Partner at Princeton, N.J. Office)
William M. Goldstein
Neil K. Haimm
Stephen D. D. Hamilton
Michael J. Holston
J. Freedley Hunsicker, Jr.
Roxanne E. Jayne (Resident Partner at Princeton, N.J. Office)
Joseph F. Johnston, Jr. (Resident Partner at Washington, D.C. Office)
Andrew C. Kassner
Sharon L. Klingelsmith
Mary E. Kohart
Samuel W. Lambert, III (Resident Partner at Princeton, N.J. Office)
Kathryn H. Levering
Michael P. Malloy
Joaquin A. Marquez (Resident Partner at Washington, D.C. Office)
Philip J. Mause (Resident Partner at Washington, D.C. Office)
Robert M. McNair, Jr.
Gregg R. Melinson
James A. Meyers (Resident Partner at Washington, D.C. Office)
M. Howard Morse (Resident Partner at Washington, D.C. Office)
John W. Pettit (Resident Partner at Washington, D.C. Office)
Thomas M. Pinney
Edward M. Posner
Lisa S. Presser (Resident Partner, Princeton, N.J. Office)
F. Douglas Raymond
Judith Reich
Michael J. Remington (Resident Partner at Washington, D.C. Office)
Paul Hewit Saint-Antoine
Pam H. Schneider
John F. Schultz
Bruce D. Shuter
Robert A. Skitol (Resident Partner at Washington, D.C. Office)
George V. Strong, III (Resident Partner at Berwyn, Pa. Office)
Clifford H. Swain
Audrey C. Talley
Charles H. Wampold, III (Resident Partner at Princeton, N.J. Office)
Thomas E. Wood (Resident Partner at Berwyn, Pa. Office)
W. Steven Woodward (Resident Partner at Berwyn, Pa. Office)
Henry S. Bryans
Harry Sarkis Cherken, Jr.
William H. Clark, Jr.
Francis J. Connell, III
Lee W. Doty
Joe D. Edge (Resident Partner at Washington, D.C. Office)
John W. Fischer (Resident Partner at Berwyn, Pa. Office)
Michael O'S. Floyd
Lawrence J. Fox
Michael L. Gassmann (Resident Partner at Washington, D.C. Office)
Richard S. Goldman (Resident Partner at Princeton, N.J. Office)
Kenneth L. Greenberg
Rush T. Haines, II
John C. Hockenbury (Resident Partner at Washington D.C. Office)
Alan J. Joaquin (Resident Partner at Washington, D.C. Office)
Morgan R. Jones
Michael B. Jordan
Marty M. Judge (Resident Partner at Princeton, N.J. Office)
Daniel W. Krane
Stuart A. Law, Jr.
William J. Lehane
Richard A. Levan
John P. Lloyd
Douglas M. Mangel (Resident Partner at Washington, D.C. Office)
Samuel Mason
David W. Maxey
W. Bruce McConnel, III
Michael J. McManus (Resident Partner at Washington, D.C. Office)
H. John Michel, Jr.
Lori A. Mills (Resident Partner, Princeton, N.J. Office)
Walter J. Mostek, Jr. (Resident Partner at Berwyn, Pa. Office)
Mark L. Pelesh (Resident Partner at Washington, D.C. Office)
Nora E. Pomerantz
Warren T. Pratt
Alfred W. Putnam, Jr.
Ellen L. Radow (Resident Partner in Princeton, N.J. Office)
Mary Jo Reilly
Jean D. Renshaw
Ralph Rodak
Michael J. Rotko
Joseph N. Schmidt, Jr. (Resident Partner at Princeton, N.J. Office)
Richard M. Singer (Resident Partner at Washington, D.C. Office)
John E. Stoddard, III (Resident Partner at Princeton, N.J. Office)
James M. Sweet
Charles J. Vinicombe (Resident Partner at Princeton, N. J. Office)
William L. Warren (Resident Partner at Princeton, N.J. Office)

COUNSEL

Sharon P. Barr
Susan G. Collings
Joseph J. Kornblum
David W. Buzzell
Carol L. Ferren
David B. Lipkin
Joan Ohlbaum Swirsky

(See Next Column)

OF COUNSEL

John P. Bankson, Jr. (Resident Of Counsel at Washington, D.C. Office)
Robert Freedman
David J. Goldberg (Resident Of Counsel at Princeton, N.J. Office)
Vernon Stanton, Jr.
Lewis H. Van Dusen, Jr.
Sylvan M. Cohen
Robert N. Cook (Resident Of Counsel, Washington, D.C. Office)
John Markle, Jr. (Resident Of Counsel at Berwyn, Pa. Office)
Kenneth E. Ryan (Resident Of Counsel at Washington, D.C. Office)

ASSOCIATES

Jeff A. Almeida
David John Antczak
Kelly Anne Beaudin
Leslie Gillin Bohner
Christopher W. Boyle
Douglas J. Brady
David R. Breck
Kieran George Brown
Christine Cartwright (Resident Associate at Princeton, N.J. Office)
Kevin M. Chu
Brian A. Coleman (Resident at Washington, D.C. Office)
David L. Coleman
Scott B. Connolly
Stephen C. Costalas
Cori E. Daggett
Christine R. Deutsch
Mark F. Dever (Resident Associate at Washington, D.C. Office)
Anthony J. Donofrio
Sara Dressler-Fiks
Don E. Felice
Regina R. Ford (Not admitted in PA)
Rachel Giuliano
Ian P. Goldstein (Resident Associate at Princeton, N.J. Office)
Alicia F. Greenaway (Resident Associate at Princeton, N.J. Office)
Barbara J. Greenwood (Resident Associate at Berwyn, Pa. Office)
Allen Harberg, Jr.
Michael D. Homans
Lori A. Jackson
Ingrid D. Johnson (Resident Associate at Princeton, N.J. Office)
Susan Marie Kennedy
David Jason Kessler
Andrew D. Klein
Christine M. Kong
Jonathan M. Kopcsik
Jessica L. Krentzman
Jonathan G. Lichtenstein
Michelle M. Lombardo
Raymond A. Lombardo
Jeffrey J. Lopez (Resident Associate at Washington, D.C. Office)
William B. Mac Knight (Resident Associate at Princeton, N.J. Office)
Nancy Harris Marvel
Frank C. Mayer
Janet R. McFadden (Resident Associate at Washington, D.C. Office)
Jon R. Mooney
Sharon A. Morgenroth (Resident Associate at Princeton, N.J. Office)
Jennifer M. Nix (Resident Associate at Princeton, N.J. Office)
Nancy P. O'Hara
Julianne L. Peck
Tina M. Pidgeon (Resident Associate at Washington, D.C. Office)
Patricia Proctor
Carolyn Purcell Reichenbach (Resident Associate at Princeton, N.J. Office)
David J. Anderson
Renee N. Battisti
Jeffrey B. Block
Dorothy E. Bolinsky (Resident Associate at Princeton, N.J. Office)
Kelly Ann Brogan
Amy E. Carroll (Resident Associate at Washington, D.C. Office)
Steven M. Chernoff (Not admitted in PA; Resident Associate at Washington, D.C. Office)
Janine Connell
William M. Connolly
Patricia A. Cullen (Resident Associate at Princeton, N.J. Office)
Daniel J. Devers
Bernard J. Diggins
Deanne L. Dissinger
Michael Dresnin
James G. Fannon
Andrew J. Flame
Jill R. Fowler
Maryanne Garber
Dina M. Gold (Resident Associate at Washington, D.C. Office)
Dean Grabelle (Resident Associate at Princeton, N.J. Office)
Kenneth J. Greenspan
Robert K. Hahm (Resident Associate at Berwyn, Pa. Office)
Kevin L. Hicks
Timothy R. Hughes (Resident Associate at Washington, D.C. Office)
Robert C. Juelke
Victoria L. Karlson (Resident Associate at Berwyn, Pa. Office)
Susan Schleck Kleiner (Resident Associate at Princeton, N.J. Office)
Shauna B. Krupnick (Resident Associate at Berwyn, Pa. Office)
Isabel C. Lopez
Patrick C. Lord
James L. Love (Not admitted in PA)
Maria Markovich
Elizabeth A. Marshall (Resident Associate at Washington, D.C. Office)
Diana E. McCarthy
Michael W. McTigue, Jr.
Mark Migliaccio
Michael F. Milone (Resident Associate at Berwyn, Pa. Office)
Ginger L. Mosier (Resident Associate at Princeton, N.J. Office)
Robert J. Osborne (Not admitted in PA)
Robert A. Particelli
Stephanie P. Pennant
Karl F. Piirimae
Amy E. Pizzutillo
Carla D. Pratt
John R. Przypyszny (Resident Associate at Washington, D.C. Office)
Terrance James Reilly

(See Next Column)

DRINKER BIDDLE & REATH LLP—*Continued*

ASSOCIATES (Continued)

David Restaino (Resident Associate at Princeton, N.J. Office)
Frances V. Ryan
Thomas D. Salus (Resident Associate, Berwyn, Pennsylvania Office)
Shane C. Siegel (Resident Associate at Princeton, N.J. Office)
Mark R. Sullivan (Resident Associate at Princeton, N.J. Office)
Jeffrey Paul Wallack
Kirke D. Weaver
Kathryn R. Williams
Rebecca S. Rimmer
MaryCatherine Roper
Stacey P. Roth (Resident Associate at Princeton, N.J. Office)
Roberta J. Sampson
James M. Scott, III
Scarlett H. Spence
Elizabeth C. Surin
Karen Steinbach (Resident Associate at Princeton, N.J. Office)
Sandy Kent Vergano
Matthew S. Weingast (Resident Associate at Princeton, N.J. Office)
David J. Woolf

LEGAL SUPPORT PERSONNEL
SPECIALIST (NON-LAWYER)

Sharon H. Bob (Higher Education Specialist on Policy and Regulation)

For full biographical listings, see the Martindale-Hubbell Law Directory

DUANE, MORRIS & HECKSCHER LLP (AV)

Suite 4200, One Liberty Place, 19103-7396
Telephone: 215-979-1000
Fax: 215-979-1020
Email: webmaster@duanemorris.com *URL:* http://www.duanemorris.com
New York, New York Office: 380 Lexington Avenue.
Telephone: 212-692-1000.
Fax: 212-692-1020.
Washington, D.C. Office: 1667 K Street NW, Suite 700.
Telephone: 202 776-7800.
Fax: 202-776-7801.
Chicago, Illinois Office: 227 West Monroe Street, Suite 3400.
Telephone: 312-499-6700.
Fax: 312-499-6701.
San Francisco, California Office: 100 Spear Street.
Telephone: 415-371-2200.
Fax: 415-371-2201.
Boston, Massachusetts Office: One International Place, 14th Floor.
Telephone: 617-598-3100.
Fax: 617-598-3101.
Miami, Florida Office: 200 South Biscayne Boulevard, Suite 3410.
Telephone: 305-960-2200.
Fax: 305-960-2201.
Wilmington, Delaware Office: 1201 Market Street, Suite 1500.
Telephone: 302-571-5550.
Fax: 302-571-5560.
Harrisburg, Pennsylvania Office: 305 North Front Street, 5th Floor, P.O. Box 1003.
Telephone: 717-237-5500.
Fax: 717-232-4015.
Wayne, Pennsylvania Office: 735 Chesterbrook Boulevard, Suite 300.
Telephone: 610-647-3555.
Fax: 610-640-2619.
Cherry Hill, New Jersey Office: 51 Haddonfield Road, Suite 340.
Telephone: 856-488-7300.
Fax: 856-488-7021.
Newark, New Jersey Office: One Riverfront Plaza.
Telephone: 973-424-2000.
Fax: 973-424-2001.
Palm Beach, Florida Office: 249 Royal Palm Way, Suite 403.
Telephone: 561-366-5400.
Fax: 561-366-5401.
Allentown, Pennsylvania Office: 968 Postal Road, Suite 200, P.O. Box 90400.
Telephone: 610-266-3650.
Fax: 610-266-3651.
Houston, Texas Office: One Greenway Plaza, Suite 500.
Telephone: 713-552-9900.
Fax: 713-552-0109.
Dover, Delaware Office: 314 S. State Street.
Telephone: 302-736-0156.
Fax: 302-736-0336.

COUNSEL

Thomas R. Bevan
John B. Felton
Thomas M. Hyndman, Jr.
Joseph W. Marshall, Jr.
James J. McCabe
David C. Toomey
John A. Clark
Maurice Heckscher
Frederick A. Levy
A. John May
Henry T. Reath
Seymour C. Wagner
Stephen V. Yarnell

(See Next Column)

MEMBERS OF FIRM

Barbara Adams
Robert L. Archie, Jr.
David R. Augustin
Michael M. Baylson
Anthony J. Bilotti
James K. Brengle
Teresa N. Cavenagh
Peter S. Clark
Frank G. Cooper
Peter J. Cronk
Robert W. Denious
Rudolph J. DiMassa, Jr.
Frederick W. Dreher
Homer L. Elliott
David M. Flynn
Abraham H. Frumkin
Elizabeth Youse Goetz
Lewis F. Gould, Jr.
David I. Haas
James J. Holman
Steven M. Janove
Bruce J. Kasten
James M. Keating, Jr.
Steven E. Koffs
Hope P. Krebs
Jonathan H. Lander
Mark Lipowicz
Patrick J. Loftus
Ralph A. Mariani
Dianne A. Meyer
William H. Murray
Frank E. Noyes, II
Thomas W. Ostrander
Gene E. K. Pratter
Margery N. Reed
Thomas B. K. Ringe, III
Robert E. Rosenthal
Andrew J. Ruck
Mark B. Schoeller
Kathleen M. Shay
Larry D. Silver
Richard C. Smith
Thomas G. Spencer
David T. Sykes
Stephen D. Teaford
Thomas J. Tumola
Diane E. Vuocolo
James L. Allison
Nolan N. Atkinson, Jr.
Donald R. Auten
Edward G. Biester, III
Sheldon M. Bonovitz
Marc D. Brookman
Lisa W. Clark
Seth v.d.H. Cooley
J. Shane Creamer, Jr.
Jane Leslie Dalton
Stephen DiBonaventura
Albert L. Doering, III
Edward M. Dunham, Jr.
Cecelia L. Fanelli
Reeder R. Fox
Vincent F. Garrity, Jr.
C. Mitchell Goldman
Stephan P. Gribok
Jeffrey S. Henderson
John F. Horstmann
Peter Jason
John W. Kauffman
Victor F. Keen
J. Scott Kramer
Jay J. Lambert
Lisa L. Lang
David E. Loder
Wayne A. Mack
Melissa H. Maxman
Roland Morris
Michael M. Mustokoff
Beatrice O'Donnell
Mark J. Packel
Robert A. Prentice
Richard W. Riley
Steve Rosenblatt (Not admitted in PA)
Thomas R. Schmuhl
Thomas G. Servodidio
Mark B. Sheppard
Elise E. Singer
John J. Soroko
Claudia Z. Springer
Matthew A. Taylor
David C. Toner
Craig F. Turet
Gary A. Wilson

ASSOCIATES

Michael E. Adler
John L. Aris
Derek J. Baker
Joel D. Beach
Marissa Boyers
Megan E. Cleghorn
Richard L. Cohen
Kimberly J. Colton
Michael I. Davidson
Monique Y. DeLapenha
Thomas Ermi
Bryan P. Fortay
Allison Z. Gifford
Hope J. Hammer
William K. Harrington
Sandra Jeskie
Matthew C. Jones
Bernadette M. Konzelman
Robert H. Kwait
Mairi V. Luce
Maura I. McInerney
Robert L. Murray, Jr.
John M. Neclerio
Deborah Tate Pecci
Edward J. Pisarcik
Elliot D. Raff
Christopher J. Redd
Randi R. Serota (Not admitted in PA)
Barry L. Small
Jonathan L. Swichar
Lauren Lonergan Taylor
Samuel W. Apicelli
Dana J. Ash
Scott A. Bank
James L. Beausoleil
Sharon L. Caffrey
Jeffrey A. Cohen
Anthony Colesanti
Gail A. Dalickas
Lauren E. DeBruicker
Kelly D. Eckel
Clare Ann Fitzgerald
Darius C. Gambino
Taryn F. Goldstein
H. Bruce Hanson
Curtis A. Hehn
Ramona Johnson
Robert E. Kelly
Michelle D. Koss
Christopher S. Lam
Stephen A. Mallozzi
Joann C. Moscariello
Robin L. Nagele
J. Manly Parks
Alison R. Petrycki
James R. Potts
R. Christopher Raphaely
John C. Ryan (Not admitted in PA)
Alisa M. Shin
James H. Steigerwald
Matthew E. Tashman
Linda D. Thomasson

SPECIAL COUNSEL

Joseph A. Battipaglia
George W. Bodenger
Richard A. Paikoff

For full biographical listings, see the Martindale-Hubbell Law Directory

F. EMMETT FITZPATRICK, P.C. (AV)

926 Public Ledger Building, 19106
Telephone: 215-925-5200
Fax: 215-925-5991
Email: info@toplaw.com *URL:* http://www.toplaw.com

(See Next Column)

F. EMMETT FITZPATRICK, P.C., *Philadelphia—Continued*

F. Emmett Fitzpatrick
F. Emmett Fitzpatrick, III

NiaLena Caravasos

LEGAL SUPPORT PERSONNEL

Doreen Howley (Paralegal)

For full biographical listings, see the Martindale-Hubbell Law Directory

FOX, ROTHSCHILD, O'BRIEN & FRANKEL, LLP (AV)

2000 Market Street, Tenth Floor, 19103-3291
Telephone: 215-299-2000
Cable Address: FROF
Fax: 215-299-2150
Email: frof@frof.com *URL:* http://www.frof.com
Atlantic City, New Jersey Office: CitiCenter Building, Suite 500, 1300 Atlantic Avenue, 08401.
Telephone: 609-348-4515.
Fax: 609-348-6834.
Doylestown, Pennsylvania Office: 102 North Main Street, P.O. Box 1589, 18901-0700.
Telephone: 215-345-7500.
Fax: 215-345-7507.
Exton, Pennsylvania Office: Eagleview Corporate Center, 760 Constitution Drive, Suite 104, P.O. Box 673, 19341-0673.
Telephone: 610-458-7500.
Fax: 610-458-7337.
Lansdale, Pennsylvania Office: 1250 South Broad Street, Suite 1000, P.O. Box 431, 19446.
Telephone: 215-699-6000.
Fax: 215-699-0231.
Sellersville, Pennsylvania Office: 64 North Main Street, 18960-0580.
Telephone: 215-257-3661.
Fax: 215-257-7999.
Trenton (Lawrenceville), New Jersey Office: Princeton Pike Corporate Center, 997 Lenox Drive, Building 3, 08648-2311.
Telephone: 609-896-3600.
Fax: 609-896-1469.
Voorhees, New Jersey Office: Laurelwood, Suite 103, 1103 Laurel Oak Road, 08043.
Telephone: 856-782-6000.
Fax: 856-346-9866.

MEMBERS OF FIRM

Alex Satinsky
Isadore A. Shrager
Robert Perry Frankel
Joseph Smukler
Samuel E. Dennis
William A. Whiteside, Jr.
James F. Young
Richard M. Kohn (Resident, Trenton (Lawrenceville), New Jersey Office)
Jay G. Ochroch
Ramon R. Obod
Louis W. Fryman (Managing Partner)
Victor Walcoff (Not admitted in PA; Resident, Trenton (Lawrenceville), New Jersey Office)
Martin G. Heckler
Owen A. Knopping
Norman Leibovitz
Herbert Bass
Stanley S. Cohen
Mark Z. Segal (Not admitted in PA; Resident, Trenton (Lawrenceville), New Jersey Office)
John D. Trainer (Resident, Doylestown, Pennsylvania Office)
Gerald J. McConomy (Resident, Exton, Pennsylvania Office)
E. Gerald Donnelly, Jr.
Barry Cooperberg (Resident, Lansdale, Pennsylvania Office)
Thomas A. Bell
Michael J. Kline (Resident, Trenton (Lawrenceville), New Jersey Office)
Steven P. Perskie (Resident, Atlantic City, New Jersey Office)
Jonathan D. Weiner (Not admitted in PA; Resident, Trenton (Lawrenceville), New Jersey Office)
Steven C. Levitt (Not admitted in PA; Resident, Trenton (Lawrenceville), New Jersey Office)
Aaron J. Beyer
Jack Gorny (Resident, Atlantic City, New Jersey Office)
Frederick C. Horn (Resident, Lansdale, Pennsylvania Office)
Stephen P. Weiss
Theodore A. Young
Howard E. Drucks (Resident, Atlantic City, New Jersey Office)
Howard R. Flaxman
Howard E. Freed (Resident, Atlantic City, New Jersey Office)
David A. Gradwohl (Resident, Lansdale, Pennsylvania Office)
Marc D. Jonas (Resident, Lansdale, Pennsylvania Office)
Kenneth H. Mack (Resident, Trenton (Lawrenceville), New Jersey Office)
David S. Rasner
William T. Renz (Resident, Doylestown, Pennsylvania Office)
David A. Sacks (Resident, Atlantic City, New Jersey Office)
Barnett Satinsky
A. Robert Degen
Phillip E. Griffin (Not admitted in PA; Resident, Trenton (Lawrenceville), New Jersey Office)
Kean K. McDonald
Abraham C. Reich
John A. Rothschild
Mark Soifer (Resident, Atlantic City, New Jersey Office)
David J. Weiss (Resident, Atlantic City, New Jersey Office)

(See Next Column)

MEMBERS OF FIRM (Continued)

Marc B. Davis (Resident, Lansdale, Pennsylvania Office)
William R. Wanger (Resident, Lansdale, Pennsylvania Office)
David S. Lieberman (Resident, Atlantic City, New Jersey Office)
Albert R. Riviezzo (Resident, Exton, Pennsylvania Office)
Thomas C. Bonner (Resident, Atlantic City, New Jersey Office)
Marvin L. Weinberg
Mary C. Helf (Resident, Sellersville, Pennsylvania Office)
Robin B. Matlin
Jack Plackter (Resident, Atlantic City, New Jersey Office)
Mark L. Silow
Peter Hansen Bach
Kevin J. Carey
Edward J. Hayes
Philip L. Hinerman
Marc L. Hurvitz (Resident, Atlantic City, New Jersey Office)
Sanford K. Mozes (Chair, Corporate Department and Member, Executive Committee)
Carl Oxholm III
Mary Ann Rossi (Resident, Exton, Pennsylvania Office)
Jeffrey T. Sultanik (Resident, Lansdale, Pennsylvania Office)
Melvyn J. Tarnopol (Resident, Atlantic City, New Jersey Office)
Mark R. Ashton (Resident, Exton, Pennsylvania Office)
William M. Honan (Resident, Atlantic City, New Jersey Office)
Elaine N. Moranz
James F. X. Rudy (Not admitted in PA; Resident, Trenton (Lawrenceville), New Jersey Office)
Gerald M. Hatfield
John P. Leon (Resident, Voorhees, New Jersey Office)
Linda Mack (Not admitted in PA; Resident, Trenton (Lawrenceville), New Jersey Office)
Ronald J. Shaffer
Michael J. Viscount, Jr. (Resident, Atlantic City, New Jersey Office)
Jeffrey H. Nicholas (Resident, Trenton (Lawrenceville), New Jersey Office)
Wendy G. Rothstein (Resident, Lansdale, Pennsylvania Office)
Anthony D. Giannascoli (Resident, Exton, Pennsylvania Office)
Matthew H. Lubart (Resident, Trenton (Lawrenceville), New Jersey Office)
Jon C. Martin (Not admitted in PA; Resident, Trenton (Lawrenceville), New Jersey Office)
Mark L. Morris
Kevin J. Thornton (Not admitted in PA; Resident, Atlantic City, New Jersey Office)
Gregory Kleiber
Steven K. Ludwig
Michael C. McBratnie (Resident, Exton, Pennsylvania Office)
Daniel S. Ojserkis (Resident, Atlantic City, New Jersey Office)
Jill T. Ojserkis (Resident, Atlantic City, New Jersey Office)
Stephanie Resnick
Tristram R. Fall III
Martin L. Monaco, Jr. (Resident, Trenton (Lawrenceville), New Jersey Office)
Marc E. Needles
Mary Elisa Reeves
Brian E. Subers (Resident, Lansdale, Pennsylvania Office)
Joseph G. Antinori (At Atlantic City and Voorhees, New Jersey Offices)
Gerald E. Arth
Mark S. Cappuccio (Resident, Lansdale, Pennsylvania Office)
Sandra L. Knapp (Resident, Exton, Pennsylvania Office)
June H. Millington (Not admitted in PA; Resident, Trenton (Lawrenceville), New Jersey Office)
Kevin B. Scott
Barbara R. Flacker
Robert W. Gundlach, Jr.
Jack L. Kolpen (Resident, Trenton (Lawrenceville), New Jersey Office)
Scott L. Vernick
Jacqueline M. Carolan
Jane E. Lessner
Thomas D. Paradise (Resident, Voorhees, New Jersey Office)
Jeffrey P. Scarpello
David B. Snyder
David J. Stutman
Joel M. Chipkin (Resident, Atlantic City, New Jersey Office)
Philip W. Fisher
Samuel H. Israel
Grace Bruther (Resident, Atlantic City, New Jersey Office)
Thomas J. Heitzman (Resident, Trenton (Lawrenceville), New Jersey Office)
R. James Kravitz (Resident, Trenton (Lawrenceville), New Jersey Office)
Lauren P. McKenna
Michael G. Menkowitz
Peter M. Sarkos (Resident, Atlantic City, New Jersey Office)
Eric M. Wood (Resident, Atlantic City, New Jersey Office)
Sally E. Heckeroth (Resident, Atlantic City, New Jersey Office)
Theodore H. Jobes
Ian D. Meklinsky (Resident, Trenton (Lawrenceville), New Jersey Office)
Bradley S. Rodos
Douglas J. Zeltt (Resident, Trenton (Lawrenceville), New Jersey Office)

ASSOCIATES

Kathryn D. Portner (Resident, Atlantic City, New Jersey Office)
Prince Altee Thomas
James A. Matthews, III
Michael F. Collins (Resident, Lansdale, Pennsylvania Office)
David J. Toll (Resident, Lansdale, Pennsylvania Office)
Susan D. Bonfield (Resident, Trenton (Lawrenceville), New Jersey Office)
Pamela M. Tobin
Holly Lichtenstein Goldberg (Resident, Trenton (Lawrenceville), New Jersey Office)

(See Next Column)

FOX, ROTHSCHILD, O'BRIEN & FRANKEL LLP—*Continued*

ASSOCIATES (Continued)

Donna M. Taylor (Resident, Atlantic City, New Jersey Office)
David J. Draganosky (Resident, Lansdale, Pennsylvania Office)
Jeffrey D. Hutton
Deborah R. Popky
Craig A. Styer (Resident, Exton, Pennsylvania Office)
Lisa Carney Eldridge
Krista Pool Harper (Resident, Doylestown, Pennsylvania Office)
Philip S. Rosenzweig (Resident, Trenton (Lawrenceville), New Jersey Office)
Randal S. White (Resident, Doylestown, Pennsylvania Office)
Michelle T. Wirtner
Lynn B. McDougall (Resident, Trenton (Lawrenceville), New Jersey Office)
Frank G. Murphy
Wendy Michelle Rosen (Resident, Doylestown, Pennsylvania Office)
Magdalena Schardt (Resident, Trenton (Lawrenceville), New Jersey Office)
Susan Jean Smith (Resident, Doylestown, Pennsylvania Office)
David S. Sokolow
Michael S. Bookbinder
Jennifer Molish Brier (Resident, Lansdale, Pennsylvania Office)
Madeleine H. Cozine (Resident, Trenton (Lawrenceville), New Jersey Office)
Michael F. Merlie (Resident, Exton, Pennsylvania Office)
Richard E. Wegryn, Jr. (Resident, Trenton (Lawrenceville), New Jersey Office)
Jacqueline M. Woolley
Amparito Arriaga (Resident, Exton, Pennsylvania Office)
Kelly Himes Brolly
Michael Scott Harrington (Resident, Exton, Pennsylvania Office)
Joshua Horn
Gina M. Merritt-Epps (Resident, Atlantic City, New Jersey Office)
Donna M. Michael-Ziereis (Resident, Atlantic City, New Jersey Office)
Mindee J. Reuben
Robert S. Tintner
Robert A. Walper (Resident, Lansdale, Pennsylvania Office)
Craig L. Finger
Maureen E. Kerns (Resident, Trenton (Lawrenceville), New Jersey Office)
Daniel G. Lyons
Lori Forter Ridyard (Resident, Exton, Pennsylvania Office)
John C. Romeo
James M. Townsend, Jr. (Resident, Doylestown, Pennsylvania Office)
Gregory B. Williams
Sherri A. Affrunti (Resident, Atlantic City, New Jersey Office)
Christina Almanzor (Resident, Trenton (Lawrenceville), New Jersey Office)
Catherine T. Barbieri
Dorothy M. Bollinger (Resident, Lansdale, Pennsylvania Office)
Samuel Edward Cohen
Michael B. Dahl (Resident, Trenton (Lawrenceville), New Jersey Office)
Hollie B. Knox
Mark R. Kossow (Resident, Trenton (Lawrenceville), New Jersey Office)
Gregory A. Petroff (Resident, Trenton (Lawrenceville), New Jersey Office)
Mark S. Rhodes
William Harold Stassen
Debra L. Swank (Resident, Lansdale, Pennsylvania Office)
Kimberley M. Wilson (Resident, Trenton (Lawrenceville), New Jersey Office)
Alicia A. Zonetti (Resident, Trenton (Lawrenceville), New Jersey Office)
Anthony Argiropoulos (Resident, Trenton (Lawrenceville), New Jersey Office)
Tess Brennan (Resident, Trenton (Lawrenceville), New Jersey Office)
Neil M. Day (Resident, Trenton (Lawrenceville), New Jersey Office)
Stephen F. Funk (Resident, Atlantic City, New Jersey Office)
Wan-Mo Kang (Resident, Trenton (Lawrenceville), New Jersey Office)
Michael J. Kornacki (Not admitted in PA)
Darin Ross Morgan
Jacqueline Gordon Snider
Ellen M. VanValkenburg (Resident, Lansdale, Pennsylvania Office)
Annamaria Vitelli
Philip N. Yannella
William Bennett Cooper, III (Resident, Exton, Pennsylvania Office)
Cara L. Levy
Judy McIntire Springer
Damon G. Tyner (Resident, Atlantic City, New Jersey Office)

SPECIAL COUNSEL

Edward R. Knight (Resident, Atlantic City, New Jersey Office)
Gerald Weinstein (Resident, Atlantic City, New Jersey Office)
Ronald E. Robinson (Resident, Lansdale, Pennsylvania Office)
Marjorie Stern Jacobs
Daniel J. Paci (Resident, Doylestown, Pennsylvania Office)
Brian J. O'Neill
Herbert K. Sudfeld, Jr. (Resident, Doylestown, Pennsylvania Office)
Elaine C. Britt (Not admitted in PA; Resident, Trenton (Lawrenceville), New Jersey Office)
Roberto A. Rivera-Soto
J. Randolph Lawlace
James W. Gerlach (Resident, Exton, Pennsylvania Office)
Nancy E. Bloomberg
Keith A. Onsdorff (Not admitted in PA)

SENIOR COUNSEL

Murray H. Shusterman
Philip M. Shiekman
Samuel G. Moyer

For full biographical listings, see the Martindale-Hubbell Law Directory

HARVEY, PENNINGTON, CABOT, GRIFFITH & RENNEISEN, LTD. (AV)

11 Penn Center, 29th Floor, 1835 Market Street, 19103
Telephone: 215-563-4470
Fax: 215-568-1044
URL: http://www.harvpenn.com
Cherry Hill, New Jersey Office: Pennington & Thompson, 135 Woodcrest Road.
Telephone: 856-795-0882.
Fax: 856-795-4907.
New York, N.Y. Office: 144 East 44th Street, Sixth Floor.
Telephone: 212-682-4900.
Fax: 212-808-9808.
Wilmington, Delaware Office: 1525 Delaware Avenue, First Floor.
Telephone: 302-428-0719.
Fax: 302-777-4682.

David L. Pennington
G. Wayne Renneisen
Glenn C. Equi
David J. Griffith
Elizabeth McKenna
Robert D. Thompson (Resident, Cherry Hill, New Jersey Office)
Stephen J. Cabot
Charles M. Weisman
Joel D. Gusky
John E. Smith
Susan McLaughlin
George A. Amacker, III (Resident, Cherry Hill, New Jersey Office)
Gary C. Chiumento (Resident, Cherry Hill, New Jersey Office)
Howard M. Cyr, III
Frederick M. Walton, Jr.
Ernest J. Bernabei, III
Carolyn B. Stevens (Resident, New York, N.Y. Office)
Mark A. Lockett
Andrew Fylypovych
Andrew K. Worek
Donald D. Bush (Not admitted in PA)
James F. Lynn
Michele Daniele
Christopher J. Murphy
Melissa Lang
Thomas Gibson

OF COUNSEL

William M. Aukamp (Not admitted in PA)
Michel Lee (Resident, New York, N.Y. Office)

Maria L. Petrillo
Patrick R. Delaney (Resident, Cherry Hill, New Jersey Office)
Victor R. Moritz (Resident, New York, N.Y. Office)
Michael E. Lignowski
William H. Dengler, Jr. (Resident, Cherry Hill, New Jersey Office)
Laurie A. Carroll
Linell M. Lukesh
John J. Winter
Toi Shields
Cynthia M. Long
Thaddeus Bechtle
Jeffrey A, Korostoff
John J. Daly
Joan Blatcher Cohen
Diem-Thy Nguyen
Robert A. Frankel
A. Christine Giordano
Erika L. Austin
Robert C. Nagle
Stephen J. Bruderle
David Marc Schwadron
Robert G. Yosua
Roberto K. Paglione (Resident, Cherry Hill, New Jersey Office)
W. J. Winterstein, Jr.
James F. Casale

For full biographical listings, see the Martindale-Hubbell Law Directory

HOYLE, MORRIS & KERR LLP (AV)

Suite 4900, One Liberty Place, 1650 Market Street, 19103
Telephone: 215-981-5700
Telecopier: 215-981-5959
Email: hoyle@hoylemk.com *URL:* http://www.hoylemk.com

MEMBERS OF FIRM

Lawrence T. Hoyle, Jr.
Alexander Kerr
Bernard J. Smolens (1916-1997)
Susan K. Herschel
Arlene Fickler
F. John Hagele
John Francis Gough
Stephen J. Mathes
Walter M. Phillips, Jr.
Henry H. Janssen
Charles B. Blakinger
Ralph A. Jacobs
Gerald Chalphin
R. Nicholas Gimbel
Bebe H. Kivitz
William R. Herman
Denise D. Colliers
Elizabeth W. Fox
Lisa M. Salazar
R. David Walk, Jr.

OF COUNSEL

Samuel W. Morris, Jr.
Arthur R. Littleton
Nathalie Martin

SENIOR ATTORNEYS

Michael T. Starczewski
Jan Fink Call
Joann M. Lytle

(See Next Column)

HOYLE, MORRIS & KERR LLP, *Philadelphia—Continued*

ASSOCIATES

Ellen M. Briggs
Nancy Stuart Portney
George Stephen Bobnak
Kevin J. Kotch
Elliot C. Fertik
Debora C. Fliegelman
Chonda Jordan Nwamu
Michael E. Plunkett
C. Scott Spear
Jeffrey D. Cohen
Todd A. Schoenhaus
Stephen P. McFate
Wendi L. Shohen

For full biographical listings, see the Martindale-Hubbell Law Directory

KLEHR, HARRISON, HARVEY, BRANZBURG & ELLERS LLP (AV)

260 South Broad Street, Suite 400, 19102
Telephone: 215-568-6060
Fax: 215-568-6603
Email: mail@klehr.com
Cherry Hill, New Jersey Office: Libertyview - Suite 510, 457 Haddonfield Road.
Telephone: 856-486-7900.
Fax: 856-486-4875.
Wilmington, Delaware Office: Mellon Bank Center, 919 Market Street, Suite 1000.
Telephone: 302-426-1189.
Fax: 302-426-9193.

MEMBERS OF FIRM

Edward S. Ellers
Morton R. Branzburg
William A. Harvey
Leonard M. Klehr
Lawrence J. Arem
Rona J. Rosen
Stephen T. Burdumy
Richard S. Roisman
Carol Ann Slocum (Resident, Cherry Hill, New Jersey Office)
Gary W. Levi (Resident, Cherry Hill, New Jersey Office)
Arnold E. Cohen
Michael C. Forman
Jeffrey Kurtzman
Michael K. Coran
Francis M. Correll, Jr.
Joanne B. Wills (Resident, Wilmington, Delaware Office)
Robert W. Cleveland
Carl S. Primavera
Keith W. Kaplan
Paul G. Nofer
Douglas F. Schleicher
Barry J. Siegel
Scott J. Fields
Richard M. Beck
Denise M. Day
Gary A. Deutsch (Resident, Cherry Hill, New Jersey Office)
David S. Eagle (Resident, Wilmington, Delaware Office)
Bradley A. Krouse
Benjamin J. Berger (Resident, Wilmington, Delaware Office)
Stephan L. Cutler
Lawrence D. Rovin
Donald M. Millinger
Domenic E. Pacitti
David Zalesne

OF COUNSEL

Donald M. Harrison
Terrance A. Kline
Lynn G. Zeitlin
Anders F. Laren (Not admitted in PA)
E. Carolyn Hochstadter Dicker
Ronald J. Patterson

ASSOCIATES

Emily M. Clay
J. Breck Smith (Resident, Wilmington, Delaware Office)
Joseph G. Gibbons
Steven A. Kaye
Steven K. Kortanek (Resident, Wilmington, Delaware Office)
Mindy Friedman
Peter J. Norman
Cynthia A. Clark
Charles A. Ercole
Donald G. Harrington (Not admitted in PA)
Fredric J. Kinkler, Jr.
William W. Matthews, III
Maria Aprile Sawczuk (Resident, Delaware Office)
Shahan G. Teberian
Shari Amster
Susan M. Dean
Glenn A. Weiner
Stephen C. Eglin
Jeffrey P. Foster (Resident, Cherry Hill, New Jersey Office)
Michael A. Iaconelli
Diana R. Ivanovic
Dimitri L. Karapelou
Heather I. Levine
Daniel P. O'Brien
Ira A. Rosenau
Julie E. Snyder
Brian I. Sopinsky
Marc H. Stofman (Resident, Cherry Hill, New Jersey Office)
Andrew L. Zivitz
Robert J. Downs, Jr.
Debra L. Markowitz
Robert L. Sichel
Craig F. Zappetti
Ronald S. Gellert
Jennifer A. Irrgang
Lee Duck Moylan
Brian E. Shanahan (Not admitted in PA)
Anthony P. Tabasso
David S. McLaughlin
Jason C. Menegakis
Randi Lynne Rubin

LEGAL SUPPORT PERSONNEL

Brian K. Ehmann
Margaret S. Fallon

For full biographical listings, see the Martindale-Hubbell Law Directory

KLEINBARD, BELL & BRECKER LLP (AV)

Suite 700, 1900 Market Street, 19103
Telephone: 215-568-2000
Facsimile: 215-568-0140
Montclair, New Jersey Office: 240 Claremont Avenue, 07042.
Telephone: 973-233-0600.
Facsimile: 973-233-9390.

(See Next Column)

Joseph S. Kleinbard (1905-1994)
Robert John Brecker (1916-1996)

COUNSEL TO THE FIRM

Arthur S. Keyser

MEMBERS OF FIRM

Paul E. Bomze
Murray I. Blackman
Howard J. Davis
Steven R. Waxman
Steven J. Engelmyer (Resident, Montclair Office)
David L. Hyman (Resident, Montclair Office)
Imogene E. Hughes
John P. Hickey
Jay R. Goldstein
Ralph J. Mauro
Thomas H. Speranza
Lisa E. Brody

ASSOCIATES

Mary Beth H. Gray
Eric J. Rothschild
Mary Vassallo Slinkard
Michael A. Frattone
Benjamin C. Graff (Not admitted in PA)
Ralph F. Salgado

COUNSEL

Joseph Bell

For full biographical listings, see the Martindale-Hubbell Law Directory

LEVIN, FISHBEIN, SEDRAN & BERMAN (AV)

Suite 500, 510 Walnut Street, 19106-3697
Telephone: 215-592-1500
Fax: 215-592-4663
Email: lfsb@psinet.com

MEMBERS OF FIRM

Arnold Levin
Michael D. Fishbein
Howard J. Sedran
Laurence S. Berman
Frederick S. Longer

Craig D. Ginsburg
Cheryl R. Brown Hill
Donald E. Haviland, Jr.
Daniel C. Levin
Terrianne Benedetto
Charles E. Schaffer
Austin B. Cohen

LEGAL SUPPORT PERSONNEL

Lee Ann Fitzpatrick
Cheryl Hesson

For full biographical listings, see the Martindale-Hubbell Law Directory

MATTIONI, LTD. (AV)

399 Market Street, 2nd Floor, 19106
Telephone: 215-629-1600
Cable Address: "Mattioni"
Fax: 215-923-2227
Email: firmmail@mattioni.com *URL:* http://www.mattioni.com
Westmont, New Jersey Office: Mattioni, LLP, Suite 100, Sentry Office Plaza, 216 Haddon Avenue, 08108.
Telephone: 856-854-6200.
Fax: 856-854-3338.
Montgomery County Office: Suite 200, 1101 Fayette Street, Conshohocken, Pennsylvania, 19428.
Telephone: 610-941-9530.
Fax: 610-940-4489.

Dante Mattioni
Faustino Mattioni
John Mattioni
Blasco Mattioni *
Eugene Mattioni
Francis X. Kelly
George R. Zacharkow
Andrew H. Quinn
Eva Helena Bleich
Robert W. Weidner, Jr.
Scott J. Schwarz
Anthony Granato
Stephen M. Martin
Stephen J. Galati
Joseph F. Bouvier
Michael Mattioni
Bruce A. O'Neill
Alan Mattioni
Itzchak E. Kornfeld
Sarah Wilson Weingast (Not admitted in PA)
Mary Alice Cleve
Paul A. Kettunen
Donald S. Sabatini
Mark David Hasenauer
Bridget C. Sciamanna
Mette Deleuran
Dante C. Rohr

Frank Carano *
Ronald R. Donatucci *
John A. DiPietro **
Kristi L. Treadway **

*Counsel to the Firm
**Of Counsel

For full biographical listings, see the Martindale-Hubbell Law Directory

McCARTER & ENGLISH, LLP (AV Ⓣ)

One Commerce Square, 2005 Market Street, Suite 3600, 19103
Telephone: 215-557-7700
Telecopier: 215-557-6544
URL: http://www.mccarter.com
Newark, New Jersey Office: Four Gateway Center, 100 Mulberry Street. P.O. Box 652.
Telephone: 973-622-4444.
Telecopier: 973-624-7070.

(See Next Column)

McCARTER & ENGLISH LLP—*Continued*

Cherry Hill, New Jersey Office: 1820 Chapel Avenue West, Suite 380.
Telephone: 609-662-8444.
Telecopier: 609-662-6203.
New York, New York Office: Suite 2247, One World Trade Center.
Telephone: 212-466-9018.
Telecopier: 212-432-6568.
Boca Raton, Florida Office: 2255 Glades Road, Suite 319-A.
Telephone: 561-994-6262.
Telecopier: 561-241-0798.
Wilmington, Delaware Office: Mellon Bank Center, 919 Market Street.
Telephone: 302-654-8010.
Telecopier: 302-654-0795.

MEMBERS OF FIRM

Glenn P. Callahan
Therese M. Keeley

SPECIAL COUNSEL

Michael J. Glasheen

ASSOCIATES

Michael A. Alfano
Anthony J. Di Marino, III
Michael N. Feder
Eric J. Kadish
Lynn L. Owens

For full biographical listings, see the Martindale-Hubbell Law Directory

MONTGOMERY, McCRACKEN, WALKER & RHOADS, LLP (AV)

123 South Broad Street, 19109
Telephone: 215-772-1500
Fax: 215-772-7620
URL: http://www.mmwr.com
Cherry Hill, New Jersey Office: LibertyView, Suite 600, 457 Haddonfield Road.
Telephone: 609-488-7700.
Facsimile: 609-488-7720.

David H. Marion
Jeremy D. Mishkin
Louis A. Petroni

PARTNERS

Arlene J. Angelo
Stephen W. Armstrong
Jeanne L. Bakker
Larry R. Barron
Howard J. Bashman
Timothy J. Bergère
Bruce H. Bikin
Steven E. Bizar
Ralph W. Brenner
Carter R. Buller
Leonard A. Busby
Baldo M. Carnecchia, Jr.
John E. Caruso
Charles B. Casper
Robert Gordon Chambers
Julie Hofmann Chelius
Christopher Scott D'Angelo
Doreen S. Davis
Gary M. Edelson
James J. Eisenhower
Edward T. Ellis
Mary Theresa Enyart
John H. Estey
H. Thomas Felix, II
Gregory J. Fox
John W. Frazier, IV
David L. Grove
Richard W. Hartmann
Gregory M. Harvey
Patrick J. Harvey
Herbert E. Hoffman
Ronald E. Hurst
Kenneth M. Jarin
John P. Judge
Sally Ackerman King
Donald W. Kramer
Jeffrey R. Lerman
John J. Levy
John H. Lewis, Jr.
Robert A. MacDonnell
David J. MacMain
Stephen A. Madva
Steven Maniloff
David H. Marion
Richard H. Martin
Frances A. McElhill
John P. McLaughlin
Joyce S. Meyers
Jeremy D. Mishkin
Arthur H. Moss
Mary Elizabeth Nagy
Francis Patrick Newell
Kathleen O'Brien
Louis A. Petroni
Richard G. Placey
Mary F. Platt
Natalie D. Ramsey
Stephen G. Rhoads
Patrick T. Ryan
Richard L. Scheff
Howard D. Scher
Nina Segré
Karen L. Senser
David Shechtman
Virginia P. Sikes
Richard M. Simins
Joseph T. Stapleton
Jennifer A. Stiller
Thomas H. Suddath, Jr.
Larry L. Turner
M. Howard Vigderman
Anthony F. Visco, Jr.
Larissa Renshaw Whitman
James A. Willhite, Jr.
John C. Wright, Jr.
Craig E. Ziegler

OF COUNSEL

Walter L. Bartholomew, Jr.
Marianne Bechtle
Martin W. Bond
Ralph H. Colflesh, Jr.
Frank S. Deming
William F. Drake, Jr.
John S. Estey
Marc R. Garber
Joseph K. Gordon
Mervin J. Hartman
Alan Reeve Hunt
Arthur Gregg Jackson
Alfred J. Kuffler
Howard H. Lewis
Clifford Scott Meyer
Harry Carl Schaub
Peter A. von Mehren (Not admitted in PA)
Nancy M. Weinman

(See Next Column)

ASSOCIATES

C. Alexa Abowitz
Christopher M. Barr
Jeffrey Adam Bartos
Peter Breslauer
David E. Brier
Samuel Z. Brown
Michael J. Butler
D. Craig Callaghan
Carol A. Cannerelli
James D. Cashel
Frank A. Chernak
Thomas L. Church
Brendan T. Conway
Christina M. Corsac
Michon L. Crawford
Richard M. Donaldson
John Ehmann
Robert W. Elias
Michael D. Epstein
Michael L. Epstein
Todd M. Felzer
Sharon O'Neill Finnegan
Wendy A. Fleming
Stacy Alison Fols
Peter J. Fontaine
A. Christina D. Frangiosa
William D. Georges
Catherine H. Gillespie
Janice A. Greenberg
Elizabeth C. Gutman
Darren L. Harrison
Gregory J. Hauck
Caridad Diego Hopkins
Michael D. Jones
Timothy F. Kennedy (Not admitted in PA)
David D. Langfitt
Patricia J. Larson
Eric Lechtzin
Michele A. Ledo
Sidney S. Liebesman
Jeanette Melendez
Erika E. Miller
Craig D. Mills
Douglas L. Overtoom
Kristin M. Palmaccio
Kristen E. Polovoy
Ellen K. Pomfret
Joseph C. Ragaglia
Glenn F. Rosenblum
Paul M. Secunda
Robert C. Seiger, III
Joanne Semeister
Douglas E. Simon
Joel S. Solomon
Min S. Suh
Charles C. Sweedler
Meghan M. Thomsen
Michael K. Twersky
Jeffrey C. Wolken
Bryan Wood
Geraldine D. Zidow

For full biographical listings, see the Martindale-Hubbell Law Directory

MORGAN, LEWIS & BOCKIUS LLP (AV)

1701 Market Street, 19103-2921
Telephone: 215-963-5000
Cable Address: "Morlebock"
Telex: 83-1315
Fax: 215-963-5299
Email: postmaster@mlb.com *URL:* http://www.mlb.com
Washington, D.C. Office: 1800 M Street, N.W., 20036-5869.
Telephone: 202-467-7000.
Fax: 202-467-7176.
New York, New York Office: 101 Park Avenue, 10178-0060.
Telephone: 212-309-6000.
Fax: 212-309-6273.
Los Angeles, California Office: 300 South Grand Avenue, 22nd Floor, 90071-3132.
Telephone: 213-612-2500.
Fax: 213-612-2554.
Miami, Florida Office: 5300 First Union Financial Center, 200 South Biscayne Boulevard, 33131-2339.
Telephone: 305-579-0300.
Fax: 305-579-0321.
Harrisburg, Pennsylvania Office: One Commerce Square, 417 Walnut Street, 17101-1904.
Telephone: 717-237-4000.
Fax: 717-237-4004.
Pittsburgh, Pennsylvania Office: One Oxford Centre, 301 Grant Street, 32nd Floor, 15219-6401.
Telephone: 412-560-3300.
Fax: 412-560-3399.
Princeton, New Jersey Office: 502 Carnegie Center, 08540.
Telephone: 609-919-6600.
Fax: 609-919-6639.
London, England Office: Morgan, Lewis & Bockius, 2 Gresham Street, London EC2V 7PE.
Telephone: 44-207-710-5500.
Fax: 44-207-710-5600.
Frankfurt, Germany Office: Guiollettstra e 54, 60325 Frankfurt am Main.
Telephone: (49-69) 71 40 07-0.
Fax: (49-69) 71 40 07-10.
Brussels, Belgium Office: 7 Rue Guimard, B-1040.
Telephone: 32-2/512.55.01.
Fax: 32-2/512.58.88.
Tokyo, Japan Office: Yurakucho Denki Building S-556, 7-1 Yurakucho 1-chome, Chiyoda-ku, Tokyo 100-0006.
Telephone: (81-3) 3216-2500.
Fax: (81-3) 3216-2501.
Singapore Office: 80 Raffles Place, #14-20 UOB Plaza 2, Singapore 048624.
Telephone: 65-438-2188.
Fax: 65-230-7100.

MEMBERS OF FIRM IN PHILADELPHIA

Alan L. Reed
John J. Lombard, Jr.
Denis V. Brenan
James W. Jennings
Kenneth R. Myers
Joseph A. O'Connor, Jr.
Howard L. Shecter
Robert S. Hodavance
Thomas M. Kittredge
William A. Macan IV
John F. Bales, III
William M. Doran
Stephen M. Goodman
George G. Loveless

(See Next Column)

MORGAN, LEWIS & BOCKIUS LLP, *Philadelphia—Continued*

MEMBERS OF FIRM IN PHILADELPHIA (Continued)

Raymond T. Cullen
Mark S. Dichter
James A. Hunter, Jr.
Jay H. Calvert, Jr.
Joseph H. Hennessy
Timothy P. O'Reilly
Marc J. Sonnenfeld
Judith E. Harris
Richard W. Grant
Lawrence H. Berger
Frederick J. M. LaValley
Mari M. Shaw
Howard L. Meyers
Edward S. G. Dennis, Jr.
Kell M. Damsgaard
David R. King
Francis M. Milone
Dennis J. Morikawa
Richard J. Sabat
Peter S. Sartorius
Robert L. Abramowitz
Michael A. Bloom
Robert J. Lichtenstein
Alan Singer
Robert D. Comfort
Thomas P. Gadsden
Thomas B. Kenworthy
Lawrence B. Fine
I. Lee Falk
Thomas J. Sharbaugh
Robert D. Lane, Jr.
David B. MacGregor
Richard F. McMenamin
Francis J. Mirabello
Steven D. Spencer
N. Jeffrey Klauder
Frank M. Thomas, Jr.
Elizabeth Hoop Fay
Kathryn A. Kapusta
Michael J. Ossip
James D. Pagliaro
Michael L. Banks
Joseph B. G. Fay
David L. Harbaugh
Jami Wintz McKeon
Eric Kraeutler
Brian J. Dougherty
Edward J. Matey, Jr.
Richard D. Martinson
(Not admitted in PA)
William P. Quinn, Jr.
Steven R. Wall
J. Gordon Cooney, Jr.
Timothy Maxwell
Thomas J. Vallone
Glen R. Stuart
Joseph J. Costello
Coleen M. Meehan
Michael L. Pillion
James W. McKenzie, Jr.
Steven J. Molitor
John C. Dodds
Michael R. Libor
Michael J. Pedrick
Brian J. Lynch
Eric L. Stern
Mark P. Edwards
Stephen A. Jannetta
Edward S. Mazurek
John J. McAleese, III
John H. Grady, Jr.
(Not admitted in PA)
Brady L. Green
John R. Washlick
Mims Maynard Zabriskie

SPECIAL COUNSEL

C. Ronald Rubley
Frederic M. Wilf

COUNSEL IN PHILADELPHIA

James M. Ballengee
(Not admitted in PA)
John S. Brittain
Richard P. Brown, Jr.
Park B. Dilks, Jr.
Donald A. Scott
Lee H. Snyder
Robert H. Young

OF COUNSEL IN PHILADELPHIA

Anthony C. DeCusatis
Michael R. Dillon
Amelia C. Kittredge
Thomas P. McCorriston, Jr.
George W. Moore
Clifford J. Peterson
Debra J. Poul
Joseph E. Ronan, Jr.
Dennis J. Valenza

ASSOCIATES IN PHILADELPHIA

Jennifer H. Adams
Richard B. Aldridge
Mitchell A. Altschuler
Nathan J. Andrisani
Melissa C. Angeline
Dominick H. Answini
Lisa J. Atkins
Edward B. Baer
(Not admitted in PA)
Ian Matheson Ballard, Jr.
Christin L. Bassett
Matthew M. Bennett
Tara L. Benson
(Not admitted in PA)
Veenita Bhatia
Lorenzo A. Bivans, Jr.
Marifrances Dant Bolger
James N. Boudreau
G. Jeffrey Boujoukos
Scott C. Bovino
Barbara L. Briggs
(Not admitted in PA)
Sean V. Burke
Michael S. Burkhardt
David K. Burton
April M. Byrd
(Not admitted in PA)
Jennifer M. Calabrese
Vincent S. Capone
Lynn Carino
Ashely M. Chan
Elaina R. Cohen
Leslie S. Cohn
Lisa Ann Cooney
Robert L. Cooney, Jr.
David W. Cromley
Bridget King Crooks
Clare D'Agostino
Aretha Delight Davis
Lauren M. DeBunda
Manya S. Deehr
(Not admitted in PA)
William J. Delany
James E. DelBello
David W. DiSabatino
Basil S. Donnelly
Amy L. Donohue-Babiak
Kevin M. Donovan
Lisa M. Dooley
Michael J. Eagles
Robert L. Ebby
Robert C. Farley, Jr.
J. Kevin Fee
Brian T. Feeney
Amy R. Feldgus
Hugh W. P. Fisher
Christina Mesires Fournaris
Anthony E. Gay
Torsten M. Geers
(Not admitted in PA)
Catharine E. Gillespie
Amanda E. Goff
(Not admitted in PA)
John C. Goodchild, III
John V. Gorman
Kimberly J. Gost
Stephanie A. Graboyes
Paul J. Greco
Jon M. Greer
B. Benjamin Haas

(See Next Column)

ASSOCIATES IN PHILADELPHIA (Continued)

Adam M. Haberfield
Catherine M. Hamberger
Andrew Hamilton
Donna M. Hill
Elke A. Hofmann
Alison D. Hoyle
Thomas Benjamin (Ben) Huggett
Jeffrey N. Hurwitz
Paul J. Jaskot
John J. Kenney, Jr.
Christine M. Kovan
Jennifer L. Kraft
David W. Laub
(Not admitted in PA)
Emily J. Lawrence
Joseph A. Levin
Timothy Levin
James J. Leyden
Raphael Licht
Bryant D. Lim
John M. Limongelli
Joseph M. Macchione
M. Kristin Malone
Michele E. Martin
John D. Martini
Gregory T. Mayes
Ralph R. Mazzeo
Vivian S. McCardell
Paul N. McCarthy
Anna Margaret McDonough
Marianne G. McLaughlin
Edward J. Meehan, Jr.
(Not admitted in PA)
Michael Migliaccio
Brian C. Miner
James A. Mirage
Lusine Moshkounian
(Not admitted in PA)
Erin F. Mulhollan
Melissa M. Mulkey
Joel R. Nied
Ellen T. Noteware
Georgina L. O'Hara
John E. Parker
Viveca D. Parker
Gregory T. Parks
Michael N. Peterson
John S. Pettibone III
(Not admitted in PA)
Karen Pieslak Pohlmann
David M. Pollard
Ajay Raju
Jeffrey M. Ramage
Susan J. Ray
Karyn K. Reed
Maureen E. Reilly
Charles J. Reitmeyer
Ursula Robinson
Richard G. Rosenblatt
Tina K. Saini
Jennifer Lobel Schneider
Mark J. Sever, Jr.
Brian W. Shaffer
Pamela Shaiman
Barbara J. Shander
Michael J. Shim
Robert N. Sobol
Joanne R. Soslow
Judith A. Sprague
R. Stephen Stigall
Sarah E. Sutor
Brendan Sweeney
Brad M. Toborowsky
Rebecca L. Weaver
Paul D. Weller
Gregg W. Winter
Guy W. Winters, Jr.
Kay Kyungsun Yu
(Not admitted in PA)
David B. Zelikoff

For full biographical listings, see the Martindale-Hubbell Law Directory

NEIL A. MORRIS ASSOCIATES, P.C. (AV)

The Widener Building, Suite 1700, One South Penn Square 1339 Chestnut Street, 19107
Telephone: 215-751-0600
Fax: 215-751-1425
URL: http://www.namapc.com
Marlton, New Jersey Office: Ten Lake Center Executive Park, 401 Route 73 North, Suite 204.
Telephone: 609-596-5656.
Telefax: 609-596-6164.

Neil A. Morris

Laurence L. Smith
Richard R. Morris
Daniel F. McLaughlin

OF COUNSEL

Jay H. Rosenfeld

LEGAL SUPPORT PERSONNEL

Jacqueline J. Ben

For full biographical listings, see the Martindale-Hubbell Law Directory

OBERMAYER, REBMANN, MAXWELL & HIPPEL LLP (AV)

One Penn Center, 1617 John F. Kennedy Boulevard, 19th Floor, 19103-1895
Telephone: 215-665-3000
Cable Address: "Edmer"
Facsimile: 215-665-3165
Haddonfield, New Jersey Office: Two Kings Highway West.
Telephone: 609-795-3300.
Harrisburg, Pennsylvania Office: 204 State Street.
Telephone: 717-234-9730.
Pittsburgh, Pennsylvania Office: USX Tower, Suite 4440, 600 Grant Street.
Telephone: 412-566-1500.

OF COUNSEL

Frank E. Hahn, Jr.
Allen Weinberg
William G. Schwartz
Jonathan H. Newman
Charles M. Taylor
Robert N.C. Nix, III
Robert Morton Dubbs
Frederick Cohen
J. Kurt Straub
Thomas Patrick Foley

MEMBERS OF FIRM

Franklin S. Edmonds (1886-1945)
Leon J. Obermayer (1886-1984)
G. Ruhland Rebmann, Jr. (1898-1983)
David F. Maxwell (1900-1985)
John F. E. Hippel (1901-1984)
George B. Clothier (1905-1992)
H. Clayton Louderback (1913-1980)
William J. Fuchs (1921-1979)

(See Next Column)

OBERMAYER, REBMANN, MAXWELL & HIPPEL LLP—*Continued*

MEMBERS OF FIRM (Continued)

Richard W. Thorington (1898-1994)
Martin Weinberg
Paul C. Heintz
Peter M. Breitling
Hugh C. Sutherland
Robert I. Whitelaw
E. Parry Warner
Jeffrey B. Rotwitt
James M. Penny, Jr.
Gregory D. Saputelli (Resident, Haddonfield, NJ Office)
Kenneth L. Oliver, Jr.
Thorley C. Mills, Jr.
John J. Ehlinger, Jr.
Warren W. Ayres
Mark A. Lublin
Charles M. Golden
James W. Baumbach
Thomas A. Leonard
Stephen D. Schrier (Resident, Haddonfield, New Jersey Office)
Ann G. Verber
Louis B. Kupperman
Joseph J. McGovern
Joseph P. Dougher
Julius M. Steiner
Paul S. Diamond
Walter W. Cohen (Resident, Harrisburg Office)
Jerome N. Kline
Marvin S. Lieber (Resident, Pittsburgh Office)
Lawrence J. Tabas
Jeffrey S. Batoff
Paul N. Allen
Scott E. Denman
Victor A. Young
Anastasius Efstratiades
Cathleen Curran Myers
Jerald S. Batoff
Charles S. K. Scudder
Daniel P. Finegan
William J. Leonard
J. Eric Rathburn
John E. Ryan
Ruth Rudbarg Wessel
Carol Brayshaw Longwell (Resident, Harrisburg Office)
Nicholas Poduslenko
Jacqueline Z. Shulman
Vahan H. Gureghian
Larry Besnoff
Richard P. Limburg
James R. Thompson (Resident, Haddonfield, New Jersey Office)
Steven A. Haber
Clare M. Diemer
Edmond M. George
John V. O'Hara
Michael P. Weinstein

ASSOCIATES

Michael C. Richman
Nina B. Stryker
Barbara Weinberg
Roger P. Cameron
Kimberly D'Arrigo Sutton (Resident, Haddonfield, NJ Office)
Steven T. Davis (Not admitted in PA)
Gary M. Samms
Catherine Pyune-McEldowney
Kirsten B. Hare
Michael S. Pepperman
Michael E. Heston (Resident, Haddonfield, NJ Office)
Cynthia A. Tedeschi
Lori A. Andreosky (Resident, Haddonfield, NJ Office)
Daniel F. Schranghamer
Andrew J. Giorgione (Resident, Harrisburg Office)
Danielle Tribuiani
Stephen W.W. Ching, Jr.
Kimberly Jardim Scott
Joseph J. Centeno
William K. Pelosi
Peter J. Oberkircher
Jason Eric Reisman
Marnie E. Simon
Christine C. Prost (Resident, Haddonfield, NJ Office)
Carolyn L. Dorazio (Resident, Pittsburgh Office)
Mathieu J. Shapiro
Hillary J. Moonay
David A. Nasatir
Dena B. Calo
Donald D. Gamburg
James T. Asali
Thomas E. Hanson, Jr.
Todd J. Glassman
Lori M. Emrick
Jonathan W. Hugg
Lori E. Halber
Kara L. Peischl
Ryan W. Decker
Michaune D. Tillman
Sean M. Reilly
Laurie Ann Urda (Resident, Pittsburgh Office)
Elisa E. Tractman
Christopher M. Brubaker
Harry Dillon Madonna

For full biographical listings, see the Martindale-Hubbell Law Directory

PELINO & LENTZ, A PROFESSIONAL CORPORATION (AV)

32nd Floor, One Liberty Place, 1650 Market Street, 19103-7393
Telephone: 215-665-1540
Fax: 215-665-1536
Email: pelino@pelino.com
Haddonfield, New Jersey Office: 30 South Haddon Avenue.
Telephone: 856-428-9484.
Fax: 856-429-7486.

John W. Pelino
Martin R. Lentz
Barry E. Bressler
Richard W. Kessler
Salvatore M. DeBunda
Kenneth J. Levin
Louis J. Sinatra
Robert A. Hanamirian
Jeanne Schubert Barnum
Howard A. Rosenthal
Victoria Page-Wooten
Gary D. Fry
Cristina G. Cavalieri
Karen A. Fahrner
Edward L. Ciemniecki
Debra Csik Kern
Patrick J. Doran

Paul R. Fitzmaurice
Jill M. Bellak
Bruce S. Pailet
Ronald L. Daugherty
James E. Miller
Michael D. Allen
Erin B. Santamaria
James C. Shah
Mark L. Rhoades
Richard J. Hoff Jr.

(See Next Column)

OF COUNSEL

Henry W. Maxmin (1914-1990)
Albert W. Schiffrin
Elliot Unterberger
Carolyn S. Nachmias

For full biographical listings, see the Martindale-Hubbell Law Directory

PEPPER HAMILTON LLP (AV)

3000 Two Logan Square, Eighteenth and Arch Streets, 19103-2799
Telephone: 215-981-4000
Telecopy: 215-981-4750
Email: phinfo@pepperlaw.com *URL:* http://www.pepperlaw.com
Washington, D.C. Office: Hamilton Square, 600 Fourteenth Street, N.W. 20005-2004.
Telephone: 202-220-1200.
Fax: 202-220-1665.
Detroit, Michigan Office: 100 Renaissance Center, 36th Floor, 48243-1157.
Telephone: 313-259-7110.
Fax: 313-259-7926.
New York, New York Office: 750 Lexington Avenue, Suite 600, 10022-1200.
Telephone: 212-813-9668.
Fax: 212-813-9802.
Wilmington, Delaware Office: 1201 Market Street, Suite 1600, P.O. Box 1709, 19899-1709.
Telephone: 302-777-6500.
Fax: 302-656-8865.
Pittsburgh, Pennsylvania Office: 500 Grant Street, 50th Floor, 15219-2502.
Telephone: 412-454-5000.
Fax: 412-281-0717.
Harrisburg, Pennsylvania Office: 200 One Keystone Plaza, North Front and Market Streets, P.O. Box 1181, 17108-1181.
Telephone: 717-255-1155.
Fax: 717-238-0575.
Berwyn, Pennsylvania Office: 1235 Westlakes Drive, Suite 400, 19312-2401.
Telephone: 610-640-7800.
Fax: 610-640-7835.
Cherry Hill, New Jersey Office: LibertyView Building, Suite 420, 457 Haddonfield Road, 08002-2220.
Telephone: 856-910-7200.
Fax: 856-665-7743.

PARTNERS

James L. Murray (Firm Executive Partner)
Barry M. Abelson (Chairman, Firm Executive Committee)
Robert E. Heideck (Managing Partner, Philadelphia Office)
Bennett L. Aaron
Matthew H. Adler
Joan C. Arnold
Jon A. Baughman
James M. Beck
Russell C. Bellavance
Jonathan D. Bennett
Norman B. Berlin
George W. Braun
James M. Brogan
Charles R. Bruton
Mitchell E. Burack
Vincent V. Carissimi
Peter O. Clauss
Deborah Fuchs Cohen
Hope A. Comisky
Julia D. Corelli
Kenneth M. Cushman
Joseph V. Del Raso
Kathryn A. Donohue
Gordon R. Downing
L. Garrett Dutton, Jr.
James D. Epstein
Eleanor N. Ewing
Salvatore R. Faia
Bruce W. Ficken
Richard W. Foltz, Jr.
David A. Franklin
Robert A. Friedel
Michael H. Friedman
W. Roderick Gagné
Michael P. Gallagher
Scott D. Godshall
M. Duncan Grant
Nina M. Gussack
Joyce K. Hackenbrach
Lois Sherman Hagarty
Anthony B. Haller
Robert L. Hickok
Susan Katz Hoffman
Franklin B. Holland
James D. Hollyday
Joel E. Horowitz
John B. Huffaker
David H. Huggler
Joann Hyle
Lisa R. Jacobs
Lisa D. Kabnick
Jonathan Kane (Berwyn, Pennsylvania Office)
Andrew E. Kantra
Philip J. Katauskas
Paul J. Kennedy
William F. Kershner
Robert A. Koons, Jr.
Nicholas M. Kouletsis
Francis J. Lawall
James S. Lawlor
Charles E. Leasure, III (Not admitted in PA)
Philip H. Lebowitz
James R. Ledwith
Susan K. Lessack (Berwyn, Pennsylvania Office)
Kenneth I. Levin
Murray S. Levin
Cary S. Levinson
Jeffrey P. Libson
Edward W. Madeira, Jr.
Barbara W. Mather
A. John May, III
Cynthia A. Metzler (Not admitted in PA)
J. Gregg Miller
Brian T. Ortelere
Lisa B. Petkun
Paul T. Porrini
A. Michael Pratt
Frank M. Rapoport
Michael H. Reed
David Richman
Andrew R. Rogoff
James D. Rosener
Andrew J. Rudolph
William A. Scari, Jr.
Ellen Kittredge Scott
Joseph J. Serritella
Laurence Z. Shiekman
Barbara T. Sicalides
Stephen J. Sundheim
Edward C. Toole, Jr.
Anthony Vale
Brian S. Vargo
Erik N. Videlock

(See Next Column)

PEPPER HAMILTON LLP, *Philadelphia—Continued*

PARTNERS (Continued)

Edward M. Watters, III
Robert J. Weinberg
Alfred H. Wilcox
Thomas E. Zemaitis
Kenneth H. Zucker

OF COUNSEL

Robert F. Cushman
Carol A. Ferri
Elam M. Hitchner, III
Edward Kessel
Edmund B. Spaeth, Jr.

ASSOCIATES

Natalie Slavens Abbott
Seth A. Abel
Joan Agran
Dorothy M. Allison
Daniel J. Anders
Helena Hadeed Astolfi (Not admitted in PA)
Timothy C. Atkins
Elizabeth D. Azari
Kathleen Shea Ballay
Stephanie Anne Bilenker (Not admitted in PA)
Noël C. Birle
J. Bradley Boericke
Barry H. Boise
Matthew J. Borger (Not admitted in PA)
Christina M. Boston
William J. Brennan, IV
Andrew J. Brookman
Joshua P. Broudy
Kelly R. Bryan
Christopher J. Camp
Natasha I. Campbell
Jodi Simme Caputo
Richard L. Chamovitz
Jennifer E. Clark
Rebecca E. Clayton
Joanna J. Cline
Chapin Cimino Cody
Thomas J. Cole, Jr.
Douglas M. Cooperberg
Kenneth Crimaldi
Daniel L. Damstra
Henry J. DeWerth-Jaffe
Katherine J. Dickinson
Sedesh Doobay
Elizabeth A. Duffy
Sean P. Fahey
Michael V. Farrell
Bruce K. Fenton
Iva Johnson Ferrell (Not admitted in PA)
David L. Fox (Not admitted in PA)
Nicole D. Galli
Jack R. Garfinkle
David L. Gollin
W. Michael Gradisek
Jeffrey E. Gross
Jacqueline V. Guynn
Matthew J. Hamilton
Stephen G. Harvey
Maria L. Henderson-Lewis
Michael S. Hino
Julie B. Holden (Not admitted in PA)
Alexis Dillett Isztwan
David M. Kaplan
Brian M. Katz
Claudia J. Keefe (Not admitted in PA)
Steven R. Klammer
Rena M. Kopelman
Laurie A. Krepto
Debra N. Kupferman
Eugene J. Kuzinski
Kim L. Lane (Not admitted in PA)
Adam L. Lantz
Kathleen M. Laubenstein
Daniel V Logue
Maureen E. Lowry
Gary L. Lozoff
Stuart D. Lurie
Alfonso Madrid
Matthew J. Maguire (Berwyn, Pennsylvania Office)
Albert H. Manwaring, IV
Robert A. Mascioli
Richard H. Maurer
Amy G. McAndrew
Enger McCartney-Smith
J.B. Todd McCoy
Claire E. McCusker
Sean P. McDevitt
Frank J. McKeaney, Jr.
Anthony J. Merhige
Joseph Milestone
Christopher S. Miller
John J. Musero III
Andrea V. Nassan
Robert S. Nix
Brian E. O'Neill
Noreen Hibbard Onimus
Julianna M. Pang
Gene Paranczak (Not admitted in PA)
Caroline J. Patterson
Russell D. Paul
Laurie H. Polinsky
Marion M. Quirk
Nancy Shane Rappaport
Michael H. Rosenthal
C. Randolph Ross (Not admitted in PA)
Christopher A. Rossi
Christopher A. Ruggiero
Jennifer Lynn Russell
Christine L. Schubert
Mindy Ellis Schwartz
Lynne Sindoni Spangler
Kathleen A. Stephenson
Michael P. Subak
Karen McDonnell Suddath
Marcia C. Sugrue
David A. Surbeck
Brett G. Sweitzer
Neil Boyden Tanner
Jeffrey K. Techentin
Michael J. Tierney
Jeffrey A. Toll
Elizabeth A. Turro
John A. Valentine
Jeffrey S. Waksman
Cuyler H. Walker
Laura Daria Warren
Christopher W. Wasson
Beth Eddinger Wesley
Arnold W. Winter
Larry R. Wood, Jr.
Matthew A. Woodward
Michelle Hart Yeary
A. Christopher Young
Marianne R. Yudes

For full biographical listings, see the Martindale-Hubbell Law Directory

SAUL, EWING, REMICK & SAUL LLP (AV)

Centre Square West, 1500 Market Street, 38th Floor, 19102-2186
Telephone: 215-972-7777
Cable Address: "Bidsal"
TWX: 83-4798
Telecopier: XEROX 7020 215-972-7725
Email: lawyers@saul.com *URL:* http://www.saul.com
Wilmington, Delaware Office: 222 Delaware Avenue, P.O. Box 1266, 19899-1266. For Courier Delivery: 222 Delaware Avenue, Suite 1200, 19801.
Telephone: 302-421-6800.
Cable Address: "Bidsal."
TWX: 83-4798.
Telecopier: XEROX 7020 302-421-6813.
New York, N.Y. Office: Twenty-first Floor, 237 Park Avenue.
Telephone: 212-551-3502.
TWX: 425170.
Telecopier: 212-697-8486.
Berwyn, Pennsylvania Office: 1055 Westlakes Drive, Suite 150.
Telephone: 610-251-5050.
Cable Address: "BIDSAL".
TWX: 83-4798.
Telecopier: 610-651-5930.
Harrisburg, Pennsylvania Office: Penn National Insurance Tower, 2 North Second Street, 7th Floor, 17101.
Telephone: 717-257-7500.
Telecopier: 717-238-4622, 717-257-7516.
Princeton, New Jersey Office: 214 Carnegie Center, Suite 202.
Telephone: 609-452-3100.
Fax: 609-452-3122.
Baltimore, Maryland Office: Saul, Ewing, Weinberg & Green, 100 South Charles Street, Suite 1500.
Telephone: 410-332-8600.
Fax: 410-332-8862.

MEMBERS OF FIRM

Stephen S. Aichele
David S. Antzis (Resident, Berwyn, Pennsylvania Office)
John J. Barrett, Jr.
James M. Becker
Earl M. Bennett (Resident, Princeton, New Jersey Office)
Gabriel L. I. Bevilacqua
Michael S. Burg (Resident, Berwyn, Pennsylvania Office)
Timothy W. Callahan, II
Timothy J. Carson
Nancy S. Cleveland
Robert N. de Luca
Carl B. Everett
Spencer W. Franck, Jr.
Richard T. Frazier
Timothy A. Frey (Resident, Wilmington, Delaware Office)
Rudolph Garcia
Pamela S. Goodwin (Managing Partner, Princeton, New Jersey Office)
Alan R. Gordon
Robert M. Greenbaum
Jeffrey C. Hampton
John L. Harrison, Jr.
Paul M. Hummer
Martha R. Hurt
Adam H. Isenberg
William Michael Janssen
Robert J. Jones
Henry L. Kent-Smith (Resident, Princeton, New Jersey Office)
John C. S. Kepner
James F. Kilcur
Sandra W. Kugler
Stanley J. Kull
Michael R. Lastowski
Maurice D. Lee, III
Mark Carlisle Levy
Robert H. Louis
Paul C. Madden
George T. Magnatta
John F. Meigs
Walter R. Milbourne
David R. Moffitt
Patrick G. Oakes (Resident, Berwyn, Pennsylvania Office)
Joseph F. O'Dea Jr.
James O'Toole, Jr.
Thomas K. Pasch
Scott D. Patterson (Resident, Berwyn, Pennsylvania Office)
Jennifer K. Peterson
John P. Pierce
George E. Rahn, Jr.
John B. Reiss
Linda Richenderfer
Gary A. Rosen
James G. Rosenberg
Robert N. Sandler
James W. Schwartz
Paula D. Shaffner
Edward F. Shay
Miles H. Shore
John F. Stoviak (Managing Partner)
Frederick D. Strober
J. Clayton Undercofler
David Unkovic
J. Scott Victor
Anthony F. Walsh
Lynanne B. Wescott
F. Michael Wysocki
Charles C. Zall

OF COUNSEL

Edward F. Beatty, Jr.
Joseph Neff Ewing, Jr. (Resident, Berwyn, Pennsylvania Office)
William R. Hudson
Robert W. Sayre
John A. Shrader
Arthur R. G. Solmssen
John R. Suria
Lowell S. Thomas, Jr.
Frederick A. Van Denbergh, Jr.
William T. Windsor, Jr.

SPECIAL COUNSEL

Donald Beckman
William A. DeStefano
David M. Felder
Charles C. Freyer
Steven D. Goldberg (Not admitted in PA)
Steven A. Goldfield
Gail Cummings Levan
John J. Mahoney (Resident, Berwyn, Pennsylvania Office)
Maria R. McGarry
Frank L. Newburger, III
James W. Patterson
Robert S. Price
Herbert S. Riband, Jr.
J. Kate Stickles
William J. Taylor

(See Next Column)

SAUL, EWING, REMICK & SAUL LLP—*Continued*

ASSOCIATES

Bruce D. Armon
Cynthia B. Bass
Lisa Galante Blackburn
Troy S. Brown
Michael F. Consedine (Resident, Harrisburg, Pennsylvania Office)
Troy Asao Kaleolani Cooper
Michele A. Daitz (Resident, Princeton, New Jersey Office)
Nicholas Day
Cathleen M. Devlin
Eric Diaz (Not admitted in PA)
Stephen M. Donweber
Martin J. Doyle
Kurt L. Ehresman (Resident, Harrisburg, Pennsylvania Office)
Todd Alan Ewan
Anthony P. Forte
Kara H. Goodchild
Risa B. Greene
Patricia A. Gritzan
David L. Hackett
J. Brent Hooker
Katayun I. Jaffari
Edward J. Kelbon, Jr.
James A. Keller
Alan V. Klein
Lisa Hwang Lanphear
Douglas M. Leavitt
Joseph R. Loverdi
Suzanne Serianni Mayes
Lawrence C. Norford
Allison L. Parlin
Robyn F. Pollack
Susan M. Rabii
Maura F. Ratigan
Francis X. Riley III (Resident, Princeton, New Jersey Office)
Frances R. Roggenbaum (Resident, Harrisburg, Pennsylvania Office)
Jeremy William Ryan
Jennifer Riddle Sletvold
Deborah Landan Spranger (Resident, Berywn, Pennsylvania Office)
Andrew P. Sutor, IV
Francis X. Taney, Jr.
Kevin L. Valentine
Sara Velazquez
Jeffrey M. Viola
Kalimah Z. White
Patrick J. Wolfe, Jr.
Allison S. Zales

For full biographical listings, see the Martindale-Hubbell Law Directory

---

SCHNADER HARRISON SEGAL & LEWIS LLP (AV)

Suite 3600, 1600 Market Street, 19103-7286
Telephone: 215-751-2000
Fax: 215-751-2205
URL: http://www.schnader.com
Washington, D.C. Office: 1300 I Street, N.W., 11th Floor East.
Telephone: 202-216-4200.
Fax: 202-775-8741.
New York, N.Y. Office: 330 Madison Avenue.
Telephone: 212-973-8000.
Fax: 212-972-8798.
San Francisco, California Office: 601 California Street, 12th Floor.
Telephone: 415-364-6700.
Fax: 415-364-6785.
Harrisburg, Pennsylvania: Suite 700, 30 North Third Street.
Telephone: 717-231-4000.
Fax: 717-231-4012.
Norristown, Pennsylvania Office: Suite 901, One Montgomery Plaza.
Telephone: 610-277-7700.
Fax: 610-277-3211.
Pittsburgh, Pennsylvania Office: Suite 2700, Fifth Avenue Place, 120 Fifth Avenue.
Telephone: 412-577-5200.
Fax: 412-765-3858.
Washington, Pennsylvania Office: 8 East Pine Street.
Telephone: 724-222-7378.
Fax: 724-222-0771.
Cherry Hill, New Jersey Office: Suite 200, Woodland Falls Corporate Park, 220 Lake Drive East.
Telephone: 856-482-5222.
Fax: 856-482-6980.
Atlanta, Georgia Office: Suite 2800, SunTrust Plaza, 303 Peachtree Street, N.E.
Telephone: 404-215-8100.
Fax: 404-223-5164.

MEMBERS OF THE FIRM

Elizabeth K. Ainslie
John M. Armstrong
Richard A. Barkasy
Edward L. Baxter
Rolin P. Bissell
T. Daniel Christenbury
Mark S. Cohen
Robert L. Collings
John J. Cunningham, III
Lisa C. Detwiler
Diana S. Donaldson
J. Allen Dougherty
Henry C. Fader
Robert D. Feder
Edward W. Ferruggia
Jerald M. Goodman
Andrew Gowa
Peter S. Greenberg
Vincent P. Haley
James M. Holston
M. Richard Kalter
Ronald E. Karam
David E. Kenty
Wilbur L. Kipnes
Philip G. Kircher
Marilyn Z. Kutler
Larry P. Laubach
William L. Leonard
Nicholas J. LePore, III
Saul Levit
Alan H. Lieblich
Theresa E. Loscalzo
William J. Maffucci
Kathy C. Mandelbaum
Michael J. Mangan
Edward J. McBride, Jr.
James R. Meyer
Louis R. Moffa, Jr. (Resident, Cherry Hill, New Jersey Office)
Albert Momjian
Mark A. Momjian
Michael G. Neri
David S. Petkun
Nicholas N. Price
Janice V. Quimby

(See Next Column)

MEMBERS OF THE FIRM (Continued)

Yves Pierre Quintin (Not admitted in PA)
Christina Rainville
Barry L. Refsin
Nicole M. Reimann
Bruce A. Rosenfield
Frank C. Sabatino
Deena Jo Schneider
Steve D. Shadowen
J. Denny Shupe
Richard J. Silpe
Samuel W. Silver
David Smith
Carl A. Solano
J. Robert Stoltzfus
Clinton A. Stuntebeck
Dennis R. Suplee
Sherry A. Swirsky
Margaret Gallagher Thompson
Michael G. Tierce
Ira P. Tiger
Gary M. Tocci
Stewart M. Weintraub
Ralph G. Wellington
Nancy Winkelman
Margaret S. Woodruff

SENIOR COUNSEL TO THE FIRM

Frank H. Abbott
William H. Brown, III
James D. Crawford
James A. Drobile
Edward W. Mullinix
George H. Nofer
Irving R. Segal
Ralph S. Snyder

COUNSEL TO THE FIRM

Arlin M. Adams
Robert S. Forster, Jr.
Paul G. Gagne
John D. Iskrant
Robin P. Lincoln
Kevin C. McCullough
Catherine M. McFadden
Austin R. Miller
Roy S. Ross
Joseph A. Sullivan

RETIRED MEMBERS OF THE FIRM

William M. Barnes
Samuel Jay Cooke
Thomas P. Glassmoyer
Bancroft D. Haviland
Ronald E. Haydanek
Charles C. Hileman, III
Arthur H. Kahn
Robert L. Kendall, Jr.
John H. Leddy
John E. Littleton
Herbert S. Mednick
Robert P. Oberly
Sanford M. Rosenbloom
Gerard J. St. John
Barry R. Spiegel
Kimber E. Vought
Martin Wald
W. Bradley Ward

ASSOCIATES

Stephen J. Anderer
Michael J. Barry
Wendy Beetlestone
Jo Bennett
Jeannette M. Brian
Aileen Camacho
Amy M. Cleary
Michael J. Colleran
Lawrence D. Dodds
Patrick J. Farley
Scott L. Fast
Sharon Fenick
Elise A. Fialkowski
Stephanie Fidler
Richard A. Fineman
Valerie J. Flocco-Hill
Armando A. Flores
David J. Glass
Denise Rubin Glatter (Not admitted in PA)
Dori F. Green
Theodore F. Haussman, Jr.
Deborah Epstein Henry
Anita K. Holm
Andrea Hyatt
Jennifer DuFault James
Kim R. Jessum (Not admitted in PA)
John W. Jones, Jr.
Jeffrey D. Kaiser
Anne E. Kane
Kimberly M. Kaplan
Nicole Perkins Kilcullen
Joan T. Kluger
Richard A. Kwait
Stacy J. Levitan
Diane L. Lisowski
Dionna K. Litvin
Joseph T. Lukens
Jane A. Makransky
Bruce P. Merenstein
Rebekah A. Z. Monson
Zanetta N. Moore-Driggers
John F. Mullen
Jonathan R. Nadler
Jennifer J. Nestle (Not admitted in PA)
Tamsin J. Newman
Michael A. Patané (Not admitted in PA)
John M. Randolph, III
Stephanie Richman
Matthew L. Rosin
Jonathan L. Ross (Not admitted in PA)
David A. Sasso (Not admitted in PA)
Kaethe B. Schumacher
H. Lee Schwartzberg Jr.
Lisa Marie Scidurlo
Ralph N. Sianni
S. Jnatel Simmons
Todd R. Steggerda
Dawn P. Stern
Karen L. Taylor-Lewis
Gillian L. Thomas
Christopher J. Waxman
Stewart M. Wiener
Denise S. Wolf

For full biographical listings, see the Martindale-Hubbell Law Directory

---

*PITTSBURGH,** Allegheny Co.

ANSTANDIG, MCDYER, BURDETTE & YURCON, P.C. (AV)

Suite 1300 Gulf Tower, 707 Grant Street, 15219-1911
Telephone: 412-765-3700
Facsimile: 412-765-3730
Email: ambylaw@usaor.net

Louis Anstandig
Daniel P. McDyer
Timothy J. Burdette
Edward A. Yurcon

John F. Deasy
Rebecca Sember
Shawn G. McMahon
Benjamin Marc Mayer

For full biographical listings, see the Martindale-Hubbell Law Directory

Pittsburgh—Continued

DAVIES MCFARLAND & CARROLL, P.C. (AV)

One Gateway Center, Tenth Floor, 15222
Telephone: 412-281-0737
Email: firm@dmcpc.com

Ralph A. Davies
Gregg P. Otto
Edward A. McFarland
Daniel P. Carroll
William D. Geiger
Francis Garger
Lynn E. Bell
James M. Poerio
C. Robert Keenan III
M.J. (Jeff) Tindall
Eric K. Falk
David E. Lamm
Clare M. Bello

Christopher Pierson
Robert P. Walter
Howard K. Hilner
Kristin L. Pieseski
Mary Kathleen Coleman
Julie L. Nord
Andrew G. Thiros
Susan Valerie Mason

LEGAL SUPPORT PERSONNEL

Karen W. Earlewine (Office Administrator)

Representative Clients: The BOC Group; Cincinnati Insurance Co.; The Goodyear Tire & Rubber Co.; Hobart Brothers Co.; LTV Steel Co.; Medical Protective Co.; Metropolitan Life Insurance Co.; Motorists Insurance Cos.; Premier Auto Insurance Co.

For full biographical listings, see the Martindale-Hubbell Law Directory

DICKIE, MCCAMEY & CHILCOTE, A PROFESSIONAL CORPORATION (AV)

Suite 400, Two PPG Place, 15222-5402
Telephone: 412-281-7272
Fax: 412-392-5367
URL: http://www.dmclaw.com
Wheeling, West Virginia Office: 1233 Main Street, Suite 2002, 26003-2839.
Telephone: 304-233-1022.
Facsimile: 304-233-1026.

J. Roy Dickie (1884-1962)
Harold E. McCamey (1894-1967)
Sanford M. Chilcote (1905-1974)
David B. Fawcett
David J. Armstrong
Richard D. Klaber
Theodore O. Struk
Wilbur McCoy Otto
Richard S. Dorfzaun
Daniel P. Stefko
M. Richard Dunlap
John Edward Wall
James R. Miller
Paul W. Roman, Jr.
Joseph S. D. Christof, II
Stewart M. Flam
Thomas P. Lutz
J. Lawson Johnston
Stephen R. Mlinac
David M. Neuhart
Robert W. Hastings
Robert J. Marino
Stephen M. Houghton
Larry A. Silverman
Arthur L. Schwarzwaelder
Frank M. Gianola
Leonard A. Costa, Jr.
Kenneth S. Mroz
James D. Strader
Ingrid Medzius Lundberg
Frederick W. Bode, III
Jeffrey T. Wiley
Richard C. Polley
Thomas M. Fallert
Gloria N. Fuehrer
William D. Clifford
Robert G. Del Greco, Jr.
Edmund L. Olszewski, Jr.
Charles G. Brown
Richard J. Federowicz
John C. Conti
L. John Argento
David J. Obermeier
Peter T. Stinson
Thomas H. May
George Monroe Schumann
Terry C. Cavanaugh
Eugene G. Berry
Anthony J. Williott
George P. Kachulis
John T. Pion
Hunter A. McGeary, Jr.
Michael J. Sweeney
Michael A. Cassidy
William M. Conwell
Joseph L. Luvara
Andrew G. Kimball
Marcelle M. Theis
W. Alan Torrance, Jr.
Howard A. Chajson
Alyson J. Kirleis
S. Jane Anderson (Resident, Wheeling, West Virginia Office)
Paul S. Mazeski
Anthony J. Rash
Peter A. Santos
Eugene A. Giotto
Vincent Scaglione, Jr.
James M. Girman
Maureen Kowalski

Michael D. Hughes
Nancy R. Winschel
Richard E. Lafferty
Michael F. Nerone
Christopher T. Lee
Ann Michailenko Wilson
Steven W. Zoffer
Robert G. Voinchet, Jr.
Rodger L. Puz
Jennifer M. Kirschler
Laurel Peters Ridener
Ralph J. Saunders, Jr.
David F. Stemmler
Lisa D. Dauer
John C. McGinley
Jason A. Archinaco
S. Manoj Jegasothy
Joseph A. DiMenno
Scott D. Clements
A. Bradley Cramer, Jr.
Pamela J. Wentz
Edward M. Vavro, Jr.
J. Matthew Horgan
Jeffrey R. Wilson
Bridget A. Murray
Kimberly L. Haddox
Christine T. McMillan
Melvin F. O'Brien (Resident, Wheeling, West Virginia Office)
Douglas C. LaSota
Brett W. Farrar

(See Next Column)

Christopher D. Stofko
Janice E. Weis
Christopher J. Gagin (Not admitted in PA)
Lisa M. Tumolo

OF COUNSEL

Charles A. DeMonaco
Herman C. Kimpel
Maria Greco Danaher
Cathy R. Gordon
Daniel R. Delaney
Daniel S. Cohen
Robert L. Kaufman
Lloyd W. Patross

For full biographical listings, see the Martindale-Hubbell Law Directory

ECKERT SEAMANS CHERIN & MELLOTT, LLC (AV)

600 Grant Street, 44th Floor, 15219
Telephone: 412-566-6000
Facsimile: 412-566-6099
Email: escm.pit.pit2.@escm.com *URL:* http://www.escm.com
Harrisburg, Pennsylvania Office: 213 Market Street, Eighth Floor.
Telephone: 717-237-6000.
Facsimile: 717-237-6019.
Philadelphia, Pennsylvania Office: 1515 Market Street, Ninth Floor.
Telephone: 215-851-8400.
Facsimile: 215-851-8383.
Boston, Massachusetts Office: One International Place, 18th Floor.
Telephone: 617-342-6800.
Facsimile: 617-342-6899.
Fort Lauderdale, Florida Office: Las Olas Centre, Suite 800, 450 East Las Olas Boulevard.
Telephone: 954-523-0400.
Facsimile: 954-523-7002.
Haddonfield, New Jersey Office: 36 Tanner Street, Second Floor.
Telephone: 609-427-6240.
Facsimile: 609-427-0611.
Washington, D.C. Office: 1250 24th Street, N.W., Suite 700.
Telephone: 202-659-6600.
Facsimile: 202-659-6699.

William Watson Smith (1871-1964)
William H. Eckert (1900-1981)
Frank L. Seamans (1914-1984)
Milton W. Lamproplos (1910-1990)
Donald C. Winson (1931-1990)
Carl F. Barger (1930-1992)
Robert M. Brown (1929-1993)
Carl Cherin (1917-1994)
Jeffrey M. Johnston (1951-1995)
Robert D. Hazlett (1924-1996)
Leon E. Hickman (1900-1999)

MEMBERS OF FIRM

Mary K. Austin
Peter C. Baggerman
Douglas K. Barth
Scott D. Cessar
Timothy S. Coon
Barton Z. Cowan
Richard K. Dandrea
Steven F. Faeth
Fred W. George
Richard W. Gladstone, II
Marcia Lucidi Grimes
John E. Hall
Richard I. Halpern
Jonathan K. Hergert
Dale Hershey
Eric L. Horne
Stuart R. Kaplan
John J. Kearns, III
William E. Kelleher, Jr.
Veronica M. Kelly
John R. Kenrick
Patrick F. Kilker
William J. Klemick
Joel L. Lennen
Elizabeth L. Lynch
William B. Mallin
C. Kent May
Dennis R. McEwen
Louis J. Moraytis
Robert P. Morgan
John J. Myers
James H. Norris
Dennis J. O'Brien
Edward G. O'Connor
Christopher R. Opalinski
John R. Owen, III
Clifford A. Pastel
Joseph M. Ramirez
Dean F. Richardson
James H. Roberts
Bryan D. Rosenberger
Timothy P. Ryan
Willis A. Siegfried
Eileen R. Sisca
Jeffrey W. Spear
David J. Strasser
Julie Fields Sweeney
Thomas J. Sweeney, Jr.
Laura K. Tate
David E. Tungate
Dennis L. Veraldi
Raymond C. Vogliano
Gregory A. Weingart
Richard S. Wiedman
Mark A. Willard
Dale E. Williams
C. Arthur Wilson, Jr.
Thomas D. Wright
Paul M. Yenerall

PATENT AND TRADEMARK MEMBERS

Daniel C. Abeles
David W. Brownlee
Robert P. Lenart
David V. Radack
Arnold B. Silverman
Alan G. Towner
Richard V. Westerhoff

SPECIAL COUNSEL

Daniel P. Cillo
Candace K. Gottschall
Edward J. Greene
David J. Mayernik
Robert F. Pugliese
Thomas L. Snyder
Robert A. Wiesemann

COUNSEL

Walter J. Blenko, Jr.
W. Gregg Kerr
Robert C. McCartney
Cloyd R. Mellott
Sidney M. Ruffin
Michael R. Stabile, Jr.

(See Next Column)

ECKERT SEAMANS CHERIN & MELLOTT LLC—*Continued*

ASSOCIATES

William E. Adams	Linda B. McClintock
Debra Z. Anderson	Daniel B. McLane
James A. Baldwin	Diane R. Meyers
Tina L. Campo	Gregg D. Michael
Nancy L. Carroll	Sandra Richetti Mihok
David A. Charapp	Cornelius J. O'Brien
Kathleen J. Davies	Daniel P. Orie
Mary Frances Dean	Brian K. Parker
Laurie S. Duchateau	Lisa M. Passarello
Kathryn A. English	William B. Pentecost, Jr.
Jon E. Evans	John D. Perkosky
Molly E. Few	Benjamin T. Queen, II
Sandy B. Garfinkel	Steven M. Quevedo
Gillian L. Hitson	Jennifer L. Rawson
Kirk D. Houser	Heather E. Rennie
Thomas M. Huber	Brian G. Ritz
Kathryn L. Hunter	James G. Seaman
David C. Jenkins	Linda S. Somerville
Michael D. Lazzara	Denise B. Springer
Lauren E. Lindh	Paul D. Steinman
Thomas D. Maxson	Jill M. Szafranski
Holly S. McCann	Mary Sue Teplitz

Jarrell D. Wright

For full biographical listings, see the Martindale-Hubbell Law Directory

GROGAN, GRAFFAM, MCGINLEY & LUCCHINO, P.C. (AV)

22nd Floor, Three Gateway Center, 15222
Telephone: 412-553-6300
Fax: 412-642-2601/2226
Email: ggml__pc@worldnet.att.mpt

Vincent J. Grogan	James A. Pellow, III
Stephen W. Graffam	Diane Barr Quinlin
John R. McGinley, Jr.	Leo Gerard Daly
Dennis A. Watson	John W. Smart
Joseph A. Macerelli	Ronald J. Brown
Dennis J. Roman	Charles A. Buechel, Jr.
William C. Passodelis	Deborah D. Olszewski

Susan M. Bicket	Edward S. McKenna
Korry Alden Greene	Stephanie M. Lester
Lori Ann Gala	Gregory A. Castelli
Eric J. Zagrocki	Gary A. Butler
Andrew F. Adomitis	Dawn M. Gust
Bethann R. Lloyd-Pittler	Jay Costa, Jr.

For full biographical listings, see the Martindale-Hubbell Law Directory

JONES, DAY, REAVIS & POGUE (AV)

500 Grant Street 31st Floor, 15219
Telephone: 412-391-3939
Telecopier: 412-394-7959
Email: counsel@jonesday.com *URL:* http://www.jonesday.com
In Atlanta, Georgia: 3500 SunTrust Plaza, 303 Peachtree Street.
Telephone: 404-521-3939.
Telecopier: 404-581-8330.
In Brussels, Belgium: Avenue Louise 480, 7th Floor, B-1050 Brussels.
Telephone: 32-2-645-14-11.
Telecopier: 32-2-645-14-45.
In Chicago, Illinois: 77 West Wacker.
Telephone: 312-782-3939.
Telecopier: 312-782-8585.
In Cleveland, Ohio: North Point, 901 Lakeside Avenue.
Telephone: 216-586-3939.
Telecopier: 216-579-0212.
In Columbus, Ohio: 1900 Huntington Center.
Telephone: 614-469-3939.
Telecopier: 614-461-4198.
In Dallas, Texas: 2727 North Harwood Street.
Telephone: 214-220-3939.
Telecopier: 214-969-5100.
In Frankfurt, Germany: Hochhaus am Park, Grüneburgweg 102, 60323 Frankfurt am Main.
Telephone: 49-69-9726-3939.
Telecopier: 49-69-9726-3993.
In Geneva, Switzerland: 20, rue de Candolle.
Telephone: 41-22-320-2339.
Telecopier: 41-22-320-1232.
In Hong Kong: 29th Floor, Entertainment Building, 30 Queen's Road Central.
Telephone: 852-2526-6895.
Telecopier: 852-2868-5871 or 852-2868-5699.
In Irvine, California: 5 Park Plaza, Suite 1100.
Telephone: 949-851-3939.
Telecopier: 949-553-7539.

(See Next Column)

In London, England: Bucklersbury House, 3 Queen Victoria Street.
Telephone: 44-171-236-3939.
Telecopier: 44-171-236-1113. 34000 Los Angeles, California: 555 West Fifth Street, Suite 4600.
Telephone: 213-489-3939.
Telecopier: 213-243-2539.
In New Delhi, India (Associate Office): Pathak & Associates (an associate firm of Jones, Day, Reavis & Pogue), 1st Floor, Dr. Gopal Das Bhaven, 28 Barakhamba Road.
Telephone: 91-11-373-8793; 91-11-335-7345.
Telecopier: 91-11-335-3761.
In New York, New York: 599 Lexington Avenue.
Telephone: 212-326-3939.
Telecopier: 212-755-7306.
In Paris, France: 120, rue du Faubourg Saint-Honoré.
Telephone: 33-1-56-59-39-39.
Telecopier: 33-1-56-59-39-38
In Riyadh, Saudi Arabia: The International Law Firm (In Association with Jones, Day, Reavis & Pogue), Sulaymaniyah, Prince Mishari IBN, Abdulaziz Street, P.O. Box 22166.
Telephone: (966-1) 462-8866.
Telecopier: (966-1) 462-9001.
In Shanghai, China: 2805 Kerry Centre, 1515 Nanjing Road West.
Telephone: 86-21-5298-6568.
Telecopier: 86-21-5298-6569.
In Sydney, Australia: Governor Phillip Tower, Level 38, 1 Farrer Place.
Telephone: 61-2-9210-6921.
Telecopier: 61-2-9210-6926.
In Taipei, Taiwan: 8th Floor, 2 Tun Hwa South Road, Section 2.
Telephone: (886-2) 2704-6808.
Telecopier: (886-2) 2704-6791.
In Tokyo, Japan: Toranomon MT Building, 4th Floor, 10-3, Toranomon 3-Chome, Minato-Ku, Tokyo 105, Japan.
Telephone: 81-3-3433-3939.
Telecopier: 81-3-5401-2725.
In Washington, D.C.: 51 Louisiana Avenue, N.W.
Telephone: 202-879-3939.
Telecopier: 202-626-1700.

MEMBERS OF FIRM IN PITTSBURGH

James J. Erb	Mary Beth Pfohl
J. W. Montgomery, III	Michael H. Ginsberg
Edward C. Schmidt	John D. Goetz
John W. Ubinger, Jr.	John E. Iole
Paul Michael Pohl	James M. Jones
Carey M. Brennan	Richard F. Shaw
Charles H. Moellenberg, Jr.	Kevin P. Holewinski
Roy A. Powell	Antonio F. Dias
Laura E. Ellsworth	Bryan D. Kocher

COUNSEL

Alan D. Chute	Curt Vazquez

Cynthia D. Driscoll

ASSOCIATES

Amy E. Dias	John M. McIntyre
Brian C. Castello	David C. Donehue
Carol Jean Gatewood	Maureen T. Taylor
Katrien A. Hemelsoet (Not admitted in the United States)	Dana Baiocco
	John W. Boyle
Peter D. Laun	Jennifer M. Bund
Ned L. Spells, Jr.	Christi L. Davis
Matthew C. Flannery	Brent A. Fewell
Robert O. Lindefjeld	Amy Kirby Pohl
Joseph P. Donohue	Mark L. Tamburri
Jennifer Brinkman Flannery	James S. Urban

STAFF ATTORNEY

Frank G. Adams

For full biographical listings, see the Martindale-Hubbell Law Directory

KABALA & GEESEMAN, A PROFESSIONAL CORPORATION (AV)

2900 CNG Tower, 625 Liberty Avenue, 15222-3115
Telephone: 412-391-1334
Fax: 412-391-6984
Email: kgmain@kglawpgh.com

Edward J. Kabala	John F. Meck
Robert G. Geeseman	James M. Meinert
Susan Foreman Jordan	Donna J. Naab
Kenneth E. Lewis	William L. Stang
William H. Maruca	Michael G. Wiethorn

Susan Brahm Gunn

OF COUNSEL

William McC. Houston	Stewart R. Snodgrass

Herbert G. Sheinberg

SPECIAL COUNSEL

John Michael Studeny

For full biographical listings, see the Martindale-Hubbell Law Directory

Pittsburgh—Continued

KIRKPATRICK & LOCKHART LLP (AV)

1500 Oliver Building, 15222
Telephone: 412-355-6500
Facsimile: 412-355-6501
URL: http://www.kl.com
Washington, D.C. Office: 1800 Massachusetts Avenue, N.W., 2nd Floor.
Telephone: 202-778-9000.
Facsimile: 202-778-9100.
Miami, Florida Office: Miami Center, 20th Floor, 201 South Biscayne Boulevard.
Telephone: 305-539-3300.
Facsimile: 305-358-7095.
Boston, Massachusetts Office: 75 State Street.
Telephone: 617-261-3100.
Facsimile: 617-261-3175.
Harrisburg, Pennsylvania Office: Payne Shoemaker Building, 240 North Third Street.
Telephone: 717-231-4500.
Facsimile: 717-231-4501.
New York, New York Office: 1251 Avenue of the Americas, 45th Floor.
Telephone: 212-536-3900.
Facsimile: 212-536-3901.

MEMBERS OF FIRM

Steven J. Adelkoff
Susan A. Apel
Kenneth M. Argentieri
Ann Morris Baker
J. Stephen Barge
John E. Beard, III
Thomas Edward Birsic
Carolyn M. Branthoover
Neal R. Brendel
David A. Brownlee
Terry Budd
Walter A. Bunt, Jr.
Robert L. Byer
George M. Cheever
David R. Cohen
William T. Cullen
Elliot S. Davis
George D. Dickos
John R. Dingess
Thomas A. Donovan
Wallace E. Edgecombe, Jr.
Thomas J. Edgington
David H. Ehrenwerth
Christine R. Ethridge
J. Michael Ewing
Keith A. Fabi
Peter N. Flocos
David L. Forney
George B. Foster
Andrew L. Gespass
Charles E. Harris, III
Janice C. Hartman
Kathleen D. Hendrickson
Judith J. Hlafcsak
Richard W. Hosking
Stuart N. Hutchison, III
Thomas R. Johnson
Peter J. Kalis
Charles Kelly
David G. Klaber
Kenneth S. Komoroski
Donald A. Kortlandt
James R. Kyper
J. Richard Lauver
David J. Lehman
Mark R. Leslie
Joseph L. Luciana, III
Michael J. Lynch
David L. McClenahan
Theodore A. McConnell
Jerry S. McDevitt
Patrick J. McElhinny
David F. McGonigle
Michael C. McLean
David Armor Murdoch
Susan M. Mussman
Thomas F. Nelson
Mary M. O'Day
Stephen M. Olson
Jerry H. Owens
Robert M. Owsiany
Richard F. Paciaroni
Andrew B. Pullman
(Not admitted in PA)
Thomas M. Reiter
Pierce Richardson
John C. Rodney
Mark A. Rush
James E. Scheuermann
Paul W. Schwendeman
James R. Segerdahl
Donald E. Seymour
Charles R. Smith, Jr.
Thomas J. Smith
Wendy E. D. Smith
W. Henry Snyder
Robert B. Sommer
Daniel J. Sponseller
Kristen Larkin Stewart
Hayes C. Stover
Ellen L. Surloff
John M. Sylvester
Chris Michael Temple
Cheryl J. Terai
Harry Woodruff Turner
J. Robert Van Kirk
Edward V. Weisgerber
Ronald D. West
Bruce Wiegand
Richard E. Wood
Robert D. Yeager
Michael G. Zanic
Robert P. Zinn

SENIOR COUNSEL

Charles J. Queenan, Jr.

COUNSEL

John U. Anderson, Jr. (1921-1996)
Robert L. Becker, Jr.
Allen H. Berkman
W. Walter Braham, Jr.
Aims C. Coney, Jr.
John F. Dugan
John G. Frazer, Jr. (1915-1996)
Charles M. Grimstad
Stuart Nye Hutchison, Jr. (1910-1985)
Thomas Phillips Johnson
David L. Ketter
Robert L. Kirkpatrick (1906-1987)
George D. Lockhart (1909-1999)
Samuel K. McCune (1921-1993)
Willis McCook Miller (1911-1990)
Richard C. Montgomery
Judd N. Poffinberger, Jr.
Thomas W. Pomeroy, Jr.

(See Next Column)

ASSOCIATES

David M. Aceto
Michael A. Agresti
Susan P. Altman
Kristin L. Anders
David P. Anderson
Roberta D. Anderson
Ronald T. Aulbach
Matthew G. Ball
Michael L. Bell
Michael G. Biro
(Not admitted in PA)
Evan A. Bloch
Carol I. Bordas
Delia A. Bouwers
Kay M. Brady
Shawn C. Bunting
Ronald J. Chleboski, Jr.
Gregory S. Collins
Brian R. Davidson
Brian E. Davis
Frank DeCarlo
Kristen M. Del Sole
Paul E. DelVecchio
Edward W. Diggs
Richard D. Dworek
Peter D. Eberhart
David Alan Edgar
Douglas J. Ellis
(Not admitted in PA)
John P. Englert
Mark D. Feczko
David T. Fisfis
Christopher C. French
April P. Gatesman
Joseph R. Gette
Jeffrey M. Gitchel
Brian J. Golias
Amy O'Connor Goodman
David J. Grecco
Jason D. Haislmaier
(Not admitted in PA)
Melody A. Hamel
James E. Hannon, Jr.
Michael A. Hart
Richard W. James
Kristin Klingenberg
Mark G. Knedeisen
Peter Leonard Kogan
Kerrin McCormick Kowach
Mark E. Kozar
Curtis B. Krasik
William E. Kuss
William J. Labovitz
Eric S. Lammers
Blaine A. Lamperski
Walter E. Lannis
George P. Long, III
Alexander Y. Loshilov
Kenneth J. Lund
Mark A. May
Karen D. Mc Kenna
Erica D. Merkow
John J. Michael
Franklin B. Molin
Heath B. Monesmith
Dean M. Naccarato
Meryl J. Neiman
Michael S. Nelson
Daniel Alan O'Connor
Lucas G. Paglia
Jonathan C. Parks
Aarti J. Patel
Jonathan W. Paul
Michael A. Pavlick
Douglas A. Pearson
Charles F. Pegher
Gregory J. Pfeifer
Marcie C. Queiser
Jason L. Richey
Brian S. Roman
Brian Scott Rudick
Usha Sadagopan
Joseph C. Safar
Jeanne M. Sauer
Brian F. Saulnier
Wade J. Savoy
David Schramm
Kimberly S. Shenk
Barbara A. Simanek
Douglas J. Simmons
Julie V. Stanier
Paul K. Stockman
Zoran Stojanovic
Timothy M. Strong
Kevin J. Stubblebine
Sean R. Sullivan
Matthew Ray Swenson
James T. Tallman
Alan W. Tamarelli
Geoffrey N. Taylor
Charles M. Tea III
Melissa J. Tea
Jennifer L. Tedjeske
Megan C. Timmins
Daniel P. Trocchio
Nicholas P. Vari
Paul R. Vittone
John T. Waldron, III
Stephanie D. Wall
Jessica C. White
Michael D. Winterhalter
Sean M. Winters
Darren E. Wolf

For full biographical listings, see the Martindale-Hubbell Law Directory

MARCUS & SHAPIRA LLP (AV)

35th Floor, One Oxford Centre, 301 Grant Street, 15219-6401
Telephone: 412-471-3490
Telecopier: 412-391-8758
Email: info@marcus-shapira.com *URL:* http://www.marcus-shapira.com

MEMBERS OF FIRM

Robert L. Allman, II
Joseph J. Barnes
Robert M. Barnes
Sylvester A. Beozzo
Estelle F. Comay
Susan Gromis Flynn
Elly Heller-Toig
Charles G. Knox
Carrie Kochenbach
James S. Larrimer
Scott D. Livingston
Bernard D. Marcus
Darlene M. Nowak
Glenn M. Olcerst
James F. Rosenberg
Daniel H. Shapira
Stephen S. Zubrow

OF COUNSEL

John M. Burkoff

ASSOCIATES

Henry G. Barr
Moira E. Cain
Traci L. McDonald
Susan H. Snively

For full biographical listings, see the Martindale-Hubbell Law Directory

MEYER, UNKOVIC & SCOTT LLP (AV)

1300 Oliver Building, 15222-2304
Telephone: 412-456-2800
Fax: 412-456-2864
Telex: 902402
URL: http://www.muslaw.com

(See Next Column)

MEYER, UNKOVIC & SCOTT LLP—*Continued*

PARTNERS

Joseph E. Bartoszewicz	James R. Mall
Thomas A. Berret	Robert Mauro
Michael J. Boyle	Kevin F. McKeegan
Laura A. Candris	Lawrence B. Niemann
Patricia L. Dodge	Russell J. Ober, Jr.
Frederick J. Francis	Joel Pfeffer
P. Christian Hague	John W. Powell
J. Robert Hanlon, Jr.	Richard F. Rinaldo
Kevin C. Hansen	Frank G. Salpietro
David L. Harnish	W. Grant Scott, II
Joel M. Helmrich	Beth Ann Slagle
Ronald L. Hicks, Jr.	Robert P. Struble
Kenneth G. Judson	Thomas E. Sweeney, Jr.
Richard G. Kotarba	Dennis Unkovic
Joseph E. Linehan	Joseph A. Vater, Jr.
John Lucas	Michael Yablonski

SPECIAL COUNSEL

William P. Getty — William A. Meyer, Jr.
Ronald D. Morelli

ASSOCIATES

Robert E. Dauer, Jr.	Kelly A. Magiske
Anthony L. DiTommaso	Peter W. McKay
Sally E. Edison	Bruce F. Rudoy
F. Timothy Grieco	Richard T. Victoria
Douglas M. Hottle	Matthew D. Whitworth

SENIOR COUNSEL

Herman S. Harvey, Jr. — W. Reid Lowe
Howard I. Scott

For full biographical listings, see the Martindale-Hubbell Law Directory

NASH & COMPANY, A PROFESSIONAL CORPORATION (AV)

Suite 700, 11 Stanwix Street, 15222
Telephone: 412-392-2333
Fax: 412-392-2343
URL: http://www.healthlawnet.com

Stephen P. Nash — Terrence J. O'Rourke
Charles G. O'Hara

Theresa Creagh — Melissa L. Staggers
Vikram Mangalmurti

For full biographical listings, see the Martindale-Hubbell Law Directory

PEPPER HAMILTON LLP (AV)

500 Grant Street, 50th Floor, 15219-2502
Telephone: 412-454-5000
Telecopy: 412-281-0717
Email: phinfo@pepperlaw.com *URL:* http://www.pepperlaw.com
Philadelphia, Pennsylvania Office: 3000 Two Logan Square, Eighteenth and Arch Streets, 19103-2799.
Telephone: 215-981-4000.
Fax: 215-981-4750.
Washington, D.C. Office: Hamilton Square, 600 Fourteenth Street, N.W. 20005-2004.
Telephone: 202-220-1200.
Fax: 202-220-1665.
Detroit, Michigan Office: 100 Renaissance Center, 36th Floor, 48243-1157.
Telephone: 313-259-7110.
Fax: 313-259-7926.
New York, New York Office: 750 Lexington Avenue, Suite 600, 10022-1200.
Telephone: 212-813-9668.
Fax: 212-813-9802.
Wilmington, Delaware Office: 1201 Market Street, Suite 1600, P.O. Box 1709, 19899-1709.
Telephone: 302-777-6500.
Fax: 302-656-8865.
Harrisburg, Pennsylvania Office: 200 One Keystone Plaza, North Front and Market Streets, P.O. Box 1181, 17108-1181.
Telephone: 717-255-1155.
Fax: 717-238-0575.
Berwyn, Pennsylvania Office: 1235 Westlakes Drive, Suite 400, 19312-2401.
Telephone: 610-640-7800.
Fax: 610-640-7835.
Cherry Hill, New Jersey Office: LibertyView Building, Suite 420, 457 Haddonfield Road, 08002-2220.
Telephone: 856-910-7200.
Fax: 856-665-7743.

PARTNERS

George M. Medved (Managing Partner, Pittsburgh Office)	Dusty Elias Kirk
Henry W. Ewalt	Dennis M. Sheedy
Charles M. Greenberg	David W. Sweet
	Barry J. Trilling
James P. Hollihan	Thomas W. Trimm

(See Next Column)

ASSOCIATES

Sharon F. DiPaolo	David J. Kolesar
Anthony Giglio	John J. Luke
John C. Hansberry	Jeffrey A. Mills
Kristin L. Ifft	David J. Montgomery

James M. Singer

For full biographical listings, see the Martindale-Hubbell Law Directory

PLOWMAN, SPIEGEL & LEWIS, P.C. (AV)

Second Floor, The Grant Building, 310 Grant Street, 15219-2201
Telephone: 412-471-8521
Fax: 412-471-4481

Jack W. Plowman — John L. Spiegel
James A. Lewis

OF COUNSEL

Harold Gondelman

Kurt F. Fernsler	Charles B. Jarrett, Jr.
Mark A. Griffith	Frank J. Kernan
William A. Houston	Kenneth W. Lee

J. Michael McCague, Jr.

Reference: Pittsburgh National Bank.

For full biographical listings, see the Martindale-Hubbell Law Directory

RILEY, MCNULTY, HEWITT & SWEITZER, A PROFESSIONAL CORPORATION (AV)

Suite 300, 650 Washingon Road, 15228
Telephone: 412-341-9300
Fax: 412-341-9177
Email: rmhs@nauticom.net

Patrick R. Riley — Patrick A. Hewitt
Sibyl S. McNulty — David E. Sweitzer

William J. Witte

For full biographical listings, see the Martindale-Hubbell Law Directory

ROSE, SCHMIDT, HASLEY & DISALLE, P.C. (AV)

900 Oliver Building, 15222-2310
Telephone: 412-434-8600
Fax: 412-263-2829
Email: rshd@rshdlaw.com
Washington, Pennsylvania Office: 7th Floor, Millcraft Center.
Telephone: 724-228-8883.

Don Rose (1881-1965)	Francis J. DiSalle
John Evans Rose (1908-1972)	Samuel L. Douglass
Robert M. DeBroff (1934-1974)	Kim D. Eaton
Harold R. Schmidt (1913-1989)	Mary Lynch Friedline
Richard DiSalle	Gail L. Gratton
Brian W. Ashbaugh	Kenneth D. Joseph
James W. Barson	Susan Hileman Malone
Raymond N. Baum	Mark E. Mazzei
Jeffrey P. Brahan	R. Stanley Mitchel
Edmund M. Carney	Keithley D. Mulvihill
Philip E. Cook	Steven M. Petrikis
Michael A. Della Vecchia	Charles L. Potter, Jr.

Charles R. Reis

Geraldine S. Skupien — Denise R. Turner
Mark D. Yablonski

COUNSEL

Daniel B. Dixon — Edward Gerjuoy
Cyril A. Fox, Jr. — Raymond G. Hasley
Andrew L. Weil

WASHINGTON, PENNSYLVANIA OFFICE PERSONNEL

Richard DiSalle

For full biographical listings, see the Martindale-Hubbell Law Directory

THE TARASI LAW FIRM, P.C. (AV)

510 Third Avenue, 15219
Telephone: 412-391-7135
Fax: 412-471-2673
Email: tarasilaw@aol.com *URL:* http://www.lawyers.com/tarasilaw

Louis M. Tarasi, Jr.

Elizabeth M. Tarasi — Christina K. Hurnyak
Craig L. Fishman — Colm William Kenny

For full biographical listings, see the Martindale-Hubbell Law Directory

Pittsburgh—Continued

THOMSON, RHODES & COWIE, P.C. (AV)

Tenth Floor, Two Chatham Center, 15219
Telephone: 412-232-3400
Fax: 412-232-3498
Email: TRC_LAW@nauticom.net

Norman J. Cowie (1929-1998)
Thomas D. Thomson (1925-1999)
John David Rhodes
Richard E. Rush
James R. Hartline
Linton L. Moyer
John K. Heisey
David R. Johnson
Jerry R. Hogenmiller
David M. McQuiston
William James Rogers
Glenn H. Gillette
Templeton Smith, Jr.
Harry W. Rosensteel
L. Jane Charlton

Francine L. Bindell
Thomas B. Anderson
Dana Weber Horton
Suzanne M. Oppman

For full biographical listings, see the Martindale-Hubbell Law Directory

ZIMMER KUNZ, PROFESSIONAL CORPORATION (AV)

3300 USX Tower, 600 Grant Street, 15219
Telephone: 412-281-8000
Fax: 412-281-1765

Harry J. Zimmer
John E. Kunz
Raymond H. Conaway
George N. Stewart
Joni M. Mangino
Joseph W. Selep
Raymond J. Conlon
Edward K. Dixon
Mark R. Hamilton
Alexander P. Bicket
John W. Zotter
Jeffrey A. Ramaley
Thomas P. McGinnis

OF COUNSEL

Andrew J. Banyas, III
Thomas A. Lazaroff

Dara A. DeCourcy
Robert W. Murdoch
Anthony C. Carone
Timothy R. Smith
Meghan Fawcett Wise
Daniel E. Krauth
George R. Farneth, II
John K. Bryan
Mark T. Caloyer
Christopher T. Yoskosky
Amy J. Brinkos
George W. Boguslawski, Jr.
Carmen A. Martucci
Tracy L. Yaggi
Kurt W. Lenz
Carl Adam Ronald
Claire A. Conaway

Attorneys For: American International Group; Cincinnati Insurance Co.; Equitable Gas Co.; Honda North America; Otis Elevator Co.; Outboard Marine Corp.; Pennsylvania Electric Co.; Travelers Insurance Co.

For full biographical listings, see the Martindale-Hubbell Law Directory

*POTTSVILLE,** Schuylkill Co.

LIPKIN, MARSHALL, BOHORAD & THORNBURG, A PROFESSIONAL CORPORATION (AV)

One Norwegian Plaza, Suite 200, P.O. Box 1280, 17901-7280
Telephone: 570-622-1811
Fax: 570-622-4850
Mahanoy City, Pennsylvania Office: 9 East Center Street.
Telephone: 570-874-4700.
Ashland, Pennsylvania Office: 1435 Arch Street.
Telephone: 570-875-2121.
Frackville, Pennsylvania Office: 44 N. Balliet Street.
Telephone: 570-874-4700.

Henry Houck (1892-1959)
James P. Bohorad (1905-1964)
H. G. Stutzman (1907-1977)
Leroy G. Adams (1946-1988)

OF COUNSEL

Alexander E. Lipkin

PARTNERS

Alvin B. Marshall
Robert N. Bohorad
Richard A. Thornburg
S. John Price, Jr.
Mark Semanchik

Dirk S. Berger
James C. Bohorad

For full biographical listings, see the Martindale-Hubbell Law Directory

ZIMMERMAN, LIEBERMAN & DERENZO (AV)

111 East Market Street, P.O. Box 238, 17901
Telephone: 570-622-1988, 622-1989
Fax: 570-622-3261
Email: zladlaw@ptd.net

MEMBERS OF FIRM

John B. Lieberman, III
Ronald T. Derenzo
Frank L. Tamulonis, Jr.
Paul J. Dufallo
Joseph G. Zerbe
Robert L. Goodman

(See Next Column)

ASSOCIATES

Wayne S. Fegley
James E. Crossen

Representative Clients: Pennsylvania Mfrs. Association Insurance Co.; Keystone Insurance Company; Erie Insurance Exchange; State Farm Mutual Automobile; Heritage National Bank; Farmers' Mutual Fire Insurance Co.; Lebanon Mutual Insurance Co.; American States Insurance Co.

For full biographical listings, see the Martindale-Hubbell Law Directory

*READING,** Berks Co.

BARLEY, SNYDER, SENFT & COHEN, LLC (AV)

Formerly: Miller and Murray, LLP
501 Washington Street, P.O. Box 942, 19603-0942
Telephone: 610-376-6651
Fax: 610-376-5243
Email: barley@barley.com *URL:* http://www.barley.com
Harrisburg, Pennsylvania Office: 240 North Third Street.
Telephone: 717-238-8263.
Fax: 717-238-8278.
Lancaster, Pennsylvania Office: 126 East King Street.
Telephone: 717-299-5201.
Fax: 717-291-4660.
York, Pennsylvania Office: 100 East Market Street.
Telephone: 717-846-8888.
Fax: 717-843-8492.
Chambersburg, Pennsylvania Office: 247 Lincoln Way East.
Telephone: 717-264-6494.
Fax: 717-264-1662.
Hanover, Pennsylvania Office: 14 Center Square.
Telephone: 717-637-6239.
Fax: 717-637-5407.
Birdsboro, Pennsylvania Office: 115 E. Main Street.
Telephone: 610-582-2735.
Hamburg, Pennsylvania Office: 239 State Street.
Telephone: 610-562-3721.
Oley, Pennsylvania Office: Route 73 and Main Street.
Telephone: 610-987-6350.
Morgantown, Pennsylvania Office: Route 23.
Telephone: 610-286-5958.

MEMBERS OF FIRM

John S. Hibschman
Charles F. Fitzpatrick
Gregory R. Young
Kathleen Ann Gray
David R. Keller
Paul G. Mattaini
Elaine Pennington Stanko
William F. Colby, Jr.
Brian R. Ott
Deborah A. Datte
Michael W. Davis
Melanie A. Zampini
Bruce J. Wolstoncroft

ASSOCIATES

Michael P. Giles
Craig T. Trebilcock

COUNSEL

James H. Murray

RETIRED

Leon A. Miller

Representative Client: Bank of Pennsylvania/All First; Conestoga Enterprises; King's Management; Blue Mountain Mushroom; Fulton Bank/Fulton Financial Corp.; Lancaster General Hospital; Summit Health; Graham Packaging; Armstrong World Industries.

For full biographical listings, see the Martindale-Hubbell Law Directory

BINGAMAN, HESS, COBLENTZ & BELL, A PROFESSIONAL CORPORATION (AV)

Suite 660, 601 Penn Street, P.O. Box 61, 19603-0061
Telephone: 610-374-8377
Fax: 610-376-3105
URL: http://www.bhcb.com
Cherry Hill, New Jersey Office: Shawn J. Lau, P.C., Building Q, Suite 14B, 1930 East Marlton Pike, 08003-4222.
Telephone: 609-751-4158.
Fax: 609-424-7112.

Llewellyn R. Bingaman (1907-1996)
James F. Bell (1921-1988)
Ralph J. Althouse, Jr. (Retired)

OF COUNSEL

Raymond K. Hess
J. Wendell Coblentz

David E. Turner
Mark G. Yoder
Carl D. Cronrath, Jr.
Kurt Althouse
Harry D. McMunigal
Patrick T. Barrett
Karen Feryo Longenecker
Shawn J. Lau

Lynne K. Beust
Elizabethanne D. McMunigal
Kevin W. Rethore
Eric J. Fabrizio
Elizabeth A. Magovern

General Counsel for: First Union National Bank; Berks Products Corp.; Utilities Employees Credit Union.

(See Next Column)

BINGAMAN, HESS, COBLENTZ & BELL A PROFESSIONAL CORPORATION—*Continued*

Local Counsel for: Erie Insurance Exchange; Liberty Mutual Insurance Co.; Old Guard Mutual Insurance Co.

For full biographical listings, see the Martindale-Hubbell Law Directory

MOGEL, SPEIDEL, BOBB & KERSHNER, A PROFESSIONAL CORPORATION (AV)

520 Walnut Street, P.O. Box 8581, 19603-8581
Telephone: 610-376-1515
Telecopier: 610-372-8710

George B. Balmer (1902-1969)
George A. Kershner (1907-1969)
Carl F. Mogel (1919-1994)
Edwin H. Kershner
Frederick R. Mogel
Michael L. Mixell
George M. Lutz
Paul M. Yatron
Stephen H. Price
Kathryn K. Harenza

Sean J. O'Brien
Matthew Earl Glinn

OF COUNSEL

Harry W. Speidel
Donald K. Bobb
Henry A. Gass

Representative Clients: Great Valley Bank; Union Township, Berks County, Pennsylvania.

For full biographical listings, see the Martindale-Hubbell Law Directory

RHODA, STOUDT & BRADLEY (AV)

Sixth Floor The Berkshire, 501 Washington Street, P.O. Box 877, 19603-0877
Telephone: 610-374-8293
Fax: 610-374-6061
Email: rsblaw@rsblaw.com *URL:* http://www.rsblaw.com
Birdsboro, Pennsylvania Office: 341A West Main Street.
Telephone: 610-582-4307.
Fleetwood, Pennsylvania Office: 42 West Main Street.
Telephone: 610-944-6334.
Kutztown, Pennsylvania Office: Main & Noble Streets.
Telephone: 610-683-8677.
Oley, Pennsylvania Office: Main Street.
Telephone: 610-987-3277.
Pottsville, Pennsylvania Office: 121 Progress Avenue, Losch Plaza Suite 340,17901.
Telephone: 717-628-5404.

MEMBERS OF FIRM

John S. Rhoda (1906-1968)
John C. Bradley (1919-1984)
Dawson H. Muth (1902-1997)
Norman E. Dettra, Jr.
Geoffrey M. Stoudt
Francis M. Mulligan
John C. Bradley, Jr.
Jerry R. Richwine
George J. Shoop
Timothy G. Dietrich
John J. Speicher
Robert R. Kreitz
Timothy J. Rowley

ASSOCIATES

Joan E. London
Eden R. Bucher
John Edward Muir
M. Theresa Johnson
Carl J. Engleman, Jr.

OF COUNSEL

James W. Stoudt
Robert H. Kauffman
D. Frederick Muth

Representative Clients: Allstate Insurance Co.; Home Insurance; CoreStates Hamilton Bank; Blue Ball National Bank; Pennsylvania National Bank; Arrow International, Inc.; Arrow Precision Products, Inc.; GPU Service, Inc.; Sweet Street Desserts, Inc.; County of Berks.

For full biographical listings, see the Martindale-Hubbell Law Directory

*SCRANTON,** Lackawanna Co.

KREDER, BROOKS, HAILSTONE & LUDWIG (AV)

Suite 200, 220 Penn Avenue, 18503
Telephone: 570-346-7922
Telecopier: 570-346-3715

Cody H. Brooks
Andrew Hailstone
Lawrence M. Ludwig
Lucille Marsh
Michael J. Donohue
David K. Brown
J. Frederick Rohrbeck
Richard G. Reed
Stephen W. Saunders

ASSOCIATES

Ann Lavelle Powell
Alyce Hailstone Farrell
Robert B. Farrell
A. James Hailstone
Suzanne T. Tighe
Lawrence A. Durkin (Not admitted in PA)

(See Next Column)

OF COUNSEL

Willard M. Henkelman
Joseph C. Kreder

Counsel For: PNC Bank; U.S. Fidelity & Guaranty Co.; Nationwide Insurance Co.; Liberty Mutual Insurance Co.; Citizens Savings Assn.; NEP Supershooters, Inc.; Moses Taylor Hospital; WEA Manufacturing, Inc.; Corestates Bank; Marywood Univ.

For full biographical listings, see the Martindale-Hubbell Law Directory

LENAHAN & DEMPSEY, A PROFESSIONAL CORPORATION (AV)

116 North Washington Avenue, 18503-0234
Telephone: 717-346-2097; 1-888-LENAHAN
Fax: 717-346-1174
Mailing Address: P.O. Box 234, Scranton, Pennsylvania, 18501-0234

John R. Lenahan, Sr. (1915-1998)
William J. Dempsey (Of Counsel)
John R. Lenahan, Jr.
Joseph P. Lenahan
Kathleen A. Lenahan
David E. Heisler
Timothy G. Lenahan
Matthew D. Dempsey

Alan P. Schoen
Brian J. Lenahan
Diane Hepford Lenahan
George E. Mehalchick
Brian Yeager
Thomas R. Daniels
Terrence E. Dempsey
Christine S. Mayernick-Lezinski
John M. Mulcahey
Margaret M. Dempsey
Lisa G. Wilson

Representative Insurance Clients: Allstate Insurance Co.; America Security Insurance Co.; Metropolitan Casualty Insurance Co.; Aetna Insurance Co.; Pennsylvania National Insurance Group; Kemper Insurance Group; American Mutual Insurance Cos.; American States Insurance, Co.

For full biographical listings, see the Martindale-Hubbell Law Directory

O'MALLEY & HARRIS, P.C. (AV)

345 Wyoming Avenue, 18503
Telephone: 570-348-3711
Fax: 570-348-4092
Email: ohpc@epix.net *URL:* http://www.ohpclaw.com
Stroudsburg, Pennsylvania Office: 111 North Seventh Street.
Telephone: 570-421-2252; 570-422-1280.
FAX: 570-422-1281. Email: cerato@ptdprolog.net.
Wilkes-Barre, Pennsylvania Office: 61 North Washington Street.
Telephone: 570-829-3232.
FAX: 570-829-4418. Email: ohpcwb@epix.net.
Williamsport, Pennsylvania Office: 321 Pine Street, Suite 308.
Telephone: 570-323-4380.

Eugene Nogi (1905-1975)
Henry Nogi (1900-1976)
Russell J. O'Malley, Sr. (1904-1993)
Norman Harris (1907-1998)
William H. Amesbury (Resident, Wilkes-Barre Office)
Paul A. Barrett
Matthew P. Barrett
J. Scott Brady (Resident, Wilkes-Barre Office)
Lori J. Cerato (Resident, Stroudsburg Office)
Bruce L. Coyer
John Q. Durkin
Gerald J. Hanchulak
Richard K. Hodges
Timothy J. Holland (Resident, Wilkes-Barre Office)
John F. Kennedy (Resident, Wilkes-Barre Office)
Daniel Morgan
Michael Perry
James M. Tressler
Joseph Timothy Healey
A. Ruth Whalen (Resident, Wilkes-Barre Office)

Representative Clients: Pennsylvania Hospital Insurance Co.; MMI Systems Agency, Inc.; State Farm Insurance Company; ITT Specialty Risk Services; St. Paul Fire & Marine Insurance Co.; Chubb Group of Insurance Companies; Geisinger System Services; Princeton Insurance Company; Northeastern Pennsylvania Physicians Organization; Catholic Healthcare Partners.

For full biographical listings, see the Martindale-Hubbell Law Directory

SCANLON, HOWLEY, SCANLON & DOHERTY (AV)

321 Spruce Street, 10th Floor, 18503
Telephone: 570-346-7651
Fax: 570-344-1542

MEMBERS OF FIRM

James M. Howley
James M. Scanlon
James A. Doherty, Jr.
Thomas R. Nealon
Thomas B. Helbig
Patrick R. Casey

Counsel for: CNA Insurance Company; The Medical Protective Co.; Harleysville Insurance Co.; The Procter & Gamble Co.; Prudential-Bach Securities, Inc.; Zurich-American Insurance Co.; The Keystone Coca-Cola Bottling Co.; The Home Insurance Co.; The Travelers Insurance Co.; Utica First Ins. Co.

For full biographical listings, see the Martindale-Hubbell Law Directory

IRWIN SCHNEIDER & ASSOCIATES, P.C. (AV)

Mellon Bank Building, 400 Spruce Street, Suite 400, 18503-1814
Telephone: 570-341-3150
Fax: 570-341-3155
Email: ischneipc@aol.com *URL:* http://www.lawyers.com/is&associates

(See Next Column)

IRWIN SCHNEIDER & ASSOCIATES, P.C., *Scranton—Continued*

Irwin Schneider

John D. Lalley | Holly B. Conway

LEGAL SUPPORT PERSONNEL

Wendy M. Schneider (Paralegal) | Jill Sensi (Legal Assistant)
Sandra L. Schneider (Legal Administrator/Paralegal)

For full biographical listings, see the Martindale-Hubbell Law Directory

WELLES & McGRATH (AV)

1117 Bank Towers, 321 Spruce Street, 18503
Telephone: 570-348-4951
Fax: 570-348-4954

MEMBERS OF FIRM

Charles H. Welles, Jr. (1876-1962)
Matthew D. Mackie (1897-1965)
Charles H. Welles (1907-1997)
Henry C. McGrath
Charles H. Welles, IV

Counsel For: Grange National Bank; Scranton Industrial Development Co.; Bear Creek Nursing Home; Northeastern Ob-Gyn Associates, P.C.; Metropolitan Life Insurance Co.; New Health Management Systems, Inc.; Chamberlin Insurance Inc.

For full biographical listings, see the Martindale-Hubbell Law Directory

SELINSGROVE, Snyder Co.

JOHN R. MOORE (AV)

719 North Market Street, 17870
Telephone: 570-374-8138
Fax: 570-374-7558
Email: moorelaw@sunlink.net *URL:* http://www.lawyers.com/jrmlaw

For full biographical listings, see the Martindale-Hubbell Law Directory

SHAMOKIN, Northumberland Co.

JACK C. YOUNKIN (AV)

One West Sunbury Street, P.O. Box 552, 17872
Telephone: 717-648-6821
Fax: 717-648-4732
Email: jcy1@Postoffice.ptd.net *URL:* http://www.lawyers.com/younkinlaw
Danville, Pennsylvania Office: 223 Mill Street.
Telephone: 717-275-7742.
Fax: 717-275-7749.

ASSOCIATES

Barbara G. Martin | Todd P. Kerstetter

LEGAL SUPPORT PERSONNEL

Patricia Janovich

For full biographical listings, see the Martindale-Hubbell Law Directory

SHARON, Mercer Co.

ROUTMAN, MOORE, GOLDSTONE & VALENTINO (AV)

194 East State Street, P.O. Box 690, 16146-0690
Telephone: 724-981-6800
Fax: 724-981-4400
Email: lawyers@rmgv.com
New Castle, Pennsylvania Office: 2656 Wilmington Road, 16105.
Telephone: 724-658-6900.

MEMBERS OF FIRM

Nathan Routman (1904-1974)
Harvey E. Moore (1903-1976)
Joseph Paul Valentino
Richard W. Epstein
Margaret T. Lucas
Ronald P. McCall
Mark A. Longietti

ASSOCIATES

Richard F. Moroco

OF COUNSEL

Bernard Goldstone

LEGAL SUPPORT PERSONNEL

Pamela Sue Sopher
Maureen A. English
Beverly J. Russo
Judy S. Erni

Representative Client: T. Bruce Campbell Construction Co. (industrial manufacturer).

For full biographical listings, see the Martindale-Hubbell Law Directory

*SOMERSET,** Somerset Co.

BARBERA, CLAPPER, BEENER, RULLO & MELVIN (AV)

(Formerly Barbera & Barbera)
146 West Main Street, P.O. Box 775, 15501-0775
Telephone: 814-443-4681
Fax: 814-443-2422

(See Next Column)

MEMBERS OF FIRM

Nathaniel A. Barbera
John J. Barbera
Samuel D. Clapper
James F. Beener
Daniel W. Rullo
Vincent J. Barbera
Matthew G. Melvin

ASSOCIATES

Patrick P. Svonavec | Annette L. Barbera

OF COUNSEL

Melanie R. Barbera

Local Counsel for: Pennsylvania Electric Co.; General Telephone Corp.

For full biographical listings, see the Martindale-Hubbell Law Directory

STATE COLLEGE, Centre Co.

LEE, MARTIN, GREEN & REITER, INC. (AV)

101 Innovation Boulevard, Suite 311, 16803
Telephone: 814-237-6291
Fax: 814-237-5861
Email: lmgrol@ibm.net
Bellefonte, Pennsylvania Office: 115 East High Street, Lock Drawer 179.
Telephone: 814-355-4769.
Fax: 814-355-5024.

Donald E. Lee
Robert L. Martin
Joseph P. Green
Dennis O. Reiter
Robert A. Mix
William T. Fleming

Representative Clients: Omega Bank, N.A.; State College Borough Water Authority; Jersey Shore State Bank; Erie Insurance Group; Centre Community Hospital; Liberty Mutual Insurance Co.; Centre Area Transportation Authority; Centre County Association of Realtors; Gregg Township; Haines Township; Boggs Township.

For full biographical listings, see the Martindale-Hubbell Law Directory

*SUNBURY,** Northumberland Co.

WIEST, SAYLOR, MUOLO, NOON & SWINEHART (AV)

244 Market Street, P.O. Box 791, 17801
Telephone: 570-286-7777
Fax: 570-286-8075

MEMBERS OF FIRM

Roger V. Wiest
Charles H. Saylor
Robert J. Muolo
David D. Noon
William R. Swinehart

References: First National Trust Bank, Sunbury; State Farm Insurance Cos.; Employers Mutual Cos.; Sunbury Motor Co.; Butter Krust Baking Co.; Zartman Construction, Inc.; John Fogarty Custom Built Homes, Inc.; Brush Industries, Inc.

For full biographical listings, see the Martindale-Hubbell Law Directory

*TUNKHANNOCK,** Wyoming Co.

FARR, DAVIS & FITZE (AV)

7 Marion Street, P.O. Box H, 18657
Telephone: 570-836-3185
Facsimile: 570-836-4991

MEMBERS OF FIRM

John B. Farr (1907-1995)
James E. Davis
Judd B. Fitze

Representative Clients: Community Bank & Trust Co.; Proctor & Gamble Paper Products Co.
Title Agents for: Commonwealth Land Title Insurance Co.
References: Mellon Bank, Tunkhannock, PA Office; First Union Bank (Tunkhannock, PA Office); Community Bank and Trust Co.; Grange National Bank of Wyoming County.

For full biographical listings, see the Martindale-Hubbell Law Directory

*WASHINGTON,** Washington Co.

MARRINER, JONES & FITCH (AV)

800 Washington Trust Building, 15301
Telephone: 724-225-6600
Fax: 724-225-8861
URL: http://www.lawyers.com/mjf-law

MEMBERS OF FIRM

Stephen D. Marriner (1917-1993)
Clarence A. Crumrine (1945-1993)
Stephen D. Marriner, Jr.
Cary D. Jones
Colin E. Fitch

Representative Clients: PNC Bank, Washington Office; Observer Publishing Co.; PennWest Farm Credit, ACA; Donegal Mutual Insurance Co.; Columbia Gas of Pennsylvania, Inc.

For full biographical listings, see the Martindale-Hubbell Law Directory

Washington—Continued

PEACOCK KELLER ECKER & CROTHERS, LLP (AV)

East Beau Building, 70 East Beau Street, 15301
Telephone: 724-222-4520
Telefax: 724-222-3318 ABA/NET ABA 34517
Email: peacock@cobweb.net
Waynesburg, Pennsylvania Office: 102 East High Street.
Telephone: 724-627-8331.
Telefax: 724-627-8025.

MEMBERS OF FIRM

Ralph W. Peacock (1902-1972)
Roger J. Ecker
Robert T. Crothers
Kenneth L. Baker
Wesley A. Cramer
Mary Drake Korsmeyer
Richard J. Amrhein
Barbara A. Rizzo
Douglas R. Nolin
Mary K. Pruss
Jonathan G. Higie
John Allan Rodgers

ASSOCIATES

Susan T. Roberts
Susan Mondik Key
Lisa J. Sciullo

OF COUNSEL

William C. Porter (1915-1988)

SENIOR COUNSEL

Davis G. Yohe
Charles C. Keller

Representative Clients: Consolidation Coal Co.; Washington School District; Monongahela Valley Hospital, Inc.; Nationwide Insurance Co.; Family Health Council, Inc.; Marianna & Scenery Hill Telephone Co.; Maternal & Family Health Services, Inc.; Pennsylvania Hospital Insurance Co.

For full biographical listings, see the Martindale-Hubbell Law Directory

WAYNE, Delaware & Chester Cos.

DUANE, MORRIS & HECKSCHER LLP (AV)

735 Chesterbrook Boulevard, Suite 300, 19087-5638
Telephone: 610-647-3555
Fax: 610-640-2619
URL: http://www.duanemorris.com
Philadelphia, Pennsylvania Office: Suite 4200, One Liberty Place.
Telephone: 215-979-1000.
Fax: 215-979-1020.
New York, New York Office: 380 Lexington Avenue.
Telephone: 212-692-1000.
Fax: 212-692-1020.
Chicago, Illinois Office: 227 West Monroe Street, Suite 3400.
Telephone: 312-499-6700.
Fax: 312-499-6701.
Washington, D.C. Office: 1667 K Street, N.W., Suite 700.
Telephone: 202-776-7800.
Fax: 202-776-7801.
San Francisco, California Office: 100 Spear Street.
Telephone: 415-371-2200.
Fax: 415-371-2201.
Boston, Massachusetts Office: One International Place, 14th Floor.
Telephone: 617-598-3100.
Fax: 617-598-3101.
Miami, Florida Office: 200 South Biscayne Boulevard, Suite 3410.
Telephone: 305-960-2200.
Fax: 305-960-2201.
Wilmington, Delaware Office: 1201 Market Street, Suite 1500.
Telephone: 302-571-5550.
Fax: 302-571-5560.
Harrisburg, Pennsylvania Office: 305 North Front Street, 5th Floor, P.O. Box 1003.
Telephone: 717-237-5500.
Fax: 717-232-4015.
Cherry Hill, New Jersey Office: 51 Haddonfield Road, Suite 340.
Telephone: 856-488-7300.
Fax: 856-488-7021.
Newark, New Jersey Office: One Riverfront Plaza.
Telephone: 973-424-2000.
Fax: 973-424-2001.
Palm Beach, Florida Office: 249 Royal Palm Way, Suite 403.
Telephone: 561-366-5400.
Fax: 561-366-5401.
Allentown, Pennsylvania Office: 968 Postal Road, Suite 200, P.O. Box 90400.
Telephone: 610-266-3650.
Fax: 610-266-3651.
Houston, Texas Office: One Greenway Plaza, Suite 500.
Telephone: 713-552-9900.
Fax: 713-552-0109.
Dover, Delaware Office: 314 S. State Street.
Telephone: 302-736-0156.
Fax: 302-736-0336.

RESIDENT PARTNERS

Edward Griffith
W. Mark Mullineaux
Lewis R. Olshin
(Partner-in-Charge, Wayne Office)
Thomas G. Thompson

(See Next Column)

RESIDENT ASSOCIATES

Gregory J. Davis
Mark E. Jakubik
Brett L. Messinger
Donna R. Monper
Michael O'Hayer

SPECIAL COUNSEL

Christopher J. Pippett
Paul M. Silver

OF COUNSEL

Frank L. White, Jr.

For full biographical listings, see the Martindale-Hubbell Law Directory

*WEST CHESTER,** Chester Co.

BUCKLEY, NAGLE, GENTRY, BRION, MCGUIRE & MORRIS (AV)

304 North High Street, 19380
Telephone: 610-436-4400
Telecopier: 610-436-8305
URL: http://www.buckleynagle.com

MEMBERS OF FIRM

C. Barry Buckley
Ronald C. Nagle
W. Richard Gentry
Joseph E. Brion
Stephen P. McGuire
Anthony Morris
Jeffrey R. Sommer

ASSOCIATES

John T. Mannato
Kristin S. Camp
Donald F. Kohler, Jr.

For full biographical listings, see the Martindale-Hubbell Law Directory

DUFFY & GREEN (AV)

10 North Church Street, Suite 307, 19380
Telephone: 610-692-0500
Fax: 610-430-6668

MEMBERS OF FIRM

John J. Duffy
Joseph P. Green, Jr.

ASSOCIATE

P.J. Redmond

For full biographical listings, see the Martindale-Hubbell Law Directory

GAWTHROP, GREENWOOD & HALSTED, A PROFESSIONAL CORPORATION (AV)

119 North High Street, P.O. Box 562, 19381-0562
Telephone: 610-696-8225
Fax: 610-344-0922
Email: gghlaw@gawthrop.com *URL:* http://www.gawthrop.com

John S. Halsted
Robert F. Adams
Kevin Holleran
George C. Zumbano
Mark L. Tunnell
Roger N. Huggins
Walter P. Eells

Andrew D.H. Rau
Jeffrey T. Baker
Miguel D. Pena

Counsel for: Chester County Hospital; Tredyffrin Township Municipal Authority; Brandywine Hospital; Easttown Township; Amica Mutual Insurance Co.; Coatesville Area School District; Penn Mutual Insurance Co.; Wooldridge Construction of Pa.

For full biographical listings, see the Martindale-Hubbell Law Directory

MACELREE, HARVEY, GALLAGHER, FEATHERMAN & SEBASTIAN, LTD. (AV)

17 West Miner Street, P.O. Box 660, 19381-0660
Telephone: 610-436-0100
Fax: 610-430-7885
Kennett Square, Pennsylvania Office: 211 E. State Street, P. O. Box 363.
Telephone 610-444-3180.
Fax: 610-444-3270.
Exton, Pennsylvania Office: 740 Springdale Drive, Suite 110.
Telephone: 610-524-7575.
Fax: 610-524-9857.

Randy L. Sebastian (1946-1997)
Joseph F. Harvey (1921-1985)

For full biographical listings, see the Martindale-Hubbell Law Directory

*WILKES-BARRE,** Luzerne Co.

HOURIGAN, KLUGER & QUINN, A PROFESSIONAL CORPORATION (AV)

700 Mellon Bank Center, 8 West Market Street, 18701-1867
Telephone: 570-825-9401
FAX: 570-829-3460
Email: hkq@epix.net
Scranton, Pennsylvania Office: Suite 200, 434 Lackawanna Avenue.
Telephone: 570-346-8414.

(See Next Column)

HOURIGAN, KLUGER & QUINN A PROFESSIONAL CORPORATION, *Wilkes-Barre—Continued*

Allentown, Pennsylvania Office: Sovereign Building, 609 Hamilton Mall. *Telephone:* 610-437-1584.

Allan M. Kluger
Joseph A. Quinn, Jr.
Richard M. Goldberg
Arthur L. Piccone
Joseph A. Lach (Managing Principal)
Richard S. Bishop (Resident, Scranton Office)
Ronald V. Santora
Eugene D. Sperazza
Neil E. Wenner (Resident, Allentown Office)
Melissa A. Scartelli
Joseph E. Kluger
Daniel J. Distasio, Jr.
James T. Shoemaker
Alexia Kita Blake (Resident, Scranton Office)
Donald C. Ligorio
John R. Hill (Resident, Allentown Office)
Michael J. Kowalski
Michelle Quinn
Patrick T. O'Connell
Jennifer L. Rogers

For full biographical listings, see the Martindale-Hubbell Law Directory

ROSENN, JENKINS & GREENWALD, L.L.P. (AV)

15 South Franklin Street, 18711-0075
Telephone: 570-826-5600
Fax: 570-826-5640
Email: rjg@rjglaw.com *URL:* http://www.rjglaw.com
Hazleton, Pennsylvania Office: P.O. Box 618, 18201-0618.
Telephone: 570-455-7112.
Fax: 570-455-8304.

Mitchell Jenkins (1896-1977)
Henry Greenwald (1908-1994)

OF COUNSEL

Harold Rosenn
Joseph J. Savitz

MEMBERS OF FIRM

Eugene Roth
Daniel G. Flannery
Marshall S. Jacobson
Murray Ufberg
Bruce C. Rosenthal
Donald H. Brobst
Anthony J. Dixon (Resident, Hazleton Office)
Joseph L. Persico
Howard M. Levinson
Alan S. Hollander
Garry S. Taroli
Richard A. Russo
James P. Valentine
Mark A. Van Loon
Lee S. Piatt
Robert D. Schaub
Robert N. Gawlas, Jr.
Steven P. Roth
James C. Oschal
George F. Shovlin
Joseph G. Ferguson
MaryJo Kishel
Patricia Ermel Lakhia

ASSOCIATES

Thomas J. MacNeely
Lawrence W. Roth
Michael K. Duricko
Ernest A. Sposto
Elizabeth C. Leo
Michael Briechle

Representative Clients: C-TEC Corp.; Chicago Title Insurance Co.; Manufacturers & Traders Trust Company; Guard Insurance Group; May Department Stores Co.; Student Loan Marketing Assn. (Sallie Mae); Penn-State Geisinger Medical Center; Subaru of America, Inc.

For full biographical listings, see the Martindale-Hubbell Law Directory

*YORK,** York Co.

BARLEY, SNYDER, SENFT & COHEN, LLC (AV)

100 East Market Street, P.O. Box 15012, 17405-7012
Telephone: 717-846-8888
Fax: 717-843-8492
Email: barley@barley.com *URL:* http://www.barley.com
Lancaster, Pennsylvania Office: 126 East King Street.
Telephone: 717-299-5201.
Fax: 717-291-4660.
Harrisburg, Pennsylvania Office: 240 North Third Street.
Telephone: 717-238-8263.
Fax: 717-238-8278.
Chambersburg, Pennsylvania Office: 247 Lincoln Way East.
Telephone: 717-264-6494.
Fax: 717-264-1662.
Reading, Pennsylvania Office: 501 Washington Street.
Telephone: 610-376-6651.
Fax: 610-376-5243.
Hanover, Pennsylvania Office: 14 Center Square.
Telephone: 717-637-6239.
Fax: 717-637-5407.
Birdsboro, Pennsylvania Office: 115 E. Main Street.
Telephone: 610-582-2735.
Hamburg, Pennsylvania Office: 239 State Street.
Telephone: 610-562-3721.
Oley, Pennsylvania Office: Route 73 and Main Street.
Telephone: 610-987-6350.
Morgantown, Pennsylvania Office: Route 23.
Telephone: 610-286-5958.

(See Next Column)

MEMBERS OF FIRM

Harry J. Rubin
Christopher W. Mattson
Frederick S. Spangler
Rees Griffiths
David R. Keller
Jeffrey D. Lobach
Steven J. Koehler
Val E. Winter
Deborah A. Datte
Michael W. Davis
Melanie A. Zampini
Bruce J. Wolstoncroft

ASSOCIATES

Craig T. Trebilcock
Beverly J. Points
John L. Senft
Paul W. Minnich
Robert J. Schefter
Kimberly J. Decker
John W. Venskus

COUNSEL

Robert J. Stewart
Lavere C. Senft

RETIRED

Donn I. Cohen

Counsel for: Franklin & Marshall College; Fulton Bank/Fulton Financial Corp.; Graham Packaging; Lancaster General Hospital; Robert A. Kinsley, Inc.; D.F. Stauffer Biscuit.
Local Counsel for: Armstrong World Industries; Susquehanna Pfaltzgraff Co.
Insurance Defense Counsel for: Medical Protective Co.; The PMA Group.

For full biographical listings, see the Martindale-Hubbell Law Directory

YOUNGWOOD, Westmoreland Co.

MILLSTEIN & KNUPP (AV)

Cherry Creek Commons Armbrust Road, P.O. Box 467, 15697-0467
Telephone: 724-837-3333
Fax: 724-837-8344

David J. Millstein
Jacquelyn A. Knupp

For full biographical listings, see the Martindale-Hubbell Law Directory

RHODE ISLAND

CRANSTON, Providence Co.

TAFT & MCSALLY (AV)

21 Garden City Drive, P.O. Box 20130, 02920
Telephone: 401-946-3800
Fax: 401-943-8859
Email: taftmcsally@ids.net

MEMBERS OF FIRM

James L. Taft (1901-1959)
Bernard F. McSally (1928-1978)
James L. Taft, Jr.

ASSOCIATES

Sarah Taft-Carter
John V. McGreen
Robert D. Murray
David H. Ferrara
Kenneth K. McKay, IV

LEGAL SUPPORT PERSONNEL

Mary T. Rochford

Representative Clients: General Motors Corp.; General Motors Acceptance Corp.; Providence Gas Co.; Fleet National Bank; Fleet Mortgage; Citizens Savings Bank; Rhode Island Hospital Trust National Bank; Town of Narragansett, Rhode Island (Bond Counsel); Brown Broadcasting Service, Inc.

For full biographical listings, see the Martindale-Hubbell Law Directory

EAST PROVIDENCE, Providence Co.

HOGAN & HOGAN (AV)

201 Waterman Avenue, 02914-3591
Telephone: 401-421-3990
Telecopier: 401-438-3460
Wakefield, Rhode Island Office: 212 Main Street, Unit #4, 02879.
Telephone: 401-782-4488.
Fax: 401-782-4496.

MEMBERS OF FIRM

Edward T. Hogan (1924-1953)
Mary C. Hogan (1928-1981)
Laurence J. Hogan (1924-1984)
Thomas S. Hogan (1951-1996)
Edward T. Hogan

Margaret L. Hogan

For full biographical listings, see the Martindale-Hubbell Law Directory

*NEWPORT,** Newport Co.

MOORE, VIRGADAMO & LYNCH, LTD. (AV)

112 Bellevue Avenue, 02840
Telephone: 401-846-0120
Telecopier: 401-848-0234

(See Next Column)

MOORE, VIRGADAMO & LYNCH LTD.—*Continued*

Cornelius C. Moore (1885-1970)
Salvatore L. Virgadamo (1914-1986)
Jeremiah C. Lynch, Jr. (1928-1987)
Laurent L. Rousseau
Stephen A. Haire
Marie Teresa Paiva Weed
Jeremiah C. Lynch, III

Counsel for: The People's Credit Union; The Portsmouth Abbey School; Salve Regina University; Newport Jai Alai Sports Theatre, Inc.

For full biographical listings, see the Martindale-Hubbell Law Directory

*PROVIDENCE,** Providence Co.

BLISH & CAVANAGH (AV)

Commerce Center, 30 Exchange Terrace, 02903
Telephone: 401-831-8900
Telecopier: 401-751-7542
Email: BLISHCAV@AOL.COM

MEMBERS OF FIRM

Joseph V. Cavanagh, Jr.
William R. Landry
Edmund L. Alves, Jr.
Stephen J. Reid, Jr.
Karen A. Pelczarski
Scott T. Spear
Raymond A. Marcaccio

Michael W. Carroll
Staci L. Sawyer
Kristin Rodgers Sullivan

OF COUNSEL

John H. Blish

Representative Clients: Providence Journal Co.; Rhode Island Hospital Trust National Bank; Fleet Bank; Metropolitan Insurance Co.; Allstate Insurance Co.; Delta Dental of Rhode Island; Colony Communications; Providence Housing Authority; Textron; A.T. Cross.

For full biographical listings, see the Martindale-Hubbell Law Directory

CARROLL, KELLY & MURPHY (AV)

The Packet Building, 155 South Main Street, 02903
Telephone: 401-331-7272
Telecopier: 401-331-4404

MEMBERS OF FIRM

Joseph A. Kelly
James E. Murphy
C. Russell Bengtson
Ruth DiMeglio
William H. Jestings
John P. McCoy
Patricia A. Buckley

ASSOCIATES

Shannon Gilheeney
Maureen L. Mallon
Paula A. Kelly
Scott D. Levesque
Andrew J. Scanlon

Representative Clients: Hartford Accident and Indemnity Co.; Atlantic Mutual Insurance Co.; St. Paul's Insurance Co.; Joint Underwriter's Association; Professional Risk Management Services, Inc.; Norcal Mutual Insurance Company; Prudential Insurance Company of America; Guaranty Fund Management Services; First State Insurance Co.
Reference: Fleet National Bank.

For full biographical listings, see the Martindale-Hubbell Law Directory

MARTIN K. DONOVAN (AV)

One Park Row, 02903-1235
Telephone: 401-831-2500
Facsimile: 401-751-7830

Reference: Fleet National Bank.

For full biographical listings, see the Martindale-Hubbell Law Directory

EDWARDS & ANGELL, LLP (AV)

A Partnership including Professional Corporations
2800 BankBoston Plaza, 02903
Telephone: 401-274-9200
Telecopier: 401-276-6611
Cable Address: "Edwangle Providence"
Telex: 952001 "E A PVD"
Email: postmaster@ealaw.com *URL:* http://www.ealaw.com
Boston, Massachusetts Office: 101 Federal Street, 02110-1800.
Telephone: 617-439-4444.
Telecopier: 617-439-4170.
New York, New York Office: 750 Lexington Avenue, 10022-1200.
Telephone: 212-308-4411.
Telecopier: 212-308-4844.
Palm Beach, Florida Office: 250 Royal Palm Way, Suite 300, 33480-4356.
Telephone: 561-833-7700.
Telecopier: 561-655-8719.
Short Hills, New Jersey Office: 51 John F. Kennedy Parkway, 07078.
Telephone: 973-376-7700.
Telecopier: 973-376-3380.

(See Next Column)

Hartford, Connecticut Office: 90 State House Square, 06103-2715.
Telephone: 860-525-5065.
Telecopier: 860-527-4198.
Newport, Rhode Island Office: 130 Bellevue Avenue, 02840.
Telephone: 401-849-7800.
Telecopier: 401-849-7887.

Bernard A. Heeke (1935-1994)
Edward F. Hindle (1918-1995)
Bancroft Littlefield (1913-1994)
Edward Winsor (1902-1998)

MEMBERS OF FIRM

Lincoln Douglas Almond
Theodore P. Augustinos (Not admitted in RI; Resident, Hartford Connecticut Office)
Edward J. Bertozzi, Jr.
Bernard V. Buonanno, Jr.
Andrew J. Chlebus
Jonathan E. Cole (Resident Palm Beach, Florida Office)
Steven M. Cowley (Not admitted in RI; Resident, Boston, Massachusetts Office)
Robert W. Curry (Not admitted in RI; Resident, Boston, Massachusetts Office)
David K. Duffell
Susan S. Egan (Not admitted in RI; Resident New York, New York Office)
Madeleine A. Estabrook (Not admitted in RI; Resident, Boston, Massachusetts Office)
Geoffrey Etherington III (Resident, New York, New York Office)
Renee A.R. Evangelista
Russell M. Finestein (Not admitted in RI; Resident, Short Hills, New Jersey Office)
Terrence M. Finn (Resident Boston, Massachusetts Office)
Andrew P. Fishkin (Not admitted in RI; New York, New York and Short Hills, New Jersey Offices)
Alan S. Flink
James G. Frangos (Not admitted in RI; Resident, New York, N.Y. Office; Partner-in-Charge, New York Office)
Donald E. Frechette (Not admitted in RI; Resident, Hartford, Connecticut Office)
Mark W. Freel
Neil N. Glazer (Not admitted in RI; Resident, Boston, Massachusetts Office)
Richard M. C. Glenn III
Christopher D. Graham
Ira G. Greenberg (Resident, New York, New York Office)
Benjamin P. Harris III
Jonathan R. Harris (Not admitted in RI; Resident, Boston, Massachusetts Office)
Mary P. Heffner
Gerald P. Hendrick (Not admitted in RI; Resident, Boston, Massachusetts Office; Partner-in-Charge)
Nicholas S. Hodge (Not admitted in RI; Resident, Boston, Massachusetts Office)
John A. Houlihan (Resident Boston, Massachusetts Office)
Kinnaird Howland
Walter C. Hunter
John G. Igoe (Resident Palm Beach, Florida Office)
V. Duncan Johnson
E. Paul Kanefsky (Not admitted in RI; Resident, New York, N.Y. Office)
Patricia L. Kantor (Not admitted in RI; Resident New York, New York Office)
Susan A. Keller
Mary Louise Kennedy
A. Max Kohlenberg
Joseph A. Kuzneski, Jr.
Stuart Lazar (Not admitted in RI)
Alan J. Levin (Not admitted in RI; Resident, Hartford, Connecticut Office)
Alfred S. Lombardi
Jonathan M. Lourie (Not admitted in RI; Resident, Boston, Massachusetts Office)
Michael D. Malloy (Not admitted in RI; Resident, Short Hills, New Jersey Office)
Christine M. Marx (Resident, Short Hills, New Jersey Office; Partner-in-Charge, New Jersey Office)
Gail E. McCann
Richard J. McCarthy (Not admitted in RI; Resident, Boston, Massachusetts Office)
Lorne W. McDougall
James D. McGinley (Not admitted in RI; Resident, Boston, Massachusetts Office)
James R. McGuirk
Stephen O. Meredith (Resident Boston, Massachusetts Office)
David T. Miele
Richard J. Miller (Not admitted in RI; Resident, Palm Beach Florida Office)
Lauren A. Mogensen (Resident, Boston, Massachusetts Office)
Barbara L. Moore (Not admitted in RI; Resident, Boston, Massachusetts Office)
Timothy T. More
Elizabeth H. Munnell (Not admitted in RI; Resident Boston, Massachusetts Office)
Arthur W. Murphy (Resident, Newport, Rhode Island Office; Partner-in-Charge, Newport Office)
G. Scott Nebergall
Eric J. Nemeth (Not admitted in RI; Resident, Short Hills, New Jersey Office)
Robert Novack (Not admitted in RI; Resident, Short Hills, New Jersey Office)
Philip D. O'Neill, Jr. (Resident Boston, Massachusetts Office)
John E. Ottaviani
Alfred R. Paliani (Not admitted in RI; New York, New York and Newark, New Jersey Offices)
Neil R. Pearson (Not admitted in RI; Resident, New York, N.Y. Office)
Richard A. Perras (Not admitted in RI; Resident Boston, Massachusetts Office)
Dana T. Pickard (Resident, Palm Beach, Florida Office)
Mark A. Pogue
Robin F. Price (Not admitted in RI; Resident, Palm Beach, Florida Office)
Stephen M. Prignano
Martin A. Purcell (Not admitted in RI; Resident, Palm Beach, Florida Office; Partner-in-Charge, Palm Beach Office)
Walter G. D. Reed
John H. Reid III (Resident, Hartford, Connecticut Office; Partner-in-Charge)
Dennis M. Reznick (Not admitted in RI; Resident, Short Hills, New Jersey Office)

(See Next Column)

EDWARDS & ANGELL LLP, *Providence—Continued*

MEMBERS OF FIRM (Continued)

Pamela S. Robertson (Resident, Palm Beach Office)
William P. Robinson III
Charles F. Rogers, Jr.
James I. Rubens (Not admitted in RI; Resident, Boston, Massachusetts Office)
Mark B. Seiger (Not admitted in RI; Resident, Hartford, Connecticut Office)
James A. Shanman (Not admitted in RI; Resident, New York, New York Office)
Deming E. Sherman
Richard A. Sherman
Susan E. Siebert (Not admitted in RI; Resident Boston, Massachusetts Office)
Robert A. S. Silberman (Not admitted in RI; Resident, Boston, Massachusetts Office)
James J. Skeffington
Leonard Q. Slap (Resident Boston, Massachusetts Office)
Richard G. Small
William E. Smith
Albert L. Sokol (Not admitted in RI; Resident Boston, Massachusetts Office)
Alan M. Spiro (Not admitted in RI; Resident, Boston, Massachusetts Office)
Justin M. Sullivan (Not admitted in RI; Resident, Hartford, Connecticut Office)
Patricia A. Sullivan
Bruce G. Tucker
Timothy P. Van Dyck (Not admitted in RI; Resident Boston, Massachusetts Office)
Vincent J. Vitkowsky (Not admitted in RI)
Kurt J. von Boeselager
Laura N. Wilkinson
Gary A. Woodfield (Not admitted in RI; Resident, Palm Beach, Florida Office)
Lynn Wright (Not admitted in RI; New York, New York and Newark, New Jersey Office)
Gregory E. Young (Not admitted in RI)

COUNSEL

Martin W. Aron (Not admitted in RI; Resident, Short Hills, New Jersey Office)
Walter E. Breen (Not admitted in RI)
Kenneth J. Cesta (Not admitted in RI; Resident, Short Hills, New Jersey Office)
Bonnie C. Dailey (Not admitted in RI; Resident, Hartford, Connecticut Office)
Edward W. Dence, Jr.
Lynne B. Dolan
Calvert C. Groton
Barry G. Hittner
Thomas F. X. Hodson (Not admitted in RI; Resident, Hartford, Connecticut Office)
Laurie B. Kirby (Resident, Newport Office)
Robert E. Lundvall (Not admitted in RI; Resident, Hartford, Connecticut Office)
Richard P. McMahon
Michael K. Miller (Not admitted in RI; Resident, Palm Beach, Florida Office)
Leonard H. Minches (Not admitted in RI; Resident, Palm Beach, Florida Office)
Charles A. Ognibene (Not admitted in RI; Resident, Boston, Massachusetts Office)
Christopher K. Pfirrman (Not admitted in RI; Resident, Hartford, Connecticut Office)
Kenneth A. Reich (Not admitted in RI; Resident, Boston, Massachusetts Office)
Paul D. Rosenberg (Not admitted in RI; Resident, Short Hills, New Jersey Office)
John B. Rosenquest III
Max Schorr (Not admitted in RI; Resident, Palm Beach, Florida Office)
Karen L. Trafford (Not admitted in RI; Resident, Palm Beach, Florida Office)
Anthony J. Viola (Not admitted in RI; Resident, New York, New York Office)

ASSOCIATES

Mark-David Adams (Not admitted in RI; Resident, Palm Beach, Florida Office)
Jon M. Anderson
Daniel D. Barnes (Resident, New York, N.Y. Office)
Lori A. Basilico
Robert J. Brener (Not admitted in RI; Resident, New York, N.Y. Office)
Virginia M. Burke
Sarah N.A. Camougis (Not admitted in RI; Resident, Boston, Massachusetts Office)
Kathleen B. Carr (Not admitted in RI; Resident, Boston, Massachusetts Office)
Kerri L. Catino-Nason
Samara J. Cooper (Not admitted in RI; Resident, Palm Beach, Florida Office)
Mary Patricia Cormier (Not admitted in RI; Resident, Boston, Massachusetts Office)
James M. Crane (Not admitted in RI)
Marc A. Crisafulli
Rosanne M. Duane (Not admitted in RI; Resident, Palm Beach, Florida Office)
Paul E. Dwyer, Jr.
Thomas C. Egg (Not admitted in RI; Resident, Short Hills, New Jersey Office)
Caroline R. Elliott (Not admitted in RI)
John N. Emmanuel (Not admitted in RI; Resident, Hartford, Connecticut Office)
Jillian L. Erdos (Not admitted in RI; Resident, Boston, Massachusetts Office)
Noreen M. Fierro (Not admitted in RI; Resident, Short Hills, New Jersey Office)
Robert J. Fitzpatrick (Resident, Boston, Massachusetts Office)
Peter J. Gillin
Mark Jay Goldberg (Not admitted in RI; Resident, New York, N.Y. Office)
Douglas G. Gray
Cheryl A. Green
Donna M. Greenspan (Not admitted in RI; Resident, Palm Beach, Florida Office)
David M. Griff (Not admitted in RI; Resident, New York, New York Office)
Michael T. Griffin (Not admitted in RI; Resident, Hartford, Connecticut Office)
Joli Lyn Gross (Not admitted in RI; New York, N.Y. and Short Hills, New Jersey Offices)

(See Next Column)

ASSOCIATES (Continued)

Mary Patricia Hagan (Not admitted in RI; Resident, Boston, Massachusetts Office)
Seth H. Handy
Michael S. Heller (Not admitted in RI; Resident, Palm Beach, Florida Office)
Janet M. Helmke-Elmore (Not admitted in RI; Resident, Hartford, Connecticut Office)
Rebecca L. Henderson (Not admitted in RI; Resident, Palm Beach, Florida Office)
Matthew J. Hoberman (Not admitted in RI; Resident, Hartford, Connecticut Office)
Soo H. Im (Not admitted in RI; Resident, New York, N.Y. Office)
Andrea B. Jacobs (Not admitted in RI; Resident, Boston, Massachusetts Office)
Carine Jean-Claude (Not admitted in RI; Resident, New York, N.Y. Office)
James Robert Joines (Not admitted in RI; Resident, Palm Beach, Florida Office)
Russell L. Kane (Not admitted in RI; Resident, Boston, Massachusetts Office)
Corrine A. LaCroix-Tighe (Not admitted in RI; Resident, Short Hills, New Jersey Office)
Brian H. Lamkin (Not admitted in RI; Resident, Boston, Massachusetts Office)
Stephen J. MacGillivray
Paul M. Mahoney, Jr. (Not admitted in RI)
Sabiha Malik (Not admitted in RI)
Peter T. Maloney (Not admitted in RI; Resident, New York, N.Y. Office)
Jason P. Marshall (Not admitted in RI)
Rosa Mazzeo (Not admitted in RI; Resident, Boston, Massachusetts Office)
Kristen K. Mead (Not admitted in RI; Resident, Boston, Massachusetts Office)
Jeffrey Joseph Medeiros (Not admitted in RI; Resident, Hartford, Connecticut Office)
Deborah A. Millum (Not admitted in RI; Resident, Hartford, Connecticut Office)
Christopher W. Nelson (Resident, Boston, Massachusetts Office)
Sharon M. O'Brien (Not admitted in RI; Resident, Boston, Massachusetts Office)
Kimberly Ann O'Connell
Mary Claire Pitocchelli (Not admitted in RI; Resident, Palm Beach, Florida Office)
Michael K. Prescott
Bruce W. Raphael (Not admitted in RI; Resident, Boston, Massachusetts Office)
Todd M. Reed (Not admitted in RI)
David G. Rickerby
John J. Rogers (Not admitted in RI)
Patrick A. Rogers
Philip S. Rosen (Not admitted in RI; Resident, Short Hills, New Jersey Office)
Dani Noam Ruran (Not admitted in RI)
Steven D. Schell (Resident, New York, N.Y. Office)
Susan M. Schiappa
Ronald J. Schott (Not admitted in RI; Resident, Short Hills, New Jersey Office)
Edward S. Shelton (Not admitted in RI)
Peter J. Sheptak (Not admitted in RI; Resident, Palm Beach, Florida Office)
Douglas W. Sichol (Not admitted in RI)
Daniel P. Silberstein (Not admitted in RI; Resident, Short Hills, New Jersey Office)
Elizabeth S. Small (Not admitted in RI)
Cathleen A. Tobin (Not admitted in RI; Resident, Hartford, Connecticut Office)
John J. Tumilty (Not admitted in RI; Resident, Boston, Massachusetts Office)
Suzanne E. Turcotte (Not admitted in RI; Resident, Boston, Massachusetts Office)
Daniel H. Wright
Stephen D. Zubiago

OF COUNSEL

Ernest N. Agresti
James H. Barnett
Philip B. Barr, Jr.
Richard M. Borod
Robert Spink Davis
James K. Edwards
Knight Edwards
Stephen A. Fanning (Retired)
Alvin M. Glazerman (Not admitted in RI)
Paul F. Greene
Gerald W. Harrington
John V. Kean
Beverly Glenn Long
George Michaels (Not admitted in RI; Resident Boston, Massachusetts Office)

For full biographical listings, see the Martindale-Hubbell Law Directory

---

HANSON, CURRAN, PARKS & WHITMAN (AV)

146 Westminster Street, 02903-2218
Telephone: 401-421-2154
Telecopier: 401-521-7040
URL: http://www.hcpw.com

Kirk Hanson (1948-1991)

MEMBERS OF FIRM

A. Lauriston Parks
David P. Whitman
Michael T. F. Wallor
Dennis J. McCarten
James T. Murphy
Seth E. Bowerman
Thomas R. Bender
Mark W. Dana

ASSOCIATES

Richard H. Burrows
Christopher J. Zangari (Resident)
Wendy J. Taylor

OF COUNSEL

William A. Curran

General Counsel for: Medical Malpractice Joint Underwriting Association of Rhode Island.

(See Next Column)

HANSON, CURRAN, PARKS & WHITMAN—*Continued*

Rhode Island Counsel for: Amica Mutual Insurance Co.; CIGNA; St. Paul Insurance Cos.; Occidental Life Insurance Co.; Exchange Mutual Insurance Co.; Aetna Casualty & Surety Co.

For full biographical listings, see the Martindale-Hubbell Law Directory

HIGGINS, CAVANAGH & COONEY (AV)

The Hay Building, Fourth Floor, 123 Dyer Street, 02903
Telephone: 401-272-3500; 800-274-5299
Telecopier: 401-273-8780

James H. Higgins, Jr. (1952-1975)
Joseph V. Cavanagh (1952-1985)
John P. Cooney, Jr. (1960-1981)
Kenneth P. Borden
Gerald C. DeMaria
John T. Walsh, Jr.
Charles A. Hambly, Jr.
Stephen B. Lang
Lawrence P. McCarthy, III
James A. Ruggieri
Michael D. Lynch
James T. Hornstein

ASSOCIATES

John F. Kelleher
Rajaram Suryanarayan
Vivian B. Dogan
Patrick B. Landers
Paul S. Callaghan
Susan Pepin Fay
Peter E. Garvey
Amy C. Vignali
Thomas F. DeVincke

For full biographical listings, see the Martindale-Hubbell Law Directory

HINCKLEY, ALLEN & SNYDER LLP (AV)

1500 Fleet Center, 02903-2393
Telephone: 401-274-2000
Fax: 401-277-9600
Email: firm@haslaw.com *URL:* http://www.haslaw.com
Boston, Massachusetts Office: 28 State Street, 30th Floor.
Telephone: 617-345-9000.
Fax: 617-345-9020. URL: http://www.haslaw.com.

MEMBERS OF FIRM

Paula K. Andrews (Not admitted in RI)
David D. Barricelli
E. Jerome Batty
Jonathan Bell
Deborah L. Benson (Not admitted in RI)
Leon C. Boghossian III
Paul Bork (Not admitted in RI)
Stephen J. Carlotti
David Barry Connolly (Not admitted in RI)
Michael J. Connolly (Not admitted in RI)
Robert Corrente
Joseph P. Curran
Michael P. DeFanti
Eric F. Eisenberg (Not admitted in RI)
Malcolm Farmer, III
Margaret D. Farrell
Noel M. Field, Jr.
Pasco Gasbarro Jr.
Bruce G. Goodman (Not admitted in RI)
Hugh J. Gorman, III (Not admitted in RI)
Alan P. Gottlieb (Not admitted in RI)
Gerard R. Goulet
William R. Grimm
Paul A. Hedstrom (Not admitted in RI)
Richard L. E. Jocelyn
Michael J. Kelly (Not admitted in RI)
Joel Lewin (Not admitted in RI)
Doris Jami Licht
Sandra Matrone Mack
Matthew T. Marcello, III
Frederick P. McClure
Elizabeth Murdock Myers
Paul F. O'Donnell, III (Not admitted in RI)
H. Peter Olsen
Julianne Palumbo (Not admitted in RI)
John J. Pendergast, III
Gerald J. Petros
Richard H. Pierce
James O. Reavis
Jeremy Ritzenberg (Not admitted in RI)
Ralph J. Rivkind (Not admitted in RI)
Lawrence R. Robins (Not admitted in RI)
David J. Rubin
Charles E. Schaub, Jr. (Not admitted in RI)
Douglas F. Seaver (Not admitted in RI)
Scott E. Sheridan (Not admitted in RI)
Paul A. Silver
Herman Snyder (Not admitted in RI)
David R. Sullivan (Not admitted in RI)
Robert F. Sylvia (Not admitted in RI)
Christopher C. Tsouros (Not admitted in RI)
Howard E. Walker
Richard D. Wayne (Not admitted in RI)
Doreen M. Zankowski (Not admitted in RI)
John R. Allen (Retired)
Richard W. Billings (Retired)
Thomas J. Hogan (Retired)
Jacques V. Hopkins (Retired)
James A. Jackson (Retired)
James E. Keeley (Retired)
Robert F. Pickard (Retired)
Robert W. Shadd (Retired)
Richard F. Staples (Retired)
Edwin G. Torrance (Retired)

ASSOCIATES

Jessica M. Bettencourt
Mark Bianchi
Charles D. Blackman
Gail Bonner (Not admitted in RI)
Alyssa V. Boss
Neil L. Brodsky (Not admitted in RI)
Alexandra K. Callam
Brent R. Canning
Clifford R. Cohen (Not admitted in RI)
Jane E. Cohen (Not admitted in RI)
Andrew D. Cummings (Not admitted in RI)
June E. Daniel
Kristine L. Donabedian
Josephine A. Giuffre (Not admitted in RI)

(See Next Column)

ASSOCIATES (Continued)

Kim Herman Goslant (Not admitted in RI)
Veronica A. Greenbaum (Not admitted in RI)
Gloria Maria Gutierrez (Not admitted in RI)
Christopher P. Hamilton (Not admitted in RI)
Kelley Jordan-Price
Catherine S. Kim (Not admitted in RI)
John P. Martin (Not admitted in RI)
Christopher W. Morog (Not admitted in RI)
Katharine Carter Noble
Elena B. Olson (Not admitted in RI)
Timothy J. Perry (Not admitted in RI)
Michael J. Pisaturo
Michael T. Renaud (Not admitted in RI)
Lynn E. Riley
Leah A. Rochwarg (Not admitted in RI)
Andrew F. Shure (Not admitted in RI)
Michael G. Tauber
Lauren Timoney Upton (Not admitted in RI)
Lawrence W. Vernaglia (Not admitted in RI)
Joseph D. Whelan

OF COUNSEL

Willard Krasnow (Not admitted in RI)
Debra Dyleski Najjar (Not admitted in RI)
Willard R. Pope (Not admitted in RI)
Bentley Tobin
Joachim A. Weissfeld

For full biographical listings, see the Martindale-Hubbell Law Directory

PEABODY & ARNOLD LLP (AV)

One Citizens Plaza Suite 1100, 02903
Telephone: 401-831-8330
Fax: 401-831-8359
URL: http://www.peabodyarnold.com
Boston, Massachusetts Office: 50 Rowes Wharf.
Telephone: 617-951-2100.
Telecopier: 617-951-2125.
Portland, Maine Office: One City Center.
Telephone: 207-773-6300.
Fax: 207-773-0609.

MEMBERS OF FIRM

Kevin C. Cain
Sean O. Coffey (Resident)
Michael P. Duffy
John R. Gowell, Jr. (Resident)
John A. Kessler, Jr.
Jeffrey B. Pine (Resident)
Frank N. Ray (Resident)
Randolph L. Smith

OF COUNSEL

Kent A. Willever (Resident)

ASSOCIATES

Tobias M. Lederberg (Resident)
Benedict A. Monachino
Joseph B. White (Resident)

For full biographical listings, see the Martindale-Hubbell Law Directory

TILLINGHAST LICHT & SEMONOFF LTD. (AV)

Historic Wayland Building, One Park Row, 02903
Telephone: 401-456-1200
Fax: 401-456-1210
Email: tlsprov@tlslaw.com *URL:* http://www.tlslaw.com

Frank Licht (1916-1987)
Ralph P. Semonoff (1918-1992)
Ellen M. Flynn Corneau
Joseph DeAngelis
Susan Leach DeBlasio
Karen S. D. Grande
Patrick A. Guida
Casby Harrison, III
John J. Hogan
Robert N. Huseby, Sr.
Richard A. Licht
George E. Lieberman
Peter J. McGinn
Norman G. Orodenker
Eustace T. Pliakas
Steven M. Richard
David T. Riedel
Lori Caron Silveira
Joseph W. Walsh
Daniel C. Waugh

Kendra L. Beaver
John J. Bolton
Douglas J. Emanuel
Glenn R. Friedemann
Robert E. Rainville

COUNSEL

Edwin H. Hastings
DeWitte T. Kersh, Jr.
Melvin L. Zurier

For full biographical listings, see the Martindale-Hubbell Law Directory

SOUTH CAROLINA

*ANDERSON,** Anderson Co.

McINTOSH, SHERARD & SULLIVAN (AV)

138 North Main Street, P.O. Box 197, 29622
Telephone: 864-225-0001
Fax: 864-225-0004
Email: mss@carol.net

(See Next Column)

McIntosh, Sherard & Sullivan, *Anderson—Continued*

MEMBERS OF FIRM

Jack F. McIntosh
Rivers Lawton McIntosh
Marshall P. Sherard, Jr.
George P. Sullivan

Representative Clients: Perpetual Bank, FSB, Anderson, South Carolina; NationsBank, Anderson, South Carolina; The Commercial Bank, Honea Path, South Carolina; People's Bank of Iva, Iva, South Carolina.

For full biographical listings, see the Martindale-Hubbell Law Directory

*BARNWELL,** Barnwell Co.

Brown, Jefferies and Boulware (AV)

FirstCitizens, P.O. Box 248, 29812
Telephone: 803-259-3532; 259-3533
Telefax: 803-259-0175

MEMBERS OF FIRM

Edgar A. Brown (1888-1975)
R. M. Jefferies, Jr. (1919-1985)
Herman I. Mazursky (1903-1970)
Thomas M. Boulware
Herman Edward Smith

Assistant Division Counsel: Southern Railway Co.
State Counsel: Kenan Transport Co.; Eagle Transport Corp.; Belue Trucking.
Local Counsel: NCNB South Carolina; Deering Milliken, Inc.; Chem-Nuclear Systems, Inc.

For full biographical listings, see the Martindale-Hubbell Law Directory

*BEAUFORT,** Beaufort Co.

Harvey & Battey, P.A. (AV)

1001 Craven Street, P.O. Drawer 1107, 29902
Telephone: 843-524-3109
Telefax: 843-524-6973

W. Brantley Harvey (1893-1981)
W. Brantley Harvey, Jr.
Colden R. Battey, Jr.
William B. Harvey, III
John M. Tatum, III
Thomas C. Davis
H. Grady Brown, III
E. Carew Rice, III
Thomas A. Holloway
Derek C. Gilbert

OF COUNSEL

Noel M. Seeburg, Jr.

Approved Attorneys for: Lawyers Title Insurance Corp.; Chicago Title Insurance Corp.
Representative Clients: Nations Bank; First Bank, F.S.B.; Pleasant Point Plantation Associates; Century 21-Carolina Realty, Inc.; Lobeco Products, Inc.; Beaufort County Association of Realtors; The Fripp Company.

For full biographical listings, see the Martindale-Hubbell Law Directory

Levin & Gilley (AV)

811 Craven Street, P.O. Box 2358, 29901-2358
Telephone: 843-522-9000
Fax: 843-524-8248
Email: dcg@hargray.com *URL:* http://www.lawyers.com/levinandgilley

Julian S. Levin
Dewey C. Gilley, Jr.

Approved Attorneys for: Old Republic National Title Insurance Company.

For full biographical listings, see the Martindale-Hubbell Law Directory

*CAMDEN,** Kershaw Co.

Savage, Royall and Sheheen, L.L.P. (AV)

1111 Church Street, P.O. Drawer 10, 29020
Telephone: 803-432-4391
Telefax: 803-425-4816

MEMBERS OF FIRM

Edward M. Royall
Robert J. Sheheen
Moultrie B. Burns, Jr.
Dana A. Morris
William David Kelly, III
William B. Cox, Jr.
Vincent Austin Sheheen

Representative Clients: Nations Bank NBSC; First Palmetto Bank; Farmers Bureau Insurance Cos.; Georgia Pacific Corp.; Carolina Power & Light Co.; Cassatt Water Co.; Bowaters Southern Paper Corp.; Kershaw County Medical Center.
Approved Attorneys for: Stewart Title Insurance; Lawyers Title.

For full biographical listings, see the Martindale-Hubbell Law Directory

*CHARLESTON,** Charleston Co.

Brockinton, Brockinton & Kerr, P.A. (AV)

51 State Street, P.O. Box 663, 29402-0663
Telephone: 843-722-8845
FAX: 843-722-3069

(See Next Column)

D. A. Brockinton (1890-1986)
D. A. Brockinton, Jr.
W. H. Brockinton
W. Harvey Brockinton, Jr.
John J. Kerr

Representative Clients: Equitable Life Assurance Society of the U.S.; The Post & Courier.

For full biographical listings, see the Martindale-Hubbell Law Directory

Buist, Moore, Smythe & McGee, P.A. (AV)

Successors to Buist, Buist, Smythe and Smythe and Moore, Mouzon and McGee.
Five Exchange Street, P.O. Box 999, 29402
Telephone: 843-722-3400
Cable Address: "Conferees"
Telex: 57-6488
Telecopier: 843-723-7398
Email: bmsm@lawyer-sc.com *URL:* http://www.lawyer-sc.com

Henry Buist (1895-1977)
Pledger M. Bishop, Jr. (1932-1987)
B. Allston Moore (1900-1988)
Augustine T. Smythe (1918-1991)
Henry B. Smythe
Benjamin Allston Moore, Jr.
Joseph H. McGee
Gordon D. Schreck
Henry B. Smythe, Jr.
Susan M. Smythe
W. Foster Gaillard
Henry E. Grimball
Kenneth F. Smith
David B. McCormack
C. Allen Gibson, Jr.
Morris A. Ellison
Charles P. Summerall, IV
James L. Parris
James D. Myrick
Douglas M. Muller
Elizabeth Henry Warner
David H. Crawford
David S. Yandle
John Marshall Allen

Shawn M. Flanagan
Julius H. Hines
David S. Cox
Jonathan D. Crumly, Sr.
Dwayne M. Green
Thomas L. Harper, Jr.
Cynthia M. Spieth
Margaret O. Dullanty
Gregory Horton

OF COUNSEL

David M. Collins
Charles J. Baker, III

Representative Clients: Nations Bank; Metropolitan Life Insurance Co.; E.I. duPont De Nemours & Co.; AIG Aviation, Inc.; ALCOA; Thomas Miller (Americas), Inc.; U.S.F.& G.; Brunswick Corp.; Daniel Island Development Co.

For full biographical listings, see the Martindale-Hubbell Law Directory

Haynsworth, Marion, McKay & Guérard, L.L.P. (AV)

134 Meeting Street, P.O. Box 1119, 29402
Telephone: 843-722-7606
Facsimile: 843-724-8016
Columbia, South Carolina Office: Suite 2400 Affinity Building, 1201 Main Street, P.O. Drawer 7157, 29202.
Telephone: 803-765-1818. Facsimile 803-765-2399.
Greenville, South Carolina Office: 75 Beattie Place, Eleventh Floor, P.O. Box 2048, 29602.
Telephone: 864-240-3200.
Facsimile: 864-240-3300.

MEMBERS OF FIRM

H.J. Haynsworth (1859-1941)
Clement Furman Haynsworth (1886-1953)
James M. Perry (1894-1964)
Eugene Bryant (1902-1969)
H.R. Stevenson, Jr. (1915-1990)
Andrew B. Marion (1920-1995)
William Francis Marion (1923-1995)
Robert S. Galloway, Jr. (1928-1997)
Theodore B. Guérard (1930-1997)
Thomas K. Johnstone, Jr. (Retired)
Fred D. Cox, Jr. (Retired)
William C. Cleveland
J. Paul Trouche
James J. Hinchey, Jr.
Robert B. Pearlman
Samuel W. Howell, IV
Carol L. Clark
Thomas S. White
James E. Lady

ASSOCIATES

M. Jean Lee
Jeremy L. Cook
Todd W. Smyth

OF COUNSEL

Julius W. McKay
Gus H. Pearlman

SPECIAL COUNSEL

Nancy Lark Schulze
John Adams Hodge
Theodore J. Hopkins Jr.

Counsel for: Healthsource of South Carolina; Allstate Insurance Co.; CSX Corp.; Lloyd's Underwriters; Coward-Hund Construction Co.; Charleston County; City of Hanahan; Duke Power Co.

For full biographical listings, see the Martindale-Hubbell Law Directory

Charleston—Continued

Hood Law Firm (AV)

172 Meeting Street, P.O. Box 1508, 29402
Telephone: 843-577-4435
Fax: 843-722-1630
Email: hlf@hoodlaw.com *URL:* http://www.hoodlaw.com

MEMBERS OF FIRM

Robert H. Hood
Louis P. Herns
G. Mark Phillips
Carl Everette Pierce, II
John K. Blincow, Jr.
James G. Kennedy
Barbara Wynne Showers
Joseph C. Wilson, IV
James Dowell Gandy, III

Dixon F. Pearce, II
Hugh Willcox Buyck
Allan Poe Sloan, III
Mary Agnes Hood Craig
Allison Snead Patrick
P. Gunnar Nistad
Robert H. Hood, Jr.
William Mullins McLeod, Jr.

For full biographical listings, see the Martindale-Hubbell Law Directory

McKay & Guérard, P.A.

(See Haynsworth, Marion, McKay & Guérard, L.L.P.)

Oberman & Oberman (AV)

38 Broad Street, 29401
Telephone: 843-577-7010
Fax: 843-722-7359

MEMBERS OF FIRM

Marvin I. Oberman
Harold A. Oberman

For full biographical listings, see the Martindale-Hubbell Law Directory

Sinkler & Boyd, P.A. (AV)

160 East Bay Street, P.O. Box 340, 29402-0340
Telephone: 843-722-3366
FAX: 843-722-2266
Email: firm@sinklerboyd.com *URL:* http://www.sinklerboyd.com
Columbia, South Carolina Office: Suite 1200 The Palmetto Center, 1426 Main Street, P.O. Box 11889.
Telephone: 803-779-3080.
FAX: 803-765-1243.
Greenville, South Carolina Office: 15 South Main Street, Insignia Financial Center on Main, Suite 500, P.O. Box 275.
Telephone: 864-467-1100.
FAX: 864-467-1521.

H. Simmons Tate, Jr. (Resident, Columbia Office)
William C. Boyd (Resident, Columbia Office)
Francis P. Mood (Resident, Columbia Office)
J. Donald Dial, Jr. (Resident, Columbia Office)
Bachman S. Smith III
Manton M. Grier (Resident, Columbia Office)
George S. King, Jr. (Resident, Columbia Office)
Thomas A. Hutcheson
Thomas R. Gottshall (Resident, Columbia Office)
Hamilton Osborne, Jr. (Resident, Columbia Office)
Stephen E. Darling
John P. Linton
Margaret Christian Pope (Resident, Columbia Office)
Harold E. Trask
Charlton deSaussure, Jr.
Marvin D. Infinger
John C. Bruton, Jr. (Resident, Columbia Office)
F. Mitchell Johnson, Jr.
Michael D. Jones
Benton D. Williamson (Resident, Columbia Office)
John B. McArthur (Resident, Columbia Office)
David M. Swanson
Robert S. Galloway, III (Resident, Greenville Office)
Clarke W. DuBose (Resident, Columbia Office)
Terri Morrill Lynch
Randolph B. Epting (Resident, Columbia Office)
Steve A. Matthews (Resident, Columbia Office)
Robert Y. Knowlton (Resident, Columbia Office)
Suzanne Hulst Clawson (Resident, Columbia Office)
William H. Short, Jr. (Resident, Columbia Office)
Theodore B. DuBose (Resident, Columbia Office)
Thomas C. Hildebrand, Jr.
John M. G. McLeod (Resident, Columbia Office)
Robert W. Buffington (Resident, Columbia Office)
Frank W. Cureton (Resident, Columbia Office)
Bert Glenn Utsey III
Charles H. Gibbs, Jr.
Stanley H. McGuffin (Resident, Columbia Office)
John K. Van Duys (Resident, Columbia Office)
John H. Tiller
Roy A. Howell III
Edward K. Pritchard III
Henry J. White (Resident, Columbia Office)
Tara Elizabeth Nauful (Resident, Columbia Office)
John F. Emerson (Resident, Columbia Office)
James Y. Becker (Resident, Columbia Office)

(See Next Column)

Joseph D. Thompson, III
Julie Oswald Medich
Joseph D. Clark (Resident, Columbia Office)
M. Todd Haynie, III (Resident, Columbia Office)
James L. Ward, Jr. (Resident, Columbia Office)
Kirsten L. Barr
B. Eric Shytle (Resident, Columbia Office)

OF COUNSEL

Martin C. McWilliams, Jr. (Resident, Columbia Office)
Paul M. Platte (Resident, Columbia Office)

Attorneys for: Wachovia Bank, N.A.; First Union National Bank; Westvaco Corp.; American Cyanamid Co.; Waste Management of North America, Inc.; Sonoco Products; Lawyers Title Insurance Corp.

For full biographical listings, see the Martindale-Hubbell Law Directory

Warren & Sinkler, L.L.P. (AV)

Suite 340 171 Church Street, P.O. Box 1254, 29402
Telephone: 843-577-0660
Fax: 843-577-6843
Email: law@warren-sinkler.com

MEMBERS OF FIRM

G. Dana Sinkler
John H. Warren, III
Henry B. Fishburne, Jr.
Scott Y. Barnes
Mark S. Sharpe
Elizabeth W. Settle
Andrea Hall Duenas
William O. Hanahan, III
Holly R. Jensen

For full biographical listings, see the Martindale-Hubbell Law Directory

*COLUMBIA,** Richland Co.

Weston Adams Law Firm (AV)

1501 Richland Street, P.O. Box 291, 29202
Telephone: 803-254-1675
Fax: 803-799-3141

Weston Adams

ASSOCIATE

Weston Adams, III

For full biographical listings, see the Martindale-Hubbell Law Directory

Barnes, Alford, Stork & Johnson, L.L.P. (AV)

1613 Main Street, P.O. Box 8448, 29202
Telephone: 803-799-1111
Telefax: 803-254-1335
Email: basj@basjlaw.com

Rudolph C. Barnes (1917-1995)
James W. Alford (Retired)
Robert E. Salane (1947-1997)
R. Lewis Johnson (1959-1996)
William C. Stork
Weldon R. Johnson
David G. Wolff
Kay Gaffney Crowe
Richard C. Thomas
Thomas C. Cofield
Robert Thomas Strickland
L. Elaine Mozingo
Curtis W. Dowling
James R. Allen

Melody Lynn James
Andrea C. Pope
Robert D. Dodson

OF COUNSEL

Alan J. Reyner
Roger A. Way, Jr.

For full biographical listings, see the Martindale-Hubbell Law Directory

Collins & Lacy, P.C. (AV)

1330 Lady Street, Suite 601, P.O. Box 12487, 29211
Telephone: 803-256-2660
Telefax: 803-771-4484
Email: TheFirm@CollinsandLacy.com *URL:* http://www.collinsandlacy.com

Joel W. Collins, Jr.
Stanford E. Lacy
Gray Thomas Culbreath
Arthur K. Aiken
Eric G. Fosmire
Ellen A. Mercer

Rebecca M. Monroy
Joseph S. McCue
Clayton B. McCullough
Peter H. Dworjanyn

LEGAL SUPPORT PERSONNEL

Joanne B. Moody

LEGAL ASSISTANTS

Jane L. Koon
Mary D. Malinaroli
Jeanne S. Volin
Leslie Edenfield
M. Larry Nelson
Victoria Allen

For full biographical listings, see the Martindale-Hubbell Law Directory

Columbia—Continued

GLENN MURPHY GRAY & STEPP, L.L.P. (AV)

B B & T Bank Building, Suite 390, 1901 Assembly Street, P.O. Box 1550, 29202-1550
Telephone: 803-765-1100
Telecopy: 803-765-0755

Terrell L. Glenn (1930-1993)

MEMBERS OF FIRM

Peter L. Murphy	Robert E. Stepp
Elizabeth Van Doren Gray	Elizabeth G. Howard
Robert C. Rhodes	Roland M. Franklin
Laura W. Robinson	C. Shawn Dryer

Reference: BB&T.

For full biographical listings, see the Martindale-Hubbell Law Directory

HAYNSWORTH, MARION, MCKAY & GUÉRARD, L.L.P. (AV)

Suite 2400 Affinity Building, 1201 Main Street, P.O. Drawer 7157, 29202
Telephone: 803-765-1818
Facsimile: 803-765-2399
Greenville, South Carolina Office: 75 Beattie Place, Eleventh Floor, P.O. Box 2048, 29602.
Telephone: 864-240-3200.
Facsimile: 864-240-3300.
Charleston, South Carolina Office: 134 Meeting Street, P.O. Box 1119, 29402.
Telephone: 843-722-7606.
Facsimile: 843-724-8016.

MEMBERS OF FIRM

H.J. Haynsworth (1859-1941)	Theodore B. Guérard (1930-1997)
Clement Furman Haynsworth (1886-1953)	Thomas K. Johnstone, Jr. (Retired)
James M. Perry (1894-1964)	Fred D. Cox, Jr. (Retired)
Eugene Bryant (1902-1969)	William P. Simpson
H.R. Stevenson, Jr. (1915-1990)	Gary W. Morris
Andrew B. Marion (1920-1995)	Steven Todd Moon
William Francis Marion (1923-1995)	Stephen F. McKinney
Robert S. Galloway, Jr. (1928-1997)	Michael R. Daniel
	Russell B. Shetterly

Edward G. Kluiters

ASSOCIATES

Gina L. Campano	Theodore D. Riley

Shiryl R. Ballard

OF COUNSEL

Julius W. McKay

SPECIAL COUNSEL

Nancy Lark Schulze	John Adams Hodge

Theodore J. Hopkins Jr.

Counsel for: St. Paul Insurance Group; Allstate Insurance Co.; Fluor-Daniel Corp.; South Carolina Jobs - Economic Development Authority; Anheuser Busch Company; CSX Transportation; Ernst & Young, LLP; Willis Corroon of South Carolina, Inc.; Westinghouse Savannah River Co.; Wachovia Bank of South Carolina, N.A.

For full biographical listings, see the Martindale-Hubbell Law Directory

KING & VERNON, P.A. (AV)

1426 Richland Street, P.O. Box 7667, 29202
Telephone: 803-779-3090
Fax: 803-779-3396
Email: TVernon@usit.net *URL:* http://www.usit.net/users/lawyer/

Kermit S. King	W. Thomas Vernon
B. Dean Pierce	David A. Root

Bradley T. Farrar

For full biographical listings, see the Martindale-Hubbell Law Directory

MCCUTCHEN, BLANTON, RHODES & JOHNSON, L.L.P. (AV)

1414 Lady Street, P.O. Drawer 11209, 29211
Telephone: 803-799-9791
Telecopier: 803-253-6084
Email: Firm1414@aol.com
Winnsboro, South Carolina Office: 120 West Washington Street, 29180.
Telephone: 803-635-6884.

MEMBERS OF FIRM

Thomas E. McCutchen	Evans Taylor Barnette
Jeter E. Rhodes, Jr.	G. D. Morgan, Jr.
T. English McCutchen, III	John C. Bradley, Jr.
Pope D. Johnson, III	Creighton B. Coleman
William R. Taylor	Ruskin C. Foster

William E. Hopkins, Jr.

(See Next Column)

ASSOCIATE

Anthony W. Livoti

OF COUNSEL

Hoover C. Blanton

Representative Clients: Allstate Insurance Co.; Sears, Roebuck and Co.; J.B. White Co.; Anchor Continental Inc.; Western Fire Insurance Co.; Liberty Mutual Insurance Co.; Southeastern Freight Lines; Continental Life Insurance Co.; State Farm Fire & Casualty Co.

For full biographical listings, see the Martindale-Hubbell Law Directory

MCKAY & GUÉRARD, P.A.

(See Haynsworth, Marion, McKay & Guérard, L.L.P.)

MCKAY & MCKAY, P.A. (AV)

1325 Laurel Street, P.O. Box 7217, 29202
Telephone: 803-256-4645
FAX: 803-765-1839

Douglas McKay, Jr.	Julius W. McKay, II
Daniel R. Settana, Jr.	John R. Delmore

Representative Clients: Americlaim Adjustment Corp.; Amoco Oil Co.; Blue Cross & Blue Shield of South Carolina; Britanco Underwriters, Inc.; Browning-Ferris Industries, Inc.; Homestead Insurance Co.; Lincoln National Life Insurance Co.; Pennsylvania Manufacturers' Association Insurance Co. (PMA); Schneider National Carriers; South Carolina Division of General Services-Insurance Reserve Fund (IRF).

For full biographical listings, see the Martindale-Hubbell Law Directory

MCNAIR LAW FIRM, P.A. (AV)

1301 Gervais Street, P.O. Box 11390, 29211
Telephone: 803-799-9800
Facsimile: 803-799-9804
Email: cfort@mcnair.net
Anderson, South Carolina Office: Carolina First Bank Building, 210 North Main Street, 29261.
Telephone: 864-226-1688.
Facsimile: 864-225-6456.
Charleston, South Carolina Office: 140 East Bay Street, P.O. Box 1431, 29402.
Telephone: 843-723-7831.
Facsimile: 843-722-3227.
Georgetown, South Carolina Office: 121 Screven Street, P.O. Drawer 418, 29442.
Telephone: 843-546-6102.
Facsimile: 843-546-0096.
Greenville, South Carolina Office: 105 East North Street, P.O. Box 447. 29602.
Telephone: 864-271-4940.
Facsimile: 864-233-0423; 864-271-4015.
Hilton Head Island, South Carolina Office: The Jade Building, Suite 204, 52 New Orleans Road, Drawer 7787, 29938.
Telephone: 843-785-5169.
Facsimile: 843-842-3310.
Myrtle Beach, South Carolina Office: Founders Centre, 2411 Oak Street, Suite 403, 29577.
Telephone: 843-444-1107.
Facsimile: 843-444-4729.
Spartanburg, South Carolina Office: Spartan Centre, Suite 306, P.O. Box 5137, 29304.
Telephone: 864-542-1300.
Facsimile: 864-542-0705.
Charlotte, North Carolina Office: Two First Union Center, 301 South Tryon Street, Suite 1615, 28282.
Telephone: 704-347-1170.
Facsimile: 704-347-4467.

Robert E. McNair	Dorothy M. Helms
O. Wayne Corley	Jane W. Trinkley
Charles Porter	Celeste Tiller Jones
Robert W. Dibble, Jr.	Joseph D. Walker
M. John Bowen, Jr.	Michael McNulty Beal
Richard L. C. Sullivan	Deborah Ann Hottel
John W. Currie	Elizabeth Bowe Anders
Hubert E. Yarborough, III	Erik P. Doerring
Carl B. Carruth	William M. Musser
M. Elizabeth Crum	Judith L. McInnis
James P. Fields, Jr.	Julianne Farnsworth
M. Craig Garner, Jr.	Ethan R. Ware
Robert T. Bockman	Jonathan Hastings Nason
John W. Foster	J. Michael Ey
Edwin W. Johnson II	Paul Daniel Harrill
Richard J. Morgan	Robert L. Widener
Sara S. "Sally" Rogers	Edward L. Grimsley

Allen F. Creighton

(See Next Column)

McNair Law Firm P.A.—*Continued*

Wayne R. Covert, Jr.
Robin Curtis Stanton
Linda K. Barr-Efird
James C. Siokos
Stephen D. Searcy
Cynthia Smith Turnipseed
Reginald Wayne Belcher
A. Victor Rawl, Jr.
Wolfgang Buchmaier
Edwin D. Givens
Michael James Seezen
Robert A. Muckenfuss

SPECIAL COUNSEL

Francenia B. Heizer
Sharon Crawley Bramlett
Margaret M. Fox

OF COUNSEL

E. McLeod Singletary
James S. Konduros
Harry M. Lightsey, Jr.
Benjamin Edward Nicholson V

Representative Clients: Fuji Photo Film, Inc.; Georgia-Pacific Corp.; Milliken & Co.; NationsBank Corp.; Norfolk Southern Corp.; Pirelli Cable Corp.; SCANA Corp.; Westinghouse Electric Corp.

For full biographical listings, see the Martindale-Hubbell Law Directory

Ernest J. Nauful, Jr., P.C. (AV)

1321 Lady Street Suite 670, P.O. Box 11866, 29211
Telephone: 803-256-4045
Facsimile: 803-256-7044
Email: nauful@aol.com

Ernest J. Nauful, Jr.

For full biographical listings, see the Martindale-Hubbell Law Directory

Nelson Mullins Riley & Scarborough, L.L.P. (AV)

A Registered Limited Liability Partnership including Professional Corporations
Keenan Building, Third Floor, 1330 Lady Street (29201-3332), P.O. Box 11070, 29211-1070
Telephone: 803-799-2000
Telecopy: 803-256-7500; 733-9499
Email: nmrs.com *URL:* HTTP://WWW.NMRS.COM
Atlanta, Georgia Office: First Union Plaza, Suite 1400, 999 Peachtree Street, N.E., 30309-3964. P.O. Box 77707, 30357-0707.
Telephone: 404-817-6000.
Telecopy: 404-817-6050.
Charleston, South Carolina Office: Liberty Center, Suite 500, 151 Meeting Street, 29401-2239. P.O. Box 1806, 29402-1806.
Telephone: 843-853-5200.
Telecopy: 843-722-8700.
Charlotte, North Carolina Office: Bank of America Corporate Center, Suite 2600, 100 North Tryon Street, 28202-4000.
Telephone: 704-417-3000.
Telecopy: 704-377-4814.
Greenville, South Carolina Office: Poinsett Plaza, 104 South Main Street, Suite 900, 29601. P.O. Box 10084, 29603-0084.
Telephone: 864-250-2300.
Telecopy: 864-232-2925.
Lexington, South Carolina Office: 955 Old Cherokee Road, 29072. P.O. Box 729, 29072.
Telephone: 803-733-9494; 803-799-2000.
Telecopy: 803-957-8226.
Myrtle Beach, South Carolina Office: Founders Centre, Suite 301 2411 North Oak Street, 29577-3165. P.O. Box 3939, 29578-3939.
Telephone: 843-448-3500.
Telecopy: 843-448-3437.
Munich, Germany Office: Brienner Strasse 9, Amiraplatz, 80333.
Telephone: 01149-89-29 09 71 57.
Fax: 01149-89-29 09 72 00.

SPECIAL COUNSEL

David W. Harwell (Resident, Myrtle Beach, SC Office)

OF COUNSEL

Rose-Marie T. Carlisle
Daniel B. Hodgson (Resident, Atlanta, GA Office)
Melissa J. Halstead-White (Resident, Atlanta, GA Office)
Julia Bennett Jagger (Resident, Atlanta, GA Office)
Brian K. Jordan (Resident, Charleston, SC Office)
Kymric Y. Mahnke (Resident, Greenville, SC Office)
Edward P. Riley, Jr. (Resident, Greenville, SC Office)
J. Kenneth Tomlinson, Sr.
Robert P. Wilkins (Resident, Lexington, SC Office)
Robert P. Wilkins, Jr. (Resident, Lexington, SC Office)
William C. Wood, Jr.

MEMBERS OF FIRM

Patrick Henry Nelson (1856-1914)
William Shannon Nelson (1881-1939)
Patrick H. Nelson (1910-1964)
F. Barron Grier, Jr. (1907-1971)
Edward W. Mullins, Sr. (1893-1989)
Claude M. Scarborough, Jr.
Edward W. Mullins, Jr.
R. Bruce Shaw
John U. Bell, III
Joe K. Bridgforth (Resident, Atlanta, GA Office)
William S. Davies, Jr.
Donald H. Stubbs
Robert M. Erwin Jr. (Resident, Myrtle Beach, SC Office)
Robert D. Pannell (Resident, Atlanta, GA Office)

(See Next Column)

MEMBERS OF FIRM (Continued)

John C. Von Lehe, Jr. (Resident, Charleston, SC Office)
Wade H. Logan, III (Resident, Charleston, SC Office)
Dwight F. Drake
Ralston B. Vanzant, II
Stephen G. Morrison
Edward E. Poliakoff
John C. Stewart, Jr. (Resident, Myrtle Beach, SC Office)
Carl B. Epps, III
Richard K. Hines, V (Resident, Atlanta, GA Office)
Philip H. Moïse (Resident, Atlanta, GA Office)
Michael T. Cole (Resident, Charleston, SC Office)
Sara S. Turnipseed (Resident, Atlanta, GA Office)
Sheryl Cudd Blenis Ortmann
John T. Moore
George S. Bailey
John M. Campbell, Jr. (Resident, Greenville, SC Office)
Kenneth L. Millwood (Resident, Atlanta, GA Office)
George B. Wolfe
George B. Cauthen
Richard B. Watson (Resident, Charleston, SC Office)
William C. Hubbard
Stanley S. Jones, Jr. (Resident, Atlanta, GA Office)
Henry M. Burwell (Resident, Greenville, SC Office)
Kenneth E. Young (Resident, Greenville, SC Office)
Jeffrey C. Baxter (Resident, Atlanta, GA Office)
James C. Gray, Jr.
Jeffrey N. Plowman (Resident, Atlanta, GA Office)
Taylor Tapley Daly (Resident, Atlanta, GA Office)
Richard B. Herzog, Jr. (Resident, Atlanta, GA Office)
Sue C. Erwin
Nina Nelson Smith
Charles R. Norris (Resident, Charleston, SC Office)
H. Bryan Ives III (Resident, Charlotte, NC Office)
William R. Asbell, Jr. (Resident, Atlanta, GA Office)
Charles D. Vaughn (Resident, Atlanta, GA Office)
William Bobo, Jr. (Resident, Charleston, SC Office)
Richard H. Willis (Resident, Atlanta, GA Office)
Joel H. Smith
David G. Traylor, Jr.
Robert W. Foster, Jr.
S. Keith Hutto
Clarence Davis
Peter C. Quittmeyer (Resident, Atlanta, GA Office)
Jane E. Jordan (Resident, Atlanta, GA Office)
James R. Kanner (Resident, Atlanta, GA Office)
Richard B. North, Jr. (Resident, Atlanta, GA Office)
Laura Callaway Hart
David E. Dukes
L. Walter Tollison, III (Resident, Greenville, SC Office)
Sylvia King Kochler (Resident, Atlanta, GA Office)
Stuart M. Andrews, Jr.
Karen Aldridge Crawford
Glenn W. Sturm (Resident, Atlanta, GA Office)
Christopher J. Daniels
Richard A. Farrier, Jr. (Resident, Charleston, SC Office)
Jane Thompson Davis (Resident, Charleston, SC Office)
Wade H. Stribling (Resident, Atlanta, GA Office)
Steven M. Wynkoop (Resident, Greenville, SC Office)
Christoph Rückel (Resident, Atlanta, GA Office)
Mark D. Romness (Resident, Charleston, SC Office)
Walter H. Hinton, II (Resident, Greenville, SC Office)
Edward D. Barnhill, Jr.
Gary R. Daves
W. Thomas Causby
Susan Pardue MacDonald (Resident, Myrtle Beach, SC Office)
C. Mark Kelly (Resident, Charlotte, NC Office)
Steven C. Ellingson (Resident, Atlanta, GA Office)
John E. Schmidt, III
Kenneth Allan Janik
John B. Hagerty (Resident, Charleston, SC Office)
Newman Jackson Smith (Resident, Charleston, SC Office)
David E. Hodge (Resident, Greenville, SC Office)
Robert O. Meriwether
Erroll Anne Y. Hodges (Resident, Greenville, SC Office)
Howard A. VanDine, III
Thomas F. Moran (Resident, Myrtle Beach, SC Office)
J. Mark Jones
Neil E. Grayson (Resident, Atlanta, GA Office)
Cherie W. Blackburn (Resident, Charleston, SC Office)
Charles B. Simmons, Jr. (Resident, Charlotte, NC Office)
Joseph M. Melchers
Robert H. Brunson
Linda Wohlbruck Phillips (Resident, Charlotte, NC Office)
Augustus M. Dixon
Lisa Sudderth Burnett (Resident, Atlanta, GA Office)
Francis B. B. Knowlton
Robert W. Pearce, Jr. (Resident, Charleston, SC Office)
Philip Paul Gura (Resident, Atlanta, GA Office)
Bradley E. Wahl (Resident, Atlanta, GA Office)
Tracy E. Tomlin (Resident, Charlotte, NC Office)
James Walker IV (Resident, Atlanta, GA Office)
Edward K. White
Jeanne N. Guest (Resident, Myrtle Beach, SC Office)
A. Marvin Quattlebaum, Jr. (Resident, Greenville, SC Office)
James F. Rogers
B. Rush Smith, III
Elizabeth Scott Moïse
Daniel J. Westbrook
John F. Kuppens
C. Mitchell Brown
Darryl D. Smalls
Sarah Link Hardy (Resident, Atlanta, GA Office)
Susan M. Glenn
Steven A. McKelvey, Jr.
Bernard F. Hawkins, Jr.
N. Keith Emge, Jr. (Resident, Charleston, SC Office)
James K. Lehman
Catherine L. Amspacher (Resident, Charlotte, NC Office)
Kevin A. Hall
Timothy P. Veith (Resident, Charlotte, NC Office)
Angus H. Macaulay, Jr.

(See Next Column)

NELSON MULLINS RILEY & SCARBOROUGH L.L.P., *Columbia—Continued*

MEMBERS OF FIRM (Continued)

Daniel J. Fritze
Deirdre Shelton McCool (Resident, Charleston, SC Office)
Michael W. Hogue
William S. Brown (Resident, Greenville, SC Office)

ASSOCIATES

D. Kay Tennyson
Don Lawrence Kristinik, III
Lisa Woodbury Caldwell (Resident, Charleston, SC Office)
Craig E. Burgess (Resident, Charleston, SC Office)
William H. Latham
R. Leonard Rowe, Jr. (Resident, Charlotte, NC Office)
Robert C. Calamari (Resident, Myrtle Beach, SC Office)
P. Mason Hogue, Jr.
James F. McCrackin (Resident, Myrtle Beach, SC Office)
Zoe Sanders Nettles
Elizabeth M. McMillan (Resident, Greenville, SC Office)
Michelle W. Johnson (Resident, Atlanta, GA Office)
Melinda L. Moseley (Resident, Atlanta, GA Office)
Carsten Alting (Resident, Atlanta, Georgia Office)
Jennifer D. Malinovsky (Resident, Atlanta, GA Office)
Barry S. Herrin (Resident, Atlanta, GA Office)
Kristie Porter Davies
Jennifer A. Gutek
Alice V. Harris
Dominic A. Starr (Resident, Myrtle Beach, SC Office)
Simpson Z. Fant
William H. Foster, III (Resident, Greenville, SC Office)
Terresa R. Tarpley (Resident, Atlanta, GA Office)
Randy A. Faigin (Resident, Atlanta, GA Office)
Susan L. Spencer (Resident, Atlanta, GA Office)
Amy Yager Jenkins (Resident, Charleston, SC Office)
Scott P. Hilsen (Resident, Atlanta, GA Office)
Jeanne M. Lyles (Resident, Charleston, SC Office)
Kimberly D. Holladay (Resident, Atlanta, GA Office)
Rivers S. Stilwell (Resident, Greenville, SC Office)
C. Russell Pickering (Resident, Atlanta, GA Office)
Melissa J. Copeland
James T. Irvin, III
Timothy M. McKissock
Maurice D. Holloway (Resident, Greenville, SC Office)
Melinda Morris Zanoni (Resident, Charlotte, NC Office)
Shonna Watson Felkel (Resident, Greenville, SC Office)
David A. Wisniewski (Resident, Atlanta, GA Office)
Gregory M. Taube (Resident, Atlanta, GA Office)
C. William McDaniel (Resident, Atlanta, GA Office)
James E. Holmes, Jr. (Resident, Atlanta GA Office)
Jonathan R. Coe (Resident, Atlanta, GA Office)
Michael T. Reynolds (Resident, Atlanta, GA Office)
Valerie Palmer Williams (Resident, Greenville, SC Office)
Shannon Smith Stuckey
William Bee Ravenel Lewis
Jason B. Sprenkle (Resident, Charlotte, NC Office)
Andrew L. Howell (Resident, Atlanta, GA Office)
Jeffrey S. Patterson
Lee R. Rimler (Resident, Charlotte, NC Office)
Eric A. Paine (Not admitted in SC)
Mark C. Fava (Resident, Charleston, SC Office)
William J. Ching (Resident, Atlanta, GA Office)
Robert E. Copps (Resident, Atlanta, GA Office)
Courtney A. Crook
Jennifer L. Mallory
Rachel G. Atkin (Not admitted in SC)
Charles S. Verdin, IV (Resident, Greenville, SC Office)
Reinhard von Hennigs (Not admitted in the United States) (Resident, Atlanta, GA Office)
Stefan Lode (Resident, Munich, Germany Office)
Stephanie B. Hope (Resident, Atlanta, GA Office)
Jennifer A. McCoid (Resident, Atlanta, GA Office)
Charles E. Watkins, III (Resident, Atlanta, GA Office)
Philip R. Elzey (Resident, Atlanta, GA Office)
Karen K. Leach (Resident, Atlanta, GA Office)
Donald L. Swift, III (Resident, Atlanta, GA Office)
Bryson M. Geer (Resident, Charleston, SC Office)
Jerome P. Doyle (Resident, Atlanta, GA Office)
Patrick K. McCarthy
John A. Stoker (Resident, Charlotte, NC Office)
J. Brennan Ryan (Resident, Atlanta, GA Office)
Katherine B. Lublin (Resident, Atlanta, GA Office)
Anthony C. Hayes (Not admitted in SC)
Patrick Jones Whelchel (Resident, Atlanta, GA Office)
Rebecca A. Culpepper (Resident, Atlanta, GA Office)
Thomas William McGee, III
Lee Ann Sparks (Resident, Atlanta, GA Office)
James A. D'Alessio
Brandy A. Bayer (Resident, Atlanta, GA Office)
Noah S. Benz (Resident, Atlanta, GA Office)
Travis Dayhuff
J. Drayton Hastie, III
Brett W. Weathersbee
Douglas Lee Lineberry (Resident, Greenville, SC Office)
Kerry D. Angus (Resident, Myrtle Beach, SC Office)
Franklin G. Daniels (Resident, Myrtle Beach, SC Office)
Jennifer L. Williams
Steven R. Wilson (Resident, Atlanta, GA Office)
Nancy W. Norris (Resident, Charlotte, NC Office)
Cristin A. Burke (Resident, Myrtle Beach, SC Office)
Jason R. Wolfersberger (Resident, Atlanta, GA Office)
Kevin J. Heiser

(See Next Column)

ASSOCIATES (Continued)

Alexandra Elizabeth Coates (Resident, Munich, Germany Office)
Janet C. Ford (Resident, Greenville, SC Office)

For full biographical listings, see the Martindale-Hubbell Law Directory

NEXSEN PRUET JACOBS & POLLARD, LLP (AV)

1441 Main Street, 15th Floor, P.O. Drawer 2426, 29202
Telephone: 803-771-8900
Facsimile: 803-253-8277
Email: NPJP@NPJP.COM *URL:* HTTP://WWW.NPJP.COM
Charleston, South Carolina Office: 200 Meeting Street, Suite 301. P.O. Box 486.
Telephone: 803-577-9440.
Facsimile: 803-720-1777.
Greenville, South Carolina Office: 201 West McBee Avenue, Fourth Floor, P.O. Box 10648.
Telephone: 864-370-2211.
Facsimile: 864-282-1177.
Myrtle Beach, South Carolina Office: 2411 Oak Street, Suite 105.
Telephone: 843-445-9688.
Facsimile: 843-445-9949.
Charlotte, North Carolina Office: 212 South Tryon Street, Suite 1700.
Telephone: 704-339-0304.
Facsimile: 704-338-5377.

Paul A. Cooper (1889-1956)
Frank B. Gary (1900-1971)
C. Alvin Brown (1940-1978)

MEMBERS OF FIRM

T. Eugene Allen, III
Mark L. Bender
Wilburn Brewer, Jr.
Henry W. Brown
Patrick F. Brown (Resident, Charlotte, NC Office)
Russell T. Burke
Robert C. Byrd (Resident, Charleston, SC Office)
David Rees Cannon (Resident, Charlotte, NC Office)
Robert D. Coble
Paul A. Dominick (Resident, Charleston, SC Office)
J. James Duggan (Resident, Charleston, SC Office)
Victoria L. Eslinger
David W. Gossett (Resident, Greenville, SC Office)
John B. Hardaway, III (Resident, Greenville, SC Office)
Leon C. Harmon (Resident, Greenville, SC Office)
J. Hayden Harrell (Resident, Charlotte, NC Office)
Robert W. Hassold, Jr. (Resident, Greenville, SC Office)
J. David Hawkins (Resident, Charleston, SC Office)
Julian Hennig, III
Timothy L. Hewson
Robert H. Hull, Jr. (Resident, Charlotte, NC Office)
Russell T. Infinger (Resident, Greenville, SC Office)
Harold W. Jacobs
Patrick Jenkins (Resident, Charlotte, NC Office)
Brian F. Kernaghan (Charleston, SC and Myrtle Beach, SC Offices)
Fred L. Kingsmore, Jr.
G. Marcus Knight
W. Thomas Lavender, Jr.
Susan Batten Lipscomb
Alan M. Lipsitz
W. Leighton Lord III
April C. Lucas
Michael A. Mann
Marcus A. Manos
William Spencer McMaster
Susan Pedrick McWilliams
Julio E. Mendoza, Jr.
Edward G. Menzie
William G. Newsome, III
Matthew J. Norton (Resident, Charleston, SC Office)
Samuel F. Painter
Thomas B. Pollard, Jr.
William A. Pollard
R. Kent Porth
James W. Potter
Pamela J. Roberts
Neil C. Robinson, Jr. (Resident, Charleston, SC Office)
John A. Sowards
Thomas L. Stephenson (Resident, Greenville, SC Office)
Val H. Stieglitz, III
B. Joel Stoudenmire (Resident, Greenville, SC Office)
M. Jeffrey Vinzani (Resident, Charleston, SC Office)
Susan Taylor Wall (Resident, Charleston, SC Office)
Richard W. Wilson (Resident, Charlotte, NC Office)

OF COUNSEL

George E. Darby (Not admitted in SC; Resident, Greenville, SC Office)
Julian J. Nexsen
Joseph Herbert O'Toole (Not admitted in SC; Resident, Greenville, SC Office)
Sean M. Phelan (Resident, Charlotte, NC Office)
Gene V. Pruet
Lee M. Robinson (Resident, Charleston, SC Office)
Charles L. Schwab (Not admitted in SC; Resident, Greenville, SC Office)
John C. B. Smith, Jr.

SPECIAL COUNSEL

Helen Elizabeth Burris (Resident, Greenville, SC Office)
Diane C. Current (Resident, Charleston, SC Office)
David C. Eckstrom
Horacio A. Farach (Not admitted in SC)
Susan A. Lake
Rose Duggan Manos
Burnet R. Maybank, III
William A. Prince
Richard Lee Tapp, Jr. (Resident, Charleston, SC Office)
Oscar A. Towler, III (Resident, Greenville, SC Office)

(See Next Column)

NEXSEN PRUET JACOBS & POLLARD LLP—*Continued*

ASSOCIATES

Beverly K. Ballinger (Resident, Charleston, SC Office)
Ralph W. Barbier III
Laurie A. Becker
Jeanne Marie Born
Daniel James Brown
Elizabeth Herlong Campbell
J. Michelle Childs
John W. Davidson
C. Jones DuBose, Jr.
Charles W. Emory, Jr. (Resident, Greenville, SC Offices)
Elizabethann Loadholt Felder
Bret Galloway (Resident, Greenville, SC Office)
Elizabeth A. Holley (Resident, Greenville, SC Office)
Laura H. Huggins
Mary L. Hughes (Resident, Charleston, SC Office)
Cynthia Bankhead Hutto (Resident, Charleston, SC Office)
Thomas C. R. Legaré, Jr.
James G. Long, III
William G. Lyles III (Resident, Charleston, SC Office)
E. Raymond Moore, III
David J. Parrish (Resident, Charleston, SC Office)
Matthew B. Roberts
Amy E. Simpson (Resident, Charlotte, NC Office)
Sandra S. Snapp (Not admitted in SC; Resident, Greenville, SC Office)
Timothy C. Thompson
Bryan L. Walpole, III (Resident, Charleston, SC Office)
John D. Watts, III (Resident, Greenville, SC Office)
Michael E. Wever

For full biographical listings, see the Martindale-Hubbell Law Directory

PARKER, POE, ADAMS & BERNSTEIN L.L.P. (AV)

1201 Main Street, Suite 1450, 29201
Telephone: 803-255-8000
Facsimile: 803-255-8017
Email: shs@ppab.com
Spartanburg, South Carolina Office: 101 W. St. John Street, Suite 203, 29306.
Telephone: 803-591-2030.
Facsimile: 803-591-2050.
Charlotte, North Carolina Offices: 2500 Charlotte Plaza, 201 South College Street, 28244.
Telephone: 704-372-9000.
Facsimile: 704-334-4706 and South Park Office: The Rotunda, 4201 Congress Street, Suite 145, 28209.
Telephone: 704-556-9600.
Facsimile: 704-556-9601.
South Park Office: The Rotunda, 4201 Congress Street, Suite 145, Charlotte, 28209.
Telephone: 704-556-9600.
Facsimile: 704-556-9601.
Raleigh, North Carolina Office: First Union Capitol Center, 150 Fayetteville Street Mall, Suite 1400, P.O. Box 389, 27602-0389.
Telephone: 919-828-0564.
Facsimile: 919-834-4564.
Frankfurt, Germany Office: Limes Park, Otto-Volger-Strasse 5B, D-65843.
Telephone: (011) (49) 6196-750081.
Telefax: (011) (49) 6196-750088.

PARTNERS

George H. Pretty II
David B. Summer, Jr.
Ronald James Tryon
Stacy K. Weinberg
Brent M. Milgrom, Jr.

ASSOCIATES

Steven J. Pugh
Ray E. Jones

SPECIAL COUNSEL

Faye A. Flowers

Representative Clients: Advantica Restaurant Group (formerly Flagstar Companies); American City Business Journals; Carolina Power and Light; Duke Energy; First Union National Bank; Georgetown Steel; GS Industries; Hoechst Corporation; Kemper National Insurance Companies;N. Schlumberger (USA), Inc.

For full biographical listings, see the Martindale-Hubbell Law Directory

QUINN, PATTERSON & WILLARD (AV)

2019 Park Street, P.O. Box 73, 29202
Telephone: 803-779-6365
Telefax: 803-779-6372
Email: qpw@bellsouth.net

MEMBERS OF FIRM

Michael H. Quinn
Grady L. Patterson, III
Theodore DuBose Willard, Jr.

Approved Attorneys for: Lawyers Title Insurance Corp.

For full biographical listings, see the Martindale-Hubbell Law Directory

RICHARDSON, PLOWDEN, CARPENTER & ROBINSON, P.A. (AV)

1600 Marion Street, P.O. Drawer 7788, 29202
Telephone: 803-771-4400
Telecopy: 803-779-0016
Email: atty@rpcrlaw.com *URL:* http://www.rpcrlaw.com
Myrtle Beach, South Carolina Office: 2103 B Farlow Street, P.O. Box 3646, 29578.
Telephone: 843-448-1008.
FAX: 843-448-1533.

Charles E. Carpenter, Jr.
Frank E. Robinson, II
George C. Beighley
Frederick A. Crawford
Francis M. Mack
Franklin Jennings Smith, Jr.
Leslie A. Cotter, Jr.
Steven W. Hamm
Douglas C. Baxter
Nina Reid Mack
S. Nelson Weston Jr.
Mary Sowell League

Marian Williams Scalise
William C. McDow
Georgia Anna Mitchell
David C. Slough
Stephen C. Lenker, Jr.
David A. Anderson
S. Elizabeth Brosnan
C. Jo Anne Wessinger
Lori S. Murray
Alexander Henry Twedt
Jeff Z. Brooker, III

OF COUNSEL

Donald V. Richardson, III
Charles N. Plowden, Jr.
Michael A. Pulliam

Representative Clients: Insurance: CNA Insurance Co.; Commercial Union Insurance Co.; The Hartford; Kemper Insurance Co.; Pennsylvania National Mutual Casualty Insurance Co.; Wausau Insurance Cos. Real Estate, Corporate and Banking: Richland Memorial Hospital; First Union Bank. Construction: S.C. Department of Transportation.

For full biographical listings, see the Martindale-Hubbell Law Directory

ROGERS TOWNSEND & THOMAS, PC (AV)

1441 Main Street, 10th Floor, P.O. Box 100200, 29202-3200
Telephone: 803-771-7900
Fax: 803-254-6305; 343-7017; 343-7019
URL: http://www.rtt-law.com

Robert Bryan Barnes
B. Michael Brackett
Sherwood M. Cleveland
Harry B. Gregory, Jr.
Clifford O. Koon, Jr.
Albert L. Moses
Eugene F. Rogers
Robert J. Thomas
Joe W. Underwood
Samuel C. Waters
W. Alex Weatherly, Jr.
Robert P. Wood
James C. Leventis
Richard M. Unger
Cheryl H. Fisher
D. Randolph Whitt
Stacey Lynch Hewson
Kendall R. Walker
Wm. Bert Brannon

Glen Paul Caulk
Thomas McRoy Shelley, III
Denis A. Brosnan, Jr.
Paul D. de Holczer

OF COUNSEL

James S. Guignard
Gwendelyn Geidel

LEGAL SUPPORT PERSONNEL

Carol A. Cummings

For full biographical listings, see the Martindale-Hubbell Law Directory

SINKLER & BOYD, P.A. (AV)

Suite 1200 The Palmetto Center, 1426 Main Street, P.O. Box 11889, 29211-1889
Telephone: 803-779-3080
FAX: 803-765-1243
Email: firm@sinklerboyd.com *URL:* http://www.sinklerboyd.com
Charleston, South Carolina Office: 160 East Bay Street, P.O. Box 340.
Telephone: 843-722-3366.
FAX: 843-722-2266.
Greenville, South Carolina Office: 15 South Main Street, Insignia Financial Center on Main, Suite 500, P.O. Box 275.
Telephone: 864-467-1100.
FAX: 864-467-1521.

H. Simmons Tate, Jr.
William C. Boyd
Francis P. Mood
J. Donald Dial, Jr.
Bachman S. Smith III (Resident, Charleston Office)
Manton M. Grier
George S. King, Jr.
Thomas A. Hutcheson (Resident, Charleston Office)
Thomas R. Gottshall
Hamilton Osborne, Jr.
Stephen E. Darling (Resident, Charleston Office)
John P. Linton (Resident, Charleston Office)
Margaret Christian Pope
Harold E. Trask (Resident, Charleston Office)
Charlton deSaussure, Jr. (Resident, Charleston Office)
Marvin D. Infinger (Resident, Charleston Office)
John C. Bruton, Jr.
F. Mitchell Johnson, Jr. (Resident, Charleston Office)
Michael D. Jones (Resident, Charleston Office)
Benton D. Williamson
John B. McArthur
David M. Swanson (Resident, Charleston Office)

(See Next Column)

SINKLER & BOYD P.A., *Columbia—Continued*

Robert S. Galloway, III (Resident, Greenville Office)
Clarke W. DuBose
Terri Morrill Lynch (Resident, Charleston Office)
Randolph B. Epting
Steve A. Matthews
Robert Y. Knowlton
Suzanne Hulst Clawson
William H. Short, Jr.
Theodore B. DuBose
Thomas C. Hildebrand, Jr. (Resident, Charleston Office)
John M. G. McLeod
Robert W. Buffington
Frank W. Cureton
Bert Glenn Utsey III (Resident, Charleston Office)
Charles H. Gibbs, Jr. (Resident, Charleston Office)
Stanley H. McGuffin
John K. Van Duys
John H. Tiller (Resident, Charleston Office)
Roy A. Howell III (Resident, Charleston Office)
Edward K. Pritchard, III (Resident, Charleston Office)
Henry J. White
Tara Elizabeth Nauful
John F. Emerson
James Y. Becker

Joseph D. Thompson, III (Resident, Charleston Office)
Julie Oswald Medich (Resident, Charleston Office)
Joseph D. Clark
M. Todd Haynie, III
James L. Ward, Jr.
Kirsten L. Barr (Resident, Charleston Office)
B. Eric Shytle

OF COUNSEL

Martin C. McWilliams, Jr.
Paul M. Platte

Attorneys for: Wachovia Bank, N.A.; First Union National Bank; Westvaco Corp.; American Cyanamid Co.; Waste Management of North America, Inc.; Sonoco Products; Lawyers Title Insurance Corp.

For full biographical listings, see the Martindale-Hubbell Law Directory

TOMPKINS AND MCMASTER (AV)

Palmetto Building, Fourth Floor, 1400 Main Street, P.O. Box 7337, 29202
Telephone: 803-799-4499
Telefax: 803-252-2240

MEMBERS OF FIRM

Frank G. Tompkins (1874-1956)
Frank G. Tompkins, Jr. (1908-1973)
Elizabeth Eldridge (1895-1976)
John Gregg McMaster
Henry Dargan McMaster
George Hunter McMaster
Frank Barnwell McMaster

ASSOCIATE

Bryan P. Stirling
Karl S. Bowers

OF COUNSEL

Joseph D. McMaster

LEGAL SUPPORT PERSONNEL

Martin J. McClellan (Office Manager)

For full biographical listings, see the Martindale-Hubbell Law Directory

TURNER, PADGET, GRAHAM & LANEY, P.A. (AV)

Seventeenth Floor, 1901 Main Street, P.O. Box 1473, 29202
Telephone: 803-254-2200
Telecopy: 803-799-3957
Florence, South Carolina Office: Fourth Floor, 1831 West Evans Street, P.O. Box 5478, 29502.
Telephone: 843-662-9008.
Fax: 843-667-0828.
Charleston, South Carolina Office: 21 Broad Street, 1st Floor, P.O. Box 836, 29402.
Telephone: 843-723-1622.
Fax: 843-577-3369.

Ronald E. Boston
W. Duvall Spruill
Charles E. Hill
Thomas C. Salane
Danny C. Crowe
R. Wayne Byrd (Resident, Florence, SC, Office)
John S. Wilkerson, III (Resident, Florence, SC, Office)
Steven W. Ouzts
David G. Fawcett
Lanneau William Lambert, Jr.
John E. Cuttino
Arthur E. Justice, Jr. (Resident, Florence, SC, Office)
Edward W. Laney, IV
Elbert S. Dorn
Hugh M. Claytor (Resident, Florence, SC, Office)
Vernon F. Dunbar
Franklin G. Shuler, Jr.
R. Todd Sherpy
J. Kenneth Carter, Jr.
Michael E. Chase
O. Carlisle Edwards, Jr.
Richard L. Hinson (Resident, Florence, SC, Office)
Jeffrey L. Payne (Resident, Florence, SC, Office)
Wilson S. Sheldon (Resident, Florence, SC, Office)
Walter H. Barefoot (Resident, Florence, SC Office)
Michael S. Hopewell (Resident, Florence, SC, Office)
Teresa A. Arnold

OF COUNSEL

Michael S. Church
Stephen A. Husman
Laura Chandler Rublee (Resident, Florence, SC, Office)

(See Next Column)

David W. Keller, Jr. (Resident, Florence, SC Office)
William O. Higgins
Jessica C. Moe (Resident, Charleston, SC, Office)
Curtis L. Ott
Julie Jeffords Moose (Resident, Florence, SC, Office)
Michael C. Abbott (Resident, Florence, SC, Office)
David S. Cobb (Resident, Charleston, SC, Office)
Donnell G. Jennings
D. Andrew Williams
Gretchen D. Holland
William C. Barnes, Jr. (Resident, Florence, SC, Office)
Cynthia C. Dooley
Richard C. Burke (Resident, Florence, SC, Office)
Steven R. LeBlanc
Tiffni Drawdy Shealy (Resident, Florence, SC, Office)
Mark B. Tinsley
Patrick W. Carr (Resident, Florence, SC, Office)
James David Smith, Jr. (Resident, Florence, SC, Office)

For full biographical listings, see the Martindale-Hubbell Law Directory

*CONWAY,** Horry Co.

MCCUTCHEON, MCCUTCHEON & BAXTER, P.A. (AV)

McCutcheon Building, 208 Elm Street, P.O. Box 1003, 29528
Telephone: 843-248-7225
Telecopier: 843-248-3568
Email: mmb4@gte.net

John Betts McCutcheon (1915-1997)
John Betts McCutcheon, Jr.
Mary Ruth M. Baxter

Lisa A. Thomas
Arrigo P. Carotti

Representative Clients: State of South Carolina, Division of General Services, Insurance Reserve Fund; South Carolina Medical Malpractice Joint Underwriters Assn.; Virginia Professional Underwriters, Inc.; Companion Property and Casualty Co.; Blue Cross and Blue Shield of South Carolina, Inc.; National Indemnity Co.; American Continental Insurance Co.; The Travelers Insurance Group.

For full biographical listings, see the Martindale-Hubbell Law Directory

THE THOMPSON LAW FIRM, P.A. (AV)

1318 Third Avenue, P.O. Box 1533, 29528
Telephone: 843-248-5741
Fax: 843-248-5112
Myrtle Beach, South Carolina Office: 1314 Professional Drive, P.O. Box 1290.
Telephone: 843-692-2628.
Fax: 843-692-0918.

John C. Thompson
John P. Henry
Linda Weeks Gangi
Emma Ruth Brittain
Lynn Gatlin Stevens
Philip C. Thompson
Catherine M. Hedgepath

Representative Clients: NationsBank; Burroughs & Chapin Co., Inc.; Canal Industries, Inc.; State Farm Mutual Automobile Insurance Co.; State Farm Fire and Casualty Insurance Co.; Horry County; Nationwide Insurance Co.; United Carolina Bank; First Union National Bank.
Reference: NationsBank.

For full biographical listings, see the Martindale-Hubbell Law Directory

*GAFFNEY,** Cherokee Co.

WINTER & RHODEN (AV)

221 East Floyd Baker Boulevard, P.O. Box 1937, 29342
Telephone: 864-489-8128; 487-2289
Fax: 864-489-8806
URL: http://www.lawyers.com/w&rlaw

William E. Winter, Jr.
William G. Rhoden

Representative Clients: NationsBank of South Carolina.
Approved Attorneys for: Chicago Title Insurance Co.; Lawyers Title Insurance Corp.; Chicago Title Insurance Co.

For full biographical listings, see the Martindale-Hubbell Law Directory

*GREENVILLE,** Greenville Co.

HAYNSWORTH, MARION, MCKAY & GUÉRARD, L.L.P. (AV)

75 Beattie Place, Eleventh Floor, P.O. Box 2048, 29602
Telephone: 864-240-3200
Facsimile: 864-240-3300
Columbia, South Carolina Office: Suite 2400 Affinity Building, 1201 Main Street, P.O. Drawer 7157, 29202
Telephone: 803-765-1818.
Facsimile: 803-765-2399.
Charleston, South Carolina Office: 134 Meeting Street, P.O. Box 1119, 29402.
Telephone: 843-722-7606.
Facsimile: 843-724-8016.

(See Next Column)

HAYNSWORTH, MARION, MCKAY & GUÉRARD L.L.P.—*Continued*

MEMBERS OF FIRM

H.J. Haynsworth (1859-1941)
Clement Furman Haynsworth (1886-1953)
James M. Perry (1894-1964)
Eugene Bryant (1902-1969)
H.R. Stevenson, Jr. (1915-1990)
Andrew B. Marion (1920-1995)
William Francis Marion (1923-1995)
Robert S. Galloway, Jr. (1928-1997)
Theodore B. Guérard (1930-1997)
Thomas K. Johnstone, Jr. (Retired)
Fred D. Cox, Jr. (Retired)
G. Dewey Oxner, Jr.
Jesse C. Belcher
Charles E. McDonald, Jr.
William E. Shaughnessy
James B. Pressly, Jr.
H. Donald Sellers
Andrew J. White, Jr.
Ellis M. Johnston, II
Joseph J. Blake, Jr.
Thomas H. Coker, Jr.
W. Francis Marion, Jr.
John B. McLeod
Bryan Francis Hickey
Richard B. Kale, Jr.
J. Wesley Crum III
Kathleen Crum McKinney
Anne S. Ellefson
Edwin Brown Parkinson, Jr.
H. Sam Mabry, III
David Hill Keller
F. Matlock Elliott
Knox H. White
Moffatt Grier McDonald
Amy Miller Snyder
Arthur Frazier McLean, III
Eric Keith Englebardt
Donna S. Kivett
J. Derrick Quattlebaum
Sarah M. (Sally) Purnell
Frank T. Davis, III
Jeffrey S. Jones

ASSOCIATES

Stephen P. Williams
Christine M. Gantt
Boyd B. Nicholson, Jr.
Matthew P. Utecht
Harold J. Willson, Jr.
William David Conner
Tracy Welsh Tiddy
Jeffrey R. Gilbert
Christopher R. Antley
Christina M. Condon
Jeremy L. Cook
Sherry L. Boswell
E. Tyler Smith
Thomas M. Sears, Jr.
J. Ben Alexander

OF COUNSEL

Julius W. McKay
Donald L. Ferguson
O. G. Calhoun, Jr.
Maye R. Johnson, Jr.

SPECIAL COUNSEL

Nancy Lark Schulze
John Adams Hodge
Theodore J. Hopkins Jr.

Counsel for: Duke Energy Corporation; Liberty Mutual Insurance Co.; Equitable Life Assurance Society of the United States; St. Paul Insurance Group; Allstate Insurance Co.; Fluor-Daniel Corp.; Synalloy Corp.; Greenville Hospital System.

For full biographical listings, see the Martindale-Hubbell Law Directory

HAYNSWORTH, PERRY, BRYANT, MARION & JOHNSTONE

(See Haynsworth, Marion, McKay & Guérard, L.L.P.)

LEATHERWOOD WALKER TODD & MANN, P.C. (AV)

100 East Coffee Street, P.O. Box 87, 29602
Telephone: 864-242-6440
FAX: 864-240-2477
Email: leatherwood@lwtm.com *URL:* http://www.lwtm.com
Spartanburg, South Carolina Office: 1451 East Main Street, P.O. Box 3188.
Telephone: 864-582-4365.
Telefax: 864-583-8961.

D. B. Leatherwood (1896-1989)
John E. Johnston
Harvey G. Sanders, Jr.
David A. Quattlebaum, III
O. Doyle Martin
Joseph E. Major
Duke K. McCall, Jr.
Earle G. Prevost
J. Richard Kelly
H. Spencer King (Resident, Spartanburg Office)
A. Marvin Quattlebaum
Jack H. Tedards, Jr.
F. Marion Hughes
Michael J. Giese
Mark R. Holmes
William L. Dennis
Bradford Neal Martin
Natalma M. McKnew
Robert A. deHoll
Richard L. Few, Jr.
Steven E. Farrar
Nancy Hyder Robinson
Robert D. Inglis
Russell D. Ghent
Samuel Wright Outten
Eugene C. McCall, Jr.
Alexander Hray, Jr. (Resident, Spartanburg Office)
H. Gibert Sanders, III
Thomas W. Epting
James L. Rogers, Jr.
Sandra L. W. Miller
Frank C. Williams III
Robert D. Moseley, Jr.
James T. Hewitt

Kurt M. Rozelsky
Cathy H. Dunn (Resident, Spartanburg Office)
J. Tod Hyche
John Patrick Riordan
Laurel R. S. Blair
Jamile J. Francis, III
Seann Anderson Gray
Daniel C. Patterson
Margaret C. McGee (Resident, Spartanburg Office)
William B. Swent
McLaurin M. McDonald
Michele Fuller Lyerly
Peter A. Rutledge

(See Next Column)

COUNSEL

Wesley M. Walker
J. D. Todd, Jr.
Fletcher C. Mann
James H. Watson
Tara H. Snyder
J. Brantley Phillips, Jr.

Counsel for: NationsBank; John D. Hollingsworth on Wheels, Inc.; Canal Insurance Co.; Hollingsworth Saco Lowell Inc.
Representative Clients: Springs Industries, Inc.; General Motors Acceptance Corp.; Suitt Construction Co.

For full biographical listings, see the Martindale-Hubbell Law Directory

LOVE, THORNTON, ARNOLD & THOMASON, P.A. (AV)

410 East Washington Street, P.O. Box 10045, 29603
Telephone: 864-242-6360
Telefax: 864-271-7972
Email: lovelaw@globalvision.net *URL:* http://www.ltatlaw.com
Greer, South Carolina Office: 1115 West Poinsett Street, P.O. Box 449, 29652-0449.
Telephone: 864-879-0144.
Telefax: 864-879-0149.

James L. Love (1892-1972)
Ben C. Thornton (1908-1968)
Belton O. Thomason, Jr. (1926-1993)
W. Harold Arnold (1907-1998)
William M. Hagood, III
Donald R. McAlister
Theron G. Cochran
Mason A. Goldsmith
S. Gray Walsh
Carroll H. Roe, Jr.
Jennings L. Graves, Jr.
Jack D. Griffeth
William A. Coates
David L. Moore, Jr.
James H. Cassidy
V. Clark Price
Marion P. Sieffert
James A. Blair, III

Judith Ward Lineback
D. Sean Faulkner
James Andrew Smith
Amy G. Richmond
Robert Scott Boatwright
Jacqueline Patterson

OF COUNSEL

Edward J. Hamilton, Jr.
John B. Duggan (Resident, Greer Office)

Counsel for: Avado Brands, Inc.; Greenville Association of Realtors, Inc.

For full biographical listings, see the Martindale-Hubbell Law Directory

WILLIAMS & HENRY, PROFESSIONAL ASSOCIATION (AV)

513 East Washington Street, P.O. Box 10307, 29603
Telephone: 864-233-1609
Fax: 864-232-7807
Email: lawfirm@williamshenry.com

Ray R. Williams (1899-1987)
J. A. Henry (1899-1971)
Ray R. Williams, Jr.
Craig H. Allen

For full biographical listings, see the Martindale-Hubbell Law Directory

*GREENWOOD,** Greenwood Co.

BURNS, MCDONALD, BRADFORD, PATRICK & TINSLEY, L.L.P. (AV)

414 Main Street, P.O. Box 1547, 29648
Telephone: 864-229-2511
Fax: 864-229-5327
Email: burnslaw@emeraldis.com

William B. Patrick, Jr.
William D. Tinsley, Jr.
Stephen D. Baggett
Kenneth W. Poston
Roy R. Hemphill
D. Welborn Adams
W. Lee Roper, II
Steven M. Pruitt

Robert W. Cone

OF COUNSEL

J. William Bradford
James E. McDonald
Howard Lamar Burns (1914-1995)

Attorney For: First Union National Bank; NationsBank; Greenwood Mills; Park Seed Co.; Self Memorial Hospital; County of Greenwood; Allstate Insurance Co.; Cincinnati Insurance Co.; Liberty Mutual Insurance Co.; Nationwide Mutual Insurance Co.; State Farm Mutual Insurance Co.

For full biographical listings, see the Martindale-Hubbell Law Directory

HILTON HEAD ISLAND, Beaufort Co.

WILLIAM M. BOWEN, P.A. (AV)

The Jade Building, 52 New Orleans Road, Suite 202, 29928
Telephone: 843-842-5000
Fax: 843-686-5990

William M. Bowen

Approved Attorneys for: Lawyers Title Ins. Co.; NationsBank; Anchor Bank; Wachovia National Bank.
References: First Union National Bank; NationsBank; The Anchor Bank; Prudential Securities; First Carolina Bank; Lighthouse Mortgage Company.

(See Next Column)

WILLIAM M. BOWEN, P.A., *Hilton Head Island—Continued*

For full biographical listings, see the Martindale-Hubbell Law Directory

MYRTLE BEACH, Horry Co.

BELLAMY, RUTENBERG, COPELAND, EPPS, GRAVELY & BOWERS, P.A. (AV)

1000 29th Avenue North, P.O. Box 357, 29578
Telephone: 843-448-2400
Telecopier: 843-448-3022

Howell V. Bellamy, Jr.
John K. Rutenberg
John E. Copeland
Claude M. Epps, Jr.
David R. Gravely
Edward B. Bowers, Jr.
Bradley D. King
Henrietta U. Golding
M. Edwin Hinds, Jr.
Jill F. Griffith
Kathryn M. Cook
David B. Miller
C. Winfield Johnson, III
Sarah A. Johnson
Douglas M. Zayicek
Jeffrey W. King
Mary Anna Malpass
Martin Charles Dawsey

Representative Clients: Dargan Construction Co.; Coastal Federal Savings Bank; Sands Investments; Wachovia Bank of South Carolina; AVX Corp.; Bank of America; Parthenon Insurance Co.; Burroughs & Chapin Co.; International Paper Co.; Hospital Corporation of America.

For full biographical listings, see the Martindale-Hubbell Law Directory

THE THOMPSON LAW FIRM, P.A. (AV)

1314 Professional Drive, P.O. Box 1290, 29578-1290
Telephone: 843-692-2628
Fax: 843-692-0918
Conway, South Carolina Office: 1318 Third Avenue, P.O. Box 1533.
Telephone: 843-248-5741.
Fax: 843-248-5112.

J. Jackson Thomas
Clay D. Brittain, III
G. Michael Smith

Russell V. Traw
Thomas C. Stanley
Stacy L. Stanley

Representative Clients: The Citizens and Southern National Bank of South Carolina; Burroughs & Collins Co.; Canal Industries, Inc.; Nationwide Mutual Insurance Co.; State Farm Mutual Automobile Insurance Co.; State Farm Fire and Casualty Insurance Co.; Horry County; United Carolina Bank; First Union National Bank; First Financial Savings Bank, Inc.

For full biographical listings, see the Martindale-Hubbell Law Directory

*ORANGEBURG,** Orangeburg Co.

HORGER, BARNWELL & REID, L.L.P. (AV)

1459 Amelia Street, P.O. Drawer 329, 29116-0329
Telephone: 803-531-3000
Facsimile: 803-531-3030
URL: http://www.lawyers.com/horgerbarnwell&reid

MEMBERS OF FIRM

Charlton B. Horger (1914-1997)
Charles Brison Barnwell, Jr.
Robert R. Horger
Samuel F. Reid, Jr.
Robert F. McCurry, Jr.
Andrew Scott Culbreath

General Counsel for: First National Bank Corp.; Farmers and Merchants Bank of S.C.; First National Bank of S.C., Holly Hill, S.C.; The Regional Medical Center of Orangeburg & Calhoun Counties.
Local Counsel for: South Carolina Electric & Gas Co.
Representative Clients: Maryland Casualty Co.; Nationwide Insurance Co.; Federated Mutual Insurance Co.

For full biographical listings, see the Martindale-Hubbell Law Directory

PAWLEYS ISLAND, Georgetown Co.

DANIEL & DANIEL (AV)

10 B Pawleys Station, 10080 Ocean Highway (US 17 S), P.O. Box 857, 29585
Telephone: 843-237-4792
Email: reesedaniel@email.msn.com

MEMBERS OF FIRM

J. Reese Daniel
Michael R. Daniel

For full biographical listings, see the Martindale-Hubbell Law Directory

ROCK HILL, York Co.

KENNEDY COVINGTON LOBDELL & HICKMAN, L.L.P. (AV)

First Union Center, 113 E. Main Street, 29730
Telephone: 803-329-7600
Fax: 803-329-7677
URL: http://www.kclh.com
Charlotte, North Carolina Office: Bank of America Corporate Center, Suite 4200, 100 North Tryon Street, 28202-4006.
Telephone: 704-331-7400.
Fax: 704-331-7598.
Raleigh, North Carolina Office: Two Hannover Square, 434 Fayetteville State Mall, P.O. Box 1070, 27602-1070.
Telephone: 919-743-7300.
Fax: 919-743-7358.

RESIDENT PARTNERS

James C. Hardin III
Stephen R. McCrae, Jr.
Herbert W. Hamilton
W. Henry Sipe III
Beverly A. Carroll

SPECIAL COUNSEL

Robert R. Carpenter
Nancy Lynne Olah

RESIDENT ASSOCIATES

Daniel J. Ballou
W. Keith Martens
Robert W. McCleave
R. Alexander Sullivan

Representative Clients: Bank of America and Subsidiaries; Crescent Resources, Inc.; Duke Energy Corp.; First Union Corp. and Subsidiaries; Fluor Daniel; Guilford Mills, Inc.; Lance, Inc.; The Lundy Packing Co.; Piedmont Health Care System; Summit Properties, Inc.

For full biographical listings, see the Martindale-Hubbell Law Directory

ROBINSON, BRADSHAW & HINSON, P.A. (AV)

The Guardian Building, 223 East Main Street, Suite 600 Post Office Drawer 12070, 29731
Telephone: 803-325-2900
FAX: 803-325-2929
Email: ylevine@rbh.com *URL:* http://www.rbh.com
Charlotte, North Carolina Office: 101 North Tryon Street, Suite 1900, 28246-1900.
Telephone: 704-377-2536.
Fax: 704-378-4000.
Telex: 802046. Internet: http://www.rbh.com.

David A. White
Carroll M. Pitts, Jr.
Benjamin A. Johnson
Duncan E. Alford
David L. Little, Jr.
Stephen M. Cox

For full biographical listings, see the Martindale-Hubbell Law Directory

SPENCER & SPENCER, PROFESSIONAL ASSOCIATION (AV)

226 East Main Street Suite 200, P.O. Box 790, 29731-6790
Telephone: 803-327-7191
Telecopier: 803-327-3868
Email: spencer@spencerfirm.com

C. E. Spencer (1849-1921)
C. W. F. Spencer (1876-1956)
C. W. F. Spencer, Jr. (1911-1985)
William C. Spencer
William L. Ferguson
Emil W. Wald
James W. Sheedy
Paul W. Dillingham
W. Mark White
W. Chaplin Spencer, Jr.

Anne Elizabeth Stelts

Representative Clients: Banking: NationsBank; Wachovia Bank of S.C., N.A.. Commercial: United Technologies Corporation; Rock Hill Zamias Limited Partnership, d/b/a Rock Hill Galleria Mall. Insurance: Hartford Accident and Indemnity Co.; Maryland Casualty Co. Local Government: City of Rock Hill; Rock Hill Economic Development Corporation.
Approved Attorneys for: Chicago Title Insurance Co.; First American Title Insurance Co.

For full biographical listings, see the Martindale-Hubbell Law Directory

*SPARTANBURG,** Spartanburg Co.

HOLCOMBE, BOMAR, GUNN AND BRADFORD, P.A. (AV)

Advantica Plaza, 203 East Main Street, P.O. Drawer 1897, 29304-1897
Telephone: 864-585-4273
Telecopier: 864-585-3844
Email: hbgb@teleplex.net

Neville Holcombe (1902-1983)
Horace L. Bomar (1912-1994)
William U. Gunn
H. Leland Bomar
Koger McIntosh Bradford
Perry D. Boulier
William B. Darwin, Jr.

S. Sterling Laney, III
Ginger D. Goforth
Walter M. White
Stacey Campbell Davis

(See Next Column)

HOLCOMBE, BOMAR, GUNN AND BRADFORD P.A.—*Continued*

OF COUNSEL

Robert L. Wynn, III

Representative Clients: Advantica Restaurant Group, Inc.; Denny's, Inc.; Wachovia Bank of South Carolina, N.A.; Community Cash Stores; Liberty Mutual Insurance Cos.; Mary Black Memorial Hospital, Inc.; Metromont Materials Corp.; S.C. Insurance Reserve Fund (State Budget and Control Board).

For full biographical listings, see the Martindale-Hubbell Law Directory

LEATHERWOOD WALKER TODD & MANN, P.C. (AV)

1451 East Main Street, P.O. Box 3188, 29304-3188
Telephone: 864-582-4365
Telefax: 864-585-8961
Email: leatherwood@lwtm.com *URL:* http://www.lwtm.com
Greenville, South Carolina Office: 100 East Coffee Street, P.O. Box 87.
Telephone: 864-242-6440.
FAX: 864-240-2477.

H. Spencer King
Alexander Hray, Jr.

Cathy H. Dunn
Margaret C. McGee

For full biographical listings, see the Martindale-Hubbell Law Directory

LYLES, DARR & CLARK (AV)

240 Magnolia Street, 29304-5726
Telephone: 864-585-4806
Telecopier: 864-585-4810
Mailing Address: P.O. Box 5726, Spartanburg, 29304-5726

William C. Lyles (Retired)
Frank A. Lyles
Terry F. Clark
Kenneth E. Darr, Jr.

ASSOCIATE

Maxie G. Jolley, II

Representative Clients: General: Triangle Ice Co. (manufacturer and distributor of ice products and fuels); ChemPro, Inc. (manufacturer of Mean Green products); Hammond-Brown-Jennings Company (retail furniture stores); Converse College. Financial: Woodruff Federal Savings and Loan Association. Real Estate Development and Construction: L.P. Pitts Development Corp.; Lanford Properties; Cannon Roofing Co., Inc.
Reference: Wachovia Bank, N.A.

For full biographical listings, see the Martindale-Hubbell Law Directory

PARKER, POE, ADAMS & BERNSTEIN L.L.P. (AV)

101 W. St. John Street, Suite 203, 29306
Telephone: 864-591-2030
Facsimile: 864-591-2050
Email: shs@ppab.com
Columbia, South Carolina Office: 1201 Main Street, Suite 1450, 29201.
Telephone: 803-255-8000.
Facsimile: 803-255-8017.
Charlotte, North Carolina Office: 2500 Charlotte Plaza, 201 South College Street, 28244.
Telephone: 704-372-9000.
Facsimile: 704-334-4706.
South Park Office: The Rotunda, 4201 Congress Street, Suite 145, Charlotte, 28209.
Telephone: 704-556-9600.
Facsimile: 704-556-9601.
Raleigh, North Carolina Office: First Union Capitol Center, 150 Fayetteville Street Mall, Suite 1400, P.O. Box 389, 27602-0389.
Telephone: 919-828-0564.
Facsimile: 919-834-4564.
Frankfurt, Germany Office: Limes Prk, Otto-Volger-Strasse 5B, D-65843.
Telephone: (011) (49) 6196-750081.
Telefax: (011) (49) 6196-750088.

PARTNERS

George H. Pretty II
T. Alexander Evins
Kevin A. Dunlap
Stacy K. Weinberg
Brent M. Milgrom, Jr.

SPECIAL COUNSEL

James B. Drennan, III

For full biographical listings, see the Martindale-Hubbell Law Directory

PERRIN, PERRIN, MANN & PATTERSON, L.L.P. (AV)

200 Library Street, P.O. Box 1655, 29304
Telephone: 864-582-5461
Fax: 864-583-5235
Email: ppm&p@teleplex.net

L. W. Perrin (1918-1980)

OF COUNSEL

Edward P. Perrin

(See Next Column)

MEMBERS OF FIRM

Franklin M. Mann
Dwight F. Patterson, Jr.
Lawrence E. Flynn, Jr.
William O. Pressley, Jr.

General Counsel for: Carolina Cash Co.; Spartanburg Sanitary Sewer District.

For full biographical listings, see the Martindale-Hubbell Law Directory

SURFSIDE BEACH, Horry Co.

THE FLOYD LAW FIRM PC (AV)

823 Surfside Drive, P.O. Drawer 14607, 29587-4607
Telephone: 843-238-5141
Fax: 843-238-9060
URL: http://www.golflaw.com
Email: dbfloyd@floydlaw.com *URL:* http://www.floydlaw.com
Lake City, South Carolina Office: 207 John Street, P.O. Box 1405.
Telephone: 843-394-2833.
Fax: 843-394-7207.

Dalton B. Floyd, Jr.

Frank J. Bryan
Ronald J. Maas
J. Matthew Dove

Representative Clients: Burroughs and Chapin Co.; The Anchor Bank; NationsBank; G. L. Sports, Inc.; Glenn's Bay, Inc.; First National South; Wachesaw Development, LLC; Thomas Management Co. (KFC).

For full biographical listings, see the Martindale-Hubbell Law Directory

*WALHALLA,** Oconee Co.

LARRY C. BRANDT, P.A. (AV)

205 West Main Street, P.O. Drawer 738, 29691
Telephone: 864-638-5406
864-638-7873
Email: lbrandt@innova.net

Larry C. Brandt

LEGAL SUPPORT PERSONNEL

Debra C. Miller

For full biographical listings, see the Martindale-Hubbell Law Directory

SOUTH DAKOTA

*DEADWOOD,** Lawrence Co.

CHRISTENSEN & FREDERICKSON LAW OFFICES (AV)

68 Sherman Street, Suite 311, 57732
Telephone: 605-578-1953; 605-347-0052; 605-644-0040
Fax: 605-578-3078
Email: cnflaw@mato.com

Steven M. Christensen
John R. Frederickson

For full biographical listings, see the Martindale-Hubbell Law Directory

LEAD, Lawrence Co.

FULLER, TELLINGHUISEN, GORDON & PERCY, P.C. (AV)

203 West Main Street, P.O. Box 898, 57754
Telephone: 605-584-2440
Fax: 605-584-1979
Email: leadlaw@mato.com
Spearfish, South Dakota Office: 132 East Illinois, 57783.
Telephone: 605-642-8080.
Fax: 605-642-1756. E-mail: spflaw@mato.com

A. P. Fuller
Roger A. Tellinghuisen
Bradley P. Gordon
Michelle Palmer Percy

Representative Clients: Homestake Mining Co.; Hotel Franklin & Gaming; Black Hills Novelty/Automatic Vending, Inc.; Northern Hills General Hospital; Lantis Enterprises, Inc.; Norwest Bank South Dakota N.A.; Lead-Deadwood Independent School District # 40-1; City of Lead.

For full biographical listings, see the Martindale-Hubbell Law Directory

*MADISON,** Lake Co.

LAMMERS, LAMMERS & KLEIBACKER, L.L.P. (AV)

108 North Egan, P.O. Box 45, 57042-0045
Telephone: 605-256-6677
FAX: 605-256-6679

(See Next Column)

LAMMERS, LAMMERS & KLEIBACKER L.L.P., *Madison—Continued*

MEMBERS OF FIRM

J. H. Lammers (1893-1983)
Jerome B. Lammers
Wilson M. Kleibacker, Jr.

Local Attorneys for: Northwestern Public Service Co., Huron, South Dakota.
Attorneys for: Madison Farmers Elevator Co.; Chester, Brant Lake, Lake Madison, Pickerel Lake and Lake Poinsett Sanitary Districts; Prostrollo Motor Co.; Norwest Bank; Green Thumb Commodities; Big Sioux and Minnehaha Rural Water Systems; Dakotaland Farm Equipment, Inc.; T & R Electric Supply.
Reference: Norwest Bank.

*PIERRE,** Hughes Co.

MAY, ADAM, GERDES & THOMPSON, L.L.P. (AV)

503 South Pierre Street, P.O. Box 160, 57501-0160
Telephone: 605-224-8803
Telecopier: 605-224-6289
Email: 2042171@mcimail.com

MEMBERS OF FIRM

Glenn W. Martens (1881-1963)
Karl Goldsmith (1885-1966)
Thomas C. Adam
David A. Gerdes
Charles M. Thompson
Robert B. Anderson
Brent A. Wilbur
Timothy M. Engel
Michael F. Shaw

OF COUNSEL

Warren W. May

General Counsel for: South Dakota Bankers Assn.; BankWest; South Dakota Medical Assn.; Dakota State Bank; South Dakota Electric Utility Companies.
Representative Clients: Travelers Insurance Co.; American States Insurance Co.; Montana-Dakota Utilities; Firemans Fund; MCI Telecommunications Corp.

For full biographical listings, see the Martindale-Hubbell Law Directory

OLINGER, LOVALD, ROBBENNOLT, MCCAHREN AND REIMERS, P.C. (AV)

117 East Capitol Avenue, P.O. Box 66, 57501-3105
Telephone: 605-224-8851
Toll Free: 1-877-225-5548
Telecopier: 605-224-8269
Email: olinger@sd-cybernex.net

Ronald D. Olinger
John S. Lovald
James Robbennolt
Lee C. (Kit) McCahren
Wade A. Reimers

General Counsel For: St. Mary's Healthcare Center of Pierre, South Dakota; South Dakota Horsemen's Association; South Dakota Real Estate Commission.
Representative Clients: South Dakota Retailers Association; Anderson Tire Co.; UST Public Affairs, Inc.; Philip Morris Management Corporation/-Miller Brewing Company; Travelers Insurance; AT&T.
Reference: American State Bank, Pierre, South Dakota.

For full biographical listings, see the Martindale-Hubbell Law Directory

RITER, MAYER, HOFER, WATTIER & BROWN, L.L.P. (AV)

Professional & Executive Building, 319 South Coteau Street, P.O. Box 280, 57501
Telephone: 605-224-5825
Fax: 605-224-7102
Email: riterlaw@sd.cybernex.net

Ernest W. Stephens (1900-1989)
Robert C. Riter (1912-1994)

MEMBERS OF FIRM

Eugene D. Mayer
Robert D. Hofer
Robert C. Riter, Jr.
Jerry L. Wattier
John L. Brown
Travis B. Jones

General Counsel for: First National Bank, Pierre, South Dakota.
State Counsel for: South Dakota Music & Vending Assn; United Parcel Service.
Local Attorneys for: United Services Automobile Assn.; Hartford Accident and Indemnity Co.; Continental Casualty Co.; Home Insurance Co.; National Farmers Union Insurance Co; Auto-Owners Insurance Co.; Church Mutual.

For full biographical listings, see the Martindale-Hubbell Law Directory

SCHMIDT, SCHROYER & MORENO, P.C. (AV)

Suite 201, Pierre Professional Plaza, 124 South Euclid, P.O. Box 1174, 57501-1174
Telephone: 605-224-0461
Fax: 605-224-1607
Email: ssmdfirm@dtgnet.com
Rapid City, South Dakota Office: 815 St. Joseph Street, P.O. Box 8007, 57709-8007.

(See Next Column)

Ronald G. Schmidt
Charles P. Schroyer
Mark A. Moreno
Ethan W. Schmidt
Brett M. Koenecke

For full biographical listings, see the Martindale-Hubbell Law Directory

*RAPID CITY,** Pennington Co.

BANGS, MCCULLEN, BUTLER, FOYE & SIMMONS, L.L.P. (AV)

818 St. Joseph Street, P.O. Box 2670, 57709
Telephone: 605-343-1040
Telecopier: 605-343-1503
URL: http://www.bangsmccullen.com

MEMBERS OF FIRM

George A. Bangs (1915-1995)
W. A. McCullen (1907-1987)
Joseph M. Butler
Thomas H. Foye
Thomas E. Simmons
Charles L. Riter
Allen G. Nelson
James P. Hurley
Michael M. Hickey
Terry L. Hofer
Rod Schlauger
Daniel F. Duffy
Jeffrey G. Hurd
John H. Raforth

ASSOCIATES

Veronica L. Bowen
Terry G. Westergaard
Steven R. Nolan
Gregory J. Erlandson

Representative Clients: Norwest Bank South Dakota, N.A., Rapid City, S.D.; Pete Lien & Sons; The Travelers Insurance Co.; Rapid City Regional Hospital; Dakota Steel & Supply Co.; Great American Insurance Co.; Fireman's Fund Insurance; United States Automobile Association; Moyle Petroleum; Rapid City Area School District 51-4.

For full biographical listings, see the Martindale-Hubbell Law Directory

DEMERSSEMAN JENSEN, L.L.P. (AV)

(Formerly, Gunderson, Farrar, Aldrich & DeMersseman)
516 Fifth Street, P.O. Box 1820, 57709-1820
Telephone: 605-342-2814
Fax: 605-342-0732
Email: law@demjen.com

MEMBERS OF FIRM

Robert W. Gunderson (1915-1994)
John C. Farrar (1914-1982)
Michael B. DeMersseman
Curtis S. Jensen
Harry W. Christianson
Frank Driscoll
Thomas W. Stanton

ASSOCIATE

Michael V. Wheeler

OF COUNSEL

Ray J. Aldrich

References: Rushmore State Bank; Norwest Bank South Dakota, N.A.; First Bank of South Dakota.

For full biographical listings, see the Martindale-Hubbell Law Directory

LYNN, JACKSON, SHULTZ & LEBRUN, P.C. (AV)

First National Bank Building Eighth Floor, 909 Saint Joseph Street, P.O. Box 8250, 57709
Telephone: 605-342-2592
Telecopier: 605-342-5185
Email: ljlawrc@lynnjackson.com *URL:* http://www.lynnjackson.com
Sioux Falls, South Dakota Office: U.S. Bank Building, Eighth Floor, P.O. Box 1920.
Telephone: 605-332-5999.
Telecopier: 605-332-4249.

Kelton S. Lynn (1916-1974)
Horace R. Jackson (1907-1987)
Donald R. Shultz
William F. Day, Jr. (Resident, Sioux Falls Office)
Gene N. Lebrun
Thomas G. Fritz
Haven L. Stuck
Lee A. Magnuson (Resident, Sioux Falls Office)
Jay C. Shultz
Jane Wipf Pfeifle
Jon C. Sogn (Resident, Sioux Falls Office)
Kurt E. Solay
R. Alan Peterson (Resident, Sioux Falls Office)
Leah J. Jeffries
Craig A. Pfeifle
Steven J. Oberg
David L. Nadolski (Resident, Sioux Falls Office)
Steven J. Morgans (Resident, Sioux Falls Office)
Daniel R. Fritz (Resident, Sioux Falls Office)

Amy H. Arndt (Resident, Sioux Falls Office)
Robert Gusinsky
Todd D. Epp (Resident, Sioux Falls Office)
Molly E. Slaughter
Todd L. Brink

Representative Clients: U.S. Bank of South Dakota; Employers Mutual of Wausau; South Dakota School of Mines & Technology; CIGNA Insurance Co.; E.D. Jones & Co.
General Counsel for: Rushmore Electric Power Cooperative; Black Hills Regional Eye Institute.

For full biographical listings, see the Martindale-Hubbell Law Directory

Rapid City—Continued

MORRILL THOMAS NOONEY & BRAUN, LLP (AV)

625 9th Street, 8th Floor, P.O. Box 8108, 57709-8108
Telephone: 605-348-7516
Fax: 605-348-5852

E. V. Morrill (1899-1974)

MEMBERS OF FIRM

Timothy L. Thomas
John K. Nooney
Lonnie R. Braun

ASSOCIATES

Penny Tibke Platnick
Gregory J. Bernard

OF COUNSEL

David E. Morrill

General Counsel for: Black Hills Corp.; Black Hills Power and Light Co.; Wyodak Resources Development Corp.; Black Hills Capital Group, Inc.; Black Hills Energy Resources, Inc.
Representative Clients: McKie Ford Inc.; Gold Key Oldsmobile, Cadillac; American Concept Insurance Co.; GMC Truck, Inc.
Reference: Norwest Bank South Dakota, N.A.

For full biographical listings, see the Martindale-Hubbell Law Directory

*SIOUX FALLS,** Minnehaha Co.

BOYCE, MURPHY, MCDOWELL & GREENFIELD, L.L.P. (AV)

Suite 600 Norwest Center, 101 North Phillips, P.O. Box 5015, 57117
Telephone: 605-336-2424
Fax: 605-334-0618

OF COUNSEL

John R. McDowell

MEMBERS OF FIRM

Jesse W. Boyce (1860-1915)
John S. Murphy (1901-1966)
Jeremiah D. Murphy
Russell R. Greenfield
David J. Vickers
Gary J. Pashby
Vance R. C. Goldammer
Thomas J. Welk
Terry N. Prendergast
James E. McMahon
Michael S. McKnight
Gregg S. Greenfield

Roger A. Sudbeck
Tamara A. Wilka
Carolyn A. Thompson
Lisa Hansen Marso
Jeffrey C. Clapper

Representative Clients: John Morrell & Co., Packers; Federal Land Bank; Citibank South Dakota, N.A.; Sears Roebuck and Co.; General Electric Co.; Ford Motor Co.; Hartford Insurance Co.; Aetna Life and Casualty Co.; Automobile Club Insurance Co.; Design Professionals Insurance Co.

For full biographical listings, see the Martindale-Hubbell Law Directory

DAVENPORT, EVANS, HURWITZ & SMITH, L.L.P. (AV)

513 South Main Avenue, P.O. Box 1030, 57101-1030
Telephone: 605-336-2880
Telecopier: 605-335-3639
Email: lawyers@dehs.com

OF COUNSEL

Louis R. Hurwitz
Lyle J. Wirt

MEMBERS OF FIRM

P. Daniel Donohue
David L. Knudson
Edwin E. Evans
Robert E. Hayes
Michael L. Luce
Charles D. Gullickson
Sarah Richardson Larson
Michael J. Schaffer
Monte R. Walz
Thomas M. Frankman
Rick W. Orr
Timothy M. Gebhart
Jonathan P. Brown
Susan Brunick Simons
Catherine A. Tanck
Roberto A. Lange
Cheryle Wiedmeier Gering
Lori Purcell Fossen
Scott Bradley Anderson
Mark W. Haigh
Sandra K. Hoglund
Dixie K. Hieb
Jean H. Bender

ASSOCIATES

Keith A. Gauer
Kristi G. Holm
Melissa C. Hinton
Kim J. Patrick
Dana M. Van Beek
Brendan W. Reilly

Counsel for: American Society of Composers, Authors and Publishers (A.S.C.A.P.); Continental Insurance Cos.; The First National Bank in Sioux Falls; Ford Motor Credit Co.; General Motors Corp.; The St. Paul Cos.; The Travelers.

For full biographical listings, see the Martindale-Hubbell Law Directory

*STURGIS,** Meade Co.

HANSEN, HUBBARD & SWANSON (AV)

1010 Ball Park Road, Suite 6, P.O. Box 580, 57785
Telephone: 605-347-2551
Fax: 605-347-4466
Email: hanslaw@sturgis.com

MEMBERS OF FIRM

Dale R. Hansen
Bruce A. Hubbard
Gordon D. Swanson

Representative Clients: Sturgis Community Health Care Center; City of Whitewood, South Dakota; Meade 46-1 School District; Newell School District 9-2; Northern Hills Federal Credit Union; New Generation Feeds; Sturgis Rally & Races, Inc.; Norwest Bank South Dakota, N.A.
References: Norwest Bank South Dakota; First Western Bank of Sturgis.

For full biographical listings, see the Martindale-Hubbell Law Directory

TENNESSEE

*BOLIVAR,** Hardeman Co.

DENTON & CARY (AV)

118 Warren Street, P.O. Box 306, 38008
Telephone: 901-658-5170
Fax: 901-658-6806

MEMBERS OF FIRM

H. B. Denton (1910-1972)
H. Morris Denton
Charles M. Cary
William Boyette Denton

LEGAL SUPPORT PERSONNEL

Janice M. Bodiford

Counsel for: Merchants & Planters Bank; Hardeman County Board of Education; Town of Whiteville; Hardeman County, Tennessee; Bolivar Electric Department; Bank of Bolivar; The Industrial Development Board of the County of Hardemen, Tennessee; City of Middleton; City of Grand Junction; Town of Saulsbury.

For full biographical listings, see the Martindale-Hubbell Law Directory

*CHATTANOOGA,** Hamilton Co.

BAKER, DONELSON, BEARMAN & CALDWELL (AV)

1800 Republic Centre, 633 Chestnut Street, 37450-1800
Telephone: 423-756-2010
Telecopier: 423-756-3447
Email: info@bdbc.com *URL:* http://www.bakerdonelson.com
Memphis, Tennessee Office: 20th Floor, First Tennessee Building, 165 Madison, 38103.
Telephone: 901-526-2000.
Telecopier: 901-577-2303.
Nashville, Tennessee Office: 1700 Nashville City Center, 511 Union Street, 37219.
Telephone: 615-726-5600.
Telecopier: 615-726-0464.
Knoxville, Tennessee Office: 2200 Riverview Tower, 900 South Gay Street, 37901.
Telephone: 423-549-7000.
Telecopier: 423-525-8569.
Johnson City, Tennessee Office: SunTrust Bank Building, 207 Mockingbird Lane, P.O. Box 3038, 37602.
Telephone: 423-928-0181.
Telecopier: 423-928-5694; 423-928-3654; Kingsport: 423-246-6191.
Huntsville, Tennessee Office: 3 Courthouse Square, 37756.
Telephone: 423-663-2321.
Telecopier: 423-663-2111.
Washington, D.C. Office: Market Square, 801 Pennsylvania Avenue, N.W., 20004.
Telephone: 202-508-3400.
Telecopier: 202-508-3402.
Jackson, Mississippi Office: Suite 500, 700 North State Street, 39202.
Telephone: 601-351-2400.
Telecopier: 601-351-2424.

MANAGING PARTNER

Susan Elliott Rich

SHAREHOLDERS

Lewis R. Donelson, III
Howard H. Baker, Jr.
Thomas A. Caldwell
John C. Mooney
Thomas O. Helton
Richard B. Gossett
Carl E. Hartley
Virginia C. Love
Richard J. McAfee
John C. Harrison
Gladys Smith Mynatt
Louann Prater Smith
Kenneth C. Beckman
J. Porter Durham, Jr.
Joe A. Conner
Robert C. Divine

(See Next Column)

BAKER, DONELSON, BEARMAN & CALDWELL, *Chattanooga—Continued*

OF COUNSEL

Randall D. Van Dolson
Robert W. Sauser
H. Allen Corey
Micheline Kelly Johnson
Michael C. Mallen
Charles N. Jolly
Jo C. Dearing

ASSOCIATES

Russell W. Gray
Cameron S. Hill
Victoria S. Childres
James H. Levine
Roddy Bailey (Not admitted in TN)
Misty Smith Kelley
Alison Tuley (Not admitted in TN)

For full biographical listings, see the Martindale-Hubbell Law Directory

FOSTER, FOSTER, ALLEN & DURRENCE, P.C. (AV)

Formerly Hall, Haynes, Lusk & Foster
801 Broad Street - Suite 515, 37402
Telephone: 423-266-1141
Telecopier: 423-266-4618
Email: dward@ffadlaw.com

George Lane Foster
William M. Foster
Craig R. Allen
Phillip M. Durrence, Jr.
David J. Ward
Clayton M. Whittaker
John M. Hull

LEGAL SUPPORT PERSONNEL

Peggy Sue Bates

Division Counsel for: Norfolk Southern Railway Co.
Attorneys for: CNA/Insurance; United States Fidelity & Guaranty Co. (USF&G); Bridgestone-Firestone, Inc.; Exxon Corp.; Murphy Oil Corp.; Chicago Title Insurance Co.; Jim Walter Homes; Mid-State Homes, Inc.

For full biographical listings, see the Martindale-Hubbell Law Directory

GEARHISER, PETERS, LOCKABY & TALLANT, PLLC (AV)

320 McCallie Avenue, 37402-2007
Telephone: 423-756-5171
Fax: 423-266-1605
Email: law@gplt.com

MEMBERS OF FIRM

Charles J. Gearhiser
R. Wayne Peters
Robert L. Lockaby, Jr.
Ralph E. Tallant, Jr.
Terry Atkin Cavett
Sam D. Elliott
Lane C. Avery
Wade K. Cannon

ASSOCIATES

Robin L. Miller
Christopher T. Varner
James C. Davey
Lee Ann Adams
Jeffrey H. Moore
Kevin T. Beck

OF COUNSEL

Richard P. Jahn, Jr.

References: First Tennessee Bank; First American National Bank.

For full biographical listings, see the Martindale-Hubbell Law Directory

LEITNER, WILLIAMS, DOOLEY & NAPOLITAN, PLLC (AV)

Third Floor-801 Broad Street - Chattanooga, 37402-2621
Telephone: 423-265-0214
Fax: 423-266-5490; 267-6625
Email: lwdn@cdc.net
Nashville, Tennessee Office: 2300 First American Center. 37238-2300.
Telephone: 615-255-7722.
FAX: 615-780-2210.
Knoxville, Tennessee Office: First American Center, Suite 1130. 507 South Gay Street, 37902.
Telephone: 423-523-0404.
Fax: 423-673-0260.
Memphis, Tennessee Office: 100 N. Main Building, Suite 2601. 38103.
Telephone: 901-527-0214.
Fax: 901-527-8224.

MEMBERS OF FIRM

W. G. M. Thomas (1856-1931)
Lavens M. Thomas (1869-1944)
Aubrey F. Folts (1901-1962)
Shelby R. Brammer (1915-1952)
Bruce Clay Bishop (1919-1968)
Paul R. Leitner
Thomas A. Williams
Charles W. Dooley
Gary S. Napolitan
William E. Godbold, III
David W. Noblit
Gregory M. Leitner
John B. Curtis, Jr.
Kelly Peters Kirkland
Steven W. Keyt
Frank Thomas (Resident, Nashville Office)
C. Douglas Dooley
Alan B. Easterly
Michael K. Alston
Marc H. Harwell
Richard C. Mangelsdorf, Jr. (Resident, Nashville Office)
D. Randall Mantooth (Resident, Nashville Office)
Dana C. Holloway (Resident, Knoxville Office)
Timothy W. Conner (Resident, Knoxville Office)
F. Scott LeRoy
Reid D. Leitner (Resident, Nashville Office)
Roy D. Campbell, III (Resident, Nashville Office)

(See Next Column)

ASSOCIATES

D. Scott Bennett
William H. Webb, Jr
Charles W. Poss
Tonya R. Willis (Resident, Knoxville Office)
Timothy L. Mickel
Molly Glover Crain (Resident, Memphis Office)
Jimmy D. Holbrook, Jr. (Resident, Knoxville Office)
Melanie Valunas Dillender (Resident, Nashville Office)
Lori D. Parish (Resident, Memphis Office)
Erin K. Brownfield
James Patrick Catalano (Resident, Knoxville Office)
Scott Safford (Resident, Nashville Office)
Thomas J. Dement, II (Resident, Nashville Office)
Jason Glenn Howell
Hal W. Wilkins (Resident, Nashville Office)
Karen Goforth Crutchfield (Resident, Knoxville Office)
Mark Andrew Pippenger
Lee Angela Holcomb
Gary M. Massey, Jr.
Robin L. Bicket (Resident, Nashville Office)
Michael Scott Shipwash (Resident, Knoxville Office)

OF COUNSEL

Charles O. McPherson (Resident, Memphis Office)
William L. Abernathy, Jr. (Resident, Nashville Office)
Richard R. Pettit
George H. Rieger, II (Resident, Nashville Office)
Mark Wayne Raines (Resident, Memphis Office)
Lawrence W. White (Resident, Memphis Office)
Ronald L. Harper (Resident, Memphis Office)
Michael D. Newton
Thomas P. Cassidy, Jr. (Resident, Memphis Office)

Representative Clients: American Home Products Corp.; Delta Air Lines; General Motors Corp.; Sears, Roebuck & Co.
Insurance Clients: Hartford Insurance Co.; Liberty Mutual Insurance Co.; Metropolitan Life Insurance Co.

For full biographical listings, see the Martindale-Hubbell Law Directory

MILLER & MARTIN LLP (AV)

Suite 1000 Volunteer Building, 832 Georgia Avenue, 37402
Telephone: 423-756-6600
Fax: 423-785-8480
URL: http://www.millermartin.com
Nashville, Tennessee Office: Miller, Martin & Trabue, 1200 First Union Tower, 150 Fourth Avenue, North.
Telephone: 615-244-9270.
Fax: 615-256-8197.
Atlanta, Georgia Office: Miller & Martin LLP, 1275 Peachtree Street N.E., Seventh Floor.
Telephone: 404-962-6100.
Fax: 404-962-6300.

Vaughn Miller (1892-1964)
Burkett Miller (1890-1977)
F. Linton Martin (1891-1979)
Jere T. Tipton (1904-1983)
James F. Waterhouse (1925-1986)
John L. Lenihan (1910-1990)

OF COUNSEL

H. James Hitching
Lowry F. Kline
Joel W. Richardson, Jr.
Whitney Durand
A. Alexander Taylor, II

MEMBERS OF FIRM

J. Guy Beatty, Jr.
Raymond R. Murphy, Jr.
Howard I. Levine
Hal F. S. Clements
Ronald G. Ingham
Richard D. Crotteau
James G. Cate, Jr.
Edward N. Boehm
James R. Buckner
Roger W. Dickson
John B. Phillips, Jr.
William L. Brown
James M. Haley, IV
W. Scott McGinness, Jr.
David F. Tugman
Alfred E. Smith, Jr.
Shelby R. Grubbs
Donald E. Morton
E. Liston Bishop III
David B. Kesler
William Alan Nichols
Jeffrey W. Guild
Allen L. McCallie
Marcia J. Meredith Eason
Shelley D. Rucker
William Randall Wilson
Douglas T. Johnson
Harry S. (Sandy) Mattice, Jr.
Hugh F. Sharber
Christopher H. Steger
Virginia Anne Sharber
Jeffrey S. Norwood
William E. Robinson
John R. Bode
Charles B. Lee
Ward W. Nelson
Franklin Miller Williams
Jonathan F. Kent
Chester Crews Townsend
Alan Ruderman
Christopher A. Crevasse
Brian E. Humphrey
Mark W. Degler
Ansley T. Moses
Daniel B. Gilmore
Nicholas W. Whittenburg
William S. Parrish
Karen M. (Sutton) Smith
R. Grant Dobson
Theodore K. Whitfield, Jr.
R. Alston Hamilton

ASSOCIATES

Odile F. Spurlock
Elisabeth B. Donnovin
James T. Williams
Matthew P. Huggins
R. Scott Ruth
Bradford G. Harvey
John Y. Elliott, III
India Marie Henson
Richard Christopher Rose
Stacie L. Caraway
E. Mattias Jannerbo
Ted S. Biderman

(See Next Column)

MILLER & MARTIN LLP—*Continued*

ASSOCIATES (Continued)

Pamela Blass Bracher
Thomas L. Hayslett III
Charles Maury Nicely
William A. Hullender
Lisa M. Szafranic
Jody L. Spencer
Carolyne S. Beaty
Stephen J. Stark
Travis R. McDonough
Evan A. Allison
Philip A. Langford
Lynda Motes Hill
Katrina Jewett

General Counsel for: Coca-Cola Enterprises, Inc.; The Krystal Co.; Olan Mills, Inc.; SunTrust Bank; Times Printing Co. (The Chattanooga Times).
Representative Clients: Chubb Group of Life Insurance Companies; John Hancock Mutual Life Insurance Co.

For full biographical listings, see the Martindale-Hubbell Law Directory

STRANG, FLETCHER, CARRIGER, WALKER, HODGE & SMITH, PLLC (AV)

400 Krystal Building, One Union Square, 37402-2514
Telephone: 423-265-2000
Telecopier: 423-756-5861

S. Bartow Strang (1882-1954)
John Storrs Fletcher (1879-1961)
John S. Fletcher, Jr. (1911-1974)
John S. Carriger (1902-1989)
Albert L. Hodge (1910-1997)
F. Thornton Strang (1920-1999)

MEMBERS OF FIRM

Carlos C. Smith
William C. Carriger
Richard T. Hudson
Frederick L. Hitchcock
Ewing Bradley Connell Strang
Larry Lee Cash
Christine Mabe Scott
J. Robin Rogers
G. Michael Luhowiak
James L. Catanzaro, Jr.

ASSOCIATES

Gregory D. Willett
Mark W. Smith
Timothy H. Nichols
Stephen D. Barham

OF COUNSEL

Robert Kirk Walker

Representative Clients: Chattanooga-Hamilton County Hospital Authority; Distributors Insurance Co.; Electric Power Board of Chattanooga; Liberty Mutual Insurance Co.; Rock-Tenn Mill Division; Tennessee Valley Public Power Assn.; Zurich-American Insurance Cos.

For full biographical listings, see the Martindale-Hubbell Law Directory

SUMMERS & WYATT, P.C. (AV)

500 Lindsay Street, 37402
Telephone: 423-265-2385
Fax: 423-266-5211
Email: summers@voy.net

Jerry H. Summers
Thomas L. Wyatt
Jeffrey W. Rufolo
Jimmy F. Rodgers, Jr.

For full biographical listings, see the Martindale-Hubbell Law Directory

WITT, GAITHER & WHITAKER, P.C. (AV)

1100 SunTrust Bank Building, 37402-2608
Telephone: 423-265-8881
Telefax: 423-266-4138; 423-756-5612

Philip B. Whitaker
John W. Murrey, III
Hugh J. Moore, Jr.
Frank P. Pinchak
John F. Henry, Jr.
Harold Alan Schwartz, Jr.
Paul Campbell, III
K. Stephen Powers
Carter J. Lynch, III
Geoffrey G. Young
Ralph M. Killebrew, Jr.
Rosemarie Luise Bryan
Douglas E. Peck
Steven R. Barrett
Philip B. Whitaker, Jr.
Jane K. Ricci

Ron D. Powers
Cynthia D. Hall
Lisa M. Pate
Stephen G. Kabalka
James Matthew Martin

Representative Clients: Chattanooga Metropolitan Airport Authority; Coca-Cola Bottling Co. Consolidated; Dean Witter Reynolds Inc.; The Dixie Group, Inc.; E.I. du Pont de Nemours & Co.; Shaw Industries, Inc.; Signal Apparel Company, Inc.; SunTrust Bank, Chattanooga, N.A.; U.S. Xpress Enterprises, Inc.

For full biographical listings, see the Martindale-Hubbell Law Directory

*CLARKSVILLE,** Montgomery Co.

BATSON, NOLAN, BRICE, HARVEY & WILLIAMSON, PLLC (AV)

622 Madison, P.O. Box 0, 37041-1334
Telephone: 931-647-1501
Fax: 931-553-0153

(See Next Column)

Richard H. Batson
Dan L. Nolan, Jr.
John R. Brice
W. Timothy Harvey
Michael K. Williamson
Steven C. Girsky
Daniel Mark Nolan
Jill Bartee Nolan

Joel D. Ragland
Suzanne Marsh Pearson
Christopher J. Pittman
David J. Silvus
Craig Hargrow
Marie Antoinette Joiner
Carol M. Joiner
J. Matthew Miller

LEGAL SUPPORT PERSONEL

Teri Blackburn (Office Legal Administrator)

Representative Clients: The City of Clarksville; Montgomery County, Tennessee; Cafaro Company; Clarksville Memorial Hospital; Farmers & Merchants Bank; First American National Bank; First Federal Savings Bank of Clarksville; Savage Zinc; Sears, Roebuck and Company; Shoney's Inc.; South Central Bell; Trans Financial Bank; The Industrial Development Board of the County of Montgomery.

For full biographical listings, see the Martindale-Hubbell Law Directory

*CLEVELAND,** Bradley Co.

DENNY E. MOBBS (AV)

55 1/2 First Street, N.E., P.O. Box 192, 37364-0192
Telephone: 423-472-7181
Fax: 423-472-7701

Representative Clients: Liberty Mutual Insurance Co.; Shelby Mutual Insurance Co.; Carolina Casualty Co.; Maytag Corp. (Magic Chef, Inc.-Hardwick Stove Co.); Industrial Development Board of Polk County; Polk County News-Citizen Advance; Ocoee Inn & Marina.

For full biographical listings, see the Martindale-Hubbell Law Directory

*COLUMBIA,** Maury Co.

WALLER LANSDEN DORTCH & DAVIS (AV)

A Professional Limited Liability Company
809 S. Main Street, Suite 300, P.O. Box 1035, 38402
Telephone: 931-388-6031
Telecopier: 931-381-7317
URL: http://www.wallerlaw.com
Nashville, Tennessee Office: Nashville City Center, 511 Union Street, Suite 2100.
Telephone: 615-244-6380.
Telecopier: 615-244-6804.

MEMBERS OF FIRM

Charles A. Trost
Thomas H. Peebles IV (Managing Partner)

RESIDENT OF COUNSEL

Robin S. Courtney

RESIDENT ASSOCIATE

Scott C. Williams

Representative Clients: Columbia Housing Authority; First Farmers and Merchants National Bank of Columbia (Offices in Centerville, Chapel Hill, Columbia, Lawrenceburg, Leoma, Lewisburg, Loretto, Mt. Pleasant, Spring Hill and White Bluff); Fly Garage, LLC; Merrill, Lynch, Pierce, Fenner & Smith, Inc.; Monsanto Co.; NationsCredit Financial Services Corp.; NationsSecurities, Inc.; Saturn Corp.; Solutia, Inc.; UCAR International.

For full biographical listings, see the Martindale-Hubbell Law Directory

*COOKEVILLE,** Putnam Co.

MADEWELL, JARED & HALFACRE (AV)

230 North Washington Avenue, P.O. Box 721, 38501
Telephone: 931-526-6101
Fax: 931-528-1909

MEMBERS OF FIRM

Eugene Jared
James D. Madewell
William E. Halfacre, III
Kenneth S. Williams

Representative Clients: State of Tennessee; Trial Counsel as Special Assistant to Attorney General; Bank of Putnam County; First Tennessee Bank, N.A. at Cookeville; The Maryland; Transamerica Ins. Group; Home Insurance Co.; Auto Owners Ins. Co.; Insurance Company of North America; Fireman's Fund Insurance Co.

For full biographical listings, see the Martindale-Hubbell Law Directory

MOORE, RADER, CLIFT AND FITZPATRICK, P.C. (AV)

46 North Jefferson Avenue, P.O. Box 3347, 38501
Telephone: 615-526-3311
Fax: 615-526-3092

L. Dean Moore
Daniel H. Rader, III
Michael E. Clift
Walter S. Fitzpatrick, III
Richard Lane Moore

(See Next Column)

MOORE, RADER, CLIFT AND FITZPATRICK P.C., *Cookeville—Continued*

General Counsel for: First Tennessee Bank.
Local Counsel for: Heritage Ford-Lincoln-Mercury, Inc.
Representative Clients: Continental Insurance Co.; Kemper Group; U.S.F.&G.; Auto Owners Insurance Co.; Wausau Insurance Cos.

For full biographical listings, see the Martindale-Hubbell Law Directory

DICKSON, Dickson Co.

WHITE, REGEN & GARTON, PLC (AV)

107 Professional Building, 110 North Mathis Drive, P.O. Box 190, 37056-0190
Telephone: 615-446-2881
Fax: 615-446-4694

MEMBERS OF FIRM

Roger G. White (1935-1980)
Barney B. Regen
Jack L. Garton
Benjamin C. Regen

General Counsel: First Federal Savings Bank, Dickson; First Service Corporation of Dickson; Mid-Cumberland Title and Abstract Co.
Representative Clients: Farmers Home Administration; Veterans Administration; General Insurance Underwriters; Tennsco, Inc.; Farm Credit Services; Turnbull-White Bluff Utility District.

For full biographical listings, see the Martindale-Hubbell Law Directory

*FAYETTEVILLE,** Lincoln Co.

STEVENS, BAGLEY & STEVENS (AV)

104 South Elk Avenue, Drawer 428, 37334
Telephone: 931-433-5704
Fax: 931-433-5788
Email: SBS-atty@Vallnet.com

MEMBER OF FIRM

R. Whitney Stevens, Jr.

OF COUNSEL

Thomas O. Bagley

Attorneys for: First Union National Bank; Colonial Bank of Tennessee; Lincoln County Bank; First National Bank; Redstone Federal Credit Union; State Farm Mutual Insurance Co.; Hartford Accident & Indemnity Co.; U.S.F.&G. Co.; CSX Transportation (Seaboard Systems Railroad); City of Fayetteville; Tennessee Farmers Mutual Insurance Co.

For full biographical listings, see the Martindale-Hubbell Law Directory

*FRANKLIN,** Williamson Co.

HARTZOG, SILVA & DAVIES (AV)

McEwen-German Building, 123 Fifth Avenue North, 37064
Telephone: 615-790-1500
Fax: 615-790-0091
Email: hsd1974@aol.com

MEMBERS OF FIRM

H. Mark Hartzog
Edward P. Silva
Robert E. Lee Davies

ASSOCIATE

Marcy S. Hardee

For full biographical listings, see the Martindale-Hubbell Law Directory

*HUNTSVILLE,** Scott Co.

BAKER, DONELSON, BEARMAN & CALDWELL (AV)

3 Courthouse Square, 37756
Telephone: 423-663-2321
Telecopier: 423-663-2111
Email: infor@bdbc.com *URL:* http://www.bakerdonelson.com
Memphis, Tennessee Office: 20th Floor, First Tennessee Building, 165 Madison, 38103.
Telephone: 901-526-2000.
Telecopier: 901-577-2303.
Nashville, Tennessee Office: 1700 Nashville City Center, 511 Union Street, 37219.
Telephone: 615-726-5600.
Telecopier: 615-726-0464.
Chattanooga, Tennessee Office: 1800 Republic Centre, 633 Chestnut Street, 37450-1800.
Telephone: 423-756-2010.
Telecopier: 423-756-3447.
Knoxville, Tennessee Office: 2200 Riverview Tower, 900 South Gay Street, 37901.
Telephone: 423-549-7000.
Telecopier: 423-525-8569.
Johnson City, Tennessee Office: SunTrust Bank Building, 207 Mockingbird Lane, P.O. Box 3038, 37602.
Telephone: 423-928-0181.
Telecopier: 423-928-5694; 423-928-3654; Kingsport: 423-246-6191.

(See Next Column)

Washington, D.C. Office: Market Square, 801 Pennsylvania Avenue, N.W., 20004.
Telephone: 202-508-3400.
Telecopier: 202-508-3402.
Jackson, Mississippi Office: Suite 500, 700 North State Street, 39202.
Telephone: 601-351-2400.
Telecopier: 601-351-2424.

MANAGING PARTNER

Ernest A. Petroff, III

PARTNERS

Lewis R. Donelson, III
Howard H. Baker, Jr.
Robert F. Worthington, Jr.
Stephen A. Marcum
P. Edward Pratt

ASSOCIATE

Mark E. Blakley

For full biographical listings, see the Martindale-Hubbell Law Directory

*JACKSON,** Madison Co.

MOSS, BENTON & WALLIS, PLLC (AV)

P.O. Box 3897, 38303-3897
Telephone: 901-668-5500
Telecopier: 901-664-2840

MEMBERS OF FIRM

William P. Moss (1897-1985)
William P. Moss, Jr. (1936-1997)
Edwin E. Wallis, Jr.
W. Stanworth Harris
Beth H. DuPree

OF COUNSEL

George O. Benton

Attorneys for: First American National Bank of Jackson; Bell South; CSX Transportation, Inc.; The Equitable Life Assurance Society of the United States; Jackson Utility Division; Allied Insurance Companies; United Services Automobile Assn.; Association of Tennessee Cola-Cola Bottlers; Central Distributors, Inc.; Scotsdale Insurance Companies.

For full biographical listings, see the Martindale-Hubbell Law Directory

JOHNSON CITY, Washington Co.

BAKER, DONELSON, BEARMAN & CALDWELL (AV)

SunTrust Bank Building, 207 Mockingbird Lane, P.O. Box 3038, 37602
Telephone: 423-928-0181
Telecopier: 423-928-5694; 928-3654; Kingsport: 423-246-6191
Email: info@bdbc.com *URL:* http://www.bakerdonelson.com
Memphis, Tennessee Office: 20th Floor, First Tennessee Building, 165 Madison, 38103.
Telephone: 901-526-2000.
Telecopier: 901-577-2303.
Nashville, Tennessee Office: 1700 Nashville City Center, 511 Union Street, 37219.
Telephone: 615-726-5600.
Telecopier: 615-726-0464.
Chattanooga, Tennessee Office: 1800 Republic Centre, 633 Chestnut Street, 37450-1800.
Telephone: 423-756-2010.
Telecopier: 423-756-3447.
Knoxville, Tennessee Office: 2200 Riverview Tower, 900 South Gay Street, 37901.
Telephone: 423-549-7000.
Telecopier: 423-525-8569.
Huntsville, Tennessee Office: 3 Courthouse Square, 37756.
Telephone: 615-663-2321.
Telecopier: 615-663-2111.
Washington, D.C. Office: Market Square, 801 Pennsylvania Avenue, N.W., 20004.
Telephone: 202-508-3400.
Telecopier: 202-508-3402.
Jackson, Mississippi Office: Suite 500, 700 North State Street, 39202.
Telephone: 601-351-2400.
Telecopier: 601-351-2424.

MANAGING PARTNER

Robert D. Van de Vuurst

PARTNERS

Linda M. Crouch
Ronald S. Range, Jr.
Robert C. Divine
Carl E. Hartley
Gary C. Shockley

ASSOCIATES

Steven H. Trent
Alice K. Corker
Jennifer P. Keller
William L. Phillips, III

For full biographical listings, see the Martindale-Hubbell Law Directory

LAW OFFICE OF EPPS AND EPPS (AV)

115 East Unaka Avenue, P.O. Drawer 2288, 37605-2288
Telephone: 423-928-7256
Fax: 423-928-0207

(See Next Column)

LAW OFFICE OF EPPS AND EPPS—*Continued*

James H. Epps, III

For full biographical listings, see the Martindale-Hubbell Law Directory

HUNTER, SMITH & DAVIS, LLP (AV)

Suite 500, First American Center, 208 Sunset Drive, 37604
Telephone: 423-283-6300
Telecopier: 423-283-6301
Email: info@hsdlaw.com *URL:* http://www.hsdlaw.com
Kingsport, Tennessee Office: 1212 North Eastman Road, P.O. Box 3740.
Telephone: 423-378-8800.
Telecopier: 423-378-8801.

MEMBERS OF FIRM

George E. Penn, Jr. (1884-1954)
E. G. Hunter (1905-1957)
Ernest F. Smith (1897-1978)
Ben C. Davis (1911-1983)
Edwin O. Norris (1926-1994)
S. Morris Hadden
T. Arthur Scott, Jr.
William C. Bovender
William T. Wray, Jr.
William C. Argabrite
Jimmie Carpenter Miller
Mark S. Dessauer
Gregory K. Haden
Michael L. Forrester
Stephen M. Darden
Edward Jennings Webb, Jr.
James N. L. Humphreys
Cynthia S. Kessler

ASSOCIATES

D. Michael Tranum
K. Jeff Luethke
Julie Poe Bennett
Suzanne Sweet Cook
John C. Bowles
Robert Morris Hadden
Leslie A. Tentler
Scott T. Powers

COUNSEL

Edwin L. Treadway
Shelburne Ferguson, Jr.
Thomas R. Wilson

LEGAL SUPPORT PERSONNEL

James R. Bowles (CPA; CFP)

Representative Clients: General Shale Products Corp.; Morrill Motors, Inc.; MiniFIBERS, Inc.; Land-O-Sun Dairies, Inc.; Paty Lumber Co.; ; Moody Dunbar, Inc.; Com-Net Construction Services, Inc.; Sprint; Government Employees Insurance Co.; SunTrust Bank, N.A.

For full biographical listings, see the Martindale-Hubbell Law Directory

KINGSPORT, Sullivan Co.

HUNTER, SMITH & DAVIS, LLP (AV)

1212 North Eastman Road, P.O. Box 3740, 37664
Telephone: 423-378-8800
Telecopier: 423-378-8801
Email: info@hsdlaw.com *URL:* http://www.hsdlaw.com
Johnson City, Tennessee Office: Suite 500 First American Center, 208 Sunset Drive, 37604.
Telephone: 423-283-6300.
Telecopier: 423-283-6301.

MEMBERS OF FIRM

George E. Penn, Jr. (1884-1954)
E. G. Hunter (1905-1967)
Ernest F. Smith (1897-1978)
Ben C. Davis (1911-1983)
Edwin O. Norris (1926-1994)
S. Morris Hadden
T. Arthur Scott, Jr.
William C. Bovender
William T. Wray, Jr.
William C. Argabrite
Jimmie Carpenter Miller
Mark S. Dessauer
Gregory K. Haden
Michael L. Forrester
Stephen M. Darden
Edward Jennings Webb, Jr.
James N. L. Humphreys
Cynthia S. Kessler

ASSOCIATES

D. Michael Tranum
K. Jeff Luethke
Julie Poe Bennett
Suzanne Sweet Cook
John C. Bowles
Robert Morris Hadden
Leslie A. Tentler
Scott T. Powers

COUNSEL

Edwin L. Treadway
Shelburne Ferguson, Jr.
Thomas R. Wilson

LEGAL SUPPORT PERSONNEL

James R. Bowles (CPA; CFP)

Representative Clients: American Electric Power; State Farm Insurance Co.; Sprint/United Telephone - Southeast, Inc.; Eastman Chemical Co.; Nationwide Insurance Co.; First Tennessee Bank National Assn.; WMX Technologies (formerly Waste Management of North America); Wellmont Health System (Bristol Regional Medical Center/Holston Valley Medical Center/-Lonesome Pine Hospital); Willamette Industries, Inc.; Bridgestone/Firestone, Inc.

For full biographical listings, see the Martindale-Hubbell Law Directory

SHINE & MASON LAW OFFICE (AV)

Suite 201, 433 East Center Street, 37660
Telephone: 423-246-8433
Fax: 423-246-7464
Email: shimas@mounet.com

(See Next Column)

MEMBERS OF FIRM

D. Bruce Shine
Donald F. Mason, Jr.

Reference: Citizens Bank, Kingsport, TN.

For full biographical listings, see the Martindale-Hubbell Law Directory

WILSON, WORLEY & GAMBLE, P.C. (AV)

Fourth Floor Heritage Building, 110 East Center Street, P.O. Box 1007, 37662-1007
Telephone: 423-246-8181
Fax: 423-246-2831
Email: wwg@tricon.net

William T. Gamble
Richard M. Currie, Jr.
Orren Taylor Pickard, Jr.
Frank A. Johnstone
Michael D. Stice
Katherine W. Singleton
Russell W. Adkins
Cherie S. Adams
James W. Holmes
Joel A. Conkin
Jill A. Rayburn

Assistant Division Counsel for: CSX Transportation, Inc.
Local Counsel for: Eastman Chemical Co.; General Motors Corp.; Holston Valley Hospital and Medical Center; United States Fidelity & Guaranty Co.; Eastman Credit Union; Vulcan Materials Co.; AFG Industries, Inc.; K Mart Corp.

For full biographical listings, see the Martindale-Hubbell Law Directory

*KNOXVILLE,** Knox Co.

AMBROSE, WILSON, GRIMM & DURAND (AV)

607 Market Street, Ninth Floor, P.O. Box 2466, 37901-2466
Telephone: 423-544-3000
Toll Free: 1-800-242-1709
Facsimile: 423-637-1709
Email: tennlaw@awgd.com

W. L. Ambrose, Jr. (1907-1992)
Wm. C. Wilson (1912-1995)

MEMBERS OF FIRM

Ronald L. Grimm
Philip P. Durand
John B. Fowler

ASSOCIATES

Lars E. Schuller
Robert B. Frost, Jr.
Mary L. Abbott

OF COUNSEL

John M. Smartt
Wallace W. Conaway

Representative Clients: Lloyd's of London; Simon Property Group L.P. (Retail Shopping Mall Devel.); East Tennessee Automobile Club (AAA); Knox-Tenn Rental & Sales Co.; Kerr-McGee Corp.; Southern Railway Employees Credit Union; National Association of Credit Management; Tellico Village Property Owners Association; First Tennessee Bank; Hertz Corp.

For full biographical listings, see the Martindale-Hubbell Law Directory

ARNETT, DRAPER & HAGOOD (AV)

Suite 2300, First Tennessee Plaza, P.O. Box 300, 37901-0300
Telephone: 865-546-7000
Telecopier: 865-546-0423
Email: adandh@aol.com

MEMBERS OF FIRM

Foster D. Arnett
Jack B. Draper
Lewis R. Hagood
Thomas S. Scott, Jr.
William A. Simms
F. Michael Fitzpatrick
Rick L. Powers
Dan D. Rhea
Steven L. Hurdle
Johanna J. McGlothlin
Robert N. Townsend
R. Kim Burnette
John Steven Collins
Keith H. Burroughs
Samuel C. Doak
Thomas M. Cole
Douglas Gerard Brehm
John A. Willis
Donald J. Farinato

Insurance Clients: Allstate Insurance Co.; Associated Aviation Underwriters; Crum & Forster Group; St. Paul Insurance Cos.; State Farm Insurance Cos; United States Aviation Underwriters.
Representative Clients: Covenant Health Systems; Phillips Petroleum Co.; Sea Ray Boats, Inc.; Vinylex Corp.

For full biographical listings, see the Martindale-Hubbell Law Directory

BAKER, DONELSON, BEARMAN & CALDWELL (AV)

2200 Riverview Tower, 900 South Gay Street, 37901
Telephone: 423-549-7000
Telecopier: 423-525-8569
Email: info@bdbc.com *URL:* http://www.bakerdonelson.com
Memphis, Tennessee Office: 20th Floor, First Tennessee Building, 165 Madison, 38103.
Telephone: 901-526-2000.
Telecopier: 901-577-2303.
Nashville, Tennessee Office: 1700 Nashville City Center, 511 Union Street, 37219.
Telephone: 615-726-5600.
Telecopier: 615-726-0464.

(See Next Column)

BAKER, DONELSON, BEARMAN & CALDWELL, *Knoxville—Continued*

Chattanooga, Tennessee Office: 1800 Republic Centre, 633 Chestnut Street, 37450-1800.
Telephone: 423-756-2010.
Telecopier: 423-756-3447.
Johnson City, Tennessee Office: SunTrust Bank Building, 207 Mockingbird Lane, P.O. Box 3038, 37602.
Telephone: 423-928-0181.
Telecopier: 423-928-5694; 423-928-3654; Kingsport: 423-246-6191.
Huntsville, Tennessee Office: 3 Courthouse Square, 37756.
Telephone: 423-663-2321.
Telecopier: 423-663-2111.
Washington, D.C. Office: Market Square, 801 Pennsylvania Avenue, N.W., 20004.
Telephone: 202-508-3400.
Telecopier: 202-508-3402.
Jackson, Mississippi Office: Suite 500, 700 North State Street, 39202.
Telephone: 601-351-2400.
Telecopier: 601-351-2424.

MANAGING PARTNER

Stephen E. Roth

PARTNERS

Lewis R. Donelson, III
Howard H. Baker, Jr.
Robert F. Worthington, Jr.
Robert G. McCullough
Richard B. Gossett
James A. McIntosh
Stephen G. Anderson
David E. Fielder
P. Edward Pratt
Mary Dillard Miller
Nelwyn W. Inman
Bruce C. Doeg
Kelli L. Thompson

ASSOCIATES

Wm. Gregory Hall, Jr.
Mary LeAnn Mynatt
Andrew L. Colocotronis
Clarence Risin
Richard D. Plumley
Jason I. Epstein
Suzanne Hefner Bauknight
David L. Morehous (Not admitted in TN)
H. Susanne Bales

For full biographical listings, see the Martindale-Hubbell Law Directory

BERNSTEIN, STAIR & MCADAMS LLP (AV)

Suite 600, 530 South Gay Street, 37902
Telephone: 423-546-8030
Telecopier: 423-522-8879
Effective October 1, 1999 Area Code will change to 865.

MEMBERS OF FIRM

Bernard E. Bernstein
L. Caesar Stair III
Thomas N. McAdams
Doris C. Allen
Celeste H. Herbert
James W. Parris

ASSOCIATES

W. Tyler Chastain
Lauren G. Strange-Boston
Margo J. Maxwell

Representative Clients: ABB Flakt, Inc.; Camel Manufacturing Company; Clayton Homes, Inc.; Horizon Physicians Group, P.C.; Modern Supply Co.; Plasti-Line, Inc.; Rafferty's Restaurants; Saks, Inc.; Vanderbilt Mortgage and Finance, Inc.; West Town Mall.

For full biographical listings, see the Martindale-Hubbell Law Directory

CARPENTER & O'CONNOR (AV)

1000 First American Center, P.O. Box 2485, 37901
Telephone: 423-546-1831
Fax: 423-546-0432

MEMBERS OF FIRM

Archie R. Carpenter
J. Gregory O'Connor
Robert A. Crawford
Charles F. Sterchi, III
Louis A. McElroy, II

ASSOCIATES

Christopher D. Heagerty
Toby R. Carpenter

Representative Clients: Allstate Insurance Co.; CNA Insurance; St. Paul Fire & Marine Insurance Co.; State Farm Insurance Co.; Farmers Insurance Group; Coca Cola Co.; Food Lion; The Hyatt Corp.; The Kroger Co.; Levi Strauss & Co.

For full biographical listings, see the Martindale-Hubbell Law Directory

DUNN, MACDONALD & COLEMAN, P.C. (AV)

1221 First Tennessee Plaza, 800 South Gay Street, 37929-1221
Telephone: 423-525-0505
Fax: 423-525-6001
Email: dmcpclaw@usit.net

Paul E. Dunn
James S. MacDonald
Gregory F. Coleman
Dallas T. Reynolds, III
Candis D. Lasley

For full biographical listings, see the Martindale-Hubbell Law Directory

FRANTZ, MCCONNELL & SEYMOUR, LLP (AV)

550 Main Avenue, Suite 500, 37902
Telephone: 423-546-9321
Fax: 423-637-5249
Mailing Address: P.O. Box 39, Knoxville, TN, 37901
Email: Lwhitfield@fmsllp.com
Effective October 1, 1999, the Area Code will change to 865.

MEMBERS OF FIRM

John H. Frantz (1869-1933)
Charles M. Seymour (1882-1958)
Thomas G. McConnell (1883-1962)
Robert M. McConnell (1890-1971)
Harris M. Harton, Jr. (1906-1978)
John William Mills (1927-1977)
E. Bruce Foster (1910-1988)
Arthur G. Seymour
Fred H. Cagle, Jr.
Arthur G. Seymour, Jr.
Francis A. Cain
Robert L. Kahn
Reggie E. Keaton
Donald D. Howell
Debra L. Fulton
Michael W. Ewell
Imogene Anderson King
John M. Lawhorn
James E. Wagner

James D. Moyers
Beverly Dean Nelms
Mary Elizabeth Maddox

Counsel For: ASARCO Incorporated; BellSouth Telecommunications, Inc.; Coca-Cola Enterprises, Inc.; Government Employees Insurance Company; Liberty Mutual Insurance Company; NBC Bank, FSB; Norfolk Southern Railway Company; Prudential Insurance Company of America; The Travelers Insurance Companies; United Services Automobile Association.

For full biographical listings, see the Martindale-Hubbell Law Directory

KRAMER, RAYSON, LEAKE, RODGERS & MORGAN, LLP (AV)

Suite 2500, First Tennessee Plaza, P.O. Box 629, 37901-0629
Telephone: 423-525-5134
Telecopier: 423-522-5723
Email: firm@kramer-rayson.com *URL:* http://www.kramer-rayson.com
Oak Ridge, Tennessee Office: 105 Donner Drive, Suite B, P.O. Box 4459, 37831.
Telephone: 423-220-5134.
Telecopier: 423-220-5132

MEMBERS OF FIRM

R. R. Kramer (1888-1966)
Carter B. Wall (1915-1968)
Andrew Johnson (1918-1985)
Erma Greenwood (1917-1991)
Jackson C. Kramer (1921-1993)
R. Arnold Kramer (1918-1993)
E. H. Rayson
John B. Rayson
David E. Rodgers
Donelson M. Leake
Hugh W. Morgan
William P. Snyder
John T. Johnson, Jr.
Warren L. Gooch
Wayne R. Kramer
Edward G. Phillips
Thomas M. Hale
Jackson G. Kramer
Beecher A. Bartlett, Jr.
Robert W. Knolton
John C. Burgin, Jr.
Adrienne L. Anderson
Charles M. Finn

ASSOCIATES

John E. Winters
Robert L. Bowman
Heidi M. Wegryn
James K. Scott
Penny A. Barton
Amanda M. Belew

OF COUNSEL

Donald C. Wood

Representative Clients: Aluminum Company of America; The Baptist Health System of East Tennessee; Levi Strauss & Co.; Lockheed Martin Energy Systems, Inc.; Methodist Medical Center of Oak Ridge; Robertshaw Controls, Inc.; Rohm & Haas Company, Inc.; Sprint; Tennessee Farmers Mutual Insurance Co.; MK-Ferguson of Oak Ridge Company.

For full biographical listings, see the Martindale-Hubbell Law Directory

LEITNER, WILLIAMS, DOOLEY & NAPOLITAN, PLLC (AV)

First American Center, Suite 1130, 507 South Gay Street, 37902
Telephone: 423-523-0404
Fax: 423-673-0260
Chattanooga, Tennessee Office: Third Floor-801 Broad Street - Chattanooga. 37402-2621.
Telephone: 423-265-0214.
Fax: 423-266-5490.
Nashville, Tennessee Office: 2300 First American Center. 37238-2300.
Telephone: 615-255-7722.
FAX: 615-780-2210.
Memphis, Tennessee Office: 100 N. Main Building, Suite 2601. 38103.
Telephone: 901-527-0214.
Fax: 901-527-8224.

MEMBERS OF FIRM

W. G. M. Thomas (1856-1931)
Lavens M. Thomas (1869-1944)
Aubrey F. Folts (1901-1962)
Shelby R. Brammer (1915-1952)
Bruce Clay Bishop (1919-1968)
Paul R. Leitner
Dana C. Holloway
Timothy W. Conner (Resident)

(See Next Column)

LEITNER, WILLIAMS, DOOLEY & NAPOLITAN PLLC—*Continued*

ASSOCIATES

Tonya R. Willis (Resident)
Jimmy D. Holbrook, Jr. (Resident)
James Patrick Catalano (Resident)
Karen Goforth Crutchfield (Resident)
Michael Scott Shipwash (Resident)

Representative Clients: American Home Products Corp.; Delta Air Lines; General Motors Corp.
Insurance Clients: Hartford Insurance Co.; Liberty Mutual Insurance Co.; Metropolitan Life Insurance Co.

For full biographical listings, see the Martindale-Hubbell Law Directory

MCCAMPBELL & YOUNG, A PROFESSIONAL CORPORATION (AV)

2021 First Tennessee Plaza, P.O. Box 550, 37901-0550
Telephone: 423-637-1440
Telecopier: 423-546-9731

Herbert H. McCampbell, Jr. (1905-1974)
F. Graham Bartlett (1920-1982)
Robert S. Young
Lindsay Young
Robert S. Stone
J. Christopher Kirk
Mark K. Williams
R. Scott Elmore
Leslie Shields

Katherine M. Hamilton

OF COUNSEL

Benét S. Theiss

For full biographical listings, see the Martindale-Hubbell Law Directory

PRYOR, FLYNN, PRIEST & HARBER (AV)

Suite 600 Two Centre Square, 625 Gay Street, P.O. Box 870, 37901
Telephone: 423-522-4191
Telecopier: 423-522-0910

Robert E. Pryor
Frank L. Flynn, Jr.
Timothy A. Priest
John K. Harber

ASSOCIATES

Mark E. Floyd
Donald R. Coffey
M. Christopher Coffey
Robert E. Pryor, Jr.

References: First Vantage Bank; Sun Trust Bank.

For full biographical listings, see the Martindale-Hubbell Law Directory

WAGNER, MYERS & SANGER, A PROFESSIONAL CORPORATION (AV)

1801 First Tennessee Plaza, P.O. Box 1308, 37901-1308
Telephone: 423-525-4600
Fax: 423-524-5731
Email: wms1801@usit.net

Sam F. Fowler, Jr.
Herbert S. Sanger, Jr.
Charles W. Van Beke
Charles A. Wagner III
William C. Myers, Jr.
M. Douglas Campbell, Jr.

Nicholas A. Della Volpe
Ronald D. Garland
Barbara D. Boulton
Robert G. Crane
John G. Brock
Kenneth C. Tucker

Representative Clients: Carolina Power & Light Co.; Cullman Electric Cooperative; Diversified Energy, Inc.; Fort Sanders Health Systems; Gatliff Coal Co.; Lockheed Martin Energy Systems, Inc.; North American Rayon Corp.; Regal Cinemas, Inc.; Roddy Vending; Sigmon Coal Company, Inc.; Skyline Coal Co.

For full biographical listings, see the Martindale-Hubbell Law Directory

WALKER & WALKER, P.C. (AV)

910 First American Center, P.O. Box 2774, 37901
Telephone: 423-523-0700
Telecopier: 423-523-4990
Email: jwalkerjr@aol.com

John A. Walker, Jr.
Kathryn D. Higginbotham

For full biographical listings, see the Martindale-Hubbell Law Directory

WATSON, HOLLOW & REEVES, P.L.C. (AV)

1700 First Tennessee Plaza, 800 South Gay Street, P.O. Box 131, 37901-0131
Telephone: 423-637-1700
Telecopier: 423-525-2514

MEMBERS OF FIRM

Robert Harmon Watson, Jr.
Richard L. Hollow
Pamela L. Reeves
Jon Gilbert Roach
John Chapman Duffy
John T. Batson, Jr.
Earl Jerome Melson

(See Next Column)

ASSOCIATES

Nathan D. Rowell
Laura C. Webb
Beverley S. Cornett
Jenny Coques Rogers

Representative Client: Union County Solid Waste Authority.

For full biographical listings, see the Martindale-Hubbell Law Directory

*LAWRENCEBURG,** Lawrence Co.

BOSTON, HOLT & SOCKWELL, PLLC (AV)

235 Waterloo Street, P.O. Box 357, 38464
Telephone: 931-762-7167
Telecopier: 931-762-5878
Email: bbhs@lorettotel.net

MEMBERS OF FIRM

William E. Boston
Charles W. Holt, Jr.
Ben Boston
Christopher V. Sockwell

Representative Clients: Murray, Inc.; Coca-Cola Bottling Co.
Reference: NationsBank of Tennessee, N.A., Lawrenceburg, TN.

For full biographical listings, see the Martindale-Hubbell Law Directory

*LEBANON,** Wilson Co.

ROCHELLE, MCCULLOCH & AULDS (AV)

109 Castle Heights Avenue, North, 37087
Telephone: 615-444-1433
Fax: 615-443-8775
Email: rma@softek.net

MEMBERS OF FIRM

Robert Rochelle
Jere N. McCulloch
Jo Ann (Jody) Aulds
Jessica Dawn Dugger
David B. Foutch

Gregory S. Gill
Alan Poindexter
Angelique P. Kane

Reference: Wilson Bank & Trust.

For full biographical listings, see the Martindale-Hubbell Law Directory

*MARYVILLE,** Blount Co.

NICHOLSON, GARNER & DUGGAN (AV)

250 High Street, P.O. Box 5059, 37802-5059
Telephone: 423-984-1460
Knoxville: 423-637-1970
Telecopier: 423-982-2595
Real Estate Fax: 423-982-2595
Litigation Fax: 423-984-9275
Email: jnicholson@earthlink.net *URL:* http://www.lawyers.com/ngdlaw

MEMBERS OF FIRM

Joe Nicholson
J. Michael Garner
David R. Duggan

ASSOCIATES

Angelia D. Morie
Daphne H. Cornwell

Representative Clients: Will be furnished upon request.

For full biographical listings, see the Martindale-Hubbell Law Directory

*MCMINNVILLE,** Warren Co.

GALLIGAN & NEWMAN (AV)

309 West Main Street, P.O. Box 289, 37111
Telephone: 931-473-8405
Fax: 931-473-1888
Email: Galligan@Blomand.Net *URL:* http://www.lawyers.com/galligan&newman

MEMBERS OF FIRM

Michael D. Galligan
Robert W. Newman

ASSOCIATE

Susan N. Marttala

Reference: City Bank & Trust Co.

For full biographical listings, see the Martindale-Hubbell Law Directory

*MEMPHIS,** Shelby Co.

ARMSTRONG ALLEN PREWITT GENTRY JOHNSTON & HOLMES, PLLC (AV)

Brinkley Plaza, Suite 700, 80 Monroe Avenue, 38103-2467
Telephone: 901-523-8211
Facsimile: 901-524-4936
Little Rock, Arkansas Office: Suite 100, 100 Morgan Keegan Drive, 72202.
Telephone: 501-280-0100.
Facsimile: 501-280-0166.
Jackson, Mississippi Office: 2525 Lakeward Drive, Suite 200, 39216.
Telephone: 601-713-1192.
Facsimile: 601-713-2049.

(See Next Column)

ARMSTRONG ALLEN PREWITT GENTRY JOHNSTON & HOLMES PLLC, *Memphis—Continued*

Jackson, Tennessee Office: 464 North Parkway, Suite A, 38305.
Telephone: 901-660-2332.
Facsimile: 901-664-1109.

MEMBERS OF FIRM

Walter Preston Armstrong (1884-1949)
John Edward McCadden (1885-1964)
James Seddon Allen (1885-1970)
Emmett W. Braden (1901-1984)
Benjamin Goodman (1904-1994)
Walter P. Armstrong, Jr. (1916-1996)
Thomas R. Prewitt
Richard H. Allen
Thomas F. Johnston
Elmore Holmes, III
Wm. Rowlett Scott
Carl H. Langschmidt, Jr.
Ross B. Clark II
Joseph Brent Walker
Thomas R. Prewitt, Jr.
Charles A. Banks (Resident, Little Rock, Arkansas Office)
Robert V. Redding (Resident, Jackson, Tennessee Office)
Prince C. Chambliss, Jr.
Paul A. Matthews
Randall D. Noel
Mark S. Norris
James Rogers (Josh) Hall, Jr.
B. Douglas Earthman
V. Ellen Morris (Resident, Jackson, Mississippi Office)
James B. McLaren, Jr.
Charles R. Crawford
David A. Thornton
James L. Pettis, III (Resident, Jackson, Mississippi Office)
Lucian T. Pera
Robertson M. Leatherman, Jr.
Cannon F. Allen
Sidney W. Farnsworth, III
Heber S. Simmons III (Resident, Jackson, Mississippi Office)
Richard R. Roberts
Thomas W. Lewis

OF COUNSEL

Gavin M. Gentry
Edward M. Kaplan

Kathy Laughter Laizure
Douglas T. Miracle (Resident, Jackson, Mississippi Office)
Martin W. Bowen (Resident, Little Rock, Arkansas Office)
Jonathan O. Steen (Resident, Jackson, Tennessee Office)
Eugene E. Tibbs, Jr.
Steven R. Regenwether (Not admitted in TN)
L. Darren Gibson
Kimberly Brown
Lawrence B. Austin (Resident, Jackson, Mississippi Office)
Sara Falkinham
C. York Craig, III (Resident, Jackson, Mississippi Office)
Parke S. Morris
Daniel W. Van Horn
E. B. Chiles, IV (Resident, Little Rock, Arkansas Office)
Paul H. Wood (Resident, Little Rock, Arkansas Office)
Franklin A. Garrison
Karen B. Hall
Clover S. Pitts (Resident, Jackson, Mississippi Office)
Eleni N. Vatsis (Not admitted in TN; Resident, Memphis, Tennessee Office)

For full biographical listings, see the Martindale-Hubbell Law Directory

BAKER, DONELSON, BEARMAN & CALDWELL (AV)

20th Floor, First Tennessee Building, 165 Madison, 38103
Telephone: 901-526-2000
Telecopier: 901-577-2303
Email: info@bdbc.com *URL:* http://www.bakerdonelson.com
Nashville, Tennessee Office: 1700 Nashville City Center, 511 Union Street, 37219.
Telephone: 615-726-5600.
Telecopier: 615-726-0464.
Chattanooga, Tennessee Office: 1800 Republic Centre, 633 Chestnut Street, 37450-1800.
Telephone: 423-756-2010.
Telecopier: 423-756-3447.
Knoxville, Tennessee Office: 2200 Riverview Tower, 900 South Gay Street, 37901.
Telephone: 423-549-7000.
Telecopier: 423-525-8569.
Johnson City, Tennessee Office: SunTrust Bank Building, 207 Mockingbird Lane, P.O. Box 3038, 37602.
Telephone: 423-928-0181.
Telecopier: 423-928-5694; 423-928-3654; Kingsport: 423-246-6191.
Huntsville, Tennessee Office: 3 Courthouse Square, 37756.
Telephone: 423-663-2321.
Telecopier: 423-663-2111.
Washington, D.C. Office: Market Square, 801 Pennsylvania Avenue, N.W., 20004.
Telephone: 202-508-3400.
Telecopier: 202-508-3402.
Jackson, Mississippi Office: Suite 500, 700 North State Street, 39202.
Telephone: 601-351-2400.
Telecopier: 601-351-2424.

MANAGING PARTNER

Robert Mark Glover

SHAREHOLDERS

Lewis R. Donelson, III
Roy Keathley
David G. Williams
Leo Bearman, Jr.
Maurice Wexler
Frank L. Watson, Jr.
Robert Walker
Boyd L. Rhodes, Jr.
W. Michael Richards
John C. Speer
Charles T. Tuggle, Jr.
Larry E. Killebrew
Jerry Stauffer
Robert C. Liddon
William H.D. Fones, Jr.
William P. Kenworthy

(See Next Column)

SHAREHOLDERS (Continued)

Allan J. Wade
Gregory G. Fletcher
Charles C. Harrell
Stephen D. Goodwin
George T. Lewis, III
Ben C. Adams, Jr.
Eugene J. Podesta, Jr.
Sam B. Blair, Jr.
Carla Peacher-Ryan
Mary Aronov
Jill M. Steinberg
Matthew S. Heiter
Michael C. Patton
Janis Wild Kesser
Stephen William Ragland
Monique A. Nassar
Bradley E. Trammell
M. Clay Bethell
Desiree M. Franklin
R. Alan Pritchard, Jr.
Peter H. Kesser

OF COUNSEL

Frierson M. Graves, Jr.
Donald A. Malmo
Lynn Ackerman Landau
Paul E. Risner (Not admitted in TN)

ASSOCIATES

Paul R. O'Rourke
Anne B. Mathes
Elizabeth Einstman Chance
Frank L. Watson, III
W. Douglas Sweet
Wm. Scott Young
Mary Ann Jackson
Angela R. Merideth
Jackie G. Prester
David L. Bearman
Clarissa M. Cissell
Robert C. McConkey, III
Jennifer R. Keown
Brett T. Parks
Cedric C.Y. Tan
Lang Wiseman
Diane Schratz Holitik
D. Benjamin Bullen
Shannon M. Hernandez
Sylvia Monique Reed
Christopher G. Boling
Louise P. Gaerig
Lori Hackleman Patterson
Lea Hall Speed

For full biographical listings, see the Martindale-Hubbell Law Directory

BOROD & KRAMER, P.C. (AV)

Beale Street Landing, 245 Wagner Place, Suite 350, 38103
Telephone: 901-524-0200
Telecopier: 901-523-0043
Email: administrator@borodankramer.com *URL:* http://www.borodandkramer.com

Marx J. Borod (1908-1998)
Bruce S. Kramer

Jeffrey C. Smith
Jeffery D. Parrish
Elaine Sheng
P. Bryan Mauldin
Steven Levy
Scott Kramer

For full biographical listings, see the Martindale-Hubbell Law Directory

BURCH, PORTER & JOHNSON (AV)

A Professional Limited Liability Company
130 North Court Avenue, 38103
Telephone: 901-524-5000
Telecopy: 901-524-5024
Email: bpjlaw.com
Other Memphis, Tennessee Office: 50 North Front Street, Suite 800, 38103.
Telephone: 901-524-5000.
Telecopy: 901-524-5026.
West Tennessee Office: 107 West Blythe, Paris, 38242.
Telephone: 901-642-2555.
Fax: 901-642-1070.

MEMBERS OF FIRM

Charles N. Burch (1868-1938)
H. D. Minor (1868-1947)
Clinton H. McKay (1889-1943)
Jesse E. Johnson, Jr. (1913-1980)
John S. Porter (1909-1990)
Lucius E. Burch, Jr. (1912-1996)
W. J. Michael Cody
Joel H. Porter
Charles Forrest Newman
C. Thomas Cates
Joe M. Duncan
John A. Stemmler
J. Brook Lathram
Jef Feibelman
DeWitt M. Shy, Jr.
R. Michael Potter
Ralph B. Lake
John W. Chandler, Jr.
David J. Harris
William A. Carson, II
Warner B. Rodda
David H. Lillard, Jr.
Sam L. Crain, Jr.
Nathan A. Bicks
Stephen D. Crawley
Laurel C. Williams
Lisa A. Krupicka
LeeAnne M. Cox
Beth Weems Bradley
Les Jones
Melissa Ann Maravich
Jay H. Lindy
Ricky E. Wilkins
Scott J. Crosby
Susan M. Clark
Todd A. Rose

ASSOCIATES

Douglas F. Halijan
Roscoe Porter Feild
Jonathan P. Lakey
Mia Gianotti Henley
Andrew B. Carter
Catherine M. McCormick
Wendy Coven Feild
G. Bailey Leopard, Jr.
Jon DeBardeleben

For full biographical listings, see the Martindale-Hubbell Law Directory

Memphis—Continued

Causey, Caywood, Taylor, McManus & Bailey (AV)

A Professional Association, Not a Partnership
Suite 2400, 100 North Main Building, 38103
Telephone: 901-526-0206
Telecopier: 901-525-1540

James D. Causey
David E. Caywood
Daniel Loyd Taylor
John E. McManus
George P. Bailey

Craig B. Flood, II
Jean E. Markowitz
Amy R. Fulton
David Shepherd Walker
John N. Bean
Susan A. Shubert
Stacy Armstrong Ingle
Glenn Keith Vines, Jr.

For full biographical listings, see the Martindale-Hubbell Law Directory

Crislip, Philip & Associates (AV)

Jefferson Plaza Building, Suite 300, 147 Jefferson Avenue, 38103
Telephone: 901-525-2427
Fax: 901-521-9306
Email: Lawgolf@aol.com

MEMBERS OF FIRM

James A. Crislip (1926-1998)
John B. Philip

ASSOCIATE

Paul N. Royal

For full biographical listings, see the Martindale-Hubbell Law Directory

Evans & Petree (AV)

81 Monroe Avenue, 38103
Telephone: 901-525-6781
Telecopier: 901-527-7756

MEMBERS OF FIRM

Marion G. Evans (1877-1957)
Jack Petree (1921-1973)
Charles Pittman Cobb (Retired)
Elwood L. Edwards (Retired)
W. Lytle Nichol IV
John W. McQuiston II
Ernest G. Kelly, Jr.
Michael C. Williams
Joseph W. Barnwell, Jr.
David C. Scruggs
Leonard C. Dunavant, Jr.
E. Woods Weathersby
C. Bradford Foster III
Andrew H. Raines
Frank N. Stockdale Carney
Paul F. T. Edwards
Percy H. Harvey
Katharine A. Jungkind
Scott A. Frick
Michael R. Marshall
Richard E.M. Nichol, Jr.

Karen Baim Reagler

For full biographical listings, see the Martindale-Hubbell Law Directory

Farris, Mathews, Branan & Hellen, P.L.C. (AV)

One Commerce Square, Suite 2000, 38103
Telephone: 901-259-7100
Fax: 901-259-7150
Email: firm@farris-law.com
East Memphis, Tennessee Office: Suite 400. First Commercial Bank Building. 5384 Poplar Avenue.
Telephone: 901-763-4000.
Fax: 901-763-4095.
Nashville, Tennessee Office: Nashville City Center, 511 Union Street, Suite 2400.
Telephone: 615-726-1200.
Fax: 615-726-1776.

MEMBERS OF FIRM

William W. Farris
Harlan Mathews
Homer B. Branan, III
Tim Wade Hellen
Edwin Dean White, III
Charles B. Welch, Jr. (Resident, Nashville Office)
G. Ray Bratton
John M. Farris
D. Edward Harvey (Resident, Nashville Office)
Rebecca Pearson Tuttle
Eugene Stone Forrester, Jr.
Dedrick Brittenum, Jr.
Barry F. White
Robert F. Miller
Robert A. McLean
Anita I. Lotz

ASSOCIATES

Gregory W. O'Neal
Steven Caines Brammer
Harold W. Fonville, II
Fred D. Thompson, Jr. (Resident, Nashville Office)
Pamela Haddock Klavon
Paul C. Peel
Garrett M. Estep
Jon F. Minkoff (Resident, Nashville Office)

OF COUNSEL

Henry H. Hancock

For full biographical listings, see the Martindale-Hubbell Law Directory

Hanover, Walsh, Jalenak & Blair, PLLC (AV)

Fifth Floor - Falls Building, 22 North Front Street, 38103-2156
Telephone: 901-526-0621
Telecopier: 901-521-9759
Email: hwj@hanover-walsh.com

MEMBERS OF FIRM

Joseph Hanover (1888-1984)
David Hanover (1899-1963)
Jay Alan Hanover
William M. Walsh
James B. Jalenak
Allen S. Blair
Michael E. Goldstein
Edward J. McKenney, Jr.
James R. Newsom III
John Kevin Walsh
James A. Johnson, Jr.
Donald S. Holm III
Barbara B. Lapides

Jason S. Wexler
E. Nicole Trail

OF COUNSEL

Helyn L. Keith

For full biographical listings, see the Martindale-Hubbell Law Directory

Harkavy, Shainberg, Kosten, Kaplan & Dunstan, PC (AV)

100 Peabody Place, Suite 1300, 38103
Telephone: 901-761-1263
Telecopier: 901-763-3340
Downtown Telecopier: 901-843-0864
Downtown Office: Memphis, Tennessee, 6060 Poplar Avenue, Suite 140, 38119.

MEMBERS AND ASSOCIATES

Ronald M. Harkavy
Raymond M. Shainberg
Alan L. Kosten
Michael D. Kaplan
Allen C. Dunstan
Neil Harkavy
Jerome A. Broadhurst
Alan M. Harkavy

OF COUNSEL

Ira D. Pruitt, Jr.
Laurie A. Cooper
G. Thomas McPherson

For full biographical listings, see the Martindale-Hubbell Law Directory

Harris, Shelton, Dunlap and Cobb, P.L.L.C. (AV)

Suite 2700, One Commerce Square, 38103-2555
Telephone: 901-525-1455
Telecopier: 901-526-4084
Email: hsdclaw@hsdclaw.com
Other Memphis Office: 6363 Poplar, Suite 430.
Telephone: 901-682-1455.
Fax: 901-682-4446.
Oxford, Mississippi Office: 428 North Lamar Boulevard, Suite 2.
Telephone: 662-238-2855.
Fax: 662-238-2895.

MEMBERS OF FIRM

Walter Chandler (1887-1967)
John H. Harris, Jr.
Max Shelton
William W. Dunlap, Jr.
M. Anderson Cobb, Jr.
James L. Kirby
James R. Garts, Jr.
George T. Wheeler, Jr.
James D. Wilson
Charles C. Drennon, III (Resident, Poplar Avenue Office)
Michael F. Rafferty
A. Neal Graham
G. Rice Byars, Jr.
Jonathan E. Scharff

ASSOCIATES

Tabitha Francisco McNabb
Brett A. Hughes
Chesney Falk McAfee
Christopher S. Campbell
Estelle C. Gaerig
Donrua Barnes-Hulsey
Shawn L. Verner

For full biographical listings, see the Martindale-Hubbell Law Directory

Humphreys Dunlap Wellford Acuff & Stanton, A Professional Corporation (AV)

Suite 2200 First Tennessee Building, 165 Madison Avenue, 38103
Telephone: 901-523-8088
Telecopier: 901-523-8261
Email: bpowell@hdwas.com
East Memphis, Tennessee Office: 600 Poplar Avenue, Suite 401, 38119.
Telephone: 901-767-2500.
Fax: 901-767-5555.

J. Fraser Humphreys, Jr.
John R. Dunlap
Alexander W. Wellford, Jr.
Fred M. Acuff, Jr.
G. Russell Stanton, Jr.
Fred M. Ridolphi, Jr.
Thomas H. Fulton
David M. Dunlap
J. Fraser Humphreys, III
James E. Bailey, III

COUNSEL

E. Brady Bartusch
W. Clary Lunsford

For full biographical listings, see the Martindale-Hubbell Law Directory

Memphis—Continued

JOHNSON, GRUSIN, KEE & SURPRISE, P.C. (AV)

An Association of Attorneys at Law
780 Ridge Lake Boulevard, Suite 202, 38120
Telephone: 901-682-3450
Fax: 901-682-3590

David J. Johnson
Martin A. Grusin
James W. Surprise

James H. Kee

OF COUNSEL

Carl N. Stokes

For full biographical listings, see the Martindale-Hubbell Law Directory

KRIVCHER MAGIDS PLC (AV)

International Place II, 6410 Poplar Avenue, Suite 300, 38119-4839
Telephone: 901-682-6431
Facsimile: 901-682-6453
Email: lawfirm@kmplc.com

James F. Arthur, III
L. Don Campbell, Jr.
Charles C. Cottam
Jack Steven Magids
Michael B. Neal
Henry C. Shelton, III

ASSOCIATES

Rachel L. Hotze
Shawn A. Tidwell
Aubrey Lee Brown, Jr.
Elizabeth J. Landrigan
Geoffrey M. Hirsch

For full biographical listings, see the Martindale-Hubbell Law Directory

LEITNER, WILLIAMS, DOOLEY & NAPOLITAN, PLLC (AV)

100 North Main Building, Suite 2601, 38103
Telephone: 901-527-0214
Fax: 901-527-8224
Chattanooga, Tennessee Office: Third Floor-801 Broad Street - Chattanooga. 37401-2621.
Telephone: 423-265-0214.
Fax: 423-266-5490.
Nashville, Tennessee Office: 2300 First American Center. 37238-2300.
Telephone: 615-255-7722.
FAX: 615-780-2210.
Knoxville, Tennessee Office: First American Center, Suite 1130, 507 South Gay Street. 37902.
Telephone: 423-523-0404.
Fax: 423-673-0260.

MEMBERS OF FIRM

W. G. M. Thomas (1856-1931)
Lavens M. Thomas (1869-1944)
Aubrey F. Folts (1901-1962)
Shelby R. Brammer (1915-1952)
Bruce Clay Bishop (1919-1968)
Paul R. Leitner

ASSOCIATES

Molly Glover Crain (Resident)
Lori D. Parish (Resident)

OF COUNSEL

Charles O. McPherson (Resident)
Mark Wayne Raines (Resident)
Lawrence W. White (Resident)
Ronald L. Harper
Thomas P. Cassidy, Jr.

Representative Clients: American Home Products Corp.; Delta Air Lines; General Motors Corp.
Insurance Clients: Hartford Insurance Co.; Liberty Mutual Insurance Co.; Metropolitan Life Insurance Co.

For full biographical listings, see the Martindale-Hubbell Law Directory

MARTIN, TATE, MORROW & MARSTON, P.C. (AV)

The Falls Building, Suite 1100, 22 North Front Street, 38103-1182
Telephone: 901-522-9000
Telecopier: 901-527-3746

John D. Martin, Jr. (1910-1984)
George E. Morrow (1922-1982)
Clare Shields (1951-1997)
S. Shepherd Tate
W. Emmett Marston
James C. Warner
Lee L. Piovarcy
W. Thomas Hutton
David Wade
Lee Welch
Jeffrey E. Thompson
Robert E. Orians
Harry J. Skefos
J. Philip Jones
Richard M. Carter
W. Price Morrison, Jr.
Ron W. McAfee
David M. Rudolph
John Anthony Williamson

McKinley C. Martin, Jr.
Shea Sisk Wellford
Mark Daniel Griffin
Brian S. Miller
Justin M. Ross
Curt R. Soefker

OF COUNSEL

Michelle M. Williams

For full biographical listings, see the Martindale-Hubbell Law Directory

MCDONALD KUHN (AV)

80 Monroe Avenue, Suite 550, P.O. Box 3160, 38173-0160
Telephone: 901-526-0606
Fax: 901-521-8397

MEMBERS OF FIRM

W. Percy McDonald (1890-1969)
W. Percy McDonald, Jr. (1921-1967)
Braxton C. Gandy (1915-1979)
Edward W. Kuhn (1904-1983)
Henry T. V. Miller
William A. Lucchesi
Carol Mills Hayden

ASSOCIATES

Loys A. "Trey" Jordan, III
Stephen P. Miller
June Kinney
Evan Nahmias

For full biographical listings, see the Martindale-Hubbell Law Directory

ROSSIE, LUCKETT, PARKER & RIDDER, P.C. (AV)

675 Oakleaf Office Lane, Suite 200, 38117-4863
Telephone: 901-763-1800
Telecopier: 901-767-6514
Email: rlpr@rlpr.com

J. Richard Rossie
William O. Luckett, Jr.
John H. Parker
Lorrie K. Ridder
William Martin Seiler
Cameron C. Jehl

COUNSEL

Harry W. Laughlin, III
Luckett Law Firm, P.A., Clarksdale, Mississippi

For full biographical listings, see the Martindale-Hubbell Law Directory

SEVIER LAW FIRM, P.C. (AV)

One Memphis Place, 200 Jefferson Avenue, Suite 975, 38103-2390
Telephone: 901-529-8888
Fax: 901-529-1234

Charles A. Sevier

Gail R. Sevier
Bruce A. Ralston

For full biographical listings, see the Martindale-Hubbell Law Directory

SMITH, SABBATINI & MCLEARY, PLLC (AV)

100 Peabody Place Suite 1250, 38103
Telephone: 901-312-5555
Fax: 901-312-5667
Mailing Address: P.O. Box 3582, Memphis, TN, 38173
URL: http://www.smithlawetal.com

Gary K. Smith
Robert L. Sabbatini
Harold W. McLeary, Jr.
William D. Domico
James F. Kyle
James T. McColgan, III
G. Edward Coleman, III
Bryant C. Witt

Representative Clients: Premier RRG Insurance; Illinois Central Railroad; Medical Assurance; Albertson's, Inc.; Med. Marc (Chiro Co.); Medical Protective Co.; Methodist Health Systems; Hartford Insurance Co.; Sentry Insurance; State Farm Insurance.

For full biographical listings, see the Martindale-Hubbell Law Directory

WARING COX, PLC (AV)

Morgan Keegan Tower, 50 North Front Street, Suite 1300, 38103-1190
Telephone: 901-543-8000
Telecopy: 901-543-8030
Email: Desk@waringcox.com

Roane Waring (1881-1958)
Sam P. Walker (1880-1957)
Allen Cox, Jr. (1902-1982)
Robert L. Cox
Jerald H. Sklar
Louis F. Allen
Samuel D. Chafetz
John E. Kruger
Saul C. Belz
William E. Frulla
Robert S. Kirk, Jr.
Shellie G. McCain, Jr.
Louis J. Miller
Charles W. Hill
Douglas P. Quay
Paul D. Amos
Earle J. Schwarz
William T. Mays, Jr.
Robert C. Starnes
Robert B.C. Hale
Michael P. Coury

Sara A. Benin
Howard Leo Beale, II
Douglas R. Pyne
Joel B. Sklar
David A. McLaughlin
Thomas Paul Brabyn
Holly L. Larkin
John C. Valas (Not admitted in TN)
Quitman R. Ledyard
William F. Burns
Tara E. Bazzone
Marcus Neil Bozeman (Not admitted in TN)
Joshua B. Lawhead

(See Next Column)

WARING COX PLC—*Continued*

OF COUNSEL

Roane Waring, Jr. James M. Manire
Richard E. Duerr, Jr.

Representative Clients: Memphis Gastroenterology Group; Delta and Pine Land Company; Bayer Corporation; Lewis Supply Company, Inc.; Hancock Fabrics; Hilliard Lyons, Inc.; Osceola Foods, Inc.; Mid-South Milling Company, Inc.; Mitsui & Co. (U.S.A.), Inc.; Helm Fertilizer Corp.

For full biographical listings, see the Martindale-Hubbell Law Directory

WEINTRAUB, STOCK, BENNETT, GRISHAM & UNDERWOOD, P.C. (AV)

Suite 2560 One Commerce Square, 38103
Telephone: 901-526-0431
1-800-467-0435
Facsimile: 901-526-8183
Email: office@weintraubstock.com *URL:* http://www.weintraubstock.com
Jackson, Tennessee Office: Towering Oaks Office Park, 2815 North Highland Avenue, Suite B, 38305.
Telephone: 901-660-4747.
Fax: 901-668-2279.
Las Vegas, Nevada Office: 4270 Decatur Boulevard, Suite B-6, 89103.
Telephone: 702-968-8050.
Fax: 702-968-8077.

Samuel J. Weintraub (1917-1993) James H. Stock, Jr.
Earl W. DeHart (1933-1977) Richard D. Bennett
Jeff Weintraub J. Gregory Grisham
Richard D. Underwood

Cecilia Suzette Barnes James Francis Barna
Keith R. Thomas

OF COUNSEL

Jay R. Robinson

For full biographical listings, see the Martindale-Hubbell Law Directory

WILSON, MCRAE, IVY, MCTYIER AND STRAIN (AV)

295 Washington Avenue, Suite 2, P.O. Box 3331, 38173
Telephone: 901-523-2364
Telecopier: 901-523-2366

MEMBERS OF FIRM

Fred E. Ivy, Jr. Alan R. Strain
Douglas A. McTyier Robert M. Nelson (1900-1967)
Albert T. McRae (Retired)

For full biographical listings, see the Martindale-Hubbell Law Directory

*NASHVILLE,** Davidson Co.

BAKER, CAMPBELL & PARSONS (AV)

Suite 300, 303 Church Street, 37201-1786
Telephone: 615-255-7701
Fax: 615-255-7704

MEMBERS OF FIRM

Kenneth L. Campbell David Bate Parsons

OF COUNSEL

Gary T. Baker

Representative Clients: Peterbilt of Nashville, Inc.; Great American Peterbilt, Inc.; Old South Peterbilt, Inc.; Cresent Enterprises, Inc.; Athens Paper Co.; Advantage Management, Inc.; Cool Springs Real Estate Associates, L.P.

For full biographical listings, see the Martindale-Hubbell Law Directory

BAKER, DONELSON, BEARMAN & CALDWELL (AV)

1700 Nashville City Center, 511 Union Street, 37219
Telephone: 615-726-5600
Telecopier: 615-726-0464
Email: info@bdbc.com *URL:* http://www.bakerdonelson.com
Memphis, Tennessee Office: 20th Floor, First Tennessee Building, 165 Madison, 38103.
Telephone: 901-526-2000.
Telecopier: 901-577-2303.
Chattanooga, Tennessee Office: 1800 Republic Centre, 633 Chestnut Street, 37450-1800.
Telephone: 423-756-2010.
Telecopier: 423-756-3447.
Knoxville, Tennessee Office: 2200 Riverview Tower, 900 South Gay Street, 37901.
Telephone: 423-549-7000.
Telecopier: 423-525-8569.
Johnson City, Tennessee Office: SunTrust Bank Building, 207 Mockingbird Lane, P.O. Box 3038, 37602.
Telephone: 423-928-0181.
Telecopier: 423-928-5694; 423-928-3654; Kingsport: 423-246-6191.
Huntsville, Tennessee Office: 3 Courthouse Square, 37756.
Telephone: 423-663-2321.
Telecopier: 423-663-2111.

(See Next Column)

Washington, D.C. Office: Market Square, 801 Pennsylvania Avenue, N.W., 20004.
Telephone: 202-508-3400.
Telecopier: 202-508-3402.
Jackson, Mississippi Office: Suite 500, 700 North State Street, 39202.
Telephone: 601-351-2400.
Telecopier: 601-351-2424.

MANAGING PARTNER

Laurence M. Papel

SHAREHOLDERS

Lewis R. Donelson, III
Howard H. Baker, Jr.
Robert F. Worthington, Jr.
Robert G. McCullough
Richard D. Bird
Thomas O. Helton
Richard B. Gossett
Robert L. Baker
Robert G. McDowell
Carl E. Hartley
William S. Painter (Not admitted in TN)
John A. Gupton, III
Claudia W. Dickerson
James A. DeLanis
Richard G. Cowart
Kenneth P. Ezell, Jr.
James L. McElroy
Robert M. Steele
Gary C. Shockley
Randal S. Mashburn
Steven J. Eisen
John S. Hicks
J. Porter Durham, Jr.
M. Kevin Outterson
J. Steven Kirkham
John H. Rowland
Philip Stuart McSween
Thomas E. Bartrum (Not admitted in TN)

ASSOCIATES

Claire F. Miley
Barbara A. Rose
John F. Rogers, Jr.
Scott D. Carey
John M. Bryant, Jr.
Kenneth A. Weber
Darwin A. Hindman III
Ann Duncan Jarvis
Lawrence S. Eastwood, Jr.
Jonathan Cole
Christopher R. Kelly
Brigid T. Miller
Christy Tosh Crider
Kelley Taylor Oliver
Richard H. Stout
J. Adin Lara
Tonya Mitchem Grindon (Not admitted in TN)
Jennifer Lynch Butler

OF COUNSEL

Peter C. Ward (Not admitted in TN)
Thomas H. Holter (Not admitted in TN)
Christy F. Batts

For full biographical listings, see the Martindale-Hubbell Law Directory

BOULT, CUMMINGS, CONNERS & BERRY, PLC (AV)

414 Union Street, Suite 1600, P.O. Box 198062, 37219
Telephone: 615-244-2582
Telecopy: 615-252-6380
Telex: 852980
Email: firminfo@bccb.com *URL:* http://www.bccb.com/

William Hume (1888-1950)
Laurence B. Howard (1900-1959)
Lindsey M. Davis (1902-1960)
Edwin F. Hunt (1902-1981)
Joseph G. Cummings (1917-1988)
Reber Fielding Boult (1907-1997)
William N. Dearborn (1916-1998)

Patrick L. Alexander
Paul A. Alexis
Andrea C. Barach
James I. Vance Berry
John Randolph Bibb, Jr.
Rebecca C. Blair
Julie A. Boswell
Michael D. Brent
Michael B. Bressman
W. Davidson Broemel
Katherine A. Brown
Karyn Crigler Bryant
Brendi Kaplan Bugalla
Eugene N. Bulso, Jr.
Kevin B. Campbell
Ann Peldo Cargile
Colin J. Carnahan
Davis H. Carr
John T. Conners, Jr.
Kim Crawford
J. Greer Cummings, Jr.
William W. Earthman III
R. Todd Ervin
Douglas C. Franck
Joseph W. Gibbs
John E. Gillmor
Michael J. Harbers
J. B. Hardcastle, Jr.
Jon E. Hastings
John R. Haynes
Scott K. Haynes
E. Berry Holt III
H. Frederick Humbracht, Jr.
April A. Ingram
Philip N. Jett
B. David Joffe
Roger G. Jones
Jennifer Sevier Kelly
William D. Leader, Jr.
Samuel D. Lipshie
Matthew C. Lonergan
Charles J. Mataya
Kathleen K. McKenney
Russell B. Morgan (Not admitted in TN)
Patricia Head Moskal
Jonathan E. Motley
John E. Murdock III
Julie C. Murphy
Gordon Earle Nichols
George H. Nolan
William L. Norton III
James Craig Oliver
Robert S. Patterson
M. Kristina Raattama
Nathan H. Ridley
David A. Rutter
Charles S. Sanger
John M. Scannapieco
Heidi L. Simmons
Barbara Hawley Smith
David K. Taylor
Robert P. Thomas
John W. Titus
J. Thomas Trent, Jr.
Thor Y. Urness
Henry M. Walker
Richard F. Warren, Jr.
Wesley G. Weeks
Cameron J. Williams

(See Next Column)

BOULT, CUMMINGS, CONNERS & BERRY PLC, *Nashville—Continued*

(Continued)

Robert E. Wood
Luther Wright Jr.
Grace S. Yu
(Not admitted in TN)

Attorneys for: St. Thomas Hospital; Williams Travel Centers; Simon Capital Corp.; Edward J. DeBartolo Corp.; Gibson Guitar Corp.; Ford Motor Co.; Genesco Inc.; MCI Telecommunications Corp.; NationsBank of Tennessee; Sholodge Inc.

For full biographical listings, see the Martindale-Hubbell Law Directory

CORNELIUS & COLLINS, LLP (AV)

Suite 2700 Nashville City Center, P.O. Box 190695, 37219-0695
Telephone: 615-244-1440
Facsimile: 615-254-9477

Charles L. Cornelius (1888-1968)
Charles L. Cornelius, Jr.
William Ovid Collins, Jr.
Charles Hampton White
Thomas I. Carlton, Jr.
Charles G. Cornelius
Noel F. Stahl
C. Bennett Harrison, Jr.
David L. Steed
Richard L. Colbert
David A. King
Blakeley D. Matthews
Joseph R. Wheeler
Kurtis J. Winstead
Rebecca Wells Demaree
Daniel P. Berexa
Jay Nelson Chamness
Leigh Ann Buckley
E. Todd Presnell
Christopher S. Dunn
J. Frank Rudy, Jr.
Beth C. Baggett

Bryan K. Williams

Representative Clients: General Motors Corp.; Tennessee Medical Assn; Tennessee Education Assn.; United Parcel Service; Hartford Insurance Group; State Volunteer Mutual Insurance Co.; Johnson & Johnson Inc.; Mercedes Benz of North American, Inc.; BIC Corp.; Pirelli Armstrong Tire Corporation.

For full biographical listings, see the Martindale-Hubbell Law Directory

EVANS, JONES & REYNOLDS, A PROFESSIONAL CORPORATION (AV)

1810 First Union Tower, 150 Fourth Avenue North, 37219-2424
Telephone: 615-259-4685
Telecopier: 615-256-4448

James Clarence Evans
Richard A. Jones
Winston S. Evans
J. Allen Reynolds III

Phillip Byron Jones
Samuel D. Payne

OF COUNSEL

Dennis J. Meaker

References: SunTrust Bank, Nashville; First American National Bank.

For full biographical listings, see the Martindale-Hubbell Law Directory

FARRIS, WARFIELD & KANADAY, PLC (AV)

18th Floor, SunTrust Center, 424 Church Street, 37219
Telephone: 615-244-5200
Fax: 615-782-2371

James G. Martin, III
W. Fred Williams, Jr.
Joseph N. Barker
Robert Norman Buchanan III
Warren H. Wild, Jr.
H. Wynne James, III
Julian L. Bibb
A. Stuart Campbell
B. Riney Green
Bradley A. MacLean
Jeffrey R. King
Charles A. Grice
Michael Hinchion
Robert C. Goodrich, Jr.
Michael L. Dagley
Alden H. Smith, Jr.
Overton Thompson III
Katherine Simpson Allen
Pamela A. Taylor
Cynthia N. Sellers
Lea Wiggins Stouffer
Elizabeth M. Adams
C. Mark Carver
Gregory D. Smith
Garry K. Grooms
Dianna Baker Shew
Stephen H. Price
N. Sue Van Sant Palmer
Steven Evans Groom
Linda C. Elam
James B. Johnson
Dwayne W. Barrett
Thomas M. Federico
Brian K. Frazier
Tara L. Swafford
Hannah K.V. Cassidy
John Bryan Echols
Warren L. Ratliff
Emily M. Smachetti
Colin Michael Daly
Andrea J. Becker
Robert C. Hannon

Andrea Taylor McKellar

OF COUNSEL

Frank M. Farris, Jr.
Charles H. Warfield

Representative Clients: SunTrust Bank, Nashville; Northern Telecom, Inc.; J.C. Bradford & Co.; Aladdin Industries, Incorporated; Kirby Building Systems; Edwin B. Raskin Co.; The Travelers Insurance; Western Sizzlin' Corp.; Insignia Financial Group.

For full biographical listings, see the Martindale-Hubbell Law Directory

HAL D. HARDIN (AV)

218 Third Avenue North, 37201
Telephone: 615-369-3377
FAX: 615-369-3333
Email: halhardin@aol.com

For full biographical listings, see the Martindale-Hubbell Law Directory

RANDOLPH B. JONES (AV)

3200 West End Avenue, Suite 500, 37203
Telephone: 615-783-1705
Facsimile: 615-783-1606

KING & BALLOW (AV)

Union Street Plaza, 315 Union Street, Suite 1100, 37201
Telephone: 615-259-3456
Fax: 615-254-7907
Email: lawfirm@king-ballow.com *URL:* http://www.king-ballow.com
San Diego, California Office: 2700 Symphony Towers, 750 B Street, 92101.
Telephone: 619-236-9401.
Fax: 619-236-9437.

MEMBERS OF FIRM

Frank S. King, Jr.
Robert L. Ballow
Richard C. Lowe
R. Eddie Wayland
Larry D. Crabtree
Alan L. Marx
Paul H. Duvall (Resident, San Diego, California Office)
Steven C. Douse
Douglas R. Pierce
Howard M. Kastrinsky
Mark E. Hunt
Lynn Siegel (Resident, San Diego California Office)
John J. Matchulat
M. Kim Vance
R. Brent Ballow
Michael D. Oesterle

Richard S. Busch

OF COUNSEL

Tonda F. Rush (Not admitted in TN)

ASSOCIATES

James P. Thompson
Dorothy L. Starnes
Patrick M. Thomas
Lynn Morrow
Stephen F. Peluso
D'Lesli M. Davis
Andrew S. Naylor
Candace Ferrell-Bhavsar
Nels Jacobson
Marcus M. Crider
Alexander J. Passantino
Denise A. Nash (Resident, San Diego, California Office)
B. Todd Vinson
David L. Wiley
James A. Crumlin, Jr.
Martina M. Stolar (Resident, San Diego, California Office)
Darin E. Playle
Elizabeth S. Washko (Not admitted in TN)
Douglas B. Janney, III
Amy C. Martin (Not admitted in TN)
Abraham F. Barker (Not admitted in TN)
R. Christopher Lowe (Not admitted in TN)

Heather Beemon Wood

Representative Clients: American Airlines, Nashville, Tennessee; Dollar General Corp.; Opryland USA, Inc.; NationsBank; Tribune Co., Chicago, Illinois; Union Tribune Publishing Co., San Diego, California; Kroger Co., Cinncinnati, OH; Young Broadcasting, New York, New York; Browning-Ferris Industries, Houston, TX; O'Charley's, Inc., Nashville, TN.

For full biographical listings, see the Martindale-Hubbell Law Directory

LEITNER, WILLIAMS, DOOLEY & NAPOLITAN, PLLC (AV)

2300 First American Center, 37238-2300
Telephone: 615-255-7722
Fax: 615-780-2210
Chattanooga, Tennessee Office: Third Floor-801 Broad Street - Chattanooga. 37402-2621.
Telephone: 423-265-0214.
Fax: 423-266-5490.
Knoxville, Tennessee Office: First American Center, Suite 1130, 507 South Gay Street. 37902.
Telephone: 423-523-0404.
Fax: 423-673-0260.
Memphis, Tennessee Office: 100 N. Main Building, Suite 2601. 38103.
Telephone: 901-527-0214.
Fax: 901-526-8224.

MEMBERS OF FIRM

W. G. M. Thomas (1856-1931)
Lavens M. Thomas (1869-1944)
Aubrey F. Folts (1901-1962)
Shelby R. Brammer (1915-1952)
Bruce Clay Bishop (1919-1968)
Paul R. Leitner
Frank Thomas (Resident)
Richard C. Mangelsdorf, Jr. (Resident)
D. Randall Mantooth (Resident)
Reid D. Leitner (Resident)
Roy D. Campbell, III (Resident)

ASSOCIATES

Thomas J. Dement, II (Resident)
Melanie Valunas Dillender (Resident)
Hal W. Wilkins (Resident)
Scott Safford (Resident)
Robin L. Bicket (Resident)

OF COUNSEL

William L. Abernathy, Jr. (Resident)
George H. Rieger, II (Resident)

Representative Clients: American Home Products Corp.; Delta Air Lines; General Motors Corp.

(See Next Column)

LEITNER, WILLIAMS, DOOLEY & NAPOLITAN PLLC—*Continued*

Insurance Clients: Hartford Insurance Co.; Liberty Mutual Insurance Co.; Metropolitan Life Insurance Co.

For full biographical listings, see the Martindale-Hubbell Law Directory

DAVID YOUNG PARKER, P.C. (AV)

131 Second Avenue North, Fifth Floor, P.O. Box 190616, 37219
Telephone: 615-242-5463
Fax: 615-244-3897

David Young Parker

For full biographical listings, see the Martindale-Hubbell Law Directory

SCHULMAN, LEROY AND BENNETT, P.C. (AV)

7th Floor, 501 Union Building, 5th Avenue, North & Union Street, P.O. Box 190676, 37219-0676
Telephone: 615-244-6670
Fax: 615-254-5407

I. R. Schulman (1908-1986)
Theodore T. McCarley, Jr. (1918-1975)
Lewis D. Pride (1933-1978)
Seymour Samuels, Jr. (1912-1992)
W. Wayne LeRoy
Angus Gillis, III
Gary S. Rubenstein
Keene W. Bartley
Barbara Jones Perutelli
J. Anthony Arena
Marian L. Kohl
Ashley Norton Arnold

OF COUNSEL

J. Carson Stone, III

Representative Clients: Allstate Insurance Co.; State Farm Insurance Co.; Kemper Insurance Company.
References: First American National Bank; Regions Bank; J.C. Bradford & Co.

For full biographical listings, see the Martindale-Hubbell Law Directory

STOKES & BARTHOLOMEW, P.A. (AV)

SunTrust Center, 424 Church Street, 28th Floor, 37219
Telephone: 615-259-1450
Telecopier: 615-259-1470
Email: stokebarth@stokebarth.com

Ogden Stokes
Samuel W. Bartholomew, Jr.
William R. Bruce
Thomas L. (Larry) Stewart
D. Reed Houk
Robert R. Campbell, Jr.
Cynthia Mitchell Barnett
Paul S. Davidson
Douglas J. Brown
D. Kirk Shaffer
William H. West
Carter R. Todd
David T. Axford
William H. Neely
Reber M. Boult
Joshua F. Aylor
Grant Charles Glassford
James H. Drescher
Elizabeth E. Moore
Darlene T. Marsh
Daniel P. Smith
Kim Harvey Looney
Guilford F. Thornton, Jr.
Charles W. Cook, III
Fred Russell Harwell
Martin Shallenberger Brown, Jr.

David N. Burn
Kevin Hunter Sharp
Albert J. Bart
Kate C. McKee
William C. Brewer, III
Joel T. Galanter
Brandon L. Hayes
Christine J. Laird
Scott J. Lynn
Charles B. Robbins (Not admitted in TN)
Bryan E. Pieper

OF COUNSEL

John L. Chambers
Lew Conner
Ruth M. Kinnard
Vaden M. Lackey, Jr.

For full biographical listings, see the Martindale-Hubbell Law Directory

WALLER LANSDEN DORTCH & DAVIS (AV)

A Professional Limited Liability Company
Nashville City Center, 511 Union Street, Suite 2100, 37219-1760
Telephone: 615-244-6380
Telecopier: 615-244-6804
URL: http://www.wallerlaw.com
Columbia, Tennessee Office: 809 S. Main Street, Suite 300, P.O. Box 1035.
Telephone: 931-388-6031.
Telecopier: 931-381-7317.

William Waller (1898-1995)
D. L. Lansden (1909-1999)
O. Lawrence Dortch (1914-1991)
William Waller Jr. (1925-1998)
Philip G. Davidson III (1927-1995)
William M. Leech Jr. (1935-1996)

MEMBERS OF FIRM

Maclin P. Davis, Jr.
Charles A. Trost
Russell H. Hippe, Jr.
James R. Cheshire III
James J. Kendig
James M. Doran, Jr.
Ames Davis
Theodore W. Lenz
Frank Grace, Jr.
Walter H. Crouch
George W. Bishop III
William H. Farmer
Stephen C. Baker
Courtney N. Pearre

(See Next Column)

MEMBERS OF FIRM (Continued)

J. Leigh Griffith
William E. Shofner
Jones W. Luna
Alexander Blackman Buchanan
J. Chase Cole
Steve Cobb
Robert E. Boston
J. Reginald Hill
G. Scott Rayson
Joseph A. Woodruff
Waverly D. Crenshaw, Jr.
Joseph A. Sowell III
E. Marlee Mitchell
Michael R. Paslay
Robert J. Martineau, Jr.
Howard W. Herndon
David E. Lemke
James W. White
Matthew Thompson Harris
Ralph W. Davis
Beth Connor Guest
Thomas H. Peebles IV (Managing Partner, Columbia Office)
James B. Bristol
Nancy S. Jones
Michael D. Pearigen
James M. Weaver
John D. Claybrook
Deborah W. Larios
L. Hunter Rost, Jr.
Neil B. Krugman
Franklin A. Berryman
Richard A. Johnson
Edward Andrew Norwood
D. Billye Sanders
Nora L. Liggett
Stephen W. Grace
Christopher L. Howard
Paul D. Gilbert

OF COUNSEL

Robin S. Courtney (Resident Of Counsel, Columbia Office)
Donald W. Fish
W. Gregory Conway

ASSOCIATES

Scott C. Williams (Resident Associate, Columbia Office)
K. Gabriel Heiser
Peter T. Dirksen
Sally Baskin Buntin
Paula D. Walker
Patricia Owen Powers
Walter H. Neilsen
Martin J. Vanek
Jeffrey A. Calk
Neal E. Miller
Lela M. Hollabaugh
Kristin Murphy Coile
Wm. Jay Harrelson
Stephanie M. Jennings
Edward Moye Callaway
Carla Fiddler Fenswick
Benjamin Cockrill Huddleston
Brian A. Lapps, Jr.
Donald Ray Moody
L. Beth Evans
Maryellen Sullivan Pickrell
Michael G. Stewart
Robert A. Guy, Jr.
E. Brent Hill
Brian R. Browder
Robert L. Harris
Stephen L. Page
David C. Head
James H. Nixon III
K. Hollyn Hollman
Thomas Hayden Lee
Michael K. Stagg
Donald B. Stuart
Ellen Frances Coughlin
Joelle James Phillips
Jennifer Clower Blankenship
Jennifer Anne Boyd
Michelle Bellamy Marsh
Charles H. Williamson
Matthew R. Burnstein
William Kenneth Marlow
Mark W. Peters
Karla R. Hyatt
Stanley E. Graham
K. Suzanne Crenshaw
Amy E. Malcolm
Michael S. Mizell
Afshin Yazdian
Paula A. Flowers
M. Sean Sullivan
Beth J. Blankenship (Not admitted in TN)
S. Gregory Cope
Christy Sawyer
Benjamin M. Sensing
Amy C. Singleton
Jane Hyatt Thorpe
David G. Wilson
Meredith M. Griffith

Representative Clients: Columbia/HCA Healthcare Co.; PhyCor, Inc.; HEALTHSOUTH Co.; Tennessee Titans; J.C. Bradford & Co.; Orthodontic Centers of America; Nissan Motor Manufacturing Co., U.S.A.; Saturn Co.; JDN Realty Co.; United Parcel Service.

For full biographical listings, see the Martindale-Hubbell Law Directory

WYATT, TARRANT & COMBS (AV)

1500 Nashville City Center, 511 Union Street, 37219-1750
Telephone: 615-244-0020
Telecopier: 615-256-1726
URL: http://www.wyattfirm.com
Music Row Office: 29 Music Square East, Nashville, 37203.
Telephone: 615-255-6161.
Telecopier: 615-254-4490.
Hendersonville, Tennessee Office: 313 E. Main Street, Suite 1, Hendersonville, 37075.
Telephone: 615-822-8822.
Telecopier: 615-824-4684.
Memphis, Tennessee Office: Crescent Center, Suite 650, 6075 Poplar Avenue, Memphis, 38119.
Telephone: 901-537-1000.
Telecopier: 901-537-1010.
Tri-Cities, Tennessee Office: Northeast Tennessee Business Park, 10368 Wallace Alley Street, Suite 6, Kingsport, Tennessee, 37663.
Telephone: 423-279-1825.
Telecopier: 423-279-9357.
Louisville, Kentucky Office: Citizens Plaza.
Telephone: 502-589-5235.
Telecopier: 502-589-0309.
Lexington, Kentucky Office: 1700 Lexington Financial Center.
Telephone: 606-233-2012.
Telecopier: 606-259-0649.
Frankfort, Kentucky Office: The Taylor-Scott Building, 311 West Main Street.
Telephone: 502-223-2104.
Telecopier: 502-227-7681.

(See Next Column)

WYATT, TARRANT & COMBS, *Nashville—Continued*

New Albany, Indiana Office: The Elsby Building, 117 East Spring Street,
Telephone: 812-945-3561.
Telecopier: 812-949-2524.

MEMBERS OF FIRM

John M. Barksdale (1903-1983)
Ward Hudgins (1910-1966)
John Donelson Whalley (1921-1991)
Harris A. Gilbert
Parker W. Duncan
Charles W. Bone
Sam J. McAllester III
W. Michael Milom (Resident, Music Row Office)
C. Michael Norton
Edwin S. Pyle
Barbara J. Moss
Christian A. Horsnell (Resident, Music Row Office)
William W. Gibson
Gail Smith Bradford
J. Graham Matherne
Keith C. Dennen (Resident, Hendersonville Office)
James C. Bradshaw III
Andrew B. Campbell

ASSOCIATES

B. Anthony Saunders
Grace H. Awh (Resident, Music Row Office)
Sharon O. Jacobs
Henry L. Hipkens
Stacey A. Garrett
Paige Waldrop Mills
Nancy A. Vincent
William J. Haynes, III
Trace Blankenship
C. Palmer Pillans, IV
Stephen J. Zralek
Charles M. Walker

COUNSEL

John Knox Walkup
Jack F. Stringham II
Daniel R. Loftus
B. Gail Reese
William L. Penny
Jerry W. Taylor
Robin Mitchell Joyce (Resident, Music Row Office)
Charles J. Biederman (Not admitted in TN)

Counsel for: Country Music Foundation; Country Radio Broadcasters; Emanuel Schatten Enterprises; Gospel Music Assn.; H.G. Hill Co., Inc.; Nashville Thermal Transfer Corp.

For full biographical listings, see the Martindale-Hubbell Law Directory

*SMITHVILLE,** DeKalb Co.

BUCK & BUCK (AV)

124 West Main Street, 37166
Telephone: 615-597-6725
Fax: 615-597-8250
Email: fbuck@dekalb.net

MEMBERS OF FIRM

Frank Buck
Lena Ann Buck

Representative Clients: Tennessee Farmers; Mutual Insurance Co.
References: City Bank & Trust.

TULLAHOMA, Coffee Co.

HAYNES, HULL, RIEDER & EWELL, P.A. (AV)

214 North Atlantic Street, P.O. Box 878, 37388
Telephone: 931-455-5478
Fax: 931-455-6148

Walter M. Haynes (1897-1967)
Thomas M. Hull
William C. Rieder
Gerald L. Ewell, Jr.

Representative Clients: First National Bank of Tullahoma; The Board of Public Utilities of the City of Tullahoma, Tenn.; Elk River Public Utility District; SSI Services, Inc.; State Farm Insurance Companies; Fireman's Fund Insurance Companies; State Volunteer Mutual Insurance Co.; Nationwide Insurance Co.; St. Paul Fire & Marine Company.

For full biographical listings, see the Martindale-Hubbell Law Directory

HENRY, MCCORD, BEAN & MILLER, P.L.L.C. (AV)

300 North Jackson Street, 37388
Telephone: 931-455-9301
Telefax: 931-455-1621
Email: hmbmpllc@edge.net

John M. McCord (1928-1996)

MEMBERS OF FIRM

James H. Henry
James H. Henry, II
Roger J. Bean
Clifton N. Miller
Richard W. Gabriel
Robert T. Carter

ASSOCIATE

Jeffrey D. Ridner

Representative Clients: Trans Financial Bank of Tennessee, FSB; South Central Bell Telephone Co.; CSX Transportation, Inc.; Coca-Cola Bottling Works, Tullahoma; Tennessee Apparel Corp.; Tennessee Dickel Distilling Co.; Wagner Division, Cooper Industries, Inc.; United Distillers, Inc.

For full biographical listings, see the Martindale-Hubbell Law Directory

*UNION CITY,** Obion Co.

ELAM & GLASGOW (AV)

Commercial Bank & Trust Building, 38261
Telephone: 901-885-2011; 901-885-2012

MEMBERS OF FIRM

Tom Elam (1909-1998)
James M. Glasgow
James M. Glasgow, Jr.
Randy N. Chism

Attorneys for: Commercial Bank, Union City; Obion, Lake & Weakley Counties; United States Fidelity & Guaranty Co.; Auto Owners Insurance Co.; C.N.A. Insurance, Union City; Travelers Insurance Co.; Goodyear Tire & Rubber Co.

For full biographical listings, see the Martindale-Hubbell Law Directory

TEXAS

*ABILENE,** Taylor Co.

BATJER & WAGSTAFF, P.C. (AV)

104 Pine Street, Suite 306, P.O. Box 888, 79601
Telephone: 915-673-2597
Fax: 915-676-9329
Email: bbatjer@camalott.com

Robert D. Batjer
Robert B. Wagstaff

LEGAL SUPPORT PERSONNEL

Pamela L. Weaver

Representative Clients: General Motors Corp.; Freightliner Corp.; Royal-Globe Insurance Cos.; USAA; Ranger Insurance Cos.; Allstate Insurance Co.; State Farm Insurancae Cos.; The Medical Protective Company; SAFECO; AIG Aviation.

For full biographical listings, see the Martindale-Hubbell Law Directory

WAGSTAFF, ALVIS, STUBBEMAN, SEAMSTER & LONGACRE, L.L.P. (AV)

290 Cedar, P.O. Box 360, 79604-0360
Telephone: 915-677-6291
Facsimile: 915-677-6313
Email: wassl@wagstafflaw.com
Dallas, Texas Office: 750 North St. Paul Street, Suite 1290.
Telephone: 214-220-9171.
Facsimile: 214-871-9327.

MEMBERS OF FIRM

J. M. Wagstaff (1862-1952)
John H. Alvis (1896-1971)
R. M. Wagstaff (1892-1973)
Robert H. Alvis (1929-1997)
David G. Stubbeman (Retired)
Don N. Seamster
Roy B. Longacre
Darrell W. Moore
Charles L. Black
John R. Saringer
Kyle D. Tatom
Diann Waddill

ASSOCIATES

Michael S. Seamster
Frederic L. Frawley
Lois A. Rockefeller
Coby Waddill

Representative Clients: Abilene Independent School District; American International Adjusting Co.; CSW Energy, Inc.; Ford New Holland, Inc.; Hardin-Simmons University; Hendrick Medical Center; NationsBank of Texas, N.A.; Sears, Roebuck & Co.; United Services Automobile Assn.; West Texas Utilites Co. (General Counsel).

For full biographical listings, see the Martindale-Hubbell Law Directory

WHITTEN & YOUNG, P.C. (AV)

500 Chestnut, Suite 1402, P.O. Box 208, 79602
Telephone: 915-672-7824
Fax: 915-672-2158
Email: wypc@camalott.com

O. Henry (Mike) Young
Gary L. Hacker
C. Terry Hagin
Donald L. Anderson, Jr.
Cynthia Rucker Allen
Charles C. Self, III

Paul R. Rotenberry

OF COUNSEL

C. G. Whitten

For full biographical listings, see the Martindale-Hubbell Law Directory

*ALICE,** Jim Wells Co.

WARBURTON, ADAMI, MCNEILL, PAISLEY & APPELL, P.C. (AV)

Norwest Bank Building, Fourth Floor, 601 East Main Street, P.O. Box 331, 78333-0331
Telephone: 361-668-8101
Fax: 361-668-8106
Beeville Office: 107 North Washington Street, P.O. Box 278, 78104-0278.
Telephone: 361-358-2525.
Fax: 361-358-2532.

Lawrence H. Warburton, Jr.
Wallis D. McNeill, Jr.
John G. "Buster" Adami, Jr.
Mark R. Paisley
R. Michael Appell

Representative Clients: Norwest Bank, Alice; Bowden Ford Lincoln Mercury Co.; Brooks County Independent School District; Jim Wells County; Lundells, Inc.; Brush County Bank; Mildred Talbert Estate; Ruth Moos Estate; John G. Kenedy Charitable Trust; San Diego Independent School District.

For full biographical listings, see the Martindale-Hubbell Law Directory

*AMARILLO,** Potter Co.

GIBSON, OCHSNER & ADKINS, LLP (AV)

701 South Taylor Street, Suite 500, 79101-2400
Telephone: 806-372-4271
Fax: 806-378-9797
URL: http://www.goa-law.com

Erwin C. Ochsner (1898-1978)
H. M. Adkins (1900-1980)
W. W. Gibson (1897-1987)

MEMBERS OF FIRM

Wayne P. Sturdivant
Richard H. Thamer
John Huffaker
David L. LeBas
Charles E. King
Kenneth S. Muncy
Danny M. Needham
Vance E. Ivy
Joel A. Howard
Robin E. Rice
Thomas C. Riney
Todd O. Lafferty
Ernest R. (Jud) Finney, Jr.
Michael G. Smith
Shyla R. Buckner

Tod Mayfield
Andrew R. Evans
Wayne R. Barnes
T. Coyt (Cody) Webb
Christopher D. Wolek
Jason R. Augustine
Julie P. Wright
Ronny H. Wall
Tiffany L. Wright

OF COUNSEL

S. Tom Morris
Robert D. Forrester
Sandra K. Webb

For full biographical listings, see the Martindale-Hubbell Law Directory

ART B. LARA, JR. (AV)

PRPC Building, Suite 30, 415 West 8th Street, 79101
Telephone: 806-358-8773
Fax: 806-376-6437
Email: abllaw@arn.net *URL:* http://www.lawyers.com/artblara

For full biographical listings, see the Martindale-Hubbell Law Directory

MULLIN HOARD & BROWN, L.L.P. (AV)

800 Amarillo National Plaza Two, 500 South Taylor, P.O. Box 31656, 79120-1656
Telephone: 806-372-5050
Fax: 806-372-5086
Email: jmerritt@mhba.com
Lubbock, Texas Office: Suite 55 City Bank Building. 5211 Brownfield Highway, P.O. Box 16646. 79490-6646.
Telephone: 806-785-0591.
Fax: 806-785-0587.
Dimmitt, Texas Office: 114 South Broadway. 79027.
Telephone: 806-647-2131.
Fax: 806-647-4535.

David Mullin
John S. Irwin
Steven L. Hoard
Jonathan S. Miller (Resident, Lubbock Office)
John M. Brown
Johnny K. Merritt
David R. Langston (Resident, Lubbock Office)
Joel R. Hogue
Jeffrey E. Ritter
John G. Turner III
Don D. Sunderland
Brad A. Chapman
J. F. "Jack" Howell, III
Vincent E. Nowak

ASSOCIATES

Jean Brown Loveall
Sherylynn A. Kime-Goodwin (Resident, Lubbock Office)
Robert R. Bell
Wolf Puckett
Michael D. Hicks (Resident, Lubbock Office)
Thomas Kevin Nelson
Mark D. Tillman

(See Next Column)

OF COUNSEL

John Mozola
Jimmy L. Ross

LEGAL SUPPORT PERSONNEL

PARALEGALS

Mary Alt
Leslie Cruger
Lori Hopson
Patricia Holt
Julie Winkelman

For full biographical listings, see the Martindale-Hubbell Law Directory

UNDERWOOD, WILSON, BERRY, STEIN & JOHNSON, P.C. (AV)

410 S. Taylor, Suite 1500, P.O. Box 9158, 79105
Telephone: 806-376-5613
Telecopier: 806-379-0316
Email: ulf@usa-soft.com *URL:* http://www.usa-soft.com/ulf/

R. E. Underwood (1877-1966)
Thomas R. Dixon, Jr.
R. A. Wilson (1905-1986)
Kelly Utsinger
Hiram A. Berry (1907-1988)
Sharon E. White
Jerome W. Johnson
Patrick B. Mosley
James A. Besselman
T. Alan Rhodes
E. T. Manning
James W. Wester
Don M. Dean
D. Lynn Tate
A. W. SoRelle III
Dan L. Schaap
Gerald G. Bybee
Sally Holt Emerson
Michael H. Loftin
Gavin J. Gadberry

OF COUNSEL

Clifford A. Stein
Winston R. Smith
Edward H. Hill

Michelle Alcon Eggleston
Michael S. Smiley
Christopher K. Wrampelmeier
Chris Wright
Charles A. Mallard
Slater Chalfant Elza
Grant Adams
Norma J. Cantu
Robert Chad Pierce
Fred A. Stormer

LEGAL SUPPORT PERSONNEL

PARALEGALS

Nancy Amburn
Carmen Hall
Rhonda Brashears
Sheri Harris
Cindy Davis
Charly Hopkins
Nancy Gormley
Jodi Maner
Mary Mitchell

Representative Clients: Allstate Insurance Co.; Amarillo Independent School District; Amarillo National Bank; ASARCO Inc.; Baptist-St. Anthony's Hospital System; Cal Farley's Boys Ranch and Affiliates; IBP, Inc.; KVII Television; Texaco, Inc.; Texas Health Care Assoc.

For full biographical listings, see the Martindale-Hubbell Law Directory

WHITTENBURG WHITTENBURG & SCHACHTER, P.C. (AV)

1010 South Harrison, P.O. Box 31718, 79120
Telephone: 806-372-5700
Facsimile: 806-372-5757
Dallas, Texas Office: 2300 Plaza of the Americas, 600 North Pearl, LB 133.
Telephone: 214-999-5700.
Facsimile: 214-999-5747.

George Whittenburg
Raymond P. Harris, Jr.
Mack Whittenburg
Deborah Ashmore Harris
Cary Ira Schachter
C. Jared Knight
Susan Lynn Burnette
Christopher W. Weber
Charles G. White
Laurel A. Siegert
Karl L. Baumgardner
Nicholas A. Taylor

For full biographical listings, see the Martindale-Hubbell Law Directory

ARLINGTON, Tarrant Co.

CRIBBS & MCFARLAND, A PROFESSIONAL CORPORATION (AV)

1000 West Abram, P.O. Box 13060, 76013
Telephone: 817-461-2000
Fax: 817-275-7810
Austin, Texas Office: 814 San Jacinto Boulevard, Suite 400.
Telephone: 512-478-1881.

James A. Cribbs
Paul F. Wieneskie
Robert McFarland
Paul Francis

Representative Clients: Bank One Arlington; Bank One Euless; Bank One Mansfield; Security Bank of Arlington; Medical Technology, Inc.; Van Zandt Realtors; City of Euless, Texas; City of Richland Hills, Texas; American Title Ins. Co.

For full biographical listings, see the Martindale-Hubbell Law Directory

*AUSTIN,** Travis Co.

AKIN, GUMP, STRAUSS, HAUER & FELD, L.L.P. (AV)

A Registered Limited Liability Partnership including Professional Corporations
Frost Bank Plaza, 816 Congress Avenue, Suite 1900, 78701
Telephone: 512-499-6200
Fax: 512-499-6290
URL: http://www.akingump.com
Dallas, Texas Office: 1700 Pacific Avenue, Suite 4100.
Telephone: 214-969-2800.
Fax: 214-969-4343.
Houston, Texas Office: 1900 Pennzoil Place-South Tower, 711 Louisiana Street.
Telephone: 713-220-5800.
Fax: 713-236-0822.
San Antonio, Texas Office: 300 Convent Street, Suite 1500.
Telephone: 210-281-7000.
Fax: 210-224-2035.
New York, New York Office: 590 Madison Avenue, 20th Floor.
Telephone: 212-872-1000.
Fax: 212-872-1002.
Philadelphia, Pennsylvania Office: One Commerce Square, 2005 Market Street, Suite 2200.
Telephone: 215-965-1200.
Fax: 215-965-1210.
Washington, D.C. Office: 1333 New Hampshire Avenue. N.W., Suite 400.
Telephone: 202-887-4000.
Fax: 202-887-4288.
Los Angeles, California Office: Century Tower Plaza, 2029 Century Park East, Suite 2600.
Telephone: 310-229-1000.
Fax: 310-229-1001.
Brussels, Belgium Office: 65 Avenue Louise, P. B. #7.
Telephone: (+32 2) 535-29-11.
Fax: (+32 2) 5 29 00.
London, England Office: One Angel Court.
Telephone: 011 44 20 7726 9600.
Fax: 011 44 20 7726 9610.
Moscow, Russia Office: Ducat Place II, 7 Gasheka Street, P.B. 20.
Telephone: 011 7 095 974 2411.
Fax: 011 7 095 974 2412.
Affiliated Office:
Law Office of Abdulaziz H. Fahad: Jarir Plaza, 4th Floor, Olaya Street, P.O. Box 15870, Riyadh, Saudi Arabia, 11454.
Telephone: 011 966 1 464 8081.
Telex: 406176 LAWS SJ.
Telecopier: 011 966 1 462 4968.

Robert N. Vedder (1945-1994) Ned Price, Sr. (1914-1999)

RETIRED

Frederick H. Young

MEMBERS

Thomas J. Bond (P.C.)
Michael R. Cannatti
James W. Cannon, Jr.
Eugene E. Elder
James B. Gambrell
Gary W. Hamilton
James W. Ingram (P.C.)
Brandon C. Janes
Glenn E. Johnson
Gary F. Kissiah
Barnett A. Kress
Timothy L. LaFrey
Larry W. Langley
Demetrius McDaniel
David W. Nelson
Yvonne K. Puig
Jody Richardson
Paul Seals
Barry R. Senterfitt
Diane B. Senterfitt
Richard J. Smith
John S. Strickland
G. Gail Watkins
Raymond E. White
Kimberly A. Yelkin (P.C.)

ASSOCIATES

Lee Ann Alexander
Patricia A. Becker
Barrett N. Bruce
Michael Chibib
Orlesia A. Duren
Richard A. Fordyce
J. Davis Gilmer
Nancy Hagquist
Mira L. Helms
Keith G. Hopkinson
Tracy L. Klinger
Richard W. Knight
Amy R. Krasner
Gregory C. Mathis
W. Brewster McCracken
Wesley A. Oliver
Lee E. Potts
Kelly A. Rittenberry
James J. Scheske
Russell C. Scott
(Not admitted in TX)
Adam D. Sheehan
Pete A. Smits
(Not admitted in TX)
Christopher H. Taylor
H. Shannon Tyson, Jr.
Mark Vane
James S. B. Whittenburg

STAFF ATTORNEY

Lisa J. Bosman (Resident)
Vera Callahan Neinast
Joe P. Reynolds

SENIOR COUNSEL

Nanette K. Beaird
James D. Bennett
(Not admitted in TX)
Robert F. Biard
James Z. Brazell
Rebecca S. Carmichael
Geoffrey Scott Connor
Dennis W. Gilstad
Diana L. Granger
Janet L. Hamilton

(See Next Column)

SENIOR COUNSEL (Continued)

Joseph H. Hart
Robert Y. Hirasuna
Tracy Walters McCormack
John R. Pitts
Dewey Poteet
Gary R. Stanford
Russell Trifovesti

COUNSEL

James D. Arbogast
Craig S. Comeaux
David L. Dawson
Melissa A. Eason
Susan Erickson Marin
Chris P. Perque

LEGAL SUPPORT PERSONNEL

Patrick Farley
(Technical Consultant)
Gloria L. Norberg
(Patent Agent)
Shayne X. Short (Patent Agent)

For full biographical listings, see the Martindale-Hubbell Law Directory

BAKER BOTTS L.L.P. (AV)

1600 San Jacinto Center, 98 San Jacinto Boulevard, 78701
Telephone: 512-322-2500
Fax: 512-322-2501
Email: postmaster@bakerbotts.com *URL:* http://www.bakerbotts.com
Houston, Texas Office: One Shell Plaza, 910 Louisiana.
Telephone: 713-229-1234.
Dallas, Texas Office: 2001 Ross Avenue.
Telephone: 214-953-6500.
Washington, D.C. Office: The Warner, 1299 Pennsylvania Avenue, N.W.
Telephone: 202-639-7700.
New York, New York Office: 599 Lexington Avenue.
Telephone: 212-705-5000.
Moscow, Russia Office: 10 ul. Bolshaya Dimitrovka (formerly Pushkinskaya), 103031.
Telephone: 7095/921-5300 (Local); 7501/929-7070 (International).
London, England Office: 45 Ludgate Hill.
Telephone: 0171-778-1400 (Local); 011-44-171-778-1400 (International).
Baku, Azerbaijan Office: 6-10 Vagif Mustafa-zadeh Street, Third Floor, Icheri Sheher, 370004.
Telephone: 994-12-97-63-88 (Local); 011-994-12-97-63-88 (International).
Fax: 994-12-97-63-61 (Local); 011-994-12-97-63-91 (International).

MEMBERS OF FIRM

Pamela M. Giblin
Aileen M. Hooks
Robert I. Howell
Jennifer Keane
Patrick O. Keel
Joseph R. Knight
Michael X. Marinelli
(Not admitted in TX)
Mark R. Robeck
Kevin M. Sadler
Robert T. Stewart
Robert W. Strauser
William F. Stutts, Jr.
Robb L. Voyles
Mark J. White
Larry F. York

SPECIAL COUNSEL

Shelley W. Austin
Thomas R. Felger
Cynthia C. Smiley

OF COUNSEL

Joe R. Greenhill
Mary F. Keller
E. Scott Lineberry
Bob E. Shannon

ASSOCIATES

David T. Arlington
Christopher T. Brown
Julie K. Buchanan
Scott King Field
Daniel S. Floyd
Susan Denmon Gusky
Sofia Harber
Robert W. Holland
Jolie M. Howard
Shannon H. Hutcheson
Christina L. Kloes
Anna Conyers Kuhn
Ann Livingston
Derek R. McDonald
Scott T. Morris
Jennifer K. Patterson
Polly F. Powell
David A. Savage
Whitney L. Swift
Gavin R. Villareal
Kelly Diane Walton
Russell W. White
Rebecca S. Whitehouse

For full biographical listings, see the Martindale-Hubbell Law Directory

DAVIS & DAVIS, P.C. (AV)

Arboretum Plaza One, 9th Floor, 9442 Capital of Texas Highway, P.O. Box 1588, 78759
Telephone: 512-343-6248
Fax: 512-343-0121
Mailing Address: P.O. Box 1588, Austin, Texas, 78767

C. Dean Davis
Fred E. Davis
Alexis J. Fuller, Jr.
Ruth Russell-Schafer
Michael L. Neely
Brian Gregory Jackson
Monte F. James

Bill Cline, Jr.
Mark Alan Keene
Kenda B. Dalrymple
Marian J. Wu
Mark S. La Spina
Paul Oveisi

For full biographical listings, see the Martindale-Hubbell Law Directory

Austin—Continued

GRAVES, DOUGHERTY, HEARON & MOODY, A PROFESSIONAL CORPORATION (AV)

Suite 2300, 515 Congress Avenue, P.O. Box 98, 78767
Telephone: 512-480-5600
Email: gdhm@gdhm.com *URL:* http://www.gdhm.com
Kerrville, Texas Office: Suite 410, 222 Sidney Baker South.
Telephone: 830-257-7311.
Fax: 830-896-7273.

SHAREHOLDERS

Ireland Graves (1885-1969)
Kathryn E. Allen
Karen J. Bartoletti
Eric G. Behrens
Diana K. Borden
Wm. Terry Bray
Boyce C. Cabaniss
Patricia A. Campbell
Carol C. Clark
Will W. Dibrell
Michael Diehl
Cliff Ernst
Eric R. Galton
John M. Harmon
R. Alan Haywood
Robert J. Hearon, Jr.
R. Clarke Heidrick, Jr.
Kevin Holcomb
Thomas B. Hudson, Jr.
G. Douglas Kilday
James M. Laughead
G. Michael Lawrence
William H. Locke, Jr.
E. Clark Lutz
(Resident, Kerrville Office)
John B. McFarland
John J. McKetta, III
Robin A. Melvin
Dan Moody, Jr.
Ron H. Moss
Preston Randall
Owen L. Roberts
Pete Schenkkan
Steven D. Smit
Roy C. Snodgrass III
Rick Triplett
Michael J. Whellan
James A. Williams

Laura Scanlan Cho
William Christian
Joan Dell Dolce
(Resident, Kerrville Office)
David H. Goodman
David Hartman
Craig Hopper
Edward S. McHorse
Erin C. Morton
Susan J. Savage

SENIOR COUNSEL

J. Chrys Dougherty

OF COUNSEL

Helen Currie Foster
David Herndon
James Noble Johnson
Donald G. Jones
Ben F. Vaughan, III, P.C.

For full biographical listings, see the Martindale-Hubbell Law Directory

HEARNE, EPPRIGHT & GEST, A PROFESSIONAL CORPORATION (AV)

700 Lavaca, Suite 1500, P.O. Box 1687, 78767
Telephone: 512-478-1500
Telecopier: 512-478-2906

Douglass D. Hearne
Charles L. Eppright
Darrell D. Gest

Douglass D. Hearne, Jr.
Allen Halbrook, Jr.
Ann R. Powers
Roger B. Williams

OF COUNSEL

Nola White

Representative Clients: Dahlstrom Corporation; EZ Pipe Paddler; Faison Stone, Inc.; Gilbane Building Supply Company; Guarantee Federal Savings; Midland Independent School District; Texas A & M University System; Temple-Inland Mortgage Corporation; University of Texas System.

For full biographical listings, see the Martindale-Hubbell Law Directory

JACKSON WALKER L.L.P. (AV)

100 Congress Avenue, Suite 1100, 78701-4099
Telephone: 512-236-2000
Fax: 512-236-2002
Email: hloftin@jw.com *URL:* http://www.jw.com
Dallas, Texas Office: 901 Main Street, Suite 6000.
Telephone: 214-953-6000.
Fax: 214-953-5822.
Fort Worth, Texas Office: 301 Commerce Street, Suite 2400.
Telephone: 817-334-7200.
Fax: 817-334-7290.
Houston, Texas Office: 1100 Louisiana, Suite 4200.
Telephone: 713-752-4200.
Fax: 713-752-4221.
Richardson, Texas Office: 2435 North Central Expressway, Suite 600.
Telephone: 972-671-2560.
Fax: 972-671-2566.
San Angelo, Texas Office: 225 West Beauregard Avenue.
Telephone: 915-481-2550.
Fax: 915-481-2552.
San Antonio, Texas Office: 112 E. Pecan Street, Suite 2100.
Telephone: 210-978-7700.
Fax: 210-978-7790.

(See Next Column)

MEMBERS OF FIRM

James M. Alsup
C. Wade Cooper
Carla J. Cox
J. Stephen Dillawn
Leonard H. Dougal
J. Matthew Dow
Aldean E. Kainz
Jeffrey T. Knebel
Harold R. Loftin, Jr.
Steven R. Martens
William R. McIlhany
Philip D. Mockford
Steven D. Moore
Robert B. Neblett, III
James M. Nias
Louis K. Obdyke, IV
Thomas T. Rogers
Thomas F. Sedberry
Michael S. Simpson
Edward C. Small
Killough Kent Smith
Peyton N. Smith
Laura Lee Stapleton
Timothy C. Taylor
Robert O. Thomas
Gary A. Thornton
Lisa K. Vaughn
Lawrence A. Waks
Gerald S. Webberman
Fred B. Werkenthin

SENIOR COUNSEL

John A. Riley

ASSOCIATES

Richard M. Crowe
Barbara B. Davenport
Carmen Symes Dusek
Kimberly A. Frost
Breck Harrison
Christine C. Heath
Sheri R. Hunter
Timothy D. Larson
Thomas M. Lipovski
Andrew Love
Jorge A. Maldonado
David A. Montoya
Joanna Kay Napp
Paulomi S. "Reena" Richtermeyer

For full biographical listings, see the Martindale-Hubbell Law Directory

MAYOR, DAY, CALDWELL & KEETON, L.L.P. (AV)

100 Congress, Suite 1500, 78701-4042
Telephone: 512-320-9200
Fax: 512-320-9292
URL: http://www.mdck.com
Houston, Texas Office: 700 Louisiana, Suite 1900.
Telephone: 713-225-7000.
FAX: 713-225-7047.

PARTNERS

Dillon J. Ferguson
(Also at Houston Office)
Stephanie Anne Kroger
Roliff H. Purrington, Jr.
(Also at Houston Office)
Rex D. VanMiddlesworth
(Also at Houston Office)

Jeffery K. Gordon
Joseph D. Hughes
Jerry V. Kyle, Jr.
C. Lane Mears
Lino Mendiola
Phillip G. Oldham
Carl S. Richie

For full biographical listings, see the Martindale-Hubbell Law Directory

MCGINNIS, LOCHRIDGE & KILGORE, L.L.P. (AV)

1300 Capitol Center, 919 Congress Avenue, 78701
Telephone: 512-495-6000
Houston, Texas Office: 3200 One Houston Center, 1221 McKinney Street.
Telephone: 713-615-8500.

OF COUNSEL

Robert W. Calvert (1905-1994)
Wade F. Spilman
Denny O. Ingram
W. James McAnelly, Jr.
(Resident, Houston Office)
David B. Young
Karla H. Bell

RETIRED OF COUNSEL

Morgan Hunter

MEMBERS OF FIRM

Robert C. McGinnis (1918-1995)
Joe M. Kilgore (1918-1999)
Lloyd Lochridge
Shannon H. Ratliff
C. Morris Davis
J. Gaylord Armstrong
Barry L. Wertz
(Resident, Houston Office)
John W. Stayton, Jr.
William H. Bingham
Robert Wilson
Steven J. Watkins
(Resident, Houston Office)
William H. Daniel
Thomas O. Barton
Julian Lockwood
Jeffrey A. Davis
(Resident, Houston Office)
Brook Bennett Brown
Marc O. Knisely
Patton G. Lochridge
Campbell McGinnis
James R. Raup
Theresa G. Eilers
W. Timothy George
Michael A. Wren
Edmond R. McCarthy, Jr.
Christine F. Miller
Jeff Bohm
Richard Kelley
Gregory S. Chanon
John R. Breihan
Ashton G. Cumberbatch, Jr.
Don Henry Magee
Douglas D. Dodds
Lin Hughes
Thomas J. Forestier
(Resident, Houston Office)
Clayton James Barton
Steve P. Turner
Karen Lynn Watkins
Penny Hobbs
John L. Wilson
Shawn P. St. Clair
Karan C. Ciotti
(Resident, Houston Office)
D. Terrence McDonald

(See Next Column)

McGINNIS, LOCHRIDGE & KILGORE L.L.P., *Austin—Continued*

ASSOCIATES

Judy Frederick
Angela Chinn Woodbury
Andrew Ramzel
(Resident, Houston Office)
Lisa A. Paulson
Donald D. Jackson
(Resident, Houston Office)
Kelly Conklin
Travis Charles Barton
Carlos R. Soltero
Scott P. Baker
Stephen E. Erickson
Joe M. Roden
(Resident, Houston Office)
Patricia D. Pope
Michael L. Navarre
Cari L. Curtis
(Resident, Houston Office)
Mark Domel
Scott S. Cooley
Samir J. Foteh
(Resident, Houston Office)
Laurie D. Tice
Kenneth C. Moursund, Jr.
(Resident, Houston Office)
Keith Strama
Ellen Beth Huchital
(Resident, Houston Office)

For full biographical listings, see the Martindale-Hubbell Law Directory

---

NAMAN, HOWELL, SMITH & LEE, A PROFESSIONAL CORPORATION (AV)

221 West Sixth Street, 1900 Bank One Tower, 78701-3485
Telephone: 512-479-0300
FAX: 512-474-1901
Email: naman@namanhowell.com *URL:* http://www.namanhowell.com
Waco, Texas Office: 900 Washington, Suite 700. P.O Box 1470.
Telephone: 254-755-4100.
FAX: 254-754-6331.
Fort Worth, Texas Office: 301 Sinclair Building, 512 Main Street.
Telephone: 817-348-0300.
Fax: 972-445-8804.
Temple, Texas Office: 6th Floor, First National Bank Building, P.O. Box 844.
Telephone: 254-778-1354.
FAX: 254-774-7254.

P. Clark Aspy
George M. Cowden
Keith E. Gamel
David G. Henry (Resident Member, Waco, Texas Office)
Allen H. King

Dennis W. Donley, Jr.
Stephen W. Sather

Representative Clients: Dow Chemical; Sabine River Authority; TXU Communications Company; TXU Communications Telephone Company; E Systems, Inc.; Monfort, Inc.; Medina Electric Cooperative, Inc.; Rayburn Country Electric Cooperative, Inc.; East Texas Fiberline Inc.; American Protective Services, Inc.

For full biographical listings, see the Martindale-Hubbell Law Directory

---

STRASBURGER & PRICE, L.L.P. (AV)

A Partnership including Professional Corporations
600 Congress Avenue, Suite 2600, 78701
Telephone: 512-499-3600
Fax: 512-499-3660
URL: http://www.strasburger.com
Dallas, Texas Office: 901 Main Street, Suite 4300.
Telephone: 214-651-4300.
Fax: 214-651-4330.
Houston, Texas Office: Suite 2800, One Houston Center, 1221 McKinney.
Telephone: 713-951-5600.
Fax: 713-951-5660.
San Antonio, Texas Office: Bank of America Plaza, 300 Convent Street, Suite 900.
Telephone: 210-250-6000.
Fax: 210-250-6100.
Mexico City Office: Montes Urales 632, Piso 3, Lomas de Chapultepec, 11000 Mexico D.F.
Telephone: 525-202-7665.
Fax: 525-202-2367.

RESIDENT MEMBERS

Mark B. Blackburn
Lloyd E. Ferguson
Bruce A. Griggs
Molly Buck Richard
Hal L. Sanders, Jr., (P.C.)
Merritt N. Spencer

OF COUNSEL

John E. Kinney
David W. Tomek

JoAnn Dalrymple
Alicia R. Duleba
Dirk M. Jordan
Jeff L. Rose
Karen S. Wright

STAFF ATTORNEY

Jane A. O'Connell

For full biographical listings, see the Martindale-Hubbell Law Directory

THOMPSON & KNIGHT L.L.P. (AV)

(Attorneys and Counselors)
1200 San Jacinto Center, 98 San Jacinto Boulevard, 78701
Telephone: 512-469-6100
Telecopy: 512-469-6180
URL: http://www.tklaw.com
Dallas, Texas Office: 1700 Pacific Avenue, Suite 3300, 75201.
Telephone: 214-969-1700.
Telecopy: 512-969-1751.
Telex: 732298.
Fort Worth, Texas Office: 801 Cherry Street, Suite 1600, 76102.
Telephone: 817-347-1700.
Telecopy: 817-347-1799.
Houston, Texas Office: Thompson Knight Brown Parker & Leahy L.L.P., 1200 Smith Street, Suite 3600, 77002-4595.
Telephone: 713-654-8111.
Telecopier: 713-654-1871.
San Pedro Garza Garcia, Nuevo León, Mexico Office: Edificio Losoles PD-4, Av. Lázaro Cárdenas No. 2400 Pte., C.P. 66220.
Telephone: (52-8) 363-0096.
Telecopy: (52-8) 363-3067.

PARTNERS

Debora Beck Alsup
Michael L. Bengtson
Jeffrey S. Boyd
Eugene W. Brees, II
Holly Claghorn
James E. Cousar
Frank L. Hill
Becky L. Jolin
James C. Morriss III
Regina C. Williams

ASSOCIATES

Kari Lavelle Arneil
Christine E. Burgess
Andrew A. Ingrum
Matthew J. Knifton
D'Ana Howard Mikeska
T. Christopher Pledger
Dale L. Roberts
Peter A. Vermillion

SENIOR ATTORNEY

Elizabeth A. Webb

OF COUNSEL

Raymond M. Galasso
(Not admitted in TX)
Mark L. Murdock

For full biographical listings, see the Martindale-Hubbell Law Directory

---

VINSON & ELKINS L.L.P. (AV)

One American Center, Suite 2700, 600 Congress Avenue, 78701-3200
Telephone: 512-495-8400
Fax: 512-495-8612
URL: http://www.velaw.com
Beijing, China Office: 20/F, Beijing Silver Tower, No. 2, Dong San Huan Bei Lu, Chaoyang District, 100027.
Telephone: +86-10-6410-6300.
Fax: +86-10-6410-6360.
Dallas, Texas Office: 3700 Trammell Crow Center, 2001 Ross Avenue, Dallas, Texas, 75201-2975.
Telephone: 214-220-7700.
Fax: 214-220-7716.
Houston, Texas Office: 2300 First City Tower, 1001 Fannin, Houston, Texas, 77002-6760.
Telephone: 713-758-2222.
Fax: 713-758-2346.
London, England Office: Regis House, 8th Floor, 45 King William Street, London, EC4R 9AN, England.
Telephone: (44-171) 618-6000.
Fax: (44-171) 618-6001.
Moscow, Russia Office: 16 Ulitsa Spiridonovka, Second Floor, 103001 Moscow, Russia.
Telephone: (7-095) 956-1995. Local
Fax: (7-095) 956-1996. U.S. Satellite
Fax: (212) 803-0142.
New York, N.Y. Office: 1325 Avenue of the Americas, 17th Floor, New York, N.Y., 10019.
Telephone: 917-206-8000.
Fax: 917-206-8100.
Singapore Office: 6 Battery Road, #39-01, Singapore, 049909.
Telephone: (65) 536-8300.
Fax: (65) 536-8311.
Washington, D.C. Office: The Willard Office Building, 1455 Pennsylvania Avenue, N.W., Washington, D.C., 20004-1008.
Telephone: 202-639-6500.
Fax: 202-639-6604.

RESIDENT PARTNERS

Robert S. Baird
James W. Boeckman
Patrick K. Breeland
Kim Edward Brightwell
Miriam M. (Dusty) Burke
Molly Cagle
Susan G. Conway
Rod T. Edens, Jr.
Christopher A. Knepp
Richard D. Milvenan
Neal A. Nichols
Beverly G. Reeves
Elizabeth P. Rippy
Willem G. Schuurman
Patrick Ford Thompson
Michael J. Tomsu
David J. Tuckfield
Jerry E. Turner
William R. Volk
Joe Bill Watkins
Donald F. Wood

(See Next Column)

VINSON & ELKINS L.L.P.—*Continued*

OF COUNSEL

O. Wade Anderson
Barry D. Burgdorf
John D. Christian
Karen J. Holody
Spikes Kangerga
Gail Weatherby

RESIDENT ASSOCIATES

Anissa A. Allbritton
J. David Bickham, Jr.
Lorin E. Bley
Jason S. Boulette
Ronald F. Bradshaw
Brian K. Buss
Charles H. Campbell, Jr.
William J. Cobb III
Alice M. Cuprill-Comas
Tracey B. Davies
Andrew DiNovo
Robert J. Dubbelde
Kelly J. Dwyer
James P. Dyer
Adam V. Floyd
Kyle K. Fox
Christopher H. Hahn
Dean W. Harvey
Robbi B. Hull
Shanna D. Jones
Katherine D. Jordan
Samuel D. Loughlin
Michael Dennis Marin
Stephen J. Moloney
Dennis W. Moore, Jr.
Jeffrey A. Mullins
Minh-Hien Nguyen
Carlos R. Peña
Jennifer Barrett Poppe
Gregory Lawrence Porter
Ann Abrams Price
Jessica L. Quinn
Elizabeth N. Rogers
Aric K. Short
Spencer Smith
Harold J. Taylor
James M. Vickery

For full biographical listings, see the Martindale-Hubbell Law Directory

WINSTEAD SECHREST & MINICK P.C. (AV)

Suite 800, 100 Congress Avenue, 78701
Telephone: 512-474-4330
Telex: 73-0051
Fax: 512-370-2850
URL: http://www.winstead.com
Dallas, Texas Office: 5400 Renaissance Tower, 1201 Elm Street.
Telephone: 214-745-5400.
Telex: 73-0051.
Fax: 214-745-5390.
Houston, Texas Office: 2400 Bank One Center, 910 Travis Street.
Telephone: 713-650-8400.
Telex: 73-0051.
Fax: 713-650-2400.
Mexico, D.F., Mexico Office: Winstead y Rivera, S.C., Av. Insurgentes Sur 1685, Piso 13-04, Torre Diamante, Colonia Guadalupe Inn, Delegacion Alvaro Obregon, 01020, Mexico, D.F., Mexico.
Telephone: (011-525) 5661-3025.
Fax: (011-525) 5661-3033.

Robert C. Bass, Jr.
Wayne W. Bost
Kent A. Caperton
Philip S. Haag
David R. Hewlett
Kelly K. Kordzik
Kelly S. Rodgers
James G. Ruiz
Berry D. Spears
Peter Winstead
Timothy E. Young

Joelle Schulze Boehle
James E. Brown II
Anthony S. Corbett
K. Samantha Engelbart Clark
Michelle Gambino
Ross S. Garsson
Karen J. Gregory
Glen A. Hodges
Mary E. Kragie
Stephanie E. Lusk
Barry S. Newberger
Michelle L. Simpkins
Stewart Whitehead

OF COUNSEL

Elbert Hooper, Jr.
Mary B. Reagan

For full biographical listings, see the Martindale-Hubbell Law Directory

BAYTOWN, Harris Co.

REID, STRICKLAND & GILLETTE, L.L.P. (AV)

A Partnership including Professional Corporations
407 Citizens Bank Tower, 1300 Rollingbrook at Garth, P.O. Box 809, 77522-0809
Telephone: 281-422-8166
Fax: 281-428-2962

Joe Reid (1887-1964)
Robert Strickland (1908-1982)
Robert L. Gillette (Retired)
John R. Sandhop (P.C.)
Everett B. Williams (P.C.)
Jon C. Pfennig (P.C.)
Stephen H. DonCarlos
Daniel D. Williams

Attorneys for: Citizens Bank & Trust Co. of Baytown, Texas; Baytown State Bank; Pasadena State Bank; Galveston County Water Control and Improvement District No. 1; The Baytown Sun.

For full biographical listings, see the Martindale-Hubbell Law Directory

*BEAUMONT,** Jefferson Co.

BENCKENSTEIN & OXFORD, L.L.P. (AV)

Community Bank Building, P.O. Box 150, 77704
Telephone: 409-833-9182
Cable Address: "Bmor"
Telex: 779485
Telefax: 409-833-8819
Email: lawfirm@benoxford.com
Houston, Texas Office: Two Post Oak Central, 1980 Post Oak Boulevard, Suite 1600, 77056.
Telephone: 713-629-0345.
Fax: 713-629-0614.

MEMBERS OF FIRM

L. J. Benckenstein (1894-1966)
F. L. Benckenstein (1918-1987)
Hubert Oxford, III
Alan G. Sampson
Frank D. Calvert
Dana Timaeus
Frances Blair Bethea
Robert J. Rose, Sr.

ASSOCIATES

F. Blair Clarke
Michael K. Eaves
Alex J. Stelly, Jr.
Robert W. Craft
Lauren Miller Robbins (Resident, Houston Office)

Representative Clients: Marine Office of American Corp. (MOAC); Moran Towing and Transportation Co., Inc.

For full biographical listings, see the Martindale-Hubbell Law Directory

MEHAFFY & WEBER, A PROFESSIONAL CORPORATION (AV)

2615 Calder Avenue, Suite 800, P.O. Box 16, 77704
Telephone: 409-835-5011
Fax: 409-835-5729; 835-5177
Email: MehaffyWeber.com
Orange, Texas Office: 1006 Green Avenue, P.O. Drawer 189.
Telephone: 409-886-7766.
Houston, Texas Office: One Allen Center, 500 Dallas, Suite 1200.
Telephone: 713-655-1200.

James W. Mehaffy (1914-1985)
Roger S. McCabe
Jim I. Graves
John Cash Smith
Arthur R. Almquist
Louis M. Scofield
Patricia Chamblin
Gene M. Williams
David B. Gaultney
Robert A. Black
Sandra F. Clark
M. C. Carrington
Kurt M. Andreason
Barbara J. Barron
Elizabeth Brandes Pratt
Joseph E. Broussard
John E. Haught
Keith W. Foley
Charles Stanton Perry
Ernest W. Boyd
Michele Y. Smith

Vickie R. Thompson
Paul R. Heyburn
James G. Martingano
Debra N. Bigler
Charles W. Goehringer, Jr.
Elizabeth C. Turley
Peter T. Gregg
E. Wade Carpenter
Nikkee E. Rutherford
Bridget M. Fuselier
Jonathan C. Allen
Chris H. Booth
Maryalyce W. Cox
Timothy A. Gasaway
Elna Nguyen Griggs
Sean Stotsky

OF COUNSEL

Otto J. Weber, Jr.
Dewey J. Gonsoulin
John J. Durkay

Representative Clients: E.I. du Pont de Nemours and Co.; Eli Lilly & Co.; Merrell Dow; Jefferson County Tax Appraisal District; W.R. Grace & Co.-Conn.; Bank of America; Christus Health; Christus St. Elizabeth; Christus St. Mary; Burlington Northern Santa Fe Railway.
Approved Attorneys for: Stewart Title Guaranty Co.

For full biographical listings, see the Martindale-Hubbell Law Directory

ORGAIN, BELL & TUCKER, L.L.P. (AV)

470 Orleans Street, 77701
Telephone: 409-838-6412
Fax: 409-838-6959
Email: obt@obt.com
URL: http://www.obt.com
Beaumont Office: 470 Orleans Street.
Telephone: 409-838-6412.
Fax: 409-838-6959.
Houston Office: 2000 West Loop South, Suite 1400.
Telephone: 713-572-8772.
Fax: 713-572-8766.
Austin Office: 1601 Rio Grande, Suite 330.
Telephone: 512-457-8797.
Fax: 512-457-8792.
Silsbee Office: 560 South Fourth Street.
Telephone: 409-386-0386.
Fax: 409-386-0900.

(See Next Column)

ORGAIN, BELL & TUCKER L.L.P., *Beaumont—Continued*

Will E. Orgain (1883-1965)
B. D. Orgain (1909-1996)
Major T. Bell (1897-1969)
John G. Tucker (Retired, 1996)
Cleve Bachman (Retired, 1994)

MEMBERS OF FIRM

James W. Hambright
Gilbert I. Low
J. Hoke Peacock, II
John Creighton, III
James H. Chesnutt, II
Jo Ben Whittenburg
Gary N. Reger
John W. Newton, III
D. Allan Jones
H. Hollis Horton, III
Robert J. Hambright
Howard L. Close
Curry L. Cooksey
Michael J. Truncale
Lance Fox
Leanne Johnson
David J. Fisher
John W. Johnson
Jack P. Carroll
Donean S. Surratt

ASSOCIATES

T. Lynn Walden
Beatrice M. Smith
Greg C. Wilkins
Dina K. Madison
Brian A. Mills
Michael L. Painter
Mary Margaret Adams
Martha R. Campbell
Jacqueline Bley Ryall

OF COUNSEL

Stanley Plettman
Benny H. Hughes

General Counsel: Gulf States Utilities Co.; Texas Commerce Bank.
Local Counsel for: Mobil Oil Corp.; General Motors Corp.; City of Beaumont; Minnesota Mining & Manufacturing Co.; Wal-Mart Stores, Inc.
Representative Insurance Clients: Kemper Group; Hartford Insurance Group; Royal Insurance.

For full biographical listings, see the Martindale-Hubbell Law Directory

STRONG, PIPKIN, NELSON, BISSELL & LEDYARD, L.L.P. (AV)

1400 San Jacinto Building, 595 Orleans, 77701-3255
Telephone: 409-981-1000
Facsimile: 409-981-1010
Houston, Texas Office: 1111 Bagby Street, Suite 2300, 77002-2546.
Telephone: 713-651-1900.
Facsimile: 713-651-1920.

Ewell Strong (1905-1974)
Charles S. Pipkin (1896-1989)
John G. Bissell (Resident Houston Office)
David W. Ledyard
Michael L. Baker
Daniel C. Ducote
Philip Babin, III
Michael T. Bridwell
John W. Bridger
Mark D. Rayburn
Greg M. Dykeman
Theodore P. Ray

Beth McGregor (Resident, Houston Office)
Daniel E. Mabry
Rocky Lawdermilk
Michael Dru Montgomery
Edward R. Batten, Jr. (Resident, Houston Office)

OF COUNSEL

Louis V. Nelson
Julie Alyssa Richardson
William J. Dyer (Resident, Houston Office)

Representative Clients: The Travelers Insurance Co.; Chevron U.S.A.; Sherwin Williams Company; The Goodyear Tire & Rubber Co.; Bituminous Insurance Companies; Exxon Corp.; The Glidden Company; Lincoln Electric Co.; Union Carbide Corp.; Occidental Chemical Corp.

For full biographical listings, see the Martindale-Hubbell Law Directory

WELLS, PEYTON, GREENBERG & HUNT, L.L.P. (AV)

6th Floor, Petroleum Building, P.O. Box 3708, 77704-3708
Telephone: 409-838-2644
Fax: 409-838-4713
Email: wellspeyton@ih2000.net

MEMBERS OF FIRM

Peter Wells (1915-1991)
George E. Duncan (1917-1979)
S. L. Greenberg
Tanner T. Hunt, Jr.
John B. Quigley
Phil Dunlap
Peter Boyd Wells, III
Bruce M. Partain
Melody G. Thomas
J. Mitchell Smith

ASSOCIATE

Julie Dyan Joffrion
Gary J. Linthicum

OF COUNSEL

Louis H. Beard

For full biographical listings, see the Martindale-Hubbell Law Directory

*BRENHAM,** Washington Co.

MOORMAN, TATE, MOORMAN, URQUHART & HALEY, L.L.P. (AV)

207 East Main Street, P.O. Box 1808, 77834-1808
Telephone: 409-836-5664
Fax: 409-830-0913
Email: hmoorman@moormantate.com *URL:* http://www.moormantate.com

George R. Moorman (Retired)
Milton Y. Tate, Jr.
R. Hal Moorman, IV
Larry P. Urquhart
Steven C. Haley

Representative Clients: Citizens State Bank, Somerville; Texas National Bank, Brenham; Brenham National Bank, Brenham; Purina Mills, Inc.; Puriina Cattle Management Services; Leggett & Platt, Inc.; Pipeline Pigging Products, Inc.; Western International Gas & Cylinders, Inc.; Blinn College.

For full biographical listings, see the Martindale-Hubbell Law Directory

*BROWNSVILLE,** Cameron Co.

RODRIGUEZ, COLVIN & CHANEY, L.L.P. (AV)

1201 East Van Buren, P.O. Box 2155, 78520
Telephone: 956-542-7441
Fax: 956-541-2170
McAllen, Texas Office: 4900 North 10th.
Telephone: 956-686-1287.
Telecopier: 956-686-6197.
Harlingen, Texas Office: 402 East Van Buren.
Telephone: 956-423-0216.
Telecopier: 956-423-2035.

MEMBERS OF FIRM

Eduardo R. Rodriguez
Norton A. Colvin, Jr.
Mitchell C. Chaney
Marjory Colvin Batsell
Jaime A. Saenz
Joseph A. (Tony) Rodriguez
Alison D. Kennamer

ASSOCIATES

Laura J. Urbis
Lecia L. Chaney
Daniel D. Herink
Robert Patrick Rodriguez
Rosa Maria Villagomez
Vanessa Garza
Teri L. Danish

OF COUNSEL

Orrin W. Johnson (Resident, Harlingen Office)
Benjamin S. Hardy (1912-1993)
Neil E. Norquest (Resident, McAllen Office)
Chris A. Brisack (Resident, McAllen Office)
Raymond A. Cowley

Division Attorneys for: Union Pacific Railroad.
Counsel for: Texas Commerce Bank-Rio Grande Valley, N.A.; Texas Commerce Bancshares, Inc.

For full biographical listings, see the Martindale-Hubbell Law Directory

ROYSTON, RAYZOR, VICKERY & WILLIAMS, L.L.P. (AV)

55 Cove Circle, 78521
Telephone: 956-542-4377
Cable Address: "Padre"
Telex: 767-817
Telecopier: 956-542-4370
Mailing Address: P.O. Box 3509, Brownsville, Texas, 78523-3509
Email: royston@roystonlaw.com *URL:* http://www.roystonlaw.com
Corpus Christi, Texas Office: 1700 Wilson Plaza West, 606 North Carancahua.
Telephone: 361-884-8808.
Cable Address: "CC PORT"
Telex: 6866625.
Telecopier: 361-884-7261.
Galveston, Texas Office: 205 Cotton Exchange Building. 2102 Mechanic Street.
Telephone: 409-763-1623.
Cable Address: "Houport"
Telex: 6869017.
Telecopier: 409-763-3853.
Houston, Texas Office: 600 Travis Street, Suite 2200.
Telephone: 713-224-8380.
Cable Address: "Houport"
Telex: 6869017.
Telecopier: 713-225-9945.
Lubbock, Texas Office: 1401 Avenue G.
Telephone: 806-763-9252.
Telex: 6869017.
Telecopier: 806-763-9254.
San Antonio, Texas Office: 2000 Riverview Towers, 111 Soledad Street.
Telephone: 210-228-0655.
Telecopier: 210-228-0839.

PARTNERS

Keith N. Uhles
James H. Hunter, Jr.

(See Next Column)

ROYSTON, RAYZOR, VICKERY & WILLIAMS L.L.P.—*Continued*

ASSOCIATES

Javier González
Ewing E. Sikes III
Daniel P. Whitworth

For full biographical listings, see the Martindale-Hubbell Law Directory

*CENTER,** Shelby Co.

FAIRCHILD, PRICE, THOMAS, HALEY & WILLINGHAM, L.L.P. (AV)

413 Shelbyville Street, P.O. Drawer 1719, 75935
Telephone: 409-598-2981
Fax: 409-598-7712
Email: wmthomas@fpthw.com
Nacogdoches, Texas Office: 1801 North Street, P. O. Box 631668, 75963-1668.
Telephone: 409-569-2327.
Fax: 409-569-7932. E-Mail: chaley@fpthw.com
Houston, Texas Office: 440 Louisiana Street, Suite 2110, 77002-4205.
Telephone: 713-426-1700.
Fax: 713-426-1717. E-Mail: mwillingham@fpthw.com

MEMBERS OF FIRM

John L. Price
W. Miller Thomas
C. Victor Haley
R. Mark Willingham
Ryan A. Beason (Resident at Houston Office)
Travis P. Clardy
David J. Fisher
Clayton H. Haley
Russell R. Smith
James A. Payne, Jr.

OF COUNSEL

Robert L. Fairchild

ASSOCIATES

David Edward Ash
Campbell Cox
Jefferson B. Davis
Thomas L. Cougill
Jeffrey Pierce Fultz
Matthew D. Mettauer

For full biographical listings, see the Martindale-Hubbell Law Directory

*CORPUS CHRISTI,** Nueces Co.

PEARSON & PRICE, PLLC (AV)

Suite 1700, South Tower, 800 North Shoreline Boulevard, 78401
Telephone: 361-885-0077
Fax: 361-885-0288
Email: INFO@PEARSON-PRICE.COM *URL:* HTTP://WWW.PEARSON-PRICE.COM

Paul C. Pearson, III
Paul O. Price
Richard E. Flint

For full biographical listings, see the Martindale-Hubbell Law Directory

ROYSTON, RAYZOR, VICKERY & WILLIAMS, L.L.P. (AV)

1700 Wilson Plaza West, 606 North Carancahua, 78476
Telephone: 361-884-8808
Cable Address: "CC PORT"
Telex: 6866625
Telecopier: 361-884-7261
Email: royston@roystonlaw.com *URL:* http://www.roystonlaw.com
Brownsville, Texas Office: 55 Cove Circle, P.O. Box 3509.
Telephone: 956-542-4377.
Cable Address: "Padre"
Telex: 767-817.
Telecopier: 956-542-4370.
Galveston, Texas Office: 205 Cotton Exchange Building, 2101 Mechanic Street.
Telephone: 409-763-1623.
Cable Address: "Houport"
Telex: 6869017.
Telecopier: 409-763-3853.
Houston, Texas Office: 600 Travis Street, Suite 2200.
Telephone: 713-224-8380.
Cable Address: "Houport"
Telex: 686-9017.
Telecopier: 713-225-9945.
Lubbock, Texas Office: 1401 Avenue G.
Telephone: 806-763-9252.
Telex: 6869017.
Telecopier: 806-763-9254.
San Antonio, Texas Office: 2000 Riverview Towers, 111 Soledad Street.
Telephone: 210-228-0655.
Telecopier: 210-228-0839.

PARTNERS

Ralph F. Meyer
Will W. Pierson
Timothy D. McMurtrie
Jack C. Partridge
Christopher Lowrance
Myra K. Morris

(See Next Column)

ASSOCIATES

Sean C. Henkel
Abel Herrero
Richard A. Mlynek
Molly P. Thomas

For full biographical listings, see the Martindale-Hubbell Law Directory

*DALLAS,** Dallas Co.

AKIN, GUMP, STRAUSS, HAUER & FELD, L.L.P. (AV)

A Registered Limited Liability Partnership including Professional Corporations
1700 Pacific Avenue Suite 4100, 75201-4675
Telephone: 214-969-2800
Fax: 214-969-4343
URL: http://www.akingump.com
Austin, Texas Office: Frost Bank Plaza, 816 Congress Avenue, Suite 1900.
Telephone: 512-499-6200.
Fax: 512-499-6290.
Houston, Texas Office: 1900 Pennzoil Place-South Tower, 711 Louisiana Street.
Telephone: 713-220-5800.
Fax: 713-236-0822.
San Antonio, Texas Office: 300 Convent Street, Suite 1500.
Telephone: 210-281-7000.
Fax: 210-224-2035.
New York, New York Office: 590 Madison Avenue, 20th Floor.
Telephone: 212-872-1000.
Fax: 212-872-1002.
Philadelphia, Pennsylvania Office: One Commerce Square, 2005 Market Street, Suite 2200.
Telephone: 215-965-1200.
Fax: 215-965-1210.
Washington, D.C. Office: 1333 New Hampshire Avenue, N.W., Suite 400.
Telephone: 202-887-4000.
Fax: 202-887-4288.
Los Angeles, California Office: Century Tower Plaza, 2029 Century Park East, Suite 2600.
Telephone: 310-229-1000.
Fax: 310-229-1001.
Brussels, Belgium Office: 65 Avenue Louise, P.B. #7.
Telephone: (+32 2) 535-29-11.
Fax: (+32 2) 535 29 00.
Moscow, Russia Office: Ducat Place II, 7 Gasheka Street, P.B. 20.
Telephone: 011 7 095 974 2411.
Fax: 011 7 095 974 2412.
London, England Office: One Angel Court.
Telephone: 011 44 20 7726 9600.
Fax: 011 44 20 7726 9610.
Affiliated Office:
Law Office of Abdulaziz H. Fahad: Jarir Plaza, 4th Floor, Olaya Street, P.O. Box 15870, Riyadh, Saudi Arabia, 11454.
Telephone: 011 966 1 464 8081.
Telex: 406176 LAWS SJ.
Telecopier: 011 966 1 462 4968.

Gary A. Herman (1942-1987)
Herbert S. Kendrick (1934-1990)
Thomas J. Raleigh (1924-1993)
Hailey A. Roberts (1931-1995)

RETIRED

Henry D. Akin
Richard A. Gump, Sr.
John L. Hauer (P.C.)
John Q. Stilwell (P.C.)

MEMBERS OF FIRM

Roger D. Arnold
Louis P. Bickel
Randall C. Brown
John M. Cone
Edward A. Copley (P.C.)
Karen C. Corallo
Walter S. Cowger
G. Michael Curran
Clarice M. Davis (P.C.)
Michael E. Dillard (P.C.)
Diana C. Dutton (P.C.)
Alan D. Feld (P.C.)
Laura M. Franze
N. Kathleen Friday (P.C.)
Lisa S. Gallerano
Charles R. Gibbs
Kenneth R. Glaser
Christopher M. Gores (P.C.)
Robin R. Green
William T. Hankinson
Terence J. Hart
John V. Jansonius
Tonya Powers Johannsen
Edward S. Koppman (P.C.)
Barnett A. Kress
Randall R. Kucera (P.C.)
Ford Lacy (P.C.)
Alan L. Laves (P.C.)
Gary M. Lawrence
Carl B. Lee (P.C.)
George T. Lee, Jr., (P.C.)
Richard C. Levin (P.C.)
Michael Lowenberg (P.C.)
David R. McAtee
Patrick F. McGowan
J. Kenneth Menges, Jr., (P.C.)
Daniel J. Micciche (P.C.)
R. Terry Miller
Seth R. Molay (P.C.)
Steven M. Morgan (P.C.)
Diane B. Muse
Mary L. O'Connor (P.C.)
Michael A. Piazza
Eliot D. Raffkind
Randall M. Ratner (P.C.)
Terry M. Schpok (P.C.)
Richard L. Schwartz
Robert S. Strauss
Michael T. Tarski (P.C.)
Timothy P. Tehan (P.C.)
J. Patrick Tielborg (P.C.)
James M. Underwood
Alan M. Utay
Antonie L. Wells Whittier

(See Next Column)

AKIN, GUMP, STRAUSS, HAUER & FELD L.L.P., *Dallas—Continued*

ASSOCIATES

Rebecca Alfert
Todd R. Amacher
Keith M. Aurzada
Richard W. Bachmann
Lori L. Baker
M. Scott Barnard
Kevin N. Barrett
Jonathan Barsade (Not admitted in TX)
Ronald Bendalin
Amy K. Bock
Eric R. Bradley
Jennifer R. Brannen
Thomas G. Buchanan, III
Stephanie A. Burris
Louisa Ann Collins
Richard Cortez, Jr.
Tracy Ann Crum
James A. Deeken
Joseph F. DePumpo
Gemma L. Descoteaux
Andrew W. Duettra
John Russell Emerson
Leigh Ann K. Epperson
Priscilla Ferguson
Edward J. Fields, Jr.
Alex Frutos
J. Eric Gambrell
Rani C. Garcia
Noel R. Gattis
Kelley M. Goes
Jeffrey M. Goldfarb
Alan O. Goodrich
Andrew M. Gould
Cynthia L. Hageman
Clay A. Hartmann
Susan Hays
Owen D. Hill
Marcia Nelson Jackson
Scott R. Jacobs
Carol Johnson
Tamara R. Jones
Daniel W. Keene
Pamela W. Kernie
Sarah B. Kight
Scott H. Kimpel
Arina Lekhe
Joseph A. Malick
Roger D. Martin
Amanda M. McMillian
Michael Meskill
Mark T. Mitchell
Marco A. Molina
Joseph L. Motes III
Kristi Ulyn Motley
David T. Norton
Firouzeh Nour
Megan M. O'Laughlin
Thomas E. Oney
Stephanie Osteen
Christina M. Pant
Christopher A. Peckham
F. Jerry Phelps
Tamara L. Reno
R. Scott Rhoades
S. Preston Ricardo
Claude D. Rich
Christopher J. Rourk
Nancy C. Rush
Aaron A. Scow
Tamara Brock Segal
Akash D. Sethi
Brian Siegal
Stephanie J. Stafford
Andrew R.A. Stewart
Mark A. Stoleson
Ian N. Trumpower
Raymond P. Turner
Jenna Vick Unell
M. Todd Williams
Scott T. Williams
Andrew Woodward
Troy D. Wuertz

SENIOR COUNSEL/ADVISOR

Diane P. Couchman
George "Russ" Schultz
Mark R. Shaw
Daniel A. Winterbottom, Jr.
Eldon L. Youngblood

COUNSEL

M. Brett Burns
Allison K. Exall
Jeffrey K. Feinglas
John L. Hendricks
Roland M. Juarez (Not admitted in TX)
Sandra K. Lauro
Cynthia Brotman Nelson
Jonathan N. Quenzer
Steven E. Ross
Shannon B. Schmoyer
Michael A. Slaney (Not admitted in TX)
David F. Staber
Kimberly O'Dawn Thompson
Katherine M. Warner

STAFF ATTORNEY

James M. McGee

MANAGER, CORPORATE SECTION TECHNOLOGY DEVELOPMENT AND FORMS

Katherine L. Squires (Not admitted in TX)

LEGAL SUPPORT PERSONNEL

Diana C. Nugent Cone (Trademark Manager)
Jose R. Matos (Patent Agent)
Michael E. Martin (Patent Agent)

For full biographical listings, see the Martindale-Hubbell Law Directory

ANDREWS & KURTH L.L.P. (AV)

Suite 3700, 1717 Main Street, 75201
Telephone: 214-659-4400
Telex: 70-9669 Ankur Dal
Telecopier: 214-659-4401
Email: webmaster@andrews-kurth.com *URL:* http://www.andrews-kurth.com
Houston, Texas Office: Suite 4200, 600 Travis, 77002.
Telephone: 713-220-4200.
Telecopier: 713-220-4285. E-Mail: webmaster@andrews-kurth.com.
The Woodlands, Texas Office: Suite 150, 2170 Buckthorne Place, 77380.
Telephone: 713-220-4801.
Telecopier: 713-220-4815.
Washington, D.C. Office: Suite 300, 1701 Pennsylvania Avenue, N.W.
Telephone: 202-662-2700.
Telecopier: 202-662-2739.
Los Angeles, California Office: Suite 4200, 601 S. Figueroa Street.
Telephone: 213-896-3100.
Telecopier: 213-896-3137.

(See Next Column)

New York, N.Y. Office: 805 Third Avenue.
Telephone: 212-850-2800.
Telecopier: 212-850-2929.
London, England Office: 2 Creed Court, 5-11 Ludgate Hill, EC4M 7AA.
Telephone: 0171-236-3456.
Telecopier: 0171-236-4276.

MEMBERS OF FIRM

David A. Barbour (Resident, London, England Office)
Gregory Haynes Bevel
Andrew L. Campbell
Gerald C. Conley
John Dugdale (Not admitted in TX)
Alan W. Harris
J. Gregory Holloway
Karen Gren Johnson
Brigitte Gawenda Kimichik
Charles T. Marshall
Peter K. McKee, Jr.
J. Van Oliver
Thomas R. Popplewell
Dennis Neil Ryan
Patrick C. Sargent
Deborah Lynn Schrier-Rape
Robert B. Weathersby
Kathleen J. Wu

OF COUNSEL

Steven R. Smith

ASSOCIATES

Katy Barklow Abel
Jules E. Angelley
J. Kevin Boardman
Jason S. Brookner (Not admitted in TX)
Tracy L. Burks
Mark W. Harris
Farley G. Houston
Kirk A. Kennedy
Kristin Jain
Michelle VonSenden Larson
Joseph E. Lednick, Jr.
Lila Clark Marsh
Bernard H. Masters
Kevin D. McCullough
Muriel C. McFarling
Scott M. McMillan
James P. Muenker
Bryan Scott Olson
Paul R. Sève
Linda R. Stahl
Darla K. Stockton
Timothy E. Taylor
Taylor D. Thaggard
Kacy J. Whitehead

SENIOR ATTORNEY

Britton B. Green

For full biographical listings, see the Martindale-Hubbell Law Directory

JOSEPH E. ASHMORE, JR., P.C. (AV)

Regency Plaza, 3710 Rawlins, Suite 1210, LB 84, 75219-4217
Telephone: 214-559-7202
Fax: 214-520-1550

Joseph E. Ashmore, Jr.

C. Gregory Shamoun
Gary M. Ashmore
Howard J. Klatsky
Lori Ashmore Peters
Brian K. Norman
Jeffrey A. Yates

For full biographical listings, see the Martindale-Hubbell Law Directory

BAKER BOTTS L.L.P. (AV)

2001 Ross Avenue, 75201
Telephone: 214-953-6500
Fax: 214-953-6503
Email: postmaster@bakerbotts.com *URL:* http://www.bakerbotts.com
Houston, Texas Office: One Shell Plaza, 910 Louisiana.
Telephone: 713-229-1234.
Washington, D.C. Office: The Warner, 1299 Pennsylvania Avenue, N.W.
Telephone: 202-639-7700.
Austin, Texas Office: 1600 San Jacinto Center, 98 San Jacinto Boulevard.
Telephone: 512-322-2500.
New York, New York Office: 599 Lexington Avenue.
Telephone: 212-705-5000.
Moscow, Russia Office: 10 ul. Bolshaya Dimitrovka (formerly Pushkinskaya), 103031.
Telephone: 7095/921-5300 (Local); 7095/929-7070.
London, England Office: 45 Ludgate Hill.
Telephone: 0171-778-1400 (Local); 011-44-171-778-1400 (International).
Baku, Azerbaijan Office: 6-10 Vagif Mustafa-zadeh Street, Third Floor, Icheri Sheher, 370004.
Telephone: 994-12-97-63-88 (Local); 011-994-12-97-63-88 (International).

MEMBERS OF FIRM

Earl B. Austin
Andrew M. Baker
Van H. Beckwith
Bryant C. Boren, Jr.
Larry D. Carlson
Robert M. Chiaviello, Jr.
Alison A. Courtwright
Henry D. DeBerry, III
Peter B. Dewar
Jonathan W. Dunlay
Timothy S. Durst
Charles S. Fish
Roderick A. Goyne
Dan Hartsfield
Robert W. Jordan
Robert W. Kantner
Jack L. Kinzie
George C. Lamb III
Stephen D. Marcus
John W. Martin
Kevin J. Meek
Jerry W. Mills
Peter A. Moir
Timothy W. Mountz
Geoffrey L. Newton
Ronald L. Palmer
Rod Phelan
Bruce D. Pingree
Sarah M. Rechter (Not admitted in TX)
Brenda T. Rhoades
Daniel J. Riley
Eric J. Senske
Bobbie T. Shell

(See Next Column)

BAKER BOTTS L.L.P.—*Continued*

MEMBERS OF FIRM (Continued)

Patricia M. Stanton
Don C. Stephenson
Edwin J. Tomko
Robb L. Voyles
Karen Leslye Wolf

SPECIAL COUNSEL

Nanette Rutka Everson (Not admitted in TX)
Thomas R. Felger
Mary L. Scott
T. Murray Smith (Not admitted in TX)
Kenneth B. Tomlinson

OF COUNSEL

Harold E. Meier
Robert J. Stokes

ASSOCIATES

David G. Adams
Curtis B. Anderson
James L. Baudino
Jeffery D. Baxter
Jay Bhattacharya
Samir A. Bhavsar
William R. Borchers
Robin Annette Brooks
Christian Brose
Randolph L. Burns
Darren W. Collins
Aaron D. Davidson
Lisa DiIorio
Rachel J. Doyle
Elizabeth E. Drigotas
David C. Druffner
Christopher D. Epperson (Not admitted in TX)
David M. Genender
Karen E. Griffin
Kelly D. Hine
Keiko Ichiye
Wei Wei Jeang
J. Atwood Jeter
Jay B. Johnson (Not admitted in TX)
William Johnson
Christopher W. Kennerly
Samara Lackman Kline
Tara D. Knapp
Jason D. Krieser (Not admitted in TX)
Douglas M. Kubehl
Michael C. Li
Jose M. Luzarraga
Rodney A. Malpert
Cheryl L. Mann
Julio Martin
Thomas J. Masterson
Randall W. Mishler (Not admitted in TX)
David G. Monk
Tyler L. Murray
Colleen B. Nabhan
Brian W. Oaks
Joel M. Overton, Jr.
K. Alan Parry
Karen B. Peck
Pamela B. Peck
Pennie Peck
Luke K. Pedersen
Chad M. Pinson
Royce P. Poinsett
Tracy L. S. Pylant
Douglass M. Rayburn
Adolfo R. Rodriguez, Jr.
Fernando Rodriguez, Jr.
Andy D. Sarwal
J. Kemp Sawers
Katrin U. Schatz
Steven G. Schortgen
Barton Earl Showalter
Alexandra L. Siegel
Anita J. Smith
Terry J. Stalford
Alfred Steiner
Brenda Levine Sutherland
Arthur C. Swanson
Matthew B. Talpis
Ardita L. Vick
David G. Wille
Bradley P. Williams
Carol R. Young

For full biographical listings, see the Martindale-Hubbell Law Directory

BAKER & MCKENZIE (AV)

4500 Trammell Crow Center, 2001 Ross Avenue, 75201
Telephone: (214) 978-3000
Intn'l. Dialing: (1-214) 978-3000
Facsimiles: (1-214) 978-3099; 978-3096
URL: http://www.bakerinfo.com
Associated Offices of Baker & McKenzie in: Almaty, Amsterdam, Bahrain, Baku, Bangkok, Barcelona, Beijing, Berlin, Bogotá, Brasília, Brussels, Budapest, Buenos Aires, Cairo, Caracas, Chicago, Düsseldorf, Frankfurt, Geneva, Hanoi, Ho Chi Minh City, Hong Kong, Houston, Hsinchu, Juárez, Kiev, London, Madrid, Manila, Melbourne, México City, Miami, Milan, Monterrey, Moscow, Münich, New York, Palo Alto, Paris, Prague, Rio de Janeiro, Riyadh, Rome, St. Petersburg, San Diego, San Francisco, Santiago, São Paulo, Singapore, Stockholm, Sydney, Taipei, Tijuana, Tokyo, Toronto, Valencia, Warsaw, Washington, D.C. and Zürich.
Correspondent Law Firm: Hadiputranto, Hadinoto & Partners, Jakarta.

MEMBERS OF FIRM

Robert H. Albaral
Robert D. Allen
R. Doak Bishop
Dan S. Boyd
David G. Glickman
Alan G. Harvey
Brian J. Hurst
Lawrence J. Johnson
Steve C. Kardell, Jr.
Sergio A. Leiseca, Jr.
Daniel W. Rabun
Mark D. Taylor

NATIONAL PARTNERS

Jordan W. Cowman
John G. Flaim

ASSOCIATES

Heiko E. Burow
Meloney J. Cargil
Kelly J. Curnutt
Mirut P. Dalal
Linda T. Dedman
Daniel P. Elms
Magdeline R. Esquivel
James E. Etri
James M. Fisher II
Jorge A. Gonzalez
Douglas R. Hafer
Holly L. Harris
Patti J. Hedgpeth
Michelle C. Johns
Larry R. Kemm
W. Crews Lott
Tamika D. Lynch
Brant C. Martin

(See Next Column)

ASSOCIATES (Continued)

Lisa A. May
Brian C. McCormack
Marilyn P. Moore
Anita L. Nesser
Jonathan B. Newton
Rakhee Patel
Melinda R. Phelan
Irina B. Plumlee
Gregory S. Porter
Christina E. Pritchard
Kimberly F. Rich
Julia L. (Jill) Stommes
Scott A. Wheatley
Timothy A. Whisler, Jr.
Roland P. Wiederaenders

For full biographical listings, see the Martindale-Hubbell Law Directory

BICKEL & BREWER (AV)

4800 Bank One Center, 1717 Main Street, 75201
Telephone: 214-653-4000
Fax: 214-653-1015
Email: counsel@bickelbrewer.com *URL:* http://www.bickelbrewer.com
Chicago, Illinois Office: 35 W. Wacker Drive, Suite 3830, 60601.
Telephone: 312-855-9200.
Fax: 312-855-1234.
New York, New York Office: 885 Third Avenue, Suite 3040, 10022.
Telephone: 212-489-1400.
Fax: 212-758-6468.

MEMBERS OF FIRM

John W. Bickel II
William A. Brewer III
Thomas C. Cronin (Not admitted in TX)
Robert P. Cummins (Not admitted in TX; Resident, Chicago, Illinois Office)
Deborah Deitsch-Perez (Resident, New York, N.Y. Office)
Porter F. Fleming (Resident, New York, N.Y. Office)
Joyce M. Hellstern
Scott S. Hershman
Paul B. Lackey
James S. Renard
William G. Todd (Resident, New York, N.Y. Office)

SENIOR ASSOCIATES

Wayne S. Ball
Kennedy Barnes
Michael S. Gardner
Jo Esta Hartwick
Kelly D. Hollingsworth
Bryan J. Wick

ASSOCIATES

Richard W. Barrett
Scott J. Bornstein (Resident, New York, N.Y. Office)
Daniel L. Brown (Resident, New York, N.Y. Office)
D. Wade Carvell
Carmela DeGruttola (Resident, New York, N.Y. Office)
Marsha L. Foulks

OF COUNSEL

Camille Reid McLeod

For full biographical listings, see the Martindale-Hubbell Law Directory

CALHOUN & STACY (AV)

Suite 5700 - Bank of America Plaza, 901 Main Street, 75202-3713
Telephone: 214-748-5000
Facsimile: 214-748-1421
Email: info@calhounstacy.com *URL:* http://www.calhounstacy.com

MEMBERS OF FIRM

Rees T. Bowen, III
Mark Alan Calhoun
Dennis D. Conder
LeAnn Wainscott Cross
David W. Elrod
Parker Nelson
Thomas E. Rosen
Shannon B. Schuster
Roy L. Stacy
Pamela J. Touchstone
Michael C. Wright

ASSOCIATES

David G. Allen
Joseph G. Barkate, Jr.
Scott S. Crocker
Sean P. Fitzgerald
Elizabeth Reding Gambrell
Leanne Capps Medford
Jonathan G. Polak
Joel W. Reese
Jennifer Young Timmons
Brad Westmoreland
Barbara L. Wohlrabe

For full biographical listings, see the Martindale-Hubbell Law Directory

CANTEY & HANGER (AV)

A Registered Limited Liability Partnership
3330 Harwood Center, 1999 Bryan Street, 75201
Telephone: 214-978-4100; Metro 972-263-7729
FAX: 214-978-4150
Email: cantey@onramp.net
Fort Worth, Texas Office: 2100 Burnett Plaza, 801 Cherry Street.
Telephone: 817-877-2800, Metro Line: 429-3815.
Telex: 758631.
FAX: 877-2807. Email: cantey@onramp.net
Austin, Texas Office: Cantey & Hanger Roan & Autrey L.L.P., 200 First State Bank Tower, 400 West Fifteenth Street.
Telephone: 512-474-4200.
FAX: 512-469-0470; 512-469-0474. Email: FIRM@ROAN-AUTREY.COM

(See Next Column)

CANTEY & HANGER, *Dallas—Continued*

MEMBERS OF FIRM

Robert P. Franke
Thomas L. Kelly, Jr.
Michael A. McClelland
Ashley Ty Parrish
Jon G. Petersen
Randall K. Price
Stephen C. Reid, III
T. Lee Wilkins

ASSOCIATES

Raymond Gilsoul
R. Douglas Scott

Represent: General Motors Corp.; Miller Brewing Co.; The Medical Protective Co.; Texas Utilities Electric Co.; Bank of America, N.A.; Union Pacific Resources Co.

For full biographical listings, see the Martindale-Hubbell Law Directory

CARRINGTON, COLEMAN, SLOMAN & BLUMENTHAL, L.L.P. (AV)

200 Crescent Court, Suite 1500, 75201
Telephone: 214-855-3000
Telecopy: 214-855-1333
Email: ccsb@ccsb.com *URL:* http://www.carringtoncoleman.com

MEMBERS OF FIRM

James E. Coleman, Jr.
Robert L. Blumenthal
Fletcher L. Yarbrough
James A. Ellis, Jr.
Peter Tierney
Lyman G. Hughes
Corbet F. Bryant, Jr.
Tyler A. Baker, III
Stephen A. Goodwin
Michael Prince
Charles C. Jordan
James E. McClain
Tim Gavin
Bruce W. Collins
David G. Drumm
Craig W. Weinlein
Rodney H. Lawson
Russell F. Nelms
Ken Carroll
Jeffrey S. Levinger
Richard A. Rohan
John W. Wesley
Tod B. Edel
Barry R. Bell
Diane M. Sumoski
Lyndon F. Bittle
James A. Cox
S. Todd Barton
Gregg R. Cannady
Mike Birrer
Allison Aranson Jacobsen

SENIOR COUNSEL

Marvin S. Sloman

COUNSEL

Don R. Hanmer
Luke Madole
Jane Makela
John Andrew Martin

ASSOCIATES

Christopher J. Akin
Cathy Lilford Altman
Ann Marie Arcadi
Bonita Carol Barksdale
Charles J. Blanchard
C. Randall Carr
David S. Coale
Gary R. Cohen
Stacy Lancaster Cozad
Stephanie M. Dooley
G. Daniel Erhard
Elisa G. Feldman
Kelli M. Hinson
Lara Hudgins Hollingsworth
Amy K. Hunt
Joshua A. Imhoff
Cheryl L. Johnson
James W. Kuntz
Brett Kutnick
Angelina LaPenotiere
Monica Wiseman Latin
Sally A. Longroy
Eric Madden
Elaine A. Manuel
Sean J. McCaffity
Jennifer Evans Morris
Christopher T. Nixon
Carolyn Konicek Raines
Jennifer A. Rangel
William A. Reece, II
Jennifer Salisbury
Christopher J. Scanlan
Roshan Zaman Selod
Sharon J. Shumway
Gregg L. Thorsen

For full biographical listings, see the Martindale-Hubbell Law Directory

CLARK, WEST, KELLER, BUTLER & ELLIS, L.L.P. (AV)

4800 Renaissance Tower, 1201 Elm Street, 75270-2146
Telephone: 214-741-1001
Telecopier: 214-760-9812

MEMBERS OF FIRM

William H. Clark (1861-1931)
William H. Clark, Jr. (1895-1943)
Robert L. Clark (1903-1963)
William L. Keller
Allen Butler
David M. Ellis
Melvyn L. Douglas
Mike M. Tabor
Mark A. Shank
Michael P. Maslanka
Kervyn B. Altaffer, Jr.
Kelly Gaffney McClure

ASSOCIATES

Veronica Cuadra
Melinda L. Eitzen
Wade A. Forsman
Theresa M. Gegen
M. Brenk Johnson
Christie A. Newkirk
Robert J. Wood, Jr.
John Peter Hagan
Sonja J. McGill

For full biographical listings, see the Martindale-Hubbell Law Directory

COWLES & THOMPSON, A PROFESSIONAL CORPORATION (AV)

901 Main Street Suite 4000, 75202
Telephone: 214-672-2000
Metro: 972-263-0005
Fax: 214-672-2020
URL: http://www.cowlesthompson.com
McKinney, Texas Office: 307 S. McDonald St., 75069-5659.
Telephone: 972-542-5000. Metro: 972-562-2270.
Fax: 972-542-5040.
Tyler, Texas Office: 1103 First Place, P.O. Box 239, 75710-0239.
Telephone: 903-593-7508.
Fax: 903-593-4057.

Charles C. Sorrells (1925-1982)
Jim E. Cowles
Hardy E. Thompson, III
Philipa M. Remington
Charles A. Green
Mark A. Stinnett
Melissa J. Pegram
Glenda O. Brewer
Stan Thiebaud
William D. Cobb, Jr.
Auston Cherry
Dwayne J. Hermes
Brian A. Mottet
Michael L. Hurst
Charles T. Frazier, Jr.
John M. Pease
Robert G. Buchanan, Jr.
David R. Woodward
Pete Eckert
B. Michael Bennett
Susan J. Snare
Russell G. Thornton
Mickie S. Bragalone
Warren Austin Gage
Sim Israeloff
David M. Hymer
Daniel D. Tostrud
Nancy Forbis Carnahan
Veronica M. Bates
Stuart B. O'Neil
Kelly N. Lovitt
John M. Hill
Julia F. Pendery
Ramona Martinez
Thomas L. Mighell
Donald B. Collins
Gregory W. Carboy
Angela K. Washington

OF COUNSEL

Kenneth C. Dippel
Kenneth J. Mighell

Christopher W. Holmes
Russell S. Newhouse
Mary E. Reyes
Shari A. Keely
Jonathan C. LaMendola
Gracelyn (Lynn) Sessions
Susan I. Nelson
Jonathan D. Campbell
Steven F. Barrett
Paula Shiroma-Bender
Ty A. Bailey
Michelle Cochran Clay
Larry W. Johnson
David E. Pomes
Ann R. Kuzel
Frank Alvarez
Pamela H. Liston
Meredith Clayton Allen
Katherine K. Elrich
Suneese R. Haywood
Michael C. Lowe
Lindsay B. Nickle
Jeff Nicodemus
Jennifer L. Nolte
David L. Ovard
Carrie Johnson Phaneuf
Jason B. Atchley
Michael A. Yanof
L. David Anderson
David Sochia
Mark D. Cronenwett
Toni Charice Miles
Kristopher Barber
Michael W. Dobbs
Christopher R. Wolfe
Brooke Hardie
Shawn M. McCaskill
Eric D. Archer

STAFF ATTORNEYS

R. Michael Northrup
Gregory J. Lensing
Camille Johnson

For full biographical listings, see the Martindale-Hubbell Law Directory

FIGARI DAVENPORT & GRAVES, L.L.P. (AV)

A Partnership including a Professional Corporation
901 Main Street, LB 125, 4800 Bank of America Plaza, 75202-3796
Telephone: 214-939-2000
Fax: 214-939-2090

MEMBERS OF FIRM

Ernest E. Figari, Jr., (P.C.)
Mark T. Davenport
Thomas A. Graves
Doug K. Butler
Donald Colleluori
Gary D. Eisenstat
Andrew G. Jubinsky
Parker D. Young
Michael G. Brown
Timothy A. Daniels
Keith R. Verges
Stephen D. Howen
Monica L. Luebker
Andrew C. Whitaker

Jill B. Davenport
Bill E. Davidoff
Amanda M. Inabnett
Dennis M. Lynch
Melissa A. Mitchell
Katherine S. Rabe
Lisa L. Traylor
Jennifer M. Trulock

For full biographical listings, see the Martindale-Hubbell Law Directory

S. STEWART FRAZER (AV)

One Turtle Creek Village, 3878 Oak Lawn Avenue, Suite 606, 75219-4498
Telephone: 214-599-9995
Fax: 214-599-9293
Email: stewartfrazer@email.msn.com

For full biographical listings, see the Martindale-Hubbell Law Directory

Dallas—Continued

GARDERE & WYNNE, L.L.P. (AV)

Thanksgiving Tower, 1601 Elm Street, Suite 3000, 75201
Telephone: 214-999-3000
Fax: 214-999-4667
Cable Address: "Garwyn Dallas"
Telex: 73-0197
Email: postmaster@gardere.com *URL:* http://www.gardere.com
Tulsa, Oklahoma Office: 100 West Fifth Street, 200 Oneok Plaza.
Telephone: 918-699-2900.
Fax: 918-699-2929.
Houston, Texas Office: Gardere Wynne Sewell & Riggs, L.L.P., 1000 Louisiana, Suite 3400.
Telephone: 713-276-5500.
Fax: 713-276-5555.
Mexico City, Mexico Office: Gardere & Wynne, Arena, Robles, Yarza, S.C., Rio Pánuco No. 7, Col Cuauhtémoc, 06500 Mèxico, D.F. Mexico.
Telèfonos: 011 (525) 546-8030.
FAX: 011 (525) 546-7796.

MEMBERS OF FIRM

Angus G. Wynne (1885-1974)
George P. Gardere (1899-1973)
Morris I. Jaffe (1912-1980)
G. Duffield Smith, Jr. (1930-1989)
Carl W. Wilson (1931-1989)
Richard F. Smith (1938-1990)
Joseph E. Nowlin (1945-1993)
Virgil Childress (1904-1990)
Paul Port (1912-1996)
Donald C. McCleary (1948-1996)
James F. Adams
M. Douglas Adkins
Val J. Albright
Michael A. Barragan
Mark W. Bayer
Steven J. Berry
Timothy A. Biggio
Stuart E. Blaugrund
Kenneth Chaim Broodo
C. Robert Butterfield
Lori M. Carr
Gary B. Clark
William J. Clay
Robert R. Cole, Jr.
David M. Curtis
Scott L. Davis
Marshall J. Doke, Jr.
Michael J. Donohue
Calman L. Donsky
Barry D. Drees
W. Robert Dyer, Jr.
David R. Earhart
Joanne Early
T. Mark Edwards
Dawn Estes
Suzan E. Fenner
Jane D. Fergason
Craig B. Florence
Curtis L. Frisbie, Jr.
Ronald M. Gaswirth
Stephen J. Gilles
D. Dale Gillette
Lawrence E. Glasgow
Beverly B. Godbey
Lawrence B. Goldstein
Stephen D. Good
Randy D. Gordon
Dan Guthrie
Douglas D. Haloftis
Susan M. Halpern
Douglas A. Harrison
Joe B. Harrison
Gregory A. Harwell
Jack W. Hawkins
D. Steven Henry
Robert M. Hoffman
Cynthia C. Hollingsworth
Richard M. Hull
William R. Keffer
Kevin L. Kelley
Paul E. Kennedy
Ronald Kirk
Roman J. Kupchynsky, II
Steven M. Ladik
Douglas S. Lang
Paul S. Leslie
Cym H. Lowell
Stephen A. McCartin
David G. McLane
Philip G. Meyers (Not admitted in TX)
Robert J. Miller
John C. Nabors
Dan L. Nicewander
Kenneth M. Niesman
Julian D. Nihill
Keith V. Novick
Neil J. O'Brien
Holland Neff O'Neil
Daniel F. Perez
Alan J. Perkins
Frances E. Phillips
James S. Pleasant
Jan M. Ramsay
Randall G. Ray
Thomas E. Reddin
James P. Reid
Michael D. Richardson
Clifford J. Risman
Richard M. Roberson
Deirdre B. Ruckman
Robert N. Rule, Jr.
Deborah Cappozzo Ryan
Larry L. Schoenbrun
Kay Lyn Schwartz
Katherine M. Seaborn
David H. Segrest
Theodore F. Shiells (Not admitted in TX)
David R. Snodgrass
John K. Sterling
B. Jane Cantrell Taber
Richard A. Tulli
Peter S. Vogel
Richard L. Waggoner
Scott C. Wallace
Sanford E. Warren, Jr.
William G. Whitehill
Robert L. Wright

OF COUNSEL

Jeffrey M. Gaba
Edward Jorgenson
John T. Kipp
Donald H. Mackaman

GENERAL COUNSEL

Harold Hoffman

SENIOR ATTORNEYS

Emily S. Barbour
Margaret E. Bond
Steven S. Camp
Thomas J. Fisher
Elizabeth Hill
Henry C. McFadyen, Jr.
Carolyn McFatridge
Thomas R. Mylott III
Stacy R. Obenhaus
Michael W. Reindollar
Stewart Wayne

(See Next Column)

ASSOCIATES

Jana Baker
Nicole S. Batten
Cynthia J. Bishop
Darcy C. Blossfeld
Jane Brown
Brent E. Bundick
Cheryl S. Camin
Neil E. Cannon, III
John Caverlee
Daniel J. Chalker, P.E.
Allison K. Chandler
Susan M. Cooper
Laurie S. Dennis
William David Dunn
Dan Feldman
Randall W. Fickel
Edwin S. Flores
Dwight M. Francis
Juan Garcia
Barry M. Golden
J. Lee Grable, Jr.
Rayna Habel
Gregory S. Heath
Carrie B. Hoffman
Elizabeth C. Jenkins
Lara S. Jitlal
Lisa S. Kennedy
Carey Patrick Kinder
H. Lisa Koh
Laurie Lamb Martin
Todd E. Landis (Not admitted in TX)
Colette M. Laycock
Eric S. Levy
Allison Freeman Logan
Connie P. Lust
Indrajit Bobby Majumder
J. Terrell Mann
Scott D. McDonald
Elaine A. Murphy
Michael Harris Newman
Shawn A. Orme
Alejandro Ortiz (Not admitted in TX)
Luis M. Ortiz (Not admitted in TX)
Mark E. Patrick
Michael D. Peay
Patrick S. Richter
Kimberly M. Robinson
Joshua S. Roseman
Telisa W. Schelin
Matthew J. Schroeder
John William Slates, III
Laurie A. Spindler (Not admitted in TX)
Christine L. Stetson
Paige L. Taylor
Monica S. Thompson
Jessica W. Thorne
David H. Timmins
Paula Tucker
Jay F. Utley
Karri L. Vinton
Kelli E. Welch
Paul T. Williamson
Amy Raney Yeager
Lawrence R. Youst
Stephanie Zapata

For full biographical listings, see the Martindale-Hubbell Law Directory

GODWIN WHITE & GRUBER, A PROFESSIONAL CORPORATION (AV)

Suite 2500, 901 Main Street, 75202-3714
Telephone: 214-939-4400
Fax: 214-760-7332

Lawrence W. Bailey
Susan Barilich
James F. Bullock
George R. Carlton, Jr.
Julia J. Dodd
Danny C. Garner
Donald E. Godwin
G. Michael Gruber
Brian N. Hail
Thomas S. Hoekstra
Michael K. Hurst
Christopher L. Kurzner
David L. Patterson
Elizabeth L. Phifer
Steven T. Polino
Ellis A. Regenbogen
Harvey M. Shapan
Bob J. Shelton
James G. Vetter, Jr.
Warren R. Westberg
David J. White

PARTICIPATING ASSOCIATES

Josephine H. Randall
G. Michael Stewart

OF COUNSEL

Joshua Mond

ASSOCIATES

Paul M. Bass, III
Mary A. Goodrich
Nick C. Inman
John F. Martin
Tonya L. Meier
Terri B. Moore
Neal M. Nagely
Guy H. Riddle
Kenneth W. Rockenbach
Debora Lynn Simon
Stephanie A. Sullins
Wes E. Wadle
Robert C. Wiegand

For full biographical listings, see the Martindale-Hubbell Law Directory

HAYNES AND BOONE, LLP (AV)

901 Main Street Suite 3100, 75202-3789
Telephone: 214-651-5000
Metro: 214-263-2310
Telecopy: 214-651-5940
Telex: 73-0187
URL: http://www.haynesboone.com
Austin, Texas Office: 600 Congress Avenue, Suite 1600.
Telephone: 512-867-8400.
Telecopy: 512-867-8470.
Fort Worth, Texas Office: 201 Main Street, Suite 2200.
Telephone: 817-347-6600. Metro: 817-654-3308.
Telecopy: 817-347-6650.
Houston, Texas Office: 1000 Louisiana Street, Suite 4300.
Telephone: 713-547-2000.
Telecopy: 713-547-2600.
San Antonio, Texas Office: 112 East Pecan Street, Suite 1600.
Telephone: 210-978-7000.
Telecopy: 210-978-7450.

(See Next Column)

HAYNES AND BOONE LLP, *Dallas—Continued*

Washington, D.C. Office: 1225 Eye Street, N.W., Suite 825.
Telephone: 202-414-1900.
Telecopy: 202-414-1920.
Mexico City, Mexico Office: Haynes & Boone, S.C., Blvd Manuel Avila Camacho, No. 40 Despacho 1801 Lomas de Chapultepec.
Telephone: (525) 540-5558.
Telecopy: 525-596-7798.

SENIOR COUNSEL

Richard D. Haynes

MEMBERS OF FIRM

Robert D. Albergotti
Paul H. Amiel
Richard D. Anigian
Hershell L. Barnes, Jr.
Kathleen McIntosh Beasley
Jeffrey M. Becker
Kenneth K. Bezozo
William L. Boeing
Michael M. Boone
Stacy L. Brainin
George W. Bramblett, Jr.
Kerry McHugh Breaux
Ronald W. Breaux
M. David Burton
Wilson Chu
John M. Collins
Randall E. Colson
Terry W. Conner
Nina Cortell
Barry W. Cowan
Greta E. (Gerberding) Cowart
Terry I. Cross
Judith Elkin
Beth L. Fancsali
Richard M. Fijolek
William P. Finegan
Sharon N. Freytag
Laurence K. Gustafson
David H. Harper
Tom D. Harris, Jr.
Robin P. Hartmann
William R. Hays, III
Tim Headley
Noel M.B. Hensley
Thomas E. Hill
Leonard A. Hirsch
Matt W. Holley
Carrie Lee Huff
Steven R. Jenkins
Stacey Cowand Jernigan
Robert R. Kibby
Warren B. Kice
Jeffrey P. King
Wm. S. Kleinman
Thomas E. Kurth
Lewis A. Lefko
C. Bradford Lowry
Ernest Martin, Jr.
Richard K. Martin
David L. McCombs
Robert A. McCulloch
Barry F. McNeil
Rona R. Mears
Robert G. Mebus
J. Mitchell Miller
Michelle McCoy Monger
Mark X. Mullin
Sue P. Murphy
Karen S. Nelson
Scott G. Night
David H. Oden
Michael D. Pegues
Stephen M. Pezanosky
Robin E. Phelan
Phillip B. Philbin
Charles F. Plenge
Timothy E. Powers
Werner A. Powers
James E. Pulis, Jr.
C. Ted Raines, Jr.
Ann M. Saegert
Gregory R. Samuel
Paul W. Searles
Janice V. Sharry
John G. Stafford, Jr.
J. Kirk Standly
William C. Strock
David R. N. Taubenfeld
Donald C. Templin
Richard L. Thurston
W. Scott Wallace
Joseph G. Werner
William C. Wilshusen
Jonathan C. Wilson
Robert E. Wilson
Taylor H. Wilson
Alan Wright

OF COUNSEL

Michael J. Balconi-Lamica
James R. Bell
Michael S. Bush
Arthur T. Carter
Alexandra Christian
Jeffrey L. Curtis
Michael Arlen Davis, Jr.
Nicholas Even (Not admitted in TX)
Chas. O. Galvin
Susie L. Hoeller
Rita Mankovich Irani
Jeffrey A. Leonard
Edward J. Lynch
Thomas Wm. Mayo (Not admitted in TX)
Maureen Frances Moore
Nina M. Orendain
Dawn C. Perotti
J. C. Pletcher
Lisa Schafroth Sootes
Paul R. Spellman
Gary Sullivan
James J. Sullivan
Jill J. Weinberg
Steven L. Wilson
Rhonda Reynolds Winslett

ASSOCIATES

John Matthew Ambler
Jeffrey B. Andrews
Heather McDaniel Bailey
Erika B. Blomquist
Steven W. Brady (Not admitted in TX)
Maurice (Marty) L. Brimmage Jr.
Russell Edward Broadway
Luis R. Campos
Roberto Cañas, Jr.
Lei Howard Chen
Doug W. Clayton
Patrick Collins
Guyanne E. Conley
LaDawn Horn Conway
Christopher J. Curtis
Martha J. Damon (Not admitted in TX)
Leila A. D'Aquin
Ruben C. DeLeon
Garrett A. Devries
David A. Dodds
Amy L. Donaldson
Lisa A. Dreishmire
Andrew S. Ehmke
Raymond S. Elliott
Scott W. Everett
Kelesha A. Fowler
Teddy Craig Friesland
Richard Fritz
Melissa M. Goodman
H. Eric Hagenswold
W. Paul Hankins
Michael L. Hood
Brian J. Hubbard
Anne McGowan Johnson
Gina M. Johnson
Cindy Kang
Patrick D. Keating

(See Next Column)

ASSOCIATES (Continued)

Charles C. Keeble, Jr.
Kathy A. King
Laura R. Kogan
Laurie G. Lang
Celeste D. Livengood
Daniel T. Mabery
Peter D. Marketos
Colin G. Martin
Vicki L. Martin
Todd D. Mattingly
David R. McAtee, II
Debra J. McComas
David P. McLean (Not admitted in TX)
Melissa A. Miles
Heath A. Miller
Walter Duval Miller
George William Morrison
Audrey E. Mross
William Bruce Newsome
Alexandria Hien Nguyen
Carey Anne O'Connor (Labor, Employment Law and Employment Benefits Section)
David M. Odell
Armando A. Olmedo
Shoshana L. Paige
Nancy Paine
Larry B. Pascal
Purvi J. Patel
Lesley Karine "Kari" Paulson
Heather L. Perttula
K. Todd Phillips
Scot Pierce
Rebecca Polak
Richard D. Rafferty
Stephanie L. Reaugh
David B. Reece
Brandi Wickline Sarfatis
Brandon N. Satterwhite
Christine Irish Sestak
David M. Shinnick
Arnold A. Spencer
Stephanie M. Staubach
Stacey Jo Stern
Erin E. Sudbury
Sarah Teachout
Eric Terry
Helen Thigpen
Debra Kay Thomas
M. Kelly Lanning Turner
Craig Scott Unterberg
A. Michael Warnecke
Paul A. Wehrmann
Kevin Wiggins
Sandra G. Wilkinson
Jennifer Thoman Wisinski
Susan K. Wisk
Susan Leonard Wittliff
Brian L. Wittneben
Zachariah Wolfe
Ann Whitley Wood
Thomas Yang
Jiannan Zhang

Representative Clients: Exxon Corp.; American Airlines (AMR Corp.); Tenet Healthcare Corp.; Bank of America; Cellstar Corp.; Sabre, Inc.; Trilogy software, Inc.; Dell U.S.A.; Tandy Corp.; USAA Realco.

For full biographical listings, see the Martindale-Hubbell Law Directory

HUGHES & LUCE, L.L.P. (AV)

A Registered Limited Liability Partnership including Professional Corporations
1717 Main Street, Suite 2800, 75201
Telephone: 214-939-5500
Fax: 214-939-6100; 214-939-5849
Email: H&L@hughesluce.com *URL:* http://www.hughesluce.com
Austin, Texas Office: 111 Congress, Suite 900.
Telephone: 512-482-6800.
Fax: 512-482-6859.
Houston, Texas Office: 1600 Smith Street, Suite 3550.
Telephone: 713-754-5200.
Fax: 713-754-5270.

MEMBERS OF FIRM

Danny S. Ashby
Kim Juanita Askew
James Hunter Birch
Bert Black
Alan J. Bogdanow
David Bryant
Craig W. Budner
Douglas A. Cawley
Michael J. Dalton
Robert Edwin Davis
Allan B. Diamond
Jeff W. Dorrill
Scott C. Drablos
Deborah J. Eichner
Zammurad Hyatt Feroze
David Lee Fields
William B. Finkelstein
Stephen G. Gleboff
David N. Guedry
Kenneth G. Hawari
Kathryn G. Henkel
Daniel K. Hennessy
Glen J. Hettinger
John B. Holden, Jr., (P.C.)
John E. Howell
Mont P. Hoyt
Vester T. Hughes, Jr.
Clifton T. Hutchinson
MaryAnn Joerres
Darrell E. Jordan
David H. Judson
David C. Kent
Ronald D. Kerridge
Jeffrey C. King
Paul M. Koning
Weston C. Loegering
David G. Luther, Jr.
James D. McCarthy
William A. McCormack
R. Matthew Molash
James A. Moomaw
Robert H. Mow, Jr. (P.C.)
Ross Clayton Mulford
Dudley W. Murrey
Gary G. Null
Cynthia Morgan Ohlenforst
Walter G. Pettey, III
Bobby M. Rubarts
Mark K. Sales
James W. Sargent
Dwight A. Shupe
David L. Sinak
Theodore Stevenson, III
Karen K. Suhre
J. Gregory Taylor
Elizabeth R. Turner
David Weitman

ASSOCIATES

Bradley L. Adams
Gregory M. Bair
James H. Billingsley
Beth W. Bivans
Julie Edwards Blend
Christopher T. Bovenkamp
Joanna H. Buck
James E. Cahill, III
J. David Clark, Jr. (Not admitted in TX)
Matthew J. Cleaves
H. Esther Cochran (Not admitted in TX)
Stefanie L. Cooper
Joseph M. Cox
Lora G. Davis

(See Next Column)

HUGHES & LUCE L.L.P.—*Continued*

ASSOCIATES (Continued)

Courtney J. Dreslin
Clifton M. Dugas, III
Tracy Eaton
Allison L. Elko
John E. Garda
Martin E. Garza
Cameron Davis Gray
Robert B. Hale
Gary W. Hays
Derek S. Hollingsworth
James W. Hryekewicz
Price L. Johnson
Samuel V. Jones
Laura M. Kalesnik
Paul J. Kardish
Chad W. King
Christopher C. Lewis (Not admitted in TX)
Michael S.J. Lozich
Richard H. Mains
Lynne A. Messina
Kelly W. Milligan (Not admitted in TX)
Christopher Munns
Bliss Burdett Pak
John W. Patton
Thomas W. Paxton
Aubrey Nick Pittman
D. Alexander Ritchie
Eric N. Roberson
Brooke Leslie Rollins
Anne-Marie Roy
Morgan A. Ryder
David J. Schenck
Matthew R. Schindel
John Sepehri
Russell B. Shelton
Bart Sloan
Anthony Gorham Soards
Margaret Laurel Stephenson
Marc H. Stone
John O. Sutton Jr.
Catherine C. Theisen
Marion Turner (Van) Van Bebber
Misty M. Ventura
Carlos P. Villota
John R. Wilcox III
Scott M. Wilson

OF COUNSEL

Paul A. Berry
André J. Brunel
Nancy Figg Duessel
Thomas W. Luce, III
Douglas A. Sorensen
Arthur A. Stewart
Matthew C. Wood

For full biographical listings, see the Martindale-Hubbell Law Directory

---

JACKSON WALKER L.L.P. (AV)

901 Main Street, Suite 6000, 75202-3797
Telephone: 214-953-6000
Fax: 214-953-5822
URL: http://www.jw.com
Austin, Texas Office: 100 Congress Avenue, Suite 1100.
Telephone: 512-236-2000.
Fax: 512-236-2002.
Fort Worth, Texas Office: 301 Commerce Street, Suite 2400.
Telephone: 817-334-7200.
Fax: 817-334-7290.
Houston, Texas Office: 1100 Louisiana, Suite 4200.
Telephone: 713-752-4200.
Fax: 713-752-4221.
Richardson, Texas Office: 2435 North Central Expressway, Suite 600.
Telephone: 972-671-2560.
Fax: 972-671-2566.
San Angelo, Texas Office: 225 West Beauregard Avenue.
Telephone: 915-481-2550.
Fax: 915-481-2552.
San Antonio, Texas Office: 112 E. Pecan Street, Suite 2100.
Telephone: 210-978-7700.
Fax: 210-978-7790.

MEMBERS OF FIRM

John Paul Jackson (1902-1960)
Conan Cantwell (1907-1977)
A. W. Walker, Jr. (1901-1987)
Samuel G. Winstead (1909-1995)
Charles L. Babcock
Larry L. Bean
Bryan C. Birkeland
Carl C. Butzer
E. Leon Carter
H. Dudley Chambers
Bryan C. Collins
Richard F. Dahlson
George L. Diamond
Emily Stacy Donahue
Jeffery P. Drummond
Daniel G. Easley
Byron F. Egan
Charles S. Gilbert
Richard B. Goodner
Alan N. Greenspan
James R. Griffin
A. David Gross
R. Thomas Groves, Jr.
Michael Patrick Haggerty
Robert F. Henderson
Leonard E. Hoffman, III
William H. Hornberger
Gary L. Ingram
Phillip Ray Jones
Mark T. Josephs
Michael L. Kaufman
John J. Klein
Michael L. Knapek
John A. Koepke
John L. Lancaster, III
Robert P. Latham
Charles D. Maguire, Jr.
Frank P. McEachern
Billy R. McGill
Retta A. Miller
David T. Moran
David C. Myers
Jack Pew, Jr.
Robert G. Richardson
Robert F. Ruckman
James S. Ryan, III
Gordon M. Shapiro
Jeffrey M. Sone
Joan Sprince Sostek
Kenneth Stohner, Jr.
Frank C. Vecella
Bradley L. Whitlock
Troy Michael Wilson

OF COUNSEL

Roy Howard Baskin, III
George C. Dunlap
Mary Emma Ackels Karam

(See Next Column)

SENIOR COUNSEL

Sarah E. Clark
Katherine A. Staton
James D. Struble

ASSOCIATES

Cami L. Dawson Boyd
Thomas A. Caswell
Kimberly J. Chastain
Ray C. Clark
Kevin T. Crocker
William D. Ellerman
Jeffrey G. Hamilton
J. Colter Harris
Collin L. Hayes
K. Janée Heizer
Ashley E. Interrante
Janie E. James
Brian A. Kilpatrick
James M. McCown
Mattew A. McMurphy
Lynden Melmed
Carrie Bowers Miller
Deborah A. Robinowitz
Tara Mackey Monroe
Jay D. Reeve
David C. Rex
Steven J. Roth
Jennifer L. Shufelt
Harry M. Singh
Michael E. Taten
Kimberly K. Taylor
Christopher A. Thompson
Janie L. Treanor
David S. Vassar
Jeffrey B. Williams
Ryan Wirtz

Representative Clients Furnished Upon Request.

For full biographical listings, see the Martindale-Hubbell Law Directory

---

JENKENS & GILCHRIST, A PROFESSIONAL CORPORATION (AV)

Suite 3200, 1445 Ross Avenue, 75202-2799
Telephone: 214-855-4500
TWX: 910-861-4047
Telex: 73-2595
Telecopy: 214-855-4300
International Telecopy: 214-855-4400
Email: jenkens@jenkens.com *URL:* http://www.jenkens.com/
Austin, Texas Office: 2200 One American Center, 600 Congress Avenue.
Telephone: 512-499-3800.
Telecopy: 512-404-3520.
Los Angeles, California Office: 12100 Wilshire Boulevard, 15th Floor.
Telephone: 310-820-8800.
Fax: 310-820-8859.
Chicago, Illinois Office: 225 West Washington, Suite 2600.
Telephone: 312-425-3900.
Telecopy: 312-425-3909.
Houston, Texas Office: 1100 Louisiana, Suite 1800.
Telephone: 713-951-3300.
Telecopy: 713-951-3314.
Washington, D.C. Office: 1919 Pennsylvania Avenue, N.W., Suite 600.
Telephone: 202-326-1500.
Telecopy: 202-326-1555.
San Antonio, Texas Office: 1800 Frost Bank Tower, 100 West Houston Street.
Telephone: 210-246-5000.
Fax: 210-246-5999.

Holman Jenkens (1918-1974)
Rodney Acker
Lawrence C. Adams
Thomas G. Adler
Michael F. Albers
James W. Bowen
William P. Bowers
Barry F. Cannaday
Thomas L. Cantrell
Thomas H. Cantrill
Lawrence Chek
George W. Coleman
T. David Cowart
William S. Dahlstrom
Theodore W. Daniel
Thomas E. Davis
Robert W. Dockery
George C. Dunlap, Jr.
William P. Durbin, Jr.
Joseph C. Edwards
John C. Eichman
Hugh W. Ferguson, III
W. Gary Fowler
Stephen E. Fox
Ronald J. Frappier
Charles A. Gall
Daniel C. Garner
Toby L. Gerber
Jeffrey W. Giese
Robert B. Gilbreath (P.C.)
John A. Gilliam
R. Kenneth Gordon
Terry P. Gorman
J. Kevin Gray
Charles E. Greef
T. Richard Handler
Drew R. Heard
Michael S. Held
Gregory Hesse
John R. Holzgraefe
Susan McMurray Hull
Harold H. Hunter
Andrew E. Jillson
Harry J. Joe
Riva T. Johnson
W. Alan Kailer
V. Elizabeth Kellow
Carolyn V. Kelly
Patrick R. Kirby
David M. Laney
L. Steven Leshin
Scott J. Luedke (Not admitted in TX)
Brian R. Marek
Stephen S. Maris
Joseph C. Mathews
Roger L. Maxwell
Joyce G. Mazero
Keith W. McGlamery
Susan Mead
Patrick E. Mitchell
Will S. Montgomery
William D. Moon
Stanley R. Moore
Richard J. Moura
P. Weston Musselman, Jr.
Robert P. Nash
Cordell M. Parvin
Pam Gates O'Quinn
John S. Rice
Robert R. Ries
Daryl B. Robertson
Ronald D. Rosener
Merlyn D. Sampels
Linda Diane Sartin
Howard E. Schreiber
Jerry R. Selinger
Robert E. Sheeder

(See Next Column)

JENKENS & GILCHRIST A PROFESSIONAL CORPORATION, *Dallas—Continued*

William L. Sladek
John J. Stenger
John M. Stephenson, Jr.
Andre Michael Szuwalski
Henry Talavera
Robert E. Thackston
William A. Thau
Mark A. Todd
Raymond Van Dyke
Mark R. Vowell
Guy I. Wade III
Edward F. Walker
James H. Wallenstein
Winston W. Walp II
Lynnette R. Warman
Paul C. Watler
Peter G. Weinstock
Gerald T. Welch
Mark D. Wigder
Tari L. Williams
J. Michael Wylie
Stephen K. Yungblut
H. Campbell Zachry

OF COUNSEL

Alan R. Bromberg
Thomas L. Crisman
Christie S. Flanagan
H. Mathews Garland
Henry Gilchrist
Joe Gray
Marshall Simmons
Vernon O. Teofan

SENIOR PATENT ATTORNEY

Stuart D. Dwork
Scott B. Stahl (Not admitted in TX)

SENIOR ATTORNEYS

Margaret S. Alford
Charles B. Cannon
Brenda Crane Salhanick
David L. Swanson
Kathryn L. Sweers
Stephen R. Voelker

Mark Charles Alfieri
Julia G. Anderson
Veretta L. Anderson
Jeffery E. Bacon
Christina G. Bartholomew
Douglas M. Berman
Cathryn Anne Berryman
Jeffry Mason Blair
Michael J. Blayney (Not admitted in TX)
Arthur J. Brady
Kandice K. Bridges
David W. Buckner
Vincent S. Carver
Carrie Cavalier
Christopher I. Clark
Tyree C. Collier
Michael Cortez
Carol A. Darling
Amy Elaine Davis
Thomas M. Dooley
Myron Dusan Dornic
Stefani Eisenstat
Jay P. Eversman (Not admitted in TX)
William F. Esser (Not admitted in TX)
Margaret L. Facklis
Jannat Thompson-Festa
Marlon W. Frazier
Terry Freeman
Delisa J. Futch
Rafael Robert Garcia
John T. Gerhart
Erin Gibbens
John R. Gillespie
E. Leigh Gillett
Timothy J. Goodwin
Brian Graham
Steven R. Greenfield
Grayson S. Hale
J. Pat Heptig
Barry S. Hersh
Craig A. Hoersten (Not admitted in TX)
Thomas M. Hoffman
Vernon C. Howerton, Jr.
Thomas A. Jolly (Not admitted in TX)
Wilson G. Jones
Craig Naveen Kakarla
Lucea Suzan Kedron-Lyn
Michael G. Keeley (Not admitted in TX)
Thomas Alexander Kulik (Not admitted in TX)
Keith L. Larney (Not admitted in TX)
Robert A. Lauer
Douglas A. Linebarger
Marc L. Lipshy
James A. Lowery, III
John J. Marcoux (Not admitted in TX)
Jacob B. Marshall
Robert W. Mason
Dena B. Mastrogiovanni
Fiona G. McCord
Robert McCormick
Amy Danise McMahon
Elizabeth A. Miller
Wm. Vincent Murchison
Richard Allen Mysliwiec
London Scott O'Dowd
Mark L. Patterson
Spencer C. Patterson
Michael J. Pendleton, Jr.
Mark A. Platt
Susan E. Powley
Michael R. Putnam
Heather Radliff
Tracy L. Reynolds
Russell N. Rippamonti
Michael D. Rist
Holly L. Rudnick
Keith W. Saunders
Gregory J. Schmitt
Ellen E. Sessions
Joel Randall Sharp
Kirk H. Sharpe (Not admitted in TX)
Gary Bruce Solomon (Not admitted in TX)
Geneva E. Stephens
J. Jay Strimel
Scott H. Thompson
Richard Michael Traynor
Leila Anne Tredemeyer
William J. Tucker
Olen Grant Underwood
Jason Villalba
Brian D. Walker
Ingrid M. Warren
Mark Weibel
Megan P. Whitten
Jason E. Winford
Melissa D. Womble
Craig D. Zips

For full biographical listings, see the Martindale-Hubbell Law Directory

JONES, DAY, REAVIS & POGUE (AV)

2727 North Harwood Street, 75201-1515
Telephone: 214-220-3939
Telecopier: 214-969-5100
Email: counsel@jonesday.com *URL:* http://www.jonesday.com
In Atlanta, Georgia: 3500 SunTrust Plaza, 303 Peachtree Street.
Telephone: 404-521-3939.
Telecopier: 404-581-8330.
In Brussels, Belgium: Avenue Louise 480, 7th Floor, B-1050 Brussels.
Telephone: 32-2-645-14-11.
Telecopier: 32-2-645-14-45.
In Chicago, Illinois: 77 West Wacker.
Telephone: 312-782-3939.
Telecopier: 312-782-8585.
In Cleveland, Ohio: North Point, 901 Lakeside Avenue.
Telephone: 216-586-3939.
Telecopier: 216-579-0212.
In Columbus, Ohio: 1900 Huntington Center.
Telephone: 614-469-3939.
Telecopier: 614-461-4198.
In Frankfurt, Germany: Hochhaus am Park, Grüneburgweg 102, 60323 Frankfurt am Main.
Telephone: 49-69-9726-3939.
Telecopier: 49-69-9726-3993.
In Geneva, Switzerland: 20, rue de Candolle.
Telephone: 41-22-320-2339.
Telecopier: 41-22-320-1232.
In Hong Kong: 29th Floor, Entertainment Building, 30 Queen's Road Central.
Telephone: 852-2526-6895.
Telecopier: 852-2868-5871.
In Irvine, California: 5 Park Plaza, Suite 1100.
Telephone: 949-851-3939.
Telecopier: 949-553-7539.
In London, England: Bucklersbury House, 3 Queen Victoria Street.
Telephone: 44-20-7236-3939.
Telecopier: 44-20-7236-1113.
In Los Angeles, California: 555 West Fifth Street, Suite 4600.
Telephone: 213-489-3939.
Telecopier: 213-243-2539.
In New York, New York: 599 Lexington Avenue.
Telephone: 212-326-3939.
Telecopier: 212-755-7306.
In Paris, France: 120, rue du Faubourg Saint-Honoré.
Telephone: 33-1-56-59-39-39.
Telecopier: 33-1-56-59-39-38.
In Pittsburgh, Pennsylvania: 500 Grant Street, 31st Floor.
Telephone: 412-391-3939.
Telecopier: 412-394-7959.
Riyadh, Saudi Arabia: The International Law Firm (In Association with Jones, Day, Reavis & Pogue), Sulaymaniyah, Prince Mishari IBN, Addulaziz Street, P.O. Box 22166.
Telephone: (966-1) 462-8866.
Telecopier: (966-1) 462-9001.
In Shanghai, China: 2805 Kerry Centre, 1515 Nanjing Road West.
Telephone: 86-21-5298-6568.
Telecopier: 86-21-5298-6569.
In Sydney, Australia: Governor Phillip Tower, Level 38, 1 Farrer Place.
Telephone: 61-2-9210-6921.
Telecopier: 61-2-9210-6926.
In Taipei, Taiwan: 8th Floor, 2 Tun Hwa South Road, Section 2.
Telephone: (886-2) 2704-6808.
Telecopier: (886-2) 2704-6791.
In Tokyo, Japan: Toranomon 45 Mori Building, 3rd Floor, 1-5, Toranomon, 5-Chome, Minato-ku, Tokyo 105, Japan.
Telephone: 81-3-3433-3939.
Telecopier: 81-3-5401-2725.
In Washington, D.C.: 51 Louisiana Avenue, N.W.
Telephone: 202-879-3939.
Telecopier: 202-626-1700.

MEMBERS OF FIRM IN DALLAS

Robert L. Meyers, III
Robert W. Turner
Francis P. Hubach, Jr.
Terence M. Murphy
Joseph L. McEntee
James F. Carey
Robert L. Estep
Frederick J. Rerko
Thomas E. Gillespie
John T. McCafferty
Sydney Bosworth McDole
Dennis B. Drapkin
Thomas E. Fennell
David E. Cowling
Bradford G. Keithley (Not admitted in TX)
Kathleen Ryan McLaurin
Henry L. Gompf
Brian D. Lafving
David J. Lowery
Martin L. Camp
Thomas R. Jackson
James P. Karen
Stanley Weiner
Jerome R. Doak
Stephen L. Fluckiger
Gregory M. Gordon
Patricia Villareal
Ronald G. Weitz
Katie J. Colopy
Alan S. Miller
Mark V. Minton
James E. O'Bannon
James S. Teater
Mark E. Betzen
Mark B. Knowles
Margaret I. Lyle
Patricia Hummel Seifert
Sally L. Crawford
Nancy MacKimm
Todd Wallace
Troy Blain Lewis

(See Next Column)

JONES, DAY, REAVIS & POGUE—*Continued*

MEMBERS OF FIRM IN DALLAS (Continued)

Michael Lyn Rice
Michael Weinberg
Roy T. Atwood
Scott W. Burt
Charles William Burton

SENIOR COUNSEL

Thomas C. Nelson

OF COUNSEL

Richard A. Freling
Richard K. Kneipper
James L. Baumoel

COUNSEL

Alfred E. Hall
James C. Kesterson
William E. Marple
W. Paul Ditto, Jr.
H. Tica Herns
Mark R. Hall
Teresa M. Cefalo
Robert D. Lochridge

ASSOCIATES

Deborah Storey Simmons
Michael C. Gibbs (Not admitted in TX)
Sharon A. Alexander
Ronald A. Antush
Jeffrey J. Joyce
Mark N. Reiter
Deborah A. Savarese
Chrysta L. Castañeda
Anna Marie Dempsey
D. Scott Hemingway
Michael D. Murphy
Michael J. Newton
Charolette F. Noel
W. Kelly Stewart
Kimberley A. Elting
Craig F. Simon
Fiona E. Arnold (Not admitted in the United States)
Hilda C. Galvan
Britt K. Latham
Shannon D. Norris
Jeffrey T. Ramsey
Matthew W. Ray
Jill E. Tananbaum
Greg L. Weselka
Stephen B. Yeager
Catherine L. Bjorck
Christopher A. Butner
John A. Conway
Lisa K. Durham
Tamara Marinkovic
David L. Pratt
Lisa A. Schiffman
Martha Wach
Kristi J. Whiteside
Todd A. Fisher
Charles C. Groves
Mark C. Nelson
Michael E. Norton
René Mario Scherr
B. Jill Timberlake Willis
Daniel P. Winikka
Kayla D. Carter
Susan C. Cox
Michael L. Davitt
Sarah K. Ettredge
Brian A. Farlow
Kerrie V. Forbes
Eric P. Harmon
Kelly J. Hunt
William J. Leatherberry
Robert M. Millimet (Not admitted in TX)
Christine L. Palmer
Paula E. Smith
Thomas C. Smith
Moses K. Song
Desmond B. Acosta
Michelle R. Berziel
David E. Colmenero
Christine M. Crase
Renna R. Embry
Julie C. Jared
Neil J. McNabnay
Melanie P. Sarwal
Dana P. Babb
Bradley K. Blackwell (Not admitted in TX)
Monica M. Brown
Susan Y. Burlazzi
Daniel T. Conrad (Not admitted in TX)
Amanda Christine Dake
La Shon Yvette Fleming
Kasey L. Huck
Matt J. Krupnick
Michelle A. Morgan
Shane P. Raley
Derek H. Sparks
Heidi K. Wambach
Kajeer Yar (Not admitted in TX)
Michael K. Blais
LeDouglas G. Johnson
Brian Jorgensen
William D. Merritt
Tracy Saffren Greenberg
James J. Savina
Michael C. Smith
Lezlie B. Willis

STAFF ATTORNEYS

Lenita L. Wilson

For full biographical listings, see the Martindale-Hubbell Law Directory

---

KANE, RUSSELL, COLEMAN & LOGAN, A PROFESSIONAL CORPORATION (AV)

3700 Thanksgiving Tower, 1601 Elm Street, 75201-7207
Telephone: 214-777-4200
Fax: 214-777-4299
Email: krcl@krcl.com

Raymond J. Kane
Gordon B. Russell
Joseph M. Coleman
Michael A. Logan
Patrick V. Stark
Kenneth W. Biermacher
David N. Condon
Karen A. Cox
William D. Elliott
Joseph A. Friedman
Robert N. LeMay
Michael L. Atchley, II
Margaret M. McLeod Jordan

Terry Flett Barakis
Harold R. Busch
Priscilla K. Davenport
Deborah A. DiMarco
Evangelos J. Gegas (Not admitted in TX)
Shelli R. Inmon
Kenneth C. Johnston
Jaqluin M. Bickmore Lloyd
Robert L. Manteuffel
David D. Ritter
Holly J. Roman

(See Next Column)

Jeffrey S. Seeburger
Jeffrey Charles Tasker
Steven M. Thornton
Karin M. Zaner

For full biographical listings, see the Martindale-Hubbell Law Directory

---

KILGORE & KILGORE, A PROFESSIONAL CORPORATION (AV)

700 McKinney Place, 3131 McKinney Avenue - LB 103, 75204-2471
Telephone: 214-969-9099
Fax: 214-953-0133; 214-953-0242; 214-953-0677

Wilmer D. Masterson, III
W. Stephen Swayze
Robert M. Thornton
Theodore C. Anderson, III
John H. Crouch, IV

D. Elizabeth Masterson

For full biographical listings, see the Martindale-Hubbell Law Directory

---

LOCKE LIDDELL & SAPP LLP (AV)

2200 Ross Avenue, Suite 2200, 75201-6776
Telephone: 214-740-8000
Fax: 214-740-8800
URL: http://www.lockeliddell.com
New Orleans, Louisiana Office: 601 Poydras Street, Suite 2400, 70130-6036.
Telephone: 504-558-5100.
Fax: 504-558-5200.
Austin, Texas Offices: 100 Congress Avenue, Suite 300, 78701-4042.
Telephone: 512-305-4700.
Fax: 512-305-4800
Houston, Texas Office: 600 Travis Street, 3400 Chase Tower, 77002-3095.
Telephone: 713-226-1200.
Fax: 713-223-3717.

Frederick W. Addison, III
Christopher F. Allison, Jr.
Jennifer Burr Altabef
James L. Armour
Thomas P. Arnold
Gabrielle M. Arrieh
Robert J. Banta
William Andrew Barr
J. Robert Beatty
J. Mitchell Bell
Earl A. Berry, Jr.
Gina E. Betts
Kenneth L. Betts
Bryan E. Bishop
George E. Bowles
Stuart M. Bumpas
E. Philip Bush
William John Bux
Kevin C. Cabaniss
Robert M. Candee
Carlyle H. Chapman, Jr.
Jerry K. Clements
R. Brent Clifton
Russell F. Coleman
Michael H. Collins
Thomas A. Connop
Roger B. Cowie
Ronald R. Cresswell
Edwin R. DeYoung
H. Gene Emery
C. W. Flynn, IV
X. Lane Folsom
Brian R. Forbes
Bradley W. Foster
Peter A. Franklin, III
Kathleen Vance Galloway
Lisa Atlas Genecov
Lawrence D. Ginsburg
Don M. Glendenning
Bryan L. Goolsby
Thomas H. Grace
Vicky Pogue Gunning
Hugh Edward Hackney
Margaret Donahue Hall
Donald A. Hammett, Jr.
Roy W. Hardin
Morris Harrell
William D. Harris, Jr.
Brad B. Hawley
Bryan Haynes
Vincent J. Hess
Jennifer G. Jackson
William D. Jackson
Jack E. Jacobsen
P. Kent Jamison
M. Charles Jennings
Van M. Jolas
C. Ronald Kalteyer
Susan L. Karamanian
Guy H. Kerr
Kirte M. Kinser
Raymond E. LaDriere, II
Elizabeth Lang-Miers
Larry M. Lesh
Janis H. Loegering
Thomas F. Loose
Gregory A. Lowry
Elizabeth E. Mack
Mark G. Magilow
John H. Marks, Jr.
Denise L. Mayfield
David G. McCracken
John P. McDonald
John H. McElhaney
John B. McKnight
Stan McMurry
Lawrence J. McNamara
Denise Clark McWatters
Harriet E. Miers
Charles M. Moore
Robert T. Mowrey
James R. Nelson
David L. Peavler
Michael P. Petersilia
Gary R. Powell
Michael V. Powell
Maurice E. Purnell, Jr.
Mark H. Ralston
Jaime Ramón
Edward A. Razim, III
Charles C. Reeder
Whit Roberts
Andrew D. Rooker
Michael K. Sanderson
Stephen L. Sapp
Michael R. Schulman
Robert F. See, Jr.
Eugene F. Segrest
Steven L. Skov
Mark M. Sloan
Cynthia M. Stamer
Frank E. Stevenson, II
Robb P. Stewart
Mark T. Story
Louis F. Strawn
Scott C. Tankersley
Robert P. Taylor, III
Cynthia Keely Timms
L. Dan Tucker
Kevin L. Twining
Donald E. Uloth
Bradley C. Weber
Toni Weinstein (Not admitted in TX)

(See Next Column)

LOCKE LIDDELL & SAPP LLP, *Dallas—Continued*

William D. White, Jr.
Linda Albright Wilkins
Barney T. Young
Thomas G. Yoxall

OF COUNSEL

L. Money Adams, Jr.
Barbara McComas Anderson
John L. Estes
James J. Laney
Charles G. Purnell
Robert E. Rain, Jr.
Talbot Rain
Trevor Wm. Rees-Jones
C. Paul Rogers, III
Phillip A. Wylie

SENIOR COUNSEL

Loral R. Conrad
Nikki Hurst Gibson
Barnett D. Hammond, Jr.
Martin Korn
Jan R. Newsom
Monty L. Ross
Charles R. Snakard
Harry J. Watson

SENIOR ATTORNEYS

Jonetta Brooks
Elizabeth A. Howard
James T. Rain

ASSOCIATES

David J. Abell (Not admitted in TX)
Arthur E. Anthony
Margaret Liu Benavente
Lori L. Bennett
Gary L. Bond, Jr.
Elizabeth Eaton Bonesio
Christopher W. Bowley
Clarence B. Brown, III
Timothy R. Brown
David G. Cabrales
John D. Carey, Jr.
Kirsten M. Castañeda
Brian A. Colao
Diana De Santos
Elizabeth B. Emerson
Andrea Meshonn Evans
Sharon R. Fancher
Evan E. Fitzmaurice
M. Matthew Fontane
Toby M. Galloway
Amy Snodgrass Genender
Kirk B. Gills
Melody Granados
Clayton E. Greenberg
Dan Gus
Christopher S. Hagge
James B. Hallmark
Kristin Jordan Harkins
W. Scott Hastings
Tricia Heaney
Michelle G. Hertzog
Susanna L. K. Hinton
Jennifer Buttross Johnson
Carolyn L. King
David W. Klaudt
Margaret Wueste Lesesne
Jason S. Lewis
Andrew P. Lustig
Paula Lynch-Griffith (Not admitted in the United States)
Khalid M. Malik
April R. Maurer
Jason P. Maxwell
Robert D. McCutchan, III
Monte J. Mitchell
Adam Moore
Denette A. Mouser (Not admitted in TX)
Paul G. Nason
Jacqueline H. Nguyen
William C. Perez (Not admitted in TX)
Jared S. Richardson
Buford H. Robertson, Jr. (Not admitted in TX)
Gina M. Romo
Kelvin L. Roquemore
Gayle E. Rosenstein
Michael P. Royal
Carl C. Scherz
Kristen Leigh Schoonover
J. Clint Schumacher
Paul F. Schuster
Derek P. Scott
David C. Sienko (Not admitted in TX)
Douglas D. Skierski
Kelly J. Thurman
Karin B. Torgerson
Eugene C. Vallow
Christine M. Vincenti
Kelli Ann Weinzierl
Kelly J. Wilhelm
Stephen D. Wilson

For full biographical listings, see the Martindale-Hubbell Law Directory

MEADOWS, OWENS, COLLIER, REED, COUSINS & BLAU, L.L.P. (AV)

901 Main Street, Suite 3700, 75202-3725
Telephone: 214-744-3700; 800-451-0093
Fax: 214-747-3732
URL: http://www.meadowsowens.com

MEMBERS OF FIRM

Charles M. Meadows, Jr.
Rodney J. Owens
Robert Don Collier
David N. Reed
Thomas G. Hineman
William R. Cousins, III
Charles W. Blau
George R. Bedell
Michael E. McCue
Fielder F. Nelms
Joel N. Crouch
Alan K. Davis
Charles D. Pulman

ASSOCIATES

Patricia King Dorey
Robert M. Bolton
M. Todd Welty
Josh O. Ungerman
Robyn A. Frohlin
Gregory A. Cardenas
Sara E. Lankford
Sarah Q. Qureshi
Bradley G. Korell
Todd A. Kraft
Alan L. Stroud
Matthew D. Richards

For full biographical listings, see the Martindale-Hubbell Law Directory

PAYNE & BLANCHARD, L.L.P. (AV)

Plaza of the Americas, 700 North Pearl Street Suite 500, LB 393, 75201-7424
Telephone: 214-953-1313
Telecopier: 214-220-0439
Email: pblaw@flash.net

(See Next Column)

MEMBERS OF FIRM

Arthur Blanchard (Retired)
James C. Allums, Jr.
John William Payne
Charles A. Girand
Bobby D. Dyess
Kevin J. Cook
Gary W. Maxfield
Jonathan A. Manning
Harold R. McKeever, Jr.

ASSOCIATES

Samuel J. Polak
David M. Walsh, IV

OF COUNSEL

Robert S. Addison

Representative Clients: AIG; American Home Products Corp.; American National Property and Casualty Co.; Liberty Mutual Insurance Co.; Maryland Casualty Co.; Mutual and United of Omaha Insurance Co.; Nationwide Insurance Cos.; Preston Chrysler-Plymouth; Texas Association of Counties; Travelers Insurance Co.; Tyler Ford, Inc.

For full biographical listings, see the Martindale-Hubbell Law Directory

SMITH, UNDERWOOD & PERKINS, A PROFESSIONAL CORPORATION (AV)

600 Two Lincoln Centre, 5420 LBJ Freeway, 75240
Telephone: 972-661-5114
Telecopier: 972-661-5691
Email: firm@suandp.com *URL:* http://www.suplaw.com

Timothy S. Perkins
David W. Ralston
G. Lynn Smith
William J. Underwood, Jr.

Christine A. McGuire
Amy K. Ratzlaff
P. Theodore Stoinoff, II
Val C. Cronin
Ellen P. Stewart
Todd W. Shadle
Ruth C. Logan
Christina L. Betanzos
Kent D. Williamson

For full biographical listings, see the Martindale-Hubbell Law Directory

STRASBURGER & PRICE, L.L.P. (AV)

A Partnership including Professional Corporations
901 Main Street, Suite 4300, 75202
Telephone: 214-651-4300
Fax: 214-651-4330
URL: http://www.strasburger.com
Austin, Texas Office: 600 Congress Avenue, Suite 2600.
Telephone: 512-499-3600.
Fax: 512-499-3660.
Houston, Texas Office: Suite 2800, One Houston Center, 1221 McKinney.
Telephone: 713-951-5600.
Fax: 713-951-5660.
San Antonio, Texas Office: Bank of America Plaza, 300 Convent Street, Suite 900.
Telephone: 210-250-6000.
Fax: 210-250-6100.
Mexico City Office: Montes Urales 632, Piso 3, Lomas de Chapultepec, 11000 Mexico D.F.
Telephone: 525-202-7665.
Fax: 525-202-2367.

MEMBERS OF FIRM

Henry W. Strasburger (1898-1972)
Hobert Price (1899-1965)
Craig A. Albert
Roland C. Anderson (P.C.)
Luke D. Bailey
Jerry L. Beane (P.C.)
Diana Joseph Bearden
Royal H. Brin, Jr., (P.C.)
Michael R. Buchanan
Daniel L. Butcher
W. Edward Carlton
E. Paul Cauley, Jr.
Duncan L. Clore (P.C.)
Deborah S. Coldwell
Deborah Cox
Gary C. Crapster (P.C.)
W. Richard Davis (P.C.)
William C. (Trey) Dowdy, III, (P.C.)
Robert Keith Drummond (P.C.)
Jack R. Dugan (P.C.)
Jeffrey R. Fine
William L. Fouché, Jr.
Frederick J. Fowler (P.C.)
Carol Glendenning
Mark E. Golman
Brian G. Hamilton
R. Chris Harvey (P.C.)
Ernest R. Higginbotham (P.C.)
Leo J. Hoffman (P.C.)
Stuart C. Hollimon (P.C.)
Charles M. Hosch
Mike Joplin (P.C.)
P. Michael Jung
Kelly Allbritton Katzman
Michael Keeley
David N. Kitner (P.C.)
D. Bradley Kizzia
David J. LaBrec
Billy G. Leonard, Jr.
Wm. Lance Lewis
Bryan J. Maedgen (P.C.)
Kevin J. Maguire
Wayne B. Mason
Sheree Lynn McCall (P.C.)
John H. McDowell, Jr.
Kurt W. Meaders
William M. Methenitis
David K. Meyercord (P.C.)
D. Randall Montgomery
James Hamilton Moody, III
David G. Moore
Elmer Murphey, III
Paul L. Myers
Marc A. Myrin
Charles S. Nichols
Jeffrey S. Osgood (P.C.)
Donald Patrick Owens
David W. Parham
Angelo P. Parker (P.C.)
James K. Peden, III, (P.C.)
J. Mark Penley
John E. Phillips (P.C.)
Mike F. Pipkin
W. Neil Rambin

(See Next Column)

STRASBURGER & PRICE L.L.P.—*Continued*

MEMBERS OF FIRM (Continued)

John R. Riddle
John K. Round
Thomas G. Rundell (P.C.)
Frank A. St. Claire (P.C.)
Mark S. Scudder
Alfredo L. Silva
Richard L. Smith, Jr.
Kirk F. Sniff
Earl Jeffery Story
Robert W. Strauss
Daniel F. Susie (P.C.)
Robert Hyer Thomas (P.C.)
Beth Pace Tiggelaar
John R. Tilly
Joseph A. Turano
John M. Vernon
Alan R. Vickery
Michael A. Walsh
W. Edward Walts, II, (P.C.)
Steven P. Watten
Kevin L. Wentz
Constance Courtney Westfall
Karen Brown Willcutts
Greg K. Winslett
S. Vance Wittie

SENIOR COUNSEL

Kenneth S. Beat
H. Michelle Caldwell
Walter D. James III
Patrick J. Larkin
Cynthia Teal Thawley
Robert E. Vinson, Jr.

OF COUNSEL

Rowland B. Foster (P.C.)
Jack M. Kinnebrew (P.C.)
Kevin H. Good
Samuel J. Hallman
Kenneth R. Matticks
(Not admitted in TX)

ASSOCIATES

Katherine Smith Anderson
Adrienne L. Baugh
George A. Boll
Melinda K. Bradley
Kay Lynn Brumbaugh
Daniel K. Burke
Thomas W. Burton
Wendi S. Campbell
Elizann Carroll
Ron Chapman, Jr.
J. Kevin Ciavarra
Nikole C. Clark
Joseph F. Coniglio
Catherine Fancher
John G. Fischer
Julie Y. Fort
Adam T. Fox
Kathryn Becker Gameros
Paul R. Genender
Michael R. Gill
Jill S. Giroir
Paul Goldean
Cynthia L. Hardy
Tiffany Gurkin Hildreth
M. Ames Hutton
Earsa R. Jackson
Courtney L. Jones
Jacqueline S. Kelley
Ashley Thomas Kisner
Lori J. Lamoreaux
(Not admitted in TX)
Jon C. Leatherberry
Joseph R. Little
Karen D. McCloud
Dewey H. McCravy, III
Kimberly S. Moore
Matthew W. Moran
David T. Morice
Craig H. Myers
Christian G. Newsom
Laura Reilly O'Hara
Kathryn E. Peterson
Matthew R. Pickelman
Leigh Campbell Porter
Kristine L. Price
Robert M. Reed, Jr.
Toni Scott Reed
Amie Richardson
Christine D. Roseveare
John N. Schwartz
Scott A. Shanes
Brian T. Smith
Dani D. Smith
Elvin E. Smith, III
Mark T. Smith
Steven M. Smith
Michael D. Stacy
Amanda Stamps
Scott E. Sullivan
Paul F. Tagg
Deron L. Wade
Jeffrey R. Ward
Melissa Webb
Carol D. Williamson
Bart M. Wyrick
Glynis L. Zavarelli

For full biographical listings, see the Martindale-Hubbell Law Directory

THOMPSON, COE, COUSINS & IRONS, L.L.P. (AV)

200 Crescent Court, Eleventh Floor, 75201-1853
Telephone: 214-871-8200
Fax: 214-871-8209
Austin, Texas Office: Suite 1500, Austin Centre, 701 Brazos, 78701.
Telephone: 512-708-8200.
Fax: 512-708-8777.

PARTNERS

Emory L. White, Jr.
Franklin H. Perry
Richard S. Geiger
Robert O. Lamb
Jack M. Cleaveland, Jr.
Randy A. Nelson
David M. Taylor
Robert B. Wellenberger
Rhonda Johnson Byrd
Rodney D. Bucker
Roger D. Higgins
John L. Ross
Alison H. Moore
Richard M. Mosher
Newton J. Jones
Beth D. Bradley
Jennifer D. Aufricht
William N. Radford
James L. Sowder
Michael W. Jones
John B. Kronenberger
Rider Scott
David F. Eriksen
Harrison H. Yoss
James Richard Harmon
Sherry L. Travers
Thomas A. Culpepper
Lisa Dreyer Ball
Aaron L. Mitchell
Kevin B. Brown
Wade C. Crosnoe
Franklin M. Kennedy
Lisa A. Songy
Bradford K. Burdette
Robin B. Seckel
Michael E. Rohde
Kevin J. Thomason
Jerry R. Gibson, Jr.

SENIOR ATTORNEY

John A. Isbell
J.E. Barry Greve

(See Next Column)

ASSOCIATES

David A. McFarland
Erin L. Williams
Ellen M. Lewis Van Meir
Michele Medlock Cassidy
Loyd Ross Earley
Catherine K. Faubion
Travis S. Gamble
Estee C. Whitaker
George N. Wilson
Darryl E. Atkinson
Barton J. Freeman
Kimberly D. Loving
Jacquelyn Chandler
Michael Barrett Jones
Kristin A. Regel
Yolanda Marie Torres
Cynthia L. Wilkinson
Michael Wilson
Elaine Tran
Patricia C. Fudzie
Jo Allison Stasney
Ryan E. Griffitts
Jason W. Snell
Abigail A. Mathews
Carie P. Pyland
Michelle E. Coburn
Coleman J. Mcallister
(Not admitted in TX)

OF COUNSEL

R. B. Cousins
Will C. Thompson (1889-1980)
David B. Irons (1917-1991)
Vernon Coe (1909-1994)
David H. Evaul

For full biographical listings, see the Martindale-Hubbell Law Directory

THOMPSON & KNIGHT L.L.P. (AV)

(Attorneys and Counselors)
1700 Pacific Avenue Suite 3300, 75201
Telephone: 214-969-1700
Telecopy: 214-969-1751
Telex: 732 298
URL: http://www.tklaw.com
Austin, Texas Office: 1200 San Jacinto Center, 98 San Jacinto Boulevard, 78701.
Telephone: 512-469-6100.
Telecopy: 512-469-6180.
Fort Worth, Texas Office: 801 Cherry Street, Suite 1600, 76102.
Telephone: 817-347-1700.
Telecopy: 817-347-1799.
Houston, Texas Office: Thompson Knight Brown Parker & Leahy L.L.P., 1200 Smith Street, Suite 3600, 77002-4595.
Telephone: 713-654-8111.
Telecopier: 713-654-1871.
San Pedro Garza Garcia, Nuevo León, Mexico Office: Edificio Losoles PD-4, Av. Lázaro Cárdenas No. 2400 Pte., C.P. 66220.
Telephone: (52-8) 363-0096.
Telecopy: (52-8) 363-3067.

PARTNERS

Craig N. Adams
G. Luke Ashley
Steven R. Baggett
P. Jefferson Ballew
William L. Banowsky
David M. Bennett
L. James Berglund, II
Buford P. Berry
Michael R. Berry
Dorothy H. Bjorck
Hugh T. Blevins, Jr.
Jane Politz Brandt
Sam P. Burford, Jr.
Beverly Ray Burlingame
Frederick W. Burnett, Jr.
Bennett W. Cervin
George C. Chapman
Steven K. Cochran
John R. Cohn
Paul E. Comeaux
O. Paul Corley, Jr.
Greg W. Curry
Lori L. Dalton
Joe Dannenmaier
F. Barrett Davis
Gregg C. Davis
Scott D. Deatherage
Andrew B. Derman
Cheryl E. Diaz
Timothy W. Dowdy
David L. Emmons
Barbara B. Ferguson
Stephen F. Fink
Frank Finn
Sharon M. Fountain
Fred W. Fulton
Howard L. Gilberg
Rachelle H. Glazer
Dennis J. Grindinger
Russell G. Gully
Herbert J. Hammond
Thornton Hardie III
James B. Harris
Martha Harris
Craig A. Haynes
M. Lawrence Hicks, Jr.
J. Mike Holt
Gregory S. C. Huffman
James L. Irish, III
Paul M. Johnston
Robert W. Jones
Marc H. Klein
Harold F. Kleinman
C. Neel Lemon III
Veronica Smith Lewis
Jack M. Little
Stephen S. Livingston
Peter A. Lodwick
John A. Mackintosh, Jr.
John H. Martin
Mia M. Martin
Timothy R. McCormick
P. Mike McCullough
James W. McKellar
Mary A. McNulty
Susan Monaco
David E. Morrison
William R. Mureiko
Maureen A. Murry
Patricia A. Nolan
Geoffrey D. Osborn
Emily A. Parker
James R. Peacock III
Joseph S. Pevsner
James R. Prince
William F. Pyne
John W. Rain
Stephen C. Rasch
Rust E. Reid
Peter J. Riley
James Y. Robb III
Harry M. Roberts, Jr.
Norman R. Rogers
James W. Rose
David M. Rosenberg
A. Kay Roska
Judith W. Ross
Joe A. Rudberg
Elizabeth A. Schartz
Stephen C. Schoettmer
Michael E. Schonberg
William J. Schuerger
Clint Shouse
Terry L. Simmons

(See Next Column)

THOMPSON & KNIGHT L.L.P., *Dallas—Continued*

PARTNERS (Continued)

Steven W. Sloan
Bruce S. Sostek
Molly Steele
Stephen E. Stein
Arlene Switzer Steinfield
Scott P. Stolley
Peter J. Thoma
Michael C. Titens
William R. Van Wagner
Debra J. Villarreal
Kenn W. Webb
Ben B. West
R. David Wheat
Bill R. Womble
Arthur J. Wright
Dawn Marie Wright
William R. Wright
Shelly A. Youree
Jeffrey A. Zlotky

SENIOR ATTORNEY

Shawna L. Brown
Ron W. Fry
David S. White

ASSOCIATES

Craig B. Anderson
Cindy W. Andrew
Christopher Lee Barnes
Charles C. Boettcher
James S. Bowie, II
Amy Brimmage
Anthony J. Campiti
J. Jeffrey Cash
Kelley Cash
Tammy Lynn Clary
Amy Cleek
Ann Marie Cowdrey
Amy Ray Curtis
Adrienne E. Dominguez
Aditi Dravid
Priscilla Lynn Dunckel
Lauren C. Felts
Marcie Y. Flores
J. Holt Foster, III
Kristy D. Freeman
Marcie J. Freeman
Susan D. Frieze
Kal Grant (Not admitted in TX)
Lawrence E. Henke
Susan G. Henry
Andrea Hyatt
Julia Elizabeth Jones
Paul A. Jorge
William M. Katz, Jr.
D. Thomas Keltner
Darin M. Klemchuk
Michelle M. Kwon
Inge A. Larish
Michael W. Lewis
Grant Clayton Lightle
Anna E. Marple
Jerry D. Mason
Laura L. McClellan
Heather E. Moulder
Neely P. Munnerlyn
Bryan P. Neal
Matthew P. Nugent
Kristin L. O'Neal
Lara M. Peirce
David M. Pryor
Katherine (Kate) Quigley
Jane E. Rast
Christopher D. Ray
Eric G. Reis
Kirsten Ellen Richesson
Jennifer A. Richie
Carolyn Ritchie
Dwain K. Rogers, Jr.
Gino J. Rossini
Rebecca T. Rutherford
G. Dawn Shawger
Jonathan R. Smith
Delia A. Spencer
Shad E. Sumrow
Jennifer Ann Taylor
William H. Underwood
Victor D. Vital
Kyle S. Volluz
Scott F. Wendorf
Deborah Lin Whalen
Lee Ann Wheelis
Richard L. Wynne, Jr.

OF COUNSEL

Johnny R. Buckles
J. W. Bullion
David C. Cain (Not admitted in TX)
Gayle E. Cannon
Laura Peterson Elkind
Julia Patterson Forrester
Sol Goodell
Samuel D. Haas
Fred L. Hamric
Jerry P. Jones
David S. Kidder
Verne H. Maxwell
Curtis W. Meadows, Jr.
William D. Neary

STAFF ATTORNEYS

Monica S. Blacker
Richard J. Lebos, Jr.
Tracy B. Liden
N. Jude Menes
Pamela Sue Ratliff

For full biographical listings, see the Martindale-Hubbell Law Directory

VIAL, HAMILTON, KOCH & KNOX, L.L.P. (AV)

A Registered Limited Liability Partnership including Professional Corporations
1717 Main Street, Suite 4400, 75201-7388
Telephone: 214-712-4400
FAX: 214-712-4402
Email: vhkk@vialaw.com *URL:* http://www.vialaw.com
Houston, Texas Office: 3700 Buffalo Speedway, Suite 550, 77098.
Telephone: 713-840-8881.
Fax: 713-840-0670.

MEMBERS OF FIRM

Robert G. Vial (P.C.)
Graham R. E. Koch (P.C.)
James A. Knox (P.C.)
Byron L. Falk (P.C.)
James H. Baumgartner, Jr., (P.C.)
George W. Fazakerly (P.C.)
Paul D. Schoonover (P.C.)
Walter L. Abbey (P.C.)
M. Leigh Bartlett (P.C.)
Stephen L. Baskind (P.C.)
James L. Deem (P.C.)
J. Raymond Chesney (P.C.)
Richard G. Dafoe (P.C.)
Jerry C. Gilmore (P.C.)
Gary L. Woolfolk (P.C.)
Paul E. Pesek (P.C.)
Stephen E. Friend (P.C.)
Richard D. Pullman (P.C.)
James M. Schendle (P.C.)
Mark A. Hendrix (P.C.)
Robert C. Wendland (P.C.)
J. Mark Hansen (P.C.)
J. Michael Colpoys (P.C.)
James A. McCorquodale (P.C.)
Robert F. Middleton (P.C.)

(See Next Column)

MEMBERS OF FIRM (Continued)

Robert W. Coleman (P.C.)
John E. Richards (P.C.)
Paula M. Romberg (P.C.)
Larry J. Bridgefarmer (P.C.)
Blake Allen Bailey (P.C.)
Eric V. Moyé(P.C.)
Drew N. Bagot (P.C.)
Martha Waters Wise (P.C.)
Scott E. Hayes (P.C.)
Karen Kohler Fitzgerald (P.C.)
Barry L. Hardin (P.C.)
Claude R. Wilson, Jr.
Elizabeth A. Hurst (P.C.)
Tracy W. Berry
Kyle E. Moore
K. Mark Vincent

ASSOCIATES

S. Brad Brown
David A. Buono, II
Hala L. Carey
S. Keenan Carter
Dawn Kahle Doherty
Eduardo S. Espinosa
Joel E. Geary
Michael G. Mahan
Christopher M. McDowell
Jamison D. Newberg
Laura S. Spangler
Jeanette A. Vloitos
Christopher Richard Ward
James M. Welch

OF COUNSEL

C. Douglas Calvert
Kerri D. Condie
William N. Hamilton
Gerald R. Powell
Cecil L. Smith

LEGAL SUPPORT PERSONNEL

William L. Evans

For full biographical listings, see the Martindale-Hubbell Law Directory

VINSON & ELKINS L.L.P. (AV)

3700 Trammell Crow Center, 2001 Ross Avenue, 75201-2975
Telephone: 214-220-7700
Fax: 214-220-7716
URL: http://www.velaw.com
Austin, Texas Office: One American Center Suite 2700, 600 Congress Avenue, Austin, Texas, 78701-3200.
Telephone: 512-495-8400.
Fax: 512-495-8612.
Beijing, China Office: 20/F, Beijing Silver Tower, No. 2, Dong San Huan Bei Lu, Chaoyang District, 100027.
Telephone: +86-10-6410-6300.
Fax: +86-10-6410-6360.
Houston, Texas Office: 2300 First City Tower, 1001 Fannin, Houston, Texas, 77002-6760.
Telephone: 713-758-2222.
Fax: 713-758-2346.
London, England Office: Regis House, 8th Floor, 45 King William Street, London, EC4R 9AN, England.
Telephone: (44-171) 618-6000.
Fax: (44-171) 618-6001.
Moscow, Russia Office: 16 Ulitsa Spiridonovka, Second Floor, 103001 Moscow, Russia.
Telephone: (7-095) 956-1995. Local
Fax: (7-095) 956-1996. U.S. Satellite
Fax: (212) 803-0142.
New York, N.Y. Office: 1325 Avenue of the Americas, 17th Floor, New York, N.Y., 10019.
Telephone: 917-206-8000.
Fax: 917-206-8100.
Singapore Office: 6 Battery Road, #39-01, Singapore, 049909.
Telephone: (65) 536-8300.
Fax: (65) 536-8311.
Washington, D.C. Office: The Willard Office Building, 1455 Pennsylvania Avenue, N.W., Washington, D.C., 20004-1008.
Telephone: 202-639-6500.
Fax: 202-639-6604.

RESIDENT PARTNERS

David P. Blanke
Michael R. Boulden
John C. Brannan, Jr.
Ben A. Brooks, III
Jeffrey A. Chapman
William H. Church, Jr.
Thomas Crichton, IV
Samuel Poage Dalton
Josiah M. Daniel III
William B. Dawson
George Harvey Dunn, III
Mark Early
Felicia A. Finston
Orrin L. Harrison, III
Paul E. Heath
Jay H. Hebert
Karen L. Hirschman
Monty Humble
E. Ray Hutchison
Stuart Brooks Johnston, Jr.
Randy R. Jurgensmeyer
Robert L. Kimball
George M. Kryder III
Thomas S. Leatherbury
Michael L. Malone
Dale Gene Markland
James S. Meyer
Garry M. Miles
Rodney L. Moore
W. Glenn Opel
A. Winston Oxley
Russell L. Reid, Jr.
George G. Rodriguez
Joel L. Ross
Michael J. Schimberg
Gary G. Short
William D. Sims, Jr.
Daniel C. Stewart
William L. Wallander
Robert C. Walters
Jim A. Watson
Michael D. Wortley
Russell Yager
William D. Young

OF COUNSEL

Mark A. Cover
Sheryl L. Hopkins
Ellis Glenn Koury
Carla N. Lindley
James S. Matthews
Geoffrey R. Polma
J. Stuart Tonkinson

(See Next Column)

VINSON & ELKINS L.L.P.—*Continued*

RESIDENT ASSOCIATES

Keefe M. Bernstein
W. Bradley Bickham
Scott W. Breedlove
Barry Bumgardner
Anthony P. Canale (Not admitted in TX)
Jon Carroll
Scott L. Cole
Robert R. Collins, III
Alexis R. Connally
Sharon M. Cooper
David C. D'Alessandro
Toni N. Dinh
Stacey H. Dore
Martha Ratnoff Fleisher
Heather Haase
Daren S. Harrell
Christine A. Hathaway
Delwin E. Hervey
Paul Gregory Hidalgo
Christopher G. Jordan
J. Christopher Kirk
James Fitzmorris Kull
Matthew L. Larsen
Robert B. Little
Paul A. Martin
J. Carter Meyer
Steven L. Miller, Jr.
John E. Mitchell
Jarod T. Moss
Clifford F. Murray
Todd A. Murray
Renn G. Neilson
Jill Oberdas
Eric M. Ostermayer
Walter R. Owens, Jr.
Carol Collins Payne
David S. Peck
Lydia T. Protopapas
Michael L. Raiff
Carrie M. Ramirez
Tonya Moffat Ramsey
Patricia F. Reilly
Tara H. Reynolds
Brian E. Robison
Christopher R. Rowley
Michael H. Ryan
Mirjam Schuller
Brad E. Seidel
Eric Stahl
Matthew R. Stammel
Mary J. Steichen
Mark W. Steirer
Ann K. Stewart
Julie I. Ungerman
Joseph G. Walker (Not admitted in TX)
John C. Wander
Jennifer L. Webster
Jennifer Lee Williams
David E. Wolfe
William Scott Wyatt
Lamar Youngblood

For full biographical listings, see the Martindale-Hubbell Law Directory

---

WHITTENBURG WHITTENBURG & SCHACHTER, P.C. (AV)

2300 Plaza of the Americas, 600 North Pearl, LB 133, 75201
Telephone: 214-999-5700
Facsimile: 214-999-5747
Amarillo, Texas Office: 1010 South Harrison.
Telephone: 806-372-5700.
Facsimile: 806-372-5757.

George Whittenburg
Mack Whittenburg
Cary Ira Schachter
Susan Lynn Burnette
Charles G. White
Karl L. Baumgardner
Raymond P. Harris, Jr.
Deborah Ashmore Harris
C. Jared Knight
Christopher W. Weber
Laurel A. Siegert
Nicholas A. Taylor

For full biographical listings, see the Martindale-Hubbell Law Directory

---

WINSTEAD SECHREST & MINICK P.C. (AV)

5400 Renaissance Tower, 1201 Elm Street, 75270-2199
Telephone: 214-745-5400
Telex: 73-0051
Fax: 214-745-5390
URL: http://www.winstead.com
Houston, Texas Office: 2400 Bank One Center, 910 Travis Street.
Telephone: 713-650-8400.
Telex: 73-0051.
Fax: 713-650-2400.
Austin, Texas Office: Suite 800, 100 Congress Avenue.
Telephone: 512-474-4330.
Telex: 73-0051.
Fax: 512-370-2850.
Mexico, D.F., Mexico Office: Winstead y Rivera, S.C., Av. Insurgentes Sur 1685, Piso 13-04, Torre Diamante, Colonia Guadalupe Inn, Delegacion Alvaro Obregon, 01020, Mexico, D.F., Mexico.
Telephone: (011-525) 5661-3025.
Fax: (011-525) 5661-3033.

Michael V. Abcarian
Thomas B. Alleman
Roger J. Allen
Arthur J. Anderson
W. Mike Baggett
John F. Bergner
P. Talmage Boston, Jr.
Bruce W. Bowman, Jr.
Nan B. Braley
Daniel H. Branch
J. David Brown
D. Forrest Brumbaugh
Bruce A. Cheatham
Charles T. Clark
Robert E. Crawford, Jr.
Dan C. Dargene
Daniel J. Davis
John C. Dickey
T. Andrew Dow
Paul V. Downey
Ira D. Einsohn
David W. Elmquist
R. Michael Farquhar
Nancy Wyman Furney
Daniel B. Gail
H. Martin Gibson
Herbert G. Gleitz
Bob C. Griffo
Jeffrey A. Hage
Craig A. Harris
Stanley G. Harvey
Thomas R. Helfand
Jerry Hicks
Michael W. Hilliard
F. Franklin Honea, II
Thomas W. Hughes

(See Next Column)

Amanda J. Jensen
Mark G. Johnson
John P. Kincade
Barry R. Knight
J. Kenneth Kopf
Keith A. Langley
James J. Lee
Diane K. Lettelleir
Jay J. Madrid
James A. Markus
T. Randall Matthews
Mike C. McWilliams
Fred J. Meier
Brian T. Morris
Keith H. Mullen
James J. Murphy
John M. Nolan
Thomas W. Oliver
Michael K. O'Neal
Robert B. Payne, Jr.
Edward A. Peterson
David C. Petruska
Stuart M. Reynolds, Jr.
Darrel A. Rice
R. Barrett Richards
Randall E. Roberts
Ted S. Schweinfurth
William B. Sechrest
John D. Smart
Connie S. Stamets (Not admitted in TX)
Robert Q. Stanton
Kevin A. Sullivan
Brice E. Tarzwell (Not admitted in TX)
J. Maxwell Tucker
Paul N. Wageman
J. Richard White
Kirk R. Williams
David L. Winston
Valinda Barrett Wolfert
Robert E. Wood
Thomas L. Woodman
Franklin E. Wright
Lynda K. Zimmerman

Michael F. Alessio
Chad M. Allen
Brian J. Bailey
Rob O. Balachandran (Not admitted in TX)
Carey L. Bertolet
Randall D. Block
C. Mark Brannum
Matthew G. Brown
Dale E. Butler
Jerald L. Butler
Donald F. Campbell
Christopher W. Carr
Shannon Cameron Carr
Scott A. Christiansen
Michael E. Coles
Lisa L. Crawford
Jay D. Crutcher (Not admitted in TX)
Jonathan J. Cunningham
Jessica Hayes Denison
Dawn M. Douthit
Jana M. Ferguson
Derek L. Fletcher
Janet E. Follstaedt
Rebecca M. Foster
Robert F. Friedman
LeAllen Frost
Stephanie Benanti Gracia
Amanda R. Grainger
James R. Griffin
James W. Hamel
Tanya D. Henderson
J. Seth Hicks
Niles W. Holmes
Matthew N. Hudnall
Thomas R. Hudnall
Laurie C. Jardine
Michael B. Johnson
Heather A. Kemble
Christopher S. Kilgore
Jennifer Dorn Knapek
Phillip L. Lamberson
Peter R. Lando
Jana K. Limer
Rosland Fisher McLeod
Christine E. Moseley
Alan K. Motes
Bill R. Naifeh
Leonard E. Nicholson
Jennifer J. Paul
Charles A. Poche, Jr.
Kendra L. Rey
Frederick W. Reynolds III
David Mace Roberts
Jason J. Rose
Owen M. Scheurich
Brian L. Shiker
Brian S. Short
Steven A. Siegel
Lisa Winston Sorrell (Not admitted in TX)
Jay M. Thompson
David M. Tobias
Kathryn D. Watson
Sheri L. Watson
Gregory M. Weinstein
Christopher D. Williams
Charles B. Wills
Douglass T. Wingo
Kimberly Frisch-Winters
Robert J. Witte
Emeline Yang

OF COUNSEL

Bill H. Brister
Don W. Davis
Joe T. Hyde
Sheryl Brantley Latham
Robert B. Payne
Lee D. (Tom) Vendig

For full biographical listings, see the Martindale-Hubbell Law Directory

---

*EASTLAND,** Eastland Co.

TURNER, SEABERRY & WARFORD (AV)

400 Exchange Building, 76448
Telephone: 254-629-1777

John Williams Turner (1886-1952)
Virgil Theodore Seaberry (1892-1960)
Tommy G. Warford

ASSOCIATE

Donald W. Reid

OF COUNSEL

Virgil T. Seaberry, Jr.

Representative Clients: Texas Utilities; Eastland National Bank; Southwestern Bell Telephone Co.; Hardware Mutuals; Peoples State Bank of Clyde, Ranger Branch.

For full biographical listings, see the Martindale-Hubbell Law Directory

*EL PASO,** El Paso Co.

CROWSON & INGRAM (AV)

Suite 706, The Cortez, 310 North Mesa, P.O. Box 862, 79945
Telephone: 915-533-7717
Telefax: 915-533-1495
Email: crowsing@huntleigh.net

MEMBERS OF FIRM

Harold E. Crowson, Jr.
Temple B. Ingram, Jr.

Reference: Bank of America, N.A.; Norwest Bank, El Paso, N.A.; Bank of the West, El Paso, Texas.

For full biographical listings, see the Martindale-Hubbell Law Directory

DELGADO, ACOSTA, BRADEN & JONES, P.C. (AV)

221 N. Kansas, Suite 1400, 79901
Telephone: 915-544-9997
Facsimile: 915-544-8544
Email: staff@delgadoacosta.com
Correspondent Offices in Ciudad Juarez, Chih., Mexico and Mexico City, Mexico.

Hector Delgado
Alejandro Acosta, Jr.
Paul A. Braden
Carlos Rincon
John R. Jones
Marco Delgado
Rene Ordoñez
Jerry R. Wallace

Rodolfo Mata
Robin J. Drake

For full biographical listings, see the Martindale-Hubbell Law Directory

JAMES, GOLDMAN & HAUGLAND, P.C. A PROFESSIONAL CORPORATION (AV)

Chase Bank of Texas, 201 East Main, Suite 800, P.O. Box 1770, 79949-1770
Telephone: 915-532-3911
Fax: 915-541-6440

Wiley F. James, III
Merton B. Goldman
Corey W. Haugland
Michael J. Hutson
Victor M. Firth
Christopher R. Johnston
Hector Phillips

Don W. Minton
Natasha Hazarian

Attorneys for: Bank of the West; United Investors Realty Trust; Ford Motor Credit Corp.; Financial Federal Credit, Inc.; First Commonwealth Mortgage Trust; Mack Massey Motors, Inc.; FCA Corp.; United Investors Realty Trust; Marvel Enterprises, Inc. (Toy Biz); Southwestern General Hospital.

For full biographical listings, see the Martindale-Hubbell Law Directory

JOHNSON & BOWEN (AV)

Suite 1600, Chase Tower, 201 East Main, 79901
Telephone: 915-532-1497
FAX: 915-532-5415

MEMBERS OF FIRM

Travis C. Johnson
Phillip C. Bowen

Representative Clients: El Paso County 911 District; Hudspeth County Conservation and Reclamation District No. 1; Southwest Airlines Co.; Chase Bank of Texas-El Paso.

For full biographical listings, see the Martindale-Hubbell Law Directory

KEMP, SMITH, DUNCAN & HAMMOND, A PROFESSIONAL CORPORATION (AV)

221 North Kansas, Suite 1700, 79901, P.O. Drawer 2800, 79999
Telephone: 915-533-4424
Fax: 915-546-5360
Email: ksdh@kempsmith.com *URL:* http://www.kempsmith.com
Austin, Texas Office: 816 Congress, Suite 1650.
Telephone: 512-320-5466.
Fax: 512-320-5431.

Christopher Allan Paul
Charles C. High, Jr.
Jim Curtis
Jack T. Chapman
Michael D. McQueen
Darrell R. Windham
Charles A. Beckham, Jr.
Margaret A. Christian
Richard A. Bonner
Milton C. Colia
Darcy Alan Frownfelter
Mitzi T. Shannon
Allan M. Goldfarb
Kathleen Campbell Walker
Mark Hedrick
Cynthia S. Anderson
Kay Cargill Jenkins
James W. Brewer
Tom Wicker, Jr.
Clara B. Burns
Gene Wolf
Mark N. Osborn
Andrew S. Miller (Resident, Austin, Texas Office)
Hunter W. Burkhalter (Resident, Austin office)
Terry G. Pasqualone
Ernesto L. Cisneros
Erich A. Morales
Alfonso Soto, III

(See Next Column)

OF COUNSEL

Tad R. Smith
Joseph P. Hammond
Bruce Hallmark

R. Shawn Oller
Kathrine E. Urban
Steven J. Blanco
Jason T. Chapman
Tammy M. Holt
Susan D. Zulkowski
Daphne M. Andritsos
Michael C. Zweber
Dustin K. Hunter
Brenda Eileen Perez
Jennifer M. Crowson
Walker F. Crowson

Attorneys for: Norwest Bank; Continental National Bank; The Leavell Company; Asarco; Petro PSC, L.P.; Tri-Gas Inc.

For full biographical listings, see the Martindale-Hubbell Law Directory

MAYFIELD & PERRENOT, P.C. (AV)

221 N. Kansas, Suite 1600, P.O. Box 2039, 79950
Telephone: 915-533-2468
Telecopier: 915-533-0620
Email: mayper@1eagle1.com

Richard B. Perrenot
Roger C. Davie
James R. Dennis
Jeffery W. McElroy

Lisa M. Power
Shelly Weatherly
Marina Mata De La Garza

OF COUNSEL

Ellis O. Mayfield
James B. McIntyre

For full biographical listings, see the Martindale-Hubbell Law Directory

MOUNCE, GREEN, MYERS, SAFI & GALATZAN, A PROFESSIONAL CORPORATION (AV)

100 N. Stanton, Suite 1700, P.O. Box 1977, 79950-1977
Telephone: 915-532-2000
Fax: 915-541-1597
Email: mouncegreenmyers@worldnet.att.net

William J. Mounce
S. Anthony Safi
H. Keith Myers
Carl H. Green
John Steven Birkelbach
Barbara Wiederstein
Kurt G. Paxson
Mark C. Walker
Steven L. Hughes
Mark D. Dore
Clyde A. Pine, Jr.
Bruce A. Koehler
Darryl S. Vereen

Carrie D. Helmcamp
James A. Martinez
Andrés E. Almanzán
Hector Andre Beltrán

OF COUNSEL

William T. Kirk

Attorneys for: El Paso Natural Gas Co.; El Paso Independent School District; Bank of the West; Norwest Bank of El Paso; Pioneer Mortgage Co.; Rocky Mountain Mortgage Co.; Stewart Title Guaranty Co.; Chicago Title Insurance Co.; R.E. Thomason General Hospital; Ticor Title Insurance Co.

For full biographical listings, see the Martindale-Hubbell Law Directory

SCOTT, HULSE, MARSHALL, FEUILLE, FINGER & THURMOND, P.C. (AV)

1100 Chase Tower, 201 East Main Drive, 79901
Telephone: 915-533-2493
Telecopier: 915-546-8333
Email: scotthulse@scotthulse.com *URL:* http://www.scotthulse.com

Louis A. Scott (1895-1974)
James F. Hulse (1905-1989)
Schuyler B. Marshall (1920-1993)
Charles R. Jones (1934-1996)
Richard H. Feuille
George W. Finger
James L. Gallagher
Richard G. Munzinger
Stephen B. Tatem, Jr.
Frank Feuille, IV
James T. McNutt, Jr.
G. Russell Hill
Myron D. Brown
W. Dean Hester
David P. Hassler
W. David Bernard
Carl E. Ryan
Terry L. Johnson
Stuart R. Schwartz
Robert R. Feuille
Joseph L. Hood, Jr.
Jeffrey C. Brown
William V. Ballew, III
Bernard D. Felsen
David R. Pierce
Jeffrey S. Alley
Scott A. Agthe
Michael D. Stell
Michael G. McLean
J. L. Jay
Gary A. Norton
Amy Stewart Sanders
Eric M. Brittain

Benjamin A. Escobar, Jr.
Rachel Anne Ekery
Robert Eric Riojas
Richard Glenn Davis
Ruth Monty Willars
Alan D. Gluth
David L. Leffman
Chantel Crews
Wesley P. Williams
Paul Pilibosian
Matthew S. Pape
Gerry M. Brown
Amy M. Stoeckl
Clint G. Bledsoe

(See Next Column)

SCOTT, HULSE, MARSHALL, FEUILLE, FINGER & THURMOND P.C.—*Continued*

Representative Clients: Chevron U.S.A.; Phelps Dodge Corp.; Southwestern Bell Telephone Co.; Dow Chemical Co.; General Motors Corp.; Allstate Insurance Co.; Kemper Insurance Group; Zurich General Accident & Liability Insurance Co.

For full biographical listings, see the Martindale-Hubbell Law Directory

STUDDARD & MELBY, A PROFESSIONAL CORPORATION (AV)

Third Floor, Franklin Plaza, 415 North Mesa, 79901
Telephone: 915-533-5938
Fax: 915-533-6225
Email: Lex@stu-mel.com
Van Horn, Texas Office: Van Horn State Bank Building.
Telephone: 915-283-2714.
Fax: 915-283-9227.

Don Studdard
John C. Melby (1939-1985)
Jonathan D. Schwartz, Jr.
Brainerd S. Parrish
Stephen L. Mitchell
Stephen H. Nickey
Lawrence M. Jordan

Patrick A. Groves

Representative Clients: Banes General Contractors, Inc.; Hunt Building Corp.; Silverton Construction Co.; Design Professionals Insurance Company; Connecticut Specialties Insurance Company; Farmers Insurance Co.; Mid-County Insurance Co.; Highlands Insurance Co.; Farmland Insurance Co.; John Deere Insurance Co.

For full biographical listings, see the Martindale-Hubbell Law Directory

*FORT WORTH,** Tarrant Co.

CANTEY & HANGER (AV)

A Registered Limited Liability Partnership
2100 Burnett Plaza, 801 Cherry Street, 76102-6899
Telephone: 817-877-2800, Metro Line: 429-3815
Telex: 758631 FAX: 877-2807
Dallas
Email: cantey@onramp.net
Dallas, Texas Office: 3330 Harwood Center, 1999 Bryan Street.
Telephone: 214-978-4100.
FAX: 214-978-4150. Email: chdallas@onramp.net
Austin, Texas Office: Cantey & Hanger Roan & Autrey L.L.P., 200 First State Bank Tower, 400 West Fifteenth Street.
Telephone: 512-474-4200.
FAX: 512-469-0470; 512-469-0474. Email: FIRM@ROAN-AUTREY.COM

MEMBERS OF FIRM

Harry E. Bartel
Mark D. Beatty
Sloan B. Blair
Donald K. Buckman
H. Carter Burdette
Perry J. Cockerell
D. Mark Daniel
Christine E. Dooling
David Bradley Dowell
Ralph H. Duggins
J. Robert Forshey
Thomas Patrick Gordon III
John F. Gray
Tolbert L. Greenwood
Richard L. Griffith
Larry Hayes
Allan Howeth
William L. Hughes, Jr.
Clay Dean Humphries
Noel C. Ice
Mary Colchin Johndroe
S. G. Johndroe III
Edward L. Kemble
J. Frank Kinsel, Jr.
Evelyn R. Leopold
Stephen A. Madsen
Kirk R. Manning
Shayne D. Moses
Kevin Norton
Jordan M. Parker
Rod Patterson
Bradley C. Poulos
Jeff P. Prostok
T. Pollard Rogers
John C. Stewart
Dean A. Tetirick
J. David Tracy
Carol J. Traylor
Estil A. Vance, Jr.
Sarah Walls
Melody McDonald Wilkinson

OF COUNSEL

W. Douglas Bailey
Whitfield J. Collins
Diego O. Giordano
Cecil E. Munn
Warren W. Shipman III
Bill J. Zimmerman

ASSOCIATES

Michael G. Appleman
Shannon Wade Bangle
Anthony N. Bishop
John B. Brown
Claudia V. Coscia
Kenneth C. Cunningham
Robert M. Doby III
Gindi L. Eckel
Timothy D. Howell
Andrew D. Keetch
Jeffrey S. McFall
David A. Palmer
Jason D. Prather
C. Matthew Terrell
Alice L. Whitten

Represent: General Motors Corp.; Miller Brewing Co.; The Medical Protective Co.; Texas Utilities Electric Co.; Bank of America, N.A.; Union Pacific Resources Company.

For full biographical listings, see the Martindale-Hubbell Law Directory

CHAPPELL, PARMELEE, JOHNSON & HILL, P.C. (AV)

1800 City Center Tower II, 301 Commerce Street, 76102-4118
Telephone: 817-332-1800
Metro: 817-654-2140
Telecopy: 817-332-1956
Email: cpjh@cmlaw.com *URL:* http://www.cmlaw.com

David F. Chappell
Robert A. Parmelee
Robert S. Johnson
Cynthia L. Hill

Suzanne K. Rosen
William F. Peters, Jr.

OF COUNSEL

James L. Williams, Jr.
Carolyn Mitchell
Christopher Cooke
C.C. "Kit" Cooke, III

For full biographical listings, see the Martindale-Hubbell Law Directory

DECKER, JONES, MCMACKIN, MCCLANE, HALL & BATES, A PROFESSIONAL CORPORATION (AV)

2500 Bank One Tower, 500 Throckmorton Street, 76102-3812
Telephone: 817-336-2400; Metro: 817-429-5260
Fax: 817-332-3043; 336-2181
Email: email@deckerjones.com *URL:* http://www.deckerjones.com

Daniel L. Bates
Robert W. Decker
Mark S. Dugan
Janet L. Hahn
Randy J. Hall
Raymond B. Kelly, III
John B. McClane
John W. McMackin
Charles B. Milliken
Gary M. Moates
Bradley H. Rice
Jeffrey W. Storie
James L. Stripling
Brian K. Yost
Tamera H. Bennett
Arthur F. Zobal
Geoffrey A. Mantooth

Representative Clients: Martin-Sprocket and Gear, Inc.; Williamson-Dickie Manufacturing Co.; MICA Corp.; Ibertech, Inc.; Harbison-Fischer Manufacturing Co.; Employers Insurance of Texas; American International Group; Medical Protective Co.; Redman Homes, Inc.; Liberty Mutual Insurance.

For full biographical listings, see the Martindale-Hubbell Law Directory

JACKSON WALKER L.L.P. (AV)

301 Commerce Street, Suite 2400, 76102
Telephone: 817-334-7200
Fax: 817-334-7290
URL: http://www.jw.com
Austin, Texas Office: 100 Congress Avenue, Suite 1100.
Telephone: 512-236-2000.
Fax: 512-236-2002.
Dallas, Texas Office: 901 Main Street, Suite 6000.
Telephone: 214-953-6000.
Fax: 214-953-5822.
Houston, Texas Office: 1100 Louisiana, Suite 4200.
Telephone: 713-752-4200.
Fax: 713-752-4221.
Richardson, Texas Office: 2435 North Central Expressway, Suite 600.
Telephone: 972-671-2560.
Fax: 972-671-2566.
San Angelo, Texas Office: 225 West Beauregard Avenue.
Telephone: 915-481-2550.
Fax: 915-481-2552.
San Antonio, Texas Office: 112 E. Pecan Street, Suite 2100.
Telephone: 210-978-7700.
Fax: 210-978-7790.

MEMBERS OF FIRM

Sheldon Anisman
Susan A. Halsey
Albon O. Head, Jr.
Gary L. Ingram
Wayne F. Malecha
Jay K. Rutherford
Kent R. Smith
Walter E. Tate
Richard S. Tucker
Jeffrey J. Wolf

SENIOR COUNSEL

Daniel L. Tatum

ASSOCIATES

Nikki H. Fanous
Jeffrey R. Grable
Lynn B. Gray
Melodee Laine Gruber
William R. Jenkins, Jr.
Daniel R. McCabe
Jason Shanks
Ginger M. Webber

For full biographical listings, see the Martindale-Hubbell Law Directory

KELLY, HART & HALLMAN, A PROFESSIONAL CORPORATION (AV)

201 Main Street, Suite 2500, 76102
Telephone: 817-332-2500
Telecopy: 817-878-9280
URL: http://www.khh.com
Austin, Texas Office: 301 Congress Avenue, Suite 2000, 78701.
Telephone: 512-495-6400.
Fax: 512-495-6401.

(See Next Column)

KELLY, HART & HALLMAN A PROFESSIONAL CORPORATION, *Fort Worth—Continued*

Dee J. Kelly
Mark L. Hart, Jr.
William P. Hallman, Jr.

Robert C. Beal
F. Richard Bernasek
Scott R. Bernhart
Mark E. Bishop
C. William Blair
Clive D. Bode
Thomas W. Briggs
Sean A. Bryan
Edward K. Clark
David P. Derber
Nancy Ebe (Resident, Austin Office)
Marc N. Epstein
Dirk E. Eshleman
Robert C. Grable
Wesley N. Harris
Alan D. Hegi
Donald E. Herrmann
Christopher E. Howe
Calvin M. Jackson
E. Glen Johnson
Paul H. Johnson, III
Dee J. Kelly, Jr.
Keith D. Kohlhepp
John T. Lee
Daniel L. Lowry
Patricia F. Meadows
Sharon S. Millians
Barbara P. Neely
Lisa A. Peterson
Cheryl Coon Roberts
Henry H. Robinson
J. Andrew Rogers
Bart A. Rue
David A. Schwarte
Marshall M. Searcy, Jr.
R. Daniel Settle, Jr.
James B. Shackelford
Dulaney G. "Dee" Steer
Wayne B. Whitham
Susan G. Zachos (Resident, Austin Office)

Derek W. Anderson
Marla Broaddus (Resident, Austin Office)
Russell D. Cawyer
Brenda L. Clayton (Resident, Austin Office)
Hugh G. Connor, II
Robin B. Connor
Beverly J. Davis
Roger C. Diseker
Mary G. Eads
John E. Frazier
Amy M. Fuqua
Greg S. Gober
Frank P. Greenhaw, IV
Lowell Winston Harrison
Heather Hitt
Brandon T. Hurley
Cheryl Poulin Leb
Theresa B. Lewis
Stephen W. Litke
Michael C. Lowder
Robert W. Lydick
Matthew A. Magidson
Mark Pittman
Randall G. Quick
David C. Reintjes
Todd W. Spake
Brian S. Stagner
Timothy J. Van Meir
William N. Warren
Lisa Martin West
Len Woodard, II

OF COUNSEL

Stephen C. Dickman (Resident, Austin Office)
Don C. Plattsmier
John J. Vay (Resident, Austin Office)

For full biographical listings, see the Martindale-Hubbell Law Directory

LAW, SNAKARD & GAMBILL, A PROFESSIONAL CORPORATION (AV)

3200 Bank One Tower, 500 Throckmorton Street, 76102
Telephone: 817-335-7373; Metro: 429-2991
Telecopier: 817-332-7473
Dallas
Dallas, Texas Office: St. Paul Place, 750 North St. Paul, Suite 1350.
Telephone: 214-871-9027; Metro: 429-2991.
Telecopier: 214-954-4476.

Rice M. Tilley (1899-1990)
Robert F. Snakard (1910-1994)
Samuel A. Denny (1937-1995)
Rice M. Tilley, Jr.
Walter S. Fortney
Dennis Swift
Jay Spencer Garrett
William F. McCann
Ed Huddleston
Vernon E. Rew, Jr.
A. Burch Waldron, III
Larry C. Bracken
Pamela Arnold Bassel
Carol Ware Bracken
Dabney D. Bassel
Lynn M. Johnson
Kelley B. Hill
B. Blake Cox
James H. Cheatham, IV
Stephen G. Wilcox
M. W. Cockrell, Jr.
Liane A. Janovsky

Christopher R. Richie
Deborah B. Morton
James O. Wyss
Laurie Dahl Babich
David F. Shurtz
Shoshana L. Thoma-Isgur

OF COUNSEL

Thos. H. Law
Lawton G. Gambill
Robert M. Randolph
Robert F. Watson
Harry Hopkins

Representative Clients: BankOne, Texas, N.A.; Southwestern Bell Telephone Co.; The Perot Group; Ford Motor Credit Co.; Prudential Securities, Inc.; Chrysler Financial Corp.
Attorneys for: Chicago Title Insurance Co.

For full biographical listings, see the Martindale-Hubbell Law Directory

NAMAN, HOWELL, SMITH & LEE, A PROFESSIONAL CORPORATION (AV)

301 Sinclair Building, 512 Main Street, 76102
Telephone: 817-348-0300
FAX: 972-445-8804
Email: naman@namanhowell.com *URL:* http://www.namanhowell.com
Waco, Texas Office: 900 Washington, Suite 700. P.O Box 1470.
Telephone: 254-755-4100.
FAX: 254-754-6331.
Austin, Texas Office: 221 West Sixth Street, 1900 Bank One Tower.
Telephone: 512-479-0300.
FAX: 512-474-1901.
Temple, Texas Office: Bowmer, Courtney, Burleson, Normand & Moore, 6th Floor, First National Bank Building, P.O. Box 844.
Telephone: 254-778-1354.
FAX: 254-774-7254.

David G. Henry (Resident Member, Waco, Texas Office)

Matthew E. Haddock

Representative Clients: Allied Mortgage Capital Corporation; Advantage Investors Mortgage Corporation; First Franklin Financial Corporation.

For full biographical listings, see the Martindale-Hubbell Law Directory

THOMPSON & KNIGHT L.L.P. (AV)

(Attorneys and Counselors)
801 Cherry Street, Suite 1600, 76102
Telephone: 817-347-1700
Telecopy: 817-347-1799
URL: http://www.tklaw.com
Dallas, Texas Office: 1700 Pacific Avenue, Suite 3300, 75201.
Telephone: 214-969-1700.
Telecopy: 214-969-1751.
Telex: 732298.
Austin, Texas Office: 1200 San Jacinto Center, 98 San Jacinto Boulevard, 78701.
Telephone: 512-469-6100.
Telecopy: 512-469-6180.
Houston, Texas Office: Thompson Knight Brown Parker & Leahy L.L.P., 1200 Smith Street, Suite 3600, 77002-4595.
Telephone: 713-654-8111.
Telecopier: 713-654-1871.
San Pedro Garza Garcia, Nuevo León, Mexico Office: Edificio Losoles PD-4, Av. Lázaro Cárdenas No. 2400 Pte., C.P. 66220.
Telephone: (52-8) 363-0096.
Telecopy: (52-8) 363-3067.

PARTNERS

R Gordon Appleman
Susan E. Coleman
Lonnie J. Copps
Jennifer Pettijohn Henry
Stephen B. Norris
E. Michael Sheehan

ASSOCIATES

Monty B. Moncrief
Jason Wylie

For full biographical listings, see the Martindale-Hubbell Law Directory

*GALVESTON,** Galveston Co.

GREER, HERZ & ADAMS, L.L.P. (AV)

A Partnership including Professional Corporations
(Formerly Dibrell & Greer)
One Moody Plaza, 18th Floor, 77550
Telephone: 409-797-3200; Houston Line: 281-480-5278
Telecopier: 409-766-6424
League City
URL: http://www.greerherz.com
League City Office: 2525 South Shore Boulevard, Suite 203, 77573.
Telephone: 281-480-5278.
Fax: 281-538-3791.

MEMBERS OF FIRM

W. E. Greer (1901-1996)
Irwin M. Herz, Jr. (P.C.)
Jerry L. Adams (P.C.)
Stephen G. Schulz (P.C.)
Debra G. James
John A. Buckley, Jr. (P.C.)
Andrew J. Mytelka
Darryl H. Levy
Frederick E. Black
Janet L. Rushing
Marilyn L. Soloway
Gregory S. Garrison
Scott D. Daniel
Joseph A. C. Fulcher
Jim Itin

ASSOCIATES

Tara B. Annweiler
Michael G. Adams
David Le Blanc
Joseph Russo, Jr.
Steve Windsor
Melissa E. Palmer
William J. Hogan
Sean Monticello

OF COUNSEL

Frank T. Crews, Jr. (P.C.)
John S. McEldowney
Charles Brown (P.C.)

General Counsel for: American National Insurance Co.; The Moody National Bank of Galveston; United States National Bank of Galveston; Transitional Learning Community of Galveston; Securities Management & Research,

(See Next Column)

GREER, HERZ & ADAMS L.L.P.—*Continued*

Inc.; American National Growth Fund, Inc.; Kempner Capital Management, Inc.; The Moody Endowment.
Counsel for: National Western Life Insurance Co.

For full biographical listings, see the Martindale-Hubbell Law Directory

McLEOD, ALEXANDER, POWEL & APFFEL, A PROFESSIONAL CORPORATION (AV)

802 Rosenberg, P.O. Box 629, 77553-0629
Telephone: 409-763-2481
Houston Line: 281-488-7150
Email: MAPAPC@AOL.COM
Houston, Texas Office: Suite 344 Onyx Building, 17225 El Camino Real, 77058.
Telephone: 281-486-1888.
Fax: 281-486-4888.

V.W. McLeod (1914-1977)	Anthony P. Brown
Robert W. Alexander (Retired)	James R. Ansell
Benjamin R. Powel (Retired)	Kenneth J. Bower
Ervin A. Apffel, Jr.	David P. Salyer
Fredrick J. Bradford	Wm. Hulse Wagner (Resident, Houston Office)
W. Daniel Vaughn	David E. Cowen
Douglas W. Poole	Genevieve Bacak McGarvey
Michael B. Hughes	Tod A. Phillips
James B. Galbraith	William R. Floyd
J. D. Bashline (Resident, Houston Office)	Bryan R. Lasswell

John V. Rabel (Resident, Houston Office)	Shana O'Neal Calderon (Resident, Houston Office)
Stacey H. Allen	Linda L. Sheets
Lyle Y. Courtney	Jeff L. Larson
Roland G. Hamilton	Mario A. Martinez

Travis Wade Hopper

Claims Attorneys: Santa Fe Lines in Texas and Louisiana.
Counsel for: Continental Insurance Cos.; Port of Galveston; Farmers Insurance Group.

For full biographical listings, see the Martindale-Hubbell Law Directory

ROYSTON, RAYZOR, VICKERY & WILLIAMS, L.L.P. (AV)

205 Cotton Exchange Building, 2102 Mechanic Street, 77550-1692
Telephone: 409-763-1623
Cable Address: "Houport"
Telex: 6869017
Telecopier: 409-763-3853
Email: royston@roystonlaw.com *URL:* http://www.roystonlaw.com
Brownsville, Texas Office: 55 Cove Circle, P.O. Box 3509.
Telephone: 956-542-4377.
Cable Address: "Padre"
Telex: 767-817.
Telecopier: 956-542-4370.
Corpus Christi, Texas Office: 1700 Wilson Plaza West, 606 North Carancahua.
Telephone: 361-884-8808.
Cable Address: "CC PORT"
Telex: 6866625.
Telecopier: 361-884-7261.
Houston, Texas Office: 600 Travis Street, Suite 2200.
Telephone: 713-224-8380.
Cable Address: "Houport"
Telex: 686-9017.
Telecopier: 713-225-9945.
Lubbock, Texas Office: 1401 Avenue G.
Telephone: 806-763-9252.
Telex: 6869017.
Telecopier: 806-763-9254.
San Antonio, Texas Office: 2000 Riverview Towers, 111 Soledad Street.
Telephone: 210-228-0655.
Telecopier: 210-228-0839.

PARTNERS
James R. Watkins
OF COUNSEL
Edward J. Patterson, Jr.

Counsel for: The United Kingdom Mutual Steamship Assurance Assn., Ltd.

For full biographical listings, see the Martindale-Hubbell Law Directory

*GEORGE WEST,** Live Oak Co.

SCHNEIDER & McWILLIAMS, P.C. (AV)

301 Bowie Street, P.O. Box 550, 78022
Telephone: 361-449-1501
Fax: 361-449-2042
Email: schneidr@speccom.net

R. E. Schneider, Jr. (1906-1976)	J. R. Schneider

Dwayne L. McWilliams

(See Next Column)

Joseph Robert Schneider, Jr.	Thomas Rex Forehand

Counsel for: First National Bank in George West; San Patricio Electric Cooperative, Inc.

For full biographical listings, see the Martindale-Hubbell Law Directory

*GREENVILLE,** Hunt Co.

MORGAN AND GOTCHER (AV)

2610-A Stonewall Street, P.O. Box 556, 75403-0556
Telephone: 903-455-3183
Metro Tel: 903-450-8800
Fax: 903-454-4654
Email: jhmorgan@koyote.com

J. Harris Morgan	Holly H. Gotcher

Representative Clients: Huffines Enterprises; Greenville Independent School District; International Cassettes, Inc.; Universal Health Services, Inc.; Hunt County Appraisal District; Bank One Greenville; Citizens Bank of Royce City.

For full biographical listings, see the Martindale-Hubbell Law Directory

*HILLSBORO,** Hill Co.

MARTIN, SHOWERS, SMITH & McDONALD, L.L.P. (AV)

62 West Elm Street, P.O. Box 257, 76645-0257
Telephone: 254-582-2536
Telecopier: 254-582-9561

MEMBERS OF FIRM

William B. Martin (1914-1999)	Stephen N. Smith
James A. Showers	Michael W. McDonald

ASSOCIATE
Andrew W. Lucas

Representative Clients: Bank of America, N.A.; First National Bank, Whitney; Norwest Bank Hillsboro and Hubbard; Whitney Independent School District; First State Bank, Mt. Calm; Towne Square Furniture, Inc.; Files Valley Water Supply Corp; Prime Group; Oakwood Industries, Inc.

For full biographical listings, see the Martindale-Hubbell Law Directory

*HOUSTON,** Harris Co.

AKIN, GUMP, STRAUSS, HAUER & FELD, L.L.P. (AV)

A Registered Limited Liability Partnership including Professional Corporations
1900 Pennzoil Place-South Tower, 711 Louisiana Street, 77002
Telephone: 713-220-5800
Fax: 713-236-0822
URL: http://www.akingump.com
Dallas, Texas Office: 1700 Pacific Avenue, Suite 4100.
Telephone: 214-969-2800.
Fax: 214-969-4343.
Austin, Texas Office: Frost Bank Plaza, 816 Congress Avenue, Suite 1900.
Telephone: 512-499-6200.
Fax: 512-499-6290.
San Antonio, Texas Office: 300 Convent Street, Suite 1500.
Telephone: 210-281-7000.
Fax: 210-224-2035.
New York, New York Office: 590 Madison Avenue, 20th Floor.
Telephone: 212-872-1000.
Fax: 212-872-1002.
Philadelphia, Pennsylvania Office: One Commerce Square, 2005 Market Street, Suite 2200.
Telephone: 215-965-1200.
Fax: 215-965-1210.
Washington, D.C. Office: 1333 New Hampshire Avenue, N.W., Suite 400.
Telephone: 202-887-4000.
Fax: 202-887-4288.
Los Angeles, California Office: Century Tower Plaza, 2029 Century Park East, Suite 2600.
Telephone: 310-229-1000.
Fax: 310-229-1001.
Brussels, Belgium Office: 65 Avenue Louise, P.B. #7.
Telephone: (+32 2) 535-29-11.
Fax: (+32 2) 535 29 00.
London, England Office: One Angel Court.
Telephone: 011 44 20 7726 9600.
Fax: 011 44 20 7726 9610.
Moscow, Russia Office: Ducat Place II, 7 Gasheka Street, P.B. 20.
Telephone: 011 7 095 974 2411.
Fax: 011 7 095 974 2412.
Affiliated Office:
Law Office of Abdulaziz H. Fahad: Jarir Plaza, 4th Floor, Olaya Street, P.O. Box 15870, Riyadh, Saudi Arabia, 11454.
Telephone: 011 966 1 464 8081.
Telex: 406176 LAWS SJ.
Telecopier: 011 966 1 462 4968.

(See Next Column)

AKIN, GUMP, STRAUSS, HAUER & FELD L.L.P., *Houston—Continued*

MEMBERS OF FIRM

Robert B. (Skip) Allen
Natalia Baratiants
(Not admitted in TX)
Kenneth R. Barrett
K. B. Battaglini
Rick L. Burdick (P.C.)
David R. Clonts
Richard D. Fladung
Karen P. Freeman
L. Todd Gremillion (P.C.)
Lester L. Hewitt
Paula W. Hinton
Randall K. Howard (P.C.)
J. Vincent Kendrick
Gregg C. Laswell
Stephen T. Miller
Charles A. Moore (P.C.)
G. Crawford Moorefield
William D. Morris
Richard M. Parr
David S. Peterman (P.C.)
Douglas W. Rommelmann
H. Rey Stroube, III, (P.C.)
Michael K. Swan (P.C.)
José L. Valera (P.C.)
S. Margie Venus
Mark T. Woolfolk
Blaine Yamagata
(Not admitted in TX)

ASSOCIATES

Jan M. Abell
J. Stephen Barrick
Brandon E. Bennett
Thomas M. Bevilacqua
Brent A. Boyd
Gregory V. Brown
Jason A. Buchman
Kurt G. Daum
Lessie G. Fitzpatrick
Shahid Ghauri
John T. Goodgame, III
Tracy L. Gostyla
Howard B. Hacker
Ann M. Hebert
Stephen S. Hodgson
Tari Lessard Hoekel
George W. Jordan, III
Julia V. Kasperski
Benita Lee
John F Luman III
Kevin P. McEnaney
Trenton T. McKenna
Louis N. Moreno
Nathan P. Murphy
Joseph John Naples, III
Kristen C. Oliver
Allen H. Rustay
Richard A. Schafer
John A. Tang
Brad Taylor
Karen C. Wehner
Joel A. Youngblood

SENIOR COUNSEL

Charles M. Cox
Bernarr Roe Pravel
Cynthia Ribas

COUNSEL

Suzanne R. Chauvin
James S.E. Cowan
Mark S. Croft
(Not admitted in TX)
J. Gail Foster
Lee C. Harwood
Gregory M. Hasley
Jeffrey A. Jansen
Yava D. Scott
Julien R. Smythe
Richard J. Wilkie

For full biographical listings, see the Martindale-Hubbell Law Directory

ANDREWS & KURTH L.L.P. (AV)

Suite 4200, 600 Travis, 77002
Telephone: 713-220-4200
Telex: 79-1208 Ankur
Telecopier: 713-220-4285
Email: webmaster@andrews-kurth.com *URL:* http://www.andrews-kurth.com
Washington, D.C. Office: Suite 300, 1701 Pennsylvania Avenue, N.W.
Telephone: 202-662-2700.
Telecopier: 202-662-2739.
Dallas, Texas Office: Suite 3700, 1717 Main Street.
Telephone: 214-659-4400.
Telecopier: 214-659-4401.
The Woodlands, Texas: Suite 150, 2170 Buckthorne Place, 77380.
Telephone: 713-220-4801.
Telecopier: 713-220-4815.
Los Angeles, California Office: Suite 4200, 601 S. Figueroa Street.
Telephone: 213-213-896-3100.
Telecopier: 213-896-3137.
New York, N.Y. Office: 805 Third Avenue.
Telephone: 212-850-2800.
Telecopier: 212-850-2929.
London, England Office: 2 Creed Court, 5-11 Ludgate Hill, EC4M 7AA.
Telephone: 0171-236-3456.
Telecopier: 0171-236-4276.

MEMBERS OF FIRM

Frank Andrews (deceased)
Howard T. Ayers
James Vernon Baird
Melissa M. Baldwin
Thomas G. Bateman, Jr.
Lawrence L. Bellatti
Michael C. Blaney
(Not admitted in TX)
Paul M. Bohannon
Michael A. Boyd
Melinda Held Brunger
John T. Cabaniss
Douglas E. Clarke
Christopher S. Collins
John P. Courtney
Douglas J. Dillon
Linda Ingols Dole
James Donnell
Rosemarie Donnelly
Alfred H. Ebert, Jr.
Jack E. Fields
William N. Finnegan, IV
Dan A. Fleckman
Thomas W. Ford, Jr.
Lori Meghan Gallagher
Suzanne E. Goss
Hal V. Haltom, Jr.
Jeffrey R. Harder
James D. Higgason, Jr.
Mark C. Hodges
A. Sidney Holderness, Jr.
(Not admitted in TX)
Jan K. Holzinger
Donald J. Horton
Robert V. Jewell
Jay D. Kelley

(See Next Column)

MEMBERS OF FIRM (Continued)

Melvin E. Kurth (deceased)
Terri Lacy
John Lee
W. Scott Locher
Thomas P. Mason
Chanse L. McLeod
Barry R. Miller
William T. Miller
James E. Myers
G. Michael O'Leary
David P. Oelman
Thomas J. Perich
Paul J. Pipitone
James M. Prince
Blake E. Rasmussen
Hugh M. Ray
Kent W. Robinson
A. Ross Rommel, Jr.
David G. Runnels
Robin Russell
Lawrence Bernard Schreve
John B. Shely
John J. Sparacino
Jeffrey E. Spiers
Michael D. Stuart
William P. Swenson
Thomas W. Taylor (Resident, London, England Office)
W. Roberts Taylor, Jr.
Darrell G. Thomas
Denton N. Thomas
Timothy J. Unger
Milton H. West, Jr.
O'Banion Williams, III
John Carlton Wynne
David A. Zdunkewicz

OF COUNSEL

John A. Adkins
J. Scott Carothers
Robert J. Collins
Patricia S. Greek
Bill E. Henry
Suzie Leggio
Walter B. Loeffler, Jr.
William C. McDonald
P. Dexter Peacock
Laurence D. Sikes, Jr.
David J. Stone
Edward W. Turley, Jr.
Hunter H. White

ASSOCIATES

Paul D. Aubert
Andrew P. Becnel
Christopher T. Boehler
Peter C. Bowden
Tammy W. Brennig
David Clyde Buck
Alan C. Buckner
William J. Cooper
Brian T. Crum
J. Todd Culwell
Edwin Theodore Davis
Gislar R. Donnenberg
J. Wesley Dorman, Jr.
Kenneth Fair
Kinloch Gill, III
Alexis J. Gómez
Ryan K. Gravelle
Kendall M. Gray
David C. Grove
Kristin L. Hamilton
Leslie M. Hansen
Thomas M. Hart III
Lance M. Harvey
Wyatt L. Hogan
Melinda M. Hough
Darren Scott Inoff
Patricia E. Lin
Heather C. McLemore
Robert J. McNamara
Joel R. Messina
Jeff D. Migit
Paul D. Moak
Michael D. Morfey
Kimberly A. Osburn
Jason M. Peters
Gillian A. Robinson
Mauricio Rondon
Omar S. Saleh
Michael R. Shaw
Steven M. Tyndall
Douglas G. Walter
(Not admitted in TX)
Benjamin H. Wells
Martha Smith Welmaker
Elizabeth Stoebner Wiley
Dimitri D. Zgourides

SENIOR ATTORNEYS

Shelley Torian Barineau
Susan Yang Gorman
George Humphrey
(Not admitted in TX)
Charles Jacaman
Peter K. Jameson
Allison Donnell Mantor
Raymond G. Randle, Jr.

For full biographical listings, see the Martindale-Hubbell Law Directory

BAKER BOTTS L.L.P. (AV)

One Shell Plaza, 910 Louisiana, 77002
Telephone: 713-229-1234
Cable Address: "Boterlove"
Fax: 713-229-1522
Email: postmaster@bakerbotts.com *URL:* http://www.bakerbotts.com
Washington, D.C. Office: The Warner, 1299 Pennsylvania Avenue, N.W.
Telephone: 202-639-7700.
New York, New York Office: 599 Lexington Avenue.
Telephone: 212-705-5000.
Austin, Texas Office: 1600 San Jacinto Center, 98 San Jacinto Boulevard.
Telephone: 512-322-2500.
Dallas, Texas Office: 2001 Ross Avenue.
Telephone: 214-953-6500.
Moscow, Russia Office: 10 ul. Bolshaya Dimitrovka (formerly Pushkinskaya), 103031.
Telephone: 7095/921-5300 (Local); 7095/929-7070 (International).
London, England Office: 45 Ludgate Hill.
Telephone: 0171-778-1400 (Local); 011-44-171-778-1400 (International).
Baku, Azerbaijan Office: 6-10 Vagif Mustafa-zadeh Street, Third Floor, Icheri Sheher, 370004.
Telephone: 994-12-97-63-88 (Local); 011-994-12-97-63-88 (International).
Fax: 994-12-97-63-91 (Local); 011-994-12-97-63-91 (International)

James A. Baker (1857-1941)
W. B. Botts (1836-1894)

MEMBERS OF FIRM

Richard C. Johnson

MEMBERS OF FIRM

Thomas H. Adolph
David F. Asmus
Louis Lee Bagwell
James Addison Baker, III
J. Michael Baldwin
Stanley C. Beyer
Jonathan T. Bickham
Maria Wyckoff Boyce

(See Next Column)

BAKER BOTTS L.L.P.—*Continued*

MEMBERS OF FIRM (Continued)

Richard R. Brann
Michael Lamar Brem
B. Daryl Bristow
David Alan Burns
Charles Tynan Buthod
Joseph D. Cheavens
Joseph A. Cialone, II
F. Walter Conrad, Jr.
Jefferson Gregory Copeland
Rufus Cormier, Jr.
Joshua Davidson
Tony M. Davis
James A. DeMent, Jr.
Gerard A. Desrochers
Fred H. Dunlop
S. Stacy Eastland
Paul R. Elliott
Pamela B. Ewen
Larry B. Feldcamp
John D. Geddes
Michael S. Goldberg
I. Jay Golub
Moulton Goodrum, Jr.
George F. Goolsby
Michael Paul Graham
Bill Hart, Jr.
Frank W. R. Hubert, Jr.
Richard Allen Husseini
Gray Jennings
Philip J. John, Jr.
Richard L. Josephson
Ronald W. Kesterson
J. David Kirkland, Jr.
Jay T. Kolb
Stephen Krebs
William Karl Kroger
Matthew L. Kuryla
Paul B. Landen
James L. Leader
Ronald C. Lewis
Marley Lott
Mitchell D. Lukin
James Edward Maloney
Stephen A. Massad
Karen Kay Maston
J. Bruce McDonald
Michael S. Moehlman
Gregory V. Nelson
John Edward Neslage
Roy L. Nolen
Rufus W. Oliver, III
Gene J. Oshman
Peter M. Oxman
Theodore William Paris
Scott F. Partridge
David R. Poage
Joe S. Poff
John W. Porter
James R. Raborn
Bradley I. Raffle
Kelly Brunetti Rose
Tony P. Rosenstein
Scott E. Rozzell
Travis James Sales
Stuart F. Schaffer
Margo S. Scholin
George T. Shipley
L. Chapman Smith
Walter J. Smith
David D. Sterling
Gail Woodson Stewart
Robert L. Stillwell
R. Joel Swanson
Charles Szalkowski
Darrell W. Taylor
Timothy S. Taylor
G. Irvin Terrell
Lewis Proctor Thomas
Stephen Gillham Tipps
Hugh Tucker
Teresa S. Valderrama
Allister M. Waldrop, Jr.
C. Michael Watson
Benjamin G. Wells
Robert M. Weylandt
Wade H. Whilden
Michael E. Wilson
Robert P. Wright

RETIRED PARTNERS

John B. Abercrombie
V. Reagan Burch
William Rufus Choate
Finis E. Cowan
Sam G. Croom, Jr.
Richard B. Dewey
C. Brien Dillon
William C. Griffith
Frank G. Harmon
William C. Harvin
John F. Heard
George H. Jewell
James P. Lee
Robert J. Malinak
Harold L. Metts
Ewell E. Murphy, Jr.
James K. Nance
Alvin Owsley
Frank B. Pugsley
James D. Randall
R. D. Richards, Jr.
John S. Sellingsloh
Ross Staine
Garrett R. Tucker, Jr.
James G. Ulmer
A. B. White
William G. Woodford
Walter E. Workman

SENIOR COUNSEL

E. William Barnett
J. Thomas Eubank

SPECIAL COUNSEL

Margaret W. Brown
W. Brad Bryan
Laura C. Higley
Tracee Kennedy Lewis
Kristine Dubiel Maclay
Carolyn Brostad Southerland
LeAnn Vaughn
Victoria Gardner Wall

OF COUNSEL

Claude E. Cooke, Jr.
Greg N. Martin
James LeGrand Read

ASSOCIATES

Aaron K. Adkins
Rebeca Aizpuru
Gretchen Gibbons Allen
Timothy Craig Allen, M.D.
John Anaipakos
Jed P. Anderson
Nancy Archer Yanochik
Christopher J. Arntzen
Mark G. Artlip
James H. Barkley
Paige K. Beach
Michael B. Bennett
Matthew D. Bekerman (Not admitted in TX)
John T. Bibb
J. Kevin Blodgett
Mark A. Bodron
Christi Bourg Brown
Laura L. Bowne
Anderson W. Brandao
Katherine Butler Brem
Michael P. Bresson
Deidre Sullivan Brod
Richard A. Brooks
Jeffrey V. Brown
Karen Skeens Caldwell
Michael L. Calhoon
T. Chuck Campbell
Dawn Lannin Carpenter
M. Andrew Chen
Karen L. Chisholm
Michael A. Choyke
Gerald W. Clanton
Samuel W. Cooper

(See Next Column)

ASSOCIATES (Continued)

Sarah Cooper
Brian D. Cororve
Cynthia Crawford
Anita Sani Damian
Tia L. Daniel
Edmund D. Daniels
Sarah Sharlot Dietrich
Roger S. Donley
Stephen T. Dyer
Brady Edwards
David Patrick Elder
Sandra K. Elzerman
Karla A. Evans
Brian P. Fenske
Kathleen S. Fenelon
Nellie Agah Fisher
Tull R. Florey
J. Robert Fowler
Roger J. Fulghum
David George
James M. Grace, Jr.
Derek S. Green
Mary Millwood Gregory
Elizabeth M. Guffy
Amy Spear Hampton
Lucy Haroutunian
Michael A. Hawes
Rennae K. Henry
Carey Jordan Hetherington
Cassandra L. Hill
Jacalyn A. Hollabaugh
Ronald E. Holmes
Keith D. Jaasma
Seshasayee Kalapatapu
Alan F. Kansas
Lori J. Khan
M. Shane Kimzey
Gregory B. Kopel
Sandra Thourot Krider
Daniel Harris Kroll
Claire Swift Kugler
Carrie C. Lancaster
Pamela Roger Laborde
Michael P. Lennon, Jr.
Michael J. Levine
Judy Y. Liu
Michael G. Locklar
Stephanie Loomis-Price
Maryanne Lyons
Amy Douthitt Maddux
Robin Lightner Maisashvili (Not admitted in TX)
Michael C. Massengale
Njeri I. Mathis
James H. Mayor
Laura B. Medina
Joel Z. Montgomery
William S. Moss, III
Denise Dardeau Muller
Marshall A. Murray
Beth K. Neese
Michelle A. Neumann
Rebecca Pacholder
Paul F. Perea
Kay M. Peterson
Paul E. Pfeffer
Felix P. Phillips
Teresa M. Potter
Sergio A. Pozzerle
Jeffrey E. Raley
Douglas B. Roberson
Rebecca L. Robertson
David M. Rodi
Cristina Espinosa Rodriguez
Elizabeth Rose
Kathryn Stegall Schueler
Robert James Sergesketter
Jessica S. Siegel
Wesley P. Shields
D'Andra Millsap Shu
J. Denmon Sigler
Katherine M. Silver
Consuella D. Simmons
Jonathan D. Simon
Amy L. Snell
Jonathan E. Sommer
Gerald M. Spedale
James R. Staley
Paul J. Stancil
Lori D. Stiffler
Macey Reasoner Stokes
Khannan Suntharam
Melissa J. Szanto
Stacey F. Tilley
Lisa M. Tilton-McCarthy
Katherine J. Traverse
Lori McFarlin Troutman
Laura Lanza Tyson
Kathryn S. Vaughn
Jennifer L. Walker Elrod
Mark L. Walters
Shelley L. Ward
Gerard Alan Witte
Hsiao-Cheng Steven Wu
Shira R. Yoshor

For full biographical listings, see the Martindale-Hubbell Law Directory

BAKER & HOSTETLER LLP (AV)

1000 Louisiana, Suite 2000, 77002-5008
Telephone: 713-751-1600
FAX: 713-751-1717
To contact an attorney on the Internet use first initial and surname followed by @baker-hostetler.com
URL: http://www.bakerlaw.com
In Cleveland, Ohio: 3200 National City Center, 1900 East Ninth Street.
Telephone: 216-621-0200.
In Cincinnati, Ohio: 312 Walnut Street, Suite 2650.
Telephone: 513-929-3400.
In Columbus, Ohio: Capitol Square, Suite 2100, 65 East State Street.
Telephone: 614-228-1541.
In Denver, Colorado: 303 East 17th Avenue, Suite 1100.
Telephone: 303-861-0600.
In Beverly Hills, California: 9150 Wilshire Boulevard, Suite 205.
Telephone: 310-385-7500.
In Long Beach, California: 300 Oceangate, Suite 620.
Telephone: 562-432-2827.
In Los Angeles, California: 600 Wilshire Boulevard.
Telephone: 213-624-2400.
In Orlando, Florida: SunBank Center, Suite 2300, 200 South Orange Avenue.
Telephone: 407-649-4000.
In Washington, D. C.: Washington Square, Suite 1100, 1050 Connecticut Avenue, N.W.
Telephone: 202-861-1500.

OFFICE MANAGING PARTNER

Kenneth R. Valka (Managing Partner-Houston Office)

(See Next Column)

BAKER & HOSTETLER LLP, *Houston—Continued*

PARTNERS

Hurlie H. Collier
Randall C. Elkins
Paul S. Francis
Shari L. Heyen
Jon David Ivey
Pamela G. Johnson
Mark C. Joye
James L. Moore
Lisa H. Pennington
Mary K. Schratwieser
William R. Whitman
James C. Winton
Robert M. Wolin
Ivan Wood, Jr.
Richard C. Yount, Jr.

ASSOCIATES

Luis E. Arri
David M. Bearden, Jr.
Blair A. Bruce
David T. Chang
Douglas D. D'Arche
Billy M. Donley
John W. Ghezzi
Tonya A. Jacobs
David R. Jarrett
Lindsay L. Lambert
Richard O. Litsey
Tina H. Mai
Joyce B. Margarce
Michele D. Mason
Lilly E. Thrower
David B. Waller
Donna Bostic Ward

OF COUNSEL

John English
Robert H. Nicholas, Jr.
William C. Stroh

For full biographical listings, see the Martindale-Hubbell Law Directory

BAKER & MCKENZIE (AV)

Two Allen Center, Suite 1200, 1200 Smith Street, 77002-4592
Telephone: (713) 427-5000
Intn'l. Dialing: (1-713) 427-5000
Facsimile: (1-713) 427-5099
URL: http://www.bakerinfo.com
Associated Offices of Baker & McKenzie in: Almaty, Amsterdam, Bahrain, Baku, Bangkok, Barcelona, Beijing, Berlin, Bogotá, Brasília, Brussels, Budapest, Buenos Aires, Cairo, Caracas, Chicago, Dallas, Düsseldorf, Frankfurt, Geneva, Hanoi, Ho Chi Minh City, Hong Kong, Hsinchu, Juárez, Kiev, London, Madrid, Manila, Melbourne, México City, Miami, Milan, Monterrey, Moscow, Münich, New York, Palo Alto, Paris, Prague, Rio de Janeiro, Riyadh, Rome, St. Petersburg, San Diego, San Francisco, Santiago, São Paulo, Singapore, Stockholm, Sydney, Taipei, Tijuana, Tokyo, Toronto, Valencia, Warsaw, Washington, D.C. and Zürich.
Correspondent Law Firm: Hadiputranto, Hadinoto & Partners, Jakarta.

MEMBERS OF FIRM

Amar N. Budarapu
John P. Cogan, Jr.
Kenneth S. Culotta
A. Duncan Gray, Jr.

NATIONAL PARTNERS

J. Richard Hammett
Jeffrey A. Schlegel
Philip R. Weems

ASSOCIATES

Scott J. Arrington
Victoria L. Branton
Raymond W. Chang
Thomas P. Dvorak
Anthony T. Fiore
Christine J. Hsieh
Nikolay Y. Isaakov (Not admitted in United States)
Roger A. Rippy
William P. M. Schwind
Laurence E. Stuart
Todd W. Taylor
Charlene H. Tsang
JoJo H. Yiu

For full biographical listings, see the Martindale-Hubbell Law Directory

BAYKO GIBSON CARNEGIE HAGAN SCHOONMAKER & MEYER LLP (AV)

Chase Tower, 65th Floor, 77002-3008
Telephone: 713-223-0101
Facsimile: 713-223-0042
Email: baykogibson@nol.net

PARTNERS

Tom Bayko
Wendy K. B. Buskop
Jack G. Carnegie
Martin P. Detloff
Larry L. Evans
Michael W. Ford
Michael M. Gibson
John L. Hagan
Robert J. Leidich
M. Michael Meyer
Linda C. Schoonmaker
Leymon Solomon

OF COUNSEL

John T. S. Williams

David M. Bays
Julia Lynn Nye
Ruth E. Piller
Melissa Brook Romine
Lauri De Brie Thanheiser

For full biographical listings, see the Martindale-Hubbell Law Directory

BEIRNE, MAYNARD & PARSONS, L.L.P. (AV)

Wells Fargo Bank Tower 25th Floor, 1300 Post Oak Boulevard, 77056-3000
Telephone: 713-623-0887
Fax: 713-960-1527
Email: info@bmpllp.com *URL:* http://www.bmpllp.com

(See Next Column)

MEMBERS OF FIRM

Martin D. Beirne
William L. Maynard
Jeffrey R. Parsons
Denise A. Acebo
Suzanne B. Baker
Brit T. Brown
Jay W. Brown
David A. Clark
Gene F. Creely, II
David S. Gamble
Timothy J. Hogan
Lisa A. Ketai
Scott D. Marrs
Roger L. McCleary
Sawnie A. McEntire
Bruce C. Morris
Edward J. Murphy
William C. Norvell, Jr.
Matthew G. Pletcher
Thomas P. Sartwelle
James E. Smith
Wm. Bruce Stanfill
Michael J. Stanley
Linda P. Wills
William N. Wilson, II

OF COUNSEL

Gerald J. Brown
Lynette Fons
Catherine Mezick Geis
Gerald T. Holtzman
Clarence E. Kendall, Jr.
Paul B. Radelat
Willard M. Tinsley
Donald W. Towe
Jack E. Urquhart

ASSOCIATES

Marissa Weitzner Arreola
R. Christopher Bell
Danya W. Blair
John E. Carlson
Ronald Patrick Chin
Pamela Anne Clark
Maria J. Courtois
Laura E. DeSantos
Jacqueline M. Houlette
Frank A. Monago
Kevin L. O'Neal
Daniel E. Pellar
Pam Rea
John Valdemar Trevino, Jr.
Mark A. Waite
Steve R. Wedemeyer
S. Ashby Williams
Marlene C. Williams

For full biographical listings, see the Martindale-Hubbell Law Directory

BRACEWELL & PATTERSON, L.L.P. (AV)

South Tower Pennzoil Place, 711 Louisiana Street, Suite 2900, 77002-2781
Telephone: 713-223-2900
Fax: 713-221-1212
Austin, Texas Office: 111 Congress Avenue, Suite 2300, 78701-4052.
Telephone: 512-472-7800.
Fax: 512-472-9123.
Corpus Christi, Texas Office: 2000 One Shoreline Plaza, South Tower, 800 North Shoreline Boulevard, 78401-3700.
Telephone: 361-882-6644.
Fax: 361-882-6659.
Dallas, Texas Office: Lincoln Plaza, 500 N. Akard Street, Suite 4000, 75201-3387.
Telephone: 214-758-1000.
Fax: 214-758-1010.
Fort Worth, Texas Office: 500 Throckmorton Street, Suite 2601, 76102-3708.
Telephone: 817-348-0700.
Fax: 817-348-0711.
San Antonio, Texas Office: 800 One Alamo Center, 106 S. St. Mary's Street, 78205-3603.
Telephone: 210-226-1166.
Fax: 210-226-1133.
Washington, D.C. Office: 2000 K Street, N.W., Suite 500, 20006-1872.
Telephone: 202-828-5800.
Fax: 202-223-1225.
London, England Office: 33 Davies Street, W1Y 1FN.
Telephone: 011-44-171-355-3330.
Telex: 261414.
Fax: 011-44-171-629-2621.
Almaty, Kazakhstan Office: 65 Kazybek bi str., Suite 410, 480091.
Telephone: 73272-581-400.
Fax: 73272-581-444.

Joseph S. Bracewell (1892-1965)
Harry W. Patterson (1922-1990)
Richard A. Royds (1938-1998)

FOUNDING PARTNERS AND SPECIAL COUNSEL

Searcy Bracewell
Fentress Bracewell

PARTNERS

William Key Wilde
Carol S. Vance (Mr.)
Carlton Wilde
V. Scott Kneese
Edgar J. Marston, III
Charles W. Giraud
Robert L. Clarke
Eugene A. Cook
J. Clifford Gunter, III
Patrick C. Oxford
Albert B. Kimball, Jr.
John L. Bland
Kelly Frels
Robert Joe Hull
Thomas D. Manford III
Thomas O. Moore, III
Gary W. Orloff
G. Waverly Vest, Jr.
Rick L Wittenbraker
Robert C. Curfiss
B. Thomas Cook
William J. Hayes
Ralph D. McBride
Michael Kuhn
Ronald Scott
R. Daniel Witschey, Jr.
J. David Thompson III
John R. Brantley
Mark C. Evans
Thomas M. Melo
William D. Gutermuth
Andrew F. Spalding
William T. Luedke IV
Roger D. Aksamit
G. Alan Rafte
Janet Little Horton
Bruce R. Jocz
Mark E. Lowes
Alfredo R. Perez
Clark G. Thompson, Jr.

(See Next Column)

BRACEWELL & PATTERSON L.L.P.—*Continued*

PARTNERS (Continued)

Marc F. Wiegand
Glenn A. Ballard, Jr.
Marcy E. Kurtz
Gray H. Muzzy
Earl D. Weed, III
William Cleland Dade
Carrin F. Patman
Laura Byrd Herring
Jeffrey John Horner
Ileana M. Blanco
Randall K. Glover
Craig L. Stahl
Jennifer W. Jacobs
Tracie J. Renfroe
Merri Schneider-Vogel
Arturo G. Michel
Robin J. Miles
Amy Karff Halevy
Tracy D. Hester
Martin J. Hunt
William Stephen Benesh
Warren Wayne Harris
Lisa A. Brown
David W. Locascio
Geoffrey A. Long
Bruce D. Oakley
Stephen B. Crain
Christopher W. Martin
David L. Ronn
Phillip D. Sharp
Robert G. Stephens
Dewey J. Gonsoulin, Jr.
Sheryl A. Gussett
W. Jackson Wisdom

SPECIAL COUNSEL

William P. Streng

OF COUNSEL

Bridget O'Toole Purdie

RETIRED PARTNERS

Bob Casey, Jr.
Joe H. Foy

ASSOCIATES

Andrew Allan Adams
John H. Barr Jr.
Mirari M. Barriola (Not admitted in TX)
Gregory M. Bopp
Christopher P. Borreca
Heather L. Brown
Jill F. Brumberger
Yuri A. Calderon
Matthew F. Carroll
Rina W. Chang
Mark J. Cole
M. Coy Connelly
Mary Donna Corso
M. Benjamin Cowan
Douglas A. Daniels
Patricia M. Daniels
Bryan S. Dumesnil
Andrew M. Edison
John J. Edmonds
Glen T. Eichelberger
Ron Israel Erlichman
Philip Fraissinet
Scott L. Franck
William Frederking
Jennifer B. Garnett
Christopher B. Gilbert
George Y. Gonzalez
Daniel S. Greenspan
Raymond L. Gregory II
Kathleen F. Harris
Catherine G. Henderson
Jon D. Hensarling
Thomas F.A. Hetherington
David B. Hodgins
Ryan Scott Holcomb
Michael D. Hopkins
Stan R. Jensen
Stephen J. Joncus
Jorge H. Kamine
Robert J. Kestelik (Not admitted in TX)
Kyung Tai Kim
Elizabeth W. King
Robert E. Kinney
Elizabeth Mata Kroger
Jeffrey T. Kuehnle
Jon Larrabee
Derek E. Leon
Paulina Lipets
Christina Loescher
Basil Mahmoud
Ryan J. Maierson
William R. Marlow
Alethia A. Martin
W. James McAnelly
Kerry Marc McMahon
Josh M. McMorrow
Marla A. Moore
Mary L. Moreland
Jeffrey J. Nichols
Keith D. Nicholson
M. Catherine Özdögan
Katherine Dunn Parsons
D. Mark Poag
Deborah E. Rank
Charlotte M. Rasche
Andrew P. Ray
Kevin S. Robins
Aaron P. Roffwarg
Jessica Rossman
Therese M. Runnels
William W. Russell
Phillip L. Sampson, Jr.
Kimberly M.O. Sanchez
Scott C. Sanders
Patricia Gail Sargent
Kwame K. Satchell
Stephen Schlather
David M. Schwab
Eden P. Sholeen
Nicholas A. Simms
Marney Collins Sims
Maureen R.M. Singleton
Jay T. Sonnenberg
Duncan W. Stewart
Margaret B. Symonds
Tracy C. Temple
Mark A. Tidwell
Thomas M. Tomlinson (Not admitted in TX)
P. Kevin Trautner
David A. Tucker
Manuel Vera (Foreign Legal Consultant — Mexico)
Gregory J. Vojack
Richard Whiteley
Timothy A. Wilkins
Anthony C. Wills
Jeffrey S. Wyman
Michael V. Young

For full biographical listings, see the Martindale-Hubbell Law Directory

EIKENBURG & STILES, P.C. (AV)

1900 One City Centre, 1021 Main Street, 77002-6603
Telephone: 713-652-2144
Fax: 713-652-2424
Email: eikensti@infohwy.com

MEMBERS OF FIRM

John J. Eikenburg (Deceased)
R. Charles Stiles
John F. Rhem, Jr.

ASSOCIATE

Joseph H. Pedigo

(See Next Column)

OF COUNSEL

Neil R. Mitchell
Cheryle R. Johnston

For full biographical listings, see the Martindale-Hubbell Law Directory

FAIRCHILD, PRICE, THOMAS, HALEY & WILLINGHAM, L.L.P. (AV)

440 Louisiana Street, Suite 2110, 77002-4205
Telephone: 713-426-1700
Fax: 713-426-1717.
Email: mwillingham@fpthw.com
Center, Texas Office: 413 Shelbyville Street, P.O. Drawer 1719, 75935.
Telephone: 409-598-2981.
Fax: 409-598-7712. E-Mail: wmthomas@fpthw.com
Nacogdoches, Texas Office: 1801 North Street, P.O. Box 631668, 75963-1668.
Telephone: 409-569-2327.
Fax: 409-569-7932. E-Mail: chaley@fpthw.com

John L. Price
W. Miller Thomas
C. Victor Haley
R. Mark Willingham
Travis P. Clardy
David J. Fisher
Clayton H. Haley
Russell R. Smith
Ryan A. Beason

OF COUNSEL

Robert L. Fairchild

James A. Payne, Jr.
David Edward Ash
Campbell Cox
Jefferson B. Davis
Thomas L. Cougill
Jeffrey Pierce Fultz
Matthew D. Mettauer

For full biographical listings, see the Martindale-Hubbell Law Directory

FULBRIGHT & JAWORSKI L.L.P. (AV)

1301 McKinney, Suite 5100, 77010-3095
Telephone: 713-651-5151
Fax: 713-651-5246
Email: info@fulbright.com *URL:* http://www.fulbright.com
Washington, D.C. Office: 801 Pennsylvania Avenue, N.W., 20004-2604.
Telephone: 202-662-0200.
Fax: 202-662-4643.
Austin, Texas Office: 600 Congress Avenue, Suite 2400, 78701.
Telephone: 512-474-5201.
Fax: 512-320-4598.
San Antonio, Texas Office: 300 Convent Street, Suite 2200, 78205.
Telephone: 210-224-5575.
Fax: 210-270-7205.
Dallas, Texas Office: 2200 Ross Avenue, Suite 2800, 75201.
Telephone: 214-855-8000.
Fax: 214-855-8200.
New York, New York Office: 666 Fifth Avenue, 31st Floor, 10103.
Telephone: 212-318-3000.
Fax: 212-752-5958.
Los Angeles, California Office: 865 South Figueroa Street, 29th Floor, 90017.
Telephone: 213-892-9200.
Fax: 213-680-4518.
London, England Office: 2 St. James's Place, SW1A 1NP.
Telephone: 011-44171-629-1207.
Fax: 011-44171-493-8259.
Hong Kong Office: The Hong Kong Club Building, Nineteenth Floor, 3A Chater Road, Central.
Telephone: 011-852-2523-3200.
Fax: 011-852-2523-3255.

R. C. Fulbright (1881-1940)
John H. Crooker (1884-1975)
John H. Freeman (1886-1980)
William B. Bates (1889-1974)
Leon Jaworski (1905-1982)

PARTNERS

William Kendall Adam
Linda Leuchter Addison
Joshua P. Agrons
John R. Allender
Eric S. Anderson
Carmody C. Baker
C. Mark Baker
Robert S. Bambace
D. Gregory Barker
John Adams Barrett
Jerry A. Bell, Jr.
Evelyn H. Biery
A. T. Blackshear, Jr.
Ronald G. Bliss
Nancy T. Bowen
John P. Bowman
William J. Boyce
Reagan M. Brown
Carol Steib Butner
W. Fred Cameron
Richard N. Carrell
Stephen K. Carroll
Winstol D. Carter, Jr.
William H. Caudill
Zack A. Clement
Lawrence H. Clore
Richard P. Colquitt
Michael W. Conlon
David Wilks Corban
Robert F. Corrigan, Jr.
R. Richard Coston
Christopher E.H. Dack
Marc L. Delflache
Otway B. Denny, Jr.
Arthur L. Dent III
Stephen C. Dillard
Harva Ruth Dockery (Also at Dallas, TX Office)
Uriel E. Dutton
Osborne J. Dykes, III
Kathleen R. Ellison
Eva Maria Fromm
Stewart W. Gagnon
Frank T. Garcia

(See Next Column)

FULBRIGHT & JAWORSKI L.L.P., *Houston—Continued*

PARTNERS (Continued)

L. Henry Gissel, Jr.
Deborah A. Gitomer
Thomas C. Godbold
Robert F. Gray, Jr.
Edmund Lee Haag III
Charles W. Hall
A. John Harper, II
Robert S. Harrell
Robert S. Hoffman
John S. Hollyfield
Henry W. Hope
Curtis W. Huff
Richard D. Huff
Charles W. Hurd
David R. Iler
Michael P. Irvin
Donald O. Jansen
Frank G. Jones
Gregg H. Jones
John L. King
Rodney C. Koenig
Arno W. Krebs, Jr.
Paul E. Krieger
Layne E. Kruse
Stephen A. Kuntz
George F. Kutzschbach
William S. Lee
Jane H. Lerner
Nancy June Locke
Gerry Lowry
C. Robert Mace
Katherine Dudas Mackillop
Barclay Arendall Manley
John G. Mauel
Daniel M. McClure
Kent H. McMahan
Claude M. McQuarrie III
Gray H. Miller
Mark Stephen Miller
John M. Mings
R. Michael Moore
Laurance C. Mosher, Jr.
Karen M. Nakfoor
Jonathan K. Newsome
D. Dudley Oldham
Cecil Jay Olmstead, III
William R. Pakalka
Stephen P. Pate
Edward J. Patterson, III
Thomas D. Paul
Gerard G. Pecht
Oliver Pennington
John Wesley Raley
Anne Rivers Reavis
James W. Repass
Steven L. Roberts
Mark A. Robertson
Arthur H. Rogers, III
Steven C. Salch
James B. Sales
John M. Sanders
David R. Schneider
Stephanie M. Schroepfer
Steven E. Segal
J. Todd Shields
Reagan W. Simpson
William B. Sing
James C. Slaughter
Joseph C. Sleeth, Jr.
Stephen William Smith
Joy M. Soloway
Charles H. Still
N. Susan Stone
Charles Louis Strauss
Samuel E. Stubbs
Charles E. Sullivan, Jr.
John F. Sullivan, III
Robert J. Swift
Hugh E. Tanner
Blake Tartt
Jasper G. Taylor, III
T. Neil Thomas
Terriann Trostle
David J. Van Susteren
Jack M. Vaughan
John A. Watson
Fredric A. Weber
Jerry L. Wickliffe
Richard J. Wilson
Robert E. Wilson
Howard Wolf
Jeffrey Stephen Wolff
William D. Wood
T. J. Wray
Alan V. Ytterberg

RETIRED PARTNERS

Ed Bluestein, Jr.
Richard P. Bogatto
Charles D. Boston
Lynn P. Carter
John H. Crooker, Jr.
Alton F. Curry
Gibson Gayle Jr.
Jefferson D. Giller
Rene P. Lavenant, Jr.
Walter J. Morrison
Charles A. Saunders
B. Dixie Smith
William A. Stout
Robert M. Welch, Jr.
C. W. Wellen
William Byron White

SPECIAL COUNSEL

Alberto Fortun (Not admitted in the United States)

SENIOR COUNSEL

Ronald W. Adzgery
Jana Banahan Cogburn
Paul L. DeVerter II
Jennifer L. Price
Ross Staine, Jr.

COUNSEL

Robert S. Ballentine
Claudia D. Christin
John P. Dillman
Warren H. Fisher
Jane Mueller Fly
Ann D. Garnett
David M. Goldberg
Roger K. Harris
Richard L. Hunn
Elaine L. Lawson
Nicole R. Martinson
Dean M. Moesser
George B. Murr
Marsha M. Nichols
Christy M. Schweikhardt
Joanna B. Walker
Claudia B. Wilkinson

SENIOR ASSOCIATES

Edward B. Adams, Jr.
David P. Ayers
Theodore G. Baroody
Philip A. Choyce
Rebecca J. Cole
Heather M. Corken
M. Carter Crow
G. Edward Deery
Martin F. Doublesin
Lucas T. Elliot
Stephen M. Fernelius
David L. Fox
Rachel S. Giesber
Christopher R. Hart
Jarvis Vincent Hollingsworth
Shauna N. Johnson
Susan H. Lawhon
David J. Levy
Edward C. Lewis
Kevin M. McDonald
Scott R. McLaughlin
Laura J. McMahon
Franklin Hobbs Newton
Andrew Price
Terry L. Radney
Anne Marie Rodgers
Ira Claborn Rogers
Lance L. Shea

(See Next Column)

SENIOR ASSOCIATES (Continued)

Jan K. Simpson
Richard T. Stilwell
Joseph G. Thompson, III
James R. Wetwiska
Kevin W. Yankowsky

ASSOCIATES

Kent Altsuler
Graig J. Alvarez
Alberto Q. Amatong, Jr.
Darryl Wade Anderson
John T. Boundas
Lance R. Bremer
Mercedes Caravello
Chelo Zepeda Carter (Not admitted in TX)
Gino Catena
Jay M. Chadha
Heather Fleniken Cochran
David S. Cook
Matthew E. Coveler
Hunter Craft
John Cyr
Christopher B. Daniels
Daniel M. Deaton
Ann DesRuisseaux
Kirk D. Dreyer
Nadelle Grossman
Eric B. Hall
Michael D. Hansen
Lara Anne Haschke
Joseph C. Henry
Melvin Houston
Warren Huang
Valerie G. Jewett
Robert S. Johnson
Tracey M. Jones
Joann Kahn
Theresa M. Kennedy
Gregory Kent Kondritz
Christopher Joseph Lallo
Hanna Liebman
Kevin W. Liles
Melissa Longin
David Mackie
Cortlan H. Maddux
Robert T. Mashburn, Jr.
Michael S. McCoy
Catrina McLean
Erica Meadough
Derrick Mitchell
Rachel Morgan
T. Neal Nobles
Shawn R. O'Brien
Nicholas Edward O'Connell
Frederick C. Ogle
Robert W. Painter
John P. Panther
Robert W. Phillpott, Jr.
Carrie A. Platt
Rick L. Rambo
Scott E. Raynes
Kathleen Rose
Charles Jason Rother
Holly A. Royce
Jason Martin Schall
Stephanie A. Schlau
Charles Rhett Shaver (Not admitted in TX)
Stacey Lynn Shawn
Michael Simons
Jody Lynn Simpson
Laura Ann Ayers Smith
Stefan Prentiss Smith
Edward D. Steakley
Stephanie Barnes Taylor
Bien C. Tran
Charles B. Walker, Jr.
Wesley R. Ward
Candice Wells
Seth D. Wexler
Ruthie White
Amy Baumann Whitworth
Richard S. Zembek
Jennifer Zucker

SENIOR STAFF ATTORNEYS

M. Patricia Prichard
Marilyn K. Scanlan
Edward W. Szczepanski (Not admitted in TX)

STAFF ATTORNEYS

William Patrick Bishop
Jeryl Annette Golub
Susan A. Logsdon
Miryam R. Mitchell
Kathleen W. Osman
Kristine Rollinson
Ann E. Webb
Deborah L. Wright

For full biographical listings, see the Martindale-Hubbell Law Directory

---

GREGG & GREGG, P.C. (AV)

16055 Space Center Boulevard Suite 150, 77062
Telephone: 281-480-1211
Fax: 281-480-1210
Email: dhgregg3@flash.net

Dick H. Gregg, Jr.
Dick H. Gregg, III

For full biographical listings, see the Martindale-Hubbell Law Directory

---

HILL & HILL (AV)

1415 Louisiana, Suite 4200, 77002-6502
Telephone: 713-651-1718
Telecopier: 713-651-1518

PRINCIPAL

J. Marcus Hill

OF COUNSEL

Jerry G. Hill
Winston E. Cochran, Jr.

Laurie C. Cobb

For full biographical listings, see the Martindale-Hubbell Law Directory

---

JACKSON WALKER L.L.P. (AV)

1100 Louisiana, Suite 4200, P.O. Box 4771, 77002
Telephone: 713-752-4200
Fax: 713-752-4221
URL: http://www.jw.com
Austin, Texas Office: 100 Congress Avenue, Suite 1100.
Telephone: 512-236-2000.
Fax: 512-236-2002.
Dallas, Texas Office: 901 Main Street, Suite 6000.
Telephone: 214-953-6000.
Fax: 214-953-5822.

(See Next Column)

JACKSON WALKER L.L.P.—*Continued*

Fort Worth, Texas Office: 301 Commerce Street, Suite 2400.
Telephone: 817-334-7200.
Fax: 817-334-7290.
Richardson, Texas Office: 2435 North Central Expressway, Suite 600.
Telephone: 972-671-2560.
Fax: 972-671-2566.
San Angelo, Texas Office: 225 West Beauregard Avenue.
Telephone: 915-481-2550.
Fax: 915-481-2552.
San Antonio, Texas Office: 112 E. Pecan Street, Suite 2100.
Telephone: 210-978-7700.
Fax: 210-978-7790.

MEMBERS OF FIRM

Charles L. Babcock
W. Todd Barnett
Barron P. Bogatto
Richard L. Burleson
Janet Douvas Chafin
John R. Clayton
Linda J. Cole
Wayne G. Dotson
David G. Dunlap
Randal S. Farber
Anne Marie Finch
Richard Earl Griffin
Nancy Wells Hamilton
Daniel J. Hayes
Mollie Cohn Lambert
Tracey Smith Lindeen
Charles G. Miller
Kurt D. Nondorf
Douglas A. Paisley, II
Michael P. Pearson
Lisa A. Powell
Norman T. Reynolds
Richard S. Roth
Bruce J. Ruzinsky
John B. Scofield
Lionel M. Schooler
Fred A. Simpson

OF COUNSEL

Frank L. Cascio, Jr.
Laurie B. Easter
Mary Lou Flynn-DuPart
Susan F. Koch
John H. Peper
Robert B. Reynolds (P.C.)
Randall L. Smith
Robert H. Walls
John R. Williford

SENIOR COUNSEL

Jennifer Adelle Bryant

ASSOCIATES

S. Priya Bharathi
Amy Catlett
Ryan Chadwick
Joel B. Daniels
David B. Deaton
John K. Edwards
Joel A. Goldberg
Robert W. Harlow
Nelita A. Hatch
C. Elaine Howard
Beth Anne Jackson
Frank G. Vlahakos
Matthew G. Zagrodzky
Shannon Savage
J. Kirk Taylor

For full biographical listings, see the Martindale-Hubbell Law Directory

MAYER, BROWN & PLATT (AV)

700 Louisiana Street, Suite 3600, 77002-2730
Telephone: (713) 221-1651
Facsimile: (713) 224-6410
Telex: 775809
Cable: LEMAYHOU
URL: http://www.mayerbrown.com
Chicago, Illinois Office: 190 South LaSalle Street, 60603-3441.
Telephone: (312) 782-0600.
Facsimile: (312) 701-7711.
Telex: 190404.
Cable: LEMAY.
Berlin, Germany Office: Breite Strasse 29, Muehlendamm, 10178.
Telephone: 011-49-30-2060-7710.
Facsimile: 011-49-30-2060-7744.
Charlotte, North Carolina Office: 100 North Tryon Street, Suite 2400.
Telephone: (704) 444-3500.
Fax: (704) 377-2033.
Cologne, Germany Office: Kaiser-Wilhelm-Ring 27-29, 50672.
Telephone: 011-49-221-5771-100.
Facsimile: 011-49-221-5771-199.
London, England Office: Bucklersbury House, 3 Queen Victoria Street, London, EC4N 8EL, England.
Telephone: 011-44-171-246-6200.
Facsimile: 011-44-171-329-4465.
Telex: 8811095.
Cable: LEMAYLDN.
Los Angeles, California Office: 350 South Grand Avenue, 25th Floor, 90071-1503.
Telephone: (213) 229-9500.
Facsimile: (213) 625-0248.
Telex: 188089.
Cable: LEMAYLA.
New York, New York Office: 1675 Broadway, 10019-5820.
Telephone: (212) 506-2500.
Facsimile: (212) 262-1910.
Telex: 701842.
Cable: LEMAYEN.
Washington, D.C. Office: 1909 K Street, N.W., 20006-1101.
Telephone: (202) 263-3000.
Facsimile: (202) 263-3300.
Telex: 892603.
Cable: LEMAYDC.

(See Next Column)

Representative Offices:
Ashgabat, Turkmenistan: 28 Gogol Street, 744000.
Telephone: 011-99-312-355247.
Facsimile: 011-99-312-510074.
Bishkek, Kyrgyz Republic: 66 Kalyka Akieva Str. 720010.
Telephone: 011-996-312-65-02-56.
Facsimile: 011-996-312-65-09-80.
Tashkent, Republic of Uzbekistan: 3rd Floor, 1 Turab Tula Street, 700003.
Telephone: 011-998-71-1206-627.
Facsimile: 011-998-71-1206-329.
Mexico City, Mexico, D.F., Independent Mexico Correspondent: Jáuregui, Navarrete, Nader y Rojas, S.C., Toros Arcos, Paseo de los Tamarindos No. 400-B. Col. Bosques de las Lomas, 05120.
Telephone: 011-525-267-45-00.
Facsimile: 011-525-267-45-99.
Paris, France, Independent Paris Correspondent: Lambert & Lee, 13 Avenue Hoche, 75008.
Telephone: 011-33-1-53-53-43-43.
Facsimile: 011-33-1-53-96-03-83.

PARTNERS

Kimberlee S. Cagle
Paul B. Clemenceau
Timothy B. Ellwood
Terri Truitt Griffiths
M. Marvin Katz
William H. Knull, III
Michael E. Niebruegge
Ronald M. Shoss
James E. Tancula
Terry Otero Vilardo
Neil A. Wasserstrom

COUNSEL

Linda H. Earle
Catherine W. Hoeg
Sultana Kaldis
Robert L. Morgan
Frank A. Perrone

ASSOCIATES

Francis R. Bradley, III
Patricia Ann Brito
Diana L. Davis
Deann Kay Feece
Eric P. Grossman
Gayle C. Hanz
Loan Anh Tran Kao
Charles S. Kelley
Terry D. Kernell
Mary B. Lemuth
Marjorie C. Nicol
Vytas A. Petrulis
Tristan E. Propst
Sara Ann Rodriguez
Timothy J. Tyler
Hoang Quan Vu

For full biographical listings, see the Martindale-Hubbell Law Directory

MAYOR, DAY, CALDWELL & KEETON, L.L.P. (AV)

700 Louisiana, Suite 1900, 77002
Telephone: 713-225-7000
Fax: 713-225-7047
URL: http://www.mdck.com
Austin, Texas Office: 100 Congress, Suite 1500.
Telephone: 512-320-9200.
Fax: 512-320-9292.

Jonathan S. Day
Richard H. Caldwell
Richard P. Keeton

PARTNERS

Mark B. Arnold
Debra L. Baker
Lorette Bauarschi
Mary M. Bearden
Roy E. Bertolatus
Gerald L. Bracht
J. Mark Breeding
Thomas A. Bres
Gary L. Bush
David W. Childress
John B. Clutterbuck
Robert M. Collie, Jr.
Michael O. Connelly
D. Michael Dalton
Jeff C. Dodd
Sylvia Matthews Egner
Thomas M. Farrell
Dillon J. Ferguson (Also at Austin Office)
Kathryn V. Garner
Robert S. Godlewski
David P. Griffith
Thomas A. Hagemann
Matthew L. Hoeg
Diana M. Hudson
Frederick D. Junkin
Walter S. Keneally
Kathleen M. Kopp
Gene L. Locke
David W. Martin
J. Gerald Martin
Jeffrey B. McClure
Daniel E. McCormick
L. Lee McMurtry III
Gail Merel
Gary C. Miller
Cheryl S. Phillips
Roliff H. Purrington, Jr. (Also at Austin Office)
Eddy J. Rogers, Jr.
Russell C. Shaw
Solace Kirkland Southwick
Cassie B. Stinson
Gregory M. Sullivan
W. Earl Touchstone
Rex D. VanMiddlesworth (Also at Austin Office)
T. Griffin Vincent
Geoffrey K. Walker
Gary J. Winston
Rick A. Witte
Earnest W. Wotring

OF COUNSEL

Richard B. Mayor

SENIOR COUNSEL

Gail A. Bartlett
Sherie Potts Beckman
Ronald J. Bigelow
Caren E. Blinka
Mindy G. Davidson
Christy M. Farrell
A. Colleen Hutchison
James L. Jackson
Gerald P. Lance
Richard H. Martin
John Muir
Nicholas H. Ro
Cheryl K. Rosenberg
Charles Manning Williams

(See Next Column)

MAYOR, DAY, CALDWELL & KEETON L.L.P., *Houston—Continued*

ASSOCIATES

Thurston C. Bailey
Brittny Bottorff
Eric P. Chenoweth
John D. Cleland
Todd H. Colvard
John R. Crosby
Glenn W. Cunningham
Patricia A. DeLaney
Leslie Ann Goldman
Cheryl L. Hagemann
Charles B. Hampton
David V. Harbach, II
James A. Hernandez
David W. Hodges
William J. Jackson
Meredith L. Johnson
George C. Jones
Trlica Lanette Cosby Kennedy
Donna Kim
Ann E. Kitzmiller
Stephen J. Maddex
Margo M. Madole
Brian Martin
Meredith Steinfeld Mouer
Michael C. Overman
Lizzette M. Palmer
Derek J. Pfaff (Not admitted in TX)
Tracy A. Phillips
Marla Thompson Poirot
C. Bonnie Rubey
Eric Save
Michael H. Smith
Justin Strother
Karen M. Thompson
Mark Trachtenberg
Laura Trenaman
Greg Waller
Lori Warner

For full biographical listings, see the Martindale-Hubbell Law Directory

McGINNIS, LOCHRIDGE & KILGORE, L.L.P. (AV)

3200 One Houston Center, 1221 McKinney Street, 77010-2009
Telephone: 713-615-8500
Austin, Texas Office: 1300 Capitol Center, 919 Congress Avenue.
Telephone: 512-495-6000.

OF COUNSEL

W. James McAnelly, Jr.

MEMBERS OF FIRM

Shannon H. Ratliff
Barry L. Wertz
Steven J. Watkins
Jeffrey A. Davis
Thomas J. Forestier
Karan C. Ciotti

ASSOCIATES

Andrew Ramzel
Donald D. Jackson
Kelly Conklin
Joe M. Roden
Cari L. Curtis
Samir J. Foteh
Kenneth C. Moursund, Jr.
Ellen Beth Huchital

For full biographical listings, see the Martindale-Hubbell Law Directory

ROYSTON, RAYZOR, VICKERY & WILLIAMS, L.L.P. (AV)

600 Travis Street, Suite 2200, 77002-2913
Telephone: 713-224-8380
Cable Address: "Houport"
Telex: 6869017
Telecopier: 713-225-9945
Email: royston@roystonlaw.com *URL:* http://www.roystonlaw.com
Brownsville, Texas Office: 55 Cove Circle, P.O. Box 3509.
Telephone: 956-542-4377.
Cable Address: "Padre"
Telex: 767-817.
Telecopier: 956-542-4370.
Corpus Christi, Texas Office: 1700 Wilson Plaza West, 606 North Carancahua.
Telephone: 361-884-8808.
Cable Address: "CC PORT"
Telex: 6866625.
Telecopier: 361-884-7261.
Galveston, Texas Office: 205 Cotton Exchange Building, 2102 Mechanic Street.
Telephone: 409-763-1623.
Cable Address: "Houport"
Telex: 6869017.
Telecopier: 409-763-3853.
Lubbock, Texas Office: 1401 Avenue G.
Telephone: 806-763-9252.
Telex: 6869017.
Telecopier: 806-763-9254.
San Antonio, Texas Office: 2000 Riverview Towers, 111 Soledad Street.
Telephone: 210-228-0655.
Telecopier: 210-228-0839.

PARTNERS

Kenneth D. Kuykendall
Ted C. Litton
Robert S. DeLange
William M. Jensen
W. Robins Brice
James Patrick Cooney
Bradley A. Jackson
Robert H. Etnyre, Jr.
James G. Blain, II
John M. Elsley
David R. Walker
John F. Unger
Mark Cohen
William R. Towns
Marilyn Tanner Hebinck
C. Scott Kinzel
Marcus R. Tucker
Chester J. Makowski
Richard L. Gorman
Jennifer S. Sickler
William P. Glenn, Jr.
Jeffrey J. Putnam
Nathan Wesely

(See Next Column)

OF COUNSEL

Edward D. Vickery
Gus A. Schill, Jr.
Ben L. Reynolds
Decatur J. Holcombe
Richard L. Lionberger

ASSOCIATES

Scott R. Breitenwischer
Michael L. Coblenz
Stephen K. Hubchen
I. Ray Kerlick
Christopher B. Ramey
Ruth Silvers
Joseph Denney Terry
Mary A. Wolter

Representative Clients: West of England Steam Ship Owners' Protection & Indemnity Assn., Ltd.; The United Kingdom Mutual Steam Ship Assurance Assn. Ltd.

For full biographical listings, see the Martindale-Hubbell Law Directory

SQUIRE, SANDERS & DEMPSEY L.L.P. (AV)

6250 Chase Tower, 600 Travis Street, 77002-3007
Telephone: 713-546-5850
Fax: 713-546-5830
URL: http://www.ssd.com
Cincinnati, Ohio Office: PNC Center, 201 East Fifth Street, Suite 1700, Cincinnati, Ohio 45202.
Telephone: 513-361-1200.
Fax: 513-361-1201.
Cleveland, Ohio Office: 4900 Key Tower, 127 Public Square, Cleveland, Ohio 44114-1304.
Telephone: 216-479-8500.
Fax: 216-479-8780.
Columbus, Ohio Office: 1300 Huntington Center, 41 South High Street, Columbus, Ohio 43215-6150.
Telephone: 614-365-2700.
Fax: 614-365-2499.
Houston, Texas Office: 6250 Chase Tower, 600 Travis Street, Houston, Texas 77002-3007.
Telephone: 713-546-5850.
Fax: 713-546-5830.
Jacksonville, Florida Office: One Enterprise Center, Suite 2100, 225 Water Street, Jacksonville, Florida 32202-4424.
Telephone: 904-366-2420.
Fax: 904-356-2986.
Miami, Florida Office: 201 South Biscayne Boulevard, 2900 Miami Center, Miami, Florida 33131-4330.
Telephone: 305-577-8700.
Fax: 305-358-1425.
New York, New York Office: 350 Park Avenue, New York, New York 10022-6002.
Telephone: 212-872-9800.
Fax: 212-872-9815.
Phoenix, Arizona Office: Two Renaissance Square, 40 North Central Avenue, Suite 2700, Phoenix, Arizona 85004-4498.
Telephone: 602-528-4000.
Fax: 602-253-8129.
Washington, D.C. Office: 1201 Pennsylvania Avenue, N.W., Suite 500, Washington, D.C. 20004-2491.
Telephone: 202-626-6600.
Fax: 202-626-6780.
Almaty, Kazakhstan Office: 141 Albay Khan Avenue, Second Floor, Almaty, Kazakhstan 480091.
Telephone: +73-27-50-11-25.
Fax: +73-27-50-11-25.
Bratislava, Slovak Republic Office: Zochova 5, 811 03 Bratislava, Slovak Republic.
Telephone: 421-7-5441-7611.
Fax: 42-1-7-6280-2212.
Brussels, Belgium Office: Avenue Louise, 165 Box 15, 1050 Brussels, Belgium.
Telephone: 32-2-627-1111.
Fax: 32-2-627-1100.
Budapest, Hungary Office: H-1062 Budapest, Andrassy ut. 64, Budapest, Hungary.
Telephone: 36-1-428-7111.
Fax: 36-1-428-7100.
Kyiv, Ukraine Office: 14A Yaroslaviv Val, Kyiv 252034, Ukraine.
Telephone: 38-044-228-8687.
Fax: 38-044-228-4938.
London, England Office: Royex House, Aldermanbury Square, London EC2V 7HR.
Telephone: 44-171-776-5200.
Fax: 44-171-776-5233.
Madrid, Spain Office: Calle Velazquez 108-110, 28006 Madrid, Spain.
Telephone: 34-91-590-2420.
Fax: 34-91-590-2421.
Moscow, Russian Federation Office: Paveletskaya Square II, 1 Valovaya Street, 5th Floor, Moscow 113054, Russian Federation.
Telephone: 7-501-258-5250.
Fax: 7-501-258-5251.
Prague, Czech Republic Office: Václavské náměst 1 57/813, 110 00 Praha 1, Czech Republic.
Telephone: 420-2-2166-2111.
Fax: 420-2-2166-2222.

(See Next Column)

SQUIRE, SANDERS & DEMPSEY L.L.P.—*Continued*

Hong Kong Office: Rooms 1101-2 St. George's Building, 2 Ice House Street, Central, Hong Kong.
Telephone: 852-2509-9732.
Fax: 852-2509-9772.
Taipei, Taiwan Office: 14F, 116 Nanking East Road, Sec. 2, Taipei, Taiwan, Republic of China.
Telephone: 886-2-2531-2888.
Fax: 886-2-2571-6199.

PARTNERS

James F. Allen
Richard C. Alsup

OF COUNSEL

Alan E. Riedel

ASSOCIATES

Farley S. Burge
Marsha L. Montgomery

For full biographical listings, see the Martindale-Hubbell Law Directory

STRASBURGER & PRICE, L.L.P. (AV)

A Partnership including Professional Corporations
Suite 2800, One Houston Center, 1221 McKinney, 77010
Telephone: 713-951-5600
Fax: 713-951-5660
URL: http://www.strasburger.com
Dallas, Texas Office: 901 Main Street, Suite 4300.
Telephone: 214-651-4300.
Fax: 214-651-4330.
Austin, Texas Office: 600 Congress Avenue, Suite 2600.
Telephone: 512-499-3600.
Fax: 512-499-3660.
San Antonio, Texas Office: Bank of America Plaza, 300 Convent Street, Suite 900.
Telephone: 210-250-6000.
Fax: 210-250-6100.
Mexico City Office: Montes Urales 632, Piso 3, Lomas de Chapultepec, 11000 Mexico D.F.
Telephone: 525-202-7665.
Fax: 525-202-2367.

RESIDENT MEMBERS OF FIRM

Paula Denney
J. Greg Dow
J. Wiley George
Layne A. Thompson
William A. Worthington

OF COUNSEL

Maryam Bani-Jamali
Jeffery J. Brashier
Barbara J. LeBarron
Gail A. Schubot
Jennings B. Thompson

RESIDENT ASSOCIATES

Karen Balter Alaniz
Debra W. Biehle
Alan B. Daughtry
Cliff Husted
Jack W. Perry
Craig P. Romero
Bryan J. Schillinger
John K. Spiller
John W. Teague
C. Patrick Waites

Representative Clients: Chrysler Corp.; General Motors Corp.; GTE; K mart Corp.; Syndicates of Lloyd's of London; NationsBank of Texas, N.A.; Rolex Watch U.S.A.; The Travelers Insurance Co.

For full biographical listings, see the Martindale-Hubbell Law Directory

THOMPSON KNIGHT BROWN PARKER & LEAHY L.L.P. (AV)

A Registered Limited Liability Partnership including Professional Corporations
(Attorneys and Counselors)
1200 Smith Street, Suite 3600, 77002-4595
Telephone: 713-654-8111
Telecopier: 713-654-1871
URL: http://www.tklaw.com
Dallas, Texas Office: Thompson & Knight L.L.P., 1700 Pacific Avenue, Suite 3300, 75201.
Telephone: 214-969-1700.
Telecopy: 214-969-1751.
Telex: 732298.
Austin, Texas Office: Thompson & Knight L.L.P., 1200 San Jacinto Center, 98 San Jacinto Boulevard, 78701.
Telephone: 512-469-6100.
Telecopy: 512-469-6180.
Fort Worth, Texas Office: Thompson & Knight L.L.P., 801 Cherry Street, Suite 1600, 76102.
Telephone: 817-347-1700.
Telecopy: 817-347-1799.
San Pedro Garza Garcia, Nuevo León, Mexico Office: Thompson & Knight L.L.P., Edificio Losoles PD-4, Av. Lázaro Cárdenas No. 2400 PTE., C.P. 66220.
Telephone: (52-8) 363-0096.
Telecopy: (52-8) 363-3067.

(See Next Column)

PARTNERS

J. Brent Baker
J. Michael Bell
Stephen M. Block
Timothy R. Brown (P.C.)
Roxella T. Cavazos
Grant Cook (P.C.)
Barry Davis
Louis J. Davis
E.F. Mano DeAyala
Andrew P. Flint
Robert L. Galloway
Regina Giovannini
Grover S. Grimes, Jr.
Marc E. Grossberg
Nancy Wilson Hargrove
William T. Heller, IV
Boris A. Hidalgo
Debbi M. Johnstone
Suzanne H. Kerr
James R. Leahy
Robert S. MacIntyre, Jr.
Gregory S. Meece
Jerry L. Metcalf
Alfred M. Meyerson
David R. Noteware
John S. Orton
Dallas Parker
Michael K. Pierce
Robert L. Pittsford
David M. Robins (P.C.)
Timothy T. Samson
Robert C. Shearer
Jon L. Tankersley
Christopher D. Thompson
Diane C. Treich
Robert C. Walker
Diana M. Woodman

SENIOR ATTORNEY

Glen F. White

ASSOCIATES

James S. Bavouset, IV
Charles J. Cain
Dax O. Faubus
Mary-Olga Ferguson
Christopher P. Hanslik
Christopher R. Hernandez
John D. Holmes, Jr.
Mark B. Hughes
Kellye R. Koehn
Jai-Prakash (J.P.) Philip Kumar
Thomas R. Lamme
W. Cameron McCulloch
Sarah E. McLean
John S. Moody, Jr.
Christopher P. Nease
Robert Paddock
Kevin J. Parks
Peter M. Roossien
Susan A. Stanton
Tony R. Taft
Jill A. Willard
Virginia Durham Young

OF COUNSEL

James B. Barnes
Gus Block
Harry R. Jones, Jr.

For full biographical listings, see the Martindale-Hubbell Law Directory

VINSON & ELKINS L.L.P. (AV)

2300 First City Tower, 1001 Fannin, 77002-6760
Telephone: 713-758-2222
Fax: 713-758-2346
Email: info@velaw.com *URL:* http://www.velaw.com
Austin, Texas Office: One American Center Suite 2700, 600 Congress Avenue, Austin, Texas, 78701-3200.
Telephone: 512-495-8400.
Fax: 512-495-8612.
Beijing, China Office: 20/F, Beijing Silver Tower, No. 2, Dong San Huan Bei Lu, Chaoyang District, 100027.
Telephone: +86-10-6410-6300.
Fax: +86-10-6410-6360.
Dallas, Texas Office: 3700 Trammell Crow Center, 2001 Ross Avenue, Dallas, Texas, 75201-2975.
Telephone: 214-220-7700.
Fax: 214-220-7716.
London, England Office: Regis House, 8th Floor, 45 King William Street, London, EC4R 9AN, England.
Telephone: (44-171) 618-6000.
Fax: (44-171) 618-6001.
Moscow, Russia Office: 16 Ulitsa Spiridonovka, Second Floor, 103001 Moscow, Russia.
Telephone: (7-095) 956-1995. Local
Fax: (7-095) 956-1996. U.S. Satellite
Fax: (212) 803-0142.
New York, N.Y. Office: 1325 Avenue of the Americas, 17th Floor, New York, N.Y., 10019.
Telephone: 917-206-8000.
Fax: 917-206-8100.
Singapore Office: 6 Battery Road, #39-01, Singapore, 049909.
Telephone: (65) 536-8300.
Fax: (65) 536-8311.
Washington, D.C. Office: The Willard Office Building, 1455 Pennsylvania Avenue, N.W., Washington, D.C., 20004-1008.
Telephone: 202-639-6500.
Fax: 202-639-6604.

MEMBERS OF FIRM

Wm. A. Vinson (1874-1951)
James A. Elkins (1879-1972)
Wharton E. Weems (1890-1961)
David T. Searls (1905-1972)
Harry M. Reasoner (Managing Partner)
William H. Drushel, Jr. (Administrative Partner)

MEMBERS OF FIRM

Joe B. Allen
Charles L. Almond
Christopher B. Amandes
Gary P. Amaon
Kenneth M. Anderson
Michael A. Andrews (Resident, Washington, D.C. Office)
David T. Andril (Resident, Washington, D.C. Office)
Ronald T. Astin
Alden L. Atkins (Resident, Washington, D.C. Office)
Scott J. Atlas
Marcia E. Backus

(See Next Column)

VINSON & ELKINS L.L.P., *Houston—Continued*

MEMBERS OF FIRM (Continued)

Alan P. Baden (Resident, New York, N.Y. Office)
Robert S. Baird (Resident, Austin, Texas Office)
Shelley A. Barber
Larry G. Barbour
John H. Barquin (Not admitted in TX)
Robert F. Barrett
Dennis M. Barry (Resident, Washington, D.C. Office)
Walker W. Beavers
Roger L. Beebe
Charles L. Berry
Bruce R. Bilger
Douglas S. Bland
David P. Blanke (Resident, Dallas, Texas Office)
Judith M. Blissard
Brian R. Bloom
James W. Boeckman (Resident, Austin, Texas Office)
David M. Bond
James A. Boone
Steven R. Borgman
Michael R. Boulden (Resident, Dallas, Texas Office)
John C. Brannan, Jr. (Resident, Dallas, Texas Office)
James Mark Brazzil (Resident, Beijing, China Office)
Patrick K. Breeland (Resident, Austin, Texas Office)
Kim Edward Brightwell (Resident, Austin, Texas Office)
Ben A. Brooks, III (Resident, Dallas, Texas Office)
David H. Brown
Miriam M. (Dusty) Burke (Resident, Austin, Texas Office)
C. Michael Buxton (Resident, Washington, D.C. Office)
Christopher W. Byrd
Molly Cagle (Resident, Austin, Texas Office)
Charles F. Caldwell
Bert L. Campbell
Boyd G. Carano (Resident, New York, N.Y. Office)
Edward A. Carr
John L. Carter
Jeffrey A. Chapman (Resident, Dallas, Texas Office)
John E. Chapoton (Resident, Washington, D.C. Office)
Michael R. Charness (Resident, Washington, D.C. Office)
William H. Church, Jr. (Resident, Dallas, Texas Office)
Christopher Clement-Davies (Resident, London, England Office)
Fielding B. Cochran, III
David B. Cohen (Resident, Washington, D.C. Office)
F.J. Hank Coleman
Susan G. Conway (Resident, Austin, Texas Office)
Morgan Lee Copeland, Jr.
Thomas Crichton, IV (Resident, Dallas, Texas Office)
James L. Cuclis
Samuel Poage Dalton (Resident, Dallas, Texas Office)
Thad T. Dameris
Josiah M. Daniel III (Resident, Dallas, Texas Office)
Platt W. Davis, III
Stephen D. Davis (Resident, Singapore Office)
John C. Dawson, Jr.
William B. Dawson (Resident, Dallas, Texas Office)
Paul C. Deemer (Resident, London, England Office)
Elena-Faye DiIorio
Joseph C. Dilg
Carol E. Dinkins
Sarah A. Duckers
Dennis C. Dunn
George Harvey Dunn, III (Resident, Dallas, Texas Office)
Phillip B. Dye, Jr.
Billy Coe Dyer
Mark Early (Resident, Dallas, Texas Office)
Rod T. Edens, Jr. (Resident, Austin, Texas Office)
Gary W. Eiland
Jeffrey E. Eldredge (Resident, London, England Office)
Jon David (J.D.) Epstein
Ky P. Ewing, Jr. (Resident, Washington, D.C. Office)
Harrell Feldt
Kenneth B. Fenelon
Michael P. Finch
Felicia A. Finston (Resident, Dallas, Texas Office)
N. Scott Fletcher
Jeffery Burton Floyd
Timothy F. Foarde (Resident, New York, N.Y. Office)
Lawrence J. Fossi
Robin S. Fredrickson
Keith R. Fullenweider
Kathleen A. Gallagher
Kevin A. Gaynor (Resident, Washington, D.C. Office)
George M. Gerachis
Steven H. Gerdes
Edward P. Gilbert (Resident, Singapore Office)
Douglas B. Glass (Resident, London, England Office)
Celso M. Gonzalez-Falla
R. Todd Greenwalt
Douglas E. Hamel
C. Michael Harrington
Orrin L. Harrison, III (Resident, Dallas, Texas Office)
David T. Harvin
Robert K. Hatcher
Paul E. Heath (Resident, Dallas, Texas Office)
Jay H. Hebert (Resident, Dallas, Texas Office)
David T. Hedges, Jr.
Max Hendrick, III
Michael J. Henke (Resident, Washington, D.C. Office)
Bruce C. Herzog
Karen L. Hirschman (Resident, Dallas, Texas Office)
Ted A. Hodges
Patricia Hunt Holmes
John B. Holstead
George C. Hopkins (Resident, Washington, D.C. Office)
Donald L. Howell
Monty Humble (Resident, Dallas, Texas Office)
Lynne B. Humphries
E. Ray Hutchison (Resident, Dallas, Texas Office)
Daniel A. Hyde
Neil W. Imus (Resident, Washington, D.C. Office)
Karen Jewell
Carol H. Jewett
David R. Johnson (Resident, Washington, D.C. Office)
Judith M. Johnson
Stuart Brooks Johnston, Jr. (Resident, Dallas, Texas Office)
William E. Joor III
W. Carl Jordan
Randy R. Jurgensmeyer (Resident, Dallas, Texas Office)
Theodore W. Kassinger (Resident, Washington, D.C. Office)
T. Mark Kelly
John E. Kennedy

MEMBERS OF FIRM (Continued)

(See Next Column)

David R. Keyes
Robert L. Kimball (Resident, Dallas, Texas Office)
Christopher A. Knepp (Resident, Austin, Texas Office)
Yolanda Chávez Knull
Gary M. Kotara (Resident, Washington, D.C. Office)
Erica L. Krennerich
George M. Kryder III (Resident, Dallas, Texas Office)
William L. LaFuze
Kathleen C. Lake
John C. LaMaster (Resident, London, England Office)
Thomas S. Leatherbury (Resident, Dallas, Texas Office)
Handel C.H. Lee (Resident, Beijing, China Office)
William Gentry Lee
John W. Leggett
Cathy A. Lewis (Resident, Washington, D.C. Office)
Kevin P. Lewis
Guy S. Lipe
Kathleen C. Little (Resident, Washington, D.C. Office)
John E. Lynch
A. Sam MacGibbon (Resident, London, England Office)
Michael L. Malone (Resident, Dallas, Texas Office)
L. Price Manford
Thomas P. Marinis, Jr.
Dale Gene Markland (Resident, Dallas, Texas Office)
Richard D. Marks (Resident, Washington, D.C. Office)
J. Clark Martin
Sharon M. Mattox
Henry S. May, Jr.
Robert A. Mazer (Resident, Washington, D.C. Office)
Louis E. McCarter
Andrew McCollam III
Frank E. McCreary, III
Thomas V. McMahan
D. Ferguson McNiel, III
Clara L. Meek
Michael W. Mengis
James S. Meyer (Resident, Dallas, Texas Office)
Garry M. Miles (Resident, Dallas, Texas Office)
Richard D. Milvenan (Resident, Austin, Texas Office)
Peter E. Mims
Elizabeth Anne Moler (Resident, Washington, D.C. Office)
H. Dixon Montague
Rodney L. Moore (Resident, Dallas, Texas Office)
John L. Murchison, Jr.
Craig W. Murray
Larry W. Nettles
Charles T. Newton, Jr.
Neal A. Nichols (Resident, Austin, Texas Office)
Penelope E. Nicholson
D. Bobbitt Noel, Jr.
Knox D. Nunnally
Larry A. Oday (Resident, Washington, D.C. Office)
Harold A. Odom III
W. Glenn Opel (Resident, Dallas, Texas Office)
Edward C. Osterberg, Jr.
Betty R. Owens
A. Winston Oxley (Resident, Dallas, Texas Office)
Richard H. Page
Glenn L. Pinkerton
Benjamin H. Powell, III
Robert René Rabalais
Barbara A. Radnofsky
Robert R. Randolph
James Arthur Reeder, Jr.
Beverly G. Reeves (Resident, Austin, Texas Office)
Russell L. Reid, Jr. (Resident, Dallas, Texas Office)
R. Glen Rigby
Elizabeth P. Rippy (Resident, Austin, Texas Office)
Alan J. Robin
W. Ronald Robins
George G. Rodriguez (Resident, Dallas, Texas Office)
Glen A. Rosenbaum
Joel L. Ross (Resident, Dallas, Texas Office)
James B. Rylander, Jr.
Robert M. Schick
Adam P. Schiffer
Michael J. Schimberg (Resident, Dallas, Texas Office)
Willem G. Schuurman (Resident, Austin, Texas Office)
Charles W. Schwartz
Russell B. Serafin
James I. Serota (Resident. New York, N.Y. Office)
Ben H. Sheppard, Jr.
Gary G. Short (Resident, Dallas, Texas Office)
August E. Shouse
Eric S. Shube (Resident, New York, N.Y. Office)
Eugene J. Silva
William D. Sims, Jr. (Resident, Dallas, Texas Office)
Shadow Sloan
Alison L. Smith
Frank F. Smith, Jr.
L. Boyd Smith, Jr.
John H. Smither
J. Brian Sokolik
Mark R. Spivak (Resident, Washington, D.C. Office)
Mark R. Spradling
Paul E. Stallings
Scott Statham
Karl S. Stern
Daniel C. Stewart (Resident, Dallas, Texas Office)
Edward T. Stockbridge
Brenda T. Strama
Mary Lou Strange
Walter B. Stuart IV
Albert S. Tabor, Jr.
Stephen C. Tarry
John D. Taurman (Resident, Washington, D. C. Office)
Charles D. Tetrault (Resident, Washington, D.C. Office)
James D. Thompson III
Patrick Ford Thompson (Resident, Austin, Texas Office)
Michael D. Thomson (Resident, Washington, D.C. Office)
James "Rell" Tipton, Jr.
Michael J. Tomsu (Resident, Austin, Texas Office)
David J. Tuckfield (Resident, Austin, Texas Office)
Mark H. Tuohey, III (Resident, Washington, D.C. Office)
Lisa Lepow Turboff
Jerry E. Turner (Resident, Austin, Texas Office)
Allan Van Fleet
Christine L. Vaughn (Resident, Washington, D.C. Office)
Eric Viehman
William R. Volk (Resident, Austin, Texas Office)
William L. Wallander (Resident, Dallas, Texas Office)
Robert C. Walters (Resident, Dallas, Texas Office)
D. Gibson Walton
Joe Bill Watkins (Resident, Austin, Texas Office)
Jim A. Watson (Resident, Dallas, Texas Office)
John S. Watson
William H. Weiland
Sanford A. Weiner
Philip D. Weller (Resident, New York, N.Y. Office)
Paul S. Wells
H. Ronald Welsh

MEMBERS OF FIRM (Continued)

(See Next Column)

VINSON & ELKINS L.L.P.—*Continued*

Adam Wenner (Resident, Washington, D.C. Office)
Robert H. Whilden, Jr.
Karen Tucker White
Anita Rutkowski Wilson (Resident, Washington, D.C. Office)
James H. Wilson
Thomas H. Wilson
Donald F. Wood (Resident, Austin, Texas Office)
Michael D. Wortley (Resident, Dallas, Texas Office)
Scott N. Wulfe
Russell Yager (Resident, Dallas, Texas Office)
Terry A. Yates
Paul L. Yde (Resident, Washington, D.C. Office)
Marie R. Yeates
William D. Young (Resident, Dallas, Texas Office)

HOUSTON OF COUNSEL

Timothy Austin
W. Scott Brown
R. Michael Bryant, Jr.
Donna Schmerin Clark
Karey Dubiel Dye
Susan M. Edwards
Hollis A. Hubenak
Robert L. Ivey
Stanley M. Johanson
Philip M. Kinkaid
John H. Kyles
Jeanne H. McDonald
Vincent S. Moreland
Catherine O'Harra
Larry J. Pechacek
James D. Penny
James David Pittman
Pamela Hays Stabler
John E. West
Julie P. Woody

AUSTIN OF COUNSEL

O. Wade Anderson
Barry D. Burgdorf
John D. Christian
Karen J. Holody
Spikes Kangerga
Gail Weatherby

DALLAS OF COUNSEL

Mark A. Cover
Sheryl L. Hopkins
Ellis Glenn Koury
Carla N. Lindley
James S. Matthews
Geoffrey R. Polma
J. Stuart Tonkinson

WASHINGTON, D.C. OF COUNSEL

Becky M. Bruner
Christopher P. B. Erckert
Tegan M. Flynn
Mark S. Laufman
William E. Lawler, III
Albert D. Shuldiner
Gregory C. Staple (Resident, Washington, D.C. Office)
Samuel B. Sterrett

NEW YORK OF COUNSEL

Michael M. Zaitz

BEIJING OF COUNSEL

Ding Jianxiang
Yong Xiao

ASSOCIATES

Anissa A. Allbritton (Resident, Austin, Texas Office)
Demetrios Anaipakos
Christopher V. Bacon
Joël Elaine Baird
Tebbie M. Barnhill
C. Dennis Barrow, Jr.
Ozgur K. Bayazitoglu
Dennis Alan Beck, Jr.
Melissa L. Beckworth
Walter Moreau Berger
Keefe M. Bernstein (Resident, Dallas, Texas Office)
Rasmani Bhattacharya
J. David Bickham, Jr. (Resident, Austin, Texas Office)
W. Bradley Bickham (Resident, Dallas, Texas Office)
Tobey D. Blanton
Bruce A. Blefeld
Lorin E. Bley (Resident, Austin, Texas Office)
Jason S. Boulette (Resident, Austin, Texas Office)
Ronald F. Bradshaw (Resident, Austin, Texas Office)
Scott W. Breedlove (Resident, Dallas, Texas Office)
Michael Curtis Brisch
Virginia Navarrete Brooks (Resident, Washington, D.C. Office)
Barry Bumgardner (Resident, Dallas, Texas Office)
Cynthia H. Burnett
Kacy S. Burnsed (Not admitted in TX)
Brian K. Buss (Resident, Austin, Texas Office)
María Luisa Cánovas (Resident, New York, N.Y. Office)
Herman Mallory Caldwell
Jeffrey M. Cameron
Charles H. Campbell, Jr. (Resident, Austin, Texas Office)
Anthony P. Canale (Resident, Dallas, Texas Office)
Ramon M. Cantu
Christopher K. Carr (Resident, Washington, D.C. Office)
Jon Carroll (Resident, Dallas, Texas Office)
Derek Chan
Trina Hill Chandler
Vanessa Y. Chandler (Resident, Washington, D.C. Office)
Merritt B. Chastain III
Luming Chen (Resident, Beijing, China Office)
David T. Cindric
Vanessa M. Clem
Stephen S. Coats
William J. Cobb III (Resident, Austin, Texas Office)
Dorene B. Cohen
Scott L. Cole (Resident, Dallas, Texas Office)
Robert R. Collins, III (Resident, Dallas, Texas Office)
Alexey L. Condratchick (Resident, Moscow, Russia Office)
Alexis R. Connally (Resident, Dallas, Texas Office)
John B. Connally, IV
S. Matthew Cook
Jeffery M. Cooper
Sharon M. Cooper (Resident, Dallas, Texas Office)
Stephanie Crain
Anissa J. Crumley
Alice M. Cuprill-Comas (Resident, Austin, Texas Office)

(See Next Column)

ASSOCIATES (Continued)

Alicia L. Curry (Not admitted in TX)
David C. D'Alessandro (Resident, Dallas, Texas Office)
Walter E. Daniel, IV
Tracey B. Davies (Resident, Austin, Texas Office)
Christopher M. Dawe (Resident, Washington, D.C. Office)
Oscar L. De la Rosa
John S. Decker (Resident, Washington, D.C. Office)
John P. DeGeeter
Timothy J. Devetski
Toni N. Dinh (Resident, Dallas, Texas Office)
Andrew DiNovo (Resident, Austin, Texas Office)
Timothy J. Dodd (Resident, New York, N.Y. Office)
Elizabeth L. Dodge
Stacey H. Dore (Resident, Dallas, Texas Office)
Katy Anne Drechsel
Robert J. Dubbelde (Resident, Austin, Texas Office)
Debra J. Duncan (Resident, Washington, D.C. Office)
Kelly J. Dwyer (Resident, Austin, Texas Office)
James P. Dyer (Resident, Austin, Texas Office)
John F. Easton
Matthew D. Eisele
Noni L. Ellison
Barry E. Engel
Joel N. Ephross
Benjamin Erulkar (Resident, Washington, D.C. Office)
Gregory Nolan Etzel
Colleen Faddick
Artem V. Faekov (Resident, London, England Office)
James R. Farnsworth (Resident, Washington, D.C. Office)
John M. Faust (Resident, Washington, D.C. Office)
Judith M. Feldt (Resident, Washington, D.C. Office)
Charles Timothy Fenn
Robert S. Field (Resident, Washington, D.C. Office)
Eric T. Finkel
Martha Ratnoff Fleisher (Resident, Dallas, Texas Office)
Adam V. Floyd (Resident, Austin, Texas Office)
Stuart J. Ford
Kyle K. Fox (Resident, Austin, Texas Office)
Shelby Scott Gaille
Alejandro E. "Alex" Garcia
Yvette Vanessa Gatling
Clayton R. Gollnick
Jennifer K. Gray
Murray A. Greene
Don C. Griffin, Jr.
Carolyn R. Guest
Heather Haase (Resident, Dallas, Texas Office)
Christopher H. Hahn (Resident, Austin, Texas Office)
Marc C. Hammerson (Resident, London, England Office)
Wallis M. Hampton
Daren S. Harrell (Resident, Dallas, Texas Office)
Dean W. Harvey (Resident, Austin, Texas Office)
Christine A. Hathaway (Resident, Dallas, Texas Office)
Lynn G. Haufrect
Kathryn L. Hays
Lisa R. Helgoe
Karl K. Hennessee
Delwin E. Hervey (Resident, Dallas, Texas Office)
Paul Gregory Hidalgo (Resident, Dallas, Texas Office)
Alan R. Hinaman
Wendy Ho
Michael C. Holmes
Tracy L. Howard
Cheryl Rylander Huffman (Resident, New York, N.Y. Office)
Robbi B. Hull (Resident, Austin, Texas Office)
Stacy Kleiner Humphries
Joseph E. Hunsader (Resident, Washington, D.C. Office)
Katrina Kaye Jackiewicz (Not admitted in United States) (Resident, New York, N.Y. Office)
Jack L. Johnson (Resident, New York, N.Y. Office)
Jeffrey S. Johnston
Shanna D. Jones (Resident, Austin, Texas Office)
Christopher G. Jordan (Resident, Dallas, Texas Office)
Katherine D. Jordan (Resident, Austin, Texas Office)
Christopher C. Juban
Sunil Kalara
Lauren J. Kares (Not admitted in TX)
Lisa J. Kaufman
Ingelisa Haskins Keeling
Mathew C. Kidwell (Resident, London, England Office)
J. Christopher Kirk (Resident, Dallas, Texas Office)
Mark Reid Klupt (Resident, Washington, D.C. Office)
Adam Miles Kramer
James Fitzmorris Kull (Resident, Dallas, Texas Office)
Joel C. Lambert
Douglas J. Lanzo (Resident, Washington, D.C. Office)
Keith W. Lapeze
Matthew L. Larsen (Resident, Dallas, Texas Office)
Camm C. "Trey" Lary, III
Dean H. Lefler
Nancy C. LeGros
Jared I. Levinthal
Greta L.H. Lichtenbaum (Resident, Washington, D.C. Office)
Benjamin S. Lippard (Resident, Washington, D.C. Office)
Barbara Popper Lipshultz
Robert B. Little (Resident, Dallas, Texas Office)
Samuel D. Loughlin (Resident, Austin, Texas Office)
Melissa E. Loyd
Jeffrey Scott Mũnoz
Margaret Maggio (Resident, Beijing, China Office)
Mary Michelle Mahony
Jeffery K. Malonson
Gerald D. Malpass, Jr.
Michael Dennis Marin (Resident, Austin, Texas Office)
Paul A. Martin (Resident, Dallas, Texas Office)
B. Scott McBride
Bruce C. McCulloch (Resident, Washington, D.C. Office)
Charles B. McFarland
Doug E. McWilliams
Christopher H. Meakin
Leah E. Medway (Resident, Washington, D.C. Office)
C. Martin Meekins
J. Carter Meyer (Resident, Dallas, Texas Office)
Steven L. Miller, Jr. (Resident, Dallas, Texas Office)
John E. Mitchell (Resident, Dallas, Texas Office)
Stephen J. Moloney (Resident, Austin, Texas Office)
William Hemingway Montjoy, II (Resident, New York, N.Y. Office)

(See Next Column)

VINSON & ELKINS L.L.P., *Houston—Continued*

ASSOCIATES (Continued)

Dennis W. Moore, Jr. (Resident, Austin, Texas Office)
Natalya V. Morozova (Resident, Moscow, Russia Office)
Brian M. Moss
Jarod T. Moss (Resident, Dallas, Texas Office)
Alexander Msimang (Resident, London, England Office)
Richard L. Muller, Jr.
Jeffrey A. Mullins (Resident, Austin, Texas Office)
George Robertson Murphy, III
Timothy M. Murphy (Resident, Washington, D.C. Office)
William J. Murphy
Clifford F. Murray (Resident, Dallas, Texas Office)
Todd A. Murray (Resident, Dallas, Texas Office)
D. John Neese, Jr.
Renn G. Neilson (Resident, Dallas, Texas Office)
Minh-Hien Nguyen (Resident, Austin, Texas Office)
Philip A. Nickles (Resident, Washington, D.C. Office)
Kevin Michael O'Gorman
Jill Oberdas (Resident, Dallas, Texas Office)
Matthew S. Okin
Eric M. Ostermayer (Resident, Dallas, Texas Office)
Walter R. Owens, Jr. (Resident, Dallas, Texas Office)
Greer Humphreys Pagan
Paige C. Patton
Carol Collins Payne (Resident, Dallas, Texas Office)
Carlos R. Peña (Resident, Austin, Texas Office)
Bryan J. Pechersky (Resident, New York, N.Y. Office)
David S. Peck (Resident, Dallas, Texas Office)
Serena L. Pelosof
Daniel A. Petalas (Resident, Washington, D.C. Office)
Laura Brodbeck Phillips (Resident, Washington, D.C. Office)
John F. Pierce (Resident, Singapore Office)
Alexander M. Popov (Not admitted in TX; Resident, Moscow, Russia Office)
Jennifer Barrett Poppe (Resident, Austin, Texas Office)
Gregory Lawrence Porter (Resident, Austin, Texas Office)
Jason M. Powers
Ann Abrams Price (Resident, Austin, Texas Office)
R. Edward Price (Resident, Washington, D.C. Office)
Christopher J. Prior (Resident, London, England Office)
S. Douglas Pritchett, Jr.
Lydia T. Protopapas (Resident, Dallas, Texas Office)
Cary D. Pugh (Resident, Washington, D.C. Office)
Jessica L. Quinn (Resident, Austin, Texas Office)
Michael L. Raiff (Resident, Dallas, Texas Office)
Jeffrey L. Raizner
Carrie M. Ramirez (Resident, Dallas, Texas Office)
Tonya Moffat Ramsey (Resident, Dallas, Texas Office)
Clifton S. Rankin
Suzanne D. Reifman (Resident, Washington, D.C. Office)
Patricia F. Reilly (Resident, Dallas, Texas Office)
Tara H. Reynolds (Resident, Dallas, Texas Office)
Donald P. Roark
Sean Alan Roberts
Stephen M. Robinson
Brian E. Robison (Resident, Dallas, Texas Office)
Mark C. Rodriguez
Sandra Garza Rodriguez
Elizabeth N. Rogers (Resident, Austin, Texas Office)
Judith M. Rosenberg (Resident, Washington, D.C. Office)
Robert J. Rothwell (Resident, Washington, D.C. Office)
Christopher R. Rowley (Resident, Dallas, Texas Office)
Michael H. Ryan (Resident, Dallas, Texas Office)
Gwen J. Samora
Carol A. Sandvick
Michael A. Sanzo (Resident, Washington, D.C. Office)
J. Gray Sasser
Mary M. Schill
Mirjam Schuller (Resident, Dallas, Texas Office)
James D. Seegers
Brad E. Seidel (Resident, Dallas, Texas Office)
Daniel B. Shilliday
James Andrew "Drew" Shirley
Aric K. Short (Resident, Austin, Texas Office)
Tomasz J. Sikora
Ashley Ann Smith
Catherine Bukowski Smith
Spencer Smith (Resident, Austin, Texas Office)
W. Creighton Smith
Kathleen Bone Spangler
Eric Stahl (Resident, Dallas, Texas Office)
Matthew R. Stammel (Resident, Dallas, Texas Office)
Julie B. Steamer (Resident, New York, N.Y. Office)
Mary J. Steichen (Resident, Dallas, Texas Office)
Mark W. Steirer (Resident, Dallas, Texas Office)
Annette Faubion Stephens
Ann K. Stewart (Resident, Dallas, Texas Office)
David Stone
Christopher B. Strong (Resident, Singapore Office)
Susanne K. Sullivan
Shantanu Surpure (Resident, Singapore Office)
Lewis C. Sutherland
Jerome A. Swindell (Resident, Washington, D.C. Office)
Harold J. Taylor (Resident, Austin, Texas Office)
Michael S. Telle
Paris Theofanidis
Kristie M. Tice
Fernando Tovar
Stacey Ann Tovino
Megan H. Troy (Resident, Washington, D.C. Office)
Julie I. Ungerman (Resident, Dallas, Texas Office)
James M. Vickery (Resident, Austin, Texas Office)
Cliff W. Vrielink
Dirk P. Walker
Joseph G. Walker (Resident, Dallas, Texas Office)
John C. Wander (Resident, Dallas, Texas Office)
Philip T. Warman
Jennifer L. Webster (Resident, Dallas, Texas Office)
George O. Wilkinson, Jr.
Fred I. Williams

ASSOCIATES (Continued)

(See Next Column)

Jennifer Lee Williams (Resident, Dallas, Texas Office)
Richard C. Williams
Rhonda Hunter Wills
Jeanne Klinefelter Wilson
David E. Wolfe (Resident, Dallas, Texas Office)
John F. Woodson, II
Andrew M. Wright (Resident, London, England Office)
William Scott Wyatt (Resident, Dallas, Texas Office)
Peter C. Yam (Resident, London, England Office)
Michael J. Yanochik
Rebecca L. Yates
Lamar Youngblood (Resident, Dallas, Texas Office)
Elizabeth Danling Yu (Not admitted in United States)
Mark R. Yzaguirre

For full biographical listings, see the Martindale-Hubbell Law Directory

WINSTEAD SECHREST & MINICK P.C. (AV)

2400 Bank One Center, 910 Travis Street, 77002-5895
Telephone: 713-650-8400
Telex: 73-0051
Fax: 713-650-2400
URL: http://www.winstead.com
Dallas, Texas Office: 5400 Renaissance Tower, 1201 Elm Street.
Telephone: 214-745-5400.
Telex: 73-0051.
Fax: 214-745-5390.
Austin, Texas Office: Suite 800, 100 Congress Avenue.
Telephone: 512-474-4330.
Telex: 73-0051.
Fax: 512-370-2850.
Mexico, D.F., Mexico Office: Winstead y Rivera, S.C., Av. Insurgentes Sur 1685, Piso 13-04, Torre Diamante, Colonia Guadalupe Inn, Delegacion Alvaro Obregon, 01020, Mexico, D.F., Mexico.
Telephone: (011-525) 5661-3025.
Fax: (011-525) 5661-3033.

Brian F. Antweil
Yasmin Islam Atasi
William W. Bell
Arthur S. Berner
Robin S. Bobbitt
Denis C. Braham
Todd B. Brewer
John G. Cannon
Steven J. Clausen
Douglas S. Craig, Jr.
James W. Doyle
Mark Eisenbraun
J. Robert Fisher
Mark C. Guthrie
William T. Johnson
Jeffrey L. Joyce
Linda D. King
David D. Knoll
Ross D. Margraves, Jr.
Dwayne L. Mason
Gail J. McDonald
W. Ted Minick
Richard H. Mourglia
R. Clyde Parker, Jr.
Charles J. Rogers
Teresa Letson Schneider
Stephen W. Schueler
Robert C. Shaddox
Cristina Portela Solomon
Paul E. Strohl
Frederick J. Tuthill
John R. Wallace
David M. Washburn
John D. White
William A. Wood, III

Glenn E. Airola
Corey C. Brown
Guinevere M. Christmann
Elliot Clark
Dena K. Creely
Jennifer M. Dinkins
Timothy M. Donoughue
Henry L. Ehrlich
Ricardo Garcia-Moreno
Mark J. Levine
Gregory S. Mathews
Chad L. Mavity
Shirat Mavligit
John H. McFarland
Duston K. McFaul
John E. McGettigan
Vincent A. Mercaldi
Donica R. Nowotny
Cindy J. Perini
David A. Pesel (Not admitted in TX)
D. Brennan Reilly
Rochelle S. Robinson
Sue D. Rosenthal
J. Keith Russell
Paul D. Strug
Yen T. Tran
Tom Van Arsdel
Hoang Vu
Thomas L. Warden
Wade Williams
Carl Wimberley
R. Joilene Wood

OF COUNSEL

Paula G. Freeman
Benny C. Pace

For full biographical listings, see the Martindale-Hubbell Law Directory

*KINGSVILLE,** Kleberg Co.

SHARPE & KRUEGER (AV)

617 East Kleberg, P.O. Box 1538, 78364
Telephone: 512-592-9361
FAX: 512-592-6547

Nelson R. Sharpe (1930-1989)
Michael J. Krueger

Representative Clients: State Bank of Kingsville; The First National Bank in Falfurrias, Texas; Greater South Texas, F.S.B.

For full biographical listings, see the Martindale-Hubbell Law Directory

*LAREDO,** Webb Co.

PERSON, WHITWORTH, RAMOS, BORCHERS & MORALES, L.L.P. (AV)

602 East Calton Road, P.O. Box 6668, 78042-6668
Telephone: 956-727-4441
Fax: 956-727-2696

MEMBERS OF FIRM

George J. Person
Stephen A. Whitworth
Donato D. Ramos
Charles R. Borchers (1943-1997)
Richard G. Morales, Jr.
Alejandro E. Villarreal, III
William E. Casey
Mark D. Willett
Martha Cigarroa Dellano
Maria Cristina Gonzalez
Baldemar Garcia, Jr.
Richard E. Morales
Katrina Borchers Mohrer

For full biographical listings, see the Martindale-Hubbell Law Directory

*LUBBOCK,** Lubbock Co.

CARR, HUNT & JOY L.L.P. (AV)

1001 Texas Avenue, P.O. Box 2585, 79408
Telephone: 806-765-7491
Fax: 806-765-0553
Email: info@chjlaw.com
Amarillo, Texas Office: Amarillo National Plaza II, Ste. 509, 500 S. Taylor Street, P.O. Box 989, Amarillo, Texas. 79105.
Telephone: 806-342-3055.
Fax: 806-342-9907.

MEMBERS OF FIRM

Marvin Warlick Carr
Donald M. Hunt
Latrelle Bright Joy
Tom H. Whiteside
Gary M. Bellair
Charles R. Watson, Jr. (Resident, Amarillo, Texas)
William R. Eichman, II
Deborah S. McClure (Resident, Amarillo, Texas)

Representative Clients: Bank of America; Beef Products, Inc.; Brown-McKee, Inc.; Burk Royalty Co.; Colorado Interstate Gas Co.; Cooper Industries, Inc.; Int'l Bank of Commerce; Monfort; Motorola, Inc.; Petrosurance; Smithlawn Maternity Home & Adoption Agency.

For full biographical listings, see the Martindale-Hubbell Law Directory

HARDING, BASS, FARGASON, BOOTH & ST. CLAIR, L.L.P. (AV)

University Plaza Building, 1901 University, Suite 500, P.O. Box 5950, 79408
Telephone: 806-744-1100
Fax: 806-744-1170
Email: thefirm@hardlaw.com

MEMBERS OF FIRM

Derry D. Harding
Roy Byrn Bass, Jr.
Ray Fargason
Monti Rice Booth
Robert W. St. Clair
Damon C. Richards

For full biographical listings, see the Martindale-Hubbell Law Directory

MCWHORTER, COBB & JOHNSON, L.L.P. (AV)

1722 Broadway, 79401
Telephone: 806-762-0214
Fax: 806-762-8014
Mailing Address: P.O. Box 2547, Lubbock, TX, 79408
Email: mcj@mcjllp.com

Owen W. McWhorter (1897-1986)
J. R. Blumrosen (1925-1996)
D. Thomas Johnson
Jack P. Driskill
D. Murray Hensley
Don R. Richards
Dulan D. Elder
Ann Manning
Sabra J. Srader
Timothy T. Pridmore

ASSOCIATES

Jamey Laney Phillips
Gary R. McLaren
R. Michael McCauley, Jr.
Gwynn P. Key

OF COUNSEL

Charles L. Cobb
Dale H. Johnson
Owen W. McWhorter, Jr.

Representative Clients: American State Bank; South Plains Electric Cooperative; Plains Cotton Cooperative Association; Plains Cooperative Oil Mill; Farmers Cooperative Compress; Lubbock Independent School District; Lubbock Avalanche Journal Newspaper; Texas Statewide Telephone Cooperatives Assn.

For full biographical listings, see the Martindale-Hubbell Law Directory

MOODY & HAYS, L.L.P. (AV)

City Bank Building, 5211 Brownfield Highway, 79407
Telephone: 806-785-0144
Fax: 806-793-0779

(See Next Column)

MEMBERS OF FIRM

Bobby J. Moody
J. Phillip Hays

For full biographical listings, see the Martindale-Hubbell Law Directory

*LUFKIN,** Angelina Co.

CLAYTON E. DARK, JR. (AV)

207 East Frank, Suite 100, P.O. Box 2207, 75902-2207
Telephone: 409-637-1733
Fax: 409-637-2897

ASSOCIATE

Michelle Wood Charanza

For full biographical listings, see the Martindale-Hubbell Law Directory

MCALLEN, Hidalgo Co.

ATLAS & HALL, L.L.P. (AV)

Professional Arts Building, 818 Pecan Avenue, P.O. Box 3725, 78502-3725
Telephone: 956-682-5501
Telecopier: 956-686-6109

MEMBERS OF FIRM

Morris Atlas
Robert L. Schwarz
Gary R. Gurwitz
Edmon G. Hall
Charles C. Murray
A. Kirby Cavin
Mike Mills
Molly Thornberry
Frederick J. Biel
Rex N. Leach
Lisa Powell
Stephen L. Crain
O. C. Hamilton, Jr.
Randy Crane
Stephen C. Haynes
Vicki M. Skaggs

ASSOCIATES

Dan K. Worthington
Valorie C. Glass
Hector J. Torres
Sofia A. Ramon
Ramona K. Kantack
Daniel G. Gurwitz
David E. Girault
José Cano
Aaron I. Vela
Adriana H. Cardenas
Gregory S. Kazen

Representative Clients: Texas Regional Bancshares, Inc.; Texas State Bank; Bentsen Development Co.; State Farm Mutual Automobile Insurance Co.; Travelers Insurance Company; Knapp Memorial Hospital; Chase Bank - McAllen; McAllen Independent School District.

For full biographical listings, see the Martindale-Hubbell Law Directory

FLORES, CASSO & PETTITT, L.L.P. (AV)

321 South 12th Street, P.O. Box 2128, 78505
Telephone: 956-686-9591
Telecopy: 956-686-9478
Email: office@f-c-p.com *URL:* http://www.f-f-p.com

Rafael H. Flores
David Casso
B. Buck Pettitt

LEGAL SUPPORT PERSONNEL

LITIGATION ADMINISTRATORS

Edmundo Martinez
Mario Garza

For full biographical listings, see the Martindale-Hubbell Law Directory

RODRIGUEZ, COLVIN & CHANEY, L.L.P. (AV)

4900 North 10th Street, 78504
Telephone: 956-686-1287
Telecopier: 956-686-6197
Brownsville, Texas Office: 1201 East Van Buren Street.
Telephone: 956-542-7441.
Telecopier: 956-541-2170.
Harlingen, Texas Office: 402 East Van Buren.
Telephone: 956-423-0216.
Telecopier: 956-423-2035.

OF COUNSEL

Neil E. Norquest
Chris A. Brisack
Raymond A. Cowley

Division Attorneys for: Union Pacific Railroad.
Counsel for: Texas Commerce Bank-Rio Grande Valley, N.A.; Texas Commerce Bancshares, Inc.

For full biographical listings, see the Martindale-Hubbell Law Directory

LAW OFFICES OF TOM WILKINS (AV)

1010 Texas State Bank, 3900 North 10th Street, P.O. Box 3609, 78501
Telephone: 956-682-4551
Fax: 956-682-4554

For full biographical listings, see the Martindale-Hubbell Law Directory

*MCKINNEY,** Collin Co.

COWLES & THOMPSON, A PROFESSIONAL CORPORATION (AV)

307 S. McDonald Street, 75069-5659
Telephone: 972-542-5000 Metro: 972-562-2270
Fax: 972-542-5040
Dallas & Tyler
URL: http://www.cowlesthompson.com
Dallas, Texas Office: 901 Main Street, Suite 4000, 75202.
Telephone: 214-672-2000; Metro: 972-263-0005.
Fax: 214-672-2020.
Tyler, Texas Office: 1103 First Place, P.O. Box 239, 75710-0239.
Telephone: 903-593-7508.
Fax: 903-593-4057.

Alan L. Campbell

Wendy A. McMillon
L. Mark McMillon

For full biographical listings, see the Martindale-Hubbell Law Directory

*MIDLAND,** Midland Co.

KERR & WARD, L.L.P. (AV)

500 W. Texas, Suite 1310, Drawer 2858, 79702
Telephone: 915-684-9990
Fax: 915-684-9997
Email: info@kerr-ward.com *URL:* http://www.kerr-ward.com

OF COUNSEL

Wm. Monroe Kerr
Theodore M. Kerr

PARTNERS

Harris E. Kerr
William E. Ward
William M. Kerr, Jr.
Brian T. McLaughlin
James Devin Alsup

For full biographical listings, see the Martindale-Hubbell Law Directory

LYNCH, CHAPPELL & ALSUP, A PROFESSIONAL CORPORATION (AV)

The Summit, Suite 700, 300 North Marienfeld, 79701
Telephone: 915-683-3351
Fax: 915-683-2587

Raymond A. Lynch (1913-1971)
James M. Alsup
Robert A. Spears
Thomas W. Ortloff
Steven C. Lindgren
Harper Estes
Steven C. Kiser
W. Scott Ryburn
L. Shane Stokes
Jeffrey D. Hewett
Richard E. Booth

Michael J. Goeke
Leslie J. Kramer
M. Michele Greene
Brandon W. Pinson
Alan J. Brown

OF COUNSEL

Clovis G. Chappell
Wm. Randall Lundy
Barbara J. Farish

Representative Clients: Tom Brown, Inc.; NationsBank of Texas, N.A.; Pioneer Natural Resources; Chevron U.S.A. Inc.; Norwest Bank Texas, Midland, N.A.; Wagner & Brown, Ltd.

For full biographical listings, see the Martindale-Hubbell Law Directory

LESLIE G. MCLAUGHLIN (AV)

1209 West Texas Avenue, 79701
Telephone: 915-687-1331
Fax: 915-687-1336

For full biographical listings, see the Martindale-Hubbell Law Directory

*NACOGDOCHES,** Nacogdoches Co.

FAIRCHILD, PRICE, THOMAS, HALEY & WILLINGHAM, L.L.P. (AV)

1801 North Street, P.O. Box 631668, 75963-1668
Telephone: 409-569-2327
Fax: 409-569-7932.
Email: chaley@fpthw.com
Center, Texas Office: 413 Shelbyville Street, P.O. Drawer 1719, 75935.
Telephone: 409-598-2981.
Fax: 409-598-7712. E-Mail: wmthomas@fpthw.com
Houston, Texas Office: 440 Louisiana Street, Suite 2110, 77002-4205.
Telephone: 713-426-1700.
Fax: 713-426-1717. E-Mail: mwillingham@fpthw.com

(See Next Column)

John L. Price
W. Miller Thomas
C. Victor Haley
R. Mark Willingham
Travis P. Clardy
David J. Fisher
Clayton H. Haley
Russell R. Smith
Ryan A. Beason

OF COUNSEL

Robert L. Fairchild

James A. Payne, Jr.
David Edward Ash
Campbell Cox
Jefferson B. Davis
Thomas L. Cougill
Jeffrey Pierce Fultz
Matthew D. Mettauer

For full biographical listings, see the Martindale-Hubbell Law Directory

*ODESSA,** Ector Co.

MCMAHON, TIDWELL, HANSEN, ATKINS & PEACOCK, P.C. (AV)

4001 East 42nd Street, Suite 200, P.O. Box 1311, 79760
Telephone: 915-367-7271
Fax: 915-363-9121

William B. Deaderick (1918-1966)
Q. B. McMahon (1918-1991)
Jack Q. Tidwell
Blake Hansen
Mike Atkins
Jimmy W. Peacock
J. T. Morgan
James M. Rush
Michael G. Kelly
Denis Dennis
Scott M. Tidwell

Darrell Wayne Corzine
Kimberly Paige Harris

Representative Clients: Bank One, Odessa; Norwest Bank, Texas, N.A.; Ector County Independent School District; State Farm Cos.; The Medical Protective Co.; The Charter Group; CGU Southwest Insurance; SouthWest Bank; Aghorn Oil & Gas, Inc.

For full biographical listings, see the Martindale-Hubbell Law Directory

SHAFER, DAVIS, ASHLEY, O'LEARY & STOKER, A PROFESSIONAL CORPORATION (AV)

Second Floor, Nations Bank Building, 700 North Grant Street, P.O. Drawer 1552, 79760
Telephone: 915-332-0893
Telecopier/Fax: 915-333-5002; 915-335-8329
E-mail: Shaferlaw@worldnet.att.net
Email: Shaferfirm@worldnet.att.net
Midland, Texas Office: 415 West Wall, Suite 1240, 79701.
Telephone: 915-498-7330.

W. O. Shafer (1917-1992)
Connell Ashley (1928-1999)
Perry Davis, Jr.
James M. O'Leary
Ray C. Stoker, Jr.
Richard E. Buck
Joel B. Locke
Bruce Bangert
Randall L. Rouse
Kathleen McCollum McCulloch
W. Stacy Trotter
Stephen C. Ashley
B. Calvin Hendrick, VII
Stephen M. Steen, Jr.
Miles R. Nelson

Representative Clients: The Continental Insurance Companies; The Fund Insurance Companies; Hartford Accident and Indemnity Co.; Halliburton Oil & Cementing Co.; TU Electric Co.; Union Pacific Railroad Co.; St. Paul Insurance Companies; Aetna Insurance Companies; The City of Odessa; Medical Center Hospital, Odessa.

For full biographical listings, see the Martindale-Hubbell Law Directory

*PAMPA,** Gray Co.

WATERS, HOLT & FIELDS (AV)

Formerly Smith, Teed, Wade & Waters
Combs-Worley Building, P.O. Box 662, 79066-0662
Telephone: 806-669-6851
FAX: 806-669-0440

MEMBERS OF FIRM

Wm. Jarrel Smith (1897-1974)
Arthur M. Teed (1904-1968)
Thos. L. Wade (1905-1972)
Bill W. Waters
David E. Holt
Kenneth W. Fields

Representative Clients: Celanese Corp.; First State Bank of Miami, Texas; Brainard Cattle Co.; Equitable Life Assurance Society of the U.S.; American General Life Insurance Co.; Beacon Insurance Group; Pampa Independent School District; Gray County Appraisal District; Arrington Cos.; Shamrock Independent School District.

For full biographical listings, see the Martindale-Hubbell Law Directory

*PERRYTON,** Ochiltree Co.

LEMON, SHEARER, EHRLICH, PHILLIPS & GOOD, A PROFESSIONAL CORPORATION (AV)

311 South Main Street, P.O. Box 1066, 79070
Telephone: 806-435-6544
FAX: 806-435-4377
Email: lsepglaw@ren.net
Booker, Texas Office: 122 South Main Street, P.O. Box 348.
Telephone: 806-658-4545.
FAX: 806-658-4524.

Robert D. Lemon
Otis C. Shearer
Mitchell Ehrlich
Randall M. Phillips
F. Keith Good

Representative Clients: The Perryton National Bank; The Perryton Equity Exchange; The North Plains Ground Water Conservation District; Natural Gas Anadarko Co.; Courson Oil & Gas, Inc.; The City of Perryton; The Booker Equity Exchange; The Follett National Bank; Unit Petroleum Co.

For full biographical listings, see the Martindale-Hubbell Law Directory

PORT ARTHUR, Jefferson Co.

BLACK & BLACK (AV)

3627 Professional Drive, P.O. Box 3286, 77642
Telephone: 409-982-9433
Fax: 409-982-0657

MEMBERS OF FIRM

Earl Black
James M. Black

For full biographical listings, see the Martindale-Hubbell Law Directory

*SAN ANGELO,** Tom Green Co.

JACKSON WALKER L.L.P. (AV)

225 West Beauregard Avenue, 76903
Telephone: 915-481-2550
Fax: 915-481-2552
Email: hloftin@jw.com *URL:* http://www.jw.com
Austin, Texas Office: 100 Congress Avenue, Suite 1100.
Telephone: 512-236-2000.
Fax: 512-236-2002.
Dallas, Texas Office: 901 Main Street, Suite 6000.
Telephone: 214-953-6000.
Fax: 214-953-5822.
Fort Worth, Texas Office: 301 Commerce Street, Suite 2400.
Telephone: 817-334-7200.
Fax: 817-334-7290.
Houston, Texas Office: 1100 Louisiana, Suite 4200.
Telephone: 713-752-4200.
Fax: 713-752-4221.
Richardson, Texas Office: 2435 North Central Expressway, Suite 600.
Telephone: 972-671-2560.
Fax: 972-671-2566.
San Antonio, Texas Office: 112 E. Pecan Street, Suite 2100.
Telephone: 210-978-7700.
Fax: 210-978-7790.

MEMBER OF FIRM

Donald W. Griffis

OF COUNSEL

Robert A. Junell

ASSOCIATES

Samuel S. Allen
Jon Mark Hogg
Jay K. Weatherby

For full biographical listings, see the Martindale-Hubbell Law Directory

*SAN ANTONIO,** Bexar Co.

AKIN, GUMP, STRAUSS, HAUER & FELD, L.L.P. (AV)

A Registered Limited Liability Partnership including Professional Corporations
300 Convent Street, Suite 1500, 78205
Telephone: 210-281-7000
Fax: 210-224-2035
URL: http://www.akingump.com
Dallas, Texas Office: 1700 Pacific Avenue, Suite 4100.
Telephone: 214-969-2800.
Fax: 214-969-4343.
Austin, Texas Office: Frost Bank Plaza, 816 Congress Avenue, Suite 1900.
Telephone: 512-499-6200.
Fax: 512-499-6290.
Houston, Texas Office: 1900 Pennzoil Place-South Tower, 711 Louisiana Street,
Telephone: 713-220-5800.
Fax: 713-236-0822.
New York, New York Office: 590 Madison Avenue, 20th Floor.
Telephone: 212-872-1000.
Fax: 212-872-1002.

(See Next Column)

Philadelphia, Pennsylvania Office: One Commerce Square, 2005 Market Street, Suite 2200.
Telephone: 215-965-1200.
Fax: 215-965-1210.
Washington, D.C. Office: 1333 New Hampshire Avenue, N.W., Suite 400.
Telephone: 202-887-4000.
Fax: 202-887-4288.
Los Angeles, California Office: Century Tower Plaza, 2029 Century Park East, Suite 2600.
Telephone: 310-229-1000.
Fax: 310-229-1001.
Brussels, Belgium Office: 65 Avenue Louise, P. B. #7.
Telephone: (+32 2) 535-29-11.
Fax: (+32 2) 535 29 00.
London, England Office: One Angel Court.
Telephone: 011 44 20 7726 9600.
Fax: 011 44 20 7726 9610.
Moscow, Russia Office: Ducat Place II, 7 Gasheka Street, P.B. 20.
Telephone: 011 7 095 974 2411.
Fax: 011 7 095 974 2412.
Affiliated Office:
Law Office of Abdulaziz H. Fahad: Jarir Plaza, 4th Floor, Olaya Street, P.O. Box 15870, Riyadh, Saudi Arabia, 11454.
Telephone: 011 966 1 464 8081.
Telex: 406176 LAWS SJ.
Telecopier: 011 966 1 462 4968.

Herbert M. Schenker (1913-1994)
Thomas H. Sharp, Jr. (1934-1989)
Mitchell S. Rosenheim (Retired)

MEMBERS OF FIRM

Robert E. Bettac
Kris J. Bird
Barry A. Chasnoff
Michael C. Elrod
Stephen L. Golden
Charles W. Hanor (P.C.)
David A. Jones
C. David Kinder
Daniel McNeel Lane, Jr.
R. Laurence Macon (P.C.)
M. Paul Martin
Pamela G. Matthews
Stephen C. Mount
Shelton E. Padgett
Kim E. Ramsey (P.C.)
Ricky H. Rosenblum
J. Patrick Ryan (P.C.)
Cecil Schenker (P.C.)
Alan Schoenbaum
Gilbert F. Vázquez
José H. Villarreal (P.C.)
W. Thomas Weir (P.C.)

ASSOCIATES

William Alberts
Nancy Belinsky
Eric W. Cernyar
Michael Sanghun Cho
Wesley L. Clarke (Not admitted in TX)
Andrew S. Cohen
Katherine Compton
Valerie L. Daniels
Jo Beth Eubanks
Michael V. Galo, Jr.
John F. Gillard
Julia G. Gokavi
Ami Gordon
Patrick Hurley
William Y. Klett, III (Not admitted in TX)
Sharla Kruger
Wilhelm E. Liebmann
Orlando R. Lopez
Kelly L. Majors
Wyre J. Marshall
William J. Maynard (Not admitted in TX)
Courtney A. Mckendrick
Christopher J. McKinney
Andrea H. Meller
Tyler Gates Mercer
Jennifer A. Munzel
David R. Nelson
Lyndon Nugent
Elizabeth M. Provencio (Not admitted in TX)
Christine E. Reinhard
Pamela J. St. John
Thomas E. Sanders
Donna K. Schneider
Theodore C. Schultz
Janie A. Shannon
Scott E. Stewart
Susan Stone
Raymond A. Suire
Michael D. Tanner
Jessica S. Taylor
Geoffrey R. Unger

SENIOR COUNSEL

Melanie Goins Cowart
Mary Claire Fischer
Winston Hankins
Frank S. Manitzas
Stephan B. Rogers
Rebecca Simmons
Sidney H. Swearingen

COUNSEL

Ruben Cantu
Karen K. Gulde
Joseph C. Martin IV
Kirt S. O'Neill
Saul H. Perloff
Roberta J. Sharp
Glenn D. Shook
David R. Stephens

STAFF ATTORNEY

Lyvonne Brittingham

For full biographical listings, see the Martindale-Hubbell Law Directory

COX & SMITH INCORPORATED (AV)

112 East Pecan Street, Suite 1800, 78205-1521
Telephone: 210-554-5500
Fax: 210-226-8395
Email: info@coxsmith.com *URL:* http://www.coxsmith.com

John J. Cox (1905-1971)
J. Burleson Smith
Paul H. Smith
Dan G. Webster, III
Richard T. Brady
Keith E. Kaiser
Jon R. Ray
Gale R. Peterson

(See Next Column)

COX & SMITH INCORPORATED, *San Antonio—Continued*

James B. Smith, Jr.
Diann M. Bartek
William H. Lester, Jr.
A. Michael Ferrill
Deborah D. Williamson
Cary Plotkin Kavy
Stephen D. Seidel
David B. West
Kevin M. Beiter
David L. Butler
Donna K. McElroy
James M. McDonough
J. Daniel Harkins
Steven R. Jacobs
Michael A. Morell
William J. McDonough, Jr.
Gardner S. Kendrick
Raymond E. Gallaway, Jr.
Robert W. Nelson
Margaret Pedrick Sullivan
Steven A. Elder
Patrick L. Huffstickler
Brett W. Schouest
R. Bradley Oxford
Harry W. Wolff, Jr.
Elizabeth Johnson Keig
Kerry T. Benedict
Ben F. Foster, Jr.
Robert D. Kilgore
Daniel R. Stern
Allan G. Paterson, Jr.
Abigail G. Kampmann
Tobin E. Olson
Carl A. Werner
Lauren M. Sheinberg
James K. Spivey
David H.O. Roth
James M. Truss
Jonathan A. Nixon
Leslie S. Hyman
W. Bradley Barnes
Peter H. Wickersham
Jeffery S. Darby
Angie D. Patrick
Matthew S. Parkin
Courtenay B. Allen
David C. Giles
Ramon D. Bissmeyer
Larry E. Gee
E. Burke Huber, Jr.
Brian N. Jaeckle
Joshua A. Sutin
Scott B. Bankler
Courtney C. Solcher
Lauren R. Huckaby
John M. Black
William ("Butch") F. Hulse, IV
H. Joseph Acosta
Michael A. Tomberg (Not admitted in TX)
Jason B. Speights
Douglas B. Kiel
Peter R. Broderick
Lisa F. Sutker

OF COUNSEL

Teresa Ereon Giltner
Jack Guenther
Stephen M. Marceau
Joe R. McFarlane, Jr.

Representative Clients: Abraxas Petroleum Corporation; Cancer Therapy & Research Center; City of San Antonio; International Bancshares Corp.; Kinetic Concepts, Inc.; San Antonio Federal Credit Union; Solo Serve Corporation.

For full biographical listings, see the Martindale-Hubbell Law Directory

EDERER & PRICE, L.L.C. (AV)

7800 IH 10 West Suite 135, 78230
Telephone: 210-341-4070
Fax: 210-892-5510 or 210-341-4459
Email: rone@edererprice.com

Ronald F. Ederer
Steven P. Price

Randall A. Parker

For full biographical listings, see the Martindale-Hubbell Law Directory

GRESHAM, DAVIS, GREGORY, WORTHY & MOORE, A PROFESSIONAL CORPORATION (AV)

Formerly Boyle, Wheeler, Gresham, Davis & Gregory
112 East Pecan Street, Ninth Floor, 78205-1542
Telephone: 210-226-4157
Telecopier: 210-226-5154

Rupert Neely Gresham (1892-1973)
Richard T. Davis (1911-1991)
Albert W. Worthy (1922-1998)
Claiborne B. Gregory
Richard B. Moore
Claiborne B. Gregory, Jr.
Moulton S. Dowler, Jr.
Marshall B. Miller, Jr.
John Wallis Harris
Nancy A. Norman
Peter E. Hosey
Brad S. Akin
Matthew D. Bradley

OF COUNSEL

Ben J. Chilcutt
Samuel H. Bayless
Ann M. Leafstedt
James E. McCutcheon, III

Raul M. Calderon

Justin G. Rice
Bart W. Huffman

For full biographical listings, see the Martindale-Hubbell Law Directory

HEARD LINEBARGER GRAHAM GOGGAN BLAIR PEÑA & SAMPSON, LLP (AV)

Tenth Floor, Tower Life Building, 310 South St. Mary's, 78205
Telephone: 210-225-6763
Facsimile: 210-225-6410
URL: http://www.publicans.com
Austin, Texas Office: 1949 South IH 35, 78741.
Telephone: 512-447-6675.
Fax: 512-443-3494.
Beaumont, Texas Office: 1148 Park, 77701.
Telephone: 409-832-9483.
Fax: 409-833-2638.

(See Next Column)

Brownsville, Texas Office: 3302 Boca Chica, Suite 105, 78521.
Telephone: 956-546-1216.
Fax: 956-546-4624.
Conroe, Texas Office: 103 W. Phillips, 77301.
Telephone: 409-760-1410.
Fax: 409-760-1285.
Corpus Christi, Texas Office: 500 N. Shoreline, Suite 1111, 78471.
Telephone: 512-888-6898.
Fax: 512-888-4405.
Corsicana, Texas Office: 1501 Northwood Boulevard, 75110.
Telephone: 903-872-3096.
Fax: 903-874-5007.
Dallas, Texas Office: 1720 Allianz Financial Centre, 2323 Bryan Street, 75201.
Telephone: 214-880-0089.
Fax: 214-754-7167.
Denton, Texas Office: 326-G East McKinney, 76201.
Telephone: 940-383-4460.
Fax: 940-382-2829.
Edinburg, Texas Office: 110 S. 12th Street, 78539.
Telephone: 956-383-4500.
Fax: 956-383-7820.
El Paso, Texas Office: 215 N. Stanton Street, 79901.
Telephone: 915-533-6637.
Fax: 915-532-7085.
Fort Worth, Texas Office: Oil & Gas Building, Suite 1414, 309 W. 7th Street, 76102.
Telephone: 817-877-4589.
Fax: 817-877-0601.
Houston, Texas Office: 1021 Main Street, Suite 1500, 77002.
Telephone: 713- 844-3400.
Fax: 713-844-3501.
Laredo, Texas Office: 1102 Scott, Suite 2B, 78041.
Telephone: 956-723-1303.
Fax: 956-723-1327.
Longview, Texas Office: 1127 Judson Road, Suite 111, 75601.
Telephone: 903-757-5448.
Fax: 903-758-3331.
Odessa, Texas Office: 1301 E. 8th Street, Suite 200, 79761.
Telephone: 915-332-9047.
Fax: 915-333-7012.
Richmond, Texas Office: 301 S. 9th Street, Suite 222, 77469.
Telephone: 281-342-9636.
Fax: 281-341-7808.
Sherman, Texas Office: 115 E. Lamar, 75091.
Telephone: 903-893-4941.
Fax: 903-868-0688.
Tyler, Texas Office: 1517 W. Front Street, Suite 202, 75702.
Telephone: 903-597-2897.
Fax: 903-597-2402.
The Woodlands, Texas Office: 10077 Grogan's Mill Road, Suite 535,v 77380-2924.
Telephone: 713-363-3632.
Fax: 281-363-3998.
New Orleans, Louisiana Office: 1515 Poydras Street, Suite 1840, 70112.
Telephone: 504-522-9100.
Fax: 504-522-9145.
Philadelphia, Pennsylvania Office: 123 S. Broad Street, Suite 1830, 19109.
Telephone: 215-790-1117.
Fax: 215-790-1197.

MEMBERS OF FIRM

Oliver S. Heard, Sr. (1915-1977)
Oliver S. Heard, Jr.
Dale Linebarger (Resident, Austin Office)
Russell R. Graham (Resident, Austin Office)
Thomas S. Goggan, III (Resident, Austin Office)
Stephen S. Blair (Resident, Austin Office)
Jim Blair (Resident, The Woodlands Office)
Juan M. Peña (Resident, Edinburg Office)
DeMetris Aquilla Sampson (Resident, Dallas Office)
David G. Aelvoet
Drew Aldinger (Resident, Philadelphia, Pennsylvania Office)
Bruce W. Anderson (Resident, Austin Office)
Kaye Applewhite (Resident, Conroe Office)
Thelma Banduch (Resident, Brownsville Office)
Gary B. Bennett (At Denton, Fort Worth and Sherman Offices)
Douglas S. Bird (Resident, Austin Office)
John R. Bolster (Resident, Tyler Office)
Phillipa L. Bowers (Resident, New Orleans, Louisiana Office)
Brian E. Brown (Resident, Austin Office)
Jeffrey K. Brown (Resident, Austin Office)
James H. Burshtyn (Resident, Austin Office)
Rebecca Bustamante
Olivero E. Canales (Resident, Laredo Office)
Paul D. Chapa (Resident, Corpus Christi Office)
Kevin D. Chester (Resident, Corsicana Office)
Cormac P. Creaven (Houston and Richmond Offices)
L. W. "Rusty" Dean (Resident, Tyler Office)
Michael W. Deeds (Resident, Houston Office)
Mary Belan Doggett
Clifton F. Douglass, III
James R. Evans, Jr. (Resident, Austin Office)
F. Duane Force (Resident, Austin Office)
Cynthia Y. Garza (Resident, Edinburg Office)
Jay T. Garrett (Resident, Austin Office)

(See Next Column)

HEARD LINEBARGER GRAHAM GOGGAN BLAIR PEÑA & SAMPSON LLP—*Continued*

MEMBERS OF FIRM (Continued)

Lucy Gonzàlez-Canales (Resident, Edinburg Office)	Pankaj R. Parmar (Resident, Houston Office)
Lee Gordon (Resident, Austin Office)	Carmen I. Perez (Resident, El Paso Office)
Sandra Griffin (Resident, Austin Office)	Monica McCoy Purdy (Resident, Dallas Office)
Eloise A. Guzman (Resident, Houston Office)	Harold D. Putman, Jr.
Judith A. Hargrove (Resident, Austin Office)	Kent M. Rider (Resident, Austin Office)
Edward Hernández (Resident, El Paso Office)	Lori Gruver Robertson (Resident, Austin Office)
Sharon N. Humble	Craig Schumacher (Resident, Tyler Office)
Pamela Pope Johnson (Resident, Dallas Office)	Michael J. Siwierka (Resident, Houston Office)
William E. King (Resident, Houston Office)	Glenn E. Smith (Resident, Fort Worth Office)
Glenn Lewis (Resident, Fort Worth Office)	Leah L. Stolar (Resident, Houston Office)
Edward Lopez, Jr. (Resident, Dallas Office)	Charles A. Sutton (Resident, Corpus Christi Office)
Clayton E. Mayfield (Resident, Beaumont Office)	Michael T. Vallandingham (Resident, Austin Office)
Russell N. McInturff (Resident, Odessa Office)	Nancy Vasquez-Perez (Resident, Corpus Christi Office)
Stephen T. Meeks (Resident, Fort Worth Office)	H. Elizabeth "Beth" Weller (Resident, Dallas Office)
Beverly Meltontree (Resident, Houston Office)	Barbara M. Williams (Resident, Fort Worth Office)
Kathleen D. Morrison (Resident, Corpus Christi Office)	Donald Lee Wolf (Resident, Tyler Office)
Harry L. Munsinger	Scott D. Wylie (Resident, Corsicana Office)
Norman J. Nelson (Resident, Houston Office)	Craig Young (Resident, Austin Office)
J. Scott Novy (Resident, Longview Office)	Lupe Zamarripa (Resident, Austin Office)

OF COUNSEL

Debra Danburg (Resident, Houston Office)	Vince Ryan (Resident, Houston Office)
Richard R. Orsinger	
Humberto Hernandez-Haddad (Not admitted in United States)	

For full biographical listings, see the Martindale-Hubbell Law Directory

JACKSON WALKER L.L.P. (AV)

112 E. Pecan Street, Suite 2100, 78205-1521
Telephone: 210-978-7700
Fax: 210-978-7790
URL: http://www.jw.com
Austin, Texas Office: 100 Congress Avenue, Suite 1100.
Telephone: 512-236-2000.
Fax: 512-236-2002.
Dallas, Texas Office: 901 Main Street, Suite 6000.
Telephone: 214-953-6000.
Fax: 214-953-5822.
Fort Worth, Texas Office: 301 Commerce Street, Suite 2400.
Telephone: 817-334-7200.
Fax: 817-334-7290.
Houston, Texas Office: 1100 Louisiana, Suite 4200.
Telephone: 713-752-4200.
Fax: 713-752-4221.
Richardson, Texas Office: 2435 North Central Expressway, Suite 600.
Telephone: 972-671-2560.
Fax: 972-671-2566.
San Angelo, Texas Office: 225 West Beauregard Avenue.
Telephone: 915-481-2550.
Fax: 915-481-2552.

MEMBERS OF FIRM

Leo D. Figueroa	Robert F. Scheihing
Dawn Bruner Finlayson	Eileen E. Scherlen
Stephen R. Fogle	Patrick B. Tobin
Richard G. Garza	James L. Walker
Jeffrey T. Harvey	William B. Nash
Eric G. Hoffman	Mark H. Miller
Janet L. King	Thomas E. Sisson
Edgar C. Morrison, Jr.	Daniel D. Chapman

ASSOCIATES

Cynthia Lopez Beverage	Patricia A. Davila
C. Dawson Bremer	Manda McMichael Kelley

Cline H. White

For full biographical listings, see the Martindale-Hubbell Law Directory

OPPENHEIMER, BLEND, HARRISON & TATE, INC. (AV)

711 Navarro, Suite 600, 78205-1796
Telephone: 210-224-2000
Telecopier: 210-224-7540
Email: obht@obht.com *URL:* http://www.obht.com
Edinburg, Texas Office: 4430 South McColl Road.
Telephone: 956-664-2963.
Fax: 956-664-2967.

Jesse H. Oppenheimer	Glen A. Yale
Reese L. Harrison, Jr.	Raymond W. Battaglia
Stanley L. Blend	Craig A. Stokes
John H. Tate, II	Bruce M. Mitchell
Kenneth M. Gindy	Cheryl K. Freed
J. David Oppenheimer	Kirk L. James
Richard N. Weinstein	David P. Stanush
Taylor S. Boone	Douglas W. Sanders

Martin I. Roos

Paul D. Barkhurst	Julie Cobb Perez
Elizabeth A. Copeland	Kathleen Quiroz
Jerome B. Cohen	Angela Marie Sanchez
Diana M. Geis	Cathy Raba Turcotte
Joe R. Hinojosa	Suzanne E. Schorlemer
A. Ryland Howard, III	W. Richey Wyatt

OF COUNSEL

Barbara Spudis de Marigny (Not admitted in TX)	Richard I. Manas
	William D. Peisen
Marshall Groce	Karen Vaughan

For full biographical listings, see the Martindale-Hubbell Law Directory

PLUNKETT & GIBSON, INC. (AV)

6243 IH-10 West, Suite 600, P.O. Box BH002, 78201
Telephone: 210-734-7092
Telecopier: 210-734-0379

Laura A. Cavaretta	Tim T. Griesenbeck, Jr.
D. Ann Comerio	John A. Heller
Richard B. Copeland	Nina E. Henderson
Joseph C. Elliott	Ronald Hornberger
Richard N. Francis, Jr.	Lewin Plunkett
Jerry A. Gibson	Cathy J. Sheehan

OF COUNSEL

Daniel Diaz, Jr.	Robert D. Reed
Marilyn G. Eades	F. Beth Morgan

William J. Baine	Gary B. Gibson
Charles L. Fridge, III	Erik V. Larson

Representative Clients: St. Paul Insurance Co.; Toyota Motor Sales, Inc.; Travelers Insurance Co.; Transport Insurance Co.; CIGNA Insurance Co.; Mazda Motor Co.; Pacificare of Texas Inc; Santa Rosa Health Care Corp.; Sisters of Mercy Health System; ANPAC.

For full biographical listings, see the Martindale-Hubbell Law Directory

*TAHOKA,** Lynn Co.

HUFFAKER, GREEN & HUFFAKER (AV)

1629 Avenue K, P.O. Box 419, 79373
Telephone: 806-998-4515
Fax: 806-998-4800

MEMBERS OF FIRM

Calloway Huffaker (1914-1988)	Harold Green

Gerald Huffaker

Representative Clients: The First National Bank, Tahoka; The Wilson State Bank, Wilson, Texas; Lyntegar Electric Cooperative, Inc.; Taylor Tractor & Equipment, Inc.

For full biographical listings, see the Martindale-Hubbell Law Directory

TEMPLE, Bell Co.

NAMAN, HOWELL, SMITH & LEE, A PROFESSIONAL CORPORATION (AV)

6th Floor, First National Bank Building, P.O. Box 844, 76503
Telephone: 254-778-1354
FAX: 254-774-7254
Email: naman@namanhowell.com *URL:* http://www.namanhowell.com
Waco, Texas Office: 900 Washington, Suite 700. P.O. Box 1470.
Telephone: 254-755-4100.
FAX: 254-754-6331. Internet: naman@namanhowell.com.
Austin, Texas Office: 221 West Sixth Street, 1900 Bank One Tower.
Telephone: 512-479-0300.
FAX: 512-474-1901.
Fort Worth, Texas Office: 301 Sinclair Building, 512 Main Street.
Telephone: 817-348-0300.
Fax: 972-445-8804.

(See Next Column)

NAMAN, HOWELL, SMITH & LEE A PROFESSIONAL CORPORATION, *Temple—Continued*

DeWitt Bowmer (1890-1940)
William R. Courtney (1923-1998)
Walker Saulsbury (1895-1944)
Jim D. Bowmer
Bob Burleson
John P. Cunningham, Jr.
Steve L. Moody
Jack M. Moore
Tom Normand

Laura R. Rayl

Counsel for: First National Bank of Temple; Wilsonart International; United States Fidelity and Guaranty Co.; KCEN-TV, Inc.; Temple Daily Telegram; Killeen Daily Herald; Scott and White Memorial Hospital; Scott, Sherwood and Brindley Foundation, Temple, Texas; King's Daugters Hospital, Temple, Texas.
Special Counsel For: Bell County, Texas.

For full biographical listings, see the Martindale-Hubbell Law Directory

TEXARKANA, Bowie Co.

ATCHLEY, RUSSELL, WALDROP & HLAVINKA, L.L.P. (AV)

1710 Moores Lane, P.O. Box 5517, 75505-5517
Telephone: 903-792-8246
Fax: 903-792-5801
Email: arwh@compuserve.com

MEMBERS OF FIRM

Otto H. Atchley (1904-1989)
Norman C. Russell (1915-1996)
Howard Waldrop
Charles J. Hlavinka
Victor F. Hlavinka
Stephen Oden
J. Dennis Chambers
Robert W. Weber
Alan D. Harrel
Josh R. Morriss, III
John R. Mercy
J. Michael Smith
Jeffrey C. Elliott
William Howard Mowery
Louise E. Tausch
Kenneth Dale Edwards (1940-1976)
Robert W. Littrell (1953-1983)
Jeffery C. Lewis

ASSOCIATES

John L. Tidwell
Shawn M. Morgan

Representative Clients: United States Fidelity & Guaranty Co.; Employer's Casualty Co.; Liberty Mutual Insurance Co.; The Home Co.; Missouri-Pacific Railway Co.; St. Louis Southwestern Railway Co.; State First National Bank in Texas; State Bank of DeKalb; St. Paul Insurance Co.; First-Bank.

For full biographical listings, see the Martindale-Hubbell Law Directory

PATTON, HALTOM, ROBERTS, MCWILLIAMS & GREER, L.L.P. (AV)

A Registered Limited Liability Partnership including Professional Corporations
700 Hibernia National Bank Building, P.O. Box 1928, 75504-1928
Telephone: 903-794-3341
Fax: 903-792-6542; 903-792-0448
URL: http://www.pattonhaltom.com

Kirk Patton (P.C.)
James N. Haltom (P.C.)
William B. Roberts
George L. McWilliams (P.C.)
John B. Greer, III, (P.C.)
Donald W. Capshaw
Phillip N. Cockrell
Kristi I. McCasland
Jennifer Haltom Doan

ASSOCIATES

Johanna Elizabeth Haltom Salter (1960-1993)
Darby Vincent Doan
Richard A. Adams
William W. Miller, Jr.
David P. Cotten

Representative Clients: Allstate Insurance Co.; Royal Insurance Group; Continental Insurance Group; Ranger/Pan American Insurance Cos.; The Hanover Insurance Group; American Mutual Liability Insurance Co.; American Hardware Mutual Insurance Co.; Kemper Insurance Co.

For full biographical listings, see the Martindale-Hubbell Law Directory

PATTON, TIDWELL & SANDEFUR, L.L.P. (AV)

4605 Texas Boulevard, P.O. Box 5398, 75505-5398
Telephone: 903-792-7080; 903-792-5859
Fax: 903-792-8233
Email: KTIDW87157@aol.com

Nicholas H. Patton
Kelly B. Tidwell
Gregory C. Sandefur

Christie G. Adams

For full biographical listings, see the Martindale-Hubbell Law Directory

YOUNG & PICKETT (AV)

4122 Texas Boulevard, P.O. Box 1897, 75504
Telephone: 870-774-3206; 903-794-1303
Facsimile: 903-792-5098; 903-794-5098
Email: YP1303@aol.com

Damon Young
John M. Pickett

ASSOCIATE

Lance Lee

Representative Clients: AT&T Corporation; AmeriSource Corporation; Bridgestone/Firestone, Inc.; Exxon Chemical Americas; Century Bank of New Boston, Texas; International Paper Company, Inc.; Lucent Technologies, Inc.; Medtronic, Inc.; Michelin North America; SmithKline Beecham Corporation.

For full biographical listings, see the Martindale-Hubbell Law Directory

*TYLER,** Smith Co.

COWLES & THOMPSON, A PROFESSIONAL CORPORATION (AV)

1103 First Place, P.O. Box 239, 75710-0239
Telephone: 903-593-7508
Fax: 903-593-4057
Email: TYLER@CTPCLAW.COM *URL:* http://www.cowlesthompson.com
Dallas, Texas Office: 901 Main Street, Suite 4000, 75202.
Telephone: 214-672-2000; Metro: 972-263-0005.
Fax: 214-672-2020.
McKinney, Texas Office: 307 S. McDonald St., 75069-5659.
Telephone: 972-542-5000; Metro: 972-562-2270.
Fax: 972-542-5040.

Stephen M. Spitzer

Mark A. Taylor
Alan W. Pigg

For full biographical listings, see the Martindale-Hubbell Law Directory

*WACO,** McLennan Co.

DUNNAM & DUNNAM, L.L.P. (AV)

4125 West Waco Drive, P.O. Box 8418, 76714-8418
Telephone: 254-753-6437
Fax: 254-753-7434

MEMBERS OF FIRM

W. V. Dunnam (1891-1974)
W. V. Dunnam, Jr.
Vance Dunnam
Vance Dunnam, Jr.
James R. Dunnam

ASSOCIATES

Alan Stucky
John Porter Mabry, Jr.
James Robert Angel

For full biographical listings, see the Martindale-Hubbell Law Directory

NAMAN, HOWELL, SMITH & LEE, A PROFESSIONAL CORPORATION (AV)

900 Washington, Suite 700, P.O. Box 1470, 76701
Telephone: 254-755-4100
FAX: 254-754-6331
Email: naman@namanhowell.com *URL:* http://www.namanhowell.com
Austin, Texas Office: 221 West Sixth Street, 1900 Bank One Tower.
Telephone: 512-479-0300.
FAX: 512-474-1901.
Fort Worth, Texas Office: 301 Sinclair Building, 512 Main Street.
Telephone: 817-348-0300.
Fax: 972-445-8804.
Temple, Texas Office: 6th Floor, First National Bank Building, P.O. Box 844.
Telephone: 254-778-1354.
FAX: 254-774-7254.

Wilford W. Naman (1887-1978)
Hilton E. Howell (1897-1968)
Hilton H. Howell (1928-1986)
P. Clark Aspy (Resident Member, Austin, Texas Office)
Roy L. Barrett
Charles K. Barrow
Frederick deB. Bostwick, III
Jim D. Bowmer (Resident Member, Temple, Texas Office)
Larry O. Brady
Richard E. Brophy, Jr.
Bob Burleson (Resident Member, Temple, Texas Office)
Jerry P. Campbell
George M. Cowden (Resident Member, Austin, Texas Office)
John P. Cunningham, Jr. (Resident Member, Temple, Texas Office)
Wesley J. Filer
Keith E. Gamel (Resident Member, Austin, Texas Office)
Kerry L. Haliburton
Alexander M. Haw
John T. Hawkins
David G. Henry
Paul H. Hubbard
Allen H. King (Resident Member, Austin, Texas Office)
J. Rodney Lee
Steve L. Moody (Resident Member, Temple, Texas Office)

(See Next Column)

NAMAN, HOWELL, SMITH & LEE A PROFESSIONAL CORPORATION—*Continued*

Jack M. Moore (Resident Member, Temple, Texas Office)
Nancy Napier Morrison
Tom Normand (Resident Member, Temple, Texas Office)
C. Patrick Nunley
John P. Palmer
Dan Pleitz
Michael L. Scanes
F. Ben Selman, Jr.
Cullen Smith
Stuart Smith
Thomas D. Swann
Enid A. Wade
Rex S. Whitaker
Albert Witcher

Nick R. Bray
Erica Littlejohn Burnette
Keith C. Cameron
Cara M. Chase
Dennis W. Donley, Jr. (Resident Member, Austin, Texas Office)
Matthew E. Haddock (Resident Member, Fort Worth, Texas Office)
Neal E. Pirkle
Laura R. Rayl (Resident Member, Temple, Texas Office)
James H. Routh, Jr.
Stephen W. Sather (Resident Member, Austin, Texas Office)
Scott M. Tschirhart

OF COUNSEL
David M. Sibley

Representative Clients: Compass Bank; Baylor University; Extraco Corporation; Texas Life Insurance Company; Methodist Children's Home; Hillcrest Baptist Medical Center; Texas Municipal League Intergovernmental Risk Pool; H. E. Butt Grocery Co.; Mid America Pipeline Company; KXXV-TV.

For full biographical listings, see the Martindale-Hubbell Law Directory

SHEEHY, LOVELACE & MAYFIELD, P.C. A PROFESSIONAL CORPORATION (AV)

510 North Valley Mills Drive, Suite 500, 76710
Telephone: 254-772-8022
Fax: 254-772-9297
Email: sheehy@slmpc.com *URL:* http://www.slmpc.com

John F. Sheehy (1898-1979)
J. Henry Lovelace (1926-1992)
John F. Sheehy, Jr.
Dan E. Mayfield
Henry W. Fielder
Philip E. McCleery
Gary K. Jordan
G. Maynard Green
Robert A. Watson
L. Hayes Fuller, III
J. David Dickson
Peter K. Rusek
Jeffrey R. Cox
John O'Herren
J. Patrick Atkins

Elisa Dillard Rainey
Erin B. Shank
Steven M. Burton
Scott V. Allen

OF COUNSEL
Michael J. Gulig

General Counsel for: American-Amicable Life Insurance Company of Texas; Community Bank & Trust; Waco Independent School District; McLennan Community College; Waco Board of REALTORS; Housing Authority of the City of Waco.
Local Counsel for: Kemper Insurance Group; United States Fidelity & Guaranty Co.; Fleetwood Enterprises, Inc.; USAA.

For full biographical listings, see the Martindale-Hubbell Law Directory

WESLACO, Hidalgo Co.

JONES, GALLIGAN, KEY & LOZANO, L.L.P. (AV)

Town Center Tower, 3300 W. Pike, Suite #300, P.O. Drawer 1247, 78599-1247
Telephone: 956-968-5402
Fax: 956-968-6089; 956-969-9402
Email: jones4@hiline.net

MEMBERS OF FIRM

Forrest L. Jones
Robert L. Galligan
Terry D. Key
Anita G. Lozano

Julie Crockett Graham
Mark W. Farris
Matthew Lee Jones
Lance Alan Kirby
Rebecca Gay Jones
Alan Troy Ozuna

For full biographical listings, see the Martindale-Hubbell Law Directory

*WICHITA FALLS,** Wichita Co.

GIBSON, HOTCHKISS, ROACH & DAVENPORT (AV)

807 8th Street, 8th Floor, 76301
Telephone: 940-322-7856
Fax: 940-322-1204
Email: ed@ghrdlaw.com *URL:* http://www.lawyers.com/ghrdlaw

MEMBERS OF FIRM

Frank Gibson
Charles A. Hotchkiss
Robert K. Roach
Erwin Davenport

(See Next Column)

ASSOCIATES

Sally E.O. Landback
Jon P. McGough
John D. Rosentreter

Representative Clients: American National Bank, Wichita Falls; First National Bank of Bowie; Wichita Falls PCA; Bennett Production Co.; Red River Authority of Texas; Burcamp Steel Co.

For full biographical listings, see the Martindale-Hubbell Law Directory

MORRISON & SHELTON, A PROFESSIONAL CORPORATION (AV)

City National Building, 807 Eighth Street, Suite 400, 76301-3316
Telephone: 940-322-2929
Telecopier: 940-322-7463

Lonny D. Morrison
Stephen R. Shelton

For full biographical listings, see the Martindale-Hubbell Law Directory

SHERRILL, CROSNOE & GOFF, A PROFESSIONAL CORPORATION (AV)

2301 Kell Boulevard, Suite 200, P.O. Box 97511, 76307-7511
Telephone: 940-322-3145
Facsimile: 940-322-8324

Joseph N. Sherrill Jr.
R. Caven Crosnoe
Robert W. Goff, Jr.
R. Ken Hines
Richard K. Bowersock

William Frank Smith

For full biographical listings, see the Martindale-Hubbell Law Directory

UTAH

CEDAR CITY, Iron Co.

HIGBEE, JENSEN & MACFARLANE, P.C. (AV)

250 South Main Street, P.O. Box 726, 84720
Telephone: 435-586-4404
Fax: 435-586-1002
Email: mtgraff@go.com *URL:* http://www.southernutahlaw.com

Thomas M. Higbee
James W. Jensen
R. Todd MacFarlane

Justin W. Wayment
Matthew T. Graff

Representative Clients: Carter Enterprises, Inc.; Cedar Land Title, Inc.; First Security Bank of Utah, N.A.; Iron County School District; New Castle Water Co.; Quality Ready Mix Concrete, Inc.; Security Title Co.; State Bank of Southern Utah; Southern Utah Title Company of Cedar City, Inc.; Elk Meadows Resort.

For full biographical listings, see the Martindale-Hubbell Law Directory

*OGDEN,** Weber Co.

VAN COTT, BAGLEY, CORNWALL & MCCARTHY, A PROFESSIONAL CORPORATION (AV)

Suite 900, 2404 Washington Boulevard, 84401
Telephone: 801-394-5783
Telecopier: 801-627-2522
Email: info@vancott.com *URL:* http://www.vancott.com
Salt Lake City, Utah Office: 50 South Main Street, Suite 1600.
Telephone: 801-532-3333.
Park City, Utah Office: 2200 Park Avenue, Suite C200-A
Telephone: 435-649-3889.

Timothy W. Blackburn (Resident)

Mara A. Brown
Sandra L. Crosland
L. Kelly Lowrey

For full biographical listings, see the Martindale-Hubbell Law Directory

PARK CITY, Summit Co.

PRINCE, YEATES & GELDZAHLER (AV)

614 Main Street, 84060
Telephone: 801-524-1000; 649-7440
Fax: 801-524-1099
Salt Lake City, Utah Office: City Centre I, Suite 900, 175 East 400 South.
Telephone: 801-524-1000.

Jon C. Heaton
John P. Ashton
J. Randall Call

Counsel for: Allstate Insurance; Deer Valley Club; Ingersoll-Rand Co.; Marker International/USA; Park City Mountain Resort; Labor Matters: Smith's Food and Drug Centers, Inc.

(See Next Column)

PRINCE, YATES & GELDZAHLER, *Park City—Continued*

For full biographical listings, see the Martindale-Hubbell Law Directory

VAN COTT, BAGLEY, CORNWALL & MCCARTHY, A PROFESSIONAL CORPORATION (AV)

2200 Park Avenue, Suite C200-A, P.O. Box 4611, 84060
Telephone: 435-649-3889
Telecopier: 435-649-3373
Email: info@vancott.com *URL:* http://www.vancott.com
Salt Lake City, Utah Office: 50 South Main Street, Suite 1600, P.O. Box 45340.
Telephone: 801-532-3333.
Telecopier: 801-534-0058.
Ogden, Utah Office: 2404 Washington Boulevard, Suite 900.
Telephone: 801-394-5783.

Thomas T. Billings

For full biographical listings, see the Martindale-Hubbell Law Directory

*PROVO,** Utah Co.

RAY, QUINNEY & NEBEKER, A PROFESSIONAL CORPORATION (AV)

92 North University Avenue, Suite 210, 84601-4420
Telephone: 801-342-2400
Fax: 801-375-8379
URL: http://www.rqn.com
Salt Lake City, Utah Office: 79 South Main Street, Suite 400, P.O. Box, 45385.
Telephone: 801-532-1500.
Fax: 801-532-7543.
Albuquerque, New Mexico Office: Suite 620, 40 First Plaza, N.W.
Telephone: 505-243-6665.
Fax: 505-764-9890.

Don B. Allen
Craig Carlile (Resident)
Larry G. Moore

For full biographical listings, see the Martindale-Hubbell Law Directory

*SALT LAKE CITY,** Salt Lake Co.

CALLISTER NEBEKER & MCCULLOUGH, A PROFESSIONAL CORPORATION (AV)

Gateway Tower East, Suite 900, 10 East South Temple, 84133
Telephone: 801-530-7300
Telecopier: 801-364-9127
Email: mjeaston@cnmlaw.com *URL:* http://www.cnmlaw.com

Louis H. Callister, Sr. (1904-1983)
Richard H. Nebeker (1924-1998)
Louis H. Callister
Gary R. Howe
Leland S. McCullough
Fred W. Finlinson
Dorothy C. Pleshe
John A. Beckstead
Jeffrey N. Clayton
James R. Holbrook
W. Waldan Lloyd
Jeffrey L. Shields
Richard T. Beard
Steven E. Tyler
Craig F. McCullough
George R. Sutton
Randall D Benson
George E. Harris, Jr.
T. Richard Davis
Paul H. Shaphren
Damon E. Coombs
Brian W. Burnett
Cass C. Butler
Lynda Cook
John H. Rees
Mark L. Callister
P. Bryan Fishburn
Martin R. Denney
Jan M. Bergeson
Laurie S. Hart
William H. Christensen
Glen F. Strong
James D. Gilson
Craig T. Jacobsen
John B. Lindsay
Douglas K. Cummings
Zachary T. Shields

Jeanene F. Patterson
David R. York
Lee S. McCullough, III
Jennifer Ward
Scott B. Finlinson

OF COUNSEL

Earl P. Staten
Lucy Knight Andre

Representative Clients: Zions First National Bank; Sears Roebuck & Company; Utah Automobile Dealers Association; Sinclair Oil Corporation (Little America); Keystone Communications; Central Valley Water Reclamation Facility Board; Citicorp; Intermountain Health Care, Inc.; Children's Miracle Network (Osmond Foundation); Nu Skin International, Inc.

For full biographical listings, see the Martindale-Hubbell Law Directory

CHAPMAN AND CUTLER (AV)

Suite 900, Key Bank Tower, 50 South Main Street, 84144
Telephone: 801-533-0066
Fax: 801-533-9595
Email: postmaster@chapman.com *URL:* http://chapman.com
Chicago, Illinois Office: 111 West Monroe Street.
Telephone: 312-845-3000.
Fax: 312-701-2361.

(See Next Column)

Phoenix, Arizona Office: Suite 1100, One Renaissance Square, 2 North Central Avenue.
Telephone: 602-256-4060.
Fax: 602-256-4099.

James C. Burr
Benjamin J. Juergens
Richard J. Scott
Rodney G. Wendt

For full biographical listings, see the Martindale-Hubbell Law Directory

HOLME ROBERTS & OWEN LLP (AV)

Suite 1100, 111 East Broadway, 84111
Telephone: 801-521-5800
Telecopier: 801-521-9639
Email: hro@hro.com *URL:* http://www.hro.com
Denver, Colorado Office: Suite 4100, 1700 Lincoln.
Telephone: 303-861-7000.
Telecopier: 303-866-0200.
Boulder, Colorado Office: Suite 400, 1401 Pearl Street.
Telephone: 303-444-5955.
Telecopier: 303-444-1063.
Colorado Springs, Colorado Office: Suite 1300, 90 South Cascade Avenue.
Telephone: 719-473-3800.
Telecopier: 719-633-1518.
London, England Office: Heathcoat House 3rd Floor, 20 Savile Row.
Telephone: 011-44-171-494-5600.
Telecopier: 011-44-171-287-9344.

PARTNERS OF FIRM

Blaine J. Benard
Mark K. Buchi
Elizabeth T. Dunning
George M. Haley, III
David H. Little
McKay Marsden (Managing Partner)
Greggory J. Savage
Robert L. Stolebarger
Gary R. Thorup

OF COUNSEL

Karen Campbell Jenson
Frank E. Moss

SPECIAL COUNSEL

Carolyn Cox

ASSOCIATES

Jennifer N. Byde
Pattie S. Christensen
Matthew N. Evans
E. Blaine Rawson
Kevin Joseph Simon
Paul M. Wilson
Steven P. Young

For full biographical listings, see the Martindale-Hubbell Law Directory

KIPP AND CHRISTIAN, P.C. (AV)

10 Exchange Place, Fourth Floor, 84111
Telephone: 801-521-3773
Fax: 801-359-9004
Email: kc1gsb@inquo.net

Carman E. Kipp
J. Anthony Eyre
Gregory J. Sanders
Heinz J. Mahler
Michael F. Skolnick
Shawn McGarry
Kirk G. Gibbs

Catherine E. Roberts

OF COUNSEL

D. Gary Christian
T. J. Tsakalos

LEGAL SUPPORT PERSONNEL

Randee Rouse LLoyd
M. Korinne Smith

Representative Clients: CNA Insurance Co; Coregis; Utah State Bar; Reliance Insurance Co.; National Farmers Union Insurance Co.; Utah Medical Insurance Association (UMIA); Utah Paper Box; Skivations, Condominium & Land Developers; Montgomery Elevators; Tim Dahle Imports/Nissan.

For full biographical listings, see the Martindale-Hubbell Law Directory

KIRTON & MCCONKIE, A PROFESSIONAL CORPORATION (AV)

1800 Eagle Gate Tower, 60 East South Temple, 84111
Telephone: 801-328-3600
Telecopier: 801-321-4893

Randy T. Austin
Lorin C. Barker
Anthony I. Bentley, Jr.
Rolf H. Berger
Berne S. Broadbent
Charles W. Dahlquist, II
Jerry W. Dearinger
Robert W. Edwards
James E. Ellsworth
Fred D. Essig
Wallace O. Felsted
Clark B. Fetzer
R. Bruce Findlay
David J. Hardy
Keith L. Hargrove
Read R. Hellewell
Dale E. Hulse
Lee Ford Hunter
Richard G. Johnson, Jr.
Von G. Keetch
Raeburn G. Kennard
Wilford W. Kirton, Jr.
Michael F. Krieger
Paul H. Matthews
Daniel S. McConkie
David M. McConkie
Oscar W. McConkie, III
Oscar W. McConkie, Jr.

(See Next Column)

KIRTON & MCCONKIE A PROFESSIONAL CORPORATION—*Continued*

Samuel D. McVey
William A. Meaders, Jr.
Thomas L. Monson
Denis Roy Morrill
Merrill F. Nelson
Richard R. Neslen
Eric C. Olson
R. Willis Orton
B. Lloyd Poelman
Robert S. Prince
Gregory M. Simonsen
Robert T. Smith (Not admitted in UT)
Myron L. Sorensen
Jon E. Waddoups
David M. Wahlquist
Thomas D. Walk
Stuart F. Weed
David A. Westerby
Todd E. Zenger

Randall C. Allen
Bryan H. Booth
Michael M. Conger
David S. Doty
Alexander Dushku
Scott C. Krieger
Melinda R. Porter
Matthew K. Richards
Dorany Rodriguez-Baltazar (Not admitted in UT)
Jeffrey Dean Stevens
Amy S. Thomas
Steven L. Whitehead

For full biographical listings, see the Martindale-Hubbell Law Directory

MANNING CURTIS BRADSHAW & BEDNAR, LLC (AV)

Third Floor, New House Building, 10 Exchange Place, 84111
Telephone: 801-363-5678
Facsimile: 801-364-5678
Email: bmanning@mc2b.com

MEMBERS OF FIRM

Brent V. Manning
LeGrand R. Curtis, Jr.
Alan C. Bradshaw
Steven C. Bednar

ASSOCIATES

Mary C. Gordon
Sean A. Monson
Candice Anderson
Jack M. Morgan, Jr.

OF COUNSEL

Thomas E. Kelly
Boyd J. Hawkins

For full biographical listings, see the Martindale-Hubbell Law Directory

MORGAN, MEYER & RICE, L.C. (AV)

Kearns Building, Eighth Floor, 136 South Main Street, 84101
Telephone: 801-531-7888
Telefax: 801-531-9732
Email: morgan@inquo.net

MEMBERS OF FIRM

Stephen G. Morgan
Cynthia K.C. Meyer
Mitchel T. Rice
Joseph E. Minnock
Jeffrey C. Miner

For full biographical listings, see the Martindale-Hubbell Law Directory

MOYLE & DRAPER, P.C. (AV)

City Centre I, Suite 900, 175 East 400 South, 84111
Telephone: 801-521-0250
Telecopier: 801-521-9015
Email: MOYLELAW@gatekeepers.com

Hardin A. Whitney
Joseph J. Palmer
O. Wood Moyle, III
Wayne G. Petty
Royal I. Hansen
Edward D. Spurgeon (Not admitted in UT)

OF COUNSEL

Prince, Yeates & Geldzahler, Salt Lake City, Utah

For full biographical listings, see the Martindale-Hubbell Law Directory

PARR WADDOUPS BROWN GEE & LOVELESS, A PROFESSIONAL CORPORATION (AV)

Suite 1300, 185 South State Street, 84111-1537
Telephone: 801-532-7840
Fax: 801-532-7750
URL: http://www.pwlaw.com

Clayton J. Parr
Clark Waddoups
Richard G. Brown
David E. Gee
Scott W. Loveless
Patricia W. Christensen
Robert B. Lochhead
Gary A. Dodge
Robert S. Clark
Kent H. Collins
Michael M. Later
Carolyn B. McHugh
Steven J. Christiansen
Victor A. Taylor
Ronald G. Russell
Roger D. Henriksen
Brian J. Romriell
Heidi E. C. Leithead
John M. Burke
Stephen E. W. Hale
Daniel A. Jensen
Brian G. Lloyd
Gregory M. Hess
Terry E. Welch
Jeffrey J. Hunt
Jonathan O. Hafen
Mark A. Wagner
Robert A. McConnell
Bentley J. Tolk
Stephen M. Sargent
D. Craig Parry
Bryan T. Allen

(See Next Column)

Eric D. Bawden
Dale T. Hansen
Brett J. Swanson
D. Kyle Sampson
Steven E. Hugie
Douglas C. Waddoups
R. Eric Smith

OF COUNSEL

Charles L. Maak
Bruce A. Maak
Brent M. Stevenson
Kent W. Larsen

For full biographical listings, see the Martindale-Hubbell Law Directory

PARSONS BEHLE & LATIMER, A PROFESSIONAL CORPORATION (AV)

One Utah Center, 201 South Main Street, Suite 1800, P.O. Box 45898, 84145-0898
Telephone: 801-532-1234
Telecopy: 801-536-6111
Email: pbl@pblutah.com *URL:* http://www.pblutah.com

James B. Lee
Gordon L. Roberts
F. Robert Reeder
J. Gordon Hansen
Lawrence E. Stevens
Daniel M. Allred
Dallin W. Jensen
W. Jeffery Fillmore
Kent W. Winterholler
Barbara K. Polich
Randy L. Dryer
Charles H. Thronson
David R. Bird
Raymond J. Etcheverry
Francis M. Wikstrom
David W. Tundermann
Chris Wangsgard
Neil Orloff
Val R. Antczak
Spencer E. Austin
Lee Kapaloski
Stephen Hull
John B. Wilson
Robert C. Hyde
Craig B. Terry
David A. Anderson
Gary E. Doctorman
Kent B. Alderman
Kent O. Roche
Patricia J. Winmill
Randy M. Grimshaw
Lawrence R. Barusch
Maxwell A. Miller
William D. Holyoak
Paul D. Veasy
Robert C. Delahunty
Stuart A. Fredman
R. Craig Johnson
Brent Christensen
Alan R. Andersen
William H. Wingo
Geoffrey W. Mangum
Daniel W. Hindert
Lois A. Baar
Jon C. Christiansen
Richard D. Clayton
Michael L. Larsen
Jonathan K. Butler
David G. Mangum
Derek Langton
Lucy B. Jenkins
Lorna Rogers Burgess
David L. Deisley
Mark E. Rinehart
Hal J. Pos
W. Mark Gavre
Scott R. Carpenter
George M. Flint, III
J. Michael Bailey
J. Thomas Beckett
M. Lindsay Ford
Jim Butler
Douglas R. Davis
Elizabeth S. Conley
Shawn C. Ferrin
Elizabeth S. Whitney
Craig D. Galli
Elisabeth R. Blattner
James E. Karkut
William J. Evans
C. Kevin Speirs
Michael J. Malmquist
Preston C. Regehr
David W. Zimmerman
H. Douglas Owens
Alan K. Flake Jr.
Lisa A. Kirschner
Michael A. Zody
Elizabeth Kitchens
David M. Bennion
Erik A. Christiansen
Matthew J. Harmer
William R. Gray
Catherine Agnoli
Jeffrey T. Sivertsen
William J. Stilling
Michael J. Tomko
R. David Grant
Margaret Niver McGann
Lisa A. Altman
James T. Blanch
Anne Whitehead Morgan
Edward B. Grandy
Laura S. Scott
Christina Jepson Schmutz
Kristine M. Edde
Kenneth E. Horton
Kerry L. Owens
Richard J. Angell
Ellen Kitzmiller
Michael J. Ziouras
Dianna M. Gibson
Sean D. Reyes
Anne E. Rice
Patrick C. Cannon
Jessica B. Woodhouse
Angie Nelson
Shane D. Hillman
Mark G. Sandbaken
Wesley L. Austin
Suzanne L. Larsen
Mark B. Durrant
Lara A. Reymann
Vicki M. Baldwin
Sandra K. Weeks
John E. Delaney, Jr.
Jared G. Parkinson (Not admitted in UT)
J. Martin Tate
Rodger M. Burge
E. Russell Vetter

OF COUNSEL

Keith E. Taylor
Roy G. Haslam
Mark A. Glick
Michael W. Devine

For full biographical listings, see the Martindale-Hubbell Law Directory

PARSONS, DAVIES, KINGHORN & PETERS, P.C. (AV)

185 South State Street, Suite 700, 84111
Telephone: 801-363-4300
Facsimile: 801-363-4378
Email: Attorneys@pdkplaw.com

(See Next Column)

PARSONS, DAVIES, KINGHORN & PETERS P.C., *Salt Lake City—Continued*

John M. Parsons
Glen E. Davies
Gerald H. Kinghorn
Bill Thomas Peters
Langdon T. Owen, Jr.
R. Kimball Mosier
John N. Brems
Ken P. Jones
David W. Scofield
Stuart W. Hinckley
John S. Bradley
Harold L. Reiser
Wm. Shane Topham
J. Scott Brown
Katherine S. Gregory
Paige Bigelow

For full biographical listings, see the Martindale-Hubbell Law Directory

PLANT, WALLACE, CHRISTENSEN & KANELL, A PROFESSIONAL CORPORATION (AV)

136 East South Temple Suite 1700, 84110-2970
Telephone: 801-363-7611
Fax: 801-531-9747
URL: http://www.pwcklaw.com

Robert R. Wallace
Scott W. Christensen
Terry M. Plant
Theodore E. Kanell
John N. Braithwaite
Mark J. Williams

Lisa Watts Baskin
Jason Max Kerr
Robert C. Olsen
Mollio L. McDonald

Representative Clients: CNA Insurance Group; Travelers Property Casualty Group; Kemper Insurance Group; Prudential Insurance; Transamerica Insurance Co.; Ranger Insurance; Guaranty National Insurance Co.; Utah Transit Authority; Western Surety.

For full biographical listings, see the Martindale-Hubbell Law Directory

PRINCE, YEATES & GELDZAHLER (AV)

City Centre I, Suite 900, 175 East 400 South, 84111
Telephone: 801-524-1000
Fax: 801-524-1099
Email: pyglaw.com
Park City, Utah Office: 614 Main Street.
Telephones: 801-524-1000; 649-7440.

MEMBERS OF FIRM

John K. Mangum (1930-1971)
F. Seaton Prince (1910-1991)
David S. Geldzahler (1932-1994)
Robert M. Yeates
Jon C. Heaton
John P. Ashton
Richard L. Blanck
D. Jay Gamble
J. Randall Call
John S. Chindlund
James A. Boevers
David K. Broadbent
Thomas J. Erbin
M. David Eckersley
Robert G. Wing
Carl W. Barton
Sally Buck McMinimee
Roger J. McConkie
Allen Sims
Michael N. Zundel
William G. Marsden
Richard H. Thornton

ASSOCIATES

Michael D. McCully
Thomas R. Barton
Cathleen Clark Gilbert
Glenn R. Bronson
Matthew T. Wirthlin

OF COUNSEL

Mark O. Van Wagoner
Moyle & Draper, Salt Lake City, Utah.

For full biographical listings, see the Martindale-Hubbell Law Directory

RAY, QUINNEY & NEBEKER, A PROFESSIONAL CORPORATION (AV)

79 South Main Street, Suite 400, P.O. Box 45385, 84145-0385
Telephone: 801-532-1500
Fax: 801-532-7543
Email: rqn@rqn.com *URL:* http://www.rqn.com
Provo, Utah Office: 92 North University Avenue, Suite 210, 84601-4420.
Telephone: 801-342-2400.
Fax: 801-375-8379.
Albuquerque, New Mexico Office: Suite 620, 40 First Plaza, N.W.
Telephone: 505-243-6665.
Fax: 505-764-9890.

Paul H. Ray (1893-1967)
A. H. Nebeker (1895-1980)
S. J. Quinney (1893-1983)
Alonzo W. Watson, Jr.
Stephen B. Nebeker
Herschel J. Saperstein
Don B. Allen
Clark P. Giles
Robert M. Graham
Narrvel E. Hall
Herbert C. Livsey
Paul S. Felt
D. Jay Curtis
Gerald T. Snow
Alan A. Enke
Weston L. Harris
Jonathan A. Dibble
Scott Hancock Clark
Steven H. Gunn
James S. Jardine
Allan T. Brinkerhoff
Janet Hugie Smith
Douglas Matsumori
Robert P. Hill
Floyd Andrew Jensen
David K. Lauritzen

(See Next Column)

Allen L. Orr
A. Robert Thorup
John P. Harrington
Larry G. Moore
Bruce L. Olson
John A. Adams
Douglas M. Monson
Craig Carlile (Resident at Provo)
Ellen J.D. Toscano
Kevin G. Glade
Lester K. Essig
Ira B. Rubinfeld
Steven T. Waterman
Gregory E. Lindley
Stephen C. Tingey
John R. Madsen
Keith A. Kelly
Michael W. Spence
Mark M. Bettilyon
Rick L. Rose
Rick B. Hoggard
Lisa A. Yerkovich
Brent D. Wride
Lorin E. Patterson
Michael E. Blue
Scott A. Hagen
Steven W. Call
Cameron M. Hancock
Elaine A. Monson
Katie A. Eccles
Calvin C. Curtis
Mark A. Cotter
R. Gary Winger
Robert O. Rice
Thomas A. Mecham
Arthur B. Berger

Kelly J. Applegate
Frederick R. Thaler, Jr.
John W. Mackay
Eric D. Barton
McKay M. Pearson
Mark W. Pugsley
Michael D. Creer
Joni J. Jones
Daniel W. Walker
Samuel C. Straight
Paul C. Burke
Elaina M. Maragakis
Joan M. Andrews
Melissa Herring Bailey
D. Zachary Wiseman
David O. Gibbon
Michael D. Mayfield

OF COUNSEL

M. John Ashton
Valerie A. Longmire

Representative Clients: First Security Bank, N.A.; Borden, Inc.; Salt Lake Organizing Committee for the Winter Olympic Games of 2002; Southern Pacific Transportation; Utah Power & Light Co.; Travelers Insurance Co.; U.S. West.

For full biographical listings, see the Martindale-Hubbell Law Directory

SNELL & WILMER L.L.P. (AV)

111 East Broadway, Suite 900, 84111-1004
Telephone: 801-237-1900
Fax: 801-237-1950
URL: http://www.swlaw.com
Phoenix, Arizona Office: One Arizona Center, 85004-2202.
Telephone: 602-382-6000.
Fax: 602-382-6070.
Tucson, Arizona Office: One South Church Avenue, Suite 1500, 85701-1612.
Telephone: 520-882-1200.
Fax: 520-884-1294.
Orange County Office: 1920 Main Street, Suite 1200, Irvine, California 92614-7230.
Telephone: 949-253-2700.
Fax: 949-955-2507.

MEMBERS OF FIRM

Greg R. Nielsen
David E. Leta
John R. Morris, Jr.
Mark O. Morris
Phillip Wm. Lear
Alan L. Sullivan
Bryon J. Benevento
Robert W. Payne
Denise A. Dragoo
Tracy H. Fowler
Bradley R. Cahoon
Matthew L. Lalli
P. Christian Anderson
Curtis J. Drake

OF COUNSEL

Carol Clawson

ASSOCIATES

Steven G. Black
Dawn M. Call
Christy L. Campbell
Brian D. Cunningham
Erik G. Davis
Daniel E. Garrison
Adrianne Goldsmith
Brent Hawkins (Not admitted in UT)
W. Brian Hulse
Michael R. Johnson
Chris D. Jones
Kari E. McCulloch
Hugh D. Odom (Not admitted in UT)
Scott C. Sandberg
Todd M. Shaughnessy
Julie A. Thomas
John G. Weston
David N. Wolf

Representative Clients: For list of Representative Clients, see end of biographical listings in the Martindale-Hubbell Law Directory.

For full biographical listings, see the Martindale-Hubbell Law Directory

SNOW, CHRISTENSEN & MARTINEAU, P.C. (AV)

Formerly Worsley, Snow & Christensen.
10 Exchange Place, Eleventh Floor, P.O. Box 45000, 84145
Telephone: 801-521-9000
Telecopier: 801-363-0400
URL: http://www.scmlaw.com

(See Next Column)

SNOW, CHRISTENSEN & MARTINEAU P.C.—*Continued*

Wood R. Worsley (1913-1975)
John H. Snow (1917-1980)
Reed L. Martineau
H. James Clegg
David W. Slagle
A. Dennis Norton
Allan L. Larson
John E. Gates
R. Brent Stephens
Kim R. Wilson
Michael R. Carlston
David G. Williams
Rex E. Madsen
Max D. Wheeler
Robert H. Henderson
Stephen J. Hill
David W. Slaughter
Stanley J. Preston
Shawn E. Draney
John R. Lund
Ryan E. Tibbitts
Rodney R. Parker
Richard A. Van Wagoner
Andrew M. Morse
Camille Neddo Johnson
Terence L. Rooney
Dennis V. Dahle
Korey D. Rasmussen
Harry H. Souvall
Linda Luinstra Baldwin

OF COUNSEL

Harold G. Christensen
Joseph Novak

David L. Pinkston
Julianne Blanch
Brian P. Miller
Judith D. Wolferts
Keith A. Call
Scott H. Martin
Heather S. White
Robert R. Harrison
Robert W. Thompson
Paxton Guymon
Kenneth L. Reich
Robert J. Shelby

Representative Clients: Novell, Inc.; General Electric Co.; American Home Products; Columbia/HCA Healthcare Corp.; Royal Insurance Co.; Federal Express; Attorneys Liability Assurance Society (ALAS).

For full biographical listings, see the Martindale-Hubbell Law Directory

STRONG & HANNI, A PROFESSIONAL CORPORATION (AV)

Sixth Floor Boston Building, 9 Exchange Place, 84111
Telephone: 801-532-7080
Fax: 801-596-1508
Email: pfishler@strongandhanni.com

Gordon R. Strong (1909-1969)
Glenn C. Hanni
Henry E. Heath
Philip R. Fishler
Roger H. Bullock
R. Scott Williams
Dennis M. Astill (Managing Partner)
Stuart H. Schultz
Paul M. Belnap
Stephen J. Trayner
Joseph J. Joyce
Bradley Wm. Bowen
Robert L. Janicki
Elizabeth L. Willey
H. Burt Ringwood
Peter H. Christensen
David R. Nielson

Kevin D. Swenson
Catherine M. Larson
Kristin Van Orman
Darren K. Nelson
Peter H. Barlow
Steven T. Densley
Jennifer C. Polley-Abramson
Shawn T. Welch

OF COUNSEL

Robert A. Burton

Representative Clients: State Farm Mutual Automobile Insurance Co.; Standard Accident Insurance Co.; United Services Automobile Assn.; Western Casualty & Surety Co.; Government Employees Insurance Co.; Guaranty Mutual Life Co.

For full biographical listings, see the Martindale-Hubbell Law Directory

VAN COTT, BAGLEY, CORNWALL & MCCARTHY, A PROFESSIONAL CORPORATION (AV)

50 South Main Street, Suite 1600, P.O. Box 45340, 84145-0340
Telephone: 801-532-3333
Telecopier: 801-534-0058
Email: info@vancott.com *URL:* http://www.vancott.com
Ogden, Utah Office: 2404 Washington Boulevard, Suite 900.
Telephone: 801-394-5783.
Park City, Utah Office: 2200 Park Avenue, Suite C200-A.
Telephone: 435-649-3889.

Robert M. Anderson (President of Firm)
Thomas T. Billings
Timothy W. Blackburn (Resident, Ogden, Utah Office)
Thomas W. Clawson
Rand L. Cook
David A. Greenwood
Jeremy M. Hoffman
H. Michael Keller
Matthew F. McNulty, III
Arthur B. Ralph
David E. Sloan
David J. Smith
Gerald H. Suniville
Stephen D. Swindle
Clark K. Taylor (On Leave)
Gregory P. Williams
Kenneth W. Yeates
John L. Young

Jennifer K. Anderson
Mara A. Brown
Stephen K. Christiansen
Kim S Colton
Sandra L. Crosland
Tacy A. Hartman
Kevin L. Jones
L. Kelly Lowrey
Inga Regenass
Kevin M. Sheff
Stephen R. Sloan
Bradley M. Strassberg

(See Next Column)

Evan S. Strassberg
Justin Toth (Not admitted in UT)
Mary E. Westby (On Leave)

OF COUNSEL

Clifford L. Ashton
William G. Fowler
Cecil R. Hedger
David E. Salisbury
Franklin N. Smith
M. Scott Woodland

For full biographical listings, see the Martindale-Hubbell Law Directory

WINDER & HASLAM, P.C. (AV)

Suite 4000, 175 West 200 South, P.O. Box 2668, 84110-2668
Telephone: 801-322-2222
Telecopier: 801-532-3706
Email: WINHAS@AROS.NET *URL:* http://www.winhas.com

Donald J. Winder
Robert D. Tingey
John W. Holt

Stewart R. Knight
Gerry B. Holman
Trystan B. Smith

OF COUNSEL

Dennis V. Haslam
William W. Downes, Jr.
Robert K. Rothfeder

Representative Clients: The Utah Jazz (NBA); The Delta Center; Larry H. Miller Group of Automotive Dealerships; Budget Rent-A-Car; Dollar Rent-A-Car; Dick Simon Trucking; Farmers Insurance Group; United Concerts; Simmons Media Group, Inc.; KJZZ TV (Channel 14).

For full biographical listings, see the Martindale-Hubbell Law Directory

VERMONT

*BURLINGTON,** Chittenden Co.

BURAK ANDERSON & MELLONI, PLC (AV)

Gateway Square, 30 Main Street, P.O. Box 787, 05402-0787
Telephone: 802-862-0500
Telecopier: 802-862-8176
Email: attorney@vtlaw1.com *URL:* http://www.vtlaw1.com

MEMBERS OF FIRM

Michael L. Burak
Jon Anderson
Thomas R. Melloni
Brian J. Sullivan
Michael B. Rosenberg

ASSOCIATES

Daniel A. Seff
Lori J. Lewis
Jeremy I. Farkas

OF COUNSEL

Vaughn A. Carney (Not admitted in VT)

LEGAL SUPPORT PERSONNEL

Stephanie Dunbar (Legal Assistant)

For full biographical listings, see the Martindale-Hubbell Law Directory

DINSE, KNAPP & MCANDREW, P.C. (AV)

209 Battery Street, P.O. Box 988, 05402-0988
Telephone: 802-864-5751
Fax: 802-862-6409
URL: http://www.dinse.com

COUNSEL

John M. Dinse

MEMBERS OF FIRM

Spencer R. Knapp
Karen McAndrew
Barbara E. Cory
Robert R. McKearin
James W. Spink
John D. Monahan, Jr.
Emily R. Morrow
Ritchie E. Berger
Austin D. Hart
Samuel Hoar, Jr.
Steven L. Knudson
Sandra A. Strempel
Molly K. Lebowitz
Pietro J. Lynn
Philip C. Woodward
Jeffrey J. Nolan
Mark A. Langan

ASSOCIATES

Douglas D. Le Brun
Shapleigh Smith, Jr.
Craig S. Nolan
Elizabeth H. Miller
Heather E. Thomas

Representative Clients: Chittenden Trust Co.; Vermont Transit Co., Inc.; Sears, Roebuck & Co.; Ford Motor Co.; Inc.; Middlebury College; Vt. Teddy Bear Co., Inc.; Key Bank.

For full biographical listings, see the Martindale-Hubbell Law Directory

Burlington—Continued

GRAVEL AND SHEA, A PROFESSIONAL CORPORATION (AV)

Corporate Plaza, 76 St. Paul Street, P.O. Box 369, 05402-0369
Telephone: 802-658-0220
Fax: 802-658-1456

Stephen R. Crampton
Stewart H. McConaughy
Robert B. Hemley
William G. Post, Jr.
Craig Weatherly
James E. Knapp
John R. Ponsetto
Dennis R. Pearson
Peter S. Erly
Robert F. O'Neill
Margaret L. Montgomery
Stephen P. Magowan
Heather Briggs

Erik B. FitzPatrick
Leigh Polk Cole
Robert H. Rushford
Johan W. E. Maitland
Michelle N. Farkas
(Not admitted in VT)

OF COUNSEL

Clarke A. Gravel
Charles T. Shea

SPECIAL COUNSEL

Norman Williams
Lucy T. Brown

For full biographical listings, see the Martindale-Hubbell Law Directory

HOFF, CURTIS, PACHT, CASSIDY & FRAME, P.C. (AV)

100 Main Street, P.O. Box 1124, 05402-1124
Telephone: 802-864-4531; 802-864-6400
Fax: 802-860-1565
Email: mail@hoffcurtis.com *URL:* http://www.hoffcurtis.com
Portland, Maine Office: 75 Pearl Street, P.O. Box 7855, 04112.
Telephone: 207-871-5750.

Richard T. Cassidy
David W. Curtis (1938-1999)
Julie A. Frame
Philip H. Hoff
Robert W. Katims
John L. Pacht
Thomas H. Somers

Michael E. Cassidy
Jennifer E. Nelson
Kerin E. Stackpole

For full biographical listings, see the Martindale-Hubbell Law Directory

MILLER, EGGLESTON & CRAMER, LTD. (AV)

150 South Champlain Street, P.O. Box 1489, 05402-1489
Telephone: 802-864-0880
Telecopier: 802-864-0328

Martin K. Miller
Jon R. Eggleston
Anne E. Cramer
Kathleen M. Boe
Mark A. Saunders
Victoria J. Brown
Scot L. Kline
Peter F. Young

OF COUNSEL

Patricia L. Rickard
Neil Wheelwright

For full biographical listings, see the Martindale-Hubbell Law Directory

ESSEX JUNCTION, Chittenden Co.

KOLVOORD, OVERTON AND WILSON (AV)

3 Main Street, 05452
Telephone: 802-878-3346
FAX: 802-879-0964
Email: kowlaw@banet.com

Alan D. Overton
Gregg H. Wilson
Daniel L. Overton

ASSOCIATES

Herbert J. Downing
Carol N. Angus

OF COUNSEL

Philip A. Kolvoord

Representative Clients: The Howard Bank; Chittenden Bank; New England Credit Union; S.T. Griswold & Company, Inc. (construction); Engineers Construction, Inc.; Champlain Water District (regional water district); Champlain Valley Exposition, Inc. (State Fair); Town of Essex School District; Town of Jericho; Town of Milton.

*MONTPELIER,** Washington Co.

THERIAULT & JOSLIN, P.C. (AV)

141 Main Street, P.O. Box 249, 05601-0249
Telephone: 802-223-2381
Fax: 802-223-1461
Email: LAWYERS@TJOSLIN.COM

William N. Theriault (1877-1961)
Peter B. Joslin
Fletcher Brian (Ted) Joslin

John Davis Buckley
Barbara R. Blackman

(See Next Column)

OF COUNSEL

Fletcher B. Joslin
Jeffry W. White

Representative Clients: Allstate Insurance Co.; American International Group; Hartford Insurance Group; St. Paul Insurance Cos.; Nationwide Insurance Cos.; Commercial Union Insurance Cos.; Prudential Insurance Cos.; PHICO Insurance Co.; Zurich Insurance Group.

For full biographical listings, see the Martindale-Hubbell Law Directory

*RUTLAND,** Rutland Co.

CLEARY SHAHI ASSOCIATES, A PROFESSIONAL CORPORATION (AV)

110 Merchants Row, P.O. Box 6740, 05702-6740
Telephone: 802-775-8800
Telefax: 802-775-8809
URL: http://www.lawyers.com/vermonttriallaw

David L. Cleary
Kaveh S. Shahi

Thomas P. Aicher
Karen S. Heald
John R. Dean

For full biographical listings, see the Martindale-Hubbell Law Directory

HULL, WEBBER & REIS, LLP (AV)

(Formerly Dick, Hackel & Hull)
60 North Main Street, P.O. Box 890, 05702-0890
Telephone: 802-775-2361
Fax: 802-775-0739
Email: WbbrReis@aol.com *URL:* http://www.webbereis.com

Donald H. Hackel (1925-1985)
John B. Webber
Robert K. Reis
John C. Holler
Frank P. Urso
Christopher Reis

ASSOCIATE

Michael C. Conroy

OF COUNSEL

Richard A. Hull (1933-1999)
Steven D. Vogl

Representative Clients: Aetna Insurance Co.; Great American Insurance Cos.

For full biographical listings, see the Martindale-Hubbell Law Directory

MILLER FAIGNANT & BEHRENS, P.C. (AV)

36 Merchants Row, P.O. Box 6688, 05702-6688
Telephone: 802-775-2521
Fax: 802-775-8274
Email: lhblaw@aol.com *URL:* http://www.lawyers.com/millerfaignantbehrenslaw

Lawrence Miller
John Paul Faignant
Lawrence H. Behrens

OF COUNSEL

Lisa L. Chalidze

LEGAL SUPPORT PERSONNEL

Marie Peck Fabian
Kim J. Miller

Representative Clients: Travelers Insurance Co.; Government Employees Insurance Co.; Utica Mutual Insurance Co.; Universal Underwriters Insurance Co.; Zurich American Acadia Insurance.
References: Travelers Insurance Co.; Universal Underwriters Insurance Co.

For full biographical listings, see the Martindale-Hubbell Law Directory

RYAN SMITH & CARBINE, LTD. (AV)

Mead Building, 98 Merchants Row, P.O. Box 310, 05702-0310
Telephone: (802)-786-1000
Fax: (802)-786-1100
Email: rsc@rsclaw.com

Charles F. Ryan (1901-1977)
R. Joseph O'Rourke
John J. Zawistoski
Thomas M. Dowling
E. Patrick Burke, Jr.
Allan R. Keyes
Harry R. Ryan, III
Glenn S. Morgan
Harold P. Berger
James B. Anderson
William A. O'Rourke, III
Elizabeth A. Glynn
Andrew H. Maass
John A. Serafino

OF COUNSEL

R. Clarke Smith
Leonard F. Wing, Jr.

Marion T. Ferguson
Ellen W. Burgess
John William Valente
Tammy Besaw Denton
Mark F. Werle
Matthew D. Gilmond
Phillip Bixby
Afi Ahmadi
Danielle E. Finck

Representative Clients: Casella Waste Management, Inc.; Central Vermont Public Service Corp.; CNA; First Vermont Bank; Killington Ltd.; Rutland Regional Medical Center; STO Industries; St. Paul Insurance Co.; Zurich American Ins. Group.

(See Next Column)

RYAN SMITH & CARBINE LTD.—*Continued*

For full biographical listings, see the Martindale-Hubbell Law Directory

SPRINGFIELD, Windsor Co.

BOYLAN & RICHARDS, P.C. (AV)

85 Main Street, P.O. Box 200, 05156-0200
Telephone: 802-885-5131
FAX: 802-885-4699
Email: triallaw@sover.net *URL:* http://www.lawyers.com/boylan-richards

John J. Boylan, III — Douglas Richards

Kimberly L. Carboneau

Representative Clients: Allstate Insurance Co.; Browning-Ferris Industries; Caliber Systems, Inc.; Casco Indemnity Co.; Commerce Insurance Co.; Commercial Union York Insurance Companies; Cressler Trucking Co.; Ford Motor Co.; General Motors Corp.; Georgia-Pacific Corp.

For full biographical listings, see the Martindale-Hubbell Law Directory

VIRGINIA

*ABINGDON,** Washington Co.

THE TATE LAW FIRM (AV)

Abingdon Professional Centre, 110 Abingdon Place, 24211
Telephone: 540-628-5185
Telecopier: 540-628-5045
Email: lynntate@naxs.com *URL:* http://www.tatelaw.com

Mary Lynn Tate

OF COUNSEL

Olen G. Haynes (Not admitted in VA)

LEGAL SUPPORT PERSONNEL

Rebecca A. Wyatt — Teresa L. Brown

For full biographical listings, see the Martindale-Hubbell Law Directory

ALEXANDRIA, (Independent City)

DIMURO, GINSBERG & MOOK, P.C. (AV)

908 King Street, Suite 200, 22314
Telephone: 703-684-4333
Telecopier: 703-548-3181
Email: dimuro@dimuro.com *URL:* http://www.dimuro.com

Bernard J. DiMuro
Nina J. Ginsberg
Jonathan R. Mook
Michael E. Barnsback
David J. Duffett

OF COUNSEL

Michael S. Lieberman

Representative Clients: Sun Healthcare Group; Ridgways, Inc.; Medtronic, Inc.; Prince William County Police; OKi Telecom.

For full biographical listings, see the Martindale-Hubbell Law Directory

LAND, CLARK, CARROLL, MENDELSON & BLAIR, P.C. (AV)

112 South Alfred Street, Suite 300, P.O. Box 19888, 22320-0888
Telephone: 703-836-1000
Fax: 703-549-3335
Email: LCCM@EROLS.COM

H. Carter Land, III
James C. Clark
F. Andrew Carroll, III
Richard S. Mendelson
Duncan Wardman Blair

Representative Clients: Bob Duncan Real Estate; Ticor Title Insurance Company; Burke and Herbert Bank and Trust Company; Crestar Bank; Don Beyer Motors; Chicago Title Insurance Co.; The Protestant Episcopal Seminary in Virginia; Pulte Home Corporation; Abramson Properties.
Reference: Burke and Herbert Bank and Trust Co.

For full biographical listings, see the Martindale-Hubbell Law Directory

REDMON, BOYKIN & BRASWELL, L.L.P. (AV)

Suite 301, 510 King Street, 22314
Telephone: 703-684-2000
Fax: 703-684-5109
Email: gredmon@redmonboykin.com *URL:* http://www.redmonboykin.com

Gant Redmon
Jerry William Boykin
John M. Braswell
W. Michael Holm
John F. Rodgers
Robert M. Gants

ASSOCIATES

E. Andrew Burcher — Kevin A. Ruby

(See Next Column)

OF COUNSEL

Roy D. Snyder, Jr. — Robert L. Calhoun

For full biographical listings, see the Martindale-Hubbell Law Directory

*BEDFORD,** Bedford Co.

LAW OFFICES GARRETT & GARRETT A PROFESSIONAL CORPORATION (AV)

116 East Main Street, P.O. Box 534, 24523
Telephone: 540-586-1034
FAX: 540-586-0545

Harry W. Garrett, Jr. — Carter B. Garrett

Representative Clients: Bedford Federal Savings Bank; Morgan Development Corp.; Piedmont Label Co., Inc.; Scott & Bond, Inc.; Roanoke Farm Credit, ACA.
Approved Attorneys for: Lawyers Title Insurance Co.; Southern Title Insurance Co.
References: Bedford Federal Savings Bank; First Union Bank.

For full biographical listings, see the Martindale-Hubbell Law Directory

BIG STONE GAP, Wise Co.

KEULING-STOUT, P.C. (AV)

125 Clinton Avenue East, P.O. Box 400, 24219
Telephone: 540-523-1676
Fax: 540-523-1608

Henry S. Keuling-Stout

For full biographical listings, see the Martindale-Hubbell Law Directory

BLACKSBURG, Montgomery Co.

GILMER, SADLER, INGRAM, SUTHERLAND & HUTTON (AV)

201 West Roanoke Street, P.O. Box 908, 24063-0908
Telephone: 540-552-1061; 888-887-9997
Telecopier: 540-552-8227
Pulaski, Virginia Office: Midtown Professional Building, 65 East Main Street, P.O. Box 878.
Telephone: 540-980-1360; 540-639-0027; 800-330-3344.
Telecopier: 540-980-5264.

MEMBERS OF FIRM

James L. Hutton
Howard C. Gilmer, Jr. (1906-1975)
Roby K. Sutherland (1909-1975)
Philip M. Sadler (1915-1994)
Robert J. Ingram
Thomas J. McCarthy, Jr.
John J. Gill
Gary C. Hancock
Jackson M. Bruce
Michael J. Barbour
Deborah Wood Dobbins
Timothy Edmond Kirtner
Robin J. Kegley

Representative Clients: Appalachian Power Co.; Magnox, Inc.; Norfolk Southern Railway Co.; Pulaski Furniture Corp.; NationsBank; Charles Lunsford Sons & Associates; First National Bank; Corning Glass Works.

For full biographical listings, see the Martindale-Hubbell Law Directory

*CHARLOTTESVILLE,** Charlottesville City Co.

MCGUIRE, WOODS, BATTLE & BOOTHE LLP (AV)

Court Square Building, 310 Fourth Street, N.E., Suite 300, P.O. Box 1288, 22902-1288
Telephone: 804-977-2500
Fax: 804-980-2222
Email: info@mwbb.com *URL:* http://www.mwbb.com
Atlanta, Georgia Office: 285 Peachtree Center Avenue, N.E., Suite 2200, Marquis Tower Two, 30303-1234.
Telephone: 404-443-5500.
Fax: 404-443-5599.
Baltimore, Maryland Office: 7 Saint Paul Street, Suite 1000, 21202-1671.
Telephone: 410-659-4400.
Fax: 410-659-4599.
Charlotte, North Carolina Offices: Bank of America Plaza, 101 South Tryon Street, 28280.
Telephone: 704-373-8999.
Fax: 704-373-8990 and Bank of America Corporate Center, Suite 2900, 100 North Tryon Street, 28202.
Telephone: 704-373-8999.
Fax: 704-373-8935.
Chicago, Illinois Office: R.R. Donnelly Building, 77 West Wacker Drive, Suite 4500, 60601-1635.
Telephone: 312-849-3699.
Fax: 312-849-3690.
Jacksonville, Florida Office: 50 North Laura Street, 32202-3635.
Telephone: 904-798-3200.
Fax: 904-798-3207.
McLean, (Tysons Corner) Virginia Office: 1750 Tysons Boulevard, Suite 1800, 22102-3892.
Telephone: 703-712-5000.
Fax: 703-712-5050.

(See Next Column)

McGuire, Woods, Battle & Boothe LLP, *Charlottesville—Continued*

Norfolk, Virginia Office: World Trade Center, 101 West Main Street, Suite 9000, 23510-1655.
Telephone: 757-640-3700.
Fax: 757-640-3701.
Richmond, Virginia Office: One James Center, 901 East Cary Street, 23219-4030.
Telephone: 804-775-1000.
Fax: 804-775-1061.
Washington, D.C. Office: Washington Square, 1050 Connecticut Avenue, N.W., Suite 1200, 20036-5317.
Telephone: 202-857-1700.
Fax: 202-857-1737.
Almaty, Republic of Kazakhstan Office: Park Palace, 41 Kazibek Bi Street, 2nd Floor, 480100.
Telephone: 7-3272-608-300.
Fax: 7-3272-608-305.
Brussels, Belgium Office: 250 Avenue Louise, Bte. 64, 1050.
Telephone: 32-2-629-42-11.
Fax: 32-2-629-42-22.
Moscow, Russia Office: Paveltskaya Square, 1 Valovaya Street, 7th Floor, 13054.
Telephone: 7-502-937-0774.
Fax: 7-502-937-0776.

RESIDENT MEMBERS

Lucius H. Bracey, Jr.
Dennis W. Good, Jr.
Kurt J. Krueger
Gary C. McGee
Leigh B. Middleditch, Jr.
D. French Slaughter III
Kristen E. Smith
Robert E. Stroud
R. Craig Wood

RETIRED PARTNER

Fred S. Landess

RESIDENT ASSOCIATES

Tracey Goyette Cote
John E. Davidson
Michael E. Derdeyn
J. Brian Jackson
James M. Johnson
John H. Kitzmann (Not admitted in VA)
Hugh M. Leavell
Valerie Wagner Long
Nancy A. McLaughlin
Christy R. Mistr
Calvin S. Spencer, Jr.
Kerri B. Taylor
Joseph W. Wright III

For full biographical listings, see the Martindale-Hubbell Law Directory

Taylor, Zunka, Milnor & Carter, Ltd. (AV)

414 Park Street, P.O. Box 1567, 22902
Telephone: 804-977-0191
FAX: 804-977-0198

John W. Zunka
Richard H. Milnor
Richard E. Carter

H. Robert Yates, III
Alvaro A. Inigo

Representative Clients: State Farm Insurance Companies; Allstate Insurance Co.; The Travelers Insurance Companies; The Harleysville Insurance Companies; Kemper Insurance Companies; Selective Insurance; Blue Cross and Blue Shield of Virginia; Crestar Bank.

For full biographical listings, see the Martindale-Hubbell Law Directory

Tremblay & Smith, LLP (AV)

105-109 East High Street, P.O. Box 1585, 22902
Telephone: 804-977-4455
Fax: 804-979-1221
Email: tslaw@esinet.net

MEMBERS OF FIRM

John K. Taggart, III
Melvin E. Gibson, Jr.
Thomas E. Albro
Christine Thomson
Patricia D. McGraw

ASSOCIATES

R. Lee Livingston
Heidi Parker
Rachel L. Rust
Christopher J. Robinette
Peter J. Caramanis

Representative Clients: Sieg Distributing Co. (Anheuser-Busch Distributors); Kloeckner Pentaplast of America, Inc.; Virginia Broadcasting Corp.; Farmington Country Club; Management Services Corporation of Charlottesville; InterTrans Carrier Co.; Wade Apartments; 360° Communications.

For full biographical listings, see the Martindale-Hubbell Law Directory

CHESAPEAKE, (Independent City)

Kaufman & Canoles, A Professional Corporation (AV)

524 Johnstown Road, 23322
Telephone: 757-547-7177
Fax: 757-436-9120
Email: kaufc@kaufcan.com *URL:* http://www.kaufmanandcanoles.com
Norfolk, Virginia Office: One Commercial Place, P.O. Box 3037, 23514-3037.
Telephone: 757-624-3000.

(See Next Column)

Virginia Beach, Virginia Office: 700 Pavilion Center, P.O. Box 626, 23451.
Telephone: 757-491-4000.
Newport News, Virginia Office: Suite 408, 11817 Canon Boulevard, 23606.
Telephone: 757-873-6300.
Williamsburg, Virginia Office: 1200 Old Colony Lane, 23187.
Telephone: 757-229-7322

RESIDENT PERSONNEL

J. Randy Forbes

Philip J. Infantino, III

Representative Clients: Bank of Tidewater; Bergeys Dairy Farm, Inc.; C & V Utilities, Inc.; Chesapeake General Hospital; Christian Broadcasting Network; City of Chesapeake School System; Crestar Bank; Greenbrier Farms; Higgerson-Buchanan, Inc.

For full biographical listings, see the Martindale-Hubbell Law Directory

DANVILLE, (Independent City)

Clement & Wheatley, A Professional Corporation (AV)

549 Main Street, P.O. Box 8200, 24543-8200
Telephone: 804-793-8200
Fax: 804-792-8200
Email: CWLAW@GAMEWOOD.NET

Rutledge C. Clement (1906-1979)
C. Stuart Wheatley (1905-1982)
Glenn W. Pulley
Whittington W. Clement
R. Lee Yancey
Patrick H. Musick
Luis A. Abreu
Harry P. Sakellaris
Ronald L. Lackey
Mark B. Holland

Debra Lynn Creasy
Michael C. Guanzon
Edward F. Hodges, Jr
M. Brent Saunders

OF COUNSEL

Joseph M. Winston, Jr.

General Counsel for: Danville Redevelopment & Housing Authority; Danville Regional Medical Center; Piedmont Broadcasting Corp.; Danville Area Chamber of Commerce; Danville Development Council; NationsBank, N.A. (Danville).
Representative Clients: American National Bank & Trust Co.; Corning, Inc.; Goodyear Tire & Rubber Co.; Dan River, Inc.

For full biographical listings, see the Martindale-Hubbell Law Directory

Gardner, Barrow & Sharpe, A Professional Corporation (AV)

494 Piney Forest Road, 25441
Telephone: 804-799-1111
Fax: 804-799-1422
Martinsville, Virginia Office: First Citizens Bank Building, 4th Floor, Church and Clay Streets, 24112.
Telephone: 540-638-2455.
Fax: 540-638-2458.

Philip G. Gardner (Resident)

For full biographical listings, see the Martindale-Hubbell Law Directory

Law Offices of Michael P. Regan, P.C. (AV)

703 Patton Street, 24541
Telephone: 804-793-9670; 793-1622
Telecopier: 804-793-6647
Email: MPRlaw@gamewood.net *URL:* http://www.lawyers.com/reganlaw

Michael P. Regan

LEGAL SUPPORT PERSONNEL

Fred N. Fitzgerald (Tax and Financial Assistant)
Janet E. Hylton (Legal Assistant)

References: First Citizens Bank; Bank of America; Virginia Bank & Trust.

For full biographical listings, see the Martindale-Hubbell Law Directory

*EASTVILLE,** Northampton Co.

Tankard and Gordon (AV)

Court Green, P.O. Box 5, 23347-0005
Telephone: 757-678-5117
Fax: 757-678-7664
Email: lawyer@esva.net

MEMBERS OF FIRM

Baxley T. Tankard
Croxton Gordon

Representative Clients: Chesapeake Bay Bridge and Tunnel District; A & N Electric Cooperative; First Virginia Bank-Tidewater, Exmore, Virginia.
Approved Attorneys for: Lawyers Title Insurance Corp.; Ticor Title Insurance Co.

For full biographical listings, see the Martindale-Hubbell Law Directory

*EMPORIA,** Greensville Co.

OUTTEN, BARRETT, BURR & SHARRETT, P.C. (AV)

314 South Main Street, P.O. Box 232, 23847-2028
Telephone: 804-634-2167
Fax: 804-634-3798
Email: www.obbs.@3rdoor.com *URL:* http://www.3rddoor.com/~obbs/
Lawrenceville, Virginia Office: 214 Court Street.
Telephone: 804-848-3184.
Fax: 804-848-0116. E-Mail: JWHITEY@JNENT.COM.

W. Curtis Outten, Jr. (Resident, Lawrenceville Office)
C. Butler Barrett
Theodore J. Burr, Jr.
W. Allan Sharrett
Joseph E. Whitby, Jr. (Resident, Lawrenceville Office)

Local Condemnation Attorneys for: Virginia Department of Highways and Transportation.
Representative Clients: The Town of Lawrenceville; City of Emporia; Town of Courtland; Georgia Pacific Corp.; Union Camp Corp.; CSX Corp.; Bank of America.

For full biographical listings, see the Martindale-Hubbell Law Directory

*FAIRFAX,** (Ind. City; Seat of Fairfax Co.)

ALLRED, BACON, HALFHILL, LANDAU & YOUNG, PC (AV)

11350 Random Hills Road, Suite 700, 22030
Telephone: 703-352-1300; 1-800-598-2965
Fax: 703-352-1301
Email: Admin@Sbhly.com *URL:* http://www.ABHLY.com

James C. Allred
James T. Bacon
Stephen D. Halfhill
Warner F. Young, III
Douglas K. W. Landau
Randolph H. Perry

Christopher B. Holley
Bruce A. Levine
Robert F. Zaniel

For full biographical listings, see the Martindale-Hubbell Law Directory

BRAULT, PALMER, GROVE, ZIMMERMAN, WHITE & STEINHILBER (AV)

10533 Main Street, P.O. Box 1010, 22030-1010
Telephone: 703-273-6400
Fax: 703-273-3514
Manassas, Virginia Office: 8567-D Sudley Road, 20110. Mailing Address: P.O. Box 534, Manassas, VA 20108.
Telephone: 703-369-7500; 631-9727.
Fax: 703-369-2285.

MEMBERS OF FIRM

Adelard L. Brault (Emeritus)
Thomas C. Palmer, Jr. (Resident, Manassas Office)
Edward H. Grove, III
Michael L. Zimmerman
Bruce D. White
August W. Steinhilber, III

ASSOCIATES

Jack A. Robbins, Jr. (Resident, Manassas Office)
C. Mark Whittington
Craig J. Franco
Bobby Puri (Resident, Manassas Office)

Representative Clients: Alamo Rent-A-Car, Inc.; CNA Insurance Companies; E.I. du Pont de Nemours and Company; Erie Insurance Group; Fidelity & Deposit Company of Maryland; Hanover Insurance Company; Harleysville Insurance Companies; Home Insurance Company; J.B. Hunt Transport, Inc.; Kemper Insurance Group.

For full biographical listings, see the Martindale-Hubbell Law Directory

JOHN A. KEATS (AV)

10511 Judicial Drive, Suite 102, 22030
Telephone: 703-273-3190
Fax: 703-383-1241
(Also of Counsel to David B. Lamb, Washington, D.C.)

For full biographical listings, see the Martindale-Hubbell Law Directory

McCANDLISH & LILLARD, A PROFESSIONAL CORPORATION (AV)

Fair Oaks Plaza, 11350 Random Hills Road, Suite 500, 22030-7429
Telephone: 703-273-2288
Fax: 703-352-4300
Email: mccand@patriot.net *URL:* http://www.mccandlaw.com
Leesburg, Virginia Office: 305 Harrison Street, S.E., Third Floor.
Telephone: 703-737-0200.
Fax: 703-737-0165.

Robert J. McCandlish, Jr. (1909-1996)
Rothwell J. Lillard (1910-1989)
Jesse B. Wilson, III
Peter A. Arntson
Gary W. Brown
Randolph A. Sutliff
Robert H. J. Loftus
William McCauley Arnold
Stephen C. Price

(See Next Column)

Stephen K. Fox
Douglas J. Sanderson
R. Peyton Mahaffey
William L. Carey
John W. Farrell
Eric J. Berghold
Ralph M. Tener
Vicki L. Layman
Adam W. Smith

Daniel P. Lyon
Lawrence J. McClafferty
Brian R. Sanderson

For full biographical listings, see the Martindale-Hubbell Law Directory

ODIN, FELDMAN & PITTLEMAN, P.C. (AV)

9302 Lee Highway, Suite 1100, 22031
Telephone: 703-218-2100
Facsimile: 703-218-2160
Email: OFP@OFPLAW.COM

Dexter S. Odin
David E. Feldman
James B. Pittleman
John S. Wisiackas
David J. Brewer
Robert K. Richardson
J. Patrick McConnell
Donald F. King
F. Douglas Ross
Bruce M. Blanchard
David A. Lawrence
Sally Ann Hostetler
Frances P. Dwornik
John P. Dedon
Leslye S. Fenton
Edward W. Cameron
Harry N. Lowe, III
Robert G. Nath
Elizabeth L. Salans
James W. Reynolds
Kevin Thomas Oliveira

Matthew J. Britton
Misti Mukherjee
Jonathan D. Frieden
Timothy S. Bird
Thomas N. Tartaro
Eric F. Horvitz
Richard D. Martindale
Thomas F. Quinn, III
Matthew Anthony Rizzo
Amy Y. Tsui
Caeli A. Keddie

OF COUNSEL

Nelson Blitz
Thomas E. Chilcott
Stephen J. O'Brien
Ronald W. Tydings
Robert C. Adams
Douglas Wyatt Bethel
John H. W. Cole

Representative Clients: Qwest Communications Corp.; Upper Occoquan Sewage Authority; James Martin & Co.; TechSpan, Inc.; Top Cow Productions, Inc.; The Hair Cuttery; F&M Bank-Northern Virginia; Stewart Title and Escrow, Inc.; Seaward International, Inc.; Capitol Building Supply, Inc.

For full biographical listings, see the Martindale-Hubbell Law Directory

FALLS CHURCH, (Independent City)

BRANDT, JENNINGS, ROBERTS, DAVIS & SNEE, PLLC (AV)

6565 Arlington Boulevard, Suite 200, 22042
Telephone: 703-536-2500
Fax: 703-536-2600
Mailing Address: P.O. Box 2908, Merrifield, Virginia, 22116-2908

MEMBERS OF FIRM

John J. Brandt
R. Craig Jennings
Walter L. O'Neal (1936-1974)
Joseph D. Roberts, II
Michael L. Davis
Tina L. Snee

ASSOCIATES

Robert S. Corish
William M. Dupray
Christopher D. Williams
Matthew J. O'Herron
David Lyndon Marks
Christopher S. Leaden
Jeffrey S. Danzig
Morgan W. Campbell
Matthew J. Parini (Not admitted in VA)
James Robert Parrish

Representative Clients: Aetna Casualty & Surety Co.; Allstate Insurance Co.; St. Paul Insurance Companies.
Reference: First Virginia Bank.

For full biographical listings, see the Martindale-Hubbell Law Directory

HOLLAND & KNIGHT LLP (AV)

3110 Fairview Park Drive, Suite 900, 22042
Telephone: 703-645-8600
Fax: 703-645-8610
Email: hklaw.com *URL:* http://www.hklaw.com
Atlanta, Georgia Office: 1201 West Peachtree Street, N.E., Suite 2000.
Telephone: 404-817-8500.
Fax: 404-881-0470.
Boston, Massachusetts Office: One Beacon Street.
Telephone: 617-523-2700.
Fax: 617-523-6850.
Fort Lauderdale, Florida Office: One East Broward Boulevard, Suite 1300.
Telephone: 954-525-1000.
Fax: 954-463-2030.
Jacksonville, Florida Office: 50 North Laura Street, Suite 3900.
Telephone: 904-353-2000.
Fax: 904-358-1872.

(See Next Column)

HOLLAND & KNIGHT LLP, *Falls Church—Continued*

Lakeland, Florida Office: 92 Lake Wire Drive.
Telephone: 941-682-1161.
Fax: 941-688-1186.
Melbourne, Florida Offices: 1499 South Harbor City Boulevard, Suite 303.
Telephone: 407-951-1776.
Fax: 407-951-1849 and Suite 400 First Union Bank Building, 700 S. Babcock Street.
Telephone: 407-984-2700.
Fax: 407-723-4092.
Miami, Florida Office: 701 Brickell Avenue, Suite 3000.
Telephone: 305-374-8500.
Fax: 305-789-7799.
New York, New York Office: 195 Broadway, 24th Floor.
Telephone: 212-513-3200.
Fax: 212-385-9010.
Orlando, Florida Office: 200 South Orange Avenue, Suite 2600.
Telephone: 407-425-8500.
Fax: 407-244-5288.
San Francisco, California Office: 44 Montgomery Street, Suite 4050.
Telephone: 415-743-6900.
Fax: 415-743-6910.
St. Petersburg, Florida Office: 200 Central Avenue, Suite 1600.
Telephone: 813-896-7171.
Fax: 813-822-8048.
Tallahassee, Florida Office: 315 South Calhoun Street, Suite 600.
Telephone: 850-224-7000.
Fax: 850-224-8832.
Tampa, Florida Office: 400 North Ashley Drive, Suite 2300.
Telephone: 813-227-8500.
Fax: 813-229-0134.
Washington, D.C. Office: 2100 Pennsylvania Avenue., N.W., Suite 400.
Telephone: 202-955-3000.
Fax: 202-955-5564.
West Palm Beach, Florida Office: 625 North Flagler Drive, Suite 700.
Telephone: 561-833-2000.
Fax: 561-650-8399.
Providence, Rhode Island Office: 50 Exchange Terrace, Suite 300, Union Station Plaza.
Telephone: 401-751-8500.
Fax: 401-553-6850.
Mexico City, Mexico Office: HOLLAND & KNIGHT-GALLÁSTEGUI Y LOZANO, S.C. (Joint Venture Office) Avenida Paseo de los Tamarindos No. 400, Torre "B" - 2° Piso, Col. Bosques d las Lomas, C.P. 05120 Mexico, D.F.
Telephone: 011-525-261-1866.
Fax: 011-525-261-1867.
Tel Aviv, Israel Office: 23 Derech Petach-Tikva, 18th Floor.
Telephone: +011 972 (3) 566 7666.
Fax: +011 972 (3) 566-7667.
Buenos Aires, Argentina Office: San Martin 323--Piso 18, 1004.
Telephone: +54-11 5324-7600.
Fax: +54-11 4324-7601. 34200 34200

FALLS CHURCH MEMBERS AND ASSOCIATES

Thomas M. Brownell
Matthew A. Clary, III
Ross W. Dembling
Richard O. Duvall
Warwick R. Furr, II
Robert E. Glenn, IV
Robert A. Hickey
James H. Rodio
John P. Rowley, III
Christopher R. Yukins

David S. Black
Jennifer A. Short

SENIOR COUNSEL

Richard G. Moore

For full biographical listings, see the Martindale-Hubbell Law Directory

REED SMITH HAZEL & THOMAS LLP (AV)

Fairfax County (Falls Church), Virginia Office Suite 1400, 3110 Fairview Park Drive, 22042
Telephone: 703-641-4200
Fax: 703-641-4340
Email: rssm@rssm.com *URL:* http://www.rssm.com
Leesburg, Virginia Office: 44084 Riverside Parkway, Suite 300.
Telephone: 703-729-8500. Metro: 703-478-1992.
Fax: 703-478-8003.
McLean, Virginia Office: Suite 1100, 8251 Greensboro Drive, 22102-3844.
Telephone: 703-734-4600.
FAX: 703-734-4699.
Richmond, Virginia Office: Suite 1700, 301 East Byrd Street.
Telephone: 804-344-3400.
Fax: 804-344-3410
Pittsburgh, Pennsylvania Office: Reed Smith Shaw & McClay LLP, 435 Sixth Avenue, 15219-1886.
Telephone: 412-288-3131.
FAX: 412-288-3063.
Philadelphia, Pennsylvania Office: Reed Smith Shaw & McClay LLP, 2500 One Liberty Place, 19103-7301.
Telephone: 215-851-8100.
FAX: 215-851-1420.

(See Next Column)

Harrisburg, Pennsylvania Office: Reed Smith Shaw & McClay LLP 213 Market Street, 17101-2132.
Telephone: 717-234-5988.
FAX: 717-236-3777.
Washington, D.C. Office: Reed Smith Shaw & McClay LLP, Suite 1100 - East Tower, 1301 K Street, N.W., 20005-3317.
Telephone: 202-414-9200.
FAX: 202-414-9299.
Princeton, New Jersey Office: Reed Smith Shaw & McClay LLP, 136 Main Street, Suite 250, 08540-5799.
Telephone: 609-987-0050.
FAX: 609-951-0824.
New York, N.Y. Office: 375 Park Avenue, 17th Floor, 10152.
Telephone: 212-521-5400.
FAX: 212-521-5450.
Newark, New Jersey Office: Reed Smith Shaw & McClay LLP, The Legal Center, One Riverfront Plaza, First Floor, 07102-5400.
Telephone: 973-621-3200.
FAX: 973-621-3199.

MEMBERS OF FIRM

Duane W. Beckhorn
Benton Burroughs, Jr.
Kathleen L. Cerveny
Bruce L. Christman
John E. Coffey
R. Mark Dare
Paul R. Dean, Jr.
Robert M. Diamond
Robert M. Dilling
Michael S. Dingman
H. Bradley Evans, Jr.
Stanley P. Fisher
Thomas R. Folk
Donald N. Goldrosen
Grayson P. Hanes
John T. Hazel, Jr.
A. Everett Hoeg, III
Carol C. Honigberg
Julia Krebs-Markrich
James S. Kurz
Robert A. Lawrence
Joseph S. Luchini
J. Howard Middleton, Jr.
Richard C. Sullivan, Jr.
William Griffith Thomas
Benjamin F. Tompkins
Mark W. Wasserman
Michael L. Zupan

COUNSEL

Thomas W. Greeson

ASSOCIATES

Jo Anne Sanderson Bitner
Aaron S. Book
James C. Brennan (Not admitted in VA)
Annemarie DiNardo Cleary
Jennifer J. Dacey
Geoffrey C. Dodson
Ellen C. Farrell
Anne M. Fraser
Heather Leigh Gunas
Lisa Marie Hughes
Paul G. Joyce
George E. Kostel
Rebecca E. Kuehn
J. Phillip London, Jr.
Michelle Lopes Maldonado
Juan Carlos A. Marquez (Not admitted in VA)
Danielle M. Stager
Julia Beecher Strickland
Steven T. Webster

For full biographical listings, see the Martindale-Hubbell Law Directory

FRANKLIN, Southampton Co.

MOYLER, MOYLER, RAINEY & COBB, P.L.C. (AV)

506 North Main Street, P.O. Box 775, 23851
Telephone: 757-562-5133
FAX: 757-562-7628
URL: http://www.lawyers.com/mmr&claw

MEMBERS OF FIRM

J. Edward Moyler (1894-1982)
J. Edward Moyler, Jr.
James E. Rainey
G. Elliott Cobb, Jr.

Representative Clients: Union Camp Corp.; Crestar Bank; Hercules, Inc.; Southampton Memorial Hospital; Appollo Plastics; Insight Communications Co.; The Village at Woods Edge; Cable Associates.

For full biographical listings, see the Martindale-Hubbell Law Directory

*GRUNDY,** Buchanan Co.

STREET, STREET, STREET, SCOTT & BOWMAN (AV)

339 West Main Street, P.O. Box 2100, 24614
Telephone: 540-935-2128
Telecopier: 540-935-4162

Eugene K. Street (1943-1990)

OF COUNSEL

H. A. Street

MEMBERS OF FIRM

N. D. Street
Thomas R. Scott, Jr.
Joseph W. Bowman
Robert J. Breimann
S. T. Mullins
James H. Street
Russell Vern Presley, II
Lucy G. Williams

ASSOCIATE

Benjamin A. Street

Representative Clients: CSX Corporation; United Coal Cos.; Jewell Coal & Coke Co.; Old Republic Insurance Co.; Appalachian Power Co.; Georgia Pacific Corp.; Vilnn Gas Company; ITT Hartford Insurance Co.
Approved Attorneys for: Lawyers Title Insurance Corp.; Southern Title Insurance Co.

For full biographical listings, see the Martindale-Hubbell Law Directory

*HARRISONBURG,** (Ind. City; Seat of Rockingham Co.)

LITTEN & SIPE, L.L.P. (AV)

410 Neff Avenue, 22801
Telephone: 540-434-5353
Fax: 540-434-6069
Email: littensipe.com *URL:* http://www.littensipe.com

MEMBERS OF FIRM

Donald D. Litten
James R. Sipe
James V. Lane
Stephen T. Heitz
Jonathan J. Litten

Stephanie R. Sipe
Melisa G. Ledbetter
Jason J. Ham
Richard A. Mahevich, II

General Counsel for: Rockingham Mutual Insurance Co.; Rockingham Casualty Co.; Nielsen Construction Co.; Shenandoah's Pride; Towns of Bridgewater and Dayton.

For full biographical listings, see the Martindale-Hubbell Law Directory

*LAWRENCEVILLE,** Brunswick Co.

OUTTEN, BARRETT, BURR & SHARRETT, P.C. (AV)

214 Court Street, 23868
Telephone: 804-848-3184
Fax: 804-848-0116
Emporia, Virginia Office: 314 South Main Street, P.O. Box 232.
Telephone: 804-634-2167.
Fax: 804-634-3798.

W. Curtis Outten, Jr.
Joseph E. Whitby, Jr.

Local Condemnation Attorneys for: Virginia Department of Highways and Transportation.
Representative Clients: Virginia Farm Bureau Mutual Insurance Co.; The Town of Lawrenceville; City of Emporia; Town of Courtland; Georgia Pacific Corp.; Union Camp Corp.; CSX Corp.; NationsBank.

For full biographical listings, see the Martindale-Hubbell Law Directory

*LEESBURG,** Loudoun Co.

REED SMITH HAZEL & THOMAS LLP (AV)

44084 Riverside Parkway, Suite 300, 20176
Telephone: 703-729-8500; Metro: 703-478-1992
Fax: 703-478-8003
Alexandria, Falls Church, Manassas, Richmond & Winchester, VA
Email: rssm@rssm.com *URL:* http://www.rssm.com
Fairfax County (Falls Church), Virginia Office: Suite 1400, 3110 Fairview Park Drive.
Telephone: 703-641-4200.
Fax: 703-641-4340.
McLean, Virginia Office: Suite 1100, 8251 Greensboro Drive.
Telephone: 703-734-4600.
FAX: 703-734-4699.
Richmond, Virginia Office: 901 East Byrd Street, Suite 1700, 23219.
Telephone: 804-344-3400.
Fax: 804-344-3410
Pittsburgh, Pennsylvania Office: Reed Smith Shaw & McClay LLP, 435 Sixth Avenue, 15219-1886.
Telephone: 412-288-3131.
FAX: 412-288-3063.
Philadelphia, Pennsylvania Office: Reed Smith Shaw & McClay LLP, 2500 One Liberty Place, 19103-7301.
Telephone: 215-851-8100.
FAX: 215-851-1420.
Harrisburg, Pennsylvania Office: Reed Smith Shaw & McClay LLP 213 Market Street, 17101-2132.
Telephone: 717-234-5988.
FAX: 717-236-3777.
Washington, D.C. Office: Reed Smith Shaw & McClay LLP, Suite 1100 - East Tower, 1301 K Street, N.W., 20005-3317.
Telephone: 202-414-9200.
FAX: 202-414-9299.
Princeton, New Jersey Office: Reed Smith Shaw & McClay LLP, 136 Main Street, Suite 250, 08540-5799.
Telephone: 609-987-0050.
FAX: 609-951-0824.
New York, N.Y. Office: 375 Park Avenue, 17th Floor, 10152.
Telephone: 212-521-5400.
FAX: 212-521-5450.
Newark, New Jersey Office: Reed Smith Shaw & McClay LLP, The Legal Center, One Riverfront Plaza, First Floor, 07102-5400.
Telephone: 973-621-3200.
FAX: 973-621-3199.

MEMBERS OF FIRM

Michael A. Banzhaf
E. William Chapman
Karen C. Fagelson
John L. McBride
Thomas W. Nalls

COUNSEL

David P. O'Brien

(See Next Column)

ASSOCIATE

Carla Blake Hook

For full biographical listings, see the Martindale-Hubbell Law Directory

SEVILA, SAUNDERS, HUDDLESTON & WHITE, A PROFESSIONAL CORPORATION (AV)

30 North King Street, 20176
Telephone: 703-777-5700
Metro: 471-9800; Fax: 703-771-4161

Robert E. Sevila
Richard R. Saunders, Jr.
Jon D. Huddleston
Craig E. White

Jeffrey A. Tuten
Jeanine M. Irving

LEGAL SUPPORT PERSONNEL

Joan Rust

For full biographical listings, see the Martindale-Hubbell Law Directory

LYNCHBURG, (Independent City)

CASKIE & FROST, A PROFESSIONAL CORPORATION (AV)

2306 Atherholt Road, P.O. Box 6360, 24505
Telephone: 804-846-2731
Fax: 804-845-1191; 804-846-0496
Email: jknakal@harris@caskie&frost.com

James Randolph Caskie (1909-1969)
E. Marshall Frost (1920-1988)
S. Bolling Hobbs (Retired)
S. J. Thompson, Jr. (1936-1994)
Joseph C. Knakal, Jr.
John R. Alford
Leighton S. Houck
Theodore J. Craddock
Gregory P. Cochran
John T. Cook
Joy Lee Price
Mark J. Peake
John R. Alford, Jr.

James Frederick Watson

General Counsel: N.B. Handy Co.; Elderberry Nursing Homes, Inc.
Local Counsel: Cincinnati Insurance Co.; General Accident Fire & Life Assurance; Nationwide Insurance Co.; Crestar Bank.

For full biographical listings, see the Martindale-Hubbell Law Directory

EDMUNDS & WILLIAMS, P.C. (AV)

800 Main Street, P.O. Box 958, 24505-0958
Telephone: 804-846-9000
Telecopier: 804-846-0337

Edmund Schaefer, III (Retired)
B. C. Baldwin, Jr. (1911-1999)
Samuel H. Williams (1890-1970)
J. Easley Edmunds, Jr. (1889-1977)
Paul H. Coffey, Jr. (Retired)
Kenneth S. White
Robert C. Wood, III
Henry M. Sackett, III
Rayner V. Snead, Jr.
Bernard C. Baldwin, III
Wm. Tracey Shaw
R. Edwin Burnette, Jr.
William E. Phillips
Kevin L. Cash
James O. Watts, IV
Eric J. Sorenson, Jr.

Kristine H. Smith
Darryl D. Whitesell
John M. Perry Jr.

Representative Clients: Appalachian Power Co.; Central Fidelity Bank; C. B. Fleet Co., Inc.; Harris Trucking; Lynchburg Foundry Co.; Norfolk Southern Corp.; Smithfield Companies; State Farm Mutual Automobile Insurance Co.; Sweet Briar College; Centra Health, Inc.

For full biographical listings, see the Martindale-Hubbell Law Directory

*MARTINSVILLE,** (Ind. City; Seat of Henry Co.)

GARDNER, GARDNER, BARROW & SHARPE, A PROFESSIONAL CORPORATION (AV)

First Citizens Bank Building, 4th Floor, Church and Clay Streets, 24112
Telephone: 540-638-2455
Fax: 540-638-2458
Danville, Virginia Office: 494 Piney Forest Road, 24541.
Telephone: 804-799-1111.
Fax: 804-799-1422.

Benjamin R. Gardner
Philip G. Gardner (Resident, Danville Office)
Hoyett L. Barrow, Jr.
B. Patrick Sharpe
George Lyle

Representative Clients: Furnished upon request.

For full biographical listings, see the Martindale-Hubbell Law Directory

MCLEAN, Fairfax Co.

HOGAN & HARTSON L.L.P. (AV)

8300 Greensboro Drive, 22102-3606
Telephone: 703-610-6100
Fax: 703-610-6200
URL: http://www.hhlaw.com
Washington, D.C. Office: Columbia Square, 555 13th Street, N.W.
Telephone: 206-637-5600.
Telex: 89-2757.
Cable Address: "Hogander Washington".
Fax: 202-637-5910.
Brussels, Belgium Office: Avenue des Arts 41, 1040.
Telephone: (32.2) 505.09.11.
Fax: (32.2) 505.09.96.
Budapest, Hungary (Affiliated Office): Nagy & Pintér, Hogan & Hartson Law Office, Bank Center, Granite Tower, 9th Floor, Budapest V., Szabadsag ter 7, 1944 Hungary.
Telephone: (36-1) 302-9050.
Fax: (36-1) 302-9060.
London, England Office: 21 Garlick Hill, EC4V 2AU.
Telephone: (44 171) 815 1200.
Fax: (44 171) 329 0299.
Moscow, Russia Office: 33/2 Usacheva Street, Building 3, 119048.
Telephone: (7095) 245-5190. Int'l
Telephone: (7501) 907-0451.
Fax: (7095) 245-5192. Int'l
Fax: (7501) 907-0462.
Paris, France (Affiliated Office): Cariddi, Mee, Rué, Avocats Associés à la Cour de Paris, 12, rue de la Paix, 75002.
Telephone: (33-1) 42.61.57.71.
Fax: (33-1) 42.61.79.21.
Prague, Czech Republic (Affiliated Office): Hogan & Hartson, Advokátní Kanceláře, Trziste 13, 118 00.
Telephone: (420-2) 2211-7111.
Fax: (420-2) 2421-5105.
Warsaw, Poland Office: Hogan & Hartson Sp.zo.o, Atrium Tower, Al. Jana Pawla II 25, 00-854.
Telephone: (48-22) 653-4200.
Fax: (48-22) 653-4250.
Baltimore, Maryland Office: 111 South Calvert Street.
Telephone: 410-659-2700.
Fax: 410-539-6981.
Rockville, Maryland Office: 600 Jefferson Plaza, Suite 203.
Telephone: 301-315-2206.
Fax: 301-315-9046.
Boulder, Colorado Office: 1800 Broadway, Suite 200.
Telephone: 720-406-5300.
Fax: 720-406-5301.
Colorado Springs, Colorado Office: Two North Cascade Avenue, Suite 1300.
Telephone: 719-448-5900.
Fax: 719-448-5922.
Denver, Colorado Office: One Tabor Center, Suite 1500, 1200 Seventeenth Street.
Telephone: 303-899-7300.
Fax: 303-899-7333.
Los Angeles, California Office: Biltmore Tower, 500 S. Grand Avenue, Suite 1900.
Telephone: 213-337-6700.
Fax: 213-337-6701.
Newport Beach, California Office: 4675 MacArthur Court, Suite 670.
Telephone: 949-250-4550.
Fax: 949-833-0976.
New York, New York Office: 885 Third Avenue, 26th Floor.
Telephone: 212-409-9800.
Fax: 212-409-9801.

MEMBERS OF FIRM

Richard K.A. Becker
Lee E. Berner
Stanley J. Brown
Robert B. Duncan
Gerald E. Gilbert
Kenneth J. Hautman
Richard T. Horan, Jr.
Duncan S. Klinedinst
Dennis K. Moyer
Richard J. Parrino (Not admitted in VA)
Philip D. Porter
Thomas E. Repke
Steven A. Robins (Not admitted in VA)
Emily M. Yinger (Not admitted in VA)

COUNSEL

Michele Sasse Harrington (Not admitted in VA)
Timothy J. Lockhart
Helen A. Nastasia (Not admitted in VA)

ASSOCIATES

Alexander D. Cobey
N. Thomas Connally, III
Claudia Marie Dobrovic
Tyler D. Duvall
Brooke E. Frewing
Katherine Marie Harman-Stokes
Lori L. Jenkins
C. Vincent Leon-Guerrero
Michael S. Long
Michael J. Lorenger
Timothy J. Lyden
Shane M. McGee
Donna E.M. McPartland
Christian O'Connor

(See Next Column)

ASSOCIATES (Continued)

Michael D. Romano
Paul Schwartz
Victoria F. Sheckler
J. Brent Singley
Celia G. Spiritos
Sharon L. Tasman
Nicole M. Thonet (Not admitted in VA)
Catherine L. Thornberry
Gretal J. Toker
Laura Eilers Tridico
Robert A. Welp
Thomas A. Wilson

For full biographical listings, see the Martindale-Hubbell Law Directory

MCGUIRE, WOODS, BATTLE & BOOTHE LLP (AV)

1750 Tysons Boulevard, Suite 1800, Tysons Corner, 22102-3892
Telephone: 703-712-5000
Fax: 703-712-5050
Email: info@mwbb.com *URL:* http://www.mwbb.com
Atlanta, Georgia Office: 285 Peachtree Center Avenue, N.E., Suite 2200, Marquis Tower Two, 30303-1234.
Telephone: 404-443-5500.
Fax: 404-443-5599.
Baltimore, Maryland Office: 7 Saint Paul Street, Suite 1000, 21202-1671.
Telephone: 410-659-4400.
Fax: 410-659-4599.
Charlotte, North Carolina Offices: 3700 Bank of America Plaza, 101 South Tryon Street, 28280.
Telephone: 704-373-8999.
Fax: 704-373-8990 and Bank of America Corporate Center, Suite 2900, 100 North Tryon Street, 28202.
Telephone: 704-373-8999.
Fax: 704-373-8935.
Charlottesville, Virginia Office: Court Square Building, 310 Fourth Street, N.E., Suite 300, P.O. Box 1288, 22902-1288.
Telephone: 804-977-2500.
Fax: 804-980-2222.
Chicago, Illinois Office: R.R. Donnelly Building, 77 West Wacker Drive, Suite 4500, 60601-1635.
Telephone: 312-849-3699.
Fax: 312-849-3690.
Jacksonville, Florida Office: 50 North Laura Street, 32202-3635.
Telephone: 904-798-3200.
Fax: 904-798-3207.
Norfolk, Virginia Office: World Trade Center, 101 West Main Street, Suite 9000, 23510-1655.
Telephone: 757-640-3700.
Fax: 757-640-3701.
Richmond, Virginia Office: One James Center, 901 East Cary Street, 23219-4030.
Telephone: 804-775-1000.
Fax: 804-775-1061.
Washington, D.C. Office: Washington Square, 1050 Connecticut Avenue, N.W., Suite 1200, 20036-5317.
Telephone: 202-857-1700.
Fax: 202-857-1737.
Almaty, Republic of Kazakhstan Office: Park Palace, 41 Kazibek Bi Street, 2nd Floor, 480100.
Telephone: 7-3272-608-300.
Fax: 7-3272-608-305.
Brussels, Belgium Office: 250 Avenue Louise, Bte. 64, 1050.
Telephone: 32-2-629-42-11.
Fax: 32-2-629-42-22.
Moscow, Russia Office: Paveltskaya Square, 1 Valovaya Street, 7th Floor, 13054.
Telephone: 7-502-937-0774.
Fax: 7-502-937-0776.

MEMBERS OF FIRM

C. Torrence Armstrong
Ronald D. Aucutt
Jocelyn West Brittin
Thomas C. Brown Jr.
Antonio J. Calabrese
Stephen M. Colangelo
J. Jay Corson IV
Curtis M. Coward
Waller T. Dudley
James Webster Dyke Jr.
Carson Lee Fifer Jr.
Michael D. Flemming (Partner in Charge)
Stanley M. Franklin
Michael J. Giguere
M. Melissa Glassman
Carol W. Hahn
Richard R. G. Hobson
David S. Houston
Catherine Veihmeyer Hughes
Christopher L. Keefer
James M. Lewis
R. Dennis McArver
John J. Michels Jr.
Sean F. Murphy
Clive R. G. O'Grady
Lawrence Eric Rifken
Stephen W. Robinson
John S. Stump
Philip Tierney
John H. Toole
Courtland L. Traver Jr.
Robert R. Vieth

RETIRED PARTNERS

Fred C. Alexander, Jr.
Minerva Wilson Andrews
Edgar Allen Prichard
Arthur P. Scibelli
Haynie Seay Trotter

RETIRED OF COUNSEL

Carrington Williams

(See Next Column)

McGuire, Woods, Battle & Boothe LLP—*Continued*

ASSOCIATES

Timothy C. Bass
John J. Bellaschi
Ronda L. Brown
Erika L. Byrd
Robert T. Cahill
Ann E. Davis
Suzanne W. Doggett
Spiros P. Fotopoulos
Molly F. James
Barry M. Johnson (Not admitted in VA)
Tammy L. Joseph
Amy Miles Kowalski
Michael L. Lefkowitz
Jackie J. Livesay (Not admitted in VA)
L. Ruth Ludeman
Gregory D. Lydon
Michael D. Moore
Amy R. Moschella
E. Kristen Moye
Susan S. Mullen
Jeffrey L. Novak
Ramona J. Sein
Christina A. Volzer
Laura C. Walker (Not admitted in VA)
David R. Weiser

For full biographical listings, see the Martindale-Hubbell Law Directory

Pledger & Feord P.L.C. (AV)

Suite 204, 1489 Chain Bridge Road, 22101
Telephone: 703-821-1250
Fax: 703-790-7250
Email: Pledger@his.com *URL:* http://www.lawyers.com/pledgerlaw

R. Harrison Pledger, Jr.
Bernard G. Feord, Jr.

Kevin D. Pledger

For full biographical listings, see the Martindale-Hubbell Law Directory

Stephens Law Firm, PLLC (AV)

1800 Old Meadow Road, P.O. Box 1096, 22101-1096
Telephone: 703-821-8700
Facsimile: 703-827-7761
Email: stelawfirm@aol.com
Washington, D.C. Office: 1029 Vermont Avenue, N.W., Suite 400, 20005.
Telephone: 202-331-8200.

MEMBERS OF FIRM

William T. Stephens
Michael A. Williams
Neil E. Graham

COUNSEL

Sean C. Connors

For full biographical listings, see the Martindale-Hubbell Law Directory

Venable Attorneys At Law Venable, Baetjer and Howard, LLP (AV)

A Partnership including Professional Corporations
Suite 400, 2010 Corporate Ridge, 22102
Telephone: 703-760-1600
Fax: 703-821-8949
URL: http://www.venable.com
Baltimore, Maryland Office: 1800 Mercantile Bank & Trust Building, 2 Hopkins Plaza.
Telephone: 410-244-7400.
Fax: 410-244-7742.
Washington, D.C. Office: Venable, Baetjer, Howard & Civiletti LLP, Suite 1000, 1201 New York Avenue, N.W.
Telephone: 202-962-4800.
Fax: 202-962-8300.
Rockville, Maryland Office: Suite 500, One Church Street, P.O. Box 1906.
Telephone: 301-217-5600.
Fax: 301-217-5617.
Towson, Maryland Office: 210 Allegheny Avenue, P. O. Box 5517.
Telephone: 410-494-6200.
Fax: 410-821-0147.

MEMBERS OF FIRM

Lars E. Anderson
Kenneth C. Bass, III (Also at Washington, D.C. Office)
John M. Bredehoft
William D. Dolan, III (P.C.)
Wm. Craig Dubishar
Ellen F. Dyke
J. Scott Hommer, III
A. Wayne Lalle, Jr.
David G. Lane
David C. Mancini
Christine M. McAnney
Douglas B. McDonald
John G. Milliken
Michael W. Robinson
Joseph C. Schmelter (Also at Baltimore, Maryland Office)
Elizabeth Corr Smedley
John L. Sullivan, III
William L. Walsh, Jr. (P.C.)
John A. Wilhelm (Also at Baltimore, Maryland Office)
M. Jay Yurow

OF COUNSEL

Lisa Harris Dean
David R. Lasso

(See Next Column)

ASSOCIATES

Laurie Curry Daugherty
Charles W. Durant
James P. Dvorak, Jr.
Thomas W. France
Linda M. Jackson
Douglas R. Kay
Sharon L. Larkin (Not admitted in VA)
Paul N. Wengert

For full biographical listings, see the Martindale-Hubbell Law Directory

NEWPORT NEWS, (Independent City)

Jones, Blechman, Woltz & Kelly, P.C. (AV)

600 Thimble Shoals Boulevard, Second Floor, P.O. Box 12888, 23612-2888
Telephone: 757-873-8000
Fax: 757-873-8103
URL: http://www.jbwk.com
Williamsburg, Virginia Office: 460 Mclaws Circle, Suite 220.
Telephone: 757-259-5700.
Fax: 757-259-5717.

Allan D. Jones (1875-1954)
Daniel Schlosser (1915-1977)
Franklin O. Blechman (1905-1986)
Arthur W. Woltz (1905-1993)
Herbert V. Kelly
Raymond H. Suttle
B. M. Millner
Ralph M. Goldstein
John T. Tompkins, III
Conway H. Sheild, III
Svein J. Lassen
David W. Otey (Resident, Williamsburg Office)
Kenneth B. Murov
Herbert V. Kelly, Jr.
Richard B. Donaldson, Jr.
David W. Otey, Jr. (Resident, Williamsburg Office)
Michael B. Ware
Robyn Hylton Hansen
Leonard C. Heath, Jr.
Raymond H. Suttle, Jr.
Gary Andrew Mills

OF COUNSEL

Thomas N. Downing

Irving B. "Chip" Goldstein
Alan J. Lee
Mai Lan Isler

Representative Clients: NationsBank of Virginia; Crestar Bank; Hampton Roads Sanitation District Commission; Peninsula Airport Commission; Ferguson Enterprises; Maida Development Co.; City of Hampton; Bell Atlantic; City of Newport News Industrial Development Authority.

For full biographical listings, see the Martindale-Hubbell Law Directory

Kaufman & Canoles, A Professional Corporation (AV)

Suite 408, 11817 Canon Boulevard, 23606
Telephone: 757-873-6300
Fax: 757-873-6359
Email: kaufc@kaufcan.com *URL:* http://www.kaufmanandcanoles.com
Norfolk, Virginia Office: One Commercial Place, P.O. Box 3037, 23514-3037.
Telephone: 757-624-3000.
Virginia Beach, Virginia Office: 700 Pavilion Center, P.O. Box 626, 23451.
Telephone: 757-491-4000.
Chesapeake, Virginia Office: 524 Johnstown Road, 23322.
Telephone: 757-547- 7177.
Williamsburg, Virginia Office: 1200 Old Colony Lane, 23187.
Telephone: 757-229-7322.

Paul W. Gerhardt
Thomas K. Norment, Jr. (Resident, Williamsburg Office)
James L. Windsor

David N. Payne
Mark Andrew Short
Curt G. Spear, Jr.
John Carl Valdivielso

Representative Clients: American Property Services; Crestar Bank; The Daily Press, Inc.; Henry S. Branscome, Inc.; NationsBank, N.A.; nVIEW Corp.; Noland Company; Old Republic National Title Insurance Company; Olympia Development Co.

For full biographical listings, see the Martindale-Hubbell Law Directory

NORFOLK, (Independent City)

Breeden, MacMillan & Green, P.L.C. (AV)

1700 First Virginia Tower, 555 Main Street, 23510-2230
Telephone: 757-622-1111
Telecopier: 757-622-4049
Email: BMGPLC@AOL.COM *URL:* http://www.hometown.aol.com/bmgplc/bmg.html

Edward L. Breeden (1905-1990)
Robert R. MacMillan (1923-1990)
Berryman Green, IV (1926-1999)
Edward L. Breeden, III
T. Jeffrey Salb
Allen W. Beasley
Darlene P. Bradberry

Cameron S. Meals

(See Next Column)

BREEDEN, MACMILLAN & GREEN P.L.C., *Norfolk—Continued*

OF COUNSEL

Michael T. Zugelder

Representative Clients: First Virginia Bank of Tidewater; A.S.C.A.P.; Metropolitan Property & Casualty Co.; Progressive Insurance Co.; Reliance Insurance Co.

For full biographical listings, see the Martindale-Hubbell Law Directory

KAUFMAN & CANOLES, A PROFESSIONAL CORPORATION (AV)

One Commercial Place, P.O. Box 3037, 23514-3037
Telephone: 757-624-3000
Fax: 757-624-3169
Email: kaufc@kaufcan.com *URL:* http://www.kaufmanandcanoles.com
Virginia Beach, Virginia Office: 700 Pavilion Center, P.O. Box 626, 23451.
Telephone: 757-491-4000.
Newport News, Virginia Office: Suite 408, 11817 Canon Boulevard, 23606.
Telephone: 757-873-6300.
Chesapeake, Virginia Office: 524 Johnstown Road, 23322.
Telephone: 757-547-7177.
Williamsburg, Virginia Office: 1200 Old Colony Lane, 23187.
Telephone: 757-229-7322.

Alvin P. Anderson (Resident, Williamsburg Office)
David Neal Anthony
Stanley G. Barr, Jr.
Robert J. Barry
R. Barrow Blackwell
Paul K. Campsen
George L. Consolvo
John R. Crumpler, Jr.
Gregory R. Davis (Resident, Williamsburgh Office)
David M. Delpierre
Pamela J. Faber (Resident, Virginia Beach Office)
Robert E. Farmer, III
J. Randy Forbes (Resident, Chesapeake Office)
Paul W. Gerhardt (Resident, Newport News Office)
Robert C. Goodman, Jr.
R. Braxton Hill, III
Barry W. Hunter
Gus J. James, II
Kirkland M. Kelley
Charles E. Land
Dennis T. Lewandowski
T. Richard Litton, Jr.
Joseph L. Lyle, Jr. (Resident, Virginia Beach Office)
Richard C. Mapp, III
Vincent J. Mastracco, Jr.
T. Braxton McKee
Charles V. McPhillips
Terence Murphy
Stephen E. Noona
Thomas K. Norment, Jr. (Resident, Williamsburg Office)
Patrick H. O'Donnell
Alfred M. Randolph, Jr. (Resident, Virginia Beach Office)
C. Edward Russell, Jr.
Winthrop A. Short, Jr.
Hunter W. Sims, Jr.
Robert E. Smartschan
J. Douglas Sorensen
W. Edgar Spivey
Jeffrey M. Stedfast
James G. Steiger
Stephen E. Story
Guy K. Tower
Winship C. Tower (Resident, Virginia Beach Office)
William R. Van Buren, III
Jody M. Wagner
Lewis W. Webb, III
Elizabeth L. White (Resident, Williamsburg Office)
Burt H. Whitt
James L. Windsor (Resident, Newport News Office)

COUNSEL

Debra Cooney Albiston (Resident, Virginia Beach Office)
Michael E. Barney (Resident, Virginia Beach Office)
Thomas C. Broyles (Resident, Virginia Beach Office)
Leroy T. Canoles, Jr.
Ann S. Dodson
Laura Geringer Gross
Harry H. Mansbach
Sherri M. Mearns
Marina Liacouras Phillips

Elizabeth J. Atkinson (Not admitted in VA)
Kristan B. Burch
Jeffrey A.D. Cohen
Eric M. Cotts
Jason Robert Davis
Brian O. Dolan
Philip J. Infantino, III (Resident, Chesapeake Office)
Scott W. Kezman
Beth V. McMahon
David N. Payne (Resident, Newport News Office)
Jonathan E. Pruden
L. Scott Seymour
Mark A. Short (Resident, Newport News Office)
Curt G. Spear, Jr. (Resident, Newport News Office)
Dale M. Truitt (Resident, Virginia Beach Office)
John Carl Valdivielso (Resident, Newport News Office)
Shepherd D. Wainger
Windley Hofler Walden

Representative Clients: Christian Broadcasting Network; Crestar Bank; The Daliy Press; Decipher, Inc.; Owens Corning; Pneumo Abex Corporation; Tarmac America; Workflow Management, Inc.

For full biographical listings, see the Martindale-Hubbell Law Directory

MCGUIRE, WOODS, BATTLE & BOOTHE LLP (AV)

World Trade Center, 101 West Main Street, Suite 9000, 23510-1655
Telephone: 757-640-3700
Fax: 757-640-3701
Email: info@mwbb.com *URL:* http://www.mwbb.com
Atlanta, Georgia Office: 285 Peachtree Center Avenue, N.E., Suite 2200, Marquis Tower Two, 30303-1234.
Telephone: 404-443-5500.
Fax: 404-443-5599.

(See Next Column)

Baltimore, Maryland Office: 7 Saint Paul Street, Suite 1000, 21202-1671.
Telephone: 410-659-4400.
Fax: 410-659-4599.
Charlotte, North Carolina Offices: 3700 Bank of America Plaza, 101 South Tryon Street, 28280.
Telephone: 704-373-8999.
Fax: 704-373-8990 and Bank of America Corporate Center, Suite 2900, 100 North Tryon Street, 28202.
Telephone: 704-373-8999.
Fax: 704-373-8935.
Charlottesville, Virginia Office: Court Square Building, 310 Fourth Street, N.E., Suite 300, P.O. Box 1288, 22902-1288.
Telephone: 804-977-2500.
Fax: 804-980-2222.
Chicago, Illinois Office: R.R. Donnelly Building, 77 West Wacker Drive, Suite 4500, 60601-1635.
Telephone: 312-849-3699.
Fax: 312-849-3690.
Jacksonville, Florida Office: 50 North Laura Street, 32202-3635.
Telephone: 904-798-3200.
Fax: 904-798-3207.
McLean, (Tysons Corner) Virginia Office: 1750 Tysons Boulevard, Suite 1800, 22102-3892.
Telephone: 703-712-5000.
Fax: 703-712-5050.
Richmond, Virginia Office: One James Center, 901 East Cary Street, 23219-4030.
Telephone: 804-775-1000.
Fax: 804-775-1061.
Washington, D.C. Office: Washington Square, 1050 Connecticut Avenue, N.W., Suite 1200, 20036-5317.
Telephone: 202-857-1700.
Fax: 202-857-1737.
Almaty, Republic of Kazakhstan Office: Park Palace, 41 Kazibek Bi Street, 2nd Floor, 480100.
Telephone: 7-3272-608-300.
Fax: 7-3272-608-305.
Brussels, Belgium Office: 250 Avenue Louise, Bte. 64, 1050.
Telephone: 32-2-629-42-11.
Fax: 32-2-629-42-22.
Moscow, Russia Office: Paveltskaya Square, 1 Valovaya Street, 7th Floor, 13054.
Telephone: 7-502-937-0774.
Fax: 7-502-937-0776.

RESIDENT MEMBERS

Page D. Cranford
Richard Joshua Cromwell
Carter B. S. Furr
Glenn W. Hampton
Patrick L. Hayden
Laura R. Lucas
Thomas M. Lucas
Robert W. McFarland
John D. Padgett
William R. Waddell
Mark D. Williamson

RESIDENT ASSOCIATES

Joseph W. Bonistalli, II
Douglas M. Foley
Lee A. Handford
Ruthie Litvin
Bryan K. Meals
Kristina H. Vaquera

For full biographical listings, see the Martindale-Hubbell Law Directory

SACKS & SACKS, A PROFESSIONAL CORPORATION (AV)

Suite 501 Town Point Center, 150 Boush Street, 23510-1615
Telephone: 757-623-2753
FAX: 757-640-7170
Email: sacks@series2000.com *URL:* http://www.lawyers.com/sacks&sacks-com

Herman A. Sacks (1886-1983)
Stanley E. Sacks
Andrew M. Sacks

LEGAL SUPPORT PERSONNEL

James S. McMahan (Litigation Manager)
Virginia S. McCann (Paralegal)
Maryjane Evans (Paralegal)
Thomas L. Gilchrist (Legal Assistant)
Marshall T. Walker, Jr. (Investigator)

For full biographical listings, see the Martindale-Hubbell Law Directory

STACKHOUSE, SMITH & NEXSEN (AV)

1600 First Virginia Tower, 555 Main Street, P.O. Box 3640, 23514
Telephone: 757-623-3555
Fax: 757-624-9245

MEMBERS OF FIRM

Robert C. Stackhouse
Peter W. Smith, IV
William W. Nexsen
R. Clinton Stackhouse, Jr.
Janice McPherson Doxey
Mary Painter Opitz

ASSOCIATES

J. Derek Turrietta
Michael T. Pangalos

Representative Clients: Heritage Bank & Trust; The Atlantic Group, Inc.; Roughton Pontiac Corp; Federal National Mortgage Association; Kemper National Insurance Cos.; Harleysville Mutual Insurance Co.; Heritage Bankshares, Inc.; Presbyterian League of the Presbytery of Eastern Virginia, Inc.; Oakwood Acceptance Corp.; Virginia Beach Plastic Surgery, L.L.C.

(See Next Column)

STACKHOUSE, SMITH & NEXSEN—*Continued*

For full biographical listings, see the Martindale-Hubbell Law Directory

TAVSS, FLETCHER, MAIDEN & KING, P.C. (AV)

Fourteenth Floor, 555 Main Street, 23510
Telephone: 757-625-1214
Fax: 757-622-7295
Mailing Address: P.O. Box 3747, 23514
Email: tavss@pilot.infi.net

Richard J. Tavss
John R. Fletcher
Ray W. King
Besianne Tavss Maiden
Michael B. Hamar
Kevin J. O'Leary

LEGAL SUPPORT PERSONNEL

Maurice J. O'Connor
Retha Rish (Paralegal)

Reference: Bank of the Commonwealth.

For full biographical listings, see the Martindale-Hubbell Law Directory

VANDEVENTER BLACK LLP (AV)

500 World Trade Center, 23510-1699
Telephone: 757-446-8600
Cable Address: "Hughsvan"
Telecopier: 757-446-8670
URL: http://www.vanblk.com
Kitty Hawk, North Carolina Office: 6 Juniper Trail.
Telephone: 252-261-5055.
Fax: 252-261-8444. E-Mail: nshearin@pinn.net.
London, England Office: Mitre House, 4th Floor, 12-14 Mitre Street.
Telephone: (0171) 623-2081.
Facsimile: (0171) 929-0043.

RETIRED PARTNERS

Hugh S. Meredith
Joseph A. Gawrys
Charles F. Tucker

PARTNERS OF FIRM

Braden Vandeventer (1878-1943)
Barron F. Black (1893-1974)
Braden Vandeventer, Jr. (1921-1998)
Walter B. Martin, Jr.
Morton H. Clark
John M. Ryan
G. William Birkhead
James S. Mathews
Geoffrey F. Birkhead
Norman W. Shearin, Jr. (Not admitted in VA; Resident Partner, Kitty Hawk, North Carolina Office)
Anita O. Poston
Robert L. O'Donnell
Carter T. Gunn
Daniel R. Weckstein
Mark T. Coberly
F. Nash Bilisoly
Michael P. Cotter
Henry P. Bouffard
R. John Barrett
Patrick W. Herman
William E. Franczek
Dean T. Buckius
Michael L. Sterling
Bryant C. McGann
Deborah Mancoll Casey
William M. Dozier
Patrick A. Genzler
Neil S. Lowenstein
Valerie J. Brodsky
Edward J. Powers
Lawrence G. Cohen
Arlene F. Klinedinst

OF COUNSEL

Richard S. Guy

ASSOCIATES

Jane D. Tucker
Kimberley Herson Timms
Howard W. Roth, III
Price M. Shapiro
Arthur Serratelli
Kelly Outten Stokes
James R. Harvey, III
Richard H. Ottinger
Christopher Ambrosio
Geoffrey G. Hemphill
John R. Lockard
Adam S. Rafal
Brian L. Sykes
Joseph T. Lamb, III (Not admitted in VA)

For full biographical listings, see the Martindale-Hubbell Law Directory

NORTON, Wise Co.

MULLINS, HARRIS & JESSEE, A PROFESSIONAL CORPORATION (AV)

The Law Building, 30 Seventh Street, P.O. Box 1200, 24273-1002
Telephone: 540-679-3110
Telecopier: 540-679-3113
Email: mh&j@naxs.com

Fred Bonham Greear (1899-1960)
William Thomas Bowen (1908-1964)
Leslie Morris Mullins (Retired)
Ronald G. Thomason (Retired)
Elsey A. Harris III
Roy M. Jessee
Kristen D. Dean
Chadwick S. Dotson

Counsel for: Old Dominion Power Co.
Local Counsel for: Allstate Insurance Co.; Norfolk-Southern Corp.; Virginia Iron, Coal & Coke Co.; Bell Atlantic Corp.; Kentucky Hospital Assn.; Canal Insurance Co.; Southern Pilot Insurance Integon.

For full biographical listings, see the Martindale-Hubbell Law Directory

ONANCOCK, Accomack Co.

AMES & AMES (AV)

Ames Building, 71 Market Street, P.O. Box 177, 23417
Telephone: 757-787-3535
Fax: 757-787-3536

MEMBERS OF FIRM

E. Almer Ames, Jr. (1903-1987)
Edward A. Ames, III

General Counsel for: Town of Onancock.
Local Counsel for: First Virginia Bank of Tidewater.

For full biographical listings, see the Martindale-Hubbell Law Directory

*ORANGE,** Orange Co.

SHACKELFORD, HONENBERGER, THOMAS, WILLIS & GREGG, P.L.C. (AV)

149 West Main Street, P.O. Box 871, 22960
Telephone: 540-672-2711
Fax: 540-672-2714
Email: shtwg1@ns.gemlink.com
Culpeper, Virginia Office: 147 West Davis Street, P.O. Box 1002.
Telephone: 540-825-0305.

OF COUNSEL

Virginius R. Shackelford, Jr.

MEMBERS OF FIRM

Virginius R. Shackelford, III
Christopher J. Honenberger
Frank A. Thomas, III
Jere M. H. Willis, III (Resident, Culpeper, Virginia Office)
Sarah Collins Honenberger
Sean D. Gregg

For full biographical listings, see the Martindale-Hubbell Law Directory

PORTSMOUTH, (Independent City)

COOPER, SPONG & DAVIS, P.C. (AV)

Wachovia Bank Building, 200 High Street Suite 500, P.O. Box 1475, 23705-1475
Telephone: 757-397-3481
Fax: 757-397-8167
Email: csdlaw@pop.erols.com

Clyde W. Cooper (1893-1980)
William B. Spong, Jr. (1920-1997)
Richard J. Davis (1921-1999)
Vincent L. Parker (1920-1989)
H. Thomas Fennell, Jr. (1937-1981)
James H. Flippen, III (1957-1996)
Robert C. Barclay, III
Albert J. Taylor, Jr.
Ralph W. Buxton
David R. Tynch
Gregory M. Pomije
Susan Taylor Hansen
Robert C. Barclay IV

Christopher S. Boynton
Branch H. Daniels, Jr.
Stephen A. Leon
Jeffrey S. Miller
C. Gerard Thompson
Paul L. Warren

OF COUNSEL

Arnold H. Leon

General Counsel: Portsmouth Redevelopment and Housing Authority; Maryview Hospital; Virga Pizza Crust of Virginia, Inc.; Tidewater Area Central Hospital Laundry, Inc.; Action Oldsmobile-Cadillac-GMC Trucks, Inc.; Don Comer Ford.
Local Counsel: Wachovia Bank; Bell Atlantic.

For full biographical listings, see the Martindale-Hubbell Law Directory

DONALD C. KILGORE (AV)

Suite 302 Wachovia Bank Building, P.O. Box 1051, 23705
Telephone: 757-397-7955
Fax: 757-393-3647

Reference: Wachovia Bank.

For full biographical listings, see the Martindale-Hubbell Law Directory

*PULASKI,** Pulaski Co.

GILMER, SADLER, INGRAM, SUTHERLAND & HUTTON (AV)

Midtown Professional Building, 65 East Main Street, P.O. Box 878, 24301-0878
Telephone: 540-980-1360; 540-639-0027; 888-330-3344
Telecopier: 540-980-5264
Blacksburg (Montgomery County), Virginia Office: 201 West Roanoke Street, P.O. Box 908.
Telephone: 540-552-1061.
Telecopier: 540-552-8227.

(See Next Column)

GILMER, SADLER, INGRAM, SUTHERLAND & HUTTON, *Pulaski—Continued*

MEMBERS OF FIRM

Howard C. Gilmer, Jr. (1906-1975)
Roby K. Sutherland (1909-1975)
Philip M. Sadler (1915-1994)
Robert J. Ingram
James L. Hutton (Resident, Blacksburg Office)
Thomas J. McCarthy, Jr.
John J. Gill
Gary C. Hancock
Jackson M. Bruce
Michael J. Barbour
Deborah Wood Dobbins
Timothy Edmond Kirtner
Robin J. Kegley

Representative Clients: Appalachian Power Co.; Norfolk Southern Railway Co.; NationsBank; Travelers Insurance Group; World Insurance; Royal Insurance; Integon Insurance.

For full biographical listings, see the Martindale-Hubbell Law Directory

RESTON, Fairfax Co.

GLENNON, GOODMAN, LUBELEY, VAUGHN & WALKER, L.L.P. (AV)

11480 Sunset Hills Road, 20190
Telephone: 703-689-2100
Telecopier: 703-471-6496

MEMBERS OF FIRM

Elizabeth Q. Glennon (Retired)
Andrew H. Goodman
Richard A. Lubeley
Robert Lee Vaughn, Jr.
Douglas D. Walker

Approved Attorneys for: Chicago Title Insurance Co.; Lawyers Title Insurance Co.; Commonwealth Title Insurance Co.; Stewart Title Insurance Co.; First American Title Insurance Co.
References: Crestar Bank; United Bank; Tysons National Bank.

For full biographical listings, see the Martindale-Hubbell Law Directory

HALL AND SICKELS, P.C. (AV)

Reston Executive Center, 12120 Sunset Hills Road, Suite 150, 20190
Telephone: 703-925-0500
Telecopier: 703-925-0501
URL: http://www.hallandsickels.com

Robert T. Hall
Charles W. Sickels

Holly Parkhurst Lear
Steven M. Frei
Donna Miller-Rostant

For full biographical listings, see the Martindale-Hubbell Law Directory

RICHMOND, (Independent City)

HUNTON & WILLIAMS (AV)

Riverfront Plaza, East Tower, 951 East Byrd Street, 23219-4074
Telephone: 804-788-8200
Cable Address: "Huntwand"
Telex: 804-684-4251
FAX: 804-788-8218; 804-788-8219; 804-788-8669
TWX: 710-956-0061
URL: http://www.hunton.com
Church Hill Office: 2300 East Marshall Street, 23223.
Telephone: 804-775-2248.
Washington, D.C. Office: 1900 K Street, N.W., 20006-1109.
Telephone: 202-955-1500.
Telex: 350 362 H&W WASH UD.
Fax: 202-778-2201 (Rapicom); 202-778-2202 (Ricoh230).
Miami, Florida Office: One Biscayne Tower, 2 South Biscayne Boulevard, 33131.
Telephone: 305-810-2500.
Fax: 305-810-2460.
Atlanta, Georgia Office: Bank of America Plaza, 600 Peachtree Street, N.E., Suite 4100, 30308-2216.
Telephone: 404-888-4000.
Fax: 404-888-4190 and Georgia-Hill Office: Southside Legal Center, 250 Georgia Avenue, S.E., Suite 211, 30312.
Telephone: 404-688-5512; 404-688-5513.
New York, New York Office: 200 Park Avenue, 10166.
Telephone: 212-309-1000. Cable Addresses: "Huntwand, New York" and "Dialboard."
Telex: 424 549 HUNT UI.
Fax: 212-309-1100.
Charlotte, North Carolina Office: Bank of America Plaza, Suite 3500, 101 South Tryon Street, 28280.
Telephone: 704-378-4700.
Telecopier: 704-378-4890.
Raleigh, North Carolina Office: 14th Floor, One Hannover Square, 421 Fayetteville Street Mall, P.O. Box 109, 27602.
Telephone: 919-899-3000.
Fax: 919-899-3096.
Knoxville, Tennessee Office: 2000 Riverview Tower, 900 South Gay Street. P.O. Box 951, 37901-0951.
Telephone: 423-549-7700.
Fax: 423-549-7704.

(See Next Column)

McLean, Virginia Office: 1751 Pinnacle Drive, Suite 1700, 22102.
Telephone: 703-714-7400.
Fax: 703-714-7410.
Norfolk, Virginia Office: Crestar Bank Building, Suite 1000, 500 East Main Street. P.O. Box 3889, 23514.
Telephone: 757-625-5501.
Fax: 757-625-7720.
Brussels, Belgium Office: Ave Louise 326, B6, 1050 Brussels, Belgium.
Telephone: 011 (32-2)-643-5800.
FAX: 011 (32-2)-643-5822.
Hong Kong Office: 23/F CITIC Tower, 1 Tim Mei Avenue, Central, Hong Kong.
Telephone: (852) 2841-9100.
Fax: (852) 2841-9191.
London, England Office: 61/63 St. John Street, London EC1M 4AN, England.
Telephone: +44 (0)20 7427 7850.
Facsimile: +44 (0)20 7427 7872.
Warsaw, Poland Office: Ul. Bagatela 14, Vp. 00-585 Warsaw, Poland.
Telephone: 011 (48-22) 690 61 00.
Telecopier: 011 (48-22) 621 83 94.
Bangkok, Thailand Office: Hunton & Williams (Thailand) Limited, 34/F Abdulrahim Place, 990 Rama IV Road, Bangkok, Thailand, 10500.
Telephone: 011 (662) 636-2366.
Fax: 011 (662) 636-2377.

SENIOR COUNSEL

Lewis T. Booker
Evans B. Brasfield
Robert P. Buford
Joseph C. Carter, Jr.
George Clemon Freeman, Jr.
H. Brice Graves
H. Merrill Pasco
David F. Peters
Jack H. Spain, Jr.
Joseph M. Spivey, III
Hugh V. White, Jr.
Walter F. Witt, Jr.

MEMBERS OF FIRM

Benjamin C. Ackerly
Robert A. Acosta-Lewis
Kenneth J. Alcott
Gerald L. Baliles (Head of the International Practice Group)
John Jennings Beardsworth, Jr.
Robert F. Brooks, Sr.
Tyler P. Brown
Kevin J. Buckley
Cynthia S. Cecil
James N. Christman
R. Noel Clinard
Cassandra C. Collins
Cameron N. Cosby
Donald L. Creach
Douglas W. Davis
Edward L. Douma
Mark S. Dray
W. Jeffery Edwards
John D. Epps
Patricia K. Epps
Lathan M. Ewers, Jr.
James E. Farnham
James W. Featherstone, III
Kevin J. Finto
Edward J. Fuhr
Richard D. Gary
Manning Gasch, Jr.
Allen C. Goolsby, III
Douglas S. Granger
John William Gray, Jr.
Anne Gordon Greever
John Owen Gwathmey
Virginia H. Hackney
Ray V. Hartwell III
Timothy G. Hayes
Mark S. Hedberg
George H. Hettrick
Louanna O. Heuhsen
Thomas Y. Hiner
George C. Howell, III
Donald P. Irwin
Matthew Dimmock Jenkins
Harry M. Johnson, III
Dan J. Jordanger
Richard G. Joynt
Joseph C. Kearfott
Steven J. Koorse
David Craig Landin
David O. Ledbetter
Darryl S. Lew
Michael J. Lockerby
David S. Lowman, Jr.
Catherine M. Marriott
Michael W. Maupin
Milby Amott McCarthy
Jack E. McClard
J. Burke McCormick
Thomas McNally Millhiser
Patrick J. Milmoe
T. Justin Moore, III
Thurston R. Moore
Dewey B. Morris
Lonnie D. Nunley, III
Michael P. Oates
John D. O'Neill, Jr.
Brian V. Otero
Randall S. Parks
R. Hewitt Pate
Robert Dean Pope
Lewis F. Powell, III
Virginia W. Powell
J. Waverly Pulley, III
Gordon F. Rainey, Jr.
William M. Richardson
James M. Rinaca
Jennings Grey Ritter, II
Gregory B. Robertson
Robert M. Rolfe
William L. S. Rowe
Marguerite R. Ruby
D. Alan Rudlin
Patricia M. Schwarzschild
Thomas G. Slater, Jr.
Andrew J. Tapscott
John Charles Thomas
Gary E. Thompson
Paul M. Thompson
Randolph F. Totten
Guy T. Tripp III
C. Porter Vaughan, III
William A. Walsh, Jr.
Harry J. Warthen, III
Hill B. Wellford, Jr.
Amy Mc Daniel Williams
David C. Wright (Not admitted in VA)

COUNSEL

Richard H. Burton
J. Kennerly Davis, Jr.
Edmund T. DeJarnette, Jr. (International Advisor)
Robert R. Merhige, Jr.
Bryar C. Nettles
Cheryl Grissom Ragsdale
James A. Schmidt
Michael R. Shebelskie
Vicki Obenchain Tucker
Jack R. Wilson, III

(See Next Column)

HUNTON & WILLIAMS—*Continued*

ASSOCIATES

Heidi Wilson Abbott
Elizabeth E. Aldridge
Cathryn L. Ammermann
Leslie Anne Argenta
Amy Louise Arnold
Kevin K. Batteh
Michele A. Baumgartner
R. Mason Bayler, Jr.
Coburn R. Beck
Michael J. Begland
Roger Gallup Bowers
Turner Anderson Broughton
Daniel M. Campbell
Curtis G. Carlson
March Dolan Coleman
Shawn A. Copeland
Paul Timothy Creeden
Cyane B. Crump
Michael T. Damgard
Brydon Mark DeWitt
E. Marie Tucker Diveley
Sean Paul Ducharme
Maya M. Eckstein
Benita W. Ellen
Edward Whitehead Elmore, Jr.
Kelly L. Faglioni
Edwin Francis Farren, IV
Alison W. Feehan
Theodore J. Fisher
Katrina Clark Forrest
Christopher L. Gaenzle
Cindy L. Gantnier
(Not admitted in VA)
Douglas M. Garrou
Raymond F. Geoffroy, III
Deborah R. Gerhardt
Louanna Godwin
Christopher R. Graham
Marie Elena Graham
Thomas Adam Gregory
Kerry Lynn Grey
Charles Tayloe Griffith
Lori Elliott Guzman
Joanna Manikas Halsey
Laura Ellen Hamm
Richard B. Harper
(Not admitted in VA)
John M. Holloway III
Cecelia Philipps Horner
Sarah C. Johnson
Scott A. Johnson
Kevin W. Jones
Daniel C. Jordan
Lindsay Brooke King
Christopher G. Kulp
Annika Kyröläinen
Sharon P. Lamb
Christopher G. Lanning
(Not admitted in VA)
Krista Latshaw
David M. Lay
Daniel M. LeBey
(Not admitted in VA)
Audrey C. Louison
Kimberly Christin Magee
McAlister C. Marshall, II
John S. Martin
Nona K. Massengill
Michael C. McCann
Jennifer L. McClellan
Kathleen McCormick
Michael J. McCullough
David T. McIndoe
Barry T. Meek
Julia B. Messersmith
David I. Meyers
Anne-Marie M. Miles
Thomas J. Mitchell
Erik D. Nadolink
Eric Reed Nowak
Andrew Richardson Park
Peter Stone Partee
Marc A. Randolph
Eric George Reeves
Sandhya Susan Reju
David B. Rich, III
Agustín E. Rodríguez
Gregory M. Romano
Caroline G. Root
James E. Sanderson, Jr.
Melissa Loughridge Savenko
James S. Seevers, Jr.
J. R. Smith
Lisa S. Spickler
Henry C. Su
C. Randolph Sullivan
Stacy Colvin Taylor
Wendell L. Taylor
William Lake Taylor, Jr.
Melvin E. Tull, III
Mark C. Van Dewsen
Michelle K. Walsh
Kevin Stark Webb
Robert S. Westermann
Charles N. Whitaker
Michael C. Whitticar
Preston Douglas Wigner
William H. Wright, Jr.

For full biographical listings, see the Martindale-Hubbell Law Directory

MALONEY, HUENNEKENS, PARKS, GECKER & PARSONS, A PROFESSIONAL CORPORATION (AV)

Bank of America Center, 1111 East Main Street, Suite 800, 23219-3103
Telephone: 804-644-0313
Telecopier: 804-783-6192

Malcolm Parks
Edward F. Parsons
Kevin R. Huennekens
Daniel A. Gecker
Joel G. Clarke
Michael A. Condyles
Yvonne Steenstra Wellford
James C. Cosby
Loc Pfeiffer
Patricia Lea Phillips
Christopher A. Jones

Fiona M. Tower
James M. Wilson
Ruth E. Nathanson
Alison V. Lennarz

OF COUNSEL

Frank C. Maloney III

Reference: First Union National Bank.

For full biographical listings, see the Martindale-Hubbell Law Directory

MCGUIRE, WOODS, BATTLE & BOOTHE LLP (AV)

One James Center, 901 East Cary Street, 23219-4030
Telephone: 804-775-1000
Fax: 804-775-1061
Email: info@mwbb.com *URL:* http://www.mwbb.com
Atlanta, Georgia Office: 285 Peachtree Center Avenue, N.E., Suite 2200, Marquis Tower Two, 30303-1234.
Telephone: 404-443-5500.
Fax: 404-443-5599.

(See Next Column)

Baltimore, Maryland Office: 7 Saint Paul Street, Suite 1000, 21202-1671.
Telephone: 410-659-4400.
Fax: 410-659-4599.
Charlotte, North Carolina Offices: 3700 Bank of America Plaza, 101 South Tryon Street, 28280.
Telephone: 704-373-8999.
Fax: 704-373-8990 and Bank of America Corporate Center, Suite 2900, 100 North Tryon Street, 28202.
Telephone: 704-373-8999.
Fax: 704-373-8935.
Charlottesville, Virginia Office: Court Square Building, 310 Fourth Street, N.E., Suite 300, P.O. Box 1288, 22902-1288.
Telephone: 804-977-2500.
Fax: 804-980-2222.
Chicago, Illinois Office: R.R. Donnelly Building, 77 West Wacker Drive, Suite 4500, 60601-1635.
Telephone: 312-849-3699.
Fax: 312-849-3690.
Jacksonville, Florida Office: 50 North Laura Street, 32202-3635.
Telephone: 904-798-3200.
Fax: 904-798-3207.
McLean, (Tysons Corner) Virginia Office: 1750 Tysons Boulevard, Suite 1800, 22102-3892.
Telephone: 703-712-5000.
Fax: 703-712-5050.
Norfolk, Virginia Office: World Trade Center, 101 West Main Street, Suite 9000, 23510-1655.
Telephone: 757-640-3700.
Fax: 757-640-3701. 23219-4030.
Washington, D.C. Office: Washington Square, 1050 Connecticut Avenue, N.W., Suite 1200, 20036-5317.
Telephone: 202-857-1700.
Fax: 202-857-1737.
Almaty, Republic of Kazakhstan Office: Park Palace, 41 Kazibek Bi Street, 2nd Floor, 480100.
Telephone: 7-3272-608-300.
Fax: 7-3272-608-305.
Brussels, Belgium Office: 250 Avenue Louise, Bte. 64, 1050.
Telephone: 32-2-629-42-11.
Fax: 32-2-629-42-22.
Moscow, Russia Office: Paveltskaya Square, 1 Valovaya Street, 7th Floor, 13054.
Telephone: 7-502-937-0774.
Fax: 7-502-937-0776.

MEMBERS OF FIRM

Russell T. Aaronson III
Robert T. Adams
George F. Allen
W. Allen Ames Jr.
Arthur E. Anderson II
David E. Anderson
Frank B. Atkinson
Terrence Mitchell Bagley
Mary Dalton Baril
John S. Barr
John W. Bates III
Dennis I. Belcher
J. William Boland
William G. Broaddus
Brickford Y. Brown
John W. Burke III
Evan A. Burkholder
Robert L. Burrus Jr.
Stephen D. Busch
James W. C. Canup
Jeffrey R. Capwell
Joseph C. Carter III
John V. Cogbill III
Richard Cullen
H. Slayton Dabney Jr.
Grace R. den Hartog
W. Birch Douglass III
Marshall H. Earl Jr.
Elizabeth Flannagan Edwards
David E. Evans
Renée B. Fain
Howard Feller
Edward L. Flippen
Bonnie M. France
Gloria L. Freye
Sam Young Garrett
Earle Duncan Getchell Jr.
Kodwo P. Ghartey-Tagoe
William F. Gieg
Larry M. Goodall
Leslie A. Grandis
T. Craig Harmon
Joanne Katsantonis
William H. King Jr.
Mark J. La Fratta
Nancy R. Little
Sandra K. Macauley
Gary S. Marshall
George Keith Martin
J. Michael Martinez de Andino
Steven C. McCallum
James P. McElligott Jr.
Robert G. McElroy
Charles W. McIntyre Jr.
Joseph P. McMenamin
Henry H. McVey III
David E. Melson
Charles L. Menges
Kenneth J. Moran
O. Forrest Morgan Jr.
Brian D. Murphy
Thomas L. Newton Jr.
David N. Oakey
John M. Oakey Jr.
John Brad O'Grady
Scott C. Oostdyk
Rosewell Page III
Robert H. Patterson Jr.
James H. Price III
Martin B. Richards
David L. Richardson II
Lloyd Macauley Richardson
Brian C. Riopelle
David W. Robertson
Thomas P. Rohman
Deborah Moreland Russell
Dana L. Rust
James L. Sanderlin
Rodney A. Satterwhite
Raymond F. Scannell
Michael J. Schewel
Gilbert E. Schill Jr.
R. Carter Scott III
George L. Scruggs Jr.
Richard H. Sedgley
Jane Whitt Sellers
Alexander H. Slaughter
Daniel K. Slone
R. Gordon Smith
Kathleen Taylor Sooy
Thomas E. Spahn
Thomas J. Stallings
Jacquelyn E. Stone
William J. Strickland
Elizabeth Butterworth Stutts
Charles R. Swartz
Eva S. Tashjian-Brown
James A. Thornhill

(See Next Column)

McGuire, Woods, Battle & Boothe LLP, *Richmond—Continued*

MEMBERS OF FIRM (Continued)

William E. Twomey Jr.
James H. Walsh
Stephen H. Watts II
John M. Weisner
Anne Marie Whittemore
Steven R. Williams
Thomas S. Word Jr.
David H. Worrell Jr.
W. Carter Younger
Warren E. Zirkle

RETIRED OF COUNSEL

Richard H. Catlett Jr.
Carle E. Davis
Thomas F. Dean
Ernest K. Geisler Jr.
Thomas C. Gordon Jr.
Kemper K. Hyers
Alexander W. Neal Jr.

OF COUNSEL

Michael G. Dowd (Not admitted in VA)
Michele A. W. McKinnon

ASSOCIATES

Todd G. Ammermann
James M. Anderson III
David E. Baker
James L. Banks Jr.
William H. Baxter II
Anne C. Bentley
F. Lewis Biggs
Jonathan T. Blank
Leo J. M. Boyd
Robert G. Boyle Jr.
Dana M. Brown
Jason C. Buckel (Not admitted in VA)
F. Paul Calamita III
Kristen M. Calleja
LaTisha O. Chatman
Eleanor Anne Chesney
Robert M. Cipolla
Scott P. Collins
Martin A. Conn
David F. Dabbs
Michael R. Daglio
Patrick A. De Ridder
Gretchen Eisenach
Bryan A. Fratkin
Joy C. Fuhr
Theofilos G. Galoozis
Pamela C. Gavin
Carol Rick Gibbons
Michael W. Graff Jr.
Sherri S. Haring
Jonathan P. Harmon
Ashley E. Harwell
Dion W. Hayes
Bethany L. Hicks
Kimberly R. Hillman
Robert L. Hodges
Patrick T. Horne
Nancy E. Huerta
William M. Hutchins
William D. James
Nancy J. Jensen
Nina L. Jezic
Peter E. Kane
Stephanie L. Karfias
A. Eric Kauders Jr.
D. Brennen Keene
Dennis R. Kiker
Kelley A. Kinney
Lee N. Kump
John M. Lain
Philip D. Lane
Maureen C. Lanning (Not admitted in VA)
Aimee D. Latimer
Mary N. Lehner
Paige G. Lester
John E. Ludlum
John H. Maddock III
Eugene Edward Mathews III
Laura Clark McCoy
Perry W. Miles, IV
James R. Miner
Tara N. Mora
Janet Selph Moyers
Robert D. Murphy Jr.
Julie A. Ortmeier
Janet P. Peyton
Godfrey T. Pinn
Edmund S. Pittman
Christopher D. Pomeroy
Laura O. Pomeroy
Joshua Hartley Rahman
Kathryn A. Ramey
H. Carter Redd
Joseph K. Reid III
Christine H. Rogerson
Gregg A. Scoggins
Scott A. Simmons
Nicholas G. Sladic
Brooks M. Smith
James A. Sonne
Anjanette Plichta Stinson
Michele L. Stoddard
Karl M. Strait
Jennifer Schooley Stringer
Samuel L. Tarry Jr.
Mark A. Taylor (Not admitted in VA)
B. Scott Tilley
Stephen S. Turley
Robert M. Tyler
J. Tracy Walker IV
Paul G. Watson IV
Mark D. Westmoreland (Not admitted in VA)
Dennis J. Whelan
Laura R. White
Neil D. Wilkin Jr.
Leslie K. Yonce IV

For full biographical listings, see the Martindale-Hubbell Law Directory

Reed Smith Hazel & Thomas LLP (AV)

901 East Byrd Street, Suite 1700, 23219
Telephone: 804-344-3400
Fax: 804-344-3410
Email: rssm@rssm.com *URL:* http://www.rssm.com
Fairfax County (Falls Church), Virginia Office: Suite 1400, 3110 Fairview Park Drive.
Telephone: 703-641-4200.
Fax: 703-641-4340.
Leesburg, Virginia Office: 44084 Riverside Parkway, Suite 300.
Telephone: 703-729-8500. Metro: 703-478-1992.
Fax: 703-478-8003
McLean, Virginia Office: Suite 1100, 8251 Greensboro Drive, 22102-3844.
Telephone: 703-734-4600.
FAX: 703-734-4699.
Pittsburgh, Pennsylvania Office: Reed Smith Shaw & McClay LLP, 435 Sixth Avenue, 15219-1886.
Telephone: 412-288-3131.
FAX: 412-288-3063.

(See Next Column)

Philadelphia, Pennsylvania Office: Reed Smith Shaw & McClay LLP, 2500 One Liberty Place, 19103-7301.
Telephone: 215-851-8100.
FAX: 215-851-1420.
Harrisburg, Pennsylvania Office: Reed Smith Shaw & McClay LLP 213 Market Street, 17101-2132.
Telephone: 717-234-5988.
FAX: 717-236-3777.
Washington, D.C. Office: Reed Smith Shaw & McClay LLP, Suite 1100 - East Tower, 1301 K Street, N.W., 20005-3317.
Telephone: 202-414-9200.
FAX: 202-414-9299.
Princeton, New Jersey Office: Reed Smith Shaw & McClay LLP, 136 Main Street, Suite 250, 08540-5799.
Telephone: 609-987-0050.
FAX: 609-951-0824.
New York, N.Y. Office: 375 Park Avenue, 17th Floor, 10152.
Telephone: 212-521-5400.
FAX: 212-521-5450.
Newark, New Jersey Office: Reed Smith Shaw & McClay LLP, The Legal Center, One Riverfront Plaza, First Floor, 07102-5400.
Telephone: 973-621-3200.
FAX: 973-621-3199.

MEMBERS OF FIRM

S. Miles Dumville
H. Lane Kneedler
D. Patrick Lacy, Jr.
Walter A. Marston, Jr.
Kathleen S. Mehfoud
Steven W. Pearson

COUNSEL

Gail D. Jaspen
Roderick B. Mathews
Patrick A. O'Hare

ASSOCIATES

Curtis Gilbert Manchester

For full biographical listings, see the Martindale-Hubbell Law Directory

Williams, Mullen, Clark & Dobbins, A Professional Corporation (AV)

Two James Center, 1021 East Cary Street, P.O. Box 1320, 23218-1320
Telephone: 804-643-1991
Fax: 804-783-6507
URL: http://www.wmcd.com
Newport News Office: Harbor Bank Center, Suite 210, One Old Oyster Point Road, 23602-7119.
Telephone: 757-249-5100.
Fax: 757-249-5109.
Virginia Beach Office: One Columbus Center, 23462-6763.
Telephone: 757-499-8800.
Fax: 757-473-0395.
Vienna Office: 1593 Spring Hill Road, Suite 510, 22182.
Telephone: 703-760-5200.
Fax: 703-748-0244.
Washington, D.C. Office: The Farragut Building, 900 17th Street, N.W., Suite 700, 20006.
Telephone: 202-293-0213.
Fax: 804-783-6507. Fax Within D.C.: 202-293-5939.
London, England Office: Blake Lodge, Bridge Lane, SW11 3AD.
Telephone: (011-44-71) 223-2756.
Fax: (011-44-71) 350-0156.
Riyadh, Saudi Arabia Affiliate Office: Saudi-American Legal Consultants Commercial Building #2, Diplomatic Quarter, P.O. Box 57270, 11574.
Telephone: (011-966-1) 488-1563.
Fax: (011-966-1) 488-0542.

Lewis C. Williams (1875-1959)
James Mullen (1876-1967)
Stuart G. Christian (1883-1967)
Morton L. Wallerstein (1890-1980)
Virgil R. Goode (1897-1972)
David D. Addison
Farhad Aghdami
Ralph L. Axselle, Jr.
R. Brian Ball
Stephen E. Baril
William D. Bayliss
William J. Benos
JoAnn Blair-Davis (Resident, Virginia Beach Office)
Paul S. Bliley, Jr.
A. Peter Brodell
Steven D. Brown
Lawrence H. Bryant (Resident, Virginia Beach Office)
James J. Burns
Michael C. Buseck
Charles L. Cabell
Theodore L. Chandler, Jr.
Mark C. Christie
Donald H. Clark (Resident, Virginia Beach Office)
Gregory P. Cirillo (Resident, Washington, D.C. Office)
David L. Dallas, Jr.
C. Richard Davis
Joseph A. Di Julio (Resident, Virginia Beach Office)
Howard W. Dobbins
Theodore J. Edlich, IV
Robert E. Eicher
Sarah Hopkins Finley
Calvin W. Fowler, Jr.
Thomas R. Frantz (Resident, Virginia Beach Office)
W. F. Drewry Gallalee
Michael J. Gardner (Resident, Virginia Beach Office)
Alexander C. Graham, Jr.
Curtis M. Hairston, Jr.
Hugh T. Harrison, II
Daniel B. Hassett (Resident, Washington, D.C. Office)
Eric A. Hauser (Resident, Virginia Beach Office)
Samuel W. Hixon, III
A. Brooks Hock
Lynn F. Jacob

(See Next Column)

WILLIAMS, MULLEN, CLARK & DOBBINS A PROFESSIONAL CORPORATION—*Continued*

Christopher H. Johnson (Resident, Washington, D.C. Office)
David R. Johnson
Reginald N. Jones
Thomas E. Knauer
Samuel M. Kroll (Resident, Virginia Beach Office)
Joseph H. Latchum, Jr. (Resident, Newport News Office)
R. Hart Lee
Randolph H. Lickey
John L. Lumpkins, Jr.
Channing J. Martin
Conard B. Mattox III
William R. Mauck, Jr.
Dana D. McDaniel
Thomas B. McVey (Resident, Washington, D.C. Office)
James V. Meath
John M. Mercer
Robert L. Musick, Jr.
Margaret Warren Swartz
Craig L. Mytelka (Resident, Virginia Beach Office)
Douglas M. Nabhan
G. Andrew Nea, Jr.
Thomas B. Nicholson
Warren E. Nowlin (Resident, Washington, D.C. Office)
John M. Paris, Jr. (Resident, Virginia Beach Office)
Robert D. Perrow
William E. Perry (Resident, Washington, D.C. Office)
William L. Pitman
Craig L. Rascoe
Robert M. Reed (Resident, Virginia Beach Office)
Jimmie V. Reyna (Resident, Washington, D.C. Office)
Robert F. Riley (Resident, Washington, D.C. Office)
Malcolm E. Ritsch, Jr.
Philip deB. Rome
Robert D. Roseman (Resident, Washington, D.C. Office)
Walter H. Ryland
Robert N. Saffelle
Robert L. Samuel, Jr. (Resident, Virginia Beach Office)
Paul G. Saunders, II
William H. Schwarzschild, III
C. Grigsby Scifres (Resident, Virginia Beach Office)
Lawrence R. Siegel (Resident, Virginia Beach Office)
Derek L. Smith
Julious P. Smith, Jr.
Thomas E. Snyder (Resident, Virginia Beach Office)
Robert E. Spicer, Jr.
Frederick T. Stant, III (Resident, Virginia Beach Office)
Andrea Rowse Stiles
W. Scott Street, III
Stephen C. Swain (Resident, Virginia Beach Office)
Stephen G. Test (Resident, Virginia Beach Office)
Janet Singletary Thomas
Ian D. Titley
Sandy T. Tucker
Abram W. VanderMeer, Jr. (Resident, Virginia Beach Office)
C. William Waechter, Jr.
John L. Walker, III
Charles E. Wall
Clayton L. Walton
B. Randolph Wellford, Jr.
Wayne A. Whitham, Jr.
Fielding L. Williams, Jr.
Russell Alton Wright

OF COUNSEL

David George Ball (Resident, Washington, D.C. Office)
A. Patrick Giles
Robert A. Marsac
Fred G. Pollard

Julia K. Bailey (Resident, Washington, D.C. Office)
Stephen M. Barnett
Wyatt S. Beazley, IV
Bradford D. Bimson (Resident, Virginia Beach Office)
Lynn K. Brugh, IV
Megan E. Burns (Resident, Virginia Beach Office)
David C. Burton
David A. Cardon (Resident, Virginia Beach Office)
John F. Carroll, IV (Resident, Virginia Beach Office)
Kimberly A. Chasteen (Resident, Newport News Office)
Andrew M. Condlin
Clifford A. Coppola (Resident, Virginia Beach Office)
Benjamin C. Crumpler
Timothy W. Dorsey (Resident, Virginia Beach Office)
David V. DuVal
Jonathan Aaron Frank
Tasos A. Galiotos (Resident, Virginia Beach Office)
Shannon P. Garbett
J. Conrad Garcia
Sean M. Gibbons
Ann Mayhew Golski (Resident, Virginia Beach Office)
Mary Eve Grandis (Resident, Virginia Beach Office)
David H. Hallock, Jr.
Patrick R. Hanes
M. Nicole Hanna (Resident, Virginia Beach Office)
Elizabeth Mason Horsley
Jeffrey B. Hubbard (Resident, Virginia Beach Office)
Michelle A. Hughes (Resident, Virginia Beach Office)
William F. Jones
A. Brent King
James Scott Kulp
Judy M. Lin
Kenneth E. Liu (Resident, Washington, D.C. Office)
Albert Lo (Resident, Washington, D.C. Office)
Stephen C. McCoy
Neil E. McCullagh
G. William Norris, Jr.
Kevin C. Nunnally
John M. Oakey, III
Dana C. M. Peluso
William D. Perun, Jr.
Daniel M. Pringle
Brian C. Purcell (Resident, Virginia Beach Office)
Andrew T. Richardson, III
Donald J. Richardson
Frances W. Russell (Resident, Virginia Beach Office)
Kathryn W. Sanborn
Patrick J. Sanderson
Kimberly A. Satterwhite
Mark S. Shepard
Allyson Martin Sladic
W. David Snead (Resident, Washington, D.C. Office)
Catherine Steffen (Resident, Virginia Beach Office)
Aisha J. Sykes
King F. Tower
John Henderson Turner III
Ingrid Ashe Watson
Jack L. Young (Resident, Virginia Beach Office)

(See Next Column)

LEGAL SUPPORT PERSONNEL

Danny W. Jackson (Executive Director of Administration)

For full biographical listings, see the Martindale-Hubbell Law Directory

---

ROANOKE, Roanoke City Co.

OSTERHOUDT, FERGUSON, NATT, AHERON & AGEE, A PROFESSIONAL CORPORATION (AV)

1919 Electric Road, S.W., 24018
Telephone: 540-774-1197
Telecopier: 540-774-0961
Mailing Address: P.O. Box 20068, Roanoke, 24018
Email: OFNNA@Roanoke.infi.net *URL:* http://www.roanoke.infi.net/~ofnaa

Charles H. Osterhoudt
Michael S. Ferguson
Edward A. Natt
Michael J. Aheron
G. Steven Agee
Mark D. Kidd
Kristen K. Johnstone

For full biographical listings, see the Martindale-Hubbell Law Directory

---

*STAUNTON,** (Ind. City; Seat of Augusta Co.)

BLACK, NOLAND & READ, P.L.C. (AV)

One Barristers Row, P.O. Box 1206, 24402-1206
Telephone: 540-885-0888
Fax: 540-885-0890
Email: bnr@cfw.com

Peyton Cochran (1880-1969)
Philip Lee Lotz (1913-1986)
Benham M. Black
N. Douglas Noland, Jr.
Susan B. Read

Philip John Markert, Jr.
J. Lori Hodge Schweller

General Counsel for: Planters Bank & Trust Co.
Representative Clients: Utica; IDA for City of Staunton; Advisory Communications Systems, Inc.; B & S Contracting, Inc.; Shenandoah Engineering Services, Inc.

For full biographical listings, see the Martindale-Hubbell Law Directory

TIMBERLAKE, SMITH, THOMAS & MOSES, P.C. (AV)

The Virginia Building, P.O. Box 108, 24402-0108
Telephone: 540-885-1517
FAX: 540-885-4537
Email: tstm@tstm.com

Wayt B. Timberlake, Jr. (1908-1989)
Richard W. Smith (Retired)
Colin J. S. Thomas, Jr.
Preston Donald Moses
John W. Sills, III
James G. Welsh
Thomas G. Bell, Jr.
B. E. Brannock
J. Ross Newell, III
C. J. Steuart Thomas, III
Rosalie V. Pemberton
Randall T. Perdue

Local Counsel for: General Motors Corp.; Commonwealth of Virginia, Division of Risk Management; Montgomery Ward & Co.; First Virginia Bank Blue Ridge; State Farm Insurance.

For full biographical listings, see the Martindale-Hubbell Law Directory

---

*TAPPAHANNOCK,** Essex Co.

DILLARD AND KATONA (AV)

Ritchie House, Prince and Cross Streets, P.O. Box 356, 22560
Telephone: 804-443-3368
Fax: 804-443-2219

A. Fleet Dillard (1912-1990)
Alexander F. Dillard, Jr.
Scot A. Katona
A. Fleet Dillard, III

Reference: Bank of Essex.

For full biographical listings, see the Martindale-Hubbell Law Directory

---

*TAZEWELL,** Tazewell Co.

GILLESPIE, HART, ALTIZER & WHITESELL, P.C. (AV)

Main Street, P.O. Box 718, 24651
Telephone: 540-988-5525; 988-5526
Fax: 988-6427
Email: ghaw@netscope.net

Carl C. Gillespie (Retired)
Carl C. Gillespie, Jr. (Retired)
Harris Hart, II
Robert B. Altizer
Eric D. Whitesell
F. Bradley Pyott
Thomas C. Givens, Jr.
Richard C. Patterson
George Robert Brittain, II

Approved Attorneys for: Lawyers Title Insurance Corp.
Representative Clients: State Farm Insurance Co.; The Travelers Insurance Co.; Virginia Farm Bureau Insurance Co.; Town of Tazewell, Virginia; Humana, Inc.; Southern States Cooperative, Inc.

(See Next Column)

GILLESPIE, HART, ALTIZER & WHITESELL P.C., *Tazewell—Continued*

For full biographical listings, see the Martindale-Hubbell Law Directory

VIRGINIA BEACH, (Independent City)

KAUFMAN & CANOLES, A PROFESSIONAL CORPORATION (AV)

700 Pavilion Center, P.O. Box 626, 23451
Telephone: 757-491-4000
Fax: 757-491-4020
Email: kaufc@kaufcan.com *URL:* http://www.kaufmanandcanoles.com
Norfolk, Virginia Office: One Commercial Place, P.O. Box 3037, 23514-3037.
Telephone: 757-624-3000.
Newport News, Virginia Office: Suite 408, 11817 Canon Boulevard, 23606.
Telephone: 757-873-6300.
Chesapeake, Virginia Office: 524 Johnstown Road, 23322.
Telephone: 757-547-7177.
Williamsburg, Virginia Office: 1200 Old Colony Lane, 23187.
Telephone: 757-229-7322.

RESIDENT PERSONNEL

Pamela J. Faber
Joseph L. Lyle, Jr.
Alfred M. Randolph, Jr.
Winship C. Tower

OF COUNSEL

Debra Cooney Albiston
Michael E. Barney
Thomas C. Broyles

Dale M. Truitt

Representative Clients: Bank of Tidewater; C.E. Thurston and Sons, Inc.; Crestar Bank; Centura Bank; Hermes Abrasives, Inc.; Jackson Hewitt; Lillian Vernon Corp.; NationsBank, N.A.

For full biographical listings, see the Martindale-Hubbell Law Directory

WOLCOTT, RIVERS, WHEARY, BASNIGHT & KELLY, P.C. (AV)

One Columbus Center, Suite 1100, 23462-6765
Telephone: 757-497-6633
FAX: 757-497-7267
Email: wolriv@series2000.com

Wilson L. Rivers
William A. Wheary, III
W. Brantley Basnight, III
Monroe Kelly, III
Carl A. Eason
Joseph R. Mayes
Samuel W. Meekins, Jr.
Edward W. Wolcott, Jr.
Barry Dorans
Leslie R. Watson
David N. Reda
Richard E. Biemiller
Cheshire I'Anson Eveleigh
M. Powell Peters
Neil L. Rose
Robert D. Marotta

David M. Bastiaans
Deborah Kirkpatrick

Counsel for: Metropolitan Life Insurance Co.; Ford Motor Co.
Approved Attorneys for: Lawyers Title Insurance Corp.

For full biographical listings, see the Martindale-Hubbell Law Directory

WHITE STONE, Lancaster Co.

DUNTON, SIMMONS & DUNTON, L.L.P (AV)

678 Rappahannock Drive, 22578
Telephone: 804-435-4000
Telecopier: 804-435-1614
Email: dsd@crosslink.net

MEMBERS OF FIRM

Ammon G. Dunton, Jr.
Craig H. Smith
William R. Curdts
John S. Martin
J. Rawleigh Simmons
Morgan Wade Alley

ASSOCIATE

John Christian Hodges

General Counsel: Bay Banks of Virginia; Bay Trust Company; Bank of Lancaster; Northern Neck Insurance Co.; Virginia Health and Accident Assn.

For full biographical listings, see the Martindale-Hubbell Law Directory

*WILLIAMSBURG,** (Ind. City; Seat of James City Co.)

KAUFMAN & CANOLES, A PROFESSIONAL CORPORATION (AV)

1200 Old Colony Lane Drawer Q, 23187
Telephone: 757-229-7322
Fax: 757-259-3838
Email: kaufc@kaufcan.com *URL:* http://www.kaufmanandcanoles.com
Norfolk, Virginia Office: One Commercial Place, P.O. Box 3037, 23514-3037.
Telephone: 757-624-3000.
Virginia Beach, Virginia Office: 700 Pavilion Center, P.O. Box 626, 23451.
Telephone: 757-491-4000.
Newport News, Virginia Office: Suite 408, 11817 Canon Boulevard, 23606.
Telephone: 757-873-6300.
Chesapeake, Virginia Office: 524 Johnstown Road, 23322.
Telephone: 757-547-7177

(See Next Column)

Alvin P. Anderson
Gregory R. Davis
Thomas K. Norment, Jr.
Elizabeth L. White

For full biographical listings, see the Martindale-Hubbell Law Directory

WASHINGTON

BELLEVUE, King Co.

PERKINS COIE LLP (AV)

Suite 1800, One Bellevue Center, 411 - 108th Avenue N.E., 98004
Telephone: 425-453-6980
Facsimile: 425-453-7350
Email: perkins@perkinscoie.com *URL:* http://www.perkinscoie.com
Seattle, Washington: 1201 Third Avenue, Suite 4800, 98101-3099.
Telephone: 206-583-8888.
Facsimile: 206-583-8500.
Anchorage, Alaska: 1029 West Third Avenue, Suite 300, 99501-1970.
Telephone: 907-279-8561.
Facsimile: 907-276-3108.
Los Angeles, California: 1620 26th Street, 6th Floor, 90404.
Telephone: 310-788-9900.
Facsimile: 310-788-3399.
Menlo Park, California: 135 Commonwealth Drive, Suite 250, 94025-1105.
Telephone: 650-752-6000.
Facsimile: 650-752-6050.
San Francisco, California: 250 Montgomery Street, Suite 1600, 94104-4448.
Telephone: 415-781-3200.
Facsimile: 415-781-2525.
Denver, Colorado: World Trade Center, 1675 Broadway, Suite 2800, 80202-062.
Telephone: 303-571-6100.
Facsimile: 303-571-6111.
Washington, D.C.: 607 Fourteenth Street, N.W., 20005-2011.
Telephone: 202-628-6600.
Telex: 44-0277 PCSO.
Facsimile: 202-434-1690.
Boise, Idaho: 714 West State Street, 83702.
Telephone: 208-343-3434.
Facsimile: 208-343-3232.
Portland, Oregon: Suite 1500, 1211 Southwest Fifth Avenue.
Telephone: 503-727-2000.
Facsimile: 503-727-2222.
Spokane, Washington: North 221 Wall Street, Suite 600, 99201-0826.
Telephone: 509-624-2212.
Facsimile: 509-458-3399.
Hong Kong: 17/F, Standard Charter Bank Building, 4 Des Voeux Road.
Telephone: 852-2878-1177.
Facsimile: 852-2524-9988.
Taipei, Taiwan, R.O.C.: 8/F Cathay United Bank Tower, 85 Jen Ai Rd., Section 5.
Telephone: 886-2-2778-1177.
Facsimile: 886-2-2777-9898.
Canada: Strategic Alliance with Russell & DuMoulin, 1700-1075 West Georgia Street. Vancouver, British Columbia, V6E 3G2.
Telephone: 604-631-3131.

PARTNERS

Kurt Becker
Joan C. Clarke
Bruce E. Dick
Charles N. Eberhardt
Craig S. Gilbert
Lawrence B. Hannah
Donald G. Kari (P.S.)
R. Gerard Lutz
Greg P. Mackay
Steven C. Marshall (P.S.)
Sherilyn Peterson
Vicki M. Pierce
Steven E. Pope
Markham A. Quehrn
Richard R. Rohde
Craig H. Shrontz
Paul E. Smith
Roger M. Tolbert
James M. Van Nostrand

OF COUNSEL

Yukio Morikubo
Lisa T. Oratz
Philip A. Thompson
F. Theodore Thomsen
Jeffrey D. Wyszynski

ASSOCIATES

Sheree Strom Carson
Kirstin S. Dodge
Andrée G. Gagnon
Donald Heyrich
Yuki Ishizuka
Melissa M. Jackson
Pamela Weidler Krueger
Anne Leahy
Michael D. Martin
William R. Maurer
Michele C. Meske
Kenneth A. Miller
Matthew G. Pearson
Kirk A. Soderquist
Brett N. Wiese
Jon M. Zieger

For full biographical listings, see the Martindale-Hubbell Law Directory

KENNEWICK, Benton Co.

LEAVY, SCHULTZ, DAVIS & FEARING, P.S. (AV)

2415 West Falls Avenue, 99336
Telephone: 509-736-1330
Fax: 509-736-1580
Email: jschultz@owt.com *URL:* http://www.tricitylaw.com

James Leavy (1915-1987)
John G. Schultz
William E. Davis
George B. Fearing
Robert G. Schultz

George E. Telquist

Representative Client: Franklin County Irrigation District.
Insurance Clients: Nationwide Insurance Co.; Safeco Insurance Co.; Grange Insurance Co.; State Farm Mutual Insurance Cos.

For full biographical listings, see the Martindale-Hubbell Law Directory

KIRKLAND, King Co.

COOLEY GODWARD LLP (AV)

5200 Carillon Point, 98033-7355
Telephone: 425-893-7700
Fax: 425-893-7777
Email: webmaster@cooley.com *URL:* http://www.cooley.com
Palo Alto, California Office: Five Palo Alto Square, 3000 El Camino Real.
Telephone: 650-843-5000.
Fax: 650-857-0663.
San Francisco, California Office: 20th Floor, One Maritime Plaza.
Telephone: 415-693-2000.
Fax: 415-951-3698 or 415-951-3699.
San Diego, California Office: 4365 Executive Drive, Suite 1100.
Telephone: 619-550-6000.
Fax: 619-453-3555.
Menlo Park, California Office: 3000 Sand Hill Road, Building 3, Suite 230.
Telephone: 650-843-5000.
Fax: 650-854-2691.
Boulder, Colorado Office: 2595 Canyon Boulevard, Suite 250.
Telephone: 303-546-4000.
Fax: 303-546-4099.
Denver, Colorado Office: One Tabor Center, 1200 17th Street, Suite 2100.
Telephone: 303-606-4800.
Fax: 303-606-4899.
Reston, Virginia Office: 2002 Edmund Halley Drive, Suite 300.
Telephone: 703-262-8000.
Fax: 703-262-8100.

PARTNERS

Gregory B. Abbott
Susan L. Preston
Christopher W. Wright

ASSOCIATES

Kevin C. Austin
Eric Scott Carnell
H. Marlow Green
Douglas H. Haeuber
Robert A. Perez
Matthew F. Roberts
Jeffry A. Shelby
Philip N. Tanaka
Thomas B. Youth

For full biographical listings, see the Martindale-Hubbell Law Directory

LAKEWOOD, Pierce Co.

McCORMICK, HOFFMAN, REES, FAUBION, VAN BUSKIRK, JOHNSON & SCHUMOCK, P.S. (AV)

Lakewood Professional Village, 5920 100th Street, S.W. Suite 25, 98499-2751
Telephone: 253-581-0660
Fax: 253-581-0894
Federal Way, Washington Office: 31919 First Avenue South, Suite 100.
Telephone: 206-946-5144.

Perry McCormick, Jr. (1921-1992)
Paul Hoffman, Jr. (Retired)
Merrifield B. Rees
Thomas K. Faubion
John J. Van Buskirk
Clint P. Johnson
Mark F. Schumock

Chong S. So

LEGAL SUPPORT PERSONNEL

Cecile Hedrick
Kathleen Pugerude
Joanne Wolf

Reference: Key Bank.

For full biographical listings, see the Martindale-Hubbell Law Directory

*OLYMPIA,** Thurston Co.

FRISTOE, TAYLOR & SCHULTZ, LTD., P.S. (AV)

Formerly Brodie, Fristoe & Taylor
Suite One Professional Arts Building, 11th & Washington Streets, 98501
Telephone: 360-357-5566
Telecopy: 360-357-5569
Email: 71231.3455@compuserve.com

H. C. Brodie (1884-1951)
H. Doane Brodie (1908-1969)
E. Robert Fristoe
Don Peter William Taylor
Theodore D. Schultz
Frank W. Groundwater

Representative Clients: Seattle-First National Bank (Olympia Branch); Kalama Telephone Co.; Tenino Telephone Co.; Yelm Telephone Co.; Thurston County Public Utility District; Great American First Savings Bank, F.S.B.; Ireco, Inc.; Memorial Clinic, Ltd., P.S.; U.S. Intelco Networks, Inc.; Select Enterprises, Inc.

For full biographical listings, see the Martindale-Hubbell Law Directory

OWENS DAVIES MACKIE, P.S. A PROFESSIONAL SERVICES CORPORATION (AV)

926 - 24th Way S.W., P.O. Box 187, 98507-0187
Telephone: 360-943-8320
Fax: 360-943-6150
Email: mail@odmlaw.com

Frank J. Owens
Burton R. Johnson (1935-1970)
Arthur L. Davies
Alexander W. Mackie, Jr.
John V. Lyman
Richard G. Phillips, Jr.
Brian L. Budsberg
Michael W. Mayberry
Robert F. Hauth
Kirk M. Veis
Matthew B. Edwards

Erik D. Price
David B. Merchant

Representative Clients: Heritage Bank, FSB; Port of Olympia; Westar Financial Services, Inc. (Vehicle Loans and Leasing); Lakeside Industries (Local Counsel); Pabst Brewing Co., Tumwater Division; Columbia Beverage Co.

For full biographical listings, see the Martindale-Hubbell Law Directory

*SEATTLE,** King Co.

BETTS, PATTERSON & MINES, P.S. (AV)

800 Financial Center, 1215 Fourth Avenue, 98161-1090
Telephone: 206-292-9988
Fax: 206-343-7053
Email: admin@bpmlaw.com *URL:* http://www.bpmlaw.com

Natalie S. Adams
Ronald D. Allen
Tracy Antley-Olander
Denise L. Ashbaugh
S. Karen Bamberger
Frederick V. Betts
Steven W. Block
John P. Braislin
Paul D. Carey
Carmen L. Cook
Deborah A. Crabbe
Andrew C. Cratsenberg, Jr.
Kathleen A.T. Dassel
Charles W. Davis
Stephen L. Day
Glenn S. Draper
William P. Fite
Jessica Jackson Fleck
Steven Goldstein
Susan K. Goplen
Lori L. Guzzo
David L. Hennings
Bruce H. Hurst
Maury A. Kroontje
Robert F. Lopez
John D. Matthews
Robert E. Matthews
Kenneth S. McEwan
Michael Mines
James D. Nelson
Thomas F. Peterson
Allison G. Pettit
Bradley J. Rorem
Jayson W. Sowers
Donald L. Thoreson
Christopher W. Tompkins
Livingston Wernecke

FOREIGN LAW CONSULTANT (JAPAN)

Toshimitsu Takaesu

Representative Clients: Associated Grocers, Incorporated; Cape Fox Corporation; COREGIS; Fleetwood Enterprises, Inc.; KeyBank National Association; Motor Cargo; Phizer, Inc.; Sofamor Danek Group; Supermarket Development Corporation.

For full biographical listings, see the Martindale-Hubbell Law Directory

CARNEY BADLEY SMITH & SPELLMAN, P.S. (AV)

701 Fifth Avenue, Suite 2200, 98104-7091
Telephone: 206-622-8020
Fax: 206-467-8215
Email: info@carneylaw.com

David W. Bever
Elvin P. Carney (1904-1984)
Mark E. Cavanagh
Charles N. Evans
Steven J. Hopp
Ted R. Katterheinrich
Patrick R. Lamb
James E. Lobsenz
Stephen L. Nourse
Richard J. Padden
Timothy J. Parker
C. Scott Penner
Frederick M. Robinson
Palmer Robinson

(See Next Column)

CARNEY BADLEY SMITH & SPELLMAN P.S., *Seattle—Continued*

Catherine A. Rothwell
B. Shana Saichek
Nicholas P. Scarpelli, Jr.
Jon M. Schorr
Milton C. Smith
Daniel W. Unti
Clifford A. Webster

Tana M. Beer
Edmund V. Caplicki, III
John C. Dippold
Peter H. Dykstra
Cynthia Grace Flynn
Charles C. Holley
Diane Kownacki
John R. McDowall
Jon A. Payne
David W. Silke

OF COUNSEL

Basil Badley
John C. Huston
Kenneth S. Kagan
John D. Spellman
Donald J. Verfurth

Insurance Clients: American Insurance Assn.; TIG (formerly Transamerica Insurance Co.); Design Professionals Insurance Co.; Acordia Northwest.
Representative Clients: Albertsons, Inc.; Carpenters Trusts of Western Washington; Manson Construction & Engineering Co.; State of Alaska.

For full biographical listings, see the Martindale-Hubbell Law Directory

FOSTER PEPPER & SHEFELMAN PLLC (AV)

A Professional Limited Liability Company including Professional Service Corporations
34th Floor, 1111 Third Avenue, 98101
Telephone: 206-447-4400
Facsimile: 206-447-9700
Email: postmaster@foster.com *URL:* http://www.foster.com
Spokane, Washington Office: W. 422 Riverside Avenue, Suite 1310.
Telephone: 509-777-1600.
Facsimile: 509-777-1616.
Portland, Oregon Office: Foster Pepper & Shefelman LLP, 15th Floor, 101 S.W. Main Street.
Telephone: 503-221-0607.
Facsimile: 503-221-1510.
Anchorage, Alaska Office: Foster Pepper Rubini & Reeves LLC, Suite 500, 601 West Fifth Avenue.
Telephone: 907-276-4411.
Facsimile: 907-276-4400.

James P. Weter (1877-1959)
F. M. Roberts (1880-1973)
W. V. Tanner (1881-1953)
John P. Garvin (1888-1972)
Paul P. Ashley (1896-1979)
Harold S. Shefelman (1898-1984)
James C. Harper (1915-1993)
Robert F. Buck (Retired)
James Gay (Retired)
Victor D. Lawrence (1913-1996)
Arthur S. Quigley (Retired)
Thomas B. Foster (Retired)
Robert G. Moch (Retired)

MEMBERS OF FIRM

Gary N. Ackerman
Thomas F. Ahearne
Christopher M. Alston
Thomas P. Amodio (Resident, Anchorage, Alaska Office)
Bradley J. Berg
Karen J. Boyle
Beth A. Clark
Bruce A. Coffey
Edward R. Coulson
Jack J. Cullen
Robert J. Diercks
P. Stephen DiJulio
James P. Dugan
Peter S. Ehrlichman
John A. Fandel
Timothy J. Filer
Gary E. Fluhrer
Linda L. Foreman
Joann H. Francis
Joseph M. Gaffney
J. Scott Galloway
Curt B. Gleaves (Resident, Portland, Oregon Office)
Lynne E. Graybeal
Camden M. Hall
John L. Hendrickson
Brian D. Hulse
Allen D. Israel
Dillon E. Jackson
Steven G. Jones
Richard E. Keefe (P.S.)
Stellman Keehnel
Michael D. Kuntz
Wade S. Leathers
Marco J. Magnano, Jr.
Roger D. Mellem
Michael G. Mitchell (Resident, Anchorage, Alaska Office)
Andrew J. Morrow, Jr. (Resident, Portland, Oregon Office)
Jonathan B. Noll
Charles P. Nomellini
Douglas S. Palmer, Jr. (P.S.)
Peter C. Partnow (Resident, Anchorage, Alaska Office)
Roger A. Pearce
Jane Pearson
Thomas M. Pors
Gregory L. Powell (Resident, Portland, Oregon Office)
Glen Price (Resident, Anchorage, Alaska Office)
Douglas R. Prince
Susan E. Reeves (Resident, Anchorage, Alaska Office)
Warren J. Rheaume
Paul V. Rieke
Kenneth E. Roberts, Jr. (Resident, Portland, Oregon Office)
Jonathan B. Rubini (Resident, Anchorage, Alaska Office)
Gail R. Schubert (Resident, Anchorage, Alaska Office)
Michael R. Silvey (Resident, Portland, Oregon Office)
Hugh D. Spitzer
Lawrence J. Steele
V. Rafael Stone
David B. Sweeney
Daniel L. Thieme
William G. Tonkin
David Utevsky
Michael K. Vaska
Lee Voorhees
Thomas M. Walsh
J. Tayloe Washburn
Judee A. Wells
Joseph P. Whitford
Alan K. Willert
Deborah S. Winter
Charles R. Wolfe

(See Next Column)

RESIDENT OF COUNSEL
AT SEATTLE, WASHINGTON OFFICE

Christine E. Allen
Mary L. Beyer
Laura J. Brackett
Jordan J. Breslow (Not admitted in WA)
Richard J. Busch
Sophia E. Chrusciel
Clifford M. Curry
Brian J. Danzig
Joseph E. Delaney
Dan D. Dixon (Not admitted in WA)
Dwight J. Drake
Gail J. Gordon
Willard Hatch
Tamara J. Hendrickson
Jon G. Hongladarom
Christopher Kane
Patrick F. Kennedy
Patrick W. Kuo
George M. Mack
Larry C. Martin
Marsha L. Martin
Patrick J. Mullaney
Mary-Alice Pomputius (Not admitted in WA)
Judith M. Runstad
Lucas D Schenck
Richard L. Settle
William V. Taylor
Anne B. Tiura
Carl J. West III, (P.S.)

RESIDENT OF COUNSEL
AT PORTLAND, OREGON OFFICE

Paul B. George
Walter W. McMonies, Jr.

RESIDENT OF COUNSEL
AT ANCHORAGE, ALASKA OFFICE

John A. Reeder
Sandra K. Saville

ASSOCIATES

Andrea D. Axel (Not admitted in WA)
Kyle L. Branum
Brian D. Buckley
Steve P. Calandrillo
Grover E. Cleveland
Gordon E. Crim (Resident, Portland, Oregon Office)
David J. Dadoun
Chryssa V. Deliganis
Steven P. Eakman
Christopher G. Emch
Bradley A. Evens
Marc R. Greenough
Stephanie Marshall Hicks
Bradley W. Hoff
Jennifer L. King
Koren T. D. Koubourlis
Jeremy R. Larson
Joseph D. Lee
Carter M. Mann (Resident, Portland, Oregon Office)
Marsha L. Martin (Resident, Bellevue Office)
Michelle K. McClure (Resident, Portland, Oregon Office)
Jeffrey S. Miller
Lori Nomura
Andrew H. Ognall (Resident, Portland, Oregon Office)
Ryan D. Rein
Robin A. Rosencrantz
Erin P. Snodgrass
Cliff E. Spencer (Resident, Portland, Oregon Office)
Kevin W. Teague

For full biographical listings, see the Martindale-Hubbell Law Directory

GARVEY, SCHUBERT & BARER (AV)

1191 Second Avenue, 18th Floor, 98101
Telephone: 206-464-3939
Cable Address: "Lex, Seattle"
Telecopier: 206-464- 0125
Washington, D.C. Office: 5th Floor, 1000 Potomac Street, N.W., 20007.
Telephone: 202-965-7880.
Telecopier: 202-965-1729.
Portland, Oregon Office: Eleventh Floor, 121 S.W. Morrison Street, 97204.
Telephone: 503-228-3939.
Telecopier: 503-226-0259.

MEMBERS OF FIRM

Joanne Thomas Blackburn
Norman J. Bruns
Timothy C. Burkart
Rodney B. Carman
Susan L. Coskey
Keven J. Davis
Jan L. Essenburg
Roger L. Hillman
John K. Hoerster
Barbara L. Holland
Stephen B. Johnson
James G. Kibble
Ronald J. Knox
Jonathan A. Kroman
David Lieberworth
Donald L. Logerwell
Bruce A. McDermott
Brian A. Morrison
Anne F. Preston
Bruce A. Robertson
Charles C. Robinson
Gregg Rodgers
E. Charles Routh
Mark A. Rowley
Lori Salzarulo
Sara P. Sandford
Kenneth L. Schubert, Jr.
William C. Severson
Alan P. Sherbrooke
Robert B. Spitzer
R. Jack Stephenson
Gary J. Strauss
Scott G. Warner
David R. West
Susan Richardson Willert

RESIDENT ASSOCIATES

Christina Barton
Karen R. Bertram
Christopher S. Brown
Jennifer D. Bucher
AnnaLisa Clar
Aline C. Flower
Ellen J. Himmel
Elizabeth Lynn Hubbard
Anne-Marie Huizinga
Kristi J. Johnson
Drake R. Kendermore
Ruth A. Kennedy
John J. Lapham, III
Berrie J. Martinis
Pegeen Mulhern
Andrea D. Orth
Donald B. Scaramastra
Amy L. Sommers
Gary D. Swearingen
Julio M. Zapata

(See Next Column)

GARVEY, SCHUBERT & BARER—*Continued*

OF COUNSEL

Craig H. Allen
Stanley H. Barer
Patricia H. Char
Gregory R. Dallaire
Steven M. Dickinson
Lucinda D. Fernald
Michael D. Garvey
David W. Gee
Kenneth L. Karlberg
Bruce A. King
Joseph A. McIntosh

Representative Clients: Foss Maritime Co.; In Focus Systems, Inc.; K2 Corporation; Nissho Iwai American Corp.; PeaceHealth; The Commerce Bank of Washington.

For full biographical listings, see the Martindale-Hubbell Law Directory

---

GRAHAM & DUNN PC (AV)

1420 Fifth Avenue, 33rd Floor, 98101-2390
Telephone: 206-624-8300
Fax: 206-340-9599
Email: solutions@grahamdunn.com
Tacoma, Washington Office: 1145 Broadway Plaza, Suite 950, 98402-3523.
Telephone: 253-572-9294.

Donald G. Graham (1894-1972)
Bryant R. Dunn (1909-1992)
W. George Bassett
Robert G. Bergquist
Douglas C. Berry
Stephen A. Crary
Robert C. Cumbow
Gary R. Duvall
K. Michael Fandel
Mark A. Finkelstein
James C. Fowler
Frederick O. Frederickson
Marcia K. Fujimoto
Ben J. Gantt, Jr.
Stephen H. Goodman
Alice F. Gustafson
John T. John
Stephen M. Klein
Mark C. Lewington (Resident, Tacoma Office)
Marisa V. Lindell
James L. Magee
Peter S. McCormick
Michael P. Mirande
Thomas H. Nelson
Mark D. Northrup
Scott B. Osborne
Edward W. Pettigrew
Irvin W. Sandman
Carmen L. Smith
Larry J. Smith
Elaine L. Spencer
Jack G. Strother
Michael J. Swofford
Michael Tobiason

COUNSEL

William E. Bartholdt, Jr.
Jeffrey A. Beaver
Wendy S. Goffe
Estera F. Gordon
George T. Hunter
Arthur J. Lachman
Nadine C. Mandel
James M. Shore

Bradford J. Axel (Not admitted in WA)
Margaret D. Christopher
Riza E. De Jesus
Kimberly S. Freise
Maren K. Gaylor
J. Andrew Jackson (Not admitted in WA)
Derek N. Ko
Michael E. Lapin
Kara M. Levis
David C. Lundsgaard
Sharon L. Rosse Fowler
Deirdre L. Runnette (Not admitted in WA)
Kumi Yamamoto

Representative Clients: The Ackerley Group; Atlantic Richfield; Fisher Companies, Inc.; Icicle Seafoods, Inc.; GeneSpan Corp.; SeaFirst; Westin Hotels and Resorts; John L. Scott Real Estate Network; US Bank; Nike Inc.

For full biographical listings, see the Martindale-Hubbell Law Directory

---

HELSELL FETTERMAN LLP (AV)

1500 Puget Sound Plaza, 1325 Fourth Avenue, P.O. Box 21846, 98111-3846
Telephone: 206-292-1144
Telecopier: 206-340-0902
Email: hf@helsell.com

MEMBERS OF FIRM

Gary F. Linden
Phillip D. Noble
David F. Jurca
John G. Bergmann
Pauline V. Smetka
David Gross
Bradley H. Bagshaw
Andrew J. Kinstler
Mark F. Rising
Kevin L. Stock
Llewelyn G. Pritchard
Robert N. Gellatly
Dirk A. Bartram
Scott E. Collins

COUNSEL

Russell V. Hokanson
Richard S. White
Harold R. Rooks
John Edward Ederer
Karen J. Vanderlaan
Laura F. Pasik
Jerry E. Thonn
Peter J. Eglick
Larry Setchell
John W. Kydd
Jennifer S. Divine

ASSOCIATES

Polly Becker-Johnson
Natalie M. Beckmann
Lisa M. Gilmore
Darla J. Goodwin
Jane S. Kiker
Catherine E. Kvistad
John D. Ferrell

Representative Clients: Allstate Insurance Cos.; Bethlehem Steel Corp.; Chevron Corp.; Chiyoda International Corp.; Farmers Insurance Group; Holland America Line-Westours Inc.; Nicholson Industries, Inc.; Star Industries, Inc.

(See Next Column)

For full biographical listings, see the Martindale-Hubbell Law Directory

---

HILLIS CLARK MARTIN & PETERSON A PROFESSIONAL SERVICE CORPORATION (AV)

500 Galland Building, 1221 Second Avenue, 98101-2925
Telephone: 206-623-1745
Facsimile: 206-623-7789
Email: info@hcmp.com *URL:* http://www.hcmp.com

D. Christian Addicott
Joseph M. Ahern
Joel N. Bodansky
Michelle S. Chang
Laurie Lootens Chyz
Mark S. Clark
Sally H. Clarke
Lynne M. Cohee
Gregory J. Duff
T. Ryan Durkan
Gary M. Fallon
Ann M. Gygi
Jerome L. Hillis
George A. Kresovich
Eric D. Lansverk
Derek W. Loeser
George W. Martin, Jr.
Melody B. McCutcheon
Mark C. McPherson
David E. Myre, Jr.
Thaddeus I. Paul
Louis D. Peterson
Richard M. Peterson
Stephen H. Roos
Gabriel S. Rosenthal
Steven R. Rovig
Michael F. Schumacher
Michael R. Scott
Matthew P. Smith
Brian D. Todd
Robert B. Van Cleve
Michael S. Wampold
Amy Williams-Derry
Richard R. Wilson

Representative Clients: Continental, Inc.; Continental Savings Bank; Horizon Air; JAMCO America, Inc.; Merrill Lynch, Pierce, Fenner & Smith Inc.; Mitsubishi International Corporation; Port of Seattle; The Quadrant Corporation; Weyerhaeuser Company.

For full biographical listings, see the Martindale-Hubbell Law Directory

---

HOLMES WEDDLE & BARCOTT, A PROFESSIONAL CORPORATION (AV)

999 Third Avenue, Suite 2600, 98104
Telephone: 206-292-8008
Telecopier: 206-340-0289
Email: INFO@SEA.HWB-LAW.COM
Anchorage, Alaska Office: 701 West Eighth Avenue, Suite 700.
Telephone: 907-274-0666.
Telecopier: 907-277-4657.

Michael M. Holmes
Michael A. Barcott
John E. Casperson
William D. De Voe
Raymond H. Warns, Jr.
James F. Whitehead
Philip W. Sanford

OF COUNSEL

Paul N. Daigle

Maribeth Conway
Christopher Y. Kim
Nina M. Mitchell
Dylan S. Jones
Jay R. Rodne

For full biographical listings, see the Martindale-Hubbell Law Directory

---

LANE POWELL SPEARS LUBERSKY LLP (AV)

Limited Liability Partnership composed of Individuals and Professional Service Corporations
1420 Fifth Avenue, Suite 4100, 98101-2338
Telephone: 206-223-7000
Facsimile: 206-223-7107
Email: information@lanepowell.com *URL:* http://www.lanepowell.com
Other Offices at: Portland, Oregon; Anchorage, Alaska; Olympia and Mount Vernon, Washington; London, England.

MANAGING PARTNERS

Michael D. Dwyer
James L. Robart

MEMBERS OF FIRM

Richard F. Allen
Glenn J. Amster
Warren E. Babb, Jr.
Clemens H. Barnes
Mark G. Beard
Stanton Phillip Beck
Randall P. Beighle
W. L. Rivers Black, III
Scott F. Campbell
Linda Blohm Clapham
Michael L. Cohen
Robert R. Davis, Jr.
Grant S. Degginger
J.C. Ditzler
Dan J. Donlan
Barbara J. Duffy
Charles R. Ekberg (P.S.)
Rudy A. Englund
Larry S. Gangnes
Jeffrey L. Gingold
D. Wayne Gittinger
Thomas F. Grohman
Charles C. Huber
David T. Hunter
D. Joseph Hurson
Robert L. Israel (P.S.)
David G. Johansen
Mark Edwin Johnson
Jim D. Johnston
Kenneth B. Kaplan
Kenyon P. Kellogg
Michael B. King
Gary M. Kirk
Dale E. Kremer
Jeffrey D. Laveson
Bruce W. Leaverton
Joseph E. Lynam
Katie Smith Matison
Gail E. Mautner
Barry N. Mesher
Suzanne Kelly Michael
Michael E. Morgan

(See Next Column)

LANE POWELL SPEARS LUBERSKY LLP, *Seattle—Continued*

MEMBERS OF FIRM (Continued)

Douglas S. Morrison
Kit G. Narodick
John R. Neeleman
Jane Rakay Nelson
Michael A. Nesteroff
Christopher W. Nicoll
Paul M. Nordsletten
Christian N. Oldham
Hartley Paul
William A. Pelandini
Ralph C. Pond
D. Michael Reilly
Charles W. Riley, Jr.
Mark A. Rossi
Michael H. Runyan
Mark P. Scheer
Reed P. Schifferman
David M. Schoeggl
Clifford D. Sethness
Richard C. Siefert
Douglas E. Smith
Stephen C. Smith
H. Peter Sorg, Jr.
Maria E. Sotirhos
David C. Spellman
Cathy A. Spicer
James B. Stoetzer
Paul D. Swanson
Gary P. Tober
Tim D. Wackerbarth
Linda D. Walton
Raymond S. Weber
Christopher B. Wells
Douglas E. Wheeler

OF COUNSEL

Meade Emory
Gordon W. Moss

COUNSEL

Mark J. Asplund (Not admitted in WA)
Minaksi Bhatt (Not admitted in WA)
Diane M. Butler
June K. Campbell
Mary Jo Heston
Eric B. Johnson
Ada Ko
Paul McCarthy
James E. Niemer
Joan E. Robinson
Emilia L. Sweeney
Thomas W. Top
John James Watson

ASSOCIATES

Stephanie R. Alexander
Gregory L. Anderson
Nancy Watkins Anderson
Gabriel Baker
Rehman H. Bashey
Ronald E. Beard
Stefan Ernst Biberfeld
David William Briggs
Daniel J. Caplinger
James D. Clack
Grant E. Courtney
Steven Clark Davis
John S. Devlin, III
Molly E. Farr
Jo M. Flannery
Timothy J. Graham
Sarah Elyse Haushild
Chris W. Higgins
June A. Jackson
Susan Brye Jahnke
Steve D. Jensen
Clarence C. Jones, Jr.
Kathleen A. Keizer (Not admitted in WA)
Gwendolyn Payton Klein
Tammy L. Lewis
William W. Lin
Matthew J. Macario
Christopher L. Marzetti
Jodi A. McDougall
Brian J. Meenaghan
Kimberly M. Meyers
Patrick R. Okell
Annmarie Petrich
Carllene M. Placide
Mack H. Shultz, Jr.
Dennis M. Strasser
Cindy A. Tramountanas
Allison S. Wallin
Eric D. Wright
Alison L. Yearsley
Masahiro "Max" Yoshimura
John E. Zehnder, Jr.
Brian D. Zeringer

Representative Clients: AT&T Corp.; Cutter & Buck; Fred Hutchinson Cancer Research Center; Mitsui & Co. (U.S.A.) Inc.; Nordstrom, Inc.; Simpson Investment Co.; Texaco Inc.; Underwriters at Lloyds, London; Wells Fargo Bank; Western Wireless Corp.

For full biographical listings, see the Martindale-Hubbell Law Directory

McNaul Ebel Nawrot Helgren & Vance P.L.L.C. (AV)

600 University Street, Suite 2700, 98101-3143
Telephone: 206-467-1816
Facsimile: 206-624-5128
Email: info@mcnaul.com *URL:* http://www.mcnaul.com

MEMBERS OF FIRM

John S. Ebel
Tyler B. Ellrodt
Barbara Hallowell
Michael D. Helgren
Jerry R. McNaul
Matthew N. Menzer
Louis F. Nawrot, Jr.
Robert D. Stewart
Robert M. Sulkin
Cyrus R. Vance, Jr.
Peter M. Vial
Marc O. Winters

OF COUNSEL

Murray B. Guterson
Barbara H. Schuknecht

RETIRED

George L. Grader

ASSOCIATES

Steven J.S. Christophersen
Gregory J. Hollon
Johnathan E. Mansfield
Ann Marie Schwartz
Nancy G. Stephenson
Christopher E. Tucker

For full biographical listings, see the Martindale-Hubbell Law Directory

Mikkelborg, Broz, Wells & Fryer, PLLC (AV)

Suite 3600, 1001 Fourth Avenue, 98154
Telephone: 206-623-5890
Facsimile: 206-623-0965
Email: mail@mbwf.com

(See Next Column)

MEMBERS OF FIRM

Robert O. Wells, Jr.
Douglas M. Fryer
Richard L. Phillips
Jeffrey L. Jernegan
Margaret Doyle Fitzpatrick
Jess G. Webster
Newell D. Smith
Mitchell A. Broz

ASSOCIATES

Victor V. Hoff
Rebecca T. White

OF COUNSEL

G. Lawrence Salkield
John E. Lenker

COUNSEL

Jacob A. Mikkelborg
Richard F. Broz

LEGAL SUPPORT PERSONNEL

M. Brigid Browne

For full biographical listings, see the Martindale-Hubbell Law Directory

Oles, Morrison, Rinker & Baker L.L.P. (AV)

3300 Columbia Center, 701 Fifth Avenue, 98104-7082
Telephone: 206-623-3427
Telecopier: 206-682-6234
Email: omr@oles.com *URL:* http://www.omr@oles.com
Anchorage, Alaska Office: 745 West 4th Avenue, Suite 502.
Telephone: 907-258-0106.
Fax: 907-277-8002.

MEMBERS OF FIRM

Stuart G. Oles (Retired)
Seth W. Morrison
David C. Stewart
Sam E. Baker, Jr.
Arthur D. McGarry
B. Michael Schestopol
Robert J. Burke
Bradley L. Powell
Douglas S. Oles
Peter N. Ralston
John Lukjanowicz
James F. Nagle
Glenn R. Nelson
J. Craig Rusk
Traeger Machetanz
David R. Chappel

ASSOCIATES

Emmanuel P. Tangas
William K. Renno (Resident, Anchorage Office)
Catherine C. Clark
Mark D. Walters
W. Gregory Guedel
Cynthia Dale Turner
C. Russell Lewis (Not admitted in WA; Resident, Anchorage, Alaska Office)
Michael R. Beyer
Laura Kleisle
Xiaoqiu Wang
Kelly Blazy
Eileen I. McKillop
Kevin G. Brady (Not admitted in WA)

For full biographical listings, see the Martindale-Hubbell Law Directory

Perkins Coie LLP (AV)

Strategic Alliance with Russell & DuMoulin
1201 Third Avenue, Suite 4800, 98101-3099
Telephone: 206-583-8888
Facsimile: 206-583-8500
Email: perkins@perkinscoie.com *URL:* http://www.perkinscoie.com
Anchorage, Alaska: 1029 West Third Avenue, Suite 300, 99501-1970.
Telephone: 907-279-8561.
Facsimile: 907-276-3108.
Los Angeles, California: 1620 26th Street, 6th Floor, 90404.
Telephone: 310-788-9900.
Facsimile: 310-788-3399.
Menlo Park, California: 135 Commonwealth Drive, Suite 250, 94025-1105.
Telephone: 650-752-6000.
Facsimile: 650-752-6050.
San Francisco, California: 180 Townsend Street, 94107-1909.
Telephone: 415-781-3200.
Facsimile: 415-781-2525.
Denver, Colorado: World Trade Center, 1675 Broadway, Suite 2800, 80202-062.
Telephone: 303-571-6100.
Facsimile: 303-571-6111.
Washington, D.C.: 607 Fourteenth Street, N.W., 20005-2011.
Telephone: 202-628-6600.
Telex: 44-0277 PCSO.
Facsimile: 202-434-1690.
Boise, Idaho: 714 West State Street, 83702.
Telephone: 208-343-3434.
Facsimile: 208-343-3232.
Portland, Oregon: Suite 1500, 1211 Southwest Fifth Avenue.
Telephone: 503-727-2000.
Facsimile: 503-727-2222.
Bellevue, Washington: Suite 1800, One Bellevue Center, 411 - 108th Avenue N.E., 98004-5584.
Telephone: 425-453-6980.
Facsimile: 425-453-7350.
Spokane, Washington: North 221 Wall Street, Suite 600, 99201-0826.
Telephone: 509-624-2212.
Facsimile: 509-458-3399.
Hong Kong: 17/F, Standard Charter Bank Building, 4 Des Voeux Road.
Telephone: 852-2878-1177.
Facsimile: 852-2524-9988.

(See Next Column)

PERKINS COIE LLP—*Continued*

Taipei, Taiwan, R.O.C.: 8/F Cathay United Bank Tower, 85 Jen Ai Rd., Section 5.
Telephone: 886-2-2778-1177.
Facsimile: 886-2-2777-9898.
Canada: Strategic Alliance with Russell & DuMoulin, 1700-1075 West Georgia Street. Vancouver, British Columbia, V6E 3G2.
Telephone: 604-631-3131.

PARTNERS

Ramsey M. Al-Salam
Elizabeth A. Alaniz
John D. Alkire
Peter B. Archie (Not admitted in WA)
John F. Aslin
Robert F. Bakemeier
Michael A. Barrett
Gregg D. Barton
Richard L. Baum (Resident, Portland Oregon Office)
George M. Beal II
Kurt Becker (Resident, Bellevue, Washington Office)
Steven Scott Bell
Thomas C. Bell
Edmund O. Belsheim, Jr.
Ronald L. Berenstain
Charles R. Blumenfeld
Thomas L. Boeder
Marc A. Boman
Andrew Bor
Scott J. Borth
Dori E. Lee Brewer
Rex C. Browning
David J. Burman
Bruce D. Campbell
David C. Clarke
Joan C. Clarke (Resident, Bellevue, Washington Office)
Bruce D. Corker
Richard C. Coyle
J. Thomas Cristy
Bruce Michael Cross
Janis A. Cunningham
David Dabroski
Christopher J. Daley-Watson
Ellen Conedera Dial
Bruce E. Dick (Resident, Bellevue, Washington Office)
Calhoun Dickinson
John D. Dillow
Charles N. Eberhardt (Resident, Bellevue, Washington Office)
Orna A. Edgar
Graham H. Fernald
Susan Fahringer
Bruce P. Flynn
Susan E. Foster
Scott L. Gelband
Keith Gerrard
Robert Edward Giles (Managing Partner)
Gregory Gorder
Ronald M. Gould
James D. Gradel (P.C.)
Stephen M. Graham
William L. Green
Steven W. Hale
Michael L. Hall
Kevin J. Hamilton
Lawrence B. Hannah (Resident, Bellevue, Washington Office)
Steven M. Hedberg
James M. Hilton (P.S.)
Michael Himes
Jeffrey A. Hollingsworth
Ramer B. Holtan, Jr.
Valerie L. Hughes
James R. Johnston
Barry M. Kaplan
Donald G. Kari (P.S.) (Resident, Bellevue, Washington Office)
Charles J. Katz, Jr.
Paul R. Katz (Resident, Santa Monica, California Office)
Roy J. Koegen (Resident, Spokane, Washington Office)
Reginald S. Koehler III
Stewart M. Landefeld
James R. Lisbakken
Douglas S. Little
R. Gerard Lutz (Resident, Bellevue, Washington Office)
Douglas S. MacBain
Greg P. Mackay (Resident, Bellevue, Washington Office)
Steven C. Marshall (P.S.) (Resident, Bellevue, Washington Office)
Richard E. McCann
Matthew B. McCutchen
Thomas J. McLaughlin
David F. McShea
Christian Moller
Philip S. Morse
Richard L. Mull
J. Shan Mullin
Bobbee J. Musgrave (Resident, Denver, Colorado Office)
Clark Reed Nichols
Richard W. Oehler
Omar S. Parker, Jr.
Russell L. Perisho
Sherilyn Peterson (Resident, Bellevue, Washington Office)
Deborah J. Phillips
Vicki M. Pierce (Resident, Bellevue, Washington Office)
Maurice J. Pirio
Thomas E. Platt
Steven E. Pope (Resident, Bellevue, Washington Office)
Richard Ottesen Prentke
Markham A. Quehrn (Resident, Bellevue, Washington Office)
Michael T. Reynvaan
Jerry A. Riedinger
Richard R. Rohde (Resident, Bellevue, Washington Office)
John S. Rossiter, Jr.
Heidi L. Sachs
Harry H. Schneider, Jr.
Mark W. Schneider
Linda A. Schoemaker
Scott F. Seablom
Benjamin S. Sharp (Resident, Washington, D.C. Office)
Michael H. Simon (Resident, Portland, Oregon Office)
Alan D. Smith
Paul E. Smith (Resident, Bellevue, Washington Office)
Michael E. Stansbury
Ben D. Straughan
David F. Taylor (Also at Santa Monica, California Office)
B. Lawrence Theis (Resident, Denver, Colorado Office)
Roger M. Tolbert (Resident, Bellevue, Washington Office)
James M. Van Nostrand (Resident, Bellevue, Washington Office)
Bart Waldman
Laura N. Whitaker
Richard A. White
Nancy Williams
V. L. Woolston
Steven R. Yentzer
D. Michael Young

(See Next Column)

COUNSEL

Richard R. Albrecht
J. David Andrews, P.S.
Wayne C. Booth, Jr.
Walter W. Eyer
H. Weston Foss, P.S.
William A. Gould
Edward W. Kuhrau (P.C.)
Harold F. Olsen
F. Theodore Thomsen (Resident, Bellevue, Washington Office)
Richard E. Walker
Andrew M. Williams (1916-1998)

OF COUNSEL

Anne F. Ackenhusen
Gene S. Anderson
Gretchen F. Baumgardner
Joseph E. Bringman
Michael D. Broaddus
Jay S. Brown
Nancy Thygesen Day
Lorri A. Dunsmore
Lisa Strauch Eggers (Not admitted in WA)
Nicholas P. Gellert
Michael W. Hoge
Karen P. Kruse
Steven D. Lawrenz
Cassandra F. Lentchner (Resident, Washington, D.C. Office)
Alice D. Leiner
Kurt E. Linsenmayer
Mark H. Lough
Bruce G. MacIntyre
Charles E. Maduell
Robert A. Maynard (Resident, Boise, Idaho Office)
Gregory K. McCall
Shannon L. McDougald
Karen M. McGaffey
Michael Edward McGowen (Not admitted in WA)
J. Sue Morgan
Yukio Morikubo (Resident, Bellevue, Washington Office)
Lisa T. Oratz (Resident, Bellevue, Washington Office)
Paul T. Parker
John T. Piper (P.S.)
John R. Price
Laurie N. Cromwell Ragen
Charles B. Roe, Jr. (Resident, Olympia, Washington Office)
Philip A. Thompson (Resident, Bellevue, Washington Office)
Lis Wiehl (Also at Washington, D.C. Office)
Faith M. Wilson
Robert G. Woolston

RESIDENT ASSOCIATES

Marie G. Aglion
Alexander T. Allen
Pamela M. Almaguer
Karla J. Axell
Ira Azulay (Resident, Menlo Park, California Office)
Melissa A. McGonigal Berry
Colonel F. Betz
Neal Black
Andrea Blander
Brian G. Bodine
Heidi B. Boone
Fiona A. Brophy (Resident, Menlo Park, California Office)
Zane A. Brown, Jr.
Michael E. Burke, IV
Mireille O. Butler
Vincent Caruso (Resident, Menlo Park, California Office)
Victor Cerda
Neil I. Chang
Donna M. Cochener
Annjanette M. Cooper
Wendy Davis Crossland
Kha Q. Dang
John P. Deery-Schmitt
John L. Dentler (Resident, Olympia, Washington Office)
Patrick J. Devine
Adrian G. Dirassar (Not admitted in the United States)
Kirstin S. Dodge (Resident, Bellevue, Washington Office)
Sarah C. Dods
Douglas J. Drennan (Resident, Menlo Park, California Office)
Iveth P. Durbin
Scott M. Edwards
Colita Ellis (Resident, San Francisco, California Office)
Nicole L. Ettinger (Resident, San Francisco, California Office)
Melisa D. Evangelos
Kirsten W. Foster
Melissa Francis (Not admitted in WA)
Andrée G. Gagnon (Resident, Bellevue, Washington Office)
Gretchen M. Gende
Danielle Wolfrom Githens
Michael R. Glaser (Resident, Menlo Park, California Office)
Martin S. Goldberg
Douglas W. Greene
Jill Marie Haley (Resident, San Francisco, California Office)
Spencer M. Gusick (Resident, San Francisco, California Office)
Christian M. Halliburton
Jason Dax Hansen
Rima Fawal Hartman
Donald Heyrich (Resident, Bellevue, Washington Office)
Troy J. Hickman
Yuki Ishizuka (Resident, Bellevue, Washington Office)
Erik H. Iverson
Mark G. Jackson
Melissa M. Jackson (Resident, Bellevue, Washington Office)
Traci A. Jarvis (Resident, Denver, Colorado Office)
Kenneth L. Kambich
Liang Leon Kan
John Stuart Kaplan
Katrina Robertson Kelly
Allison Roseman Kendrick
Leigh S. Kilcline
Holly Blair Kjerulff
Steve Y. Koh
Elizabeth W. Korrell
Pamela Weidler Krueger (Resident, Bellevue, Washington Office)
Patricia C. Lally
Heidi Lantz
Sonja L. Lengnick
Jessica Stone Levy
James O. Lyons
Taraneh Maghamé
Robert L. Mahon
Lalitha Mani (Not admitted in WA)
Michael D. Martin (Resident, Bellevue, Washington Office)
Laura E. Mate
William R. Maurer (Resident, Bellevue, Washington Office)
Maurin K. McBroom
James McCullagh
Elizabeth McDougall-Tural
Ann L. McGuire
Joseph Michael McMillan
Brian P. McQuillen
Thomas G. Melling
Michele C. Meske (Resident, Bellevue, Washington Office)
Kenneth A. Miller (Resident, Bellevue, Washington Office)
Andrew B. Moore
John P. Morgan
Sarah Kanwit Morehead

(See Next Column)

PERKINS COIE LLP, *Seattle—Continued*

RESIDENT ASSOCIATES (Continued)

Andrew Moriarty
Kenneth Morrissette, Jr.
Teresa L. Nauta
Melissa Morgan Nelson
Kurt B. Opsahl (Resident, Menlo Park, California)
Kevin C. Osborn
Kathleen M. O'Sullivan
Sean Pak (Resident, San Francisco, California Office)
Julia L. Parsons
Shannon E. Phillips
Barbara Prowant-Hircock (Not admitted in WA)
Theresa E. Pruett
Kelly Reinholdtsen
P. Amy Reischauer
A. Paul Rimas (Resident, San Francisco, California Office)
Frederick B. Rivera
Bridget G. Rodden
Todd W. Rosencrans
Tuhin Roy (Resident, San Francisco, California Office)
Patrick W. Ryan
Brent Sanders
James Sanders
S. Paul Sassalos
Peter K. Schalestock
Galen G. Schuler
Grant Josiah Silvernale, III
Jennifer S. Sim (Resident, Menlo Park, California Office)
Carrie C. Simchuk
Alan C. Smith
Brent C. Snyder
Kirk A. Soderquist (Resident, Bellevue, Washington Office)
Erika Jongejan Starrs
John C. Stewart
Eric Thoreson
Catherine Hong Tran
Kathryn L. Tucker
Kari Anne Tuohy
Daniel F. Vaughn
Sarah H. Villanueva
Douglas M. Walker
Kurt R. Walters
Donald E. Walther
Amy L. Watson
Wayt T. (Tim) Watterson
John M. Wechkin
Leecia Welch
Melvin E. Wheaton
Curtrice M. White
James A.D. White
Stephen C. Willey
James Fitzgerald Williams
Michael P. Witek
Georges H.G. Yates
Jon M. Zieger (Resident, Bellevue, Washington Office)

Counsel for: AT&T Wireless; The Boeing Co.; General Motors Corp.; Lloyd's of London (Aviation); Puget Sound Power & Light Co.; Seattle School District; Shurgard Capital Group; Sierra On-Line, Inc.; U.S. West; Weyerhaeuser Co.

For full biographical listings, see the Martindale-Hubbell Law Directory

REED MCCLURE (AV)

Two Union Square, 601 Union Street, Suite 4800, 98101-3900
Telephone: 206-292-4900
Telecopier: 206-223-0152
ABA/Net 1429
Email: info@rmlaw.com

SHAREHOLDERS

Stuart C. Allen
Keith Gormley Baldwin
Katharine Witter Brindley
Steven L. Burgon
Mary R. DeYoung
Marilee C. Erickson
Kathryn L. Feldman
Geoffrey Groshong
Bruce E. Heller
William R. Hickman
William L. Holder
Mark M. Hough
Ross D. Jacobson
Robert D. Johns
Vanessa Lee
C. Dean Little
Michael P. Monroe
Greg Montgomery
Pamela A. Okano
R. Thomas Olson
Mary S. Petersen
Beth Mattler Picardo
John W. Rankin, Jr.
Petrea Knudsen Reilly
Michael S. Rogers
GailAnn Y. Stargardter
Earl M. Sutherland
Guy Towle
George S. Treperinas
Robert J. Walerius
Mark Weakley

OF COUNSEL

Bradley D. Grisham

PRINCIPALS

Kent A. Caputo
John P. Erlick
Darrell S. Mitsunaga
Sherry H. Rogers
Brian J. Todd
J. Todd Tracy
Janice Sue Wang

ASSOCIATES

Cynthia L. Alderete-Medjo
Steven Beeghly
David S. Cottnair
Hilary S. Franz
Anamaria Gil
Julie Goldsmith
Danielle A. Hess
Dana Livingstone Kenny
Nicole M. Rendahl
Mark A. Rowland
David G. Schoolcraft
Jennifer L. Scully

Representative Clients: Allstate; McCormick Land Co.; Northwest Hospital; Seattle University; State Farm Insurance Companies; W & H Pacific, Inc.; Wards Cove Packing Co.; Washington Federal Savings; Washington Casualty Co.

For full biographical listings, see the Martindale-Hubbell Law Directory

SAYRE LAW OFFICES (AV)

1016 Jefferson Street, 98104-2435
Telephone: 206-625-0092
Facsimile: 206-625-9040
URL: http://www.lawyers.com/sayrelaw
Email: sayrelaw@seanet.com *URL:* http://www.lawyers.com/sayre

(See Next Column)

MEMBERS OF FIRM

Matt Sayre
Jeffrey M. Sayre

ASSOCIATE

Karin S. Treadwell

Reference: Seattle-First National Bank.

For full biographical listings, see the Martindale-Hubbell Law Directory

*SPOKANE,** Spokane Co.

WITHERSPOON, KELLEY, DAVENPORT & TOOLE, P.S. (AV)

1100 U.S. Bank Building, 422 West Riverside, 99201
Telephone: 509-624-5265
Fax: 509-458-2728
Coeur d'Alene, Idaho Office: 608 Northwest Boulevard, Suite 401.
Telephone: 208-667-4000.
Fax: 208-667-8470.

Robert L. Magnuson
Ned M. Barnes
William D. Symmes
Robert H. Lamp
K. Thomas Connolly
Thomas D. Cochran
Duane M. Swinton
Joseph H. Wessman
Jeffrey L. Supinger
Donald J. Lukes
Leslie R. Weatherhead
Michael D. Currin
Brian T. Rekofke
R. Max Etter, Jr.
Stanley R. Schultz
Michael F. Nienstedt
John M. Riley, III
F. J. Dullanty, Jr.
Daniel E Finney
Mary R. Giannini

Timothy M. Lawlor
William M. Symmes
Robert S. Magnuson
David M. Knutson
Jody M. McCormick
Paul C. Swainston
Eric J. Roth
Shelley N. Swanson

OF COUNSEL

William A. Davenport
John E. Heath, Jr.
William V. Kelley
Allan H. Toole
Karl K Krogue

Representative Clients: Boeing Commerical Airplanes; Cowles Publishing Co. (The Spokesman-Review); Doctor's Co.; First Security Bank of Idaho; Inland Empire Paper Co.; Shopko Stores, Inc.; Sterling Savings Assn.; Travelers Insurance Co.; U.S. Bank of Washington, N.A.; Western Union Telegraph Co.

For full biographical listings, see the Martindale-Hubbell Law Directory

*TACOMA,** Pierce Co.

VANDEBERG JOHNSON & GANDARA (AV)

A Partnership of Professional Service Corporations
1201 Pacific Avenue, Suite 1900, P.O. Box 1315, 98402
Telephone: 253-383-3791
Facsimile: 253-383-6377
Seattle, Washington Office: One Union Square, Suite 2424, 600 University Street, 98101-1192.
Telephone: 206-464-0404.

Darrel B. Addington
John H. Binns, Jr.
Kerry E. Brink
Robert J. Burnett
Charles R. Bush (Resident, Seattle Office: See Biographical Card at Seattle, Washington)
James H. Bush
Lucy Russell Clifthorne
William A. Coats
Sherie L. Coons
George T. Cowan (Resident, Seattle Office; See Biographical Card at Seattle Washington)
H. Frank Crawford
Daniel Gandara (Resident, Seattle Office; See Biographical Card at Seattle, Washington)
Greg W. Haffner
Kinne F. Hawes (Resident, Seattle Office: See Biographical Card at Seattle, Washington)
Danferd W. Henke (Resident, Seattle Office: See Biographical Card at Seattle, Washington)
Joanne Henry
John A. Holmes (Resident, Seattle Office; See Biographical Card at Seattle, Washington)
Mark A. Hood
W. Roger Johnson
James A. Krueger
Daniel C. Montopoli
John L. Nichols
Vicki E. Orrico (Resident, Seattle Office: See Biographical Card at Seattle, Washington)
Mark R. Patterson
H. Andrew Saller, Jr.
Andrew L. Seiple (Resident, Seattle Office; See Biographical Card at Seattle Washington)
James L. Vandeberg (Resident, Seattle Office; See Biographical Card at Seattle Washington)
G. Perrin Walker
Chapin E. (Shea) Wilson, III (Resident, Seattle Office: See Biographical Card at Seattle, Washington)

OF COUNSEL

Harold T. Hartinger
Elvin J. Vandeberg

For full biographical listings, see the Martindale-Hubbell Law Directory

*VANCOUVER,** Clark Co.

BLAIR, SCHAEFER, HUTCHISON & WOLFE, LLP (AV)

105 West Evergreen Boulevard, Suite 200, P.O. Box 1148, 98666-1148
Telephone: Vancouver: 360-693-5883; Portland: 503-285-4103
Telecopier Only: 360-693-1777
Email: inquiry@bshw-law.com

MEMBERS OF FIRM

John F. Wynne (1920-1988)
Donald C. Blair (1921-1996)
Brian H. Wolfe
Hugh J. Potter
James D. Horton
James D. Mullins
Donald Russo
Michael C. Simon
David W. Christel
Steven N. Bogdon
Scott W. Swindell

ASSOCIATES

Denise J. Lukins
Lucinda R. Giorgetti
Juliet C. Laycoe

OF COUNSEL

Robert M. Schaefer
Terrance D. Hannan
David C. Hutchison

For full biographical listings, see the Martindale-Hubbell Law Directory

MORSE & BRATT (AV)

Sixth Floor, Main Place, 1111 Main Street, P.O. Box 61566, 98666
Telephone: 360-699-4780
Portland, Oregon: 503-286-2520
Washington: 800-945-4084
Fax: 360-699-4839

MEMBERS OF FIRM

John E. Morse
Douglas J. Bratt
John David Morse
Ben Shafton
J. D. Nellor
William D. Robison
Gideon D. Caron
Diane Marie Woolard
Don Thacker
Gimi D. Page
Nancy A. Nellor
Bruce R. Colven
Charles D. Carlson
Michael W. Brace
Robert C. Russell

ASSOCIATES

William G. Hagedorn
Paul H. Finkelstein
Gregory M. Abel

OF COUNSEL

Douglas G. Combs (Not admitted in WA)

Reference: West Coast Bank.

For full biographical listings, see the Martindale-Hubbell Law Directory

*WENATCHEE,** Chelan Co.

JEFFERS, DANIELSON, SONN & AYLWARD, P.S. (AV)

317 North Mission, P.O. Box 1688, 98807
Telephone: 509-662-3685
Fax: 509-662-2452
Email: postmaster@jdsa.org
Moses Lake, Washington Office: 515 N. Stratford Road.
Telephone: 509-765-9705.
Fax: 509-765-5060.

Garfield R. Jeffers
James M. Danielson
David E. Sonn
J. Patrick Aylward
J. Kirk Bromiley
Gregory A. Lair
Douglas J. Takasugi
Peter A. Spadoni
Robert C. Nelson
Donald L. Dimmitt
Robert R. Siderius, Jr.
Stanley A. Bastian
Mitchell P. Delabarre
Theodore A. Finegold

Todd M. Kiesz
Kari Danielson-Kube
Brian C. Huber

OF COUNSEL

William F. Baldwin
Joseph L. Hughes (1905-1982)
Richard G. Jeffers (1910-1976)

Attorneys for: Public Utility District No. 1 of Douglas County; Wells Hydroelectric Project; Eye and Ear Clinic of Wenatchee, Inc.; Kemper Insurance Group; Auvil Fruit Co.; Wenatchee Reclamation District.

For full biographical listings, see the Martindale-Hubbell Law Directory

*YAKIMA,** Yakima Co.

HALVERSON & APPLEGATE, P.S. (AV)

311 North Fourth Street, P.O. Box 22730, 98907-2715
Telephone: 509-575-6611
Telecopier: 509-457-2419
Email: haps@halversonlaw.com *URL:* http://www.halversonlaw.com

(See Next Column)

Frederick N. Halverson
Terry C. Schmalz
J. Lawrence Wright
Don W. Schussler
Gerard L. Sandersen
Timothy J. Carlson
James S. Berg
Donald A. Boyd
Lawrence E. Martin
Brad L Englund
Ryan M. Edgley
Linda A. Sellers
Michael F. Shinn
Gregory S. Lighty

Kenneth W. Harper
Roger William Bailey
Kirk A. Ehlis
James S. Elliot
Kathy L. Bona

OF COUNSEL

C. W. Halverson (1903-1995)
J. S. Applegate (Retired)
Donald H. Bond
Thomas B. Grahn
Richard L. Wiehl

Representative Clients: Allstate Insurance; Seafirst; Pacificorp (local counsel); Tree Top, Inc.; Snokist Growers; Hogue Cellars Winery; S.S. Steiner (Hop Dealer/Broker); Holtzinger Fruit, Inc.; Inland Fruit & Produce Co.; S. Martinez Livestock, Inc.

For full biographical listings, see the Martindale-Hubbell Law Directory

LYON, WEIGAND & GUSTAFSON, P.S. (AV)

222 North Third Street, 98901
Telephone: 509-248-7220
Fax: 509-575-1883
Mailing Address: P.O. Box 1689, Yakima, Washington, 98907-1689
URL: http://www.lyon@lyon-law.com

Charles R. Lyon (1914-1997)
William L. Weigand, Jr.
J. Eric Gustafson
Robert M. Boggs
Jeanie R. Zimmerman
Russell Gilbert
Eric R. Vargas

William D. Pickett
Bryan P. Myre

Representative Clients: Washington State Fruit Commission; Wells Fargo Bank; J. R. Simplot Co.; West Valley School District No. 208; Pepsi-Cola Bottling Company of Yakima, Inc.; Fidelity Title Co.

For full biographical listings, see the Martindale-Hubbell Law Directory

MEYER, FLUEGGE AND TENNEY, P.S. (AV)

230 South Second Street, P.O. Box 22680, 98907
Telephone: 509-575-8500
Fax: 509-575-4676
Email: maxjd@wolfenet.com *URL:* http://www.wolfenet.com/~maxjd/genmft.html

Walter G. Meyer
Dennis L. Fluegge
Robert C. Tenney
Mark D. Watson
Jerome R. Aiken
John A. Maxwell, Jr.

Jeffrey M. Kreutz
Ellen M. McLaughlin

Representative Clients: Albertson's, Inc.; Caterpillar Tractor Co.; FMC Corp.; Hyster Co.; J.R. Simplot Co.; Farmers Insurance Group; Fireman's Fund Insurance; The St. Paul Companies; Safeco Insurance Co.; Washington Casualty Co.

For full biographical listings, see the Martindale-Hubbell Law Directory

WEST VIRGINIA

*BECKLEY,** Raleigh Co.

FILE, PAYNE, SCHERER & FILE (AV)

Law Building, 130 Main Street, P.O. Drawer L, 25802
Telephone: 304-253-3358
Fax: 304-255-5136
Email: filepayne@mtneer.net

MEMBERS OF FIRM

Edward M. Payne, III
John Payne Scherer
Robert N. File
William H. File, III

ASSOCIATE

Floyd M. Sayre, III

OF COUNSEL

William Henry File, Jr.

Representative Clients: City National Bank; City Holding Co.; Norfolk and Western Railway Co.; A. T. Massey Coal Co.; State Automobile Mutual Insurance Co.; Continental Insurance Group; Professional Medical Insurance Co.; Natiowide Insurance Company.

For full biographical listings, see the Martindale-Hubbell Law Directory

BLUEFIELD, Mercer Co.

KATZ, KANTOR & PERKINS (AV)

Suite 502-17 Law & Commerce Building, P.O. Box 727, 24701
Telephone: 304-327-3551
Fax: 304-325-7495

MEMBERS OF FIRM

Norris Kantor
Guy W. Perkins

ASSOCIATES

Wayne L. Evans
Wayne S. Stonestreet
Robert H. Miller, II
David B. Kelly
James J. Palmer, III
LeRoy H. Katz (1917-1994)

General Counsel for: Bluefield Regional Medical Center, Inc.; Mercer County Building Commission; Bluefield Health Systems, Inc.; Mountaineer Resources, Inc.; Cumberland Care Center, Inc.; Bluefield Regional Medical Center Foundation, Inc.; Sanitary Board of Bluefield.
References: First Century Bank, N.A.; First Community Bank, Inc.

For full biographical listings, see the Martindale-Hubbell Law Directory

*CHARLESTON,** Kanawha Co.

BOWLES RICE MCDAVID GRAFF & LOVE, PLLC (AV)

600 Quarrier Street, P.O. Box 1386, 25325-1386
Telephone: 304-347-1100
Fax: 304-343-2867
Email: bowles@bowlesrice.com *URL:* http://www.bowlesrice.com
Fairmont, West Virginia Office: 1000 Technology Drive, Suite 2310.
Telephone: 304-368-4000.
Fax: 304-368-4040.
Martinsburg, West Virginia Office: (Serves Berkeley Springs and Charles Town, West Virginia). 105 West Burke Street, P.O. Drawer 1419.
Telephone: 304-263-0836.
Fax: 304-267-3822.
Morgantown, West Virginia Office: 7000 Hampton Center, Suite K.
Telephone: 304-599-1390.
Fax: 304-599-1308.
Parkersburg, West Virginia Office: 501 Avery Street, Fifth Floor, P.O. Box 49.
Telephone: 304-485-8500.
Fax: 304-485-7973.
Lexington, Kentucky Office: 1200 World Trade Center, 333 West Vine Street.
Telephone: 606-225-8700.
Fax: 606-225-8418.

MEMBERS OF FIRM

Paul N. Bowles (1921-1986)
F. Thomas Graff, Jr.
Charles M. Love, III
P. Michael Pleska
Gary G. Markham
Michael E. Caryl
Carl D. Andrews
Edward D. McDevitt
Ricklin Brown
J. Thomas Lane
Gerard R. Stowers
P. Nathan Bowles, Jr.
Sarah E. Smith
Richard M. Francis
George A. Patterson, III
Phyllis M. Potterfield
John W. Woods, III
Thomas A. Heywood
Camden P. Siegrist
Sandra M. Murphy
Julia A. Chincheck
Leonard Knee
Marc A. Monteleone
Lesley A. Russo
Ellen Maxwell-Hoffman
Lynn Photiadis
Fazal A. Shere
Charles B. Dollison
Kenneth E. Webb, Jr.
Michael J. Schessler
John R. Teare, Jr.
Elizabeth D. Harter
Joseph J. Starsick, Jr.
Mark B. D'Antoni

ASSOCIATES

Robert G. Lilly
Ronda L. Harvey
Stuart A. McMillan
Geoffry Alan Haddad
Maria W. Hughes
James E. White, Jr.
Sarah Rebekah Carden
Tracy L. Webb
Robert L. Burns, Jr.
Jeffrey K. Matherly
Gary O. Kinder, Jr.
Corey Palumbo
David E. Potters
Gregory W. Bailey

SPECIAL COUNSEL

Giles D. H. Snyder
John S. Moore
David P. Lambert

OF COUNSEL

William R. McDavid

For full biographical listings, see the Martindale-Hubbell Law Directory

CAMPBELL, WOODS, BAGLEY, EMERSON, MCNEER & HERNDON, P.L.L.C. (AV)

810 One Valley Square, P.O. Box 2393, 25328-2393
Telephone: 304-346-2391
Fax: 304-346-2433
Huntington, West Virginia Office: 14th Floor, Coal Exchange Building, P.O. Box 1835, 25719.
Telephone: 304-529-2391.
Fax: 304-529-1832.

(See Next Column)

Ashland, Kentucky Office: 1608 Carter Avenue, P.O. Box 1862, 41105-1832.
Telephone: 606-329-1974
Fax: 606-324-2025

MEMBERS OF FIRM

Milton T. Herndon
David A. Mohler
Charles I. Jones, Jr.
John F. Hussell, IV

ASSOCIATES

Phillip C. Monroe
Michael A. Olivio

OF COUNSEL

James Hornor Davis, III

Representative Clients: Corporate: Federal Deposit Insurance Corp. (FDIC); The Matewan National Bank; Prestera Center for Mental Health Services, Inc.; Valley Health Systems, Inc.; Dingess-Rum Coal Co.; Cole & Crane Real Estate Trust. Insurance: State Farm Mutual Automobile Insurance Co.; Continental Casualty Co.; Liberty Mutual Insurance Co.

For full biographical listings, see the Martindale-Hubbell Law Directory

GOODWIN & GOODWIN (AV)

1500 One Valley Square, 25301
Telephone: 304-346-7000
Fax: 304-344-9692
Email: g&glaw@goodwin.goodwin.com *URL:* http://www.goodwingoodwin.com
Ripley, West Virginia Office: 500 Church Street, P.O. Box 349.
Telephone: 304-372-2651.
Parkersburg, West Virginia Office: 201 Third Street, Town Square.
Telephone: 304-485-2345.
Fax: 304-485-3459.

Robert B. Goodwin (1909-1955)

OF COUNSEL

C. E. Goodwin

MEMBERS OF FIRM

Thomas R. Goodwin
Stephen P. Goodwin
Michael I. Spiker
Steven F. White
Richard E. Rowe
Leonard S. Coleman
Susan C. Wittemeier
Robert W. Full (Resident at Parkersburg Office)
Richard D. Owen
Tammy J. Owen
J. David Fenwick
Alexander Macia

ASSOCIATES

Suzanne Jett Trowbridge
William K. Bragg, Jr.
George M. Smith
John N. Ellem (Resident, Parkersburg Office)
Lisa A. Tackett
Robert (Booth) Goodwin, II
Carrie Goodwin Fenwick
Tiffany E. Davis

Representative Clients: Bucyrus-Erie Co.; CSX Corp.; Eastern American Energy Corp.; The Eureka Pipe Line Co.

For full biographical listings, see the Martindale-Hubbell Law Directory

HUDDLESTON, BOLEN, BEATTY, PORTER & COPEN (AV)

One Bridge Place, 10 Hale Street, P.O. Box 3786, 25337
Telephone: 304-344-9869
Telecopier: 304-344-4309
Huntington, West Virginia Office: 611 Third Avenue, P.O. Box 2185.
Telephone: 304-529-6181
Telecopier: 304-522-4312.
Ashland, Kentucky Office: 1422 Winchester Avenue, P.O. Box 770.
Telephone: 606-329-8771
Telecopier: 606-324-4651.

MEMBERS OF FIRM

William C. Beatty (1925-1994)
Noel P. Copen
R. Kemp Morton
Richard J. Bolen
Fred Adkins
John R. Fowler (Resident)
Thomas H. Gilpin
Thomas J. Murray
Andrew S. Zettle
Bruce L. Stout
Christopher J. Plybon
Mary H. Sanders (Resident)
Marc E. Williams
R. Russell Alexander
Daniel J. Konrad
Scott K. Sheets
Luke A. Lafferre
Janet Smith Holbrook
James Wade Turner
Angela Wynn Konrad
Robert L. Massie

ASSOCIATES

Daniel A. Earl
Melissa G. Foster
James C. Stebbins
Kathleen H. Jones
Blake Benton Westfall
Robert B. Warner
James R. Akers, II

For full biographical listings, see the Martindale-Hubbell Law Directory

Charleston—Continued

JACKSON & KELLY (AV)

1600 Laidley Tower, P.O. Box 553, 25322
Telephone: 304-340-1000
Fax: 304-340-1130
Email: info@jacksonkelly.com *URL:* http://www.jacksonkelly.com
Martinsburg, West Virginia Office: 300 Foxcroft Avenue, P.O. Box 1068.
Telephone: 304-263-8800.
Fax: 304-263-7110.
Morgantown, West Virginia Office: 6000 Hampton Center, P.O. Box 619.
Telephone: 304-599-3000.
Fax: 304-285-2040.
New Martinsville, West Virginia Office: 256 Russell Avenue, P.O. Box 68.
Telephone: 304-455-1751.
Fax: 304-455-6314.
Parkersburg, West Virginia Office: 412 Market Street, Suite 202, P.O. Box 1144.
Telephone: 304-424-3490.
Fax: 304-424-3499.
Fairmont, West Virginia Office: 1000 Technology Drive, Suite 1310.
Telephone: 304-368-2000.
Fax: 304-368-2020.
Lexington, Kentucky Office: 175 East Main Street, Suite 500, P.O. Box 2150.
Telephone: 606-255-9500.
Fax: 606-281-6478.
Washington, D. C. Office: 2401 Pennsylvania Avenue, N.W., Suite 400.
Telephone: 202-973-0200.
Fax: 202-973-0232.
Denver, Colorado Office: Suite 2710, 1660 Lincoln Street.
Telephone: 303-390-0003.
Fax: 303-390-0040.
Wheeling, West Virginia Office: 1144 Market Street.
Telephone: 304-233-4000.
Fax: 304-233-4077.

MEMBERS OF FIRM

Thomas B. Jackson (1892-1966)
Robert G. Kelly (1898-1979)
Homer A. Holt (1898-1975)
William T. O'Farrell (1906-1983)
J. S. Francis (Resident, New Martinsville, West Virginia Office)
James Knight Brown
John L. McClaugherty
Thomas E. Potter
Lee O. Hill
John R. Lukens
W. Warren Upton
Louis S. Southworth, II
John M. Slack, III
Charles Q. Gage
Michael A. Albert
Stephen R. Crislip
William F. Dobbs, Jr.
Thomas G. Freeman, II
Roger A. Wolfe
Harvey Alan Siler
W. Henry Jernigan, Jr.
Michael D. Foster
A. L. Emch
William A. Hoskins, III (Administrative Manager, Lexington, Kentucky Office)
Taunja Willis Miller
Charles M. Surber, Jr.
Robert J. Busse
James R. Snyder
Thomas N. McJunkin
David Allen Barnette
Barbara D. Little
Laura E. Beverage (Administrative Manager, Denver, Colorado Office)
Ellen S. Cappellanti
Allen R. Prunty
Cheryl Harris Wolfe
Dennis C. Sauter
James W. Thomas
Larry W. Blalock (Administrative Manager, New Martinsville and Wheeling, West Virginia Offices)
Mary Clare Eros (Administrative Manager, Martinsburg and Charles Town, West Virginia Offices)
Gary W. Hart
Robert G. McLusky
George E. Roeder, III (Resident, Morgantown, West Virginia Office)
Douglas A. Smoot
Jeff Chandler Woods
Jeffrey J. Yost (Resident, Lexington, Kentucky Office)
Daniel L. Stickler (Administrative Manager)
A. Stuart Bennett (Resident, Lexington, Kentucky Office)
Samme L. Gee
Thomas J. Hurney, Jr.
John Philip Melick
Lynn Oliver Frye
Gale Reddie Lea
William E. Doll, Jr. (Resident, Lexington, Kentucky Office)
Stephen M. LaCagnin (Administrative Manager, Morgantown, West Virginia Office)
James I. Manion (Resident, Martinsburg and Charles Town, West Virginia Offices)
Charles D. Dunbar
Thad S. Huffman (Administrative Manager, Washington, D.C. Office)
Martin E. Hall (Resident, Lexington, Kentucky Office)
Kevin M. McGuire (Resident, Lexington, Kentucky Office)
W. Rodes Brown (Resident, Lexington, Kentucky Office)
Timothy E. Huffman
Charles W. Loeb, Jr.
G. Lindsay Simmons (Resident, Washington, D.C. Office)
Natalie D. Brown (Resident, Lexington, Kentucky Office)
L. Anthony George (Resident, Denver, Colorado Office)
William J. Powell
Wendel B. Turner
Albert F. Sebok
William S. Mattingly (Resident, Morgantown, West Virginia Office)
Ann Brannon Rembrandt
David J. Hardy
Mary Jane Curran (Resident, Fairmont, West Virginia Office)
Eric H. London (Morgantown, West Virginia Office)
Stanton L. Cave (Resident, Lexington, Kentucky Office)
Bradley A. Crouser
Elizabeth Osenton Lord

(See Next Column)

MEMBERS OF FIRM (Continued)

John K. McDonald (Resident, Washington, D.C. Office)
Robert L. Johns (Resident, Wheeling, West Virginia Office)
William Prentice Young (Martinsburg and Charles Town, West Virginia Offices)
Anthony J. Ferrise
Dana Franklin Eddy
David M. Flannery
Robert D. Fluharty
Kathy G. Beckett
John A. Mairs
Julia M. Chico (Resident, Morgantown, West Virginia Office)
Melissa Mize Robinson
Charles J. Crooks (Resident, Morgantown, West Virginia Office)
J. Rudy Martin
Michael B. Victorson

ASSOCIATES

Brooks K. Barkwill (Resident, New Martinsville, West Virginia Office)
Jennifer Z. Cain (Resident, Parkersburg, West Virginia Office)
Jacqueline Syers Duncan (Resident, Lexington, Kentucky Office)
Mary Rich Lewis Maloy
Dennis N. Broglio
Lucinda Fluharty Fitch (Resident, Wheeling, West Virginia Office)
Maris E. McCambley
Patience Ann Alexander
Christopher L. Callas
Erin Magee Condaras
Christopher Kenneth Robertson (Resident, Martinsburg, West Virginia Office)
Mychal S. Schulz
Kathy L. Snyder (Resident, Morgantown, West Virginia Office)
William C. Miller, II
Michael T. Cimino
Sannie Overly (Resident, Lexington, Kentucky Office)
James Eric Whytsell (Resident, Fairmont Office)
Robert G. Tweel
Katherine Venti
Whitney G. Clegg (Resident, New Martinsville, West Virginia Office)
M. Shane Harvey
Kelley L. Mount
Debra A. Bowers (Resident, Morgantown, West Virginia Office)
Monika Hussell
Steven M. Condaras
Robert F. Duncan
Shawn L. Reed (Resident, Wheeling, West Virginia Office)
Allan William Brown (Resident, Wheeling, West Virginia Office)
Gretchen M. Callas
David B. Mattingly (Resident, Lexington, Kentucky Office)
David Z. Myerberg, M.D. (Resident, Morgantown, West Virginia Office)
Victoria J. Sopranik (Resident, Lexington, Kentucky Office)
Rob J. Aliff
Karen M. Rexing Weber
Julia K. Shreve
Karen L. Johnston (Resident, Denver, Colorado Office)
Jay E. Ingle (Resident, Lexington, Kentucky Office)
Peter Moyson (Resident, Denver, Colorado Office)
Lorna M. Waddell
Gretchen E. Pyles
Thomas J. Hodge (Resident, Lexington, Kentucky Office)
Lee Van Egmond
Brent P. Copenhaver (Resident, Morgantown, West Virginia Office)
Christina L. Townsend
Scott David Goldman
Joseph M. Sellaro
Beth R. Lewis
I. William Snider III
Cortland Christopher Putbrese

OF COUNSEL

Andrew L. Blair (Retired)
Philip B. Cardi (Resident, Denver, Colorado Office)
Robert L. Elkins (Retired)
Louis J. Ferrara (Resident, Washington, D.C. Office)
David D. Johnson (Retired)
Katherine Shand Larkin (Resident, Denver, Colorado Office)
Edward W. Rugeley, Jr. (Retired)
Winfield T. Shaffer (Retired)

LEGAL SUPPORT PERSONNEL

James A Lowen
Robin Smith Claudio
Sara P. Walker
Lana H. Thomas (Office Manager) (At Lexington, Kentucky Office)
Tonya Doby (Resident, Washington, DC Office)
Mary Ann Baker
Ruth L. Williams
Janette G. Gidley
Melody Somers
Darren T. Olofson
Alan Y. Etter

Representative Clients: Consol Inc.; Go-Mart, Inc.; Monongahela Power Co.; One Valley Bancorp of West Virginia; Pittston Coal Co.; Rhone-Poulenc AG Co.; Thomas Memorial Hospital; Union Carbide Corp.; United Parcel Service; West Virginia-American Water Co.

For full biographical listings, see the Martindale-Hubbell Law Directory

KAY CASTO & CHANEY PLLC (AV)

1600 Bank One Center, P.O. Box 2031, 25327
Telephone: 304-345-8900
Telefax: 304-345-8909; 304-343-9833
Email: kcc@kaycasto.com *URL:* http://www.kaycasto.com
Morgantown, West Virginia Office: Suite C, 3000 Hampton Center.
Telephone: 304-599-8900.
Telefax: 304-599-8901.

OF COUNSEL

John B. Carrico
John O. Kizer

(See Next Column)

KAY CASTO & CHANEY PLLC, *Charleston—Continued*

MEMBERS OF FIRM

Charles E. Barnett
William W. Booker
Michael T. Chaney
Barney W. Frazier, Jr.
George W. S. Grove, Jr.
Ann L. Haight
Steven C. Hanley
Elliot G. Hicks
John R. Hoblitzell
Craig M. Kay
John T. Kay, Jr.
John R. McGhee, Jr.
Dina M. Mohler
W. Michael Moore
Kevin A. Nelson
Jonathan Nicol
Harry M. Rubenstein (Morgantown, West Virginia Office)
Howard G. Salisbury, Jr.
Steven L. Thomas
Stephen A. Weber

ASSOCIATES

Aaron B. Alexander
Robert L. Bandy
Rita Massie Biser
Richard E. Boyle, Jr.
Hannah Bishop Curry
William F. Foster, II
Katherine A. Jones
Kelly J. Kimble (Morgantown, West Virginia Office)
Daniel A. Oliver (Morgantown, West Virginia Office)
David M. Thomas (Morgantown, West Virginia Office)
Susan B. Tucker
Constance H. Weber
Robert P. Welsh

Attorneys for: Bank One, West Virginia; Wausau Insurance Cos,; West Virginia Contractors Bargaining Assn.; Charleston Area Medical Center, Inc.; Wal-Mart Stores, Inc.; University of Charleston; Ford Motor Credit Co.; The Huntington National Bank; West Virginia Hospital Assn.; Appalachian Regional Healthcare, Inc.

For full biographical listings, see the Martindale-Hubbell Law Directory

SHUMAN ANNAND BAILEY WYANT & EARLES (AV)

Suite 1007, 405 Capitol Street, P.O. Box 3953, 25339
Telephone: 304-345-1400
Telecopier: 304-343-1826
Email: shuman@newwave.net
Wheeling, West Virginia Office: Suite 3002, 1233 Main Street, 26003.
Telephone: 304-233-3100.
Telecopier: 304-233-0201.

MEMBERS OF FIRM

David L. Shuman
Stephen Darley Annand
Charles R. Bailey
Richard L. Earles
David L. Wyant (Resident, Wheeling, West Virginia Office)
Mark William Browning
William R. Slicer
George J. Joseph
Thomas E. Buck (Resident at Wheeling, West Virginia Office)

ASSOCIATES

DesiréeHalkias Divita
Roberta F. Green
Paul Kipling Reese
Heidi A. Kossuth (Resident, Wheeling, West Virginia Office)
Lou Ann S. Cassell
Dwayne E. Cyrus
Eric W. Santos (Not admitted in WV; Resident, Wheeling, West Virginia Office)
John T. Molleur
Mark A. Kepple (Resident, Wheeling, West Virginia Office)
David J. Mincer
Karen M. Tracy
Virginia Ann Grottendieck
Arden J. Cogar
Melissa A. Morris
Stacie L. Price (Resident, Wheeling, West Virginia Office)
J. Parker Bazzle
Lisa Bray
Darin C. James
Brian D. Morrison

OF COUNSEL

John F. McCuskey

Representative Clients: American International/Companies (AIG); CNA Insurance Companies; Insurance Corporation of America; Metropolitan Property & Liability Insurance Co.; MMI Companies, Inc.; Motorists Insurance Cos.; Travelers Insurance Cos.; Westfield Companies.
Reference: One Valley Bank.

For full biographical listings, see the Martindale-Hubbell Law Directory

SPILMAN THOMAS & BATTLE, PLLC (AV)

Spilman Center, 300 Kanawha Boulevard, East, P.O. Box 273, 25321-0273
Telephone: 304-340-3800
Fax: 304-340-3801
Email: stb@spilmanlaw.com *URL:* http://www.spilmanlaw.com
Morgantown, West Virginia Office: 990 Elmer Prince Drive, Suite 205, P.O. Box 4474, 26504-4474.
Telephone: 304-599-8175.
Fax: 304-599-8229.
Parkersburg, West Virginia Office: PM Center, 417 Grand Park Drive, Suite 203, P.O. Box 1469, 26102-1469.
Telephone: 304-422-6700.
Fax: 304-422-6733.

(See Next Column)

Martinsburg, West Virginia Office: 100 North Maple Avenue, Suite 200, P.O. Box 5129, 25402-5129.
Telephone: 304-263-4100.
Fax: 304-263-2993.
Weirton, West Virginia Office: 333 Penco Road, Suite A, P.O. Box 2435, 26062-2435.
Telephone: 304-723-6980.
Fax: 304-723-6986.

MEMBERS OF FIRM

Hawthorne D. Battle (1901-1984)
Howard R. Klostermeyer (1904-1983)
W. Victor Ross (1913-1992)
James P. Robinson (1914-1993)
Thomas W. Bayley (1915-1996)
William T. Brotherton, Jr. (1926-1997)
G. Thomas Battle
John H. Tinney
William C. Payne
F. Richard Hall
Lee F. Feinberg
Charles L. Woody
K. Paul Davis
Ward D. (Jerry) Stone, Jr. (Resident, Morgantown, West Virginia Office)
John J. Nesius
David B. Shapiro
William T. Brotherton, III
M. Ann Bradley
Joyce Fleming Ofsa
Robert J. O'Neil
T. Randolph Cox, Jr.
William A. Trainer (Resident, Parkersburg, West Virginia Office)
William M. Herlihy
Carl H. Cather, III (Resident, Morgantown, West Virginia Office)
Richard A. Hudson (Also at Parkersburg, West Virginia Office)
J. Michael Weber (Resident, Parkersburg, West Virginia Office)
David P. Ferretti
F. Thomas Rubenstein (Resident, Morgantown, West Virginia Office)
Lynn S. Clarke
John F. Allevato
Heather Heiskell Jones
David G. Hammond
Eric M. James
Neva G. Lusk
Gray Silver, III (Resident, Martinsburg, West Virginia Office)
Niall A. Paul
Paula Durst Gillis
Nancy A. Green (Resident, Morgantown and Weirton, West Virginia Office)
Michael J. Basile

SENIOR ATTORNEYS

Kimberley R. Fields
Robert A. Lockhart
Dean A. Furner (Resident, Parkersburg, West Virginia)

ASSOCIATES

Bruce M. Jacobs
John G. Byrd
Clifford F. Kinney, Jr.
Eric W. Iskra
Don C. A. Parker
Kate Wilson Fife
Kevin L. Carr
James T. Carey (Resident, Weirton, West Virginia Office)
Corey T. Zurbuch
Jill C. Bentz
Jeffrey L. Hare
Michael H. Spencer
Jamie S. Alley
Gordon C. F. Chin
H. Dill Battle, III
Marcy Elizabeth Aber
Nicole Renee Allman
Karin L. Weingart (Not admitted in WV)
Susan J. Riggs

OF COUNSEL

Frederick L. Thomas, Jr.
William B. Maxwell, III
Charles B. Stacy
Kenneth E. Kincaid (Resident, Morgantown, West Virginia Office)

LEGAL SUPPORT PERSONNEL
EXECUTIVE DIRECTOR

Donald O. Gatewood
Deborah M. Ashworth (Marketing/Administrative Assistant)
Karen T. Orlando (Librarian)

Representative Clients: Allied-Signal, Inc.; Anker Group, Inc.; Baxter Healthcare Corp.; Berwind Land Co.; Charleston Area Medical Center, Inc.; E.I. du Pont de Nemours and Company; Pittsburgh Corning Corporation; State Farm Insurance Companies; United National Bank; Weirton Steel Corp.

For full biographical listings, see the Martindale-Hubbell Law Directory

*CLARKSBURG,** Harrison Co.

MCNEER, HIGHLAND, MCMUNN AND VARNER, L.C. (AV)

One Valley Bank Building, P.O. Drawer 2040, 26302-2040
Telephone: 304-626-1100
Facsimile: 304-623-3035
Martinsburg Office: 2520 Aikens Center, P.O. Box 2509.
Telephone: 304-264-4621.
Fax: 304-264-8623.
Parkersburg Office: 404 Market Street, Suite 204, P.O. Box 1507.
Telephone: 304-422-7193.
Facsimile: 304-422-7196.

C. David McMunn
J. Cecil Jarvis
James A. Varner
Robert W. Trumble (Resident, Martinsburg Office)
Catherine D. Munster
James N. Riley
Steven R. Bratke (Resident, Parkersburg Office)
Michael J. Novotny (Resident, Martinsburg Office)
Dennis M. Shreve
Geraldine S. Roberts

(See Next Column)

McNeer, Highland, McMunn and Varner L.C.—*Continued*

William F. Rohrbaugh (Resident, Martinsburg Office)
Gregory H. Schillace
Judy L. Shanholtz
Tiffany R. Durst
Gene W. Bailey, II

OF COUNSEL

James E. McNeer
Cecil B. Highland, Jr.
William L. Fury

Representative Clients: One Valley Bank of Clarksburg, National Assn.; Bruceton Bank; Harrison County Bank; Nationwide Mutual Insurance Cos.; Clarksburg Publishing Co.; C.I.T. Financial Services; State Automobile Mutual Insurance Co.; United Hospital Center, Inc.; West Virginia Coals, Inc.; Swanson Plating Co.

For full biographical listings, see the Martindale-Hubbell Law Directory

Waters, Warner & Harris, PLLC (AV)

Formerly Stathers & Cantrall
701 Goff Building, P.O. Box 1716, 26301
Telephone: 304-624-5571
Fax: 304-624-7228
Email: wwh.atty@northnap.citynet.net

Birk S. Stathers (1884-1945)
W. G. Stathers (1889-1970)
Arch M. Cantrall (1896-1967)
Stuart R. Waters
Boyd L. Warner
James A. Harris
Scott E. Wilson
James C. Turner
G. Thomas Smith

ASSOCIATES

D. Andrew McMunn
David C. Glover

Representative Clients: Bethlehem Steel Corp.; Davis-Weaver Funeral Home, Inc.; Dowell Schlumberger, Inc.; Grafton Coal Co.; Harry Green Chevrolet, Inc.; Emax Oil Co.; Southern Steel Products Co.; Hartland Planing Mill Co.; Gas Flame Federal Credit Union; City of Clarksburg Federal Credit Union.

For full biographical listings, see the Martindale-Hubbell Law Directory

*FAIRMONT,** Marion Co.

Bowles Rice McDavid Graff & Love, PLLC (AV)

Alan B. Mollohan Innovation Center, 1000 Technology Drive, Suite 2310, 26554
Telephone: 304-368-4000
Fax: 304-368-4040
Email: bowles@bowlesrice.com *URL:* http://www.bowlesrice.com
Charleston, West Virginia Office: 600 Quarrier Street, P.O. Box 1386.
Telephone: 304-347-1100.
Fax: 304-343-2867.
Martinsburg, West Virginia Office: (Serves Berkeley Springs and Charles Town, West Virginia). 105 West Burke Street, P.O. Drawer 1419.
Telephone: 304-263-0836.
Fax: 304-267-3822.
Morgantown, West Virginia Office: 7000 Hampton Center, Suite K.
Telephone: 304-599-1390.
Fax: 304-599-1308.
Parkersburg, West Virginia Office: 501 Avery Street, Fifth Floor, P.O. Box 49.
Telephone: 304-485-7973.
Fax: 304-485-7973.
Lexington, Kentucky Office: 1200 World Trade Center, 333 West Vine Street.
Telephone: 606-225-8700.
Fax: 606-225-8418.

MEMBERS OF FIRM

Paul E. Frampton (Resident)
Charles C. Wise, III (Resident)

RESIDENT ASSOCIATES

Susan Woods Coffindaffer
Charles T. Berry

For full biographical listings, see the Martindale-Hubbell Law Directory

Furbee, Amos, Webb & Critchfield (AV)

132 Adams Street, P.O. Box 1189, 26555
Telephone: 304-363-8800
Telecopier: 304-366-3783
Morgantown, West Virginia Office: 5000 Hampton Center, Suite 4.
Telephone: 304-598-0900.
Telecopier: 304-598-2712.

MEMBERS OF FIRM

Russell L. Furbee (1898-1978)
John D. Amos
Benjamin Hays Webb
Charles Vincent Critchfield
Alfred J. Lemley
Billy Atkins
Kenneth R. Miller
Stephen R. Brooks
William T. Holmes
Debra Hodges Scudiere (Resident at Morgantown Office)
Rebecca J. Zuleski
Tamara J. DeFazio

(See Next Column)

ASSOCIATE

Peter T. DeMasters

Attorneys for: Consolidation Coal Co.; Westinghouse Electric Co.; Monongahela Power Co.; Eastern Associated Coal Corp.; West Virginia Community Television Association; Continental Casualty Co.; State Farm Insurance Co.; Nationwide Insurance Co.

For full biographical listings, see the Martindale-Hubbell Law Directory

HUNTINGTON, Cabell & Wayne Cos.

Campbell, Woods, Bagley, Emerson, McNeer & Herndon, P.L.L.C. (AV)

14th Floor, Coal Exchange Building, P.O. Box 1835, 25719-1835
Telephone: 304-529-2391
Fax: 304-529-1832
Email: info@campbellwoods.com
Charleston, West Virginia Office: 810 One Valley Square, P.O. Box 2393, 25328-2393.
Telephone: 304-346-2391.
Fax: 304-346-2433.
Ashland, Kentucky Office: 1608 Carter Avenue, P.O. Box 1862, 41105-1862.
Telephone: 606-329-1974
Fax: 606-324-2025

MEMBERS OF FIRM

Rolla D. Campbell (1895-1987)
Selden S. McNeer (1894-1963)
Robert K. Emerson (1922-1991)
Luther E. Woods (Retired)
Richard Gregory McNeer
Howard Ross Crews, Jr.
Charles F. Bagley, III
Edward M. Kowal, Jr.
J. Patrick Jones
W. Nicholas Reynolds
R. Carter Elkins
Cheryl Lynne Connelly
J. Grant McGuire
David C. Ray
Laura L. Gray
W. Joseph Bronosky
Robert A. Wilson, Jr.

ASSOCIATES

Roy F. Layman
Dustin C. Haley
Erik W. Legg

OF COUNSEL

Charles F. Bagley, Jr.
Selden S. McNeer, Jr.

Representative Clients: Corporate: Federal Deposit Insurance Corp. (FDIC); Ashland Oil, Inc.; Ashland Coal, Inc.; Blazer Energy, Inc.; Huntington National Bank, W.Va.; The Matewan National Bank; Valley Health Systems, Inc.; Huntington Internal Medicine Group, Inc. Insurance; State Farm Mutual Automobile Insurance Co.; Continental Casualty Co.

For full biographical listings, see the Martindale-Hubbell Law Directory

Huddleston, Bolen, Beatty, Porter & Copen (AV)

611 Third Avenue, P.O. Box 2185, 25722
Telephone: 304-529-6181
Telecopier: 304-522-4312
Ashland, Kentucky Office: 1422 Winchester Avenue, P.O. Box 770.
Telephone: 606-329-8771.
Telecopier: 606-324-4651.
Charleston, West Virginia Office: One Bridge Place, 10 Hale Street, P.O. Box 3786.
Telephone: 304-344-9869.
Telecopier: 304-344-4309.

MEMBERS OF FIRM

Jackson N. Huddleston (1908-1977)
William C. Beatty (1925-1994)
Amos A. Bolen (1909-1996)
Noel P. Copen
R. Kemp Morton
Richard J. Bolen
Fred Adkins
John R. Fowler (Resident at Charleston Office)
Thomas H. Gilpin
James E. Cleveland, III (Resident at Ashland, Kentucky Office)
Thomas J. Murray
Andrew S. Zettle
Bruce L. Stout
Christopher J. Plybon
Mary H. Sanders (Resident at Charleston Office)
Marc E. Williams
R. Russell Alexander
Daniel J. Konrad
Scott K. Sheets
Luke A. Lafferre
Janet Smith Holbrook
James Wade Turner
Angela Wynn Konrad
Robert L. Massie

ASSOCIATES

Daniel A. Earl
Melissa G. Foster
James C. Stebbins
Craig R. Banford
John H. Mahaney
Rodney L. Baker II
Kathleen H. Jones (Resident at Charleston Office)
Audy M. Perry Jr.
William H. Harkins Jr.
Melissa Dodd Veltri
Tracy D. Frye
Paul J. Loftus
Jon B. Orndorff
Marvin (Chip) Capehart II
Blake Benton Westfall (Resident at Charleston Office)
Robert B. Warner (Resident at Charleston Office)
James R. Akers, II (Resident, Charleston Office)
M. Edward Cunningham, II

(See Next Column)

HUDDLESTON, BOLEN, BEATTY, PORTER & COPEN, *Huntington—Continued*

OF COUNSEL

Paul C. Hobbs (Resident at Ashland, Kentucky Office)
James O. Porter

Representative Clients: CSX Transportation Inc.; Norfolk and Western Railway Co.; Banc One West Virginia Corp.; The Herald-Dispatch, Huntington, WV; Ashland Inc.; Metropolitan Life Insurance Co.; Insurance Company of North America.

For full biographical listings, see the Martindale-Hubbell Law Directory

*LEWISBURG,** Greenbrier Co.

FORD & RICHARDSON (AV)

Formerly Haynes, Ford & Rowe
203 West Randolph Street, 24901
Telephone: 304-645-1858; 645-1859
Fax: 304-645-1918
Email: fordlaw@inetone.net

MEMBERS OF FIRM

Richard E. Ford
Richard E. Ford, Jr.
Robert E Richardson

Representative Clients: Greenbrier Valley Medical Center; First National Bank in Ronceverte; Greenbrier Valley National Bank; Federal Land Bank of Baltimore; America Fore Loyalty Group; The Greenbrier Hotel; Westvaco; Georgia Pacific Corp.

For full biographical listings, see the Martindale-Hubbell Law Directory

*MARTINSBURG,** Berkeley Co.

BOWLES RICE MCDAVID GRAFF & LOVE, PLLC (AV)

(Formerly Rice, Douglas & Shingleton)
105 West Burke Street, P.O. Drawer 1419, 25401
Telephone: 304-263-0836
Fax: 304-267-3822
Email: bowles@bowlesrice.com *URL:* http://www.bowlesrice.com
Charleston, West Virginia Office: 600 Quarrier Street, P.O. Box 1386.
Telephone: 304-347-1100.
Fax: 304-343-2867.
Fairmont, West Virginia Office: 1000 Technology Drive, Suite 2310.
Telephone: 304-368-4000.
Fax: 304-368-4040.
Morgantown, West Virginia Office: 7000 Hampton Center, Suite K.
Telephone: 304-599-1390.
Fax: 304-599-1308.
Parkersburg, West Virginia Office: 501 Avery Street, Fifth Floor, P.O. Box 49.
Telephone: 304-485-7973.
Fax: 304-485-7973.
Lexington, Kentucky Office: 1200 World Trade Center, 333 West Vine Street.
Telephone: 606-225-8700.
Fax: 606-225-8418.

MEMBERS OF FIRM

Lacy I. Rice (1901-1974)
J. Oakley Seibert (Resident)
Michael B. Keller (Resident)
Michael E. Caryl
Charles F. Printz, Jr. (Resident)
Michael D. Lorensen (Resident)
M. Shannon Brown (Resident)
Norwood Bentley (Resident)
Claudia W. Bentley (Resident)
David A. DeJarnett (Resident)
Curtis G. Power III (Resident)
Stephen McDowell Mathias

RESIDENT ASSOCIATES

Amy R. Lamp
Susan Mosser Caperton
Brian M. Peterson
Tracey A. Rohrbaugh

RESIDENT OF COUNSEL

Lacy I. Rice, Jr.

For full biographical listings, see the Martindale-Hubbell Law Directory

JACKSON & KELLY (AV)

300 Foxcroft Avenue, P.O. Box 1068, 25401
Telephone: 304-263-8800
Fax: 304-263-7110
Email: info@jacksonkelly.com *URL:* http://www.jacksonkelly.com
Charleston, West Virginia Office: 1600 Laidley Tower, P.O. Box 553.
Telephone: 304-340-1000.
Fax: 304-340-1130.
Morgantown, West Virginia Office: 6000 Hampton Center, P.O. Box 619.
Telephone: 304-599-3000.
Fax: 304-285-2040.
New Martinsville, West Virginia Office: 256 Russell Avenue, P.O. Box 68.
Telephone: 304-455-1751.
Fax: 304-455-6314.
Parkersburg, West Virginia Office: 412 Market Street, Suite 202, P.O. Box 1144.
Telephone: 304-424-3490.
Fax: 304-424-3499.

(See Next Column)

Fairmont, West Virginia Office: 1000 Technology Drive, Suite 1310.
Telephone: 304-368-2000.
Fax: 304-368-2020.
Lexington, Kentucky Office: 175 East Main Street, Suite 500, P.O. Box 2150.
Telephone: 606-255-9500.
Fax: 606-281-6478.
Washington, D. C. Office: 2401 Pennsylvania Avenue, N.W., Suite 400.
Telephone: 202-973-0200.
Fax: 202-973-0232.
Denver, Colorado Office: Suite 2710, 1660 Lincoln Street.
Telephone: 303-390-0003.
Fax: 303-390-0040.
Wheeling, West Virginia Office: 1144 Market Street.
Telephone: 304-233-4000.
Fax: 304-233-4077.

MEMBERS OF FIRM

Mary Clare Eros (Administrative Manager)
James I. Manion
William Prentice Young

ASSOCIATE

Christopher Kenneth Robertson

Representative Clients: Anthem Personal Insurance Co.; Blue Ridge Bank; CNA Insurance Companies; GEICO; Home Insurance Co.; Huntington National Bank of West Virginia; One Valley Bank of Martinsburg, N.A.; State Automobile Mutual Insurance Co.; First Empire Federal; Prudential Property and Casualty Ins. Co.

For full biographical listings, see the Martindale-Hubbell Law Directory

*MORGANTOWN,** Monongalia Co.

BOWLES RICE MCDAVID GRAFF & LOVE, PLLC (AV)

7000 Hampton Center, Suite K, 26505
Telephone: 304-599-1390
Fax: 304-599-1308
Email: bowles@bowlesrice.com *URL:* http://www.bowlesrice.com
Charleston, West Virginia Office: 600 Quarrier Street, P.O. Box 1386.
Telephone: 304-347-1100.
Fax: 304-343-2867.
Fairmont, West Virginia Office: 1000 Technology Drive, Suite 2310.
Telephone: 304-368-4000.
Fax: 304-368-4040.
Martinsburg, West Virginia Office: (Serves Berkeley Springs and Charles Town, West Virginia). 105 West Burke Street, P.O. Drawer 1419.
Telephone: 304-263-0836.
Fax: 304-267-3822.
Parkersburg, West Virginia Office: 501 Avery Street, Fifth Floor, P.O. Box 49.
Telephone: 304-485-8500.
Fax: 304-485-7973.
Lexington, Kentucky Office: 1200 World Trade Center, 333 West Vine Street.
Telephone: 606-225-8700.
Fax: 606-225-8418.

MEMBER OF FIRM

Robert W. Dinsmore
Kimberly S. Croyle

For full biographical listings, see the Martindale-Hubbell Law Directory

FURBEE, AMOS, WEBB & CRITCHFIELD (AV)

5000 Hampton Center, Suite 4, 26505
Telephone: 304-598-0900
Telecopier: 304-598-2712
Fairmont, West Virginia Office: 132 Adams Street, P.O. Box 1189.
Telephone: 304-363-8800.

MEMBERS OF FIRM

Billy Atkins
Debra Hodges Scudiere (Resident)
Rebecca J. Zuleski

ASSOCIATE

Peter T. DeMasters

Attorneys for: Consolidation Coal Co.; Westinghouse Electric Co.; Monongahela Power Co.; C & P Telephone Co.; Eastern Associated Coal Corp.; Continental Casualty Co.; State Farm Insurance Co.; Nationwide Insurance Co.; Aetna Life & Casualty.

For full biographical listings, see the Martindale-Hubbell Law Directory

THE FUSCO LEGAL GROUP, L.C. (AV)

2400 Cranberry Square, 26505-9209
Telephone: 304-594-1000
Telecopier: 304-594-1181
URL: http://www.fuscolegalgroup.com
Email: fnlaw@wvlaw.com *URL:* http://www.wvlaw.com

Andrew G. Fusco

(See Next Column)

THE FUSCO LEGAL GROUP, L.C.—*Continued*

William J. Leon, Jr. | Steven M. Prunty
Jeffrey A. Ray

For full biographical listings, see the Martindale-Hubbell Law Directory

JACKSON & KELLY (AV)

6000 Hampton Center, P.O. Box 619, 26507
Telephone: 304-599-3000
Fax: 304-285-2040
Email: info@jacksonkelly.com *URL:* http://www.jacksonkelly.com
Charleston, West Virginia Office: 1600 Laidley Tower, P.O. Box 553.
Telephone: 304-340-1000.
Fax: 304-340-1130.
Martinsburg, West Virginia Office: 300 Foxcroft Avenue, P.O. Box 1068.
Telephone: 304-263-8800.
Fax: 304-263-7110.
New Martinsville, West Virginia Office: 256 Russell Avenue, P.O. Box 68.
Telephone: 304-455-1751.
Fax: 304-455-6314.
Parkersburg, West Virginia Office: 412 Market Street, Suite 202, P.O. Box 1144.
Telephone: 304-424-3490.
Fax: 304-424-3499.
Fairmont, West Virginia Office: 1000 Technology Drive, Suite 1310.
Telephone: 304-368-2000.
Fax: 304-368-2020.
Lexington, Kentucky Office: 175 East Main Street, Suite 500, P.O. Box 2150.
Telephone: 606-255-9500.
Fax: 606-281-6478.
Washington, D. C. Office: 2401 Pennsylvania Avenue, N.W., Suite 400.
Telephone: 202-973-0200.
Fax: 202-973-0232.
Denver, Colorado Office: Suite 2710, 1660 Lincoln Street.
Telephone: 303-390-0003.
Fax: 303-390-0040.
Wheeling, West Virginia Office: 1144 Market Street.
Telephone: 304-233-4000.
Fax: 304-233-4077.

MEMBERS OF FIRM

George E. Roeder, III
Stephen M. LaCagnin (Administrative Partner)
William S. Mattingly
Eric H. London
Julia M. Chico
Charles J. Crooks

ASSOCIATES

Kathy L. Snyder
David Z. Myerberg, M.D.
Brent P. Copenhaver
Debra A. Bowers
Francesca Tan

LEGAL SUPPORT PERSONNEL

Janette G. Gidley

Representative Clients: One Valley Bank, Inc.; West Virginia University Hospitals, Inc.; Monongalia General Hospital; Chico Dairy; Greer Industries, Inc.; Swanson Plating Co. Inc.; Integra Bank; Fed One Bank; T & T Pump Company, Inc.; Asplundh Tree Expert Co.

For full biographical listings, see the Martindale-Hubbell Law Directory

*NEW MARTINSVILLE,** Wetzel Co.

JACKSON & KELLY (AV)

256 Russell Avenue, P.O. Box 68, 26155
Telephone: 304-455-1751
Fax: 304-455-6314
Email: info@jacksonkelly.com *URL:* http://www.jacksonkelly.com
Charleston, West Virginia Office: 1600 Laidley Tower, P.O. Box 553.
Telephone: 304-340-1000.
Fax: 304-340-1130.
Martinsburg, West Virginia Office: 300 Foxcroft Avenue, P.O. Box 1068.
Telephone: 304-263-8800.
Fax: 304-263-7110.
Morgantown, West Virginia Office: 6000 Hampton Center, P.O. Box 619.
Telephone: 304-599-3000.
Fax: 304-285-2040.
Parkersburg, West Virginia Office: 412 Market Street, Suite 202, P.O. Box 1144.
Telephone: 304-424-3490.
Fax: 304-424-3499.
Fairmont, West Virginia Office: 1000 Technology Drive, Suite 1310.
Telephone: 304-368-2000.
Fax: 304-368-2020.
Lexington, Kentucky Office: 175 East Main Street, Suite 500, P.O. Box 2150.
Telephone: 606-255-9500.
Fax: 606-281-6478.
Washington, D. C. Office: 2401 Pennsylvania Avenue, N.W., Suite 400.
Telephone: 202-973-0200.
Fax: 202-973-0232.

(See Next Column)

Denver, Colorado Office: Suite 2710, 1660 Lincoln Street.
Telephone: 303-390-0003.
Fax: 303-390-0040.
Wheeling, West Virginia Office: 1144 Market Street.
Telephone: 304-233-4000.
Fax: 304-233-4077.

MEMBERS OF FIRM

J. S. Francis
Larry W. Blalock (Administrative Manager, New Martinsville and Wheeling, WV Offices)

ASSOCIATES

Brooks K. Barkwill
Whitney G. Clegg

LEGAL SUPPORT PERSONNEL

Mary Ann Baker

Representative Clients: Bayer Corp; PPG Industries, Inc.; Wetzel County Hospital; Olin Corp.; Allstate Insurance Co.; State Farm Insurance Co.; Hartford Insurance Co.; Physicians Insurance Co. of Ohio; Huntington National Bank, West Virginia; Crum & Forster Insurance Co.

For full biographical listings, see the Martindale-Hubbell Law Directory

*PARKERSBURG,** Wood Co.

BOWLES RICE MCDAVID GRAFF & LOVE, PLLC (AV)

(Formerly Davis, Bailey, Pfalzgraf & Hall)
501 Avery Street, Fifth Floor, P.O. Box 49, 26102-0048
Telephone: 304-485-8500
Fax: 304-485-7973
Email: bowles@bowlesrice.com *URL:* http://www.bowlesrice.com
Charleston, West Virginia Office: 600 Quarrier Street, P.O. Box 1386.
Telephone: 304-347-1100.
Fax: 304-343-2867.
Fairmont, West Virginia Office: 1000 Technology Drive, Suite 2310.
Telephone: 304-368-4000.
Fax: 304-368-4040.
Martinsburg, West Virginia Office (Serves Berkeley Springs and Charles Town, West Virginia): 105 West Burke Street, P.O. Drawer 1419.
Telephone: 304-263-0836.
Fax: 304-267-3822.
Morgantown, West Virginia Office: 7000 Hampton Center, Suite K.
Telephone: 304-599-1390.
Fax: 304-599-1308.
Lexington, Kentucky Office: 1200 World Trade Center, 333 West Vine Street.
Telephone: 606-225-8700.
Fax: 606-225-8418.

MEMBERS OF FIRM

Howard E. Seufer, Jr. (Resident)
Robert J. Kent (Resident)
Steven R. Hardman (Resident)
Robert L. Bays (Resident)

RESIDENT ASSOCIATES

Ellen L. Medaglio
Kevin A. Rings
Charles E. McDonough

RESIDENT OF COUNSEL

John S. Bailey, Jr.

For full biographical listings, see the Martindale-Hubbell Law Directory

GOODWIN & GOODWIN (AV)

201 Third Street, Town Square, 26101
Telephone: 304-485-2345
Fax: 304-485-3459
URL: http://www.goodwingoodwin.com
Charleston, West Virginia Office: 1500 One Valley Square.
Telephone: 304-346-7000
Fax: 304-344-9692
Ripley, West Virginia Office: 500 Church Street, P.O. Box 349.
Telephone: 304-372-2651.

RESIDENT PARTNER

Robert W. Full

RESIDENT ASSOCIATE

John N. Ellem

For full biographical listings, see the Martindale-Hubbell Law Directory

*PETERSBURG,** Grant Co.

DUKE A. MCDANIEL (AV)

304 Virginia Avenue, P.O. Box 417, 26847
Telephone: 304-257-4377
Telefax: 304-257-4033

Reference: Potomac Valley Bank, Petersburg, W. Va.

For full biographical listings, see the Martindale-Hubbell Law Directory

*PRINCETON,** Mercer Co.

JOHNSTON, HOLROYD & ASSOCIATES (AV)

1438 Main Street, 24740
Telephone: 304-425-2103
Fax: 304-425-5385
Email: mlawdog@inet1.net

MEMBERS OF FIRM

W. Broughton Johnston (1905-1978)
Robert E. Holroyd
Anthony Bisaha
Michael A. Lawrence
Scott A. Ash

Representative Clients: McDowell-Pocahontas Coal Co.; One Valley Bank; Princeton Community Hospital.

For full biographical listings, see the Martindale-Hubbell Law Directory

*RIPLEY,** Jackson Co.

GOODWIN & GOODWIN (AV)

500 Church Street, P.O. Box 349, 25271
Telephone: 304-372-2651
URL: http://www.goodwingoodwin.com
Charleston, West Virginia Office: 1500 One Valley Square.
Telephone: 304-346-7000.
Fax: 304-344-9692
Parkersburg, West Virginia Office: 201 Third Street, Town Square.
Telephone: 304-485-2345.
Fax: 304-485-3459.

Robert B. Goodwin (1909-1955)

OF COUNSEL

C. E. Goodwin

MEMBERS OF FIRM

Stephen P. Goodwin
Michael I. Spiker
Steven F. White
Richard E. Rowe

For full biographical listings, see the Martindale-Hubbell Law Directory

WEIRTON, Hancock & Brooke Cos.

FRANKOVITCH, ANETAKIS, COLANTONIO & SIMON (AV)

337 Penco Road, 26062
Telephone: 304-723-4400
Fax: 304-723-5892
Email: fanda@1stnet
Wheeling, West Virginia Office: United National Bank Building, Suite 504, 21 Twelfth Street.
Telephone: 304-233-1212.
Fax: 304-233-1251.
Chester, West Virginia Office: 529 Carolina Avenue, 26034.
Telephone: 304-387-4400.
Fax: 304-387-4412.

MEMBERS OF FIRM

George J. Anetakis
Carl N. Frankovitch
John J. Anetakis
M. Eric Frankovitch
Mark A. Colantonio
Michael G. Simon

ASSOCIATES

Bryan S. Neft
Thomas J. Decapio
J. George (Jack) Anetakis

OF COUNSEL

Carl Frankovitch
John H. Kamlowsky

For full biographical listings, see the Martindale-Hubbell Law Directory

*WELLSBURG,** Brooke Co.

WILLIAM E. WATSON & ASSOCIATES (AV)

800 Main Street, P.O. Box 111, 26070
Telephone: 304-737-0881
Fax: 304-737-9853
Email: wewalaw@aol.com

Marc B. Chernenko
Christine Machel

General Counsel For: Advance Financial Savings Bank, F.S.B.
Local Counsel For: Scott Lumber Co.; First Federal Savings and Loan Assn. of Greene County, Waynesburg, Pa. and Uniontown, Pa.; Stone Container Corp.; WesBanco Bank, Wheeling; Eagle Manufacturing Co.; Cattrell Cos; The Louis Berkman Co.; Wheeling-Nisshin, Inc.; WV Annual Conference, United Methodist Church.

For full biographical listings, see the Martindale-Hubbell Law Directory

*WHEELING,** Ohio Co.

BACHMANN, HESS, BACHMANN & GARDEN, P.L.L.C. (AV)

1226 Chapline Street, P.O. Box 351, 26003-0046
Telephone: 304-233-3511
Fax: 304-233-3199
Email: info@bhbglaw.com *URL:* http://www.bhbglaw.com

(See Next Column)

MEMBERS OF FIRM

Carl G. Bachmann (1890-1980)
Lester C. Hess (1903-1971)
John B. Garden (1925-1994)
Gilbert S. Bachmann
Lester C. Hess, Jr.
John L. Allen
Paul T. Tucker
George E. McLaughlin
Jeffrey R. Miller
Anthony Ira Werner
Jeffrey A. Grove
Elizabeth Abraham Delk

ASSOCIATE

David L. Delk, Jr.

Representative Clients: American Electric Power; Ohio Power Co.; United National Bank; Wheeling Housing Authority; Windsor Coal Co.

For full biographical listings, see the Martindale-Hubbell Law Directory

PHILLIPS, GARDILL, KAISER & ALTMEYER (AV)

61 Fourteenth Street, 26003
Telephone: 304-232-6810
Fax: 304-232-4918

OF COUNSEL

John D. Phillips (Retired)
Robert J. Samol

MEMBERS OF FIRM

James C. Gardill
Charles J. Kaiser, Jr.
H. Brann Altmeyer
William A. Kolibash
Edward M. George III

ASSOCIATES

Denise H. Knouse-Snyder
Todd M. Kildow (Not admitted in WV)
Mary C. Schaffer
Richard N. Beaver

General Counsel for: WesBanco Inc.; Wheeling Park Commission (Oglebay); Belmont Bancorp; Mull Industries, Inc.; Altmeyer Funeral Homes, Inc.; Strauss Industries, Inc.; Catholic Diocese of Wheeling-Charleston.
Local Counsel For: Ormet Corp.; Consolidation Coal, Inc.

For full biographical listings, see the Martindale-Hubbell Law Directory

SCHRADER BYRD & COMPANION, PLLC (AV)

(A Professional Limited Liability Company)
The Maxwell Centre, 32-20th Street, Suite 500, P.O. Box 6336, 26003
Telephone: 304-233-3390
Fax: 304-233-2769
URL: http://www.schraderlaw.com
Martins Ferry, Ohio Office: 205 North Fifth Street, P.O. Box 309, 43935.
Telephone: 740-633-9976.
Fax: 740-633-0400.
Weirton, West Virginia Office: 3205 Pennsylvania Avenue, Suite 103, Penn Place, P.O. Box 2785, 26062.
Telephone: 304-723-2674.
Fax: 304-723-2876.

MEMBERS

Ray A. Byrd
James F. Companion
Frank X. Duff
Teresa Rieman-Camilletti
Yolonda G. Lambert
Daniel P. Fry (Resident Partner, Martins Ferry, Ohio Office)
James P. Mazzone (Resident Member, Weirton, West Virginia Office)
Sandra K. Law
D. Kevin Coleman

SPECIAL COUNSEL

Thomas B. Miller

ASSOCIATES

Denise D. Klug
Michael A. Adams
John Porco
Aimee Morgan Stern
Kimberly R. Wilson
Christopher J. Adams

OF COUNSEL

James A. Byrum, Jr.

General Counsel: Reynolds Memorial Hospital; WesBanco Bank-Elm Grove.
Representative Clients: American Cyanamid Company; Bank One; Matlack Systems, Inc.; Moutaineer Gas Co.; Ohio County Board of Education; PHICO Insurance Co.; Wheeling Hospital; Wheeling-Pittsburg Steel Corp.

For full biographical listings, see the Martindale-Hubbell Law Directory

WISCONSIN

*EAGLE RIVER,** Vilas Co.

O'BRIEN, ANDERSON, BURGY, GARBOWICZ & BROWN, LLP (AV)

Arbutus Court, P.O. Box 639, 54521
Telephone: 715-479-6444
FAX: 715-479-3021
Boulder Junction, Wisconsin Office: County Highway M, 54512.
Telephone: 715-385-2047.
Fax: 715-385-2344.

(See Next Column)

O'BRIEN, ANDERSON, BURGY, GARBOWICZ & BROWN LLP—*Continued*

Edmund H. Drager (1894-1988)

MEMBERS OF FIRM

John L. O'Brien
William W. Anderson
Dennis M. Burgy
Steven C. Garbowicz
Alexander E. Brown

Representative Clients: First National Bank of Eagle River; M&I Bank of Three Lakes, Wisconsin; M&I Bank of Eagle River; Northern Title Corp., Eagle River, Wisconsin; Cranberry Products, Inc.
Reference: First National Bank.

For full biographical listings, see the Martindale-Hubbell Law Directory

*EAU CLAIRE,** Eau Claire Co.

GARVEY, ANDERSON, JOHNSON, GABLER & GERACI, S.C. (AV)

402 Graham Avenue, P.O. Box 187, 54702-0187
Telephone: 715-834-3425
FAX: 715-834-9240

Frank L. Morrow (1905-1969)
James E. Garvey
David G. Anderson
Douglas M. Johnson
William M. Gabler
Sebastian J. Geraci
Joseph R. Mirr
Carol S. Dittmar
Jane E. Lokken
Linda M. Danielson
Randi L. Osberg
Steven V. Schlitz
John D. Leary
Christopher M. Seelen

Representative Clients: Bauer Built, Inc.; Grace Lutheran Foundation; Grassland Dairy Products, Inc.; M&I Community State Bank; Silver Spring Gardens, Inc.; Northern States Power Company; Commonweal Development; Market & Johnson, Inc.- general contractors; Royal Credit Union; Goldridge Group-Developer.

For full biographical listings, see the Martindale-Hubbell Law Directory

WILCOX, WILCOX, ENRIGHT, HALLSTEIN, MCMAHON & ADLER, LLC (AV)

Limited Liability Company
1030 Regis Court, P.O. Box 128, 54701
Telephone: 715-832-6645
Fax: 715-832-8438
Email: willaw@win.bright.net

MEMBERS OF FIRM

Roy P. Wilcox (1873-1946)
Francis J. Wilcox
Roy S. Wilcox
Daniel A. Enright
John F. Wilcox
Howard G. McMahon
George W. Hallstein
Timothy J. Adler

Attorneys for: Aetna Insurance Group; Medical Protective Assn.; American Surety Co.; Viking Insurance Co.; American Mutual Liability Ins. Co.; Continental Cas. Co.; Farmers Insurance Group.

For full biographical listings, see the Martindale-Hubbell Law Directory

*FOND DU LAC,** Fond du Lac Co.

EDGARTON, ST. PETER, PETAK, MASSEY & BULLON (AV)

10 Forest Avenue, P.O. Box 1276, 54936-1276
Telephone: 920-922-0470
Fax: 920-922-9091

MEMBERS OF FIRM

Allan L. Edgarton (1908-1994)
Thomas L. Massey (1935-1995)
George M. St. Peter (Retired)
Neil Hobbs (Retired)
A. D. Edgarton
Robert V. Edgarton
Ronald L. Petak
John A. St. Peter
Kathryn M. Bullon
Paul W. Rosenfeldt

Representative Clients: Firstar Bank Fond du Lac, N.A.; The Combination Door Co.; Ready Mix Concrete, Inc.; Mayville Engineering Co., Inc.; J. F. Ahern Co.; Giddings & Lewis; Moraine Park Technical College; Fond du Lac School District.

For full biographical listings, see the Martindale-Hubbell Law Directory

*GREEN BAY,** Brown Co.

EVERSON, WHITNEY, EVERSON & BREHM, S.C. (AV)

Suite 106, 125 South Jefferson Street, P.O. Box 22248, 54305-2248
Telephone: 920-435-3734
Fax: 920-435-0126
Email: eweb@execpc.com

John C. Whitney (1915-1994)
Philip R. Brehm
John E. Herald
Rodney A. Charnholm
George F. Savage
Peter J. Hickey
Susan J. Reigel
John M. Thompson, IV
Jeffrey T. DeMeuse
John H. Heide

OF COUNSEL

James L. Everson

(See Next Column)

Peter C. Brehm
Katherine L. Pleger
Erik J. Pless

LEGAL SUPPORT PERSONNEL

PARALEGAL

Cheryl Lynn Morin

Counsel for: American Family Insurance; Bank One; Rural Mutual Medical Protective; U.S. Fidelity & Guaranty Co.; Employers Insurance of Wausau; State Farm Mutual Cos.; Travelers Insurance Co.; Farmers Insurance Group; Liberty Mutual Insurance Co.

For full biographical listings, see the Martindale-Hubbell Law Directory

GODFREY & KAHN, S.C. (AV)

333 Main Street, Suite 600, P.O. Box 13067, 54307-3067
Telephone: 920-432-9300
Telecopier: 920-436-7988
Email: sdavis@gklaw.com *URL:* http://www.gklaw.com
Milwaukee, Wisconsin Office: 780 North Water Street, 53202.
Telephone: 414-273-3500.
Madison, Wisconsin Office: 131 West Wilson Street, Suite 700, 53703.
Telephone: 608-251-4670.
Oshkosh, Wisconsin Office: 219 Washington Avenue, 54901.
Telephone: 920-233-6050.
Appleton, Wisconsin Office: 100 West Lawrence Street, 54911.
Telephone: 920-830-2800.

Benjamin W. Laird
Ronald T. Pfeifer
Joseph M. Nicks
Winston A. Ostrow
Robert W. Burns
Dennis W. Rader
William J. Plummer
Donald L. Romundson
Timothy J. McCoy
John A. Haase
Scott M. Fuhr

For full biographical listings, see the Martindale-Hubbell Law Directory

*JANESVILLE,** Rock Co.

BRENNAN, STEIL, BASTING & MACDOUGALL, S.C. (AV)

One East Milwaukee Street, P.O. Box 1148, 53547
Telephone: 608-756-4141
Facsimile: 608-756-9000
Email: brennan@bsbmlaw.com *URL:* http://www.bsbmlaw.com
Madison, Wisconsin Office: 22 East Mifflin Street, Suite 400, P.O. Box 990.
Telephone: 608-251-7770.
Facsimile: 608-251-6626.
Monroe, Wisconsin Office: 1628 11th Street, P.O. Box 739.
Telephone: 608-325-2131.
Facsimile: 608-325-9546.
Delavan, Wisconsin Office: 512 East Walworth Avenue.
Telephone: 414-728-5591.
Facsimile: 414-728-1780.

Glen R. Campbell (1927-1972)
Paul M. Ryan (1931-1986)
George K. Steil, Sr.
Thomas J. Basting, Sr.
David J. MacDougall
Thomas S. Hornig
James E. Hartwig
George K. Steil, Jr.
John R. Steil
William B. Vogt
Michael E. Grubb
Dennis M. White (Resident, Madison Office)
Edward A. Corcoran (Resident, Madison Office)
Peter B. Kelly (Resident, Monroe Office)
Michael R. Fitzpatrick
Clarence F. Asmus (Resident, Monroe Office)
Marc T. McCrory
Bryan D. Woods (Resident, Madison Office)
Howard Goldberg (Resident, Madison Office)
Margery Mebane Tibbetts
Kevin C. Potter (Resident at Madison Office)
Jonathan W. Groessl

David B. Williams (Resident, Delavan Office)
Terry J. Finman-Pince
Dennis E. Robertson (Resident at Madison Office)
Nancy B. Johnson
Robert E. Mahoney (Resident, Delavan Office)
Christine M. Witherill
Caryl Shortridge Peters
Stephen M. Compton
Dale L. Thorpe (Resident, Delavan Office)
Scott T. Christian (Resident, Delavan Office)
Jeffry R. Schwartz
Beth Eyster Shore
John A. Kassner (Resident, Madison Office)

OF COUNSEL

James E. Brennan
Robert M. Berg

Counsel for: Heritage Bank, Rock County; Blain Supply, Inc.; Farm and Fleet Stores.
Local Counsel for: Fireman's Fund Insurance Co.; Insurance Company of North America; Heritage Mutual Insurance Co.; PICW; CIVMIC; Capitol Indemnity Corp.

For full biographical listings, see the Martindale-Hubbell Law Directory

*KENOSHA,** Kenosha Co.

Rose & Rose (AV)

5529 Sixth Avenue, 53140
Telephone: 262-658-8550, 657-7556
Fax: 262-658-1313

MEMBERS OF FIRM

William S. Rose (1914-1994)
Terry W. Rose
Christopher W. Rose

For full biographical listings, see the Martindale-Hubbell Law Directory

*LA CROSSE,** La Crosse Co.

Fitzpatrick, Blackey & Devanie (AV)

123 South 7th Street, P.O. Box 0519, 54602-0519
Telephone: 608-784-4370
Fax: 608-784-4908
Email: law@fitzpatricklaw.com *URL:* http://centuryinter.net/fitzpatricklaw/

Thomas M. Fitzpatrick
Michael J. Devanie
T. David Blackey
Elizabeth A. Wright
David J. Fitzpatrick

For full biographical listings, see the Martindale-Hubbell Law Directory

Johns, Flaherty & Rice, S.C. (AV)

205 Fifth Avenue South Suite 600, P.O. Box 1626, 54602-1626
Telephone: 608-784-5678
Fax: 608-784-0557
Sparta, Wisconsin Office: 112 West Oak Street, P.O. Box 255, 54656.
Telephone: 608-269-2174.
Fax: 608-269-1134.

Daniel T. Flaherty
Richard J. Heitman
Robert D. Johns, Jr.
Brent P. Smith
J. David Rice
Peder G. Arneson
Maureen L. Kinney
Ellen M. Frantz
Janet A. Jenkins
Gregory S. Bonney
Michael L. Stoker

Brian G. Weber
Terry A. Davis
Matthew E. Valley
Joseph G. Veenstra

Representative Clients: Aetna C & S Co.; Allstate Insurance Co.; CNA; INA; Norwest Bank, La Crosse, N.A.; St. Paul Cos.; U.S.F. & G. Co.; Gundersen Clinic, Ltd.; Altec International, Inc.

For full biographical listings, see the Martindale-Hubbell Law Directory

Moen, Sheehan, Meyer, Ltd. (AV)

Suite 700, First Bank Place, 201 Main Street, P.O. Box 0786, 54602-0786
Telephone: 608-784-8310
FAX: 608-782-6611
Email: msm_ltd@centuryinter.net

Leon E. Sheehan
David F. Stickler
Paul W. Henke, Jr.
James L. Kroner, Jr.
Michael S. Moen
Joseph J. Skemp, Jr.
Michael E. Ehrsam
Kara M. Burgos
James Naugler
Daniel J. Lilly
G. Jeffrey George
Michelle M. Guillien
Margaret E. Ebner

OF COUNSEL

William E. Meyer

Representative Clients: Allstate Insurance Co.; Mathy Construction Co.; St. Paul Insurance Cos; State Farm Insurance Co.
References: First Bank, N.A.; First Wisconsin Trust Co. (Milwaukee); La Crosse Trust Co.; Marshall & Ilsley Bank (Milwaukee).

For full biographical listings, see the Martindale-Hubbell Law Directory

*MADISON,** Dane Co.

Axley Brynelson, LLP (AV)

(Formerly Brynelson, Herrick, Bucaida, Dorschel & Armstrong Including the former Easton & Assoc., S.C.)
2 East Mifflin Street, P.O. Box 1767, 53701-1767
Telephone: 608-257-5661
Fax: 608-257-5444
Email: law@axley.com *URL:* http://www.axley.com

MEMBERS OF FIRM

Bradley D. Armstrong
Peter Weisenberger (1946-1992)
John H. Schmid, Jr.
Curtis C. Swanson
Timothy D. Fenner
Michael S. Anderson
John C. Mitby
Patricia M. Gibeault
Daniel T. Hardy
Michael J. Westcott
John Walsh
Larry K. Libman
Bruce L. Harms
Richard E. Petershack
David Easton
Steven A. Brezinski

(See Next Column)

MEMBERS OF FIRM (Continued)

Steven M. Streck
Edith F. Merila
Joy L. O'Grosky
Michael J. Modl
Arthur E. Kurtz
Guy J. DuBeau
Gregory C. Collins

ASSOCIATES

John T. Payette
Nicholas S. Harned
Leslie A. Fiskey
Kevin Trost
Andrew J. Clarkowski
Matthew C. Carlson
Jan A. Erickson
Derek R. Kritzer
Steven E. Grimm
Timothy Cesar
Judd A. Genda
Joseph C. Copa
Lori M. Lubinsky
Timothy R. Verhoff
Aaron R. Gary
Lisa R. Foerst
Mark Edward O'Neill
Sarah K. Frost
Paul D. Curtis

OF COUNSEL

Ralph E. Axley (1902-1995)
James C. Herrick
Floyd A. Brynelson (1914-1998)
Frank J. Bucaida
Griffin G. Dorschel

For full biographical listings, see the Martindale-Hubbell Law Directory

DeWitt Ross & Stevens S.C. (AV)

2 East Mifflin Street, Suite 600, 53703
Telephone: 608-255-8891
Facsimile: 608-252-9243
West Madison Office: 8000 Excelsior Drive, Suite 401, Madison, WI 53717.
Telephone: 608-831-2100.
Telecopier: 608-831-2106.

Philip H. Porter (1891-1976)
Wrede H. Smith, Jr.
Frank A. Ross (1901-1990)
Frederic J. Brouner
Myron Stevens (1902-1994)
Donald Leo Bach
A.J. McAndrews (1903-1990)
Stuart C. Herro
James W. Morgan (1932-1988)
Anthony R. Varda
Donald R. Huggett (1933-1993)
Ronald R. Ragatz
Jack R. DeWitt
Gregory E. Scallon
Charles P. Seibold
Eric A. Farnsworth
Duane P. Schumacher
Richard J. Lewandowski
Thomas D. Zilavy
Joseph A. Ranney
Peter R. Dohr
Douglas L. Flygt
Daniel W. Hildebrand
Brian L. Anderson
John Rashke
William E. McCardell
John Koeppl
Charles S. Sara
Jon P. Axelrod
Dennis P. Birke
Peter A. Peshek
Christopher D. Daniels
John Duncan Varda
Timm P. Speerschneider
Henry J. Handzel, Jr.
Bradley W. Hauck
Ronald W. Kuehn
Robert E. Shumaker
Jayne K. Kuehn
Troy A. Mayne
Anne Taylor Wadsack
Stephen A. DiTullio
Paul A. Croake
Joseph T. Leone
Denis P. Bartell
Todd E. Palmer
Michael R. Davis
Craig A. Fieschko

OF COUNSEL

Norman C. Herro
John H. Lederer
Jean G. Setterholm
David W. Kruger
Stephen E. Bablitch

Scott K. Petersen
Amy C. Heckmann
Jacob P. Westerhof
M. Elizabeth Winters
Bryan C. Esch
Bradley W. Raaths
Bradley C. Fulton
Mary E. Eberle

Representative Clients: American Family Insurance Group; Dean Foundation for Health, Research and Education, Inc.; Firstar Bank Wisconsin; Independent Insurance Agents; Kennecott Corp.; Northern Engraving Corp.; Perry Printing Corp.; Promega Corp.; Wisconsin Association of Manufacturers and Commerce Transportation, Mining and Environmental Advisory Committees; Wisconsin Alumni Research Foundation.

For full biographical listings, see the Martindale-Hubbell Law Directory

Foley & Lardner (AV)

Verex Plaza, 150 East Gilman Street, P.O. Box 1497, 53701-1497
Telephone: 608-257-5035
Facsimile: 608-258-4258
Email: foleylardner@worldnet.att.net *URL:* http://www.foleylardner.com
Los Angeles, California Office: 2029 Century Park East, 35th Floor.
Telephone: 310-277-2223.
Fax: 310-557-8475.
Sacramento, California Office: 300 Capitol Mall, Suite 1125.
Telephone: 916-443-8005.
Fax: 916-443-2240.
San Diego, California Office: 402 West Broadway, 23rd Floor.
Telephone: 619-234-6655.
Fax: 619-234-3510.
San Francisco, California Office: One Maritime Plaza, Sixth Floor.
Telephone: 415-434-4484.
Fax: 415-434-4507.

(See Next Column)

FOLEY & LARDNER—*Continued*

Denver, Colorado Office: 1999 Broadway, Suite 2560.
Telephone: 303-297-0260.
Fax: 303-297-0266.
Washington, D.C. Office: Washington Harbour, Suite 500, 3000 K Street, N.W.
Telephone: 202-672-5300.
Telex: 904136 (Foley Lard Wash).
Facsimile: 202-672-5399.
Jacksonville, Florida Office: The Greenleaf Building, 200 Laura Street. P.O. Box 240.
Telephone: 904-359-2000.
Facsimile: 904-359-8700.
Orlando, Florida Office: Suite 1800, 111 North Orange Avenue, P.O. Box 2193.
Telephone: 407-423-7656.
Facsimile: 407-648-1743.
Tallahassee, Florida Office: 300 East Park Avenue, P.O. Box 1454.
Telephone: 850-222-6100.
Facsimile: 850-561-6475.
Tampa, Florida Offices: Suite 2700, One Hundred N. Tampa Street, P.O. Box 3391.
Telephones: 813-229-2300; Pinellas County: 813-442-3296.
Facsimile: 813-221-4210.
West Palm Beach, Florida Office: Suite 200, Phillips Point East Tower, 777 South Flagler Drive.
Telephone: 561-655-5050.
Facsimile: 561-655-6925.
Chicago, Illinois Office: Suite 3300, One IBM Plaza, 330 N. Wabash Avenue.
Telephone: 312-755-1900.
Facsimile: 312-755-1925.
Annapolis, Maryland Office: Suite 102, 175 Admiral Cochrane Drive.
Telephone: 410-266-8077.
Telex: 899149 (Oldtownpat).
Facsimile: 410-266-8664.
Milwaukee, Wisconsin Office: Firstar Center, 777 East Wisconsin Avenue.
Telephone: 414-271-2400.
Telex: 26-819 (Foley Lard Mil).
Facsimile: 414-297-4900.
Brussels, Belgium Office: Avenue Louise, 283.
Telephone: 32-2-646-2777.
Facsimile: 32-2-646-7574.

PARTNERS

Allen A. Arntsen
Michael H. Auen
Christopher S. Berry
Douglas B. Clark (Resident)
William M. Conley
Charles G. Curtis, Jr.
Gordon Davenport III
Joan L. Eads (Resident)
Harry C. Engstrom
Henry A. Gempeler
David J. Harth
Joseph P. Hildebrandt
Roberta F. Howell (Resident)
Bradley D. Jackson (Resident)
Allan R. Koritzinsky
Michael G. Laskis
Wayman C. Lawrence, IV
Timothy J. Radelet
Thomas G. Ragatz
David W. Reinecke
Blaine Renfert (Resident)
Anne Elizabeth Ross
John S. Skilton
Leonard S. Sosnowski
Gisèle M. Sutherland
Harvey L. Temkin
Michael B. Van Sicklen
David G. Walsh (Firm Management Committee, 1993—, Partner-in-Charge, Madison Office, 1988-1996)
Robert M. Whitney

RESIDENT SPECIAL COUNSEL

Megan J. Ballard
Ann E. Baxter
Raymond R. Carey
James R. Conohan
Michael S. Heffernan
Arthur W. Jorgensen III
Mark L. Langenfeld
Terry D. Nelson
Anita M. Sorensen

ASSOCIATES

Sandy M. Ballou
Christopher C. Cain
Susan L. Collins
Michael Falk
Bernard P. Friedrichsen
Catherine M. Gillman
Emily R. Gnam
Anat Hakim
Christopher Hanewicz
Wayne Omar Hanewicz
Steven A. Heinzen
Thomas W. Henshue (Resident)
Daniel A. Kaplan
Mark A. Kassel
Christopher L. Kopecky
Peter J. Manghera
William S. McClenahan
Marta T. Meyers
Sharon Mollman Elliott
Gregory F. Monday
Mark Neuser
Andrew L. Nelson
David V. Northcutt
Antonina Prestigiacomo
Lori A. Ringhand
Katherine Stadler
Michelle M. Umberger

For full biographical listings, see the Martindale-Hubbell Law Directory

GODFREY & KAHN, S.C. (AV)

131 West Wilson Street, Suite 700, P.O. Box 1110, 53701-1110
Telephone: 608-251-4670
Telecopier: 608-251-2983
Email: sdavis@gklaw.com *URL:* http://www.gklaw.com
Milwaukee, Wisconsin Office: 780 North Water Street, 53202.
Telephone: 414-273-3500.

(See Next Column)

Green Bay, Wisconsin Office: 333 Main Street, Suite 600, 54301.
Telephone: 920-432-9300.
Oshkosh, Wisconsin Office: 219 Washington Avenue, 54901.
Telephone: 920-233-6050.
Appleton, Wisconsin Office: 100 West Lawrence Street, 54911.
Telephone: 920-830-2800.

Jon E. Anderson
Peter L. Albrecht
Brandon Krueger

For full biographical listings, see the Martindale-Hubbell Law Directory

LATHROP & CLARK, LLP (AV)

Suite 400, 740 Regent Street, P.O. Box 1507, 53701-1507
Telephone: 608-257-7766
FAX: 608-257-1507
URL: http://www.lathropclark.com
Poynette, Wisconsin Office: 111 North Main Street, P.O. Box 128.
Telephone: 608-635-4324.
FAX: 608-635-4690.
Lodi, Wisconsin Office: 108 Lodi Street, P.O. Box 256.
Telephone: 608-592-3877.
FAX: 608-592-5844.
Belleville, Wisconsin Office: 27 West Main.
Telephone: 608-424-3404.

MEMBERS OF FIRM

G. Burgess Ela (1904-1976)
Leon E. Isaksen (1903-1979)
San W. Orr (1906-1991)
Trayton L. Lathrop (1923-1998)
Edmund J. Hart (1914-1998)
Donald M. Ryan (1914-1998)
Donald L. Heaney
Theodore J. Long
Ronald J. Kotnik
Jerry E. McAdow
David S. Uphoff
John C. Frank
Michael J. Lawton
William L. Fahey
Michael J. Julka
Shelley J. Safer
Jeffrey P. Clark
Kenneth B. Axe
David E. Rohrer
Marjorie H. Schuett
Jill Weber Dean
Jeffrey S. Ward
Kirk D. Strang
David R. J. Stiennon
Jeffry W. Smith
Heidi S. Tepp
Patrick J. G. Stiennon
Peter A. Martin
Daniel L. Dooge
Paul A. Johnson
Frank C. Sutherland

OF COUNSEL

John H. Esch
James F. Clark

ASSOCIATES

James E. Zylstra
Shannon L. Day

Representative Clients: Associated Bank South Central; The Richard E. Jacobs Group; Roman Catholic Diocese of Madison; Mid-West Management, Inc.; Research Products Corp.; Kayser Ford, Inc.; Metropolitan Life Insurance Co.; Wisconsin Association of School Boards, Inc.; American Family Mutual Insurance Co.

For full biographical listings, see the Martindale-Hubbell Law Directory

MELLI, WALKER, PEASE & RUHLY, S.C. (AV)

Suite 900, Ten East Doty, P.O. Box 1664, 53701-1664
Telephone: 608-257-4812
Telefax: 608-258-7470
URL: http://www.melliwalker.com

Jack D. Walker
James K. Pease, Jr.
James K. Ruhly
Thomas R. Crone
Philip J. Bradbury
JoAnn M. Hart
Susan C. Sheeran
Douglas E. Witte
Dana J. Erlandsen
Devon R. Baumbach
Daniel D. Barker
Jenifer L. Kraemer

OF COUNSEL

Joseph A. Melli

Representative Clients: Wisconsin Transportation Builders Assn.; Associated Builders & Contractors of Wisconsin, Inc.; Marshall Erdman & Associates, Inc.; Research Products Corp.; Kraemer Brothers, LLC.; Covance Laboratories; JJ Protective Services, Inc.; Racine Unified School District; Green Bay Area School District.

For full biographical listings, see the Martindale-Hubbell Law Directory

MICHAEL BEST & FRIEDRICH LLP (AV)

One South Pinckney Street, Firstar Plaza, P.O. Box 1806, 53701-1806
Telephone: 608-257-3501
Telecopier: 608-283-2275
Email: info@mbf-law.com *URL:* http://www.mbf-law.com
Milwaukee, Wisconsin Office: 100 East Wisconsin Avenue. 53202-4108.
Telephone: 414-271-6560.
Telecopier: 414-277-0656.
Manitowoc, Wisconsin Office: 1000 Maritime Drive, 54220.
Telephone: 920-686-2800.
Fax: 920-686-2810.
Chicago, Illinois Office: Michael Best & Friedrich LLC, 77 West Wacker Drive, Suite 4300, 60601-1635.
Telephone: 312-845-5800.
Telecopier: 312-845-5828.

(See Next Column)

MICHAEL BEST & FRIEDRICH LLP, *Madison—Continued*

PARTNERS

Tod B. Linstroth
David J. Hanson
Nelson D. Flynn
James R. Troupis
William F. White
Richard J. Langer
Thomas P. Godar
Charles V. Sweeney
Teresa J. Welch
Grady J. Frenchick
Ann Ustad Smith
Richard A. Latta
Thomas E. Klancnik
Linda H. Bochert
Raymond P. Taffora
Steven L. Ritt
David A. Crass
J. Donald Best
Thomas Patrick Heneghan
Richard Z. Kabaker
Jon G. Furlow
Steven P. Means
Paul J. Dombrowski
Susan V. Kelley
Linda L. Lilledahl
Timothy S. Crisp

ASSOCIATES

Eric M. McLeod
Amy O. Bruchs
Lauren L. Azar
Ian A. Pitz
Gregory J. Lynch
Linda Blair Meier
Sheila Boothby Stevens
Jordan J. Hemaidan
Matthew L. Storms
John C. Scheller
Michael S. Green
Gregory P. Meier
Paul F. Donovan
Karen B. King
H. Nia Enemuoh-Trammell
Karla M. Davis
Mary C. Turke
Porter J. Martin
Erik J. Phelps
Christine Cooney Mansour

SPECIAL COUNSEL

Judith M. Hecker

For full biographical listings, see the Martindale-Hubbell Law Directory

MURPHY & DESMOND, S.C. (AV)

Manchester Place, Suite 800, 2 East Mifflin Street, P.O. Box 2038, 53701-2038
Telephone: 608-257-7181
Telecopier: 608-257-2508
Email: email@murphydesmond.com *URL:* http://www.murphydesmond.com

Robert B. L. Murphy
William F. Mundt
Michael R. Vaughan
Richard W. Pitzner
William J. Rameker
James D. Sweet
Stephen L. Morgan
Robert A. Pasch
Debbie Garten
William Smoler
Stephen C. Beilke
Catherine J. Furay
Stephen R. Tumbush
Lawrence E. Bechler
Pamela J. Schmelzer
Leslie D. Shear
Jane F. (Ginger) Zimmerman

Gregory P. Seibold
Robert R. Studt
Charles G. Center
Daniel J. Lipman
Ronald M. Trachtenberg
Marinus (Rick) J.W. Petri
Vernon J. Jesse
Diane M. Pica
Daniel G. Jardine
Teresa A. Mueller
Robert J. Lightfoot II
Rebecca R. DeMarb
Kimberly P. Sebranek

OF COUNSEL

John P. Desmond
Harvey L. Wendel
Tim R. Valentyn

Representative Clients: Anheuser-Busch Co.; Bank of Sun Prairie; Coordinated Capital Securities; Mapco Gas Products, Inc.; The Multicare Companies, Inc.; R.J. Reynolds Tobacco Co.; Samuels Recycling Co.; Shockley Communications Corp.; Village of McFarland; Wisconsin Bankers Assn.

For full biographical listings, see the Martindale-Hubbell Law Directory

QUARLES & BRADY LLP (AV)

Firstar Plaza, One South Pinckney Street, P.O. Box 2113, 53701-2113
Telephone: 608-251-5000
Fax: 608-251-9166
URL: http://www.quarles.com
Milwaukee, Wisconsin Office: 411 East Wisconsin Avenue, 53202-4497.
Telephone: 414-277-5000.
Fax: 414-271-3552.
West Palm Beach, Florida Office: 222 Lakeview Avenue, 4th Floor, 33401.
Telephone: 561-653-5000.
Fax: 561-653-5333.
Naples, Florida Office: Barnett Center, 4501 Tamiami Trail North, Suite 300, 34103-3060.
Telephone: 941-262-5959.
Fax: 941-434-4999.
Phoenix, Arizona Office: One Camelback Building, One East Camelback Road, Suite 400, 85012-1649.
Telephone: 602-230-5500.
Fax: 602-230-5598.
Chicago, Illinois Office: Quarles & Brady LLC, Citicorp Center, 500 West Madison Street, Suite 3700.
Telephone: 312-715-5000.
Fax: 312-715-5155.

(See Next Column)

PARTNERS

Anthony S. Earl
Jeremy C. Shea
John S. Holbrook, Jr.
Michael L. Zaleski
Jeffrey B. Bartell
James R. Cole
Michael S. Weiden
Anthony H. Driessen
Roy L. Prange, Jr.
Fred Gants
Peter C. Christianson
Nicholas J. Seay
John T. Whiting
Waltraud A. Arts
Donald K. Schott
Ralph V. Topinka
William J. Toman
Jane F. Clokey
Kevin A. Delorey
Kenneth J. Hansen
Jennifer V. Powers
Anthony A. Tomaselli
Jean C. Baker

ASSOCIATES

Lauri D. Morris
Brian W. Blanchard
Gregory T. Everts
Valerie L. Bailey-Rihn
Bennett J. Berson
Sarah Edelman Coyne
Jennifer S. McGinnity
Kristin Graham Noel
Thomas N. Shorter
Jill A. Fahrlander
Elizabeth A. Hartman
David M. Kettner

LEGAL SUPPORT PERSONNEL

Lisa V. Boyce (Government Relations Advisor)
Thomas J. Fonfara (Government Relations Advisor)

LEGAL ASSISTANTS

Richard P. Carney
Laura Marie Herberg
Heidi Manni-Johnson
April L. Trickel

For full biographical listings, see the Martindale-Hubbell Law Directory

STROUD, WILLINK & HOWARD, LLC (AV)

25 West Main Street, Suite 300, P.O. Box 2236, 53701
Telephone: 608-257-2281
Fax: 608-257-7643
Email: email@stroudlaw.com

MEMBERS OF FIRM

C. Vernon Howard
Ronald W. Todd
Robert R. Stroud
H. Dale Peterson
Robert J. Schwab
Carolyn A. Hegge
James F. Gebhart
Joseph P. Bartol

OF COUNSEL

Seward Ritchey Stroud
Donald R. Stroud
Donald D. Willink
Dale R. Thompson

ASSOCIATES

Sverre David Roang
Peter J. Richter
Norman D. Farnam

General Counsel for: Temperature Systems, Inc.; Wisconsin Farm Bureau Federation; Anchor Bank, SSB; The Wisconsin Cheeseman, Inc.; J.H. Findorff & Son, Inc.; Edward Kraemer & Sons, Inc.; Hilldale Shopping Center; American T.V. & Appliance of Madison, Inc.; Demco, Inc.; Schoep's Ice Cream Co., Inc.

For full biographical listings, see the Martindale-Hubbell Law Directory

*MILWAUKEE,** Milwaukee Co.

COOK & FRANKE S.C. (AV)

660 East Mason Street, 53202
Telephone: 414-271-5900
Facsimile: 414-271-2002

Thomas J. Drought
Francis R. Croak
L. William Staudenmaier
Robert F. Johnson
Kevin J. Lyons
William A. Jennaro
Margaret T. Lund
Thomas N. Harrington
Brian R. Wanasek
Charles I. Henderson
Pamela H. Schaefer
John M. Swietlik, Jr.
Philip C. Reid
Sandra J. Janssen
Lawrence Clancy
Laura E. Schuett
John G. Gehringer
Michael J. Lund
David J. Hase
Ann M. Rieger
Alexander T. Pendleton
Christopher J. Jaekels
Kaye K. Vance
Thomas J. Lonzo
Jane C. Schlicht
Heidi L. Vogt
Steven L. Nelson
Dennis P. Coffey
Stacy Gerber Ward
Lee Anne N. Conta
Patrick G. McBride
Jason R. Handal
Timothy E. Kronquist
Denasha A. Scott
Raymond D. Jamieson
Roslyn J. Kitchen
Lynne M. Mueller
Scott S. Fensin
Thomas H. Kister

OF COUNSEL

Robert E. Cook
Harry F. Franke
Joseph E. Tierney, Jr.

Representative Clients: Bradley Center Corp.; CH2M Hill; Svedala Industries, Inc.; Wisconsin Electric Power Co.; Safeco Insurance Co.; General Casualty Company of Wisconsin; Payne & Dolan, Inc.; City of Cedarburg.

For full biographical listings, see the Martindale-Hubbell Law Directory

Milwaukee—Continued

FOLEY & LARDNER (AV)

Firstar Center, 777 East Wisconsin Avenue, 53202-5367
Telephone: 414-271-2400
Telex: 26-819 (Foley Lard Mil)
Facsimile: 414-297-4900
Email: foleylardner@worldnet.att.net *URL:* http://www.foleylardner.com
Los Angeles, California Office: 2029 Century Park East, 35th Floor.
Telephone: 310-277-2223.
Fax: 310-557-8475.
Sacramento, California Office: 300 Capitol Mall, Suite 1125.
Telephone: 916-443-8005.
Fax: 916-443-2240.
San Diego, California Office: 402 West Broadway, 23rd Floor.
Telephone: 619-234-6655.
Fax: 619-234-3510.
San Francisco, California Office: One Maritime Plaza, Sixth Floor.
Telephone: 415-434-4484.
Fax: 415-434-4507.
Denver, Colorado Office: 1999 Broadway, Suite 2560.
Telephone: 303-297-0260.
Fax: 303-297-0266.
Washington, D.C. Office: Washington Harbour, Suite 500, 3000 K Street, N.W.
Telephone: 202-672-5300.
Telex: 904136 (Foley Lard Wash).
Facsimile: 202-672-5399.
Jacksonville, Florida Office: The Greenleaf Building, 200 Laura Street. P.O. Box 240.
Telephone: 904-359-2000.
Facsimile: 904-359-8700.
Orlando, Florida Office: Suite 1800, 111 North Orange Avenue, P.O. Box 2193.
Telephone: 407-423-7656.
Facsimile: 407-648-1743.
Tallahassee, Florida Office: 300 East Park Avenue, P.O. Box 1454.
Telephone: 850-222-6100.
Facsimile: 850-561-6475.
Tampa, Florida Offices: Suite 2700, One Hundred N. Tampa Street, P.O. Box 3391.
Telephones: 813-229-2300; Pinellas County: 813-442-3296.
Facsimile: 813-221-4210.
West Palm Beach, Florida Office: Suite 200, Phillips Point East Tower, 777 South Flagler Drive.
Telephone: 561-655-5050.
Facsimile: 561-655-6925.
Chicago, Illinois Office: Suite 3300, One IBM Plaza, 330 N. Wabash Avenue.
Telephone: 312-755-1900.
Facsimile: 312-755-1925.
Annapolis, Maryland Office: Suite 102, 175 Admiral Cochrane Drive.
Telephone: 410-266-8077.
Telex: 899149 (Oldtownpat).
Facsimile: 410-266-8664.
Madison, Wisconsin Office: Verex Plaza, 150 East Gilman Street, P.O. Box 1497.
Telephone: 608-257-5035.
Facsimile: 608-258-4258.
Brussels, Belgium Office: Avenue Louise, 283.
Telephone: 32-2-646-2777.
Facsimile: 32-2-646-7574.

PARTNERS

Leon F. Foley (1894-1978)
Lynford Lardner, Jr. (1915-1973)
William J. Abraham, Jr.
Benjamin J. Abrohams
Russell J. Barron
Steven R. Barth
Linda E. Benfield
Charles A. Benner
Michael M. Biehl
Robert L. Binder
Elizabeth S. Blutstein
Bernard J. Bobber
Ralf-Reinhard Böer
Robert J. Bonner
Larry J. Bonney
Wendy Reed Bosworth
Michael A. Bowen
John W. Brahm
Joseph C. Branch
Mary Kathryn Braza
Carolyn C. Burrell
John F. Callan
James M. Caragher
Harry V. Carlson, Jr.
Richard H. Casper
Jon P. Christiansen
Keith A. Christiansen
James R. Clark
James P. Connelly
John C. Cooper, III
George D. Cunningham
John R. Dawson
Lloyd J. Dickinson
George A. Dionisopoulos
Benn S. DiPasquale
Gregg H. Dooge
Rodney H. Dow
Robert A. DuPuy
Patrick P. Fee
Michael Fischer
Stephen M. Fisher
Kevin G. Fitzgerald
Michael D. Flanagan
Richard S. Florsheim
Mark F. Foley
Carl D. Fortner
Timothy C. Frautschi
Laura J. Gage
Richard S. Gallagher
Benjamin F. Garmer, III
Michael A. Gehl
C. Frederick Geilfuss, II
Michael W. Grebe
Reed Groethe
Barry L. Grossman
Edward J. Hammond
Phillip J. Hanrahan
Steven T. Hartung
Michael W. Hatch
James O. Huber
Marsha E. Huff
James L. Huston

(See Next Column)

PARTNERS (Continued)

Emory Ireland
Stanley S. Jaspan
Sarah O. Jelencic
Jeffrey J. Jones
Michael J. Kelly
Joan F. Kessler
W. David Knox, II
Harvey A. Kurtz
Patricia J. Lane
Benjamin D. Levin
David Lucey
Wayne R. Lueders
Lawrence T. Lynch
Susan R. Maisa
Martin D. Mann
Marc J. Marotta
Jere D. McGaffey
Maureen A. McGinnity
Brian W. McGrath
Richard J. McKenna
James T. McKeown
Maurice J. (Marc) McSweeney
Kurt S. Meckstroth
James G. Morrow
Lisa Stephens Neubauer
Michael S. Nolan
Hugh J. O'Halloran
John M. Olson
Jamshed J. Patel
Ulice Payne, Jr.
Thomas C. Pence
Patrick G. Quick
Michael D. Regenfuss
David M. Reicher
Greg W. Renz
Jay O. Rothman
David B. Ryan
Russell E. Ryba
Richard L. Schwaab (Not admitted in WI)
Nancy J. Sennett
Timothy J. Sheehan
Thomas L. Shriner, Jr.
Luke E. Sims
Christian G. Steinmetz
James F. Stern
Peter J. Stone
Richard L. Teigen
Mark A. Thimke
James T. Tynion III
Joseph B. Tyson, Jr.
Ronald L. Walter
Ronald M. Wawrzyn
Robert G. Weber
Richard A. Weiss
Kevin P. Whaley
Edwin P. Wiley
Trevor J. Will
Allen W. Williams, Jr.
Edward B. Witte
Patrick M. Zabrowski
Lynette M. Zigman

RETIRED PARTNERS

Paul M. Barnes
David E. Beckwith
Robert B. Bradley
James P. Brody
George M. Chester
Eugene C. Daly
Robert K. Drummond
David H. Fleck
Richard L. Harrington
William J. Kiernan, Jr.
Marvin E. Klitsner
Bernard S. Kubale
F. Anthony Maio
Harrold J. McComas
Richard H. Miller
Lyman A. Precourt
Orin Purintun
Allen M. Taylor
Harry L. Wallace
Edwin Fitch Walmer
Herbert P. Wiedemann
William J. Willis

SPECIAL COUNSEL

Karen A. Balistreri
Edward W. Brown
James H. Gormley, Jr.
Richard B. O'Planick (Not admitted in WI)
Ann E. Reinke
James L. Vana (Not admitted in WI)
Mark M. Velguth
James A. Wilke

ASSOCIATES

Brian P. Akers
Jason W. Allen
Chad R. Anderson
Scott D. Anderson
Michael J. Aprahamian
Travis L. Bachman
Paul Bargren
Ann C. Becker
Steven C. Becker
Stephen W. Boettinger
Charles G. Carter (Not admitted in WI)
Alistair K. Chan
Kristine Susan Cherek
Scott D. Cheskiewicz
Roxana E. Cook
Lafayette L. Crump
Mark J. Diliberti
Victoria A. Dukatz
Peter D. Fetzer
Cynthia J. Franecki
David J.B. Froiland
G. Michael Halfenger
Mary Ann C. Halloin
Rachelle R. Hart
Thomas E. Hartman
Daniel M. Hess
Caroline A. Hogan
Paul S. Hunter
Melissa Jackson
Paul J. Jones
Brian S. Kaas
Jason M. Katz
Anne Berleman Kearney
Joshua T. Keleske
Jennifer J. Kent
Bruce A. Keyes
Cynthia M. Klots
Maria E. Gonzalez Knavel
Deborah L. Koconis
Carl R. Kugler
Dana Marie Lach
Katherine D. Lee
Zhu Lee
Keith Lindenbaum
Michelle Andreshak Lloyd
H. Timothy Lopez
Brett H. Ludwig
Morten Lund
Eric L. Maassen
Kevin D. Makowski
Marti L.S. Marquart
Susan Ham Martin
Ann I. Mennell
Michael Mishlove
Thomas McCann Mullooly
Eric C. Nelson
Kara E. Nelson
Stephen Michael Patton
John T. Pienkos
Mark T. Plichta
Todd A. Rathe
Kelly B. Reilly
Leigh C. Riley
Bartholomew F. Reuter
Thomas M. Rose
Joseph S. Rupkey
Timothy J. Saviano
Andrew R. Schiesl
Bryan S. Schultz
Kevin R. Schulz
Elizabeth A. Shepard
David W. Simon
M. Reed Staheli
Brent A. Stork
Kenny Tatum
Leslie M. Tector
Jennifer M. Tenhaeff

(See Next Column)

FOLEY & LARDNER, *Milwaukee—Continued*

ASSOCIATES (Continued)

James G. Topetzes (Not admitted in WI)	Frederic J. Vorlop
Timothy M. Truel	Brian N. Wanek
Christopher M. Turoski	Rebecca E. W. Wegner
Peter C. Underwood	Adam J. Wiensch
Jonathan J. Van Handel	Gerry Lee Williams
Peter J. Vogel	John K. Wilson
Timothy L. Voigtman	Andrew J. Wronski
	Joseph N. Ziebert

Walter E. Zimmerman

For full biographical listings, see the Martindale-Hubbell Law Directory

GODFREY & KAHN, S.C. (AV)

780 North Water Street, 53202-3590
Telephone: 414-273-3500
Telecopier: 414-273-5198
Email: sdavis@gklaw.com *URL:* http://www.gklaw.com
Green Bay, Wisconsin Office: 333 Main Street, Suite 600, 54301.
Telephone: 920-432-9300.
Oshkosh, Wisconsin Office: 219 Washington Avenue, 54901.
Telephone: 920-233-6050.
Madison, Wisconsin Office: 131 West Wilson Street, Suite 700, 53703.
Telephone: 608-251-4670.
Appleton, Wisconsin Office: 100 West Lawrence Street, 54911.
Telephone: 920-830-2800.

Dudley J. Godfrey, Jr.	Elliot H. Berman
Gerald J. Kahn	Shawn G. Rice
John M. Byers	Michael P. Waxman
Joseph M. Bernstein	Susan M. Hoaglund
William H. Alverson	Carol Muratore Dehler
Andrew R. Lauritzen	Steven S. Bartelt
William H. Levit, Jr.	Daniel B. Geraghty
Peter M. Sommerhauser	Kristine M. Strodthoff
Henry E. Fuldner	Kelley Kimmel Falkner
Terrence K. Knudsen	David G. Peterson
Michael Ash	Joan D. Klimpel
Stephen L. Chernof	John L. Clancy
Charles G. Vogel	Daniel A. Ryan
Howard A. Pollack	Pamela M. Krill
Richard S. Marcus	Mark C. Witt
Richard J. Bliss	Kristin N. Schelwat
Kenneth C. Hunt	John J. Kalter
Howard A. Schoenfeld	Kristin S. Dalen-Bard
Arthur J. Harrington	Barbara Doty Gurican
Michael J. Dwyer	Stephanie A. Lyons
Robert L. Kamholz, Jr.	Sarah Burlison Ludwick
Debra Sadow Koenig	Paul E. Guttormsson
James N. Phillips	Jennifer L. Beaty
Pamela E. Barker	Dennis F. Connolly
James A. Sheriff	David R. Navarre
Nicholas A. Kees	Douglas J. Patch
John A. Dickens	Brian G. Gilpin
Bradden C. Backer	John J. Lott
Michael B. Apfeld	David H. Patzer
John F. Gaebler	Judith L. Carlson (Not admitted in WI)
Thomas E. Griggs	Jeremy D. Newman
Melanie N. Aska Knox	Sean O'D. Bosack
Kristi E. Leswing	Renee Hardt Torr
Christopher B. Noyes	Anthony S. Baish
Randall J. Erickson	William K. Baxter
Mark T. Ehrmann	Timothy J. Randall
Larry D. Lieberman	Domingo G. Cruz
Paul A. Lucey	Angela M. Rogers
Daniel T. Flaherty	Heather Reed
Patricia L. Leiker	Jennifer R. Schmidt
John L. Kirtley	Ellen Drought
Robert C. Risch, Jr.	Thomas R. Homberg
Daniel D. Seibel	Rebecca L. Himmelspach
J. Gardner Govan	Keith D. Carpenter (Not admitted in WI)
William E. Duffin	Steven J. Ziesmann
Scott M. Fabry	Paul W. Griepentrog
Adam L. Brookman	Tara J. Bohling
Scott A. Moehrke	Andrew S. Gollin
Anna M. Geyso	Kristi A. Hayek
Kim E. Patterson	Michael D. Huitink
Kristin A. Roeper	Donald E. Laverdure
Thomas P. DeMuth	John Braxton Neiman
Nicholas P. Wahl	Tonya A. Trumm
Diane M. Marchik	
Carol A. Gehl	

RESEARCH

Mary J. Koshollek

For full biographical listings, see the Martindale-Hubbell Law Directory

MICHAEL BEST & FRIEDRICH LLP (AV)

100 East Wisconsin Avenue, 53202-4108
Telephone: 414-271-6560
Telecopier: 414-277-0656
Cable Address: "Mibef"
Email: info@mbf-law.com *URL:* http://www.mbf-law.com
Madison, Wisconsin Office: One South Pinckney Street, Firstar Plaza, P.O. Box 1806, 53701-1806.
Telephone: 608-257-3501.
Telecopier: 283-2275.
Manitowoc, Wisconsin Office: 1000 Maritime Drive, 54220.
Telephone: 920-686-2800.
Fax: 920-686-2810.
Chicago, Illinois Office: Michael Best & Friedrich LLC, 77 West Wacker Drive, Suite 4300, 60601-1635.
Telephone: 312-845-5800.
Telecopier: 312-845-5828.

PARTNERS

John K. MacIver	Robert D. Rothacker
Frank J. Pelisek	Bret A. Roge
K. Thor Lundgren	John E. Flanagan
John R. Sapp	Bartlett C. Petersen
Thomas E. Obenberger	Michael A. Gral
Robert A. Teper	Casimir F. Laska
W. Charles Jackson	Hal Karas
Richard J. Canter	Nathaniel A. Hoffman
Marshall R. Berkoff	Sean Lanphier
Robert A. Schnur	José A. Olivieri
John A. Busch	David L. De Bruin
Jerome H. Kringel	Paul G. Hoffman
Robert J. Johannes	Jonathan O. Levine
David B. Smith	Scott C. Beightol
Joseph A. Gemignani	Roger D. Strode, Jr.
David W. Croysdale	Joshua L. Gimbel
Scott H. Engroff	Saul N. Winsten
Robert W. Mulcahy	Jonathan H. Margolies
Thomas W. Scrivner	Donald F. Kiesling
J. Lewis Perlson	Robyn S. Shapiro
Raymond R. Krueger	Timothy M. Kelley
Michael E. Husmann	Eric H. Rumbaugh
F. William Haberman	Lynda R. Templen
David R. Olson	Grant C. Killoran
David J. Cannon	Mark S. Poker
David E. Leichtfuss	Debra H. Zarne
Lorna J. Granger	Joseph A. Pickart
Charles P. Graupner	Mitchell W. Quick
Jeffrey L. Abraham	Paul E. Benson
David R. Price	Douglas P. Dehler
Lee J. Geronime	David A. Krutz
David V. Meany	Peter K. Richardson
Donald A. Schoenfeld	Mark E. Toth
Paul E. Prentiss	Dyann L. Kostello
Nancy Leary Haggerty	Cathleen S. Biehl
John C. Lapinski	Paul R. Riegel
Gary A. Ahrens	Wanda L. Hurr
Donald P. Gallo	Michael J. McDonagh
Geoffrey R. Morgan	Charles P. Stevens
Peter L. Coffey	Gilbert L. Southwell, III
Chris J. Trebatoski	Barbara K. Boxer
Peggy E. Brever	Donald A. Daugherty, Jr.
Eric E. Hobbs	Gerald L. Fellows
Timothy G. Schally	Miriam S. Fleming
Paul F. Linn	Teresa M. Levy
Michael P. Dunn	Thomas A. Miller
Gordon K. Miller	Kevin P. Moran
Toni Lee Bonney	David W. Runke
Kristine H. Cleary	Billie Jean Strandt

OF COUNSEL

Joseph R. Filachek	Robert E. Clemency
James C. Mallatt	Jackson M. Bruce, Jr.
Bayard H. Michael	Roy C. LaBudde
Jacob L. Bernheim	Steven S. Gensler

ASSOCIATES

Julie Gorens-Winston	Lori Kaczynski Hoch
Gordon P. Giampietro	Edward R. Lawson, Jr.
Jorge A. Gomez	Kathleen M. O'Toole
Cynthia E. Smith	Colleen O'Connor Patzer
James Patrick Thomas	Andrew R. Peret
Mark C. Treter	Stacie J. Andritsch
Alexander P. Fraser	E. Troy Blanchard
David K. Hoover	Claudia Egan
Linda Sauser Moroney	Amy Schmidt Jones
Kathleen A. Rinehart	Daniel S. Jones
Katherine W. Schill	Brenda S. Kasper
Pamela L. Gergens	Amy D. Katarincic
Patrick J. Marget	Leslie C. Mastey
James P. Peterson	Sara Purtell Scullen
Christopher B. Austin	Kristina E. Somers
Nathaniel Cade, Jr.	Steve R. Battenberg
Kenneth R. Dortzbach	Randall W. Fieldhack

(See Next Column)

MICHAEL BEST & FRIEDRICH LLP—*Continued*

ASSOCIATES (Continued)

Matthew S. MacLean
Deborah J. Powers
Reince R. Priebus
S. Edward Sarskas
Jesús J. Villa
Timothy J. Voeller
Roberta A. Harris
Melinda Mann Mitchell
Joshua M. Erickson
Derek C. Stettner
Matthew E. Gabrys
David A. Dixon
Allan M. Foeckler
Gregory J. Hartwig
Richard L. Kaiser
Leah M. Krider (Not admitted in WI)
Julie M. Maslowski
Christopher C. Mohrman
Carrie L. Norbin
Joseph E. Tierney, IV
Sheldon L. Wolfe

For full biographical listings, see the Martindale-Hubbell Law Directory

QUARLES & BRADY LLP (AV)

411 East Wisconsin Avenue, 53202-4497
Telephone: 414-277-5000
Fax: 414-271-3552
URL: http://www.quarles.com
Madison, Wisconsin Office: Firstar Plaza, One South Pinckney Street, P.O. Box 2113, 53701-2113.
Telephone: 608-251-5000.
Fax: 608-251-9166.
West Palm Beach, Florida Office: 222 Lakeview Avenue, 4th Floor, 33401.
Telephone: 561-653-5000.
Fax: 561-653-5333.
Naples, Florida Office: Barnett Center, 4501 Tamiami Trail North, Suite 300, 34103-3060.
Telephone: 941-262-5959.
Fax: 941-434-4999.
Phoenix, Arizona Office: One Camelback Building, One East Camelback Road, Suite 400, 85012-1649.
Telephone: 602-230-5500.
Fax: 602-230-5598.
Chicago, Illinois Office: Quarles & Brady LLC, Citicorp Center, 500 West Madison Street, Suite 3700.
Telephone: 312-715-5000.
Fax: 312-715-5155.

Louis Quarles (1883-1972) Bernard V. Brady (1891-1977)

MEMBERS OF FIRM
(ALPHABETICALLY BY YEAR OF ADMISSION TO BAR)

Harry G. Holz
Charles Q. Kamps
Thomas W. Ehrmann
Anthony S. Earl (Resident, Madison Office)
Fred G. Groiss
Richard C. Ninneman
Samuel J. Recht
Jeremy C. Shea (Resident, Madison Office)
Donald S. Taitelman
John A. Hazelwood
John S. Holbrook, Jr. (Resident, Madison Office)
Peter J. Lettenberger
John A. McDonald (Resident, Chicago, Illinois Office)
Arthur B. Harris
Richard L. Horn (Resident, Chicago, Illinois Office)
Henry J. Loos
Hugh S. McManus
Michael J. Spector
George K. Whyte, Jr.
Robert H. Diaz, Jr.
David L. Kinnamon
Gary H. Kline (Resident, Chicago, Illinois Office)
J. Rodman Steele, Jr. (Resident, West Palm Beach, Florida Office)
Michael L. Zaleski (Resident, Madison Office)
Anthony W. Asmuth, III
Wayne E. Babler, Jr.
Thomas E. Maloney (Resident, Naples, Florida Office)
W. Stuart Parsons
Jeffrey B. Bartell (Resident, Madison Office)
Frank J. Daily
Charles W. Herf (Resident, Phoenix, Arizona Office)
David E. Jarvis
Larry J. Martin
Kendall R. Meyer (Resident, Chicago, Illinois Office)
David L. Petersen (Resident, Naples, Florida Office)
Thomas A. Polachek (Resident, Chicago, Illinois Office)
James R. Cole (Resident, Madison Office)
Thomas E. Chomicz (Resident, Chicago, Illinois Office)
Steven R. Duback
Conrad G. Goodkind
Lawrence J. Jost
Patrick M. Ryan
Barry E. Sammons
Ronald L. Wallenfang
Michael S. Weiden (Resident, Madison Office)
John A. Casey
Bruce C. Davidson
Robert F. Forrer (Resident, Chicago, Illinois Office)
P. Robert Moya (Resident, Phoenix, Arizona Office)
Stephen E. Richman
Gerald E. Connolly
Anthony H. Driessen
James D. Friedman
J. Paul Jacobson
Peter C. Karegeannes
John R. Maynard
William M. Shattuck (Resident, Phoenix, Arizona Office)
James H. Baxter III
Quinn W. Martin
Michael J. McGovern
F. Joseph McMackin, III (Resident, Naples, Florida Office)
Ned R. Nashban (Resident, West Palm Beach, Florida Office)
Robert L. Titley
Thomas J. Phillips
James D. Vieregg (Resident, Phoenix, Arizona Office)
Robert T. Bailes (Resident, Phoenix, Arizona Office)
Bruce R. Bauer
Darryl S. Bell
Michael J. Conlan
James F. Daly
John W. Daniels, Jr.

(See Next Column)

MEMBERS OF FIRM
(ALPHABETICALLY BY YEAR OF ADMISSION TO BAR) (Continued)

James J. Gatziolis (Resident, Chicago, Illinois Office)
George E. Haas
Timothy G. Hains (Resident, Naples, Florida Office)
Alyce C. Katayama
John H. Lhost
Michael L. Roshar
Peter A. Sarasek (Resident, Chicago, Illinois Office)
Leonard S. Shifflett (Resident, Chicago, Illinois Office)
Thomas Armstrong
Andrew M. Barnes
Robert E. Doyle, Jr. (Resident, Naples, Florida Office)
Matthew J. Flynn
David A. Paige (Resident, Phoenix, Arizona Office)
Roy L. Prange, Jr. (Resident, Madison Office)
Michael H. Schaalman
Patrick W. Schmidt
John T. Bannen
Fred Gants (Resident, Madison Office)
Mary Pat Ninneman
Jon E. Pettibone (Resident, Phoenix, Arizona Office)
Phillip E. Recht
Janice E. Rodgers (Resident, Chicago, Illinois Office)
Roger K. Spencer (Resident, Phoenix, Arizona Office)
Eric J. Van Vugt
Patricia K. Ballman
Warren S. Blumenthal
Peter C. Christianson
Patrick J. Goebel
Thomas J. Magill (Resident, Chicago, Illinois Office)
Michael S. McCauley
Nicholas J. Seay (Resident, Madison Office)
Alexander Terras (Resident, Chicago, Illinois Office)
John T. Whiting (Resident, Madison Office)
Joseph D. Masterson
Carl R. Schwartz
Peter A. Terry (Resident, Phoenix, Arizona Office)
Paul J. Tilleman
James L. Adashek
Waltraud A. Arts (Resident, Madison Office)
David B. Kern
Ely A. Leichtling
Jeffrey Morris
Ann M. Murphy
John A. Rothstein
Arthur A. Vogel, Jr.
Kenneth V. Hallett
William H. Harbeck
Charles H. McMullen
Sally C. Merrell
Elizabeth A. Orelup
Gary M. Ruesch
Leo J. Salvatori (Resident, Naples, Florida Office)
Donald K. Schott (Resident, Madison Office)
Ralph V. Topinka (Resident, Madison Office)
John P. Vail (Resident, Chicago, Illinois Office)
David B. Bartel
David G. Beauchamp (Resident, Phoenix, Arizona Office)
David R. Cross
Julianna Ebert
Mary N. Fertl
Glenn Spencer Bacal (Resident, Phoenix, Arizona Office)
Kimberly Leach Johnson (Resident, Naples, Florida Office)
Nancy Meissner Kennedy
Brian G. Lanser
Daniel L. Muchow (Resident, Phoenix, Arizona Office)
Dennis P. Reis
Thomas A. Simonis
David D. Wilmoth
Michael J. Gonring
Kathleen A. Gray
Douglas R. Hoffman (Resident, Chicago, Illinois Office)
Michael A. Levey
Elizabeth G. Nowakowski
David A. Selden (Resident, Phoenix, Arizona Office)
Stephanie B. Shellenback (Resident, Chicago, Illinois Office)
William J. Toman (Resident, Madison Office)
Ann K. Comer
John D. Franzini
Marta S. Levine
Thomas P. McElligott
Gregory A. Nelson (Resident, West Palm Beach, Florida Office)
Nancy K. Peterson
Keith M. Baxter
Jane F. Clokey (Resident, Madison Office)
Robert H. Duffy
Steven P. Emerick
Sarah M. Linsley (Resident, Chicago, Illinois Office)
Dana L. O'Brien
Michael D. Zeka
Mark A. Kircher
Fredrick G. Lautz
David P. Olson
Sheila M. Reynolds
Gerald L. Shelley (Resident, Phoenix, Arizona Office)
Richard P. Blessen (Resident, Chicago, Illinois Office)
Robert S. Bornhoft (Resident, Phoenix, Arizona Office)
Kathryn M. Buono
Daniel E. Conley
Kevin A. Delorey (Resident, Madison Office)
Jeffrey L. Elverman
John D. Humphreville (Resident, Naples, Florida Office)
Scott L. Langlois
Francis H. LoCoco
Jeffrey O. Davis
Kenneth J. Hansen (Resident, Madison, Wisconsin Office)
John A. Klages (Resident, Chicago, Illinois Office)
Benjamin R. Norris (Resident, Phoenix, Arizona Office)
Jennifer V. Powers
Joseph E. Puchner
David L. Bourne
Nancy Berz Colman (Resident, West Palm Beach, Florida Office)
Marie K. Eitrheim (Resident, Chicago, Illinois Office)
Timothy S. Harris (Resident, Chicago, Illinois Office)
Anthony A. Tomaselli (Resident, Madison Office)
Margaret C. Kelsey
Todd A. Rowden (Resident, Chicago, Illinois Office)
Colleen A. Scherkenbach (Resident, Phoenix, Arizona Office)
Jeffrey K. Spoerk
Charles M. Weber
Joseph W. Bain (Resident, West Palm Beach, Florida Office)
Jean C. Baker
Patrick J. Bitterman (Resident, Chicago, Illinois Office)
Michael J. Ostermeyer
George J. Marek
Robert J. Sacco (Resident, West Palm Beach, Florida Office)
Walter J. Skipper
Rebecca A. Speckhard

(See Next Column)

QUARLES & BRADY LLP, *Milwaukee—Continued*

OF COUNSEL

Paul Noelke
Patrick W. Cotter
A. William Asmuth, Jr.
Richard W. Cutler
James C. Mallien
John T. Harrington
Laurence E. Gooding, Jr.
Elwin J. Zarwell
Neal E. Madisen
Dale L. Sorden
Laurence C. Hammond, Jr.
John S. Sammond (Resident, West Palm Beach, Florida Office)
David L. MacGregor
James Urdan
Roger P. Paulsen
Robert J. Kalupa
Thad F. Kryshak
Thomas O. Kloehn
Thomas W. O'Brien

ASSOCIATES

Neil E. Hamilton
Patrick J. Schoen
Lauri D. Morris (Resident, Madison Office)
Michael G. Galloway (Resident, Phoenix, Arizona Office)
Chris K. Gawart
Brian W. Blanchard (Resident, Madison Office)
Susan A. Cerbins
Michael Aldana
Gregory T. Everts (Resident, Madison Office)
Samara S. Holland (Resident, Naples, Florida Office)
Carmella A. Huser
Catherine Stevens Powell
David B. Altman (Resident, Chicago, Illinois Office)
Valerie L. Bailey-Rihn (Resident, Madison Office)
Mitchell S. Moser
Mark Hubert Muller (Resident, Naples, Florida Office)
David T. Barton (Resident, Phoenix, Arizona Office)
Bennett J. Berson (Resident, Madison, Wisconsin Office)
David G. Bray (Resident, Phoenix, Arizona Office)
Sean D. Garrison (Resident, Phoenix, Arizona Office)
Michael A. Jaskolski
Daniel J. La Fave
Kevin M. Long
Lisa A. Lyons
Mary Beth Miller Orson (Resident, Phoenix, Arizona Office)
Julie A. Pace (Resident, Phoenix, Arizona Office)
Nora M. Platt
David G. Ryser
Kurt T. Temple (Resident, Chicago, Illinois Office)
Guri Ademi
Michael M. Grebe
Daniel M. Janssen
Cheryl A. Johnson
Michael Lappin
Jennifer A. Lazewski
Pamela M. Ploor
Mark K. Briggs (Resident, Phoenix, Arizona Office)
Bonnie J. Buhrow
Maureen Henry (Resident, Phoenix, Arizona Office)
Patricia A. Hintz
Lisa Carozza Lottes (Resident, Naples, Florida Office)
Panna P. Patel (Resident, Chicago, Illinois Office)
Richard T. Roche
Brenda J. Stugelmeyer
Stephen R. White
Joel A. Brodsky (Resident, Chicago, Illinois Office)
James T. Demarest (Resident, Naples, Florida Office)
Sarah Edelman Coyne (Resident, Madison, Wisconsin Office)
Shannon B. Farrell
Michael J. Fischer
Michael A. Hatfield, Jr.
Jason N. Kaplan (Resident, Chicago, Illinois Office)
Susan Kubar (Resident, Naples, Florida Office)
Douglas P. Martin (Resident, Phoenix, Arizona Office)
Jennifer S. McGinnity (Resident, Madison Office)
Mark D. Passler (Resident, West Palm Beach, Florida Office)
Heidi B. Retzlaff
Steven M. Schindhelm
Gregory J. Stanton (Resident, Phoenix, Arizona Office)
David C. Swanson
D. Scott Watson (Resident, Chicago, Illinois Office)
C. Christine Burns (Resident, Phoenix, Arizona Office)
Alicia M. Dagosta (Resident, Phoenix, Arizona Office)
Richard G. Frohling
Leezie Kim (Resident, Phoenix, Arizona Office)
Edmond E. Koester (Resident, Naples, Florida Office)
Linda K. Menzel
David P. Muth
Cory L. Nettles
Kristin Graham Noel (Resident, Madison, Wisconsin Office)
Rachel A. Schneider
Thomas N. Shorter (Resident, Madison, Wisconsin Office)
Janice L. Tucker
Brian D. Winters
James Y. Wu (Resident, Chicago, Illinois Office)
Paul D. Bauer
Frank C. DeGuire, Jr.
Jill A. Fahrlander (Resident, Madison, Wisconsin Office)
Kelly A. Hardy
Sean D. Johnson (Resident, Phoenix, Arizona Office)
Mireya Castillo Martin (Resident, Phoenix, Arizona Office)
Allen J. Moss (Resident, Phoenix, Arizona Office)
Daniel G. Radler
Hoyt R. Stastney
Luis I. Arroyo
Jessamyn L. Bagley (Resident, Chicago, Illinois Office)
Lisa L. Behm
Keith A. Bruett
Jennifer Clements
Marcia E. Facey
Sherylynn Fiandaca (Resident, Phoenix, Arizona Office)
William B. Gaschler
Elizabeth A. Hartman (Resident, Madison, Wisconsin Office)
Matthew J. Kading
David M. Kettner (Resident, Madison, Wisconsin Office)
Stanley A. Kim (Resident, West Palm Beach, Florida Office)
Scott D. Paul (Resident, West Palm Beach, Florida Office)
Jeffrey D. Peelen
Steven J. Wietrzny
C. Lane Wood (Resident, Naples, Florida Office)
Ana M. Alfonso
Judith T. Beckler (Resident, Naples, Florida Office)
Nicole E. Dorsey (Resident, Phoenix, Arizona Office)
Matthew J. Duchemin
Stephen Fahey

(See Next Column)

ASSOCIATES (Continued)

Steven M. Greenberg (Resident, West Palm Beach, Florida Office)
Michelle L. Atkins Head
Jennifer A. Johnson
Nicole M. Marginian (Resident, Naples, Florida Office)
Sean K. Murphy
Brian T. Vandervest

LEGAL SUPPORT PERSONNEL

LEGAL ASSISTANTS

Mary J. Achterhof
Susan T. Barker
James M. Benware
Tracy A. Berrones
Ronald J. Burtch
Carrie L. Caan
Teresa M. Como
Richard Feedar
Mary McBride Gerkin
Diane C. Haase
Janine M. Jaeschke
Jyll E. Jordan
Cynthia Z. Jorgensen
Barbara A. Juran
Katherine Karamalegos
Kaye E. Kern
Carolyn P. Kinney
Marie E. Koster
Susan M. Lacourt
Janet Harry Litscher
Patricia M. Murphy
Susan M. Nygren
Rose M. Reitz
Kenneth M. Smith
Julie A. Sullivan-Mielke
Deborah A. Thomson
Cynthia Vick
Sonja Vujatovic
Corrine L. Weber
Susan M. Weber

PARALEGALS

Tracey A. Baxter
Cheryl Smukowski

BUSINESS MANAGEMENT SUPPORT GROUP

John J. Peterburs (Executive Director)
Heather M. Barrie (Director, Client Development and Communications)
Jill M. Miller (Director, Human Resources)
Thomas R. Schoewe
Jack H. Washow

For full biographical listings, see the Martindale-Hubbell Law Directory

---

REINHART, BOERNER, VAN DEUREN, NORRIS & RIESELBACH, S.C. (AV)

1000 North Water Street, P.O. Box 92900, 53202-0900
Telephone: 414-298-1000
Facsimile: 414-298-8097
URL: http://www.reinhartlaw.com
Denver, Colorado Office: One Norwest Center, 1700 Lincoln Street, Suite 3725, 80203.
Telephone: 303-831-0909.
Fax: 303-831-4805.
Madison, Wisconsin Office: 22 East Mifflin Street, P.O. Box 2020, 53701-2020.
Telephone: 608-229-2200.
Fax: 608-229-2100.

John M. Reinhart (1923-1982)
Richard H. Norris III (1930-1996)
Richard A. Van Deuren
Allen N. Rieselbach
Paul V. Lucke
Robert E. Meldman
Arthur F. Lubke, Jr.
Donald J. Christl
Thomas E. Funk
David A. Erne
Robert E. Bellin
William R. Steinmetz
Burton A. Wagner (Resident, Madison, Wisconsin Office)
Frederick G. Meyer (Resident, Denver, Colorado Office)
Gary A. Hollman
John A. Erich
Jeffrey R. Fuller
Arnold R. Kaplan (Resident, Denver, Colorado Office)
Frederic G. Friedman
Delos N. Lutton
Robert E. Dallman
Mary A. Brauer (Resident, Denver, Colorado Office)
Stephen T. Jacobs
Scott W. Hansen
Michael H. Simpson
John L. Schliesmann
Steven D. Huff
Mary H. Michal (Resident, Madison, Wisconsin Office)
William F. Flynn
Peter C. Blain
Thomas A. Myers
Bruce T. Block
Jeffrey P. Clark
Daniel J. Brink
Michael T. Pepke
John H. Zawadsky (Resident, Madison, Wisconsin Office)
Peter L. Gardon (Resident, Madison, Wisconsin Office)
Richard P. Carr
Robert F. Henkle, Jr.
Richard W. Graber
Anne Willis Reed
Robert K. Sholl
Kristin M. Bergstrom
Lawrence J. Burnett
John A. Herbers
Francis W. Deisinger
Jerome M. Janzer
Jesse S. Ishikawa
Ralph A. Weber
Kevin J. Howley
Anthony J. Handzlik
Mark L. Metz
Steven P. Bogart
Joseph J. Balistreri
Timothy G. Atkinson (Resident, Denver, Colorado Office)
Timothy A. Nettesheim
John M. Van Lieshout
James M. Bedore
Michael R. Smith
Robert J. Heath
Denise P. Goergen
Albert S. Orr
R. Timothy Muth
William T. Shroyer
Kathleen S. Donius
Martin J. McLaughlin
Larri J. Broomfield
Timothy P. Reardon
Michael D. Jankowski
Lynn M. Stathas (Resident, Madison, Wisconsin Office)
Rodney D. DeKruif
William C. Niemann

(See Next Column)

REINHART, BOERNER, VAN DEUREN, NORRIS & RIESELBACH S.C.—*Continued*

Raymond M. Roder (Resident, Madison, Wisconsin Office)
Michael P. Erhard (Resident, Madison, Wisconsin Office)
Otto K. Hilbert, II (Resident, Denver, Colorado Office)
Elizabeth Crewson Paris (Resident, Denver, Colorado Office)
Mark A. Cameli
Tracey L. Klein
James F. Lorimer (Resident, Madison Office)
Carrie Raymond Bedore
Leslie S. Miller
John Cardinal Parks (Resident, Denver, Colorado Office)
Mark K. Osbeck (Resident, Denver, Colorado, Office)
David R. Krosner
William R. Cummings
Bennett E. Choice
David M. Sanders
John R. Austin
Catherine L. Davies
David J. Sisson
Patrick J. Hodan
John E. Mossberg
Martin G. Flyke
Margaret M. Derus
Vincent J. Beres
Peter W. Becker
Dean E. Mabie

Anne M. Hlavacka
Sandra L. Botcher
Gail M. Olsen
Carolyn A. Sullivan
Colleen D. Ball
David G. Hanson
Benjamin G. Lombard
Allen C. Schlinsog, Jr.
Michael R. Miller (Resident, Denver, Colorado Office)
Michael G. Goller
Laura A. Brenner
Dorothy J. Clarke (Resident, Madison, Wisconsin Office)
Gregory A. Fedders (Resident, Madison, Wisconsin Office)
K.C. Groves (Resident, Denver, Colorado Office)
Troy A. Hilliard
Deborah C. Tomczyk
John N. Kurowski
Steven D. Mayer
Christopher P. Banaszak
Marcia MacKenzie
Thomas F. Walker, Jr.
Paul R. Seifert
Daniel Kelly
James A. Pellegrini
David M. Naples (Resident, Denver, Colorado Office)
Stephanie L. Mott
David B. Schulz
John G. Pawley
Amelia L. McCarthy
Kristi Blumhardt (Resident, Denver, Colorado Office)
Daniel R. Plane (Resident, Madison Office)
Robert J. Misey
Heather L. Fields (Not admitted in WI)
Douglas J. Mitchell (Resident, Denver, Colorado Office)
Steven E. Grieb
Nancy A. Noet
Michael J. Frazier
John R. Loew
Terri S. Flynn
Megan Paris Rundlet (Resident, Denver, Colorado Office)
Beth E. Hanan
Laura A. Gramling (Not admitted in WI)
John L. Barlament
Anthony C. Marino
Walter J. Lemanski
Peter D. Turke
Michael E. Dell
William H. Tobin
Bryan K. Nowicki
Jon D. Anderson
Andrew W. Erlandson (Resident, Madison, Wisconsin Office)
Masud E. Khan
Gregory A. Storm
Robert J. Muten
Nora E. Gierke
Sherilyn R. Whitmoyer
Jeremy T. Whitt
Inna Pullin
Jon D. Becker (Resident, Madison, Wisconsin Office)
Kurt D. Dykstra
Catherine E. Levinson
Thomas J. O'Brien
Amy F. Copeland (Resident, Madison, Wisconsin Office)
Jason E. Pauls
Daniel P Cooper
Shawn K. Stevens
Michael T. Flynn
Marcus A. Payson
Elizabeth M. Drew
Todd Cleary
David E. Osswald
Thomas E. Ravn
Amy Schoeffel
James J. Killean
James S. Swiderski
Meredith P. Steinberg
Daryll J. Neuser (Resident, Madison, Wisconsin Office)
Mark D. Griepentrog
Joshua A. Blakely
Thomas H. Shanley (Resident, Denver, Colorado Office)
Daniel S. Galligan

RETIRED

Roger L. Boerner

STAFF ATTORNEY

Richard A. Petrie

LEGAL SUPPORT PERSONNEL

Elaine S. Anderson
Tanya Braga
Margaret M. Chase
Sheryl M. Deer
Juliene Devor
Merlene DeZur
Ellen Heib
Jayette Kerkman
Julienne King
Dwayne Krager
Richard Laswell
Lori Lentz
Gregory M. Levesque
Eileen Linzmeyer
Susan K. Lipson
Mears M. McCarthy
Kathy Mintner
Susan B. Mixdorf
David Nabors
Laurie Noble
James D. Oldham
Donna Paulsen
Mary Ellen Raney
Jeanne Scherkenbach
Colleen McGuire Schmitz
Gwen Shotwell

(See Next Column)

LEGAL SUPPORT PERSONNEL (Continued)

Nancy Stanton
Julie Tjugum-Rasmussen
Kathryn Wein
Kathleen C. Wessels

For full biographical listings, see the Martindale-Hubbell Law Directory

NEENAH, Winnebago Co.

DI RENZO AND BOMIER, LLC (AV)

231 East Wisconsin Avenue, P.O. Box 788, 54957-0788
Telephone: 920-725-8464
Fax: 920-725-8568
Email: direnzolaw@aol.com

MEMBERS OF FIRM

Robert C. Di Renzo
Dennis L. Simon
Philip A. Munroe
Howard T. Healy
Roy N. Fine
Samuel J. Bomier

OF COUNSEL

Jerome T. Bomier

ASSOCIATES

Denise R. Burkett
Steven R. Schilke
Jesse R. Ostrom
Troy D. Thompson
Eric S. Gissel

Representative Clients: Associated Bank, N.A., Neenah, WI; Associated Realty & Management, Inc., Appleton, WI; Neenah Downtown Redevelopment Associates, LTD Partnership, Neenah, WI; Radiology Associates of the Fox Valley, S.C., Neenah, WI; Valley VNA Health Systems, Inc., Neenah, WI; Bergstrom Corporation, Neenah, WI; Alexander Eye Institute, S.C., Appleton, WI; TEC Graphics, Inc., Neenah, WI; First National Bank-Fox Valley, Neenah, WI; Becher Engineering, Inc., Menasha, WI.

For full biographical listings, see the Martindale-Hubbell Law Directory

*OSHKOSH,** Winnebago Co.

GODFREY & KAHN, S.C. (AV)

219 Washington Avenue, P.O. Box 1278, 54903-1278
Telephone: 920-233-6050
Telecopier: 920-233-8528
Email: sdavis@gklaw.com *URL:* http://www.gklaw.com
Milwaukee, Wisconsin Office: 780 North Water Street, 53202.
Telephone: 414-273-3500.
Green Bay, Wisconsin Office: 333 Main Street, Suite 600, 54301.
Telephone: 920-432-9300.
Madison, Wisconsin Office: 131 West Wilson Street, Suite 700, 53703.
Telephone: 608-251-4670.
Appleton, Wisconsin Office: 100 West Lawrence Street, 54911.
Telephone: 920-830-2800.

Edward J. Williams
James R. Macy
Rebecca L. Kent
Tony J. Renning
Alysia C. Hopper

For full biographical listings, see the Martindale-Hubbell Law Directory

*RACINE,** Racine Co.

HOSTAK, HENZL & BICHLER, S.C. (AV)

840 Lake Avenue, P.O. Box 516, 53401-0516
Telephone: 262-632-7541
Fax: 262-632-1256

Robert R. Henzl
Robert H. Bichler
James W. Hill
Stephen J. Smith
Thomas M. Devine
Timothy J. Pruitt
Susan M. Perry
David A. Wolfe
JoAnne Breese-Jaeck
Kristin M. Cafferty
Cheryl A. Hagen

OF COUNSEL

Kenneth F. Hostak

Representative Clients: Advance Mechanical Contractors, Inc.; Andis Co.; Christ Iron Works, Inc.; Warren Industries, Inc.; M & I Bank of Racine; American Family Mutual Insurance Co.; Wisconsin Health Care Liability Plan; Bud Orth & Associates, Inc.; St. Luke's Memorial Hospital, Inc.; Greene Manufacturing Co.

For full biographical listings, see the Martindale-Hubbell Law Directory

*RHINELANDER,** Oneida Co.

ECKERT KOST & VOCKE (AV)

1285 Lincoln Street, P.O. Box 1247, 54501-1247
Telephone: 715-369-1624
FAX: 715-369-1273
Email: ecklaw@newnorth.net *URL:* http://www.ecklaw.com

Michael L. Eckert
Keith K. Kost
Timothy L. Vocke
Mitchell R. Olson

Reference: M & I Merchants Bank.

For full biographical listings, see the Martindale-Hubbell Law Directory

Rhinelander—Continued

JOHNSON & HOULIHAN, S.C. (AV)

28 North Stevens Street, P.O. Box 1148, 54501
Telephone: 715-365-5060
FAX: 715-365-5066
Email: jandhlaw@newnorth.net
Minocqua, Wisconsin Office: Professional & Financial Plaza, Highway 51 and 70, PO Box 630.
Telephone: 715-356-1422.
FAX: 715-356-1446.

James A. Johnson
John C. Houlihan
D. G. Graff
Martha J. Milanowski

For full biographical listings, see the Martindale-Hubbell Law Directory

*STEVENS POINT,** Portage Co.

ANDERSON, SHANNON, O'BRIEN, RICE & BERTZ (AV)

1257 Main Street, P.O. Box 228, 54481
Telephone: 715-344-0890
Fax: 715-344-1012; 344-2892
URL: http://www.andlaw.com
Plover, Wisconsin Office: 2840 Post Road, 54467.
Telephone: 715-341-2560.
Fax: 715-341-2676.

OF COUNSEL

Hiram D. Anderson, Jr.
John E. Shannon, Jr.

PARTNERS

Gerald M. O'Brien
Maurice G. Rice, Jr.
Thomas W. Bertz
Ronald T. Skrenes
Russell T. Golla
Robert F. Konkol (Resident at Plover Office)
Torren K. Pies
Nadine I. Davy
Rick A. Flugaur
Robert J. Shannon
Brian G. Formella (Resident, Plover Office)

ASSOCIATES

William K. Hlavac
Steven E. Viner
Brian P. Hodgkiss

General Attorneys for: M&I Mid-State Bank, N.A.; F & M Bank - Portage County; Rice Clinic, S.C.; The Copps Corp.; Wisconsin Interscholastic Athletic Assn.; Heritage Mutual Ins. Co.; Ellis Stone Construction Co.

For full biographical listings, see the Martindale-Hubbell Law Directory

*WAUPACA,** Waupaca Co.

HANSEN, MEAGHER, SHAMBEAU & MARONEY, S.C. (AV)

204 South Main Street, P.O. Box 111, 54981
Telephone: 715-258-4000
FAX: 715-258-4015
Toll Free: 800-675-4013
Iola, Wisconsin Office: 169 North Main Street, P.O. Box 335, 54945.
Telephone: 715-445-7000.
Fax: 715-445-3979.

Stephen F. Hansen
Steven D. Shambeau
Thomas A. Maroney
Bruce J. Meagher (Resident, Iola office)
Kaye E. Anderson

Eric D. Hendrickson

OF COUNSEL

Richard E. Johnson

Representative Clients: First National Bank of Waupaca, Wisconsin; Riverside Medical Center; Neuville Motors, Inc.; Tigerton Lumber Co.; Krause Publications, Inc.; City of Waupaca; Central Wis. Electric Co-op; Towns of Farmington and Dayton; Villages of Iola and Fremont; First National Bank of Iola.

For full biographical listings, see the Martindale-Hubbell Law Directory

WYOMING

*BUFFALO,** Johnson Co.

KIRVEN & KIRVEN, P.C. (AV)

104 Fort Street, P.O. Box 640, 82834
Telephone: 307-684-2248
Fax: 307-684-2242
Email: tkirven@wyo.com

William J. Kirven (Retired)
Dennis M. Kirven
Timothy J. Kirven

Representative Clients: Texaco Inc.; Wyoming Bank and Trust Co.; Buffalo Federal Savings & Loan Assn.; Reeves Concrete Products; Gordon Ranch; Powder River Corporation Reservoir; TR Ranch; School District Coalition; City of Buffalo.

(See Next Column)

For full biographical listings, see the Martindale-Hubbell Law Directory

*CASPER,** Natrona Co.

BROWN, DREW & MASSEY, LLP (AV)

Casper Business Center, Suite 800, 123 West First Street, 82601-2486
Telephone: 307-234-1000
800-877-6755
Telefax: 307-265-8025
Email: brwndrew@coffey.com

MEMBERS OF FIRM

William H. Brown (1913-1991)
William F. Drew (1925-1995)
Morris R. Massey
Harry B. Durham, III
Donn J. McCall
Thomas F. Reese
J. Kenneth Barbe
Jeffrey C. Brinkerhoff
Rex O. Arney
P. Jaye Rippley
Courtney Robert Kepler

ASSOCIATES

Scott P. Klosterman
Timothy M. Stubson

OF COUNSEL

B. J. Baker
Hampton K. O'Neill

RETIRED

George M. Apostolos

Attorneys for: Norwest Bank Wyoming, N.A.; The CIT Group/Equpment Financing; The Doctor's Co.; MEDMARC; Westech, Inc.; Chevron USA; Enron Group of Energy Companies; North American Resources Co.

For full biographical listings, see the Martindale-Hubbell Law Directory

WILLIAMS, PORTER, DAY & NEVILLE, P.C. (AV)

159 North Wolcott Street Suite 400, P.O. Box 10700, 82602
Telephone: 307-265-0700
Fax: 307-266-2306
Email: wpdn@trib.com

Houston G. Williams
Richard E. Day
Frank D. Neville
Barry G. Williams
Patrick J. Murphy
Stuart R. Day
Ann M. Rochelle
Mark L. Carman
Stephenson D. Emery
Scott E. Ortiz
Margo Harlan Sabec
Scott W. Skavdahl
Kevin D. Huber
Susan Chapin Stubson

Representative Clients: Attorneys Liability Protection Society; Wyoming Medical Center; Casper College; ITT Hartford Insurance Cos.; PacifiCorp; Amoco Corp.; Texaco Inc.; Conoco Inc.; True Industries; First American title Insurance Company.

For full biographical listings, see the Martindale-Hubbell Law Directory

*CHEYENNE,** Laramie Co.

HICKEY, MACKEY, EVANS & WALKER (AV)

1800 Carey Avenue, Suite 700, P.O. Drawer 467, 82003
Telephone: 307-634-1525
Telecopier: 307-638-7335
URL: http://www.hickeymackey.com

MEMBERS OF FIRM

Paul J. Hickey
Terry W. Mackey
David F. Evans
John M. Walker
Roger C. Fransen
Richard D. Tim Bush
Mary A. Throne

A List of Representative Clients will be furnished upon request.
Reference: Norwest Bank, Cheyenne, N.A.

For full biographical listings, see the Martindale-Hubbell Law Directory

LATHROP & RUTLEDGE, A PROFESSIONAL CORPORATION (AV)

Suite 500 City Center Building, 1920 Thomes Avenue, P.O. Box 4068, 82003-4068
Telephone: 307-632-0554
Telecopier: 307-635-4502
Email: mail@lathropandrutledge.com

Carl L. Lathrop
J. Kent Rutledge
Corinne E. Rutledge
James T. Dinneen

Lou Piccioni
Scott W. Meier
Kevin C. Cook

General Counsel for: Laramie County School District No. 2; Cheyenne Newspapers, Inc.; Wyoming Hospital Assn.; Cheyenne Medical Specialists, P.C.; Emergency Medical Physicians.
Insurance Clients: The Doctor's Company; CUMIS Insurance Society; Gainsco, Inc.; The St. Paul Companies; Infinity Insurance Co.

For full biographical listings, see the Martindale-Hubbell Law Directory

*CODY,** Park Co.

SIMPSON, KEPLER & EDWARDS, LC (AV)

1135 14th Street, P.O. Box 490, 82414
Telephone: 307-527-7891
Fax: 307-527-7897
Email: skeatty@wavecom.net

Milward L. Simpson (1897-1993)
Charles G. Kepler
William L. Simpson
Colin M. Simpson
Chris D. Edwards

OF COUNSEL

Alan K. Simpson

References: Community First National Bank-Cody; Shoshone-First National Bank; Jackson State Bank.

For full biographical listings, see the Martindale-Hubbell Law Directory

*JACKSON,** Teton Co.

SPENCE, MORIARITY & SCHUSTER, LLC (AV)

15 South Jackson Street, P.O. Box 548, 83001
Telephone: 307-733-7290
Fax: 307-733-5248
Salt Lake City, Utah Office: 39 Exchange Place, Suite 101, 84111.
Telephone: 801-521-0811.
Fax: 801-521-0437.

MEMBERS OF FIRM

Gerry L. Spence, P.C.
Edward P. Moriarity
Robert P. Schuster
Gary L. Shockey
J. Douglas McCalla
Roy A. Jacobson, Jr.
Kent W. Spence
Robert A. Krause

ASSOCIATES

Glen G. Debroder
R. Daniel Fleck
G. Bryan Ulmer, III
Laura N. MacPherson (Not admitted in WY)
David M. Gosar
Gerard R. Bosch
Jeffrey Gooch

Reference: First Interstate Bank, Casper, Wyoming.

For full biographical listings, see the Martindale-Hubbell Law Directory

ROCK SPRINGS, Sweetwater Co.

BUSSART, WEST, ROSSETTI, PIAIA & TYLER, P.C. (AV)

Suite A, 409 Broadway, P.O. Box 1020, 82902-1020
Telephone: 307-362-3300; 307-875-4080
Telecopier: 307-362-3309

Ford T. Bussart
L. Galen West
John D. Rossetti
Marvin L. Tyler
David M. Piaia

Representative Clients: Memorial Hospital of Sweetwater Co.; Horace Mann Insurance; American Hardware Insurance; Lancer Claims; The Home Insurance; Black Butte Coal Co.; Bridger Coal Co.; Castle Rock Hospital District; City of Green River, Wyoming.

For full biographical listings, see the Martindale-Hubbell Law Directory

*WHEATLAND,** Platte Co.

JONES, JONES, VINES & HUNKINS (AV)

An Association of Lawyers
Ninth and Maple, P.O. Drawer 189, 82201
Telephone: 307-322-2882
Fax: 307-322-4827; 322-3075

W. B. Jones (1896-1964)
Raymond B. Hunkins
William H. Vines

OF COUNSEL

William R. Jones

Representative Clients: Wyoming Realty; Metropolitan Life Ins. Co.; Prudential Insurance Co.; State of Wyoming (Special Assistant Attorney General)
Counsel for: Platte County School Districts #1 and #2; Wheatland Irrigation District; Banner Associates (Architects and Engineers).

For full biographical listings, see the Martindale-Hubbell Law Directory

PUERTO RICO

PONCE, Ponce Dist.

PARRA, DEL VALLE, FRAU & LIMERES

Second Floor, Banco Popular Building, P.O. Box 331429, 00733-1429
Telephone: 787-848-4900
Telecopier: 787-840-2022
Email: parralaw@prtc.net

(See Next Column)

MEMBERS OF FIRM

Francisco J. Parra-Toro (1904-1985)
Waldemar Del Valle-López (1927-1996)
Waldemar Del Valle-Armstrong
Manuel A. Frau-Pietri
Miguel Limeres-Grau
Ramon I. Ortiz-Palmieri
Maria M. Del Valle-Armstrong
Alys M. Collazo-Bougeois

Representative Clients: Banco Popular de Puerto Rico; Banco Santander-Puerto Rico; Integrand Assurance Company; Island Finance, Puerto Rico, Inc.; Hospital de Damas; Puerto Rican Cement Company, Inc.; El Día, Inc.; Ferré Development Co., Inc.; Caribbean Photo Imaging Co., Inc.; IDI Holdings PR, Inc.

For full biographical listings, see the Martindale-Hubbell Law Directory

SAN JUAN, San Juan Dist.

FIDDLER GONZÁLEZ & RODRÍGUEZ, LLP

254 Muñoz Rivera Avenue (Hato Rey), P.O. Box 363507, 00936-3507
Telephone: 787-753-3113
Telecopier: 787-759-3123
Email: fiddler@fgrlaw.com *URL:* http://www.fgrlaw.com

OF COUNSEL

Ileana Fernández-Buitrago

MEMBERS OF FIRM

Rafael R. Vizcarrondo
Salvador Antonetti-Zequeira
Pedro Pumarada
Rafael Cortés-Dapena
Julio L. Aguirre
Aurelio Emanuelli-Belaval
Antonio R. Sifre
Jay A. García-Gregory
Roberto B. Suárez
Leopoldo J. Cabassa-Sauri
Juan Carlos Pérez-Otero
Tristán Reyes-Gilestra
Eduardo M. Negrón-Navas
José A. Silva-Cofresí
Pedro J. Polanco
José A. Acosta-Grubb
Teodoro Peña-García
Mario Arroyo-Dávila
Arturo Bauermeister-Baldrich
Diego A. Ramos
José Julián Alvarez-Maldonado
Raúl J. Vilá-Sellés
José J. Santiago
Pedro A. Cantero-Frau
Ricardo F. Casellas
Juan Carlos Gómez Escarce
César Gómez Negrón
Armando Martínez-Fernández
Heriberto J. Burgos-Pérez
Aurelio Emanuelli Freese
Rafael E. Dávila-Thomas
José E. González-Borgos
María del Carmen Taboas
José R. Jiménez del Valle
Carlos V. J. Dávila
Lolita J. Semidey Garcia
Charles Bimbela-Quiñones
Rosa M. Méndez-Santoni
César T. Alcover-Acosta
María Luisa González-Hernández
Pedro J. Reyes-Bibiloni
Pedro I. Vidal-Cordero
Arline V. Bauzá-Figueroa
Alberto Luis Toro-Suarez
Ricardo L. Ortíz-Colón
Pedro J. Manzano-Yates

JUNIOR PARTNERS

Fernando Van Derdys
José Alberto Sosa-Lloréns
María Teresa Szendrey Ramos
Minerva I. Centeno-Rossy
Carmen Rosa Juarbe
Miguel Agustín Blanco Fuertes
Juan C. Salichs Pou
Luis A. Oliver

SENIOR ASSOCIATES

Rebecca Páez-Rodríguez
Orlando Cabrera-Rodriguez
Luis L. Torres-Marrero
José R. Negrón Fernandez
Yldebrando Suárez Martínez
Carlos A. Padilla-Velez
Irializ Vélez Quiñones

ASSOCIATES

César Vázquez-Morales
Rafael S. Bonilla
María-Isabel Rey-Cancio
Guillermo Zúñiga López
Beatriz M. Rodríguez-Burgos
Clotilde Rexach-Beníitez
Dirma M. Valentín-Capeles
Diana M. Batlle-Barasorda
Luis F. Colón-Conde
Ricardo E. Soto-Miranda
Luz Nereida Carrero
Lilliam Torres-Marín
Enrique R. Ubarri
Vivian I. Neptune-Rivera
Etienne Totti del Toro
María I. Santos

STAFF ATTORNEYS

Maritza Silva-Cofresí
Luis M. Rodríguez-Lopez
Carmen Irizarry de Domínguez
María del Pilar Rivera
Héctor Jiménez-Juarbe

Representative Clients: The Chase Manhattan Bank, N.A.; The Equitable Life Assurance Society of the U.S.; Westinghouse Electric Corp.; Pfizer, Inc.; Merck & Co., Inc.; American Cyanamid Co.; Metropolitan Life Insurance Co.; Bacardi Corp.; Banco Bilbao Vizcaya.

For full biographical listings, see the Martindale-Hubbell Law Directory

GOLDMAN ANTONETTI & CÓRDOVA

American International Plaza Fourteenth & Fifteenth Floors, 250 Muñoz Rivera Avenue (Hato Rey), P.O. Box 70364, 00936-0364
Telephone: 787-759-8000
Telecopiers: 787-767-9333 (Main)
787-767-9177 (Litigation Department)
787-767-8660 (Labor & Corporate Law Departments)
787-767-9325 (Tax & Environmental Law Departments)
URL: http://www.gaclaw.com

(See Next Column)

GOLDMAN ANTONETTI & CÓRDOVA, *San Juan—Continued*

MEMBERS OF FIRM

Enrique Córdova Díaz (1911-1998)
Vicente J. Antonetti
Roberto Montalvo Carbia
Luis F. Antonetti
Jorge Souss
Francisco de Jesús-Schuck
Luis D. Ortiz-Abreu
Edgar Cartagena-Santiago
Pedro Morell Losada
Ramón E. Dapena
Francis Torres-Fernández
Jorge L. Martinez
Carlos A. Rodríguez-Vidal
Thelma Rivera-Miranda
Jorge Segurola
Edgardo Colón Arrarás
Jesús E. Cuza
Howard Pravda
Braulio García Jiménez
Karín G. Díaz-Toro
Jorge R. Rodriguez-Micheo
Antonio Bauza-Santos
Georgiana S. Colón
Migdalia Davila-Garcia

OF COUNSEL

Max Goldman
Charles P. Adams
Heber E. Lugo-Rigau
Fernando Castro

SPECIAL COUNSEL

Jaime Morgan-Stubbe

ASSOCIATES

Mildred Cabán
Wilda Rodriguez Plaza
Gretchen M. Mendez-Vilella
María Patricia Lake
Ina M. Berlingeri Vincenty
Mayra Del C. Doble-Ruiz
Vivian Nuñez
Hector Perez
Claribel Ortiz-Rodríguez
Joanna Bocanegra Ocasio
Vanessa Bayonet-Tartak
Raul Negron Casasnovas
Guillermo J. Silva-Wiscovich
Frances R. Colon-Rivera
Veronica Olivieri-Barreto
Aida Barrios-Castellanos
Edna E. Perez-Roman
Michelle Feria-Cestero
Nilsa Flores-Sola
Eugenia I. Orsini-Herencia
Yvette De Luna-Colon
Ricardo Pizarro
Ruben Rivera-Rosa
Maura Santiago-Ducos
Lizzie M. Padro
Rosalie Irizarry-Silvestrini
Alicia Lamboy
Angel Berberena
Sara Vazquez
Rebeca Vargas-Ruiz

Representative Clients: Borden, Inc.; Crown Cork de Puerto Rico, Inc.; Maidenform, Inc.; Philip Morris, Inc.; Seven Up Flavors Mfg. Co.; Xerox Corp.

For full biographical listings, see the Martindale-Hubbell Law Directory

JIMÉNEZ, GRAFFAM & LAUSELL

Suite 505, Midtown Building, 421 Muñoz Rivera Avenue, Hato Rey, P.O. Box 366104, 00936-6104
Telephone: 787-767-1030; 767-1000; 767-1061; 767-1064
Telefax: 787-751-4068;
Cable: "Nezte"
RCA Telex: 325-2730
Email: manager@jgl.com *URL:* http://www.jgl.com

OF COUNSEL

Nicolás Jiménez

MEMBERS OF FIRM

William A. Graffam
Steven C. Lausell
J. Ramón Rivera-Morales
José Juan Torres-Escalera
Raquel M. Dulzaides
Manolo T. Rodríguez-Bird

ASSOCIATES

Patricia A. Garrity
Isabel J. Vélez-Serrano
Edgardo A. Vega-López
José Luis Suárez-Villafañe
Jorge F. Blasini
Ruy V. Díaz-Díaz
Rafael A. Rosado-Marrero

Representative Clients: Sea-Land Service, Inc.; McAllister Brothers, Inc.; Crowley Maritime Corp.; General Motors Overseas Distribution Corp.; HIH Casualty & General Insurance Ltd.; University of Puerto Rico.

For full biographical listings, see the Martindale-Hubbell Law Directory

JORGE R. JIMENEZ LAW OFFICES

Suite 807 IBM Building, 654 Muñoz Rivera Avenue (Hato Rey), 00918
Telephone: 787-763-0106
Fax: 787-763-0574

MEMBERS OF FIRM

Jorge R. Jimenez
Juan F. Doval

For full biographical listings, see the Martindale-Hubbell Law Directory

MARTÍNEZ ODELL & CALABRIA

Banco Popular Center, 209 Muñoz Rivera Avenue, Suite 1600 (Hato Rey), P.O. Box 190998, 00919-0998
Telephone: 787-753-8914
Facsimile: 787-753-8402; 787-759-9075; 787-764-5664
Email: postmaster@mocpr.com

MEMBERS OF FIRM

Fred H. Martínez
Lawrence Odell
Jose R. Cestero
Juan Ramón Cancio-Ortiz
Francisco M. Ramirez-Rivera
Luis E. Lopez Correa
Patrick D. O'Neill
Graciela J. Belaval
Luis Morales-Steinmann
Anabelle Rodriguez-Rodriguez

(See Next Column)

MEMBERS OF FIRM (Continued)

Fernando A. Pérez-Colon
Alberto Rodríguez-Ramos
Angel S. Ruiz-Rodriguez
Javier E. Ferrer-Canals
Juan Carlos Fierres
Arnaldo Villamil
Humberto Guzmán-Rodríguez
Roberto E. Vega Pacheco
Francisco L. Acevedo-Nogueras
Carlos Berreteaga
Maria del Carmen Garriga
Eric Perez Ochoa
Ramón Eugenio-Meléndez
María I. De Mier
Rafael Kodesh-Baragaño
Manuel E. Lopez-Fernandez
Jose Antonio Fernandez-Jaquete
Ivonne Palerm-Cruz
Brunilda Rodríguez-Vélez
Jose G. Fagot-Diaz
Jose David Medina-Rivera
Jorge J. Garcia-Diaz
Ignacio M. Arbona-Arbona
Carlos P. Santiago-Sarkis

OF COUNSEL

Jose L. Calabria
Jose B. Diaz Asencio
Dominic T. Longo
Hernan R. Franco
Francisco Orsini-Capo

ASSOCIATES

Carmen J. Rocafort
Amelia Fortuño-Ruiz
Brunilda R. Santiago-Acevedo
Jorge L. Covas-Mendoza
Fernando J. Gierbolini-Gonzalez
Charles P. Gilmore
Dora L. Monserrate-Peñagaricano
Carmen T. Ubarri-Nevares
Jaime L. Vazquez-Bernier
Jennifer Odell-Gonzalez
Luis J. Mongil-Casasnovas
Mariela Garcia-Colberg
Juan A. Frau-Escudero
Jose Luis Baez-Rivera
Luis A. Hernandez-Vivoni
Gustavo J. Umpierre-Ponton
Julio D. Vazquez-Rodriguez
Mildred L. Santana-Mejias
Jose Carlos Diaz-Vega
Jose G. Diaz-Tejera
Roxana M. Viera-Canales
Brigitte S. Krumhansl
Mario Loyola

Representative Clients: Banco Popular de Puerto Rico; Daewoo Motor Corporation; Eckerd Corporation; Empresas Fonalledas; Hilton International; L'Aire Liquide, S.A.; Loctile Corporation; Lucent Technologies; Lutron Electronics Co., Inc.; Waste Management, Inc.

For full biographical listings, see the Martindale-Hubbell Law Directory

MCCONNELL VALDÉS

270 Muñoz Rivera Avenue, 9th Floor (Hato Rey), 00918
Telephone: 787-759-9292
Cable Address: "Macval"
Telex (ITT): 345-0067 (Easylink 6243678)
Telecopier: 787-759-9225 or 787-759-8282
Mailing Address: P.O. Box 364225, San Juan, Puerto Rico, 00936-4225
Email: aev@mcvpr.com *URL:* http://www.mcvpr.com

MEMBERS OF FIRM

Herbert S. McConnell (1905-1971)
Gonzalo Sifre (1913-1995)
Odette Portuondo-Díaz (1951-1999)
Samuel T. Céspedes
Antonio Escudero-Viera
Silvestre M. Miranda
Miguel Palou-Sabater
Rubén T. Nigaglioni
Jorge R. González
Radamés (Rudy) A. Torruella
Antonio J. Rodríguez
Carlos O. Souffront
Rafael Pérez-Bachs
Francisco G. Bruno
Ana Matilde Nin-Torregrosa
Aníbal Irizarry-Rivera
Frederick E. Hulser
José R. González-Irizarry
Néstor Durán-González
Harry O. Cook
Manuel Moreda-Toledo
Maggie Correa-Avilés
Arturo J. García-Solá
Mario L. Paniagua
Esteban R. Bengoa
Richard M. Graffam-Rodríguez
Roberto L. Cabañas
Rafael Fernández-Suárez
Rossell Barrios-Amy
Ernesto N. Mayoral-Megwinoff
Paul R. Cortés-Rexach
Jaime E. Toro-Monserrate
Salvador F. Casellas
Alfredo M. Hopgood-Jovet
William A. Power
Samuel T. Céspedes Jr.
Antonio A. Arias-Larcada
Gilberto J. Marxuach-Torrós
James D. Noel III
Angel Rafael Marrero
Manuel Fernández-Bared
Dora M. Peñagarícano-Suárez
David Muñoz-Ocasio
Lilia R. Rodríquez-Ruiz
Carmencita Velázquez-Márquez
Pedro E. Ruiz-Meléndez
Gerardo J. Rivera-Fourquet
Jorge Antonio Antongiorgi-Betancourt
José A. B. Nolla-Mayoral
Jeanne Habib
Rafael A. Ruiz-Ayala
Carlos González-Padró
Amaya Iraolagoitia
Raúl M. Arias-Marxuach
Carlos J. Fernández-Lugo
Luis E. Palou Balsa
Roberto C. Quiñones-Rivera

SPECIAL COUNSEL

Robert S. Griggs
Isis Carballo
Francisco Chévere
Mari Carmen Bosch
Armando Llorens (Not admitted in PR)

SPECIAL TAX COUNSEL

Soledad Reichard-Megwinoff

OF COUNSEL

Adolfo Valdés
Fernando Ruiz-Suria
Abelardo Ruiz-Suria
Daniel F. Kelley, Jr.
Robert W. Van Kirk
Walter G. McConnell
Joseph T. Wynne
Aurelio Torres Ponsa

(See Next Column)

McConnell Valdés—*Continued*

ASSOCIATES

Leonor M. Aguilar-Guerrero
Joan Mulet
(Not admitted in PR)
Anita Montaner-Sevillano
María T. Juan-Urrutia
Maria Antongiorgi
Maria L. Fuster-Zalduondo
Ariadna Álvarez
Elaine Maldonado-Matías
Jorge Calero Blanco
Ivette M. López
Vanessa Elías
Denise M. Rexach González
Javier Rivera-Carbone
Cecile A. Armstrong
María L. Quintana
Rica López de Alós
Luis R. Amadeo
Francisco X. Pascual-Amadeo
Carlos E. Serrano
Agustin Fortuño-Fas
Pedro J. Torres-Diaz
Carmen H. Busó-García
Veronica Ferraiuoli
Ivan G. Marrero
Salvador J. Antonetti-Stutts
Eduardo H. Martinez-Echeverría
Maria Eugenia Ramirez
Vanessa Conde Aymerich
Francisco Arrivi Silva
Juan A. Marqués
Berenice B. Bellotti
Lee Sepulvado-Ramos
Henry O. Freese Souffront
Katherine González-Valentín
Maria Alejandra Mercado-Betancourt
Eugenio J. Torres-Oyola
Angélica T. Toro-Lavergne
María Victoria Múnera-Pascual
Arturo J. Vélez
Carlos Diaz Vivo
Marta M. Kury Latorre
Fernando J. Roviva Rullan
Carmen A. Valdés Alvarez
Cynthia M. Gonzalez-Aranguren
Helen A. Salichs
(Not admitted in PR)
Sandra L. Negrón-Monge

Representative Clients: American Home Products Corp.; Chrysler Corp.; Eli Lilly & Co.; ITT; The Shell Co.; Union Carbide Corp.

For full biographical listings, see the Martindale-Hubbell Law Directory

Barry A. Woods

Capital Center Building, 239 Arterial Hostos, Suite 706, 00918-1476
Telephone: 787-759-8181
Fax: 787-751-3115
Email: baw@canibe.net/bawbat@cs.com

For full biographical listings, see the Martindale-Hubbell Law Directory

U.S. PACIFIC TERRITORIES

SAIPAN, Mariana Islands

Carlsmith Ball

A Partnership including Law Corporations
Carlsmith Building, Capitol Hill, P.O. Box 5241, 96950-5241
Telephone: 670-322-3455
Fax: 670-322-3368
Email: execdirector@carlsmith.com *URL:* http://www.carlsmith.com
Honolulu, Hawaii Office: Suite 2200, Pacific Tower, 1001 Bishop Street. P.O. Box 656, 96809-3402.
Telephone: 808-523-2500.
Fax: 808-523-0842.
Kapolei, Hawaii Office: Suite 318, Kapolei Building, 1001 Kamokila Boulevard, 96707.
Telephone: 808-523-2500.
Fax: 808-674-0850.
Wailuku, Maui Hawaii Office: Suite 400, One Main Plaza, 2200 Main Street, P.O. Box 1086, 96793-1086.
Telephone: 808-242-4535.
Fax: 808-244-4974.
Kailua-Kona, Hawaii Office: Suite 209, 75-1000 Henry Street, 96740.
Telephone: 808-329-6464.
Fax: 808-329-9450.
Hilo, Hawaii Office: 121 Waianuenue Avenue, P.O. Box 686, 96721-0686.
Telephone: 808-935-6644.
Fax: 808-935-7975.
Hagatna, Guam Office: Suite 401, Bank of Hawaii Building, 134 West Soledad Avenue, P.O. Box BF, 96932-5027.
Telephone: 671-472-6813.
Fax: 671-477-4375.
Telex: 721-6445 CWCMI GM.
Los Angeles, California Office: 9th Floor, 444 South Flower Street, 90071-2901.
Telephone: 213-955-1200.
Fax: 213-623-0032.
Washington, D.C. Office: Suite 300, 1201 Pennsylvania Avenue, N.W., 20004-2401.
Telephone: 202-628-2228.
Fax: 202-628-2071.
Mexico City, Mexico Office: Sierra Nevada 119, Lomas de Chapultepec, 11000 Mexico, D.F.
Telephone: 52-5-520-8514, 52-5-520-8757.
Fax: 52-5-540-1545.

(See Next Column)

Mexico, D.F. Office of Carlsmith Ball, S.C. (Authorized to practice as foreign legal consultants in Mexico): Sierra Nevada 119, Lomas de Chapultepec, 11000 Mexico, D.F.
Telephone: 52-5-520-8514, 52-5-520-8757.
Fax: 52-5-540-1545.

RESIDENT PARTNERS

John F. Biehl
David R. Nevitt
(Not admitted in TT)
John D. Osborn
Marcia K. Schultz

OF COUNSEL

Robert B. Dunlap, II

For full biographical listings, see the Martindale-Hubbell Law Directory

VIRGIN ISLANDS

*CHARLOTTE AMALIE, ST. THOMAS,** St. Thomas

Grunert Stout & Bruch (BV)

24-25 Kongensgade, P.O. Box 1030, 00804
Telephone: 340-774-1320
Fax: 340-774-7839
Email: gsbusvi@viaccess.net
Affiliated with: Solomon Pearl Blum & Quinn LLP, New York, New York and Denver, Colorado.

MEMBERS OF FIRM

John E. Stout
Susan Bruch Moorehead

ASSOCIATE

Gabriel J. Villegas

OF COUNSEL

William L. Blum

For full biographical listings, see the Martindale-Hubbell Law Directory

Stryker, Duensing, Casner & Dollison (AV)

A Partnership of Professional Corporations
Upper Level Drake's Passage, P.O. Box 6785, 00804
Telephone: 340-774-6011
Telefax: 340-776-8520
Email: vilaw@viaccess.net

MEMBERS OF FIRM

John W. Stryker (P.C.)
Matthew J. Duensing (P.C.)
A. James Casner III, (P.C.)
Richard H. Dollison

ASSOCIATES

T. Lee Mason
Garry E. Garten
Ishmael A. Meyers, Jr.
Anne-Marie Storm
(Not admitted in VI)

OF COUNSEL

Margaret A. Duensing (P.C.)
Mary R. Weber (P.C.)

For full biographical listings, see the Martindale-Hubbell Law Directory

CANADA
ALBERTA

*CALGARY,** Calgary Jud. Dist.

Bennett Jones (AV)

4500 Bankers Hall East, 855-2nd Street S.W., T2P 4K7
Telephone: 403-298-3100
Facsimile: 403-265-7219
Email: firmwatch@bennettjones.ca *URL:* http://www.bennettjones.ca
Edmonton, Alberta Office: 1000, 10035-105 Street.
Telephone: 780-421-8133.
Facsimile: 780-421-7951.
Toronto, Ontario Office: 3400 1 First Canadian Place, P.O. Box 130.
Telephone: 416-863-1200.
Facsimile: 416-863-1716.

MEMBERS OF FIRM

Rt. Hon. R. B. Bennett, P.C., K.C. (1870-1947)
Walter B. O'Donoghue, Q.C.
William L. Britton, Q.C.
John F. Curran, Q.C.
David H. McDermid
Lenard M. Sali, Q.C.
Donald G. Anderson
Richard B. Low
J. D. Bruce McDonald
Wayne R. Whitlock
Brian K. O'Ferrall
Donnel O. Sabey, Q.C.
W. Gordon Brown, Q.C.
Clifton D. O'Brien, Q.C.
John C. Armstrong, Q.C.
Lawrence A. Johnson
John S. Burns, Q.C.
John G. Martland, Q.C.
H. Martin Kay, Q.C.
Roland K. Laing, Q.C.
William S. Rice
Douglas A. Ast
Alan W. Rubin

(See Next Column)

BENNETT JONES, *Calgary—Continued*

MEMBERS OF FIRM (Continued)

C. Michael Ryer
Philip D. Backman
Bradley G. Nemetz
Daniel T. Gallagher
David M. Lennox
Grant N. Stapon
Tim D. Kerrigan
Martin A. Lambert
Robert W. Thompson
Paul M. Farion
Margaret G. Lemay
James G. Smeltzer
Jo'Anne Strekaf
D. Alan Ross
James A. D'Andrea
Blair C. Yorke-Slader
Robert A. Lehodey
Kim D. Nixon
J. David D. Steele
John W. Gulak
John E. E. Lowe
John N. Craig
John L. Townley
Peter R. S. Leveque
Donald M. Boykiw
David J. Macaulay
Valerie R. Prather
John D. MacNeil
Karen J. Middleton
Noralee M. Bradley
Robert P. Desbarats
Anthony L. Friend, Q.C.
John F. Cordeau
Robert T. Booth
Frank R. Dearlove
Garnet M. Schulhauser
R. Vance Milligan
Lawrence E. Smith
Donald E. Greenfield
William F. Quigley
Lorne W. Carson
Karen M. Horner
Loyola G. Keough
J. Douglas Foster
Neil H. Stevenson
C. Perry Spitznagel
Robert R. Rooney
Michael J. Hopkins
Patrick J. Brennan
Martin P. J. Kratz
Renée M. Ratke
David J. Corry
Nicholas M. Gretener
Darcy D. Moch
Shawn H. T. Denstedt
Ronald M. Barron
Stanley R. Ebel
Nick P. Fader
Donald G. MacDiarmid
E. Bruce Mellett
D. Mitchell Williams

Jeffrey T. Daines
Brad D. Markel
Scott H.D. Bower
John Kousinioris
Kenneth T. Lenz
Heather I. Forester
Indra L. Maharaj
Catherine J. Valestuk
James D. Roberts
Filomena Lerede
Brent J. Ludwig
(Not admitted in AB)
Kevin L. Zemp
John R. Gilmore
Erin R. Bourgeault
Bryan C.G. Haynes
Steven T. Robertson
Josef W. Hocher
Steven L. Major
Brent A. Molesky
John C. Batzel
Murray G. Coleman
Mary E. Barroll
Bradley S. Gilmour
Alice C. Woolley
George W. Wowk
(Not admitted in AB)
S. Farouk Adatia
Michel H. Bourque
S. Ashley Evans
Chistopher D. Simard
Kelly R. Nicholson
Kenton G.C. Rein
Jon C. Truswell
L. Blair Jordan
Kenneth R. Davidson
Andrea L. Neufeld
Jason T. Marino
Gregory M. Johnson
Michael A. Waite
Shannon E. Young
Christopher S. Davis
Philip B. Hodge
Mark T. Houston
Tara L. Whidden
Jennifer J. Edwards
Geeta Bharadia
Brenda J. Johnson
Heather J. Smith
Christopher R. Skelton
Kim P. Nayyer
Christopher A. Brown
Shawn M. Munro
K. Louise Redmond
Robert J. Hawkes
Debbie E. Bryden
Denise D. Bright
Darrell R. Peterson
Timothy J. Robson
Maureen E. Killoran
Gerald A. Grenon
William S. Osler
W. Chipman Johnston
Scott M. Reeves
George M. Vlavianos
Michael P. Theroux
Janice D.L. Buckingham
Conan J. Taylor
Jacqueline D. Cullen
Sharon J. Cartmill
(Not admitted in AB)
Took B.P.E. Whiteley
Tean-Rae Kerr
Y. Beth Riley
Denis R. Rajotte
Russell N. Watterson
Paul A. Bolger
Denise C. Jakal
April D. Grosse
Jean-Pierre Pham
Thomas W. McInerney
Suzanne C. Vickers

OF COUNSEL

Maclean E. Jones, Q.C.
Hon. E. Peter Lougheed, P.C., C.C., Q.C.
Herbert D. Wyman, Q.C.

For full biographical listings, see the Martindale-Hubbell Law Directory

---

BLAKE, CASSELS & GRAYDON LLP (AV)

Suite 3500, East Tower, Bankers Hall, 855 - 2nd Street South West, T2P 4J8
Telephone: 403-260-9600
Facsimile: 403-260-9700
Email: calgary@blakes.com *URL:* http://www.blakes.com
The Firm maintains other offices in: Toronto, Ontario, Ottawa, Ontario, Vancouver, British Columbia, London, England and Beijing, China.

(See Next Column)

PARTNERS

A. Webster Macdonald, Jr., Q.C.
Gerald M. Deyell
Dallas L. Droppo
Wally Y. Shaw
Mitchell B. Cohen
Ken Mills
Mungo Hardwicke-Brown
Jacqueline S. Moore
Bryan C. Duguid
Aleck H. Trawick, Q.C.
Richard L. Dawson
A. Robert Anderson
Daniel P.E. Fournier
Patrick C. Finnerty
Brock W. Gibson
Joni R. Paulus
Dalton W. McGrath
Christa Nicholson
Ronald W.K. Mar

COUNSEL

Charalee F. Graydon
Dawn Giebelhaus Mains

For full biographical listings, see the Martindale-Hubbell Law Directory

---

HOWARD, MACKIE (AV)

Barristers, Solicitors, Notaries
1000 Canterra Tower, 400 Third Avenue, S.W., T2P 4H2
Telephone: 403-232-9500
Telecopier: 403-266-1395
Email: postmaster@howardmackie.com *URL:* http://www.howardmackie.com

William Arnold Howard, C.M.M., C.M., C.D., Q.C. (Retired)
Douglas H. Mitchell, Q.C.
Hugh D. Williamson, Q.C.
George E. Anderson
Frank R. Foran, Q.C.
Allan D. Nielsen
John P. Petch, Q.C. *
Terence G. Lidster *
Ross A. Reaburn
Patrick T. McCarthy, Q.C.
James W. Surbey
Frederick W. T. Somerville *
Brian E. Roberts *
John L. Ircandia
Ross D. Freeman *
Larry M. Kwinter
Andrew K. Maciag
John Poetker
David R. Wright, Q.C.
William C. Guinan
Jeffrey D. Vallis
Stephen W. Wilson
Frank P. J. Cahill
Katherine L. Milani
David C. Whelan
Randall W. Block
Brad J. Pierce
Colin P. MacDonald
Ruth M. Spetz
David T. Madsen
M. Scott Wilson
Daniel G. Kolibar
R. Craig Steele
Marilyn D. Paterson
Michael G. Massicotte
Jonathan M. Liteplo

ASSOCIATES

William R. Blain, Q.C.
D. George Kelly
John E. Tyrrell
N. L. Golding
Susan I. Dumont
Peter J. Major
Derek A. Kurrant, C.A., LL.B.
Julie G. Hopkins
Maria S. Doerksen
Stephen C. Lee
Karen A. McHugh
Laurie M. Robson
Darwin A. Schofer
Mark A. Klassen
Jeffrey A. Helper
Julio N. Arboleda Ramirez
Keith R. Chatwin
Greg S. Lilles
Patricia L. Morrison
Lauren J.M. Warrack
Derrick K. Auch
Brent W. Kraus
Michael A. Marion
Cora S. Miller
Edward A. Wooldridge
Josef G.A. Krüger

COUNSEL

John Hopwood, Q.C.
William D. Dickie, Q.C.
Hon. Roger P. Kerans

Reference: The Royal Bank of Canada, Main Branch, Calgary.
*Denotes Lawyer Whose Professional Corporation is a Member of the Partnership.

For full biographical listings, see the Martindale-Hubbell Law Directory

---

MCCARTHY TÉTRAULT (AV)

Suite 3300, 421 7th Avenue, S.W., T2P 4K9
Telephone: 403-260-3500
Facsimile: 403-260-3501
Email: calgary@mccarthy.ca *URL:* http://www.mccarthy.ca
Vancouver, British Columbia Office: Suite 1300, 777 Dunsmuir Street, P.O. Box 10424, Vancouver, British Columbia V7Y 1K2.
Telephone: 604-643-7100.
Facsimile: 604-643-7900.
Surrey, British Columbia Office: Suite 1300, Station Tower, Gateway 13401-108th Avenue, Surrey, British Columbia V3T 5T3.
Telephone: 604-583-9100.
Fax: 604-583-9150.
London, Ontario Office: Suite 2000, One London Place, 255 Queens Avenue, London, Ontario N6A 5R8.
Telephone: 519-660-3587.
Facsimile: 519-660-3599.
Toronto, Ontario Office: Suite 4700, Toronto Dominion Bank Tower, Toronto, Ontario M5K 1E6.
Telephone: 416-362-1812.
Facsimile: 416-868-0673.
Ottawa, Ontario Office: The Chambers, Suite 1400, 40 Elgin Street, Ottawa, Ontario K1P 5K6.
Telephone: 613-238-2000.
Facsimile: 613-563-9386.

(See Next Column)

McCarthy Tétrault—*Continued*

Montréal, Québec Office: Le Windsor, 1170 rue Peel, Montréal, Québec H3B 4S8.
Telephone: 514-397-4100.
Facsimile: 514-875-6246.
Québec, Québec Office: Le Complexe St-Amable 1150, rue Claire-Fontaine, 7e étage, Québec, Québec G1R 5G4.
Telephone: 418-521-3000.
Facsimile: 418-521-3098, 418-521-3099.
United Kingdom and Europe Office: Pountney Hill House, 6 Laurence Pountney Hill, London, England EC4R 0BL.
Telephone: 011-144-71-618-2888.
Facsimile: 011-144-71-618-2880.

PARTNERS

I. Michael Robison, Q.C.
Gwen K. Randall, Q.C.
Douglas S. Ewens, Q.C.
Ross O. Drysdale
Patricia L. Daunais, Q.C.
Kieth R. Mullback
William H. Smith, Q.C.
Michael J. Flatters
Clifford D. Johnson
Stuart F. Blyth
Bruce L. MacPhail
David F. Phillips
J. Michael McIntosh
Timothy S. J. Ellam
Robert J. S. Hanf
Thomas H. Ferguson, Q.C.
Richard A. Wilson, Q.C.
David H. Field
Richard A. Shaw, Q.C. (Managing Partner)
David W. Ross
C. Anne Simpson
Philippe V. Lalonde
James L. Lebo, Q.C.
Mendy M. Chernos
Douglas G. Cole
Dale E. Skinner
Karen L. Wiwchar
John S. Osler
Andrew D. Grasby
David J. Stanford

ASSOCIATES

Tim P. Chick
Michele H. Hollins
Douglas M. Singerman (Not admitted in AB)
Lyle S. Yuzdepski (Not admitted in AB)
LLoyd E. Symons
Michael D. Briggs
James P. Flanagan
James E.R. Lord
Hugo Prud'Homme
Michelle A. Epp
Johanna C. Price
Cathy Villeneuve
Charlene Brownlee
David C. Maxwell
Mark G. Eade
John MacKay
Olivia Colic
Kristine A. Kennedy
Michael J. Bennett
Crispin J. Arthur
Greg A. Liakopoulos
Elizabeth J. Osler
Shawn M. Belecki
Deanna H. Kolibar
Annie C. Tétrault
Graham M. Young

COUNSEL

Robert W. Calvert
John B. Zaozirny, Q.C.
Robert N. Depoe
Robert M. Perrin
Terence Dalgleish, Q.C.
Cheryl L. James
Kerry M. Smyth Osler

For full biographical listings, see the Martindale-Hubbell Law Directory

Miller Thomson (AV)

700 Ninth Avenue S.W., Suite 3000, T2P 3V4
Telephone: 403-298-2400
Fax: 403-262-0007
Email: calgary@millerthomson.ca *URL:* http://www.millerthomson.ca
Edmonton, Alberta Office: 2700 Commerce Place, 10155-102 Street, Edmonton, Alberta, T5J 4G8.
Telephone: 780-429-1751.
Fax: 780-424-5866.
Toronto, Ontario Office: 2500, 20 Queen Street West, Toronto, Ontario, M5H 3S1.
Telephone: 416-595-8500.
Fax: 905-415-6777.
York Region, Ontario Office: 60 Columbia Way, Suite 600, Markham, Ontario, L3R 0C9.
Telephone: 905-415-6700.
Fax: 905-415-6777.
Law Firm Affiliations/Associations:
Campney & Murphy - Vancouver, British Columbia, Canada
McCarter Grespan Robson Beynon - Kitchener, Ontario
Azevedo Sette Advogados - Sao Paulo and Belo Horizonte, Brazil, South America
Estudio Faraggi, Sateler & CIA - Santiago, Chile
Davis Arnold Cooper - London, England (Offices also in Manchester, Brussels, Vienna, Zurich, Madrid and Hong Kong)
Schürmann & Partners - Germany (Offices in Frankfurt, Berlin, Bonn, Dresden, Leipzig, Munich, Brussels, Milan, New York, Paris and Prague)
CONTACT: JOHN A. PETERS.
Telephone: 403-298-2434. E-mail: jpeters@millerthomson.ca.

Larry B. Robinson
Michael F. Hayduk
Kent R. Anderson
Glen G. Ortt
Paddy-Jo Davis
John A. Middleton
Marvin R. Koochin
E. Jane Sidnell
Sandra Mah
Brian J. Evans
John A. Peters
Richard L.G. Gushue
Michael J. Bailey
William J. Fowlis
Gregory P. Shannon
Sean F. Collins
Alex J. Kotkas
Michael J. Morcom

(See Next Column)

Michael A. Rasmuson
R. Benson Rogers
Michael D. Aasen
Katharine Saether

OF COUNSEL

Cheryl C. Gottselig
Joachim (Joe) Pfaefflin

For full biographical listings, see the Martindale-Hubbell Law Directory

Osler, Hoskin & Harcourt LLP (AV)

Barristers & Solicitors
Patent and Trade-Mark Agents
Suite 1900, Toronto Dominion Square, 333 - 7th Avenue S.W., T2P 2Z1
Telephone: 403-260-7000
Fax: 403-260-7024
Email: counsel@osler.com *URL:* http://www.osler.com
Toronto, Ontario Office: P.O. Box 50, 1 First Canadian Place M5X 1B8
Telephone: 416-362-2111.
Fax: 416-862-6666.
Ottawa, Ontario Office: Suite 1500, 50 O'Connor Street, K1P 6L2.
Telephone: 613-235-7234.
FAX: 613-235-2867.
New York, N.Y. Office: 280 Park Avenue-30W, 10017.
Telephone: 212-867-5800.
Fax: 212-867-5802.

MEMBERS OF FIRM

Francis R. Allen
Ariel Z. Breitman
John H. Macfarlane (Not admitted in AB)
Tristram J. Mallett
Christopher W. Nixon
Richard H. Peters
Raymond E. Quesnel
Jack A. Silverson
Mark R. Smith
R. John (Jack) Thrasher

ASSOCIATES

Kenneth B. Flowers
Sherri L. Fountain
Alyson F. Goldman
Andrew D. Little (Not admitted in AB)
Sean S. Smyth
David T. Weyant

For full biographical listings, see the Martindale-Hubbell Law Directory

Parlee McLaws (AV)

3400 Petro-Canada Centre, 150 - 6th Avenue, SW, T2P 3Y7
Telephone: 403-294-7000
Telecopier: 403-265-8263
Email: lawyers@parlee.com *URL:* http://www.parlee.com
Edmonton, Alberta Office: 15th Floor Manulife Place, 10180 101st Street.
Telephone: 403-423-8500.
Telecopier: 403-423-2870.

MEMBERS OF FIRM

Donald P. McLaws, Q.C.
Everett L. Bunnell, Q.C.
Gordon M. Adams
Dale R. Spackman, Q.C.
Bruce Churchill-Smith
Nancy M. Penner
Patrick J. McGovern
Aldo P. Argento
Andrew P. Bedford
George L. Crawford, Q.C.
William R. Pieschel, Q.C.
Lindsay J. Holmes
Richard B. Mask
Bruce A. Lawrence
Gregory D. M. Stirling
G. Scott Watson
Terry R. Davis
Nancy M. Carruthers

ASSOCIATES

Dennis J. Pelkie
Paul J. Mason
Elaine A. Thompson
Brenda M. Tsukishima
Morey D. Sair
Anne Marie Godin
Angela M. Tripathy
Seema S. Johal
H. David McLellan
Donald A. Young
Ariane E. Young
Barbara E. Janzen
Alec N. Silenzi
Peter W. Cline
Erin A. MacPherson
Susan E. Hrychuk
Tasha D. Backus
Kathryn Trenerry-Harker
Jon W. Arnott

COUNSEL

Jeffrey H. Selby

For full biographical listings, see the Martindale-Hubbell Law Directory

*EDMONTON,** Edmonton Jud. Dist.

Bennett Jones (AV)

1000, 10035-105 Street, T5J 3T2
Telephone: 780-421-8133
Facsimile: 780-421-7951
Email: firmwatch@bennettjones.ca *URL:* http://www.bennettjones.ca
Calgary, Alberta Office: 4500 Bankers Hall East, 855-2nd Street S.W.
Telephone: 403-298-3100.
Facsimile: 403-265-7219.
Toronto, Ontario Office: 3400 1 First Canadian Place, P.O. Box 130.
Telephone: 416-863-1200.
Facsimile: 416-863-1716.

MEMBERS OF FIRM

Glyn K. Edwards, Q.C.
Donald R. Cranston
Frank P. Layton, Q.C.
Enzo J. Barichello
Rose M. Carter

(See Next Column)

BENNETT JONES, *Edmonton—Continued*

Brian D. Heck	Mark P. Kortbeek
Simon D. Johnson	James J. Heelan
Barbara J. Stratton	Edward T. Yoo
Jennifer A. Miller	Tracey L. Howell
Carole L. Hunt	Angela E. Weaver
Tara S. Mah	George F. Chivers

For full biographical listings, see the Martindale-Hubbell Law Directory

EMERY JAMIESON (AV)

1700 Oxford Tower, 10235 - 101 Street, T5J 3G1
Telephone: 780-426-5220
Fax: 780-420-6277
Email: general@emeryjamieson.com *URL:* http://www.emeryjamieson.com
Calgary, Alberta Office: 206 Kensington House, 1167 Kensington Crescent, N.W., T2N 1X7.
Telephone: 403-543-6010.
Fax: 403-270-8080. E-mail: ejcalg@emeryjamieson.com

MEMBERS OF FIRM

Howard T. Emery, Q.C. (1899-1990)	G. Bruce Comba
	Rex M. Nielsen
John H. Jamieson, Q.C. (Retired)	Donna Carson Read
	Susan L. Bercov
Sydney A. Bercov, Q.C.	Bruce F. Hughson
Henry B. Martin, Q.C.	Murray F. Tait
Richard B. Drewry	Robert D. McDonald
W. Paul Sharek, Q.C.	Jeffrey K. Friesen
Robert W. Thompson	Blair E. Maxston
Phyllis A. Smith, Q.C.	Frederica L. Schutz
Gordon D. Sustrik	Janet N. Alexander-Smith
Shirley A. McNeilly	Claire M. Klassen
Michael J. Penny	Earl J. Evaniew

ASSOCIATES

Regina M. Corrigan (Resident, Calgary Office)	Michael D. Cooper (Resident at Calgary Office)
Stuart J. Weatherill	Patrick G. Nugent
Scott H. Chen	Heidi K. Robinson

Christopher R. Ontkean

Reference: Canadian Imperial Bank of Commerce.

For full biographical listings, see the Martindale-Hubbell Law Directory

LUCAS BOWKER & WHITE (AV)

Scotia 2 Tower - Scotia Place, 1201-10060 Jasper Avenue, T5J 4E5
Telephone: 780-426-5330
Fax: 780-428-1066
Email: Lucas@lbw.ab.ca *URL:* http://www.lbw.ab.ca
Calgary, Alberta Office: Suite 3800, Bankers Hall, 855 2nd Street S.W., T2P 4J8.
Telephone: 403-218-1795.
Fax: 403-264-2993. Email: Lucas@lbw.ab.ca. URL: http://www.lbw.ab.ca

MEMBERS OF FIRM

Gerald A. I. Lucas, Q.C.	Alan R. Gray
George E. Bowker, Q.C.	Robert A. Seidel, Q.C.
Robert B. White, Q.C.	Robert P. Bruce
David J. Stratton, Q.C.	David J. Stam
John Reginald Day, Q.C.	Donald J. Wilson
Norman J. Pollock, Q.C.	Kevin J. Smith
Robert C. Dunseith	Gordon V. Garside
Douglas H. Shell	Debbie L. Hughes
Kent H. Davidson	Douglas A. Bodner

COUNSEL

Joseph J. Stratton, Q.C.

Reference: Canadian Imperial Bank of Commerce.

For full biographical listings, see the Martindale-Hubbell Law Directory

MCLENNAN ROSS (AV)

A Partnership including Professional Corporations
600 West Chambers, 12220 Stony Plain Road, T5N 3Y4
Telephone: 780-482-9200
Fax: 780-482-9100; 780-482-9101; 780-482-9102
Email: edmonton@mross.com *URL:* http://www.mross.com
Calgary, Alberta Office: 1801 Altius Centre, 500 - 4th Avenue S.W, T2P 2V6.
Telephone: 403-543-9120.
Fax: 403-543-9150. Email: calgary@mross.com
Yellowknife, Northwest Territory Office: 802 Precambrian Building, 4920-52nd Street, X1A 3T1.
Telephone: 867-873-5968.
Fax: 867-873-5972

(See Next Column)

Roderick A. McLennan, Q.C. *	Christopher J. Lane
David J. Ross, Q.C.	Shawn W. McLeod
Peter P. Taschuk, Q.C.	Clay K. Hamdon
Havelock B. Madill, Q.C.	Stephen J. Livingstone
Darren B. Becker, Q.C. *	Sandra J. Weber
Frederick A. Day, Q.C. *	Robert R. Chappell
Hugh J. D. McPhail	Doreen C. Mueller
Charles P. Russell *	Karen J. A. Metcalfe
Karen A. Platten	David D. Risling
Jonathan P. Rossall *	Corbin D. Devlin
Graham McLennan	Andrew J. Haynes
Glenn D. Tait	Charles R. Dalton
William S. Rosser *	Kenneth W. Fitz
Yolanda S. Van Wachem	Vicki L. Giles
Ronald M. Kruhlak	Neal A. McLennan
Michelle G. Crighton	Bernard C. Grenon
Gerhard J. Seifner	Carole P. Karbonik
Rodney R. Neys	Pierre R. Dagenais
Donald J. McGarvey	J. Jay Haugen

Stuart W. Chambers

*Denotes Lawyer Whose Professional Corporation is a Member of the Partnership.

For full biographical listings, see the Martindale-Hubbell Law Directory

MILLER THOMSON (AV)

Suite 2700, Commerce Place, 10155 102nd Street, T5J 4G8
Telephone: 780-429-1751
Fax: 780-424-5866
Email: edmonton@millerthomson.ca *URL:* http://www.millerthomson.ca
Calgary, Alberta Office: Suite 3000, 700 Ninth Avenue S.W., Calgary, Alberta, T2P 3V4.
Telephone: 403-298-2400.
Fax: 403-262-0007.
Toronto, Ontario Office: 2500, 20 Queen Street West, Toronto, Ontario, M5H 3S1.
Telephone: 416-595-8500.
Fax: 905-415-6777.
York Region, Ontario Office: 60 Columbia Way, Suite 600, Markham, Ontario, L3R 0C9.
Telephone: 905-415-6700.
Fax: 905-415-6777.
Law Firm Affiliations/Associations:
Campney & Murphy - Vancouver, British Columbia, Canada
McCarter Grespan Robson Beynon - Kitchener, Ontario
Azevedo Sette Advogados - Sao Paulo and Belo Horizonte, Brazil, South America
Estudio Faraggi, Sateler & CIA - Santiago, Chile
Davis Arnold Cooper - London, England (Offices also in Manchester, Brussels, Vienna, Zurich, Madrid and Hong Kong)
Schürmann & Partners - Germany (Offices in Frankfurt, Berlin, Bonn, Dresden, Leipzig, Munich, Brussels, Milan, New York, Paris and Prague)
CONTACT: BRIAN W. L. TOD.
Telephone: 780-429-9723. E-mail: btod@millerthomson.ca.

Jack N. Agrios, Q.C.	Edwin S. Cook, Q.C.
John D. Neilson	Robert L. Duke
Brian W. L. Tod	William J. Kenny
Daniel C. Stachnik	John A. Cross
Richard H. Kennedy	James A. Duke
Joseph W. Yurkovich	Lorne A. Smart
Joanne H. Goss	Kathryn L. Dykstra
Constance I. Taylor	Frank H. Monaghan
Janice A. Agrios	Terrence M. Warner
D. A. Chankasingh	Scott J. Hammel
Marjorie E. Simington	Bruce N. Geiger
Ronald H. Haggett	Annette E. Koski
Douglas J. Forer	Anthony A. Morris
Darin J. Hannaford	Colleen F. Kinsella
Michael J. Pucylo	Jeff S. Paetz
G. James Thorlakson	Jordan A. Slator
Wendi P. Crowe	Sandra L. Hawes
Katrina M. Haymond	James L. Hutson
Lisa M. Balsillie	Stacey A. Denham

Kevin J. Klaassen

OF COUNSEL

The Hon. Samuel S. Lieberman, Q.C.	Gary G. Campbell, Q.C.
	David R. Percy

For full biographical listings, see the Martindale-Hubbell Law Directory

PARLEE MCLAWS (AV)

15th Floor Manulife Place, 10180 101st Street, T5J 4K1
Telephone: 403-423-8500
Telecopier: 403-423-2870
Email: lawyers@parlee.com *URL:* http://www.parlee.com
Calgary, Alberta Office: 3400 Petro-Canada Centre, 150 - 6th Avenue, SW.
Telephone: 403-294-7000.
Telecopier: 403-265-8263.

(See Next Column)

PARLEE MCLAWS—*Continued*

MEMBERS OF FIRM

Colin H. Kerr, Q.C.
Michael D. MacDonald
Kenneth F. Bailey, Q.C.
H. Douglas Montemurro
Roderick B. Davison, Q.C.
David G. Finlay
Richard W. Wilson
Robert G. McBean
Douglas L. Kennedy
David C. Rolf
Allan A. Garber
Robert P. James
Walter J. Pavlic
Jerri L. Cairns
Marco S. Poretti
R. Johnson Billingsley
John W. McClure
David S. Tam
Robert A. Newton, Q.C.
Terence A. Cockrall, Q.C.
Frank J. Niziol
F. Richard Haldane, Q.C.
Bruce D. Hirsche, Q.C.
Ian L. MacLachlan
James K. McFadyen
James T. Neilson
Jeremy H. H. Hockin
James F. McGinnis
Gregory W. Jaycock
Dane C. Wintermute
Brian J. Curial
Anthony W. Slemko
Kevin L. Lynch
Paul A. Shenher
Karen A. Smith
Galan T. Lund

ASSOCIATES

Christopher R. Head
Priscilla E. S. J. Kennedy
Sandra L. Corbett
Jamie E. Pytel
Rolinda D. Y. Mack
Shawn M. Johanson
Kim D. Watamaniuk
Carla L. Lamash
K. Colleen Verville
David L. Sharko
Diana W. Kwan
Lorne J. Ruzicka
Norah B. Ramsay
Bryan Maruyama
Thomas L.B. Carbone
George E. Flemming
Deborah J. Polny
J. Kristin Bryson
Gregory P. Nakonechny
Wendy N. Moody
Donn MacDougall
Sean P. Tindale
Randy S. Shapiro

COUNSEL

Edward H. Molstad, Q.C.

For full biographical listings, see the Martindale-Hubbell Law Directory

CANADA BRITISH COLUMBIA

*VANCOUVER,** Vancouver Co.

ALEXANDER, HOLBURN, BEAUDIN & LANG (AV)

P.O. Box 10057 2700 Toronto Dominion Bank Tower, 700 West Georgia Street, V7Y 1B8
Telephone: 604-688-1351
Fax: 604-669-7642
URL: http://www.ahbl.bc.ca
Hong Kong Office, In Association with Ong & Chung: Room 2101, 21/F Tower II, Admiralty Centre, No. 18 Harcourt Road.
Telephone: (852) 2526-1171.
Fax: (852) 2845-0686.

PARTNERS

Ernest A. Alexander, Q.C. (1918-1983)
F. Stuart Lang
James A. Dowler
Robert B. Kennedy
Michael V. Roche
Jo Ann Carmichael
David B. Wende
Gary M. Nijman
Ross Shamenski
Michel E. Giasson
Andrew S. MacKay
Sharleen L. Dumont
David A. Garner
D. Christopher Fong
William M. Holburn, Q.C.
Michael P. Ragona, Q.C.
Lawrance J. Gwozd
Michael C. Scholz
Roger M. Bourbonnais
R. Patrick Saul
Bruno De Vita
Terry C. Vos
Judith P. Kennedy
J. Dale Stewart
Darcie A. Laurient
Barbara L. Devlin
Eileen E. Vanderburgh
Todd R. Davies
David T. McKnight

CONTRACT LAWYER IN HONG KONG

Calvin Kam-Wing Chung

ASSOCIATES

David A. Gooderham
Sharon M. Urquhart
Brian D. Rhodes
Robert A. McLennan
Joseph P. Cahan
Peter V. Snell
Moira C. Wong
Susan Sangha
C. Larry Kyle
Dianna S. Hwang
Raymond C. K. Ho
Gregory S. Pun
Judy A. Rost
Parrish Kang-Kwan Kwan
Jeremy M. Poole
Christopher E. Hirst
Christine M. York
Desmond M. Balakrishnan
Norman D. Streu
Kirsten D. Hume
Melissa A. Apprill

(See Next Column)

Reference: The Toronto-Dominion Bank.
A list of Representative Clients will be furnished on request.

For full biographical listings, see the Martindale-Hubbell Law Directory

BLAKE, CASSELS & GRAYDON LLP (AV)

Suite 2600, Three Bentall Centre, 595 Burrard Street, V7X 1L3
Telephone: 604-631-3300
Facsimile: 604-631-3309
Email: vancouvr@blakes.com *URL:* http://www.blakes.com
The Firm maintains other offices in: Toronto and Ottawa, Ontario, Calgary, Alberta, London, England and Beijing, China.

PARTNERS

Josiah Wood, Q.C.
Anne M. Stewart, Q.C.
William C. Kaplan
Peter J. O'Callaghan
Jocelyn M. Kelley
Catherine E. H. Wade
Randy J. Kaardal
Scott A. Turner
Gayle Hunter
Wendy S. Morrison
Roger G. Howay
Peter C. Kalbfleisch
Paul R. Cassidy
Joanne B. Payne
Maria A. Morellato
Bill S. Maclagan
Joanne R. Lysyk
Jeffrey Merrick
Jennifer J. Lynch
Geoffrey S. Belsher
Peter A. Juk

COUNSEL

Marvin R.V. Storrow, Q.C.
Barbara L. Fisher

For full biographical listings, see the Martindale-Hubbell Law Directory

BULL, HOUSSER & TUPPER (AV)

Patent and Trade Mark Agents
A Member of McMillan Bull Casgrain
1055 West Georgia Street, Suite 3000, P.O. Box 11130, V6E 3R3
Telephone: 604-687-6575
Fax: 604-641-4949
Email address for each lawyer = lawyer's three initials@bht.com
Shanghai, China Office: 17/E2 Zhaofeng Universe Building, No. 1800, Zhong Shan West Road, Shanghai 200233, China.
Telephone: 86-21-6440-0015.
Fax: 86-21-6440-0021.

MEMBERS OF FIRM

Hamish C. Cameron
Barry O'N. Dryvynsyde, Q.C.
Daniel A. Webster, Q.C.
Philip B. Webber
R. Eric P. Maurice
Nils E. Daugulis
Alan N. Robertson
Douglas G. Morrison
William J. McFetridge
R. John Kearns
Elliott M. Myers
Christopher G. Speakman
George D. Burke (Managing Partner)
Herbert B. Regehr
Simon B. Margolis
Catherine L. Woods
Brian E. Taylor
E. Jane Milton
Penny A. Washington
John M. Sibley
Shelley F. O'Callaghan
Carmen S. Thériault (Partner)
Gregory D. Lewis (Partner)
William S. Garton (Partner)
William C. Bice, Q.C.
J.D. Lach Morrison
William G. Gooderham
William M. Burris
D. Larry Page
R. Brian Wallace
Grant K. Weaver
Robert W. Hunter
C. Decatur Howe
Judith B. Downes
John S. Haythorne
Ann Gourley
N. Victoria Gray, Q.C.
Howard L. Ehrlich
Lynda C. Darling
David R. Bain
David W. Bursey
R.S. Jindy Bhalla
Angela T.F. Mong
Karen Martin
Herbert J. Isherwood
Margaret H. Mason
Daniel R. Bennett
Marion V. Shaw
Clive M. Ansley (Resident, Shanghai, China Office)

ASSOCIATES

Vincent H. Kou (Resident, Shanghai, China Office)
Tim W. Clarke
I. Shane Nossal
M. Patti Towler
James H. Goulden
H. Beth Allard
Michael I. Burgar
John C.Y. Fang
Neva R. Beckie
Joshua B. Hauser
Joseph M. G. Shaw
Melody Robens-Paradise
Elizabeth M. Araujo
James (Jay) J. Lemoine
R. Max Collett
Wendy E. Woloshyn
Christopher S. Wilson
Craig E. Jones
Lloyd H. Hong
Lorne G. Milne
Michael B. Hetherington
Jean F. Billing
James E. Sutcliffe
Janet P. Grove
Sandra Carter
William E. Cascadden
Gwendoline C. Allison
David M. Hunter
Robin A. Wotherspoon
Scott R. Gibner
Sharon Dos Remedios
Jennie F. Yap
Eva K. Weclaw
Steve R. McKoen
Angela L. Grams
Tanya J. Rothe
Jacqueline A. Tahara
Julie A. Mosher
Kristine E. MacTaggart
Jennifer A. Scott

(See Next Column)

BULL, HOUSSER & TUPPER, *Vancouver—Continued*

ASSOCIATE COUNSEL

Wilfred J. Wallace, Q.C.
Edward F. Horsey, Q.C.
David Brander-Smith, Q.C.
Frank Low-Beer

For full biographical listings, see the Martindale-Hubbell Law Directory

CAMPNEY & MURPHY (AV)

2100-1111 West Georgia Street, P.O. Box 48800, V7X 1K9
Telephone: 604-688-8022
Facsimile: 604-688-0829
Email: cmlaw@campney.com *URL:* http://www.campney.com

MEMBERS OF FIRM

Marshall M. Soule
David P. Roberts, Q.C.
Robert F. Hungerford
Peter G. Bernard
Henning W. Wiebach
Robert J. MacRae
Robert D. Standerwick
Timothy J. Nichols
W. Bruce Tattrie
Christopher K. Haines
Colin M. Emslie
Deborah D. Anderson
Howie A. Caldwell
Paul C. MacNeill
Lynn C. Waterman
Ian M. Lawrenson
Shelley C. Fitzpatrick
Heather M. B. Ferris
Nevin L. Fishman
Andrew G. Kadler
Murray L. Smith
W. Gary Wharton
Paula M. Palyga
Elaine E. Reynolds
James P. Shumka
H. Peter Swanson
Thomas S. Hawkins
Iain R. Mant
Mark W. Hilton
Nicole J. Garson
Rupert M. Shore

ASSOCIATE COUNSEL

Denis W. H. Creighton (Retired)
John R. Cunningham, Q.C. (Retired)
W. Donald C. Tuck (Retired)
R. I. A. Smith (Retired)
John D. Montgomery

Reference: Bank of Montreal.

For full biographical listings, see the Martindale-Hubbell Law Directory

DAVIS & COMPANY (AV)

Lawyers
Patent & Trade Mark Agents
2800 Park Place, 666 Burrard Street, V6C 2Z7
Telephone: 604-687-9444
Facsimile: 604-687-1612
URL: http://www.davis.ca
Toronto, Ontario Office: 1 First Canadian Place, Suite 5300, P.O. Box 367, 100 King Street West, M5X 1E2.
Telephone: 416-365-6188.
Facsimile: 416-365-7886.
Montreal, Quebec Office: Davis Hara Rothschild, 1010 de la Gauchetière Street West, Place du Canada, Suite 2250, H3B 2N2.
Telephone: 514-392-1991.
Facsimile: 514-392-1999. URL: http://www.hara-rothschild.ca.
Whitehorse, Yukon Territory Office: Suite 200, 304 Jarvis Street, Y1A 2H2.
Telephone: 867-393-5100.
Facsimile: 867-667-2669.
Yellowknife, Northwest Territories Office: Suite 802 Northwest Tower, 5201 50th Avenue, X1A 3S9.
Telephone: 867-669-8400.
Facsimile: 867-669-8420.
Tokyo, Japan Office: New ATT Building 7F, 11-7, Akasaka 2-Chome, Minato-ku, 107-0052.
Telephone: 011-81-3-5563-0354.
Facsimile: 011-81-3-5563-2996.

MEMBERS OF FIRM

Arnold M. Abramson
Paul R. Albi
Robert T. Banno
Donald R. M. Bell
Matthew S. Bingham
Peter W. Bogardus
Frank S. Borowicz
Douglas Blair Buchanan
Michael P. Carroll, Q.C.
D. Ross Clark
Donald W. Cooper
David C. Davenport
Rhys Davies, Q.C.
Kathryn I. Denhoff
Warren H. Downs
Scott Dunlop
W. Ross Ellison
Robert A. Fashler
Patrick J. Furlong
Maria F. Giardini
Tracey P. Gibb
Robert T. Groves
Brian F. Hiebert
Albert J. Hudec
John J.L. Hunter, Q.C.
Rolf N. Kaplun
Jacqueline A. Kelly
Winston P. Kiang
Paul D. Lailey
P. John Landry
Peter C. Lee
Brian D. MacKay
Malcolm O. Maclean
Garry E. Mancell, R.P.F.
Robert E. Marriott
P. Anthony McArthur
John I. McLean
Rowland K. McLeod
Cynthia A. Millar
Keith E. W. Mitchell
R. Glenn Morgan
Vincent Morgan
Douglas C. Morley
Stuart B. Morrow
Linda Parsons
James I. Reynolds
Mary L. Ruhl
Dale G. Sanderson, Q.C.
John Saunders
Mark A. Schmidt
Wolfgang Schwegler
David H. Searle, C.M., Q.C.

(See Next Column)

MEMBERS OF FIRM (Continued)

Blair Shaw
Douglas G. Shields
Allen A. Soltan
James M. Sullivan
Robert B.D. Swift
Franco E. Trasolini
Peter G. Voith
Stanley Wong

ASSOCIATES

Lorne H. Beiles
Catherine J. Branch
Luciana Brasil
Robert F. Brookfield
Sandra L. Case
Grace G. Choi
Dean A. Crawford
Matthew K. Desharnais
Diana L. Dorey
Anneke Driessen van der Lieck
Emmet Duncan
Martin Ertl
David A. Fewer
Monika Gehlen
Catherine Gibson
Jason K. Herbert
Tamara L. Hunter
Tom Kaweski
Suzanne Marie Kennedy
David C. Knoll
Roger Douglas Lee
Marie H. LeFebvre
Leah D. Matthews
Elizabeth (Lisa) G. McDonald
Stephanie McHugh
Brent Allan Meckling
Craig Kisa Ngai-Natsuhara
Lisa Christine Osoba
Ingrid M. Otto
Sarah Pike
Michelle B. Pockey
Richard Press
Brian N. Radnoff
David Redford
Douglas Arthur Scullion
Kelly E. Slade-Kerr
Anna E. Stavrakov
K. Michael Stephens
Euan R. Taylor
Michael J. Todd
Jeffrey B. Waatainen
Simon Robert Wells
Daniel J. Wilgosh
J. Kevin Wright

ASSOCIATE COUNSEL

Brenda J. Brown
William H. Cooper
Janine A. S. Thomas
Rosanna Wong

COUNSEL

D.S.D. Hossie
David M. Johnston
D. H. C. Paterson
Alexander C. Robertson, Q.C.
Martin R. Taylor, Q.C.
L. Allan Williams, Q.C.

For full biographical listings, see the Martindale-Hubbell Law Directory

FARRIS, VAUGHAN, WILLS & MURPHY (AV)

P.O. Box 10026, Pacific Centre South Toronto Dominion Bank Tower, 2600-700 West Georgia Street, V7Y 1B3
Telephone: 604-684-9151
Telex: 04-507819
Fax: 604-661-9349
Cable Address: "Farem"
Email: info@farris.com

Hon. John Wallace deBeque Farris, Q.C. (1903-1970)

COUNSEL

C. Francis Murphy, Q.C.

MEMBERS OF FIRM

Peter Woods Butler, Q.C.
Jack M. Giles, Q.C.
R. Christopher Holmes
A. Keith Mitchell, Q.C.
Elizabeth J. Harrison, Q.C.
Alan J. Hamilton
George K. Macintosh, Q.C.
Mitchell H. Gropper, Q.C.
Hugh M. Matthews
Barry T. Gibson
Charles G. Pearson
Herbert D. Dodd
R. Hector MacKay-Dunn
Peter F. Parsons
Paul S. Richardson
Jeffrey J. Kay
Robert S. Anderson
Judy Jansen
Robert P. Sloman
Robert J. McDonell
Brock R. Rowland
Geoffrey N. M. Lewis
David I. McBride
Rupert A. Legge
James P. Hatton
Dean A. O'Leary
Donald L. Richards
Gordon A. Love
J. Kenneth McEwan
Cameron G. Belsher
Alison H. Narod
Marylee A. Davies
Maria K. McKenzie
Lisa A. Warren
M. Kevin Woodall

ASSOCIATES

Karen Shirley-Paterson
Michael Gianacopoulos
Brian R. Canfield
Ronald A. Chin
Heather L. Jones
Douglas A. Holl
Andre J. Cyr
Scott A. Dawson
Jennifer A. Farac
F. Derek Lew
Michael H. Korbin
Judith MacFarlane
Susan B. Horne
David J. Selley
Craig T. Munroe
Christine E. Coleman
Alan M. Shuster
Doug B. Muir
Teresa P. Budd
Trevor R. Scott
Ludmila B. Herbst
John A. McLachlan
Wendy K. Chan

Reference: The Toronto-Dominion Bank.

For full biographical listings, see the Martindale-Hubbell Law Directory

Vancouver—Continued

FASKEN MARTINEAU DUMOULIN (AV)

2100-1075 West Georgia Street, V6E 3G2
Telephone: 604-631-3131
Fax: 604-631-3232
Email: info@van.fasken.com *URL:* www.fasken.com
Fasken Martineau DuMoulin is a leading Canadian firm with a national and international practice and having offices in Toronto, Montreal, Quebec, Vancouver, New York and London. Please refer to listings in the respective city sections.
Toronto, Ontario Office: Toronto-Dominion Centre, Toronto Dominion Bank Tower, P.O. Box 20, M5K 1N6.
Telephone: 416-366-8381. Toll Free: 1-800-268-8424 (Ontario & Quebec).
Facsimile: 416-364-7813. EMail: info@tor.fasken.com. Website: www.fasken.com.
Montreal, Quebec Office: Stock Exchange Tower, Suite 3400, P.O. Box 242. 800 Place-Victoria H4Z 1E9.
Telephone: 514-397-7400. Toll-Free: 1-800-361-6266 (Ontario & Quebec).
Facsimile: 514-397-7600.
Telex: 05-24610 BUOY MTL. EMail: info@mlt.fasken.com. Website: www.fasken.com
Quebec City, Quebec Office: Immeuble Le Saint-Patrick, 140, rue Grande Allée est, bureau 800, G1R 5M8.
Telephone: 418-640-2000. Toll Free: 1-800-463-2827 (Ontario & Quebec).
Facsimile: 418-647-2455. EMail: info@qc.fasken.com. Website: www.fasken.com
New York, New York Office: Seagram Building, 375 Park Avenue, Suite 2608, 10152.
Telephone: 212-935-3203.
Facsimile: 212-935-4822. EMail: info@nyc.fasken.com. Website: www.fasken.com.
London, England Office: 10 Arthur Street, 5th Floor, EC4R 9AY.
Telephone: 71-929-2894.
Facsimile: 71-929-3634. EMail: info@lon.fasken.com. Website: www.fasken.com.

MEMBERS OF FIRM

Michael S. Allen
Leopold Amighetti, Q.C.
Richard J. Berrow
Andrew D. Borrell
James G. Carphin
W. Ian Cassie
Brian L. Child
Simon R. Coval
Donald M. Dalik
Michael A. Fitch
John F. Grieve
Andrew G. Haring
Christopher Harvey, Q.C.
Gavin H. Hume, Q.C.
Patricia L. Janzen
Cal B. Johnson
Anne L. B. Kober
Helen H. Low
J. Geoffrey Lyster
W. Stanley Martin
John S. McKercher
Robert A. Millar
William T. Morley
James S. Mutter
Richard J. Olson
Gary W. Ott
Marcel J. Peerson
James D. Piers
Lori Price
Frank S. Schober
Merrill W. Shepard
Peter H. Stafford, Q.C.
Barbara Vanderburgh
William Westeringh
Charles F. Willms
Alan D. Winter
Henri C. Alvarez
Mark D. Andrews
Murray B. Blok
H. Laing Brown
Lata Casciano
Gary Catherwood
Tracey M. Cohen
D. Geoffrey G. Cowper, Q.C.
Peter H. Finley
Edgar A. Frechette
Bruce R. Grist
Charles G. Harrison
Gregory J. Heywood
Michael W. Hunter
Helmut K. Johannsen
David W. Kington
Brent J. Lewis
Elizabeth B. Lyall
Thomas Manson
J. M. (Mitch) McCormick
Avon M. Mersey
Joyce A. Mitchell
Brent G. Mullin
Lorene A. Novakowski
Kevin P. O'Neill
Susan I. Paish
Scott L. Perrin
Marina A. Pratchett
Douglas G. S. Rae, Q.C.
Allan P. Seckel
Keith E. Spencer
Norman K. Trerise
Donald J. Weaver
Darrell J. Wickstrom
Paul C. Wilson
David Wotherspoon

ASSOCIATES

Stephen C. Best
Lynne M. Charbonneau
David Crerar
R. Paul Fairweather
Rebecca A. Finlay
Jennifer L. Harry
Theresa T. Johannsen
Clark B. Ledingham
David W. Little
Robert M. Lonergan
Gavin Marshall
David McDonald
Mark D. Okerstrom
W. Simon Patey
Felicity Schweitzer
Lisa J. Southern
Waldemar Braul
Lucas A. Corwin
Ron Ezekiel
Anna Feglerska
Brook Greenberg
Andrew P. Jackson
John M. Lauinger
Josh D. Lewis
Andrew Loh
Edmond C. C. Luke
Albert J. McClean
Andrew I. Nathanson
Alison J. Oxtoby
Kevin I. Price
Thora A. Sigurdson
George Waggott

(See Next Column)

ASSOCIATE COUNSEL

Holly A. Brinton
B. W. F. Fodchuk
Peter S. Hyndman
Lauri Ann Fenlon
D. M. M. Goldie
Steven G. Lukas
William R. McIntyre, C.C., Q.C.

For full biographical listings, see the Martindale-Hubbell Law Directory

FRASER MILNER (AV)

15th Floor, The Grosvenor Building, 1040 West Georgia Street, V6E 4H8
Telephone: 604-687-4460
Telecopier: 604-683-5214
Email: webmaster@frasermilner.com *URL:* http://www.frasermilner.com
Toronto, Ontario Office: 1 First Canadian Place, 100 King Street West, M5X 1B2.
Telephone: 416-863-4511.
Telecopier: 416-863-4592.
Fax: 416-367-6787.
Calgary, Alberta Office: 30th Floor, Fifth Avenue Place. 237 4 Avenue, S.W., T2P 4X7.
Telephone: 403-268-7000.
Fax: 403-268-3100.
Edmonton, Alberta Office: 2900 Manulife Place, 10180 - 101 Street, T5J 3V5.
Telephone: 780-423-7100.
Fax: 780-423-7276.
Ottawa, Ontario Office: 180 Elgin Street, Suite 1200, K2P 2K7.
Telephone: 613-783-9600.
Telecopier: 613-783-9690.

PARTNERS, CONSULTANTS AND ASSOCIATES

Michael R. Axford
Tim T. Bezeredi
Clayton W. Caverly
Alan W. Dabb
Jeevyn Dhaliwal
Gordon W. Esau
Gordon S. Funt
Robert A. Goodrich
G. Lisa Heddema
Benjamin J. Ingram
Howard J. Kellough, Q.C.
Alexander T. Levine
Lori Anne Mathison
Sara K. McCracken
Colin J. McIver
Robert G. Nikelski
Valorie A. Pawson
Jeffrey A. Read
Gary R. Sollis
Jason C. Stevens
Andrea J. Wales
James D. Beeby
Mary I.A. Buttery
Gary T. Clarke
Arnon A. Dachner
J. Thomas English, Q.C.
Paul D.K. Fraser, Q.C.
Kelly L. Geddes
Susan A. Griffin
Blair Horn
Stephanie A. Jackson
Douglas I. Knowles
Thomas M. Lutes
J. Donald Mawhinney, Q.C.
Michael J. McDonald
Bruce M. McKay
Joel A. Nitikman
Nicholas J. Preovolos
Juliet D.W. Smith
Neal S. Steinman
John G. R. Third
David A. Zacks

For full biographical listings, see the Martindale-Hubbell Law Directory

LADNER DOWNS (AV)

1200 Waterfront Centre, 200 Burrard Street, P.O. Box 48600, V7X 1T2
Telephone: 604-687-5744
Fax: 604-687-1415
Email: ldmaster@ladner-downs.com *URL:* http://www.ladner-downs.com

FIRM MEMBERS

Stephen Antle
Kenneth M. Bagshaw, Q.C.
Clive S. Bird
Jonty Bogardus
Ron L. Bozzer
David K. Camp
Nigel P.H. Cave
Barry D. Chase
Edward C. Chiasson, Q.C., F.C.I.Arb.,C.Arb.
G. Sidney Cross
Bradley W. Dixon
Martin D. Donner
Debra J. Finlay
Bradley J. Freedman
P. Craig Godsoe
Noel Z. Golden
Do-Ellen S. Hansen
Jonathan K.M. Jeske
Vincent P. Johnston
Joseph P.C. Lee
Sandy Lloyd
Paul J. Lowry
Mary Locke Macaulay
Heidi E. Massel
D. Ross McGowan
Jennifer D. McNaught
David L. Miachika
Shelley-Mae Mitchell
Stephen J. Mulhall
Otto Hans Nowak
Vincent R. K. Orchard
Peter M. Archibald, Q.C.
Diana D. Batts
Donald G. Bird
Barbara E. Boytinck
Jason J. Brooks
Mary Jo E. Campbell
Joan C. Chambers
Valli Chettiar
Michael A. Coady
Douglas G. Copland
Neil de Gelder, Q.C.
G. Eric Doherty
Douglas R. Eyford
Patrick G. Foy, Q.C.
Gerald W. J. Ghikas, F.C.I.ARB.
Angus M. Gunn, Jr.
Larry R. Jackie
Gordon R. Johnson
Warren B. Learmonth
Mark V. Lewis
David C.S. Longcroft
Russell W. Lusk, Q.C.
P. Donald MacDonald
Roger D. McConchie
John C. McLeod
William K. McNaughton
William R. Miles
Sean A. Muggah
David P. L. Mydske
Christopher J. O'Connor
Stephanie Jane Osatenko

(See Next Column)

LADNER DOWNS, *Vancouver—Continued*

FIRM MEMBERS (Continued)

Deborah H. Overholt
Sudhir K. Padmanabhan
Katrina K. Pierce
David R. Poore
Siobhan H. Sams
Douglas R. Sanders
Timothy R. Sehmer
Robert D. Shaw
Robert R. Shouldice
Debra L. Sing, Q.C.
Michael A. Skene
Ambrose H.Y. Sung
Evan R. Taylor
Jeffrey S. Thomas
Shelley M. Tratch
Magnus C. Verbrugge
Graham B. Walker
Ian A. Webb
Trevor J. Wiebe
Warren T. Wilson, Q.C.
Jann M. Winters
Robert G. Owen
C. R. Laurence Peers
Fred R. Pletcher
John L. Sampson
Oren Samuel
Larry R. Sandrin
Catherine Shaley
Key-Yong Shin
David C. Sinclair
William F. Sirett
Barbara E. Smith
G. Ross Switzer
Brian W. Thom
Geoffrey Thompson
Kenneth J. Tyler
Deron P. Waldock
Mark A. Wang
Max J. Weder
Gary J. Wilson
Steve M. Winder
Andrew C. Wood
P. James Zibarras

ASSOCIATE COUNSEL

Charles C. Locke, Q.C.

For full biographical listings, see the Martindale-Hubbell Law Directory

LAWSON LUNDELL LAWSON & MCINTOSH (AV)

1600 Cathedral Place, 925 West Georgia Street, V6C 3L2
Telephone: 604-685-3456
Facsimile: 604-669-1620
Email: genmail@lawsonlundell.com *URL:* http://www.lawsonlundell.com
Calgary, Alberta Office: Suite 850, 300 - 5th Avenue S.W., T2P 3C4.
Telephone: 403-269-6900.
Facsimile: 403-269-9494.
Yellowknife, Northwest Territories Office: Suite 204, 4817 - 49th Street, X1A 3S7. Telephone 867-669-9990.
Facsimile: 867-669-9991.

SENIOR COUNSEL

Reginald J. Gibbs, Q.C. (Resident, Calgary, Alberta Office)

MEMBERS AND ASSOCIATES

James H. Lawson, Q.C. (1955)
David A. Lawson (1975)
John M. Tennant (Retired 1998)
David J. Smith
John O.E. Lundell
John G. Trueman
William F. Dickson
Alastair G. Miller
William M. Everett, Q.C.
Stephen McCullough
Anthony W. Ryan
Walter G. Rilkoff
M. Patricia Gallivan
Chris W. Sanderson
J. Edward Gouge, Q.C.
Brian D. Fulton
Gordon C. Weatherill
David L. Adderley
Edward L. Wilson
Rodney L. Hayley
Murray T.A. Campbell
Irving D. Laskin
Gordon R. Chambers
K. Alan Blair
David A. Allard
Thomas S. Woods
Ian C. MacLeod
Lisa A. Peters
Clifford G. Proudfoot
Craig A.B. Ferris
Michael J. Low
Lisa A. Bugry
John T.C. Christian
Valerie C. Mann
Cecilia A. Low (Resident, Calgary, Alberta Office)
Jeff Christian
Anne M. Dobson-Mack
Peggy Grace
Patricia D. Burchmore
Elissa F. Amighetti
John M. Olynyk
Karl J. Bomhof (Resident, Calgary, Alberta Office)
Keith B. Bergner
Catherine A. Graham
Oscar F. Lundell, Q.C. (1982)
G. Buchan McIntosh, Q.C. (Retired 1992)
Robert J. Mair, Q.C.
Lorne D. Peterson
Brian J. Wallace, Q.C.
Gregory T.W. Bowden, Q.C.
David L. Rice
Douglas F. Robinson, Q.C.
John H. Fraser
Paul D. Bradley
Christopher G. Baldwin
J. Martin Kyle
Gordon M. Craig
Kelly R. Doyle
L. Neil Marshall
S. Bradley Armstrong
John Smith
Peter D. Feldberg
M.J. (Peggy) O'Brien
A.W. (Sandy) Carpenter
Randolph G. Klarenbach
Jerrold W. Schramm
Maureen E. Baird
Ron A. Skolrood
Rita C. Andreone
H. Jane Murdoch
Melanie C. Samuels
Leslee J. Warren (Not admitted in BC)
Leonard Glass
Robert A. Sider
Christine A. MacLean
Clara Y.K. Tsang
James D. Fraser
Reinhold G. Krahn
Diana Valiela
Jill M. Shore
Khaled S. Abdel-Barr
Andrew G. Stephens
Treva D. London
Cydney J. Elofson (Resident, Calgary, Alberta Office)
Catherine Davies
Michael L. Lee
Steven W. Lesiuk

(See Next Column)

MEMBERS AND ASSOCIATES (Continued)

Tanya N. Punjabi
Kenneth E. Burns
Benjamin P. Slager
Michael E. Tenta
John C. Kleefeld
Karen L. MacMillan
Laura J. Mills
Suzanne R. Mercier
Katherine H. Stephens
Sheri Allen-Fawkes
Charles B. Hotel
Tania Tomaszewska
Maria D. Preovolos
Anne E. Fitzpatrick
D. Michael Bain
Michael B. Morgan

For full biographical listings, see the Martindale-Hubbell Law Directory

MACKENZIE FUJISAWA BREWER STEVENSON (AV)

1800 - 400 Burrard Street, V6C 3A6
Telephone: 604-689-3281
Facsimile: 604-685-6494

PARTNERS

George K. Fujisawa, Q.C. (1928-1998)
Graham C. MacKenzie
Robert W. Brewer
Robert W. Stevenson
Ken V. Krohman
Perry A. Mazzone
Michael D. Tatchell
Michael D. Murphy
Judy G. Williams
Patrick M. Holmes
Robert V. Wickett

ASSOCIATES

Brian J. Konst
Raymond D. Leong
Pamela J. Quesnel
Brian C. Poston

ASSOCIATE COUNSEL

Robert H. Wynick

Reference: The Royal Bank of Canada.

For full biographical listings, see the Martindale-Hubbell Law Directory

MCCARTHY TÉTRAULT (AV)

P.O. Box 10424, Pacific Centre, Suite 1300, 777 Dunsmuir Street, V7Y 1K2
Telephone: 604-643-7100
Fax: 604-643-7900
Email: vancouver@mccarthy.ca *URL:* http://www.mccarthy.ca
Surrey, British Columbia Office: Suite 1300, Station Tower, Gateway, 13401-108th Avenue, Surrey, British Columbia V3T 5T3.
Telephone: 604-583-9100.
Fax: 604-583-9150.
Calgary, Alberta Office: Suite 3300, 421 7th Avenue, S.W., Calgary, Alberta T2P 4K9.
Telephone: 403-260-3500.
Facsimile: 403-260-3501.
London, Ontario Office: Suite 2000, One London Place, 255 Queens Avenue, London, Ontario N6A 5R8.
Telephone: 519-660-3587.
Facsimile: 519-660-3599.
Toronto, Ontario Office: Suite 4700, Toronto Dominion Bank Tower, Toronto, Ontario M5K 1E6.
Telephone: 416-362-1812.
Facsimile: 416-868-0673.
Ottawa, Ontario Office: The Chambers, Suite 1400, 40 Elgin Street, Ottawa, Ontario K1P 5K6.
Telephone: 613-238-2000.
Facsimile: 613-563-9386.
Montréal, Québec Office: Le Windsor, 1170 rue Peel, Montréal, Québec H3B 4S8.
Telephone: 514-397-4100.
Facsimile: 514-875-6246.
Québec, Québec Office: Le Complexe St-Amable 1150, Claire-Fontaine, 7e étage Québec, Québec G1R 5G4. Telephone 418-521-3000.
Facsimile: 418-521-3098, 418-521-3099.
United Kingdom and Europe Office: Pountney Hill House, 6 Laurence Pountney Hill, London, England EC4R 0BL.
Telephone: 011-44-171-216-2888.
Facsimile: 011-44-171-216-2888.

PARTNERS

Sholto Hebenton, Q.C.
Winton K. Derby, Q.C.
John W. Pearson
Trevor W. Bell (Managing Partner)
Ashley F. Hilliard
D. Anthony Knox
A. Brent Kerr
R. Barry Fraser
Earl G. Phillips
Peter D. Fairey
Alan H. Brown
Richard J. Balfour
Peter Kenward
Robin Sirett
Karen M. Gilmore
Sally Dennis
John A. Doolan
Linda G. Parker
Timothy P. McCafferty
R. Paul Beckmann, Q.C.
Robert Sewell
Byran Gibson
Rosemarie Wertschek, Q.C.
James A. Titerle
Keith E. Burrell
Derek Winnett
Michael E. Mitchell
Peter A. Pagnan
Donna J. Cooke
Gabriel M. Somjen
Brian E. Vick
Elaine J. Adair
Elizabeth M. Vogt
Robert W. Cooper
Herman Van Ommen
Scott A. Griffin
Ted I. Koffman
Bronson Toy
Kevin Wright

(See Next Column)

McCARTHY TÉTRAULT—*Continued*

PARTNERS (Continued)

Dawn P. Whittaker
Russell G. Benson
B. Glenn Leung
Nicholas R. Hughes
Linda Brown
Timothy S. Kwan
H. William Veenstra
Julie L. Owen
Warren B. Milman
George W. Holloway
Ariel DeJong
Colin S. McIvor
Ed Kroft
Beverly G. Ellingson
K. Beth Macdonald
Thomas D. Ciz
Lisa Martz
Christopher L.T. Falk

ASSOCIATES

Noreen V. Brox
Elizabeth H. Yip
Naomi M. Youngson
Sandra Draibye
Matthew D. Peters
Carolyn Ritchie
Kathryn Lever
Scott Smythe
Marja Bulmer
Laura E. Bliss
Michelle S. Lawrence
Daniel J. Lipetz
Nancy A. Trott
Maureen S. Boyd
Joyce Lee
Michael Wilhelmson
Justine G. Mercer
Jenifer C. Gentle
Brenda Lightbody
Michael G. Urbani
Tina Thomas
John M. Cameron
Sylvia R. Lee
Peter L. Regier

COUNSEL

John B. Zaozirny, Q.C.
Nicolaas A. Blom

ASSOCIATE COUNSEL

John Lutes
Leonard T. Doust, Q.C.

For full biographical listings, see the Martindale-Hubbell Law Directory

OGILVY RENAULT (AV)

800 Park Place, 666 Burrard Street, V6C 3P3
Telephone: 604-806-0922
Fax: 604-806-0933
Email: info@ogilvyrenault.com *URL:* http://www.ogilvyrenault.com
Montréal, Québec Office: Suite 1100, 1981 McGill College Avenue, H3A 3C1.
Telephone: 514-847-4747.
Fax: 514-286-5474. Email: info@ogilvyrenault.com
Ottawa, Ontario Office: Suite 1600, 45 O'Connor Street, K1P 1A4.
Telephone: 613-780-8661.
Fax: 613-230-5459. Email: ottawa@ogilvyrenault.com
Québec, Québec Office: Suite 520, 500 Grande Allée est, G1R 2J7.
Telephone: 418-640-5000.
Fax: 418-640-1500. Email: quebec@ogilvyrenault.com
Toronto, Ontario Office: Suite 2100, P.O. Box 141, Royal Trust Tower, TD Centre, M5K 1H1.
Telephone: 416-216-4000.
Fax: 416-216-3930. Email: toronto@ogilvyrenault.com
London, England Office: 38 Charterhouse Square, EC1M 6EQ, England.
Telephone: 44 (0) 207-600-9005.
Fax: 44 (0) 207-600-9006. Email: info@ogilvyrenault.com

Matthew Cooperwilliams
Patrick A. McE. Gilligan-Hackett
Julie D. Platz
Delayne M. Sartison
Kim G. Thorne
David W. Garner
Graeme Michael McFarlane
Gregory J. Nash
Thomas A. Roper, Q.C.
Randy C. Sutton
Michael A. Wagner

For full biographical listings, see the Martindale-Hubbell Law Directory

OWEN, BIRD (AV)

Affiliated with Aird & Berlis, Toronto, Ontario.
29th Floor Three Bentall Centre, 595 Burrard Street, P.O. Box 49130, V7X 1J5
Telephone: 604-688-0401
Telecopier: 604-688-2827
URL: http://www.owenbird.com

MEMBERS OF FIRM

Walter S. Owen, Q.C. (1904-1981)
John I. Bird, Q.C. (Retired)
William E. Ireland, Q.C.
Derek H. Standfield
D. Barry Kirkham, Q.C.
Robin C. Macfarlane
J. David Dunn
Richard H. Hamilton, Q.C.
Douglas R. Johnson
Michael J. Bird
William G. Farish
Ronald J. Argue
Tobin S. Robbins
Katherine J. Heller
Josephine Margolis Nadel
Florence T. Wong
Jack H. Grant
James A. Hall
Ian W. Muirhead
Daniel W. Burnett
Harvey S. Delaney
Christopher P. Weafer
James L. Carpick
Paul J. Brown
Michael G. Demers
Patrick J. Haberl
Sara E. Pope
James Brennan
Gregory J. Tucker
Valerie L. Strike
Nazeer T. Mitha

(See Next Column)

ASSOCIATES

Allison R. Kuchta
Heather E. Maconachie
David C. Hendricks
Harley J. Harris
Cheryl M. Teron
Christopher Forguson
Catherine Vrabec
Shelan R. Miller
Nancy M. Deshaw (Not admitted in BC)
Brett S. Baker
Mark J. Morabito

For full biographical listings, see the Martindale-Hubbell Law Directory

PAINE EDMONDS (AV)

Suite 1100, 510 Burrard Street, V6C 3A8
Telephone: 604-683-1211
Facsimile: 604-681-5084
Email: law@paine-edmonds.com

W. H. Kemp Edmonds, Q.C. (1916-1986)

MEMBERS OF FIRM

J. Lyle Woodley, Q.C.
James C. Taylor
Elmer A. Yusep
Owen G. Jones
Henry D. M. Edmonds
Steven H. Heringa
John J. Hyde
Bradford D. S. Garside
Kirsten J. Madsen

ASSOCIATES

John Bancroft-Jones
P. L. (Lee) Quinton
S. Jane Clasby
Siobhan Elizabeth Rea
Gary Michael Hagel

OF COUNSEL

Leonard C. Dudley

Reference: Toronto Dominion Bank.

For full biographical listings, see the Martindale-Hubbell Law Directory

SINGLETON URQUHART (AV)

1200 - 1125 Howe Street, V6Z 2K8
Telephone: 604-682-7474
Fax: 604-682-1283
Email: reception@singleton.com *URL:* http://www.singleton.com

John R. Singleton, Q.C.
Derek A. Brindle
Dale B. Pope
David G. Butcher
Mark D. Nordman
Jeffery A. Hand
C. L. (Kate) Mclean
Michael J. Hewitt

ASSOCIATE COUNSEL

Glenn A. Urquhart, Q.C.
Bonita J. Thompson, Q.C.
Rolf Weddigen
J. M. (Tim) Mackenzie
Susan Grattan-Doyle
Roger E. Holland

Representative Clients: Agra Industries; Architectural Institute of British Columbia; Attorney General of British Columbia; Attorney General of Canada; British Columbia Hydro and Power Authority; B.C. Rail Ltd; B.C. Gas Utility Ltd.; Chubb Insurance Company of Canada; ENCON Group Inc.

For full biographical listings, see the Martindale-Hubbell Law Directory

STIKEMAN ELLIOTT (AV)

666 Burrard Street, Suite 1700, Park Place, V6C 2X8
Telephone: 604-631-1300
Fax: 604-681-1825
Email: info@stikeman.com *URL:* http://www.stikeman.com
Montreal, Quebec Office: 1155 René-Lévesque Boulevard West, 40th Floor, H3B 3V2.
Telephone: 514-397-3000.
Fax: 514-397-3222.
Toronto, Ontario Office: Commerce Court West, 53rd Floor, M5L 1B9.
Telephone: 416-869-5500.
Fax: 416-947-0866.
Ottawa, Ontario Office: 50 O'Connor Street, Suite 914, K1P 6L2.
Telephone: 613-234-4555.
Fax: 613-230-8877.
Calgary, Alberta Office: 855 - 2nd Street S.W., 1500 Bankers Hall, T2P 4J7.
Telephone: 403-266-9000.
Fax: 403-266-9034.
New York, New York Office: 126 East 56th Street, 14th Floor, Tower 56, 10022.
Telephone: 212-371-8855.
Fax: 212-371-7087.
London, England Office: Regis House, 45 King William Street, EC4R 9AN.
Telephone: +44 (0) 20 7648 1300.
Fax: +44 (0) 20 7648 1400.
Hong Kong Office: 29 Queen's Road Central, Suite 1103, Aon China Building.
Telephone: 852-22305200.
Fax: 852-2845-9076.
Singapore Office: 1 Shenton Way, #13-07 Robina House, Singapore 068803.
Telephone: 65-532-3556.
Fax: 65-532-3557.

(See Next Column)

STIKEMAN ELLIOTT, *Vancouver—Continued*

Sydney, Australia Office: Level 40, The Chifley Tower, 2 Chifley Square.
Telephone: 61-2-9232-7199.
Fax: 61-2-9232-6908.

RESIDENTS IN VANCOUVER

John F. Anderson
R. Stuart (Tookie) Angus
David R. Brown
Janis D. Busse
Jonathan S. Drance
Deborah A. Fahy
David P. Farrell
David E. Gillanders
Richard J. Jackson
Eugene H. Kwan
Susan E. Lloyd
Ross A. MacDonald
Stuart A. MacKenzie
Neville McClure
David A. Martin
John N. Paton
Gordon D. Phillips
Hein Poulus
Bruce D. Woolley

For full biographical listings, see the Martindale-Hubbell Law Directory

CANADA MANITOBA

*WINNIPEG,** Eastern Jud. Dist.

AIKINS, MACAULAY & THORVALDSON (AV)

Thirtieth Floor, Commodity Exchange Tower, 360 Main Street, R3C 4G1
Telephone: 204-957-0050
Fax: 204-957-0840
Email: amt@aikins.com *URL:* http://www.aikins.com

Sir James Aikins, K.B., K.C., LL.D. (1879-1929)
G.H. Aikins, D.S.O., Q.C., LL.D. (1910-1954)
John A. MacAulay, C.C., Q.C., LL.D. (1919-1978)
Hon. G.S. Thorvaldson, Q.C., LL.D. (1925-1969)

COUNSEL

Arthur V. Mauro, O.C., Q.C., KSG, LL.D., D.Comm.

MEMBERS OF FIRM

A. Lorne Campbell, O.C., C.D., LL.D., D.C.L., Q.C.
John S. Lamont, Q.C.
Roger J. Hansell, Q.C.
Michael J. Mercury, Q.C.
Hon. Duncan J. Jessiman, Q.C., LL.D.
A.J. Mercury, Q.C.
Martin H. Freedman, Q.C., C.Arb.
James E. Foran, Q.C.
Knox B. Foster, Q.C.
Raymond H.G. Flett, Q.C.
J. Timothy Samson, Q.C.
Winston F. Smith, Q.C.
Cyril G. Labman
Larry R. Crane, Q.C.
Bryan D. Klein
Charles L. Chappell
Colin R. MacArthur, Q.C.
Thomas P. Dooley
Rod E. Stephenson, Q.C.
Gerald D. Parkinson
Joel A. Weinstein, Q.C.
Duncan D. Jessiman, Q.C.
Edward L. Warkentin
E. Bruce Parker
Judith M. Blair
E. Wells Peever, Q.C.
David L. Voechting
Robert Gordon Sly
Daryl J. Rosin
James A. Ferguson
Kevin R. Bolt
G. Bruce Taylor
Richard L. Yaffe
Frank Lavitt
Herbert J. Peters
G. Todd Campbell
J. Milton Christiansen
Lori T. Spivak
David M. Carrick
Barbara M. Shields
Betty A. Johnstone
Fay-Lynn Katz
L. William Bowles
Jonathan B. Kroft
Kristin L. Gibson
J. Douglas Sigurdson
John R. Braun
Catherine E. Carlson
William K.A. Emslie
Allan F. Foran
Keith Ferbers
J. Guy Joubert
Thor J. Hansell
Brian D. Lerner
James C.R. Ludlow
Marianne Rivoalen
Michael E. Guttormson
Carmele N. Peter
Robert L. Tyler
Theodor E. Bock
Helga D. Van Iderstine
Barbara S. MacDonald
Philip T. Samyn
Nigel J. Thompson
Harley C. Boles
Graham E. Robson
Michelle R. Redekopp
David C. Filmon
Tyler J. Kochanski
Steven J. Kohn
David P. Negus
R. Reis Pagtakhan
David M. Wright
Robert C. Lee
Kathryn J. Durkin
Jennifer (JJ) Burnell
Gregory M. Fleetwood
Nicole M. Watson
Steven M. London
Rachel E. R. Margolis
Sonya C. McCoshen
Colin Pewarchuk
Gordon M. Peters
Lucia M. Stuhldreier
Adam R. Herstein
Brent C. Ross
Marla S. Singer
Todd W. Thomson
Curtis M. Unfried
Keith C. Eyrikson

Counsel for: Air Canada; Bank of Montreal; Boeing of Canada; Canada Safeway Limited; Canadian Medical Protective Assn.; The Great West Life Assurance Co.; John Labatt Limited; Russel Metals Inc.; Winnipeg Free Press.

For full biographical listings, see the Martindale-Hubbell Law Directory

CANADA NEW BRUNSWICK

*FREDERICTON,** York Co.

COX HANSON O'REILLY MATHESON (AV)

(Formerly Hanson Hashey)
Suite 400, Phoenix Square, P.O. Box 310, E3B 4Y9
Telephone: 506-453-7771
Fax: 506-453-9600
Email: fredericton@coxhanson.ca *URL:* http://www.coxhanson.ca
Halifax, Nova Scotia Office: Suite 1100, Purdy's Wharf Tower 1, P.O. Box 2380 Station Central RPO, B3J 3E5.
Telephone: 902-421-6262.
Fax: 902-421-3130. E-Mail: halifax@coxhanson.ca
Saint John, New Brunswick Office: 1212-One Brunswick Square, 1 Germain St. E2L 4V1.
Telephone: 506-652-7771.
Fax: 506-632-9600.
St. John's, Newfoundland Office: Scotia Centre, 401-235 Water Street, A1C 1B6.
Telephone: 709-726-3321.
Fax: 709-726-2992. E-Mail: stjohns@coxhanson.ca
Charlottetown, Prince Edward Island Office: Queen Square, Suite 202, 119 Queen Street, P.O. Box 875, Station Central, C1A 7L9.
Telephone: 902-894-7051.
Fax: 902-368-3762. E-Mail: charlottetown@coxhanson.ca

MEMBERS OF FIRM

H. A. Hanson, Q.C. (1909-1985)
David T. Hashey, Q.C.
David M. Norman, Q.C.
J. Ian M. Whitcomb, Q.C.
John M. Hanson, Q.C.
Walter D. Vail, Q.C.
Michael E. Bowlin
John D. Larlee, Q.C.
Bruce D. Hatfield, Q.C.
Julian A. G. Dickson, Q.C.
Anne D. Wooder
Terrence J. Morrison
Lucie Richard
Catherine M. Bowlen
J. Marc Richard

ASSOCIATES

Amanda J. Frenette
Monika M. L. Zauhar
Jade A. Spalding
William E. Gould
Christopher R. DeLong
Deborah M. Power
Corinne A. Godbout
Marc-Antoine Chiasson

For full biographical listings, see the Martindale-Hubbell Law Directory

MCINNES COOPER (AV)

Suite 600, 570 Queen Street, P.O. Box 610, E3B 5A6
Telephone: 506-458-8572
Fax: 506-458-9903
Email: mcrfton@mcrlaw.com *URL:* http://www.mcrlaw.com
Halifax, Nova Scotia Office: Summit Place, 1601 Lower Water Street, P.O. Box 730, B3J 2V1.
Telephone: 902-425-6500.
Fax: 902-425-6350. Email: mcrhfx@mcrlaw.com.
St. John's, Newfoundland Office: Baine Johnston Centre, 5th Floor, 10 Fort William Place, P.O. Box 5939, A1C 5X4.
Telephone: 709-722-8735.
Telecopier: 709-722-1763. Email: mcrsj@mcrlaw.com.
Moncton, New Brunswick Office: Place Moncton Place, 655 Main Street, P.O. Box 1368, E1C 8T6.
Telephone: 506-857-8970.
Fax: 506-857-4095. Email: mcrmctn@mcrlaw.com.
Charlottetown, Prince Edward Island Office: BDC Place, Suite 620, 119 Kent Street, C1A 1N3.
Telephone: 902-368-8473.
Fax: 902-368-8346. Email: mcrpei@mcrlaw.com.

PARTNERS

R. Bruce Eddy, Q.C.
David Duncan Young
Leonard T. Hoyt
Carol J. Downs

ASSOCIATES

David D. Eidt
Alan Rockwell
Patrick V. Windle
Steven D. Christie
Lise C. Landry

For full biographical listings, see the Martindale-Hubbell Law Directory

STEWART MCKELVEY STIRLING SCALES (AV)

Suite 600, Frederick Square, 77 Westmorland Street, P.O. Box 730, E3B 5B4
Telephone: 506-458-1970
Telecopier: 506-444-8974
Email: fredericton@smss.com *URL:* http://www.smss.com
Moncton, New Brunswick Office: Suite 601, Blue Cross Centre, 644 Main Street, P.O. Box 28051, E1C 9N4.
Telephone: 506-853-1970.
Telecopier: 506-858-8454. Email: moncton@smss.com

(See Next Column)

STEWART MCKELVEY STIRLING SCALES—*Continued*

Saint John, New Brunswick Office: 10th Floor, Brunswick House, 44 Chipman Hill, P.O. Box 7289 Station "A," E2L 4S6.
Telephone: 506-632-1970.
Telecopier: 506-652-1989. Email: saint-john@smss.com
Halifax, Nova Scotia Office: Suite 900, Purdy's Wharf Tower One, 1959 Upper Water Street, P.O. Box 997, B3J 2X2.
Telephone: 902-420-3200.
Telecopier: 902-420-1417. Email: halifax@smss.com
Sydney, Nova Scotia Office: 50 Dorchester Street, P.O. Box 820, B1P 6J1.
Telephone: 902-539-5135.
Telecopier: 902-539-8256. Email: sydney@smss.com
St. John's, Newfoundland Office: Cabot Place, 100 New Gower Street, P.O. Box 5038, A1C 5V3.
Telephone: 709-722-4270.
Telecopier: 709-722-4565. Email: st-johns@smss.com
Charlottetown, Prince Edward Island Office: 65 Grafton Street, P.O. Box 2140, C1A 8B9.
Telephone: 902-892-2485.
Telecopier: 902-566-5283. Email: charlottetown@smss.com

LAWYERS PRACTICING IN FREDERICTON, NEW BRUNSWICK OFFICE

J. Gordon Petrie, Q.C. — J.E. Britt Dysart
William B. Goss, Q.C. — Hugh J. Cameron
Frederick C. McElman — Allison J. McCarthy
Richard G. Petrie

COUNSEL

Hon. Gérard V. La Forest, Q.C. — Catherine A. Walsh

For full biographical listings, see the Martindale-Hubbell Law Directory

---

*MONCTON,** Westmorland Co.

MCINNES COOPER (AV)

Barristers, Solicitors & Trade Mark Agents
Place Moncton Place, 655 Main Street, P.O. Box 1368, E1C 8T6
Telephone: 506-857-8970
Fax: 506-857-4095
Email: mcrmctn@mcrlaw.com *URL:* http://www.mcrlaw.com
Halifax, Nova Scotia Office: Summit Place, 1601 Lower Water Street, P.O. Box 730, B3J 2V1.
Telephone: 902-425-6500.
Fax: 902-425-6350. Email: mcrhfx@mcrlaw.com.
St. John's, Newfoundland Office: Baine Johnston Centre, 5th Floor, 10 Fort William Place, P.O. Box 5939, A1C 5X4.
Telephone: 709-722-8735.
Telecopier: 709-722-1763. Email: mcrsj@mcrlaw.com.
Charlottetown, Prince Edward Island Office: BDC Place, Suite 620, 119 Kent Street, C1A 1N3.
Telephone: 902-368-8473.
Fax: 902-368-8346. Email: mcrpei@mcrlaw.com.
Fredericton, New Brunswick Office: Suite 600, 570 Queen Street, P.O. Box 610.
Telephone: 506-458-8572.
Fax: 506-458-9903. Email: mcrfton@mcrlaw.com.

PARTNERS

Eric LeDrew — Bernard F. Miller
Donna MacEwen

ASSOCIATES

John C. Friel, Q.C. — Christa A. Bourque
Christopher A. Borden — Sylvie C. Roussel

ASSOCIATED ATTORNEY

Robert E. Radford, Q.C.

COUNSEL

J. Fernand Landry, Q.C. — Frank J. McKenna

For full biographical listings, see the Martindale-Hubbell Law Directory

---

STEWART MCKELVEY STIRLING SCALES (AV)

Suite 601, Blue Cross Centre, 644 Main Street, P.O. Box 28051, E1C 9N4
Telephone: 506-853-1970
Telecopier: 506-858-8454
Email: moncton@smss.com *URL:* http://www.smss.com
Saint John, New Brunswick Office: 10th Floor, Brunswick House, 44 Chipman Hill, P.O. Box 7289 Station "A", E2L 4S6.
Telephone: 506-632-1970.
Telecopier: 506-652-1989. Email: saint-john@smss.com
Halifax, Nova Scotia Office: Suite 900, Purdy's Wharf Tower One, 1959 Upper Water Street, P.O. Box 997, B3J 4S6.
Telephone: 902-420-3200.
Telecopier: 902-420-1417. Email: halifax@smss.com
Fredericton, New Brunswick Office: Suite 600, Frederick Square, 77 Westmorland Street, P.O. Box 730, E3B 5B4.
Telephone: 506-458-1970.
Fax: 506-444-8974. Email: fredericton@smss.com
Sydney, Nova Scotia Office: 50 Dorchester Street, P.O. Box 820, B1P 6J1.
Telephone: 902-539-5135.
Telecopier: 902-539-8256. Email: sydney@smss.com

(See Next Column)

St. John's, Newfoundland Office: Cabot Place, 100 New Gower Street, P.O. Box 5038, A1C 5V3.
Telephone: 709-722-4270.
Telecopier: 709-722-4565. Email: st-johns@smss.com
Charlottetown, Prince Edward Island Office: 65 Grafton Street, P.O. Box 2140, C1A 8B9.
Telephone: 902-892-2485.
Telecopier: 902-566-5283. Email: charlottetown@smss.com

LAWYERS PRACTICING IN MONCTON, NEW BRUNSWICK OFFICE

Levi E. Clain, Q.C. — Stephen J. McNally
John E. Pöllabauer — Marie-Claude Bélanger-Richard
André G. Richard — Micheline T. Doiron
Jolène M. Richard

For full biographical listings, see the Martindale-Hubbell Law Directory

---

*SAINT JOHN,** Saint John Co.

CLARK DRUMMIE (AV)

40 Wellington Row, P.O. Box 6850, E2L 4S3
Telephone: 506-633-3800
Telecopier (Automatic): 506-633-3811
Email: cd@nbnet.nb.ca

MEMBERS OF FIRM

Thomas B. Drummie, Q.C. — Deno P. Pappas, Q.C.
Donald F. MacGowan, Q.C. — Willard M. Jenkins
M. Robert Jette — Barry R. Morrison, Q.C.
Terrence W. Hutchinson — Norman J. Bossé
W. Andrew LeMesurier — J. George Byrne
Ross A. Pierce — William B. Richards
Frederick A. Welsford — Sherrie R. Boyd
William C. Kean — Peter H. MacPhail
Ewan W. Clark — François M. Beaulieu
Mélanie Cyr — Michelle S. Brzak
Jonathan Westphal

OF COUNSEL

Richard W. Bird, Q.C. — L. Paul Zed

Reference: Royal Bank of Canada.

For full biographical listings, see the Martindale-Hubbell Law Directory

---

GILBERT, MCGLOAN, GILLIS (AV)

Suite 710, Mercantile Centre, 55 Union Street, P.O. Box 7174, E2L 4S6
Telephone: 506-634-3600
Telecopier: 506-634-3612
Mailing Address: P.O. Box 7174, Station "A", Saint John, New Brunswick, E2L 4S6
Email: gmg@gmglaw.com

T. Louis McGloan, Q.C. (1896-1986) — Adrian B. Gilbert, Q.C. (1895-1986)

MEMBERS OF FIRM

Donald M. Gillis, Q.C. — Douglas A. M. Evans, Q.C.
Thomas L. McGloan, Q.C. — Brenda J. Lutz, Q.C.
A. G. Warwick Gilbert, Q.C. — David N. Rogers
Rodney J. Gillis, Q.C. — Mark A. Canty

ASSOCIATES

Edward Veitch — Nathalie L. Godbout
Hugh J. Flemming, Q.C. — Bruce D. Grant
Anne F. MacNeill — J. Danie Roy
Nancy E. Forbes — Catherine A. Fawcett
Guy C. Spavold — Danys R.X. Delaquis
Claire B.N. Porter — James M. Barry

Representative Clients: Bank of Montreal; Canada Packers Ltd.; McCain Foods Ltd.; The Sunderland Steamship Protecting & Indemnity Association; Steamship Mutual Underwriting Association (Bermuda) Limited; Royal Insurance Co.; Wawanesa Mutual Insurance Co.; Dominion of Canada General Insurance Co.; Canadian General Insurance Co.

For full biographical listings, see the Martindale-Hubbell Law Directory

---

STEWART MCKELVEY STIRLING SCALES (AV)

10th Floor, Brunswick House, 44 Chipman Hill, P.O. Box 7289 Station "A", E2L 4S6
Telephone: 506-632-1970
Telecopier: 506-652-1989
Email: saint-john@smss.com *URL:* http://www.smss.com
Moncton, New Brunswick Office: Suite 601, Blue Cross Centre, 644 Main Street, P.O. Box 28051, E1C 9N4.
Telephone: 506-853-1970.
Telecopier: 506-858-8454. Email: moncton@smss.com
Fredericton, New Brunswick Office: Suite 600, Frederick Square, 77 Westmorland Street, P.O. Box 730, E3B 5B4.
Telephone: 506-458-1970.
Fax: 506-444-8974. Email: fredericton@smss.com
Halifax, Nova Scotia Office: Suite 900, Purdy's Wharf Tower One, 1959 Upper Water Street, P.O. Box 997, B3J 2X2.
Telephone: 902-420-3200.
Telecopier: 902-420-1417. Email: halifax@smss.com

(See Next Column)

STEWART MCKELVEY STIRLING SCALES, *Saint John—Continued*

Sydney, Nova Scotia Office: 50 Dorchester Street, P.O. Box 820, B1P 6J1.
Telephone: 902-539-5135.
Telecopier: 902-539-8256. Email: sydney@smss.com
St. John's, Newfoundland Office: Cabot Place, 100 New Gower Street, P.O. Box 5038, A1C 5V3.
Telephone: 709-722-4270.
Telecopier: 709-722-4565. Email: st-johns@smss.com
Charlottetown, Prince Edward Island Office: 65 Grafton Street, P.O. Box 2140, C1A 8B9.
Telephone: 902-892-2485.
Telecopier: 902-566-5283. Email: charlottetown@smss.com

LAWYERS PRACTICING IN SAINT JOHN, NEW BRUNSWICK OFFICE

Wayne R. Chapman, Q.C.
D. Hayward Aiton
Frederick D. Toole, Q.C.
Robert G. Vincent, Q.C.
Gerald S. McMackin
John D. Wallace
Kenneth B. McCullogh, Q.C.
Lynne M. Burnham
Michael D. Wennberg
Gregory S. Sinclair
James F. LeMesurier
Peter M. Klohn
Charles A. LeBlond
Stephen J. Hutchison
Rodney D. Gould
Darrell J. Stephenson
James D. Murphy
C. Paul W. Smith
Christopher J. Stewart
J. Paul M. Harquail
Cynthia J. Benson
Catherine A. Lahey

COUNSEL

E. Neil McKelvey, O.C., Q.C.

For full biographical listings, see the Martindale-Hubbell Law Directory

CANADA
NEWFOUNDLAND

*ST. JOHN'S,**

COX HANSON O'REILLY MATHESON (AV)

(Formerly O'Reilly Noseworthy)
Scotia Centre, 401-235 Water Street, A1C 1B6
Telephone: 709-726-3321
Telecopier: 709-726-2992
Email: stjohns@coxhanson.ca *URL:* http://www.coxhanson.ca
Fredericton, New Brunswick Office: Suite 400, Phoenix Square, P.O. Box 310, E3B 4Y9.
Telephone: 506-453-7771.
Fax: 506-453-9600.
Saint John, New Brunswick Office: 1212-One Brunswick Square, 1 Germain St. E2L 4V1.
Telephone: 506-652-7771.
Fax: 506-632-9600.
Halifax, Nova Scotia Office: Suite 1100, Purdy's Wharf Tower 1, P.O. Box 2380 Station Central RPO, B3J 3E5.
Telephone: 902-421-6262.
Fax: 902-421-3130. E-Mail: halifax@coxhanson.ca
Charlottetown, Prince Edward Island Office: Queen Square, 119 Queen Street, P.O. Box 875, Station Central, C1A 7L9.
Telephone: 902-894-7051.
Fax: 902-368-3762. E-Mail: charlottetown@coxhanson.ca

MEMBERS OF FIRM

Thomas J. O'Reilly, Q.C.
Ronald S. Noseworthy, Q.C.
John F. Roil, Q.C.
Reginald H. Brown, Q.C.
Roland C. Snelgrove
D. Richard Robbins
Randall W. Smith
Robert P. Stack
Paul M. McDonald
Sandra R. Chaytor
Jorge P. Segovia
F. Richard Gosse
Griffith D. Roberts
Peter D. Shea
H. Jason Hickman
Michelle A. Willette

For full biographical listings, see the Martindale-Hubbell Law Directory

MCINNES COOPER (AV)

Barristers, Solicitors & Trade Mark Agents
Baine Johnston Centre, 5th Floor, 10 Fort William Place, P.O. Box 5939, A1C 5X4
Telephone: 709-722-8735
Telecopier: 709-722-1763
Email: mcrsj@mcrlaw.com *URL:* http://www.mcrlaw.com
Halifax, Nova Scotia Office: Summit Place, 1601 Lower Water Street, P.O. Box 730, B3J 2V1.
Telephone: 902-425-6500.
Fax: 902-425-6350. Email: mcrhfx@mcrlaw.com.
Moncton, New Brunswick Office: Place Moncton Place, 655 Main Street, P.O. Box 1368, E1C 8T6.
Telephone: 506-857-8970.
Fax: 506-857-4095. Email: mcrmctn@mcrlaw.com.
Charlottetown, Prince Edward Island Office: BDC Place, Suite 620, 119 Kent Street, C1A 1N3.
Telephone: 902-368-8473.
Fax: 902-368-8346. Email: mcrpei@mcrlaw.com.

(See Next Column)

Fredericton, New Brunswick Office: Suite 600, 570 Queen Street, P.O. Box 610.
Telephone: 506-458-8572.
Fax: 506-458-9903. Email: mcrfton@mcrlaw.com.

PARTNER, HALIFAX OFFICE

Wylie Spicer, Q.C.

PARTNERS

James R. Chalker, Q.C.
W. Gary Rowe, Q.C.
Christine A. Fagan, Q.C.
John V. O'Dea
Deborah L. J. Hutchings
Caroline C. Watton
John M. Green, Q.C.
Thomas R. Kendell
J. David B. Eaton
Michael J. Crosbie
Philip J. Buckingham
Denis J. Mahoney

ASSOCIATES

Brock Myles
Genevieve M. Dawson
Jacqueline S. Bartlett
Gerrie N. Smith
Sandra A. Gogal
Dennis N. Clarke
D. Scott Worsfold
Jennifer Dawn Blackmore
William James O'Keefe

For full biographical listings, see the Martindale-Hubbell Law Directory

STEWART MCKELVEY STIRLING SCALES (AV)

Cabot Place, 100 New Gower Street, P.O. Box 5038, A1C 5V3
Telephone: 709-722-4270
Telecopier: 709-722-4565
Email: st-johns@smss.com *URL:* http://www.smss.com
Halifax, Nova Scotia Office: Suite 900, Purdy's Wharf Tower One, 1959 Upper Water Street, P.O. Box 997, B3J 2X2.
Telephone: 902-420-3200.
Telecopier: 902-420-1417. Email: halifax@smss.com
Sydney, Nova Scotia Office: 50 Dorchester Street, P.O. Box 820, B1P 6J1.
Telephone: 902-539-5135.
Telecopier: 902-539-8256. Email: sydney@smss.com
Fredericton, New Brunswick Office: Suite 600, Frederick Square, 77 Westmorland Street, P.O. Box 730, E3B 5B4.
Telephone: 506-458-1970.
Fax: 506-444-8974. Email: fredericton@smss.com
Moncton, New Brunswick Office: Suite 601, Blue Cross Centre, 644 Main Street, P.O. Box 28051, E1C 9N4.
Telephone: 506-853-1970.
Telecopier: 506-858-8454. Email: moncton@smss.com
Saint John, New Brunswick Office: 10th Floor, Brunswick House, 44 Chipman Hill, P.O. Box 7289 Station "A", E2L 4S6.
Telephone: 506-632-1970.
Telecopier: 506-652-1989. Email: saint-john@smss.com
Charlottetown, Prince Edward Island Office: 65 Grafton Street, P.O. Box 2140, C1A 8B9.
Telephone: 902-892-2485.
Telecopier: 902-566-5283. Email: charlottetown@smss.com

LAWYERS PRACTICING IN ST. JOHN'S, NEWFOUNDLAND OFFICE

Gordon M. Stirling, C.M., Q.C., LL.D. (1907-1985)
Francis J. Ryan, Q.C. (1926-1997)
Ernest G. Reid, Q.C.
Michael F. Harrington, Q.C.
Lewis B. Andrews, Q.C.
Augustus G. Lilly, Q.C.
Harold M. Smith
Geoffrey E. J. Brown
Janet M. Henley Andrews
Bruce C. Grant
Kenneth A. Templeton
William H. Goodridge
Colm St. Roch Seviour
Dennis J. Ryan
Neil L. Jacobs
Ian C. Wallace
R. Wayne Bruce
Daniel M. Boone
Paul L. Coxworthy
Maureen E. Ryan
Cecily Y. Strickland
Rodney J. Zdebiak

For full biographical listings, see the Martindale-Hubbell Law Directory

CANADA
NOVA SCOTIA

*HALIFAX,** Regional Munic. of Halifax

COX HANSON O'REILLY MATHESON (AV)

(Formerly Cox Downie)
Suite 1100, Purduy's Wharf Tower 1, P.O. Box 2380 Stn Central RPO, B3J 3E5
Telephone: 902-421-6262
Fax: 902-421-3130
Email: halifax@coxhanson.ca *URL:* http://www.coxhanson.ca
Fredericton, New Brunswick Office: Suite 400, Phoenix Square, P.O. Box 310, E3B 4Y9.
Telephone: 506-453-7771.
Fax: 506-453-9600.
Saint John, New Brunswick Office: 1212-One Brunswick Square, 1 Germain St. E2L 4V1.
Telephone: 506-652-7771.
Fax: 506-632-9600.

(See Next Column)

COX HANSON O'REILLY MATHESON—*Continued*

St. John's, Newfoundland Office: Scotia Centre, 401-235 Water Street, A1C 1B6.
Telephone: 709-726-3321.
Fax: 709-726-2992. E-Mail: stjohns@coxhanson.ca
Charlottetown, Prince Edward Island Office: Queen Square, Suite 202, 119 Queen Street, P.O. Box 875, Station Central, C1A 7L9.
Telephone: 902-894-7051.
Fax: 902-368-3762. E-Mail: charlottetown@coxhanson.ca

MEMBERS OF FIRM

George M. Mitchell, Q.C.
Robert G. MacKeigan, Q.C.
Michael S. Ryan, Q.C.
Daniel M. Campbell, Q.C.
John Arnold, Q.C.
Gregory I. North, Q.C.
Daniel F. Gallivan, Q.C.
Peter W. Gurnham, Q.C.
Thomas P. Donovan, Q.C.
Frederick P. Crooks, Q.C.
Terry L. Roane, Q.C.
Anthony L. Chapman, Q.C.
Michael E. Dunphy
J. Craig McCrea
Leslie J. Dellapinna
Brian W. Downie
Jamie S. Campbell
Robert W. Carmichael
Alan J. Dickson
A. James Musgrave
Lorraine P. Lafferty
Jan McKenzie
D. Kevin Latimer
Jocelyn M. Campbell
Jonathan R. Gale
Brian A. Tabor
Karen A. Fitzner
Daniel W. Ingersoll
Marc J. Belliveau
Colin J. Clarke

ASSOCIATES

David A. Mombourquette
P. Robert Arkin
John Anselm Keith
Sandra Olga Arab
D. Kevin Burke
George A. Monroe
Richard S. Niedermayer
John B. MacIsaac
Joey D. Palov
Michael B. Ganley
Jeffrey A. Hoyt
Michael James Messenger
Tim S. O'Leary

OF COUNSEL

Ronald J. Downie, Q.C.

Representative Clients: Air Canada; Association of Professional Engineers of N.S.; Canadian Imperial Bank of Commerce; Camp Hill Medical Centre; Canadian Medical Protective Association; Canadian Surety Co.; Coca Cola Ltd.; Institute of Chartered Accountants of N.S.; Maritime Telegraph & Telephone Co., Ltd.; Metropolitan Authority of Halifax-Dartmouth.

For full biographical listings, see the Martindale-Hubbell Law Directory

DALEY, BLACK & MOREIRA (AV)

400-The TD Centre, 1791 Barrington Street, P.O. Box 355, B3J 2N7
Telephone: 902-423-7211
Fax: 902-420-1744
Email: dbm@dbm.ns.ca *URL:* http://www.daleyblack.com

PARTNERS

John W. Alward, Q.C.
Edwin C. Harris, Q.C.
Richard W. Cregan, Q.C.
B. William Piercey, Q.C.
Peter J. MacKeigan, Q.C.
Alexander S. Beveridge, Q.C.
M. Gerard Tompkins, Q.C.
A. William Moreira, Q.C.
Robert L. Mellish
Wayne R. Marryatt
Marjorie A. Hickey, Q.C.
Gregory H. Cooper
David A. Cameron
Diana M. Musgrave
Kelly L. Greenwood

ASSOCIATES

Hayley E. Clarke
Raymond G. Adlington
Matthew G. Williams
M. Michelle Higgins

For full biographical listings, see the Martindale-Hubbell Law Directory

MCINNES COOPER (AV)

Barristers, Solicitors & Trade Mark Agents
Summit Place, 1601 Lower Water Street, P.O. Box 730, B3J 2V1
Telephone: 902-425-6500
Fax: 902-425-6350
Email: mcrhfx@mcrlaw.com *URL:* http://www.mcrlaw.com
St. John's, Newfoundland Office: Baine Johnston Centre, 5th Floor, 10 Fort William Place, P.O. Box 5939, A1C 5X4.
Telephone: 709-722-8735.
Telecopier: 709-722-1763. Email: mcrsj@mcrlaw.com.
Moncton, New Brunswick Office: Place Moncton Place, 655 Main Street, P.O. Box 1368, E1C 8T6.
Telephone: 506-857-8970.
Fax: 506-857-4095. Email: mcrmctn@mcrlaw.com.
Charlottetown, Prince Edward Island Office: BDC Place, Suite 620, 119 Kent Street, C1A 1N3.
Telephone: 902-368-8473.
Fax: 902-368-8346. Email: mcrpei@mcrlaw.com.
Fredericton, New Brunswick Office: Suite 600, 570 Queen Street, P.O. Box 610.
Telephone: 506-458-8572.
Fax: 506-458-9903. Email: mcrfton@mcrlaw.com.

(See Next Column)

PARTNERS

Reginald A. Cluney, Q.C.
Stewart McInnes, P.C., Q.C.
Alan J. Stern, Q.C.
George T. H. Cooper, Q.C.
David H. Reardon, Q.C.
George W. MacDonald, Q.C.
Robert G. Belliveau, Q.C.
Lawrence A. Freeman
F. Van W. Penick
Christopher C. Robinson, Q.C.
Thomas E. Hart
Peter M. S. Bryson
Scott C. Norton
Fae J. Shaw
Stephen Kingston
John H. (Jack) Graham
David S. Mac Dougall
Barry D. Horne
Harry E. Wrathall, Q.C.
Lawrence J. Hayes, Q.C.
Joseph A. F. Macdonald, Q.C.
Peter J. E. McDonough, Q.C.
James E. Gould, Q.C.
Eric Durnford, Q.C.
Peter McLellan, Q.C.
Wylie Spicer, Q.C.
John D. Stringer, Q.C.
Harvey L. Morrison
David A. Graves
Marcia L. Brennan
Deborah K. Smith
Malcolm D. Boyle
John Kulik
Aidan J. Meade
Noella Martin
G. Grant Machum
Michelle C. Awad

ASSOCIATES

Bruce S. Russell
Hugh Wright
Henry A. Visser
Paul McLean
Tara A. Miller
Jennifer A. Healy
Bernadine MacAulay
Janet Clark
Brenda L. Rice-Thomson
Frank E. Hughes
Jeffrey R. Blucher
Tara A. Erskine
Rebecca Saturley
Matthew O'Halloran
Jane O'Neill
Kristi Sebalj

COUNSEL

Hector McInnes, Q.C.

For full biographical listings, see the Martindale-Hubbell Law Directory

STEWART MCKELVEY STIRLING SCALES (AV)

Suite 900, Purdy's Wharf Tower One, 1959 Upper Water Street, P.O. Box 997, B3J 2X2
Telephone: 902-420-3200
Telecopier: 902-420-1417
Email: halifax@smss.com *URL:* http://www.smss.com
Sydney, Nova Scotia Office: 50 Dorchester Street, P.O. Box 820, B1P 6J1.
Telephone: 902-539-5135.
Telecopier: 902-539-8256. Email: sydney@smss.com
Fredericton, New Brunswick Office: Suite 600, Frederick Square, 77 Westmorland Street, P.O. Box 730, E3B 5B4.
Telephone: 506-458-1970.
Fax: 506-444-8974. Email: fredericton@smss.com
Moncton, New Brunswick Office: Suite 601, Blue Cross Centre, 644 Main Street, P.O. Box 28051, E1C 9N4.
Telephone: 506-853-1970.
Telecopier: 506-858-8454. Email: moncton@smss.com
Saint John, New Brunswick Office: 10th Floor, Brunswick House, 44 Chipman Hill, P.O. Box 7289 Station "A", E2L 4S6.
Telephone: 506-632-1970.
Telecopier: 506-652-1989. Email: saint-john@smss.com
St. John's, Newfoundland Office: Cabot Place, 100 New Gower Street, P.O. Box 5038, A1C 5V3.
Telephone: 709-722-4270.
Telecopier: 709-722-4565. Email: st-johns@smss.com
Charlottetown, Prince Edward Island Office: 65 Grafton Street, P.O. Box 2140, C1A 8B9.
Telephone: 902-892-2485.
Telecopier: 902-566-5283. Email: charlottetown@smss.com

LAWYERS PRACTICING IN HALIFAX, NOVA SCOTIA OFFICE

J. William E. Mingo, Q.C.
John D. Moore, Q.C.
J. Thomas MacQuarrie, Q.C.
George A. Caines, Q.C.
David A. Stewart, Q.C.
James S. Cowan, Q.C.
Donald H. McDougall, Q.C.
John S. McFarlane, Q.C.
Richard K. Jones, Q.C.
Douglas J. Mathews, Q.C.
Carman G. McCormick, Q.C.
William L. Ryan, Q.C.
David Miller, Q.C.
John D. Murphy, Q.C.
John D. Plowman
Jonathan C. K. Stobie, Q.C.
Robert P. Dexter, Q.C.
Timothy C. Matthews, Q.C.
Karin A. McCaskill
Robert G. Grant, Q.C.
Brian G. Johnston, Q.C.
Mark E. MacDonald, Q.C.
Glen V. Dexter
Nancy I. Murray
T. Arthur Barry
Elizabeth M. Haldane
Charles S. Reagh
D. Geoffrey Machum
John MacL. Rogers
Lawrence J. Stordy
Richard A. Hirsch
D. Fraser MacFadyen
R. Blois Colpitts
James M. Dickson
David P. S. Farrar
Paul W. Festeryga
Elizabeth Jollimore
Maurice P. Chiasson
Virve Sandstrom
Mark S. Bursey
M. Ross Langley
Roderick H. Rogers
Andrew V. Burke
James L. Chipman
Nancy G. Rubin

(See Next Column)

STEWART MCKELVEY STIRLING SCALES, *Halifax—Continued*

COUNSEL

Sir Graham Day
Hugh K. Smith, Q.C.

Representative Clients: The Royal Bank of Canada; Canadian General Insurance; Prudential Insurance; Guardian Insurance; Allstate Insurance; Sun Life Assurance Company of Canada; Royal Insurance; Victoria Insurance; Bowater Mersey Paper Co.; Eastern Telephone and Telegraph Co.

For full biographical listings, see the Martindale-Hubbell Law Directory

*SYDNEY,** Cape Breton Co.

STEWART MCKELVEY STIRLING SCALES (AV)

50 Dorchester Street, P.O. Box 820, B1P 6J1
Telephone: 902-539-5135
Telecopier: 902-539-8256
Email: sydney@smss.com *URL:* http://www.smss.com
Halifax, Nova Scotia Office: Suite 900, Purdy's Wharf Tower One, 1959 Upper Water Street, P.O. Box 997, B3J 2X2.
Telephone: 902-420-3200.
Telecopier: 902-420-1417. Email: halifax@smss.com
Moncton, New Brunswick Office: Suite 601, Blue Cross Centre, 644 Main Street, P.O. Box 28051, E1C 9N4.
Telephone: 506-853-1970.
Telecopier: 506-858-8454. Email: moncton@smss.com
Fredericton, New Brunswick Office: Suite 600, Frederick Square, 77 Westmorland Street, P.O. Box 730, E3B 5B4.
Telephone: 506-458-1970.
Fax: 506-444-8974. Email: fredericton@smss.com
Saint John, New Brunswick Office: 10th Floor, Brunswick House, 44 Chipman Hill, P.O. Box 7289 Station "A", E2L 4S6.
Telephone: 506-632-1970.
Telecopier: 506-652-1989. Email: saint-john@smss.com
St. John's, Newfoundland Office: Cabot Place, 100 New Gower Street, P.O. Box 5038, A1C 5V3.
Telephone: 709-722-4270.
Telecopier: 709-722-4565. Email: st-johns@smss.com
Charlottetown, Prince Edward Island Office: 65 Grafton Street, P.O. Box 2140, C1A 8B9.
Telephone: 902-892-2485.
Telecopier: 902-566-5283. Email: charlottetown@smss.com

LAWYERS PRACTICING IN SYDNEY, NOVA SCOTIA OFFICE

Guy LaFosse, Q.C.
Glenn F. Gouthro
Patrick J. Murray
Lee Anne MacLeod-Archer

For full biographical listings, see the Martindale-Hubbell Law Directory

CANADA ONTARIO

*LONDON,** Middlesex Co.

MCCARTHY TÉTRAULT (AV)

Suite 2000, One London Place, 255 Queens Avenue, N6A 5R8
Telephone: 519-660-3587
Facsimile: 519-660-3599
Email: london@mccarthy.ca *URL:* http://www.mccarthy.ca
Vancouver, British Columbia Office: Suite 1300, 777 Dunsmuir Street, P.O. Box 10424, Vancouver, British Columbia V7Y 1K2.
Telephone: 604-643-7100.
Facsimile: 604-643-7900.
Surrey, British Columbia Office: Suite 1300, Station Tower, Gateway 13401-108th Avenue, Surrey, British Columbia V3T 5T3.
Telephone: 604-583-9100.
Fax: 604-583-9150.
Calgary, Alberta Office: Suite 3300, 421 7th Avenue, S.W., Calgary, Alberta T2P 4K9.
Telephone: 403-260-3500.
Facsimile: 403-260-3501.
Toronto, Ontario Office: Suite 4700, Toronto Dominion Bank Tower, Toronto, Ontario M5K 1E6.
Telephone: 416-362-1812.
Facsimile: 416-868-0673.
Ottawa, Ontario Office: The Chambers, Suite 1400, 40 Elgin Street, Ottawa, Ontario K1P 5K6.
Telephone: 613-238-2000.
Facsimile: 613-563-9386.
Montréal, Québec Office: Le Windsor, 1170 rue Peel, Montréal, Québec H3B 4S8.
Telephone: 514-397-4100.
Facsimile: 514-875-6246.
Québec, Québec Office: Le Complexe St-Amable 1150, rue Claire-Fontaine, 7e étage Québec, Québec G1R 5G4.
Telephone: 418-521-3000.
Facsimile: 418-521-3098, 418-521-3099.

(See Next Column)

United Kingdom and Europe Office: Pountney Hill House, 6 Laurence Pountney Hill, London, England EC4R 0BL.
Telephone: 011-44-171-618-2888.
Facsimile: 011-44-171-618-2880.

PARTNERS

T. David Little
Daniel R. Ross (Managing Partner)
Peter Christopher Johnson
A. Duncan Grace
Christopher C. White
Anthony G.J. Van Klink
Alissa Kathleen Mitchell
Gordon B. Carmichael
R. Gregory Hatt
F. Glenn Jones
David I.W. Hamer
Alec S. Bildy
Catherine M. Patterson
Jane E. Ferguson
Stephen H. Shantz

ASSOCIATES

Andrea H. Plumb
Arlene B. Alvares
M. Kathleen Robb
John K. Downing
Kristina M. Shaw

COUNSEL

Stephen N. Adams, Q.C.
E. Lindsey Elwood
W. Duncan Leggett
Alan W. Bryant
Brian T. Daly
Gregory K.G. Clark

For full biographical listings, see the Martindale-Hubbell Law Directory

MARKHAM, Regional Munic. of York

MILLER THOMSON (AV)

60 Columbia Way Suite 600, L3R 0C9
Telephone: 905-415-6700
Fax: 905-415-6777
Email: markham@millerthomson.ca *URL:* http://www.millerthomson.ca
Toronto, Ontario Office: 20 Queen Street West, Suite 2500, M5H 3S1.
Telephone: 416-595-8500.
Fax: 416-595-8695.
Edmonton, Alberta Office: 2700, Commerce Place, 10155-102 Street, Edmonton, Alberta, T5J 4G8.
Telephone: 780-429-1751.
Fax: 780-424-5866.
Calgary, Alberta Office: 3000, 700-9th Avenue S.W., Calgary, Alberta, T2P 3V4.
Telephone: 403-298-2400.
Fax: 403-262-0007.
Law Firm Affiliations/Associations:
Campney & Murphy - Vancouver, British Columbia, Canada
McCarter Grespan Robson Beynon - Kitchener, Ontario
Azevedo Sette Advogados - Sao Paulo and Belo Horizonte, Brazil, South America
Estudio Faraggi, Sateler & CIA - Santiago, Chile
Davis Arnold Cooper - London, England (Offices also in Manchester, Brussels, Vienna, Zurich, Madrid and Hong Kong)
Schürmann & Partners - Germany (Offices in Frankfurt, Berlin, Bonn, Dresden, Leipzig, Munich, Brussels, Milan, New York, Paris and Prague)
CONTACT: JUDSON D. WHITESIDE.
Telephone: 905-415-6701. E-mail: jwhitesi@millerthomson.ca.

Eric M. Lane
David J. Moxon, Q.C.
Eduardo M. Barradas
John L. Martin
Michael L. Shell
J. Bruce McMeekin
Roderick M. McLeod, Q.C.
Judson D. Whiteside
Paul E. Brace
Peter F. Kiborn
John R. Tidball
Eamonn J. Flaherty

For full biographical listings, see the Martindale-Hubbell Law Directory

NIAGARA FALLS, Regional Munic. of Niagara

SULLIVAN, MAHONEY (AV)

4780 Portage Road, L2E 6A8
Telephone: 905-357-0500
Facsimile: 905-357-0501
Email: lawyers@sullivan-mahoney.com
St. Catherines, Ontario Office: 40 Queen Street, P.O. Box 1360, L2R 6Z2.
Telephone: 905-688-6655.
Fax: 905-688-5814.

MEMBERS OF FIRM

P. H. Sullivan (1909-1988)
Peter B. Bedard
Philip M. Sheehan
Joseph M. Gottli
Bruce A. Macdonald
Victor F. Muratori, Q.C.
Thomas A. Richardson
Joseph Dallal
Robert B. Culliton
C. H. Mahoney, Q.C.
Peter T. Banwell, Q.C.
Douglas A. Goslin
J. Rodney Bush
Glen W. McCann
Gordon A. Wiggins
Woodward B. McKaig
Catherine Anne Bain
Peter A. Mahoney
Michael J. Bonomi

ASSOCIATES

Leanne P. McClay
Sara J. Premi
Rocco Vacca
Carmelina D'Angelo

(See Next Column)

SULLIVAN, MAHONEY—*Continued*

OF COUNSEL
Marvin D. Kriluck

*OTTAWA,** Regional Munic. of Ottawa-Carleton

BLAKE, CASSELS & GRAYDON LLP (AV)

World Exchange Tower, 20th Floor, 45 O'Connor Street, K1P 1A4
Telephone: 613-788-2200
Facsimile: 613-788-2247
Email: ottawa@blakes.com *URL:* http://www.blakes.com
The Firm maintains other offices in: Toronto, Ontario, Calgary, Alberta, Vancouver, British Columbia, London, England and Beijing, China.

PARTNERS

Eric R. Elvidge
Gordon K. Cameron
Matthew J. Halpin
Donald M. Greenfield
Gary O. Jessop

COUNSEL
George E. Fisk

For full biographical listings, see the Martindale-Hubbell Law Directory

FRASER MILNER (AV)

Suite 1200, 180 Elgin Street, K2P 2K7
Telephone: 613-783-9600
Telecopier: 613-783-9690
Email: webmaster@frasermilner.com *URL:* http://www.frasermilner.com
Toronto, Ontario Office: 1 First Canadian Place, 100 King Street West, M5X 1B2.
Telephone: 416-863-4511.
Telecopier: 416-863-4592.
Fax: 416-367-6787.
Calgary, Alberta Office: 30th Floor, Fifth Avenue Place. 237 4 Avenue, S.W., T2P 4X7.
Telephone: 403-268-7000.
Fax: 403-268-3100.
Edmonton, Alberta Office: 2900 Manulife Place, 10180 - 101 Street, T5J 3V5.
Telephone: 780-423-7100.
Fax: 780-423-7276.
Vancouver, British Columbia Office: 15th Floor, The Grosvenor Building, 1040 West Georgia Street.
Telephone: 604-687-4460.
Telecopier: 604-683-5214.

PARTNERS AND CONSULTANTS

John F. Blakney
William T. Houston
Richard J. Mahoney
John I. Tavel, Q.C.
Thomas A. Houston
David P. Little
Philip M. Rimer
Karen D. Zypchen

For full biographical listings, see the Martindale-Hubbell Law Directory

LANG MICHENER (AV)

Suite 300, 50 O'Connor Street, K1P 6L2
Telephone: 613-232-7171
Telecopier: 613-231-3191
URL: http://www.langmichener.ca
Toronto, Ontario Office: BCE Place, Suite 2500, 181 Bay Street, P.O. Box 747, M5J 2T7.
Telephone: 416-360-8600.
Vancouver, British Columbia Office: 1500 Royal Centre, P.O. Box 11117, 1055 West Georgia Street, V6E 4N7.
Telephone: 604-232-7171.
Telecopier: 604-685-7084.

RESIDENT MEMBERS

John G.M. Hooper, Q.C.
John M. Connolly
Pierre Richard, Q.C.
Norman M. Fera
Charles Saikaley
Michael S. Rankin
Barbara J. Sinclair
Edward L. Gladu, Q.C.
Terry W. Peterman
Eugene Meehan
Emanuel Montenegrino
David A. Bertschi
James M. Canapini
Ronald S. Petersen
Andrea R. Camacho

OF COUNSEL

John H. Nichols
Morris M. Kertzer

RESIDENT ASSOCIATES

Jennifer Ward
Clifford Z. Sosnow
Norman W. Carroll
Edward A. Pundyk
Debbie Orth
Karen J. Cooper
Patricia B. Simpson
Jeffrey W. Beedell
J. Robeert Allan
David M. Attwater
Daniel J. Leduc
Jacqueline V. Loignon
Kenenth S. Purchase
Julie G. Parent

For full biographical listings, see the Martindale-Hubbell Law Directory

MCCARTHY TÉTRAULT (AV)

The Chambers, Suite 1400, 40 Elgin Street, K1P 5K6
Telephone: 613-238-2000
Facsimile: 613-563-9386
Email: ottawa@mccarthy.ca *URL:* http://www.mccarthy.ca
Vancouver, British Columbia Office: Suite 1300, 777 Dunsmuir Street, P.O. Box 10424, Vancouver, British Columbia V7Y 1K2.
Telephone: 604-643-7100.
Facsimile: 604-643-7900.
Surrey, British Columbia Office: Suite 1300, Station Tower, Gateway 13401-108th Avenue, Surrey, British Columbia V3T 5T3.
Telephone: 604-583-9100.
Fax: 604-583-9150.
Calgary, Alberta Office: Suite 3300, 421 7th Avenue S.W., Calgary, Alberta T2P 4K9.
Telephone: 403-260-3500.
Facsimile: 403-260-3501.
London, Ontario Office: Suite 2000, One London Place, 255 Queens Avenue, London, Ontario N6A 5R8.
Telephone: 519-660-3587.
Facsimile: 519-660-3599.
Toronto, Ontario Office: Suite 4700, Toronto Dominion Bank Tower, Toronto, Ontario M5K 1E6.
Telephone: 416-362-1812.
Facsimile: 416-868-0673.
Montréal, Québec Office: Le Windsor, 1170 rue Peel, Montréal, Québec H3B 4S8.
Telephone: 514-397-4100.
Facsimile: 514-875-6246.
Québec, Québec Office: Le Complexe St-Amable 1150, rue Claire-Fontaine, 7e étage, Québec, Québec G1R 5G4.
Telephone: 418-521-3000.
Facsimile: 418-521-3098, 418-521-3099.
United Kingdom and Europe Office: Pountney Hill House, 6 Laurence Pountney Hill, London, England EC4R 0BL.
Telephone: 011-44-171-618-2888.
Facsimile: 011-44-171-618-2880.

MANAGING PARTNER
Barbara A. McIsaac, Q.C.

PARTNERS

Robert D. Chapman
William J. Honeywell
Michael S. Polowin
Thomas G. Conway
Anthony H.A. (Tony) Keenleyside
Anna M. Tosto
Colin S. Baxter

ASSOCIATES

Rick Shields
Marie-José Régimbal
Debra J. Henke
Kris Klein
D. Lynne Watt
Virginia K. Schweitzer
Sabrina F. Magro
Gregory S. Tzemenakis
Elisabeth S. Preston

For full biographical listings, see the Martindale-Hubbell Law Directory

OGILVY RENAULT (AV)

Suite 1600, 45 O'Connor Street, K1P 1A4
Telephone: 613-780-8661
Fax: 613-230-5459
Email: ottawa@ogilvyrenault.com *URL:* http://www.ogilvyrenault.com
Montréal, Québec Office: Suite 1100, 1981 McGill College Avenue, H3A 3C1.
Telephone: 514-847-4747.
Fax: 514-286-5474. Email: info@ogilvyrenault.com
Québec, Québec Office: Suite 520, 500 Grande Allée est, G1R 2J7.
Telephone: 418-640-5000.
Fax: 418-640-1500. Email: quebec@ogilvyrenault.com
Toronto, Ontario Office: Suite 2100, P.O. Box 141, Royal Trust Tower, TD Centre, M5K 1H1.
Telephone: 416-216-4000.
Fax: 416-216-3930. Email: toronto@ogilvyrenault.com
Vancouver, British Columbia Office: 800 Park Place, 666 Burrard Street, V6C 3P3.
Telephone: 604-806-0922.
Fax: 604-806-0933. Email: info@ogilvyrenault.com
London, England Office: 38 Charterhouse Square, EC1M 6EQ, England.
Telephone: 44 (0) 207-600-9005.
Fax: 44- (0) 207-600-9006. Email: info@ogilvyrenault.com

Rowena Borenstein
C. Ross Carson
Andrew A. Foti
Mary J. Gleason
Marcia A. Green
Patricia M. Harrison
Laurel A. Johnson
Terrance J. McManus
D. John Naccarato
Michael L. Phelan
Kenneth E. Sharpe
Brenda C. Swick-Martin
Marion J. Breen
Katherine A. Evans
I. H. Fraser
Sally A. Gomery
Bryan J. Handsley
Charles E. Hurdon
Norman B. Lieff
Cindy A. Morantz
Dan G. Palayew
Stephanie I. Rich
Peter J. Stanford
Richard A. Wagner

For full biographical listings, see the Martindale-Hubbell Law Directory

Ottawa—Continued

OSLER, HOSKIN & HARCOURT LLP (AV)

Barristers & Solicitors
Patent and Trade-Mark Agents
Suite 1500, 50 O'Connor Street, K1P 6L2
Telephone: 613-235-7234
FAX: 613-235-2867
Email: counsel@osler.com *URL:* http://www.osler.com
Toronto, Ontario Office: P.O. Box 50, 1 First Canadian Place M5X 1B8
Telephone: 416-362-2111.
Fax: 416-862-6666.
Calgary, Alberta Office: Suite 1900, Toronto Dominion Square, 333 - 7th Avenue S.W., T2P 2Z1.
Telephone: 403-260-7000.
Fax: 403-260-7024.
New York, N.Y. Office: 280 Park Avenue-30W, 10017.
Telephone: 212-867-5800.
Fax: 212-867-5802.

MEMBERS OF FIRM

Lorne H. Abugov
David W. Aitken
Stephen G. Blair
Glen A. Bloom
Kenneth L. W. Boland
Ronald C. Cheng
Diane E. Cornish
Kirsten R. Embree
K. Scott McLean
Kent H.E. Plumley
J. Andrew Pritchard
James H. Smellie
Gregory O. Somers
Elizabeth M. Walker
Donna G. White
David K. Wilson
Patricia J. Wilson
J. Craig Wright

ASSOCIATES

Benjamin P. Bedard
Darlene Carreau
Cheryl D.M. Emberley
Martha A. Healey
Christine E. Hicks
Derek S. Keay
Thomas Gresham Kelley (Not admitted in ON)
Leigh Ann Kirby
Allan Millard
Melanie A. Polowin
Y. Monica Song
M. Lynn Starchuk
Ed Vandenberg

PATENT AGENT

James R. Keneford

For full biographical listings, see the Martindale-Hubbell Law Directory

STIKEMAN ELLIOTT (AV)

50 O'Connor Street, Suite 914, K1P 6L2
Telephone: 613-234-4555
Fax: 613-230-8877
Email: info@stikeman.com *URL:* http://www.stikeman.com
Montreal, Quebec Office: 1155 René-Lévesque Boulevard West, 40th Floor, H3B 3V2.
Telephone: 514-397-3000.
Fax: 514-397-3222.
Toronto, Ontario Office: Commerce Court West, Suite 5300, M5L 1B9.
Telephone: 416-869-5500.
Fax: 416-947-0866.
Calgary, Alberta Office: 1500 Bankers Hall, 855 - 2nd Street S.W., T2P 4J7.
Telephone: 403-266-9000.
Fax: 403-266-9034.
Vancouver, British Columbia Office: Suite 1700, Park Place, 666 Burrard Street, V6C 2X8.
Telephone: 604-631-1300.
Fax: 604-681-1825.
New York, N.Y. Office: Tower 56, 126 East 56th Street, 14th Floor, 10022.
Telephone: 212-371-8855.
Fax: 212-371-7087.
London, England Office: Regis House, 45 King William Street, EC4R 9AN.
Telephone: +44 (0) 20 7648 1300.
Fax: +44 (0) 20 7648 1400.
Hong Kong Office: 29 Queen's Road Central, Suite 1103, Aon China Building.
Telephone: 852-22305200.
Fax: 852-2845-9076.
Singapore Office: 1 Shenton Way, #13-07 Robina House, Singapore 068803.
Telephone: 65-532-3556.
Fax: 65-532-3557.
Sydney, Australia Office: Level 40, The Chifley Tower, 2 Chifley Square.
Telephone: 61-2-9232-7199.
Fax: 61-2-9232-6908.

SENIOR ASSOCIATES AND PARTNERS IN OTTAWA

Tamra Alexander
Jonathan A. Blakey
Randall J. Hofley
Susan M. Hutton
Donald A. Kubesh
Nicholas P. McHaffie
Mirko Bibic
Nicole Brousseau
Lawson A. W. Hunter, Q.C.
T. Gregory Kane, Q.C.
Stuart C. McCormack
Thurlow Bradbrooke Smith, Q.C.

(See Next Column)

For full biographical listings, see the Martindale-Hubbell Law Directory

*ST. CATHARINES,** Regional Munic. of Niagara

SULLIVAN, MAHONEY (AV)

40 Queen Street, P.O. Box 1360, L2R 6Z2
Telephone: 905-688-6655
Facsimile: 905-688-5814
Email: lawyers@sullivan-mahoney.com
Niagara Falls, Ontario Office: 4780 Portage Road, L2E 6A8.
Telephone: 905-357-0500.
Fax: 905-357-0501.

MEMBERS OF FIRM

P. H. Sullivan, Q.C. (1909-1988)
Victor F. Muratori, Q.C.
Gordon A. Wiggins
Thomas A. Richardson
Woodward B. McKaig
Douglas A. Goslin
Joseph M. Gottli
J. Rodney Bush
Bruce A. Macdonald
C. H. Mahoney, Q.C.
Peter B. Bedard
Peter T. Banwell, Q.C.
Philip M. Sheehan
Joseph Dallal
Catherine Anne Bain
Robert B. Culliton
Peter A. Mahoney
Michael J. Bonomi
Glen W. McCann

ASSOCIATES

Sara J. Premi
Carmelina D'Angelo
Leanne P. McClay
Rocco Vacca

OF COUNSEL

Marvin D. Kriluck

For full biographical listings, see the Martindale-Hubbell Law Directory

*TORONTO,** Regional Munic. of Toronto

AIRD & BERLIS (AV)

Suite 1800 BCE Place, Bay Wellington Tower P.O. Box 754, 181 Bay Street, M5J 2T9
Telephone: 416-863-1500
Telecopier: 416-863-1515
Email: contact@airdberlis.com

The Honourable John Black Aird, C.C., Q.C. (1923-1995)
Douglas A. Berlis, Q.C. (1920-1995)

MEMBERS OF FIRM

J. Paul Terry
Harold R. Berry, Q.C.
James G. Matthews
Albert J. Milstein
Edmund C. D. Smith
Garry W. Dawson
Robert G. Doumani
Donald L. West
Diane Harris
Eldon J. Bennett
Grant H. Doak
Leo F. Longo
Lloyd F. Cornett
Douglas A. Palmateer
Brian G. Wright
K. John Harild
David Malach
Lindsay Ann Histrop
Jay A. Lefton
R. Grant Cansfield
Nick Torchetti
Stephen K. Young
Michael J. Bourassa
Barbra H. Miller
Margaret T. Nelligan
Philip P. Healey
R. Scott MacKendrick
Kristin J. Morch
Thomas A. Fenton
Ronald M. Kosonic
Andrew R.C. Webster
John J. Longo
Kevin G. Rooney
Steven L. Graff
Jennifer Ann Wainwright
David T. Takenaka
Carol J. Burns
Sonia M. Yung
David W. Dembroski
Jill P. Fraser
Dennis Miller
Andrew J. Wilder
Richard M. Kimel
David I. Matheson, Q.C.
W. Stearns ("Steve") Vaughan
Jerry H. Farrell
N. Jane Pepino, Q.C.
William G. VanderBurgh
Harry M. Fogul
Martin E. Kovnats
Jack Bernstein
Paul V. McCallen
Lawrence J. Crozier
Norman I. Kahn
Frederick D. Cass
Bernard McGarva
Christopher J. Williams
Donald M. Cameron
Barbara J. Lawrie
Michael D. Smith
Marilyn G. Lee
Helen T. Soudek
Martin J. Henderson
Barbara J. Worndl
Andy Ayotte
Steven P. Kelman
Cecilia M. Moffat
Harold S. Springer
Kim M. Kovar
Josephine A. Matera
Allan S. Bronstein
Timothy J. Hill
John W. Torrey
Randy T. Hooke
Eric M. Carmona
Louise R. Summerhill
Steven A. Zakem
Patricia A. Foran
Paul H. Bachand
William A. Chalmers
Lisa M. Assaf
Allyson Whyte
Christie A. McNeill
Joel D. Watson
Judy E. Cotte
Michael McCloskey
Hayden A. Solomons

(See Next Column)

AIRD & BERLIS—*Continued*

ASSOCIATES

Joseph Philip Dawson
Tracy O'Donnell
Jeffrey Board
Jeffrey Hewitt
David Stevens
Jennifer Goldman
Lisa E. Moreau
Harjinder (Jim) S. Sahdra
Lindsay Burry
Caroline Kim
Moe Sangani
S. Michael Brooks
Janet Ozembloski
Aaron Detlor
Lisa M. Marcuzzi
Kimberly A. Thomas
Tom Halinski
Boris Muchalov
Sandra Barton
Andrea Cotroneo
Rebecca Murphy
Bobby Stoller

For full biographical listings, see the Martindale-Hubbell Law Directory

BAKER & MCKENZIE (AV)

BCE Place, 181 Bay Street, Suite 2100, P.O. Box 874, M5J 2T3
Telephone: (416) 863-1221
Intn'l. Dialing: (1-416) 863-1221
Facsimile: (1-416) 863-6275
URL: http://www.bakerinfo.com
Associated Offices of Baker & McKenzie in: Almaty, Amsterdam, Bahrain, Baku, Bangkok, Barcelona, Beijing, Berlin, Bogotá, Brasília, Brussels, Budapest, Buenos Aires, Cairo, Caracas, Chicago, Dallas, Düsseldorf, Frankfurt, Geneva, Hanoi, Ho Chi Minh City, Hong Kong, Houston, Hsinchu, Juárez, Kiev, London, Madrid, Manila, Melbourne, México City, Miami, Milan, Monterrey, Moscow, Münich, New York, Palo Alto, Paris, Prague, Rio de Janeiro, Riyadh, Rome, St. Petersburg, San Diego, San Francisco, Santiago, São Paulo, Singapore, Stockholm, Sydney, Taipei, Tijuana, Tokyo, Valencia, Warsaw, Washington, D.C. and Zürich.
Correspondent Law Firm: Hadiputranto, Hadinoto & Partners, Jakarta.

PARTNERS

Salvador M. Borraccia
Joseph F. Caruso
Kevin B. Coon
Cheryl J. Elliott
Caleb J. Hayhoe
Roy K. Kusano
Stewart D. Saxe
Schuyler M. Sigel, Q.C.
Allan H. Turnbull
Paul D. Burns
J. Brian Casey
David T. A. Côté
Mary C. Hall
Edward J. Kowal, Q.C.
S. Janice McAuley
Brian D. Segal
Hubert J. Stitt, Q.C.
William R. Watson

LOCAL PARTNERS

Blair W. M. Bowen
Charles M. Magerman
Susan G. Seller
Marina M. Stephens (Not admitted in ON)
Lisa Kirby
Kathleen M. Orysiuk
James R. Sennema
Kanta L. Wadhwan
Jonathan H. Wigley

ASSOCIATES

Christopher Aide
Dawn C. Benson
Lisa Douglas
James J. Holloway
Joanne N. Horibe
Mitchell E. Kowalski
Matthew J. Latella
Janet E. Mills
Gabriela Ramó
Jillian B. Robins
D. Paul Tackaberry
Adam I. Balinsky
Richard M. Brooks
Keenan H. Hohol (Not admitted in ON)
Hartley M. Isenberg
Andrée Lambert-Dubois
Theodore C. Ling
Motria Onyschuk-Morozov
David Douglas Robertson
Neal B. Sommer
Stephanie E. Vaccari
Karen J. Weisz

For full biographical listings, see the Martindale-Hubbell Law Directory

BENNETT JONES (AV)

3400 One First Canadian Place, P.O. Box 130, M5X 1A4
Telephone: 416-863-1200
Facsimile: 416-863-1716
Email: firmwatch@bennettjones.ca *URL:* http://www.bennettjones.ca
Calgary, Alberta Office: 4500 Bankers Hall East, 855-2nd Street S.W.
Telephone: 403-298-3100.
Facsimile: 403-265-7219.
Edmonton, Alberta Office: 1000, 10035-105 Street.
Telephone: 780-421-8133.
Facsimile: 780-421-7951.

RESIDENT MEMBERS OF FIRM

Benjamin J. Hutzel
J. Fraser Mann, Q.C.
Hugh L. Mackinnon (Not admitted in ON)
Steve J. Suarez
David M. McIntyre
D. Bernard Morris
Jacques Bernier
Robert W. Staley
Robyn M. Bell
Heidi Visser
Mark S. Laugesen

Mark W. S. Bain
J. Scott Martyn
David J. Bannon
Julia E. Schatz
Susan E. Mann
Michelle L. Schwartzberg
Alan M. Gahtan
Pamela C. Spencer
Nita L. Major
Laurel C. Broten
Patrick Ko
David R. Price

(See Next Column)

COUNSEL

Stephen Paddon, Q.C.

For full biographical listings, see the Martindale-Hubbell Law Directory

BLAKE, CASSELS & GRAYDON LLP (AV)

Box 25, Commerce Court West, 199 Bay Street, 28th Floor, M5L 1A9
Telephone: 416-863-2400
Facsimile: 416-863-2653
Email: toronto@blakes.com *URL:* http://www.blakes.com
The Firm maintains other offices in: Ottawa, Ontario, Calgary, Alberta, Vancouver, British Columbia, London, England and Beijing, China.

PARTNERS

Edward L. Donegan, Q.C.
Brian C. Westlake
Timothy N. Unwin
John M. Stewart
Robert E.H. Macdonald
J. Anthony Doyle
J. Rob Collins
Peter W. Gilchrist
John D. DeSipio
Glenn F. Leslie
Richard C. McIvor
Derek L. Rogers
Greg M. Frenette
Barry G. McGee
Paul K. Tamaki
James R. Christie
Joan C. G. Kennedy
Edward M. Perlmutter
Philip W. Slayton
Sheldon Burshtein
Pamela S. Hughes
Joel Richler
T. Nigel M. Campbell
Timothy W. Bermingham
C. Dawn Jetten
Thomas A. McKee
Mark J. Selick
John M. Tuzyk
Robert M. Granatstein
Alison B. Woodbury
Kathryn M. Bush
Jeffrey Kerbel
David O'Brien
Andrea D. Vabalis
Gordon A. M. Currie
Jeremy J. Forgie
Anne C. McNeely
Kenneth Pearce
Michael W. Sharp
Bliss A. White
Henry Bertossi
Allan J. Gelkopf
Robert E. Kwinter
Paul B. Schabas
Caroline L. Helbronner
Pamela L.J. Huff
J.A. Prestage
Craig C. Thorburn
Robert H. Wilkes
Michael E. Burke
Jeffrey W. Galway
Anna I. MacMillan
Ernest McNee
Gary T. Daniel
Christopher C. Hale
Michael R. Stephenson
Frank P. Arnone
Mark J. Nicholson
David J. Toswell
Barbara J. Austin
Jeffrey Glass
Jeffrey R. Lloyd
Steven J. Weisz
Peter S. MacGowan
Bryson A. Stokes
Milly Chow
James S. Hausman
David J. Kee
James P. Dube
Robert A. Bondy
John M. Solursh
Martin Fingerhut
Elizabeth L. McNaughton
Robert S. Bruser
J. David A. Jackson
Alan Bell
William G. Horton
John W. Teolis
James S. Hilton
Robin J. McGillis
Dorothy Wahl
Brian W. Gray
Leslie J. Morgan
Gary R. Shiff
Gerald S. Swinkin
Susan M. Grundy
Gail D. Lilley
Alan F. Brown
Deborah H. Rowat
Ben A. Jetten
Kevin P. McElcheran
Samuel J. Principi
Mary Jane Stitt
Randy V. Bauslaugh
W. Ross F. McKee
J. Alan Aucoin
Michael R. Harquail
Sheila A. Murray
Connie Reeve
David D. Valentine
Robert M. Fishlock
Christopher A. Huband
William D. Mugford
James J. Shanks
Susan E. Slattery
Judy L. Wilson
Gwen Chamberlain
Frank D. Guarascio
John J. Quinn
Nathan Cheifetz
Christopher A. Hewat
Alfred A. Macchione
Lee Shouldice
Thomas P.B. von Hahn
Paul Belanger
Lisa S. Corne
Jonathan W. Kahn
S. Gordon McKee
Sharon S. Wong
Elizabeth M. Gearing
Kathleen V. Penny
R. Seumas M. Woods
Greg Kanargelidis
Anthony M. Prenol
Stephen R. Ashbourne
Silvana M. D'Alimonte
Monica C. Kowal
Jeffrey Trossman
Elizabeth H. Boyd
Dirk E. Rueter
Jill M. Lawrie
Rachel J. Ingram

COUNSEL

V. Richard E. Perry, Q.C.
Samuel R. Hill
Christopher R.J. Van Loan
Garry D. Watson, Q.C. (Part-time Director of Professional Development)

COUNSEL

Donald J.M. Brown, Q.C.
Ronald C. Brown, Q.C.
George W. Hately, Q.C.
John F. Howard, Q.C.
Robert A. Kingston, Q.C.
James F. McCallum, Q.C.
Desmond M. O'Rorke
John B. Tinker, Q.C.
John W. Brown, Q.C.
Warren Grover, Q.C.
John M. Hodgson, Q.C.
Burton H. Kellock, Q.C.
Edwin S. Langdon
W. O. Chris Miller, Q.C.
Robert W. Stevens, Q.C.
J. Roy Weir, Q.C.

(See Next Column)

BLAKE, CASSELS & GRAYDON LLP, *Toronto—Continued*

For full biographical listings, see the Martindale-Hubbell Law Directory

BLANEY McMURTRY LLP (AV)

Suite 1400, 20 Queen Street West, M5H 2V3
Telephone: 416-593-1221
Telecopier: 416-593-5437
URL: http://WWW.BLANEY.COM

MEMBERS OF FIRM

James W. Blaney, Q.C. *
Richard H. Krempulec, Q.C. *
Gary E. Siskind
Barry T. Grant *
Robert J. Potts *
Roderick S. W. Winsor *
Michael J. Penman
Arthur L. Shapero
Geza R. Banfai *
D. Barry Prentice
Joan H. Garson *
Michael J. Bennett *
Stephen R. Moore *
Mark E. Geiger *
Steven P. Jeffery
Timothy P. Alexander *
Deborah S. Grieve
Brett Tkatch *
Maria Scarfo
Robert Muir
Harry W. McMurtry
Tim Farrell
William R. McMurtry, Q.C. *
Alex A. Mesbur, Q.C. *
Rodney L. K. Smith, Q.C. *
Robert Cohen, Q.C. *
Jeffery L. Freelan *
Jack Ditkofsky
Stanley Kugelmass *
Stephen I. Selznick *
Elizabeth J. Forster
Crawford W. Spratt *
David S. Wilson
H. Todd Greenbloom *
Ian S. Epstein *
Jess C. Bush *
Katherine L. Higginson
Roger J. Horst *
Mirilyn R. Selznick *
S. Steve Popoff
Andrew J. Heal
William D. Anderson
Chris J. Clapperton
Eugene G. Mazzuca

ASSOCIATES

Murray A. Thompson, Q.C.
Karen A. Henein
W. Fraser McDonald
Mona R. Taylor
Giovanna Asaro
Brinley Evans
Michele A. Hecke
David Epstein
Eric Golden
Larry Reimer
Nathan Chan
Kevin Robinson
Bruno Soucy
Bradley Phillips
Paul L. Schnier
Maureen E. Merrill
Suzanne Bailey
Alva Orlando
Elizabeth A. Hyde
Minami Ganaha
Arlene O'Neill
Felix Semberov
Daniel Condon
Eric Boehm
Mark Zwegers
John Polyzogopoulis
Russell Hatch
Tanya Litzenburger
Linda E. Misetich

COUNSEL

Murray H. Chusid, Q.C.

*Denotes Member of Firm

For full biographical listings, see the Martindale-Hubbell Law Directory

BORDEN & ELLIOT (AV)

Barristers & Solicitors
Scotia Plaza, 40 King Street West, M5H 3Y4
Telephone: 416-367-6000
Telecopier: 416-367-6749
Email: info@borden.com *URL:* http://www.borden.com
Ottawa, Ontario Office: Borden Elliot Scott & Aylen, 1000-60 Rue Queen Street.
Telephone: 613-237-5160; 800-661-4237. General
Facsimile: 613-230-8842. IP Dept.
Facsimile: 613-787-3558. Email: ottinfo@scottaylen.com. URL: http://www.borden.com.

David A. L. Britnell, Q.C.
John D. Holding, Q.C.
George Cihra, Q.C.
John D. Hylton, Q.C.
J. D'Arcy P. Brooks, Q.C.
Simon B. Scott, Q.C.
Morton G. Gross, Q.C.
Hans J. B. A. Dickie, Q.C.
John F. T. Warren
A. Winn Oughtred
W. Paul McCarten
Peter R. Braund
Edmund F. Merringer
William S. Robertson
Charles Simon
Nigel H. Frawley
Martin Sclisizzi
Brian C. Keith
William D. T. Carter
M. Jeffrey Dermer
Robert P. Hutchison
Evelyn Goldfarb
Eva M. Krasa
Kenneth W. Scott, Q.C.
W. Ross Murray, Q.C.
David M. Harley, Q.C.
Rino A. Stradiotto, Q.C.
James H. McC. McNair
R. Lee Woods
Terrance A. Sweeney
Donald L. Macdonald, Q.C.
Frank J. C. Newbould, Q.C.
Brent J. Lisowski
Edward A. Ayers, Q.C.
L. (Lou) Kozak, Q.C.
Gordon A. Park
William T. Pashby
Richard A. Applebaum
Thomas W. Ouchterlony
Steven N. Iczkovitz
Timothy P. D. Bates (Manager, Litigation Department)
Randall Scott Echlin
John D. Marshall
Robert W. Kitchen
Paul G. Findlay

(See Next Column)

D. Bruce Garrow
Andrew J. Skinner
W. Douglas R. Beamish
Barry H. Bresner
Marguerite P. Mooney
Anne C. Corbett
Mary Margaret Fox
Paul A. D. Mingay
Alfred L. J. Page
Sean Weir (Executive Committee Member)
Barry S. Corbin
Gordon J. Zimmerman
Joanne E. Foot
R. Bruce Reynolds
Wendy J. Earle
Rosalind Morrow
Catherine E. Bray
Robert S. Russell
Robert W. Traves
Daphne G. Jarvis
Shelley L. Timms
James R. Elder
Mary Lynn Gleason
Joanne M. Poljanowski
Bruce E. Fowler
Noella M. Milne
Neil C. Saxe
M. Christine Fotopoulos
Freya J. Kristjanson
Malcolm J. MacKillop
Anne E. Spafford
Christine A. Zablocki
Douglas M. Worndl
F.F. (Rick) Coburn
Melany V. Franklin
Carole E. Hoglund
Craig J. Hill
Murray B. Shopiro
Stephen F. Waqué
Robert B. Bell
Michael K. McKelvey
Thomas G. Andrews
James D. G. Douglas
Daniel Frederick Hirsh
Brian D. Mulroney
Larissa V. Tkachenko
Robert N. Black
Frank S. Callaghan
James W. Mathers
Timothy O. Buckley
John J. Morris
Christopher D. Bredt
Sean L. Gosnell
Winnie C. W. Tse
Julie K. Hannaford
Richard H. Shaban
Carol E. Derk
John K. Rodgers
Matthew R. Alter
Ronald Foerster
Andrew W. Kingsmill
Eric M. Roher
David A. Huctwith
James D. Patterson
Paul B. Scargall
R. Andrew G. Harrison
Norman Letalik
Robert B. MacLellan
William A. McClelland
John J. Tobin
Keith N. Batten
Ian J. Houston
Barry L. Glaspell
Lynn M. McGrade
Kevin A. McGivney

John R. Wood
Colleen Shannon
Carole A. Lindsay
Rebecca A. Clements
Patrick J. Hawkins
May J. Sproat
Prema K. R. Thiele
Barbara J. Caplan
Michael P. Fitzgibbon
Michael D. Shadbolt
Craig J. Webster
Tess DiPonio
Robert L. Love
Aïda Van Wees
Aaron A. Blumenfeld
Matthew L. O. Certosimo
Anne Marie Kendall
Salvatore Mirandola
Douglas Owen Smith
Michael J. Calich
Adam F. Fanaki
Stephen J. Redican
Kathleen E. Church
Garri Benjamin Hendell
Christine Elizabeth Long
Richard Joseph Morelli
Jonathan F. Dyck
David G. Gore
Jeffery P. Mitchell
Michael C. Smith
Kimberley A. Vooro
Stephen Alsace
Cynthia Dawn Clarke
Aimee Ilysse Israel
Markus F. Kremer
David R. Surat
Melanie A. Warner
Jacinthe I. Boudreau
Margaret J. M. Atkinson
Andre George Poles
Howard S. Silverman
Gabrielle K. Kramer
Carolyn L. Tate
Denise L. Bambrough
Daniel J. Dochylo
Benjamin T. Glustein
Sharon C. Vogel
Dolores Di Felice
Eric R. Hoaken
Laleh Moshiri
Brian D. Behrman
J. Lincoln J. Caylor
Orlando V. R. Da Silva
James W. Maclellan
Ira Nishisato
Christine M. Thomlinson
Victoria Cowling
J. Pitman Patterson
Randy M. Zettle
Laurie J. Cook
Michael R. Holder
H. Scott McEvoy
David M. Di Paolo
Kevin F. Fritz
John S. Lutz
Victor R. Peter
Donna Spagnolo
Cheryl M. Woodin
Robert H. Brent
Michael C. Decosimo
Elizabeth A. Jordan
Ivy Lam
Christopher J. Toal
Christiane Vachon (Not admitted in ON)

OF COUNSEL

William L. N. Somerville, Q.C.
M.E. (Libby) Burnham, Q.C.
Wayne D. Barton
John E. Hall
Stephen J. Fyfe
Richard H. Ling
Stephen S. Heller
Richard C. Meech, Q.C.
P. Jeffrey S. Graham
Linda L. Bertoldi
Trevor Whiffen
Victoria Prince
Sonia T. Mak
J. Mark Rodger
Alan Martin Sless

PATENT AND TRADEMARK COUNSEL

G. James M. Shearn

For full biographical listings, see the Martindale-Hubbell Law Directory

Toronto—Continued

CASSELS BROCK & BLACKWELL LLP (AV)

Suite 2100, Scotia Plaza, 40 King Street West, M5H 3C2
Telephone: 416-869-5300
Toll Free: 1-888-869-5344
Fax: 416-360-8877
Email: postmaster@casselsbrock.com *URL:* http://www.casselsbrock.com
Member of International Affiliation: Cassels Pouliot Douglas Noriega, Toronto, Montreal, Vancouver, Mexico City.

MEMBERS OF FIRM

Gordon G. Dickson	Bruce Alexander Thomas, Q.C.
Walter M. Bowen, Q.C.	Vernol I. Rogers
Crawford R. Spencer, Q.C.	M. Virginia MacLean, Q.C.
David R. Peterson, P.C., Q.C.	Philip Spencer, Q.C.
Donald Robert Arthurs	E. Bruce Leonard
Peter E. Steinmetz, Q.C.	John H. Craig
Harvey J. Kirsh	Ralph E. Lean, Q.C.
Lorne H. Saltman	D. Rick Angelson
Ian Blue, Q.C.	John W. R. Day
Bruce T. McNeely	James M. Parks
William Johnson Burden	John S. McKeown
Lanning J. Abramson	Maxwell Gotlieb
Stanley M. Makuch	Frank P. Monteleone
Sheldon Plener	Alison R. Manzer
Robert D. Kligman	S. John Page
Timothy Pinos	Mark I. Young
Bruce C. Bell	W. Bruce Clark
Leilah Edroos	Gary Steinhart
Cameron A. Mingay	J. Brian Reeve
James Rossiter	Christopher B. Norton
Gregory J. Peebles	Lori A. Roth
Paul M. Stein	Glenn M. Zakaib
Donald G. Gray	Renate Diane Herbst
Lorne E. Silver	Christopher W. Besant
Stephen R. Morrison	Leonard Glickman
Ian H. Gold	B. Robin Moodie
Anne-Marie Widner	Peter Marrone
John P. McGowan	Cathy L. Mercer
Jeffrey P. Roy	Geoffrey B. Shaw
Timothy Wach	Diane E. Klukach
M. Janine Kovach	David A. Redmond
L. Michael Shannon	Lawrence Wilder
Peter E. Dunne	Norman F. Findlay
Ian A. Mair	William H. Steele
Brian P. Dominique	Lori A. Prokopich
Ann L. Watterworth	Lawrence M. Weinberg
Stevan Novoselac	Julie A. Thorburn
Robert Cohen	Gordon P. Goodman
Alexander David Pettingill	David S. Ward

ASSOCIATES

Roberta McGill	Robyn Collver
Sari Springer	D'Arcy D. McGoey
A. Neil Craik	Tom Koutoulakis
John Jacques Abdo	Catherine M. Dennis
Thomas A. J. Harley	Andrew Reback
Christopher John Schnarr	Mark Bennett
Audrey Fennell	John C. O'Reilly
Frank Spizzirri	John Vettese
Claire Walker	Roger J. Gillott
David R. Kerr	Jody McCormack
Firaz Mohamed	Jacqueline Laura Wall
Richard John Wyruch	John N. Birch
W. Colin Empke	Arthur L. Hamilton
Jordan M. Jacobs	Nadine Nasr
Daniel B. Green	Stephanie E. Kirsh
Alexandra Iliopoulos	Carol Anne O'Brien
Moira C. Urbanski	Michele Ann Wright
S. Jason Arbuck	Jason Kenneth Spero Bullen
Thomas Joseph Donnelly	Mindy Beth Gilbert
Brian P. Koscak	Sarah Robertson

Candice D.F. Solomon

COUNSEL

H. Donald Guthrie, Q.C., L.S.M., LL.B.	Robert Law, Q.C.
	Marshall A. Cohen, O.C., Q.C.
Sanford World, Q.C.	Aubrey A. Russell, Q.C.

Albert Abramson, Q.C.

ASSOCIATE COUNSEL

Lawrence L. Herman

For full biographical listings, see the Martindale-Hubbell Law Directory

DAVIES, WARD & BECK (AV)

1 First Canadian Place, M5X 1B1
Telephone: 416-863-0900
Fax: 416-863-0871
Email: info@dwb.com *URL:* http://www.dwb.com

(See Next Column)

PARTNERS AND ASSOCIATES

David A. Ward, Q.C.	David W. Smith, Q.C.
Mark Q. Connelly	Nicholas J. Leblovic
Donald C. Stanbury	Timothy G. Youdan
William M. O'Reilly	Jay A. Swartz
Robert T. Bauer	Calvin S. Goldman, Q.C.
I. Berl Nadler	Arthur S. Shiff
Jean-Paul Bisnaire	Ronald S. Wilson
John A. Zinn	Patricia L. Olasker
Gray E. Taylor	Michael Disney
Gregory J. Howard	John M. Ulmer
William M. Ainley	Carol D. Pennycook
Colin Campbell	Neil Finkelstein
A. Gerold Goldlist	Edward C. Hannah
Jeffrey O. Palmer	Catherine G. Ross
Neal H. Armstrong	Duncan C. Card
Jeremy M. Freedman	Mark S. Hayes
Paul M. Kennedy	D. Shawn McReynolds
Kevin J. Thomson	Michael Creery
K. A. Siobhan Monaghan	Ian D. Johnson
Joel T. Kissack	John D. Bodrug
James J. Lawson	Thomas A. Smee
Paul S. Crampton	R. Ian Crosbie
Carol Hansell	Mark C. Katz
Ian R. McBride	Vincent A. Mercier
Cameron M. Rusaw	Matthew P. Gottlieb
Timothy H. Moran	Michael W. Clifford
Maureen Y. Berry	Richard F. D. Corley
David A. Dell	James W. E. Doris
Sandra A. Forbes	Milos Barutciski
Catherine A. MacNeill	Patrick G. Barry
Melanie L. Aitken	Geoffrey S. Turner
Sarbjit S. Basra	Kent F. Beattie
Christine J. Prudham	Gillian R. Stacey
Andrew L. Welsh	Paolo Boni
Gabriella Lombardi	Lori A. Cornwall
Brian A. Facey	Sarah V. Powell
Jennifer A. Pfuetzner	Julianna S. Ahn
Dany H. Assaf	Delphine Brooker
Andrea L. Burke	Andrea E. Daly
Sabrina Gherbaz	Terrance J. Ritchie
Mitchell P. Finkelstein	Warren M. Katz
Claire M. C. Kennedy	Russell Cohen
Paul W. Golding	Steven M. Harris
Jennifer D. Howard	Christopher H. Jones
Jennifer L. Toone	Richard J. Fullerton
Domenic Marciano	Alana G. McPhee
Patrick E. Moyer	Rosemary A. Newman
James R. Reid	Gregory G. Southam
David Stevens	Robin G. Tessier
Derek R. G. Vesey	Tarne P. Whiteley
Paul A. Beauregard	Andrée M. Blais
R. Michael Brisson	Michael S. Brown
Donald S. Harrison	Robert S. Murphy
Erinn E. Somerville	Lori K. Sullivan
Rachel J. Urman	John M. Walsh

COUNSEL

Willard Z. Estey, Q.C.

For full biographical listings, see the Martindale-Hubbell Law Directory

FASKEN MARTINEAU DUMOULIN (AV)

Toronto-Dominion Centre Toronto-Dominion Bank Tower, P.O. Box 20, M5K 1N6
Telephone: 416-366-8381
Toll Free: 1-800-268-8424 (Ontario & Quebec)
Facsimile: 416-364-7813
Email: info@tor.fasken.com *URL:* http://www.fasken.com
Fasken Martineau DuMoulin is a leading Canadian firm with a national and international practice and having offices in Toronto, Montreal, Quebec, Vancouver, New York and London. Please refer to listings in the respective city sections.
Montreal, Quebec Office: Stock Exchange Tower, Suite 3400, P.O. Box 242. 800 Place-Victoria H4Z 1E9.
Telephone: 514-397-7400. Toll-Free: 1-800-361-6266 (Ontario & Quebec).
Facsimile: 514-397-7600.
Telex: 05-24610 BUOY MTL. EMail: info@mtl.fasken.com. Website: www.fasken.com
Quebec City, Quebec Office: Immeuble Le Saint-Patrick, 140, rue Grande Allée est, bureau 800, G1R 5M8.
Telephone: 418-640-2000. Toll Free: 1-800-463-2827 (Ontario & Quebec).
Facsimile: 418-647-2455. EMail: infor@qc.fasken.com. Website: www.fasken.com.
Vancouver, British Columbia Office: 2100-1075 West Georgia Street.
Telephone: 604-631-3131.
Fax: 604-631-3232. EMail: info@van.fasken.com. Website: www.fasken.com.
New York, New York Office: Seagram Building, 375 Park Avenue, Suite 2608, 10152.
Telephone: 212-935-3203.
Facsimile: 212-935-4822. Website: www.fasken.com. EMail: info@nyc.fasken.com.

(See Next Column)

FASKEN MARTINEAU DuMOULIN, *Toronto—Continued*

London, England Office: 10 Arthur Street, 5th Floor, EC4R 9AY.
Telephone: 71-929-2894.
Facsimile: 71-929-3634. EMail: info@lon.fasken.com.

MEMBERS

Robert M. Sutherland, Q.C.
James A. Bradshaw, Q.C.
Claude R. Thomson, Q.C., FCIArb.
Donald J. Steadman
J. Michael Robinson, Q.C.
David M. Doubilet
Stephen T. P. Risk
Robert E. Smolkin
George C. Glover, Jr.
Stephen S. Ruby
John A. Campion
Robert W. Cosman
Kenneth C. Morlock
Esther L. Lenkinski
Walter J. Palmer
Samuel R. Rickett
Donald E. Short
Douglas C. New
Peter L. Roy
John H. Loosemore
David N. Corbett
Beryl B. Green
Ronald J. McCloskey
Constance L. Sugiyama
Philip J. Wolfenden
Anthony F. Baldanza
Douglas E. Grundy
Elizabeth J. Johnson
Douglas A. Cannon
Barbara Miller
Neal J. Smitheman
Jeffrey A. Kaufman
C. Ian Kyer
Bruce Salvatore
Ronald J. Walker
W. Thomas Barlow
J. Mark Stinson
Nigel P. J. Johnston
Gerald L. R. Ranking
Scott D. Conover
David C. Rosenbaum
David G. Allsebrook
Peter A. Downard
Michael J. W. Round
Paul F. Monahan
Belinda J. James
Katherine M. Pollock
Richard J. Steinberg
Alan L. W. D'Silva
B. Lynne Golding
Neil M. Smiley
Janne M. Duncan
Kelley M. McKinnon
Joel E. Binder
David Hausman
T. Anthony Ball
Garth J. Foster
Edmond F.B. Lamek
Peggy A. McCallum
Laura F. Cooper
Andrew B. Laidlaw
Ronald N. Robertson, Q.C.
Robert L. Shirriff, Q.C.
George Tiviluk, Q.C.
Ian MacGregor
John H. Hough, Q.C.
Arthur R. Kitamura
John T. Morin, Q.C.
Alan M. Schwartz, Q.C.
David W. Salomon
Robert W. McDowell
Douglas R. Scott
Howard M. Carr
Robert S. Harrison
S. Bruce Blain
Jonathan A. Levin
Mark A. Richardson
Leslie H. Rose
William J. Bies
Brian A. T. O'Byrne
Rand A. Lomas
Craig R. Carter
Stephen I. Erlichman
Jeffrey S. Leon
Edward W. Purdy
Peter W. Vair
Colleen Spring Zimmerman
Elizabeth A. Fisher
M. Elena Hoffstein
Allan G. Beach
Jon J. Holmstrom
Donald E. Milner
J. David Vincent
Paul R. King
Roxanne E. McCormick
Sheryl E. Seigel
John D. Abraham
Richard E. Johnston
J. Steven Follett
Paul J. Martin
Eric C. Belli-Bivar
Gary S. Fogler
Liana L. Turrin
Peter S. Ascherl
Michael J. MacNaughton
Cathy Singer
David Koichi Moritsugu
Daniel R. Law
Robert N. Spiegel
Steven K. D'Arcy
Mark J. Fecenko
Peter J. Pliszka
John S. M. Turner
Kathryn L. Knight
Ralph N. Nero
Rosalind H. Cooper
Richard B. Swan
Martin K. Denyes
C. William Hourigan
David F. O'Connor
Robert E. Elliott
David J. Coultice
Bruce C. Treichel

ASSOCIATES

Ronald W. McInnes
Mary Ellen Cavett
Murray J. Braithwaite
Norman D. Kribs
May M. Cheng
Cynthia L. Heinz
Gregory Ho Yuen
Elizabeth G. Beattie
Ronald E. Nobrega
Yvonne B. Chisholm
Gideon C. Forrest
Tracy A. Pratt
Corina S. Weigl
Angela Di Padova
J. Alex Pankratz
Mitchell Thaw
Lisa M. Tracey
Duane E. Schippers
Katharine A. Evans
Eric C. Haslett
Andrea T. Horton
Darrell L. Kloeze
Lori A. McMillan
Scott K. Wallace
Mary J. Gersht
Scott K. Fenton
Pandora D. Strasler
Andrew D. Burns
Louise J.A. Greig
Jonathan F. Lancaster
Greg M. Dee
Kathryn J. Daniels
Brian D. Wylynko
Lena Crawford
Maureen Helt
Harry J. Thompson
Christine M.S. Chen
Barbara F. Lippett
Robin Roddey
Ian C. Whan Tong
L. Catherine Eckenswiller
Kelly A. Callon-McLean
Annie M. Finn
Tracy L. Hooey
C. Brent Jay
Melissa J. MacKewn
Robyn D. Mendelson
John G. Webster

(See Next Column)

ASSOCIATES (Continued)

Anil Aggarwal
Brian J. Budden
Rochelle S. Fox
Janice J. Javier
Sara A. Levine
Scott Rollwagen
Steven J. Blackburn
Christopher J. Edwards
Anuradha Iyer
Vince Kazmierski
John Marsalek
James W. Murdoch
John P. Beardwood
Heather C. Devine
Patrick T. J. Gannon
Stephen B. Kerr
Marinela Mostic
Berkley D. Sells
Mark E. Burton
Claudia D. Feldkamp
Jodi Katz
Jeffrey A. Legault
Jennifer A. Mazin
Sean Stevens
Rene Zanin

COUNSEL

Hon. John M. Godfrey, Q.C.
Roger G. Doe, Q.C.
Jay W. Huckle, Q.C.
Alexander D. T. Givens, Q.C.
Richard B. Potter, Q.C.
John L. Bowles
David G. C. Menzel, Q.C.
Robert B. Tuer, Q.C.
Karl J. C. Harries, Q.C.
Fraser M. Fell, Q.C.
Rudolph W. Gardner, Q.C.
Roger D. Wilson, Q.C.
Ronald J. Rolls, Q.C., L.S.M.

For full biographical listings, see the Martindale-Hubbell Law Directory

---

FRASER MILNER (AV)

1 First Canadian Place, 100 King Street West, M5X 1B2
Telephone: 416-863-4511
Telecopier: 416-863-4592
Fax: 416-367-6787
Email: webmaster@frasermilner.com *URL:* http://www.frasermilner.com
Calgary, Alberta Office: 30th Floor, Fifth Avenue Place. 237 4 Avenue, S.W., T2P 4X7.
Telephone: 403-268-7000.
Fax: 403-268-3100.
Edmonton, Alberta Office: 2900 Manulife Place, 10180 - 101 Street, T5J 3V5.
Telephone: 780-423-7100.
Fax: 780-423-7276.
Ottawa, Ontario Office: 180 Elgin Street, Suite 1200, K2P 2K7.
Telephone: 613-783-9600.
Telecopier: 613-783-9690.
Vancouver, British Columbia Office: 15th Floor, The Grosvenor Building, 1040 West Georgia Street.
Telephone: 604-687-4460.
Telecopier: 604-683-5214.

PARTNERS, CONSULTANTS AND COUNSEL

John W. Adams, Q.C.
Paul F. Baston
Janet L. Bobechko
Patrick J. Boyle
David I. Bristow, Q.C.
Peter J. Cavanagh
Barbara A. Conway
Ian C. B. Currie, Q.C.
Robert E. Dickson
James A. S. Dunbar
John S. Elder, Q.C.
P. Martin Emmons
Alan J. Frank
William Fung
Ronald A. Goldenberg
Karen B. Groulx
Robb C. Heintzman
Michael G. Horan
Victor Y. Hum
James J. Janetos
Jeremy G. N. Johnston
Elizabeth Keenan
James G. Knight
R. Shayne Kukulowicz
N. Anneli LeGault
Jules L. Lewy
W. Macdonald Macintosh
Joseph Marin
Ronald J. Matheson
Yvonne L. McAndrew
John Lorn McDougall, Q.C.
Raymond H. Mikkola
Aaron Milrad
Peter E. Murphy
Albert Page, Q.C.
Roger J. Pead
R. Jamie Plant
Karen V. Ray
Doug Scott
Paul D. Shantz
Hon. David P. Smith, P.C., Q.C.
Mark W. Stewart
Riccardo C. Trecroce
Graham Turner
Peter L. Van Loan
Jeffery A. Barnes
Michael G. Beairsto
Frank E. P. Bowman
Maggie A. Brady
Brian R. Carr
William D. Chambers
Ralph Cuervo-Lorens
Joseph C. Debono
Daniel R. Dowdall
Stanley E. Edwards, Q.C.
Norman J. Emblem
Fred Ernst
David G. Fuller
Paul P. Ginou
Barbara L. Grossman
Peter W. Hand
Richard C. Hoffman
Randal T. Hughes
Thomas J. Hunter
Leslie Ann Johnson
Michael N. Kaplan
Rick H. Kesler
Russel Z. Kowalyk
John M. Langs
Brian R. Leonard
J. Blair MacAulay (Counsel)
Audrey H. Mak
Ronald H. Marshall
Christopher J. Matthews
P. David McCutcheon
R. Marc Mercier
David L. Miller
David J. T. Mungovan
M. Catherine Osborne
Susan E. Paul
Mary M. Picard
Rubin Rapuch
Robert Rueter
Richard A. Scott
Peter A. Shiroky
Christopher J. Steeves
Roy D. R. Stewart
Jennifer S. Trent
Christopher Turney
Ross W. Walker

(See Next Column)

FRASER MILNER—*Continued*

PARTNERS, CONSULTANTS AND COUNSEL (Continued)

Dennis R. Wiebe
Christopher D. Woodbury
Patricia J. Williams
Michael Wunder

For full biographical listings, see the Martindale-Hubbell Law Directory

LANG MICHENER (AV)

BCE Place Suite 2500, 181 Bay Street, P.O. Box 747, M5J 2T7
Telephone: 416-360-8600
Telecopier: 416-365-1719
Email: langinfo@toronto.langmichener.ca *URL:* http://www.langmichener.ca
Vancouver, British Columbia Office: 1500 Royal Centre, P.O. Box 11117, 1055 West Georgia Street, V6E 4N7.
Telephone: 604-689-9111.
Telecopier: 604-685-7084.
Ottawa, Ontario Office: Suite 300, 50 O'Connor Street, K1P 6L2.
Telephone: 613-232-7171.
Telecopier: 613-231-3191.

RESIDENT MEMBERS

Gordon M. Farquharson, Q.C.
Gerhard K. Selzer, Q.C.
Warren S.R. Seyffert, Q.C.
Donald H. MacOdrum
Wayne F. Carney
J. Douglas Wilson
R. Nairn Waterman
Marni M.K. Whitaker
David Hager
Bruce A. McKenna
Peter E.J. Wells
Robert E. Glass
Geofrey Myers
David E. Thring
Nancy M. Johnston
William A. Rowlands
F. Paul Collins
J. Mark Richardson
Mark S. Mitchell
Joseph C. D'Angelo
John S. Contini
Daniel G. Edmondstone
Arnold Englander
Donald N. Plumley, Q.C.
Albert Gnat, Q.C.
Kalle Soomer, Q.C.
William J. V. Sheridan
John L. Dillman
Martin D. Rabinovitch
Robert R. Cranston
David M. W. Young
Frank Palmay
Mark E.P. Cavanaugh
Alexandra Hoy
Jeffrey B. Simpson
Howard M. Drabinsky
Patrick J. Phelan
David Burstein
James B. Musgrove
Carl A. De Vuono
Philippe Tardif
Carol Virginia Lyons
Eric B. Friedman
Helen L. Siwanowicz
Dale E. Schlosser

RESIDENT ASSOCIATES

Linda C. McCaffrey, Q.C.
Constance Olsheski
Vincent Berry
Stephanie Chong
Marie Lussier
Carmen Diges
Kimberly L. Townley-Smith
Christopher J. Garrah
Melynda E. A. Layton
Anne E. Butler
Neil V. Puddicombe
Timothy M. Squire
John C. Payne
Maria Scullion
Keith Bird
Craig Manuel
Kevin P. von Bargen
Arnold Ceballos
Cynthia Cross
Erik Penz
Arshia Tabrizi
Israel Balter
J. Michael Mulroy
Clive Elkin
Kenneth A. Krupat
Mark Morgan Mulima
D. Brent McPherson
Brian Ferstman
Nicolette Mueller
Marsha M. Lindsay
J. Lindsay Kertland
Martha Rafuse
Nicole Gerrard
François Potvin
Annelies I. Weiser
Peter Giddens
Gavin Smyth
F. (Beau) Zahrai
John Conway
Stephan Luciw
Lesley Rapaport
R. Scott Whitley

NON-LEGAL SUPPORT PERSONNEL

David H. Atkins
Madeline A. Courey
Susannah Rolston

COUNSEL

Robert J. Wright, Q.C.
Donald J. Wright, Q.C.
Louis H. Milrad
Robert A. Cranston, Q.C.
Robert M. McDerment, Q.C.
Howard A. Levitt
Lawrence Levenstein

For full biographical listings, see the Martindale-Hubbell Law Directory

MCCARTHY TÉTRAULT (AV)

Suite 4700 Toronto Dominion Bank Tower, M5K 1E6
Telephone: 416-362-1812
Facsimile: 416-868-0673
Email: toronto@mccarthy.ca *URL:* http://www.mccarthy.ca
Vancouver, British Columbia Office: Pacific Centre, P.O. Box 10424, Suite 1300, 777 Dunsmuir Street, Vancouver, British Columbia V7Y 1K2.
Telephone: 604-643-7100.
Facsimile: 604-643-7900.
Surrey, British Columbia Office: Suite 1300, Station Tower, Gateway 13401-108th Avenue, Surrey, British Columbia V3T 5T3.
Telephone: 604-583-9100.
Fax: 604-583-9150.

(See Next Column)

Calgary, Alberta Office: Suite 3300, 421 7th Avenue, S.W., Calgary, Alberta T2P 4K9.
Telephone: 403-260-3500.
Facsimile: 403-260-3501.
London, Ontario Office: Suite 2000, One London Place, 255 Queens Avenue, London, Ontario N6A 5R8.
Telephone: 519-660-3587.
Facsimile: 519-660-3599.
Ottawa, Ontario Office: The Chambers, Suite 1400, 40 Elgin Street, Ottawa, Ontario K1P 5K6.
Telephone: 613-238-2000.
Facsimile: 613-563-9386.
Montréal, Québec Office: Le Windsor, 1170 rue Peel, Montréal, Québec H3B 4S8.
Telephone: 514-397-4100.
Facsimile: 514-875-6246.
Québec, Québec Office: Le Complexe St-Amable 1150, rue Claire-Fontaine, 7e étage Québec, Québec G1R 5G4.
Telephone: 418-521-3000.
Facsimile: 418-521-3098, 418-521-3099
United Kingdom and Europe Office: Pountney Hill House, 6 Laurence Pountney Hill, London, England EC4R 0BL.
Telephone: 011-44 171-618-2888.
Facsimile: 011-44 171-618-2880.

PARTNERS

Peter G. Beattie, Q.C.
John H. Francis, Q.C.
L. Thomas Forbes, Q.C.
Bradley Crawford, Q.C.
Arthur R. A. Scace, Q.C.
David H. Gordon
Alan Peters
Peter S. Grant
Daryl E. McLean
Donald G. Gibson
D. Murray Paton
Edward P. Kerwin
W. Niels F. Ortved (Managing Partner)
Christopher S. L. Hoffmann
Henry J. P. Wiercinski
David M. Harley
F. David Rounthwaite
Judith M. Woods
Eric Gertner
Eric F. Spindler
Stephen D. A. Clark
Garth M. Girvan
Gerald P. Sadvari
René R. Sorell
Elizabeth M. Stewart
Thomas B. Akin
Gordon S. Sato
Gordon F. Willcocks
Richard B. Miner
Kirby Chown
Owen A. Johnson
Brian P. Smeenk
Harry C. G. Underwood
Abraham Costin
Brian C. Kelsall
Michael C. Nicholas
Gabrielle M. R. Richards
R. Paul Steep
Michael Weizman
Philip C. Moore
David M. Porter
William G. Scott
Mary M. Thomson
Jane A. Ford
Malcolm M. Mercer
David B. Tennant
Mark J. Freiman
Godyne N. L. Sibay
Ian W. Arellano
J. Thomas Curry
William H. Richardson
M. Philip Tunley
Barbara J. Boake
Jay M. Hoffman
David A. N. Lever
Brian C. Pel
John L. Walker
Oliver J. Borgers
Bernadette Dietrich
John R. Jason
William C. McDowell
Jenny P. Stephenson
William D. Black
Danny C. Grandilli
James G. Morand
Timothy J. Murphy
Sean D. Sadler
Neil E. Bass
H. J. Michael Croghan, Q.C.
C. Edward Walden
Donald E. Smith, Q.C.
James C. McCartney, Q.C.
Burton Tait, Q.C.
Thomas G. Heintzman, Q.C.
Terence M. Dolan
Peter H. Harris, Q.C.
Thomas H. Bjarnason
James B. Noonan
Dennis H. Wood
Glen G. MacArthur
G. Blair Cowper-Smith
Peter D. Quinn
Lorne P. Salzman
James R. Wilson
Henry G. (Hank) Intven
Adam D. Vereshack
Robert E. Forbes
F. Paul Morrison
James H. Archer
Stephen H. Diamond
Shanon O. N. Grauer
Phillip L. Sanford
Robert W. F. Stephenson
Frances B. Wright
Linda J. Betts
W. Iain C. Scott
David M. Armstrong
Michael G. Quigley
Brian D. Edmonds
Robert A. Macpherson
Alan Brad Teichman
Michael E. Barrack
Graham P. C. Gow
Kevin C. McLoughlin
Richard J. Nixon
Barry B. Sookman
Doug R. Thomson
John P. Brown
S. Richard Orzy
Barry J. Ryan
F. Gordon Thompson
Riyaz Dattu
William D. McCullough
Steven F. Rosenhek
Mary Beth Currie
Dean T. Palmer
George S. Takach
Nancy J. Carroll
Cynthia A. MacDougall
Fred M. Rubinoff
Christa C. Wessel
Suzanne M. Duncan
Douglas J. Klaassen
Marta O. Lewycky
Ronald R. Schwass
Jillian M. Welch
Mary K. Bull
Delee A. Fromm
Sheena J. MacAskill
Jeremy A. Oliver
Gregory James Winfield
Cindy J. Findlay
Jacqueline E.H. Lord
Iain R. Morton
Steven J. Rapkin
Leneo E. Sdao
Steven Baum

(See Next Column)

McCarthy Tétrault, *Toronto—Continued*

PARTNERS (Continued)

Danielle Marie Bush
David Judson
Marc J. MacMullin
Dana M. Peebles
Andrew J. Reddon
Gordon D. Baird
Darryl R. Ferguson
Gina Papageorgiou
Jerald M. Wortsman
Darryl A. Cruz
Jonathan C. Lisus
Kevin Zych
Robert J. Brant
Geoff R. Hall
Robert J. Richardson
Anthony M. C. Alexander
Julie Garner-Smith
Lorenzo Lisi
Frank McLaughlin
Paul J. Peterson
Caroline R. Zayid
John A. R. Dawson
Jonathan R. Grant
David E. Woollcombe
Lisa A. Clarkson
Susan L. Gratton
Linda Pieterson
Paul A. Boniferro
James D. Gage
Tanneke Heersche
Gregory B. Shepherd
J. Stephen Furlan

ASSOCIATES

Leslie A. Sigurdson
John W. Boscariol
Sacha C. Fraser
Lisa Constantine
Jeremy J. Devereux
Francois Gilbert
David E. Leonard
Michael W. Dunleavy
Naomi Morisawa De Koven
W. Ian Palm
Laura M. Porter
(Not admitted in ON)
Michael S. Valihora
John C. Yuan
S. Daniel Black
Mary Catherine Chambers
Bernice Fan
David M.G. Klassen
Robin C. MacAulay
Andrew C. Parker
Stephen D.E. Walters
John C. Currie
Brian C. Graves
Jane A. Langford
Andrew de L. McDougall
Angela M. Ross
Christopher A. Wayland
Andrew Armstrong
Erin K. Carley
(Not admitted in ON)
Rasha H. El Sissi
Peter C. Goode
John-David R.C. Humphreys
Stuart M. Miller
Stephanie L. Smith
Susan J. Spence
Lesley Arbus
Lia M. Bramwell
Brenda L. Cowie
William G. Ford
Avi E. Goldstein
Lori Anne Heckbert
Philip S. Kurtz
Dean Masse
John J. Salmas
Sean Sorensen
Gwendolyn G. Watson
Jonathan D. Gitlin
Kori J. Levitt
Debra R. MacIntyre
Glynnis P. Burt
France M. Tenaille
(Not admitted in ON)
Robert Fenton
Navin Khanna
Steven Mason
John Inglis
Peter Murphy
Ella Plotkin
Norma M. Priday
Adam L. Slater
Teresa J. Walsh
Lorraine Allard
Sally P. Bryant
Silvio A. D'Addario
Oliver Hobday
Cecilia C. Lee
Peter M. Neumann
Karen M. Sargeant
Norie Campbell
Jasprit Gill
Samantha R. Hans
Iain A.C. MacKinnon
Danielle T. Miller
Susan Rothfels
Elspeth M. Williams
Cynthia L. Cammidge
Suzanne Clapp
Hugh J. Craig
Dwight Gomes
Kathryn L. Hamill
Naizam Kanji
Craig Mitchell
Federico Soda
Thomas N.T. Sutton
Mary Lou Brady
Sarah M. Chesworth
Daniela Dos Santos
Alpana Garg
Robert O. Hansen
Michally A. Iny
Christopher Langdon
Dean Novak
Tiina K. Salo
Paula Trattner
Sarit E. Batner
Coreen Lawton
Blaise Szolgyemy

COUNSEL

Douglas G. Milne, Q.C.
A. S. Peter Kingsmill, Q.C.
Thomas E. (Tim) Armstrong
James W. McCutcheon, Q.C.
R. Barry Fillimore
Heather A. Howe
Stephen G. Rawson
Richard T. Pfohl
(Not admitted in ON)
Basil R. Cheeseman, Q.C.
The Hon. Donald S. Macdonald, P.C.
John M. Fingret
Stephen Grant
Nancy A. Eber
Sarah Boulby

ASSOCIATE COUNSEL

Ian Douglas, Q.C.
John H. C. Clarry, Q.C.
G. Patrick H. Vernon, Q.C.
Philip H. G. Walker, Q.C.
John B. Lawson, Q.C.
Harry W. Macdonell, Q.C.
Donald J. Donahue, Q.C.

For full biographical listings, see the Martindale-Hubbell Law Directory

McMillan Binch (AV)

Royal Bank Plaza Suite 3800 South Tower, M5J 2J7
Telephone: 416-865-7000
Fax: 416-865-7048
URL: http://www.mcbinch.com

(See Next Column)

MEMBERS OF FIRM

Peter G. Cathcart, Q.C.
W. David McCordic
Graham W. S. Scott, Q.C.
John W. Craig
Michael M. Peterson
J. William F. Rowley QC
John G. Armstrong
Donald E. Salisbury
Bruce C. Barker
George K.S. Payne
Joseph Chertkow
Andrew J. F. Kent
Francis A. Archibald
Thomas E. Scott
Paul J. Avis
David N. Ross
Catherine F. Nixon
Dennis A. Trinaistich
David S. Elenbaas
David W. Kent
Paul G. F. Macdonald
James D. Scarlett
Dalton J. Albrecht
Kathleen S.M. Hanly
Hilary E. Clarke
Margaret C. McNee
Catherine A. Roberts
Robert M. Scavone
Diana Cafazzo
Nancy J. Iadeluca
Tony Reyes
Sandra L. Walker
David R. Dunlop
Warren Kinsella
E. Jane Richardson
Joel Joseph Robichaud
A. Neil Campbell
Martha A. McCarthy
James H.M. Warnock
Vickie S. Wong
Shelley L. Munro
Sean M. Farrell
Melanie A. Yach
W. Brad Hanna
John T. Kalm
Jeffrey P. Roode
Elizabeth Alexandra Hall
Z. Edward Akkawi
Alexander M. Gay
Mark Lobsinger
Sandra Richmond
Stephen M. Tilly
Robert Wisner
Bruce A. Chapple
Pasquale (Pat) Forgione
Jacqueline Kwaga Masaba
Victoria B. Wilson
Michael J. Campbell
Sonia D. Keshwar
Tracy L. McPhee
Mark Opashinov
Kimberly J. Poster
Michelle M. Sloan
Jennifer Dent
Natalie M.R. Girard
Pollyanna Lord
Joanna L. Radbord
Cheryl Stacey
Steven R. Willard
John A. Paterson
Robert K. McDermott
William Woloshyn
Robert N. Gilmore
Richard B. Thomas
William V. Sasso
Alice Anne Morlock
David G. Butler
Douglas Barrett
Mickey M. Yaksich
Harold P. Rolph
Luigi (Lou) Macchione
Heather R. Douglas
Jean E. Anderson
Leonard Ricchetti
Simon Chester
Michael D. Templeton
David G. Wentzell
Jeffrey B. Gollob
Daniel V. MacDonald
Peter E. Milligan
David G. Woolford
Teresa M. Dufort
David H. Stewart
Mary-Ann E. Haney
Bruce N. McWilliam
Gary K. Ostoich
Michael P. Whitcombe
Chris N. Germanakos
Markus Koehnen
Esther Shainblum
John F. Clifford
Scott A. Horner
J. Scott Maidment
Richard T. Higa
Earl Stuart
John S. Liotta
Stephen C. E. Rigby
Peter A. Willis
Edward (Ted) Kelterborn
Lisa H. Kerbel Caplan
Tracey A. Lazareth
Tracey L. Durand
Glen R. Johnson
R.D. Jeffrey Rogers
John Fox
Todd A. Miller
Timothy Baron
Darryl R. Hiscocks
Estelle Richmond
David E. Slan
Omar K. Wakil
Ari Blicker
Alexander J. Du
Karen L. Liebesman
Kristin E. Maw
Lisa T. Wong
Thomas H. Kapsales
Kathryn J. Manning
Susan L. Nickerson
Claudette G. Pennesi
Karen R. Rosen
Bruno Battista
Robin Nicole Frew
Richard Koo
Andrew E.C. McFarlane
David Rinaldo
Shaul Tarek
Tara D'Andrea
Don Waters

For full biographical listings, see the Martindale-Hubbell Law Directory

Meighen Demers (AV)

Suite 1100, Merrill Lynch Canada Tower, 200 King Street West, P.O. Box 11, M5H 3T4
Telephone: 416-340-6000
Telecopier: 416-977-5239
Email: general@meighen.com *URL:* http://www.meighendemers.com

MEMBERS OF FIRM

Hon. Michael A. Meighen, Q.C.
John D. Pennal
Peter E. Lockie
John D. Stirling
James R. Cade
Richard S. Sutin
Jacques Demers
Alan Whiteley
Robert L. Armstrong
Dana B. Fuller
Derrick C. Tay
Peter S. Newell
Robert A. Kozlov
Ian A. Ness
John T. Porter
Mark A. Convery
Geoffrey Walker
Kevin J. Morley
Nicholas C. Williams
Merie-Anne E. Beavis
Rahul K. Bhardwaj
Charlie A. MacCready
M. Lynne O'Brien
Orestes Pasparakis

(See Next Column)

MEIGHEN DEMERS—*Continued*

MEMBERS OF FIRM (Continued)

Gil I. Cornblum
Barbara I.M. Crawley
Ashutosh Gupta
Wendy W. Choy
Virginie Gauthier
Jennifer F. Bensky
Elizabeth S. Lai-Fook
Susan T.C. Morais
Alan B. Merskey

For full biographical listings, see the Martindale-Hubbell Law Directory

MILLER THOMSON (AV)

20 Queen Street West, Suite 2500, M5H 3S1
Telephone: 416-595-8500
Fax: 416-595-8695
URL: http://www.millerthomson.ca
York Region, Ontario Office: 60 Columbia Way, Suite 600, Markham, Ontario, L3R 0C9.
Telephone: 905-415-6700.
Fax: 905-415-6777.
Edmonton, Alberta Office: 2700 Commerce Place, 10155-102 Street, Edmonton, Alberta, T5J 4G8.
Telephone: 780-429-1751.
Fax: 780-424-5866.
Calgary, Alberta Office: 3000, 700-9th Avenue S.W., Calgary, Alberta, T2P 3V4.
Telephone: 403-298-2400.
Fax: 403-262-0007.
Law Firm Affiliations/Associations:
Campney & Murphy - Vancouver, British Columbia, Canada
McCarter Grespan Robson Beynon - Kitchener, Ontario
Azevedo Sette Advogados - Sao Paulo and Belo Horizonte, Brazil, South America
Estudio Faraggi, Sateler & CIA - Santiago, Chile
Davis Arnold Cooper - London, England (Offices also in Manchester, Brussels, Vienna, Zurich, Madrid and Hong Kong)
Schürmann & Partners - Germany (Offices in Frankfurt, Berlin, Bonn, Dresden, Leipzig, Munich, Brussels, Milan, New York, Paris and Prague)
CONTACT: JUDSON D. WHITESIDE.
Telephone: 905-415-6701. E-mail: jwhitesi@millerthomson.ca.

A. David Churchill-Smith, Q.C.
John N. Turner, P.C., C.C., Q.C.
George A. Rolston
Hugh M. Kelly, Q.C.
Lawrence H. Iron, Q.C.
Adrian A. Phillips
Arthur D. Angus
Robert J. Fuller, Q.C.
B. Franklin Shostack
Franklin T. Richmond
Andrew J. Roman
James T. Beamish
David B. Buchanan
James D.M. Fraser
Brian M. Dourley
John R. Varley
Harold W.D. Cares
Michael C. Birley
Rosanne T. Rocchi
Michael J. Pace
Michael W. Kerr
John R. Sproat
Lawrence M. Foy
Peter D. Lauwers
R. Paul Edmonds
Michael T. Tamblyn
Kenneth W. Chalmers
Constance M. Brothers
Robert W. England
Susan Adam Metzler
Steven F. Hartley
John M. Campbell
Douglas F. Best
Hugh R. Dyer
Elizabeth K. Ackman
Paul Jones
Nancy M. Avison
Robert M. Stewart
Clifford J. Hart
Mark R. Frederick
Gita Anand
Bryan J. Buttigieg
Novalea Jarvis
Nora F. Osbaldeston
Derek J. Ferris
Anthony D. Scane
M. Christine O'Donohue
Nishan Swais
Marla N. Cox
Tamara Farber
Brent K. Duguid
Jennifer N. Maron
K. Duncan Finlayson, Q.C.
Jeffrey K. Smith
Gerald C. Hollyer, Q.C.
Lloyd D. Cadsby, Q.C.
Ivan Fleischmann
Eric B. Russell, Q.C.
Andrew M. Robinson
Robert L. Falby, Q.C.
Anthony K. Crossley
Peter J. Clarke
T. Keith Billings
Peter H. Smith
Lawrence A. Bertuzzi
Norman S. Rankin
Peter A. Daley
F. Max E. Maréchaux
Linda S. Bohnen
Effie J. Triantafilopoulos
D. Bruce McCartney
William M. Pigott
Wayne D. Gray
Jane A. Roffey
J. Jody Morrison
Gerald D. Courage
M. Stephen Georgas
Charles R. Robertson
Peter K. Foulds
Barbara R.C. Doherty
Jennifer E. Babe
S. Brian Levett
Michael J. Wren
John J. Chapman
Jeffrey C. Carhart
Susan M. Manwaring
Peter F. Chauvin
James A. Proskurniak
Gregory T. Callahan
Steven L. Wesfield
Chris T.J. Blom
Thomas R. Whitby
E. Peter Auvinen
Ani M. Abdalyan
Douglas J.R. Moodie
Wendy G. Hulton
Drazen F. Bulat
M. Jasmine Sweatman
Neil W. Henderson
Dirk L. Van de Kamer
Aleem Bharmal
Janice M. Duggan
Kirsten A. Ramage
Douglas Y. Han
Peter Prattas

(See Next Column)

Robert B. Hayhoe
Craig A. Mills
Alfred May
Lisa M. Dwyer

For full biographical listings, see the Martindale-Hubbell Law Directory

O'DONOHUE & O'DONOHUE (AV)

Suite 210, 330 Bay Street, M5H 2S8
Telephone: 416-361-3231
Fax: 416-361-3472
Email: odonohue@pathcom.com

MEMBERS OF FIRM

Melville O'Donohue, Q.C.
Stephen O'Donohue

ASSOCIATE

A. Sean Graham

For full biographical listings, see the Martindale-Hubbell Law Directory

OGILVY RENAULT (AV)

Suite 2100, P.O. Box 141 Royal Trust Tower, TD Centre, M5K 1H1
Telephone: 416-216-4000
Fax: 416-216-3930
Email: toronto@ogilvyrenault.com *URL:* http://www.ogilvyrenault.com
Montréal, Québec Office: Suite 1100, 1981 McGill College Avenue, H3A 3C1.
Telephone: 514-847-4747.
Fax: 514-286-5474. Email: info@ogilvyrenault.com
Ottawa, Ontario Office: Suite 1600, 45 O'Connor Street, K1P 1A4.
Telephone: 613-780-8661.
Fax: 613-230-5459. Email: ottawa@ogilvyrenault.com
Québec, Québec Office: Suite 520, 500 Grande Allée est, G1R 2J7.
Telephone: 418-640-5000.
Fax: 418-640-1500. Email: quebec@ogilvyrenault.com
Vancouver, British Columbia Office: 800 Park Place, 666 Burrard Street, V6C 3P3.
Telephone: 604-806-0922.
Fax: 604-806-0933. Email: info@ogilvyrenault.com
London, England Office: 38 Charterhouse Square, EC1M 6EQ, England.
Telephone: 44 (0) 207-600-9005.
Fax: 44 (0) 207-600-9006. Email: info@ogilvyrenault.com

Andrew J. Ahonen
Thomas I. A. Allen, Q.C.
Michael Bennett
D. Michael Brown
Charlotte E. Conlin
Nadine D. D'Aguiar
Terence S. Dobbin
Andrew Fleming (Not admitted in ON)
David C. Gavsie
Michael F. Horvat
Mary E. Kelly
Patrick E. Kierans
Julie A. Lane
Michael J. Lang
Barn-Yen Li
John Mastoras
Michael D. Matheson
Michael G. McFadden
William W. McNamara
Sandra Nissan
Darren Noseworthy
Stephanie L. Parkin
James A. Riley
Doug Sanderson
Stephen A. Scholtz
Charles F. Scott
Susan J. Serena
Michael G. Sherrard
C. Nicole Sigouin
Bogdan A. Teofilovici
Wendy D. Warhaft
Kirsten F. Watson
Michael A. Weinczok
John B. West
Ava G. Yaskiel

For full biographical listings, see the Martindale-Hubbell Law Directory

OSLER, HOSKIN & HARCOURT LLP (AV)

Barristers & Solicitors
Patent and Trade-Mark Agents
1 First Canadian Place, P.O. Box 50, M5X 1B8
Telephone: 416-362-2111
FAX: 416-862-6666
Email: counsel@osler.com *URL:* http://www.osler.com
Ottawa, Ontario Office: Suite 1500, 50 O'Connor Street, K1P 6L2.
Telephone: 613-235-7234.
FAX: 613-235-2867.
Calgary, Alberta Office: Suite 1900, Toronto Dominion Square, 333 - 7th Avenue S.W., T2P 2Z1.
Telephone: 403-260-7000.
Fax: 403-260-7024.
New York, N.Y. Office: 280 Park Avenue-30W, 10017.
Telephone: 212-867-5800.
Fax: 212-867-5802.

MEMBERS OF FIRM

Ahab Abdel-Aziz
S. Firoz Ahmed
David W. Aitken (Resident in Ottawa, Ontario)
Stephen V. Arnold
Ronald G. Atkey, P.C., Q.C.
Andrew W. Aziz
Laurie E. Barrett
Monica E. Biringer
Lorne H. Abugov (Resident in Ottawa, Ontario)
Deborah M. Alexander
Francis R. Allen (Resident in Calgary, Alberta)
Sean C. Aylward
Lyndon A. J. Barnes
D. Robert Beaumont
Arthur Birnbaum

(See Next Column)

OSLER, HOSKIN & HARCOURT LLP, *Toronto—Continued*

MEMBERS OF FIRM (Continued)

John M. Bishop
Glen A. Bloom
(Resident in Ottawa, Ontario)
Penelope S. Bonner
Michael H. D. Bowman
Brian D. Bucknall
Terrence R. Burgoyne
Rupert H. Chartrand
Richard J. Coleman
Maurice J. Coombs
John C. Cotter
Linda G. Currie
Jean M. De Marco
Anthony J. Devir
Valerie A. E. Dyer
John T. Evans
Marilyn M.M. Field-Marsham
Peter H. G. Franklyn
Mark A. Gelowitz
Deborah A. Glendinning
Steven G. Golick
Michael J. Gough
W. Jason M. Hanson
James R. Hassell
Laurence D. Hebb, Q.C.
David Hunter
John A. Kazanjian
J. Timothy Kennish
(Co-Managing Partner)
A. Michelle Lally
Allyson C. Landy (On Leave)
J. Brett G. Ledger
Jolie Lin
Paul W. Litner
Norman C. Loveland
Stephen W. Luff
Andrew J. MacDougall
Daniel Macintosh
Tristram J. Mallett
(Resident in Calgary, Alberta)
Donald L. Marston
Barbara J. McGregor
Heather R. McKean
(Co-Managing Partner)
Ian J. F. McSweeney
Paul J. Morassutti
David S. Morritt
Blake M. Murray
Frederick L. Myers
Shelley W. Obal
Eden M. Oliver
Randy A. Pepper (On Leave)
Richard H. Peters
(Resident in Calgary, Alberta)
Dale R. Ponder
Christopher Portner
J. Andrew Pritchard
(Resident in Ottawa, Ontario)
Lawrence E. Ritchie
Linda D. Robinson
John F. Rook
Tracy C. Sandler
Timothy P. Schumacher
Edward A. Sellers
Jack A. Silverson
(Resident in Calgary, Alberta)
James H. Smellie
(Resident in Ottawa, Ontario)
Steven W. Smith
David A. Stamp
Stanley B. Stein
John W. Stevens
(Resident in New York, N.Y.)
R. John (Jack) Thrasher
(Resident in Calgary Alberta)
Richard G. Tremblay
Steven J. Trumper
Susan Van Der Hout
Elizabeth M. Walker
(Resident in Ottawa, Ontario)
W. Lee Webster
Donna G. White
(Resident in Ottawa, Ontario)
David K. Wilson
(Resident in Ottawa, Ontario)
J. Craig Wright
(Resident in Ottawa, Ontario)
Stephen G. Blair
(Resident in Ottawa, Ontario)
Kenneth L. W. Boland
(Resident in Ottawa, Ontario)
Ariel Z. Breitman
(Resident in Calgary, Alberta)
Nancy D. Chaplick
Ronald C. Cheng
(Resident in Ottawa, Ontario)
Diane E. Cornish
(Resident in Ottawa, Ontario)
Michael J. Davies
J. Mark DesLauriers
Jennifer Dolman
Kirsten R. Embree
(Resident in Ottawa, Ontario)
James E. Fordyce
Jean M. Fraser
Donald G. Gilchrist
Peter L. Glossop
Clara M. González-Martin
Donald D. Hanna
Adrian P. Hartog
Philip J. B. Heath
H. B. Clay Horner
Sushma Jobanputra
James F. Kennedy, Q.C.
Andrew H. Kingissepp
C. W. Daniel Kirby
Robert C. Lando
John F. Layton
Julie Y. Lee
James H. Lisson
Richard A. Lococo
Larry P. Lowenstein
John A. MacDonald
John H. Macfarlane
Stanley Magidson
R. Gordon Marantz, Q.C.
Douglas R. Marshall
Edward T. McDermott
Andrew S. McGuffin
K. Scott McLean
(Resident in Ottawa, Ontario)
Kelly L. Moffatt
Brian G. Morgan
G. Lee Muirhead
Christopher S. Murray
Christopher W. Nixon
(Resident in Calgary, Alberta)
Arthur J. Peltomaa
John F. Petch, Q.C.
(Vice-Chair of the Firm)
Kent H.E. Plumley
(Resident in Ottawa, Ontario)
Randall W. Pratt
(Resident in New York, N.Y.)
Raymond E. Quesnel
(Resident in Calgary, Alberta)
John M.M. Roland, Q.C.
Donald C. Ross
Scott L. Scheuermann
E.A. (Ward) Sellers
Stephen P. Sigurdson
Janet E. Sim
Stephen B. Smart
Mark R. Smith
(Resident in Calgary, Alberta)
Gregory O. Somers
(Resident in Ottawa, Ontario)
Joseph M. Steiner
Geoffrey K. Taber
David T. Tetreault
Terrence J. Tone
Mark A. Trachuk (Resident in London, England)
George M. Valentini
Ruth I. Wahl
Don Watkins
(Not admitted in ON)
Karen J. Weinstein (On leave)
Peter White
Scott Wilkie
Patricia J. Wilson
(Resident in Ottawa, Ontario)
Robert M. Yalden
Frank Zaid
H. Alec Zimmerman

(See Next Column)

ASSOCIATES

Kevin Ackhurst
Leonard Arnold
Mark Austin
(Not admitted in ON)
Dov B. Begun
Lauralee Bielert
John A. Black
Ian D. Bock
Richard Borins
Patrick J. Callaghan
Anne C. Carty
Peter J. Chapin
Samuel Delbert Clark
Jacqueline Code
Julie A. Colden
Jason Comerford
K. Monica Creery
Carl J.A. DeLuca
(Resident in New York, N.Y.)
Jason Dubchak
(Not admitted in ON)
Alexandra Eshelman
Michael G. G. Fekete
F. Susan Fisher
Kim Forwell
Sherri L. Fountain
(Resident in Calgary, Alberta)
Andraya C. Frith
Tanya M. Goldberg
Alyson F. Goldman
(Resident in Calgary, Alberta)
Julia M. Graham
Rosemary Grenside
John Groenewegen
Kelly J. Harbridge
Martha A. Healey
(Resident in Ottawa, Ontario)
Yi-Wen Hsu
Mahmud Jamal
Peter S. Janicki
Thomas T. Jurkovic
Thomas Gresham Kelley
(Resident in Ottawa, Ontario)
Terra Klinck
Stephen Lamont
Desmond M. Lee
Sean Love
Jonathan Lundy
Natasha MacParland
Robin L. Martin
Allan Millard
(Resident in Ottawa, Ontario)
Christopher P. Naudie
Bonnie C. Oldham
Susan M. Paré
David V. Pathe
Melanie A. Polowin
(Resident in Ottawa, Ontario)
Douglas J. Rienzo
John C. Roberts
Patricia Ross
M. Janet Salter
Steve Sansom
Robin B. Schwill
Paul W. A. Severin
Daniel Shap
Elizabeth R. Shriver
Stephen Solursh
Y. Monica Song
(Resident in Ottawa, Ontario)
Joseph A. Starkman
(Not admitted in ON)
Nancy J. Stitt
Caroline L.M. Thomas
Elizabeth Topp
Ed Vandenberg
(Resident in Ottawa, Ontario)
David T. Weyant
(Resident in Calgary, Alberta)
Rani Wong
(Not admitted in ON)
Sandra Adams
(Not admitted in ON)
Benjamin P. Bedard
(Resident in Ottawa, Ontario)
Paulo Berard
Sonia L. Bjorkquist
Stephen Blimkie
Janet E. Bolton
Douglas A. Bryce
Darlene Carreau
(Resident in Ottawa, Ontario)
Eugene A.G. Cipparone
(Resident in New York, N.Y.)
Michael Cody
Allan Coleman
Paul Conlin
Jeremy Dacks
Andrew M. Diamond
Sarah Downie
Cheryl D.M. Emberley
(Resident in Ottawa, Ontario)
Eleanor K. Farrell
Gregory M. Firnau
Kenneth B. Flowers
(Resident in Calgary, Alberta)
Sivan A. Fox
Laura K. Fric
Karen E. Galpern
Matthew H. Golden
Kevin J. Gormely
Alexis Gosselin
Benjamin Gray
G.Dean Gresdal
Katty Habib
Michael S. Hart
Christine E. Hicks
(Resident in Ottawa, Ontario)
Michael Innes
Tara James
Adam W. Joseph
Derek S. Keay
(Resident in Ottawa, Ontario)
Leigh Ann Kirby
(Resident in Ottawa, Ontario)
John Leddy
Andrew D. Little
(Resident in Calgary, Alberta)
Camilla A. Mackenzie
Patrick W. Marley
Eddy Mezzetta
Lynn L. Mitchell
Frank W.B. Morison
Cameron G. Negraiff
Donald Padget
Marion F.B. Passmore
Shari A. Pinkus
Michal Lynne Pomotov
Richard S. Pratt
Damian J. Rigolo
Nancy L. Roberts
Tal Sagorsky
Lisa Sand
Daniel L. Scholes
Rocco M. Sebastiano
Dale Seymour
Christine A. Sharp
Sean S. Smyth
(Resident, Calgary, Alberta)
M. Lynn Starchuk
(Resident in Ottawa, Ontario)
Paul H. Starkman
Daniel E. Steiner
Carla R. Swansburg
Mark L. Thompson
Marc A. Valencia
Frank Vivacqua
Allan C. Wells
Kimberley J. Wharram
Andrew Wong
Sabrina W.Y. Wong
Gregory R. Wylie
Landon P. Young

DEPARTMENT OF LEGAL EDUCATION

Mara L. Nickerson

PATENT AGENT

James R. Keneford
(Resident in Ottawa, Ontario)

For full biographical listings, see the Martindale-Hubbell Law Directory

Toronto—Continued

SHIBLEY RIGHTON (AV)

Suite 1900 The Simpson Tower, 401 Bay Street, P.O. Box 32, M5H 2Z1
Telephone: 416-363-9381
Telecopier: 416-214-5438
Affiliated Offices: Windsor, Ontario

MEMBERS AND ASSOCIATES

Harold H. Elliott, Q.C.
Barry S. Wortzman, Q.C.
Leslie S. Mason
John P. Bell
Michael M. K. Fitzpatrick, Q.C.
Peter C. Williams
Peter G. Neilson
Jonathan H. Flanders
Charles Simco
William L. Northcote
Helder M. Travassos
Peter V. Raytek
Charles Gastle
Sheila M. MacKinnon
J. Paul R. Howard
Sandra E. Dawe
Janis E. Ingram
Thomas McRae
Cinda M. Serianni
Marion Hoffer
Byrdena M. MacNeil
Elizabeth Bennett-Martin
Richard D. LeBlanc
M. Hannah Lee

COUNSEL

Richard E. Shibley, Q.C.
John F. O'Donnell
Martin L. O'Brien, Q.C.

For full biographical listings, see the Martindale-Hubbell Law Directory

SMITH LYONS (AV)

Suite 5800, Scotia Plaza, 40 King Street, West, M5H 3Z7
Telephone: 416-369-7200
Facsimile: 416-369-7250
URL: http://www.smithlyons.ca
Ottawa, Ontario Office: Suite 2300, 150 Metcalfe Street.
Telephone: 613-230-3988.
Facsimile: 613-230-7085.
Kyiv, Ukraine Office: Suite 507, 26 Lesia Ukrainka Boulevard, 252133.
Telephone: 380 44-573-8858.
Facsimile: 380 44-295-5240.

MEMBERS OF FIRM AND ASSOCIATES

H. Bernard Mayer, Q.C.
John D. Stevenson, Q.C.
Thomas R. Hawkins
Bohdan S. Onyschuk, Q.C.
John G. Myers
J. Thomas Brett
Robert E. Milnes
Frank N. Marrocco, Q.C.
William J. McNaughton
Leslie T. Gord
Ronald M. Richler
S. Paul Mantini
Bruce M. Graham
Peter A. Magnus
(At Ottawa and Kyiv Offices)
Louise S. Pelly, Q.C.
David F. Bell
C. Michael Harpur
Evelyn P. Moskowitz
Kathryn M. Tamaki
Grant W. Gold
David B. Light
Lilly A. Wong
Franklin L. Davis
Mark A. McHughan
Graeme Mew
Dean J. Blain
Elise Orenstein
Elizabeth E. Breen
Robert D. Muncaster
Daniel W. Sooley
Steven I. Sofer
Pamela D. Horton
K. Lynn Mahoney
John E. Callaghan
Richard C. Owens
Peter E. Manderville
Tina M. Woodside
David F.W. Cohen
Maxine M. Kerr
Gordon R. Pansegrau
Ariane Siegel
Myron B. Dzulynsky
Todd M. May
Barbara Jo Caruso
Lesley R. Charkow
Jane M. Waechter
Moira J. Callahan
Karen P. Earl
Lisa R. Lifshitz
Aaron Schwartz
Noona R.A. Barlow
Debra M. Haak
Melissa J. Catalano
Robert A. Smith, Q.C.
John R. Finley, Q.C.
D. William Mutch, Q.C.
Michael J. Anderson
Brian G. Armstrong, Q.C.
Robert D. Finlayson
Arthur P. Tarasuk
David J. McFadden, Q.C.
Rodney W.J. Seyffert
C. Barry Tarshis
Glenn A. Hainey
Alan P.C. Dean
Donald B. Johnston
Michael S.F. Watson
Nicholas E.J. Dietrich
Jeffrey Wm. Strype
Allen V. Craig
Paul H. Harricks
R. Bruce Smith
Andrew D. Brands
Robert G.S. Hull
James D. Tomlinson
Christopher J. Bardsley
Carolyn J. Horkins
Terence A. McNally
Merle D. Rosenhek
Hugh A. Christie
Katherine M. van Rensburg
Phillip P. Macdonald
Stephen A. Pike
Justin R.G. Fogarty
Martha L. McKinnon
John T. Kruk
Heather E. Perkins-McVey
Daniel R. Hayhurst
Darryl J. Brown
Jane V. Nelson
John W. Petrykanyn
James E. Fisher
David E. Liblong
Joel M. Scoler
Emily C. Cole
Gloria J. Geddes
Hilda W. Wong
Seanna L. Callaghan
Michael G. Kovacevic
Yuri V. Zaichuck
(Not admitted in ON)
D. Chad Hutchison
John P. Ormston
Mark J. Travers
Daniella E. Dimitrov
Nicole Y. Himel
Seán C. O'Neill

(See Next Column)

MEMBERS OF FIRM AND ASSOCIATES (Continued)

Kim Silvestri
Eric J. Adelson
Belinda A. Bain
Robert L. Percival
Kathleen M. Ritchie
Ned Djordjevic
William A. Schnurr
Corina O. Zatreanu
Aaron Del Rizzo
Katherine M. Gurney
Tony R. Linardi
Fraser D. Rowand
E. Patrick Shea
Christopher N. Alam
Boyd Balogh
Susan P. Redmayne
Simon P. Crawford
Bryce A. Kraeker
C. Michelle Small
Shani Briffa
Ryan R. Farquhar
Andrea J. Himel
Elana J. Lipstein
Leisa A. Stangret
Troy B. Ungerman

PATENT AND TRADE-MARK AGENTS

Christopher B. Barlow
June M. Baigent
Gerald A. Gowan

IMMIGRATION CONSULTANTS

Harry Goslett
Gary Moore

URBAN PLANNER

Brian Parker

G.S.T. SPECIALIST

Allan Taitz

For full biographical listings, see the Martindale-Hubbell Law Directory

STIKEMAN ELLIOTT (AV)

Commerce Court West, Suite 5300, M5L 1B9
Telephone: 416-869-5500
Fax: 416-947-0866
Email: info@stikeman.com *URL:* http://www.stikeman.com
Montreal, Quebec Office: 1155 René-Lévesque Boulevard West, 40th Floor, H3B 3V2.
Telephone: 514-397-3000.
Telex: 05-267316.
Fax: 514-397-3222.
Ottawa, Ontario Office: 50 O'Connor Street, Suite 914, K1P 6L2.
Telephone: 613-234-4555.
Fax: 613-230-8877.
Calgary, Alberta Office: 1500 Bankers Hall, 855 - 2nd Street S.W., T2P 4J7.
Telephone: 403-266-9000.
Fax: 403-266-9034.
Vancouver, British Columbia Office: Suite 1700, Park Place, 666 Burrard Street, V6C 2X8.
Telephone: 604-631-1300.
Fax: 604-681-1825.
New York, N.Y. Office: Tower 56, 126 East 56th Street, 14th Floor, 10022.
Telephone: 212-371-8855.
Fax: 212-371-7087.
London, England Office: Regis House, 45 King William Street, EC4R 9AN.
Telephone: +44 (0) 20 7648 1300.
Fax: +44 (0) 20 7648 1400.
Hong Kong Office: 29 Queen's Road Central, Suite 1103, Aon China Building.
Telephone: 852-22305200.
Fax: 852-2845-9076.
Singapore Office: 1 Shenton Way, #13-07 Robina House, Singapore 068803.
Telephone: 65-532-3556.
Fax: 65-532-3557.
Sydney, Australia Office: Level 40, The Chifley Tower, 2 Chifley Square.
Telephone: 61-2-9232-7199.
Fax: 61-2-9232-6908.

SENIOR ASSOCIATES AND PARTNERS IN TORONTO

Roderick F. Barrett
William J. Braithwaite
David R. Byers
Stuart S. Carruthers
Richard E. Clark
Paul Collins
Curtis Cusinato
James C. Davis
John R. Dow
Ronald K. Durand
Ron A. Ferguson
David Glicksman
Margaret E. Grottenthaler
James W. Harbell
Brenda Hebert
Ruth A. C. Horn
Peter F.C. Howard
Karen E. Jackson
Katherine L. Kay
Kevin B. Kelly
Dean A. Kraus
Jennifer G. Legge
John G. Lorito
Christopher T. Bean
David M. Brown
Michael R. Carman
Kathryn I. Chalmers
Larry Cobb
Christopher J. Cosgriffe
Lorna A. Cuthbert
Rocco M. Delfino
Sean F. Dunphy
R. Fraser Elliott, C.M., Q.C.
David N. Finkelstein
Kimberley M. Graham
Peter E. Hamilton
Douglas F. Harrison
L. Milton Hess, Q.C.
Samantha G. Horn
Lawson A. W. Hunter, Q.C.
John A. M. Judge
Jay C. Kellerman
Eliot N. Kolers
Martin Langlois
F. Daniel H. Logan
Daphne J. MacKenzie

(See Next Column)

STIKEMAN ELLIOTT, *Toronto—Continued*

SENIOR ASSOCIATES AND PARTNERS IN TORONTO (Continued)

David R. McCarthy
E. Lianne Miller
Edgar D. Moss
Robert W. A. Nicholls
Jennifer L. Northcote
Patrick J. O'Kelly
C. Mario Paura
Sharon C. Polan
Dana Porter
Dee Rajpal
Anne L. Ristic
W. Brian Rose
Michael D. Rumball
Wayne E. Shaw
Kenneth Harold Swain
Ashley John Taylor
Thomas Vowinckel
Kathleen G. Ward
Marvin Yontef
Nathalie Mercure
Shawna M. Miller
Gary F. Nachshen
Angelo Nikolakakis
Kieran O'Donnell
Mark Osbaldeston
Elizabeth Pillon
R. Bruce Pollock
Brian M. Pukier
Darin R. Renton
Simon A. Romano
David M. Ross
William A. Scott
John M. Stransman
Joanne E. Swystun
Mihkel E. Voore
Edward J. Waitzer
Edward Weidberg
Alison J. Youngman

For full biographical listings, see the Martindale-Hubbell Law Directory

THOMSON, ROGERS (AV)

Suite 3100 390 Bay Street, M5H 1W2
Telephone: 416-868-3100
Fax: 416-868-3134

PARTNERS

Lawrence H. Mandel, Q.C.
Desmond H. Dixon
Patrick D. Schmidt
Alan A. Farrer
Stephen J. D'Agostino
Leonard H. Kunka
Jeffrey J. Wilker
Roger T. Beaman
David R. Neill
L. Craig Brown
Sharon E. Ramsden
Richard C. Halpern
David R. Tenszen
David F. MacDonald

ASSOCIATES

Michelle E. Gill
Sloan H. Mandel
Wendy M. Moore Johns
Leah K. Bowness
Graham F. Sirman

COUNSEL

Kenneth E. Howie, Q.C.
Ralph O. Howie, Q.C.

For full biographical listings, see the Martindale-Hubbell Law Directory

TORYS (AV)

Suite 3000, Maritime Life Tower, Toronto-Dominion Centre, P.O. Box 270, M5K 1N2
Telephone: 416-865-0040; 800-505-8679
Fax: 416-865-7380
URL: http://www.torys.com
Affiliated With:
Desjardins Ducharme Stein Monast-Montreal, Quebec City, Quebec.
New York, N.Y. Office: 237 Park Avenue, 10017.
Telephone: 212-880-6000.
Facsimile: 212-682-0200.
Beijing, China Office: China Merchants Tower, Suite C, 29/F, 2 Dong Huan Nan Lu, Jianguomenwai, Chaoyang District, 100022.
Telephone: 011-8610-6566-9088.
Facsimile: 011-8610-6566-9096.

PARTNERS AND ASSOCIATES

James M. Tory, Q.C.
Brian W. Shields, Q.C.
Ross L. Kennedy
James C. Baillie, Q.C.
Paul M. Moore, Q.C.
Sidney P. H. Robinson
Brian M. Flood
Gabor G. S. Takach
Sheila R. Block
Wilfred M. Estey
Stephen R. Richardson
James E. A. Turner
Herman J. Wilton-Siegel
Michael B. Rotsztain
Patricia D. S. Jackson
John W. McIninch
Donald B. Roger
Richard J. Balfour
Katherine Christie
Jacqueline R. Bryers
Roger Cotton
Sandra J. Geddes
W. Kenneth McCarter
R. John Cameron
Patricia A. Koval
Les M. Viner
Brian A. Davis
Michael K. Feldman
Robert H. Karp
William J. DesLauriers, Q.C.
David E. Baird, Q.C.
H. Lorne Morphy, Q.C.
Michael G. Thorley, Q.C.
Robert P. Armstrong, Q.C.
Robin D. Walker, Q.C.
Charles M. Dalfen (Not admitted in ON)
Peter E. S. Jewett
Laurence A. Pattillo
Barry A. Leon
Geoffrey J. R. Dyer
Barry J. Reiter
Marlene J. Davidge
John B. Laskin
Stephen J. Donovan
John Unger
Heather G. Hisey
Kathleen L. Keller-Hobson
Richard A. Conway
Geoffrey D. Creighton
Karen A. Malatest
Cheryl L. Waldrum
Corrado Cardarelli
James C. Tory
James W. Welkoff
Beth DeMerchant
Judith E. Harris
Sharon C. Pel

(See Next Column)

PARTNERS AND ASSOCIATES (Continued)

Michael A. Penny
Kent E. Thomson
Peter D. Ballantyne
R. Jay Holsten
Gary S. A. Solway
Donald P. Wright
Peter K. Fritze
Christina H. Medland
David A. Chaikof
Mario J. Forte
Edwin B. Nordholm
Mary H. Mullens
Cheryl L.C. Lewis
Tony DeMarinis
Blair W. Keefe
Rose T. Bailey
Adam E. Delean
Peter B. Birkness
S. Wendy Del Mul
Hugh M. O'Reilly
John A. Terry
Julia E. Holland
Jonathan B. Weisz
David P. Chernos
Wendy J. Gross
Kevin M. Morris
David A. Steele
Graeme A. Coffin
Jane S. Bailey
Trevor C.W. Farrow
Suh W. Kim
Sarah L. MacKenzie
Ann Marie McGovern
Natalie A. Ochrym
Faeron K. Trehearne
Kyle Genga
Christopher J. Fowles
Peter A.M. Kalins
Cameron D. Koziskie
Salil Munjal
Karrin A. Powys-Lybbe
Danny N. Dagan
K. Vanessa A. Grant
R. Randy MacEwen
M. Paul Michell
Michael C.J. Padfield
Nicole S. Rosenberg
Michael D. Amm
Christophe G. Bondy
Kelly L. Brown
Donna J. Clark
Ronit Florence
Cheryl L. Graden
Alexandra Kau
Tanya C. Mushynski
Philip de L. Panet
Samantha J. Sheen
Darren D. Baccus
Michael R. Barrett
Andrew E. Bernstein
Antonio Di Tullio
John E. Emanoilidis
Darcy L. Macpherson
Melanie A. Shishler
Andrew G. Spence
Dawn V. Scott
Robert M. Aziz
Leonard J. Griffiths
Philip Mohtadi
Lucia M. ten Kortenaar
Philip J. Brown
Robert Mansell
Edward J. Babin
Debbie De Girolamo
Jane C. Helmstadter
Alison Lacy
Sharon C. Geraghty
Wendy M. Matheson
Daniel R. Donnelly
Lillian Y. Pan
William A. Charnetski
Philip D.A. Symmonds
Clare E. Burns
Donna L. Parish
Ilene R. Shiller
J. James Duffield
Steve J. Tenai
Peter A. Aziz
Patrick D. Flaherty
John P. Koch
John C. Sheedy
Patrice S. Walch-Watson
A. Douglas Harris
Matthew W. Cockburn
Sharon M. Haward-Laird
Melissa T. G. LaFlair
Dennis E. Mahony
Carolyn N. Naiman
Michael J. Siltala
Antonella Deo
David W. Foulds
Krista F. Hill
Simon C. Knowling
Tycho M.J. Manson
Linda M. Plumpton
Darren E. Sukonick
Jeffrey M. Davis
Sherri Kreisman
Rhonda L. Maines
Paul V. Noble
Paul O. Petrelli
Cynthia L. Tape
Adam S. Armstrong
Sophie R. Boulakia
Alexandra S. Clark
Elizabeth J. Evans
Geoffrey G. Gilbert
Jennifer E. Guerard
Judith H. Kim
Nanci M. Nickerson
David A. Seville
Michael F.E. Akkawi
Peter Balasubramanian
Shawn L. Beber
Amanda C. Chester
Paul Dufays
Christina E. Litz
Michael T. Pickersgill
Crawford G. Smith
Arlen K. Sternberg
Jamie R.D. Todd

COUNSEL

Hon. Charles L. Dubin, O.C., O.Ont., Q.C., LL.D.
Hon. William G. Davis, P.C., C.C., Q.C.

PROFESSIONAL DEVELOPMENT DEPARTMENT

Janet M. Hoyt (Not admitted in ON; Director, Professional Development)

For full biographical listings, see the Martindale-Hubbell Law Directory

*WINDSOR,** Essex Co.

MCTAGUE LAW FIRM (AV)

455 Pelissier Street, N9A 6Z9
Telephone: 519-255-4300
Detroit, Michigan Telephone: 313-965-1332
Fax: 519-255-4360(Corporate/Labor)
Fax: 519-255-4384 (Litigation/Real Estate)

MEMBERS OF FIRM

H. M. McTague, Miss, Q.C. (1900-1986)
Alexander R. Szalkai, Q.C.
Peter J. Kuker
George W. King
J. Douglas Lawson, Q.C.
Roger A. Skinner
Daniel K. Moorhouse
Jerry B. Udell
Michael K. Coughlin

(See Next Column)

McTAGUE LAW FIRM—*Continued*

MEMBERS OF FIRM (Continued)

Josephine Stark
Tom Serafimovski
John D. Leslie
Marilee Marcotte

ASSOCIATES

Kevin G. Fanick
Michael A. Wills
Dana J. Young
Jeffrey W. MacKinnon
Brian L. Chillman

For full biographical listings, see the Martindale-Hubbell Law Directory

SUTTS, STROSBERG LLP (AV)

600 Westcourt Place, 251 Goyeau Street, P.O. Box 670, N9A 6V4
Telephone: 519-258-9333
Detroit Michigan: 313-962-0137
Facsimile: Windsor 519-258-9527
Detroit 313-962-0139

MEMBERS OF FIRM

Achille F. Gignac, Q.C. (1902-1984)
Robert E. Barnes, Q.C.
Clifford N. Sutts, Q.C.
Harvey T. Strosberg, Q.C.
Gary V. Wortley
James K. Ball
John C. Holland
Mary M. S. Fox
William C. Chapman
Donald M. Gordon
Paul C. Nesseth
Heather Rumble Peterson
Patricia A. Speight
Edward W. Ducharme
Michelle A. Gagnon
Craig J. Allen
Werner H. Keller
Francine A. Herlehy
Paul Simard
Jasminka Kalajdzic

COUNSEL FOR CRIMINAL MATTERS

Patrick J. Ducharme

For full biographical listings, see the Martindale-Hubbell Law Directory

CANADA PRINCE EDWARD ISLAND

*CHARLOTTETOWN,** Queen's Co.

CAMPBELL, LEA, MICHAEL, McCONNELL & PIGOT (AV)

15 Queen Street, P.O. Box 429, C1A 7K7
Telephone: 902-566-3400
Telecopier: 902-566-9266
Email: www.office@campbelllea.com

MEMBERS OF FIRM

William G. Lea, Q.C.
Robert A. McConnell
M. Jane Ralling
Paul D. Michael, Q.C.
Ross D. Pigot
Kenneth L. Godfrey
Karolyn M. Godfrey

General Counsel in Prince Edward Island for: Canadian Imperial Bank of Commerce; Maritime Electric Co., Ltd.; Michelin Tires (Canada) Ltd.; Newsco Investments Ltd. (Dundas Farms); Imperial Oil Limited; General Motors of Canada; Co-op Atlantic; Liberty Mutual; Employers Reinsurance Group.

For full biographical listings, see the Martindale-Hubbell Law Directory

McINNES COOPER (AV Ⓣ)

Barristers, Solicitors & Trade Mark Agents
BDC Place, Suite 620, 119 Kent Street, C1A 1N3
Telephone: 902-368-8473
Fax: 902-368-8346
Email: mcrpei@mcrlaw.com *URL:* http://www.mcrlaw.com
Halifax, Nova Scotia Office: Summit Place, 1601 Lower Water Street, P.O. Box 730, B3J 2V1.
Telephone: 902-425-6500.
Fax: 902-425-6350. Email: mcrhfx@mcrlaw.com.
St. John's, Newfoundland Office: Baine Johnston Centre, 5th Floor, 10 Fort William Place, P.O. Box 5939, A1C 5X4.
Telephone: 709-722-8735.
Telecopier: 709-722-1763. Email: mcrsj@mcrlaw.com.
Moncton, New Brunswick Office: Place Moncton Place, 655 Main Street, P.O. Box 1368, E1C 8T6.
Telephone: 506-857-8970.
Fax: 506-857-4095. Email: mcrmctn@mcrlaw.com.
Fredericton, New Brunswick Office: Suite 600, 570 Queen Street, P.O. Box 610.
Telephone: 506-458-8572.
Fax: 506-458-9903. Email: mcrfton@mcrlaw.com.

PARTNER, HALIFAX OFFICE

Reginald A. Cluney, Q.C.

PARTNERS

Horace B. Carver, Q.C.
Mark Ledwell
Michele M. Murphy

(See Next Column)

ASSOCIATES

L. Charles Keizer
Murray L. Murphy
Kevin J. Kiley
Paul Kiley
Kim Petrie

For full biographical listings, see the Martindale-Hubbell Law Directory

STEWART McKELVEY STIRLING SCALES (AV)

65 Grafton Street, P.O. Box 2140, C1A 8B9
Telephone: 902-892-2485
Telecopier: 902-566-5283
Email: charlottetown@smss.com *URL:* http://www.smss.com
Halifax, Nova Scotia Office: Suite 900, Purdy's Wharf Tower One, 1959 Upper Water Street, P.O. Box 997, B3J 2X2.
Telephone: 902-420-3200.
Telecopier: 902-420-1417. Email: halifax@smss.com
Sydney, Nova Scotia Office: 50 Dorchester Street. P.O. Box 820, B1P 6J1.
Telephone: 902-539-5135.
Telecopier: 902-539-8256. Email: sydney@smss.com
Fredericton, New Brunswick Office: Suite 600, Frederick Square, 77 Westmorland Street, P.O. Box 730, E3B 5B4.
Telephone: 506-458-1970.
Fax: 506-444-8974. Email: fredericton@smss.com
Moncton, New Brunswick Office: Suite 601, Blue Cross Centre, 644 Main Street, P.O. Box 28051, E1C 9N4.
Telephone: 506-853-1970.
Telecopier: 506-858-8454. Email: moncton@smss.com
Saint John, New Brunswick Office: 10th Floor, Brunswick House, 44 Chipman Hill, P.O. Box 7289 Station "A", E2L 4S6.
Telephone: 506-632-1970.
Telecopier: 506-652-1989. Email: saint-john@smss.com
St. John's, Newfoundland Office: Cabot Place, 100 New Gower Street, P.O. Box 5038, A1C 5V3.
Telephone: 709-722-4270.
Telecopier: 709-722-4565. Email: st-johns@smss.com

LAWYERS PRACTICING IN CHARLOTTETOWN, PRINCE EDWARD ISLAND OFFICE

Alan K. Scales, Q.C.
Shawn A. Murphy, Q.C.
Eugene P. Rossiter, Q.C.
Rosemary Scott, Q.C.
James C. Travers, Q.C.
Gordon L. Campbell
J. Scott MacKenzie
John K. Mitchell, Q.C.
Brian L. Waddell
Keith M. Boswell
Ronald J. Keefe
Sean J. Casey
James W. Gormley
D. Spencer Campbell
Barbara E. Smith
Tracey L. Clements

For full biographical listings, see the Martindale-Hubbell Law Directory

CANADA QUEBEC

*MONTREAL,** Montreal Dist.

BYERS CASGRAIN (AV)

A Member of McMillan Bull Casgrain
Suite 3900, 1 Place Ville-Marie, H3B 4M7
Telephone: 514-878-8800
Telecopier: 514-866-2241

PARTNERS

Philippe Casgrain, Q.C.
Herbert B. McNally, Q.C.
Paul F. Dingle, Q.C.
Marc Bourgeois
Claude E. Leduc
Robert S. Carswell
Hon. Jean Bazin, Q.C.
Ray E. Lawson
Pierre Langlois
Jean-Pierre Dépelteau
Luc Giroux
John F. Lemieux
Allan A. Mass
Céline April
Neil L. Bindman
Michel A. Brunet
Michel Towner
John Hurley
Gérard Dugré
Louis Dumont
Denis Manzo
Nicolas Beaudin
Martin Bernard
Guy Lavoie
Alain Roberge
Guy A. Gagnon
Christian J. Brossard
Charles R. Spector
Richard B. Epstein
Constantine Kyres
Laurent Nahmiash
Daniel Garant
Stéphane Dansereau
Constantine Troulis
Jean-Pierre Huard
Ronald Audette
Jean M. Gagnon
Pierre D. Grenier
Christian Létourneau
Mathilde Carrière
Yves Turgeon
Louis Clément

ASSOCIATES

Jean Lefrançois
Josée Lefebvre
Bernard Colas
Nicole Cloutier
Michel Jodoin
Jean Groleau
Patrice Beaudin
Julie Desrochers
Claude Morency
Stéphane W. Miron
Catherine Pilon
Sébastien Grammond

(See Next Column)

BYERS CASGRAIN, *Montreal—Continued*

ASSOCIATES (Continued)

Stephen Lloyd
Marc Lussier
Joseph Mastrogiuseppe
Karine Martin
Stefan Martin
Emil Vidrascu
Éric Allard-Pouliot
Sophie-Emmanuelle Chebin
Neil Katz
Geneviève Pharand
Charles-André Sauvé
Joanie Schwartz
Pascale Dionne-Bourassa
Sylvain Dorais
Hion Kou
Margaret Weltrowska
Barbara Farina
Marie-Hélène Béland
Francois Brais
Vitale A. Santoro
Valéry Zamuner

OF COUNSEL

Gil Rémillard
Jean-Claude Bachand
E. Paul Legault

LEGAL SUPPORT PERSONNEL

Myriam Sarrazin

For full biographical listings, see the Martindale-Hubbell Law Directory

COLBY, MONET, DEMERS, DELAGE & CREVIER (AV)

McGill College Tower, 1501 McGill College Avenue Suite 2900, H3A 3M8
Telephone: 514-284-3663
Telecopier: 514-284-1961

PARTNERS AND ASSOCIATES

Jean Monet, Q.C.
Paul Michael Demers
Jean Delage
Monique Dionne
David Crevier
Michael C. Martin
Marek Nitoslawski
Katherine M. Peacocke
Campbell J. Stuart
Valérie A. Miglia
Lyne Carrier
Julie D. Gagnon
Christian R. Leblanc
Jean-Philippe Mikus
Robert Scalesse
Stephanie Séguin
Isabelle Pierre
Myriam Fortin

For full biographical listings, see the Martindale-Hubbell Law Directory

DE GRANDPRÉ CHAIT (AV)

1000, De La Gauchetière Street West, Suite 2900, H3B 4W5
Telephone: 514-878-4311
Fax: 514-878-4333
Email: info@degrandpre-chait.com

PARTNERS OF FIRM

Founding Partner Samuel Chait, Q.C. (1904-1982)

Christiane Alary
Normand Amyot
Jacques L. Archambault
André P. Asselin
François Beauchamp
Marc Beauchemin
Jean Benoît
Jacques Bourque
Arthur I. Bronstein
Pierre Brossoit
J. Brian Cornish
Louis Demers
Jean-Pierre Desmarais
Gilles Fafard
Jean-Jacques Gagnon
Guy Gilain
Jean François Giroux
Gilles Godin, Q.C.
Andrée Gosselin
Frederica Jacobs
David H. Kauffman
Sandor J. Klein
Gabriel Kordovi
Pierre Labelle
Diane Lajeunesse
Eric Lalanne
Virginia K. H. Lam
Benoît Larose
Philippe Leclercq
Daniel Lessard
Ronald H. Levy
C. Ralph Lipper
Jean-François Ménard
Pierre Mercille
Benoît Pelchat
Yves Poirier
Olivier Prat, Q.C.
Alain Robichaud
Marc J. Rubin
Louis Samuel
Ronald L. Stein
Mark E. Turcot

For full biographical listings, see the Martindale-Hubbell Law Directory

DESJARDINS DUCHARME STEIN MONAST (AV)

600 de La Gauchetière Street West, Suite 2400, H3B 4L8
Telephone: 514-878-9411
Telecopier: 514-878-9092
Email: avocat@ddsm.ca *URL:* http://www.ddsm.ca
Quebec, Quebec Office: Suite 300, 1150 Claire Fontaine Street, G1R 5G4.
Telephone: 418-529-6531.
Telecopier: 418-523-5391.
Affiliated Offices:
Torys:
Toronto: Suite 3000, Aetna Tower, Toronto-Dominion Centre, P.O. Box 270, Toronto (Ontario) M5K 1N2.
Telephone: 416-865-0040.
Telecopier: 416-865-7398.
New York, New York Office: 237 Park Avenue, 10017-3142.
Telephone: 212-880-6000.
Fax: 212-682-0200.

(See Next Column)

Beijing, China Office: China Merchants Tower, Suite C, 29F 2 Dong Huan Nan Lu, Jianguomenwai, Chaoyang District, 100022.
Telephone: 8610 6566 9088.
Fax: 8610 6566 9096.

PARTNERS AND ASSOCIATES OF FIRM

Pierre Bourque, Q.C.
Michel Roy
Daniel Bellemare, Q.C.
Denis St-Onge
Jacques Paquin
Gérard Coulombe, Q.C.
Marc Rochefort
Michel Benoit
Robert Dorion
Luc Bigaouette
Serge Gloutnay
Pierre-Yves Châtillon
Pierre Legault
Michèle St-Onge
Paul Marcotte
François Garneau
Michel Legendre
Marie St-Pierre
Marcel Racicot
Joanne Biron
Robert Y. Girard
André Vautour
Lucia Bourbonnais
Dominique Bélisle
Mason Poplaw
Richard Comtois
Christian Drapeau
Patrice Picard
Lucie Letendre
Sonia Paradis
Jocelyne Gagné
Patrice Benoit
Josée Dumoulin
François Ouellette
Jacques Lemieux
Fabrice Benoît
Benoit V. Morel
François Parent
Annie Turcotte
Natalie Gosselin
Nadine Landry
Patrick Theoret
Francois Parizeau
Pascale Pageau
Caroline Boutin
Eric Verret
Melanie B. Forcier
Patrick Elfassy
Jean-Paul Zigby
Claude Bédard
Réjean Lizotte
C. François Couture
Marc A. Léonard
Jean-Maurice Saulnier
Louis Payette
Roger Page, Q.C.
Robert J. Phénix
Paul R. Granda
Maurice Mongrain
Michel McMillan
Jean-Francois Cloutier
Odette Nadon
Danièle Mayrand
Sylvain Lussier
Louise Lalonde
Johanne Savard
Benoit Emery
Eugène Czolij
Daniel Majeau
Johanne Bérubé
Marc Beauchemin
François Renaud
Nicole Nobert
Joëlle Boisvert
Claude Dallaire
Lucie Guimond
Sophie Picard
Paule Hamelin
Paule Tardif
Martin Rolland
Marc Lapointe
Sylvie Champagne
Tiziana Di Donato
Jean-Pierre Chamberland
Marie-France Gagnon
Marie-Julie Croteau
Ilinca Ghibu
Hatzikiriakos Kiriakoula
Patricia Fourcand
Diane Bouchard
Francois Viau
Lyne Perron
Olivier Therrien
Christian Meighen
Véronik Bonneville-Pesant
Dominique Babin

COUNSEL

Adrien Bordua
Claude Ducharme, Q.C.
André E. Gadbois, Q.C.
Guy Desjardins, Q.C.
Georges Emery, Q.C.
Alain Lortie

For full biographical listings, see the Martindale-Hubbell Law Directory

FASKEN MARTINEAU DUMOULIN (AV)

Stock Exchange Tower, Suite 3400, 800 Place-Victoria, P.O. Box 242, H4Z 1E9
Telephone: 514-397-7400
Toll Free: 1-800-361-6266 (Ontario & Quebec)
Facsimile: 514-397-7600.
Telex: 05-24610 BUOY MTL
Email: info@mlt.fasken.com *URL:* www.fasten.com
Fasken Martineau DuMoulin is a leading Canadian firm with a national and international practice and having offices in Toronto, Montreal, Quebec, Vancouver, New York and London. Please refer to listings in the respective city sections.
Quebec City, Quebec Office: 140, rue Grande Allée est, bureau 800, G1R 5M8.
Telephone: 418-640-2000. Toll Free: 1-800-463-2827 (Ontario & Quebec).
Facsimile: 418-647-2455. EMail: info@qc.fasken.com
Toronto, Ontario Office: Toronto-Dominion Centre, Toronto Dominion Bank Tower, P.O. Box 20, M5K 1N6.
Telephone: 416-366-8381. Toll Free: 1-800-268-8424 (Ontario & Quebec).
Facsimile: 416-364-7813. EMail: info@tor.fasken.com.
Vancouver, British Columbia Office: 2100-1075 West Georgia Street.
Telephone: 604-631-3131.
Fax: 604-631-3232. EMail: info@van.fasken.com. Website: www.fasken.com.
New York, New York Office: Seagram Building, 375 Park Avenue, Suite 2608, 10152.
Telephone: 212-935-3203.
Facsimile: 212-935-4822. EMail: info@nyc.fasken.com. Website: www.fasken.com.
London, England Office: 10 Arthur Street, 5th Floor, EC4R 9AY.
Telephone: 71-929-2894.
Facsimile: 71-929-3634. EMail: info@lon.fasken.com.

(See Next Column)

FASKEN MARTINEAU DUMOULIN—*Continued*

MEMBERS OF FIRM

Jean H. Lafleur, Q.C.
C. Stephen Cheasley
Robert M. Skelly
Richard Martel
Lawrence P. Yelin
Réal A. Forest
Serge Guérette
Louis Bernier
Jean Masson
Gilles Carli
Claude Gendron
Xenophon C. Martis
Robert Paré
Pierre J. Deslauriers
Denis Paquin
Jacques Rajotte
George Artinian
Marc-André Fabien
Marc Généreux
Alain Ranger
Louise Béchamp
Marie Lafleur
Dominique Monet
Nathalie Bonneau
Alain Riendeau
Marie-José Roux-Fauteux
Claude Marseille
Peter Villani
Suzanne Anfousse
Sylvie Bourdeau
René Cadieux
Louis-François Hogue
Stéphane Létourneau
Dominique Gibbens
Robert J. Stocks
Pierre B. Meunier
Maurice A. Forget
Rolland Forget
Yvon Martineau
Paul Martel
Jean-Francois Buffoni
Dennis P. Griffin
André Durocher
Denis Lachance
Richard J. Clare
Ronald J. McRobie
Richard Lacoursière
Daniel Picotte
Karl Delwaide
Francois Brissette
R. Andrew Ford
Louis H. Séguin
Pierre Y. Lefebvre
Claude Auger
Claudette Allard
Edith Bonnot
Benoit Turmel
Bernard J. Bussières
Paul Mayer
Peter E. Kirby
Pierre Setlakwe
Eric Ménard
Nathalie Faucher
Marc Novello
Éric Bédard
Charles Kazaz
Julie Desrosiers
Martin Sheehan

MEMBERS OF FIRM (Continued)

Stéphane Gilker
Angela C. Onesi
Gilles Leclerc
Louis Tassé
Jean Yeong-Gin Yoon

ASSOCIATES

Carole Larivière
Lucie Rivest
Isabelle Dongier
Linda Facchin
David Lemieux
Frédéric Despars
Marie-Josée Neveu
Jean-François Perreault
Patrick Beauger
Philippe J. Laurin
Christian Mindru
Sunny Handa (Not admitted in QU)
Enrico Forlini
Kiriakos Vanikiotis
Mathieu Desforges
Diane Bertrand
Karine Martel
Marc Savard
Stéphane Grégoire
Lise Szmigielski
Daniel J. Martin
Hervé Paul-Marie Le Pierres (Not admitted in QU)
Nathalie Y. Provost
Tamara Gitto
Stuart S. Aronovitch
Louis Mousseau
Hélène V. Gagnon
Marianne Messier
Lise Rochette
Maxime Bédard
Marie-Hélène Constantin
Christine Malenfant
Gilda Villaran
Caroline Thomassin
Clifford Feldstein
Sabah Mirza
Christina Scott
Catherine L'Écuyer
Pierre-Yves Leduc

COUNSEL

Bâtonnier Marcel Cinq-Mars, Q.C.
Lambert Toupin, Q.C.
Hon. Céline Hervieux-Payette,
Peter R. D. MacKell, Q.C.
Guy Gagnon, Q.C.
Francis Fox, P.C., Q.C.
Robert P. Godin

For full biographical listings, see the Martindale-Hubbell Law Directory

GOODMAN PHILLIPS & VINEBERG (AV)

1501 McGill College, 26th Floor, H3A 3N9
Telephone: 514-841-6400; 1-888-841-6400
Telecopier: 514-841-6499; 1-888-841-6499
Email: gpv@mtl.gpv.com
Beijing, People's Republic of China Office: 1612 Office Tower One, Henderson Center, 18 Jianguomennei Avenue, Dongcheng District, Beijing, China, 100005.
Telephone: 86-10-6518-6201.
Telecopier: 86-10-6518-6205.
Hong Kong Office: 8/F AON China Building, 29 Queen's Road Central, Hong Kong.
Telephone: (852) 2522-1061.
Telecopier: (852) 2845-9089.
New York, New York Office: 430 Park Avenue, 10th Floor, New York, New York, 10022.
Telephone: 212-308-8866.
Telecopier: 212-308-0132.
Paris, France Office: 13, avenue Hoche, 75008, Paris, France.
Telephone: (33) 01 53 53 44 44.
Telecopier: (33) 01 53 96 04 20.

(See Next Column)

Singapore Office: 40-A Tras Street, Singapore, 078979.
Telephone: (65) 323-6770.
Telecopier: (65) 323-4337.
Toronto, Ontario Office: 250 Yonge Street, Suite 2400, Toronto, Ontario, Canada M5B 2M6.
Telephone: 416-979-2211.
Telecopier: 416-979-1234.
Vancouver, British Columbia Office: Suite 1900, 355 Burrard Street, Vancouver, British Columbia, Canada V6C 2G8.
Telephone: 604-682-7737.
Telecopier: 604-682-7131.

MEMBERS AND ASSOCIATES

The Hon. Lazarus Phillips, O.B.E., Q.C., LL.D. (1895-1986)
François Barette
Daniel Belleau
Maryse Bertrand
Marc-André Boutin
Mark D. Brender
Richard Cherney
Silvana Conte
Rita Lc de Santis
Geneviève Dufour
Lloyd Perry Feldman
Janet Ferrier
Leon P. Garfinkle
The Hon. Alan B. Gold, O.C., O.Q., Q.C., LL.D.
Shahir Guindi
George R. Hendy
Robert B. Issenman
Claude E. Jodoin
Neil Kravitz
Claudel Lacroix
Geneviève Lefebvre
Sandra Mastrogiuseppe
Daniel S. Miller
Marisol L. Miro
Louis-Martin O'Neill
Michel Pelletier
Douglas C. Robertson
Francis-Ian Rojas
Rhonda Rudick
Brian G. Salpeter
Ève-Stéphanie Sauvé
Alan J. Shragie
Sébastien Thériault
Justin D. Vineberg
Philip F. Vineberg, O.C., Q.C., LL.D. (1914-1987)
Robert J. Abrams
Nathalie Beauregard
Elias Benhamou
Nathan Boidman
Marie Brault
William Brock
Nicolas Cloutier
Sylvain Cossette
Laurence Detière
Guy Du Pont
Denis Ferland
Michèle Gamache
Alain Gaul
Alan Z. Golden
Qin Hua Joseph Gu
Paul Harris
Sidney M. Horn
Joseph Jarjour
Mitchell H. Klein
Jodi A. Lackman
Marie-Andrée Latreille
Marie-Christine Lemerise
Peter Mendell
Scott D. Miller
Robert Mongeon
Louise Patry
Robert Raizenne
Nick Rodrigo
Hillel W. Rosen
Monique Ryan
Jacqueline Sanderson
Sébastien Savage
Pierre-André Themens
Marie-Emmanuelle Vaillancourt
Michael D. Vineberg
Robert S. Vineberg

For full biographical listings, see the Martindale-Hubbell Law Directory

HEENAN BLAIKIE (AV)

Suite 2500, 1250 René-Lévesque Boulevard West, H3B 4Y1
Telephone: 514-846-1212
Telecopier: 514-846-3427
URL: http://www.heenanblaikie.com
Toronto, Ontario Office: Suite 2600 South Tower, Royal Bank Plaza, 200 Bay Street, P.O. Box 185, M5J 2J4.
Telephone: 416-360-6336.
Telecopier: 416-360-8425.
Vancouver, British Columbia Office: Suite 2200, 1055 West Hastings Street, V6E 2E9.
Telephone: 604-669-0011.
Telecopier: 604-669-5101.
Québec, Québec Office: Heenan Blaikie Aubut, Suite 600, 900 René-Lévesque Boulevard East, G1R 2B5.
Telephone: 418-524-5131.
Telecopier: 418-524-1717.
Sherbrooke, Québec Office: Suite 210, 455 King Street West, J1H 6E9.
Telephone: 819-346-5058.
Telecopier: 819-346-5007.
Trois-Rivières, Québec Office: Suite 360, 1500 Royale Street, G9A 6E6.
Telephone: 819-373-7000.
Telecopier: 819-373-0943.
Ottawa, Ontario Office: 270 Albert Street, 14th Floor, K1P 5G8.
Telephone: 613-567-9348.
Kelowna, British Columbia Office: 1626 Richter, V1Y 2M3.
Telephone: 250-862-3277.
Telecopier: 205-862-5045.
Affiliated Office: Marusyk Miller & Swain, Ottawa, Ontario, 270 Albert Street, 14th Floor, K1P 5G8.
Telephone: 613-567-0762.
Telecopier: 613-563-7671.
Affiliated Office: Heenan Blaikie, Beverly Hills, California, Suite 1100, 9401 Wilshire Boulevard, 90210-2924.
Telephone: 310-275-3600.
Telecopier: 310-724-8340.

COUNSEL

The Right Honourable Pierre Elliott Trudeau, P.C., Q.C.
James W. Hemens, Q.C.
Pierre Marc Johnson
André Bureau, O.C.
Pierre C. Lemoine

(See Next Column)

HEENAN BLAIKIE, *Montreal—Continued*

MEMBERS

Bernard Amyot
Kenneth S. Atlas
Sam Berliner
Yvan M. Bolduc
Jean Boulet (Resident Partner, Trois-Rivières Office)
Jean E. Clerk, Q.C.
Andrew M. Cohen
Nicola Di Iorio
Etienne Dubreuil
Robert Dupont
Ralph D. Farley
Serge Gaudet
Joel H. Goldberg
Roy L. Heenan, O.C.
Louise Houle
Bernard Jolin
Chantal Lamarche
Eric M. Maldoff
Auguste Masson
Gary D.D. Morrison
Sylvain Poirier
Karen M. Rogers
André Roy (Resident Partner, Trois-Rivières Office)
Manon Thivierge
Christopher Atchison
Claudette Bellemare
Max R. Bernard
Robert Bonhomme
Benoit G. Bourgon
Thomas E.F. Brady (Not admitted in QU)
Corrado De Stefano
Norman A. Dionne
Guy Dufort
Sophie Émond
Clément Gascon
André P. Gauthier
Yves Hébert
Marie-Josée Hogue
Manon Jolicoeur
Danny J. Kaufer
Louis Leclerc
Claude Martin
M. Bruce McNiven
Sylvi Plante
François A. Raymond
Gary S. Rosen
Guy Sarault
Suzanne Thibaudeau, Q.C.
Guy Tremblay

MEMBERS (Continued)

Pierre Trépanier
Patrice Vachon
Jean Trudel
Neil Wiener
Keith D. Wilson

ASSOCIATES

Poupak Bahamin
Annie Beaudin (Resident Associate, Sherbrooke Office)
Geneviève Bérubé
Daniel Bourque
Richard G.R. Brabander
Elizabeth Camiré
Sébastien Caron
Catherine Conides
Andrew G. Deere
Mélanie Rose De Souza
Véronique Dubois
Fawaz Elmalki
Simon Gagné
Danielle Gauthier (Resident Associate, Sherbrooke Office)
Martin Hébert
Marie-Josée Hétu (Resident Associate, Trois-Rivières Office)
Anny Lafrance (Resident Associate, Sherbrooke Office)
Nathalie Lecoq
Laurent Lesage
Eric Levy
Troy McEachren
Patrick A. Molinari
Jacques A. Nadeau
Hubert Pépin (Resident Associate, Sherbrooke Office)
Michel Perreault (Resident Associate, Trois-Rivières Office)
Sylvain Provencher (Resident Associate, Sherbrooke Office)
Pascal Rochefort
Shari L. Segal
Philippe Tremblay
Michèle Veilleux
Christine Baudouin
Carl Bélanger
Nathalie-Anne Béliveau
Peter M. Blaikie, Q.C.
Glen A. Bowman
Alexandre Buswell
Robert D. Campbell
Dean J. Chenoy
Magali Cournoyer-Proulx
Martine Desjardins
Louise Dubé
Nancy Dubuc
Stéphane Fillion
Richard Gaudreault
Jean-Éric Guindon (Resident Associate, Trois-Rivières Office)
Veronique Iezzoni
David Joanisse
Dominique Lafleur
Pierre Lajoie
Elisabeth Laroche
Francine Legault
Daniel J. Levinson
Corinne P. Levy
Geneviève Marcotte
Lise Morissette
Annie Pagé (Resident Associate, Trois-Rivières Office)
David R.P. Perez
Rhéaume Perreault
Nicolas Plourde
Michel Poirier
Normand Quesnel
Vincent Regnault
Lucie Roy
Ronald W. Silverson
Daniel Urbas
Yanick Vlasak (Resident Associate, Sherbrooke Office)

For full biographical listings, see the Martindale-Hubbell Law Directory

LAFLEUR BROWN (AV)

1 Place Ville Marie, 37th Floor, H3B 3P4
Telephone: 514-878-9641
Cable Address: "Mankin"
Telex: 05-25610
Telecopier: 514-878-1450
Email: lawyers@lafleurbrown.ca *URL:* http://www.loginnet.com
Toronto, Ontario Office: Suite 920 P.O. Box 359 1, First Canadian Place.
Telephone: 416-869-0994.
Telecopier: 416-362-5818. Email: lbtor@tor.lafleurbrown.ca

MEMBERS OF FIRM

Paul Bédard
Marc-André Blanchard
Pierre Boyer
Yvon Brisson
Mark Bantey
Martin D. Boily
Charles S. Bradeen, Q.C.
Thierry Carriere

(See Next Column)

MEMBERS OF FIRM (Continued)

John Brooke Claxton, Q.C.
L.-P. de Grandpré, O.C., Q.C.
Luc Deshaies
Anik Fontaine
Robert A. Fyfe
Ysolde Gendreau
Martine J. Guimond
Julie Himo
Francois L'Heureux
Marc Laflèche
Henri Lanctôt
Jacques Laurent, Q.C.
Pierre-Denis Leroux
Pierre Lissoir
Véronique Mariani
Claude J. Melançon
Alain Morin
John A. Penhale
Isabelle Reinhardt
Richard J. Roy
Gilles Séguin
Jean M. Tardif
Reno Vaillancourt
Olivier Désilets
Marc De Wever
Philippe Ferland
Marzia Frascadore
Benoit Gascon
Benoit Groleau
Pierre-André Hamel
David B. Kierans
Daniel Lacelle
Alain Lalonde
Hubert Larose
Jean-François Lemay
Luc Lissoir
Julie-Martine Loranger
Francine Martel
Ronald Montcalm, Q.C.
Yves Ouellette
Guy Poitras
André Rivest
Ann-Marie Ryan
Leonard Serafini
Pierre Tourigny
Donald B. Wilkie

OF COUNSEL

Jack Greenstein, Q.C.

For full biographical listings, see the Martindale-Hubbell Law Directory

LAVERY, DE BILLY (AV)

1 Place Ville Marie, 40th Floor, H3B 4M4
Telephone: 514-871-1522
Facsimile: 514-871-8977
Email: info@lavery.qc.ca *URL:* http://www.laverydebilly.com
Quebec City, Quebec Office: 925 Chemin St-Louis, Suite 500, Quebec, Quebec G1S 1C1.
Telephone: 418-688-5000.
Facsimile: 418-688-3458.
Ottawa, Ontario Office: 45 O'Connor, 20th Floor, Ottawa, Ontario K1P 1A4.
Telephone: 613-594-4936.
Facsimile: 613-594-8783.
Laval, Quebec Office: Suite 500, 3080 Boul. Le Carrefour, Laval, Quebec H7T 2R5.
Telephone: 450-978-8100.
Facsimile: 450-978-8111.
Associate Office: Blake, Cassels & Graydon, Box 25, Commerce Court West, Toronto, Ontario M5L 1A9.
Telephone: 416-863-2400.
Facsimile: 416-863-2653.

MEMBERS OF FIRM AND ASSOCIATES

Jerome C. Smyth, Q.C.
Anthime Y. Bergeron, Q.C.
Georges Dubé
Robert W. Mason
Michel Blouin
Jacques Nols
Edouard Baudry
Pierre Caron
Paul Cartier
Jean Pomminville
Gerald Stotland
André Champagne
Ian Rose
Claude Baillargeon
Michel Caron
Denis Charest
Réal Favreau
Pierre L. Baribeau
Jacques Paul-Hus
Jacques Audette
Jean Martel
David M. Eramian
Richard Wagner
Jocelyne Forget
Odette Jobin-Laberge
Marie Gaudreau
Jean Beauregard
Pierre Denis
Pamela McGovern
Pierre Cadotte
Marie-Andrée Gravel
Hélène Lauzon
Anne Bélanger
Lucie Desjardins
Élise Poisson
Monique Brassard
Yves St-Cyr
Carl Lessard
John Mavridis
Jean-Francois Michaud
Andre Paquette
J. Vincent O'Donnell, Q.C.
Serge Bourque
Douglas S. Pryde
Jean Bélanger
Guy Lemay
André René
Raphael H. Schachter, Q.C.
André Laurin (Managing Partner)
Monique Lagacé
Jean-Pierre Casavant
René Paquette
Johanne L. Rémillard
Jean Hébert
Michel Yergeau
Pierre Daviault
Richard A. Hinse
Louis André Leclerc
Marc Talbot
Alain Gascon
Michel Gélinas
Daniel Alain Dagenais
Louise Cérat
Jean Saint-Onge
Jean-Francois Hotte
Gilles Paquette
Raymond Doray
Francois Duprat
René Branchaud
Philippe Frère
Yvan Biron
Yves Jobin
Fabienne Benoit
Véronique Morin
Julie Veilleux
Catherine Papineau
Dominique Vézina
Jean-Yves Simard
Luc Pariseau
Philip Nolan
Nicolas Gagnon

(See Next Column)

LAVERY, DE BILLY—*Continued*

MEMBERS OF FIRM AND ASSOCIATES (Continued)

Marie-Claude Cantin
Francois Charette
Nicole Messier
Erik Sabbatini
Martin Joyal
Isabelle Lamarre
Andre D'Amours
Michel Servant
Bernard Larocque
Charles A. Nieto
Stephanie Lefebvre
Francois Touchette
Luc Thibaudeau
Janet Oh
Alexandra C. Lee
Tania F. Smith
Beatrice van Rutten
Julie Anne Brien
Hind Merabet
Dina Raphael
Marie-Claude Perreault
Marc Cigana
Patrick Buchholz
Marie-Claude Armstrong
Evelyne Verrier
Yann Bernard
Catherine H. Maheu
Louis Charette
Dominique L. L'Heureux
Andrea Daniels
Larry Markowitz
Julie Bédard
Claudine Décarie
Isabelle Gosselin
Jean-Francois LePage
Tania Maria Tretiak
Lisa Miller
Sébastien Vezina
Alexis-Francois Charette
Anne Boyer

For full biographical listings, see the Martindale-Hubbell Law Directory

McCARTHY TÉTRAULT (AV)

Le Windsor, 1170 rue Peel, H3B 4S8
Telephone: 514-397-4100
Facsimile: 514-875-6246 or 514-397-4187
Email: montreal@mccarthy.ca *URL:* http://www.mccarthy.ca
Vancouver, British Columbia Office: Suite 1300, 777 Dunsmuir Street, P.O. Box 10424, Vancouver, British Columbia V7Y 1K2.
Telephone: 604-643-7100.
Facsimile: 604-643-7900.
Surrey, British Columbia Office: Suite 1300, Station Tower, Gateway 13401-108th Avenue, Surrey, British Columbia V3T 5T3.
Telephone: 604-583-9100.
Fax: 604-583-9150.
Calgary, Alberta Office: Suite 3300, 421 7th Avenue, S.W., Calgary, Alberta T2P 4K9.
Telephone: 403-260-3500.
Facsimile: 403-260-3501.
London, Ontario Office: Suite 2000, One London Place, 255 Queens Avenue, London, Ontario N6A 5R8.
Telephone: 519-660-3587.
Facsimile: 519-660-3599.
Toronto, Ontario Office: Suite 4700, Toronto Dominion Bank Tower, Toronto, Ontario M5K 1E6.
Telephone: 416-362-1812.
Facsimile: 416-868-0673.
Ottawa, Ontario Office: The Chambers, Suite 1400, 40 Elgin Street, Ottawa, Ontario K1P 5K6.
Telephone: 613-238-2000.
Facsimile: 613-563-9386.
Québec, Québec Office: Le Complexe St-Amable 1150, rue Claire-Fontaine, 7e étage, Québec, Québec G1R 5G4.
Telephone: 418-521-3000.
Facsimile: 418-521-3098,418-521-3099.
United Kingdom and Europe Office: Pountney Hill House, 6 Laurence Pountney Hill, London, England EC4R 0BL.
Telephone: 011-44-171-618-2888.
Facsimile: 011-44-171-618-2880.

PARTNERS

Michael Dennis
Claude P. Desaulniers
Yves Bériault
Paul Dupuy Leblanc
Michael D. Levinson
André J. Payeur
Michel Racicot
Ann Maryse Bigué
Louis Lacoursière
Peter S. Martin
Robert B. Schubert
Daniel Bénay
J. Robert Doyle
Hubert Graton
Warren M. Goodman
Geoffrey Lawson
R. Timothé Huot
Daniel W. Payette
Jacques Rousse
John T. Sullivan
Marc Benoit
Cherine Cheftechi
Christiane Jodoin
Louis Brousseau
Marc Dufour
Elaine Marchand
Carole Tremblay
Marc Lemieux
Madeleine Renaud
Graham Nesbitt
Richard A. Beaulieu
Gérald R. Tremblay, Q.C.
J. Michel Deschamps
William J. Atkinson (Managing Partner)
Thomas R.M. Davis
Robert-Jean Chénier
Carol Anne Laramée
André Prévost
Sylvain Deslauriers
Hubert T. Lacroix
Lorna Jean Telfer
Louis Terriault
Jacques Jeansonne
Martin Boodman
Sylvie Lachapelle
Jean-François Lehoux
Benjamin H. Silver
Laurent M. Themens
Jean-Pierre Bertrand
Sylvain A. Vauclair
Robert P. Metcalfe
Julie Chenette
Michel Laplante
Franziska Ruf
Martine Kaigle
Chantal Masse
Sonia Jacqueline Struthers

(See Next Column)

PARTNERS (Continued)

Philippe Henri Bélanger
Michel Gagné
Laurent R. Debrun
François Grondin
Catherine D. Mandeville
Pierre Saint-Aubin, Q.C.
Marc-André Blanchard
Lonnie J. Brodkin-Schneider
Christiane Larouche
G. Scot Diamond
Jean Lortie
David E. Platts
Anne-Marie Sheahan
Alain Tardif

ASSOCIATES

Dominique Têtu
Michel D. Bergeron
Alida Gualtieri
Daniel A. Artola
Eric Gelinas
Chloé Archambault
Mireille Fontaine
Marie-Anne Paquette
Bruno Caron
Vanessa Dumoulin
Eric Gosselin
Mark Phillips
Chantal C. Tremblay
Jean-François Boisvenu
Jessica M. Elbaz
Emmanuelle Lamarre-Cliche
Josianne Turcotte
Martine Boucher
Catherine Dagenais
Christian Giner
Caroline Morin
E. Marian Tremblay
Frédéric Gascon
Charles S. Morgan
Jacques Papy
Karl Tabbakh
Alain F. Dussault
P. Martin Dumas
Isabelle Grégoire
Fany O'Bomsawin
Marie Mandeville
André Goyer
Stephen Gerard Schenke
Donald Bisson
Lambert Perron
Ilan Dunsky
Nathalie Gagnon
Philippe Trudel
Yves Comtois
Stéphanie Gilcher
Marc-André LeChasseur
Emmanuelle Poupart
Mireille Tremblay
Patrick Boucher
Francois Giroux
Catherine Ross
Athanassia Bitzakidis
Martin-Pierre Boulianne
Stéphane Duval
Fred W. Headon
Isabelle Synnott
Patrice Bonneau
Tracey Luttrell
Katia Opalka
Frédéric Pérodeau
Marc Tremblay
Juliette D'Hollander
Geneviève Gagnon
Stephanie Johnson
Jane Ross
Véronique Wattiez-Larose

COUNSEL

Jacques Tétrault, Q.C.
Richard R. Drouin, O.C., Q.C.
Claude Bisson, O.C.
Luc Plamondon
Daniel Johnson

For full biographical listings, see the Martindale-Hubbell Law Directory

McMASTER GERVAIS (AV)

A General Partnership
1000 de La Gauchetière Street West, Suite 900, H3B 5H4
Telephone: 514-879-1212
Fax: 514-954-1905
Email: info@mcmastergervais.com *URL:* http://www.mcmastergervais.com

MEMBERS OF FIRM

Alex K. Paterson, O.C., O.Q., Q.C.
Lionel J. Blanshay
Paul R. Marchand
Sean J. Harrington
Brian M. Schneiderman
Daniel Ayotte
Georges R. Thibaudeau
Peter Richardson
Robert E. Charbonneau
Elizabeth A. Mitchell
Jean-René Ranger
Virgile A. Buffoni
Benoît M. Provost
Michael Patry
Thomas M. Davis
Yves A. Dubois
Marilyn Ann Piccini Roy
Pierre Trudeau
Pierre B. Côté
Sylvie Bouvette
André Royer
François Morin
Peter G. Pamel
H. John Godber
Michael Bantey
John G. Murphy
Amélia A. Salehabadi
Lise Fortier
Jacques S. Darche
Jacques Beaumier
Patrice Martin
Julie Normand
Stéphanie Moffatt
Avi Levy
Valérie Dufour
William E. Stavert
Timothy R. Carsley
Peter C. Casey
Alexis P. Bergeron
Norman A. Saibil
Luc LaRochelle
Ian B. Taylor
Pierre Flageole
Richard W. Shannon
Raymond Picard
Pierre Gattuso
P. Jeremy Bolger
Johanne Thomas
Philippe C. Vachon
Roger P. Simard
François Rioux
Charles P. Marquette
Janet Casey
André Dufour
Jacques Gauthier
Rosaire S. Houde
Bruno Duguay
D. James Papadimitriou
P. Vivian Cyriacopoulos
Yvan Houle
François Longpré
Christine Duchaine
Éric Beaulieu
Darren E.G. McGuire
Marie Audren
Elana Weissbach
Patricia Galella
Caroline Matte
Brigitte Brathwaite
Patrice Morin
Virginia Chan

(See Next Column)

McMaster Gervais, *Montreal—Continued*

MEMBERS OF FIRM (Continued)

Robert Fosco
Manon Gauthier
David Torralbo
Geneviève Bergeron
Marc-Antoine La Rochelle
Tammy J. Shulman
Joel M. Cabelli
Grégoire Baillargeon
Mylany David
Rhonda Friesen
Gary Rivard
Catherine Guertin
Antoine Leduc
Roderick Darrock Elliott
Sophia Tolias
Sébastien Lormeau
Sébastien Berthelet
Melanie Charbonneau
Daniel Ferreira
Patricia Gagnon
Stéphane Pitre

COUNSEL

Maurice D. Godbout, Q.C.
David Mackenzie, Q.C.
Thomas C. Camp, Q.C.
P. André Gervais, Q.C.
Richard J. Riendeau, Q.C.
Raymond D. LeMoyne
Daniel O'Connel Doheny, Q.C.
A. Stuart Hyndman, Q.C.
Hon. Lawrence A. Poitras, Q.C.
Tass G. Grivakes, Q.C.
Jacques Brien
Bartha M. Knoppers
Marc Laperrière

For full biographical listings, see the Martindale-Hubbell Law Directory

Ogilvy Renault (AV)

Suite 1100, 1981 McGill College Avenue, H3A 3C1
Telephone: 514-847-4747
Fax: 514-286-5474
Email: info@ogilvyrenault.com *URL:* http://www.ogilvyrenault.com
Ottawa, Ontario Office: Suite 1600, 45 O'Connor Street, K1P 1A4.
Telephone: 613-780-8661.
Fax: 613-230-5459. Email: ottawa@ogilvyrenault.com
Québec, Québec Office: Suite 520, 500 Grande Allée est, G1R 2J7.
Telephone: 418-640-5000.
Fax: 418-640-1500. Email: quebec@ogilvyrenault.com
Toronto, Ontario Office: Suite 2100, P.O. Box 141, Royal Trust Tower, TD Centre, M5K 1H1.
Telephone: 416-216-4000.
Fax: 416-216-3930. Email: toronto@ogilvyrenault.com
Vancouver, British Columbia Office: 800 Park Place, 666 Burrard Street, V6C 3P3.
Telephone: 604-806-0922.
Fax: 604-806-0933. Email: info@ogilvyrenault.com
London, England Office: 38 Charterhouse Square, EC1M 6EQ, England.
Telephone: 44 (0) 207-600-9005.
Fax: 44 (0) 207-600-9006. Email: info@ogilvyrenault.com

Jean R. Allard
Christian J. Beaudry
Lise Bergeron
Pierre Bienvenu
Jane Bogaty
Gregory B. Bordan
Luc Boucher
Danièle Boutet
Claude Brunet
Isabelle Cantin
Mario M. Caron
Christine A. Carron
Jules Charette
Joanne Chriqui
Joan Clark, Q.C.
John A. Coleman
Jean-Pierre Colpron
François Côté
Benoît-Carl Coulombe
François Courteau
Leigh D. Crestohl
Louis-Paul Cullen
Brian R. Daley
Claudia Déry
Annick Désy
Emmanuelle J. Doyon
Stephen L. Drymer
Éric Dunberry
Carmen M. Fernandez
Claude Fontaine, Q.C.
L. Yves Fortier, C.C., Q.C.
Guy Fortin
Rémi Gagnon
Denis Gascon
Thomas S. Gillespie
André C. Giroux
Louis J. Gouin
Manon Guesthier
Sylvie Hébert
William Hesler, Q.C.
Gail R. Jaffe
Stephen J. Kelly
Daniel I. Lack
Anne-Louise Lamarre
Frédérique Amrouni
R. Luc Beaulieu
Jean G. Bertrand
Casper M. Bloom, Q.C.
Charles J. Boivin
Robert G. Borduas
Martine S. Boucher
Natalie Brown
Yves W. Brunet, Q.C.
Michel G. Carle
Sandra E. Carr
Sandro Cellucci
Robert P. Charlton
Nicolas Cimon
Benoît Clermont
David R. Collier
Alain Côté
Pierre G. Côté
Renaud Coulombe
Robert J. Cowling
Raymond Crevier, Q.C.
Jean Daigle
Françoise Cécile Denault
Richard L. Desgagnés
Thierry Dorval
Daniel S. Drapeau
Christine Dubé
Marc Duquette
Laura A. Fish
François Fontaine
Dominique Fortin
Michel A. Gagnon
Nadine Ganesan
Johanne Gauthier
Sébastien Gingras
Michel Goudreau
Dominic Gourgues
Pierre Hébert
Antonio Henriquez
Marianne Ignacz
Marie-Hélène Jetté
Olivier F. Kott
Marc Lacourcière
Pierre Y. Lamarre

(See Next Column)

J. Nelson Landry
Christine LeBrun
Daniel Leduc
Wilfrid Lefebvre, Q.C.
André Legrand
George R. Locke
Miguel F. Manzano
Christine M. Marsan
Lindsay Matthews
Clemens Mayr
Sophie Melchers
The Rt. Hon. Brian Mulroney, P.C., C.C., LL.D.
Josée Noiseux
André Papillon
Priscille Pelletier
Jean Piette
Simon V. Potter
Pierre Pronovost
Francine Proulx
Paul Raymond
Donald A. Riendeau
Judith M. Robinson
Gérard Rochon
Bernard A. Roy, Q.C.
Solomon Sananes
Manon Savard
Kathy Shakibnia
Leanne Souquet
Norman M. Steinberg
Michel G. Sylvestre
Martin Thériault
Marc Tremblay
Louise Laplante
Amar Leclair-Ghosh
Hélène Lefebvre
Francis R. Legault
Pierre Legrand, Q.C.
Steve Malakassiotis
Véronique E. Marquis
Alessandra Massobrio
Philip R. Matthews
Malcolm E. McLeod
Robert Monette
Shannon Myre
Angelo Noce
John J. O'Connor
Daniel J. Paul
Sophie Perreault
Caroline Pillon
Marc Prévost
Paul Prosterman
Bernard P. Quinn
Jean-Charles René
Sylvain Rigaud
Martin Rochette
Sylvie Rodrigue
Claudine Roy
Jean A. Savard, Q.C.
Michelle Setlakwe
Christian P. Sioufi
Martine St-Louis
Eric Stevens
Douglas H. Tees
Gilles Touchette
Anouk Violette

COUNSEL

Paul M. Amos
Alphonse Giard, Q.C.
Donald F. Cope
John A. Ogilvy, Q.C.
Peter D. Walsh, Q.C.

For full biographical listings, see the Martindale-Hubbell Law Directory

Pouliot, Mercure (AV)

CIBC Tower, 31st Floor, 1155 René-Lévesque Boulevard, West, H3B 3S6
Telephone: 514-875-5210
Telecopier: 514-875-4308
Email: POUMER@CEDEP.COM
Genève, Suisse Office: 8, Rue de la Rôtisserie, 1204 Geneva, Switzerland.
Telephone: +41 22-28 79 40.
Telecopier: +41 22-21 23 67.

MEMBERS OF FIRM

Georges A. Pouliot, Q.C.
Gilles Brunelle
Luc Gratton
Brian Riordan
Pierre Paquet
Anne-Marie Gauthier
Yvon Brizard
Robert Tessier
Daniel Gagné
Lilia Pouliot
Marco Veilleux
Alain Nadon
Jean H. Gagnon
Richard Fontaine
Normand Royal
Gilles Bertrand
Jean Larivière
Louis-Michel Tremblay
David I. Johnston
Stéphane Hébert
Jacques LeBel, Q.C.
Joel A. Silcoff
Ronald M. Auclair
Philippe Roy
Maxime B. Rhéaume
Serge Desrochers
C. Keenan LaPierre
Alain Bond
Louis Coallier
Nicole Chouinard
Stéphane Teasdale

ASSOCIATES

Micheline Perrault
Caroline Lemoine
Béatrice Arronis
Yvan Nantel
Sylvie Boulanger
Vincent Frenette
Robert Cardin
Alexandre Henri
Brent J. Muir
Louise Tremblay
Chantal Joubert
Normand D'Amour
Pascale Cloutier
Eric Couture
Frédéric Chatel
Mary-Lynn Breton
Alexandre Ajami

For full biographical listings, see the Martindale-Hubbell Law Directory

Robinson Sheppard Shapiro, G.P. (AV)

800 Place Victoria Suite 4700, H4Z 1H6
Telephone: 514-878-2631
Telecopier: 514-878-1865
Email: info@rsslex.com *URL:* http://www.rsslex.com

PARTNERS AND ASSOCIATES

Jonathan J. Robinson
Claude-Armand Sheppard
Barry H. Shapiro
Charles E. Flam
Michel J. Green
Herbert Z. Pinchuk
Theodore Goloff
Yves Cousineau
Patrick Henry
Louise Baillargeon
Eric Boulva
Jean-Denis Boucher
Lynne Kassie
Claude-Henri Grignon

(See Next Column)

ROBINSON SHEPPARD SHAPIRO G.P.—*Continued*

PARTNERS AND ASSOCIATES (Continued)

Céline Trudeau
Jean-François Lamoureux
Jacques Bélanger
Karen Kear-Jodoin
Jacques Bouchard, Jr.
Steve McInnes
Andrey Hollinger
François Marseille
Martin Lord
Brigitte Nadeau
Jean-Pierre Sheppard
Nicholas John Krnjevic
Dominique Poulin
Normand Laurendeau
Mariella De Stefano
Pascale Nolin
Brigitte Roy
Rhona Luger
Chantal Noël
Caroline Biron
Annick Bergeron
Brigitte B. Garceau
Francine Nantel
Allison P. Turner
Micheline Del Vecchio
Patrick Goudreau
Carole Goyette
Isabelle Bourgeau
Andrée Chamberland
Jean-François Fortin
Alexandre Cousineau
Fabienne Léonard
Josée Bouret
Luc Pelletier
Geneviève Goulet
Kimberly Wenger
Valérie Lagacé
Katherine Delage
Geneviève Henry
Piero Iannuzzi
Marc André Robert
Patrick Lebel
Anthony Molle

COUNSEL

Samuel Greenblatt, Q.C.
Jules Allard
Marcel Gerbeau

For full biographical listings, see the Martindale-Hubbell Law Directory

STIKEMAN ELLIOTT (AV)

1155 René-Lévesque Boulevard West, 40th Floor, H3B 3V2
Telephone: 514-397-3000
Fax: 514-397-3222
Email: info@mtl.stikeman.com *URL:* http://www.stikeman.com/
Toronto, Ontario Office: Commerce Court West, 53rd Floor, M5L 1B9.
Telephone: 416-869-5500.
Fax: 416-947-0866.
Ottawa, Ontario Office: 50 O'Connor Street, Suite 914, K1P 6L2.
Telephone: 613-234-4555.
Fax: 613-230-8877.
Calgary, Alberta Office: 855 - 2nd Street S.W., 1500 Bankers Hall, T2P 4J7.
Telephone: 403-266-9000.
Fax: 403-266-9034.
Vancouver, British Columbia Office: 666 Burrard Street, Suite 1700, Park Place, V6C 2X8.
Telephone: 604-631-1300.
Fax: 604-681-1825.
New York, New York Office: 126 East 56th Street, 14th Floor, Tower 56, 10022.
Telephone: 212-371-8855.
Fax: 212-371-7087.
London, England Office: Regis House, 45 King William Street, EC4R 9AN.
Telephone: +44 (0) 20 7648 1300.
Fax: +44 (0) 20 7648 1400.
Hong Kong Office: 29 Queen's Road Central, Suite 1103, Aon China Building.
Telephone: 852-2230-5200.
Fax: 852-2845-9076.
Singapore Office: 1 Shenton Way, #13-07 Robina House, Singapore 068803.
Telephone: 65-532-3556.
Fax: 65-532-3557.
Sydney, New South Wales Office: Level 40, The Chifley Tower, 2 Chifley Square, Sydney, NSW 2000.
Telephone: 61-2-9232-7199.
Fax: 61-2-9232-6908.

PARTNERS AND ASSOCIATES

Hon. W. David Angus, Q.C.
Marc Barbeau
Louis P. Bélanger
Patrick L. Benaroche
Sylvie Bordet
Jean Carrier
Lyse Charette
Edward B. Claxton
Suzanne Côté
Glenn A. Cranker
R. Michel Décary, Q.C.
Sterling Harrison Dietze
Jean Farley
Laurent G. Fortier
Mortimer G. Freiheit
Michel Gélinas
Lily Germain
Josée G. Gravel
Stephen W. Hamilton
Robert Hogan
Sydney J. Isaacs
Louis Juneau
M. Bruno Arnould
France Margaret Bélanger
Jean-Pierre Belhumeur
Lise Bertrand
Hélène Bussières
Peter Castiel
Viateur Chénard
Stuart H. (Kip) Cobbett
Marc-André Coulombe
Peter J. Cullen
Christine Desaulniers
Bruno Étienne Duguay
Jean Fontaine
Donald Francoeur
Arden Furlotte
Michel Généreux
James A. Grant, Q.C.
Benjamin J. Greenberg
Frédéric Harvey
Jean Marc Huot
Catherine A. Jenner
Kevin Kyte

(See Next Column)

PARTNERS AND ASSOCIATES (Continued)

Hon. Marc Lalonde, P.C., O.C., Q.C.
John W. Leopold
Monique Lussier
Yves Martineau
Étienne Massicotte
Francine Matte
François Mercier, O.C., Q.C.
Louis Morisset
Peter R. O'Brien
Ron Peck
François Picard
Éveline Poirier
Richard W. Pound, O.C., O.Q., Q.C.
Pierre A. Raymond
Michael L. Richards
Erik Richer La Fleche
James A. Robb, Q.C.
Anna Romano
Howard Rosenoff
André Roy
Victor Salvaggio
Paul J. Setlakwe
Pierrette Sinclair
Mireille A. Tabib
Serge Tousignant
Michel Vennat, Q.C.
Marc Laurin
Geneviève Lavertu
Martin Claude Lepage
Pierre Martel
Alain Massicotte
R. Guy Masson
Bertrand P. Ménard
Éric Mongeau
Marie-France Nantel
François H. Ouimet
J. Anthony Penhale
Frédéric Pierrestiger
Isabel Pouliot
Vincent M. Prager
Stephen M. Raicek
Maurice A. Régnier
Elinore J. Richardson
Hon. Maurice Riel, P.C., Q.C.
Steeve Robitaille
William B. Rosenberg
Calin Rovinescu
Richard J. Rusk
Martin H. Scheim
Margo R. Siminovitch
Diane C. Skiejka
Louise Touchette
Anik Trudel
François Vincent

For full biographical listings, see the Martindale-Hubbell Law Directory

WOODS & PARTNERS (AV)

2000 McGill College Avenue, Suite 1100, H3A 3H3
Telephone: 514-982-4545
Telecopier: 514-284-2046
Email: general@woods.qc.ca

MEMBERS OF FIRM

James A. Woods
Christian Immer
Julien Cools-Lartigue
Nathalie Chalifour
Christopher Lund Richter
Annie Galarneau
Sébastien Richemont
Kathleen Beaugé
Marjorie Delagrave

For full biographical listings, see the Martindale-Hubbell Law Directory

*QUEBEC,** Quebec Dist.

DESJARDINS DUCHARME STEIN MONAST (AV)

Suite 300, 1150 Claire Fontaine Street, G1R 5G4
Telephone: 418-529-6531
Telecopier: 418-523-5391
Email: avocat@ddsm.ca *URL:* http://www.ddsm.ca
Montréal, Quebec Office: 600 de la Gauchetiere Street West, Suite 2400, H3B 4L8.
Telephone: 514-878-9411.
Telecopier: 514-878-9092.
Affiliated Offices:
Torys:
Toronto: Suite 3000, Aetna Tower, Toronto-Dominion Centre, P.O. Box 270, Toronto (Ontario) M5K 1N2.
Telephone: 416-865-0040;
Telecopier: 416-865-7380.
New York, New York Office: 237 Park Avenue, 10017-3142.
Telephone: 212-880-6000.
Fax: 212-682-0200.
Beijing, China Office: China Merchants Tower, Suite C, 29F 2 Dong Huan Nan Lu, Jianguomenwai, Chaoyang District, 100022.
Telephone: 8610 6566 9088.
Fax: 8610 6566 9096.

MEMBERS OF FIRM

Pierre Marseille, Q.C.
Jean Marier
Roger Vallières
Louis Huot
Pierre Pelletier
Michel-C. Chabot
Michel Dupont
Henri-Louis Fortin
Jean Brunet
René Delorme
Edward Gosselin
Jean-François Drolet
Charles G. Gagnon
Martin Roy
Julie-Suzanne Doyon
Karine Brassard
Stéphanie Rheault
Charles Taschereau
Sébastien Guy
Pierre LaRue, Q.C.
Pierre Lesage
Hon. Paule Gauthier, P.C., O.C., Q.C.
Jean F. Keable
Claude Girard
Michel Demers
Claude Rochon
André Johnson
Claude L. Gravel
Christian Racicot
Eric Lemay
Marie A. Pettigrew
Jacques Boulanger
Marie Vezina
Odette St-Laurent
Jocelyn Auger
Nancy Fournier
Philippe Chouinard-Rousseau

(See Next Column)

DESJARDINS DUCHARME STEIN MONAST, *Quebec—Continued*

COUNSEL

Charles Stein, Q.C., LL.D.

For full biographical listings, see the Martindale-Hubbell Law Directory

FASKEN MARTINEAU DUMOULIN (AV)

140, rue Grande Allée est Bureau 800, G1R 5M8
Telephone: 418-640-2000
Toll Free: 1-800-463-2827 (Ontario & Quebec)
Facsimile: 418-647-2455
Email: info@qc.fasken.com *URL:* www.fasken.com
Fasken Martineau DuMoulin is a leading Canadian firm with a national and international practice and having offices in Toronto, Montreal, Quebec, Vancouver, New York and London. Please refer to listings in the respective city sections.
Montreal, Quebec Office: Tour De La Bourse, Suite 800 Place Victoria Suite 3400, P.O. Box 242 , Montreal (Quebec) Canada, H4Z 1E9.
Telephone: 514-397-7400. Toll Free: 1-800-361-6266 (Ontario & Quebec).
Facsimile: 514-397-7600.
Telex: 05-24610 BUOY MTL. EMail: info@mtl.fasken.com.
Toronto, Ontario Office: Toronto-Dominion Centre, Toronto Dominion Bank Tower, P.O. Box 20, M5K 1N6.
Telephone: 416-366-8381. Toll Free: 1-800-268-8424 (Ontario & Quebec).
Facsimile: 416-364-7813. EMail: info@torfasken.com.
Vancouver, British Columbia Office: 2100-1075 West Georgia Street.
Telephone: 604-631-3131.
Fax: 604-631-3232. EMail: info@van.fasken.com. Website: www..fasken.com.
New York, New York Office: Seagram Building, 375 Park Avenue, Suite 2608, 10152.
Telephone: 212-935-3203.
Facsimile: 212-935-4822. EMail: info@nyc.fasken.com. Website: www.fasken.com.
London, England Office: 10 Arthur Street, 5th Floor, EC4R 9AY.
Telephone: 71-929-2894.
Facsimile: 71-929-3634. EMail: info@lon.fasken.com.

MEMBERS OF FIRM

P.-Michel Bouchard
Jean G. Morency
Jean M. Gagné
Guy C. Dion
Martin R. Gagné
Pierre Lamontagne
André Asselin
Guy Samson
Guy Leblanc
François Duchesneau
Michel Heroux
Benoit Mailloux

ASSOCIATES

Claudette Tessier-Couture
Stéphane Lalancette
Valérie Lemaire
Hans Bois
Frédéric Boucher
Charles Mercier
Sophie Sénéchal
Jean-François Hébert
Jasmin Marcotte
Simon Marchand-Fortier
Jacques Cossette-Lesage
Ann Quigley
Christian Trépanier

For full biographical listings, see the Martindale-Hubbell Law Directory

LAVERY, DE BILLY (AV)

925 Chemin St-Louis, Suite 500, G1S 1C1
Telephone: 418-688-5000
Facsimile: 418-688-3458
Email: info@lavery.qc.ca *URL:* http://www.laverydebilly.com
Montreal, Quebec Office: 1 Place Ville Marie, 40th Floor, Montreal, Quebec H3B 4M4.
Telephone: 514-871-1522.
Facsimile: 514-871-8977.
Ottawa, Ontario Office: 45 O'Connor, 20th Floor, Ottawa, Ontario K1P 1A4.
Telephone: 613-594-4936.
Facsimile: 613-594-8783.
Laval, Quebec Office: Suite 500, 3080 Boul. Le Carrefour, Laval, Quebec H7T 2R5.
Telephone: 450-978-8100.
Facsimile: 450-978-8111.
Associate Office: Blake, Cassels & Graydon, Box 25, Commerce Court West, Toronto, Ontario M5L 1A9.
Telephone: 416-863-2400.
Facsimile: 416-863-2653.

MEMBERS OF FIRM AND ASSOCIATES

Jacques de Billy, Q.C.
André Gagnon, Q.C.
Pierre Beaudoin
Pierre Cantin
Pierre-C. Gagnon
Martin J. Edwards
Christian R. Drolet
Claude M. Jarry
Pierre F. Carter
Danielle Côté
Louis Rochette
Judith Rochette
Claudia P. Prémont
Stephane Labrie
Gilles de Billy, Q.C.
Jules Brière
Jean-Pierre Roy
Jacques R. Gingras
Claude Larose
Hélène Gauvin
Serge Letourneau
Élisabeth Pinard
Francois Houde
Pierre Gourdeau
Jean-Francois Fournier
Bernard Jacob
Marie-Elaine Racine
Michele Bernier

(See Next Column)

MEMBERS OF FIRM AND ASSOCIATES (Continued)

Daniel Bouchard
Simon Lemay
Francois Vallieres
Philippe Cantin
Sylvie Harbour
Jean-Francois Pichette
Kim Thomassin
Laurier Gauthier

For full biographical listings, see the Martindale-Hubbell Law Directory

MCCARTHY TÉTRAULT (AV)

Le Complexe St-Amable, 1150, rue Claire Fontaine 7e Étage, G1R 5G4
Telephone: 418-521-3000
Facsimile: 418-521-3098; 418-521-3099
Email: quebec@mccarthy.ca *URL:* http://www.mccarthy.ca
Vancouver, British Columbia Office: Suite 1300, 777 Dunsmuir Street, P.O. Box 10424, Vancouver, British Columbia V7Y 1K2.
Telephone: 604-643-7100.
Facsimile: 604-643-7900.
Surrey, British Columbia Office: Suite 1300, Station Tower, Gateway 13401-108th Avenue, Surrey, British Columbia V3T 5T3.
Telephone: 604-583-9100.
Fax: 604-583-9150.
Calgary, Alberta Office: Suite 3300, 421 7th Avenue, S.W., Calgary, Alberta T2P 3K9.
Telephone: 403-260-3500.
Facsimile: 403-260-3501.
London, Ontario Office: Suite 2000, One London Place, 255 Queens Avenue, London, Ontario N6A 5R8.
Telephone: 519-660-3587.
Facsimile: 519-660-3599.
Toronto, Ontario Office: Suite 4700, Toronto Dominion Bank Tower, Toronto, Ontario M5K 1E6.
Telephone: 416-362-1812.
Facsimile: 416-868-0673.
Ottawa, Ontario Office: The Chambers, Suite 1400, 40 Elgin Street, Ottawa, Ontario K1P 5K6.
Telephone: 613-238-2000.
Facsimile: 613-563-9386.
Montréal, Québec Office: Le Windsor, 1170 rue Peel, Montréal, Québec H3B 4S8.
Telephone: 514-397-4100.
Facsimile: 514-875-6246.
United Kingdom and Europe Office: Pountney Hill House, 6 Laurence Pountney Hill, London, England EC4R 0BL.
Telephone: 011-44-171-618-2888.
Facsimile: 011-44-171-618-2880.

PARTNERS

Richard R. Drouin, O.C., Q.C.
Marc Germain
François Amyot (Managing Partner)
Bernard Tremblay
Pierre Jolin
Marc N. Dorion, Q.C.
Mario Lacombe
France Bonsaint
Denis Roy
Philippe Leclerc

ASSOCIATES

Pierre Boivin
Jean Berthelot
Christian Roy
Philippe Boivin
Doris Dion
Marie-Paule Gagnon
Pascal Paradis
Louise Gauthier
Caroline Fontaine

For full biographical listings, see the Martindale-Hubbell Law Directory

OGILVY RENAULT (AV)

Suite 520, 500 Grande Allée est, G1R 2J7
Telephone: 418-640-5000
Fax: 418-640-1500
Email: quebec@ogilvyrenault.com *URL:* http://www.ogilvyrenault.com
Montréal, Québec Office: Suite 1100, 1981 McGill College Avenue, H3A 3C1.
Telephone: 514-847-4747.
Fax: 514-286-5474. Email: info@ogilvyrenault.com
Ottawa, Ontario Office: Suite 1600, 45 O'Connor Street, K1P 1A4.
Telephone: 613-780-8661.
Fax: 613-230-5459. Email: ottawa@ogilvyrenault.com
Toronto, Ontario Office: Suite 2100, P.O. Box 141, Royal Trust Tower, TD Centre, M5K 1H1.
Telephone: 416-216-4000.
Fax: 416-216-3930. Email: toronto@ogilvyrenault.com
Vancouver, British Columbia Office: 800 Park Place, 666 Burrard Street, V6C 3P3.
Telephone: 604-806-0922.
Fax: 604-806-0933. Email: info@ogilvyrenault.com
London, England Office: 38 Charterhouse Square, EC1M 6EQ.
Telephone: 44 (0) 207-600-9005.
Fax: 44 (0) 207-600-9006. Email: info@ogilvyrenault.com

François Arsenault
Julie Branchaud
Bernard Choquette
Louis-M. Cossette
Pierre Déry
Claude A. Blanchard
Maxime Cantin
Pierre Cimon
Jacques Côté
Roger Duval

(See Next Column)

OGILVY RENAULT—*Continued*

Sylvain Gendron	Yves Gonthier
Ian Gosselin	Éric Hardy
Jean Houle	Anne-Marie Naud
Marc Paradis	Claude Paré
Lucie Pariseau	Jean Piette
Jocelyn F. Rancourt	Martin Rochette
Louis Roy	Nicolas Sapp
Jean Setlakwe	Louis Ste-Marie
Carl Tremblay	Louis Vaillancourt

For full biographical listings, see the Martindale-Hubbell Law Directory

CANADA
SASKATCHEWAN

*REGINA,** Regina Jud. Centre

BALFOUR MOSS (AV)

Bank of Montreal Building, 700-2103 11th Avenue, S4P 4G1
Telephone: 306-347-8300
Fax: 306-347-8350
Email: balfourmoss.regina@dlcwest.com *URL:* http://www.dlcwest.com/~balfourmoss
Saskatoon, Saskatchewan Office: #600-123-2nd Avenue South.
Telephone: 306-665-7844.
Fax: 306-652-1586.

PARTNERS

A. John Beke, Q.C.	Rick M. Van Beselaere
Fredrick C. McBeth	George E. Nystrom
Brian J. Scherman (Resident Saskatoon)	Jeff N. Grubb
Roger J.F. Lepage	David G. Gerecke (Resident Saskatoon)
Reginald A. Watson	Raymond J. Dean
Glen S. Lekach	Bob P. Hrycan

COUNSEL

E. John Moss, Q.C.	Robert A. Milliken, Q.C.
Hon. R. James Balfour, Q.C.	Roy B. Laschuk, Q.C.

ASSOCIATES

Michael D. Crosbie	Kathleen Á. Richardson
Peter T. Bergbusch	Stewart J.O. Berringer
Kerri A. Froc	Yens Pedersen
Heather MacMillan-Brown (Resident, Saskatoon Office)	

Representative Clients: Bank of Montreal; Saskatchewan Wheat Pool; Cable Regina; Cameco; Wascana Centre Authority; Regina Regional Health District; Canadian Western Bank; Coopers & Lybrand; Southland Canada; Walmart Canada Limited.

For full biographical listings, see the Martindale-Hubbell Law Directory

MACPHERSON LESLIE & TYERMAN (AV)

1500-1874 Scarth Street, S4P 4E9
Telephone: 306-347-8000
Telecopier: 306-352-5250
Email: mltreg@mlt.com
Saskatoon, Saskatchewan Office: 1500-410 22nd Street East, S7K 5T6.
Telephone: 306-975-7100.
Telecopier: 306-975-7145.

MEMBERS OF FIRM

Harold H. MacKay, Q.C.	Dennis P. Ball, Q.C.
Robert B. Pletch, Q.C.	A. Robson Garden, Q.C. (Resident, Saskatoon Office)
Maurice O. Laprairie, Q.C.	Larry B. LeBlanc, Q.C.
Donald K. Wilson, Q.C.	Leonard D. Andrychuk
R. Neil MacKay (Resident, Saskatoon Office)	Bruce W. Wirth (Resident, Saskatoon Office)
Garret J. Oledzki	Robert G. Richards, Q.C.
Alain J. Gaucher (Resident, Saskatoon Office)	Douglas A. Ballou
Melissa A. Brunsdon (Resident, Saskatoon Office)	Brian J. Kenny
	Danny R. Anderson (Resident, Saskatoon Office)
Douglas C. Hodson (Resident, Saskatoon Office)	Robert W. Leurer
James S. Kerby (Resident, Saskatoon Office)	Randy U. Brunet
	John A. Dipple
Jeffrey M. Lee (Resident, Saskatoon Office)	Kevin C. Wilson (Resident, Saskatoon Office)
Conrad D. Hadubiak	Curtis R. Stewart (Resident, Saskatoon Office)
Eileen V. Libby	
Scott A. Exner	Todd M. Rosenberg (Resident, Saskatoon Office)

ASSOCIATES

R. M. Louise Simard, Q.C.	David B. Jahnke (Resident, Saskatoon Office)
Michael D. Tochor	
Jeffrey D. Scott	F. Neil Turcotte (Resident, Saskatoon Office)

(See Next Column)

Linda A. Christensen

ASSOCIATES (Continued)

Paul A. Beke (Resident, Saskatoon Office)	Vanessa Monar Enweani (Resident, Saskatoon Office)
Michele T. Klebuc-Simes	Scott D. Whitby
Grant D. Marshak (Resident, Saskatoon Office)	Barclay A. Laughland (Resident, Saskatoon Office)
M. Jean Torrens (Resident, Saskatoon Office)	Wendy Y. Martin White (Resident, Saskatoon Office)
Aaron D. Runge	Jordan P. Hardy
Rachelle M. Verret	James D. Camplin
Kurt G. Wintermute (Resident, Saskatoon Office)	Dana D.J. Schindelka
	Heather D. Heavin
Kevin D. Trumpour (Resident, Saskatoon Office)	Michael J. Clark (Resident, Saskatoon Office)
Kenton J. Gray	Charita N. Parchewsky
Deron A. Kuski	Scott A. Newell (Resident, Saskatoon Office)
R. Allen Kirk (Resident, Saskatoon Office)	Crystal L. Taylor (Resident, Saskatoon Office)
Bradley N. Vance	

Meghan R. McCreary

COUNSEL

William M. Elliott, Q.C.	W. Thomas Molloy, O.C., Q.C. (Resident, Saskatoon Office)

For full biographical listings, see the Martindale-Hubbell Law Directory

*SASKATOON,** Saskatoon Jud. Centre

GAULEY & CO. (AV)

701 Broadway Avenue, P.O. Box 638, S7K 3L7
Telephone: 306-653-1212
Telecopier: 306-652-1323
Email: gauleyco@gauleyco.com
Regina, Saskatchewan Office: Suite 400, 2201 11th Avenue S4P 0J8.
Telephone: 306-352-1643.
Telecopier: 306-525-8499.

MEMBERS OF FIRM

David E. "Tom" Gauley, Q.C.	Ian A. Sutherland
Harry H. Dahlem, Q.C.	J. J. (Joe) Dierker, Q.C.
Larry F. Seiferling, Q.C.	Peter Foley, Q.C.
Pat A. Kelly, Q.C. (Resident, Regina Office)	William J. Shaw
	David J. McKeague, Q.C.
Nancy E. Hopkins, Q.C. (Hon.) C.A.	Rex M. Beaton
	Gary A. Zabos
James Russell	Raymond Wiebe

ASSOCIATES

Dale G. Linn	Neal W. Caldwell
Chris C. Boychuk	Warren D. Martinson
Leah A. Schatz	Neil B. Fisher
Eugene T. Harmel (Resident, Regina Office)	Stephanie L. Tynan
	William A. Nickel

Reference: Royal Bank of Canada.

For full biographical listings, see the Martindale-Hubbell Law Directory

ARGENTINA

*BUENOS AIRES,**

American Lawyers In Buenos Aires

BAKER & MCKENZIE

Avenida Leandro N. Alem 1110, Piso 13, 1001 Buenos Aires
Telephone: 4310-2200
Intn'l Dialing: (54-11) 4310-2200
Facsimile: (54-11) 4310-2299
URL: http://www.bakerinfo.com
Associated Offices of Baker & McKenzie in: Almaty, Amsterdam, Bahrain, Baku, Bangkok, Barcelona, Beijing, Berlin, Bogotá, Brasília, Brussels, Budapest, Cairo, Caracas, Chicago, Dallas, Düsseldorf, Frankfurt, Geneva, Hanoi, Ho Chi Minh City, Hong Kong, Houston, Hsinchu, Juárez, Kyiv, London, Madrid, Manila, Melbourne, México City, Miami, Milan, Monterrey, Moscow, Münich, New York, Palo Alto, Paris, Prague, Rio de Janeiro, Riyadh, Rome, St. Petersburg, San Diego, San Francisco, Santiago, São Paulo, Singapore, Stockholm, Sydney, Taipei, Tijuana, Tokyo, Toronto, Valencia, Warsaw, Washington, D.C. and Zürich.
Correspondent Law Firm: Hadiputranto, Hadinoto & Partners, Jakarta.

PARTNERS

Gonzalo E. Cáceres	Miguel Menegazzo Cané
Carlos A. A. Dodds	Alejandro J. Olivera
Pablo Dukarevich	Avelino Rolon

Horacio C. Soares

(See Next Column)

BAKER & MCKENZIE, *Buenos Aires—Continued*

LOCAL PARTNERS

Rafael E. Ayerza
Martín J. Barreiro
Gustavo A. Boruchowicz
Adolfo Durañona
Gabriela López Cremaschi
Bernard W. Malone
Ricardo Truppel

OF COUNSEL

Pedro Julio Agote

ASSOCIATES

Juan Ignacio Achaval Dodero
Alba Avila Quintana
Josep Maria Balcells (Not admitted in Argentina)
Marcos J. Basso
Albino Juan Bazzanella
Alejandra Verónica Bugna
María Vanina Caniza
Guillermo Jose Cervio
Fernando Emiliano Córdoba
Carolina V. Correa Crovetto
Valentin Miguel Di Sisto
Nicolas Garcia Pinto
Micaela Inés Geiderman
Pablo Gonzalez del Solar
María Patricia González Presedo
Alberto J. González Torres
Roberto Grané (On Leave)
Graciela Alba Haggi
María Gabriela Hahan
Dr. Emilio R. Itzcovich(h)
Juan Martin Jovanovich (On Leave)
Alexis Kook Weskott
Mariana Rosa Laurence
Maria Beatriz Lopez Provera
Claudio A. Luqui
Martín Pedro Marpegán
Verónica Melián
Ronaldo Agustin Negri
Sebastian L. Nordemann
Maria Eugenia Oliver
Jorge Daniel Orlansky
Hernán Didier Pantaleón
Javier G. Pereira Amigo
Isabela Pucci
Martín R. Quintanar
Inés Amparo Riobó
Esteban Pablo Rópolo
Marcelo Slonimsky
Juan M. Steverlynck
Diego Fernando Viviani

For full biographical listings, see the Martindale-Hubbell Law Directory

AUSTRALIA

MELBOURNE, VICTORIA,

BAKER & MCKENZIE

Level 39 Rialto, 525 Collins Street, Melbourne, Victoria 3000
Telephone: (03) 9617-4200
Intn'l Dialing: (61-3) 9617-4200
Facsimile: (61-3) 9614-2103
URL: http://www.bakerinfo.com
Associated Offices of Baker & McKenzie in: Almaty, Amsterdam, Bahrain, Baku, Bangkok, Barcelona, Beijing, Berlin, Bogotá, Brasília, Brussels, Budapest, Buenos Aires, Cairo, Caracas, Chicago, Dallas, Düsseldorf, Frankfurt, Geneva, Hanoi, Ho Chi Minh City, Hong Kong, Houston, Hsinchu, Juárez, Kyiv, London, Madrid, Manila, México City, Miami, Milan, Monterrey, Moscow, Münich, New York, Palo Alto, Paris, Prague, Rio de Janeiro, Riyadh, Rome, St. Petersburg, San Diego, San Francisco, Santiago, São Paulo, Singapore, Stockholm, Sydney, Taipei, Tijuana, Tokyo, Toronto, Valencia, Warsaw, Washington, D.C. and Zürich.
Correspondent Law Firm: Hadiputranto, Hadinoto & Partners, Jakarta.
Postal Address: P.O. Box 2119T, G.P.O., Melbourne, Victoria 3001

MEMBERS OF FIRM

Ian M. Dixon
Leigh W. Duthie
Kenneth W. Gray
Theodore Kindynis
Paul D. McSweeney
Christopher B. Penman
Graham V. Sherry

LOCAL PARTNERS

David N. Carter
Christopher J. Connor
Gillad Dalal
Anne Maree Moon
Donna Pelka
Michael F. Selth
Bruce C. Webb
Anthony B. Whelan

ASSOCIATES

John T. Abrahamson
Meaghan Bare
Catherine J. Bell
Anthony Brearley
Sophie Callander
Rebecca A. Carroll
Chad K. de Souza
Jacinda de Witts
Venita Dimos
Edwina Garrisson
Samuel J. Golding
Kirsti Hanson
Alexander A. Hartmann
Rashpal K. Hartmann (Not admitted in Australia)
Timothy V. Jackson
Roger S. Johnson
Jane L. Kirsner
Junko Kobayashi
Peter G. Little
Joshua L. Magennis
Darren P. Marx
Patrick J. McGrath
John J. McNeill
Alan D. Moyle
Scott L. Munro
Nicholas D. Power
Daniel J. Roberts
Antonia Skondras
Mini Menon Vandepol
Peter G. Vitale
Christina S. Wilhelm
Ashley Graham Woods
Benedict Wei Wen Yong
Timothy J. Young

For full biographical listings, see the Martindale-Hubbell Law Directory

SULLIVAN & CROMWELL

101 Collins Street, Melbourne, Victoria 3000
Telephone: (011)(613)9654-1500
Telecopier: (011)(613)9654-2422
URL: http://www.sullcrom.com
New York City Office: 125 Broad Street, 10004-2498.
Telephone: 212-558-4000.
Telex: 62694.
Telecopier: 212-558-3588 or 212-514-5706.
Washington, D.C. Office: 1701 Pennsylvania Avenue, N.W., 20006-5805.
Telephone: 202-956-7500.
Telecopier: 202-293-6330.
Los Angeles, California Office: 1888 Century Park East, 90067-1725.
Telephone: 310-712-6600.
Telecopier: 310-712-8800.
Paris Office: 8, Place Vendôme, 75001 Paris, France.
Telephone: (011)(331) 44 50 60 00.
Telex: 240654.
Telecopier: (011)(331) 44 50 60 60 or (011)(331) 42 60 56 36.
London Office: St. Olave's House, 9a Ironmonger Lane, London EC2V 8EY, England.
Telephone: (011)(44207) 710 6500.
Telecopier: (011)(44207) 710 6565.
Tokyo Office: Sullivan & Cromwell, Gaikokuho Jimu Bengoshi Jimusho, Akai Law Offices (Registered Associated Offices), Otemachi First Square East Tower 16F, 5-1, Otemachi 1-chome, Chiyoda-ku, Tokyo 100-0004, Japan.
Telephone: (011)(813) 3213-6140.
Telecopier: (011)(813) 3213-6470 or (011)(813) 3213-6477.
Hong Kong Office: 28th Floor, Nine Queen's Road, Central, Hong Kong.
Telephone: (011)(852) 2826-8688.
Telecopier: (011)(852) 2522-2280.
Frankfurt Office: Neue Mainzer Strasse 52, 60322 Frankfurt, Germany.
Telephone: (011)(4969) 7191 26-0.
Telecopier: (011)(4969) 7191 26-10.
Beijing Office: The Beijing Representative Office of Sullivan & Cromwell, Suite 501, China World Trade Center, No. 1 Jianguo Menwai Avenue, Beijing 100004, P.R.C.
Telephone: (011)(86) 10 6505 6120.
Telecopier: (011)(86) 10 6505 6136.

PARTNER IN MELBOURNE

Jeffrey F. Browne

SPECIAL COUNSEL IN MELBOURNE

Burr Henly (Not admitted in Australia)
Waldo D. Jones, Jr. (Not admitted in Australia)

ASSOCIATES IN MELBOURNE

Jack J. Chen (Not admitted in Australia)
John E. Capps (Not admitted in Australia)

For full biographical listings, see the Martindale-Hubbell Law Directory

SYDNEY, NEW SOUTH WALES,

BAKER & MCKENZIE

Level 26, A.M.P. Centre, 50 Bridge Street, P.O. Box R126, Royal Exchange, Sydney, New South Wales 1223
Telephone: (02) 9225-0200
Intn'l Dialing: (61-2) 9225-0200
Facsimile: (61-2) 9223-7711
URL: http://www.bakerinfo.com
Associated Offices of Baker & McKenzie in: Almaty, Amsterdam, Bahrain, Baku, Bangkok, Barcelona, Beijing, Berlin, Bogotá, Brasília, Brussels, Budapest, Buenos Aires, Cairo, Caracas, Chicago, Dallas, Düsseldorf, Frankfurt, Geneva, Hanoi, Ho Chi Minh City, Hong Kong, Houston, Hsinchu, Juárez, Kyiv, London, Madrid, Manila, Melbourne, México City, Miami, Milan, Monterrey, Moscow, Münich, New York, Palo Alto, Paris, Prague, Rio de Janeiro, Riyadh, Rome, St. Petersburg, San Diego, San Francisco, Santiago, São Paulo, Singapore, Stockholm, Taipei, Tijuana, Tokyo, Toronto, Valencia, Warsaw, Washington, D.C. and Zürich.
Correspondent Law Firm: Hadiputranto, Hadinoto & Partners, Jakarta.
Postal Address: Box R126, Royal Exchange P.O., Sydney.

MEMBERS OF FIRM

Michael C. Ahrens
Paul G. Brown
Frank Cahill
Frank J. Castiglia
Mark D. Chapple
John A. Connors
Graeme J. Dickson
Peter T. Dwight
John R. Fabbro
Joan T. Fitzhenry
Anthony J. Foley
Steven M. Glanz
Richard T. Gough
George C. Harris
David L. Jacobs
Michael J. Kunstler
Robert Leacock
Benjamin T. McLaughlin
Ross G. McLean
Roy E. Melick
Spiro Mellos
James H. Momsen
Timothy P. O'Doherty
Ralph B. Pliner
Timothy J. Reed
Andrew M. Salgo
Christopher J. Saxon
David R. Shannon
Robert I. Simpson
Rodney Stone
Penelope J. Ward
Timothy A. Woodhouse
Edwin J. Zemancheff

(See Next Column)

BAKER & MCKENZIE—*Continued*

LOCAL PARTNERS

Anne-Marie L. Allgrove
John C. Balazs
Stephanie M. Bronk
Andrew Christopher
Julieanne E. Cox
Brett C. Doyle
John A. Ellis
Howard H. Fraser
Bill Fuggle
James A. Hamilton
E. Amrit Macintyre
Michael Michalandos
Karen J. Ryder
Guy J. Sanderson
Stephen J. Watts

ASSOCIATES

Nicola Adams (Not admitted in Australia)
Sarah Aitken
Richard Amos
Mark Bennett
Susan E. Beaumont
Paul Boyle (Not admitted in Australia)
Jennifer A. Brookman
Peter Brudenall
Seamus J. Burke
Stephanie Burton
Alison Carrigan (Not admitted in Australia)
Craig Cawood
David L. Cleland
Elizabeth Coffey
Andrew Lloyd Connolly (Not admitted in Australia)
Jacqueline Cormack (Not admitted in Australia)
Celina Creek
Elizabeth J. Crowhurst (Not admitted in Australia)
Ursula E. Crowley
Deborah Cubeddu
Paul H. Curnow
Claire H. Dombkins
Gavin Douglas
Richard D. Doyle
David Egan (Not admitted in Australia)
Fleur Findlay
Anne Flahvin
Hayden C. Fox
Michael D. French
Peter Harrison (Not admitted in Australia)
Caroline M. K. Ho
Barbara Hugh
Amanda Hutton
Teresa Ientile
Dominic Instone (Not admitted in Australia)
Brian D. Jebb
Lindsey Joffe
Jonathan M. Kelt
Lindsay Kyle (Not admitted in Australia)
Frances A. Kyrikos
Paul Anthony Lanzone
Janine Lapworth
Adrian J. Lawrence
Felicity Lee-Young
Jonathon N. Leek
James K. Leeken
Belinda Lin
Caroline M. Long
John B. MacPhail
Mary Frances Maher
David C. McCredie
Brett McGuire (Not admitted in Australia)
David John McIntyre
Mark McNamara
Andrew J. McNee
Louise J. Muldoon (Not admitted in Australia)
Rebecca Ng
Danh V. Nguyen
Maria F. C. O'Brien
Margaret Pavey
Astrid Raetze
Elizabeth Raper
Evan Wynn Rees
David J. Russell
David M. Ryan (Not admitted in Australia)
Kenneth Saurajen
Tracey M. Savage
Samantha A. Selmes
Adrian Smith (Not admitted in Australia)
Lynne-Maree Sproule
Anita Spudic
Gillian M. Stals
Catherine J. M. Tan
Melissa J. Taylor
Annette Teckemeier
Kate Temple (Not admitted in Australia)
Richard E. Tripp (Not admitted in Australia)
Ginta Viliunas
Linda Michelle Vogel
Thomas D. Wait
Kirstin Warley (Not admitted in Australia)
Robert J. Wilcher
Martijn B.D. Wilder
Jacqueline Williams
Christopher Wong (Not admitted in Australia)

For full biographical listings, see the Martindale-Hubbell Law Directory

American Lawyers In Sydney, New South Wales

JONES, DAY, REAVIS & POGUE

Governor Phillip Tower, Level 38, 1 Farrer Place, Sydney, New South Wales 2000
Telephone: 61-2-9210-6921
Telecopier: 61-2-9210-6926
URL: http://www.jonesday.com
In Atlanta, Georgia: 3500 SunTrust Plaza, 303 Peachtree Street.
Telephone: 404-521-3939.
Telecopier: 404-581-8330.
In Brussels, Belgium: Avenue Louise 480, 7th Floor. B-1050 Brussels.
Telephone: 32-2-645-14-11.
Telecopier: 32-2-645-14-45.
In Chicago, Illinois: 77 West Wacker.
Telephone: 312-782-3939.
Telecopier: 312-782-8585.
In Cleveland, Ohio: North Point, 901 Lakeside Avenue.
Telephone: 216-586-3939.
Telecopier: 216-579-0212.
In Columbus, Ohio: 1900 Huntington Center.
Telephone: 614-469-3939.
Telecopier: 614-461-4198.

(See Next Column)

In Dallas, Texas: 2727 North Harwood Street.
Telephone: 214-220-3939.
Telecopier: 214-969-5100.
In Frankfurt, Germany: Hochhaus am Park, Grüneburgweg 102, 60323 Frankfurt am Main.
Telephone: 49-69-9726-3939.
Telecopier: 49-69-9726-3993.
In Geneva, Switzerland: 20, rue de Candolle.
Telephone: 41-22-320-2339.
Telecopier: 41-22-320-1232.
In Hong Kong: 29th Floor, Entertainment Building, 30 Queen's Road Central.
Telephone: 852-2526-6895.
Telecopier: 852-2868-5871.
In Irvine, California: 5 Park Plaza, Suite 1100.
Telephone: 949-851-3939.
Telecopier: 949-553-7539.
In London, England: Bucklersbury House, 3 Queen Victoria Street.
Telephone: 44-20-7236-3939
Telecopier: 44-20-7236-1113.
In Los Angeles, California: 555 West Fifth Street, Suite 4600.
Telephone: 213-489-3939.
Telecopier: 213-243-2539.
In New York, New York: 599 Lexington Avenue.
Telephone: 212-326-3939.
Telecopier: 212-755-7306.
In Paris, France: 120, rue du Faubourg Saint-Honoré.
Telephone: 33-1-56-59-39-39.
Telecopier: 33-1-56-59-39-38
In Pittsburgh, Pennsylvania: 500 Grant Street, 31st Floor.
Telephone: 412-391-3939.
Telecopier: 412-394-7959.
In Riyadh, Saudi Arabia: The International Law Firm (In Association with Jones, Day, Reavis & Pogue), Sulaymaniyah, Prince Mishari IBN, Abdulaziz Street, P.O. Box 22166.
Telephone: (966-1) 462-8866.
Telecopier: (966-1) 462-9001.
In Shanghai, China: 2805 Kerry Centre, 1515 Nanjing Road West.
Telephone: 86-21-5298-6568.
Telecopier: 86-21-5298-6569.
In Taipei, Taiwan: 8th Floor, 2 Tun Hwa South Road, Section 2.
Telephone: (886-2) 2704-6808.
Telecopier: (886-2) 2704-6791.
In Tokyo, Japan: Toranomon 45 Mori Building, 3rd Floor, 1-5, Toranomon 5-Chome, Minato-Ku, Tokyo 105, Japan.
Telephone: 81-3-3433-3939.
Telecopier: 81-3-5401-2725.
In Washington, D.C.: 51 Louisiana Avenue, N.W.
Telephone: 202-879-3939.
Telecopier: 202-626-1700.

MEMBER OF FIRM

Kevin D. Cramer (Not admitted in Australia)

ASSOCIATES

Jamie A. Benson (Not admitted in Australia)
Andrew S. Reilly (Not admitted in Australia)

For full biographical listings, see the Martindale-Hubbell Law Directory

AZERBAIJAN

BAKU,

BAKER & MCKENZIE

The Landmark Building, 96 Nizami Street, 6th Floor, Baku 370010
Telephone: (8-8922) 98-24-80 Intn'l Dialing: (99412) 97-18-01
Facsimile: (w/in CIS): (8-8922) 97-18-05
(Outside CIS): (99412) 97-18-05
Chgo., IL
Email: baku.info@bakernet.com *URL:* http://www.bakerinfo.com
Associated Offices of Baker & McKenzie in: Almaty, Amsterdam, Bahrain, Bangkok, Barcelona, Beijing, Berlin, Bogotá, Brasília, Brussels, Budapest, Buenos Aires, Cairo, Caracas, Chicago, Dallas, Düsseldorf, Frankfurt, Geneva, Hanoi, Ho Chi Minh City, Hong Kong, Houston, Hsinchu, Juárez, Kyiv, London, Madrid, Manila, Melbourne, México City, Miami, Milan, Monterrey, Moscow, Münich, New York, Palo Alto, Paris, Prague, Rio de Janeiro, Riyadh, Rome, St. Petersburg, San Diego, San Francisco, Santiago, São Paulo, Singapore, Stockholm, Sydney, Taipei, Tijuana, Tokyo, Toronto, Valencia, Warsaw, Washington, D.C. and Zürich.
Correspondent Law Firm: Hadiputranto, Hadinoto & Partners, Jakarta.

LOCAL PARTNER

Daniel R. Matthews (Not admitted in Azerbaijan)

ASSOCIATES

Aykhan I. Asadov
Samira S. Moussayeva

For full biographical listings, see the Martindale-Hubbell Law Directory

BAHRAIN

MANAMA,*

American Lawyers In Manama

BAKER & MCKENZIE

Al Salam Tower, 6th Floor, P.O. Box 11981 Diplomatic Area, Manama
Telephone: (973) 538800
Facsimile: (973) 533379
URL: http://www.bakerinfo.com
Associated Offices of Baker & McKenzie in: Almaty, Amsterdam, Baku, Bangkok, Barcelona, Beijing, Berlin, Bogotá, Brasília, Brussels, Budapest, Buenos Aires, Cairo, Caracas, Chicago, Dallas, Düsseldorf, Frankfurt, Geneva, Hanoi, Ho Chi Minh City, Hong Kong, Houston, Hsinchu, Juárez, Kyiv, London, Madrid, Manila, Melbourne, México City, Miami, Milan, Monterrey, Moscow, Münich, New York, Palo Alto, Paris, Prague, Rio de Janeiro, Riyadh, Rome, St. Petersburg, San Diego, San Francisco, Santiago, São Paulo, Singapore, Stockholm, Sydney, Taipei, Tijuana, Tokyo, Toronto, Valencia, Warsaw, Washington, D.C. and Zürich.
Correspondent Law Firm: Hadiputranto, Hadinoto & Partners, Jakarta.

LOCAL PARTNER

Ian R. Siddell (Not admitted in Bahrain; Also at Riyadh, Saudi Arabia Office of Legal Advisors Torki A. Al-Shubaiki)

ASSOCIATES

Matthew B. Hansen (Not admitted in Bahrain)
Rasha Sabkar (Not admitted in Bahrain)

For full biographical listings, see the Martindale-Hubbell Law Directory

BELGIUM

BRUSSELS,*

AKIN, GUMP, STRAUSS, HAUER & FELD

(Brussels office of Akin, Gump, Strauss, Hauer & Feld, L.L.P.)
65 Avenue Louise P.B.7, 1050 Brussels
Telephone: (+32 2) 535-29-11
Telefax: (+32 2) 535 29 00
URL: http://www.akingump.com
Dallas, Texas Office: Akin, Gump, Strauss, Hauer & Feld, L.L.P., 1700 Pacific Avenue, Suite 4100, 75201-4675.
Telephone: (1) 214-969-2800.
Fax: (1) 214-969-4343.
Austin, Texas Office: Akin, Gump, Strauss, Hauer & Feld, L.L.P., Frost Bank Plaza, 816 Congress Avenue, Suite 1900, 78701.
Telephone: (1) 512-499-6200.
Fax: (1) 512-499-6290.
Houston, Texas Office: Akin, Gump, Strauss, Hauer & Feld, L.L.P., 1900 Pennzoil Place-South Tower, 711 Louisiana Street, 77002.
Telephone: (1) 713-220-5800.
Fax: (1) 713-236-0822.
San Antonio, Texas Office: Akin, Gump, Strauss, Hauer & Feld, L.L.P., Nationsbank Plaza, 300 Convent Street, Suite 1500, 78205.
Telephone: (1) 210-281-7000.
Fax: (1) 210-224-2035.
New York, New York Office: Akin, Gump, Strauss, Hauer & Feld, L.L.P., 590 Madison Avenue, 10022.
Telephone: (1) 212-872-1000.
Fax: (1) 212-872-1002.
Washington, D.C. Office: Akin, Gump, Strauss, Hauer & Feld, L.L.P., 1333 New Hampshire Avenue, N.W., Suite 400, 20036.
Telephone: (1) 202-887-4000.
Fax: (1) 202-887-4288.
Philadelphia, Pennsylvania Office: Akin, Gump, Strauss, Hauer & Feld, L.L.P., One Commerce Square, 2005 Market Street, Suite 2200, 19103.
Telephone: (1) 215-965-1200.
Fax: (1) 215-965-1210.
Moscow, Russia Office: Akin, Gump, Strauss, Hauer & Feld, Ducat Place II, 7 Gasheka Street, Moscow 123056.
Telephone: 7095-974-2411 or (1) 202 887-4545.
Fax: 7095-974-2412 or (1) 202 887-4544.
London, United Kingdom Office: Akin, Gump, Strauss, Hauer & Feld, One Angel Court, London EC2R 7HJ.
Telephone: (44) 20-7726-9600.
Fax: (44) 20-7726-9610.
Los Angeles, California Office: Akin, Gump, Strauss, Hauer & Feld, L.L.P., 2029 Century Park East, Suite 2600, CA 90067.
Telephone: (1) 310-229-1000.
Fax: (1) 310-229-1001.
Affiliated Office:
Law Office of Abdulaziz H. Fahad: Jarir Plaza, 4th Floor, Olaya Street, P.O. Box 15870, Riyadh, Saudi Arabia, 11454.
Telephone: (011) 966-1-464-8081.
Telex: 406176 LAWS SJ.
Telecopier: (011) 966-1-462-4968.

(See Next Column)

PARTNERS

Jacques H.J. Bourgeois
Jack J. Langlois (P.C.)
Martine De Witte

COUNSEL

Laura M. Reifschneider

ASSOCIATES

Margaret D. Chisholm
N. Köhncke

For full biographical listings, see the Martindale-Hubbell Law Directory

BAKER & MCKENZIE

149 Avenue Louise—Louizalaan 149, Eighth Floor, 1050 Brussels
Telephone: (02) 639-36-11
Intn'l Dialing: (32-2) 639-36-11
Facsimile: (32-2) 639-36-99
URL: http://www.bakerinfo.com
Associated Offices of Baker & McKenzie in: Almaty, Amsterdam, Bahrain, Baku, Bangkok, Barcelona, Beijing, Berlin, Bogotá, Brasília, Budapest, Buenos Aires, Cairo, Caracas, Chicago, Dallas, Düsseldorf, Frankfurt, Geneva, Hanoi, Ho Chi Minh City, Hong Kong, Houston, Hsinchu, Juárez, Kyiv, London, Madrid, Manila, Melbourne, México City, Miami, Milan, Monterrey, Moscow, Münich, New York, Palo Alto, Paris, Prague, Rio de Janeiro, Riyadh, Rome, St. Petersburg, San Diego, San Francisco, Santiago, São Paulo, Singapore, Stockholm, Sydney, Taipei, Tijuana, Tokyo, Toronto, Valencia, Warsaw, Washington, D.C. and Zürich.
Correspondent Law Firm: Hadiputranto, Hadinoto & Partners, Jakarta.

François Gabriel
Jacques Ghysbrecht
Arne Gutermann
Paul G. Herten
Luc Hinnekens
Alain Huyghe
Aristotelis Kaplanidis
Thomas Lampert
Anne Laurent
Dominique Lechien
Peter Leys
Ignace M. Maes
Pierre Sculier
Jozef Slootmans
Koen Vanhaerents

Annabelle Bruyndonckx
Karoline Capon
Erik Daems
Kim Dassesse
Mia Declercq
Thibaut De Haene
Antoine De Raeve
David Du Pont
Rudy Dupont
Daniel Fesler
Christophe Geys
Kurt Haegeman
Axelle Heuvelmans
Nancy Luyten
Dominique Maes
Roel Meers
Luc Meeus
Xavier Michel
Isabelle Pérignon (Not admitted in Belgium)
Benoit Philippart de Foy
Quentin Rutsaert
Jeroen Smets
Timothy Speelman
Jean-François Vandenberghe
Annick Van Hoorebeke
Stephane Wilmes
Arnaud Wtterwulghe

For full biographical listings, see the Martindale-Hubbell Law Directory

American Lawyers In Brussels

CLEARY, GOTTLIEB, STEEN & HAMILTON

Rue de la Loi 23, 1040 Brussels
Telephone: 32/2/287.20.00
Fax: 32/2/231.16.61
New York, New York Office: One Liberty Plaza, New York, N.Y. 10006.
Telephone: 212-225-2000.
Washington, D.C. Office: 2000 Pennsylvania Avenue, N.W., Suite 9000, Washington, D.C. 20006-1801.
Telephone: 202-974-1500.
Paris, France Office: 41, Avenue de Friedland, 75008 Paris, France.
Telephone: 33-1-40-74-68-00.
London, England Office: City Place House, 55 Basinghall Street, London EC2V 5EH England.
Telephone: 44-71-614-2200.
Hong Kong Office: 39th Floor, Bank of China Tower, One Garden Road, Hong Kong.
Telephone: 852-2521-4122.
Tokyo, Japan Office: Cleary, Gottlieb, Steen & Hamilton Gaikokuho Jimubengoshi Jimusho, 20th Floor, Shin Kasumigaseki Building, 3-2, Kasumigaseki 3-Chome, Chiyoda-Ku, Tokyo 100-0013, Japan.
Telephone: 81-3-3595-3911.
Frankfurt, Germany Office: Main Tower, Neue Mainzer Strasse 52, 60311 Frankfurt am Main, Germany.
Telephone: 49-69-971-03-0.
Rome, Italy Office: Piazza di Spagna 15, 00187 Rome, Italy.
Telephone: 39-06-69-52-22-1.

COUNSEL

Donald L. Holley
Bavo Cool (Resident)
Etienne P. de Rossius d'Humain (Resident)
Walter W. Oberreit (Resident)

(See Next Column)

CLEARY, GOTTLIEB, STEEN & HAMILTON—*Continued*

PARTNERS

Mario Siragusa
Wolfgang Knapp (Resident)
George L. Bustin (Resident)
Jean-Louis Joris (Resident)
Jan Meyers (Resident)
Dirk Vandermeersch (Resident)
Jacques Reding (Resident)
Antoine Winckler
Maurits J.F.M. Dolmans (Resident)
James R. Modrall (Resident)
Giuseppe Scassellati-Sforzolini
Romano Francesco Subiotto (Resident)
Nicholas Levy (Resident)

RESIDENT SPECIAL COUNSEL

Jan Van Gysegem
Till Müller-Ibold
Annette Luise Schild

RESIDENT ASSOCIATES

Claudia Allatta
Steven Allcock
Filippo Amato
Claudia Annacker
Matteo F. Bay
Matteo Beretta
Silvio Cappellari
Laura De Sanctis
Adelina Ferrara
Rogier Groen
Stephanie Hallouët
Sophie Hulthén
Deborah Janssens
Konstantin J. Joergens
Paul Laikin
Damien Levie
Leanne M. Mader
Paul D. Marquardt
Pamela G. Meisel
Geraldine Nolens
Kristina B. Nordlander
Robert O'Donoghue
Simon Priddis
Xavier Reumont
Ingrid Rossi
Laurent A. Ruzette
Robbert Snelders
Sergio Sorinas
Despina A. Spanou
David E. Stiepleman
Henri Tack
Evelyne Terryn
Karen Vandekerckhove
Annet Van Hooft
Marc Waha
Andrew Ward
Peter Werdmuller

For full biographical listings, see the Martindale-Hubbell Law Directory

DECHERT PRICE & RHOADS

65 Avenue Louise, 1050 Brussels
Telephone: (02) 535-5411
Telefax: (02) 535-5400
URL: http://www.dechert.com
Philadelphia, Pennsylvania: 4000 Bell Atlantic Tower, 1717 Arch Street, 19103-2793.
Telephone: 215-994-4000.
New York, New York: 30 Rockefeller Plaza, 10112.
Telephone: 212-698-3500.
Washington, D.C.: 1775 Eye Street, N.W., 20006.
Telephone: 202-261-3300.
Harrisburg, Pennsylvania: Thirty North Third Street, 17101-1603.
Telephone: 717-237-2000.
Princeton, New Jersey: Princeton Pike Corporate Center, P.O. Box 5218, 08543-5218.
Telephone: 609-620-3200.
Boston, Massachusetts: Ten Post Office Square South, 02109-4603.
Telephone: 617-728-7100.
Hartford, Connecticut: 90 State House Square, 06103-3702.
Telephone: 860-524-3999.
London, England: 2 Serjeants' Inn, EC4Y 1LT.
Telephone: (0171) 583-5353. (Also see Titmuss Sainer Dechert).
Paris, France: 55, avenue Kléber, 76116.
Telephone: 33-(0) 1-53 65 05 00.
Fax: 33-(0) 1-53 65 05 05.

RESIDENT PARTNERS

Richard J. Temko

COUNSEL

A. Claude Delcorde
Jean-Louis Jaspar

RESIDENT ASSOCIATES

Jean-Pierre Magremanne
Benedikte Verdegem
Karin Winters

(Not admitted to practice in Belgian courts)

For full biographical listings, see the Martindale-Hubbell Law Directory

HOGAN & HARTSON L.L.P.

Avenue des Arts 41, 1040 Brussels
Telephone: (32.2) 505.09.11
Fax: (32.2) 505.09.96
URL: www.hhlaw.com
Washington, D.C. Office: Columbia Square, 555 13th Street, N.W.
Telephone: 202-637-5600.
Telex: 89-2757.
Cable Address: "Hogander Washington".
Fax: 202-637-5910.
Budapest, Hungary (Affiliated Office): Nagy & Pintér, Hogan & Hartson Law Office, Bank Center, Granite Tower, 9th Floor, Budapest V., Szabadsag ter 7, 1944 Hungary.
Telephone: (36-1) 302-9050.
Fax: (36-1) 302-9060.

(See Next Column)

London, England Office: One Angel Court, EC2R 7HJ.
Telephone: +(44) 207-367-0200.
Fax: +(44) 207-367-0220.
Moscow, Russia Office: 33/2 Usacheva Street, Building 3, 119048.
Telephone: (7095) 245-5190. Int'l
Telephone: (7501) 907-0451.
Fax: (7095) 245-5192. Int'l
Fax: (7501) 907-0462.
Paris, France (Affiliated Office): Cariddi, Mee, Rué, Avocats Associés à la Cour de Paris, 12, rue de la Paix, 75002.
Telephone: (33-1) 42.61.57.71.
Fax: (33-1) 42.61.79.21.
Prague, Czech Republic (Affiliated Office): Hogan & Hartson, Advokátní Kanceláře, v.o.s., Trziste 13, 118 00.
Telephone: (420-2) 2211-7111.
Fax: (420-2) 2211-7222.
Warsaw, Poland Office: Hogan & Hartson Sp.zo.o, Atrium Tower, Al. Jana Pawla II 25, 00-854.
Telephone: (48-22) 653-4200.
Fax: (48-22) 653-4250.
Baltimore, Maryland Office: 111 South Calvert Street.
Telephone: 410-659-2700.
Fax: 410-539-6981.
Rockville, Maryland Office: 600 Jefferson Plaza, Suite 203.
Telephone: 301-315-2206.
Fax: 301-315-9046.
Boulder, Colorado Office: 1800 Broadway, Suite 200.
Telephone: 720-406-5300.
Fax: 720-406-5301.
Colorado Springs, Colorado Office: Two North Cascade Avenue, Suite 1300.
Telephone: 719-448-5900.
Fax: 719-448-5922.
Denver, Colorado Office: One Tabor Center, Suite 1500, 1200 Seventeenth Street.
Telephone: 303-899-7300.
Fax: 303-899-7333.
Los Angeles, California Office: Biltmore Tower, 500 S. Grand Avenue, Suite 1900.
Telephone: 213-337-6700.
Fax: 213-337-6701.
Newport Beach, California Office: 4675 MacArthur Court, Suite 670.
Telephone: 949-250-4550.
Fax: 949-833-0976.
McLean, Virginia Office: 8300 Greensboro Drive.
Telephone: 703-610-6100.
Fax: 703-610-6200.
New York, New York Office: 885 Third Avenue, 26th Floor.
Telephone: 212-409-9800.
Fax: 212-409-9801.

PARTNERS

Claud v. S. Eley
Catriona Hatton (Not admitted in Belgium)
Dirk Leermakers
Gerald E. Oberst, Jr.
Richard L.A. Weiner (Not admitted in Belgium)

ASSOCIATES

Laure Courtin (Not admitted in Belgium)
Filip Tuytschaever
Lisa W. Zannoni

For full biographical listings, see the Martindale-Hubbell Law Directory

JONES, DAY, REAVIS & POGUE

Avenue Louise 480 Louizalaan 480, B-1050 Brussels
Telephone: 32-2-645-14-11
Telecopier: 32-2-645-14-45
Email: counsel@jonesday.com *URL:* http://www.jonesday.com
In Atlanta, Georgia: 3500 SunTrust Plaza, 303 Peachtree Street.
Telephone: 404-521-3939.
Telecopier: 404-581-8330.
In Chicago, Illinois: 77 West Wacker.
Telephone: 312-782-3939.
Telecopier: 312-782-8585.
In Cleveland, Ohio: North Point, 901 Lakeside Avenue.
Telephone: 216-586-3939.
Telecopier: 216-579-0212.
In Columbus, Ohio: 1900 Huntington Center.
Telephone: 614-469-3939.
Telecopier: 614-461-4198.
In Dallas, Texas: 2727 North Harwood Street.
Telephone: 214-220-3939.
Telecopier: 214-969-5100.
In Frankfurt, Germany: Hochhaus am Park, Grüneburgweg 102, 60323 Frankfurt am Main.
Telephone: 49-69-9726-3939.
Telecopier: 49-69-9726-3993.
In Geneva, Switzerland: 20, rue de Candolle.
Telephone: 41-22-320-2339.
Telecopier: 41-22-320-1232.
In Hong Kong: 29th Floor, Entertainment Building, 30 Queen's Road Central.
Telephone: 852-2526-6895.
Telecopier: 852-2868-5871.

(See Next Column)

JONES, DAY, REAVIS & POGUE, *Brussels—Continued*

In Irvine, California: 5 Park Plaza, Suite 1100.
Telephone: 949-851-3939.
Telecopier: 949-553-7539.
In London, England: Bucklersbury House, 3 Queen Victoria Street.
Telephone: 44-20-7236-3939.
Telecopier: 44-20-7236-1113.
In Los Angeles, California: 555 West Fifth Street, Suite 4600.
Telephone: 213-489-3939.
Telecopier: 213-243-2539.
In New York, New York: 599 Lexington Avenue.
Telephone: 212-326-3939.
Telecopier: 212-755-7306.
In Paris, France: 120, rue du Faubourg Saint-Honoré.
Telephone: 33-1-56-59-39-39.
Telecopier: 33-1-56-59-39-38
In Pittsburgh, Pennsylvania: 500 Grant Street, 31st Floor.
Telephone: 412-391-3939.
Telecopier: 412-394-7959.
In Riyadh, Saudi Arabia: The International Law Firm (In Association with Jones, Day, Reavis & Pogue), Sulaymaniyah, Prince Ishari IBN, Abdulaziz Street, P.O. Box 22166.
Telephone: (966-1) 462-8866.
Telecopier: (966-1) 462-9001.
In Shanghai, China: 2805 Kerry Centre, 1515 Nanjing Road West.
Telephone: 86-21-5298-6568.
Telecopier: 86-21-5298-6569.
In Sydney, Australia: Governor Phillip Tower, Level 38, 1 Farrer Place.
Telephone: 61-2-9210-6921.
Telecopier: 61-2-9210-6926.
In Taipei, Taiwan: 8th Floor, 2 Tun Hwa South Road, Section 2.
Telephone: (886-2) 2704-6808.
Telecopier: (886-2) 2704-6791.
In Tokyo, Japan: Toranomon 45 Mori Building, 3rd Floor, 1-5, Toranomon 5-Chome,Minato-Ku, Tokyo 105, Japan.
Telephone: 81-3-3433-3939.
Telecopier: 81-3-5401-2725.
In Washington, D.C.: 51 Louisiana Avenue, N.W.
Telephone: 202-879-3939.
Telecopier: 202-626-1700.

MEMBERS OF FIRM IN BRUSSELS

Ghislain Joseph
Luc G. Houben
Bernard E. Amory
Alexandre G. Verheyden

CONSULTANT

Norbert Koch

OF COUNSEL

Thierry G. F. Buytaert
Isabelle M. Rahman

ASSOCIATES

Werner Derijcke
David Walsh
Saskia S. Bellinkx
Sébastien Champagne
Dimitri A. Mertens de Wilmars
Marie-Evelyne Lukoff
Thomas De Muynck
Yvan N. Desmedt
Cédric J. Malherbe

(Not admitted to practice in Belgian courts)

For full biographical listings, see the Martindale-Hubbell Law Directory

SQUIRE, SANDERS & DEMPSEY L.L.P.

Avenue Louise, 165, Box 15, 1050 Brussels
Telephone: 32-2-627-1111
Cable Address: "Coxsquire"
TLX: 61961 Brussels Squire B
Fax: 32-2-627-1100
URL: http://www.ssd.com
Cincinnati, Ohio Office: PNC Center, 201 East Fifth Street, Suite 1700, Cincinnati, Ohio 45202.
Telephone: 513-361-1200.
Fax: 513-361-1201.
Cleveland, Ohio Office: 4900 Key Tower, 127 Public Square, Cleveland, Ohio 44114-1304.
Telephone: 216-479-8500.
Fax: 216-479-8780.
Columbus, Ohio Office: 1300 Huntington Center, 41 South High Street, Columbus, Ohio 43215-6150.
Telephone: 614-365-2700.
Fax: 614-365-2499.
Jacksonville, Florida Office: One Enterprise Center, Suite 2100, 225 Water Street, Jacksonville, Florida 32202-4424.
Telephone: 904-366-2420.
Fax: 904-356-2986.
Miami, Florida Office: 201 South Biscayne Boulevard, 2900 Miami Center, Miami, Florida 33131-4330.
Telephone: 305-577-8700.
Fax: 305-358-1425.
New York, New York Office: 350 Park Avenue, New York, New York 10022-6002.
Telephone: 212-872-9800.
Fax: 212-872-9815.

(See Next Column)

Phoenix, Arizona Office: Two Renaissance Square, 40 North Central Avenue, Suite 2700, Phoenix, Arizona 85004-4498.
Telephone: 602-528-4000.
Fax: 602-253-8129.
Washington, D.C. Office: 1201 Pennsylvania Avenue, N.W., Suite 500, Washington, D.C. 20004-2491.
Telephone: 202-626-6600.
Fax: 202-626-6780.
Almaty, Kazakhstan Office: 141 Albay Khan Avenue, Second Floor, Almaty, Kazakhstan 480091.
Telephone: +73-27-50-11-25.
Fax: +73-27-50-11-25.
Bratislava, Slovak Republic Office: Zochova 5, 811 03 Bratislava, Slovak Republic.
Telephone: 421-7-5441-7611.
Fax: 42-1-7-6280-2212.
Brussels, Belgium Office: Avenue Louise, 165-Box 15, 1050 Brussels, Belgium.
Telephone: 32-2-627-1111.
Fax: 32-2-627-1100.
Budapest, Hungary Office: H-1062 Budapest, Andrassy ut. 64, Budapest, Hungary.
Telephone: 36-1-428-7111.
Fax: 36-1-428-7100.
Kyiv, Ukraine Office: 14A Yaroslaviv Val, Kyiv 252034, Ukraine.
Telephone: 38-044-228-8687.
Fax: 38-044-228-4938.
London, England Office: Royex House, Aldermanbury Square, London EC2V 7HR.
Telephone: 44-171-776-5200.
Fax: 44-171-776-5233.
Madrid, Spain Office: Calle Velazquez 108-110, 28006 Madrid, Spain.
Telephone: 34-91-590-2420.
Fax: 34-91-590-2421.
Moscow, Russian Federation Office: Paveletskaya Square II, 1 Valovaya Street, 5th Floor, Moscow 113054, Russian Federation.
Telephone: 7-501-258-5250.
Fax: 7-501-258-5251.
Prague, Czech Republic Office: Václavské náměst 1 57/813, 110 00 Praha 1, Czech Republic.
Telephone: 420-2-2166-2111.
Fax: 420-2-2166-2222.
Hong Kong Office: Rooms 1101-2 St. George's Building, 2 Ice House Street, Central, Hong Kong.
Telephone: 852-2509-9732.
Fax: 852-2509-9772.
Taipei, Taiwan Office: 14F, 116 Nanking East Road, Sec. 2, Taipei, Taiwan, Republic of China.
Telephone: 886-2-2531-2888.
Fax: 886-2-2571-6199.

PARTNERS

Peter Alexiadis
Brian Hartnett
(Not admitted in Belgium)
Thomas J. Ramsey
(Not admitted in Belgium)

OF COUNSEL

Pius Alexander Benczek
(Not admitted in Belgium)
Maria José Cabeza
(Not admitted in Belgium)
Carter Eltzroth
(Not admitted in Belgium)

ASSOCIATES

Karel D'Hulst
David Dillon
Christele Fewkes
(Not admitted in Belgium)
Alexandre A. Mencik von Zebinsky
Rebecca O'Donnell
(Not admitted in Belgium)
Ana-Isabel Perez Ocon
Flip J. Petillion
Cristiana Spontoni
Jonathan N.T. Uphoff

(Not admitted to practice in Belgian courts)

For full biographical listings, see the Martindale-Hubbell Law Directory

WILMER, CUTLER & PICKERING

Rue de la Loi 15# Wetstraat, B-1040 Brussels
Telephone: +32 (2) 285 49 00
Fax: +32 (2) 285 49 49
Email: Law@Wilmer.Com *URL:* http://www.wilmer.com
Washington, D.C. Office: 2445 M Street, N.W., 20037-1420.
Telephone: 202-663-6000.
Fax: 202-663-6363. Internet: Law@Wilmer.Com.
Baltimore, Maryland Office: 100 Light Street, 21202.
Telephone: 410-986-2800.
Fax: 410-986-2828.
New York, New York Office: 520 Madison Avenue, 10022.
Telephone: 212-230-8800.
Fax: 212-230-8888.
London, England Office: 4 Carlton Gardens, London, SW1Y 5AA.
Telephone: +44 (20) 7 872 1000.
Fax: +44 (20) 7 839 3537.
Berlin, Germany Office: Friedrichstrasse 95, D-10117.
Telephone: +49 (30) 20 22 64 00.
Fax: +49 (30) 20 22 65 00.

(See Next Column)

WILMER, CUTLER & PICKERING—*Continued*

PARTNERS

James S. Venit (Not admitted in Belgium)
Dr. Andreas Weitbrecht (Not admitted in Belgium)
John H. Ratliff (Not admitted in Belgium; Resident)
Paul A. von Hehn (Not admitted in Belgium)
Marc C. Hansen (Not admitted in Belgium)
Thomas Mueller (Not admitted in Belgium)
Christian L. Duvernoy (Not admitted in Belgium)

COUNSEL

Patricia A. Sherman (Not admitted in Belgium)
John J. Kallaugher (Not admitted in Belgium)

ASSOCIATES

Andreas Bardong
Jean-Michel Coumes (Not admitted in Belgium)
Andrea De Matteis (Not admitted in Belgium)
Flavia Distefano (Not admitted in Belgium; Resident)
Justin Menezes (Not admitted in Belgium; Not admitted in Belgium)
Sophie Moonen
Jean Paul M. Poitras (Not admitted in Belgium)
Sven B. Völcker (Not admitted in Belgium; Not admitted in Belgium)

For full biographical listings, see the Martindale-Hubbell Law Directory

BRAZIL

*BRASÍLIA,** Distrito Federal

TRENCH, ROSSI E WATANABE

(Associated Office of Baker & McKenzie)
SCN, Centro Empresarial ENCOL, Torre A, Conj. 1126, 70710-500 Brasília
Telephone: (061) 327-3273
Intn'l Dialing: (55-61) 327-3273
Facsimile: (55-61) 327-3274
Email: brasilia.info@bakernet.com *URL:* http://www.bakerinfo.com
Associated Offices of Baker & McKenzie in: Almaty, Amsterdam, Bahrain, Baku, Bangkok, Barcelona, Beijing, Berlin, Bogotá, Brussels, Budapest, Buenos Aires, Cairo, Caracas, Chicago, Dallas, Düsseldorf, Frankfurt, Geneva, Hanoi, Ho Chi Minh City, Hong Kong, Houston, Hsinchu, Juárez, Kyiv, London, Madrid, Manila, Melbourne, México City, Miami, Milan, Monterrey, Moscow, Münich, New York, Palo Alto, Paris, Prague, Rio de Janeiro, Riyadh, Rome, St. Petersburg, San Diego, San Francisco, Santiago, São Paulo, Singapore, Stockholm, Sydney, Taipei, Tijuana, Tokyo, Toronto, Valencia, Warsaw, Washington, D.C. and Zürich.
Correspondent Law Firm: Hadiputranto, Hadinoto & Partners, Jakarta.

MANAGING PARTNER

Tulio Freitas do Egito Coelho

LOCAL PARTNER

Fabio de Sousa Coutinho

ASSOCIATES

Carla Lobão Barroso de Souza
Luciano Costa
Alessandro Marius Oliveira Martins
Leandro da Silva Soares
Francisco Ribeiro Todorov

For full biographical listings, see the Martindale-Hubbell Law Directory

RIO DE JANEIRO, Rio de Janeiro, RJ

TRENCH, ROSSI E WATANABE

(Associated Office of Baker & McKenzie)
Av. Rio Branco, 1 19th Floor, Sector B, 20090-003 Rio de Janeiro
Telephone: (021) 206-4900
Intn'l Dialing: (55-21) 206-4900
Facsimile: (55-21) 206-4949; 516-6422
Postal Address: Caixa Postal 1470, Rio de Janeiro, RJ
URL: http://www.bakerinfo.com
Associated Offices of Baker & McKenzie in: Almaty, Amsterdam, Bahrain, Baku, Bangkok, Barcelona, Beijing, Berlin, Bogotá, Brasília, Brussels, Budapest, Buenos Aires, Cairo, Caracas, Chicago, Dallas, Düsseldorf, Frankfurt, Geneva, Hanoi, Ho Chi Minh City, Hong Kong, Houston, Hsinchu, Juárez, Kyiv, London, Madrid, Manila, Melbourne, México City, Miami, Milan, Monterrey, Moscow, Münich, New York, Palo Alto, Paris, Prague, Riyadh, Rome, St. Petersburg, San Diego, San Francisco, Santiago, São Paulo, Singapore, Stockholm, Sydney, Taipei, Tijuana, Tokyo, Toronto, Valencia, Warsaw, Washington, D.C. and Zürich.
Correspondent Law Firm: Hadiputranto, Hadinoto & Partners, Jakarta.

PARTNERS

Alfredo Ruy Barbosa
Gabriel Araujo de Lacerda
Luis Fernando Ayres de Mello Pacheco
Ricardo Coelho Salles

(See Next Column)

OF COUNSEL

Pierre J. d'Incelli

RESIDENT ASSOCIATES

Ana Tereza Palhares Basílio
Andrea Z. Brick
Renata de Saboyo Chagas
Ana Luiza David
Maria Gabriela Prestes Fróes
Márcia Gomes Lencastre
Leonardo Alfradique Martins
Maria Fernanda da Rosa Martins
Marianna de Assumpção Medeiros
Anna Tavares de Mello
Gustavo Fróes Mendonça
Nilo Cunha Furtado de Mendonça
Carlos Eduardo Rangel de Menezes Côrtes
Joaquim Tavares de Paiva Muniz
Monica Araujo de Castro Pereira
Flavia Gouvêa de Almeida e Souza
Maristella D.M. Caldas Tocantins
Ana Paula F. Vizintini

For full biographical listings, see the Martindale-Hubbell Law Directory

SÃO PAULO, São Paulo

TRENCH, ROSSI E WATANABE

(Associated Office of Baker & McKenzie)
Av. Dr. Chucri Zaidan 920, 8th Floor, Market Place Tower, 04583-904 São Paulo
Telephone: (011) 3048-6800
Intn'l Dialing: (55-11) 3048-6800
Facsimile: (55-11) 5506-3455
Postal Address: Caixa Postal 2673. CEP: 01060-970
URL: http://www.bakerinfo.com
Associated Offices of Baker & McKenzie in: Almaty, Amsterdam, Bahrain, Baku, Bangkok, Barcelona, Beijing, Berlin, Bogotá, Brasília, Brussels, Budapest, Buenos Aires, Cairo, Caracas, Chicago, Dallas, Düsseldorf, Frankfurt, Geneva, Hanoi, Ho Chi Minh City, Hong Kong, Houston, Hsinchu, Juárez, Kyiv, London, Madrid, Manila, Melbourne, México City, Miami, Milan, Monterrey, Moscow, Münich, New York, Palo Alto, Paris, Prague, Rio de Janeiro, Riyadh, Rome, St. Petersburg, San Diego, San Francisco, Santiago, Singapore, Stockholm, Sydney, Taipei, Tijuana, Tokyo, Toronto, Valencia, Warsaw, Washington, D.C. and Zürich.
Correspondent Law Firm: Hadiputranto, Hadinoto & Partners, Jakarta.

PARTNERS

Sérgio Paula Souza Caiuby
Virgílio Garcia Cassemunha
Hércules Celescuekci
Augusto Marianno Dias Netto
Antonio Carlos Farroco Jr.
Antonio Carlos de Queiroz Ferreira
Esther Miriam Flesch
Eduardo de Cerqueira Leite
Dagmar da Silva Lisboa
Claudia Farkouh Prado
Carlos Alberto de Souza Rossi
Luiz Antonio D'Arace Vergueiro
Juliana Laura Bruna Viegas
Kazuo Watanabe

LOCAL PARTNERS

Fátima Aparecida Carr
Antonio Urbino Penna Jr.
Léa Maria De Souza Ribeiro

ASSOCIATES

Virgínia Viana Arrais
Claudete Valentim Bastos
Roberta Chaves Sá Borges
Maria Augusta Sadi Buarraj
Mary Lane Bulhões Dortas
Marcia Assis Calafate
Ricardo Valim Camargo
Silvana Benincasa de Campos
Fernanda Zacharias Fauze Carlos
Jorge Gutiérrez Chamlati (Not admitted in Brazil)
Carla Chisman
Priscilla Archur Coscarelli
Brian J. Cronin (Not admitted in Brazil)
Ana Martha de Carmargo Bueno Cunha
Claudia C. Derenusson
Simone Dias Musa
Augusto Carvalho Faria
FlAvio Machado Ferreira
Renata Karvelis Franco
Naoka Sera Furuiti
Alvaro Schmidt Gallo Neto
Antonio S. Giacomini, Jr.
Denise Correia GonÇalves
Marcio S. Grandchamp
Mário Massanori Iwamizu
Thomas J. Karsten (Not admitted in Brazil)
Ana Beatriz Marchioni Kesselring
Juliana de Sampaio Lemos
Alessandra Certo Lopes
Claudia Possi Lopes
Ana Maria Sales Loureiro
Clarissa G. Machado
Osmar Marsilli, Jr.
José Augusto Martins
José Roberto Baldoini Martins
Adriana Garcia dos Santos Bandeira Mello
Maria Beatriz Guedes Machado Mello
Alberto Mori
Graciana Stella Mussi
Rodrigo Zingales do Nascimento
Carla Raynal de Passos
Victor Moraes de Paula
Alexandre Simões Pinto
João Francisco Rebello Regos
Leocadio Geraldo Rocha Filho
Carlos Eduardo Leme Romeiro
Anamaria Favero Rosenthal
Rodrigo Sales
Paula Rios Bastos Santos
Valéria K. Schramm
Paulo César Pereira da Silva
Regina Gargiulo Neves da Silva
Marcio de Souza Polto
Mary Hessemann Swanson (Not admitted in Brazil)
Nazir Takieddini
Bruno de Souza Vichi
Mariana Neves de Vito
Alessandra Saraceni Machado Villas Bôas

(See Next Column)

TRENCH, ROSSI E WATANABE, *Sjo Paulo—Continued*

ASSOCIATES (Continued)

Christian Heinz de Andrade Wiesenthal	FlÃvia Black Wortsman
	Karina Klabinska Yunan

Mira Lopes Zimmermann

For full biographical listings, see the Martindale-Hubbell Law Directory

CHILE

*SANTIAGO,**

BAKER & MCKENZIE

(Cruzat, Ortúzar & Mackenna)
Nueva Tajamar 481, Torre Norte, Piso 21 Las Condes, Santiago
Telephone: (2) 367-7000
Intn'l Dialing: (56-2) 367-7000
Facsimile: (56-2) 362-9875; 362-9876; 362-9877; 362-9878
URL: http://www.bakerinfo.com
Associated Offices of Baker & McKenzie in: Almaty, Amsterdam, Bahrain, Baku, Bangkok, Barcelona, Beijing, Berlin, Bogotá, Brasília, Brussels, Budapest, Buenos Aires, Cairo, Caracas, Chicago, Dallas, Düsseldorf, Frankfurt, Geneva, Hanoi, Ho Chi Minh City, Hong Kong, Houston, Hsinchu, Juárez, Kyiv, London, Madrid, Manila, Melbourne, México City, Miami, Milan, Monterrey, Moscow, Münich, New York, Palo Alto, Paris, Prague, Rio de Janeiro, Riyadh, Rome, St. Petersburg, San Diego, San Francisco, São Paulo, Singapore, Stockholm, Sydney, Taipei, Tijuana, Tokyo, Toronto, Valencia, Warsaw, Washington, D.C. and Zürich.
Correspondent Law Firm: Hadiputranto, Hadinoto & Partners, Jakarta.

Carlos Cruzat P. (1924-1993)

PARTNERS

León Larrain A.	Antonio Ortúzar, Jr.
Domingo Irarrázaval M.	Raimundo Pérez de Arce L.

Andrés Wagner M-M.

LOCAL PARTNERS

Oscar Contreras	Fernando Sáenz de Santa María M.
Vicente Eguiguren	

OF COUNSEL

Luis Fernando Mackenna, Sr.	Antonio Ortúzar, Sr.

ASSOCIATES

Rodrigo Cuchacovich	Jaime Munro
Ignacio García	Ricardo Ovalle
Arturo Garnham B.	Karen Paz
Luis Fernando Mackenna, Jr.	Sean Rush (Not admitted in Chile)
Militza Marinkovic	
Rodrigo Marré G.	Pedro Felipe Vial L.

For full biographical listings, see the Martindale-Hubbell Law Directory

CHINA

*BEIJING,**

American Lawyers in Beijing

BAKER & MCKENZIE

Suite 2526 China World Tower China World Trade Center, 1 Jianguomenwai Dajie, 100004 Beijing
Telephone: 6505-0591; 6505-0592; 6505-4867; 6505-4967; *6505-4969; 6505-2288, Ext. 2526*
Intn'l Dialing: +86-10 6505-0591; 6505-0592; 6505-4867; *6505-4967; 6505-4969; 6505-2288, Ext. 2526*
Cable: ABOGADO BEIJING
Facsimiles: +86-10 6505-2309; 6505-0378
URL: http://www.bakerinfo.com
Associated Offices of Baker & McKenzie in: Almaty, Amsterdam, Bahrain, Baku, Bangkok, Barcelona, Berlin, Bogotá, Brasília, Brussels, Budapest, Buenos Aires, Cairo, Caracas, Chicago, Dallas, Düsseldorf, Frankfurt, Geneva, Hanoi, Ho Chi Minh City, Hong Kong, Houston, Hsinchu, Juárez, Kyiv, London, Madrid, Manila, Melbourne, México City, Miami, Milan, Monterrey, Moscow, Münich, New York, Palo Alto, Paris, Prague, Rio de Janeiro, Riyadh, Rome, St. Petersburg, San Diego, San Francisco, Santiago, São Paulo, Singapore, Stockholm, Sydney, Taipei, Tijuana, Tokyo, Toronto, Valencia, Warsaw, Washington, D.C. and Zürich.
Correspondent Law Firm: Hadiputranto, Hadinoto & Partners, Jakarta.

LOCAL PARTNER

Danian Zhang (Not admitted in China)

ASSOCIATES

Song Huang (Not admitted in China)	John W. Sullivan (Not admitted in China)

(See Next Column)

CONSULTANT

Xiangyang Ge

For full biographical listings, see the Martindale-Hubbell Law Directory

PAUL, WEISS, RIFKIND, WHARTON & GARRISON

Beijing Office 2918 China World Tower II, No.1 Jianguomenwai Dajie, Beijing 100004
Telephone: 86-10 6505-6822
Facsimile: 86-10 6505-6830
Email: mailbox@paulweiss.com *URL:* http://www.paulweiss.com
New York, N.Y. Office: 1285 Avenue of the Americas, 10019-6064.
Telephones: 212-373-3000, TDD 212-373-2000.
Facsimile: 212-757-3990.
Washington, D.C. Office: 1615 L Street, NW, Suite 1300, 20036-5694.
Telephones: 202-223-7300, TDD 202-223-7490.
Facsimile: 202-223-7420.
Paris, France Office: 62, rue du Faubourg Saint-Honoré, 75008.
Telephone: 33-1 53.43.14.14.
Facsimile: 33-1 53-43.00.23.
Tokyo, Japan Office: Fukoku Seimei Building, 2-2 Uchisaiwaicho 2-chome, Chiyoda-ku, Tokyo 100-0011, Japan.
Telephone: 81-3 3597-8101.
Facsimile: 81-3 3597-8120.
Hong Kong, China Office: 12th Floor, Hong Kong Club Building, 3A Chater Road, Central Hong Kong.
Telephone: 011-852 2536-9933.
Facsimile: 011 852 2536-9622.

RESIDENT PARTNER

Nicholas C. Howson

RESIDENT ASSOCIATES

Angela Hendricks Davis	Gangliang Qiao
Charles F. Goldsmith	Lester Ross
Andrea Goodman	Libin Zhang

For full biographical listings, see the Martindale-Hubbell Law Directory

SHEARMAN & STERLING

Suite #2205, Capital Mansion, No. 6, Xin Yuan Nan Road Chao Yang District, Beijing 100004
Telephone: (86-10) 6465-2299
Fax: (86-10) 6465-4578
URL: http://www.shearman.com
New York, N.Y. Office: 599 Lexington Avenue, New York, New York, 10022-6069.
Telephone: (212) 848-4000.
Telex: 667290. Num Lau.
Fax: (212) 848-7179.
Abu Dhabi, United Arab Emirates Office: Butti Al Otaiba Building, 13th Floor, Suite 1302, Sheikh Khalifa Street, P.O. Box 2948.
Telephone: (971-2) 6274477.
Fax: (971-2) 6268933.
Düsseldorf, Federal Republic of Germany Office: Couvenstrasse 8 40211 Düsseldorf.
Telephone: (49 211) 178 88-0.
Fax: (49 211) 178 88-88.
Frankfurt, Federal Republic of Germany Office: Trianon Building, Mainzer Landstrasse 16, 60325 Frankfurt am Main.
Telephone: (49-69) 9711-1000.
Fax: (49-69) 9711-1100.
Hong Kong Office: Standard Chartered Bank Building, 4 Des Voeux Road, Central.
Telephone: (852) 2978-8000.
Fax: (852) 2978-8099.
London, England Office: Broadgate West, 9 Appold Street, London EC2A 2AP.
Telephone: 011-44-20-7655-5000.
Fax: 011-44-20-7655-5500.
Menlo Park, California Office: 1550 El Camino Real, 94025-4100.
Telephone: (650) 330-2200.
Fax: (650) 330-2299.
Paris, France Office: 114, avenue des Champs-Elysées, 75008.
Telephone: (33-1) 53-89-7000.
Fax: (33-1) 53-89-7070.
San Francisco, California Office: 555 California Street, 94104-1522.
Telephone: (415) 616-1100.
Fax: (415) 616-1199.
Singapore Office: 6 Battery Road #25-03. Singapore 049909.
Telephone: (65) 230-3800.
Fax: (65) 230-3899.
Tokyo, Japan Office: Fukoku Seimei Building, 5th Fl. 2-2-2, Uchisaiwaicho, Chiyoda-ku, Tokyo 100-0011. Japan.
Telephone: (81 3) 5251-1601.
Fax: (81 3) 5251-1602.
Toronto, Ontario, Canada Office: Commerce Court West, Suite 4405, P.O. Box 247, M5L 1E8.
Telephone: (416) 360-8484.
Fax: (416) 360-2958.
Washington, D.C. Office: 801 Pennsylvania Avenue, N.W., 20004-2604.
Telephone: (202) 508-8000.
Fax: (202) 508-8100.

(See Next Column)

SHEARMAN & STERLING—*Continued*

PARTNER

Edward L. Turner III (Not admitted in China; Managing Partner, Beijing and Hong Kong)

RESIDENT ASSOCIATES

Lee Edwards (Not admitted in China)
Zhigeng (David) Fu

For full biographical listings, see the Martindale-Hubbell Law Directory

THE BEIJING REPRESENTATIVE OFFICE OF SULLIVAN & CROMWELL

Suite 501, China World Trade Center, No. 1 Jianguo Menwei Avenue, Beijing 100004
Telephone: (011)(813) 3213-6140
Telecopier: (011)(813) 3213-6470 or (011)(813) 3213-6477
URL: http://www.sullcrom.com
New York City Office: Sullivan & Cromwell, 125 Broad Street, 10004-2498.
Telephone: 212-558-4000.
Telex: 62694.
Telecopier: 212-558-3588 or 212-514-5706.
Washington, D.C. Office: Sullivan & Cromwell, 1701 Pennsylvania Avenue, N.W., 20006-5805.
Telephone: 202-956-7500.
Telecopier: 202-293-6330.
Los Angeles, California Office: Sullivan & Cromwell, 1888 Century Park East, 90067-1725.
Telephone: 310-712-6600.
Telecopier: 310-712-8800.
Paris Office: Sullivan & Cromwell, 8, Place Vendôme, 75001 Paris, France.
Telephone: (011)(331) 44 50 60 00.
Telex: 240654.
Telecopier: (011)(331) 44 50 60 60 or (011)(331) 42 60 56 36.
London Office: Sullivan & Cromwell, St. Olave's House, 9a Ironmonger Lane, London EC2V 8EY, England.
Telephone: (011)(44207) 710 6500.
Telecopier: (011)(44207) 710 6565.
Melbourne Office: Sullivan & Cromwell, 101 Collins Street, Melbourne, Victoria 3000, Australia.
Telephone: (011)(613) 9635-1500.
Telecopier: (011)(613) 9654-2422.
Tokyo Office: Sullivan & Cromwell, Gaikokuho Jimu Bengoshi Jimusho, Akai Law Offices (Registered Associated Offices), Otemachi First Square East Tower 16F, 5-1, Otemachi 1-chome, Chiyoda-ku, Tokyo 100-0004, Japan.
Telephone: (011)(813) 3213-6140.
Telecopier: (011)(813) 3213-6470 or (011)(813) 3213-6477.
Hong Kong Office: Sullivan & Cromwell, 28th Floor, Nine Queen's Road, Central, Hong Kong.
Telephone: (011)(852) 2826-8688.
Telecopier: (011)(852) 2522-2280.
Frankfurt Office: Sullivan & Cromwell, Neue Mainzer Strasse 52, 60322 Frankfurt, Germany.
Telephone: (011)(4969) 7191 26-0.
Telecopier: (011)(4969) 7191 26-10.

PARTNER

Chun Wei (Not admitted in China)

For full biographical listings, see the Martindale-Hubbell Law Directory

Canadian Lawyers in Beijing

BLAKE, CASSELS & GRAYDON LLP

Suite A-1, 21st Floor, Hanwei Plaza, 7 Guanghua Road, Beijing 100004
Telephone: (011) 861-06-561-1515
Facsimile: (011) 861-06-561-0667
URL: http://www.blakes.com
The Firm maintains other offices in: Toronto and Ottawa, Ontario, Calgary, Alberta, Vancouver, British Columbia and London, England.

PARTNER

Robert Y.M. Kwauk (Not admitted in China)

ASSOCIATES

Andrea E. Redway (Not admitted in China)
Tong Wu

For full biographical listings, see the Martindale-Hubbell Law Directory

HONG KONG,

BAKER & MCKENZIE

14th Floor, Hutchison House, 10 Harcourt Road, Hong Kong
Telephone: 2846-1888
Intn'l Dialing: 852 2846-1888
Cable Address: ABO GA DO
Telex: 76416
Answer Back: 76416 ABOG HX
Facsimiles: 852 2845-0476; 2845-0487; 2845-0490
URL: http://www.bakerinfo.com
Associated Offices of Baker & McKenzie in: Almaty, Amsterdam, Bahrain, Baku, Bangkok, Barcelona, Beijing, Berlin, Bogotá, Brasília, Brussels, Budapest, Buenos Aires, Cairo, Caracas, Chicago, Dallas, Düsseldorf, Frankfurt, Geneva, Hanoi, Ho Chi Minh City, Houston, Hsinchu, Juárez, Kyiv, London, Madrid, Manila, Melbourne, México City, Miami, Milan, Monterrey, Moscow, München, New York, Palo Alto, Paris, Prague, Rio de Janeiro, Riyadh, Rome, St. Petersburg, San Diego, San Francisco, Santiago, São Paulo, Singapore, Stockholm, Sydney, Taipei, Tijuana, Tokyo, Toronto, Valencia, Warsaw, Washington, D.C. and Zürich.
Correspondent Law Firm: Hadiputranto, Hadinoto & Partners, Jakarta.

Robert A. Arnold
Barry W. M. Cheng
Pius Kai-Wah Cheng
Yuk Tong Cheung
Neil M. Donoghue
Stephen R. Eno
David J. Fleming
Patrick B. Fontaine
George Forrai
Graeme R. Halford
William Kuo
Angela W. Y. Lee
Lawrence K. H. Lee
Nancy Leigh
Cheuk-Yan Leung
David R. Martin
John M. Morgans
Michael A. Olesnicky
Fiona Jeannie Smith
Paul C. Y. Tan
Poh Lee Tan
Christopher J. Wilson

Clifford Borg-Marks (Not admitted in China)
Stephen M. Nelson (Not admitted in China)
David E. Neuville (Not admitted in China)
Richard L. Weisman (Not admitted in China)
Winston K. T. Zee (Not admitted in China)

LOCAL PARTNERS

Andrew J. L. Aglionby
Christopher M. Buchan
Kathileena M. Carpio
Milton W. M. Cheng
Debbie F. Cheung
Anna W. T. Chong
Hilary Cordell
Dow P. Famulak
William K. K. Ho
Junri Konii
Anita P. F. Leung
Karen L. Linker
Andrew W. Lockhart
Anthony K. S. Poon
Phillip K. Smith
Loke-Khoon Tan
Ernest K. T. Wong

Scott D. Clemens (Not admitted in China)
John V. Grobowski (Not admitted in China)
Andreas W. Lauffs (Not admitted in China)

ASSOCIATES

A. Michael Abbott
Victor Kwok-Yiu Au
Brian K. Barron
Daniel L. F. Chan
Edmond L.Y. Chan
Edward P. Chan
Elsa Chan
Grace L. S. Chan
Rico W. K. Chan
May M. W. Chang
Lisa P. Chen
Cynthia Cheng
Kwun-Yee Cheung (Not admitted in China)
Peggy P. Y. Cheung
Michael G. Chin
Mason P. C. Ching
Edward S.Y. Chiu
Patrice Choi Wai Ying
Maureen Chow Tze Wing
Angela F. Y. Chu
Anne Man Kwan Chu
Nicholas Y. Chua
Timothy L. Clarke
Sally A. Durant
Wesley Fung
Paul D. Gleghorn
Timothy S. Haynes
Yvonne Y. M. Ho
Susie Hui Wai Yee
Anthony P. Jacobsen
Susan C. A. Kendall
Dorothea G. Koo
Joseph Kwan
Suk-Fun Funny Kwan
Stephen K.P. Kwong
Harvey Lau
Vivian W. W. Lau
Chiang Ling Li
Paul Liu
Gary C. O. Lo
Jackie F. K. Lo
Shara K. Y. Lo
Jacqueline J.C. Loh (Not admitted in China)
Ben Yiu Fai Lui
Carol K.F. Lui
Justin Ma Man Kit
Keith K.H. Mak
Sally A. Marsden
David Mao
Siobhán McKeating
Siu John Morris
Rosa C. S. Pang
Tanya Prew
Diana J. Purdy-Tsang
Iain C. L. Seow
David W. Smith
Douglas C. T. So
Cindy S. C. Tam
Martin Chi Wai Tam
Helen Tang
Karen F. To
Derek Tsang
Hai Yin Scarlet Tsao
Jennifer Van Dale
Dominic S. C. Wai
William Ho Pang Wang
Choo Hua Wee
Yu Yuen Wong

(See Next Column)

BAKER & MCKENZIE, *Hong Kong—Continued*

ASSOCIATES (Continued)

Chi Kuen Wu
Tracy O. C. Wut
Winnie C.W. Yeung
Ricky C. W. Yiu
Pessy P. D. Yu
Priscilla H. S. Yu
Karen Yung

Gregory Buhyoff (Not admitted in China)
Stephen P. Chan (Not admitted in China)
Gigi K.C. Cheah (Not admitted in China)
Chi Ming Chee (Not admitted in China)
Damian Cottier (Not admitted in China)
Stanley D. Jia (Not admitted in China)
Sun H. Kim (Not admitted in China)
Andrew Wai Kit Lai (Not admitted in China)
Andy K.H. Leck (Not admitted in China)
Ingrid L. Lenhardt (Not admitted in China)
Richard C. Lee (Not admitted in China)
Stephen Pei-jing Lin (Not admitted in China)
Shih Yann Loo (Not admitted in China)
Karen Hoi Yee Man (Not admitted in China)
Patrice Marceau (Not admitted in China)
Douglas J. Masson (Not admitted in China)
Jason Ng (Not admitted in China)
An Ning (Not admitted in China)
Julie J. Peng (Not admitted in China)
Sophie C. Roseveare (Not admitted in China)
Steven R. Sieker (Not admitted in China)
Brian P. Spires (Not admitted in China)
Wang Su (Not admitted in China)
Mao Tan (Not admitted in China)
Marcus H. Vass (Not admitted in China)
Danchi Wang (Not admitted in China)
Janice R. Wingo (Not admitted in China)
Kevin M. Wolf (Not admitted in China)
Pei Kwun Yap (Not admitted in China)
Dene T. Yeaman (Not admitted in China)
Simone Wen Tsan Yew (Not admitted in China)
Carman Y. Young (Not admitted in China)
Yulin Zhang (Not admitted in China)

For full biographical listings, see the Martindale-Hubbell Law Directory

SQUIRE, SANDERS & DEMPSEY L.L.P.

Rooms 1101-2 St. George's Building, 2 Ice House Street Central, Hong Kong
Telephone: 852-2509-9732
Fax: 852-2509-9772
URL: http://www.ssd.com
Cincinnati, Ohio Office: PNC Center, 201 East Fifth Street, Suite 1700, Cincinnati, Ohio 45202.
Telephone: 513-361-1200.
Fax: 513-361-1201.
Cleveland, Ohio Office: 4900 Key Tower, 127 Public Square, Cleveland, Ohio 44114-1304.
Telephone: 216-479-8500.
Fax: 216-479-8780.
Columbus, Ohio Office: 1300 Huntington Center, 41 South High Street, Columbus, Ohio 43215-6150.
Telephone: 614-365-2700.
Fax: 614-365-2499.
Houston, Texas Office: 6250 Chase Tower, 600 Travis Street, Houston, Texas 77002-3007.
Telephone: 713-546-5850.
Fax: 713-546-5830.
Jacksonville, Florida Office: One Enterprise Center, Suite 2100, 225 Water Street, Jacksonville, Florida 32202-4424.
Telephone: 904-366-2420.
Fax: 904-356-2986.
Miami, Florida Office: 201 South Biscayne Boulevard, 2900 Miami Center, Miami, Florida 33131-4330.
Telephone: 305-577-8700.
Fax: 305-358-1425.
New York, New York Office: 350 Park Avenue, New York, New York 10022-6002.
Telephone: 212-872-9800.
Fax: 212-872-9815.
Phoenix, Arizona Office: Two Renaissance Square, 40 North Central Avenue, Suite 2700, Phoenix, Arizona 85004-4498.
Telephone: 602-528-4000.
Fax: 602-253-8129.
Washington, D.C. Office: 1201 Pennsylvania Avenue, N.W., Suite 500, Washington, D.C. 20004-2491.
Telephone: 202-626-6600.
Fax: 202-626-6780.
Almaty, Kazakhstan Office: 141 Albay Khan Avenue, Second Floor, Almaty, Kazakhstan 480091.
Telephone: +73-27-50-11-25.
Fax: +73-27-50-11-25.

(See Next Column)

Bratislava, Slovak Republic Office: Zochova 5, 811 03 Bratislava, Slovak Republic.
Telephone: 421-7-5441-7611.
Fax: 42-1-7-6280-2212.
Brussels, Belgium Office: Avenue Louise, 165 Box 15, 1050 Brussels, Belgium.
Telephone: 32-2-627-1111.
Fax: 32-2-627-1100.
Budapest, Hungary Office: H-1062 Budapest, Andrassy ut. 64, Budapest, Hungary.
Telephone: 36-1-428-7111.
Fax: 36-1-428-7100.
Kyiv, Ukraine Office: 14A Yaroslaviv Val, Kyiv 252034, Ukraine.
Telephone: 38-044-228-8687.
Fax: 38-044-228-4938.
London, England Office: Royex House, Aldermanbury Square, London EC2V 7HR.
Telephone: 44-171-776-5200.
Fax: 44-171-776-5233.
Madrid, Spain Office: Calle Velazquez 108-110, 28006 Madrid, Spain.
Telephone: 34-91-590-2420.
Fax: 34-91-590-2421.
Moscow, Russian Federation Office: Paveletskaya Square II, 1 Valovaya Street, 5th Floor, Moscow 113054, Russian Federation.
Telephone: 7-501-258-5250.
Fax: 7-501-258-5251.
Prague, Czech Republic Office: Václavské námĕst 1 57/813, 110 00 Praha 1, Czech Republic.
Telephone: 420-2-2166-2111.
Fax: 420-2-2166-2222.
Taipei, Taiwan Office: 14F, 116 Nanking East Road, Sec. 2, Taipei, Taiwan, Republic of China.
Telephone: 886-2-2531-2888.
Fax: 886-2-2571-6199.

PARTNERS

Mao Tong (Not admitted in China)
James S. Tsang (Not admitted in China)

OF COUNSEL

Antony Corel (Not admitted in China)
Sang Bin Xue (Not admitted in China)

ASSOCIATE

Nicholas H. Chan (Not admitted in China)

For full biographical listings, see the Martindale-Hubbell Law Directory

SULLIVAN & CROMWELL (AV)

28th Floor, Nine Queen's Road, Central, Hong Kong
Telephone: (011)(852)2826-8688
Telecopier: (011)(852)2522-2280
URL: http://www.sullcrom.com
New York City Office: 125 Broad Street, 10004-2498.
Telephone: 212-558-4000.
Telex: 62694.
Telecopier: 212-558-3588 or 212-514-5706.
Washington, D.C. Office: 1701 Pennsylvania Avenue, N.W., 20006-5805.
Telephone: 202-956-7500.
Telecopier: 202-293-6330.
Los Angeles, California Office: 1888 Century Park East, 90067-1725.
Telephone: 310-712-6600.
Telecopier: 310-712-8800.
Paris Office: 8, Place Vendôme, 75001 Paris, France.
Telephone: (011)(331) 44 50 60 00.
Telex: 240654.
Telecopier: (011)(331) 44 50 60 60 or (011)(331) 42 60 56 36.
London Office: St. Olave's House, 9a Ironmonger Lane, London EC2V 8EY, England.
Telephone: (011)(44207) 710 6500.
Telecopier: (011)(44207) 710 6565.
Melbourne Office: 101 Collins Street, Melbourne, Victoria 3000, Australia.
Telephone: (011)(613) 9635-1500.
Telecopier: (011)(613) 9654-2422.
Tokyo Office: Sullivan & Cromwell, Gaikokuho Jimu Bengoshi Jimusho, Akai Law Offices (Registered Associated Offices), Otemachi First Square East Tower 16F, 5-1, Otemachi 1-chome, Chiyoda-ku, Tokyo 100-0004, Japan.
Telephone: (011)(813) 3213-6140.
Telecopier: (011)(813) 3213-6470 or (011)(813) 3213-6477.
Frankfurt Office: Neue Mainzer Strasse 52, 60322 Frankfurt, Germany.
Telephone: (011)(4969) 7191 26-0.
Telecopier: (011)(4969) 7191 26-10.
Beijing Office: The Beijing Representative Office of Sullivan & Cromwell, Suite 501, China World Trade Center, No. 1 Jianguo Menwai Avenue, Beijing 100004, P.R.C.
Telephone: (011)(86) 10 6505 6120.
Telecopier: (011)(86) 10 6505 6136.

PARTNERS IN HONG KONG

Robert G. DeLaMater (Not admitted in China)
Chun Wei (Not admitted in China)
John D. Young, Jr. (Not admitted in China)

(See Next Column)

SULLIVAN & CROMWELL—*Continued*

ASSOCIATES IN HONG KONG

Yunfei Chen (Not admitted in China)
William Y. Chua (Not admitted in China)
Michael G. DeSombre (Not admitted in China)
Tao Jin (Not admitted in China)
Elana P. Kermaier (Not admitted in China)
Calvin C. Lai (Not admitted in China)
Stuart B. Leichenko (Not admitted in China)
Rebecca J. Li (Not admitted in China)
George Y. Liu (Not admitted in China)
Xiaoyu Greg Liu (Not admitted in China)
Dolly Mirchandani (Not admitted in China)
Terrence L. Shen (Not admitted in China)

For full biographical listings, see the Martindale-Hubbell Law Directory

American Lawyers In Hong Kong

CHADBOURNE & PARKE LLP

1701A The Hong Kong Club Building, 3A Chater Road, Central, Hong Kong
Telephone: 852-2842-5400
Facsimile: 852-2521-7527
New York, N.Y. Office: 30 Rockefeller Plaza, 10112.
Telephone: 212-408-5100.
Facsimile: 212-541-5369.
Washington, D.C. Office: 1200 New Hampshire Avenue, N.W., 20036.
Telephone: 202-974-5600.
Facsimile: 202-974-5602.
Los Angeles, California Office: 601 South Figueroa Street, 90017.
Telephone: 213-892-1000.
Facsimile: 213-622-9865.
London, England Affiliate Office: Chadbourne & Parke, a multinational partnership of Registered Foreign Lawyers and Solicitors: Regis House, 45 King William Street, London, EC4R 9AN.
Telephone: 44-171-337-8000.
Facsimile: 44-171-337-8001.
Moscow, Russia Office: 52/5 Kosmodamianskaya Nab., 113054.
Telephone: 7095-974-2424.
Facsimile: 7095-974-2425. International satellite lines via U.S.:
Telephone: 212-408-1190.
Facsimile: 212-408-1199.

PARTNERS

Kerin Cantwell (Not admitted in China)

For full biographical listings, see the Martindale-Hubbell Law Directory

CLEARY, GOTTLIEB, STEEN & HAMILTON

39th Floor Bank of China Tower, One Garden Road, Hong Kong
Telephone: 852-2521-4122
Cable Address: "Cleargolaw, Hong Kong"
Fax: 852-2845-9026
New York, New York Office: One Liberty Plaza, New York, N.Y. 10006.
Telephone: 212-225-2000.
Washington, D.C. Office: 2000 Pennsylvania Avenue, N.W., Suite 9000, Washington, D.C. 20006-1801.
Telephone: 202-974-1500.
Paris, France Office: 41, Avenue de Friedland, 75008 Paris, France.
Telephone: 33-1-40-74-68-00.
Brussels, Belgium Office: Rue de la Loi 23, 1040 Brussels, Belgium.
Telephone: 32-2-287-2000.
London, England Office: City Place House, 55 Basinghall Street, London, EC2V 5EH, England.
Telephone: 44-71-614-2200.
Tokyo, Japan Office: Cleary, Gottlieb, Steen & Hamilton Gaikokuho Jimu Bengoshi Jimusho, 20th Floor, Shin Kasumigaseki Building, 3-2, Kasumigaseki 3-Chome, Chiyoda-Ku, Tokyo 100-0013, Japan.
Telephone: 81-3-3595-3911.
Frankfurt, Germany Office: Main Tower, Neue Mainzer Strasse 52, 60311 Frankfurt am Main, Germany.
Telephone: 49-69-971-03-0.
Rome, Italy Office: Piazza di Spagna 15, 00187 Rome, Italy.
Telephone: 39-06-69-52-22-1.

PARTNERS

Richard S. Lincer (Not admitted in China)
Michael M. Hickman (Not admitted in China)
Jinduk Han (Not admitted in China)
David W. Hirsch (Not admitted in China)

SPECIAL COUNSEL

David F. Johnson (Not admitted in China)

ASSOCIATES

Ya Qin (Not admitted in China)
Sung Kwan Kang (Not admitted in China)
Anne Chrun (Not admitted in China)
Pao-Ann Phua (Not admitted in China)
Bobby Liu (Not admitted in China)
Robert K. Williams (Not admitted in China)
Jay Hoon Choi (Not admitted in China)

(See Next Column)

(Not admitted to practice in Hong Kong courts)

For full biographical listings, see the Martindale-Hubbell Law Directory

CRAVATH, SWAINE & MOORE

Suite 2609, Asia Pacific Finance Tower, 3 Garden Road, Central, Hong Kong
Telephone: 852-2509-7200
Facsimile: 852-2509-7272
URL: http://www.cravath.com
New York City Office: Worldwide Plaza, 825 Eighth Avenue, 10019.
Telephone: 212-474-1000.
Facsimile: 212-474-3700.
London, England Office: 33 King William Street, London, EC4R 9DU.
Telephone: 171-453-1000.
Facsimile: 171-860-1150.

RESIDENT PARTNERS

W. Clayton Johnson (Not admitted in China)
Timothy G. Massad (Not admitted in China)

For full biographical listings, see the Martindale-Hubbell Law Directory

DEBEVOISE & PLIMPTON

13/F Entertainment Building, 30 Queen's Road Central, Hong Kong
Telephone: 852-2160-9800
Fax: 852-2810-9828
New York, N.Y. Office: 875 Third Avenue, 10022.
Telephone: 212-909-6000,
Telex: (Domestic) 148377 DEBSTEVE NYK.
Telecopier: 210-909-68363.
Washington, D.C. Office: 555 13th Street, N.W., 20004.
Telephone: 202-383-8000.
Telex: 405586 DPDC WUUD.
Telecopier: (202) 383-8118.
Paris, France Office: 21 Avenue George V 75008.
Telephone: (33-1) 40 73 12 12.
Telecopier: (33-1) 47 20 50 82.
Telex: 648141F DPPAR.
London, England Office: Old Broad Street, EC2N 1HQ.
Telephone: (44-171) 786-9000.
Telex: 88 4569 DPLON G.
Facsimile: (44-171) 588-4180.
Moscow, Russia Representative Office: Debevoise & Plimpton, LLC, Bolshoi Palashevsky Pereulok 13/2, 4th Floor, 103104.
Telephone: 7 (095 or 503) 956-3858.
Fax: 7 (095 or 503) 956-3868.

RESIDENT PARTNERS

Jeffrey S. Wood
Andrew M. Ostrognai

ASSOCIATES

Elizabeth G. Bynum
Pierre Maugüé
Kathryn E. Sun
Richard Yun Xu

For full biographical listings, see the Martindale-Hubbell Law Directory

JONES, DAY, REAVIS & POGUE

29th Floor, Entertainment Building, 30 Queen's Road Central, Hong Kong
Telephone: 852-2526-6895
Telecopier: 852-2868-5871 or 852-2868-5699
Email: jdrphk@jonesday.com *URL:* http://www.jonesday.com
In Atlanta, Georgia: 3500 SunTrust Plaza, 303 Peachtree Street.
Telephone: 404-521-3939.
Telecopier: 404-581-8330.
In Brussels, Belgium: Avenue Louise 480, 7th Floor. B-1050 Brussels.
Telephone: 32-2-645-14-11.
Telecopier: 32-2-645-14-45.
In Chicago, Illinois: 77 West Wacker.
Telephone: 312-782-3939.
Telecopier: 312-782-8585.
In Cleveland, Ohio: North Point, 901 Lakeside Avenue.
Telephone: 216-586-3939.
Telecopier: 216-579-0212.
In Columbus, Ohio: 1900 Huntington Center.
Telephone: 614-469-3939.
Telecopier: 614-461-4198.
In Dallas, Texas: 2727 North Harwood Street.
Telephone: 214-220-3939.
Telecopier: 214-969-5100.
In Frankfurt, Germany: Hochhaus am Park, Grüneburgweg 102, 60323 Frankfurt am Main.
Telephone: 49-69-9726-3939.
Telecopier: 49-69-9726-3993.
In Geneva, Switzerland: 20, rue de Candolle.
Telephone: 41-22-320-2339.
Telecopier: 41-22-320-1232.
In Irvine, California: 5 Park Plaza, Suite 1100.
Telephone: 949-851-3939.
Telecopier: 949-553-7539.
In London, England: Bucklersbury House, 3 Queen Victoria Street.
Telephone: 44-20-7236-3939.
Telecopier: 44-20-7236-1113.

(See Next Column)

JONES, DAY, REAVIS & POGUE, *Hong Kong—Continued*

In Los Angeles, California: 555 West Fifth Street, Suite 4600.
Telephone: 213-489-3939.
Telecopier: 213-243-2539.
In New York, New York: 599 Lexington Avenue.
Telephone: 212-326-3939.
Telecopier: 212-755-7306.
In Paris, France: 120, rue du Faubourg Saint-Honoré.
Telephone: 33-1-56-59-39-39.
Telecopier: 33-1-56-59-39-38
In Pittsburgh, Pennsylvania: 500 Grant Street, 31st Floor.
Telephone: 412-391-3939.
Telecopier: 412-394-7959.
In Riyadh, Saudi Arabia: The International Law Firm (In Association with Jones, Day, Reavis & Pogue), Sulaymaniyah, Prince Mishari IBN, Abdulaziz Street, P.O. Box 22166.
Telephone: (966-1) 462 8866.
Telecopier: (966-1) 462-9001.
In Shanghai, China: 2805 Kerry Centre, 1515 Nanjing Road West.
Telephone: 86-21-5298-6568.
Telecopier: 86-21-5298-6569.
In Sydney, Australia: Governor Phillip Tower, Level 38, 1 Farrer Place.
Telephone: 61-2-9210-6921.
Telecopier: 61-2-9210-6926.
In Taipei, Taiwan: 8th Floor, 2 Tun Hwa South Road, Section 2.
Telephone: (886-2) 2704-6808.
Telecopier: (886-2) 2704-6791.
In Tokyo, Japan: Toranomon 45 Mori Building, 3rd Floor, 1-5, Toranomon 5-Chome, Minato-Ku, Tokyo 105, Japan.
Telephone: 81-3-3433-3939.
Telecopier: 81-3-5401-2725.
In Washington, D.C.: 51 Louisiana Avenue, N.W.
Telephone: 202-879-3939.
Telecopier: 202-626-1700.

MEMBERS OF FIRM IN HONG KONG

William Anthony Stewart
Barbara Wai Kun Mok

OF COUNSEL

John Y. Lo
Sharon J. Mann

ASSOCIATES

Zhiyang Zhang (Not admitted in China)
Anne Ko
Jeffrey H. Chen (Not admitted in China)
Nicola J. Won
Justina Tin Yee Chan
Nancy Po-Yi Lau

For full biographical listings, see the Martindale-Hubbell Law Directory

KAYE, SCHOLER, FIERMAN, HAYS & HANDLER, LLP

A New York Limited Liability Partnership
Suite 2006-2010, One International Finance Centre, No. 1 Harbor View Street, Central, Hong Kong
Telephone: 852-28458989
Facsimile: 852-28452389
New York, N.Y.: 425 Park Avenue, 10022-3598.
Telephone: 212-836-8000.
Telex: 234860 KAY UR.
Facsimile: 212-836-8689.
Washington, D.C.: McPherson Building, 901 Fifteenth Street, N.W., Suite 1100, 20005- 2327.
Telephone: 202-682-3500.
Facsimile: 202-682-3580.
Los Angeles, California: 1999 Avenue of the Stars, Suite 1600, 90067-6048.
Telephone: 310-788-1000.
Facsimile: 310-788-1200.
West Palm Beach, Florida: Phillips Point, West Tower 1002, 777 South Flagler Drive, 33401.
Telephone: 561-802-3230.
Facsimile: 561-802-3217.
Shanghai, China: Suite 405 Shanghai Centre, 1376 Nanjing Xi Lu, 200040.
Telephone: 86-21-62797356.
Facsimile: 86-21-62797351.

PARTNERS

Franklin D. Chu (Not admitted in China)
Kenneth G. M. Mason (Not admitted in China)
David T. Zhang (Not admitted in China)

RESIDENT ASSOCIATES

Maurice L. Hoo (Not admitted in China)
Shuang Hu (Not admitted in China)
Melanie A. Moore (Not admitted in China)

(Not admitted to practice in Hong Kong courts)

For full biographical listings, see the Martindale-Hubbell Law Directory

MILBANK, TWEED, HADLEY & MCCLOY LLP

3007 Alexandra House, 16 Chater Road, Hong Kong
Telephone: 852-2971-4888
Fax: 852-2840-0792, 852-2845-9046
Email: postmaster@milbank.com *URL:* http://www.milbank.com
New York, New York Office: 1 Chase Manhattan Plaza, 10005-1413.
Telephone: 212-530-5000.
Fax: 212- 530-5219.
Midtown Office: 375 Park Avenue, Suite 3601, 10152.
Telephone: 212-530-5800.
Fax: 212-530-0158.
Los Angeles, California Office: 601 South Figueroa Street, 90017.
Telephone: 213-892-4000.
Fax: 213-629-5063.
Washington, D.C. Office: International Square Building, Suite 1100, 1825 Eye Street, N.W., 20006.
Telephone: 202-835-7500.
Fax: 202-835-7586.
Tokyo, Japan Office: Fukoku Seimei Building, 2-2, Uchisaiwai-cho 2-Chome, Chiyoda-ku, Tokyo 100-0011, Japan.
Telephone: 81-3-3504-1050.
Fax: 81-3-3595-2790, 81-3-3595-2840.
London, England Office: Dashwood House, 69 Old Broad Street, London, EC2M 1QS.
Telephone: 44-207-448-3000.
Fax: 44-207-448-3029.
Singapore Office: 14-00 Caltex House, 30 Raffles Place, 048622.
Telephone: 65-428-2400.
Fax: 65-428-2500.
Moscow, Russia Office: 24/27 Sadovaya-Samotyochnaya, Moscow, 103051.
Telephone: 7-501-258-5015.
Fax: 7-501-258-5014.

PARTNERS

Caroline G. Angoorly (Not admitted in China)
Anthony Root (Not admitted in China)
Douglas A. Tanner (Not admitted in China)
Caroline Sang-Un Han (Not admitted in China)

ASSOCIATES

Jacqueline S. Leung (Not admitted in China)
Tracey L. Schell
Bing Song (Not admitted in China)
Desiree Woo (Not admitted in China)

(Not admitted to practice in Hong Kong courts)

For full biographical listings, see the Martindale-Hubbell Law Directory

PAUL, WEISS, RIFKIND, WHARTON & GARRISON

12th Floor, Hong Kong Club Building, 3A Chater Road (Central), Hong Kong
Telephone: (852) 2536-9933
Facsimile: (852) 2536-9622
Email: mailbox@paulweiss.com *URL:* http://www.paulweiss.com
New York, N.Y. Office: 1285 Avenue of the Americas, 10019-6064.
Telephones: 212-373-3000, TDD 212-373-2000;
Facsimile: 212-757-3990
Washington, D.C. Office: 1615 L Street, NW, Suite 1300, 20036-5694.
Telephones: 202-223-7300. TDD 202-223-7490.
Facsimile: 202-223-7420.
Paris, France Office: 62, rue du Faubourg Saint-Honoré, 75008.
Telephone: (33-1) 53.43.14.14.
Facsimile: (33-1) 53.43.00.23.
Tokyo, Japan Office: Fukoku Seimei Building, 2-2 Uchisaiwaicho 2-chome, Chiyoda-ku, Tokyo 100-0011, Japan.
Telephone: (81-3) 3597-8101.
Facsimile: (81-3) 3597-8120.
Beijing, China Office: 2918 China World Tower II, No. 1 Jianguomenwai Dajie, 100004.
Telephones: (86-10) 6505-6882.
Facsimile: (86-10) 6505-6830.

RESIDENT PARTNERS

Jeanette K. Chan
G. Frederick Kinmonth
John E. Lange

COUNSEL

Michael D. Gertler

RESIDENT ASSOCIATES

Marcia L. Ellis (Not admitted in China)
Kevin Fung
Gayle M. Hyman
Deborah K. Johns (Not admitted in China)
Jean Lau
Peter Man
Lisa Mather
Philip Millward
Miriam Tong
Corinna Yu

For full biographical listings, see the Martindale-Hubbell Law Directory

SHEARMAN & STERLING

Standard Chartered Bank Building, 4 Des Voeux Road Central, Hong Kong
Telephone: (852) 2978-8000
Fax: (852) 2978-8099
URL: http://www.shearman.com
New York, N.Y. Office: 599 Lexington Avenue, New York, New York, 10022-6069.
Telephone: (212) 848-4000.
Telex: 667290. Num Lau.
Fax: (212) 848-7179.
Abu Dhabi, United Arab Emirates Office: Butti Al Otaiba Building, 13th Floor, Suite 1302, Sheikh Khalifa Street, P.O. Box 2948.
Telephone: (971-2) 6274477.
Fax: (971-2) 6268933.
Beijing, People's Republic of China Office: Suite #2205, Capital Mansion, No. 6, Xin Yuan Nan Road. Chao Yang District, Beijing, 100004.
Telephone: (86-10) 6465-2299.
Fax: (86-10) 6465-4578.
Düsseldorf, Federal Republic of Germany Office: Couvenstrasse 8 40211 Düsseldorf.
Telephone: (49 211) 178 88-0.
Fax: (49 211) 178 88-88.
Frankfurt, Federal Republic of Germany Office: Trianon Building, Mainzer Landstrasse 16, 60325 Frankfurt am Main.
Telephone: (49-69) 9711-1000.
Fax: (49-69) 9711-1100.
London, England Office: Broadgate West, 9 Appold Street, London EC2A 2AP.
Telephone: 011-44-20-7655-5000.
Fax: 011-44-20-7655-5500.
Menlo Park, California Office: 1550 El Camino Real, 94025-4100.
Telephone: (650) 330-2200.
Fax: (650) 330-2299.
Paris, France Office: 114, avenue des Champs-Elysées, 75008.
Telephone: (33-1) 53-89-7000.
Fax: (33-1) 53-89-7070.
San Francisco, California Office: 555 California Street, 94104-1522.
Telephone: (415) 616-1100.
Fax: (415) 616-1199.
Singapore Office: 6 Battery Road #25-03. Singapore 049909.
Telephone: (65) 230-3800.
Fax: (65) 230-3899.
Tokyo, Japan Office: Fukoku Seimei Building, 5th Fl. 2-2-2, Uchisaiwaicho, Chiyoda-ku, Tokyo 100-0011. Japan.
Telephone: (81 3) 5251-1601.
Fax: (81 3) 5251-1602.
Toronto, Ontario, Canada Office: Commerce Court West, Suite 4405, P.O. Box 247, M5L 1E8.
Telephone: (416) 360-8484.
Fax: (416) 360-2958.
Washington, D.C. Office: 801 Pennsylvania Avenue, N.W., 20004-2604.
Telephone: (202) 508-8000.
Fax: (202) 508-8100.

PARTNERS

Edward L. Turner III (Not admitted in China; Managing Partner, Hong Kong and Beijing)
Matthew D. Bersani (Not admitted in China)
Hsiao-chiung Li (Not admitted in China)
Clark T. Randt, Jr.

COUNSEL

Mark J. Harty (Not admitted in China)
Chu Liu (Senior Asia Counsel)
Paul G. Prince (Not admitted in China)

RESIDENT ASSOCIATES

Leiming Chen (Not admitted in China)
Adlai Hardin (Not admitted in China)
Barker C. Keith (Not admitted in China)
Seong Soo Kim (Not admitted in China)
Lesley B. Lahm (Not admitted in China)
Kala K. Mulqueeny (Not admitted in China)
Stephen Peepels (Not admitted in China)
Andrew D. Ruff (Not admitted in China)
Alan D. Seem (Not admitted in China)
Bowon Suk (Not admitted in China)
Stephanie S. L. Wong (Not admitted in China)
Chuanjie Zhou

For full biographical listings, see the Martindale-Hubbell Law Directory

SIMPSON THACHER & BARTLETT

Asia Pacific Finance Tower - 7th Floor, 3 Garden Road, Central, Hong Kong
Telephone: 852-2514-7600
Telecopier: 852-2869-7694
URL: http://www.simpsonthacher.com
New York, NY Office: 425 Lexington Avenue, 10017-3954.
Telephone: 212-455-2000.
Telecopier: 212-455-2502. ESL 62928462.
Columbus, Ohio Office: One Riverside Plaza, 43215.
Telephone: 614-461-7799.
Telecopier: 614-461-0040.

(See Next Column)

Los Angeles, California Office: 10 Universal City Plaza, Suite 1850, Universal City, CA, 91608.
Telephone: 818-755-7000.
Fax: 818-755-7009.
Palo Alto, California Office: 3373 Hillview Avenue, 94304.
Telephone: 650-251-5000.
Telecopier: 650-251-5002.
London Office: 99 Bishopsgate, London EC2M 3YH, England.
Telephone: 207 422-4000.
Telecopier: 207 422-4022.
Tokyo Office: Ark Mori Building, 30th Floor, 12-32, Akasaka 1-Chome, Minato-Ku, Tokyo 107, Japan.
Telephone: 81-3-5562-8601.
Telecopier: 81-3-5562-8606. ESL 62765846.
Singapore Office: Suntec Tower One, 33rd Floor, 7 Temasek Boulevard, Singapore 038987.
Telephone: 65-430-5100.
Fax: 65-430-5151.

PARTNERS

John E. Riley (Not admitted in China)

COUNSEL

Helen Pak (Not admitted in China)
Karen Mieko Sakanashi (Not admitted in China)

RESIDENT ASSOCIATES

Joshua Ford Bonnie (Not admitted in China)
Amy I. Chen (Not admitted in China)
Wayne W. Chen (Not admitted in China)
Philip M. J. Culhane (Not admitted in China)
Amy F. Halverson (Not admitted in China)
Kuang-Hsiang (Chris) Lin (Not admitted in China)
Homer Sun (Not admitted in China)

For full biographical listings, see the Martindale-Hubbell Law Directory

WHITE & CASE, SOLICITORS

9th Floor, Gloucester Tower, The Landmark, 11 Pedder Street, Central, Hong Kong
Telephone: (852) 2822-8700
Facsimile: (852) 2845-9070
URL: http://www.whitecase.com
Los Angeles, California:
Telephone: 213-620-7700.
Facsimile: 213-687-0758; 213-452-2330; 213-452-2331.
Palo Alto, California:
Telephone: 650-213-0300.
Facsimile: 650-213-8158.
San Francisco, California:
Telephone: 415-544-1100.
Facsimile: 415-544-0202.
Miami, Florida:
Telephone: 305-371-2700.
Facsimile: 305-358-5744; 305-358-5766.
New York, New York:
Telephone: 212-819-8200.
Facsimile: 212-354-8113.
Washington, D.C.:
Telephone: 202-626-3600.
Facsimile: 202-639-9355.
Bratislava, Slovak Republic:
Telephone: (421-7) 5441-5100.
Facsimile: (421-7) 5441-6100.
Brussels, Belgium:
Telephone: (32-2) 219-16-20.
Facsimile: (32-2) 219-16-26.
Budapest, Hungary: Réczicza Law Firm White & Case.
Telephone: (36-1) 488-5200.
Facsimile: (36-1) 488-5299.
Frankfurt, Germany: White & Case (Rechtsanwälte).
Telephone: (49-69) 713-77-(0).
Facsimile: (49-69) 713-77-100.
Helsinki, Finland: Asianajotoimisto White & Case OY.
Telephone: (358-9) 228-641.
Facsimile: (358-9) 228-64228.
Istanbul, Turkey:
Telephone: (90-212) 275-75-33.
Facsimile: (90-212) 275-75-43.
London, England:
Telephone: (44-20) 7600-7300.
Facsimile: (44-20) 7600-7030.
Moscow, Russia:
Telephone: (7-095) 787-3000.
Facsimile: (7-095) 787-3001.
Paris, France:
Telephone: (33-1) 55-04-15-15.
Facsimile: (33-1) 55-04-15-16.
Prague, Czech Republic:
Telephone: (420-2) 2481-0808; 2481-1796.
Facsimile: (420-2) 2481-0330; 2481-0252.
Stockholm, Sweden: White & Case Advokat AB.
Telephone: (46-8) 506-323-00.
Facsimile: (46-8) 611-21-22.

(See Next Column)

WHITE & CASE, SOLICITORS, *Hong Kong—Continued*

Warsaw, Poland: White & Case (Poland) Sp. z o.o.
Telephone: (48-22) 625-33-33; (48-22) 622-67-67; (48-39) 12-19-06.
Facsimile: (48-22) 628-22-28.
Johannesburg, Republic of South Africa:
Telephone: 27 (11) 884-7689.
Facsimile: 27 (11) 884-7229.
Almaty, Kazakhstan:
Telephone: (7-3272) 50-74-91.
Facsimile: (7-3272) 50-74-93.
Ankara, Turkey:
Telephone: (90-312) 442-5680.
Facsimile: (90-312) 442-5691/4.
Bangkok, Thailand: White & Case (Thailand) Limited.
Telephone: (662) 656-1721 to 32.
Facsimile: (662) 656-1733/34.
Bombay/Mumbai, India: Liaison Office, (91-22) 282-6300/01/02/03.
Facsimile: (91-22) 282-6305.
Hanoi, Vietnam:
Telephone: (84-4) 934-5355.
Facsimile: (84-4) 934-5356.
Ho Chi Minh City, Vietnam:
Telephone: (84-8) 821-0888.
Facsimile: (84-8) 823-6902.
Singapore, Republic of Singapore:
Telephone: (65) 225-6000.
Facsimile: (65) 225-6009.
Tokyo, Japan: White & Case Kandabashi Law Offices.
Telephone: (81-3) 3259-0200.
Facsimile: (81-3) 3259-0150.
Manama, Bahrain:
Telephone: (973) 9610105; (973) 9610119; (973) 535965.
Facsimile: (973) 590962; (973) 532342.
Jeddah, Saudi Arabia: Law Office of Hassan Mahassni,
Telephone: (966-2) 665-4353.
Facsimile: (966-2) 669-2996.
Riyadh, Saudi Arabia: Law Office of Hassan Mahassni,
Telephone: (966-1) 464-4006.
Facsimile: (966-1) 465-1348.
Mexico City, Mexico: White & Case, S.C.
Telephone: (52) 5-540-9600.
Facsimile: (52) 5-540-9699.
São Paulo, SP, Brazil:
Telephone: (55-11) 3171-0011.
Facsimile: (55-11) 3171-0041.
Associated Law Firm(s):
Bombay/Mumbai, India: India Law Services (ILS).
Telephones: (91-22) 284-1995; (91-22) 284-1847.
Facsimile: (91-22) 285-0824.
New Delhi, India: India Law Services (ILS).
Telephone: (91-11) 697-1602/3/4.
Facsimile: (91-11) 698-8860.
Jakarta, Indonesia: Ali Budiardjo, Nugroho, Reksodiputro, Counsellors at Law.
Telephone: (62-21) 250-5125; 250-5136.
Facsimile: (62-21) 250-5392; 250-5122; 250-5001.
Associated Consultancies:
Jakarta, Indonesia: PT WCI Konsultan.
Telephone: (62-21) 577-1527.
Facsimile: (62-21) 577-1535/6.

HONG KONG RESIDENT PARTNERS

George K. Crozer, IV
Allan L. Gropper (Not admitted in China)
Sharon E. Hartline (Not admitted in China)
John T. Kuzmik (Not admitted in China)
Eric S. Yoon (Not admitted in China)

LOCAL PARTNERS
HONG KONG, WHITE & CASE, SOLICITORS

Sandra P. S. Fan
Philip B. Gilligan
Kim M. Rooney

COUNSEL

James B. Griffiths

ASSOCIATES

Juan Andres D. Bautista (Not admitted in China)
Xia Chao (Not admitted in China)
Ying Woo Chung
Victor Ho (Not admitted in China)
Raymund G. Kawasaki (Not admitted in China)
Bernadette Mak Lomas
Douglas B. Miller (Not admitted in China)
Ka Lam Karen Ng
Yvonne Pang
Pan Qi (Not admitted in China)
Dennis G. Soliven (Not admitted in China)
William A. Thomson
Lydia J. Wingrad (Not admitted to practice in Hong Kong courts)

For full biographical listings, see the Martindale-Hubbell Law Directory

WINTHROP, STIMSON, PUTNAM & ROBERTS

2505 Asia Pacific Finance Tower Citibank Plaza, 3 Garden Road, Central, Hong Kong
Telephone: 011-852-2530-3400
Fax: 011-852-2530-3355
URL: http://www.winstim.com
New York Main Office: One Battery Park Plaza, New York, N.Y. 10004-1490.
Telephone: 212-858-1000.
Fax: 212-858-1500.
Stamford, Connecticut Office: Financial Centre, 695 East Main Street, P.O. Box 6760, 06904-6760.
Telephone: 203-348-2300.
Fax: 203-965-8226.
Washington, D.C. Office: 1133 Connecticut Avenue, N.W., 20036.
Telephone: 202-775-9800.
Fax: 202-833-8491.
Palm Beach, Florida Office: 125 Worth Avenue, Suite 310, 33480.
Telephone: 561-655-7297.
Fax: 561-833-6726.
London Office: 54 Lombard Street, London EC3V 9DH, England.
Telephone: 011-44207-648-9200.
Fax: 011-44207-283-1656.
Tokyo, Japan Office: 608 Atagoyama Bengoshi Building 6-7, Atago 1-chome, Minato-ku, Tokyo 105 Japan.
Telephone: 011-813-3437-9740.
Fax: 011-813-3437-9261.
Singapore Office: 6 Battery Road #38-01/B, Singapore 049909.
Telephone: 65-227-4700.
Fax: 65-227-4711.

PARTNERS

Yeow Ming Choo (Not admitted in China)
Andrew H. Lo (Not admitted in China)

For full biographical listings, see the Martindale-Hubbell Law Directory

Canadian Lawyers In Hong Kong

GOODMAN PHILLIPS & VINEBERG

8/F AON China Building, 29 Queen's Road Central, Hong Kong
Telephone: (852) 2522-1061
Telecopier: (852) 2845-9089
Beijing, People's Republic of China Office: 1612 Office Tower One, Henderson Center, 18 Jianguomennei Avenue, Dongcheng District, Beijing, China, 100005.
Telephone: 86-10-6518-6201.
Telecopier: 86-10-6518-6205.
Montreal, Quebec Office: 1501 McGill College, 26th Floor, Montreal, Quebec, Canada H3A 3N9.
Telephone: 514-841-6400; 1-888-841-6400.
Telecopier: 514-841-6499; 1-888-841-6499.
New York, New York Office: 430 Park Avenue, 10th Floor, New York, New York, 10022.
Telephone: 212-308-8866.
Telecopier: 212-308-0132.
Paris, France Office: 13, avenue Hoche, 75008, Paris, France.
Telephone: (33) 01 53 53 44 44.
Telecopier: (33) 01 53 96 04 20.
Singapore Office: 40-A Tras Street, Singapore, 078979.
Telephone: (65) 323-6770.
Telecopier: (65) 323-4337.
Toronto, Ontario Office: 250 Yonge Street, Suite 2400, Toronto, Ontario, Canada M5H 2M6.
Telephone: 416-979-2211.
Telecopier: 416-979-1234.
Vancouver, British Columbia Office: Suite 1900, 355 Burrard Street, Vancouver, British Columbia Canada V6C 2G8.
Telephone: 604-682-7737.
Telecopier: 604-682-7131.

PARTNERS

Olivia S. M. Lee
Ermanno Pascutto
Scott D. Lau (Not admitted in China)
Anne O.Y. Louie
Douglas G. Smith

For full biographical listings, see the Martindale-Hubbell Law Directory

STIKEMAN ELLIOTT

29 Queen's Road Central, Suite 1103, Aon China Building, Hong Kong
Telephone: 852-22305200
Fax: 852-2845-9076
Email: lawyers@hkg.stikeman.com *URL:* http://www.stikeman.com/
Montreal, Quebec Office: 1155 René-Lévesque Boulevard West, 40th Floor, H3B 3V2.
Telephone: 514-397-3000.
Fax: 514-397-3222.
Toronto, Ontario Office: Commerce Court West, 53rd Floor, M5L 1B9.
Telephone: 416-869-5500.
Fax: 416-947-0866.

(See Next Column)

STIKEMAN ELLIOTT—*Continued*

Ottawa, Ontario Office: 50 O'Connor Street, Suite 914, K1P 6L2.
Telephone: 613-234-4555.
Fax: 613-230-8877.
Calgary, Alberta Office: 855 - 2nd Street S.W., 1500 Bankers Hall, T2P 4J7.
Telephone: 403-266-9000.
Fax: 403-266-9034.
Vancouver, British Columbia Office: 666 Burrard Street, Suite 1700, Park Place, V6C 2X8.
Telephone: 604-631-1300.
Fax: 604-681-1825.
New York, New York Office: 126 East 56th Street, 14th Floor, Tower 56, 10022.
Telephone: 212-371-8855.
Fax: 212-371-7087.
London, England Office: Regis House, 45 King William Street, EC4R 9AN.
Telephone: +44 (0) 20 7648 1300.
Fax: +44 (0) 20 7648 1400.
Singapore Office: 1 Shenton Way, #13-07 Robina House, Singapore 068803.
Telephone: 65-532-3556.
Fax: 65-532-3557.
Sydney, Australia Office: Level 40, The Chifley Tower, 2 Chifley Square.
Telephone: 61-2-9232-7199.
Fax: 61-2-9232-6908.

PRINCIPALS AND SENIOR ASSOCIATES

Clifford Sau Man Ng (Not admitted in China) (Not admitted to practice in Hong Kong courts)
Guanxi Zheng

For full biographical listings, see the Martindale-Hubbell Law Directory

---

QINGDAO,

American Lawyers In Qingdao

BAKER & DANIELS

Room C, 13th Floor, Qingdao Beer Building, May 4th Square 35 Donghai Road, 266071 Qingdao
Telephone: +011-86-532-575-1051
Fax: +011-86-532-575-1055
URL: http://www.bakerdaniels.com
Indianapolis, Indiana Office: 300 North Meridian Street, 46204.
Telephone: 317-237-0300.
South Bend, Indiana Office: First Bank Building, 205 West Jefferson Boulevard, 46601.
Telephone: 219-234-4149.
Elkhart, Indiana Office: 301 B South Main Street, Suite 307, 46516.
Telephone: 219-296-6000.
Fort Wayne, Indiana Office: 111 East Wayne Street, Suite 800, 46802.
Telephone: 219-424-8000.
Washington, D.C. Office: 805 15th Street, Suite 700, 20005.
Telephone: 202-312-7440.

MEMBERS OF FIRM

Gregory N. Dale (Not admitted in China)
Michael R. Maine (Not admitted in China)
John Joseph Tanner (Not admitted in China)

ASSOCIATES

Ji-Qing Liu (Not admitted in China)
Courtney F. Ren (Not admitted in China)
Xiang Wang (Not admitted in China)

RESIDENT CONSULTANT

David M. T. Wang

For full biographical listings, see the Martindale-Hubbell Law Directory

COLOMBIA

*BOGOTÁ,**

RAISBECK, LARA, RODRIGUEZ & RUEDA

(Associated Office of Baker & McKenzie)
Calle 35 No. 7-25, 4th Floor, Bogotá D.C.
Telephone: 285-1400
Intn'l Dialing: (57-1) 285-1400
Telex: 43282
Answer Back: 43282 ABOGA CO
Facsimile: (57-1) 285-6908
URL: http://www.bakerinfo.com
Associated Offices of Baker & McKenzie in: Almaty, Amsterdam, Bahrain, Baku, Bangkok, Barcelona, Beijing, Berlin, Brasília, Brussels, Budapest, Buenos Aires, Cairo, Caracas, Chicago, Dallas, Düsseldorf, Frankfurt, Geneva, Hanoi, Ho Chi Minh City, Hong Kong, Houston, Hsinchu, Juárez, Kyiv, London, Madrid, Manila, Melbourne, México City, Miami, Milan, Monterrey, Moscow, Münich, New York, Palo Alto, Paris, Prague, Rio de Janeiro, Riyadh, Rome, St. Petersburg, San Diego, San Francisco, Santiago, São Paulo, Singapore, Stockholm, Sydney, Taipei, Tijuana, Tokyo, Toronto, Valencia, Warsaw, Washington, D.C. and Zürich.
Correspondent Law Firm: Hadiputranto, Hadinoto & Partners, Jakarta.
Postal Address: Apartado Aereo No. 3746

Alvaro Correa O.
Antonio Duarte A.
Jorge Lara-Urbaneja
Jorge Rodríguez R.
Sergio Rueda F.
Eduardo Zuleta J.

LOCAL PARTNERS

Juan Manuel Garrido
Maria Clara López
Jaime Trujillo-Caicedo

Bibiana Agudelo-Aguillon
William J. Araque
Rubby Esperanza Aristizabal
Alvaro Camacho
Maria Fernanda Carvajal
Juan Pablo Concha
Dr. Camilo Duarte-Marin
Tatiana Garces-Carvajal
Daniel Garcia
Paola Vasquez Garcia
Santiago Jaramillo
Cristina Matiz Mejia
Alejandro Mesa Neira
Clare Montgomery
Carlos R. Olarte-Garcia
Pedro Osman-Gomez
Olga Georgette Otero
Carolina Pardo Cuellar
Monica Plazas-Navarrete
Rosa L. Rodriguez
Cristina Rueda
Maria Claudia Rueda
Sylvia Rueda
Juan Camilo Santamaria
Carolina Suarez-Marin
Jaime H. Tobar Ordoñez
Luz Helena Villamil
Andrés Williamson

For full biographical listings, see the Martindale-Hubbell Law Directory

CZECH REPUBLIC

PRAGUE,

American Lawyers In Prague

BAKER & MCKENZIE

Praha City Center, Klimentská 46, Prague
Telephone: Telephone: (02) 2185 5001
Intn'l Dialing: (420-2) 2185 5001
Facsimile: (420-2) 2185 5055
Chgo., IL
URL: http://www.bakerinfo.com
Associated Offices of Baker & McKenzie in: Almaty, Amsterdam, Bahrain, Baku, Bangkok, Barcelona, Beijing, Berlin, Bogotá, Brasília, Brussels, Budapest, Buenos Aires, Cairo, Caracas, Chicago, Dallas, Düsseldorf, Frankfurt, Geneva, Hanoi, Ho Chi Minh City, Hong Kong, Houston, Hsinchu, Juárez, Kyiv, London, Madrid, Manila, Melbourne, México City, Miami, Milan, Monterrey, Moscow, Münich, New York, Palo Alto, Paris, Rio de Janeiro, Riyadh, Rome, St. Petersburg, San Diego, San Francisco, Santiago, São Paulo, Singapore, Stockholm, Sydney, Taipei, Tijuana, Tokyo, Toronto, Valencia, Warsaw, Washington, D.C. and Zürich.
Correspondent Law Firm: Hadiputranto, Hadinoto & Partners, Jakarta.

PARTNER

John P. Hewko

ASSOCIATES

Andrea Bednaříková
Alexandr César
Benjamin John Gray (Not admitted in Czech Republic)
Martin [illegible]rodek
Marek Kreisl
Karolina Peake
Ondřej Sekanina
Tomáš Skoumal
Pavla TlouŠtovÁ
Gabriela Vendlova

For full biographical listings, see the Martindale-Hubbell Law Directory

HOGAN & HARTSON

(Advokátnií Kanceláře, v.o.s.)
Trziste 13, 118 00 Prague
Telephone: (420-2) 2211-7111
Fax: (420-2) 2211-7222
URL: www.hhlaw.com
Washington, D.C. Office: Columbia Square, 555 13th Street, N.W.
Telephone: 206-637-5600.
Telex: 89-2757.
Cable Address: "Hogander Washington".
Fax: 202-637-5910.
Brussels, Belgium Office: Avenue des Arts 41, 1040.
Telephone: (32.2) 505.09.11.
Fax: (32.2) 505.09.96.
Budapest, Hungary (Affiliated Office): Nagy & Pintér, Hogan & Hartson Law Office, Bank Center, Granite Tower, 9th Floor, Budapest V., Szabadsag ter 7, 1944 Hungary.
Telephone: (36-1) 302-9050.
Fax: (36-1) 302-9060.
London, England Office: One Angel Court, EC2R 7HJ.
Telephone: +(44) 207-367-0200.
Fax: +(44) 207-367-0220.
Moscow, Russia Office: 33/2 Usacheva Street, Building 3, 119048.
Telephone: (7095) 245-5190. Int'l
Telephone: (7501) 907-0451.
Fax: (7095) 245-5192. Int'l
Fax: (7501) 907-0462.
Paris, France (Affiliated Office): Cariddi, Mee, Rué, Avocats Associés à la Cour de Paris, 12, rue de la Paix, 75002.
Telephone: (33-1) 42.61.57.71.
Fax: (33-1) 42.61.79.21.
Warsaw, Poland Office: Hogan & Hartson Sp.zo.o, Atrium Tower, Al. Jana Pawla II 25, 00-854.
Telephone: (48-22) 653-4200.
Fax: (48-22) 653-4250.
Baltimore, Maryland Office: 111 South Calvert Street.
Telephone: 410-659-2700.
Fax: 410-539-6981.
Rockville, Maryland Office: 600 Jefferson Plaza, Suite 203.
Telephone: 301-315-2206.
Fax: 301-315-9046.
Boulder, Colorado Office: 1800 Broadway, Suite 200.
Telephone: 720-406-5300.
Fax: 720-406-5301.
Colorado Springs, Colorado Office: Two North Cascade Avenue, Suite 1300.
Telephone: 719-448-5900.
Fax: 719-448-5922.
Denver, Colorado Office: One Tabor Center, Suite 1500, 1200 Seventeenth Street.
Telephone: 303-899-7300.
Fax: 303-899-7333.
Los Angeles, California Office: Biltmore Tower, 500 S. Grand Avenue, Suite 1900.
Telephone: 213-337-6700.
Fax: 213-337-6701.
Newport Beach, California Office: 4675 MacArthur Court, Suite 670.
Telephone: 949-250-4550.
Fax: 949-833-0976.
McLean, Virginia Office: 8300 Greensboro Drive.
Telephone: 703-610-6100.
Fax: 703-610-6200.
New York, New York Office: 885 Third Avenue, 26th Floor.
Telephone: 212-409-9800.
Fax: 212-409-9801.

PARTNERS

Colin W. Craik
Milan Lovíšek
Jan Tanzer

EUROPEAN COUNSEL

Pavel Bradác

ASSOCIATES

Silvia Belovicova (Not admitted in Czech Republic)
Jana Hrstková
Karin Luftmanová

For full biographical listings, see the Martindale-Hubbell Law Directory

SQUIRE, SANDERS & DEMPSEY V. O. S. ADVOKATNI KANCEPAF

Václavské náměst 1 57/813, 110 00 Prague
Telephone: 420-2-2166-2111
Fax: 420-2-2166-2222
URL: http://www.ssd.com
Cincinnati, Ohio Office: PNC Center, 201 East Fifth Street, Suite 1700, Cincinnati, Ohio 45202.
Telephone: 513-361-1200.
Fax: 513-361-1201.
Cleveland, Ohio Office: 4900 Key Tower, 127 Public Square, Cleveland, Ohio 44114-1304.
Telephone: 216-479-8500.
Fax: 216-479-8780.

(See Next Column)

Columbus, Ohio Office: 1300 Huntington Center, 41 South High Street, Columbus, Ohio 43215-6150.
Telephone: 614-365-2700.
Fax: 614-365-2499.
Houston, Texas Office: 62590 Chase Tower, 600 Travis Street, Houston, Texas 77002-3007.
Telephone: 713-546-5850.
Fax: 713-546-5830.
Jacksonville, Florida Office: One Enterprise Center, Suite 2100, 225 Water Street, Jacksonville, Florida 32202-4424.
Telephone: 904-366-2420.
Fax: 904-356-2986.
Miami, Florida Office: 201 South Biscayne Boulevard, 2900 Miami Center, Miami, Florida 33131-4330.
Telephone: 305-577-8700.
Fax: 305-358-1425.
New York, New York Office: 350 Park Avenue, New York, New York 10022-6002.
Telephone: 212-872-9800.
Fax: 212-872-9815.
Phoenix, Arizona Office: Two Renaissance Square, 40 North Central Avenue, Suite 2700, Phoenix, Arizona 85004-4498.
Telephone: 602-528-4000.
Fax: 602-253-8129.
Washington, D.C. Office: 1201 Pennsylvania Avenue, N.W., Suite 500, Washington, D.C. 20004-2491.
Telephone: 202-626-6600.
Fax: 202-626-6780.
Almaty, Kazakhstan Office: 141 Ablay Khan Avenue, Second Floor, Almaty, Kazakhstan 480091.
Telephone: +73-27-50-11-25.
Fax: +73-27-50-11-25.
Bratislava, Slovak Republic Office: Zochova 5, 811 03 Bratislava, Slov k Republic.
Telephone: 421-7-5441-7611.
Fax: 42-1-7-6280-2212.
Brussels, Belgium Office: Avenue Louise, 165-Box 15, 1050 Brussels, Belgium.
Telephone: 32-2-627-1111.
Fax: 32-2-627-1100.
Budapest, Hungary Office: H-1062 Budapest, Andrassy ut. 64, Budapest, Hungary.
Telephone: 36-1-428-7111.
Fax: 36-1-428-7100.
Kyiv, Ukraine Office: 14A Yaroslaviv Val, Kyiv 252034, Ukraine.
Telephone: 38-044-228-8687.
Fax: 38-044-228-4938.
London, England Office: Royex House, Aldermanbury Square, London EC2V 7HR.
Telephone: 44-171-776-5200.
Fax: 44-171-776-5233.
Madrid, Spain Office: Calle Velazquez 108-110, 28006 Madrid, Spain.
Telephone: 34-91-590-2420.
Fax: 34-91-590-2421.
Moscow, Russian Federation Office: Paveletskaya Square II, 1 Valovaya Street, 5th Floor, Moscow 113054, Russian Federation.
Telephone: 7-501-258-5250.
Fax: 7-501-258-5251.
Prague, Czech Republic Office: Václavské náměst 1 57/813, 110 00 Praha 1, Czech Republic.
Telephone: 420-2-2166-2111.
Fax: 420-2-2166-2222.
Hong Kong Office: Rooms 1101-2 St. George's Building, 2 Ice House Street, Central, Hong Kong.
Telephone: 852-2509-9732.
Fax: 852-2509-9772.
Taipei, Taiwan Office: 14F, 116 Nanking East Road, Sec. 2, Taipei, Taiwan, Republic of China.
Telephone: 886-2-2531-2888.
Fax: 886-2-2571-6199.

PARTNERS

John M. Clapp
Gerald L. Jacobs
Jeffrey A. McGehee
Vladimira N. Papirnik
Luboš Tichý

OF COUNSEL

Milan Ganik (Not admitted in Czech Republic)
Jaromír Růžička

ASSOCIATES

Marketa Bendova
Alexander V. Borovik
Robert F. Gage
Mark J. Gardberg
Radek Janeček
Julian Juhasz
Zdeněk Rosický
Jaroslav Salač
Petr Slach
Iva Wright

(Not admitted to practice in Czech courts)

For full biographical listings, see the Martindale-Hubbell Law Directory

EGYPT

*CAIRO,**

BAKER & MCKENZIE

World Trade Center, 1191 Cornich El Nil Eighteenth Floor, Cairo
Telephone: 579-1801 to 1806
Intn'l Dialing: (20-2) 579-1801 to 1806
Facsimile: (20-2) 579-1808
URL: http://www.bakerinfo.com
Associated Offices of Baker & McKenzie in: Almaty, Amsterdam, Bahrain, Baku, Bangkok, Barcelona, Beijing, Berlin, Bogotá, Brasília, Brussels, Budapest, Buenos Aires, Caracas, Chicago, Dallas, Düsseldorf, Frankfurt, Geneva, Hanoi, Ho Chi Minh City, Hong Kong, Houston, Hsinchu, Juárez, Kyiv, London, Madrid, Manila, Melbourne, México City, Miami, Milan, Monterrey, Moscow, Münich, New York, Palo Alto, Paris, Prague, Rio de Janeiro, Riyadh, Rome, St. Petersburg, San Diego, San Francisco, Santiago, São Paulo, Singapore, Stockholm, Sydney, Taipei, Tijuana, Tokyo, Toronto, Valencia, Warsaw, Washington, D.C. and Zürich.
Correspondent Law Firm: Hadiputranto, Hadinoto & Partners, Jakarta.

PARTNERS

Mohamed A. Ghannam
Samir M. Hamza
M. Taher Helmy
Hazim A. Rizkana
Mohammad B. Talaat

ASSOCIATES

Mohamed Abdalla
Kamel I. El-Wakil
Abdel Moneim Emara
Samer Youssef Faragalla (Not admitted in Egypt)
Suzan E. Farid (Not admitted in Egypt)
Marzouk M. Hegazy
Shirin Ikram (Not admitted in Egypt)
Nader R. Kamel
Hatem M. Soliman
Saber I. A. W. Soliman

For full biographical listings, see the Martindale-Hubbell Law Directory

ENGLAND

*LONDON,**

PAUL, HASTINGS, JANOFSKY & WALKER LLP

A Limited Liability Partnership including Professional Corporations
Firm Established in 1951; Office in 1997
The International Financial Centre 25 Old Broad Street, London EC2N 1HQ
Telephone: (011) 44-171-562-4000
Facsimile: (011) 44-171-628-4444
Email: info@phjw.com *URL:* http://www.phjw.com
Atlanta, Georgia Office: 24th Floor, 600 Peachtree Street, N.E.
Telephone: 404-815-2400.
Los Angeles, California Office: 555 South Flower Street.
Telephone: 213-683-6000.
New York, New York Office: 399 Park Avenue.
Telephone: 212-318-6000.
Orange County, California Office: 695 Town Center Drive, Costa Mesa.
Telephone: 714-668-6200.
San Francisco, California Office: 345 California Street.
Telephone: 415-835-1600.
Stamford, Connecticut Office: 1055 Washington Boulevard.
Telephone: 203-961-7400.
Washington, D.C. Office: 1299 Pennsylvania Avenue, N.W.
Telephone: 202-508-9500.
Tokyo, Japan Office: Ark Mori Building, 12-32 Akasaka, P.O. Box 577, 1-Chome, Minato-Ku.
Telephone: (03) 3586-4711.
ATTORNEY E-MAIL ADDRESSES: first initial middle initial last name @phjw.com (e.g. rmasbill@phjw.com)

MEMBERS OF FIRM

Wayne McArdle
Keith T. Ott (Not admitted in England)

OF COUNSEL

Robert L. Gross

ASSOCIATES

Ian R. Burton
June L. Lin (Not admitted in England)
Wendy Lotter (Not admitted in England)
Jeremy Tarsh
Marie-Laure Ducamp Weisberg (Not admitted in England)

For full biographical listings, see the Martindale-Hubbell Law Directory

American Lawyers In London

BINGHAM DANA LLP

39 Victoria Street, London SWIH 0EE
Telephone: 011-44-171-799-2646
Telecopy: 011-44-171-799-2654
Email: info@bingham.com *URL:* http://www.bingham.com
Boston, Massachusetts Office: 150 Federal Street, 02110.
Telephone: 617-951-8000.
Telecopy: 617-951-8736.
Hartford, Connecticut Office: One State Street.
Telephone: 860-240-2700.
Fax: 860-240-2800.
Washington, D.C. Office: 1120 20th Street, N.W.
Telephone: 202-778-6150.
Fax: 202-778-6155.
Los Angeles, California Office: 444 South Flower Street, Suite 4500.
Telephone: 213-817-3700.
Fax: 213-817-3701.
New York, New York Office: 399 Park Avenue.
Telephone: 212-318-7700.
Fax: 212-752-5378.
Singapore Office: Level 15 Prudential Tower, 30 Cecil Street, 049712.
Telephone: 65 232-2768/2769.
Fax: 65 232-2888.

MEMBERS OF FIRM

Barry G. Russell (Not admitted in England)
James C. Stokes (Not admitted in England)
Jay S. Zimmerman (Not admitted in England; Managing Partner)

ASSOCIATES

John M. Casanova (Not admitted in England)
Robert J. Keough, Jr. (Not admitted in England)
Patrick A. Piscatelli (Not admitted in England)
Andrew L. Rotenberg (Not admitted in England)

(Not admitted to practice in English courts)

For full biographical listings, see the Martindale-Hubbell Law Directory

CHADBOURNE & PARKE

A multinational partnership of Registered Foreign Lawyers and Solicitors
Regis House, 45 King William Street, EC4R 9AN London
Telephone: 44-171-337-8000
Facsimile: 44-171-337-8001
New York, N.Y. Office: Chadbourne & Parke LLP, 30 Rockefeller Plaza, 10112.
Telephone: 212-408-5100.
Facsimile: 212-541-5369.
Washington, D.C. Office: Chadbourne & Parke LLP, 1200 New Hampshire Avenue, N.W., 20036.
Telephone: 202-974-5600.
Facsimile: 202-974-5602.
Los Angeles, California Office: Chadbourne & Parke LLP, 601 South Figueroa Street, 90017.
Telephone: 213-892-1000.
Facsimile: 213-622-9865.
Moscow, Russia Office: Chadbourne & Parke LLP, 52/5 Kosmodamianskaya Nab., 113054.
Telephone: 7095-974-2424.
Facsimile: 7095-974-2425, International satellite lines via U.S.:
Telephone: 212-408-1190.
Facsimile: 212-408-1199.
Hong Kong, China Office: Chadbourne & Parke LLP, 1701A The Hong Kong Club Building, 3A Chater Road, Central, Hong Kong.
Telephone: 852-2842-5400.
Facsimile: 852-2521-7527.

ADMINISTRATIVE PARTNERS

William Greason (Not admitted in England)
Thomas C. Meriam (Not admitted in England)
Paul L. Weber (Not admitted in England)

RESIDENT COUNSEL

Lynne E. Gedanken (Not admitted in England)
Anna McConnell

RESIDENT ASSOCIATES

Stephanie A. Conaghan (Not admitted in England)
Sarah L. Empson
Kevin Jordan
Robin Mizrahi (Not admitted in England)

For full biographical listings, see the Martindale-Hubbell Law Directory

CLEARY, GOTTLIEB, STEEN & HAMILTON

City Place House, 55 Basinghall Street, London EC2V 5EH
Telephone: 44-171-614-2200
Cable Address: "Cleargolaw London"
Facsimile: Gps. 3 44-171-600-1698; 44-171-588-5163
New York, New York Office: One Liberty Plaza, New York, N.Y. 10006.
Telephone: 212-225-2000.
Washington, D.C. Office: 2000 Pennsylvania Avenue, N.W., Suite 9000, Washington, D.C. 20006-1801.
Telephone: 202-974-1500.
Paris, France Office: 41, Avenue de Friedland, 75008 Paris, France.
Telephone: 33-1-40-74-68-00.
Brussels, Belgium Office: Rue de la Loi 23, 1040 Brussels, Belgium.
Telephone: 32-2-287-2000.
Hong Kong Office: 39th Floor, Bank of China Tower, One Garden Road, Hong Kong.
Telephone: 852-2521-4122.
Tokyo, Japan Office: Cleary, Gottlieb, Steen & Hamilton Gaikokuho Jimubengoshi Jimusho, 20th Floor, Shin Kasumigaseki Building, 3-2, Kasumigaseki 3-Chome, Chiyoda-Ku, Tokyo 100-0013, Japan.
Telephone: 81-3-3595-3911.
Frankfurt, Germany Office: Main Tower, Neue Mainzer Strasse 52, 60311 Frankfurt am Main, Germany.
Telephone: 49-69-971-03-0.
Rome, Italy Office: Piazza di Spagna 15, 00187 Rome, Italy.
Telephone: 39-06-69-52-22-1.

PARTNERS

Manley O. Hudson, Jr. (Not admitted in England)
Edward F. Greene (Not admitted in England)
Andrew Curran
James A. Duncan (Not admitted in England)
Simon Jay
Daniel A. Braverman (Not admitted in England)
Glen M. Scarcliffe
Sebastian R. Sperber (Not admitted in England)
Ashar Qureshi (Not admitted in England)

ASSOCIATES

Andrew C. Shutter (Resident)
Farmida Bi (Resident)
Thomas K. Kopp (Not admitted in England)
Thomas Mayer (Not admitted in England)
Stuart Grider (Not admitted in England; Resident)
Steven C. Planchard (Not admitted in England; Resident)
Gordon L. Mullis, III (Not admitted in England)
Dmitri B. Shevtsov (Not admitted in England)
Michael F. Rinzler (Not admitted in England; Resident)
Yvonne Braun (Not admitted in England)
Claire Timmins
Sarah A. Barth (Not admitted in England; Resident)
Simon R. Bell (Resident)
David G. F. Sefton (Resident)
Raj S. Panasar (Resident)
David E. Arroyo (Not admitted in England)
Diane Brayton (Not admitted in England; Resident)
Charles Henry Hawes (Not admitted in England; Resident)
Sharon Gillon (Not admitted in England; Resident)
Daniel Coppel (Resident)
Fiona Doyle (Resident)
Christopher Wyeth Kirkham (Not admitted in England; Resident)
Elizabeth A. Harwick (Resident)
Daniel Lewin (Not admitted in England; Resident)

For full biographical listings, see the Martindale-Hubbell Law Directory

CRAVATH, SWAINE & MOORE

33 King William Street, London EC4R 9DU
Telephone: 171-453-1000
Facsimile: 171-860-1150
URL: http://www.cravath.com
New York City Office: Worldwide Plaza, 825 Eighth Avenue, 10019.
Telephone: 212-474-1000.
Facsimile: 212-474-3700.
Hong Kong, China Office: Suite 2609, Asia Pacific Finance Tower, 3 Garden Road, Central, Hong Kong, China.
Telephone: 852-2509-7200.
Facsimile: 852-2509-7272.

RESIDENT PARTNERS

David O. Brownwood (Not admitted in England)
Paul Michalski (Not admitted in England)

(Not admitted to practice in English courts)

For full biographical listings, see the Martindale-Hubbell Law Directory

CROWELL & MORING

Registered Foreign Lawyers and Solicitors
180 Fleet Street, London EC4A 2HG
Telephone: 44-207-413-0011
Fax: 44-207-413-0333
URL: http://www.crowellmoring.com
Washington, D.C. Office: Crowell & Moring LLP, 1001 Pennsylvania Avenue, N.W., 20004-2595.
Telephone: 202-624-2500.
Fax: 202-628-5116.

(See Next Column)

Irvine, California Office: Crowell & Moring LLP, 2010 Main Street, Suite 1200, 92614-7217.
Telephone: 949-263-8400.
Fax: 949-263-8414.

RESIDENT PARTNERS

Peter A. D. Teare
James Ashe-Taylor

RESIDENT ASSOCIATES

Kate Rowson (Not admitted in United States)
Nicholas Clarke (Not admitted in England)
Heidi H. Lamer (Not admitted in England)
Suzanne McNulty (Not admitted in England)

For full biographical listings, see the Martindale-Hubbell Law Directory

CURTIS, MALLET-PREVOST, COLT & MOSLE LLP

Two Throgmorton Avenue, London EC2N 2DL
Telephone: 0207-638-7957
Telecopier: 0207-638-5512
Email: info@cm-p.com *URL:* http://www.cm-p.com
New York, New York Office: 101 Park Avenue.
Telephone: 212-696-6000.
Telecopier: 212-697-1559.
Newark, New Jersey Office: One Gateway Center, Suite 403.
Telephone: 973-622-0605.
Telecopier: 973-622-5646.
Washington, D.C. 20006 Office: Suite 1205L, 1801 K Street, N.W.
Telephone: 202-452-7373.
Telecopier: 202-452-7333.
Houston, Texas Office: 2 Houston Center, 909 Fannin Street, Suite 3725.
Telephone: 713-759-9555.
Telecopier: 713-759-0712.
Stamford, Connecticut Office: One Canterbury Green.
Telephone: 203-359-6200.
Telecopier: 203-328-2617.
Mexico City, D.F., Mexico Office: Curtis, Mallet-Prevost, Colt & Mosle, Ruben Dario 281, Piso 9, Col. Bosque de Chapultepec, 11530 Mexico, D.F.
Telephone: 525-282-0444.
Telecopier: 525-282-0637.
Paris, France Office: 15 rue d'Astorg, 75008.
Telephone: 42-66-39-10.
Telecopier: 42-66-39-62.
Frankfurt am Main 1, Germany Office: Staufenstrasse 42.
Telephone: 69-971-4420.
Telecopier: 69-17 33 99.
Muscat, Sultanate of Oman Office: Jewel Beach-134.
Telephone: 968-607-725.
Telecopier: 968-607-724.
Milan, Italy Office: Curtis, Mallet-Prevost & Gilioli, Piazzale Principessa Clotilde 8, 20121.
Telephone: (39) 02 29 00 29 32.
Telefax: (39) 02 65 75 969.

RESIDENT PARTNER

Bruce B. Palmer (Not admitted in England)

RESIDENT ASSOCIATE

Amy Coyle Norman (Not admitted in England)

For full biographical listings, see the Martindale-Hubbell Law Directory

DAVIS POLK & WARDWELL

99 Gresham Street, London EC2V 7NG
Telephone: 44-171-418-1300
Fax: 44-171-418-1400
URL: http://www.dpw.com
New York, N.Y. Office: 450 Lexington Avenue, 10017.
Telephone: 212-450-4000.
Fax: 212-450-4800.
Washington, D.C. Office: 1300 I Street, N.W., 20005.
Telephone: 202-962-7000.
Fax: 202-962-7111.
Menlo Park, California Office: 1600 El Camino Real, Menlo Park, California, 94025.
Telephone: 650-752-2000.
Fax: 650-752-2195.
Paris, France Office: 15, avenue Matignon, 75008 Paris, France.
Telephone: 33-01-56-59-36-00.
Fax: 33-01-56-59-36-90.
Tokyo, Japan Office: Akasaka Twin Tower East, 11th Floor, 17-22, Akasaka 2-Chome, Minato-ku, Tokyo 107-0052, Japan.
Telephone: 81-3-5561-4421.
Fax: 81-3-5561-4425.
Frankfurt, Germany Office: MesseTurm, 60308 Frankfurt am Main, Germany.
Telephone: 49-69-97-57-03-0.
Fax: 49-69-74-77-44.
Hong Kong, China Office: The Hong Kong Club Building, 3A Chater Road, Hong Kong.
Telephone: 852-2533-3300.
Fax: 852-2533-3388.

SENIOR COUNSEL

Joseph Chubb (Not admitted in England)

(See Next Column)

DAVIS POLK & WARDWELL—*Continued*

MEMBERS OF FIRM

John W. Banes (Not admitted in England)
Jeffrey D. Berman (Not admitted in England)
Keith L. Kearney (Not admitted in England)
Paul E. Kumleben (Not admitted in England)
John J. McCarthy, Jr. (Not admitted in England)
Jeffrey M. Oakes (Not admitted in England)
John D. Paton (Not admitted in England)
Thomas J. Reid (Not admitted in England)
Margaret Tahyar (Not admitted in England)
David M. Wells (Not admitted in England)

RESIDENT ASSOCIATES

John D. Amorosi (Not admitted in England)
Alexander A. Bafi (Not admitted in England)
Richard M. Baumann (Not admitted in England)
Dina T. Brewer (Not admitted in England)
Donna M. Chambers (Not admitted in England)
Eric R. Dann (Not admitted in England)
Chinedu Reginald Ezetah (Not admitted in England)
Avrohom C. Gelber (Not admitted in England)
Brian J. Gill (Not admitted in England)
Sonia K. Han (Not admitted in England)
Ethan T. James (Not admitted in England)
Marcelle R. Joseph (Not admitted in England)
Mira Kothari
Joyce McCarthy (Not admitted in England)
Catherine Moroz (Not admitted in England)
Ebelechukwu A. Okobi
David W. Parento (Not admitted in England)
Ryan F. Pearson (Not admitted in England)
Daniel Rabinowitz (Not admitted in England)
Simona Spazzini (Not admitted in England)
Jennifer A. Spiegel (Not admitted in England)
Eva H. Studenny (Not admitted in England)
Anna Torstensson (Not admitted in England)
Amy L. Valley (Not admitted in England)
Michael J. Willisch (Not admitted in England)

(Not admitted to practice in English courts)

For full biographical listings, see the Martindale-Hubbell Law Directory

DEBEVOISE & PLIMPTON

Tower 42 The International Financial Centre, Old Broad Street, London EC2N 1HQ
Telephone: (44-171) 786 9000
Telecopier: (44-171) 588 4180
New York Office: 875 Third Avenue, 10022.
Telephone: 212-909-6000.
Telex: (Domestic) 148377 DEBSTEVE NYK.
Telecopier: (212) 909-6836.
Washington, D.C. Office: 555 13th Street, N.W., 20004.
Telephone: 202-383-8000.
Telex: 405586 DPDC WUUD.
Telecopier: (202) 383-8118.
Paris, France Office: 21 Avenue George V, 75008.
Telephone: (33-1) 40 73 12 12.
Telecopier: (33-1) 47 2050 82.
Telex: 648141F DPPAR.
Hong Kong Office: 13/F Entertainment Building, 30 Queen's Road Central.
Telephone: (852) 2610-9800.
Fax: (852) 2810-9828.
Moscow, Russia Representative Office: Debevoise & Plimpton, LLC, Bolshoi Palashevsky Pereulok 13/2, 4th Floor, 103104.
Telephone: 7 (095 or 503) 956-3858.
Fax: 7 (095 or 503) 956-3868.

RESIDENT PARTNERS

James A. Kiernan III (Also at Paris, France Office)
Robert R. Bruce
Arthur L. Marriott, QC *
Katherine Ashton *

INTERNATIONAL COUNSEL

Colin William Bogie

RESIDENT ASSOCIATES

Nicholas James Boyle
Scott C. Budlong
Geoffrey P. Burgess
Erin Callahan
Sally Fitzgerald
Tzechien Goh
Giselle P. Hantz
Matthew E. Kaplan
Vera Losonci
Wendy A. Semel

For full biographical listings, see the Martindale-Hubbell Law Directory

DECHERT PRICE & RHOADS

(also see Titmuss Sainer Dechert)
2 Serjeants' Inn, London EC4Y 1LT
Telephone: (0171) 583-5353
Telefax: (0171) 353-3683
URL: http://www.dechert.com
Philadelphia, Pennsylvania: 4000 Bell Atlantic Tower, 1717 Arch Street, 19103-2793.
Telephone: 215-994-4000.
Telefax: 215-994-2222.
New York, New York: 30 Rockefeller Plaza, 10112.
Telephone: 212-698-3500.
Washington, D.C.: 1775 Eye Street, N.W., 20006.
Telephone: 202-261-3300.
Harrisburg, Pennsylvania: Thirty North Third Street, 17101-1603.
Telephone: 717-237-2000.
Princeton, New Jersey: Princeton Pike Corporate Center, P.O. Box 5218, 08543-5218.
Telephone: 609-620-3200.
Boston, Massachusetts: Ten Post Office Square South, 02109-4603.
Telephone: 617-728-7100.
Hartford, Connecticut: 90 State House Square, 06103-3702.
Telephone: 860-524-3999.
Brussels, Belgium: 65 Avenue Louise, 1050.
Telephone: (02) 535-5411.
Paris, France: 55, avenue Kléber, 76116.
Telephone: 33-(0) 1-53 65 05 00.
Fax: 33-(0) 1-53 65 05 05.

RESIDENT PARTNERS

Peter David Astleford
Peter Draper
Edward L. Kling
David E. Schulman

RESIDENT ASSOCIATES

Brian M. McCall

(Not admitted to practice in English courts)

For full biographical listings, see the Martindale-Hubbell Law Directory

FAEGRE BENSON HOBSON AUDLEY

A Multi-national Partnership of Registered Foreign Lawyers and Solicitors
7 Pilgrim Street, London EC4V 6DR
Telephone: 0171-450-4510
Facsimile: 0171-450-4544
Email: lawyers@faegre.co.uk *URL:* http://www.faegre.com/offices/off_lond.html
Associated with Faegre & Benson LLP with offices in Minneapolis, Minnesota; Denver, Colorado, Des Moines, Iowa, and Frankfurt, Germany.
Associated with Hobson Audley Hopkins & Wood with offices in London.

LAWYERS AND SOLICITORS IN LONDON

U.S. LAWYER

Scott M. James (Not admitted in England; Partner, Faegre & Benson LLP)

ENGLISH SOLICITORS

Gerald A. Hobson
Roger C. B. Hopkins
Maxwell C. Audley
Simon J.J. Smith
Berry G. C. Holding-Parsons
Godfrey M. Bruce-Radcliffe
Andrew L. Joyce
Rupert M. A. Connell
Caroline L. Whiteley
David A. Walter
Malcolm Peter Robson
Anthony L. Brockbank
Robert T.J. Bond

For full biographical listings, see the Martindale-Hubbell Law Directory

FRIED, FRANK, HARRIS, SHRIVER & JACOBSON

4 Chiswell Street, London EC1Y 4UP
Telephone: 011-44-171-972-9600
Fax: 011-44-171-972-9602
Telex: 011-44-171-972-9602
Email: info@ffhsj.com
Other London, England Office: International Securities Unit, 21 Wilson Street, London EC2M 2TX.
Telephone: 011-44-171-825-3093.
New York, New York Office: One New York Plaza, 10004.
Telephone: 212-859-8000.
Cable Address: "Steric New York." W.U. Intl.
Telex: 662119. W.U. Domestic: 128173.
Telecopier: 212-859-4000 (Dex 6200).
Washington, D.C. Office: Suite 800, 1001 Pennsylvania Avenue, N.W., 20004-2505.
Telephone: 202-639-7000.
Los Angeles, California Office: 350 South Grand Avenue, 32nd Floor.
Telephone: 213-473-2000.
Paris, France Office: 7, Rue Royale, 75008.
Telephone: (011 331) 40 17 04 04.
Fax: (011 331) 40 17 08 30.

(See Next Column)

FRIED, FRANK, HARRIS, SHRIVER & JACOBSON, *London—Continued*

PARTNERS

Jerry L. Smith (Not admitted in England)
Robert P. Mollen (Not admitted in England)
Timothy E. Peterson (Not admitted in England; International Securities Unit)
Karen C. Wiedemann (Not admitted in England)

RESIDENT ASSOCIATES

Daniel J. Bursky (Not admitted in England)
Sean M. Flynn (Not admitted in England)
Alon Harnoy (Not admitted in England)
Angelique C. Mamby (Not admitted in England)
Angelique C. Mamby (Not admitted in England)
Michael B. Robinson (Not admitted in England)
Federico Salinas (Not admitted in England)
Federico Salinas (Not admitted in England)
Steven R. Schultz (Not admitted in England)
Brian Whaley (Not admitted in England)

(Not admitted to practice in English courts)

For full biographical listings, see the Martindale-Hubbell Law Directory

HOGAN & HARTSON L.L.P.

One Angel Court, London
Telephone: +(44) 207-367-0200
Fax: +(44) 207-367-0220
URL: www.hhlaw.com
Washington, D.C. Office: Columbia Square, 555 13th Street, N.W.
Telephone: 206-637-5600.
Telex: 89-2757.
Cable Address: "Hogander Washington".
Fax: 202-637-5910.
Brussels, Belgium Office: Avenue des Arts 41, 1040.
Telephone: (32.2) 505.09.11.
Fax: (32.2) 505.09.96.
Budapest, Hungary (Affiliated Office): Nagy & Pintér, Hogan & Hartson Law Office, Bank Center, Granite Tower, 9th Floor, Budapest V., Szabadsag ter 7, 1944 Hungary.
Telephone: (36-1) 302-9050.
Fax: (36-1) 302-9060.
Moscow, Russia Office: 33/2 Usacheva Street, Building 3, 119048.
Telephone: (7095) 245-5190. Int'l
Telephone: (7501) 907-0451.
Fax: (7095) 245-5192. Int'l
Fax: (7501) 907-0462.
Paris, France (Affiliated Office): Cariddi, Mee, Rué, Avocats Associés à la Cour de Paris, 12, rue de la Paix, 75002.
Telephone: (33-1) 42.61.57.71.
Fax: (33-1) 42.61.79.21.
Prague, Czech Republic (Affiliated Office): Hogan & Hartson, Advokátní Kanceláře, v.o.s., Trziste 13, 118 00.
Telephone: (420-2) 2211-7111.
Fax: (420-2) 2211-7222.
Warsaw, Poland Office: Hogan & Hartson Sp.zo.o, Atrium Tower, Al. Jana Pawla II 25, 00-854.
Telephone: (48-22) 653-4200.
Fax: (48-22) 653-4250.
Baltimore, Maryland Office: 111 South Calvert Street.
Telephone: 410-659-2700.
Fax: 410-539-6981.
Rockville, Maryland Office: 600 Jefferson Plaza, Suite 203.
Telephone: 301-315-2206.
Fax: 301-315-9046.
Boulder, Colorado Office: 1800 Broadway, Suite 200.
Telephone: 720-406-5300.
Fax: 720-406-5301.
Colorado Springs, Colorado Office: Two North Cascade Avenue, Suite 1300.
Telephone: 719-448-5900.
Fax: 719-448-5922.
Denver, Colorado Office: One Tabor Center, Suite 1500, 1200 Seventeenth Street.
Telephone: 303-899-7300.
Fax: 303-899-7333.
Los Angeles, California Office: Biltmore Tower, 500 S. Grand Avenue, Suite 1900.
Telephone: 213-337-6700.
Fax: 213-337-6701.
Newport Beach, California Office: 4675 MacArthur Court, Suite 670.
Telephone: 949-250-4550.
Fax: 949-833-0976.
McLean, Virginia Office: 8300 Greensboro Drive.
Telephone: 703-610-6100.
Fax: 703-610-6200.
New York, New York Office: 885 Third Avenue, 26th Floor.
Telephone: 212-409-9800.
Fax: 212-409-9801.

PARTNERS

Raymond J. Batla, Jr. (Not admitted in England)
Colin W. Craik
Daniel H. Maccoby
Michael A. Proett (Not admitted in England)

(See Next Column)

ASSOCIATE

Susan S. Namkung (Not admitted in England)

For full biographical listings, see the Martindale-Hubbell Law Directory

HOLME ROBERTS & OWEN LLP

U.S. Counsellors at Law
Heathcoat House, 3rd Floor, 20 Savile Row, London W1X 1AE
Telephone: 011-44-171-494-5600
Telecopier: 011-44-171-287-9344
Email: hro@hro.com *URL:* http://www.hro.com
Denver, Colorado Office: Suite 4100, 1700 Lincoln, 80203.
Telephone: 303-861-7000.
Telecopier: 303-866-0200.
Boulder, Colorado Office: Suite 400, 1401 Pearl Street, 80302.
Telephone: 303-444-5955.
Telecopier: 303-444-1063.
Colorado Springs, Colorado Office: Suite 1300, 90 South Cascade Avenue, 80903.
Telephone: 719-473-3800.
Telecopier: 719-633-1518.
Salt Lake City, Utah Office: Suite 1100, 111 East Broadway, 84111.
Telephone: 801-521-5800.
Telecopier: 801-521-9639.

PARTNERS OF FIRM

Bruce R. Kohler (Not admitted in England; Managing Partner)
Michael H. Prosser
Martha Traudt Collins Rolle (Not admitted in England)
Paul G. Thompson (Not admitted in England)

ASSOCIATES

Lisa McGee Allen (Not admitted in England)
Karen J. Ebert (Not admitted in England)
Tara M. Schiller
Annette M. Schüller (Not admitted in England)

(Not admitted to practice in English courts)

For full biographical listings, see the Martindale-Hubbell Law Directory

JONES, DAY, REAVIS & POGUE

Bucklersbury House, 3 Queen Victoria Street, London EC4N 8NA
Telephone: 44-20-7236-3939
Telecopier: 44-20-7236-1113
Email: counsel@jonesday.com *URL:* http://www.jonesday.com
In Atlanta, Georgia: 3500 SunTrust Plaza, 303 Peachtree Street.
Telephone: 404-521-3939.
Telecopier: 404-581-8330.
In Brussels, Belgium: Avenue Louise 480, 7th Floor. B-1050 Brussels.
Telephone: 32-2-645-14-11.
Telecopier: 32-2-645-14-45.
In Chicago, Illinois: 77 West Wacker.
Telephone: 312-782-3939.
Telecopier: 312-782-8585.
In Cleveland, Ohio: North Point, 901 Lakeside Avenue.
Telephone: 216-586-3939.
Telecopier: 216-579-0212.
In Columbus, Ohio: 1900 Huntington Center.
Telephone: 614-469-3939.
Telecopier: 614-461-4198.
In Dallas, Texas: 2727 North Harwood Street.
Telephone: 214-220-3939.
Telecopier: 214-969-5100.
In Frankfurt, Germany: Hochhaus am Park, Grüneburgweg 102, 60323 Frankfurt am Main.
Telephone: 49-69-9726-3939.
Telecopier: 49-69-9726-3993.
In Geneva, Switzerland: 20, rue de Candolle.
Telephone: 41-22-320-2339.
Telecopier: 41-22-320-1232.
In Hong Kong: 29th Floor, Entertainment Building, 30 Queen's Road Central.
Telephone: 852-2526-6895.
Telecopier: 852-2868-5871.
In Irvine, California: 5 Park Plaza, Suite 1100.
Telephone: 949-851-3939.
Telecopier: 949-553-7539.
In Los Angeles, California: 555 West Fifth Street, Suite 4600.
Telephone: 213-489-3939.
Telecopier: 213-243-2539.
In New York, New York: 599 Lexington Avenue.
Telephone: 212-326-3939.
Telecopier: 212-755-7306.
In Paris, France: 120, rue du Faubourg Saint-Honoré.
Telephone: 33-1-56-59-39-39.
Telecopier: 33-1-56-59-39-38
In Pittsburgh, Pennsylvania: 500 Grant Street, 31st Floor.
Telephone: 412-391-3939.
Telecopier: 412-394-7959.

(See Next Column)

JONES, DAY, REAVIS & POGUE—*Continued*

In Riyadh, Saudi Arabia: The International Law Firm (In Association with Jones, Day, Reavis & Pogue), Sulaymaniyah, Prince Mishari IBN, Abdulaziz Street, P.O. Box 22166.
Telephone: (966-1) 462-8866.
Telecopier: (966-1 462-9001.
In Shanghai, China: 2805 Kerry Centre, 1515 Nanjing Road West.
Telephone: 86-21-5298-6568.
Telecopier: 86-21-5298-6569.
In Sydney, Australia: Governor Phillip Tower, Level 38, 1 Farrer Place.
Telephone: 61-2-9210-6921.
Telecopier: 61-2-9210-6926.
In Taipei, Taiwan: 8th Floor, 2 Tun Hwa South Road, Section 2.
Telephone: (886-2) 2704-6808.
Telecopier: (886-2) 2704-6791.
In Tokyo, Japan: Toranomon 45 Mori Building, 3rd Floor, 1-5, Toranomon 5-Chome, Minato-Ku, Tokyo 105, Japan.
Telephone: 81-3-3433-3939.
Telecopier: 81-3-5401-2725.
In Washington, D.C.: 51 Louisiana Avenue, N.W.
Telephone: 202-879-3939.
Telecopier: 202-626-1700.

MEMBERS OF FIRM IN LONDON

Hugh W. Chapman	Robert L. Thomson
Peter E. Faber	Jai S. Pathak (Not admitted in England)
Stephen E. Fiamma (Not admitted in England)	Keith Featherstone

ASSOCIATES

Elizabeth A. Oberle-Robertson	Martin J.C. Scott
Nicholas M. Alfille	Annabel M. Grout
Jane D. Wessel	Hugh Naylor
Maryann Clemente (Not admitted in England)	Jeremy R. Davis
Linda E. Fletcher	Nicholas D. Smith
Guy B. Abbiss	Laura E. Hegedus (Not admitted in England)
Lee M. Coffey	Nicholas P. Cotter
Vimal Tilakapala	Rachel C. Smith
Donald C. Irvine	Rachel E. Evans
Martin S. Rowley (Not admitted in England)	Alper Deniz
Robert E. Gaut	Karen B. Elizaga (Not admitted in England)

STAFF ATTORNEY

Mary-Beth L. Hawrish	Penelope I. Richardson (Not admitted in England)

(Not admitted to practice in English courts)

For full biographical listings, see the Martindale-Hubbell Law Directory

KIRKLAND & ELLIS

A Partnership including Professional Corporations
International Financial Centre, Old Broad Street, London EC2N 1HQ
Telephone: 171-816-8700; New Telephone Effective April 1, 2000: 207-816-8700
Facsimile: 171-816-8800
Chicago, IL, Los Angeles, CA, Washington, DC & New York, NY
URL: http://www.kirkland.com
Chicago, Illinois Office: 200 East Randolph Drive.
Telephone: 312-861-2000.
Facsimile: 312-861-2200.
Telex: 25-4361.
Los Angeles, California Office: 777 South Figueroa Street.
Telephone: 213-680-8400.
Facsimile: 213-680-8500.
Washington, D.C. Office: 655 Fifteenth Street, N.W.
Telephone: 202-879-5000.
Facsimile: (202) 879-5200.
New York, New York Office: Citicorp Center, 153 East 53rd Street.
Telephone: 212-446-4800.
Facsimile: 212-446-4900.

RESIDENT PARTNERS

Samuel A. Haubold (P.C.) (Not admitted in England)	Stuart L. Mills (Not admitted in England)
Barbara Ann Jones (Not admitted in England)	M. Gilbey Strub (Not admitted in England)

RESIDENT ASSOCIATES

Aaron Edward Alt (Not admitted in England)	Caroline Paranikas (Not admitted in England)
Pragati "Peggy" Balsawer (Not admitted in England)	Mark S. Silver (Not admitted in England)
Allison I. Brown (Not admitted in England)	John B. Van de North, III (Not admitted in England)
Srinivas S. Kaushik (Not admitted in England)	Candace E. Wilhelm (Not admitted in England)
Siyamak (Sam) Pakbaz (Not admitted in England)	

(Not admitted to practice in English Courts)

For full biographical listings, see the Martindale-Hubbell Law Directory

MAYER, BROWN & PLATT

(Mayer, Friedlich, Spiess, Tierney, Brown & Platt)
Bucklersbury House, 3 Queen Victoria Street, London EC4N 8EL
Telephone: 011-44-171-246-6200
Facsimile: 011-44-171-329-4465
Telex: 8811095
Cable: LEMAYLDN
URL: http://www.mayerbrown.com
Berlin, Germany Office: Breite Strasse 29, Muehlendamm, 10178.
Telephone: 011-49-30-2060-7710.
Facsimile: 011-49-30-2060-7744.
Chicago, Illinois Office: 190 South LaSalle Street, 60603-3441.
Telephone: (312) 782-0600.
Facsimile: (312) 701-7711.
Telex: 190404.
Cable: LEMAY.
Charlotte, North Carolina Office: 100 North Tryon Street, Suite 2400.
Telephone: (704) 444-3500.
Fax: (704) 377-2033.
Cologne, Germany Office: Kaiser-Wilhelm-Ring 27-29, 50672.
Telephone: 011-49-221-5771-100.
Facsimile: 011-49-221-5771-199.
Houston, Texas Office: 700 Louisiana Street, Suite 3600, 77002-2730.
Telephone: (713) 221-1651.
Facsimile: (713) 224-6410.
Telex: 775809.
Cable: LEMAYHOU.
Los Angeles, California Office: 350 South Grand Avenue, 25th Floor, 90071-1503.
Telephone: (213) 229-9500.
Facsimile: (213) 625-0248.
Telex: 188089.
Cable: LEMAYLA.
New York, New York Office: 1675 Broadway, 10019-5820.
Telephone: (212) 506-2500.
Facsimile: (212) 262-1910.
Telex: 701842.
Cable: LEMAYEN.
Washington, D.C. Office: 1909 K Street, N.W., 20006-1101.
Telephone: (202) 263-3000.
Facsimile: (202) 263-3300.
Telex: 892603.
Cable: LEMAYDC.
Representative Offices:
Ashgabat, Turkmenistan: 28 Gogol Street, 744000.
Telephone: 011-99-312-355247.
Facsimile: 011-99-312-510074.
Bishkek, Kyrgyz Republic: 66 Kalyka Akieva Str. 720010.
Telephone: 011-996-312-65-02-56.
Facsimile: 011-996-312-65-09-80.
Tashkent, Republic of Uzbekistan: 3rd Floor, 1 Turab Tula Street, 700003.
Telephone: 011-998-71-1206-627.
Facsimile: 011-998-71-1206-329.
Mexico City, Mexico, D.F., Independent Mexico Correspondent: Jáuregui, Navarrete, Nader y Rojas, S.C., Torre Arcos, paseo de los Tamarindos No. 400-B. Col. Bosques de las Lomas, 05120.
Telephone: 011-525-267-45-00.
Facsimile: 011-525-267-45-99.
Paris, France, Independent Paris Correspondent: Lambert & Lee, 13 Avenue Hoche, 75008.
Telephone: 011-33-1-53-53-43-43.
Facsimile: 011-33-1-53-96-03-83.

PARTNERS

Richard A. Cole (Not admitted in England)	Denis Petkovic
Ian R. Coles	Mark R. Uhrynuk (Not admitted in England)
Steven P. Janes	Nigel Weiss
Nabil L. Khodadad (Not admitted in England)	Nigel A. Wright

COUNSEL

Robert M. Lyons

ASSOCIATES

Christopher A. Badham	Benedict P. O'Halloran
Lela C. Bristol (Not admitted in England)	Michael Pabst (Not admitted in England)
Kimberly J. Heimert (Not admitted in England)	Martin Reid
Romanie Jade Hollingworth	Adam Sanitt
Sergei A. Lomako (Not admitted in England)	Francis John Sergejew
Anna Lilley	Dominic Spacie
Sally N. Mills	Zane Tominna
Stephen G. Milne	Stuart Tyler
	Annika L. Westling (Not admitted in England)

For full biographical listings, see the Martindale-Hubbell Law Directory

Milbank, Tweed, Hadley & McCloy LLP

Dashwood House, 69 Old Broad Street, London EC2M 1QS
Telephone: 44-207-448-3000
Fax: 44-207-448-3029
Email: postmaster@milbank.com *URL:* http://www.milbank.com
Offices of an Affiliated Partnership:
New York, New York Office: 1 Chase Manhattan Plaza, 10005-1413.
Telephone: 212-530-5000.
Fax: 212- 530-5219.
Midtown Office: 375 Park Avenue, Suite 3601, 10152.
Telephone: 212-530-5800.
Fax: 212-530-0158.
Los Angeles, California Office: 601 South Figueroa Street, 90017.
Telephone: 213-892-4000.
Fax: 213-629-5063.
Washington, D.C. Office: International Square Building, Suite 1100, 1825 Eye Street, N.W., 20006.
Telephone: 202-835-7500.
Fax: 202-835-7586.
Tokyo, Japan Office: Fukoku Seimei Building, 2-2, Uchisaiwai-cho 2-chome, Chiyoda-ku, Tokyo 100-0011, Japan.
Telephone: 81-3-3504-1050.
Fax: 81-3-3595-2790; 81-3-3595-2840.
Hong Kong Office: 3007 Alexandra House, 16 Chater Road.
Telephone: 852-2971-4888.
Fax: 852-2840-0792; 852-2845-9046.
Singapore Office: 14-00 Caltex House, 30 Raffles Place, 048622.
Telephone: 65-428-2400.
Fax: 65-428-2500.
Moscow, Russia Office: 24/27 Sadovaya-Samotyochnaya, Moscow, 103051.
Telephone: 7-501-258-5015.
Fax: 7-501-258-5014.

PARTNERS

John Dewar
Phillip D. Fletcher (Not admitted in England)
Mark Frewin
Michael W. Goroff (Not admitted in England)
Thomas B. Siebens (Not admitted in England)
Jane Templeton-Knight

ASSOCIATES

Elizabeth E. Bauza (Not admitted in England)
Henry J. Cort
Lonnie S. Keene (Not admitted in England)
Agnieszka Klich (Not admitted in England)
Jonathan W. Nash
Swati Patel
Delia Poon (Not admitted in England)
Ronald D. Stuber
Andrew Welbourn
Melanie J. Wilson (Not admitted in England)

(Not admitted to practice in English courts)

For full biographical listings, see the Martindale-Hubbell Law Directory

Shearman & Sterling

Broadgate West, 9 Appold Street, London EC2A 2AP
Telephone: 011-44-20-7655-5000
Fax: 011-44-20-7655-5500
URL: http://www.shearman.com
New York, N.Y. Office: 599 Lexington Avenue, New York, New York, 10022-6069.
Telephone: (212) 848-4000.
Telex: 667290. Num Lau.
Fax: (212) 848-7179.
Abu Dhabi, United Arab Emirates Office: Butti Al Otaiba Building, 13th Floor, Suite 1302, Sheikh Khalifa Street, P.O. Box 2948.
Telephone: (971-2) 6274477.
Fax: (971-2) 6268933.
Beijing, People's Republic of China Office: Suite #2205, Capital Mansion, No. 6, Xin Yuan Nan Road. Chao Yang District, Beijing, 100004.
Telephone: (86-10) 6465-2299.
Fax: (86-10) 6465-4578.
Düsseldorf, Federal Republic of Germany Office: Couvenstrasse 8 40211 Düsseldorf.
Telephone: (49 211) 178 88-0.
Fax: (49 211) 178 88-88.
Frankfurt, Federal Republic of Germany Office: Trianon Building, Mainzer Landstrasse 16, 60325 Frankfurt am Main.
Telephone: (49-69) 9711-1000.
Fax: (49-69) 9711-1100.
Hong Kong Office: Standard Chartered Bank Building, 4 Des Voeux Road, Central.
Telephone: (852) 2978-8000.
Fax: (852) 2978-8099.
Menlo Park, California Office: 1550 El Camino Real, 94025-4100.
Telephone: (650) 330-2200.
Fax: (650) 330-2299.
Paris, France Office: 114, avenue des Champs-Elysées, 75008.
Telephone: (33-1) 53-89-7000.
Fax: (33-1) 53-89-7070.
San Francisco, California Office: 555 California Street, 94104-1522.
Telephone: (415) 616-1100.
Fax: (415) 616-1199.

(See Next Column)

Singapore Office: 6 Battery Road #25-03. Singapore 049909.
Telephone: (65) 230-3800.
Fax: (65) 230-3899.
Tokyo, Japan Office: Fukoku Seimei Building, 5th Fl. 2-2-2, Uchisaiwaicho, Chiyoda-ku, Tokyo 100-0011. Japan.
Telephone: (81 3) 5251-1601.
Fax: (81 3) 5251-1602.
Toronto, Ontario, Canada Office: Commerce Court West, Suite 4405, P.O. Box 247, M5L 1E8.
Telephone: (416) 360-8484.
Fax: (416) 360-2958.
Washington, D.C. Office: 801 Pennsylvania Avenue, N.W., 20004-2604.
Telephone: (202) 508-8000.
Fax: (202) 508-8100.

RESIDENT PARTNERS

Pamela M. Gibson (Not admitted in England; Managing Partner)
Clifford Atkins
James M. Bartos (Not admitted in England)
David J. Beveridge (Not admitted in England)
Nicholas Buckworth
Iain M. Goalen
Adrian Knight
W. Jeffrey Lawrence (Not admitted in England)
Kenneth MacRitchie
Stephen Mostyn-Williams
Stephen Peppiatt
Bernie J. Pistillo, Jr. (Not admitted in England)
Nigel J. Thompson
Rupert D.E. Walker
Anthony Ward
William J. Wiegmann (Not admitted in England)
John D. Wilson (Not admitted in England)

RESIDENT ASSOCIATES

Rajinder Bassi
Vanessa Beever
Amy C Bevacqua
Nicola Blair
Michael S. Bosco (Not admitted in England)
Sarah Brufal
Philip T. Chase, II (Not admitted in England)
Christopher G. Colbridge
Rebecca A. Connolly
Robin S. Dinning
Philippa Dodd
Boris Dolgonos (Not admitted in England)
Jaquelyn Fahey
Nicola Ferguson (Not admitted in England)
Janet R. Firkin
Simon Fraser (Not admitted in England)
Leonard Shui-Kei Fung
Shobha V. George (Not admitted in England)
Bruce A. Hendry (Not admitted in England)
Leigh Hoolihan
Beatriz P. Kanitz (Not admitted in England)
Stephen L. Kenyon-Slade (Not admitted in England)
Kelly Anne Knight
Caroline Leeds
Gabrielle C. Lese
Karen Madorsky (Not admitted in England)
David S. Manny
Marco A. Martins (Not admitted in England)
Kevin A. McGuire (Not admitted in England)
J. Warden McKimm (Not admitted in England)
Mary Jo Naples Miller (Not admitted in England)
Laura S. Miller (Not admitted in England)
Dr. Gábor Molnár (Not admitted in England)
Stephanus J. Naudé (Not admitted in England)
Julia Newlove
Gregor D. Page
Edward J. Park (Not admitted in England)
Duncan Perry
Penny A. Pilzer (Not admitted in England)
Andrew R. Powell
Shaun Rixon
Shalini Sequeira
Ben Shorten
Sanja L. Udovicic
Ann H. Wagner (Not admitted in England)
Robert Watt (Not admitted in England)
Leigh White
Gabrielle C. Wong (Not admitted in England)
Peter J. T. Wright
Peter J. Young

(Not admitted to practice in English courts)

For full biographical listings, see the Martindale-Hubbell Law Directory

Simpson Thacher & Bartlett

99 Bishopsgate, London EC2M 3YH
Telephone: 207 422-4000
Telecopier: 207 422-4022
URL: http://www.simpsonthacher.com
New York, NY Office: 425 Lexington Avenue, 10017-3954.
Telephone: 212-455-2000.
Telecopier: 212-455-2502. ESL 62928462.
Columbus, Ohio Office: One Riverside Plaza, 43215.
Telephone: 614-461-7799.
Telecopier: 614-461-0040.
Los Angeles, California Office: 10 Universal City Plaza, Suite 1850, Universal City, CA, 91608.
Telephone: 818-755-7000.
Fax: 818-755-7009.
Palo Alto, California Office: 3373 Hillview Avenue, 94304.
Telephone: 650-251-5000.
Telecopier: 650-251-5002.
Tokyo Office: Ark Mori Building, 30th Floor, 12-32, Akasaka 1-Chome, Minato-Ku, Tokyo 107, Japan.
Telephone: 81-3-5562-8601.
Telecopier: 81-3-5562-8606. ESL 62765846.

(See Next Column)

SIMPSON THACHER & BARTLETT—*Continued*

Hong Kong Office: Asia Pacific Finance Tower - 7th Floor, 3 Garden Road, Central, Hong Kong.
Telephone: 852-2514-7600.
Telecopier: 852-2869-7694.
Singapore Office: Suntec Tower One, 33rd Floor, 7 Temasek Boulevard, Singapore 038987.
Telephone: 65-430-5100.
Fax: 65-430-5151.

RESIDENT PARTNERS

Gregory W. Conway (Not admitted in England)
William R. Dougherty (Not admitted in England)
Walter A. Looney Jr. (Not admitted in England)
Michael O. Wolfson (Not admitted in England)

RESIDENT ASSOCIATES

Monte H. Baier (Not admitted in England)
Christopher Evison (Not admitted in England)
Michael T. Fahey (Not admitted in England)
Gregory M. King (Not admitted in England)
Karen Matsushima King (Not admitted in England)
Bradley Joseph Kurkowski (Not admitted in England)

(Not admitted to practice in English courts)

For full biographical listings, see the Martindale-Hubbell Law Directory

SQUIRE, SANDERS & DEMPSEY

Royex House, Aldermanbury Square, London EC2V 7HR
Telephone: 44-171-776-5200
Fax: 44-171-776-5233
URL: http://www.ssd.com
Cincinnati, Ohio Office: PNC Center, 201 East Fifth Street, Suite 1700, Cincinnati, Ohio 45202.
Telephone: 513-361-1200.
Fax: 513-361-1201.
Cleveland, Ohio Office: 4900 Key Tower, 127 Public Square, Cleveland, Ohio 44114-1304.
Telephone: 216-479-8500.
Fax: 216-479-8780.
Columbus, Ohio Office: 1300 Huntington Center, 41 South High Street, Columbus, Ohio 43215-6150.
Telephone: 614-365-2700.
Fax: 614-365-2499.
Houston, Texas Office: 6250 Chase Tower, 600 Travis Street, Houston, Texas 77002-3007.
Telephone: 713-546-5850.
Fax: 713-546-5830.
Jacksonville, Florida Office: One Enterprise Center, Suite 2100, 225 Water Street, Jacksonville, Florida 32202-4424.
Telephone: 904-366-2420.
Fax: 904-356-2986.
Miami, Florida Office: 201 South Biscayne Boulevard, 2900 Miami Center, Miami, Florida 33131-4330.
Telephone: 305-577-8700.
Fax: 305-358-1425.
New York, New York Office: 350 Park Avenue, New York, New York 10022-6002.
Telephone: 212-872-9800.
Fax: 212-872-9815.
Phoenix, Arizona Office: Two Renaissance Square, 40 North Central Avenue, Suite 2700, Phoenix, Arizona 85004-4498.
Telephone: 602-528-4000.
Fax: 602-253-8129.
Washington, D.C. Office: 1201 Pennsylvania Avenue, N.W., Suite 500, Washington, D.C. 20004-2491.
Telephone: 202-626-6600.
Fax: 202-626-6780.
Almaty, Kazakhstan Office: 141 Albay Khan Avenue, Second Floor, Almaty, Kazakhstan 480091.
Telephone: +73-27-50-11-25.
Fax: +73-27-50-11-25.
Bratislava, Slovak Republic Office: Zochova 5, 811 03 Bratislava, Slovak Republic.
Telephone: 421-7-5441-7611.
Fax: 42-1-7-6280-2212.
Brussels, Belgium Office: Avenue Louise, 165 Box 15, 1050 Brussels, Belgium.
Telephone: 32-2-627-1111.
Fax: 32-2-627-1100.
Budapest, Hungary Office: H-1062 Budapest, Andrassy ut. 64, Budapest, Hungary.
Telephone: 36-1-428-7111.
Fax: 36-1-428-7100.
Kyiv, Ukraine Office: 14A Yaroslaviv Val, Kyiv 252034, Ukraine.
Telephone: 38-044-228-8687.
Fax: 38-044-228-4938.
Madrid, Spain Office: Calle Velazquez 108-110, 28006 Madrid, Spain.
Telephone: 34-91-590-2420.
Fax: 34-91-590-2421.
Moscow, Russian Federation Office: Paveletskaya Square II, 1 Valovaya Street, 5th Floor, Moscow 113054, Russian Federation.
Telephone: 7-501-258-5250.
Fax: 7-501-258-5251.

(See Next Column)

Prague, Czech Republic Office: Václavské náměst 1 57/813, 110 00 Praha 1, Czech Republic.
Telephone: 420-2-2166-2111.
Fax: 420-2-2166-2222.
Hong Kong Office: Rooms 1101-2 St. George's Building, 2 Ice House Street, Central, Hong Kong.
Telephone: 852-2509-9732.
Fax: 852-2509-9772.
Taipei, Taiwan Office: 14F, 116 Nanking East Road, Sec. 2, Taipei, Taiwan, Republic of China.
Telephone: 886-2-2531-2888.
Fax: 886-2-2571-6199.

PARTNERS

Cathy B. Horton (Not admitted in England)
Joseph P. Markoski (Not admitted in England)
James A. Nimmo
Richard Sterling Surrey
Carol M. Welu

OF COUNSEL

Michael J. Sussman (Not admitted in England)

ASSOCIATES

Abayomi Akinjide
Miranda L. Cole
Sara Johns
Ann Marie Kearney
Deborah Robson

For full biographical listings, see the Martindale-Hubbell Law Directory

SULLIVAN & CROMWELL

St. Olave's House, 9a Ironmonger Lane, London EC2V 8EY
Telephone: (011)(44171)710-6500
Telecopier: (011)(44171)710-6565
URL: http://www.sullcrom.com
New York City Office: 125 Broad Street, 10004-2498.
Telephone: 212-558-4000.
Telex: 62694.
Telecopier: 212-558-3588 or 212-514-5706.
Washington, D.C. Office: 1701 Pennsylvania Avenue, N.W., 20006-5805.
Telephone: 202-956-7500.
Telecopier: 202-293-6330.
Los Angeles, California Office: 1888 Century Park East, 90067-1725.
Telephone: 310-712-6600.
Telecopier: 310-712-8800.
Paris Office: 8, Place Vendôme, 75001 Paris, France.
Telephone: (011)(331) 44 50 60 00.
Telex: 240654.
Telecopier: (011)(331) 44 50 60 60 or (011)(331) 42 60 56 36.
Melbourne Office: 101 Collins Street, Melbourne, Victoria 3000, Australia.
Telephone: (011)(613) 9635-1500.
Telecopier: (011)(613) 9654-2422.
Tokyo Office: Sullivan & Cromwell, Gaikokuho Jimu Bengoshi Jimusho, Akai Law Offices (Registered Associated Offices), Otemachi First Square East Tower 16F, 5-1, Otemachi 1-chome, Chiyoda-ku, Tokyo 100-0004, Japan.
Telephone: (011)(813) 3213-6140.
Telecopier: (011)(813) 3213-6470 or (011)(813) 3213-6477.
Hong Kong Office: 28th Floor, Nine Queen's Road, Central, Hong Kong.
Telephone: (011)(852) 2826-8688.
Telecopier: (011)(852) 2522-2280.
Frankfurt Office: Neue Mainzer Strasse 52, 60322 Frankfurt, Germany.
Telephone: (011)(4969) 7191 26-0.
Telecopier: (011)(4969) 7191 26-10.
Beijing Office: The Beijing Representative Office of Sullivan & Cromwell, Suite 501, China World Trade Center, No. 1 Jianguo Menwai Avenue, Beijing 100004, P.R.C.
Telephone: (011)(86) 10 6505 6120.
Telecopier: (011)(86) 10 6505 6136.

PARTNERS IN LONDON

Robert M. Osgood
William A. Plapinger
George H. White III (Also at Frankfurt Office)
Richard C. Morrissey
Scott D. Miller
Kathryn Ann Campbell

EUROPEAN COUNSEL IN LONDON

John O'Connor
Stephen C. Connor

ASSOCIATES IN LONDON

Christopher B. Bernard
Jennifer E. Brady
Selene Brett
Roberto Bruno
Daniel G. Dufner, Jr.
Nina R. Evison
Matthew M. Friestedt (Not admitted in England)
Sherry K. Holbrook (Not admitted in England)
Craig Joffe
Craig Jones
Antony G. Page
Thomas W. Laryea
Carl B. McCarthy
Samuel Neal McKnight
Ivan J. Presant
Robert M. Schlein
Benjamin H. Schwartz
Christine A. Spillane
Kimberly Woolley (Not admitted in England)

SPECIAL COUNSEL

Michael B. Miller

For full biographical listings, see the Martindale-Hubbell Law Directory

VINSON & ELKINS

Registered Foreign Lawyers and Solicitors
Regis House, 8th Floor, 45 King William Street, London EC4R 9AN
Telephone: (44-171) 618-6000
Fax: (44-171) 618-6001
URL: http://www.velaw.com
Austin, Texas Office: One American Center Suite 2700, 600 Congress Avenue, Austin, Texas, 78701-3200.
Telephone: 512-495-8400.
Fax: 512-495-8612.
Beijing, China Office: 20/F, Beijing Silver Tower, No. 2, Dong San Huan Bei Lu, Chaoyang District, 100027.
Telephone: +86-10-6410-6300.
Fax: +86-10-6410-6360.
Dallas, Texas Office: 3700 Trammell Crow Center, 2001 Ross Avenue, Dallas, Texas, 75201-2975.
Telephone: 214-220-7700.
Fax: 214-220-7716.
Houston, Texas Office: 2300 First City Tower, 1001 Fannin, Houston, Texas, 77002-6760.
Telephone: 713-758-2222.
Fax: 713-758-2346.
Moscow, Russia Office: 16 Ulitsa Spiridonovka, Second Floor, 103001 Moscow, Russia.
Telephone: (7-095) 956-1995. Local
Fax: (7-095) 956-1996. U.S. Satellite
Fax: (212) 803-0142.
New York, N.Y. Office: 1325 Avenue of the Americas, 17th Floor, New York, N.Y., 10019.
Telephone: 917-206-8000.
Fax: 917-206-8100.
Singapore Office: 6 Battery Road, #39-01, Singapore, 049909.
Telephone: (65) 536-8300.
Fax: (65) 536-8311.
Washington, D.C. Office: The Willard Office Building, 1455 Pennsylvania Avenue, N.W., Washington, D.C., 20004-1008.
Telephone: 202-639-6500.
Fax: 202-639-6604.

RESIDENT PARTNERS

Christopher Clement-Davies
Paul C. Deemer
(Not admitted in England)
Jeffrey E. Eldredge
(Not admitted in England)
Douglas B. Glass
(Not admitted in England)
John C. LaMaster
(Not admitted in England)
A. Sam MacGibbon

RESIDENT ASSOCIATES

Artem V. Faekov
(Not admitted in England)
Marc C. Hammerson
Mathew C. Kidwell
Alexander Msimang
Christopher J. Prior
Andrew M. Wright
(Not admitted in England)
Peter C. Yam

For full biographical listings, see the Martindale-Hubbell Law Directory

WHITE & CASE

7-11 Moorgate, London EC2R 6HH
Telephone: (44-20) 7600-7300
Facsimile: (44-20) 7600-7030
URL: http://www.whitecase.com
Los Angeles, California:
Telephone: 213-620-7700.
Facsimile: 213-687-0758; 213-452-2330; 213-452-2331.
Palo Alto, California:
Telephone: 650-213-0300.
Facsimile: 650-213-8158.
San Francisco, California:
Telephone: 415-544-1100.
Facsimile: 415-544-0202.
Miami, Florida:
Telephone: 305-371-2700.
Facsimile: 305-358-5744; 305-358-5766.
New York, New York:
Telephone: 212-819-8200.
Facsimile: 212-354-8113.
Washington, D.C.:
Telephone: 202-626-3600.
Facsimile: 202-639-9355.
Bratislava, Slovak Republic:
Telephone: (421-7) 5441-5100.
Facsimile: (421-7) 5441-6100.
Brussels, Belgium:
Telephone: (32-2) 219-16-20.
Facsimile: (32-2) 219-16-26.
Budapest, Hungary: Réczicza Law Firm White & Case.
Telephone: (36-1) 488-5200.
Facsimile: (36-1) 488-5299.
Frankfurt, Germany: White & Case (Rechtsanwälte).
Telephone: (49-69) 713-77-(0).
Facsimile: (49-69) 713-77-100.
Helsinki, Finland: Asianajotoimisto White & Case Oy.
Telephone: (358-9) 228-641.
Facsimile: (358-9) 228-64228.

(See Next Column)

Istanbul, Turkey:
Telephone: (90-212) 275-75-33.
Facsimile: (90-212) 275-75-43.
Moscow, Russia:
Telephone: (7-095) 787-3000.
Facsimile: (7-095) 787-3001.
Paris, France:
Telephone: (33-1) 55-04-15-15.
Facsimile: (33-1) 55-04-15-16.
Prague, Czech Republic:
Telephone: (420-2) 2481-0808; 2481-1796.
Facsimile: (420-2) 2481-0330; 2481-0252.
Stockholm, Sweden: White & Case Advokat AB.
Telephone: (46-8) 506-323-00.
Facsimile: (46-8) 611-21-22.
Warsaw, Poland: White & Case (Poland) Sp. z o.o.
Telephone: (48-22) 625-33-33; (48-22) 622-67-67; (48-39) 12-19-06.
Facsimile: (48-22) 628-22-28.
Johannesburg, Republic of South Africa:
Telephone: 27 (11) 884-7689.
Facsimile: 27 (11) 884-7229.
Almaty, Kazakhstan:
Telephone: (7-3272) 50-74-91.
Facsimile: (7-3272) 50-74-93.
Ankara, Turkey:
Telephone: (90-312) 442-5680.
Facsimile: (90-312) 442-5691/4.
Bangkok, Thailand: White & Case (Thailand) Limited.
Telephone: (662) 656-1721 to 32.
Facsimile: (662) 656-1733/34.
Bombay/Mumbai, India: Liaison Office, (91-22) 282-6300/01/02/03.
Facsimile: (91-22) 282-6305.
Hanoi, Vietnam:
Telephone: (84-4) 934-5355.
Facsimile: (84-4) 934-5356.
Ho Chi Minh City, Vietnam:
Telephone: (84-8) 821-0888.
Facsimile: (84-8) 823-6902.
Hong Kong: White & Case, Solicitors.
Telephone: (852) 2822-8700.
Facsimile: (852) 2845-9070.
Singapore, Republic of Singapore:
Telephone: (65) 225-6000.
Facsimile: (65) 225-6009.
Tokyo, Japan: White & Case Kandabashi Law Offices.
Telephone: (81-3) 3259-0200.
Facsimile: (81-3) 3259-0150.
Manama, Bahrain:
Telephone: (973) 9610105; (973) 9610119; (973) 535965.
Facsimile: (973) 590962; (973) 532342.
Jeddah, Saudi Arabia: Law Office of Hassan Mahassni,
Telephone: (966-2) 665-4353.
Facsimile: (966-2) 669-2996.
Riyadh, Saudi Arabia: Law Office of Hassan Mahassni,
Telephone: (966-1) 464-4006.
Facsimile: (966-1) 465-1348.
Mexico City, Mexico: White & Case, S.C.
Telephone: (52) 5-540-9600.
Facsimile: (52) 5-540-9699.
São Paulo, SP, Brazil:
Telephone: (55-11) 3171-0011.
Facsimile: (55-11) 3171-0041.
Associated Law Firm(s):
Bombay/Mumbai, India: India Law Services (ILS).
Telephones: (91-22) 284-1995; (91-22) 284-1847.
Facsimile: (91-22) 285-0824.
New Delhi, India: India Law Services (ILS).
Telephone: (91-11) 697-1602/3/4.
Facsimile: (91-11) 698-8860.
Jakarta, Indonesia: Ali Budiardjo, Nugroho, Reksodiputro, Counsellors at Law.
Telephone: (62-21) 250-5125; 250-5136.
Facsimile: (62-21) 250-5392; 250-5122; 250-5001.
Associated Consultancies:
Jakarta, Indonesia: PT WCI Konsultan.
Telephone: (62-21) 577-1527.
Facsimile: (62-21) 577-1535/6.

RESIDENT PARTNERS

Alasdair Bell
(Not admitted in England)
John M. H. Bellhouse
Jonathan M. Clark, Jr.
(Not admitted in England)
Margaret B. Cole
Margaret R. Cole
David M. Eisenberg
(Not admitted in England)
Peter Finlay
Francis Fitzherbert-Brockholes
Gregory J. Hammond
Jon Lang
David Llewelyn
Mats Sacklén
(Not admitted in England)
H. Philip T. Stopford

COUNSEL

Hugh Brett
John F. Runeckles
(Not admitted in England)

(See Next Column)

WHITE & CASE—*Continued*

ASSOCIATES

David G. Baker
Ellis D. Baker
Jane M.Q. Ballantyne
Richard J. Bamforth
Robyn A. Chew
Paul Christensen (Not admitted in England)
Marcus Collins
Nicholas Collins
Rebecca Cox
Aydin A. Düren (Not admitted in England)
Gilead Halevy
Adrian Horne
Jason Kerr
Joshua G. Kiernan (Not admitted in England)
Thomas Leo Madden (Not admitted in England)
Paul A. Marchand
Richard G. Marlin (Not admitted in England)
Craig R. Nethercott
Christine Poyer (Not admitted in England)
Kaya H. Proudian (Not admitted in England)
Aloke Ray
Diane Mage Roberts
Zurina Saban (Not admitted in England)
Sirak Solomon (Not admitted in England)
Julie Breene Smith
Miles Thomas
Seema Shah Wadhwani (Not admitted in England)
Andrew C. Weiler (Not admitted in England)
Stuart Weir
Anuita Woodhull
Andrew Wright

For full biographical listings, see the Martindale-Hubbell Law Directory

---

WHITMAN BREED ABBOTT & MORGAN LLP

A Multi-National Partnership
11 Waterloo Place, London SW1Y 4AU
Telephone: 71-839-3226
Cable Address: "Whitsom London SW1"
Telex: 917881
Telecopier: 71-839-6741
Email: wbam@wbam.com *URL:* http://www.wbam.com
New York, N.Y. Office: 200 Park Avenue, 10166.
Telephone: 212-351-3000.
Los Angeles, California Office: 633 West Fifth Street, 90071.
Telephone: 213-896-2400.
Greenwich, Connecticut Office: 100 Field Point Road, 06830.
Telephone: 203-869-3800.
Newark, New Jersey Office: One Gateway Center, 07102-5398.
Telephone: 973-621-2230.
Palm Beach, Florida Office: 220 Sunrise Avenue, 33480.
Telephone: 407-832-5458.
Tokyo, Japan Office: Suite 450, New Otemachi Building, 2-2-1 Otemachi, Chiyoda-Ku, Tokyo 100.
Telephone: 81-3-3242-1289.
Beirut, Lebanon Office: Tyan & Associes, 22, La Sagesse Street-Rmeil, Lebanon.
Telephone: (961) (1) 56 16 73; (961) (1) 56 16 74.
Fax: (961) (1) 56 14 35

MEMBERS OF FIRM

Graeme H. Clark
Jon H. I. Grouf (Not admitted in England)
Michael J. McNulty (Not admitted in England)
Berge Setrakian
Elton Shane

COUNSEL

Gordon L. Jaynes (Not admitted in England)

For full biographical listings, see the Martindale-Hubbell Law Directory

---

WILLKIE FARR & GALLAGHER

35 Wilson Street, London EC2M 2SJ
Telephone: 011-44-171-696-9060
Fax: 011-44-171-417-9191
New York, N.Y. Office: The Equitable Center, 787 Seventh Avenue, 10019-6099.
Telephone: 212-728-8000.
Fax: 212-728-8111.
Washington, D.C. Office: Three Lafayette Centre, 1155 21st Street, N.W., 20036-3384.
Telephone: 202-328-8000.
Fax: 202-887-8979; 202-331-8187.
Paris, France Office: 21-23 rue de la Ville l' Evêque, 75008.
Telephone: 011-33-1-53-43-45-00.
Fax: 011-33-1-40-06-96-06.

PARTNER

William N. Dye (Not admitted in England)

(Not admitted to practice in English courts)

For full biographical listings, see the Martindale-Hubbell Law Directory

---

WILMER, CUTLER & PICKERING

Registered Foreign Lawyers and Solicitors
4 Carlton Gardens, London SW1Y 5AA
Telephone: +44 (20) 7 872 1000
Fax: +44 (20) 7 839 3537
Email: Law@Wilmer.Com *URL:* http://www.wilmer.com
Washington, D.C. Office: 2445 M Street, N.W., 20037-1420.
Telephone: 202-663-6000.
Fax: 202-663-6363. Internet: Law@Wilmer.Com.
Baltimore, Maryland Office: 100 Light Street, 21202.
Telephone: 410-986-2800.
Fax: 410-986-2828.
New York, New York Office: 520 Madison Avenue, 10022.
Telephone: 212-230-8800.
Fax: 212-230-8888.
Brussels, Belgium Office: Rue de la Loi 15# Wetstraat. B-1040.
Telephone: +32 (2) 285 49 00.
Fax: +32 (2) 285 49 49.
Berlin, Germany Office: Friedrichstrasse 95, D-10117.
Telephone: +49 (30) 20 22 64 00.
Fax: +49 (30) 20 22 65 00.

RESIDENT PARTNERS

Dieter G. F. Lange (Not admitted in England)
Paul Mitchard
Gary B. Born (Not admitted in England)
Andrew K. Parnell
Michael R. Holter

COUNSEL

John J. Kallaugher

ASSOCIATES

Joseph R. Profaizer
Reinhard Schu (Not admitted in England)

For full biographical listings, see the Martindale-Hubbell Law Directory

---

WINTHROP, STIMSON, PUTNAM & ROBERTS

54 Lombard Street, London EC3V HDH
Telephone: 011-44207-648-9200
Telefax: 011-44207-283-1656
Cable Address: "Winstim, London EC2"
Telex: 8950511 ONEONE G BOX 24723001
URL: http://www.winstim.com
New York Main Office: One Battery Park Plaza, New York, N.Y., 10004-1490.
Telephone: 212-858-1000.
Fax: 212-858-1500.
Stamford, Connecticut Office: Financial Centre, 695 East Main Street, P.O. Box 6760, 06904-6760.
Telephone: 203-348-2300.
Fax: 203-965-8226.
Washington, D.C. Office: 1133 Connecticut Avenue, N.W., 20036.
Telephone: 202-775-9800.
Fax: 202-833-8491.
Palm Beach, Florida Office: 125 Worth Avenue, Suite 310, 33480.
Telephone: 561-655-7297.
Fax: 561-833-6726.
Tokyo, Japan Office: 608 Atagoyama Bengoshi Building 6-7, Atago 1-chome, Minato-ku, Tokyo 105 Japan.
Telephone: 011-813-3437-9740.
Fax: 011-813-3437-9261.
Hong Kong, China Office: 2505 Asia Pacific Finance Tower, Citibank Plaza, 3 Garden Road, Central.
Telephone: 011-852-2530-3400.
Fax: 011-852-2530-3355.
Singapore Office: 6 Battery Road #38-01/B, Singapore 049909.
Telephone: 65-227-4700.
Fax: 65-227-4711.

RESIDENT PARTNERS

Peter S. Brown (Not admitted in England)
John D. White

RESIDENT ASSOCIATES

Timothy Fanning (Not admitted [illegible] the United States) (Legal [illegible]onsultant on the Laws of [illegible]ngland)
Stefanie L. Roth (Not adm[illegible] England)
Jo Scotnery

(Not admitted to practice in English courts)

For full biographical listings, see the Martindale-Hubbell Law Directory

Canadian Lawyers In London

BLAKE, CASSELS & GRAYDON LLP

7th Floor, 10 Lloyd's Avenue, London EC3N 3AX
Telephone: (011) 44-171-680-4600
Facsimile: (011) 44-171-680-4646
Email: blakes@bcg-mail.win-uk.net *URL:* http://www.blakes.com
The Firm maintains other offices in: Toronto and Ottawa, Ontario, Calgary, Alberta, Vancouver, British Columbia and Beijing, China.

(See Next Column)

CARIDDI, MEE, RUÉ, AVOCATS ASSOCIÉS à LA COUR DE PARIS, *Paris—Continued*

AVOCATS á LA COUR
(MEMBERS OF PARIS BAR)
ALSO PARTNERS IN HOGAN & HARTSON L.L.P.

Alan F. Cariddi
Bijan-Emmanuel Eghbal
Bruce C. Mee
Fabrice Rué

COUNSEL TO CARIDDI, MEE, RUm
(NOT MEMBERS OF PARIS BAR)
PARTNERS IN HOGAN & HARTSON L.L.P.

Mark E. Mazo

INTERNATIONAL COUNSEL

Christine Bougis
Vuong Van Bac (Counsel and International Counsel to Hogan & Hartson L.L.P.)

RESIDENT ASSOCIATES

Delphine Benabou
Estelle Créteur
Hervé De Kervasdoué
Frédérique Schlumberger
David W. Smail
Carol A. F. Umhoefer (Not admitted in France)

For full biographical listings, see the Martindale-Hubbell Law Directory

CLEARY, GOTTLIEB, STEEN & HAMILTON

41, Avenue de Friedland, 75008 Paris
Telephone: 33-1-40-74-68-00
Facsimile: 33-1-45-63-66-37
New York, New York Office: One Liberty Plaza, New York, N.Y. 10006.
Telephone: 212-225-2000.
Washington, D.C. Office: 2000 Pennsylvania Avenue, N.W., Suite 9000, Washington, D.C. 20006-1801.
Telephone: 202-974-1500.
Brussels, Belgium Office: Rue de la Loi 23, 1040 Brussels, Belgium.
Telephone: 32-2-287-2000.
London, England Office: City Place House, 55 Basinghall Street, London EC2V 5EH England.
Telephone: 44-71-614-2200.
Hong Kong Office: 39th Floor, Bank of China Tower, One Garden Road, Hong Kong.
Telephone: 852-2521-4122.
Tokyo, Japan Office: Cleary, Gottlieb, Steen & Hamilton Gaikokuho Jimubengoshi Jimusho, 20th Floor, Shin Kasumigaseki Building, 3-2, Kasumigaseki 3-Chome, Chiyoda-Ku, Tokyo 100-0013, Japan.
Telephone: 81-3-3595-3911.
Frankfurt, Germany Office: Main Tower, Neue Mainzer Strasse 52, 60311 Frankfurt am Main, Germany.
Telephone: 49-69-971-03-0.
Rome, Italy Office: Piazza di Spagna 15, 00187 Rome, Italy.
Telephone: 39-06-69-52-22-1.

COUNSEL

Richard H. Moore
Donald L. Holley
Bernard Josien
Roger J. Benrubi

PARTNERS

Jean-Michel Tron
Jean-Pierre Vignaud
Gilles Entraygues
William B. McGurn, III
Robert Bordeaux-Groult
François Jonemann
Jean-Marcel Cheyron
Antoine Winckler
Laurent Cohen-Tanugi
Arnaud de Brosses
Jean-Marie Ambrosi
Andrew A. Bernstein
Pierre-Yves Chabert
Jean-Yves Garaud
Fabrice Baumgartner
Francois Brunet

RESIDENT ASSOCIATES

Mark A. Adams (Not admitted in France)
Stephanie Beghe
Sacha Benichou
Bruno Bertrand
Nathalie Bouche
Manuela Caruso
Stephane Chaouat
Austin B. Clayton (Not admitted in France)
Philippe Despres
Karina Dimidjian (Not admitted in France)
Estelle Dougier
Emmanuel Dresch
Alexandre Duval-Stalla
Daniel Ehrmann
Madeleine Fabre
Romain Ferla
Chantal Genermont (Not admitted in France)
Frederic Grillier
Sebastien Guyot de la Pommeraye
Vanessa Jaeger
Patrick Ledoux
Thierry Leleu
Valerie Lemaitre
Ayélé V. Locoh-Donou
François Mary
Elodie Maxime-Leclere
Gwenaël Muguet-Poullennec (Not admitted in France)
Catherine Peulve
Claire Picard
Laurence Remond
Olivier Renault
Mark D. Rollinger (Not admitted in France)
Isabelle Simon
Renaud Thominette (Not admitted in France)
Marie-Laurence Tibi
Antoine Verny
Olivier de Vilmorin

For full biographical listings, see the Martindale-Hubbell Law Directory

CURTIS, MALLET-PREVOST, COLT & MOSLE LLP

15 rue d'Astorg, 75008 Paris
Telephone: +33-1 42-66-39-10
Fax: +33-1 42-66-39-62.
Email: info@cm-p.com *URL:* http://www.cm-p.com
New York, New York Office: 101 Park Avenue.
Telephone: 212-696-6000.
Telecopier: 212-697-1559.
Newark, New Jersey Office: One Gateway Center, Suite 403.
Telephone: 973-622-0605.
Telecopier: 973-622-5646.
Washington, D.C. Office: Suite 1205L, 1801 K Street, N.W.
Telephone: 202-452-7373.
Telecopier: 202-452-7333.
Houston, Texas Office: 2 Houston Center, 909 Fannin Street, Suite 3725.
Telephone: 713-759-9555.
Telecopier: 713-759-0712.
Stamford, Connecticut Office: One Canterbury Green.
Telephone: 203-359-6200.
Telecopier: 203-328-2617.
Mexico City, D.F., Mexico Office: Curtis, Mallet-Prevost, Colt & Mosle, Ruben Dario 281, Piso 9, Col. Bosque de Chapultepec, 11530 Mexico, D.F.
Telephone: 525-282-0444.
Telecopier: 525-282-0637.
London, England Office: Two Throgmorton Avenue, EC2N 2DL.
Telephone: 0207-638-7957.
Telecopier: 0207-638-5512.
Frankfurt am Main 1, Germany Office: Staufenstrasse 42.
Telephone: 69-971-4420.
Telecopier: 69-17 33 99.
Muscat, Sultanate of Oman Office: Jewel Beach-134.
Telephone: 968-607-725.
Telecopier: 968-607-724.
Milan, Italy Office: Curtis, Mallet-Prevost & Gilioli, Piazzale Principessa Clotilde 8, 20121.
Telephone: (39) 02 29 00 29 32.
Telefax: (39) 02 65 75 969.

PARTNERS

Geoffroy P. Lyonnet
Peter M. Wolrich

RESIDENT ASSOCIATE

Emmanuel R. Buet

For full biographical listings, see the Martindale-Hubbell Law Directory

DAVIS POLK & WARDWELL

Paris Office Established in 1962
15, avenue Matignon, 75008 Paris
Telephone: 33-01-56-59-36-00
Fax: 33-01-56-59-36-90
URL: http://www.dpw.com
New York, N.Y. Office: 450 Lexington Avenue, 10017.
Telephone: 212-450-4000.
Fax: 212-450-4800.
Washington, D.C. Office: 1300 I Street, N.W., 20005.
Telephone: 202-962-7000.
Fax: 202-962-7111.
Menlo Park, California Office: 1600 El Camino Real, Menlo Park, California, 94025.
Telephone: 650-752-2000.
Fax: 650-752-2195.
London, England Office: 99 Gresham Street, London EC2V 7NG, England.
Telephone: 44-171-418-1300.
Fax: 44-171-418-1400.
Tokyo, Japan Office: Akasaka Twin Tower East, 11th Floor, 17-22, Akasaka 2-Chome, Minato-ku, Tokyo 107-0052, Japan.
Telephone: 81-3-5561-4421.
Fax: 81-3-5561-4425.
Frankfurt, Germany Office: MesseTurm, 60308 Frankfurt am Main, Germany.
Telephone: 49-69-97-57-03-0.
Telecopier: 49-69-74-77-44.
Hong Kong, China Office: The Hong Kong Club Building, 3A Chater Road, Hong Kong.
Telephone: 852-2533-3300.
Fax: 852-2533-3388.

MEMBERS OF FIRM

Patrick S. Kenadjian (Not admitted in France)
Thomas J. Reid (Not admitted in France)

COUNSEL

Nancy J. Marchand

RESIDENT ASSOCIATES

Kathleen de Carbuccia
Pippa F. Tubman (Not admitted in France)

(Firm not admitted to practice in French Courts reserved for Avocats)

For full biographical listings, see the Martindale-Hubbell Law Directory

DEBEVOISE & PLIMPTON

21 Avenue George V, 75008 Paris
Telephone: (33-1) 40 73 12 12
Telecopier: (33-1) 47 20 50 82.
Telex: 648141F DPPAR
New York Office: 875 Third Avenue, 10022.
Telephone: 212-909-6000.
Telex: (Domestic) 148377 DEBSTEVE NYK.
Telecopier: (212) 909-6836.
Washington, D.C. Office: 555 13th Street, N.W., 20004.
Telephone: 202-383-8000.
Telex: 405586 DPDC WUUD.
Telecopier: (202) 383-8118.
London, England Office: Old Broad Street, EC2N 1HQ.
Telephone: (44-171) 786-9000.
Telex: 884569 DPLON G
Facsimile: (44-171) 588-4180.
Hong Kong Office: 13/F Entertainment Building, 30 Queen's Road Central.
Telephone: (852) 2160-9800.
Fax: (852) 2810-9828.
Moscow, Russia Representative Office: Debevoise & Plimpton, LLC, Bolshoi Palashevsky Pereulok 13/2, 4th Floor, 103104.
Telephone: 7 (095 or 503) 956-3858.
Fax: 7 (095 or 503) 956-3868.

James A. Kiernan III (Also at London, England Office)
David F. Hickok
Antoine F. Kirry

INTERNATIONAL COUNSEL

James Cecil Swank
Ann G. Baker
Antoine d'Ornano

ASSOCIATES

Gérard Dufrêne
Sylvie DeParis-Maze
Mariana Gonatas
Geoffrey Kittredge (Not admitted in France)
Jean-Louis Martin
Michael M. Ostrove (Not admitted in France)
Pascal Bine
Charles E. Malone (Not admitted in France)
Melanie Johnson (Not admitted in France)
Marc Castagnède
Wolfgang T. Hohensee (Not admitted in France)
Julie Perchenet
Etienne Pujol
David M. Reilly (Not admitted in France)
Julie Rosaz
Philippe Raybaud

For full biographical listings, see the Martindale-Hubbell Law Directory

DECHERT PRICE & RHOADS

Correspondance Organique
55, avenue Kléber, 76116 Paris
Telephone: 33-(0) 1-53 65 05 00
Fax: 33-(0) 1-53 65 05 05
URL: http://www.dechert.com
Philadelphia, Pennsylvania: 4000 Bell Atlantic Tower, 1717 Arch Street, 19103-2793.
Telephone: (215) 994-4000.
New York, New York: 30 Rockefeller Plaza, 10112.
Telephone: (212) 698-3500.
Washington, D.C.: 1775 Eye Street, N.W., 20006.
Telephone: (202) 261-3300.
Boston, Massachusetts: Ten Post Office Square South, 02109-4603.
Telephone: (617) 728-7100.
Princeton, New Jersey: Princeton Pike Corporate Center, P.O. Box 5218, 08543-5218.
Telephone: (609) 620-3200.
Harrisburg, Pennsylvania: Thirty North Third Street, 17101-1603.
Telephone: (717) 237-2000.
Hartford, Connecticut: 90 State House Square, 06103-3702.
Telephone: 860-524-3999.
London, England: 2 Serjeants' Inn, EC4Y 1LT.
Telephone: (44 171) 583-5353. (Also see Titmuss Sainer Dechert).
Brussels, Belgium: 65 Avenue Louise 1050.
Telephone: (32 2) 535-5411.

RESIDENT PARTNERS

Kathie D. Claret
Joseph J. Smallhoover

ASSOCIATES

Christian Cano
Vincent Coq

For full biographical listings, see the Martindale-Hubbell Law Directory

FRIED, FRANK, HARRIS, SHRIVER & JACOBSON

Correspondance Organique
7, Rue Royale, Paris 75008
Telephone: (011 331) 40 17 04 04
Fax: (011 331) 40 17 08 30
New York, New York Office: One New York Plaza, 10004.
Telephone: 212-859-8000.
Cable Address: "Steric New York." W.U. Int.
Telex: 662119. W.U. Domestic: 128173.
Telecopier: 212-859-4000 (Dex 6200).

(See Next Column)

Washington, D.C. Office: Suite 800, 1001 Pennsylvania Avenue, N.W., 20004-2505.
Telephone: 202-639-7000.
Los Angeles, California Office: 350 South Grand Avenue, 32nd Floor.
Telephone: 213-473-2000.
London, England Office: 4 Chiswell Street, London EC1Y 4UP.
Telephone: 011-44-171-972-9600.
Fax: 011-44-171-972-9602.
Other London, England Office: International Securities Unit, 21 Wilson Street, London EC2M 2TX.
Telephone: 011-44-171-825-3093.

PARTNER

Eric M. Cafritz

ASSOCIATES

Laurent Assaya
FrédériqueJais Emery
Patrick Guerin (Not admitted in France)
Melanie Lanoë (Not admitted in France)
Thomas E. Moore (Not admitted in France)
Erwan Heurtel
J. Christian Nahr (Not admitted in France)
Elisabeth Villame (Not admitted in France)

For full biographical listings, see the Martindale-Hubbell Law Directory

JONES, DAY, REAVIS & POGUE

120, rue du Faubourg Saint-Honoré, 75008 Paris
Telephone: 33-1-56-59-39-39
Telecopier: 33-1-56-59-39-38
Email: counsel@jonesday.com *URL:* http://www.jonesday.com
InAtlanta, Georgia: 3500 SunTrust Plaza, 303 Peachtree Street.
Telephone: 404-521-3939.
Telecopier: 404-581-8330.
In Brussels, Belgium: Avenue Louise 480, 7th Floor. B-1050 Brussels.
Telephone: 32-2-645-14-11.
Telecopier: 32-2-645-14-45.
In Chicago, Illinois: 77 West Wacker.
Telephone: 312-782-3939.
Telecopier: 312-782-8585.
In Cleveland, Ohio: North Point, 901 Lakeside Avenue.
Telephone: 216-586-3939.
Telecopier: 216-579-0212.
In Columbus, Ohio: 1900 Huntington Center.
Telephone: 614-469-3939.
Telecopier: 614-461-4198.
In Dallas, Texas: 2727 North Harwood Street.
Telephone: 214-220-3939.
Telecopier: 214-969-5100.
In Frankfurt, Germany: Hochhaus am Park, Grüneburgweg 102, 60323 Frankfurt am Main.
Telephone: 49-69-9726-3939.
Telecopier: 49-69-9726-3993.
In Geneva, Switzerland: 20, rue de Candolle.
Telephone: 41-22-320-2339.
Telecopier: 41-22-1232.
In Hong Kong: 29th Floor, Entertainment Building, 30 Queen's Road Central.
Telephone: 852-2526-6895.
Telecopier: 852-2868-5871.
In Irvine, California: 5 Park Plaza, Suite 1100.
Telephone: 949-851-3939.
Telecopier: 949-553-7539.
In London, England: Bucklersbury House, 3 Queen Victoria Street.
Telephone: 44-20-7236-3939.
Telecopier: 44-20-7236-1113.
In Los Angeles, California: 555 West Fifth Street, Suite 4600.
Telephone: 213-489-3939.
Telecopier: 213-243-2539.
In New York, New York: 599 Lexington Avenue.
Telephone: 212-326-3939.
Telecopier: 212-755-7306.
In Pittsburgh, Pennsylvania: 500 Grant Street, 31st Floor.
Telephone: 412-391-3939.
Telecopier: 412-394-7959.
In Riyadh, Saudi Arabia: The International Law Firm (In Association with Jones, Day, Reavis & Pogue), Sulaymaniyah, Prince Mishari IBN, Abdulaziz Street, P.O. Box 22166.
Telephone: (966-1) 462-8866.
Telecopier: (966-1) 462-9001.
In Shanghai, China: 2805 Kerry Centre, 1515 Nanjing Road West.
Telephone: 86-21-5298-6568.
Telecopier: 86-21-5298-6569.
In Sydney, Australia: Governor Phillip Tower, Level 38, 1 Farrer Place.
Telephone: 61-2-9210-6921.
Telecopier: 61-2-9210-6926.
In Taipei, Taiwan: 8th Floor, 2 Tun Hwa South Road, Section 2.
Telephone: (886-2) 2704-6808.
Telecopier: (886-2) 2704-6791.
In Tokyo, Japan: Toranomon 45 Mori Building, 3rd Floor, 1-5, Toranomon 5-Chome, Minato-Ku, Tokyo 105 Japan.
Telephone: 81-3-3433-3939.
Telecopier: 81-3-5401-2725.

(See Next Column)

JONES, DAY, REAVIS & POGUE, *Paris—Continued*

In Washington, D.C.: 51 Louisiana Avenue, N.W.
Telephone: 202-879-3939.
Telecopier: 202-626-1700.

MEMBERS OF FIRM IN PARIS

John F. Crawford	Michael W. Bühler
Pierre Ullmann	Gael P. Saint Olive
Philippe Billot	Peter R. Sternberg
Wesley R. Johnson, Jr.	François Bonteil
Edward J. Nalbantian	Sophie Hagège

OF COUNSEL

Anne C. Boileau

COUNSEL

Marie-Laure Larget-Bozonnet	Carroll S. Dorgan

Lucie A. Carswell Parmentier

ASSOCIATES

Agnès L. Férey	Adrien Moser
Pierre-Nicolas Ferrand	My Linh X. Vu-Gregoire
Carol Khoury (Not admitted in France)	Herminie Monmignaut
Arnaud G. Vanbremeersch	Paul-Emmanuel Benachi
Anne G. Vrignaud	Marine Guyon
Vincent Agulhon	Alexa Sempiana
Emmanuelle Rivez-Domont	Roland Guény
Sonia de Kondserovsky	Frédérique Protin
Gabriel M. Klarsfeld (Not admitted in France)	Nataline Zarifiau
	Helen A. Conybeare Williams

For full biographical listings, see the Martindale-Hubbell Law Directory

PAUL, WEISS, RIFKIND, WHARTON & GARRISON

62, rue du Faubourg Saint-Honoré, 75008 Paris
Telephone: (33-1) 53.43.14.14
Facsimile: (33-1) 53.43.00.23
Email: mailbox@paulweiss.com *URL:* http://www.paulweiss.com
NewYork, N.Y. Office: 1285 Avenue of the Americas, 10019-6064.
Telephones: 212-373-3000, TDD 212-373-2000;
Facsimile: 212-757-3990.
Washington, D.C. Office: 1615 L Street, NW, Suite 1300, 20036-5694.
Telephones: 202-223-7300, TDD 202-223-7490.
Facsimile: 202-223-7420.
Tokyo, Japan Office: Fukoku Seimei Building, 2-2 Uchisaiwaicho 2-chome, Chiyoda-ku, Tokyo 100-0011, Japan.
Telephone: (81-3) 3597-8101.
Facsimile: (81-3) 3597-8120.
Beijing, China Office: 2918 China World Tower II, No. 1 Jianguomenwai Dajie, 100004.
Telephones: (86-10) 6505-6882.
Facsimile: (86-10) 6505-6830.
Hong Kong, China Office: 12th Floor, Hong Kong Club Building, 3A Chater Road, (Central) Hong Kong.
Telephone: (852) 2536-9933.
Facsimile: (852) 2536-9622.

RESIDENT PARTNERS

Dominique Fargue	Steven E. Landers

Steven L. Wolfram

COUNSEL

Joseph S. Iseman

RESIDENT ASSOCIATES

Katia Chéron	Kate V. Romain (Not admitted in France)
Tania Glowinski	
Stephanie Leclaire	Naïma Zitouni

(Firm registered as Conseils Juridiques, not admitted to practice in French Courts reserved for Avocats)

For full biographical listings, see the Martindale-Hubbell Law Directory

SHEARMAN & STERLING

114, avenue des Champs-Elysées, 75008 Paris
Telephone: (33-1) 53-89-7000
Fax: (33-1) 53-89-7070
URL: http://www.shearman.com
New York, N.Y. Office: 599 Lexington Avenue, New York, New York, 10022-6069.
Telephone: (212) 848-4000.
Telex: 667290. Num Lau.
Fax: (212) 848-7179.
Abu Dhabi, United Arab Emirates Office: Butti Al Otaiba Building, 13th Floor, Suite 1302, Sheikh Khalifa Street, P.O. Box 2948.
Telephone: (971-2) 6274477.
Fax: (971-2) 6268933.
Beijing, People's Republic of China Office: Suite #2205, Capital Mansion, No. 6, Xin Yuan Nan Road. Chao Yang District, Beijing, 100004.
Telephone: (86-10) 6465-2299.
Fax: (86-10) 6465-4578.
Düsseldorf, Federal Republic of Germany Office: Couvenstrasse 8 40211 Düsseldorf.
Telephone: (49 211) 178 88-0.
Fax: (49 211) 178 88-88.

(See Next Column)

Frankfurt, Federal Republic of Germany Office: Trianon Building, Mainzer Landstrasse 16, 60325 Frankfurt am Main.
Telephone: (49-69) 9711-1000.
Fax: (49-69) 9711-1100.
Hong Kong Office: Standard Chartered Bank Building, 4 Des Voeux Road, Central.
Telephone: (852) 2978-8000.
Fax: (852) 2978-8099.
London, England Office: Broadgate West, 9 Appold Street, London EC2A 2AP.
Telephone: 011-44-20-7655-5000.
Fax: 011-44-20-7655-5500.
Menlo Park, California Office: 1550 El Camino Real, 94025-4100.
Telephone: (650) 330-2200.
Fax: (650) 330-2299.
San Francisco, California Office: 555 California Street, 94104-1522.
Telephone: (415) 616-1100.
Fax: (415) 616-1199.
Singapore Office: 6 Battery Road #25-03. Singapore 049909.
Telephone: (65) 230-3800.
Fax: (65) 230-3899.
Tokyo, Japan Office: Fukoku Seimei Building, 5th Fl. 2-2-2, Uchisaiwaicho, Chiyoda-ku, Tokyo 100-0011. Japan.
Telephone: (81 3) 5251-1601.
Fax: (81 3) 5251-1602.
Toronto, Ontario, Canada Office: Commerce Court West, Suite 4405, P.O. Box 247, M5L 1E8.
Telephone: (416) 360-8484.
Fax: (416) 360-2958.
Washington, D.C. Office: 801 Pennsylvania Avenue, N.W., 20004-2604.
Telephone: (202) 508-8000.
Fax: (202) 508-8100.
Budapest, Hungary Associated Office: Szerb Utca 17-19, 1056 Budapest.
Telephone: 36.1.266.3522.
Telefax: 36.1.266.3523.

RESIDENT PARTNERS

Isabelle Chauvet	Hervé Letréguilly
Emmanuel Gaillard (Managing Partner)	Cyrille Niedzielski
Robert C. Treuhold (Deputy Managing Partner)	Manuel A. Orillac
Christophe Dugué	John Savage
Jacques-Henri Epstein	Hubertus V. Sulkowski
	Sami L. Toutounji (Not admitted in France)

Jacques Wantz

OF COUNSEL

Robert A. MacCrindle	David T. McGovern

EUROPEAN COUNSEL

Bernard Carrez	Lee D. Neumann (Not admitted in France)
Eric Teynier	

CONSULTANT

Dominique Carreau (Not admitted in France)	Herve Synvet (Not admitted in France)

RESIDENT ASSOCIATES

Yas Banifatemi	Theresa M. Hinz (Not admitted in France)
Thomas Bieder	Michèle Hulin
Denis Boulianne (Not admitted in France)	Anne Sophie Kerfant
Nathalie Bouri	Francoise Sylvie Labrousse
Aline V. Cardin (Not admitted in France)	Rebekah Le Magny (Not admitted in France)
Colin D. Chang (Not admitted in France)	Sylvie Magnaval
Francesca Cinotti (Not admitted in France)	Yann Martin-Lavigne
B. Neil S. Clarke (Not admitted in France)	Marcia T. Moffat (Not admitted in France)
Christophe Clerc	Michèle F. Moss
Carlo Daneo (Not admitted in France)	Jacques Naquet-Radiguet
Julie de Cazenove	Pierre Pic
Severine de la Courtie	Philippe Pinsolle
Jenny A. Edelstein (Not admitted in France)	Bruno Ranger
Troy Edward Elder	David Reed (Not admitted in France)
Robert M. Ellison	Mathieu Remy
John Andre Felitti	Elodie Ribardiere-Le May
Jennifer B. Flanigan (Not admitted in France)	Armelle Santamans
Robert M. Flanigan (Not admitted in France)	Bertrand Senechal (Not admitted in France)
Valérie Gaillard	Luigi Sensi (Not admitted in France)
German Garcia-Cordero (Not admitted in France)	Casey Slamani
Sophie Gilg	Barbara C. Streichenberger
Arnaud-Tadzio Granger	Renée Thériault (Not admitted in France)
Peter R. Griffin	Emmanuelle Van Den Broucke
Linda A. Hesse (Not admitted in France)	Campbell Walker (Not admitted in France)
	Todd J. Wetmore (Not admitted in France)
	Anthony R. Wilson (Not admitted in France)

For full biographical listings, see the Martindale-Hubbell Law Directory

SULLIVAN & CROMWELL

8, Place Vendôme, 75001 Paris
Telephone: (011)(331)4450-6000
Telex: 240654
Telecopier: (011)(331)4450-6060
URL: http://www.sullcrom.com
New York City Office: 125 Broad Street, 10004-2498.
Telephone: 212-558-4000.
Telex: 62694.
Telecopier: 212-558-3588 or 212-514-5706.
Washington, D.C. Office: 1701 Pennsylvania Avenue, N.W., 20006-5805.
Telephone: 202-956-7500.
Telecopier: 202-293-6330.
Los Angeles, California Office: 1888 Century Park East, 90067-1725.
Telephone: 310-712-6600.
Telecopier: 310-712-8800.
London Office: St. Olave's House, 9a Ironmonger Lane, London EC2V 8EY, England.
Telephone: (011)(44207) 710 6500.
Telecopier: (011)(44207) 710 6565.
Melbourne Office: 101 Collins Street, Melbourne, Victoria 3000, Australia.
Telephone: (011)(613) 9635-1500.
Telecopier: (011)(613) 9654-2422.
Tokyo Office: Sullivan & Cromwell, Gaikokuho Jimu Bengoshi Jimusho, Akai Law Offices (Registered Associated Offices), Otemachi First Square East Tower 16F, 5-1, Otemachi 1-chome, Chiyoda-ku, Tokyo 100-0004, Japan.
Telephone: (011)(813) 3213-6140.
Telecopier: (011)(813) 3213-6470 or (011)(813) 3213-6477.
Hong Kong Office: 28th Floor, Nine Queen's Road, Central, Hong Kong.
Telephone: (011)(852) 2826-8688.
Telecopier: (011)(852) 2522-2280.
Frankfurt Office: Neue Mainzer Strasse 52, 60322 Frankfurt, Germany.
Telephone: (011)(4969) 7191 26-0.
Telecopier: (011)(4969) 7191 26-10.
Beijing Office: The Beijing Representative Office of Sullivan & Cromwell, Suite 501, China World Trade Center, No. 1 Jianguo Menwai Avenue, Beijing 100004, P.R.C.
Telephone: (011)(86) 10 6505 6120.
Telecopier: (011)(86) 10 6505 6136.

PARTNERS IN PARIS

Richard G. Asthalter
David F. Morrison (Also at Frankfurt Office)
Pierre Servan-Schreiber

EUROPEAN COUNSEL IN PARIS

Richard A. Kahn (Not admitted in France)

ASSOCIATES IN PARIS

Erwan Barre (Not admitted in United States)
Jean-Christophe Beaury
Daniel A. Cord (Not admitted in France)
Krystian Marek Czerniecki (Not admitted in France)
Kurt M. Lebakken (Not admitted in France)
Elise C. Masiée (Not admitted in France)
Brian J. Pierce (Not admitted in France)
Mark D. Wiseman (Not admitted in France)

(Firm not admitted to practice in French Courts reserved for Avocats)

For full biographical listings, see the Martindale-Hubbell Law Directory

WHITE & CASE

Limited Liability Partnership
11, Boulevard de la Madeleine, 75001 Paris
Telephone: +(33-1) 55-04-15-15
Facsimile: +(33-1) 55-04-15-16
URL: http://www.whitecase.com
Los Angeles, California:
Telephone: 213-620-7700.
Facsimile: 213-687-0758; 213-452-2330; 213-452-2331.
Palo Alto, California:
Telephone: 650-213-0300.
Facsimile: 650-213-8158.
San Francisco, California:
Telephone: 415-544-1100.
Facsimile: 415-544-0202.
Miami, Florida:
Telephone: 305-371-2700.
Facsimile: 305-358-5744; 305-358-5766.
New York, New York:
Telephone: 212-819-8200.
Facsimile: 212-354-8113.
Washington, D.C.:
Telephone: 202-626-3600.
Facsimile: 202-639-9355.
Bratislava, Slovak Republic:
Telephone: (421-7) 5441-5100.
Facsimile: (421-7) 5441-6100.
Brussels, Belgium:
Telephone: (32-2) 219-16-20.
Facsimile: (32-2) 219-16-26.

(See Next Column)

Budapest, Hungary: Réczicza Law Firm White & Case.
Telephone: (36-1) 488-5200.
Facsimile: (36-1) 488-5299.
Frankfurt, Germany: White & Case (Rechtsanwälte).
Telephone: (49-69) 713-77-(0).
Facsimile: (49-69) 713-77-100.
Helsinki, Finland: Asianajotoimisto White & Case Oy.
Telephone: (358-9) 228-641.
Facsimile: (358-9) 228-64228.
Istanbul, Turkey:
Telephone: (90-212) 275-75-33.
Facsimile: (90-212) 275-75-43.
London, England:
Telephone: (44-20) 7600-7300.
Facsimile: (44-20) 7600-7030.
Moscow, Russia:
Telephone: (7-095) 787-3000.
Facsimile: (7-095) 787-3001.
Prague, Czech Republic:
Telephone: (420-2) 2481-0808; 2481-1796.
Facsimile: (420-2) 2481-0330; 2481-0252.
Stockholm, Sweden: White & Case Advokat AB.
Telephone: (46-8) 506-323-00.
Facsimile: (46-8) 611-21-22.
Warsaw, Poland: White & Case (Poland) Sp. z o.o.
Telephone: (48-22) 625-33-33; (48-22) 622-67-67; (48-39) 12-19-06.
Facsimile: (48-22) 628-22-28.
Johannesburg, Republic of South Africa:
Telephone: 27 (11) 884-7689.
Facsimile: 27 (11) 884-7229.
Almaty, Kazakhstan:
Telephone: (7-3272) 50-74-91.
Facsimile: (7-3272) 50-74-93.
Ankara, Turkey:
Telephone: (90-312) 442-5680.
Facsimile: (90-312) 442-5691/4.
Bangkok, Thailand: White & Case (Thailand) Limited.
Telephone: (662) 656-1721 to 32.
Facsimile: (662) 656-1733/34.
Bombay/Mumbai, India: Liaison Office, (91-22) 282-6300/01/02/03.
Facsimile: (91-22) 282-6305.
Hanoi, Vietnam:
Telephone: (84-4) 934-5355.
Facsimile: (84-4) 934-5356.
Ho Chi Minh City, Vietnam:
Telephone: (84-8) 821-0888.
Facsimile: (84-8) 823-6902.
Hong Kong: White & Case, Solicitors.
Telephone: (852) 2822-8700.
Facsimile: (852) 2845-9070.
Singapore, Republic of Singapore:
Telephone: (65) 225-6000.
Facsimile: (65) 225-6009.
Tokyo, Japan: White & Case Kandabashi Law Offices.
Telephone: (81-3) 3259-0200.
Facsimile: (81-3) 3259-0150.
Manama, Bahrain:
Telephone: (973) 9610105; (973) 9610119; (973) 535965.
Facsimile: (973) 590962; (973) 532342.
Jeddah, Saudi Arabia: Law Office of Hassan Mahassni,
Telephone: (966-2) 665-4353.
Facsimile: (966-2) 669-2996.
Riyadh, Saudi Arabia: Law Office of Hassan Mahassni,
Telephone: (966-1) 464-4006.
Facsimile: (966-1) 465-1348.
Mexico City, Mexico: White & Case, S.C.
Telephone: (52) 5-540-9600.
Facsimile: (52) 5-540-9699.
São Paulo, SP, Brazil:
Telephone: (55-11) 3171-0011.
Facsimile: (55-11) 3171-0041.
Associated Law Firm(s):
Bombay/Mumbai, India: India Law Services (ILS).
Telephones: (91-22) 284-1995; (91-22) 284-1847.
Facsimile: (91-22) 285-0824.
New Delhi, India: India Law Services (ILS).
Telephone: (91-11) 697-1602/3/4.
Facsimile: (91-11) 698-8860.
Jakarta, Indonesia: Ali Budiardjo, Nugroho, Reksodiputro, Counsellors at Law.
Telephone: (62-21) 250-5125; 250-5136.
Facsimile: (62-21) 250-5392; 250-5122; 250-5001.
Associated Consultancies:
Jakarta, Indonesia: PT WCI Konsultan.
Telephone: (62-21) 577-1527.
Facsimile: (62-21) 577-1535/6.

RESIDENT PARTNERS

Paule Biensan
Stephen R. Bond
Jean-Luc Boussard
Nicholas Budd
Reinhard Dammann
Anthony Giustini
Rayner M. Hamilton (Not admitted in France)
François Leloup
Rosine Lorotte
Norbert Majerholc
Thomas J. McDonald

(See Next Column)

WHITE & CASE, *Paris—Continued*

RESIDENT PARTNERS (Continued)

Philippe Métais
Vincent Morin
Gilles Peigney
John H. Riggs
Christopher R. Seppala

RESIDENT COUNSEL

Michael T. Hancock

ASSOCIATES

Catherine Andrieux
Thierry Arachtingi
Jacques Bouillon
Nikko Chaudry
(Not admitted in France)
Paul Edouard Clos
(Not admitted in France)
Isabelle Combes
Edouard De Chavagnac
Christopher Dempsey
Laurent Develle
Suzanne Durdevic
John H. Elovson
(Not admitted in France)
François Farmine
Nicolas Huet
Alexandre Ippolito
John R. W. D. Jones
(Not admitted in France)
Beatrice Joyaud
Frederic Lafond
Pierre J. Lastenouse
(Not admitted in France)
Jean-Francois Le Corre
Serge Levine
Robert F. Mayo
(Not admitted in France)
Virginie Mosse
Mark B. Richards
(Not admitted in France)
Lola Schaufuss
Damien Schmitt
Monika Seidel-Moreau
Patrick Sergant
Kirk E. Sheriff
(Not admitted in France)
Gilles Veuillot
Anne Vincent
David Wadham
(Not admitted in France)
Sophie Waldberg

For full biographical listings, see the Martindale-Hubbell Law Directory

WILLKIE FARR & GALLAGHER

21-23 rue de la Ville l'Evêque, 75008 Paris
Telephone: 011-33-1-53-43-45-00
Fax: 011-33-1-40-06-96-06
URL: http://www.willkie.com
New York, N.Y. Office: The Equitable Center, 787 Seventh Avenue, 10019-6099.
Telephone: 212-728-8000.
Fax: 212-728-8111.
Washington, D.C. Office: Three Lafayette Centre, 1155 21st Street, N.W., 20036-3384.
Telephone: 202-328-8000.
Fax: 202-887-8979; 331-8787. 89-2762.
London, England Office: 35 Wilson Street, EC2M 2SJ.
Telephone: 011-44-171-696-9060.
Fax: 011-44-171-417-9191.

RESIDENT PARTNERS

Jean-Luc Cuadrado
Allard De Waal
Laurent Faugérolas
Michel Frieh
Daniel Hurstel
Jay F. Leary
Bernard Le-Pezron
Daniel Payan
Annette Peron
Emmanuel Rosenfeld

SPECIAL COUNSEL

Laurent Ménière

SPECIAL EUROPEAN COUNSEL

Pascal Chadenet
Jeffrey W. Fouts
Inès Le Gris

ASSOCIATES

Denis Barat
Christophe Bouchez
(Not admitted in France)
Etienne Boursican
Benedicte Bremond
Maud Bruchon
Sandrine Carteron
(Not admitted in France)
Anne Noëlle Charvillat-Carrez
Maxine Delpy
(Not admitted in France)
Estelle Dion
(Not admitted in France)
Guillaume Durand
Isabelle Eid
Amélie Fayet
Christophe Garaud
Jean-Marc Grosperrin
Philippe Grudé
Cedric Hajage
François d'Hautefeuille
(Not admitted in France)
Genevieve A. Helleringer
(Not admitted in France)
Clotilde Jurges
Laure Lagarde Seknadje
François Le Roquais
David Lussigny
Nicolas Ménard-Durand
(Not admitted in France)
Dominique Mondoloni
Tatiana Nourrissat
Véronique Prévôt-Leygonie
Stéphane Sabatier
Emmanuel Scialom
Franck Sekri
Muriel Serre
Gisela Suss
David Swinburne
(Not admitted in France)
Jean-Marie Valentin
Philippe Arnaud Zannier

(Firm registered as Conseils Juridiques, not admitted to practice in French Courts reserved for Avocats)

For full biographical listings, see the Martindale-Hubbell Law Directory

GERMANY

BERLIN,

BAKER & MCKENZIE DÖSER AMERELLER NOACK

Friedrichstrasse 79-80, D-10117 Berlin
Telephone: (030) 20387-600
Intn'l Dialing: (49-30) 20387-600
Facsimile: (49-30) 20387-699
URL: http://www.bakerinfo.com
Düsseldorf, Germany Office: Neuer Zollhof 3, D-40221 Düsseldorf.
Telephone: (49-211) 31116-0.
Facsimile: (49-211) 31116-199.
Frankfurt/Main, Germany Office: Bethmannstrasse 50-54, D-60311 Frankfurt/Main.
Telephone: (49-69) 29908-0.
Facsimile: (49-69) 29908-108.
Munich, Germany Office: Palais am Lenbachplatz, Ottostrasse 8, D-80333 Munich.
Telephone: (49-89) 55238-0.
Facsimile: (49-89) 55238-199.

PARTNERS

Carl H. Andres *
Wilhelm B. Hebing *
Ulrich Hennings *

LOCAL PARTNERS

Andre Sayatz
Frank-Rainer Töpfer
Frank Vogel
Peter Wessels

ASSOCIATES

Ulrike Moog
Hannes Schloemann

*Also Partner of Baker & McKenzie, Chicago, Illinois, U.S.A.

For full biographical listings, see the Martindale-Hubbell Law Directory

MAYER, BROWN & PLATT

Breite Strasse 29 Muehlendamm, 10178 Berlin
Telephone: 011-49-30-2060-7710
Facsimile: 011-49-30-2060-7744
URL: http://www.mayerbrown.com
Chicago, Illinois Office: 190 South LaSalle Street, 60603-3441.
Telephone: (312) 782-0600.
Facsimile: (312) 701-7711.
Telex: 190404.
Cable: LEMAY
Charlotte, North Carolina Office: 100 North Tryon Street, Suite 2400.
Telephone: (704) 444-3500.
Fax: (704) 377-2033.
Cologne, Germany Office: Kaiser-Wilhelm-Ring 27-29, 50672.
Telephone: 011-49-221-5771-100.
Facsimile: 011-49-221-5771-199.
Houston, Texas Office: 700 Louisiana Street, Suite 3600, 77002-2730.
Telephone: (713) 221-1651.
Facsimile: (713) 224-6410.
Telex: 775809.
Cable: LEMAYHOU.
London, England Office: Bucklersbury House, 3 Queen Victoria Street, London, EC4N 8EL, England.
Telephone: 011-44-171-246-6200.
Facsimile: 011-44-171-329-4465.
Telex: 8811095.
Cable: LEMAYLDN.
Los Angeles, California Office: 350 South Grand Avenue, 25th Floor, 90071-1503.
Telephone: (213) 229-9500.
Facsimile: (213) 625-0248.
Telex: 188089.
Cable: LEMAYLA.
New York, New York Office: 1675 Broadway, 10019-5820.
Telephone: (212) 506-2500.
Facsimile: (212) 262-1910.
Telex: 701842.
Cable: LEMAYEN.
Washington, D.C. Office: 1909 K Street, N.W., 20006-1101.
Telephone: (202) 263-3000.
Facsimile: (202) 263-3300.
Telex: 892603.
Cable: LEMAYDC.
Representative Offices:
Ashgabat, Turkmenistan: 28 Gogol Street, 744000.
Telephone: 011-99-312-355247.
Facsimile: 011-99-312-510074.
Bishkek, Kyrgyz Republic: 66 Kalyka Akieva Str. 720010.
Telephone: 011-996-312-65-02-56.
Facsimile: 011-996-312-65-09-80.
Tashkent, Republic of Uzbekistan: 3rd Floor, 1 Turab Tula Street, 700003.
Telephone: 011-998-71-1206-627.
Facsimile: 011-998-71-1206-329.

(See Next Column)

MAYER, BROWN & PLATT—*Continued*

Mexico City, Mexico, D.F., Independent Mexico Correspondent: Jáuregui, Navarrete, Nader y Rojas, S.C., Torre Arcos, paseo de los Tamarindos No. 400-B. Col. Bosques de las Lomas, 05120.
Telephone: 011-525-267-45-00.
Facsimile: 011-525-267-45-99.
Paris, France, Independent Paris Correspondent: Lambert & Lee, 13 Avenue Hoche, 75008.
Telephone: 011-33-1-53-53-43-43.
Facsimile: 011-33-1-53-96-03-83.

PARTNERS

C. Mark Nicolaides (Not admitted in Germany)
John P. Schmitz (Not admitted in Germany)

SENIOR COUNSEL

Wolfgang Pfletschinger

For full biographical listings, see the Martindale-Hubbell Law Directory

WILMER, CUTLER & PICKERING

Friedrichstrasse 95, D-10117 Berlin
Telephone: +49 (30) 20 22 64 00
Fax: +49 (30) 20 22 65 00
Email: Law@Wilmer.Com *URL:* http://www.wilmer.com
Washington, D.C. Office: 2445 M Street, N.W., 20037-1420.
Telephone: 202-663-6000.
Fax: 202-663-6363. Internet: Law@Wilmer.Com.
Baltimore, Maryland Office: 100 Light Street, 21202.
Telephone: 410-986-2800.
Fax: 410-986-2828.
New York, New York Office: 520 Madison Avenue, 10022.
Telephone: 212-230-8800.
Fax: 212-230-8888.
London, England Office: 4 Carlton Gardens, London, SW1Y 5AA.
Telephone: +44 (20) 7 872 1000.
Fax: +44 (20) 7 839 3537.
Brussels, Belgium Office: Rue de la Loi 15# Wetstraat, B-1040.
Telephone: +32 (2) 285 49 00.
Fax: +32 (2) 285 49 49.

RESIDENT PARTNERS

Matthias Wissmann
Gary B. Born (Not admitted in Germany)
Dr. Andreas Weitbrecht
Paul A. von Hehn
Dr. Natalie Lübben
Dr. Roland Steinmeyer

COUNSEL

Martin Seyfarth

ASSOCIATES

Dr. Britta Delmas
Wilhelm M.A. Hartung
Dr. Thorsten Seidel
Esmée Gräfin Von Der Groeben
Jutta von Falkenhausen

For full biographical listings, see the Martindale-Hubbell Law Directory

COLOGNE,

MAYER, BROWN & PLATT

Kaiser-Wilhelm-Ring 27-29, Cologne 50672
Telephone: 011-49-221-5771-100
Facsimile: 011-49-221-5771-199
URL: http://www.mayerbrown.com
Chicago, Illinois Office: 190 South LaSalle Street, 60603-3441.
Telephone: (312) 782-0600.
Facsimile: (312) 701-7711.
Telex: 190401.
Cable: LEMAY.
Berlin, Germany Office: Breite Strasse 29, Muehlendamm, 10178.
Telephone: 011-49-30-2060-7710.
Facsimile: 011-49-30-2060-7744.
Charlotte, North Carolina Office: 100 North Tryon Street, Suite 2400.
Telephone: (704) 444-3500.
Fax: (704) 377-2033.
Houston, Texas Office: 700 Louisiana Street, Suite 3600, 77002-2730.
Telephone: (713) 221-1651.
Facsimile: (713) 224-6410.
Telex: 775809.
Cable: LEMAYHOU.
London, England Office: Bucklersbury House, 3 Queen Victoria Street, London, EC4N 8EL, England.
Telephone: 011-44-171-246-6200.
Facsimile: 011-44-171-329-4465.
Telex: 8811095.
Cable: LEMAYLDN.
Los Angeles, California Office: 350 South Grand Avenue, 25th Floor, 90071-1503.
Telephone: (213) 229-9500.
Facsimile: (213) 625-0248.
Telex: 188089.
Cable: LEMAYLA.

(See Next Column)

New York, New York Office: 1675 Broadway, 10019-5820.
Telephone: (212) 506-2500.
Facsimile: (212) 262-1910.
Telex: 701842.
Cable: LEMAYEN.
Washington, D.C. Office: 1909 K Street, N.W., 20006-1101.
Telephone: (202) 263-3000.
Facsimile: (202) 263-3300.
Telex: 892603.
Cable: LEMAYDC.
Representative Offices:
Ashgabat, Turkmenistan: 28 Gogol Street, 744000.
Telephone: 011-99-312-355247.
Facsimile: 011-99-312-510074.
Bishkek, Kyrgyz Republic: 66 Kalyka Akieva Str. 720010.
Telephone: 011-996-312-65-02-56.
Facsimile: 011-996-312-65-09-80.
Tashkent, Republic of Uzbekistan: 3rd Floor, 1 Turab Tula Street, 700003.
Telephone: 011-998-71-1206-627.
Facsimile: 011-998-71-1206-329.
Mexico City, Mexico, D.F., Independent Mexico Correspondent: Jáuregui, Navarrete, Nader y Rojas, S.C., Torre Arcos, paseo de los Tamarindos No. 400-B. Col. Bosques de las Lomas, 05120.
Telephone: 011-525-267-45-00.
Facsimile: 011-525-267-45-99.
Paris, France, Independent Paris Correspondent: Lambert & Lee, 13 Avenue Hoche, 75008.
Telephone: 011-33-1-53-53-43-43.
Facsimile: 011-33-1-53-96-03-83.

MEMBERS OF FIRM

Werner J. Hein
C. Mark Nicolaides (Not admitted in Germany)
John P. Schmitz (Not admitted in Germany; Washington, D.C. and Berlin & Cologne, Germany Offices)

ASSOCIATES

Christof Gaudig
Antje Günther

For full biographical listings, see the Martindale-Hubbell Law Directory

DÜSSELDORF,

American Lawyers In Düsseldorf

BAKER & MCKENZIE DÖSER AMERELLER NOACK

Neuer Zollhof 3, D-40221 Düsseldorf
Telephone: (0211) 31116-0
Intn'l Dialing: (49-211) 31116-0
Facsimile: (49-211) 31116-199
URL: http://www.bakerinfo.com
Berlin, Germany Office: Friedrichstrasse 79-80, D-10117 Berlin.
Telephone: (49-30) 20387-600.
Facsimile: (49-30) 20387-699.
Frankfurt/Main, Germany Office: Bethmannstrasse 50-54, D-60311 Frankfurt/Main.
Telephone: (49-69) 29908-0.
Facsimile: (49-69) 29908-108.
Munich, Germany Office: Palais am Lenbachplatz, Ottostrasse 8, D-80333 Munich.
Telephone: (49-89) 55238-0.
Facsimile: (49-89) 55238-199.

PARTNERS

Jürgen Mark *
Hans-Jörg Ziegenhain *

LOCAL PARTNER

Barbara Deilmann

ASSOCIATES

Angela Dechow
Thomas Görgemanns
Heiko Plameier
Marc-Roger Schlieper
Benedikt von Schorlemer
Ernst-Markus Schuberth
Oliver Schultz

*Also Partner of Baker & McKenzie, Chicago, Illinois, U.S.A.

For full biographical listings, see the Martindale-Hubbell Law Directory

SHEARMAN & STERLING

Couvenstrasse 8, 40211 Düsseldorf
Telephone: 49 (211) 178 88-0
Fax: 49 (211) 178 88-88
URL: http://www.shearman.com
New York, N.Y. Office: 599 Lexington Avenue, New York, New York, 10022-6069.
Telephone: (212) 848-4000.
Telex: 667290. Num Lau.
Fax: (212) 848-7179.
Abu Dhabi, United Arab Emirates Office: Butti Al Otaiba Building, 13th Floor, Suite 1302, Sheikh Khalifa Street, P.O. Box 2948.
Telephone: (971-2) 6274477.
Fax: (971-2) 6268933.
Beijing, People's Republic of China Office: Suite #2205, Capital Mansion, No. 6, Xin Yuan Nan Road. Chao Yang District, Beijing, 100004.
Telephone: (86-10) 6465-2299.
Fax: (86-10) 6465-4578.

(See Next Column)

SHEARMAN & STERLING, *Düsseldorf—Continued*

Frankfurt, Federal Republic of Germany Office: Trianon Building, Mainzer Landstrasse 16, 60325 Frankfurt am Main.
Telephone: (49-69) 9711-1000.
Fax: (49-69) 9711-1100.
Hong Kong Office: Standard Chartered Bank Building, 4 Des Voeux Road, Central.
Telephone: (852) 2978-8000.
Fax: (852) 2978-8099.
London, England Office: Broadgate West, 9 Appold Street, London EC2A 2AP.
Telephone: 011-44-20-7655-5000.
Fax: 011-44-20-7655-5500.
Menlo Park, California Office: 1550 El Camino Real, 94025-4100.
Telephone: (650) 330-2200.
Fax: (650) 330-2299.
Paris, France Office: 114, avenue des Champs-Elysées, 75008.
Telephone: (33-1) 53-89-7000.
Fax: (33-1) 53-89-7070.
San Francisco, California Office: 555 California Street, 94104-1522.
Telephone: (415) 616-1100.
Fax: (415) 616-1199.
Singapore Office: 6 Battery Road #25-03. Singapore 049909.
Telephone: (65) 230-3800.
Fax: (65) 230-3899.
Tokyo, Japan Office: Fukoku Seimei Building, 5th Fl. 2-2-2, Uchisaiwaicho, Chiyoda-ku, Tokyo 100-0011. Japan.
Telephone: (81 3) 5251-1601.
Fax: (81 3) 5251-1602.
Toronto, Ontario, Canada Office: Commerce Court West, Suite 4405, P.O. Box 247, M5L 1E8.
Telephone: (416) 360-8484.
Fax: (416) 360-2958.
Washington, D.C. Office: 801 Pennsylvania Avenue, N.W., 20004-2604.
Telephone: (202) 508-8000.
Fax: (202) 508-8100.

PARTNER

Georg F. Thoma (Managing Partner, Europe; Managing Partner, Düsseldorf and Frankfurt)

RESIDENT PARTNERS

Dr. Hans Diekmann
Dr. Anton Klösters
Dr. Alfred L. Kossmann
Dr. Hans Jürgen Meyer-Lindemann

RESIDENT ASSOCIATES

Olaf Benning
Andrea Eggenstein
Katharina Hartwig
Dr. Hanno F. Kaiser
Boris Körner
Dr. Dieter Leuering
Patrick Mittmann
Dr. Joachim J. Modlich
Dr. Olaf Müller-Michaels
Dr. Kerstin Prange
Birgit Reese
Jens Peter Schmidt
Marina von Achten
Dr. Klaus-Peter Weber

For full biographical listings, see the Martindale-Hubbell Law Directory

FRANKFURT/MAIN,

BAKER & MCKENZIE DÖSER AMERELLER NOACK

Bethmannstrasse 50-54, D-60311 Frankfurt/Main
Telephone: (069) 29908-0
Intn'l Dialing: (49-69) 29908-0
Facsimile: (49-69) 29908-108
URL: http://www.bakerinfo.com
Berlin, Germany Office: Friedrichstrasse 79-80, D-10117 Berlin.
Telephone: (49-30) 20387-600.
Facsimile: (49-30) 20387-699.
Düsseldorf, Germany Office: Neuer Zollhof 3, D-40221 Düsseldorf.
Telephone: (49-211) 31116-0.
Facsimile: (49-211) 31116-199.
Munich, Germany Office: Palais am Lenbachplatz, Ottostrasse 8, D-80333 Munich.
Telephone: (49-89) 55238-0.
Facsimile: (49-89) 55238-199.

PARTNERS

Horst Amereller *
Christian Brodersen *
Michael A. Fammler *
Hans-Georg Feick *
Peter Ficht *
Wolfgang Fritzemeyer *
Sebastian Gronstedt *
Axel Hamm *
Günther Heckelmann *
Stephen J. Hodgson *
Matthias G. Jaletzke *
Markus O. Kappenhagen *
Jörg K. Kirchner *
Karl-Ludwig Koenen *
Manuel Lorenz *
Rainer Magold *
Werner Müller *
Ulrich Ränsch *
Thilo Räpple *
Joachim Scherer *
Matthias P. Scholz
Jörg-Martin Schultze *
Claudia Seibel *
Rainer Stachels *
Joachim Treeck *
Franz J. Waltermann *
Ulf Wauschkuhn *

LOCAL PARTNERS

Matthias Götz
Laurenti Kiszczuk
Thomas Lampert
Günter Pickrahn
Eleonore Ronge
Constanze Ulmer-Eilfort

(See Next Column)

OF COUNSEL

Wulf H. Döser
Carl Otto Lenz
Hilmar Noack

ASSOCIATES

Christopher Aide (Not admitted in Germany)
Klaus-Georg Baier
Yvonne Gräfin von Bassewitz
Torsten Bartsch
Martin Bünning
Stefan Dittmer
Gregor Dornbusch
Ulrich Ellinghaus
Regina Engelstädter
Mathias Fischer
Georg Freiherr von und zu Franckenstein
Olaf Gebler
Thomas Gilles
Bettina Goldmann
Dietmar Helms
Truiken Heydn
Frank Hölscher
Christian Kessel
Michèle Klein
Sonja G. Klein
Ursula Königer
Jan-Mathias Kuhr
Matthias Limmeroth
J. F. Hannes Meckel
Antje Michel
Rembert Niebel
Eva-Maria Pils
Klaus Pilz
Jacqueline Piran
Kirsten Reich
Christian Reichel
Beate Hanne Rickert
Christoph F. Rittweger
Hein-Jürgen Schramke
Kerstin Schweizer
Clemens Tobias Steins
Christina Ungeheuer
Dominique Wagener
Thomas Wernicke
Bijan Yazdani
Andrea Ziegler

*Also Partner of Baker & McKenzie, Chicago, Illinois, U.S.A.

For full biographical listings, see the Martindale-Hubbell Law Directory

CLEARY, GOTTLIEB, STEEN & HAMILTON

Main Tower, Neue Mainzer Strasse 52, 60311 Frankfurt/Main
Telephone: 49-69-971 03-0
Facsimile: 49-69-971 03 199
New York, New York Office: One Liberty Plaza, New York, N.Y. 10006.
Telephone: 212-225-2000.
Washington, D.C. Office: 2000 Pennsylvania Avenue, N.W., Suite 9000, Washington, D.C. 20006-1801.
Telephone: 202-974-1500.
Paris, France Office: 41, Avenue de Friedland, 75008 Paris, France.
Telephone: 33-1-40-74-68-00.
Brussels, Belgium Office: Rue de la Loi 23, 1040 Brussels, Belgium.
Telephone: 32-2-287-2000.
London, England Office: City Place House, 55 Basinghall Street, London EC2V 5EH England.
Telephone: 44-71-614-2200.
Hong Kong Office: 39th Floor, Bank of China Tower, One Garden Road, Hong Kong.
Telephone: 852-2521-4122.
Tokyo, Japan Office: Cleary, Gottlieb, Steen & Hamilton Gaikokuho Jimubengoshi Jimusho, 20th Floor, Shin Kasumigaseki Building, 3-2, Kasumigaseki 3-Chome, Chiyoda-Ku, Tokyo 100-0013, Japan.
Telephone: 81-3-3595-3911.
Rome, Italy Office: Piazza di Spagna 15, 00187 Rome, Italy.
Telephone: 39-06-69-52-22-1.

RESIDENT PARTNERS

Alan S. Dunning (Not admitted in Germany)
Christof von Dryander
Thomas M. Buhl
John Palenberg (Not admitted in Germany)
Stephan Barthelmess
Gottfried E. Breuninger
Ward A. Greenberg (Not admitted in Germany)

RESIDENT SPECIAL COUNSEL

Werner Meier

ASSOCIATES

Monica Aguilar (Not admitted in Germany)
Gabriele Apfelbacher
Klaus Banke
Yvonne Braun
Michael Brems
Johannes Frey
Jörg Häring
Jens Heimann
Alexander R. Klett
Thomas K. Kopp
Astrid Krüger
Hans Peter Leube
Frank Lohrmann
Jochen W. Mann
Thomas Mayer (Not admitted in Germany)
Tobias Nauth
Karen A. Robertson (Not admitted in Germany)
Jennifer L. Schmid (Not admitted in Germany; Resident)
Robert Schulz
Ramón Sieveking
Hanno Sperlich
Jonathan V. Wallenberger (Not admitted in Germany)
Peter Wand
Daniel Weyde
Ulrike Willoughby

For full biographical listings, see the Martindale-Hubbell Law Directory

American Lawyers In Frankfurt/Main

CURTIS, MALLET-PREVOST, COLT & MOSLE LLP

Staufenstrasse 42, 60323 Frankfurt/Main 1
Telephone: +49-69-971-4420
Telecopier: +49-69-17 33 99
Email: info@cm-p.com *URL:* http://www.cm-p.com
New York, New York Office: 101 Park Avenue.
Telephone: 212-696-6000.
Telecopier: 212-697-1559.
Newark, New Jersey Office: One Gateway Center, Suite 403.
Telephone: 973-622-0605.
Telecopier: 973-622-5646.
Washington, D.C. Office: Suite 1201L, 1801 K Street, N.W.
Telephone: 202-452-7373.
Telecopier: 202-452-7333.
Houston, Texas Office: 2 Houston Center, 909 Fannin Street, Suite 3725.
Telephone: 713-759-9555.
Telecopier: 713-759-0712.
Stamford, Connecticut Office: One Canterbury Green.
Telephone: 203-359-6200.
Telecopier: 203-328-2617.
Mexico City, D.F., Mexico Office: Curtis, Mallet-Prevost, Colt & Mosle, Ruben Dario 281, Piso 9, Col. Bosque de Chapultepec, 11530 Mexico, D.F.
Telephone: 525-282-0444.
Telecopier: 525-282-0637.
London, England Office: Two Throgmorton Avenue, EC2N 2DL.
Telephone: 0207-638-7957.
Telecopier: 0207-638-5512.
Paris, France Office: 15 rue d'Astorg, 75008.
Telephone: 42-66-39-10.
Telecopier: 42-66-39-62.
Muscat, Sultanate of Oman Office: Jewel Beach-134.
Telephone: 968-607-725.
Telecopier: 968-607-724.
Milan, Italy Office: Curtis, Mallet-Prevost & Gilioli, Piazzale Principessa Clotilde 8, 20121.
Telephone: (39) 02 29 00 29 32.
Telefax: (39) 02 65 75 969.

PARTNER

Marie-Therese Allen (Not admitted in Germany)

COUNSEL

Eric Stenshoel (Not admitted in Germany)

RESIDENT ASSOCIATES

Ute Tünnermann-Kasch

For full biographical listings, see the Martindale-Hubbell Law Directory

JONES, DAY, REAVIS & POGUE

Hochhaus am Park, Grüneburgweg 102, 60323 Frankfurt/Main
Telephone: 49-69-9726-3939
Telecopier: 49-69-9726-3993
Email: counsel@jonesday.com *URL:* http://www.jonesday.com
In Atlanta, Georgia: 3500 SunTrust Plaza, 303 Peachtree Street.
Telephone: 404-521-3939.
Telecopier: 404-581-8330.
In Brussels, Belgium: Avenue Louise 480, 7th Floor. B-1050 Brussels.
Telephone: 32-2-645-14-11.
Telecopier: 32-2-645-14-45.
In Chicago, Illinois: 77 West Wacker.
Telephone: 312-782-3939.
Telecopier: 312-782-8585.
In Cleveland, Ohio: North Point, 901 Lakeside Avenue.
Telephone: 216-586-3939.
Telecopier: 216-579-0212.
In Columbus, Ohio: 1900 Huntington Center.
Telephone: 614-469-3939.
Telecopier: 614-461-4198.
In Dallas, Texas: 2727 North Harwood Street.
Telephone: 214-220-3939.
Telecopier: 214-969-5100.
In Geneva, Switzerland: 20, rue de Candolle.
Telephone: 41-22-320-2339.
Telecopier: 41-22-320-1232.
In Hong Kong: 29th Floor, Entertainment Building, 30 Queen's Road Central.
Telephone: 852-2526-6895.
Telecopier: 852-2868-5871.
In Irvine, California: 5 Park Plaza, Suite 1100.
Telephone: 949-851-3939.
Telecopier: 949-553-7539.
In London, England: Bucklersbury House, 3 Queen Victoria Street.
Telephone: 44-20-7236-3939.
Telecopier: 44-20-7236-1113.
In Los Angeles, California: 555 West Fifth Street, Suite 4600.
Telephone: 213-489-3939.
Telecopier: 213-243-2539.

(See Next Column)

In New York, New York: 599 Lexington Avenue.
Telephone: 212-326-3939.
Telecopier: 212-755-7306.
In Paris, France: 120, rue du Faubourg Saint-Honoré.
Telephone: 33-1-56-59-39-39.
Telecopier: 33-1-56-59-39-38
In Pittsburgh, Pennsylvania: 500 Grant Street, 31st Floor.
Telephone: 412-391-3939.
Telecopier: 412-394-7959.
In Riyadh, Saudi Arabia: The International Law Firm (In Association with Jones, Day, Reavis & Pogue), Sulaymaniyah, Prince Mishari IBN, Abdulaziz Street, P.O. Box 22166.
Telephone: (966-1) 462-8866.
Telecopier: (966-1) 462-9001.
In Shanghai, China: 2805 Kerry Centre, 1515 Nanjing Road West.
Telephone: 86-21-5298-6568.
Telecopier: 86-21-5298-6569.
In Sydney, Australia: Governor Phillip Tower, Level 38, 1 Farrer Place.
Telephone: 61-2-9210-6921.
Telecopier: 61-2-9210-6926.
In Taipei, Taiwan: 8th Floor, 2 Tun Hwa South Road, Section 2.
Telephone: (886-2) 2704-6808.
Telecopier: (886-2) 2704-6791.
In Tokyo, Japan: Toranomon 45 Mori Building, 3rd Floor, 1-5, Toranomon 5-Chome, Minato-Ku, Tokyo 105, Japan.
Telephone: 81-3-3433-3939.
Telecopier: 81-3-5401-2725.
In Washington, D.C.: 51 Louisiana Avenue, N.W.
Telephone: 202-879-3939.
Telecopier: 202-626-1700.

MEMBERS OF FIRM IN FRANKFURT

Karl G. Herold
Joachim Borggräfe
Richard H. Kreindler
Dr. Helga Elizabeth Kroeger
Oliver Passavant
Douglas J. Whipple (Not admitted in Germany)

OF COUNSEL

Eckart C. Hild
Walther Karl-Joh VonWietzlow

EUROPEAN COUNSEL

Thomas C. Mahlich
Ansgar C. Rempp
Juergen R.H. Reemers
DR. Carsten T. Gromotke
Sina R. Hekmat, Jr.

ASSOCIATES

Andreas Koester-Boeckenfoerde
Timothy J. Kautz (Not admitted in Germany)
Juergen A. Heilbock
Jan D. Bayer
Holger Hecklau
Peter Lotz
Ercan Acikel
Marijon Kaysser
Jens Boeck

STAFF ATTORNEYS

Georg Mikes
Andreas Metzner
Alexandra C. Breuer
Janin V. Ahnefeld

For full biographical listings, see the Martindale-Hubbell Law Directory

PARKER, POE, ADAMS & BERNSTEIN GMBH-IG

Limes Park, Otto-Volger-Strasse 5B, D-65843 Frankfurt/Main
Telephone: (011)(49) 6196-750081
Telefax: (011)(49) 6196-750088
Email: info@parkerpoe.com *URL:* http://www.parkerpoe.com
Charlotte, North Carolina Office: 2500 Charlotte Plaza, 201 South College Street, 28244.
Telephone: 704-372-9000.
Facsimile: 704-334-4706.
South Park Office: The Rotunda, 4201 Congress Street, Suite 145, Charlotte, 28209.
Telephone: 704-556-9600.
Facsimile: 704-556-9601.
Raleigh, North Carolina Office: First Union Capitol Center, 150 Fayetteville Street Mall, Suite 1400, P.O. Box 389, 27602-0389.
Telephone: 919-828-0564.
Facsimile: 919-834-4564.
Columbia, South Carolina Office: 1201 Main Street, Suite 1450, 29201.
Telephone: 803-255-8000.
Facsimile: 803-255-8017.
Spartanburg, South Carolina Office: 101 W. St. John Street, Suite 203, 29306.
Telephone: 803-591-2030.
Facsimile: 803-591-2050.

PARTNER

I. Faison Hicks (Also at Charlotte, North Carolina Office)

ASSOCIATE

Andreas Gottlieb

For full biographical listings, see the Martindale-Hubbell Law Directory

SHEARMAN & STERLING

Trianon Building, Mainzer Landstrasse 16, 60325 Frankfurt/Main
Telephone: (49-69) 9711-1000
Fax: (49-69) 9711-1100
URL: http://www.shearman.com
New York, N.Y. Office: 599 Lexington Avenue, New York, New York, 10022-6069.
Telephone: (212) 848-4000.
Telex: 667290. Num Lau.
Fax: (212) 848-7179.
Abu Dhabi, United Arab Emirates Office: Butti Al Otaiba Building, 13th Floor, Suite 1302, Sheikh Khalifa Street, P.O. Box 2948.
Telephone: (971-2) 6274477.
Fax: (971-2) 6268933.
Beijing, People's Republic of China Office: Suite #2205, Capital Mansion, No. 6, Xin Yuan Nan Road. Chao Yang District, Beijing, 100004.
Telephone: (86-10) 6465-2299.
Fax: (86-10) 6465-4578.
Düsseldorf, Federal Republic of Germany Office: Couvenstrasse 8 40211 Düsseldorf.
Telephone: (49 211) 178 88-0.
Fax: (49 211) 178 88-88.
Hong Kong Office: Standard Chartered Bank Building, 4 Des Voeux Road, Central.
Telephone: (852) 2978-8000.
Fax: (852) 2978-8099.
London, England Office: Broadgate West, 9 Appold Street, London EC2A 2AP.
Telephone: 011-44-20-7655-5000.
Fax: 011-44-20-7655-5500.
Menlo Park, California Office: 1550 El Camino Real, 94025-4100.
Telephone: (650) 330-2200.
Fax: (650) 330-2299.
Paris, France Office: 114, avenue des Champs-Elysées, 75008.
Telephone: (33-1) 53-89-7000.
Fax: (33-1) 53-89-7070.
San Francisco, California Office: 555 California Street, 94104-1522.
Telephone: (415) 616-1100.
Fax: (415) 616-1199.
Singapore Office: 6 Battery Road #25-03. Singapore 049909.
Telephone: (65) 230-3800.
Fax: (65) 230-3899.
Tokyo, Japan Office: Fukoku Seimei Building, 5th Fl. 2-2-2, Uchisaiwaicho, Chiyoda-ku, Tokyo 100-0011. Japan.
Telephone: (81 3) 5251-1601.
Fax: (81 3) 5251-1602.
Toronto, Ontario, Canada Office: Commerce Court West, Suite 4405, P.O. Box 247, M5L 1E8.
Telephone: (416) 360-8484.
Fax: (416) 360-2958.
Washington, D.C. Office: 801 Pennsylvania Avenue, N.W., 20004-2604.
Telephone: (202) 508-8000.
Fax: (202) 508-8100.

MANAGING PARTNER

Georg F. Thoma (Managing Partner, Europe; Managing Partner, Düsseldorf and Frankfurt)

RESIDENT PARTNERS

Dr. Hanno Berger
Dr. Stephan Hutter (Not admitted in Germany)
Dr. Thomas N. König
Michael A. Leppert
Johann Georg Mühlmann
Reinhard Stockum
Wolfgang Tischbirek

OF COUNSEL

Dr. Michael Gruson (Not admitted in Germany)

RESIDENT ASSOCIATES

Mark Devlin (Not admitted in Germany)
Bernhard Gemmel
Matthias Hertel
Friedrich von Holst
Martin Hunstein
Stefanie Klappenbach
Markus Mayer
Robert Michels
Michael Môlling
Markus Müller-Dott
Sandra Pfister
Beatrice Prauschke
Dr. Georg Scherl
Hans Martin Schmid
Dr. Susanne Strelau
Florian Stürwald
Dr. Stefan Wagner

For full biographical listings, see the Martindale-Hubbell Law Directory

---

SULLIVAN & CROMWELL

Oberlindau 54-56, 60323 Frankfurt/Main
Telephone: (011)(4969)7191-260
Telecopier: (011)(4969)7191-2610
URL: http://www.sullcrom.com
New York City Office: 125 Broad Street, 10004-2498.
Telephone: 212-558-4000.
Telex: 62694.
Telecopier: 212-558-3588 or 212-514-5706.
Washington, D.C. Office: 1701 Pennsylvania Avenue, N.W., 20006-5805.
Telephone: 202-956-7500.
Telecopier: 202-293-6330.
Los Angeles, California Office: 1888 Century Park East, 90067-1725.
Telephone: 310-712-6600.
Telecopier: 310-712-8800.

(See Next Column)

Paris Office: 8, Place Vendôme, 75001 Paris, France.
Telephone: (011)(331) 44 50 60 00.
Telex: 240654.
Telecopier: (011)(331) 44 50 60 60 or (011)(331) 42 60 56 36.
London Office: St. Olave's House, 9a Ironmonger Lane, London EC2V 8EY, England.
Telephone: (011)(44207) 710 6500.
Telecopier: (011)(44207) 710 6565.
Melbourne Office: 101 Collins Street, Melbourne, Victoria 3000, Australia.
Telephone: (011)(613) 9635-1500.
Telecopier: (011)(613) 9654-2422.
Tokyo Office: Sullivan & Cromwell, Gaikokuho Jimu Bengoshi Jimusho, Akai Law Offices (Registered Associated Offices), Otemachi First Square East Tower 16F, 5-1, Otemachi 1-chome, Chiyoda-ku, Tokyo 100-0004, Japan.
Telephone: (011)(813) 3213-6140.
Telecopier: (011)(813) 3213-6470 or (011)(813) 3213-6477.
Hong Kong Office: 28th Floor, Nine Queen's Road, Central, Hong Kong.
Telephone: (011)(852) 2826-8688.
Telecopier: (011)(852) 2522-2280.
Beijing Office: The Beijing Representative Office of Sullivan & Cromwell, Suite 501, China World Trade Center, No. 1 Jianguo Menwai Avenue, Beijing 100004, P.R.C.
Telephone: (011)(86) 10 6505 6120.
Telecopier: (011)(86) 10 6505 6136.

PARTNERS IN FRANKFURT

David F. Morrison (Not admitted in Germany; Also at Paris Office)
George H. White III (Not admitted in Germany)
David B. Rockwell

ASSOCIATE IN FRANKFURT

Sven O. Riethmueller

For full biographical listings, see the Martindale-Hubbell Law Directory

---

MUNICH,

BAKER & MCKENZIE DÖSER AMERELLER NOACK

Palais am Lenbrachplatz, Ottostrasse 8, D-80333 Munich
Telephone: (089) 55238-0
Intn'l Dialing: (49-89) 55238-0
Facsimile: (49-89) 55238-199
URL: http://www.bakerinfo.com
Berlin, Germany Office: Friedrichstrasse 79-80, D-10117 Berlin.
Telephone: (49-30) 20387-600.
Facsimile: (49-30) 20387-699.
Düsseldorf, Germany Office: Neuer Zollhof 3, D-40221 Düsseldorf.
Telephone: (49-211) 31116-0.
Facsimile: (49-211) 31116-199.
Frankfurt/Main, Germany Office: Bethmannstrasse 50-54, D-60311 Frankfurt/Main.
Telephone: (49-69) 29908-0.
Facsimile: (49-69) 29908-108.

PARTNERS

Walter Henle *
Stephan J. Spehl *
Uwe H. Steininger *

LOCAL PARTNERS

André Gloede
Claudia Heins
Bernhard Trappehl
Peter Veranneman

ASSOCIATES

Justus Binder
Volkmar Bruckner
Katja Heuterkes
Andreas Lohner
Sonya Margaret Willimsky (Not admitted in Germany)
Jörg Wössner
Lutz Zimmer

*Also Partner of Baker & McKenzie, Chicago, Illinois, U.S.A.

For full biographical listings, see the Martindale-Hubbell Law Directory

---

HUNGARY

BUDAPEST,

American Lawyers In Budapest

MARTONYI ÈS KAJTÁR BAKER & MCKENZIE

Andrássy-út 102, 1062 Budapest
Telephone: (1) 302-3330
Intn'l Dialing: (36-1) 302-3330
Facsimile: (36-1) 302-3331
URL: http://www.bakerinfo.com
Associated Offices of Baker & McKenzie in: Almaty, Amsterdam, Bahrain, Baku, Bangkok, Barcelona, Beijing, Berlin, Bogotá, Brasília, Brussels, Buenos Aires, Cairo, Caracas, Chicago, Dallas, Düsseldorf, Frankfurt, Geneva, Hanoi, Ho Chi Minh City, Hong Kong, Houston, Hsinchu, Juárez, Kyiv, London, Madrid, Manila, Melbourne, México City, Miami, Milan, Monterrey, Moscow, Münich, New York, Palo Alto, Paris, Prague, Rio de Janeiro, Riyadh, Rome, St. Petersburg, San Diego, San Francisco, Santiago, São Paulo, Singapore, Stockholm, Sydney, Taipei, Tijuana, Tokyo, Toronto, Valencia, Warsaw, Washington, D.C. and Zürich.

(See Next Column)

MARTONYI ÉS KAJTÁR BAKER & MCKENZIE—*Continued*

Correspondent Law Firm: Hadiputranto, Hadinoto & Partners, Jakarta.

PARTNERS

Dr. Géza Kajtár
Ines K. Radmilovic (Not admitted in Hungary)

LOCAL PARTNERS

Dr. Zoltán Hegymegi-Barakonyi
Dr. Konrád Siegler
Dr. Pál P. Takács

SENIOR COUNSEL

Dr. Kálmán Gyárfás

ASSOCIATES

Dr. Pál Csanády
Dr. Ákos Fehérváry
Dr. Zita Fekete
Anne-Marie Fortier (Not admitted in Hungary)
Dr. Mónika K. Hajdú
Dr. Kinga M. Hetényi
Dr. Attila S. Horváth
Dr. Ildikó Jóna
Dr. Gabriella Kicska
Dr. Zoltán Lengyel
Dr. Zita Orbán

For full biographical listings, see the Martindale-Hubbell Law Directory

NAGY & PINTÉR HOGAN & HARTSON LAW OFFICE

Bank Center Granite Tower, 9th Floor, Budapest V., Szabadsag ter 7
1944 Hungary, Budapest
Telephone: (36-1) 302-9050
Fax: (36-1) 302-9060
URL: www.hhlaw.com
Washington, D.C. Office: Columbia Square, 555 13th Street, N.W.
Telephone: 206-637-5600.
Telex: 89-2757.
Cable Address: "Hogander Washington".
Fax: 202-637-5910.
Brussels, Belgium Office: Avenue des Arts 41, 1040.
Telephone: (32.2) 505.09.11.
Fax: (32.2) 505.09.96.
London, England Office: One Angel Court, EC2R 7HJ.
Telephone: +(44) 207-367-0200.
Fax: +(44) 207-367-0220.
Moscow, Russia Office: 33/2 Usacheva Street, Building 3, 119048.
Telephone: (7095) 245-5190. Int'l
Telephone: (7501) 907-0451.
Fax: (7095) 245-5192. Int'l
Fax: (7501) 907-0462.
Paris, France (Affiliated Office): Cariddi, Mee, Rué, Avocats Associés à la Cour de Paris, 12, rue de la Paix, 75002.
Telephone: (33-1) 42.61.57.71.
Fax: (33-1) 42.61.79.21.
Prague, Czech Republic (Affiliated Office): Hogan & Hartson, Advokátní Kanceláře, v.o.s., Trziste 13, 118 00.
Telephone: (420-2) 2211-7111.
Fax: (420-2) 2211-7222.
Warsaw, Poland Office: Hogan & Hartson Sp.zo.o, Atrium Tower, Al. Jana Pawla II 25, 00-854.
Telephone: (48-22) 653-4200.
Fax: (48-22) 653-4250.
Baltimore, Maryland Office: 111 South Calvert Street.
Telephone: 410-659-2700.
Fax: 410-539-6981.
Rockville, Maryland Office: 600 Jefferson Plaza, Suite 203.
Telephone: 301-315-2206.
Fax: 301-315-9046.
Boulder, Colorado Office: 1800 Broadway, Suite 200.
Telephone: 720-406-5300.
Fax: 720-406-5301.
Colorado Springs, Colorado Office: Two North Cascade Avenue, Suite 1300.
Telephone: 719-448-5900.
Fax: 719-448-5922.
Denver, Colorado Office: One Tabor Center, Suite 1500, 1200 Seventeenth Street.
Telephone: 303-899-7300.
Fax: 303-899-7333.
Los Angeles, California Office: Biltmore Tower, 500 S. Grand Avenue, Suite 1900.
Telephone: 213-337-6700.
Fax: 213-337-6701.
Newport Beach, California Office: 4675 MacArthur Court, Suite 670.
Telephone: 949-250-4550.
Fax: 949-833-0976.
McLean, Virginia Office: 8300 Greensboro Drive.
Telephone: 703-610-6100.
Fax: 703-610-6200.
New York, New York Office: 885 Third Avenue, 26th Floor.
Telephone: 212-409-9800.
Fax: 212-409-9801.

MEMBERS OF FIRM

Raymond J. Batla, Jr. (Not admitted in Hungary)
Kornelia Nagy-Koppany

COUNSEL

Ildiko Laszlo (Not admitted in Hungary)
Aurel Pinter

(See Next Column)

ASSOCIATES

Annamaria Csenterics
Rita Bársony
Tamás I. Kovács (Not admitted in Hungary)
G. Péter Nagy (Not admitted in Hungary)

For full biographical listings, see the Martindale-Hubbell Law Directory

SQUIRE, SANDERS & DEMPSEY L.L.P.

H-1062 Budapest Andrassy ut. 64, Budapest
Telephone: 36-1-428-7111
Fax: 36-1-428-7100
URL: http://www.ssd.com
Cincinnati, Ohio Office: PNC Center, 201 East Fifth Street, Suite 1700, Cincinnati, Ohio 45202.
Telephone: 513-361-1200.
Fax: 513-361-1201.
Cleveland, Ohio Office: 4900 Key Tower, 127 Public Square, Cleveland, Ohio 44114-1304.
Telephone: 216-479-8500.
Fax: 216-479-8780.
Columbus, Ohio Office: 1300 Huntington Center, 41 South High Street, Columbus, Ohio 43215-6150.
Telephone: 614-365-2700.
Fax: 614-365-2499.
Houston, Texas Office: 6250 Chase Tower, 600 Travis Street, Houston, Texas 77002-3007.
Telephone: 713-546-5850.
Fax: 713-546-5830.
Jacksonville, Florida Office: One Enterprise Center, Suite 2100, 225 Water Street, Jacksonville, Florida 32202-4424.
Telephone: 904-366-2420.
Fax: 904-356-2986.
Miami, Florida Office: 201 South Biscayne Boulevard, 2900 Miami Center, Miami, Florida 33131-4330.
Telephone: 305-577-8700.
Fax: 305-358-1425.
New York, New York Office: 350 Park Avenue, New York, New York 10022-6002.
Telephone: 212-872-9800.
Fax: 212-872-9815.
Phoenix, Arizona Office: Two Renaissance Square, 40 North Central Avenue, Suite 2700, Phoenix, Arizona 85004-4498.
Telephone: 602-528-4000.
Fax: 602-253-8129.
Washington, D.C. Office: 1201 Pennsylvania Avenue, N.W., Suite 500, Washington, D.C. 20004-2491.
Telephone: 202-626-6600.
Fax: 202-626-6780.
Almaty, Kazakhstan Office: 141 Albay Khan Avenue, Second Floor, Almaty, Kazakhstan 480091.
Telephone: +73-27-50-11-25.
Fax: +73-27-50-11-25.
Brussels, Belgium Office: Avenue Louise, 165-Box 15, 1050 Brussels, Belgium.
Telephone: 32-2-627-1111.
Fax: 32-2-627-1100.
Kyiv, Ukraine Office: 14A Yaroslaviv Val, Kyiv 252034, Ukraine.
Telephone: 38-044-228-8687.
Fax: 38-044-228-4938.
London, England Office: Royex House, Aldermanbury Square, London EC2V 7HR.
Telephone: 44-171-776-5200.
Fax: 44-171-776-5233.
Madrid, Spain Office: Calle Velazquez 108-110, 28006 Madrid, Spain.
Telephone: 34-91-590-2420.
Fax: 34-91-590-2421.
Moscow, Russian Federation Office: Paveletskaya Square II, 1 Valovaya Street, 5th Floor, Moscow 113054, Russian Federation.
Telephone: 7-501-258-5250.
Fax: 7-501-258-5251.
Prague, Czech Republic Office: Václavské námĕst 1 57/813, 110 00 Praha 1, Czech Republic.
Telephone: 420-2-2166-2111.
Fax: 420-2-2166-2222.
Hong Kong Office: Rooms 1101-2 St. George's Building, 2 Ice House Street, Central, Hong Kong.
Telephone: 852-2509-9732.
Fax: 852-2509-9772.
Taipei, Taiwan Office: 14F, 116 Nanking East Road, Sec. 2, Taipei, Taiwan, Republic of China.
Telephone: 886-2-2531-2888.
Fax: 886-2-2571-6199.

PARTNER

Blaise G. A. Pasztory

OF COUNSEL

Péter Komáromi

(See Next Column)

SQUIRE, SANDERS & DEMPSEY L.L.P., *Budapest—Continued*

ASSOCIATES

Gyöngyi Bozzay
Paul L. Csiszár
Ágnes Divinyi
Péter Gaál
Attila Lotz

For full biographical listings, see the Martindale-Hubbell Law Directory

INDIA

*NEW DELHI,**

PATHAK & ASSOCIATES

1st Fl., Dr. Gopal Das Bhavan, 28 Barakhamba Rd., New Delhi 110-001
Telephone: 91-11-373-8793, 911-11-335-7345, 91-11-373-7636 and 91-11-335-0416
Telecopier: 91-11-335-3761

MEMBER OF FIRM

Jai S. Pathak

ASSOCIATES

Freyan Desai
Sandip Bhagat
Abhimanyu Jalan
Sanjeev Adlakha
Darpan Wadhwa
Saugata Mukherjee

For full biographical listings, see the Martindale-Hubbell Law Directory

INDONESIA

*JAKARTA,**

HADIPUTRANTO, HADINOTO & PARTNERS

The Jakarta Stock Exchange Building Tower II, 21st Floor Sudirman Central Business District, Jl. Jendral Sudirman Kav. 52-53, Jakarta 12190
Telephone: (21) 515-5090; 515-5091; 515-5092; 515-5093
Intn'l Dialing: (62-21) 515-5090; 515-5091; 515-5092; 515-5093
Facsimiles: (62-21) 515-4840; 515-4845; 515-4850; 515-4855; 515-4860; 515-4865

MEMBERS OF FIRM

Tuti Dewi Hadinoto
Sri Indrastuti Hadiputranto
Timur Sukirno

LOCAL PARTNERS

Melli Nuraini Darsa
Erwandi Hendarta
Yandri Hendarta
Erna Letty Kusoy
Enny Melanita
Erika Chiko Noveni
Indah N. Respati
Christian Budianto Teo
Wimbanu Widyatmoko

ASSOCIATES

Bono Daru Adji
Ignatius Andy
Ike Andriani
Mardalena Arleen
Ibrahim S. Assegaf
Chairiyah
Salomo Rahmatuah Damanik
Sarina Sutadisastra Danuningrat
Dwi Anita Daruherdani
Garnasih A. Dharmaputra
Mochamad Fachri
Yeni Fatmawati
Daniel Ginting
Katherine Grace
Heidy Handriati
Satrya H. Harefa
Rudy Kusmanto
Daru Lukiantono
Rico J. Moegandi
Siendy Katirachmadiah Musmar
Hendri Naldi
Nadia H. Nasoetion
Ratih Nawangsari
Mohamad Kadri Nizaroeddin
Sugianto Osman
Ervin L. Pakpahan
Indri Pramitaswari
Sri Hartati Rahayu
Mutia Rivayanthi
Unggul Santoso
Dini Shanti
Amalia Sianti
Elizabeth S. Silalahi
Hendronoto Soesabdo
Nia K. Harimatara Sujani
Zoraida Syarfuan
Ilya Utama
Veronika
Alvira M. Wahjosoedibjo
Dorothea Nawang Wulan
Said Zaidansyah
Andi Zulfikar

FOREIGN LEGAL CONSULTANTS

Catherine J. Boggs (Not admitted in Indonesia)
Peter C.H.M. Hilders (Not admitted in Indonesia)
Mark C. Innis (Not admitted in Indonesia)

For full biographical listings, see the Martindale-Hubbell Law Directory

ITALY

MILAN,

BAKER & MCKENZIE

3 Piazza Meda, 20121 Milan
Telephone: (02) 76.231.1
Intn'l Dialing: (39-02) 76.231.1
Facsimiles: (39-02) 76.231.620 - 76.231.623 - 76.231.679
Email: milan.info@bakernet.com *URL:* http://www.bakerinfo.com
Associated Offices of Baker & McKenzie in: Almaty, Amsterdam, Bahrain, Baku, Bangkok, Barcelona, Beijing, Berlin, Bogotá, Brasília, Brussels, Budapest, Buenos Aires, Cairo, Caracas, Chicago, Dallas, Düsseldorf, Frankfurt, Geneva, Hanoi, Ho Chi Minh City, Hong Kong, Houston, Hsinchu, Juárez, Kyiv, London, Madrid, Manila, Melbourne, México City, Miami, Monterrey, Moscow, Münich, New York, Palo Alto, Paris, Prague, Rio de Janeiro, Riyadh, Rome, St. Petersburg, San Diego, San Francisco, Santiago, São Paulo, Singapore, Stockholm, Sydney, Taipei, Tijuana, Tokyo, Toronto, Valencia, Warsaw, Washington, D.C. and Zürich.
Correspondent Law Firm: Hadiputranto, Hadinoto & Partners, Jakarta.

PARTNERS

Corrado Bartoli
Gerardo M. Boniello
Claudio Camilli
Gianfranco Di Garbo
Pierfrancesco L. Federici
Alberto Semeria
Alberto Maria Fornari

LOCAL PARTNERS

Francesco Adami
Andrea Cicala
Lorenzo De Martinis
Gianmarco Mileni Munari
Silvia Picchetti
Giuliana Polacco

OF COUNSEL

Lorenzo De Angelis

ASSOCIATES

Antonella Alfonsi
Lorenzo F. Bertola
Luisa Bianchi
Massimiliano Biolchini
Roberto Camilli
Carlo Carta
Paola Colarossi
Bianca Del Genio
Ombretta Faggiano
Maria Cristina Ferradini
Pietro Fiori
Francesco Florenzano
Luca Lippolis
Raffaella Marzi
Uberto Percivalle
Patrizia Pirro

For full biographical listings, see the Martindale-Hubbell Law Directory

American Lawyers In Milan

GRAHAM & JAMES LLP

Piazza San Babila, 3, 20122 Milan
Telephone: 39-02-77721511
Telecopier: 39-02-77721515
E-Mail: gjmilan@gj.com
Email: gjmilan@tin.it *URL:* http://www.gj.com
Other offices located in: San Francisco, Los Angeles, Orange County and Palo Alto, California; Washington, D.C.; New York, New York; Beijing, China; Tokyo, Japan; London, England; Düsseldorf, Germany.
Associated Offices: Deacons Graham & James, Hong Kong, Sydney, Melbourne, Brisbane, Perth and Canberra, Australia.
Affiliated Offices: Deacons Graham & James, Hanoi and Ho Chi Minh City, Vietnam; Taipei, Taiwan and Bangkok, Thailand; In association with Dewi Soeharto & Rekan, Jakarta, Indonesia; Graham & James in affiliation with Taylor Joynson Garrett, London, England, Bucharest, Romania and Brussels, Belgium; Kau, Dusseldorf, Germany; Mishare M. Al-Ghazali & Partners, Safat, Kuwait; Law Firm of Salah Al-Hejailan, Jeddah and Riyadh, Saudi Arabia; Yeo Wee Kiong & Partners, Singapore.

PARTNERS

Gabriele Bernascone
Alessandro Bossi
Paolo A. Grondona
Fabrizia Maurici

ASSOCIATES

Cristina Corsetto
Pierluigi Congedo
Salvatore Di Salvatore
Ivo Formigaro
Manuela Rumsey (Not admitted in Italy)
Paola Sangiovanni
Cristina Iori Uchikawa (Resident in Tokyo)

RESIDENT OF COUNSEL

Wolfgang M. Kau
Francesco Maurici

RESIDENT TAX COUNSEL

Marco Busalini

For full biographical listings, see the Martindale-Hubbell Law Directory

*ROME,**

BAKER & MCKENZIE

Via Degli Scipioni, 288, 00192 Rome
Telephone: (06) 3225162
Intn'l Dialing: (39-06) 322-5162
Facsimile: (39-06) 320-3502
URL: http://www.bakerinfo.com
Associated Offices of Baker & McKenzie in: Almaty, Amsterdam, Bahrain, Baku, Bangkok, Barcelona, Beijing, Berlin, Bogotá, Brasília, Brussels, Budapest, Buenos Aires, Cairo, Caracas, Chicago, Dallas, Düsseldorf, Frankfurt, Geneva, Hanoi, Ho Chi Minh City, Hong Kong, Houston, Hsinchu, Juárez, Kyiv, London, Madrid, Manila, Melbourne, México City, Miami, Milan, Monterrey, Moscow, Münich, New York, Palo Alto, Paris, Prague, Rio de Janeiro, Riyadh, St. Petersburg, San Diego, San Francisco, Santiago, São Paulo, Singapore, Stockholm, Sydney, Taipei, Tijuana, Tokyo, Toronto, Valencia, Warsaw, Washington, D.C. and Zürich.
Correspondent Law Firm: Hadiputranto, Hadinoto & Partners, Jakarta.

RESIDENT PARTNERS

Fabio Brembati
Raffaele Giarda
Aurelio Giovannelli
G. Franco Macconi

LOCAL PARTNERS

Gianluca Benedetti
Guido Brocchieri
Giorgio Gallenzi
Alfredo Lucente
Antonio Petraglia

ASSOCIATES

Claudia Barsotti
Sandro Campilongo
Cristina Capitanio
Giada Cortesi
Caterina Errigo
Paola Giacovelli
Cecilia Mambrini
Maria Mariniello
Anna Sofia N. Mauro
Dolores Mugherli
Rocco Panetta
Giovanni Parrillo
Francesco Pau
Francesco Portolano
Eugenio Prosperetti
Massimo Riccio
Massimiliano Russo
Valerio Salce
Elvezio Santarelli
Corinna Sciarretta
Riccardo Sensi
Eugenio Tranchino
Michele Vitale

For full biographical listings, see the Martindale-Hubbell Law Directory

American Lawyers In Rome

CLEARY, GOTTLIEB, STEEN & HAMILTON

Piazza di Spagna 15, 00187 Rome
Telephone: 39-06-69-52-22-1
Fax: 39-06-69-20-06-65
New York, New York Office: One Liberty Plaza, New York, N.Y. 10006.
Telephone: 212-225-2000.
Washington, D.C. Office: 2000 Pennsylvania Avenue, N.W., Suite 9000, Washington, D.C. 20006-1801.
Telephone: 202-974-1500.
Paris, France Office: 41, Avenue de Friedland, 75008 Paris, France.
Telephone: 33-1-40-74-68-00.
Brussels, Belgium Office: Rue de la Loi 23, 1040 Brussels, Belgium.
Telephone: 32-2-287-2000.
London, England Office: City Place House, 55 Basinghall Street, London EC2V 5EH England.
Telephone: 44-71-614-2200.
Hong Kong Office: 39th Floor, Bank of China Tower, One Garden Road, Hong Kong.
Telephone: 852-2521-4122.
Tokyo, Japan Office: Cleary, Gottlieb, Steen & Hamilton Gaikokuho Jimubengoshi Jimusho, 20th Floor, Shin Kasumigaseki Building, 3-2, Kasumigaseki 3-Chome, Chiyoda-Ku, Tokyo 100-0013, Japan.
Telephone: 81-3-3595-3911.
Frankfurt, Germany Office: Main Tower, Neue Mainzer Strasse 52, 60311 Frankfurt am Main, Germany.
Telephone: 49-69-971-03-0.

PARTNERS

Mario Siragusa
Peter H. Darrow
(Not admitted in Italy)
Giuseppe Scassellati-Sforzolini

RESIDENT ASSOCIATES

Roberto Bonsignore
Giancarlo Capolino
Nicola Ceraolo
Francisco L. Cestero
(Not admitted in Italy)
Stefano Ciullo
Francesco De Biasi
Claudio Di Falco
Fabio Filocamo
Pietro M. Fioruzzi
Tommaso Foco
Francesca M. Moretti
Stefania Pelusi
(Not admitted in Italy)
Vania Petrella
Stefano Sciolla

For full biographical listings, see the Martindale-Hubbell Law Directory

LOEB & LOEB LLP

A Limited Liability Partnership including Professional Corporations
Piazza Digione 1, Rome 00197
Telephone: 011-3906-808-8456
Facsimile: 011-3906-808-8288
Email: info@loeb.com *URL:* http://www.loeb.com
Los Angeles, California Office: Suite 1800, 1000 Wilshire Boulevard, 90017-2475.
Telephone: 213-688-3400.
Facsimile: 213-688-3460.
Century City (Los Angeles), California Office: Suite 2200, 10100 Santa Monica Boulevard, Los Angeles, 90067-4164.
Telephone: 310-282-2000.
Facsimile: 310-282-2192.
New York, N.Y. Office: 345 Park Avenue, 10154-0037.
Telephone: 212-407-4000.
Facsimile: 212-407-4990.
Nashville, Tennessee Office: 45 Music Square West, 37203-3205.
Telephone: 615-749-8300.
Facsimile: 615-749-8308.

MEMBERS OF FIRM

Lorenzo De Sanctis
Guendalina Ponti

ASSOCIATE

Riccardo Siciliani

For full biographical listings, see the Martindale-Hubbell Law Directory

JAPAN

*TOKYO,**

TOKYO AOYAMA LAW OFFICE

Attorneys at Law
BAKER & MCKENZIE
Attorney at Foreign Law Office
Qualified Joint Enterprise Offices
410 Aoyama Building, 2-3, Kita Aoyama 1 Chome, Tokyo 107-0061
Telephone: (03) 3403-5281
Intn'l Dialing: (81-3) 3403-5281
Cable Address: ABOGADO TOKYO
Telex: 28249
Answer Back: ABOGADO J28249
Facsimiles: (81-3) 3470-3152; 3470-3658; 3479-4224; 3479-4386
URL: http://www.bakerinfo.com
Associated Offices of Baker & McKenzie in: Almaty, Amsterdam, Bahrain, Baku, Bangkok, Barcelona, Beijing, Berlin, Bogotá, Brasília, Brussels, Budapest, Buenos Aires, Cairo, Caracas, Chicago, Dallas, Düsseldorf, Frankfurt, Geneva, Hanoi, Ho Chi Minh City, Hong Kong, Houston, Hsinchu, Juárez, Kyiv, London, Madrid, Manila, Melbourne, México City, Miami, Milan, Monterrey, Moscow, Münich, New York, Palo Alto, Paris, Prague, Rio de Janeiro, Riyadh, Rome, St. Petersburg, San Diego, San Francisco, Santiago, São Paulo, Singapore, Stockholm, Sydney, Taipei, Tijuana, Toronto, Valencia, Warsaw, Washington, D.C. and Zürich.
Correspondent Law Firm: Hadiputranto, Hadinoto & Partners, Jakarta.
Postal Address: C.P.O Box 1576, Tokyo, 100-91, Japan

Paul A. Davis
Naoaki Eguchi
John Kakinuki
Hiroshi Kondo
Yasushi Murofushi
Nobuko Narita
Kiyoshi Odaka
Hideo Ohta
Jeremy D. Pitts
Shinichi Saito
Hidetaka Sekine
Masatsugu Suzuki
Yukinori Watanabe

LOCAL PARTNERS

Yasuyoshi Goto
Anne K.T. Hung
Shimon Takagi
Edwin T. Whatley

OF COUNSEL

Mikako Fujiki
Kohji Mori
Yoshio Ohara

SENIOR FOREIGN ASSOCIATES

Kelli S. Longworth
Jean-Denis Marx
(Not admitted in Japan)

ASSOCIATES

Toshio Ishikawa
Yoshiya Ishimura
Takeru Ito
Masako Iwamoto
Akimoto Kawamura
Shinichi Kobayashi
Kazutaka Mizuochi
Yoshiaki Muto
Miho Niunoya
Masayoshi Odaka
Toshio Sasaki
Norihiro Sekiguchi
Akiko Sozu
Kaoruko Suzuki
Takeshi Takahashi
Shinji Toyohara
Akiko Tsukatani
Hideyuki Yamamoto

(See Next Column)

TOKYO AOYAMA LAW OFFICE, *Tokyo—Continued*

Mina Arai-Ito
(Not admitted in Japan)
Christopher M. Hodgens
(Not admitted in Japan)
Delphine F. Laisney-Dreux
Erin V. McKenzie
(Not admitted in Japan)
Cheryl A. Muller
(Not admitted in Japan)
James C. Plaisted
(Not admitted in Japan)
Safari Watanabe
(Not admitted in Japan)

For full biographical listings, see the Martindale-Hubbell Law Directory

American Lawyers In Tokyo

CLEARY, GOTTLIEB, STEEN & HAMILTON

(Cleary, Gottlieb, Steen & Hamilton Gaikokuho Jimubengoshi Jimusho)
In Tokyo since 1987.
Shin Kasumigaseki Building, 20th Floor, 3-2, Kasumigaseki 3-Chome, Chiyoda-ku, Tokyo 100-0013
Telephone: 81-3-3595-3911
Facsimile: 81-3-3595-3910
New York, New York Office: One Liberty Plaza, New York, N.Y. 10006.
Telephone: 212-225-2000.
Washington, D.C. Office: 2000 Pennsylvania Avenue, N.W., Suite 9000, Washington, D.C. 20006-1801.
Telephone: 202-974-1500.
Paris, France Office: 41, Avenue de Friedland, 75008 Paris, France.
Telephone: 33-1-40-74-68-00.
Brussels, Belgium Office: Rue de la Loi 23, Bte 5, 1040 Brussels, Belgium.
Telephone: 32-2-287-2000.
London, England Office: City Place House, 55 Basinghall Street, London EC2V 5EH England.
Telephone: 44-171-614-2200.
Hong Kong Office: 39th Floor, Bank of China Tower, One Garden Road, Hong Kong.
Telephone: 852-2521-4122.
Frankfurt, Germany Office: Main Tower, Neue Mainzer Strasse 52, 60311 Frankfurt am Main, Germany.
Telephone: 49-69-971-03-0.
Rome, Italy Office: Piazza di Spagna 15, 00187 Rome, Italy.
Telephone: 39-06-69-52-22-1.

RESIDENT PARTNER
Christopher H. Lunding

RESIDENT ASSOCIATES

Kimberly Brown Blacklow
(Not admitted in Japan)
Masahisa Ikeda
(Not admitted in Japan)
Laurie N. Lebrun
(Not admitted in Japan)
Brian A. Yeager
(Not admitted in Japan)

For full biographical listings, see the Martindale-Hubbell Law Directory

JONES, DAY, REAVIS & POGUE

(Jones, Day, Reavis & Pogue Gaikokuho Jimu Bengoshi Jimusho)
Toranomon 45 Mori Building, 3rd Floor, 1-5, Toranomon 5-Chome, Tokyo 105-0001
Telephone: 81-3-3433-3939
Telecopier: 81-3-5401-2725
Email: counsel@jonesday.com *URL:* http://www.jonesday.com
In Atlanta, Georgia: 3500 SunTrust Plaza, 303 Peachtree Street.
Telephone: 404-521-3939.
Telecopier: 404-581-8330.
In Brussels, Belgium: Avenue Louise 480, 7th Floor. B-1050 Brussels.
Telephone: 32-2-645-14-11.
Telecopier: 32-2-645-14-45.
In Chicago, Illinois: 77 West Wacker.
Telephone: 312-782-3939.
Telecopier: 312-782-8585.
In Cleveland, Ohio: North Point, 901 Lakeside Avenue.
Telephone: 216-586-3939.
Telecopier: 216-579-0212.
In Columbus, Ohio: 1900 Huntington Center.
Telephone: 614-469-3939.
Telecopier: 614-461-4198.
In Dallas, Texas: 2727 North Harwood Street.
Telephone: 214-220-3939.
Telecopier: 214-969-5100.
In Frankfurt, Germany: Hochhaus am Park, Grüneburgweg 102, 60323 Frankfurt am Main.
Telephone: 49-69-9726-3939.
Telecopier: 49-69-9726-3993.
In Geneva, Switzerland: 20, rue de Candolle.
Telephone: 41-22-320-2339.
Telecopier: 49-22-320-1232.
In Hong Kong: 29th Floor, Entertainment Building, 30 Queen's Road Central.
Telephone: 852-2526-6895.
Telecopier: 852-2868-5871.

(See Next Column)

In Irvine, California: 5 Park Plaza, Suite 1100.
Telephone: 949-851-3939.
Telecopier: 949-553-7539.
In London, England: Bucklersbury House, 3 Queen Victoria Street.
Telephone: 44-20-7236-3939.
Telecopier: 44-20-7236-1113.
In Los Angeles, California: 555 West Fifth Street, Suite 4600.
Telephone: 213-489-3939.
Telecopier: 213-243-2539.
In New York, New York: 599 Lexington Avenue.
Telephone: 212-326-3939.
Telecopier: 212-755-7306.
In Paris, France: 120, rue du Faubourg Saint-Honoré.
Telephone: 33-1-56-59-39-39.
Telecopier: 33-1-56-59-39-38
In Pittsburgh, Pennsylvania: 500 Grant Street, 31st Floor.
Telephone: 412-391-3939.
Telecopier: 412-394-7959.
In Riyadh, Saudi Arabia: The International Law Firm (In Association with Jones, Day, Reavis & Pogue), Sulaymaniyah, Prince Mishari IBN, Abdulaziz Street, P.O. Box 22166.
Telephone: (966-1) 462-8866.
Telecopier: (966-1) 462-9001.
In Shanghai, China: 2805 Kerry Centre, 1515 Nanjing Road West.
Telephone: 86-21-5298-6568.
Telecopier: 86-21-5298-6569.
In Sydney, Australia: Governor Phillip Tower, Level 38, 1 Farrer Place.
Telephone: 61-2-9210-6921.
Telecopier: 61-2-9210-6926.
In Taipei, Taiwan: 8th Floor, 2 Tun Hwa South Road, Section 2.
Telephone: (886-2) 2704-6808.
Telecopier: (886-2) 2704-6791.
In Washington, D.C.: 51 Louisiana Avenue, N.W.
Telephone: 202-879-3939.
Telecopier: 202-626-1700.

MEMBER OF FIRM
John C. Roebuck

OF COUNSEL
Masatami Otsuka

ASSOCIATE

David R. Nelson
(Not admitted in Japan)
Patricia Ginsberg
(Not admitted in Japan)

For full biographical listings, see the Martindale-Hubbell Law Directory

MILBANK, TWEED, HADLEY & McCLOY LLP

(Gaikokuho Jimu Bengoshi Jimusho)
Fukoku Seimei Building, 2-2, Uchisaiwai-cho 2-Chome, Chiyoda-ku, Tokyo 100-0011
Telephone: 81-3-3504-1050
Fax: 81-3-3595-2790; 81-3-3595-2840
Email: postmaster@milbank.com *URL:* http://www.milbank.com
New York, New York Office: 1 Chase Manhattan Plaza, 10005-1413.
Telephone: 212-530-5000.
Fax: 212-530-5219.
Midtown Office: 375 Park Avenue, Suite 3601, 10152.
Telephone: 212-530-5800.
Fax: 212-530-0158.
Los Angeles, California Office: 601 South Figueroa Street, 90017.
Telephone: 213-892-4000.
Fax: 213-629-5063.
Washington, D.C. Office: International Square Building, Suite 1100, 1825 Eye Street, N.W., 20006.
Telephone: 202-835-7500.
Fax: 202-835-7586.
London, England Office: Dashwood House, 69 Old Broad Street, London, EC2M 1QS.
Telephone: 44-207-448-3000.
Fax: 44-207-448-3029.
Hong Kong Office: 3007 Alexandra House, 16 Chater Road.
Telephone: 011-852-2971-4888.
Fax: 852-2840-0792; 852-2845-9046.
Singapore Office: 14-00 Caltex House, 30 Raffles Place, 048622.
Telephone: 65-428-2400.
Fax: 65-428-2500.
Moscow, Russia Office: 24/27 Sadovaya-Samotyochnya, Moscow, 103051.
Telephone: 7-501-258-5015.
Fax: 7-501-258-5014.

PARTNERS

Young Joon Kim
Jonathan A. Maizel
(Not admitted in Japan)

ASSOCIATES

William B. Bice
(Not admitted in Japan)
Thomas C. Lee
(Not admitted in Japan)
Yasufumi Nakamori
(Not admitted in Japan)
Susan A. Young
(Not admitted in Japan)

For full biographical listings, see the Martindale-Hubbell Law Directory

Paul, Hastings, Janofsky & Walker LLP

Gaikokuho-Jimu-Bengoshi Jimusho
A Limited Liability Partnership including Professional Corporations
Firm Established in 1951; Office in 1988
Taiyo Law Office (Registered Association)
Ark Mori Building, 12-32, Akasaka 1-Chome, Minato-Ku, P.O. Box 577, Tokyo 107
Telephone: (03) 3586-4711
Facsimile: (03) 3586-4705
Email: info@phjw.com
Atlanta, Georgia Office: 24th Floor, 600 Peachtree Street, N.E., 30308-2222.
Telephone: 404-815-2400.
Los Angeles, California Office: 555 South Flower Street, 90071-2371.
Telephone: 213-683-6000
New York, New York Office: 399 Park Avenue, 10022-4697.
Telephone: 212-318-6000.
Orange County, California Office: 695 Town Center Drive, Costa Mesa, 92626-1924.
Telephone: 714-668-6200.
San Francisco, California Office: 345 California Street, San Francisco, 94104-2635.
Telephone: 415-835-1600.
Stamford, Connecticut Office: 1055 Washington Boulevard, 06901-2217.
Telephone: 203-961-7400.
Washington, D.C. Office: 1299 Pennsylvania Avenue, N.W., 20036-5331.
Telephone: 202-508-9500.
London, England Office: The International Financial Centre, 25 Old Broad Street.
Telephone: (011) 44-171-562-4000.
ATTORNEY E-MAIL ADDRESSES: first initial middle initial last name @phjw.com (e.g. rmasbill@phjw.com)

MEMBERS OF FIRM

Mark L. Bronson (Not admitted in Japan)
Joel M. Simon (Not admitted in Japan)
John H. Steed
Kaoru Umino (Not admitted in Japan)

OF COUNSEL

James Che-Ming Hsu (Not admitted in Japan)
Tetsuya Ogawa
Joel H. Rothstein

ASSOCIATES

Atsuko Matsui
Keisuke Mochizuki
Asako Yamagami

For full biographical listings, see the Martindale-Hubbell Law Directory

Paul, Weiss, Rifkind, Wharton & Garrison

Gaikokuho Jimu Bengoshi Jimusho
Fukoku Seimei Building, 2-2 Uchisaiwaicho 2-chome, Chiyoda-ku, Tokyo 100-0011
Telephone: (81-3) 3597-8101
Facsimile: (81-3) 3597-8120
Email: mailbox@paulweiss.com *URL:* http://www.paulweiss.com
New York, N.Y. Office: 1285 Avenue of the Americas, 10019-6064.
Telephones: (212) 373-3000, TDD 212-373-2000;
Facsimile: 212-757-3990.
Washington, D.C. Office: 1615 L Street, NW, Suite 1300, 20036-5694.
Telephones: 202-223-7300, TDD 202-223-7490.
Facsimile: 202-223-7420.
Paris, France Office: 62, rue du Faubourg Saint-Honoré, 75008.
Telephone: (33-1) 53.43.14.14.
Facsimile: (33-1) 53.43.00.23.
Beijing, China: 2918 China World Tower II, No. 1 Jianguomenwai Dajie, 100004.
Telephones: (86-10) 6505-6882.
Facsimile: (86-10) 6505-6830.
Hong Kong Office: 12th Floor, Hong Kong Club Building, 3A Chater Road, (Central) Hong Kong.
Telephone: (852) 2536-9933.
Facsimile: (852) 2536-9622.

RESIDENT PARTNERS

Russell E. Colwell
Lionel H. Olmer

RESIDENT ASSOCIATES

Hans E. Kim (Not admitted in Japan)
Leza S. Tellam (Not admitted in Japan)

For full biographical listings, see the Martindale-Hubbell Law Directory

Shearman & Sterling

Fukoku Seimei Building, 5th Floor, 2-2-2, Uchisaiwaicho, Tokyo 100-0011
Telephone: (81-3) 5251-1601
Fax: (81-3) 5251-1602
URL: http://www.shearman.com
New York, N.Y. Office: 599 Lexington Avenue, New York, New York, 10022-6069.
Telephone: (212) 848-4000.
Telex: 667290. Num Lau.
Fax: (212) 848-7179.

(See Next Column)

Abu Dhabi, United Arab Emirates Office: Butti Al Otaiba Building, 13th Floor, Suite 1302, Sheikh Khalifa Street, P.O. Box 2948.
Telephone: (971-2) 6274477.
Fax: (971-2) 6268933.
Beijing, People's Republic of China Office: Suite #2205, Capital Mansion, No. 6, Xin Yuan Nan Road. Chao Yang District, Beijing, 100004.
Telephone: (86-10) 6465-2299.
Fax: (86-10) 6465-4578.
Düsseldorf, Federal Republic of Germany Office: Couvenstrasse 8 40211 Düsseldorf.
Telephone: (49 211) 178 88-0.
Fax: (49 211) 178 88-88.
Frankfurt, Federal Republic of Germany Office: Trianon Building, Mainzer Landstrasse 16, 60325 Frankfurt am Main.
Telephone: (49-69) 9711-1000.
Fax: (49-69) 9711-1100.
Hong Kong Office: Standard Chartered Bank Building, 4 Des Voeux Road, Central.
Telephone: (852) 2978-8000.
Fax: (852) 2978-8099.
London, England Office: Broadgate West, 9 Appold Street, London EC2A 2AP.
Telephone: 011-44-20-7655-5000.
Fax: 011-44-20-7655-5500.
Menlo Park, California Office: 1550 El Camino Real, 94025-4100.
Telephone: (650) 330-2200.
Fax: (650) 330-2299.
Paris, France Office: 114, avenue des Champs-Elysées, 75008.
Telephone: (33-1) 53-89-7000.
Fax: (33-1) 53-89-7070.
San Francisco, California Office: 555 California Street, 94104-1522.
Telephone: (415) 616-1100.
Fax: (415) 616-1199.
Singapore Office: 6 Battery Road #25-03. Singapore 049909.
Telephone: (65) 230-3800.
Fax: (65) 230-3899.
Toronto, Ontario, Canada Office: Commerce Court West, Suite 4405, P.O. Box 247, M5L 1E8.
Telephone: (416) 360-8484.
Fax: (416) 360-2958.
Washington, D.C. Office: 801 Pennsylvania Avenue, N.W., 20004-2604.
Telephone: (202) 508-8000.
Fax: (202) 508-8100.

RESIDENT PARTNER

David D. Deck (Not admitted in Japan; Managing Partner)

COUNSEL

Chieko Eda (Not admitted in Japan)

RESIDENT ASSOCIATES

Clifford J. Bernstein (Not admitted in Japan)
Isamu Paul Watson (Not admitted in Japan)

For full biographical listings, see the Martindale-Hubbell Law Directory

Simpson Thacher & Bartlett

David Sneider Gaikokuho Jimu Bengoshi Jimusho
Ark Mori Building, 30th Floor, 12-32, Akasaka 1-Chome, Minato-Ku, Tokyo 107
Telephone: 81-3-5562-8601
Telecopier: 81-3-5562-8606
ESL 62765846
URL: http://www.simpsonthacher.com
New York, NY Office: 425 Lexington Avenue, 10017-3954.
Telephone: 212-455-2000.
Telecopier: 212-455-2502. ESL 62928462.
Columbus, Ohio Office: One Riverside Plaza, 43215.
Telephone: 614-461-7799.
Telecopier: 614-461-0040.
Los Angeles, California Office: 10 Universal City Plaza, Suite 1850, Universal City, CA, 91608.
Telephone: 818-755-7000.
Fax: 818-755-7009.
Palo Alto, California Office: 3373 Hillview Avenue, 94304.
Telephone: 650-251-5000.
Telecopier: 650-251-5002.
London Office: 99 Bishopsgate, London EC2M 3YH, England.
Telephone: 207 422-4000.
Telecopier: 207 422-4022.
Hong Kong Office: Asia Pacific Finance Tower - 7th Floor, 3 Garden Road, Central, Hong Kong.
Telephone: 852-2514-7600.
Telecopier: 852-2869-7694.
Singapore Office: Suntec Tower One, 33rd Floor, 7 Temasek Boulevard, Singapore 038987.
Telephone: 65-430-5100.
Fax: 65-430-5151.

PARTNER

David A. Sneider

(See Next Column)

SIMPSON THACHER & BARTLETT, *Tokyo—Continued*

RESIDENT ASSOCIATES

Tomoko Akashi (Not admitted in Japan)
Colin P. A. Jones (Not admitted in Japan)
Alan G. Cannon (Not admitted in Japan)
Jin H. Park (Not admitted in Japan)
Jon R. Gray (Not admitted in Japan)

For full biographical listings, see the Martindale-Hubbell Law Directory

SULLIVAN & CROMWELL

Gaikokuho Jimu Bengoshi Jimusho
AKAI LAW OFFICES
(Registered Associated Offices)
Otemachi First Square East Tower 16, 5-1, Otemachi 1-chome, Chiyoda-ku, Tokyo 100-0004
Telephone: (011)(813)3213-6140
Telecopier: (011)(813)3213-6470
URL: http://www.sullcrom.com
New York City Office: 125 Broad Street, 10004-2498.
Telephone: 212-558-4000.
Telex: 62694.
Telecopier: 212-558-3588 or 212-514-5706.
Washington, D.C. Office: 1701 Pennsylvania Avenue, N.W., 20006-5805.
Telephone: 202-956-7500.
Telecopier: 202-293-6330.
Los Angeles, California Office: 1888 Century Park East, 90067-1725.
Telephone: 310-712-6600.
Telecopier: 310-712-8800.
Paris Office: 8, Place Vendôme, 75001 Paris, France.
Telephone: (011)(331) 44 50 60 00.
Telex: 240654.
Telecopier: (011)(331) 44 50 60 60 or (011)(331) 42 60 56 36.
London Office: St. Olave's House, 9a Ironmonger Lane, London EC2V 8EY, England.
Telephone: (011)(44207) 710 6500.
Telecopier: (011)(44207) 710 6565.
Melbourne Office: 101 Collins Street, Melbourne, Victoria 3000, Australia.
Telephone: (011)(613) 9635-1500.
Telecopier: (011)(613) 9654-2422.
Hong Kong Office: 28th Floor, Nine Queen's Road, Central, Hong Kong.
Telephone: (011)(852) 2826-8688.
Telecopier: (011)(852) 2522-2280.
Frankfurt Office: Neue Mainzer Strasse 52, 60322 Frankfurt, Germany.
Telephone: (011)(4969) 7191 26-0.
Telecopier: (011)(4969) 7191 26-10.
Beijing Office: The Beijing Representative Office of Sullivan & Cromwell, Suite 501, China World Trade Center, No. 1 Jianguo Menwai Avenue, Beijing 100004, P.R.C.
Telephone: (011)(86) 10 6505 6120.
Telecopier: (011)(86) 10 6505 6136.

PARTNER IN TOKYO

Robert G. DeLaMater (Not admitted in Japan; Also at Hong Kong Office)

ASSOCIATES IN TOKYO

Darin A. Bifani (Not admitted in Japan)
Eric C. Sibbitt (Not admitted in Japan)
Mark D. Hunsaker (Not admitted in Japan)
Yoichiro Taniguchi

AFFILIATED FIRM LAWYERS

Izumi Akai
Takashi Shimokado

For full biographical listings, see the Martindale-Hubbell Law Directory

WHITE & CASE

Limited Liability Partnership
KANDABASHI LAW OFFICES
(Registered Association)
Kandabashi Park Building, 19-1 Kanda-Nishikicho 1-Chome, Chiyoda-Ku, Tokyo 101-0054
Telephone: (81-3) 3259-0200
Facsimile: (81-3) 3259-0150
URL: http://www.whitecase.com
Los Angeles, California:
Telephone: 213-620-7700.
Facsimile: 213-687-0758; 213-452-2330; 213-452-2331.
Palo Alto, California:
Telephone: 650-213-0300.
Facsimile: 650-213-8158.
San Francisco, California:
Telephone: 415-544-1100.
Facsimile: 415-544-0202.
Miami, Florida:
Telephone: 305-371-2700.
Facsimile: 305-358-5744; 305-358-5766.
New York, New York:
Telephone: 212-819-8200.
Facsimile: 212-354-8113.

(See Next Column)

Washington, D.C.:
Telephone: 202-626-3600.
Facsimile: 202-639-9355.
Bratislava, Slovak Republic:
Telephone: (421-7) 5441-5100.
Facsimile: (421-7) 5441-6100.
Brussels, Belgium:
Telephone: (32-2) 219-16-20.
Facsimile: (32-2) 219-16-26.
Budapest, Hungary: Réczicza Law Firm White & Case.
Telephone: (36-1) 488-5200.
Facsimile: (36-1) 488-5299.
Frankfurt, Germany: White & Case (Rechtsanwälte).
Telephone: (49-69) 713-77-(0).
Facsimile: (49-69) 713-77-100.
Helsinki, Finland: Asianajotoimisto White & Case Oy.
Telephone: (358-9) 228-641.
Facsimile: (358-9) 228-64228.
Istanbul, Turkey:
Telephone: (90-212) 275-75-33.
Facsimile: (90-212) 275-75-43.
London, England:
Telephone: (44-20) 7600-7300.
Facsimile: (44-20) 7600-7030.
Moscow, Russia:
Telephone: (7-095) 787-3000.
Facsimile: (7-095) 787-3001.
Paris, France:
Telephone: (33-1) 55-04-15-15.
Facsimile: (33-1) 55-04-15-16.
Prague, Czech Republic:
Telephone: (420-2) 2481-0808; 2481-1796.
Facsimile: (420-2) 2481-0330; 2481-0252.
Stockholm, Sweden: White & Case Advokat AB.
Telephone: (46-8) 506-323-00.
Facsimile: (46-8) 611-21-22.
Warsaw, Poland: White & Case (Poland) Sp. z o.o.
Telephone: (48-22) 625-33-33; (48-22) 622-67-67; (48-39) 12-19-06.
Facsimile: (48-22) 628-22-28.
Johannesburg, Republic of South Africa:
Telephone: 27 (11) 884-7689.
Facsimile: 27 (11) 884-7229.
Almaty, Kazakhstan:
Telephone: (7-3272) 50-74-91/2.
Facsimile: (7-3272) 50-74-93.
Ankara, Turkey:
Telephone: (90-312) 442-5680.
Facsimile: (90-312) 442-5691/4.
Bangkok, Thailand: White & Case (Thailand) Limited.
Telephone: (662) 656-1721 to 32.
Facsimile: (662) 656-1733/34.
Bombay/Mumbai, India: Liaison Office, (91-22) 282-6300/01/02/03.
Facsimile: (91-22) 282-6305.
Hanoi, Vietnam:
Telephone: (84-4) 934-5355.
Facsimile: (84-4) 934-5356.
Ho Chi Minh City, Vietnam:
Telephone: (84-8) 821-0888.
Facsimile: (84-8) 823-6902.
Hong Kong: White & Case, Solicitors.
Telephone: (852) 2822-8700.
Facsimile: (852) 2845-9070.
Singapore, Republic of Singapore:
Telephone: (65) 225-6000.
Facsimile: (65) 225-6009.
Manama, Bahrain:
Telephone: (973) 9610105; (973) 9610119; (973) 535965.
Facsimile: (973) 590962; (973) 532342.
Jeddah, Saudi Arabia: Law Office of Hassan Mahassni,
Telephone: (966-2) 665-4353.
Facsimile: (966-2) 669-2996.
Riyadh, Saudi Arabia: Law Office of Hassan Mahassni,
Telephone: (966-1) 464-4006.
Facsimile: (966-1) 465-1348.
Mexico City, Mexico: White & Case, S.C.
Telephone: (52) 5-540-9600.
Facsimile: (52) 5-540-9699.
São Paulo, SP, Brazil:
Telephone: (55-11) 3171-0011.
Facsimile: (55-11) 3171-0041.
Associated Law Firm(s):
Bombay/Mumbai, India: India Law Services (ILS).
Telephones: (91-22) 284-1995; (91-22) 284-1847.
Facsimile: (91-22) 285-0824.
New Delhi, India: India Law Services (ILS).
Telephone: (91-11) 697-1602/3/4.
Facsimile: (91-11) 698-8860.
Jakarta, Indonesia: Ali Budiardjo, Nugroho, Reksodiputro, Counsellors at Law.
Telephone: (62-21) 250-5125; 250-5136.
Facsimile: (62-21) 250-5392; 250-5122; 250-5001.

(See Next Column)

WHITE & CASE—*Continued*

Associated Consultancies:
Jakarta, Indonesia: PT WCI Konsultan.
Telephone: (62-21) 577-1527.
Facsimile: (62-21) 577-1535/6.

RESIDENT PARTNERS

Burton H. Fohrman	Eric N. Roose
Robert F. Grondine	Gary M. Thomas
Gregory J. Ossi (Not admitted in Japan)	Christopher P. Wells
	Michael J. Yoshii (Not admitted in Japan)

JAPANESE COUNSEL

Hisao Hirose	Mizuho Yamada
Tetsuya Morimoto	Koichiro Ohashi
Keiko Tashiro	Kouji Ishikawa
Mika Suzuki	Michihiro Maeda
Yoshiko Yasuda	Chiho Saito

ASSOCIATES

Keld O. Conradsen (Not admitted in Japan)
Metavee Eiamkachorn (Not admitted in Japan)
Gerald M. Fujii
George J. Hibbert
Reiko Hiramatsu (Not admitted in Japan)
Junko Iijima (Not admitted in Japan)
Charles N. Koyama (Not admitted in Japan)
Yvette S. Lanneaux (Not admitted in Japan)
Kenneth J. Lebrun (Not admitted in Japan)
Joshua Margolis (Not admitted in Japan)
Todd M. McHenry
Robert E. Melson, Jr. (Not admitted in Japan)
Sergey J. Milanov
Samantha D. Naik (Not admitted in Japan)
Jeffrey K. Natori
Linda L. Ng
Brent O'Leary (Not admitted in Japan)
Clovis Peryer (Not admitted in Japan)
Dmitri Rezchikov (Not admitted in Japan)
Michael H. Shikuma (Not admitted in Japan)
Glen E. Sugimoto (Not admitted in Japan)
Ichizo Takayama
Yukiko Tanaka (Not admitted in Japan)
Jonathan A. Tyler (Not admitted in Japan)

For full biographical listings, see the Martindale-Hubbell Law Directory

WINTHROP, STIMSON, PUTNAM & ROBERTS

(Gaikokuho Jimu Bengoshi Jimusho)
608 Atagoyama Bengoshi Building, 6-7, Atago 1-Chome, Minato-Ku, Tokyo 105
Telephone: 011-813-3437-9740
Telefax: 011-813-3437-9261
URL: http://www.winstim.com
New York Main Office: One Battery Park Plaza, New York, N.Y. 10004-1490.
Telephone: 212-858-1000.
Fax: 212-858-1500.
Stamford, Connecticut Office: Financial Centre, 695 East Main Street, P.O. Box 6760, 06904-6760.
Telephone: 203-348-2300.
Fax: 203-965-8226.
Washington, D.C. Office: 1133 Connecticut Avenue, N.W., 20036.
Telephone: 202-775-9800.
Fax: 202-833-8491.
Palm Beach, Florida Office: 125 Worth Avenue, Suite 310, 33480.
Telephone: 561-655-7297.
Fax: 561-833-6726.
London Office: 54 Lombard Street, London EC3V 9DH, England.
Telephone: 011-44207-648-9201.
Fax: 011-44207-648-1656.
Hong Kong, China Office: 2505 Asia Pacific Finance Tower, Citibank Plaza, 3 Garden Road, Central.
Telephone: 011-852-2530-3400.
Fax: 011-852-2530-3355.
Singapore Office: 6 Battery Road #38-01/B, Singapore 049909.
Telephone: 65-227-4700.
Fax: 65-227-4711.

PARTNER

Jeffrey L. Pote

For full biographical listings, see the Martindale-Hubbell Law Directory

KAZAKHSTAN

ALMATY,

American Lawyers In Almaty

BAKER & MCKENZIE

8th Floor, 155 Abai Avenue, Almaty
Telephone: 50-99-45
Int'l Dialing: (7-3272) 50-99-45
Facsimile: (7-3272) 50-95-79
Email: almaty.info@bakernet.com *URL:* http://www.bakerinfo.com
Associated Offices of Baker & McKenzie in: Amsterdam, Bahrain, Baku, Bangkok, Barcelona, Beijing, Berlin, Bogotá, Brasília, Brussels, Budapest, Buenos Aires, Cairo, Caracas, Chicago, Dallas, Düsseldorf, Frankfurt, Geneva, Hanoi, Ho Chi Minh City, Hong Kong, Houston, Hsinchu, Juárez, Kyiv, London, Madrid, Manila, Melbourne, México City, Miami, Milan, Monterrey, Moscow, Münich, New York, Palo Alto, Paris, Prague, Rio de Janeiro, Riyadh, Rome, St. Petersburg, San Diego, San Francisco, Santiago, São Paulo, Singapore, Stockholm, Sydney, Taipei, Tijuana, Tokyo, Toronto, Valencia, Warsaw, Washington, D.C. and Zürich.
Correspondent Law Firm: Hadiputranto, Hadinoto & Partners, Jakarta.

PARTNERS

Mark A. Lockwood (Not admitted in Kazakhstan)	Curtis B. Masters (Not admitted in Kazakhstan)

ASSOCIATES

Elina A. Boldina (Not admitted in Kazakhstan)
Natalia V. Bulekbayeva
Giorgi Gelovani (Not admitted in Kazakhstan)
Alexander G. Korchagin (Not admitted in Kazakhstan)
Azamat A. Kuatbekov
Laila T. Nazarbekova
Igor A. Novikov
Vakhid Y. Saparov
Robert F. Taylor (Not admitted in Kazakhstan)
Mark T. Urban (Not admitted in Kazakhstan)
Mariya N. Zikeyeva

For full biographical listings, see the Martindale-Hubbell Law Directory

SQUIRE, SANDERS & DEMPSEY

141 Ablay Khan Avenue, Second Floor, Almaty 480091
Telephone: +73-27-50-11-25
Fax: +73-27-50-11-25
URL: http://www.ssd.com
Cincinnati, Ohio Office: PNC Center, 201 East Fifth Street, Suite 1700, Cincinnati, Ohio 45202.
Telephone: 513-361-1200.
Fax: 513-361-1201.
Cleveland, Ohio Office: 4900 Key Tower, 127 Public Square, Cleveland, Ohio 44114-1304.
Telephone: 216-479-8500.
Fax: 216-479-8780.
Columbus, Ohio Office: 1300 Huntington Center, 41 South High Street, Columbus, Ohio 43215-6150.
Telephone: 614-365-2700.
Fax: 614-365-2499.
Houston, Texas Office: 6250 Chase Tower, 600 Travis Street, Houston, Texas 77002-3007.
Telephone: 713-546-5850.
Fax: 713-546-5830.
Jacksonville, Florida Office: One Enterprise Center, Suite 2100, 225 Water Street, Jacksonville, Florida 32202-4424.
Telephone: 904-366-2420.
Fax: 904-356-2986.
Miami, Florida Office: 201 South Biscayne Boulevard, 2900 Miami Center, Miami, Florida 33131-4330.
Telephone: 305-577-8700.
Fax: 305-358-1425.
New York, New York Office: 350 Park Avenue, New York, New York 10022-6002.
Telephone: 212-872-9800.
Fax: 212-872-9815.
Phoenix, Arizona Office: Two Renaissance Square, 40 North Central Avenue, Suite 2700, Phoenix, Arizona 85004-4498.
Telephone: 602-528-4000.
Fax: 602-253-8129.
Washington, D.C. Office: 1201 Pennsylvania Avenue, N.W., Suite 500, Washington, D.C. 20004-2491.
Telephone: 202-626-6600.
Fax: 202-626-6780.
Bratislava, Slovak Republic Office: Zochova 5, 811 03 Bratislava, Slov k Republic.
Telephone: 421-7-5441-7611.
Fax: 42-1-7-6280-2212.
Brussels, Belgium Office: Avenue Louise, 165 Box 15, 1050 Brussels, Belgium.
Telephone: 32-2-627-1111.
Fax: 32-2-627-1100.
Budapest, Hungary Office: H-1062 Budapest, Andrassy ut. 64, Budapest, Hungary.
Telephone: 36-1-428-7111.
Fax: 36-1-428-7100.

(See Next Column)

SQUIRE, SANDERS & DEMPSEY, *Almaty—Continued*

Kyiv, Ukraine Office: 14A Yaroslaviv Val, Kyiv 252034, Ukraine.
Telephone: 38-044-228-8687.
Fax: 38-044-228-4938.
London, England Office: Royex House, Aldermanbury Square, London, EC2V 7HR England.
Madrid, Spain Office: Calle Velazquez 108-110, 28006 Madrid, Spain.
Telephone: 34-91-590-2420.
Fax: 34-91-590-2421.
Moscow, Russian Federation Office: Paveletskaya Square II, 1 Valovaya Street, 5th Floor, Moscow 113054, Russian Federation.
Telephone: 7-501-258-5250.
Fax: 7-501-258-5251.
Prague, Czech Republic Office: Václavské náměst 1 57/813, 110 00 Praha 1, Czech Republic.
Telephone: 420-2-2166-2111.
Fax: 420-2-2166-2222.
Hong Kong Office: Rooms 1101-2 St. George's Building, 2 Ice House Street, Central, Hong Kong.
Telephone: 852-2509-9732.
Fax: 852-2509-9772.
Taipei, Taiwan Office: 14F, 116 Nanking East Road, Sec. 2, Taipei, Taiwan, Republic of China.
Telephone: 886-2-2531-2888.
Fax: 886-2-2571-6199.

PARTNERS

Sarah C. Carey (Not admitted in Kazakhstan)

ASSOCIATES

James M. Higbee (Not admitted in Kazakhstan)
Nurlan Dostanov
Zhanar Iskhakova
Marat Kabdikulov
Elshat Seksembayeva

For full biographical listings, see the Martindale-Hubbell Law Directory

KYRGYZSTAN

BISHKEK,

MAYER, BROWN & PLATT

66 Kalyka Akieva Street, Bishkek 720010
Telephone: 011-996-312-65-02-56
Facsimile: 011-996-312-620-980
Email: nic@mbp.bishkek.su *URL:* http://www.mayerbrown.com
Berlin, Germany Office: Breite Strasse 29, Muehlendamm, 10178.
Telephone: 011-49-30-2060-7710.
Facsimile: 011-49-30-2060-7744.
Chicago, Illinois Office: 190 South LaSalle Street, 60603-3441.
Telephone: (312) 782-0600.
Facsimile: (312) 701-7711.
Telex: 190404.
Cable: LEMAY
Charlotte, North Carolina Office: 100 North Tryon Street, Suite 2400.
Telephone: (704) 444-3500.
Fax: (704) 377-2033.
Cologne, Germany Office: Kaiser-Wilhelm-Ring 27-29, 50672.
Telephone: 011-49-221-5771-100.
Facsimile: 011-49-221-5771-199.
Houston, Texas Office: 700 Louisiana Street, Suite 3600, 77002-2730.
Telephone: (713) 221-1651.
Facsimile: (713) 224-6410.
Telex: 775809.
Cable: LEMAYHOU.
London, England Office: Bucklersbury House, 3 Queen Victoria Street, London, EC4N 8EL, England.
Telephone: 011-44-171-246-6200.
Facsimile: 011-44-171-329-4465.
Telex: 8811095.
Cable: LEMAYLDN.
Los Angeles, California Office: 350 South Grand Avenue, 25th Floor, 90071-1503.
Telephone: (213) 229-9500.
Facsimile: (213) 625-0248.
Telex: 188089.
Cable: LEMAYLA.
New York, New York Office: 1675 Broadway, 10019-5820.
Telephone: (212) 506-2500.
Facsimile: (212) 262-1910.
Telex: 701842.
Cable: LEMAYEN.
Washington, D.C. Office: 1909 K Street, N.W., 20006-1101.
Telephone: (202) 263-3000.
Facsimile: (202) 263-3300.
Telex: 892603.
Cable: LEMAYDC.
Representative Offices:
Ashgabat, Turkmenistan: 28 Gogol Street, 744000.
Telephone: 011-99-312-355247.
Facsimile: 011-99-312-510074.

(See Next Column)

Tashkent, Republic of Uzbekistan: 3rd Floor, 1 Turab Tula Street, 700003.
Telephone: 011-998-71-1206-627.
Facsimile: 011-998-71-1206-329.
Mexico City, Mexico, D.F., Independent Mexico Correspondent: Jáuregui, Navarrete, Nader y Rojas, S.C., Torre Arcos, Paseo de los Tamarindos No. 400-B. Col. Bosques de las Lomas, 05120.
Telephone: 011-525-267-45-00.
Facsimile: 011-525-267-45-99.
Paris, France, Independent Paris Correspondent: Lambert & Lee, 13 Avenue Hoche, 75008.
Telephone: 011-33-1-53-53-43-43.
Facsimile: 011-33-1-53-96-03-83.

ASSOCIATE

Gulnara A. Kalikova

For full biographical listings, see the Martindale-Hubbell Law Directory

LEBANON

*BEIRUT,** (Beyrouth)

TYAN & ASSOCIES

22, La Sagesse Street-Rmeil, Beirut
Telephone: (961) (1) 561 673; (961) (1) 561 674
Fax: (961) (1) 561 435
Email: tyanasso@dm.net.lb
Paris, France Office: Law Offices of Nady Tyan, 12, Avenue Pierre ler de Serbie, 75116 Paris.
Telephone: 01 47.20.18.50.
Fax: 01 47.20.06.28.
Associated with Whitman Breed Abbott & Morgan LLP, 200 Park Avenue, New York, N.Y. Telephone: 212-351-3000. 212-351-3022.
Fax: 212-351-3131. 212-351-3003.

MEMBERS OF FIRM

Nady Tyan
Maurice Absi
Souheil Elias
Chamel Bassile
Mireille Richa
Graziella Saliba
Fady Ibrahim
Ghada Yazbeck
Claudia Karam
Ariette Khairallah

OF COUNSEL

Berge Setrakian

For full biographical listings, see the Martindale-Hubbell Law Directory

MEXICO

CIUDAD JUAREZ, CHIHUAHUA,

BAKER & MCKENZIE

P.T. de la Republica 3304, Piso 2, 32330 Ciudad Juarez, Chihuahua
Telephone: (16) 29-1300
Intn'l Dialing: (52-16) 29-1300
Facsimile: (52-16) 29-1399
Mailing Address: P.O. Box 9338, El Paso, Texas, 79995
URL: http://www.bakerinfo.com
Associated Offices of Baker & McKenzie in: Almaty, Amsterdam, Bahrain, Baku, Bangkok, Barcelona, Beijing, Berlin, Bogotá, Brasília, Brussels, Budapest, Buenos Aires, Cairo, Caracas, Chicago, Dallas, Düsseldorf, Frankfurt, Geneva, Hanoi, Ho Chi Minh City, Hong Kong, Houston, Hsinchu, Kyiv, London, Madrid, Manila, Melbourne, México City, Miami, Milan, Monterrey, Moscow, Münich, New York, Palo Alto, Paris, Prague, Rio de Janeiro, Riyadh, Rome, St. Petersburg, San Diego, San Francisco, Santiago, São Paulo, Singapore, Stockholm, Sydney, Taipei, Tijuana, Tokyo, Toronto, Valencia, Warsaw, Washington, D.C. and Zürich.
Correspondent Law Firm: Hadiputranto, Hadinoto & Partners, Jakarta.

PARTNERS

Carlos Angulo Parra
Jaime Gonzalez-Bendiksen
Raul Jaquez-Madrid
Eduardo Romero-Ramos
Jorge L. Ruiz

LOCAL PARTNERS

Graciela M. Punete De Diedrich
Edmundo Elias-Fernandez
Francisco Javier Legarreta-Martinez
Fidencio Martínez-Buenrostro
Manuel Padron-Castillo

ASSOCIATES

Roberto Anaya-Moreno
Luis Clemente Carbajo
Rafael Cereceres Ronquillo
Alejandro Enriquez-Mariscal
Hector Granados-Hernández
Jesus E. Gutierrez Colomo
David H. Huie-Gamboa
Cesar Humberto Lara-Godina
Ricardo C. Leon-Santacruz
Juan Levario-Gebbia
Manuel Renato Martinez Quezada

(See Next Column)

BAKER & MCKENZIE—*Continued*

ASSOCIATES (Continued)

Daniel Mendez-Antillon
Juan E. Muñoz-Rivera
Arturo Muñoz-Vázquez
Mariana Ruiz Linares
Max E. Salazar-Quintana
Claudia Tabuenca-Orozco
Benjamin Torres-Barron
Irlanda Torres-Lara
Juan-Carlos Valles-Zavala
Karla Venzor-Crabtree
Martha Villalobos-Murillo
Victor Yanar-Rios
Paulina Zubikarai-Espinosa

For full biographical listings, see the Martindale-Hubbell Law Directory

GARZA GARCIA, NUEVO LEON,

American Lawyers in Garza Garcia

THOMPSON & KNIGHT L.L.P.

(Attorneys and Counselors)
Edificio Losoles PD-4, Av. Lázaro Cárdenas No. 2400 PTE San Pedro Garza Garcia, Garza Garcia, Nuevo Leon 66220
Telephone: (52-8) 363-0096
Telecopy: (52-8) 363-3067
URL: http://www.tklaw.com
Dallas, Texas Office: 1700 Pacific Avenue, Suite 3300, 75201.
Telephone: 214-969-1700.
Telecopy: 214-969-1751.
Telex: 732298.
Austin, Texas Office: 1200 San Jacinto Center, 98 San Jacinto Boulevard, 78701.
Telephone: 512-469-6100.
Telecopy: 512-469-6180.
Fort Worth, Texas Office: 801 Cherry Street, Suite 1600, 76102.
Telephone: 817-347-1700.
Telecopy: 817-347-1799.
Houston, Texas Office: Thompson Knight Brown Parker & Leahy L.L.P., 1200 Smith Street, Suite 3600.
Telephone: 713-654-8111.
Telecopier: 713-654-1871.

PARTNERS

J. Galdino Canseco-Quintanilla
Joe A. Rudberg
Michael C. Titens

For full biographical listings, see the Martindale-Hubbell Law Directory

*MEXICO, D.F.,**

BAKER & MCKENZIE

Edificio Plaza Inverlat Blvd. M. Avila Camacho No. 1-12°, Col. Lomas de Chapultepec, 11560 Mexico, D.F.
Telephone: (5) 230-2900
Intn'l Dialing: (52-5) 230-2900
Facsimiles: (52-5) 557-8829; 580-1795; 230-2999
URL: http://www.bakerinfo.com
Associated Offices of Baker & McKenzie in: Almaty, Amsterdam, Bahrain, Baku, Bangkok, Barcelona, Beijing, Berlin, Bogotá, Brasília, Brussels, Budapest, Buenos Aires, Cairo, Caracas, Chicago, Dallas, Düsseldorf, Frankfurt, Geneva, Hanoi, Ho Chi Minh City, Hong Kong, Houston, Hsinchu, Juárez, Kyiv, London, Madrid, Manila, Melbourne, Miami, Milan, Monterrey, Moscow, Münich, New York, Palo Alto, Paris, Prague, Rio de Janeiro, Riyadh, Rome, St. Petersburg, San Diego, San Francisco, Santiago, São Paulo, Singapore, Stockholm, Sydney, Taipei, Tijuana, Tokyo, Toronto, Valencia, Warsaw, Washington, D.C. and Zürich.
Correspondent Law Firm: Hadiputranto, Hadinoto & Partners, Jakarta.

Abraham G. Alegría Martínez
Jorge A. de Regil
Raymundo E. Enriquez
Carlos R. Grimm
Gaspar Gutiérrez-Centeno
Manuel Limón Aguirre-B.
Ricardo Martinez-Rojas
Genaro Martinez-Siller
Jorge Narváez-Hasfura
Jorge Peláez-Bolaños
Luis M. Ruiz de Velasco
Alejandro Sepúlveda de la Fuente

LOCAL PARTNERS

José Antonio Ambrosi
Perla D. Arreola Carbajal
María Casas Lopez
Miguel Angel Ruggeri-Correa
Gerardo Saavedra Silva
Reynaldo Vizcarra-Méndez

Peter Michael Bostock
Francisco Escutia Rodriguez
Claudia Freyre Castaneda
Enrique A. Hernández-Villegas
Alfredo Kupfer Dominguez
María del Rosario Lombera-Gonzalez
Luis F. Lozano-Olivares
Francisco Luna-Anaya
Guillermo Massieu-Urquiza
Jose Juan Mendez-Cortes
Maria Teresa Muñoz-Berrones
Javier Pandal Perez
Salvador Pasquel-Villegas
Jose A. Postigo-Uribe
Alejandro Resendiz-Tellez
Jose Luis Ruiz Sotres
Ma. de la Luz Sánchez-de la Concha
Adriana Velasco-Tarelo
Luis Gerardo Villazón-Méndez

For full biographical listings, see the Martindale-Hubbell Law Directory

CARLSMITH BALL

A Partnership including Law Corporations
Sierra Nevada 119, Col. Lomas de Chapultepec, 11000 Mexico, D.F.
Telephone: 52-5-520-8514, 52-5-520-8757
Fax: 52-5-540-1545
Email: execdirector@carlsmith.com *URL:* http://www.carlsmith.com
Honolulu, Hawaii Office: Suite 2200, Pacific Tower, 1001 Bishop Street. P.O. Box 656, 96809-3402.
Telephone: 808-523-2500.
Fax: 808-523-0842.
Kapolei, Hawaii Office: Suite 318, Kapolei Building, 1001 Kamokila Boulevard, 96707.
Telephone: 808-523-2500.
Fax: 808-674-0850.
Wailuku, Maui Hawaii Office: Suite 400, One Main Plaza, 2200 Main Street, P.O. Box 1086, 96793-1086.
Telephone: 808-242-4535.
Fax: 808-244-4974.
Kailua-Kona, Hawaii Office: 75-1000 Henry Street, Suite 209, 96740.
Telephone: 808-329-6464.
Fax: 808-329-9450.
Hilo, Hawaii Office: 121 Waianuenue Avenue, P.O. Box 686, 96721-0686.
Telephone: 808-935-6644.
Fax: 808-935-7975.
Hagatna, Guam Office: Suite 401, Bank of Hawaii Building, 134 West Soledad Avenue, P.O. Box BF, 96932-5027.
Telephone: 671-472-6813.
Fax: 671-477-4375.
Telex: 721-6445 CWCMI GM.
Saipan, Commonwealth of the Northern Mariana Islands Office: Carlsmith Building, Capitol Hill, P.O. Box 5241, 96950-5241.
Telephone: 670-322-3455.
Fax: 670-322-3368.
Los Angeles, California Office: 9th Floor, 444 South Flower Street, 90071-2901.
Telephone: 213-955-1200.
Fax: 213-623-0032.
Washington, D.C. Office: Suite 300, 1201 Pennsylvania Avenue, N.W., 20004-2401.
Telephone: 202-628-2228.
Fax: 202-628-2071.
Mexico, D.F. Office of Carlsmith Ball, S.C. (Authorized to practice as foreign legal consultants in Mexico): Sierra Nevada 119, Lomas de Chapultepec, 11000 Mexico, D.F.
Telephone: 52-5-520-8514, 52-5-520-8757.
Fax: 52-5-540-1545.

RESIDENT PARTNER

John E. Rogers (Not admitted in Mexico)

For full biographical listings, see the Martindale-Hubbell Law Directory

CURTIS, MALLET-PREVOST, COLT & MOSLE

Ruben Dario 281 Piso 9 Col. Bosque de Chapultepec, Mexico, D.F. 11530
Telephone: 525-282-0444
Telecopier: 525-282-0637
Email: info@cm-p.com *URL:* http://www.cm-p.com
New York, New York Office: Curtis, Mallet-Prevost, Colt & Mosle LLP, 101 Park Avenue.
Telephone: 212-696-6000.
Telecopier: 212-697-1559.
Newark, New Jersey Office: Curtis, Mallet-Prevost, Colt & Mosle LLP, One Gateway Center, Suite 403.
Telephone: 973-622-0605.
Telecopier: 973-622-5646.
Washington, D.C. Office: Curtis, Mallet-Prevost, Colt & Mosle LLP, Suite 1205L, 1801 K Street, N.W.
Telephone: 202-452-7373.
Telecopier: 202-452-7333.
Houston, Texas Office: Curtis, Mallet-Prevost, Colt & Mosle LLP, 2 Houston Center, 909 Fannin Street, Suite 3725.
Telephone: 713-759-9555.
Telecopier: 713-759-0712.
Stamford, Connecticut Office: Curtis, Mallet-Prevost, Colt & Mosle LLP, One Canterbury Green.
Telephone: 203-359-6200.
Telecopier: 203-328-2617.
London, England Office: Curtis, Mallet-Prevost, Colt & Mosle LLP, Two Throgmorton Avenue. EC2N 2DL.
Telephone: 0207-633-7957.
Telecopier: 0207-638-5512.
Paris, France Office: Curtis, Mallet-Prevost, Colt & Mosle LLP, 15 rue d'Astorg, 75008.
Telephone: 42-66-39-10.
Telecopier: 42-66-39-62.
Frankfurt am Main 1, Germany Office: Curtis, Mallet-Prevost, Colt & Mosle LLP, Staufenstrasse 42.
Telephone: 69-971-4420.
Telecopier: 69-17 33 99.
Muscat, Sultanate of Oman Office: Curtis, Mallet-Prevost, Colt & Mosle LLP, Jewel Beach-134.
Telephone: 968-607-725.
Telecopier: 968-607-724.

(See Next Column)

CURTIS, MALLET-PREVOST, COLT & MOSLE, *Mexico, D.F.—Continued*

Milan, Italy Office: Curtis, Mallet-Prevost & Gilioli, Piazzale Principessa Clotilde 8, 20121.
Telephone: (39) 02 29 00 29 32.
Telecopier: (39) 02 65 75 969.

PARTNERS

Eloy Barbará-de-Parres
Mark H. O'Donoghue (Not admitted in Mexico)
Charles L. O. Buderi (Not admitted in Mexico)
Frank A. Russo

COUNSEL

Alexander C. Hoagland, Jr.

For full biographical listings, see the Martindale-Hubbell Law Directory

STRASBURGER & PRICE, L.L.P.

A Partnership including Professional Corporations
Montes Urales 632, Piso 3, Lomas de Chapultepec, 11000 Mexico, D.F.
Telephone: 525-202-7665
Fax: 525-202-2367
URL: http://www.strasburger.com
Dallas, Texas Office: 901 Main Street, Suite 4300.
Telephone: 214-651-4300.
Fax: 214-651-4330.
Austin, Texas Office: 600 Congress Avenue, Suite 2600.
Telephone: 512-499-3600.
Fax: 512-499-3660.
Houston, Texas Office: Suite 2800, One Houston Center, 1221 McKinney.
Telephone: 713-951-5600.
Fax: 713-951-5660.
San Antonio, Texas Office: Bank of America Plaza, 300 Convent Street, Suite 900.
Telephone: 210-250-6000.
Fax: 210-250-6100.

Jane Woods LaFranchi (Not admitted in Mexico)
Susan A. Fletcher (Not admitted in Mexico)
James A. Lawton (Not admitted in Mexico)

For full biographical listings, see the Martindale-Hubbell Law Directory

MONTERREY, NUEVO LEÓN,

BAKER & MCKENZIE

Oficinas en el Parque- piso 10, Blvd. Antonio L. Rodríguez 1884 Pte., 64650 Monterrey, Nuevo León
Telephone: (8) 399-1300
Intn'l Dialing: (52-8) 399-1300
Facsimile: (52-8) 399-1399
URL: http://www.bakerinfo.com
Associated Offices of Baker & McKenzie in: Almaty, Amsterdam, Bahrain, Baku, Bangkok, Barcelona, Beijing, Berlin, Bogotá, Brasília, Brussels, Budapest, Buenos Aires, Cairo, Caracas, Chicago, Dallas, Düsseldorf, Frankfurt, Geneva, Hanoi, Ho Chi Minh City, Hong Kong, Houston, Hsinchu, Juárez, Kyiv, London, Madrid, Manila, Melbourne, México City, Miami, Milan, Moscow, Münich, New York, Palo Alto, Paris, Prague, Rio de Janeiro, Riyadh, Rome, St. Petersburg, San Diego, San Francisco, Santiago, São Paulo, Singapore, Stockholm, Sydney, Taipei, Tijuana, Tokyo, Toronto, Valencia, Warsaw, Washington, D.C. and Zürich.
Correspondent Law Firm: Hadiputranto, Hadinoto & Partners, Jakarta.

PARTNERS

Javier Luis Navarro-Velasco
Andrés Ochoa-Bünsow

LOCAL PARTNERS

Ricardo Castro-Garza
Mauricio Martinez D'Meza Violante
Carol S. Osmond (Not admitted in Mexico)
Gerardo Prado-Hernández

ASSOCIATES

Alfonso C. Cortez-Fernandez
Deyanira Flores-Rodriguez
Juan Bernardo Garcia-Garza
Alfonso García-Lozano
Mario Emilio Gutiérrez-Caballero
José Enrique Guzmán-Quiroga
Carlos Leal-Isla Garza
Ricardo C. Leon-Santacruz
Cynthia Marcela Ortega Arredondo
Carrie L. Osman (Not admitted in Mexico)
Ana Margarita Ríos-Farjat
Sergio Rodriguez Castillo
Ernesto F. Silvas Medina
Gerardo Treviño-Gil
Fernando Treviño Martinez
Rafael Villamar-Ramos

For full biographical listings, see the Martindale-Hubbell Law Directory

TIJUANA, BAJA CALIFORNIA,

BAKER & MCKENZIE

Blvd. Agua Caliente no. 10611 - 1er.Piso, Edificio Centura, 22420 Tijuana, Baja California
Telephone: (6) 633-4300
Intn'l Dialing: (52-6) 633-4300
Facsimile: (52-6) 633-4399
URL: http://www.bakerinfo.com
Associated Offices of Baker & McKenzie in: Almaty, Amsterdam, Bahrain, Baku, Bangkok, Barcelona, Beijing, Berlin, Bogotá, Brasília, Brussels, Budapest, Buenos Aires, Cairo, Caracas, Chicago, Dallas, Düsseldorf, Frankfurt, Geneva, Hanoi, Ho Chi Minh City, Hong Kong, Houston, Hsinchu, Juárez, Kyiv, London, Madrid, Manila, Melbourne, México City, Miami, Milan, Monterrey, Moscow, Münich, New York, Palo Alto, Paris, Prague, Rio de Janeiro, Riyadh, Rome, St. Petersburg, San Diego, San Francisco, Santiago, São Paulo, Singapore, Stockholm, Sydney, Taipei, Tokyo, Toronto, Valencia, Warsaw, Washington, D.C. and Zürich.
Correspondent Law Firm: Hadiputranto, Hadinoto & Partners, Jakarta.
Postal Address: P.O. Box 1205, Chula Vista, California 91912.

PARTNERS

Jose M. Larroque
René X. Pérez-Ruíz

LOCAL PARTNER

Federico Ruanova Guinea

ASSOCIATES

Alicia Corona-Beltran
Juan Carlos Gastelum-Treviño
Maria O. Guajardo Calvillo
Eduardo Moel Modiano
Carlos Fernando Perez-Gautrin
Florentina E. Reyes-Retana Villalobos
Juan Ygnacio Reyes-Retana Villalobos
Leobardo Tenorio-Malof

For full biographical listings, see the Martindale-Hubbell Law Directory

NETHERLANDS

*AMSTERDAM,**

CARON & STEVENS/BAKER & MCKENZIE

(Associated Office of Baker & McKenzie)
Leidseplein 29, 1017 PS Amsterdam
Telephone: (020) 5517555
Intn'l Dialing: (31-20) 5517555
Facsimiles: (31-20) 6267949; 6232884
Mailing Address: P.O. Box 2720, 1000, CS Amsterdam,
URL: http://www.bakerinfo.com

Mark P. Bongard
Jan-Kees Brandse
Mic van Bremen
M. H. Frank van Buuren
Ton H. M. Daniels
Peter Dekker
Eduard J. Ferman
Carla Hamburger
Albert van Herk
Frank R. Herreveld
Fred C. de Hosson
Norbert R. Jansen
Maarten L. B. van der Lande
Gijsbert Loos
Theo L. van Maaren
Dick M. N. Schonis
Piet L. A. M. Schroeder
Willem F. C. Stevens
Joseph F. van Vlijmen
Willem C. B. Van Wettum
Henk van Wilsum

LOCAL PARTNERS

Pieter G. van Druten
Serge J. H. Gijrath
Roelof O. N. van Holthe tot Echten
Alexander R. T. Odle
Wouter A. Paardekooper
Hélène A. M. Stuijt
Barend W. J. M. de Roy van Zuidewijn
Eric T. H. Scheer

Boris M. van Beek
Carolina J.M. van Beek
Misha G. lutje Beerenbroek
Jaap Willem Bellingwout
Frank de Beÿer (Not admitted in Netherlands)
Susan C. Bienfait (Not admitted in Netherlands)
Mirjam A. de Blécourt-Wouterse
Karin W. M. Bodewes
Hélène M. J. Bogaard
Emile Bongers
Frank M. M. de Bont (Not admitted in Netherlands)
Michael A. Broeders
Lidwyn M. M. Brokx (Not admitted in Netherlands)
C. J. M. van Bronkhorst
Marc J.L. van Campen
Hendrikje S. C. Crebolder
Mariëlle Daudt
Ingrid A. F. Depijper
Frank T.M. Deurvorst
Marloes Diepenbach
Jeroen N.A. Dijkman
Stephanie A. van Gelderen
Paul Gerrits
Jan-Willem A. M. Gerritsen
Bart-Jan E. Gorissen
Alexandra F. van de Griendt
Michiel A. van Haelst
Menno J. Heerma van Voss
Johannes C. Hintzen
Jeroen O. Hoekstra
Nathalie A. Hollestelle
Caroline Holtrop-Bun
Esther M. Hovenier
Sander Huisjes
Allard A. H. J. Huizing
Michiel A. de Jager
Piet-Hein C. de Jager
Mike Jansen

(See Next Column)

CARON & STEVENS/BAKER & MCKENZIE—*Continued*

Anita A. de Jong	Peter Roos
Alexandra F. Jonker	Esther H.M. Rosenberg
Herman L. Kaemingk	Florian F.J. Ruyten
Helger Kamerman	Eduard Scheenstra
Bob van der Kamp	Marc Schoolmeesters (Not admitted in Netherlands)
Karianne Kas	
Marc G. Kelder	Marie Christine Schoute (Not admitted in Netherlands)
Laurentein K.A. Kok (Not admitted in Netherlands)	Rosalien R. Schreuder
Claudia Koken	Harro F.K. Schulz
Bernd F.G. van Kooten	Rieke M. P. J. Smakman
Svenne N. Korthals Altes	Karin J. T. Smit
Chr. Frank Kroes	Jan L. N. Snel
Antal S. van der Laken	Pamela L. N. Spaans
Pieter Reinien Leguit (Not admitted in Netherlands)	Niels C. van Steÿn (Not admitted in Netherlands)
Lenet T. Leusink	Fedor L. Tanke
Martyn Roelof Maathuis	J.A. Tempelman
Jean-Paul M. van Marissing	Anthony S.K. Terng
Ruud Mars	Carina M.J. Tielemans (Not admitted in Netherlands)
Ciel Meewis (Not admitted in Netherlands)	Jacobus William de Tombe (Not admitted in Netherlands)
Sabine H. Merkus	
L. van Middelkoop	Nynke Vegter (Not admitted in Netherlands)
Hans Mouthaan	
Hubertus W. van Osch	Raymond Verhage
Christa A.M. van de Paverd	Irene H. Vermeeren-Keijzers
Therry K. M. Penners	David Verstraten
Eline Polak	Suzanne J. Verver
J.A.A.J. Raijmakers	Margot M. van Vuurden (Not admitted in Netherlands)
Mariëlle M.P.E. Reints	
Anouk S. Reitsma	Klaas-Jan Visser
Solange van Rens (Not admitted in Netherlands)	Marco Wallart
	Robert van Warmerdam
Charles G. A. van Rijckevorsel	M. L. Webb
Cees J. A. F. Rijssenbeek	Menno Weij

Redmar A. Wolf

For full biographical listings, see the Martindale-Hubbell Law Directory

PHILIPPINES

*METRO MANILA,**

QUISUMBING TORRES

(Associated with Baker & McKenzie)
11th Floor, Pacific Star Building, Makati Ave. corner Sen. Gil. J. Puyat Ave. Makati City 1200, Metro Manila
Telephone: 817-3016; 878-6900; 811-5925
Intn'l Dialing: (63-2) 817-3016; 878-6900; 811-5925
Cable Address: ABOGADO MANILA
Facsimiles: (63-2) 811-5640; 811-5641
Mailing Address: MCPO Box 327, Makati City 1299, Philippines,
URL: http://www.bakerinfo.com
Associated Offices of Baker & McKenzie in: Almaty, Amsterdam, Bahrain, Baku, Bangkok, Barcelona, Beijing, Berlin, Bogotá, Brasília, Brussels, Budapest, Buenos Aires, Cairo, Caracas, Chicago, Dallas, Düsseldorf, Frankfurt, Geneva, Hanoi, Ho Chi Minh City, Hong Kong, Houston, Hsinchu, Juárez, Kyiv, London, Madrid, Melbourne, México City, Miami, Milan, Monterrey, Moscow, Münich, New York, Palo Alto, Paris, Prague, Rio de Janeiro, Riyadh, Rome, St. Petersburg, San Diego, San Francisco, Santiago, São Paulo, Singapore, Stockholm, Sydney, Taipei, Tijuana, Tokyo, Toronto, Valencia, Warsaw, Washington, D.C. and Zürich.
Correspondent Law Firm: Hadiputranto, Hadinoto & Partners, Jakarta.

Juan G. Collas	Christopher L. Lim
Edgardo M. de Vera	Lucas M. Nunag
Leo G. Dominguez	Ramon J. Quisumbing
Natividad B. Kwan	Romeo L. Salonga

Jose R. Sandejas

LOCAL PARTNERS

Arthur P. Autea	Pearl T. Liu
Emmanuel S. Buenaventura	Ma. Ruby Sarah S. Nitorreda
Ricardo P. C. Castro, Jr.	Rodrigo Lope S. Quimbo
Dennis G. Dimagiba	Gil Roberto L. Zerrudo

OF COUNSEL

Vicente A. Torres

Cornelio B. Abuda	Anthony D. Bengzon
Maria Franchette M. Acosta	André Philippe G. Betita
Shirley F. Alinea	Raymond Peter C. de Castro
Ariel R. Arriola	Kenneth L. Chua
Laurence Hector B. Arroyo	Jose Jaime V. Cruz
John Maynard G. Atotubo	Alejandre C. Dueñas II
Genaro Jehremiah W. C. Asis	Jonathan C. Flaminiano

(See Next Column)

May R. Flores	Gregory G. Macaltao
Ma. Carolina V. Fuentes	Ma. Christina J. Macasaet
Ma. Jamea Assumpta S. Garcia	Esteban Y. Mendoza
Katrina V. Goli	Ferdinand M. Negre
Jocelyn Anne J. Gregorio	Elizabeth B. Opeña
Richard C. Gutierrez	Franklin A. Prestousa
Teodoro Alejandro Y. Kalaw IV	Lourdes Marivic K. Punzalan-Espiritu
Calvin L. Kohchet-Chua	Jonathan P. Serrano
Alfredo R. Lagamon, Jr.	Nina Patricia D. Sison
Larissa G. Lambino	Felix T. Sy, Jr.
Yvonne Angeli C. Lee	Shennan A. Sy

Ulfredo A. Tuyac

For full biographical listings, see the Martindale-Hubbell Law Directory

POLAND

WARSAW,

American Lawyers In Warsaw

BAKER & MCKENZIE GRUSZCZYSKI & PARTNERS LAW OFFICES

ul. Dluga 26/28, 00-238 Warsaw
Telephone: (22) 635 3521; 635 4111; 635 0521; 635 8611; 635 9611; 39121203 (Komertel/satellite)
Intn'l Dialing: (48-22) 635 3521; 635 4111; 635 0521; 635 8611; *635 9611; (48) 39121203 (Komertel/satellite)*
Facsimiles: (48-22) 635 9447; (48) 39121213 (Komertel/satellite)
URL: http://www.bakerinfo.com
Associated Offices of Baker & McKenzie in: Almaty, Amsterdam, Bahrain, Baku, Bangkok, Barcelona, Beijing, Berlin, Bogotá, Brasília, Brussels, Budapest, Buenos Aires, Cairo, Caracas, Chicago, Dallas, Düsseldorf, Frankfurt, Geneva, Hanoi, Ho Chi Minh City, Hong Kong, Houston, Hsinchu, Juárez, Kyiv, London, Madrid, Manila, Melbourne, México City, Miami, Milan, Monterrey, Moscow, Münich, New York, Palo Alto, Paris, Prague, Rio de Janeiro, Riyadh, Rome, St. Petersburg, San Diego, San Francisco, Santiago, São Paulo, Singapore, Stockholm, Sydney, Taipei, Tijuana, Tokyo, Toronto, Valencia, Washington, D.C. and Zürich.
Correspondent Law Firm: Hadiputranto, Hadinoto & Partners, Jakarta.

RESIDENT PARTNERS

Wojciech T. Bialik	Jerzy Skrzypowski
Robert A. O. Fröman (Not admitted in Poland)	Piotr Święcicki (Not admitted in Poland)
Jur Gruszczyński	Tomasz Ujejski (Not admitted in Poland)

LOCAL PARTNERS

Slawomir Boruc	Konrad Konarski
Agnieszka Duda	Nicholas H. Richardson
Marcin R. Gmaj	(Not admitted in Poland)

Piotr Strawa

OF COUNSEL

Andrzej Tynel

RESIDENT ASSOCIATES

Andrzej Foltyn	Ireneusz Matusielański
Dariusz C. Bach	Dariusz Nasilowski
Slawomir Chmielewski	Ignatjew Pawel
Carole Ditty (Not admitted in Poland)	Wojciech Pfadt
	Krzysztof Pisarek
Wojciech Dmoch	Roberto Rios-Herran (Not admitted in Poland)
Michèle Fajtmann (Not admitted in Poland)	Marcin RomaŃczuk
Przemystaw Filipowicz	Waleria K. Skarzyńska
Agata Klimek-Cortinovis	Sylwia Sobowiec
Krzysztof Korzeniewski	Pawel Świrski
Pawel Magierowski	Ewa Zalewska

For full biographical listings, see the Martindale-Hubbell Law Directory

HOGAN & HARTSON SP.ZO.O.

Atrium Tower, Al. Jana Pawla II 25, 00-854 Warsaw
Telephone: (48 22) 653-4200
Fax: (48 22) 653-4250
URL: www.hhlaw.com
Washington, D.C. Office: Columbia Square, 555 13th Street, N.W.
Telephone: 206-637-5600.
Telex: 89-2757.
Cable Address: "Hogander Washington".
Fax: 202-637-5910.
Brussels, Belgium Office: Avenue des Arts 41, 1040.
Telephone: (32.2) 505.09.11.
Fax: (32.2) 505.09.96.
Budapest, Hungary (Affiliated Office): Nagy & Pintér, Hogan & Hartson Law Office, Bank Center, Granite Tower, 9th Floor, Budapest V., Szabadsag ter 7, 1944 Hungary.
Telephone: (36-1) 302-9050.
Fax: (36-1) 302-9060.

(See Next Column)

HOGAN & HARTSON SP.ZO.O., *Warsaw—Continued*

London, England Office: One Angel Court, EC2R 7HJ.
Telephone: +(44) 207-367-0200.
Fax: +(44) 207-367-0220.
Moscow, Russia Office: 33/2 Usacheva Street, Building 3, 119048.
Telephone: (7095) 245-5190. Int'l
Telephone: (7501) 907-0451.
Fax: (7095) 245-5192. Int'l
Fax: (7501) 907-0462.
Paris, France (Affiliated Office): Cariddi, Mee, Rué, Avocats Associés à la Cour de Paris, 12, rue de la Paix, 75002.
Telephone: (33-1) 42.61.57.71.
Fax: (33-1) 42.61.79.21.
Prague, Czech Republic (Affiliated Office): Hogan & Hartson, Advokátní Kanceláře, v.o.s., Trziste 13, 118 00.
Telephone: (420-2) 2211-7111.
Fax: (420-2) 2211-7222.
Baltimore, Maryland Office: 111 South Calvert Street.
Telephone: 410-659-2700.
Fax: 410-539-6981.
Rockville, Maryland Office: 600 Jefferson Plaza, Suite 203.
Telephone: 301-315-2206.
Fax: 301-315-9046.
Boulder, Colorado Office: 1800 Broadway, Suite 200.
Telephone: 720-406-5300.
Fax: 720-406-5301.
Colorado Springs, Colorado Office: Two North Cascade Avenue, Suite 1300.
Telephone: 719-448-5900.
Fax: 719-448-5922.
Denver, Colorado Office: One Tabor Center, Suite 1500, 1200 Seventeenth Street.
Telephone: 303-899-7300.
Fax: 303-899-7333.
Los Angeles, California Office: Biltmore Tower, 500 S. Grand Avenue, Suite 1900.
Telephone: 213-337-6700.
Fax: 213-337-6701.
Newport Beach, California Office: 4675 MacArthur Court, Suite 670.
Telephone: 949-250-4550.
Fax: 949-833-0976.
McLean, Virginia Office: 8300 Greensboro Drive.
Telephone: 703-610-6100.
Fax: 703-610-6200.
New York, New York Office: 885 Third Avenue, 26th Floor.
Telephone: 212-409-9800.
Fax: 212-409-9801.

PARTNERS

Joseph C. Bell	Nevin J. Kelly
Michael L. Cheroutes	Krzysztof Stefanowicz
Aleksander Galos	Zdzislaw W. Wieckowski
Maciej Jamka (Adwokat)	(Not admitted in Poland)

OF COUNSEL

Iwo Byczewski	Bogudar Kordasiewicz

ASSOCIATES

Stefan Jaworski	Lech Najbauer
Robert W. Karwowski	Agnieszka Suchecka-Tarnacka

For full biographical listings, see the Martindale-Hubbell Law Directory

RUSSIA

MOSCOW,

SQUIRE, SANDERS & DEMPSEY

Paveletskaya Square II, 1 Valovaya Street, 5th Floor, 113054 Moscow
Telephone: 7-501-258-5250
Fax: 7-501-258-5251
Email: ssdinfo@ssd.com *URL:* http://www.ssd.com
Cincinnati, Ohio Office: PNC Center, 201 East Fifth Street, Suite 1700, Cincinnati, Ohio 45202.
Telephone: 513-361-1200.
Fax: 513-361-1201.
Cleveland, Ohio Office: 4900 Key Tower, 127 Public Square, Cleveland, Ohio 44114-1304.
Telephone: 216-479-8500.
Fax: 216-479-8780.
Columbus, Ohio Office: 1300 Huntington Center, 41 South High Street, Columbus, Ohio 43215-6150.
Telephone: 614-365-2700.
Fax: 614-365-2499.
Houston, Texas Office: 6250 Chase Tower, 600 Travis Street, Houston, Texas 77002-3007.
Telephone: 713-546-5850.
Fax: 713-546-5830.

(See Next Column)

Jacksonville, Florida Office: One Enterprise Center, Suite 2100, 225 Water Street, Jacksonville, Florida 32202-4424.
Telephone: 904-366-2420.
Fax: 904-356-2986.
Miami, Florida Office: 201 South Biscayne Boulevard, 2900 Miami Center, Miami, Florida 33131-4330.
Telephone: 305-577-8700.
Fax: 305-358-1425.
New York, New York Office: 350 Park Avenue, New York, New York 10022-6002.
Telephone: 212-872-9800.
Fax: 212-872-9815.
Phoenix, Arizona Office: Two Renaissance Square, 40 North Central Avenue, Suite 2700, Phoenix, Arizona 85004-4498.
Telephone: 602-528-4000.
Fax: 602-253-8129.
Washington, D.C. Office: 1201 Pennsylvania Avenue, N.W., Suite 500, Washington, D.C. 20004-2491.
Telephone: 202-626-6600.
Fax: 202-626-6780.
Almaty, Kazakhstan Office: 141 Albay Khan Avenue, Second Floor, Almaty, Kazakhstan 480091.
Telephone: +73-27-50-11-25.
Fax: +73-27-50-11-25.
Bratislava, Slovak Republic Office: Zochova 5, 811 03 Bratislava, Slovak Republic.
Telephone: 421-7-5441-7611.
Fax: 42-1-7-6280-2212.
Brussels, Belgium Office: Avenue Louise, 165 Box 15, 1050 Brussels, Belgium.
Telephone: 32-2-627-1111.
Fax: 32-2-627-1100.
Budapest, Hungary Office: H-1062 Budapest, Andrassy ut. 64, Budapest, Hungary.
Telephone: 36-1-428-7111.
Fax: 36-1-428-7100.
Kyiv, Ukraine Office: 14A Yaroslaviv Val, Kyiv 252034, Ukraine.
Telephone: 38-044-228-8687.
Fax: 38-044-228-4938.
London, England Office: Royex House, Aldermanbury Square, London EC2V 7HR.
Telephone: 44-171-776-5200.
Fax: 44-171-776-5233.
Madrid, Spain Office: Calle Velazquez 108-110, 28006 Madrid, Spain.
Telephone: 34-91-590-2420.
Fax: 34-91-590-2421.
Prague, Czech Republic Office: Václavské náměst 1 57/813, 110 00 Praha 1, Czech Republic.
Telephone: 420-2-2166-2111.
Fax: 420-2-2166-2222.
Hong Kong Office: Rooms 1101-2 St. George's Building, 2 Ice House Street, Central, Hong Kong.
Telephone: 852-2509-9732.
Fax: 852-2509-9772.
Taipei, Taiwan Office: 14F, 116 Nanking East Road, Sec. 2, Taipei, Taiwan, Republic of China.
Telephone: 886-2-2531-2888.
Fax: 886-2-2571-6199.

PARTNERS

A. Randolph Bregman	Sarah C. Carey

OF COUNSEL

Laurence C.T. George	Tatiana K. Kovaleva

Michael J. Sussman

ASSOCIATES

Olga Bezrukova	Marina A. Kaldina

Anna Proshina

For full biographical listings, see the Martindale-Hubbell Law Directory

American Lawyers In Moscow

BAKER & MCKENZIE

Bolshoi Strochenovsky Pereulok, 22/25, 113054 Moscow
Telephone: Telephone: (095) 230-60-36
Intn'l Dialing: (1-212) 891-3799* (7-095) 230-60-36
Telex: 413671
Answer Back: 413671 BAKER SU
Facsimile: (7-095) 230-60-47
**This number is available as a telephone line from 9:* 00 a.m. to 9:00 p.m. Moscow time. After 9:00 p.m. Moscow time, the number is switched to serve as a facsimile line.
URL: http://www.bakerinfo.com
Associated Offices of Baker & McKenzie in: Almaty, Amsterdam, Bahrain, Baku, Bangkok, Barcelona, Beijing, Berlin, Bogotá, Brasília, Brussels, Budapest, Buenos Aires, Cairo, Caracas, Chicago, Dallas, Düsseldorf, Frankfurt, Geneva, Hanoi, Ho Chi Minh City, Hong Kong, Houston, Hsinchu, Juárez, Kyiv, London, Madrid, Manila, Melbourne, México City, Miami, Milan, Monterrey, Münich, New York, Palo Alto, Paris, Prague, Rio de Janeiro, Riyadh, Rome, St. Petersburg, San Diego, San Francisco, Santiago, São Paulo, Singapore, Stockholm, Sydney, Taipei, Tijuana, Tokyo, Toronto, Valencia, Warsaw, Washington, D.C. and Zürich.
Correspondent Law Firm: Hadiputranto, Hadinoto & Partners, Jakarta.

PARTNERS

Eugene A. Arievich
Alexander Chmelev (Not admitted in Russia)
Max B. Gutbrod (Not admitted in Russia)
Paul J. Melling (Not admitted in Russia)
Adrian S. Moore (Not admitted in Russia)
Carol A. M. Patterson (Not admitted in Russia)

ASSOCIATES

Evgeny V. Astakhov
Dr. Sergei V. Avramov
Julia Vassilievna Borozdna
Jean A. Brough (Not admitted in Russia)
Alexander A. Bychkov
Vladimir V. Dragunov
Nikolay Y. Isaakov
Vladimir V. Khvalei (Not admitted in Russia)
Elena Sergeevna Mossina
Marat V. Mouradov
Ilya Stanislavovich Petukhov
William E. Pomeranz (Not admitted in Russia)
Dr. Andrey Vladimirovich Popov
Igor B. Pozhitkov
Evgueni L. Reizman
Vladimir N. Schitikov
Andrei V. Soukhomlinov
Maxim S. Tikhonov
Sergei P. Voitishkin

For full biographical listings, see the Martindale-Hubbell Law Directory

CHADBOURNE & PARKE LLP

52/5 Kosmodamianskaya Naberezhnaya, Moscow 113054
Telephone: 7095-974-2424 Facsimile: 7095-974-2425
International satellite lines via U.S.: Telephone: 212-408-1190. Facsimile: 212-408-1199
New York, N.Y. Office: 30 Rockefeller Plaza, 10112.
Telephone: 212-408-5100.
Facsimile: 212-541-5369.
Los Angeles, California Office: 601 South Figueroa Street, 90017.
Telephone: 213-892-1000.
Facsimile: 213-622-9865.
Washington, D.C. Office: 1200 New Hampshire Avenue, N.W., 20036.
Telephone: 202-974-5600.
Facsimile: 202-974-5602.
London, England Affiliate Office: Chadbourne & Parke, a multinational partnership of Registered Foreign Lawyers and Solicitors, Regis House, 45 King William Street, London, EC4R 9AN.
Telephone: 44-171-337-8000.
Facsimile: 44-171-337-8001.
Hong Kong, China Office: 1701A The Hong Kong Club Building, 3A Chater Road, Central, Hong Kong.
Telephone: 852-2842-5400.
Facsimile: 852-2521-7527.

PARTNERS

Laura M. Brank
Mikhail A. Rozenberg

RESIDENT GENERAL DIRECTOR

Genrikh P. Padva

RESIDENT COUNSEL

Shane R. DeBeer (Not admitted in Russia)

RESIDENT ASSOCIATES

Anastasia Efimova
Ilya Y. Glotin
Konstantin Konstantinov
Eugeniya Korotkova
Alexander Kozlovski
Natasha Menshikova
Julia Romanova
Eleonora E. Sergeeva
Andrei V. Zalivako

For full biographical listings, see the Martindale-Hubbell Law Directory

DEBEVOISE & PLIMPTON LLC

Bolshoi Palashevsky Pereulok 13/2, 4th Floor, Moscow 103104
Telephone: 7 (095 or 503) 956-3858
Fax: 7 (095 or 503) 956-3868
Email: 2225346@mcimail.com
New York, N.Y.: Debevoise & Plimpton, 875 Third Avenue, 10022.
Telephone: 212-909-6000.
Telex: (Domestic) 148377 DEBSTEVE NYK.
Telecopier: (212) 909-6836.
Washington, D.C.: 555 13th Street, N.W., 20004.
Telephone: 202-383-8000.
Telecopier: (202) 383-8118.
Paris, France: 21 Avenue George V 75008.
Telephone: (33-1) 40 73 12 12.
Telecopier: (33-1) 47 20 50 82.
Telex: 648141F DPPAR.
London, England: Old Broad Street, EC2N 1HQ.
Telephone: (44-171) 786-9000.
Telex: 88 4569 DPLON G.
Telecopier: (44-171) 588-4180.
Hong Kong: 13/F Entertainment Building, 30 Queen's Road Central.
Telephone: (852) 2810-7918.
Fax: (852) 2160-9800.

RESIDENT PARTNER

Roswell B. Perkins

RESIDENT INTERNATIONAL COUNSEL

Dr. Dmitri V. Nikiforov (Also at New York, New York Office)

RESIDENT ASSOCIATES

Kenneth Schneider
Nadia Y. Rendak
Innokenty Y. Alekseev
Olga Frolova

INTERNATIONAL COUNSEL

Jonathan H. Hines

For full biographical listings, see the Martindale-Hubbell Law Directory

HOGAN & HARTSON L.L.P.

33/2 Usacheva Street, Building 3, 119048 Moscow
Telephone: (7095) 245-5190
Int'l Telephone: (7501) 907-0451
Fax: (7095) 245-5192
Int'l Fax: (7501) 907-0462
URL: www.hhlaw.com
Washington, D.C. Office: Columbia Square, 555 13th Street, N.W.
Telephone: 206-637-5600.
Telex: 89-2757.
Cable Address: "Hogander Washington".
Fax: 202-637-5910.
Brussels, Belgium Office: Avenue des Arts 41, 1040.
Telephone: (32.2) 505.09.11.
Fax: (32.2) 505.09.96.
Budapest, Hungary (Affiliated Office): Nagy & Pintér, Hogan & Hartson Law Office, Bank Center, Granite Tower, 9th Floor, Budapest V., Szabadsag ter 7, 1944 Hungary.
Telephone: (36-1) 302-9050.
Fax: (36-1) 302-9060.
London, England Office: One Angel Court, EC2R 7HJ.
Telephone: +(44) 207-367-0200.
Fax: +(44) 207-367-0220.
Paris, France (Affiliated Office): Cariddi, Mee, Rué, Avocats Associés à la Cour de Paris, 12, rue de la Paix, 75002.
Telephone: (33-1) 42.61.57.71.
Fax: (33-1) 42.61.79.21.
Prague, Czech Republic (Affiliated Office): Hogan & Hartson, Advokátní Kanceláře, v.o.s., Trziste 13, 118 00.
Telephone: (420-2) 2211-7111.
Fax: (420-2) 2211-7222.
Warsaw, Poland Office: Hogan & Hartson Sp.zo.o, Atrium Tower, Al. Jana Pawla II 25, 00-854.
Telephone: (48-22) 653-4200.
Fax: (48-22) 653-4250.
Baltimore, Maryland Office: 111 South Calvert Street.
Telephone: 410-659-2700.
Fax: 410-539-6981.
Rockville, Maryland Office: 600 Jefferson Plaza, Suite 203.
Telephone: 301-315-2206.
Fax: 301-315-9046.
Boulder, Colorado Office: 1800 Broadway, Suite 200.
Telephone: 720-406-5300.
Fax: 720-406-5301.
Colorado Springs, Colorado Office: Two North Cascade Avenue, Suite 1300.
Telephone: 719-448-5900.
Fax: 719-448-5922.
Denver, Colorado Office: One Tabor Center, Suite 1500, 1200 Seventeenth Street.
Telephone: 303-899-7300.
Fax: 303-899-7333.
Los Angeles, California Office: Biltmore Tower, 500 S. Grand Avenue, Suite 1900.
Telephone: 213-337-6700.
Fax: 213-337-6701.

(See Next Column)

HOGAN & HARTSON L.L.P., *Moscow—Continued*

Newport Beach, California Office: 4675 MacArthur Court, Suite 670.
Telephone: 949-250-4550.
Fax: 949-833-0976.
McLean, Virginia Office: 8300 Greensboro Drive.
Telephone: 703-610-6100.
Fax: 703-610-6200.
New York, New York Office: 885 Third Avenue, 26th Floor.
Telephone: 212-409-9800.
Fax: 212-409-9801.

PARTNERS

Rebecca B. Bronson (Not admitted in Russia)
Todd D. Schafer (Not admitted in Russia)

COUNSEL

Robert C. Satrom (Not admitted in Russia)

ASSOCIATES

Sergei V. Terentiev
Zarina Tsomaeva

For full biographical listings, see the Martindale-Hubbell Law Directory

MILBANK, TWEED, HADLEY & MCCLOY LLP

24/27 Sadovaya-Samotyochnaya, Moscow 103051
Telephone: 7-501-258-5015
Fax: 7-501-258-5014
Email: postmaster@milbank.com *URL:* http://www.milbank.com
New York, New York Office: 1 Chase Manhattan Plaza, 10005-1413.
Telephone: 212-530-5000.
Fax: 212-530-5219.
Midtown Office: 375 Park Avenue, Suite 3601, 10152.
Telephone: 212-530-5800.
Fax: 212-530-0158.
Los Angeles, California Office: 601 South Figueroa Street, 90017.
Telephone: 213-892-4000.
Fax: 213-629-5063.
Washington, D.C. Office: International Square Building, Suite 1100, 1825 Eye Street, N.W., 20006.
Telephone: 202-835-7500.
Fax: 202-835-7586.
Tokyo, Japan Office: Fukoku Seimei Building, 2-2, Uchisaiwai-cho 2-Chome, Chiyoda-ku, Tokyo 100-0011, Japan.
Telephone: 81-3-3504-1050.
Fax: 81-3-3595-2790, 81-3-3595-2840.
London, England Office: Dashwood House, 69 Old Broad Street, London, EC2M 1QS.
Telephone: 44-207-448-3000.
Fax: 44-207-448-3029.
Hong Kong Office: 3007 Alexandra House, 16 Chater Road.
Telephone: 852-2971-4888.
Fax: 852-2840-0792, 852-2845-9046.
Singapore Office: 14-00 Caltex House, 30 Raffles Place, 048622.
Telephone: 65-428-2400.
Fax: 65-428-2500.

PARTNER

Holly A. Nielsen (Not admitted in Russia)

ASSOCIATE

Elena A. Kuryatnikova

For full biographical listings, see the Martindale-Hubbell Law Directory

ST. PETERSBURG,

American Lawyers In St. Petersburg

BAKER & MCKENZIE

Bolshaya Morskaya, 57, 190000 St. Petersburg
Telephone: Telephone: (812) 325-83-08
Int'l Dialing: (7-812) 325-83-08 (Satellite)
Facsimile: (7-812) 325-60-13 (Satellite)
Email: office@bm.spb.ru *URL:* http://www.bakerinfo.com
Associated Offices of Baker & McKenzie in: Almaty, Amsterdam, Bahrain, Baku, Bangkok, Barcelona, Beijing, Berlin, Bogotá, Brasília, Brussels, Budapest, Buenos Aires, Cairo, Caracas, Chicago, Dallas, Düsseldorf, Frankfurt, Geneva, Hanoi, Ho Chi Minh City, Hong Kong, Houston, Hsinchu, Juárez, Kyiv, London, Madrid, Manila, Melbourne, México City, Miami, Milan, Monterrey, Moscow, Münich, New York, Palo Alto, Paris, Prague, Rio de Janeiro, Riyadh, Rome, San Diego, San Francisco, Santiago, São Paulo, Singapore, Stockholm, Sydney, Taipei, Tijuana, Tokyo, Toronto, Valencia, Warsaw, Washington, D.C. and Zürich.
Correspondent Law Firm: Hadiputranto, Hadinoto & Partners, Jakarta.

PARTNER

James T. Hitch, III (Not admitted in Russia)

ASSOCIATES

Maxim V. Kalinin
Igor N. Makarov
Sergey K. Nosov
Alexey A. Trusov

For full biographical listings, see the Martindale-Hubbell Law Directory

SAUDI ARABIA

JEDDAH,

LAW OFFICE OF HASSAN MAHASSNI

In Association with White & Case LLP
Al-Nakheel Center, 3rd Floor, Medina Road on Palestine Circle, P.O. Box 2256, Jeddah
Telephone: (966-2) 665-4353
Facsimile: (966-2) 669-2996
Los Angeles, California:
Telephone: 213-620-7700.
Facsimile: 213-687-0758; 213-452-2330; 213-452-2331.
Palo Alto, California:
Telephone: 650-213-0300.
Facsimile: 650-213-8158.
San Francisco, California:
Telephone: 415-544-1100.
Facsimile: 415-544-0202.
Miami, Florida:
Telephone: 305-371-2700.
Facsimile: 305-358-5744; 305-358-5766.
New York, New York:
Telephone: 212-819-8200.
Facsimile: 212-354-8113.
Washington, D.C.:
Telephone: 202-626-3600.
Facsimile: 202-639-9355.
Bratislava, Slovak Republic:
Telephone: (421-7) 5441-5100.
Facsimile: (421-7) 5441-6100.
Brussels, Belgium:
Telephone: (32-2) 219-16-20.
Facsimile: (32-2) 219-16-26.
Budapest, Hungary: Réczicza Law Firm White & Case.
Telephone: (36-1) 488-5200.
Facsimile: (36-1) 488-5299.
Frankfurt, Germany: White & Case (Rechtsanwälte).
Telephone: (49-69) 713-77-(0).
Facsimile: (49-69) 713-77-100.
Helsinki, Finland: Asianajotoimisto White & Case Oy.
Telephone: (358-6) 228-641.
Facsimile: (358-9) 228-64228.
Istanbul, Turkey:
Telephone: (90-212) 275-75-33.
Facsimile: (90-212) 275-75-43.
London, England:
Telephone: (44-20) 7600-7300.
Facsimile: (44-20) 7600-7030.
Moscow, Russia:
Telephone: (7-095) 787-3000.
Facsimile: (7-095) 787-3001.
Paris, France:
Telephone: (33-1) 55-04-15-15.
Facsimile: (33-1) 55-04-15-16.
Prague, Czech Republic:
Telephone: (420-2) 2481-0808; 2481-1796.
Facsimile: (420-2) 2481-0330; 2481-0252.
Stockholm, Sweden: White & Case Advokat AB.
Telephone: (46-8) 506-323-00.
Facsimile: (46-8) 611-21-22.
Warsaw, Poland: White & Case (Poland) Sp. z o.o.
Telephone: (48-22) 625-33-33; (48-22) 622-67-67; (48-39) 12-19-06.
Facsimile: (48-22) 628-22-28.
Johannesburg, Republic of South Africa:
Telephone: 27 (11) 884-7689.
Facsimile: 27 (11) 884-7229.
Almaty, Kazakhstan:
Telephone: (7-3272) 50-74-91.
Facsimile: (7-3272) 50-74-93.
Ankara, Turkey:
Telephone: (90-312) 442-5680.
Facsimile: (90-312) 442-5691/4.
Bangkok, Thailand: White & Case (Thailand) Limited.
Telephone: (662) 656-1721 to 32.
Facsimile: (662) 656-1733/34.
Bombay/Mumbai, India: (91-22) 282-6300/01/02/03.
Facsimile: (91-22) 282-6305.
Hanoi, Vietnam:
Telephone: (84-4) 934-5355.
Facsimile: (84-4) 934-5356.
Ho Chi Minh City, Vietnam:
Telephone: (84-8) 821-0888.
Facsimile: (84-8) 823-6902.
Hong Kong: White & Case, Solicitors.
Telephone: (852) 2822-8700.
Facsimile: (852) 2845-9070.
Singapore, Republic of Singapore:
Telephone: (65) 225-6000.
Facsimile: (65) 225-6009.

(See Next Column)

LAW OFFICE OF HASSAN MAHASSNI—*Continued*

Tokyo, Japan: White & Case Kandabashi Law Offices.
Telephone: (81-3) 3259-0200.
Facsimile: (81-3) 3259-0150.
Manama, Bahrain:
Telephone: (973) 9610105; (973) 9610119; (973) 535965.
Facsimile: (973) 590962; (973) 532342.
Riyadh, Saudi Arabia: Law Office of Hassan Mahassni,
Telephone: (966-1) 464-4006.
Facsimile: (966-1) 465-1348.
Mexico City, Mexico: White & Case, S.C.
Telephone: (52) 5-540-9600.
Facsimile: (52) 5-540-9699.
São Paulo, SP, Brazil:
Telephone: (55-11) 3171-0011.
Facsimile: (55-11) 3171-0041.
Associated Law Firm(s):
Bombay/Mumbai, India: India Law Services (ILS).
Telephones: (91-22) 284-1995; (91-22) 284-1847.
Facsimile: (91-22) 285-0824.
New Delhi, India: India Law Services (ILS).
Telephone: (91-11) 697-1602/3/4.
Facsimile: (91-11) 698-8860.
Jakarta, Indonesia: Ali Budiardjo, Nugroho, Reksodiputro, Counsellors at Law.
Telephone: (62-21) 250-5125; 250-5136.
Facsimile: (62-21) 250-5392; 250-5122; 250-5001.
Associated Consultancies:
Jakarta, Indonesia: PT WCI Konsultan.
Telephone: (62-21) 577-1527.
Facsimile: (62-21) 577-1535/6.

RESIDENT PARTNER

Hassan M.S. Mahassni

ASSOCIATES

Brian L. Conway (Not admitted in Saudi Arabia)
Imad El-Dine Ghazi (Not admitted in Saudi Arabia)
Anas Keilani (Not admitted in Saudi Arabia; Legal Consultant)
Ayman Abdel Khaleq (Not admitted in Saudi Arabia)
M. Farouk Kouatli (Not admitted in Saudi Arabia; Legal Consultant)
Gassim Zanoon (Not admitted in Saudi Arabia)

For full biographical listings, see the Martindale-Hubbell Law Directory

RIYADH,

LEGAL ADVISORS TORKI A. AL-SHUBAIKI

License No. 501
(In Association with Baker & McKenzie)
King Faisal Foundation Building, King Fahad Road, P.O. Box 4288, Riyadh 11491
Telephone: (01) 462-9886
Intn'l Dialing: (966-1) 462-9886
Facsimile: (966-1) 463-2657
URL: http://www.bakerinfo.com
In Association with Baker & McKenzie with offices in:
Chicago, Illinois: One Prudential Plaza, 130 East Randolph Drive, 60601.
Dallas, Texas: 4500 Trammell Crow Center, 2001 Ross Avenue, 75201.
Miami, Florida: 1200 Brickell Avenue, 19th Floor, 33131-2827.
New York, New York: 805 Third Avenue, 10022.
Palo Alto, California: 660 Hansen Way, P.O. Box 60309, 94304-0309.
San Diego, California: 101 West Broadway, Twelfth Floor, 92101.
San Francisco, California: Two Embarcadero Center, 24th Floor, 94111-3909.
Washington, D.C.: 815 Connecticut Avenue, N.W., 20006-4078.

MEMBERS OF FIRM

George Sayen (Not admitted in Saudi Arabia)
John E. Xefos (Not admitted in Saudi Arabia)

LOCAL PARTNER

Ian R. Siddell (Not admitted in Saudi Arabia; Also at Manama, Bahrain Office of Baker & McKenzie)

Nasser Alfaraj
Zaid Al-Farisi (Not admitted in Saudi Arabia)
Walid S. Hegazy (Not admitted in Saudi Arabia)
Karim Nassar (Not admitted in Saudi Arabia)

For full biographical listings, see the Martindale-Hubbell Law Directory

THE INTERNATIONAL LAW FIRM

(In Association with Jones, Day, Reavis & Pogue)
Sulaymaniyah Prince Mishari IBN, Abdulaziz Street, P.O. Box 22166, Riyadh 11495
Telephone: (966-1) 462-8866
Telecopier: (966-1) 462-9001
URL: http://www.jonesday.com
In Atlanta, Georgia: 3500 SunTrust Plaza, 303 Peachtree Street.
Telephone: 404-521-3939.
Cable Address: "Attorneys Atlanta".
Telex: 54-2711.
Telecopier: 404-581-8330.
In Brussels, Belgium: Avenue Louise 480, 7th Floor. B-1050 Brussels.
Telephone: 32-2-645-14-11.
Telecopier: 32-2-645-14-45.
In Chicago, Illinois: 77 West Wacker.
Telephone: 312-782-3939.
Telecopier: 312-782-8585.
In Cleveland, Ohio: North Point, 901 Lakeside Avenue.
Telephone: 216-586-3939.
Cable Address: "Attorneys Cleveland."
Telex: 980389.
Telecopier: 216-579-0212.
In Columbus, Ohio: 1900 Huntington Center.
Telephone: 614-469-3939.
Cable Address: "Attorneys Columbus."
Telecopier: 614-461-4198.
In Dallas, Texas: 2727 North Harwood Street.
Telephone: 214-220-3939.
Cable Address: "Attorneys Dallas."
Telex: 730852.
Telecopier: 214-969-5100.
In Frankfurt, Germany: Hochhaus am Park, Grüneburgweg 102, 60323, Frankfurt am Main.
Telephone: 49-69-9726-3939.
Telecopier: 49-69-9726-3993.
In Geneva, Switzerland: 20, rue de Candolle.
Telephone: 41-22-320-2339.
Telecopier: 41-22-320-1232.
In Hong Kong: 29th Floor, Entertainment Building, 30 Queens's Road Central.
Telephone: 852-2526-6895.
Telecopier: 852-2868-5871.
In Irvine, California: 5 Park Plaza, Suite 1100.
Telephone: 949-851-3939.
Telex: 194911 Lawyers LSA.
Telecopier: 949-553-7539.
In London, England: Bucklersbury House, 3 Queen Victoria Street.
Telephone: 44-20-7236-3939.
Telecopier: 44-20-7236-1113.
In Los Angeles, California: 555 West Fifth Street, Suite 4600.
Telephone: 213-489-3939.
Telex: 181439 UD.
Telecopier: 213-243-2539.
In New York, New York: 599 Lexington Avenue.
Telephone: 212-326-3939.
Cable Address: "JONESDAY NEWYORK."
Telex: 237013 JDRP UR.
Telecopier: 212-755-7306.
In Paris, France: 120, rue du Faubourg Saint-Honoré.
Telephone: 33-1-56-59-39-39.
Telecopier: 33-1-56-59-39-38
In Pittsburgh, Pennsylvania: 500 Grant Street, 31st Floor.
Telephone: 412-391-3939.
Cable Address: "Attorneys Pittsburgh".
Telecopier: 412-394-7959.
In Shanghai, China: 2805 Kerry Centre, 1515 Nanjing Road West.
Telephone: 86-21-5298-6568.
Telecopier: 86-21-5298-6569.
In Sydney, Australia: Governor Phillip Tower, Level 38, 1 Farrer Place.
Telephone: 61-2-9210-6921.
Telecopier: 61-2-9210-6926.
In Taipei, Taiwan: 8th Floor, 2 Tun Hwa South Road, Section 2.
Telephone: (886-2) 2704-6808.
Telecopier: (886-2) 2704-6791.
In Tokyo, Japan: Toranomon 45 Mori Building, 3rd Floor, 1-5, Toranomon 5-chome, Minato-Ku.
Telephone: 81-3-3433-3939.
Telecopier: 81-3-5401-2725.
In Washington, D.C.: 51 Louisiana Avenue, N.W.
Telephone: 202-879-3939.
Telecopier: 202-626-1700.

RESIDENT LAWYERS

Osama Mohammed Al Sulaim, Saudi National
Ghassan Ibrahim Al Awaji, Saudi National
Ali Abdullah Al-Ahmari
Vernon Cassin, Jr. (Not admitted in Saudi Arabia)
Yusuf Giansiracusa (Not admitted in Saudi Arabia)

For full biographical listings, see the Martindale-Hubbell Law Directory

SINGAPORE

SINGAPORE,

WONG & LEOW

(Associated with Baker & McKenzie)
1 Temasek Avenue #27-01, Millenia Tower, Singapore 039192
Telephone: 3381888
Intn'l Dialing: (65) 3381888
Facsimile: (65) 3375100
URL: http://www.bakerinfo.com
Associated Offices of Baker & McKenzie in: Almaty, Amsterdam, Bahrain, Baku, Bangkok, Barcelona, Beijing, Berlin, Bogotá, Brasília, Brussels, Budapest, Buenos Aires, Cairo, Caracas, Chicago, Dallas, Düsseldorf, Frankfurt, Geneva, Hanoi, Ho Chi Minh City, Hong Kong, Houston, Hsinchu, Juárez, Kyiv, London, Madrid, Manila, Melbourne, México City, Miami, Milan, Monterrey, Moscow, Münich, New York, Palo Alto, Paris, Prague, Rio de Janeiro, Riyadh, Rome, St. Petersburg, San Diego, San Francisco, Santiago, São Paulo, Stockholm, Sydney, Taipei, Tijuana, Tokyo, Toronto, Valencia, Warsaw, Washington, D.C. and Zürich.
Correspondent Law Firm: Hadiputranto, Hadinoto & Partners, Jakarta.

Kien Keong Wong
Edmund H. M. Leow

James T. O. Huang
Kok Wah Koh
Kok Keng Lau
Ai Ai Wong

Joyce Chen
Felicia J. L. Chua
Kenny T.L. Foo
Nicholas C. H. How
Maisie Koh
Leng Fong Lai
Jonathan T.B. Lim
Mark F. C. Lim
Su-Fen Lim
Kelvin T.W. Poa
Jane S. Quek
Lorraine Anne Tay
Sophy Y.F. Teng
Kwong Weng Wan
Wily Wan
Shirley S. Wong
Jih-Shian Yeo
Rebecca M.S. Tai-Yeo

For full biographical listings, see the Martindale-Hubbell Law Directory

American Lawyers In Singapore

BAKER & MCKENZIE

#27-01 Millenia Tower, 1 Temasek Avenue, Singapore 039192
Telephone: 3381888
Intn'l Dialing: (65) 3381888
Facsimile: (65) 3375100
URL: http://www.bakerinfo.com
Associated Offices of Baker & McKenzie in: Almaty, Amsterdam, Bahrain, Baku, Bangkok, Barcelona, Beijing, Berlin, Bogotá, Brasília, Brussels, Budapest, Buenos Aires, Cairo, Caracas, Chicago, Dallas, Düsseldorf, Frankfurt, Geneva, Hanoi, Ho Chi Minh City, Hong Kong, Houston, Hsinchu, Juárez, Kyiv, London, Madrid, Manila, Melbourne, México City, Miami, Milan, Monterrey, Moscow, Münich, New York, Palo Alto, Paris, Prague, Rio de Janeiro, Riyadh, Rome, St. Petersburg, San Diego, San Francisco, Santiago, São Paulo, Stockholm, Sydney, Taipei, Tijuana, Tokyo, Toronto, Valencia, Warsaw, Washington, D.C. and Zürich.
Correspondent Law Firm: Hadiputranto, Hadinoto & Partners, Jakarta.

Timothy C. Garrood (Not admitted in Singapore)
David J. Howell (Not Admitted in Singapore)
Graeme S. M. Johnston (Not admitted in Singapore)
Edmund H. M. Leow *
Nicholas J. Serwer (Not admitted in Singapore)
Kien Keong Wong *

OF COUNSEL

Paul S. Elliott (Not admitted in Singapore)

LOCAL PARTNERS

William B. Abraham (Not admitted in Singapore)
James T. O. Huang *
Kok Wah Koh *
Kok Keng Lau *
Michael M. McNeill (Not admitted in Singapore)
G. Matthew Sheridan (Not admitted in Singapore)
Ai Ai Wong *

Joyce Chen *
Kenneth Chia (Not admitted in Singapore)
Felicia J. L. Chua *
Luke D. Devine (Not admitted in Singapore)
Kenny T.L. Foo
Yasuhiro Fujii (Not admitted in Singapore)
Nicholas C. H. How *
Mariam Anna John (Not admitted in Singapore)
Maisie Koh *
Leng Fong Lai *
Jonathan T.B. Lim *
Mark F.C. Lim *
Su-Fen Lim *
Kelvin T.W. Poa *
Meng Yi Ong (Not admitted in Singapore)
Jane S. Quek *
Niels Reder (Not admitted in Singapore)
Matthew P. Richards (Not admitted in Singapore)
Gordon Smith (Not admitted in Singapore)
Rebecca M.S. Tai-Yeo *
Lorraine Anne Tay *

(See Next Column)

Steven S. Y. Tee (Not admitted in Singapore)
Sophy Y.F. Teng *
Kwong Weng Wan *
Wily Wan *
Shirley S. Wong *
Jih-Shian Yeo *

(Not authorized to appear before the Singapore courts)
*Practising with Wong & Leow, Singapore advocates and solicitors

For full biographical listings, see the Martindale-Hubbell Law Directory

MILBANK, TWEED, HADLEY & MCCLOY LLP

14-00 Caltex House, 30 Raffles Place, Singapore 048622
Telephone: 65-428-2400
Fax: 65-428-2500
Email: milbank@pacific.net.5g *URL:* http://www.milbank.com
New York, New York Office: 1 Chase Manhattan Plaza, 10005-1413.
Telephone: 212-530-5000.
Fax: 212- 530-5219.
Midtown Office: 375 Park Avenue, Suite 3601, 10152.
Telephone: 212-530-5800.
Fax: 212-530-0158.
Los Angeles, California Office: 601 South Figueroa Street, 90017.
Telephone: 213-892-4000.
Fax: 213-629-5063.
Washington, D.C. Office: International Square Building, Suite 1100, 1825 Eye Street, N.W., 20006.
Telephone: 202-835-7500.
Fax: 202-835-7586.
Tokyo, Japan Office: Fukoku Seimei Building, 2-2 Uchisaiwai-cho 2-Chome, Chiyoda-ku, Tokyo 100-0011, Japan.
Telephone: 81-3-3504-1050.
Fax: 81-3-3595-2790, 81-3-3595-2840.
London, England Office: Dashwood House, 69 Old Broad Street, London, EC2M 1QS.
Telephone: 44-207-448-3000.
Fax: 44-207-448-3029.
Hong Kong Office: 3007 Alexandra House, 16 Chater Road.
Telephone: 852-2791-4888.
Fax: 852-2840-0792, 852-2845-9046.
Moscow, Russia Office: 24/27 Sadovaya-Samotyochnaya, Moscow, 103051.
Telephone: 7-501-258-5015.
Fax: 7-501-258-5014.

PARTNERS

Oren B. Azar (Not admitted in Singapore)
Richard M. Gray (Not admitted in Singapore)
Gary S. Wigmore (Not admitted in Singapore)

ASSOCIATES

Leigh Kim Borrello (Not admitted in Singapore)
Shelli M. Ching (Not admitted in Singapore)
Vanessa Wai Shan Hui (Not admitted in Singapore)
Edward Pearson (Not admitted in Singapore)
Cary B. Schmelzer (Not admitted in Singapore)
Megan Siau Feng Tang (Not admitted in Singapore)
Susan E. Turner (Not admitted in Singapore)
David H. Zemans (Not admitted in Singapore)

(Not authorized to appear before the Singapore courts)

For full biographical listings, see the Martindale-Hubbell Law Directory

SHEARMAN & STERLING

6 Battery Road #25-03, Singapore 049909
Telephone: (65) 230-3800
Fax: (65) 230-3899
URL: http://www.shearman.com
New York, N.Y. Office: 599 Lexington Avenue, New York, New York, 10022-6069.
Telephone: (212) 848-4000.
Telex: 667290. Num Lau.
Fax: (212) 848-7179.
Abu Dhabi, United Arab Emirates Office: Butti Al Otaiba Building, 13th Floor, Suite 1302, Sheikh Khalifa Street, P.O. Box 2948.
Telephone: (971-2) 6274477.
Fax: (971-2) 6268933.
Beijing, People's Republic of China Office: Suite #2205, Capital Mansion, No. 6, Xin Yuan Nan Road. Chao Yang District, Beijing, 100004.
Telephone: (86-10) 6465-2299.
Fax: (86-10) 6465-4578.
Düsseldorf, Federal Republic of Germany Office: Couvenstrasse 8 40211 Düsseldorf.
Telephone: (49 211) 178 88-0.
Fax: (49 211) 178 88-88.
Frankfurt, Federal Republic of Germany Office: Trianon Building, Mainzer Landstrasse 16, 60325 Frankfurt am Main.
Telephone: (49-69) 9711-1000.
Fax: (49-69) 9711-1100.
Hong Kong Office: Standard Chartered Bank Building, 4 Des Voeux Road, Central.
Telephone: (852) 2978-8000.
Fax: (852) 2978-8099.

(See Next Column)

SHEARMAN & STERLING—*Continued*

London, England Office: Broadgate West, 9 Appold Street, London EC2A 2AP.
Telephone: 011-44-20-7655-5000.
Fax: 011-44-20-7655-5500.
Menlo Park, California Office: 1550 El Camino Real, 94025-4100.
Telephone: (650) 330-2200.
Fax: (650) 330-2299.
Paris, France Office: 114, avenue des Champs-Elysées, 75008.
Telephone: (33-1) 53-89-7000.
Fax: (33-1) 53-89-7070.
San Francisco, California Office: 555 California Street, 94104-1522.
Telephone: (415) 616-1100.
Fax: (415) 616-1199.
Tokyo, Japan Office: Fukoku Seimei Building, 5th Fl. 2-2-2, Uchisaiwaicho, Chiyoda-ku, Tokyo 100-0011. Japan.
Telephone: (81 3) 5251-1601.
Fax: (81 3) 5251-1602.
Toronto, Ontario, Canada Office: Commerce Court West, Suite 4405, P.O. Box 247, M5L 1E8.
Telephone: (416) 360-8484.
Fax: (416) 360-2958.
Washington, D.C. Office: 801 Pennsylvania Avenue, N.W., 20004-2604.
Telephone: (202) 508-8000.
Fax: (202) 508-8100.

RESIDENT PARTNERS

Calvert C. Miller (Not admitted in Singapore)
Richard J. B. Price (Not admitted in Singapore)

RESIDENT ASSOCIATES

Clodagh M. Curran (Not admitted in Singapore)
Barbara A. Edwards
Marc B. Hankin (Not admitted in Singapore)
Jessica Jennings-Mares
William McCormack (Not admitted in Singapore)
Min Yee Ng
Stephen Phillips (Not admitted in Singapore)
Catherine M. Poyen (Not admitted in Singapore)
Alexander M. Regan (Not admitted in Singapore)

For full biographical listings, see the Martindale-Hubbell Law Directory

SIMPSON THACHER & BARTLETT

Suntec Tower One, 33rd Floor, 7 Temasek Boulevard, Singapore 038987
Telephone: 011-65-430-5100
Fax: 011-65-430-5151
URL: http://www.simpsonthacher.com
New York, NY Office: 425 Lexington Avenue, 10017-3954.
Telephone: 212-455-2000.
Telecopier: 212-455-2502. ESL: 62928462.
Columbus, Ohio Office: One Riverside Plaza, 43215.
Telephone: 614-461-7799.
Telecopier: 614-461-0040.
Los Angeles, California Office: 10 Universal City Plaza, Suite 1850, Universal City, CA, 91608.
Telephone: 818-755-7000.
Fax: 818-755-7009.
Palo Alto, California Office: 3373 Hillview Avenue, 94304.
Telephone: 650-251-5000.
Telecopier: 650-251-5002.
London Office: 99 Bishopsgate, London EC2M 3YH, England.
Telephone: 207 422-4000.
Telecopier: 207 422-4022.
Tokyo Office: Ark Mori Building, 30th Floor, 12-32 Akasaka 1-Chome, Minato-Ku, Tokyo 107, Japan.
Telephone: 81-3-5562-8601.
Telecopier: 81-3-5562-8606. ESL 62765846.
Hong Kong Office: Asia Pacific Finance Tower - 7th Floor, 3 Garden Road, Central, Hong Kong.
Telephone: 852-2514-7600.
Telecopier: 852-2869-7694.

RESIDENT PARTNERS

Alan G. Brenner (Not admitted in Singapore)

RESIDENT ASSOCIATES

Joseph E. Bauerschmidt (Not admitted in Singapore)
Melinda M. Good (Not admitted in Singapore)
Anuradha M. Shastri (Not admitted in Singapore)
Christopher M. Wilson (Not admitted in Singapore)
Marianne C. Yang (Not admitted in Singapore)

(Not admitted to practice in Singapore courts)

For full biographical listings, see the Martindale-Hubbell Law Directory

WHITE & CASE

Limited Liability Partnership
50 Raffles Place #30-00, Singapore Land Tower, Singapore 048623
Telephone: (65) 225-6000
Facsimile: (65) 225-6009
URL: http://www.whitecase.com
Los Angeles, California:
Telephone: 213-620-7700.
Facsimile: 213-687-0758; 213-452-2330; 213-452-2331.
Palo Alto, California:
Telephone: 650-213-0300.
Facsimile: 650-213-8158.
San Francisco, California:
Telephone: 415-544-1100.
Facsimile: 415-544-0202.
Miami, Florida:
Telephone: 305-371-2700.
Facsimile: 305-358-5744; 305-358-5766.
New York, New York:
Telephone: 212-819-8200.
Facsimile: 212-354-8113.
Washington, D.C.:
Telephone: 202-626-3600.
Facsimile: 202-639-9355.
Bratislava, Slovak Republic:
Telephone: (421-7) 5441-5100.
Facsimile: (421-7) 5441-6100.
Brussels, Belgium:
Telephone: (32-2) 219-16-20.
Facsimile: (32-2) 219-16-26.
Budapest, Hungary: Réczicza Law Firm White & Case.
Telephone: (36-1) 488-5200.
Facsimile: (36-1) 488-5299.
Frankfurt, Germany: White & Case (Rechtsanwälte).
Telephone: (49-69) 713-77-(0).
Facsimile: (49-69) 713-77-100.
Helsinki, Finland: Asianajotoimisto White & Case Oy.
Telephone: (358-9) 228-641.
Facsimile: (358-9) 228-64228.
Istanbul, Turkey:
Telephone: (90-212) 275-75-33.
Facsimile: (90-212) 275-75-43.
London, England:
Telephone: (44-20) 7600-7300.
Facsimile: (44-20) 7600-7030.
Moscow, Russia:
Telephone: (7-095) 787-3000.
Facsimile: (7-095) 787-3001.
Paris, France:
Telephone: (33-1) 55-04-15-15.
Facsimile: (33-1) 55-04-15-16.
Prague, Czech Republic:
Telephone: (420-2) 2481-0808; 2481-1796.
Facsimile: (420-2) 2481-0330; 2481-0252.
Stockholm, Sweden: White & Case Advokat AB.
Telephone: (46-8) 506-323-00.
Facsimile: (46-8) 611-21-22.
Warsaw, Poland: White & Case (Poland) Sp. z o.o.
Telephone: (48-22) 625-33-33; (48-22) 622-67-67; (48-39) 12-19-06.
Facsimile: (48-22) 628-22-28.
Johannesburg, Republic of South Africa:
Telephone: 27 (11) 884-7689.
Facsimile: 27 (11) 884-7229.
Almaty, Kazakhstan:
Telephone: (7-3272) 50-74-91.
Facsimile: (7-3272) 50-74-93.
Ankara, Turkey:
Telephone: (90-312) 442-5680.
Facsimile: (90-312) 442-5691/4.
Bangkok, Thailand: White & Case (Thailand) Limited.
Telephone: (662) 656-1721 to 32.
Facsimile: (662) 656-1733/34.
Bombay/Mumbai, India: Liaison Office, (91-22) 282-6300/01/02/03.
Facsimile: (91-22) 282-6305.
Hanoi, Vietnam:
Telephone: (84-4) 934-5355.
Facsimile: (84-4) 934-5356.
Ho Chi Minh City, Vietnam:
Telephone: (84-8) 821-0888.
Facsimile: (84-8) 823-6902.
Hong Kong: White & Case, Solicitors.
Telephone: (852) 2822-8700.
Facsimile: (852) 2845-9070.
Tokyo, Japan: White & Case Kandabashi Law Offices.
Telephone: (81-3) 3259-0200.
Facsimile: (81-3) 3259-0150.
Manama, Bahrain:
Telephone: (973) 9610105; (973) 9610119; (973) 535965.
Facsimile: (973) 590962; (973) 532342.
Jeddah, Saudi Arabia: Law Office of Hassan Mahassni,
Telephone: (966-2) 665-4353.
Facsimile: (966-2) 669-2996.

(See Next Column)

WHITE & CASE, *Singapore—Continued*

Riyadh, Saudi Arabia: Law Office of Hassan Mahassni,
Telephone: (966-1) 464-4006.
Facsimile: (966-1) 465-1348.
Mexico City, Mexico: White & Case, S.C.
Telephone: (52) 5-540-9600.
Facsimile: (52) 5-540-9699.
São Paulo, SP, Brazil:
Telephone: (55-11) 3171-0011.
Facsimile: (55-11) 3171-0041.
Associated Law Firm(s):
Bombay/Mumbai, India: India Law Services (ILS).
Telephones: (91-22) 284-1995; (91-22) 284-1847.
Facsimile: (91-22) 285-0824.
New Delhi, India: India Law Services (ILS).
Telephone: (91-11) 697-1602/3/4.
Facsimile: (91-11) 698-8860.
Jakarta, Indonesia: Ali Budiardjo, Nugroho, Reksodiputro, Counsellors at Law.
Telephone: (62-21) 250-5125; 250-5136.
Facsimile: (62-21) 250-5392; 250-5122; 250-5001.
Associated Consultancies:
Jakarta, Indonesia: PT WCI Konsultan.
Telephone: (62-21) 577-1527.
Facsimile: (62-21) 577-1535/6.

PARTNERS

K. Minh Dang (Not admitted in Singapore)
Alistair A. Duffield (Not admitted in Singapore)
Kenneth C. Ellis (Not admitted in Singapore)
Bertie M. Mehigan (Not admitted in Singapore)
Brian M. Miller (Not admitted in Singapore)
Raj Pande (Not admitted in Singapore)
Jeffrey Washenko (Not admitted in Singapore)

COUNSEL

Anand S. Dayal (Not admitted in Singapore)

ASSOCIATES

Guan Feng Chen
Daniel Chung (Not admitted in Singapore)
John W. Creighton, III (Not admitted in Singapore)
Shonu S.K. Das (Not admitted in Singapore)
Clarinda Tjia Dharmadi (Not admitted in Singapore)
Ashok K. Lalwani (Not admitted in Singapore)
Rudy Lim (Not admitted in Singapore)
Sin Teck Lim (Not admitted in Singapore)
Mary Ng (Not admitted in Singapore)
Iwan Nurjadin (Not admitted in Singapore)
Xiao-Shan Peh
Niket Rele (Not admitted in Singapore)
Edmund W. Sim (Not admitted in Singapore)
Nelson L. Y. Suit (Not admitted in Singapore)
Dipa Swaminathan (Not admitted in Singapore)
Su Ann Teoh (Not admitted in Singapore)
Huey Yann Thong
Brian J. Wesol (Not admitted in Singapore)
Yen-Wen Yu (Not admitted in Singapore)

(Not authorized to appear before the Singapore courts)

For full biographical listings, see the Martindale-Hubbell Law Directory

SLOVAKIA

BRATISLAVA,

American Lawyers In Bratislava

SQUIRE, SANDERS & DEMPSEY L.L.P.

Zochova 5, 811 03 Bratislava
Telephone: 421-7-5441-7611
Fax: 42-1-7-6280-2212
URL: http://www.ssd.com
Cincinnati, Ohio Office: PNC Center, 201 East Fifth Street, Suite 1700, Cincinnati, Ohio 45202.
Telephone: 513-361-1200.
Fax: 513-361-1201.
Cleveland, Ohio Office: 4900 Key Tower, 127 Public Square, Cleveland, Ohio 44114-1304.
Telephone: 216-479-8500.
Fax: 216-479-8780.
Columbus, Ohio Office: 1300 Huntington Center, 41 South High Street, Columbus, Ohio 43215-6150.
Telephone: 614-365-2700.
Fax: 614-365-2499.
Houston, Texas Office: 6250 Chase Tower, 600 Travis Street, Houston, Texas 77002-3007.
Telephone: 713-546-5850.
Fax: 713-546-5830.

(See Next Column)

Jacksonville, Florida Office: One Enterprise Center, Suite 2100, 225 Water Street, Jacksonville, Florida 32202-4424.
Telephone: 904-366-2420.
Fax: 904-356-2986.
Miami, Florida Office: 201 South Biscayne Boulevard, 2900 Miami Center, Miami, Florida 33131-4330.
Telephone: 305-577-8700.
Fax: 305-358-1425.
New York, New York Office: 350 Park Avenue, New York, New York 10022-6002.
Telephone: 212-872-9800.
Fax: 212-872-9815.
Phoenix, Arizona Office: Two Renaissance Square, 40 North Central Avenue, Suite 2700, Phoenix, Arizona 85004-4498.
Telephone: 602-528-4000.
Fax: 602-253-8129.
Washington, D.C. Office: 1201 Pennsylvania Avenue, N.W., Suite 500, Washington, D.C. 20004-2491.
Telephone: 202-626-6600.
Fax: 202-626-6780.
Almaty, Kazakhstan Office: 141 Albay Khan Avenue, Second Floor, Almaty, Kazakhstan 480091.
Telephone: +73-27-50-11-25.
Fax: +73-27-50-11-25.
Brussels, Belgium Office: Avenue Louise, 165 Box 15, 1050 Brussels, Belgium.
Telephone: 32-2-627-1111.
Fax: 32-2-627-1100.
Budapest, Hungary Office: H-1062 Budapest, Andrassy ut. 64, Budapest, Hungary.
Telephone: 36-1-428-7111.
Fax: 36-1-428-7100.
Kyiv, Ukraine Office: 14A Yaroslaviv Val, Kyiv 252034, Ukraine.
Telephone: 38-044-228-8687.
Fax: 38-044-228-4938.
London, England Office: Royex House, Aldermanbury Square, London EC2V 7HR.
Telephone: 44-171-776-5200.
Fax: 44-171-776-5233.
Madrid, Spain Office: Calle Velazquez 108-110, 28006 Madrid, Spain.
Telephone: 34-91-590-2420.
Fax: 34-91-590-2421.
Moscow, Russian Federation Office: Paveletskaya Square II, 1 Valovaya Street, 5th Floor, Moscow 113054, Russian Federation.
Telephone: 7-501-258-5250.
Fax: 7-501-258-5251.
Prague, Czech Republic Office: Václavské náměst 1 57/813, 110 00 Praha 1, Czech Republic.
Telephone: 420-2-2166-2111.
Fax: 420-2-2166-2222.
Hong Kong Office: Rooms 1101-2 St. George's Building, 2 Ice House Street, Central, Hong Kong.
Telephone: 852-2509-9732.
Fax: 852-2509-9772.
Taipei, Taiwan Office: 14F, 116 Nanking East Road, Sec. 2, Taipei, Taiwan, Republic of China.
Telephone: 886-2-2531-2888.
Fax: 886-2-2571-6199.

PARTNER

Kevin T. Connor (Not admitted in Slovakia)

COUNSEL

Nataša Nikitinová

ASSOCIATES

Peter Czúdor
Julian Juhasz
Peter Šuba
Matthew Charles Vernon (Not admitted in Slovakia)

For full biographical listings, see the Martindale-Hubbell Law Directory

SPAIN

BARCELONA,

BAKER & MCKENZIE

Avda. Diagonal, 652, Edif. D, 8th Floor, 08034 Barcelona
Telephone: (93) 280 59 00
Intn'l Dialing: (34) 93 280 59 00
Facsimile: (34) 93 205 49 59
URL: http://www.bakerinfo.com
Associated Offices of Baker & McKenzie in: Almaty, Amsterdam, Bahrain, Baku, Bangkok, Beijing, Berlin, Bogotá, Brasília, Brussels, Budapest, Buenos Aires, Cairo, Caracas, Chicago, Dallas, Düsseldorf, Frankfurt, Geneva, Hanoi, Ho Chi Minh City, Hong Kong, Houston, Hsinchu, Juárez, Kyiv, London, Madrid, Manila, Melbourne, México City, Miami, Milan, Monterrey, Moscow, Münich, New York, Palo Alto, Paris, Prague, Rio de Janeiro, Riyadh, Rome, St. Petersburg, San Diego, San Francisco, Santiago, São Paulo, Singapore, Stockholm, Sydney, Taipei, Tijuana, Tokyo, Toronto, Valencia, Warsaw, Washington, D.C. and Zürich.
Correspondent Law Firm: Hadiputranto, Hadinoto & Partners, Jakarta.

(See Next Column)

BAKER & MCKENZIE—*Continued*

PARTNERS

Pedro Aguarón
Jesús M. de Alfonso
Alvaro Espinós
Rafael Jiménez-Gusi
Xavier Junquera
Alejandro Valls

ASSOCIATES

Silvia Abelló
Mariona Baldo
Cristina Calvo
Angela Toro Cebada
Valeria Enrich SchrÖder
Ferran Escayola
Manel Garcia Rodriguez
Beatriz Henriquez
Silvia Lorente
Marta Martin
Francisco Javier Merino
Andrés Millán
Rafael Navarro
Maria Mercè Pujadas
Eusebio Pujol
Claudi Rossell Piedrafita
Ana Royuela
Jordi Sanchez Sanchez-Crespo
Pilar Tellez
Montserrat Llopart Vidal

For full biographical listings, see the Martindale-Hubbell Law Directory

*MADRID,**

SQUIRE, SANDERS & DEMPSEY

Calle Velazquez 108-110, 28006 Madrid
Telephone: 34-91-590-2420
Fax: 34-91-590-2421
URL: http://www.ssd.com
Cincinnati, Ohio Office: PNC Center, 201 East Fifth Street, Suite 1700, Cincinnati, Ohio 45202.
Telephone: 513-361-1200.
Fax: 513-361-1201.
Cleveland, Ohio Office: 4900 Key Tower, 127 Public Square, Cleveland, Ohio 44114-1304.
Telephone: 216-479-8500.
Fax: 216-479-8780.
Columbus, Ohio Office: 1300 Huntington Center, 41 South High Street, Columbus, Ohio 43215-6150.
Telephone: 614-365-2700.
Fax: 614-365-2499.
Houston, Texas Office: 6250 Chase Tower, 600 Travis Street, Houston, Texas 77002-3007.
Telephone: 713-546-5850.
Fax: 713-546-5830.
Jacksonville, Florida Office: One Enterprise Center, Suite 2100, 225 Water Street, Jacksonville, Florida 32202-4424.
Telephone: 904-366-2420.
Fax: 904-356-2986.
Miami, Florida Office: 201 South Biscayne Boulevard, 2900 Miami Center, Miami, Florida 33131-4330.
Telephone: 305-577-8700.
Fax: 305-358-1425.
New York, New York Office: 350 Park Avenue, New York, New York 10022-6002.
Telephone: 212-872-9800.
Fax: 212-872-9815.
Phoenix, Arizona Office: Two Renaissance Square, 40 North Central Avenue, Suite 2700, Phoenix, Arizona 85004-4498.
Telephone: 602-528-4000.
Fax: 602-253-8129.
Washington, D.C. Office: 1201 Pennsylvania Avenue, N.W., Suite 500, Washington, D.C. 20004-2491.
Telephone: 202-626-6600.
Fax: 202-626-6780.
Almaty, Kazakhstan Office: 141 Ablay Khan Avenue, Second Floor, Almaty, Kazakhstan 480091.
Telephone: +73-27-50-11-25.
Fax: +73-27-50-11-25.
Bratislava, Slovak Republic Office: Zochova 5, 811 03 Bratislava, Slov k Republic.
Telephone: 421-7-5441-7611.
Fax: 42-1-7-6280-2212.
Brussels, Belgium Office: Avenue Louise, 165-Box 15, 1050 Brussels, Belgium.
Telephone: 32-2-627-1111.
Fax: 32-2-627-1100.
Budapest, Hungary Office: H-1062 Budapest, Andrassy ut. 64, Budapest, Hungary.
Telephone: 36-1-428-7111.
Fax: 36-1-428-7100.
Kyiv, Ukraine Office: 14A Yaroslaviv Val, Kyiv 252034, Ukraine.
Telephone: 38-044-228-8687.
Fax: 38-044-228-4938.
London, England Office: Royex House, Aldermanbury Square, London EC2V 7HR.
Telephone: 44-171-776-5200.
Fax: 44-171-776-5233.
Moscow, Russian Federation Office: Paveletskaya Square II, 1 Valovaya Street, 5th Floor, Moscow 113054, Russian Federation.
Telephone: 7-501-258-5250.
Fax: 7-501-258-5251.

(See Next Column)

Prague, Czech Republic Office: Václavské náměst 1 57/813, 110 00 Praha 1, Czech Republic.
Telephone: 420-2-2166-2111.
Fax: 420-2-2166-2222.
Hong Kong Office: Rooms 1101-2 St. George's Building, 2 Ice House Street, Central, Hong Kong.
Telephone: 852-2509-9732.
Fax: 852-2509-9772.
Taipei, Taiwan Office: 14F, 116 Nanking East Road, Sec. 2, Taipei, Taiwan, Republic of China.
Telephone: 886-2-2531-2888.
Fax: 886-2-2571-6199.

PARTNER

Juan Picón

OF COUNSEL

Gonzalo Aranzabal
Javier Santos

ASSOCIATES

Rodrigo Achirica
Vicente Arias
Javier Berrocal
Diego Colchero
María Pillar García Guijarro
Josep Maria Julià
Paul Hitchings
Santiago Mediano
Manuel Mingot

For full biographical listings, see the Martindale-Hubbell Law Directory

American Lawyers In Madrid

BAKER & MCKENZIE

Paseo de la Castellana, 33, Edificio Fénix—6th Floor, 28046 Madrid
Telephone: (91) 391-5950
Intn'l Dialing: (34-91) 391-5950
Facsimiles: (34-91) 391-5145; 391-5149
Email: madrid.reception@bakernet.com *URL:* http://www.bakerinfo.com
Associated Offices of Baker & McKenzie in: Almaty, Amsterdam, Bahrain, Baku, Bangkok, Barcelona, Beijing, Berlin, Bogotá, Brasília, Brussels, Budapest, Buenos Aires, Cairo, Caracas, Chicago, Dallas, Düsseldorf, Frankfurt, Geneva, Hanoi, Ho Chi Minh City, Hong Kong, Houston, Hsinchu, Juárez, Kyiv, London, Manila, Melbourne, México City, Miami, Milan, Monterrey, Moscow, Münich, New York, Palo Alto, Paris, Prague, Rio de Janeiro, Riyadh, Rome, St. Petersburg, San Diego, San Francisco, Santiago, São Paulo, Singapore, Stockholm, Sydney, Taipei, Tijuana, Tokyo, Toronto, Valencia, Warsaw, Washington, D.C. and Zürich.
Correspondent Law Firm: Hadiputranto, Hadinoto & Partners, Jakarta.

José A. Arcila
Cristina Bustillo
Eduardo García Calleja
Antonio López Barrio

OF COUNSEL

Carlos E. Rubio

LOCAL PARTNERS

Maite Díez
Javier Fernandez-Lasquetty
Fermin Guardiola
Cecilia Pastor
Miguel Pintos

ASSOCIATES

Esteban Barreda
Raquel Blanco
Jose A. de la Calle
Maria Teresa Delia Candel (Not admitted in Spain)
David Diaz Zaforas
Mario De Echevarria
Gabriel Gamazo
Jorge Gorostegut
Concepción Martín
Maria Merino
María del Olmo
Isabel de Otaola Ubieta
Raquel Perez-Arana
Julia Esther Leo Rubio
José F. Ruiz-Cámara
Alvaro Sánchez López-Chicheri
Cristina Sanz
Teresa Serrano
Mercedes Tort
Enrique Valera

For full biographical listings, see the Martindale-Hubbell Law Directory

SWEDEN

*STOCKHOLM,**

BAKER & MCKENZIE ADVOKATBYRA

Linnégatan 18, P.O. Box 5719, SE-114 87 Stockholm
Telephone: +46-8-566 177 00
Intn'l Dialing: +46-8-566 177 00
Facsimile: +46-8-566 177 99
Email: stockholm@bakernet.com *URL:* http://www.bakerinfo.com
Associated Offices of Baker & McKenzie in: Almaty, Amsterdam, Bahrain, Baku, Bangkok, Barcelona, Beijing, Berlin, Bogotá, Brasília, Brussels, Budapest, Buenos Aires, Cairo, Caracas, Chicago, Dallas, Düsseldorf, Frankfurt, Geneva, Hanoi, Ho Chi Minh City, Hong Kong, Houston, Hsinchu, Juárez, Kyiv, London, Madrid, Manila, Melbourne, México City, Miami, Milan, Monterrey, Moscow, Münich, New York, Palo Alto, Paris, Prague, Rio de Janeiro, Riyadh, Rome, St. Petersburg, San Diego, San Francisco, Santiago, São Paulo, Singapore, Sydney, Taipei, Tijuana, Tokyo, Toronto, Valencia, Warsaw, Washington, D.C. and Zürich.
Correspondent Law Firm: Hadiputranto, Hadinoto & Partners, Jakarta.

(See Next Column)

BAKER & MCKENZIE ADVOKATBYRÅ, *Stockholm—Continued*

MEMBERS OF FIRM

Sten H. Bauer
Jonas K. V. Benedictsson
Claes R. S. Cronstedt
Leif G. Gustafsson
Bo W. Lindqvist
Johan Norman
Mauritz Silfverstolpe

LOCAL PARTNERS

Stefan M. Bessman
Stefan Brandt
Carl M. Svernlöv

COUNSEL

Sven Harald F. Bauer
Sigvard Norman

ASSOCIATES

Jan A. Alexanderson
Kristin K. A. Baer
Cecilia Bjelle
Carl Bökwall
Anders Fast
Mattias Hedwall
Jenny Jilmstad
Cecilia Kindgren-Bengtsson
Fredrik S. B. Niklasson
Michael C. B. Nyman
Tomas C. Rudenstam
Charlotta Tajthy
Johan H. Widholm
Ola Wälimaa

For full biographical listings, see the Martindale-Hubbell Law Directory

WHITE & CASE ADVOKAT AB

Nybrogatan 3, Box 5573, S-114 85 Stockholm
Telephone: (46-8) 506-323-00.
Facsimile: (46-8) 611-21-22
URL: http://www.whitecase.com
Los Angeles, California:
Telephone: 213-620-7700.
Facsimile: 213-687-0758; 213-452-2330; 213-452-2331.
Palo Alto, California:
Telephone: 650-213-0300.
Facsimile: 650-213-8158.
San Francisco, California:
Telephone: 415-544-1100.
Facsimile: 415-544-0202.
Miami, Florida:
Telephone: 305-371-2700.
Facsimile: 305-358-5744; 305-358-5766.
New York, New York:
Telephone: 212-819-8200.
Facsimile: 212-354-8113.
Washington, D.C.:
Telephone: 202-626-3600.
Facsimile: 202-639-9355.
Bratislava, Slovak Republic:
Telephone: (421-7) 5441-5100.
Facsimile: (421-7) 5441-6100.
Brussels, Belgium:
Telephone: (32-2) 219-16-20.
Facsimile: (32-2) 219-16-26.
Budapest, Hungary: Réczicza Law Firm White & Case.
Telephone: (36-1) 488-5200.
Facsimile: (36-1) 488-5299.
Frankfurt, Germany: White & Case (Rechtsanwälte).
Telephone: (49-69) 713-77-(0).
Facsimile: (49-69) 713-77-100.
Helsinki, Finland: Asianajotoimisto White & Case Oy.
Telephone: (358-9) 228-641.
Facsimile: (358-9) 228-64228.
Istanbul, Turkey:
Telephone: (90-212) 275-75-33.
Facsimile: (90-212) 275-75-43.
London, England:
Telephone: (44-20) 7600-7300.
Facsimile: (44-20) 7600-7030.
Moscow, Russia:
Telephone: (7-095) 787-3000.
Facsimile: (7-095) 787-3001.
Paris, France:
Telephone: (33-1) 55-04-15-15.
Facsimile: (33-1) 55-04-15-16.
Prague, Czech Republic:
Telephone: (420-2) 2481-0808; 2481-1796.
Facsimile: (420-2) 2481-0330; 2481-0252.
Warsaw, Poland: White & Case (Poland) Sp. z o.o.
Telephone: (48-22) 625-33-33; (48-22) 622-67-67; (48-39) 12-19-06.
Facsimile: (48-22) 628-22-28.
Johannesburg, Republic of South Africa:
Telephone: 27 (11) 884-7689.
Facsimile: 27 (11) 884-7229.
Almaty, Kazakhstan:
Telephone: (7-3272) 50-74-91.
Facsimile: (7-3272) 50-74-93.
Ankara, Turkey:
Telephone: (90-312) 442-5680.
Facsimile: (90-312) 442-5691/4.
Bangkok, Thailand: White & Case (Thailand) Limited.
Telephone: (662) 656-1721 to 32.
Facsimile: (662) 656-1733/34.

(See Next Column)

Bombay/Mumbai, India: Liaison Office, (91-22) 282-6300/01/02/03.
Facsimile: (91-22) 282-6305.
Hanoi, Vietnam:
Telephone: (84-4) 934-5355.
Facsimile: (84-4) 934-5356.
Ho Chi Minh City, Vietnam:
Telephone: (84-8) 821-0888.
Facsimile: (84-8) 823-6902.
Hong Kong: White & Case, Solicitors.
Telephone: (852) 2822-8700.
Facsimile: (852) 2845-9070.
Singapore, Republic of Singapore:
Telephone: (65) 225-6000.
Facsimile: (65) 225-6009.
Tokyo, Japan: White & Case Kandabashi Law Offices.
Telephone: (81-3) 3259-0200.
Facsimile: (81-3) 3259-0150.
Manama, Bahrain:
Telephone: (973) 9610105; (973) 9610119; (973) 535965.
Facsimile: (973) 590962; (973) 532342.
Jeddah, Saudi Arabia: Law Office of Hassan Mahassni,
Telephone: (966-2) 665-4353.
Facsimile: (966-2) 669-2996.
Riyadh, Saudi Arabia: Law Office of Hassan Mahassni,
Telephone: (966-1) 464-4006.
Facsimile: (966-1) 465-1348.
Mexico City, Mexico: White & Case, S.C.
Telephone: (52) 5-540-9600.
Facsimile: (52) 5-540-9699.
São Paulo, SP, Brazil:
Telephone: (55-11) 3171-0011.
Facsimile: (55-11) 3171-0041.
Associated Law Firm(s):
Bombay/Mumbai, India: India Law Services (ILS).
Telephones: (91-22) 284-1995; (91-22) 284-1847.
Facsimile: (91-22) 285-0824.
New Delhi, India: India Law Services (ILS).
Telephone: (91-11) 697-1602/3/4.
Facsimile: (91-11) 698-8860.
Jakarta, Indonesia: Ali Budiardjo, Nugroho, Reksodiputro, Counsellors at Law.
Telephone: (62-21) 250-5125; 250-5136.
Facsimile: (62-21) 250-5392; 250-5122; 250-5001.
Associated Consultancies:
Jakarta, Indonesia: PT WCI Konsultan.
Telephone: (62-21) 577-1527.
Facsimile: (62-21) 577-1535/6.

RESIDENT PARTNERS

Göran Åseborn
Ulf Johansson
Rolf S. Olofsson
Clas Romander
Claes Zettermarck

ASSOCIATES

Magnus W. Eriksson (Not admitted in Sweden)
Frida Grundberg (Not admitted in Sweden)
Johan Holgersson
Tomas Jonasson
Anna Martinez (Not admitted in Sweden)
Anders Relden (Not admitted in Sweden)
Tony Rydén (Not admitted in Sweden)
Fredrik Schultz
Katarina Segerståhl
Anna Smieszek (Not admitted in Sweden)
Anna Sundberg (Not admitted in Sweden)
Henrik Thyselius (Not admitted in Sweden)
Maria Trolén (Not admitted in Sweden)

For full biographical listings, see the Martindale-Hubbell Law Directory

SWITZERLAND

GENEVA, (Genève)

ETUDE BAKER & MCKENZIE

Rue Bellot 6, 1206 Geneva
Telephone: 022 346 76 08; 346 70 70
Intn'l Dialing: 41-22 346 76 08; 346 70 70
Facsimile: 41-22 347 02 84
Email: geneva.info@bakernet.com *URL:* http://www.bakerinfo.com

MEMBERS OF FIRM

Martin Anderson
Denis Berdoz
Daniel Peregrina
Philippe Preti
Alain Stehlé

RESIDENT ASSOCIATES

Frédéric Bétrisey
Valérie Delerue
Christophe Germann
Prod'hom Per
Christian Thill

(See Next Column)

ETUDE BAKER & MCKENZIE—*Continued*

OF COUNSEL

Thomas Cottier | Donald Etienne
Alfons A.E. Noll

For full biographical listings, see the Martindale-Hubbell Law Directory

American Lawyers In Geneva

JONES, DAY, REAVIS & POGUE

20, rue de Candolle, CH-1205 Geneva
Telephone: 41-22-320-2339
Telecopier: 41-22-320-1232
Email: counsel@jonesday.com *URL:* http://www.jonesday.com
In Atlanta, Georgia: 3500 SunTrust Plaza, 303 Peachtree Street.
Telephone: 404-521-3939.
Telecopier: 404-581-8330.
In Brussels, Belgium: Avenue Louise 480, 7th Floor. B-1050 Brussels.
Telephone: 32-2-645-14-11.
Telecopier: 32-2-645-14-45.
In Chicago, Illinois: 77 West Wacker.
Telephone: 312-782-3939.
Telecopier: 312-782-8585.
In Cleveland, Ohio: North Point, 901 Lakeside Avenue.
Telephone: 216-586-3939.
Telecopier: 216-579-0212.
In Columbus, Ohio: 1900 Huntington Center.
Telephone: 614-469-3939.
Telecopier: 614-461-4198.
In Dallas, Texas: 2727 North Harwood Street.
Telephone: 214-220-3939.
Telecopier: 214-969-5100.
In Frankfurt, Germany: Hochhaus am Park, Grüneburgweg 102, 60323 Frankfurt am Main.
Telephone: 49-69-9726-3939.
Telecopier: 49-69-9726-3993.
In Hong Kong: 29th Floor, Entertainment Building, 30 Queen's Road Central.
Telephone: 852-2526-6895.
Telecopier: 852-2868-5871.
In Irvine, California: 5 Park Plaza, Suite 1100.
Telephone: 949-851-3939.
Telecopier: 949-553-7539.
In London, England: Bucklersbury House, 3 Queen Victoria Street.
Telephone: 44-20-7236-3939.
Telecopier: 44-20-7236-1113.
In Los Angeles, California: 555 West Fifth Street, Suite 4600.
Telephone: 213-489-3939.
Telecopier: 213-243-2539.
In New York, New York: 599 Lexington Avenue.
Telephone: 212-326-3939.
Telecopier: 212-755-7306.
In Paris, France: 120, rue du Faubourg Saint-Honoré.
Telephone: 33-1-56-59-39-39.
Telecopier: 33-1-56-59-39-38
In Pittsburgh, Pennsylvania: 500 Grant Street, 31st Floor.
Telephone: 412-391-3939.
Telecopier: 412-394-7959.
In Riyadh, Saudi Arabia: The International Law Firm (In Association with Jones, Day, Reavis & Pogue), Sulaymaniyah, Prince Mishari IBN, Abdulaziz Street, P.O. Box 22166.
Telephone: (966-1) 462-8866.
Telecopier: (966-1) 462-9001.
In Shanghai, China: 2805 Kerry Centre, 1515 Nanjing Road West.
Telephone: 86-21-5298-6568.
Telecopier: 86-21-5298-6569.
In Sydney, Australia: Governor Phillip Tower, Level 38, 1 Farrer Place.
Telephone: 61-2-9210-6921.
Telecopier: 61-2-9210-6926.
In Taipei, Taiwan: 8th Floor, 2 Tun Hwa South Road, Section 2.
Telephone: (886-2) 2704-6808.
Telecopier: (886-2) 2704-6791.
In Tokyo, Japan: Toranomon 45 Mori Building, 3rd Floor, 1-5, Toranomon 5-Chome, Minato-Ku, Tokyo 105, Japan.
Telephone: 81-3-3433-3939.
Telecopier: 81-3-5401-2725.
In Washington, D.C.: 51 Louisiana Avenue, N.W.
Telephone: 202-879-3939.
Telecopier: 202-626-1700.

MEMBERS OF FIRM IN GENEVA

Roy F. Ryan, III (Not admitted in Switzerland)
Vernon Cassin, Jr. (Not admitted in Switzerland)

ASSOCIATE

Christophe de Kalbermatten

For full biographical listings, see the Martindale-Hubbell Law Directory

ZÜRICH,

BAKER & MCKENZIE

(Formerly Achermann, Müller, Heini & Wehrli)
Zollikerstrasse 225, 8034 Zürich
Telephone: (01) 384 14 14
Intn'l Dialing: (41-1) 384 14 14
Facsimile: (41-1) 384 12 84
Email: zurich.info@bakernet.com *URL:* http://www.bakerinfo.com
Associated Offices of Baker & McKenzie in: Almaty, Amsterdam, Bahrain, Baku, Bangkok, Barcelona, Beijing, Berlin, Bogotá, Brasília, Brussels, Budapest, Buenos Aires, Cairo, Caracas, Chicago, Dallas, Düsseldorf, Frankfurt, Geneva, Hanoi, Ho Chi Minh City, Hong Kong, Houston, Hsinchu, Juárez, Kyiv, London, Madrid, Manila, Melbourne, México City, Miami, Milan, Monterrey, Moscow, Münich, New York, Palo Alto, Paris, Prague, Rio de Janeiro, Riyadh, Rome, St. Petersburg, San Diego, San Francisco, Santiago, São Paulo, Singapore, Stockholm, Sydney, Taipei, Tijuana, Tokyo, Toronto, Valencia, Warsaw and Washington, D.C.
Correspondent Law Firm: Hadiputranto, Hadinoto & Partners, Jakarta.

PARTNERS

Dr. Markus Affentranger
Dr. Markus H. Berni
Fürsprecher Martin Frey
Philip Marcovici (Not admitted in Switzerland)
Dr. Franz Schenker
Dr. Urs Schenker
Dr. Thomas Stäheli
Dr. Michael Treis

LOCAL PARTNERS

Lic.Iur. Hans-Andrée Koch (Not admitted in Switzerland)

OF COUNSEL

Lic. iur. Peter Achermann
Prof. Dr. Anton C. Heini
Dr. Johannes J. Müller
Prof. Dr. Oscar Vogel

ASSOCIATES

Dr. Alexander Appel (Not admitted in Switzerland)
Dr. Joachim G. Frick
Dr. Martin P. Furrer
Dr. Richard Gassmann
Dr. Marcel Giger
Dr. Lukas Glanzmann
Lic. Iur. Maria Heer
Frano Koslar
Teresa Lewis (Not admitted in Switzerland)
David McLellan (Not admitted in Switzerland)
Marnin J. Michaels (Not admitted in Switzerland)
Lic. Iur. Kilian Perroulaz
Lic. Iur. Philippe M. Reich
Dr. Peter U. Reinert
Dr. Urs Zenhäusern

For full biographical listings, see the Martindale-Hubbell Law Directory

TAIWAN

HSINCHU,

BAKER & MCKENZIE

3F, No. 11, Park Avenue II, Hsinchu Science-based Industrial Park, Hsinchu
Telephone: (03) 564-1177
Intn'l Dialing: (886-3) 564-1177
Facsimile: (886-3) 564-1561
Email: hsinchu.info@bakernet.com *URL:* http://www.bakerinfo.com
Associated Offices of Baker & McKenzie in: Almaty, Amsterdam, Bahrain, Baku, Bangkok, Barcelona, Beijing, Berlin, Bogotá, Brasília, Brussels, Budapest, Buenos Aires, Cairo, Caracas, Chicago, Dallas, Düsseldorf, Frankfurt, Geneva, Hanoi, Ho Chi Minh City, Hong Kong, Houston, Juárez, Kyiv, London, Madrid, Manila, Melbourne, México City, Miami, Milan, Monterrey, Moscow, Münich, New York, Palo Alto, Paris, Prague, Rio de Janeiro, Riyadh, Rome, St. Petersburg, San Diego, San Francisco, Santiago, São Paulo, Singapore, Stockholm, Sydney, Taipei, Tijuana, Tokyo, Toronto, Valencia, Warsaw, Washington, D.C. and Zürich.
Correspondent Law Firm: Hadiputranto, Hadinoto & Partners, Jakarta.

Daniel Lee
Lillian Li-Ling Huang

For full biographical listings, see the Martindale-Hubbell Law Directory

*TAIPEI,**

BAKER & MCKENZIE

15th Floor, Hung Tai Center, No. 168, Tun Hwa North Road, Taipei 105
Telephone: (02) 2712-6151
Intn'l Dialing: (886-2) 2712-6151
Facsimiles: (886-2) 2716-9250; 2712-8292
Email: taipei.info@bakernet.com *URL:* http://www.bakerinfo.com
Associated Offices of Baker & McKenzie in: Almaty, Amsterdam, Bahrain, Baku, Bangkok, Barcelona, Beijing, Berlin, Bogotá, Brasília, Brussels, Budapest, Buenos Aires, Cairo, Caracas, Chicago, Dallas, Düsseldorf, Frankfurt, Geneva, Hanoi, Ho Chi Minh City, Hong Kong, Houston, Hsinchu, Juárez, Kyiv, London, Madrid, Manila, Melbourne, México City, Miami, Milan, Monterrey, Moscow, Münich, New York, Palo Alto, Paris, Prague, Rio de Janeiro, Riyadh, Rome, St. Petersburg, San Diego, San Francisco, Santiago, São Paulo, Singapore, Stockholm, Sydney, Tijuana, Tokyo, Toronto, Valencia, Warsaw, Washington, D.C. and Zürich.
Correspondent Law Firm: Hadiputranto, Hadinoto & Partners, Jakarta.

Lindy L. Y. Chern
Remington Huang
Tiffany T. F. Huang
John S. Lee
David T. Liou
James T. T. Tseng
David H. J. Yang

Michelle Y. L. Gon
Michael Wong

Joseph C.S. Fu
Stacey G. M. Lee
Justin C. Liang
Seraphim G. R. Mar
Joy C. H. Pan
Keye S. Wu

H. Henry Chang
Yuan-San Lu
Kevin Y. H. Wang

Charlie C.L. Chang
Catherine Chen
Hazel C.Y. Chen
Kevin Chen
Helen I. C. Chou
Justin S. J. Ding
Shelley H.L. Fan
Jessy Y. C. Hong
Sylvia S.L. Hong
Carole C.P. Hsu
Sonya S. Y. Hsu
Steven Hsu
Margaret Huang
Tess Szu-Yin Kuo
Min-Hui Li
Victoria H. Y. Lin
Besson P.T. Lu
May J. Lu
Sylvia S. C. Sun
Vincent L. C. Shih
William Te-Yang Tsai
Jansen D. J. Wu
Jason T.S. Wu
Wayne W. Y. Yang

Stan (Shih) C. Chang (Not admitted in Taiwan)
Sheana Hsin Yi Chen
Peter X. Huang (Not admitted in Taiwan)
John B. Kehoe (Not admitted in Taiwan)
Stephen Y. Tan (Not admitted in Taiwan)
Bee Leay Teo (Not admitted in Taiwan)
Robin Y. Wang
Kuang-Chang Yeh (Not admitted in Taiwan)

For full biographical listings, see the Martindale-Hubbell Law Directory

JONES, DAY, REAVIS & POGUE

8th Floor, 2 Tun Hwa South Road Section 2, Taipei 10654
Telephone: (886-2) 2704-6808
Telecopier: (886-2) 2704-6791
Email: counsel@jonesday.com *URL:* http://www.jonesday.com
In Atlanta, Georgia: 3500 SunTrust Plaza, 303 Peachtree Street.
Telephone: 404-521-3939.
Telecopier: 404-581-8330.
In Brussels, Belgium: Avenue Louise 480, 7th Floor, B-1050 Brussels.
Telephone: 32-2-645-14-11.
Telecopier: 32-2-645-14-45.
In Chicago, Illinois: 77 West Wacker.
Telephone: 312-782-3939.
Telecopier: 312-782-8585.
In Cleveland, Ohio: North Point, 901 Lakeside Avenue.
Telephone: 216-586-3939.
Telecopier: 216-579-0212.
In Columbus, Ohio: 1900 Huntington Center.
Telephone: 614-469-3939.
Telecopier: 614-461-4198.
In Dallas, Texas: 2727 North Harwood Street.
Telephone: 214-220-3939.
Telecopier: 214-969-5100.
In Frankfurt, Germany: Hochhaus am Park, Grüneburgweg 102, 60323 Frankfurt am Main.
Telephone: 49-69-9726-3939.
Telecopier: 49-69-9726-3993.
In Geneva, Switzerland: 20, rue de Candolle.
Telephone: 41-22-320-2339.
Telecopier: 41-22-320-1232.

(See Next Column)

In Hong Kong: 29th Floor, Entertainment Building, 30 Queen's Road Central.
Telephone: 852-2526-6895.
Telecopier: 852-2868-5871.
In Irvine, California: 5 Park Plaza, Suite 1100.
Telephone: 949-851-3939.
Telecopier: 949-553-7539.
In London, England: Bucklersbury House, 3 Queen Victoria Street.
Telephone: 44-20-7236-3939.
Telecopier: 44-20-7236-1113.
In Los Angeles, California: 555 West Fifth Street, Suite 4600.
Telephone: 213-489-3939.
Telecopier: 213-243-2539.
In New York, New York: 599 Lexington Avenue.
Telephone: 212-326-3939.
Telecopier: 212-755-7306.
In Paris, France: 120, rue du Faubourg Saint-Honoré.
Telephone: 33-1-56-59-39-39.
Telecopier: 33-1-56-59-39-38
In Pittsburgh, Pennsylvania: 500 Grant Street, 31st Floor.
Telephone: 412-391-3939.
Telecopier: 412-394-7959.
In Riyadh, Saudi Arabia: The International Law Firm (In Association with Jones, Day, Reavis & Pogue), Sulaymaniyah, Prince Mishari IBN, Abdulaziz Street, P.O. Box 22166.
Telephone: (966-1) 462-8866.
Telecopier: (966-1) 462-9001.
In Shanghai, China: 2805 Kerry Centre, 1515 Nanjing Road West.
Telephone: 86-21-5298-6568.
Telecopier: 86-21-5298-6569.
In Sydney, Australia: Governor Phillip Tower, Level 38, 1 Farrer Place.
Telephone: 61-2-9210-6921.
Telecopier: 61-2-9210-6926.
In Tokyo, Japan: Toranomon 45 Mori Building, 3rd Floor, 1-5, Toranomon 5-Chome, Minato-Ku, Tokyo 105, Japan.
Telephone: 81-3-3433-3939.
Telecopier: 81-3-5401-2725.
In Washington, D.C.: 51 Louisiana Avenue, N.W.
Telephone: 202-879-3939.
Telecopier: 202-626-1700.

MEMBERS OF FIRM IN TAIPEI

Jack Jih-Tsan Huang
William E. Bryson, Jr. (Not admitted in Taiwan)

ASSOCIATES

Ke-Wei William Hsu (Not admitted in Taiwan)
Marianne Mei-Chun Chao
Kevin Chih-Feng Lin
Hong John Kao (Not admitted in Taiwan)
James L. Hsu (Not admitted in Taiwan)
Thomas Tai-Ming Chen (Not admitted in Taiwan)
Michael Shang-Jen Chiang (Not admitted in Taiwan)
Jill Y. Niu
Hsin-Chu Wang
Chung-ping Liu (Not admitted in Taiwan)

ASIA ATTORNEYS

Phoebe Yun Chen Ho
Phoebe Hui-Ying Li

For full biographical listings, see the Martindale-Hubbell Law Directory

MCCUTCHEN, DOYLE, BROWN & ENERSEN, LLP

International Trade Building, Tenth Floor, 333 Keelung Road, Section 1, Taipei 110
Telephone: 886-2-2723-5000
Facsimile: 886-2-2757-6070
Email: postmaster@mdbe.com *URL:* http://www.mccutchen.com
San Francisco, California Office: Three Embarcadero Center, 94111-4067.
Telephone: 415-393-2000.
Facsimile: 415-393-2286.
Los Angeles, California Office: 355 South Grand Avenue, Suite 4400, 90071-1560.
Telephone: 213-680-6400.
Facsimile: 213-680-6499.
Walnut Creek, California Office: 1331 North California Boulevard. Post Office Box V, 94596-4502.
Telephone: 510-937-8000.
Facsimile: 510-975-5390.
Palo Alto, California Office: 3150 Porter Drive, 94304.
Telephone: 650-849-4400.
Fax: 650-849-4800.

Joan C. Y. Chen
David D. Chow (Not admitted in Taiwan)
Jacqueline C. Fu

ASSOCIATES

Winnie L. Chern
Alex C. Hung
Claire T. Lin

For full biographical listings, see the Martindale-Hubbell Law Directory

Taipei—Continued

SQUIRE, SANDERS & DEMPSEY L.L.C.

14F, 116 Nanking East Road, Section 2, Taipei
Telephone: 886-2-2531-2888
Fax: 886-2-2571-6199
URL: http://www.ssd.com
Cincinnati, Ohio Office: PNC Center, 201 East Fifth Street, Suite 1700, Cincinnati, Ohio 45202.
Telephone: 513-361-1200.
Fax: 513-361-1201.
Cleveland, Ohio Office: 4900 Key Tower, 127 Public Square, Cleveland, Ohio 44114-1304.
Telephone: 216-479-8500.
Fax: 216-479-8780.
Columbus, Ohio Office: 1300 Huntington Center, 41 South High Street, Columbus, Ohio 43215-6150.
Telephone: 614-365-2700.
Fax: 614-365-2499.
Houston, Texas Office: 6250 Chase Tower, 600 Travis Street, Houston, Texas 77002-3007.
Telephone: 713-546-5850.
Fax: 713-546-5830.
Jacksonville, Florida Office: One Enterprise Center, Suite 2100, 225 Water Street, Jacksonville, Florida 32202-4424.
Telephone: 904-366-2420.
Fax: 904-356-2986.
Miami, Florida Office: 201 South Biscayne Boulevard, 2900 Miami Center, Miami, Florida 33131-4330.
Telephone: 305-577-8700.
Fax: 305-358-1425.
New York, New York Office: 350 Park Avenue, New York, New York 10022-6002.
Telephone: 212-872-9800.
Fax: 212-872-9815.
Phoenix, Arizona Office: Two Renaissance Square, 40 North Central Avenue, Suite 2700, Phoenix, Arizona 85004-4498.
Telephone: 602-528-4000.
Fax: 602-253-8129.
Washington, D.C. Office: 1201 Pennsylvania Avenue, N.W., Suite 500, Washington, D.C. 20004-2491.
Telephone: 202-626-6600.
Fax: 202-626-6780.
Almaty, Kazakhstan Office: 141 Albay Khan Avenue, Second Floor, Almaty, Kazakhstan 480091.
Telephone: +73-27-50-11-25.
Fax: +73-27-50-11-25.
Bratislava, Slovak Republic Office: Zochova 5, 811 03 Bratislava, Slovak Republic.
Telephone: 421-7-5441-7611.
Fax: 42-1-7-6280-2212.
Brussels, Belgium Office: Avenue Louise, 165 Box 15, 1050 Brussels, Belgium.
Telephone: 32-2-627-1111.
Fax: 32-2-627-1100.
Budapest, Hungary Office: H-1062 Budapest, Andrassy ut. 64, Budapest, Hungary.
Telephone: 36-1-428-7111.
Fax: 36-1-428-7100.
Kyiv, Ukraine Office: 14A Yaroslaviv Val, Kyiv 252034, Ukraine.
Telephone: 38-044-228-8687.
Fax: 38-044-228-4938.
London, England Office: Royex House, Aldermanbury Square, London EC2V 7HR.
Telephone: 44-171-776-5200.
Fax: 44-171-776-5233.
Madrid, Spain Office: Calle Velazquez 108-110, 28006 Madrid, Spain.
Telephone: 34-91-590-2420.
Fax: 34-91-590-2421.
Moscow, Russian Federation Office: Paveletskaya Square II, 1 Valovaya Street, 5th Floor, Moscow 113054, Russian Federation.
Telephone: 7-501-258-5250.
Fax: 7-501-258-5251.
Prague, Czech Republic Office: Václavské náměst 1 57/813, 110 00 Praha 1, Czech Republic.
Telephone: 420-2-2166-2111.
Fax: 420-2-2166-2222.
Hong Kong Office: Rooms 1101-2 St. George's Building, 2 Ice House Street, Central, Hong Kong.
Telephone: 852-2509-9732.
Fax: 852-2509-9772.

PARTNER

Nicholas V. G. Chen (Not admitted in Taiwan)

OF COUNSEL

Yen-Wei Jiang

SENIOR CONSULTANT

Julie Chu

ASSOCIATE

Michael D. Lee (Not admitted in Taiwan)

(See Next Column)

LEGAL SUPPORT PERSONNEL

Silvia Peng (Legal Assistant)
Nancy Wu (Research Specialist)

For full biographical listings, see the Martindale-Hubbell Law Directory

THAILAND

*BANGKOK,**

BAKER & MCKENZIE

25th Floor, 990 Rama IV, Rama IV Road, Bangkok 10500
Telephone: 636-2000; 636-2222
Intn'l Dialing: (66-2) 636-2000; 636-2222
Facsimile: (66-2) 636-2111
Postal Address: G.P.O. Box 2815, Bangkok 10501, Thailand
URL: http://www.bakerinfo.com
Associated Offices of Baker & McKenzie in: Almaty, Amsterdam, Bahrain, Baku, Barcelona, Beijing, Berlin, Bogotá, Brasília, Brussels, Budapest, Buenos Aires, Cairo, Caracas, Chicago, Dallas, Düsseldorf, Frankfurt, Geneva, Hanoi, Ho Chi Minh City, Hong Kong, Houston, Hsinchu, Juárez, Kyiv, London, Madrid, Manila, Melbourne, México City, Miami, Milan, Monterrey, Moscow, Münich, New York, Palo Alto, Paris, Prague, Rio de Janeiro, Riyadh, Rome, St. Petersburg, San Diego, San Francisco, Santiago, São Paulo, Singapore, Stockholm, Sydney, Taipei, Tijuana, Tokyo, Toronto, Valencia, Warsaw, Washington, D.C. and Zürich.
Correspondent Law Firm: Hadiputranto, Hadinoto & Partners, Jakarta.

MEMBERS OF FIRM

Jakkarin Bantathong
Thinawat Bukhamana
Suchint Chaimungkalanont
John W. Hancock
(Not admitted in Thailand)
Hatasakdi Na Pombejra
Chirachai Okanurak
Sawanee Amoradhat Sethsathira
Siripong Silpakul
Dhiraphol Suwanprateep
Pornapa L. Thaicharoen
Anurat Tiyaphorn
Kitipong Urapeepatanapong
Kanit Vallayapet

LOCAL PARTNERS

Supparut Allapach
Choopun Chaiprabha
Prechaya Ebrahim
Chaipat Kamchadduskorn
Wisit Kanjanopas
Kulkanist Khamsirivatchara
Suttiphat Khamsirivatchara
Komkrit Kietduriyakul
Charin Satchayan
Taj Singusaha
Sunpasiri Sunpa-a-sa
Prachern Tiyapunjanit
Peerapan Tungsuwan
Suriyong Tungsuwan

Avuth Aksornpan
Sorachon Boonsong
Montien Bunjarnondha
Michael S. Carl
(Not admitted in Thailand)
Pattarasupang Chalermnon
Warangkarat Chalermnon
Isorn Chandrawong
Manoon Changchumni
Pantip Chirakarnjanakorn
Khemajit Choomwattana
Kidhanan Choomwattana
Nirut Dej-udom
Nont Horyangura
Sasiwimol Kasemsri
Punn Kasemsup
Jongtip Kenthaworn
Theppachol Kosol
Wittaya Luengsukcharoen
Chotikorn Luesumpunt
Pravith Mangklatanakul
Pilaipan Mekaratana
Kulachet Na Nakorn
Kitti Netprasat
Chaiyong Ngampravatdee
Wynn Pakdeejit
Piyapong Panyachiva
Phakapon Phokaviboon
Dutdao Phuttasuatta
Chumpol Praphanont
Manu Rakwattanakul
Supoj Ratanasirivilai
Duangjai Sae-Ung
Asawin Sangchay
Thaloengsak Siriratsadon
Yuthana Sivaraks
Weena Siwanansakul
Achchareeya Songvatthana
Kru Sukcharoen
Sawanan Suwankota
Nattaya Techrochanarit
Ornanong Tesabamroong
Tang Thongpakdee
Vit Vatanayothin
Wanee Visitvudhikul
Yoh Wiwatthanopas
Wanchai Yiamsamatha

For full biographical listings, see the Martindale-Hubbell Law Directory

TURKEY

*ANKARA,**

American Lawyers In Ankara

WHITE & CASE

Müşavirlik Ltd. Şti.
Piyade Sokak No. 18, Portakal Çiçeği Apt. C Blok Kat 2 06550 Çankaya, Ankara
Telephone: (90-312) 442-5680
Facsimile: (90-312) 442-5691/4
URL: http://www.whitecase.com
Los Angeles, California:
Telephone: 213-620-7700.
Facsimile: 213-687-0758; 213-452-2330; 213-452-2331.
Palo Alto, California:
Telephone: 650-213-0300.
Facsimile: 650-213-8158.
San Francisco, California:
Telephone: 415-544-1100.
Facsimile: 415-544-0202.
Miami, Florida:
Telephone: 305-371-2700.
Facsimile: 305-358-5744; 305-358-5766.
New York, New York:
Telephone: 212-819-8200.
Facsimile: 212-354-8113.
Washington, D.C.:
Telephone: 202-626-3600.
Facsimile: 202-639-9355.
Bratislava, Slovak Republic:
Telephone: (421-7) 5441-5100.
Facsimile: (421-7) 5441-6100.
Brussels, Belgium:
Telephone: (32-2) 219-16-20.
Facsimile: (32-2) 219-16-26.
Budapest, Hungary: Réczicza Law Firm White & Case.
Telephone: (36-1) 488-5200.
Facsimile: (36-1) 488-5299.
Frankfurt, Germany: White & Case (Rechtsanwälte).
Telephone: (49-69) 713-77-(0).
Facsimile: (49-69) 713-77-100.
Helsinki, Finland: Asianajotoimisto White & Case Oy.
Telephone: (358-9) 228-641.
Facsimile: (358-9) 228-64228.
Istanbul, Turkey:
Telephone: (90-212) 275-75-33.
Facsimile: (90-212) 275-75-43.
London, England:
Telephone: (44-20) 7600-7300.
Facsimile: (44-20) 7600-7030.
Moscow, Russia:
Telephone: (7-095) 787-3000.
Facsimile: (7-095) 787-3001.
Paris, France:
Telephone: (33-1) 55-04-15-15.
Facsimile: (33-1) 55-04-15-16.
Prague, Czech Republic:
Telephone: (420-2) 2481-0808; 2481-1796.
Facsimile: (420-2) 2481-0330; 2481-0252.
Stockholm, Sweden: White & Case Advokat AB.
Telephone: (46-8) 506-323-00.
Facsimile: (46-8) 611-21-22.
Warsaw, Poland: White & Case (Poland) Sp. z o.o.
Telephone: (48-22) 625-33-33; (48-22) 622-67-67; (48-39) 12-19-06.
Facsimile: (48-22) 628-22-28.
Johannesburg, Republic of South Africa:
Telephone: 27 (11) 884-7689.
Facsimile: 27 (11) 884-7229.
Almaty, Kazakhstan:
Telephone: (7-3272) 50-74-91.
Facsimile: (7-3272) 50-74-93.
Bangkok, Thailand: White & Case (Thailand) Limited.
Telephone: (662) 656-1721 to 32.
Facsimile: (662) 656-1733/34.
Bombay/Mumbai, India: Liaison Office, (91-22) 282-6300/01/02/03.
Facsimile: (91-22) 282-6305.
Hanoi, Vietnam:
Telephone: (84-4) 934-5355.
Facsimile: (84-4) 934-5356.
Ho Chi Minh City, Vietnam:
Telephone: (84-8) 821-0888.
Facsimile: (84-8) 823-6902.
Hong Kong: White & Case, Solicitors.
Telephone: (852) 2822-8700.
Facsimile: (852) 2845-9070.
Singapore, Republic of Singapore:
Telephone: (65) 225-6000.
Facsimile: (65) 225-6009.

(See Next Column)

Tokyo, Japan: White & Case Kandabashi Law Offices.
Telephone: (81-3) 3259-0200.
Facsimile: (81-3) 3259-0150.
Manama, Bahrain:
Telephone: (973) 9610105; (973) 9610119; (973) 535965.
Facsimile: (973) 590962; (973) 532342.
Jeddah, Saudi Arabia: Law Office of Hassan Mahassni,
Telephone: (966-2) 665-4353.
Facsimile: (966-2) 669-2996.
Riyadh, Saudi Arabia: Law Office of Hassan Mahassni,
Telephone: (966-1) 464-4006.
Facsimile: (966-1) 465-1348.
Mexico City, Mexico: White & Case, S.C.
Telephone: (52) 5-540-9600.
Facsimile: (52) 5-540-9699.
São Paulo, SP, Brazil:
Telephone: (55-11) 3171-0011.
Facsimile: (55-11) 3171-0041.
Associated Law Firm(s):
Bombay/Mumbai, India: India Law Services (ILS).
Telephones: (91-22) 284-1995; (91-22) 284-1847.
Facsimile: (91-22) 285-0824.
New Delhi, India: India Law Services (ILS).
Telephone: (91-11) 697-1602/3/4.
Facsimile: (91-11) 698-8860.
Jakarta, Indonesia: Ali Budiardjo, Nugroho, Reksodiputro, Counsellors at Law.
Telephone: (62-21) 250-5125; 250-5136.
Facsimile: (62-21) 250-5392; 250-5122; 250-5001.
Associated Consultancies:
Jakarta, Indonesia: PT WCI Konsultan.
Telephone: (62-21) 577-1527.
Facsimile: (62-21) 577-1535/6.

FOREIGN LAW AND INTERNATIONAL LAW CONSULTANTS

RESIDENT PARTNER

Gwynne H. Wales (Not admitted in Turkey)

OF COUNSEL

Dr. T. Nurkut Inan

CONSULTANT

Dr. Gamze Öz

For full biographical listings, see the Martindale-Hubbell Law Directory

ISTANBUL,

American Lawyers In Istanbul

WHITE & CASE

Müşavirlik Ltd. Şti.
Maya Akar Center Büyükdere Caddesi 101-102, B Blok, Kat 23 80280 Esentepe, Istanbul
Telephone: (90-212) 275-75-33
Facsimile: (90-212) 275-75-43
URL: http://www.whitecase.com
Los Angeles, California:
Telephone: 213-620-7700.
Facsimile: 213-687-0758; 213-452-2330; 213-452-2331.
Palo Alto, California:
Telephone: 650-213-0300.
Facsimile: 650-213-8158.
San Francisco, California:
Telephone: 415-544-1100.
Facsimile: 415-544-0202.
Miami, Florida:
Telephone: 305-371-2700.
Facsimile: 305-358-5744; 305-358-5766.
New York, New York:
Telephone: 212-819-8200.
Facsimile: 212-354-8113.
Washington, D.C.:
Telephone: 202-626-3600.
Facsimile: 202-639-9355.
Bratislava, Slovak Republic:
Telephone: (421-7) 5441-5100.
Facsimile: (421-7) 5441-6100.
Brussels, Belgium:
Telephone: (32-2) 219-16-20.
Facsimile: (32-2) 219-16-26.
Budapest, Hungary: Réczicza Law Firm White & Case.
Telephone: (36-1) 488-5200.
Facsimile: (36-1) 488-5299.
Frankfurt, Germany: White & Case (Rechtsanwälte).
Telephone: (49-69) 713-77-(0).
Facsimile: (49-69) 713-77-100.
Helsinki, Finland: Asianajotoimisto White & Case Oy.
Telephone: (358-9) 228-641.
Facsimile: (358-9) 228-64228.
London, England:
Telephone: (44-20) 7600-7300.
Facsimile: (44-20) 7600-7030.

(See Next Column)

WHITE & CASE—*Continued*

Moscow, Russia:
Telephone: (7-095) 787-3000.
Facsimile: (7-095) 787-3001.
Paris, France:
Telephone: (33-1) 55-04-15-15.
Facsimile: (33-1) 55-04-15-16.
Prague, Czech Republic:
Telephone: (420-2) 2481-0808; 2481-1796.
Facsimile: (420-2) 2481-0330; 2481-0252.
Stockholm, Sweden: White & Case Advokat AB.
Telephone: (46-8) 506-323-00.
Facsimile: (46-8) 611-21-22.
Warsaw, Poland: White & Case (Poland) Sp. z o.o.
Telephone: (48-22) 625-33-33; (48-22) 622-67-67; (48-39) 12-19-06.
Facsimile: (48-22) 628-22-28.
Johannesburg, Republic of South Africa:
Telephone: 27 (11) 884-7689.
Facsimile: 27 (11) 884-7229.
Almaty, Kazakhstan:
Telephone: (7-3272) 50-74-91.
Facsimile: (7-3272) 50-74-93.
Ankara, Turkey:
Telephone: (90-312) 442-5680.
Facsimile: (90-312) 442-5691/4.
Bangkok, Thailand: White & Case (Thailand) Limited.
Telephone: (662) 656-1721 to 32.
Facsimile: (662) 656-1733/34.
Bombay/Mumbai, India: Liaison Office, (91-22) 282-6300/01/02/03.
Facsimile: (91-22) 282-6305.
Hanoi, Vietnam:
Telephone: (84-4) 934-5355.
Facsimile: (84-4) 934-5356.
Ho Chi Minh City, Vietnam:
Telephone: (84-8) 821-0888.
Facsimile: (84-8) 823-6902.
Hong Kong: White & Case, Solicitors.
Telephone: (852) 2822-8700.
Facsimile: (852) 2845-9070.
Singapore, Republic of Singapore:
Telephone: (65) 225-6000.
Facsimile: (65) 225-6009.
Tokyo, Japan: White & Case Kandabashi Law Offices.
Telephone: (81-3) 3259-0200.
Facsimile: (81-3) 3259-0150.
Manama, Bahrain:
Telephone: (973) 9610105; (973) 9610119; (973) 535965.
Facsimile: (973) 590962; (973) 532342.
Jeddah, Saudi Arabia: Law Office of Hassan Mahassni,
Telephone: (966-2) 665-4353.
Facsimile: (966-2) 669-2996.
Riyadh, Saudi Arabia: Law Office of Hassan Mahassni,
Telephone: (966-1) 464-4006.
Facsimile: (966-1) 465-1348.
Mexico City, Mexico: White & Case, S.C.
Telephone: (52) 5-540-9600.
Facsimile: (52) 5-540-9699.
São Paulo, SP, Brazil:
Telephone: (55-11) 3171-0011.
Facsimile: (55-11) 3171-0041.
Associated Law Firm(s):
Bombay/Mumbai, India: India Law Services (ILS).
Telephones: (91-22) 284-1995; (91-22) 284-1847.
Facsimile: (91-22) 285-0824.
New Delhi, India: India Law Services (ILS).
Telephone: (91-11) 697-1602/3/4.
Facsimile: (91-11) 698-8860.
Jakarta, Indonesia: Ali Budiardjo, Nugroho, Reksodiputro, Counsellors at Law.
Telephone: (62-21) 250-5125; 250-5136.
Facsimile: (62-21) 250-5392; 250-5122; 250-5001.
Associated Consultancies:
Jakarta, Indonesia: PT WCI Konsultan.
Telephone: (62-21) 577-1527.
Facsimile: (62-21) 577-1535/6.

RESIDENT PARTNER

Asli F. Basgoz (Not admitted in Turkey)

RESIDENT COUNSEL

M. Fadlullah Cerrahoglu — Serap Zuvin

ASSOCIATES

Leigh J. Hall (Not admitted in Turkey)

For full biographical listings, see the Martindale-Hubbell Law Directory

TURKMENISTAN

ASHGABAT,

MAYER, BROWN & PLATT

28 Gogol Street, Ashgabat 744000
Telephone: 011-99-312-355247
Facsimile: 011-99-312-510074
URL: http://www.mayerbrown.com
Chicago, Illinois Office: 190 South LaSalle Street. 60603-3441.
Telephone: (312) 782-0600.
Facsimile: (312) 701-7711.
Telex: 190404.
Cable: LEMAY.
Berlin, Germany Office: Breite Strasse 29, Muehlendamm, 10178.
Telephone: 011-49-30-2060-7710.
Facsimile: 011-49-30-2060-7744.
Charlotte, North Carolina Office: 100 North Tryon Street, Suite 2400.
Telephone: (704) 444-3500.
Fax: (704) 377-2033.
Cologne, Germany Office: Kaiser-Wilhelm-Ring 27-29, 50672.
Telephone: 011-49-221-5771-100.
Facsimile: 011-49-221-5771-199.
Houston, Texas Office: 700 Louisiana Street, Suite 3600, 77002-2730.
Telephone: (713) 221-1651.
Facsimile: (713) 224-6410.
Telex: 775809.
Cable: LEMAYHOU.
London, England Office: Bucklersbury House, 3 Queen Victoria Street, London, EC4N 8EL, England.
Telephone: 011-44-171-246-6200.
Facsimile: 011-44-171-329-4465.
Telex: 8811095.
Cable: LEMAYLDN.
Los Angeles, California Office: 350 South Grand Avenue, 25th Floor, 90071-1503.
Telephone: (213) 229-9500.
Facsimile: (213) 625-0248.
Telex: 188089.
Cable: LEMAYLA.
New York, New York Office: 1675 Broadway, 10019-5820.
Telephone: (212) 506-2500.
Facsimile: (212) 262-1910.
Telex: 701842.
Cable: LEMAYEN.
Washington, D.C. Office: 1909 K Street, N.W., 20006-1101.
Telephone: (202) 263-3000.
Facsimile: (202) 263-3300.
Telex: 892603.
Cable: LEMAYDC.
Representative Offices:
Bishkek, Kyrgyz Republic: 66 Kalyka Akieva Str. 720010.
Telephone: 011-996-312-65-02-56.
Facsimile: 011-996-312-65-09-80.
Tashkent, Republic of Uzbekistan: 3rd Floor, 1 Turab Tula Street, 700003.
Telephone: 011-998-71-1206-627.
Facsimile: 011-998-71-1206-329.
Mexico City, Mexico, D.F., Independent Mexico Correspondent: Jáuregui, Navarrete, Nader y Rojas, S.C., Torre Arcos, Paseo de los Tamarindos No. 400-B. Col. Bosques de las Lomas, 05120.
Telephone: 011-525-267-45-00.
Facsimile: 011-525-267-45-99.
Paris, France, Independent Paris Correspondent: Lambert & Lee, 13 Avenue Hoche, 75008.
Telephone: 011-33-1-53-53-43-43.
Facsimile: 011-33-1-53-96-03-83.

ASSOCIATE

Ashir K. Abdullaev

For full biographical listings, see the Martindale-Hubbell Law Directory

UKRAINE

*KYIV (KIEV),**

American Lawyers in Kyiv (Kiev)

BAKER & MCKENZIE

48 Bohdana Khmelnytskoho Street, Kyiv (Kiev) 01030
Telephone: Telephone: (044) 490-7070
Int'l Dialing: (380-44) 490-7070
Facsimile: (380-44) 490-6787
URL: http://www.bakerinfo.com
Associated Offices of Baker & McKenzie in: Almaty, Amsterdam, Bahrain, Baku, Bangkok, Barcelona, Beijing, Berlin, Bogotá, Brasília, Brussels, Budapest, Buenos Aires, Cairo, Caracas, Chicago, Dallas, Düsseldorf, Frankfurt, Geneva, Hanoi, Ho Chi Minh City, Hong Kong, Houston, Hsinchu, Juárez, London, Madrid, Manila, Melbourne, México City, Miami, Milan, Monterrey, Moscow, München, New York, Palo Alto, Paris, Prague, Rio de Janeiro, Riyadh, Rome, St. Petersburg, San Diego, San Francisco, Santiago, São Paulo, Singapore, Stockholm, Sydney, Taipei, Tijuana, Tokyo, Toronto, Valencia, Warsaw, Washington, D.C. and Zürich.
Correspondent Law Firm: Hadiputranto, Hadinoto & Partners, Jakarta.

PARTNERS

Borys Y. Dackiw (Not admitted in Ukraine)
David I. Scott (Not admitted in Ukraine)

LOCAL PARTNERS

Serhiy V. Chorny
Alexander P. Martinenko

ASSOCIATES

Yulia Andrusiv
Vladimir Goutsaliouk
Iryna Nagayets
Ihor Nazarchuk
Vyacheslav Petrashenko
Serhiy V. Piontkovsky
Mykhailo Tymoshenko
Vadym Vasko

For full biographical listings, see the Martindale-Hubbell Law Directory

SQUIRE, SANDERS & DEMPSEY L.L.P. (AV)

14A Yaroslaviv Val, 252034 Kyiv (Kiev)
Telephone: 38-044-228-8687
Fax: 38-044-228-4938
URL: http://www.ssd.com
Cincinnati, Ohio Office: PNC Center, 201 East Fifth Street, Suite 1700, Cincinnati, Ohio 45202.
Telephone: 513-361-1200.
Fax: 513-361-1201.
Cleveland, Ohio Office: 4900 Key Tower, 127 Public Square, Cleveland, Ohio 44114-1304.
Telephone: 216-479-8500.
Fax: 216-479-8780.
Columbus, Ohio Office: 1300 Huntington Center, 41 South High Street, Columbus, Ohio 43215-6150.
Telephone: 614-365-2700.
Fax: 614-365-2499.
Houston, Texas Office: 6250 Chase Tower, 600 Travis Street, Houston, Texas 77002-3007.
Telephone: 713-546-5850.
Fax: 713-546-5830.
Jacksonville, Florida Office: One Enterprise Center, Suite 2100, 225 Water Street, Jacksonville, Florida 32202-4424.
Telephone: 904-366-2420.
Fax: 904-356-2986.
Miami, Florida Office: 201 South Biscayne Boulevard, 2900 Miami Center, Miami, Florida 33131-4330.
Telephone: 305-577-8700.
Fax: 305-358-1425.
New York, New York Office: 350 Park Avenue, New York, New York 10022-6002.
Telephone: 212-872-9800.
Fax: 212-872-9815.
Phoenix, Arizona Office: Two Renaissance Square, 40 North Central Avenue, Suite 2700, Phoenix, Arizona 85004-4498.
Telephone: 602-528-4000.
Fax: 602-253-8129.
Washington, D.C. Office: 1201 Pennsylvania Avenue, N.W., Suite 500, Washington, D.C. 20004-2491.
Telephone: 202-626-6600.
Fax: 202-626-6780.
Almaty, Kazakhstan Office: 141 Albay Khan Avenue, Second Floor, Almaty, Kazakhstan 480091.
Telephone: +73-27-50-11-25.
Fax: +73-27-50-11-25.
Bratislava, Slovak Republic Office: Zochova 5, 811 03 Bratislava, Slovak Republic.
Telephone: 421-7-5441-7611.
Fax: 42-1-7-6280-2212.
Brussels, Belgium Office: Avenue Louise, 165-Box 15, 1050 Brussels, Belgium.
Telephone: 32-2-627-1111.
Fax: 32-2-627-1100.

(See Next Column)

Budapest, Hungary Office: H-1062 Budapest, Andrassy ut. 64, Budapest, Hungary.
Telephone: 36-1-428-7111.
Fax: 36-1-428-7100.
London, England Office: Royex House, Aldermanbury Square, London EC2V 7HR.
Telephone: 44-171-776-5200.
Fax: 44-171-776-5233.
Madrid, Spain Office: Calle Velazquez 108-110, 28006 Madrid, Spain.
Telephone: 34-91-590-2420.
Fax: 34-91-590-2421.
Moscow, Russian Federation Office: Paveletskaya Square II, 1 Valovaya Street, 5th Floor, Moscow 113054, Russian Federation.
Telephone: 7-501-258-5250.
Fax: 7-501-258-5251.
Prague, Czech Republic Office: Václavské námĕst 1 57/813, 110 00 Praha 1, Czech Republic.
Telephone: 420-2-2166-2111.
Fax: 420-2-2166-2222.
Hong Kong Office: Rooms 1101-2 St. George's Building, 2 Ice House Street, Central, Hong Kong.
Telephone: 852-2509-9732.
Fax: 852-2509-9772.
Taipei, Taiwan Office: 14F, 116 Nanking East Road, Sec. 2, Taipei, Taiwan, Republic of China.
Telephone: 886-2-2531-2888.
Fax: 886-2-2571-6199.

PARTNER

Sarah C. Carey (Not admitted in Ukraine)
Helen Z. Kryshtalowych

COUNSEL

Evgeny V. Goussev

ASSOCIATES

William Smith Greig (Not admitted in Ukraine)
Armen G. Khachaturyan
Nazar Kovalenko
Vyacheslav Yakymchuk

For full biographical listings, see the Martindale-Hubbell Law Directory

UNITED ARAB EMIRATES

ABU DHABI,

American Lawyers In Abu Dhabi

SHEARMAN & STERLING

Butti Al Otaiba Building 13th Floor, Suite 1302, Sheikh Khalifa Street, P.O. Box 2948, Abu Dhabi
Telephone: (971-2) 6274477
Fax: (971-2) 6268933
Telex: 22662 Num Lat
URL: http://www.shearman.com
New York, N.Y. Office: 599 Lexington Avenue, New York, New York, 10022-6069.
Telephone: (212) 848-4000.
Telex: 667290. Num Lau.
Fax: (212) 848-7179.
Beijing, People's Republic of China Office: Suite #2205, Capital Mansion, No. 6, Xin Yuan Nan Road. Chao Yang District, Beijing, 100004.
Telephone: (86-10) 6465-2299.
Fax: (86-10) 6465-4578.
Düsseldorf, Federal Republic of Germany Office: Couvenstrasse 8 40211 Düsseldorf.
Telephone: (49 211) 178 88-0.
Fax: (49 211) 178 88-88.
Frankfurt, Federal Republic of Germany Office: Trianon Building, Mainzer Landstrasse 16, 60325 Frankfurt am Main.
Telephone: (49-69) 9711-1000.
Fax: (49-69) 9711-1100.
Hong Kong Office: Standard Chartered Bank Building, 4 Des Voeux Road, Central.
Telephone: (852) 2978-8000.
Fax: (852) 2978-8099.
London, England Office: Broadgate West, 9 Appold Street, London EC2A 2AP.
Telephone: 011-44-20-7655-5000.
Fax: 011-44-20-7655-5500.
Menlo Park, California Office: 1550 El Camino Real, 94025-4100.
Telephone: (650) 330-2200.
Fax: (650) 330-2299.
Paris, France Office: 114, avenue des Champs-Elysées, 75008.
Telephone: (33-1) 53-89-7000.
Fax: (33-1) 53-89-7070.
San Francisco, California Office: 555 California Street, 94104-1522.
Telephone: (415) 616-1100.
Fax: (415) 616-1199.
Singapore Office: 6 Battery Road #25-03. Singapore 049909.
Telephone: (65) 230-3800.
Fax: (65) 230-3899.

(See Next Column)

SHEARMAN & STERLING—*Continued*

Tokyo, Japan Office: Fukoku Seimei Building, 5th Fl. 2-2-2, Uchisaiwaicho, Chiyoda-ku, Tokyo 100-0011. Japan.
Telephone: (81 3) 5251-1601.
Fax: (81 3) 5251-1602.
Toronto, Ontario, Canada Office: Commerce Court West, Suite 4405, P.O. Box 247, M5L 1E8.
Telephone: (416) 360-8484.
Fax: (416) 360-2958.
Washington, D.C. Office: 801 Pennsylvania Avenue, N.W., 20004-2604.
Telephone: (202) 508-8000.
Fax: (202) 508-8100.

MANAGING PARTNER

Philip B. Dundas, Jr. (Not admitted in United Arab Emirates)
(Not admitted to practice in United Arab Emirates courts)

For full biographical listings, see the Martindale-Hubbell Law Directory

UZBEKISTAN

*TASHKENT,**

American Lawyers in Tashkent

MAYER, BROWN & PLATT

3rd Floor, 1 Turab Tula Street, Tashkent 700003
Telephone: 011-998-71-1206-627
Facsimile: 011-998-71-1206-329
URL: http://www.mayerbrown.com
Berlin, Germany Office: Breite Strasse 29, Muehlendamm, 10178.
Telephone: 011-49-30-2060-7710.
Facsimile: 011-49-30-2060-7744.
Chicago, Illinois Office: 190 South LaSalle Street, 60603-3441.
Telephone: (312) 782-0600.
Facsimile: (312) 701-7711.
Telex: 190404.
Cable: LEMAY.
Charlotte, North Carolina Office: 100 North Tryon Street, Suite 2400.
Telephone: (704) 444-3500.
Fax: (704) 377-2033.
Cologne, Germany Office: Kaiser-Wilhelm-Ring 27-29, 50672.
Telephone: 011-49-221-5771-100.
Facsimile: 011-49-221-5771-199.
Houston, Texas Office: 700 Louisiana Street, Suite 3600, 77002-2730.
Telephone: (713) 221-1651.
Facsimile: (713) 224-6410.
Telex: 775809.
Cable: LEMAYHOU.
London, England Office: Bucklersbury House, 3 Queen Victoria Street, London, EC4N 8EL, England.
Telephone: 011-44-171-246-6200.
Facsimile: 011-44-171-329-4465.
Telex: 8811095.
Cable: LEMAYLDN.
Los Angeles, California Office: 350 South Grand Avenue, 25th Floor, 90071-1503.
Telephone: (213) 229-9500.
Facsimile: (213) 625-0248.
Telex: 188089.
Cable: LEMAYLA.
New York, New York Office: 1675 Broadway, 10019-5820.
Telephone: (212) 506-2500.
Facsimile: (212) 262-1910.
Telex: 701842.
Cable: LEMAYEN.
Washington, D.C. Office: 1909 K Street, N.W., 20006-1101.
Telephone: (202) 263-3000.
Facsimile: (202) 263-3300.
Telex: 892603.
Cable: LEMAYDC.
Representative Offices:
Ashgabat, Turkmenistan: 28 Gogol Street, 744000.
Telephone: 011-99-312-355247.
Facsimile: 011-99-312-510074.
Bishkek, Kyrgyz Republic: 66 Kalyka Akieva Str. 720010.
Telephone: 011-996-312-65-02-56.
Facsimile: 011-996-312-65-09-80.
Mexico City, Mexico, D.F., Independent Mexico Correspondent: Jáuregui, Navarrete, Nader y Rojas, S.C., Torre Arcos, paseo de los Tamarindos No. 400-B. Col. Bosques de las Lomas, 05120.
Telephone: 011-525-267-45-00.
Facsimile: 011-525-267-45-99.
Paris, France, Independent Paris Correspondent: Lambert & Lee, 13 Avenue Hoche, 75008.
Telephone: 011-33-1-53-53-43-43.
Facsimile: 011-33-1-53-96-03-83.

(See Next Column)

ASSOCIATES

Jamol A. Askarov
Yegor A. Boyarkin
Aleksey Yu Katulevskiy
Mwanajuma P. Lugogo (Not admitted in Uzbekistan)
Alexander V. Voronin

For full biographical listings, see the Martindale-Hubbell Law Directory

VENEZUELA

*CARACAS,**

BAKER & MCKENZIE

Torre Edicampo, P.H. Avenida Francisco de Miranda, cruce con Avenida Del Parque Urbanización Campo Alegre, Caracas
Telephone: (02) 276-5111; 276-5112
Intn'l Dialing: (58-2) 276-5111; 276-5112
Facsimile: (58-2) 264-1532; 264-1637
Modem: (58-2) 265-5515; 265-0255; 265-2463
Cable: ABOGADO-CARACAS
URL: http://www.bakerinfo.com
U.S. Mailing Address: Baker & McKenzie, M-287, Jet Cargo International, P.O. Box 020010, Miami, Florida 33102-0010, U.S.A.
Associated Offices of Baker & McKenzie in: Almaty, Amsterdam, Bahrain, Baku, Bangkok, Barcelona, Beijing, Berlin, Bogotá, Brasília, Brussels, Budapest, Buenos Aires, Cairo, Chicago, Dallas, Düsseldorf, Frankfurt, Geneva, Hanoi, Ho Chi Minh City, Hong Kong, Houston, Hsinchu, Juárez, Kyiv, London, Madrid, Manila, Melbourne, México City, Miami, Milan, Monterrey, Moscow, Münich, New York, Palo Alto, Paris, Prague, Rio de Janeiro, Riyadh, Rome, St. Petersburg, San Diego, San Francisco, Santiago, São Paulo, Singapore, Stockholm, Sydney, Taipei, Tijuana, Tokyo, Toronto, Valencia, Warsaw, Washington, D.C. and Zürich.
Correspondent Law Firm: Hadiputranto, Hadinoto & Partners, Jakarta.
Postal Address: P.O. Box 1286, Caracas 1010-A, Venezuela

PARTNERS

Alejandro Alfonzo-Larrain R.
Pedro Pablo Benedetti
Humberto J. Briceño León
Diego Bustillos
Malcolm Caplan (Not admitted in Venezuela)
Raúl Curiel
José H. D'Apollo
Manuel Díaz Mujica
Gilberto Haiek-Wülff
Eugenio Hernández-Bretón
Eduardo Machado I.
Roberto J. Mendoza
Maritza Mészáros Reyes
Francisco I. Palma
Freddy Paván V.
Carlos A. Plaza Anselmi
Emilio J. Roche
Henry Torrealba Ledesma
Luis Miguel Vicentini
Miguel A. Zaldívar

LOCAL PARTNERS

Nedo E. Boccardo
Carlos E. Delgado A.
Ronald E. Evans
Carlos A. Felce
Fernando M. Fernández
José Alfredo Giral
Carolina Lanao de la Sota
Alejandro B. Lares Díaz
Leopoldo Enrique Olavarría
Alvaro J. Posada
María Eugenia Reyes
Leopoldo E. Ustáriz C.

Yanet C. Aguiar
Juan Carlos Andrade
María Teresa Arcaya
Juan Carlos Balzán
José P. Barnola
Juan Carlos Blanco
Sergio Casinelli
Gaiskale Castillejo
Mario Calosso Castillo
María De Los Angeles Celis
Norma Cigala
Martha Esther Cohen
Pedro José Crisafulli
Gabriel De Jesús
Manuel E. D'Empaire Parra
Rossanna D'Onza
Alberto Galuppo
Luis Eduardo González
René Gutiérrez Robles
Margot Huen
Daniela Jaimes Cifuentes
Aníbal Latuff
Manuel Emilio Marin
Andrea Márquez Bottome
Edmundo Martinez Rivero
Miguel Mónaco
Emma Isabel Neher
Gustavo I. Nieto
Gabriela Palmieri
Erasmo A. Pérez Fernández
Dianne R. Phoebus
Armando J. Planchart
Eduardo J. Quintero
Hector Jose Ramírez CH
Irene B. Rivas Gómez
Liliana Salazar Medina
Mariá E. Salazar Furiati
Shirley Sanquiz
Antonella D. Sciubba
María Gabriela Sosa Reber
Juan Carlos Varela
Carlos Alfonso Vivi
María Fernanda Zajía Tobía

For full biographical listings, see the Martindale-Hubbell Law Directory

VALENCIA,

BAKER & MCKENZIE

Edificio Torre Venezuela, Piso No. 4 Av. Bolivar cruce con Calle 154 (Misael Delgado), Urbanizacion La Alegria, Valencia
Telephone: (41) 248711
Intn'l Dialing: (58-41) 248711
Facsimile: (58-41) 246166
Postal Address: P.O. Box 1155 Valencia, Estado Carabobo, Venezuela
URL: http://www.bakerinfo.com
Associated Offices of Baker & McKenzie in: Almaty, Amsterdam, Bahrain, Baku, Bangkok, Barcelona, Beijing, Berlin, Bogotá, Brasília, Brussels, Budapest, Buenos Aires, Cairo, Caracas, Chicago, Dallas, Düsseldorf, Frankfurt, Geneva, Hanoi, Ho Chi Minh City, Hong Kong, Houston, Hsinchu, Juárez, Kyiv, London, Madrid, Manila, Melbourne, México City, Miami, Milan, Monterrey, Moscow, Münich, New York, Palo Alto, Paris, Prague, Rio de Janeiro, Riyadh, Rome, St. Petersburg, San Diego, San Francisco, Santiago, São Paulo, Singapore, Stockholm, Sydney, Taipei, Tijuana, Tokyo, Toronto, Warsaw, Washington, D.C. and Zürich.
Correspondent Law Firm: Hadiputranto, Hadinoto & Partners, Jakarta.

RESIDENT PARTNER

Omar Benítez

RESIDENT ASSOCIATES

Monica Guerrero
Carlos Enrique Lüdert León
Douvelin J. Serra Gonzalez
Francisco J. Velasquez Arcay

For full biographical listings, see the Martindale-Hubbell Law Directory

VIETNAM

HANOI,

BAKER & MCKENZIE

Hanoi Branch Office
3rd Floor, 63 Ly Thai To Street Hoan Kiem District, Hanoi
Telephone: (4) 825-1428; 825-1429; 825-1430
Intn'l Dialing: (84-4) 825-1428; 825-1429; 825-1430
Facsimile: (84-4) 825-1432
URL: http://www.bakerinfo.com
Associated Offices of Baker & McKenzie in: Almaty, Amsterdam, Bahrain, Baku, Bangkok, Barcelona, Beijing, Berlin, Bogotá, Brasília, Brussels, Budapest, Buenos Aires, Cairo, Caracas, Chicago, Dallas, Düsseldorf, Frankfurt, Geneva, Ho Chi Minh City, Hong Kong, Houston, Hsinchu, Juárez, Kyiv, London, Madrid, Manila, Melbourne, México City, Miami, Milan, Monterrey, Moscow, Münich, New York, Palo Alto, Paris, Prague, Rio de Janeiro, Riyadh, Rome, St. Petersburg, San Diego, San Francisco, Santiago, São Paulo, Singapore, Stockholm, Sydney, Taipei, Tijuana, Tokyo, Toronto, Valencia, Warsaw, Washington, D.C. and Zürich.
Correspondent Law Firm: Hadiputranto, Hadinoto & Partners, Jakarta.

PARTNER

Frederick R. Burke (Not admitted in Vietnam)

ASSOCIATES

Oliver Massmann
Hien Truc Nguyen

For full biographical listings, see the Martindale-Hubbell Law Directory

HO CHI MINH CITY,

BAKER & MCKENZIE

Ho Chi Minh City Branch Office
12th Floor, Saigon Tower, 29 Le Duan Boulevard District 1, Ho Chi Minh City
Telephone: (08) 829-5585; 829-5601; 829-5602; 829-5613
Intn'l Dialing: (84-8) 829-5585; 829-5601; 829-5602; 829-5613
Facsimile: (84-8) 829-5618
URL: http://www.bakerinfo.com
Associated Offices of Baker & McKenzie in: Almaty, Amsterdam, Bahrain, Baku, Bangkok, Barcelona, Beijing, Berlin, Bogotá, Brasília, Brussels, Budapest, Buenos Aires, Cairo, Caracas, Chicago, Dallas, Düsseldorf, Frankfurt, Geneva, Hanoi, Hong Kong, Houston, Hsinchu, Juárez, Kyiv, London, Madrid, Manila, Melbourne, México City, Miami, Milan, Monterrey, Moscow, Münich, New York, Palo Alto, Paris, Prague, Rio de Janeiro, Riyadh, Rome, St. Petersburg, San Diego, San Francisco, Santiago, São Paulo, Singapore, Stockholm, Sydney, Taipei, Tijuana, Tokyo, Toronto, Valencia, Warsaw, Washington, D.C. and Zürich.
Correspondent Law Firm: Hadiputranto, Hadinoto & Partners, Jakarta.

PARTNER

Frederick R. Burke (Not admitted in Vietnam)

ASSOCIATES

Net Le
Oanh Hoang Kim Nguyen
Yee Chung Seck (Not admitted in Vietnam)

For full biographical listings, see the Martindale-Hubbell Law Directory

GOVERNMENT CONTRACTS

MISSISSIPPI

*GULFPORT,** Harrison Co.

BOYCE HOLLEMAN A PROFESSIONAL CORPORATION (AV)

1913 15th Street, P.O. Drawer 1030, 39502
Telephone: 228-863-3142; 1-800-863-3140
Telecopier: 228-863-9829
Email: boyce1913@aol.com

Boyce Holleman

Timothy C. Holleman
Leslie Dean Holleman
David J. "Jeff" White

References: Hancock Bank, Gulfport; Merchants Bank & Trust Co., Gulfport; Bank of Wiggins, Wiggins, Mississippi.

For full biographical listings, see the Martindale-Hubbell Law Directory

*PASCAGOULA,** Jackson Co.

COLINGO, WILLIAMS, HEIDELBERG, STEINBERGER & McELHANEY, P.A. (AV)

711 Delmas Avenue, P.O. Box 1407, 39568-1407
Telephone: 228-762-8021
FAX: 228-762-7589
Email: info@colingowilliams.com *URL:* http://www.ColingoWilliams.com

Roy C. Williams
James H. Heidelberg
Karl R. Steinberger
Stephen W. Burrow

Representative Clients: International Paper Co.; R.J. Reynolds; CBS Corp.; Kemper Group; Singing River Hospital System; Mississippi Gulf Coast Regional Wastewater Authority; Medical Assurance Company of Mississippi; Mutual Assurance of Alabama; Dole Food Co.

For full biographical listings, see the Martindale-Hubbell Law Directory

NEW JERSEY

MOORESTOWN, Burlington Co.

FREDERICK W. HARDT (AV)

Suite 101, 300 Chester Avenue, P.O. Box 840, 08057-2512
Telephone: 609-234-4141
Fax: 609-273-8617

ASSOCIATE

Pamela A. Moy

For full biographical listings, see the Martindale-Hubbell Law Directory

NEW MEXICO

*ALBUQUERQUE,** Bernalillo Co.

FAIRFIELD, FARROW, FLOWERS, PIERSON & STROTZ, P.C. (AV)

2400 Louisiana N.E., AFC 3, Suite 100, P.O. Box 35400, 87176-5400
Telephone: 505-881-8300
Fax: 505-889-0553
Email: fairlaw@nm.net

Raymond R. (Dick) Flowers, Jr.

Representative Clients: David Montoya Construction; Jamco Constructors; F2 Associates, Inc.; TPL, Inc.; Data Trac; Voss Scientific; Science & Engineering Associates; Otero County Electrical Corp.; Commodore Advanced Sciences, Inc.; Zuni Public School District.

For full biographical listings, see the Martindale-Hubbell Law Directory

NEW YORK

*NEW YORK,** New York Co.

POSTNER & RUBIN (AV)

17 Battery Place, 10004
Telephone: 212-269-2510
Fax: 212-425-0968
Email: postner@aol.com
Holmdel, New Jersey Office: 42 West Main Street,
Telephone: 732-946-9001.
Fax: 732-946-9005.

Robert A. Rubin
William J. Postner
Robert J. MacPherson
Jeffrey R. Cruz

ASSOCIATES

Patricia M. Caplicki
Dana Wordes
Michael W. Bautz

NEW JERSEY RESIDENT COUNSEL

Sarah B. Biser

For full biographical listings, see the Martindale-Hubbell Law Directory

SACKS MONTGOMERY, P.C. (AV)

800 Third Avenue, 10022
Telephone: 212-355-4660
Telecopier: 212-593-7257
Email: sm@sacksmontgomery.com
Westport, Connecticut Office: Sacks, Montgomery, Pastore & Levine, P.C., 1071 Post Road East, Suite 3.
Telephone: 203-291-6844.

Harry P. Sacks
David E. Montgomery
Stuart M. Levine (Resident, Westport, Connecticut Office)
Jeffrey A. Aronson
Frederick R. Rohn
Scott D. St. Marie
Stephen A. Stallings

Thomas F. Giordano
Amy S. Cohen
Kathleen M. Fay

OF COUNSEL

Steven J. Brill

For full biographical listings, see the Martindale-Hubbell Law Directory

SOUTH CAROLINA

*COLUMBIA,** Richland Co.

TURNER, PADGET, GRAHAM & LANEY, P.A. (AV)

Seventeenth Floor, 1901 Main Street, P.O. Box 1473, 29202
Telephone: 803-254-2200
Telecopy: 803-799-3957
Florence, South Carolina Office: Fourth Floor, 1831 West Evans Street, P.O. Box 5478, 29502.
Telephone: 843-662-9008.
Fax: 843-667-0828.
Charleston, South Carolina Office: 21 Broad Street, 1st Floor, P.O. Box 836, 29402.
Telephone: 843-723-1622.
Fax: 843-577-3369.

Thomas C. Salane

Donnell G. Jennings

For Complete List of Firm Personnel, See General Section

For full biographical listings, see the Martindale-Hubbell Law Directory

TENNESSEE

*DYERSBURG,** Dyer Co.

ASHLEY, ASHLEY & ARNOLD (AV)

322 Church Avenue, P.O. Box H, 38024
Telephone: 901-285-5074
Telecopier: 901-285-5089
Email: aaafirm@usit.net *URL:* http://www.lawyers.com/ashleylaw

MEMBERS OF FIRM

Barret Ashley
Randolph A. Ashley, Jr.
S. Leo Arnold
Marianna Williams
Anthony Lee Winchester
Jason G. Yarbro

(See Next Column)

ASHLEY, ASHLEY & ARNOLD, *Dyersburg—Continued*

OF COUNSEL

Joree G. Brownlow

Representative Clients: Illinois Central Gulf Railroad; Bekeart Steel Wire Corp.; Fidelity and Deposit Company of Maryland; St. Paul Fire and Marine Insurance Co.
Construction Company Clients: Chancellor & Sons, Inc.; Davco Corp; Dumey Excavation, Inc.; Folk Construction Co.; Ford Construction Co.; Fordice Construction Co.

For full biographical listings, see the Martindale-Hubbell Law Directory

TEXAS

*EL PASO,** El Paso Co.

AINSA PARTNERS, LLP (AV)

5809 Acacia Circle, 79912
Telephone: 915-845-5300
Fax: 915-845-7800
Email: fain@acaciapark.com *URL:* http://www.ainsa.com

Francis S. Ainsa, Jr.
Michael F. Ainsa
David M. Driscoll

For full biographical listings, see the Martindale-Hubbell Law Directory

*HOUSTON,** Harris Co.

BELL, RYNIKER & LETOURNEAU, P.C. (AV)

Five Post Oak Park, Suite 1300, 77027
Telephone: 713-871-8822
Fax: 713-871-8844
URL: http://www.brlpc.com
Email: mkbell@brlpc.com *URL:* http://www.lawyers.com/brlpc

Michael K. Bell
Keith B. Letourneau
Robert J. Ryniker
Thomas R. Nork

Douglas J. Shoemaker
Deborah T. Busby
Wesley T. Welmaker

For full biographical listings, see the Martindale-Hubbell Law Directory

UTAH

*SALT LAKE CITY,** Salt Lake Co.

VAN COTT, BAGLEY, CORNWALL & MCCARTHY, A PROFESSIONAL CORPORATION (AV)

50 South Main Street, Suite 1600, P.O. Box 45340, 84145-0340
Telephone: 801-532-3333
Telecopier: 801-534-0058
Email: info@vancott.com *URL:* http://www.vancott.com
Ogden, Utah Office: 2404 Washington Boulevard, Suite 900.
Telephone: 801-394-5783.
Park City, Utah Office: 2200 Park Avenue, Suite C200-A.
Telephone: 435-649-3889.

David A. Greenwood
John L. Young

Jennifer K. Anderson
Evan S. Strassberg

OF COUNSEL

Franklin N. Smith

For Complete List of Firm Personnel, See General Section

For full biographical listings, see the Martindale-Hubbell Law Directory

WEST VIRGINIA

*CHARLESTON,** Kanawha Co.

GOODWIN & GOODWIN (AV)

1500 One Valley Square, 25301
Telephone: 304-346-7000
Fax: 304-344-9692
Email: g&glaw@goodwin.goodwin.com *URL:* http://www.goodwingoodwin.com
Ripley, West Virginia Office: 500 Church Street, P.O. Box 349.
Telephone: 304-372-2651.

(See Next Column)

Parkersburg, West Virginia Office: 201 Third Street, Town Square.
Telephone: 304-485-2345.
Fax: 304-485-3459.

Robert B. Goodwin (1909-1955)

OF COUNSEL

C. E. Goodwin

MEMBERS OF FIRM

Thomas R. Goodwin
Stephen P. Goodwin
Michael I. Spiker
Steven F. White
Richard E. Rowe
Leonard S. Coleman
Susan C. Wittemeier
Robert W. Full (Resident at Parkersburg Office)
Richard D. Owen
Tammy J. Owen
J. David Fenwick
Alexander Macia

ASSOCIATES

Suzanne Jett Trowbridge
William K. Bragg, Jr.
George M. Smith
John N. Ellem (Resident, Parkersburg Office)
Lisa A. Tackett
Robert (Booth) Goodwin, II
Carrie Goodwin Fenwick
Tiffany E. Davis

Representative Clients: Bucyrus-Erie Co.; CSX Corp.; Eastern American Energy Corp.; The Eureka Pipe Line Co.

For full biographical listings, see the Martindale-Hubbell Law Directory

CANADA
NEW BRUNSWICK

*FREDERICTON,** York Co.

MCINNES COOPER (AV)

Suite 600, 570 Queen Street, P.O. Box 610, E3B 5A6
Telephone: 506-458-8572
Fax: 506-458-9903
Email: mcrfton@mcrlaw.com *URL:* http://www.mcrlaw.com
Halifax, Nova Scotia Office: Summit Place, 1601 Lower Water Street, P.O. Box 730, B3J 2V1.
Telephone: 902-425-6500.
Fax: 902-425-6350. Email: mcrhfx@mcrlaw.com.
St. John's, Newfoundland Office: Baine Johnston Centre, 5th Floor, 10 Fort William Place, P.O. Box 5939, A1C 5X4.
Telephone: 709-722-8735.
Telecopier: 709-722-1763. Email: mcrsj@mcrlaw.com.
Moncton, New Brunswick Office: Place Moncton Place, 655 Main Street, P.O. Box 1368, E1C 8T6.
Telephone: 506-857-8970.
Fax: 506-857-4095. Email: mcrmctn@mcrlaw.com.
Charlottetown, Prince Edward Island Office: BDC Place, Suite 620, 119 Kent Street, C1A 1N3.
Telephone: 902-368-8473.
Fax: 902-368-8346. Email: mcrpei@mcrlaw.com.

PARTNERS

R. Bruce Eddy, Q.C.
Leonard T. Hoyt

For Complete List of Firm Personnel, See General Section

For full biographical listings, see the Martindale-Hubbell Law Directory

CANADA
NOVA SCOTIA

*HALIFAX,** Regional Munic. of Halifax

MCINNES COOPER (AV)

Barristers, Solicitors & Trade Mark Agents
Summit Place, 1601 Lower Water Street, P.O. Box 730, B3J 2V1
Telephone: 902-425-6500
Fax: 902-425-6350
Email: mcrhfx@mcrlaw.com *URL:* http://www.mcrlaw.com
St. John's, Newfoundland Office: Baine Johnston Centre, 5th Floor, 10 Fort William Place, P.O. Box 5939, A1C 5X4.
Telephone: 709-722-8735.
Telecopier: 709-722-1763. Email: mcrsj@mcrlaw.com.
Moncton, New Brunswick Office: Place Moncton Place, 655 Main Street, P.O. Box 1368, E1C 8T6.
Telephone: 506-857-8970.
Fax: 506-857-4095. Email: mcrmctn@mcrlaw.com.
Charlottetown, Prince Edward Island Office: BDC Place, Suite 620, 119 Kent Street, C1A 1N3.
Telephone: 902-368-8473.
Fax: 902-368-8346. Email: mcrpei@mcrlaw.com.

(See Next Column)

McInnes Cooper—*Continued*

Fredericton, New Brunswick Office: Suite 600, 570 Queen Street, P.O. Box 610.
Telephone: 506-458-8572.
Fax: 506-458-9903. Email: mcrfton@mcrlaw.com.

PARTNERS

Stewart McInnes, P.C., Q.C. Joseph A. F. Macdonald, Q.C.
Lawrence A. Freeman

For Complete List of Firm Personnel, See General Section

For full biographical listings, see the Martindale-Hubbell Law Directory

HEALTH CARE LAW

MINNESOTA

*ST. CLOUD,** Stearns Co.

HUGHES, MATHEWS & DIDIER, P.A. (AV)

110 Sixth Avenue South, Suite 205, P.O. Box 548, 56302-0548
Telephone: 320-251-4399
Fax: 320-251-5781

Kevin J. Hughes
Thomas E. Mathews
Paul R. Harris

Suzanne M. Johnson

Representative Clients: The St. Cloud Hospital; CentraCare Health System; Tri-County Hospital; Elder Care of Bemidji, Inc.; Horizon Health, Inc.; Lutheran Senior Care Center.

For full biographical listings, see the Martindale-Hubbell Law Directory

MISSISSIPPI

*JACKSON,** Hinds Co.

BAKER, DONELSON, BEARMAN & CALDWELL (AV)

Suite 500, 700 North State Street, 39202
Telephone: 601-351-2400
Telecopier: 601-351-2424
Email: info@bdbc.com *URL:* http://www.bakerdonelson.com
Memphis, Tennessee Office: 20th Floor, First Tennessee Building, 165 Madison, 38103.
Telephone: 901-526-2000.
Telecopier: 901-577-2303.
Nashville, Tennessee Office: 1700 Nashville City Center, 511 Union Street, 37219.
Telephone: 615-726-5600.
Telecopier: 615-726-0464.
Chattanooga, Tennessee Office: 1800 Republic Centre, 633 Chestnut Street, 37450-1800.
Telephone: 423-756-2010.
Telecopier: 423-756-3447.
Knoxville, Tennessee Office: 2200 Riverview Tower, 900 South Gay Street, 37901.
Telephone: 423-549-7000.
Telecopier: 423-525-8569.
Johnson City, Tennessee Office: SunTrust Bank Building, 207 Mockingbird Lane, P.O. Box 3038, 37602.
Telephone: 423-928-0181.
Telecopier: 423-928-5694; 423-928-3654; Kingsport: 423-246-6191.
Huntsville, Tennessee Office: 3 Courthouse Square, 37756.
Telephone: 423-663-2321.
Telecopier: 423-663-2111.
Washington, D.C. Office: Market Square, 801 Pennsylvania Avenue, N.W., 20004.
Telephone: 202-508-3400.
Telecopier: 202-508-3402.

PARTNERS

William S. Painter
James L. Jones
William N. Reed
Richard G. Cowart
Barry K. Cockrell
Jonell B. Williamson

ASSOCIATES

Philip W. Thomas
Bradley W. Smith
Charles W. Ferguson
Charles R. Galloway
Tiffanee N. Wade
Michael R. Hess
Michelle Dawn Alexander (Not admitted in MS)
Scott W. Bates

OF COUNSEL

John B. Beard

For Complete List of Firm Personnel, See General Section

For full biographical listings, see the Martindale-Hubbell Law Directory

MISSOURI

KANSAS CITY, Jackson, Clay, Platte & Cass Cos.

BARTIMUS, FRICKLETON & PRESLEY, A PROFESSIONAL CORPORATION (AV)

23rd Floor City Center Square, 1100 Main Street, 64196
Telephone: 816-842-2300
Fax: 816-421-2111
Email: bfplaw@bfplaw.com *URL:* http://www.bfplaw.com
Jefferson City, Missouri Office: 122 East High, Suite 200, 65101.
Telephone: 573-659-4454.

James R. Bartimus
James P. Frickleton
Kirk R. Presley
Peter S. Obetz

Stephen M. Gorny
Christopher A. Wright

OF COUNSEL

Edward D. Robertson, Jr. (Resident, Jefferson City Office)
Julie C. Frickleton

LEGAL SUPPORT PERSONNEL

LEGAL ASSISTANTS

Tammy J. Gilliams
Laura M. Burbach
Patricia E. Cook
Martha C. Fann

For full biographical listings, see the Martindale-Hubbell Law Directory

ST. LOUIS, (Independent City)

THE LOWENBAUM PARTNERSHIP, L.L.C. (AV)

222 South Central Avenue, Suite 901 (Clayton), 63105
Telephone: 314-863-0092
Facsimile: 314-746-4848
Email: rml@lowenbaumlaw.com

Timothy L. Elliott
J. Timothy Gorman

Representative Clients: Unity Health; NextCare, Inc.; RehabCare Group.

For full biographical listings, see the Martindale-Hubbell Law Directory

THE STOLAR PARTNERSHIP (AV)

7th Floor, 911 Washington Avenue, 63101
Telephone: 314-231-2800
Telex: 880984
Telecopier: 314-436-8400
Belleville, Illinois Office: 7 North High Street.
Telephone: 618-277-1030.

MEMBERS OF FIRM

Doreen D. Dodson
Dale E. Hermeling
Randall A. Martin

For full biographical listings, see the Martindale-Hubbell Law Directory

WEINHAUS AND DOBSON (AV)

Suite 900, 906 Olive Street, 63101
Telephone: 314-621-8363
Telecopier: 314-621-8366
Email: weidob@nela.org

MEMBERS OF FIRM

S. Sheldon Weinhaus
Jerome J. Dobson
Michael Craig Goldberg
Mark E. Moreland

ASSOCIATES

Jonathan Charles Berns
Gregory Alan Rich
Scott P. Holwitt

Reference: The Boatmen's National Bank of St. Louis.

For full biographical listings, see the Martindale-Hubbell Law Directory

MONTANA

*BILLINGS,** Yellowstone Co.

CROWLEY, HAUGHEY, HANSON, TOOLE & DIETRICH, P.L.L.P. (AV)

500 Transwestern II, 490 North 31st Street, P.O. Box 2529, 59103
Telephone: 406-252-3441
Fax: 406-259-4159
Email: crowley@crowleylaw.com
Helena, Montana Office: IBM Building, 100 North Park Avenue, Suite 300, 59601.
Telephone: 406-449-4165.
Fax: 406-449-5149.

(See Next Column)

CROWLEY, HAUGHEY, HANSON, TOOLE & DIETRICH P.L.L.P., *Billings—Continued*

Kalispell, Montana Office: 431 1st Avenue West, 59901.
Telephone: 406-752-6644.
Fax: 406-752-5108.
Williston, North Dakota Office: 113 East Broadway, 58801.
Telephone: 701-572-2200.
Fax: 701-572-7072.

OF COUNSEL

John M. Dietrich
Gareld F. Krieg

MEMBERS OF FIRM

Herbert I. Pierce, III
Lawrence B. Cozzens
Steven J. Lehman
Daniel N. McLean (Resident, Helena, Montana Office)
John R. Alexander
Michael S. Dockery
Mary Scrim Dyre (Resident, Kalispell, Montana Office)

Representative Clients: Deaconess Medical Center of Billings; Deaconess Care Corporation; Deaconess Research Institute; The Billings Clinic; Trinity Hospital Association.

For Complete List of Firm Personnel, See General Section

For full biographical listings, see the Martindale-Hubbell Law Directory

*HELENA,** Lewis and Clark Co.

BROWNING, KALECZYC, BERRY & HOVEN, P.C. (AV)

139 North Last Chance Gulch, P.O. Box 1697, 59624
Telephone: 406-443-6820
Telefax: 406-443-6882
Email: BKBH@BKBH.COM *URL:* http://www.BKBH.com

R. Stephen Browning
J. Daniel Hoven
Katharine S. Donnelley

Kimberly A. Beatty
Kimberly Lewis Towe

Representative Clients: Montana Hospital Association; MHA Ventures, Inc.; Northern Montana Hospital; Stillwater Community Hospital; Pondera Medical Center; Teton Medical Center; St. John's Lutheran Home; Helena Health Alliance; Community Hospital of Anaconda; St. Luke Community Hospital; PHICO Insurance Company; Liberty County Hospital; North Valley Hospital; Powell County Memorial; Sidney Health Center; Montana Pharmaceutical Association; Missouri River Medical Center; Deaconess Billings Clinic.

For full biographical listings, see the Martindale-Hubbell Law Directory

NEBRASKA

*LINCOLN,** Lancaster Co.

CLINE, WILLIAMS, WRIGHT, JOHNSON & OLDFATHER (AV)

1900 U.S. Bank Building, 233 South 13th Street, 68508
Telephone: 402-474-6900
Fax: 402-474-5393
Email: postmaster@cline-law.com *URL:* http://www.cline-law.com
Omaha, Nebraska Office: Suite 720, One Pacific Place, 1125 South 103rd Street, 68124.
Telephone: 402-397-1700.
Fax: 402-397-1806.

ATTORNEYS

Allen L. Graves
Charles M. Pallesen, Jr.
Fredric H. Kauffman
Donald F. Burt
Alan E. Peterson
Stephen E. Gehring
Robert J. Routh
Kevin Colleran
L. Bruce Wright
James M. Bausch
Larry A. Holle
David R. Buntain
Stephen H. Nelsen
Michael C. Mueller
Lauren W. Wismer
Daniel R. Stogsdill
Scott D. Kelly
Terry R. Wittler
Pamela Hastings Carrier
Mark A. Christensen
Richard P. Garden, Jr.
Shawn D. Renner
John C. Miles
Mary Kay Frank
Thomas C. Huston
Sonya S. Ekart
Don R. Janssen
Susan Kubert Sapp
Kevin J. Schneider
Andrew D. Strotman
Jill Gossin Jensen
Rochelle A. Mullen
John L. Horan
Bryan S. Hatch
Steven C. Likes
Tracy A. Oldemeyer
Jolene M. Papa
Timothy G. Aschoff
Eric N. Bergquist
Janis J. Winterhof
Andrea Dylan Snowden

OF COUNSEL

Charles E. Wright
Richard P. Jeffries
Mary M. Campbell

(See Next Column)

RETIRED PARTNERS

Flavel A. Wright (Retired)
Warren C. Johnson (Retired)
Charles E. Oldfather (1927-1998)

Representative Clients: U.S. Bank National Association; University of Nebraska; Nebraska Medical Assn.; Saint Elizabeth Regional Medical Center; Media of Nebraska; Cargill Inc.; State Farm Insurance Cos.; Wal-Mart Stores, Inc.; Textron/Cushman; Isco, Inc.

For full biographical listings, see the Martindale-Hubbell Law Directory

ERICKSON & SEDERSTROM, P.C. (AV)

Suite 400, Cornhusker Plaza, 301 South 13th Street, 68508
Telephone: 402-476-1000
Fax: 402-476-6167
Omaha, Nebraska Office: Regency Westpointe, 10330 Regency Parkway Drive, Suite 100, 68114-3761.
Telephone: 402-397-2200.
Fax: 402-390-7137.

Linda W. Rohman

Representative Clients: Lincoln General Hospital; Health Lincoln; Alegent Health; Gramercy Hill Enterprises; Gateway Manor.

For Complete List of Firm Personnel, See General Section

For full biographical listings, see the Martindale-Hubbell Law Directory

JOHNSON, FLODMAN, GUENZEL, ESKE & WIDGER (AV)

1227 Lincoln Mall, P.O. Box 81686, 68501-1686
Telephone: 402-475-4240
Fax: 402-475-0329
URL: http://www.linclaw.com

MEMBER OF FIRM

Abbie J. Widger

Special Counsel: Nebraska Public Power District.
Representative Clients: Atlanta Casualty; Chubb/Pacific Indemnity Group; Citizens State Bank, Polk, Nebraska; Crum & Foster; Federated Rural Electric Insurance Corp.; Runza Drive-Inns of America; State Farm Insurance Cos.; Viking Insurance Company of Wisconsin.

For full biographical listings, see the Martindale-Hubbell Law Directory

*OMAHA,** Douglas Co.

CLINE, WILLIAMS, WRIGHT, JOHNSON & OLDFATHER (AV)

One Pacific Place, 1125 South 103rd Street, Suite 720, 68124
Telephone: 402-397-1700
Fax: 402-397-1806
Email: postmaster@cline-law.com *URL:* http://www.cline-law.com
Lincoln, Nebraska Office: 1900 U.S. Bank Building, 233 South 13th Street, 68508.
Telephone: 402-474-6900.
Fax: 402-474-5393.

ATTORNEYS

Donald F. Burt
Stephen E. Gehring
James M. Bausch
Michael C. Mueller
Daniel R. Stogsdill
Scott D. Kelly
John C. Miles
Mary Kay Frank
Andrew D. Strotman
Rochelle A. Mullen
Steven C. Likes
Tracy A. Oldemeyer
Timothy G. Aschoff

OF COUNSEL

Richard P. Jeffries

Representative Clients: U.S. Bank National Association; University of Nebraska; Nebraska Medical Assn.; Saint Elizabeth Regional Medical Center; Media of Nebraska; Cargill Inc.; State Farm Insurance Cos.; Wal-Mart Stores, Inc.; Textron/Cushman; ISCO, Inc.

For full biographical listings, see the Martindale-Hubbell Law Directory

DWYER, SMITH, GARDNER, LAZER, POHREN, ROGERS & FORREST (AV)

Suite 400, 8712 West Dodge Road, 68114
Telephone: 402-392-0101
Telefax: 402-392-1011
Email: dwyerlaw@dwyer-smith.com *URL:* http://www.dwyer-smith.com

MEMBERS OF FIRM

Robert V. Dwyer, Jr.
H. Daniel Smith
Edward F. Pohren
John L. Apker

Representative Clients: Nebraska Health System; Nebraska Hospital Association subsidiary Bio Electronics, Lincoln, Nebraska; Community Hospital Association, McCook, Nebraska; Faith Regional Health Services, Norfolk, Nebraska; Western Nebraska Health Systems, Sidney, Nebraska.

For Complete List of Firm Personnel, See General Section

For full biographical listings, see the Martindale-Hubbell Law Directory

Omaha—Continued

McGill, Gotsdiner, Workman & Lepp, P.C. (AV)

Suite 500 - First National Plaza, 11404 West Dodge Road, 68154
Telephone: 402-492-9200
Telecopier: 402-492-9222
Email: mgwl@mgwl.com

Robert L. Lepp

Representative Clients: Vetter Health Services, Inc.; Aksarben Nursing Centers, Inc.; Bethesda Living Centers; Quality Care Physicians; Ambassador Group; Care Center Management; Rose Blumkin Jewish Home; Sunrise Country Manor; Consultants in Cardiology; Omaha Orthopedic Clinic and Sports Medicine.

For Complete List of Firm Personnel, See General Section

For full biographical listings, see the Martindale-Hubbell Law Directory

NEVADA

HENDERSON, Clark Co.

Rooker & Gibson (AV)

Suite 105, 701 North Green Valley Parkway, 89014
Telephone: 702-990-8100
Telecopier: 702-932-5266

C. Keith Rooker James B. Gibson

Reference: BankWest of Nevada.

For full biographical listings, see the Martindale-Hubbell Law Directory

*LAS VEGAS,** Clark Co.

Hale Lane Peek Dennison Howard and Anderson (AV)

Nevada Financial Center, 2300 West Sahara Avenue, Eighth Floor, Box 8, 89102
Telephone: 702-222-2500
Fax: 702-365-6940
Email: info@halelane.com
Reno, Nevada Office: 100 West Liberty Street, Tenth Floor, P.O. Box 3237.
Telephone: 775-327-3000.
Telefax: 775-786-6179.
Carson City, Nevada Office: 777 East William Street, Suite 200, P.O. Box 2620.
Telephone: 775-684-6000.
Telefax: 775-684-6001.

MEMBERS OF FIRM

Robert C. Anderson (Resident, Reno, Nevada)
Kelly Testolin
Norman Patrick Flanagan (Resident, Reno, Nevada)

Representative Clients: Madera Community Hospital; Primary Care Associates.

For Complete List of Firm Personnel, See General Section

For full biographical listings, see the Martindale-Hubbell Law Directory

Pico & Mitchell (AV)

2000 South Eastern Avenue, 89104
Telephone: 702-457-9099
FAX: 702-457-8451
Email: lawyers@picomitchell.com

MEMBERS OF FIRM

James F. Pico
Bert O. Mitchell
Christy Brad Escobar
James R. Rosenberger
E. Breen Arntz

ASSOCIATES

Michelle Schwarz
Rebecca L. Mastrangelo
Jill M. Chase
Daniel E. Carvalho
Stephen H. Rogers

Representative Clients: Home Insurance Co.; State Farm Mutual Insurance Co.; Industrial Indemnity Insurance Co.; Great American Insurance Co.; Argonaut Insurance Cos.; Clark County Medical Society; Rose de Lima Hospital; Fairway Chevrolet; American States Insurance Co.; The Hartford Insurance Co.

For full biographical listings, see the Martindale-Hubbell Law Directory

Wright, Judd & Winckler (AV)

302 East Carson Avenue, 3rd Floor, 89101
Telephone: 702-382-4004
FAX: 702-382-4800
Email: wjw@netxs.net

(See Next Column)

MEMBERS OF FIRM

Richard A. Wright
Bruce M. Judd
Karen C. Winckler

For full biographical listings, see the Martindale-Hubbell Law Directory

*RENO,** Washoe Co.

Hale Lane Peek Dennison Howard and Anderson (AV)

100 West Liberty Street, Tenth Floor, P.O. Box 3237, 89505
Telephone: 775-327-3000
Telefax: 775-786-6179
Email: info@halelane.com
Las Vegas, Nevada Office: Nevada Financial Center, 2300 West Sahara Avenue, Eighth Floor, Box 8.
Telephone: 702-222-2500.
Fax: 702-365-6940.
Carson City, Nevada Office: 777 East William Street, Suite 200, P.O. Box 2620.
Telephone: 775-684-6000.
Telefax: 775-684-6001.

MEMBERS OF FIRM

Robert C. Anderson
Kelly Testolin
Norman Patrick Flanagan

ASSOCIATE

James Newman

Representative Clients: Madera Community Hospital; Primary Care Associates.

For Complete List of Firm Personnel, See General Section

For full biographical listings, see the Martindale-Hubbell Law Directory

Walther, Key, Maupin, Oats, Cox & LeGoy, A Professional Corporation (AV)

Lakeside Professional Plaza, 3500 Lakeside Court, 89509
Telephone: 775-827-2000
Facsimile: 775-827-2185
Mailing Address: P.O. Box 30000, Reno, Nevada, 89520

Steven T. Walther
Jon J. Key
Ernest J. Maupin
C. Robert Cox
L. Robert LeGoy, Jr.
Michael E. Malloy
G. Barton Mowry
Kim G. Rowe
Procter J. Hug
Donald A. Lattin
Gustave J. Rossi
Robert A. Winkel
Kurt O. Hunsberger
Michael A. Nivinskus
Christopher D. Jaime

Rick R. Hsu
Michaelle D. Rafferty

Representative Clients: Associated Anesthesiologists; Home Town Health; Humboldt General Hospital; Luthern Health Services/Churchill Community Hospital; Radiation Oncology Associates; Reno Heart Physicians; Reno Radiological; Sierra Anesthesia; Washoe Health System; Washoe Medical Center.

For full biographical listings, see the Martindale-Hubbell Law Directory

NEW JERSEY

CHERRY HILL, Camden Co.

Flaster/Greenberg, P.C. (AV)

Commerce Center, 1810 Chapel Avenue West, Third Floor, 08002-4609
Telephone: 856-661-1900
Telecopier: 856-661-1919
Email: FIRM@FLASTERGREENBERG.COM *URL:* http://www.flastergreenberg.com

Richard J. Flaster
Stephen M. Greenberg
Laura B. Wallenstein
Allen P. Fineberg
Markley S. Roderick
Peter R. Spirgel
Alan H. Zuckerman
William S. Skinner
J. Philip Kirchner
Paul J. Russoniello
Carl S. Bisgaier
Steven B. Sacharow
E. Richard Dressel
Kenneth S. Goodkind
Frank H. Wisniewski
Alma L. Saravia

OF COUNSEL

Peter M. Dolinger
James J. Binns

Elizabeth J. Hampton
Jeffrey Herskowitz
Christopher E. Kaltenbach
Steven J. Abrams
Julie A. Williamson
Donna T. Urban
Amelia Carolla
Matthew Azoulay
Elaine J. Petruzziello (Not admitted in NJ)
Ann Marie Iannone
Pasquale Guglietta

(See Next Column)

FLASTER/GREENBERG P.C., *Cherry Hill—Continued*

LEGAL SUPPORT PERSONNEL

PARALEGALS

Ann Gorman | Theresa Cooke
Patricia D'Alessio | Rosemary Dunaif

For full biographical listings, see the Martindale-Hubbell Law Directory

FLORHAM PARK, Morris Co.

DRINKER BIDDLE & SHANLEY LLP (AV)

A Pennsylvania Limited Liability Partnership
500 Campus Drive, 07932-1047
Telephone: 973-360-1100
Fax: 973-285-1625; 360-9831
URL: http://www.dbr.com
Philadelphia, Pennsylvania Office: Drinker Biddle & Reath LLP, One Logan Square, 18th & Cherry Streets.
Telephone: 215-988-2700.
Telefax: 215-988-2757.
Cable Address: "Debemac."
Washington, D.C. Office: Drinker Biddle & Reath LLP, 1500 K Street, N.W., Suite 1100.
Telephone: 202-842-8800.
Telefax: 202-842-8465.
Princeton, New Jersey Office: Suite 300, 105 College Road East.
Telephone: 609-716-6500.
Telefax: 609-799-7000.
Berwyn, Pennsylvania Office: Drinker Biddle & Reath LLP, Suite 300, 1000 Westlakes Drive.
Telephone: 610-993-2200.
Telefax: 610-993-8585.
New York, New York Office: Drinker Biddle & Reath LLP, 89th Floor, One World Trade Center.
Telephone: 212-321-1812.
Telecopier: 1-212-466-0569.

James H. Freis | Daniel F. O'Connell

Christina Butler Murphy | Amy E. Watkins
Decanda M. Faulk | Brenda Eady Stafford

For Complete List of Firm Personnel, See General Section

For full biographical listings, see the Martindale-Hubbell Law Directory

SCHWARTZ SIMON EDELSTEIN CELSO & KESSLER (AV)

A Partnership including a Professional Corporation
Ten James Street, 07932
Telephone: 973-301-0001
Fax: 973-301-0203
Email: sseck1@aol.com

Stephen J. Edelstein | John B. Mariano, Jr.
Donald A. Kessler | Raymond W. Fisher
Burton Zitomer

OF COUNSEL

Glenn C. Guritzky | Scott A. Elk (P.A.)
Miguel A. Maza | (Not admitted in NJ)

For full biographical listings, see the Martindale-Hubbell Law Directory

LIBERTY CORNER, Somerset Co.

KALISON, MCBRIDE & JACKSON, P.A. (AV)

Liberty Corner Executive Center, 645 Martinsville Road, P.O. Box 814, 07938
Telephone: 908-647-4600
Telecopier: 908-647-6226

Michael J. Kalison | John Zen Jackson
Andrew F. McBride III | James V. Hetzel
Paul R. Murphy | James Acre Robertson, IV

Barry Liss | Daniel R. Esposito
Sloane S. Belitz | Alison Wholey Mynick
Todd Schaper | Jennifer Candace Weissman

OF COUNSEL

Wendy C. Tomey

LEGAL SUPPORT PERSONNEL

Susan R. Buchanan | Roman Bohoslawec

Representative Clients: University Health System of New Jersey, Inc.; Hunterdon Healthcare, LLC; Direct Care Medical Services, LLC; Central Jersey Individual Practice Association, P.A.; The Matheny School and Hospital; Princeton Individual Practice Association, P.C.; Hackensack University Medical Center; Cooper Hospital/University Medical Center; St. Elizabeth Hospital; University Health Plans, Inc.; Magellan Public Solutions; Meridian Health System (Jersey Shore Medical Center, Medical Center of Ocean County, Riverview Medical Center).

For full biographical listings, see the Martindale-Hubbell Law Directory

LIVINGSTON, Essex Co.

GENOVA, BURNS & VERNOIA (AV)

Eisenhower Plaza II, 354 Eisenhower Parkway, 07039
Telephone: 973-533-0777
Facsimile: 973-533-1112
URL: http://www.gbvlaw.com
Trenton, New Jersey Office: The Princeton House, 160 West State Street.
Telephone: 609-393-1131.

MEMBERS OF FIRM

Angelo J. Genova | John C. Petrella
James M. Burns | James J. McGovern, III
Francis J. Vernoia | Carmel Joy Decker

ASSOCIATES

Sandro Polledri | J. Frank Vespa-Papaleo
Celia S. Bosco | Susan B. Burns
Lynn S. Degen | Bruno Genova
Elizabeth A. Daly | Robert C. Gifford, Jr.
Brian O. Lipman | Courtney Gaccione

For full biographical listings, see the Martindale-Hubbell Law Directory

*NEWARK,** Essex Co.

CARPENTER, BENNETT & MORRISSEY (AV)

Three Gateway Center, 17th Floor, 100 Mulberry Street, 07102-4079
Telephone: 973-622-7711
New York City: 212-943-6530
Telex: 139405
Telecopier: 973-622-5314
Email: cbm@carpben.com

MEMBERS OF FIRM

Laurence Reich | Irving L. Hurwitz
James J. Crowley, Jr. | John D. Goldsmith
Donald A. Romano | James Peter Lidon

ASSOCIATE

Hans G. Polak

Representative Clients: Summit Medical Group, P.A.; The Center for Molecular Medicine and Immunology, Inc.; Valley Hospital; Aetna U.S. Healthcare; Robert Wood Johnson University Hospital at Hamilton; Carrier Foundation.

For Complete List of Firm Personnel, See General Section

For full biographical listings, see the Martindale-Hubbell Law Directory

MCCARTER & ENGLISH, LLP (AV)

Four Gateway Center, 100 Mulberry Street, P.O. Box 652, 07101-0652
Telephone: 973-622-4444
Telecopier: 973-624-7070
URL: http://www.mccarter.com
Cherry Hill, New Jersey Office: 1820 Chapel Avenue West, Suite 380.
Telephone: 609-662-8444.
Telecopier: 609-662-6203.
New York, New York Office: Suite 2247, One World Trade Center.
Telephone: 212-466-9018.
Telecopier: 212-432-6568.
Boca Raton, Florida Office: 2255 Glades Road, Suite 319-A.
Telephone: 561-994-6262.
Telecopier: 561-241-0798.
Wilmington, Delaware Office: Mellon Bank Center, 919 Market Street.
Telephone: 302-654-8010.
Telecopier: 302-654-0795.
Philadelphia, Pennsylvania Office: One Commerce Square, 2005 Market Street, Suite 3600.
Telephone: 215-557-7700.
Telecopier: 215-557-6544.

MEMBERS OF FIRM

Charles R. Merrill | Richard J. Webb
Frederick B. Lehlbach | Scott A. Kobler
George H. Kendall

COUNSEL

Beth Yingling

SPECIAL COUNSEL

Robert A. Mintz

ASSOCIATES

David W. Opderbeck | Susan M. Mello
Audrey A. Hale

For Complete List of Firm Personnel, See General Section

For full biographical listings, see the Martindale-Hubbell Law Directory

Newark—Continued

SILLS CUMMIS RADIN TISCHMAN EPSTEIN & GROSS, A PROFESSIONAL CORPORATION (AV)

One Riverfront Plaza, 07102-5400
Telephone: 973-643-7000
Fax: 973-643-6500
Telex: 820630 Sillsbeck Nwk
Email: sillsmail@sillscummis.com *URL:* http://www.sillscummis.com
Atlantic City, New Jersey Office: 17 Gordon's Alley.
Telephone: 609-344-2800.
New York, N.Y. Office: 712 Fifth Avenue.
Telephone: 212-643-7000.
Washington, D.C. Office: 1800 K Street, N.W.
Telephone: 202-296-4750.

MEMBERS OF FIRM

Clive S. Cummis
Steven S. Radin
Michael B. Tischman
Barry M. Epstein
Stephen J. Moses
Steven M. Goldman
James M. Hirschhorn

OF COUNSEL

Mitchel E. Ostrer

Noel D. Humphreys
Barbara Quackenbos
Gary W. Herschman

Representative Clients: Blue Cross/Blue Shield of New Jersey; Bristol-Myers Squibb Corporation; Jersey City Medical Center; Englewood Hospital; Ciba Geigy Pharmaceuticals; Becton Dickinson & Company; Johnson & Johnson; First Option Health Care; Olsten Kimberly Quality Care.

For Complete List of Firm Personnel, See General Section

For full biographical listings, see the Martindale-Hubbell Law Directory

PARAMUS, Bergen Co.

STRASSER & ASSOCIATES, A PROFESSIONAL CORPORATION (AV)

Paramus Plaza I, 140 Route 17 North, Suite 265, 07652-2816
Telephone: 201-262-7177
Fax: 201-262-3113

William I. Strasser

Conrad M. Olear
Constantinos J. Ballas

Representative Clients: Consumer Value Stores (CVS); Melville Corp.; Melville Realty Corp.; Linens 'N Things, Inc.; This End Up Furniture Co., Inc.; Universal Foods Corp.; Essex Computers, Inc.; Polevoy Associates; Footstar, Inc.; Bob's Stores.

For full biographical listings, see the Martindale-Hubbell Law Directory

PRINCETON, Mercer Co.

STEELE R. CHADWELL (AV)

134 Nassau Street, 08542
Telephone: 609-924-8262
Fax: 609-921-9468
URL: http://www.lawyers.com/steelerchadwell

For full biographical listings, see the Martindale-Hubbell Law Directory

ROSELAND, Essex Co.

BRACH, EICHLER, ROSENBERG, SILVER, BERNSTEIN, HAMMER & GLADSTONE, A PROFESSIONAL CORPORATION (AV)

101 Eisenhower Parkway, 07068
Telephone: 973-228-5700
Telecopier: 973-228-7852
Email: law@bracheichler.com *URL:* http://www.bracheichler.com

Todd C. Brower
Burton L. Eichler
John D. Fanburg
Joseph M. Gorrell
Susan Y. Leonard

Carol Grelecki
Richard B. Robins
Brian Kalver
Simone E. Handler Hutchinson
Mark E. Manigan
Alexis Goldberger
Mark Sblendorio

Representative Clients: Capital Health System; East Orange General Hospital; Emergency Medical Associates; Hackettstown Community Hospital; Home Health Assembly of New Jersey; New Jersey Academy of Ophthalmology; The New Jersey Society of Pathologists; New Jersey State Society of Anesthesiologists; Physician Health Care Plan of New Jersey; Radiological Society of New Jersey; Saint Barnabas Health Care System.

For Complete List of Firm Personnel, See General Section

For full biographical listings, see the Martindale-Hubbell Law Directory

SPRINGFIELD, Union Co.

HARDIN, KUNDLA, MCKEON, POLETTO & POLIFRONI, P.A., A PROFESSIONAL CORPORATION (AV)

673 Morris Avenue, P.O. Box 730, 07081
Telephone: 973-912-5222
Fax: 973-912-9212
Email: info@HKMPP.com
New York, New York Office: 55 John Street, 10038.
Telephone: 212-571-0111.
Fax: 212-571-1117.

George R. Hardin
Robert L. Polifroni
Janet L. Poletto
Mark S. Kundla
John F. McKeon
James R. Greene
Nicea J. D'Annunzio
John Samuel Favate
Patrick J. Clare
Anna Marie Strand

Jeffrey A. Oshin
Joseph R. Lowicky
Tracy C. Forsyth
Joseph A. DeFuria
John G. Kilbride
Jeffrey H. Goldsmith
Jeffrey Roth
Nora J. Grimbergen
William C. Sullivan, Jr.
Paul Daly
V. Christopher Hirsch
Richard S. Reig
Sam A. Dotro
Brian K. Kaiser
David M. Steiner
Lani M. D'Agostino
Sheila A. Glackin
Michael S. Schwartz
Kirsten L. McCaw
Sanjoy Mukherjee
Louisa B. Sargent
Michael A. Cifelli
James J. A. Mulhall
Kevin M. Regan
Lisa D. Chanel
Maria-Milagros Herrero
Brian A. King
Christina Fichera Dente
Andrea L. Strack
Roger J. Imhof
John P. Monaghan
Stephen J. Donahue
Cindy L. Thompson
Lisa A. Ganzhorn

Representative Clients: St. Paul Fire and Marine Insurance Co.; CNA Insurance; Princeton Ins. Co.; Healthcare Ins. Exchange; Hospital Center at Orange; St. Barnabus Healthcare System; Montclair Community Hospital.

For full biographical listings, see the Martindale-Hubbell Law Directory

*TRENTON,** Mercer Co.

SCHRAGGER, LAVINE & NAGY (AV)

Mountainview Office Park, 840 Bear Tavern Road, Suite 307, 08628
Telephone: 609-771-0700
Fax: 609-771-9535

Bruce M. Schragger
Raymond L. Nagy
James A. Schragger
Jonathan S. Robinson
Michael E. Sullivan

OF COUNSEL

Henry C. Schragger
Alan S. Lavine
Frank P. Reiche
A. Jerome Moore

LEGAL SUPPORT PERSONNEL

Annemarie Saccani (Office Administrator)

Representative Clients: New Jersey Manufacturers Insurance Co.; Mercer County Community College; Mercer Mutual Insurance Co.; New Jersey Optometric Association; Allentown Caging; Dick Greenfield Dodge.

For full biographical listings, see the Martindale-Hubbell Law Directory

WESTFIELD, Union Co.

LINDABURY, MCCORMICK & ESTABROOK, P.A. (AV)

53 Cardinal Drive, P.O. Box 2369, 07091
Telephone: 908-233-6800
Fax: 908-233-5078
New York, N.Y. Office: 26 Broadway, Suite 2300.
Telephone: 212-742-3390.
Fax: 212-269-5016.

Richard R. Width
Peter A. Somers
William R. Watkins
Donald F. Nicolai
Bruce P. Ogden
Robert S. Burney

Kelly A. Briganti
Jennifer F. Barry

Representative Clients: Bayonne Hospital; Central New Jersey Medical Group; Central New Jersey Maternal and Child Health Consortium; Chilton Memorial Hospital; Elizabeth General Medical Center; Helene Fuld Medical Center; HIP/Rutgers Health Plan; Kessler Institute for Rehabilitation; Memorial Hospital of Burlington County; Meridian Health System.

For Complete List of Firm Personnel, See General Section

For full biographical listings, see the Martindale-Hubbell Law Directory

WOODBRIDGE, Middlesex Co.

DEUTCH & FALK, A PROFESSIONAL CORPORATION (AV)

843 Rahway Avenue, 07095-3699
Telephone: 732-636-4200
Fax: 732-636-3575
URL: http://www.deutchfalk.com
URL: http://www.lawyers.com/dflaw
Linden, New Jersey Office: 924 North Wood Avenue, Second Floor, 07036.
Telephone: 908-486-2422.
New York, N.Y. Office: 2 Pennsylvania Plaza, Suite 1910, 10121.
Telephone: 212-319-7332.

Victor A. Deutch
Kenneth B. Falk

John F. Kwasnik
Monica Kowalski

OF COUNSEL

Kenneth A. Wallach

Representative Clients: In-Step Podiatry; Women's Health Care Specialists, P.A.

For full biographical listings, see the Martindale-Hubbell Law Directory

WILENTZ, GOLDMAN & SPITZER, A PROFESSIONAL CORPORATION (AV)

90 Woodbridge Center Drive Suite 900, Box 10, 07095
Telephone: 732-636-8000
Telecopier: 732-855-6117
URL: http://www.newjerseylaw.com
Eatontown, New Jersey Office: Meridian Center I, Two Industrial Way West, 07724.
Telephone: 732-542-4500.
Telecopier: 732-493-8387.
New York, New York Office: Wall Street Plaza, 88 Pine Street, 9th Floor, 10005.
Telephone: 212-267-3091.
Telecopier: 212-267-3828.

Francis V. Bonello
Gordon J. Golum
Michael F. Schaff
Hesser G. McBride, Jr.
Robert C. Kautz
Steven P. Marshall
Douglas Watson Lubic

Jonathan P. Falk
Brett R. Harris
Helen C. Lee
Christopher W. Hager
Nicole Huberfeld

Representative Clients: Amerada Hess Corp.; Chevron, U.S.A.; Co-Steel Raritan; Cumberland Farms, Inc.; Middlesex County Utilities Authority; New Jersey Automobile Dealers Assn.; The Rouse Co.

For Complete List of Firm Personnel, See General Section

For full biographical listings, see the Martindale-Hubbell Law Directory

NEW MEXICO

*ALBUQUERQUE,** Bernalillo Co.

DINES, GROSS & ESQUIVEL, P.C. (AV)

6301 Indian School Road, N.E., Suite 900, 87110
Telephone: 505-889-4050
Fax: 505-889-4049
Email: law@dge.psemail.com *URL:* http://www.lawyers.com/dgelaw

Michael A. Gross

For full biographical listings, see the Martindale-Hubbell Law Directory

KREHBIEL, BANNERMAN & HORN, P.A. (AV)

6400 Uptown Boulevard, N.E., Suite 310 East, 87110
Telephone: 505-837-1900
Fax: 505-837-1800
Email: kbh@kbh-lawfirm.com *URL:* http://www.kbh-lawfirm.com

Phil Krehbiel
John A. Bannerman
Barry D. Williams

Rikki L. Quintana
Carol Lisa Smith
David H. Johnson
Lucinda R. Bovee

OF COUNSEL

Ronald F. Horn

For full biographical listings, see the Martindale-Hubbell Law Directory

RODEY, DICKASON, SLOAN, AKIN & ROBB, P.A. (AV)

Albuquerque Plaza, Suite 2200, 201 Third Street, N.W., P.O. Box 1888, 87103-1888
Telephone: 505-765-5900
Fax: 505-768-7395
Email: info@rodey.com *URL:* http://www.rodey.com
Santa Fe, New Mexico Office: Suite 101 Marcy Plaza, 123 East Marcy Street, P.O. Box 1357, 87504-1357.
Telephone: 505-984-0100.
Fax: 505-989-9542.

W. Robert Lasater, Jr.
Edward Ricco
W. Mark Mowery (Resident, Santa Fe Office)
Ellen T. Skrak
Theresa W. Parrish
Susan K. Barger

Deborah E. Mann

For Complete List of Firm Personnel, See General Section

For full biographical listings, see the Martindale-Hubbell Law Directory

*LAS CRUCES,** Dona Ana Co.

REEVES, CHAVEZ, GREENFIELD & WALKER, P.A. (AV)

300 South Water Street, P.O. Box 2769, 88004-2769
Telephone: 505-524-9617
Fax: 505-524-1954
Email: rcgw@zianet.com

B. James Reeves
Frank N. Chavez
Charlotte Greenfield
William A. Walker, Jr.
Kelly P. Albers
Joyce A. Montes
William R. Anderson
Carolyn J. Baca

Glenn D. Hall
CaraLyn Banks

For full biographical listings, see the Martindale-Hubbell Law Directory

*SANTA FE,** Santa Fe Co.

HERRERA, LONG & POUND, P.A. (AV)

2200 Brothers Road, P.O. Box 5098, 87502-5098
Telephone: 505-982-8405
Fax: 505-982-8513
Email: hlplaw@aol.com

Judith C. Herrera
Nancy R. Long
John B. Pound

Mark E. Komer

LEGAL SUPPORT PERSONNEL

Shauna Allen Metzo

Reference: Bank of America.

For full biographical listings, see the Martindale-Hubbell Law Directory

NEW YORK

*ALBANY,** Albany Co.

COUCH WHITE, LLP (AV)

540 Broadway, P.O. Box 22222, 12201
Telephone: 518-426-4600
Telecopier: 518-426-0376
Email: CouchWhiteBrenn@Global2000.net *URL:* http://www.couchwhite.com
Washington, D.C. Office: 700 Thirteenth Street, N.W., Suite 950.
Telephone: 202-434-4503.
Fax: 202-434-4562.

MEMBERS OF FIRM

Leslie F. Couch
Algird F. White, Jr.
Barbara S. Brenner
Joel M. Howard, III
Paul A. Feigenbaum
Robert M. Loughney
Harold N. Iselin
Leonard H. Singer
Keith B. Rose
Christopher A. Cernik
Michael B. Mager
Mark F. Glaser
Pamela A. Madeiros
James J. Barriere
Doreen Unis Saia

SENIOR COUNSEL

Lawrence H. Cooke

ASSOCIATES

David G. Anderson
Tricia A. Asaro
James S. King
Marc A. Madia

For full biographical listings, see the Martindale-Hubbell Law Directory

Albany—Continued

Hinman, Straub, Pigors & Manning, P.C. (AV)

121 State Street, 12207-1622
Telephone: 518-436-0751
Fax: 518-436-4751
Email: Reception@hspm.com *URL:* http://www.hspm.com
Washington, D.C. Office: 50 E Street Southeast.
Telephone: 202-863-0806.

John J. Lynch
Stephen M. Cleary
Bartley J. Costello, III
Philip T. Dunne
David John Oakley
Bruce N. Gyory
Christopher C. Booth
Sean M. Doolan
Carolyn Shearer
Beverly Cohen
Robin Lynch Sise
Kimberly C. Lawrence
Kevin P. Quinn
Matthew P. Amodeo
Cheryl Potvin Hogan
E. Raymond Kolarsey

Paul A. Gillan, Jr.
Jane Bello Burke
Philip J. Murphy

OF COUNSEL

Joseph Boochever
Richard E. Casagrande

Representative Clients: New York State Conference of Blue Cross and Blue Shield Plans; North Country Oncology, P.C.; Maplewood Pathology, P.C.; Everest Dialysis Services; Meadowplace Dental; Hudson Mohawk Dental Practice Association.

For full biographical listings, see the Martindale-Hubbell Law Directory

Iseman, Cunningham, Riester & Hyde, LLP (AV)

9 Thurlow Terrace, 12203
Telephone: 518-462-3000
Telecopier: 518-462-4199
Email: lawfirm@icrh.com *URL:* http://www.icrh.com
Canandaigua, New York Office: 37 East Gibson Street, P.O. Box 179, 14424.
Telephone: 716-394-1450.
Fax: 716-394-5121.

MEMBERS OF FIRM

Frederick C. Riester
Michael J. Cunningham
Robert Hall Iseman
Carol Ann Hyde
Linda J. Clark

Brian M. Culnan
Kihyun S. Kim
Richard A. Frankel
Stephanie E. Moriarty
Valerie R. Lape Handy
Marcia B. Smith
Ellen Gillerman Cox
Jennifer A. Grego
Cara E. Johnson

OF COUNSEL

Michael J. McNeil
Deborah A. Kirby

For full biographical listings, see the Martindale-Hubbell Law Directory

O'Connell and Aronowitz, P.C. (AV)

100 State Street, 12207-1885
Telephone: 518-462-5601
Telecopier: 518-462-2670
Email: info@oalaw.com
Plattsburgh, New York Office: 206 West Bay Plaza.
Telephone: 518-562-0600.
Fax: 518-562-0657.
Saratoga Springs, New York Office: Suite 204, 358 Broadway.
Telephone: 518-587-0425.

Cornelius D. Murray
Sarah Walker Birn
Gloria Herron Arthur
Pamela A. Nichols

OF COUNSEL

Philip J. Sgarlata

Representative Client: New York State Health Facilities Association.

For full biographical listings, see the Martindale-Hubbell Law Directory

*BUFFALO,** Erie Co.

Damon & Morey LLP (AV)

(Formerly Damon, Morey, Sawyer & Moot)
1000 Cathedral Place, 298 Main Street, 14202-4096
Telephone: 716-856-5500
Facsimile: 716-856-5510
Email: apinder@damonmorey.com *URL:* http://www.damonmorey.com
Rochester, New York Office: Powers Building, Suite 507, 16 West Main Street, 14614.
Telephone: 716-232-3640.
Fax: 716-232-8448.

MEMBERS OF FIRM

Mason O. Damon (1905-1983)
Robert J. Plache
James N. Schmit
Christopher T. Greene
Franklin W. Heller
Gregory C. Yungbluth
James W. Gormley
James M. Mucklewee

(See Next Column)

MEMBERS OF FIRM (Continued)

Melinda G. Disare
Robert J. Portin
Joseph J. Schoellkopf, Jr.
William F. Savino
Thomas J. Drury
Patrick B. Curran
Peter S. Marlette
Vincent J. Moore
Gust P. Pullman
Barbara L. Schifeling
Michael J. Willett
Carol Guck Snider
Joseph W. Dunbar
Kenneth W. Africano
Julie M. Bargnesi
Arthur A. Marrapese III (Resident, Rochester Office)
Sharyn G. Rogers
Daniel F. Brown
David L. Edmunds, Jr.
Charles S. Carra
Hedwig Maria Auletta
Marylou K. Roshia
Maryjo C. Falcone
Charles E. Telford, III
Timothy C. Cashmore
Anthony L. Eugeni
Amy Archer Flaherty
Kathleen M. Reilly
Steven I. Rubinstein
Diane C. Zarlock

ASSOCIATES

Brian Alan Birenbach
Daniel T. Cavarello
Michelle A. Crew
Anne C. Evans
Michael Thomas Feeley
Judy S. Hernandez
David S. Kelly
Joseph J. Manna
Rosalie A. Melisz
Mary C. Raymond
Vincent George Saccomando
Allison Fields Stravino
Kellie Muffoletto Ulrich

OF COUNSEL

Joseph H. Morey, Jr.

SPECIAL COUNSEL

Richard E. Moot
George F. Gabel, Jr.
G. Steven Pigeon
Susan A. Benz
Edward Yankelunas

Counsel For: Advanced Refractory Technologies; Catholic Health East; D.A. Elia Construction Corporation; Kaleida Health; Town of Cheektowaga; Bagel Brothers Amherst, Inc.; Burt Rigid Box, Inc.; Lake Shore Health Care Center; County of Cattaraugus; Commonwealth Land Title Insurance; Diocese of Buffalo; Baker Victory Services; Niagara Lutheran Home and Rehabilitation, Inc.; Sheehan Memorial Hospital; Robert James Sales, Inc.; Olean General Hospital; Wendt Corporation; Aria Wireless Systems, Inc.; Buffalo Sewer Authority; City of Tonawanda; Roswell Park Cancer Institute; Ivoclar North America, Inc.; Olean Medical Group; Cold Spring Construction Company; Buffalo Municipal Housing Authority.
Local Counsel For: Healthcare Underwriters Mutual Insurance Company; AIG Companies; Owens-Corning Fiberglas; Unigard Insurance Group; Key Tronic Corporation; Medical Liability Insurance; Risk Enterprise Management Limited; Wintherthur International; Hanover Insurance Company; National Casualty Company; Marine Midland Mortgage Corporation; Acordia Resort Services; Medical Malpractice Insurance Association; OUM & Associates; Ohio Casualty Company; PACCAR, Inc.; Frontier Insurance Company; The Limited, Inc.; Zurich-American Insurance Group; Allstate Insurance Company; Universal Studios, Inc.

For full biographical listings, see the Martindale-Hubbell Law Directory

Feldman, Kieffer & Herman, LLP (AV)

110 Pearl Street, Suite 400, 14202
Telephone: 716-852-5875
Fax: 716-852-4253
Email: info@fkhattys.com *URL:* http://www.fkhattys.com

PRINCIPALS OF THE FIRM

Andrew Feldman
James M. Kieffer
Ann W. Herman
Mark F. Scarcello
Gordon D. Tresch
Mary Jo Herrscher

For full biographical listings, see the Martindale-Hubbell Law Directory

GARDEN CITY, Nassau Co.

Jacobson and Goldberg, LLP (AV)

585 Stewart Avenue, 11530
Telephone: 516-222-2330
Telex: 80-4294 BARRISTER
Fax: 516-222-2339
Email: JacobsonandGoldberg@worldnet.att.net

MEMBERS OF FIRM

Arthur I. Goldberg
Miles R. Jacobson
Amy T. Kulb
Daniel M. Goldberg
Jeffrey A. Granat

For full biographical listings, see the Martindale-Hubbell Law Directory

Montfort, Healy, McGuire & Salley (AV)

1140 Franklin Avenue, 11530
Telephone: 516-747-4082
Telecopier: 516-746-0748

MEMBERS OF FIRM

E. Richard Rimmels, Jr. (1930-1999)
Frank J. Cafaro
Philip J. Catapano
Fredric C. Montfort
Donald S. Neumann, Jr.
James J. Keefe, Jr.
Michael A. Baranowicz
James Michael Murphy

(See Next Column)

MONTFORT, HEALY, MCGUIRE & SALLEY, *Garden City—Continued*

OF COUNSEL

Fredric H. Montfort
Edward M. Salley, Jr.
David J. Fleming
Robert J. Mettalia

ASSOCIATES

Claudia C. Glacken
Marcie K. Glasser
Bruce A. Cook
Jeffrey D. Present
Joan E. Resnik
Susan H. Dempsey
Camille L. Hansen
Christopher T. Cafaro
Kathleen Dumont
Jeffrey B. Siler
Michael G. Kruzynski
Karen J. Cooper

For full biographical listings, see the Martindale-Hubbell Law Directory

GREAT NECK, Nassau Co.

GARFUNKEL, WILD & TRAVIS, P.C. (AV)

111 Great Neck Road, Suite 503, P.O. Box 220602, 11021
Telephone: 516-393-2200
Fax: 516-466-5964

George M. Garfunkel
Robert Andrew Wild (Chairman of Firm)
Norton L. Travis
Richard A. Dennett
Fredrick I. Miller
Judith A. Eisen
Joel M. Greenberg
Leonard M. Rosenberg
David J. Biehl
Greg E. Bloom
Andrew E. Blustein
Steven J. Chananie
Michael J. Keane
Doris L. Martin
Allan E. Silver
Hayden S. Wool

Jeffry Adest
Suzanne M. Brackley
Roy W. Breitenbach
Caryn Block Gibson
Debra A. Hamerman
Peter M. Hoffman
Barbara D. Knothe
Eve Green Koopersmith
John P. Kraljic
Erris Langer
David A. Langner
Peter B. Mancino
Lourdes Martinez
Lauren E. Matejka
Joseph E. Oliva
Jordy E. Rabinowitz
Gregg D. Reisman
Andrew J. Schulson
Alexandra Trinkoff
Christina Van Vort

SENIOR ATTORNEY

Debra Ann Silverman

OF COUNSEL

David E. Steckler

For full biographical listings, see the Martindale-Hubbell Law Directory

MELVILLE, Suffolk Co.

LAMB & BARNOSKY, LLP (AV)

534 Broadhollow Road-CS 9034, 11747-9034
Telephone: 631-694-2300
Telecopier: 631-694-2309
Email: thefirm@lambbarnosky.com *URL:* http://www.lambbarnosky.com

PARTNERS

Eugene R. Barnosky
Robert H. Cohen
Marcia Lyn Finkelstein
Michael J. Heller
Gary Holman
Scott M. Karson
P. L. Lamb
Arthur A. Lane
Joel M. Markowitz
Gerald P. Rosenberg
Patrice Dowd Shenn

OF COUNSEL

Louis E. Black
James F. Gesualdi
Howard W. Newman
Joseph J. Salvatore
Joseph H. Wishod

COUNSEL

Lloyd K. Chanin
Scott P. McBride

ASSOCIATES

Cathleen D. Allen
Catherine Healy Kanzler
Rita Fishman Sheena
Shari Lee Sugarman

For full biographical listings, see the Martindale-Hubbell Law Directory

*NEW YORK,** New York Co.

ROBERT P. BORSODY, P.C. (AV)

909 Third Avenue, 17th Floor, 10022
Telephone: 212-453-2727
Fax: 212-644-7485
Email: rborsody@fbwhlaw.com

Robert P. Borsody

For full biographical listings, see the Martindale-Hubbell Law Directory

KING, PAGANO & HARRISON (AV)

425 Park Avenue, 10022
Telephone: 212-223-4000
Fax: 212-223-4134
URL: http://www.kph.com
Washington, D.C. Office: 1730 Pennsylvania Avenue, N.W., 20006.
Telephone: 202-371-6800.
FAX: 202-371-6770.

MEMBERS OF FIRM

Jeffrey W. King (Resident, Washington, D.C. Office)
Jeffrey W. Pagano
Keith J. Harrison (Resident, Washington, D.C. Office)
James E. Kellett
Steven Schaars (Resident, Washington, D.C. Office)
Jeffrey L. Poston (Resident, Washington, D.C. Office)
Ira M. Saxe

OF COUNSEL

Herbert I. Meyer

ASSOCIATES

Cheryl A. Maier (Resident, Washington, D.C. Office)
Christopher Flynn (Resident, Washington, D.C. Office)
Emily B. Zuckerman
Thomas W. Jones, Jr. (Resident, Washington, D.C. Office)
Eric M. Carr

Representative Clients: Brink's, Inc.; The Pittston Co.; BAX Global; GEO Logistics; Air Transport International, L.L.C.; GAB Robbins, Inc.; SGS Control Services, Inc.; COMSAT; The Union Corp.; Kaiser Permanente.

For full biographical listings, see the Martindale-Hubbell Law Directory

MCALOON & FRIEDMAN, P.C. (AV)

116 John Street, 10038
Telephone: 212-732-8700
Fax: 212-227-2903

Edward H. McAloon (1908-1986)
Stanley D. Friedman
Gunther H. Kilsch
Theodore B. Rosenzweig
Gary A. Greenfield
Brendan J. Lantier
Lawrence W. Mumm
Laura R. Shapiro
Lisa B. Goldstein
Thomas Medardo Oliva
Adam R. Goldsmith
Wayne M. Roth
Kenneth S. Oliver
Stephen S. York

Jennifer D. Correale
Mark Gregory Duncan
Kenneth Gordon Ellison
Ilene R. Fish
Gillian Fisher
Kenneth Fox
Evette E. Harrison
Alex Johnson
Ross Katz
Sherry Levin
Robin P. Lorell
Carolan Magnoli
Linda P. McMillan
Douglas M. Nadjari
Timothy O'Shaugnessy
Matthew Luke Prisco
Caryn Rosen
Corey Lee Wishner

LEGAL SUPPORT PERSONNEL

Robyn L. Reyes (Firm Administrator)

For full biographical listings, see the Martindale-Hubbell Law Directory

NEIMAN GINSBURG & MAIRANZ P.C. (AV)

39 Broadway, 25th Floor, 10006-3003
Telephone: 212-269-1000
Telecopier: 212-635-9302
Email: ngmpc@concentric.net *URL:* http://www.ngmpc.com

Marvin Neiman
Theodore T. Mairanz
Gary Ginsburg

Betsy R. Malik
Susie Chovev

For full biographical listings, see the Martindale-Hubbell Law Directory

*ROCHESTER,** Monroe Co.

UNDERBERG & KESSLER LLP (AV)

1800 Chase Square, 14604
Telephone: 716-258-2800
Fax: 716-258-2821
Email: INFO@UNDERBERG-KESSLER.COM
Buffalo, New York Office: 1100 Main Place Tower. 14202.
Telephone: 716-848-9000.
Fax: 716-847-6004.

MEMBERS OF FIRM

Alan J. Underberg (1929-1998)
Irving L. Kessler
Michael J. Beyma
James A. Coniglio
Frank T. Crego
Robert W. Croessmann
John W. Crowe
Patrick L. Cusato
Michael C. Dwyer
Bernard A. Frank
Steven R. Gersz
Katherine Howk Karl
Lawrence P. Keller
Gordon J. Lipson
Anna E. Lynch
Robert F. Mechur
Paul V. Nunes
Terry M. Richman

(See Next Column)

UNDERBERG & KESSLER LLP—*Continued*

MEMBERS OF FIRM (Continued)

J. David Sampson (Resident, Buffalo Office)
Sharon P. Stiller
Stephen H. Waite
Russell I. Zuckerman

OF COUNSEL

Andrew M. Greenstein

SENIOR ATTORNEYS

Duncan R. Farney
Ronald G. Hull

ASSOCIATES

James F. Armstrong (Resident, Buffalo Office)
Karen A. DiNardo
Lise C. Hamilton
Jeffrey D. Hummel
Paul F. Keneally
Ella L. Krzanowicz
Maureen E. Mulholland
Suzanne D. Nott
Kelly L. Odorisi
Thomas A. Rall

For full biographical listings, see the Martindale-Hubbell Law Directory

*SYRACUSE,** Onondaga Co.

COSTELLO COONEY & FEARON, LLP (AV)

Salina Place, 205 South Salina Street, 13202
Telephone: 315-422-1152
Fax: 315-422-1139
Email: ccf-law.com *URL:* http://www.ccf-law.com

MEMBERS OF FIRM

Donald L. Nicholas
Timothy J. Conan

ASSOCIATE

W. Scott Gambee

General Counsel for: Auburn Memorial Hospital; Crouse Hospital; Health Services Association of Central New York; St. Joseph's Hospital Health Center.
Local Counsel for: Deere & Co.; New York Telephone Co.; Crum & Forster Insurance Co.; The Travelers Insurance Companies; Caterpillar, Inc.; Otis Elevator.

For Complete List of Firm Personnel, See General Section

For full biographical listings, see the Martindale-Hubbell Law Directory

DELANEY AND O'CONNOR LLP (AV)

Suite 275, Lincoln Center, 13202
Telephone: 315-476-8450
Telecopier: 315-476-8730
Email: deloco@dreamscape.com *URL:* http://www.dreamscape.com/deloco

MEMBERS OF FIRM

John M. DeLaney
Michael E. O'Connor
Denise P. Cambs

ASSOCIATES

Carol Currie Olech
Karin Sloan

For full biographical listings, see the Martindale-Hubbell Law Directory

NORTH CAROLINA

*CHARLOTTE,** Mecklenburg Co.

VAN HOY, REUTLINGER & TAYLOR (AV)

737 East Boulevard, 28203
Telephone: 704-375-6022
Fax: 704-375-6024
URL: http://www.lawyers.com/vrtlawfirm

MEMBERS OF FIRM

Philip M. Van Hoy
Craig A. Reutlinger
Paul B. Taylor

ASSOCIATE

Stephen J. Dunn

Representative Clients: McDowell Hospital; Medical Review of North Carolina; Beverly Enterprises; Cape Fear Valley Medical Center; Southeast Radiation Oncology Group; University Medical Associates; Total Care Home Health; Cabarrus Nursing Center; Miller Orthopedic Clinic; Heart Group of the Carolinas.

For full biographical listings, see the Martindale-Hubbell Law Directory

*RALEIGH,** Wake Co.

HOLLOWELL, PEACOCK & MEYER, P.A. (AV)

Crosspointe Plaza, 2840 Plaza Place, Suite 300, 27612
Telephone: 919-783-5657; 800-662-7403
Facsimile: 919-787-1833
Email: attorney@nchealthlaw.com *URL:* http://www.nchealthlaw.com

(See Next Column)

Edward E. Hollowell
Erle E. Peacock, Jr.
Deborah N. Meyer
Barry H. Bloch
Steven K. Sanborn
William E. Parker, III
Kevin S. Joyner
Dorothy L. Donaldson

OF COUNSEL

Roland S. Jones, Jr.
Mark A. Bernat

For full biographical listings, see the Martindale-Hubbell Law Directory

WOMBLE CARLYLE SANDRIDGE & RICE (AV)

A Professional Limited Liability Company
2100 First Union Capitol Center, 150 Fayetteville Street Mall, P.O. Box 831, 27602
Telephone: 919-755-2100
Fax: 919-755-2150
Email: lawyers@wcsr.com *URL:* http://www.wcsr.com
Charlotte, North Carolina Office: 3300 One First Union Center, 301 South College Street.
Telephone: 704-331-4900.
Fax: 704-331-4955.
Winston-Salem, North Carolina Office: 200 West Second Street, P.O. Drawer 84.
Telephone: 336-721-3600.
Fax: 336-721-3660.
Research Triangle Park, North Carolina Office: 2505 Meridian Parkway, Suite 300 (Durham), 27713.
Telephone: 919-484-2300.
Fax: 919-484-2340.
Atlanta, Georgia Office: One Atlantic Center, 1201 West Peachtree Street, Suite 3500.
Telephone: 404-872-7000.
Fax: 404-888-7490.
Other Atlanta, Georgia Office: Suite 404, 2296 Henderson Mill Road, N.E.
Telephone: 770-492-9030.
Fax: 770-492-9609.
Washington, D.C. Office: 1120 Nineteenth Street, N.W., Eighth Floor.
Telephone: 202-857-4400.
Fax: 202-467-6910.
Greenville, South Carolina Office: 15 South Main Street, Suite 601, P.O. Box 10208.
Telephone: 864-255-5400.
Fax: 864-255-5440.

RESIDENT MEMBER

Alexander P. Sands, III

RESIDENT ASSOCIATE

Samuel M. Taylor

RESIDENT OF COUNSEL

E. Lawrence Davis, III

Representative Clients: Aetna Casualty and Surety Co., Inc.; ALSCO/AmeriMark Building Products, Inc.; Aoki Corporation America, Inc.; Hackney Brothers, Inc.; Lawyers Mutual Liability Insurance Company of North Carolina; Meredith College; Regency Park Corp.; Wachovia Bank, N.A.

For Complete List of Firm Personnel, See General Section

For full biographical listings, see the Martindale-Hubbell Law Directory

*WILMINGTON,** New Hanover Co.

KAUFMAN & GREEN, L.L.P. (AV)

Landfall Park North, 1985 Eastwood Road, Suite 200, 28403
Telephone: 910-256-5135
Fax: 910-256-6451

James J. Kaufman
Michael A. Green

Owen D. Lewis, Jr.

Representative Clients: Steven P. Braff, M.D., P.C.; Boro Medical, P.C.; Boro Health Care of Union, P.C.; Boro Medical of New York, Inc.; Boro Medical of Westchester, Inc.; Atlantic Dermatology Assoc., P.A.; Southtech Orthopedics, Inc.; Thomas G. Pottle, M.D., P.C.; Old Nassau Imaging, P.C.

For full biographical listings, see the Martindale-Hubbell Law Directory

*WINSTON-SALEM,** Forsyth Co.

WOMBLE CARLYLE SANDRIDGE & RICE (AV)

A Professional Limited Liability Company
200 West Second Street, P.O. Drawer 84, 27102
Telephone: 336-721-3600
Fax: 336-721-3660
Email: lawyers@wcsr.com *URL:* http://www.wcsr.com
Charlotte, North Carolina Office: 3300 One First Union Center, 301 South College Street.
Telephone: 704-331-4900.
Fax: 704-331-4955.

(See Next Column)

WOMBLE CARLYLE SANDRIDGE & RICE, *Winston-Salem—Continued*

Raleigh, North Carolina Office: 2100 First Union Capitol Center, 150 Fayetteville Street Mall, P.O. Box 831.
Telephone: 919-755-2100.
Fax: 919-755-2150.
Research Triangle Park, North Carolina Office: 2505 Meridian Parkway, Suite 300 (Durham), 27713.
Telephone: 919-484-2300.
Fax: 919-484-2340.
Atlanta, Georgia Office: One Atlantic Center, 1201 West Peachtree Street, Suite 3500.
Telephone: 404-872-7000.
Fax: 404-888-7490.
Other Atlanta, Georgia Office: Suite 404, 2296 Henderson Mill Road, N.E.
Telephone: 770-492-9030.
Fax: 770-492-9609.
Washington, D.C. Office: 1120 Nineteenth Street, N.W., Eighth Floor.
Telephone: 202-857-4400.
Fax: 202-467-6910.
Greenville, South Carolina Office: 15 South Main Street, Suite 601, P.O. Box 10208.
Telephone: 864-255-5400.
Fax: 864-255-5440.

RESIDENT MEMBERS

Anthony H. Brett
Roddey M. Ligon, Jr.

RESIDENT ASSOCIATE

Joel M. Leander

Representative Clients: Brad Ragan, Inc.; Brenner Companies; Food Lion, Inc.; Hanes Companies, Inc.; North Carolina Baptist Hospitals, Inc.; R.J. Reynolds Tobacco Co.; Thomasville Furniture Industries, Inc.; Wachovia Corp.; Wake Forest University.

For Complete List of Firm Personnel, See General Section

For full biographical listings, see the Martindale-Hubbell Law Directory

OHIO

*CINCINNATI,** Hamilton Co.

BROWN, CUMMINS & BROWN CO., L.P.A. (AV)

3500 Carew Tower, 441 Vine Street, 45202
Telephone: 513-381-2121
Fax: 513-381-2125

Robert S. Brown
James R. Cummins
Donald S. Mendelsohn
Lynne Skilken
Amy G. Applegate
Kathryn Knue Przywara

OF COUNSEL

Gilbert Bettman

Counsel for: The University of Cincinnati.
Reference: Star Bank of Cincinnati.

For full biographical listings, see the Martindale-Hubbell Law Directory

FROST & JACOBS LLP (AV)

2500 PNC Center, 201 East Fifth Street, 45202
Telephone: 513-651-6800
Telecopier: 513-651-6981
URL: http://www.frojac.com
Columbus, Ohio Office: One Columbus, 10 West Broad Street, 43215.
Telephone: 614-464-1211.
Telecopier: 614-464-1737.
Lexington, Kentucky Office: 1100 Vine Center Tower, 333 West Vine Street, 40507.
Telephone: 606-254-1100.
Telecopier: 606-253-2990.
Middletown, Ohio Office: 400 First National Bank Building, 2 North Main Street, 45042.
Telephone: 513-422-2001.
Telecopier: 513-422-3010.
Frankfort, Kentucky Office: 201 W. Main Street, 40601.
Telephone: 502-223-1400.
Telecopier: 502-223-1410.

MEMBERS OF FIRM

Ronald E. Heinlen
Frederick J. McGavran
Jeffery R. Rush
William H. Hawkins II
Myron L. Dale
Walter E. Haggerty
David T. Croall
Douglas D. Thomson

SENIOR ATTORNEY

Daniel W. Scharff

ASSOCIATES

Caryn Franklin Gleich
Bill J. Paliobeis

OF COUNSEL

Clayton R. Sanders Jr. (Not admitted in OH)
Diane S. Shank

(See Next Column)

LEXINGTON, KENTUCKY OFFICE
OF COUNSEL

David C. Trimble

Representative Clients: Catholic Healthcare Partners; Mercy Health Partners-Greater Cincinnati Region; Bethesda Hospital; Mercy Health Partners-Western Ohio; Deaconess Hospital; University of Cincinnati Medical Center; Good Samaritan; Kentucky Medical Insurance; Pacificare of Ohio; Middletown Regional Hospital; Adena Regional Medical Center.

For Complete List of Firm Personnel, See General Section

For full biographical listings, see the Martindale-Hubbell Law Directory

GOODMAN & GOODMAN A LEGAL PROFESSIONAL ASSOCIATION (AV)

123 East Fourth Street, 45202
Telephone: 513-621-1505; 1-800-494-4529
Fax: 513-621-6900
URL: http://www.goodlaw.com

Sol Goodman (1906-1971)
Stanley Goodman
Ronald J. Goodman

Donald P. Morrisroe
John E. Stillpass
Reneé S. Frankel
Jeffrey S. Goodman

For full biographical listings, see the Martindale-Hubbell Law Directory

KATZ, TELLER, BRANT & HILD A LEGAL PROFESSIONAL ASSOCIATION (AV)

2400 Chemed Center, 255 East Fifth Street, 45202-4724
Telephone: 513-721-4532
Telecopier: 513-721-7120
Email: corp@ktbh.com

Reuven J. Katz
Jerome S. Teller
Robert E. Brant
Andrew R. Berger
Mark J. Jahnke
William F. Russo

Tedd H. Friedman

For Complete List of Firm Personnel, See General Section

For full biographical listings, see the Martindale-Hubbell Law Directory

*CLEVELAND,** Cuyahoga Co.

WALTER & HAVERFIELD, P.L.L. (AV)

1300 Terminal Tower, 44113-2253
Telephone: 216-781-1212
Telecopier: 216-575-0911
Email: law@walterhav.com *URL:* http://www.walterhav.com
Columbus, Ohio Office: 88 East Broad Street.
Telephone: 614-898-1096.

MEMBERS OF FIRM

Robert J. Crump
Charles R. Schaefer
Michael J. Jordan
Mark P. McGrievy

ASSOCIATES

Amy Leopard Woodhall
Mary E. Zeit

Representative Clients: Applied Medical Technology, Inc.; Northern Ohio Otolaryngology Network Ltd.; Edgepark Surgical, Inc.; Multi-Care Management; Health Force; Dettman Speech Therapy; Lifebanc; Lake County Primary Care Physicians, Ltd.

For Complete List of Firm Personnel, See General Section

For full biographical listings, see the Martindale-Hubbell Law Directory

*COLUMBUS,** Franklin Co.

BRICKER & ECKLER LLP (AV)

100 South Third Street, 43215-4291
Telephone: 614-227-2300
Telecopy: 614-227-2390
Email: info@be.bricker.com *URL:* http://www.bricker.com

James J. Hughes
Edward A. Matto
Michael K. Gire
David C. Spialter
Randall Edwin Moore
Elisabeth A. Squeglia
Diane M. Signoracci
Martha Post Baxter
Gretchen A. McBeath
Catherine M. Ballard
Scott W. Taebel
James F. Flynn
Harry Wright, IV

Lisa E. Hanger
Elizabeth H. Watts
Karen D. Smith

Representative Clients: OHA: The Association for Hospitals and Health Systems; ProMedica Health System; Ohio Health Corporation; Ohio Dental Association.

(See Next Column)

BRICKER & ECKLER LLP—*Continued*

For Complete List of Firm Personnel, See General Section

For full biographical listings, see the Martindale-Hubbell Law Directory

KEGLER, BROWN, HILL & RITTER (AV)

Capitol Square Suite 1800, 65 East State Street, 43215-4294
Telephone: 614-462-5400
Telecopier: 614-464-2634
Cable Address: "Law KBHR"
Telex: 246671
Email: info@kbhr.com *URL:* http://www.kbhr.com
Marion, Ohio Office: 250 Executive Drive, Suite B, P.O. Box 919.
Telephone: 614-387-3501.
Facsimile: 614-387-3630.

Donald A. Antrim
William J. Brown
Daniel G. Hilson
R. Kevin Kerns
R. Douglas Wrightsel

Stephen D. Dunson

Representative Clients: Arbor Health Care Company; Magellan Health Services, Inc.; Medco Containment Services, Inc.; Meridia Health System; Ohio Council for Home Care.

For Complete List of Firm Personnel, See General Section

For full biographical listings, see the Martindale-Hubbell Law Directory

SCHOTTENSTEIN, ZOX & DUNN A LEGAL PROFESSIONAL ASSOCIATION (AV)

The Huntington Center, 41 South High Street, 43215
Telephone: 614-462-2700
Telecopier: 614-462-5135
Telex: 650 24 444 365
URL: http://www.szd.com
Cincinnati, Ohio Office: Bank One Towers, 8044 Montgomery Road, Suite 700, 45236-2926.
Telephone: 513-792-2730.
Cleveland, Ohio Office: One Cleveland Center, 1375 East 9th Street, Suite 950.
Telephone: 216-621-6501.
Fax: 216-621-6502.

Peter A. Pavarini
Catherine T. Dunlay
Kris M. Dawley
Susan Porter
Edwin L. Skeens
John M. Latsko

William P. Zox
Nancy A. Brigner
Frank W. Carsonie
Marcia J. Myers (Resident, Cincinnati Office)
Lisa G. Han
Ara Mekhjian
Katrina L. Trimble Coffaro (Resident, Cincinnati Office)

Reference: Bank One of Columbus, N.A.

For Complete List of Firm Personnel, See General Section

For full biographical listings, see the Martindale-Hubbell Law Directory

GEOFFREY E. WEBSTER (AV)

17 South High Street, Suite 600, 43215
Telephone: 614-461-1156
Fax: 614-461-7168
Email: gewlaw@aol.com

ASSOCIATES

J. Randall Richards
Eric B. Hershberger

Representative Clients: The Ohio Academy of Nursing Homes, Inc.; Suburban Nursing & Mobile Homes, Inc.; Silver Circles of Care, Inc.; St. Rita's Home for the Aged, Inc.; St. Raphaels Home for the Aged, Inc.; St. Catherine's Health Care Centers, Inc.; Soroka Telle & Associates, Inc.; Marketing Services by Vectra, Inc.; Ohio Full Court Press, Ltd.; Oscar Jarnicki, Inc.

For full biographical listings, see the Martindale-Hubbell Law Directory

*DAYTON,** Montgomery Co.

PICKREL, SCHAEFFER & EBELING (AV)

2700 Kettering Tower, 45423-2700
Telephone: 937-223-1130
Facsimile: 937-223-0339
URL: http://www.pselaw.com

Paul E. Zimmer

Jeffrey S. Senney
Cara W. Powers

Representative Clients: Maria-Joseph Living Care Center; Miami Valley Cardiologists; Valley Pathologists, Inc.; Midstate Radiology Consultants, Inc.

For full biographical listings, see the Martindale-Hubbell Law Directory

SEBALY, SHILLITO & DYER A LEGAL PROFESSIONAL ASSOCIATION (AV)

1300 Courthouse Plaza, NE, P.O. Box 220, 45402-0220
Telephone: 937-222-2500
Telefax: 937-222-6554; 222-8279
URL: http://www.ssdlaw.com

Martin A. Beyer
Daniel A. Brown
James A. Dyer
Gale S. Finley
John R. Glankler
Deborah D. Hunt
Michael P. Moloney
Jon M. Sebaly
Beverly F. Shillito
Jeffrey B. Shulman
Karl R. Ulrich
Lawrence S. Walter
Nita S. Yates

OF COUNSEL

William W. Lambert

Michael A. Booth
Robert E. Goff, Jr.
Leslie Blair Graden
Joseph V. Hatala
J. David Ruffner, II
Kendra F. Thompson

Representative Clients: Children's Medical Center; The Dartmouth Hospital; Imaging Physicians, Inc.; Anesthesia Associates of Cincinnati, Inc.; Ohio Psychiatric Institutes, Inc.; Patient First Imaging Network.

For full biographical listings, see the Martindale-Hubbell Law Directory

*LIMA,** Allen Co.

ROBENALT & ROBENALT (AV)

211-215 North Elizabeth Street, 45801-4302
Telephone: 419-229-0054
Telecopier: 419-228-3631
Nokomis, Florida Office: 2440 Tamiami Trail North. P.O. Box 1608. 34275.
Telephone: 941-966-7755.
Fax: 941-966-6678.

MEMBERS OF FIRM

John A. Robenalt (Resident)
John F. Robenalt (Resident, Nokomis, Florida Office)

Representative Clients: National Health Investors, Inc. (listed New York Stock Exchange); National Health Corp. L.P. (listed AMEX); Dot Lines, Inc.; Warehouse Associates, Inc.; The Green and Sawyer Company; Ohio Automobile Club (OAC); Gooding Gallery of Homes; Allen County Regional Transit Authority.
Approved Attorney for: Guardian Title Insurance Co.
Reference: Bank One, Lima, Ohio.

For full biographical listings, see the Martindale-Hubbell Law Directory

*TOLEDO,** Lucas Co.

EASTMAN & SMITH LTD. (AV)

One Seagate, Twenty-Fourth Floor, P.O. Box 10032, 43699-0032
Telephone: 419-241-6000
Telecopier: 419-247-1777
Columbus, Ohio Office: 65 East State Street, Suite 1000, 43215.
Telephone: 614-460-3556.
Telecopier: 614-228-5371.

MEMBERS OF FIRM

Bruce L. Smith
David L. Kuhl
Gary M. Harden
Dirk P. Plessner

ASSOCIATE

Kevin D. Devaney

Counsel for: Riverside Hospital; Memorial Hospital (Fremont); The Toledo Clinic, Inc.; Medicare Equipment Supply Co.; Medical Protective Co.; The PM Group, Inc.; Magruder Hospital; Van Wert County Hospital.

For Complete List of Firm Personnel, See General Section

For full biographical listings, see the Martindale-Hubbell Law Directory

OKLAHOMA

*NORMAN,** Cleveland Co.

CROWE & DUNLEVY (AV)

A Professional Corporation
2500 South McGee, Suite 140, 73072-6705
Telephone: 405-321-7317
Fax: 405-360-4002
Email: marketing@crowedunlevy.com *URL:* http://www.crowedunlevy.com
Oklahoma City, Oklahoma Office: Crowe & Dunlevy, A Professional Corporation, 1800 Mid-America Tower, 20 North Broadway, 73102-8273.
Telephone: 405-235-7700.
Fax: 405-239-6651.

(See Next Column)

CROWE & DUNLEVY, *Norman—Continued*

Tulsa, Oklahoma Office: Crowe & Dunlevy, A Professional Corporation, 500 Kennedy Building, 321 South Boston Avenue, 74103-3313.
Telephone: 918-592-9800.
Fax: 918-592-9801.

Gary C. Rawlinson

Christopher R. Graves

For Complete List of Firm Personnel, See General Section

For full biographical listings, see the Martindale-Hubbell Law Directory

*OKLAHOMA CITY,** Oklahoma Co.

ANDREWS DAVIS LEGG BIXLER MILSTEN & PRICE, A PROFESSIONAL CORPORATION (AV)

500 West Main, Suite 500, 73102
Telephone: 405-272-9241
FAX: 405-235-8786
Email: andrewsdavis@andrewsdavis.com *URL:* http://www.andrewsdavis.com

J. Edward Barth
Alan C. Durbin
John F. Fischer, II
Timothy M. Larason
Mark H. Price
D. Joe Rockett
R. Brown Wallace

For Complete List of Firm Personnel, See General Section

For full biographical listings, see the Martindale-Hubbell Law Directory

CROWE & DUNLEVY, A PROFESSIONAL CORPORATION (AV)

1800 Mid-America Tower, 20 North Broadway, 73102-8273
Telephone: 405-235-7700
Fax: 405-239-6651
Email: marketing@crowedunlevy.com *URL:* http://www.crowedunlevy.com
Tulsa, Oklahoma Office: 500 Kennedy Building, 321 South Boston Avenue, 74103-3313.
Telephone: 918-592-9800.
Fax: 918-592-9801.
Norman, Oklahoma Office: Crowe & Dunlevy, 2500 South McGee, Suite 140, 73072-6705.
Telephone: 405-321-7317.
Fax: 405-360-4002.

J. Lawrence Blankenship
Earl A. Skarky
James H. Holloman, Jr.
Brooke Smith Murphy
Michael M. Stewart
Leonard Court
Michael S. Laird
Karen S. Rieger
Kevin D. Gordon
Roger A. Stong
Robert G. McCampbell

Cori Hook Loomis
Eric S. Fisher

For Complete List of Firm Personnel, See General Section

For full biographical listings, see the Martindale-Hubbell Law Directory

DAY, EDWARDS, FEDERMAN, PROPESTER & CHRISTENSEN, P.C. (AV)

Suite 2900 Oklahoma Tower, 210 Park Avenue, 73102-5605
Telephone: 405-239-2121
Telecopier: 405-236-1012
URL: http://lawlinks.com/attys/ok/defpc.html

Bruce W. Day
D. Wade Christensen
Joe E. Edwards
J. Clay Christensen

Representative Clients: Horizon Healthcare Corporation; Metropolitan Health Care; Southwest Healthcare.

For Complete List of Firm Personnel, See General Section

For full biographical listings, see the Martindale-Hubbell Law Directory

HARTZOG CONGER & CASON, A PROFESSIONAL CORPORATION (AV)

1600 Bank of Oklahoma Plaza 201 Robert S. Kerr, 73102
Telephone: 405-235-7000
Facsimile: 405-235-7329

Larry D. Hartzog
J. William Conger
Len Cason
James C. Prince
Steven C. Davis
Joseph P. Hogsett
John D. Robertson
Kurt M. Rupert
Laura Haag McConnell
Linda G. Scoggins
Susan B. Shields
Ryan S. Wilson
Amy J. Sine
Jon H. Trudgeon
Charles E. Geister, III
Phillip G. Whaley
Armand Paliotta

(See Next Column)

J. Christian Guzzy
Stacey D. Spivey
Melissa Beeson Heindselman
Christin V. Adkins
Byron K. Linkous

OF COUNSEL

Kent F. Frates
Kenneth R. Davis
Alan Newman

For full biographical listings, see the Martindale-Hubbell Law Directory

*TULSA,** Tulsa Co.

BOESCHE, MCDERMOTT & ESKRIDGE (AV)

Suite 800 Oneok Plaza, 100 West Fifth Street, 74103
Telephone: 918-583-1777
Fax: 918-592-5809
Email: bme@intellex.com
Muskogee, Oklahoma Office: 1111 West Broadway, P.O. Box 2669, 74402.
Telephone: 918-683-6100.
Fax: 918-683-2303.

MEMBERS OF FIRM

R. Casey Cooper
David B. McKinney
R. Kevin Layton
Sheila M. Powers

ASSOCIATES

Byron E. (Rusty) Brown
Christopher K. Woosley

OF COUNSEL

Clifford K. Cate, Jr. (Resident at Muskogee)

Representative Clients: Tulsa Regional Medical Center; Springer Clinic; Community Physicians Group.

For Complete List of Firm Personnel, See General Section

For full biographical listings, see the Martindale-Hubbell Law Directory

BOONE, SMITH, DAVIS, HURST & DICKMAN, A PROFESSIONAL CORPORATION (AV)

500 Oneok Plaza, 100 West 5th Street, 74103
Telephone: 918-587-0000
Fax: 918-599-9317
URL: http://www.boonesmith.com

Byron V. Boone (1908-1988)
Teresa Meinders Burkett
John A. Burkhardt
Paul J. Cleary
Reuben Davis
J. Jerry Dickman
Monica Goodman
David J. Hyman
William C. Kellough
Donald A. Lepp
Mary Lohrke
Kimberly Lambert Love
Scott R. Rowland
Frederic N. (Nick) Schneider III
Jeffrey R. Schoborg
Stephen Schuller
L. K. Smith
Paul E. Swain III

OF COUNSEL

Edwin S. Hurst
Lloyd G. Minter

Representative Clients: American Airlines; BP Amoco Corp.; Chevron U.S.A., Inc.; Ford Motor Co.; Hillcrest Medical Center; PricewaterhouseCoopers; Phillips Petroleum Co.; The Boeing Company; Sears, Roebuck & Co.; World Publishing Co; Whirlpool Corp.

For full biographical listings, see the Martindale-Hubbell Law Directory

CROWE & DUNLEVY, A PROFESSIONAL CORPORATION (AV)

500 Kennedy Building, 321 South Boston Avenue, 74103-3313
Telephone: 918-592-9800
Fax: 918-592-9801
Email: marketing@crowedunlevy.com *URL:* http://www.crowedunlevy.com
Oklahoma City, Oklahoma Office: 1800 Mid-America Tower, 20 North Broadway, 73102-8273.
Telephone: 405-235-7700.
Fax: 405-239-6651.
Norman, Oklahoma Office: Crowe & Dunlevy, 2500 South McGee, Suite 140, 73072-6705.
Telephone: 405-321-7317.
Fax: 405-360-4002.

Lon Foster, III
Gary L. Betow
Malcolm E. Rosser IV

Nancy Lynn Roberts

For Complete List of Firm Personnel, See General Section

For full biographical listings, see the Martindale-Hubbell Law Directory

RHODES, HIERONYMUS, JONES, TUCKER & GABLE, P.L.L.C. (AV)

Oneok Plaza, 100 West 5th Street, Suite 400, P.O. Box 21100, 74121-1100
Telephone: 918-582-1173
Fax: 918-592-3390
URL: http://www.rhodesokla.com

(See Next Column)

RHODES, HIERONYMUS, JONES, TUCKER & GABLE P.L.L.C.—*Continued*

MEMBERS OF FIRM

Kevin D. Berry
Jo Anne Deaton
Richard M. Eldridge
E. D. Hieronymus (1908 -1994)
Bert M. Jones
William S. Leach
Michael W. McGivern
William D. Perrine
Mary Quinn-Cooper
Robert P. Redemann
David P. Reid
Chris L. Rhodes, III
Thomas E. Steichen
Catherine C. Taylor
John H. Tucker
Wilson T. White
Harold C. Zuckerman

Ann E. Allison
Steven K. Bunting
Robert P. Coffey, Jr.
J. Christopher Davis
Andrew D. Downing
Dana L. Gish
Kerry R. Lewis
Andrew L. Richardson
Michael F. Smith
Leslie J. Southerland
Kimberly E. West
Keith A. Wilkes

OF COUNSEL

George W. Gable (Retired Partner)
Larry J. Fulton
Kelly M. Greenough

Representative Clients: American International Companies; Bechtel; Chubb Group of Insurance Companies; General Motors Corporation; Merrill, Lynch; Nissan Motor Corporation in U.S.A.; Pfizer, Inc.; Volkswagen of America, Volkswagen, A.G.; Zurich U.S.

For full biographical listings, see the Martindale-Hubbell Law Directory

OREGON

*EUGENE,** Lane Co.

WATKINSON LAIRD RUBENSTEIN LASHWAY & BALDWIN, P.C. (AV)

101 East Broadway, Suite 200, P.O. Box 10567, 97440
Telephone: 541-484-2277
Fax: 541-484-2282
Roseburg, Oregon Office: 2750 West Harvard Boulevard.
Telephone: 541-672-2755.
FAX: 541-672-6379.

Steve C. Baldwin
B. Kevin Burgess
Donald R. Laird
J. Lee Lashway
Barry Rubenstein
John C. Watkinson

Leonard A. Hagen
Tami S. P. Carroll
Amanda Tracey Walkup
Daniel J. Drazan

OF COUNSEL

R. Sande Tomlinson

Representative Clients: Lane Individual Practice Association; Douglas County Independent Practice Association, Inc.; Womens Health Care Associates, P.C.; Sure HealthPlans, Inc.; Advantage Dental Plans, Inc.; Roseburg Dental Services, LLC; Doctors of Clackawas County, Inc.; Southwest Oregon IPA, Inc.; Treasure Valley Physicians Management Corp.; South Coast Dental Services, LLC.

For full biographical listings, see the Martindale-Hubbell Law Directory

PENNSYLVANIA

BLUE BELL, Montgomery Co.

KAPLIN STEWART MELOFF REITER & STEIN, PROFESSIONAL CORPORATION (AV)

350 Sentry Parkway, Building 640, P.O. Box 3037, 19422-0765
Telephone: 610-260-6000
Telecopier: 610-260-1240
Cherry Hill, New Jersey Office: 900 Dudley Avenue, #250, 08002-4426.
Telephone: 856-486-1044.
Fax: 856-486-1074.

MEMBER OF FIRM

Barry A. Furman

For full biographical listings, see the Martindale-Hubbell Law Directory

*CHAMBERSBURG,** Franklin Co.

BARLEY, SNYDER, SENFT & COHEN, LLC (AV)

247 Lincoln Way East, 17201
Telephone: 717-264-6494
Fax: 717-264-1662
Email: barley@barley.com *URL:* http://www.barley.com
Harrisburg, Pennsylvania Office: 240 North Third Street.
Telephone: 717-238-8263.
Fax: 717-238-8278.
Lancaster, Pennsylvania Office: 126 East King Street.
Telephone: 717-299-5201.
Fax: 717-291-4660.
York, Pennsylvania Office: 100 East Market Street.
Telephone: 717-846-8888.
Fax: 717-843-8492.
Reading, Pennsylvania Office: 501 Washington Street.
Telephone: 610-376-6651.
Fax: 610-376-5243.
Hanover, Pennsylvania Office: 14 Center Square.
Telephone: 717-637-6239.
Fax: 717-637-5407.
Birdsboro, Pennsylvania Office: 115 E. Main Street.
Telephone: 610-582-2735.
Hamburg, Pennsylvania Office: 239 State Street.
Telephone: 610-562-3721.
Oley, Pennsylvania Office: Route 73 and Main Street.
Telephone: 610-987-6350.
Morgantown, Pennsylvania Office: Route 23.
Telephone: 610-286-5958.

MEMBERS OF FIRM

Martha B. Walker
Christopher W. Mattson
Kathleen Ann Gray
David R. Keller
Carol E. Van Horn
Timothy P. Brown
Lynn Y. MacBride
Michael W. Davis
Melanie A. Zampini

ASSOCIATES

Anne S. Johnson
John W. Venskus

For full biographical listings, see the Martindale-Hubbell Law Directory

*HARRISBURG,** Dauphin Co.

KEEFER WOOD ALLEN & RAHAL, LLP (AV)

210 Walnut Street, P.O. Box 11963, 17108-1963
Telephone: 717-255-8000
Telecopier: 717-255-8050
Email: info@keeferwood.com *URL:* http://www.keeferwood.com
Camp Hill, Pennsylvania Office: 415 Fallowfield Road.
Telephone: 717-612-5800.
Telecopier: 717-612-5805.

MEMBERS OF FIRM

Thomas E. Wood
Bradford Dorrance
Wayne M. Pecht

SENIOR ATTORNEY

Donald M. Lewis, III

ASSOCIATE

John A. Feichtel

Representative Clients: Central Pennsylvania Blood Bank; Highmark, Inc.; Homeland Center; Keystone Health Plan Central; Physicians' and Dentists' Professional Corporations; Pinnacle Health Systems.

For Complete List of Firm Personnel, See General Section

For full biographical listings, see the Martindale-Hubbell Law Directory

THOMAS, THOMAS & HAFER, LLP (AV)

305 North Front Street, 6th Floor, P.O. Box 999, 17108
Telephone: 717-237-7100
Fax: 717-237-7105
Verify: 717-255-7642
Bethlehem, Pennsylvania Office: 12 East Market Street, P.O. Box 1172, 12016.
Telephone: 610-868-1675.
Fax: 610-868-1702.

MEMBERS OF FIRM

Joseph P. Hafer
James K. Thomas, II
Robertson B. Taylor
Jeffrey B. Rettig
Peter J. Curry
R. Burke McLemore, Jr.
Edward H. Jordan, Jr.
C. Kent Price
Randall G. Gale
David L. Schwalm
Peter J. Speaker
Douglas B. Marcello
Paul J. Dellasega

OF COUNSEL

James K. Thomas

(See Next Column)

THOMAS, THOMAS & HAFER LLP, *Harrisburg—Continued*

Timothy I. Mark
Daniel J. Gallagher
Robert A. Taylor
Sarah W. Arosell
Eugene N. McHugh
Stephen E. Geduldig
Karen S. Coates
Gary T. Lathrop
Todd B. Narvol
James J. Dodd-o
Kenneth A. Rapp
Kevin C. McNamara
Brooks R. Foland
John Flounlacker
John M. Popilock
Michele J. Thorp

Representative Clients: Aetna Casualty & Surety Co.; Commercial Union Insurance Companies; Geisinger Medical Center; Hartford Insurance Group; Liberty Mutual Insurance Co.; Medical Inter-Insurance Exchange; Medical Protective Co.; Pennsylvania Hospital Insurance Co.; Pennsylvania Medical Society Liability Insurance Co.; Weis Markets, Inc.

For full biographical listings, see the Martindale-Hubbell Law Directory

*LANCASTER,** Lancaster Co.

BARLEY, SNYDER, SENFT & COHEN, LLC (AV)

126 East King Street, 17602-2893
Telephone: 717-299-5201
Fax: 717-291-4660
Email: barley@barley.com *URL:* http://www.barley.com
Reading, Pennsylvania Office: 501 Washington Street.
Telephone: 610-376-6651.
Fax: 610-376-5243.
Harrisburg, Pennsylvania Office: 240 North Third Street.
Telephone: 717-238-8263.
Fax: 717-238-8278.
York, Pennsylvania Office: 100 East Market Street.
Telephone: 717-846-8888.
Fax: 717-843-8492.
Chambersburg, Pennsylvania Office: 247 Lincoln Way East.
Telephone: 717-264-6494.
Fax: 717-264-1662.
Hanover, Pennsylvania Office: 14 Center Square.
Telephone: 717-637-6239.
Fax: 717-637-5407.
Birdsboro, Pennsylvania Office: 115 E. Main Street.
Telephone: 610-582-2735.
Hamburg, Pennsylvania Office: 239 State Street.
Telephone: 610-562-3721.
Oley, Pennsylvania Office: Route 73 and Main Street.
Telephone: 610-987-6350.
Morgantown, Pennsylvania Office: Route 23.
Telephone: 610-286-5958.

MEMBERS OF FIRM

John O. Shirk
James R. Adams
W. Jeffrey Sidebottom
Christopher W. Mattson
Jesse C. Robinson
Paul M. Browning
Kathleen Ann Gray
George C. Werner, Jr.
David R. Keller
Caroline M. Hoffer
Paul G. Mattaini
Elaine Pennington Stanko
Paul D. Clouser
Michael A. Moore
Kendra D. McGuire
Anne E. Doliner
Timothy P. Brown
Deborah A. Datte
Ronald H. Pollock, Jr.
Michael S. Butler
Michael W. Davis
Katherine Betz Kravitz
Bruce J. Wolstoncroft

ASSOCIATES

Nancy Mayer Hughes
Craig T. Trebilcock
Leigh A. J. Ellis
Hanna-Aurelia Dunlap
Barbara M. Boben
Jennifer L. Craighead
Scott F. Landis
Robert A. Evarts
James F. Devine, III
Philip A. Wolgemuth
Theresa M. Melchiorre
John T. Reed
Gene P. Otto
Cynthia A. Otto
Stephanie Carfley
Kurt W. McCabe
Daniel M. Lieberman

RETIRED

Paul A. Mueller, Jr.
Charles R. Cooper, Jr.
John T. Barber

Counsel for: Fulton Bank/Fulton Financial Corp.; Lancaster General Hospital; Robert A. Kinsley, Inc.; Summit Health.
Local Counsel for: Armstrong World Industries; South Central Community Health.
Insurance Defense Counsel for: Medical Protective Co.; The PMA Group; Medical Inter-Insurance Exchange.

For full biographical listings, see the Martindale-Hubbell Law Directory

*PHILADELPHIA,** Philadelphia Co.

BALLARD SPAHR ANDREWS & INGERSOLL, LLP (AV)

1735 Market Street, 51st Floor, 19103-7599
Telephone: 215-665-8500
Fax: 215-864-8999
URL: http://www.ballardspahr.com
Baltimore, Maryland Office: 300 East Lombard Street. 19th Floor.
Telephone: 410-528-5600.
Fax: 410-528-5650.
Camden, New Jersey Office: 800 Hudson Square, 5th Floor.
Telephone: 856-541-5577.
Fax: 856-541-8272.
Denver, Colorado Office: Seventeenth Street Plaza Building, Suite 2300, 1225 17th Street.
Telephone: 303-292-2400.
Fax: 303-296-3956.
Salt Lake City, Utah Office: One Utah Center, Suite 1200, 201 South Main Street.
Telephone: 801-531-3000.
Fax: 801-531-3001.
Voorhees, New Jersey Office: Suite 100, 1101 Laurel Oak Drive.
Telephone: 856-627-8555.
Fax: 856-627-1153.
Washington, D.C. Office: Suite 1000 South, 601 13th Street, N.W.
Telephone: 202-661-2200.
Fax: 202-661-2299.

Kevin R. Cunningham
Peter M. Mattoon
John B. Langel
William P. Scott
Matthew M. Strickler

OF COUNSEL

Jean C. Hemphill
Deborah J. Zateeny

For Complete List of Firm Personnel, See General Section

For full biographical listings, see the Martindale-Hubbell Law Directory

MCKISSOCK & HOFFMAN, P.C. (AV)

1700 Market Street, Suite 3000, 19103
Telephone: 215-246-2100
Fax: 215-246-2144
Westmont, New Jersey Office: 216 Haddon Avenue, Suite 603.
Telephone: 609-858-1650.
Fax: 609-858-1466.
Doylestown, Pennsylvania Office: 16 North Franklin Street, Suite 300.
Telephone: 215-345-4501.
Fax: 215-246-4503.
Harrisburg, Pennsylvania Office: 105 North Front Street, Suite 205.
Telephone: 717-234-0103.
Fax: 717-234-1350.
West Chester, Pennsylvania Office: 31 South High Street, P.O. Box 3086.
Telephone: 610-738-8850.
Fax: 610-738-9121.

J. Bruce McKissock
Peter J. Hoffman
Leslie Anne Miller
Jeffrey B. Albert
Jill Baratz Clarke
John J. McGrath (Resident, Westmont, New Jersey Office)
Donald J. Brooks, Jr.
William J. Mundy
Bryan Craig Black (Resident, Harrisburg Office)
Eileen Lampe
Christopher Thomson (Resident Shareholder, West Chester Office)
K. Reed Haywood
Maureen P. Fitzgerald

For full biographical listings, see the Martindale-Hubbell Law Directory

PERRY, FIALKOWSKI & PERRY (AV)

Suite 1600 One Penn Square West, 30 South 15th Street, 19102
Telephone: 215-561-4110
Fax: 215-561-4177
Email: pfp@pfplaw.com *URL:* http://www.pfplaw.com
Clementon, New Jersey Office: 180 White Horse Pike.
Telephone: 609-627-1005.

MEMBERS OF FIRM

David Perry
Anne E. Fialkowski
Sherryl R. Perry
Marcia F. Rosenbaum

LEGAL SUPPORT PERSONNEL

Lisa Garrett

For full biographical listings, see the Martindale-Hubbell Law Directory

ROSENTHAL AND WEISBERG, P.C. (AV)

Two Logan Square Suite 1565, 18th & Arch Streets, 19103
Telephone: 215-656-4100
Fax: 215-656-4119

Brian D. Rosenthal
Michael Stuart Weisberg

Neil T. Murray
Margaret M. Foley

(See Next Column)

ROSENTHAL AND WEISBERG P.C.—*Continued*

LEGAL SUPPORT PERSONNEL

Wendy Frost (Paralegal) Lynn Gibbs (Paralegal)

For full biographical listings, see the Martindale-Hubbell Law Directory

SCHUBERT, BELLWOAR, CAHILL & QUINN, A PROFESSIONAL CORPORATION (AV)

Two Penn Center, Suite 1400, 1500 John F. Kennedy Boulevard, 19102-1890
Telephone: 215-569-3535
Fax: 215-557-7426
Email: attorneys@sbcq.com
Haddon Township, New Jersey Office: 311 West Cuthbert Boulevard, 08108.
Telephone: 856-854-5757.

Thomas M. Schubert (1924-1989)
William E. Schubert, Jr. (1921-1998)
Harry J. J. Bellwoar, III
John P. Quinn
John J. Cahill, Jr.
Robert T. Lynch
Robert G. Bellwoar
John P. Gallagher
James O. Hausch
Deborah E. Kolodner
Richard T. Mulcahey, Jr.
James M. Tyler
Jan M. Ritchie

Joseph W. Cunningham
Michael S. Piotrowicz
Patricia Farrell Kerelo
Christopher B. Hogan
Kathleen M. O'Connell
Mark Pfeiffer
Eric A. Feldhake

OF COUNSEL

John D. Lucey, Jr. Robert F. Blanck

For full biographical listings, see the Martindale-Hubbell Law Directory

*PITTSBURGH,** Allegheny Co.

FELDSTEIN GRINBERG STEIN & MCKEE, A PROFESSIONAL CORPORATION (AV)

428 Boulevard of the Allies, 15219
Telephone: 412-471-0677
Fax: 412-263-6129
URL: http://www.fgsmlaw.com
Elizabeth, Pennsylvania Office: 400 Second Street.
Telephone: 412-384-6111.

Edwin I. Grinberg Stanley M. Stein
Robert E. McKee, Jr.

For full biographical listings, see the Martindale-Hubbell Law Directory

HORTY, SPRINGER & MATTERN, P.C. (AV)

4614 5th Avenue, 15213
Telephone: 412-687-7677
Fax: 412-687-7692
URL: http://www.hortyspringer.com

John Horty
Clara L. Mattern (1931-1981)
Barbara A. Blackmond
Linda Haddad
Daniel M. Mulholland III
Charlotte S. Jefferies
Henry M. Casale
Paul A. Verardi
Alan J. Steinberg
Susan M. Lapenta
Lauren M. Massucci

Nicholas J. Calabrese Philip W. Zarone

OF COUNSEL

Eric W. Springer

For full biographical listings, see the Martindale-Hubbell Law Directory

NASH & COMPANY, A PROFESSIONAL CORPORATION (AV)

Suite 700, 11 Stanwix Street, 15222
Telephone: 412-392-2333
Fax: 412-392-2343
URL: http://www.healthlawnet.com

Stephen P. Nash Terrence J. O'Rourke
Charles G. O'Hara

Theresa Creagh Melissa L. Staggers
Vikram Mangalmurti

For full biographical listings, see the Martindale-Hubbell Law Directory

PLYMOUTH, Luzerne Co.

MUSTO & SAUNDERS, P.C. (AV)

117 W. Main Street, 18651-2926
Telephone: 570-779-5122
Fax: 570-719-0306
Enola, Pennsylvania Office: Suite 208 North Enola Drive.
Telephone: 717-732-8114.

Joseph J. Musto Keith J. Saunders

Fortunata G. Musto
Daniel J. Balutis
Camille H. Jescavage (Not admitted in PA)
Christopher J. O'Donnell

For full biographical listings, see the Martindale-Hubbell Law Directory

*WEST CHESTER,** Chester Co.

GAWTHROP, GREENWOOD & HALSTED, A PROFESSIONAL CORPORATION (AV)

119 North High Street, P.O. Box 562, 19381-0562
Telephone: 610-696-8225
Fax: 610-344-0922
Email: gghlaw@gawthrop.com *URL:* http://www.gawthrop.com

John S. Halsted
Robert F. Adams
Kevin Holleran
George C. Zumbano
Mark L. Tunnell
Roger N. Huggins
Walter P. Eells

Andrew D.H. Rau Jeffrey T. Baker
Miguel D. Pena

Counsel for: Chester County Hospital; Brandywine Hospital.

For full biographical listings, see the Martindale-Hubbell Law Directory

*YORK,** York Co.

BARLEY, SNYDER, SENFT & COHEN, LLC (AV)

100 East Market Street, P.O. Box 15012, 17405-7012
Telephone: 717-846-8888
Fax: 717-843-8492
Email: barley@barley.com *URL:* http://www.barley.com
Lancaster, Pennsylvania Office: 126 East King Street.
Telephone: 717-299-5201.
Fax: 717-291-4660.
Harrisburg, Pennsylvania Office: 240 North Third Street.
Telephone: 717-238-8263.
Fax: 717-238-8278.
Chambersburg, Pennsylvania Office: 247 Lincoln Way East.
Telephone: 717-264-6494.
Fax: 717-264-1662.
Reading, Pennsylvania Office: 501 Washington Street.
Telephone: 610-376-6651.
Fax: 610-376-5243.
Hanover, Pennsylvania Office: 14 Center Square.
Telephone: 717-637-6239.
Fax: 717-637-5407.
Birdsboro, Pennsylvania Office: 115 E. Main Street.
Telephone: 610-582-2735.
Hamburg, Pennsylvania Office: 239 State Street.
Telephone: 610-562-3721.
Oley, Pennsylvania Office: Route 73 and Main Street.
Telephone: 610-987-6350.
Morgantown, Pennsylvania Office: Route 23.
Telephone: 610-286-5958.

MEMBERS OF FIRM

Harry J. Rubin
Christopher W. Mattson
Frederick S. Spangler
Rees Griffiths
David R. Keller
Jeffrey D. Lobach
Steven J. Koehler
Val E. Winter
Deborah A. Datte
Michael W. Davis
Melanie A. Zampini
Bruce J. Wolstoncroft

ASSOCIATES

Craig T. Trebilcock
Beverly J. Points
John L. Senft
Paul W. Minnich
Robert J. Schefter
Kimberly J. Decker
John W. Venskus

COUNSEL

Robert J. Stewart Lavere C. Senft

RETIRED

Donn I. Cohen

Counsel for: Fulton Bank/Fulton Financial Corp.; Lancaster Chamber of Commerce and Industry; Lancaster General Hospital; Robert A. Kinsley, Inc.; Summit Health.
Local Counsel for: Armstrong World Industries; South Central Community Health.
Insurance Defense Counsel for: Medical Protective Co.; The PMA Group; Medical Inter-Insurance Exchange.

(See Next Column)

BARLEY, SNYDER, SENFT & COHEN LLC, *York—Continued*

For full biographical listings, see the Martindale-Hubbell Law Directory

RHODE ISLAND

*PROVIDENCE,** Providence Co.

CAMERON & MITTLEMAN LLP (AV)

56 Exchange Terrace, 02903
Telephone: 401-331-5700
Telecopier: 401-331-5787

Richard S. Mittleman
E. Colby Cameron
Amy L. Mower
David L. Mayer
Bruce W. Gladstone
Justin T. Shay
Joseph F. Whinery, Jr.
Don E. Wineberg
Robert A. Migliaccio
Karen G. DelPonte

Catherine T. Schneider
John W. Wolfe
Charles S. Beal
Kathy J. Kushnir

Representative Clients: PHO of South County; South County Hospital; St. Joseph Hospital; RIH Medical Foundation; University Cardiology Foundation; New England Physicians Alliance; VNS of Greater Rhode Island; Northern RI Community Mental Health Center; Neighborhood Health Plan of RH.

For full biographical listings, see the Martindale-Hubbell Law Directory

HINCKLEY, ALLEN & SNYDER LLP (AV)

1500 Fleet Center, 02903-2393
Telephone: 401-274-2000
Fax: 401-277-9600
Email: firm@haslaw.com *URL:* http://www.haslaw.com
Boston, Massachusetts Office: 28 State Street, 30th Floor.
Telephone: 617-345-9000.
Fax: 617-345-9020. URL: http://www.haslaw.com.

MEMBERS OF FIRM

E. Jerome Batty
Jonathan Bell
Leon C. Boghossian III
Paul Bork (Not admitted in RI)
Stephen J. Carlotti
Eric F. Eisenberg (Not admitted in RI)
Malcolm Farmer, III
Bruce G. Goodman (Not admitted in RI)
Alan P. Gottlieb (Not admitted in RI)
Gerard R. Goulet
William R. Grimm
Paul A. Hedstrom (Not admitted in RI)
Richard L. E. Jocelyn
Michael J. Kelly (Not admitted in RI)
Frederick P. McClure
H. Peter Olsen
Julianne Palumbo (Not admitted in RI)
John J. Pendergast, III
James O. Reavis
Douglas F. Seaver (Not admitted in RI)
Robert F. Sylvia (Not admitted in RI)
Howard E. Walker
Richard D. Wayne (Not admitted in RI)

ASSOCIATES

Brent R. Canning
Michael G. Tauber
Lawrence W. Vernaglia (Not admitted in RI)

OF COUNSEL

Willard Krasnow (Not admitted in RI)

For Complete List of Firm Personnel, See General Section

For full biographical listings, see the Martindale-Hubbell Law Directory

SOUTH CAROLINA

*CHARLESTON,** Charleston Co.

BARNWELL WHALEY PATTERSON & HELMS, LLC (AV)

134 Meeting Street, Suite 300, P.O. Drawer H, 29402
Telephone: 843-577-7700
Telecopier: 843-577-7708
Email: bwph@barnwell-whaley.com *URL:* http://barnwell-whaley.com

MEMBERS OF FIRM

M. Dawes Cooke, Jr.
Bruce E. Miller
Matthew H. Henrikson
James E. Reeves

ASSOCIATES

J. Matthew Dillon
Lucinda Gardner Wichmann

Representative Clients: Caroria Corporation; Colleton Medical Center; Columbis/HCA Healthcare Corporation; GranCare; Grand Strand Regional Medical Center; Health Care Indemnity, Inc.; Medical Claims Management; Group Steadfast Insurance Company; Summerville Medical Center; Trident Ambulatory Surgery Center.

(See Next Column)

For full biographical listings, see the Martindale-Hubbell Law Directory

BUIST, MOORE, SMYTHE & MCGEE, P.A. (AV)

Successors to Buist, Buist, Smythe and Smythe and Moore, Mouzon and McGee.
Five Exchange Street, P.O. Box 999, 29402
Telephone: 843-722-3400
Cable Address: "Conferees"
Telex: 57-6488
Telecopier: 843-723-7398
Email: bmsm@lawyer-sc.com *URL:* http://www.lawyer-sc.com

Susan M. Smythe
Kenneth F. Smith
Morris A. Ellison
James L. Parris
John Marshall Allen

Representative Clients: East Cooper Regional Medical Center; Palmetto Physicians Association, Inc.; Medical Anesthesia Associates, LLC; Orthopaedic Specialists of Charleston, P.A.; Charleston Plastic Surgery, P.A.; Charleston ENT Associates, LLC; Palmetto Specialty Care Physicians, LLC; Southeastern Fertility Center, P.A.; Coastal Anesthesia Associates, LLC; Carolina Eye Care Physicians, LLC.

For Complete List of Firm Personnel, See General Section

For full biographical listings, see the Martindale-Hubbell Law Directory

HAYNSWORTH, MARION, MCKAY & GUÉRARD, L.L.P. (AV)

134 Meeting Street, P.O. Box 1119, 29402
Telephone: 843-722-7606
Facsimile: 843-724-8016
Columbia, South Carolina Office: Suite 2400 Affinity Building, 1201 Main Street, P.O. Drawer 7157, 29202.
Telephone: 803-765-1818. Facsimile 803-765-2399.
Greenville, South Carolina Office: 75 Beattie Place, Eleventh Floor, P.O. Box 2048, 29602.
Telephone: 864-240-3200.
Facsimile: 864-240-3300.

MEMBERS OF FIRM

James J. Hinchey, Jr.
Thomas S. White

Representative Clients: Greenville Hospital System; Baker Hospital; Roper Hospital; Oconee; Memorial Hospital; Beauford Memorial Hospital; Cooper Hall Nursing Home; Clemson Health Center; Medical Society Health Systems, Inc.; HealthSource of South Carolina.

For Complete List of Firm Personnel, See General Section

For full biographical listings, see the Martindale-Hubbell Law Directory

*COLUMBIA,** Richland Co.

NEXSEN PRUET JACOBS & POLLARD, LLP (AV)

1441 Main Street, 15th Floor, P.O. Drawer 2426, 29202
Telephone: 803-771-8900
Facsimile: 803-253-8277
Email: NPJP@NPJP.COM *URL:* HTTP://WWW.NPJP.COM
Charleston, South Carolina Office: 200 Meeting Street, Suite 301. P.O. Box 486.
Telephone: 803-577-9440.
Facsimile: 803-720-1777.
Greenville, South Carolina Office: 201 West McBee Avenue, Fourth Floor, P.O. Box 10648.
Telephone: 864-370-2211.
Facsimile: 864-282-1177.
Myrtle Beach, South Carolina Office: 2411 Oak Street, Suite 105.
Telephone: 843-445-9688.
Facsimile: 843-445-9949.
Charlotte, North Carolina Office: 212 South Tryon Street, Suite 1700.
Telephone: 704-339-0304.
Facsimile: 704-338-5377.

MEMBERS OF FIRM

David Rees Cannon (Resident, Charlotte, NC Office)
Robert D. Coble
Timothy L. Hewson
William A. Pollard

SPECIAL COUNSEL

Susan A. Lake
William A. Prince

ASSOCIATES

Ralph W. Barbier III
Jeanne Marie Born
Cynthia Bankhead Hutto (Resident, Charleston, SC Office)
Matthew B. Roberts

For Complete List of Firm Personnel, See General Section

For full biographical listings, see the Martindale-Hubbell Law Directory

Columbia—Continued

RICHARDSON, PLOWDEN, CARPENTER & ROBINSON, P.A. (AV)

1600 Marion Street, P.O. Drawer 7788, 29202
Telephone: 803-771-4400
Telecopy: 803-779-0016
Email: atty@rpcrlaw.com *URL:* http://www.rpcrlaw.com
Myrtle Beach, South Carolina Office: 2103 B Farlow Street, P.O. Box 3646, 29578.
Telephone: 843-448-1008.
FAX: 843-448-1533.

George C. Beighley
Frederick A. Crawford

OF COUNSEL

Donald V. Richardson, III

Representative Clients: Richland Memorial Hospital; Anesthesiologist of Columbia, P.A.; Cardiovascular Associates, P.A.; Carolina Health Choice Network; Newberry County Memorial Hospital.

For Complete List of Firm Personnel, See General Section

For full biographical listings, see the Martindale-Hubbell Law Directory

TURNER, PADGET, GRAHAM & LANEY, P.A. (AV)

Seventeenth Floor, 1901 Main Street, P.O. Box 1473, 29202
Telephone: 803-254-2200
Telecopy: 803-799-3957
Florence, South Carolina Office: Fourth Floor, 1831 West Evans Street, P.O. Box 5478, 29502.
Telephone: 843-662-9008.
Fax: 843-667-0828.
Charleston, South Carolina Office: 21 Broad Street, 1st Floor, P.O. Box 836, 29402.
Telephone: 843-723-1622.
Fax: 843-577-3369.

Charles E. Hill
John S. Wilkerson, III (Resident, Florence, SC, Office)
Teresa A. Arnold

OF COUNSEL

Laura Chandler Rublee (Resident, Florence, SC, Office)

William C. Barnes, Jr. (Resident, Florence, SC, Office)
Richard C. Burke (Resident, Florence, SC, Office)
Tiffni Drawdy Shealy (Resident, Florence, SC, Office)

For Complete List of Firm Personnel, See General Section

For full biographical listings, see the Martindale-Hubbell Law Directory

*GREENVILLE,** Greenville Co.

HAYNSWORTH, MARION, MCKAY & GUÉRARD, L.L.P. (AV)

75 Beattie Place, Eleventh Floor, P.O. Box 2048, 29602
Telephone: 864-240-3200
Facsimile: 864-240-3300
Columbia, South Carolina Office: Suite 2400 Affinity Building, 1201 Main Street, P.O. Drawer 7157, 29202
Telephone: 803-765-1818.
Facsimile: 803-765-2399.
Charleston, South Carolina Office: 134 Meeting Street, P.O. Box 1119, 29402.
Telephone: 843-722-7606.
Facsimile: 843-724-8016.

MEMBERS OF FIRM

G. Dewey Oxner, Jr.
Joseph J. Blake, Jr.
Edwin Brown Parkinson, Jr.
Donna S. Kivett
Sarah M. (Sally) Purnell

ASSOCIATE

Stephen P. Williams

Representative Clients: Greenville Hospital System; Roper Health Systems, Inc.; Oconee Memorial Hospital; Wallace Thompson Hospital; Health Management Services; Clemson Health Center; Georgetown Memorial Hospital; Conway Hospital, Inc.; Health First, Inc.; Upstate Teleservices, Inc.

For Complete List of Firm Personnel, See General Section

For full biographical listings, see the Martindale-Hubbell Law Directory

LEATHERWOOD WALKER TODD & MANN, P.C. (AV)

100 East Coffee Street, P.O. Box 87, 29602
Telephone: 864-242-6440
FAX: 864-240-2477
Email: leatherwood@lwtm.com *URL:* http://www.lwtm.com
Spartanburg, South Carolina Office: 1451 East Main Street, P.O. Box 3188.
Telephone: 864-582-4365.
Telefax: 864-583-8961.

Sandra L. W. Miller

(See Next Column)

McLaurin M. McDonald

Representative Clients: Carolina Multispecialty Associates, P.A.; Vaughn Buchanan Sheally & Associates, Inc.; Jennie Ware Family Medical Services, Inc.; Family Health Care Center, P.A.

For Complete List of Firm Personnel, See General Section

For full biographical listings, see the Martindale-Hubbell Law Directory

SOUTH DAKOTA

*RAPID CITY,** Pennington Co.

BANGS, MCCULLEN, BUTLER, FOYE & SIMMONS, L.L.P. (AV)

818 St. Joseph Street, P.O. Box 2670, 57709
Telephone: 605-343-1040
Telecopier: 605-343-1503
URL: http://www.bangsmccullen.com

MEMBERS OF FIRM

Charles L. Riter
Daniel F. Duffy
Jeffrey G. Hurd
John H. Raforth

Representative Clients: Norwest Bank South Dakota, N.A., Rapid City, S.D.; Pete Lien & Sons; The Travelers Insurance Co.; Rapid City Regional Hospital; Dakota Steel & Supply Co.; Great American Insurance Co.; Fireman's Fund Insurance; United States Automobile Association; Moyle Petroleum; Rapid City Area School District 51-4.

For Complete List of Firm Personnel, See General Section

For full biographical listings, see the Martindale-Hubbell Law Directory

*SIOUX FALLS,** Minnehaha Co.

HUGHES LAW OFFICES (AV)

412 West Ninth Street, 57104-3602
Telephone: 605-339-3939
Fax: 605-339-3940

John R. Hughes

LeeAnn Larson LaFave

For full biographical listings, see the Martindale-Hubbell Law Directory

TENNESSEE

*CHATTANOOGA,** Hamilton Co.

BAKER, DONELSON, BEARMAN & CALDWELL (AV)

1800 Republic Centre, 633 Chestnut Street, 37450-1800
Telephone: 423-756-2010
Telecopier: 423-756-3447
Email: info@bdbc.com *URL:* http://www.bakerdonelson.com
Memphis, Tennessee Office: 20th Floor, First Tennessee Building, 165 Madison, 38103.
Telephone: 901-526-2000.
Telecopier: 901-577-2303.
Nashville, Tennessee Office: 1700 Nashville City Center, 511 Union Street, 37219.
Telephone: 615-726-5600.
Telecopier: 615-726-0464.
Knoxville, Tennessee Office: 2200 Riverview Tower, 900 South Gay Street, 37901.
Telephone: 423-549-7000.
Telecopier: 423-525-8569.
Johnson City, Tennessee Office: SunTrust Bank Building, 207 Mockingbird Lane, P.O. Box 3038, 37602.
Telephone: 423-928-0181.
Telecopier: 423-928-5694; 423-928-3654; Kingsport: 423-246-6191.
Huntsville, Tennessee Office: 3 Courthouse Square, 37756.
Telephone: 423-663-2321.
Telecopier: 423-663-2111.
Washington, D.C. Office: Market Square, 801 Pennsylvania Avenue, N.W., 20004.
Telephone: 202-508-3400.
Telecopier: 202-508-3402.
Jackson, Mississippi Office: Suite 500, 700 North State Street, 39202.
Telephone: 601-351-2400.
Telecopier: 601-351-2424.

MANAGING PARTNER

Susan Elliott Rich

(See Next Column)

BAKER, DONELSON, BEARMAN & CALDWELL, *Chattanooga—Continued*

SHAREHOLDERS

Lewis R. Donelson, III
Howard H. Baker, Jr.
Thomas A. Caldwell
John C. Mooney
Thomas O. Helton
Richard B. Gossett
Carl E. Hartley
Virginia C. Love
Richard J. McAfee
John C. Harrison
Gladys Smith Mynatt
Louann Prater Smith
Kenneth C. Beckman
J. Porter Durham, Jr.
Joe A. Conner
Robert C. Divine

OF COUNSEL

Randall D. Van Dolson
Robert W. Sauser
H. Allen Corey
Micheline Kelly Johnson
Michael C. Mallen
Charles N. Jolly
Jo C. Dearing

ASSOCIATES

Russell W. Gray
Cameron S. Hill
Victoria S. Childres
James H. Levine
Roddy Bailey (Not admitted in TN)
Misty Smith Kelley
Alison Tuley (Not admitted in TN)

For full biographical listings, see the Martindale-Hubbell Law Directory

*KNOXVILLE,** Knox Co.

EGERTON, MCAFEE, ARMISTEAD & DAVIS, P.C. (AV)

500 First American National Bank Center, P.O. Box 2047, 37901
Telephone: 423-546-0500
Fax: 423-525-5293
URL: http://emadlaw.com

Lewis C. Foster, Jr.
Herbert H. Slatery III
Stephen A. McSween

Representative Clients: The Baptist Health System of East Tennessee, Inc.; Baptist Hospital of East Tennessee, Inc.; Baptist Hospital of Cocke County, Inc.; Cookeville General Hospital; The Health Education and Housing Facilities Board of Knox County; Holston Long Term Care Corporation; Albers, Inc.

For full biographical listings, see the Martindale-Hubbell Law Directory

WAGNER, MYERS & SANGER, A PROFESSIONAL CORPORATION (AV)

1801 First Tennessee Plaza, P.O. Box 1308, 37901-1308
Telephone: 423-525-4600
Fax: 423-524-5731
Email: wms1801@usit.net

William C. Myers, Jr.
M. Douglas Campbell, Jr.

Representative Clients: Covenant Health System; Orthopedic Associates of Knoxville, P.C.; Blount Orthopedics Associates, P.C.; Allergy Associates, P.A.; Fort Sanders Regional Medical Center; Fort Sanders Parkwest Medical Center; Fort Sanders Sevier Medical Center; Fort Sanders London Medical Center; Fort Sanders West Outpatient Surgery Center.

For Complete List of Firm Personnel, See General Section

For full biographical listings, see the Martindale-Hubbell Law Directory

*MEMPHIS,** Shelby Co.

ARMSTRONG ALLEN PREWITT GENTRY JOHNSTON & HOLMES, PLLC (AV)

Brinkley Plaza, Suite 700, 80 Monroe Avenue, 38103-2467
Telephone: 901-523-8211
Facsimile: 901-524-4936
Little Rock, Arkansas Office: Suite 100, 100 Morgan Keegan Drive, 72202.
Telephone: 501-280-0100.
Facsimile: 501-280-0166.
Jackson, Mississippi Office: 2525 Lakeward Drive, Suite 200, 39216.
Telephone: 601-713-1192.
Facsimile: 601-713-2049.
Jackson, Tennessee Office: 464 North Parkway, Suite A, 38305.
Telephone: 901-660-2332.
Facsimile: 901-664-1109.

MEMBERS OF FIRM

Elmore Holmes, III
Thomas R. Prewitt, Jr.
Robert V. Redding (Resident, Jackson, Tennessee Office)
Paul A. Matthews
V. Ellen Morris (Resident, Jackson, Mississippi Office)
Charles R. Crawford
Heber S. Simmons III (Resident, Jackson, Mississippi Office)

For Complete List of Firm Personnel, See General Section

For full biographical listings, see the Martindale-Hubbell Law Directory

BAKER, DONELSON, BEARMAN & CALDWELL (AV)

20th Floor, First Tennessee Building, 165 Madison, 38103
Telephone: 901-526-2000
Telecopier: 901-577-2303
Email: info@bdbc.com *URL:* http://www.bakerdonelson.com
Nashville, Tennessee Office: 1700 Nashville City Center, 511 Union Street, 37219.
Telephone: 615-726-5600.
Telecopier: 615-726-0464.
Chattanooga, Tennessee Office: 1800 Republic Centre, 633 Chestnut Street, 37450-1800.
Telephone: 423-756-2010.
Telecopier: 423-756-3447.
Knoxville, Tennessee Office: 2200 Riverview Tower, 900 South Gay Street, 37901.
Telephone: 423-549-7000.
Telecopier: 423-525-8569.
Johnson City, Tennessee Office: SunTrust Bank Building, 207 Mockingbird Lane, P.O. Box 3038, 37602.
Telephone: 423-928-0181.
Telecopier: 423-928-5694; 423-928-3654; Kingsport: 423-246-6191.
Huntsville, Tennessee Office: 3 Courthouse Square, 37756.
Telephone: 423-663-2321.
Telecopier: 423-663-2111.
Washington, D.C. Office: Market Square, 801 Pennsylvania Avenue, N.W., 20004.
Telephone: 202-508-3400.
Telecopier: 202-508-3402.
Jackson, Mississippi Office: Suite 500, 700 North State Street, 39202.
Telephone: 601-351-2400.
Telecopier: 601-351-2424.

OF COUNSEL

Paul E. Risner (Not admitted in TN)

For Complete List of Firm Personnel, See General Section

For full biographical listings, see the Martindale-Hubbell Law Directory

HALE HEADRICK DEWEY & WOLF, PLLC (AV)

One Memphis Place, 200 Jefferson Avenue Suite 1450, 38103
Telephone: 901-523-1123
Fax: 901-523-7472
Nashville, Tennessee Office: Suntrust Bank Building, 201 Fourth Avenue North, Suite 1450, 37219.
Telephone: 615-843-5160.
Fax: 615-843-5165

Stephen P. Hale
S. Russell Headrick
H. Tucker Dewey
Herbert B. Wolf, Jr.
John S. Golwen

OF COUNSEL

Steven L. Gill

Jennifer Ziegenhorn
Wendy A. Geurin
John W. Campbell
Joseph M. Koury
Holly N. Knight
Charles S. Blatteis
Jennifer S. Kiesewetter
J. William Williams

For full biographical listings, see the Martindale-Hubbell Law Directory

HARRIS, SHELTON, DUNLAP AND COBB, P.L.L.C. (AV)

Suite 2700, One Commerce Square, 38103-2555
Telephone: 901-525-1455
Telecopier: 901-526-4084
Email: hsdclaw@hsdclaw.com
Other Memphis Office: 6363 Poplar, Suite 430.
Telephone: 901-682-1455.
Fax: 901-682-4446.
Oxford, Mississippi Office: 428 North Lamar Boulevard, Suite 2.
Telephone: 662-238-2855.
Fax: 662-238-2895.

MEMBERS OF FIRM

Walter Chandler (1887-1967)
John H. Harris, Jr.
Max Shelton
William W. Dunlap, Jr.
M. Anderson Cobb, Jr.
James L. Kirby
James R. Garts, Jr.
George T. Wheeler, Jr.
James D. Wilson
Charles C. Drennon, III (Resident, Poplar Avenue Office)
Michael F. Rafferty
A. Neal Graham
G. Rice Byars, Jr.
Jonathan E. Scharff

ASSOCIATES

Tabitha Francisco McNabb
Brett A. Hughes
Chesney Falk McAfee
Christopher S. Campbell
Estelle C. Gaerig
Donrua Barnes-Hulsey
Shawn L. Verner

For full biographical listings, see the Martindale-Hubbell Law Directory

Austin—Continued

JACKSON WALKER L.L.P. (AV)

100 Congress Avenue, Suite 1100, 78701-4099
Telephone: 512-236-2000
Fax: 512-236-2002
Email: hloftin@jw.com *URL:* http://www.jw.com
Dallas, Texas Office: 901 Main Street, Suite 6000.
Telephone: 214-953-6000.
Fax: 214-953-5822.
Fort Worth, Texas Office: 301 Commerce Street, Suite 2400.
Telephone: 817-334-7200.
Fax: 817-334-7290.
Houston, Texas Office: 1100 Louisiana, Suite 4200.
Telephone: 713-752-4200.
Fax: 713-752-4221.
Richardson, Texas Office: 2435 North Central Expressway, Suite 600.
Telephone: 972-671-2560.
Fax: 972-671-2566.
San Angelo, Texas Office: 225 West Beauregard Avenue.
Telephone: 915-481-2550.
Fax: 915-481-2552.
San Antonio, Texas Office: 112 E. Pecan Street, Suite 2100.
Telephone: 210-978-7700.
Fax: 210-978-7790.

MEMBERS OF FIRM

Carla J. Cox
J. Stephen Dillawn
Gary A. Thornton

For Complete List of Firm Personnel, See General Section

For full biographical listings, see the Martindale-Hubbell Law Directory

THOMPSON & KNIGHT L.L.P. (AV)

(Attorneys and Counselors)
1200 San Jacinto Center, 98 San Jacinto Boulevard, 78701
Telephone: 512-469-6100
Telecopy: 512-469-6180
URL: http://www.tklaw.com
Dallas, Texas Office: 1700 Pacific Avenue, Suite 3300, 75201.
Telephone: 214-969-1700.
Telecopy: 512-969-1751.
Telex: 732298.
Fort Worth, Texas Office: 801 Cherry Street, Suite 1600, 76102.
Telephone: 817-347-1700.
Telecopy: 817-347-1799.
Houston, Texas Office: Thompson Knight Brown Parker & Leahy L.L.P., 1200 Smith Street, Suite 3600, 77002-4595.
Telephone: 713-654-8111.
Telecopier: 713-654-1871.
San Pedro Garza Garcia, Nuevo León, Mexico Office: Edificio Losoles PD-4, Av. Lázaro Cárdenas No. 2400 Pte., C.P. 66220.
Telephone: (52-8) 363-0096.
Telecopy: (52-8) 363-3067.

PARTNERS

Eugene W. Brees, II
James E. Cousar
Frank L. Hill

For Complete List of Firm Personnel, See General Section

For full biographical listings, see the Martindale-Hubbell Law Directory

*DALLAS,** Dallas Co.

JOSEPH E. ASHMORE, JR., P.C. (AV)

Regency Plaza, 3710 Rawlins, Suite 1210, LB 84, 75219-4217
Telephone: 214-559-7202
Fax: 214-520-1550

Joseph E. Ashmore, Jr.

C. Gregory Shamoun

For Complete List of Firm Personnel, See General Section

For full biographical listings, see the Martindale-Hubbell Law Directory

CALHOUN & STACY (AV)

Suite 5700 - Bank of America Plaza, 901 Main Street, 75202-3713
Telephone: 214-748-5000
Facsimile: 214-748-1421
Email: info@calhounstacy.com *URL:* http://www.calhounstacy.com

MEMBERS OF FIRM

Dennis D. Conder
LeAnn Wainscott Cross
David W. Elrod
Roy L. Stacy
Michael C. Wright

For Complete List of Firm Personnel, See General Section

For full biographical listings, see the Martindale-Hubbell Law Directory

FERNANDEZ & KNEBEL, A PROFESSIONAL CORPORATION (AV)

Bank One Center, 1717 Main Street, Suite 2100, 75201
Telephone: 214-747-2100
Fax: 214-747-2144

Bennett I. Abramowitz
Clint A. Corrie
Raymond R. Fernandez, Jr.
Delbert L. Gibbs
Robert L. Knebel, Jr.
Mary Jo Vida

Barbara F. Blaylock
Herbert J. Gilles
Maria Isabel Roman
Jon M. Payne
Joseph L. Mira

For full biographical listings, see the Martindale-Hubbell Law Directory

FRALEY & FRALEY, L.L.P. (AV)

901 Main Street, Suite 6510, 75202
Telephone: 214-761-6460
Fax: 214-761-6469
Email: info@fraleyandfraley.com *URL:* http://www.fraleyandfraley.com

R. Scott Fraley
Elizabeth Masters Fraley
J. Patrick Bredehoft

J. David Criss

For full biographical listings, see the Martindale-Hubbell Law Directory

JACKSON WALKER L.L.P. (AV)

901 Main Street, Suite 6000, 75202-3797
Telephone: 214-953-6000
Fax: 214-953-5822
URL: http://www.jw.com
Austin, Texas Office: 100 Congress Avenue, Suite 1100.
Telephone: 512-236-2000.
Fax: 512-236-2002.
Fort Worth, Texas Office: 301 Commerce Street, Suite 2400.
Telephone: 817-334-7200.
Fax: 817-334-7290.
Houston, Texas Office: 1100 Louisiana, Suite 4200.
Telephone: 713-752-4200.
Fax: 713-752-4221.
Richardson, Texas Office: 2435 North Central Expressway, Suite 600.
Telephone: 972-671-2560.
Fax: 972-671-2566.
San Angelo, Texas Office: 225 West Beauregard Avenue.
Telephone: 915-481-2550.
Fax: 915-481-2552.
San Antonio, Texas Office: 112 E. Pecan Street, Suite 2100.
Telephone: 210-978-7700.
Fax: 210-978-7790.

MEMBERS OF FIRM

Jeffery P. Drummond
James S. Ryan, III

OF COUNSEL

Mary Emma Ackels Karam

Representative Clients Furnished Upon Request.

For Complete List of Firm Personnel, See General Section

For full biographical listings, see the Martindale-Hubbell Law Directory

CHRISTOPHER G. SHARP, P.C. (AV)

6116 North Central Expressway, Suite 520, 75206
Telephone: 214-368-3600
Fax: 214-368-3632
Email: CGSPC@Prodigy.com *URL:* http://www.lawyers.com/christophergsharplaw

Christopher G. Sharp

For full biographical listings, see the Martindale-Hubbell Law Directory

THOMPSON & KNIGHT L.L.P. (AV)

(Attorneys and Counselors)
1700 Pacific Avenue Suite 3300, 75201
Telephone: 214-969-1700
Telecopy: 214-969-1751
Telex: 732 298
URL: http://www.tklaw.com
Austin, Texas Office: 1200 San Jacinto Center, 98 San Jacinto Boulevard, 78701.
Telephone: 512-469-6100.
Telecopy: 512-469-6180.
Fort Worth, Texas Office: 801 Cherry Street, Suite 1600, 76102.
Telephone: 817-347-1700.
Telecopy: 817-347-1799.
Houston, Texas Office: Thompson Knight Brown Parker & Leahy L.L.P., 1200 Smith Street, Suite 3600, 77002-4595.
Telephone: 713-654-8111.
Telecopier: 713-654-1871.

(See Next Column)

Memphis—Continued

SMITH, SABBATINI & MCLEARY, PLLC (AV)

100 Peabody Place Suite 1250, 38103
Telephone: 901-312-5555
Fax: 901-312-5667
Mailing Address: P.O. Box 3582, Memphis, TN, 38173
URL: http://www.smithlawetal.com

Gary K. Smith
Robert L. Sabbatini
Harold W. McLeary, Jr.
William D. Domico
James F. Kyle
James T. McColgan, III
G. Edward Coleman, III
Bryant C. Witt

Representative Clients: Premier RRG Insurance; Illinois Central Railroad; Medical Assurance; Albertson's, Inc.; Med. Marc (Chiro Co.); Medical Protective Co.; Methodist Health Systems; Hartford Insurance Co.; Sentry Insurance; State Farm Insurance.

For full biographical listings, see the Martindale-Hubbell Law Directory

*NASHVILLE,** Davidson Co.

BAKER, DONELSON, BEARMAN & CALDWELL (AV)

1700 Nashville City Center, 511 Union Street, 37219
Telephone: 615-726-5600
Telecopier: 615-726-0464
Email: info@bdbc.com *URL:* http://www.bakerdonelson.com
Memphis, Tennessee Office: 20th Floor, First Tennessee Building, 165 Madison, 38103.
Telephone: 901-526-2000.
Telecopier: 901-577-2303.
Chattanooga, Tennessee Office: 1800 Republic Centre, 633 Chestnut Street, 37450-1800.
Telephone: 423-756-2010.
Telecopier: 423-756-3447.
Knoxville, Tennessee Office: 2200 Riverview Tower, 900 South Gay Street, 37901.
Telephone: 423-549-7000.
Telecopier: 423-525-8569.
Johnson City, Tennessee Office: SunTrust Bank Building, 207 Mockingbird Lane, P.O. Box 3038, 37602.
Telephone: 423-928-0181.
Telecopier: 423-928-5694; 423-928-3654; Kingsport: 423-246-6191.
Huntsville, Tennessee Office: 3 Courthouse Square, 37756.
Telephone: 423-663-2321.
Telecopier: 423-663-2111.
Washington, D.C. Office: Market Square, 801 Pennsylvania Avenue, N.W., 20004.
Telephone: 202-508-3400.
Telecopier: 202-508-3402.
Jackson, Mississippi Office: Suite 500, 700 North State Street, 39202.
Telephone: 601-351-2400.
Telecopier: 601-351-2424.

MANAGING PARTNER

Laurence M. Papel

SHAREHOLDERS

Lewis R. Donelson, III
Howard H. Baker, Jr.
Robert F. Worthington, Jr.
Robert G. McCullough
Richard D. Bird
Thomas O. Helton
Richard B. Gossett
Robert L. Baker
Robert G. McDowell
Carl E. Hartley
William S. Painter (Not admitted in TN)
John A. Gupton, III
Claudia W. Dickerson
James A. DeLanis
Richard G. Cowart
Kenneth P. Ezell, Jr.
James L. McElroy
Robert M. Steele
Gary C. Shockley
Randal S. Mashburn
Steven J. Eisen
John S. Hicks
J. Porter Durham, Jr.
M. Kevin Outterson
J. Steven Kirkham
John H. Rowland
Philip Stuart McSween
Thomas E. Bartrum (Not admitted in TN)

ASSOCIATES

Claire F. Miley
Barbara A. Rose
John F. Rogers, Jr.
Scott D. Carey
John M. Bryant, Jr.
Kenneth A. Weber
Darwin A. Hindman III
Ann Duncan Jarvis
Lawrence S. Eastwood, Jr.
Jonathan Cole
Christopher R. Kelly
Brigid T. Miller
Christy Tosh Crider
Kelley Taylor Oliver
Richard H. Stout
J. Adin Lara
Tonya Mitchem Grindon (Not admitted in TN)
Jennifer Lynch Butler

OF COUNSEL

Peter C. Ward (Not admitted in TN)
Thomas H. Holter (Not admitted in TN)
Christy F. Batts

For full biographical listings, see the Martindale-Hubbell Law Directory

BASS, BERRY & SIMS PLC (AV)

2700 First American Center, 37238-2700
Telephone: 615-742-6200
Telecopy: 615-742-6293
URL: http://www.bassberry.com
Knoxville, Tennessee Office: 1700 Riverview Tower, 900 S. Gay Street, 37902 and P.O. Box 1509, 37901-1509.
Telephone: 423-521-6200.
Telecopy: 423-521-6234.
Memphis, Tennessee Office: 119 S. Main Street, Suite 500, 38103.
Telephone: 901-312-9100.
Fax: 901-312-9101.

MEMBERS OF FIRM

Leigh Walton
T. Andrew Smith
G. Mark Mamantov (Resident, Knoxville, Tennessee Office)
Cynthia Y. Reisz

ASSOCIATES

T. Scott Noonan
Randall E. Bruce

Representative Clients: American Healthcorp, Inc.; American retirement Corporation; AmSurg Corp.; Arcon HealthCare, Inc.; Columbia/HCA Healthcare Corp.; Concentra Managed Care, Inc.; Dialysis Clinic, Inc.; Hemophilia Health Services, Inc.; Meridian Occupational Healthcare Services, Inc.; Physicians Reliance Network, Inc.; PrincipalCare Inc.; Vanderbilt University Medical Center.

For full biographical listings, see the Martindale-Hubbell Law Directory

TEXAS

*AUSTIN,** Travis Co.

DAVIS & DAVIS, P.C. (AV)

Arboretum Plaza One, 9th Floor, 9442 Capital of Texas Highway, P.O. Box 1588, 78759
Telephone: 512-343-6248
Fax: 512-343-0121
Mailing Address: P.O. Box 1588, Austin, Texas, 78767

C. Dean Davis
Fred E. Davis
Alexis J. Fuller, Jr.
Ruth Russell-Schafer
Michael L. Neely
Brian Gregory Jackson
Monte F. James

Bill Cline, Jr.
Mark Alan Keene
Kenda B. Dalrymple
Marian J. Wu
Mark S. La Spina

For Complete List of Firm Personnel, See General Section

For full biographical listings, see the Martindale-Hubbell Law Directory

DAVIS & WILKERSON, P.C. (AV)

1801 South Mopac, Suite 300, P.O. Box 2283, 78768-2283
Telephone: 512-482-0614
Fax: 512-482-0342
Email: dwlaw@dwlaw.com *URL:* http://www.dwlaw.com
Alpine Office: 1110 East Holland, P.O. Box 777.
Telephone: 915-837-5547.

David M. Davis
Steven R. Welch
Glen Wilkerson
David A. Wright
Leonard W. Woods
Kevin A. Reed
J. Mark Holbrook
Brian E. Riewe
Brian McElroy
Robert L. Hargett
Michael Wilson
Frances W. Hamermesh
Fletcher H. Brown

Jennifer B. Claymon
David M. Coffey
Hollis Hudson Gaston
Steven C. Levatino
Diana Maldonado
Erin E. Matherne
Joel S. Pace
Stephen G. Wohleb
Michael P. Young

OF COUNSEL

Pete P. Gallego (Resident, Alpine Office)
Peter R. Meeker

For full biographical listings, see the Martindale-Hubbell Law Directory

THOMAS GEORGE, P.C. (AV)

2310 Westgate Building, 1122 Colorado Street, 78701
Telephone: 512-477-9651
Fax: 512-477-6586
Email: tomwgeorge@aol.com

Thomas William George

For full biographical listings, see the Martindale-Hubbell Law Directory

THOMPSON & KNIGHT L.L.P.—*Continued*

San Pedro Garza Garcia, Nuevo León, Mexico Office: Edificio Losoles PD-4, Av. Lázaro Cárdenas No. 2400 Pte., C.P. 66220.
Telephone: (52-8) 363-0096.
Telecopy: (52-8) 363-3067.

PARTNERS

Susan Monaco
William R. Van Wagner
Norman R. Rogers
Bill R. Womble

For Complete List of Firm Personnel, See General Section

For full biographical listings, see the Martindale-Hubbell Law Directory

*FORT WORTH,** Tarrant Co.

LAW OFFICES OF PATRICK H. O'NEILL (AV)

110 West 7th Street, Suite 1100, 76102
Telephone: 817-878-3333
Fax: 817-878-3672

Patrick H. O'Neill

James L. Jackson, Jr.
Glenn T. Lupo

For full biographical listings, see the Martindale-Hubbell Law Directory

THOMPSON & KNIGHT L.L.P. (AV)

(Attorneys and Counselors)
801 Cherry Street, Suite 1600, 76102
Telephone: 817-347-1700
Telecopy: 817-347-1799
URL: http://www.tklaw.com
Dallas, Texas Office: 1700 Pacific Avenue, Suite 3300, 75201.
Telephone: 214-969-1700.
Telecopy: 214-969-1751.
Telex: 732298.
Austin, Texas Office: 1200 San Jacinto Center, 98 San Jacinto Boulevard, 78701.
Telephone: 512-469-6100.
Telecopy: 512-469-6180.
Houston, Texas Office: Thompson Knight Brown Parker & Leahy L.L.P., 1200 Smith Street, Suite 3600, 77002-4595.
Telephone: 713-654-8111.
Telecopier: 713-654-1871.
San Pedro Garza Garcia, Nuevo León, Mexico Office: Edificio Losoles PD-4, Av. Lázaro Cárdenas No. 2400 Pte., C.P. 66220.
Telephone: (52-8) 363-0096.
Telecopy: (52-8) 363-3067.

PARTNERS

R Gordon Appleman
Jennifer Pettijohn Henry
E. Michael Sheehan

For Complete List of Firm Personnel, See General Section

For full biographical listings, see the Martindale-Hubbell Law Directory

*HOUSTON,** Harris Co.

PATRICIA KAY DUBE, P.C. (AV)

4140 Bank of America Center, 700 Louisiana Street, 77002
Telephone: 713-225-2297
Facsimile: 713-225-2298
Email: pkdube@wt.net *URL:* http://www.lawyers.com/dubelaw

Patricia Kay Dube
Clare I. Vetters
Lee Broze

OF COUNSEL

Alan J. Winters
Harold J. Eisenman

For full biographical listings, see the Martindale-Hubbell Law Directory

THOMPSON KNIGHT BROWN PARKER & LEAHY L.L.P. (AV)

A Registered Limited Liability Partnership including Professional Corporations
(Attorneys and Counselors)
1200 Smith Street, Suite 3600, 77002-4595
Telephone: 713-654-8111
Telecopier: 713-654-1871
URL: http://www.tklaw.com
Dallas, Texas Office: Thompson & Knight L.L.P., 1700 Pacific Avenue, Suite 3300, 75201.
Telephone: 214-969-1700.
Telecopy: 214-969-1751.
Telex: 732298.
Austin, Texas Office: Thompson & Knight L.L.P., 1200 San Jacinto Center, 98 San Jacinto Boulevard, 78701.
Telephone: 512-469-6100.
Telecopy: 512-469-6180.
Fort Worth, Texas Office: Thompson & Knight L.L.P., 801 Cherry Street, Suite 1600, 76102.
Telephone: 817-347-1700.
Telecopy: 817-347-1799.

(See Next Column)

San Pedro Garza Garcia, Nuevo León, Mexico Office: Thompson & Knight L.L.P., Edificio Losoles PD-4, Av. Lázaro Cárdenas No. 2400 PTE., C.P. 66220.
Telephone: (52-8) 363-0096.
Telecopy: (52-8) 363-3067.

PARTNER

Debbi M. Johnstone

For Complete List of Firm Personnel, See General Section

For full biographical listings, see the Martindale-Hubbell Law Directory

*MIDLAND,** Midland Co.

KERR & WARD, L.L.P. (AV)

500 W. Texas, Suite 1310, Drawer 2858, 79702
Telephone: 915-684-9990
Fax: 915-684-9997
Email: info@kerr-ward.com *URL:* http://www.kerr-ward.com

OF COUNSEL

Wm. Monroe Kerr
Theodore M. Kerr

PARTNERS

Harris E. Kerr
William M. Kerr, Jr.
William E. Ward
Brian T. McLaughlin
James Devin Alsup

For full biographical listings, see the Martindale-Hubbell Law Directory

*SAN ANTONIO,** Bexar Co.

COX & SMITH INCORPORATED (AV)

112 East Pecan Street, Suite 1800, 78205-1521
Telephone: 210-554-5500
Fax: 210-226-8395
Email: info@coxsmith.com *URL:* http://www.coxsmith.com

Dan G. Webster, III
J. Daniel Harkins
James B. Smith, Jr.
Steven A. Elder
David L. Butler
Peter H. Wickersham
Lisa F. Sutker

OF COUNSEL

Joe R. McFarlane, Jr.

Representative Clients: Abraxas Petroleum Corporation; Cancer Therapy & Research Center; City of San Antonio; International Bancshares Corp.; Kinetic Concepts, Inc.; San Antonio Federal Credit Union; Solo Serve Corporation.

For Complete List of Firm Personnel, See General Section

For full biographical listings, see the Martindale-Hubbell Law Directory

JACKSON WALKER L.L.P. (AV)

112 E. Pecan Street, Suite 2100, 78205-1521
Telephone: 210-978-7700
Fax: 210-978-7790
URL: http://www.jw.com
Austin, Texas Office: 100 Congress Avenue, Suite 1100.
Telephone: 512-236-2000.
Fax: 512-236-2002.
Dallas, Texas Office: 901 Main Street, Suite 6000.
Telephone: 214-953-6000.
Fax: 214-953-5822.
Fort Worth, Texas Office: 301 Commerce Street, Suite 2400.
Telephone: 817-334-7200.
Fax: 817-334-7290.
Houston, Texas Office: 1100 Louisiana, Suite 4200.
Telephone: 713-752-4200.
Fax: 713-752-4221.
Richardson, Texas Office: 2435 North Central Expressway, Suite 600.
Telephone: 972-671-2560.
Fax: 972-671-2566.
San Angelo, Texas Office: 225 West Beauregard Avenue.
Telephone: 915-481-2550.
Fax: 915-481-2552.

MEMBERS OF FIRM

Janet L. King
Edgar C. Morrison, Jr.

For Complete List of Firm Personnel, See General Section

For full biographical listings, see the Martindale-Hubbell Law Directory

*TYLER,** Smith Co.

RAMEY & FLOCK, A PROFESSIONAL CORPORATION (AV)

500 First Place, P.O. Box 629, 75710
Telephone: 903-597-3301
Telecopier: 903-597-2413
Email: Ramey@Ramey-Flock.com *URL:* http://www.RameyFlock.com

(See Next Column)

BENNETT BIGELOW & LEEDOM P.S., *Seattle—Continued*

Teresa V. Bigelow
Stephen I. Pentz
Carla M. DewBerry
Anne M. Redman (Managing Partner)
Carol S. Gown
David B. Robbins
Sanford E. Pitler
Elizabeth A. Leedom
William J. Leedom
Michael Madden

OF COUNSEL

David A. Bennett

Teri M. Dettmer
Susan L. Fine
Mark C. Gary
Wade J. Harman
Carol Sue Janes
Elizabeth A. McFall
Bruce W. Megard, Jr.
Karen Olson Rasmussen
Karen L. Tyler
Vickie J. Williams

Reference: US Bank.

For full biographical listings, see the Martindale-Hubbell Law Directory

TARUTIS & BARRON, P.S. (AV)

Bank of California, Suite 3900, 900 Fourth Avenue, 98164
Telephone: 206-223-1515
Fax: 206-223-1325

Gerald R. Tarutis
Kathryn R. Barron

Joline M. Recknaged
Laura E Twitchell

For full biographical listings, see the Martindale-Hubbell Law Directory

WEST VIRGINIA

*CHARLESTON,** Kanawha Co.

ALLEN GUTHRIE & McHUGH (AV)

1300 Bank One Center, P.O. Box 3394, 25333
Telephone: 304-345-7250
Telecopier: 304-345-9941
Email: kagwv@kagww.com

George G. Guthrie
Robert B. Allen
Thomas E. McHugh
R. Terrance Rodgers
S. Benjamin Bryant
Wm. Scott Wickline
Pamela Lynn Kandzari
James P. McHugh

John K. McHugh
Charles W. Pace, Jr.

For full biographical listings, see the Martindale-Hubbell Law Directory

JACKSON & KELLY (AV)

1600 Laidley Tower, P.O. Box 553, 25322
Telephone: 304-340-1000
Fax: 304-340-1130
Email: info@jacksonkelly.com *URL:* http://www.jacksonkelly.com
Martinsburg, West Virginia Office: 300 Foxcroft Avenue, P.O. Box 1068.
Telephone: 304-263-8800.
Fax: 304-263-7110.
Morgantown, West Virginia Office: 6000 Hampton Center, P.O. Box 619.
Telephone: 304-599-3000.
Fax: 304-285-2040.
New Martinsville, West Virginia Office: 256 Russell Avenue, P.O. Box 68.
Telephone: 304-455-1751.
Fax: 304-455-6314.
Parkersburg, West Virginia Office: 412 Market Street, Suite 202, P.O. Box 1144.
Telephone: 304-424-3490.
Fax: 304-424-3499.
Fairmont, West Virginia Office: 1000 Technology Drive, Suite 1310.
Telephone: 304-368-2000.
Fax: 304-368-2020.
Lexington, Kentucky Office: 175 East Main Street, Suite 500, P.O. Box 2150.
Telephone: 606-255-9500.
Fax: 606-281-6478.
Washington, D. C. Office: 2401 Pennsylvania Avenue, N.W., Suite 400.
Telephone: 202-973-0200.
Fax: 202-973-0232.
Denver, Colorado Office: Suite 2710, 1660 Lincoln Street.
Telephone: 303-390-0003.
Fax: 303-390-0040.
Wheeling, West Virginia Office: 1144 Market Street.
Telephone: 304-233-4000.
Fax: 304-233-4077.

(See Next Column)

MEMBERS OF FIRM

W. Warren Upton
William A. Hoskins, III (Administrative Manager, Lexington, Kentucky Office)
Taunja Willis Miller
James W. Thomas
Larry W. Blalock (Administrative Manager, New Martinsville and Wheeling, West Virginia Offices)
Thomas J. Hurney, Jr.
William E. Doll, Jr. (Resident, Lexington, Kentucky Office)

ASSOCIATE

Jacqueline Syers Duncan (Resident, Lexington, Kentucky Office)

Representative Clients: Thomas Memorial Hospital; Camden-Clark Memorial Hospital; Wetzel County Hospital; Preston Memorial Hospital; Shawnee Hills, Inc.; St. Joseph's Hospital; Res-Care, Inc.; Genisis Affiliated Health Services, Inc.

For Complete List of Firm Personnel, See General Section

For full biographical listings, see the Martindale-Hubbell Law Directory

HUNTINGTON, Cabell & Wayne Cos.

BAKER, LANCIANESE, CAMPBELL & CONATY (AV)

The River Tower, 1108 Third Avenue, Suite 300, 25701-1578
Telephone: 304-522-6906
Facsimile: 304-522-6910
Email: BLCC@BLCCLAW.COM *URL:* http://www.BLCCLAW.COM
Washington, D.C. Office: 1090 Vermont Avenue, N.W. Suite 800.
Telephone: 202-966-1500.
Fax: 202-966-7075. E-Mail: BLCC@BLCCLAW.COM.
Lexington, Kentucky Office: 2265 Harrodsburg Road, Suite 200, 40504-3517.
Telephone: 606-278-0297.
Fax: 206-278-0334. E-Mail: BLCC@BLCCLAW.COM.

Roy D. Baker, Jr.
Richard L. Lancianese
David L. Campbell
Brian P. Conaty
Janice P. Epperly

OF COUNSEL

Margaret M. Brizzolara (Not admitted in WV)

For full biographical listings, see the Martindale-Hubbell Law Directory

*MORGANTOWN,** Monongalia Co.

THE FUSCO LEGAL GROUP, L.C. (AV)

2400 Cranberry Square, 26505-9209
Telephone: 304-594-1000
Telecopier: 304-594-1181
URL: http://www.fuscolegalgroup.com
Email: fnlaw@wvlaw.com *URL:* http://www.wvlaw.com

Andrew G. Fusco

William J. Leon, Jr.

For Complete List of Firm Personnel, See General Section

For full biographical listings, see the Martindale-Hubbell Law Directory

WISCONSIN

*MADISON,** Dane Co.

QUARLES & BRADY LLP (AV)

Firstar Plaza, One South Pinckney Street, P.O. Box 2113, 53701-2113
Telephone: 608-251-5000
Fax: 608-251-9166
URL: http://www.quarles.com
Milwaukee, Wisconsin Office: 411 East Wisconsin Avenue, 53202-4497.
Telephone: 414-277-5000.
Fax: 414-271-3552.
West Palm Beach, Florida Office: 222 Lakeview Avenue, 4th Floor, 33401.
Telephone: 561-653-5000.
Fax: 561-653-5333.
Naples, Florida Office: Barnett Center, 4501 Tamiami Trail North, Suite 300, 34103-3060.
Telephone: 941-262-5959.
Fax: 941-434-4999.
Phoenix, Arizona Office: One Camelback Building, One East Camelback Road, Suite 400, 85012-1649.
Telephone: 602-230-5500.
Fax: 602-230-5598.
Chicago, Illinois Office: Quarles & Brady LLC, Citicorp Center, 500 West Madison Street, Suite 3700.
Telephone: 312-715-5000.
Fax: 312-715-5155.

(See Next Column)

QUARLES & BRADY LLP—*Continued*

PARTNERS

John S. Holbrook, Jr.
Michael S. Weiden
Anthony H. Driessen
Nicholas J. Seay
John T. Whiting
Ralph V. Topinka

For Complete List of Firm Personnel, See General Section

For full biographical listings, see the Martindale-Hubbell Law Directory

*MILWAUKEE,** Milwaukee Co.

BECK, CHAET, MOLONY & BAMBERGER, S.C. (AV)

Two Plaza East, 330 East Kilbourn Avenue, Suite 1085, 53202
Telephone: 414-273-4200
Fax: 414-273-7786
Email: bcmb@execpc.com *URL:* http://www.bcmblaw.com
Madison, Wisconsin Office: 44 East Mifflin Street, Suite 304.
Telephone: 608-255-1140.
Fax: 608-255-0160.

Arthur E. Beck
Barry L. Chaet
Maureen A. Molony (Resident, Madison, Wisconsin Office)
Michael Bamberger
E. Vanessa Jones
Katherine L. Williams
Christopher J. Johnson
Kevin L. Keeler
Joshua B. Levy
LouAnn Koval
Daniel M. Lowndes
Edward B. Matkom

Drew J. Cochrane

OF COUNSEL

Robert P. Mandel

For full biographical listings, see the Martindale-Hubbell Law Directory

EHLINGER & KRILL, S.C. (AV)

316 North Milwaukee Street, Suite 410, 53202-5803
Telephone: 414-272-8085
Facsimile: 414-272-8290
Email: ehlinger@execpc.com

Ralph J. Ehlinger
R. Jeffrey Krill

For full biographical listings, see the Martindale-Hubbell Law Directory

MEISSNER TIERNEY FISHER & NICHOLS S.C. (AV)

The Milwaukee Center, 111 East Kilbourn Avenue, 19th Floor, 53202-6622
Telephone: 414-273-1300
Facsimile: 414-273-5840
URL: http://www.mtfn.com

Joseph E. Tierney III
Dennis L. Fisher
Thomas J. Nichols
Randal J. Brotherhood
Michael J. Cohen

Michael A. Kallas
Justin B. Nelsen
Jeffrey A. Ellis
Adam J. Tutaj

For full biographical listings, see the Martindale-Hubbell Law Directory

QUARLES & BRADY LLP (AV)

411 East Wisconsin Avenue, 53202-4497
Telephone: 414-277-5000
Fax: 414-271-3552
URL: http://www.quarles.com
Madison, Wisconsin Office: Firstar Plaza, One South Pinckney Street, P.O. Box 2113, 53701-2113.
Telephone: 608-251-5000.
Fax: 608-251-9166.
West Palm Beach, Florida Office: 222 Lakeview Avenue, 4th Floor, 33401.
Telephone: 561-653-5000.
Fax: 561-653-5333.
Naples, Florida Office: Barnett Center, 4501 Tamiami Trail North, Suite 300, 34103-3060.
Telephone: 941-262-5959.
Fax: 941-434-4999.
Phoenix, Arizona Office: One Camelback Building, One East Camelback Road, Suite 400, 85012-1649.
Telephone: 602-230-5500.
Fax: 602-230-5598.
Chicago, Illinois Office: Quarles & Brady LLC, Citicorp Center, 500 West Madison Street, Suite 3700.
Telephone: 312-715-5000.
Fax: 312-715-5155.

MEMBERS OF FIRM

(ALPHABETICALLY BY YEAR OF ADMISSION TO BAR)

Michael S. Weiden (Resident, Madison Office)
Anthony H. Driessen
James D. Friedman
Alyce C. Katayama
Warren S. Blumenthal
Ralph V. Topinka (Resident, Madison Office)
Sheila M. Reynolds

(See Next Column)

OF COUNSEL

Thad F. Kryshak
Thomas W. O'Brien

ASSOCIATE

Lisa A. Lyons

For Complete List of Firm Personnel, See General Section

For full biographical listings, see the Martindale-Hubbell Law Directory

CANADA
ALBERTA

*CALGARY,** Calgary Jud. Dist.

BENNETT JONES (AV)

4500 Bankers Hall East, 855-2nd Street S.W., T2P 4K7
Telephone: 403-298-3100
Facsimile: 403-265-7219
Email: firmwatch@bennettjones.ca *URL:* http://www.bennettjones.ca
Edmonton, Alberta Office: 1000, 10035-105 Street.
Telephone: 780-421-8133.
Facsimile: 780-421-7951.
Toronto, Ontario Office: 3400 1 First Canadian Place, P.O. Box 130.
Telephone: 416-863-1200.
Facsimile: 416-863-1716.

MEMBER OF FIRM

John G. Martland, Q.C.

For Complete List of Firm Personnel, See General Section

For full biographical listings, see the Martindale-Hubbell Law Directory

CANADA
NEWFOUNDLAND

*ST. JOHN'S,**

MCINNES COOPER (AV)

Barristers, Solicitors & Trade Mark Agents
Baine Johnston Centre, 5th Floor, 10 Fort William Place, P.O. Box 5939, A1C 5X4
Telephone: 709-722-8735
Telecopier: 709-722-1763
Email: mcrsj@mcrlaw.com *URL:* http://www.mcrlaw.com
Halifax, Nova Scotia Office: Summit Place, 1601 Lower Water Street, P.O. Box 730, B3J 2V1.
Telephone: 902-425-6500.
Fax: 902-425-6350. Email: mcrhfx@mcrlaw.com.
Moncton, New Brunswick Office: Place Moncton Place, 655 Main Street, P.O. Box 1368, E1C 8T6.
Telephone: 506-857-8970.
Fax: 506-857-4095. Email: mcrmctn@mcrlaw.com.
Charlottetown, Prince Edward Island Office: BDC Place, Suite 620, 119 Kent Street, C1A 1N3.
Telephone: 902-368-8473.
Fax: 902-368-8346. Email: mcrpei@mcrlaw.com.
Fredericton, New Brunswick Office: Suite 600, 570 Queen Street, P.O. Box 610.
Telephone: 506-458-8572.
Fax: 506-458-9903. Email: mcrfton@mcrlaw.com.

PARTNER

Denis J. Mahoney

For Complete List of Firm Personnel, See General Section

For full biographical listings, see the Martindale-Hubbell Law Directory

CANADA ONTARIO

*TORONTO,** Regional Munic. of Toronto

BORDEN & ELLIOT (AV)

Barristers & Solicitors
Scotia Plaza, 40 King Street West, M5H 3Y4
Telephone: 416-367-6000
Telecopier: 416-367-6749
Email: info@borden.com *URL:* http://www.borden.com
Ottawa, Ontario Office: Borden Elliot Scott & Aylen, 1000-60 Rue Queen Street.
Telephone: 613-237-5160; 800-661-4237. General
Facsimile: 613-230-8842. IP Dept.
Facsimile: 613-787-3558. Email: ottinfo@scottaylen.com. URL: http://www.borden.com.

Rino A. Stradiotto, Q.C.

For Complete List of Firm Personnel, See General Section

For full biographical listings, see the Martindale-Hubbell Law Directory

CANADA PRINCE EDWARD ISLAND

*CHARLOTTETOWN,** Queen's Co.

McINNES COOPER (AV⊤)

Barristers, Solicitors & Trade Mark Agents
BDC Place, Suite 620, 119 Kent Street, C1A 1N3
Telephone: 902-368-8473
Fax: 902-368-8346
Email: mcrpei@mcrlaw.com *URL:* http://www.mcrlaw.com
Halifax, Nova Scotia Office: Summit Place, 1601 Lower Water Street, P.O. Box 730, B3J 2V1.
Telephone: 902-425-6500.
Fax: 902-425-6350. Email: mcrhfx@mcrlaw.com.
St. John's, Newfoundland Office: Baine Johnston Centre, 5th Floor, 10 Fort William Place, P.O. Box 5939, A1C 5X4.
Telephone: 709-722-8735.
Telecopier: 709-722-1763. Email: mcrsj@mcrlaw.com.
Moncton, New Brunswick Office: Place Moncton Place, 655 Main Street, P.O. Box 1368, E1C 8T6.
Telephone: 506-857-8970.
Fax: 506-857-4095. Email: mcrmctn@mcrlaw.com.
Fredericton, New Brunswick Office: Suite 600, 570 Queen Street, P.O. Box 610.
Telephone: 506-458-8572.
Fax: 506-458-9903. Email: mcrfton@mcrlaw.com.

PARTNER

Mark Ledwell

ASSOCIATES

Kevin J. Kiley — Kim Petrie

For Complete List of Firm Personnel, See General Section

For full biographical listings, see the Martindale-Hubbell Law Directory

CANADA QUEBEC

*MONTREAL,** Montreal Dist.

McMASTER GERVAIS (AV)

A General Partnership
1000 de La Gauchetière Street West, Suite 900, H3B 5H4
Telephone: 514-879-1212
Fax: 514-954-1905
Email: info@mcmastergervais.com *URL:* http://www.mcmastergervais.com

MEMBERS OF FIRM

Alex K. Paterson, O.C., O.Q., Q.C.
Robert E. Charbonneau
Philippe C. Vachon
Thomas M. Davis
Janet Casey
Rosaire S. Houde
Stéphanie Moffatt
William E. Stavert
Timothy R. Carsley
Jean-René Ranger
Michael Patry
Yves A. Dubois
Jacques Gauthier
André Royer
Manon Gauthier
Geneviève Bergeron

COUNSEL

Bartha M. Knoppers

For Complete List of Firm Personnel, See General Section

For full biographical listings, see the Martindale-Hubbell Law Directory

CANADA SASKATCHEWAN

*REGINA,** Regina Jud. Centre

MacPHERSON LESLIE & TYERMAN (AV)

1500-1874 Scarth Street, S4P 4E9
Telephone: 306-347-8000
Telecopier: 306-352-5250
Email: mltreg@mlt.com
Saskatoon, Saskatchewan Office: 1500-410 22nd Street East, S7K 5T6.
Telephone: 306-975-7100.
Telecopier: 306-975-7145.

MEMBER OF FIRM

Robert G. Richards, Q.C.

ASSOCIATE

R. M. Louise Simard, Q.C.

For Complete List of Firm Personnel, See General Section

For full biographical listings, see the Martindale-Hubbell Law Directory

IMMIGRATION AND NATURALIZATION

MINNESOTA

*MINNEAPOLIS,** Hennepin Co.

BORENE LAW FIRM, P.A. (AV)

4602 IDS Center, 55402
Telephone: 612-321-0082
Fax: 612-332-8368
URL: http://www.borene.com
Rochester Office: Kahler Mezzanine, 20 Second Avenue S.
Telephone: 507-287-9761.

Scott M. Borene
Renee Mueller Steinle
Robin R. Spencer

Special Immigration Counsel For: Mayo Clinic/Mayo Foundation; Medtronic, Inc.; University of Minnesota; Unisys Corporation; ACT/American College Testing; Schwan's Sales Enterprises; North Dakota State University; Luther College; Trinity Medical Center; St. Paul Pioneer Press.

For full biographical listings, see the Martindale-Hubbell Law Directory

INGBER & ARONSON, P.A. (AV)

Suite 506, 1221 Nicollet Mall, 55403
Telephone: 612-339-0517
Fax: 612-349-6059
Email: immigration@Immlawyer.com *URL:* http://www.ilw.com/ingber/

Jerome Ingber
Robert Aronson

LEGAL SUPPORT PERSONNEL

Valerie L. Long (Administrator)

For full biographical listings, see the Martindale-Hubbell Law Directory

MISSOURI

ST. LOUIS, (Independent City)

BROWN & WICHMER, P.C. (AV)

7700 Clayton Road, Suite 306, 63117
Telephone: 314-646-1144
Fax: 314-646-8855
URL: http://www.lawyers.com/immigrationlawyers

Suzanne Brown
Timothy E. Wichmer
Susan Cho Figenshau

For full biographical listings, see the Martindale-Hubbell Law Directory

MONTANA

*BILLINGS,** Yellowstone Co.

CROWLEY, HAUGHEY, HANSON, TOOLE & DIETRICH, P.L.L.P. (AV)

500 Transwestern II, 490 North 31st Street, P.O. Box 2529, 59103
Telephone: 406-252-3441
Fax: 406-259-4159
Email: crowley@crowleylaw.com
Helena, Montana Office: IBM Building, 100 North Park Avenue, Suite 300, 59601.
Telephone: 406-449-4165.
Fax: 406-449-5149.
Kalispell, Montana Office: 431 1st Avenue West, 59901.
Telephone: 406-752-6644.
Fax: 406-752-5108.
Williston, North Dakota Office: 113 East Broadway, 58801.
Telephone: 701-572-2200.
Fax: 701-572-7072.

MEMBER OF FIRM

James P. Sites

Representative Clients: Norfolk Energy, Inc.; Billings Clinic; Billings Cardiology Associates, P.C.; Dutch Brothers Bakery.

For Complete List of Firm Personnel, See General Section

For full biographical listings, see the Martindale-Hubbell Law Directory

*HELENA,** Lewis and Clark Co.

BROWNING, KALECZYC, BERRY & HOVEN, P.C. (AV)

139 North Last Chance Gulch, P.O. Box 1697, 59624
Telephone: 406-443-6820
Telefax: 406-443-6882
Email: BKBH@BKBH.COM *URL:* http://www.BKBH.com

R. Stephen Browning
Stanley T. Kaleczyc

Mary K. Giddings

Representative Clients: Foster Wheeler; Montana Hospital Association; Watkins and Shepard Trucking, Inc.

For full biographical listings, see the Martindale-Hubbell Law Directory

NEBRASKA

*OMAHA,** Douglas Co.

KRIEGER & KRIEGER (AV)

Suite 302, 9290 West Dodge Road, 68114
Telephone: 402-392-1280
Fax: 402-392-1563
Email: kriegers@compuserve.com

MEMBERS OF FIRM

Stanley A. Krieger
M. Angela Krieger

Reference: Norwest Bank Omaha, N.A.

For full biographical listings, see the Martindale-Hubbell Law Directory

NEVADA

*LAS VEGAS,** Clark Co.

ALVERSON, TAYLOR, MORTENSEN, NELSON & SANDERS (AV)

7401 West Charleston Boulevard, 89117
Telephone: 702-384-7000
FAX: 702-385-7000
Email: alverson@intermind.net
Reno, Nevada Office: 245 East Liberty, Suite 520, 89505.
Telephone: 775-329-0473.
Fax: 775-329-3303.

MEMBERS OF FIRM

J. Bruce Alverson
Eric K. Taylor
David J. Mortensen
Erven T. Nelson
LeAnn Sanders

OF COUNSEL

Jack C. Cherry
Kurt D. Anderson
Philip C. Van Alstyne

ASSOCIATES

Rebecca Hopkins Miller
Sandra Smagac
Victoria L. Nelson
Aaron D. Lovaas
Diane Obritsch
Michael A. Olsen
Randal D. Shimon
Catherine A. Olendorff
Monica L. Pierce
Gabriel D. Lither
Kurt R. Bonds
Darius F. Rafie
Mark J. King, IV
Shell L. Mercer
Carrie S. Bourdeau
Jason Lane Earnest
Nathan R. Reinmiller
Donn C. Alexander
Afshin Tadayon
Eric O. Freeman
Lindsay L. Stadtlander
Julie M. Sueoka

Representative Clients: Citibank (Nevada), N.A.; First Interstate Bank of Nevada; The CIT Group; Federal Deposit Insurance Corporation/Resolution Trust Corporation (TRTC); General Electric Company; St. Paul Fire & Marine Insurance Co.; The Doctors Company; University Medical Center of So. Nevada; Chubb Group of Insurance Companies.

For full biographical listings, see the Martindale-Hubbell Law Directory

NEW JERSEY

EDISON, Middlesex Co.

WONG FLEMING, P.C. (AV)

Edison Square West, Suite 1050, 2035 Lincoln Highway, 08817
Telephone: 732-248-4111
Fax: 732-248-8665
Mailing Address: P.O. Box 985, 08818-0985
Email: info@wongfleming.com *URL:* http://www.wongfleming.com
Philadelphia, Pennsylvania Office: 230 South Broad Street, Suite 601, 19102.
Telephone: 215-546-2776.
Fax: 215-546-3206.
New York, New York Office: The Empire State Building, 350 Fifth Avenue, Suite 5411, 10118.
Telephone: 212-643-9668.
Fax: 212-643-9640.

Linda Wong
Daniel C. Fleming
Katherine C. Lee

Andrew J. Bayne
Stephen Tsai
Theresa Homisak
Paul J. Young
Wenjun Zhang (Not admitted in NJ)
Tanya E. Lawrence
Fei F. Lam

For full biographical listings, see the Martindale-Hubbell Law Directory

*NEWARK,** Essex Co.

MEYNER AND LANDIS (AV)

One Gateway Center, Suite 2500, 07102-5311
Telephone: 973-624-2800
Fax: 973-624-0356
Email: attys@meyner.com *URL:* http://www.meyner.com

Robert B. Meyner (1908-1990)
Edwin C. Landis, Jr.
John N. Malyska
William J. Fiore
Anthony F. Siliato
Francis R. Perkins
Howard O. Thompson
Scott T. McCleary
Linda Townley Snyder
William H. Schmidt, Jr.
David B. Grantz

For full biographical listings, see the Martindale-Hubbell Law Directory

RUBIN & DORNBAUM (AV)

Suite 1300, 744 Broad Street, 07102
Telephone: 973-623-4444
Fax: 973-623-6839
Email: 73032.51@compuserve.com

MEMBERS

Edwin R. Rubin
Neil S. Dornbaum

OF COUNSEL

Kathleen M. Peregoy

For full biographical listings, see the Martindale-Hubbell Law Directory

NEW YORK

*BUFFALO,** Erie Co.

HODGSON, RUSS, ANDREWS, WOODS & GOODYEAR, LLP (AV)

A Registered Limited Liability Partnership including Professional Associations
One M & T Plaza, Suite 2000, 14203
Telephone: 716-856-4000
Fax: 716-849-0349
Email: info@hodgsonruss.com *URL:* www.hodgsonruss.com
Albany, New York Office: Three City Square, 12207.
Telephone: 518-465-2333.
Fax: 518-465-1567.
Boca Raton, Florida Office: Suite 400, 2000 Glades Road, 33431.
Telephone: 561-394-0500.
Fax: 561-394-3862.
Toronto, Ontario, Canada Office: 150 King Street West, Suite 2309, M5H 1J9, P.O. Box 30.
Telephone: 416-595-5100.
Fax: 416-595-5021.
New York, New York Office: 65 East 55th Street, 10th Floor, 10022.
Telephone: 212-751-4300.
Fax: 212-751-0928.
Gloversville, New York Office: 6 Fremont Street, 12078.
Telephone: 518-725-6347.
Fax: 518-773-7350.

(See Next Column)

Newark, New Jersey Office: One Gateway Center, Suite 2600, 07102.
Telephone: 973-645-0577.
Fax: 973-645-0551.

MEMBER OF FIRM
(ALPHABETICALLY BY YEAR OF ADMISSION TO BAR)

Lance J. Madden

SENIOR COUNSEL

James G. Meagley

ASSOCIATES
(ALPHABETICALLY BY YEAR OF ADMISSION TO BAR)

Alice F. Jacobs
Margot L. Watt
Rosanna Berardi (Not admitted in NY)

For Complete List of Firm Personnel, See General Section

For full biographical listings, see the Martindale-Hubbell Law Directory

*NEW YORK,** New York Co.

LAW OFFICES OF FRANCES C. BERGER (AV)

335 Broadway, Suite 1103, 10013
Telephone: 212-925-6688
Fax: 212-925-6987
Email: franberger@compuserve.com

Laura L. Vea

For full biographical listings, see the Martindale-Hubbell Law Directory

LAW OFFICES OF RICHARD S. GOLDSTEIN, P.C. (AV)

145 West 57th Street, 10019
Telephone: 212-957-0500
Fax: 212-957-2020
Email: lawoffices@lorsg.com *URL:* http://www.lawyers.com/richardsgoldsteinpc
London, England Office: 96A Mount Street, First Floor, Mayfair, London W1Y 5HG.
Telephone: +44-(0) 207-499-8200.
Fax: +44-(0) 207-499-8300. Email: richardgoldstein@goldsteinvisa.com

Richard S. Goldstein

Stephen B. Horton (Not admitted in NY)
Tammy M. Lee
Sara B. Levin
Anastasia Tonello

For full biographical listings, see the Martindale-Hubbell Law Directory

ALLEN E. KAYE, P.C. (AV)

11 Park Place, 10007
Telephone: 212-964-5858
Fax: 212-608-3734
URL: http://www.aeklaw.com

Allen E. Kaye

Louise S. Cavanaugh (Not admitted in NY)

OF COUNSEL

Ira Fieldsteel
Sandi DiMola (Not admitted in NY)

For full biographical listings, see the Martindale-Hubbell Law Directory

NORTH CAROLINA

*CHARLOTTE,** Mecklenburg Co.

DOZIER, MILLER, POLLARD & MURPHY (AV)

Cameron Brown Building, 301 South McDowell Street, Suite 700, 28204
Telephone: 704-372-6373
Fax: 704-347-0674
URL: http://www.dmpm.com

MEMBERS OF FIRM

W. Joseph Dozier, Jr.
R. Craig Miller, Jr.
Scott T. Pollard
Gary L. Murphy
William Patrick Hobson
Timothy H. Graham
George N. Miller
Richard S. Gordon
Thomas J. Falish
Kristin L. Smith

For full biographical listings, see the Martindale-Hubbell Law Directory

*RALEIGH,** Wake Co.

ALLEN AND PINNIX, P.A. (AV)

333 Fayetteville Street, Mall, Suite 1200, 27601
Telephone: 919-755-0505
Facsimile: 919-829-8098

(See Next Column)

ALLEN AND PINNIX P.A.—*Continued*

John L. Pinnix
C. Lynn Calder
Alice S. Glover

For full biographical listings, see the Martindale-Hubbell Law Directory

OHIO

*CLEVELAND,** Cuyahoga Co.

BAKER & HOSTETLER LLP (AV)

3200 National City Center, 1900 East Ninth Street, 44114-3485
Telephone: 216-621-0200
Telecopier: 216-696-0740
TWX: 810 421 8375
RCA Telex: 215032
To contact an attorney on the Internet use first initial and surname followed by @baker-hostetler.com
URL: http://www.bakerlaw.com
In Cincinnati, Ohio: 312 Walnut Street, Suite 2650.
Telephone: 513-929-3400.
In Columbus, Ohio: Capitol Square, Suite 2100, 65 East State Street.
Telephone: 614-228-1541.
In Denver, Colorado: 303 East 17th Avenue, Suite 1100.
Telephone: 303-861-0600.
In Houston, Texas: 1000 Louisiana, Suite 2000.
Telephone: 713-751-1600.
In Beverly Hills, California: 9150 Wilshire Boulevard, Suite 205.
Telephone: 310-385-7500.
In Long Beach, California: 300 Oceangate, Suite 620.
Telephone: 562-432-2827.
In Los Angeles, California: 600 Wilshire Boulevard.
Telephone: 213-624-2400.
In Orlando, Florida: SunBank Center, Suite 2300, 200 South Orange Avenue.
Telephone: 407-649-4000.
In Washington, D.C.: Washington Square, Suite 1100, 1050 Connecticut Avenue, N.W.
Telephone: 202-861-1500.

PARTNERS

John H. M. Fenix
John H. Wilharm, Jr.

For Complete List of Firm Personnel, See General Section

For full biographical listings, see the Martindale-Hubbell Law Directory

MARGARET W. WONG & ASSOCIATES (AV)

1128 Standard Building, 44113
Telephone: 216-566-9908
Fax: 216-566-1125
URL: http://www.lawyers.com/wonglaw
Email: wong@immwong.com *URL:* http://www.imwong.com

ASSOCIATES

Michael H. Sharon
William J. Nickerson, Jr. (Not admitted in OH)
Aniko T. Kalnoki
Michelle A. Rahija

Reference: National City Bank.

For full biographical listings, see the Martindale-Hubbell Law Directory

*COLUMBUS,** Franklin Co.

KEGLER, BROWN, HILL & RITTER (AV)

Capitol Square Suite 1800, 65 East State Street, 43215-4294
Telephone: 614-462-5400
Telecopier: 614-464-2634
Cable Address: "Law KBHR"
Telex: 246671
Email: info@kbhr.com *URL:* http://www.kbhr.com
Marion, Ohio Office: 250 Executive Drive, Suite B, P.O. Box 919.
Telephone: 614-387-3501.
Facsimile: 614-387-3630.

S. Martijn Steger

For Complete List of Firm Personnel, See General Section

For full biographical listings, see the Martindale-Hubbell Law Directory

OKLAHOMA

*OKLAHOMA CITY,** Oklahoma Co.

T. DOUGLAS STUMP (AV)

50 Penn Place, Suite 1320, 73118
Telephone: 405-879-0800
Fax: 405-879-0303
Email: tdstumplaw@aol.com *URL:* http://www.tds-immigration.com
Representative Clients: Amoco; Hilti, Inc.; Unit Parts; Braden Manufacturing; MidFirst Bank; UroCor; C.H. Guernsey.

For full biographical listings, see the Martindale-Hubbell Law Directory

WINNINGHAM & STEIN (AV)

The Registry, 2200 Northwest 50th Street, Suite 240, 73112-8044
Telephone: 405-843-1037
Fax: 405-848-2463
Email: mail@americanvisas.com *URL:* http://www.americanvisas.com

MEMBERS OF FIRM

E. Vance Winningham
Rance G. Stein

Representative Institutional Clients: General Motors Corp.; Hilton International Hotels; Marriott Corp.; Oklahoma State University; University of Oklahoma; Department of Veteran Affairs Medical Center; Oklahoma State Department of Health.

For full biographical listings, see the Martindale-Hubbell Law Directory

OREGON

*PORTLAND,** Multnomah Co.

BLACK HELTERLINE LLP (AV)

1200 Union Bank of California Tower, 707 S.W. Washington Street, 97205
Telephone: 503-224-5560
Telecopier: 503-224-6148
URL: http://www.bhlaw.com

MEMBERS OF FIRM

Robert W. Donaldson
Paul R. Hribernick
David G. Newhall

ASSOCIATES

Amy P. Alexander
Judith Woo Poutasse (Not admitted in OR)

OF COUNSEL

Gerald H. Robinson (Retired)

Representative Clients: C H 2 M Hill; ESCO Corp.; IDC; NACCO Materials Handling Group, Inc.; NIKE, Inc.; Portland Trailblazers; S.E.H. America, Inc.; Sacramento Kings; Tektronix, Inc.; Wieden & Kennedy.

For Complete List of Firm Personnel, See General Section

For full biographical listings, see the Martindale-Hubbell Law Directory

PENNSYLVANIA

*PHILADELPHIA,** Philadelphia Co.

ORLOW AND ORLOW, P.C. (AV)

600 Chestnut Street Suite 1156, 19106
Telephone: 215-922-1183
Telecopier: 215-922-0516
Email: jorlow@orlow.com

Abram Orlow (1900-1950)
Lena Orlow Ginsburg (1908-1998)
James J. Orlow

Joan Katz Betesh

For full biographical listings, see the Martindale-Hubbell Law Directory

STEEL, RUDNICK & RUBEN (AV)

1608 Walnut Street Suite 1500, 19103
Telephone: 215-546-4333
Fax: 215-546-4222
Email: SRR936@aol.com *URL:* http://www.steelrudnickruben.com
Pittsburgh, Pennsylvania Office: Law & Finance Building, 429 Fourth Avenue.
Telephone: 412-391-4719.

(See Next Column)

STEEL, RUDNICK & RUBEN, *Philadelphia—Continued*

MEMBERS OF FIRM

Richard D. Steel
Lawrence H. Rudnick
Ann A. Ruben

ASSOCIATE

Roberta Shaner

LEGAL SUPPORT PERSONNEL

Aida Mendez (Paralegal)
Elena Tchoumandrine (Paralegal)

For full biographical listings, see the Martindale-Hubbell Law Directory

SOUTH CAROLINA

*SPARTANBURG,** Spartanburg Co.

EDWARDS, BALLARD, BISHOP, STURM, CLARK & KEIM, P.A. (AV)

International Center, Suite 400, 101 North Pine Street, P.O. Box 5398, 29304-5398
Telephone: 864-542-8612
Fax: 864-542-8712
Email: lawfirm@ebbsck.com
Winston-Salem, North Carolina Office: Edwards, Ballard, Clark, Barrett and Carlson, P.A., 380 Knollwood, Suite 730, P.O. Box 1708. 27102-1708.
Telephone: 336-750-0707.
Fax: 336-750-0711.

James F. Edwards, Jr.
Wade E. Ballard
Michael W. Bishop
Kevin W. Sturm
Terry A. Clark (Resident Partner, Edwards, Ballard, Clark, Barrett and Carlson, P.A., Winston-Salem, North Carolina)
Thomas H. Keim, Jr.
Karen M. Tyner
Roger G. Chandler
Patrick L. Cont

S. Clay Keim
Krishna Y. McVey
W. Allen Myrick, Jr.
Penny Correll Wofford

Representative Clients: Texfi Industries, Inc.; Coca-Cola Bottling Co. Consolidated; Kobe Copper Products, Inc.; Van Waters & Rogers, Inc.; Spartanburg Steel Products, Inc.; Century Furniture Co.; Grimes Aerospace Corp.; Sulzer Ruti, Inc.; Comm/Scope, Inc.; South Carolina Insurance Reserve Fund.

For full biographical listings, see the Martindale-Hubbell Law Directory

TENNESSEE

*CHATTANOOGA,** Hamilton Co.

BAKER, DONELSON, BEARMAN & CALDWELL (AV)

1800 Republic Centre, 633 Chestnut Street, 37450-1800
Telephone: 423-756-2010
Telecopier: 423-756-3447
Email: info@bdbc.com *URL:* http://www.bakerdonelson.com
Memphis, Tennessee Office: 20th Floor, First Tennessee Building, 165 Madison, 38103.
Telephone: 901-526-2000.
Telecopier: 901-577-2303.
Nashville, Tennessee Office: 1700 Nashville City Center, 511 Union Street, 37219.
Telephone: 615-726-5600.
Telecopier: 615-726-0464.
Knoxville, Tennessee Office: 2200 Riverview Tower, 900 South Gay Street, 37901.
Telephone: 423-549-7000.
Telecopier: 423-525-8569.
Johnson City, Tennessee Office: SunTrust Bank Building, 207 Mockingbird Lane, P.O. Box 3038, 37602.
Telephone: 423-928-0181.
Telecopier: 423-928-5694; 423-928-3654; Kingsport: 423-246-6191.
Huntsville, Tennessee Office: 3 Courthouse Square, 37756.
Telephone: 423-663-2321.
Telecopier: 423-663-2111.
Washington, D.C. Office: Market Square, 801 Pennsylvania Avenue, N.W., 20004.
Telephone: 202-508-3400.
Telecopier: 202-508-3402.
Jackson, Mississippi Office: Suite 500, 700 North State Street, 39202.
Telephone: 601-351-2400.
Telecopier: 601-351-2424.

(See Next Column)

SHAREHOLDERS

Robert C. Divine

For Complete List of Firm Personnel, See General Section

For full biographical listings, see the Martindale-Hubbell Law Directory

*MEMPHIS,** Shelby Co.

BAKER, DONELSON, BEARMAN & CALDWELL (AV)

20th Floor, First Tennessee Building, 165 Madison, 38103
Telephone: 901-526-2000
Telecopier: 901-577-2303
Email: info@bdbc.com *URL:* http://www.bakerdonelson.com
Nashville, Tennessee Office: 1700 Nashville City Center, 511 Union Street, 37219.
Telephone: 615-726-5600.
Telecopier: 615-726-0464.
Chattanooga, Tennessee Office: 1800 Republic Centre, 633 Chestnut Street, 37450-1800.
Telephone: 423-756-2010.
Telecopier: 423-756-3447.
Knoxville, Tennessee Office: 2200 Riverview Tower, 900 South Gay Street, 37901.
Telephone: 423-549-7000.
Telecopier: 423-525-8569.
Johnson City, Tennessee Office: SunTrust Bank Building, 207 Mockingbird Lane, P.O. Box 3038, 37602.
Telephone: 423-928-0181.
Telecopier: 423-928-5694; 423-928-3654; Kingsport: 423-246-6191.
Huntsville, Tennessee Office: 3 Courthouse Square, 37756.
Telephone: 423-663-2321.
Telecopier: 423-663-2111.
Washington, D.C. Office: Market Square, 801 Pennsylvania Avenue, N.W., 20004.
Telephone: 202-508-3400.
Telecopier: 202-508-3402.
Jackson, Mississippi Office: Suite 500, 700 North State Street, 39202.
Telephone: 601-351-2400.
Telecopier: 601-351-2424.

ASSOCIATE

Cedric C.Y. Tan

For Complete List of Firm Personnel, See General Section

For full biographical listings, see the Martindale-Hubbell Law Directory

TEXAS

*DALLAS,** Dallas Co.

COHEN DARNELL & COHEN (AV)

A Professional Limited Liability Company
302 North Market Street, Suite 200, 75202
Telephone: 214-655-2600
Telecopier: 214-655-2601
Email: cdc@cohen-law.com *URL:* http://www.connect.net/cdc
Oklahoma City, Oklahoma Office: 5530 N. Western.
Telephone: 405-840-9049.
Fax: 405-840-9187.

Mark A. Cohen

For full biographical listings, see the Martindale-Hubbell Law Directory

LAW OFFICES OF RICHARD A. GUMP, JR., P.C. (AV)

One Galleria Tower, Suite 1940, 13355 Noel Road, Lock Box 39, 75240
Telephone: 972-386-9544
FAX: 972-386-9547
Email: rickgump@rickgump.com *URL:* http://www.lawyers.com/rickgump

Richard A. Gump, Jr.

Charla Truett

For full biographical listings, see the Martindale-Hubbell Law Directory

THOMPSON & KNIGHT L.L.P. (AV)

(Attorneys and Counselors)
1700 Pacific Avenue Suite 3300, 75201
Telephone: 214-969-1700
Telecopy: 214-969-1751
Telex: 732 298
URL: http://www.tklaw.com
Austin, Texas Office: 1200 San Jacinto Center, 98 San Jacinto Boulevard, 78701.
Telephone: 512-469-6100.
Telecopy: 512-469-6180.

(See Next Column)

THOMPSON & KNIGHT L.L.P.—*Continued*

Fort Worth, Texas Office: 801 Cherry Street, Suite 1600, 76102.
Telephone: 817-347-1700.
Telecopy: 817-347-1799.
Houston, Texas Office: Thompson Knight Brown Parker & Leahy L.L.P., 1200 Smith Street, Suite 3600, 77002-4595.
Telephone: 713-654-8111.
Telecopier: 713-654-1871.
San Pedro Garza Garcia, Nuevo León, Mexico Office: Edificio Losoles PD-4, Av. Lázaro Cárdenas No. 2400 Pte., C.P. 66220.
Telephone: (52-8) 363-0096.
Telecopy: (52-8) 363-3067.

PARTNER
Marc H. Klein
STAFF ATTORNEY
Tracy B. Liden

For Complete List of Firm Personnel, See General Section

For full biographical listings, see the Martindale-Hubbell Law Directory

*EL PASO,** El Paso Co.

MAYFIELD & PERRENOT, P.C. (AV)

221 N. Kansas, Suite 1600, P.O. Box 2039, 79950
Telephone: 915-533-2468
Telecopier: 915-533-0620
Email: mayper@1eagle1.com

Richard B. Perrenot — James R. Dennis
Roger C. Davie — Jeffery W. McElroy

Lisa M. Power — Shelly Weatherly
Marina Mata De La Garza

OF COUNSEL
Ellis O. Mayfield — James B. McIntyre

For full biographical listings, see the Martindale-Hubbell Law Directory

*HOUSTON,** Harris Co.

TINDALL & FOSTER, P.C. (AV)

600 Travis, Suite 2800, 77002-3094
Telephone: 713-229-8733
Fax: 713-228-1303
Email: info@tindallfoster.com *URL:* http://www.tindallfoster.com

Charles C. Foster — Robert F. Loughran

H. Richard Sindelar, III (Not admitted in TX) — Robert G. Nadalin
Matthew G. Thompson — Kay-Linh H. Pham
Alice Margaret Gruber — Lisa M. Reed
Karen Katz Feldman

Reference: Texas Commerce Bank, N.A., Houston, Texas.

For full biographical listings, see the Martindale-Hubbell Law Directory

UTAH

*SALT LAKE CITY,** Salt Lake Co.

VAN COTT, BAGLEY, CORNWALL & MCCARTHY, A PROFESSIONAL CORPORATION (AV)

50 South Main Street, Suite 1600, P.O. Box 45340, 84145-0340
Telephone: 801-532-3333
Telecopier: 801-534-0058
Email: info@vancott.com *URL:* http://www.vancott.com
Ogden, Utah Office: 2404 Washington Boulevard, Suite 900.
Telephone: 801-394-5783.
Park City, Utah Office: 2200 Park Avenue, Suite C200-A.
Telephone: 435-649-3889.

Mara A. Brown

For Complete List of Firm Personnel, See General Section

For full biographical listings, see the Martindale-Hubbell Law Directory

VERMONT

*BURLINGTON,** Chittenden Co.

GRAVEL AND SHEA, A PROFESSIONAL CORPORATION (AV)

Corporate Plaza, 76 St. Paul Street, P.O. Box 369, 05402-0369
Telephone: 802-658-0220
Fax: 802-658-1456

Leigh Polk Cole
OF COUNSEL
Clarke A. Gravel

For Complete List of Firm Personnel, See General Section

For full biographical listings, see the Martindale-Hubbell Law Directory

MILLER, EGGLESTON & CRAMER, LTD. (AV)

150 South Champlain Street, P.O. Box 1489, 05402-1489
Telephone: 802-864-0880
Telecopier: 802-864-0328

Victoria J. Brown

For Complete List of Firm Personnel, See General Section

For full biographical listings, see the Martindale-Hubbell Law Directory

VIRGINIA

*ARLINGTON,** Arlington Co.

LEVINE AND YATES, P.C. (AV)

4001 North 9th Street, Suite 224, 22203
Telephone: 703-524-8500
703-524-9009 (Spanish)
703-284-7586 (Korean)
703-284-7588 (Chinese)
Telecopier: 703-527-4473
Email: law@visa-usa.com *URL:* http://www.visa-usa.com

Samuel Jay Levine — Kenneth Yates
Irene S. Chang

For full biographical listings, see the Martindale-Hubbell Law Directory

NORFOLK, (Independent City)

VANDEVENTER BLACK LLP (AV)

500 World Trade Center, 23510-1699
Telephone: 757-446-8600
Cable Address: "Hughsvan"
Telecopier: 757-446-8670
URL: http://www.vanblk.com
Kitty Hawk, North Carolina Office: 6 Juniper Trail.
Telephone: 252-261-5055.
Fax: 252-261-8444. E-Mail: nshearin@pinn.net.
London, England Office: Mitre House, 4th Floor, 12-14 Mitre Street.
Telephone: (0171) 623-2081.
Facsimile: (0171) 929-0043.

PARTNERS OF FIRM
Walter B. Martin, Jr. — Mark T. Coberly
Valerie J. Brodsky

For Complete List of Firm Personnel, See General Section

For full biographical listings, see the Martindale-Hubbell Law Directory

RICHMOND, (Independent City)

LECLAIR RYAN, A PROFESSIONAL CORPORATION (AV)

707 East Main Street, 11th Floor, 23219
Telephone: 804-783-2003
Facsmile: 804-783-2294
Email: email@leclairryan.com
Glen Allen, Virginia Office: 4201 Dominion Boulevard, Suite 200, 23060.
Telephone: 804-270-0070.
Facsimile: 804-270-4715.
Blacksburg, Virginia Office: 1872 Pratt Drive, Suite 1865, 24060.
Telephone: 540-961-2762.
Fax: 540-961-2781.
Norfolk, Virginia Office: 999 Waterside Drive, Suite 2025.
Telephone: 757-624-1454.
Facsimile: 757-624-3773.
Alexandria, Virginia Office: 225 Reinekers Lane, Suite 290, 22314.
Telephone: 703-684-8007.
Facsimile: 703-684-8075.

(See Next Column)

LeClair Ryan A Professional Corporation, *Richmond—Continued*

Charlottesville, Virginia Office: 108 S.E. Second Street, P.O. Box 2017, 22902.
Telephone: 804-971-7771.
Facsimile: 804-296-0905.

Debra J.C. Dowd

For full biographical listings, see the Martindale-Hubbell Law Directory

Williams, Mullen, Clark & Dobbins, A Professional Corporation (AV)

Two James Center, 1021 East Cary Street, P.O. Box 1320, 23218-1320
Telephone: 804-643-1991
Fax: 804-783-6507
URL: http://www.wmcd.com
Newport News Office: Harbor Bank Center, Suite 210, One Old Oyster Point Road, 23602-7119.
Telephone: 757-249-5100.
Fax: 757-249-5109.
Virginia Beach Office: One Columbus Center, 23462-6763.
Telephone: 757-499-8800.
Fax: 757-473-0395.
Vienna Office: 1593 Spring Hill Road, Suite 510, 22182.
Telephone: 703-760-5200.
Fax: 703-748-0244.
Washington, D.C. Office: The Farragut Building, 900 17th Street, N.W., Suite 700, 20006.
Telephone: 202-293-0213.
Fax: 804-783-6507. Fax Within D.C.: 202-293-5939.
London, England Office: Blake Lodge, Bridge Lane, SW11 3AD.
Telephone: (011-44-71) 223-2756.
Fax: (011-44-71) 350-0156.
Riyadh, Saudi Arabia Affiliate Office: Saudi-American Legal Consultants Commercial Building #2, Diplomatic Quarter, P.O. Box 57270, 11574.
Telephone: (011-966-1) 488-1563.
Fax: (011-966-1) 488-0542.

William J. Benos

Daniel M. Pringle
Allyson Martin Sladic

For Complete List of Firm Personnel, See General Section

For full biographical listings, see the Martindale-Hubbell Law Directory

SPRINGFIELD, Fairfax Co.

Becker, Hicks, Irving & Hadeed, P.C. (AV)

5501 Backlick Road, Suite 220, 22151
Telephone: 703-256-1300
Fax: 703-256-3467
Email: mail@bhihlaw.com *URL:* http://www.bhihlaw.com

Larry E. Becker
B. R. Hicks
James V. Irving
Michael Mitry Hadeed, Jr.
Mark E. Kellogg, P.C.
Lynn E. Berry
Scott R. Sexauer

May Shallal Kheder
Alix L. Mattingly
Ashraf W. Nubani

For full biographical listings, see the Martindale-Hubbell Law Directory

WISCONSIN

*MILWAUKEE,** Milwaukee Co.

Jerome G. Grzeca, S.C. (AV)

525 East Wells Street Suite 250, 53202-3815
Telephone: 414-271-1400
Fax: 414-271-1414
Email: jgrzeca@compuserve.com *URL:* http://www.lawyers.com/jggimmigration

Jerome G. Grzeca

For full biographical listings, see the Martindale-Hubbell Law Directory

Quarles & Brady LLP (AV)

411 East Wisconsin Avenue, 53202-4497
Telephone: 414-277-5000
Fax: 414-271-3552
URL: http://www.quarles.com
Madison, Wisconsin Office: Firstar Plaza, One South Pinckney Street, P.O. Box 2113, 53701-2113.
Telephone: 608-251-5000.
Fax: 608-251-9166.

(See Next Column)

West Palm Beach, Florida Office: 222 Lakeview Avenue, 4th Floor, 33401.
Telephone: 561-653-5000.
Fax: 561-653-5333.
Naples, Florida Office: Barnett Center, 4501 Tamiami Trail North, Suite 300, 34103-3060.
Telephone: 941-262-5959.
Fax: 941-434-4999.
Phoenix, Arizona Office: One Camelback Building, One East Camelback Road, Suite 400, 85012-1649.
Telephone: 602-230-5500.
Fax: 602-230-5598.
Chicago, Illinois Office: Quarles & Brady LLC, Citicorp Center, 500 West Madison Street, Suite 3700.
Telephone: 312-715-5000.
Fax: 312-715-5155.

MEMBERS OF FIRM

(ALPHABETICALLY BY YEAR OF ADMISSION TO BAR)

Alyce C. Katayama
Jeffrey Morris
Joseph E. Puchner

ASSOCIATES

Julie A. Pace (Resident, Phoenix, Arizona Office)
Patricia A. Hintz
Shannon B. Farrell

For Complete List of Firm Personnel, See General Section

For full biographical listings, see the Martindale-Hubbell Law Directory

PUERTO RICO

SAN JUAN, San Juan Dist.

Fiddler González & Rodríguez, LLP

254 Muñoz Rivera Avenue (Hato Rey), P.O. Box 363507, 00936-3507
Telephone: 787-753-3113
Telecopier: 787-759-3123
Email: fiddler@fgrlaw.com *URL:* http://www.fgrlaw.com

MEMBER OF FIRM

Lolita J. Semidey Garcia

For Complete List of Firm Personnel, See General Section

For full biographical listings, see the Martindale-Hubbell Law Directory

CANADA
ALBERTA

*EDMONTON,** Edmonton Jud. Dist.

Parlee McLaws (AV)

15th Floor Manulife Place, 10180 101st Street, T5J 4K1
Telephone: 403-423-8500
Telecopier: 403-423-2870
Email: lawyers@parlee.com *URL:* http://www.parlee.com
Calgary, Alberta Office: 3400 Petro-Canada Centre, 150 - 6th Avenue, SW.
Telephone: 403-294-7000.
Telecopier: 403-265-8263.

MEMBER OF FIRM

David S. Tam

ASSOCIATE

George E. Flemming

For Complete List of Firm Personnel, See General Section

For full biographical listings, see the Martindale-Hubbell Law Directory

CANADA
PRINCE EDWARD ISLAND

*CHARLOTTETOWN,** Queen's Co.

McInnes Cooper (AV(T))

Barristers, Solicitors & Trade Mark Agents
BDC Place, Suite 620, 119 Kent Street, C1A 1N3
Telephone: 902-368-8473
Fax: 902-368-8346
Email: mcrpei@mcrlaw.com *URL:* http://www.mcrlaw.com
Halifax, Nova Scotia Office: Summit Place, 1601 Lower Water Street, P.O. Box 730, B3J 2V1.
Telephone: 902-425-6500.
Fax: 902-425-6350. Email: mcrhfx@mcrlaw.com.

(See Next Column)

McInnes Cooper—*Continued*

St. John's, Newfoundland Office: Baine Johnston Centre, 5th Floor, 10 Fort William Place, P.O. Box 5939, A1C 5X4.
Telephone: 709-722-8735.
Telecopier: 709-722-1763. Email: mcrsj@mcrlaw.com.
Moncton, New Brunswick Office: Place Moncton Place, 655 Main Street, P.O. Box 1368, E1C 8T6.
Telephone: 506-857-8970.
Fax: 506-857-4095. Email: mcrmctn@mcrlaw.com.
Fredericton, New Brunswick Office: Suite 600, 570 Queen Street, P.O. Box 610.
Telephone: 506-458-8572.
Fax: 506-458-9903. Email: mcrfton@mcrlaw.com.

ASSOCIATE

Kevin J. Kiley

For Complete List of Firm Personnel, See General Section

For full biographical listings, see the Martindale-Hubbell Law Directory

CANADA
QUEBEC

*MONTREAL,** Montreal Dist.

McMaster Gervais (AV)

A General Partnership
1000 de La Gauchetière Street West, Suite 900, H3B 5H4
Telephone: 514-879-1212
Fax: 514-954-1905
Email: info@mcmastergervais.com *URL:* http://www.mcmastergervais.com

MEMBERS OF FIRM

Darren E.G. McGuire
Valérie Dufour

For Complete List of Firm Personnel, See General Section

For full biographical listings, see the Martindale-Hubbell Law Directory

INSURANCE DEFENSE

MINNESOTA

*DULUTH,** St. Louis Co.

HALVERSON, WATTERS, DOWNS, REYELTS & BATEMAN, LTD. (AV)

700 Providence Building, 55802
Telephone: 218-727-6833
Fax: 218-727-4632
Email: hwdrb@computerpro.com

W. D. Watters (1926-1995)
Anthony S. Downs
Steven L. Reyelts
Charles B. Bateman
Steven W. Schneider
Eric L. D. Hylden
Sonia M. Sturdevant

Richard J. Leighton
Aaron Bransky
Diana B. Dodge
Anne L. Roeser

OF COUNSEL
G. W. Halverson

Representative Clients: American States Insurance Co.; CNA Group; Minnesota Lawyer's Mutual Insurance Co.; Midwest Medical Insurance Co.; Mutual Service Insurance Co.; Reinsurance Association of Minnesota; St. Paul Cos.; Wausau; Westfield Cos.

For full biographical listings, see the Martindale-Hubbell Law Directory

HANFT, FRIDE, O'BRIEN, HARRIES, SWELBAR & BURNS, P.A. (AV)

1000 U.S. Bank Place, 130 West Superior Street, 55802-2094
Telephone: 218-722-4766
Fax: 218-529-2401
Email: firm@hanftlaw.com

John D. Kelly
John R. Baumgarth
Tim A. Strom
R. Thomas Torgerson
Cheryl M. Prince
Robin C. Merritt

OF COUNSEL
Gaylord W. Swelbar

Representative Clients: American International Adjustment Companies, Inc./American International Group, Inc.; Auto-Owners Insurance; Continental Loss Adjusting; Employers Mutual Companies; Federated Insurance Company; Great American Insurance Company; Maryland Casualty Company; Ohio Casualty Insurance Company; United States Fidelity and Guarantee Company; Western National Insurance Company.

For Complete List of Firm Personnel, See General Section

For full biographical listings, see the Martindale-Hubbell Law Directory

MAGIE, ANDRESEN, HAAG, PACIOTTI, BUTTERWORTH & McCARTHY, P.A. (AV)

1000 Alworth Building, P.O. Box 745, 55801
Telephone: 218-722-1411
Telecopier: 218-720-6817
Email: lawduluth@aol.com

Robert H. Magie, III
Michael W. Haag
James P. Paciotti
Brian R. McCarthy
Robert C. Barnes
Steven J. Sheridan

Representative Clients: State Farm Insurance Comapnies; Allstate Insurance Company; Western National Insurance Company; Horace Mann Insurance Company; Farmers Home Group; Austin Mutual Insurance Company; Allied Group Insurance; Colonial Penn Insurance Company; Lumbermen's Underwriting Alliance; Progressive Group.

For Complete List of Firm Personnel, See General Section

For full biographical listings, see the Martindale-Hubbell Law Directory

*GRAND RAPIDS,** Itasca Co.

LANO, NELSON, O'TOOLE & BENGTSON, LTD. (AV)

515 NE 2nd Avenue, 55744
Telephone: 218-326-9603
Fax: 218-326-1565
Email: info@lanolaw.com

Neal Lano
Leif Nelson
Dennis O'Toole
Brian Bengtson

Representative Clients: State Farm Mutual Automobile Insurance Co.; Allstate Insurance Co.; American West Insurance Co.; Farmers Home Group; Cuna Mutual Insurance Group; Coregis Insurance; Austin Mutual Insurance Company; Midwest Family Ins. Co.; Horace Mann Ins. Co.; Allied Group Insurance.

(See Next Column)

For full biographical listings, see the Martindale-Hubbell Law Directory

*HALLOCK,** Kittson Co.

BRINK, SOBOLIK, SEVERSON, MALM & ALBRECHT, P.A. (AV)

217 South Birch Avenue, P.O. Box 790, 56728
Telephone: 218-843-3686
FAX: 218-843-2724
Email: brink@rural-access.com

Lyman A. Brink (1909-1972)
Dennis M. Sobolik
Robert K. Severson
Roger C. Malm
Robert M. Albrecht
Blake S. Sobolik
Jeffrey W. Hane

Representative Clients: Northwestern State Bank, Hallock, Minn.; Prime Security Bank, Karlstad, Minn.; Argyle State Bank, Argyle, Minn.; City of Hallock; American Federal Savings & Loan Assn.; State Farm Insurance Co.; Minnesota Rice Growers, Inc.

For full biographical listings, see the Martindale-Hubbell Law Directory

*MANKATO,** Blue Earth Co.

FARRISH, JOHNSON & MASCHKA, P.L.L.P. (AV)

Union Square Business Center, 201 North Broad Street, P.O. Box 550, 56002-0550
Telephone: 507-387-3002
Telecopier: 507-625-4002
Mailing Address: P.O. Box 550, 56002-0550
Email: farrish@mctcnet.net *URL:* http://www.fjm-law.com

MEMBERS OF FIRM
Gerald L. Maschka
John M. Riedy
Scott V. Kelly
William S. Partridge
Kenneth R. White

ASSOCIATES
Paul J. Simonett
Renee C. Rubish

OF COUNSEL
Robert G. Johnson

Representative Clients: Travelers Insurance Co.; CNA Insurance Co.; Hartford Accident and Indemnity Co.; St. Paul Insurance Cos.; Employers Mutual Companies; State Farm Co.; Federated Insurance Co.; Fireman's Fund Insurance Co.; Maryland Casualty Co.; American Family Insurance Group.

For Complete List of Firm Personnel, See General Section

For full biographical listings, see the Martindale-Hubbell Law Directory

*MINNEAPOLIS,** Hennepin Co.

AAFEDT, FORDE, GRAY & MONSON, P.A. (AV)

150 South Fifth Street, Suite 3100, 55402
Telephone: 612-339-8965
Fax: 612-349-6839

Curtis C. Gilmore (Retired)
John R. de Lambert (Retired)
Michael D. Aafedt
Michael Forde
James R. Gray
Janet Monson
Mary Marvin Hager
Peter M. Banovetz
Robin D. Simpson
Kirk C. Thompson
Kathy A. Endres
Janet Scheel Stellpflug
David J. Klaiman

Jessica Lipsky Roe
Krista L. Twesme
Anne F. Knipe

Representative Clients: Aetna Casualty and Surety Company; CIGNA Companies; Crawford Risk Management Service; Kemper Insurance Group; Liberty Mutual Insurance Group; Sentry Insurance Company; St. Paul Companies; United States Fidelity and Guaranty; U.S. Insurance Group/Crum and Forster Commercial Insurance; Western National Insurance Group.

For full biographical listings, see the Martindale-Hubbell Law Directory

ABRAMS & SMITH, A PROFESSIONAL ASSOCIATION (AV)

700 Northstar West, 55402
Telephone: 612-332-4273; 800-659-2679
Fax: 612-342-2107
Email: abrams@pclink.com

Harold J. Carroll (1901-1978)
Frank X. Cronan (1912-1975)
Jerome B. Abrams
Paul R. Smith
Lauris Heyerdahl
Bradford J. Roegge

Representative Clients: Hawkeye Security Insurance Co.; CNA Insurance; Employer's Mutual Insurance Co.

For full biographical listings, see the Martindale-Hubbell Law Directory

BASSFORD, LOCKHART, TRUESDELL & BRIGGS, P.A. (AV)

(Formerly Richards, Montgomery, Cobb & Bassford, P.A.)
3550 Multifoods Tower, 55402-3787
Telephone: 612-333-3000
Telecopier: 612-333-8829

(See Next Column)

BASSFORD, LOCKHART, TRUESDELL & BRIGGS P.A., *Minneapolis—Continued*

Greer E. Lockhart
Frederick E. Finch
John M. Degnan
Lewis A. Remele, Jr.
Kevin P. Keenan
James O. Redman
Rebecca Egge Moos
John M. Anderson
Charles E. Lundberg
Gregory P. Bulinski
Dale M. Wagner
Louis J. Speltz
Laura J. McKnight
Mark P. Hodkinson
Thomas J. Niemiec
Andrew L. Marshall
Michael A. Klutho
Gregory W. Deckert
Kevin P. Hickey
Stanford P. Hill
Mark R. Whitmore
Fred B. Snyder (1859-1951)
Edward C. Gale (1862-1943)
Frank A. Janes (1908-1959)
Nathan A. Cobb, Sr. (1905-1976)
Bergmann Richards (1888-1978)
Edmund T. Montgomery (1904-1987)
Charles A. Bassford (1914-1990)
Jerome C. Briggs (Retired)
Lynn G. Truesdell (Retired)

Dani M. Shimon
Christopher R. Morris
Kelly A. Putney
Jennifer L. Hill
Robin Ann Williams
Michael A. Switzer
Shalanda Denise Ballard

Representative Clients: Chubb/Pacific Indemnity Group; Employers Reinsurance Corporation; John Hancock Mutual Life Insurance Co.; Medical Protective Co.; Safeco Insurance Co.; The Travelers Insurance Cos.; The St. Paul Insurance Cos.; Utica Mutual Insurance Co.

For full biographical listings, see the Martindale-Hubbell Law Directory

COUSINEAU, MCGUIRE & ANDERSON, CHARTERED (AV)

600 Travelers Express Tower, 1550 Utica Avenue South, 55416-5318
Telephone: 612-546-8400
Facsimile: 612-546-0628
Email: cma@cousineaulaw.com
Ironwood, Michigan Office: 225 East Aurora Street, 49938.
Telephone: 800-877-8661. Email: kinneyl@up.lib.mi.us.

Henry A. Cousineau, Jr. (Retired)
Craig H. Anderson (Retired)
Robert J. McGuire
William F. Davern
Peter G. Van Bergen
James R. Waldhauser
Thomas P. Kieselbach
Barbara A. Burke
James L. Haigh
Michael W. McNee
Mark A. Gwin
John T. Thul
Bruce D. Elliott
Mark A. Kleinschmidt
Thomas F. Coleman
Susan M. Pasch
Michael D. Barrett
Richard W. Schmidt
Dale J. Evensen
Andrea E. Reisbord
Thomas V. Maguire
Lisa F. Kinney

Thomas J. Peterson
David M. Bialke
Jo Ann Strauss
Kevin T. McGrath
Eric R. Lee
Barton C. Gernander
Sarah J. Batzli
Patricia A. Garberg

Representative Clients: American Family Insurance; CNA; GAB Business Services; General Casualty; Great West Casualty; Minnesota Insurance Guaranty Assn.; Sedgwick James; St. Paul Cos.; Western National; Zurich American.

For full biographical listings, see the Martindale-Hubbell Law Directory

FETTERLY & GORDON, P.A. (AV)

1800 U.S. Bank Place, 650 Third Avenue South, 55402
Telephone: 612-288-2501
800-288-2501
Fax: 612-288-2551
Email: mail@Fetterly.com *URL:* http://www.fetterly.com

James L. Fetterly
Gary J. Gordon
Keith A. Hanson

Stephen G. Lickteig
Diane B. Bratvold
Timothy J. Fetterly
Thomas J. Basting, Jr.
Katherine A. Killen Hall
Christopher J. Sorenson
Stephen M. Warner

Reference: National City Bank.

For full biographical listings, see the Martindale-Hubbell Law Directory

FLYNN & GASKINS, L.L.P. (AV)

29th Floor, Metropolitan Centre, 333 South Seventh Street, 55402
Telephone: 612-333-9500
Fax: 612-333-9579
Email: mail@flynngaskins.com *URL:* http://www.flynngaskins.com

(See Next Column)

MEMBERS OF FIRM

George W. Flynn
Steve Gaskins
Jeannine L. Lee
Barbara Jean D'Aquila
Thomas Klosowski
Randall J. Pattee
Bradley J. Ayers
Hal A. Shillingstad
David A. Wikoff

ASSOCIATES

Scott M. Rusert
Jennifer F. Rosemark
Karen Reierson
Patrick R. Martin
John J. Laravuso
Gregory J. Wiley
Stephanie D. Sarantopoulos
Cory A. Kallheim
Craig D. Sandok (Not admitted in MN)

For full biographical listings, see the Martindale-Hubbell Law Directory

HANSON, LULIC & KRALL (AV)

Suite 500, 920 Second Avenue South, 55402
Telephone: 612-333-2530
FAX: 612-334-5955

MEMBERS OF FIRM

Jon A. Hanson
Joseph F. Lulic
Tony R. Krall
Kevin J. Kennedy

ASSOCIATES

John F. Cook
William M. Drinane
E. Curtis Roeder
Mark S. Brown
J. Robert Keena
Betsy L. Marstad
Kristin M. Nimsger
Randall E. Gottschalk

For full biographical listings, see the Martindale-Hubbell Law Directory

LOMMEN, NELSON, COLE & STAGEBERG, P.A. (AV)

1800 IDS Center, 80 South 8th Street, 55402
Telephone: 612-339-8131
Fax: 612-339-8064
Email: postmaster@email.lommen.com *URL:* http://www.lommen.com
Hudson, Wisconsin Office: Grandview Professional Building, 400 South Second Street, Suite 210.
Telephones: 715-386-8217 and 612-436-8085.

W. Wyman Smith (1914-1994)
Henry H. Feikema (1926-1996)
V. Owen Nelson (1928-1998)
John P. Lommen (1927-1988)
Michael P. Shroyer (1953-1993)
Leonard T. Juster
Alvin S. Malmon
Ronald L. Haskvitz
Phillip A. Cole
Roger V. Stageberg
Glenn R. Kessel
Thomas R. Jacobson (Resident, Hudson, Wisconsin Office)
John M. Giblin
John R. McBride
J. Christopher Cuneo
Thomas F. Dougherty
Stacey A. DeKalb
Kay N. Hunt
Richard L. Plagens
Ehrich L. Koch
Margie R. Bodas
James M. Lockhart
Stephen C. Rathke
James C. Searls
Paul L. Dinger
Sherri D. Ulland
Reid R. Lindquist
James R. Johnson (Resident, Hudson, Wisconsin Office)
Marc A. Johannsen
Barry A. O'Neil

Scott M. Nelson
Scott N. Ross
Mary I. King
David M. Hudson
Sheila A. Bjorklund
David S. Ezrilov
Susan Hayes Stephan
Geraint D. Powell
Brent R. Johnson (Resident, Hudson, Wisconsin Office)
Laura L. Enga
Christopher R. Grote

OF COUNSEL

Thomas F. Miller

Representative Clients: Midwest Medical Insurance Company; The St. Paul Companies; State Farm Insurance Companies.

For full biographical listings, see the Martindale-Hubbell Law Directory

MAHONEY, DOUGHERTY AND MAHONEY, P.A. PROFESSIONAL ASSOCIATION (AV)

801 Park Avenue, 55404-1189
Telephone: 612-339-5863; 888-339-5863
Fax: 612-339-1529
Email: mail@mahoney-law.com *URL:* http://www.lawinfo.com/law/mn/mahoney

Richard P. Mahoney
John (Jack) M. Miller
James M. Mahoney
Randee S. Held
Mark J. Manderfeld
Patrick E. Mahoney
James M. Lehman
Gregory A. Zinn
Kelley R. Lorix
Victor E. Lund
Paul E. D. Darsow

Representative Insurance Clients: GCU; Great American Insurance Co.; Guidant Insurance Group (Formerly Preferred Risk Group); John Deere Insurance Co.; Maryland Casualty Co.; Milwaukee Insurance Co.; National Farmers Union Insurance Cos.; Park Glen National Insurance Co.; Scottsdale Insurance Co.; Wausau Insurance Co.

For full biographical listings, see the Martindale-Hubbell Law Directory

Minneapolis—Continued

McCollum, Crowley, Vehanen, Moschet & Miller, Ltd. (AV)

1300 Norwest Financial Center, 7900 Xerxes Avenue South, 55431
Telephone: 612-831-4980
Fax: 612-831-2942
Rice Lake, Wisconsin Office: 3013 South Main Street.
Telephone: 715-234-2656.
Facsimile: 715-234-1491.

Robert L. McCollum
Jerome D. Vehanen
Deborah L. Crowley
Robyn N. Moschet
Michael D. Miller
William G. Laak

Nancy E. Lamo
Jerry D. Van Cleave
Cynthia K. Thurston
David C. Higgs
William Nathan Schieken
Elizabeth Anne Skinner

For full biographical listings, see the Martindale-Hubbell Law Directory

Waldeck & Lind, P.A. (AV)

Suite 730, TCF Tower, 121 South Eighth Street, 55402
Telephone: 612-375-1550
Facsimilie: 612-375-0647

Timothy W. Waldeck
Peter E. Lind

Steven D. Pattee

For full biographical listings, see the Martindale-Hubbell Law Directory

*ST. CLOUD,** Stearns Co.

Rajkowski Hansmeier Ltd. (AV)

Daniel Building, 11 Seventh Avenue North, P.O. Box 1433, 56302-1433
Telephone: 320-251-1055
Toll Free: 800-445-9617
Fax: 320-251-5896
Email: rajhan@cloudnet.com

Frank J. Rajkowski
Gordon H. Hansmeier
Frederick L. Grunke
Thomas G. Jovanovich
John H. Scherer
Paul A. Rajkowski
Kevin F. Gray
William J. Cashman
Richard W. Sobalvarro
Lotte Rose Hansen
Beth S. Thompson
Mark E. Arneson

Patrick J. Larkin

Representative Clients: The Travelers Ins. Co.; American Family Insurance Co.; Allstate Insurance Co.; Milbank/State Auto Insurance Companies; Safeco Insurance Co.; Employers Mutual Co.; Farmland Insurance Co.; Grinnell Mutual Reinsurance Mutual Service Insurance; Chubb Group Insurance Co.

For full biographical listings, see the Martindale-Hubbell Law Directory

*ST. PAUL,** Ramsey Co.

Collins, Buckley, Sauntry and Haugh, P.L.L.P. (AV)

West 1100 First National Bank Building, 332 Minnesota Street, 55101
Telephone: 651-227-0611
Telecopier: 651-227-0758
Email: info@cbsh.net *URL:* http://www.cbsh.net

MEMBERS OF FIRM

Eugene D. Buckley (Retired)
Michael J. Sauntry
William E. Haugh, Jr.
Mark W. Gehan, Jr.
Patrick T. Tierney
Thomas J. Germscheid
John R. Schulz
Thomas R. O'Connell
Dan C. O'Connell
Christine L. Stroemer
Thomas E. McEllistrem

OF COUNSEL

Theodore J. Collins

For Complete List of Firm Personnel, See General Section

For full biographical listings, see the Martindale-Hubbell Law Directory

Geraghty, O'Loughlin & Kenney, Professional Association (AV)

1400 Ecolab University Center, 386 North Wabasha Street, 55102-1308
Telephone: 651-291-1177
Fax: 651-291-9477
Email: gok@pclink.com

Terence J. O'Loughlin
Robert M. Mahoney
David C. Hutchinson
William H. Leary, III
Mary H. Alcorn
Matthew J. Hanzel
Ann D. Bray
Jean B. Hoppe
Kyle M. Thomas

(See Next Column)

OF COUNSEL

James H. Geraghty (Retired)
James W. Kenney (Retired)

Representative Clients: St. Paul Cos.; Allina Health System; Fairview Hospital and Healthcare Services; HealthEast; HealthPartners; MMI Cos.; Midwest Medical Insurance Co.; North Memorial Hospital; Aspen Medical Group.

For full biographical listings, see the Martindale-Hubbell Law Directory

Spence, Ricke & Thurmer, P.A. (AV)

Suite 600, Degree of Honor Building, 325 Cedar Street, 55101
Telephone: 651-223-8000
Fax: 651-223-8003
Email: meganr@srtpa.com

Thomas W. Spence
Megan Korfhage Ricke
Susan D. Thurmer

Patrick J. Sweeney
Julius W. Gernes
Glenn Olander-Quamme
Timothy K. Masterson
Rodney A. Honkanen
Scott H. Rauser

Representative Clients: Burlington Northern Sante Fe Railroad; Glacier Park Co.

For full biographical listings, see the Martindale-Hubbell Law Directory

MISSISSIPPI

BILOXI, Harrison Co.

Brown, Watt & Buchanan, P.A. (AV)

115 Main Street, P.O. Box 1377, 39533-1377
Telephone: 228-374-2999
Telecopier: 228-435-7090
Email: mail@bwblaw.com *URL:* http://www.bwblaw.com
Pascagoula, Mississippi Office: 3112 Canty Street, P.O. Box 2220.
Telephone: 228-762-0035.
Fax: 228-762-0299.

Raymond L. Brown
W. Lee Watt
Patrick R. Buchanan
W. Mark Edwards
A. Kelly Sessoms, III
Alan K. Sudduth

General Counsel for: Mississippi Export Railroad Co.; Pascagoula Municipal Separate School District.
Representative Clients: United States Fidelity & Guaranty Co.; The Travelers Companies; The Home Insurance Co.; CSX Transportation, Inc.; Blue Cross-Blue Shield of Mississippi; Burlington Insurance Co.; Continental Insurance; Deere & Co.

For full biographical listings, see the Martindale-Hubbell Law Directory

Corban & Gunn (AV)

770 Water Street, P.O. Drawer 1916, 39533-1916
Telephone: 228-432-7826
Telecopier: 228-435-5702

MEMBERS OF FIRM

Lawrence C. Corban, Jr.
Clyde H. Gunn, III

Representative Clients: Dees Chevrolet Co.; First Federal Savings & Loan Association of Pascagoula-Moss Point; Frank P. Corso & Co., Inc.; Munro Petroleum & Terminal Corp.; Ship Services Corp.

For full biographical listings, see the Martindale-Hubbell Law Directory

Page, Mannino, Peresich & McDermott (AV)

A Professional Limited Liability Company
759 Vieux Marché Mall, P.O. Drawer 289, 39533
Telephone: 228-374-2100
Facsimile: 228-432-5539
Email: pmp@pmp.org

MEMBERS OF FIRM

Lyle M. Page (Resident)
Frederick J. Mannino (Resident)
Ronald G. Peresich (Resident)
Stephen G. Peresich (Resident)
Michael B. McDermott (Resident)
Tere Richardson Steel (Resident)
Michael E. Whitehead (Resident)
Mary Alexander Nichols (Resident)
David M. Allen (Resident)

ASSOCIATES

Henry N. Dick, III
Les W. Smith (Resident)
Emilie Whitehead
Kaara L. Liskow
Joel L. Blackledge

Representative Clients: United States Fidelity & Guaranty Co.; St. Paul Fire & Marine Insurance Co.; Crawford & Co.; Anheuser-Busch Corp.
General Counsel for: Peoples Bank of Biloxi, Mississippi; Biloxi Regional Medical Center; Bank of Mississippi (Gulf Coast Division).

For full biographical listings, see the Martindale-Hubbell Law Directory

*BROOKHAVEN,** Lincoln Co.

ALLEN, ALLEN, BOERNER & BREELAND (AV)

214 Justice Street, P.O. Box 751, 39602-0751
Telephone: 601-833-4361
Fax: 601-833-6647
Email: aabblaw@tislink.com

Emmette P. Allen (1915-1999)
Robert O. Allen
William D. Boerner
Durwood J. Breeland

ASSOCIATE

Sally Burchfield Doty

For full biographical listings, see the Martindale-Hubbell Law Directory

*CLARKSDALE,** Coahoma Co.

HENKE-BUFKIN, A PROFESSIONAL ASSOCIATION (AV)

408 Hopson Street, P.O. Box 39, 38614
Telephone: 601-624-8500
Telecopier: 601-624-8040

W. Kurt Henke
Elizabeth T. Bufkin
Michael D. Stevens
Jeffrey S. Dilley
Roy Jefferson Allen

OF COUNSEL

William Cliff Heaton

Reference: United Southern Bank, Clarksdale, Mississippi.

For full biographical listings, see the Martindale-Hubbell Law Directory

HOLCOMB DUNBAR, A PROFESSIONAL ASSOCIATION (AV)

152 Delta Avenue, P.O. Box 368, 38614
Telephone: 601-627-2241
Facsimile: 601-627-9788
Email: mchaffin@clarksdale.com *URL:* http://www.holcombdunbar.com
Oxford, Mississippi Office: 1217 Jackson Avenue, P.O. Drawer 707, 38655.
Telephone: 601-234-8775.
Facsimile: 601-238-7552.
Southaven, Mississippi Office: Suite 1, 728 Goodman Road East, P.O. Box 190, 38671.
Telephone: 601-349-0664.
Facsimile: 601-349-2432.

William M. Chaffin
Michael K. Graves
Edward (Ted) P. Connell, Jr.
Daniel M. Czamanske, Jr.

Representative Clients: Southern Farm Bureau Casualty Insurance Co.; State Farm Mutual Fire & Casualty Insurance Co.; Fireman's Fund Insurance Cos.; The Employers Group Insurance Co.; Central Mutual Insurance Co.; Commercial Union Insurance Cos; Federated Mutual Insurance Co.; Shelter Insurance Co.; Atlanta Casualty Insurance Cos.; United Southern Assurance Corp.

For Complete List of Firm Personnel, See General Section

For full biographical listings, see the Martindale-Hubbell Law Directory

LUCKETT LAW FIRM, A PROFESSIONAL ASSOCIATION (AV)

143 Yazoo Avenue, P.O. Drawer 1000, 38614-1000
Telephone: 601-624-2591
Telecopier: 601-627-5403
Email: llf@gmi.net

William O. Luckett (1922-1996)
William O. Luckett, Jr.

John B. Gillis
Rivers H. Humber
Robert M. Tyner, Jr.
Jonathan S. Masters

District and Local Counsel for: Liberty Mutual Insurance Co.; CNA Group; Deere & Co.; Indiana Lumbermens Insurance Co.; Texas Gas Transmission Corp.; American Interstate Insurance Company of Georgia; Elliston, Inc.; Graward General Insurance; Wal-Mart Stores, Inc.; Grand Casinos, Inc.

For full biographical listings, see the Martindale-Hubbell Law Directory

*CLEVELAND,** Bolivar Co.

GRIFFITH & GRIFFITH (AV)

123 South Court Street, Post Office Drawer 1680, 38732
Telephone: 662-843-6100
Telecopier: 662-843-8153
Email: griffith@tecinfo.com *URL:* http://www.vralitigator.com

MEMBERS OF FIRM

L. Ellis Griffith (1926-1987)
Benjamin E. Griffith
Daniel J. Griffith

Reference: The Cleveland State Bank.

For full biographical listings, see the Martindale-Hubbell Law Directory

JACKS, ADAMS & WESTERFIELD, P.A. (AV)

106 South Pearman Avenue, P.O. Box 1209, 38732
Telephone: 662-843-6171
FAX: 662-843-6176
Email: jaws@tecinfo.com

Gerald H. Jacks
William S. Adams, Jr.
Andrew M. W. Westerfield
S. David Norquist
Thomas B. Janoush

Representative Clients: United States Fidelity & Guaranty Co.; Audubon Insurance Co.; State Farm Mutual Automobile Ins. Co.; State Farm Fire & Casualty Co.; New Hampshire Insurance Co.; Southern Guaranty Co.; Zurich Insurance Co.; Providence Washington Ins. Co.; Aetna Life & Casualty Co.; Baxter-Travenol, Inc.

For full biographical listings, see the Martindale-Hubbell Law Directory

*COLUMBIA,** Marion Co.

AULTMAN, TYNER, RUFFIN & YARBOROUGH, LTD., A PROFESSIONAL LAW CORPORATION (AV)

329 Church Street, P.O. Drawer 707, 39429
Telephone: 601-736-2222
FAX: 601-736-9884
Email: rfyjr@cblink.com
Hattiesburg, Mississippi Office: 315 Hemphill Street, P.O. Drawer 750.
Telephone: 601-583-2671.
FAX: 601-583-2677.
Gulfport, Mississippi Office: 1201 25th Avenue, Suite 300, P.O. Box 607.
Telephone: 228-863-6913.
FAX: 228-868-8505. Email: atmr@digiscape.com.
New Orleans, Louisiana Office: The Texaco Center, 400 Poydras Street, Suite 2250.
Telephone: 504-528-9616.
FAX: 504-528-9640.

Richard F. Yarborough, Jr.

OF COUNSEL

Ernest Ray Duff

Representative Clients: Hercules, Inc.; United States Steel Corp.; Ford Motor Co.; International Paper Co.; Phillips Petroleum Co.; Aetna Casualty & Surety Co.; CNA Group; Liberty Mutual Insurance Co.; St. Paul Fire & Marine Insurance Co.; Fireman's Fund.

For full biographical listings, see the Martindale-Hubbell Law Directory

*GREENWOOD,** Leflore Co.

UPSHAW, WILLIAMS, BIGGERS, BECKHAM & RIDDICK, LLP (AV)

309 Fulton Street, 38930
Telephone: 662-455-1613
Facsimile: 662-453-9245
Mailing Address: P.O. Drawer 8230, Greenwood, Mississippi, 38935-8230
Email: lexgwd@uwbbr.com
Jackson, Mississippi Office: Suite 300 Plaza One, 715 South Pear Orchard Road, P.O. Box 9147, 39286-9147.
Telephone: 601-978-1996.
Facsimile: 601-978-1949. Email: lexjax@uwbbr.com.

MEMBERS OF FIRM

James E. Upshaw
Tommie G. Williams
Marc A. Biggers
Glenn F. Beckham
Roger C. Riddick (Resident, Jackson Office)
F. Ewin Henson III
Lonnie D. Bailey
Robert S. Upshaw
Clinton M. Guenther
Richard C. Williams, Jr. (Resident, Jackson Office)
Richard L. Kimmel
Mark C. Carroll (Resident, Jackson Office)
W. Hugh Gillon IV (Resident, Jackson Office)
Paul L. Goodman
Walter C. Morrison IV (Resident, Jackson Office)

ASSOCIATES

Steven H. Funderburg (Resident, Jackson Office)
Bonnie Bridgers Smith (Resident, Jackson Office)
Patrick M. Tatum (Resident, Jackson Office)
Craig R. Sessums (Resident, Jackson Office)
James K. Warrington
Cecil D. McClellan, III (Resident, Jackson Office)
J. L. Wilson, IV

OF COUNSEL

Ben L. Riddick (Resident, Jackson Office)
John R. Countiss III (Resident, Jackson Office)

Representative Clients: United States Fidelity & Guaranty Co.; State Farm Mutual Automobile Insurance Co.; CNA Insurance Cos.; St. Paul Fire & Marine Insurance Co.; Travelers/Aetna Property and Casualty Corp.; Kemper Insurance Co.; Zurich-American Insurance Group; Risk Enterprise Management, Ltd.; Allstate Insurance Co.

For Complete List of Firm Personnel, See General Section

For full biographical listings, see the Martindale-Hubbell Law Directory

*GULFPORT,** Harrison Co.

ALLEN, VAUGHN, COBB & HOOD, P.A. (AV)

One Hancock Plaza, Suite 1209, P.O. Drawer 4108, 39502-4108
Telephone: 601-864-4011
Fax: 601-864-4852
Email: avchlaw@sunherald.infinet.com

Harry R. Allen	Benjamin U. Bowden
Thomas E. Vaughn	Richard B. Tubertini
David L. Cobb	Rodney Douglas Robinson
Billy W. Hood	E. Colette Towles
Joy Lambert Phillips	David W. Crane
Robert W. Atkinson	John A. Foxworth, Jr.

J. Adrian Smith — Michael J. Casano

OF COUNSEL

D. Knox White

LEGAL SUPPORT PERSONNEL

Kevin C. Stachowski (Paralegal)

For full biographical listings, see the Martindale-Hubbell Law Directory

AULTMAN, TYNER, RUFFIN & YARBOROUGH, LTD., A PROFESSIONAL LAW CORPORATION (AV)

1201 25th Avenue, Suite 300, P.O. Box 607, 39502
Telephone: 228-863-6913
FAX: 228-868-8505
Email: atmr@digiscape.com
Hattiesburg, Mississippi Office: 315 Hemphill Street, P.O. Drawer 750.
Telephone: 601-583-2671.
FAX: 601-583-2677.
Columbia, Mississippi Office: 329 Church Street, P.O. Drawer 707.
Telephone: 601-736-2222.
FAX: 601-736-9884. Email: rfyjr@cblink.com.
New Orleans, Louisiana Office: The Texaco Center, 400 Poydras Street, Suite 2250.
Telephone: 504-528-9616.
FAX: 504-528-9640.

Ben E. Sheely — Dorrance (Dee) Aultman, Jr.

For Complete List of Firm Personnel, See General Section

For full biographical listings, see the Martindale-Hubbell Law Directory

DUKES, DUKES, KEATING AND FANECA, P.A. (AV)

2909 13th Street, 6th Floor, P.O. Drawer W, 39501
Telephone: 228-868-1111
Fax: 228-863-2886
Email: ddkf@ddkf.com

William F. Dukes	Hugh D. Keating
Walter W. Dukes	Phillip W. Jarrell

W. Edward Hatten, Jr.	Trace D. McRaney
Thomas William Busby	Stephen M. Cozart

For Complete List of Firm Personnel, See General Section

For full biographical listings, see the Martindale-Hubbell Law Directory

FRANKE, RAINEY & SALLOUM, PLLC (AV)

2605 14th Street, P.O. Drawer 460, 39502
Telephone: 228-868-7070
Telecopier: 228-868-7090
Email: frs@diversicomm.com

Paul M. Franke, Jr.	Paul B. Howell
William M. Rainey	Fredrick B. Feeney, II
Richard P. Salloum	Traci M. Castille

Donald P. Moore

Kaleel G. Salloum, Jr.	Brandi C. Schwartz

James C. Simpson, Jr.

For full biographical listings, see the Martindale-Hubbell Law Directory

HOPKINS, CRAWLEY, BAGWELL & UPSHAW, P.L.L.C. (AV)

2701 24th Avenue, P.O. Box 1510, 39501-4941
Telephone: 228-864-2200
Mississippi and USA Wats: 1-800-421-3629
Fax: 228-868-9358; 228-863-4227
Email: Hopkins@MSLawyer.com
Jackson, Mississippi Office: 499 South President Street, Second Floor, Suite 1.
Telephone: 601-355-6510.
Fax: 601-355-6503. Email: TCrawley@MSLawyer.com.

(See Next Column)

MEMBERS OF FIRM

Alben N. Hopkins	Douglas Bagwell
Timothy D. Crawley	Jessica Sibley Upshaw

Thomas Alan Waller

ASSOCIATES

Raymond D. Carter	David E. Wilson
Kenneth S. Womack	Laura Faye Paulk
Mary Benton-Shaw	Ronald C. Small
Pat Sharkey Burke, Jr.	(Not admitted in MS)

Representative Clients: Coregis Group; General Cable Corp.; Insurance Company of North America; Liberty Mutual Insurance Group; Reliance Insurance Co.; USX Corp.; Employers Insurance of Wausau; American International Group (AIG); Quaker Chemical Corp.

For full biographical listings, see the Martindale-Hubbell Law Directory

*HATTIESBURG,** Forrest Co.

AULTMAN, TYNER, RUFFIN & YARBOROUGH, LTD., A PROFESSIONAL LAW CORPORATION (AV)

315 Hemphill Street, P.O. Drawer 750, 39403-0750
Telephone: 601-583-2671
FAX: 601-583-2677
Email: aultyn@c-gate.net
Columbia, Mississippi Office: 329 Church Street, P.O. Drawer 707.
Telephone: 601-736-2222.
FAX: 601-736-9884. Email: rfyjr@cblink.com.
Gulfport, Mississippi Office: 1201 25th Avenue, Suite 300, P.O. Box 607.
Telephone: 228-863-6913.
FAX: 228-868-8505. Email: atmr@digiscape.com.
New Orleans, Louisiana Office: The Texaco Center, 400 Poydras Street, Suite 2250.
Telephone: 504-528-9616.
FAX: 504-528-9640.

Dorrance Aultman	Ben E. Sheely (Resident, Gulfport Office)
Thomas W. Tyner	R. Curtis Smith, II
Louie F. Ruffin	Dorrance (Dee) Aultman, Jr. (Resident, Gulfport Office)
Richard F. Yarborough, Jr. (Resident, Columbia Office)	

William Nelson Graham

Victor A. DuBose

OF COUNSEL

Ernest Ray Duff (Resident, Columbia Office)

Representative Clients: Hercules, Inc.; U.S. Steel Corp.; Ford Motor Co.; Phillips Petroleum Co.; Aetna Casualty & Surety Co.; CNA Group; Liberty Mutual Insurance Co.; St. Paul Fire & Marine Insurance Co.; Fireman's Fund; L & A Contracting Co.

For Complete List of Firm Personnel, See General Section

For full biographical listings, see the Martindale-Hubbell Law Directory

*JACKSON,** Hinds Co.

THE ALLRED LAW FIRM (AV)

1911 Dunbarton Drive, P.O. Box 3828, 39216-5002
Telephone: 601-713-1414
Telefax: 601-713-3259
Email: ALLRED_Lawfirm@MSN.com

MEMBERS OF FIRM

Michael S. Allred — Ottowa E. Carter, Jr.

OF COUNSEL

Kenneth A. Rutherford

For full biographical listings, see the Martindale-Hubbell Law Directory

BAKER, DONELSON, BEARMAN & CALDWELL (AV)

Suite 500, 700 North State Street, 39202
Telephone: 601-351-2400
Telecopier: 601-351-2424
Email: info@bdbc.com *URL:* http://www.bakerdonelson.com
Memphis, Tennessee Office: 20th Floor, First Tennessee Building, 165 Madison, 38103.
Telephone: 901-526-2000.
Telecopier: 901-577-2303.
Nashville, Tennessee Office: 1700 Nashville City Center, 511 Union Street, 37219.
Telephone: 615-726-5600.
Telecopier: 615-726-0464.
Chattanooga, Tennessee Office: 1800 Republic Centre, 633 Chestnut Street, 37450-1800.
Telephone: 423-756-2010.
Telecopier: 423-756-3447.
Knoxville, Tennessee Office: 2200 Riverview Tower, 900 South Gay Street, 37901.
Telephone: 423-549-7000.
Telecopier: 423-525-8569.

(See Next Column)

BAKER, DONELSON, BEARMAN & CALDWELL, *Jackson—Continued*

Johnson City, Tennessee Office: SunTrust Bank Building, 207 Mockingbird Lane, P.O. Box 3038, 37602.
Telephone: 423-928-0181.
Telecopier: 423-928-5694; 423-928-3654; Kingsport: 423-246-6191.
Huntsville, Tennessee Office: 3 Courthouse Square, 37756.
Telephone: 423-663-2321.
Telecopier: 423-663-2111.
Washington, D.C. Office: Market Square, 801 Pennsylvania Avenue, N.W., 20004.
Telephone: 202-508-3400.
Telecopier: 202-508-3402.

PARTNERS

Walker W. (Bill) Jones, III
William N. Reed

ASSOCIATES

Stacy E. Thomas
Jody Brian Martin

For Complete List of Firm Personnel, See General Section

For full biographical listings, see the Martindale-Hubbell Law Directory

BENNETT LOTTERHOS SULSER & WILSON, P.A. (AV)

One Jackson Place Suite 1400, 188 East Capitol Street, P.O. Box 98, 39205-0098
Telephone: 601-944-0466
Telecopier: 601-944-0467

Richard T. Bennett
Joseph E. Lotterhos
Marcus M. Wilson
Edward E. Lawler, Jr.
Mary E. McAlister
J. Mark Franklin, III
Ronald Keith Foreman
John L. Pannier

OF COUNSEL

Floyd M. Sulser, Jr.

Representative Clients: Agristor Leasing; Chubb Group of Insurance Companies; 84 Lumber Company; European American Bank; FSLIC; Great Southern Federal Savings; Hibernia National Bank; Holiday Inns, Inc; Masonite Corp.

For full biographical listings, see the Martindale-Hubbell Law Directory

COPELAND COOK TAYLOR & BUSH, A PROFESSIONAL ASSOCIATION (AV)

200 Concourse, Suite 200, 1062 Highland Colony Parkway, P.O. Box 2132, 39225-2132
Telephone: 601-856-7200
Facsimile: 601-856-7626
Email: mail@cctb.com *URL:* http://www.cctb.com
Ridgeland, Mississippi Office: Post Office Box 6020, 39158.
Telephone: 601-856-7200.
Facsimile: 601-856-7626.

Charles G. Copeland
Thomas A. Cook
Glenn Gates Taylor
C. Glen Bush
Thomas C. Gerity
James T. Knight
James R. Moore, Jr.
J. Tucker Mitchell
Robert P. Thompson
Thomas R. Hudson
R. Nash Neyland
Michael W. Baxter
C. Ted Sanderson, Jr.
Monte L. Barton, Jr.
W. Shan Thompson
C. Dale Shearer
Robert C. Richardson
Lee Howell, III
John M. Breland
Jefferson P.W. Skelton
Patricia H. Cottingham
Samuel S. Goza
Amanda L. Baham
Samuel O. Morris, IV
Michelle C. Partridge
John E. Gough, Jr.
Victor Donald Hunt
Donald J. Blackwood, Jr.
Rhonda Lea McCullough

OF COUNSEL

James P. Knight, Jr.
Robert L. Goza

For full biographical listings, see the Martindale-Hubbell Law Directory

CURRIE JOHNSON GRIFFIN GAINES & MYERS, PLLC (AV)

Mississippi Valley Title Building, 315 Tombigbee Street, P.O. Box 750, 39205-0750
Telephone: 601-969-1010
Telecopier: 601-969-5120
URL: http://www.curriejohnson.com

MEMBERS OF FIRM

Edward J. Currie, Jr.
Whitman B. Johnson, III
William C. Griffin
Philip W. Gaines
Michael F. Myers
Frances R. Shields
William H. Creel, Jr.

Lisa L. Williams
James F. Noble, III
William W. McKinley, Jr.
Timothy D. Moore
Trent L. Walker
Robert B. Ogletree
James M. Priest, Jr.
Shelly G. Burns
Yumeka C. Burt
Kristi A. Duncan

For full biographical listings, see the Martindale-Hubbell Law Directory

EDMONSON, BIGGS & MOZINGO, P.A. (AV)

Deposit Guaranty Bank Building, 200 East Capitol, Suite 1500, P.O. Box 865, 39205
Telephone: 601-944-1900
Telecopier: 601-944-1906
Email: ebmh@misnet.com *URL:* http://www.ebmh.com

Richard M. Edmonson
Robert A. Biggs, III
James R. Mozingo
Fred W. Johnson, Jr.
Craig D. Smith
Todd A. Coker

Representative Clients: Andover Cos; Combined Insurance Co.; Design Professional Insurance Co.; Bituminous Insurance Co.; Lexington Insurance Co.; Mississippi State Medical Association Benefit Plan; Coregis; USF&G; Utica Mutual Insurance Co.; Trustmark National Bank, Union Planters Bank.

For full biographical listings, see the Martindale-Hubbell Law Directory

MARKOW, WALKER & REEVES, P.A. (AV)

Atrium North Building, 805 South Wheatley, Suite 400, P.O. Box 13669, 39236-3669
Telephone: 601-956-8500
Telecopier: 601-956-8423
Oxford, Mississippi Office: 1006 Van Buren Avenue, 38655.
Telephone: 601-234-9899.
Telecopier: 601-234-9762.

Peter J. Markow, Jr.
Christopher J. Walker
William C. Reeves
Terry B. Germany
Richard C. Coker
Gilson Davis (Dave) Peterson
Alfonso Nuzzo
Richard M. Edmonson, Jr.
Hubert Wesley Williams, III
L. Pepper Cossar
J. Hale Freeland (Resident, Oxford Office)

Delia R. Owens
T.G. Bolen, Jr.
Holly Bridges Wiggs
Michael D. Young
S. Deann Thomas
Robert Niles Hooper
L. Abraham Rowe, Jr.
Andrew D. Shull (Resident, Oxford Office)

Reference: Trustmark National Bank, Jackson, Miss.

For full biographical listings, see the Martindale-Hubbell Law Directory

MCCOY, WILKINS, STEPHENS & TIPTON, P.A. (AV)

1 LeFleur Square, 4735 Old Canton Road, P.O. Box 13429, 39211
Telephone: 601-366-4343
Telecopier: 601-981-7608
Email: mwst@mccoywilkins.com

Joseph L. McCoy
Joseph T. Wilkins, III
Senith C. Tipton
Robert M. Carpenter
William A. Patterson
Leland S. Smith, III
Mark C. Carlson
Betty Burton Arinder
Daniel M. Baker
Diane V. Pradat

Christopher H. Hughes
John D. Brady
Craig D. Bluntson
Roxanne P. Case
Jay R. McLemore
Chandra T. Lee
John Hall

OF COUNSEL

Joseph T. Stephens

Representative Client: Insurance Company of North America.

For full biographical listings, see the Martindale-Hubbell Law Directory

RHODEN, LACY, DOWNEY & COLBERT (AV)

111 Park Circle Drive, P.O. Box 13762, 39236
Telephone: 601-932-1155
Telecopier: 601-936-2515
Email: rldclaw@netdoor.com *URL:* http://www.Thrhoden-law.com

MEMBERS OF FIRM

John H. Downey
William L. Colbert, Jr.

For full biographical listings, see the Martindale-Hubbell Law Directory

SHELL, BUFORD, BUFKIN, CALLICUTT & PERRY (AV)

920 Trustmark Building, P.O. Box 157, 39205
Telephone: 601-948-2291
Facsimile: 601-352-6968

MEMBERS OF FIRM

Cary E. Bufkin
Kenneth G. Perry
Douglas R. Duke
James N. Bullock
Ken R. Adcock
Eugene R. Naylor

ASSOCIATES

E. Frank Goodman
Mark D. Morrison

(See Next Column)

SHELL, BUFORD, BUFKIN, CALLICUTT & PERRY—*Continued*

OF COUNSEL

K. Hayes Callicutt

Representative Clients: Mississippi Baptist Medical Center; Mississippi Chemical Corp.; Aetna Casualty and Surety Co.; American International Group; Atlantic Mutual Insurance Co.; Commercial Union Insurance Co.; United States Fidelity and Guaranty Co.; Home Insurance Co.; The Chubb Group; Trustmark National Bank.

For full biographical listings, see the Martindale-Hubbell Law Directory

STEEN REYNOLDS & DALEHITE, LLP (AV)

Heritage Building, 401 East Capitol Street, Suite 415, P.O. Box 900, 39201
Telephone: 601-969-7054
Telecopier: 601-353-3782
Email: firm@Steenrd.com

Jerome B. Steen (1933-1997)

MEMBERS OF FIRM

Jimmie B. Reynolds, Jr.
William M. Dalehite, Jr.
Michael V. Cory, Jr.
Lee Ann Rikard
Lanny R. Pace
Heather L. Saum

Representative Clients: Allstate Insurance Co.; St. Paul Insurance Cos.; Indiana Lumbermens Mutual Insurance Co.; United Services Automobile Assn.; Empire Fire & Marine Insurance Co.; Sears Roebuck & Co.; State Farm Mutual Co.; State Farm Fire & Casualty Co.
Reference: Trustmark National Bank, Jackson, Mississippi.

For full biographical listings, see the Martindale-Hubbell Law Directory

UPSHAW, WILLIAMS, BIGGERS, BECKHAM & RIDDICK, LLP (AV)

Suite 300 Plaza One, 715 South Pear Orchard Road (Ridgeland), 39147
Telephone: 601-978-1996
Facsimile: 601-978-1949
Mailing Address: P.O. Box 9147, Jackson, Mississippi, 39286-9147
Email: lexjax@uwbbr.com
Greenwood, Mississippi Office: 309 Fulton Street, P.O. Drawer 8230, 38935-8230.
Telephone: 662-455-1613.
Facsimile: 662-453-9245. Email: lexgwd@uwbbr.com.

MEMBERS OF FIRM

James E. Upshaw (Resident, Greenwood Office)
Tommie G. Williams (Resident, Greenwood Office)
Marc A. Biggers (Resident, Greenwood Office)
Glenn F. Beckham (Resident, Greenwood Office)
Roger C. Riddick
F. Ewin Henson III (Resident, Greenwood Office)
Lonnie D. Bailey (Resident, Greenwood Office)
Robert S. Upshaw (Resident, Greenwood Office)
Clinton M. Guenther (Resident, Greenwood Office)
Richard C. Williams, Jr.
Richard L. Kimmel (Resident, Greenwood Office)
Mark C. Carroll
W. Hugh Gillon IV
Paul L. Goodman (Resident, Greenwood Office)
Walter C. Morrison IV

ASSOCIATES

Steven H. Funderburg
Bonnie Bridgers Smith
Patrick M. Tatum
Craig R. Sessums
James K. Warrington (Resident, Greenwood Office)
Cecil D. McClellan, III
J. L. Wilson, IV (Resident, Greenwood Office)

OF COUNSEL

Ben L. Riddick
John R. Countiss III

Representative Clients: United States Fidelity & Guaranty Co.; State Farm Mutual Automobile Insurance Co.; CNA Insurance Cos.; St. Paul Fire & Marine Insurance Co.; Travelers/Aetna Property and Casualty Corp.; Kemper Insurance Co.; Zurich-America Insurance Group; Risk Enterprise Management, Ltd.; Allstate Insurance Co.

For Complete List of Firm Personnel, See General Section

For full biographical listings, see the Martindale-Hubbell Law Directory

WATKINS & EAGER (AV)

A Professional Limited Liability Company
Suite 300 The Emporium Building, 400 East Capitol Street, P.O. Box 650, 39205
Telephone: 601-948-6470
Facsimile: 601-354-3623

MEMBERS OF FIRM

James A. Becker, Jr.
Clifford B. Ammons
Richard T. Lawrence
Robert H. Pedersen
Rebecca Lee Wiggs
Susan Latham Steffey

Representative Clients: Audubon Insurance Group; AVEMCO Aviation Insurance Co.; CGU Insurance Co.; Cigna Property and Casualty Cos.; CNA Insurance; Medical Assurance Company of Mississippi; Mississippi Insurance Guaranty Assn.; New York Life Insurance Co.; Tokio Marine and Fire Insurance Group.

(See Next Column)

For Complete List of Firm Personnel, See General Section

For full biographical listings, see the Martindale-Hubbell Law Directory

*LAUREL,** Jones Co.

GIBBES GRAVES MULLINS HORTMAN HARLOW MARTINDALE & JONES, PLLC (AV)

414 West Oak Street, P.O. Drawer 1409, 39441-1409
Telephone: 601-649-8611
FAX: 601-649-6062

MEMBERS OF FIRM

William S. Mullins, III
Norman Gene Hortman, Jr.
Eugene M. Harlow
David L. Martindale
Deidra D. Jones

ASSOCIATES

Brett W. Robinson
Leslie P. Barry

Representative Clients: St. Paul Insurance; The Virginia Insurance Reciprocal; BellSouth; Liberty Mutual Ins. Co.; Southern Guaranty Insurance Co.; Utica Mutual Insurance Co.; The Fireman's Fund Insurance Cos.; State Auto Insurance Co.; American Bankers Insurance Co.; Audubon Insurance Group; AmFed Companies, LLC.

For full biographical listings, see the Martindale-Hubbell Law Directory

*MERIDIAN,** Lauderdale Co.

GLOVER, YOUNG, WALTON, PHILLIPS & TUCKER, PLLC (AV)

Jefferson Square Office Plaza, 1724-A 23rd Avenue, P.O. Box 5514, 39302-5514
Telephone: 601-693-1301
Telecopy: 601-693-1363
Email: gywptpsp@hotmail.com

H. Wingfield Glover, Jr.
Ralph E. Young, Jr.
Ronnie L. Walton
P. Scott Phillips
Judson T. Tucker

Representative Clients: Alfa Insurance Companies; American States Insurance Co.; Deposit Guaranty National Bank; General Agents Insurance Company of America, Inc.; Great River Insurance; Jeff Anderson Regional Medical Center; Liberty National Life Insurance Co.; Mississippi Power Co.; State Auto Insurance Companies; Universal Underwriters.

For Complete List of Firm Personnel, See General Section

For full biographical listings, see the Martindale-Hubbell Law Directory

*NATCHEZ,** Adams Co.

GWIN, LEWIS & PUNCHES, LLP (AV)

319 Market Street, P.O. Box 1344, 39120-3465
Telephone: 601-446-6621
FAX: 601-442-6175
Email: gwin1p@bkbank.com
Woodville, Mississippi Office: 457 Main Street.
Telephone: 601-446-6621.

MEMBERS OF FIRM

Lucien C. Gwin, Jr.
W. Bruce Lewis
Robert R. Punches
Lucien C. Gwin, III
Christopher E. Kelley

Mississippi Counsel for: International Paper Company.
Representative Clients: Sammons Communications, Inc.; Britton & Koontz First National Bank; Mississippi Farm Bureau Insurance Co.

For full biographical listings, see the Martindale-Hubbell Law Directory

*OXFORD,** Lafayette Co.

FREELAND & FREELAND (AV)

1013 Jackson Avenue, P.O. Box 269, 38655
Telephone: 662-234-3414
Telecopier: 662-234-0604
Email: thf4@watervalley.net

MEMBERS OF FIRM

T. H. Freeland, III
T. H. Freeland, IV

Representative Clients: American Republic Insurance Co.; Carolina Casualty Insurance Co.; John Deere Insurance Co.; Express Insurance Co.; Fireman's Fund Insurance; Northwestern Mutual Life Insurance Co.; Sentry Insurance; American Insurance Co.; Ohio Casualty Group; Home Insurance Co.

For full biographical listings, see the Martindale-Hubbell Law Directory

Oxford—Continued

HOLCOMB DUNBAR, A PROFESSIONAL ASSOCIATION (AV)

1217 Jackson Avenue P.O. Drawer 707, 38655
Telephone: 601-234-8775
Facsimile: 601-238-7552
Email: hdccw@holcombdunbar.com *URL:* http://www.holcombdunbar.com
Clarksdale, Mississippi Office: 152 Delta Avenue, P.O. Box 368, 38614.
Telephone: 601-627-2241.
Facsimile: 601-627-9788.
Southaven, Mississippi Office: Suite 1, 728 Goodman Road East, P.O. Box 190, 38671.
Telephone: 601-349-0664.
Facsimile: 601-349-2432.

Jack F. Dunbar
Edward A. Moss
Thomas J. Suszek
Michael N. Watts
Marjorie T. O'Donnell
David D. O'Donnell
T. Swayze Alford
R. Bradley Best
Angela M. Spivey
Walter Alan Davis
Mark R. Smith

Representative Clients: Southern Farm Bureau Casualty Insurance Co.; State Farm Mutual Fire & Casualty Insurance Co.; Fireman's Fund Insurance Cos.; The Employers Group Insurance Co.; Central Mutual Insurance Co.; Commercial Union Insurance Cos; Federated Mutual Insurance Co.; Shelter Insurance Co.; Atlanta Casualty Insurance Cos.; United Southern Assurance Corp.

For Complete List of Firm Personnel, See General Section

For full biographical listings, see the Martindale-Hubbell Law Directory

*PASCAGOULA,** Jackson Co.

BROWN, WATT & BUCHANAN, P.A. (AV)

3112 Canty Street, P.O. Box 2220, 39569-2220
Telephone: 228-762-0035
Telecopier: 228-762-0299
Email: mail@bwblaw.com *URL:* http://www.bwblaw.com
Biloxi, Mississippi Office: 115 Main Street, P.O. Box 1377.
Telephone: 228-374-2999.
Fax: 228-435-7090.

Raymond L. Brown
W. Lee Watt
Patrick R. Buchanan
W. Mark Edwards
A. Kelly Sessoms, III
Alan K. Sudduth

General Counsel for: Mississippi Export Railroad Co.; Pascagoula Municipal Separate School District.
Representative Clients: United States Fidelity & Guaranty Co.; The Travelers Companies; The Home Insurance Co.; CSX Transportation, Inc.; Blue Cross-Blue Shield of Mississippi; Burlington Insurance Co.; Continental Insurance; Deere & Co.

For full biographical listings, see the Martindale-Hubbell Law Directory

BRYAN, NELSON, SCHROEDER, CASTIGLIOLA & BANAHAN (AV)

1103 Jackson Avenue, P.O. Drawer 1529, 39568-1529
Telephone: 228-762-6631
Fax: 228-769-6392
Email: bns@datasync.com

MEMBERS OF FIRM

E. S. Ned Nelson (1928-1985)
John F. Bryan, III (1915-1994)
Ernest R. Schroeder
Vincent J. Castigliola, Jr.
John A. Banahan
H. Benjamin Mullen

ASSOCIATES

Melinda O. Johnson
Scott Corlew

For full biographical listings, see the Martindale-Hubbell Law Directory

COLINGO, WILLIAMS, HEIDELBERG, STEINBERGER & MCELHANEY, P.A. (AV)

711 Delmas Avenue, P.O. Box 1407, 39568-1407
Telephone: 228-762-8021
FAX: 228-762-7589
Email: info@colingowilliams.com *URL:* http://www.ColingoWilliams.com

Joe R. Colingo
Roy C. Williams
James H. Heidelberg
Karl R. Steinberger
James H. Colmer, Jr.

Representative Clients: International Paper Co.; R.J. Reynolds; CBS Corp.; Kemper Group; Singing River Hospital System; Mississippi Gulf Coast Regional Wastewater Authority; Medical Assurance Company of Mississippi; Mutual Assurance of Alabama; Dole Food Co.

For full biographical listings, see the Martindale-Hubbell Law Directory

SOUTHAVEN, De Soto Co.

HOLCOMB DUNBAR, A PROFESSIONAL ASSOCIATION (AV)

Suite 1, 728 Goodman Road East, P.O. Box 190, 38671
Telephone: 601-349-0664
Facsimile: 601-349-2432
Email: hdccw@holcombdunbar.com *URL:* http://www.holcombdunbar.com
Clarksdale, Mississippi Office: 152 Delta Avenue, P.O. Box 368, 38614.
Telephone: 601-627-2241.
Facsimile: 601-627-9788.
Oxford, Mississippi Office: 1217 Jackson Avenue, P.O. Drawer 707, 38655.
Telephone: 601-234-8775.
Facsimile: 601-238-7552.

William A. Baskin
John Ramsey McCarroll, III
Michael K. Graves
Billy C. Campbell, Jr.

Representative Clients: Southern Farm Bureau Casualty Insurance Co.; State Farm Mutual Fire & Casualty Insurance Co.; Fireman's Fund Insurance Cos.; The Employers Group Insurance Co.; Central Mutual Insurance Co.; Commercial Union Insurance Cos; Federated Mutual Insurance Co.; Shelter Insurance Co.; Atlanta Casualty Insurance Cos.; United Southern Assurance Corp.

For Complete List of Firm Personnel, See General Section
For full biographical listings, see the Martindale-Hubbell Law Directory

*TUPELO,** Lee Co.

WEBB, SANDERS, BALDUCCI & SMITH, P.L.L.C. (AV)

363 North Broadway, P.O. Box 496, 38802-0496
Telephone: 662-844-2137
Fax: 662-842-3863
Email: webbsand@webbsanders.com *URL:* http://www.webbsanders.com
Oxford, Mississippi Office: 405 South Lamar Boulevard, P.O. Box 148, 38655.
Telephone: 662-236-5700.
Fax: 662-236-5800.

Dan W. Webb
Timothy R. Balducci
Kent E. Smith
B. Wayne Williams
Sherrie L. Moore
Sammye S. Tharp
K. Kathy Brown
Guthrie T. Abbott, Jr.
Emily D. Wade

OF COUNSEL

Rachael Howell Webb
Benjamin H. Sanders (1942-1999)

Representative Clients: Farm Bureau; Mississippi Farm Bureau; Southern Farm Bureau; GAB Business Services, Inc.; Gulf Guaranty Life Insurance; Phillips and Assocs.; State Farm Fire & Casualty Co.; State Farm Mutual Automobile Insurance Company.

For full biographical listings, see the Martindale-Hubbell Law Directory

MISSOURI

CAPE GIRARDEAU, Cape Girardeau Co.

OLIVER, OLIVER & WALTZ, P.C. (AV)

400 Broadway, P.O. Box 559, 63702-0559
Telephone: 573-335-8278
Fax: 573-334-6375
Email: oliver@ldd.net

John L. Oliver, Jr.
James Frederick Waltz

Representative Clients: Mercantile Bank of Southern Missouri; Union Electric Co.; Southwestern Bell Corp.; Ford Motor Co.; Consolidated Drainage District; MOMEDICO; The Travelers; The Hartford; The Kemper Group; AAA of Missouri.

For Complete List of Firm Personnel, See General Section
For full biographical listings, see the Martindale-Hubbell Law Directory

*COLUMBIA,** Boone Co.

KNIGHT, FORD, ATWILL, PARSHALL & BAKER (AV)

609 East Walnut Street, P.O. Box 1097, 65205
Telephone: 573-449-2613
Telecopier: 573-875-8154
Email: kfwapb@computerland.com

MEMBERS OF FIRM

David L. Knight
Hamp Ford
Daniel K. Atwill
Jeffrey O. Parshall
Michael R. Baker
Susan Ford Robertson
Jeffrey H. Blaylock
David W. Walker
Mariam W. Decker
Edward L. Guinn
Richard L. Montgomery, Jr.

(See Next Column)

KNIGHT, FORD, ATWILL, PARSHALL & BAKER—*Continued*

ASSOCIATES

Justin R. Davis
Elizabeth Hodge Weber
Daniel E. Himmelberg
Robert J. Buckley
Jordan M. Humphreys

OF COUNSEL

James R. Green

Representative Clients: Aetna Insurance; Alexsis, Inc.; Allied Group; American Med. Int.; American States/Western Insurance Cos.; Argonaut Insurance Co.; Automobile Club Inter-Insurance Exchange; The Bar Plan; Cameron Mutual Insurance Co.; Casualty Indemnity Exchange.

For full biographical listings, see the Martindale-Hubbell Law Directory

OLIVER, WALKER, WILSON & EHRHARDT, LLC (AV)

Suite 406, 401 Locust Street, P.O. Box 977, 65205
Telephone: 573-443-3134
Telecopier: 573-442-6323
Email: owwe@socket.net

MEMBERS OF FIRM

David A. Oliver
Roland P. Walker
Betty K. Wilson
Glen R. Ehrhardt
Cynthia Barchet
Ronald N. Sweet

Representative Clients: Aetna Insurance Co.; Allied Group; American Family Insurance Group; Safeco; CNA Insurance; Federated Insurance Co.; Old Republic; Shelter Insurance Cos.

For full biographical listings, see the Martindale-Hubbell Law Directory

*JEFFERSON CITY,** Cole Co.

CARSON & COIL, P.C. (AV)

515 East High, P.O. Box 28, 65102
Telephone: 573-636-2177
Telecopier: 573-636-7119
Email: general@carsoncoil.com

Forrest P. Carson (1910-1981)
Cullen Coil (1907-1989)
Michael P. Riley
Ronald R. McMillin
Eugene G. Bushmann
James W. Gallaher
Lori J. Levine
Rudolph L. Veit
Michael Madsen
R. Max Humphreys
Mark A. Ludwig
Dana L. Frese
Edward C. Clausen
Carla G. Holste
Kent L. Brown
Douglas W. Hennon
Charles J. McPheeters
Paul T. Graham

Jack C. Hauser, Jr.
Charles A. "Chip" Gentry
James W. "Jamie" Gallaher, Jr.

General Counsel for: Capital Reserve Life Insurance Co.; Missouri Farm Bureau; Healthcare Services Group.
Reference: Central Trust Bank.

For full biographical listings, see the Martindale-Hubbell Law Directory

HENDREN AND ANDRAE (AV)

Riverview Office Center, 221 Bolivar Street, Suite 300, P.O. Box 1069, 65102
Telephone: 573-636-8135
Telecopier: 573-636-5226
Email: henand@socket.net

OF COUNSEL

Henry Andrae

MEMBERS OF FIRM

Charles H. Howard (1925-1970)
John E. Burruss, Jr. (1933-1985)
John H. Hendren (1907-1988)
Gerald E. Roark (1956-1995)
Richard S. Brownlee, III
Michael A. Dallmeyer
Duane E. Schreimann
Douglas L. Van Camp
Michael G. Berry
John W. Kuebler
Susan M. Turner
Christopher P. Rackers

ASSOCIATES

Sara C. Michael
Patricia D. Perkins
Brian K. Francka

Representative Clients: United States Fidelity & Guaranty; CNA; Travelers-/Aetna; Zurich; State Farm Insurance Companies; GEICO; Liberty Mutual; United State Automobile Association; AAA.

For full biographical listings, see the Martindale-Hubbell Law Directory

INGLISH & MONACO, P.C. (AV)

Monroe House Law Center, 237 East High Street, P.O. Box 67, 65102
Telephone: 573-634-2522
Telecopier: 573-634-4526
Email: inglishmonaco-jc@socket.net
California, Missouri Office: 329 South Oak.
Telephone: 573-796-4333.

(See Next Column)

Lake Ozark, Missouri Office: Cliffside Office Center, 2140 Bagnell Dam Boulevard, 65049.
Telephone: 573-964-6211.
Telecopier: 573-964-6787.

John W. Inglish
Nicholas M. Monaco
Ann Monaco Warren
Mark G. R. Warren
Lewis Z. Bridges
Timothy R. Cisar
David G. Bandré
Daniel E. Hunt
Daniel C. Mizell
Stephen W. Richey
William Barton
Charles P. Dribben (1929-1991)

OF COUNSEL

Andrew Jackson Higgins

References: Central Trust Bank; Jefferson Bank.

For full biographical listings, see the Martindale-Hubbell Law Directory

JOPLIN, Jasper Co.

BLANCHARD, ROBERTSON, MITCHELL & CARTER, P.C. (AV)

320 West Fourth Street, P.O. Box 1626, 64802
Telephone: 417-623-1515
Facsimile: 417-623-6865

Malcolm L. Robertson
Karl W. Blanchard, Jr.
Ronald E. Mitchell
Greg B. Carter

Ronald G. Sparlin

Representative Clients: Chubb Group; First National Bank of Sarcoxie; First State Bank; Liberty Mutual Insurance Co.; Missouri Southern State College; St. Paul Insurance Co.; State Farm Insurance Cos.; Southwestern Bell Telephone Co.; Tamko Asphalt Products; United States Fidelity & Guaranty Co..

For Complete List of Firm Personnel, See General Section

For full biographical listings, see the Martindale-Hubbell Law Directory

KANSAS CITY, Jackson, Clay, Platte & Cass Cos.

FRANKE & SCHULTZ, A PROFESSIONAL CORPORATION (AV)

1312 Commerce Tower, 911 Main Street, 64105
Telephone: 816-421-7100
Telecopier: 816-421-7915
Email: Franke.Schultz@Micro.com
Springfield, Missouri Office: 300 John Q. Hammons Pkwy., Suite 701, 65806.
Telephone: 417-863-0040.
Fax: 417-863-6286.
Overland Park, Kansas Office: 5340 College, 66211.
Telephone: 913-327-7661.
Fax: 913-327-7669.

John E. Franke
John G. Schultz
John L. Mullen
Bradley C. Nielsen
Ryan E. Karaim
Jill Frost
Keith A. Cary
Wendell E. Koerner, Jr.

Cari F. Walsh
Michael J. Tubbesing
Andrew D. Hennier
Laurel Stevenson
Shawn G. Foster
John H. Kizer
Edward J. Barbosa

For full biographical listings, see the Martindale-Hubbell Law Directory

*KIRKSVILLE,** Adair Co.

OSWALD, COTTEY & TEMPLETON, A PROFESSIONAL CORPORATION (AV)

Suite A, 210 North Elson, P.O. Box K, 63501
Telephone: 660-665-5628
Fax: 660-665-6035
Email: oswaldcotteytempleton@yahoo.com

Louis F. Cottey (1931-1999)
Thomas R. Oswald
Scott L. Templeton

Brenda Wall-Swedberg
Theresa L. Kenney
Susan R. Barrow
David Briggs

For full biographical listings, see the Martindale-Hubbell Law Directory

ST. LOUIS, (Independent City)

AMELUNG, WULFF & WILLENBROCK, P.C. (AV)

17th Floor, 515 Olive Street, 63101
Telephone: 314-436-6757 Telecopier: 314-231-7305
Email: info@awwstl.com
Belleville, Illinois Office: P.O. Box 368, 62222.
Telephone: 618-233-9765.

(See Next Column)

AMELUNG, WULFF & WILLENBROCK P.C., *St. Louis—Continued*

Robert A. Wulff
Ronald C. Willenbrock
Stephen D. Hoyne
Michael C. Margherio
Robert J. Foley
A. Stephen Pernoud
Robert J. Wulff
Edward J. Bippen
Ann Marie Piana

OF COUNSEL

James J. Amelung

William J. Magrath
Julie A. Stoff
Rhonda K. Jenkins
Christopher A. Allen
Scott J. Dickenson
Harry M. Stockman

Representative Clients: American Family Insurance Group; Farm Bureau Town & Country Insurance Company of Missouri; Farmers Alliance Mutual Insurance Co.; Great Central Insurance Co.; Insurance Company of North America; Pennsylvania National Insurance Group; Ranger/Pan American Insurance Cos.; St. Paul Insurance Cos.; U.S.A.A.; Medical Defense Assn.

For full biographical listings, see the Martindale-Hubbell Law Directory

BEHR, MANTOVANI, MCCARTER & POTTER, P.C. (AV)

7777 Bonhomme Avenue, Suite 1810, 63105
Telephone: 314-862-3800
Fax: 314-862-3953

Anthony R. Behr
Mark P. Mantovani
W. Dudley McCarter
Stephen J. Potter
John W. Maupin
Thomas J. Hayek

Darren E. Daley
Christopher L. Kanzler
Michael J. Zarrilli
James T. Corrigan
JulieAnn M. Broyles

For full biographical listings, see the Martindale-Hubbell Law Directory

BRINKER & DOYEN, L.L.P. (AV)

120 South Central, Suite 700, 63105
Telephone: 314-863-6311
Telecopier: 314-863-8197
Email: brinkerandoyen@earthlink.net

PARTNERS

Bernard C. Brinker
John G. Doyen
Gary P. Paul
Jeffrey J. Brinker
Scott C. Harper
Lawrence R. Smith
James C. Thoele
Kevin M. Hazlett

ASSOCIATES

Aaron I. Mandel
Jon R. Sanner
Karen Marie Speiser
David N. Bohrer
Scot C. Allen

OF COUNSEL

Michael E. Magliari

LEGAL SUPPORT PERSONNEL

Jacqueline L. Hunstein (Office Administrator)

Representative Clients: Farmers Insurance Group; State Farm Insurance Cos.; Transamerica Insurance Group; The Medical Protective Co.; Millers Mutual Insurance Co.; United States Fidelity & Guaranty Co.

For full biographical listings, see the Martindale-Hubbell Law Directory

EVANS & DIXON, L.L.C. (AV)

1200 Saint Louis Place, 200 North Broadway, 63102-2749
Telephone: 314-621-7755
URL: http://www.evans-dixon.com
Kansas City, Missouri Office: City Center Square, 1100 Main Street, Suite 2000, 64105-2119.
Telephone: 816-472-4600.
Edwardsville, Illinois Office: 17 Ginger Creek Meadows, P.O. Box 405. 62025-3508.
Telephone: 618-656-8505.
Leawood, Kansas Office: 8016 State Line Road, Suite 207. 66208-3713.
Telephone: 913-649-5386.

MEMBERS OF FIRM

Robert M. Evans
Robert W. Wilson (Resident, Edwardsville, Illinois Office)
Sam P. Rynearson
Edward M. Vokoun
Harvey G. Schneider
James B. Kennedy
Jeffry S. Thomsen
James A. Thoenen
Gerre S. Langton
John A. Michener
Raymond J. Flunker
Stefan J. Glynias
James M. Gallen
Robert E. Bidstrup
Edward S. Meyer
Bradley V. Spaunhorst
Robert J. Krehbiel
Robert N. Hendershot, II
Robert P. Numrich (Kansas City, Missouri and Leawood, Kansas Offices)
William F. Ringer (Resident, Kansas City, Missouri Office)
Marilyn C. Phillips
David S. Ware
George T. Floros
Robert W. Haeckel
Michael F. Banahan
Carl D. Lothman
Betsy J. Levitt

(See Next Column)

MEMBERS OF FIRM (Continued)

Michael Reda (Resident, Edwardsville, Illinois Office)
Brian J. Fowler (Kansas City, Missouri and Leawood, Kansas Offices)
Thomas Clinkenbeard (Resident, Kansas City, Missouri Office)
Priscilla F. Gunn
Jeffrey K. Suess
Kevin P. Schnurbusch
Adrian P. Sulser
Paul D. Larimore
Joy Urbom Taylor
Debbie C. Snyder
Patrick A. Patterson
Timothy M. Tierney
Kim M. Parks
John S. McCollough
Mark R. Kornblum

OF COUNSEL

William W. Evans
Rex R. Redhair (Resident, Kansas City, Missouri Office)
Edward W. Warner

ASSOCIATES

Christine A. Alsop
Scott C. Annunziata
Todd L. Beekley
Joan B. Bernstein
Joseph F. Callahan
Clinton D. Collier (Resident, Kansas City, Missouri and Leawood, Kansas Offices)
Lynn M. Curtis (Resident, Kansas City, Missouri Office)
Kristan M. Dames
Raymond B. Flojo
Patricia B. Frank
Mitchell A. Gibson
Lisa A. Green
Jennifer K. Greene
Brent W. Halbleib
Cynthia Hamilton
Rhonda J. Henry-Webb
Susan M. Herold
Robert L. Hinson
John W. Hoffman (Resident, Edwardsville, Illinois Office)
J. Lee Johnson
Paul F. Keeven
John P. Kemppainen, Jr.
Daniel J. Kertz
Carl Kessinger
Martin A. Klug
John Joseph Lee
Mary Anne Lindsey
Jay Lory
Kevin J. Marquitz
Cynthia A. Masterson
Erin M. Matis
Jacqueline E. Moore
Terry J. Mort (Not admitted in MO)
Karen A. Mulroy
Cristina Clare Nolan
Matthew P. O'Grady
James D. O'Leary
Jeffrey M. Proske
David J. Reynolds, Jr.
Michele G. Roy
David Louis Schrader
Steven R. Sharp
David K. Simkins
Dean A. Stark
William B. Starnes, II (Resident, Edwardsville, Illinois Office)
Elizabeth S. Stumpf
Douglas S. Teasdale
Carol Marie Crandall Van Sambeek
Ethan Vaughan (Resident, Kansas City, Missouri Office)
Helen J.S. White (Not admitted in MO)
Betsy S. Willer
Wendellyn S. Wright

Attorneys for: Allstate Insurance Co.; Chrysler Corp.; Chubb & Son, Inc.; CNA Insurance Co.; Crawford and Co.; Gallagher Bassett Services, Inc.; Kemper Insurance Group; Southwestern Bell Telephone Co.; Travelers Insurance Co.; Zurich Insurance Co.

For full biographical listings, see the Martindale-Hubbell Law Directory

GODFREY, VANDOVER & BURNS, INC., A PROFESSIONAL CORPORATION (AV)

21st Floor, 720 Olive Street, 63101
Telephone: 314-421-1857
FAX: 314-421-1912
Cable Address: "Jogo"

Samuel T. Vandover
Denis C. Burns

John B. Singleton

References: Bank of St. Louis; Farm and Home Savings & Loan; Boatmen's National Bank; Southside National Bank.

For full biographical listings, see the Martindale-Hubbell Law Directory

GOFFSTEIN, RASKAS, POMERANTZ, KRAUS, SHERMAN, RUTHMEYER & SUSMAN, L.L.C. (AV)

7701 Clayton Road (Clayton), 63117-1371
Telephone: 314-721-7171
Telecopier: 314-721-7765

Sanford Goffstein
Don R. Sherman
Robert M. Susman

Lawrence J. Permuter
Edward L. Adelman
Dana D. Eilers
Lori R. Koch
Robert E. Tucker
Grant T. Williams
Craig S. Redler
Brian Robert Seigel

Reference: Truman Bank.

For full biographical listings, see the Martindale-Hubbell Law Directory

HALE LAW FIRM (AV)

1221 Locust Street, Suite 310, 63103
Telephone: 314-231-3168
Fax: 314-231-4072

(See Next Column)

HALE LAW FIRM—*Continued*

MEMBER OF FIRM

Larry D. Hale

ASSOCIATES

Gloria J. Reno
Andrew T. Pickens

For full biographical listings, see the Martindale-Hubbell Law Directory

MOSER AND MARSALEK, P.C. (AV)

Suite 700, St. Louis Place, 200 North Broadway, 63102-2730
Telephone: 314-421-5364
Telecopier: 314-421-5640
Email: postmaster@moser.com
Kansas City Office: 1101 Walnut Street, Suite 1510, 64106.
Telephone: 816-471-6060.
Telecopier: 816-471-7744.
Belleville, Illinois Office: 23 South First Street, 62204.
Telephone: 618-234-1408.

W. Edwin Moser (1894-1969)
G. W. Marsalek (1913-1963)
Frank X. Cleary (1900-1975)
John S. Marsalek (1887-1980)
Julian C. Jaeckel (1924-1984)
Joseph H. Mueller
F. Douglas O'Leary
William L. Davis
David L. Zwart
Peter F. Spataro
Brian R. Plegge
Philip L. Willman
Thomas J. Magee
Doreen A. Graham
Kevin M. Leahy
Robyn G. Fox
Brian D. Winer
Jeffrey W. Wright
Terry L. Pijut
Stephen G. Reuter

Ann Gaylor Rucker
Karie E. Casey
Mark A. Cordes
Mark D. Madden
Thomas Edward Fagan
Catherine M. Vale
Neal J. Wallace
Stephen J. Telken
Matthew S. Hendricks

OF COUNSEL

John J. Horgan
Parks G. Carpenter

Representative Clients: Aetna Casualty & Surety; American Indemnity Group; American International Group; Chubb Group Insurance Cos.; Fireman's Fund Insurance Co.; Goodyear Tire & Rubber Co.; Medical Protective Insurance Co.

For full biographical listings, see the Martindale-Hubbell Law Directory

NOCE & BUCKLEY, L.L.C. (AV)

515 Olive Street - Suite 800, 63101-1839
Telephone: 314-621-3434
Fax: 314-621-3485
Email: nocebuck@anet-stl.com

PARTNERS

Gerard T. Noce
Martin J. Buckley
Thomas M. Buckley

ASSOCIATES

Kevin Francis Hormuth
Christiana M. Rush
Brett W. Batty

OF COUNSEL

Eugene K. Buckley

For full biographical listings, see the Martindale-Hubbell Law Directory

THE LAW OFFICES OF THOMAS J. NOONAN, P.C. (AV)

Gateway One, 701 Market Street, Suite 425, 63101
Telephone: 314-241-4747
Facsimile: 314-241-2039
Email: attorneytn@thomasnoonan.com

Thomas J. Noonan

Kathryn E. Van Voorhees
Gary E. Wiseman
Amy T. Tucker
Stephen J. Barber
Tammie J. Philbrick
Andrew D. Ryan

OF COUNSEL

John G. Schultz

For full biographical listings, see the Martindale-Hubbell Law Directory

THE O'MALLEY LAW FIRM, P.C. (AV)

Suite 102, Ten South Brentwood Boulevard, 63105
Telephone: 314-721-8001
Telecopier: 314-721-3754
Email: omalfirm@stlnet.com

Kevin F. O'Malley
John F. Cooney
Mary L. Reitz
Debra Stachowski Pierce
Linda Cary Hinshaw
Weldon N. Johnson

For full biographical listings, see the Martindale-Hubbell Law Directory

RABBITT, PITZER & SNODGRASS, P.C. (AV)

One NationsBank Plaza, Suite 2300, 800 Market Street, 63101-2608
Telephone: 314-421-5545
Facsimile: 314-421-3144
Email: rps@rabbittlaw.com *URL:* http://www.rabbittlaw.com
Belleville, Illinois Office: 23 South First Street.

Daniel T. Rabbitt
Michael J. Pitzer
Gary E. Snodgrass
Richard J. Zalasky
Peter J. Dunne
Steven J. Hughes
Jerome C. Simon
Donald L. O'Keefe
Seth G. Gausnell
William S. Thomas
Douglas S. Dove
Kimberly Cates Wiseman
James J. Bentivoglio
Jason L. Call
Paula Jane Coughlin
James A. Hansen
Mark M. Anson
Daniel D. Bennett
Elizabeth P. Schott
Christopher J. Lang
J. Phillip Bryant
James Jonathan Rosemergy

For full biographical listings, see the Martindale-Hubbell Law Directory

ROBERTS, PERRYMAN, BOMKAMP & MEIVES, P.C. (AV)

Suite 2300, One Mercantile Center, 63101
Telephone: 314-421-1850
Cable Address: "Henrogo"
Telecopier: 314-421-4346
Email: rpbm@istnet.net
Belleville, Illinois Office: 23 Public Square, Suite 402.
Telephone: 618-277-9955.

Ted L. Perryman
Gary W. Bomkamp
John I. Schaberg
John L. Walker
Thomas J. Kernell
Robert C. Anderson
James D. Maschoff

Reference: Boatmen's National Bank.

For full biographical listings, see the Martindale-Hubbell Law Directory

WUESTLING & JAMES, L.C. (AV)

Suite 730, The Locust Building, 1015 Locust Street, 63101
Telephone: 314-421-6565
FAX: 314-421-4724

MEMBERS OF FIRM

Richard C. Wuestling, III (1928-1984)
William F. James
R. C. Wuestling
James G. Onder

ASSOCIATES

Lindsay A. Dibler
Michael W. Shelton
Elizabeth G. Roper
Heejun "Jay" Kim

Reference: Mercantile Trust Co.

For full biographical listings, see the Martindale-Hubbell Law Directory

*SPRINGFIELD,** Greene Co.

HALL, ANSLEY, RODGERS & CONDRY, A PROFESSIONAL CORPORATION (AV)

Suite A, 1370 East Primrose, 65804
Telephone: 417-890-8700
Fax: 417-890-8855
Email: harcpc@intrcom.com *URL:* http://www.harcpc.com

Fred L. Hall
David W. Ansley
Lynn C. Rodgers
James B. Condry
D. Patrick Sweeney
Jan Y. Millington
Michael P. Mergen
Deborah K. Dodge

Daniel B. Johnson
Lisa McKay
Benjamin A. Stringer

Reference: Commerce Bank of Springfield (Trust Department).

For full biographical listings, see the Martindale-Hubbell Law Directory

MONTANA

*BILLINGS,** Yellowstone Co.

BROWN LAW FIRM, P.C. (AV)

315 North 24th Street, P.O. Drawer 849, 59103-0849
Telephone: 406-248-2611
FAX: 406-248-3128
URL: http://www.brownfirm.com
Bozeman, Montana Office: 510 South 23rd Street.
Telephone: 406-587-8486.
Fax: 406-587-4524.

(See Next Column)

BROWN LAW FIRM P.C., *Billings—Continued*

Rockwood Brown
Steven J. Harman
John J. Russell
Michael P. Heringer
Guy W. Rogers
Scott G. Gratton
Don M. Hayes
Lisa A. Rodeghiero
James E. Roberts
Margy Bonner
William A. D'Alton

For Complete List of Firm Personnel, See General Section

For full biographical listings, see the Martindale-Hubbell Law Directory

CROWLEY, HAUGHEY, HANSON, TOOLE & DIETRICH, P.L.L.P. (AV)

500 Transwestern II, 490 North 31st Street, P.O. Box 2529, 59103
Telephone: 406-252-3441
Fax: 406-259-4159
Email: crowley@crowleylaw.com
Helena, Montana Office: IBM Building, 100 North Park Avenue, Suite 300, 59601.
Telephone: 406-449-4165.
Fax: 406-449-5149.
Kalispell, Montana Office: 431 1st Avenue West, 59901.
Telephone: 406-752-6644.
Fax: 406-752-5108.
Williston, North Dakota Office: 113 East Broadway, 58801.
Telephone: 701-572-2200.
Fax: 701-572-7072.

OF COUNSEL

Bruce R. Toole
Neil S. Keefer
George C. Dalthorp

MEMBERS OF FIRM

Herbert I. Pierce, III
Ronald R. Lodders
Lawrence B. Cozzens
Carolyn S. Ostby
Steven J. Lehman
Donald L. Harris
William J. Mattix
Peter F. Habein
Jon T. Dyre (Resident, Kalispell, Montana Office)
Bruce A. Fredrickson
Janice L. Rehberg
Joe C. Maynard, Jr.
Steven Robert Milch
Leonard H. Smith
Neil G. Westesen

Representative Clients: Aetna; CNA Insurance; Connecticut Mutual Life; St. Paul Insurance Cos.; The Doctor's Company; The Home Insurance Cos.; Farmers Insurance Group; Fireman's Fund Insurance Co.; Kemper Insurance Group; Metropolitan Life Insurance Co.

For Complete List of Firm Personnel, See General Section

For full biographical listings, see the Martindale-Hubbell Law Directory

STACEY & WALEN (AV)

The Grand, 100 North 27th Street, Suite 700, 59103
Telephone: 406-259-4545
Fax: 406-259-4540

MEMBERS OF FIRM

Calvin J. Stacey
James D. Walen

ASSOCIATE

Kevin M. Funyak

References: First Bank, Billings, Montana; Norwest Bank, Billings, Montana.

For full biographical listings, see the Martindale-Hubbell Law Directory

WRIGHT, TOLLIVER AND GUTHALS A PROFESSIONAL SERVICE CORPORATION (AV)

Windsor Court, 10 North 27th Street, P.O. Box 1977, 59103-1977
Telephone: 406-245-3071
Telecopier: 406-245-3074
Email: lawfirm@mcn.net

Ralph S. Wright (1939-1985)
Kenneth D. Tolliver
Joel E. Guthals
Virginia A. Bryan
Susan Fisher Stevens
J. Reuss
Jeffery A. Hunnes
James W. Thompson

David Paul Wilkins

For full biographical listings, see the Martindale-Hubbell Law Directory

*HELENA,** Lewis and Clark Co.

BROWNING, KALECZYC, BERRY & HOVEN, P.C. (AV)

139 North Last Chance Gulch, P.O. Box 1697, 59624
Telephone: 406-443-6820
Telefax: 406-443-6882
Email: BKBH@BKBH.COM *URL:* http://www.BKBH.com

Stanley T. Kaleczyc
J. Daniel Hoven
Oliver H. Goe
Leo S. Ward
Catherine A. Laughner
Mark D. Etchart

(See Next Column)

Kimberly A. Beatty
Steven T. Wade
Kimberly Lewis Towe
G. Andy Adamek
Robert Cameron

Representative Clients: Montana Municipal Insurance Authority; Montana School Groups Insurance Authority; The Doctors Company; Golden Bear Insurance Company; Montana Hospital Association Workers' Compensation Trust; Montana State Compensation Mutual Insurance Fund; PHICO Group; Travelers Group; CIGNA; Continental Western Insurance; Utah Medical Insurance Association; CNA Surety; Crawford and Company; New West Health Plan.

For full biographical listings, see the Martindale-Hubbell Law Directory

KELLER, REYNOLDS, DRAKE, JOHNSON & GILLESPIE, P.C. (AV)

38 South Last Chance Gulch, 59601
Telephone: 406-442-0230
Fax: 406-449-2256
Email: firm@kellerlawmt.com

P. Keith Keller
Thomas Q. Johnson
Richard E. Gillespie
G. Curt Drake
Jacqueline T. Lenmark
Robert R. Throssell
Charles J. Seifert

Gregory A. Van Horssen
Charles G. Adams

OF COUNSEL

Glen L. Drake

Representative Clients: Northwestern National Insurance Group; Government Employees Insurance Co.; Commercial Union Assurance Cos.; Kemper Insurance Group; Crum and Forster Group; CNA Insurance Cos.; Safeco Insurance; Allstate Insurance Co.; USF&G; American Insurance Assoc.

For full biographical listings, see the Martindale-Hubbell Law Directory

*KALISPELL,** Flathead Co.

HASH & O'BRIEN, PLLP (AV)

Plaza West, 136 First Avenue, West, P.O. Box 1178, 59901
Telephone: 406-755-6919
Fax: 406-755-6911
Email: cmhash@digisys.net

MEMBERS OF FIRM

Charles L. Hash
Kenneth E. O'Brien
C. Mark Hash

General Counsel for: Glacier Bancorp, Inc; Glacier Bank, Eureka and Whitefish; First National Bank of Eureka; Vortex Fishing Systems.
Representative Clients: Western Surety Co.; Liberty Mutual Insurance Co.; Allstate Insurance Co.; Lincoln Electric Cooperative; Read Enterprises.
Reference: Glacier Bancorp, Inc.

For full biographical listings, see the Martindale-Hubbell Law Directory

*MISSOULA,** Missoula Co.

PHILLIPS & BOHYER, P.C. (AV)

Suite 301 River Front Place, 283 W. Front Street, P.O. Box 8569, 59807-8569
Telephone: 406-721-7880
Telecopier: 406-549-2253
Email: phillips@montana.com

Robert J. Phillips
John E. Bohyer
Tammy Wyatt-Shaw
Fred Simpson, Jr.
John F. Jenks

LEGAL SUPPORT PERSONNEL

Mary J. Maynard
Elaine LaPointe-Vetter
Martin Suda

For full biographical listings, see the Martindale-Hubbell Law Directory

NEBRASKA

*GERING,** Scotts Bluff Co.

HOLTORF, KOVARIK, ELLISON & MATHIS, P.C. (AV)

1715 11th Street, P.O. Box 340, 69341-0340
Telephone: 308-436-5297
Fax: 308-436-2297
Email: hkem@prairieweb.com *URL:* http://www.prairieweb.com/hkem

Hans J. Holtorf, Jr. (1914-1992)
Leland K. Kovarik
James W. Ellison
James M. Mathis

Representative Clients: Travelers Insurance Co.; State Farm Mutual Auto Insurance Co.; Allied Group; Hawkeye Security Insurance Co.; Aetna Life & Casualty Co.; Casualty Underwriters.; Farmers Mutual Insurance Co.

(See Next Column)

HOLTORF, KOVARIK, ELLISON & MATHIS P.C.—*Continued*

Counsel: North Platte Natural Resources District; Farmers Mutual Ins. Co.; Wausau Ins. Co.
References: First State Bank of Gering; Gering State Bank.

For full biographical listings, see the Martindale-Hubbell Law Directory

*LINCOLN,** Lancaster Co.

CLINE, WILLIAMS, WRIGHT, JOHNSON & OLDFATHER (AV)

1900 U.S. Bank Building, 233 South 13th Street, 68508
Telephone: 402-474-6900
Fax: 402-474-5393
Email: postmaster@cline-law.com *URL:* http://www.cline-law.com
Omaha, Nebraska Office: Suite 720, One Pacific Place, 1125 South 103rd Street, 68124.
Telephone: 402-397-1700.
Fax: 402-397-1806.

ATTORNEYS

Allen L. Graves
Charles M. Pallesen, Jr.
Fredric H. Kauffman
Donald F. Burt
Alan E. Peterson
Stephen E. Gehring
Robert J. Routh
Kevin Colleran
L. Bruce Wright
James M. Bausch
Larry A. Holle
David R. Buntain
Stephen H. Nelsen
Michael C. Mueller
Lauren W. Wismer
Daniel R. Stogsdill
Scott D. Kelly
Terry R. Wittler
Pamela Hastings Carrier
Mark A. Christensen
Richard P. Garden, Jr.
Shawn D. Renner
John C. Miles
Mary Kay Frank
Thomas C. Huston
Sonya S. Ekart
Don R. Janssen
Susan Kubert Sapp
Kevin J. Schneider
Andrew D. Strotman
Jill Gossin Jensen
Rochelle A. Mullen
John L. Horan
Bryan S. Hatch
Steven C. Likes
Tracy A. Oldemeyer
Jolene M. Papa
Timothy G. Aschoff
Eric N. Bergquist
Janis J. Winterhof
Andrea Dylan Snowden

OF COUNSEL

Charles E. Wright
Richard P. Jeffries
Mary M. Campbell

RETIRED PARTNERS

Flavel A. Wright (Retired)
Warren C. Johnson (Retired)
Charles E. Oldfather (1927-1998)

Representative Clients: U.S. Bank National Association; University of Nebraska; Nebraska Medical Assn.; Saint Elizabeth Regional Medical Center; Media of Nebraska; Cargill Inc.; State Farm Insurance Cos.; Wal-Mart Stores, Inc.; Textron/Cushman; Isco, Inc.

For full biographical listings, see the Martindale-Hubbell Law Directory

ERICKSON & SEDERSTROM, P.C. (AV)

Suite 400, Cornhusker Plaza, 301 South 13th Street, 68508
Telephone: 402-476-1000
Fax: 402-476-6167
Omaha, Nebraska Office: Regency Westpointe, 10330 Regency Parkway Drive, Suite 100, 68114-3761.
Telephone: 402-397-2200.
Fax: 402-390-7137.

Charles D. Humble
David C. Mussman

Representative Clients: Cornhusker Casualty Co.; Columbia Insurance Group.

For Complete List of Firm Personnel, See General Section

For full biographical listings, see the Martindale-Hubbell Law Directory

JOHNSON, FLODMAN, GUENZEL, ESKE & WIDGER (AV)

1227 Lincoln Mall, P.O. Box 81686, 68501-1686
Telephone: 402-475-4240
Fax: 402-475-0329
URL: http://www.linclaw.com

MEMBERS OF FIRM

Robert A. Barlow (1921-1986)
Kile W. Johnson
Steven J. Flodman
Steven E. Guenzel
James A. Eske

Special Counsel: Nebraska Public Power District.
Representative Clients: Atlanta Casualty; Chubb/Pacific Indemnity Group; Citizens State Bank, Polk, Nebraska; Crum & Foster; Federated Rural Electric Insurance Corp.; Runza Drive-Inns of America; State Farm Insurance Cos.; Viking Insurance Company of Wisconsin.

For full biographical listings, see the Martindale-Hubbell Law Directory

WOLFE, SNOWDEN, HURD, LUERS & AHL (AV)

Suite 830, NBC Center, 68508-1424
Telephone: 402-474-1507
Fax: 402-474-3170

MEMBERS OF FIRM

Jack G. Wolfe
James A. Snowden
John C. Hurd
James B. Luers
Stephen L. Ahl
Dean J. Sitzmann

ASSOCIATES

Douglas L. Kluender
Thomas B. Wood

For full biographical listings, see the Martindale-Hubbell Law Directory

*OMAHA,** Douglas Co.

ERICKSON & SEDERSTROM, P.C. (AV)

Regency Westpointe, 10330 Regency Parkway Drive, Suite 100, 68114-3761
Telephone: 402-397-2200
Fax: 402-390-7137
Lincoln, Nebraska Office: Suite 400, Cornhusker Plaza, 301 South 13th Street, 68508-2571.
Telephone: 402-476-1000.
Fax: 402-476-6167.

Donald H. Erickson
Daniel D. Koukol
Wm. E. Morrow, Jr.
Soren S. Jensen
Daniel B. Kinnamon
Virgil K. Johnson
Charles V. Sederstrom, Jr.
Michael C. Washburn
John C. Brownrigg
Thomas J. Culhane
Richard J. Gilloon
Samuel Earle Clark
Gary L. Hoffman
J Russell Derr
Jerald L. Rauterkus
William T. Foley
David C. Mussman

Andrea M. Jahn
Kevin R. McManaman
Michelle B. Miller

OF COUNSEL

Lewis R. Leigh
Leo Eisenstatt
Roland J. Santoni

Representative Clients: Nebraska State Bank of Omaha; Berkshire Hathaway, Inc.; Bozell, Inc.; IBP, Inc.; Quaker Oats Co.; United A-G Cooperative, Inc.; Immanuel Medical Center; Cornhusker Casualty Co.; Hartford Accident & Indemnity Co.; Mortgage Guaranty Insurance Corp. (MGIC).

For Complete List of Firm Personnel, See General Section

For full biographical listings, see the Martindale-Hubbell Law Directory

FRASER, STRYKER, VAUGHN, MEUSEY, OLSON, BOYER & BLOCH, P.C. (AV)

500 Energy Plaza, 409 South 17th Street, 68102
Telephone: 402-341-6000
Telecopier: 402-341-8290
Email: fraserstryker.com

Joseph K. Meusey
Wayne J. Mark
Joseph E. Jones
Robert F. Rossiter, Jr.
Michael F. Coyle
Rex A. Rezac
Mark C. Laughlin

Representative Clients: State Farm Insurance Cos.; Shand Morahan & Co.; Prudential Property and Casualty Insurance.

For Complete List of Firm Personnel, See General Section

For full biographical listings, see the Martindale-Hubbell Law Directory

KATSKEE, HENATSCH & SUING (AV)

10404 Essex Court, Suite 100, 68114
Telephone: 402-391-1697
Fax: 402-391-8932
Email: katskee@uswest.net

MEMBERS OF FIRM

Milton A. Katskee
Dean F. Suing
Jerry W. Katskee

ASSOCIATES

Francis T. Belsky
David A. Castello
John B. Henley
Todd W. Weidemann

OF COUNSEL

Harry R. Henatsch

Reference: Mid-City Bank.

For full biographical listings, see the Martindale-Hubbell Law Directory

McGRATH, NORTH, MULLIN & KRATZ, P.C. (AV)

Suite 1400, One Central Park Plaza, 68102
Telephone: 402-341-3070
Fax: 402-341-0216

(See Next Column)

McGrath, North, Mullin & Kratz P.C., *Omaha—Continued*

John E. North
Robert D. Mullin, Sr.
James P. Fitzgerald
Leo A. Knowles
Terrence D. O'Hare
Timothy J. Pugh
Robert D. Mullin, Jr.
Thomas C. McGowan
William F. Hargens
Edward G. Warin
Michael G. Mullin
Steven P. Case
James G. Powers
Douglas E. Quinn
J. Scott Paul
James J. Frost
Martel J. Bundy
Patrick E. Brookhouser, Jr.
James M. Sulentic
William J. Birkel
John J. Schirger
Aaron A. Clark

General Counsel for: ConAgra, Inc.; InaCom Corp.; Omaha Airport Authority; Physicians Mutual Insurance Co.; Supertel Hospitality, Inc.; Valmont Industries, Inc.
Representative Clients: Clarkson Hospital; Omaha Chamber of Commerce.
Insurance Clients: American Family Insurance Group; Blue Cross-Blue Shield of Nebraska.

For Complete List of Firm Personnel, See General Section

For full biographical listings, see the Martindale-Hubbell Law Directory

NEVADA

*LAS VEGAS,** Clark Co.

Albright, Stoddard, Warnick & Albright, A Professional Corporation (AV)

Quail Park I, Building D-4, 801 South Rancho Drive, 89106
Telephone: 702-384-7111
Fax: 702-384-0605
URL: http://www.aswalaw.com

G. Vern Albright
William H. Stoddard
Whitney B. Warnick
G. Mark Albright

D. Chris Albright
Tami C. Budo
Corey D. Randall (Not admitted in NV)

Representative Clients: Tokio Marine and Fire Insurance Co.; INAPRO, a CIGNA Co.; Nevada Ready Mix; North American Health Care, Inc. (Nursing Home); Royal Insurance; First Security Bank of Utah; Nevada Community Bank; Nationwide Insurance Co.; Liberty Mutual Insurance; CB Commercial.

For full biographical listings, see the Martindale-Hubbell Law Directory

Alverson, Taylor, Mortensen, Nelson & Sanders (AV)

7401 West Charleston Boulevard, 89117
Telephone: 702-384-7000
FAX: 702-385-7000
Email: alverson@intermind.net
Reno, Nevada Office: 245 East Liberty, Suite 520, 89505.
Telephone: 775-329-0473.
Fax: 775-329-3303.

MEMBERS OF FIRM

J. Bruce Alverson
Eric K. Taylor
David J. Mortensen
Erven T. Nelson
LeAnn Sanders

OF COUNSEL

Jack C. Cherry
Kurt D. Anderson
Philip C. Van Alstyne

ASSOCIATES

Rebecca Hopkins Miller
Sandra Smagac
Victoria L. Nelson
Aaron D. Lovaas
Diane Obritsch
Michael A. Olsen
Randal D. Shimon
Catherine A. Olendorff
Monica L. Pierce
Gabriel D. Lither
Kurt R. Bonds
Darius F. Rafie
Mark J. King, IV
Shell L. Mercer
Carrie S. Bourdeau
Jason Lane Earnest
Nathan R. Reinmiller
Donn C. Alexander
Afshin Tadayon
Eric O. Freeman
Lindsay L. Stadtlander
Julie M. Sueoka

Representative Clients: St. Paul Fire & Marine Insurance Company; Chubb Group of Insurance Companies; Employers of Wausau Insurance Company; Farmers Home Group; General Accident Insurance; Kemper National Insurance Company; Nationwide Insurance Company; Reliance/United Pacific Insurance Company; Scottsdale Insurance Company; United States Fidelity & Guaranty.

For full biographical listings, see the Martindale-Hubbell Law Directory

Leland Eugene Backus & Associates Ltd. (AV)

2810 West Charleston Boulevard, Suite H-74, P.O. Box 28700, 89126-2700
Telephone: 702-872-5555
Facsimile: 702-872-5545
Email: backuslaw@earthlink.net *URL:* http://www.backuslaw.com

Leland Eugene Backus

John S. Delikanakis
Edgar Carranza
Robert Earl Werbicky
John L. Krieger
Megan Mahoney

For full biographical listings, see the Martindale-Hubbell Law Directory

Barker, Brown, Busby, Chrisman & Thomas, A Professional Corporation (AV)

800 Bank of America Plaza, 300 South Fourth Street, 89101
Telephone: 702-386-1086
Fax: 702-384-5386
Email: BAR-BRO@IX.NETCOM.COM

William S. Barker
Janice J. Brown
Jerry S. Busby
James P. Chrisman
David L. Thomas
Robert A. Winner

Robert D. Tarte
Brent A. Carson
Marino A. Cesaretti
Ann C. Elworth
Michael D. Demman
Curtis J. Busby
J. Scott Ralston

LEGAL SUPPORT PERSONNEL

David A. Ross (Not admitted in NV)
Michael W. Salend
Michael Allen Davis
Britt K. Beckstrom

Representative Clients: Fireman's Fund; Liberty Mutual; Southwest Airlines; Colonial Penn; Metropolitan, Inc.; Uniroyal Tire; Del E. Webb Corp.

For full biographical listings, see the Martindale-Hubbell Law Directory

DeLanoy, English, Schuetze & McGaha, A Professional Corporation (AV)

Suite One, 1000 East Sahara Avenue, 89104
Telephone: 702-369-3225
Fax: 702-369-2110
Email: motovegas@aol.com

Drake DeLanoy
Damon A. Schuetze
William W. McGaha

For full biographical listings, see the Martindale-Hubbell Law Directory

Edwards, Sooy & Byron, A Professional Corporation (AV®)

3960 Howard Hughes Parkway Fifth Floor, 89109
Telephone: 702-474-0861
Fax: 702-474-4538
Email: esb-legal.com *URL:* http://www.esb-legal.com
San Diego, California Office: 101 West Broadway, Ninth Floor, 92101.
Telephone: 619-231-1500.
Fax: 619-231-1588.

Michael M. Edwards (Not admitted in NV)
Richard R. Sooy
Thomas W. Byron

Alfred Paul Centofanti, III
Bart M. Blechschmidt
Michael M. Edwards, Jr.

For full biographical listings, see the Martindale-Hubbell Law Directory

Joel F. Hansen & Associates (AV)

Suite 200, 415 South Sixth Street, 89101-6937
Telephone: 702-385-5533
Fax: 702-382-8891
Email: HansenLaw@aol.com *URL:* http://www.ins.lawnt.com

LEGAL SUPPORT PERSONNEL

Carole F. Chapman
Karen Quick

Representative Clients: American Drug Stores; Motel 6; Kemper Insurance Group; State Farm Fire and Casualty Company; American National Property and Casualty Company; E & O Professionals; American States Insurance; United States Fidelity & Guaranty Company; State Farm Mutual Automobile Insurance Company.

For full biographical listings, see the Martindale-Hubbell Law Directory

Kravitz, Schnitzer & Sloane, Chartered, A Professional Corporation (AV)

2300 West Sahara Avenue, Suite 500, 89102
Telephone: 702-362-6666
Fax: 702-362-2203
Email: KRAVSCHNIT@AOL.COM

(See Next Column)

Kravitz, Schnitzer & Sloane, Chartered A Professional Corporation—*Continued*

Martin J. Kravitz
Gary E. Schnitzer
Jeffrey G. Sloane
Michael Bradley Johnson
Jane Eberhardy
Marisa C. Guarino

David J. Feldman
Jerry R. Graf

LEGAL SUPPORT PERSONNEL

Sandye Smith (Legal Administrator)

Representative Clients: State Farm Fire and Casualty Co.; State Farm Automobile Insurance Co.; MGM Grand Hotel and Casino; Hilton Hotels Corporation; Circus Circus Enterprises; Yellow Cab Co.; Checker Cab Co.; Star Cab Co.; CNA Insurance; G.R.E. Insurance Group; Allstate Insurance Company.

For full biographical listings, see the Martindale-Hubbell Law Directory

Kummer Kaempfer Bonner & Renshaw (AV)

Seventh Floor, 3800 Howard Hughes Parkway, 89109-0907
Telephone: 702-792-7000
Fax: 702-796-7181
Email: nvlaw@kkbr.com

MEMBERS OF FIRM

John C. Renshaw
Thomas F. Kummer
Christopher L. Kaempfer
Michael J. Bonner
Kathleen Jane England
John N. Brewer
Gerald D. Waite
Sherwood N. Cook
Shari Cassin Patterson
John C. Jeppsen
Mark H. Fiorentino
John A. Curtas

OF COUNSEL

H. Gregory Nasky
James H. Bilbray
Michael W. Brimley

ASSOCIATES

Thomas D. Amick
Sean L. Anderson (Not admitted in NV)
Nikki L. Baker
George J. Claseman
L. Joe Coppedge
Gregory S. Gilbert
Robert J. Gronauer
Robert C. Kim
Kurt C. Lambeth
Angela Turriciano Otto
Elizabeth A. Savage
Lyssa M. Simonelli
James E. Smyth II
Gregg R. Vermeys
Anthony A. Zmaila

For full biographical listings, see the Martindale-Hubbell Law Directory

Lefebvre, Barron & Vivone, Chtd. (AV)

1404 South Jones Boulevard, 89146-1231
Telephone: 702-383-8668
Facsimile: 702-383-6828
Email: lb@coam.net

Alan J. Lefebvre
David L. Barron
Thomas J. Vivone
Raymond W. Holland
Michelle O. Tobler
William Howard Pruitt
Bradley V. Gibbons
Jared Casper (Not admitted in NV)
Kevin S. Smith

LEGAL SUPPORT PERSONNEL

Jennifer L. Hageman

For full biographical listings, see the Martindale-Hubbell Law Directory

Pearson, Patton, Shea, Foley & Kurtz, P.C. (AV)

Bank of America West, 6900 Westcliff Drive, Suite 800, 89128
Telephone: 702-228-7717
FAX: 702-228-8824

Niels L. Pearson
W. Randolph Patton
Randa Reiff Shea
George Foley, Jr.
Theodore J. Kurtz
John P. Skalak
Douglas M. Rowan
Gina Gilbert Winspear

Ryan L. Dennett
Michele A. Kiraly
Jennifer Newton Taylor
Tina Louise Amodeo
Bruce A. Brown

For full biographical listings, see the Martindale-Hubbell Law Directory

Perry & Spann, A Professional Corporation (AV)

1701 West Charleston Suite 200, 89102
Telephone: 702-870-2400
Fax: 702-870-8220
Email: perryspann@perryspann.com
Reno, Nevada Office: 6130 Plumas Street, 89509.
Telephone: 775-829-2002.
Facsimile: 775-829-1808.

Victor A. Perry
Charles W. Spann

Reference: Pioneer Citizens Bank.

For full biographical listings, see the Martindale-Hubbell Law Directory

Pico & Mitchell (AV)

2000 South Eastern Avenue, 89104
Telephone: 702-457-9099
FAX: 702-457-8451
Email: lawyers@picomitchell.com

MEMBERS OF FIRM

James F. Pico
Bert O. Mitchell
Christy Brad Escobar
James R. Rosenberger
E. Breen Arntz

ASSOCIATES

Michelle Schwarz
Rebecca L. Mastrangelo
Jill M. Chase
Daniel E. Carvalho
Stephen H. Rogers

Representative Clients: Home Insurance Co.; State Farm Mutual Insurance Co.; Industrial Indemnity Insurance Co.; Great American Insurance Co.; Argonaut Insurance Cos.; Clark County Medical Society; Rose de Lima Hospital; Fairway Chevrolet; American States Insurance Co.; The Hartford Insurance Co.

For full biographical listings, see the Martindale-Hubbell Law Directory

Rawlings, Olson, Cannon, Gormley & Desruisseaux, A Professional Corporation (AV)

301 East Clark Avenue, Suite 1000, 89101
Telephone: 702-384-4012
Telecopier: 702-383-0701

Henry H. Rawlings, Jr.
James R. Olson
Walter R. Cannon
John D. Nitz
John E. Gormley
Richard E. Desruisseaux
Dana Jonathon Nitz
Bryan W. Lewis
Michael E. Stoberski

Yvette D. Robichaud
Peter M. Angulo
Don F. Shreve, Jr.
Craig B. Friedberg
Marsha H. Tarte

For full biographical listings, see the Martindale-Hubbell Law Directory

Ryan Marks Johnson Todd & Broder (AV®)

1160 Town Center Drive, Suite 300, 89134
Telephone: 702-341-7870
Facsimile: 702-341-8049
San Diego, California Office: Wingert Grebing Brubaker & Ryan LLP, One America Plaza, Seventh Floor, 600 West Broadway, 92101-3370.
Telephone: 619-232-8151.
Facsimile: 619-232-4665.

MEMBERS OF FIRM

Norman A. Ryan
Eileen Mulligan Marks
Robert L. Johnson
Christopher W. Todd
James P. Broder

ASSOCIATES

Stephen C. Grebing
Jay A. Kenyon

For full biographical listings, see the Martindale-Hubbell Law Directory

Smith Larsen & Wixom, Chartered (AV)

3360 West Sahara Avenue, Suite 175, 89102
Telephone: 702-252-5002
Fax: 702-252-5006
Email: slwlaw@slwlaw.com

Jay Earl Smith
Kent F. Larsen
Michael B. Wixom

Stewart C. Fitts

Representative Clients: Norwest Bank Nevada, N.A.; Wells Fargo Bank; General Star Management Company; Northwestern National Casualty Co.; Circus Circus Hotel & Casino; Luxor Hotel & Casino; Excalibur Hotel & Casino; Colorado Belle Hotel & Casino; Monte Carlo Hotel & Casino; Gold Strike Hotel & Gambling Hall.

For full biographical listings, see the Martindale-Hubbell Law Directory

Thorndal, Armstrong, Delk, Balkenbush & Eisinger, A Professional Corporation (AV)

1100 East Bridger Avenue, P.O. Box 2070, 89125-2070
Telephone: 702-366-0622
Fax: 702-366-0327
Email: info@thorndal.com *URL:* http://www.thorndal.com
Reno, Nevada Office: Suite 200, 888 West Second Street.
Telephone: 775-786-2882.
Fax: 775-786-8004.
Elko, Nevada Office: 919 Idaho Street, P.O. Box 5508.
Telephone: 775-777-3011.
Fax: 775-786-8004.

(See Next Column)

THORNDAL, ARMSTRONG, DELK, BALKENBUSH & EISINGER A PROFESSIONAL CORPORATION, *Las Vegas—Continued*

John L. Thorndal
James G. Armstrong
Craig R. Delk
Stephen C. Balkenbush (Resident, Reno Office)
Paul F. Eisinger
Charles Lee Burcham (Resident, Reno Office)
Brian K. Terry
Brent Thomas Kolvet (Resident, Reno Office)
Blair C. Parker
William R. Killip, Jr.
Robert F. Balkenbush (Resident, Reno Office)

Michael E. Sullivan (Resident, Reno Office)
Philip Goodhart
Deborah L. Elsasser
James J. Jackson
Gavin C. Jangard
R. Scott Rasmussen
Christopher J. Curtis
Alyssa A. Martini
Susan E. Frasca
Daniel D. Norr
David P. Lane
William R. Jones
Katherine F. Bobier (Resident, Reno Office)
C. Scott Wormsley
Renee E. Jensen
Thierry V. Barkley (Resident, Reno Office)

Representative Clients: Allied Insurance Group; American Hardware; California Casualty; Cigna; Employer's Reinsurance; Farmers Insurance Exchange; Federated Group; Nationwide Insurance; Reliance Insurance Co., Inc.; Zurich-American Insurance.

For full biographical listings, see the Martindale-Hubbell Law Directory

VANNAH COSTELLO CANEPA RIEDY & RUBINO (AV)

A Partnership including a Professional Corporation
Greystone, 1850 East Flamingo, Suite 236, 89119
Telephone: 702-369-4161
Fax: 702-369-0104
Email: vannahnet@vannahnet.com

MEMBERS OF FIRM

Robert D. Vannah (Chartered)
Nathan M. Costello
Scott K. Canepa
Terry W. Riedy
Michael C. Rubino

ASSOCIATES

Connie J. Forsythe
Shawn D. Dorman
Adam Ganz
Denise M. Cooper
Jeffrey Ferguson
Matthew Vannah
Ronald J. Flinders
Russell M. Rowe
Jonathan G. Lattie (Not admitted in NV)

Representative Clients: Prudential Property and Casualty Insurance Co.; Continental Insurance Health Care; Chubb Group of Insurance; Reliance Insurance Co.; Transamerica Insurance Group; Foremost Insurance Co.; CNA Insurance Co.; Scottsdale Insurance Co.; The Maryland Insurance Group; Insurance Company of the West.

For full biographical listings, see the Martindale-Hubbell Law Directory

*RENO,** Washoe Co.

ERICKSON, THORPE & SWAINSTON, LTD. (AV)

99 West Arroyo Street, P.O. Box 3559, 89505
Telephone: 702-786-3930
Fax: 702-786-4160
Email: etsreno@aol.com

Roger L. Erickson
Donald A. Thorpe
George W. Swainston
William G. Cobb
Gary A. Cardinal
Thomas Peter Beko
John A. Aberasturi
Paul M. Bertone
Lisa E. Bruce
John C. Boyden

Representative Clients: Allstate Insurance Co.; Coregis Insurance; Country Companies; American National Property and Casualty Company; Kemper Insurance Company; State Farm Fire & Casualty; TIG (Transamerica); Willis, Corroon Administrative Services; Associated Aviation Underwriters; CNA; Hawkeye Insurance Company; Hartford Insurance Company.

For full biographical listings, see the Martindale-Hubbell Law Directory

GEORGESON, THOMPSON & ANGARAN, CHARTERED (AV)

100 West Grove Street, Suite 500, 89509
Telephone: 775-827-6440
Fax: 775-827-9256
Mailing Address: P.O. Box 3257, Reno, Nevada, 89505

C. James Georgeson
Harold B. Thompson
Jack G. Angaran

Whitney J. Selert
Tina M. Chartraw
Richard A. Salvatore

Representative Clients: California State Automobile Assn.; Consolidated Freightways; Employers Insurance of Wausau; Hawkeye-Security Insurance Co.; Industrial Indemnity Co.; Liberty Mutual; National Chiropractic Mutual Ins. Co.; Scottsdale Insurance Companies; St. Paul Insurance Co.; State Farm Insurance Co.

(See Next Column)

For full biographical listings, see the Martindale-Hubbell Law Directory

PERRY & SPANN, A PROFESSIONAL CORPORATION (AV)

6130 Plumas Street, 89509
Telephone: 775-829-2002
Fax: 775-829-1808
Email: perryspann@perryspann.com *URL:* http://www.perryspann.com
Las Vegas, Nevada Office: 1701 West Charleston, Suite 200, 89102.
Telephone: 702-870-2400.
Facsimile: 702-870-8220.

Victor A. Perry
Charles W. Spann

Reference: Pioneer Citizens Bank.

For full biographical listings, see the Martindale-Hubbell Law Directory

FRANK H. ROBERTS (AV)

290 South Arlington Avenue, Suite 250, 89501
Telephone: 775-329-4041
Facsimile: 775-329-9019

For full biographical listings, see the Martindale-Hubbell Law Directory

NEW HAMPSHIRE

*CONCORD,** Merrimack Co.

RATH, YOUNG AND PIGNATELLI, PROFESSIONAL ASSOCIATION (AV)

One Capital Plaza, P.O. Box 1500, 03302-1500
Telephone: 603-226-2600
Telecopier: 603-226-2700; 228-2294; 225-9774
Email: ryp@rathlaw.com *URL:* http://www.rathlaw.com
Nashua, New Hampshire Office: The Glass Tower, 20 Trafalgar Square.
Telephone: 603-889-9952.
Telecopier: 603-595-7489.

Thomas D. Rath
Michael A. Pignatelli
Andrew W. Serell
Brian T. Tucker

Claire W. Rouillard

For Complete List of Firm Personnel, See General Section

For full biographical listings, see the Martindale-Hubbell Law Directory

*DOVER,** Strafford Co.

BURNS, BRYANT, HINCHEY, COX & ROCKEFELLER, P.A. (AV)

Burns Building, 255 Washington Street, P.O. Box 608, 03820
Telephone: 603-742-2332
Fax: 603-749-4970
Email: bbhcr@concentric.net

George T. Hughes (1873-1943)
Stanley M. Burns (1902-1967)
Robert P. Shea (1936-1983)
Robert E. Hinchey (Retired)
Paul Richard Cox
Donald R. Bryant (Of Counsel)
Christine M. Rockefeller
Gregory J. Wenger

Matthew B. Cox
Carolyn F. Dickson

Representative Clients: Metropolitan Life Insurance Co.; Prudential Insurance Company of America; Concord Group Insurance Cos.

For full biographical listings, see the Martindale-Hubbell Law Directory

*MANCHESTER,** Hillsborough Co.

SHEEHAN PHINNEY BASS + GREEN, PROFESSIONAL ASSOCIATION (AV)

Hampshire Plaza, 1000 Elm Street, P.O. Box 3701, 03105-3701
Telephone: 603-668-0300
800-625-SPBG
Fax: 603-627-8121
Email: postmaster@sheehan.com *URL:* http://www.sheehan.com
Portsmouth, New Hampshire Office: Old City Hall, 126 Daniel Street.
Telephone: 603-433-2111.
Fax: 603-433-3126.
Concord, New Hampshire Office: 143 North Main Street.
Telephone: 603-223-2020.
Fax: 603-224-8899.

James E. Higgins
Peter F. Kearns
James Q. Shirley
William J. Donovan
Claudia Cords Damon
Edward A. Haffer
Michael C. Harvell
Stephen E. Weyl
Peter S. Cowan
Katherine M. Hanna
Douglas G. Verge
Christopher Cole
David W. McGrath
James F. Ogorchock

(See Next Column)

SHEEHAN PHINNEY BASS + GREEN PROFESSIONAL ASSOCIATION—*Continued*

Representative Clients: Anheuser-Busch, Inc.; Bank of New Hampshire Corp.; The Elliot Hospital of Manchester; Granite State Packing Co.; Moore Business Forms, Inc.; New Hampshire College; New Hampshire Dental Service Corp.; New Hampshire Yankee Electric Corp.; Numerica Financial Corp.

For Complete List of Firm Personnel, See General Section

For full biographical listings, see the Martindale-Hubbell Law Directory

WIGGIN & NOURIE, P.A. (AV)

20 Market Street, P.O. Box 808, 03105
Telephone: 603-669-2211
Facsimile: 603-623-8442
Email: attys@wiggin-nourie.com *URL:* http://www.wiggin-nourie.com

J. Walker Wiggin (1901-1995)
Paul E. Nourie (1908-1978)
T. William Bigelow (Retired)
Dort S. Bigg
William S. Orcutt
W. Wright Danenbarger
L. Jonathan Ross
John R. Monson
Jeffrey B. Osburn
Benjamin F. Gayman
Gordon A. Rehnborg, Jr.
Douglas R. Chamberlain
Wilfred J. Desmarais
Richard B. McNamara
Gregory A. Holmes
Gary Ellis Hicks
Andrew A. Merrill
Thomas John Pappas
Dennis T. Ducharme
Gary M. Burt
Doreen F. Connor
Scott Ames Ewing
Stephanie A. Bray
Shari M. Jankowski
Ellen M. Joseph
Andrea Grilli Chatfield
David W. Johnston

Stephen A. Gould
Jean M. Long
James V. Ferro, Jr.
Daniel Duckett
Elizabeth Maher Leonard
Gail E. Bakis
Douglas J. Wenners
Meredith P. Cook
Ralph Suozzo
Brian G. Vaughan
Erik T. Barstow
Jodi L. Nourse
Carol L. Kunz

LEGAL SUPPORT PERSONNEL

Richard D. M. Strawbridge

Representative Clients: Associated Anesthesiologists of Manchester, PA; Atomic Ski USA; Eckman Construction, Inc.; Fleet Financial Group; Keane, Inc.; New Hampshire Automobile Dealers Association; State Farm; Wausau; Zurich-American.

For full biographical listings, see the Martindale-Hubbell Law Directory

NASHUA, Hillsborough Co.

RATH, YOUNG AND PIGNATELLI, PROFESSIONAL ASSOCIATION (AV)

The Glass Tower, 20 Trafalgar Square, 03063
Telephone: 603-889-9952
Telecopier: 603-595-7489
Email: ryp@rathlaw.com *URL:* http://www.rathlaw.com
Concord, New Hampshire Office: One Capital Plaza, P.O. Box 1500.
Telephone: 603-226-2600.
Telecopier: 603-226-2700.

Thomas D. Rath
Michael A. Pignatelli

For full biographical listings, see the Martindale-Hubbell Law Directory

NEW JERSEY

ASBURY PARK, Monmouth Co.

CARTON, WITT, ARVANITIS & BARISCILLO, L.L.C. (AV)

(Formerly Durand, Ivins & Carton)
4001 Route 66 At Garden State Parkway, P.O. Box 1229, 07712
Telephone: 732-922-9500
Telecopier: 732-922-1625
Manasquan, New Jersey Office: 40 Union Avenue, P.O. Box 367.
Telephones: 908-223-1800; 449-5311.

MEMBERS OF FIRM

George N. Arvanitis
James D. Carton, III (Manasquan Office)
John C. Carton (Manasquan Office)
Stephen C. Carton
H. Frank Carpentier
Dana C. Argeris
Martin J. McGreevy
Albert A. Zager
Mark R. Aikins
K. Edward Jacobi
Joseph J. Colao, Jr.
James D. Carton (1868-1943)
Forman T. Bailey (1887-1964)
J. Victor Carton (1900-1982)
Thomas D. Nary (1904-1985)
Robert R. Witt (1921-1988)

(See Next Column)

ASSOCIATES

Thomas F. Heaney, Jr.
Peter V. Koenig
Susan J. F. Weiss
James D. Carton, IV
Aaron J. Rosenfeld
Russell J. Malta
Janice B. Venables
Marc J. Comer

OF COUNSEL

Francis X. Crahay
Henry E. Kordes
George A. Bariscillo, Jr.
Robert V. Carton

Attorneys for: New Jersey Bell Telephone Co.; Garden State Indemnity Co.; Jersey Shore Medical Center, Inc.
Local Attorneys for: Travelers Insurance Co.; Aetna Casualty & Surety Co.; New Jersey Manufacturers Insurance Co.; Liberty Mutual; Prudential Insurance Co.; Chubb & Son.

For full biographical listings, see the Martindale-Hubbell Law Directory

BEDMINSTER, Somerset Co.

PURCELL, RIES, SHANNON, MULCAHY & O'NEILL (AV)

One Pluckemin Way, P.O. Box 754, 07921
Telephone: 908-658-3800
Fax: 908-658-4659
Email: general@prsmo.com *URL:* http://www.prsmo.com
Philadelphia, Pennsylvania Office: 12th Floor, East Tower, Centre Square, 1500 Market Square.
Telephone: 215-665-5602.
Fax: 215-569-8228.

MEMBERS OF FIRM

Eugene M. Purcell
William P. Ries
John J. Shannon
Thomas M. Mulcahy
Michael F. O'Neill
David M. Hawkins
Joseph R. Purcell
Kevin R. Brotz
John M. Bowens
Kevin Kovacs
Kenneth D. Merin
Valerie K. Bollheimer
Andrew L. Indeck
Joseph M. Donegan
Mark Mattia

ASSOCIATES

Rita F. Barone
Kathleen J. Devlin
Paul L. Gallagher
Gary Grabas
John R. Haggerty
William T. Hilliard
Eric J. Konecke
Susan Lawless
Michael J. McCaffrey
Kathleen M. Quinn
Thomas Charles Savoth
Donna M. Stephan-Nolan
Barbara C. Zimmerman

OF COUNSEL

David D. Furman
C. Judson Hamlin

LEGAL SUPPORT PERSONNEL

Gary Molloy

Reference: Somerset Trust Co.

For full biographical listings, see the Martindale-Hubbell Law Directory

BRICK, Ocean Co.

GROSSMAN, KRUTTSCHNITT, HEAVEY & JACOB, A PROFESSIONAL CORPORATION (AV)

Brick Professional Plaza, 1608 Highway 88 West, Suite 200, 08724
Telephone: 732-206-0200
Facsimile: 732-206-0205

Richard A. Grossman
Herbert Kruttschnitt, III
Thomas J. Heavey
Barbara Ann Jacob

Roberta Di Biase
Bradley F. Randell

References: First Fidelity Bank, N.A. New Jersey; The Bank of New York, National Community Division.

For full biographical listings, see the Martindale-Hubbell Law Directory

*CAMDEN,** Camden Co.

BROWN & CONNERY, LLP (AV)

518 Market Street, P.O. Box 1449, 08101
Telephone: 609-365-5100
Facsimile: 609-858-4967
Westmont, New Jersey Office: 360 Haddon Avenue, P.O. Box 539.
Telephone: 609-854-8900.

MEMBERS OF FIRM

Thomas F. Connery, Jr.
Warren W. Faulk
Steven G. Wolschina
Paul Mainardi
Michael J. Vassalotti
Dennis P. Blake
William M. Tambussi
Mark P. Asselta
Stephen J. DeFeo
Joseph M Nardi, III

(See Next Column)

BROWN & CONNERY LLP, *Camden—Continued*

ASSOCIATES

Joseph A. Zechman
Karen A. McGuinness
Jeffrey E. Ugoretz
Christine O'Hearn
Christine A. Campbell
Joseph T. Carney
Richard C. Belli, Jr.
Stephanie E. Nolan
Shawn C. Huber
Susan M. Leming
Beth L. Marlin
Louis R. Lessig
Kevin C. Heil

Representative Clients: Camden County Health Services Center; Delaware River Port Authority; Federal Deposit Insurance Corp.; Mercedes-Benz Credit Corp.; Philadelphia Newspaper, Inc.; Philip Morris Inc.; Pollution Control Financing Authority of Camden County; Underwood-Memorial Hospital.

For Complete List of Firm Personnel, See General Section

For full biographical listings, see the Martindale-Hubbell Law Directory

CEDAR KNOLLS, Morris Co.

LEARY, BRIDE, TINKER & MORAN, A PROFESSIONAL CORPORATION (AV)

7 Ridgedale Avenue, 07927
Telephone: 973-539-2090
Fax: 973-539-0806

W. Stephen Leary
James D. Bride
John G. Tinker, Jr.
Glenn R. Moran
James T. Gill
William H. Mergner, Jr.
Mark Bongiovanni

Tracey L. VanWiemokly
James P. McHugh III
Brian Peoples
Marguerite Anne Leary
Mark J. Brancato
Wendy Allyson Reek
David J. Dering
Peter M. Bouton
Christopher H. Frick
Mark A. Trudeau

For full biographical listings, see the Martindale-Hubbell Law Directory

CHERRY HILL, Camden Co.

GREEN, LUNDGREN & RYAN, A PROFESSIONAL CORPORATION (AV)

1010 Kings Highway South, Building Two, 08034
Telephone: 609-428-5800
Telecopier: 609-428-9802
Mailing Address: P.O. Box 70, Haddonfield, NJ, 08033-0085

Peter P. Green
William L. Lundgren, III
Francis X. Ryan
Daniel J. DiStasi
Charles F. Blumenstein, II
James E. Mulroy

Laurence Todd Bennett
Matthew K. Mitchell
Karen L. Eisele
Frank P. Brennan
Mark A. Leonetti
Michele A. Naipawer
Jennifer Hiller
Jeffrey R. Owens
Pina M. Vricella
Thomas L. Wilkinson
David A. Grabowski
Patrick W. Conner
Danielle J. Skypala
Janet Law
Gregory S. Soffian
Tobin A. Butler
Robert Fraser Miller

Representative Clients: Allstate Insurance Company; Amtrack; Bell Atlantic Corporation; Borough of Haddonfield; Coolidge Mortgage Service; CNA Insurance Companies, Gloucester, Salem, Cumberland Counties Municipal Joint Insurance Fund; Pettinaro Enterprises, Inc.; Prudential Insurance Company; Modern Plastics Techniques, Inc.; Market Transition Facility.

For full biographical listings, see the Martindale-Hubbell Law Directory

JAMES L. MCKENNA, P.C. (AV)

Woodcrest Pavilion, Ten Melrose Avenue, Suite 450, 08003
Telephone: 856-429-6662
Telecopier: 856-429-0064
Email: jlmpcnj@erols.com
Wynnewood, Pennsylvania Office: 30-31 Hampstead Circle.
Telephone: 610-642-5768.
Fax: 610-642-1130.

James L. McKenna

Joanne M. Walker
Arnold E. Capriotti, Jr.
Mary L. Russell

OF COUNSEL

Deborah M. Wilson

For full biographical listings, see the Martindale-Hubbell Law Directory

FLORHAM PARK, Morris Co.

D'ALESSANDRO, JACOVINO & GERSON (AV)

147 Columbia Turnpike, 07932
Telephone: 201-966-1910
Fax: 201-966-6774
URL: http://www.lawyers.com/djgattys
New York, N.Y. Office: 321 Broadway, 4th Floor.
Telephone: 212-608-7500.

MEMBERS OF FIRM

Edward G. D'Alessandro
Amedeo C. Jacovino
Frederick E. Gerson

ASSOCIATES

Edward G. D'Alessandro, Jr.
Anthony J. Bianciella

Reference: Midatlantic Bank.

For full biographical listings, see the Martindale-Hubbell Law Directory

HACK, PIRO, O'DAY, MERKLINGER, WALLACE & MCKENNA, P.A. (AV)

30 Columbia Turnpike, P.O. Box 941, 07932-0941
Telephone: 973-301-6500
Fax: 973-301-0094
Email: hpom@ix.netcom.com

Peter A. Piro
William J. O'Day
M. Richard Merklinger
Joseph V. Wallace
Peter T. Melnyk
Patrick M. Sages
Robert G. Alencewicz
John T. West
Thomas M. Madden

Michael J. Leegan
Joanne Vos
Peter Nastasi
Carol A. Rankin

For Complete List of Firm Personnel, See General Section

For full biographical listings, see the Martindale-Hubbell Law Directory

RYAN AND GANNON (AV)

Suite 201, 147 Columbia Turnpike, 07932
Telephone: 201-966-1000
Fax: 201-966-6215
URL: http://www.lawyers.com/ryanandgannon

MEMBERS OF FIRM

William J. Gannon
Gerald J. Helfrich

ASSOCIATE

Edward George Fattell, III

OF COUNSEL

George P. Helfrich
Edward V. Ryan
Thomas A. Shepard, Jr.

For full biographical listings, see the Martindale-Hubbell Law Directory

*HACKENSACK,** Bergen Co.

HEIN, SMITH, BEREZIN, MALOOF & JACOBS, L.L.C. (AV)

Court Plaza East, 19 Main Street, 07601-7023
Telephone: 201-487-7400
Telecopier: 201-487-4228
Email: counsel@heinsmith.com

MEMBERS OF FIRM

Robert J. Maloof
Robert L. Baum
Lawrence H. Jacobs
Ellen W. Smith
Carla H. Madnick

ASSOCIATES

John L. Shanahan
Douglas V. Sanchez
Robert J. Logan

Representative Clients: Bergen County Joint Municipal Insurance Fund; Commercial General Union Insurance Cos. of New York; Crawford & Co.; Health Care Insurance Co.; Princeton Insurance Co.; St. Paul Fire & Marine Insurance Co.; Pro Mutual Insurance Company; NJ Cure.
Reference: Summit Bank.

For Complete List of Firm Personnel, See General Section

For full biographical listings, see the Martindale-Hubbell Law Directory

HADDONFIELD, Camden Co.

WILBRAHAM, LAWLER & BUBA, A PROFESSIONAL CORPORATION (AV Ⓣ)

24 Kings Highway West, 08033-2122
Telephone: 856-795-4422
Fax: 856-795-4699
Philadelphia, Pennsylvania Office: 1818 Market Street, Suite 3100.
Telephone: 215-564-4141.
Fax: 215-564-4385.

(See Next Column)

WILBRAHAM, LAWLER & BUBA A PROFESSIONAL CORPORATION—*Continued*

Wilmington, Delaware Office: Stoney Batter Office Building, 5301 Limestone Road, Suite 221.
Telephone: 302-234-8217.
Fax: 302-234-8218.

Edward J. Wilbraham | Michael J. Block
Mary S. Cook

For full biographical listings, see the Martindale-Hubbell Law Directory

LIVINGSTON, Essex Co.

GENOVA, BURNS & VERNOIA (AV)

Eisenhower Plaza II, 354 Eisenhower Parkway, 07039
Telephone: 973-533-0777
Facsimile: 973-533-1112
URL: http://www.gbvlaw.com
Trenton, New Jersey Office: The Princeton House, 160 West State Street.
Telephone: 609-393-1131.

MEMBERS OF FIRM

Angelo J. Genova
James M. Burns
Francis J. Vernoia
John C. Petrella
James J. McGovern, III
Carmel Joy Decker

ASSOCIATES

Sandro Polledri
Celia S. Bosco
Lynn S. Degen
Elizabeth A. Daly
Brian O. Lipman
J. Frank Vespa-Papaleo
Susan B. Burns
Bruno Genova
Robert C. Gifford, Jr.
Courtney Gaccione

For full biographical listings, see the Martindale-Hubbell Law Directory

PHILIP M. LUSTBADER & DAVID LUSTBADER A PROFESSIONAL CORPORATION (AV)

615 West Mount Pleasant Avenue, 07039
Telephone: 973-740-1000
Fax: 973-740-1520
URL: http://www.lawyers.com/lustbader,law

Philip M. Lustbader | David Lustbader

John L. Riordan, Jr. | James S. Colavito

For full biographical listings, see the Martindale-Hubbell Law Directory

MANASQUAN, Monmouth Co.

CARTON, WITT, ARVANITIS & BARISCILLO, L.L.C. (AV)

(Formerly Durand, Ivins & Carton)
40 Union Avenue, P.O. Box 367, 08736
Telephone: 908-223-1800
Asbury Park, New Jersey Office: 4001 Route 66 at Garden State Parkway, P.O. Box 1229.
Telephone: 732-922-9500.
Telecopier: 732-922-1625.

RESIDENT PARTNERS

James D. Carton, III | John C. Carton

Attorneys for: New Jersey Bell Telephone Co.; Jersey Shore Medical Center, Inc.
Local Attorneys for: Travelers Insurance Co.; Aetna Casualty & Surety Co.; New Jersey Manufacturers Insurance Co.; Liberty Mutual; Prudential Insurance Co.; Chubb & Son.; Princeton Insurance Co.; Garden State Indemnity Co.

For full biographical listings, see the Martindale-Hubbell Law Directory

MILLBURN, Essex Co.

McDERMOTT & McGEE (AV)

75 Main Street, P.O. Box 192, 07041-0192
Telephone: 973-467-8080
Fax: 973-376-8669

MEMBERS OF FIRM

John L. McDermott
John P. McGee
Richard P. Maggi
Thomas A. Wester
Richard M. Tango
Frank P. Leanza
John L. McDermott, Jr.
David J. Dickinson
A. Charles Lorenzo
Robert A. McDermott
Kevin John McGee

ASSOCIATES

Anthony John Verardi
Lindsay K. O'Shaughnessy
Andre L. McGuire

OF COUNSEL

Daniel K. Van Dorn

Representative Clients: Affiliated Building Service, Inc.; Allstate Insurance Co.; General Agents Insurance Company of America; Greater New York Mutual; General Accident Group; ISS International Service System, Inc.; Zurich-American Insurance Co.; Penn National Insurance Co.; Tokio Marine & Fire Insurance Co.; Medical Inter-Insurance Exchange of New Jersey.

(See Next Column)

For full biographical listings, see the Martindale-Hubbell Law Directory

LAW OFFICES OF STEPHEN H. SCHECHNER (AV)

75 Main Street, 07041
Telephone: 973-376-6200
Fax: 973-376-5620

ASSOCIATE

Virginia T. Shea

For full biographical listings, see the Martindale-Hubbell Law Directory

MOORESTOWN, Burlington Co.

CHIERICI, CHIERICI & SMITH, A PROFESSIONAL CORPORATION (AV)

Blason Campus - III, 509 South Lenola Road Building Six, 08057-1561
Telephone: 856-234-6300
Fax: 856-234-9490

Donald R. Chierici, Jr. | Elizabeth Coleman Chierici
Julie C. Smith

Carolyn J. Kornas
Mark G. Esposito
Richard D. DiTomaso
Melvin McDowell
David J. Karbasian
Peter P. Sanchez
Donald R. Chierici, III

For full biographical listings, see the Martindale-Hubbell Law Directory

*MORRISTOWN,** Morris Co.

COLQUHOUN & COLQUHOUN, A PROFESSIONAL CORPORATION (AV)

165 South Street, 07960
Telephone: 973-540-0500
FAX: 973-540-0550
Cable Address: "Lawscot"
URL: http://www.lawyers.com/colqhounlaw

Robert F. Colquhoun
Kevin F. Colquhoun
Robert F. Colquhoun, II
Sean F. Colquhoun
Moira E. Colquhoun

Reference: The Andover Companies.

For full biographical listings, see the Martindale-Hubbell Law Directory

McELROY, DEUTSCH AND MULVANEY (AV)

1300 Mount Kemble Avenue, P.O. Box 2075, 07962-2075
Telephone: 973-993-8100
Fax: 973-425-0161
URL: http://www.MDMlaw.com
Denver, Colorado Office: 1099 18th Street, Suite 3120.
Telephone: 303-293-8800.
Fax: 303-293-3116.
New York, New York Office: Wall Street Plaza, 88 Pine Street.
Telephone: 212-766-1807.
Fax: 212-483-9129.
Ridgewood, New Jersey Office: 40 West Ridgewood Avenue.
Telephone: 201-445-6722.
Fax: 201-445-8075.

MEMBERS OF FIRM

Lorraine M. Armenti (Resident Partner, Denver Colorado Office)
Grace C. Bertone
John P. Beyel
William C. Carey
Stephen H. Cohen (1938-1992)
Kevin T. Coughlin
John F. Darcy (Resident, Ridgewood Office)
Edward B. Deutsch
Timothy I. Duffy
Kevin P. Galvin
Robert J. Kelly
Joseph P. La Sala
James P. Lisovicz
Paul A. Lisovicz
Fred A. Manley, Jr.
Michael J. Marone
Nancy McDonald
William T. McElroy
Laurence M. McHeffey (Resident Partner, Denver, Colorado Office)
Robert W. Muilenburg
James M. Mulvaney
Alfred S. Nugent, Jr. (1925-1989)
Octavius A. Orbe (Resident, Ridgewood Office)
Loren L. Pierce
Warren K. Racusin
Mark A. Rosen
Thomas P. Scrivo
John H. Suminski
Walter F. Timpone
Kevin E. Wolff

COUNSEL TO THE FIRM

Robert L. Clifford

OF COUNSEL

John K. Bradley | John F. Whitteaker

(See Next Column)

McElroy, Deutsch and Mulvaney, *Morristown—Continued*

ASSOCIATES

Susan Freeman Anthony
H. George Avery
Elizabeth Addison Barrow
Joseph F. Bermudez
Thomas Richard Calcagni
Patrick J. Casey (Resident Associate, Denver, Colorado Office)
Lisbeth W. Cload (Resident, Ridgewood Office)
Daniel J. Cohen
Craig J. Compoli, Jr.
John P. Cookson (Resident Associate, New York, NY Office)
John Thomas Coyne
Andrew J. D'Arcy
Andrew M. Csaszar
Michael B. Devins
John W. DiNicola, II
Robin A. Donato
Rebecca Ward Donohue
Steven F. Dorry
Julienne S. Duncan
Brian F. Fowler (Resident, Ridgewood Office)
Aaron C. Foy (Not admitted in NJ; Resident, Denver, Colorado Office)
Christopher S. Frangeš
Lorna A. Friel
Kevin P. Harkins (Resident, Ridgewood Office)
Sarah C. Herzog
Eric J. Hughes
George A. Kelman
Justin N. Kinney
Linda F. Kitz
John P. Leonard
Joseph J. McGlone
Robert McGuire
Kaneez Fatema Madraswalla
Nadine Maleski
Faith Martin
Suzanne Cocco Midlige
Heidi S. Minuskin
Louis A. Modugno
Florina A. Moldovan
John W. Morris
Francis C. Porada (Resident Associate, Denver, Colorado Office)
Robert J. Re
Vincent E. Reilly
Jay R. Ruble
Craig T. Sashihara
Adam R. Schwartz
Peter W. Smith
Timothy P. Smith
Ronnie H. Spring
Michael J. Sullivan
Catharine Acker Vaughan
Meredith A. Walling
Richard J. Williams, Jr.

Representative Clients: Crum & Forster Insurance Co.; Fireman's Fund Insurance Cos.; New Jersey Manufacturers Insurance Co.; The Home Indemnity Co.; Hartford Accident & Indemnity Co.; Harleysville Insurance Co.; Highlands Insurance Group; Kemper Insurance Co.; Zurich Insurance Group; St. Paul Insurance Companies.

For full biographical listings, see the Martindale-Hubbell Law Directory

Stephen S. Weinstein A Professional Corporation (AV)

20 Park Place, Suite 301, 07960
Telephone: 973-267-5200
Fax: 973-538-1779
Email: skippy@sswpa.com *URL:* http://www.sswpa.com

Stephen S. Weinstein

Gail S. Boertzel
William G. Johnson
Melissa H. Luce

For full biographical listings, see the Martindale-Hubbell Law Directory

*NEWARK,** Essex Co.

McCarter & English, LLP (AV)

Four Gateway Center, 100 Mulberry Street, P.O. Box 652, 07101-0652
Telephone: 973-622-4444
Telecopier: 973-624-7070
URL: http://www.mccarter.com
Cherry Hill, New Jersey Office: 1820 Chapel Avenue West, Suite 380.
Telephone: 609-662-8444.
Telecopier: 609-662-6203.
New York, New York Office: Suite 2247, One World Trade Center.
Telephone: 212-466-9018.
Telecopier: 212-432-6568.
Boca Raton, Florida Office: 2255 Glades Road, Suite 319-A.
Telephone: 561-994-6262.
Telecopier: 561-241-0798.
Wilmington, Delaware Office: Mellon Bank Center, 919 Market Street.
Telephone: 302-654-8010.
Telecopier: 302-654-0795.
Philadelphia, Pennsylvania Office: One Commerce Square, 2005 Market Street, Suite 3600.
Telephone: 215-557-7700.
Telecopier: 215-557-6544.

MEMBERS OF FIRM

Richard M. Eittreim
B. John Pendleton, Jr.
Penelope M. Taylor

COUNSEL

Joseph F. Falgiani

For Complete List of Firm Personnel, See General Section

For full biographical listings, see the Martindale-Hubbell Law Directory

St. John & Wayne, L.L.C. (AV)

Two Penn Plaza East, 07105-2249
Telephone: 973-491-3600
Fax: 973-491-3555
Email: firm@nwk.stjohn-law.com *URL:* http://www.stjohn-law.com
Rochester, New York Office: St. John & Curtin, L.L.C., First Federal Plaza.
Telephone: 716-262-6780.
Fax: 716-262-6755.
New York, New York Office: Heron Tower, 70 East 55th. Street.
Telephone: 212-446-5000.
Fax: 212-446-5055.

Bruce S. Edington

For Complete List of Firm Personnel, See General Section

For full biographical listings, see the Martindale-Hubbell Law Directory

Sills Cummis Radin Tischman Epstein & Gross, A Professional Corporation (AV)

One Riverfront Plaza, 07102-5400
Telephone: 973-643-7000
Fax: 973-643-6500
Telex: 820630 Sillsbeck Nwk
Email: sillsmail@sillscummis.com *URL:* http://www.sillscummis.com
Atlantic City, New Jersey Office: 17 Gordon's Alley.
Telephone: 609-344-2800.
New York, N.Y. Office: 712 Fifth Avenue.
Telephone: 212-643-7000.
Washington, D.C. Office: 1800 K Street, N.W.
Telephone: 202-296-4750.

MEMBERS OF FIRM

Steven S. Radin
Thomas J. Demski
Thomas S. Novak
Alan J. Cohen (Resident at Atlantic City, N.J. Office)

Steven S. Katz
Paul F. Doda
Adam J. Kaiser

Representative Clients: International Fidelity Insurance Co.; Integrity Insurance Co. in Liquidation; EMAR, Ltd.; American Bankers Insurance Co.; American Casualty Co.; Fidelity Mutual Life Insurance Co.; Motor Club of America; American Home Assurance Co.

For Complete List of Firm Personnel, See General Section

For full biographical listings, see the Martindale-Hubbell Law Directory

Tompkins, McGuire, Wachenfeld & Barry (AV)

A New Jersey Limited Liability Partnership including a Professional Association
Four Gateway Center, 100 Mulberry Street, 07102-4070
Telephone: 973-622-3000
Telecopier: 973-623-7780
Email: attorneys@tompkinsmcguire.com
New York, New York Office: 1 Bankers Trust Plaza. 130 Liberty Street, Suite 2707. 10006.
Telephone: 212-714-1720.

MEMBERS OF FIRM

William F. Tompkins (1913-1989)
William J. Prout, Jr. (1947-1996)
William B. McGuire (P.A.)
Howard G. Wachenfeld
Theodore L. Abeles
John J. Barry
Rex K. Harriott
James F. Flanagan, III
Marianne Espinosa Murphy
Eugene J. Sullivan
Frederic S. Kessler
Michael F. Nestor
Marianne M. DeMarco
Patrick M. Callahan
Paul S. Werther
Mark Falk
Michael S. Miller
Douglas E. Motzenbecker
Evelyn R. Storch
Ellen Nunno Corbo
William H. Trousdale
George G. Campion
Joseph K. Cobuzio
Richard F. Connors, Jr.
Richard A. Ulsamer
Madeline E. Cox
Nadia Walker Brunetto
Angelo R. Giacchi
Adam N. Saravay

OF COUNSEL

Michael F. DeCapua
Frances S. Margolis
Paul B. Thompson
Raymond W. Troy (1911-1992)
William T. Wachenfeld

COUNSEL

Peter A. Bogaard
Brian M. English
Leonore C. Lewis

ASSOCIATES

Christopher A. Barbarisi
Thomas A. Callahan, Jr.
Joann K. Dobransky
Thomas F. Doherty
Robert Leonardo
Stephen C. Matthews
Grant W. McGuire
Matthew P. O'Malley
Michael P. Pasquale
Colleen Duffy Shiarella

Representative Clients: Corbo Jewelers, Inc.; General Electric Co.; Hartford Insurance Group; Marriott Corp.; National Indemnity Co., Inc.; National Union Fire Insurance Co.; Underwriters at Lloyd's, London.

(See Next Column)

TOMPKINS, MCGUIRE, WACHENFELD & BARRY—*Continued*

For full biographical listings, see the Martindale-Hubbell Law Directory

*NEW BRUNSWICK,** Middlesex Co.

HOAGLAND, LONGO, MORAN, DUNST & DOUKAS (AV)

40 Paterson Street, P.O. Box 480, 08903
Telephone: 732-545-4717
Fax: 732-545-4579
Email: info@hlmdd.com

MEMBERS OF FIRM

Bartholomew A. Longo
James B. Moran
Alan I. Dunst
Kenneth J. Doukas, Jr.
Michael John Stone
Donald D. Davidson
Thaddeus J. Hubert, III
Joan Alster Weisblatt
Karen M. Buerle
Robert G. Kenny
Michael J. Baker
Andrew J. Carlowicz, Jr.
Gary J. Hoagland
Jeffrey S. Intravatola
Jamie D. Happas
Thomas J. Walsh, Jr.
Robert S. Helwig
Michael F. Dolan
Douglas M. Fasciale
Marc S. Gaffrey
John Charles Simons
Susan K. O'Connor
Stephen G. Perrella
Jacquelyn L. Poland
Douglas Susan
Patrick J. McDonald

OF COUNSEL

John J. Hoagland
Herman L. Breitkopf
Richard S. Cohen

ASSOCIATES

Andrew N. Kessler
John P. Barnes
Christopher M. Longo
Nancy A. Freedman
Tiffany C. Chong
Michael Dermody
Diane Hoagland
Michael T. Kearns
Keith C. Northridge
Andrew J. DiMarsico
Edward J. Rebenack
Paul N. Harris
Denis A. Gooding
Kevin J. Musiakiewicz
Michael N. Porter
Kenneth Sisco
M. Stephanie Beaty

Representative Clients: CNA/Continental Casualty; National Indemnity Company; Providence Washington Insurance Company; The Mutual Fire, Marine & Inland Insurance Company; INAPRO/CIGNA; Allstate Insurance Company; Home Depot; American Reliance Insurance Company; Shand, Morahan & Company; CPC International.

For full biographical listings, see the Martindale-Hubbell Law Directory

NORTH BRUNSWICK, Middlesex Co.

BUSCH AND BUSCH, LLP (AV)

215 North Center Drive, Commerce Center - U.S. #1 South, P.O. Box 7448, 08902-7448
Telephone: 732-821-2300
Telecopier: 732-821-5588
Email: busch@ifu.net

MEMBERS OF FIRM

Lewis D. Busch (1901-1986)
Henry Busch (Retired)
Malcolm R. Busch
Ronald J. Busch
Bertram E. Busch
Mark N. Busch
Leonard R. Busch
Steven F. Satz
Donald J. Sears

ASSOCIATE

Paul Alan VanBuskirk

Representative Clients: Littman Jewelers; Utica Mutual Insurance Co.; New Brunswick Tomorrow; Township of South Brunswick; Township of Monroe, Board of Education; Township of East Brunswick; Minnesota Mutual Life Insurance Co.; Middlesex County Joint Insurance Fund; Cincinnati Insurance Co.

For full biographical listings, see the Martindale-Hubbell Law Directory

LYNCH, MARTIN, KANE, KUPER, KEEFE & BARTELS, LLC (AV)

1368 How Lane, P.O. Box 6022, 08902-6022
Telephone: 732-545-0745
Fax: 732-545-4780
Email: LYNCHMRTN@aol.com

John A. Lynch, Sr. (1908-1978)
John A. Lynch
James D. Martin, Jr.
John J. Kane
Eric Kuper
John E. Keefe, Jr.
Patrick J. Bartels
Carl W. Swanson
James Den Uyl
John W. Harding
Lori A. Dvorak
Bernard P. Hvozdovic, Jr.
Joseph J. LaCosta
Timothy E. Annin

Laura M. Shea
Robyn M. Mitchell
Christine Klimczuk

OF COUNSEL

Robert T. Quackenboss (Retired Superior Court Judge)

(See Next Column)

LEGAL SUPPORT PERSONNEL

Sharon Stewart (Administrator)

For full biographical listings, see the Martindale-Hubbell Law Directory

NORTHFIELD, Atlantic Co.

McALLISTER, HYBERG & WHITE (AV)

Executive Plaza, 2111 New Road, Suite 105, 08225
Telephone: 609-407-1000
Fax: 609-407-1010
Email: McAllister-Hyberg@prodigy.net

Robert N. McAllister
Lars S. Hyberg
Joseph B. White

ASSOCIATE

Keith T. Smith

For full biographical listings, see the Martindale-Hubbell Law Directory

OCEAN TOWNSHIP, Monmouth Co.

EVANS, OSBORNE & KREIZMAN (AV)

CN 7808 1500 Lawrence Avenue, 07712-7808
Telephone: 732-643-0300
Fax: 732-643-0340
New York, New York Office: Suite 7967, One World Trade Center.
Telephone: 212-466-1207.

MEMBERS OF FIRM

Harry S. Evans
Harry V. Osborne, II
Joel N. Kreizman
Mary O'Keefe Massey
Kevin E. Hoffman

ASSOCIATES

Marie A. Accardi
James F. McDonough
Kenneth P. Skibinski

Representative Clients: United Kingdom P&I Club (Thomas R. Miller Insurance Services); American Marine Underwriters, Inc.; Continental Insurance Cos.; Hartford Insurance Cos.; CIGNA Cos.; Jersey Central Power & Light Co.; First Union Bank; CNA Insurance Cos.; Prudential Property and Casualty Ins. Co.; General Public Utilities, Inc.

For full biographical listings, see the Martindale-Hubbell Law Directory

PARSIPPANY, Morris Co.

CUYLER BURK (AV)

Parsippany Corporate Center, Four Century Drive, 07054-4663
Telephone: 973-734-3200
Telex: 429071
Telecopier: 973-734-3201
Email: Main@Cuyler.com *URL:* http://www.cuyler.com
New York, New York Office: 350 Fifth Avenue, Suite 3304. 10018.
Telephone: 212-645-4039.

MEMBERS OF FIRM

Stephen D. Cuyler
Jo Ann Burk
Stefano Calogero
David L. Menzel
Peter Petrou
Richard A. Crooker
Michael J. Jones

COUNSEL

Anne M. Mohan
Frank J. Miele

ASSOCIATES

Jan C. Walker
Kathleen Jane Olear
Claudia L. Marchese
Mark G. Eliades
Kimberly A. Joel
Christy A. Ramunno
Catherine E. Youngman
Andrew K. Craig
Mark S. Winter
Thomas J. Castano
Hugo A. Hilgendorff, IV

LEGAL SUPPORT PERSONNEL

Frederick M. H. Currie, Jr.

For full biographical listings, see the Martindale-Hubbell Law Directory

GENNET, KALLMANN, ANTIN & ROBINSON, A PROFESSIONAL CORPORATION (AV)

6 Campus Drive, 07054-4406
Telephone: 973-285-1919
Fax: 973-285-1177
Email: gkar@nac.net
New York, New York Office: Litman Suite, 45 Broadway Atrium, 10006.
Telephone: 212-406-1919.

Stanley W. Kallmann
Mark L. Antin
Harry Robinson, III
Richard S. Nichols

William Gary Hanft
Thomas J. Olsen, IV
Francie E. Joseph
Paul A. Tumbleson

(See Next Column)

GENNET, KALLMANN, ANTIN & ROBINSON A PROFESSIONAL CORPORATION, *Parsippany—Continued*

LEGAL SUPPORT PERSONNEL
Eleanor Dawalt (Administrator)

Representative Clients: Aetna Insurance Co.; Hartford Fire; Lloyds of London; New England Mutuals.
Reference: United Jersey Bank.

For full biographical listings, see the Martindale-Hubbell Law Directory

REISEMAN SHARP KELSEY & BROWN LLP (AV)

4 Campus Drive, P.O. Box 431, 07054-0431
Telephone: 973-267-3600
Fax: 973-267-2332

MEMBERS OF FIRM

Neil Reiseman
James B. Sharp
Jane S. Kelsey
Kenneth M. Brown
Sam Rosenberg
Meghan E. Walsh

John C. Macce
Jayne E. Turner
Everett E. Gale, III
Robert T. Gunning
Gregory A. Bush

Representative Clients: Medical Inter-Insurance Exchange of New Jersey; Princeton Insurance Company; Health Care Insurance Company; Home Depot; United Capitol Insurance Company; New Jersey Property-Liability Insurance Guaranty Association; New Jersey Joint Underwriting Association; Franciscan Health Systems; Zurich American; Avis.

For full biographical listings, see the Martindale-Hubbell Law Directory

RARITAN, Somerset Co.

LAW OFFICES OF LAUB & FRANCHINO, L.L.C. (AV)

901 U.S. Highway 202, 08869-1419
Telephone: 908-725-1411
Fax: 908-725-9303
URL: http://www.lawyers.com/laub&franchino

Salvatore L. Franchino
Peter N. Laub

James J. Pieper
Peter J. O'Connor

OF COUNSEL

Daniel A. Lime, II
William J. Salmond

For full biographical listings, see the Martindale-Hubbell Law Directory

RED BANK, Monmouth Co.

WHITE, FLEISCHNER & FINO (AV)

272 Broad Street, 07701
Telephone: 732-530-7787
Telecopier: 732-530-8552
New York, New York Office: 140 Broadway.
Telephone: 212-487-9700.
Telecopier: 212-487-9777.

Benjamin A. Fleischner
Sheri E. Holland

ASSOCIATES

Daniel MacLaren Stewart
Elaine N. Chou

Representative Clients: Empire Fire & Marine Ins. Co.; Marriott International; Avis Rent A Car; Chicago Insurance Company; Holyoke Mutual Insurance Co.; AIU; Lloyd's Syndicates; Markel Insurance Company; Gerling Insurance Company; News Corp.

For full biographical listings, see the Martindale-Hubbell Law Directory

ROSELAND, Essex Co.

BRACH, EICHLER, ROSENBERG, SILVER, BERNSTEIN, HAMMER & GLADSTONE, A PROFESSIONAL CORPORATION (AV)

101 Eisenhower Parkway, 07068
Telephone: 973-228-5700
Telecopier: 973-228-7852
Email: law@bracheichler.com *URL:* http://www.bracheichler.com

Alan H. Bernstein
Richard J. Driver
Charles X. Gormally
Alan S. Pralgever

Stuart Jeffrey Polkowitz
John P. Wyciskala, III

OF COUNSEL

Lance A. Posner

COUNSEL

David J. Klein
David S. Bernstein

Representative Clients: American USF&G; Central Mutual Zurich; Great American Insurance Co.; Motor Club of America; Ohio Casualty Insurance Group.

(See Next Column)

For Complete List of Firm Personnel, See General Section

For full biographical listings, see the Martindale-Hubbell Law Directory

CONNELL, FOLEY & GEISER LLP (AV)

85 Livingston Avenue, 07068
Telephone: 973-535-0500
Telefax: 973-535-9217
Email: info@cfglaw.com *URL:* http://www.cfglaw.com

MEMBERS OF FIRM

George W. Connell
Adrian M. Foley, Jr.
Theodore W. Geiser
John B. La Vecchia
George J. Kenny
Samuel Darrow Lord
Richard D. Catenacci
Richard J. Badolato
Peter D. Manahan
Mark L. Fleder
Linda A. Palazzolo
John F. Neary
Thomas S. Cosma
Kathleen S. Murphy
Patrick J. McAuley
Peter J. Pizzi
Kevin R. Gardner
Robert Emmett Ryan
Michael X. McBride
Jeffrey W. Moryan
Patricia J. Pindar
Peter J. Smith
Brian G. Steller
Judith A. Wahrenberger
Karen Munster Cassidy
Karen Painter Randall
Liza M. Walsh
Timothy E. Corriston
Ernest W. Schoellkopff
Heidi Willis Currier

Representative Clients: Bethlehem Steel Corp.; Borden Inc.; Chase Manhattan Bank; CNA Insurance; Conrail; Hilton Hotels Corp.; Merrill Lynch; Microsoft; New Jersey Manufacturers Insurance.

For Complete List of Firm Personnel, See General Section

For full biographical listings, see the Martindale-Hubbell Law Directory

SELLAR RICHARDSON, P.C. (AV)

Six Becker Farm Road, 07068-1735
Telephone: 973-535-1400
Fax: 973-535-6522
Email: info@sellarrichardson.com

James P. Richardson
Wendy H. Smith
John M. Kearney
Denise M. Luckenbach
Shawn R. Stowell

Patricia R. Carley
Julia C. Talarick
Deborah M. Taub
Albert N. Montano
Jennifer R. Sentivan
Victoria F. Pratt

OF COUNSEL

Alastair J. Sellar
E. Scott Garrett
Anthony C. Stuart

For full biographical listings, see the Martindale-Hubbell Law Directory

WALDER, SONDAK & BROGAN, A PROFESSIONAL CORPORATION (AV)

5 Becker Farm Road, P.O. Box 901, 07068
Telephone: 973-992-5300
Telecopier: 973-992-1505; 992-1006
Email: general@wsbesqs.com *URL:* http://www.wsbesqs.com

Barry A. Kozyra
James A. Plaisted
Jeffrey A. Walder

Representative Clients: Old Republic Insurance; Chicago Underwriting Group, Inc.

For Complete List of Firm Personnel, See General Section

For full biographical listings, see the Martindale-Hubbell Law Directory

SECAUCUS, Hudson Co.

STEVENS & MINTER (AV)

One Harmon Plaza, 7th Floor, 07094
Telephone: 201-319-5700
Fax: 201-319-0151

STAFF COUNSEL
AMERICAN INTERNATIONAL COMPANIES
MANAGING ATTORNEY
Claude J. Minter
SUPERVISING ATTORNEY
Barbara A. Schwab
SENIOR TRIAL SPECIALIST
Frederick W. Stevens
SENIOR TRIAL ATTORNEYS

Gary J. Chester
John P. Gillespie
John S. Sawicki
Victoria A. Schwartz

For full biographical listings, see the Martindale-Hubbell Law Directory

SHIP BOTTOM, Ocean Co.

SHACKLETON, HAZELTINE AND BISHOP (AV)

22nd Street and Long Beach Boulevard, P.O. Box 410, 08008
Telephone: 609-494-2136
Telefax: 609-494-0870
Fairfield, New Jersey Office: One Passaic Avenue.
Telephone: 201-882-4646.
Telefax: 201-882-4620.

MEMBERS OF FIRM

Richard J. Shackleton
Colin R. Hazeltine
James E. Bishop

ASSOCIATES

Laura M. O'Regan
Marc Baden Powell
Robert Emmet Rue

OF COUNSEL

Kenneth L. Leiby, Jr. (Resident, Fairfield Office)

References: Commerce Bank/Shore N/A; Summit Bank Corp.

For full biographical listings, see the Martindale-Hubbell Law Directory

SHORT HILLS, Essex Co.

EDWIN R. MATTHEWS, P.C. (AV)

150 John F. Kennedy Parkway CN 5008, 07078-2707
Telephone: 973-912-9500
Telecopier: 973-912-9411
Email: mwgf@mail.att.net

Edwin R. Matthews

Robert J. Pansulla
Drew D. Krause
Daniel J. Bonner
Lisa A. Grattan

For full biographical listings, see the Martindale-Hubbell Law Directory

SPRINGFIELD, Union Co.

HARDIN, KUNDLA, MCKEON, POLETTO & POLIFRONI, P.A., A PROFESSIONAL CORPORATION (AV)

673 Morris Avenue, P.O. Box 730, 07081
Telephone: 973-912-5222
Fax: 973-912-9212
Email: info@HKMPP.com
New York, New York Office: 55 John Street, 10038.
Telephone: 212-571-0111.
Fax: 212-571-1117.

George R. Hardin
Robert L. Polifroni
Janet L. Poletto
Mark S. Kundla
John F. McKeon
James R. Greene
Nicea J. D'Annunzio
John Samuel Favate
Patrick J. Clare
Anna Marie Strand

Jeffrey A. Oshin
Joseph R. Lowicky
Tracy C. Forsyth
Joseph A. DeFuria
John G. Kilbride
Jeffrey H. Goldsmith
Jeffrey Roth
Nora J. Grimbergen
William C. Sullivan, Jr.
Paul Daly
V. Christopher Hirsch
Richard S. Reig
Sam A. Dotro
Brian K. Kaiser
David M. Steiner
Lani M. D'Agostino
Sheila A. Glackin
Michael S. Schwartz
Kirsten L. McCaw
Sanjoy Mukherjee
Louisa B. Sargent
Michael A. Cifelli
James J. A. Mulhall
Kevin M. Regan
Lisa D. Chanel
Maria-Milagros Herrero
Brian A. King
Christina Fichera Dente
Andrea L. Strack
Roger J. Imhof
John P. Monaghan
Stephen J. Donahue
Cindy L. Thompson
Lisa A. Ganzhorn

Representative Clients: Crum & Forster Insurance; St. Paul Fire and Marine Insurance Co.; Wausau Insurance Cos.; CNA Insurance; Envision Claims Mgmt.; Royal Insurance Co.; U.S.F.&G.; Princeton Insurance Company; Healthcare Insurance Exchange; Prudential Property and Casualty Co.; Risk Enterprise Mgmt.

For full biographical listings, see the Martindale-Hubbell Law Directory

MCDONOUGH, KORN & EICHHORN, A PROFESSIONAL CORPORATION (AV)

Park Place Legal Center, 959 South Springfield Avenue, P.O. Box 712, 07081-0712
Telephone: 973-912-9099
Fax: 973-912-8604

Peter L. Korn
R. Scott Eichhorn
James R. Korn
William S. Mezzomo
Timothy J. Jaeger
Wilfred P. Coronato

(See Next Column)

Julia A. Klubenspies
Matthew S. Schorr
Danielle M. Verrastro
Jeffrey John Berezny

OF COUNSEL

Robert P. McDonough

Representative Clients: Chubb Insurance; Medical Inter-Insurance Exchange of New Jersey; Medical Liability Mutual Insurance Co.; GRE Insurance; The Travelers; State Volunteer Insurance; Wausau Insurance; Continental Insurance; The Home.
Reference: First Union, Summit, N.J.

For full biographical listings, see the Martindale-Hubbell Law Directory

*TOMS RIVER,** Ocean Co.

LOMELL, MUCCIFORI, ADLER, RAVASCHIERE, AMABILE & PEHLIVANIAN, A PROFESSIONAL CORPORATION (AV)

250 Washington Street, P.O. Box 787, 08754
Telephone: 732-349-2443
Fax: 732-349-6917
Email: thefirm@lomell.com *URL:* http://www.lomell.com

Herman A. Adler
Dominic Ravaschiere
John S. Pehlivanian
Ronald E. Prusek
Jeffrey R. Surenian
James M. McKenna
Teresa K. Gierla
Arthur F. Leyden, III

Marc S. Galella
Robyn A. Belluardo
Janet Zaorski Kalapos
James S. Braaten
Regina M. Butler
Paul J Capotorto

Representative Clients: Commercial Union Insurance Co.; Kemper Insurance Co.; New Jersey Manufacturers Insurance Co.; The Ohio Casualty Insurance Co.; Cumberland Insurance Co.; Farmers Mutual Fire Assurance Assoc. of New Jersey; Professional Risk Management Co.; Showboat Hotel and Casino; Caesar's World Hotel and Casino; Tropworld Hotel and Casino.

For Complete List of Firm Personnel, See General Section

For full biographical listings, see the Martindale-Hubbell Law Directory

NOVINS, YORK & PENTONY, A PROFESSIONAL CORPORATION (AV)

202 Main Street, 08753
Telephone: 732-349-7100
Email: info@nyplaw.com

Robert J. Novins (1910-1973)
Robert F. Novins
Harvey L. York
Kenneth R. Pentony
Ann K. Haskell
Robert M. McKeon

W. Mark Bayles
Robert J. Roth

OF COUNSEL

William E. O'Connor
Lorna S. Scanlon

Counsel for: Allstate Insurance Co.; Motor Club of America.

For Complete List of Firm Personnel, See General Section

For full biographical listings, see the Martindale-Hubbell Law Directory

STARKEY, KELLY, BLANEY & WHITE (AV)

2 Hooper Avenue, 08753
Telephone: 732-240-3600
Fax: 732-240-3777
Brick, New Jersey Office: 459 Jack Martin Boulevard, 08724.
Telephone: 732-840-5900.
Fax: 732-840-5901.
Manasquan, New Jersey Office: 23 Route 71, 08736.
Telephone: 732-223-7328.
Fax: 732-240-3777.

MEMBERS OF FIRM

Charles E. Starkey
William V. Kelly
James M. Blaney

ASSOCIATES

Natalie Pouch
Anthony Mancuso
Robert A. Bauer
Scott W. Kenneally
Susan K. White
Brent D. Miller

Representative Clients: Hartford Insurance Co.; New Jersey Education Assn.; New Jersey Psychiatric Assn.; Ocean County Utilities Authority; Brick Township Municipal Utilities Authority; Manasquan River Regional Sewerage Authority; Hanover Insurance Co.; John Hancock Insurance Co.; Rider Inc. Co.

For full biographical listings, see the Martindale-Hubbell Law Directory

Albuquerque—Continued

MADISON, HARBOUR, MROZ & BRENNAN, P.A. (AV)
Suite 1800 Albuquerque Plaza, 201 Third Street, N.W., P.O. Box 25467, 87102
Telephone: 505-242-2177
Fax: 505-242-7184
URL: http://www.madisonlaw.com
Santa Fe, New Mexico Office: Coronado Building, 2nd Floor, 141 East Palace Avenue, P.O. Box 1234.
Telephone: 505-992-8933.
Facsimile: 505-988-2987.

William C. Madison
Michael W. Brennan
Michael H. Harbour
Robert J. Mroz
Neils L. Thompson
M. Eliza Stewart
Lorri Krehbiel
Gregory D. Steinman

Michael Joseph Dekleva
Michele U. Estrada
Scott E. Turner
Shannon A. Parden
Corey A. Goldsand
Jude A. Cisneros

For full biographical listings, see the Martindale-Hubbell Law Directory

MILLER, STRATVERT & TORGERSON, P.A. (AV)
500 Marquette Avenue, N.W., Suite 1100, P.O. Box 25687, 87102
Telephone: 505-842-1950
Facsimile: 505-243-4408
Email: info@mstLAW.com *URL:* http://www.mstLAW.com
Farmington, New Mexico Office: 300 West Arrington, Suite 300, P.O. Box 869.
Telephone: 505-326-4521.
Facsimile: 505-325-5474.
Las Cruces, New Mexico Office: 500 South Main, Suite 800, P.O. Box 1209.
Telephone: 505-523-2481.
Facsimile: 505-526-2215.
Santa Fe, New Mexico Office: 150 Washington Avenue, Suite 300, P.O. Box 1986.
Telephone: 505-989-9614.
Facsimile: 505-989-9857.

Ranne B. Miller
Alan C. Torgerson
Alice Tomlinson Lorenz
Gregory W. Chase
Lyman G. Sandy
Stephen M. Williams
Stephan M. Vidmar
Robert C. Gutierrez
Seth V. Bingham (Resident at Farmington Office)
James B. Collins (Resident at Farmington Office)
Timothy Ray Briggs
Rudolph A. Lucero
Deborah A. Solove
Gary L. Gordon
Lawrence R. White (Resident at Las Cruces Office)
Virginia Anderman
Thomas R. Mack
Terri L. Sauer
Joel T. Newton (Resident at Las Cruces Office)
Thomas M. Domme
Ruth O. Pregenzer
Jeffrey E. Jones (Resident at Santa Fe Office)
Manuel I. Arrieta (Resident at Las Cruces Office)
Robin A. Goble
James R. Wood
Kirk R. Allen
Ruth M. Fuess
Kyle M. Finch (Resident at Farmington Office)
Henry Brook Laskey
Katherine Weeks Hall (Resident at Santa Fe Office)
Lara L. White (Resident at Las Cruces Office)
Paula G. Maynes (Resident at Santa Fe Office)
Katherine N. Blackett
Jennifer L. Stone
Andrew M. Sanchez
Amina Quargnali-Linsley

COUNSEL

William K. Stratvert

Representative Clients: Mutual Insurance Corp. of America; Massachusetts Mutual Life Insurance; Medical Protective Co.; Farmers Insurance Group; United States Fidelity & Guaranty Co.; St. Paul Insurance Cos.; State Farm Mutual Automobile Insurance Co.; Sentry Dairyland Insurance Co.; The Travelers.

For Complete List of Firm Personnel, See General Section

For full biographical listings, see the Martindale-Hubbell Law Directory

RODEY, DICKASON, SLOAN, AKIN & ROBB, P.A. (AV)
Albuquerque Plaza, Suite 2200, 201 Third Street, N.W., P.O. Box 1888, 87103-1888
Telephone: 505-765-5900
Fax: 505-768-7395
Email: info@rodey.com *URL:* http://www.rodey.com
Santa Fe, New Mexico Office: Suite 101 Marcy Plaza, 123 East Marcy Street, P.O. Box 1357, 87504-1357.
Telephone: 505-984-0100.
Fax: 505-989-9542.

James C. Ritchie
Joseph J. Mullins
Robert G. McCorkle
Bruce Hall
Jonathan W. Hewes
W. Robert Lasater, Jr.
Mark C. Meiering
Travis R. Collier

(See Next Column)

W. Mark Mowery (Resident, Santa Fe Office)
Patrick M. Shay
David C. Davenport, Jr. (Resident, Santa Fe Office)
Tracy McGee Jenks
Henry M. Bohnhoff
Charles K. Purcell
John M. Brant
Susan S. Throckmorton
R. Nelson Franse
Paul R. Koller
David W. Bunting
Susan K. Barger
MacDonnell Gordon (Resident, Santa Fe Office)

Paul C. Collins
Kevin Lynn Wildenstein
Deborah E. Mann
Glenn A. Beard
Lisa A. Chavez

COUNSEL

Thomas P. Gulley

For Complete List of Firm Personnel, See General Section

For full biographical listings, see the Martindale-Hubbell Law Directory

SIMONE, ROBERTS & WEISS, P.A. (AV)
8102 Menaul Boulevard N.E., 87110
Telephone: 505-298-9400
Fax: 505-298-7070

Stephen M. Simone
Randal W. Roberts
Norman F. Weiss
Michelle Lalley Blake
Thomas E. Perkins
Ashley Gauthier
Megan Day Hill

For full biographical listings, see the Martindale-Hubbell Law Directory

*LAS CRUCES,** Dona Ana Co.

REEVES, CHAVEZ, GREENFIELD & WALKER, P.A. (AV)
300 South Water Street, P.O. Box 2769, 88004-2769
Telephone: 505-524-9617
Fax: 505-524-1954
Email: rcgw@zianet.com

B. James Reeves
Frank N. Chavez
Charlotte Greenfield
William A. Walker, Jr.
Kelly P. Albers
Joyce A. Montes
William R. Anderson
Carolyn J. Baca

Glenn D. Hall
CaraLyn Banks

For full biographical listings, see the Martindale-Hubbell Law Directory

SANDENAW, CARRILLO & PIAZZA, P.C. (AV)
2951 Roadrunner Parkway, Suite A, 88011
Telephone: 505-522-7500
Fax: 505-522-5544
URL: http://www.lawyers.com/insurancedefenselaw

SHAREHOLDERS

Thomas A. Sandenaw, Jr.
Leonard J. Piazza
Raúl A. Carrillo, Jr.

Carlos M. Quiñones

OF COUNSEL

James T. Martin

For full biographical listings, see the Martindale-Hubbell Law Directory

*ROSWELL,** Chaves Co.

ATWOOD, MALONE, TURNER & SABIN, A PROFESSIONAL ASSOCIATION (AV)
400 North Pennsylvania Avenue Suite 1100, P.O. Drawer 700, 88202-0700
Telephone: 505-622-6221
Fax: 505-624-2883
Email: atwood@nm.net
Albuquerque, New Mexico Office: 500 Marquette N.W., Suite 750, P.O. Box 20.
Telephone: 505-842-5715.
Fax: 505-842-5713.

Jefferson Davis Atwood (1883-1960)
Ross L. Malone (1910-1974)
Robert E. Sabin (Resident)
Steven Lynn Bell (Resident)
Rod M. Schumacher (Resident)
John S. Nelson (Resident)
Lee M. Rogers, Jr. (Resident)
Timothy A. Lucas (Resident)
Victoria Davis Armstrong (Resident)
Remo E. Gay (Resident, Albuquerque Office)
Bryan Evans (Resident)
Timothy L. White (Resident, Albuquerque Office)
Barbara A. Reddy (Resident)

David J. Jaramillo (Resident, Albuquerque Office)
Bryon R. Hammer

(See Next Column)

ATWOOD, MALONE, TURNER & SABIN A PROFESSIONAL ASSOCIATION—*Continued*

OF COUNSEL

Charles F. Malone (1923-1999) Bob F. Turner (Resident)

Representative Clients: State Farm Insurance Cos.; Allstate Insurance Co.; The Travelers Insurance Co.; Farmers Alliance Mutual Insurance Company; The Aetna Insurance Co.; Mountain States Mutual Casualty Co.; New Mexico Physicians Insurance Services; Houston General Insurance Co.; Federated Insurance Co.; Royal Insurance; ITT Hartford.

For full biographical listings, see the Martindale-Hubbell Law Directory

*SANTA FE,** Santa Fe Co.

COMEAU, MALDEGEN, TEMPLEMAN & INDALL, L.L.P. (AV)

Coronado Building, 141 East Palace Avenue, P.O. Box 669, 87504-0669
Telephone: 505-982-4611
Telecopier: 505-988-2987
Email: cmtilaw@earthlink.net

MEMBERS OF FIRM

Michael R. Comeau
Larry D. Maldegen
William P. Templeman
Jon J. Indall
Stephen J. Lauer
Paula Ann Cook
Grey Handy
Joseph E. Manges

Michael C. Smith
Christian A. Hatfield

OF COUNSEL

Jeffrey R. Brannen

Representative Clients: Great American Insurance Co.; Agricultural Insurance Co.; American National Fire Insurance; UNIRISC; Vanliner Insurance Co.

For full biographical listings, see the Martindale-Hubbell Law Directory

HERRERA, LONG & POUND, P.A. (AV)

2200 Brothers Road, P.O. Box 5098, 87502-5098
Telephone: 505-982-8405
Fax: 505-982-8513
Email: hlplaw@aol.com

Judith C. Herrera
Nancy R. Long
John B. Pound

Mark E. Komer

LEGAL SUPPORT PERSONNEL

Shauna Allen Metzo

Reference: Bank of America.

For full biographical listings, see the Martindale-Hubbell Law Directory

HUFFAKER & CONWAY, A PROFESSIONAL CORPORATION (AV)

155 Grant Avenue, P.O. Box 1868, 87504-1868
Telephone: 505-988-8921
Fax: 505-983-3927
Email: sfstaff@sisna.com
Albuquerque, New Mexico Office: 201 Third Street, N.W., Suite 1910.
Telephone: 505-244-0021.
Facsimile: 505-244-1372.

Gregory D. Huffaker, Jr.
Ann Maloney Conway
Lisa A. Joynes
Seth L. Sparks
Edward C. Bagley

Representative Clients: State Farm Insurance Cos.; Royal Insurance Co. of America; The St. Paul/Seaboard; St. Paul Fire & Marine Ins. Co.; The Alliance Group; Universal Surety Co.; Mid-Continent Ins. Group.; National American Insurance Co.; Insurance Company of the West Group; Frontier Insurance Co.

For full biographical listings, see the Martindale-Hubbell Law Directory

MONTGOMERY & ANDREWS, PROFESSIONAL ASSOCIATION (AV)

325 Paseo de Peralta, P.O. Box 2307, 87504-2307
Telephone: 505-982-3873
Fax: 505-982-4289
Email: montand@montand.com

Walter J. Melendres
Sarah Michael Singleton
Stephen S. Hamilton
Carolyn Wolf
Grace Philips
Jennifer Lynn Weed

Representative Clients: American Insurance Association; American International Group; Hartford Insurance Company; Kemper Insurance Company; Travelers Insurance Company; United States Fidelity & Guaranty Company.

For Complete List of Firm Personnel, See General Section

For full biographical listings, see the Martindale-Hubbell Law Directory

SIMONS, CUDDY & FRIEDMAN, LLP (AV)

1701 Old Pecos Trail, P.O. Box 4160, 87502-4160
Telephone: 505-988-4476
Fax: 505-984-1807

Thomas A. Simons, IV
John F. Kennedy
Charlotte H. Hetherington
Robert D. Sckalor

Representative Clients: Old Republic National Title Insurance Company; State Farm Fire & Casualty Co.; Aetna Life & Casualty Companies; Lawyers Title Insurance Corporation; Ticor Title Insurance Co.; Fidelity National Title Insurance Co.; TIG Insurance Group; Commonwealth Land Title Insurance Co.; State Farm Mutual Automobile Insurance Co.

For full biographical listings, see the Martindale-Hubbell Law Directory

WHITE, KOCH, KELLY & MCCARTHY, A PROFESSIONAL ASSOCIATION (AV)

433 Paseo De Peralta, P.O. Box 787, 87504-0787
Telephone: 505-982-4374
ABA/NET: 1154
Fax: 505-982-0350; 984-8631
Email: WKKM@NM.NET

Albert V. Gonzales
M. Karen Kilgore

Representative Clients: City of Albuquerque, New Mexico; City of Santa Fe, New Mexico; Nationwide Insurance Company; Clarendon.

For Complete List of Firm Personnel, See General Section

For full biographical listings, see the Martindale-Hubbell Law Directory

NEW YORK

*ALBANY,** Albany Co.

AINSWORTH, SULLIVAN, TRACY, KNAUF, WARNER & RUSLANDER, P.C. (AV)

Brandon Place, 403 New Karner Road, P.O. Box 12849, 12212-2849
Telephone: 518-464-0600
Fax: 518-464-0679
Email: foc@brokerlaw.com *URL:* http://www.brokerlaw.com

Danforth E. Ainsworth (1908-1927)
Charles B. Sullivan (1881-1975)
Thomas F. Tracy (1914-1994)
John E. Knauf (1914-1996)
Frank J. Warner, Jr.
Robert K. Ruslander
James E. McHenry
John W. Bailey
Frank M. Pell
Elizabeth M. Dumas
Margaret Comard Lynch
Michael J. Murphy
Timothy J. O'Connor
Dennis W. Habel
Maria C. Tebano

Colleen M. O'Connell
Anthony V. Cardona, Jr.
Rebecca A. Slezak
Scott R. Almas

OF COUNSEL

Bruce R. Sullivan

Local Counsel for: Liberty Insurance Co.; United Service Auto Assn.; Continental Insurance Cos.; American International Insurance Co.; Aetna Insurance Co.; Kemper Insurance Co.; Sears Roebuck & Co.; Yamaha Motor Corp.; Chubb & Sons, Inc.; Grand Union Co.

For full biographical listings, see the Martindale-Hubbell Law Directory

DONOHUE, SABO, VARLEY & ARMSTRONG, P.C. (AV)

1 Winner's Circle Drive, P.O. Box 15056, 12212-5056
Telephone: 518-458-8922
Telecopier: 518-438-4349
Email: kvarley@dsvalaw.com

Paul F. Donohue, Sr. (Retired)
Alvin O. Sabo
Kenneth Varley, Jr.
Robert J. Armstrong
Fred J. Hutchison
Bruce S. Huttner
Kathleen L. Werther

Walter M.B. Spiro
Andrew R. Ferguson
Joshua A. Sabo
Gerald D. D'Amelia, Jr.

Representative Clients: CNA Insurance Cos.; Continental Loss Adjusting Services; Electric Insurance Co.; Electric Mutual Insurance Co.; General Accident Assurance Co.; General Electric Co.; NY Central Mutual Fire Insurance Co.; Preferred Mutual Insurance Co.; State Insurance Fund; Zurich-American Insurance Co.

For full biographical listings, see the Martindale-Hubbell Law Directory

Albany—Continued

MAYNARD, O'CONNOR, SMITH & CATALINOTTO, LLP (AV)

Seventh Floor, 80 State Street, 12207
Telephone: 518-465-3553
Fax: 518-465-5845
Saugerties, New York Office: Route 9W, P.O. Box 180.
Telephone: 914-246-3666.
Fax: 914-246-0390.

MEMBERS OF FIRM

William C. Maynard (1883-1972)
Gerald W. O'Connor (1896-1965)
J. Vincent Smith (1916-1991)
Michael E. Catalinotto
Stephen C. Prudente
Christopher K.H. Dressler
Thomas G. Daley
James R. Schultz
Bruce A. Bell
Concetta R. Lomanto
Edwin J. Tobin, Jr.

ASSOCIATES

Michael E. Catalinotto, Jr.
Robert A. Rausch
Teresa M. Morrisey
Aaron M. Baldwin
Laurel L. Bohl

OF COUNSEL

Earl S. Jones, Jr.

Local Counsel for: Utica Mutual Insurance Co.; General Motors; Medical Liability Mutual Insurance; Metropolitan Insurance Co.

For full biographical listings, see the Martindale-Hubbell Law Directory

O'CONNOR, O'CONNOR, MAYBERGER & FIRST, P.C. (AV)

20 Corporate Woods Boulevard, 12211-0400
Telephone: 518-465-0400
Facsimile: 518-465-0015
Email: info@1stlaw.com *URL:* http://www.1stlaw.com

Michael J. O'Connor
Terence P. O'Connor
Dianne Bresee Mayberger
Dennis A. First
Michele M. Monserrate
Cynthia Ann Platt

Justin O. Corcoran
Michael P. Cavanagh
Christopher D. Drake
Eugene N. Sarfoh
Francis J. Brennan
Colleen D. Galligan

For full biographical listings, see the Martindale-Hubbell Law Directory

ROCHE CORRIGAN McCOY & BUSH (AV)

The Wilem Van Zandt Building, 36 South Pearl Street, 12207
Telephone: 518-436-9370
Fax: 518-436-8233

MEMBERS OF FIRM

Robert P. Roche
Peter J. Corrigan
Joseph M. McCoy
Scott W. Bush

For full biographical listings, see the Martindale-Hubbell Law Directory

*BINGHAMTON,** Broome Co.

O'CONNOR, GACIOCH, POPE & TAIT, L.L.P. (AV)

One Marine Midland Plaza, East Tower-Seventh Floor, P.O. Box 1964, 13902
Telephone: 607-772-9262
Fax: 607-724-6002
Email: ogplaw@compuserve.com

Thomas F. O'Connor
James C. Gacioch
Alan J. Pope
Jeffrey A. Tait
Hugh B. Leonard
Robert N. Nielsen, Jr.
Stephen B. Atkinson
Kurt D. Schrader
Richard M. Hill
Patricia A. Cummings
Robert C. Murphy

OF COUNSEL

Walter T. Gorman
Cheryl Insinga

For full biographical listings, see the Martindale-Hubbell Law Directory

*BUFFALO,** Erie Co.

BROWN & KELLY, L.L.P. (AV)

1500 Liberty Building, 14202-3663
Telephone: 716-854-2620
Fax: 716-854-0082
Email: mail@brownkelly.com *URL:* http://www.brownkelly.com

MEMBERS OF FIRM

Thomas J. Kelly
Rodney O. Personius
Frederick D. Turner
Paul Michael Hassett
Peter E. Klaassez
Donald B. Eppers
Andrew D. Merrick
William P. Wiles
William D. Harrington
Joseph M. Schnitter
Paula L. Feroleto
Daniel J. Marren
Lisa T. Sofferin

(See Next Column)

OF COUNSEL

Ogden R. Brown
Charles F. Harrington
James T. Duggan
Karen Cook Serotte
Roland R. Benzow
Philip B. Abramowitz
Elizabeth R. O'Connor
Catherine E. Marra

ASSOCIATES

David S. Zygaj
Olney H. Clowe
Brian M. Melber
David O. Teach
Patricia S. Ciccarelli
Susan J. Schmidt

Representative Clients: Selective Insurance Co.; Fidelity & Deposit Company of Maryland; Zurich Insurance Group; New York Central Mutual; Metropolitan Property & Casualty; Progressive Insurance Co.; Nationwide Insurance Company; CGU; GNA Insurance Co.; Travelers Indemnity Co.

For full biographical listings, see the Martindale-Hubbell Law Directory

COHEN & LOMBARDO, P.C. (AV)

343 Elmwood Avenue, P.O. Box 5204, 14213-5204
Telephone: 716-881-3010
Fax: 716-881-2755
Email: law@cohenlombardo.com *URL:* http://www.cohenlombardo.com

Joseph Cohen (1909-1966)
Ernest Lombardo (1913-1993)
Richard N. Blewett
Rocco Lucente, II
Stuart Brian Shapiro
Neil R. Sherwood
Douglas S. Cream

Mark S. Nemeth
Thomas J. Navarro, Jr.
Jennifer D. Bowen
Christopher A. Zampogna

For Complete List of Firm Personnel, See General Section

For full biographical listings, see the Martindale-Hubbell Law Directory

DAMON & MOREY LLP (AV)

(Formerly Damon, Morey, Sawyer & Moot)
1000 Cathedral Place, 298 Main Street, 14202-4096
Telephone: 716-856-5500
Facsimile: 716-856-5510
Email: apinder@damonmorey.com *URL:* http://www.damonmorey.com
Rochester, New York Office: Powers Building, Suite 507, 16 West Main Street, 14614.
Telephone: 716-232-3640.
Fax: 716-232-8448.

MEMBERS OF FIRM

Mason O. Damon (1905-1983)
Robert J. Plache
James N. Schmit
Christopher T. Greene
Franklin W. Heller
Gregory C. Yungbluth
James W. Gormley
James M. Mucklewee
Melinda G. Disare
Robert J. Portin
Joseph J. Schoellkopf, Jr.
William F. Savino
Thomas J. Drury
Patrick B. Curran
Peter S. Marlette
Vincent J. Moore
Gust P. Pullman
Barbara L. Schifeling
Michael J. Willett
Carol Guck Snider
Joseph W. Dunbar
Kenneth W. Africano
Julie M. Bargnesi
Arthur A. Marrapese III (Resident, Rochester Office)
Sharyn G. Rogers
Daniel F. Brown
David L. Edmunds, Jr.
Charles S. Carra
Hedwig Maria Auletta
Marylou K. Roshia
Maryjo C. Falcone
Charles E. Telford, III
Timothy C. Cashmore
Anthony L. Eugeni
Amy Archer Flaherty
Kathleen M. Reilly
Steven I. Rubinstein
Diane C. Zarlock

ASSOCIATES

Brian Alan Birenbach
Daniel T. Cavarello
Michelle A. Crew
Anne C. Evans
Michael Thomas Feeley
Judy S. Hernandez
David S. Kelly
Joseph J. Manna
Rosalie A. Melisz
Mary C. Raymond
Vincent George Saccomando
Allison Fields Stravino
Kellie Muffoletto Ulrich

OF COUNSEL

Joseph H. Morey, Jr.

SPECIAL COUNSEL

Richard E. Moot
George F. Gabel, Jr.
G. Steven Pigeon
Susan A. Benz
Edward Yankelunas

Counsel For: Advanced Refractory Technologies; Catholic Health East; D.A. Elia Construction Corporation; Kaleida Health; Town of Cheektowaga; Bagel Brothers Amherst, Inc.; Burt Rigid Box, Inc.; Lake Shore Health Care Center; County of Cattaraugus; Commonwealth Land Title Insurance; Diocese of Buffalo; Baker Victory Services; Niagara Lutheran Home and Rehabilitation, Inc.; Sheehan Memorial Hospital; Robert James Sales, Inc.; Olean General Hospital; Wendt Corporation; Aria Wireless Systems, Inc.; Buffalo Sewer Authority; City of Tonawanda; Roswell Park Cancer Institute; Ivoclar North America, Inc.; Olean Medical Group; Cold Spring Construction Company; Buffalo Municipal Housing Authority.

(See Next Column)

DAMON & MOREY LLP—*Continued*

Local Counsel For: Healthcare Underwriters Mutual Insurance Company; AIG Companies; Owens-Corning Fiberglas; Unigard Insurance Group; Key Tronic Corporation; Medical Liability Insurance; Risk Enterprise Management Limited; Wintherthur International; Hanover Insurance Company; National Casualty Company; Marine Midland Mortgage Corporation; Acordia Resort Services; Medical Malpractice Insurance Association; OUM & Associates; Ohio Casualty Company; PACCAR, Inc.; Frontier Insurance Company; The Limited, Inc.; Zurich-American Insurance Group; Allstate Insurance Company; Universal Studios, Inc.

For full biographical listings, see the Martindale-Hubbell Law Directory

FELDMAN, KIEFFER & HERMAN, LLP (AV)

110 Pearl Street, Suite 400, 14202
Telephone: 716-852-5875
Fax: 716-852-4253
Email: info@fkhattys.com *URL:* http://www.fkhattys.com

PRINCIPALS OF THE FIRM

Andrew Feldman
James M. Kieffer
Ann W. Herman
Mark F. Scarcello
Gordon D. Tresch
Mary Jo Herrscher

For full biographical listings, see the Martindale-Hubbell Law Directory

O'SHEA, REYNOLDS & CUMMINGS (AV)

237 Main Street, Suite 500, 14203
Telephone: 716-853-6341-2-3
Fax: 716-852-3880
Email: info@oshea-reynolds.com

MEMBERS OF FIRM

Frank Gibbons (1869-1953)
Henry W. Pottle (1872-1943)
Willard M. Pottle (1901-1967)
Philip J. O'Shea (1909-1984)
William S. Reynolds
C. DeForest Cummings, Jr.
David M. Stillwell
Gerard E. O'Connor
William A. Long, Jr.
Nelson E. Schule, Jr.

ASSOCIATES

Kevin D. Cox
Nicole A. Heary

Local Attorneys for: Amica Mutual Insurance Co.; Continental National American Group; Nationwide Mutual Insurance Co.; The Continental Insurance Cos.
Reference: Key Bank.

For full biographical listings, see the Martindale-Hubbell Law Directory

QUINN, MCGARRY & CAFFERY, P.C. (AV)

1600 Statler Towers, 14202
Telephone: 716-856-6066
Fax: 716-856-2914

David C. Quinn
Francis P. McGarry
Michael P. Caffery
John P. Quinn, Jr.
Kenneth A. Patricia
Thomas J. DeBoy

Reference: Key Bank.

For full biographical listings, see the Martindale-Hubbell Law Directory

ROACH, BROWN, MCCARTHY & GRUBER, P.C. (AV)

1620 Liberty Building, 420 Main Street, 14202-3511
Telephone: 716-852-0400
Fax: 716-852-2535
Email: roachbrown@roachbrown.com

Daniel T. Roach
Edmund S. Brown, Jr.
T. Alan Brown
Joseph V. McCarthy
J. Mark Gruber
Mary J. Murray
John P. Danieu
Elizabeth G. Redmond
Gregory T. Miller
Teresa C. Brophy Bair
Jason A. Botticelli
Jennifer L. Noah
Joel J. Java, Jr.

OF COUNSEL

Arthur J. Maloney
John Y. Gallup

Local Attorneys for: American International Group; Chubb Group of Insurance Co.; Healthcare Underwriters Mutual Insurance Co.; Peter J. McBreen and Associates; Frontier Insurance Co.; Medical Liability Mutual Insurance Co.; Medical Malpractice Insurance Assn.; Merrill Dow; Reliance Insurance Group; Travelers Group.

For full biographical listings, see the Martindale-Hubbell Law Directory

SUGARMAN, WALLACE, MANHEIM & SCHOENWALD (AV)

1720 Rand Building, 14 Lafayette Square, 14203
Telephone: 716-847-2523
Fax: 716-847-2589
Email: sugarmanlaw.com *URL:* http://www.sugarmanlaw.com
Syracuse Office: HSBC Center, Fifth Floor, 360 South Warren Street.
Telephone: 315-474-2943.
Fax: 315-474-0235.

(See Next Column)

MEMBER OF FIRM

Brian Sutter

ASSOCIATES

James E. Hanlon
Tasha T. Dandridge

Representative Clients: Allstate Insurance Co.; CNA Insurance Companies; Chubb & Son; Liberty Mutual Insurance Co.; Carpenter Manufacturing Co., Inc.; General Accident Group; Hartford Accident & Indemnity Co.; Firemans Fund; New York Central Mutual; Progressive Insurance Co.
Reference: HSBC.

For full biographical listings, see the Martindale-Hubbell Law Directory

WILLIAMS & WILLIAMS (AV)

237 Main Street Suite 1400, 14203
Telephone: 716-856-8200
Fax: 716-856-0559
Email: wmswmsfirm@aol.com

Mark W. Kerwood
Roger J. Edel
Mary Meyer Russo

Robert D. Leary
Lynette M. Gohr
Ellen Shanahan Becker
Boyd L. Earl
Wayne D. Schiffhauer
Julie A. Houghtaling
Melissa A. Day
Dawn M. Netzel
Christina M. Hassler

OF COUNSEL

Clyde M. Williams
Paul D. Williams (1910-1993)

A List of Representative Clients and References will be furnished upon request.

For full biographical listings, see the Martindale-Hubbell Law Directory

*CATSKILL,** Greene Co.

JOHN P. KINGSLEY, P.C. (AV)

329 Main Street, 12414
Telephone: 518-943-3399
Telecopier: 518-943-3049
URL: http://www.lawyers.com/kingsley

John P. Kingsley

OF COUNSEL

Oreste Vincent

For full biographical listings, see the Martindale-Hubbell Law Directory

FARMINGDALE, Nassau Co.

CARMAN, CALLAHAN & INGHAM (AV)

Carman Building, 280 Main Street, 11735
Telephone: 516-249-3450
Telecopier: 516-249-3782

Willis B. Carman, Jr.
Robert M. Callahan
Michael F. Ingham
Gregory W. Carman, Jr.
James M. Carman

ASSOCIATE

Stephanie L. Boden

For full biographical listings, see the Martindale-Hubbell Law Directory

GARDEN CITY, Nassau Co.

GALLAGHER GOSSEEN FALLER KAPLAN & CROWLEY (AV)

1010 Franklin Avenue, Suite 400, 11530-2927
Telephone: 516-742-2500
Fax: 516-742-2516
Email: GGFKC_Postmaster@GGFKC.com
New York, New York Office: 350 Fifth Avenue, Suite 603.
Telephone: 212-947-5800.
Fax: 212-967-4965.

MEMBERS OF FIRM

James A. Gallagher, Jr.
Robert I. Gosseen (Resident, New York City Office)
Robert A. Faller
Alan D. Kaplan
Michael J. Crowley
William E. Vita
Brian P. Morrissey

ASSOCIATES

David H. Arntsen
Joseph A. Latasso
Amy L. Ruina
Gerald A. Corallo, Jr.

OF COUNSEL

John P. Coogan
Peter F. Vetro
William A. Bales, Jr.

For full biographical listings, see the Martindale-Hubbell Law Directory

Garden City—Continued

L'ABBATE, BALKAN, COLAVITA & CONTINI, L.L.P. (AV)

1050 Franklin Avenue, 11530
Telephone: 516-294-8844
Telecopier: 516-294-8202; 742-6563
Email: law@labbatebalkan.com *URL:* http://www.labbatebalkan.com
Livingston, New Jersey Office: 7 Regent Street, Suite 711, 07039.
Telephone: 973-422-0422.
Telecopier: 973-422-0420.

MEMBERS OF FIRM

Donald R. L'Abbate
Anthony P. Colavita
Peter L. Contini
Monte E. Sokol
Douglas L. Pintauro
Richard P. Byrne
Jane M. Myers
Paula M. Gart
Anna M. DiLonardo
David B. Kosakoff
Lewis A. Bartell
Marian C. Rice
Ralph A. Catalano
Douglas R. Halstrom
Steven R. Goldstein
Gary Petropoulos
Domingo R. Gallardo
Mercedes Colwin

COUNSEL TO THE FIRM

Kenneth J. Balkan

SPECIAL COUNSEL

Arthur D. Bromberg (Resident, Livingston, New Jersey Office)
Jonathan M. Kuller (Resident, Livingston, New Jersey Office)

OF COUNSEL

Marianne S. Conklin
Joanne C. Watson
Marie Ann Hoenings

ASSOCIATES

Colleen M. Cronin
Wendy S. Van Dorn
Nicholas Toumbekis
Andrew Marc Warshauer
Michelle J. Simon
Annalee J. Cataldo-Barile
Martin A. Schwartzberg
Louis M. Goldberg
Scott Evan Kossove
Peter D. Rigelhaupt
Orin J. Ketyer
Anthony T. Battaglia
Christopher B. Block (Resident, Livingston, New Jersey Office)
James S. Montano (Resident, Livingston, New Jersey Office)
Maureen E. Scott
John D. McKenna
Michael B. Curan
Jeffrey E. Edelman (Resident, Livingston, New Jersey Office)
Matthew K. Flanagan
Claudia M. Kessler

Representative Clients: Chicago Underwriting Group, Inc.; CNA; DPIC Insurance Cos.; Evanston Insurance Co.; General Accident Insurance Co.; The Home Insurance Co.; Imperial Casualty and Indemnity Co.; Markel American Insurance Co.; Shand, Morahan & Co., Inc.; Utica Mutual Insurance Co.

For full biographical listings, see the Martindale-Hubbell Law Directory

MONTFORT, HEALY, MCGUIRE & SALLEY (AV)

1140 Franklin Avenue, 11530
Telephone: 516-747-4082
Telecopier: 516-746-0748

MEMBERS OF FIRM

E. Richard Rimmels, Jr. (1930-1999)
Frank J. Cafaro
Philip J. Catapano
Fredric C. Montfort
Donald S. Neumann, Jr.
James J. Keefe, Jr.
Michael A. Baranowicz
James Michael Murphy

OF COUNSEL

Fredric H. Montfort
Edward M. Salley, Jr.
David J. Fleming
Robert J. Mettalia

ASSOCIATES

Claudia C. Glacken
Marcie K. Glasser
Bruce A. Cook
Jeffrey D. Present
Joan E. Resnik
Susan H. Dempsey
Camille L. Hansen
Christopher T. Cafaro
Kathleen Dumont
Jeffrey B. Siler
Michael G. Kruzynski
Karen J. Cooper

For full biographical listings, see the Martindale-Hubbell Law Directory

HEMPSTEAD, Nassau Co.

DEEGAN & DEEGAN, L.L.P. (AV)

550 Front Street, 11550
Telephone: 516-486-9400
Telecopier: 516-486-8680
Email: deegan550@aol.com

MEMBERS OF FIRM

Donald E. Deegan
James V. Deegan

ASSOCIATES

Michael A. Wolf
James M. Hayes
Robert H. Doud
Mary E. Hayes
Gregg M. McGrath

(See Next Column)

OF COUNSEL

Diane Klaum Farrell
Thomas G. Nolan
John S. White
George Planos
Donald F. McCarthy
Gregory M. Maurer
George A. Boehling
Theresa Rho

For full biographical listings, see the Martindale-Hubbell Law Directory

JERICHO, Nassau Co.

FIEDELMAN & MCGAW (AV)

Two Jericho Plaza, Wing B, Third Floor, 11753-1681
Telephone: 516-822-8900
Fax: 516-822-8919

STAFF COUNSEL
AMERICAN INTERNATIONAL COMPANIES

Robert I. Fiedelman

For full biographical listings, see the Martindale-Hubbell Law Directory

MARTIN, VAN DE WALLE, DONOHUE, MCGAHAN, CATALANO & FAIRGRIEVE (AV)

555 North Broadway, P.O. Box 350, 11753
Telephone: 516-681-3100
Telecopier: 516-681-5357

MEMBERS OF FIRM

Jules Martin (1928-1995)
Charles R. Van de Walle
Joseph A. Guarino (1946-1991)
Nicholas J. Donohue
James M. McGahan
Thomas C. Catalano, Jr.
Scott Fairgrieve
Michael Belitsis

ASSOCIATES

Randi M. Seidner
Laurie Ann Corallo

Representative Clients: Biener Pontiac-Nissan, Inc.; Festo Corp.; New York State Land Title Association, Inc.; New York Schools Insurance Reciprocal; New York Municipal Insurance Reciprocal; Leo and Arnstein Agency; Liberty Mutual Insurance Company; Northeast Adjustment Co., Inc.; Long Island Community Newspapers.

For full biographical listings, see the Martindale-Hubbell Law Directory

*KINGSTON,** Ulster Co.

COOK, TUCKER, NETTER & CLOONAN, P.C. (AV)

85 Main Street, P.O. Box 3939, 12401
Telephone: 914-331-0702
Fax: 914-331-1003
Email: ctnc@prodigy.net

Andrew J. Cook (1884-1958)
Francis X. Tucker (1923-1987)
Andrew J. Cook, Jr. (1918-1997)
Robert E. Netter
William N. Cloonan
Robert D. Cook
Eric M. Kurtz
Thomas A. Murphy
Michael T. Cook

Counsel for: Town of Rochester.
Representative Clients: Central Hudson Gas & Electric Corp.; CNA Insurance Co.; Covenant Group; Hanover Insurance Co.; Metropolitan Property & Liability Insurance Co.; Norstar Bank; USF&G; Allstate Insurance Co.; AIA Insurance Group; Universal Underwriters.

For full biographical listings, see the Martindale-Hubbell Law Directory

LAKE SUCCESS, Nassau Co.

IVONE, DEVINE & JENSEN, LLP (AV)

2001 Marcus Avenue, Suite N100, 11042
Telephone: 516-326-2400
Telecopier: 516-352-4952
Email: idjlaw@aol.com *URL:* http://www.lawyers.com/idjlaw

MEMBERS OF FIRM

Michael T. Ivone
Robert Devine
Richard C. Jensen
Brian E. Lee
Michael Ferguson

ASSOCIATES

Debora G. Nobel
Ellin M. Regis
Jonathan Rubin
Veronica Henry
Patrick G. Toner
Keith C. Jewell

For full biographical listings, see the Martindale-Hubbell Law Directory

LIBERTY, Sullivan Co.

EISENBERG & KIRSCH (AV)

33 Chestnut Street, P.O. Box 715, 12754
Telephone: 914-292-4412
Fax: 914-292-1636
Email: kirschair@aol.com

(See Next Column)

EISENBERG & KIRSCH—*Continued*

Bertram W. Eisenberg
Jeffrey Kirsch

For full biographical listings, see the Martindale-Hubbell Law Directory

*MALONE,** Franklin Co.

FISCHER, BESSETTE & MULDOWNEY, L.L.P. (AV)

Country Club Road, P.O. Box 420, 12953
Telephone: 518-481-5000
Fax: 518-481-5203
Email: fbm@northnet.org *URL:* http://www.lawyers.com/fb&mlaw

William J. Herron (1905-1993)

OF COUNSEL

Henry A. Fischer

MEMBERS OF FIRM

James P. Bessette
John J. Muldowney
Richard F. Hunter

For full biographical listings, see the Martindale-Hubbell Law Directory

MIDDLETOWN, Orange Co.

MACVEAN, LEWIS, SHERWIN & MCDERMOTT, P.C. (AV)

34 Grove Street, P.O. Box 310, 10940
Telephone: 914-343-3000
Fax: 914-343-3866

Kenneth A. MacVean (1926-1999)
Kermit W. Lewis
Louis H. Sherwin
Paul T. McDermott
Jeffrey D. Sherwin
Thomas P. Clarke, Jr.
John M. Clancy

SENIOR TRIAL COUNSEL

George F. Roesch, III

Kevin F. Preston
Ferol Reed McDermott
Anthony R. LoBiondo
James V. Galvin

OF COUNSEL

Samuel W. Eager, Jr.

Counsel for: Orange County Trust Co.; Middletown Savings Bank; First Federal Savings & Loan Association of Middletown; Goshen Savings Bank; Advest Bank.

For full biographical listings, see the Martindale-Hubbell Law Directory

*MINEOLA,** Nassau Co.

FUREY, KERLEY, WALSH, MATERA & CINQUEMANI, A PROFESSIONAL CORPORATION (AV)

200 Old Country Road, Suite 660, 11501
Telephone: 516-248-8880
Fax: 516-873-8786

Raymond J. Furey
Brian P. Kerley
Jeffrey G. Walsh
Rosemary A. Cinquemani
Glenn J. Matera

Lauren B. Bristol
Jeffrey M. Di Luccio
Peter X. Dodge
Kathleen Lindsay
MaryAnne Powers Richardson
Bryan L Salamone
William Scott Matlin
Alejandro Monroy

LEGAL SUPPORT PERSONNEL

Arthetta Baldock

For full biographical listings, see the Martindale-Hubbell Law Directory

GALLAGHER, WALKER, BIANCO & PLASTARAS (AV)

98 Willis Avenue, 11501
Telephone: 516-248-2002
Fax: 516-248-2394

Gerard M. Gallagher
Robert J. Walker
Dominic P. Bianco
Thomas E. Plastaras

ASSOCIATES

Ann Willoughby
William P. Nolan

OF COUNSEL

Stephen P. Burke

For full biographical listings, see the Martindale-Hubbell Law Directory

HATTER, DONOVAN & MCFAUL, LLP (AV)

47 Mineola Boulevard, 11501
Telephone: 516-873-8800
Fax: 516-873-1418
Email: law@hdmlaw.com
URL: http://www.hdmlaw.com

(See Next Column)

MEMBERS OF FIRM

James R. Hatter
Thomas J. Donovan
John M. McFaul

Lawrence J. Freeze, III

For full biographical listings, see the Martindale-Hubbell Law Directory

KELLY, RODE & KELLY, LLP (AV)

330 Old Country Road, Suite 305, 11501
Telephone: 516-739-0400
FAX: 516-739-0434
Email: krk@i-2000.com
Riverhead, New York Office: 631 Griffing Avenue.
Telephone: 516-727-0110.

MEMBERS OF FIRM

Joseph F. O'Brien (1956-1968)
George L. Ryan (1968-1976)
John D. Kelly
John Kenneth Rode
Shawn P. Kelly
George J. Wilson
John W. Hoefling

ASSOCIATES

Michael D. Abneri
Bridget Beyer
Bruce M. Cohn
Gary E. Dvoskin
Elyse R. Farrell-Ulino
I. Paul Howansky
Kevin G. Lencki
Katherine A. McDonough
William P. Pawlow
Joann M. Scifo
Beverly A. Smith
John J. Stewart, Jr.
Daniel R. Wasp
Cheryl M. Wendt
Loris Zeppieri

Representative Clients: State Farm Mutual Automobile Insurance Company; State Farm Fire & Casualty Insurance Company; Nationwide Insurance Company; New York Hospital Medical Center of Queens; Medical Liability Mutual Insurance Company; Domino's Pizza; New York State Insurance Dept.-Liquidation Bureau; McDonnell-Douglas Corp. Physicians' Reciprocal Insurers; Preferred Physicians Medical Risk Retention Group; United Community Insurance Co.
Reference: Citibank.

For full biographical listings, see the Martindale-Hubbell Law Directory

MCCABE, COLLINS, MCGEOUGH & FOWLER, LLP (AV)

114 Old Country Road, P.O. Box 855, 11501
Telephone: 516-741-6266
Fax: 516-873-9496
Email: MCMF4LAW@aol.com

MEMBERS OF FIRM

Stephen M. McCabe
Brian J. McGeough
James J. Collins
David T. Fowler
Patrick M. Murphy
Thomas J. Nogan
Michael S. Levine

Scott L. Mathias
Mark L. Weisenreder
Lawrence J. Buchman
Barry L. Manus
John Joseph Connelly
Jason C. Altman
Chris P. Termini
Brian P. Hickey, Jr.
Patrick J. Engle
Clifford D. Gabel
Richard B. Brown
Frank V. Pesce
Doron Rosenheck
Martha S. Henley
John E. McLoughlin
Joseph T. Roccanova
Ben Niderberg

OF COUNSEL

Alfred S. Robbins

LEGAL SUPPORT PERSONNEL

Christine Taliercio (Paralegal)

For full biographical listings, see the Martindale-Hubbell Law Directory

NICOLINI & PARADISE (AV)

114 Old Country Road Suite 500, 11501
Telephone: 516-741-6355

MEMBERS OF FIRM

Anthony J. Nicolini
Vincent J. Paradise

Representative Clients: Long Island Railroad; NYS Liquidation Bureau; Avis Rent-A-Car System, Inc.; County of Nassau; Continental Excess & Select.

For full biographical listings, see the Martindale-Hubbell Law Directory

SHAYNE, DACHS, STANISCI, CORKER & SAUER (AV)

250 Old Country Road, 11501
Telephone: 516-747-1100
Telecopier: 516-747-1185

MEMBERS OF FIRM

Moe Levine (1908-1974)
Neil T. Shayne (1932-1998)
Norman H. Dachs
W. Russell Corker
Brian J. Sauer
Kenneth J. Landau
Jonathan A. Dachs

(See Next Column)

SHAYNE, DACHS, STANISCI, CORKER & SAUER, *Mineola—Continued*

Naomi R. Nathan

For full biographical listings, see the Martindale-Hubbell Law Directory

*NEW YORK,** New York Co.

ABRAMS, GORELICK, FRIEDMAN & JACOBSON, P.C. (AV)

120 Wall Street, 10005
Telephone: 212-422-1200
Fax: 212-968-7573
Email: insurancelaw@fgfj.com
Livingston, New Jersey Office: 70 South Orange Avenue, 07039.
Telephone: 973-597-0920.
Fax: 973-535-1760.

Henry H. Abrams (1910-1977)
Mark E. Abrams
Michael E. Gorelick
Daniel J. Friedman
Glenn A. Jacobson

Melvin P. Meyer
Kevin J. Spencer
Pamela R. Wolff Cohen
Martin I. Nagel
Eric E. Rothstein
Jonathan Schaerf
Patrick J. Hayes
Ahmed Elzoghby

OF COUNSEL

Harold A. Craig, Jr.

LEGAL SUPPORT PERSONNEL

Manna Cheng

Representative Clients: Underwriters at Lloyds; New York Property Insurance Underwriting Assn.; American International Group; Jefferson Insurance Co.; Wausau Insurance Co.; Reliance National Insurance Co.; Home Depot, Inc.

For full biographical listings, see the Martindale-Hubbell Law Directory

AHMUTY, DEMERS & McMANUS (AV)

123 William Street, 10038
Telephone: 212-513-7788
Facsimile: 212-513-7843
Email: Information@admlaw.com
Albertson, New York Office: 200 I.U. Willets Road.
Telephone: 516-294-5433.
Facsimile: 516-294-5387.
Riverhead, New York Office: 750 Roanoke Avenue.
Telephone: 516-727-2340.
Facsimile: 516-727-8198.
White Plains, New York Office: One North Broadway.
Telephone: 914-686-5050.
Facsimile: 914-686-5960.

MEMBERS OF FIRM

William R. Ahmuty, III (Resident, Albertson Office)
Philip J. McManus
Henri A. Demers (Resident, Albertson Office)
Vincent S. Ambrosino
Janice Berkowitz (Resident, Albertson Office)
Peter F. Broderick
Nicholas M. Cardascia (Resident, White Plains Office)
Maureen Casey (Resident, Albertson Office)
Frank A. Cecere (Resident, Albertson Office)
Richard J. DaVolio (Resident, Riverhead Office)
Brian J. Donnelly
James A. Edwards
Robert J. Hindman (Resident, Riverhead Office)
Diane E. Inbody (Resident, Riverhead Office)
Christopher Kendric (Resident, Albertson Office)
Edward G. Lukoski (Resident, Riverhead Office)
Kenneth R. Maguire (Resident, Albertson Office)
Thomas V. McMahon (Resident, Riverhead Office)
Kevin G. McMorrow (Resident, Albertson Office)
John A. McPhilliamy (Resident, Albertson Office)
Gary P. Muhlstock (Resident, Albertson Office)
Frank J. Pecorelli, Jr. (Resident, Albertson Office)
Michael J. Rabus
William E. Rosa
William F. Ryan
Daniel G. Sergiacomi (Resident, Albertson Office)
Robert A. Shaw
Steven L. Sidney (Resident, Albertson Office)
Frederick B. Simpson (Resident, Albertson Office)

COUNSEL

Robert E. Hirsch (Resident, Riverhead Office)
Patrick J. Kenny

ASSOCIATES

Suzanne J. Adams
Neil H. Angel (Resident, Albertson Office)
Frederick C. Aranki
Matthew T. Brown
Carmine J. Carolei (Resident, White Plains Office)
Christopher P. Cartier (Resident, Albertson Office)
Jennifer A. Casey (Resident, Albertson Office)
Steven M. Christman (Resident, Albertson Office)
Thomas J. Colameo

(See Next Column)

ASSOCIATES (Continued)

David S. Conklin (Resident, Albertson Office)
Mark John Connolly
Christopher J. Conover
Patrick J. Cooney (Resident, Albertson Office)
Deborah A. DelSordo
Michael Gerard Dempsey
Thomas M. DeSimone (Resident, White Plains Office)
Matthew P. Donohue (Resident, White Plains Office)
Debra Ann Edwards (Resident, Albertson Office)
Paul Eschmann
George S. Evans, Jr.
Brendan T. Fitzpatrick (Resident, Albertson Office)
Emilio F. Grillo
Keith A. Guarnuccio
Michael A. Heran (Resident, White Plains Office)
Moriah A. Heuer (Resident, Albertson Office)
Daniel I. Hirsch
Glenn A. Kaminska (Resident, Albertson Office)
Andria Simone Kelly (Resident, Albertson Office)
William A. Klaus
Peter G. Lavrenchik (Resident, Riverhead Office)
Leslie Leonick (Resident, Albertson Office)
Jeffrey M. Malsch
Matthew J. McDermott
Joseph M. O'Connor (Resident, Albertson Office)
Erin M. O'Hanlon
Joseph A. Oliva
Sean J. O'Sullivan (Resident, Albertson Office)
Gary J. Robbins
John J. Ryan (Resident, Albertson Office)
Michael C. Salvo
Diane R. Silvergleid
John R. Sordi (Resident, Albertson Office)
Alexandra Vandoros
Cindy Varrecchia

For full biographical listings, see the Martindale-Hubbell Law Directory

BADIAK WILL & RUDDY (AV)

Suite 1040, 120 Broadway, 10271
Telephone: 212-376-6767
Telecopier: 212-376-6777
Telex: 6716686 BANDW
Email: admiralaw@aol.com
North Miami Beach, Florida Office: Badiak, Will & Kallen, 17071 West Dixie Highway, P.O. Box 600550.
Telephone: 305-945-1851.

MEMBERS OF FIRM

Roman Badiak
Alfred J. Will
James J. Ruddy
John D. Kallen (Resident, North Miami, Florida Office)
David L. Maloof (1924-1992)

ASSOCIATES

Stephen A. Frank
Nicholas Kalfa
James P. Krauzlis
Martin L. Lindahl
Lisa A. Scognamillo
Deborah R. Reid

OF COUNSEL

Charles C. Goodenough

For full biographical listings, see the Martindale-Hubbell Law Directory

BARRY, McTIERNAN & MOORE (AV)

25 Broadway, 10004
Telephone: 212-509-8999
Fax: 212-509-5258
White Plains, New York Office: 175 Main Street.
Telephone: 914-946-1030.
Fax: 914-946-3814.
Jersey City, New Jersey Office: 75 Montgomery Street, 07302.
Telephone: 201-333-0300.
Fax: 201-333-0639.

MEMBERS OF FIRM

Desmond T. Barry (1906-1975)
Roger P. McTiernan
Roger Paul McTiernan, Jr.
Patricia A. Sullivan
James L. Moran
Suzanne M. Halbardier

ASSOCIATES

Katherine Hargas
William E. Fay, III
Kevin Gerard Maguire
Patricia A. McTiernan-Moore
Richard Wayne Wedinger
Dennis A. Breen
John V. Wynne
Regine Dely-Lazard
Mark A. Collesano
Mark P. Hannafey
Suey K. Chung
Michael E. Jones
Diana DeCesare-Treitler
William D. Joyce, III
Jeffrey Miller
Laurel Wedinger-Gyimesi
William A. Cooney
Christopher Sommer
Edwin F. Lambert, Jr.
Anthony J. McNulty

OF COUNSEL

John J. Moore

For full biographical listings, see the Martindale-Hubbell Law Directory

BEATIE AND OSBORN LLP (AV)

599 Lexington Avenue, 42nd Floor, 10022
Telephone: 212-888-9000
Fax: 212-888-9664
Email: bandolaw@aol.com *URL:* http://www.bandolaw@aol.com

Russel H. Beatie, Jr.
Daniel A. Osborn

(See Next Column)

BEATIE AND OSBORN LLP—*Continued*

ASSOCIATES

Curt D. Marshall | Eduard Korsinsky

OF COUNSEL

Richard M. Cummings

For full biographical listings, see the Martindale-Hubbell Law Directory

BIGHAM ENGLAR JONES & HOUSTON (AV)

40 Wall Street, 10005-2301
Telephone: 212-269-5500
Telefax: 212-269-4030; 212-269-4031
Email: bejh.com
London, England Office: 107/112 Lendenhall Street, EC3A 4AH.
Telephone: 171-891-2504.
Telefax: 171-891-2401.
Newark, New Jersey Office: One Gateway Center, Suite 2600, 07102-5315.
Telephone: 973-799-8545.
Telecopier: 973-799-8546.

MEMBERS OF FIRM

James S. McMahon, Jr.
Louis G. Juliano
Jay Levine
George R. Daly
John MacCrate, III
Robert J. Phillips, Jr.
Stephen M. Marcusa
William R. Connor, III
Helen M. Benzie
Paul Ambos
Karin A. Schlosser
Patrick J. Corbett

COUNSEL

Laurence W. Levine | Joseph A. Kilbourn

ASSOCIATES

R. Brent English
Jon D. Miller
Douglas E. Szulman
Joseph A. Yamali
Bryce A. Larrabee
Eric D. Suben

For full biographical listings, see the Martindale-Hubbell Law Directory

BRODY FABIANI & COHEN (AV)

570 Lexington Avenue, 10022
Telephone: 212-644-4420
Telex: 149546 LAW NYK UD
FAX: 212-207-8182

MEMBERS OF FIRM

Neil Brody
John V. Fabiani, Jr.
Kevin B. Pollak
Stephen M. Cohen
Michael E. Shay

ASSOCIATES

Wayne S. Stanton
Thomas J. Hall
Christopher R. Toppo
Daniel O. Dietchweiler
Eugene Patrick Devany
Steven P. Orlowski
Jeffrey C. Nagle
Sander N. Rothchild
Thomas G. Connolly
Ann-Gail Bregianes Hult
John A. Ortiz
Jody C. Benard
Tanya M. Branch
Christopher J. Crawford
Joanna R. Rosenblut
Denise A. Palmeri
Richard Adam

For full biographical listings, see the Martindale-Hubbell Law Directory

CALLAN, REGENSTREICH, KOSTER & BRADY (AV)

One Whitehall Street 10th Floor, 10004
Telephone: 212-248-8800
Fax: 212-248-6815
Shrewsbury, New Jersey Office: 740 Broad Street.
Telephone: 732-345-9333.
Fax: 732-345-9444.
Garden City, New York Office: 1205 Franklin Avenue.
Telephone: 516-294-4383.
Fax: 516-294-4386.

MEMBERS OF FIRM

Paul F. Callan
Bruce N. Regenstreich
Warren S. Koster
Bruce M. Brady
William L. Brennan
Vincent A. Nagler
Scott W. Bermack

ASSOCIATES

Kenneth S. Merber
Michael P. Kandler
Vincent D. Finnegan
Stephanie Palermo
Walter Paterson Burrell
Beth S. Block
Meredith B. Borg
Pamela Patton Fynes
Mara J. Sibley
Eric A. Wasserfall
Amie Catherine Kalac (Resident, Shrewsbury, New Jersey Office)
Lisa B. Katz

For full biographical listings, see the Martindale-Hubbell Law Directory

CONWAY, FARRELL, CURTIN & KELLY, P.C. (AV)

63 Wall Street, 10005
Telephone: 212-785-2929
Fax: 212-785-7229

(See Next Column)

James A. Flood (1912-1962)
James S. Conway
Joseph H. Farrell
John W. Walsh (1912-1971)
Patrick E. Curtin, Jr.
Kevin J. Kelly
Angela Pantony
John A. McManus
Thomas P. Gorton
Michael T. Blumenfeld
Anne P. Richter
Kristin G. Shea
Jonathan T. Uejio

Eugene M. Maloney
John J. Mullaney
Patricia A. Murphy
Eileen Monahan Carroll
Dierdre James
Teresa A. Klaum
Brian P. Murphy (1965-1997)
Thomas S. Reilly
Kathleen M. O'Gara Buckley
Gail M. Kelly
Dana Carroll
Debora A. Pitman
Robert S. Delmond
Mary A. Fallon
Eileen Donovan
Michael J. Toolan
Arturo M. Boutin
Susan Chun
Debra Takakjian
Richard W. Dawson
Susan M. Johnson
Peter D. Suglia
Patrick T. O'Malley
Ann Marie Forte

Representative Clients: U.S.F.& G.; General Star Management Company; Crum & Foster; Roman Catholic Diocese of Brooklyn; The Travelers; Farm Family Mutual Insurance Company.

For full biographical listings, see the Martindale-Hubbell Law Directory

THE LAW OFFICES OF MICHAEL E. CURAN, P.C. (AV)

59 John Street, Third Floor, 10038
Telephone: 212-513-1578
Fax: 212-513-1592

Michael E. Curan

Anthony Van Zwaren
Robert J. Callahan
Steven R. Mitlitzky

OF COUNSEL

William H. Maloney, Jr.

For full biographical listings, see the Martindale-Hubbell Law Directory

D'AMATO & LYNCH (AV)

70 Pine Street, 10270-0110
Telephone: 212-269-0927
Cable Address: "Damcosh"
Telex: 960085 DCOS UI NYK
Telefax: 212-269-3559

Luke D. Lynch (1921-1999)

MEMBERS OF FIRM

George G. D'Amato
Kenneth A. Sagat
Luke D. Lynch, Jr.
Robert E. Kushner
Richard George
Robert M. Makla
Richard F. Russell
Ronald H. Alenstein
Harry J. Arnold, Jr.
Philip J. Bergan
Robert W. Lang
Neal M. Glazer
Andrew R. Simmonds
John P. Higgins
Thomas F. Breen
Alfred A. D'Agostino, Jr.
William P. Larsen, III
Robert D. Lang
David A. Boyar
Mary Jo Barry
Barbara R. Seymour
Bill V. Kakoullis
Thomas Ward Hanlon, Jr.
John H. FitzSimons
Michael Latham Manire
Kevin J. Windels
Samuel F. Paniccia
William C. Burton
Harvey Barrison

ASSOCIATES

Laurie P. Beatus
Anna E. Bomstein
Frances Buckley
Carla S. Caliendo
Roy T. Caplinger
Kevin P. Carroll
Catherine L. Casavant
Liza A. Chafiian
James D. Christo
Judy Y. Chung
Deborah M. Collins
Mary Lee Cunningham
Daniel J. Curry
Thomas G. Darmody
Michael J. Devereaux
Daniel J. Dolcetti, Jr.
Jan H. Duffalo
Maria T. Ehrlich
Richard F. Ferrigno
Robert S. Fraser
Deeanna M. Galla
Jeffrey R. Gaylord
Lloyd J. Herman
Donna Marie Hughes
David J. Kuffler
Jason M. Lesko
Shari H. Lichtman
Cindy Liu
John J. Maalouf
Annemarie J. Mazzone
Brendon M. McNamara
Neil R. Morrison
Victor F. Mustelier
Anthony C. Pace
John J. Patterson
Edward M. Roth
Sanjit S. Shah
Jennifer G. Smith
Arthur Steinberg
Peter A. Stroili
Maryann Taylor
James E. Tolan, II
Richard S. Trostle
Humphrey O. Uddoh
Johnston de Forest Whitman, Jr
Stephen F. Willig
Robert M. Yellen

(See Next Column)

D'AMATO & LYNCH, *New York—Continued*

COUNSEL

Robert E. Gilroy
Richard G. McGahren
Peter J. Thumser
John J. Cullen
Albert B. Lewis
Charles H. Witherwax
Charles Bramham

For full biographical listings, see the Martindale-Hubbell Law Directory

DE ORCHIS, WALKER & CORSA, LLP (AV)

One Battery Park Plaza, Second Floor, 10004-1480
Telephone: 212-344-4700
MCI Telex: 673-4608
Telefax: 212-509-7886
Email: DW&C@MCIMAIL.COM *URL:* http://www.marinelex.com
Union, New Jersey Office: 1495 Morris Avenue, P.O. Box 1718.
Telephone: 973-467-4740.
Telefax: 908-687-0255.
Stamford, Connecticut Office: 999 Summer Street.
Telephone: 203-323-9120.
Telefax: 203-323-9015.
Boston, Massachusetts Office: One Boston Place, 5th Floor, 02180.
Telephone: 617-619-3610.
Telefax: 617-619-3924.
Miami, Florida Office: De Orchis, Corsa & Hillerbrand, LLP, 2650 Biscayne Boulevard, 33137.
Telephone: 305-571-9200.
Telefax: 305-571-9250.

PARTNERS

LeRoy S. Corsa
Vincent M. De Orchis
Christopher H. Mansuy
Alexander V. Sansone
John A. Orzel
Michael E. Unger
Cary R. Wiener

ASSOCIATES

R. Brett Kelly
William E. Lakis
Marc I. Kunkin
Francesco A. Di Pietro

RESIDENT COUNSEL

M. E. De Orchis

OF COUNSEL

Ara A. Shimshidian
Bruce H. Neuman

For full biographical listings, see the Martindale-Hubbell Law Directory

DONOVAN PARRY CARBIN MCDERMOTT & RADZIK (AV)

Wall Street Plaza, 88 Pine Street, 10005-1801
Telephone: 212-376-6400
Telecopier: 212-376-6490
Email: DONOVANLAW@AOL.COM

MEMBERS OF FIRM

James J. Donovan (1915-1988)
Richard E. Repetto (1935-1988)
Thomas P. Parry
James W. Carbin
Daniel G. McDermott
Edward C. Radzik

OF COUNSEL

Patrick J. Foley

ASSOCIATES

John K. McElligott
John F. Ryan

For full biographical listings, see the Martindale-Hubbell Law Directory

GARSON GERSPACH DECORATO & COHEN, LLP (AV)

One Whitehall Street, Tenth Floor, 10004
Telephone: 212-742-8700
Fax: 212-742-1471
Email: ASGGGDC@aol.com *URL:* http://www.MEDILAW@aol.com

Andrew S. Garson
Thomas J. Gerspach
Linda J. DeCorato
Joshua R. Cohen

For full biographical listings, see the Martindale-Hubbell Law Directory

GOLDBERGER AND DUBIN, P.C. (AV)

401 Broadway, 10013
Telephone: 212-431-9380
Fax: 212-966-0588
Email: GND401@aol.com *URL:* http://www.ny-attorney.com

Paul A. Goldberger
Lawrence Dubin

Robert A. Horne

For full biographical listings, see the Martindale-Hubbell Law Directory

HEIDELL, PITTONI, MURPHY & BACH, LLP (AV)

99 Park Avenue, 10016
Telephone: 212-286-8585
Telecopier: 212-490-8966
Email: hpmb@hpmb.com
Stamford, Connecticut Office: 24 Richmond Hill Avenue.
Telephone: 203-327-1800. Email: hpmb@hpbm.com

Luke M. Pittoni
Raymond W. Murphy
Charles L. Bach, Jr.
Rosary A. Morelli
Bruce F. Gilpatrick
Robin R. Dolsky
Elizabeth Cornacchio
Austa S. Devlin
Michael D. Shalhoub
Stephen R. Marshall
Louise A. Derevlany
John F. Costa
E. Marc Hyman
Cheryl A. Harris
John J. Murphy, Jr.
Terrence P. St. John
Daniel S. Ratner

OF COUNSEL

Robert C. Heidell

Linda M. Ruma
Janice Kirsten Lunde
Geraldine Koeneke Russell
Carol L. Morris-Fox
Raphael J. Berman
Michael S. Coulston
Daniel Newman
Sandra Erica Ann Dwyer
Matthew S. Hirsch
Elizabeth D. Stuart
Holly Anne Brown
Anne Margaret Bracken
Stacey L. Mahdavian
Robert W. Finke
Tracey J. Knuckles
Theresann J. Potter
Paul Sean Curtin
Lori Wallace-Fischler
Ronit Rubin
Joseph A. Sack
Karen T. Grottalio
Tonya M Lindsey
Harold Clement Baker, III
Suzanne R. Byrne
Daryl Paxson
Ellen Griffel
Fern H Block
Andrea L. Crawford
William A. Elder
Arthur J. Robb
Leah J. Terranova (Not admitted in NY)
Bill P. Chimos
Amgad Michael Sabongui
David N. Esterman
Danielle L. Sullivan
Russell S. Jamison

For full biographical listings, see the Martindale-Hubbell Law Directory

INGRAM YUZEK GAINEN CARROLL & BERTOLOTTI, LLP (AV)

250 Park Avenue, 10177
Telephone: 212-907-9600
Facsimile: 212-907-9681

MEMBERS OF FIRM

Ernest J. Bertolotti (1942-1999)
Daniel L. Carroll
Roger Cukras
David G. Ebert
Larry F. Gainen
Samuel W. Ingram, Jr.
Paulette Kendler
Steven Mastbaum
Shane O'Neill
Dean G. Yuzek

ASSOCIATES

Warren E. Barrows
Amy Bertolotti
Patricia Hewitt
Theodore M. Kakoyiannis
Jeanne F. Pucci
Leigh A. Roveda
Jennifer E. Schwartz
Paul H. Slaney

OF COUNSEL

Karin J. Barkhorn
Beverly L. Deickler
Mark E. Klein
Paulette Lemay Peters
Cory L. Weiss

For full biographical listings, see the Martindale-Hubbell Law Directory

JACOBOWITZ, GARFINKEL & LESMAN (AV)

Seven Hanover Square, Ninth Floor, 10004-2594
Telephone: 212-809-8000
Fax: 212-344-8263

MANAGING ATTORNEYS

Edward A. Garfinkel
Michael S. Lesman

For full biographical listings, see the Martindale-Hubbell Law Directory

JONES, DAY, REAVIS & POGUE (AV)

599 Lexington Avenue, 10022
Telephone: 212-326-3939
Telecopier: 212-755-7306
Email: counsel@jonesday.com *URL:* http://www.jonesday.com
In Atlanta, Georgia: 3500 SunTrust Plaza, 303 Peachtree Street.
Telephone: 404-521-3939.
Telecopier: 404-581-8330.
In Brussels, Belgium: Avenue Louise 480, 7th Floor, B-1050 Brussels.
Telephone: 32-2-645-14-11.
Telecopier: 32-2-645-14-45.
In Chicago, Illinois: 77 West Wacker.
Telephone: 312-782-3939.
Telecopier: 312-782-8585.
In Cleveland, Ohio: North Point, 901 Lakeside Avenue.
Telephone: 216-586-3939.
Telecopier: 216-579-0212.

(See Next Column)

JONES, DAY, REAVIS & POGUE—*Continued*

In Columbus, Ohio: 1900 Huntington Center.
Telephone: 614-469-3939.
Telecopier: 614-461-4198.
In Dallas, Texas: 2727 North Harwood Street.
Telephone: 214-220-3939.
Telecopier: 214-969-5100.
In Frankfurt, Germany: Hochhaus am Park, Grüneburgweg 102, 60323 Frankfurt am Main.
Telephone: 49-69-9726-3939.
Telecopier: 49-69-9726-3993.
In Geneva, Switzerland: 20, rue de Candolle.
Telephone: 41-22-320-2339.
Telecopier: 41-22-320-1232.
In Hong Kong: 29th Floor, Entertainment Building, 30 Queen's Road Central.
Telephone: 852-2526-6895.
Telecopier: 852-2868-5871.
In Irvine, California: 5 Park Plaza, Suite 1100.
Telephone: 949-851-3939.
Telecopier: 949-553-7539.
In London, England: Bucklersbury House, 3 Queen Victoria Street.
Telephone: 44-20-7236-3939
Telecopier: 44-20-7236-1113.
In Los Angeles, California: 555 West Fifth Street, Suite 4600.
Telephone: 213-489-3939.
Telecopier: 213-243-2539.
In Paris, France: 120, rue du Faubourg Saint-Honoré.
Telephone: 33-1-56-59-39-39.
Telecopier: 33-1-56-59-39-38
In Pittsburgh, Pennsylvania: 500 Grant Street, 31st Floor.
Telephone: 412-391-3939.
Telecopier: 412-394-7959.
In Riyadh, Saudi Arabia: The International Law Firm (In Association with Jones, Day, Reavis & Pogue), Sulaymaniyah, Prince Mishari IBN, Abdulaziz Street, P.O. Box 22166.
Telephone: (966-1) 462-8866.
Telecopier: (966-1) 462-9001.
In Shanghai, China: 2805 Kerry Centre, 1515 Nanjing Road West.
Telephone: 86-21-5298-6568.
Telecopier: 86-21-5298-6569.
In Sydney, Australia: Governor Phillip Tower, Level 38, 1 Farrer Place.
Telephone: 61-2-9210-6921.
Telecopier: 61-2-9210-6926.
In Taipei, Taiwan: 8th Floor, 2 Tun Hwa South Road, Section 2.
Telephone: (886-2) 2704-6808.
Telecopier: (886-2) 2704-6791.
In Tokyo, Japan: Toranomon 45 Mori Building, 3rd Floor, 1-5, Toranomon 5-Chome, Minato-Ku, Tokyo 105, Japan.
Telephone: 81-3-3433-3939.
Telecopier: 81-3-5401-2725.
In Washington, D.C.: 51 Louisiana Avenue, N.W.
Telephone: 202-879-3939.
Telecopier: 202-626-1700.

MEMBER OF FIRM IN NEW YORK

Thomas H. Sear

For Complete List of Firm Personnel, See General Section

For full biographical listings, see the Martindale-Hubbell Law Directory

KENNY & STEARNS (AV)

26 Broadway, 10004-1882
Telephone: 212-422-6111
Fax: 212-422-6544
Email: kenny-stearns@erols.com
Newark, New Jersey Office: 56 Park Place.
Telephone: 201-624-7779.

MEMBERS OF FIRM

James M. Kenny
Joseph T. Stearns
Gino A. Zonghetti

ASSOCIATES

Michael C. Mulé
Christina M. Kenny (Not admitted in NY)
John D. Blomquist

For full biographical listings, see the Martindale-Hubbell Law Directory

LAVIN, COLEMAN, O'NEIL, RICCI, FINARELLI & GRAY (AV)

7th Floor, 767 Third Avenue, 10017
Telephone: 212-319-6898
Fax: 212-319-6932
Philadelphia, Pennsylvania Office: Suite 1000, 510 Walnut Street.
Telephone: 215-627-0303.
Fax: 215-627-2551.
Mount Laurel, New Jersey Office: 8000 Midlantic Drive, Suite 201 South.
Telephone: 609-778-5544.
Fax: 609-778-3383.

(See Next Column)

Francis F. Quinn
William J. Ricci
Edward A. Gray
Joseph A. McGinley
Michael D. Brophy

Jessica Faden (Resident, Mount Laurel, New Jersey Office)
Margot L. Ludlam
Leona C. McFadden
Timothy J. McHugh
Michelle S. Regan
Elizabeth A. Weill
Christopher P. Yodice

For full biographical listings, see the Martindale-Hubbell Law Directory

LEAHEY & JOHNSON, P.C. (AV)

Suite 2220, 120 Wall Street, 10005
Telephone: 212-269-7308
Facsimile: 212-422-4751
Email: Leaheylaw@Aol.com

Peter James Johnson
Peter James Johnson, Jr.
William G. Murphy
Kevin Brian Lynch

James P. Tenney
Steven Martin
William J. Gordon
Christopher Delamere Clarke
Vincent L. Gallo, Jr.
Joseph Francis Ferrette
Gregory Wilson
Michael Cannella
James Gerard Mcgovern
Nadine M. Duhamel
Sharon A. Toussaint
Melissa Ann Weinberg
Edward J. White
Daniel Michael Sullivan
Lennon C. Edwards
Carmen M. Vasquez
Eric L. Horn
Sean T. O'Leary (Not admitted in NY)

For full biographical listings, see the Martindale-Hubbell Law Directory

LEDY-GURREN & BLUMENSTOCK, L.L.P. (AV)

150 East 52nd Street-30th Floor, 10022
Telephone: 212-753-4444
Fax: 212-753-1003
Email: ledygurren@aol.com

Nancy Ledy-Gurren
John U. H. Blumenstock
Deborah Bass
Daniel E. Siff

Elissa L. Shechter

OF COUNSEL

Elizabeth Marion Young

For full biographical listings, see the Martindale-Hubbell Law Directory

LIEBER & LIEBER (AV)

111 John Street, 10038
Telephone: 212-608-5844
Fax: 212-608-5848

MEMBERS OF FIRM

Joel M. Lieber (1953-1992)
Eugene H. Lieber

Representative Clients: Johnson Controls, Inc.; The Manitowoc Co., Inc.; Bucyrus-Erie Co.; Wausau Insurance Cos.; General Accident Group; The Heil Co.; Manitowoc-Forsythe Corp.; Kemper Group; Lexington Insurance Co.

For full biographical listings, see the Martindale-Hubbell Law Directory

LOCKE & HERBERT (AV)

A Partnership including a Professional Corporation
900 Third Avenue, 10022
Telephone: 212-355-7493
Telecopier: 212-355-7674
Stamford, Connecticut Office: 1100 Summer Street. 06905.
Telephone: 203-969-6030.
Facsimile: 203-324-3607.

MEMBERS OF FIRM

Charles T. Locke (P.C.)
Stephen R. Herbert

Representative Clients: Mutual of Omaha Insurance Co.; National Benefit Life Insurance Co.; Companion Life Insurance Co.
Reference: The Bank of New York.

For full biographical listings, see the Martindale-Hubbell Law Directory

LONDON FISCHER LLP (AV)

59 Maiden Lane, 10038
Telephone: 212-972-1000
Facsimile: 212-972-1030
Email: Law@LondonFischer.com

(See Next Column)

LONDON FISCHER LLP, *New York—Continued*

MEMBERS OF FIRM

Bernard London
James L. Fischer
Daniel Zemann, Jr.
John E. Sparling
Richard S. Endres
Leah Campbell
Marvin B. Segal
James Walsh
Anthony F. Tagliagambe

For full biographical listings, see the Martindale-Hubbell Law Directory

MARSHALL CONWAY & WRIGHT, P.C. (AV)

116 John Street, 10038
Telephone: 212-619-4444
Fax: 212-962-2647
Jersey City, New Jersey Office: One Exchange Place, Suite 1000, 07302.
Telephone: 201-521-3170.
Fax: 201-521-3180.

Jeffrey A. Marshall
Robert J. Conway
John R. Wright
Christopher T. Bradley
Norman J. Golub (Resident, Jersey City, New Jersey Office)

George J. Carpenter
Steven Lee Sonkin
Michael J. Pearsall
Joseph J. Andriola
John C. Szewczuk
Sandro Attilio Battaglia
John DeMatteo, III
Robert P. Fumo
Clara M. Villarreal
David F. Tavella
Gerald A. Greenberger
Stacey H. Snyder
Maria E. Cannon
Kenneth P. Horenstein
Steven R. Vaccaro
Keith L. Kaplan
Penelope G. Stothers
Irwin H. Haut
Christopher L. Perry
Alan E. Kleinberger

For full biographical listings, see the Martindale-Hubbell Law Directory

MENDES & MOUNT, LLP (AV)

750 Seventh Avenue, 10019-6829
Telephone: 212-261-8000
Fax: 212-261-8750
Los Angeles, California Office: Citicorp Plaza, 725 South Figueroa Street, Nineteenth Floor.
Telephone: 213-955-7700.
Fax: 213-955-7725.
Newark, New Jersey Office: 1 Newark Center.
Telephone: 973-639-7300.
Fax: 973-639-7350.

EQUITY PARTNERS

William Blanc Mendes (1891-1957)
Russell Theodore Mount (1881-1962)
John R. Arscott
Daniel M. Bianca
Mark F. Bruckmann
Charles G. Carluccio, III (Resident, Los Angeles, California Office)
Frank J. Chiarchiaro
Ellen R. Clarke
Mary Ann D'Amato
James J. Finnerty, Jr.
Garrett J. Fitzpatrick
Robert M. Flannery
Leo W. Fraser, III
Ronald R. Houdlett
James W. Hunt (Resident, Los Angeles, California Office)
John F. Larkin, III
Henry Lee (Resident, Los Angeles, California Office)
George C. Lock
Edward M. Manganiello
Robert M. Mangino, Jr.
John G. McAndrews
William J. McAndrews
Eileen T. McCabe
James A. McGuire
Edward J. McMurrer
Mary D. Melvin
Richard C. Milazzo
Dennis R. Mullins
Robert F. Priestley (Resident, Newark, New Jersey Office)
Thomas J. Quinn
Anthony P. Spain
Raymond R. Trismen
Stephen Tucker
Arthur J. Washington, III

NON-EQUITY PARTNERS

Steven P. Agosta
R. James Bradford, III
Robert J. Brown
John A. Catania
Alan H. Collier (Resident, Los Angeles, California Office)
Kevin F. Cook
Joseph M. Coppola
Bruce H. Davidson
Joseph A. Deliso
Matthew G. Dineen
Mark S. Facer (Resident, Los Angeles, California Office)
John P. Falcone
Robert P. Firriolo
Kevin G. Fitzgerald
Kevin G. Flynn
Michael C. Giordano
William G. Goldsmith
John A. Guarascio
Joseph G. Hynes
Michael F. Klag
Brendan J. Malley
George L. Maniatis
Shalem A. Massey (Resident, Los Angeles, California Office)
Suzanne Naatz McNulty (Resident, Los Angeles, California Office)
William A. Meehan
Joseph K. Molloy
Michael E. Morley
Paul E. Moran
Eugene P. Murphy
Richard R. Nelson (Resident, Los Angeles, California Office)
Daniel T. O'Neil
Ralph V. Pagano
Kevin J. Philbin
Stephen V. Rible
Stephen Thomas Roberts
Lawrence W. Rose

(See Next Column)

NON-EQUITY PARTNERS (Continued)

Nancy Newton Sipp
Joseph F. Uvino
Ty S. Vanderford (Resident, Los Angeles, California Office)
Arjang Victory
Dean J. Vigliano
William S. Wachenfeld (Resident, Newark, New Jersey Office)
Robert B. Wall
Bruce R. Wildermuth
Joseph J. Winowiecki

OF COUNSEL

Harold J. Levy

Steven A. Accinelli
Garth W. Aubert (Resident, Los Angeles, California Office)
Felix Avila (Resident, Los Angeles, California Office)
M. Kathleen Beatley
Kathleen Browne-Pindilli (Resident, Newark, New Jersey Office)
Christopher J. Butler
Matthew J. Byrne
Eileen S. Carlton
Alice Chan
Evelyn Y. Cheh
Dominick Cirelli, Jr. (Resident, Newark, New Jersey Office)
William J. Cleary
Victoria Cuttita
Olympia Daskalakis
Elizabeth Anne Dee
Steven R. DeGeorge
Michael R. Delhagen
Diane DiFranco
Mark A. DiTaranto
Patrick J. Donohue
Cory D. Esters (Resident, Los Angeles, California Office)
Anthony R. Filiato
Michael A. Fleming
Matthew G. Foglia
Joseph L. Francoeur
Christine Gagliano
Gary A. Gardner
Catherine D. Glover
Julie M. Granser
Ann E. Halden
John D. Haller
Christopher S. Hickey (Resident, Los Angeles, California Office)
Marcy Hillman
Toby Holbreich (Resident, Newark, New Jersey Office)
Jeff Imeri
Mark R. Irvine (Resident, Los Angeles, California Office)
Robert J. Keane
Kipp A. Landis (Resident, Los Angeles, California Office)
Stacey A. Lara
Danielle M. Leventhal
Kyle B. Levine (Resident, Los Angeles, California Office)
Lori M. Linger
Gerald M. Lynch, Jr.
Jennifer L. Malin
Patrick J. Maloney
Shari R. Marko (Resident, Newark, New Jersey Office)
Raymond S. Mastrangelo
Dennis J. McEnery
Janice L. McGuckin
Allen R. McKay
Christine M. McNicholas
Wendy B. Millman
Maria Moukides
Francesca V. Naso
Christopher C. Novak
John D. O'Byrne
Diane J. O'Neil (Resident, Newark, New Jersey Office)
Thomas R. Pantino
Paul Piantino III (Resident, Newark, New Jersey Office)
Howard R. Rabin
David A. Robinson (Resident, Los Angeles, California Office)
Maritza Eliane Rodriguez
Peter S. Samaan
Andrew J. Shaw
Melissa C. Shea
Yvonne T. Simon (Resident, Los Angeles, California Office)
Sean R. Simpson (Resident, Los Angeles, California Office)
Adam M. Smith (Resident, Newark, New Jersey Office)
Edward T. Smith
Marla A. Smith (Resident, Los Angeles, California Office)
Jennifer A. Snyder
Richard J. Sprock
Geoffrey E. Stein
Irene C. Sun (Resident, Los Angeles, California Office)
Stacy J. Sussman
Pandora Thompson (Resident, Newark, New Jersey Office)
Jason Vincent

For full biographical listings, see the Martindale-Hubbell Law Directory

MOUND, COTTON & WOLLAN (AV)

One Battery Park Plaza, 10004
Telephone: 212-804-4200
Facsimile: 212-344-8066
San Francisco, California Office: 1700 California Street, Suite 470.
Telephone: 415-434-4301.
Telecopier: 415-434-4303.
London, England Office: Longbow House, 14-20 Chiswell Street.
Telephone: 0071-638-3688.
Newark, New Jersey Office: The Legal Center, One Riverfront Plaza, 8th Floor, 07102-5497.
Telephone: 973-242-2050.
Telecopier: 973-242-4244.

Arthur N. Brook (1933-1997)

MEMBERS OF FIRM

Stuart Cotton
Jeffrey C. Crawford
Leonard S. Dome
Wayne R. Glaubinger
Michael H. Goldstein
Lawrence S. Greengrass
Lloyd A. Gura
Bruce R. Kaliner
Michael R. Koblenz
Daniel Markewich
John C. Mezzacappa
Frederic R. Mindlin
Francis A. Montbach
David A. Silva
Philip C. Silverberg
Costantino P. Suriano
James D. Veach
Jeffrey S. Weinstein

COUNSEL

Eugene A. Leiman
Eugene Wollan

(See Next Column)

MOUND, COTTON & WOLLAN—*Continued*

RESIDENT OF COUNSEL
SAN FRANCISCO, CALIFORNIA OFFICE

Anna Maria Martin (Not admitted in NY)
Joseph M. Rimac, Jr. (Not admitted in NY)

RESIDENT MEMBER
NEWARK, NEW JERSEY OFFICE

William D. Wilson

ASSOCIATES

Michael Altman
Emilie L. Bakal
Todd A. Bakal
Kevin F. Buckley
Doreen A. Cronin
Frank J. DeAngelis
Alyssa DeSimone
Lauren G. Dome
Douglas K. Eisenstein
Maria Fazzolari
Joseph W. Ferraro
Aaron F. Fishbein
Elisa T. Gilbert
Diana E. Goldberg
Hilary M. Henkind
Mark S. Katz
David W. Kenna
David S. Mahaffey
Mark D. Marino
Catherine F. Megret
Mitchell D. Otto
Albert J. Pinzon
Renee M. Plessner
Jon Quint
Ronnie A. Rifkin
Mark J. Weber
Christina M. Wood

For Complete List of Firm Personnel, See General Section

For full biographical listings, see the Martindale-Hubbell Law Directory

---

NEWMAN FITCH ALTHEIM MYERS, P.C. (AV)

14 Wall Street, 22nd Floor, 10005
Telephone: 212-619-4350
Fax: 212-619-3622
Email: lawfirm@nfam.com
Newark, New Jersey Office: 744 Broad Street, Suite 2109.
Telephone: 201-824-2600.
Fax: 201-824-2993.

Robert A. Fitch
Abraham S. Altheim
Jan Kevin Myers
Charles W. Kreines
Floyd G. Cottrell (Resident Partner, Newark, New Jersey Office)
Olivia M. Gross
Ian F. Harris

COUNSEL

Laura M. Mattera
Charles Dewey Cole, Jr.
William A. Prinsell

Vanessa M. Corchia
Harry Steinberg
Alex M. Grant
James Sawicki
Jeffrey A. Lesser
Peter C. Bobchin
Elisa Cullen Schorr
Robin B. Baer
Ian R. Grodman (Resident, Newark, New Jersey Office)
Francine Scotto
Susan A. Karp
Jaimi Berliner
John F. Raio Jr.
Rhonda D. Thompson
Steven Bandel
Anita Bowen
Carolyn M. Walsh
Peter DeNoto
Susan A. Romano
Stephanie Monaco (Resident, Newark, New Jersey Office)
Paul Romano (Resident, Newark, New Jersey Office)
Joseph A. Orlando
Lon V. Hughes
Eric Cheng
Richard B. Polner
Colleen A. Tan
Julie C. Chodos
Stephen M. Bigham
Rosario Chetta

Reference: Chase Manhattan Bank, New York.

For full biographical listings, see the Martindale-Hubbell Law Directory

---

OHRENSTEIN & BROWN, L.L.P. (AV)

One World Trade Center 85th Floor, 10048
Telephone: 212-682-4500
Facsimile: 212-839-0854
Garden City, New York Office: 1050 Franklin Avenue.
Telephone: 516-873-6334.
Telecopier: 516-873-8912.

MEMBERS OF FIRM

Manfred Ohrenstein
Michael D. Brown
Peter J. Biging
Joseph Francis Fields
Abraham E. Havkins
Geoffrey W. Heineman
Christopher B. Hitchcock
Andrew L. Margulis
Steven H. Rosenfeld
Abe M. Rychik
John R. Sachs, Jr.

COUNSEL

Anne J. Coploff
Stanley M. Kolber
Paul L. Dillon
Gail L. Ritzert

ASSOCIATES

Joseph G. Colbert
Jonathan A. Judd
Bennett R. Katz
Kenneth M. Labbate
Jennifer A. Lowitt
John A. McGrath
Tessie M. Perrini (Resident, Garden City, New York)
Jennifer R. Robinson
Sharon Portnof Russ
Philip Touitou
Carla Varriale

(See Next Column)

ASSOCIATES (Continued)

Brian D. Waller
Cristin L. Flynn
Jason A. Advocate
Timothy F. Finnerty (Resident, Garden City Office)
Michelle Maerov
Stacey Niditch
Brian A. Smith
Theresa Brennan Murphy
Thomas Brian Ferris (Resident at Garden City Office)

LEGAL SUPPORT PERSONNEL

Christine A. Maguire (Office Manager)

For full biographical listings, see the Martindale-Hubbell Law Directory

---

PARKER CHAPIN LLP (AV)

Chrysler Building, 405 Lexington Avenue, 10017
Telephone: 212-704-6000
Telecopier: 212-704-6288
URL: http://www.parkerchapin.com
Great Neck, New York Office: 175 Great Neck Road.
Telephone: 516-482-4422.
Telecopier: 516-482-4469.
Hackensack, New Jersey: 190 Morre Street, Suite 307.
Telephone: 210-883-6400.
Telecopier: 210-883-6404.
Beverly Hills, California: 9454 Wilshire Boulevard.
Telephone: 310-288-8367.
Telecopier: 310-288-8365.

MEMBERS OF FIRM

Mark Abramowitz
Robert M. Carmen
Elliot Cohen
Michael D. Friedman
Charles P. Greenman
Alvin M. Stein
Lee W. Stremba

OF COUNSEL

Katherine Cooney Ash
Daniel S. Greenfeld
Mark I. Schlesinger

For Complete List of Firm Personnel, See General Section

For full biographical listings, see the Martindale-Hubbell Law Directory

---

PELTZ & WALKER (AV)

222 Broadway - 25th Floor, 10038
Telephone: 212-349-6775
Cable Address: "Dypelaw New York"
Telex: 230199 SWIFTUR ATTDPW
Telefax: (212) 227-4002
Email: Pelzwalker@aol.com

MEMBERS OF FIRM

Alexander Peltz
Paul E. Walker
Edward M. Schoenman
Miles S. Reiner
Bhalinder L. Rikhye
Jaymie L. Einhorn
Robert A. Rosenfeld

ASSOCIATES

Steven M. Silverman
L. Ruby Rey
Patrice R. McKenna
Sharon Elmaleh
Mitchel Lidowsky

OF COUNSEL

John J. O'Donnell
Edward V. Schwendemann
Jane Himelfarb

LEGAL SUPPORT PERSONNEL

PARALEGALS

Joseph Lipari
Melissa Jamison
H. Steven Ortiz
Maria D. Corvaia

For full biographical listings, see the Martindale-Hubbell Law Directory

---

POSTNER & RUBIN (AV)

17 Battery Place, 10004
Telephone: 212-269-2510
Fax: 212-425-0968
Email: postner@aol.com
Holmdel, New Jersey Office: 42 West Main Street,
Telephone: 732-946-9001.
Fax: 732-946-9005.

Robert A. Rubin
William J. Postner
Robert J. MacPherson
Jeffrey R. Cruz

ASSOCIATES

Patricia M. Caplicki
Dana Wordes
Michael W. Bautz

NEW JERSEY RESIDENT COUNSEL

Sarah B. Biser

For full biographical listings, see the Martindale-Hubbell Law Directory

---

QUIRK AND BAKALOR, P.C. (AV)

845 Third Avenue, 10022
Telephone: 212-319-1000

(See Next Column)

QUIRK AND BAKALOR P.C., *New York—Continued*

Robert E. Quirk
Richard H. Bakalor
Stephen K. Blunda
Jeffrey J. Ellis
Richard M. Freiman
Scott P. Taylor
Henry Nicholas Goodman
Timothy J. Keane

Alice J. Jaffe
Loretta A. Redmond
Michael W. Hecht
Debra E. Seidman
Dominic S. Curcio
A. Lorenzo Bryan
Steven A. Lee
Anoushka Sharifi-Bayley
Brian P. Sexton
Donna Hope Bakalor
Alyssa M. Cohen
James M. Andriola
Liza R. Berliner
Pablo A. Sosa
Christopher J. Gray
Anne E. Pettit
Todd A. Paradeis
Andrew M. Premisler

For full biographical listings, see the Martindale-Hubbell Law Directory

JEFFREY SAMEL & PARTNERS (AV)

150 Broadway, 20th Floor, 10038
Telephone: 212-587-9690
Fax: 212-587-9673

Jeffrey Samel
David S. Gary
Dorothy Samel

ASSOCIATES

Robert G. Spevack
David M. Samel
Stacey L. Schwartz

OF COUNSEL

Richard A. Soberman

Representative Clients: New York City Transit Authority; New York City Housing Authority; Empire Insurance Co.; National General Insurance Co.; Federal Express Corp.; Shell Oil Corp.; American Building Maintenance Corp; United Fidelity & Guaranty Corp.; Little Caesar Enterprises, Inc.; Showbiz Pizza Time, Inc.

For full biographical listings, see the Martindale-Hubbell Law Directory

SCHNEIDER, KLEINICK, WEITZ, DAMASHEK & SHOOT (AV)

233 Broadway, Fifth Floor, 10279-0003
Telephone: 212-553-9000
Fax: 212-804-0820
Email: mail@lawyer1.com *URL:* http://www.lawyer1.com

Ivan S. Schneider
Arnold L. Kleinick
Harvey Weitz
Philip M. Damashek
Brian J. Shoot
Robert B. Jackson
Clifford J. Stern
Gregory J. Cannata
Keith A. Kleinick
Richard B. Ancowitz
Charles J. Nolet, Jr.
Leslie Debra Kelmachter
Louis J. Mitchell

John Kieran Daly
Jonathan S. Damashek
Thomas V. Deffina
Dawn S. DeWeil
David W. Druker
Steven Gold
Keith H. Gross
Erin K. Hurley
Judy Keenan
Paul A. Marber
Lloyd M. Roberts
Joseph S. Rosato
Derek S. Sells
Lawrence A. Wilson, II
James M. Lane
Donald D. Casale

For full biographical listings, see the Martindale-Hubbell Law Directory

SMITH MAZURE DIRECTOR WILKINS YOUNG YAGERMAN & TARALLO, P.C. (AV)

111 John Street, 10038
Telephone: 212-964-7400
Fax: 212-374-1935 (Not for Legal Service)

Gerald Director
David E. Mazure
Stanley Wilkins
Nicholas Tarallo
Jacob J. Young
Mark S. Yagerman

Irwin D. Miller
Marc H. Pillinger
Michael K. Berman
John Kevin Reilly
Cary Maynard
Robert P. Siegel
John Colucci
Haydn J. Brill
Jeffrey T. Miller
Corey A. Tavel
Mark D. Levi
Howard S. Shafer
Peter H. Graber
Irwin Bloom
Michael S. Livow
Steven I. Brizel
Joel M. Simon
Frank J. Keenan
Melissa S. Romano
Paul L. LaClair
Constantine Vlavianos
Joseph A. Schwarzenberg
Stephanie Morfesis
Stacy I. Oberman
Dawn McNamara
David A. Glazer
Lara Jill Miller
Andrew J. Funk
Angela Lurie Milch
Seth M. Katz

(See Next Column)

Michael G. Brown
Christopher M. FitzPatrick
Neil Thomas Veilleux
Doris M. Carrasquillo
Alan C. Kelhoffer
Howard J. Snyder

For full biographical listings, see the Martindale-Hubbell Law Directory

VERNER SIMON LLP (AV)

1350 Broadway, Suite 818, 10018
Telephone: 212-696-1600
Facsimile: 212-696-1670
Email: goodlaw@msn.com
Audubon, New Jersey Office: 601 White Horse Pike, 80106.
Telephone: 609-546-9100.
Facsimile: 609-546-6725.

Richard S. Kaye

For full biographical listings, see the Martindale-Hubbell Law Directory

WADE CLARK MULCAHY (AV)

111 Broadway, 10006
Telephone: 212-267-1900
Fax: 212-267-9470
Email: info@wcmlaw.com *URL:* http://www.wcmlaw.com
Westfield, New Jersey Office: 211 North Avenue East, 07090.
Telephone: 908-789-1681.
Fax: 908-789-0984.

PARTNERS

Dennis M. Wade
Paul F. Clark
John Mulcahy
Owen B. Carragher, Jr.

ASSOCIATES

Kathleen M. Mulholland
Rose M. McGrinder
Andrea E. Sacco
Christopher C. Mauro
Linda D. Werbel
Nicole Y. Brown
Suzanne M. O'Keefe

For full biographical listings, see the Martindale-Hubbell Law Directory

WHITE, FLEISCHNER & FINO (AV)

140 Broadway, 10005
Telephone: 212-487-9700
Telecopier: 212-487-9777
Email: infor@wff-law.com
Red Bank, New Jersey Office: 272 Broad Street.
Telephone: 732-530-7787.
Telecopier: 732-530-8552.

MEMBERS OF FIRM

Allan P. White
Benjamin A. Fleischner
Paul A. Fino, Jr.
Patti F. Potash
Wendy K. Carrano
Stephanie M. Holzback
Sheri E. Holland
James A. Robbins

ASSOCIATES

Deanna E. Hazen
Dionne G. Sinclair
Daniel MacLaren Stewart
Joanne Carlozzi
Elaine N. Chou

OF COUNSEL

Gil M. Coogler

Representative Clients: Empire Fire & Marine Ins. Co.; Marriott International; Avis Rent A Car; Chicago Insurance Company; Holyoke Mutual Insurance Co.; AIU; Lloyd's Syndicates; News Corp.; Markel Insurance Company; Gerling Insurance Company.

For Complete List of Firm Personnel, See General Section
For full biographical listings, see the Martindale-Hubbell Law Directory

WILSON, ELSER, MOSKOWITZ, EDELMAN & DICKER LLP (AV)

150 East 42nd Street, 10017-5639
Telephone: 212-490-3000
Telex: 177679
Facsimile: 212-490-3038; 212-557-7810
URL: http://www.wemed.com
Los Angeles, California, San Diego, California, San Francisco, California, Washington, D.C., Newark, New Jersey, Philadelphia, Pennsylvania, Baltimore, Maryland, Miami, Florida, Chicago, Illinois, White Plains, New York, Dallas, Texas, Houston, Texas, Albany, New York, Garden City, New York, London, England.
Affiliates: Paris, France: Honig Buffat Mettetal., Munich, Germany: Bach, Langheid Dallmayr, Cologne, Germany: Bach, Langheid Dallmayr, Frankfurt/Main, Germany: Bach, Langheid Dallmayr, Wiesbaden, Germany: Bach, Langheid Dallmayr, Berlin, Germany: Bach, Langheid Dallmayr.

MEMBERS OF FIRM

Thomas W. Wilson
John T. Elser
Harold J. Moskowitz
Max Edelman (1906-1989)
Herbert Dicker
Michael D. Glatt
Martin M. Ween
Marshal S. Endick
Richard S. Klein
Stephen A. Postelnek
Thomas W. Hyland
Vincent R. Fontana

(See Next Column)

WILSON, ELSER, MOSKOWITZ, EDELMAN & DICKER LLP—*Continued*

MEMBERS OF FIRM (Continued)

Patrick M. Kelly * (Resident Partner in Charge, Los Angeles Office)
James P. Donovan
Stephen M. Marcellino
Perry I. Kreidman
Philip J. Walsh
Edward J. Boyle
Anthony J. Mercorella
Robert M. Weber
Paul J. Bottari
Michael N. Stevens
Mark K. Anesh
Steven Kent
Harry P. Brett
Glenn J. Fuerth
Phillip A. Tumbarello
Thomas M. Gambardella
Thomas W. Tobin
Robert F. Roarke
Glen S. Feinberg
Arnold Kideckel
Francis P. Manchisi
H. Michael O'Brien
Steven L. Young
Richard H. Rubenstein
Thomas A. Leghorn
Ricki Roer
Thomas R. Manisero
Jerry B. Black
Richard S. Oelsner
Carl J. Pernicone
Carolyn Karp Schwartz
Alan Kaminsky
Robert W. Littleton
Edward A. Taylor
Rosario M. Vignali
James C. Ughetta
Robert L. Joyce
Scott R. Schaffer
Timothy J. Sheehan
John D. Morio
Yongjin Park
Robert T. Adams
Helmut Beron
Michael L. Boulhosa
Brian T. Del Gatto
Julie R. Evans
Lawrence H. Lum
Richard T. Mermelstein
Frederick W. Reif
Carl L. Steccato
Steven Verveniotis
Louis C. Roberts
Eric J. Sauter
David S. Sheiffer
Debra Tama
Lawrence B. Brennan
David A. Jones

*(Not admitted in New York)

For full biographical listings, see the Martindale-Hubbell Law Directory

NYACK, Rockland Co.

MACCARTNEY, MACCARTNEY, KERRIGAN & MACCARTNEY (AV)

MacCartney Building, 13 North Broadway, P.O. Box 350, 10960
Telephone: 914-358-0074
Fax: 914-358-0793

MEMBERS OF FIRM

Harold Y. MacCartney (1901-1988)
Harold Y. MacCartney, III (1968-1996)
Harold Y. MacCartney, Jr.
John D. MacCartney
William K. Kerrigan

Representative Clients: Action Auto Rental, Inc.; American Fidelity; American International Adjusting Co.; The Andover Cos.; Associated Mutual Insurance Company; Atlantic Mutual Ins. Co.; Avis Rent a Car; Bay State Insurance; Callicoon Co-operative Insurance Company; Cambridge Mutual Fire Insurance Company.

For full biographical listings, see the Martindale-Hubbell Law Directory

*ROCHESTER,** Monroe Co.

CONNORS & CORCORAN, L.L.P. (AV)

Suite 250, 45 Exchange Street, 14614-2002
Telephone: 716-232-5885
Fax: 716-546-3631
Email: buholtz@frontiernet.net *URL:* http://www.connorscorcoran.com

MEMBERS OF FIRM

Herbert J. LePage
Roger W. Avery
Joseph G. Fritsch, Jr.
James E. Maslyn
Eileen E. Buholtz
Cheryl Loria-Dinolfo
Gregory T. Phillips

Attorneys for: Allstate Insurance Co.; Continental National American Group; Criterion Insurance Co.; General Accident Group; Ideal Mutual Insurance Co.; Prudential Property & Casualty Co.; SAFECO; Sentry Insurance; Travelers Property Casualty.
Reference: Marine Midland Bank.

For full biographical listings, see the Martindale-Hubbell Law Directory

TREVETT, LENWEAVER & SALZER, P.C. (AV)

700 Reynolds Arcade, 16 East Main Street, 14614
Telephone: 716-454-2181
Telecopier: 716-454-4026

Oscar J. Brown (1884-1958)
Melvin H. Zurett (1905-1967)
Eric P. Smith (1900-1967)
Thomas W. Sullivan (1916-1981)
William V. Gough (1922-1985)
Walter C. Eves (Retired)
Robert T. Skipworth (Retired)
Ronald James Summers (Retired)
Thomas N. Trevett
Bohdan Wenglowskyj
Thomas E. Lenweaver
Kenneth Bersani
Richard M. Doyle
James A. Valenti
Karl F. Salzer
Peter A. Jacobson
Louis B. Cristo

(See Next Column)

Cynthia A. Constantino
Henry L. Jesserer, III
Lawrence J. Andolina
James C. Gocker

John C. Palermo
Jon Paul Getz
Nicole L. Black

Representative Clients: American Motorists Insurance Co.; Lumbermens Mutual Casualty Co.; Nationwide Mutual Insurance Co.; Interboro Mutual Indemnity Insurance Co.; Michigan Mutual Liability Insurance Co.; Virginia Surety Co.; Allstate Insurance Co.; American Hardware Insurance Co.; Pearl Assurance Co., Ltd.

For full biographical listings, see the Martindale-Hubbell Law Directory

UNDERBERG & KESSLER LLP (AV)

1800 Chase Square, 14604
Telephone: 716-258-2800
Fax: 716-258-2821
Email: INFO@UNDERBERG-KESSLER.COM
Buffalo, New York Office: 1100 Main Place Tower. 14202.
Telephone: 716-848-9000.
Fax: 716-847-6004.

MEMBERS OF FIRM

Alan J. Underberg (1929-1998)
Irving L. Kessler
Michael J. Beyma
James A. Coniglio
Frank T. Crego
Robert W. Croessmann
John W. Crowe
Patrick L. Cusato
Michael C. Dwyer
Bernard A. Frank
Steven R. Gersz
Katherine Howk Karl
Lawrence P. Keller
Gordon J. Lipson
Anna E. Lynch
Robert F. Mechur
Paul V. Nunes
Terry M. Richman
J. David Sampson (Resident, Buffalo Office)
Sharon P. Stiller
Stephen H. Waite
Russell I. Zuckerman

OF COUNSEL

Andrew M. Greenstein

SENIOR ATTORNEYS

Duncan R. Farney
Ronald G. Hull

ASSOCIATES

James F. Armstrong (Resident, Buffalo Office)
Karen A. DiNardo
Lise C. Hamilton
Jeffrey D. Hummel
Paul F. Keneally
Ella L. Krzanowicz
Maureen E. Mulholland
Suzanne D. Nott
Kelly L. Odorisi
Thomas A. Rall

For full biographical listings, see the Martindale-Hubbell Law Directory

ROCKVILLE CENTRE, Nassau Co.

JACOBSON & SCHWARTZ (AV)

510 Merrick Road, P.O. Box 46, 11571
Telephone: 516-536-0900
Telecopier: 516-536-2371

Jacob N. Schwartz
Ronald A. Jacobson (1935-1993)
Gary R. Schwartz
Robert M. Bridges

Paul Goodovitch
Eric P. Tosca
Jeffrey D. Kadushin
Walter P. Wagner
Rhonda Hammer Barry
Susan B. Mandiberg
Anthony Eugene Graziani
Marc G. Schultz

OF COUNSEL

Bernard Adler

For full biographical listings, see the Martindale-Hubbell Law Directory

*SYRACUSE,** Onondaga Co.

ANDREWS LAW OFFICES (AV)

217 South Salina Street, Sixth Floor, 13202
Telephone: 315-471-2413
Telecopier: 315-471-7849
Email: andrews@servtech.com

William S. Andrews

For full biographical listings, see the Martindale-Hubbell Law Directory

GREENE AND REID (AV)

Brighton Hill, 892 East Brighton Avenue, 13205
Telephone: 315-492-9665
FAX: 315-492-9741
Toll Free: 1-800-886-9665
Email: cajansen@worldnet.att.net *URL:* http://www.nofaultlawyer.com
Newark, New York Office: 330 East Avenue.
Telephone: 315-331-5633.
Sackets Harbor, New York Office: 101 East Main Street.
Telephone: 315-646-2500.
Fax: 315-646-1732.

(See Next Column)

GREENE AND REID, *Syracuse—Continued*

MEMBERS OF FIRM

Arthur M. Greene
James E. Reid

LEGAL SUPPORT PERSONNEL

John F. Hogan
Polly Spring

Reference: M&T Bank.

For full biographical listings, see the Martindale-Hubbell Law Directory

PINSKY & SKANDALIS (AV)

5790 Widewaters Parkway, P.O. Box 250, 13214-0250
Telephone: 315-446-2384
Fax: 315-446-3016
Email: pinskyskan@aol.com
Albany, New York Office: 111 Washington Avenue, Suite 409.
Telephone: 518-432-4265.
Fax: 518-432-4267.

Norman M. Pinsky (1912-1980)
Philip C. Pinsky
Roy D. Pinsky
George Skandalis

Robert A. Kent (Resident, Albany Office)
Ellen S. Weinstein
John F. Pfeifer
Bradley M. Pinsky
Pamela M. Pozzi

For full biographical listings, see the Martindale-Hubbell Law Directory

SUGARMAN, WALLACE, MANHEIM & SCHOENWALD (AV)

HSBC Center, Fifth Floor, 360 South Warren Street, 13202-2680
Telephone: 315-474-2943
Fax: 315-474-0235
URL: http://www.sugarmanlaw.com
Buffalo Office: 1720 Rand Building, 14 Lafayette Square, 14203.
Telephone: 716-847-2523.
Fax: 716-847-2589.

MEMBERS OF FIRM

James G. Stevens, Jr.
David A. Kalabanka
Kevin T. Hunt

OF COUNSEL

Donald L. Schoenwald

Representative Clients: Allstate Insurance Co.; CNA Insurance Companies; Chubb & Son; Liberty Mutual Insurance Co.; Carpenter Manufacturing Co., Inc.; General Accident Group; Hartford Accident & Indemnity Co.; Firemans Fund; New York Central Mutual; Progressive Insurance Co.
Reference: HSBC.

For full biographical listings, see the Martindale-Hubbell Law Directory

*UTICA,** Oneida Co.

PETRONE & PETRONE, P.C. (AV)

1624 Genesee Street, 13502
Telephone: 315-735-7566
Fax: 315-735-5368
Email: pnp@borg.com *URL:* http://www.lawyers.com/petrone
Rochester, New York Office: 929 Times Square Building, 45 Exchange Street.
Telephone: 800-521-1260.
FAX: 716-232-7788.
Syracuse, New York Office: 314 East Fayette Street, 13202.
Telephone: 800-521-1260.
Fax: 315-735-5368.
Buffalo, New York Office: 1606 Liberty Building.
Telephone: 800-521-1260.
FAX: 716-852-6216.

Marcus M. Curry (1924-1996)
Louis S. Petrone
John R. Petrone, II
Lori E. Petrone

Reynolds E. Hahn (Resident, Rochester Office)
Edward J. Taublieb (Resident, Buffalo Office)
Mark J. Halpin
James P. Godemann
Frank Leonard Madia

For full biographical listings, see the Martindale-Hubbell Law Directory

ROSSI, MURNANE & HUGHES (AV)

209 Elizabeth Street, P.O. Box 209, 13503-0209
Telephone: 315-733-4671
Fax: 315-733-4609

Vincent J. Rossi
Don P. Murnane
Vincent J. Rossi, Jr.
Thomas P. Hughes

ASSOCIATE

Douglas M. DeMarché, Jr.

General Counsel for: Utica First Insurance Co.
Reference: Chase Bank, Utica, New York.

For full biographical listings, see the Martindale-Hubbell Law Directory

*WATERTOWN,** Jefferson Co.

CONBOY, MCKAY, BACHMAN & KENDALL, LLP (AV)

407 Sherman Street, 13601-3998
Telephone: 315-788-5100
Fax: 315-788-3463
Email: conboy@imcnet.net *URL:* http://www.gisco.net/conboy
Carthage, New York Office: 307 State Street.
Telephone: 315-493-0030.
Fax: 315-493-7549.
Canton, New York Office: 2 Judson Street.
Telephone: 315-386-8544.
Fax: 315-379-0126.

OF COUNSEL

Joanne M. Novak (Resident, Canton Office)

MEMBERS OF FIRM

Floyd J. Chandler
Lawrence D. Hasseler (Resident, Carthage Office)
Stephen W. Gebo
Arthur C. Stever, III
Peter L. Walton
David B. Geurtsen
Gerald J. Ducharme (Resident, Canton, New York Office)

ASSOCIATES

Scott B. Goldie
Edward A. Gibson
John V. Hartzell
Kimberly A. Wood

Attorneys for: Travelers Indemnity Co.; Royal Insurance Co.; Niagara Mohawk Power Corp.; Marine Midland Bank, N.A.; Community Bank, N.A.; State Farm Insurance; Hartford; CNA; Utica Mutual Insurance; New York Casualty.

For full biographical listings, see the Martindale-Hubbell Law Directory

*WHITE PLAINS,** Westchester Co.

BOEGGEMAN, GEORGE, HODGES & CORDE, P.C. (AV)

11 Martine Avenue, 10606
Telephone: 914-761-2252
Telecopier: 914-761-5211
Email: boeggeman@bghc-law.com *URL:* http://www.bghc-law.com
Albany, New York Office: 46 Columbia Street, 12207-2716.
Telephone: 518-465-1100.
Fax: 518-465-1800.

George S. Hodges
Richard G. Corde
John J. Walsh, II
Harold L. Moroknek
Robert S. Ondrovic
Thomas A. Sica (Resident Managing Attorney, Albany Office)

Karen A.D. Jockimo
William M. Wingertzahn
Elizabeth C. Mirisola
Cynthia Dolan
Marcella M. Green
Paul A. Hurley
Leslie K. Arfine
John T. Holden
James J. Lofrese
Jeanne M. Hurley
Ira H. Lapp
Matt Randolph Belkin
Cynthia K. Messemer

OF COUNSEL

Joseph H. George
John E. Boeggeman (1919-1993)

Representative Clients: American Telephone & Telegraph; Anheuser-Busch Companies, Inc.; Lowe's Home Centers; Great Atlantic & Pacific Tea Company; Reliance National Insurance Company; Metropolitan Property & Casualty Insurance Company; Fisher Price, Inc.; CGU Insurance Company; United Services Automobile Association; New York Central Mutual Fire Insurance Company.

For full biographical listings, see the Martindale-Hubbell Law Directory

ANTHONY J. CAPUTO, P.C. (AV)

175 Main Street, 10601
Telephone: 914-948-5151
Fax: 914-761-1246

Anthony J. Caputo

OF COUNSEL

Bruce F. Caputo

References: The Bank of New York; Chemical Bank; Citicorp.

For full biographical listings, see the Martindale-Hubbell Law Directory

CERUSSI & SPRING, A PROFESSIONAL CORPORATION (AV)

One North Lexington Avenue, 10601-1700
Telephone: 914-948-1200
Facsimile: 914-948-1579
Greenwich, Connecticut Office: 66 Field Point Road.
Telephone: 203-661-4000.
Facsimile: 203-661-1197.

MEMBERS OF FIRM

Michael A. Cerussi, Jr.
Thomas F. Cerussi
Ronald G. Crispi
Arthur J. Spring

(See Next Column)

CERUSSI & SPRING A PROFESSIONAL CORPORATION—*Continued*

ASSOCIATES

Laura Morrison Allen
Donald S. Campbell
Michael F. Cavolo (Not admitted in NY)
Lisa Conte
Thomas M. Crispi
Frank J. DeSalvo, Jr.
Laura M. Garcia
Gregg P. Garneau
Thomas M. Giangrande
Evy L. Kazansky
Peter Riggs
John A. Risi
D. Bradford Sessa
Kevin P. Westerman

SENIOR COUNSEL

Richard D. Bentzen

OF COUNSEL

Alfred E. Page, Jr.

For full biographical listings, see the Martindale-Hubbell Law Directory

DELBELLO DONNELLAN WEINGARTEN & TARTAGLIA, LLP (AV)

One North Lexington Avenue, 10601
Telephone: 914-681-0200
Telecopier: 914-684-0288
Email: general@ddwt.com

Alfred B. DelBello
Alfred E. Donnellan (Managing Partner)
Mark P. Weingarten
Daniel D. Tartaglia
Peter J. Wise
Lee S. Wiederkehr
Patrick M. Reilly
Robert A. Korren

ASSOCIATES

William E. Dumke
Christine Moccia
Suzanne Bogdanoff
Allyse B. Dunefsky
Jerry F. Kebrdle, II
Bradley D. Wank
Ann Farrissey Carlson
Janet J. Giris

OF COUNSEL

J. David Jutkowitz
Andrew J. Balint
Robert C. Epstein

For full biographical listings, see the Martindale-Hubbell Law Directory

ROGAN GUIDA & ORENSTEIN (AV)

235 Mamaroneck Avenue, 10605
Telephone: 1-888-WIN-WITH-US; 914-328-4480
Fax: 914-328-4479
URL: http://www.NYlawyers.com
Email: RoganGO@aol.com *URL:* http://www.lawyers.com/personalinjury

Jeffrey P. Rogan
Toni M. Guida
David L. Orenstein

Representative Clients: Recore One Mortgage Corp.; LEASCO; Pappas Enterprises Inc.; Steelcase, Inc.; Printing Center of Westchester Inc.; Corporate Imaging, Inc.; King Jolo's Flowers, Inc.; Systems Exchange, Inc.; Domus Realty.
Reference: Fleet Bank.

For full biographical listings, see the Martindale-Hubbell Law Directory

VOUTÉ, LOHRFINK, MAGRO & COLLINS, LLP (AV)

170 Hamilton Avenue, 10601-1789
Telephone: 914-946-1400
Facsimile: 914-946-8024

Arthur J. Vouté, Jr.
Richard L. Magro
Charles D. Lohrfink, Jr.
Charles A. Collins, Jr.

Elliot A. Cristantello
Stephen F. Fischer
Ralph F. Schoene
Kevin P. Fitzpatrick
Catherine F. Gale
Hal Roberts
Stephen J. Riebling, Jr.
John A. Howard
Michael A. Sonkin
Kelly E. Cardany

Representative Clients: Aetna Casualty & Surety Co.; Allstate Insurance Co.; Chubb Group; CNA Companies; Medical Liability Mutual Insurance Co.; National Car Rental System, Inc.; Physicians Reciprocal Insurance Co.; Preferred Physicians Medical Insurance Co.; Risk Enterprise Management; St. Josephs Medical Center.

For full biographical listings, see the Martindale-Hubbell Law Directory

WILSON, BAVE, CONBOY, COZZA & COUZENS, P.C. (AV)

Two William Street, 10601
Telephone: 914-686-9010
Telecopier: 914-686-0873
Email: wbcc@aol.com

(See Next Column)

William H. Bave (1919-1991)
Donald C. Wilson (1917-1994)
R. Kevin Conboy
William H. Bave, Jr.
Michael J. Cozza
John C. Couzens, Jr.
Patricia Bave-Planell
Kevin D. Odell
Leo T. McGrath
Alexandra C. Karamitsos
Joel A. Hirshfield
Megan J. Conboy
Teresa A. Gruber

LEGAL SUPPORT PERSONNEL

PARALEGAL

John R. Pearsall

Representative Clients: State Farm Mutual Automobile Insurance Co.; Continental National American Group; Medical Liability Mutual Insurance Co.; General Accident Insurance Co.; Metropolitan Property and Liability; Royal Insurance; County of Westchester; City of Yonkers.

For full biographical listings, see the Martindale-Hubbell Law Directory

NORTH CAROLINA

AHOSKIE, Hertford Co.

BAKER, JENKINS, JONES & DALY, P.A. (AV)

304 West Sunset Street, P.O. Box 986, 27910-0986
Telephone: 252-332-2181
Fax: 252-332-8354; Real Estate
Fax: 252-209-0046
Email: bjjdlaw@ahoskienc.com
Rocky Mount, North Carolina Office: 140 North Franklin Street, P.O. Box 68.
Telephone: 252-442-1977.
Facsimile: 252-442-5175.

Ronald G. Baker
Robert C. Jenkins
W. Hugh Jones, Jr.
Roswald B. Daly, Jr.
Ernie K. Murray
Roger Allan Askew
Ernest R. Carter, Jr.
Kevin Neil Lewis
Bruce L. Daughtry

Representative Clients: North Carolina Farm Bureau Mutual Insurance Co.; Nationwide Mutual Insurance Co.; Great American Insurance Cos.; Integon Insurance Corporation; Grain Dealers Mutual Insurance Co.; Lawyers Mutual Insurance Company of North Carolina; Traverers Insurance company; Employers Mutual Insurance Group; Universal Insurance Company; Travelers Property Casualty.

For full biographical listings, see the Martindale-Hubbell Law Directory

*ASHEVILLE,** Buncombe Co.

BALL, BARDEN & BELL, P.A. (AV)

18-20 North Spruce Street, P.O. Box 7157, 28802
Telephone: 828-252-0682
Fax: 828-251-5784
Email: BalBarBel@aol.com

Ervin L. Ball, Jr.
Stephen L. Barden, III
Thomas R. Bell, Jr.

Representative Clients: Allstate Insurance Co.; Bituminous Casualty Co.; The Concord Group Insurance Co.
Approved Attorneys for: Federal Deposit Insurance Corp.; Lawyers Title Insurance Co.

For full biographical listings, see the Martindale-Hubbell Law Directory

VAN WINKLE, BUCK, WALL, STARNES AND DAVIS, P.A. (AV)

11 North Market Street, P.O. Box 7376, 28801
Telephone: 828-258-2991
FAX: 828-255-0255; 257-2767
Hendersonville, North Carolina Office: 422 South Main Street.
Telephone: 828-697-6196.
Fax: 828-693-3999.

Kingsland Van Winkle (1879-1972)
Charles G. Buck (Retired)
Robertson Wall (1913-1996)
O. E. Starnes
Roy W. Davis, Jr.
Brian F. D. Lavelle
Larry S. McDevitt
Philip J. Smith
Barry B. Kempson
Albert L. Sneed, Jr.
Robert H. Haggard (Resident, Hendersonville)
Marla Tugwell Adams
Jones Pharr Byrd
Allan R. Tarleton
Larry C. Harris, Jr.
Michelle Rippon
William Perry Fisher, II
Michael M. Thompson (Resident, Hendersonville, North Carolina Office)
Mark A. Pinkston
Stephen J. Grabenstein
Craig D. Justus
Cynthia W. Eller
Stephen B. Williamson
Adam Langdon Shealy
John G. Kelso
Dale A. Curriden
W. Carleton Metcalf
David G. Redding

(See Next Column)

VAN WINKLE, BUCK, WALL, STARNES AND DAVIS P.A., *Asheville—Continued*

W. Kevin McLaughlin, Jr.
Jennifer Wayland Moore
Robert J. Fedder
Juliet M. Sarkessian
Carolyn Lloyd Coward

Western Region General Counsel for: Wachovia Bank & Trust Co.
Attorneys for: Carolina Power & Light Co.; Charles D. Owen Manufacturing Co.; Clyde Savings and Loan Assn.; Continental Telephone Company of N.C.; Gerber Products Co.; Liberty Mutual Insurance Co.; Reliance Insurance Co.; State Farm Mutual Automobile Insurance Co.; United States Fidelity & Guaranty Co.

For full biographical listings, see the Martindale-Hubbell Law Directory

*CHARLOTTE,** Mecklenburg Co.

CANSLER, LOCKHART, CAMPBELL, EVANS, BRYANT & GARLITZ, P.A. (AV)

2030 The Carillon, 227 West Trade Street, 28202
Telephone: 704-372-1282
Fax: 704-372-1621
URL: http://www.canslerlockhart.com

Hugh B. Campbell, Jr.
George K. Evans, Jr.
Frank L. Bryant
Thomas D. Garlitz
W. Lewis Smith, Jr.
R. Michael Allen
Stacy C. Cordes
Kristin D. Decker

Drupti P. Chauhan

OF COUNSEL

Thomas Ashe Lockhart
James B. Craighill

Representative Insurance Clients: Blue Cross/Blue Shield of North Carolina, Inc.; Companion Property & Casualty Insurance Co.; Equitable Life Assurance Society of U.S.; Guaranty National Insurance Cos.; Hartford Accident & Indemnity Co.; Integon Corp.; Metropolitan Life Insurance Co.; New York Life Insurance Co.; UNUM Life Insurance Co.; USAA Life Insurance Co.

For full biographical listings, see the Martindale-Hubbell Law Directory

CAUDLE & SPEARS, P.A. (AV)

2600 Interstate Tower, 121 West Trade Street, 28202
Telephone: 704-377-1200
Telecopier: 704-338-5858
Email: caudlespears@caudlespears.com

Lloyd C. Caudle
Harold C. Spears
L. Cameron Caudle, Jr.
Timothy T. Leach
Christopher J. Loebsack
Michael J. Selle

Counsel For: Auto-Owners Insurance; Bituminous Casualty Corp.; The A. G. Boone Co.; Consolidated Freightways; Employers Mutual Casualty Co.; Great American Insurance Company; N.C. Farm Bureau Mutual Insurance Co.; S.C. Farm Bureau.

For Complete List of Firm Personnel, See General Section

For full biographical listings, see the Martindale-Hubbell Law Directory

CREWS & KLEIN, P.C. (AV)

4500 Cameron Valley Parkway, Suite 120, P.O. Box 221648, 28222-1648
Telephone: 704-442-0660
Facsimile: 704-364-2295
Email: croftmill@aol.com

James P. Crews
Paul I. Klein
Andrew W. Lax
James N. Freeman, Jr.

For full biographical listings, see the Martindale-Hubbell Law Directory

DEAN & GIBSON, L.L.P. (AV)

Suite 900, Cameron Brown Building, 301 South McDowell Street, 28204-2686
Telephone: 704-372-2700
Facsimile: 704-372-1804
Email: info@deanandgibson.com

Rodney A. Dean
Michael G. Gibson
Brien D. Stockman
Christopher J. Culp

ASSOCIATES

John Whitelaw Ong
Colin E. Scott
Kimberly A. Gossage
Thomas G. Nance, II

OF COUNSEL

Barbara J. Dean

Representative Clients: Liberty Mutual; Nationwide Ins. Co.; St. Paul Ins. Co.; Kemper Ins. Co.; Hartford Ins. Co.; CNA Ins. Co.; Royal Ins. Co.; Travelers Ins. Co.; Firemans Fund Ins. Co.

For full biographical listings, see the Martindale-Hubbell Law Directory

GOLDING HOLDEN COSPER POPE & BAKER, L.L.P. (AV)

Suite 1200, Cameron Brown Building, 301 South McDowell Street, 28204
Telephone: 704-374-1600
Fax: 704-374-1103

MEMBERS OF FIRM

John G. Golding
C. Byron Holden
Harvey L. Cosper, Jr.
James W. Pope
Lawrence M. Baker

ASSOCIATES

Chip Holmes, Jr.
Betsy J. Jones
Tricia Y. Morvan
Robert J. Aylward
John H. Beyer
J. Timothy Sparks

Representative Clients: State Farm Insurance Companies; St. Paul Insurance Companies; Allstate Insurance Company; Integon Insurance Co.; Nationwide Mutual Insurance Companies.

For full biographical listings, see the Martindale-Hubbell Law Directory

MORRIS YORK WILLIAMS SURLES & BARRINGER, L.L.P. (AV)

525 North Tryon Street, Suite 1400, 28202
Telephone: 704-375-4480
Facsimile: 704-375-6895
URL: http://www.morrisyork.com

John F. Morris
Gregory C. York
Thomas E. Williams
Martha W. Surles
John P. Barringer
George Lee Martin
Robert Gregory Lewis
Cynthia Michelle Sain
Anna L. Baird
Paul Joseph Osowski
Demetrius L. Worley

Susan Hunt Briggs
Kevin D. Elliott
J. Huntington Wofford
John H. Capitano
Jennefer J. Cross
Hans H. Huang
L. Stephen Kushner
Elizabeth F. Schwanz
Mark D. Gustafson
Christa C. Pratt

OF COUNSEL

Jennifer S. Brearley

For full biographical listings, see the Martindale-Hubbell Law Directory

STILES BYRUM & HORNE, L.L.P. (AV)

Suite 610, Cameron Brown Building, 301 South McDowell Street, 28204
Telephone: 704-332-2830
Fax: 704-332-3281
URL: http://www.lawyers.com/sb&h

MEMBERS OF FIRM

Ned A. Stiles
Henry C. Byrum, Jr.
Terry D. Horne

ASSOCIATES

D. Lane Matthews
Mark O. Crowther

For full biographical listings, see the Martindale-Hubbell Law Directory

WOMBLE CARLYLE SANDRIDGE & RICE (AV)

A Professional Limited Liability Company
3300 One First Union Center, 301 South College Street, 28202-6025
Telephone: 704-331-4900
Fax: 704-331-4955
Email: lawyers@wcsr.com *URL:* http://www.wcsr.com
Winston-Salem, North Carolina Office: 200 West Second Street, P.O. Drawer 84.
Telephone: 336-721-3600.
Fax: 336-721-3660.
Raleigh, North Carolina Office: 2100 First Union Capitol Center, 150 Fayetteville Street Mall, P.O. Box 831.
Telephone: 919-755-2100.
Fax: 919-755-2150.
Research Triangle Park, North Carolina Office: 2505 Meridian Parkway, Suite 300 (Durham), 27713.
Telephone: 919-484-2300.
Fax: 919-484-2340.
Atlanta, Georgia Office: One Atlantic Center, 1201 West Peachtree Street, Suite 3500.
Telephone: 404-872-7000.
Fax: 404-888-7490.
Other Atlanta, Georgia Office: Suite 404, 2296 Henderson Mill Road, N.E.
Telephone: 770-492-9030.
Fax: 770-492-9609.
Washington, D.C. Office: 1120 Nineteenth Street, N.W., Eighth Floor.
Telephone: 202-857-4400.
Fax: 202-467-6910.
Greenville, South Carolina Office: 15 South Main Street, Suite 601, P.O. Box 10208.
Telephone: 864-255-5400.
Fax: 864-255-5440.

RESIDENT MEMBER

G. Michael Barnhill

(See Next Column)

WOMBLE CARLYLE SANDRIDGE & RICE—*Continued*

RESIDENT ASSOCIATE

W. Clark Goodman

Representative Clients: Childress Klein Properties, Inc.; Food Lion, Inc.; J.A. Jones Construction Co.; Parkdale Mills, Inc.; Pillowtex; Duke Power Co.; Bowles Hollowell Conner & Co.; ALLTEL Carolina, Inc.; Belk Store Services, Inc.; Philip Holzmann A.G.

For Complete List of Firm Personnel, See General Section

For full biographical listings, see the Martindale-Hubbell Law Directory

*CONCORD,** Cabarrus Co.

HARTSELL, HARTSELL & WHITE, PA (AV)

77 McCachern Boulevard, S.E., P.O. Box 368, 28025
Telephone: 704-786-5161
Facsimile: 704-788-8058
Email: HHWPA@CTC.NET

Luther T. Hartsell (1870-1961)
Luther T. Hartsell, Jr. (1902-1961)
Fletcher L. Hartsell, Jr.
J. Merritt White, III
Herbert J. White
Marilyn D. Porter
David C. Williams

OF COUNSEL

John Sharpe Hartsell (Retired)
J. Maxton Elliott (Retired)

Representative Clients: First Charter National Bank; Southern Railway Co.; Nationwide Insurance Co.; Travelers Indemnity Co.; The Shoe Show, Inc.; S & D Coffee, Inc.; Cabarrus County Board of Education; North East Medical Center; Lawyers Title Insurance Corp.; Cabarrus County.

For full biographical listings, see the Martindale-Hubbell Law Directory

*FAYETTEVILLE,** Cumberland Co.

ANDERSON, JOHNSON, LAWRENCE, BUTLER & BOCK (AV)

Suite 204 First-Citizens Bank Building, P.O. Drawer 2737, 28302-2737
Telephone: 910-483-1171
FAX: 910-483-5005

MEMBERS OF FIRM

Henry L. Anderson (1911-1986)
Hal W. Broadfoot (1929-1994)
Lee Best Johnson
John Huske Anderson, II
Steven C. Lawrence
J. Stewart Butler, III
A. David Bock

ASSOCIATES

Catherine Ross Dunham
Robert A. Hasty, Jr.

Representative Clients: North Carolina Farm Bureau Mutual Insurance Co.; Integon; Nationwide Insurance Company; GEICO; Allstate Insurance Company; Shelter Insurance Company; Canal Insurance Company; Providian Insurance Company; Professional Risk Management Services, Inc.; TIG.

For full biographical listings, see the Martindale-Hubbell Law Directory

*GREENSBORO,** Guilford Co.

BURTON & SUE, L.L.P. (AV)

419 North Elm Street, P.O. Box 20083, 27420
Telephone: 336-275-0512
Facsimile: 336-378-1390

MEMBERS OF FIRM

Gary K. Sue
Walter K. Burton

ASSOCIATES

James D Secor, III
William T. Corbett, Jr.
William L. Hill
Kurt A. Seeber

For full biographical listings, see the Martindale-Hubbell Law Directory

HENSON & HENSON, L.L.P. (AV)

Suite 600, The Piedmont Building, 114 North Elm Street, 27401
Telephone: 336-275-0587
Facsimile: 336-273-2585
Mailing Address: P.O. Box 3525, 27402,
Email: hensnlaw@bellsouth.net

MEMBERS OF FIRM

Perry C. Henson
Perry C. Henson, Jr.

ASSOCIATE

Clayton B. Krohn

Representative Clients: Canal Ins. Company; Employers Mutual Insurance Companies; Erie Insurance Group; Fireman's Fund Ins. Company; Frontier Risk Managers; IHDS Corporation; K & K Insurance Group; Kentucky Medical Insurance Company; Kmart Corporation; Lawyers Mutual Liability Ins. Co.

For full biographical listings, see the Martindale-Hubbell Law Directory

PINTO COATES KYRE & BROWN, PLLC (AV)

3203 Brassfield Road, 27410
Telephone: 336-282-8848
Facsimile: 336-282-8409
Mailing Address: P.O. Box 4848, Greensboro, N.C., 27404
Email: PCKB@Interpath.com

Richard L. Pinto
Paul D. Coates
Kenneth Kyre, Jr.
David L. Brown
Martha P. Brown
Nancy R. Meyers
John I. Malone, Jr.
Deborah J. Bowers

Representative Clients: Travelers; Grain Dealers Mutual Insurance Co.; N.C. Farm Bureau Insurance Co.; Southern Pilot Insurance Co.; Peerless Insurance Co.; Penn National Insurance Co.; Virginia Mutual Insurance Co.; GAB Business Services; Harleysville Mutual Insurance Co.; Selective Insurance.

For full biographical listings, see the Martindale-Hubbell Law Directory

*GREENVILLE,** Pitt Co.

GAYLORD, MCNALLY, STRICKLAND & SNYDER, L.L.P. (AV)

498 Red Banks Road, P.O. Drawer 545, 27835-0545
Telephone: 252-321-7111
Fax: 252-321-7112

MEMBERS OF FIRM

Louis W. Gaylord, Jr. (Retired)
Danny D. McNally
D. Michael Strickland
Vernon G. Snyder, III

ASSOCIATE

Emma Stallings Holscher

Representative Clients: Wachovia Bank, N.A.; Nationsbank, N.A.; Garris Evans Lumber Co., Inc.; United States Fidelity and Guaranty Co.; The Daily Reflector, Inc.; Hastings Ford, Inc.; Nationwide Mutual Insurance Co.; U.S. Cellular; Ironwood Development, Inc.

For full biographical listings, see the Martindale-Hubbell Law Directory

*LOUISBURG,** Franklin Co.

DAVIS, STURGES & TOMLINSON (AV)

DSS Building, 101 North Church Street, P.O. Drawer 708, 27549
Telephone: 919-496-2137
Telecopier: 919-496-6291

MEMBERS OF FIRM

Charles M. Davis
Conrad B. Sturges, Jr.
Aubrey S. Tomlinson, Jr.
John Wyatt Davis

ASSOCIATE

C. Boyd Sturges, III

General Counsel for: National American Corp.
Representative Clients: Kemper Insurance Co.; Union Camp Corp.
Approved Attorneys for: Lawyers Title Insurance Corp.; Fidelity National Insurance Co.
References: First Citizens Bank & Trust Co.; United Carolina Bank.

For full biographical listings, see the Martindale-Hubbell Law Directory

*RALEIGH,** Wake Co.

BAILEY & DIXON, L.L.P. (AV)

2500 Two Hannover Square, 434 Fayetteville Street Mall, P.O. Box 1351, 27602
Telephone: 919-828-0731
Facsimile: 919-828-6592
Email: info@bdixon.com *URL:* http://www.bdixon.com

MEMBERS OF FIRM

Ralph McDonald
Gary S. Parsons
Carson Carmichael, III
Alan J. Miles
Patricia P. Kerner
Cathleen M. Plaut
David S. Coats
M. Denise Stanford
Kenyann Brown Stanford

OF COUNSEL

J. Ruffin Bailey
Wright T. Dixon, Jr. (Retired)
James H. Walker (1920-1994)
David M. Britt

ASSOCIATES

David Scott Wisz
Warren Tobin Savage, IV
Rita Lane Hanshumaker
Dayatra T. King
Philip Todd Gray
Ali John Hoomani

Representative Clients: North Carolina League of Municipalities Risk Management Services; Lawyers Mutual Liability Insurance Company of North Carolina; Interlocal Risk Financing Fund of North Carolina; Nationwide Insurance Company; Liberty Mutual Insurance Co.; Erie Insurance Company; Southern Pilot Insurance Co.; Hartford Insurance Group; Scottsdale Insurance Co.; State Auto Insurance Companies.

For full biographical listings, see the Martindale-Hubbell Law Directory

Raleigh—Continued

CRANFILL, SUMNER & HARTZOG, L.L.P. (AV)

Hillsborough Place, 225 Hillsborough Street, Suite 300, P.O. Box 27808, 27611-7808
Telephone: 919-828-5100
Fax: 919-828-2277
Charlotte, North Carolina Office: 301 South McDowell Street, Suite 1100.
Telephone: 704-332-8300.
Fax: 704-332-9994.

MEMBERS OF FIRM

Paul L. Cranfill
Robert W. Sumner
Dan M. Hartzog, Managing Partner
Alene M. Mercer
Richard T. Boyette
David D. Ward
Patricia L. Holland
David H. Batten
H. Lee Evans, Jr.
C. D. Taylor Pace
Samuel H. Poole, Jr. (Resident, Charlotte Office)
Susan K. Burkhart
Buxton S. Copeland
P. Collins Barwick, III
Robert H. Griffin
David A. Rhoades
Kari Russwurm Johnson
Stephanie Hutchins Autry
M. Andrew Avram (Resident, Charlotte Office)
Gregory M. Kash
Joseph B. Chambliss, Jr.
Anthony T. Lathrop (Resident, Charlotte Office)
Robin H. Terry
William W. Pollock
Patrick H Flanagan
Emerson M. Thompson III
Brady W. Wells
Scott J. Lasso
W. Scott Fuller

ASSOCIATES

Nicholas Peter Valaoras (Resident, Charlotte Office)
William J. Garrity (Resident, Charlotte Office)
Edward C. Lecarpentier III
Leigh Ann G. Smith
Jonathan C. Anders
Maranda J. Freeman
H. Vance Barnette, III
Colleen N. Shea
Kirk D. Kuhns
Gregory W. Brown
Jaye Elizabeth Bingham
David D. Larson, Jr.
Beth R. Fleishman
Jeffrey C. Thompson (Resident, Charlotte Office)
Ann Smith Estridge
Gregory Newton
Donna R. Rascoe
Norwood P. Blanchard, III
C. Houston Foppiano
James Bell Black, IV
Erin E. Fleming
Elizabeth K. Freeman
F. Marshall Wall

Representative Clients: American International Group; CNA Insurance Cos.; Great American Insurance Group; ITT Hartford; The Kemper Group; Liberty Mutual Insurance Co.; The Medical Protective Co.; The PMA Group; Safeco Insurance Co.; St. Paul Insurance Co.

For full biographical listings, see the Martindale-Hubbell Law Directory

LEWIS & ROBERTS, P.L.L.C. (AV)

1305 Navaho Drive, Suite 400, 27609-7482
Telephone: 919-981-0191
888-981-0939
Facsimile: 919-981-0199
Mailing Address: P.O. Box 17529, Raleigh, N.C., 27619-7529
Rock Hill, South Carolina Office: 448 Lakeshore Parkway, Suite 200.
Telephone: 803-324-8118.
Facsimile: 803-324-2093.

Richard M. Lewis
James A. Roberts, III
Steven M. Rudisill (Resident, Rock Hill, South Carolina Office)
Winston L. Page, Jr.
Timothy S. Riordan
Jack Spain Holmes
Daniel K. Bryson
John D. Elvers
A. Graham Shirley
Brian D. Lake
John H. Ruocchio
Robert L. Pratt
Garth Hinsdale White (Resident, Rock Hill, South Carolina Office)
Devin Ferree Thomas
James T. Johnson
Daniel T. Tower

For full biographical listings, see the Martindale-Hubbell Law Directory

PATTERSON, DILTHEY, CLAY & BRYSON, L.L.P. (AV)

4020 Westchase Boulevard, Suite 550, 27607
Telephone: 919-821-4020
Fax: 919-829-0055
URL: HTTP://WWW.PDCB.COM
Wilmington, North Carolina Office: 2214-C Wrightsville Avenue.
Telephone: 910-762-6544.
Fax: 910-762-4241.

MEMBERS OF FIRM

Grady S. Patterson, Jr. (Retired)
Ronald C. Dilthey
Robert M. Clay
E. C. Bryson, Jr.
Reid Russell
Stuart L. Egerton (Resident, Wilmington Office)
Mark E. Anderson
Donna Renfrow Rutala
Phillip J. Anthony
G. Lawrence Reeves, Jr.
Jonathan E. Hall

(See Next Column)

ASSOCIATES

Charles George
Mary McHugh Webb
Charles A. Madison
Claire A. Modlin
Scott B. Goodson
Sean A.B. Cole
Christian Michael Kennedy
Christopher J. Derrenbacher
J. Scott Lewis
Christopher M. Hinnant (Resident, Wilmington Office)
Patrick M. Meacham
Daniel M. Gaylord

Representative Clients: Amica Mutual Insurance Co.; Great American Insurance Group; Kemper Insurance Group; Medical Protective Insurance Co.

For full biographical listings, see the Martindale-Hubbell Law Directory

TEAGUE, CAMPBELL, DENNIS & GORHAM, L.L.P. (AV)

1621 Midtown Place, 27609
Telephone: 919-873-0166
Facsimile: 919-873-1814
URL: http://www.tcdg.com
Lumberton, North Carolina Office: 408 North Chestnut Street, P.O. Box 1424.
Telephone: 910-738-8534.

MEMBERS OF FIRM

C. Woodrow Teague
George W. Dennis III
Henry W. Gorham
Dayle A. Flammia
Linda Stephens
Thomas M. Clare
Robert C. Kerner, Jr.
John A. Tomei
Bruce Alan Hamilton
George H. Pender

ASSOCIATES

Donald F. Lively
Bryan T. Simpson
J. Matthew Little
Gregory M. Willis
Mallory A. Taylor
Jan N. Pittman
Kurt F. Hausler
John R. Green, Jr.
Melissa R. Garrell
Heather L. Aberle
Michael P. Williams
Tracey L. Jones

OF COUNSEL

John Wishart Campbell (Resident at Lumberton Office)
Marilyn Ellison Tomei

LEGAL SUPPORT PERSONNEL

William H. Stephenson

Representative Clients: AIG; Budget Rent-A-Car Corp.; Winn-Dixie Stores, Inc.; CNA Insurance Companies; Bituminous Insurance Co.; Orion Auto, Inc.; Seibels Bruce and Company; Southern Guaranty Insurance Co.; Weyerhaeuser Company; Universal Insurance Company.

For full biographical listings, see the Martindale-Hubbell Law Directory

WOMBLE CARLYLE SANDRIDGE & RICE (AV)

A Professional Limited Liability Company
2100 First Union Capitol Center, 150 Fayetteville Street Mall, P.O. Box 831, 27602
Telephone: 919-755-2100
Fax: 919-755-2150
Email: lawyers@wcsr.com *URL:* http://www.wcsr.com
Charlotte, North Carolina Office: 3300 One First Union Center, 301 South College Street.
Telephone: 704-331-4900.
Fax: 704-331-4955.
Winston-Salem, North Carolina Office: 200 West Second Street, P.O. Drawer 84.
Telephone: 336-721-3600.
Fax: 336-721-3660.
Research Triangle Park, North Carolina Office: 2505 Meridian Parkway, Suite 300 (Durham), 27713.
Telephone: 919-484-2300.
Fax: 919-484-2340.
Atlanta, Georgia Office: One Atlantic Center, 1201 West Peachtree Street, Suite 3500.
Telephone: 404-872-7000.
Fax: 404-888-7490.
Other Atlanta, Georgia Office: Suite 404, 2296 Henderson Mill Road, N.E.
Telephone: 770-492-9030.
Fax: 770-492-9609.
Washington, D.C. Office: 1120 Nineteenth Street, N.W., Eighth Floor.
Telephone: 202-857-4400.
Fax: 202-467-6910.
Greenville, South Carolina Office: 15 South Main Street, Suite 601, P.O. Box 10208.
Telephone: 864-255-5400.
Fax: 864-255-5440.

RESIDENT MEMBER

Robert H. Sasser, III

RESIDENT ASSOCIATES

Mark A. Davis
G. Christopher Olson

Representative Clients: Aetna Casualty and Surety Co., Inc.; ALSCO/AmeriMark Building Products, Inc.; Aoki Corporation America, Inc.; Hackney Brothers, Inc.; Lawyers Mutual Liability Insurance Company of North Carolina; Meredith College; Regency Park Corp.; Wachovia Bank, N.A.

(See Next Column)

WOMBLE CARLYLE SANDRIDGE & RICE—*Continued*

For Complete List of Firm Personnel, See General Section

For full biographical listings, see the Martindale-Hubbell Law Directory

YATES, McLAMB & WEYHER, L.L.P. (AV)

One Hannover Square, 421 Fayetteville Street Mall, Suite 1200, 27601
Telephone: 919-835-0900
Fax: 919-835-0910
Mailing Address: P.O. Box 2889, 27602-2889

MEMBERS OF FIRM

R. Scott Brown
Derek M. Crump
Dan J. McLamb
John W. Minier
Rodney E. Pettey
O. Craig Tierney, Jr.
Andrew A. Vanore, III
Kirk G. Warner
Barbara B. Weyher
Joseph W. Yates, III (Retired)

ASSOCIATES

Virginia Green Adams
Michael J. Byrne
Hunt K. Choi
Barry S. Cobb
Renee Billings Crawford
Susan T. Fountain
Gwenda L. Laws
Michael E. McDaniel
Travis K. Morton
Shirley Maring Pruitt
Beth Y. Smoot
Diane S. Tilley
Michael W. Washburn

OF COUNSEL

Michael C. Hurley

Representative Clients: Aetna Casualty & Surety Co.; Allstate Insurance Co.; CIGNA Cos.; Kemper Insurance Group; Nationwide Insurance Co.; North Carolina Farm Bureau Mutual Insurance Co.; Shelby Mutual Insurance Co.; St. Paul Insurance Cos.; Zurich Insurance Group.

For full biographical listings, see the Martindale-Hubbell Law Directory

*SALISBURY,** Rowan Co.

KLUTTZ, REAMER, BLANKENSHIP, HAYES & RANDOLPH, L.L.P. (AV)

131 North Main Street, P.O. Drawer 1617, 28145-1617
Telephone: 704-636-7100
Telecopier: 704-636-2284
Email: kluttzlaw@salisbury.net

Wm. Clarence Kluttz (1917-1996)
Lewis P. Hamlin, Jr. (1919-1988)
Richard R. Reamer
Malcolm B. Blankenship, Jr.
William C. Kluttz, Jr.
Glenn S. Hayes
James D.K.F. Randolph

ASSOCIATE

Roman C. Pibl

Representative Clients: Nationwide Mutual Insurance Company; Kemper National Insurance Companies; N.C. Farm Bureau Insurance Company; Va. Mutual Insurance Company; AETNA; USAA Property & Casualty Insurance; Auto Owners; Harleysville Mutual Insurance Company.

For full biographical listings, see the Martindale-Hubbell Law Directory

*WILKESBORO,** Wilkes Co.

WILLARDSON & LIPSCOMB, LLP (AV)

206 East Main Street, 28697
Telephone: 336-838-5129
Fax: 336-838-8959

MEMBERS OF FIRM

John S. Willardson
William F. Lipscomb

Representative Clients: Travelers Insurance; North Carolina Farm Bureau Mutual Insurance Co.; Allstate Insurance Company; Nationwide Insurance Company; Integon General Insurance.

For full biographical listings, see the Martindale-Hubbell Law Directory

*WILMINGTON,** New Hanover Co.

HOGUE, HILL, JONES, NASH AND LYNCH, L.L.P. (AV)

101 S. Third Street, P.O. Drawer 2178, 28402
Telephone: 910-763-4565
Telecopier: 910-762-6687

MEMBERS OF FIRM

Cyrus D. Hogue (1888-1960)
W. Talmage Jones
David A. Nash
William O. J. Lynch
James B. Snow, III
Wayne A. Bullard

OF COUNSEL

Cyrus D. Hogue, Jr.
William L. Hill, II
Roy C. Bain

ASSOCIATE

Stacey L. Fuller

Representative Clients: Lancer Claims Service; Cigna Insurance Company; Horace Mann Insurance Co.; Canal Insurance Co.; Federated Mutual Insurance Co.; Colonial Penn Insurance Co.; World Insurance Co.; Colonia Insurance Co.; Underwriters Service Co.; CNL Insurance America.

(See Next Column)

For full biographical listings, see the Martindale-Hubbell Law Directory

JOHNSON & LAMBETH (AV)

232 Princess Street, P.O. Box 660, 28402
Telephone: 910-763-0481
Fax: 910-251-1276
Email: johnlam@wilmington.net

MEMBERS OF FIRM

Robert White Johnson
Carter Tate Lambeth
Maynard M. Brown
Beth M. Bryant
John Gregory Tillery, III

References: BB & T; NationsBank.

For full biographical listings, see the Martindale-Hubbell Law Directory

*WINSTON-SALEM,** Forsyth Co.

BENNETT & GUTHRIE, P.L.L.C. (AV)

3334 Healy Drive, Suite 203, 27103-1476
Telephone: 336-765-3121
Fax: 336-765-8622

Richard V. Bennett
Rodney A. Guthrie
Stanley P. Dean

Kevin J. Williams

Representative Clients: American Continental Insurance Company; Commercial Union Insurance Company; Integon Insurance; Kentucky Medical Insurance Company; Medtronic, Inc.; Montgomery Mutual Insurance Company; Novant Health, Inc.; Pennsylvania Lumberman's Mutual Insurance Company; St. Paul Fire & Marine Insurance Company; Zurich Insurance Company.

For full biographical listings, see the Martindale-Hubbell Law Directory

CRAIGE, BRAWLEY, LIIPFERT & WALKER, L.L.P. (AV)

500 West Fourth Street, Suite 200, P.O. Box 1666, 27102-1666
Telephone: 336-725-0583
Fax: 336-725-4677

MEMBERS OF FIRM

Cowles Liipfert
William W. Walker
B. Bailey Liipfert, III

ASSOCIATES

John A. Keiger
J. Laross Ketner
Robert A. Lefkowitz
Brent Wayne Stephens
Robert Martin Addison

Approved Attorneys for: Lawyers Title Insurance Corp.; Chicago Title Insurance Co.; Commonwealth Land Title Insurance Co.; First American Title Insurance Co.; Jefferson-Pilot Title Insurance Co.

For full biographical listings, see the Martindale-Hubbell Law Directory

WOMBLE CARLYLE SANDRIDGE & RICE (AV)

A Professional Limited Liability Company
200 West Second Street, P.O. Drawer 84, 27102
Telephone: 336-721-3600
Fax: 336-721-3660
Email: lawyers@wcsr.com *URL:* http://www.wcsr.com
Charlotte, North Carolina Office: 3300 One First Union Center, 301 South College Street.
Telephone: 704-331-4900.
Fax: 704-331-4955.
Raleigh, North Carolina Office: 2100 First Union Capitol Center, 150 Fayetteville Street Mall, P.O. Box 831.
Telephone: 919-755-2100.
Fax: 919-755-2150.
Research Triangle Park, North Carolina Office: 2505 Meridian Parkway, Suite 300 (Durham), 27713.
Telephone: 919-484-2300.
Fax: 919-484-2340.
Atlanta, Georgia Office: One Atlantic Center, 1201 West Peachtree Street, Suite 3500.
Telephone: 404-872-7000.
Fax: 404-888-7490.
Other Atlanta, Georgia Office: Suite 404, 2296 Henderson Mill Road, N.E.
Telephone: 770-492-9030.
Fax: 770-492-9609.
Washington, D.C. Office: 1120 Nineteenth Street, N.W., Eighth Floor.
Telephone: 202-857-4400.
Fax: 202-467-6910.
Greenville, South Carolina Office: 15 South Main Street, Suite 601, P.O. Box 10208.
Telephone: 864-255-5400.
Fax: 864-255-5440.

RESIDENT MEMBERS

Reid C. Adams, Jr.
S. Fraley Bost
Clayton M. Custer
Tyrus V. Dahl, Jr.
Allan R. Gitter
James R. Morgan, Jr.
Richard T. Rice

(See Next Column)

WOMBLE CARLYLE SANDRIDGE & RICE, *Winston-Salem—Continued*

RESIDENT ASSOCIATES

Alison R. Bost
Andrew C. Buckner
Philip J. Mohr
Stacey M. Stone
Jack M. Strauch

MEMBER OF COUNSEL

Dewey W. Wells

Representative Clients: Brad Ragan, Inc.; Brenner Companies; Food Lion, Inc.; Hanes Companies, Inc.; North Carolina Baptist Hospitals, Inc.; R.J. Reynolds Tobacco Co.; Thomasville Furniture Industries, Inc.; Wachovia Corp.; Wake Forest University.

For Complete List of Firm Personnel, See General Section

For full biographical listings, see the Martindale-Hubbell Law Directory

WRIGHTSVILLE BEACH, New Hanover Co.

ANDERSON, DANIEL & COXE (AV)

527 Causeway Drive, P.O. Box 1309, 28480
Telephone: 910-256-6896
Fax: 910-256-3472
Email: bcoxe@wilmington.net

Henry L. Anderson, Jr.
A. L. Butler Daniel
Bradley A. Coxe

For full biographical listings, see the Martindale-Hubbell Law Directory

NORTH DAKOTA

*BISMARCK,** Burleigh Co.

PEARCE AND DURICK, PLLP (AV)

314 East Thayer Avenue, P.O. Box 400, 58502
Telephone: 701-223-2890
Fax: 701-223-7865
Email: law.office@pearce-durick.com *URL:* http://www.pearce-durick.com

MEMBERS OF FIRM

Patrick W. Durick
B. Timothy Durick
Gary R. Thune
David E. Reich
Jerome C. Kettleson
Larry L. Boschee

ASSOCIATE

Jonathan P. Sanstead

Representative Clients: American Insurance Assn.; Attorneys Liability Protection Society; Cigna-INA Insurance Co.; Millers First Insurance Companies; North Dakota Insurance Reserve Fund; Royal Insurance Co.; Travelers Insurance Co.; United Fire and Casualty Co.; Zurich-American Insurance Group.

For Complete List of Firm Personnel, See General Section

For full biographical listings, see the Martindale-Hubbell Law Directory

*FARGO,** Cass Co.

NILLES, HANSEN & DAVIES, LTD. (AV)

1800 Radisson Tower, P.O. Box 2626, 58108
Telephone: 701-237-5544
Facsimile: 701-280-0762
Williston, North Dakota Office: Energy Resource Building, 504 East Broadway, Suite 101, P.O. Box 1525.
Telephone: 701-572-5544.
Fax: 701-572-5561.

Timothy Q. Davies
Duane H. Ilvedson
E. Thomas Conmy, III
Stephen W. Plambeck
Leo F. J. Wilking
Richard Henderson
William P. Harrie
Mark R. Hanson
Harry M. Pippin
Douglas W. Gigler
Joel M. Fremstad

Representative Clients: Fireman's Fund Insurance Group Companies; Blue Cross and Blue Shield; CNA Insurance Companies; Nodak Mutual Insurance Company; Farmers Insurance Group; U.S. Fidelity & Guaranty Company; Coregis; Aetna Life & Casualty Group; U.S.A.A.; Employers Mutual Companies.

For Complete List of Firm Personnel, See General Section

For full biographical listings, see the Martindale-Hubbell Law Directory

VOGEL, WEIR, BYE, HUNKE & MCCORMICK, LTD. (AV)

502 First Avenue North, P.O. Box 1389, 58107
Telephone: 701-237-6983
Facsimile: 701-237-0847
Email: vogellaw@vogellaw.com *URL:* http://www.vogellaw.com

(See Next Column)

Carlton J. Hunke
Mart Daniel Vogel
W. Todd Haggart
Bruce Douglas Quick
Wayne W. Carlson

Representative Clients: Acceptance Insurance Company; All Nation Insurance Company; Allied Group Insurance; American Family Insurance Group; American Life & Casualty Company; American West Insurance Company; Auto Owners Insurance Company; Automobile Club Insurance Company; Center Mutual Insurance Company; Chubb Group of Insurance Companies.

For Complete List of Firm Personnel, See General Section

For full biographical listings, see the Martindale-Hubbell Law Directory

OHIO

*AKRON,** Summit Co.

OLDHAM & DOWLING (AV)

195 South Main Street Suite 300, 44308
Telephone: 330-762-7377
Telecopier: 330-762-7390
Email: wdowling@oldham-dowling.com *URL:* http://www.lawyers.com/oldham&dowling

William M. Oldham
William D. Dowling, Jr.
Hamilton DeSaussure, Jr.
Martin R. Hulthen
Joseph K. Oldham
Raymond C. Mueller
Blake R. Gerney

Representative Clients: State Farm Mutual Automobile Insurance Co.; State Farm Mutual Fire Insurance Co.; Ohio Casualty Group Insurance Companies; Step II Corp.; WCI Steel Inc.; American States Insurance Co.; Taco Bell Corp.; May Company Department Stores; National City Bank, Masco.
Reference: Key Bank.

For full biographical listings, see the Martindale-Hubbell Law Directory

PERANTINIDES & NOLAN CO., L.P.A. (AV)

300 Courtyard Square, 80 South Summit Street, 44308-1736
Telephone: 330-253-5454
Telecopier: 330-253-6524
Email: pn@perantinides.com

Paul G. Perantinides
Chris T. Nolan

James J. Gutbrod
Christopher L. Parker
Peter D. Janos
Antonios P. Tsarouhas
Christina Simoudis
Sophie Mitsopoulos

References: First National Bank of Akron; National City Bank, Akron; Society Bank; Charter One Bank.

For full biographical listings, see the Martindale-Hubbell Law Directory

ASHTABULA, Ashtabula Co.

WARREN AND YOUNG PLL (AV)

134 West 46th Street, P.O. Box 2300, 44005-2300
Telephone: 440-997-6175
Facsimile: 440-992-9114
URL: http://www.warrenyoung.com

William E. Riedel
Carl F. Muller

For Complete List of Firm Personnel, See General Section

For full biographical listings, see the Martindale-Hubbell Law Directory

*BATAVIA,** Clermont Co.

ELY AND TRUE (AV)

322 Main Street, 45103
Telephone: 513-732-2140
Fax: 513-732-0692

MEMBERS OF FIRM

Forrest E. Ely (1901-1981)
John S. Moore (1914-1991)
Rex E. Ely
J. Robert True
Gary D. Ostendarp
James C. Henderson
Richard P. Ferenc

Counsel for: The Cincinnati Gas & Electric Co.; American States Insurance Cos.; GRE Insurance Group; Heritage Mutual Insurance Co.; Motorists Mutual Insurance Co.; Nationwide Mutual Insurance Co.; State Automobile Mutual Insurance Co.; Travelers Insurance Co.; United Ohio Insurance Co.

For full biographical listings, see the Martindale-Hubbell Law Directory

*CANTON,** Stark Co.

BAKER, DUBLIKAR, BECK, WILEY & MATHEWS (AV)

205 Mellett Building, 115 DeWalt Avenue, N.W., 44702
Telephone: 330-453-4999
Telecopier: 330-455-0333

MEMBERS OF FIRM

Jack R. Baker
Ralph F. Dublikar
Gregory A. Beck
Donald P. Wiley
James F. Mathews
Mel L. Lute, Jr.

ASSOCIATES

Melissa S. Ulrich
Daniel J. Funk
Stephen E. Matasich
Elizabeth Ann Warg

For full biographical listings, see the Martindale-Hubbell Law Directory

*CINCINNATI,** Hamilton Co.

ROBERT J. GEHRING CO., L.P.A. (AV)

4th Floor, 105 East Fourth Street, 45202
Telephone: 513-721-2758
Fax: 513-621-9285

Robert J. Gehring

For full biographical listings, see the Martindale-Hubbell Law Directory

KEATING, MUETHING & KLEKAMP, P.L.L. (AV)

1400 Provident Tower, One East Fourth Street, 45202
Telephone: 513-579-6400
Facsimile: 513-579-6457
URL: http://www.kmklaw.com

MEMBERS OF FIRM

W. Keith Noel
Daniel J. Donnellon
Daniel E. Izenson
Gail King
Pamela Morgan Hodge

Representative Clients: American Financial Group; BP America Inc.; Chiquita Brands International, Inc.; Cintas Corporation; Comair Holdings, Inc.; Duke Realty Limited Partnership; LSI Industries Inc.; Mosler Inc.; Provident Financial Group Inc.

For Complete List of Firm Personnel, See General Section

For full biographical listings, see the Martindale-Hubbell Law Directory

LINDHORST & DREIDAME CO., L.P.A. (AV)

312 Walnut Street, Suite 2300, 45202-4091
Telephone: 513-421-6630
Telecopier: 513-421-0212

Ambrose H. Lindhorst (1913-1997)
Robert F. Dreidame (1914-1978)
William J. Walsh (1919-1996)

SENIOR COUNSEL

Leo J. Breslin
James L. O'Connell
William M. Cussen
Charles J. Kelly
John A. Goldberg
William N. Kirkham
James M. Moore
James H. Smith, III
Jay R. Langenbahn
Thomas E. Martin
James F. Brockman
Michael F. Lyon
Edward S. Dorsey
Harold L. Anness
Dale A. Stalf
Gary F. Franke

Peter C. Newberry

Representative Clients: CNA; CSX Corp.; Fireman's Fund-American Group; Medical Protective Co.; Norfolk Southern Corp.; Roadway Express, Inc.; Sibcy Cline, Inc.; Jewish Hospital; T.W. Smith Aircraft, Inc.; U.S.F.&G.

For Complete List of Firm Personnel, See General Section

For full biographical listings, see the Martindale-Hubbell Law Directory

STRAUSS & TROY A LEGAL PROFESSIONAL ASSOCIATION (AV)

The Federal Reserve Building, 150 East Fourth Street, 45202-4018
Telephone: 513-621-2120
Telecopier: 513-241-8259
URL: http://www.strauss-troy.com
Northern Kentucky Office: Suite 1400, 50 East Rivercenter Boulevard, Covington, Kentucky, 41011.
Telephone: 513-621-8900; 513-621-2120.
Telecopier: 513-629-9444.

R. Guy Taft
Paul B. Calico

OF COUNSEL

Charles G. Atkins

Representative Clients: PNC Bank, N.A. (Ohio and Kentucky); Corporex Companies, Inc.; Mercantile Stores Co., Inc.; Star Bank, N.A. (Ohio and Kentucky).

(See Next Column)

For Complete List of Firm Personnel, See General Section

For full biographical listings, see the Martindale-Hubbell Law Directory

*CLEVELAND,** Cuyahoga Co.

DAVIS & YOUNG (AV)

A Legal Professional Association
1700 Midland Building, 44115
Telephone: 216-348-1700
Fax: 216-621-0602
Cable: DANDY CLE
Email: atty@davisyoung.com *URL:* http://www.davisyoung.com
Akron, Ohio Office: 1015 Society Building, 159 South Main Street. Telephone 216-376-1717.
Fax: 216-376-1797.
Youngstown, Ohio Office: 406 Wick Building, 34 Federal Plaza West, 44503.
Telephone: 330-743-1717.

George W. Lutjen
Martin J. Murphy
C. Richard McDonald
Paul D. Eklund
Jan L. Roller
Thomas W. Wright
David J. Fagnilli
Gregory H. Collins
William Vance
Patrick F. Roche

David G. Utley
Timothy L. Kerwin
Marc A. Sanchez
Ann Marie O'Brien
Susan L. Fricker
Michele Y. Wharton
Larry D. Wilkes
Timothy G. Welsh

OF COUNSEL

R. Emmett Moran

Counsel for: Aetna Insurance Co.; Alliance Insurance Co.; Amerisure Companies; Cincinnati Insurance Co.; Central Mutual Insurance Co.; Great American Insurance Co.; John Hancock Property & Casualty Co.; Motorist Mutual Insurance Co.; St. Paul Property & Liability; Unigard Insurance Group.

For Complete List of Firm Personnel, See General Section

For full biographical listings, see the Martindale-Hubbell Law Directory

GALLAGHER, SHARP, FULTON & NORMAN (AV)

(Formerly Hauxhurst, Sharp, Mollison & Gallagher)
Bulkley Building, Seventh Floor, 1501 Euclid Avenue, 44115
Telephone: 216-241-5310
Telecopier: 216-241-1608
Email: gsfn.com *URL:* http://www.gsfn.com

MEMBERS OF FIRM

H. Austin Hauxhurst (1881-1962)
Frank X. Cull (1887-1965)
I. Walter Sharp (1884-1966)
Clarence L. Mollison (1906-1981)
Robert C. Horrigan (1916-1993)
Forrest A. Norman
Edward J. Cass
John B. Robertson
Thomas E. Betz
Alan M. Petrov
Alton L. Stephens, Jr.
Virginia L. Heidloff
Jay Clinton Rice
Joseph W. Pappalardo
Thomas E. Dover
James F. Koehler
Robert H. Eddy
Thomas J. Kaiser
D John Travis
Paul J. Schumacher, Jr.
William F. Gibson
Gary L. Nicholson
Lynn L. Moore
Ernest W. Auciello, Jr.
Patrick M. Foy
Kevin C. Alexandersen
Stanley M. Dub
Timothy T. Brick
Sheila A. McKeon
Thomas J. Cabral
Timothy J. Fitzgerald
Mark A. Greer

OF COUNSEL

Michael R. Gallagher
Robert W. Sharp
George W. Stuhldreher
Burt J. Fulton
James F. Sweeney
James G. Gowan
James L. Ryhal, Jr.

Edward G. Kagels
John T. Murphy
M. Terence Cawley
Todd M. Haemmerle
Brian R. McGraw
Timothy P. Whitford
Daniel J. Michalec
Alexander E. Goetsch
Joseph J. Santoro
Monica A. Sansalone
John A. Simon
Dennis G. Rehor
Beth A. Nagel
Timothy Patrick Roth
Gregory K. Boop
Janice Aitken
Gary F. Werner
Mark Joseph Savage
Catherine A. Davis
Charles Allston Bowers
Pamela S. Schremp
James T. Tyminski, Jr.
Matthew J. Hatchadorian

STAFF ATTORNEY

Daniel L. Herak

Counsel for: Associated Aviation Underwriters; Conrail; The Continental Insurance Cos.; Continental National American Group; Fireman's Fund Insurance Cos.; The Home Insurance Co.; Motorist Ins. Co.; Norfolk Southern Corp.; Royal Insurance Co.; United States Aviation Underwriters.

(See Next Column)

GALLAGHER, SHARP, FULTON & NORMAN, *Cleveland—Continued*

For full biographical listings, see the Martindale-Hubbell Law Directory

HERMANN, CAHN & SCHNEIDER (AV)

Suite 500, 1301 East Ninth Street, 44114
Telephone: 216-781-5515
Facsimile: 216-781-1030
Email: hcs@en.com

MEMBERS OF FIRM

Gary D. Hermann
Kerry S. Volsky
Anthony J. Hartman
Peter J. Krembs

ASSOCIATES

Jay H. Salamon
Thomas P. Marotta
Romney B. Cullers

Representative Clients: Allstate Insurance Co.; Farmers Insurance Companies; Great Central Insurance Co.; Foremost Insurance Co.; Transamerica Insurance Co.; Wausau Insurance Cos.; Maryland Casualty Co.; Occidental Fire & Casualty Co.; Progressive Insurance Co.

For full biographical listings, see the Martindale-Hubbell Law Directory

JANIK & FORBES (AV)

Building Two, 8223 Brecksville Road, 44141-1371
Telephone: 440-838-7600
Fax: 440-838-7601

MEMBERS OF FIRM

Steven G. Janik
Steven Forbes

For Complete List of Firm Personnel, See General Section

For full biographical listings, see the Martindale-Hubbell Law Directory

JOHNSON AND ANGELO (AV)

1001 Lakeside Avenue, Suite 1700, 44114
Telephone: 216-696-5222
Fax: 216-696-5288

MEMBERS OF FIRM

Gary C. Johnson
Michael J. Angelo

ASSOCIATES

James A. Budzik
Gina A. Kuhlman
Thomas L. Colaluca
William F. Schmitz
Jack P. DeSario
Jeffrey C. Miller
Jack L. Petronelli
Amy L. Phillips

For full biographical listings, see the Martindale-Hubbell Law Directory

JONES, DAY, REAVIS & POGUE (AV)

North Point, 901 Lakeside Avenue, 44114
Telephone: 216-586-3939
Telecopier: 216-579-0212
Email: counsel@jonesday.com *URL:* http://www.jonesday.com
In Columbus, Ohio: 1900 Huntington Center.
Telephone: 614-469-3939.
Telecopier: 614-461-4198.
In Atlanta, Georgia: 3500 SunTrust Plaza, 303 Peachtree Street.
Telephone: 404-521-3939.
Telecopier: 404-581-8330.
In Brussels, Belgium: Avenue Louise 480, 7th Floor. B-1050 Brussels.
Telephone: 32-2-645-14-11.
Telecopier: 32-2-645-14-45.
In Chicago, Illinois: 77 West Wacker.
Telephone: 312-782-3939.
Telecopier: 312-782-8585.
In Dallas, Texas: 2727 North Harwood Street.
Telephone: 214-220-3939.
Telecopier: 214-969-5100.
In Frankfurt, Germany: Hochhaus am Park, Grüneburgweg 102, 60323 Frankfurt am Main.
Telephone: 49-69-9726-3939.
Telecopier: 49-69-9726-3993.
In Geneva, Switzerland: 20, rue de Candolle.
Telephone: 41-22-320-2339.
Telecopier: 41-22-320-1232.
In Hong Kong, China: 29th Floor, Entertainment Building, 30 Queen's Road Central.
Telephone: 852-2526-6895.
Telecopier: 852-2868-5871 or 852-2868-5699.
In Irvine, California: 5 Park Plaza, Suite 1100.
Telephone: 949-851-3939.
Telecopier: 949-553-7539.
In London, England: Bucklersbury House, 3 Queen Victoria Street.
Telephone: 44-171-236-3939.
Telecopier: 44-171-236-1113.
In Los Angeles, California: 555 West Fifth Street, Suite 4600.
Telephone: 213-489-3939.
Telecopier: 213-243-2539.

(See Next Column)

In New Delhi, India (Associate Office): Pathak & Associates (an associate firm of Jones, Day, Reavis & Pogue), 1st Floor, Dr. Gopal Das Bhaven, 28 Barakhamba Road.
Telephone: 91-11-373-8793; 91-11-335-7345.
Telecopier: 91-11-335-3761.
In New York, N.Y.: 599 Lexington Avenue.
Telephone: 212-326-3939.
Telecopier: 212-755-7306.
In Paris, France: 120, rue du Faubourg Saint-Honoré.
Telephone: 33-1-56-59-39-39.
Telecopier: 33-1-56-59-39-38
In Pittsburgh, Pennsylvania: 500 Grant Street, 31st Floor.
Telephone: 412-391-3939.
Telecopier: 412-394-7959.
In Riyadh, Saudi Arabia: The International Law Firm (In Association with Jones, Day, Reavis & Pogue), Sulaymaniyah, Prince Mishari IBN, Abdulaziz Street, P.O. Box 22166.
Telephone: (966-1) 462-8866.
Telecopier: (966-1) 462-9001.
In Shanghai, China: 2805 Kerry Centre, 1515 Nanjing Road West.
Telephone: 86-21-5298-6568.
Telecopier: 86-21-5298-6569.
In Sydney, Australia: Governor Phillip Tower, Level 38, 1 Farrer Place.
Telephone: 61-2-9210-6921.
Telecopier: 61-2-9210-6926.
In Taipei, Taiwan: 8th Floor, Tun Hwa South Road, Section 2.
Telephone: (886-2) 2704-6808.
Telecopier: (886-2) 2704-6791.
In Tokyo, Japan: Toranomon MT Building, 4th Floor, 10-3, Toranomon 3-Chome, Minato-ku, Tokyo 105, Japan.
Telephone: 81-3-3433-3939.
Telecopier: 81-3-5401-2725.
In Washington, D.C.: 51 Louisiana Avenue, N.W.
Telephone: 202-879-3939.
Telecopier: 202-626-1700.

MEMBERS OF FIRM IN CLEVELAND

Brian F. Toohey
Steven E. Sigalow

For Complete List of Firm Personnel, See General Section

For full biographical listings, see the Martindale-Hubbell Law Directory

KELLER AND CURTIN CO., L.P.A. (AV)

Suite 330 The Hanna Building, 44115-1901
Telephone: 216-566-7100
Fax: 216-566-5430
Email: keller@en.com
Akron, Ohio Office: 920 Key Building, 159 South Main Street, 44308-1318.
Telephone: 330-376-7245.
Fax: 330-376-8128. Email: kcakron@en.com.
Elyria, Ohio Office: 120 East Avenue, 44035-5228.
Telephone: 440-323-8662.
Fax: 440-323-6610.

Stanley S. Keller
Thomas M. Coughlin, Jr.
G. Michael Curtin
John Swansinger
Walter H. Krohngold
Camille D. Kuri
James M. Johnson
Franklin C. Malemud
Joseph G. Ritzler
Brian D. Spitz
Deena Charisse Miller

Reference: Bank One, Cleveland.

For full biographical listings, see the Martindale-Hubbell Law Directory

MEYERS, HENTEMANN & REA CO., L.P.A. (AV)

21st Floor, Superior Building, 815 Superior Avenue, N.E., 44114
Telephone: 216-241-3435
Telecopier: 216-241-6568
Elyria, Ohio Office: 301 Fifth Street, 44035.
Telephone: 216-323-6920.

Kent H. Meyers (1902-1970)
John S. Rea
Richard F. Stevens (1915-1981)
Henry A. Hentemann
David S. Meyers (1928-1983)
Gerald L. Jeppe
Eugene J. Gilroy (1926-1984)
Lynn A. Lazzaro

J. Michael Creagan
Ronald J. Ziehm
John J. Reagan
Cornelius J. O'Sullivan, Jr.

OF COUNSEL

Richard C. Talbert
Timothy R. Sweeney
Donald E. Worthing

Representative Clients: State Farm Mutual Insurance Co.; Travelers Insurance Co.; Lloyds Underwriters, London, England; Preferred Risk Mutual Insurance Co.; Detroit Automobile Inter-Insurance Exchange; Electrical Mutual.

For full biographical listings, see the Martindale-Hubbell Law Directory

Cleveland—Continued

QUANDT, GIFFELS & BUCK CO., L.P.A. (AV)

800 Leader Building, 526 Superior Avenue, E., 44114-1460
Telephone: 216-241-2025
Telecopier: 216-241-2080
Email: attys@qgb.com

Robert G. Quandt (1925-1998)
Walter R. Matchinga
Joseph R. Tira
Beth A. Sebaugh
Laurence F. Buzzelli
Larry C. Greathouse
Hunter S. Havens
Timothy G. Sweeney
Richard A. Hoenigman
Jeffrey A. Schenk
Edward J. Stoll, Jr.
Ernest C. Pisanelli
Richard L. Warren, Jr.
Daniel A. Romaine

OF COUNSEL

Stephen D. Richman

Representative Clients: Physicians Insurance Company of Ohio; Royal Insurance; CNA Insurance Co.; Heritage Mutual Insurance Co.; Reliance Insurance Co.; Safeco Insurance Co.; American International Group.

For full biographical listings, see the Martindale-Hubbell Law Directory

RODGERS AND CO., L.P.A. (AV)

1750 Guildhall, Landmark Office Towers, 45 Prospect Avenue, West, 44115
Telephone: 216-861-6191
Fax: 216-861-4699
Email: attys@rodgers-lpa.com

Walter A. Rodgers

Jeffrey M. Elzeer
Shawn A. Cormier

For full biographical listings, see the Martindale-Hubbell Law Directory

SEELEY, SAVIDGE AND EBERT A LEGAL PROFESSIONAL ASSOCIATION (AV)

800 Bank One Center, 600 Superior Avenue, East, 44114-2655
Telephone: 216-566-8200
Fax-Telecopier: 216-566-0213
URL: http://www.sse-law.com

Keith A. Savidge

Matthew K. Seeley
Michael E. Stinn

Reference: KeyBank.

For Complete List of Firm Personnel, See General Section

For full biographical listings, see the Martindale-Hubbell Law Directory

SMITH, MARSHALL, WEAVER AND VERGON (AV)

500 National City East Sixth Building, 1965 East Sixth Street, 44114
Telephone: 216-781-4994
Telecopier: 216-781-9448
Email: smw@multiverse.com.

MEMBERS OF FIRM

Wentworth J. Marshall, Jr.
Philip J. Weaver, Jr.
Frederick P. Vergon, Jr.

ASSOCIATES

R. Eric Smearman
Gretchen A. Hirschauer
Jason W. Richards

Representative Clients: American States Insurance Co.; Federated Mutual Group; Hartford Insurance Group; State Automobile Mutual Insurance Co.

For full biographical listings, see the Martindale-Hubbell Law Directory

WESTON HURD FALLON PAISLEY & HOWLEY L.L.P. (AV)

2500 Terminal Tower, 50 Public Square, 44113-2241
Telephone: 216-241-6602;
Ohio Toll Free: 800-336-4952
FAX: 216-621-8369
Email: Hurd2500@westonhurd.com

MEMBERS OF FIRM

Mark O'Neill
John W. Jeffers
John M. Baker
Ronald A. Rispo
Carolyn M. Cappel
Hilary Sheldon Taylor
Kenneth A. Torgerson
John S. Kluznik
Jeffrey D. Fincun
William H. Baughman, Jr.
Stephen D. Walters
Gary W. Johnson
Deirdre G. Henry
Harry Sigmier
Warren Rosman
Timothy D. Johnson
Dana A. Rose
Hernan N. Visani
John G. Farnan
Gregory E. O'Brien
Scott C. Smith
Timothy P. Ristau
David C. Lamb

(See Next Column)

ASSOCIATES

Lisa M. Chesler
Maria A. Kortan-Sampson
Daniel A. Richards
John A. Albers
Forrest A. Norman III
Christopher M. Ernst
Marilyn Miller Crisafi
Martin J. Fallon
Mark S. Bennett
Randy L. Taylor
Jeremy R. Sayre
Dennis R. Fogarty
Thomas J. Connick
Jason R. Sussman

For Complete List of Firm Personnel, See General Section

For full biographical listings, see the Martindale-Hubbell Law Directory

*COLUMBUS,** Franklin Co.

BRENNER, BROWN, GOLIAN & MCCAFFREY CO., L.P.A. (AV)

1654 East Broad Street, 43203-2079
Telephone: 614-258-6000
Telecopier: 614-258-6006
Email: bbgm@netwalk.com

Philip F. Brown
Joseph J. Golian
Todd Austin Brenner
Patrick McCaffrey, Jr.

For full biographical listings, see the Martindale-Hubbell Law Directory

CRABBE, BROWN, JONES, POTTS & SCHMIDT (AV)

500 South Front Street, Suite 1200, 43215
Telephone: 614-228-5511
Telecopier: 614-229-4559
URL: HTTP://WWW.CBJPS.COM
Cincinnati, Ohio Office: 30 Garfield Place, Suite 940, 45202.
Telephone: 513-784-1525.
Telecopier: 513-784-1250. Email: BHurley@Psinet.com
Lancaster, Ohio Office: 111 South Broad Street, Suite 209, 43130.
Telephone: 740-689-1743.
Telecopier: 740-689-1746. Email: sdavis@greenapple.com

MEMBERS OF FIRM

William Page Lewis (1914-1998)
Robert C. Potts (1913-1994)
William T. McCracken (1929-1993)
J. Roth Crabbe (1906-1989)
Charles E. Brown
Theodore D. Sawyer
Vincent J. Lodico
Steven B. Ayers
Keith H. Jung
Jeffrey M. Brown
Larry H. James
Brian E. Hurley (Resident, Cincinnati Office)
Gilbert J. Gradisar
Richard D. Wetzel, Jr.
Jerry A. Eichenberger
James D. Gilbert
Luis M. Alcalde
John C. Albert
George R. McCue, III
Michael R. Henry
Robert C. Buchbinder
Catherine L. Worley
Steven A. Davis (Resident, Lancaster Office)

ASSOCIATES

Francesca Tosi Ward
Todd William Collis
Kristen H. Smith
Daniel J. Hurley
Beth Wayne (Resident, Cincinnati Office)
Heather W. Guthrie
Christina L. Corl
Steven E. Miller
Darlene E. Chavers
Amy M. Fulmer Stevenson
Phillip A. Templeton

OF COUNSEL

William H. Jones
Wilbur W. Jones (1913-1999)
William L. Schmidt

Representative Clients: Allstate Insurance Co.; American States Insurance Co.; General Electric.

For full biographical listings, see the Martindale-Hubbell Law Directory

HAMMOND & SEWARDS (AV)

22 East Gay Street - Suite 700, 43215
Telephone: 614-461-5300
Telephone: 1-800-842-5475
Fax: 614-461-8285
Email: pmartz@hammondsewards.com *URL:* http://www.lawyers.com/hammondlawoffice

MEMBERS OF FIRM

Gary W. Hammond
Frederick A. Sewards

ASSOCIATE

Scott E. Williams

LEGAL SUPPORT PERSONNEL

Heather Vekasy (Secretary to Attorney Williams and Attorney Sewards)
Heather Rodgers (Secretary to Attorney Hammond)
Prindall H. Martz (Office Manager)

For full biographical listings, see the Martindale-Hubbell Law Directory

Columbus—Continued

KEENER DOUCHER CURLEY & PATTERSON A LEGAL PROFESSIONAL ASSOCIATION (AV)

88 East Broad Street, Suite 1750, 43215
Telephone: 614-280-1100
Fax: 614-280-9503
Email: KDCP@IWAYNET.NET

Thomas J. Keener
W. Charles Curley
Paul M. Doucher
David T. Patterson
Kevin R. Bush

Michael J. Kelley
Kimberley A. Doucher
Amy K. Schermer

For full biographical listings, see the Martindale-Hubbell Law Directory

MCNAMARA AND MCNAMARA (AV)

Suite 1250, 88 East Broad Street, 43215-3558
Telephone: 614-228-6131
FAX: 614-228-6126

MEMBERS OF FIRM

J. Paul McNamara (1908-1994)
John L. Miller
John J. Petro
William H. Woods
Lisa Weekley Coulter

ASSOCIATE

Jonathan M. Bryan

OF COUNSEL

Dennis D. Liston
Keith McNamara

References: BancOhio National Bank; The City National Bank & Trust Co.; Huntington National Bank.

For full biographical listings, see the Martindale-Hubbell Law Directory

NEMETH, CABORN & BUTAUSKI (AV)

21 East Frankfort Street, 43206-1069
Telephone: 614-443-4866
Fax: 614-443-4860
URL: http://www.lawyers.com/nemeth
Email: nemeth@nemethlaw.com *URL:* http://www.nemethlaw.com

John C. Nemeth
David A. Caborn
Joseph A. Butauski

ASSOCIATES

David A. Herd
Michael J. Collins

Representative Clients: Anheuser-Busch, Inc.; TCO Ins. Services; Crawford & Co.; Erie Insurance Group; Home Insurance Co.; Safeco Insurance Co.; The Hartford Group; Citizens Insurance Co.; State Farm Insurance Co.; Zurich American Group.

For full biographical listings, see the Martindale-Hubbell Law Directory

WILES, BOYLE, BURKHOLDER & BRINGARDNER CO., L.P.A. (AV)

115 West Main Street, Suite 100, 43215-5043
Telephone: 614-221-5216
Fax: 614-221-5692
Email: mail@wiles-lawfirm.com

Daniel G. Wiles
Bruce H. Burkholder
James W. Wheeler
Jay B. Eggspuehler
James M. Wiles
John T. Kelly
Thomas E. Boyle
William B. Benson
Michael L. Close
Samuel M. Pipino
Richard D. Bringardner
C. William Klausman
Mark C. Melko

OF COUNSEL

Stanley K. Van Buren

Representative Insurance Clients: Aetna Life & Casualty Co.; All-state Insurance Co.; Associated Aviation Underwriters, Inc.; Kemper Insurance Co.; Physician's Insurance Company of America; United States Aviation Underwriters, Inc.; Zurich-American Insurance Co.; Carolina Casualty Ins. Co.; Travel Air Ins. Co.; Underwriters at Lloyd's of London.

For full biographical listings, see the Martindale-Hubbell Law Directory

ROBERT H. WILLARD (AV)

500 South Front Street, Suite 125, 43215
Telephone: 614-228-9494
Fax: 614-228-7766
Email: robertwillard@sprintmail.com

ASSOCIATE

Elizabeth A. Ayers

For full biographical listings, see the Martindale-Hubbell Law Directory

*DAYTON,** Montgomery Co.

FREUND, FREEZE & ARNOLD A LEGAL PROFESSIONAL ASSOCIATION (AV)

Suite 1800 One Dayton Centre, One South Main Street, 45402-2017
Telephone: 937-222-2424
Telecopier: 937-222-5369
Email: ffalawda@ffalaw.com *URL:* http://www.ffalaw.com
Cincinnati, Ohio Office: 8805 Governor's Hill Drive, Suite 300, 45249-3313.
Telephone: 513-583-3700.
FAX: 513-583-3703. Email: ffalawci@ffalaw.com.

Neil F. Freund
Shawn M. Blatt
Stephen V. Freeze
Ray C. Freudiger
Gordon D. Arnold
Kevin C. Connell
Patrick J. Janis
Margaret R. Young
Stephen C. Findley
Jennifer L. Kirkpatrick
Robert N. Snyder
Lynnette Pisone Ballato
Christopher W. Carrigg
Timothy B. Schenkel
Susan Blasik-Miller
Daniel D. Ernst
Scott F. McDaniel
Julie R. Lewis
Wayne E. Waite
John J. Garvey, III
Thomas B. Bruns
David J. Cusack
John G. Witherspoon, Jr.
Marc G. Pera
Lisa A. Hesse
Julie M. Olson
Mark L. Schumacher
T. Andrew Vollmar
Robert W. Young

Local Counsel for: Auto-Owners Insurance Co.; CNA Insurance Co.; Employers Reinsurance Corp.; Farmers Insurance Group; General Accident Ins. Co.; Lloyds of London; Medical Protective; Ohio Insurance Co.; Motorists Mutual Ins.

For full biographical listings, see the Martindale-Hubbell Law Directory

PICKREL, SCHAEFFER & EBELING (AV)

2700 Kettering Tower, 45423-2700
Telephone: 937-223-1130
Facsimile: 937-223-0339
URL: http://www.pselaw.com

Paul J. Winterhalter
Andrew C. Storar
John W. Slagle
James W. Kelleher

L. Michael Bly
Michael W. Sandner
Gregory S. Page

Representative Clients: Allstate Insurance Co.; American Mutual Liability Co.; Church Mutual Insurance Co.; Grange Mutual Insurance Co.; Grange Mutual; Metropolitan Property & Casualty Insurance Co.; Transport Insurance Co.; Western Reserve Mutual; Wausau Insurance Cos.; Amerisure Cos.

For full biographical listings, see the Martindale-Hubbell Law Directory

YOUNG & ALEXANDER CO., L.P.A. (AV)

367 West Second Street, Suite 100, 45402
Telephone: 937-224-9291
Telecopier: 937-224-9679
Cincinnati, Ohio Office: 110 Boggs Lane, Suite 350.
Telephone: 513-326-5555.
FAX: 513-326-5550.

James M. Brennan
Steven O. Dean
Mark R. Chilson
James K. Hemenway

Counsel for: The Children's Medical Center, Dayton, Ohio; The Colonial Stair & Woodwork Co.; The Greater Dayton Area Hospital Assn.; Mike-Sell's Potato Chip Co.; Moorman Pontiac, Inc.
Local Counsel for: Colonial Penn Insurance Co.; John Hancock Mutual Life Insurance Co.; Hertz Corp.; State Farm Insurance Co.

For full biographical listings, see the Martindale-Hubbell Law Directory

*FINDLAY,** Hancock Co.

OXLEY, MALONE, FITZGERALD & HOLLISTER (AV)

301 East Main Cross Street, P.O. Box 1086, 45840
Telephone: 419-422-8713
Fax: 419-422-6495
Email: oxleylaw@bright.net

MEMBERS OF FIRM

Michael J. Malone
Dennis M. Fitzgerald
Robert B. Hollister

ASSOCIATES

Michael E. Gilb
Bradley S. Warren
Bret A. Spaeth

OF COUNSEL

Julie A. Davenport

Representative Clients: CNA Insurance Co.; American States Insurance Co.; Allstate Insurance Co.; Auto-Owners Insurance Co.; Western Reserve Group; Buckeye State Mutual Insurancce Co.; OHIC Insurance Co.; Ohio Mutual Insurance Co.; Cinncinati Insurance.

(See Next Column)

OXLEY, MALONE, FITZGERALD & HOLLISTER—*Continued*

For Complete List of Firm Personnel, See General Section

For full biographical listings, see the Martindale-Hubbell Law Directory

HOLLAND, Lucas Co.

JONES & BAHRET CO., L.P.A. (AV)

Attorneys at Law
7050 Spring Meadows West, 43528
Telephone: 419-861-7800
Fax: 419-861-7808

Willis P. Jones, Jr.
Robert J. Bahret

Keith J. Watkins
Jeffrey B. Charles
Peter C. Munger
Marie E. Findish
Kathleen M Malkoski

LEGAL SUPPORT PERSONNEL

Denise M. Schmidt (Paralegal)
Shannon R. Tilton (Paralegal)
Susan J. Masson (Paralegal)

Representative Clients: American Modern Homes Insurance Company; Auto-Owners Insurance Co.; German Mutual Insurance Company; Michigan Millers Mutual Insurance Company; Motorists Insurance Companies; Podiatry Insurance Co.; Progressive Insurance Co.; Utica National Insurance Group; Western Reserve Mutual Casualty Co.; Westfield Companies.

For full biographical listings, see the Martindale-Hubbell Law Directory

*LIMA,** Allen Co.

GOODING, HUFFMAN, KELLEY & BECKER (AV)

127-129 North Pierce Street, P.O. Box 546, 45802
Telephone: 419-227-3423
Fax: 419-228-1937
URL: http://www.ghkb.com

Fred Wemmer Gooding (1914-1972)
Lawrence S. Huffman

ASSOCIATES

C. Bradford Kelley
Matthew C. Huffman
Lawrence A. Huffman
John C. Huffman
Stephen L. Becker
T. Blain Brock, II
Craig A. Gottschalk

LEGAL SUPPORT PERSONNEL

Carol L. Swem (Probate Paralegal)

Representative Clients: The Medical Protective Co.; Physicians Insurance Company of Ohio; Hamilton Mutual Insurance Co.; Bank One, Lima, Ohio; Lima Contracting Co.; Otis Wright & Sons Trucking, Inc.; Superior Metal Products; Frontier Insurance Co.; Zurich-American Insurance Group; Urology Assoc. of Ohio, Inc.

For full biographical listings, see the Martindale-Hubbell Law Directory

*MANSFIELD,** Richland Co.

BROWN, BEMILLER, MURRAY & MCINTYRE (AV)

70 Park Avenue West, P.O. Box 728, 44901-0728
Telephone: 419-525-1611
FAX: 419-525-3810

MEMBERS OF FIRM

John T. Brown
J. Jeffrey Heck
F. Loyal Bemiller
William T. McIntyre
D. Kim Murray
Jeffrey Molyet
Adam Vetter, Jr.

Local Counsel for: Royal-Globe Group; Westfield Companies; Ohio Edison Co.; Grange Mutual Casualty Co.; Buckeye Union Insurance Co.; Maryland Casualty Co.; Shelby Insurance; Montgomery Ward & Co.; Continental Insurance Group; Artesian Industries, Inc.

For Complete List of Firm Personnel, See General Section

For full biographical listings, see the Martindale-Hubbell Law Directory

*TOLEDO,** Lucas Co.

DOYLE, LEWIS & WARNER (AV)

202 North Erie Street, P.O. Box 2168, 43603
Telephone: 419-248-1500
Fax: 419-248-2002
Email: dlw1@primenet.com

MEMBERS OF FIRM

Steven Timonere
Michael E. Hyrne
Richard F. Ellenberger
Michael A. Bruno
David W. Doerner

(See Next Column)

ASSOCIATES

Kevin A. Pituch
Maureen O. Atkins

Representative Clients: Prudential Insurance Company of America; Equitable Life Assurance Society of U.S.; Metropolitan Life Insurance Co.; Northwestern Mutual Life Insurance Co.; John Hancock Life Insurance; Connecticut General Life Insurance Co.; National Life & Accident Insurance Co.; Fireman's Fund Insurance Cos.; Hanover Insurance; Leader National Insurance Co.

For Complete List of Firm Personnel, See General Section

For full biographical listings, see the Martindale-Hubbell Law Directory

EASTMAN & SMITH LTD. (AV)

One Seagate, Twenty-Fourth Floor, P.O. Box 10032, 43699-0032
Telephone: 419-241-6000
Telecopier: 419-247-1777
Columbus, Ohio Office: 65 East State Street, Suite 1000, 43215.
Telephone: 614-460-3556.
Telecopier: 614-228-5371.

MEMBERS OF FIRM

James F. Nooney
Rudolph A. Peckinpaugh, Jr.
David M. Jones
Barry W. Fissel
Peter R. Casey, III
John D. Willey, Jr.
David F. Cooper
Stuart J. Goldberg

ASSOCIATES

Timothy C. Kuhlman
Michael W. Regnier

OF COUNSEL

Richard E. Antonini
M. Donald Carmin

For Complete List of Firm Personnel, See General Section

For full biographical listings, see the Martindale-Hubbell Law Directory

MANAHAN, PIETRYKOWSKI, BAMMAN & DELANEY (AV)

(Formerly Finn, Manahan & Pietrykowski)
414 North Erie Street, P.O. Box 2328, 43603-2328
Telephone: 419-243-6148
Fax: 419-241-7759
Email: mpbd@mindspring.com
Port Clinton Office: 125 Jefferson Street.
Telephone: 419-734-5516.
Fax: 419-732-8246.

MEMBERS OF FIRM

William A. Finn (1898-1980)
Gerald R. Kowalski
Thomas J. Manahan (1923-1988)
Michael J. Manahan
John A. Pietrykowski (1931-1993)
Glenn E. Wasielewski
William F. Pietrykowski (Resident, Port Clinton Office)
Cormac B. DeLaney
George C. Ward
Larry P. Meyer
Stephen F. Ahern
Ted B. Riley

ASSOCIATES

Jeffrey Jon Madrzykowski
Stephen E. House

OF COUNSEL

H. William Bamman (Retired)

For full biographical listings, see the Martindale-Hubbell Law Directory

RITTER, ROBINSON, MCCREADY & JAMES (AV)

1850 National City Bank Building, 405 Madison Avenue, 43624
Telephone: 419-241-3213
FAX: 419-241-4925

MEMBERS OF FIRM

Ellis F. Robinson (Retired)
William S. McCready
Milton C. Boesel, Jr. (Retired)
Timothy C. James

Counsel for: Chrysler Corp.; Rubini Motors, Inc.; Ohio Casualty Insurance Co.; National Mutual Insurance Co.; Celina Mutual Insurance Co.; Westfield Insurance Co.; Northwestern National Insurance Co.; Midwestern Insurance Co.; United Ohio Insurance Co.; Toledo Auto Electric Co.

For Complete List of Firm Personnel, See General Section

For full biographical listings, see the Martindale-Hubbell Law Directory

ROHRBACHERS, LIGHT, CRON, ZMUDA & TRIMBLE CO., L.P.A. (AV)

National City Bank Building 8th Floor, 405 Madison Avenue, 43604-1243
Telephone: 419-248-2600
Telecopier: 419-248-2614
URL: http://www.rlczt.com
URL: http://www.lawyers.com/rlcztcom

Vernon E. Rohrbacher (1920-1978)
C. Randolph Light
Nicholas J. Cron
David J. Rohrbacher
Gene A. Zmuda
Matthew J. Rohrbacher
J. Mark Trimble

(See Next Column)

ROHRBACHERS, LIGHT, CRON, ZMUDA & TRIMBLE CO. L.P.A., *Toledo—Continued*

Beverly J. St. Clair
Diane J. Knoblauch
Todd M. Zimmerman

OF COUNSEL

Brent B. Nicholson

LEGAL SUPPORT PERSONNEL

PARALEGAL

Anne E. Scott

For full biographical listings, see the Martindale-Hubbell Law Directory

SCHNORF & SCHNORF CO., L.P.A. A PROFESSIONAL CORPORATION (AV)

1400 National City Bank Building, 405 Madison Avenue, 43604
Telephone: 419-248-2646
Facsimile: 419-248-2889

David M. Schnorf
Christopher F. Parker
Johna M. Bella

Representative Clients: Universal Underwriters Group; Medical Mutual of Ohio; Bankers Multiple Line Insurance Company; GRE Insurance Group; Reliance Insurance.

For Complete List of Firm Personnel, See General Section

For full biographical listings, see the Martindale-Hubbell Law Directory

TWINSBURG, Summit Co.

WILLIAMS, SENNETT & SCULLY CO., L.P.A. (AV)

2241 Pinnacle Parkway, 44087-2367
Telephone: 330-405-5061
Fax: 330-405-5586
Email: attorneys@wsslaw.com
Cleveland, Ohio Office: 113 St. Clair Building, Suite 430.
Telephone: 216-771-8660.
Fax: 216-771-8831.

Roger H. Williams
James A. Sennett
William F. Scully, Jr.
Adam E. Carr
Louis R. Moliterno
Gina K. Desiderio
Matthew J. Grimm

OF COUNSEL

Charles F. Cichocki

Representative Clients: Allstate Insurance Co.; Giant Eagle, Inc.; Goodyear Tire & Rubber Co.; Nationwide Mutual Insurance Co.; Safeco Insurance Co.; Simon DeBartolo Group, Inc.; State Farm Insurance Cos.; Toys "R" Us; Universal Underwriters Insurance Co.; Senty Insurance Co.;

For full biographical listings, see the Martindale-Hubbell Law Directory

*WARREN,** Trumbull Co.

CHARLES L. RICHARDS (AV)

159 East Market Street, Suite 300, 44481-1122
Telephone: 330-373-1000
Fax: 330-394-5291

ASSOCIATES

Robert C. Maynard
Maureen E. Richards
Vincent E. Cononico

For full biographical listings, see the Martindale-Hubbell Law Directory

*ZANESVILLE,** Muskingum Co.

MICHELI, BALDWIN, BOPELEY & NORTHRUP CO., L.P.A. (AV)

2806 Bell Street, P.O. Box 788, 43702-0788
Telephone: 614-454-2545
Fax: 614-454-6372

Frank J. Micheli
Michael J. Micheli
James C. Micheli (1956-1992)
Steven R. Baldwin
Thomas R. Bopeley
Michael A. Northrup

Eric D. Martin

Representative Clients: Bank One Cambridge, N.A.; Consolidated Rail Corp.; Medical Protective Co.; Nationwide Insurance Cos.; Continental Insurance Cos.; Motorists Mutual Insurance Co.; Frontier Insurance Co.
Reference: Mutual Federal Savings Bank

For full biographical listings, see the Martindale-Hubbell Law Directory

OKLAHOMA

*ADA,** Pontotoc Co.

DEATON, DAVISON & KESSINGER, A PROFESSIONAL CORPORATION (AV)

300 South Rennie, P.O. Box 1219, 74820
Telephone: 580-332-1752
Fax: 580-332-0827
Email: ddkesq@chickasaw.com

Austin R. Deaton, Jr.
Denver N. Davison
C. Steven Kessinger

For full biographical listings, see the Martindale-Hubbell Law Directory

*ANTLERS,** Pushmataha Co.

STAMPER, HADLEY & REASOR (AV)

112 North High Street, P.O. Box 100, 74523
Telephone: 580-298-3153; 580-298-3332
Fax: 580-298-3263
Email: joestamper@yahoo.com
Atoka, Oklahoma Office: 209 East Court, P.O. Box 393.
Telephone: 580-889-3343
Fax: 580-889-9334.

MEMBERS OF FIRM

Joe Stamper
Thomas J. Hadley
Shannon Reasor (Resident, Atoka Office)

Representative Clients: Farmers Exchange Bank, Antlers, Okla.; First National Bank at Antlers, Okla.; Town of Antlers; U. S. F. & G. Co.

For full biographical listings, see the Martindale-Hubbell Law Directory

*OKLAHOMA CITY,** Oklahoma Co.

ABOWITZ, RHODES & DAHNKE, P.C. (AV)

Tenth Floor 15 North Robinson, P.O. Box 1937, 73101
Telephone: 405-236-4645
Telecopier: 405-239-2843

Murray E. Abowitz
Sarah Jackson Rhodes
George W. Dahnke

Lisa Luschen Dietrich
Janice M. Dansby
Kayce L. Gisinger
Stephen S. Parker
Andrew D. Schwartz
Blake A. Bittel

Representative Clients: Admiral Insurance Company; Atlanta Casualty Companies; Colorado Western Insurance Company; Harbor Insurance Company; Liberty Mutual Insurance Company; Oklahoma Attorneys Mutual Insurance Company; Oklahoma Farmers Union Mutual Insurance Company; The Travelers Insurance Group; Carolina Casualty Insurance Company; United Wisconsin Life Insurance Company.

For full biographical listings, see the Martindale-Hubbell Law Directory

CHUBBUCK SMITH & RHODES, A PROFESSIONAL CORPORATION (AV)

Robinson Renaissance, Suite 820, 119 North Robinson, 73102
Telephone: 405-236-8282
Fax: 405-236-2828

Gary Mitchell Chubbuck
Curtis L. Smith
Scott M. Rhodes
June L. Chubbuck
William B. Blew III
Jeffrey A. Curran
Paul G. Summars
John Dexter Marble
Debra A. Charles

OF COUNSEL

David C. Johnston, Jr.

For full biographical listings, see the Martindale-Hubbell Law Directory

DAY, EDWARDS, FEDERMAN, PROPESTER & CHRISTENSEN, P.C. (AV)

Suite 2900 Oklahoma Tower, 210 Park Avenue, 73102-5605
Telephone: 405-239-2121
Telecopier: 405-236-1012
URL: http://lawlinks.com/attys/ok/defpc.html

Rodney J. Heggy

Kenneth A. Brokaw
Stuart W. Emmons
Gary L. Farnum

OF COUNSEL

Robert S. Baker

Representative Clients: AIG Aviation, Inc.; Allied Group Insurance; BASF Corporation; Colony Insurance Company; COMAV Managers, Inc.; Eagle Star Insurance Co., Empire Insurance Group; Employers Mutual Casualty

(See Next Column)

DAY, EDWARDS, FEDERMAN, PROPESTER & CHRISTENSEN P.C.—*Continued*

Company; Gallagher Bassett Services, Inc.; General Star Management; Generali Insurance Company.

For Complete List of Firm Personnel, See General Section

For full biographical listings, see the Martindale-Hubbell Law Directory

DURBIN, LARIMORE & BIALICK, P.C. (AV)

920 North Harvey, 73102-2610
Telephone: 405-235-9584
Fax: 405-235-0551
Email: DLB@Telepath.com

Gerald E. Durbin, II
James K. Larimore
Mark E. Bialick
Jerry John Hager, Jr.
David B. Donchin
Micheal L. Darrah

Rodney D. Stewart
Bill M. Roberts
Katherine Taylor Loy
J. Logan Johnson
Hilary S. Allen
Frances J. Stanton
Amy L. Alden
R. Brad Miller
Susanna M. Gattoni

For full biographical listings, see the Martindale-Hubbell Law Directory

HUCKABY, FLEMING, FRAILEY, CHAFFIN, CORDELL, GREENWOOD & PERRYMAN, L.L.P. (AV)

1215 Classen Drive, P.O. Box 60130, 73146
Telephone: 405-235-6648
Fax: 405-235-1533
URL: http://www.FlemingLaw@aol.com
Chickasha, Oklahoma Office: 201 North 4th, P.O. Box 533.
Telephone: 405-224-0237.
Fax: 405-222-2319.

MEMBERS OF FIRM

Owen Vaughn (1900-1981)
Clarence McElroy (1903-1970)
Steve Stack (1946-1979)
Richard A. Procter (1932-1980)
Kent Fleming
Tom A. Frailey
Michael R. Chaffin
F. Thomas Cordell, Jr.
William D. Greenwood
David L. Perryman
Deborah A. Sterkel
Brently C. Olsson
Stephen R. McCalla

ASSOCIATES

D. Renée Hildebrant
Rodney Dean Fergason
Jason L. West
Jeromy E. Brown

Representative Clients: American Indemnity Group; Bituminous Insurance Company; Chubb Group of Insurance Companies; Hartford Insurance Company; Home Insurance Company; National Casualty Insurance Company; Scottsdale Insurance Company; Travelers Insurance Company; Vanliner Insurance Company; Wausau Insurance Companies.

For full biographical listings, see the Martindale-Hubbell Law Directory

KERR, IRVINE, RHODES & ABLES, A PROFESSIONAL CORPORATION (AV)

201 Robert S. Kerr Avenue, Suite 600, 73102-4267
Telephone: 405-272-9221
Fax: 405-236-3121
Email: kira201@aol.com

Horace G. Rhodes
J. Angela Ables
James W. Rhodes

Kevin R. Wisner

Representative Clients: Allstate Insurance Co.; Foundation Health, an Oklahoma Health Plan; Community Care HMO; Life Assurance Co, Inc.; United Teachers Association Insurance Co.; Trafalgar Insurance Co.

For Complete List of Firm Personnel, See General Section

For full biographical listings, see the Martindale-Hubbell Law Directory

KING LAW FIRM (AV)

15 North Robinson, Suite 1100, 73102
Telephone: 405-239-6143
Fax: 405-236-3934
Email: kinglaw@flash.net

Tom L. King

ASSOCIATES

Richard M. Glasgow
Scott F. McKinney
Scott K. Suchy
John J. Foley

(See Next Column)

OF COUNSEL

Donald E. DeSpain

Representative Clients: CGU Insurance Co.; AIG/American International Group; Gainsco/MGA Insurance; Republic Insurance; GAB Business Services; Montgomery Kone; DowElanco; All-American Bottling Co.; C.L. Frates & Co.; Fred Jones Companies.

For full biographical listings, see the Martindale-Hubbell Law Directory

LEE, DUROCHER, KISNER, WALKER & REID (AV)

An Association of Professional Associations
5532 North Western, 73118
Telephone: 405-848-5532
Facsimile: 405-848-5502

Jim W. Lee
Daniel L. Durocher
David W. Kisner
David A. Walker
James M. Reid

For full biographical listings, see the Martindale-Hubbell Law Directory

MANCHESTER & PIGNATO, P.C. (AV)

Suite 900, Robinson Renaissance Building, 119 North Robinson, 73102
Telephone: 405-235-2222
Fax: 405-235-2204
Email: mplaw@manchesterandpignato.com

Robert Edward Manchester
Gerard F. Pignato
Shannon K. Emmons
Susan Ann Knight

ASSOCIATES

R. Thompson Cooper
Jenny L. Evans

OF COUNSEL

Stacey Haws Felkner

Representative Clients: Electric Mutual Liability Insurance Co.; Otis Elevator Co.; Budget Rent-A-Car Systems, Inc.; Essex Insurance Co.; American Bankers Insurance Company of Florida; Motors Insurance Co.; Lexington Insurance Co.; City of Oklahoma City; Clint Williams Co.

For full biographical listings, see the Martindale-Hubbell Law Directory

THE MILLS LAW FIRM, P.C. (AV)

500 One Leadership Square, 211 North Robinson, 73102
Telephone: 405-239-2501
Fax: 405-239-2575
Email: millsfirm@attymail.com

Earl D. Mills
Robert B. Mills
W. Wayne Mills
Barbara K. Buratti

Margaret K. Myers
Daniel K. Jones
J. Drew Houghton
Carole L. Dulisse

For full biographical listings, see the Martindale-Hubbell Law Directory

PIERCE COUCH HENDRICKSON BAYSINGER & GREEN, L.L.P. (AV)

1109 North Francis, P.O. Box 26350, 73126
Telephone: 405-235-1611
Fax: 405-235-2904
Tulsa, Oklahoma Office: Suite 707, 100 W. 5th, ONEOK Plaza, 74103.
Telephone: 918-583-8100.
Fax: 918-583-8107.

MEMBERS OF FIRM

Calvin W. Hendrickson
Hugh A. Baysinger
Gerald P. Green
Stephen L. Olson
James B. Durant (Resident, Tulsa Office)
D. Lynn Babb
Inona Jane Harness
Russell L. Hendrickson
John Roger Hurt
Frances E. Patton
Charles A. Brandt
Robert S. Lafferandre
John Christopher Condren
Peter L. Wheeler
G. Calvin Sharpe
Todd Estes

ASSOCIATES

Susan A. Doke
Bradley T. Hollar
E. Marissa Lane
Haven Tobias
Edwin J. Carlton
Rachel K. Jackson
Victoria D. Ford
Stefan K. Doughty
Linda Prine Brown
Angela J. O'Dell
Brandy Kearney Isom
Ted D. Rossier

OF COUNSEL

Kathleen J. Adler
Michael W. Hinkle
Scott A. Law

Representative Clients: CNA Insurance; Hartford Accident and Indemnity Co.; Lloyd's of London; Physicians Liability Insurance Co.; Shelter Insurance Co.; Chubb Insurance Group; CUNA Mutual; Brotherhood Mutual Insurance Co.; United Services Automobile Assn.; Foremost Insurance Co.

For full biographical listings, see the Martindale-Hubbell Law Directory

Oklahoma City—Continued

WELCH, JONES & SMITH, P.C. (AV)

2601 Northwest Expressway 601 Oil Center West, 73112
Telephone: 405-848-2000
Fax: 405-848-2029
Email: WJSPC@AOL.COM

Mort G. Welch
Laurie Walker Jones
Sherry L. Smith
Robin A. Wiens

Representative Clients: Oklahoma Farmers Union Mutual Insurance Co.; Trinity Universal Insurance Co.; U.S.F. & G. Co.; Great American Insurance Co.; Oklahoma Attorneys Mutual Insurance Co.; Evanston Insurance Co.; CNA Insurance Cos.; Highlands Insurance Group; Grain Dealers Mutual Insurance Co.; Avis Rent-A-Car Systems, Inc.

For full biographical listings, see the Martindale-Hubbell Law Directory

WHITTEN, MCGUIRE, WOOD, TERRY, ROSELIUS & DITTRICH A PROFESSIONAL LIMITED LIABILITY COMPANY (AV)

Suite 400, One Leadership Square, 211 North Robinson, 73102
Telephone: 405-239-2522
Fax: 405-239-2573
Email: whitten@whitten-mcguire.com
Tulsa, Oklahoma Office: 3600 First Place Tower, 15 East Fifth Street.
Telephone: 918-582-9903.

Reggie N. Whitten
Kent R. McGuire
Douglas A. Terry
Jason E. Roselius

Simone Gosnell Fulmer
Philip W. Anderson
R. Gregory Kirby
Derrick T. Dewitt

Representative Clients: The St. Paul Insurance Cos.; Crum & Forster Commercial Insurance Co.; OML Municipal Assurance Group; Progressive Casualty; Shelter Ins. Co.; Fireman's Fund Ins. Co.; Travelers Ins. Co.

For full biographical listings, see the Martindale-Hubbell Law Directory

*TULSA,** Tulsa Co.

ATKINSON, HASKINS, NELLIS, BOUDREAUX, HOLEMAN, PHIPPS & BRITTINGHAM, A PROFESSIONAL CORPORATION (AV)

1500 ParkCentre, 525 South Main Street, 74103
Telephone: 918-582-8877
Fax: 918-585-8096
Email: ahnmail@ahn-law.com

Michael P. Atkinson, P.C.
Walter D. Haskins, P.C.
Gregory D. Nellis, P.C.
Paul T. Boudreaux, P.C.
Daniel E. Holeman, P.C.
K. Clark Phipps
Galen Lee Brittingham, P.C.
John S. Gladd
John J. Carwile
Martha J. Phillips
William A. Fiasco
Jon D. Starr
Mark W. Maguire
Marthanda J. Beckworth
James N. Edmonds

Kirsten E. Pace
Scott R. Hall
Jeffrey L. Wilson
Whitney M. Eschenheimer
Margaret M. Clarke
Margaret A. Nunnery
Jeffrey A. Risch
Jennifer Annis
Eric J. Begin
Roni S. Rierson
Christine M. Benson
Bret A. Sanders

Representative Clients: Allstate Insurance Co.; Bayer Corp.; Crum & Forster Insurance Co.; Hartford Insurance Company; National American Insurance Co.; Federated Insurance Co.; Liberty Mutual Insurance Co.; Physicians Liability Insurance Co.; State Farm Mutual Automobile Insurance Co.; United States Aviation Underwriters.

For full biographical listings, see the Martindale-Hubbell Law Directory

BEST & SHARP, A PROFESSIONAL CORPORATION (AV)

Oneok Plaza, 100 W. 5th, Suite 808, 74103-4225
Telephone: 918-582-1234
Fax: 918-585-9447
Email: Webmaster@BestSharp.com *URL:* http://www.BestSharp.com

Joseph M. Best
Joseph A. Sharp
Timothy G. Best
Daniel S. Sullivan
Amy E. Kempfert
Karen M. Grundy
Terry S. O'Donnell

Catherine L. Campbell
Malcom D. Smith, Jr.
Jeffrey W. Swanson
Dan W. Ernst
Thomas A. Le Blanc

For full biographical listings, see the Martindale-Hubbell Law Directory

RHODES, HIERONYMUS, JONES, TUCKER & GABLE, P.L.L.C. (AV)

Oneok Plaza, 100 West 5th Street, Suite 400, P.O. Box 21100, 74121-1100
Telephone: 918-582-1173
Fax: 918-592-3390
URL: http://www.rhodesokla.com

MEMBERS OF FIRM

Kevin D. Berry
Jo Anne Deaton
Richard M. Eldridge
E. D. Hieronymus (1908 -1994)
Bert M. Jones
William S. Leach
Michael W. McGivern
William D. Perrine
Mary Quinn-Cooper
Robert P. Redemann
David P. Reid
Chris L. Rhodes, III
Thomas E. Steichen
Catherine C. Taylor
John H. Tucker
Wilson T. White
Harold C. Zuckerman

Ann E. Allison
Steven K. Bunting
Robert P. Coffey, Jr.
J. Christopher Davis
Andrew D. Downing
Dana L. Gish
Kerry R. Lewis
Andrew L. Richardson
Michael F. Smith
Leslie J. Southerland
Kimberly E. West
Keith A. Wilkes

OF COUNSEL

George W. Gable (Retired Partner)
Larry J. Fulton
Kelly M. Greenough

Representative Clients: American International Companies; Bechtel; Chubb Group of Insurance Companies; General Motors Corporation; Merrill, Lynch; Nissan Motor Corporation in U.S.A.; Pfizer, Inc.; Volkswagen of America, Volkswagen, A.G.; Zurich U.S.

For full biographical listings, see the Martindale-Hubbell Law Directory

RICHARDS & CONNOR (AV)

9 East 4th Street, Suite 910, 74103-5103
Telephone: 918-585-2394
Fax: 918-585-1449

MEMBERS OF FIRM

Phil R. Richards
James W. Connor, Jr.

ASSOCIATES

Rachel Carver Mathis
Malinda S. Matlock
Thomas D. Hird
Jan L. Heister
Jason Lee Glass
John A.L. Campbell

For full biographical listings, see the Martindale-Hubbell Law Directory

THE ROACH LAW FIRM, P.C. (AV)

Park Centre, Suite 660, 525 South Main Street, 74103-4521
Telephone: 918-587-2544
Fax: 918-582-0551

Loyal J. Roach, III

Reference: Nations Bank, Tulsa.

For full biographical listings, see the Martindale-Hubbell Law Directory

THE ROBINSON LAW FIRM (AV)

15 West Sixth Street Suite 1850, 74119
Telephone: 918-587-2311
Fax: 918-587-2317

Eugene Robinson

ASSOCIATE

Kenneth M. Yates

For full biographical listings, see the Martindale-Hubbell Law Directory

SECREST, HILL & FOLLUO (AV)

7134 South Yale, Suite 900, 74136-6342
Telephone: 918-494-5905
Fax: 918-494-2847
Email: jksecrest@webzone.net

MEMBERS OF FIRM

James K. Secrest, II
W. Michael Hill
Dan S. Folluo

Richard C. Honn
Edward John Main
Roger N. Butler, Jr.
Nathan E. Clark
David A. Russell
John Jay Bowling
J. Derek Ingle
Brian J. Goree
Bradley A. Jackson

Representative Clients: Travelers/Aetna Casualty and Surety Co.; Allstate Insurance Co.; American States Insurance Co.; CNA Insurance Cos.; The Hanover Insurance Co.; Kemper Group; Maryland Casualty; United Services Automobile Association; Mid-Continent Casualty Group; Chubb Group of Insurance Cos.

For full biographical listings, see the Martindale-Hubbell Law Directory

Tulsa—Continued

SNEED LANG, P.C. (AV)

2300 Williams Center Tower II, Two West Second Street, 74103
Telephone: 918-583-3145
Telecopier: 918-582-0410

James C. Lang
D. Faith Orlowski
Brian S. Gaskill
G. Steven Stidham
Stephen R. McNamara
Thomas E. Black, Jr.
Robbie Emery Burke
Patrick O. Waddel
Randolph P. Stainer
Steven K. Balman
Brian T. Inbody
D. Michael McBride III

OF COUNSEL

James L. Sneed

Representative Clients: Amoco Production Co.; Bank One, Texas; Enron Corp.; Halliburton Energy Services; Helmerich & Payne, Inc.; Shell Oil Co.; State Farm Mutual Automobile Insurance Co.; The Williams Companies.

For full biographical listings, see the Martindale-Hubbell Law Directory

WILBURN, MASTERSON & SMILING (AV)

Executive Center II, 7134 South Yale, Suite 560, 74136-6337
Telephone: 918-494-0414
Fax: 918-493-3455
Email: wmslaw@ionet.net

Ray H. Wilburn
Michael J. Masterson
A. Mark Smiling

ASSOCIATES

Rhett Henry Wilburn
Scott R. Taylor
Jane R. Cowdery
Thomas J. Sullivent, Jr.
Elizabeth A. Ballard

For full biographical listings, see the Martindale-Hubbell Law Directory

OREGON

BEAVERTON, Washington Co.

CASE & DUSTERHOFF, LLP (AV)

9800 SW Beaverton Hillsdale Highway, Suite 200, 97005
Telephone: 503-641-7222
Facsimile: 503-643-5522
Email: jcase@case-dusterhoff.com

James D. Case
R. Bruce Dusterhoff

Leo A. Reinikka

For full biographical listings, see the Martindale-Hubbell Law Directory

*EUGENE,** Lane Co.

BROWN, ROSETA, LONG, McCONVILLE, KILCULLEN & CARLSON (AV)

210 Northbank Building, 44 Club Road, 97401
Telephone: 541-686-1883
Fax: 541-686-2008
Email: brownros@rio.com

MEMBERS OF FIRM

Larry A. Brown
Richard A. Roseta
Michael H. Long
Philip R. McConville
John F. Kilcullen
Charles D. Carlson
Thomas A. Ped

Representative Clients: All Nation Insurance Co.; Allstate Insurance Co.; American States Insurance Co.; Crawford & Co.; Grange Mutual Insurance; Heritage Life Insurance Co.; Insurance Corp. of America; Mutual of Enumclaw; Northwest Physicians Mutual Insurance Co.

For full biographical listings, see the Martindale-Hubbell Law Directory

CALKINS & CALKINS (AV)

1163 Olive Street, 97401
Telephone: 541-345-0371
FAX: 541-342-1220

MEMBERS OF FIRM

Windsor Calkins (1910-1989)
S. M. Calkins (1872-1969)
W. W. Calkins (1860-1945)
Win Calkins
Judy Ann Calkins

Josephine H. Mooney
Eric S. DeFreest

Counsel for: Eugene Water & Electric Board; Sacred Heart Medical Center; Lane County Medical Society; Oregon Automobile Insurance Co.; North Pacific Insurance Co.; St. Paul Insurance Cos.; American States Insurance Co.; Northwest Physicians Mutual Insurance Co.; General Accident Insurance Co.; Farmers Insurance Group.

For full biographical listings, see the Martindale-Hubbell Law Directory

*MEDFORD,** Jackson Co.

FROHNMAYER, DEATHERAGE, PRATT, JAMIESON, CLARKE & MOORE, P.C. (AV)

Larson Creek Professional Center, 2592 E. Barnett Road, 97504
Telephone: 541-779-2333
Fax: 541-779-6379
Email: fdfirm@internetcds.com

Otto J. Frohnmayer
William V. Deatherage
Steven H. Pratt
Stephen G. Jamieson
Mark D. Clarke
Bernard S. Moore
Thomas F. Armosino, Jr.

Tracy M. McGovern
Frederick H. Lundblade
Christian Oelke

Local Counsel for: Allstate Insurance Company; CNA; Farmers Insurance Group; Northwest Physicians Mutual Insurance Company; Professional Liability Fund.
General Counsel for: Lithia Motors, Inc.

For full biographical listings, see the Martindale-Hubbell Law Directory

*PORTLAND,** Multnomah Co.

BODYFELT, MOUNT, STROUP & CHAMBERLAIN (AV)

300 Powers Building, 65 S.W. Yamhill Street, 97204-3377
Telephone: 503-243-1022
Fax: 503-243-2019
Email: bmsc@bmsc-law.com

MEMBERS OF FIRM

Barry M. Mount
Roger K. Stroup
Peter R. Chamberlain
Richard A. Lee
Mark A. Hiefield

ASSOCIATES

Molly Jo Mullen
Eric "Skip" Winters
Aaron M. Brian

OF COUNSEL

Cathy E. Smith

Representative Clients: American International Group; Catholic Health Initiatives; Chrysler Corp.; Genuine Parts Co.; Georgia-Pacific Corp.; Hartford Insurance Co.; Oregon Mutual Insurance Company; Otis Elevator Co.; Safeway Stores, Inc.; Tokio Marine Insurance Co.

For full biographical listings, see the Martindale-Hubbell Law Directory

KEATING JONES BILDSTEIN & HUGHES, P.C. (AV)

800 Benjamin Franklin Plaza, One Southwest Columbia, 97258-2095
Telephone: 503-222-9955
Fax: 503-796-0699
Email: partners@keatingjones.com

Jeffrey W. Bildstein
Lindsey H. Hughes
Steven P. Jones
Robert M. Keating

Robert H. Beatty-Walters
Scott G O'Donnell
Katherine R. Heekin
Sheri C. Browning

OF COUNSEL

Richard E. Talbott
Molly K. Marcum

For full biographical listings, see the Martindale-Hubbell Law Directory

LEHNER, MITCHELL, RODRIGUES AND SEARS (AV)

Suite 1015 Crown Plaza, 1500 S.W. First Avenue, 97201
Telephone: 503-226-2225
Facsimle: 503-226-2418

MEMBERS OF FIRM

Michael A. Lehner
Michael C. Mitchell
Carl R. Rodrigues
Edward L. Sears

LEGAL SUPPORT PERSONNEL

Julie K. West
Barbara A. Bariletti

For full biographical listings, see the Martindale-Hubbell Law Directory

MOSCATO & HALLOCK (AV)

A Partnership including a Professional Corporation
1100 Union Bank of California Tower, 707 S.W. Washington Street, 97205
Telephone: 503-241-1442
FAX: 503-241-1458
Email: info@moscatolaw.com

Steven D. Hallock
Frank A. Moscato (P.C.)

(See Next Column)

MOSCATO & HALLOCK, *Portland—Continued*

OF COUNSEL

Paul L. Roess

ASSOCIATE

Matthew A. Borrillo

For full biographical listings, see the Martindale-Hubbell Law Directory

SATHER, BYERLY & HOLLOWAY, LLP (AV)

621 Southwest Morrison Street, Suite 650, 97205
Telephone: 503-225-5858
Fax: 503-721-9272
Email: sbh@teleport.com *URL:* http://www.teleport.com/~sbh/sbh.htm

Deborah L. Sather
Bruce L. Byerly
Ronald C. Holloway
Krishna Balasubramani
Tracy J. White
Constance Lynn Wold

For full biographical listings, see the Martindale-Hubbell Law Directory

*SALEM,** Marion Co.

ASHCROFT WILES, LLP (AV)

Formerly Rhoten, Rhoten & Speerstra
201 Pioneer Trust Building, 117 Commercial Street N.E., 97301
Telephone: 503-364-6734
Fax: 503-364-6735
Email: ashcroftwiles@uswest.net

MEMBERS OF FIRM

Lynn E. Ashcroft
David B. Wiles

ASSOCIATE

Mark Allen Ronning

OF COUNSEL

Timothy G. Bickler
J. Ray Rhoten (Retired)
Geo. A. Rhoten (1906-1988)
Sam F. Speerstra (1913-1994)

A list of representative clients will be furnished upon request.

For full biographical listings, see the Martindale-Hubbell Law Directory

PENNSYLVANIA

*ALLENTOWN,** Lehigh Co.

FONZONE & ASHLEY (AV)

33 South Seventh Street, P.O. Box 4180, 18105-4180
Telephone: 610-433-0121
Fax: 610-434-8440
Email: fonzlaw@aol.com

MEMBERS OF FIRM

Charles J. Fonzone
John W. Ashley

OF COUNSEL

James L. Weirbach

ASSOCIATES

Christopher W. Gittinger
Brian R. Longenhagen
Frances Ann Fruhwirth
Maryann E. Higgins
Frank G. Procyk

Representative Clients: Erie Insurance Exchange; State Farm Mutual Automobile Insurance Co.; Selective Insurance Co.; Mutual Benefit Insurance Co.; Brethren; Public Service Mutual Insurance Co.; Cumis Insurance Co; The PMA Insurance Group; The Medical Protective Co.

For full biographical listings, see the Martindale-Hubbell Law Directory

STEVENS & JOHNSON (AV)

(Successors to Butz & Rupp)
740 Hamilton Mall, 18101
Telephone: 610-439-1451
Telecopier: 610-439-1733

MEMBERS OF FIRM

Richard F. Stevens
Howard S. Stevens
Timothy T. Stevens
Paul F. Laughlin

OF COUNSEL

Robert J. Johnson
Herbert M. Rafner

General Counsel for: Lehigh Valley Hospital, Inc.
Representative Client: Phico Insurance Co.

For full biographical listings, see the Martindale-Hubbell Law Directory

BLUE BELL, Montgomery Co.

KELLEY & MURPHY (AV)

Union Meeting Corporate Center V, Suite 160 925 Harvest Drive, 19422
Telephone: 215-643-6500
Fax: 215-643-8356
Cable Address: "BIGTIME"
Email: kmlaw@counsel.com

Joseph T. Kelley, Jr.
Patrick G. Murphy
Joseph T. Kelley, III

LEGAL SUPPORT PERSONNEL

Marianne Rowen
Tanja M.Z. Barron

For full biographical listings, see the Martindale-Hubbell Law Directory

ELKINS PARK, Montgomery Co.

MONAGHAN & GOLD, P.C. (AV)

Manor Professional Building, 7837 Old York Road, 19027
Telephone: 215-782-1800
Fax: 215-782-1010
URL: http://www.MNG-LAW.com

Alan S. Gold
John F. X. Monaghan, Jr.

Murray R. Glickman
Tanya M. Sweet
Mitchell K. Brudno
Robert F. Fortin
Sean Robins
Kenneth W. Taylor
Francis D. Hennessy, Jr.

OF COUNSEL

Alan L. Butkovitz
Steven M. Zelitch
Barbara Malett Weitz

LEGAL SUPPORT PERSONNEL

Andrew Logan (Paralegal)
Carol Veach (Paralegal)
Janet McCrossen (Registered Nurse)

For full biographical listings, see the Martindale-Hubbell Law Directory

*ERIE,** Erie Co.

MARSH, SPAEDER, BAUR, SPAEDER & SCHAAF, LLP (AV)

Suite 300, 300 State Street, 16507
Telephone: 814-456-5301
Fax: 814-456-1112
Email: MSBSS@AOL.COM

MEMBERS OF FIRM

James E. Marsh, Sr. (1908-1988)
Ritchie T. Marsh (1870-1947)
John A. Spaeder (1902-1994)
Robert N. Spaeder (1915-1993)
Byron A. Baur (Retired)
Will J. Schaaf
Ritchie T. Marsh
William J. Schaaf
James E. Marsh, Jr.
John P. Eppinger
John C. Brydon
Thomas E. Kuhn
Thomas M. Lent
Francis J. Klemensic
John B. Fessler
Eugene C. Sundberg, Jr.
James R. Fryling
Donald F. Fessler, Jr.
Kurt L. Sundberg

Jeffrey Scibetta

Representative Clients: Borough of Edinboro; Cincinnati Insurance; Donegal Mutual Insurance Co.; Progressive Insurance; Erie Parking Authority; Home Insurance Co.; Marquette Savings Assn.; Motorists Insurance Co.; Northwest Savings Bank; Risk Enterprise and Management, Ltd.

For full biographical listings, see the Martindale-Hubbell Law Directory

*HARRISBURG,** Dauphin Co.

GOLDBERG, KATZMAN & SHIPMAN, P.C. (AV)

320 Market Street - Strawberry Square, P.O. Box 1268, 17108-1268
Telephone: 717-234-4161
Telecopier: 717-234-6808; 717-234-6810
Email: gks@gkslaw.com

F. Lee Shipman
Thomas E. Brenner
John A. Statler
Guy H. Brooks
Jefferson J. Shipman
Michael J. Crocenzi

Evan J. Kline
John R. Ninosky

Representative Clients: Cincinnati Insurance Co.; Atlantic Mutual Cos.; Erie Insurance Co.; Merchant's & Businessmen's Insurance Co.; State Auto Mutual Insurance Co.; Crawford & Co.; Foremost Insurance Co.; Virginia Mutual Insurance Co.; Zurich Commercial Insurance Group.
Reference: Fulton Bank.

For Complete List of Firm Personnel, See General Section
For full biographical listings, see the Martindale-Hubbell Law Directory

Harrisburg—Continued

METZGER, WICKERSHAM, KNAUSS & ERB, P.C. (AV)

3211 North Front Street, P.O. Box 5300, 17110-0300
Telephone: 717-238-8187
Telefax: 717-234-9478
Other Harrisburg, Pennsylvania Office: 4813 Jonestown Road, P.O. Box 5300, 17110-0300.
Telephone: 717-652-7020.

Maurice R. Metzger (1918-1980)
F. Brewster Wickersham (1918-1974)
Edward E. Knauss, III (Retired)
Christian S. Erb, Jr.
Robert E. Yetter
James F. Carl
Edward E. Knauss, IV
Jered L. Hock
Karl R. Hildabrand
Richard B. Druby
Steven P. Miner

Clark DeVere
Carrie L. Carroll

Representative Clients: Allstate Insurance Co.; Chubb Group of Insurance Companies; Fireman's Fund American Insurance Group; Liberty Mutual Insurance Co.; Crum & Forster; CNA Insurance; Prudential Insurance Co.

For full biographical listings, see the Martindale-Hubbell Law Directory

PETERS & WASILEFSKI (AV)

2931 North Front Street, 17110
Telephone: 717-238-7555
Fax: 717-238-7750
Email: pwlaw@redrose.net

MEMBERS OF FIRM

William J. Peters
Charles E. Wasilefski
Dennis J. Bonetti
Joseph C. Phillips
Michael R. Bonshock
Thomas A. Lang

ASSOCIATES

Pamela S. Parascandola
Stephen F. Moore
Cindy J. Murphy
James A. Garver

Reference: Commonwealth National Bank.

For full biographical listings, see the Martindale-Hubbell Law Directory

THOMAS, THOMAS & HAFER, LLP (AV)

305 North Front Street, 6th Floor, P.O. Box 999, 17108
Telephone: 717-237-7100
Fax: 717-237-7105
Verify: 717-255-7642
Bethlehem, Pennsylvania Office: 12 East Market Street, P.O. Box 1172, 12016.
Telephone: 610-868-1675.
Fax: 610-868-1702.

MEMBERS OF FIRM

Joseph P. Hafer
James K. Thomas, II
Robertson B. Taylor
Jeffrey B. Rettig
Peter J. Curry
R. Burke McLemore, Jr.
Edward H. Jordan, Jr.
C. Kent Price
Randall G. Gale
David L. Schwalm
Peter J. Speaker
Douglas B. Marcello
Paul J. Dellasega

OF COUNSEL

James K. Thomas

Timothy I. Mark
Daniel J. Gallagher
Robert A. Taylor
Sarah W. Arosell
Eugene N. McHugh
Stephen E. Geduldig
Karen S. Coates
Gary T. Lathrop
Todd B. Narvol
James J. Dodd-o
Kenneth A. Rapp
Kevin C. McNamara
Brooks R. Foland
John Flounlacker
John M. Popilock
Michele J. Thorp

Representative Clients: Aetna Casualty & Surety Co.; CIGNA; Commercial Union Insurance Companies; General Accident Group; Hartford Insurance Group; Liberty Mutual Insurance Co.; Maryland Casualty Co.; Ohio Casualty Co.; Pennsylvania Hospital Insurance Co.; Pennsylvania Medical Society Liability Insurance Co.

For full biographical listings, see the Martindale-Hubbell Law Directory

*MEDIA,** Delaware Co.

BEATTY, CRAMP, KAUFFMAN & LINCKE (AV)

215 North Olive Street, P.O. Box 901, 19063
Telephone: 610-565-8800
Fax: 610-565-8127
Email: BCKLLaw@aol.com

MEMBERS OF FIRM

Lewis B. Beatty, Jr.
Joseph W. Kauffman
David J. Otis
David G. Blake
William P. Lincke
Natalie M. Habert
Peter W. Dicce

(See Next Column)

ASSOCIATES

Regina M. MacKenzie
Bereth K. Graeff
Daniel J. McCusker
Kelly A. Barnes

OF COUNSEL

John F. Cramp
Ralph B. D'Iorio
Robert C. Grasberger

Joseph R. Young (1921-1993)

Representative Clients: Prudential; USAA; Zurich American; Geico, AIG.

For full biographical listings, see the Martindale-Hubbell Law Directory

*NEW CASTLE,** Lawrence Co.

LUXENBERG, GARBETT, KELLY & SAPIENZA, P.C. (AV)

303 Central Building, 16101-3763
Telephone: 724-658-8535
Fax: 724-658-8013
Ellwood City, Pennsylvania Office: 317 Seventh Street.
Telephone: 412-758-7581.
Fax: 412-758-0690.

Charles W. Garbett
Lawrence M. Kelly
Charles P. Sapienza, Jr.

Representative Clients: Erie Insurance Exchange; Ellwood Federal Savings Bank; Ohio Casualty Insurance Co.; Beneficial Consumer Discount Co.; Keystone Insurance Co.; Ellwood City Hospital.

For full biographical listings, see the Martindale-Hubbell Law Directory

*NORRISTOWN,** Montgomery Co.

MCTIGHE, WEISS, O'ROURKE & MILNER, P.C. (AV)

Eleven East Airy Street, P.O. Box 510, 19404
Telephone: 610-275-8800
Telecopier: 610-272-5325
Email: mctighe@montcolawyer.com *URL:* http://www.montcolawyer.com

Desmond J. McTighe (1902-1990)
Philip D. Weiss (Retired)
John R. O'Rourke, Jr.
Kenneth P. Milner
Julia Going Becker
Cynthia Weiss Stein

Philip A. Downey

Representative Clients: Colonial Penn Insurance Cos.; Co.; Penn Mutual Insurance Co.; National Grange Mutual Insurance Co.; Connecticut Specialty Insurance Co.; Celina Group; Penna; Medical Professional Liability Catastrophe Loss Fund; Liberty Mutual Insurance Co.; Zurich-American Insurance Co.; Colony Management Services, Inc.; Executive Risk Insurance Co.

For full biographical listings, see the Martindale-Hubbell Law Directory

MURPHY, OLIVER, CAIOLA & GOWEN, A PROFESSIONAL LAW CORPORATION (AV)

43 East Marshall Street, 19401-4828
Telephone: 610-272-4222; 610-279-3838
Fax: 610-272-2549; 610-275-0140
Email: molaw@injury-law.com *URL:* http://www.injury-law.com
Spring City, Pennsylvania Office: 500 S. Main Street, 19475.
Telephone: 610-948-3770.
Pottstown, Pennsylvania Office: 5 Sunnybrook Road, 19464.
Telephone: 610-323-3480.
West Chester, Pennsylvania Office: 1534 McDaniel Drive, Westtown Business Center, 19250.
Telephone: 610-272-4222.

James J. Oliver
Frank P. Murphy
Frank L. Caiola
Thomas L. Gowen, Jr.
Carla E. Connor
Barbara A. Barnes

John F. Haskins, Jr.
Cynthia Love Dengler
Carol A. Crisci

LEGAL SUPPORT PERSONNEL

Patricia A. Talese (Paralegal)
Kathleen Nicholson

For full biographical listings, see the Martindale-Hubbell Law Directory

*PHILADELPHIA,** Philadelphia Co.

BRITT, HANKINS, SCHAIBLE & MOUGHAN (AV)

Suite 515, Two Penn Center Plaza, 15th Street and John F. Kennedy Boulevard, 19102
Telephone: 215-569-6900
Fax: 215-569-3711
Email: bhsm@bhsm.com
Plymouth Meeting, Pennsylvania Office: 633 West Germantown Pike, Suite 202.
Telephone: 610-832-9339.
Fax: 610-832-9342. E-Mail: bhsm-pm@bhsm-pm.com.

(See Next Column)

BRITT, HANKINS, SCHAIBLE & MOUGHAN, *Philadelphia—Continued*

MEMBERS OF FIRM

Earl T. Britt
Joseph M. Hankins
Wayne A. Schaible
James T. Moughan (Resident Partner, Plymouth Meeting Office)
Joseph D. Mancano
Teresa Ficken Sachs
Lise Luborsky
Brian A. Wall, Jr.

ASSOCIATES

William S. Fox
Steven T. Williams
Elizabeth Schuetz Gallard
Edward Bradley
Richard L. Stutman
Gary A. Drakas
William J. McDonough
Charles J. Galvin
Christopher J. Urban
Christopher D. Strunk
Eric S. Scher

For full biographical listings, see the Martindale-Hubbell Law Directory

CHRISTIE, PABARUE, MORTENSEN AND YOUNG, A PROFESSIONAL CORPORATION (AV)

1880 JFK Boulevard - Tenth Floor, 19103
Telephone: 215-587-1600
Fax: 215-587-1699
Email: cpmy@cpmy.com *URL:* http://www.cpmy.com
Cherry Hill, New Jersey Office: Woodland Falls Corporate Park, 200 Lake Drive East.
Telephone: 609-482-7887.
Fax: 609-482-7438.
New York, N.Y. Office: 20 Exchange Place, 31st Floor.
Telephone: 212-366-1310.
Fax: 212-797-3545.
Boston, Massachusetts, Office: One State Street, Fifteenth Floor.
Telephone: 617-854-8315.
Fax: 617-854-8311.
Radnor, Pennsylvania Office: Radnor Station Building No. 2, Suite 222, 290 King of Prussia Road.
Telephone: 610-688-5778.
Fax: 610-688-5788.

James W. Christie
Bradley J. Mortensen
James A. A. Pabarue, Jr.
James A. Young
Jerome E. Bogutz
Marc L. Bogutz
John D. Frumer (Resident, Boston, Massachusetts Office)
Ralph J. Luongo
Peter J. Lynch
Stella M. Tsai
Brian C. Vance

Anthony J. Arena
Carolyn Bates
Rex F. Brien
K. Tia Burke
Michael J. Burns
Michael E. DiFebbo, Jr.
John C. Falls (Resident, Cherry Hill, New Jersey Office)
Christie L. Gamble
Nadine M. Hunt
Elaine Whiteman Klinger
Randy J. Maniloff
Richard S. Margulies
Christopher M. Martin
Etienne C. Maumus
William F. McDevitt
Catherine O. Raymond
Heather A. Salko
Marie T. Sarkees
Barbara L. Schmuck
Paul V. Shehadi
Randee Lynn Strair
June A. Taima
Christina G. Tershakovec
Thaddeus J. Weaver
Marybeth Smith Werb
Lisa B. Zucker

For full biographical listings, see the Martindale-Hubbell Law Directory

COZEN AND O'CONNOR, A PROFESSIONAL CORPORATION (AV)

1900 Market Street, 19103
Telephone: 215-665-2000
800-523-2900
Fax: 215-665-2013
Email: postmaster@cozen.com *URL:* http://www.cozen.com
Charlotte, North Carolina Office: One First Union Center, Suite 2100, 301 S. College Street, 28202.
Telephones: 704-376-3400; 800-762-3575.
Fax: 704-334-3351.
Dallas, Texas Office: 2300 BankOne Center, 1717 Main Street, 75201.
Telephones: 214-462-3000; 800-448-1207.
Fax: 214-462-3299.
New York, N.Y. Office: 45 Broadway Atrium, 16th Floor, 10006.
Telephones: 212-509-9400; 800-437-7040.
Fax: 212-509-9492.
West Conshohocken, Pennsylvania Office: 200 Four Falls Corporate Center, Suite 400, P.O. Box 800, 19428.
Telephone: 610-941-5400.
Fax: 610-941-0711.
San Diego, California Office: Suite 1610, 501 West Broadway, 92101.
Telephones: 619-234-1700; 800-782-3366.
Fax: 619-234-7831.
Los Angeles, California Office: 777 Tower, 777 South Figueroa Street, Suite 2850, 90017.
Telephones: 213-892-7900; 800-563-1027.
Fax: 213-892-7999.

(See Next Column)

Seattle, Washington Office: Suite 5200, Washington Mutual Tower, 1201 Third Avenue, 98101.
Telephones: 206-340-1000; 800-423-1950.
Fax: 206-621-8783.
Westmont, New Jersey Office: 316 Haddon Avenue, 08108.
Telephones: 609-854-4900; 800-523-2900.
Fax: 609-854-1782.
Newark, New Jersey Office: One Newark Center, Suite 1900, 1085 Raymond Boulevard, 07102.
Telephone: 973-286-1200; 888-200-9521.
Fax: 973-242-2121.
Atlanta, Georgia Office: Suite 2200, SunTrust Plaza, 303 Peachtree Street, N.E., 30308.
Telephones: 404-572-2000; 800-890-1393.
Fax: 404-572-2199.
London, England Office: Cozen and O'Connor at Radcliffes, 5 Great College Street, Westminster, SW1P 3SJ.
Telephone: 011-44-207-654-7600.
Fax: 011-44-207-654-7613.
Wilmington, Delaware Office: Chase Manhattan Centre, 1201 North Market Street, Suite 1400, 19801.
Telephone: 302-295-2000; 888-207-2440.
Fax: 302-295-2013.
Mt. Laurel, New Jersey Office: 10,000 Midlantic Drive, Suite 301, 08054.

FIRM MEMBERS IN PHILADELPHIA

Stephen A. Cozen
Joseph J. Bellew
Denise Brinker Bense
John Dwyer
Ann Thornton Field
Thomas F. Gallagher
Josh M. Greenbaum
Dexter R. Hamilton
Ronald B. Hamilton
James H. Heller
Denise H. Houghton
Patrick J. O'Connor
William H. Howard
Richard M. Mackowsky
Michael R. McCarty
Deborah Melamut Minkoff
Joseph H. Riches
John T. Salvucci
William F. Stewart
Jeffrey R. Stoner
John T. Thorn
Joshua Wall
Anita B. Weinstein

Representative Clients: Available upon request.

For Complete List of Firm Personnel, See General Section

For full biographical listings, see the Martindale-Hubbell Law Directory

DEASEY, MAHONEY & BENDER, LTD. (AV)

1800 John F. Kennedy Boulevard, Suite 1300, 19103-2978
Telephone: 215-587-9400
Facsimile: 215-587-9456
Email: dmbphila@aol.com
Haddonfield, New Jersey Office: 80 Tanner Street, 08033-2419.
Telephone: 609-429-6331.
Facsimile: 609-429-6562.

William R. Deasey (1917-1993)
James G. Barnes (1961-1997)
Francis J. Deasey
Harry G. Mahoney
James W. Daly, IV

K. Craig McChesney
Gerald J. Valentini
James B. Burns
Jane A. North
Thomas C. Sullivan
John P. Kamstra
Pamela J. Devine
Jane G. O'Donnell
Barbara Corr Morrow
Henri Marcel

OF COUNSEL

Frank C. Bender

For full biographical listings, see the Martindale-Hubbell Law Directory

JOHN GERARD DEVLIN & ASSOCIATES, P.C. (AV)

1515 Market Street Suite 2010, 19102
Telephone: 215-564-6740
Telefax: 215-564-6732
Email: devlinlaw@aol.com
Allentown, Pennsylvania Office: The Sovereign Building, Executive Suite 103, 609 Hamilton Mall.
Telephone: 215-820-6422.
Westmont, New Jersey Office: 216 Haddon Avenue, Suite 103.
Telephone: 609-858-1690.
Fax: 609-858-8998.
East Brunswick, New Jersey Office: 190 Route 18, Suite 3000.
Telephone: 908-214-2621.
Fax: 908-246-2917.
Wilkes-Barre, Pennsylvania Office: Cross Creek Pointe, 1065 Hwy 315, Suite H.
Telephone: 610-820-6422.

John Gerard Devlin
James B. Corrigan, Jr.
Joseph T. Murphy, Jr.
Thomas Paschos
Michael Malarick
Suzanne Curran Murphy
Arthur F. Wheeler
Paul A. Lawless, Jr.

Representative Clients: Lloyds of London; Commercial Union; John Hancock Property and Casualty Insurance Co.; Wausau Insurance Co.; Hanseco Insurance Co.; American Family Insurance Co.; Liberty Mutual Insurance Co.; Linberg Adjustment Co.

(See Next Column)

JOHN GERARD DEVLIN & ASSOCIATES, P.C.—*Continued*

For full biographical listings, see the Martindale-Hubbell Law Directory

GALLAGHER, REILLY, LACHAT & EGBERT, P.C. (AV)

Suite 1300, 2000 Market Street, 19103
Telephone: 215-299-3000
Fax: 215-299-3010
Email: grllaw@erols.com
Pennsauken, New Jersey Office: Kevon Office Center, Suite 130, 2500 McClellan Boulevard, 09109.
Telephone: 856-663-8200.
Fax: 856-663-1923.
Colonia, New Jersey Office: 800 Inman Avenue, 07067.
Telephone: 908-382-4660.
Facsimile: 908-382-3338.
Wilmington, Delaware Office: 800 Delaware Avenue, The Corporate Plaza, 7th Floor, 19801.
Telephone: 302-652-4477.
Fax: 302-652-8405.

Paul F. X. Gallagher
Thomas F. Reilly
Frederick T. Lachat, Jr.
James Emerson Egbert
Maureen Rowan

Wilfred T. Mills, Jr.
Sean F. Kennedy
Julie Cavanagh
John A. Livingood, Jr.
Lawrence Farnese, Jr.
Holly L. McReynolds
C. Curtis Staropoli
Ellen Wilber Fulker

SPECIAL COUNSEL

Dolores Rocco Kulp

For full biographical listings, see the Martindale-Hubbell Law Directory

GOLDFEIN & JOSEPH, A PROFESSIONAL CORPORATION (AV)

1600 Market Street 33rd Floor, 19103-7288
Telephone: 215-979-8200
Fax: 215-979-8201
URL: http://www.goldfeinlaw.com
Princeton, New Jersey Office: Princeton Metro Center, Suite 115, 5 Vaughn Drive.
Telephone: 609-520-0400.
Fax: 609-520-1450.
Wilmington, Delaware Office: PNC Bank Center, Suite 1110, P.O. Box 2206, 222 Delaware Avenue.
Telephone: 302-656-3301.
Fax: 302-656-0643.
New York, New York Office: 150 Broadway, Suite 1212, 10038.
Telephone: 212-791-0340.
Fax: 212-791-0347.

Edward B. Joseph
Fredric L. Goldfein
E. Chandler Hosmer, III
David C. Weinberg
Bernard L. Levinthal
Roseann Lynn Brenner
Gary H. Kaplan
John A. Turlik

Michael A. Billotti
Medford J. Brown, III
Robert P. Coleman
Robert T. Connor
Charles D. Cooper
Kelly A. Costello
Lawrence E. Currier
Janet E. Golup
Christine Renee Guiliano
David M. Katzenstein
Matthew A Kelly, III
Deborah M. Knight
Pamela A. Post
Thomas M. Savon
Julie M. Sebring (Not admitted in PA)
Robert M. Stroh
Marc R. Wilner
Anthony F. Zabicki, Jr.

For full biographical listings, see the Martindale-Hubbell Law Directory

HARAD, GITTLEMAN, GREENBERG, BRUNNER & LOVE (AV)

1310 Two Penn Center Plaza 15th & John F. Kennedy Boulevard, 19102-1722
Telephone: 215-561-9999
Fax: 215-561-7369

MEMBERS OF FIRM

Charles A. Harad
Gary V. Gittleman
Michael E. Greenberg
Gail A. Brunner
Judith A. Love

D. Scott Bonebrake
Maria R. Granaudo
Thomas A. McCormack

For full biographical listings, see the Martindale-Hubbell Law Directory

KELLEY, JASONS, McGUIRE & SPINELLI, L.L.P. (AV)

One Penn Center, Suite 1400, 1617 JFK Boulevard, 19103
Telephone: 215-854-0658
Fax: 215-854-8434; 215-854-0777
Marlton, New Jersey Office: One Greentree Centre, Suite 201, 08053.
Telephone: 609-988-5543.
Fax: 609-988-9165.

(See Next Column)

Wilmington, Delaware Office: 800 Delaware Avenue, P.O. Box 194, 19899.
Telephone: 302-652-8560.
Fax: 302-652-8405.

MEMBERS OF FIRM

John Patrick Kelley
Catherine N. Jasons
Joseph W. McGuire
Armand J. Della Porta, Jr.
Christopher N. Santoro
Robert N. Spinelli
Thomas P. Hanna
Thomas J. Johanson
Michael L. Turner
Richard L. Walker, II
Timothy McGowan

ASSOCIATES

Neal C. Glenn
W. Matthew Reber
Ann C. Lebowitz
Anthony J. Ryan

OF COUNSEL

Matthew D. Blum

For full biographical listings, see the Martindale-Hubbell Law Directory

KITTREDGE, DONLEY, ELSON, FULLEM & EMBICK, LLP (AV)

Fifth Floor, The Bank Building, 421 Chestnut Street, 19106-2416
Telephone: 215-829-9900
Fax: 215-829-9888
Email: lawoffice@kdefe.com *URL:* http://www.kdefe.com

MEMBERS OF FIRM

Patrick W. Kittredge
Joseph M. Donley
Barry R. Elson
Joseph W. Fullem, Jr.
John R. Embick
Keith E. Johnston

ASSOCIATES

Glenn E. Davis
Michael S. Soule
Patricia Powers
Brendan P. McGlynn
Lisa G. Miller
Edward Bigham
Michael K. Smith (1963-1995)

OF COUNSEL

Richard B. Pearl

For full biographical listings, see the Martindale-Hubbell Law Directory

LAVIN, COLEMAN, O'NEIL, RICCI, FINARELLI & GRAY (AV)

Suite 1000, 510 Walnut Street, 19106
Telephone: 215-627-0303
Fax: 215-627-2551
Mount Laurel, New Jersey Office: 8000 Midlantic Drive, Suite 201 South.
Telephone: 609-778-5544.
Fax: 609-778-3383.
New York, New York Office: 7th Floor, 767 Third Avenue.
Telephone: 212-319-6898.
Fax: 212-319-6932.

George J. Lavin, Jr.
Thomas Finarelli
William V. Coleman
Francis F. Quinn
Joseph E. O'Neil
Francis P. Burns, III
William J. Ricci
Edward A. Gray
Basil A. DiSipio
Wayne A. Graver
Gerard Cedrone
Mary Grace Maley
Christine O. Boyd
Michael D. Brophy
Joseph A. McGinley
Robert J. Hafner
Robert J. Martin
Susan Ellyn Satkowski
Henry Michael Clinton
Francis J. Grey, Jr.
Richard B. Wickersham, Jr.
John J. Bateman
Ronald W. Boak
Michael T. Droogan, Jr.
Eugene Hamill
Michael P. Kinkopf
Stephen E. Moore
Michael J. Quinn
William E. Staas, III
Denise Carroll Chaplin
Marsha E. Flora
Peter M. Newman
John J. O'Donnell
Jo E. Peifer

Valerie Aabdollah
Lee R. Allman
Jennifer M. Brooks
Jessica Faden (Resident, Mount Laurel, New Jersey Office)
Frank C. B. Friestedt
Louis Giansante
Julie M. Holland
Leland I. Kellner
George J. Lavin, III
Margot L. Ludlam (Resident, New York, New York Office)
Daniel P. Lynch
Leona C. McFadden
Lorraine B. McGlynn
Henry James Noye
Michael J. O'Neill
Monica Tamar Proffitt
Sheila Marie Raftery
Michelle S. Regan (Resident, New York, New York Office)
Robert L. Sanzo
William E. Schaefer
Richard J. Sexton
Gregory Steven Spizer
Susan L. Troxell
Fiona J. Van Dyck
Anne E. Walters
Dennis P. Ziemba

For full biographical listings, see the Martindale-Hubbell Law Directory

Philadelphia—Continued

MANTA AND WELGE, A PROFESSIONAL CORPORATION (AV)

2000 Market Street, 6th Floor, 19103
Telephone: 215-851-6600
Telecopy: 215-851-6644
URL: http://www.mantalaw.com
Allentown, Pennsylvania Office: Suite 204, 5000 Tilghman Street.
Telephone: 610-395-7499.
Fax: 610-366-5096.
Harrisburg, Pennsylvania Office: Governors Row, 27 North Front Street.
Telephone: 717-236-8420.
West Trenton, New Jersey Office: 810 Bear Tavern Road, Suite 301.
Telephone: 609-883-6990.
Fax: 609-883-7730.
Wilmington, Delaware Office: Suite 1400, Mellon Bank Center, 919 Market Street.
Telephone: 302-655-7460.
Fax: 302-655-7004.

MEMBERS OF FIRM

William R. Hourican
Albert L. Piccerilli
Margaret E. Wenke
Kim Hollaender
Albert M. Saltz

Joseph B. Silverstein
Ellen R. Tarrington
Daniel C. Moraglia
Robert M. Cavalier
Denise Adamucci
Jennifer M. Welding
Robert S. Stickley
Michael A. Green

For full biographical listings, see the Martindale-Hubbell Law Directory

---

MARKS, O'NEILL, REILLY, O'BRIEN & COURTNEY, P.C. (AV)

1880 John F. Kennedy Boulevard Suite 1200, 19103
Telephone: 215-564-6688
Fax: 215-564-2526
Email: moro1@morocpa.com
Norristown, Pennsylvania Office: 411 Cherry Street.
Telephone: 215-277-7601.
Pittsburgh, Pennsylvania Office: 707 Grant Street, Gulf Tower, Suite 3200.
Telephone: 412-391-6171.
Fax: 412-391-8804.
Westmont, New Jersey Office: 216 Haddon Avenue, Suite 500.
Telephone: 856-858-6110.
Fax: 856-858-3687. E-Mail: moro1@morocnj.com
Wilmington, Delaware Office: 2004 Foulk Road, Suite 7.
Telephone: 302-475-5500.
Fax: 302-475-5584.

Jerome E. Marks
Joseph M. O'Neill
Vincent F. Reilly
Kevin J. O'Brien
Dawn R. Courtney
Sean Xavier Kelly
Gino P. Mecoli
John J. Repcheck (Resident, Pittsburgh Office)

David P. Helwig (Resident, Pittsburgh Office)
Maureen Murray-O'Toole
Patrick C. Lamb
Christine G. Boyle
Nancy E. Mancheski
Michael T. Hamilton
Kelly L. Bracken
Tracey Marie McDevitt
Sharon A. Connors (Resident, Westmont, New Jersey Office)
Malissa A. Richetti
Patricia M. Henrich
Judith H. Ring
Gary Weinberg (Resident, Westmont, New Jersey Office)
Lee J. Janiczek
Wendy D. Testa (Resident, Westmont, New Jersey Office)
Gary F. Sharlock (Resident, Pittsburgh Office)
Robert Dale Leidigh (Resident, Pittsburgh Office)
Joseph L. Orszulak, II (Resident, Pittsburgh Office)
Diane Beckman Carvell
Karen J. Stanzione
Michael A. Kosar
Susan D. Grant (Resident, Westmont, New Jersey Office)
Frances Wang-Deveney (Resident, Westmont, New Jersey)
Courtney E. Passin
Stephanie Victoria Shreibman
Megan Kochell D'Iorio (Resident, Wilmington, Delaware Office)
Megan Trocki Mantzavinos (Resident, Wilmington, Delaware Office)
Toni Anderson Moore
Natalie M. Nugent
Frank Gattuso
Michael A. Ring (Resident, Westmont, New Jersey Office)
Ann M. Madden (Not admitted in PA)
Matthew J. Zamites
Salvatore A. Clemente

LEGAL SUPPORT PERSONNEL

PARALEGALS

Gregory P. Sabo
Elisa LaRosa
Frances P. Rossi
Heather Feenan
Jerry Ezekiel
Steven Randisi
Sharon Williams
Melanie Gaskins

For full biographical listings, see the Martindale-Hubbell Law Directory

MCCORMICK & PRIORE, P.C. (AV)

One Penn Square West, 30 S. 15th Street, Suite 1500, 19102
Telephone: 215-972-0161
Fax: 215-972-5580
Email: mccormick5@aol.com
Marlton, New Jersey Office: One Greentree Centre, Suite 201, 08053.
Telephone: 609-988-5452.
Fax: 609-596-8359.

David M. McCormick
Philip D. Priore
Stephen M. McManus

OF COUNSEL

Harry A. Short, Jr.

Wendy L. Schmidt-Levin
H. Joseph Byron
Michelle Nick Rossi
Christina A. Toriello
Jill Schneider
John P. Lock

LEGAL SUPPORT PERSONNEL

Deborah Stefan
Jane Coley

For full biographical listings, see the Martindale-Hubbell Law Directory

---

MCKISSOCK & HOFFMAN, P.C. (AV)

1700 Market Street, Suite 3000, 19103
Telephone: 215-246-2100
Fax: 215-246-2144
Westmont, New Jersey Office: 216 Haddon Avenue, Suite 603.
Telephone: 609-858-1650.
Fax: 609-858-1466.
Doylestown, Pennsylvania Office: 16 North Franklin Street, Suite 300.
Telephone: 215-345-4501.
Fax: 215-246-4503.
Harrisburg, Pennsylvania Office: 105 North Front Street, Suite 205.
Telephone: 717-234-0103.
Fax: 717-234-1350.
West Chester, Pennsylvania Office: 31 South High Street, P.O. Box 3086.
Telephone: 610-738-8850.
Fax: 610-738-9121.

J. Bruce McKissock
Peter J. Hoffman
Leslie Anne Miller
Jeffrey B. Albert
Jill Baratz Clarke
John J. McGrath (Resident, Westmont, New Jersey Office)
Donald J. Brooks, Jr.
William J. Mundy
Bryan Craig Black (Resident, Harrisburg Office)
Eileen Lampe
Christopher Thomson (Resident Shareholder, West Chester Office)
K. Reed Haywood
Maureen P. Fitzgerald

For full biographical listings, see the Martindale-Hubbell Law Directory

---

REMICK MARTONE, A PROFESSIONAL CORPORATION (AV)

1608 Walnut Street, Suite 703, 19103
Telephone: 215-772-3010
Fax: 215-772-3017
URL: http://remick-martone.com
Hammonton, New Jersey Office: P.O. Box 1172. 110 Route 206, 08037.
Telephone: 609-567-4500.
Fax: 609-567-7524.

Lloyd Zane Remick
Lauren Remick Martone
Margaret Loud Charendoff
Marjorie Singer Ochroch
Jacqueline Borock
Ernest De Stefano
Gregory M. Pedicin (Not admitted in PA)
Charles Sovel
Paul A. Leodori

LEGAL SUPPORT PERSONNEL

Amanda Rae Gross

For full biographical listings, see the Martindale-Hubbell Law Directory

---

RYAN, BROWN, MCDONNELL, BERGER GIBBONS & LAROCCA, LLP (AV)

1600 Market Street, Suite 2500, 19103-7240
Telephone: 215-564-3800
Facsimile: 215-564-1301
Email: lawfirm@ryanbrown.com
Cherry Hill, New Jersey Office: 500 Kings Highway South, 08034.
Telephone: 609-216-8155.
Facsimile: 609-429-7726.

Daniel J. Ryan
John R. Brown
Michael T. McDonnell, III
Mitchell S. Berger
Patrick J. Gibbons
Robert J. LaRocca

For full biographical listings, see the Martindale-Hubbell Law Directory

Philadelphia—Continued

SILVERMAN FRIMMER BERNHEIM & MCDONNELL, A PROFESSIONAL CORPORATION (AV)

Two Penn Center Plaza, Suite 910, 19102
Telephone: 215-569-0000
Fax: 215-636-3999
Email: lawyers@scf-law.com *URL:* http://www.scf-law.com
Westmont, New Jersey Office: Sentry Office Plaza, Suite 704. 216 Haddon Avenue, 08108-2815.
Telephone: 609-858-9499.
Fax: 609-858-4606.

Lawrence M. Silverman
Daniel S. Bernheim, 3rd
Patrick J. McDonnell
Jonathan S. Ziss
Jeffrey A. Krawitz
Jill Fisher

Jonathan J. Bart
David J. Gaier
Courtney Seda
Marc D. Weinberg
Jonathan A. Cass
Karen L. Green

Representative Clients: Boat Owners Association of the United States; Delta Air Lines, Inc.; John Deere Transporation Insurance; Princeton Insurance Co.; Rider Insurance Co.; U.S. Aviation Underwriters, Inc.; Robinson Bus Service, Inc./Educo Transit; Temple University Health System; Wal-Mart Stores Inc.; Protective National Insurance Co.

For full biographical listings, see the Martindale-Hubbell Law Directory

CLAYTON H. THOMAS, JR. (AV)

37th Floor, Bell Atlantic Tower Building, 1717 Arch Street, 19103-2793
Telephone: 215-994-5290
Fax: 215-994-5296

Benjamin Rose

For full biographical listings, see the Martindale-Hubbell Law Directory

WILBRAHAM, LAWLER & BUBA, A PROFESSIONAL CORPORATION (AV)

1818 Market Street, Suite 3100, 19103-3631
Telephone: 215-564-4141
Fax: 215-564-4385
Email: @wlbdeflaw.com
Haddonfield, New Jersey Office: 24 Kings Highway West.
Telephone: 856-795-4422.
Fax: 856-795-4699.
Wilmington, Delaware Office: Stoney Batter Office Building, 5301 Limestone Road, Suite 221.
Telephone: 302-234-8217.
Fax: 302-234-8218.

Edward J. Wilbraham
Robert B. Lawler
Barbara J. Buba
Michael J. Block

R. Erick Chizmar
Kevin J. Maginnis
InSook Kim
Sandra D. Terry-Crawford
John S. Howarth
David M. Maselli
Renee E. Berger
Edward T. Finch
Sean P. Buggy

OF COUNSEL

Walter J. Timby, Jr.
Daniel J. Allan

Representative Clients: GAF Corporation; Armstrong World Industries, Inc.; U.S. Gypsum Company; Georgia-Pacific Corporation; ARCO; Shell; Royal; AIG; Chubb; Keystone.

For full biographical listings, see the Martindale-Hubbell Law Directory

YOST & TRETTA (AV)

2 Penn Center Plaza, Suite, 610, 1500 John F. Kennedy Boulevard, 19102
Telephone: 215-972-6600
Telecopier: 215-972-6609

Richard W. Yost
Christopher M. Tretta
John M. Campbell
Donald I. Wall
Jill A. Maslynsky
Charles W. Spitz

For full biographical listings, see the Martindale-Hubbell Law Directory

ZARWIN, BAUM, DEVITO, KAPLAN & O'DONNELL, P.C. (AV)

1515 Market Street, Suite 1200, 19102
Telephone: 215-569-2800
Fax: 215-569-1606
Cherry Hill, New Jersey Office: Woodland Falls Corporate Center, Suite 105, 220 Lake Drive East, 08002.
Telephone: 609-667-3434.
Fax: 609-667-2491.
Jersey City, New Jersey Office: 75 Montgomery Street, Suite 200, 07302.
Telephone: 201-432-7840.
Fax: 201-432-3945.

(See Next Column)

Norman P. Zarwin
E. Harris Baum
John R. O'Donnell
Mitchell S. Kaplan
Gary A. DeVito
Theodore M. Schaer
Lionel A. Prince
Joseph M. Toddy
Kenneth J. Fleisher

Gary Alan Zlotnick
Edward J. McKenna
Jay L. Solnick
Lisa M. Zinn
Michelle R. Sergent
Joseph W. Denneler
Xavier P. Hayden
Mindy L. Feldstein
David R. Joseph
Glori A. Friedman

OF COUNSEL

Joseph F. Busacca
Ronald J. Bayer
Dennis L. Friedman
Mario F. Driggs

For full biographical listings, see the Martindale-Hubbell Law Directory

*PITTSBURGH,** Allegheny Co.

ANSTANDIG, MCDYER, BURDETTE & YURCON, P.C. (AV)

Suite 1300 Gulf Tower, 707 Grant Street, 15219-1911
Telephone: 412-765-3700
Facsimile: 412-765-3730
Email: ambylaw@usaor.net

Louis Anstandig
Daniel P. McDyer
Timothy J. Burdette
Edward A. Yurcon

John F. Deasy
Rebecca Sember
Shawn G. McMahon
Benjamin Marc Mayer

For full biographical listings, see the Martindale-Hubbell Law Directory

DAVIES MCFARLAND & CARROLL, P.C. (AV)

One Gateway Center, Tenth Floor, 15222
Telephone: 412-281-0737
Email: firm@dmcpc.com

Ralph A. Davies
Daniel P. Carroll
William D. Geiger
Francis Garger
Lynn E. Bell
C. Robert Keenan III
M.J. (Jeff) Tindall
Eric K. Falk
David E. Lamm
Clare M. Bello

Howard K. Hilner
Kristin L. Pieseski
Mary Kathleen Coleman
Julie L. Nord
Andrew G. Thiros

Representative Clients: Cincinnati Insurance Co.; GAB Business Services, Inc.; John Deere Insurance Co.; Motorists Insurance Cos.; The Travelers; Physicians Insurance Co.; CNA Insurance Cos.; PA Medical Society Liability Ins. Co.; The Medical Protective Co.; PHICO Insurance Co.; Metropolitan Life Insurance Co.; Premier Auto Insurance Co.; Pharmacists Mutual Ins. Co.

For Complete List of Firm Personnel, See General Section
For full biographical listings, see the Martindale-Hubbell Law Directory

FELDSTEIN GRINBERG STEIN & MCKEE, A PROFESSIONAL CORPORATION (AV)

428 Boulevard of the Allies, 15219
Telephone: 412-471-0677
Fax: 412-263-6129
URL: http://www.fgsmlaw.com
Elizabeth, Pennsylvania Office: 400 Second Street.
Telephone: 412-384-6111.

Jay H. Feldstein
Stanley M. Stein
Gary M. Lang

James C. Heneghan
David S. Bloom
Cory Owen Daschbach
Regis J. Moeller

For full biographical listings, see the Martindale-Hubbell Law Directory

HEINTZMAN, WARREN, WISE & FORNELLA, P.C. (AV)

The 35th Floor, Gulf Tower, 707 Grant Street, 15219
Telephone: 412-394-7810
Fax: 412-263-5222
Email: hww@hwwlaw.com *URL:* http://www.hwwlaw.com

Michael D. Heintzman
Charles S. Warren
Roger L. Wise
Leonard Fornella
Joseph R. Schaper
Kenneth F. Klanica

Jeanine L. Fonner
Jeanne Welch Sopher
Max T. Busatto

For full biographical listings, see the Martindale-Hubbell Law Directory

Pittsburgh—Continued

JONES, DAY, REAVIS & POGUE (AV)

500 Grant Street 31st Floor, 15219
Telephone: 412-391-3939
Telecopier: 412-394-7959
Email: counsel@jonesday.com *URL:* http://www.jonesday.com
In Atlanta, Georgia: 3500 SunTrust Plaza, 303 Peachtree Street.
Telephone: 404-521-3939.
Telecopier: 404-581-8330.
In Brussels, Belgium: Avenue Louise 480, 7th Floor, B-1050 Brussels.
Telephone: 32-2-645-14-11.
Telecopier: 32-2-645-14-45.
In Chicago, Illinois: 77 West Wacker.
Telephone: 312-782-3939.
Telecopier: 312-782-8585.
In Cleveland, Ohio: North Point, 901 Lakeside Avenue.
Telephone: 216-586-3939.
Telecopier: 216-579-0212.
In Columbus, Ohio: 1900 Huntington Center.
Telephone: 614-469-3939.
Telecopier: 614-461-4198.
In Dallas, Texas: 2727 North Harwood Street.
Telephone: 214-220-3939.
Telecopier: 214-969-5100.
In Frankfurt, Germany: Hochhaus am Park, Grüneburgweg 102, 60323 Frankfurt am Main.
Telephone: 49-69-9726-3939.
Telecopier: 49-69-9726-3993.
In Geneva, Switzerland: 20, rue de Candolle.
Telephone: 41-22-320-2339.
Telecopier: 41-22-320-1232.
In Hong Kong: 29th Floor, Entertainment Building, 30 Queen's Road Central.
Telephone: 852-2526-6895.
Telecopier: 852-2868-5871 or 852-2868-5699.
In Irvine, California: 5 Park Plaza, Suite 1100.
Telephone: 949-851-3939.
Telecopier: 949-553-7539.
In London, England: Bucklersbury House, 3 Queen Victoria Street.
Telephone: 44-171-236-3939.
Telecopier: 44-171-236-1113. 34000 Los Angeles, California: 555 West Fifth Street, Suite 4600.
Telephone: 213-489-3939.
Telecopier: 213-243-2539.
In New Delhi, India (Associate Office): Pathak & Associates (an associate firm of Jones, Day, Reavis & Pogue), 1st Floor, Dr. Gopal Das Bhaven, 28 Barakhamba Road.
Telephone: 91-11-373-8793; 91-11-335-7345.
Telecopier: 91-11-335-3761.
In New York, New York: 599 Lexington Avenue.
Telephone: 212-326-3939.
Telecopier: 212-755-7306.
In Paris, France: 120, rue du Faubourg Saint-Honoré.
Telephone: 33-1-56-59-39-39.
Telecopier: 33-1-56-59-39-38
In Riyadh, Saudi Arabia: The International Law Firm (In Association with Jones, Day, Reavis & Pogue), Sulaymaniyah, Prince Mishari IBN, Abdulaziz Street, P.O. Box 22166.
Telephone: (966-1) 462-8866.
Telecopier: (966-1) 462-9001.
In Shanghai, China: 2805 Kerry Centre, 1515 Nanjing Road West.
Telephone: 86-21-5298-6568.
Telecopier: 86-21-5298-6569.
In Sydney, Australia: Governor Phillip Tower, Level 38, 1 Farrer Place.
Telephone: 61-2-9210-6921.
Telecopier: 61-2-9210-6926.
In Taipei, Taiwan: 8th Floor, 2 Tun Hwa South Road, Section 2.
Telephone: (886-2) 2704-6808.
Telecopier: (886-2) 2704-6791.
In Tokyo, Japan: Toranomon MT Building, 4th Floor, 10-3, Toranomon 3-Chome, Minato-Ku, Tokyo 105, Japan.
Telephone: 81-3-3433-3939.
Telecopier: 81-3-5401-2725.
In Washington, D.C.: 51 Louisiana Avenue, N.W.
Telephone: 202-879-3939.
Telecopier: 202-626-1700.

MEMBER OF FIRM IN PITTSBURGH

J. W. Montgomery, III

For Complete List of Firm Personnel, See General Section

For full biographical listings, see the Martindale-Hubbell Law Directory

KIGER & ALPERN (AV)

1404 Grant Building, 15219
Telephone: 412-765-1811
Fax: 412-765-0440

MEMBERS OF FIRM

Jerome W. Kiger
Charles H. Alpern

For full biographical listings, see the Martindale-Hubbell Law Directory

MARCUS & SHAPIRA LLP (AV)

35th Floor, One Oxford Centre, 301 Grant Street, 15219-6401
Telephone: 412-471-3490
Telecopier: 412-391-8758
Email: info@marcus-shapira.com *URL:* http://www.marcus-shapira.com

MEMBERS OF FIRM

Robert L. Allman, II
Robert M. Barnes
James S. Larrimer
Scott D. Livingston
Bernard D. Marcus
Daniel H. Shapira
Stephen S. Zubrow

OF COUNSEL

John M. Burkoff

ASSOCIATE

Henry G. Barr

For Complete List of Firm Personnel, See General Section

For full biographical listings, see the Martindale-Hubbell Law Directory

MOLLICA & MURRAY (AV)

450 Trimont Plaza, 1305 Grandview Avenue, 15211
Telephone: 412-381-7000
Fax: 412-381-7111
Email: firm@mollicamurray.com *URL:* http://www.mollicamurray.com

MEMBERS OF FIRM

James A. Mollica, Jr.
Dr. John E. Murray, Jr.
Cathy Ann Chromulak
Timothy Murray
William J. Moorhead, Jr.

Michael E. Flaherty
Michelle D. Smith

For full biographical listings, see the Martindale-Hubbell Law Directory

PLOWMAN, SPIEGEL & LEWIS, P.C. (AV)

Second Floor, The Grant Building, 310 Grant Street, 15219-2201
Telephone: 412-471-8521
Fax: 412-471-4481

Jack W. Plowman
John L. Spiegel

Frank J. Kernan
Kenneth W. Lee

Reference: Pittsburgh National Bank.

For Complete List of Firm Personnel, See General Section

For full biographical listings, see the Martindale-Hubbell Law Directory

WAYMAN, IRVIN & McAULEY (AV)

Suite 1624 Frick Building, 15219
Telephone: 412-566-2970
Fax: 412-391-1464
Email: wayman@nauticom.net

MEMBERS OF FIRM

Michael L. Magulick
Mark J. Gesk
Kate J. Fagan
Francis X. McTiernan, Jr.
Warren L. Siegfried
Dale K. Forsythe
John Sieminski

ASSOCIATES

David A. Neely
Susan K. Dirks
Paul M. Mannix
John C. Bogut, Jr.
Krista M. Kochosky
Craig A. Briggs
Scott W. Stephan
Mark J. Scorpion

Representative Clients: Allstate Insurance Company; American International Group; American National Property & Casualty Company; American Nuclear Insurers; Associated Aviation Underwriters; Atlantic Mutual Companies; Carolina Casualty Insurance Company; Chubb & Son Insurance Group; Clarenden National Insurance Company; CNA Insurance Company.

For full biographical listings, see the Martindale-Hubbell Law Directory

WILLMAN & ARNOLD, LLP (AV)

Suite 705-708, 700 McKnight Park Drive, 15237
Telephone: 412-366-3333
Fax: 412-366-3462
Email: RANTINON@IX.NETCOM.COM *URL:* http://www.wilandarn.com

MEMBERS OF FIRM

Gene E. Arnold
R. Kenneth Willman
James W. Young, Jr.
Ruth A. Antinone
Concetta A. Silvaggio

ASSOCIATES

Glenn A. Huetter, Jr.
Lola M. James
Joseph D. Silvaggio
Thomas A. Smolinski
Steven G. Blackmer
Maureen A. Shannon
Robert Anthony Conroy
Jeffrey Thomas Strittmatter

For full biographical listings, see the Martindale-Hubbell Law Directory

Pittsburgh—Continued

ZIMMER KUNZ, PROFESSIONAL CORPORATION (AV)

3300 USX Tower, 600 Grant Street, 15219
Telephone: 412-281-8000
Fax: 412-281-1765

Harry J. Zimmer
John E. Kunz
Raymond H. Conaway
George N. Stewart
Joni M. Mangino
Joseph W. Selep
Raymond J. Conlon
Edward K. Dixon
Mark R. Hamilton
Alexander P. Bicket
John W. Zotter
Jeffrey A. Ramaley
Thomas P. McGinnis

OF COUNSEL

Andrew J. Banyas, III
Thomas A. Lazaroff

Dara A. DeCourcy
Robert W. Murdoch
Anthony C. Carone
Timothy R. Smith
Meghan Fawcett Wise
Daniel E. Krauth
George R. Farneth, II
John K. Bryan
Mark T. Caloyer
Christopher T. Yoskosky
Amy J. Brinkos
George W. Boguslawski, Jr.
Carmen A. Martucci
Tracy L. Yaggi
Kurt W. Lenz
Carl Adam Ronald
Claire A. Conaway

Attorneys For: American International Group; Cincinnati Insurance Co.; Equitable Gas Co.; Honda North America; Otis Elevator Co.; Outboard Marine Corp.; Pennsylvania Electric Co.; Travelers Insurance Co.

For full biographical listings, see the Martindale-Hubbell Law Directory

---

PLYMOUTH, Luzerne Co.

MUSTO & SAUNDERS, P.C. (AV)

117 W. Main Street, 18651-2926
Telephone: 570-779-5122
Fax: 570-719-0306
Enola, Pennsylvania Office: Suite 208 North Enola Drive.
Telephone: 717-732-8114.

Joseph J. Musto
Keith J. Saunders

Fortunata G. Musto
Daniel J. Balutis
Camille H. Jescavage (Not admitted in PA)
Christopher J. O'Donnell

For full biographical listings, see the Martindale-Hubbell Law Directory

---

*SCRANTON,** Lackawanna Co.

FOLEY, COGNETTI, COMERFORD & CIMINI (AV)

Suite 700 Scranton Electric Building, 507 Linden Street, 18503-1666
Telephone: 570-346-0745
Fax: 570-346-0776

MEMBERS OF FIRM

Gomer W. Morgan (1890-1969)
Carlon M. O'Malley, Sr. (1905-1978)
Timothy E. Foley
Sal Cognetti, Jr.
Thomas P. Comerford
Vincent S. Cimini

Mary C. Welby
Daniel E. Cummins

OF COUNSEL

John W. Bour
Joseph E. Gallagher

Representative Clients: Royal Insurance Cos.; Pennsylvania Gas & Water Co.; State Farm Mutual Automobile Insurance Co.; The Travelers Insurance Co.; Liberty Mutual Insurance Co.; Aetna Casualty & Surety Co.; Medical Protective Co.; Prudential Property and Casualty Co.; The Stanley Works; MEDMARC.

For full biographical listings, see the Martindale-Hubbell Law Directory

---

KREDER, BROOKS, HAILSTONE & LUDWIG (AV)

Suite 200, 220 Penn Avenue, 18503
Telephone: 570-346-7922
Telecopier: 570-346-3715

Cody H. Brooks
Lucille Marsh
Michael J. Donohue

ASSOCIATES

Alyce Hailstone Farrell
Robert B. Farrell

Counsel For: U.S. Fidelity & Guaranty Co.; Nationwide Insurance Co.; Liberty Mutual Insurance Co.; United States Automobile Assn.; Reliance Insurance Co.; Harleyville Insurance Co.; Maryland Casualty Insurance Co.

For Complete List of Firm Personnel, See General Section

For full biographical listings, see the Martindale-Hubbell Law Directory

LENAHAN & DEMPSEY, A PROFESSIONAL CORPORATION (AV)

116 North Washington Avenue, 18503-0234
Telephone: 717-346-2097; 1-888-LENAHAN
Fax: 717-346-1174
Mailing Address: P.O. Box 234, Scranton, Pennsylvania, 18501-0234

John R. Lenahan, Sr. (1915-1998)
William J. Dempsey (Of Counsel)
John R. Lenahan, Jr.
Joseph P. Lenahan
Kathleen A. Lenahan
David E. Heisler
Timothy G. Lenahan
Matthew D. Dempsey

Alan P. Schoen
Brian J. Lenahan
Diane Hepford Lenahan
George E. Mehalchick
Brian Yeager
Thomas R. Daniels
Terrence E. Dempsey
Christine S. Mayernick-Lezinski
John M. Mulcahey
Margaret M. Dempsey
Lisa G. Wilson

Representative Insurance Clients: Allstate Insurance Co.; America Security Insurance Co.; Metropolitan Casualty Insurance Co.; Aetna Insurance Co.; Pennsylvania National Insurance Group; Kemper Insurance Group; American Mutual Insurance Cos.; American States Insurance, Co.

For full biographical listings, see the Martindale-Hubbell Law Directory

---

O'MALLEY & HARRIS, P.C. (AV)

345 Wyoming Avenue, 18503
Telephone: 570-348-3711
Fax: 570-348-4092
Email: ohpc@epix.net *URL:* http://www.ohpclaw.com
Stroudsburg, Pennsylvania Office: 111 North Seventh Street.
Telephone: 570-421-2252; 570-422-1280.
FAX: 570-422-1281. Email: cerato@ptdprolog.net.
Wilkes-Barre, Pennsylvania Office: 61 North Washington Street.
Telephone: 570-829-3232.
FAX: 570-829-4418. Email: ohpcwb@epix.net.
Williamsport, Pennsylvania Office: 321 Pine Street, Suite 308.
Telephone: 570-323-4380.

Eugene Nogi (1905-1975)
Henry Nogi (1900-1976)
Russell J. O'Malley, Sr. (1904-1993)
Norman Harris (1907-1998)
William H. Amesbury (Resident, Wilkes-Barre Office)
Paul A. Barrett
Matthew P. Barrett
J. Scott Brady (Resident, Wilkes-Barre Office)
Lori J. Cerato (Resident, Stroudsburg Office)
Bruce L. Coyer
John Q. Durkin
Gerald J. Hanchulak
Richard K. Hodges
Timothy J. Holland (Resident, Wilkes-Barre Office)
John F. Kennedy (Resident, Wilkes-Barre Office)
Daniel Morgan
Michael Perry
James M. Tressler
Joseph Timothy Healey
A. Ruth Whalen (Resident, Wilkes-Barre Office)

Representative Clients: Pennsylvania Hospital Insurance Co.; MMI Systems Agency, Inc.; State Farm Insurance Company; ITT Specialty Risk Services; St. Paul Fire & Marine Insurance Co.; Chubb Group of Insurance Companies; Geisingen System Services; Princeton Insurance Company; Northeastern Pennsylvania Physicians Organization; Catholic Healthcare Partners.

For full biographical listings, see the Martindale-Hubbell Law Directory

---

SCANLON, HOWLEY, SCANLON & DOHERTY (AV)

321 Spruce Street, 10th Floor, 18503
Telephone: 570-346-7651
Fax: 570-344-1542

MEMBERS OF FIRM

James M. Howley
James M. Scanlon
James A. Doherty, Jr.
Thomas R. Nealon
Thomas B. Helbig
Patrick R. Casey

Counsel for: CNA Insurance Company; The Medical Protective Co.; Harleysville Insurance Co.; The Procter & Gamble Co.; Prudential-Bach Securities, Inc.; Zurich-American Insurance Co.; The Keystone Coca-Cola Bottling Co.; The Home Insurance Co.; The Travelers Insurance Co.; Utica First Ins. Co.

For full biographical listings, see the Martindale-Hubbell Law Directory

---

*WILLIAMSPORT,** Lycoming Co.

MITCHELL, MITCHELL, GRAY & GALLAGHER, A PROFESSIONAL CORPORATION (AV)

10 West Third Street, 17701-6513
Telephone: 570-323-8404
Fax: 570-323-8585
Email: mmggpc@csrlink.net

Jacob Neafie Mitchell (1919-1996)
C. Edward S. Mitchell
Richard A. Gray
Robert A. Gallagher
Gary L. Weber
Bret J. Southard

(See Next Column)

MITCHELL, MITCHELL, GRAY & GALLAGHER A PROFESSIONAL CORPORATION, *Williamsport—Continued*

Darryl R. Wishard

For full biographical listings, see the Martindale-Hubbell Law Directory

RHODE ISLAND

*PROVIDENCE,** Providence Co.

BOYER, REYNOLDS & DEMARCO, LTD. (AV)

Suite 200, 170 Westminster Street, 02903
Telephone: 401-861-5522
Telecopier: 401-331-4861
Email: boyrendem@aol.com

Paul V. Reynolds
Anthony F. DeMarco
John M. Boland
Gregory L. Boyer
Mark T. Reynolds

Representative Clients: Lumbermens Mutual Casualty Co.; American Motorists Insurance Co.; B. F. Goodrich Co.; Andover Group; Insurance Company of North America; Nationwide Mutual Insurance Co.; Worcester Co.; Amica Mutual Insurance Co.; Casco Indemnity Co.; Farmers Insurance Co.

For full biographical listings, see the Martindale-Hubbell Law Directory

MARTIN K. DONOVAN (AV)

One Park Row, 02903-1235
Telephone: 401-831-2500
Facsimile: 401-751-7830

Reference: Fleet National Bank.

For full biographical listings, see the Martindale-Hubbell Law Directory

HANSON, CURRAN, PARKS & WHITMAN (AV)

146 Westminster Street, 02903-2218
Telephone: 401-421-2154
Telecopier: 401-521-7040
URL: http://www.hcpw.com

Kirk Hanson (1948-1991)

MEMBERS OF FIRM

A. Lauriston Parks
David P. Whitman
Michael T. F. Wallor
Dennis J. McCarten
James T. Murphy
Seth E. Bowerman
Thomas R. Bender
Mark W. Dana

ASSOCIATES

Richard H. Burrows
Christopher J. Zangari (Resident)
Wendy J. Taylor

OF COUNSEL

William A. Curran

General Counsel for: Medical Malpractice Joint Underwriting Association of Rhode Island.
Rhode Island Counsel for: Amica Mutual Insurance Co.; CIGNA; St. Paul Insurance Cos.; Occidental Life Insurance Co.; Exchange Mutual Insurance Co.; Aetna Casualty & Surety Co.

For full biographical listings, see the Martindale-Hubbell Law Directory

HIGGINS, CAVANAGH & COONEY (AV)

The Hay Building, Fourth Floor, 123 Dyer Street, 02903
Telephone: 401-272-3500; 800-274-5299
Telecopier: 401-273-8780

James H. Higgins, Jr. (1952-1975)
Joseph V. Cavanagh (1952-1985)
John P. Cooney, Jr. (1960-1981)
Kenneth P. Borden
Gerald C. DeMaria
John T. Walsh, Jr.
Charles A. Hambly, Jr.
Stephen B. Lang
Lawrence P. McCarthy, III
James A. Ruggieri
Michael D. Lynch
James T. Hornstein

ASSOCIATES

John F. Kelleher
Rajaram Suryanarayan
Vivian B. Dogan
Patrick B. Landers
Paul S. Callaghan
Susan Pepin Fay
Peter E. Garvey
Amy C. Vignali
Thomas F. DeVincke

For full biographical listings, see the Martindale-Hubbell Law Directory

WILLIAM T. MURPHY LAW OFFICES, INC. (AV)

The Calart Tower, 400 Reservoir Avenue, Suite 3L, 02907
Telephone: 401-461-7740
Telecopier: 401-461-7753

(See Next Column)

William T. Murphy

Charles A. Pisaturo, Jr.
Steven T. Hayes

Reference: Citizens Bank.

For full biographical listings, see the Martindale-Hubbell Law Directory

VETTER & WHITE, INCORPORATED (AV)

20 Washington Place, 02903
Telephone: 401-421-3060
Telecopier: 401-272-6803
Email: vetlit@aol.com

Benjamin V. White, III
Gordon P. Cleary
Howard A. Merten, Jr.
Brooks R. Magratten

OF COUNSEL

George Vetter

Kimberly A. Simpson
Michael W. Long

For full biographical listings, see the Martindale-Hubbell Law Directory

SOUTH CAROLINA

*BEAUFORT,** Beaufort Co.

DAVIS, TUPPER & GRIMSLEY, L.L.P. (AV)

611 Bay Street, P.O. Box 2055, 29901-2055
Telephone: 843-524-1116
Facsimile: 843-524-1463
Email: DTGS@Hargray.com

MEMBERS OF FIRM

Hutson S. Davis, Jr.
Ralph E. Tupper
James A. Grimsley, III
Erin D. Dean
R. Gerald Chambers, Jr.
Virginia D. Meeks

For full biographical listings, see the Martindale-Hubbell Law Directory

*CHARLESTON,** Charleston Co.

BARNWELL WHALEY PATTERSON & HELMS, LLC (AV)

134 Meeting Street, Suite 300, P.O. Drawer H, 29402
Telephone: 843-577-7700
Telecopier: 843-577-7708
Email: bwph@barnwell-whaley.com *URL:* http://barnwell-whaley.com

MEMBERS OF FIRM

Robert A. Patterson
William C. Helms, III
M. Dawes Cooke, Jr.
Bruce E. Miller
Matthew H. Henrikson
Frank E. Grimball
James E. Reeves

ASSOCIATES

J. Matthew Dillon
James H. Elliott, Jr.

Representative Clients: Continental Insurance Group; General Accident Group; Hartford Insurance Cos; The Home Insurance Co.; Kemper Insurance Group; Liberty Mutual Insurance; Nationwide; State Farm Fire; United States Aviation Underwriters.

For full biographical listings, see the Martindale-Hubbell Law Directory

BUIST, MOORE, SMYTHE & MCGEE, P.A. (AV)

Successors to Buist, Buist, Smythe and Smythe and Moore, Mouzon and McGee.
Five Exchange Street, P.O. Box 999, 29402
Telephone: 843-722-3400
Cable Address: "Conferees"
Telex: 57-6488
Telecopier: 843-723-7398
Email: bmsm@lawyer-sc.com *URL:* http://www.lawyer-sc.com

Benjamin Allston Moore, Jr.
Joseph H. McGee
Gordon D. Schreck
Henry B. Smythe, Jr.
Henry E. Grimball
David B. McCormack
C. Allen Gibson, Jr.
James D. Myrick
Douglas M. Muller
Elizabeth Henry Warner
David S. Yandle

Julius H. Hines
David S. Cox
Jonathan D. Crumly, Sr.
Dwayne M. Green
Margaret O. Dullanty
Gregory Horton

OF COUNSEL

David M. Collins
Charles J. Baker, III

Representative Clients: Allstate Insurance Company; Associated Aviation Underwriters; Chicago Title Insurance Company; Liberty Mutual Insurance Company; Seaboard Surety; U.S.F.&G.; U.S. Aviation Underwriters, Inc.; State Farm Insurance Co.; MOAC/Continental; St. Paul Fire and Marine

(See Next Column)

BUIST, MOORE, SMYTHE & MCGEE P.A.—*Continued*

Insurance Co.; Zurich-American Insurance Group; Lancer Insurance Co.; Horace Mann Insurance Co.; Universal Underwriters Insurance Co.; Reliance Insurance Co.; Frontier Insurance Co.

For Complete List of Firm Personnel, See General Section

For full biographical listings, see the Martindale-Hubbell Law Directory

HAYNSWORTH, MARION, MCKAY & GUÉRARD, L.L.P. (AV)

134 Meeting Street, P.O. Box 1119, 29402
Telephone: 843-722-7606
Facsimile: 843-724-8016
Columbia, South Carolina Office: Suite 2400 Affinity Building, 1201 Main Street, P.O. Drawer 7157, 29202.
Telephone: 803-765-1818. Facsimile 803-765-2399.
Greenville, South Carolina Office: 75 Beattie Place, Eleventh Floor, P.O. Box 2048, 29602.
Telephone: 864-240-3200.
Facsimile: 864-240-3300.

MEMBER OF FIRM

James E. Lady

For Complete List of Firm Personnel, See General Section

For full biographical listings, see the Martindale-Hubbell Law Directory

HOOD LAW FIRM (AV)

172 Meeting Street, P.O. Box 1508, 29402
Telephone: 843-577-4435
Fax: 843-722-1630
Email: hlf@hoodlaw.com *URL:* http://www.hoodlaw.com

MEMBERS OF FIRM

Robert H. Hood
John K. Blincow, Jr.
Louis P. Herns
James G. Kennedy
G. Mark Phillips
Barbara Wynne Showers
Carl Everette Pierce, II
Joseph C. Wilson, IV
James Dowell Gandy, III

Dixon F. Pearce, II
Allison Snead Patrick
Hugh Willcox Buyck
P. Gunnar Nistad
Allan Poe Sloan, III
Robert H. Hood, Jr.
Mary Agnes Hood Craig
William Mullins McLeod, Jr.

For full biographical listings, see the Martindale-Hubbell Law Directory

*COLUMBIA,** Richland Co.

BARNES, ALFORD, STORK & JOHNSON, L.L.P. (AV)

1613 Main Street, P.O. Box 8448, 29202
Telephone: 803-799-1111
Telefax: 803-254-1335
Email: basj@basjlaw.com

Weldon R. Johnson
Thomas C. Cofield
Kay Gaffney Crowe
Robert Thomas Strickland
Richard C. Thomas
L. Elaine Mozingo
Curtis W. Dowling

Melody Lynn James
Andrea C. Pope
Robert D. Dodson

Representative Clients: First Union National Bank; Travelers/Aetna; M.B. Kahn Construction Co., Inc.

For Complete List of Firm Personnel, See General Section

For full biographical listings, see the Martindale-Hubbell Law Directory

FINKEL & ALTMAN, L.L.C. (AV)

Suite 1800, 1201 Main Street, P.O. Box 1799, 29202
Telephone: 803-765-2935
Fax: 803-252-0786
Email: webmaster@finkellaw.com *URL:* http://www.finkellaw.com
Charleston, South Carolina Office: 12 Exchange Street, P.O. Box 225.
Telephone: 843-577-5460.
Fax: 843-577-5135.

Gerald M. Finkel
Harry L. Goldberg
Howard S. Sheftman

Representative Clients: First Union National Bank; Banc One Mortgage Co.; Motorola Communications & Electronics Corp.; Colonia Insurance Company; Aetna Insurance Company.

For full biographical listings, see the Martindale-Hubbell Law Directory

HAYNSWORTH, MARION, MCKAY & GUÉRARD, L.L.P. (AV)

Suite 2400 Affinity Building, 1201 Main Street, P.O. Drawer 7157, 29202
Telephone: 803-765-1818
Facsimile: 803-765-2399
Greenville, South Carolina Office: 75 Beattie Place, Eleventh Floor, P.O. Box 2048, 29602.
Telephone: 864-240-3200.
Facsimile: 864-240-3300.
Charleston, South Carolina Office: 134 Meeting Street, P.O. Box 1119, 29402.
Telephone: 843-722-7606.
Facsimile: 843-724-8016.

MEMBERS OF FIRM

William P. Simpson
Steven Todd Moon
Stephen F. McKinney

ASSOCIATE

Gina L. Campano

Counsel for: St. Paul Insurance Group; Allstate Insurance Co.; Fluor-Daniel Corp.; South Carolina Jobs - Economic Development Authority; Anheuser Busch Company; CSX Transportation; Ernst & Young, LLP; Willis Corroon of South Carolina, Inc.; Westinghouse Savannah River Co.; Wachovia Bank of South Carolina, N.A.

For Complete List of Firm Personnel, See General Section

For full biographical listings, see the Martindale-Hubbell Law Directory

HOWSER, NEWMAN & BESLEY, L.L.C. (AV)

1508 Washington Street, P.O. Box 12009, 29211
Telephone: 803-758-6000
Fax: 803-758-4445
Email: rdhowser@hnblaw.com

R. Davis Howser
William G. Besley
James P. Newman, Jr.
Benjamin D. McCoy

Kelley S. Shull
Andrew E. Haselden
Janet Brooks

Representative Clients: American Modern Home Company; Clayton Homes; CNA Risk Management Group; DPIC Companies, Inc.; Horace Mann Insurance Company; Zurich Companies; Selective Insurance Company; South Carolina School Boards Insurance Trust; State Auto Insurance Company; Utica National Insurance Group.

For full biographical listings, see the Martindale-Hubbell Law Directory

MCCUTCHEN, BLANTON, RHODES & JOHNSON, L.L.P. (AV)

1414 Lady Street, P.O. Drawer 11209, 29211
Telephone: 803-799-9791
Telecopier: 803-253-6084
Email: Firm1414@aol.com
Winnsboro, South Carolina Office: 120 West Washington Street, 29180.
Telephone: 803-635-6884.

MEMBERS OF FIRM

Thomas E. McCutchen
Evans Taylor Barnette
Jeter E. Rhodes, Jr.
G. D. Morgan, Jr.
T. English McCutchen, III
John C. Bradley, Jr.
Pope D. Johnson, III
Creighton B. Coleman
William R. Taylor
Ruskin C. Foster
William E. Hopkins, Jr.

ASSOCIATE

Anthony W. Livoti

OF COUNSEL

Hoover C. Blanton

Representative Clients: Allstate Insurance Co.; Sears, Roebuck and Co.; J.B. White Co.; Anchor Continental Inc.; Western Fire Insurance Co.; Liberty Mutual Insurance Co.; Southeastern Freight Lines; Continental Life Insurance Co.; State Farm Fire & Casualty Co.

For full biographical listings, see the Martindale-Hubbell Law Directory

RICHARDSON, PLOWDEN, CARPENTER & ROBINSON, P.A. (AV)

1600 Marion Street, P.O. Drawer 7788, 29202
Telephone: 803-771-4400
Telecopy: 803-779-0016
Email: atty@rpcrlaw.com *URL:* http://www.rpcrlaw.com
Myrtle Beach, South Carolina Office: 2103 B Farlow Street, P.O. Box 3646, 29578.
Telephone: 843-448-1008.
FAX: 843-448-1533.

Charles E. Carpenter, Jr.
Leslie A. Cotter, Jr.
George C. Beighley
Douglas C. Baxter
Frederick A. Crawford
Nina Reid Mack
Francis M. Mack
S. Nelson Weston Jr.
Franklin Jennings Smith, Jr.
Mary Sowell League

(See Next Column)

RICHARDSON, PLOWDEN, CARPENTER & ROBINSON P.A., *Columbia—Continued*

Marian Williams Scalise
William C. McDow
Georgia Anna Mitchell
David C. Slough
Stephen C. Lenker, Jr.
David A. Anderson
S. Elizabeth Brosnan

OF COUNSEL

Donald V. Richardson, III
Michael A. Pulliam

Representative Clients: Insurance: CNA Insurance Co.; The Hartford; Kemper Insurance Co.; Pennsylvania National Mutual Casualty Insurance Co.; Wausau Insurance Cos.; The Reudlinger Cos. Real Estate, Corporate and Banking: First Union Bank. Construction: S.C. Department of Transportation.

For Complete List of Firm Personnel, See General Section

For full biographical listings, see the Martindale-Hubbell Law Directory

TURNER, PADGET, GRAHAM & LANEY, P.A. (AV)

Seventeenth Floor, 1901 Main Street, P.O. Box 1473, 29202
Telephone: 803-254-2200
Telecopy: 803-799-3957
Florence, South Carolina Office: Fourth Floor, 1831 West Evans Street, P.O. Box 5478, 29502.
Telephone: 843-662-9008.
Fax: 843-667-0828.
Charleston, South Carolina Office: 21 Broad Street, 1st Floor, P.O. Box 836, 29402.
Telephone: 843-723-1622.
Fax: 843-577-3369.

Ronald E. Boston
W. Duvall Spruill
Charles E. Hill
Thomas C. Salane
Danny C. Crowe
John S. Wilkerson, III (Resident, Florence, SC, Office)
John E. Cuttino
Arthur E. Justice, Jr. (Resident, Florence, SC, Office)
Edward W. Laney, IV
Elbert S. Dorn
Hugh M. Claytor (Resident, Florence, SC, Office)
Vernon F. Dunbar
J. Kenneth Carter, Jr.
O. Carlisle Edwards, Jr.
Richard L. Hinson (Resident, Florence, SC, Office)
Jeffrey L. Payne (Resident, Florence, SC, Office)
Wilson S. Sheldon (Resident, Florence, SC, Office)
Michael S. Hopewell (Resident, Florence, SC, Office)
Teresa A. Arnold

OF COUNSEL

Laura Chandler Rublee (Resident, Florence, SC, Office)

Jessica C. Moe (Resident, Charleston, SC, Office)
Curtis L. Ott
Michael C. Abbott (Resident, Florence, SC, Office)
David S. Cobb (Resident, Charleston, SC, Office)
Donnell G. Jennings
D. Andrew Williams
Cynthia C. Dooley
Richard C. Burke (Resident, Florence, SC, Office)
Steven R. LeBlanc
Patrick W. Carr (Resident, Florence, SC, Office)
James David Smith, Jr. (Resident, Florence, SC, Office)

For Complete List of Firm Personnel, See General Section

For full biographical listings, see the Martindale-Hubbell Law Directory

*CONWAY,** Horry Co.

MCCUTCHEON, MCCUTCHEON & BAXTER, P.A. (AV)

McCutcheon Building, 208 Elm Street, P.O. Box 1003, 29528
Telephone: 843-248-7225
Telecopier: 843-248-3568
Email: mmb4@gte.net

John Betts McCutcheon (1915-1997)
John Betts McCutcheon, Jr.
Mary Ruth M. Baxter

Lisa A. Thomas
Arrigo P. Carotti

Representative Clients: State of South Carolina, Division of General Services, Insurance Reserve Fund; South Carolina Medical Malpractice Joint Underwriters Assn.; Virginia Professional Underwriters, Inc.; Companion Property and Casualty Co.; Blue Cross and Blue Shield of South Carolina, Inc.; National Indemnity Co.; American Continental Insurance Co.; The Travelers Insurance Group.

For full biographical listings, see the Martindale-Hubbell Law Directory

THE THOMPSON LAW FIRM, P.A. (AV)

1318 Third Avenue, P.O. Box 1533, 29528
Telephone: 843-248-5741
Fax: 843-248-5112
Myrtle Beach, South Carolina Office: 1314 Professional Drive, P.O. Box 1290.
Telephone: 843-692-2628.
Fax: 843-692-0918.

John C. Thompson
John P. Henry
Linda Weeks Gangi
Emma Ruth Brittain
Lynn Gatlin Stevens
Philip C. Thompson
Catherine M. Hedgepath

Representative Clients: NationsBank; Burroughs & Chapin Co., Inc.; Canal Industries, Inc.; State Farm Mutual Automobile Insurance Co.; State Farm Fire and Casualty Insurance Co.; Horry County; Nationwide Insurance Co.; United Carolina Bank; First Union National Bank.
Reference: NationsBank.

For full biographical listings, see the Martindale-Hubbell Law Directory

*FLORENCE,** Florence Co.

CLARKE, JOHNSON, PETERSON & MCLEAN, A PROFESSIONAL ASSOCIATION (AV)

620 West Evans Street, P.O. Box 1865, 29503
Telephone: 843-669-2401
Fax: 843-662-1779

Finley B. Clarke
Brown W. Johnson
James W. Peterson, Jr.
Joseph P. McLean

Clients: General Motors Corp; Liberty Mutual Insurance Co.; The Home Indemnity Co.; Canal Insurance Co.; Employers Insurance of Wausau; South Carolina Budget and Control Board; Citizens Insurance Co.; Royal Insurance Co.; State Farm Insurance Co.; American Southern Insurance Co.

For full biographical listings, see the Martindale-Hubbell Law Directory

MCINTOSH & LEE (AV)

234 West Cheves Street, P.O. Box 1831, 29503
Telephone: 803-662-4328; 662-4329
Fax: 803-661-5183

MEMBERS OF FIRM

Jack J. Wright (1904-1991)
C. Dexter Powers (1921-1989)
D. Laurence McIntosh
Robert E. Lee

LEGAL SUPPORT PERSONNEL

Pam J. Jordan

Attorneys for: Allstate; American States Insurance; Fireman's Fund American Co.; First Union National Bank of S.C.; Amerisure Cos.; Florence School District No. 1; McLeod Regional Medical Center; South Carolina Medical Malpractice Joint Underwriting Assoc.; Stone Container Corp.; S.C. Insurance Reserve Fund.

For full biographical listings, see the Martindale-Hubbell Law Directory

*GREENVILLE,** Greenville Co.

CLARKSON, FORTSON, WALSH & RHENEY, P.A. (AV)

117 Manly Street, P.O. Box 6186, 29606
Telephone: 864-232-4400
Fax: 864-235-4399
Email: cfwr@cfwr.com

Rebecca R. Wray
Samuel C. Weldon

For full biographical listings, see the Martindale-Hubbell Law Directory

GRANT, LEATHERWOOD & PITTS, P.A. (AV)

Palmetto Bank Building, 306 East North Street, 2nd Floor, P.O. Box 10367, 29603-0367
Telephone: 864-242-2300
Facsimile: 864-242-2280
Email: attorneys@grantleatherwood.com

William M. Grant, Jr.
Judith A. Leatherwood
Michael S. Pitts

Langdon Cheves, III
Paul C. Rathke

LEGAL SUPPORT PERSONNEL

Jackie L. Carver (Litigation Paralegal)
Sarah A. Carmichael (Paralegal)
Mary A. Fuller (Paralegal)

For full biographical listings, see the Martindale-Hubbell Law Directory

Greenville—Continued

HAYNSWORTH, MARION, MCKAY & GUÉRARD, L.L.P. (AV)

75 Beattie Place, Eleventh Floor, P.O. Box 2048, 29602
Telephone: 864-240-3200
Facsimile: 864-240-3300
Columbia, South Carolina Office: Suite 2400 Affinity Building, 1201 Main Street, P.O. Drawer 7157, 29202
Telephone: 803-765-1818.
Facsimile: 803-765-2399.
Charleston, South Carolina Office: 134 Meeting Street, P.O. Box 1119, 29402.
Telephone: 843-722-7606.
Facsimile: 843-724-8016.

MEMBERS OF FIRM

G. Dewey Oxner, Jr.
William E. Shaughnessy
James B. Pressly, Jr.
H. Donald Sellers
Ellis M. Johnston, II
W. Francis Marion, Jr.
John B. McLeod
Richard B. Kale, Jr.
Edwin Brown Parkinson, Jr.
H. Sam Mabry, III
David Hill Keller
F. Matlock Elliott
Moffatt Grier McDonald
Amy Miller Snyder
Eric Keith Englebardt
J. Derrick Quattlebaum
Sarah M. (Sally) Purnell
Jeffrey S. Jones

ASSOCIATES

Boyd B. Nicholson, Jr.
Matthew P. Utecht
Harold J. Willson, Jr.
William David Conner
J. Ben Alexander

Representative Clients: Travelers Insurance Co.; United States Fidelity & Guaranty; Allstate Insurance Co.; Wausau Insurance; Liberty Mutual Ins. Co.; Fireman's Fund Insurance Co.; Companion Property & Casualty Co.; Hartford Accident & Indemnity Co.; Prudential Property & Casualty; St. Paul Insurance Group.

For Complete List of Firm Personnel, See General Section

For full biographical listings, see the Martindale-Hubbell Law Directory

LEATHERWOOD WALKER TODD & MANN, P.C. (AV)

100 East Coffee Street, P.O. Box 87, 29602
Telephone: 864-242-6440
FAX: 864-240-2477
Email: leatherwood@lwtm.com *URL:* http://www.lwtm.com
Spartanburg, South Carolina Office: 1451 East Main Street, P.O. Box 3188.
Telephone: 864-582-4365.
Telefax: 864-583-8961.

John E. Johnston
O. Doyle Martin
Joseph E. Major
Duke K. McCall, Jr.
Michael J. Giese
Bradford Neal Martin
Samuel Wright Outten

Kurt M. Rozelsky
John Patrick Riordan
Laurel R. S. Blair
William B. Swent
Peter A. Rutledge

COUNSEL

Fletcher C. Mann
James H. Watson

Counsel for: NationsBank; John D. Hollingsworth on Wheels, Inc.; Canal Insurance Co.; Hollingsworth Saco Lowell Inc.
Representative Clients: Springs Industries, Inc.; General Motors Acceptance Corp.; Suitt Construction Co.

For Complete List of Firm Personnel, See General Section

For full biographical listings, see the Martindale-Hubbell Law Directory

LOVE, THORNTON, ARNOLD & THOMASON, P.A. (AV)

410 East Washington Street, P.O. Box 10045, 29603
Telephone: 864-242-6360
Telefax: 864-271-7972
Email: lovelaw@globalvision.net *URL:* http://www.ltatlaw.com
Greer, South Carolina Office: 1115 West Poinsett Street, P.O. Box 449, 29652-0449.
Telephone: 864-879-0144.
Telefax: 864-879-0149.

William M. Hagood, III
Theron G. Cochran
Mason A. Goldsmith
Jack D. Griffeth
William A. Coates
David L. Moore, Jr.
V. Clark Price
James A. Blair, III

James Andrew Smith
Amy G. Richmond
Robert Scott Boatwright

OF COUNSEL

John B. Duggan (Resident, Greer Office)

Counsel for: Selective Insurance Co.; Risk Enterprise Management (Formerly The Home Insurance Co.); Kemper Insurance Group; State Farm Fire and Casualty; Government Employees Insurance Co.; Reliance Insurance Companies Group; South Carolina Farm Bureau Mutual Insurance Co.; St. Paul Fire and Marine Insurance Company.

(See Next Column)

For Complete List of Firm Personnel, See General Section

For full biographical listings, see the Martindale-Hubbell Law Directory

MYRTLE BEACH, Horry Co.

BELLAMY, RUTENBERG, COPELAND, EPPS, GRAVELY & BOWERS, P.A. (AV)

1000 29th Avenue North, P.O. Box 357, 29578
Telephone: 843-448-2400
Telecopier: 843-448-3022

Howell V. Bellamy, Jr.
John K. Rutenberg
John E. Copeland
Claude M. Epps, Jr.
David R. Gravely
Edward B. Bowers, Jr.
Bradley D. King
Henrietta U. Golding
M. Edwin Hinds, Jr.
Jill F. Griffith
Kathryn M. Cook
David B. Miller
C. Winfield Johnson, III
Sarah A. Johnson
Douglas M. Zayicek
Jeffrey W. King
Mary Anna Malpass
Martin Charles Dawsey

Representative Clients: Dargan Construction Co.; Coastal Federal Savings Bank; Sands Investments; Wachovia Bank of South Carolina; AVX Corp.; Bank of America; Parthenon Insurance Co.; Burroughs & Chapin Co.; International Paper Co.; Hospital Corporation of America.

For full biographical listings, see the Martindale-Hubbell Law Directory

THE THOMPSON LAW FIRM, P.A. (AV)

1314 Professional Drive, P.O. Box 1290, 29578-1290
Telephone: 843-692-2628
Fax: 843-692-0918
Conway, South Carolina Office: 1318 Third Avenue, P.O. Box 1533.
Telephone: 843-248-5741.
Fax: 843-248-5112.

J. Jackson Thomas
Clay D. Brittain, III
G. Michael Smith

Russell V. Traw
Thomas C. Stanley
Stacy L. Stanley

Representative Clients: The Citizens and Southern National Bank of South Carolina; Burroughs & Collins Co.; Canal Industries, Inc.; Nationwide Mutual Insurance Co.; State Farm Mutual Automobile Insurance Co.; State Farm Fire and Casualty Insurance Co.; Horry County; United Carolina Bank; First Union National Bank; First Financial Savings Bank, Inc.

For full biographical listings, see the Martindale-Hubbell Law Directory

*SPARTANBURG,** Spartanburg Co.

LEATHERWOOD WALKER TODD & MANN, P.C. (AV)

1451 East Main Street, P.O. Box 3188, 29304-3188
Telephone: 864-582-4365
Telefax: 864-585-8961
Email: leatherwood@lwtm.com *URL:* http://www.lwtm.com
Greenville, South Carolina Office: 100 East Coffee Street, P.O. Box 87.
Telephone: 864-242-6440.
FAX: 864-240-2477.

H. Spencer King

Cathy H. Dunn

For Complete List of Firm Personnel, See General Section

For full biographical listings, see the Martindale-Hubbell Law Directory

*SUMTER,** Sumter Co.

LEE, ERTER, WILSON, HOLLER & SMITH, L.L.C. (AV)

126 North Main Street, P.O. Box 580, 29150
Telephone: 803-778-2471
Telecopier: 803-778-1643

MEMBERS OF FIRM

John Dozier Lee, Jr. (1921-1999)
Jack W. Erter, Jr.
Harry C. Wilson, Jr.
David Cornwell Holler
G. Murrell Smith, Jr.

Representative Clients: South Carolina National Bank; Carolina Power and Light Co.; Peoples Natural Gas Company of South Carolina; BB&T; Allstate Insurance Co.; American Surety Co.; Prudential Insurance Company of America; General Telephone; Korn Industries, Inc.; V-B William Furniture Co., Inc.

For full biographical listings, see the Martindale-Hubbell Law Directory

SOUTH DAKOTA

*ABERDEEN,** Brown Co.

BANTZ, GOSCH, CREMER, PETERSON & SOMMERS (AV)

305 Sixth Avenue, S.E., P.O. Box 970, 57402-0970
Telephone: 605-225-2232
Fax: 605-225-2497
Email: bantzlaw@midco.net

MEMBERS OF FIRM

Douglas W. Bantz (1909-1983)
Kennith L. Gosch
James M. Cremer
Greg L. Peterson
Richard A. Sommers
Ronald A. Wager

General Counsel for: Dacotah Banks, Inc.
Attorneys for: Northwestern Mutual Life Insurance Co.; Northwestern National Insurance Group; Transamerica Insurance Group; United Pacific Insurance Co.

For full biographical listings, see the Martindale-Hubbell Law Directory

*RAPID CITY,** Pennington Co.

DELANEY & SUMNER (AV)

623 Quincy Street Suite 103, 57701
Telephone: 605-388-3153
Fax: 605-388-3155
Mailing Address: P.O. Box 8305, Rapid City, SD, 57709-8305
Email: toogoodoo1@aol.com

MEMBERS OF FIRM

John J. Delaney
Scott Sumner

For full biographical listings, see the Martindale-Hubbell Law Directory

JOHNSON EIESLAND HUFFMAN & CLAYBORNE LAW FIRM, LLP (AV)

2201 Jackson Boulevard, Suite 200, P.O. Box 6900, 57709-6900
Telephone: 605-348-7300; 800-998-3998
FAX: 605-348-4757
Email: jehc22@aol.com *URL:* http://www.jehc-law.com

Glen H. Johnson
Gregory A. Eiesland
Richard E. Huffman
Courtney R. Clayborne

Kristi K. Wammen

For full biographical listings, see the Martindale-Hubbell Law Directory

WHITING, HAGG & HAGG (AV)

1220 Mt. Rushmore Road, Suite Two, P.O. Box 8008, 57701
Telephone: 605-348-1125
Fax: 605-348-9744
URL: http://www.amatteroflaw.com

MEMBERS OF FIRM

Brian D. Hagg
Rexford A. Hagg
John Stanton Dorsey

ASSOCIATES

Kent R. Hagg
Robert J. Hollan
Kevin W. Klapprodt

LEGAL SUPPORT PERSONNEL

Beverly J. McCracken
Becky J. Buhmann

For full biographical listings, see the Martindale-Hubbell Law Directory

*SIOUX FALLS,** Minnehaha Co.

DAVENPORT, EVANS, HURWITZ & SMITH, L.L.P. (AV)

513 South Main Avenue, P.O. Box 1030, 57101-1030
Telephone: 605-336-2880
Telecopier: 605-335-3639
Email: lawyers@dehs.com

MEMBERS OF FIRM

Edwin E. Evans
Michael L. Luce
Michael J. Schaffer
Thomas M. Frankman
Rick W. Orr
Timothy M. Gebhart
Susan Brunick Simons
Roberto A. Lange
Cheryle Wiedmeier Gering
Lori Purcell Fossen
Mark W. Haigh
Sandra K. Hoglund

ASSOCIATES

Keith A. Gauer
Kristi G. Holm
Dana M. Van Beek

Counsel for: American Society of Composers, Authors and Publishers (A.S.C.A.P.); Continental Insurance Cos.; The First National Bank in Sioux Falls; Ford Motor Credit Co.; General Motors Corp.; The St. Paul Cos.; The Travelers.

For Complete List of Firm Personnel, See General Section

For full biographical listings, see the Martindale-Hubbell Law Directory

TENNESSEE

*CHATTANOOGA,** Hamilton Co.

FOSTER, FOSTER, ALLEN & DURRENCE, P.C. (AV)

Formerly Hall, Haynes, Lusk & Foster
801 Broad Street - Suite 515, 37402
Telephone: 423-266-1141
Telecopier: 423-266-4618
Email: dward@ffadlaw.com

George Lane Foster
William M. Foster
Craig R. Allen
Phillip M. Durrence, Jr.
David J. Ward
Clayton M. Whittaker
John M. Hull

LEGAL SUPPORT PERSONNEL

Peggy Sue Bates

Division Counsel For: Norfolk Southern Railway Co.
Attorneys For: CNA/Insurance; United States Fidelity and Guaranty Co. (USF&G); Bridgestone-Firestone, Inc.; State Volunteer Mutual Insurance Co. (SVMIC); Exxon Corp.; Murphy Oil Corp.; Chicago Title Insurance Co.; Jim Walter Homes; Mid-State Homes, Inc.

For full biographical listings, see the Martindale-Hubbell Law Directory

FRANKLIN, COOPER & MARCUS, PLLC (AV)

837 Fort Wood Street, 37403
Telephone: 423-756-3596
Telecopier: 423-756-3597

David L. Franklin
Gary A. Cooper
H. Richard Marcus

For full biographical listings, see the Martindale-Hubbell Law Directory

LUTHER, ANDERSON, PLLP (AV)

1110 Market Street, Suite 500, P.O. Box 151, 37401-0151
Telephone: 423-756-5034
Fax: 423-265-9903

William B. Luther (Retired)
Samuel R. Anderson
Gerard M. Siciliano
Alaric A. Henry
Daniel J. Ripper

ASSOCIATES

Thomas M. Horne
J. Christopher Clem
Lisa E. Ferraro
Mary Sullivan Moore
Christian Scott Johnson
Carl T. Huskins

For full biographical listings, see the Martindale-Hubbell Law Directory

NELSON, MCMAHAN & NOBLETT (AV)

(An Association of Attorneys)
400 Pioneer Bank Building, 37402
Telephone: 423-756-2291
Fax: 423-756-0737

Randall L. Nelson
Michael A. McMahan
Phillip A. Noblett
Douglas M. Cox
Kenneth O. Fritz
Lawrence W. Kelly

For full biographical listings, see the Martindale-Hubbell Law Directory

*CLARKSVILLE,** Montgomery Co.

BATSON, NOLAN, BRICE, HARVEY & WILLIAMSON, PLLC (AV)

622 Madison, P.O. Box 0, 37041-1334
Telephone: 931-647-1501
Fax: 931-553-0153

Richard H. Batson
Dan L. Nolan, Jr.
John R. Brice
W. Timothy Harvey
Michael K. Williamson
Steven C. Girsky
Daniel Mark Nolan
Jill Bartee Nolan

Joel D. Ragland
Suzanne Marsh Pearson
Christopher J. Pittman
David J. Silvus
Craig Hargrow
Marie Antoinette Joiner
Carol M. Joiner
J. Matthew Miller

LEGAL SUPPORT PERSONEL

Teri Blackburn (Office Legal Administrator)

Representative Clients: The City of Clarksville; Montgomery County, Tennessee; Cafaro Company; Clarksville Memorial Hospital; Farmers & Merchants Bank; First American National Bank; First Federal Savings Bank of Clarksville; Savage Zinc; Sears, Roebuck and Company; Shoney's Inc.; South Central Bell; Trans Financial Bank; The Industrial Development Board of the County of Montgomery.

For full biographical listings, see the Martindale-Hubbell Law Directory

*CLEVELAND,** Bradley Co.

DENNY E. MOBBS (AV)

55 1/2 First Street, N.E., P.O. Box 192, 37364-0192
Telephone: 423-472-7181
Fax: 423-472-7701

Representative Clients: Liberty Mutual Insurance Co.; Shelby Mutual Insurance Co.; Carolina Casualty Co.; Maytag Corp. (Magic Chef, Inc.-Hardwick Stove Co.); Industrial Development Board of Polk County; Polk County News-Citizen Advance; Ocoee Inn & Marina.

For full biographical listings, see the Martindale-Hubbell Law Directory

*COOKEVILLE,** Putnam Co.

MADEWELL, JARED & HALFACRE (AV)

230 North Washington Avenue, P.O. Box 721, 38501
Telephone: 931-526-6101
Fax: 931-528-1909

MEMBERS OF FIRM

James D. Madewell
William E. Halfacre, III

Representative Clients: State of Tennessee; Trial Counsel as Special Assistant to Attorney General; Bank of Putnam County; First Tennessee Bank, N.A. at Cookeville; The Maryland; Transamerica Ins. Group; Home Insurance Co.; Auto Owners Ins. Co.; Insurance Company of North America; Fireman's Fund Insurance Co.

For Complete List of Firm Personnel, See General Section

For full biographical listings, see the Martindale-Hubbell Law Directory

MOORE, RADER, CLIFT AND FITZPATRICK, P.C. (AV)

46 North Jefferson Avenue, P.O. Box 3347, 38501
Telephone: 615-526-3311
Fax: 615-526-3092

L. Dean Moore
Michael E. Clift
Daniel H. Rader, III
Walter S. Fitzpatrick, III
Richard Lane Moore

General Counsel for: First Tennessee Bank.
Local Counsel for: Heritage Ford-Lincoln-Mercury, Inc.
Representative Clients: Continental Insurance Co.; Kemper Group; U.S.F.&G.; Auto Owners Insurance Co.; Wausau Insurance Cos.

For full biographical listings, see the Martindale-Hubbell Law Directory

*GALLATIN,** Sumner Co.

MCCLELLAN, POWERS, EHMLING & DIX, P.C. (AV)

McClellan Building, 116 Public Square, 37066-2887
Telephone: 615-452-5872
Fax: 615-452-0054
Murfreesboro, Tennessee Office: Suite 201, Court Square Building, 201 West Main Street.
Telephone: 615-895-2529.
FAX: 615-896-7254.

Arthur E. McClellan
Dennis Wade Powers
M. Allen Ehmling

Jade A. Rogers

Representative Clients: First Independent Bank; Tennessee Farmers Mutual Insurance Co.; Travelers Insurance Co.; Blue Cross and Blue Shield of Tennessee; Aetna Casualty & Surety Co.

For full biographical listings, see the Martindale-Hubbell Law Directory

*JACKSON,** Madison Co.

MOSS, BENTON & WALLIS, PLLC (AV)

P.O. Box 3897, 38303-3897
Telephone: 901-668-5500
Telecopier: 901-664-2840

MEMBERS OF FIRM

William P. Moss (1897-1985)
Edwin E. Wallis, Jr.
William P. Moss, Jr. (1936-1997)
W. Stanworth Harris
Beth H. DuPree

OF COUNSEL

George O. Benton

Attorneys for: First American National Bank of Jackson; Bell South; CSX Transportation, Inc.; The Equitable Life Assurance Society of the United States; Jackson Utility Division; Allied Insurance Companies; United Services Automobile Assn.; Association of Tennessee Cola-Cola Bottlers; Central Distributors, Inc.; Scotsdale Insurance Companies.

For full biographical listings, see the Martindale-Hubbell Law Directory

KINGSPORT, Sullivan Co.

FULLER, VAUGHN AND GOTT (AV)

215 E. Sullivan Street, 37660
Telephone: 423-246-8158
Fax: 423-246-2592
Email: fvglaw@usit.net

MEMBERS OF FIRM

Joseph O. Fuller (1929-1995)
Jack M. Vaughn
Steven G. Gott

Guyton O. Terry, III

LEGAL SUPPORT PERSONNEL

R. Anne Flatt

Reference: Bank of Tennessee.

For full biographical listings, see the Martindale-Hubbell Law Directory

WEST & ROSE (AV)

537 East Center Street, P.O. Box 1404, 37660
Telephone: 423-246-8176
Fax: 423-246-4028

MEMBERS OF FIRM

M. Lacy West
Steven C. Rose
Julia C. West

For full biographical listings, see the Martindale-Hubbell Law Directory

*KNOXVILLE,** Knox Co.

AMBROSE, WILSON, GRIMM & DURAND (AV)

607 Market Street, Ninth Floor, P.O. Box 2466, 37901-2466
Telephone: 423-544-3000
Toll Free: 1-800-242-1709
Facsimile: 423-637-1709
Email: tennlaw@awgd.com

W. L. Ambrose, Jr. (1907-1992)
Wm. C. Wilson (1912-1995)

MEMBERS OF FIRM

Ronald L. Grimm
Philip P. Durand
John B. Fowler

ASSOCIATES

Lars E. Schuller
Robert B. Frost, Jr.
Mary L. Abbott

OF COUNSEL

John M. Smartt
Wallace W. Conaway

Representative Clients: Lloyd's of London; Utica Mutual Insurance Co.; Georgia Casualty and Surety Co.; Sentry Insurance Co.; Shand, Morahan & Co., Inc.; Ranger Insurance Co.; Horace Mann Insurance Cos.; The Tokio Marine & Fire Insurance Co. Ltd.; Guardian Royal Exchange Insurance Group; Agora Syndicate.

For full biographical listings, see the Martindale-Hubbell Law Directory

CARPENTER & O'CONNOR (AV)

1000 First American Center, P.O. Box 2485, 37901
Telephone: 423-546-1831
Fax: 423-546-0432

MEMBERS OF FIRM

Archie R. Carpenter
Robert A. Crawford
J. Gregory O'Connor
Charles F. Sterchi, III
Louis A. McElroy, II

ASSOCIATES

Christopher D. Heagerty
Toby R. Carpenter

Representative Clients: Allstate Insurance Co.; CNA Insurance; St. Paul Fire & Marine Insurance Co.; State Farm Insurance Co.; Farmers Insurance Group; Coca Cola Co.; Food Lion; The Hyatt Corp.; The Kroger Co.; Levi Strauss & Co.

For full biographical listings, see the Martindale-Hubbell Law Directory

DUNN, MACDONALD & COLEMAN, P.C. (AV)

1221 First Tennessee Plaza, 800 South Gay Street, 37929-1221
Telephone: 423-525-0505
Fax: 423-525-6001
Email: dmcpclaw@usit.net

Paul E. Dunn
Gregory F. Coleman
James S. MacDonald
Dallas T. Reynolds, III
Candis D. Lasley

For full biographical listings, see the Martindale-Hubbell Law Directory

Knoxville—Continued

FRANTZ, MCCONNELL & SEYMOUR, LLP (AV)

550 Main Avenue, Suite 500, 37902
Telephone: 423-546-9321
Fax: 423-637-5249
Mailing Address: P.O. Box 39, Knoxville, TN, 37901
Email: Lwhitfield@fmsllp.com
Effective October 1, 1999, the Area Code will change to 865.

MEMBERS OF FIRM

Fred H. Cagle, Jr.
Arthur G. Seymour, Jr.
Francis A. Cain
Reggie E. Keaton
Donald D. Howell
Debra L. Fulton
Michael W. Ewell
Imogene Anderson King
John M. Lawhorn
James E. Wagner

Beverly Dean Nelms
Mary Elizabeth Maddox

References: Bituminous Casualty Corporation; Colonial Penn Insurance Company; Electric Mutual Liability Insurance Co.; Government Employees Insurance Company (GEICO); Liberty Mutual Insurance Company; Old Republic Insurance Company; Provident Life & Accident Insurance Company; Prudential Insurance Company of America; The Travelers Insurance Companies; United Service Automobile Association (USAA).

For Complete List of Firm Personnel, See General Section

For full biographical listings, see the Martindale-Hubbell Law Directory

WATSON, HOLLOW & REEVES, P.L.C. (AV)

1700 First Tennessee Plaza, 800 South Gay Street, P.O. Box 131, 37901-0131
Telephone: 423-637-1700
Telecopier: 423-525-2514

MEMBERS OF FIRM

Robert Harmon Watson, Jr.
Richard L. Hollow
Pamela L. Reeves
Jon Gilbert Roach
John Chapman Duffy
John T. Batson, Jr.
Earl Jerome Melson

ASSOCIATES

Nathan D. Rowell
Laura C. Webb
Beverley S. Cornett
Jenny Coques Rogers

Representative Clients: Tennessee Municipal League Insurance Pool; State Volunteer Mutual Insurance; Frontier Insurance Co.; Titan Indemnity Co.; Insbrok Insurance Company; CIGNA; Colonial Trust Self Insured; State Farm Mutual Automobile Insurance Co.; American National Property & Casualty Co.; State Farm Fire and Casualty Co.

For full biographical listings, see the Martindale-Hubbell Law Directory

*LAWRENCEBURG,** Lawrence Co.

HARWELL & PLANT (AV)

225 Mahr Avenue, P.O. Box 399, 38464
Telephone: 931-762-7528
Fax: 931-762-7520
Email: harwellplant@lawrenceburg.com *URL:* http://www.lawyers.com/harwellplant

W. A. Harwell (1917-1982)
Paul B. Plant

ASSOCIATE

Stacey Lemley Grooms

LEGAL SUPPORT PERSONNEL

Kim Davenport (Certified Professional Legal Secretary)
Diane Springer (Accredited Legal Secretary)

General Counsel For: Southland Express Inc. and Related Companies; Title and Escrow of Lawrence County, LLC; Counce/Hooper Realty & Auction; Pro-Rac, Inc.; Beckman Lumber Industries; City of St. Joseph, Tenn.; Lawrence County School Board.
Reference: First Farmers & Merchants National Bank.
Representative Clients: Tennessee Farmers Mutual Insurance Co.; Liberty National Insurance Co.; General Accident Insurance Co.

For full biographical listings, see the Martindale-Hubbell Law Directory

*MEMPHIS,** Shelby Co.

ARMSTRONG ALLEN PREWITT GENTRY JOHNSTON & HOLMES, PLLC (AV)

Brinkley Plaza, Suite 700, 80 Monroe Avenue, 38103-2467
Telephone: 901-523-8211
Facsimile: 901-524-4936
Little Rock, Arkansas Office: Suite 100, 100 Morgan Keegan Drive, 72202.
Telephone: 501-280-0100.
Facsimile: 501-280-0166.
Jackson, Mississippi Office: 2525 Lakeward Drive, Suite 200, 39216.
Telephone: 601-713-1192.
Facsimile: 601-713-2049.
Jackson, Tennessee Office: 464 North Parkway, Suite A, 38305.
Telephone: 901-660-2332.
Facsimile: 901-664-1109.

(See Next Column)

MEMBERS OF FIRM

Thomas F. Johnston
Charles A. Banks (Resident, Little Rock, Arkansas Office)
Prince C. Chambliss, Jr.
Paul A. Matthews
Randall D. Noel
Cannon F. Allen

OF COUNSEL

Gavin M. Gentry

For Complete List of Firm Personnel, See General Section

For full biographical listings, see the Martindale-Hubbell Law Directory

BAKER, DONELSON, BEARMAN & CALDWELL (AV)

20th Floor, First Tennessee Building, 165 Madison, 38103
Telephone: 901-526-2000
Telecopier: 901-577-2303
Email: info@bdbc.com *URL:* http://www.bakerdonelson.com
Nashville, Tennessee Office: 1700 Nashville City Center, 511 Union Street, 37219.
Telephone: 615-726-5600.
Telecopier: 615-726-0464.
Chattanooga, Tennessee Office: 1800 Republic Centre, 633 Chestnut Street, 37450-1800.
Telephone: 423-756-2010.
Telecopier: 423-756-3447.
Knoxville, Tennessee Office: 2200 Riverview Tower, 900 South Gay Street, 37901.
Telephone: 423-549-7000.
Telecopier: 423-525-8569.
Johnson City, Tennessee Office: SunTrust Bank Building, 207 Mockingbird Lane, P.O. Box 3038, 37602.
Telephone: 423-928-0181.
Telecopier: 423-928-5694; 423-928-3654; Kingsport: 423-246-6191.
Huntsville, Tennessee Office: 3 Courthouse Square, 37756.
Telephone: 423-663-2321.
Telecopier: 423-663-2111.
Washington, D.C. Office: Market Square, 801 Pennsylvania Avenue, N.W., 20004.
Telephone: 202-508-3400.
Telecopier: 202-508-3402.
Jackson, Mississippi Office: Suite 500, 700 North State Street, 39202.
Telephone: 601-351-2400.
Telecopier: 601-351-2424.

MANAGING PARTNER

Robert Mark Glover

SHAREHOLDERS

Lewis R. Donelson, III
Roy Keathley
David G. Williams
Leo Bearman, Jr.
Maurice Wexler
Frank L. Watson, Jr.
Robert Walker
Boyd L. Rhodes, Jr.
W. Michael Richards
John C. Speer
Charles T. Tuggle, Jr.
Larry E. Killebrew
Jerry Stauffer
Robert C. Liddon
William H.D. Fones, Jr.
William P. Kenworthy
Allan J. Wade
Gregory G. Fletcher
Charles C. Harrell
Stephen D. Goodwin
George T. Lewis, III
Ben C. Adams, Jr.
Eugene J. Podesta, Jr.
Sam B. Blair, Jr.
Carla Peacher-Ryan
Mary Aronov
Jill M. Steinberg
Matthew S. Heiter
Michael C. Patton
Janis Wild Kesser
Stephen William Ragland
Monique A. Nassar
Bradley E. Trammell
M. Clay Bethell
Desiree M. Franklin
R. Alan Pritchard, Jr.
Peter H. Kesser

OF COUNSEL

Frierson M. Graves, Jr.
Donald A. Malmo
Lynn Ackerman Landau
Paul E. Risner (Not admitted in TN)

ASSOCIATES

Paul R. O'Rourke
Anne B. Mathes
Elizabeth Einstman Chance
Frank L. Watson, III
W. Douglas Sweet
Wm. Scott Young
Mary Ann Jackson
Angela R. Merideth
Jackie G. Prester
David L. Bearman
Clarissa M. Cissell
Robert C. McConkey, III
Jennifer R. Keown
Brett T. Parks
Cedric C.Y. Tan
Lang Wiseman
Diane Schratz Holitik
D. Benjamin Bullen
Shannon M. Hernandez
Sylvia Monique Reed
Christopher G. Boling
Louise P. Gaerig
Lori Hackleman Patterson
Lea Hall Speed

For full biographical listings, see the Martindale-Hubbell Law Directory

EVANS & PETREE (AV)

81 Monroe Avenue, 38103
Telephone: 901-525-6781
Telecopier: 901-527-7756

(See Next Column)

EVANS & PETREE—*Continued*

MEMBERS OF FIRM

Marion G. Evans (1877-1957)
Jack Petree (1921-1973)
Charles Pittman Cobb (Retired)
Elwood L. Edwards (Retired)
W. Lytle Nichol IV
John W. McQuiston II
Ernest G. Kelly, Jr.
Michael C. Williams
Joseph W. Barnwell, Jr.
David C. Scruggs
Leonard C. Dunavant, Jr.
E. Woods Weathersby
C. Bradford Foster III
Andrew H. Raines
Frank N. Stockdale Carney
Paul F. T. Edwards
Percy H. Harvey
Katharine A. Jungkind
Scott A. Frick
Michael R. Marshall
Richard E.M. Nichol, Jr.

Karen Baim Reagler

For full biographical listings, see the Martindale-Hubbell Law Directory

FARRIS, MATHEWS, BRANAN & HELLEN, P.L.C. (AV)

One Commerce Square, Suite 2000, 38103
Telephone: 901-259-7100
Fax: 901-259-7150
Email: firm@farris-law.com
East Memphis, Tennessee Office: Suite 400. First Commercial Bank Building. 5384 Poplar Avenue.
Telephone: 901-763-4000.
Fax: 901-763-4095.
Nashville, Tennessee Office: Nashville City Center, 511 Union Street, Suite 2400.
Telephone: 615-726-1200.
Fax: 615-726-1776.

MEMBERS OF FIRM

Tim Wade Hellen
G. Ray Bratton
D. Edward Harvey (Resident, Nashville Office)
Rebecca Pearson Tuttle
Eugene Stone Forrester, Jr.

ASSOCIATES

Gregory W. O'Neal
Pamela Haddock Klavon
Paul C. Peel
Garrett M. Estep

For Complete List of Firm Personnel, See General Section

For full biographical listings, see the Martindale-Hubbell Law Directory

GLASSMAN, JETER, EDWARDS & WADE, P.C. (AV)

26 North Second Street Building, 38103
Telephone: 901-527-4673
Telecopier: 901-521-0940
Email: GJEWW@Memphisonline.com

Richard Glassman
William M. Jeter
Tim Edwards
B. J. Wade
Carl K. Wyatt, Jr.
Dale H. Tuttle
John Barry Burgess
Robert A. Cox
Rebecca Adelman
Lori J. Keen
James F. Horner, Jr.
Richard E. Sorin

Todd Britton Murrah
Heather Walters Thompson

For full biographical listings, see the Martindale-Hubbell Law Directory

HARRIS, SHELTON, DUNLAP AND COBB, P.L.L.C. (AV)

Suite 2700, One Commerce Square, 38103-2555
Telephone: 901-525-1455
Telecopier: 901-526-4084
Email: hsdclaw@hsdclaw.com
Other Memphis Office: 6363 Poplar, Suite 430.
Telephone: 901-682-1455.
Fax: 901-682-4446.
Oxford, Mississippi Office: 428 North Lamar Boulevard, Suite 2.
Telephone: 662-238-2855.
Fax: 662-238-2895.

MEMBERS OF FIRM

Walter Chandler (1887-1967)
John H. Harris, Jr.
Max Shelton
William W. Dunlap, Jr.
M. Anderson Cobb, Jr.
James L. Kirby
James R. Garts, Jr.
George T. Wheeler, Jr.
James D. Wilson
Charles C. Drennon, III (Resident, Poplar Avenue Office)
Michael F. Rafferty
A. Neal Graham
G. Rice Byars, Jr.
Jonathan E. Scharff

ASSOCIATES

Tabitha Francisco McNabb
Brett A. Hughes
Chesney Falk McAfee
Christopher S. Campbell
Estelle C. Gaerig
Donrua Barnes-Hulsey
Shawn L. Verner

For full biographical listings, see the Martindale-Hubbell Law Directory

KRIVCHER MAGIDS PLC (AV)

International Place II, 6410 Poplar Avenue, Suite 300, 38119-4839
Telephone: 901-682-6431
Facsimile: 901-682-6453
Email: lawfirm@kmplc.com

Michael B. Neal

ASSOCIATES

Aubrey Lee Brown, Jr.
Elizabeth J. Landrigan

For Complete List of Firm Personnel, See General Section

For full biographical listings, see the Martindale-Hubbell Law Directory

MCDONALD KUHN (AV)

80 Monroe Avenue, Suite 550, P.O. Box 3160, 38173-0160
Telephone: 901-526-0606
Fax: 901-521-8397

MEMBERS OF FIRM

W. Percy McDonald (1890-1969)
W. Percy McDonald, Jr. (1921-1967)
Braxton C. Gandy (1915-1979)
Edward W. Kuhn (1904-1983)
Henry T. V. Miller
William A. Lucchesi
Carol Mills Hayden

ASSOCIATES

Loys A. "Trey" Jordan, III
Stephen P. Miller
June Kinney
Evan Nahmias

For full biographical listings, see the Martindale-Hubbell Law Directory

ROSSIE, LUCKETT, PARKER & RIDDER, P.C. (AV)

675 Oakleaf Office Lane, Suite 200, 38117-4863
Telephone: 901-763-1800
Telecopier: 901-767-6514
Email: rlpr@rlpr.com

William O. Luckett, Jr.
Lorrie K. Ridder
Cameron C. Jehl

For Complete List of Firm Personnel, See General Section

For full biographical listings, see the Martindale-Hubbell Law Directory

SEVIER LAW FIRM, P.C. (AV)

One Memphis Place, 200 Jefferson Avenue, Suite 975, 38103-2390
Telephone: 901-529-8888
Fax: 901-529-1234

Charles A. Sevier

Gail R. Sevier
Bruce A. Ralston

Representative Clients: Nationwide Insurance Co.; Colonial Insurance Co.; TML Risk Management; State Farm Insurance Co.; Worldwide Insurance Co.; Amerisure.

For full biographical listings, see the Martindale-Hubbell Law Directory

SMITH, SABBATINI & MCLEARY, PLLC (AV)

100 Peabody Place Suite 1250, 38103
Telephone: 901-312-5555
Fax: 901-312-5667
Mailing Address: P.O. Box 3582, Memphis, TN, 38173
URL: http://www.smithlawetal.com

Gary K. Smith
Robert L. Sabbatini
Harold W. McLeary, Jr.
William D. Domico
James F. Kyle
James T. McColgan, III
G. Edward Coleman, III
Bryant C. Witt

Representative Clients: Premier RRG Insurance; Illinois Central Railroad; Medical Assurance; Albertson's, Inc.; Med. Marc (Chiro Co.); Medical Protective Co.; Methodist Health Systems; Hartford Insurance Co.; Sentry Insurance; State Farm Insurance.

For full biographical listings, see the Martindale-Hubbell Law Directory

WARING COX, PLC (AV)

Morgan Keegan Tower, 50 North Front Street, Suite 1300, 38103-1190
Telephone: 901-543-8000
Telecopy: 901-543-8030
Email: Desk@waringcox.com

Louis F. Allen
William E. Frulla
Louis J. Miller
Charles W. Hill
Robert B.C. Hale

Representative Clients: Federal Express Corp.; South Central Bell Telephone Co.; American States Insurance; Central Benefits National Life Insurance Co.; ICAROM, PLC; Primerica Life Insurance Co.; Miles Inc.; Underwriters at Lloyds.

For Complete List of Firm Personnel, See General Section

For full biographical listings, see the Martindale-Hubbell Law Directory

Memphis—Continued

WILSON, MCRAE, IVY, MCTYIER AND STRAIN (AV)

295 Washington Avenue, Suite 2, P.O. Box 3331, 38173
Telephone: 901-523-2364
Telecopier: 901-523-2366

MEMBERS OF FIRM

Fred E. Ivy, Jr.
Douglas A. McTyier
Alan R. Strain
Robert M. Nelson (1900-1967)
Albert T. McRae (Retired)

For full biographical listings, see the Martindale-Hubbell Law Directory

*NASHVILLE,** Davidson Co.

COX, LEVAN, SPRADER & PATTON, P.L.L.C. (AV)

172 Second Avenue, North Suite 214, 37201
Telephone: 615-843-0300
Telecopier: 615-843-0310
URL: http://www.lawyers.com/clsp

MEMBERS OF FIRM

Stephen E. Cox
Mark S. LeVan
Paul L. Sprader
C. Benton Patton

For full biographical listings, see the Martindale-Hubbell Law Directory

DAVIES & HUMPHREYS (AV)

150 Second Avenue North, Suite 225, P.O. Box 190609, 37219-0609
Telephone: 615-256-8125
Fax: 615-242-7853
Email: davies_h@bellsouth.net

MEMBERS OF FIRM

Ed Reynolds Davies
Jerry R. Humphreys
Robert R. Davies
E. Reynolds Davies, Jr.

ASSOCIATE

John T. Horton

Representative Clients: Bituminous Insurance Companies; Carrier Corporation; E.B.I. Companies (Orion Group); Liberty Mutual Insurance Company; Ohio Casualty Insurance Group; Otis Elevator Company; St. Paul/United States Fidelity & Guaranty Company; State Volunteer Mutual Insurance Company; United HealthCare Corporation; Wausau Insurance Companies.

For full biographical listings, see the Martindale-Hubbell Law Directory

GLASGOW AND VEAZEY (AV)

Washington Square, 222 Second Avenue, North Suite 312, 37201-1649
Telephone: 615-244-4693
Fax: 615-256-0499
Email: g&v@nashville.com

MEMBERS OF FIRM

S. McPheeters Glasgow, Jr.
Randolph A. Veazey

ASSOCIATES

Connie Jones
Warren M. Smith
James R. Tomkins

Representative Clients: The Travelers Insurance Co.; Westfield Insurance Companies; Royal Insurance Companies; Ryder Truck Rental, Inc.; Worldwide Insurance Group; GRE Insurance Group; TAB Service Corporation; MSI Insurance Group; Motors Insurance Group; North American Life Insurance Company.

For full biographical listings, see the Martindale-Hubbell Law Directory

HOLLINS, WAGSTER & YARBROUGH, P.C. (AV)

22nd Floor SunTrust Center, 424 Church Street, 37219
Telephone: 615-256-6666
Telecopier: 615-254-4254

John J. Hollins
John W. Wagster
Edward M. Yarbrough
John L. Norris
David L. Raybin
James L. Weatherly, Jr.
John J. Hollins, Jr.
Patrick T. McNally

Jacqueline B. Dixon

References: First American National Bank; Sun Trust Bank.

For full biographical listings, see the Martindale-Hubbell Law Directory

MINK & BLAIR (AV)

Suite 400, 219 Second Avenue, North, P.O. Box 190584, 37219-0584
Telephone: 615-256-0138
Fax: 615-726-8796
Lawrenceburg, Tennessee Office: 316 Waterloo Street, P.O. Box 707.
Telephone: 931-762-7112.
Fax: 931-762-1318. Email: tmink@lorettotel.net.
Smithville, Tennessee Office: 110 Market Street, 37166.
Telephone: 615-597-3065.
Fax: 615-597-3066.

(See Next Column)

MEMBERS OF FIRM

Thomas F. Mink, II
Keith W. Blair
M. Wallace Coleman

For full biographical listings, see the Martindale-Hubbell Law Directory

ORTALE, KELLEY, HERBERT & CRAWFORD (AV)

Third Floor, Noel Place, 200 Fourth Avenue North, P.O. Box 198985, 37219-8985
Telephone: 615-256-9999
Fax: 615-726-1494
Email: GENERAL@ortalekelley.com *URL:* http://www.ortalekelley.com

MEMBERS OF FIRM

John W. Kelley, Jr. (1931-1985)
William P. Ortale
David B. Herbert
William H. Crawford, Jr.
Thomas C. Corts
Douglas A. Brace
William M. Billips
Joseph B. Klockenkemper, II
Paul M. Buchanan
Michael Gigandet
Wendy Lynne Longmire
Gerald C. Wigger
David B. Scott
J. Michael Morgan

ASSOCIATES

Joseph M. Huffaker
Richard W. Sebastian
W. Carl Spining
Cynthia D. Plymire
John C. Rochford
Todd A. Bricker
Randi Yvette Greene

OF COUNSEL

Elaine M. Youngblood

For full biographical listings, see the Martindale-Hubbell Law Directory

PARKER, LAWRENCE, CANTRELL & DEAN (AV)

Fifth Floor, 200 Fourth Avenue North, 37219
Telephone: 615-255-7500
Telecopy: 615-242-1515
Email: plcd@plcd.com *URL:* http://www.plcd.com

MEMBERS OF FIRM

Robert E. Parker
Thomas W. Lawrence, Jr.
Rose Park Cantrell
George A. Dean
Richard K. Smith
Louis Marshall Albritton
M. Bradley Gilmore
Garrett E. Asher
R. Blake Menzel

ASSOCIATE

Richard F. Russell

Representative Clients: Regions Bank; Wal-Mart Stores, Inc.; State Volunteer Mutual Insurance Co.; Harpeth Valley Utility District; Steinhouse Supply Co.

For full biographical listings, see the Martindale-Hubbell Law Directory

PRINCE & HELLINGER, P.C. (AV)

150 Second Avenue North, Suite 300, 37201-1902
Telephone: 615-244-8630
Fax: 615-244-8644

Raymond G. Prince
John R. Hellinger

For full biographical listings, see the Martindale-Hubbell Law Directory

STEWART, ESTES & DONNELL (AV)

SunTrust Financial Center, 424 Church Street Suite 1401, 37219
Telephone: 615-244-6538
Telecopier: 615-256-8386

MEMBERS OF FIRM

H. Francis Stewart (1915-1991)
Robert L. (Larry) Estes
Thomas M. Donnell, Jr.
Philip M. Kirkpatrick
Stephen K. Heard
M. Reid Estes, Jr.
Jerry W. Carnes
Martin Douglas Holmes
Peter F. Klett
W. Stuart Scott
Jeffrey L. Peterson

ASSOCIATES

John Edward Anderson
Jeffrey M. Beemer
Jennifer A. Lawrence
Leah K. Shearin
Jennifer L. Novak
Andrew C. Matteson

For full biographical listings, see the Martindale-Hubbell Law Directory

*SHELBYVILLE,** Bedford Co.

ANDREW C. RAMBO, P.C. (AV)

104 Depot Street, P.O. Box 129, 37162
Telephone: 931-684-6213
Fax: 931-684-6227
Email: arambo@cafes.net *URL:* http://www.lawyers.com/rambolaw

Andrew C. Rambo

Representative Clients: State Farm Insurance; Nationwide Insurance.

For full biographical listings, see the Martindale-Hubbell Law Directory

*UNION CITY,** Obion Co.

ELAM & GLASGOW (AV)

Commercial Bank & Trust Building, 38261
Telephone: 901-885-2011; 901-885-2012

MEMBERS OF FIRM

Tom Elam (1909-1998)
James M. Glasgow
James M. Glasgow, Jr.
Randy N. Chism

Attorneys for: Commercial Bank, Union City; Obion, Lake & Weakley Counties; United States Fidelity & Guaranty Co.; Auto Owners Insurance Co.; C.N.A. Insurance, Union City; Travelers Insurance Co.; Goodyear Tire & Rubber Co.

For full biographical listings, see the Martindale-Hubbell Law Directory

TEXAS

*ABILENE,** Taylor Co.

BATJER & WAGSTAFF, P.C. (AV)

104 Pine Street, Suite 306, P.O. Box 888, 79601
Telephone: 915-673-2597
Fax: 915-676-9329
Email: bbatjer@camalott.com

Robert D. Batjer
Robert B. Wagstaff

LEGAL SUPPORT PERSONNEL

Pamela L. Weaver

Representative Clients: General Motors Corp.; Freightliner Corp.; Royal-Globe Insurance Cos.; USAA; Ranger Insurance Cos.; Allstate Insurance Co.; State Farm Insurancae Cos.; The Medical Protective Company; SAFECO; AIG Aviation.

For full biographical listings, see the Martindale-Hubbell Law Directory

RUSSELL C. (RUSTY) BEARD (AV)

Bank of America Tower, 500 Chestnut Street, Suite 1716, P.O. Box 1401, 79604
Telephone: 915-670-9011
Fax: 915-670-9525
Email: rustybeardattorney@abilene.com

ASSOCIATES

Tami Ratliff Morris
Tami Ratliff Morris

For full biographical listings, see the Martindale-Hubbell Law Directory

WAGSTAFF, ALVIS, STUBBEMAN, SEAMSTER & LONGACRE, L.L.P. (AV)

290 Cedar, P.O. Box 360, 79604-0360
Telephone: 915-677-6291
Facsimile: 915-677-6313
Email: wassl@wagstafflaw.com
Dallas, Texas Office: 750 North St. Paul Street, Suite 1290.
Telephone: 214-220-9171.
Facsimile: 214-871-9327.

MEMBERS OF FIRM

J. M. Wagstaff (1862-1952)
John H. Alvis (1896-1971)
R. M. Wagstaff (1892-1973)
Robert H. Alvis (1929-1997)
David G. Stubbeman (Retired)
Don N. Seamster
Roy B. Longacre
Darrell W. Moore
Charles L. Black
John R. Saringer
Kyle D. Tatom
Diann Waddill

ASSOCIATES

Michael S. Seamster
Frederic L. Frawley
Lois A. Rockefeller
Coby Waddill

Representative Clients: Abilene Independent School District; American International Adjusting Co.; CSW Energy, Inc.; Ford New Holland, Inc.; Hardin-Simmons University; Hendrick Medical Center; NationsBank of Texas, N.A.; Sears, Roebuck & Co.; United Services Automobile Assn.; West Texas Utilites Co. (General Counsel).

For full biographical listings, see the Martindale-Hubbell Law Directory

ADDISON, Dallas Co.

GERARD SINGER & LEVICK, P.C. (AV)

16200 Addison Road Suite 140, 75001-5350
Telephone: 972-380-5533
Fax: 972-380-5748
Email: bcgerard@flash.net

(See Next Column)

Bretton C. Gerard
Gregory Z. Singer
Larry A. Levick
Michael I. Kahn
Robert J. Mabel
I. Richard Levy

For full biographical listings, see the Martindale-Hubbell Law Directory

*AUSTIN,** Travis Co.

BROYLES & PRATT, A PROFESSIONAL CORPORATION (AV)

One Northpoint Centre, Suite 250, 6836 Austin Center Boulevard, 78731
Telephone: 361-886 6200
Fax: 361-886 6262
Corpus Christi, Texas Office: 1001 Bank of America Center North. 500 North Shoreline Boulevard, 78471.
Telephone: 361-886-6200.
Fax: 361-886-6262.

R. Michael Anderson
Larry W. Brewer
Mark Held
Joe N. Pratt
Davison W. Grant
Mason L. Terry

Dudley McClellan

OF COUNSEL

Richard H. Cory

For full biographical listings, see the Martindale-Hubbell Law Directory

BURNS ANDERSON JURY & BRENNER, L.L.P. (AV)

A Limited Liability Partnership including a Professional Corporation
4807 Spicewood Springs Road, Building 4, P.O. Box 26300, 78755-6300
Telephone: 512-338-5322
Facsimile: 512-338-5363
Email: lmackey@bajb.com

Robert B. Burns, Jr. (P.C.)
Joe R. Anderson
Jeffrey R. Jury
David L. Brenner
Michael J. Donovan

Gilbert Atkinson
Arturo M. Aviles
Lea M. Burleson
Kenton P. Campbell
Cristina Mireles Cooper
Paul Gonzalez
Kristin Lee Lemke
Danielle M. Harsany
David L. Swanson

For full biographical listings, see the Martindale-Hubbell Law Directory

CANTEY & HANGER ROAN & AUTREY L.L.P. (AV)

200 First State Bank Tower, 400 West Fifteenth Street, 78701-4200
Telephone: 512-474-4200
FAX: 512-469-0470; 512-469-0474
Email: FIRM@ROAN-AUTREY.COM *URL:* http://www.Roan-Autrey.com
Fort Worth, Texas Office: Cantey & Hanger, 2100 Burnett Plaza, 801 Cherry Street.
Telephone: 817-877-2800, Metro Line: 429-3815.
Telex: 758631.
FAX: 877-2807. Email: cantey@onramp.net
Dallas, Texas Office: Cantey & Hanger, 3330 Harwood Center, 1999 Bryan Street.
Telephone: 214-978-4100.
FAX: 214-978-4150. Email: chdallas@onramp.net

Forrest C. Roan
Jeff W. Autrey
Stephen L. Phillips
Brian C. Newby
Julie K. Lane

OF COUNSEL

Tieman H. Dippel, Jr.

LEGAL SUPPORT PERSONNEL

Mary B. Jordan
Mary Perroni Blevins

Representative Clients: American Insurance Assn.; American Bankers Insurance Group; Manufactures Life Insurance Co.; Prudential Insurance Co.; Zenith Insurance Co.; Zurich American Life Insurance Company; Commercial General Union Insurance Co.; Tokio Marine & Fire Insurance Co.

For full biographical listings, see the Martindale-Hubbell Law Directory

DAVIS & DAVIS, P.C. (AV)

Arboretum Plaza One, 9th Floor, 9442 Capital of Texas Highway, P.O. Box 1588, 78759
Telephone: 512-343-6248
Fax: 512-343-0121
Mailing Address: P.O. Box 1588, Austin, Texas, 78767

C. Dean Davis
Fred E. Davis
Alexis J. Fuller, Jr.
Ruth Russell-Schafer
Michael L. Neely
Brian Gregory Jackson
Monte F. James

(See Next Column)

DAVIS & DAVIS P.C., *Austin—Continued*

Bill Cline, Jr.
Mark Alan Keene
Kenda B. Dalrymple
Marian J. Wu
Mark S. La Spina

For Complete List of Firm Personnel, See General Section
For full biographical listings, see the Martindale-Hubbell Law Directory

DAVIS & WILKERSON, P.C. (AV)

1801 South Mopac, Suite 300, P.O. Box 2283, 78768-2283
Telephone: 512-482-0614
Fax: 512-482-0342
Email: dwlaw@dwlaw.com *URL:* http://www.dwlaw.com
Alpine Office: 1110 East Holland, P.O. Box 777.
Telephone: 915-837-5547.

David M. Davis
Steven R. Welch
Glen Wilkerson
David A. Wright
Leonard W. Woods
Kevin A. Reed
J. Mark Holbrook
Brian E. Riewe
Brian McElroy
Robert L. Hargett
Michael Wilson
Frances W. Hamermesh
Fletcher H. Brown

Jennifer B. Claymon
David M. Coffey
Hollis Hudson Gaston
Steven C. Levatino
Diana Maldonado
Erin E. Matherne
Joel S. Pace
Stephen G. Wohleb
Michael P. Young

OF COUNSEL

Pete P. Gallego (Resident, Alpine Office)
Peter R. Meeker

For full biographical listings, see the Martindale-Hubbell Law Directory

DELEON, BOGGINS & ICENOGLE, A PROFESSIONAL CORPORATION (AV)

Bank One Tower, 221 West 6th Street, Suite 1050, 78701
Telephone: 512-478-5308
Fax: 512-482-8628
Email: deleon@dandb.com

Hector DeLeon
Anthony Icenogle
Thomas P. Washburn

OF COUNSEL

Joseph C. Boggins
Waggoner Carr
L. Dean Coff

Reference: Bank One, Austin.

For full biographical listings, see the Martindale-Hubbell Law Directory

HANNA & PLAUT, L.L.P. (AV)

The Littlefield Building, 106 East Sixth Street, Suite 520, 78701
Telephone: 512-472-7700
Facsimile: 512-472-0205
Email: hannaplaut.com

Catherine L. Hanna
David L. Plaut

Lynn E. Carter
Jeff Glass
Eric S. Peabody
Tara L Dale

For full biographical listings, see the Martindale-Hubbell Law Directory

HENSLEE, FOWLER, HEPWORTH & SCHWARTZ, L.L.P. (AV)

800 Frost Bank Plaza, 816 Congress Avenue, 78701-2443
Telephone: 512-708-1804; 800-969-7444
Fax: 512-708-9037
URL: http://www.Insurance-Defense.com
URL: http://www.school-law.com
Houston Office: 3200 Southwest Freeway, Suite 2355.
Telephone: 713-552-1693.
Tyler Office: 1114 Plaza Tower, 110 North College Avenue.
Telephone: 903-593-0454.
Fax: 903-593-0193.
Dallas Office: 4131 North Central Expressway, Suite 680.
Telephone: 214-219-8833; 800-690-5456.
Fax: 214-219-8866.
Rio Grande Valley (McAllen) Office: 6521 N. 10th Street, Suite C.
Telephone: 956-631-8883.
Fax: 956-631-8188.

Donald G. Henslee
Laura S. Fowler
Roger D. Hepworth
Susan Abbott Schwartz (Resident, Dallas Office)
C. Mark Stratton
V. Jay Youngblood (Resident, Tyler Office)
Trey L. Dolezal

(See Next Column)

Rhonda Cagle Barfield
Peter C. Blomquist
Robert Penn Fowler
Michael B. Gerstle (Resident, Dallas Office)
Teresa V. Harris
Jason E. Kipness
John C. Koechel
Kirk Kuykendall
Sue M. Lee
D. Roderick MacRae, II
Dana L. Minissale (Resident, Dallas Office)
Stephen Jon Moss
Barry A. Moscowitz
J. Erik Nichols
George J. Petras, IV
Keena L. Smotherman
Mark P. Tilley
H. Lee Veness
Robert J. West

OF COUNSEL

Cindy Ann Lopez Garcia
J. Malcolm Harris
George J. (Dick) Stengel (Resident, San Antonio Office)

For full biographical listings, see the Martindale-Hubbell Law Directory

HOHMANN & TAUBE, L.L.P. (AV)

100 Congress Avenue, Suite 1600, 78701-4042
Telephone: 512-472-5997
Fax: 512-472-5248
Email: bille@ht-law.com *URL:* http://www.ht-law.com

Guy M. Hohmann
Robert Summers
Gary N. Schumann

Cristina B. McGarr
Robert D. Thomas
T. Wade Jefferies
Neal Meinzer
Scott B. Herlihy

For full biographical listings, see the Martindale-Hubbell Law Directory

LONG, BURNER, PARKS & SEALY, A PROFESSIONAL CORPORATION (AV)

515 Congress Avenue, Suite 1500, P.O. Box 2212, 78768-2212
Telephone: 512-474-1587
Fax: 512-322-0301

Larry Parks
Earl W. (Rusty) Sealy
Jane G. Noble

For full biographical listings, see the Martindale-Hubbell Law Directory

SCHWARTZ & EICHELBAUM, P.C. (AV)

One Commodore Plaza, 800 Brazos, Suite 870, 78701
Telephone: 512-476-9944
Fax: 512-472-2599
Email: info@edlaw.com
San Antonio, Texas Office: 700 N. St. Mary's, Suite 1850, 78205.
Telephone: 210-228-9944.
Fax: 210-228-9950.
Plano, Texas Office, D/FW Metroplex: P.O. Box 250025, 75025.
Telephone: 972-377-7900.
Fax: 972-377-7277.

Leonard J. Schwartz
Dennis J. Eichelbaum (Resident, D/FW Metroplex, Texas)
Kelli Hamm Karczewski
Robert A. Schulman (Resident, San Antonio, Texas)
Cobby A. Caputo
Stacy C. Ferguson (Resident, San Antonio, Texas)

Holly Boyd Wardell
Cheryl Tremaine Mehl
Kaye Knox Feist
Suzanne Stephens Becker (Resident, San Antonio, Texas)
Deirdre Vasquez (Resident, San Antonio, Texas)

For full biographical listings, see the Martindale-Hubbell Law Directory

THOMPSON & KNIGHT L.L.P. (AV)

(Attorneys and Counselors)
1200 San Jacinto Center, 98 San Jacinto Boulevard, 78701
Telephone: 512-469-6100
Telecopy: 512-469-6180
URL: http://www.tklaw.com
Dallas, Texas Office: 1700 Pacific Avenue, Suite 3300, 75201.
Telephone: 214-969-1700.
Telecopy: 512-969-1751.
Telex: 732298.
Fort Worth, Texas Office: 801 Cherry Street, Suite 1600, 76102.
Telephone: 817-347-1700.
Telecopy: 817-347-1799.
Houston, Texas Office: Thompson Knight Brown Parker & Leahy L.L.P., 1200 Smith Street, Suite 3600, 77002-4595.
Telephone: 713-654-8111.
Telecopier: 713-654-1871.
San Pedro Garza Garcia, Nuevo León, Mexico Office: Edificio Losoles PD-4, Av. Lázaro Cárdenas No. 2400 Pte., C.P. 66220.
Telephone: (52-8) 363-0096.
Telecopy: (52-8) 363-3067.

(See Next Column)

THOMPSON & KNIGHT L.L.P.—*Continued*

PARTNERS

Debora Beck Alsup
Eugene W. Brees, II

For Complete List of Firm Personnel, See General Section

For full biographical listings, see the Martindale-Hubbell Law Directory

WALSH, ANDERSON, BROWN, SCHULZE & ALDRIDGE, P.C. (AV)

La Costa Centre, 6300 La Calma, Suite 200, P.O. Box 2156, 78768
Telephone: 512-454-6864
Fax: 512-467-9318
San Antonio, Texas Office: Renaissance Plaza, Suite 800, 70 N.E. Loop 410. P.O. Box 460606, 78246-0606.
Telephone: 210-979-6633.
Fax: 210-979-7024.
Irving, Texas Office: 511 E. John Carpenter Freeway, Suite 430, P.O. Box 168046, 75062.
Telephone: 214-574-8800.
Fax: 214-574-8801.

Jim Walsh
Denise Howell Anderson
Judy Brown
Eric W. Schulze
John S. Aldridge
Paul William Hunn
Elena M. Gallegos
Nan Porett Hundere (Resident, San Antonio Office)
Joe B. Hairston
Dorcas A. Green
Therold I. Farmer
Robert Russo (Resident, San Antonio Office)
Paige C. Kyle (Resident, San Antonio Office)
Oscar G. Treviño
Bridget R. Robinson
Mark C. Goulet
Susan B. Graham (Resident, Irving Office)

Nona C. Matthews (Resident, Irving Office)
Denise Hays
Paula Maddox Roalson (Resident, San Antonio Office)
Daniel M. (Matt) Burns
Terry L. Kyle (Resident, San Antonio Office)
JoAnn S. Wright (Resident, Irving Office)
Liza M. Crow (Resident, San Antonio Office)
Stacy Tuer Castillo (Resident, San Antonio Office)
Jennifer A. Childress
Joe A. De Los Santos
Marie K. Williams
George E. Grimes, Jr. (Resident, San Antonio Office)
Sharon E. Ramage (Resident, Irving, Texas Office)
Yvonnilda G. Muñiz
Marquette M. Maresh

LEGAL SUPPORT PERSONNEL

Diana Stangl (Office Manager)

For full biographical listings, see the Martindale-Hubbell Law Directory

WILSON GROSENHEIDER MOORE & JACOBS, L.L.P. (AV)

A Limited Liability Partnership including Professional Corporations
One Northpoint Centre, 6836 Austin Center Boulevard, Suite 280, 78731
Telephone: 512-478-1657
Fax: 512-478-9016
Mailing Address: P.O. Box 1584, 78767
Email: wgmj@wgmj.com

John C. Wilson (P.C.)
Delno J. Grosenheider (P.C.)
David M. Moore
Richard F. Jacobs
L. Kim Basinger
Jane Lipscomb Stone
Joseph Loiacono, II

Jacqueline L. Wood
James M. Loughlin

Representative Clients: CNA Insurance Cos.; Continental Insurance Cos.; Farmers Insurance Cos.; GAB Business Services; ITT Hartford Insurance Group; Lawyers Title Insurance Corporation; Liberty Mutual Insurance Co.; SAFECO Insurance Cos.; Texas Hospital Insurance Exchange; Texas Workers' Compensation Insurance Fund; The Travelers Companies.

For full biographical listings, see the Martindale-Hubbell Law Directory

*BEAUMONT,** Jefferson Co.

BENCKENSTEIN, NORVELL & NATHAN, L.L.P. (AV)

550 Fannin, Suite 200, P.O. Box 551, 77704
Telephone: 409-833-4309
Telecopier: 409-833-9558
Email: bmtlaw@aol.com
Houston, Texas Office: One Riverway, Suite 100
Telephone: 713-871-8081.
Fax: 713-871-1509.

MEMBERS OF FIRM

Lipscomb Norvell, Jr.
Gerald W. Riedmueller
Michael J. Reviere (Resident, Houston Office)
Paul A. Scheurich
Craig H. Clendenin (Resident, Houston Office)

(See Next Column)

ASSOCIATES

Floyd F. McSpadden, Jr.
Dennis S. Dresden (Resident, Houston Office)
David A. Oubre (Resident, Houston Office)
J. Keith Stanley

OF COUNSEL

Jerry J. Nathan

Representative Clients: Chubb/Pacific Indemnity Group; Mobil Oil Corp.; Travelers; Wausau; American International Group; CNA; Kemper Insurance Group; E.I. DuPont; Zurich American; Fina Oil & Chemical Co.

For full biographical listings, see the Martindale-Hubbell Law Directory

LEWIS & ASSOCIATES (AV)

The Courtyard, 4180 Delaware, Suite 402, 77706
Telephone: 409-899-5600
Fax: 409-899-5682

Clint W. Lewis

Edward B. Chatelain, III
James W. Henges

For full biographical listings, see the Martindale-Hubbell Law Directory

MEHAFFY & WEBER, A PROFESSIONAL CORPORATION (AV)

2615 Calder Avenue, Suite 800, P.O. Box 16, 77704
Telephone: 409-835-5011
Fax: 409-835-5729; 835-5177
Email: MehaffyWeber.com
Orange, Texas Office: 1006 Green Avenue, P.O. Drawer 189.
Telephone: 409-886-7766.
Houston, Texas Office: One Allen Center, 500 Dallas, Suite 1200.
Telephone: 713-655-1200.

James W. Mehaffy (1914-1985)
Roger S. McCabe
Jim I. Graves
John Cash Smith
Arthur R. Almquist
Louis M. Scofield
Patricia Chamblin
Gene M. Williams
David B. Gaultney
Robert A. Black
Sandra F. Clark
M. C. Carrington
Barbara J. Barron
Elizabeth Brandes Pratt
John E. Haught
Keith W. Foley
Charles Stanton Perry
Ernest W. Boyd
Michele Y. Smith

Vickie R. Thompson
Paul R. Heyburn
James G. Martingano
Debra N. Bigler
Elizabeth C. Turley
Peter T. Gregg
E. Wade Carpenter
Nikkee E. Rutherford
Bridget M. Fuselier
Jonathan C. Allen
Chris H. Booth
Maryalyce W. Cox
Timothy A. Gasaway
Elna Nguyen Griggs
Sean Stotsky

OF COUNSEL

Otto J. Weber, Jr.
Dewey J. Gonsoulin
John J. Durkay

Representative Clients: E.I. du Pont de Nemours and Co.; Eli Lilly & Co.; Merrell Dow; Jefferson County Tax Appraisal District; W.R. Grace & Co.-Conn.; Bank of America; Christus Health; Christus St. Elizabeth; Christus St. Mary; Burlington Northern Santa Fe Railway.
Approved Attorneys for: Stewart Title Guaranty Co.

For Complete List of Firm Personnel, See General Section

For full biographical listings, see the Martindale-Hubbell Law Directory

PATE & DODSON (AV)

470 Orleans Building, Suite 1201, 77701
Telephone: 409-838-6578
Fax: 409-838-6922

MEMBERS OF FIRM

Gordon R. Pate
Joe Michael Dodson
Karen L. Spivey
Christy Amuny

ASSOCIATE

Mark William Frasher

Representative Clients: Allstate Insurance Co.; The Travelers Insurance Co.; Universal Underwriters Insurance Co.; City Coach Lines, Inc.; Commercial Union Insurance Co.; Scottsdale Insurance Co.; GAINSCO; Hartford Insurance Co.; American International Adjustment Co., Inc.; Fidelity and Deposit Company of Maryland.

For full biographical listings, see the Martindale-Hubbell Law Directory

WELLER, GREEN, TOUPS & TERRELL, L.L.P. (AV)

2615 Calder Street, Suite 400, P.O. Box 350, 77704
Telephone: 409-838-0101
Telecopy: 409-838-6780
Houston, Texas Office: 4265 San Felipe, Suite 1045.
Telephone: 713-626-1126.
Fax: 713-626-1363.

(See Next Column)

FIGARI DAVENPORT & GRAVES L.L.P., *Dallas—Continued*

Jill B. Davenport
Bill E. Davidoff
Amanda M. Inabnett
Dennis M. Lynch
Melissa A. Mitchell
Katherine S. Rabe
Lisa L. Traylor
Jennifer M. Trulock

For full biographical listings, see the Martindale-Hubbell Law Directory

FRALEY & FRALEY, L.L.P. (AV)

901 Main Street, Suite 6510, 75202
Telephone: 214-761-6460
Fax: 214-761-6469
Email: info@fraleyandfraley.com *URL:* http://www.fraleyandfraley.com

R. Scott Fraley
Elizabeth Masters Fraley
J. Patrick Bredehoft

J. David Criss

For full biographical listings, see the Martindale-Hubbell Law Directory

GIBSON, MCCLURE & WALLACE, L.L.P. (AV)

8080 North Central Expressway, Suite 1300, LB50, 75206
Telephone: 214-891-8040
Fax: 214-891-8010

MEMBERS OF FIRM

Dennis D. Gibson
Wade L. McClure
Jay M. Wallace
Gabrielle Honore Kickham
Ruth Ann Norton Daniels
James M. McCoy
Alan L. Rucker
Bryan D. Perkins

Evelyn A. Yeager
Connie Kay Wilhite

For full biographical listings, see the Martindale-Hubbell Law Directory

GODWIN WHITE & GRUBER, A PROFESSIONAL CORPORATION (AV)

Suite 2500, 901 Main Street, 75202-3714
Telephone: 214-939-4400
Fax: 214-760-7332

George R. Carlton, Jr.
Elizabeth L. Phifer
Warren R. Westberg

PARTICIPATING ASSOCIATE

Josephine H. Randall

ASSOCIATES

Paul M. Bass, III
Terri B. Moore
Debora Lynn Simon
Wes E. Wadle

For Complete List of Firm Personnel, See General Section

For full biographical listings, see the Martindale-Hubbell Law Directory

JACKSON WALKER L.L.P. (AV)

901 Main Street, Suite 6000, 75202-3797
Telephone: 214-953-6000
Fax: 214-953-5822
URL: http://www.jw.com
Austin, Texas Office: 100 Congress Avenue, Suite 1100.
Telephone: 512-236-2000.
Fax: 512-236-2002.
Fort Worth, Texas Office: 301 Commerce Street, Suite 2400.
Telephone: 817-334-7200.
Fax: 817-334-7290.
Houston, Texas Office: 1100 Louisiana, Suite 4200.
Telephone: 713-752-4200.
Fax: 713-752-4221.
Richardson, Texas Office: 2435 North Central Expressway, Suite 600.
Telephone: 972-671-2560.
Fax: 972-671-2566.
San Angelo, Texas Office: 225 West Beauregard Avenue.
Telephone: 915-481-2550.
Fax: 915-481-2552.
San Antonio, Texas Office: 112 E. Pecan Street, Suite 2100.
Telephone: 210-978-7700.
Fax: 210-978-7790.

MEMBERS OF FIRM

Charles L. Babcock
E. Leon Carter
H. Dudley Chambers
Michael L. Knapek
John L. Lancaster, III
Robert P. Latham
Billy R. McGill
Retta A. Miller
David T. Moran
David C. Myers
Robert F. Ruckman
Frank C. Vecella
Troy Michael Wilson

Representative Clients Furnished Upon Request.

For Complete List of Firm Personnel, See General Section

For full biographical listings, see the Martindale-Hubbell Law Directory

JOHNSON & SYLVAN, P.C. (AV)

4440 Renaissance Tower, P.O. Box 50189, 75250
Telephone: 214-748-4747
Telecopier: 214-748-3191

Stephen W. Johnson
W. Coleman Sylvan
Stephen D. McKimmey
Benjamin H. Read
Charles W. Arnold

Charles B. Mitchell, Jr.
James K. Campbell
James E. Johnson
Robert C. Brown
Shelly S. Jock
Susan C. Austin
Ruben Rios
Travis B. Hulka
Heather A Hohmann

For full biographical listings, see the Martindale-Hubbell Law Directory

MIDDLEBERG, RIDDLE & GIANNA (AV)

2323 Bryan Street, Suite 1600, 75201
Telephone: 214-220-6300
Telecopier: 214-220-2785
New Orleans, Louisiana Office: 201 St. Charles Avenue, Suite 3100.
Telephone: 504-525-7200.
Telecopier: 504-581-5983.
Austin, Texas Office: 1300 South Mopac Expressway, First Floor.
Telephone: 512-434-8334.
Houston, Texas Office: 7676 Woodway, Suite 325.
Telephone: 713-430-5000.
Telecopier: 713-430-5090.

Ira Joel Middleberg (Not admitted in TX)
Michael Lee Riddle
Dominic J. Gianna (Not admitted in TX)

Kay A. King
Laura C. LaRaia
Angela R. Maverick
Lisa E. Minkoff
Carol J. Riddle
Robert A. Schlanger
Alexandra Smith
Marsha L. Williams
Christina R. Wommack

OF COUNSEL

Richard S. Wilensky
Robert M. Duval

For full biographical listings, see the Martindale-Hubbell Law Directory

NICHOLS, JACKSON, DILLARD, HAGER & SMITH, L.L.P. (AV)

(formerly Nichols, Jackson, Kirk & Dillard)
1800 Lincoln Plaza, 75201
Telephone: 214-965-9900
Telecopier: 214-965-0010
Email: NJDHS@NJDHS.COM

MEMBERS OF FIRM

R. E. L. Saner (1871-1938)
John C. Saner (1874-1948)
W. Harry Jack (1899-1984)
Robert L. Dillard, III
Robert E. Hager
Peter G. Smith
David M. Berman

ASSOCIATES

Bruce A. Stockard
John F. Roehm, III
Jason C. Marshall
John David Dodd, III

OF COUNSEL

R. L. Dillard, Jr.
H. Louis Nichols
Lawrence W. Jackson

Representative Clients: City of Richardson; City of Duncanville; City of University Park; City of Lancaster; Dallas Central Appraisal District; City of Coppell; Gallagher-Bassett; Texas Municipal League Intergovernmental Risk; City of DeSoto Pool.

For full biographical listings, see the Martindale-Hubbell Law Directory

SIFFORD & ANDERSON, L.L.P. (AV)

A Partnership including Professional Corporations
6300 NationsBank Plaza, 901 Main Street, 75202-3771
Telephone: 214-742-1200
Fax: 214-220-0206

MEMBERS OF FIRM

Lewis R. Sifford (P.C.)
L. W. Anderson
John L. Ratcliffe (P.C.)

Michele A. Ratcliffe
Kevin W. Vice
Ron G. MacFarlane, Jr.

For full biographical listings, see the Martindale-Hubbell Law Directory

Dallas—Continued

SMITH & MOORE (AV)

A Registered Limited Liability Partnership
4242 Lincoln Plaza, 500 N. Akard Street, 75201-6606
Telephone: 214-740-4200
Cable "PALADIN" Telex: 4630225
Facsimile: 214-740-4242
Email: cable_paladin@compuserve.com

Charles H. Smith
John W. Moore
April Robbins

Daniel Lee Alford, IV
Jennifer N. Cook
David Denny
Andrew M. Gilbert
Todd W. Hutton
John J. Reenan

Representative Clients: AI Transport; AIG Aviation, Inc.; Associated Aviation Underwriters, Inc.; Avemco Insurance Co.; Aviation & Marine Insurance Group, Inc.; Evanston Insurance Co.; National Marine Underwriters; Phoenix Aviation Insurance Managers, Inc.; United States Aviation Underwriters, Inc.; Underwriters at Lloyds, London.

For full biographical listings, see the Martindale-Hubbell Law Directory

SMITH, UNDERWOOD & PERKINS, A PROFESSIONAL CORPORATION (AV)

600 Two Lincoln Centre, 5420 LBJ Freeway, 75240
Telephone: 972-661-5114
Telecopier: 972-661-5691
Email: firm@suandp.com *URL:* http://www.suplaw.com

Timothy S. Perkins
David W. Ralston
G. Lynn Smith
William J. Underwood, Jr.

Christine A. McGuire
Amy K. Ratzlaff
P. Theodore Stoinoff, II
Val C. Cronin
Ellen P. Stewart
Todd W. Shadle
Ruth C. Logan
Christina L. Betanzos
Kent D. Williamson

For full biographical listings, see the Martindale-Hubbell Law Directory

STRADLEY & WRIGHT (AV)

9330 LBJ Freeway Suite 1400, 75243
Telephone: 972-231-6001
Telecopier: 972-231-7004

PARTNERS

Fred S. Stradley
Edwin E. Wright, III
Mark E. Stradley
Henry Wehrmann
Andrew T. Fifield

ASSOCIATES

L. Scot Dailey
George E. Crumley
Stephen C. Pipkin
William Marcus Toles

OF COUNSEL

Susan B. Burroughs
Thomas V. Murto III

For full biographical listings, see the Martindale-Hubbell Law Directory

THOMPSON, COE, COUSINS & IRONS, L.L.P. (AV)

200 Crescent Court, Eleventh Floor, 75201-1853
Telephone: 214-871-8200
Fax: 214-871-8209
Austin, Texas Office: Suite 1500, Austin Centre, 701 Brazos, 78701.
Telephone: 512-708-8200.
Fax: 512-708-8777.

PARTNERS

Franklin H. Perry
Robert O. Lamb
Randy A. Nelson
David M. Taylor
Robert B. Wellenberger
Rhonda Johnson Byrd
Roger D. Higgins
John L. Ross
Alison H. Moore
Richard M. Mosher
Newton J. Jones
Beth D. Bradley
Jennifer D. Aufricht
James L. Sowder
John B. Kronenberger
David F. Eriksen
Harrison H. Yoss
James Richard Harmon
Thomas A. Culpepper
Lisa Dreyer Ball
Kevin B. Brown
Franklin M. Kennedy
Bradford K. Burdette

ASSOCIATES

Catherine K. Faubion
Travis S. Gamble
Estee C. Whitaker

OF COUNSEL

R. B. Cousins

Representative Clients: Allstate Insurance Co.; American International Group; First State Insurance Co.; Lexington Insurance Co.; The London Agency; TIG Insurance Company; Zurich American.

(See Next Column)

For Complete List of Firm Personnel, See General Section

For full biographical listings, see the Martindale-Hubbell Law Directory

THOMPSON & KNIGHT L.L.P. (AV)

(Attorneys and Counselors)
1700 Pacific Avenue Suite 3300, 75201
Telephone: 214-969-1700
Telecopy: 214-969-1751
Telex: 732 298
URL: http://www.tklaw.com
Austin, Texas Office: 1200 San Jacinto Center, 98 San Jacinto Boulevard, 78701.
Telephone: 512-469-6100.
Telecopy: 512-469-6180.
Fort Worth, Texas Office: 801 Cherry Street, Suite 1600, 76102.
Telephone: 817-347-1700.
Telecopy: 817-347-1799.
Houston, Texas Office: Thompson Knight Brown Parker & Leahy L.L.P., 1200 Smith Street, Suite 3600, 77002-4595.
Telephone: 713-654-8111.
Telecopier: 713-654-1871.
San Pedro Garza Garcia, Nuevo León, Mexico Office: Edificio Losoles PD-4, Av. Lázaro Cárdenas No. 2400 Pte., C.P. 66220.
Telephone: (52-8) 363-0096.
Telecopy: (52-8) 363-3067.

PARTNERS

Rachelle H. Glazer
Craig A. Haynes
Stephen C. Rasch
Scott P. Stolley

SENIOR ATTORNEY

David S. White

For Complete List of Firm Personnel, See General Section

For full biographical listings, see the Martindale-Hubbell Law Directory

TOOLEY & VOSS (AV)

8214 Westchester Drive, Suite 420, 75225
Telephone: 214-368-2224
Fax: 214-368-8307
Email: JCToutfit@aol.com

Joe C. Tooley
Edwin P. Voss Jr.

For full biographical listings, see the Martindale-Hubbell Law Directory

WOODRUFF & ASSOCIATES (AV)

8144 Walnut Hill Lane Suite 1550, 75231
Telephone: 214-932-2750
Fax: 214-932-2775

STAFF COUNSEL
AMERICAN INTERNATIONAL COMPANIES

MANAGING ATTORNEY

Katherine D. Woodruff

SENIOR TRIAL ATTORNEY

Joe D. Anderson

For full biographical listings, see the Martindale-Hubbell Law Directory

*EL PASO,** El Paso Co.

DUDLEY, DUDLEY & WINDLE (AV)

310 North Mesa, Suite 823, 79901
Telephone: 915-544-3090
Fax: 915-542-2651

MEMBER OF FIRM

Wayne Windle

OF COUNSEL

William C. (Pat) Dudley
Paul W. Dudley

ASSOCIATES

Troy C. Brown
Bobbie Marie Guerra

Representative Clients: A.I.G. Group; The Charter Group; Chubb Group of Insurance Companies; CNA Insurance Co.; Crawford & Co.; The Medical Protective Company; Texas Workers' Compensation Insurance Fund.

For full biographical listings, see the Martindale-Hubbell Law Directory

HICKS & LUCKY, A PROFESSIONAL CORPORATION (AV)

5812 Cromo Drive, 79912-5502
Telephone: 915-834-8400
Fax: 915-587-8401
Toll Free: 888-738-8401
Email: info@hicksandlucky.com *URL:* http://www.hicksandlucky.com

Larry W. Hicks
Jeffrey T. Lucky
Hadley A. Huchton

(See Next Column)

HICKS & LUCKY A PROFESSIONAL CORPORATION, *El Paso—Continued*

John Scott Mann
Cynthia C. Llamas
Jennifer F. Callan
Melissa A. Dorman
Laura Montalvo

For full biographical listings, see the Martindale-Hubbell Law Directory

JAMES, GOLDMAN & HAUGLAND, P.C. A PROFESSIONAL CORPORATION (AV)

Chase Bank of Texas, 201 East Main, Suite 800, P.O. Box 1770, 79949-1770
Telephone: 915-532-3911
Fax: 915-541-6440

Wiley F. James, III
Christopher R. Johnston
Hector Phillips

Don W. Minton

Attorneys for: John Deere Insurance Co.; Mission Claims; Lone Star General Agency; Colonial Insurance Company of California; Crawford & Company; Coldwell International; Allstate Insurance; Amerisure Insurance Co.; Insurance Company of the West.

For Complete List of Firm Personnel, See General Section

For full biographical listings, see the Martindale-Hubbell Law Directory

MAYFIELD & PERRENOT, P.C. (AV)

221 N. Kansas, Suite 1600, P.O. Box 2039, 79950
Telephone: 915-533-2468
Telecopier: 915-533-0620
Email: mayper@1eagle1.com

Richard B. Perrenot
Roger C. Davie
James R. Dennis
Jeffery W. McElroy

Lisa M. Power
Shelly Weatherly
Marina Mata De La Garza

OF COUNSEL

Ellis O. Mayfield
James B. McIntyre

For full biographical listings, see the Martindale-Hubbell Law Directory

MOUNCE, GREEN, MYERS, SAFI & GALATZAN, A PROFESSIONAL CORPORATION (AV)

100 N. Stanton, Suite 1700, P.O. Box 1977, 79950-1977
Telephone: 915-532-2000
Fax: 915-541-1597
Email: mouncegreenmyers@worldnet.att.net

H. Keith Myers
Carl H. Green
Barbara Wiederstein
Kurt G. Paxson
Mark C. Walker
Steven L. Hughes
Bruce A. Koehler
Darryl S. Vereen

Carrie D. Helmcamp
James A. Martinez
Andrés E. Almanzán
Hector Andre Beltrán

Attorneys for: State Farm Mutual Automobile Insurance Co.; Safeco; Farmers Insurance Group; CGU Insurance Co.; Texas Lawyers' Insurance Exchange; Professional Liability Ins. Co.; Nationwide Insurance; Reliance Insurance Co.; Scottsdale Insurance Co.; Zurich-US.

For Complete List of Firm Personnel, See General Section

For full biographical listings, see the Martindale-Hubbell Law Directory

RAY, MCCHRISTIAN & JEANS, A PROFESSIONAL CORPORATION (AV)

5822 Cromo Drive, Suite 400, 79912
Telephone: 915-832-7200
Fax: 915-832-7333
Email: rmj@rmjfirm.com

Jeff Ray
John W. McChristian, Jr.
David S. Jeans
James A. Mounts, III
Eduardo Miranda
Robin Collins
Leticia Nuñez

Daniel H. Hernandez
Michael K. Dean
Angelica B. Carreon
Todd E. Marshall
Stacy Bearden Zavala

Representative Clients: Carolina Casualty Insurance Co.; Cigna Property and Casualty Insurance Co.; CNA Insurance Cos.; Commercial Union Insurance Cos; Houston General Insurance Co.; Kemper National Insurance Cos.; Occidental Fire and Casualty Company of North Carolina; Reliance Insurance Co.; St. Paul Fire & Marine Insurance Co.; Travelers Indemnity Co. and Aetna Casualty & Surety Co.

For full biographical listings, see the Martindale-Hubbell Law Directory

*FORT WORTH,** Tarrant Co.

BENNETT & HALL, L.L.P. (AV)

2300 Bank One Tower, 500 Throckmorton, 76102-3708
Telephone: 817-870-2300
Fax: 817-338-1915

James Gordon Bennett
Randy J. Hall

Representative Client: The Travelers.

For full biographical listings, see the Martindale-Hubbell Law Directory

CANTEY & HANGER (AV)

A Registered Limited Liability Partnership
2100 Burnett Plaza, 801 Cherry Street, 76102-6899
Telephone: 817-877-2800, Metro Line: 429-3815
Telex: 758631 FAX: 877-2807
Dallas
Email: cantey@onramp.net
Dallas, Texas Office: 3330 Harwood Center, 1999 Bryan Street.
Telephone: 214-978-4100.
FAX: 214-978-4150. Email: chdallas@onramp.net
Austin, Texas Office: Cantey & Hanger Roan & Autrey L.L.P., 200 First State Bank Tower, 400 West Fifteenth Street.
Telephone: 512-474-4200.
FAX: 512-469-0470; 512-469-0474. Email: FIRM@ROAN-AUTREY.COM

MEMBERS OF FIRM

Mark D. Beatty
D. Mark Daniel
David Bradley Dowell
Thomas Patrick Gordon III
John F. Gray
Tolbert L. Greenwood
William L. Hughes, Jr.
Stephen A. Madsen
Bradley C. Poulos
John C. Stewart

ASSOCIATE

Andrew D. Keetch

Represent: CNA; Houston General Insurance Company; Winn Dixie Stores; Ohio Casualty Insurance; Inspire Insurance Solutions; Underwriters at Lloyd's; Insurance Company of the West.

For Complete List of Firm Personnel, See General Section

For full biographical listings, see the Martindale-Hubbell Law Directory

DECKER, JONES, MCMACKIN, MCCLANE, HALL & BATES, A PROFESSIONAL CORPORATION (AV)

2500 Bank One Tower, 500 Throckmorton Street, 76102-3812
Telephone: 817-336-2400; Metro: 817-429-5260
Fax: 817-332-3043; 336-2181
Email: email@deckerjones.com *URL:* http://www.deckerjones.com

Daniel L. Bates
Robert W. Decker
Mark S. Dugan
Janet L. Hahn
Randy J. Hall
Raymond B. Kelly, III
John B. McClane
John W. McMackin
Charles B. Milliken
Gary M. Moates
Bradley H. Rice
Jeffrey W. Storie
James L. Stripling
Brian K. Yost
Tamera H. Bennett
Arthur F. Zobal
Geoffrey A. Mantooth

Representative Clients: Employers Insurance of Texas; American International Group; Medical Protective Co.; Redman Homes, Inc.; Liberty Mutual Insurance; Texas Medical Liability Trust; MIIX Insurance Group; The St. Paul Insurance Cos.; Royal Sun Alliance; Champion Homebuilders.

For full biographical listings, see the Martindale-Hubbell Law Directory

JACKSON WALKER L.L.P. (AV)

301 Commerce Street, Suite 2400, 76102
Telephone: 817-334-7200
Fax: 817-334-7290
URL: http://www.jw.com
Austin, Texas Office: 100 Congress Avenue, Suite 1100.
Telephone: 512-236-2000.
Fax: 512-236-2002.
Dallas, Texas Office: 901 Main Street, Suite 6000.
Telephone: 214-953-6000.
Fax: 214-953-5822.
Houston, Texas Office: 1100 Louisiana, Suite 4200.
Telephone: 713-752-4200.
Fax: 713-752-4221.
Richardson, Texas Office: 2435 North Central Expressway, Suite 600.
Telephone: 972-671-2560.
Fax: 972-671-2566.
San Angelo, Texas Office: 225 West Beauregard Avenue.
Telephone: 915-481-2550.
Fax: 915-481-2552.
San Antonio, Texas Office: 112 E. Pecan Street, Suite 2100.
Telephone: 210-978-7700.
Fax: 210-978-7790.

(See Next Column)

JACKSON WALKER L.L.P.—*Continued*

MEMBERS OF FIRM

Albon O. Head, Jr.
Jeffrey J. Wolf

For Complete List of Firm Personnel, See General Section

For full biographical listings, see the Martindale-Hubbell Law Directory

MCMULLEN LAW FIRM (AV)

6300 Ridglea Place Suite 509, 76116-5731
Telephone: 817-731-4163
Fax: 817-731-4340
Email: wademcmullen@msn.com

Wade H. McMullen

For full biographical listings, see the Martindale-Hubbell Law Directory

THOMPSON & KNIGHT L.L.P. (AV)

(Attorneys and Counselors)
801 Cherry Street, Suite 1600, 76102
Telephone: 817-347-1700
Telecopy: 817-347-1799
URL: http://www.tklaw.com
Dallas, Texas Office: 1700 Pacific Avenue, Suite 3300, 75201.
Telephone: 214-969-1700.
Telecopy: 214-969-1751.
Telex: 732298.
Austin, Texas Office: 1200 San Jacinto Center, 98 San Jacinto Boulevard, 78701.
Telephone: 512-469-6100.
Telecopy: 512-469-6180.
Houston, Texas Office: Thompson Knight Brown Parker & Leahy L.L.P., 1200 Smith Street, Suite 3600, 77002-4595.
Telephone: 713-654-8111.
Telecopier: 713-654-1871.
San Pedro Garza Garcia, Nuevo León, Mexico Office: Edificio Losoles PD-4, Av. Lázaro Cárdenas No. 2400 Pte., C.P. 66220.
Telephone: (52-8) 363-0096.
Telecopy: (52-8) 363-3067.

PARTNER

Lonnie J. Copps

For Complete List of Firm Personnel, See General Section

For full biographical listings, see the Martindale-Hubbell Law Directory

FRISCO, Collin & Denton Cos.

WINIKATES & WINIKATES (AV)

Prosper State Bank Building, 7700 Main Street, P.O. Box 249, 75034-0249
Telephone: 972-335-1122
Fax: 972-335-1125

MEMBERS OF FIRM

Charles J. Winikates
Charles J. Winikates, Jr.
Regina W. Mentesana
Frances A. Fazio

For full biographical listings, see the Martindale-Hubbell Law Directory

*GALVESTON,** Galveston Co.

MILLS, SHIRLEY, ECKEL & BASSETT, L.L.P. (AV)

400 Washington Building, 2228 Mechanic Street, P.O. Box 1943, 77553
Telephone: 409-763-2341; Houston Line: 281-488-8716
Facsimile: 409-763-2879
Houston
Email: msebllp@ibm.net
Houston, Texas Office: 3950 Chase Tower, 600 Travis, 77002.
Telephone: 713-225-0547.
Facsimile: 713-225-0844.

MEMBERS OF FIRM

Preston Shirley (1912-1990)
Ballinger Mills, Jr. (1914-1992)
John Eckel
Jack C. Brock
Carla Cotropia (Resident, Houston Office)
Fred D. Raschke
Grant G. Gealy (Resident, Houston Office)
William E. Griffey
Finis E. Cowan, III
Robert A. Davee
Christopher S. Cahill
George W. Vie, III
Christopher D. Bertini
Maureen Kuzik McCutchen

ASSOCIATES

Scott Lyford
Taylor Townsend Schwab
Sherrill H. Tompkins
Molly Baer (Resident, Houston Office)
Belinda A. Beek
David Toney (Resident, Houston Office)
Christopher C. Garcia
Pamela D. Tyner
Maya Nicollier Schlegel (Resident, Houston Office)

(See Next Column)

OF COUNSEL

Roland L. Bassett

General Attorneys for: American Indemnity Group.
General Counsel for: Galveston Independent School District.
Counsel for: CNA Insurance Group; INA Insurance Group; Hartford Insurance; Fireman's Fund; The St. Paul Cos.

For full biographical listings, see the Martindale-Hubbell Law Directory

HARLINGEN, Cameron Co.

ADAMS & GRAHAM, L.L.P. (AV)

222 East Van Buren, West Tower, 78550
Telephone: 956-428-7495
Fax: 956-428-2954
Email: office@adamsgraham.com *URL:* http://www.adamsgraham.com
Affiliate Austin, Texas Office: Hill Gilstrap Adams & Graham, L.L.P., 1005 Congress Avenue, Suite 880, 78701.
Telephone: 512-457-9806.
Fax: 512-457-9066.

John Q. Adams (1900-1968)
Marshall W. Graham (1924-1988)
James S. Graham, Jr. (1922-1990)
Ferriel C. Hamby, Jr.
Tom A. Lockhart
Jim Denison
Leo C. Salzman
Roger W. Hughes
Craig H. Vittitoe
William L. Pope
Patricia Kelly
Jaime Balli
Gina M. Benavides
Charlie J. Cilfone
Juan A. Gonzalez
Barry Ray
Wilbert (Will) Hughes
Trinidad P. Galdean

Representative Clients: State Farm Insurance Companies; Texas Workers' Compensation Insurance Fund; W.R. Grace; American International Companies; Gallagher-Bassett; CIGNA; Federated Insurance Company; Texas General Agency; Highlands Insurance Co,; Texas Municipal League.

For full biographical listings, see the Martindale-Hubbell Law Directory

*HOUSTON,** Harris Co.

BELL, RYNIKER & LETOURNEAU, P.C. (AV)

Five Post Oak Park, Suite 1300, 77027
Telephone: 713-871-8822
Fax: 713-871-8844
URL: http://www.brlpc.com
Email: mkbell@brlpc.com *URL:* http://www.lawyers.com/brlpc

Michael K. Bell
Robert J. Ryniker
Keith B. Letourneau
Thomas R. Nork

Douglas J. Shoemaker
Deborah T. Busby
Wesley T. Welmaker

For full biographical listings, see the Martindale-Hubbell Law Directory

BREWER & PRITCHARD, A PROFESSIONAL CORPORATION (AV)

24th Floor, Heritage Plaza, 1111 Bagby, 77002
Telephone: 713-209-2950
Facsimile: 713-659-5302
Email: info@bplaw.com *URL:* http://www.bplaw.com

J. Mark Brewer
Patrick E. Gaas

Heather E. Nelson

For full biographical listings, see the Martindale-Hubbell Law Directory

BROWN, SIMS, WISE & WHITE, A PROFESSIONAL CORPORATION (AV)

One Post Oak Central, 21st Floor, 2000 Post Oak Boulevard, 77056-4496
Telephone: 713-629-1580
Fax: 713-629-5027
Telex: 775557
Email: bsww@neosoft.com *URL:* http://www.neosoft.com/~bsww/bsww.htm

G. Byron Sims
James D. Wise, Jr.
Ronald L. White
Kenneth G. Engerrand
Innes Alexander Henderson Mackillop
James N. Isbell
Thomas O. Deen
Michael D. Williams
Thomas W. Burch, III
Ronnie W. Baham, Jr.
Polly A. Kinnibrugh
Deanna H. Brewer
Mark C. Clemer
James R. Koecher
John R. Walker
William A. Galerston
Cynthia A. Galvan
Michael A. Varner
Walter Joseph Gallant
Philip Robert Brinson
Monica A. Fekete
Gregory L. Deans
Nelson D. Skyler
James A. Tatem, III
Sheri E. Moore

(See Next Column)

BROWN, SIMS, WISE & WHITE A PROFESSIONAL CORPORATION, *Houston—Continued*

Lisa L. Gambrell
Jeromy D. Hughes
Robbie A. Moehlmann
Hal Davis Hale, Jr.
Thomas A. Brown (1932-1997)

For full biographical listings, see the Martindale-Hubbell Law Directory

DAVIS, ORETSKY & GUILFOYLE, P.C. (AV)

1415 Louisiana, Suite 4200, 77002
Telephone: 713-659-1010
Facsimile: 713-659-1122
Email: doglawfirm@dog.pc *URL:* http://www.dogpc.com
Affiliated Law Firm: Wommack Law Firm, P.C., 7 West Way Court, Suite A, P.O. Box 420, Lake Jackson, Texas 77566.
Telephone: 409-297-9755. Houston
Telephone: 713-355-5737.
Fax: 409-297-9761. Email: wdm-george@computron.net.

Tom M. Davis, Jr.
Andrew S. Oretsky
Matthew C. Guilfoyle
Juliann H. Panagos
Curt M. Langley
George T. Wommack, Jr.
David C. Redford

M. Lucille Anderson
Kristin Bauer
Robert M. Browning
Paige Black Larrabee
Norman W. Peters, Jr.
Jonathan L. Phillips
William R. Pilat

For full biographical listings, see the Martindale-Hubbell Law Directory

PATRICIA KAY DUBE, P.C. (AV)

4140 Bank of America Center, 700 Louisiana Street, 77002
Telephone: 713-225-2297
Facsimile: 713-225-2298
Email: pkdube@wt.net *URL:* http://www.lawyers.com/dubelaw

Patricia Kay Dube
Clare I. Vetters
Lee Broze

OF COUNSEL

Alan J. Winters
Harold J. Eisenman

For full biographical listings, see the Martindale-Hubbell Law Directory

FAIRCHILD, PRICE, THOMAS, HALEY & WILLINGHAM, L.L.P. (AV)

440 Louisiana Street, Suite 2110, 77002-4205
Telephone: 713-426-1700
Fax: 713-426-1717.
Email: mwillingham@fpthw.com
Center, Texas Office: 413 Shelbyville Street, P.O. Drawer 1719, 75935.
Telephone: 409-598-2981.
Fax: 409-598-7712. E-Mail: wmthomas@fpthw.com
Nacogdoches, Texas Office: 1801 North Street, P.O. Box 631668, 75963-1668.
Telephone: 409-569-2327.
Fax: 409-569-7932. E-Mail: chaley@fpthw.com

John L. Price
W. Miller Thomas
C. Victor Haley
R. Mark Willingham
Travis P. Clardy
David J. Fisher
Clayton H. Haley
Russell R. Smith
Ryan A. Beason

OF COUNSEL

Robert L. Fairchild

James A. Payne, Jr.
David Edward Ash
Campbell Cox
Jefferson B. Davis
Thomas L. Cougill
Jeffrey Pierce Fultz
Matthew D. Mettauer

For full biographical listings, see the Martindale-Hubbell Law Directory

FJELDAL & ASSOCIATES, A PROFESSIONAL CORPORATION (AV)

1225 North Loop West, Suite 1111, 77008
Telephone: 713-869-9690
Fax: 713-869-6777
Email: fjeldlaw@aol.com

Timothy A. Fjeldal

Scott T. Burkett

For full biographical listings, see the Martindale-Hubbell Law Directory

GILPIN, PAXSON & BERSCH (AV)

A Registered Limited Liability Partnership
Attorney at Law
1900 West Loop South, Suite 2000, 77027-3259
Telephone: 713-623-8800
Telecopier: 713-993-8451
Email: gpb@gpblaw.com *URL:* http://www.texinslaw.com

PARTNERS

Gary M. Alletag
Timothy R. Bersch
John D. Gilpin
Darryl W. Malone
Michael J. Pappert
Stephen Paxson
Kevin F. Risley

OF COUNSEL

Harless R. Benthul
David F. Webb

ASSOCIATES

Joseph D. Batson
Jeri Pharis Wechsler

Representative Clients: BMW of North America, Inc.; Federal Deposit Insurance Corporation; Greater Houston Builders Association; Owens Corning Fiberglas Corporation; Shaw Industries, Inc.; Southwest Guaranty Trust Company, N.A.; Sprint Communications Company L.P.; Volkswagen of America, Inc.; Volvo North America Corporation; Wells Fargo Bank (Texas), N.A.

For full biographical listings, see the Martindale-Hubbell Law Directory

HANDLIN & ASSOCIATES (AV)

5444 Westheimer Road, Suite 1750, 77056
Telephone: 713-585-6444
Fax: 713-585-6456

STAFF COUNSEL
AMERICAN INTERNATIONAL COMPANIES

MANAGING ATTORNEY

Terry J. Handlin

SENIOR TRIAL ATTORNEYS

Andrea N. Moore
Paul R. Tinsley
Sandra K. Williams

For full biographical listings, see the Martindale-Hubbell Law Directory

HANEN, ALEXANDER, JOHNSON & SPALDING, L.L.P. (AV)

910 Travis, Suite 1700, 77002
Telephone: 713-222-2323
Fax: 713-222-2226

Andrew S. Hanen
Joseph R. Alexander, Jr.
Brian P. Johnson
John E. Spalding
Frank A. Doyle
Lawrence J. West
T. Christopher Trent

Geoffrey C. Guill
Tamara M. Madden
Richard Todd Marshall
Raphael (Rafe) Taylor
Lisa M. Moran
Shashi Patel
Annette Sepulveda Kenefick
Craig A. Choate

For full biographical listings, see the Martindale-Hubbell Law Directory

HAYS, MCCONN, RICE & PICKERING (AV)

400 Two Allen Center, 1200 Smith Street, 77002
Telephone: 713-654-1111
Fax: 713-650-0027
Email: HMRP@HaysMcConn.com *URL:* http://www.haysmcconn.com

MEMBERS OF FIRM

Michael S. Hays
James J. McConn, Jr.
B. Stephen Rice
Michael R. Pickering
Mark A. Padon
Bruce Gaible
Susan Crowley Stevenson
Allen Till
Craig S. Wolcott
Naomi S. Ostfeld
Margaret Twomey Brenner
W. Michael Scott
Jeffery Allen Addicks
J. Philip Griffis
A. Scott Kidd
Robert E. Purgatorio
Brian Tew
Steven M. Duble
Lance K. Thomas
Michael W. Magee

ASSOCIATES

Troy A. Williams
Shannon D. Robbie
Staton M. Childers
Timothy R. Hightower
William Jason Walker
Michael A. Durr
Leslie M. Henry
Amanda F. Bell
David Wilson, II

OF COUNSEL

John T. Golden

For full biographical listings, see the Martindale-Hubbell Law Directory

Houston—Continued

JACKSON WALKER L.L.P. (AV)

1100 Louisiana, Suite 4200, P.O. Box 4771, 77002
Telephone: 713-752-4200
Fax: 713-752-4221
URL: http://www.jw.com
Austin, Texas Office: 100 Congress Avenue, Suite 1100.
Telephone: 512-236-2000.
Fax: 512-236-2002.
Dallas, Texas Office: 901 Main Street, Suite 6000.
Telephone: 214-953-6000.
Fax: 214-953-5822.
Fort Worth, Texas Office: 301 Commerce Street, Suite 2400.
Telephone: 817-334-7200.
Fax: 817-334-7290.
Richardson, Texas Office: 2435 North Central Expressway, Suite 600.
Telephone: 972-671-2560.
Fax: 972-671-2566.
San Angelo, Texas Office: 225 West Beauregard Avenue.
Telephone: 915-481-2550.
Fax: 915-481-2552.
San Antonio, Texas Office: 112 E. Pecan Street, Suite 2100.
Telephone: 210-978-7700.
Fax: 210-978-7790.

MEMBERS OF FIRM

Janet Douvas Chafin
John R. Clayton
Anne Marie Finch
Richard Earl Griffin
Mollie Cohn Lambert
Lisa A. Powell
Fred A. Simpson

OF COUNSEL

Mary Lou Flynn-DuPart
Randall L. Smith

For Complete List of Firm Personnel, See General Section

For full biographical listings, see the Martindale-Hubbell Law Directory

KILLEEN & FIERRO (AV)

1717 St. James Place, Suite 620, 77056
Telephone: 713-626-5100
Facsimile: 713-626-4545

Robert Joseph Killeen, Jr.
John M. Longoria
L. Byron Wilson

Candace A. Ourso

OF COUNSEL

Gerald M. Johnson, III

For full biographical listings, see the Martindale-Hubbell Law Directory

MARKLE, RAMOS & ZITO, A PROFESSIONAL CORPORATION (AV)

777 Post Oak Boulevard, Suite 350, 77056
Telephone: 713-861-9595
Facsimile: 713-861-8368
Email: mrz@marzpc.com

Spencer G. Markle
Dion Ramos
Nicholas E. Zito

Nathan A. Hardee
Shelley V. Hutson
Andrea Frey Lopes
Heather L. Nistler
Angela Nolan

For full biographical listings, see the Martindale-Hubbell Law Directory

MATTHIESEN, CHASE & ERWIN, L.L.P. (AV)

3003 Eleven Greenway Plaza, 77046
Telephone: 713-877-8522
Fax: 713-877-8822

David G. Matthiesen
A. Scot Chase
R. Harding Erwin, Jr.
Aaron Pool

R. Todd Carpenter
Trevor R. Jefferies
Deborah M. Wotring Landis
Ronald A. Wasinger

For full biographical listings, see the Martindale-Hubbell Law Directory

MEHAFFY & WEBER, A PROFESSIONAL CORPORATION (AV)

One Allen Center, 500 Dallas, Suite 1200, 77002
Telephone: 713-655-1200
Fax: 713-655-0222
Email: MehaffyWeber.com
Beaumont, Texas Office: 2615 Calder Avenue, Suite 800, P.O. Box 16.
Telephone: 409-835-5011.
Orange, Texas Office: 1006 Green Avenue, P.O. Drawer 189.
Telephone: 409-886-7766.

(See Next Column)

Jim I. Graves
Arthur R. Almquist
Charles Stanton Perry

Paul R. Heyburn
James G. Martingano
Debra N. Bigler
Peter T. Gregg
Elna Nguyen Griggs

Representative Clients: E.I. duPont de Nemours and Co.; W.R. Grace & Co.-Conn.; Merrill Dow; Eli Lilly & Company; Burlington, Northen, Santa Fe Railway Company; Christus Health.

For full biographical listings, see the Martindale-Hubbell Law Directory

MILLS, SHIRLEY, ECKEL & BASSETT, L.L.P. (AV)

3950 Chase Tower, 600 Travis, 77002
Telephone: 713-225-0547
Facsimile: 713-225-0844
Galveston, Texas Office: 400 Washington Building, 2228 Mechanic Street, P.O. Box 1943.
Telephone: 409-763-2341; Houston Line: 281-488-8716.
Facsimile: 409-763-2879.

MEMBERS OF FIRM

Carla Cotropia (Resident)
Grant G. Gealy (Resident)
William E. Griffey

ASSOCIATES

Molly Baer (Resident)
David Toney (Resident)
Maya Nicollier Schlegel (Resident)

General Attorneys for: American Indemnity Group.
Counsel for: CNA Insurance Group; INA Insurance Group; Crawford & Co.; Allright Parking Texas, Inc.; PM Realty Group, Ltd.; American Builders Supply.

For full biographical listings, see the Martindale-Hubbell Law Directory

RAMSEY & MURRAY, A PROFESSIONAL CORPORATION (AV)

10000 Memorial Drive, Suite 700, 77024-3412
Telephone: 713-613-5400
Fax: 713-613-5414

Ben Ramsey
John A. Murray, Jr.
Russell J. Ramsey
Mark Ramsey
Curtis D. Collette
Michael Stout Wright
Rick McRory

Joseph W. Gagnon
R. Russell Hollenbeck
Adrian V. Villacorta
Brenda Renee Ferguson

Representative Clients: Great Central Insurance Co.; Republic Insurance Co.

For full biographical listings, see the Martindale-Hubbell Law Directory

ROBERTS, MARKEL & FOLGER, L.L.P. (AV)

A Limited Liability Partnership of Professional Corporations
Weslayan Tower, Suite 2000, 24 Greenway Plaza, 77046
Telephone: 713-840-1666
Telecopier: 713-840-9404

MEMBERS OF FIRM

Jeffrey D. Roberts
Alan B. Folger
Theodore L. Guerry, Jr.

ASSOCIATES

John Bradley Mitchell
Ross Asher

For full biographical listings, see the Martindale-Hubbell Law Directory

SCHWARTZ JUNELL CAMPBELL & OATHOUT, L.L.P. (AV)

Two Houston Center, 909 Fannin, Suite 2000, 77010
Telephone: 713-752-0017
Telecopier: 713-752-0327
Email: dschwartz@schwartz-junell.com

Richard A. Schwartz
William Edward Junell, Jr.
Marshall S. Campbell
Monica F. Oathout
Steven R. Rech

Phillip W. Bechter
J. Parker Fauntleroy, Jr.

OF COUNSEL

Joe H. Reynolds
A. R. Schwartz

LEGAL SUPPORT PERSONNEL

PARALEGALS

Nannette Koger
Maria Woods
Shelly A. Savage, CLA

For full biographical listings, see the Martindale-Hubbell Law Directory

Houston—Continued

TEKELL, BOOK, MATTHEWS & LIMMER, L.L.P. (AV)

4300 One Houston Center, 1221 McKinney, 77010
Telephone: 713-222-9542
Fax: 713-655-7727
Email: tbml@tbml.com
Corpus Christi, Texas Office: 711 North Carancahua, Suite 902, 78475.
Telephone: 361-883-6100.
Fax: 361-883-6103. Email: cctbml@swbell.net.

Kenneth Tekell
William Book
Raymond T. Matthews
James H. Limmer
Mark K. Allen
Michael P. Morris
Todd A. Kissner
Matt W. Childs
Jeff Murphrey

Michele E. Taylor
David W. Burns
Kevin D. Didway
Kathleen Carney
WC "Trey" Book
Kenneth L. Tekell, Jr.
J. Gregory McEldowney
Robin T. Balette

OF COUNSEL

Danny L. Van Winkle

Representative Clients: Royal-Globe Insurance Group; Minnesota Mining and Manufacturing; Chubb Insurance Co.; CIGNA Companies; Fireman's Fund; Mobil Oil Co.; Arco Oil Co.

For full biographical listings, see the Martindale-Hubbell Law Directory

THOMPSON KNIGHT BROWN PARKER & LEAHY L.L.P. (AV)

A Registered Limited Liability Partnership including Professional Corporations
(Attorneys and Counselors)
1200 Smith Street, Suite 3600, 77002-4595
Telephone: 713-654-8111
Telecopier: 713-654-1871
URL: http://www.tklaw.com
Dallas, Texas Office: Thompson & Knight L.L.P., 1700 Pacific Avenue, Suite 3300, 75201.
Telephone: 214-969-1700.
Telecopy: 214-969-1751.
Telex: 732298.
Austin, Texas Office: Thompson & Knight L.L.P., 1200 San Jacinto Center, 98 San Jacinto Boulevard, 78701.
Telephone: 512-469-6100.
Telecopy: 512-469-6180.
Fort Worth, Texas Office: Thompson & Knight L.L.P., 801 Cherry Street, Suite 1600, 76102.
Telephone: 817-347-1700.
Telecopy: 817-347-1799.
San Pedro Garza Garcia, Nuevo León, Mexico Office: Thompson & Knight L.L.P., Edificio Losoles PD-4, Av. Lázaro Cárdenas No. 2400 PTE., C.P. 66220.
Telephone: (52-8) 363-0096.
Telecopy: (52-8) 363-3067.

PARTNERS

Nancy Wilson Hargrove
Robert L. Pittsford

For Complete List of Firm Personnel, See General Section

For full biographical listings, see the Martindale-Hubbell Law Directory

TUCKER, HENDRYX, TAUNTON, SNYDER & SLADE, P.C. (AV)

8 Greenway Plaza, Suite 1200, 77046
Telephone: 713-961-5800
FAX: 713-993-2308; 993-2309
Email: lawfirm@thtss.com

Jack W. Tucker, Jr.
Michael Hendryx
Norman E. Snyder, Jr.
L. Keith Slade
Keith R. Taunton
Steven C. Howard
Wade B. Reese

Brian Holland
Margaret R. Banks
Bradley E. Chambers
Carolyn S. Schultz
Tory Taylor
Gregory A. Holloway

For full biographical listings, see the Martindale-Hubbell Law Directory

*LONGVIEW,** Gregg Co.

MERRIMAN, PATTERSON & ALLISON, L.L.P. (AV)

A Partnership of Professional Corporations
402 Austin Bank Building, 3400 West Marshall Avenue, P.O. Box 4237, 75606
Telephone: 903-297-7676
Fax: 903-297-7682

E. Lawrence Merriman (P.C.)
Stephen R. Patterson (P.C.)
George Thomas Allison, III, (P.C.)

(See Next Column)

ASSOCIATES

Charles P. Connolly
James E. Hughes
Timothy G. Moore
Brian T. Hoyle
W. Mark Bennett

For full biographical listings, see the Martindale-Hubbell Law Directory

*LUBBOCK,** Lubbock Co.

CARR, HUNT & JOY L.L.P. (AV)

1001 Texas Avenue, P.O. Box 2585, 79408
Telephone: 806-765-7491
Fax: 806-765-0553
Email: info@chjlaw.com
Amarillo, Texas Office: Amarillo National Plaza II, Ste. 509, 500 S. Taylor Street, P.O. Box 989, Amarillo, Texas. 79105.
Telephone: 806-342-3055.
Fax: 806-342-9907.

MEMBERS OF FIRM

Tom H. Whiteside
William R. Eichman, II

Representative Clients: Alexis Risk Management; SAFECO; CNA; Crawford and Company; Crum & Forrester; GAB Robins; Gainsco Companies; Gallagher Bassett; Medical Protective; Medmarc; MIIX; Progressive County Mutual Insurance; Zurich-American Insurance.

For Complete List of Firm Personnel, See General Section

For full biographical listings, see the Martindale-Hubbell Law Directory

CRENSHAW, DUPREE & MILAM, L.L.P. (AV)

Norwest Center, 1500 Broadway, 10th Floor, P.O. Box 1499, 79408-1499
Telephone: 806-762-5281
Fax: 806-762-3510
Email: attorney@cdmlaw.com

Chas. C. Crenshaw (1886-1964)
Geo. W. Dupree (1890-1973)
James H. Milam (1911-1994)

MEMBERS OF FIRM

Cecil C. Kuhne
John Crews
William J. Wade
Jack McCutchin, Jr.
W C Bratcher
Layton Z. Woodul
David R. Cobb
Robert L. Duncan
W. Chris Boyer
Robert L. Jones
Mark W. Harmon
Mark O. Blankenship
Charlotte D. Bingham

ASSOCIATES

Sheila M. Kidwell
Matt D. Matzner
Jeff R. Lashaway
Taylor L. Pope

OF COUNSEL

Tom S. Milam
William R. Moss

For full biographical listings, see the Martindale-Hubbell Law Directory

THOMPSON & THOMAS, A PROFESSIONAL CORPORATION (AV)

4412 74th Street, Suite A-100, P.O. Box 65150, 79464
Telephone: 806-793-7600
Fax: 806-793-6882

George L. Thompson, III
Michael A. Thomas

Molly Forsyth

For full biographical listings, see the Martindale-Hubbell Law Directory

*LUFKIN,** Angelina Co.

CLAYTON E. DARK, JR. (AV)

207 East Frank, Suite 100, P.O. Box 2207, 75902-2207
Telephone: 409-637-1733
Fax: 409-637-2897

ASSOCIATE

Michelle Wood Charanza

For full biographical listings, see the Martindale-Hubbell Law Directory

MCALLEN, Hidalgo Co.

DALE & KLEIN, L.L.P. (AV)

A Partnership including Professional Corporations
6301 North Tenth Street, 78504
Telephone: 956-687-8700
FAX: 956-687-2416
Brownsville Office: 815 Ridgewood.
Telephone: 956-546-5100.

Roy S. Dale (P.C.)
Katie Pearson Klein (P.C.)
Martin E. Morris
William D. Mount, Jr.

(See Next Column)

DALE & KLEIN L.L.P.—*Continued*

A. Peter Thaddeus, Jr.
Kathryn M. Flagg
Catherine Anderson Garcia
Marina Garcia

For full biographical listings, see the Martindale-Hubbell Law Directory

RODRIGUEZ, COLVIN & CHANEY, L.L.P. (AV)

4900 North 10th Street, 78504
Telephone: 956-686-1287
Telecopier: 956-686-6197
Brownsville, Texas Office: 1201 East Van Buren Street.
Telephone: 956-542-7441.
Telecopier: 956-541-2170.
Harlingen, Texas Office: 402 East Van Buren.
Telephone: 956-423-0216.
Telecopier: 956-423-2035.

OF COUNSEL

Neil E. Norquest
Chris A. Brisack
Raymond A. Cowley

Division Attorneys for: Union Pacific Railroad.
Counsel for: Texas Commerce Bank-Rio Grande Valley, N.A.; Texas Commerce Bancshares, Inc.

For full biographical listings, see the Martindale-Hubbell Law Directory

*MIDLAND,** Midland Co.

LESLIE G. McLAUGHLIN (AV)

1209 West Texas Avenue, 79701
Telephone: 915-687-1331
Fax: 915-687-1336

For full biographical listings, see the Martindale-Hubbell Law Directory

*NACOGDOCHES,** Nacogdoches Co.

FAIRCHILD, PRICE, THOMAS, HALEY & WILLINGHAM, L.L.P. (AV)

1801 North Street, P.O. Box 631668, 75963-1668
Telephone: 409-569-2327
Fax: 409-569-7932.
Email: chaley@fpthw.com
Center, Texas Office: 413 Shelbyville Street, P.O. Drawer 1719, 75935.
Telephone: 409-598-2981.
Fax: 409-598-7712. E-Mail: wmthomas@fpthw.com
Houston, Texas Office: 440 Louisiana Street, Suite 2110, 77002-4205.
Telephone: 713-426-1700.
Fax: 713-426-1717. E-Mail: mwillingham@fpthw.com

John L. Price
W. Miller Thomas
C. Victor Haley
R. Mark Willingham
Travis P. Clardy
David J. Fisher
Clayton H. Haley
Russell R. Smith
Ryan A. Beason

OF COUNSEL

Robert L. Fairchild

James A. Payne, Jr.
David Edward Ash
Campbell Cox
Jefferson B. Davis
Thomas L. Cougill
Jeffrey Pierce Fultz
Matthew D. Mettauer

For full biographical listings, see the Martindale-Hubbell Law Directory

*ORANGE,** Orange Co.

MEHAFFY & WEBER, A PROFESSIONAL CORPORATION (AV)

1006 Green Avenue, P.O. Drawer 189, 77630
Telephone: 409-886-7766
Fax: 409-886-7790
Email: MehaffyWeber.com
Beaumont, Texas Office: 2615 Calder Avenue, Suite 800, P.O. Box 16.
Telephone: 409-835-5011.
Houston, Texas Office: One Allen Center, 500 Dallas, Suite 1200.
Telephone: 713-655-1200.

John Cash Smith

Representative Clients: Sabine River Authority of Texas; Equitable Bag Co., Southern Division; Texas Farm Bureau; City of Orange; CNA Insurance, Maryland Casualty/Zurich Insurance Co.

For full biographical listings, see the Martindale-Hubbell Law Directory

*SAN ANTONIO,** Bexar Co.

ADAMI, GOLDMAN & SHUFFIELD, INCORPORATED (AV)

9311 San Pedro Avenue, Suite 900, 78216
Telephone: 210-344-0500
Fax: 210-344-7228

(See Next Column)

Grant E. Adami, III
Larry J. Goldman
E. Wayne Shuffield

Peter J. Beverage
Michelle M. Copeland
David Wes Holland
Douglas E. Pennebaker
Martin J. Phipps
R. Scott Westlund
Kevin S. Baker

For full biographical listings, see the Martindale-Hubbell Law Directory

BROCK & PERSON, A PROFESSIONAL CORPORATION (AV)

Union Square Building, 10101 Reunion Place, Suite 1000, 78216-4157
Telephone: 210-979-0100
Fax: 210-979-7810

Roy C. Brock
Stephen L. Dittlinger
John A. Guerra
Audrey A. Haake
David B. Person
Ricardo R. Reyna

O. Rene Diaz
A.J. Dimaline, IV
Julie K. Hogenauer
Mark R. Strandmo
Jorge Albert Tuckler

For full biographical listings, see the Martindale-Hubbell Law Directory

GENDRY & SPRAGUE, P.C. (AV)

645 Lockhill Selma, 78216-5057
Telephone: 210-349-0511
Fax: 210-349-2760
Email: genspr@aol.com

Thomas W. Gendry
Ron A. Sprague
Neil H Stone
R. Matt Lair
Blanca P. Galo
Timothy R. Price
Claudia D. Brown

Reference: NCNB Texas National Bank, San Antonio.

For full biographical listings, see the Martindale-Hubbell Law Directory

JACKSON WALKER L.L.P. (AV)

112 E. Pecan Street, Suite 2100, 78205-1521
Telephone: 210-978-7700
Fax: 210-978-7790
URL: http://www.jw.com
Austin, Texas Office: 100 Congress Avenue, Suite 1100.
Telephone: 512-236-2000.
Fax: 512-236-2002.
Dallas, Texas Office: 901 Main Street, Suite 6000.
Telephone: 214-953-6000.
Fax: 214-953-5822.
Fort Worth, Texas Office: 301 Commerce Street, Suite 2400.
Telephone: 817-334-7200.
Fax: 817-334-7290.
Houston, Texas Office: 1100 Louisiana, Suite 4200.
Telephone: 713-752-4200.
Fax: 713-752-4221.
Richardson, Texas Office: 2435 North Central Expressway, Suite 600.
Telephone: 972-671-2560.
Fax: 972-671-2566.
San Angelo, Texas Office: 225 West Beauregard Avenue.
Telephone: 915-481-2550.
Fax: 915-481-2552.

MEMBERS OF FIRM

Leo D. Figueroa
Stephen R. Fogle
Jeffrey T. Harvey
Robert F. Scheihing
James L. Walker

For Complete List of Firm Personnel, See General Section

For full biographical listings, see the Martindale-Hubbell Law Directory

JONES, ROGERS & NAVARRO (AV)

200 Scobek Square, 14526 Jones Maltsberger, 78247
Telephone: 210-495-3505
Fax: 210-495-3533
Email: JRNLAW@email.msn.com

Scott P. Jones
Craig A. Rogers
Martin J. Navarro

ASSOCIATES

William R. Hintze
Edward J. Garcia

For full biographical listings, see the Martindale-Hubbell Law Directory

San Antonio—Continued

LANE, GANNON & TALIAFERRO, L.L.P. (AV)

8620 North New Braunfels, Suite 310, 78217
Telephone: 210-829-1545
Telecopier: 210-829-1633
Email: gannon@lgtlaw.com
Austin, Texas Office: 816 Congress Avenue, Suite 1100, 78701.
Telephone: 512-485-4595.
Fax: 512-485-4594.

MEMBERS OF FIRM

Gregory Gannon
John R. Lane, Jr.
William Craig Taliaferro

ASSOCIATES

Sharon Denise Hobbs
Frederick D. Schraub
Georganne G. Leonard
John R. Resendez
Brent Austin Biggs
Alfred Michael Casillas
Christia M. Antolik
Hella V. Caldera

OF COUNSEL

C. Gilbert House
James B. House

For full biographical listings, see the Martindale-Hubbell Law Directory

LINDOW & TREAT, L.L.P. (AV)

27th Floor 112 East Pecan, 78205
Telephone: 210-227-4195
Telecopier: 210-227-4602
Email: firm@lindow-treat.com

Mark A. Lindow
David L. Treat
Michael R. Salinas
Carlos E. Solis

OF COUNSEL

Martha J. Hess

For full biographical listings, see the Martindale-Hubbell Law Directory

O'CONNELL, BENJAMIN & COGHLAN, L.L.P. (AV)

153 Treeline Park, Suite 200, 78209
Telephone: 210-824-0009
Fax: 210-824-9429
Email: obcllp@oconben.com

Keith B. O'Connell
David P. Benjamin
G. Thomas Coghlan
Ernest F. Avery
Les Katona, Jr.
Dan Vana

Gayla S. Corley
Cathrin J. Martinez

For full biographical listings, see the Martindale-Hubbell Law Directory

PLUNKETT & GIBSON, INC. (AV)

6243 IH-10 West, Suite 600, P.O. Box BH002, 78201
Telephone: 210-734-7092
Telecopier: 210-734-0379

Laura A. Cavaretta
D. Ann Comerio
Richard B. Copeland
Joseph C. Elliott
Richard N. Francis, Jr.
Jerry A. Gibson
Tim T. Griesenbeck, Jr.
John A. Heller
Nina E. Henderson
Ronald Hornberger
Lewin Plunkett
Cathy J. Sheehan

OF COUNSEL

Daniel Diaz, Jr.
Marilyn G. Eades
Robert D. Reed
F. Beth Morgan

William J. Baine
Charles L. Fridge, III
Gary B. Gibson
Erik V. Larson

Representative Clients: St. Paul Insurance Co.; Toyota Motor Sales, Inc.; Travelers Insurance Co.; Transport Insurance Co.; CIGNA Insurance Co.; Mazda Motor Co.; Pacificare of Texas Inc; Santa Rosa Health Care Corp.; Sisters of Mercy Health System; ANPAC.

For full biographical listings, see the Martindale-Hubbell Law Directory

SHELTON & VALADEZ, P.C. (AV)

112 East Pecan Street, Suite 2600, 78205
Telephone: 210-349-0515
Facsimile: 210-349-3666
Email: shelton-valadez.com

Wade B. Shelton
Robert A. Valadez
Mark A. Giltner
Robert J. Perez

Stephen D. Navarro
Brandon T. Hudson
Michael I. Ramirez

OF COUNSEL

K. Blake Coffee

For full biographical listings, see the Martindale-Hubbell Law Directory

TEXARKANA, Bowie Co.

GOODING & DODSON, P.C. (AV)

300 Hibernia National Bank Building, P.O. Box 1877, 75504
Telephone: 903-794-3121
Fax: 903-793-4801
Email: GandDLaw@cs.com

William C. Gooding
Robert E. Dodson
Robert S. McGinnis, Jr.
Michael F. Jones
Lisa R. Crittenden

Jeffrey S. Young

Representative Clients: American General Insurance Co.; Kansas City Southern Railway Co.; Maryland Casualty Co.; North Texas Production Credit Assn.; The Travelers Indemnity Company/The Aetna Casualty; Wadely Regional Medical Center; Hibernia National Bank; Resolution Trust Corp.

For full biographical listings, see the Martindale-Hubbell Law Directory

PATTON, HALTOM, ROBERTS, MCWILLIAMS & GREER, L.L.P. (AV)

A Registered Limited Liability Partnership including Professional Corporations
700 Hibernia National Bank Building, P.O. Box 1928, 75504-1928
Telephone: 903-794-3341
Fax: 903-792-6542; 903-792-0448
URL: http://www.pattonhaltom.com

James N. Haltom (P.C.)
George L. McWilliams (P.C.)
John B. Greer, III, (P.C.)
Kristi I. McCasland
Jennifer Haltom Doan

ASSOCIATES

Darby Vincent Doan
William W. Miller, Jr.
David P. Cotten

Representative Clients: Allstate Insurance Co.; Royal Insurance Group; Continental Insurance Group; Ranger/Pan American Insurance Cos.; The Hanover Insurance Group; American Mutual Liability Insurance Co.; American Hardware Mutual Insurance Co.; Kemper Insurance Co.

For Complete List of Firm Personnel, See General Section

For full biographical listings, see the Martindale-Hubbell Law Directory

*TYLER,** Smith Co.

IRELAND, CARROLL & KELLEY, P.C. (AV)

6101 South Broadway, Suite 500, P.O. Box 7879, 75711
Telephone: 903-561-1600
Fax: 903-581-1071
Email: ICKLAW@AOL.COM

H. Kelly Ireland (Retired)
Donald Carroll (1929-1992)
Otis W. Carroll
Patrick Kelley
Marcus Carroll
Michael G. Carroll

Deborah Race

For full biographical listings, see the Martindale-Hubbell Law Directory

SAMMONS & PARKER, A PROFESSIONAL CORPORATION (AV)

218 North College, 75702
Telephone: 903-595-4541
FAX: 903-595-2864

Martin Z. Sammons, Jr.
Jerry C. Parker
Clay M. White
Jeffery J. Shaver
Reid Wm. Martin
J. Chad Parker

W. Todd Parker
Alan D. Wharton
John F. (Jack) Walker, III
Vanessa L. Vance

Representative Clients: A list of Representative Clients will be furnished upon request.

For full biographical listings, see the Martindale-Hubbell Law Directory

*VICTORIA,** Victoria Co.

WALKER, KEELING & CARROLL, L.L.P. (AV)

210 East Constitution, P.O. Box 108, 77902
Telephone: 361-576-6800
Fax: 361-576-6196
Email: wkc@wkcfirm.com

Ronald B. Walker
Terry M. Carroll, Jr.
W. Lee Keeling
Patricia L. Hayden
Donna K. Grafe

(See Next Column)

WALKER, KEELING & CARROLL L.L.P.—*Continued*

LEGAL SUPPORT PERSONNEL

Sue A. Comstock (Legal Assistant)

For full biographical listings, see the Martindale-Hubbell Law Directory

UTAH

*SALT LAKE CITY,** Salt Lake Co.

KIPP AND CHRISTIAN, P.C. (AV)

10 Exchange Place, Fourth Floor, 84111
Telephone: 801-521-3773
Fax: 801-359-9004
Email: kc1gsb@inquo.net

Carman E. Kipp
J. Anthony Eyre
Gregory J. Sanders
Heinz J. Mahler
Michael F. Skolnick
Shawn McGarry
Kirk G. Gibbs

OF COUNSEL

D. Gary Christian

Representative Clients: CNA Insurance Co; Coregis; Utah State Bar; Reliance Insurance Co.; National Farmers Union Insurance Co.; Utah Medical Insurance Association (UMIA); Utah Paper Box; Skivations, Condominium & Land Developers; Montgomery Elevators; Tim Dahle Imports/Nissan.

For Complete List of Firm Personnel, See General Section

For full biographical listings, see the Martindale-Hubbell Law Directory

KIRTON & MCCONKIE, A PROFESSIONAL CORPORATION (AV)

1800 Eagle Gate Tower, 60 East South Temple, 84111
Telephone: 801-328-3600
Telecopier: 801-321-4893

Randy T. Austin
Lorin C. Barker
Anthony I. Bentley, Jr.
Rolf H. Berger
Berne S. Broadbent
Charles W. Dahlquist, II
Jerry W. Dearinger
Robert W. Edwards
James E. Ellsworth
Fred D. Essig
Wallace O. Felsted
Clark B. Fetzer
R. Bruce Findlay
David J. Hardy
Keith L. Hargrove
Read R. Hellewell
Dale E. Hulse
Lee Ford Hunter
Richard G. Johnson, Jr.
Von G. Keetch
Raeburn G. Kennard
Wilford W. Kirton, Jr.
Michael F. Krieger
Paul H. Matthews
Daniel S. McConkie
David M. McConkie
Oscar W. McConkie, III
Oscar W. McConkie, Jr.
Samuel D. McVey
William A. Meaders, Jr.
Thomas L. Monson
Denis Roy Morrill
Merrill F. Nelson
Richard R. Neslen
Eric C. Olson
R. Willis Orton
B. Lloyd Poelman
Robert S. Prince
Gregory M. Simonsen
Robert T. Smith (Not admitted in UT)
Myron L. Sorensen
Jon E. Waddoups
David M. Wahlquist
Thomas D. Walk
Stuart F. Weed
David A. Westerby
Todd E. Zenger

Randall C. Allen
Bryan H. Booth
Michael M. Conger
David S. Doty
Alexander Dushku
Scott C. Krieger
Melinda R. Porter
Matthew K. Richards
Dorany Rodriguez-Baltazar (Not admitted in UT)
Jeffrey Dean Stevens
Amy S. Thomas
Steven L. Whitehead

For full biographical listings, see the Martindale-Hubbell Law Directory

MORGAN, MEYER & RICE, L.C. (AV)

Kearns Building, Eighth Floor, 136 South Main Street, 84101
Telephone: 801-531-7888
Telefax: 801-531-9732
Email: morgan@inquo.net

MEMBERS OF FIRM

Stephen G. Morgan
Cynthia K.C. Meyer
Mitchel T. Rice
Joseph E. Minnock
Jeffrey C. Miner

Representative Clients: Albertson's Inc.; Smith Food and Drug Centers, Inc.; Colorado Casualty; Farmers Insurance Group; SLC Airport Authority; St. Paul Fire and Marine Insurance Co.; State Farm Fire and Casualty; State Farm Mutual Automobile Insurance Co.; Utah Farm Bureau Insurance Co.; Utah Local Government's Insurance Trust.

For full biographical listings, see the Martindale-Hubbell Law Directory

PARR WADDOUPS BROWN GEE & LOVELESS, A PROFESSIONAL CORPORATION (AV)

Suite 1300, 185 South State Street, 84111-1537
Telephone: 801-532-7840
Fax: 801-532-7750
URL: http://www.pwlaw.com

Patricia W. Christensen
Bentley J. Tolk

OF COUNSEL

Bruce A. Maak

For Complete List of Firm Personnel, See General Section

For full biographical listings, see the Martindale-Hubbell Law Directory

PLANT, WALLACE, CHRISTENSEN & KANELL, A PROFESSIONAL CORPORATION (AV)

136 East South Temple Suite 1700, 84110-2970
Telephone: 801-363-7611
Fax: 801-531-9747
URL: http://www.pwcklaw.com

Robert R. Wallace
Scott W. Christensen
Terry M. Plant
Theodore E. Kanell
John N. Braithwaite
Mark J. Williams

Lisa Watts Baskin
Jason Max Kerr
Robert C. Olsen
Mollio L. McDonald

Representative Clients: CNA Insurance Group; Travelers Property Casualty Group; St. Paul Fire & Marine; Kemper Insurance Group; Prudential Insurance; Transamerica Insurance Co.; Ranger Insurance; Guaranty National Ins. Co.; Utah Transit Authority; Western Surety.

For full biographical listings, see the Martindale-Hubbell Law Directory

RAY, QUINNEY & NEBEKER, A PROFESSIONAL CORPORATION (AV)

79 South Main Street, Suite 400, P.O. Box 45385, 84145-0385
Telephone: 801-532-1500
Fax: 801-532-7543
Email: rqn@rqn.com *URL:* http://www.rqn.com
Provo, Utah Office: 92 North University Avenue, Suite 210, 84601-4420.
Telephone: 801-342-2400.
Fax: 801-375-8379.
Albuquerque, New Mexico Office: Suite 620, 40 First Plaza, N.W.
Telephone: 505-243-6665.
Fax: 505-764-9890.

Stephen B. Nebeker
Paul S. Felt
John A. Adams
Rick L. Rose
Rick B. Hoggard

Eric D. Barton

Representative Clients: Aetna Casualty & Surety Co.; Cigna Cos.; Educator's Mutual Insurance Co.; Great American Insurance Co.; Home Insurance Co.; New York Life Insurance Co.; Teachers Insurance and Annuity; Travelers Insurance Co.

For Complete List of Firm Personnel, See General Section

For full biographical listings, see the Martindale-Hubbell Law Directory

SCALLEY & READING, A PROFESSIONAL CORPORATION (AV)

261 East 300 South, Second Floor, 84111
Telephone: 801-531-7870
Fax: 801-531-7968
Email: law@scalleyreading.com

Ford G. Scalley
J. Bruce Reading
Marlon L. Bates
John Edward Hansen
Scott N. Rasmussen
Steven B. Smith

Wesley D. Hutchins
Kami L. Peterson
Amy D. Kraus
Darwin H. Bingham
Lisa A. Jones

For full biographical listings, see the Martindale-Hubbell Law Directory

STRONG & HANNI, A PROFESSIONAL CORPORATION (AV)

Sixth Floor Boston Building, 9 Exchange Place, 84111
Telephone: 801-532-7080
Fax: 801-596-1508
Email: pfishler@strongandhanni.com

Gordon R. Strong (1909-1969)
Glenn C. Hanni
Henry E. Heath
Philip R. Fishler
Roger H. Bullock
R. Scott Williams
Dennis M. Astill (Managing Partner)
Stuart H. Schultz
Paul M. Belnap
Stephen J. Trayner
Joseph J. Joyce

(See Next Column)

STRONG & HANNI A PROFESSIONAL CORPORATION, *Salt Lake City—Continued*

Bradley Wm. Bowen
Robert L. Janicki
Elizabeth L. Willey
H. Burt Ringwood
Peter H. Christensen
David R. Nielson

Kevin D. Swenson
Catherine M. Larson
Kristin Van Orman
Darren K. Nelson
Peter H. Barlow
Steven T. Densley
Jennifer C. Polley-Abramson
Shawn T. Welch

OF COUNSEL
Robert A. Burton

Representative Clients: State Farm Mutual Automobile Insurance Co.; Standard Accident Insurance Co.; United Services Automobile Assn.; Western Casualty & Surety Co.; Government Employees Insurance Co.; Guaranty Mutual Life Co.

For full biographical listings, see the Martindale-Hubbell Law Directory

VAN COTT, BAGLEY, CORNWALL & McCARTHY, A PROFESSIONAL CORPORATION (AV)

50 South Main Street, Suite 1600, P.O. Box 45340, 84145-0340
Telephone: 801-532-3333
Telecopier: 801-534-0058
Email: info@vancott.com *URL:* http://www.vancott.com
Ogden, Utah Office: 2404 Washington Boulevard, Suite 900.
Telephone: 801-394-5783.
Park City, Utah Office: 2200 Park Avenue, Suite C200-A.
Telephone: 435-649-3889.

Robert M. Anderson (President of Firm)
Kenneth W. Yeates
John L. Young

OF COUNSEL
Franklin N. Smith

For Complete List of Firm Personnel, See General Section

For full biographical listings, see the Martindale-Hubbell Law Directory

WEISS BERRETT PETTY, L.C. (AV)

Key Bank Tower, 50 South Main Street, Suite 530, 84144
Telephone: 801-531-7733
Facsimile: 801-531-7711

Loren E. Weiss
Barbara K. Berrett
Ralph C. Petty

Bret M. Hanna

OF COUNSEL
Charles F. Loyd

For full biographical listings, see the Martindale-Hubbell Law Directory

VERMONT

*BURLINGTON,** Chittenden Co.

DINSE, KNAPP & McANDREW, P.C. (AV)

209 Battery Street, P.O. Box 988, 05402-0988
Telephone: 802-864-5751
Fax: 802-862-6409
URL: http://www.dinse.com

COUNSEL
John M. Dinse

MEMBERS OF FIRM

Spencer R. Knapp
Karen McAndrew
Barbara E. Cory
Robert R. McKearin
James W. Spink
John D. Monahan, Jr.
Emily R. Morrow
Ritchie E. Berger
Austin D. Hart
Samuel Hoar, Jr.
Steven L. Knudson
Sandra A. Strempel
Molly K. Lebowitz
Pietro J. Lynn
Philip C. Woodward
Jeffrey J. Nolan
Mark A. Langan

ASSOCIATES

Douglas D. Le Brun
Shapleigh Smith, Jr.
Craig S. Nolan
Elizabeth H. Miller
Heather E. Thomas

Representative Clients: Chittenden Trust Co.; Vermont Transit Co., Inc.; Sears, Roebuck & Co.; Ford Motor Co.; Inc.; CNA; PHICO; Royal Ins.; Middlebury College.

For full biographical listings, see the Martindale-Hubbell Law Directory

*MONTPELIER,** Washington Co.

THERIAULT & JOSLIN, P.C. (AV)

141 Main Street, P.O. Box 249, 05601-0249
Telephone: 802-223-2381
Fax: 802-223-1461
Email: LAWYERS@TJOSLIN.COM

William N. Theriault (1877-1961)
Peter B. Joslin
Fletcher Brian (Ted) Joslin

John Davis Buckley
Barbara R. Blackman

OF COUNSEL

Fletcher B. Joslin
Jeffry W. White

Representative Clients: Allstate Insurance Co.; American International Group; Hartford Insurance Group; St. Paul Insurance Cos.; Nationwide Insurance Cos.; Commercial Union Insurance Cos.; Prudential Insurance Cos.; PHICO Insurance Co.; Zurich Insurance Group.

For full biographical listings, see the Martindale-Hubbell Law Directory

*RUTLAND,** Rutland Co.

MILLER FAIGNANT & BEHRENS, P.C. (AV)

36 Merchants Row, P.O. Box 6688, 05702-6688
Telephone: 802-775-2521
Fax: 802-775-8274
Email: lhblaw@aol.com *URL:* http://www.lawyers.com/millerfaignantbehrenslaw

Lawrence Miller
John Paul Faignant
Lawrence H. Behrens

OF COUNSEL
Lisa L. Chalidze

LEGAL SUPPORT PERSONNEL

Marie Peck Fabian
Kim J. Miller

Representative Clients: Travelers Insurance Co.; Government Employees Insurance Co.; Utica Mutual Insurance Co.; Universal Underwriters Insurance Co.; Zurich American Acadia Insurance.
References: Travelers Insurance Co.; Universal Underwriters Insurance Co.

For full biographical listings, see the Martindale-Hubbell Law Directory

VIRGINIA

ALEXANDRIA, (Independent City)

CARTER & COLEMAN (AV)

602 Cameron Street, 22314
Telephone: 703-739-4200
Fax: 703-739-4210
Email: rcarter@cartercoleman.com *URL:* http://www.lawyers.com/carter&coleman
Washington, D.C. Office: 900 Seventeenth Street, N.W., Suite 900, 20006.
Telephone: 202-326-8600.
Fax: 202-289-0184.

Richard D. Carter
Douglas M. Coleman
David C. Simmons (Not admitted in VA)
James M. Loots (Not admitted in VA)

ASSOCIATES

Juliane C. Miller
Mercedes Madole (Not admitted in VA)
Paul A. Daniels

For full biographical listings, see the Martindale-Hubbell Law Directory

HUDGINS LAW FIRM (AV)

515 King Street, Suite 400, 22314
Telephone: 703-739-3300
Telefax: 703-739-3700
URL: http://www.hudginslawfirm.com
Norfolk, Virginia Office: 125 Saint Paul's Boulevard, Suite 600, 23510.
Washington, D.C. Office: 1510 H Street, N.W., 4th Floor, 20005.
Baltimore, Maryland Office: 201 North Charles Street, Suite 600, 21201-4110.

PARTNERS

David D. Hudgins
Mary K. Gogoel

ASSOCIATES

Ann S. Hudgins
John Christopher McDonough
Paul T. Emerick
Kevin A. Kernan
Sean C. E. McDonough

(See Next Column)

HUDGINS LAW FIRM—*Continued*

OF COUNSEL

Robert B. Scarlett (Not admitted in VA; Resident, Baltimore, Maryland Office)

Representative Clients: Interstate Insurance Group; Chicago Insurance Company; National Association of Realtors; Professional Insurance Underwriters, Inc.; Scottsdale Insurance Company; Homestead Ins. Co.; AIG Claims Services, Inc.; Argenbright Holdings, Ltd.; TIG Insurance Company; Zurich-American Insurance Company.

For full biographical listings, see the Martindale-Hubbell Law Directory

BLACKSBURG, Montgomery Co.

GILMER, SADLER, INGRAM, SUTHERLAND & HUTTON (AV)

201 West Roanoke Street, P.O. Box 908, 24063-0908
Telephone: 540-552-1061; 888-887-9997
Telecopier: 540-552-8227
Pulaski, Virginia Office: Midtown Professional Building, 65 East Main Street, P.O. Box 878.
Telephone: 540-980-1360; 540-639-0027; 800-330-3344.
Telecopier: 540-980-5264.

MEMBERS OF FIRM

James L. Hutton
Howard C. Gilmer, Jr. (1906-1975)
Roby K. Sutherland (1909-1975)
Philip M. Sadler (1915-1994)
Robert J. Ingram
Thomas J. McCarthy, Jr.
John J. Gill
Gary C. Hancock
Jackson M. Bruce
Michael J. Barbour
Deborah Wood Dobbins
Timothy Edmond Kirtner
Robin J. Kegley

Representative Clients: Appalachian Power Co.; Liberty Mutual Insurance Co.; Norfolk Southern Railway Co.; Travelers Insurance Group; NationsBank; Charles Lunsford Sons & Associates; First National Bank; Corning Glass Works.

For full biographical listings, see the Martindale-Hubbell Law Directory

*CHARLOTTESVILLE,** Charlottesville City Co.

TAYLOR, ZUNKA, MILNOR & CARTER, LTD. (AV)

414 Park Street, P.O. Box 1567, 22902
Telephone: 804-977-0191
FAX: 804-977-0198

John W. Zunka
Richard H. Milnor
Richard E. Carter

H. Robert Yates, III
Alvaro A. Inigo

Representative Clients: State Farm Insurance Companies; Allstate Insurance Co.; The Travelers Insurance Companies; The Harleysville Insurance Companies; Kemper Insurance Companies; Selective Insurance; Blue Cross and Blue Shield of Virginia; Crestar Bank.

For full biographical listings, see the Martindale-Hubbell Law Directory

*FAIRFAX,** (Ind. City; Seat of Fairfax Co.)

BRAULT, PALMER, GROVE, ZIMMERMAN, WHITE & STEINHILBER (AV)

10533 Main Street, P.O. Box 1010, 22030-1010
Telephone: 703-273-6400
Fax: 703-273-3514
Manassas, Virginia Office: 8567-D Sudley Road, 20110. Mailing Address: P.O. Box 534, Manassas, VA 20108.
Telephone: 703-369-7500; 631-9727.
Fax: 703-369-2285.

MEMBERS OF FIRM

Adelard L. Brault (Emeritus)
Thomas C. Palmer, Jr. (Resident, Manassas Office)
Edward H. Grove, III
Michael L. Zimmerman
Bruce D. White
August W. Steinhilber, III

ASSOCIATES

Jack A. Robbins, Jr. (Resident, Manassas Office)
C. Mark Whittington
Craig J. Franco
Bobby Puri (Resident, Manassas Office)

Representative Clients: Alamo Rent-A-Car, Inc.; CNA Insurance Companies; E.I. du Pont de Nemours and Company; Erie Insurance Group; Fidelity & Deposit Company of Maryland; Hanover Insurance Company; Harleysville Insurance Companies; Home Insurance Company; J.B. Hunt Transport, Inc.; Kemper Insurance Group.

For full biographical listings, see the Martindale-Hubbell Law Directory

DOHERTY & SHERIDAN, L.L.P. (AV)

8408 Arlington Boulevard, Suite 200, 22031
Telephone: 703-698-7700
Facsimile: 703-641-9645
Email: d&s.law@erols.com
Washington, D.C. Office: 1050 17th Street, Suite 1250, 20036-5510.
Bethesda, Maryland Office: 4701 Sangamore Road, Suite S-225, 20816.
Vero Beach, Florida Office: 1701 Highway AIA, Suite 220, 32963.

MEMBERS OF FIRM

Cornelius H. Doherty, Jr.
Edwin A. Sheridan
Eric M. Persian

Representative Clients: CGU Insurance Companies; Canal Insurance Company; Claims Control, Inc.; First Financial Insurance; The Hartford; Ruder TRS; North Carolina Farm Bereau; Burlington Insurance; Enterprise; Travelers Property & Casualty.

For full biographical listings, see the Martindale-Hubbell Law Directory

GODARD, WEST & ADELMAN, P.C. (AV)

3975 University Drive, P.O. Box 1287, 22030
Telephone: 703-273-4800
Facsimile: 703-691-0804
URL: http://www.gwadrlaw.com

Gary A. Godard
Norman A. West (Retired)
Thomas M. Hogan
Roger W. Heald
Mark R. Lightfoot
Patricia C. Karppi
Marc A. Brown

LEGAL SUPPORT PERSONNEL

Leslie C. Jelacic
Jean K. Wheelock
Marla J. Burn, R.N.
Betty Servaites

For full biographical listings, see the Martindale-Hubbell Law Directory

TRICHILO, BANCROFT, MCGAVIN, HORVATH & JUDKINS, P.C. (AV)

F & M Bank Building, Suite 400, 4117 Chain Bridge Road, P.O. Box 22, 22030-0022
Telephone: 703-385-1000
Telecopier: 703-385-1555

Benjamin J. Trichilo
Steven W. Bancroft
John D. McGavin
Stephen A. Horvath
Julia B. Judkins
Melissa Hogue Katz
Dawn E. Boyce

Heather Kathleen Bardot
Michael J. Carita
Michael Earle Thorsen
Barry J. Waldman

References: Virginia Farm Bureau Insurance Cos.; Amoco Oil Co.; Erie Insurance Exchange; Hartford Insurance Co.; State Farm Insurance Cos.; Ohio Casualty Group; Chubb Group of Insurance Cos.; Atlantic Mutual Insurance Co.; USAA; Allstate Insurance Co.; CNA; Reliance Insurance co.; K-Mart Corp.; Farmer's Insurance Co.; CIGNA Insurance Co.

For full biographical listings, see the Martindale-Hubbell Law Directory

FALLS CHURCH, (Independent City)

GARNIER & GARNIER, P.C. (AV)

109 Rowell Court, 22046
Telephone: 703-237-2010
Fax: 703-237-9738
URL: http://members.aol.com/garnierlaw

Jean-Pierre Garnier
Michael J. Garnier

Robert L. Garnier

Representative Clients: The Schering-Plough Corp.; Key Pharmaceutical, Inc.; Warner-Lambert Company ; Glaxo Wellcome Inc.; Ciba-Geigy Corp.; Otis Elevator Co.; Montgomery KONE, Inc.; The Hertz Corp.; The Coca-Cola Company; General Elevator Company, Inc.

For full biographical listings, see the Martindale-Hubbell Law Directory

MCLEAN, Fairfax Co.

PLEDGER & FEORD P.L.C. (AV)

Suite 204, 1489 Chain Bridge Road, 22101
Telephone: 703-821-1250
Fax: 703-790-7250
Email: Pledger@his.com *URL:* http://www.lawyers.com/pledgerlaw

R. Harrison Pledger, Jr.
Bernard G. Feord, Jr.

Kevin D. Pledger

For full biographical listings, see the Martindale-Hubbell Law Directory

NORFOLK, (Independent City)

DAVEY & BROGAN, P.C. (AV)

101 Granby Street, Suite 300, 23510
Telephone: 757-622-0100
Telecopier: 757-622-4924
Email: daveylaw@pilot.infi.net *URL:* http://www.lawyers.com/davey&associates

Philip N. Davey
Patrick M. Brogan
R. Arthur Jett, Jr.

Representative Clients: GRE Insurance Group; Marine Office of America Corp.; Spliethoff's Bevrachtingskantoor B.V.; W.F. Magann Corp.; The North of England Protecting and Indemnity Association Limited; Evergreen America Corporation; Sveriges Angfartygs Assurans Forening "The Swedish Club"; Mediterranean Shipping Co., S.A.
Reference: Crestar Bank.

For full biographical listings, see the Martindale-Hubbell Law Directory

HARRIS, FEARS, DAVIS, LYNCH & McDANIEL (AV)

5735 Poplar Hall Drive, P.O. Box 12756, 23502
Telephone: 757-461-4100
Fax: 757-455-5115
Email: HFDL5735@AOL.COM

MEMBERS OF FIRM

Preston P. Taylor (1891-1964)
Terry Hunter Davis, Jr.
Benjamin P. Lynch, Jr.

OF COUNSEL

J. Carroll Fears, Jr.
William M. Harris

ASSOCIATE

Catherine J. Rogers

For full biographical listings, see the Martindale-Hubbell Law Directory

HEILIG, McKENRY, FRAIM & LOLLAR, A PROFESSIONAL CORPORATION (AV)

700 Newtown Road, 23502-3999
Telephone: 757-461-2500
Fax: 757-461-2341

James R. McKenry
John A. Heilig
Paul D. Fraim
George J. Dancigers
Charles M. Lollar
Carolyn P. Oast
Teresa R. Warner
Thomas C. Dawson, Jr.
Peter S. Lake
Todd M. Fiorella
Robert E. Moreland
A. William Charters

Debra Mosley Evans
Joseph T. McFadden, Jr.
Jason Evans Dodd
J. Andrew Basham
Deborah S. Prince
Patrick M. Mayette
Todd David Anderson

For full biographical listings, see the Martindale-Hubbell Law Directory

PAYNE, GATES, FARTHING & RADD, P.C. (AV)

15th Floor, Dominion Tower, 999 Waterside Drive, Suite 1515, 23510-3309
Telephone: 757-640-1500
Facsimile: 757-627-6583
URL: http://www.paynegates.com

Ronald M. Gates
Philip R. Farthing
Anthony F. Radd
Glen M. Robertson
Brian R. Dinning
Todd J. Preti
Marshall A. Winslow, Jr.

C. Arthur Robinson, II
Stephen E. Heretick
Raymond L. Hogge, Jr.

OF COUNSEL

Charles E. Payne

For full biographical listings, see the Martindale-Hubbell Law Directory

REYNOLDS, SMITH & WINTERS, P.C. (AV)

500 East Plume Street, Suite 800, 23510
Telephone: 757-622-3111
Fax: 757-623-6951

Allan S. Reynolds
Robert G. Winters
Allan S. Reynolds, Jr.

Representative Clients: General Motors Corp.; The Travelers Cos.; Allstate Insurance Co.; Selective Insurance Co. of America; Werner Co.

For full biographical listings, see the Martindale-Hubbell Law Directory

STACKHOUSE, SMITH & NEXSEN (AV)

1600 First Virginia Tower, 555 Main Street, P.O. Box 3640, 23514
Telephone: 757-623-3555
Fax: 757-624-9245

MEMBERS OF FIRM

Robert C. Stackhouse
Peter W. Smith, IV
William W. Nexsen
R. Clinton Stackhouse, Jr.
Janice McPherson Doxey
Mary Painter Opitz

ASSOCIATES

J. Derek Turrietta
Michael T. Pangalos

Representative Clients: Heritage Bank & Trust; The Atlantic Group, Inc.; CNA Insurance Co.; Federal National Mortgage Association; Kemper National Insurance Cos.; Harleysville Mutual Insurance Co.; Southern Insurance Company of Virginia; Oakwood Acceptance Corp.; The Travelers; Argonaut Insurance Co.

For full biographical listings, see the Martindale-Hubbell Law Directory

TAYLOR & WALKER, P.C. (AV)

1300 First Virginia Tower, 555 Main Street, P.O. Box 3490, 23514-3490
Telephone: 757-625-7300
Telefax: 757-625-1504
URL: http://www.TAYWAL.com
Richmond, Virginia Office: 6802 Paragon Place, Suite 126, 23230.
Telephone: 804-673-0341.
Facsimile: 804-673-2001.

OF COUNSEL

J. Hume Taylor, Jr.

PARTNERS

William C. Walker
Gerard E. W. Voyer
James E. Brydges, Jr.
John Franklin, III
F. Bradford Stillman
Henry M. Massie, Jr.
James E. Vaiden
Brian N. Casey
James C. McCaa, III

Donna White Kearney
Mary Margaret Callahan Lyons
Richard W. Zahn, Jr.
Bradford Clark Jacob
Mark B. Kilduff
Stephen B. Royalty
Patricia C. Arrighi
Douglas Eugene Penner

LEGAL SUPPORT PERSONNEL

Diana L. White (Director of Administration)

For full biographical listings, see the Martindale-Hubbell Law Directory

NORTON, Wise Co.

MULLINS, HARRIS & JESSEE, A PROFESSIONAL CORPORATION (AV)

The Law Building, 30 Seventh Street, P.O. Box 1200, 24273-1002
Telephone: 540-679-3110
Telecopier: 540-679-3113
Email: mh&j@naxs.com

Fred Bonham Greear (1899-1960)
William Thomas Bowen (1908-1964)
Leslie Morris Mullins (Retired)
Ronald G. Thomason (Retired)
Elsey A. Harris III
Roy M. Jessee
Kristen D. Dean
Chadwick S. Dotson

Counsel for: Old Dominion Power Co.
Local Counsel for: Allstate Insurance Co.; Norfolk-Southern Corp.; Virginia Iron, Coal & Coke Co.; Bell Atlantic Corp.; Kentucky Hospital Assn.; Canal Insurance Co.; Southern Pilot Insurance Integon.

For full biographical listings, see the Martindale-Hubbell Law Directory

*PULASKI,** Pulaski Co.

GILMER, SADLER, INGRAM, SUTHERLAND & HUTTON (AV)

Midtown Professional Building, 65 East Main Street, P.O. Box 878, 24301-0878
Telephone: 540-980-1360; 540-639-0027; 888-330-3344
Telecopier: 540-980-5264
Blacksburg (Montgomery County), Virginia Office: 201 West Roanoke Street, P.O. Box 908.
Telephone: 540-552-1061.
Telecopier: 540-552-8227.

MEMBERS OF FIRM

Howard C. Gilmer, Jr. (1906-1975)
Roby K. Sutherland (1909-1975)
Philip M. Sadler (1915-1994)
Robert J. Ingram
James L. Hutton (Resident, Blacksburg Office)
Thomas J. McCarthy, Jr.
John J. Gill
Gary C. Hancock
Jackson M. Bruce
Michael J. Barbour
Deborah Wood Dobbins
Timothy Edmond Kirtner
Robin J. Kegley

Representative Clients: Appalachian Power Co.; Norfolk Southern Railway Co.; NationsBank; Travelers Insurance Group; World Insurance; Royal Insurance; Integon Insurance.

For full biographical listings, see the Martindale-Hubbell Law Directory

RICHMOND, (Independent City)

BRENNER, DOHNAL, EVANS & YOFFY, P.C. (AV)

411 East Franklin Street, Suite 200, P.O. Box 470, 23218-0470
Telephone: 804-644-1300
Facsimile: 804-644-1354
Email: bdeyp@erols.com

Theodore I. Brenner
Dennis W. Dohnal
Ronald S. Evans
James S. Yoffy

Jay O. Millman
Gregory S. Hooe
Kathryn Spruill Lingle
Mary J. Bennett
Thomas D. Stokes, III

For full biographical listings, see the Martindale-Hubbell Law Directory

HARMAN, CLAYTOR, CORRIGAN & WELLMAN, A PROFESSIONAL CORPORATION (AV)

P.O. Box 70280, 23255
Telephone: 804-747-5200
Telecopier: 804-747-6085
Email: hccw@hccw.com

Michael E. Harman
John M. Claytor
David P. Corrigan
Stanley P. Wellman
Lynne Jones Blain
Elizabeth E. S. Skilling

OF COUNSEL

Michelle Preston Wiltshire

Glen Andrew Lea
Stephanie P. Karn

Representative Clients: Amerisure Companies; Anthem Insurance Companies; Cincinnati Insurance Company; Erie Insurance Group; Essex Insurance Company; Estes Express Lines; Federated Mutual Insurance Company.

For full biographical listings, see the Martindale-Hubbell Law Directory

SMITH & JENSEN, P.C. A PROFESSIONAL CORPORATION (AV)

The Campbell Building, Suite 415, 8002 Discovery Drive, 23229
Telephone: 804-285-2742
Fax: 282-8738
Email: sonofyens@aol.com

Nathan H. Smith
Eric S. Jensen

Mark S. Paullin

For full biographical listings, see the Martindale-Hubbell Law Directory

WILLIAMS, MULLEN, CLARK & DOBBINS, A PROFESSIONAL CORPORATION (AV)

Two James Center, 1021 East Cary Street, P.O. Box 1320, 23218-1320
Telephone: 804-643-1991
Fax: 804-783-6507
URL: http://www.wmcd.com
Newport News Office: Harbor Bank Center, Suite 210, One Old Oyster Point Road, 23602-7119.
Telephone: 757-249-5100.
Fax: 757-249-5109.
Virginia Beach Office: One Columbus Center, 23462-6763.
Telephone: 757-499-8800.
Fax: 757-473-0395.
Vienna Office: 1593 Spring Hill Road, Suite 510, 22182.
Telephone: 703-760-5200.
Fax: 703-748-0244.
Washington, D.C. Office: The Farragut Building, 900 17th Street, N.W., Suite 700, 20006.
Telephone: 202-293-0213.
Fax: 804-783-6507. Fax Within D.C.: 202-293-5939.
London, England Office: Blake Lodge, Bridge Lane, SW11 3AD.
Telephone: (011-44-71) 223-2756.
Fax: (011-44-71) 350-0156.
Riyadh, Saudi Arabia Affiliate Office: Saudi-American Legal Consultants Commercial Building #2, Diplomatic Quarter, P.O. Box 57270, 11574.
Telephone: (011-966-1) 488-1563.
Fax: (011-966-1) 488-0542.

Stephen E. Baril
William D. Bayliss
Theodore J. Edlich, IV
Calvin W. Fowler, Jr.
W. F. Drewry Gallalee
Andrea Rowse Stiles
John L. Walker, III

OF COUNSEL

David George Ball (Resident, Washington, D.C. Office)

Kevin C. Nunnally

For Complete List of Firm Personnel, See General Section

For full biographical listings, see the Martindale-Hubbell Law Directory

ROANOKE, Roanoke City Co.

JOHNSON, AYERS & MATTHEWS (AV)

Southwest Virginia Savings Bank Building Second Floor, 302 Second Street, S.W., P.O. Box 2200, 24009
Telephone: 540-982-3666
Fax: 540-982-1552
Email: jamlaw@swva.net

MEMBERS OF FIRM

James F. Johnson
Ronald M. Ayers
Joseph A. Matthews, Jr.
John D. Eure
William P. Wallace, Jr.
Kenneth J. Ries
Jonnie L. Speight
David B. Carson
Robert S. Ballou

ASSOCIATES

Bryan Grimes Creasy
Clark H. Worthy
Lori Elizabeth Jones
Michael R. Gray

Representative Clients: Bell Atlantic-Virginia, Inc.; Trigon Blue Cross and Blue Shield; Federated Mutual Insurance Co.; Nationwide Mutual Insurance Co.; Norfolk Southern Railway Co.; Progressive Insurance Cos.; Royal Insurance Cos.; State Farm Insurance Cos.; The Travelers Cos.

For full biographical listings, see the Martindale-Hubbell Law Directory

WOOTEN & HART, A PROFESSIONAL CORPORATION (AV)

707 Building, Suite 300, P.O. Box 12247, 24024-2247
Telephone: 540-343-2451; 540-342-9672
Telecopier: 540-345-6417
URL: http://www.wootenhart.com

George W. Wooten
David B. Hart
L. Thompson Hanes
Susan A. Waddell
Bradley D. McGraw
John L. Cooley
Thomas W. Farrell
Paul C. Kuhnel
Peter D. Vieth

David W. Hearn
John Mark Cooley
Christopher W. Stevens
Elizabeth D. Guilbert
Eunice Park Austin

OF COUNSEL

M. Lanier Woodrum

Representative Clients: Wachovia Bank; St. Paul Insurance Cos.
Approved Attorneys for: Lawyers Title Insurance Corp.
Reference: First Union National Bank.

For full biographical listings, see the Martindale-Hubbell Law Directory

WASHINGTON

*SEATTLE,** King Co.

GARDNER BOND TRABOLSI ST. LOUIS & CLEMENT, PLLC (AV)

Denny Building, Suite 600, 2200 Sixth Avenue, 98121
Telephone: 206-256-6309
Facsimile: 206-256-6318

Michael J. Bond
W. Scott Clement
Ronald C. Gardner
Lynn R. McDonald
Gary A. Trabolsi

Robert Meyers
Jennifer L. Whatley

For full biographical listings, see the Martindale-Hubbell Law Directory

LEE, SMART, COOK, MARTIN & PATTERSON, P.S., INC. (AV)

800 Puget Sound Plaza, 1325 Fourth Avenue, 98101-2585
Telephone: 206-624-7990
Facsimile: 206-624-5944

David L. Martin
Michael A. Patterson
Joel E. Wright
Philip B. Grennan
Steven J. Jager
Jeffrey P. Downer
Richard C. Robinson
Joseph P. Lawrence, Jr.
August G. Cifelli
Duncan K. Fobes
Rebecca S. Ringer
Sam B. Franklin
Creighton S. Hutchins
John C. Versnel, III
Kathleen F. Cochran
Gregory P. Turner
Patricia K. Fenske Buchanan

(See Next Column)

LEE, SMART, COOK, MARTIN & PATTERSON P.S., INC., *Seattle—Continued*

Christopher S. Clemenson
Michelle A. Corsi
Shawn M. Farrell
Kenneth E. Hepworth
Lisa A. Hollomon
Jennifer M. Ilenstine
Laurie L. Johnston
Karen A. Kalzer
Craig L. McIvor
Dirk J. Muse
Tisha F. Pagalilauan
Jason D. Ryning
Justin D. Sudweeks
Tamera L. Williams
Kelly M. Willig

OF COUNSEL

John P. Cook

For full biographical listings, see the Martindale-Hubbell Law Directory

MADDEN, POLIAK, MACDOUGALL & WILLIAMSON (AV)

1001 Fourth Avenue Plaza, Suite 2800, 98154
Telephone: 206-621-1011
Telecopier: 206-622-6805
Email: maddenpoliak@msn.com

William J. Madden (1908-1987)
Paul M. Poliak
Allan L. MacDougall
Michael H. Williamson
Rodney Q. Fonda
Craig L. Watson
Bradley P. Scarp
Tom Montgomery

Representative Clients: American International Marine Agency; Chubb Pacific Indemnity; CIGNA; Colony Insurance Company; Commercial Fisherman's Inter-Insurance Exchange; Commercial Union; Fireman's Fund Insurance Company; GRE (Albany); Great American Insurance Company; Highlands Insurance Company.

For full biographical listings, see the Martindale-Hubbell Law Directory

MURRAY, DUNHAM & MURRAY (AV)

3200 Union Bank of California Center, 900 Fourth Avenue, 98164-1001
Telephone: 206-622-2655
Fax: 206-684-6924
Email: murrayz@ibm.net

MEMBERS OF FIRM

(Retired) Wayne Murray
Roger E. Dunham
Matt Murray
Harold B. Field
William W. Spencer
Jeffory E. Adams
Vali M. Somers
Michael K. Taylor
Michael J. McGurn

ASSOCIATES

Ronald L. Unger
Deborah S.C. Sheldon
John E. Schaefers
Andrea E. Holburn
Satwant K. Atwal
Theodore G. Bryant

Representative Clients: Mutual of Enumclaw Insurance Co.; United States Fidelity and Guaranty Co.; St. Paul Fire & Marine Insurance Co.; Allstate Insurance Co.; Federated American Insurance Co.; National Merit Insurance Co.; California State Automobile Assn.; Liberty Mutual Insurance Co.; Orion Auto, Inc.; Nevada General Ins. Co.

For full biographical listings, see the Martindale-Hubbell Law Directory

OLES, MORRISON, RINKER & BAKER L.L.P. (AV)

3300 Columbia Center, 701 Fifth Avenue, 98104-7082
Telephone: 206-623-3427
Telecopier: 206-682-6234
Email: omr@oles.com *URL:* http://www.omr@oles.com
Anchorage, Alaska Office: 745 West 4th Avenue, Suite 502.
Telephone: 907-258-0106.
Fax: 907-277-8002.

MEMBERS OF FIRM

Seth W. Morrison
Arthur D. McGarry
Bradley L. Powell
Traeger Machetanz

ASSOCIATES

William K. Renno (Resident, Anchorage Office)
Catherine C. Clark
Mark D. Walters
W. Gregory Guedel

For Complete List of Firm Personnel, See General Section

For full biographical listings, see the Martindale-Hubbell Law Directory

PREG O'DONNELL & GILLETT PLLC (AV)

The Financial Center, Suite 920, 1215 Fourth Avenue, 98161-1008
Telephone: 206-287-1775
Facsimile: 206-287-9113
Anchorage, Alaska Office: 310 K Street, Suite 405, 99501.
Telephone: 907-274-1544.
Fax: 907-276-5291.

Theodore L. Preg
Mark F. O'Donnell
Eric P. Gillett
Charles A. Willmes
Larry E. Leggett

(See Next Column)

Susan E. Spuller
Bennett J. Hansen
Jeffrey W. Daly
Aaron Dean
Lori K. O'Tool
Tyler M. Johnson

For full biographical listings, see the Martindale-Hubbell Law Directory

TODD & WAKEFIELD (AV)

2100 Century Square, 1501 Fourth Avenue, 98101-1662
Telephone: 206-622-3585
Fax: 206-583-8980
Email: twlaw@twlaw.com

Stephen M. Todd
Scott Channing Wakefield

ASSOCIATES

Robert A. Mannheimer
Mark R. Koenig

LEGAL SUPPORT PERSONNEL

Ellen Roberts
Barbara Erickson

For full biographical listings, see the Martindale-Hubbell Law Directory

WEST VIRGINIA

*BECKLEY,** Raleigh Co.

FILE, PAYNE, SCHERER & FILE (AV)

Law Building, 130 Main Street, P.O. Drawer L, 25802
Telephone: 304-253-3358
Fax: 304-255-5136
Email: filepayne@mtneer.net

MEMBERS OF FIRM

Edward M. Payne, III
John Payne Scherer
Robert N. File
William H. File, III

ASSOCIATE

Floyd M. Sayre, III

OF COUNSEL

William Henry File, Jr.

Representative Clients: Federal Insurance Co.; Globe Indemnity Co.; Nationwide Insurance Co.; Horace Mann Insurance Co.; Metropolitan Property and Liability Insurance Co.; Prudential Insurance; Federated Insurance; Kemper Insurance; Professional Medical Insurance Company; Lloyd's of London.

For full biographical listings, see the Martindale-Hubbell Law Directory

*CHARLESTON,** Kanawha Co.

JACKSON & KELLY (AV)

1600 Laidley Tower, P.O. Box 553, 25322
Telephone: 304-340-1000
Fax: 304-340-1130
Email: info@jacksonkelly.com *URL:* http://www.jacksonkelly.com
Martinsburg, West Virginia Office: 300 Foxcroft Avenue, P.O. Box 1068.
Telephone: 304-263-8800.
Fax: 304-263-7110.
Morgantown, West Virginia Office: 6000 Hampton Center, P.O. Box 619.
Telephone: 304-599-3000.
Fax: 304-285-2040.
New Martinsville, West Virginia Office: 256 Russell Avenue, P.O. Box 68.
Telephone: 304-455-1751.
Fax: 304-455-6314.
Parkersburg, West Virginia Office: 412 Market Street, Suite 202, P.O. Box 1144.
Telephone: 304-424-3490.
Fax: 304-424-3499.
Fairmont, West Virginia Office: 1000 Technology Drive, Suite 1310.
Telephone: 304-368-2000.
Fax: 304-368-2020.
Lexington, Kentucky Office: 175 East Main Street, Suite 500, P.O. Box 2150.
Telephone: 606-255-9500.
Fax: 606-281-6478.
Washington, D. C. Office: 2401 Pennsylvania Avenue, N.W., Suite 400.
Telephone: 202-973-0200.
Fax: 202-973-0232.
Denver, Colorado Office: Suite 2710, 1660 Lincoln Street.
Telephone: 303-390-0003.
Fax: 303-390-0040.
Wheeling, West Virginia Office: 1144 Market Street.
Telephone: 304-233-4000.
Fax: 304-233-4077.

MEMBERS OF FIRM

John M. Slack, III
A. L. Emch
William A. Hoskins, III (Administrative Manager, Lexington, Kentucky Office)
Larry W. Blalock (Administrative Manager, New Martinsville and Wheeling, West Virginia Offices)

(See Next Column)

JACKSON & KELLY—*Continued*

MEMBERS OF FIRM (Continued)

Gary W. Hart
Lynn Oliver Frye
Gale Reddie Lea
Stephen M. LaCagnin (Administrative Manager, Morgantown, West Virginia Office)
William Prentice Young (Martinsburg and Charles Town, West Virginia Offices)

Representative Clients: Home Insurance Company; ITT Hartford; Reliance Insurance Company; USAA Property & Casualty Insurance Company; Government Employees Insurance Company; Metropolitan Life Insurance Company; Prudential Insurance Company of America; Medical Assurance of West Virginia, Inc.; Anthem Personal Insurance Co.

For Complete List of Firm Personnel, See General Section

For full biographical listings, see the Martindale-Hubbell Law Directory

SHUMAN ANNAND BAILEY WYANT & EARLES (AV)

Suite 1007, 405 Capitol Street, P.O. Box 3953, 25339
Telephone: 304-345-1400
Telecopier: 304-343-1826
Email: shuman@newwave.net
Wheeling, West Virginia Office: Suite 3002, 1233 Main Street, 26003.
Telephone: 304-233-3100.
Telecopier: 304-233-0201.

MEMBERS OF FIRM

David L. Shuman
Stephen Darley Annand
Charles R. Bailey
Richard L. Earles
David L. Wyant (Resident, Wheeling, West Virginia Office)
Mark William Browning
William R. Slicer
George J. Joseph
Thomas E. Buck (Resident at Wheeling, West Virginia Office)

ASSOCIATES

DesireéHalkias Divita
Roberta F. Green
Paul Kipling Reese
Heidi A. Kossuth (Resident, Wheeling, West Virginia Office)
Lou Ann S. Cassell
Dwayne E. Cyrus
Eric W. Santos (Not admitted in WV; Resident, Wheeling, West Virginia Office)
John T. Molleur
Mark A. Kepple (Resident, Wheeling, West Virginia Office)
David J. Mincer
Karen M. Tracy
Virginia Ann Grottendieck
Arden J. Cogar
Melissa A. Morris
Stacie L. Price (Resident, Wheeling, West Virginia Office)
J. Parker Bazzle
Lisa Bray
Darin C. James
Brian D. Morrison

OF COUNSEL

John F. McCuskey

Representative Clients: American International/Companies (AIG); CNA Insurance Companies; Insurance Corporation of America; Metropolitan Property & Liability Insurance Co.; MMI Companies, Inc.; Motorists Insurance Cos.; Travelers Insurance Cos.; Westfield Companies.
Reference: One Valley Bank.

For full biographical listings, see the Martindale-Hubbell Law Directory

*CLARKSBURG,** Harrison Co.

MCNEER, HIGHLAND, MCMUNN AND VARNER, L.C. (AV)

One Valley Bank Building, P.O. Drawer 2040, 26302-2040
Telephone: 304-626-1100
Facsimile: 304-623-3035
Martinsburg Office: 2520 Aikens Center, P.O. Box 2509.
Telephone: 304-264-4621.
Fax: 304-264-8623.
Parkersburg Office: 404 Market Street, Suite 204, P.O. Box 1507.
Telephone: 304-422-7193.
Facsimile: 304-422-7196.

C. David McMunn
J. Cecil Jarvis
James A. Varner
Robert W. Trumble (Resident, Martinsburg Office)
Catherine D. Munster
James N. Riley
Steven R. Bratke (Resident, Parkersburg Office)
Michael J. Novotny (Resident, Martinsburg Office)
Dennis M. Shreve
Geraldine S. Roberts
William F. Rohrbaugh (Resident, Martinsburg Office)
Gregory H. Schillace
Judy L. Shanholtz
Tiffany R. Durst
Gene W. Bailey, II

OF COUNSEL

James E. McNeer
Cecil B. Highland, Jr.
William L. Fury

Representative Clients: One Valley Bank of Clarksburg, National Assn.; Bruceton Bank; Harrison County Bank; Nationwide Mutual Insurance Cos.; Clarksburg Publishing Co.; C.I.T. Financial Services; State Automobile Mutual Insurance Co.; United Hospital Center, Inc.; West Virginia Coals, Inc.; Swanson Plating Co.

For full biographical listings, see the Martindale-Hubbell Law Directory

WATERS, WARNER & HARRIS, PLLC (AV)

Formerly Stathers & Cantrall
701 Goff Building, P.O. Box 1716, 26301
Telephone: 304-624-5571
Fax: 304-624-7228
Email: wwh.atty@northnap.citynet.net

Birk S. Stathers (1884-1945)
W. G. Stathers (1889-1970)
Arch M. Cantrall (1896-1967)
Stuart R. Waters
Boyd L. Warner
James A. Harris
Scott E. Wilson
James C. Turner
G. Thomas Smith

ASSOCIATES

D. Andrew McMunn
David C. Glover

Representative Clients: United States Fidelity and Guaranty Co.; State Farm Insurance Companies; Westfield Insurance Company; Nationwide Insurance Company; The Shelby Mutual Insurance Co.

For full biographical listings, see the Martindale-Hubbell Law Directory

*FAIRMONT,** Marion Co.

FURBEE, AMOS, WEBB & CRITCHFIELD (AV)

132 Adams Street, P.O. Box 1189, 26555
Telephone: 304-363-8800
Telecopier: 304-366-3783
Morgantown, West Virginia Office: 5000 Hampton Center, Suite 4.
Telephone: 304-598-0900.
Telecopier: 304-598-2712.

MEMBERS OF FIRM

Russell L. Furbee (1898-1978)
John D. Amos
Benjamin Hays Webb
Charles Vincent Critchfield
Alfred J. Lemley
Billy Atkins
Kenneth R. Miller
Stephen R. Brooks
William T. Holmes
Debra Hodges Scudiere (Resident at Morgantown Office)
Rebecca J. Zuleski
Tamara J. DeFazio

ASSOCIATE

Peter T. DeMasters

Representative Clients: CNA Insurance Co.; Aetna Life and Casualty; Prudential Insurance Company of America; Continental Casualty Co.; State Farm Insurance Co.; Nationwide Insurance Co.; Insurance Company of North America; Fireman's Fund; Employers Liability Insurance Co.; U.S.F. & G. Hartford Accident & Indemnity Co.

For full biographical listings, see the Martindale-Hubbell Law Directory

HUNTINGTON, Cabell & Wayne Cos.

BAKER, LANCIANESE, CAMPBELL & CONATY (AV)

The River Tower, 1108 Third Avenue, Suite 300, 25701-1578
Telephone: 304-522-6906
Facsimile: 304-522-6910
Email: BLCC@BLCCLAW.COM *URL:* http://www.BLCCLAW.COM
Washington, D.C. Office: 1090 Vermont Avenue, N.W. Suite 800.
Telephone: 202-966-1500.
Fax: 202-966-7075. E-Mail: BLCC@BLCCLAW.COM.
Lexington, Kentucky Office: 2265 Harrodsburg Road, Suite 200, 40504-3517.
Telephone: 606-278-0297.
Fax: 206-278-0334. E-Mail: BLCC@BLCCLAW.COM.

Roy D. Baker, Jr.
Richard L. Lancianese
David L. Campbell
Brian P. Conaty
Janice P. Epperly

OF COUNSEL

Margaret M. Brizzolara (Not admitted in WV)

For full biographical listings, see the Martindale-Hubbell Law Directory

OFFUTT, FISHER & NORD (AV)

949 Third Avenue, Suite 300, P.O. Box 2868, 25728-2868
Telephone: 304-529-2868; Toll Free: 1-800-529-2868
Fax: 304-529-2999
Charleston
Email: oefn@earthlink.net
Charleston, West Virginia Office: 208 Capitol Street, Suite 400, 25530.
Telephone: 304-343-2869.
Fax: 304-343-3053.

MEMBERS OF FIRM

D. C. Offutt, Jr.
Michael M. Fisher
Steven K. Nord

(See Next Column)

OFFUTT, FISHER & NORD, *Huntington—Continued*

ASSOCIATES

Scott W. Andrews
Sonja L. Carpenter
Perry W. Oxley
Tammy R. Harvey
Monica L. Robinson

Representative Clients: St. Paul Insurance Co.; Home Insurance Co.; Federal Kemper Insurance Co.; Insurance Corporation of America; Erie Insurance Co.; Continental Insurance Co.; Liberty Mutual Insurance Co.; Colonial Insurance Company of California; CIGNA Insurance Cos.; Westfield Insurance Co.

For full biographical listings, see the Martindale-Hubbell Law Directory

*WHEELING,** Ohio Co.

BACHMANN, HESS, BACHMANN & GARDEN, P.L.L.C. (AV)

1226 Chapline Street, P.O. Box 351, 26003-0046
Telephone: 304-233-3511
Fax: 304-233-3199
Email: info@bhbglaw.com *URL:* http://www.bhbglaw.com

MEMBERS OF FIRM

Carl G. Bachmann (1890-1980)
Lester C. Hess (1903-1971)
John B. Garden (1925-1994)
Gilbert S. Bachmann
Lester C. Hess, Jr.
John L. Allen
Paul T. Tucker
George E. McLaughlin
Jeffrey R. Miller
Anthony Ira Werner
Jeffrey A. Grove
Elizabeth Abraham Delk

ASSOCIATE

David L. Delk, Jr.

Representative Clients: Allstate Insurance Co.; Anthem Casualty Insurance Group; The Cincinnati Insurance Co.; Worldwide Insurance Co.; Horace Mann Insurance Co.; Canal Insurance Co.; Metropolitan Life Insurance Co.; Nationwide Insurance Co.; The Travelers Insurance Co.

For full biographical listings, see the Martindale-Hubbell Law Directory

SCHRADER BYRD & COMPANION, PLLC (AV)

(A Professional Limited Liability Company)
The Maxwell Centre, 32-20th Street, Suite 500, P.O. Box 6336, 26003
Telephone: 304-233-3390
Fax: 304-233-2769
URL: http://www.schraderlaw.com
Martins Ferry, Ohio Office: 205 North Fifth Street, P.O. Box 309, 43935.
Telephone: 740-633-9976.
Fax: 740-633-0400.
Weirton, West Virginia Office: 3205 Pennsylvania Avenue, Suite 103, Penn Place, P.O. Box 2785, 26062.
Telephone: 304-723-2674.
Fax: 304-723-2876.

MEMBERS

Ray A. Byrd
James F. Companion
Frank X. Duff
Teresa Rieman-Camilletti
Yolonda G. Lambert
Daniel P. Fry (Resident Partner, Martins Ferry, Ohio Office)
James P. Mazzone (Resident Member, Weirton, West Virginia Office)
Sandra K. Law
D. Kevin Coleman

SPECIAL COUNSEL

Thomas B. Miller

ASSOCIATES

Denise D. Klug
Michael A. Adams
John Porco
Aimee Morgan Stern
Kimberly R. Wilson
Christopher J. Adams

OF COUNSEL

James A. Byrum, Jr.

General Counsel: Reynolds Memorial Hospital; WesBanco Bank-Elm Grove.
Representative Clients: American Cyanamid Company; Bank One; Matlack Systems, Inc.; Moutaineer Gas Co.; Ohio County Board of Education; PHICO Insurance Co.; Wheeling Hospital; Wheeling-Pittsburg Steel Corp.

For full biographical listings, see the Martindale-Hubbell Law Directory

WISCONSIN

*APPLETON,** Outagamie Co.

MCCANNA, KONZ, DUDAS, KEWLEY & PAPENDORF, S.C. (AV)

Forty Seven Park Place, P.O. Box 1857, 54913-1857
Telephone: 920-734-2825
Fax: 920-734-9770
Email: mkdlegal@aol.com

(See Next Column)

Michael R. McCanna
Michael P. Konz
David G. Dudas
Richard Kewley, Jr.
Jarrod J. Papendorf

Representative Clients: American States Insurance Co.; Auto Owners Insurance Co.; Custom Marine Engineering, Inc.; Economy Fire & Casualty Co.; C. R. Meyer & Sons Company; Northbrook Property & Casualty Co.; State Farm Cos.; West Bend Mutual Insurance Co.; Montgomery Elevator Inc.

For full biographical listings, see the Martindale-Hubbell Law Directory

BROOKFIELD, Waukesha Co.

NELSON, DRIES, CONNELL & KRAMER, S.C. (AV)

150 North Sunnyslope Road, Suite 305, 53005
Telephone: 262-789-5880
Facsimile: 262-789-5888
Email: ndck@execpc.com

Christine K. Nelson
Craig W. Nelson
James J. Dries
Robert W. Connell
Mark S. Nelson
Mark R. Kramer
Christopher J. Conrad
Philip J. Tallmadge
Jennifer C. Tierney

For full biographical listings, see the Martindale-Hubbell Law Directory

*EAU CLAIRE,** Eau Claire Co.

GARVEY, ANDERSON, JOHNSON, GABLER & GERACI, S.C. (AV)

402 Graham Avenue, P.O. Box 187, 54702-0187
Telephone: 715-834-3425
FAX: 715-834-9240

James E. Garvey
Douglas M. Johnson
William M. Gabler
Carol S. Dittmar
Steven V. Schlitz

Representative Clients: Chubb Group of Insurance Co.; Midwest Family Mutual Ins. Co.; General Casualty Insurance Co.; Grinnell Mutual Insurance Co.; Heritage Mutual Insurance Co.; Horace Mann Insurance Co.; Milwaukee Mutual Insurance Co.; Progressive Casualty Insurance Co.; Society Insurance a Mutual Company; United Fire & Casualty Co.

For Complete List of Firm Personnel, See General Section

For full biographical listings, see the Martindale-Hubbell Law Directory

WILCOX, WILCOX, ENRIGHT, HALLSTEIN, MCMAHON & ADLER, LLC (AV)

Limited Liability Company
1030 Regis Court, P.O. Box 128, 54701
Telephone: 715-832-6645
Fax: 715-832-8438
Email: willaw@win.bright.net

MEMBERS OF FIRM

Roy P. Wilcox (1873-1946)
Francis J. Wilcox
Roy S. Wilcox
Daniel A. Enright
John F. Wilcox
Howard G. McMahon
George W. Hallstein
Timothy J. Adler

Attorneys for: Aetna Insurance Group; Medical Protective Assn.; American Surety Co.; Viking Insurance Co.; American Mutual Liability Ins. Co.; Continental Cas. Co.; Farmers Insurance Group.

For full biographical listings, see the Martindale-Hubbell Law Directory

*FOND DU LAC,** Fond du Lac Co.

HERRICK LAW OFFICE, S.C. (AV)

45 Sheboygan Street, P.O. Box 1378, 54936-1378
Telephone: 920-923-6522
Fax: 920-923-6388

James C. Herrick, Jr.
John W. Herrick

For full biographical listings, see the Martindale-Hubbell Law Directory

*GREEN BAY,** Brown Co.

EVERSON, WHITNEY, EVERSON & BREHM, S.C. (AV)

Suite 106, 125 South Jefferson Street, P.O. Box 22248, 54305-2248
Telephone: 920-435-3734
Fax: 920-435-0126
Email: eweb@execpc.com

John C. Whitney (1915-1994)
Philip R. Brehm
John E. Herald
Rodney A. Charnholm
George F. Savage
Peter J. Hickey
Susan J. Reigel
John M. Thompson, IV
Jeffrey T. DeMeuse
John H. Heide

OF COUNSEL

James L. Everson

(See Next Column)

EVERSON, WHITNEY, EVERSON & BREHM S.C.—*Continued*

Peter C. Brehm
Katherine L. Pleger
Erik J. Pless

LEGAL SUPPORT PERSONNEL

PARALEGAL

Cheryl Lynn Morin

Counsel for: American Family Insurance; Bank One; Rural Mutual Medical Protective; U.S. Fidelity & Guaranty Co.; Employers Insurance of Wausau; State Farm Mutual Cos.; Travelers Insurance Co.; Farmers Insurance Group; Liberty Mutual Insurance Co.

For full biographical listings, see the Martindale-Hubbell Law Directory

*MADISON,** Dane Co.

AXLEY BRYNELSON, LLP (AV)

(Formerly Brynelson, Herrick, Bucaida, Dorschel & Armstrong Including the former Easton & Assoc., S.C.)
2 East Mifflin Street, P.O. Box 1767, 53701-1767
Telephone: 608-257-5661
Fax: 608-257-5444
Email: law@axley.com *URL:* http://www.axley.com

MEMBERS OF FIRM

Bradley D. Armstrong
John H. Schmid, Jr.
Timothy D. Fenner
John C. Mitby
Daniel T. Hardy
John Walsh
Bruce L. Harms
David Easton
Curtis C. Swanson
Michael S. Anderson
Patricia M. Gibeault
Michael J. Westcott
Larry K. Libman
Richard E. Petershack
Steven A. Brezinski
Steven M. Streck
Joy L. O'Grosky
Arthur E. Kurtz
Edith F. Merila
Michael J. Modl

OF COUNSEL

Ralph E. Axley (1902-1995)
Floyd A. Brynelson (1914-1998)
James C. Herrick
Frank J. Bucaida
Griffin G. Dorschel

For Complete List of Firm Personnel, See General Section

For full biographical listings, see the Martindale-Hubbell Law Directory

KAY & ANDERSEN, S.C. (AV)

One Point Place, Suite 201, 53719
Telephone: 608-833-0077
Fax: 608-833-3901
Email: KandA@execpc.com

Robert J. Kay
Randall J. Andersen

James N. Graham
Robert A. Mich, Jr.

For full biographical listings, see the Martindale-Hubbell Law Directory

*MILWAUKEE,** Milwaukee Co.

BRENNAN & COLLINS (AV)

Suite 700, 788 North Jefferson Street, 53202
Telephone: 414-276-2066
Fax: 414-276-1476
Email: bren-col@execpc.com

MEMBERS OF FIRM

James P. Brennan
Charles W. Collins

Russell D. Bohach
Joseph E. Schubert
Meghan M. O'Callaghan

For full biographical listings, see the Martindale-Hubbell Law Directory

FELLOWS, PIPER & SCHMIDT (AV)

733 North Van Buren Street, 53202-4705
Telephone: 414-225-4060
Fax: 414-271-6196
Email: fpslaw.com

MEMBERS OF FIRM

Donald H. Piper
Richard E. Schmidt
Terry J. Booth
Robert E. Neville
Joseph M. Wirth
Steven T. Caya

ASSOCIATES

Daniel J. Jungen
Allen M. Ratkowski
Ronald W. Harmeyer
Amy E. Wochos
Shannon M. Whitworth
Lisa M. Wilson

(See Next Column)

OF COUNSEL

Donald C. Fellows

Representative Clients: The Atlantic Companies; Blue Cross & Blue Shield United of Wisconsin; Church Mutual Insurance Co.; Economy Fire & Casualty Co.; Farmers Insurance Group; General Casualty Cos.

For full biographical listings, see the Martindale-Hubbell Law Directory

GUTGLASS ERICKSON & BONVILLE, S.C. (AV)

Suite 1400, 735 North Water Street, 53202-4267
Telephone: 414-273-1144
Fax: 414-273-3821
Email: GUTGLASS@mixcom.com

James R. Gutglass
Paul R. Erickson
Kathleen E. Bonville
Mark E. Larson
Colleen M. Fleming

Sharon R. Long
Peter W. McCombs
Maria K. Schneider

For full biographical listings, see the Martindale-Hubbell Law Directory

KASDORF, LEWIS & SWIETLIK, S.C. (AV)

1551 South 108th Street, 53214
Telephone: 414-257-1055
Facsimile: 414-257-3759
Green Bay, Wisconsin Office: 727 East Walnut Street, 54301.
Telephone: 920-436-0304.
Wausau, Wisconsin Office: 2100 Stewart Avenue, Suite 230, 54401.
Telephone: 715-848-9250.
Facsimile: 715-849-2017.

James P. Reardon
Werner E. Scherr
Terrance E. Davczyk
Jeff Schmeckpeper
Gregory J. Cook
Michael J. Cieslewicz
Michael A. Mesirow
Joseph J. Ferris
James J. Kriva
David L. Styer
Robert J. Lauer
James M. Ryan
Robert P. Ochowicz

Michael C. Frohman
Charles G. Maris
Vicki L. Arrowood
Michael S. Murray
Peter J. Eckardt (Resident)
Christine D. Esser
Thomas A. Cabush
John K. Garofani
Bonni D. Fredrick
Christopher A. Duesing
Daniel W. Varline
(Resident, Wausau Office)
Jerome A. Long
(Resident, Wausau Office)

OF COUNSEL

Clifford C. Kasdorf
John M. Swietlik
Hugh E. Russell
Patti J. Kurth

Representative Clients: State Farm Insurance Cos.; Crum & Forster; Kemper Insurance Cos.; Allstate Insurance Cos.; Employers Mutual Insurance Cos.; Fireman's Fund Insurance Cos.; American International Group; Liberty Mutual Insurance; Progressive Insurance Cos.

For full biographical listings, see the Martindale-Hubbell Law Directory

KRAVIT, GASS, HOVEL & LEITNER S.C. (AV)

825 North Jefferson, 53202-3737
Telephone: 414-271-7100
Fax: 414-271-8135
Email: Info@kravit-gass.com

Stephen E. Kravit
J. Ric Gass
Mark M. Leitner
Mary S. Ogorchock
Thomas K. Mullins
Jay R. Starrett
John J. Laffey
Brian D. Trexell
Michael D. Rosenberg
Marilyn M. Carroll
Molly J. Zillig
C. Claibourne Greene
Karen Tidwall
Susan A. Philpott

Representative Clients: Acceptance Insurance; Bituminous Insurance; The Cincinnati Insurance Companies; Cooper Industries; Fireman's Fund Insurance Companies; Great American Insurance; Midland National Life Insurance; Northland Insurance; Progressive Insurance; Reliance Insurance.

For full biographical listings, see the Martindale-Hubbell Law Directory

MUELLER, GOSS & POSSI, S.C. (AV)

Suite 600 Commerce Center, 744 North Fourth Street, 53203-2177
Telephone: 414-278-0303
Facsimile: 414-278-0367

Richard T. Mueller
Thomas E. Goss, Jr.
John C. Possi, Jr.

Kevin T. Roach

OF COUNSEL

Thomas J. Mueller

For full biographical listings, see the Martindale-Hubbell Law Directory

Milwaukee—Continued

OTJEN, VAN ERT, LIEB & WEIR, S.C. (AV)

First Financial Centre, 700 North Water Street, Suite 800, 53202-4206
Telephone: 414-271-7271
Fax: 414-271-7272
Madison, Wisconsin Office: 450 Science Drive, Suite 110, 53711.
Telephone: 608-238-9500.
Fax: 608-238-9599.

Wayne R. Van Ert
Donald M. Lieb
Todd M. Weir
Lori Gendelman
Paul J. Pytlik
Thomas J. Binder
Stephen O. Murray (Resident, Madison Office)
Thomas M. Rohe
Theodore T. Balistreri
Joseph Berger

Rhonda Devorkin
Jeffrey J. P. Conta
Jennifer Anne Slater Carlson
Brett D. Stacey
Matthew C. Siderits
Terri Weber (Resident, Madison Office)
Jason Franckowiak

OF COUNSEL

Carl N. Otjen

Representative Clients: International Harvester Co.; Continental Insurance Companies.
Reference: Marine Bank, N.A.

For full biographical listings, see the Martindale-Hubbell Law Directory

QUALE, FELDBRUEGGE, CALVELLI, THOM & CROKE, S.C. (AV)

(Formerly Prosser, Wiedabach & Quale, S.C.)
710 North Plankinton Avenue, 9th Floor, 53203-2404
Telephone: 414-271-2266
FAX: 414-276-0417
Email: qfctc@execpc.com

Frederick H. Prosser (1901-1981)
David M. Quale (1932-1997)
John E. Feldbruegge
Rocke A. Calvelli
Terrence C. Thom
William P. Croke
Dorothy H. Dey

Bradley S. Foley

OF COUNSEL

Jack R. Wiedabach

For full biographical listings, see the Martindale-Hubbell Law Directory

SCHELLINGER & DOYLE, S.C. (AV)

Stone Ridge II, Suite 280, N14 W23777 Stone Ridge Drive (Waukesha), 53188-1158
Telephone: 262-523-2080
Fax: 262-523-2088

Stanley F. Schellinger (1923-1983)
James G. Doyle
Timothy J. Strattner
Paul J. Kelly
Linda Vogt Meagher

Donald P. Schneider
Amy J. Doyle

Representative Clients: Wisconsin Health Care Liability Insurance Plan; Wausau Insurance Cos.; The Medical Protective Co.; Admiral Insurance Co.; Fireman's Fund Insurance Cos.; Unigard Insurance Co.; Commercial Union; Carolina Casualty Insurance Co.

For full biographical listings, see the Martindale-Hubbell Law Directory

LAW OFFICES OF SCOTT G. THOMAS (AV)

411 East Wisconsin Avenue, Suite 1040, 53202
Telephone: 414-291-7680
Fax: 414-291-7688
Email: sgtesq@execpc.com

STAFF COUNSEL
AMERICAN INTERNATIONAL COMPANIES
MANAGING ATTORNEY

Scott G. Thomas

For full biographical listings, see the Martindale-Hubbell Law Directory

NEENAH, Winnebago Co.

DI RENZO AND BOMIER, LLC (AV)

231 East Wisconsin Avenue, P.O. Box 788, 54957-0788
Telephone: 920-725-8464
Fax: 920-725-8568
Email: direnzolaw@aol.com

MEMBERS OF FIRM

Philip A. Munroe
Samuel J. Bomier

(See Next Column)

ASSOCIATES

Steven R. Schilke
Troy D. Thompson

Representative Clients: Aetna Casualty and Surety Company; Employers Mutual Companies; General Casualty Insurance Co. of Wisconsin; Harco National Insurance Company; United Heartland Insurance Company; Evergreen National Indemnity Co.; Economy Fire & Casualty Co.; St. Paul Fire and Marine Insurance Co.; Secura Insurance, Appleton, WI.

For Complete List of Firm Personnel, See General Section

For full biographical listings, see the Martindale-Hubbell Law Directory

*RACINE,** Racine Co.

JEFFREY LEAVELL, S.C. (AV)

723 South Main Street, 53403
Telephone: 414-633-7322
Fax: 414-633-7323
Email: 102661.3312@compuserve.com

Jeffrey L. Leavell

ASSOCIATES

Michael R. Vescio
Christine M. Genthner

For full biographical listings, see the Martindale-Hubbell Law Directory

*RHINELANDER,** Oneida Co.

ECKERT KOST & VOCKE (AV)

1285 Lincoln Street, P.O. Box 1247, 54501-1247
Telephone: 715-369-1624
FAX: 715-369-1273
Email: ecklaw@newnorth.net *URL:* http://www.ecklaw.com

Michael L. Eckert
Keith K. Kost
Timothy L. Vocke
Mitchell R. Olson

Reference: M & I Merchants Bank.

For full biographical listings, see the Martindale-Hubbell Law Directory

*WAUSAU,** Marathon Co.

TERWILLIGER, WAKEEN, PIEHLER & CONWAY, S.C. (AV)

555 Scott Street, P.O. Box 8063, 54402-8063
Telephone: 715-845-2121
Fax: 715-845-3538
Email: twpc@execpc.com *URL:* http://www.lawyers.com/twpc

W. Thomas Terwilliger
Walter Gene Lew
Robert D. Reid
John P. Runde
John R. Shull, Jr.

For full biographical listings, see the Martindale-Hubbell Law Directory

WYOMING

*CASPER,** Natrona Co.

BROWN, DREW & MASSEY, LLP (AV)

Casper Business Center, Suite 800, 123 West First Street, 82601-2486
Telephone: 307-234-1000
800-877-6755
Telefax: 307-265-8025
Email: brwndrew@coffey.com

MEMBERS OF FIRM

Donn J. McCall
J. Kenneth Barbe
Jeffrey C. Brinkerhoff
Rex O. Arney
Courtney Robert Kepler

ASSOCIATES

Scott P. Klosterman
Timothy M. Stubson

OF COUNSEL

Hampton K. O'Neill

Attorneys for: Aetna Casualty & Surety Co.; Bituminous Insurance Companies; CIGNA; Commercial Union Insurance Co.; Crum & Forster Managers Corp.; ITT Hartford Insurance Co.; The Doctor's Co.; MEDMARC; State Farm Mutual Automobile Insurance Co.; United Pacific Insurance.

For Complete List of Firm Personnel, See General Section

For full biographical listings, see the Martindale-Hubbell Law Directory

WILLIAMS, PORTER, DAY & NEVILLE, P.C. (AV)

159 North Wolcott Street Suite 400, P.O. Box 10700, 82602
Telephone: 307-265-0700
Fax: 307-266-2306
Email: wpdn@trib.com

(See Next Column)

WILLIAMS, PORTER, DAY & NEVILLE P.C.—*Continued*

Richard E. Day
Frank D. Neville
Patrick J. Murphy
Stuart R. Day
Ann M. Rochelle
Mark L. Carman
Stephenson D. Emery
Scott E. Ortiz
Scott W. Skavdahl

Representative Clients: ITT Hartford Insurance Group; Fireman's Fund Insurance Co.; Continental Insurance Co.; Wausau Insurance Co.; Home Insurance Co.; The Doctors Company; Ohio Casualty Insurance Co.; Guaranty National Insurance Co.; Bituminous Insurance Companies; Attorneys Liability Protection Society.

For Complete List of Firm Personnel, See General Section

For full biographical listings, see the Martindale-Hubbell Law Directory

*CHEYENNE,** Laramie Co.

LATHROP & RUTLEDGE, A PROFESSIONAL CORPORATION (AV)

Suite 500 City Center Building, 1920 Thomes Avenue, P.O. Box 4068, 82003-4068
Telephone: 307-632-0554
Telecopier: 307-635-4502
Email: mail@lathropandrutledge.com

Carl L. Lathrop
J. Kent Rutledge
Corinne E. Rutledge
James T. Dinneen

Lou Piccioni
Scott W. Meier
Kevin C. Cook

General Counsel for: Laramie County School District No. 2; Cheyenne Newspapers, Inc.; Wyoming Hospital Assn.; Cheyenne Medical Specialists, P.C.; Emergency Medical Physicians.
Insurance Clients: The Doctor's Company; CUMIS Insurance Society; Gainsco, Inc.; The St. Paul Companies; Infinity Insurance Co.

For full biographical listings, see the Martindale-Hubbell Law Directory

SUNDAHL, POWERS, KAPP & MARTIN, L.L.C. (AV)

1725 Carey Avenue, P.O. Box 328, 82001
Telephone: 307-632-6421
Fax: 307-632-7216
Email: atty@spkm.org

MEMBERS OF FIRM

John Alan Sundahl
George E. Powers, Jr.
Paul Kapp
Raymond W. Martin

ASSOCIATES

John A. Coppede
Kay Lynn Bestol
Deborah G. M. Kellam
Brian J. Hanify

A list of Representative Clients will be furnished upon request.

For full biographical listings, see the Martindale-Hubbell Law Directory

PUERTO RICO

SAN JUAN, San Juan Dist.

FIDDLER GONZÁLEZ & RODRÍGUEZ, LLP

254 Muñoz Rivera Avenue (Hato Rey), P.O. Box 363507, 00936-3507
Telephone: 787-753-3113
Telecopier: 787-759-3123
Email: fiddler@fgrlaw.com *URL:* http://www.fgrlaw.com

MEMBERS OF FIRM

Pedro J. Polanco
César T. Alcover-Acosta
Pedro I. Vidal-Cordero

Representative Clients: John Hancock; The Prudential Insurance Co.; Allstate Insurance Co.

For Complete List of Firm Personnel, See General Section

For full biographical listings, see the Martindale-Hubbell Law Directory

JIMÉNEZ, GRAFFAM & LAUSELL

Suite 505, Midtown Building, 421 Muñoz Rivera Avenue, Hato Rey, P.O. Box 366104, 00936-6104
Telephone: 787-767-1030; 767-1000; 767-1061; 767-1064
Telefax: 787-751-4068;
Cable: "Nezte"
RCA Telex: 325-2730
Email: manager@jgl.com *URL:* http://www.jgl.com

MEMBERS OF FIRM

William A. Graffam
Steven C. Lausell
J. Ramón Rivera-Morales
José Juan Torres-Escalera
Manolo T. Rodríguez-Bird

(See Next Column)

ASSOCIATES

Patricia A. Garrity
Isabel J. Vélez-Serrano
Edgardo A. Vega-López
Jorge F. Blasini
Ruy V. Díaz-Díaz
Rafael A. Rosado-Marrero

Representative Clients: Underwriters at Lloyds; Ropner Insurance Co.; Evanston Insurance Co.; Continental Insurance/Commercial Life Insurance Co.; The United Kingdom Steamship P & I Association.

For Complete List of Firm Personnel, See General Section

For full biographical listings, see the Martindale-Hubbell Law Directory

VIRGIN ISLANDS

*CHRISTIANSTED, ST. CROIX,** St. Croix

R. ERIC MOORE (AV)

2108 Company Street, P.O. Box 3086, 00822
Telephone: 340-773-4150
Fax: 340-778-7168
Email: rericmoore@worldnet.att.net

ASSOCIATES

Edgar A. Christensen
Ivan A. Guzman
Odis Simpson Mingus, II
Franklin G. Quow

For full biographical listings, see the Martindale-Hubbell Law Directory

*CHARLOTTE AMALIE, ST. THOMAS,** St. Thomas

GRUNERT STOUT & BRUCH

24-25 Kongensgade, P.O. Box 1030, 00804
Telephone: 340-774-1320
Fax: 340-774-7839
Email: gsbusvi@viaccess.net
Affiliated with: Solomon Pearl Blum & Quinn LLP, New York, New York and Denver, Colorado.

MEMBERS OF FIRM

John E. Stout
Susan Bruch Moorehead

ASSOCIATE

Gabriel J. Villegas

OF COUNSEL

William L. Blum

For full biographical listings, see the Martindale-Hubbell Law Directory

CANADA ALBERTA

*CALGARY,** Calgary Jud. Dist.

PARLEE MCLAWS (AV)

3400 Petro-Canada Centre, 150 - 6th Avenue, SW, T2P 3Y7
Telephone: 403-294-7000
Telecopier: 403-265-8263
Email: lawyers@parlee.com *URL:* http://www.parlee.com
Edmonton, Alberta Office: 15th Floor Manulife Place, 10180 101st Street.
Telephone: 403-423-8500.
Telecopier: 403-423-2870.

MEMBERS OF FIRM

Everett L. Bunnell, Q.C.
Patrick J. McGovern
Bruce Churchill-Smith
Aldo P. Argento
Nancy M. Carruthers

ASSOCIATES

Donald A. Young
Brenda M. Tsukishima
Morey D. Sair
Susan E. Hrychuk
Paul J. Mason
Alec N. Silenzi
Erin A. MacPherson
H. David McLellan

For Complete List of Firm Personnel, See General Section

For full biographical listings, see the Martindale-Hubbell Law Directory

*EDMONTON,** Edmonton Jud. Dist.

PARLEE MCLAWS (AV)

15th Floor Manulife Place, 10180 101st Street, T5J 4K1
Telephone: 403-423-8500
Telecopier: 403-423-2870
Email: lawyers@parlee.com *URL:* http://www.parlee.com
Calgary, Alberta Office: 3400 Petro-Canada Centre, 150 - 6th Avenue, SW.
Telephone: 403-294-7000.
Telecopier: 403-265-8263.

(See Next Column)

PARLEE MCLAWS, *Edmonton—Continued*

MEMBERS OF FIRM

Michael D. MacDonald
Roderick B. Davison, Q.C.
James K. McFadyen
James T. Neilson
James F. McGinnis
Gregory W. Jaycock
Dane C. Wintermute
Anthony W. Slemko
Karen A. Smith
Kenneth F. Bailey, Q.C.
Richard W. Wilson
Robert G. McBean
David C. Rolf
Allan A. Garber
Robert P. James
Jerri L. Cairns
R. Johnson Billingsley
Galan T. Lund

ASSOCIATES

Norah B. Ramsay
Jamie E. Pytel
Rolinda D. Y. Mack
Kim D. Watamaniuk
Carla L. Lamash
Wendy N. Moody
Sandra L. Corbett
Thomas L.B. Carbone
Shawn M. Johanson
J. Kristin Bryson
K. Colleen Verville
Sean P. Tindale

COUNSEL

Edward H. Molstad, Q.C.

For Complete List of Firm Personnel, See General Section

For full biographical listings, see the Martindale-Hubbell Law Directory

CANADA
BRITISH COLUMBIA

*VANCOUVER,** Vancouver Co.

ALEXANDER, HOLBURN, BEAUDIN & LANG (AV)

P.O. Box 10057 2700 Toronto Dominion Bank Tower, 700 West Georgia Street, V7Y 1B8
Telephone: 604-688-1351
Fax: 604-669-7642
URL: http://www.ahbl.bc.ca
Hong Kong Office, In Association with Ong & Chung: Room 2101, 21/F Tower II, Admiralty Centre, No. 18 Harcourt Road.
Telephone: (852) 2526-1171.
Fax: (852) 2845-0686.

PARTNERS

William M. Holburn, Q.C.
James A. Dowler
R. Patrick Saul
Bruno De Vita
Terry C. Vos
Judith P. Kennedy
J. Dale Stewart
Barbara L. Devlin
Eileen E. Vanderburgh
Todd R. Davies
Michael P. Ragona, Q.C.
Robert B. Kennedy
Jo Ann Carmichael
David B. Wende
Gary M. Nijman
Ross Shamenski
Darcie A. Laurient
Sharleen L. Dumont
David A. Garner
D. Christopher Fong
David T. McKnight

ASSOCIATES

David A. Gooderham
Brian D. Rhodes
Robert A. McLennan
Jeremy M. Poole
Moira C. Wong
Susan Sangha
Gregory S. Pun
Judy A. Rost
Joseph P. Cahan
Christopher E. Hirst
Christine M. York
C. Larry Kyle

A list of Representative Clients will be furnished on request.

For Complete List of Firm Personnel, See General Section

For full biographical listings, see the Martindale-Hubbell Law Directory

PAINE EDMONDS (AV)

Suite 1100, 510 Burrard Street, V6C 3A8
Telephone: 604-683-1211
Facsimile: 604-681-5084
Email: law@paine-edmonds.com

W. H. Kemp Edmonds, Q.C. (1916-1986)

MEMBERS OF FIRM

J. Lyle Woodley, Q.C.
James C. Taylor
Elmer A. Yusep
Owen G. Jones
Henry D. M. Edmonds
Steven H. Heringa
John J. Hyde
Bradford D. S. Garside
Kirsten J. Madsen

ASSOCIATES

John Bancroft-Jones
P. L. (Lee) Quinton
S. Jane Clasby
Siobhan Elizabeth Rea
Gary Michael Hagel

(See Next Column)

OF COUNSEL

Leonard C. Dudley

Reference: Toronto Dominion Bank.

For full biographical listings, see the Martindale-Hubbell Law Directory

SINGLETON URQUHART (AV)

1200 - 1125 Howe Street, V6Z 2K8
Telephone: 604-682-7474
Fax: 604-682-1283
Email: reception@singleton.com *URL:* http://www.singleton.com

John R. Singleton, Q.C.
Derek A. Brindle
Jeffery A. Hand
C. L. (Kate) Mclean

ASSOCIATE COUNSEL

Glenn A. Urquhart, Q.C.

Representative Clients: Allianz Canada; Canadian Northern Shield; CGU Insurance; Chubb Insurance Company of Canada; Commonwealth Insurance Company; ENCON Group Inc.; Insurance Corporation of British Columbia; Municipal Insurance Association of British Columbia; Royal Sun Alliance Insurance Company of Canada; St. Paul Fire and Marine Insurance Company.

For Complete List of Firm Personnel, See General Section

For full biographical listings, see the Martindale-Hubbell Law Directory

CANADA
MANITOBA

*WINNIPEG,** Eastern Jud. Dist.

AIKINS, MACAULAY & THORVALDSON (AV)

Thirtieth Floor, Commodity Exchange Tower, 360 Main Street, R3C 4G1
Telephone: 204-957-0050
Fax: 204-957-0840
Email: amt@aikins.com *URL:* http://www.aikins.com

MEMBERS OF FIRM

Knox B. Foster, Q.C.
Rod E. Stephenson, Q.C.
Daryl J. Rosin
G. Todd Campbell
Lori T. Spivak
L. William Bowles
Keith Ferbers
Thor J. Hansell
Helga D. Van Iderstine
Sonya C. McCoshen

Representative Clients: Canadian Medical Protective Assn.; Cigna Insurance Co.; Zurich Insurance Co.; Great-West Life Assurance Co.; Sovereign General Insurance Co.; Wawanesa Mutual Insurance Co.; Royal Insurance Co.; American Home Insurance Co.; Paul Revere Insurance Co.; Dominion of Canada Group.

For Complete List of Firm Personnel, See General Section

For full biographical listings, see the Martindale-Hubbell Law Directory

CANADA
NEW BRUNSWICK

*FREDERICTON,** York Co.

COX HANSON O'REILLY MATHESON (AV)

(Formerly Hanson Hashey)
Suite 400, Phoenix Square, P.O. Box 310, E3B 4Y9
Telephone: 506-453-7771
Fax: 506-453-9600
Email: fredericton@coxhanson.ca *URL:* http://www.coxhanson.ca
Halifax, Nova Scotia Office: Suite 1100, Purdy's Wharf Tower 1, P.O. Box 2380 Station Central RPO, B3J 3E5.
Telephone: 902-421-6262.
Fax: 902-421-3130. E-Mail: halifax@coxhanson.ca
Saint John, New Brunswick Office: 1212-One Brunswick Square, 1 Germain St. E2L 4V1.
Telephone: 506-652-7771.
Fax: 506-632-9600.
St. John's, Newfoundland Office: Scotia Centre, 401-235 Water Street, A1C 1B6.
Telephone: 709-726-3321.
Fax: 709-726-2992. E-Mail: stjohns@coxhanson.ca
Charlottetown, Prince Edward Island Office: Queen Square, Suite 202, 119 Queen Street, P.O. Box 875, Station Central, C1A 7L9.
Telephone: 902-894-7051.
Fax: 902-368-3762. E-Mail: charlottetown@coxhanson.ca

(See Next Column)

COX HANSON O'REILLY MATHESON—*Continued*

MEMBERS OF FIRM

H. A. Hanson, Q.C. (1909-1985)
David T. Hashey, Q.C.
David M. Norman, Q.C.
J. Ian M. Whitcomb, Q.C.
John M. Hanson, Q.C.
Walter D. Vail, Q.C.
Michael E. Bowlin
John D. Larlee, Q.C.
Bruce D. Hatfield, Q.C.
Julian A. G. Dickson, Q.C.
Anne D. Wooder
Terrence J. Morrison
Lucie Richard
Catherine M. Bowlen
J. Marc Richard

ASSOCIATES

Amanda J. Frenette
Monika M. L. Zauhar
Jade A. Spalding
William E. Gould
Christopher R. DeLong
Deborah M. Power
Corinne A. Godbout
Marc-Antoine Chiasson

For full biographical listings, see the Martindale-Hubbell Law Directory

*MONCTON,** Westmorland Co.

McINNES COOPER (AV)

Barristers, Solicitors & Trade Mark Agents
Place Moncton Place, 655 Main Street, P.O. Box 1368, E1C 8T6
Telephone: 506-857-8970
Fax: 506-857-4095
Email: mcrmctn@mcrlaw.com *URL:* http://www.mcrlaw.com
Halifax, Nova Scotia Office: Summit Place, 1601 Lower Water Street, P.O. Box 730, B3J 2V1.
Telephone: 902-425-6500.
Fax: 902-425-6350. Email: mcrhfx@mcrlaw.com.
St. John's, Newfoundland Office: Baine Johnston Centre, 5th Floor, 10 Fort William Place, P.O. Box 5939, A1C 5X4.
Telephone: 709-722-8735.
Telecopier: 709-722-1763. Email: mcrsj@mcrlaw.com.
Charlottetown, Prince Edward Island Office: BDC Place, Suite 620, 119 Kent Street, C1A 1N3.
Telephone: 902-368-8473.
Fax: 902-368-8346. Email: mcrpei@mcrlaw.com.
Fredericton, New Brunswick Office: Suite 600, 570 Queen Street, P.O. Box 610.
Telephone: 506-458-8572.
Fax: 506-458-9903. Email: mcrfton@mcrlaw.com.

PARTNER

Eric LeDrew

ASSOCIATES

John C. Friel, Q.C.
Christa A. Bourque

For Complete List of Firm Personnel, See General Section

For full biographical listings, see the Martindale-Hubbell Law Directory

*SAINT JOHN,** Saint John Co.

CLARK DRUMMIE (AV)

40 Wellington Row, P.O. Box 6850, E2L 4S3
Telephone: 506-633-3800
Telecopier (Automatic): 506-633-3811
Email: cd@nbnet.nb.ca

MEMBERS OF FIRM

Barry R. Morrison, Q.C.
J. George Byrne
Norman J. Bossé
Ewan W. Clark

Reference: Royal Bank of Canada.

For Complete List of Firm Personnel, See General Section

For full biographical listings, see the Martindale-Hubbell Law Directory

GILBERT, McGLOAN, GILLIS (AV)

Suite 710, Mercantile Centre, 55 Union Street, P.O. Box 7174, E2L 4S6
Telephone: 506-634-3600
Telecopier: 506-634-3612
Mailing Address: P.O. Box 7174, Station "A", Saint John, New Brunswick, E2L 4S6
Email: gmg@gmglaw.com

T. Louis McGloan, Q.C. (1896-1986)
Adrian B. Gilbert, Q.C. (1895-1986)

MEMBERS OF FIRM

Donald M. Gillis, Q.C.
Thomas L. McGloan, Q.C.
A. G. Warwick Gilbert, Q.C.
Rodney J. Gillis, Q.C.
Douglas A. M. Evans, Q.C.
Brenda J. Lutz, Q.C.
David N. Rogers
Mark A. Canty

ASSOCIATES

Edward Veitch
Hugh J. Flemming, Q.C.
Anne F. MacNeill
Nancy E. Forbes
Guy C. Spavold
Claire B.N. Porter
Nathalie L. Godbout
Bruce D. Grant
J. Danie Roy
Catherine A. Fawcett
Danys R.X. Delaquis
James M. Barry

(See Next Column)

Representative Clients: Bank of Montreal; Canada Packers Ltd.; McCain Foods Ltd.; The Sunderland Steamship Protecting & Indemnity Association; Steamship Mutual Underwriting Association (Bermuda) Limited; Royal Insurance Co.; Wawanesa Mutual Insurance Co.; Dominion of Canada General Insurance Co.; Canadian General Insurance Co.

For full biographical listings, see the Martindale-Hubbell Law Directory

CANADA NEWFOUNDLAND

*ST. JOHN'S,**

COX HANSON O'REILLY MATHESON (AV)

(Formerly O'Reilly Noseworthy)
Scotia Centre, 401-235 Water Street, A1C 1B6
Telephone: 709-726-3321
Telecopier: 709-726-2992
Email: stjohns@coxhanson.ca *URL:* http://www.coxhanson.ca
Fredericton, New Brunswick Office: Suite 400, Phoenix Square, P.O. Box 310, E3B 4Y9.
Telephone: 506-453-7771.
Fax: 506-453-9600.
Saint John, New Brunswick Office: 1212-One Brunswick Square, 1 Germain St. E2L 4V1.
Telephone: 506-652-7771.
Fax: 506-632-9600.
Halifax, Nova Scotia Office: Suite 1100, Purdy's Wharf Tower 1, P.O. Box 2380 Station Central RPO, B3J 3E5.
Telephone: 902-421-6262.
Fax: 902-421-3130. E-Mail: halifax@coxhanson.ca
Charlottetown, Prince Edward Island Office: Queen Square, 119 Queen Street, P.O. Box 875, Station Central, C1A 7L9.
Telephone: 902-894-7051.
Fax: 902-368-3762. E-Mail: charlottetown@coxhanson.ca

MEMBERS OF FIRM

Thomas J. O'Reilly, Q.C.
Ronald S. Noseworthy, Q.C.
John F. Roil, Q.C.
Reginald H. Brown, Q.C.
Roland C. Snelgrove
D. Richard Robbins
Randall W. Smith
Robert P. Stack
Paul M. McDonald
Sandra R. Chaytor
Jorge P. Segovia
F. Richard Gosse
Griffith D. Roberts
Peter D. Shea
H. Jason Hickman
Michelle A. Willette

For full biographical listings, see the Martindale-Hubbell Law Directory

McINNES COOPER (AV)

Barristers, Solicitors & Trade Mark Agents
Baine Johnston Centre, 5th Floor, 10 Fort William Place, P.O. Box 5939, A1C 5X4
Telephone: 709-722-8735
Telecopier: 709-722-1763
Email: mcrsj@mcrlaw.com *URL:* http://www.mcrlaw.com
Halifax, Nova Scotia Office: Summit Place, 1601 Lower Water Street, P.O. Box 730, B3J 2V1.
Telephone: 902-425-6500.
Fax: 902-425-6350. Email: mcrhfx@mcrlaw.com.
Moncton, New Brunswick Office: Place Moncton Place, 655 Main Street, P.O. Box 1368, E1C 8T6.
Telephone: 506-857-8970.
Fax: 506-857-4095. Email: mcrmctn@mcrlaw.com.
Charlottetown, Prince Edward Island Office: BDC Place, Suite 620, 119 Kent Street, C1A 1N3.
Telephone: 902-368-8473.
Fax: 902-368-8346. Email: mcrpei@mcrlaw.com.
Fredericton, New Brunswick Office: Suite 600, 570 Queen Street, P.O. Box 610.
Telephone: 506-458-8572.
Fax: 506-458-9903. Email: mcrfton@mcrlaw.com.

PARTNERS

J. David B. Eaton
Michael J. Crosbie
Philip J. Buckingham

ASSOCIATES

D. Scott Worsfold
Jennifer Dawn Blackmore

For Complete List of Firm Personnel, See General Section

For full biographical listings, see the Martindale-Hubbell Law Directory

CANADA NOVA SCOTIA

*HALIFAX,** Regional Munic. of Halifax

McINNES COOPER (AV)

Barristers, Solicitors & Trade Mark Agents
Summit Place, 1601 Lower Water Street, P.O. Box 730, B3J 2V1
Telephone: 902-425-6500
Fax: 902-425-6350
Email: mcrhfx@mcrlaw.com *URL:* http://www.mcrlaw.com
St. John's, Newfoundland Office: Baine Johnston Centre, 5th Floor, 10 Fort William Place, P.O. Box 5939, A1C 5X4.
Telephone: 709-722-8735.
Telecopier: 709-722-1763. Email: mcrsj@mcrlaw.com.
Moncton, New Brunswick Office: Place Moncton Place, 655 Main Street, P.O. Box 1368, E1C 8T6.
Telephone: 506-857-8970.
Fax: 506-857-4095. Email: mcrmctn@mcrlaw.com.
Charlottetown, Prince Edward Island Office: BDC Place, Suite 620, 119 Kent Street, C1A 1N3.
Telephone: 902-368-8473.
Fax: 902-368-8346. Email: mcrpei@mcrlaw.com.
Fredericton, New Brunswick Office: Suite 600, 570 Queen Street, P.O. Box 610.
Telephone: 506-458-8572.
Fax: 506-458-9903. Email: mcrfton@mcrlaw.com.

PARTNERS

Harry E. Wrathall, Q.C.
George W. MacDonald, Q.C.
Christopher C. Robinson, Q.C.
Peter M. S. Bryson
Deborah K. Smith
John Kulik
G. Grant Machum
Stewart McInnes, P.C., Q.C.
Robert G. Belliveau, Q.C.
David A. Graves
Scott C. Norton
Stephen Kingston
Aidan J. Meade
Michelle C. Awad

ASSOCIATES

Hugh Wright
Tara A. Miller

For Complete List of Firm Personnel, See General Section

For full biographical listings, see the Martindale-Hubbell Law Directory

CANADA ONTARIO

*HAMILTON,** Regional Munic. of Hamilton-Wentworth

THOMAN SOULE GAGE (AV)

46 Jackson Street East, P.O. Box 187, L8N 3C5
Telephone: 905-529-8195
Fax: 905-529-7906

J. Douglas Thoman, Q.C.
John A. Soule
George S. Gage
J. Neil Smith
S. Stuart Aird
David J. Sherman
Lesley G. Matthewson
William F. Bastien
James Scott Greve
Catherine A. Korte

For full biographical listings, see the Martindale-Hubbell Law Directory

KITCHENER, Regional Munic. of Waterloo

GIFFEN LEE (AV)

50 Queen Street North, P.O. Box 2396, N2H 6M3
Telephone: 519-578-4150
Fax: 519-578-8740
Email: info@GiffenLeeLaw.com *URL:* http://www.GiffenLeeLaw.com

MEMBERS OF FIRM

J. Peter Giffen, Q.C.
Bruce L. Lee
J. Scott Morley
Brian R. Wagner
Philip A. Garbutt
Daniel J. Fife

ASSOCIATES

(Ms.) Milena Protich
Cindy L. Dickinson
Edward J. Vanderkloet
Graham M. Bennett
Mitra Golnaraghi
Donald C. Olson

For full biographical listings, see the Martindale-Hubbell Law Directory

*TORONTO,** Regional Munic. of Toronto

BORDEN & ELLIOT (AV)

Barristers & Solicitors
Scotia Plaza, 40 King Street West, M5H 3Y4
Telephone: 416-367-6000
Telecopier: 416-367-6749
Email: info@borden.com *URL:* http://www.borden.com
Ottawa, Ontario Office: Borden Elliot Scott & Aylen, 1000-60 Rue Queen Street.
Telephone: 613-237-5160; 800-661-4237. General
Facsimile: 613-230-8842. IP Dept.
Facsimile: 613-787-3558. Email: ottinfo@scottaylen.com. URL: http://www.borden.com.

Edward A. Ayers, Q.C.

For Complete List of Firm Personnel, See General Section

For full biographical listings, see the Martindale-Hubbell Law Directory

HUGHES, AMYS (AV)

1 First Canadian Place, Suite 5050, P.O. Box 401, M5X 1E3
Telephone: 416-367-1608
Toll Free: 1-800-565-1713
Fax: 416-367-8821
Hamilton
Email: mail@hughesamys.com *URL:* http://www.hughesamys.com
Hamilton, Ontario Office: One King Street, West, Suite 1401.
Telephone: 905-577-4050; Toll Free: 1-877-858-8234.
Fax: 905-577-6301.

MEMBERS OF FIRM

Wendell S. Wigle, Q.C.
Darcy G. Duke, Q.C.
Lloyd G. Harlock, Q.C.
Michael T. J. McGoey, Q.C.
Paul J. French
James J. Keaney
Richard F. Horak
Pamela M. Stevens
Jack F. Fitch
Michael S. Teitelbaum
Weir H. Milne
William J. McCorriston
Mario R. Pietrangeli
Michael E. Girard
Albert M. Conforzi
A. Jarvis Scott
William S. Chalmers
Martha S. Binks
Jamie K. Trimble
Barbara McAfee

ASSOCIATES

Bruce L. Desmond
Mary Ann Teal
Caroline P. Gronke
James V. Maloney
Mark T. Koyama
Lorella Giliberti

For full biographical listings, see the Martindale-Hubbell Law Directory

KELLY AFFLECK GREENE (AV)

One First Canadian Place, Suite 840, P.O. Box 489, M5X 1E5
Telephone: 416-360-2800
Fax: 416-360-5960
Email: info@kag.net *URL:* http://www.kag.net

MEMBERS OF FIRM

W. Anthony Kelly, Q.C.
Donald S. Affleck, Q.C.
Peter R. Greene
Donald B. Houston
James C. Orr
Peter C. Wardle
Helen A. Daley
Melissa J. Kennedy

ASSOCIATES

Kenneth A. Dekker
W. Michael G. Osborne
Jason C. Markwell
Patrice F. Band

For full biographical listings, see the Martindale-Hubbell Law Directory

LILLY, ANDERSON, MORGAN (AV)

330 Bay Street, Suite 900, M5H 2S8
Telephone: 416-365-6300
Telefax: 416-368-7965
Email: LAM@Inforamp.net

MEMBERS OF FIRM

W. Donald Lilly, Q.C.
Thomas B. Anderson
Christopher J. Morgan

ASSOCIATES

Murray A. MacDonald
Mark S. Wilson
Victor T. Bulger

For full biographical listings, see the Martindale-Hubbell Law Directory

*WINDSOR,** Essex Co.

McTAGUE LAW FIRM (AV)

455 Pelissier Street, N9A 6Z9
Telephone: 519-255-4300
Detroit, Michigan Telephone: 313-965-1332
Fax: 519-255-4360(Corporate/Labor)
Fax: 519-255-4384 (Litigation/Real Estate)

(See Next Column)

McTague Law Firm—*Continued*

MEMBERS OF FIRM

J. Douglas Lawson, Q.C.
Alexander R. Szalkai, Q.C.
Peter J. Kuker
George W. King
Josephine Stark
Tom Serafimovski
Roger A. Skinner
Daniel K. Moorhouse
Jerry B. Udell
Michael K. Coughlin
John D. Leslie
Marilee Marcotte

ASSOCIATES

Kevin G. Fanick
Michael A. Wills
Dana J. Young
Jeffrey W. MacKinnon
Brian L. Chillman

For Complete List of Firm Personnel, See General Section

For full biographical listings, see the Martindale-Hubbell Law Directory

Sutts, Strosberg LLP (AV)

600 Westcourt Place, 251 Goyeau Street, P.O. Box 670, N9A 6V4
Telephone: 519-258-9333
Detroit Michigan: 313-962-0137
Facsimile: Windsor 519-258-9527
Detroit 313-962-0139

MEMBERS OF FIRM

Achille F. Gignac, Q.C. (1902-1984)
Robert E. Barnes, Q.C.
Clifford N. Sutts, Q.C.
Harvey T. Strosberg, Q.C.
Gary V. Wortley
James K. Ball
John C. Holland
Mary M. S. Fox
William C. Chapman
Donald M. Gordon
Paul C. Nesseth
Heather Rumble Peterson
Patricia A. Speight
Edward W. Ducharme
Michelle A. Gagnon
Craig J. Allen
Werner H. Keller
Francine A. Herlehy
Paul Simard
Jasminka Kalajdzic

COUNSEL FOR CRIMINAL MATTERS

Patrick J. Ducharme

For full biographical listings, see the Martindale-Hubbell Law Directory

CANADA PRINCE EDWARD ISLAND

*CHARLOTTETOWN,** Queen's Co.

Campbell, Lea, Michael, McConnell & Pigot (AV)

15 Queen Street, P.O. Box 429, C1A 7K7
Telephone: 902-566-3400
Telecopier: 902-566-9266
Email: www.office@campbelllea.com

MEMBERS OF FIRM

William G. Lea, Q.C.
Robert A. McConnell
Paul D. Michael, Q.C.
Kenneth L. Godfrey

General Counsel in Prince Edward Island for: Canadian Imperial Bank of Commerce; Maritime Electric Co., Ltd.; Michelin Tires (Canada) Ltd.; Newsco Investments Ltd. (Dundas Farms); Imperial Oil Limited; General Motors of Canada; Co-op Atlantic; Liberty Mutual; Employers Reinsurance Group.

For Complete List of Firm Personnel, See General Section

For full biographical listings, see the Martindale-Hubbell Law Directory

McInnes Cooper (AV Ⓣ)

Barristers, Solicitors & Trade Mark Agents
BDC Place, Suite 620, 119 Kent Street, C1A 1N3
Telephone: 902-368-8473
Fax: 902-368-8346
Email: mcrpei@mcrlaw.com *URL:* http://www.mcrlaw.com
Halifax, Nova Scotia Office: Summit Place, 1601 Lower Water Street, P.O. Box 730, B3J 2V1.
Telephone: 902-425-6500.
Fax: 902-425-6350. Email: mcrhfx@mcrlaw.com.
St. John's, Newfoundland Office: Baine Johnston Centre, 5th Floor, 10 Fort William Place, P.O. Box 5939, A1C 5X4.
Telephone: 709-722-8735.
Telecopier: 709-722-1763. Email: mcrsj@mcrlaw.com.
Moncton, New Brunswick Office: Place Moncton Place, 655 Main Street, P.O. Box 1368, E1C 8T6.
Telephone: 506-857-8970.
Fax: 506-857-4095. Email: mcrmctn@mcrlaw.com.
Fredericton, New Brunswick Office: Suite 600, 570 Queen Street, P.O. Box 610.
Telephone: 506-458-8572.
Fax: 506-458-9903. Email: mcrfton@mcrlaw.com.

ASSOCIATE

Kim Petrie

For Complete List of Firm Personnel, See General Section

For full biographical listings, see the Martindale-Hubbell Law Directory

CANADA QUEBEC

*MONTREAL,** Montreal Dist.

McMaster Gervais (AV)

A General Partnership
1000 de La Gauchetière Street West, Suite 900, H3B 5H4
Telephone: 514-879-1212
Fax: 514-954-1905
Email: info@mcmastergervais.com *URL:* http://www.mcmastergervais.com

MEMBERS OF FIRM

Alex K. Paterson, O.C., O.Q., Q.C.
P. Jeremy Bolger
Bruno Duguay
Yvan Houle
Darren E.G. McGuire
Stéphanie Moffatt
Robert Fosco
Daniel Ayotte
Robert E. Charbonneau
Jacques Gauthier
Peter G. Pamel
John G. Murphy
Caroline Matte
Patrice Morin
Manon Gauthier

COUNSEL

Hon. Lawrence A. Poitras, Q.C.
P. André Gervais, Q.C.
Jacques Brien

For Complete List of Firm Personnel, See General Section

For full biographical listings, see the Martindale-Hubbell Law Directory

CANADA SASKATCHEWAN

*REGINA,** Regina Jud. Centre

MacPherson Leslie & Tyerman (AV)

1500-1874 Scarth Street, S4P 4E9
Telephone: 306-347-8000
Telecopier: 306-352-5250
Email: mltreg@mlt.com
Saskatoon, Saskatchewan Office: 1500-410 22nd Street East, S7K 5T6.
Telephone: 306-975-7100.
Telecopier: 306-975-7145.

MEMBERS OF FIRM

Maurice O. Laprairie, Q.C.
Robert G. Richards, Q.C.
Brian J. Kenny
Robert W. Leurer
Jeffrey M. Lee
Bruce W. Wirth (Resident, Saskatoon Office)
Douglas C. Hodson (Resident, Saskatoon Office)
Eileen V. Libby

ASSOCIATES

Paul A. Beke (Resident, Saskatoon Office)
M. Jean Torrens (Resident, Saskatoon Office)
Heather D. Heavin
Charita N. Parchewsky
Vanessa Monar Enweani (Resident, Saskatoon Office)
Jordan P. Hardy
Kurt G. Wintermute (Resident, Saskatoon Office)
Deron A. Kuski

For Complete List of Firm Personnel, See General Section

For full biographical listings, see the Martindale-Hubbell Law Directory

INTELLECTUAL PROPERTY LAW

MINNESOTA

*MINNEAPOLIS,** Hennepin Co.

NAWROCKI, ROONEY & SIVERTSON, P.A. (AV)

Suite 401, Broadway Place East, 3433 Broadway Street Northeast, 55413
Telephone: 612-331-1464
Fax: 612-331-2239
Email: ip@nrslaw.com

Wayne A. Sivertson
John L. Rooney
Lawrence M. Nawrocki

Donald A. Jacobson
Lew Schwartz (Retired)

Representative Clients: Micro Component Technology, Inc.; Crown Iron Works Co.; Marvin Windows; Tandem Products, Inc.; UNISYS; SciMed Life Systems, Inc.; International Hairgoods, Inc.; Twin City Fan & Blower Co.; Flavorite Laboratories, Inc.; Great Plains Supply, Inc.

For full biographical listings, see the Martindale-Hubbell Law Directory

OPPENHEIMER WOLFF & DONNELLY LLP (AV)

3400 Plaza VII, 45 South Seventh Street, 55402
Telephone: 612-607-7000
FAX: 612-607-7100
URL: http://www.owdlaw.com
Amsterdam, The Netherlands Office: Keizergracht 241.
Telephone: 31-20-423-4555.
FAX: 31-20-423-4545.
Brussels, Belgium Office: Avenue Louise 240, Box 5, 1050.
Telephone: 32-2-626-0500.
FAX: 32-2-626-0510.
Geneva, Switzerland Office: Rue Gabriel Eynard, 6, 1205.
Telephone: (41/22) 311-7410.
FAX: (41/22) 311-7407.
New York, N.Y. Office: Citicorp Center, 153 East 53rd Street, 10022.
Telephone: 212-826-5000.
FAX: 212-486-0708.
Newport Beach, California Office: 500 Newport Center Drive, Suite 700, 92660.
Telephone: 949-719-6000.
FAX: 949-719-6020.
Paris, France Office: 53 Avenue Montaigne, 75008.
Telephone: (33/1) 44 95 03 50.
FAX: (33/1) 44 95 03 40.
St. Paul, Minnesota Office: 1700 First National Bank Building, 55101.
Telephone: 651-605-2000.
FAX: 651-605-2100.
Washington, D.C. Office: Oppenheimer Wolff Donnelly & Bayh LLP, 1350 Eye Street, N.W., Suite 200, 20005.
Telephone: 202-312-8000.
FAX: 202-312-8100.
Los Angeles, California Office: 2029 Century Park East, 38th Floor, 90067.
Telephone: 310-788-5000.
FAX: 310-277-1297.
San Jose, California Office: 101 Park Center Plaza, Suite 300, 95113.
Telephone: 408-795-3000.
FAX: 408-795-3100.
Chicago, Illinois Office: Oppenheimer Wolff & Donnelly (Illinois), Two Prudential Plaza, 45th Floor, 180 North Stetson Avenue, 60601.
Telephone: 312-616-1800.
Fax: 312-616-5800.

RESIDENT PARTNERS

Harold D. Jastram
James E. Schatz
Edward M. Laine
Barbara J. Grahn
Jake M. Holdreith
Craig J. Lervick

RESIDENT ASSOCIATES

Alan D. Kamrath
Chad A. Klingbeil
Erika S. Koster
Ernest W. Grumbles, III
Bridget A. Sullivan
Daniel G. Chapik
Cyrus A. Morton

For Complete List of Firm Personnel, See General Section

For full biographical listings, see the Martindale-Hubbell Law Directory

MISSOURI

KANSAS CITY, Jackson, Clay, Platte & Cass Cos.

SWANSON MIDGLEY, LLC (AV)

Crown Center, 2420 Pershing Road, Suite 400, 64108
Telephone: 816-842-6100
Fax: 816-842-0013
Email: mail@swansonmidgley.com *URL:* http://www.swansonmidgley.com
Overland Park, Kansas Office: Commerce Plaza I, 7th Floor, 7300 W. 110th Street.
Telephone: 913-317-2717.
FAX: 913-317-1505.

Wm. Bruce Day

Counsel For: Ifra-Red Technologies, Inc.; Scot Young Research, Inc.; Ash Grove Cement Co.; Dynamic Fastener Service, Inc.; Xantech Corp.; AFM Corporation; Bruason Instrument Co.

For Complete List of Firm Personnel, See General Section

For full biographical listings, see the Martindale-Hubbell Law Directory

ST. LOUIS, (Independent City)

HELFREY, SIMON & JONES, P.C. (AV)

120 South Central Avenue Suite 1500, 63105
Telephone: 314-725-9100
Facsimile: 314-725-5754

David B. B. Helfrey
Michael H. Musich

Gregory M. Power

For full biographical listings, see the Martindale-Hubbell Law Directory

SUMMERS, COMPTON, WELLS AND HAMBURG, PROFESSIONAL CORPORATION (AV)

8909 Ladue Road, 63124
Telephone: 314-991-4999
Fax: 314-991-2413
URL: http://www.scwh.com

Robert F. Summers
Ronald N. Compton
Richard H. Ulrich
Stephen L. Wells
Steven M. Hamburg
Michael M. Sayers
David A. Sosne
Susan Z. Gamble
Michael W. Newport
Carol Stanton Fiala

Christopher J. Rausch
Brian K. Rull
Jill R. Van Meter

OF COUNSEL

Pamela D. Perdue
G. Lane Roberts
James P. Gamble

LEGAL SUPPORT PERSONNEL

Donna L. Hudson (Office Manager)
Ronda G. Rutherford (Paralegal)
Suzanne L. Schmitt (Paralegal)

For full biographical listings, see the Martindale-Hubbell Law Directory

NEBRASKA

*LINCOLN,** Lancaster Co.

CLINE, WILLIAMS, WRIGHT, JOHNSON & OLDFATHER (AV)

1900 U.S. Bank Building, 233 South 13th Street, 68508
Telephone: 402-474-6900
Fax: 402-474-5393
Email: postmaster@cline-law.com *URL:* http://www.cline-law.com
Omaha, Nebraska Office: Suite 720, One Pacific Place, 1125 South 103rd Street, 68124.
Telephone: 402-397-1700.
Fax: 402-397-1806.

ATTORNEYS

Allen L. Graves
Charles M. Pallesen, Jr.
Fredric H. Kauffman
Donald F. Burt
Alan E. Peterson
Stephen E. Gehring
Robert J. Routh
Kevin Colleran
L. Bruce Wright
James M. Bausch
Larry A. Holle
David R. Buntain
Stephen H. Nelsen
Michael C. Mueller
Lauren W. Wismer
Daniel R. Stogsdill
Scott D. Kelly
Terry R. Wittler
Pamela Hastings Carrier
Mark A. Christensen

(See Next Column)

CLINE, WILLIAMS, WRIGHT, JOHNSON & OLDFATHER, *Lincoln—Continued*

ATTORNEYS (Continued)

Richard P. Garden, Jr.	Jill Gossin Jensen
Shawn D. Renner	Rochelle A. Mullen
John C. Miles	John L. Horan
Mary Kay Frank	Bryan S. Hatch
Thomas C. Huston	Steven C. Likes
Sonya S. Ekart	Tracy A. Oldemeyer
Don R. Janssen	Jolene M. Papa
Susan Kubert Sapp	Timothy G. Aschoff
Kevin J. Schneider	Eric N. Bergquist
Andrew D. Strotman	Janis J. Winterhof

Andrea Dylan Snowden

OF COUNSEL

Charles E. Wright	Richard P. Jeffries

Mary M. Campbell

RETIRED PARTNERS

Flavel A. Wright (Retired)	Warren C. Johnson (Retired)

Charles E. Oldfather (1927-1998)

Representative Clients: U.S. Bank National Association; University of Nebraska; Nebraska Medical Assn.; Saint Elizabeth Regional Medical Center; Media of Nebraska; Cargill Inc.; State Farm Insurance Cos.; Wal-Mart Stores, Inc.; Textron/Cushman; Isco, Inc.

For full biographical listings, see the Martindale-Hubbell Law Directory

*OMAHA,** Douglas Co.

McGRATH, NORTH, MULLIN & KRATZ, P.C. (AV)

Suite 1400, One Central Park Plaza, 68102
Telephone: 402-341-3070
Fax: 402-341-0216

John P. Passarelli	Patrick C. Stephenson
Gary F. Wence	James M. Sulentic

Meredith M. Wilkes

General Counsel for: ConAgra, Inc.; InaCom Corp.; Omaha Airport Authority; Physicians Mutual Insurance Co.; Supertel Hospitality, Inc.; Valmont Industries, Inc.
Representative Clients: Clarkson Hospital; Omaha Chamber of Commerce.
Insurance Clients: American Family Insurance Group; Blue Cross-Blue Shield of Nebraska.

For Complete List of Firm Personnel, See General Section

For full biographical listings, see the Martindale-Hubbell Law Directory

SUITER & ASSOCIATES P.C. (AV)

11516 Nicholas Street, Suite 205, 68154-4409
Telephone: 402-496-0300
Facsimile: 402-496-0333
URL: http://www.suiter.com

Sean Patrick Suiter

Kenneth J. Cool	Kevin E. West
Scott C. Rand	William J. Breen, III

LEGAL SUPPORT PERSONNEL

Nancy S. Husarik (Patent Agent)

For full biographical listings, see the Martindale-Hubbell Law Directory

NEVADA

*RENO,** Washoe Co.

McDONALD CARANO WILSON McCUNE BERGIN FRANKOVICH & HICKS LLP (AV)

241 Ridge Street, 89501
Telephone: 775-788-2000
Telecopier: 775-788-2020
URL: http://www.mcdonaldcarano.com
Las Vegas, Nevada Office: Suite 1000, 2300 West Sahara Avenue.
Telephone: 702-873-4100.
Telecopier: 702-873-9966.

MEMBERS OF FIRM

Thomas R. C. Wilson	James C. Giudici
William A. S. Magrath, II	Scott A. Swain

ASSOCIATE

Bonnie Fleischer Drinkwater

Representative Clients: Mills Lane; Eldorado Hotel & Casino; Silver Legacy Hotel & Casino; Scolaris Warehouse Markets, Inc.; Jackpot Enterprises, Inc.; Calculated Industries, Inc.; Ferrari Carrano Winery.

(See Next Column)

For Complete List of Firm Personnel, See General Section

For full biographical listings, see the Martindale-Hubbell Law Directory

NEW JERSEY

ENGLEWOOD CLIFFS, Bergen Co.

BARRY I. FREDERICKS (AV)

560 Sylvan Avenue, 07632
Telephone: 201-871-7484
Telecopier: 201-871-8428
New York, N.Y. Office: Empire State Building, 350 Fifth Avenue, Suite 6011.
Telephone: 212-586-5042.

For full biographical listings, see the Martindale-Hubbell Law Directory

MOORESTOWN, Burlington Co.

ESTELLA S. GOLD (AV)

Blason II, 505 South Lenola Road, 08057
Telephone: 609-234-1004
Telecopier: 609-234-7836
Email: esglaw@aol.com

Representative Clients: South Jersey Processing, Inc.; OM Assn., Inc.

For full biographical listings, see the Martindale-Hubbell Law Directory

*NEWARK,** Essex Co.

HELLRING LINDEMAN GOLDSTEIN & SIEGAL LLP (AV)

One Gateway Center, 07102-5386
Telephone: 973-621-9020
Fax: 973-621-7406
Englewood, New Jersey Office: 32-40 North Dean Street.
Telephone: 201-871-3060.

Joel D. Siegal	Stephen L. Dreyfuss
Jonathan L. Goldstein	Judah I. Elstein
Richard D. Shapiro	Matthew E. Moloshok
Robert S. Raymar	Rachel N. Davidson

Robert B. Rosen

For Complete List of Firm Personnel, See General Section

For full biographical listings, see the Martindale-Hubbell Law Directory

NEW PROVIDENCE, Union Co.

COOPER & STIELER (AV)

A Partnership including a Professional Corporation
(Formerly Smith & Stieler)
27 Murray Hill Square, 07974
Telephone: 908-665-2828
Fax: 908-771-7792
Cable Address: "Cooper Stieler"
Email: info@cooperstieler.com
Mailing Address: 41 Mountain Avenue, P.O. Box Box 125, New Providence, New Jersey, 07974
Email: cooperstieler@lawyers.com *URL:* http://www.lawyers.com/cooperstieler
Summit, New Jersey Office: Harper Plaza, Suite 100, 34 River Road, P.O. Box 361.
Telephone: 908-467-0900.
Fax: 908-467-0911.

MEMBERS OF FIRM

Carol Cooper *
Scott R. Stieler III (Not admitted in NJ; Resident, Summit Office)

LEGAL SUPPORT PERSONNEL

Sandra L. Harris (Paralegal)	Paul G. Rispoli, Jr. (Patent Agent)

Representative Clients: Lucent Corp.; Apple Corp.; Datascape, Inc.; TelCom 1, Inc.; Ameritech Corp.; America On Line, Inc.; Compuserve Corp.
*A Professional Corporation

For full biographical listings, see the Martindale-Hubbell Law Directory

PARSIPPANY, Morris Co.

HOFFMANN & BARON, LLP (AV)

1055 Parsippany Boulevard, 07054
Telephone: 973-331-1700
Fax: 973-331-1717
Syosset, New York Office: 6900 Jericho Turnpike, 11791.
Telephone: 516-822-3550.
Telecopier: 516-822-3582.

(See Next Column)

HOFFMANN & BARON LLP—*Continued*

MEMBER OF FIRM

Daniel A. Scola, Jr. — Salvatore J. Abbruzzese

ASSOCIATES

Kirk M. Miles
Robert F. Chisholm (Not admitted in NJ)
Mark E. Baron
Kellyanne Merkel
John S. Sopko
Barry H. Jacobsen

LEGAL SUPPORT PERSONNEL
PATENT AGENTS

Keith R. Lange — Gloria K. Szakiel

For full biographical listings, see the Martindale-Hubbell Law Directory

PRINCETON, Mercer Co.

MATHEWS, COLLINS, SHEPHERD & GOULD, A PROFESSIONAL CORPORATION (AV)

100 Thanet Circle Suite 306, 08540
Telephone: 609-924-8555
Fax: 609-924-3036
Telex: 642948
Email: Attorneys@MathewsLaw.Com

H. Hume Mathews (1911-1989)
Bruce M. Collins
Robert G. Shepherd
Ronald Gould
Diane Dunn McKay
Glen E. Books
Brooks R. Bruneau
Anastasia P. Winslow
Todd A. Denys
Dr. Charles Joseph Brumlik (Not admitted in NJ)

Representative Clients: Novartis Corp.; Ciba Speciality Chemicals; Medtronic, Inc.; Stiefel Laboratories, Inc.; Celgene Corp.; Princeton University; Genetics Institute; Summit Bank; Church & Dwight, Inc.; UMDNJ;

For full biographical listings, see the Martindale-Hubbell Law Directory

RED BANK, Monmouth Co.

WHITE, FLEISCHNER & FINO (AV)

272 Broad Street, 07701
Telephone: 732-530-7787
Telecopier: 732-530-8552
New York, New York Office: 140 Broadway.
Telephone: 212-487-9700.
Telecopier: 212-487-9777.

Benjamin A. Fleischner

For full biographical listings, see the Martindale-Hubbell Law Directory

NEW YORK

*ALBANY,** Albany Co.

HESLIN & ROTHENBERG, P.C. (AV)

5 Columbia Circle, 12203
Telephone: 518-452-5600
Facsimile: 518-452-5579
Email: hesroth@hriplaw.com

Robert E. Heslin
Jeff Rothenberg
Kevin P. Radigan
Susan E. Farley
Nicholas Mesiti
Blanche E. Schiller
Wayne F. Reinke

Jeffrey R. Klembczyk
Martha L. Boden
Candice J. Clement
Kathy Smith Dias
Mary Louise Gioeni
Michael J. Bendel (Not admitted in NY)
David A. Pascarella
Leo M. Loughlin
Daniel H. Beaty
Victor A. Cardona

PATENT AGENT

Philip E. Hansen

For full biographical listings, see the Martindale-Hubbell Law Directory

*BUFFALO,** Erie Co.

DAMON & MOREY LLP (AV)

(Formerly Damon, Morey, Sawyer & Moot)
1000 Cathedral Place, 298 Main Street, 14202-4096
Telephone: 716-856-5500
Facsimile: 716-856-5510
Email: apinder@damonmorey.com *URL:* http://www.damonmorey.com
Rochester, New York Office: Powers Building, Suite 507, 16 West Main Street, 14614.
Telephone: 716-232-3640.
Fax: 716-232-8448.

(See Next Column)

MEMBERS OF FIRM

Mason O. Damon (1905-1983)
Robert J. Plache
James N. Schmit
Christopher T. Greene
Franklin W. Heller
Gregory C. Yungbluth
James W. Gormley
James M. Mucklewee
Melinda G. Disare
Robert J. Portin
Joseph J. Schoellkopf, Jr.
William F. Savino
Thomas J. Drury
Patrick B. Curran
Peter S. Marlette
Vincent J. Moore
Gust P. Pullman
Barbara L. Schifeling
Michael J. Willett
Carol Guck Snider
Joseph W. Dunbar
Kenneth W. Africano
Julie M. Bargnesi
Arthur A. Marrapese III (Resident, Rochester Office)
Sharyn G. Rogers
Daniel F. Brown
David L. Edmunds, Jr.
Charles S. Carra
Hedwig Maria Auletta
Marylou K. Roshia
Maryjo C. Falcone
Charles E. Telford, III
Timothy C. Cashmore
Anthony L. Eugeni
Amy Archer Flaherty
Kathleen M. Reilly
Steven I. Rubinstein
Diane C. Zarlock

ASSOCIATES

Brian Alan Birenbach
Daniel T. Cavarello
Michelle A. Crew
Anne C. Evans
Michael Thomas Feeley
Judy S. Hernandez
David S. Kelly
Joseph J. Manna
Rosalie A. Melisz
Mary C. Raymond
Vincent George Saccomando
Allison Fields Stravino
Kellie Muffoletto Ulrich

OF COUNSEL

Joseph H. Morey, Jr.

SPECIAL COUNSEL

Richard E. Moot
George F. Gabel, Jr.
G. Steven Pigeon
Susan A. Benz
Edward Yankelunas

Counsel For: Advanced Refractory Technologies; Catholic Health East; D.A. Elia Construction Corporation; Kaleida Health; Town of Cheektowaga; Bagel Brothers Amherst, Inc.; Burt Rigid Box, Inc.; Lake Shore Health Care Center; County of Cattaraugus; Commonwealth Land Title Insurance; Diocese of Buffalo; Baker Victory Services; Niagara Lutheran Home and Rehabilitation, Inc.; Sheehan Memorial Hospital; Robert James Sales, Inc.; Olean General Hospital; Wendt Corporation; Aria Wireless Systems, Inc.; Buffalo Sewer Authority; City of Tonawanda; Roswell Park Cancer Institute; Ivoclar North America, Inc.; Olean Medical Group; Cold Spring Construction Company; Buffalo Municipal Housing Authority.
Local Counsel For: Healthcare Underwriters Mutual Insurance Company; AIG Companies; Owens-Corning Fiberglas; Unigard Insurance Group; Key Tronic Corporation; Medical Liability Insurance; Risk Enterprise Management Limited; Wintherthur International; Hanover Insurance Company; National Casualty Company; Marine Midland Mortgage Corporation; Acordia Resort Services; Medical Malpractice Insurance Association; OUM & Associates; Ohio Casualty Company; PACCAR, Inc.; Frontier Insurance Company; The Limited, Inc.; Zurich-American Insurance Group; Allstate Insurance Company; Universal Studios, Inc.

For full biographical listings, see the Martindale-Hubbell Law Directory

GARDEN CITY, Nassau Co.

SCULLY, SCOTT, MURPHY & PRESSER, A PROFESSIONAL CORPORATION (AV)

400 Garden City Plaza, 11530
Telephone: 516-742-4343
Facsimile: 516-742-4366
Email: intprop@ssmp.com

John F. Scully (Retired)
Anthony C. Scott (1931-1994)
William E. McNulty (1927-1993)
Stephen D. Murphy
Leopold Presser
Kenneth L. King
Frank S. DiGiglio
Paul J. Esatto, Jr.
John S. Sensny
Mark J. Cohen
Richard L. Catania
Edward W. Grolz
William C. Roch

Peter I. Bernstein
Marvin Bressler
Steven Fischman
Ann R. Pokalsky
Thomas Spinelli, Sr.
John F. Vodopia
Patricia A. Wilczynski

COUNSEL

Allen R. Morganstern — Stephen A. Young

LEGAL SUPPORT PERSONNEL
PROFESSIONAL TECHNICAL ASSOCIATE

Leslie S. Szivos, Ph.D.
Alexander G. Vodovozov
Xiaochun Zhu, Ph.D.

For full biographical listings, see the Martindale-Hubbell Law Directory

*NEW YORK,** New York Co.

BERGER STERN & WEBB, LLP (AV)

900 Third Avenue, 10022
Telephone: 212-319-1900
Telecopier: (212) 319-2017
URL: http://www.bswny.com

MEMBERS OF FIRM

Steven A. Berger
Peter R. Stern
Charles S. Webb, III
John R. Cahill

Thomas E. Hone
Jonathan Rogin
Kenneth J. Applebaum

For full biographical listings, see the Martindale-Hubbell Law Directory

COBRIN & GITTES (AV)

750 Lexington Avenue, 10022
Telephone: 212-486-4000
Telecopier: 212-486-4007
Email: cgpats@ix.netcom.com

Peter T. Cobrin
Marvin S. Gittes
Richard M. Lehrer
David W. Denenberg

Robert J. Hess
Michael A. Adler
Gerald J. Cechony (Not admitted in NY)
Oren J. Warshavsky
Clyde Alvin Shuman
Lawrence E. Russ

Representative Clients: Northern Telecom, Inc.; DataPoint, Corporation; Magnivision, Inc.; Atico; Global Direct Mail Corporation; MW; Oxigene, Inc.; Horphag Research, LTD.

For full biographical listings, see the Martindale-Hubbell Law Directory

FURGANG & ADWAR, LLP (AV)

205 Lexington Avenue, 10016
Telephone: 212-725-1818
Telecopier: Group III, 212-941-9711; 914-353-1996
Email: info@furgang.com *URL:* http://www.furgang.com
White Plains, New York Office: 11 Martine Avenue.
Telephone: 914-428-5000.
Facsimile: 914-353-1996.
West Nyack, New York Office: Suite 210 Centerock East, 2 Crosfield Avenue.
Telephone: 914-353-1818.
Facsimile: 914-353-1996.

Philip Furgang
Stephanie Furgang Adwar

Ainslee Ann Schreiber

OF COUNSEL

Leo C. Krazinski
Bertrand M. Lanchner
Sheldon Palmer

For full biographical listings, see the Martindale-Hubbell Law Directory

GRAHAM, CAMPAIGN P.C. (AV)

The Bar Building, 36 West 44th Street, 10036-8178
Telephone: 212-354-5650
Cable Address: "Forbland"
Telex: 6502048313 MCI UW
MCI Mail: 204-8313
Telecopier: 212-354-6354
Email: gracam@aol.com *URL:* http://www.lawyers.com/trademarks

Andrew J. Graham (1911-1986)
William L. McGuire, Sr. (1926-1992)
H. John Campaign
John M. Keene
Charles H. Knull
Gail E. Nickols
William C. Wright

OF COUNSEL

Gerard H. Davis

For full biographical listings, see the Martindale-Hubbell Law Directory

HOPGOOD, CALIMAFDE, KALIL & JUDLOWE LLP (AV)

A Partnership including Professional Corporations
Lincoln Building, 60 East 42nd Street, 10165
Telephone: 212-551-5000
Telecopier: 212-949-2795; 212-949-9623

MEMBERS OF FIRM

Roy C. Hopgood
John M. Calimafde (P.C.)
Eugene J. Kalil
Stephen B. Judlowe (P.C.)
Dennis J. Mondolino
Ira B. Winkler
James M. Bollinger
Brian P. Murphy
Janet B. Linn
Bradley N. Ruben (Not admitted in NY)
Robert G. Gibbons
Lisa M. Ferri

(See Next Column)

ASSOCIATES

Eve Kunen
Michael F. Hurley
Edward M. Reisner
Jason A. Lief
Richard C. Pettus
Gordon F. Belcher
Keith T. Takeda
John F. Gallagher III
Steven R. Bartholomew (Not admitted in NY)
G. Michael Bryner
Jeffrey M. Gold
Dennis C. Hopkins
Vivek S. Suri
Michael H. Imbacuan
David J. Garrod
Frank Chesky (Not admitted in NY)
Douglas R. Weider (Not admitted in NY)
Vincent A. Sireci
Anthony L. Meola, Jr.
Richard McCormick (Not admitted in NY)
Esther H. Steinhauer
Philip L. Hirschhorn

For full biographical listings, see the Martindale-Hubbell Law Directory

KALOW, SPRINGUT & BRESSLER LLP (AV)

488 Madison Avenue, 10022-5702
Telephone: 212-813-1600
Fax: 212-813-9600
Email: info@creativity-law.com

David A. Kalow
Milton Springut
Kenneth L. Bressler
Jay S. Rand

ASSOCIATES

Scott D. Locke
Gary R. Molnar
Karin J. Norton
David Petroff
Laura E. Smith
Christina M. Thompson

OF COUNSEL

Philip A. Byler
J. David Ellett, Jr.
John J. Santalone, Jr.

SCIENCE ADVISOR

Donna Robertson-Chow

For full biographical listings, see the Martindale-Hubbell Law Directory

KING, PAGANO & HARRISON (AV)

425 Park Avenue, 10022
Telephone: 212-223-4000
Fax: 212-223-4134
URL: http://www.kph.com
Washington, D.C. Office: 1730 Pennsylvania Avenue, N.W., 20006.
Telephone: 202-371-6800.
FAX: 202-371-6770.

MEMBERS OF FIRM

Jeffrey W. King (Resident, Washington, D.C. Office)
Jeffrey W. Pagano
Keith J. Harrison (Resident, Washington, D.C. Office)
James E. Kellett
Steven Schaars (Resident, Washington, D.C. Office)
Jeffrey L. Poston (Resident, Washington, D.C. Office)
Ira M. Saxe

OF COUNSEL

Herbert I. Meyer

ASSOCIATES

Cheryl A. Maier (Resident, Washington, D.C. Office)
Christopher Flynn (Resident, Washington, D.C. Office)
Emily B. Zuckerman
Thomas W. Jones, Jr. (Resident, Washington, D.C. Office)
Eric M. Carr

Representative Clients: Brink's, Inc.; The Pittston Co.; BAX Global; COMSAT; Kaiser Permanente; Medica; Del Laboratories; E-Systems; Renaissance International Hotels and Resorts.

For full biographical listings, see the Martindale-Hubbell Law Directory

KOSTELANETZ & FINK, LLP (AV)

530 Fifth Avenue, 22nd Floor, 10036
Telephone: 212-808-8100
Fax: 212-808-8108
Email: mail@kostelanetzfink.com

SENIOR COUNSEL

Boris Kostelanetz

MEMBERS OF FIRM

Robert S. Fink
Kevin M. Flynn
Bryan C. Skarlatos

COUNSEL

Norman Sinrich
Theodore F. Dickson
Caroline Rule
Brian C. Wille
William F. Cuozzi, III
Dawn Ngo

For full biographical listings, see the Martindale-Hubbell Law Directory

MARSHALL LAW FIRM (AV)

1065 Avenue of the Americas, 10018
Telephone: 212-382-2044
Fax: 212-382-3610

Paul G. Marshall

(See Next Column)

MARSHALL LAW FIRM—*Continued*

ASSOCIATES

David E. Benjamin | Rebecca M. Heller
Scott F. Brown | Francois Mobasser
George T. Gilbert | Lawrence J. Studnicky, III

OF COUNSEL

Marilyn G. Haft

For full biographical listings, see the Martindale-Hubbell Law Directory

McGuire, Kehl & Nealon, LLP (AV)

230 Park Avenue, Suite 2830, 10169
Telephone: 212-557-0040
Telecopier: 212-953-0768

MEMBERS OF FIRM

Harold F. McGuire, Jr. | Jeffrey A. Kehl
Arthur V. Nealon

OF COUNSEL

Andrea Green | Shelley Sanders Kehl
Marion C. Katzive | Terri E. Simon

For full biographical listings, see the Martindale-Hubbell Law Directory

Nims, Howes, Collison, Hansen & Lackert (AV)

605 Third Avenue, Suite 3500, 10158
Telephone: 212-661-9700
Cable Address: "Nims"
Telex: 237665
Facsimile: 212-661-9213
Email: nims@nimslaw.com

MEMBERS OF FIRM

Oliver P. Howes, Jr. | Elizabeth Atkins
William R. Hansen | Thomas H. Curtin
Clark W. Lackert | Keith E. Sharkin
William J. Sapone

OF COUNSEL

Bert A. Collison | Bruce J. Grossman
Karen P. Clancy | Robert P. Schwartz
Irving N. Stein | Robert J. O'Hare
August G. Maron, Jr. | Robert E. Isner (1921-1993)

ASSOCIATES

Robert L. Powley | Larry H. Tronco
Edwin J. Lubin | Richard P. Georget

For full biographical listings, see the Martindale-Hubbell Law Directory

Oppenheimer Wolff & Donnelly LLP (AV)

The Chrysler East Building 19th Floor, 666 Third Avenue, 10017
Telephone: 212-826-5000
FAX: 212-486-0708
URL: http://www.oppenheimer.com
Minneapolis, Minnesota Office: 3300 Plaza VII, 45 South Seventh Street. 55402.
Telephone: 612-607-7000.
FAX: 612-607-7100.
Amsterdam, The Netherlands Office: Keizergracht 241.
Telephone: 31-20-423-4555.
FAX: 312-20-423-4545.
Brussels, Belgium Office: Avenue Louise 240, Box 5, 1050.
Telephone: 32-2-626-0500.
FAX: 32-2-626-0510.
Geneva, Switzerland Office: Rue Gabriel Eynard, 6, 1205.
Telephone: (41/22) 311-7410.
FAX: (41/22) 311-4707.
Newport Beach, California Office: 500 Newport Center Drive, Suite 700, 92660.
Telephone: 949-823-6000.
FAX: 949-823-6100.
Paris, France Office: 35 Boulevard des Capucines, 75002.
Telephone: (33/1) 53 45 40 00.
FAX: (33/1) 53 45 40 10.
St. Paul, Minnesota Office: 1700 First National Bank Building, 55101.
Telephone: 651-605-2000.
FAX: 651-605-2100.
Washington, D.C. Office: Oppenheimer Wolff Donnelly & Bayh LLP, 1350 Eye Street, N.W., Suite 200, 20005.
Telephone: 202-312-8000.
FAX: 202-312-8100.
Los Angeles, California Office: 2029 Century Park East, 38th Floor, 90067.
Telephone: 310-788-5000.
FAX: 310-277-1297.
Palo Alto, California Office: 3373 Hillview Avenue, Suite 200, 94304.
Telephone: 650-320-4000.
FAX: 650-320-4100.
Chicago, Illinois Office: Oppenheimer Wolff & Donnelly (Illinois), Two Prudential Plaza, 45th Floor, 180 North Stetson Avenue, 60601.
Telephone: 312-616-1800.
Fax: 312-616-5800.

(See Next Column)

RESIDENT PARTNERS

Joseph J. Vicinanza (Resident Managing Partner) | Herbert C. Ross, Jr.

RESIDENT ASSOCIATES

Kimberley K. Adams | Joseph E. Petersen

For full biographical listings, see the Martindale-Hubbell Law Directory

Parker Chapin LLP (AV)

Chrysler Building, 405 Lexington Avenue, 10017
Telephone: 212-704-6000
Telecopier: 212-704-6288
URL: http://www.parkerchapin.com
Great Neck, New York Office: 175 Great Neck Road.
Telephone: 516-482-4422.
Telecopier: 516-482-4469.
Hackensack, New Jersey: 190 Morre Street, Suite 307.
Telephone: 210-883-6400.
Telecopier: 210-883-6404.
Beverly Hills, California: 9454 Wilshire Boulevard.
Telephone: 310-288-8367.
Telecopier: 310-288-8365.

MEMBER OF FIRM

Michael D. Friedman

OF COUNSEL

Karl M. Zielaznicki

For Complete List of Firm Personnel, See General Section

For full biographical listings, see the Martindale-Hubbell Law Directory

Piliero Goldstein Jenkins & Sullivan, LLP (AV)

292 Madison Avenue, 10017
Telephone: 212-213-8200
Fax: 212-685-2028
Email: lawyers@pgjhlaw.com *URL:* http://www.pgjhlaw.com
Carlstadt, New Jersey Office: One Palmer Terrace.
Telephone: 201-507-5157.
FAX: 201-507-5221.
Washington, D.C. Office: 888 17th Street, N.W., Suite 1100.
Telephone: 202-467-6991.
FAX: 202-467-6703.
San Francisco, California Office: 507 Howard Street, Suite 200.
Telephone: 415-281-3631.
Fax: 415-281-3630.

MEMBERS OF FIRM

Kimberlee S. Bogen | Marc A. Lebowitz
Edward J. Goldstein | Robert D. Piliero
Jon Mark Jenkins | George O. Richardson, III
Michael T. Sullivan

ASSOCIATES

Craig Avedisian | Eric M. Kogan
Rosemary G. Feit | Mariano Schwed

OF COUNSEL

Kenneth D. Arbeeny | Christopher P. Hall

For full biographical listings, see the Martindale-Hubbell Law Directory

White, Fleischner & Fino (AV)

140 Broadway, 10005
Telephone: 212-487-9700
Telecopier: 212-487-9777
Email: infor@wff-law.com
Red Bank, New Jersey Office: 272 Broad Street.
Telephone: 732-530-7787.
Telecopier: 732-530-8552.

MEMBERS OF FIRM

Allan P. White | Benjamin A. Fleischner

For Complete List of Firm Personnel, See General Section

For full biographical listings, see the Martindale-Hubbell Law Directory

SYOSSET, Nassau Co.

Hoffmann & Baron, LLP (AV)

6900 Jericho Turnpike, 11791
Telephone: 516-822-3550
Telecopier: 516-822-3582
Parsippany, New Jersey Office: 1055 Parsippany Blvd., 07054.
Telephone: 973-331-1700.
Telecopier: 973-331-1717.

MEMBERS OF FIRM

Charles R. Hoffmann | A. Thomas Kammer
Ronald J. Baron | Salvatore J. Abbruzzese (Resident, Parsippany, New Jersey Office)
Gerald T. Bodner | Alan M. Sack
Daniel A. Scola, Jr. (Resident, Parsippany, New Jersey Office) | Irving N. Feit

(See Next Column)

HOFFMANN & BARON LLP, *Syosset—Continued*

ASSOCIATES

R. Glenn Schroeder
Glenn T. Henneberger
Kirk M. Miles (Resident, Parsippany, New Jersey Office)
Anthony E. Bennett
Robert Francis Chisholm (Not admitted in NY; Resident, Parsippany, New Jersey Office)
Gregory W. Bachmann
Mark E. Baron (Resident, Parsippany, New Jersey Office)
Steven T. Zuschlag
Kellyanne Merkel (Resident, Parsippany, New Jersey Office)
Susan A. Sipos
Samir R. Patel
James F. Harrington
Kevin E. McDermott
Robert C. Morriss
Roderick S.W. Turner
John S. Sopko (Resident, Parsippany, New Jersey Office)
Barry H. Jacobsen (Resident, Parsippany, New Jersey Office)
Richard LaCava
Robert L. Bernstein
Justin K. Holmes

LEGAL SUPPORT PERSONNEL
PATENT AGENTS

Keith R. Lange (Resident, Parsippany, New Jersey Office)
Gloria K. Szakiel (Resident, Parsippany, New Jersey Office)

OF COUNSEL

Joseph J. Catanzaro

For full biographical listings, see the Martindale-Hubbell Law Directory

NORTH CAROLINA

*DURHAM,** Durham Co.

JENKINS & WILSON, P.A. (AV)

Suite 1400 University Tower, 3100 Tower Boulevard, 27707-6226
Telephone: 919-493-8000
Fax: 919-419-0383
URL: http://www.jenkinsandwilson.com

Richard E. Jenkins
Jeffrey L. Wilson

Jennifer L. Skord
Arles A. Taylor, Jr.
David P. Gloekler (Not admitted in NC)
Gregory A. Hunt

Representative Clients: Bell and Howell Mail Processing Systems; Duke University; Freudenberg Spunweb Co. (The Lutravil Co.); Glaxo Wellcome, Inc.; Huesker, Inc.; North Carolina State University; Rhone-Poulenc AG Co.; Sumitomo Electric Lightwave Corp.; The University of North Carolina at Chapel Hill; Vanderbilt University.

For full biographical listings, see the Martindale-Hubbell Law Directory

MOORE & VAN ALLEN, PLLC (AV)

Suite 800, 2200 West Main Street, 27705
Telephone: 919-286-8000
Fax: 919-286-8199
URL: http://www.mvalaw.com
Charleston, South Carolina Office: 40 Calhoun Street, Suite 300.
Telephone: 843-579-7000.
Fax: 843-579-7099.
Charlotte, North Carolina Office: 100 North Tryon Street, Floor 47.
Telephone: 704-331-1000.
Fax: 704-331-1159.
Raleigh, North Carolina Office: One Hannover Square, Suite 1700, P.O. Box 26507.
Telephone: 919-821-6200.
Fax: 919-821-6500.

Dominic J. Chiantera
David A. Harlow

OF COUNSEL

William G. Dossé
William L. London, III

COUNSEL

Rita M.K. Purut

ASSOCIATES

Arlene D. Hanks
Michael G. Johnston
Laura Keohane
Scott W. Reid
Mark H. Webbink

For full biographical listings, see the Martindale-Hubbell Law Directory

OLIVE AND OLIVE, P.A. (AV)

500 Memorial Street, P.O. Box 2049, 27702-2049
Telephone: 919-683-5514
Fax: 919-688-3781
Email: iplaw@oliveandolive.com *URL:* http://oliveandolive.com

(See Next Column)

B. B. Olive
Susan Freya Olive

Michael R. Philips
Tara J. Williams
Bruce Vrana
Vedia Jones-Richardson

LEGAL SUPPORT PERSONNEL

Barbara Porterfield (Administrator)

Reference: North Carolina Bar Assn.

For full biographical listings, see the Martindale-Hubbell Law Directory

OHIO

*AKRON,** Summit Co.

RENNER, KENNER, GREIVE, BOBAK, TAYLOR & WEBER A LEGAL PROFESSIONAL ASSOCIATION (AV)

Sixteenth Floor, First National Tower, 44308-1456
Telephone: 330-376-1242; 330-376-1034
Facsimile: 330-376-9646
Email: patlaw@rennerkenner.com *URL:* http://www.rennerkenner.com
Westlake, Ohio Office: 24500 Center Ridge Road, Suite 280, 44145.
Telephone: 440-808-0011.
Fax: 440-808-0657.

Reese Taylor
Phillip L. Kenner
Edward G. Greive
Donald J. Bobak
Ray L. Weber
Joseph G. Curatolo (Resident, Westlake, Ohio Office)
Rodney Lee Skoglund

Andrew B. Morton
Arthur M. Reginelli
Laura J. Gentilcore
Shannon V. McCue

OF COUNSEL

Jack L. Renner
Sylvia A. Petrosky

LEGAL SUPPORT PERSONNEL

Michael F. Morgan (Patent Agent)
Salvatore A. Sidoti (Patent Agent) (Resident, Westlake Office)

Reference: Key Bank.

For full biographical listings, see the Martindale-Hubbell Law Directory

*CANTON,** Stark Co.

RENNER, KENNER, GREIVE, BOBAK, TAYLOR & WEBER A LEGAL PROFESSIONAL ASSOCIATION

(See Akron)

*CINCINNATI,** Hamilton Co.

FROST & JACOBS LLP (AV)

2500 PNC Center, 201 East Fifth Street, 45202
Telephone: 513-651-6800
Telecopier: 513-651-6981
URL: http://www.frojac.com
Columbus, Ohio Office: One Columbus, 10 West Broad Street, 43215.
Telephone: 614-464-1211.
Telecopier: 614-464-1737.
Lexington, Kentucky Office: 1100 Vine Center Tower, 333 West Vine Street, 40507.
Telephone: 606-254-1100.
Telecopier: 606-253-2990.
Middletown, Ohio Office: 400 First National Bank Building, 2 North Main Street, 45042.
Telephone: 513-422-2001.
Telecopier: 513-422-3010.
Frankfort, Kentucky Office: 201 W. Main Street, 40601.
Telephone: 502-223-1400.
Telecopier: 502-223-1410.

PATENT, TRADEMARK AND COPYRIGHT ATTORNEYS
MEMBERS OF FIRM

David E. Schmit
Steven J. Goldstein
Kenneth B. Germain
Edwin R. Acheson, Jr.
Louis K. Ebling

ASSOCIATES

Ann Gallagher Robinson
Kevin S. Sprecher
Sean P. Hodge
Karen E. Kreider
Katherine F. Horvath

OF COUNSEL

Stephen E. Gillen
Gretchen R. Blum
Glenn D. Bellamy

Representative Clients: AK Steel Corporation; Chiquita; Cincinnati Bell Inc.; Cincinnati Machine; B.F. Goodrich-Hilton Davis Inc.; Hillenbrand Industries; Lexmark International; Senco Products, Inc.; Standard Textile Company, Inc.; University of Cincinnati.

(See Next Column)

FROST & JACOBS LLP—*Continued*

For Complete List of Firm Personnel, See General Section

For full biographical listings, see the Martindale-Hubbell Law Directory

*CLEVELAND,** Cuyahoga Co.

FAY, SHARPE, FAGAN, MINNICH & MCKEE, LLP (AV)

1100 Superior Avenue, Seventh Floor, 44114
Telephone: 216-861-5582
FAX: 216-241-1666
Email: fs@faysharpe.com *URL:* http://www.faysharpe.com

MEMBERS OF FIRM

Albert P. Sharpe, III
Christopher B. Fagan
Richard J. Minnich
James W. McKee
Patrick R. Roche
Thomas E. Kocovsky, Jr.
Timothy E. Nauman
Richard M. Klein
Jay F. Moldovanyi
Philip J. Moy, Jr.
Mark S. Svat
Joseph D. Dreher
Scott Andrew McCollister
Mark E. Bandy
Michael E. Hudzinski

ASSOCIATES

Sandra M. Koenig
Jude A. Fry
Colleen Flynn Goss
Brian E. Kondas
Steven M. Auvil
R. Scott Speroff
Steven M. Haas
John P. Cornely
Ann M. Skerry
James E. Scarbrough
W. Scott Harders
Brian G. Bembenick
Christopher P. Harris

OF COUNSEL

Sue Ellen Phillips

For full biographical listings, see the Martindale-Hubbell Law Directory

RANKIN, HILL, PORTER & CLARK LLP (AV)

700 Huntington Building, 925 Euclid Avenue, 44115-1405
Telephone: 216-566-9700
Fax: 216-566-9711
Email: rankin@rhpc.com

Carl A. Rankin
Stephen A. Hill
Wayne D. Porter, Jr.
Kenneth A. Clark
Randolph E. Digges, III

For full biographical listings, see the Martindale-Hubbell Law Directory

RENNER, OTTO, BOISSELLE & SKLAR, P.L.L. (AV)

Nineteenth Floor, 1621 Euclid Avenue, 44115-2183
Telephone: 216-621-1113
Cable: "Oldpat"
Telex: 8104212034 Oldpat Clv
Fax: 216-621-6165
Email: mailroom@rennerotto.com

John F. Oberlin (1880-1971)
Edwin E. Donnelly, Jr. (1925-1976)

MEMBERS OF FIRM

John W. Renner
Donald L. Otto
Armand P. Boisselle
Warren A. Sklar
Neil A. DuChez
Don W. Bulson
Gordon D. Kinder
William C. Tritt
Jay R. Campbell
Mark D. Saralino

ASSOCIATES

Cynthia S. Murphy
Thomas W. Adams
Christopher B. Jacobs
Joseph J. Crimaldi
Jonathan A Platt
Paul R. Steffes

OF COUNSEL

Walter Maky
Charles S. Lynch (Not admitted in OH; Retired)

For full biographical listings, see the Martindale-Hubbell Law Directory

*COLUMBUS,** Franklin Co.

SCHOTTENSTEIN, ZOX & DUNN A LEGAL PROFESSIONAL ASSOCIATION (AV)

The Huntington Center, 41 South High Street, 43215
Telephone: 614-462-2700
Telecopier: 614-462-5135
Telex: 650 24 444 365
URL: http://www.szd.com
Cincinnati, Ohio Office: Bank One Towers, 8044 Montgomery Road, Suite 700, 45236-2926.
Telephone: 513-792-2730.
Cleveland, Ohio Office: One Cleveland Center, 1375 East 9th Street, Suite 950.
Telephone: 216-621-6501.
Fax: 216-621-6502.

(See Next Column)

Felix C. Wade
John P. Gilligan
John C. McDonald
Susan Darnell Rector
Bridgette C. Roman
Phillip G. Lilly

Reference: Bank One of Columbus, N.A.

For Complete List of Firm Personnel, See General Section

For full biographical listings, see the Martindale-Hubbell Law Directory

*TOLEDO,** Lucas Co.

EMCH, SCHAFFER, SCHAUB & PORCELLO CO., L.P.A. (AV)

One Seagate, Suite 1980, P.O. Box 916, 43697-0916
Telephone: 419-243-1294
Fax: 419-243-8502
Email: EMCHETAL@COMPUSERVE.COM

Mark C. Schaffer
Charles R. Schaub
James F. Porcello, Jr.
Catherine B. Martineau
Gregg W. Emch
Philip M. Rice
Patrick P. Pacella

OF COUNSEL

Richard D. Emch

For full biographical listings, see the Martindale-Hubbell Law Directory

OKLAHOMA

*OKLAHOMA CITY,** Oklahoma Co.

CROWE & DUNLEVY, A PROFESSIONAL CORPORATION (AV)

1800 Mid-America Tower, 20 North Broadway, 73102-8273
Telephone: 405-235-7700
Fax: 405-239-6651
Email: marketing@crowedunlevy.com *URL:* http://www.crowedunlevy.com
Tulsa, Oklahoma Office: 500 Kennedy Building, 321 South Boston Avenue, 74103-3313.
Telephone: 918-592-9800.
Fax: 918-592-9801.
Norman, Oklahoma Office: Crowe & Dunlevy, 2500 South McGee, Suite 140, 73072-6705.
Telephone: 405-321-7317.
Fax: 405-360-4002.

D. Kent Meyers
Bill D. McCarthy
John J. Griffin, Jr.
Brooke Smith Murphy
Mack J. Morgan III
Daniel S. Hodgins
Reeder E. Ratliff
Roger A. Stong
Joseph J. Ferretti

Phillip L. Free, Jr.
Randall K. McCarthy
Mary Hirth Tolbert
Paige S. Bass
Radha Masilamani

OF COUNSEL

Ruth Gana Okediji (Not admitted in OK)

For Complete List of Firm Personnel, See General Section

For full biographical listings, see the Martindale-Hubbell Law Directory

DAY, EDWARDS, FEDERMAN, PROPESTER & CHRISTENSEN, P.C. (AV)

Suite 2900 Oklahoma Tower, 210 Park Avenue, 73102-5605
Telephone: 405-239-2121
Telecopier: 405-236-1012
URL: http://lawlinks.com/attys/ok/defpc.html

Joe E. Edwards
Rodney J. Heggy

Stuart W. Emmons

Representative Clients: Applied Thermal Systems, Inc.

For Complete List of Firm Personnel, See General Section

For full biographical listings, see the Martindale-Hubbell Law Directory

*TULSA,** Tulsa Co.

CROWE & DUNLEVY, A PROFESSIONAL CORPORATION (AV)

500 Kennedy Building, 321 South Boston Avenue, 74103-3313
Telephone: 918-592-9800
Fax: 918-592-9801
Email: marketing@crowedunlevy.com *URL:* http://www.crowedunlevy.com
Oklahoma City, Oklahoma Office: 1800 Mid-America Tower, 20 North Broadway, 73102-8273.
Telephone: 405-235-7700.
Fax: 405-239-6651.

(See Next Column)

CROWE & DUNLEVY A PROFESSIONAL CORPORATION, *Tulsa—Continued*

Norman, Oklahoma Office: Crowe & Dunlevy, 2500 South McGee, Suite 140, 73072-6705.
Telephone: 405-321-7317.
Fax: 405-360-4002.

Michael J. Gibbens

For Complete List of Firm Personnel, See General Section

For full biographical listings, see the Martindale-Hubbell Law Directory

OREGON

*PORTLAND,** Multnomah Co.

MARGER, JOHNSON & MCCOLLOM, P.C. (AV)

1030 S.W. Morrison Street, 97205
Telephone: 503-222-3613
FAX: 503-274-4622
Email: inquiry@techlaw.com *URL:* http://www.techlaw.com
Bend, Oregon Office: 777 N.W. Wall, Suite 308, 97702.
Telephone: 541-312-2500.
Fax: 541-312-8900.

Alexander C. Johnson, Jr.
Alan T. McCollom
Glenn C. Brown
Stephen S. Ford

Scott A. Schaffer
Joseph S. Makuch
Graciela G. Cowger
Hosoon Lee
Ariel S. Rogson
Gregory T. Kavounas
James E. Harris
James G. Stewart
Craig R. Rogers

LEGAL SUPPORT PERSONNEL

PARALEGAL

Kimberly A. Hubbell

OF COUNSEL

Jerome S. Marger

Representative Clients: Adidas; Advanced Power Technology; Analog Devices; Baker Hughes Inc.; Battelle Pacific Northwest Laboratories; Cisco Systems; Columbia Machine, Inc.; Elmers Restaurants, Inc.; Hanson Natural Resources Co.; Hewlett-Packard Co.

For full biographical listings, see the Martindale-Hubbell Law Directory

PENNSYLVANIA

*HARRISBURG,** Dauphin Co.

MCNEES, WALLACE & NURICK (AV)

100 Pine Street, P.O. Box 1166, 17108-1166
Telephone: 717-232-8000
Fax: 717-237-5300
Email: info@mwn.com *URL:* http://www.mwn.com
Columbus, Ohio Office: 21 East State Street, Suite 1700, 43215.
Telephone: 614-469-8000.
Fax: 614-469-4653.
Washington, D.C. Office: 1200 G Street, N.W., 20005.
Telephone: 202-434-8991.
Fax: 202-434-8707.
Hazleton, Pennsylvania Office: 1 South Church Street, Suite 302, 18201.
Telephone: 570-455-8300.
Fax: 570-455-8390.

MEMBERS OF THE FIRM

Alan R. Boynton, Jr.
Louis A. Dejoie
Michael A. Doctrow
Harvey Freedenberg
Louise Hutchinson
W. Jeffry Jamouneau
Franklin A. Miles, Jr.
Carmen Santa Maria
Dana Stevens Scaduto

OF COUNSEL

Kathleen A. Dunst

ASSOCIATES

Marc J. Farrell
Linda J. Laub
Ellen K. McDonnell (Not admitted in PA)
Mitchell A. Smolow (Resident, Hazleton Office)

For Complete List of Firm Personnel, See General Section

For full biographical listings, see the Martindale-Hubbell Law Directory

*PHILADELPHIA,** Philadelphia Co.

CAESAR, RIVISE, BERNSTEIN, COHEN & POKOTILOW, LTD. (AV)

12th Floor, 1635 Market Street, 19103-2212
Telephone: 215-567-2010
Telecopier: 215-751-1142
Email: gatekeeper@Caesarrivise.com

Alan H. Bernstein
Stanley H. Cohen
Manny D. Pokotilow
Barry A. Stein
Martin L. Faigus
Eric S. Marzluf
Robert S. Silver
Michael J. Berkowitz
Scott M. Slomowitz
Mona Gupta
David M. Tener
James J. Kozuch
Salvatore Guerriero (Not admitted in PA)
William J. Castillo (Not admitted in PA)
Francis M. Linguiti

OF COUNSEL

Max Goldman

For full biographical listings, see the Martindale-Hubbell Law Directory

DANN, DORFMAN, HERRELL AND SKILLMAN, A PROFESSIONAL CORPORATION (AV)

Suite 720, 1601 Market Street, 19103-2307
Telephone: 215-563-4100
Fax: 215-563-4044
Email: internet:email@ddhs.com

John C. Dorfman
Henry H. Skillman
Roger W. Herrell
Patrick J. Hagan
Donald R. Piper, Jr.
Vincent T. Pace
Janet E. Reed
Stephen H. Eland
Craig M. Bell
Clement A. Berard (Not admitted in PA)
Alfred W. Zaher

OF COUNSEL

C. Marshall Dann
John S. Child, Jr.
Charles N. Quinn

LEGAL SUPPORT PERSONNEL

PATENT AGENTS

John B. Berryhill
Kathleen D. Rigaut

TECHNICAL ADVISOR

Ellen Klann
Niels Haun (Technical Advisor)

For full biographical listings, see the Martindale-Hubbell Law Directory

PAUL & PAUL (AV)

2900 Two Thousand Market Street, 19103
Telephone: 215-568-4900
Cable Address: "Caveat"
Telex: 710-670-1352 Dex
Telecopier: 215-567-5057
Email: paulandpaul@compuserve.com

MEMBERS OF FIRM

James C. McConnon
John F. McNulty
Alex R. Sluzas

ASSOCIATES

Frank J. Bonini, Jr.
Paul A. Taufer
Gary A. Greene

For full biographical listings, see the Martindale-Hubbell Law Directory

SYNNESTVEDT & LECHNER LLP (AV)

2600 Aramark Tower, 1101 Market Street, 19107-2950
Telephone: 215-923-4466
Facsimile: 215-923-2189
Email: synnlech@synnlech.com *URL:* http://www.synnlech.com

Paul Synnestvedt (1870-1950)
Harvey L. Lechner (1885-1954)
Raymond H. Synnestvedt (1902-1986)
Andrew R. Klein (1928-1987)
Albert L. Free (1922-1996)
William H. Elliott, Jr. (1918-1997)

MEMBERS OF FIRM

John T. Synnestvedt
Charles H. Lindrooth
Alexis Barron
Joseph F. Posillico
Bryna S. Silver
Gary A. Hecht
Theodore Naccarella

SENIOR COUNSEL

Irving Newman (Not admitted in PA)

ASSOCIATES

Lisa B. Lane
Stephen J. Driscoll
Joshua R. Slavitt
Mark D. Simpson
Patrick John Kelly
John A. Chionchio
Gregory S. Bernabeo
Stephen James Weed (Not admitted in PA)
Peter J. Butch III (Not admitted in PA)

OF COUNSEL

Richard D. Weber

(See Next Column)

SYNNESTVEDT & LECHNER LLP—*Continued*

LEGAL SUPPORT PERSONNEL

SCIENTIFIC ADVISORS

Brett T. Freeman
Gene J. Yao

For full biographical listings, see the Martindale-Hubbell Law Directory

WOODCOCK WASHBURN KURTZ MACKIEWICZ & NORRIS LLP (AV)

One Liberty Place - 46th Floor, 17th & Market Streets, 19103
Telephone: 215-568-3100
Fax: 215-568-3439
URL: http://www.woodcock.com

Virgil E. Woodcock (1905-1974)
Lawrence T. Phelan (1900-1969)
Robert B. Washburn
Richard E. Kurtz
John J. Mackiewicz
Norman L. Norris
Dale M. Heist
Philip S. Johnson
John W. Caldwell
Gary H. Levin
Steven J. Rocci
Dianne B. Elderkin
Francis A. Paintin
John P. Donohue, Jr.
Henrik D. Parker
Suzanne E. Miller
Lynn Bavaro Morreale
Mark DeLuca
Laura Genovese Miller
Joseph Lucci
Michael P. Dunnam
Michael D. Stein
Albert J. Marcellino
David R. Bailey
Doreen Y. Trujillo

ASSOCIATES

Barbara Lynn Mullin
Kevin M. Flannery
Lynn A. Malinoski
Michael P. Straher
David A. Cherry
Michael J. Swope
Michael J. Bonella
Harold H. Fullmer
William R. Richter
John E. McGlynn
Kimberly R. Hild
Lawrence A. Aaronson
Jonathan M. Waldman
Chad E. Ziegler
Gwilym J.O. Attwell
David N. Farsiou
Paul K. Legaard
Maureen S. Gibbons
Steven H. Meyer
Thomas D. Smith
Paul B. Milcetic
Joseph R. Condo
Michael K. Jones
Frank T. Carroll
Hans J. Crosby
Mark J. Rosen
Camille M. Miller
Rena Patel
Mitchell R. Brustein
Thomas E. Watson (Not admitted in PA)
Eric H. Vance
Peter M. Ullman
Richard B. LeBlanc (Not admitted in PA)
Vincent J. Roccia
Denise Incorvaia Mroz (Not admitted in PA)

COUNSEL

Albert W. Preston, Jr.

OF COUNSEL

Anthony J. Rossi
Kathleen A. Milsark

LEGAL SUPPORT PERSONNEL

Christine A. Goddard (Scientific Advisor)

Representative Clients: Crown Cork & Seal Co.; Johnson & Johnson; ARAMARK CORPORATION; W. R. Grace & Co. - Conn.; Mobil Oil Corporation; Iomega Corp.; Asea Brown Boveri (ABB) Power T&D Company Inc.; Microsoft; Denstply International Inc.; Pharmacia & Upjohn, Inc.

For full biographical listings, see the Martindale-Hubbell Law Directory

*PITTSBURGH,** Allegheny Co.

PAUL A. BECK & ASSOCIATES (AV)

1106 Frick Building, 437 Grant Street, 15219-6101
Telephone: 412-261-4599
Fax: 412-471-6068
Email: pbeck46571@aol.com

OF COUNSEL

Floyd B. Carothers
William L. Krayer
George Raynovich, Jr.

LEGAL SUPPORT PERSONNEL

Amanda M. Dunyak (Legal Assistant)
John C. Thomas (Law Clerk)

For full biographical listings, see the Martindale-Hubbell Law Directory

*READING,** Berks Co.

BARLEY, SNYDER, SENFT & COHEN, LLC (AV)

Formerly: Miller and Murray, LLP
501 Washington Street, P.O. Box 942, 19603-0942
Telephone: 610-376-6651
Fax: 610-376-5243
Email: barley@barley.com *URL:* http://www.barley.com
Harrisburg, Pennsylvania Office: 240 North Third Street.
Telephone: 717-238-8263.
Fax: 717-238-8278.

(See Next Column)

Lancaster, Pennsylvania Office: 126 East King Street.
Telephone: 717-299-5201.
Fax: 717-291-4660.
York, Pennsylvania Office: 100 East Market Street.
Telephone: 717-846-8888.
Fax: 717-843-8492.
Chambersburg, Pennsylvania Office: 247 Lincoln Way East.
Telephone: 717-264-6494.
Fax: 717-264-1662.
Hanover, Pennsylvania Office: 14 Center Square.
Telephone: 717-637-6239.
Fax: 717-637-5407.
Birdsboro, Pennsylvania Office: 115 E. Main Street.
Telephone: 610-582-2735.
Hamburg, Pennsylvania Office: 239 State Street.
Telephone: 610-562-3721.
Oley, Pennsylvania Office: Route 73 and Main Street.
Telephone: 610-987-6350.
Morgantown, Pennsylvania Office: Route 23.
Telephone: 610-286-5958.

MEMBERS OF FIRM

John S. Hibschman
Charles F. Fitzpatrick
Gregory R. Young
Paul G. Mattaini
Elaine Pennington Stanko
William F. Colby, Jr.
Brian R. Ott
Melanie A. Zampini
Bruce J. Wolstoncroft

ASSOCIATE

Michael P. Giles

COUNSEL

James H. Murray

Representative Client: Bank of Pennsylvania/AllFirst; Conestoga Enterprises; Graham Packaging; Kerr Group; Lancaster General Hospital; King's Management; Blue Mountain Mushroom.

For Complete List of Firm Personnel, See General Section

For full biographical listings, see the Martindale-Hubbell Law Directory

RHODE ISLAND

*PROVIDENCE,** Providence Co.

HINCKLEY, ALLEN & SNYDER LLP (AV)

1500 Fleet Center, 02903-2393
Telephone: 401-274-2000
Fax: 401-277-9600
Email: firm@haslaw.com *URL:* http://www.haslaw.com
Boston, Massachusetts Office: 28 State Street, 30th Floor.
Telephone: 617-345-9000.
Fax: 617-345-9020. URL: http://www.haslaw.com.

MEMBERS OF FIRM

Paula K. Andrews (Not admitted in RI)
David D. Barricelli
Jonathan Bell
Deborah L. Benson (Not admitted in RI)
Paul Bork (Not admitted in RI)
Stephen J. Carlotti
Eric F. Eisenberg (Not admitted in RI)
Malcolm Farmer, III
Margaret D. Farrell
William R. Grimm
Paul A. Hedstrom (Not admitted in RI)
Richard L. E. Jocelyn
Elizabeth Murdock Myers
Paul F. O'Donnell, III (Not admitted in RI)
H. Peter Olsen
Julianne Palumbo (Not admitted in RI)
John J. Pendergast, III
Gerald J. Petros
James O. Reavis
Lawrence R. Robins (Not admitted in RI)
David R. Sullivan (Not admitted in RI)
Robert F. Sylvia (Not admitted in RI)
Howard E. Walker
Richard D. Wayne (Not admitted in RI)

ASSOCIATES

Mark Bianchi
Neil L. Brodsky (Not admitted in RI)
Jane E. Cohen (Not admitted in RI)
Kelley Jordan-Price
Joseph D. Whelan

OF COUNSEL

Willard Krasnow (Not admitted in RI)
Bentley Tobin
Joachim A. Weissfeld

For Complete List of Firm Personnel, See General Section

For full biographical listings, see the Martindale-Hubbell Law Directory

WM. W. RYMER (AV)

400 South Main Street, 02903
Telephone: 401-331-0181
Telecopier: 401-274-5070

For full biographical listings, see the Martindale-Hubbell Law Directory

Providence—Continued

VETTER & WHITE, INCORPORATED (AV)

20 Washington Place, 02903
Telephone: 401-421-3060
Telecopier: 401-272-6803
Email: vetlit@aol.com

Benjamin V. White, III
Gordon P. Cleary
Howard A. Merten, Jr.
Brooks R. Magratten

OF COUNSEL

George Vetter

Kimberly A. Simpson
Michael W. Long

For full biographical listings, see the Martindale-Hubbell Law Directory

SOUTH CAROLINA

*COLUMBIA,** Richland Co.

NEXSEN PRUET JACOBS & POLLARD, LLP (AV)

1441 Main Street, 15th Floor, P.O. Drawer 2426, 29202
Telephone: 803-771-8900
Facsimile: 803-253-8277
Email: NPJP@NPJP.COM *URL:* HTTP://WWW.NPJP.COM
Charleston, South Carolina Office: 200 Meeting Street, Suite 301. P.O. Box 486.
Telephone: 803-577-9440.
Facsimile: 803-720-1777.
Greenville, South Carolina Office: 201 West McBee Avenue, Fourth Floor, P.O. Box 10648.
Telephone: 864-370-2211.
Facsimile: 864-282-1177.
Myrtle Beach, South Carolina Office: 2411 Oak Street, Suite 105.
Telephone: 843-445-9688.
Facsimile: 843-445-9949.
Charlotte, North Carolina Office: 212 South Tryon Street, Suite 1700.
Telephone: 704-339-0304.
Facsimile: 704-338-5377.

MEMBERS OF FIRM

John B. Hardaway, III (Resident, Greenville, SC Office)
Michael A. Mann
Marcus A. Manos

OF COUNSEL

George E. Darby (Not admitted in SC; Resident, Greenville, SC Office)
Joseph Herbert O'Toole (Not admitted in SC; Resident, Greenville, SC Office)
Charles L. Schwab (Not admitted in SC; Resident, Greenville, SC Office)

SPECIAL COUNSEL

Oscar A. Towler, III (Resident, Greenville, SC Office)

ASSOCIATES

Sandra S. Snapp (Not admitted in SC; Resident, Greenville, SC Office)
Michael E. Wever

For Complete List of Firm Personnel, See General Section

For full biographical listings, see the Martindale-Hubbell Law Directory

TENNESSEE

*CHATTANOOGA,** Hamilton Co.

BAKER, DONELSON, BEARMAN & CALDWELL (AV)

1800 Republic Centre, 633 Chestnut Street, 37450-1800
Telephone: 423-756-2010
Telecopier: 423-756-3447
Email: info@bdbc.com *URL:* http://www.bakerdonelson.com
Memphis, Tennessee Office: 20th Floor, First Tennessee Building, 165 Madison, 38103.
Telephone: 901-526-2000.
Telecopier: 901-577-2303.
Nashville, Tennessee Office: 1700 Nashville City Center, 511 Union Street, 37219.
Telephone: 615-726-5600.
Telecopier: 615-726-0464.
Knoxville, Tennessee Office: 2200 Riverview Tower, 900 South Gay Street, 37901.
Telephone: 423-549-7000.
Telecopier: 423-525-8569.

(See Next Column)

Johnson City, Tennessee Office: SunTrust Bank Building, 207 Mockingbird Lane, P.O. Box 3038, 37602.
Telephone: 423-928-0181.
Telecopier: 423-928-5694; 423-928-3654; Kingsport: 423-246-6191.
Huntsville, Tennessee Office: 3 Courthouse Square, 37756.
Telephone: 423-663-2321.
Telecopier: 423-663-2111.
Washington, D.C. Office: Market Square, 801 Pennsylvania Avenue, N.W., 20004.
Telephone: 202-508-3400.
Telecopier: 202-508-3402.
Jackson, Mississippi Office: Suite 500, 700 North State Street, 39202.
Telephone: 601-351-2400.
Telecopier: 601-351-2424.

OF COUNSEL

Micheline Kelly Johnson

For Complete List of Firm Personnel, See General Section

For full biographical listings, see the Martindale-Hubbell Law Directory

*KNOXVILLE,** Knox Co.

LUEDEKA, NEELY & GRAHAM, P.C. (AV)

Suite 1871, Riverview Tower, 900 South Gay Street, P.O. Box 1871, 37901-1871
Telephone: 423-546-4305
Fax: 423-523-4478
Email: firm@lng-patent.com *URL:* http://www.LNG-patent.com

Edwin M. Luedeka (1920-1999)
Andrew S. Neely
Mark S. Graham
Robert O. Fox
David E. LaRose
Michael E. Sellers
Richard W. Barnes, Jr.

Jason L. Hornkohl
Mark P. Crockett

OF COUNSEL

J. Frederick Thomsen

For full biographical listings, see the Martindale-Hubbell Law Directory

*MEMPHIS,** Shelby Co.

WARING COX, PLC (AV)

Morgan Keegan Tower, 50 North Front Street, Suite 1300, 38103-1190
Telephone: 901-543-8000
Telecopy: 901-543-8030
Email: Desk@waringcox.com

John E. Kruger
Saul C. Belz

Sara A. Benin
David A. McLaughlin
Thomas Paul Brabyn
John C. Valas (Not admitted in TN)

OF COUNSEL

Richard E. Duerr, Jr.

Representative Clients: Memphis Gastroenterology Group; Delta and Pine Land Company; Bayer Corporation; Lewis Supply Company, Inc.; Hancock Fabrics; Hilliard Lyons, Inc.; Osceola Foods, Inc.; Mid-South Milling Company, Inc.; Mitsui & Co. (U.S.A.), Inc.; Helm Fertilizer Corp.

For Complete List of Firm Personnel, See General Section

For full biographical listings, see the Martindale-Hubbell Law Directory

TEXAS

*DALLAS,** Dallas Co.

HUGHES & LUCE, L.L.P. (AV)

A Registered Limited Liability Partnership including Professional Corporations
1717 Main Street, Suite 2800, 75201
Telephone: 214-939-5500
Fax: 214-939-6100; 214-939-5849
Email: H&L@hughesluce.com *URL:* http://www.hughesluce.com
Austin, Texas Office: 111 Congress, Suite 900.
Telephone: 512-482-6800.
Fax: 512-482-6859.
Houston, Texas Office: 1600 Smith Street, Suite 3550.
Telephone: 713-754-5200.
Fax: 713-754-5270.

MEMBERS OF FIRM

Craig W. Budner
Douglas A. Cawley
Stephen G. Gleboff
David N. Guedry
Darrell E. Jordan
David H. Judson
R. Matthew Molash
Theodore Stevenson, III

(See Next Column)

HUGHES & LUCE L.L.P.—*Continued*

ASSOCIATES

Christopher T. Bovenkamp
Chad W. King
John W. Patton
Aubrey Nick Pittman

OF COUNSEL

André J. Brunel
Douglas A. Sorensen

For Complete List of Firm Personnel, See General Section

For full biographical listings, see the Martindale-Hubbell Law Directory

SMITH, UNDERWOOD & PERKINS, A PROFESSIONAL CORPORATION (AV)

600 Two Lincoln Centre, 5420 LBJ Freeway, 75240
Telephone: 972-661-5114
Telecopier: 972-661-5691
Email: firm@suandp.com *URL:* http://www.suplaw.com

Timothy S. Perkins
David W. Ralston
G. Lynn Smith
William J. Underwood, Jr.

Christine A. McGuire
Amy K. Ratzlaff
P. Theodore Stoinoff, II
Val C. Cronin
Ellen P. Stewart
Todd W. Shadle
Ruth C. Logan
Christina L. Betanzos
Kent D. Williamson

For full biographical listings, see the Martindale-Hubbell Law Directory

THOMPSON & KNIGHT L.L.P. (AV)

(Attorneys and Counselors)
1700 Pacific Avenue Suite 3300, 75201
Telephone: 214-969-1700
Telecopy: 214-969-1751
Telex: 732 298
URL: http://www.tklaw.com
Austin, Texas Office: 1200 San Jacinto Center, 98 San Jacinto Boulevard, 78701.
Telephone: 512-469-6100.
Telecopy: 512-469-6180.
Fort Worth, Texas Office: 801 Cherry Street, Suite 1600, 76102.
Telephone: 817-347-1700.
Telecopy: 817-347-1799.
Houston, Texas Office: Thompson Knight Brown Parker & Leahy L.L.P., 1200 Smith Street, Suite 3600, 77002-4595.
Telephone: 713-654-8111.
Telecopier: 713-654-1871.
San Pedro Garza Garcia, Nuevo León, Mexico Office: Edificio Losoles PD-4, Av. Lázaro Cárdenas No. 2400 Pte., C.P. 66220.
Telephone: (52-8) 363-0096.
Telecopy: (52-8) 363-3067.

PARTNERS

Jane Politz Brandt
Beverly Ray Burlingame
Joe Dannenmaier
Cheryl E. Diaz
Frank Finn
Herbert J. Hammond
Veronica Smith Lewis
William J. Schuerger
Bruce S. Sostek
Stephen E. Stein
Peter J. Thoma

ASSOCIATES

Julia Elizabeth Jones
Darin M. Klemchuk
Richard L. Wynne, Jr.

OF COUNSEL

David C. Cain (Not admitted in TX)
Gayle E. Cannon
Laura Peterson Elkind

For Complete List of Firm Personnel, See General Section

For full biographical listings, see the Martindale-Hubbell Law Directory

TIMMONS & KELLY (AV)

The White House on Turtle Creek, 2401 Turtle Creek Boulevard, 75219-4760
Telephone: 214-528-1881 Fax: 214-528-1882
URL: http://www.ippractice.com

MEMBERS OF FIRM

W. Thomas Timmons
H. Dennis Kelly

ASSOCIATES

Jeffrey T. Hubbard
John S. Torkelson

OF COUNSEL

Daniel Rubin

For full biographical listings, see the Martindale-Hubbell Law Directory

*FORT WORTH,** Tarrant Co.

DECKER, JONES, MCMACKIN, MCCLANE, HALL & BATES, A PROFESSIONAL CORPORATION (AV)

2500 Bank One Tower, 500 Throckmorton Street, 76102-3812
Telephone: 817-336-2400; Metro: 817-429-5260
Fax: 817-332-3043; 336-2181
Email: email@deckerjones.com *URL:* http://www.deckerjones.com

Daniel L. Bates
Robert W. Decker
Mark S. Dugan
Janet L. Hahn
Randy J. Hall
Raymond B. Kelly, III
John B. McClane
John W. McMackin
Charles B. Milliken
Gary M. Moates
Bradley H. Rice
Jeffrey W. Storie
James L. Stripling
Brian K. Yost
Tamera H. Bennett
Arthur F. Zobal
Geoffrey A. Mantooth

Representative Clients: Martin-Sprocket and Gear, Inc.; Williamson-Dickie Manufacturing Co.; MICA Corp.; Ibertech, Inc.; Harbison-Fischer Manufacturing Co.; Employers Insurance of Texas; American International Group; Medical Protective Co.; Redman Homes, Inc.

For full biographical listings, see the Martindale-Hubbell Law Directory

*HOUSTON,** Harris Co.

CUNNINGHAM, DARLOW, ZOOK & CHAPOTON, LLP (AV)

1000 Louisiana, Suite 6900, 77002
Telephone: 713-659-5522
Fax: 713-659-4466
Email: sgosslee@cdzc.com

Tom Alan Cunningham
Debbie Crupain Darlow
Richard J. Zook
John E. Chapoton, Jr.

ASSOCIATES

Kelley M. Keller
Jon T. Powell

For full biographical listings, see the Martindale-Hubbell Law Directory

ROSENTHAL & OSHA, L.L.P. (AVⓣ)

700 Louisiana Street, Suite 4550, 77002
Telephone: 713-228-8600
Fax: 713-228-8778

Alan D. Rosenthal
Jonathan P. Osha

ASSOCIATES

Richard A. Fagin
K. Karan Reed
David E. Mixon

OF COUNSEL

L. Wayne White

LEGAL SUPPORT PERSONNEL

Adenike A. Adewuya (Patent Agent)
Daniel G. Nguyen (Patent Agent)
Thomas K. Scherer (Patent Agent)
Y. Renee Alsandor (Patent Engineer)
Jeffrey S. Bergman (Patent Engineer)
Scott W. Hejny (Patent Engineer)
W. Thomas Morrow (Patent Engineer)
Daniel H. Watanabe, Ph.D. (Japan Practice Specialist)

For full biographical listings, see the Martindale-Hubbell Law Directory

THOMPSON KNIGHT BROWN PARKER & LEAHY L.L.P. (AV)

A Registered Limited Liability Partnership including Professional Corporations
(Attorneys and Counselors)
1200 Smith Street, Suite 3600, 77002-4595
Telephone: 713-654-8111
Telecopier: 713-654-1871
URL: http://www.tklaw.com
Dallas, Texas Office: Thompson & Knight L.L.P., 1700 Pacific Avenue, Suite 3300, 75201.
Telephone: 214-969-1700.
Telecopy: 214-969-1751.
Telex: 732298.
Austin, Texas Office: Thompson & Knight L.L.P., 1200 San Jacinto Center, 98 San Jacinto Boulevard, 78701.
Telephone: 512-469-6100.
Telecopy: 512-469-6180.
Fort Worth, Texas Office: Thompson & Knight L.L.P., 801 Cherry Street, Suite 1600, 76102.
Telephone: 817-347-1700.
Telecopy: 817-347-1799.
San Pedro Garza Garcia, Nuevo León, Mexico Office: Thompson & Knight L.L.P., Edificio Losoles PD-4, Av. Lázaro Cárdenas No. 2400 PTE., C.P. 66220.
Telephone: (52-8) 363-0096.
Telecopy: (52-8) 363-3067.

(See Next Column)

THOMPSON KNIGHT BROWN PARKER & LEAHY L.L.P., *Houston—Continued*

PARTNER

Jon L. Tankersley

For Complete List of Firm Personnel, See General Section

For full biographical listings, see the Martindale-Hubbell Law Directory

UTAH

*SALT LAKE CITY,** Salt Lake Co.

CLAYTON, HOWARTH & CANNON, P.C.

(See Sandy)

MADSON & METCALF, A PROFESSIONAL CORPORATION (AV)

900 Gateway Tower West, 15 West South Temple, 84101
Telephone: 801-537-1700
Facsimile: 801-537-1799
Email: info@mmlaw.com *URL:* http://www.mmlaw.com

Craig J. Madson
L. Craig Metcalf
Evan R. Witt
A. John (Jack) Pate
Gary D.E. Pierce
David B. Fonda

John R. Thompson
Brian C. Kunzler
Barton W. Giddings
Hal D. Baird
Eric M. Barzee
Kory Christensen

For full biographical listings, see the Martindale-Hubbell Law Directory

PARR WADDOUPS BROWN GEE & LOVELESS, A PROFESSIONAL CORPORATION (AV)

Suite 1300, 185 South State Street, 84111-1537
Telephone: 801-532-7840
Fax: 801-532-7750
URL: http://www.pwlaw.com

Robert B. Lochhead
Brian J. Romriell
Brian G. Lloyd
Gregory M. Hess
Terry E. Welch
Jeffrey J. Hunt
Jonathan O. Hafen
Mark A. Wagner
D. Craig Parry

For Complete List of Firm Personnel, See General Section

For full biographical listings, see the Martindale-Hubbell Law Directory

SNELL & WILMER L.L.P. (AV)

111 East Broadway, Suite 900, 84111-1004
Telephone: 801-237-1900
Fax: 801-237-1950
URL: http://www.swlaw.com
Phoenix, Arizona Office: One Arizona Center, 85004-2202.
Telephone: 602-382-6000.
Fax: 602-382-6070.
Tucson, Arizona Office: One South Church Avenue, Suite 1500, 85701-1612.
Telephone: 520-882-1200.
Fax: 520-884-1294.
Orange County Office: 1920 Main Street, Suite 1200, Irvine, California 92614-7230.
Telephone: 949-253-2700.
Fax: 949-955-2507.

MEMBERS OF FIRM

John R. Morris, Jr.
Alan L. Sullivan
Bryon J. Benevento
Robert W. Payne
P. Christian Anderson

Representative Clients: For list of Representative Clients, see end of biographical listings in the Martindale-Hubbell Law Directory.

For Complete List of Firm Personnel, See General Section

For full biographical listings, see the Martindale-Hubbell Law Directory

VAN COTT, BAGLEY, CORNWALL & McCARTHY, A PROFESSIONAL CORPORATION (AV)

50 South Main Street, Suite 1600, P.O. Box 45340, 84145-0340
Telephone: 801-532-3333
Telecopier: 801-534-0058
Email: info@vancott.com *URL:* http://www.vancott.com
Ogden, Utah Office: 2404 Washington Boulevard, Suite 900.
Telephone: 801-394-5783.
Park City, Utah Office: 2200 Park Avenue, Suite C200-A.
Telephone: 435-649-3889.

David J. Smith

(See Next Column)

Jennifer K. Anderson
Stephen K. Christiansen
Tacy A. Hartman

For Complete List of Firm Personnel, See General Section

For full biographical listings, see the Martindale-Hubbell Law Directory

WORKMAN, NYDEGGER & SEELEY, A PROFESSIONAL CORPORATION (AV)

1000 Eagle Gate Tower, 60 East South Temple, 84111
Telephone: 801-533-9800
Telecopier: 801-328-1707
Email: info@wnspat.com *URL:* http://www.wnspat.com

Rick D. Nydegger
David O. Seeley
Brent P. Lorimer
Thomas R. Vuksinick
Larry R. Laycock
Jonathan W. Richards
David R. Wright
John C. Stringham
Bradley K. DeSandro
John M. Guynn
Charles L. Roberts
Gregory M. Taylor
Dana L. Tangren
Kevin B. Laurence
Eric L. Maschoff
Charles J. Veverka
Robyn L. Phillips
Richard C. Gilmore (Not admitted in UT)
David B. Dellenbach
Kevin K. Johanson
L. David Griffin
R. Burns Israelsen
David R. Todd
Fraser D. Roy
Carl T. Reed
Jesús Juanós i Timoneda
Stephen D. Prodnuk
R. Parrish Freeman, Jr.
Peter F. Malen, Jr.
Adrian J. Lee
Kyle H. Flindt

OF COUNSEL

H. Ross Workman

For full biographical listings, see the Martindale-Hubbell Law Directory

SANDY, Salt Lake Co.

CLAYTON, HOWARTH & CANNON, P.C. (AV)

10150 South Centennial Parkway, Suite 400, P.O. Box 1909, 84091
Telephone: 801-255-5335
Fax: 801-256-2043
Email: patlaw@chcpat.com

Grant R. Clayton
Alan J. Howarth
Karl R. Cannon

For full biographical listings, see the Martindale-Hubbell Law Directory

THORPE, NORTH & WESTERN, L.L.P. (AV)

A Partnership including a Professional Corporation
8180 South 700 East, Suite 200, 84070
Telephone: 801-566-6633
Fax: 801-566-0750
Mailing Address: P.O. Box 1219, Sandy, Utah, 84091
Email: patlaw@tnw.com *URL:* http://www.tnw.com
Las Vegas, Nevada Office: 2345 Red Rock Street, Suite 310. Telephone 702-368-7767.

Calvin E. Thorpe (1938-1999)
Vaughn W. North
M. Wayne Western

ASSOCIATES

Michael W. Starkweather (Not admitted in UT)
Clifton W. Thompson (Not admitted in UT)
Garron M. Hobson
Peter M. deJonge
Weili Cheng, PhD.
David R. McKinney
Steve M. Perry
Gary P. Oakeson
David W. Osborne

TECHNICAL CONSULTANT

Loren Hulse

OF COUNSEL

Neil J. Beller (Resident, Las Vegas, Nevada Office)

For full biographical listings, see the Martindale-Hubbell Law Directory

VIRGINIA

ALEXANDRIA, (Independent City)

ROGERS & KILLEEN (AV)

Suite 400, 510 King Street, 22314
Telephone: 703-836-0400
Telex: 283843 LAWR UR
Cable Address: "LAWROGERS"
Facsimile: 703-836-1539
Email: ideas@randk.com

(See Next Column)

ROGERS & KILLEEN—*Continued*

MEMBERS OF FIRM

Joseph M. Killeen (1947-1998)
L. Lawton Rogers, III
Mark Charles Comtois
D. Joseph English
Patrick Dennis McPherson (Not admitted in VA)

ASSOCIATES

Howard N. Shipley
Patrick J. Wells (Not admitted in VA)
Donna D. King (Not admitted in VA)

For full biographical listings, see the Martindale-Hubbell Law Directory

*ARLINGTON,** Arlington Co.

ANTONELLI, TERRY, STOUT & KRAUS, LLP (AV)

1300 North Seventeenth Street, Suite 1800, 22209
Telephone: 703-312-6600
Telefacsimile: 703-312-6666
Email: email@antonelli.com

Donald R. Antonelli
David T. Terry
Melvin Kraus
William I. Solomon (Not admitted in VA)
Gregory E. Montone
Ronald J. Shore
Donald E. Stout
Alan E. Schiavelli
James N. Dresser
Carl I. Brundidge (Not admitted in VA)
Paul J. Skwierawski (Not admitted in VA)

Randall S. Svihla
David S. Lee (Not admitted in VA)
Robert M. Bauer
Demetra J. Mills
Hung H. Bui (Not admitted in VA)
R. Edward Brake (Not admitted in VA)
George N. Stevens (Not admitted in VA)
Frederick D. Bailey
Henry M. Zykorie (Not admitted in VA)

OF COUNSEL

Dale Curtis Hogue, Sr.
James H. Laughlin, Jr.

LEGAL SUPPORT PERSONNEL

PATENT AGENT

Larry N. Anagnos

For full biographical listings, see the Martindale-Hubbell Law Directory

BERGERT & BERGERT (AV)

Suite 706, 2121 Crystal Drive, 22202
Telephone: 703-521-6590
Facsimile: 703-521-8928
Email: bertlaw1@aol.com

MEMBERS OF FIRM

Frederick L. Bergert *
Thomas F. Bergert

*Admission in Virginia limited to Patent, Trademark, Copyright and Unfair Competition Causes only.

For full biographical listings, see the Martindale-Hubbell Law Directory

ROPER & QUIGG (AV)

Three Crystal Park, 2231 Crystal Drive, Suite 410, 22202
Telephone: 703-920-8910
Facsimile: 703-979-5227
URL: http://www.roperandquigg.com
Chicago, Illinois Office: 200 South Michigan Avenue, Suite 1000.
Telephone: 312-408-0855.
Facsimile: 312-408-0865.

MEMBERS OF FIRM

Harry J. Roper (Not admitted in VA)
Donald J. Quigg
Archie W. Umphlett (Not admitted in VA)

For full biographical listings, see the Martindale-Hubbell Law Directory

*FAIRFAX,** (Ind. City; Seat of Fairfax Co.)

MCCANDLISH & LILLARD, A PROFESSIONAL CORPORATION (AV)

Fair Oaks Plaza, 11350 Random Hills Road, Suite 500, 22030-7429
Telephone: 703-273-2288
Fax: 703-352-4300
Email: mccand@patriot.net *URL:* http://www.mccandlaw.com
Leesburg, Virginia Office: 305 Harrison Street, S.E., Third Floor.
Telephone: 703-737-0200.
Fax: 703-737-0165.

Robert J. McCandlish, Jr. (1909-1996)
Rothwell J. Lillard (1910-1989)
Jesse B. Wilson, III
Peter A. Arntson
Gary W. Brown
Randolph A. Sutliff
Robert H. J. Loftus
William McCauley Arnold
Stephen C. Price
Stephen K. Fox
Douglas J. Sanderson

(See Next Column)

R. Peyton Mahaffey
William L. Carey
John W. Farrell
Eric J. Berghold
Ralph M. Tener
Vicki L. Layman
Adam W. Smith

Daniel P. Lyon
Lawrence J. McClafferty
Brian R. Sanderson

For full biographical listings, see the Martindale-Hubbell Law Directory

ODIN, FELDMAN & PITTLEMAN, P.C. (AV)

9302 Lee Highway, Suite 1100, 22031
Telephone: 703-218-2100
Facsimile: 703-218-2160
Email: OFP@OFPLAW.COM

Dexter S. Odin
Bruce M. Blanchard
Leslye S. Fenton
Kevin Thomas Oliveira

Thomas N. Tartaro

OF COUNSEL

Thomas E. Chilcott

For Complete List of Firm Personnel, See General Section

For full biographical listings, see the Martindale-Hubbell Law Directory

NORFOLK, (Independent City)

PAYNE, GATES, FARTHING & RADD, P.C. (AV)

15th Floor, Dominion Tower, 999 Waterside Drive, Suite 1515, 23510-3309
Telephone: 757-640-1500
Facsimile: 757-627-6583
URL: http://www.paynegates.com

Ronald M. Gates
Philip R. Farthing
Anthony F. Radd
Glen M. Robertson
Brian R. Dinning
Todd J. Preti
Marshall A. Winslow, Jr.

C. Arthur Robinson, II
Stephen E. Heretick
Raymond L. Hogge, Jr.

OF COUNSEL

Charles E. Payne

For full biographical listings, see the Martindale-Hubbell Law Directory

RESTON, Fairfax Co.

WHITHAM, CURTIS & WHITHAM, PLC (AV)

Suite 900 11800 Sunrise Valley Drive, 20191
Telephone: 703-391-2510
Facsimile: 703-391-9035
Email: Patents1@IX.Netcom.com *URL:* http://www.wcw-law.com

C. Lamont Whitham
Marshall M. Curtis
Michael E. Whitham

Kevin A. Reif
Elizabeth W. Cook
Samuel W. Ntiros
Andrew Michael Calderon
Joni D. Stutman
Gregory Scott Discher

OF COUNSEL

Clyde R Christofferson

For full biographical listings, see the Martindale-Hubbell Law Directory

RICHMOND, (Independent City)

WILLIAMS, MULLEN, CLARK & DOBBINS, A PROFESSIONAL CORPORATION (AV)

Two James Center, 1021 East Cary Street, P.O. Box 1320, 23218-1320
Telephone: 804-643-1991
Fax: 804-783-6507
URL: http://www.wmcd.com
Newport News Office: Harbor Bank Center, Suite 210, One Old Oyster Point Road, 23602-7119.
Telephone: 757-249-5100.
Fax: 757-249-5109.
Virginia Beach Office: One Columbus Center, 23462-6763.
Telephone: 757-499-8800.
Fax: 757-473-0395.
Vienna Office: 1593 Spring Hill Road, Suite 510, 22182.
Telephone: 703-760-5200.
Fax: 703-748-0244.
Washington, D.C. Office: The Farragut Building, 900 17th Street, N.W., Suite 700, 20006.
Telephone: 202-293-0213.
Fax: 804-783-6507. Fax Within D.C.: 202-293-5939.
London, England Office: Blake Lodge, Bridge Lane, SW11 3AD.
Telephone: (011-44-71) 223-2756.
Fax: (011-44-71) 350-0156.

(See Next Column)

WILLIAMS, MULLEN, CLARK & DOBBINS A PROFESSIONAL CORPORATION, *Richmond—Continued*

Riyadh, Saudi Arabia Affiliate Office: Saudi-American Legal Consultants Commercial Building #2, Diplomatic Quarter, P.O. Box 57270, 11574.
Telephone: (011-966-1) 488-1563.
Fax: (011-966-1) 488-0542.

Craig L. Mytelka (Resident, Virginia Beach Office)

Bradford D. Bimson (Resident, Virginia Beach Office)
Megan E. Burns (Resident, Virginia Beach Office)
John F. Carroll, IV (Resident, Virginia Beach Office)
Clifford A. Coppola (Resident, Virginia Beach Office)

For Complete List of Firm Personnel, See General Section

For full biographical listings, see the Martindale-Hubbell Law Directory

WASHINGTON

*SEATTLE,** King Co.

SEED AND BERRY LLP (AV)

6300 Columbia Center, 98104-7092
Telephone: 206-622-4900
Facsimile: 206-682-6031
URL: http://www.seed-berry.com

MEMBERS OF FIRM

Richard W. Seed
Robert J. Baynham
Edward W. Bulchis
George C. Rondeau, Jr.
David H. Deits
William O. Ferron, Jr.
Paul T. Meiklejohn
David J. Maki
David V. Carlson
Richard G. Sharkey
Karl R. Hermanns
David D. McMasters (Managing Partner)
Michael J. Donohue

OF COUNSEL

Ellen M. Bierman
Jane E. R. Potter

ASSOCIATES

David W. Parker
Frank Abramonte
E. Russell Tarleton
Stephen J. Rosenman
Thomas E. Loop
Dale C. Barr
Kevin S. Costanza
Brian L. Johnson
Susan D. Betcher
Mark Roberts
Dennis M. de Guzman
Kimton N. Eng
Andrew F. Pratt
William T. Christiansen II
Timothy L. Boller
Robert Iannucci
Gary M. Myles
Brian C. Park
Kenneth H. Tarbet (Not admitted in WA)

For full biographical listings, see the Martindale-Hubbell Law Directory

WISCONSIN

BROOKFIELD, Waukesha Co.

RYAN KROMHOLZ & MANION, S.C. (AV)

3360 Gateway Road, 53045
Telephone: 262-797-6700
Facsimile: 262-797-9600
Toll No: 800-686-9333
URL: http://www.rkmiplaw.com

Daniel D. Ryan
Joseph A. Kromholz
John M. Manion

Patricia Gollhardt Jones
Laura A. Dable
Daniel R. Johnson

SENIOR COUNSEL

Allan O. Maki
Paul R. Puerner

OF COUNSEL

Arnold J. Ericsen
Henry C. Fuller, Jr.
Ralph G. Hohenfeldt (Emeritus)
Allan B. Wheeler (Emeritus)

For full biographical listings, see the Martindale-Hubbell Law Directory

*MADISON,** Dane Co.

NEIDER & BOUCHER, S.C. (AV)

440 Science Drive, P.O. Box 5510, 53705-0510
Telephone: 608-661-4500
Facsimile: 608-661-4510
URL: http://www.neiderboucher.com
URL: http://www.lawyers.com/neider&boucher-sc

(See Next Column)

Ronald C. Berman
Joseph W. Boucher
Charles E. Neider
Steven C. Underwood

Susan M. De Groot
Erik W. Ibele
Rana Kang
Cynthia L. Richson
Matthew L. Schemmel
Kent L. Schlienger
Dean T. Stange

OF COUNSEL

Ralph M. Cagle
Ronald R. Smith

For full biographical listings, see the Martindale-Hubbell Law Directory

CANADA
ALBERTA

*CALGARY,** Calgary Jud. Dist.

PARLEE MCLAWS (AV)

3400 Petro-Canada Centre, 150 - 6th Avenue, SW, T2P 3Y7
Telephone: 403-294-7000
Telecopier: 403-265-8263
Email: lawyers@parlee.com *URL:* http://www.parlee.com
Edmonton, Alberta Office: 15th Floor Manulife Place, 10180 101st Street.
Telephone: 403-423-8500.
Telecopier: 403-423-2870.

ASSOCIATE

Ariane E. Young

For Complete List of Firm Personnel, See General Section

For full biographical listings, see the Martindale-Hubbell Law Directory

*EDMONTON,** Edmonton Jud. Dist.

PARLEE MCLAWS (AV)

15th Floor Manulife Place, 10180 101st Street, T5J 4K1
Telephone: 403-423-8500
Telecopier: 403-423-2870
Email: lawyers@parlee.com *URL:* http://www.parlee.com
Calgary, Alberta Office: 3400 Petro-Canada Centre, 150 - 6th Avenue, SW.
Telephone: 403-294-7000.
Telecopier: 403-265-8263.

MEMBER OF FIRM

Bruce D. Hirsche, Q.C.

ASSOCIATE

Gregory P. Nakonechny

For Complete List of Firm Personnel, See General Section

For full biographical listings, see the Martindale-Hubbell Law Directory

CANADA
BRITISH COLUMBIA

*VANCOUVER,** Vancouver Co.

SMART & BIGGAR (AV)

Box 11560, Vancouver Centre, 2200 - 650 West Georgia Street, V6B 4N8
Telephone: 604-682-7295
Facsimile: 604-682-0274
Email: vancouver@smart-biggar.ca *URL:* http://www.smart-biggar.ca
Ottawa, Ontario Office: Suite 900, 55 Metcalfe Street, P.O. Box 2999, Station D, K1P 5Y6.
Telephone: 613-232-2486.
Facsimile: 613-232-8440. Email: ottawa@smart-biggar.ca.
Toronto, Ontario Office: Box 111, The First Century Tower, 1500-438 University Avenue, M5G 2K8.
Telephone: 416-593-5514.
Facsimile: 416-591-1690. Email: toronto@smart-biggar.ca.
Montreal, Quebec Office: 1000 De La Gauchetière Street West, Suite 3400, H3B 4W5.
Telephone: 514-954-1500.
Facsimile: 514-954-1396. Email: montreal@smart-biggar.ca.

MEMBERS OF FIRM

Michael D. Manson (Resident)
Brian G. Kingwell (Resident)
J. Christopher Robinson (Resident)

ASSOCIATES

Otto Zsigmond
Theodore W. Sum (Resident)
Timothy P. Lo (Resident)
Stephen J. Ferance (Resident)

(See Next Column)

SMART & BIGGAR—*Continued*

PATENT & TRADEMARK AGENTS

Brian J. Wood (Resident) John W. Knox (Resident)
Neil S. Clark (Resident)

For full biographical listings, see the Martindale-Hubbell Law Directory

CANADA NEWFOUNDLAND

*ST. JOHN'S,**

MCINNES COOPER (AV)

Barristers, Solicitors & Trade Mark Agents
Baine Johnston Centre, 5th Floor, 10 Fort William Place, P.O. Box 5939, A1C 5X4
Telephone: 709-722-8735
Telecopier: 709-722-1763
Email: mcrsj@mcrlaw.com *URL:* http://www.mcrlaw.com
Halifax, Nova Scotia Office: Summit Place, 1601 Lower Water Street, P.O. Box 730, B3J 2V1.
Telephone: 902-425-6500.
Fax: 902-425-6350. Email: mcrhfx@mcrlaw.com.
Moncton, New Brunswick Office: Place Moncton Place, 655 Main Street, P.O. Box 1368, E1C 8T6.
Telephone: 506-857-8970.
Fax: 506-857-4095. Email: mcrmctn@mcrlaw.com.
Charlottetown, Prince Edward Island Office: BDC Place, Suite 620, 119 Kent Street, C1A 1N3.
Telephone: 902-368-8473.
Fax: 902-368-8346. Email: mcrpei@mcrlaw.com.
Fredericton, New Brunswick Office: Suite 600, 570 Queen Street, P.O. Box 610.
Telephone: 506-458-8572.
Fax: 506-458-9903. Email: mcrfton@mcrlaw.com.

ASSOCIATE

Jacqueline S. Bartlett

For Complete List of Firm Personnel, See General Section

For full biographical listings, see the Martindale-Hubbell Law Directory

CANADA NOVA SCOTIA

*HALIFAX,** Regional Munic. of Halifax

MCINNES COOPER (AV)

Barristers, Solicitors & Trade Mark Agents
Summit Place, 1601 Lower Water Street, P.O. Box 730, B3J 2V1
Telephone: 902-425-6500
Fax: 902-425-6350
Email: mcrhfx@mcrlaw.com *URL:* http://www.mcrlaw.com
St. John's, Newfoundland Office: Baine Johnston Centre, 5th Floor, 10 Fort William Place, P.O. Box 5939, A1C 5X4.
Telephone: 709-722-8735.
Telecopier: 709-722-1763. Email: mcrsj@mcrlaw.com.
Moncton, New Brunswick Office: Place Moncton Place, 655 Main Street, P.O. Box 1368, E1C 8T6.
Telephone: 506-857-8970.
Fax: 506-857-4095. Email: mcrmctn@mcrlaw.com.
Charlottetown, Prince Edward Island Office: BDC Place, Suite 620, 119 Kent Street, C1A 1N3.
Telephone: 902-368-8473.
Fax: 902-368-8346. Email: mcrpei@mcrlaw.com.
Fredericton, New Brunswick Office: Suite 600, 570 Queen Street, P.O. Box 610.
Telephone: 506-458-8572.
Fax: 506-458-9903. Email: mcrfton@mcrlaw.com.

PARTNERS

David H. Reardon, Q.C. Peter M. S. Bryson

ASSOCIATES

Jennifer A. Healy Janet Clark
Kristi Sebalj

For Complete List of Firm Personnel, See General Section

For full biographical listings, see the Martindale-Hubbell Law Directory

CANADA ONTARIO

*OTTAWA,** Regional Munic. of Ottawa-Carleton

SMART & BIGGAR (AV)

Suite 900, 55 Metcalfe Street, P.O. Box 2999, Station D, K1P 5Y6
Telephone: 613-232-2486
Facsimile: 613-232-8440
Email: ottawa@smart-biggar.ca *URL:* http://www.smart-biggar.ca
Toronto, Ontario Office: Box 111, The First Century Tower, 1500-438 University Avenue, M5G 2K8.
Telephone: 416-593-5514.
Facsimile: 416-591-1690. Email: toronto@smart-biggar.ca.
Montreal, Quebec Office: 1000 De La Gauchetière Street West, Suite 3400, H3B 4W5.
Telephone: 514-954-1500.
Facsimile: 514-954-1396. Email: montreal@smart-biggar.ca.
Vancouver, British Columbia Office: Box 11560, Vancouver Centre, 2200 - 650 West Georgia Street, V6B 4N8.
Telephone: 604-682-7295.
Facsimile: 604-682-0274. Email: vancouver@smart-biggar.ca.

MEMBERS OF FIRM

James D. Kokonis, Q.C.
Alan R. Campbell
Robert D. Gould
Raymond Trudeau
**(Not admitted in ON)
Joy D. Morrow
Gunars A. Gaikis *
Michael D. Manson ***
Ronald D. Faggetter *
Mark K. Evans *
Alistair G. Simpson *
Steven B. Garland
Nicholas H. Fyfe, Q.C.
A. David Morrow
John R. Morrissey *
Thomas R. Kelly
John Bochnovic
François Guay
**(Not admitted in ON)
Keltie R. Sim *
Glen B. Tremblay
J. Christopher Robinson ***
Brian P. Isaac
J. Sheldon Hamilton *
Brian G. Kingwell ***

ASSOCIATES

Donald F. Phenix
Yoon Kang *
Matthew Zischka *
Christian Bolduc
**(Not admitted in ON)
Elliott S. Simcoe
Theodore W. Sum ***
Grant W. Lynds
Shonagh L. McVean *
Kohji Suzuki
Kevin K. Graham
Marc-André Huot
**(Not admitted in ON)
Daphne L. Maravei
Stephen J. Ferance ***
Peter R. Wilcox *
Philip Lapin
Otto Zsigmond ***
Dennis S.K. Leung
Ywe J. Looper
Timothy P. Lo ***
Marc Gagnon
**(Not admitted in ON)
Nancy P. Pei *
Christine N. Genge
Geneviève M. Prévost *
Mark G. Biernacki *
Robert Guay
Kevin A. O'Neil *
Jean-Sébastien Brière **
Ekaterina K. Tsimberis **

COUNSEL

Immanuel Goldsmith, Q.C. *

PATENT & TRADEMARK AGENTS

Hugh O'Gorman
James McGraw
Michael E. Wheeler
Tokuo Hirama
John W. Knox ***
Brian J. Wood ***
A. Dennis Armstrong
R. John Haley
Stephan P. Georgiev **
Neil S. Clark ***
R. Allan Brett

*Toronto Office
**Montreal Office
***Vancouver Office

For full biographical listings, see the Martindale-Hubbell Law Directory

*TORONTO,** Regional Munic. of Toronto

DEETH WILLIAMS WALL, LLP (AV)

National Bank Building, 150 York Street, Suite 400, M5H 3S5
Telephone: 416-941-9440
Facsimile: 416-941-9443
Email: info@dww.com *URL:* http://www.dww.com

MEMBERS OF FIRM

Douglas N. Deeth
Amy-Lynne Williams
Gervas W. Wall
A. Marijo Coates
Victor V. Butsky
Michael Erdle

ASSOCIATES

Gordon S. Jepson
Diane M. LaCalamita
Noel A. Courage
Shereen Hamdy
Aílbe C. Flynn

For full biographical listings, see the Martindale-Hubbell Law Directory

Toronto—Continued

KELLY AFFLECK GREENE (AV)

One First Canadian Place, Suite 840, P.O. Box 489, M5X 1E5
Telephone: 416-360-2800
Fax: 416-360-5960
Email: info@kag.net *URL:* http://www.kag.net

MEMBERS OF FIRM

W. Anthony Kelly, Q.C.
Donald S. Affleck, Q.C.
Peter R. Greene
Donald B. Houston
James C. Orr
Peter C. Wardle
Helen A. Daley
Melissa J. Kennedy

ASSOCIATES

Kenneth A. Dekker
W. Michael G. Osborne
Jason C. Markwell
Patrice F. Band

For full biographical listings, see the Martindale-Hubbell Law Directory

SIM, HUGHES, ASHTON & MCKAY (AV)

Sixth Floor, 330 University Avenue, M5G 1R7
Telephone: 416-595-1155
Cable Address: "Simbas" Toronto
Telex: 065-24567
Telecopier: 416-595-1163
Email: mailsim@sim-mcburney.com *URL:* http://www.sim-mcburney.com

Roger T. Hughes, Q.C.
Toni B. Polson Ashton
Kenneth D. McKay
Timothy M. Lowman
Stephen M. Lane
Arthur B. Renaud
Patricia A. Rae
Barbara J. Murchie

ASSOCIATES

John N. Allport
Steven L. Nemetz
Robert C. T. Liang
Kamleh J. Nicola
Gillian M. Smith
L. E. Trent Horne

For full biographical listings, see the Martindale-Hubbell Law Directory

SMART & BIGGAR (AV)

Box 111, The First Century Tower, 1500-438 University Avenue, M5G 2K8
Telephone: 416-593-5514
Facsimile: 416-591-1690
Email: toronto@smart-biggar.ca *URL:* http://www.smart-biggar.ca
Ottawa, Ontario Office: Suite 900, 55 Metcalfe Street, P.O. Box 2999, Station D, K1P 5Y6.
Telephone: 613-232-2486.
Facsimile: 613-232-8440. Email: ottawa@smart-biggar.ca.
Montreal, Quebec Office: 1000 De La Gauchetière Street West, Suite 3400, H3B 4W5.
Telephone: 514-954-1500.
Facsimile: 514-954-1396. Email: montreal@smart-biggar.ca.
Vancouver, British Columbia Office: Box 11560, Vancouver Centre, 2200 - 650 West Georgia Street, V6B 4N8.
Telephone: 604-682-7295.
Facsimile: 604-682-0274. Email: vancouver@smart-biggar.ca.

MEMBERS OF FIRM

John R. Morrissey (Resident)
Keltie R. Sim (Resident)
Mark K. Evans (Resident)
Gunars A. Gaikis (Resident)
Ronald D. Faggetter (Resident)
Alistair G. Simpson (Resident)
J. Sheldon Hamilton (Resident)

ASSOCIATES

Peter R. Wilcox (Resident)
Matthew Zischka (Resident)
Nancy P. Pei (Resident)
Mark G. Biernacki (Resident)
Yoon Kang (Resident)
Shonagh L. McVean (Resident)
Geneviève M. Prévost (Resident)
Kevin A. O'Neil (Resident)

COUNSEL

Immanuel Goldsmith, Q.C. (Resident)

For full biographical listings, see the Martindale-Hubbell Law Directory

CANADA
QUEBEC

*MONTREAL,** Montreal Dist.

MCMASTER GERVAIS (AV)

A General Partnership
1000 de La Gauchetière Street West, Suite 900, H3B 5H4
Telephone: 514-879-1212
Fax: 514-954-1905
Email: info@mcmastergervais.com *URL:* http://www.mcmastergervais.com

MEMBERS OF FIRM

Timothy R. Carsley
Raymond Picard
Michael Patry
Michael Bantey
Lionel J. Blanshay
Pierre Gattuso
H. John Godber
Patrice Martin
Geneviève Bergeron

COUNSEL

Bartha M. Knoppers

For Complete List of Firm Personnel, See General Section

For full biographical listings, see the Martindale-Hubbell Law Directory

POULIOT, MERCURE (AV)

CIBC Tower, 31st Floor, 1155 René-Lévesque Boulevard, West, H3B 3S6
Telephone: 514-875-5210
Telecopier: 514-875-4308
Email: POUMER@CEDEP.COM
Genève, Suisse Office: 8, Rue de la Rôtisserie, 1204 Geneva, Switzerland.
Telephone: +41 22-28 79 40.
Telecopier: +41 22-21 23 67.

MEMBERS OF FIRM

Georges A. Pouliot, Q.C.
Gilles Brunelle
Luc Gratton
Brian Riordan
Pierre Paquet
Anne-Marie Gauthier
Yvon Brizard
Robert Tessier
Daniel Gagné
Lilia Pouliot
Marco Veilleux
Alain Nadon
Jean H. Gagnon
Richard Fontaine
Normand Royal
Gilles Bertrand
Jean Larivière
Louis-Michel Tremblay
David I. Johnston
Stéphane Hébert
Jacques LeBel, Q.C.
Joel A. Silcoff
Ronald M. Auclair
Philippe Roy
Maxime B. Rhéaume
Serge Desrochers
C. Keenan LaPierre
Alain Bond
Louis Coallier
Nicole Chouinard
Stéphane Teasdale

ASSOCIATES

Micheline Perrault
Caroline Lemoine
Béatrice Arronis
Yvan Nantel
Sylvie Boulanger
Vincent Frenette
Robert Cardin
Alexandre Henri
Brent J. Muir
Louise Tremblay
Chantal Joubert
Normand D'Amour
Pascale Cloutier
Eric Couture
Frédéric Chatel
Mary-Lynn Breton
Alexandre Ajami

For full biographical listings, see the Martindale-Hubbell Law Directory

INTERNATIONAL BUSINESS LAW

MINNESOTA

*MINNEAPOLIS,** Hennepin Co.

HAUGEN LAW FIRM, PLLP (AV)

121 South Eighth Street, Suite 1130, 55402
Telephone: 612-339-8300
Fax: 612-339-8200
Email: ohaugen@haugenlaw.com *URL:* http://www.haugenlaw.com

Orrin M. Haugen
Eric O. Haugen

OF COUNSEL

Douglas E. Mackenzie

For full biographical listings, see the Martindale-Hubbell Law Directory

NIKOLAI, MERSEREAU & DIETZ, P.A. (AV)

820 International Centre, 900 Second Avenue South, 55402
Telephone: 612-339-7461
Telecopier: 612-349-6556
Email: tnikolai@prodigy.net

Thomas J. Nikolai
James T. Nikolai
Charles G. Mersereau
Paul T. Dietz

Reference: Norwest Bank.

For full biographical listings, see the Martindale-Hubbell Law Directory

MISSOURI

ST. LOUIS, (Independent City)

HELFREY, SIMON & JONES, P.C. (AV)

120 South Central Avenue Suite 1500, 63105
Telephone: 314-725-9100
Facsimile: 314-725-5754

OF COUNSEL

Martin T. Sigillito

For full biographical listings, see the Martindale-Hubbell Law Directory

SCHRAMM & PINES, L.L.C. (AV)

Suite 950 The Bemiston Tower, 231 South Bemiston Avenue, 63105
Telephone: 314-721-5321
Telecopier: 314-721-0790

MEMBERS OF FIRM

Paul H. Schramm
M. Harvey Pines
Daniel R. Schramm

Timothy I. Nicholson
Dean A. Schramm

Reference: Magna Bank.

For full biographical listings, see the Martindale-Hubbell Law Directory

NEBRASKA

*OMAHA,** Douglas Co.

McGILL, GOTSDINER, WORKMAN & LEPP, P.C. (AV)

Suite 500 - First National Plaza, 11404 West Dodge Road, 68154
Telephone: 402-492-9200
Telecopier: 402-492-9222
Email: mgwl@mgwl.com

R. Thomas Workman

Representative Clients: Behlen Mfg. Co.

For Complete List of Firm Personnel, See General Section

For full biographical listings, see the Martindale-Hubbell Law Directory

NEVADA

*LAS VEGAS,** Clark Co.

ALVERSON, TAYLOR, MORTENSEN, NELSON & SANDERS (AV)

7401 West Charleston Boulevard, 89117
Telephone: 702-384-7000
FAX: 702-385-7000
Email: alverson@intermind.net
Reno, Nevada Office: 245 East Liberty, Suite 520, 89505.
Telephone: 775-329-0473.
Fax: 775-329-3303.

MEMBERS OF FIRM

J. Bruce Alverson
Eric K. Taylor
David J. Mortensen
Erven T. Nelson
LeAnn Sanders

OF COUNSEL

Jack C. Cherry
Kurt D. Anderson
Philip C. Van Alstyne

ASSOCIATES

Rebecca Hopkins Miller
Sandra Smagac
Victoria L. Nelson
Aaron D. Lovaas
Diane Obritsch
Michael A. Olsen
Randal D. Shimon
Catherine A. Olendorff
Monica L. Pierce
Gabriel D. Lither
Kurt R. Bonds
Darius F. Rafie
Mark J. King, IV
Shell L. Mercer
Carrie S. Bourdeau
Jason Lane Earnest
Nathan R. Reinmiller
Donn C. Alexander
Afshin Tadayon
Eric O. Freeman
Lindsay L. Stadtlander
Julie M. Sueoka

Representative Clients: Citibank (Nevada), N.A.; First Interstate Bank of Nevada; The CIT Group; Federal Deposit Insurance Corporation/Resolution Trust Corporation (TRTC); General Electric Company; St. Paul Fire & Marine Insurance Co.; The Doctors Company; University Medical Center of So. Nevada; Chubb Group of Insurance Companies.

For full biographical listings, see the Martindale-Hubbell Law Directory

LELAND EUGENE BACKUS & ASSOCIATES LTD. (AV)

2810 West Charleston Boulevard, Suite H-74, P.O. Box 28700, 89126-2700
Telephone: 702-872-5555
Facsimile: 702-872-5545
Email: backuslaw@earthlink.net *URL:* http://www.backuslaw.com

Leland Eugene Backus

John S. Delikanakis
Edgar Carranza
Robert Earl Werbicky
John L. Krieger
Megan Mahoney

For full biographical listings, see the Martindale-Hubbell Law Directory

GOOLD PATTERSON DEVORE ALES & ROADHOUSE (AV)

4496 South Pecos Road, 89121
Telephone: 702-436-2600
Telecopier: 702-436-2650
URL: http://www.gooldpatterson.com

Barry Stephen Goold
Jeffrey D. Patterson
Thomas J. DeVore
Barney C. Ales
Wilbur M. Roadhouse

ASSOCIATES

Bryan K. Day
E. Bruce Jorgensen
James A. Kohl

Representative Clients: Adams Management; The Allen Group; Archon Financial, L.P.; Desert Oak Development; Lockheed Martin Corporation; Newcourt Financial Corporation; Olympic Land Corporation; Presley Homes; Red Rock Land, LLC; Sunrise Company.

For full biographical listings, see the Martindale-Hubbell Law Directory

NEW JERSEY

*NEWARK,** Essex Co.

McCARTER & ENGLISH, LLP (AV)

Four Gateway Center, 100 Mulberry Street, P.O. Box 652, 07101-0652
Telephone: 973-622-4444
Telecopier: 973-624-7070
URL: http://www.mccarter.com
Cherry Hill, New Jersey Office: 1820 Chapel Avenue West, Suite 380.
Telephone: 609-662-8444.
Telecopier: 609-662-6203.

(See Next Column)

McCARTER & ENGLISH LLP, *Newark—Continued*

New York, New York Office: Suite 2247, One World Trade Center.
Telephone: 212-466-9018.
Telecopier: 212-432-6568.
Boca Raton, Florida Office: 2255 Glades Road, Suite 319-A.
Telephone: 561-994-6262.
Telecopier: 561-241-0798.
Wilmington, Delaware Office: Mellon Bank Center, 919 Market Street.
Telephone: 302-654-8010.
Telecopier: 302-654-0795.
Philadelphia, Pennsylvania Office: One Commerce Square, 2005 Market Street, Suite 3600.
Telephone: 215-557-7700.
Telecopier: 215-557-6544.

MEMBERS OF FIRM

Richard C. Cooper
James F. Hammill (Resident Partner, Cherry Hill, New Jersey Office)
William S. Greenberg
Bart J. Colli
John J. Scally, Jr.
Roslyn S. Harrison
Seth T. Taube
Peter S. Twombly

For Complete List of Firm Personnel, See General Section

For full biographical listings, see the Martindale-Hubbell Law Directory

SILLS CUMMIS RADIN TISCHMAN EPSTEIN & GROSS, A PROFESSIONAL CORPORATION (AV)

One Riverfront Plaza, 07102-5400
Telephone: 973-643-7000
Fax: 973-643-6500
Telex: 820630 Sillsbeck Nwk
Email: sillsmail@sillscummis.com *URL:* http://www.sillscummis.com
Atlantic City, New Jersey Office: 17 Gordon's Alley.
Telephone: 609-344-2800.
New York, N.Y. Office: 712 Fifth Avenue.
Telephone: 212-643-7000.
Washington, D.C. Office: 1800 K Street, N.W.
Telephone: 202-296-4750.

MEMBERS OF FIRM

Steven E. Gross
Jeffrey J. Greenbaum
Simon Levin
Stanley U. North, III
Richard J. Sapinski
Steven R. Kamen

Representative Clients: Blue Cross/Blue Shield of New Jersey; Bristol-Myers Squibb Co.; Circuit City Stores; Eastman Kodak; New Jersey Performing Arts Center; Six Flags Corporation; WWOR-TV, Inc.; PNC Bank Corp.

For Complete List of Firm Personnel, See General Section

For full biographical listings, see the Martindale-Hubbell Law Directory

SADDLE BROOK, Bergen Co.

KRUGMAN & KAILES LLP (AV)

Park 80 West-Plaza Two, 07663-5835
Telephone: 201-845-3434; 212-695-3262
Telecopier: 201-845-9627
Email: counsel@krugmankailes.com
New York, New York Office: 99 Park Avenue, Suite 2200.
Telephone: 212-599-1060.
Telecopier: 212-599-6282.
London, England Office: 90 Fetter Lane, London EC4A-1PT.
Telephone: 011 (44) 171-421-7918.
Telecopier: 011 (44) 171-831-6407.

MEMBERS OF FIRM

Martin Krugman (1916-1994)
Howard Kailes
Thomas J. Goodwin
Ward C. Laracy
Robert I. Wexler
Alan H. Fox
Joy M. Mercer
Kerry B. Flowers

OF COUNSEL

James D. Krugman

COUNSEL

Judith S. Musicant

ASSOCIATES

Anne M. Wallace (Not admitted in NJ)
April A. Savoye
Lisa Ann Miller
Patrizia E. DeBari
David J. Hanley, Jr.
Anjana D. Patel
W. Mark O'Brien

For full biographical listings, see the Martindale-Hubbell Law Directory

NEW MEXICO

*ALBUQUERQUE,** Bernalillo Co.

RODEY, DICKASON, SLOAN, AKIN & ROBB, P.A. (AV)

Albuquerque Plaza, Suite 2200, 201 Third Street, N.W., P.O. Box 1888, 87103-1888
Telephone: 505-765-5900
Fax: 505-768-7395
Email: info@rodey.com *URL:* http://www.rodey.com
Santa Fe, New Mexico Office: Suite 101 Marcy Plaza, 123 East Marcy Street, P.O. Box 1357, 87504-1357.
Telephone: 505-984-0100.
Fax: 505-989-9542.

John P. Burton (Resident, Santa Fe Office)
DeWitt Michael Morgan
Leslie McCarthy Apodaca

COUNSEL

S. I. Betzer, Jr.

For Complete List of Firm Personnel, See General Section

For full biographical listings, see the Martindale-Hubbell Law Directory

NEW YORK

MELVILLE, Suffolk Co.

LAMB & BARNOSKY, LLP (AV)

534 Broadhollow Road-CS 9034, 11747-9034
Telephone: 631-694-2300
Telecopier: 631-694-2309
Email: thefirm@lambbarnosky.com *URL:* http://www.lambbarnosky.com

PARTNERS

Eugene R. Barnosky
Robert H. Cohen
Marcia Lyn Finkelstein
Michael J. Heller
Gary Holman
Scott M. Karson
P. L. Lamb
Arthur A. Lane
Joel M. Markowitz
Gerald P. Rosenberg
Patrice Dowd Shenn

OF COUNSEL

Louis E. Black
James F. Gesualdi
Howard W. Newman
Joseph J. Salvatore
Joseph H. Wishod

COUNSEL

Lloyd K. Chanin
Scott P. McBride

ASSOCIATES

Cathleen D. Allen
Catherine Healy Kanzler
Rita Fishman Sheena
Shari Lee Sugarman

For full biographical listings, see the Martindale-Hubbell Law Directory

*NEW YORK,** New York Co.

BLATT, HAMMESFAHR & EATON (AV)

45 Broadway 12th Floor, 10006
Telephone: 212-363-1900
Fax: 212-363-2600
Email: bhe@bhelaw.com *URL:* HTTP://WWW.BHELAW.COM
Chicago, Illinois Office: 333 W. Wacker Drive, Suite 1900.
Telephone: 312-849-8000.
FAX: 312-357-0198. Email: BHE@BHELAW.COM. URL: HTTP://WWW.BHELAW.COM.

MEMBERS OF FIRM

Robert W. Hammesfahr
Elliot S. Orol
Scott W. Wright

ASSOCIATES

Veronica K. Danko
Dana Loughran

For full biographical listings, see the Martindale-Hubbell Law Directory

CHIMEL DORADO (AV)

1180 Avenue of the Americas, Suite 1459, 10036
Telephone: 212-899-5454
Fax: 212-899-5459
Email: cd@cdlawfirm.com *URL:* http://www.lawyers.com/cdlawfirm

Rita A. Chimel
Marianne Gaertner Dorado

OF COUNSEL

Samuel M. Hung

For full biographical listings, see the Martindale-Hubbell Law Directory

New York—Continued

Curtis, Mallet-Prevost, Colt & Mosle LLP (AV)

101 Park Avenue, 10178-0061
Telephone: 212-696-6000
Telecopier: 212-697-1559
Email: info@cm-p.com *URL:* http://www.cm-p.com
Washington, D.C. Office: Suite 1205L, 1801 K Street, N.W.
Telephone: 202-452-7373.
Telecopier: 202-452-7333.
Newark, New Jersey Office: One Gateway Center, Suite 403.
Telephone: 973-622-0605.
Telecopier: 973-622-5646.
Houston, Texas Office: 2 Houston Center, 909 Fannin Street, Suite 3725.
Telephone: 713-759-9555.
Telecopier: 713-759-0712.
Stamford, Connecticut Office: One Canterbury Green.
Telephone: 203-359-6200.
Telecopier: 203-328-2617.
Mexico City, D.F., Mexico Office: Curtis, Mallet-Prevost, Colt & Mosle, Ruben Dario 281, Piso 9, Col. Bosque de Chapultepec, 11530 Mexico, D.F.
Telephone: 525-282-0444.
Telecopier: 525-282-0637.
Paris, France Office: 15 rue d'Astorg, 75008.
Telephone: +33-1 42-66-39-10.
Telecopier: +33-1 42-66-39-62.
London, England Office: Two Throgmorton Avenue, EC2N 2DL.
Telephone: 0207-638-7957.
Telecopier: 0207-638-5512.
Frankfurt am Main 1, Germany Office: Staufenstrasse 42.
Telephone: +49-69-971-4420.
Telecopier: +49-69-17 33 99.
Muscat, Sultanate of Oman Office: Jewel Beach-134.
Telephone: 968-607-725.
Telecopier: 968-607-724.
Milan, Italy Office: Curtis, Mallet-Prevost & Gilioli, Piazzale Principessa Clotilde 8, 20121.
Telephone: +(39) 02 29 00 29 32.
Telefax: +(39) 02 65 75 969.

MEMBERS OF FIRM

J. Dinsmore Adams, Jr.
Marie-Therese Allen
Mark H. Barth
Alan Berlin
Marco A. Blanco
Roman A. Bninski
William L. Bricker, Jr.
Preston Brown (Resident Partner, Washington, D.C. Office)
Charles L. O. Buderi (Resident Partner, Mexico City, Mexico Office)
Eduardo A. Cukier
Ricardo J. Diez Hidalgo (Resident Partner, Houston, Texas Office)
John F. Egan
Anthony W. Fitzgerald (Co-Resident Partner, Newark, New Jersey Office)
Peter E. Fleming Jr.
Edgar H. Garza-Morales
Eric L. Gilioli
Lawrence Goodman
Robert J. Gruendel
Lynn P. Harrison, III
George Kahale, III
Peter A. Kalat
T. Barry Kingham
Townsend J. Knight
Eliot Lauer
Daniel R. Lenihan
Yves E. Lepage
Robert S. Lipton
Herbert M. Lord
Geoffroy P. Lyonnet (Resident, Paris, France Office)
Jeffrey D. Mamorsky
Eileen P. Matthews
Jeremiah T. Mulligan
Mark H. O'Donoghue
Jeffrey N. Ostrager
Bruce B. Palmer (Resident Partner, London, England Office)
Joseph D. Pizzurro
Benard V. Preziosi, Jr.
Steven J. Reisman
Charles D. Riviezzo
Samuel Rosenthal (Resident Partner, Washington, D.C. Office)
Carl A. Ruggiero
Frank A. Russo (Resident Partner, Mexico City, Mexico Office)
Jacques Semmelman
Robert W. Sheehan
Turner P. Smith
Matias Alfonso Vega
Martin Wendel (Resident Partner, Newark, New Jersey Office)
Robert D. Whoriskey
Peter M. Wolrich (Resident Partner, Paris, France Office)
Victor L. Zimmermann, Jr. (Resident Partner, Stamford, Connecticut Office)
Jeffrey I. Zuckerman (Resident Partner, Washington, D.C. Office)

COUNSEL

John P. Campbell
Morgan A. Casey, Jr.
Antoinette N. Ceisler
Miner D. Crary, Jr.
Nancy E. Delaney
Peter E. Fleming, III (Resident Counsel, Stamford, Connecticut Office)
Albert Francke
Alexander C. Hoagland, Jr.
Michael J. Moscato
Bruce Ashley Mullins (Resident Counsel, Muscat, Oman Office)
Susan F. Pollack
Kemal A. Sheikh
David B. Spanier
Michael K. Stanton, Jr. (Resident Counsel, Stamford, Connecticut Office)
Eric Stenshoel
Herbert Stoller

(See Next Column)

INTERNATIONAL COUNSEL

Eloy Barbará-de-Parres
Miguel I. Estrada Sámano
Daniel E. Gilioli
Enrico S. Gilioli
Ivano C. Mazzoleni
Antonio M. Prida

OF COUNSEL

Benjamin H. Balkind
C. Thomas Godfrey
Kenneth N. LaVine

ASSOCIATES

Kathryn Alisbah
Zoubida Arfaoui
Juan Avendaño (Not Admitted in the United States)
Catherine M. Baecher
Brian Bandler
James R. Banko
Myles K. Bartley
David Bayrock
Mehdi Bennani (Not admitted in the United States)
Evan S. Borenstein
Michael J. Brown
Carter A. Bundy
Elizabeth E. Butler
Joseph F. Clyne
Brett B. Coffee
James E. Connelly
Christina Corona, Not Admitted in the United States
Gary L. Cutler
Rena G. Donin
John C. Dworkin
Terry Eder-Kaufman
Mark Feldman
Enrique Felices, Not Admitted in the United States
José A. Fernandez
Orietta Fraenkel (Not Admitted in the United States)
Alexia M. Garamfalvi
Timothy A. Geishecker
Alison C. Gilbert (Not admitted in NY)
Christopher M. Goebel
Steven Goldberg
Ali R. Gursel
David R. Hesse
Brendan P. Kearse
Ian L. Kelley
Daniel Kheel
Heather W. Lane
Catalina Legarre (Foreign Legal Consultant) (Not Admitted in the United States)
Jae W. Lee
Jane E. Lee
Sergio M. Marxuach
Gabriel Monzon-Cortarelli (Foreign Legal Consultant) (Not Admitted in the United States)
Askar N. Moukhitdinov (Foreign Legal Consultant) (Not Admitted in the United States)
Susana M. Namnum
Paul R. Niehaus
John D. Nielson
John P. Paraschos
Jorge Enrique Paúl, Not Admitted in the United States
Michael C. Quinn
Claudia Rachadell
Diane Rapisarda
Shalini Sharma
Jerrold A. Siskin
Caryn B. Sobelman
Stephen Z. Starr
Guillermo Ulke
Harold Ullman
Philip T. von Mehren
Jonathan J. Walsh
Debra M. Wisdom
Yanira G. Wong (Not admitted in NY)

For full biographical listings, see the Martindale-Hubbell Law Directory

Fox Horan & Camerini LLP (AV)

One Broadway, 10004
Telephone: 212-480-4800
Telecopier: 212-269-2383; 212-709-0248
Email: webmaster@foxhoran.com *URL:* http://www.foxhoran.com

MEMBERS OF FIRM

Donald T. Fox
John R. Horan
Ezequiel A. Camerini
Patrick L. Ferriere
Rafael A. Ginebra
Alan R. Johnson
Michael F. Johnston
Kathleen M. Kundar
Robert Courtney Mangone
Edward C. Marschner
Clifford A. Rathkopf, Jr.
Oleg Rivkin
Christopher H. Seymour
Eduardo L. Tabio

OF COUNSEL

Rafael Urquia II

ASSOCIATES

David C. Camerini
Drew G.L. Chapman
William S. Kogan
Eric Lindquist
V. David Rivkin

For full biographical listings, see the Martindale-Hubbell Law Directory

Gold & Associates (AV)

400 Park Avenue, 10022
Telephone: 212-876-4000
Telecopier: 212-876-0400
URL: http://www.GoldAssociates.com

MEMBER OF THE FIRM

Matthew Aaron Gold

ASSOCIATE

William Emmett Dwyer (Not admitted in NY)

For full biographical listings, see the Martindale-Hubbell Law Directory

New York—Continued

MILLER, CANFIELD, PADDOCK AND STONE, P.L.C. (AV(T))

A Professional Limited Liability Company
Founded in 1852 by Sidney Davy Miller
1450 Broadway, 41st Floor, 10018
Telephone: 212-704-4400
Fax: 212-704-4410
URL: http://www.millercanfield.com
Detroit, Michigan Office: 150 West Jefferson, Suite 2500, 48226-4415.
Telephone: 313-963-6420.
Fax: 313-496-7500.
Cable Address: "Stem Detroit."
Ann Arbor, Michigan Office: 101 North Main Street, 7th Floor, 48104-1400.
Telephone: 734-663-2445.
Fax: 734-747-7147.
Troy, Michigan Office: 840 West Long Lake Road, Suite 200, 48098.
Telephone: 248-879-2000.
Fax: 248-879-2001.
Grand Rapids, Michigan Office: 99 Monroe, N.W., Suite 1200, 49503-2639.
Telephone: 616-454-8656.
Fax: 616-776-6322.
Howell, Michigan Office: 121 South Barnard Street, Suite 4, 48843-2305.
Telephone: 517-546-7600.
Telecopier: 517-546-6974.
Kalamazoo, Michigan Office: 444 West Michigan Avenue, 49007-3752.
Telephone: 616-381-7030.
Fax: 616-382-0244.
Lansing, Michigan Office: One Michigan Avenue, Suite 900, 48933-1609.
Telephone: 517-487-2070.
Fax: 517-374-6304.
Monroe, Michigan Office: 214 East Elm Avenue, Suite 100, 48162-2682.
Telephone: 734-243-2000.
Fax: 734-243-0901.
Washington, D.C. Office: 1900 K Street, N.W., Suite 1150. 20006.
Telephone: 202-429-5575; 785-0600.
Fax: 202-331-1118; 785-1234.
Pensacola, Florida Office: 25 West Cedar, 32501.
Telephone: 850-469-1088.
Fax: 850-432-0677.
Gdynia, Poland Office: UL. Slaska 21, 81-319.
Telephone: 011-485-831-2808.
Fax: 011-48-58-628 6411.
Warsaw, Poland Office: UL. Nowogrodzkall, 5th Floor, 00-513.
Telephone: 011-4822 529 0200.
Fax: 011-4822 529 0201.
Katowice, Poland Office: UL. Francuska 35/37, 40-027.
Telephone: 011 (48-32) 757-2414.
Fax: 011 (48-32) 757-2483.

OF COUNSEL/SENIOR COUNSEL

Geoffrey M. Chinn

Representative Firm Clients: Chrysler Corp.; Comerica, Inc.; City of Detroit, Mich.; Detroit Tigers, Inc.; First of Michigan; Fretter, Inc.; Ford Motor Co.; Ford Motor Credit Co.; Great Lakes Bancorp; Henry Ford Hospital.

For Complete List of Firm Personnel, See General Section

For full biographical listings, see the Martindale-Hubbell Law Directory

MOUND, COTTON & WOLLAN (AV)

One Battery Park Plaza, 10004
Telephone: 212-804-4200
Facsimile: 212-344-8066
San Francisco, California Office: 1700 California Street, Suite 470.
Telephone: 415-434-4301.
Telecopier: 415-434-4303.
London, England Office: Longbow House, 14-20 Chiswell Street.
Telephone: 0071-638-3688.
Newark, New Jersey Office: The Legal Center, One Riverfront Plaza, 8th Floor, 07102-5497.
Telephone: 973-242-2050.
Telecopier: 973-242-4244.

Arthur N. Brook (1933-1997)

MEMBERS OF FIRM

Stuart Cotton
Jeffrey C. Crawford
Leonard S. Dome
Wayne R. Glaubinger
Michael H. Goldstein
Lawrence S. Greengrass
Lloyd A. Gura
Bruce R. Kaliner
Michael R. Koblenz
Daniel Markewich
John C. Mezzacappa
Frederic R. Mindlin
Francis A. Montbach
David A. Silva
Philip C. Silverberg
Costantino P. Suriano
James D. Veach
Jeffrey S. Weinstein

COUNSEL

Eugene A. Leiman
Eugene Wollan

RESIDENT OF COUNSEL
SAN FRANCISCO, CALIFORNIA OFFICE

Anna Maria Martin (Not admitted in NY)
Joseph M. Rimac, Jr. (Not admitted in NY)

(See Next Column)

RESIDENT MEMBER
NEWARK, NEW JERSEY OFFICE

William D. Wilson

ASSOCIATES

Michael Altman
Emilie L. Bakal
Todd A. Bakal
Kevin F. Buckley
Doreen A. Cronin
Frank J. DeAngelis
Alyssa DeSimone
Lauren G. Dome
Douglas K. Eisenstein
Maria Fazzolari
Joseph W. Ferraro
Aaron F. Fishbein
Elisa T. Gilbert
Diana E. Goldberg
Hilary M. Henkind
Mark S. Katz
David W. Kenna
David S. Mahaffey
Mark D. Marino
Catherine F. Megret
Mitchell D. Otto
Albert J. Pinzon
Renee M. Plessner
Jon Quint
Ronnie A. Rifkin
Mark J. Weber
Christina M. Wood

For Complete List of Firm Personnel, See General Section

For full biographical listings, see the Martindale-Hubbell Law Directory

OTTERBOURG, STEINDLER, HOUSTON & ROSEN, P.C. (AV)

230 Park Avenue, 29th Floor, 10169
Telephone: 212-661-9100
Telecopier: 212-682-6104

Donald N. Gellert
William M. Silverman
Alan R. Weiskopf
Daniel Wallen
Albert F. Reisman
David W. Morse

For Complete List of Firm Personnel, See General Section

For full biographical listings, see the Martindale-Hubbell Law Directory

PILIERO GOLDSTEIN JENKINS & SULLIVAN, LLP (AV)

292 Madison Avenue, 10017
Telephone: 212-213-8200
Fax: 212-685-2028
Email: lawyers@pgjhlaw.com *URL:* http://www.pgjhlaw.com
Carlstadt, New Jersey Office: One Palmer Terrace.
Telephone: 201-507-5157.
FAX: 201-507-5221.
Washington, D.C. Office: 888 17th Street, N.W., Suite 1100.
Telephone: 202-467-6991.
FAX: 202-467-6703.
San Francisco, California Office: 507 Howard Street, Suite 200.
Telephone: 415-281-3631.
Fax: 415-281-3630.

MEMBERS OF FIRM

Kimberlee S. Bogen
Edward J. Goldstein
Jon Mark Jenkins
Marc A. Lebowitz
Robert D. Piliero
George O. Richardson, III
Michael T. Sullivan

ASSOCIATES

Craig Avedisian
Rosemary G. Feit
Eric M. Kogan
Mariano Schwed

OF COUNSEL

Kenneth D. Arbeeny
Christopher P. Hall

For full biographical listings, see the Martindale-Hubbell Law Directory

SERKO & SIMON LLP (AV)

Suite 3371, 1 World Trade Center, 10048
Telephone: 212-775-0055
Facsimile: 212-839-9103
Email: serko-simon@customs-law.com *URL:* http://www.customs-law.com

MEMBERS OF FIRM

David Serko
Joel K. Simon
Daniel J. Gluck
Christopher M. Kane

SPECIAL COUNSEL

Melvyn N. Minsky

ASSOCIATES

Despina Keegan
Jerome L. Hanifin (Not admitted in NY)

OF COUNSEL-NEW YORK

David S. Chang
Rafael F. Castro-Lang (Not admitted in NY)

TECHNICAL ADVISORS

Joseph Raul
Martin L. Weiss

For full biographical listings, see the Martindale-Hubbell Law Directory

New York—Continued

Yerushalmi & Associates, L.L.P. (AV)

Empire State Building, 350 Fifth Avenue, 60th Floor Suite 6011, 10118-6096
Telephone: 212-244-2400
Fax: 212-967-3403

Joseph Yerushalmi

OF COUNSEL

Fran Mulnick Parker
Richard H. Wender

For full biographical listings, see the Martindale-Hubbell Law Directory

NORTH CAROLINA

*CHARLOTTE,** Mecklenburg Co.

Womble Carlyle Sandridge & Rice (AV)

A Professional Limited Liability Company
3300 One First Union Center, 301 South College Street, 28202-6025
Telephone: 704-331-4900
Fax: 704-331-4955
Email: lawyers@wcsr.com *URL:* http://www.wcsr.com
Winston-Salem, North Carolina Office: 200 West Second Street, P.O. Drawer 84.
Telephone: 336-721-3600.
Fax: 336-721-3660.
Raleigh, North Carolina Office: 2100 First Union Capitol Center, 150 Fayetteville Street Mall, P.O. Box 831.
Telephone: 919-755-2100.
Fax: 919-755-2150.
Research Triangle Park, North Carolina Office: 2505 Meridian Parkway, Suite 300 (Durham), 27713.
Telephone: 919-484-2300.
Fax: 919-484-2340.
Atlanta, Georgia Office: One Atlantic Center, 1201 West Peachtree Street, Suite 3500.
Telephone: 404-872-7000.
Fax: 404-888-7490.
Other Atlanta, Georgia Office: Suite 404, 2296 Henderson Mill Road, N.E.
Telephone: 770-492-9030.
Fax: 770-492-9609.
Washington, D.C. Office: 1120 Nineteenth Street, N.W., Eighth Floor.
Telephone: 202-857-4400.
Fax: 202-467-6910.
Greenville, South Carolina Office: 15 South Main Street, Suite 601, P.O. Box 10208.
Telephone: 864-255-5400.
Fax: 864-255-5440.

RESIDENT MEMBER

J. Carlton Fleming

Representative Clients: Childress Klein Properties, Inc.; Food Lion, Inc.; J.A. Jones Construction Co.; Parkdale Mills, Inc.; Pillowtex; Duke Power Co.; Bowles Hollowell Conner & Co.; ALLTEL Carolina, Inc.; Belk Store Services, Inc.; Philip Holzmann A.G.

For Complete List of Firm Personnel, See General Section

For full biographical listings, see the Martindale-Hubbell Law Directory

*RALEIGH,** Wake Co.

Allen and Pinnix, P.A. (AV)

333 Fayetteville Street, Mall, Suite 1200, 27601
Telephone: 919-755-0505
Facsimile: 919-829-8098

Noel L. Allen
John L. Pinnix
C. Lynn Calder
M. Jackson Nichols
D. James Jones, Jr.
Michael L. Weisel
Alice S. Glover

For full biographical listings, see the Martindale-Hubbell Law Directory

Womble Carlyle Sandridge & Rice (AV)

A Professional Limited Liability Company
2100 First Union Capitol Center, 150 Fayetteville Street Mall, P.O. Box 831, 27602
Telephone: 919-755-2100
Fax: 919-755-2150
Email: lawyers@wcsr.com *URL:* http://www.wcsr.com
Charlotte, North Carolina Office: 3300 One First Union Center, 301 South College Street.
Telephone: 704-331-4900.
Fax: 704-331-4955.

(See Next Column)

Winston-Salem, North Carolina Office: 200 West Second Street, P.O. Drawer 84.
Telephone: 336-721-3600.
Fax: 336-721-3660.
Research Triangle Park, North Carolina Office: 2505 Meridian Parkway, Suite 300 (Durham), 27713.
Telephone: 919-484-2300.
Fax: 919-484-2340.
Atlanta, Georgia Office: One Atlantic Center, 1201 West Peachtree Street, Suite 3500.
Telephone: 404-872-7000.
Fax: 404-888-7490.
Other Atlanta, Georgia Office: Suite 404, 2296 Henderson Mill Road, N.E.
Telephone: 770-492-9030.
Fax: 770-492-9609.
Washington, D.C. Office: 1120 Nineteenth Street, N.W., Eighth Floor.
Telephone: 202-857-4400.
Fax: 202-467-6910.
Greenville, South Carolina Office: 15 South Main Street, Suite 601, P.O. Box 10208.
Telephone: 864-255-5400.
Fax: 864-255-5440.

RESIDENT MEMBERS

M. Christopher Bolen
Donald A. Donadio

RESIDENT OF COUNSEL

E. Lawrence Davis, III

Representative Clients: Aetna Casualty and Surety Co., Inc.; ALSCO/AmeriMark Building Products, Inc.; Aoki Corporation America, Inc.; Hackney Brothers, Inc.; Lawyers Mutual Liability Insurance Company of North Carolina; Meredith College; Regency Park Corp.; Wachovia Bank, N.A.

For Complete List of Firm Personnel, See General Section

For full biographical listings, see the Martindale-Hubbell Law Directory

*WINSTON-SALEM,** Forsyth Co.

Womble Carlyle Sandridge & Rice (AV)

A Professional Limited Liability Company
200 West Second Street, P.O. Drawer 84, 27102
Telephone: 336-721-3600
Fax: 336-721-3660
Email: lawyers@wcsr.com *URL:* http://www.wcsr.com
Charlotte, North Carolina Office: 3300 One First Union Center, 301 South College Street.
Telephone: 704-331-4900.
Fax: 704-331-4955.
Raleigh, North Carolina Office: 2100 First Union Capitol Center, 150 Fayetteville Street Mall, P.O. Box 831.
Telephone: 919-755-2100.
Fax: 919-755-2150.
Research Triangle Park, North Carolina Office: 2505 Meridian Parkway, Suite 300 (Durham), 27713.
Telephone: 919-484-2300.
Fax: 919-484-2340.
Atlanta, Georgia Office: One Atlantic Center, 1201 West Peachtree Street, Suite 3500.
Telephone: 404-872-7000.
Fax: 404-888-7490.
Other Atlanta, Georgia Office: Suite 404, 2296 Henderson Mill Road, N.E.
Telephone: 770-492-9030.
Fax: 770-492-9609.
Washington, D.C. Office: 1120 Nineteenth Street, N.W., Eighth Floor.
Telephone: 202-857-4400.
Fax: 202-467-6910.
Greenville, South Carolina Office: 15 South Main Street, Suite 601, P.O. Box 10208.
Telephone: 864-255-5400.
Fax: 864-255-5440.

RESIDENT MEMBERS

Conrad C. Baldwin, Jr.
Karen Estelle Carey
William A. Davis, II
Gusti W. Frankel
James K. Phillips
Michael E. Ray
Greg L. Smith
Ashley O. Thrift
Robert A. West

MEMBER OF COUNSEL

Susan P. Strommer

Representative Clients: Brad Ragan, Inc.; Brenner Companies; Food Lion, Inc.; Hanes Companies, Inc.; North Carolina Baptist Hospitals, Inc.; R.J. Reynolds Tobacco Co.; Thomasville Furniture Industries, Inc.; Wachovia Corp.; Wake Forest University.

For Complete List of Firm Personnel, See General Section

For full biographical listings, see the Martindale-Hubbell Law Directory

OHIO

*CINCINNATI,** Hamilton Co.

WAITE, SCHNEIDER, BAYLESS & CHESLEY CO., L.P.A. (AV)

1513 Central Trust Tower, Fourth and Vine Streets, 45202
Telephone: 513-621-0267
Fax: 513-381-2375; 621-0262

Stanley M. Chesley

Thomas F. Rehme
Robert A. Steinberg
Fay E. Stilz
Louise M. Roselle
D. Arthur Rabourn
Jerome L. Skinner
Janet G. Abaray
Paul M. De Marco
Terrence L. Goodman
Colleen M. Hegge
Jane H. Walker
Renée Infante
James F. Keller
Jean M. Geoppinger
Robert Heuck II

For full biographical listings, see the Martindale-Hubbell Law Directory

*CLEVELAND,** Cuyahoga Co.

WALTER & HAVERFIELD, P.L.L. (AV)

1300 Terminal Tower, 44113-2253
Telephone: 216-781-1212
Telecopier: 216-575-0911
Email: law@walterhav.com *URL:* http://www.walterhav.com
Columbus, Ohio Office: 88 East Broad Street.
Telephone: 614-898-1096.

MEMBER OF FIRM

David P.N. Silk

Representative Clients: AGA Gas, Inc.; A.J. Rose Manufacturing Co.; Applied Medical Technology, Inc.; Arabica Cafes, Inc.; Braden Sutphin Ink Co.; Choice Construction Company; Cooper Tire & Rubber Company; Morse Diesel Internatl; Multi-Care Management; WJW-TV (Cleveland).

For Complete List of Firm Personnel, See General Section

For full biographical listings, see the Martindale-Hubbell Law Directory

*COLUMBUS,** Franklin Co.

CHAPPANO WOOD PLL (AV)

145 North High Street, 12th Floor, 43215-3006
Telephone: 614-228-4422; 800-377-4537
Fax: 614-228-4423
URL: http://www.cwpll.com
Email: cwpll@cwpll.com *URL:* http://www.lawyers.com/chappanowood
Dublin, Ohio Office: 6457 Reflections Drive. Suite 200. 43017.
Telephone: 614-485-9356.
Fax: 614-228-4423.

Perry M. Chappano
Lee M. Wood

Margaret (Peggy) M. Blaha
Wendi S. Bootes

OF COUNSEL

Robert E. Schuerman
David L. Petitjean

For full biographical listings, see the Martindale-Hubbell Law Directory

CHESTER, WILLCOX AND SAXBE LLP (AV)

17 South High Street, Suite 900, 43215-3413
Telephone: 614-221-4000
Fax: 614-221-4012
Email: cwslaw.com

PARTNERS

J. Richard Emens
J. Anthony Kington

ASSOCIATE

Thomas H. Mallory, Jr.

For full biographical listings, see the Martindale-Hubbell Law Directory

OKLAHOMA

*OKLAHOMA CITY,** Oklahoma Co.

DAY, EDWARDS, FEDERMAN, PROPESTER & CHRISTENSEN, P.C. (AV)

Suite 2900 Oklahoma Tower, 210 Park Avenue, 73102-5605
Telephone: 405-239-2121
Telecopier: 405-236-1012
URL: http://lawlinks.com/attys/ok/defpc.html

(See Next Column)

Joe E. Edwards

Representative Clients: Applied Thermal Systems; BancFirst Corporation; Bank of America Corporation; LSB Industries, Inc.; Peripheral Enhancements Corporation.

For Complete List of Firm Personnel, See General Section

For full biographical listings, see the Martindale-Hubbell Law Directory

*TULSA,** Tulsa Co.

BOESCHE, MCDERMOTT & ESKRIDGE (AV)

Suite 800 Oneok Plaza, 100 West Fifth Street, 74103
Telephone: 918-583-1777
Fax: 918-592-5809
Email: bme@intellex.com
Muskogee, Oklahoma Office: 1111 West Broadway, P.O. Box 2669, 74402.
Telephone: 918-683-6100.
Fax: 918-683-2303.

MEMBERS OF FIRM

R. Casey Cooper
David A. Johnson

OF COUNSEL

Clifford K. Cate, Jr. (Resident at Muskogee)

Representative Clients: Occidental Petroleum; CEALC; Bartec.

For Complete List of Firm Personnel, See General Section

For full biographical listings, see the Martindale-Hubbell Law Directory

PENNSYLVANIA

NARBERTH, Montgomery Co.

EDWARD M. MEZVINSKY (AV)

815 Woodbine Avenue, 19072
Telephone: 610-664-7115
Fax: 610-664-7225
Email: emmez@aol.com *URL:* http://www.lawyers.com/edwardmmezvinsky

For full biographical listings, see the Martindale-Hubbell Law Directory

*PHILADELPHIA,** Philadelphia Co.

BRUCE G. CASSIDY & ASSOCIATES, P.A. (AV)

Suite 1040, 21 South 12th Street, 19107
Telephone: 215-568-6700
Fax: 215-568-4077
Email: bgclaw@aol.com
Princeton, New Jersey Office: 345 Witherspoon Street, 08542.
Telephone: 609-252-9800.
Fax: 609-252-9111.

Bruce G. Cassidy

David E. Breslau

OF COUNSEL

Dr. Peter H. Feuerstein (Not admitted United States)
Halina Pilarska (Not Admitted in United States)

For full biographical listings, see the Martindale-Hubbell Law Directory

F. EMMETT FITZPATRICK, P.C. (AV)

926 Public Ledger Building, 19106
Telephone: 215-925-5200
Fax: 215-925-5991
Email: info@toplaw.com *URL:* http://www.toplaw.com

F. Emmett Fitzpatrick
F. Emmett Fitzpatrick, III

NiaLena Caravasos

LEGAL SUPPORT PERSONNEL

Doreen Howley (Paralegal)

For full biographical listings, see the Martindale-Hubbell Law Directory

RHODE ISLAND

*PROVIDENCE,** Providence Co.

HINCKLEY, ALLEN & SNYDER LLP (AV)

1500 Fleet Center, 02903-2393
Telephone: 401-274-2000
Fax: 401-277-9600
Email: firm@haslaw.com *URL:* http://www.haslaw.com
Boston, Massachusetts Office: 28 State Street, 30th Floor.
Telephone: 617-345-9000.
Fax: 617-345-9020. URL: http://www.haslaw.com.

MEMBERS OF FIRM

Jonathan Bell
Paul Bork (Not admitted in RI)
Stephen J. Carlotti
Margaret D. Farrell
Gerard R. Goulet
William R. Grimm
Joel Lewin (Not admitted in RI)
Sandra Matrone Mack
Matthew T. Marcello, III
Frederick P. McClure
Paul F. O'Donnell, III (Not admitted in RI)
James O. Reavis
Herman Snyder (Not admitted in RI)
Robert F. Sylvia (Not admitted in RI)

OF COUNSEL

Willard Krasnow (Not admitted in RI)
Joachim A. Weissfeld

For Complete List of Firm Personnel, See General Section

For full biographical listings, see the Martindale-Hubbell Law Directory

TEXAS

*AUSTIN,** Travis Co.

CANTEY & HANGER ROAN & AUTREY L.L.P. (AV)

200 First State Bank Tower, 400 West Fifteenth Street, 78701-4200
Telephone: 512-474-4200
FAX: 512-469-0470; 512-469-0474
Email: FIRM@ROAN-AUTREY.COM *URL:* http://www.Roan-Autrey.com
Fort Worth, Texas Office: Cantey & Hanger, 2100 Burnett Plaza, 801 Cherry Street.
Telephone: 817-877-2800, Metro Line: 429-3815.
Telex: 758631.
FAX: 877-2807. Email: cantey@onramp.net
Dallas, Texas Office: Cantey & Hanger, 3330 Harwood Center, 1999 Bryan Street.
Telephone: 214-978-4100.
FAX: 214-978-4150. Email: chdallas@onramp.net

Forrest C. Roan
Jeff W. Autrey
Stephen L. Phillips
Brian C. Newby
Julie K. Lane

OF COUNSEL

Tieman H. Dippel, Jr.

LEGAL SUPPORT PERSONNEL

Mary B. Jordan
Mary Perroni Blevins

For full biographical listings, see the Martindale-Hubbell Law Directory

THOMPSON & KNIGHT L.L.P. (AV)

(Attorneys and Counselors)
1200 San Jacinto Center, 98 San Jacinto Boulevard, 78701
Telephone: 512-469-6100
Telecopy: 512-469-6180
URL: http://www.tklaw.com
Dallas, Texas Office: 1700 Pacific Avenue, Suite 3300, 75201.
Telephone: 214-969-1700.
Telecopy: 512-969-1751.
Telex: 732298.
Fort Worth, Texas Office: 801 Cherry Street, Suite 1600, 76102.
Telephone: 817-347-1700.
Telecopy: 817-347-1799.
Houston, Texas Office: Thompson Knight Brown Parker & Leahy L.L.P., 1200 Smith Street, Suite 3600, 77002-4595.
Telephone: 713-654-8111.
Telecopier: 713-654-1871.
San Pedro Garza Garcia, Nuevo León, Mexico Office: Edificio Losoles PD-4, Av. Lázaro Cárdenas No. 2400 Pte., C.P. 66220.
Telephone: (52-8) 363-0096.
Telecopy: (52-8) 363-3067.

PARTNERS

Michael L. Bengtson
Holly Claghorn

For Complete List of Firm Personnel, See General Section

For full biographical listings, see the Martindale-Hubbell Law Directory

*DALLAS,** Dallas Co.

BURT BARR & ASSOCIATES, L.L.P. (AV)

304 South Record Street, 75202
Telephone: 214-742-8001
Telefax: 214-741-6744
Email: jhbarr@onramp.net

Burt Barr (1907-1988)
John Holman Barr
G. Scott Damuth
M. Forest Nelson
Alicia Hayes Curran
Morton J. Fogelman
Price Stone
John Howell House
Leonard H. Plog II
Bryan D. Wendt
Kenneth A. Mayfield
Jason Graham
Clifford A. Lawrence, Jr.
William B. Lofland

For full biographical listings, see the Martindale-Hubbell Law Directory

JACKSON WALKER L.L.P. (AV)

901 Main Street, Suite 6000, 75202-3797
Telephone: 214-953-6000
Fax: 214-953-5822
URL: http://www.jw.com
Austin, Texas Office: 100 Congress Avenue, Suite 1100.
Telephone: 512-236-2000.
Fax: 512-236-2002.
Fort Worth, Texas Office: 301 Commerce Street, Suite 2400.
Telephone: 817-334-7200.
Fax: 817-334-7290.
Houston, Texas Office: 1100 Louisiana, Suite 4200.
Telephone: 713-752-4200.
Fax: 713-752-4221.
Richardson, Texas Office: 2435 North Central Expressway, Suite 600.
Telephone: 972-671-2560.
Fax: 972-671-2566.
San Angelo, Texas Office: 225 West Beauregard Avenue.
Telephone: 915-481-2550.
Fax: 915-481-2552.
San Antonio, Texas Office: 112 E. Pecan Street, Suite 2100.
Telephone: 210-978-7700.
Fax: 210-978-7790.

MEMBERS OF FIRM

Larry L. Bean
Bryan C. Birkeland
William H. Hornberger
Gordon M. Shapiro

Representative Clients Furnished Upon Request.

For Complete List of Firm Personnel, See General Section

For full biographical listings, see the Martindale-Hubbell Law Directory

SMITH, UNDERWOOD & PERKINS, A PROFESSIONAL CORPORATION (AV)

600 Two Lincoln Centre, 5420 LBJ Freeway, 75240
Telephone: 972-661-5114
Telecopier: 972-661-5691
Email: firm@suandp.com *URL:* http://www.suplaw.com

Timothy S. Perkins
David W. Ralston
G. Lynn Smith
William J. Underwood, Jr.

Christine A. McGuire
Amy K. Ratzlaff
P. Theodore Stoinoff, II
Val C. Cronin
Ellen P. Stewart
Todd W. Shadle
Ruth C. Logan
Christina L. Betanzos
Kent D. Williamson

For full biographical listings, see the Martindale-Hubbell Law Directory

THOMPSON & KNIGHT L.L.P. (AV)

(Attorneys and Counselors)
1700 Pacific Avenue Suite 3300, 75201
Telephone: 214-969-1700
Telecopy: 214-969-1751
Telex: 732 298
URL: http://www.tklaw.com
Austin, Texas Office: 1200 San Jacinto Center, 98 San Jacinto Boulevard, 78701.
Telephone: 512-469-6100.
Telecopy: 512-469-6180.
Fort Worth, Texas Office: 801 Cherry Street, Suite 1600, 76102.
Telephone: 817-347-1700.
Telecopy: 817-347-1799.
Houston, Texas Office: Thompson Knight Brown Parker & Leahy L.L.P., 1200 Smith Street, Suite 3600, 77002-4595.
Telephone: 713-654-8111.
Telecopier: 713-654-1871.
San Pedro Garza Garcia, Nuevo León, Mexico Office: Edificio Losoles PD-4, Av. Lázaro Cárdenas No. 2400 Pte., C.P. 66220.
Telephone: (52-8) 363-0096.
Telecopy: (52-8) 363-3067.

(See Next Column)

THOMPSON & KNIGHT L.L.P., *Dallas—Continued*

PARTNERS

Dorothy H. Bjorck
Sam P. Burford, Jr.
Frederick W. Burnett, Jr.
John R. Cohn
Andrew B. Derman
David L. Emmons
Gregory S. C. Huffman
David E. Morrison
Peter J. Riley
Joe A. Rudberg
Molly Steele
Stephen E. Stein
Michael C. Titens

ASSOCIATE

Ann Marie Cowdrey

For Complete List of Firm Personnel, See General Section

For full biographical listings, see the Martindale-Hubbell Law Directory

*FORT WORTH,** Tarrant Co.

THOMPSON & KNIGHT L.L.P. (AV)

(Attorneys and Counselors)
801 Cherry Street, Suite 1600, 76102
Telephone: 817-347-1700
Telecopy: 817-347-1799
URL: http://www.tklaw.com
Dallas, Texas Office: 1700 Pacific Avenue, Suite 3300, 75201.
Telephone: 214-969-1700.
Telecopy: 214-969-1751.
Telex: 732298.
Austin, Texas Office: 1200 San Jacinto Center, 98 San Jacinto Boulevard, 78701.
Telephone: 512-469-6100.
Telecopy: 512-469-6180.
Houston, Texas Office: Thompson Knight Brown Parker & Leahy L.L.P., 1200 Smith Street, Suite 3600, 77002-4595.
Telephone: 713-654-8111.
Telecopier: 713-654-1871.
San Pedro Garza Garcia, Nuevo León, Mexico Office: Edificio Losoles PD-4, Av. Lázaro Cárdenas No. 2400 Pte., C.P. 66220.
Telephone: (52-8) 363-0096.
Telecopy: (52-8) 363-3067.

PARTNER

Stephen B. Norris

For Complete List of Firm Personnel, See General Section

For full biographical listings, see the Martindale-Hubbell Law Directory

*HOUSTON,** Harris Co.

BELL, RYNIKER & LETOURNEAU, P.C. (AV)

Five Post Oak Park, Suite 1300, 77027
Telephone: 713-871-8822
Fax: 713-871-8844
URL: http://www.brlpc.com
Email: mkbell@brlpc.com *URL:* http://www.lawyers.com/brlpc

Michael K. Bell
Robert J. Ryniker
Keith B. Letourneau
Thomas R. Nork

Douglas J. Shoemaker
Deborah T. Busby
Wesley T. Welmaker

For full biographical listings, see the Martindale-Hubbell Law Directory

JACKSON WALKER L.L.P. (AV)

1100 Louisiana, Suite 4200, P.O. Box 4771, 77002
Telephone: 713-752-4200
Fax: 713-752-4221
URL: http://www.jw.com
Austin, Texas Office: 100 Congress Avenue, Suite 1100.
Telephone: 512-236-2000.
Fax: 512-236-2002.
Dallas, Texas Office: 901 Main Street, Suite 6000.
Telephone: 214-953-6000.
Fax: 214-953-5822.
Fort Worth, Texas Office: 301 Commerce Street, Suite 2400.
Telephone: 817-334-7200.
Fax: 817-334-7290.
Richardson, Texas Office: 2435 North Central Expressway, Suite 600.
Telephone: 972-671-2560.
Fax: 972-671-2566.
San Angelo, Texas Office: 225 West Beauregard Avenue.
Telephone: 915-481-2550.
Fax: 915-481-2552.
San Antonio, Texas Office: 112 E. Pecan Street, Suite 2100.
Telephone: 210-978-7700.
Fax: 210-978-7790.

MEMBER OF FIRM

Douglas A. Paisley, II

(See Next Column)

OF COUNSEL

Frank L. Cascio, Jr.

For Complete List of Firm Personnel, See General Section

For full biographical listings, see the Martindale-Hubbell Law Directory

LIPSTET & HIRSCH, L.L.P. (AV)

A Partnership including a Professional Corporation
Suite 1780, Two Post Oak Central, 1980 Post Oak Boulevard, 77056
Telephone: 713-961-7800
Fax: 713-961-3453

MEMBERS OF FIRM

Robert Leighton Lipstet (P.C.)
Reginald A. Hirsch

For full biographical listings, see the Martindale-Hubbell Law Directory

*SAN ANTONIO,** Bexar Co.

HEARD LINEBARGER GRAHAM GOGGAN BLAIR PEÑA & SAMPSON, LLP (AV)

Tenth Floor, Tower Life Building, 310 South St. Mary's, 78205
Telephone: 210-225-6763
Facsimile: 210-225-6410
URL: http://www.publicans.com
Austin, Texas Office: 1949 South IH 35, 78741.
Telephone: 512-447-6675.
Fax: 512-443-3494.
Beaumont, Texas Office: 1148 Park, 77701.
Telephone: 409-832-9483.
Fax: 409-833-2638.
Brownsville, Texas Office: 3302 Boca Chica, Suite 105, 78521.
Telephone: 956-546-1216.
Fax: 956-546-4624.
Conroe, Texas Office: 103 W. Phillips, 77301.
Telephone: 409-760-1410.
Fax: 409-760-1285.
Corpus Christi, Texas Office: 500 N. Shoreline, Suite 1111, 78471.
Telephone: 512-888-6898.
Fax: 512-888-4405.
Corsicana, Texas Office: 1501 Northwood Boulevard, 75110.
Telephone: 903-872-3096.
Fax: 903-874-5007.
Dallas, Texas Office: 1720 Allianz Financial Centre, 2323 Bryan Street, 75201.
Telephone: 214-880-0089.
Fax: 214-754-7167.
Denton, Texas Office: 326-G East McKinney, 76201.
Telephone: 940-383-4460.
Fax: 940-382-2829.
Edinburg, Texas Office: 110 S. 12th Street, 78539.
Telephone: 956-383-4500.
Fax: 956-383-7820.
El Paso, Texas Office: 215 N. Stanton Street, 79901.
Telephone: 915-533-6637.
Fax: 915-532-7085.
Fort Worth, Texas Office: Oil & Gas Building, Suite 1414, 309 W. 7th Street, 76102.
Telephone: 817-877-4589.
Fax: 817-877-0601.
Houston, Texas Office: 1021 Main Street, Suite 1500, 77002.
Telephone: 713- 844-3400.
Fax: 713-844-3501.
Laredo, Texas Office: 1102 Scott, Suite 2B, 78041.
Telephone: 956-723-1303.
Fax: 956-723-1327.
Longview, Texas Office: 1127 Judson Road, Suite 111, 75601.
Telephone: 903-757-5448.
Fax: 903-758-3331.
Odessa, Texas Office: 1301 E. 8th Street, Suite 200, 79761.
Telephone: 915-332-9047.
Fax: 915-333-7012.
Richmond, Texas Office: 301 S. 9th Street, Suite 222, 77469.
Telephone: 281-342-9636.
Fax: 281-341-7808.
Sherman, Texas Office: 115 E. Lamar, 75091.
Telephone: 903-893-4941.
Fax: 903-868-0688.
Tyler, Texas Office: 1517 W. Front Street, Suite 202, 75702.
Telephone: 903-597-2897.
Fax: 903-597-2402.
The Woodlands, Texas Office: 10077 Grogan's Mill Road, Suite 535,v 77380-2924.
Telephone: 713-363-3632.
Fax: 281-363-3998.
New Orleans, Louisiana Office: 1515 Poydras Street, Suite 1840, 70112.
Telephone: 504-522-9100.
Fax: 504-522-9145.
Philadelphia, Pennsylvania Office: 123 S. Broad Street, Suite 1830, 19109.
Telephone: 215-790-1117.
Fax: 215-790-1197.

(See Next Column)

HEARD LINEBARGER GRAHAM GOGGAN BLAIR PEÑA & SAMPSON LLP—*Continued*

MEMBERS OF FIRM

Oliver S. Heard, Sr. (1915-1977)
Oliver S. Heard, Jr.
Dale Linebarger (Resident, Austin Office)
Russell R. Graham (Resident, Austin Office)
Thomas S. Goggan, III (Resident, Austin Office)
Stephen S. Blair (Resident, Austin Office)
Jim Blair (Resident, The Woodlands Office)
Juan M. Peña (Resident, Edinburg Office)
DeMetris Aquilla Sampson (Resident, Dallas Office)
David G. Aelvoet
Drew Aldinger (Resident, Philadelphia, Pennsylvania Office)
Bruce W. Anderson (Resident, Austin Office)
Kaye Applewhite (Resident, Conroe Office)
Thelma Banduch (Resident, Brownsville Office)
Gary B. Bennett (At Denton, Fort Worth and Sherman Offices)
Douglas S. Bird (Resident, Austin Office)
John R. Bolster (Resident, Tyler Office)
Phillipa L. Bowers (Resident, New Orleans, Louisiana Office)
Brian E. Brown (Resident, Austin Office)
Jeffrey K. Brown (Resident, Austin Office)
James H. Burshtyn (Resident, Austin Office)
Rebecca Bustamante
Olivero E. Canales (Resident, Laredo Office)
Paul D. Chapa (Resident, Corpus Christi Office)
Kevin D. Chester (Resident, Corsicana Office)
Cormac P. Creaven (Houston and Richmond Offices)
L. W. "Rusty" Dean (Resident, Tyler Office)
Michael W. Deeds (Resident, Houston Office)
Mary Belan Doggett
Clifton F. Douglass, III
James R. Evans, Jr. (Resident, Austin Office)
F. Duane Force (Resident, Austin Office)
Cynthia Y. Garza (Resident, Edinburg Office)
Jay T. Garrett (Resident, Austin Office)
Lucy Gonzàlez-Canales (Resident, Edinburg Office)
Lee Gordon (Resident, Austin Office)
Sandra Griffin (Resident, Austin Office)
Eloise A. Guzman (Resident, Houston Office)
Judith A. Hargrove (Resident, Austin Office)
Edward Hernández (Resident, El Paso Office)
Sharon N. Humble
Pamela Pope Johnson (Resident, Dallas Office)
William E. King (Resident, Houston Office)
Glenn Lewis (Resident, Fort Worth Office)
Edward Lopez, Jr. (Resident, Dallas Office)
Clayton E. Mayfield (Resident, Beaumont Office)
Russell N. McInturff (Resident, Odessa Office)
Stephen T. Meeks (Resident, Fort Worth Office)
Beverly Meltontree (Resident, Houston Office)
Kathleen D. Morrison (Resident, Corpus Christi Office)
Harry L. Munsinger
Norman J. Nelson (Resident, Houston Office)
J. Scott Novy (Resident, Longview Office)
Pankaj R. Parmar (Resident, Houston Office)
Carmen I. Perez (Resident, El Paso Office)
Monica McCoy Purdy (Resident, Dallas Office)
Harold D. Putman, Jr.
Kent M. Rider (Resident, Austin Office)
Lori Gruver Robertson (Resident, Austin Office)
Craig Schumacher (Resident, Tyler Office)
Michael J. Siwierka (Resident, Houston Office)
Glenn E. Smith (Resident, Fort Worth Office)
Leah L. Stolar (Resident, Houston Office)
Charles A. Sutton (Resident, Corpus Christi Office)
Michael T. Vallandingham (Resident, Austin Office)
Nancy Vasquez-Perez (Resident, Corpus Christi Office)
H. Elizabeth "Beth" Weller (Resident, Dallas Office)
Barbara M. Williams (Resident, Fort Worth Office)
Donald Lee Wolf (Resident, Tyler Office)
Scott D. Wylie (Resident, Corsicana Office)
Craig Young (Resident, Austin Office)
Lupe Zamarripa (Resident, Austin Office)

OF COUNSEL

Debra Danburg (Resident, Houston Office)
Richard R. Orsinger
Humberto Hernandez-Haddad (Not admitted in United States)
Vince Ryan (Resident, Houston Office)

For full biographical listings, see the Martindale-Hubbell Law Directory

UTAH

*SALT LAKE CITY,** Salt Lake Co.

PARR WADDOUPS BROWN GEE & LOVELESS, A PROFESSIONAL CORPORATION (AV)

Suite 1300, 185 South State Street, 84111-1537
Telephone: 801-532-7840
Fax: 801-532-7750
URL: http://www.pwlaw.com

Clayton J. Parr
David E. Gee
Scott W. Loveless
Terry E. Welch
D. Craig Parry

For Complete List of Firm Personnel, See General Section

For full biographical listings, see the Martindale-Hubbell Law Directory

VERMONT

*BURLINGTON,** Chittenden Co.

GABEL INTERNATIONAL LAW FIRM (AV)

189 Battery Street, 3rd Floor, 05401
Telephone: 802-865-2300
Fax: 802-865-3625
Email: pgabel@gabel-law.com

Patricia Gabel

For full biographical listings, see the Martindale-Hubbell Law Directory

VIRGINIA

*ARLINGTON,** Arlington Co.

SCHWARTZ AND ELLIS, LTD. (AV)

6950 North Fairfax Drive, 22213
Telephone: 703-532-9300
Telex: 892320
Facsimile: 703-534-0329
Email: schwellis@aol.com *URL:* http://www.lawyers.com/schwartzandellis

Philip Schwartz
John P. Ellis

John S. Petrillo

References: First Virginia Bank; Bank of America; First Union National Bank.

For full biographical listings, see the Martindale-Hubbell Law Directory

*FAIRFAX,** (Ind. City; Seat of Fairfax Co.)

DOUGLAS R. MARVIN, P.C. (AV)

9675 Main Street, Suite C, 22031
Telephone: 703-426-7200
Fax: 703-426-7210
Email: dmarvin@erols.com *URL:* http://www.lawyers.com/dmarvinlaw

Douglas R. Marvin

For full biographical listings, see the Martindale-Hubbell Law Directory

ODIN, FELDMAN & PITTLEMAN, P.C. (AV)

9302 Lee Highway, Suite 1100, 22031
Telephone: 703-218-2100
Facsimile: 703-218-2160
Email: OFP@OFPLAW.COM

Dexter S. Odin
David A. Lawrence
John P. Dedon
Leslye S. Fenton
Kevin Thomas Oliveira

Thomas N. Tartaro

For Complete List of Firm Personnel, See General Section

For full biographical listings, see the Martindale-Hubbell Law Directory

MCLEAN, Fairfax Co.

WATT, TIEDER, HOFFAR & FITZGERALD, L.L.P. (AV)

7929 Westpark Drive, Suite 400, 22102
Telephone: 703-749-1000
Telecopier: 703-893-8029
Email: contactus@wthf.com *URL:* http://www.wthf.com
Washington, D.C. Office: 601 Pennsylvania Ave, N.W., Suite 900.
Telephone: 703-749-1000.
Irvine, California Office: 3 Park Plaza, Suite 1500.
Telephone: 949-852-6700.

MEMBERS OF FIRM

John B. Tieder, Jr.
Robert G. Watt
Julian F. Hoffar
Robert M. Fitzgerald
Robert K. Cox
Charles E. Raley
Lewis J. Baker
Benjamin T. Riddles, II
Wayne G. Tatusko
Richard G. Mann, Jr.
Henry D. Danforth
Carter B. Reid
Mark A. Sgarlata
Michael G. Long (Resident, Irvine, California Office)
Thomas J. Powell
Edward Parrott
Steven J. Weber
Paul A. Varela
Vivian Katsantonis
Kathleen Olden Barnes
Christopher P. Pappas (Resident, Irvine, California Office)
Shelly L. Ewald
Christopher J. Brasco
John G. Lavoie
Robert C. Niesley (Resident, Irvine, California Office)
Colin J. Smith
Fred A. Mendicino
Timothy E. Heffernan (Not admitted in VA)

OF COUNSEL

Avv. Roberto Tassi

ASSOCIATES

Robert G. Barbour
Keith C. Phillips
Marybeth Z. Gaul
William Drew Mallender
Joseph W. Rasnic
Heidi B. Hering
James M. Donahue
Bennett J. Lee (Not admitted in VA)
Todd R. Metz (Not admitted in VA)
Joseph S. Guarino
Lewis I. Askew, Jr.
Erica S. Beardsley
Robert James Lloyd, III
Harish C. Mirchandani (Not admitted in VA)
William Kennedy
Michael J. Kirwin (Not admitted in VA)
Peter L. Vanderloo
Scott W. Kowalski
Carol Kelly Skrabak
J. Brian Cashmere
Michele Mintz
David A. Leib (Not admitted in VA)
Denis W. Kohl
Elizabeth A. Hall

For full biographical listings, see the Martindale-Hubbell Law Directory

NORFOLK, (Independent City)

PAYNE, GATES, FARTHING & RADD, P.C. (AV)

15th Floor, Dominion Tower, 999 Waterside Drive, Suite 1515, 23510-3309
Telephone: 757-640-1500
Facsimile: 757-627-6583
URL: http://www.paynegates.com

Ronald M. Gates
Philip R. Farthing
Anthony F. Radd
Glen M. Robertson
Brian R. Dinning
Todd J. Preti
Marshall A. Winslow, Jr.

C. Arthur Robinson, II
Stephen E. Heretick
Raymond L. Hogge, Jr.

OF COUNSEL

Charles E. Payne

For full biographical listings, see the Martindale-Hubbell Law Directory

RICHMOND, (Independent City)

WILLIAMS, MULLEN, CLARK & DOBBINS, A PROFESSIONAL CORPORATION (AV)

Two James Center, 1021 East Cary Street, P.O. Box 1320, 23218-1320
Telephone: 804-643-1991
Fax: 804-783-6507
URL: http://www.wmcd.com
Newport News Office: Harbor Bank Center, Suite 210, One Old Oyster Point Road, 23602-7119.
Telephone: 757-249-5100.
Fax: 757-249-5109.
Virginia Beach Office: One Columbus Center, 23462-6763.
Telephone: 757-499-8800.
Fax: 757-473-0395.
Vienna Office: 1593 Spring Hill Road, Suite 510, 22182.
Telephone: 703-760-5200.
Fax: 703-748-0244.

(See Next Column)

Washington, D.C. Office: The Farragut Building, 900 17th Street, N.W., Suite 700, 20006.
Telephone: 202-293-0213.
Fax: 804-783-6507. Fax Within D.C.: 202-293-5939.
London, England Office: Blake Lodge, Bridge Lane, SW11 3AD.
Telephone: (011-44-71) 223-2756.
Fax: (011-44-71) 350-0156.
Riyadh, Saudi Arabia Affiliate Office: Saudi-American Legal Consultants Commercial Building #2, Diplomatic Quarter, P.O. Box 57270, 11574.
Telephone: (011-966-1) 488-1563.
Fax: (011-966-1) 488-0542.

William J. Benos
Theodore L. Chandler, Jr.
Alexander C. Graham, Jr.
David R. Johnson
Thomas B. McVey (Resident, Washington, D.C. Office)
William E. Perry (Resident, Washington, D.C. Office)
Jimmie V. Reyna (Resident, Washington, D.C. Office)
Julious P. Smith, Jr.

Julia K. Bailey (Resident, Washington, D.C. Office)
W. David Snead (Resident, Washington, D.C. Office)

For Complete List of Firm Personnel, See General Section

For full biographical listings, see the Martindale-Hubbell Law Directory

WISCONSIN

*MILWAUKEE,** Milwaukee Co.

QUARLES & BRADY LLP (AV)

411 East Wisconsin Avenue, 53202-4497
Telephone: 414-277-5000
Fax: 414-271-3552
URL: http://www.quarles.com
Madison, Wisconsin Office: Firstar Plaza, One South Pinckney Street, P.O. Box 2113, 53701-2113.
Telephone: 608-251-5000.
Fax: 608-251-9166.
West Palm Beach, Florida Office: 222 Lakeview Avenue, 4th Floor, 33401.
Telephone: 561-653-5000.
Fax: 561-653-5333.
Naples, Florida Office: Barnett Center, 4501 Tamiami Trail North, Suite 300, 34103-3060.
Telephone: 941-262-5959.
Fax: 941-434-4999.
Phoenix, Arizona Office: One Camelback Building, One East Camelback Road, Suite 400, 85012-1649.
Telephone: 602-230-5500.
Fax: 602-230-5598.
Chicago, Illinois Office: Quarles & Brady LLC, Citicorp Center, 500 West Madison Street, Suite 3700.
Telephone: 312-715-5000.
Fax: 312-715-5155.

MEMBERS OF FIRM

(ALPHABETICALLY BY YEAR OF ADMISSION TO BAR)

Harry G. Holz
Arthur B. Harris
Anthony W. Asmuth, III
James D. Friedman
Robert L. Titley
Thomas J. Phillips
Darryl S. Bell
John W. Daniels, Jr.
Alyce C. Katayama
Andrew M. Barnes
Jeffrey Morris
Kenneth V. Hallett
Thomas A. Simonis
David D. Wilmoth
John D. Franzini
Steven P. Emerick
Joseph E. Puchner
Rebecca A. Speckhard

OF COUNSEL

Robert J. Kalupa
Thad F. Kryshak

ASSOCIATES

Patricia A. Hintz
Steven M. Schindhelm

For Complete List of Firm Personnel, See General Section

For full biographical listings, see the Martindale-Hubbell Law Directory

VIRGIN ISLANDS

*CHARLOTTE AMALIE, ST. THOMAS,** St. Thomas

GRUNERT STOUT & BRUCH

24-25 Kongensgade, P.O. Box 1030, 00804
Telephone: 340-774-1320
Fax: 340-774-7839
Email: gsbusvi@viaccess.net
Affiliated with: Solomon Pearl Blum & Quinn LLP, New York, New York and Denver, Colorado.

(See Next Column)

GRUNERT STOUT & BRUCH—*Continued*

MEMBERS OF FIRM

John E. Stout Susan Bruch Moorehead

ASSOCIATE

Gabriel J. Villegas

OF COUNSEL

William L. Blum

For full biographical listings, see the Martindale-Hubbell Law Directory

CANADA ALBERTA

*CALGARY,** Calgary Jud. Dist.

BENNETT JONES (AV)

4500 Bankers Hall East, 855-2nd Street S.W., T2P 4K7
Telephone: 403-298-3100
Facsimile: 403-265-7219
Email: firmwatch@bennettjones.ca *URL:* http://www.bennettjones.ca
Edmonton, Alberta Office: 1000, 10035-105 Street.
Telephone: 780-421-8133.
Facsimile: 780-421-7951.
Toronto, Ontario Office: 3400 1 First Canadian Place, P.O. Box 130.
Telephone: 416-863-1200.
Facsimile: 416-863-1716.

MEMBERS OF FIRM

John F. Curran, Q.C. Robert R. Rooney

For Complete List of Firm Personnel, See General Section

For full biographical listings, see the Martindale-Hubbell Law Directory

*EDMONTON,** Edmonton Jud. Dist.

PARLEE MCLAWS (AV)

15th Floor Manulife Place, 10180 101st Street, T5J 4K1
Telephone: 403-423-8500
Telecopier: 403-423-2870
Email: lawyers@parlee.com *URL:* http://www.parlee.com
Calgary, Alberta Office: 3400 Petro-Canada Centre, 150 - 6th Avenue, SW.
Telephone: 403-294-7000.
Telecopier: 403-265-8263.

MEMBERS OF FIRM

David G. Finlay Ian L. MacLachlan

For Complete List of Firm Personnel, See General Section

For full biographical listings, see the Martindale-Hubbell Law Directory

CANADA NOVA SCOTIA

*HALIFAX,** Regional Munic. of Halifax

MCINNES COOPER (AV)

Barristers, Solicitors & Trade Mark Agents
Summit Place, 1601 Lower Water Street, P.O. Box 730, B3J 2V1
Telephone: 902-425-6500
Fax: 902-425-6350
Email: mcrhfx@mcrlaw.com *URL:* http://www.mcrlaw.com
St. John's, Newfoundland Office: Baine Johnston Centre, 5th Floor, 10 Fort William Place, P.O. Box 5939, A1C 5X4.
Telephone: 709-722-8735.
Telecopier: 709-722-1763. Email: mcrsj@mcrlaw.com.
Moncton, New Brunswick Office: Place Moncton Place, 655 Main Street, P.O. Box 1368, E1C 8T6.
Telephone: 506-857-8970.
Fax: 506-857-4095. Email: mcrmctn@mcrlaw.com.
Charlottetown, Prince Edward Island Office: BDC Place, Suite 620, 119 Kent Street, C1A 1N3.
Telephone: 902-368-8473.
Fax: 902-368-8346. Email: mcrpei@mcrlaw.com.
Fredericton, New Brunswick Office: Suite 600, 570 Queen Street, P.O. Box 610.
Telephone: 506-458-8572.
Fax: 506-458-9903. Email: mcrfton@mcrlaw.com.

PARTNER

Joseph A. F. Macdonald, Q.C.

For Complete List of Firm Personnel, See General Section

For full biographical listings, see the Martindale-Hubbell Law Directory

CANADA ONTARIO

*TORONTO,** Regional Munic. of Toronto

BORDEN & ELLIOT (AV)

Barristers & Solicitors
Scotia Plaza, 40 King Street West, M5H 3Y4
Telephone: 416-367-6000
Telecopier: 416-367-6749
Email: info@borden.com *URL:* http://www.borden.com
Ottawa, Ontario Office: Borden Elliot Scott & Aylen, 1000-60 Rue Queen Street.
Telephone: 613-237-5160; 800-661-4237. General
Facsimile: 613-230-8842. IP Dept.
Facsimile: 613-787-3558. Email: ottinfo@scottaylen.com. URL: http://www.borden.com.

Norman Letalik

For Complete List of Firm Personnel, See General Section

For full biographical listings, see the Martindale-Hubbell Law Directory

CANADA QUEBEC

*MONTREAL,** Montreal Dist.

MCMASTER GERVAIS (AV)

A General Partnership
1000 de La Gauchetière Street West, Suite 900, H3B 5H4
Telephone: 514-879-1212
Fax: 514-954-1905
Email: info@mcmastergervais.com *URL:* http://www.mcmastergervais.com

MEMBERS OF FIRM

Lionel J. Blanshay
Norman A. Saibil
François Rioux
André Dufour
H. John Godber
Peter C. Casey
Daniel Ayotte
Charles P. Marquette
Peter G. Pamel
Amélia A. Salehabadi

COUNSEL

Hon. Lawrence A. Poitras, Q.C. P. André Gervais, Q.C.

For Complete List of Firm Personnel, See General Section

For full biographical listings, see the Martindale-Hubbell Law Directory

MEXICO

GARZA GARCIA, NUEVO LEON,

American Lawyers in Garza Garcia

THOMPSON & KNIGHT L.L.P.

(Attorneys and Counselors)
Edificio Losoles PD-4, Av. Lázaro Cárdenas No. 2400 PTE San Pedro Garza Garcia, Garza Garcia, Nuevo Leon 66220
Telephone: (52-8) 363-0096
Telecopy: (52-8) 363-3067
URL: http://www.tklaw.com
Dallas, Texas Office: 1700 Pacific Avenue, Suite 3300, 75201.
Telephone: 214-969-1700.
Telecopy: 214-969-1751.
Telex: 732298.
Austin, Texas Office: 1200 San Jacinto Center, 98 San Jacinto Boulevard, 78701.
Telephone: 512-469-6100.
Telecopy: 512-469-6180.
Fort Worth, Texas Office: 801 Cherry Street, Suite 1600, 76102.
Telephone: 817-347-1700.
Telecopy: 817-347-1799.
Houston, Texas Office: Thompson Knight Brown Parker & Leahy L.L.P., 1200 Smith Street, Suite 3600.
Telephone: 713-654-8111.
Telecopier: 713-654-1871.

(See Next Column)

THOMPSON & KNIGHT L.L.P., *Garza Garcia, Nuevo Leon—Continued*

PARTNERS

Joe A. Rudberg Michael C. Titens

For Complete List of Firm Personnel, See General Section

For full biographical listings, see the Martindale-Hubbell Law Directory

INTERNATIONAL TRADE LAW

MISSOURI

KANSAS CITY, Jackson, Clay, Platte & Cass Cos.

MILLER & COMPANY P.C. (AV)

4929 Main Street, 64112
Telephone: 816-561-4999
Fax: 816-561-5999
Email: intllaw@millerco.com *URL:* http://www.millerco.com
Washington, D.C. Office: 1825 "I" Street, N.W., Suite 400, 20006.
Telephone: 202-429-2017.
Fax: 202-659-6848.

Marshall V. Miller

Sean T. Murray | Scott S. Taylor

OF COUNSEL

Lebert D. Shultz

Representative Clients: Bristol Myers Squibb; Kawaski Motors Corporation; Eastman Kodak Company; Hewlett-Packard Company; Citgo Petroleum Corporation; Gateway 2000; Government of Puerto Rico; Intel Corporation; Merck & Co., Inc.; Onkyo Manufacturing Co.

For full biographical listings, see the Martindale-Hubbell Law Directory

NEW JERSEY

*NEWARK,** Essex Co.

SILLS CUMMIS RADIN TISCHMAN EPSTEIN & GROSS, A PROFESSIONAL CORPORATION (AV)

One Riverfront Plaza, 07102-5400
Telephone: 973-643-7000
Fax: 973-643-6500
Telex: 820630 Sillsbeck Nwk
Email: sillsmail@sillscummis.com *URL:* http://www.sillscummis.com
Atlantic City, New Jersey Office: 17 Gordon's Alley.
Telephone: 609-344-2800.
New York, N.Y. Office: 712 Fifth Avenue.
Telephone: 212-643-7000.
Washington, D.C. Office: 1800 K Street, N.W.
Telephone: 202-296-4750.

MEMBERS OF FIRM

Steven E. Gross | Jeffrey Barton Cahn
Jeffrey J. Greenbaum | Stanley U. North, III

Jennifer L. Borofsky

For Complete List of Firm Personnel, See General Section

For full biographical listings, see the Martindale-Hubbell Law Directory

NEW YORK

HUNTINGTON STATION, Suffolk Co.

FOLLICK & BESSICH, P.C. (AV)

33 Walt Whitman Road, Suite 204, 11746
Telephone: 516-549-1938
Facsimile: 516-549-2189
Email: customs@idt.net
Email: tarifflaw@aol.com *URL:* http://www.fbcustomslaw.com
Jersey City, New Jersey Office: One Exchange Place, Suite 915, 07302.
Telephone: 201-946-1200.
Facsimile: 201-946-1242.
New York, New York Office: 225 Broadway, Suite 500, 10007.
Telephone: 212-233-6630.
Fax: 212-233-5759.

Robert L. Follick | John A. Bessich

For full biographical listings, see the Martindale-Hubbell Law Directory

*NEW YORK,** New York Co.

GOLD & ASSOCIATES (AV)

400 Park Avenue, 10022
Telephone: 212-876-4000
Telecopier: 212-876-0400
URL: http://www.GoldAssociates.com

MEMBER OF THE FIRM

Matthew Aaron Gold

ASSOCIATE

William Emmett Dwyer (Not admitted in NY)

For full biographical listings, see the Martindale-Hubbell Law Directory

PILIERO GOLDSTEIN JENKINS & SULLIVAN, LLP (AV)

292 Madison Avenue, 10017
Telephone: 212-213-8200
Fax: 212-685-2028
Email: lawyers@pgjhlaw.com *URL:* http://www.pgjhlaw.com
Carlstadt, New Jersey Office: One Palmer Terrace.
Telephone: 201-507-5157.
FAX: 201-507-5221.
Washington, D.C. Office: 888 17th Street, N.W., Suite 1100.
Telephone: 202-467-6991.
FAX: 202-467-6703.
San Francisco, California Office: 507 Howard Street, Suite 200.
Telephone: 415-281-3631.
Fax: 415-281-3630.

MEMBERS OF FIRM

Kimberlee S. Bogen | Marc A. Lebowitz
Edward J. Goldstein | Robert D. Piliero
Jon Mark Jenkins | George O. Richardson, III
Michael T. Sullivan

ASSOCIATES

Craig Avedisian | Eric M. Kogan
Rosemary G. Feit | Mariano Schwed

OF COUNSEL

Kenneth D. Arbeeny | Christopher P. Hall

For full biographical listings, see the Martindale-Hubbell Law Directory

SERKO & SIMON LLP (AV)

Suite 3371, 1 World Trade Center, 10048
Telephone: 212-775-0055
Facsimile: 212-839-9103
Email: serko-simon@customs-law.com *URL:* http://www.customs-law.com

MEMBERS OF FIRM

David Serko | Daniel J. Gluck
Joel K. Simon | Christopher M. Kane

SPECIAL COUNSEL

Melvyn N. Minsky

ASSOCIATES

Despina Keegan | Jerome L. Hanifin (Not admitted in NY)

OF COUNSEL-NEW YORK

David S. Chang | Rafael F. Castro-Lang (Not admitted in NY)

TECHNICAL ADVISORS

Joseph Raul | Martin L. Weiss

For full biographical listings, see the Martindale-Hubbell Law Directory

YERUSHALMI & ASSOCIATES, L.L.P. (AV)

Empire State Building, 350 Fifth Avenue, 60th Floor Suite 6011, 10118-6096
Telephone: 212-244-2400
Fax: 212-967-3403

Joseph Yerushalmi

OF COUNSEL

Fran Mulnick Parker | Richard H. Wender

For full biographical listings, see the Martindale-Hubbell Law Directory

OKLAHOMA

*TULSA,** Tulsa Co.

BOESCHE, MCDERMOTT & ESKRIDGE (AV)

Suite 800 Oneok Plaza, 100 West Fifth Street, 74103
Telephone: 918-583-1777
Fax: 918-592-5809
Email: bme@intellex.com
Muskogee, Oklahoma Office: 1111 West Broadway, P.O. Box 2669, 74402.
Telephone: 918-683-6100.
Fax: 918-683-2303.

MEMBER OF FIRM

David A. Johnson

Representative Clients: CEALC; Bartec; Occidental Petroleum, CRL-Evans Pipeline International, Inc.

For Complete List of Firm Personnel, See General Section

For full biographical listings, see the Martindale-Hubbell Law Directory

PENNSYLVANIA

NARBERTH, Montgomery Co.

EDWARD M. MEZVINSKY (AV)

815 Woodbine Avenue, 19072
Telephone: 610-664-7115
Fax: 610-664-7225
Email: emmez@aol.com *URL:* http://www.lawyers.com/edwardmmezvinsky

For full biographical listings, see the Martindale-Hubbell Law Directory

*PHILADELPHIA,** Philadelphia Co.

DONOHUE AND DONOHUE (AV)

232 South Fourth Street, 19106
Telephone: 215-574-1080
Fax: 215-574-1255
URL: http://www.lawyers.com/donohuelaw
New York, N.Y. Office: 26 Broadway.
Telephone: 212-269-2330.
Telecopier: 212-269-5016.

John P. Donohue (Resident)

Patrick J. Egan
Melissa G. Pinheiro

For full biographical listings, see the Martindale-Hubbell Law Directory

F. EMMETT FITZPATRICK, P.C. (AV)

926 Public Ledger Building, 19106
Telephone: 215-925-5200
Fax: 215-925-5991
Email: info@toplaw.com *URL:* http://www.toplaw.com

F. Emmett Fitzpatrick
F. Emmett Fitzpatrick, III

NiaLena Caravasos

LEGAL SUPPORT PERSONNEL

Doreen Howley (Paralegal)

For full biographical listings, see the Martindale-Hubbell Law Directory

RHODE ISLAND

*PROVIDENCE,** Providence Co.

HINCKLEY, ALLEN & SNYDER LLP (AV)

1500 Fleet Center, 02903-2393
Telephone: 401-274-2000
Fax: 401-277-9600
Email: firm@haslaw.com *URL:* http://www.haslaw.com
Boston, Massachusetts Office: 28 State Street, 30th Floor.
Telephone: 617-345-9000.
Fax: 617-345-9020. URL: http://www.haslaw.com.

MEMBERS OF FIRM

Paula K. Andrews (Not admitted in RI)
E. Jerome Batty
Jonathan Bell
Paul Bork (Not admitted in RI)
Stephen J. Carlotti
David Barry Connolly (Not admitted in RI)
Joseph P. Curran
Michael P. DeFanti

(See Next Column)

MEMBERS OF FIRM (Continued)

Eric F. Eisenberg (Not admitted in RI)
Malcolm Farmer, III
Margaret D. Farrell
Hugh J. Gorman, III (Not admitted in RI)
William R. Grimm
Michael J. Kelly (Not admitted in RI)
Matthew T. Marcello, III
Frederick P. McClure
Elizabeth Murdock Myers
Paul F. O'Donnell, III (Not admitted in RI)
Gerald J. Petros
Robert F. Sylvia (Not admitted in RI)
Howard E. Walker

ASSOCIATES

Mark Bianchi
Andrew D. Cummings (Not admitted in RI)
June E. Daniel
Gloria Maria Gutierrez (Not admitted in RI)
Kelley Jordan-Price

OF COUNSEL

Joachim A. Weissfeld

For Complete List of Firm Personnel, See General Section

For full biographical listings, see the Martindale-Hubbell Law Directory

TEXAS

*EL PASO,** El Paso Co.

MAYFIELD & PERRENOT, P.C. (AV)

221 N. Kansas, Suite 1600, P.O. Box 2039, 79950
Telephone: 915-533-2468
Telecopier: 915-533-0620
Email: mayper@1eagle1.com

Richard B. Perrenot
Roger C. Davie
James R. Dennis
Jeffery W. McElroy

Lisa M. Power
Shelly Weatherly
Marina Mata De La Garza

OF COUNSEL

Ellis O. Mayfield
James B. McIntyre

For full biographical listings, see the Martindale-Hubbell Law Directory

UTAH

*SALT LAKE CITY,** Salt Lake Co.

VAN COTT, BAGLEY, CORNWALL & MCCARTHY, A PROFESSIONAL CORPORATION (AV)

50 South Main Street, Suite 1600, P.O. Box 45340, 84145-0340
Telephone: 801-532-3333
Telecopier: 801-534-0058
Email: info@vancott.com *URL:* http://www.vancott.com
Ogden, Utah Office: 2404 Washington Boulevard, Suite 900.
Telephone: 801-394-5783.
Park City, Utah Office: 2200 Park Avenue, Suite C200-A.
Telephone: 435-649-3889.

David J. Smith
Stephen D. Swindle

Mara A. Brown
Kim S Colton

For Complete List of Firm Personnel, See General Section

For full biographical listings, see the Martindale-Hubbell Law Directory

CANADA
NOVA SCOTIA

*HALIFAX,** Regional Munic. of Halifax

MCINNES COOPER (AV)

Barristers, Solicitors & Trade Mark Agents
Summit Place, 1601 Lower Water Street, P.O. Box 730, B3J 2V1
Telephone: 902-425-6500
Fax: 902-425-6350
Email: mcrhfx@mcrlaw.com *URL:* http://www.mcrlaw.com
St. John's, Newfoundland Office: Baine Johnston Centre, 5th Floor, 10 Fort William Place, P.O. Box 5939, A1C 5X4.
Telephone: 709-722-8735.
Telecopier: 709-722-1763. Email: mcrsj@mcrlaw.com.

(See Next Column)

McInnes Cooper—*Continued*

Moncton, New Brunswick Office: Place Moncton Place, 655 Main Street, P.O. Box 1368, E1C 8T6.
Telephone: 506-857-8970.
Fax: 506-857-4095. Email: mcrmctn@mcrlaw.com.
Charlottetown, Prince Edward Island Office: BDC Place, Suite 620, 119 Kent Street, C1A 1N3.
Telephone: 902-368-8473.
Fax: 902-368-8346. Email: mcrpei@mcrlaw.com.
Fredericton, New Brunswick Office: Suite 600, 570 Queen Street, P.O. Box 610.
Telephone: 506-458-8572.
Fax: 506-458-9903. Email: mcrfton@mcrlaw.com.

PARTNER

Joseph A. F. Macdonald, Q.C.

For Complete List of Firm Personnel, See General Section

For full biographical listings, see the Martindale-Hubbell Law Directory

---

CANADA
QUEBEC

*MONTREAL,** Montreal Dist.

Gottlieb & Pearson (AV)

Suite 1600, 2020 University Street, H3A 2A5
Telephone: 514-288-1744
Fax: 514-288-6629
URL: http://www.gottliebpearson.ca
Toronto, Ontario Office: The Madison Centre, 4950 Yonge Street, Suite 1800, Toronto, M2N 6K1.
Telephone: 416-250-1550.
Fax: 416-250-7889.

MEMBERS OF FIRM

Richard S. Gottlieb
Darrel H. Pearson (Resident, Ontario, Toronto Office)
Laurier Beauchamp
Jeffery D. Jenkins (Resident, Toronto, Ontario Office)
Jesse I. Goldman (Not admitted in QU)
J. Peter Jarosz (Not admitted in QU)
Robert J. Bertrand, Q.C.
A. L. C. de Mestral
Marc de Man
Andrea J. Sterling
Hynek Zikovsky
Alfredo Moreira
Armand A. Kazandjian
André K. Baby

For full biographical listings, see the Martindale-Hubbell Law Directory

LABOR AND EMPLOYMENT LAW

MINNESOTA

*MINNEAPOLIS,** Hennepin Co.

BURK & SEATON, P.A. (AV)

7301 Ohms Lane (Edina), Suite 320, 55439
Telephone: 612-896-1700
Fax: 612-896-1704
Email: bsc@pconline.com

Robert S. Burk
Douglas P. Seaton

Carole B. Grossman
Elizabeth M. McDowell
Robin N. Kelleher
Gregory L. Peters

OF COUNSEL

Robert L. Grossman

For full biographical listings, see the Martindale-Hubbell Law Directory

FELHABER, LARSON, FENLON & VOGT, PROFESSIONAL ASSOCIATION (AV)

601 2nd Avenue South, Suite 4200, 55402-4302
Telephone: 612-339-6321
800-989-6321
Facsimile: 612-338-0535
St. Paul, Minnesota Office: 30 East Seventh Street, 2100 Minnesota World Trade Center.
Telephone: 651-222-6321; 800-229-6321.
Facsimile: 651-222-8905.

Robert L. Bach
Richard A. Beens
Edward J. Bohrer
Stephen J. Burton
James J. Cronin
James M. Dawson
Robert J. Fenlon
Jan Douglas Halverson
Catharine F. Haukedahl
David R. Hols
Katherine A. Jones
Dennis J. Merley
Penelope J. Phillips
Karen G. Schanfield
Thomas R. Trachsel
Frederick W. Vogt
Thomas M. Vogt
Paul J. Zech

For Complete List of Firm Personnel, See General Section

For full biographical listings, see the Martindale-Hubbell Law Directory

FLYNN & GASKINS, L.L.P. (AV)

29th Floor, Metropolitan Centre, 333 South Seventh Street, 55402
Telephone: 612-333-9500
Fax: 612-333-9579
Email: mail@flynngaskins.com *URL:* http://www.flynngaskins.com

MEMBERS OF FIRM

Barbara Jean D'Aquila
Randall J. Pattee

ASSOCIATES

Karen Reierson
Patrick R. Martin
John J. Laravuso
Gregory J. Wiley
Stephanie D. Sarantopoulos
Cory A. Kallheim
Craig D. Sandok (Not admitted in MN)

For full biographical listings, see the Martindale-Hubbell Law Directory

HESSIAN & McKASY, P.A. (AV)

4700 IDS Center, 80 South Eighth Street, 55402-2228
Telephone: 612-330-3000
Telecopier: 612-371-0653
St. Paul, Minnesota Offices: 2050 Piper Jaffray Plaza, 444 Cedar Street, 55101.
Telephone: 612-330-3071.
Fax: 651-228-9161.

Lee A. Henderson
William A. Cumming

SHAREHOLDERS

David W. Larson

For full biographical listings, see the Martindale-Hubbell Law Directory

MANSFIELD TANICK & COHEN, P.A. (AV)

1560 International Centre, 900 Second Avenue South, 55402
Telephone: 612-339-4295
Fax: 612-339-3161
Email: tanick@mansfieldtanick.com *URL:* http://www.mansfieldtanick.com

(See Next Column)

Seymour J. Mansfield
Marshall H. Tanick
Earl H. Cohen
Robert A. Johnson
Teresa J. Ayling
Richard J. Fuller

Phillip J. Trobaugh
Debra S. Lepert
Ann M. Zewiske
V. John Ella

OF COUNSEL

James P. Cullen
Sholly A. Blustin

For full biographical listings, see the Martindale-Hubbell Law Directory

PARSINEN KAPLAN LEVY ROSBERG & GOTLIEB P.A. (AV)

100 South 5th Street Suite 1100, 55402-1298
Telephone: 612-333-2111
Fax: 612-333-6798

John Parsinen
Robert A. Levy
Sidney Kaplan
Jack A. Rosberg
David Gotlieb
Karen A. Ciegler Hansen
Joseph M. Sokolowski
Howard J. Rubin
David A. Orenstein
John C. Levy
Steven R. Katz
Kathleen Doar
Brian R. Martens
Rebecca J. McDaniel
Stephen M. Hickok
Ann Marks Sanford
Jude Anne Carluccio
Pamela A. Curran
David B. Gollin

Theresa M. Kowalski
Joan P. Kurlander
Bryan D. Biesterfeld
Daniel W. Eck
Nels E. Carlson
John Scott De Lanoy
Ann S. Grayson
Kimberley Ste. Marie Becker
Heidi E. Pergament

For full biographical listings, see the Martindale-Hubbell Law Directory

SPRENGER & LANG, P.L.L.C. (AV)

325 Ridgewood Avenue, 55403-3542
Telephone: 612-871-8910
Fax: 612-871-9270
Washington, D.C. Office: Sprenger & Lang, P.L.L.C., 1614 Twentieth Street, N.W.
Telephone: 202-265-8010.
Fax: 202-332-6652.

MEMBERS OF FIRM

Paul C. Sprenger (Resident, Washington, D.C. Office)
Jane Lang (Resident, Washington, D.C. Office)
Lawrence P. Schaefer (Resident)
James R. Behrenbrinker (Resident)
Eli Gottesdiener (Not admitted in MN; Resident, Washington, D.C. Office)
Susan E. Stokes (Resident)

Lisa C. Stratton (Resident)

OF COUNSEL

Jean M. Boler (Resident)
Mara R. Thompson (Resident)

For full biographical listings, see the Martindale-Hubbell Law Directory

*ST. CLOUD,** Stearns Co.

HUGHES, MATHEWS & DIDIER, P.A. (AV)

110 Sixth Avenue South, Suite 205, P.O. Box 548, 56302-0548
Telephone: 320-251-4399
Fax: 320-251-5781

Kevin J. Hughes
Thomas E. Mathews
Paul R. Harris

Suzanne M. Johnson

Representative Clients: The St. Cloud Hospital; CentraCare Health System; St. John's University; College of St. Benedict; Tanner Systems, Inc.; Anderson Trucking Service, Inc.

For full biographical listings, see the Martindale-Hubbell Law Directory

*ST. PAUL,** Ramsey Co.

BANNIGAN & KELLY, P.A. (AV)

Suite 1750, North Central Life Tower, 445 Minnesota Street, 55101
Telephone: 651-224-3781
Fax: 651-223-8019

John F. Bannigan, Jr.
Patrick J. Kelly

Song Lo Fawcett
Stephen Kelly
Sia Lo

St. Paul—Continued

GERAGHTY, O'LOUGHLIN & KENNEY, PROFESSIONAL ASSOCIATION (AV)

1400 Ecolab University Center, 386 North Wabasha Street, 55102-1308
Telephone: 651-291-1177
Fax: 651-291-9477
Email: gok@pclink.com

Terence J. O'Loughlin
Robert M. Mahoney
David C. Hutchinson
William H. Leary, III
Mary H. Alcorn
Matthew J. Hanzel
Ann D. Bray
Jean B. Hoppe
Kyle M. Thomas

OF COUNSEL

James H. Geraghty (Retired)
James W. Kenney (Retired)

Representative Clients: St. Paul Cos.; Allina Health System; Fairview Hospital and Healthcare Services; HealthEast; HealthPartners; MMI Cos.; Midwest Medical Insurance Co.; North Memorial Hospital; Aspen Medical Group.

For full biographical listings, see the Martindale-Hubbell Law Directory

SPENCE, RICKE & THURMER, P.A. (AV)

Suite 600, Degree of Honor Building, 325 Cedar Street, 55101
Telephone: 651-223-8000
Fax: 651-223-8003
Email: meganr@srtpa.com

Thomas W. Spence
Megan Korfhage Ricke
Susan D. Thurmer

Patrick J. Sweeney
Julius W. Gernes
Glenn Olander-Quamme
Timothy K. Masterson
Rodney A. Honkanen
Scott H. Rauser

Representative Clients: Burlington Northern Sante Fe Railroad; Glacier Park Co.

For full biographical listings, see the Martindale-Hubbell Law Directory

MISSISSIPPI

*ABERDEEN,** Monroe Co.

PATTERSON & PATTERSON (AV)

304 East Jefferson Street, P.O. Box 663, 39730
Telephone: 662-369-2476
Fax: 662-369-9806
Email: JPP@ebicom.net

MEMBERS OF FIRM

Robert D. Patterson
Jan P. Patterson
Peter T. Martin

Local Counsel for: National Bank of Commerce of Mississippi; American Colloid Company; Condea Vista Company; Pruet Production Co.; Arco Oil & Gas Co.; Chemical Corporation; Unimin Corporation.
Approved Title Attorneys for: First American Title Insurance Co.; Mississippi Valley Title Insurance Co.

For full biographical listings, see the Martindale-Hubbell Law Directory

*BROOKHAVEN,** Lincoln Co.

ALLEN, ALLEN, BOERNER & BREELAND (AV)

214 Justice Street, P.O. Box 751, 39602-0751
Telephone: 601-833-4361
Fax: 601-833-6647
Email: aabblaw@tislink.com

Emmette P. Allen (1915-1999)
Robert O. Allen
William D. Boerner
Durwood J. Breeland

ASSOCIATE

Sally Burchfield Doty

For full biographical listings, see the Martindale-Hubbell Law Directory

*GULFPORT,** Harrison Co.

DUKES, DUKES, KEATING AND FANECA, P.A. (AV)

2909 13th Street, 6th Floor, P.O. Drawer W, 39501
Telephone: 228-868-1111
Fax: 228-863-2886
Email: ddkf@ddkf.com

William F. Dukes
Hugh D. Keating
Cy Faneca
Phillip W. Jarrell

For Complete List of Firm Personnel, See General Section

For full biographical listings, see the Martindale-Hubbell Law Directory

*JACKSON,** Hinds Co.

BAKER, DONELSON, BEARMAN & CALDWELL (AV)

Suite 500, 700 North State Street, 39202
Telephone: 601-351-2400
Telecopier: 601-351-2424
Email: info@bdbc.com *URL:* http://www.bakerdonelson.com
Memphis, Tennessee Office: 20th Floor, First Tennessee Building, 165 Madison, 38103.
Telephone: 901-526-2000.
Telecopier: 901-577-2303.
Nashville, Tennessee Office: 1700 Nashville City Center, 511 Union Street, 37219.
Telephone: 615-726-5600.
Telecopier: 615-726-0464.
Chattanooga, Tennessee Office: 1800 Republic Centre, 633 Chestnut Street, 37450-1800.
Telephone: 423-756-2010.
Telecopier: 423-756-3447.
Knoxville, Tennessee Office: 2200 Riverview Tower, 900 South Gay Street, 37901.
Telephone: 423-549-7000.
Telecopier: 423-525-8569.
Johnson City, Tennessee Office: SunTrust Bank Building, 207 Mockingbird Lane, P.O. Box 3038, 37602.
Telephone: 423-928-0181.
Telecopier: 423-928-5694; 423-928-3654; Kingsport: 423-246-6191.
Huntsville, Tennessee Office: 3 Courthouse Square, 37756.
Telephone: 423-663-2321.
Telecopier: 423-663-2111.
Washington, D.C. Office: Market Square, 801 Pennsylvania Avenue, N.W., 20004.
Telephone: 202-508-3400.
Telecopier: 202-508-3402.

ASSOCIATE

J. Randall Patterson

For Complete List of Firm Personnel, See General Section

For full biographical listings, see the Martindale-Hubbell Law Directory

PHELPS DUNBAR, L.L.P. (AV)

Suite 500, SkyTel Centre, 200 South Lamar Street, P.O. Box 23066, 39225-3066
Telephone: 601-352-2300
Telecopier: 601-360-9777
Email: info@phelps.com
New Orleans, Louisiana Office: Texaco Center, 400 Poydras Street.
Telephone: 504-566-1311.
Telecopier: 504-568-9130; 504-568-9007.
Cable Address: "Howspencer."
Telex: 584125 WU.
Telex: 6821155 WUI.
Baton Rouge, Louisiana Office: Suite 701, 445 North Boulevard, P.O. Box 4412.
Telephone: 225-346-0285.
Telecopier: 225-381-9197.
Tupelo, Mississippi Office: Seventh Floor, One Mississippi Plaza, P.O. Box 1220.
Telephone: 662-842-7907.
Telecopier: 662-842-3873.
Houston, Texas Office: Suite 900, 3040 Post Oak Boulevard.
Telephone: 713-626-1386.
Telecopier: 713-626-1388.
London, England Office: Suite 731, Level 7, Lloyd's, 1 Lime Street, London EC3M 7DQ England.
Telephone: 011-44-207-929-4765.
Telecopier: 011-44-207-929-0046.
Telex: 987321.

RESIDENT PARTNERS

R. Pepper Crutcher, Jr.
Gary E. Friedman
Paul O. Miller, III
Armin J. Moeller, Jr.
W. Thomas Siler, Jr.
David M. Thomas, II

RESIDENT ASSOCIATES

Joseph Lee Adams
Ken Fairly
Mark Fijman
A. Matt Pesnell
Chelye E. Prichard
E. Russell Turner

Representative Clients: Associated Builders and Contractors; BellSouth Telecommunications, Inc.; First Mississippi Corp.; General Motors Corporation; The Kroger Co.; Mississippi Hospital Association; Mississippi Municipal Liability Plan; Philip Morris Incorporated; Raytheon Aerospace, Inc.; Southern Farm Bureau Life Insurance Company.

For Complete List of Firm Personnel, See General Section

For full biographical listings, see the Martindale-Hubbell Law Directory

Jackson—Continued

WATKINS & EAGER (AV)

A Professional Limited Liability Company
Suite 300 The Emporium Building, 400 East Capitol Street, P.O. Box 650, 39205
Telephone: 601-948-6470
Facsimile: 601-354-3623

MEMBERS OF FIRM

Kenneth E. Milam
Walter J. Brand

ASSOCIATE

W. Thomas McCraney, III

Representative Clients: UPS; MTEL; La-Z-Boy; Mississippi Baptist Health Systems, Inc.; South Mississippi Electrical Power Assn.

For Complete List of Firm Personnel, See General Section

For full biographical listings, see the Martindale-Hubbell Law Directory

*MERIDIAN,** Lauderdale Co.

GLOVER, YOUNG, WALTON, PHILLIPS & TUCKER, PLLC (AV)

Jefferson Square Office Plaza, 1724-A 23rd Avenue, P.O. Box 5514, 39302-5514
Telephone: 601-693-1301
Telecopy: 601-693-1363
Email: gywptpsp@hotmail.com

H. Wingfield Glover, Jr.
Ronnie L. Walton
Ralph E. Young, Jr.
P. Scott Phillips
Judson T. Tucker

Representative Clients: Alfa Insurance Companies; American States Insurance Co.; Deposit Guaranty National Bank; General Agents Insurance Company of America, Inc.; Great River Insurance; Jeff Anderson Regional Medical Center; Liberty National Life Insurance Co.; Mississippi Power Co.; State Auto Insurance Companies; Universal Underwriters.

For Complete List of Firm Personnel, See General Section

For full biographical listings, see the Martindale-Hubbell Law Directory

*OXFORD,** Lafayette Co.

HOLCOMB DUNBAR, A PROFESSIONAL ASSOCIATION (AV)

1217 Jackson Avenue P.O. Drawer 707, 38655
Telephone: 601-234-8775
Facsimile: 601-238-7552
Email: hdccw@holcombdunbar.com *URL:* http://www.holcombdunbar.com
Clarksdale, Mississippi Office: 152 Delta Avenue, P.O. Box 368, 38614.
Telephone: 601-627-2241.
Facsimile: 601-627-9788.
Southaven, Mississippi Office: Suite 1, 728 Goodman Road East, P.O. Box 190, 38671.
Telephone: 601-349-0664.
Facsimile: 601-349-2432.

Jack F. Dunbar
Marjorie T. O'Donnell
Edward A. Moss
David D. O'Donnell
Thomas J. Suszek
R. Bradley Best
Michael N. Watts
Walter Alan Davis
Mark R. Smith

Counsel for: Union Planters Bank, National Association; Mississippi Power & Light Co.; Mississippi Valley Gas Co.; South Central Bell Telephone Co.; State Farm Mutual Fire & Casualty Insurance Co.; Fireman's Fund Insurance Cos.; Deere & Co.; Drexel Chemical Co.; Fruit of the Loom.

For Complete List of Firm Personnel, See General Section

For full biographical listings, see the Martindale-Hubbell Law Directory

MISSOURI

CHESTERFIELD, St. Louis Co.

LAWRENCE J. ALTMAN (AV)

Suite 502, 14500 South Outer Forty Road, 63017
Telephone: 314-205-9544
Fax: 314-205-9545
Email: ljalaw@aol.com

For full biographical listings, see the Martindale-Hubbell Law Directory

*INDEPENDENCE,** Jackson Co.

WHITE, ALLINDER & GRAHAM, L.L.C. (AV)

Hidden Creek Office Park, 14801 East 42nd Street, 64055
Telephone: 816-373-9080
Fax: 816-373-9319

(See Next Column)

MEMBERS OF FIRM

Steven W. White
John K. Allinder
Gene P. Graham, Jr.

ASSOCIATE

Mary Beth Clune

For full biographical listings, see the Martindale-Hubbell Law Directory

KANSAS CITY, Jackson, Clay, Platte & Cass Cos.

BIOFF SINGER AND FINUCANE, LLP (AV)

Suite 400 The Stilwell Building, 104 West Ninth Street, 64105-1718
Telephone: 816-842-8770
Telefax: 816-842-8767

MEMBERS OF FIRM

Allan L. Bioff
Brian J. Finucane
Leonard Singer
J. Randall Coffey

James R. Holland, II
Jill Waldman (Not admitted in MO)
Gregory D. Ballew
Von E. Hays
Jennifer L. Robinson
Nancy M. Leonard
Stacie M. Johnson

OF COUNSEL

Martha A. Halvordson

Representative Clients: United Parcel Service, Inc.; Bunge Corporation; Sprint Corporation; Sutherland Lumber Company; Interstate Brands Corporation; GTE Corporation; Farmers Insurance Group of Companies; Neighbors Construction Company; Hill's Pet Nutrition; Kansas City Southern Industries, Inc.

For full biographical listings, see the Martindale-Hubbell Law Directory

SHUGHART THOMSON & KILROY, A PROFESSIONAL CORPORATION (AV)

Twelve Wyandotte Plaza, 120 West 12th Street, 64105
Telephone: 816-421-3355
Email: Solutions@KC.STKLAW.COM *URL:* http://www.STKLAW.COM
Overland Park, Kansas Office: Suite 1100, 32 Corporate Woods, 9225 Indian Creek Parkway 66210.
Telephone: 913-451-3355.
Springfield, Missouri Office: Suite 1200, Hammons Tower, 901 St. Louis, 65806.
Telephone: 417-869-3353.
Denver, Colorado Office: 1050 17th Street, Suite 2350. 80265.
Telephone: 303-572-9300.
Fax: 303-572-7883.

Jack L. Campbell
John R. Cleary
W. Terrence Kilroy
Karen J. Halbrook
Gregory M. Bentz
James C. Sullivan

Linda J. Sheppard
Julie B. Tincknell

For Complete List of Firm Personnel, See General Section

For full biographical listings, see the Martindale-Hubbell Law Directory

SPENCER FANE BRITT & BROWNE LLP (AV)

1000 Walnut Street, Suite 1400, 64106-2140
Telephone: 816-474-8100
URL: http://www.spencerfane.com
Overland Park, Kansas Office: Suite 700, 40 Corporate Woods, 9401 Indian Creek Parkway.
Telephone: 913-345-8100.

MEMBERS OF FIRM

J. Nick Badgerow (Resident, Overland Park, Kansas Office)
Denise K. Drake (Clemow)
Elaine Drodge Koch
James G. Baker (Resident, Overland Park, Kansas Office)
William C. Martucci
Michaela M. Warden (Resident, Overland Park, Kansas Office)
Daniel B. Boatright (Resident, Overland Park, Kansas Office)
Jack L. Whitacre
Stanley E. Craven
James R. Willard (Resident, Overland Park, Kansas Office)
Gardiner B. Davis
Michael F. Delaney
David L. Wing

OF COUNSEL

Jill Galbreath Smith (Resident, Overland Park, Kansas Office)
Sue K. Willman

ASSOCIATES

Jeannie M. DeVeney (Resident, Overland Park, Kansas Office)
James C. Holland
Jeffrey M. Place
Michael Brett Fulkerson
Joyce R. Rosenberg
Eric W. Smith

Representative Clients: AlliedSignal Federal Manufacturing & Technologies; Armour Swift-Eckrich, Inc.; Farmland Industries, Inc.; Health Midwest; Sprint; Universal Underwriters Group; The Woolworth Corporation.

For full biographical listings, see the Martindale-Hubbell Law Directory

Kansas City—Continued

SWANSON MIDGLEY, LLC (AV)

Crown Center, 2420 Pershing Road, Suite 400, 64108
Telephone: 816-842-6100
Fax: 816-842-0013
Email: mail@swansonmidgley.com *URL:* http://www.swansonmidgley.com
Overland Park, Kansas Office: Commerce Plaza I, 7th Floor, 7300 W. 110th Street.
Telephone: 913-317-2717.
FAX: 913-317-1505.

Henry R. Cox — James A. Durbin
John J. Kitchin

Rebecca S. Bihr

OF COUNSEL

Ronald E. Sandhaus

Counsel For: TWA; Lee Apparel Co.; Circle K; AFC Enterprises; HNTB Corp.; Reynolds Metal; Yellow (Freight) Corp.; Acoustics Development Corp.; Armed Forces Insurance Exchange; IMC Global.

For Complete List of Firm Personnel, See General Section

For full biographical listings, see the Martindale-Hubbell Law Directory

ST. LOUIS, (Independent City)

ARMSTRONG TEASDALE LLP (AV)

A Partnership including Professional Corporations
One Metropolitan Square, 63102-2740
Telephone: 314-621-5070
Facsimile: 314-621-5065
Twx: 910 761-2246
Cable: ATKV LAW
Email: armstrongteasdale@armstrongteasdale.com *URL:* http://www.armstrongteasdale.com
Kansas City, Missouri Office: 2345 Grand Boulevard, Suite 2000, 64108.
Telephone: 816-221-3420.
Facsimile: 816-221-0786.
Jefferson City, Missouri Office: 3405 W. Truman Blvd., Suite 210, 65109.
Telephone: 573-636-8394.
Washington, D.C. Office: 1747 Pennsylvania Avenue, N.W., Suite 300, 20006.
Telephone: 202-347-0259.
Belleville, Illinois Office: 23 South First Street, 62220.
Telephone: 618-397-4411.
Olathe, Kansas Office: 100 East Park, 66061.
Telephone: 913-345-0706.
Shanghai, China Office: A-T International Consultants, LLC, Suite 310, No. 12 Zhongshan Road (E1), Shanghai 200002 P.R.C.
Telephone: 86-21-6326-7001.
Facsimile: 86-21-6326-0626.

MEMBERS OF FIRM

Joan Z. Cohen — John H. Quinn, III, (P.C.)
Robert A. Kaiser — Mark J. Rubinelli
Fred Leicht, Jr., (P.C.) — Wilbur L. Tomlinson (P.C.)
Vance D. Miller — Paul N. Venker
Daniel K. O'Toole — David W. Welch

ASSOCIATES

Jennifer Lee Arendes — C. Wayne Davis

Representative Clients: AmerenUE; Cass Bank & Trust Company; Citicorp Mortgage, Inc.; Manna Pro Corporation; Southwest Bank; Spartech Corporation; St. Louis Cardinals, L.P.; St. Louis Community College; United Parcel Service.

For Complete List of Firm Personnel, See General Section

For full biographical listings, see the Martindale-Hubbell Law Directory

BEARDEN, BRECKENRIDGE & GIDLOW (AV)

Suite 1250 University Club Tower, 1034 South Brentwood Boulevard, 63117-1212
Telephone: 314-726-6618
Telecopier: 314-726-6757
URL: http://www.lawyers.com/laborrelations

MEMBERS OF FIRM

Thomas G. Bearden — Catherine S. Gidlow
Ray E. Breckenridge — W. Steven Winter

For full biographical listings, see the Martindale-Hubbell Law Directory

BOBROFF, HESSE, LINDMARK & MARTONE, P.C. (AV)

7730 Forsyth, Suite 200, 63105
Telephone: 314-862-0300
Fax: 314-862-7010

(See Next Column)

Michael J. Bobroff — Marvin L. Lindmark, III
James Christopher Hesse — Andrew J. Martone

OF COUNSEL

Gail Gaus Renshaw — Thomas B. Tobin

For full biographical listings, see the Martindale-Hubbell Law Directory

HARRIS, DOWELL, FISHER & HARRIS, L.C. (AV)

Suite 202 15400 South Outer Forty (Chesterfield), 63017-2063
Telephone: 314-532-0300
Fax: 314-532-0246

John O. Harris — Diana Richards Francis
John H. Dowell — (Not admitted in MO)
Ronald K. Fisher — George L. Lenard
Michael F. Harris — David Charles Nelson
James M. Paul

For full biographical listings, see the Martindale-Hubbell Law Directory

KOHN, SHANDS, ELBERT, GIANOULAKIS & GILJUM, LLP (AV)

24th Floor, One Mercantile Center, 63101
Telephone: 314-241-3963
Telecopier: 314-241-2509
Email: attys@ksegg.com

Alan C. Kohn — Charles S. Elbert
John Gianoulakis — Robert A. Useted
Mark J. Bremer — Lisa A. Pake
Robert F. Murray

ASSOCIATES

David A. Castleman — Jennifer S. Forsythe

For full biographical listings, see the Martindale-Hubbell Law Directory

LEWIS, RICE & FINGERSH (AV)

A Limited Liability Company
500 North Broadway, Suite 2000, 63102-2147
Telephone: 314-444-7600
Telecopier: 314-241-6056
URL: http://www.lrf.com
Belleville, Illinois Office: 325 South High Street.
Telephone: 618-234-8636.
Leawood, Kansas Office: Suite 375, 8900 State Line Road.
Telephone: 913-381-8898.
Creve Coeur, Missouri Office: 700 Office Parkway, Suite 15.
Telephone: 314-569-2262.
Kansas City, Missouri Office: 1010 Walnut, Suite 500.
Telephone: 816-421-2500.
Washington, Missouri Office: 216 West Main, P.O. Box 1040.
Telephone: 636-239-7747.

RESIDENT MEMBERS

John J. Gazzoli, Jr. — Curtis C. Calloway
John J. Moellering — Robert J. Golterman
Gary M. Smith

For Complete List of Firm Personnel, See General Section

For full biographical listings, see the Martindale-Hubbell Law Directory

THE LOWENBAUM PARTNERSHIP, L.L.C. (AV)

222 South Central Avenue, Suite 901 (Clayton), 63105
Telephone: 314-863-0092
Facsimile: 314-746-4848
Email: rml@lowenbaumlaw.com

R. Michael Lowenbaum — Karen E. Milner
Julie A. Bregande — Gerald M. Richardson

Representative Clients: Sinclair Broadcast Group; Unity Health; St. Louis Zoological Park; LaserSight Incorporated; Drury Inns, Inc.; St. Clair-Madison Automotive Association.

For full biographical listings, see the Martindale-Hubbell Law Directory

MCCARTHY, LEONARD, KAEMMERER, OWEN, LAMKIN & MCGOVERN, L.C. (AV)

16141 Swingley Ridge Road (Chesterfield), Suite 300, 63017
Telephone: 636-532-7100
Telecopier: 636-532-0857
Email: info@mlklaw.com

Thomas W. McCarthy, III — Brian E. McGovern
Michael E. Kaemmerer — Diana K. Wieland
Andrew B. Leonard — James P. Towey, Jr.
James C. Owen — Todd A. Massa
Walter R. Lamkin — Paula M. Young
Robert W. Hoffman

(See Next Column)

McCarthy, Leonard, Kaemmerer, Owen, Lamkin & McGovern L.C.—*Continued*

E. Megan Kinsella
Elaine M. Moss
Katherine S. Walsh
Kevin T. McLaughlin
Tami Zeisler Morrissey
Robert A. Miller
Christopher C. O'Connell
James R. Walsh

For full biographical listings, see the Martindale-Hubbell Law Directory

McMahon, Berger, Hanna, Linihan, Cody & McCarthy, A Professional Corporation (AV)

Suite 200, 2730 North Ballas Road, 63131
Telephone: 314-567-7350
Telecopier: 314-567-5968
Email: lawfirm@mcmanberger.com

Alan I. Berger (1933-1999)
Thomas M. Hanna
D. Michael Linihan
William W. Cody
Thomas O. McCarthy
Robert W. Stewart
James N. Foster, Jr.
Daniel R. Begian
John B. Renick
Patricia M. McFall
Fred A. Ricks, Jr.
Kevin J. Lorenz
Thomas E. Berry
Stanley G. Schroeder
Shelley M. Roither
Geoffrey M. Gilbert

Michelle M. Cain
Stephen B. Maule
Timothy O. Schranck
Stephanie O. Zorn
William M. Lawson
William B. Jones
Thomas L. Bell
Burton D. Garland, Jr.
Mary Carter Duncan
Robert D. Younger
Gregory A. Shoemaker

OF COUNSEL

Ralph E. Kennedy

Representative Clients: Emerson Electric Co.; Mallinckrodt Inc.; Monsanto Co.

For full biographical listings, see the Martindale-Hubbell Law Directory

MONTANA

*BILLINGS,** Yellowstone Co.

Crowley, Haughey, Hanson, Toole & Dietrich, P.L.L.P. (AV)

500 Transwestern II, 490 North 31st Street, P.O. Box 2529, 59103
Telephone: 406-252-3441
Fax: 406-259-4159
Email: crowley@crowleylaw.com
Helena, Montana Office: IBM Building, 100 North Park Avenue, Suite 300, 59601.
Telephone: 406-449-4165.
Fax: 406-449-5149.
Kalispell, Montana Office: 431 1st Avenue West, 59901.
Telephone: 406-752-6644.
Fax: 406-752-5108.
Williston, North Dakota Office: 113 East Broadway, 58801.
Telephone: 701-572-2200.
Fax: 701-572-7072.

OF COUNSEL

Gareld F. Krieg

MEMBERS OF FIRM

Terry B. Cosgrove (Resident, Helena, Montana Office)
Steven J. Lehman
William J. Mattix
Joe C. Maynard, Jr.
Michael S. Lahr (Resident, Helena, Montana Office)

Representative Clients: Xerox Corporation; Valley Motor Supply; Montana Power Company; Armstrong World Industries; Peabody Coal Co.; United Parcel Service; Billings Clinic; Yellowstone County; MDU Resources Group, Inc.; General Electric Co.

For Complete List of Firm Personnel, See General Section

For full biographical listings, see the Martindale-Hubbell Law Directory

Wright, Tolliver and Guthals A Professional Service Corporation (AV)

Windsor Court, 10 North 27th Street, P.O. Box 1977, 59103-1977
Telephone: 406-245-3071
Telecopier: 406-245-3074
Email: lawfirm@mcn.net

(See Next Column)

Ralph S. Wright (1939-1985)
Kenneth D. Tolliver
Joel E. Guthals
Virginia A. Bryan
Susan Fisher Stevens
J. Reuss
Jeffery A. Hunnes
James W. Thompson

David Paul Wilkins

For full biographical listings, see the Martindale-Hubbell Law Directory

*BOZEMAN,** Gallatin Co.

Kirwan & Barrett, P.C. (AV)

215 West Mendenhall, P.O. Box 1348, 59771-1348
Telephone: 406-586-1553
Fax: 406-586-8971

Peter M. Kirwan
Stephen M. Barrett

For full biographical listings, see the Martindale-Hubbell Law Directory

NEBRASKA

*LINCOLN,** Lancaster Co.

Cline, Williams, Wright, Johnson & Oldfather (AV)

1900 U.S. Bank Building, 233 South 13th Street, 68508
Telephone: 402-474-6900
Fax: 402-474-5393
Email: postmaster@cline-law.com *URL:* http://www.cline-law.com
Omaha, Nebraska Office: Suite 720, One Pacific Place, 1125 South 103rd Street, 68124.
Telephone: 402-397-1700.
Fax: 402-397-1806.

ATTORNEYS

Allen L. Graves
Charles M. Pallesen, Jr.
Fredric H. Kauffman
Donald F. Burt
Alan E. Peterson
Stephen E. Gehring
Robert J. Routh
Kevin Colleran
L. Bruce Wright
James M. Bausch
Larry A. Holle
David R. Buntain
Stephen H. Nelsen
Michael C. Mueller
Lauren W. Wismer
Daniel R. Stogsdill
Scott D. Kelly
Terry R. Wittler
Pamela Hastings Carrier
Mark A. Christensen
Richard P. Garden, Jr.
Shawn D. Renner
John C. Miles
Mary Kay Frank
Thomas C. Huston
Sonya S. Ekart
Don R. Janssen
Susan Kubert Sapp
Kevin J. Schneider
Andrew D. Strotman
Jill Gossin Jensen
Rochelle A. Mullen
John L. Horan
Bryan S. Hatch
Steven C. Likes
Tracy A. Oldemeyer
Jolene M. Papa
Timothy G. Aschoff
Eric N. Bergquist
Janis J. Winterhof
Andrea Dylan Snowden

OF COUNSEL

Charles E. Wright
Richard P. Jeffries
Mary M. Campbell

RETIRED PARTNERS

Flavel A. Wright (Retired)
Warren C. Johnson (Retired)
Charles E. Oldfather (1927-1998)

Representative Clients: U.S. Bank National Association; University of Nebraska; Nebraska Medical Assn.; Saint Elizabeth Regional Medical Center; Media of Nebraska; Cargill Inc.; State Farm Insurance Cos.; Wal-Mart Stores, Inc.; Textron/Cushman; Isco, Inc.

For full biographical listings, see the Martindale-Hubbell Law Directory

Erickson & Sederstrom, P.C. (AV)

Suite 400, Cornhusker Plaza, 301 South 13th Street, 68508
Telephone: 402-476-1000
Fax: 402-476-6167
Omaha, Nebraska Office: Regency Westpointe, 10330 Regency Parkway Drive, Suite 100, 68114-3761.
Telephone: 402-397-2200.
Fax: 402-390-7137.

Mark M. Schorr

Representative Clients: Nash Finch Co.; Sun-Husker Foods, Inc.; Sandoz Pharmaceuticals Corp.; Sioux City Foundry; Orthman Manufacturing; TG (U.S.A.) Corp.; K-Mart Corp.; Central Confinement Services, Ltd.; Arrow Gear Co.

For Complete List of Firm Personnel, See General Section

For full biographical listings, see the Martindale-Hubbell Law Directory

*OMAHA,** Douglas Co.

ANDERSEN, BERKSHIRE, LAURITSEN & BROWER (AV)

A Partnership including a Professional Corporation
Suite 200, 8805 Indian Hills Drive, 68114-4070
Telephone: 402-397-0666
Facsimile: 402-397-4633

Thomas C. Lauritsen
John C. Hewitt

Representative Clients: Wilson Trailer Co.; U.S. Cold Storage; Affiliated Foods Cooperative, Inc.; KMTV; United Affiliated Grocers; Lisle Corp.; CMI-Load King; Owen Industries, Inc.; Goodkind & Goodkind, Inc.; Interstate Printing, Inc.

For Complete List of Firm Personnel, See General Section

For full biographical listings, see the Martindale-Hubbell Law Directory

BERENS & TATE, P.C. (AV)

Suite 400, 10050 Regency Circle, 68114
Telephone: 402-391-1991
Fax: 402-391-7363
Email: Berems@Berenstate.com

Kelvin C. Berens
Joseph Dreesen
Timothy D. Loudon
Christopher E. Hoyme
Mark E. McQueen
Donna S. Colley
Jerylyn R. Bridgeford
Timothy M. Welsh
William M. Muth, Jr.
Nancy A. Wood
David D. Gale

Michaelle L. Behrns

OF COUNSEL

John E. Tate
Donald E. Leonard (1933-1994)

For full biographical listings, see the Martindale-Hubbell Law Directory

CLINE, WILLIAMS, WRIGHT, JOHNSON & OLDFATHER (AV)

One Pacific Place, 1125 South 103rd Street, Suite 720, 68124
Telephone: 402-397-1700
Fax: 402-397-1806
Email: postmaster@cline-law.com *URL:* http://www.cline-law.com
Lincoln, Nebraska Office: 1900 U.S. Bank Building, 233 South 13th Street, 68508.
Telephone: 402-474-6900.
Fax: 402-474-5393.

ATTORNEYS

Donald F. Burt
Stephen E. Gehring
James M. Bausch
Michael C. Mueller
Daniel R. Stogsdill
Scott D. Kelly
John C. Miles
Mary Kay Frank
Andrew D. Strotman
Rochelle A. Mullen
Steven C. Likes
Tracy A. Oldemeyer
Timothy G. Aschoff

OF COUNSEL

Richard P. Jeffries

Representative Clients: U.S. Bank National Association; University of Nebraska; Nebraska Medical Assn.; Saint Elizabeth Regional Medical Center; Media of Nebraska; Cargill Inc.; State Farm Insurance Cos.; Wal-Mart Stores, Inc.; Textron/Cushman; ISCO, Inc.

For full biographical listings, see the Martindale-Hubbell Law Directory

DWYER, SMITH, GARDNER, LAZER, POHREN, ROGERS & FORREST (AV)

Suite 400, 8712 West Dodge Road, 68114
Telephone: 402-392-0101
Telefax: 402-392-1011
Email: dwyerlaw@dwyer-smith.com *URL:* http://www.dwyer-smith.com

MEMBERS OF FIRM

Michael L. Lazer
Edward F. Pohren
John L. Apker

Representative Clients: Nebraska Health System; Ford Motor Credit Company, Dearborn, Michigan; Nebraska Hospital Association subsidiary Bio Electronics, Lincoln, Oak Bancorporation; Lynn Roberts International; Elliot Equipment Co.; Design Plastics, Inc.

For Complete List of Firm Personnel, See General Section

For full biographical listings, see the Martindale-Hubbell Law Directory

ERICKSON & SEDERSTROM, P.C. (AV)

Regency Westpointe, 10330 Regency Parkway Drive, Suite 100, 68114-3761
Telephone: 402-397-2200
Fax: 402-390-7137
Lincoln, Nebraska Office: Suite 400, Cornhusker Plaza, 301 South 13th Street, 68508-2571.
Telephone: 402-476-1000.
Fax: 402-476-6167.

Soren S. Jensen
J Russell Derr

Kevin R. McManaman

Representative Clients: A T & T; Boise Cascade Corp.; Dubuque Packing Co.; Eaton Corp.; General Motors Corp.; Hershey Foods, Inc.; IBP, Inc.; Mutual of Omaha; Omaha World Herald.

For Complete List of Firm Personnel, See General Section

For full biographical listings, see the Martindale-Hubbell Law Directory

FRASER, STRYKER, VAUGHN, MEUSEY, OLSON, BOYER & BLOCH, P.C. (AV)

500 Energy Plaza, 409 South 17th Street, 68102
Telephone: 402-341-6000
Telecopier: 402-341-8290
Email: fraserstryker.com

George C. Rozmarin
Robert F. Rossiter, Jr.
Roger L. Shiffermiller

For Complete List of Firm Personnel, See General Section

For full biographical listings, see the Martindale-Hubbell Law Directory

MCGILL, GOTSDINER, WORKMAN & LEPP, P.C. (AV)

Suite 500 - First National Plaza, 11404 West Dodge Road, 68154
Telephone: 402-492-9200
Telecopier: 402-492-9222
Email: mgwl@mgwl.com

Robert L. Lepp
Mary L. Hewitt

Representative Clients: Metz Baking Company; Behlen Mfg. Co.; Vetter Health Services, Inc.; Mutual of Omaha; Midlands Food Systems, Inc.; Wright Printing; College of St. Mary; Service Data Corporation; Better Quality Cassettes; Crawford & Co.

For Complete List of Firm Personnel, See General Section

For full biographical listings, see the Martindale-Hubbell Law Directory

MCGRATH, NORTH, MULLIN & KRATZ, P.C. (AV)

Suite 1400, One Central Park Plaza, 68102
Telephone: 402-341-3070
Fax: 402-341-0216

Dean G. Kratz
Roger J. Miller
A. Stevenson Bogue
Patrick J. Barrett
Jean E. Connolly
Christopher M. Bikus

General Counsel for: ConAgra, Inc.; InaCom Corp.; Omaha Airport Authority; Physicians Mutual Insurance Co.; Supertel Hospitality, Inc.; Valmont Industries, Inc.
Representative Clients: Clarkson Hospital; Omaha Chamber of Commerce.
Insurance Clients: American Family Insurance Group; Blue Cross-Blue Shield of Nebraska.

For Complete List of Firm Personnel, See General Section

For full biographical listings, see the Martindale-Hubbell Law Directory

NEVADA

HENDERSON, Clark Co.

ROOKER & GIBSON (AV)

Suite 105, 701 North Green Valley Parkway, 89014
Telephone: 702-990-8100
Telecopier: 702-932-5266

C. Keith Rooker
James B. Gibson

Reference: BankWest of Nevada.

For full biographical listings, see the Martindale-Hubbell Law Directory

*LAS VEGAS,** Clark Co.

BARKER, BROWN, BUSBY, CHRISMAN & THOMAS, A PROFESSIONAL CORPORATION (AV)

800 Bank of America Plaza, 300 South Fourth Street, 89101
Telephone: 702-386-1086
Fax: 702-384-5386
Email: BAR-BRO@IX.NETCOM.COM

William S. Barker
Janice J. Brown
Jerry S. Busby
James P. Chrisman
David L. Thomas
Robert A. Winner

Robert D. Tarte
Brent A. Carson
Marino A. Cesaretti
Ann C. Elworth
Michael D. Demman
Curtis J. Busby
J. Scott Ralston

LEGAL SUPPORT PERSONNEL

David A. Ross (Not admitted in NV)
Michael W. Salend
Michael Allen Davis
Britt K. Beckstrom

Representative Clients: Fireman's Fund; Liberty Mutual; Southwest Airlines; Colonial Penn; Metropolitan, Inc.; Uniroyal Tire; Del E. Webb Corp.

For full biographical listings, see the Martindale-Hubbell Law Directory

JOLLEY, URGA, WIRTH & WOODBURY (AV)

3800 Howard Hughes Parkway Suite 1600, 89109
Telephone: 702-699-7500
Facsimile: 702-699-7555
URL: http://www.juww.com
Boulder City, Nevada Office: Suite 105, 1000 Nevada Highway, 89005.
Telephone: 702-293-3674.

MEMBERS OF FIRM

William R. Urga
Allen D. Emmel

ASSOCIATE

Kelly J. Brinkman

Representative Clients: Wells Fargo Bank and its predecessor, First Interstate Bank of Nevada; Nevada State Bank; Chicago Title Insurance Co.; Melvin Simon & Associates, Inc.; General Motors Acceptance Corp.; Toyota Motor Credit Corporation; Champion Home Builders Co.; Circus Circus Casinos, Inc.

For Complete List of Firm Personnel, See General Section

For full biographical listings, see the Martindale-Hubbell Law Directory

KAMER & ZUCKER (AV)

3000 West Charleston Boulevard Suite 3, 89102
Telephone: 702-259-8640
Fax: 702-259-8646

MEMBERS OF FIRM

Gregory J. Kamer
Carol Davis Zucker
Scott M. Abbott

ASSOCIATES

Barbara Dillon De Souza
Edwin A. Keller, Jr.
Jody M. Florence
Susan L. Gray

For full biographical listings, see the Martindale-Hubbell Law Directory

KIRSHMAN, HARRIS & BRANTON, A PROFESSIONAL CORPORATION (AV)

411 East Bonneville Avenue Suite 300, 89101
Telephone: 702-384-3877
Fax: 702-384-7057; 702-384-4250
Email: Kirshman@Juno.com
Beverly Hills, California Office: 315 South Beverly Drive, Suite 315.
Telephone: 310-277-2323.
Telecopier: 310-277-6701.

Norman H. Kirshman
Michael S. Harris
Gary G. Branton
Roger L. Grandgenett, II

Mary F. Chapman

Representative Clients: American Nevada Corp.; City of Henderson; Printronix; Caesars Palace; Nevada Ready Mix; Contractors Wardrobe, Inc; Lewis Homes/Kaufman & Broad; Sands Expo and Convention Center; Republic Silver State Disposal Service, Inc.

For full biographical listings, see the Martindale-Hubbell Law Directory

LIONEL SAWYER & COLLINS (AV)

1700 Bank of America Plaza, 300 South Fourth Street, 89101
Telephone: 702-383-8888
Fax: 702-383-8845
Email: first initial last@lionelsawyer.com
Reno, Nevada Office: Suite 1100, Bank of America Plaza, 50 West Liberty Street.
Telephone: 702-788-8666.
Fax: 702-788-8682.

MEMBERS OF FIRM

Dan C. Bowen (Resident, Reno Office)
Howard E. Cole

ASSOCIATES

Madelene C. Amendola (Resident, Reno Office)
Robert P. Spretnak
Todd E. Kennedy
Laura J. Thalacker

Representative Clients: Aztar Corporation; Caesars Palace; Citicorp; General Motors Corporation; Hilton Hotels Corporation; Humana, Inc.; Kerr McGee Corporation; Lewis Homes of Nevada; Sunrise Hospital and Medical Center.

For Complete List of Firm Personnel, See General Section

For full biographical listings, see the Martindale-Hubbell Law Directory

PICO & MITCHELL (AV)

2000 South Eastern Avenue, 89104
Telephone: 702-457-9099
FAX: 702-457-8451
Email: lawyers@picomitchell.com

MEMBERS OF FIRM

James F. Pico
Bert O. Mitchell
Christy Brad Escobar
James R. Rosenberger
E. Breen Arntz

ASSOCIATES

Michelle Schwarz
Rebecca L. Mastrangelo
Jill M. Chase
Daniel E. Carvalho
Stephen H. Rogers

Representative Clients: Home Insurance Co.; State Farm Mutual Insurance Co.; Industrial Indemnity Insurance Co.; Great American Insurance Co.; Argonaut Insurance Cos.; Clark County Medical Society; Rose de Lima Hospital; Fairway Chevrolet; American States Insurance Co.; The Hartford Insurance Co.

For full biographical listings, see the Martindale-Hubbell Law Directory

RICCIARDI & PAUSTIAN (AV)

2300 West Sahara Avenue Suite 680, Box 19, 89102
Telephone: 702-252-3131; 800-245-1611
Fax: 702-252-7411
Email: info@ricciardilaw.com *URL:* http://www.Ricciardilaw.com

Mark J. Ricciardi
Kathleen M. Paustian

ASSOCIATE

Donna L. Sternicki (Not admitted in NV)

For full biographical listings, see the Martindale-Hubbell Law Directory

SCHRECK MORRIS (AV)

1200 Bank of America Plaza, 300 South Fourth Street, 89101
Telephone: 702-382-2101
Fax: 702-382-8135; 702-474-9422
URL: http://www.schreckmorris.com
Reno, Nevada Office: 100 West Liberty, Suite 940, 89501.
Telephone: 775-322-7777.
Facsimile: 775-322-7791.

MEMBERS OF FIRM

Frank A. Schreck
Steve Morris
Andrew S. Brignone
Leslie Terry Jones
Mary Kristina Pickering
John A. Godfrey
Ann Morgan
Sean T. McGowan
Ellen Schulhofer
James J. Pisanelli
Clark V. Vellis
Todd L. Bice

ASSOCIATES

James R. Chamberlain
Dennis V. Gallagher
Margaret L. Sanner
F. Edward Mulholland, II
Elizabeth M. Fielder
Elayna Youchah
Sonia C. Vermeys
Denise Michaelides
Mary J. Drury
John P. Desmond
Adam P. Segal
Matthew McCaughey
Amelia R. De Los Santos
Wendy Medura
Robert J. Grasso
Shawn G. Pearson
David Dornak
Matthew L. Heinhold
Paul D. Colton

For full biographical listings, see the Martindale-Hubbell Law Directory

*RENO,** Washoe Co.

ERICKSON, THORPE & SWAINSTON, LTD. (AV)

99 West Arroyo Street, P.O. Box 3559, 89505
Telephone: 702-786-3930
Fax: 702-786-4160
Email: etsreno@aol.com

Roger L. Erickson	Thomas Peter Beko
Donald A. Thorpe	John A. Aberasturi
George W. Swainston	Paul M. Bertone
William G. Cobb	Lisa E. Bruce
Gary A. Cardinal	John C. Boyden

Representative Clients: Airport Authority of Washoe County; Club Cal Neva; Comstock Hotel Casino; Nevada Public Agency Group; Peppermill Casinos, Inc.; Reno Toyota; Silver Club Casinos; Smiths Food and Drug Centers; Sears Roebuck & Co.

For full biographical listings, see the Martindale-Hubbell Law Directory

ERWIN THOMPSON & HASCHEFF (AV)

A Partnership including Professional Corporations
Suite 424, One East Liberty Street, P.O. Box 40817, 89501-2123
Telephone: 775-786-9494
Facsimile: 775-786-1180
Email: erwin@renolaw.com *URL:* http://www.renolaw.com

Pierre A. Hascheff	Frank W. Thompson

Thomas P. Erwin

Reference: U.S. Bank (Reno, Nevada, Main Office).

For full biographical listings, see the Martindale-Hubbell Law Directory

McDONALD CARANO WILSON McCUNE BERGIN FRANKOVICH & HICKS LLP (AV)

241 Ridge Street, 89501
Telephone: 775-788-2000
Telecopier: 775-788-2020
URL: http://www.mcdonaldcarano.com
Las Vegas, Nevada Office: Suite 1000, 2300 West Sahara Avenue.
Telephone: 702-873-4100.
Telecopier: 702-873-9966.

MEMBERS OF FIRM

John J. McCune	Timothy E. Rowe
Thomas R. C. Wilson	James W. Bradshaw
Larry R. Hicks	Pat Lundvall
William A. S. Magrath, II	Bryan R. Clark

ASSOCIATES

Paul J. Georgeson	Bonnie Fleischer Drinkwater
Miranda M. Du	Jeffrey A. Silvestri

Judy P. Osgood

Representative Clients: Associated General Contractors of America; Clark & Sullivan Constructors, Inc.; Eldorado Hotel & Casino; Hamilton Group of Companies; Jackpot Enterprises, Inc.; Regional Emergency Medical Services Authority; Sierra Nevada Production Credit Association; Amerigas, Inc.; Carter Hawley Hale Co.; Sentinel Real Estate Corporation.

For Complete List of Firm Personnel, See General Section

For full biographical listings, see the Martindale-Hubbell Law Directory

NEW HAMPSHIRE

*CONCORD,** Merrimack Co.

DOUGLAS, ROBINSON, LEONARD & GARVEY, P.C. (AV)

6 Loudon Road Suite 502, 03301
Telephone: 603-224-1988
Fax: 603-229-1988
Email: drlg@grolen.com *URL:* http://www.lawyers.com/drl&glaw

Charles G. Douglas, III	C. Kevin Leonard
Timothy I. Robinson	Carolyn S. Garvey

Susanna G. Robinson

For full biographical listings, see the Martindale-Hubbell Law Directory

*MANCHESTER,** Hillsborough Co.

SHEEHAN PHINNEY BASS + GREEN, PROFESSIONAL ASSOCIATION (AV)

Hampshire Plaza, 1000 Elm Street, P.O. Box 3701, 03105-3701
Telephone: 603-668-0300
800-625-SPBG
Fax: 603-627-8121
Email: postmaster@sheehan.com *URL:* http://www.sheehan.com
Portsmouth, New Hampshire Office: Old City Hall, 126 Daniel Street.
Telephone: 603-433-2111.
Fax: 603-433-3126.
Concord, New Hampshire Office: 143 North Main Street.
Telephone: 603-223-2020.
Fax: 603-224-8899.

James E. Higgins	Michael C. Harvell
James Q. Shirley	Peter S. Cowan
Bradford E. Cook	James P. Reidy
Alan P. Cleveland	Robert R. Lucic
Claudia Cords Damon	David W. McGrath

OF COUNSEL

Raymond S. Perry, Jr.

Representative Clients: Anheuser-Busch, Inc.; Bank of New Hampshire Corp.; The Elliot Hospital of Manchester; Granite State Packing Co.; Moore Business Forms, Inc.; New Hampshire College; New Hampshire Dental Service Corp.; New Hampshire Yankee Electric Corp.; Numerica Financial Corp.

For Complete List of Firm Personnel, See General Section

For full biographical listings, see the Martindale-Hubbell Law Directory

PORTSMOUTH, Rockingham Co.

SHEEHAN PHINNEY BASS + GREEN, PROFESSIONAL ASSOCIATION (AV)

Old City Hall, 126 Daniel Street, 03801
Telephone: 603-433-2111
Fax: 603-433-3126
Email: postmaster@sheehan.com *URL:* http://www.sheehan.com
Manchester, New Hampshire Office: Hampshire Plaza, 1000 Elm Street, P.O. Box 3701.
Telephone: 603-668-0300.
Fax: 603-627-8121.
Concord, New Hampshire Office: 143 North Main Street.
Telephone: 603-223-2020.
Fax: 603-224-8899.

Michael C. Harvell

For full biographical listings, see the Martindale-Hubbell Law Directory

NEW JERSEY

BEDMINSTER, Somerset Co.

PURCELL, RIES, SHANNON, MULCAHY & O'NEILL (AV)

One Pluckemin Way, P.O. Box 754, 07921
Telephone: 908-658-3800
Fax: 908-658-4659
Email: general@prsmo.com *URL:* http://www.prsmo.com
Philadelphia, Pennsylvania Office: 12th Floor, East Tower, Centre Square, 1500 Market Square.
Telephone: 215-665-5602.
Fax: 215-569-8228.

MEMBERS OF FIRM

Eugene M. Purcell	Kevin R. Brotz
William P. Ries	John M. Bowens
John J. Shannon	Kevin Kovacs
Thomas M. Mulcahy	Kenneth D. Merin
Michael F. O'Neill	Valerie K. Bollheimer
David M. Hawkins	Andrew L. Indeck
Joseph R. Purcell	Joseph M. Donegan

Mark Mattia

ASSOCIATES

Rita F. Barone	Eric J. Konecke
Kathleen J. Devlin	Susan Lawless
Paul L. Gallagher	Michael J. McCaffrey
Gary Grabas	Kathleen M. Quinn
John R. Haggerty	Thomas Charles Savoth
William T. Hilliard	Donna M. Stephan-Nolan

Barbara C. Zimmerman

OF COUNSEL

David D. Furman	C. Judson Hamlin

(See Next Column)

PURCELL, RIES, SHANNON, MULCAHY & O'NEILL—*Continued*

LEGAL SUPPORT PERSONNEL

Gary Molloy

Reference: Somerset Trust Co.

For full biographical listings, see the Martindale-Hubbell Law Directory

CHERRY HILL, Camden Co.

FLASTER/GREENBERG, P.C. (AV)

Commerce Center, 1810 Chapel Avenue West, Third Floor, 08002-4609
Telephone: 856-661-1900
Telecopier: 856-661-1919
Email: FIRM@FLASTERGREENBERG.COM *URL:* http://www.flastergreenberg.com

Richard J. Flaster
Stephen M. Greenberg
Laura B. Wallenstein
Allen P. Fineberg
Markley S. Roderick
Peter R. Spirgel
Alan H. Zuckerman
William S. Skinner
J. Philip Kirchner
Paul J. Russoniello
Carl S. Bisgaier
Steven B. Sacharow
E. Richard Dressel
Kenneth S. Goodkind
Frank H. Wisniewski
Alma L. Saravia

OF COUNSEL

Peter M. Dolinger
James J. Binns

Elizabeth J. Hampton
Jeffrey Herskowitz
Christopher E. Kaltenbach
Steven J. Abrams
Julie A. Williamson
Donna T. Urban
Amelia Carolla
Matthew Azoulay
Elaine J. Petruzziello (Not admitted in NJ)
Ann Marie Iannone
Pasquale Guglietta

LEGAL SUPPORT PERSONNEL

PARALEGALS

Ann Gorman
Patricia D'Alessio
Theresa Cooke
Rosemary Dunaif

For full biographical listings, see the Martindale-Hubbell Law Directory

KENNEY & KEARNEY LLP (AV)

Woodland Falls Corporate Park, Suite 210, 220 Lake Drive East, P.O. Box 5034, 08034-0421
Telephone: 856-779-7000
Telecopier: 856-779-1342

Joseph H. Kenney
John B. Kearney
John A. Miller, Jr.
Allen A. Etish
Michele Mareschi Fox
Thomas J. Hagner
William J. DeSantis
Charles J. Connery
John A. Zohlman, III

ASSOCIATES

John J. Bannan
David A. Haworth
Paul F. Jenkins
Margaret J. Quinn
Laura D. Ruccolo

OF COUNSEL

Jane A. Kenney
Joel B. Korin

For full biographical listings, see the Martindale-Hubbell Law Directory

TOMAR, SIMONOFF, ADOURIAN, O'BRIEN, KAPLAN, JACOBY & GRAZIANO, A PROFESSIONAL CORPORATION (AV)

20 Brace Road, 08034
Telephone: 609-429-1100
Telecopier: 609-429-8164
Email: TOMAR@TOMARLAW.COM *URL:* http://www.tomarlaw.com
Atlantic City, New Jersey Office: Commerce Building, Suite 220, 1200 Atlantic Avenue.
Telephone: 609-348-5900.
Camden, New Jersey Office: 200 North Fifth Street.
Telephone: 609-338-0553.
Northfield, New Jersey Office: The Executive Plaza, Suite 101, 2111 New Road.
Telephone: 609-485-0800.
Telecopier: 609-484-9388.
Wilmington, Delaware Office: Tomar, Simonoff, Adourian, O'Brien, Kaplan, Jacoby & Graziano, The Mellon Bank Center, Suite 1701, 919 Market Street.
Telephone: 302-655-0500.
Telecopier: 302-428-0963.
Media, Pennsylvania Office: 334 West Front Street.
Telephone: 215-574-0635.

Howard S. Simonoff
Robert F. O'Brien
Ronald A. Graziano
Mary L. Crangle
James Katz
Mark E. Belland
Theodore M. Lieverman
Richard M. Schall

For full biographical listings, see the Martindale-Hubbell Law Directory

EDISON, Middlesex Co.

HANLON & LAVIGNE, A PROFESSIONAL CORPORATION (AV)

Suite 200, Executive Plaza, 10 Parsonage Road, 08837
Telephone: 732-549-9880
North Jersey Number: 973-808-0186
Fax: 732-549-3068
Email: larry@hlt-law.com *URL:* http://HanlonLavigne.com
New York, New York Office: One Word Trade Center, Suite 7967, 10048.
Telephone: 212-775-7142 and 212-775-7187.
Marysville, Pennsylvania Office: 505 Maple Avenue, P.O. Box 149, 17053-0149.
Telephone: 717-957-4292.
Fax: 717-957-4293.

William F. Hanlon (1901-1972)
Robert M. Hanlon
Lawrence N. Lavigne
Bonnie H. Hanlon

Richard P. Grossman, Jr.
Robert Michael Hanlon, Jr.
Robert M. Cook
Christine Giordano Hanlon

For full biographical listings, see the Martindale-Hubbell Law Directory

WONG FLEMING, P.C. (AV)

Edison Square West, Suite 1050, 2035 Lincoln Highway, 08817
Telephone: 732-248-4111
Fax: 732-248-8665
Mailing Address: P.O. Box 985, 08818-0985
Email: info@wongfleming.com *URL:* http://www.wongfleming.com
Philadelphia, Pennsylvania Office: 230 South Broad Street, Suite 601, 19102.
Telephone: 215-546-2776.
Fax: 215-546-3206.
New York, New York Office: The Empire State Building, 350 Fifth Avenue, Suite 5411, 10118.
Telephone: 212-643-9668.
Fax: 212-643-9640.

Linda Wong
Daniel C. Fleming
Katherine C. Lee

Andrew J. Bayne
Stephen Tsai
Theresa Homisak
Paul J. Young
Wenjun Zhang (Not admitted in NJ)
Tanya E. Lawrence
Fei F. Lam

For full biographical listings, see the Martindale-Hubbell Law Directory

FLORHAM PARK, Morris Co.

CARLIN, MADDOCK, FAY & CERBONE, P.C. (AV)

25 Vreeland Road, P.O. Box 751, 07932
Telephone: 201-377-3350
Fax: 201-377-5626
URL: http://www.lawyers.com/cmfclaw

John J. Carlin, Jr.
Laurence R. Maddock
Donald J. Fay
Richard R. Cerbone

Arthur G. Warden, III

For full biographical listings, see the Martindale-Hubbell Law Directory

DRINKER BIDDLE & SHANLEY LLP (AV)

A Pennsylvania Limited Liability Partnership
500 Campus Drive, 07932-1047
Telephone: 973-360-1100
Fax: 973-285-1625; 360-9831
URL: http://www.dbr.com
Philadelphia, Pennsylvania Office: Drinker Biddle & Reath LLP, One Logan Square, 18th & Cherry Streets.
Telephone: 215-988-2700.
Telefax: 215-988-2757.
Cable Address: "Debemac."
Washington, D.C. Office: Drinker Biddle & Reath LLP, 1500 K Street, N.W., Suite 1100.
Telephone: 202-842-8800.
Telefax: 202-842-8465.
Princeton, New Jersey Office: Suite 300, 105 College Road East.
Telephone: 609-716-6500.
Telefax: 609-799-7000.
Berwyn, Pennsylvania Office: Drinker Biddle & Reath LLP, Suite 300, 1000 Westlakes Drive.
Telephone: 610-993-2200.
Telefax: 610-993-8585.
New York, New York Office: Drinker Biddle & Reath LLP, 89th Floor, One World Trade Center.
Telephone: 212-321-1812.
Telecopier: 1-212-466-0569.

Paul G. Nittoly
Kathleen B. Harden

(See Next Column)

DRINKER BIDDLE & SHANLEY LLP, *Florham Park—Continued*

John M. Blumers
Scott C. Carroll
Benjamin L. Siegel

For Complete List of Firm Personnel, See General Section

For full biographical listings, see the Martindale-Hubbell Law Directory

SCHWARTZ SIMON EDELSTEIN CELSO & KESSLER (AV)

A Partnership including a Professional Corporation
Ten James Street, 07932
Telephone: 973-301-0001
Fax: 973-301-0203
Email: sseck1@aol.com

Lawrence S. Schwartz (P.C.)
Stephen J. Edelstein
Nathanya Guritzky Simon
Nicholas Celso, III
Donald A. Kessler
Raymond W. Fisher
Paul H. Green
Allan P. Dzwilewski

Marc H. Zitomer
Stefani C Schwartz
Denis G. Murphy

COUNSEL

Jacob Green

OF COUNSEL

Glenn C. Guritzky
Miguel A. Maza
Scott A. Elk (P.A.)
(Not admitted in NJ)

For full biographical listings, see the Martindale-Hubbell Law Directory

*HACKENSACK,** Bergen Co.

PASHMAN STEIN, A PROFESSIONAL CORPORATION (AV)

45 Essex Street, 07601-5415
Telephone: 201-488-8200
Fax: 201-488-5556
Email: info@pashmanstein.com *URL:* http://www.lawyers.com/pashmanstein

Louis Pashman
Samuel J. Samaro
Dennis T. Smith
Michael S. Stein

Amy E. Whitteaker
John T. Whipple

SPECIAL COUNSEL

Morris Pashman

For full biographical listings, see the Martindale-Hubbell Law Directory

THURBER CAPPELL, L.L.C. (AV)

235 Main Street, Suite 300, 07601
Telephone: 201-488-0594
Telecopier: 201-488-5283
Email: thurblaw@aol.com *URL:* http://www.lawyers.com/thurber,cappell,law

Mary F. Thurber
Cynthia A. Cappell

ASSOCIATES

Allison Turley Madden
Anne Marie Fox

OF COUNSEL

Frank Huttle, III

For full biographical listings, see the Martindale-Hubbell Law Directory

ISELIN, Middlesex Co.

MCMORAN & ASSOCIATES, P.C. (AV)

120 Wood Avenue South Suite 515, 08830
Telephone: 732-452-0200
Fax: 732-452-0295
Email: mcmoranlaw@aol.com *URL:* http://www.lawyers.com/mcmoran&associates

Bruce P. McMoran

Michael F. O'Connor
Jeremy G. Weiss

For full biographical listings, see the Martindale-Hubbell Law Directory

LAWRENCEVILLE, Mercer Co.

SZAFERMAN, LAKIND, BLUMSTEIN, WATTER & BLADER, P.C. (AV)

Suite 104 Quakerbridge Executive Center, 101 Grovers Mill Road, 08648
Telephone: 609-275-0400
Telefax: 609-275-4511

(See Next Column)

Arnold C. Lakind
Barry D. Szaferman
Jeffrey P. Blumstein
Paul N. Watter
Steven Blader
Sidney H. Lehmann
Gerald B. Schenkman
David B. Beckett
Scott P. Borsack
Mary Lou Delahanty

Jennifer Weisberg Millner
Cathyanne A. Pisciotta
Jason N. Fruhschein
Demery J. Roberts
Stuart A. Tucker
Brian G. Paul
Victoria Rivera-Cruz
Thomas J. Burns III

LEGAL SUPPORT PERSONNEL

Paula M. Rossi (Office Administrator)
Patricia Hallstrum (Controller)

Representative Clients: Sun National Bank; First Washington Bank; Gilmore Securities & Co.; Communication Workers of America; The Eagle Group; Water's Edge Convalescent Center; Ronson Aviation, Inc.; Holmdel Township Board of Adjustment; Public Service Managers Association; Chemical Leaman Tank Lines.

For full biographical listings, see the Martindale-Hubbell Law Directory

LIBERTY CORNER, Somerset Co.

APRUZZESE, MCDERMOTT, MASTRO & MURPHY, A PROFESSIONAL CORPORATION (AV)

25 Independence Boulevard, P.O. Box 112, 07938
Telephone: 908-580-1776
Fax: 908-647-1492
Email: firmmail@ammm.com *URL:* http://www.firmmail@ammm.com

OF COUNSEL

Vincent J. Apruzzese
Frank X. McDermott

Francis A. Mastro
James F. Murphy (1938-1990)
Frederick T. Danser, III
Maurice J. Nelligan, Jr.
Barry Marell
Robert T. Clarke
Mark J. Blunda
James L. Plosia, Jr.

J. Andrew Kinsey
John P. Harrington
Robert J. Merryman
Kathleen Barnett Einhorn
Joseph C. DeBlasio

COUNSEL

Lisa Barré-Quick

Representative Clients: General Public Utilities Corp.; Public Service Electric & Gas Co.; Jersey Central Power & Light Co.; Saint Barnabas Health Care System; Schering Plough Corp.; New Jersey Transit Corporation; SmithKline Beecham; U.S. Metals & Refining Co.; Asea Brown-Boveri; Foster Wheeler Corp.

For full biographical listings, see the Martindale-Hubbell Law Directory

LIVINGSTON, Essex Co.

GENOVA, BURNS & VERNOIA (AV)

Eisenhower Plaza II, 354 Eisenhower Parkway, 07039
Telephone: 973-533-0777
Facsimile: 973-533-1112
URL: http://www.gbvlaw.com
Trenton, New Jersey Office: The Princeton House, 160 West State Street.
Telephone: 609-393-1131.

MEMBERS OF FIRM

Angelo J. Genova
James M. Burns
Francis J. Vernoia
John C. Petrella
James J. McGovern, III
Carmel Joy Decker

ASSOCIATES

Sandro Polledri
Celia S. Bosco
Lynn S. Degen
Elizabeth A. Daly
Brian O. Lipman
J. Frank Vespa-Papaleo
Susan B. Burns
Bruno Genova
Robert C. Gifford, Jr.
Courtney Gaccione

For full biographical listings, see the Martindale-Hubbell Law Directory

*MORRISTOWN,** Morris Co.

PITNEY, HARDIN, KIPP & SZUCH LLP (AV)

P.O. Box 1945, 07962-1945
Telephone: 973-966-6300
New York City: 212-687-6000
Telex: 642014
Telecopier: 973-966-1550
URL: http://www.phks.com
New York, New York Office: 711 Third Avenue, 10017-4014.
Telephone: 212-687-6000.
Fax: 212-682-3485.

(See Next Column)

PITNEY, HARDIN, KIPP & SZUCH LLP—*Continued*

MEMBERS OF FIRM

S. Joseph Fortunato
Edward P. Lynch
Gregory C. Parliman
Patrick J. McCarthy
Kathy A. Lawler
Theresa Donahue Egler
David P. Doyle
Michael T. Bissinger

COUNSEL

Theresa A. Kelly
Jonathan E. Hill
Michael J. Duane (Not admitted in NJ)
Mary B. Rogers

ASSOCIATES

Rosalie J. Shoeman
Amanda Berlowe Jaffe
Wendy Johnson Lario
Glenn Eric Butash (Not admitted in NJ)
Kristine J. Feher
Jonathan J. Harper
Marjorie F. Sheron
Maureen B. O'Neill
Lisa Ness Seidman

Representative Clients: AlliedSignal Inc.; Atlantic States Cast Iron Pipes; Lucent Technologies; United Parcel Post.

For Complete List of Firm Personnel, See General Section

For full biographical listings, see the Martindale-Hubbell Law Directory

RAND, ALGEIER, TOSTI & WOODRUFF, A PROFESSIONAL CORPORATION (AV)

60 Washington Street, 07960
Telephone: 973-539-2600
Telecopier: 973-984-0430
Email: randlaw@bellatlantic.net

Gary C. Algeier
David B. Rand
Robert M. Tosti
Robert B. Woodruff
John F. McDonnell
John E. Croot, Jr.

Kathryn J. Kingree
Deborah A. White

OF COUNSEL

Ronald M. Pflug
Ellen S. Bass
Tamara Krikorian

For full biographical listings, see the Martindale-Hubbell Law Directory

STANTON, HUGHES, DIANA, SALSBERG, CERRA & MARIANI, P.C. (AV)

10 Madison Avenue, Suite 402, 07960
Telephone: 973-656-1600
Fax: 973-656-1611
Email: stantonmail@stantonhughes.com *URL:* http://www.stantonhughes.com

Patrick M. Stanton
Richard M. Salsberg
Richard C. Mariani
Sharon P. Margello
Peter O. Hughes
Mark Diana
Suzanne M. Cerra

Matthew J. Giacobbe
Kimberly E. Robertson
Robin H. Rome
Carmen J. Di Maria

For full biographical listings, see the Martindale-Hubbell Law Directory

*NEWARK,** Essex Co.

APRUZZESE, MCDERMOTT, MASTRO & MURPHY, A PROFESSIONAL CORPORATION

(See Liberty Corner)

BALK, OXFELD, MANDELL & COHEN, A PROFESSIONAL CORPORATION (AV)

50 Commerce Street, 07102-4003
Telephone: 973-623-0353
Fax: 973-802-1055
Elizabeth, New Jersey Office: 27 Prince Street, 07208.
Telephone: 908-353-0500.
Fax: 908-353-1495.

Louis David Balk
Sanford R. Oxfeld
Jack Mandell
Arnold Shep Cohen
Nancy Iris Oxfeld
Denzil R. Dunkley
Daniel Geddes

Randi Doner April
Gail Oxfeld Kanef
Sherri Litt Goldman
Henry J. Cistrelli

OF COUNSEL

Jacob L. Balk
Dora P. Rothschild

For full biographical listings, see the Martindale-Hubbell Law Directory

BISCEGLIE & FRIEDMAN, LLC (AV)

One Newark Center, 07102
Telephone: 973-624-7500
Telecopier: 973-624-9494
URL: http://www.lawyers.com/bisceglie friedmanlaw

Angelo R. Bisceglie, Jr.
Paul A. Friedman

Thomas C. Martin
Matthew A. Siebel
Andrew J. Zuckerman

OF COUNSEL

Judy L. Cavet

For full biographical listings, see the Martindale-Hubbell Law Directory

CARPENTER, BENNETT & MORRISSEY (AV)

Three Gateway Center, 17th Floor, 100 Mulberry Street, 07102-4079
Telephone: 973-622-7711
New York City: 212-943-6530
Telex: 139405
Telecopier: 973-622-5314
Email: cbm@carpben.com

MEMBERS OF FIRM

James J. Crowley, Jr.
Donald A. Romano
Francis X. Dee
Irving L. Hurwitz
John J. Peirano
Linda B. Celauro
Patrick G. Brady
Kevin C. Donovan
James Peter Lidon
David J. Reilly
Vincent P. Browne

OF COUNSEL

Edward F. Ryan

ASSOCIATES

Joseph Gerard Lee
David A. Cohen
Vimal K. Shah
Linda Pope Torres
David B. Beal
Thomas C. Bigosinski
Gary S. Prish
Yvette M. Gordon
Paula M. Castaldo
Mason C. Miller
Stephanie J. Hart
Ivanyla D. Vargas (Not admitted in NJ)
George M. Macchia
Catherine Brennan Rinaldi
Seth Ptasiewicz
George P. Barbatsuly
Lisa E. Stern
Michael D. Thompson (Not admitted in NJ)
Cindy E. Switzer (Not admitted in the United States)

Representative Clients: General Motors Corp.; AT&T; Bell Atlantic; Litton Industries; Merck & Co.; Johnson & Johnson; Lucent Technologies Inc.; International Flavors & Fragrances Inc.; Prudential Insurance Company of America; Rutgers, The State University.

For Complete List of Firm Personnel, See General Section

For full biographical listings, see the Martindale-Hubbell Law Directory

DEMARIA ELLIS & BAUCH L.L.C. (AV)

Suite 1400, 744 Broad Street, 07102-3805
Telephone: 973-623-1699
Telecopier: 973-623-0954
Email: firm@demariaellis.com

MEMBERS OF FIRM

H. Reed Ellis
Ronald H. DeMaria
Richard H. Bauch
Joanne M. Maxwell

OF COUNSEL

B. Frank Flaherty (Not admitted in NJ)

ASSOCIATES

Kathryn Van Deusen Hatfield
Alex E. Bernstein
Davin Paul Cellura
Matthew A. Kaplan

Representative Clients: Arkansas Best Freight, Inc.; Citgo Petroleum; Cookson America, Inc.; County of Union; Merck & Co.; Mobil Chemical Co.; Roadway Express, Inc.; Sun Chemical Corporation; The Hertz Corporation; USF Red Star, Inc.

For full biographical listings, see the Martindale-Hubbell Law Directory

HELLRING LINDEMAN GOLDSTEIN & SIEGAL LLP (AV)

One Gateway Center, 07102-5386
Telephone: 973-621-9020
Fax: 973-621-7406
Englewood, New Jersey Office: 32-40 North Dean Street.
Telephone: 201-871-3060.

Jonathan L. Goldstein
Richard D. Shapiro
Stephen L. Dreyfuss
Matthew E. Moloshok
Rachel N. Davidson

Joanne M. Frasca

For Complete List of Firm Personnel, See General Section

For full biographical listings, see the Martindale-Hubbell Law Directory

Newark—Continued

McCarter & English, LLP (AV)

Four Gateway Center, 100 Mulberry Street, P.O. Box 652, 07101-0652
Telephone: 973-622-4444
Telecopier: 973-624-7070
URL: http://www.mccarter.com
Cherry Hill, New Jersey Office: 1820 Chapel Avenue West, Suite 380.
Telephone: 609-662-8444.
Telecopier: 609-662-6203.
New York, New York Office: Suite 2247, One World Trade Center.
Telephone: 212-466-9018.
Telecopier: 212-432-6568.
Boca Raton, Florida Office: 2255 Glades Road, Suite 319-A.
Telephone: 561-994-6262.
Telecopier: 561-241-0798.
Wilmington, Delaware Office: Mellon Bank Center, 919 Market Street.
Telephone: 302-654-8010.
Telecopier: 302-654-0795.
Philadelphia, Pennsylvania Office: One Commerce Square, 2005 Market Street, Suite 3600.
Telephone: 215-557-7700.
Telecopier: 215-557-6544.

MEMBERS OF FIRM

Richard C. Cooper
William S. Greenberg
John E. Flaherty
John B. Brescher, Jr.
Rosemary Alito
Theodore D. Moskowitz
Mark A. Daniele
B. John Pendleton, Jr.
John C. McGuire

For Complete List of Firm Personnel, See General Section

For full biographical listings, see the Martindale-Hubbell Law Directory

Reed Smith Shaw & McClay LLP (AV)

The Legal Center, One Riverfront Plaza, First Floor, 07102-5400
Telephone: 973-621-3200
FAX: 973-621-3199
Email: rssm@rssm.com *URL:* http://www.rssm.com
Pittsburgh, Pennsylvania Office: 435 Sixth Avenue, 15219-1886.
Telephone: 412-288-3131.
FAX: 412-288-3063.
Washington, D.C. Office: Suite 1100 - East Tower, 1301 K Street, N.W., 20005-3317.
Telephone: 202-414-9200.
FAX: 202-414-9299.
Philadelphia, Pennsylvania Office: 2500 One Liberty Place, 19103-7301.
Telephone: 215-851-8100.
FAX: 215-851-1420.
Harrisburg, Pennsylvania Office: 213 Market Street, 17101-2132.
Telephone: 717-234-5988.
FAX: 717-236-3777.
Princeton, New Jersey Office: 136 Main Street, Suite 250, 08540-5799.
Telephone: 609-987-0050.
FAX: 609-951-0824.
New York, N.Y. Office: 375 Park Avenue, 17th Floor, 10152.
Telephone: 212-521-5400.
FAX: 212-521-5450.
McLean, Virginia Office: Reed Smith Hazel & Thomas LLP, Suite 1100, 8251 Greensboro Drive, 22102-3844.
Telephone: 703-734-4600.
FAX: 703-734-4699.
Falls Church, Virginia Office: Reed Smith Hazel & Thomas, Suite 1400, 3110 Fairview Park Drive, P.O. Box 12001.
Telephone: 703-641-4200.
Fax: 703-641-4340.
Leesburg, Virginia Office: Reed Smith Hazel & Thomas LLP, 44084 Riverside Parkway, Suite 300.
Telephone: 703-729-8500. Metro: 703-478-1992.
Fax: 703-478-8003.
Richmond, Virginia Office: Reed Smith Hazel & Thomas LLP, Suite 600, 411 East Franklin Street, P.O. Box 788.
Telephone: 804-344-3400.
Fax: 804-344-3410.

MEMBERS OF FIRM

Gerard S. DiFiore
John J. Fahy
James A. Kosch
Anthony J. Laura
Marilyn Sneirson

COUNSEL

Jeff Ellentuck
Andrea A. Lipuma
Kurt D. Olender

ASSOCIATES

David B. Cosgrove
Michelle G. Darvin
Thomas A. Della Croce
Joseph R. Donahue
Donna H. Hartman
Christopher P. Minnetian

For full biographical listings, see the Martindale-Hubbell Law Directory

St. John & Wayne, L.L.C. (AV)

Two Penn Plaza East, 07105-2249
Telephone: 973-491-3600
Fax: 973-491-3555
Email: firm@nwk.stjohn-law.com *URL:* http://www.stjohn-law.com
Rochester, New York Office: St. John & Curtin, L.L.C., First Federal Plaza.
Telephone: 716-262-6780.
Fax: 716-262-6755.
New York, New York Office: Heron Tower, 70 East 55th. Street.
Telephone: 212-446-5000.
Fax: 212-446-5055.

James P. Anelli

Christopher R. Welgos

For Complete List of Firm Personnel, See General Section

For full biographical listings, see the Martindale-Hubbell Law Directory

Sills Cummis Radin Tischman Epstein & Gross, A Professional Corporation (AV)

One Riverfront Plaza, 07102-5400
Telephone: 973-643-7000
Fax: 973-643-6500
Telex: 820630 Sillsbeck Nwk
Email: sillsmail@sillscummis.com *URL:* http://www.sillscummis.com
Atlantic City, New Jersey Office: 17 Gordon's Alley.
Telephone: 609-344-2800.
New York, N.Y. Office: 712 Fifth Avenue.
Telephone: 212-643-7000.
Washington, D.C. Office: 1800 K Street, N.W.
Telephone: 202-296-4750.

MEMBERS OF FIRM

Lester Aron
Trent S. Dickey
David W. Garland
Beth S. Rose
Linda Badash Katz

OF COUNSEL

Cherie L. Maxwell

Lynne Anne Anderson
Philip Edward Stern
Daniel A. Schlein
Kelly Ann Guariglia
Elnardo J. Webster, II
Brigette N. Shrank

Representative Clients: Becton Dickinson & Company; Allied Signal; McKinsey & Co.; Melvin Simon; N.J.. Nets; P.S.E.& G.; Rutgers University; Syms; WWOR-TV.

For Complete List of Firm Personnel, See General Section

For full biographical listings, see the Martindale-Hubbell Law Directory

Zazzali, Zazzali, Fagella & Nowak, A Professional Corporation (AV)

One Riverfront Plaza, 07102-5410
Telephone: 973-623-1822
Telecopier: 973-623-2209
URL: http://www.lawyers.com/zazzali
Trenton, New Jersey Office: 150 West State Street.
Telephone: 609-392-8172.
Facsimile: 609-392-8933.
New York, New York Office: 15 West 72nd Street.
Telephone: 212-529-3927.
Facsimile: 212-875-8275.

Andrew F. Zazzali (1925-1969)
Andrew F. Zazzali, Jr.
James R. Zazzali
Robert A. Fagella
Kenneth I. Nowak
Paul L. Kleinbaum
Richard A. Friedman

Kathleen Anne Naprstek
Aileen M. O'Driscoll
Edward H. O'Hare
Jason Solowkowski

For full biographical listings, see the Martindale-Hubbell Law Directory

NORTHFIELD, Atlantic Co.

Tomar, Simonoff, Adourian, O'Brien, Kaplan, Jacoby & Graziano, A Professional Corporation (AV)

The Executive Plaza, Suite 101, 2111 New Road, 08225
Telephone: 609-485-0800
Telecopier: 609-484-9388
Cherry Hill, New Jersey Office: 20 Brace Road.
Telephone: 609-429-1100.
Telecopier: 609-429-8164.
Atlantic City, New Jersey Office: Commerce Building, Suite 220, 1200 Atlantic Avenue.
Telephone: 609-348-5900.
Camden, New Jersey Office: 200 North Fifth Street.
Telephone: 609-338-0553.

(See Next Column)

TOMAR, SIMONOFF, ADOURIAN, O'BRIEN, KAPLAN, JACOBY & GRAZIANO A PROFESSIONAL CORPORATION—*Continued*

Wilmington, Delaware Office: Tomar, Simonoff, Adourian, O'Brien, Kaplan, Jacoby & Graziano, The Mellon Bank Center, Suite 1701, 919 Market Street.
Telephone: 302-655-0500.
Telecopier: 302-428-0963.
Media, Pennsylvania Office: 334 West Front Street.
Telephone: 215-574-0635.

Howard S. Simonoff
Robert F. O'Brien
Ronald A. Graziano
Mary L. Crangle
James Katz
Mark E. Belland
Theodore M. Lieverman
Richard M. Schall

For full biographical listings, see the Martindale-Hubbell Law Directory

PRINCETON, Mercer Co.

BERGMAN & BARRETT (AV)

9 Tamarack Circle, Montgomery Knoll, U.S. Highway 206 North, P.O. Box 1273, 08542
Telephone: 609-921-1502
Fax: 609-683-0288

Edward J. Bergman
Michael T. Barrett

LEGAL SUPPORT PERSONNEL

Kelli E. Murphy (Paralegal)

For full biographical listings, see the Martindale-Hubbell Law Directory

REED SMITH SHAW & MCCLAY LLP (AV)

136 Main Street, Suite 250, 08540-5799
Telephone: 609-987-0050
FAX: 609-951-0824
Email: rssm@rssm.com *URL:* http://www.rssm.com
Pittsburgh, Pennsylvania Office: 435 Sixth Avenue, 15219-1886.
Telephone: 412-288-3131.
FAX: 412-288-3063.
Washington, D.C. Office: Suite 1100 - East Tower, 1301 K Street, N.W., 20005-3317.
Telephone: 202-414-9200.
FAX: 202-414-9299.
Philadelphia, Pennsylvania Office: 2500 One Liberty Place, 19103-7301.
Telephone: 215-851-8100.
FAX: 215-851-1420.
Harrisburg, Pennsylvania Office: 213 Market Street, 17101-2132.
Telephone: 717-234-5988.
FAX: 717-236-3777.
New York, N.Y. Office: 375 Park Avenue, 17th Floor, 10152.
Telephone: 212-521-5400.
FAX: 212-521-5450.
Newark, New Jersey Office: The Legal Center, One Riverfront Plaza, First Floor, 07102-5400.
Telephone: 973-621-3200.
FAX: 973-621-3199.
McLean, Virginia Office: Reed Smith Hazel & Thomas LLP, Suite 1100, 8251 Greensboro Drive, 22102-3844.
Telephone: 703-734-4600.
FAX: 703-734-4699.
Falls Church, Virginia Office: Reed Smith Hazel & Thomas, Suite 1400, 3110 Fairview Park Drive, P.O. Box 12001.
Telephone: 703-641-4200.
Fax: 703-641-4340.
Leesburg, Virginia Office: Reed Smith Hazel & Thomas LLP, 44084 Riverside Parkway, Suite 300.
Telephone: 703-729-8500. Metro: 703-478-1992.
Fax: 703-478-8003.
Richmond, Virginia Office: Reed Smith Hazel & Thomas LLP, Suite 600, 411 East Franklin Street, P.O. Box 788.
Telephone: 804-344-3400.
Fax: 804-344-3410.

MEMBERS OF FIRM

Don A. Innamorato (Also at Princeton, New Jersey)
Stephanie Wilson

For full biographical listings, see the Martindale-Hubbell Law Directory

RAHWAY, Union Co.

DORF & DORF, A PROFESSIONAL CORPORATION (AV)

2376 St. Georges Avenue, 07065
Telephone: 732-574-9700
Fax: 732-574-0340
Boca Raton, Florida Office: 7764 Wind Key Drive.
Telephone: 561-488-3122.

Gerald L. Dorf
Mitchell L. Dorf

For full biographical listings, see the Martindale-Hubbell Law Directory

RIVER EDGE, Bergen Co.

PECKAR & ABRAMSON, A PROFESSIONAL CORPORATION (AV)

70 Grand Avenue, 07661
Telephone: 201-343-3434
Fax: 201-343-6306
Email: mail@pecklaw.com *URL:* http://www.pecklaw.com
New York, N.Y. Office: Peckar & Abramson, P.C., 1185 Avenue of the Americas.
Telephone: 212-382-0909.
Fax: 212-382-3456.
San Francisco, California Office: Peckar & Abramson, P.C., 601 Montgomery Street, Suite 325.
Telephone: 415-837-1968.
Fax: 415-837-1320.

David Lew

Gregory R. Begg
Jeffrey M. Daitz
Steven N. Davi
Aaron Charles Schlesinger

For full biographical listings, see the Martindale-Hubbell Law Directory

ROSELAND, Essex Co.

POST, POLAK, GOODSELL & MACNEILL, P.A. (AV)

75 Livingston Avenue, 07068-3701
Telephone: 973-994-1100
Telecopier: 973-994-1705
Email: administrator@ppgm.com
New York, New York Office: 575 Madison Avenue, Suite 1006.
Telephone: 212-486-1455.

John N. Post
Frederick B. Polak

Loretta B. Critchley
Franca D. Maiorano
Christopher O. Eriksen

For Complete List of Firm Personnel, See General Section

For full biographical listings, see the Martindale-Hubbell Law Directory

SPRINGFIELD, Union Co.

APRUZZESE, MCDERMOTT, MASTRO & MURPHY, A PROFESSIONAL CORPORATION

(See Liberty Corner)

JARDINE & PAGANO, A PROFESSIONAL CORPORATION (AV)

11 Cleveland Place, 07081
Telephone: 201-467-1620
Fax: 201-467-5562
Email: jandp@interserv.com *URL:* http://www.lawyers.com/jandplaw

Thomas V. Jardine
Joseph R. Pagano

For full biographical listings, see the Martindale-Hubbell Law Directory

*TRENTON,** Mercer Co.

NEEDELL, SIEKERKA & CASTELLANI, A PROFESSIONAL CORPORATION (AV)

Quakerbridge Commons, 2681 Quakerbridge Road, 08619-1625
Telephone: 609-584-7700
Fax: 609-584-0123
Email: nsclaw@aol.com

Stanley H. Needell
Michele N. Siekerka
Anthony P. Castellani

John M. Cinti
Dean C. Gresek

LEGAL SUPPORT PERSONNEL

PARALEGALS

Marlene Griesbach
Carolyn D. Shaw
Veronica A. Mitchell

For full biographical listings, see the Martindale-Hubbell Law Directory

VINELAND, Cumberland Co.

GRUCCIO, PEPPER GIOVINAZZI, DESANTO & FARNOLY, P.A. (AV)

817 Landis Avenue, P.O. Box 1501, 08362
Telephone: 856-691-0100
Fax: 856-692-4095
Email: Gruccio1@eticomm.net
Woodbury, New Jersey Office: 21 Delaware Street.
Telephone: 856-848-5558.
Fax: 856-384-1181.

(See Next Column)

GRUCCIO, PEPPER GIOVINAZZI, DESANTO & FARNOLY, P.A., *Vineland—Continued*

Bridgeton, New Jersey Office: 120 West Broad Street.
Telephone: 856-459-3334.
Fax: 856-692-4095.

James J. Gruccio, Sr. | Lawrence Pepper, Jr.
Cosmo A. Giovinazzi, III

Stephen D. Barse

Representative Clients: State Farm Mutual Automobile Insurance Cos.; United States Fidelity & Guaranty Co.; South Jersey Transportation Authority; County of Salem; County of Cape May; Cumberland County Guidance Center; City of Millville; Garden State Parkway Authority; Cape May County Welfare Board; Cape May County Bridge Commission.

For Complete List of Firm Personnel, See General Section

For full biographical listings, see the Martindale-Hubbell Law Directory

WAYNE, Passaic Co.

GERBER & SAMSON, L.L.C. (AV)

155 Willowbrook Boulevard, 07470
Telephone: 973-256-9000
Fax: 973-256-9001
Email: njlaw@gerberlaw.com *URL:* http://www.gerberlaw.com

MEMBERS OF FIRM

Steven Gerber | Linda H. Samson
Mary Patricia Gallagher

ASSOCIATES

Mark J. Semeraro | Keith A. Bregman
Patti A. Scott | N. Noelle Letcher

OF COUNSEL

Richard P. Weiss

Representative Clients: Federal Express Corp.; New Jersey Institute of Technology; Prestige Capital Corp.

For full biographical listings, see the Martindale-Hubbell Law Directory

WESTFIELD, Union Co.

LINDABURY, MCCORMICK & ESTABROOK, P.A. (AV)

53 Cardinal Drive, P.O. Box 2369, 07091
Telephone: 908-233-6800
Fax: 908-233-5078
New York, N.Y. Office: 26 Broadway, Suite 2300.
Telephone: 212-742-3390.
Fax: 212-269-5016.

Peter A. Somers | Donald F. Nicolai
John R. Blasi | James K. Estabrook
John H. Schmidt, Jr. | Anthony P. Sciarrillo
Richard J. Cino

Kathleen M. Connelly | Athina Lekas Cornell

OF COUNSEL

Kenneth L. Estabrook

Representative Clients: Elizabeth General Medical Center; Kessler Institute for Rehabilitation; Mechanical Contractors Association of New Jersey, Inc.; St. Joseph's Hospital and Medical Center; DeDietrich (USA), Inc.; Plunkett-Webster, Inc.; Princeton Insurance Companies; Union Trucking Co.; Visiting Nurse Association of Trenton, Inc.

For Complete List of Firm Personnel, See General Section

For full biographical listings, see the Martindale-Hubbell Law Directory

WOODBRIDGE, Middlesex Co.

WILENTZ, GOLDMAN & SPITZER, A PROFESSIONAL CORPORATION (AV)

90 Woodbridge Center Drive Suite 900, Box 10, 07095
Telephone: 732-636-8000
Telecopier: 732-855-6117
URL: http://www.newjerseylaw.com
Eatontown, New Jersey Office: Meridian Center I, Two Industrial Way West, 07724.
Telephone: 732-542-4500.
Telecopier: 732-493-8387.
New York, New York Office: Wall Street Plaza, 88 Pine Street, 9th Floor, 10005.
Telephone: 212-267-3091.
Telecopier: 212-267-3828.

Alan M. Darnell | Stephen A. Spitzer

(See Next Column)

Fred Hopke | Joseph M. Accardi
Roberto Benites | Elizabeth Siso Bair

Representative Clients: Suburban Transit Corp.; Co-Steel Raritan; Local 358 International Brotherhood of Electrical Workers.

For Complete List of Firm Personnel, See General Section

For full biographical listings, see the Martindale-Hubbell Law Directory

NEW MEXICO

*ALBUQUERQUE,** Bernalillo Co.

BUTT, THORNTON & BAEHR, P.C. (AV)

4101 Indian School Road N.E., Suite 300S, P.O. Box 3170, 87190
Telephone: 505-884-0777
Fax: 505-889-8870

J. Duke Thornton | J. Douglas Compton
Carlos G. Martinez | David N. Whitham
Norman L. Gagne | Emily A. Franke
Alfred L. Green, Jr. | Jane A. Laflin
James H. Johansen | Paul T. Yarbrough
Rodney L. Schlagel | Glenna Hayes Long
Martin Diamond | Michael P. Clemens

Sherrill K. Filter | Monica R. Garcia
Agnes Fuentevilla Padilla | Laura J. Ramos
Gregory P. Williams | Robert Tabor Booms
Louis N. Colón | J. Scott Steinberger

OF COUNSEL

Paul L. Butt | Raymond A. Baehr
John A. Klecan

Representative Clients: Ford Motor Co.; Home Insurance Co.; Reliance Insurance Cos.; Royal Insurance Co.; CIGNA; Norwest Bank; Mayflower Transit; Federal Express Corp.
Reference: Norwest Bank.

For full biographical listings, see the Martindale-Hubbell Law Directory

DINES, GROSS & ESQUIVEL, P.C. (AV)

6301 Indian School Road, N.E., Suite 900, 87110
Telephone: 505-889-4050
Fax: 505-889-4049
Email: law@dge.psemail.com *URL:* http://www.lawyers.com/dgelaw

James M. Dines | Michael A. Gross
Martin R. Esquivel

For full biographical listings, see the Martindale-Hubbell Law Directory

GILKEY, STEPHENSON & WEESE, P.A. (AV)

500 Marquette N.W., Suite 505, P.O. Box 25566, 87125
Telephone: 505-242-4466
Fax: 505-242-3145
Email: duane@gilkeylaw.com

Duane C. Gilkey | Barbara G. Stephenson
Charles W. Weese

Mary A. Woodward | Carol Lee Dominguez

Representative Clients: United Parcel Service; Southwest Airlines; Westinghouse Electric Corporation; Intel Corporation; Phillips Electronics; University of New Mexico; U.S. West Communications, Inc.; Bowlin, Inc.; Home Depot; Raley's Supermarkets.

For full biographical listings, see the Martindale-Hubbell Law Directory

NOEDING & MOODY, P.C. (AV)

San Mateo Corporate Center, 4300 San Mateo Boulevard NE Suite B260, 87110
Telephone: 505-878-0515
Fax: 505-878-0398

Nicholas J. Noeding | Christopher M. Moody

Anne Marie Turner | Whitney Warner

Representative Clients: CVI Laser, Inc.; Elastimold, a Division of Thomas & Betts; Ethicon, Inc., a Johnson & Johnson Company; New Century Energies; NM Building Branch, Associated General Contractors of America; Nobel/-Sysco Food Services Co.; Plains Electric Generationand Transmissionn Cooperative, Inc.; Pres byterian Medical Services; Quixx Power Services, Inc.; St. Vincent Hospital.

For full biographical listings, see the Martindale-Hubbell Law Directory

Albuquerque—Continued

LAW OFFICES OF K. LEE PEIFER (AV)

108 Wellesley SE, 87106
Telephone: 505-266-4335
Fax: 505-266-1915

ASSOCIATE

Angela B. Cornell

For full biographical listings, see the Martindale-Hubbell Law Directory

RODEY, DICKASON, SLOAN, AKIN & ROBB, P.A. (AV)

Albuquerque Plaza, Suite 2200, 201 Third Street, N.W., P.O. Box 1888, 87103-1888
Telephone: 505-765-5900
Fax: 505-768-7395
Email: info@rodey.com *URL:* http://www.rodey.com
Santa Fe, New Mexico Office: Suite 101 Marcy Plaza, 123 East Marcy Street, P.O. Box 1357, 87504-1357.
Telephone: 505-984-0100.
Fax: 505-989-9542.

Robert M. St. John
Jo Saxton Brayer
Patrick M. Shay
David C. Davenport, Jr. (Resident, Santa Fe Office)
Scott D. Gordon
Theresa W. Parrish
James P. Bieg (Resident, Santa Fe Office)
Charles J. Vigil
Thomas L. Stahl

Jeffrey L. Lowry
Amy E. Badger
Thomas A. Outler
Glenn A. Beard
Jocelyn C. Drennan

For Complete List of Firm Personnel, See General Section

For full biographical listings, see the Martindale-Hubbell Law Directory

SÍLVA, RIEDER & MAESTAS, P.C. (AV)

Albuquerque Plaza, Suite 1700, 201 3rd Street, N.W., P.O. Box 1670, 87103-1670
Telephone: 505-767-9800
Facsimile: 505-767-9807
Email: srmlaw@srmlaw.com *URL:* http://www.lawyers.com/srmlaw

Benjamin Sílva, Jr.
Geoffrey D. Rieder
Paul Maestas

Wayne R. Suggett
Christopher A. Riehl
Richard A. Allen

Representative Clients: American Contractors Insurance Group, Inc.; CIGNA; GSL Properties, Inc.; Honeywell, Inc.; Hubbard Broadcasting Company; Intel Corporation; John Q. Hammons, Inc.; KOB-TV, Inc.; Prudential Securities, Inc.; Tandy Corporation.

For full biographical listings, see the Martindale-Hubbell Law Directory

WATROUS & REARDON (AV)

A Partnership of Professional Associations
3733 Eubank Boulevard, N.E., 87111-3536
Telephone: 505-293-7000
Fax: 505-293-0831

MEMBERS OF FIRM

Thomas S. Watrous (P.A.)
Walter L. Reardon, Jr., (P.A.)

Representative Clients: U.S. West, Inc.; State Street Bank and Trust Co.; Angel Fire Ski Area and Resort; Air Touch Cellular; American Linen; Rio Pecos Oil Company; First Health Plan (FHP); Albuquerque Title Co.; Furrow Building materials; Melloy Nissan.

For full biographical listings, see the Martindale-Hubbell Law Directory

*SANTA FE,** Santa Fe Co.

MONTGOMERY & ANDREWS, PROFESSIONAL ASSOCIATION (AV)

325 Paseo de Peralta, P.O. Box 2307, 87504-2307
Telephone: 505-982-3873
Fax: 505-982-4289
Email: montand@montand.com

Bruce Herr
Sarah Michael Singleton
Carolyn Wolf
Grace Philips

Representative Clients: El Paso Corp.; ENMR Telephone Cooperative, Inc.; Giant Industries Arizona, Inc.; Johnson Controls Northern New Mexico, L.L.C.; Los Alamos Technical Associates, Inc.; Protection Technology Los Alamos; St. Vincent Hospital; State of New Mexico, Risk Management Division of the State of New Mexico; St. John's College; U S WEST Communications, Inc.

For Complete List of Firm Personnel, See General Section

For full biographical listings, see the Martindale-Hubbell Law Directory

SCHEUER, YOST & PATTERSON, A PROFESSIONAL CORPORATION (AV)

125 Lincoln Avenue, Suite 223, P.O. Drawer 9570, 87504
Telephone: 505-982-9911
505-989-7500
Fax: 505-982-1621
Email: firm@santafelawyers.com

Melvin T. Yost (Retired)
Ralph H. Scheuer
Mel E. Yost
John N. Patterson
Byron L. Treaster
Donald A. Walcott
Christopher M. Grimmer
Daniel J. Monte

OF COUNSEL

Reverdy Johnson

Representative Clients: American Challenge Enterprises, Inc.; Cyprus-AMAX, Inc.; Century Bank, FSB; Chicago Title Insurance Co.; Davis Selected Venture Advisors; GEICO; St. John's College; School of American Research; Sun Loan Companies; Territorial Abstract & Title Co.

For full biographical listings, see the Martindale-Hubbell Law Directory

SIMONS, CUDDY & FRIEDMAN, LLP (AV)

1701 Old Pecos Trail, P.O. Box 4160, 87502-4160
Telephone: 505-988-4476
Fax: 505-984-1807

Daniel H. Friedman
John F. Kennedy
Frank J. Albetta
Patricia Salazar Ives
Jacquelyn Archuleta-Staehlin

Tanya M. Trujillo

OF COUNSEL

Frank M. Bond

Representative Clients: Los Alamos National Laboratory; New Mexico Public School Insurance Authority; Western New Mexico University; Sandia National Laboratory.

For full biographical listings, see the Martindale-Hubbell Law Directory

WHITE, KOCH, KELLY & MCCARTHY, A PROFESSIONAL ASSOCIATION (AV)

433 Paseo De Peralta, P.O. Box 787, 87504-0787
Telephone: 505-982-4374
ABA/NET: 1154
Fax: 505-982-0350; 984-8631
Email: WKKM@NM.NET

David F. Cunningham
Albert V. Gonzales
Janet Clow
M. Karen Kilgore

Representative Clients: Santa Fe Community College; La Fonda Hotel; Pueblo of Zuni; State and Local Governments; Local School Districts.

For Complete List of Firm Personnel, See General Section

For full biographical listings, see the Martindale-Hubbell Law Directory

NEW YORK

*ALBANY,** Albany Co.

ROBERT S. CATAPANO-FRIEDMAN, P.C. (AV)

744 Broadway, 12207
Telephone: 518-463-7501; 518-463-7502
Fax: 518-463-1948
Email: catapan@worldnet.att.net

Robert S. Catapano-Friedman

For full biographical listings, see the Martindale-Hubbell Law Directory

FEATHERSTONHAUGH, CONWAY, WILEY & CLYNE, L.L.P. (AV)

99 Pine Street, Suite 207, 12207
Telephone: 518-436-0786
Fax: 518-427-0452
URL: http://www.fcwc-law.com

MEMBERS OF FIRM

James D. Featherstonhaugh
Thomas A. Conway
Stephen J. Wiley
Elizabeth K. Clyne

ASSOCIATES

Nadine Feiden Shadlock
Denis R. Hurley, Jr.
Andrew W. Kirby
William F. Conway, IV
Gerard L. Conway, Jr.
Steven M. Connolly

OF COUNSEL

William F. Conway
Jeffrey J. Conklin
David Weinraub
Randall J. Ezick

(See Next Column)

FEATHERSTONHAUGH, CONWAY, WILEY & CLYNE L.L.P., *Albany—Continued*

LEGAL SUPPORT PERSONNEL
GOVERNMENTAL RELATIONS

John L. Hardy
John P. Griffin
Daniel G. Plummer
David F. Fleming

For full biographical listings, see the Martindale-Hubbell Law Directory

HINMAN, STRAUB, PIGORS & MANNING, P.C. (AV)

121 State Street, 12207-1622
Telephone: 518-436-0751
Fax: 518-436-4751
Email: Reception@hspm.com *URL:* http://www.hspm.com
Washington, D.C. Office: 50 E Street Southeast.
Telephone: 202-863-0806.

Bartley J. Costello, III
William P. Golderman
William F. Sheehan
John R. Saccocio
Lawrence H. Schaefer
Keith R. Jacques
Edward J. Greene, Jr.

OF COUNSEL

Richard E. Casagrande
Nancy L. Burritt

Representative Clients: New York State Troopers Benevolent Association; School Administrators' Association of New York; Organization of Managerial / Confidential Employees, Inc.; National Troopers Coalition; New York State Park Police PBA; New York State Correctional Officers and Police Benevolent Association, Inc.

For full biographical listings, see the Martindale-Hubbell Law Directory

O'CONNELL AND ARONOWITZ, P.C. (AV)

100 State Street, 12207-1885
Telephone: 518-462-5601
Telecopier: 518-462-2670
Email: info@oalaw.com
Plattsburgh, New York Office: 206 West Bay Plaza.
Telephone: 518-562-0600.
Fax: 518-562-0657.
Saratoga Springs, New York Office: Suite 204, 358 Broadway.
Telephone: 518-587-0425.

Cornelius D. Murray
Gloria Herron Arthur

Representative Clients: The New York State Health Facilities Association, Inc.; Time Warner Entertainment; First Albany Corporation (Retirement Plan Counsel).

For full biographical listings, see the Martindale-Hubbell Law Directory

RUBERTI, GIRVIN & FERLAZZO, P.C. (AV)

120 State Street, 2nd Floor, 12207-2829
Telephone: 518-462-0300
Fax: 518-462-5037
Email: attorneys@rgflaw.com

PARTNERS

E. Michael Ruberti
Kristine Amodeo Lanchantin
James E. Girvin
Jeffrey D. Honeywell
Salvatore D. Ferlazzo
M. Cornelia Cahill
Gregg Tyler Johnson

ASSOCIATES

Patrick J. McKenna
Christopher P. Langlois
Kathy Ann Wolverton
Bruce I. Kopf
Maureen Finnegan Harris

SPECIAL COUNSEL

Mary Helen Moses
Elaine M. Pers
James A. P. McCarthy
Karen S. Norlander

For full biographical listings, see the Martindale-Hubbell Law Directory

*BINGHAMTON,** Broome Co.

ASWAD & INGRAHAM (AV)

46 Front Street, 13905
Telephone: 607-722-3495
Fax: 607-722-2566; 607-722-7269
Email: office@AILAW.COM

MEMBERS OF FIRM

Richard N. Aswad
James F. Haley, Jr.
Charles O. Ingraham
Angelina C. Cutrona
Thomas A. Saitta
William M. Thomas

SPECIAL COUNSEL

James F. Moran

ASSOCIATE

Jeffrey Husisian

Reference: Charter One Bank.

For full biographical listings, see the Martindale-Hubbell Law Directory

HINMAN, HOWARD & KATTELL, LLP (AV)

700 Security Mutual Building, 80 Exchange Street, P.O. Box 5250, 13902-5250
Telephone: 607-723-5341
Fax: 607-723-6605
Email: jworband@hhk.com *URL:* http://www.hhk.com
Norwich, New York Office: 48 Hale Street, 13815-2039.
Telephone: 607-334-5896.
Fax: 607-336-1628.
Oneonta, New York Office: 12 South Main Street, 13820-2542.
Telephone: 607-432-5331.
Fax: 607-432-2683.
New York, N.Y. Office: 500 5th Avenue, Suite 1725, 10110.
Telephone: 212-840-3017.
Fax: 212-840-2345.

MEMBERS OF FIRM

James S. Gleason
Peter J. Vivona
John C. Fish
James R. Franz
Leslie Prechtl Guy

Representative Clients: BSB Bank & Trust Co.; International Business Machines Corp.; Universal Instruments Corp.; Security Mutual Life Insurance Company of New York; Bell Atlantic; Preferred Mutual Insurance Company; New York State Electric & Gas Corp.; Lourdes Hospital; United Health Services; The Hospital (Sydney).

For Complete List of Firm Personnel, See General Section

For full biographical listings, see the Martindale-Hubbell Law Directory

HOGAN & SARZYNSKI, L.L.P. (AV)

20 Hawley Street, P.O. Box 660, 13902-0660
Telephone: 607-723-7413
Fax: 607-723-0129
Email: hsatty@pronetisp.net

MEMBERS OF FIRM

John B. Hogan
John P. Lynch
Edward J. Sarzynski
Michael G. Surowka

Wendy K. DeWind

For full biographical listings, see the Martindale-Hubbell Law Directory

O'CONNOR, GACIOCH, POPE & TAIT, L.L.P. (AV)

One Marine Midland Plaza, East Tower-Seventh Floor, P.O. Box 1964, 13902
Telephone: 607-772-9262
Fax: 607-724-6002
Email: ogplaw@compuserve.com

Thomas F. O'Connor
Robert N. Nielsen, Jr.
James C. Gacioch
Stephen B. Atkinson
Alan J. Pope
Kurt D. Schrader
Jeffrey A. Tait
Richard M. Hill
Hugh B. Leonard
Patricia A. Cummings
Robert C. Murphy

OF COUNSEL

Walter T. Gorman
Cheryl Insinga

For full biographical listings, see the Martindale-Hubbell Law Directory

*BUFFALO,** Erie Co.

BROWN & KELLY, L.L.P. (AV)

1500 Liberty Building, 14202-3663
Telephone: 716-854-2620
Fax: 716-854-0082
Email: mail@brownkelly.com *URL:* http://www.brownkelly.com

MEMBERS OF FIRM

Thomas J. Kelly
Andrew D. Merrick
Rodney O. Personius
William P. Wiles
Frederick D. Turner
William D. Harrington
Paul Michael Hassett
Joseph M. Schnitter
Peter E. Klaasesz
Paula L. Feroleto
Donald B. Eppers
Daniel J. Marren
Lisa T. Sofferin

OF COUNSEL

Ogden R. Brown
Roland R. Benzow
Charles F. Harrington
Philip B. Abramowitz
James T. Duggan
Elizabeth R. O'Connor
Karen Cook Serotte
Catherine E. Marra

ASSOCIATES

David S. Zygaj
David O. Teach
Olney H. Clowe
Patricia S. Ciccarelli
Brian M. Melber
Susan J. Schmidt

For full biographical listings, see the Martindale-Hubbell Law Directory

Buffalo—Continued

DAMON & MOREY LLP (AV)

(Formerly Damon, Morey, Sawyer & Moot)
1000 Cathedral Place, 298 Main Street, 14202-4096
Telephone: 716-856-5500
Facsimile: 716-856-5510
Email: apinder@damonmorey.com *URL:* http://www.damonmorey.com
Rochester, New York Office: Powers Building, Suite 507, 16 West Main Street, 14614.
Telephone: 716-232-3640.
Fax: 716-232-8448.

MEMBERS OF FIRM

Mason O. Damon (1905-1983)
Robert J. Plache
James N. Schmit
Christopher T. Greene
Franklin W. Heller
Gregory C. Yungbluth
James W. Gormley
James M. Mucklewee
Melinda G. Disare
Robert J. Portin
Joseph J. Schoellkopf, Jr.
William F. Savino
Thomas J. Drury
Patrick B. Curran
Peter S. Marlette
Vincent J. Moore
Gust P. Pullman
Barbara L. Schifeling
Michael J. Willett
Carol Guck Snider
Joseph W. Dunbar
Kenneth W. Africano
Julie M. Bargnesi
Arthur A. Marrapese III (Resident, Rochester Office)
Sharyn G. Rogers
Daniel F. Brown
David L. Edmunds, Jr.
Charles S. Carra
Hedwig Maria Auletta
Marylou K. Roshia
Maryjo C. Falcone
Charles E. Telford, III
Timothy C. Cashmore
Anthony L. Eugeni
Amy Archer Flaherty
Kathleen M. Reilly
Steven I. Rubinstein
Diane C. Zarlock

ASSOCIATES

Brian Alan Birenbach
Daniel T. Cavarello
Michelle A. Crew
Anne C. Evans
Michael Thomas Feeley
Judy S. Hernandez
David S. Kelly
Joseph J. Manna
Rosalie A. Melisz
Mary C. Raymond
Vincent George Saccomando
Allison Fields Stravino
Kellie Muffoletto Ulrich

OF COUNSEL

Joseph H. Morey, Jr.

SPECIAL COUNSEL

Richard E. Moot
George F. Gabel, Jr.
G. Steven Pigeon
Susan A. Benz
Edward Yankelunas

Counsel For: Advanced Refractory Technologies; Catholic Health East; D.A. Elia Construction Corporation; Kaleida Health; Town of Cheektowaga; Bagel Brothers Amherst, Inc.; Burt Rigid Box, Inc.; Lake Shore Health Care Center; County of Cattaraugus; Commonwealth Land Title Insurance; Diocese of Buffalo; Baker Victory Services; Niagara Lutheran Home and Rehabilitation, Inc.; Sheehan Memorial Hospital; Robert James Sales, Inc.; Olean General Hospital; Wendt Corporation; Aria Wireless Systems, Inc.; Buffalo Sewer Authority; City of Tonawanda; Roswell Park Cancer Institute; Ivoclar North America, Inc.; Olean Medical Group; Cold Spring Construction Company; Buffalo Municipal Housing Authority.
Local Counsel For: Healthcare Underwriters Mutual Insurance Company; AIG Companies; Owens-Corning Fiberglas; Unigard Insurance Group; Key Tronic Corporation; Medical Liability Insurance; Risk Enterprise Management Limited; Wintherthur International; Hanover Insurance Company; National Casualty Company; Marine Midland Mortgage Corporation; Acordia Resort Services; Medical Malpractice Insurance Association; OUM & Associates; Ohio Casualty Company; PACCAR, Inc.; Frontier Insurance Company; The Limited, Inc.; Zurich-American Insurance Group; Allstate Insurance Company; Universal Studios, Inc.

For full biographical listings, see the Martindale-Hubbell Law Directory

HODGSON, RUSS, ANDREWS, WOODS & GOODYEAR, LLP (AV)

A Registered Limited Liability Partnership including Professional Associations
One M & T Plaza, Suite 2000, 14203
Telephone: 716-856-4000
Fax: 716-849-0349
Email: info@hodgsonruss.com *URL:* www.hodgsonruss.com
Albany, New York Office: Three City Square, 12207.
Telephone: 518-465-2333.
Fax: 518-465-1567.
Boca Raton, Florida Office: Suite 400, 2000 Glades Road, 33431.
Telephone: 561-394-0500.
Fax: 561-394-3862.
Toronto, Ontario, Canada Office: 150 King Street West, Suite 2309, M5H 1J9, P.O. Box 30.
Telephone: 416-595-5100.
Fax: 416-595-5021.
New York, New York Office: 65 East 55th Street, 10th Floor, 10022.
Telephone: 212-751-4300.
Fax: 212-751-0928.

(See Next Column)

Gloversville, New York Office: 6 Fremont Street, 12078.
Telephone: 518-725-6347.
Fax: 518-773-7350.
Newark, New Jersey Office: One Gateway Center, Suite 2600, 07102.
Telephone: 973-645-0577.
Fax: 973-645-0551.

MEMBERS OF FIRM

(ALPHABETICALLY BY YEAR OF ADMISSION TO BAR)

David E. Hall
Karl W. Kristoff
Anne Smith Simet
David A. Farmelo
Joseph L. Braccio
John J. Christopher

COUNSEL

Arnold T. Olena

ASSOCIATES

(ALPHABETICALLY BY YEAR OF ADMISSION TO BAR)

Jeffrey F. Swiatek
Lynda M. Tarantino
Peter C. Godfrey
Kimberly M. Sebastian
Tracie L. Lopardi

For Complete List of Firm Personnel, See General Section

For full biographical listings, see the Martindale-Hubbell Law Directory

PHILLIPS, LYTLE, HITCHCOCK, BLAINE & HUBER LLP (AV)

(Formerly Kenefick, Letchworth, Baldy, Phillips & Emblidge)
3400 HSBC Center, 14203
Telephone: 716-847-8400
Telecopier: 716-852-6100
Email: info@phillipslytle.com *URL:* http://www.phillipslytle.com
Jamestown, New York Office: 307 Chase Bank Building, 8 E. Third Street.
Telephone: 716-664-3906.
Telecopier: 716-664-4230.
Rochester, New York Office: 1400 First Federal Plaza.
Telephone: 716-238-2000.
Telecopier: 716-232-3141.
New York, New York Office: 437 Madison Avenue.
Telephone: 212-759-4888.
Telecopier: 212-308-9079.
Fredonia, New York Office: 11 East Main Street.
Telephone: 716-672-2164.
FAX: 716-672-7979.

OF COUNSEL

John F. Donovan

PARTNERS

James D. Donathen
James R. Grasso
Michael R. Moravec

ASSOCIATE

Sharon A. Swift

General Counsel for: Astronics Corp.; Bryant & Stratton Business Institute; Canisius College; Chase Manhattan Bank, N.A.; Columbus McKinnon Corp.
Local Counsel for: A.O. Smith Corp.; Allied Signal; Bethlehem Steel Corp.; Chrysler Motor Corp.; E.I. DuPont deNemours Co., Inc.

For Complete List of Firm Personnel, See General Section

For full biographical listings, see the Martindale-Hubbell Law Directory

RAICHLE, BANNING, WEISS & STEPHENS (AV)

410 Main Street, 14202
Telephone: 716-852-7587
Telecopier: 716-852-7599
Email: RBWS@MSN.COM

MEMBERS OF FIRM

Frank G. Raichle (1898-1986)
Derrick C. Banning (1916-1995)
Arnold Weiss
R. William Stephens

ASSOCIATES

Lisa Parlato Neff
R. Hugh Stephens

Representative Clients: General Motors Corp.; Cliffstar Corp.; Blue Cross & Blue Shield of Michigan; Sony Picture Releasing Inc.; Superior Jamestown Corp., Adanlock Office Environments Division; Permclip Products Corp.; Living Monuments Inc.

For full biographical listings, see the Martindale-Hubbell Law Directory

GARDEN CITY, Nassau Co.

COLLERAN, O'HARA & MILLS (AV)

1225 Franklin Avenue, Suite 450, 11530
Telephone: 516-248-5757; 212-614-9119
Telecopier: 516-742-1765

Walter M. Colleran (1912-1998)
Richard L. O'Hara
John F. Mills
Edward J. Groarke
Christopher P. O'Hara
Carol L. O'Rourke

(See Next Column)

New York—Continued

O'DONNELL, SCHWARTZ, GLANSTEIN, ROSEN, DI PRETA & GOLDSTEIN, L.L.P. (AV)

Suite 1022, 60 East 42nd Street, 10165
Telephone: 212-370-5100
Fax: 212-697-6299
Email: odsgr@worldnet.att.net
Washington, D.C. Offices: O'Donnell, Schwartz & Anderson, Suite 1200, 1300 L Street, N.W.
Telephone: 202-898-1707.
Telex: 202-429-8928 and Suite 707, 1900 L Street, N.W.
Telephone: 202-898-1824.

RESIDENT MEMBERS

John F. O'Donnell (1907-1993)
Asher W. Schwartz
Joel C. Glanstein
David B. Rosen
Malcolm A. Goldstein
Manlio Di Preta

RESIDENT ASSOCIATES

Edmond V. Pendleton
David M. Glanstein

OF COUNSEL

Suzanne McCarthy

For full biographical listings, see the Martindale-Hubbell Law Directory

PARKER CHAPIN LLP (AV)

Chrysler Building, 405 Lexington Avenue, 10017
Telephone: 212-704-6000
Telecopier: 212-704-6288
URL: http://www.parkerchapin.com
Great Neck, New York Office: 175 Great Neck Road.
Telephone: 516-482-4422.
Telecopier: 516-482-4469.
Hackensack, New Jersey: 190 Morre Street, Suite 307.
Telephone: 210-883-6400.
Telecopier: 210-883-6404.
Beverly Hills, California: 9454 Wilshire Boulevard.
Telephone: 310-288-8367.
Telecopier: 310-288-8365.

MEMBER OF FIRM

Aurora Cassirer

OF COUNSEL

Norman Alexander Jenkins, III

For Complete List of Firm Personnel, See General Section

For full biographical listings, see the Martindale-Hubbell Law Directory

PILIERO GOLDSTEIN JENKINS & SULLIVAN, LLP (AV)

292 Madison Avenue, 10017
Telephone: 212-213-8200
Fax: 212-685-2028
Email: lawyers@pgjhlaw.com *URL:* http://www.pgjhlaw.com
Carlstadt, New Jersey Office: One Palmer Terrace.
Telephone: 201-507-5157.
FAX: 201-507-5221.
Washington, D.C. Office: 888 17th Street, N.W., Suite 1100.
Telephone: 202-467-6991.
FAX: 202-467-6703.
San Francisco, California Office: 507 Howard Street, Suite 200.
Telephone: 415-281-3631.
Fax: 415-281-3630.

MEMBERS OF FIRM

Kimberlee S. Bogen
Edward J. Goldstein
Jon Mark Jenkins
Marc A. Lebowitz
Robert D. Piliero
George O. Richardson, III
Michael T. Sullivan

ASSOCIATES

Craig Avedisian
Rosemary G. Feit
Eric M. Kogan
Mariano Schwed

OF COUNSEL

Kenneth D. Arbeeny
Christopher P. Hall

For full biographical listings, see the Martindale-Hubbell Law Directory

PROSKAUER ROSE LLP (AV)

1585 Broadway, 10036-8299
Telephone: 212-969-3000
Fax: 212-969-2900
Telex: TRT 175719 ROPUT NY
URL: http://www.proskauer.com
Washington, D.C. Office: 1233 Twentieth Street, N.W., Suite 800.
Telephone: 202-416-6800.
Fax: 202-416-6899.
Los Angeles, California Office: 2049 Century Park East, Suite 3200.
Telephone: 310-557-2900.
Fax: 310-557-2193.

(See Next Column)

Boca Raton, Florida Office: One Boca Place, Suite 340 West, 2255 Glades Road.
Telephone: 561-241-7400.
Fax: 561-241-7145.
Newark, New Jersey Office: One Newark Center.
Telephone: 973-274-3200.
Fax: 973-274-3299.
Paris, France Office: Proskauer Rose, 68, rue du Faubourg Saint-Honoré.
Telephone: +33-1-53-05-60-00.
Fax: +33-1-53-05-60-05.

MEMBERS OF FIRM

Neil H. Abramson
Rory Judd Albert
L. Robert Batterman
Joseph Baumgarten
Edward A. Brill
Peter D. Conrad
David H. Diamond
Allen I. Fagin
Howard L. Ganz
Murray Gartner
Ira M. Golub
Daniel R. Halem
Jerold D. Jacobson
Alan S. Jaffe
Kathleen M. McKenna
Carole O'Blenes
Martin J. Oppenheimer
Bettina B. Plevan
Bernard M. Plum
Myron D. Rumeld
Paul Salvatore
Donald W. Savelson
Neal S. Schelberg
Aaron J. Schindel
Ronald F. Storette
M. David Zurndorfer

RETIRED PARTNERS

Marvin Dicker
Bernard Gold
Saul G. Kramer
Sara S. Portnoy
Edward Silver

SENIOR COUNSEL

Roberta K. Chevlowe
Fredric C. Leffler
Richard A. Levin
Michael H. Roffer
Steven D. Weinstein

CONSULTANT

Carole Simon

ASSOCIATES

Michael W. Arseneault
James M. Beach
Charlotte L. Behrendt
Craig A. Bitman
Lloyd B. Chinn
Denise M. Clark (Not admitted in NY)
Christopher J. Collins
John E. Daly
Matthew E. Feiner
Jo-Ann W. Fox-Weingarten
James Scott Frazier (Not admitted in NY)
John F. Fullerton, III
Maria F. Gandarez
Jennifer Rosar Gefsky
Loren M. Gesinsky
Sheri L. Gilbert
Jonathan M. Glassman
Jeffrey A. Goldstein
Andrew S. Goodstadt
Deidre A. Grossman
Andrew M. Gutterman
Amanda D. Haverstick
S. Jean Kim
Naoko Kumada-Lawrence
Michael J. Lebowich
Laurie S. Leonard
Kelly B. Levi
Tracey I. Levy
Gwen J. Lourie
Marc A. Mandelman
Frank F. Martinez
Nina Massen
Francine E. Menaker
Paul V. Mifsud, Jr.
Ravi B. Motwani
Andrea B. Neuman
Vera M. Ovadia
Katharine H. Parker
Robert M. Projansky
Xan Raskin
Howard Z. Robbins
Alyce Rogers-Goodstein
Eric D. Roth
Sally L. Schneider
David T. Seiden
Regina E. Shannahan
Karen Steffire
Joshua H. Sternoff
Priscilla Steward
Joshua Zuckerberg

WASHINGTON, D.C. ASSOCIATE

Timothy E. Delahunt

LOS ANGELES, CALIFORNIA
MEMBERS OF FIRM

Harold M. Brody
Bernard D. Gold
Arthur F. Silbergeld
Scott J. Witlin

LOS ANGELES, CALIFORNIA ASSOCIATES

Gloria C. Jan
Mark R. Rehe
Stephanie T. Sasaki
Tracy L. Turner
Carolyn R. Young

BOCA RATON, FLORIDA
MEMBERS OF FIRM

Jay S. Blumenkopf
Allan H. Weitzman

BOCA RATON, FLORIDA ASSOCIATES

Jonathan M. Fordin
Joshua B. Frank
Wendy L. Furman
Walter J. Harvey
Jeannine Cline Jacobson
Michael S. Metta
Julie M. Mihelich
Justin Michael Senior
Susan H. Stern
Michael R. Tricarico
David Todd Zieper

NEWARK, NEW JERSEY
MEMBERS OF FIRM

Marvin M. Goldstein
Kathleen M. McKenna

NEWARK, NEW JERSEY SENIOR COUNSEL

Joseph C. O'Keefe
Donald B. Shanin

(See Next Column)

PROSKAUER ROSE LLP—*Continued*

NEWARK, NEW JERSEY ASSOCIATES

Jeremy M. Brown
Jennifer Morris Cohen
John Joseph Dabney
Wanda L. Ellert
Elana Gilaad
Gregg S. Kahn
Devora L. Lindeman
David W. MacGregor
Michael MacManus
Anne N. Smith
Steven Yarusinsky

For Complete List of Firm Personnel, See General Section

For full biographical listings, see the Martindale-Hubbell Law Directory

REED SMITH SHAW & McCLAY LLP (AV⓵)

375 Park Avenue, 17th Floor, 10152
Telephone: 212-521-5400
FAX: 212-521-5450
Email: rssm@rssm.com *URL:* http://www.rssm.com
Pittsburgh, Pennsylvania Office: 435 Sixth Avenue, 15219-1886.
Telephone: 412-288-3131.
FAX: 412-288-3063.
Washington, D.C. Office: Suite 1100 - East Tower, 1301 K Street, N.W., 20005-3317.
Telephone: 202-414-9200.
FAX: 202-414-9299.
Philadelphia, Pennsylvania Office: 2500 One Liberty Place, 19103-7301.
Telephone: 215-851-8100.
FAX: 215-851-1420.
Harrisburg, Pennsylvania Office: 213 Market Street, 17101-2132.
Telephone: 717-234-5988.
FAX: 717-236-3777.
Princeton, New Jersey Office: 136 Main Street, Suite 250, 08540-5799.
Telephone: 609-987-0050.
FAX: 609-951-0824.
Newark, New Jersey Office: The Legal Center, One Riverfront Plaza, First Floor, 07102-5400.
Telephone: 973-621-3200.
FAX: 973-621-3199.
McLean, Virginia Office: Reed Smith Hazel & Thomas LLP, Suite 1100, 8251 Greensboro Drive, 22102-3844.
Telephone: 703-734-4600.
FAX: 703-734-4699.
Falls Church, Virginia Office: Reed Smith Hazel & Thomas, Suite 1400, 3110 Fairview Park Drive, P.O. Box 12001.
Telephone: 703-641-4200.
Fax: 703-641-4340.
Leesburg, Virginia Office: Reed Smith Hazel & Thomas LLP, 44084 Riverside Parkway, Suite 300.
Telephone: 703-729-8500. Metro: 703-478-1992.
Fax: 703-478-8003.
Richmond, Virginia Office: Reed Smith Hazel & Thomas LLP, Suite 600, 411 East Franklin Street, P.O. Box 788.
Telephone: 804-344-3400.
Fax: 804-344-3410.

MEMBERS OF FIRM

Alan A. D'Ambrosio
Ruth S. Perfido (Not admitted in NY; Also at Pittsburgh, Pennsylvania)
David L. Weissman
Jonathan Young

COUNSEL

Adria De Landri
Andrew B. Messite
Marlene A. Zarfes

ASSOCIATES

Werner S. Achatz
Feini Ardelean
Ellen McPhillips Baumann
John F. Curran, Jr.
Annmarie D'Amour
Joseph M. Marger
Scott S. McKessy
Andre T. Nobles
Kipling Oren
Darren M. Sharlach
William R. Wright

For full biographical listings, see the Martindale-Hubbell Law Directory

SEHAM SEHAM MELTZ & PETERSEN, LLP (AV)

380 Madison Avenue, Suite 17, 10017-2513
Telephone: 212-557-9577
Email: ssmpls@aol.com

Martin C. Seham
Lee Seham
Louis S. Meltz
Scott C. Petersen

For full biographical listings, see the Martindale-Hubbell Law Directory

SKADDEN, ARPS, SLATE, MEAGHER & FLOM LLP (AV)

Four Times Square, 10036
Telephone: 212-735-3000
Fax: 212-735-2000
URL: http://www.sasmf.com
Firm/Affiliate Offices:
Boston, Massachusetts: One Beacon Street, 02108.
Telephone: 617-573-4800.
Fax: 617-573-4822.

(See Next Column)

Washington, D.C.: 1440 New York Avenue, N.W., 20005.
Telephone: 202-371-7000.
Fax: 202-393-5760.
Wilmington, Delaware: One Rodney Square, P.O. Box 636, 19899.
Telephone: 302-651-3000.
Fax: 302-651-3001.
Los Angeles, California: 300 South Grand Avenue, 90071.
Telephone: 213-687-5000.
Fax: 213-687-5600.
Chicago, Illinois: Skadden, Arps, Slate, Meagher & Flom (Illinois), 333 West Wacker Drive, 60606.
Telephone: 312-407-0700.
Fax: 312-407-0411.
San Francisco, California: Four Embarcadero Center, 94111.
Telephone: 415-984-6400.
Fax: 415-984-2698.
Houston, Texas: 1600 Smith Street, Suite 4460, 77002.
Telephone: 713-655-5100.
Fax: 713-655-5181.
Newark, New Jersey: One Newark Center, 07102.
Telephone: 973-639-6800.
Fax: 973-639-6858.
Palo Alto, California: 525 University Avenue, Suite 220, 94301.
Telephone: 650-470-4500.
Fax: 650-470-4570.
Tokyo, Japan: ATT Main Tower 12F, 2-17-22, Akasaka, Minato-ku, 107-0052.
Telephone: 011-813-3568-2600.
Fax: 011-813-3568-2626.
London, England: One Canada Square, Canary Wharf, E14 5DS.
Telephone: 011-44-207-519-7000.
Fax: 011-44-207-519-7070.
Hong Kong, China: 30/F Tower Two, Lippo Centre, 89 Queensway, Central.
Telephone: 011-852-2820-0700.
Fax: 011-852-2820-0727.
Sydney, New South Wales 2000, Australia: Skadden, Arps, Slate, Meagher & Flom (International), Level 13, 131 Macquarie Street.
Telephone: 011-61-2-9253-6000.
Fax: 011-61-2-9253-6044.
Toronto, Ontario, Canada: Suite 1820, North Tower, P.O. Box 189, Royal Bank Plaza, M5J 2J4.
Telephone: 416-777-4700.
Fax: 416-777-4747.
Brussels, Belgium: 523 avenue Louise, Box 30, 1050.
Telephone: 011-32-2-639-0300.
Fax: 011-32-2-639-0339.
Frankfurt am Main, Germany: MesseTurm, 27th Floor, 60308.
Telephone: 011-49-69-742200.
Fax: 011-49-69-74220300.
Paris, France: 68, rue du Faubourg Saint-Honoré, 75008.
Telephone: 011-331-55-27-11-00.
Fax: 011-331-55-27-11-99.
Beijing, China: East Wing Office, Level 4, China World Trade Center, No. 1 Jian Guo Men Wai Avenue, 100004.
Telephone: 011-86-10-6505-5511.
Fax: 011-86-10-6505-5522.
Moscow, Russia: Degtyarniy Pereulok 4, Building 1, 103009.
Telephone: 011-7-501-797-4600.
Fax: 011-7-501-797-4601.
Singapore, Singapore: Skadden, Arps, Slate, Meagher & Flom (International), 9 Temasek Boulevard, Suite 29-01, Suntec Tower Two, 038989.
Telephone: 011-65-434-2900.
Fax: 011-65-434-2988.

MEMBERS OF FIRM/AFFILIATES

Michael M. Connery
John P. Furfaro
Jay S. Berke

OF COUNSEL

Henry P. Baer

LOS ANGELES, CALIFORNIA

PARTNER

Karen L. Corman

NEWARK, NEW JERSEY

COUNSEL

Stephen D. Kinnard

NEW YORK, NEW YORK

ASSOCIATES

Lisa R. D'Avolio
Carl G. Guida
Ragini Gupta
Christian G. Hildenbrand
Brian S. Kaplan
David E. Schwartz
Neal A. Stern

LOS ANGELES, CALIFORNIA

ASSOCIATES

Rhonda Bethea
John A. Makarewich
Barbara C. Sousa

PALO ALTO, CALIFORNIA

ASSOCIATE

Calvin Siemer

(See Next Column)

SKADDEN, ARPS, SLATE, MEAGHER & FLOM LLP, *New York—Continued*

NEWARK, NEW JERSEY

ASSOCIATES

Aney K. Chandy | Gary J. Ruckelshaus
Ellen O'Connell | Michael A. Shipp

WASHINGTON, D.C.

ASSOCIATES

Ellen L. Lyons | August J. Matteis, Jr.

For Complete List of Firm Personnel, See General Section

For full biographical listings, see the Martindale-Hubbell Law Directory

SLADE & ASSOCIATES, P.C. (AV)

11 Vestry Street, 5th Floor, 10013
Telephone: 212-226-8787
Fax: 212-226-3619
URL: http://www.lawyers.com/slade&associatespc

Jeffrey C. Slade

Marianne Yen | Bridget Connolly

OF COUNSEL

Douglas E. Grover | Norman A. Bloch

For full biographical listings, see the Martindale-Hubbell Law Directory

VLADECK, WALDMAN, ELIAS & ENGELHARD, P.C. (AV)

1501 Broadway, Suite 800, 10036
Telephone: 212-403-7300
Fax: 212-221-3172

Stephen C. Vladeck (1920-1979)
Sylvan H. Elias (1909-1998)
Judith P. Vladeck
Anne C. Vladeck
Karen Honeycutt
Linda E. Rodd
Debra L. Raskin
Julian R. Birnbaum
Larry Cary
James I. Wasserman
Jay P. Levy-Warren
Ivan D. Smith
Anne L. Clark
James D. Esseks
Margaret L. Watson
Maureen M. Stampp
Charles Pergue

SENIOR ATTORNEY

Robert H. Stroup

Genevieve A. Felix
Andrew H. Tarsy (Not admitted in NY)
Karen Kithan Yau
Laura Matlow
Walter M. Kane
Key Alexandra Mendes
Kevin Mintzer
Laren E. Spirer
Elaine Grant

OF COUNSEL

Seymour M. Waldman | Sheldon Engelhard

For full biographical listings, see the Martindale-Hubbell Law Directory

WHITE, FLEISCHNER & FINO (AV)

140 Broadway, 10005
Telephone: 212-487-9700
Telecopier: 212-487-9777
Email: infor@wff-law.com
Red Bank, New Jersey Office: 272 Broad Street.
Telephone: 732-530-7787.
Telecopier: 732-530-8552.

MEMBERS OF FIRM

Patti F. Potash | Wendy K. Carrano

For Complete List of Firm Personnel, See General Section

For full biographical listings, see the Martindale-Hubbell Law Directory

*POUGHKEEPSIE,** Dutchess Co.

HANKIN, HANIG, STALL, CAPLICKI, REDL & CURTIN, LLP (AV)

319 Main Mall Rear, P.O. Box 911, 12602-0911
Telephone: 914-471-7177
FAX: 914-471-0105
Email: hhscrc@aol.com *URL:* http://www.hvlaw.com
Newburgh, New York Office: 6 Jeanne Drive, P.O. Box 7229, 12550.
Telephone: 914-566-8888.
Fax: 914-566-3886.
LaGrangeville, New York Office: Lexington Park, Route 55, P.O. Box 15, LaGrangeville, New York.
Telephone: 914-473-1200.

MEMBERS OF FIRM

Jerard S. Hankin
Joel D. Hanig
Todd S. Stall
Edmund V. Caplicki, Jr.
Frank E. Redl
Daniel F. Curtin

(See Next Column)

Lynn M. Smookler | David V. Hasin

For full biographical listings, see the Martindale-Hubbell Law Directory

*ROCHESTER,** Monroe Co.

DOLIN & ASSOCIATES, P.C. (AV)

135 Corporate Woods, 14623
Telephone: 716-272-0540
Telecopier: 716-272-0574
TTY: 716-292-0606
URL: http://www.lawyers.com/dolin

Lonny H. Dolin

Donald G. Rehkopf, Jr.

LEGAL SUPPORT PERSONNEL

Dawn M. Stiles (Paralegal) | Laura P. Wagner (Paralegal)

For full biographical listings, see the Martindale-Hubbell Law Directory

TREVETT, LENWEAVER & SALZER, P.C. (AV)

700 Reynolds Arcade, 16 East Main Street, 14614
Telephone: 716-454-2181
Telecopier: 716-454-4026

Oscar J. Brown (1884-1958)
Melvin H. Zurett (1905-1967)
Eric P. Smith (1900-1967)
Thomas W. Sullivan (1916-1981)
William V. Gough (1922-1985)
Walter C. Eves (Retired)
Robert T. Skipworth (Retired)
Ronald James Summers (Retired)
Thomas N. Trevett
Bohdan Wenglowskyj
Thomas E. Lenweaver
Kenneth Bersani
Richard M. Doyle
James A. Valenti
Karl F. Salzer
Peter A. Jacobson
Louis B. Cristo
Cynthia A. Constantino
Henry L. Jesserer, III
Lawrence J. Andolina
James C. Gocker

John C. Palermo | Jon Paul Getz
Nicole L. Black

Representative Clients: American Motorists Insurance Co.; Lumbermens Mutual Casualty Co.; Nationwide Mutual Insurance Co.; Interboro Mutual Indemnity Insurance Co.; Michigan Mutual Liability Insurance Co.; Virginia Surety Co.; Allstate Insurance Co.; American Hardware Insurance Co.; Pearl Assurance Co., Ltd.

For full biographical listings, see the Martindale-Hubbell Law Directory

UNDERBERG & KESSLER LLP (AV)

1800 Chase Square, 14604
Telephone: 716-258-2800
Fax: 716-258-2821
Email: INFO@UNDERBERG-KESSLER.COM
Buffalo, New York Office: 1100 Main Place Tower. 14202.
Telephone: 716-848-9000.
Fax: 716-847-6004.

MEMBERS OF FIRM

Alan J. Underberg (1929-1998)
Irving L. Kessler
Michael J. Beyma
James A. Coniglio
Frank T. Crego
Robert W. Croessmann
John W. Crowe
Patrick L. Cusato
Michael C. Dwyer
Bernard A. Frank
Steven R. Gersz
Katherine Howk Karl
Lawrence P. Keller
Gordon J. Lipson
Anna E. Lynch
Robert F. Mechur
Paul V. Nunes
Terry M. Richman
J. David Sampson (Resident, Buffalo Office)
Sharon P. Stiller
Stephen H. Waite
Russell I. Zuckerman

OF COUNSEL

Andrew M. Greenstein

SENIOR ATTORNEYS

Duncan R. Farney | Ronald G. Hull

ASSOCIATES

James F. Armstrong (Resident, Buffalo Office)
Karen A. DiNardo
Lise C. Hamilton
Jeffrey D. Hummel
Paul F. Keneally
Ella L. Krzanowicz
Maureen E. Mulholland
Suzanne D. Nott
Kelly L. Odorisi
Thomas A. Rall

For full biographical listings, see the Martindale-Hubbell Law Directory

*SYRACUSE,** Onondaga Co.

COSTELLO COONEY & FEARON, LLP (AV)

Salina Place, 205 South Salina Street, 13202
Telephone: 315-422-1152
Fax: 315-422-1139
Email: ccf-law.com *URL:* http://www.ccf-law.com

MEMBERS OF FIRM

David F. Costello (1872-1934)
Charles E. Cooney (1873-1958)
George R. Fearon (1883-1976)
Donald L. Nicholas
Warren W. Bader
Robert D. Essig
Kevin M. Gilligan
Robert J. Smith
Michael A. Tremont
Alicia S. Calagiovanni
James J. Gascon
Paul G. Ferrara
Maureen G. Fatcheric
Timothy J. Conan
John R. Langey
Daniel Fletcher

ASSOCIATES

Robert W. Connolly
W. Scott Gambee
David S. Grasso
Edmund J. Gegan
Louis J. Viviani
Michael P. McCarthy
Joseph N. Bulko
Edward G. Melvin
Lauren M. Mumford
Samuel C. Young

OF COUNSEL

Vincent A. O'Neil
Richard D. Hillman

General Counsel for: Auburn Memorial Hospital; Crouse Hospital; Health Services Association of Central New York; St. Joseph's Hospital Health Center.
Local Counsel for: Deere & Co.; New York Telephone Co.; Crum & Forster Insurance Co.; The Travelers Insurance Companies; Caterpillar, Inc.; Otis Elevator.

For full biographical listings, see the Martindale-Hubbell Law Directory

FERRARA, FIORENZA, LARRISON, BARRETT & REITZ, P.C. (AV)

5010 Campuswood Drive, 13057
Telephone: 315-437-7600
Fax: 315-437-7744

Benjamin J. Ferrara
Nicholas J. Fiorenza
David W. Larrison
Dennis T. Barrett
Marc H. Reitz
Henry F. Sobota
Susan T. Johns
Frank W. Miller
Craig M. Atlas

Norman H. Gross
Miles G. Lawlor
Michael L. Dodd
Marina L.C. Bottone
Jennifer G. Speller
Perri Karen Rosenfeld Guido

For full biographical listings, see the Martindale-Hubbell Law Directory

*WHITE PLAINS,** Westchester Co.

JACKSON, LEWIS, SCHNITZLER & KRUPMAN (AV)

One North Broadway, 10601
Telephone: 914-328-0404
Facsimile: 914-328-1882; 914-328-7921
Email: wp@jacksonlewis.com *URL:* http://www.jacksonlewis.com
Other offices located in: Atlanta, Georgia; Boston, Massachusetts; Chicago, Illinois; Dallas, Texas; Greenville, South Carolina; Hartford, Connecticut; Long Island, New York; Los Angeles, California; Miami, Florida; Minneapolis, Minnesota; Morristown, New Jersey; New York, New York; Orlando, Florida; Pittsburgh, Pennsylvania; Sacramento, California; San Francisco, California; Seattle, Washington; Stamford, Connecticut; Washington, D.C.

MEMBERS OF FIRM

Steven D. Baderian
Susan M. Corcoran
Robert Heiferman
Richard D. Landau
E. Johan Lubbe
Joseph M. Martin
Martin F. Payson
Andrew A. Peterson
Thomas P. Piekara
Joseph A. Saccomano, Jr.
Thomas P. Schnitzler
Bruce H. Schwartz
Lewis H. Silverman
Donna R. Tsamis
Patrick L. Vaccaro (Managing Partner, White Plains Office)
Thomas V. Walsh
Margaret Armstrong Weiner

OF COUNSEL

William J. Manning

ASSOCIATES

Margaret R. Bryant (Not admitted in NY)
Anthony J. DiOrio
Loren L. Forrest, Jr. (Not admitted in NY)
Sean G. Hanagan
Cody Jaffe
Susanne Kantor
Jonathan M. Kozak
Thomas P. McDonough
Mark W. Pawlak
Greg A. Riolo

For full biographical listings, see the Martindale-Hubbell Law Directory

KEANE & BEANE, P.C. (AV)

One North Broadway, 10601
Telephone: 914-946-4777
Telecopier: 914-946-6868
Rye, New York Office: 15 Elm Place.
Telephone: 914-967-3936.

Thomas F. Keane, Jr. (1932-1991)
Edward F. Beane
Donna E. Frosco
David Glasser
Lance H. Klein
Ronald A. Longo
Richard L. O'Rourke
Lawrence Praga
Joel H. Sachs
Steven A. Schurkman
Judson K. Siebert

Stephanie L. Burns
Eric L. Gordon
Jonathan Kornblatt
Stephanie M. Orefice
Patrick J. O'Sullivan
Frances M. Pantaleo
Nicholas M. Ward-Willis

OF COUNSEL

Peter A. Borrok
John F. Burkhardt
Eric F. Jensen

LEGAL SUPPORT PERSONNEL

Lenny Amodeo (Legal Assistant)
Barbara S. Durkin (Office Manager)
Sylvia J. Zuckerman (Legal Assistant)

For full biographical listings, see the Martindale-Hubbell Law Directory

NORTH CAROLINA

*CHARLOTTE,** Mecklenburg Co.

FERGUSON, STEIN, WALLAS, ADKINS, GRESHAM & SUMTER, P.A. (AV)

741 Kenilworth Avenue, Suite 300, 28204-2828
Telephone: 704-375-8461
Fax: 704-334-5654
Mailing Address: P.O. Box 36486, 28236-6486
Email: FSWAGS@aol.com
Chapel Hill, North Carolina Office: Suite 2, 312 West Franklin Street.
Telephone: 919-933-5300.
Fax: 919-967-4953.

James E. Ferguson, II
Adam Stein (Resident, Chapel Hill Office)
Jonathan Wallas
Karl Adkins
John W. Gresham
Geraldine Sumter
Henderson Hill
Thomas M. Stern (Resident, Chapel Hill Office)
C. Margaret Errington
Stephen Luke Largess

Rebecca Ann Thorne
James E. Ferguson, III
Corie Diane Pauling
Ann C. Todd

For full biographical listings, see the Martindale-Hubbell Law Directory

HAYNSWORTH BALDWIN JOHNSON & GREAVES LLC (AV)

Federal Plaza Building, 400 West Trade Street, 28202
Telephone: 704-342-2588
Facsimile: 704-342-4379
Greenville, South Carolina Office: 918 South Pleasantburg Drive, P.O. Box 10888.
Telephone: 864-271-7410.
Columbia, South Carolina Office: 1201 Main Street, Suite 1230.
Telephone: 803-799-5858.
Raleigh, North Carolina Office: 3605 Glenwood Avenue, Suite 210, P.O. Box 10035.
Telephone: 919-782-3340.
Greensboro, North Carolina Office: 2709 Henry Street, P.O. Box 13310.
Telephone: 336-375-9737.
Jacksonville, Florida Office: 1301 Riverplace Boulevard, Suite 800, P.O. Box 40593.
Telephone: 904-396-3000.
Tampa, Florida Office: 600 North Westshore Boulevard, Suite 200.
Telephone: 813-289-1247.

Knox L. Haynsworth, Jr. (Not admitted in NC)
James B. Spears, Jr. (Resident)
Robert S. Phifer (Resident)
Stephen D. Dellinger (Resident)
Jacob J. Modla (Resident)
John D. Cole (Resident)

Amy K. Reynolds (Resident)
Jerry H. Walters, Jr. (Resident)
Linda M. Fox (Resident)
Elizabeth J. M. Caldwell (Resident)

(See Next Column)

HAYNSWORTH BALDWIN JOHNSON & GREAVES LLC, *Charlotte—Continued*

OF COUNSEL

James J. Baldwin (Not admitted in NC)

Representative Clients: Belk Stores Services, Inc.; Carolina Panthers; Charlotte Pipe and Foundry Co.; Drexel Heritage Furnishings, Inc.; Harris Teeter; Interstate Johnson Lane; Nucor Steel Corp.; Sears, Roebuck and Co.

For full biographical listings, see the Martindale-Hubbell Law Directory

VAN HOY, REUTLINGER & TAYLOR (AV)

737 East Boulevard, 28203
Telephone: 704-375-6022
Fax: 704-375-6024
URL: http://www.lawyers.com/vrtlawfirm

MEMBERS OF FIRM

Philip M. Van Hoy
Craig A. Reutlinger
Paul B. Taylor

ASSOCIATE

Stephen J. Dunn

Representative Clients: Duke Power Company; AAA Carolina Motor Club; Verbatim Corporation; Pic 'N Pay Stores, Inc.; City of Charlotte, North Carolina; International Paper Co.; New York Life Insurance Co.; Cato Corp.; Sanger Clinic; Revlon Consumer Products.

For full biographical listings, see the Martindale-Hubbell Law Directory

WOMBLE CARLYLE SANDRIDGE & RICE (AV)

A Professional Limited Liability Company
3300 One First Union Center, 301 South College Street, 28202-6025
Telephone: 704-331-4900
Fax: 704-331-4955
Email: lawyers@wcsr.com *URL:* http://www.wcsr.com
Winston-Salem, North Carolina Office: 200 West Second Street, P.O. Drawer 84.
Telephone: 336-721-3600.
Fax: 336-721-3660.
Raleigh, North Carolina Office: 2100 First Union Capitol Center, 150 Fayetteville Street Mall, P.O. Box 831.
Telephone: 919-755-2100.
Fax: 919-755-2150.
Research Triangle Park, North Carolina Office: 2505 Meridian Parkway, Suite 300 (Durham), 27713.
Telephone: 919-484-2300.
Fax: 919-484-2340.
Atlanta, Georgia Office: One Atlantic Center, 1201 West Peachtree Street, Suite 3500.
Telephone: 404-872-7000.
Fax: 404-888-7490.
Other Atlanta, Georgia Office: Suite 404, 2296 Henderson Mill Road, N.E.
Telephone: 770-492-9030.
Fax: 770-492-9609.
Washington, D.C. Office: 1120 Nineteenth Street, N.W., Eighth Floor.
Telephone: 202-857-4400.
Fax: 202-467-6910.
Greenville, South Carolina Office: 15 South Main Street, Suite 601, P.O. Box 10208.
Telephone: 864-255-5400.
Fax: 864-255-5440.

RESIDENT MEMBERS

Jim D. Cooley
Richard L. Rainey

Representative Clients: Childress Klein Properties, Inc.; Food Lion, Inc.; J.A. Jones Construction Co.; Parkdale Mills, Inc.; Pillowtex; Duke Power Co.; Bowles Hollowell Conner & Co.; ALLTEL Carolina, Inc.; Belk Store Services, Inc.; Philip Holzmann A.G.

For Complete List of Firm Personnel, See General Section

For full biographical listings, see the Martindale-Hubbell Law Directory

*GREENSBORO,** Guilford Co.

HAYNSWORTH BALDWIN JOHNSON & GREAVES LLC (AV)

2709 Henry Street, P.O. Box 13310, 27415
Telephone: 336-375-9737
Facsimile: 336-375-4430
Greenville, South Carolina Office: 918 South Pleasantburg Drive, P.O. Box 10888.
Telephone: 864-271-7410.
Columbia, South Carolina Office: 1201 Main Street, Suite 1230.
Telephone: 803-799-5858.
Raleigh, North Carolina Office: 3605 Glenwood Avenue, Suite 210, P.O. Box 10035.
Telephone: 919-782-3340.
Charlotte, North Carolina Office: 400 West Trade Street.
Telephone: 704-342-2588.
Jacksonville, Florida Office: 1301 Riverplace Boulevard, Suite 800, P.O. Box 40593.
Telephone: 904-396-3000.

(See Next Column)

Tampa, Florida Office: 600 North Westshore Boulevard, Suite 200.
Telephone: 813-289-1247.

Knox L. Haynsworth, Jr. (Not admitted in NC)
James M. Powell (Resident)
Brian M. Freedman (Resident)
Lucretia D. Guia (Resident)
D. Ross Hamilton, Jr. (Resident)
J. Nathan Duggins III (Resident)
Linda B. Rogers (Resident)

OF COUNSEL

James J. Baldwin (Not admitted in NC)

Representative Clients: Coca-Cola Bottling Co. Consolidated; Cone Mills Corp.; Dan River Inc.; GKN Automotive, Inc.; Kmart Corp.; Laboratory Corp of America; LifeStyle Furnishings International; Owens Corning Corp.; Unifi, Inc.; VF Corp.

For full biographical listings, see the Martindale-Hubbell Law Directory

STERN & KLEPFER, L.L.P. (AV)

600 NationsBank Building, P.O. Box 3112, 27402
Telephone: 336-373-1500
Fax: 336-272-8258

Sidney J. Stern, Jr. (1914-1991)
John L. Rendleman (1932-1983)

MEMBERS OF FIRM

Robert O. Klepfer, Jr.
James W. Miles, Jr.
John T. Higgins, Jr.
Brinton D. Wright
William A. Eagles

ASSOCIATES

Melanie H. Rodenbough
Ronda Leigh Lowe
Maureen Breen Gerhardt
Douglas M. Heberle

Representative Clients: Bankers Trust of North Carolina; NationsBank of North Carolina, N.A.; Tannenbaum-Sternberger Foundation; Bennett College; Endura Products, Inc.; Carlyle & Co. Jewelers.

For full biographical listings, see the Martindale-Hubbell Law Directory

*RALEIGH,** Wake Co.

HAYNSWORTH BALDWIN JOHNSON & GREAVES LLC (AV)

3605 Glenwood Avenue, Suite 210, P.O. Box 10035, 27605
Telephone: 919-782-3340
Facsimile: 919-782-3346
Greenville, South Carolina Office: 918 South Pleasantburg Drive, P.O. Box 10888.
Telephone: 864-271-7410.
Columbia, South Carolina Office: 1201 Main Street, Suite 1230.
Telephone: 803-799-5858.
Greensboro, North Carolina Office: 2709 Henry Street, P.O. Box 13310.
Telephone: 336-375-9737.
Charlotte, North Carolina Office: 400 West Trade Street.
Telephone: 704-342-2588.
Jacksonville, Florida Office: 1301 Riverplace Boulevard, Suite 800, P.O. Box 40593.
Telephone: 904-396-3000.
Tampa, Florida Office: 600 North Westshore Boulevard, Suite 200.
Telephone: 813-289-1247.

Knox L. Haynsworth, Jr. (Not admitted in NC)
Bruce A. Petesch (Resident)
Gregory P. McGuire (Resident)
Rodolfo R. Agraz (Resident)

Sarah Helen Berdahl

OF COUNSEL

James J. Baldwin (Not admitted in NC)

Representative Clients: Cone Mills Corp.; Consolidated Diesel Company; Drexel Heritage Furnishings, Inc.; GKN Automotive, Inc.; Harris Teeter, Inc.; Kmart Corporation; Perdue Farms, Inc.

For full biographical listings, see the Martindale-Hubbell Law Directory

MAUPIN TAYLOR & ELLIS, P.A. (AV)

Highwoods Tower One, Suite 500, 3200 Beechleaf Court, P.O. Drawer 19764, 27619
Telephone: 919-981-4000
Telecopier: 919-981-4300
URL: http://www.maupinlaw.com
Research Triangle Park, North Carolina Office: 480 Beta Building, Headquarters Park, Post Office Box 13646, 27709-3646.
Telephone: 919-361-4900.

Robert A. Valois
James C. Dever, III
Frank P. Ward, Jr.
John W. (Jack) Marin
Margie Toy Case
Joel H. Katz
Thomas A. Farr
Laura A. Edgerton
Gretchen W. Ewalt
Joshua M. Krasner
Michael C. Lord
Terence D. Friedman
William P. Barrett
Robert B. Jones, Jr.

(See Next Column)

MAUPIN TAYLOR & ELLIS P.A.—*Continued*

Representative Clients: Ball-Foster Glass Containers Co., L.L.C.; Bandag, Inc.; Blue Cross & Blue Shield of NC; Flour Daniel; Glaxo Wellcome, Inc.; Lenox, Inc.; McDonald's Corp.; Northern Telcom; Reichhold Chemical; Smithfield Foods.

For Complete List of Firm Personnel, See General Section

For full biographical listings, see the Martindale-Hubbell Law Directory

OGLETREE, DEAKINS, NASH, SMOAK & STEWART, P.C. (AV)

4101 Lake Boone Trail, Suite 511, P.O. Box 31608, 27622
Telephone: 919-787-9700
Facsimile: 919-783-9412
Email: Raleigh@odnss.com *URL:* http://www.Ogletreedeakins.com
Atlanta, Georgia Office: 600 Peachtree Street, N.E., Suite 2100.
Telephone: 404-881-1300.
Washington, D.C. Office: Fifth Floor, 2400 N Street, N.W.
Telephone: 202-887-0855.
Winston-Salem, North Carolina Office: 150 South Stratford Road, Suite 350.
Telephone: 336-725-2110.
Houston, Texas Office: One Allen Center, 500 Dallas Street, Suite 3000.
Telephone: 713-655-0855.
Chicago, Illinois Office: Twenty-Fifth Floor, Two First National Plaza, 20 South Clark Street.
Telephone: 312-558-1220.
Nashville, Tennessee Office: SunTrust Center, Suite 800, 424 Church Street.
Telephone: 615-254-1900.
Birmingham, Alabama Office: 1900 SouthTrust Tower, 420 North 20th Street.
Telephone: 205-328-1900.
Greenville, South Carolina Office: The Ogletree Building, 300 North Main Street, P.O. Box 2757.
Telephone: 864-271-1300.
Charleston, South Carolina Office: 134 Meeting Street, Suite 500, P.O. Box 1808.
Telephone: 843-853-1300.
Columbia, South Carolina Office: 1501 Main Street, Suite 600, P.O. Box 11206.
Telephone: 803-252-1300.

L. Gray Geddie, Jr. (Not admitted in NC)
Stuart M. Vaughan, Jr.
John S. Burgin
Guy F. Driver, Jr.
A. Bruce Clarke
Mary Lou Hill
C. Matthew Keen
Michael T. Brittingham (Not admitted in NC)
Brian J. Reilly
Andrew W. Merrills

H. Bernard Tisdale III
Keith E. Coltrain
Robert A. Sar
Marifrances Morrison
John F. Quill
Arthur C. Stone, Jr.

OF COUNSEL

Todd M. Rubin

Representative Clients: Boddie-Noell Enterprises, Inc.; Burlington Industries, Inc.; Duke Energy Corp.; Duke University; General Electric Co.; GlaxoWellcome Inc.; Deere and Company; Northern Telecom Inc.; SAS Institute Inc.; Wachovia Corporation.

For full biographical listings, see the Martindale-Hubbell Law Directory

MARVIN SCHILLER (AV)

Two Hannover Square, Suite 1250, 434 Fayetteville Street Mall, 27601
Telephone: 919-836-8800
Fax: 919-836-8838
URL: http://www.lawyers.com/marvinschiller

For full biographical listings, see the Martindale-Hubbell Law Directory

WOMBLE CARLYLE SANDRIDGE & RICE (AV)

A Professional Limited Liability Company
2100 First Union Capitol Center, 150 Fayetteville Street Mall, P.O. Box 831, 27602
Telephone: 919-755-2100
Fax: 919-755-2150
Email: lawyers@wcsr.com *URL:* http://www.wcsr.com
Charlotte, North Carolina Office: 3300 One First Union Center, 301 South College Street.
Telephone: 704-331-4900.
Fax: 704-331-4955.
Winston-Salem, North Carolina Office: 200 West Second Street, P.O. Drawer 84.
Telephone: 336-721-3600.
Fax: 336-721-3660.
Research Triangle Park, North Carolina Office: 2505 Meridian Parkway, Suite 300 (Durham), 27713.
Telephone: 919-484-2300.
Fax: 919-484-2340.

(See Next Column)

Atlanta, Georgia Office: One Atlantic Center, 1201 West Peachtree Street, Suite 3500.
Telephone: 404-872-7000.
Fax: 404-888-7490.
Other Atlanta, Georgia Office: Suite 404, 2296 Henderson Mill Road, N.E.
Telephone: 770-492-9030.
Fax: 770-492-9609.
Washington, D.C. Office: 1120 Nineteenth Street, N.W., Eighth Floor.
Telephone: 202-857-4400.
Fax: 202-467-6910.
Greenville, South Carolina Office: 15 South Main Street, Suite 601, P.O. Box 10208.
Telephone: 864-255-5400.
Fax: 864-255-5440.

RESIDENT MEMBER

Charles A. Edwards

RESIDENT ASSOCIATES

Richard M. Feathers
Jeffrey M. Hahn
M. Todd Sullivan

Representative Clients: Aetna Casualty and Surety Co., Inc.; ALSCO/AmeriMark Building Products, Inc.; Aoki Corporation America, Inc.; Hackney Brothers, Inc.; Lawyers Mutual Liability Insurance Company of North Carolina; Meredith College; Regency Park Corp.; Wachovia Bank, N.A.

For Complete List of Firm Personnel, See General Section

For full biographical listings, see the Martindale-Hubbell Law Directory

*WINSTON-SALEM,** Forsyth Co.

OGLETREE, DEAKINS, NASH, SMOAK & STEWART, P.C. (AV)

150 South Stratford Road, Suite 350, 27104
Telephone: 336-725-2110
Facsimile: 336-725-2505
Email: WinstonSalem@odnss.com *URL:* http://www.Ogletreedeakins.com
Atlanta, Georgia Office: 600 Peachtree Street, N.E., Suite 2100.
Telephone: 404-881-1300.
Washington, D.C. Office: Fifth Floor, 2400 N Street, N.W.
Telephone: 202-887-0855.
Houston, Texas Office: One Allen Center, 500 Dallas Street, Suite 3000.
Telephone: 713-655-0855.
Chicago, Illinois Office: Twenty-Fifth Floor, Two First National Plaza, 20 South Clark Street.
Telephone: 312-558-1220.
Birmingham, Alabama Office: 1900 SouthTrust Tower, 420 North 20th Street.
Telephone: 205-328-1900.
Nashville, Tennessee Office: SunTrust Center, Suite 800, 424 Church Street.
Telephone: 615-254-1900.
Raleigh, North Carolina Office: 4101 Lake Boone Trail, Suite 511, P.O. Box 31608.
Telephone: 919-787-9700.
Greenville, South Carolina Office: The Ogletree Building, 300 North Main Street, P.O. Box 2757.
Telephone: 864-271-1300.
Charleston, South Carolina Office: 134 Meeting Street, Suite 500, P.O. Box 1808.
Telephone: 843-853-1300.
Columbia, South Carolina Office: 1501 Main Street, Suite 600, P.O. Box 11206.
Telephone: 803-252-1300.

Guy F. Driver, Jr.

Representative Clients: A.T. Williams Oil (WILCO); Antech Diagnostics; Duke University; Elon College; The Home Depot; Kelly Services; Laboratory Corporation of America; Pike Electric, Inc.; Salem Electric; Veterinary Centers of America.

For full biographical listings, see the Martindale-Hubbell Law Directory

WOMBLE CARLYLE SANDRIDGE & RICE (AV)

A Professional Limited Liability Company
200 West Second Street, P.O. Drawer 84, 27102
Telephone: 336-721-3600
Fax: 336-721-3660
Email: lawyers@wcsr.com *URL:* http://www.wcsr.com
Charlotte, North Carolina Office: 3300 One First Union Center, 301 South College Street.
Telephone: 704-331-4900.
Fax: 704-331-4955.
Raleigh, North Carolina Office: 2100 First Union Capitol Center, 150 Fayetteville Street Mall, P.O. Box 831.
Telephone: 919-755-2100.
Fax: 919-755-2150.
Research Triangle Park, North Carolina Office: 2505 Meridian Parkway, Suite 300 (Durham), 27713.
Telephone: 919-484-2300.
Fax: 919-484-2340.

(See Next Column)

WOMBLE CARLYLE SANDRIDGE & RICE, *Winston-Salem—Continued*

Atlanta, Georgia Office: One Atlantic Center, 1201 West Peachtree Street, Suite 3500.
Telephone: 404-872-7000.
Fax: 404-888-7490.
Other Atlanta, Georgia Office: Suite 404, 2296 Henderson Mill Road, N.E.
Telephone: 770-492-9030.
Fax: 770-492-9609.
Washington, D.C. Office: 1120 Nineteenth Street, N.W., Eighth Floor.
Telephone: 202-857-4400.
Fax: 202-467-6910.
Greenville, South Carolina Office: 15 South Main Street, Suite 601, P.O. Box 10208.
Telephone: 864-255-5400.
Fax: 864-255-5440.

RESIDENT MEMBERS

Gusti W. Frankel — David A. Irvin

RESIDENT ASSOCIATE

Lisa M. Drabik (Not admitted in NC)

Representative Clients: Brad Ragan, Inc.; Brenner Companies, Inc.; Food Lion, Inc.; Hanes Companies, Inc.; North Carolina Baptist Hospitals, Inc.; R.J. Reynolds Tobacco Company; Thomasville Furniture Industries, Inc.; Wachovia Bank of North Carolina, National Association; Wake Forest University.

For Complete List of Firm Personnel, See General Section

For full biographical listings, see the Martindale-Hubbell Law Directory

NORTH DAKOTA

*BISMARCK,** Burleigh Co.

PEARCE AND DURICK, PLLP (AV)

314 East Thayer Avenue, P.O. Box 400, 58502
Telephone: 701-223-2890
Fax: 701-223-7865
Email: law.office@pearce-durick.com *URL:* http://www.pearce-durick.com

MEMBERS OF FIRM

Gary R. Thune — David E. Reich

ASSOCIATE

Jonathan P. Sanstead

Representative Clients: General Motors Corp.; Kensington Management Group; North Dakota School Boards Assn.; Royal Insurance Co.

For Complete List of Firm Personnel, See General Section

For full biographical listings, see the Martindale-Hubbell Law Directory

*FARGO,** Cass Co.

NILLES, HANSEN & DAVIES, LTD. (AV)

1800 Radisson Tower, P.O. Box 2626, 58108
Telephone: 701-237-5544
Facsimile: 701-280-0762
Williston, North Dakota Office: Energy Resource Building, 504 East Broadway, Suite 101, P.O. Box 1525.
Telephone: 701-572-5544.
Fax: 701-572-5561.

Richard Henderson — Douglas W. Gigler

Representative Clients: Altru Health Systems; Red River Valley and Western Railroad; Cass Clay Creamery, Inc.; Maintenance Engineering; The Village Family Service Center.

For Complete List of Firm Personnel, See General Section

For full biographical listings, see the Martindale-Hubbell Law Directory

VOGEL, WEIR, BYE, HUNKE & MCCORMICK, LTD. (AV)

502 First Avenue North, P.O. Box 1389, 58107
Telephone: 701-237-6983
Facsimile: 701-237-0847
Email: vogellaw@vogellaw.com *URL:* http://www.vogellaw.com

Jerilynn Brantner Adams — Lisa Kay Edison-Smith

Representative Clients: Associated General Contractors of North Dakota; Blue Shield of North Dakota; Cass County Electric Cooperative, Inc.; Clark Equipment Co.; Forum Communications Company; Merit Care Medical Group; Northern Improvement Co.; Dakota Clinic Ltd.; United Parcel Service; Gateway Chevrolet, Inc.

For Complete List of Firm Personnel, See General Section

For full biographical listings, see the Martindale-Hubbell Law Directory

OHIO

*AKRON,** Summit Co.

FORTNEY & KLINGSHIRN (AV)

100 Commonwealth Square, 300 North Cleveland-Massillon Road, 44333-2484
Telephone: 330-665-5445
Telefax: 330-665-5446
URL: http://www.fklaborlaw.com

Michael L. Fortney — Neil E. Klingshirn

For full biographical listings, see the Martindale-Hubbell Law Directory

WHALEN & COMPTON A LEGAL PROFESSIONAL ASSOCIATION (AV)

565 Wolf Ledges Parkway, P.O. Box 2020, 44309-2020
Telephone: 330-376-1112; 1-800-376-1112 in Ohio
Telecopier: 330-376-3200

Dennis M. Whalen — G. Frederick Compton, Jr.
R. Brent Minney

Elizabeth Grooms Taylor — Craig A. Robinson
Helen S. Carroll

References: Bank One Akron.

For full biographical listings, see the Martindale-Hubbell Law Directory

ASHTABULA, Ashtabula Co.

WARREN AND YOUNG PLL (AV)

134 West 46th Street, P.O. Box 2300, 44005-2300
Telephone: 440-997-6175
Facsimile: 440-992-9114
URL: http://www.warrenyoung.com

Carl F. Muller

For Complete List of Firm Personnel, See General Section

For full biographical listings, see the Martindale-Hubbell Law Directory

*CANTON,** Stark Co.

BLACK, MCCUSKEY, SOUERS & ARBAUGH A LEGAL PROFESSIONAL ASSOCIATION (AV)

1000 United Bank Plaza, 220 Market Avenue South, 44702
Telephone: 330-456-8341; 877-656-8341
Telecopier: 330-456-5756
Email: info@bmsa.com *URL:* http://www.bmsa.com
Dover Office: 130 West Third Street, P.O. Box 2330, 44622.
Telephone: 330-364-6553; 877-564-6553.
Fax: 330-364-2739.

Ronald K. Bennington
Charles J. Tyburski
Anthony E. Efremoff
Robert I. Friedman
Arnold R. Shifman
Victor R. Marsh
Daniel M. Jonas
Randolph L. Snow (Managing Director)
Stephen D. Thompson
Terrence P. Kessler
James R. Strawn
Joel K. Dayton
Scott P. Sandrock
Gust Callas
Bruce M. Soares
James P. Kamerer
Karen S. Reiland
Richard D. Dodez
Mary E. Randall
John J. Rambacher
Thomas W. Connors
Terrence L. Seeberger
Robert E. Soles, Jr.
Tod T. Morrow
Francis G. Centrone
David M. Hanhart (Resident, Dover Office)
C. Jason Deeds (Resident, Dover Office)
Erick L. Bauer (Resident, Dover Office)

Brenda S. Schwartz
Jane Murphy Timken
Brian C. Cich
Gregory L. Taddonio
Mark E. Owens
Gordon D. Woolbert, II
Edward C. Redder

OF COUNSEL

John D. Jolliffe — Richard M. Hanhart (Resident, Dover Office)
Gene Barnhart

Representative Clients: The Hoover Co.; Diebold, Inc.; Travelers Insurance Co.

For full biographical listings, see the Martindale-Hubbell Law Directory

*CINCINNATI,** Hamilton Co.

BROWN, CUMMINS & BROWN CO., L.P.A. (AV)

3500 Carew Tower, 441 Vine Street, 45202
Telephone: 513-381-2121
Fax: 513-381-2125

(See Next Column)

BROWN, CUMMINS & BROWN CO. L.P.A.—*Continued*

Robert S. Brown
Lynne Skilken
Kathryn Knue Przywara
Melanie S. Corwin

Counsel for: Paramount's Kings Island; Squeri Food Products; Public Library of Cincinnati and Hamilton County; Maisonette-LaNormandie; United Air Specialists, Inc.; Cincinnati Gardens, Inc.; WYZZ-TV; WSMH-TV; Clarke Detroit Diesel-Allison, Inc.; Ethicon Endo-Surgery, Inc.
Reference: Star Bank of Cincinnati.

For full biographical listings, see the Martindale-Hubbell Law Directory

DENLINGER, ROSENTHAL & GREENBERG A LEGAL PROFESSIONAL ASSOCIATION (AV)

2310 Firstar Tower, 425 Walnut Street, 45202
Telephone: 513-621-3440
Fax: 513-621-4449

Daniel G. Rosenthal
Gary L. Greenberg
John W. Fischer, II
Mark E. Lutz
James A. Mills
Robert M. Lamb

D. Scott Poley
Michael S. Roe
Martin I. Fish

OF COUNSEL

Dean E. Denlinger

Representative Clients: Columbia Sussex Corp.; Duro Bag Manufacturing Co.; Georgia-Pacific Corp.; The City of Kettering; The Kroger Co.; Moraine Materials Co.; The Ohio Masonic Home; Riverwood International Corp.; Spectra Precision, Inc.; The Standard Textile Co.

For full biographical listings, see the Martindale-Hubbell Law Directory

FROST & JACOBS LLP (AV)

2500 PNC Center, 201 East Fifth Street, 45202
Telephone: 513-651-6800
Telecopier: 513-651-6981
URL: http://www.frojac.com
Columbus, Ohio Office: One Columbus, 10 West Broad Street, 43215.
Telephone: 614-464-1211.
Telecopier: 614-464-1737.
Lexington, Kentucky Office: 1100 Vine Center Tower, 333 West Vine Street, 40507.
Telephone: 606-254-1100.
Telecopier: 606-253-2990.
Middletown, Ohio Office: 400 First National Bank Building, 2 North Main Street, 45042.
Telephone: 513-422-2001.
Telecopier: 513-422-3010.
Frankfort, Kentucky Office: 201 W. Main Street, 40601.
Telephone: 502-223-1400.
Telecopier: 502-223-1410.

MEMBERS OF FIRM

James K. L. Lawrence
Robert A. Dimling
John H. Appel
George E. Yund
David T. Croall
Deborah S. Adams
Gregory P. Adams
William C. Strangfeld
William W. Ford, III
Raymond D. Neusch
Hilla M. Zerbst
Douglas Halpert

ASSOCIATES

David A. Skidmore, Jr.
Joanne Wissman Glass
Rachel E. Hansen
Mark J. Chumley
Lorie J. Kravetsky
Katherine Cook Morgan
Matthew P. Gunn
Kenton K. Pettit (Not admitted in OH)
Kevin S. Reeve

COLUMBUS, OHIO OFFICE
MEMBERS OF FIRM

Thomas V. Williams
Jeffrey N. Lindemann

COLUMBUS, OHIO OFFICE
ASSOCIATE

Jeffrey G. Rupert

LEXINGTON, KENTUCKY OFFICE
ASSOCIATE

Catherine S. Wright

LEXINGTON, KENTUCKY OFFICE
OF COUNSEL

Susan C. Sears

MIDDLETOWN, OHIO OFFICE
MEMBERS OF FIRM

Thomas A. Swope
Donald L. Crain

Representative Clients: AK Steel Corporation; Armco Inc.; Arthur Andersen & Co.; Catholic Healthcare Partners; Champion International; Cincinnati Bell Inc.; Cincinnati Machine; Federated Department Stores Inc.; Mercy Regional Healthcare System-Greater Cincinnati; PNC Bank, National Association.

For Complete List of Firm Personnel, See General Section

For full biographical listings, see the Martindale-Hubbell Law Directory

GOODMAN & GOODMAN A LEGAL PROFESSIONAL ASSOCIATION (AV)

123 East Fourth Street, 45202
Telephone: 513-621-1505; 1-800-494-4529
Fax: 513-621-6900
URL: http://www.goodlaw.com

Donald P. Morrisroe

For full biographical listings, see the Martindale-Hubbell Law Directory

KATZ, TELLER, BRANT & HILD A LEGAL PROFESSIONAL ASSOCIATION (AV)

2400 Chemed Center, 255 East Fifth Street, 45202-4724
Telephone: 513-721-4532
Telecopier: 513-721-7120
Email: corp@ktbh.com

Robert A. Pitcairn, Jr.
James F. McCarthy, III
Cynthia Loren Gibson

For Complete List of Firm Personnel, See General Section

For full biographical listings, see the Martindale-Hubbell Law Directory

SIRKIN PINALES MEZIBOV & SCHWARTZ (AV)

920 Fourth & Race Tower, 105 West Fourth Street, 45202-2776
Telephone: 513-721-4876
Telecopier: 513-721-0876
Email: spms@fuse.net

MEMBER OF FIRM

Marc D. Mezibov

Reference: The Huntington National Bank.

For full biographical listings, see the Martindale-Hubbell Law Directory

WAITE, SCHNEIDER, BAYLESS & CHESLEY CO., L.P.A. (AV)

1513 Central Trust Tower, Fourth and Vine Streets, 45202
Telephone: 513-621-0267
Fax: 513-381-2375; 621-0262

Stanley M. Chesley

Thomas F. Rehme
Robert A. Steinberg
Fay E. Stilz
Louise M. Roselle
D. Arthur Rabourn
Jerome L. Skinner
Janet G. Abaray
Paul M. De Marco
Terrence L. Goodman
Colleen M. Hegge
Jane H. Walker
Renée Infante
James F. Keller
Jean M. Geoppinger
Robert Heuck II

For full biographical listings, see the Martindale-Hubbell Law Directory

*CLEVELAND,** Cuyahoga Co.

ARTER & HADDEN LLP (AV)

1100 Huntington Building, 925 Euclid Avenue, 44115-1475
Telephone: 216-696-1100
Fax: 216-696-2645
Telex: 98-5384
URL: http://www.arterhadden.com
In Columbus, Ohio: Suite 1200, One Columbus, 10 West Broad Street. 43215-3422.
Telephone: 614-221-3155.
Fax: 614-221-0479.
In Dayton, Ohio: Kettering Tower, Suite 2310, 40 North Main Street. 45423.
Telephone: 937-223-4701.
Fax: 937-223-0170.
In Washington, D.C.: 1801 K Street, N.W., Suite 400K. 20006-3480.
Telephone: 202-775-7100.
Fax: 202-857-0172.
In Dallas, Texas: 1717 Main Street, Suite 4100. 75201-4605.
Telephone: 214-761-2100.
Fax: 214-741-7139.
In Los Angeles, California: 725 South Figueroa Street, Suite 3400. 90017.
Telephone: 213-430-3000.
Fax: 213-617-9255.
In Irvine, California: Five Park Plaza, Suite 1000, Jamboree Center, 92714.
Telephone: 949-252-7500.
Fax: 949-833-9604.
In Austin, Texas: 100 Congress Avenue, Suite 1800.
Telephone: 512-479-6403.
Fax: 512-469-5505.
In San Antonio, Texas: One Riverwalk Place, 700 North Saint Mary's Street, Suite 800, 78205.
Telephone: 210-805-8497.
Fax: 210-805-8519.

(See Next Column)

ARTER & HADDEN LLP, *Cleveland—Continued*

In San Francisco, California: Two Embarcadero Center, 5th Floor, 94111.
Telephone: 415-617-2100.
Fax: 415-912-3636.
In Sacramento, California: Wells Fargo Center, 400 Capitol Mall, Suite 900, 95814.
Telephone: 916-449-3917.
Fax: 916-449-8249.
In San Diego, California: 402 West Broadway, Sixth Floor, 92102.
Telephone: 619-238-0001.
Fax: 619-238-8333.
In Woodland Hills, California: 5959 Topanga Canyon Boulevard, Suite 244, 91367.
Telephone: 818-712-0036.
Fax: 818-346-6502.

MEMBERS OF FIRM

John B. Lewis   Gregory V. Mersol

RETIRED PARTNER

Joseph A. Rotolo

ASSOCIATES

Thomas J. Piatak   David S. Winston

For Complete List of Firm Personnel, See General Section

For full biographical listings, see the Martindale-Hubbell Law Directory

BAKER & HOSTETLER LLP (AV)

3200 National City Center, 1900 East Ninth Street, 44114-3485
Telephone: 216-621-0200
Telecopier: 216-696-0740
TWX: 810 421 8375
RCA Telex: 215032
To contact an attorney on the Internet use first initial and surname followed by @baker-hostetler.com
URL: http://www.bakerlaw.com
In Cincinnati, Ohio: 312 Walnut Street, Suite 2650.
Telephone: 513-929-3400.
In Columbus, Ohio: Capitol Square, Suite 2100, 65 East State Street.
Telephone: 614-228-1541.
In Denver, Colorado: 303 East 17th Avenue, Suite 1100.
Telephone: 303-861-0600.
In Houston, Texas: 1000 Louisiana, Suite 2000.
Telephone: 713-751-1600.
In Beverly Hills, California: 9150 Wilshire Boulevard, Suite 205.
Telephone: 310-385-7500.
In Long Beach, California: 300 Oceangate, Suite 620.
Telephone: 562-432-2827.
In Los Angeles, California: 600 Wilshire Boulevard.
Telephone: 213-624-2400.
In Orlando, Florida: SunBank Center, Suite 2300, 200 South Orange Avenue.
Telephone: 407-649-4000.
In Washington, D.C.: Washington Square, Suite 1100, 1050 Connecticut Avenue, N.W.
Telephone: 202-861-1500.

PARTNERS

Elliot Stephen Azoff   W. James Ollinger
John H. M. Fenix   Robert C. Petrulis
Paula L. Friedman   Charles T. Price
Tom A. King   Thomas M. Seger
Earl M. Leiken   Victor Strimbu, Jr.
Richard H. Leukart, II   John H. Wilharm, Jr.
John A. Zangerle

RETIRED PARTNERS

William L. Calfee   John F. Novatney, Jr.

For Complete List of Firm Personnel, See General Section

For full biographical listings, see the Martindale-Hubbell Law Directory

CHATTMAN, GAINES & STERN (AV)

1400 Renaissance Center, 1350 Euclid Avenue, 44115-1817
Telephone: 216-781-1700; 800-321-1700
Telecopier: 216-781-1972
Lorain, Ohio Office: 5300 Baumhart Road.
Telephone: 216-282-4598.
Fax: 216-960-1298.

Gerald B. Chattman   Douglas J. Paul
Harold S. Stern   Neal E. Shapero
Lawrence Friedlander   Loreen M. Robinson

Dale A. Nowak   Leslie Moore Jenny

For full biographical listings, see the Martindale-Hubbell Law Directory

DINN, HOCHMAN AND POTTER, LLC (AV)

5910 Landerbrook Drive, Suite 200 (Mayfield Heights), 44124
Telephone: 440-446-1100
Fax: 440-446-1240
Email: dhp@dhplaw.com

(See Next Column)

MEMBERS OF FIRM

Irwin J. Dinn   Steven B. Potter
David B. Hochman   Gregg S. Levy

ASSOCIATES

Robert R. Lucarelli   Beth Dworken Krasnow
Thomas A. Barni   Shawn Marie Czuprun
Mitchell I. Cohen

COUNSEL

Eric R. Hoffman   John A. Podgurski
Linda Rocker

For full biographical listings, see the Martindale-Hubbell Law Directory

DUVIN, CAHN & HUTTON A LEGAL PROFESSIONAL ASSOCIATION (AV)

Erieview Tower, 20th Floor, 1301 East Ninth Street, 44114
Telephone: 216-696-7600
Facsimile: 216-696-2038
Email: attorneys@duvin.com *URL:* http://www.duvinlaw.com
Southfield, Michigan Office: 26211 Central Park Boulevard, Suite 500, 48076.
Telephone: 248-945-1977.
Fax: 248-945-1162.

Robert P. Duvin   Martin T. Wymer
Stephen J. Cahn   Robert M. Wolff
Lee J. Hutton   Steven W. Albert
Marc J. Bloch   Stephen J. Sferra
Andrew C. Meyer   Christine C. Covey
Martin S. List   Richard C. Hubbard, III
Craig M. Brown   Jon M. Dileno
Frank W. Buck   Suellen Oswald
Neal B. Wainblat   David A. Posner
Kenneth B. Stark   Janette McCarthy Louard

Lisa Froimson Mann   Bradley A. Sherman
David W. Neel   Jonathan S. Forman
Kathleen M. Kordeleski   Mark F. Humenik
Michael T. Pearson   Robert C. Pivonka
Kenneth D. Schwartz   Fredrick W Englehart
Brett S. Krantz   Jonathan T. Hyman
Barry Y. Freeman   Latha M. Srinivasan
Shannon K. Patton

OF COUNSEL

Mark V. Webber

Representative Clients: Ameritech; City of Cleveland; Cleveland-Akron-Canton Supermarket Industry; The Scott-Fetzer Co.; Forest City Enterprises, Inc.; Electronic Data Systems; The Cleveland Clinic; Progressive Insurance Companies; LTV Steel; Lincoln Electric.

For full biographical listings, see the Martindale-Hubbell Law Directory

BERNARD S. GOLDFARB (AV)

55 Public Square, Suite 1500, 44113
Telephone: 216-696-0606
Fax: 216-696-0732
Email: resconet@multiverse.com

For full biographical listings, see the Martindale-Hubbell Law Directory

JANIK & FORBES (AV)

Building Two, 8223 Brecksville Road, 44141-1371
Telephone: 440-838-7600
Fax: 440-838-7601

MEMBERS OF FIRM

Steven G. Janik   Steven Forbes

For Complete List of Firm Personnel, See General Section

For full biographical listings, see the Martindale-Hubbell Law Directory

JOHNSON AND ANGELO (AV)

1001 Lakeside Avenue, Suite 1700, 44114
Telephone: 216-696-5222
Fax: 216-696-5288

MEMBERS OF FIRM

Gary C. Johnson   Michael J. Angelo

ASSOCIATES

James A. Budzik   Gina A. Kuhlman
Thomas L. Colaluca   William F. Schmitz
Jack P. DeSario   Jeffrey C. Miller
Jack L. Petronelli   Amy L. Phillips

For full biographical listings, see the Martindale-Hubbell Law Directory

Cleveland—Continued

JONES, DAY, REAVIS & POGUE (AV)

North Point, 901 Lakeside Avenue, 44114
Telephone: 216-586-3939
Telecopier: 216-579-0212
Email: counsel@jonesday.com *URL:* http://www.jonesday.com
In Columbus, Ohio: 1900 Huntington Center.
Telephone: 614-469-3939.
Telecopier: 614-461-4198.
In Atlanta, Georgia: 3500 SunTrust Plaza, 303 Peachtree Street.
Telephone: 404-521-3939.
Telecopier: 404-581-8330.
In Brussels, Belgium: Avenue Louise 480, 7th Floor. B-1050 Brussels.
Telephone: 32-2-645-14-11.
Telecopier: 32-2-645-14-45.
In Chicago, Illinois: 77 West Wacker.
Telephone: 312-782-3939.
Telecopier: 312-782-8585.
In Dallas, Texas: 2727 North Harwood Street.
Telephone: 214-220-3939.
Telecopier: 214-969-5100.
In Frankfurt, Germany: Hochhaus am Park, Grüneburgweg 102, 60323 Frankfurt am Main.
Telephone: 49-69-9726-3939.
Telecopier: 49-69-9726-3993.
In Geneva, Switzerland: 20, rue de Candolle.
Telephone: 41-22-320-2339.
Telecopier: 41-22-320-1232.
In Hong Kong, China: 29th Floor, Entertainment Building, 30 Queen's Road Central.
Telephone: 852-2526-6895.
Telecopier: 852-2868-5871 or 852-2868-5699.
In Irvine, California: 5 Park Plaza, Suite 1100.
Telephone: 949-851-3939.
Telecopier: 949-553-7539.
In London, England: Bucklersbury House, 3 Queen Victoria Street.
Telephone: 44-171-236-3939.
Telecopier: 44-171-236-1113.
In Los Angeles, California: 555 West Fifth Street, Suite 4600.
Telephone: 213-489-3939.
Telecopier: 213-243-2539.
In New Delhi, India (Associate Office): Pathak & Associates (an associate firm of Jones, Day, Reavis & Pogue), 1st Floor, Dr. Gopal Das Bhaven, 28 Barakhamba Road.
Telephone: 91-11-373-8793; 91-11-335-7345.
Telecopier: 91-11-335-3761.
In New York, N.Y.: 599 Lexington Avenue.
Telephone: 212-326-3939.
Telecopier: 212-755-7306.
In Paris, France: 120, rue du Faubourg Saint-Honoré.
Telephone: 33-1-56-59-39-39.
Telecopier: 33-1-56-59-39-38
In Pittsburgh, Pennsylvania: 500 Grant Street, 31st Floor.
Telephone: 412-391-3939.
Telecopier: 412-394-7959.
In Riyadh, Saudi Arabia: The International Law Firm (In Association with Jones, Day, Reavis & Pogue), Sulaymaniyah, Prince Mishari IBN, Abdulaziz Street, P.O. Box 22166.
Telephone: (966-1) 462-8866.
Telecopier: (966-1) 462-9001.
In Shanghai, China: 2805 Kerry Centre, 1515 Nanjing Road West.
Telephone: 86-21-5298-6568.
Telecopier: 86-21-5298-6569.
In Sydney, Australia: Governor Phillip Tower, Level 38, 1 Farrer Place.
Telephone: 61-2-9210-6921.
Telecopier: 61-2-9210-6926.
In Taipei, Taiwan: 8th Floor, Tun Hwa South Road, Section 2.
Telephone: (886-2) 2704-6808.
Telecopier: (886-2) 2704-6791.
In Tokyo, Japan: Toranomon MT Building, 4th Floor, 10-3, Toranomon 3-Chome, Minato-ku, Tokyo 105, Japan.
Telephone: 81-3-3433-3939.
Telecopier: 81-3-5401-2725.
In Washington, D.C.: 51 Louisiana Avenue, N.W.
Telephone: 202-879-3939.
Telecopier: 202-626-1700.

MEMBER OF FIRM IN CLEVELAND

James A. Rydzel

For Complete List of Firm Personnel, See General Section

For full biographical listings, see the Martindale-Hubbell Law Directory

---

KELLEY, MCCANN & LIVINGSTONE, LLP (AV)

3500 BP Tower, 200 Public Square, 44114-2302
Telephone: 216-241-3141
Fax: 216-241-3707
Email: Attorneys@kmlegal.com

MEMBERS OF FIRM

Donna M. Flammang
Mark J. Valponi
Mary Grace Balazs
David H. Wallace
Peter M. Poulos

(See Next Column)

ASSOCIATES

Corinne Katz Moore
Colleen G. Treml
Laurie H. Goetz
Gregory J. O'Brien
Andrew Agati

For Complete List of Firm Personnel, See General Section

For full biographical listings, see the Martindale-Hubbell Law Directory

---

ROSS, BRITTAIN & SCHONBERG CO., L.P.A. (AV)

6000 Freedom Square Drive, Suite 540, 44131
Telephone: 216-447-1551
Telecopier: 216-447-1554
URL: http://www.rbslaw.com

Alan G. Ross
Brian K. Brittain
Evelyn P. Schonberg
Richard E. Walters

Brian A. Paton
David P. Pavlik
David T. Andrews
Jennifer A. Bennett
Karen C. Cecere
Steven R. Yoo
Fred Seleman
Patrick J. Harrington
Thomas J. Stefanik, Jr.

LEGAL SUPPORT PERSONNEL

PARALEGALS

Renee M. Mezera
Kelly M. Shaffer-Fraatz
Arlene M. Stanek
Janice M. Michaels
Cishma Haines
Buffy L. Hathaway
Christine H. Grenig
Erin L. DiRocco
Lori A. Adger
Nicole Bukovian

For full biographical listings, see the Martindale-Hubbell Law Directory

---

SEELEY, SAVIDGE AND EBERT A LEGAL PROFESSIONAL ASSOCIATION (AV)

800 Bank One Center, 600 Superior Avenue, East, 44114-2655
Telephone: 216-566-8200
Fax-Telecopier: 216-566-0213
URL: http://www.sse-law.com

Keith A. Savidge
Gary A. Ebert

Andrew D. Bemer
Matthew K. Seeley
Michael E. Stinn

Reference: KeyBank.

For Complete List of Firm Personnel, See General Section

For full biographical listings, see the Martindale-Hubbell Law Directory

---

TIMOTHY A. SHIMKO & ASSOCIATES A LEGAL PROFESSIONAL ASSOCIATION (AV)

2010 Huntington Building, 925 Euclid Avenue, 44115
Telephone: 216-241-8300
Fax: 216-241-2702
Email: taslaw@ix.netcom.com *URL:* http://www.netcom.com/~taslaw

Timothy A. Shimko

Frank E. Piscitelli, Jr.

Reference: National City Bank, Cleveland.

For full biographical listings, see the Martindale-Hubbell Law Directory

---

SPIETH, BELL, MCCURDY & NEWELL CO., L.P.A. (AV)

2000 Huntington Building, 925 Euclid Avenue, 44115-1496
Telephone: 216-696-4700
Fax: 216-696-2706
Email: law@spiethbell.com

Glen O. Smith, Jr.
Stanley Dan Pace
Bruce G. Hearey
Dianne Foley Hearey
Wade M. Fricke

Jennifer Cook Jontz
Jennifer Welfley Nohra

Representative Clients: American Greetings Corp.; Cleveland Cavaliers; Nationwide Advertising Services, Inc.; Independent Steel Co.; Baldwin Wallace College; The Tool-Die Engineering Co.
Representative Labor Relations Clients (Management Only): Parker Hannifin Corp.; Brush Wellman Co.; Elsag Bailey; M.A. Hanna Co.

For Complete List of Firm Personnel, See General Section

For full biographical listings, see the Martindale-Hubbell Law Directory

Cleveland—Continued

ULMER & BERNE LLP (AV)

Ninth Floor, Bond Court Building, 1300 East Ninth Street, 44114-1583
Telephone: 216-621-8400
FAX: 216-621-7488
Email: infocleveland@ulmer.com
Email: infocolumbus@ulmer.com *URL:* http://www.ulmer.com/
Columbus, Ohio Office: 88 East Broad Street, Suite 1980.
Telephone: 614-228-8400.
FAX: 614-228-8561.

MEMBERS OF FIRM

Thomas H. Barnard
Barton A. Bixenstine
Ronald H. Isroff
Ronald L. Kahn
Mark D. Katz
Bruce P. Mandel
Stephen A. Markus
Patricia A. Shlonsky
Stephanie E. Trudeau

ATTORNEY IN COLUMBUS, OHIO OFFICE (SEE LISTING)

MEMBER OF FIRM

Thomas L. Rosenberg

For Complete List of Firm Personnel, See General Section

For full biographical listings, see the Martindale-Hubbell Law Directory

VORYS, SATER, SEYMOUR AND PEASE LLP (AV)

2100 One Cleveland Center, 1375 East Ninth Street, 44114
Telephone: 216-479-6100
Telecopier: 216-479-6060
URL: http://www.vssp.com
Columbus, Ohio Office: 52 East Gay Street, P.O. Box 1008, 43216-1008.
Telephone: 614-464-6400.
Telex: 241348.
Telecopier: 614-464-6350.
Cincinnati, Ohio Office: Suite 2100, 221 East Fourth Street, P.O. Box 0236, 45201-0236.
Telephone: 513-723-4000.
Telecopier: 513-723-4056.
Washington, D.C. Office: Suite 1111, 1828 L Street, N.W., 20036-5104.
Telephone: 202-467-8800.
Telex: 440693.
Telecopier: 202-467-8900.
Alexandria, Virginia Office: 277 South Washington Street, Suite 310, 22314.
Telephone: 703-549-4282.
Facsimile: 703-549-4492.

MEMBERS OF FIRM

F. Daniel Balmert (Resident)
John W. Read
Drew T. Parobek
Anthony J. O'Malley
David J. Tocco

RESIDENT ASSOCIATES

Julie M. Larson
Jerome C. Webbs
K. Ellen Toth
Margaret Dodane Everett
Bruce P. Batista
Amanda Martinsek
Lisa Babish Forbes
Marcel C. Duhamel
Anthony O. Calabrese, III
Kenneth A. Stump

COUNSEL

Karen A. Seawall
John M. Saganich
Joshua S. Berger

For full biographical listings, see the Martindale-Hubbell Law Directory

WALTER & HAVERFIELD, P.L.L. (AV)

1300 Terminal Tower, 44113-2253
Telephone: 216-781-1212
Telecopier: 216-575-0911
Email: law@walterhav.com *URL:* http://www.walterhav.com
Columbus, Ohio Office: 88 East Broad Street.
Telephone: 614-898-1096.

MANAGING PARTNER

Michael T. McMenamin

MEMBERS OF FIRM

Nancy A. Noall
Jonathan D. Greenberg
R. Todd Hunt

ASSOCIATES

Barbara Rhodes Marburger
Patricia F. Weisberg
Randal G. Ammons
Katherine A. Friedell
Susan M. Zidek
Vincent L. Cheverine
Darrell A. Clay

Representative Clients: Andrews Moving & Storage Company; Allen Medical Systems, Inc.; Beverly Enterprises, Inc.; Cooper Tire & Rubber Co.; Dairy Mart Convenience Stores Inc.; The Keebler Company; Industrial Security Service, Inc.; Phoenix Insurance Group; Vantage Financial Group, Inc.; Multi Care, Inc.

For Complete List of Firm Personnel, See General Section

For full biographical listings, see the Martindale-Hubbell Law Directory

*COLUMBUS,** Franklin Co.

BAKER & HOSTETLER LLP (AV)

Capitol Square, Suite 2100, 65 East State Street, 43215-4260
Telephone: 614-228-1541
Telecopier: 614-462-2616
To contact an attorney on the Internet use first initial and surname followed by @baker-hostetler.com
URL: http://www.bakerlaw.com
In Cleveland, Ohio: 3200 National City Center, 1900 East Ninth Street.
Telephone: 216-621-0200.
In Cincinnati, Ohio: 312 Walnut Street, Suite 2650.
Telephone: 513-929-3400.
In Denver, Colorado: 303 East 17th Avenue, Suite 1100.
Telephone: 303-861-0600.
In Houston, Texas: 1000 Louisiana, Suite 2000.
Telephone: 713-751-1600.
In Beverly Hills, California: 9150 Wilshire Boulevard, Suite 205.
Telephone: 310-385-7500.
In Long Beach, California: 300 Oceangate, Suite 620.
Telephone: 562-432-2827.
In Los Angeles, California: 600 Wilshire Boulevard.
Telephone: 213-624-2400.
In Orlando, Florida: SunBank Center, Suite 2300, 200 South Orange Avenue.
Telephone: 407-649-4000.
In Washington, D. C.: Washington Square, Suite 1100, 1050 Connecticut Avenue, N.W.
Telephone: 202-861-1500.

PARTNERS

M.J. Asensio, III
R. Christopher Doyle
Ellen J. Garling
Ronald G. Linville
David M. Selcer

For Complete List of Firm Personnel, See General Section

For full biographical listings, see the Martindale-Hubbell Law Directory

BRICKER & ECKLER LLP (AV)

100 South Third Street, 43215-4291
Telephone: 614-227-2300
Telecopy: 614-227-2390
Email: info@be.bricker.com *URL:* http://www.bricker.com

Jerry E. Nathan
Donald R. Keller
Charles D. Smith
Betsy A. Swift

James G. Petrie
Bobbie S. Sprader

Representative Clients: Nationwide Insurance Companies; City of Columbus, Ohio; OHA: The Association for Hospitals and Health Systems; YSK Corp.; Weyerhauser Paper Co.; Laidlaw Transit, Inc.; Kraft General Foods, Inc.; National Federation of Independent Business (Ohio); Mill's Pride, Inc.

For Complete List of Firm Personnel, See General Section

For full biographical listings, see the Martindale-Hubbell Law Directory

JONES, DAY, REAVIS & POGUE (AV)

1900 Huntington Center, 43215
Telephone: 614-469-3939
Telecopier: 614-461-4198
Email: counsel@jonesday.com *URL:* http://www.jonesday.com
In Cleveland, Ohio: North Point, 901 Lakeside Avenue.
Telephone: 216-586-3939.
Telecopier: 216-579-0212.
In Atlanta, Georgia: 3500 SunTrust Plaza, 303 Peachtree Street.
Telephone: 404-521-3939.
Telecopier: 404-581-8330.
In Brussels, Belgium: Avenue Louise 480, 7th Floor, B-1050 Brussels.
Telephone: 32-2-645-14-11.
Telecopier: 32-2-645-14-45.
In Chicago, Illinois: 77 West Wacker.
Telephone: 312-782-3939.
Telecopier: 312-782-8585.
In Dallas, Texas: 2727 North Harwood Street.
Telephone: 214-220-3939.
Telecopier: 214-969-5100.
In Frankfurt, Germany: Hochhaus am Park, Grüneburgweg 102, 60323 Frankfurt am Main.
Telephone: 49-69-9726-3939.
Telecopier: 49-69-9726-3993.
In Geneva, Switzerland: 20, rue de Candolle.
Telephone: 41-22-320-2339.
Telecopier: 41-22-320-1232.
In Hong Kong: 29th Floor, Entertainment Building, 30 Queen's Road Central.
Telephone: 852-2526-6895.
Telecopier: 852-2868-5871 or 852-2868-5699.
In Irvine, California: 5 Park Plaza, Suite 1100.
Telephone: 949-851-3939.
Telecopier: 949-553-7539.

(See Next Column)

JONES, DAY, REAVIS & POGUE—*Continued*

In London, England: Bucklersbury House, 3 Queen Victoria Street.
Telephone: 44-171-236-3939.
Telecopier: 44-171-236-1113.
In Los Angeles, California: 555 West Fifth Street, Suite 4600.
Telephone: 213-489-3939.
Telecopier: 213-243-2539.
In New Delhi, India (Associate Office): Pathak & Associates (an associate firm of Jones, Day, Reavis & Pogue), 1st Floor, Dr. Gopal Das Bhaven, 28 Barakhamba Road.
Telephone: 91-11-373-8793; 91-11-335-7345.
Telecopier: 91-11-335-3761.
In New York, New York: 599 Lexington Avenue.
Telephone: 212-326-3939.
Telecopier: 212-755-7306.
In Paris, France: 120, rue du Faubourg Saint-Honoré.
Telephone: 33-1-56-59-39-39.
Telecopier: 33-1-56-59-39-38
In Pittsburgh, Pennsylvania: 500 Grant Street, 31st Floor.
Telephone: 412-391-3939.
Telecopier: 412-394-7959.
In Riyadh, Saudi Arabia: The International Law Firm (In Association with Jones, Day, Reavis & Pogue), Sulaymaniyah, Prince Mishari IBN, Abdulaziz Street, P.O. Box 22166.
Telephone: (966-1) 462-8866.
Telecopier: (966-1) 462-9001.
In Shanghai, China: 2805 Kerry Centre, 1515 Nanjing Road West.
Telephone: 86-21-5298-6568.
Telecopier: 86-21-5298-6569.
In Sydney, Australia: Governor Phillip Tower, Level 38, 1 Farrer Place.
Telephone: 61-2-9210-6921.
Telecopier: 61-2-9210-6926.
In Taipei, Taiwan: 8th Floor, 2 Tun Hwa South Road, Section 2.
Telephone: (886-2) 2704-6808.
Telecopier: (886-2) 2704-6791.
In Tokyo, Japan: Toranomon MT Building, 4th Floor, 10-3, Toranomon 3-Chome, Minato-ku, Tokyo 105, Japan.
Telephone: 81-3-3433-3939.
Telecopier: 81-3-5401-2725.
In Washington, D.C.: 51 Louisiana Avenue, N.W.
Telephone: 202-879-3939.
Telecopier: 202-626-1700.

MEMBER OF FIRM IN COLUMBUS

G. Roger King

For Complete List of Firm Personnel, See General Section

For full biographical listings, see the Martindale-Hubbell Law Directory

KEGLER, BROWN, HILL & RITTER (AV)

Capitol Square Suite 1800, 65 East State Street, 43215-4294
Telephone: 614-462-5400
Telecopier: 614-464-2634
Cable Address: "Law KBHR"
Telex: 246671
Email: info@kbhr.com *URL:* http://www.kbhr.com
Marion, Ohio Office: 250 Executive Drive, Suite B, P.O. Box 919.
Telephone: 614-387-3501.
Facsimile: 614-387-3630.

Lawrence F. Feheley
Ronald L. Mason
Timothy T. Tullis

COUNSEL

Joseph M. Millious (Retired)

Thomas M. L. Metzger

Representative Clients: Associated Builders & Contractors, Inc.; Borden, Inc.; Columbus Metropolitan Housing Authority; Diocese of Columbus; Farmers Insurance Group; The Fishel Co.

For Complete List of Firm Personnel, See General Section

For full biographical listings, see the Martindale-Hubbell Law Directory

PORTER WRIGHT MORRIS & ARTHUR LLP (AV)

41 South High Street, 43215-6194
Telephone: 614-227-2000; (800-533-2794)
Fax: 614-227-2100
Email: cmh@porterwright.com *URL:* http://www.porterwright.com
Cincinnati, Ohio Office: 250 E. Fifth Street, Suite 2200, 45202-4199.
Telephones: 513-381-4700; (800-582-5813).
Fax: 513-421-0991. Internet: cvg@porterwright.com.
Cleveland, Ohio Office: 925 Euclid Avenue, Suite 1700, 44115-1483.
Telephones: 216-443-9000; (800-824-1980).
Fax: 216-443-9011. Internet: cle@porterwright.com.
Dayton, Ohio Office: One Dayton Centre, One South Main Street, Suite 1600, 45402-2028.
Telephones: 937-449-6810; (800-533-4434).
Fax: 937-449-6820. Internet: day@porterwright.com.
Naples, Florida Office: 5801 Pelican Bay Boulevard, Suite 300, 34108-2709.
Telephones: 941-593-2900; (800-876-7962).
Fax: 941-593-2990. Internet: apf@porterwright.com.

(See Next Column)

Washington, D.C. Office: 1667 K Street, N.W., Suite 1100, 20006-1605.
Telephones: 202-778-3000; (800-456-7962).
Fax: 202-778-3063. Internet: dca@porterwright.com.

MEMBERS OF FIRM
COLUMBUS, OHIO OFFICE

Stuart M. Gordon
Kevin E. Griffith
Brian D. Hall
David A. Laing
Alvin J. McKenna
Adele E. O'Conner
Fred G. Pressley, Jr.
Diane C. Reichwein
Christopher C. Russell
Bradd N. Siegel
Mark S. Stemm
John M. Stephen
Michael J. Underwood
Charles C. Warner
Franck G. Wobst

ASSOCIATES
COLUMBUS, OHIO OFFICE

Priscilla Hapner
Barbara A. North
Melissa A. Romig

DAYTON, OHIO OFFICE
RESIDENT MEMBERS

John J. Heron
R. Bruce Snyder

CINCINNATI, OHIO OFFICE
RESIDENT ASSOCIATE

Duane A. Boggs

CLEVELAND, OHIO OFFICE
RESIDENT MEMBER

Paul J. Corrado

For Complete List of Firm Personnel, See General Section

For full biographical listings, see the Martindale-Hubbell Law Directory

SCHOTTENSTEIN, ZOX & DUNN A LEGAL PROFESSIONAL ASSOCIATION (AV)

The Huntington Center, 41 South High Street, 43215
Telephone: 614-462-2700
Telecopier: 614-462-5135
Telex: 650 24 444 365
URL: http://www.szd.com
Cincinnati, Ohio Office: Bank One Towers, 8044 Montgomery Road, Suite 700, 45236-2926.
Telephone: 513-792-2730.
Cleveland, Ohio Office: One Cleveland Center, 1375 East 9th Street, Suite 950.
Telephone: 216-621-6501.
Fax: 216-621-6502.

James M. L. Ferber
Robert D. Weisman
Felix C. Wade
James E. Davidson
Roger L. Sabo
David A. Kadela
Susan Porter
William J. Barath
Corey V. Crognale
Robert M. Robenalt
Patrick A. Devine

Michael A. Womack
Denise L. Hanson
Daniel W. Srsic
Angelique M. Paul
Alison M. Day
Kyle J. Stroh
Michael T. Short

OF COUNSEL

Melissa L. Zox

Reference: Bank One of Columbus, N.A.

For Complete List of Firm Personnel, See General Section

For full biographical listings, see the Martindale-Hubbell Law Directory

VORYS, SATER, SEYMOUR AND PEASE LLP (AV)

52 East Gay Street, P.O. Box 1008, 43216-1008
Telephone: 614-464-6400
Telecopier: 614-464-6350
URL: http://www.vssp.com
Washington, D.C. Office: 1828 L Street, N.W., 20036-5109.
Telephone: 202-467-8800.
Telex: 440693.
Telecopier: 202-467-8900.
Cleveland, Ohio Office: 2100 One Cleveland Center, 1375 East Ninth Street, 44114-1724.
Telephone: 216-479-6100.
Telecopier: 216-479-6060.
Cincinnati, Ohio Office: Suite 2100, 221 East Fourth Street, P.O. Box 0236, 45201-0236.
Telephone: 513-723-4000.
Telecopier: 513-723-4056.
Alexandria, Virginia Office: 277 South Washington St., Suite 310, 22314.
Telephone: 703-549-4282.
Telecopier: 703-549-4492.

(See Next Column)

VORYS, SATER, SEYMOUR AND PEASE LLP, *Columbus—Continued*

MEMBERS OF FIRM

James P. Friedt
Thomas M. Tarpy
G. Ross Bridgman
Robert A. Minor
Jonathan M. Norman
Chris J. North
Jonathan R. Vaughn
Andrew C. Smith
Bradley K. Sinnott

OF COUNSEL

Lester S. Lash

Local Counsel: Anheuser-Busch, Inc.; Bob Evans Farms, Inc.; Borden, Inc.; Eaton Corporation; General Motors Corp.; Pitney Bowes, Inc.; The Limited, Inc.; The Kroger Co.; Ohio Manufacturers Assn.; Ranco Inc.

For Complete List of Firm Personnel, See General Section

For full biographical listings, see the Martindale-Hubbell Law Directory

*DAYTON,** Montgomery Co.

PICKREL, SCHAEFFER & EBELING (AV)

2700 Kettering Tower, 45423-2700
Telephone: 937-223-1130
Facsimile: 937-223-0339
URL: http://www.pselaw.com

Thomas J. Harrington
Janet K. Cooper
David C. Korte

Diane L. Gentile
Michelle Depew Bach
Melissa Green Azallion

Representative Clients: Appleton Paper; E.G. and G.; Archdiocese of Cincinnati; Kettering Board of Education; Sinclair Community College; American Aggregates; Sears, Roebuck and Co.; Midmark Corp.; International Paper Co.

For full biographical listings, see the Martindale-Hubbell Law Directory

SEBALY, SHILLITO & DYER A LEGAL PROFESSIONAL ASSOCIATION (AV)

1300 Courthouse Plaza, NE, P.O. Box 220, 45402-0220
Telephone: 937-222-2500
Telefax: 937-222-6554; 222-8279
URL: http://www.ssdlaw.com

Martin A. Beyer
Daniel A. Brown
James A. Dyer
Gale S. Finley
John R. Glankler
Deborah D. Hunt
Michael P. Moloney
Jon M. Sebaly
Beverly F. Shillito
Jeffrey B. Shulman
Karl R. Ulrich
Lawrence S. Walter
Nita S. Yates

OF COUNSEL

William W. Lambert

Michael A. Booth
Robert E. Goff, Jr.
Leslie Blair Graden
Joseph V. Hatala
J. David Ruffner, II
Kendra F. Thompson

For full biographical listings, see the Martindale-Hubbell Law Directory

DUBLIN, Franklin Co.

BLAUGRUND, HERBERT & MARTIN, INCORPORATED (AV)

5455 Rings Road, Suite 500, 43017-7517
Telephone: 614-764-0681
Fax: 614-764-0774
Email: bhm@bhmlaw.net

David S. Blaugrund
Sharon Cason-Adams
John W. Herbert
John S. Jones
David S. Kessler
Emily J. Lewis
Marc E. Myers
Stephen P. Postalakis

For full biographical listings, see the Martindale-Hubbell Law Directory

*TOLEDO,** Lucas Co.

FRITZ BYERS (AV)

Suite 824 The Spitzer Building, 43604
Telephone: 419-241-8013
Telecopier: 419-241-4215
Email: fbyers@accesstoledo.com

General Counsel for: Blade Communications, Inc.; Toledo Blade Co.; Buckeye Cablevision, Inc.; Pittsburgh Post Gazette.
Reference: Capital Bank N.A.

For full biographical listings, see the Martindale-Hubbell Law Directory

EASTMAN & SMITH LTD. (AV)

One Seagate, Twenty-Fourth Floor, P.O. Box 10032, 43699-0032
Telephone: 419-241-6000
Telecopier: 419-247-1777
Columbus, Ohio Office: 65 East State Street, Suite 1000, 43215.
Telephone: 614-460-3556.
Telecopier: 614-228-5371.

MEMBERS OF FIRM

Patrick J. Johnson
John T. Landwehr
Robert J. Gilmer, Jr.
Thomas A. Dixon
Thomas J. Gibney

ASSOCIATES

Margaret A. Mattimoe
Michael J. Spisak
Katharine M. Thomas
Natacha M. Vincent-Kolcun

Counsel for: Chrysler Corp.; Roadway Express, Inc.; Dana Corp.; A P Parts Co.; City of Wauseon; Fayette Tubular Products, Inc.; Fulton Industries; Ludlow Composites Corp.; Coulton Chemical Co., L.P.

For Complete List of Firm Personnel, See General Section

For full biographical listings, see the Martindale-Hubbell Law Directory

LACKEY, NUSBAUM, HARRIS, RENY & TORZEWSKI A LEGAL PROFESSIONAL ASSOCIATION (AV)

Two Maritime Plaza Third Floor, 43604
Telephone: 419-243-1105
Fax: 419-243-8953

Joan Torzewski

John D. Franklin

References: Fifth Third Bank; Society Bank.

For full biographical listings, see the Martindale-Hubbell Law Directory

ROHRBACHERS, LIGHT, CRON, ZMUDA & TRIMBLE CO., L.P.A. (AV)

National City Bank Building 8th Floor, 405 Madison Avenue, 43604-1243
Telephone: 419-248-2600
Telecopier: 419-248-2614
URL: http://www.rlczt.com
URL: http://www.lawyers.com/rlcztcom

Vernon E. Rohrbacher (1920-1978)
David J. Rohrbacher
Matthew J. Rohrbacher
C. Randolph Light
Nicholas J. Cron
Gene A. Zmuda
J. Mark Trimble

Beverly J. St. Clair
Diane J. Knoblauch
Todd M. Zimmerman

OF COUNSEL

Brent B. Nicholson

LEGAL SUPPORT PERSONNEL

PARALEGAL

Anne E. Scott

For full biographical listings, see the Martindale-Hubbell Law Directory

SCHNORF & SCHNORF CO., L.P.A. A PROFESSIONAL CORPORATION (AV)

1400 National City Bank Building, 405 Madison Avenue, 43604
Telephone: 419-248-2646
Facsimile: 419-248-2889

David M. Schnorf
Christopher F. Parker
Johna M. Bella
Barry F. Hudgin

Representative Clients: American Federation of Teachers, AFL-CIO; Ohio Federation of Teachers, AFL-CIO; Toledo Federation of Teachers, AFL-CIO.

For Complete List of Firm Personnel, See General Section

For full biographical listings, see the Martindale-Hubbell Law Directory

OKLAHOMA

*ANTLERS,** Pushmataha Co.

STAMPER, HADLEY & REASOR (AV)

112 North High Street, P.O. Box 100, 74523
Telephone: 580-298-3153; 580-298-3332
Fax: 580-298-3263
Email: joestamper@yahoo.com
Atoka, Oklahoma Office: 209 East Court, P.O. Box 393.
Telephone: 580-889-3343.
Fax: 580-889-9334.

(See Next Column)

STAMPER, HADLEY & REASOR—*Continued*

MEMBERS OF FIRM

Joe Stamper
Thomas J. Hadley
Shannon Reasor (Resident, Atoka Office)

Representative Clients: Farmers Exchange Bank, Antlers, Okla.; First National Bank at Antlers, Okla.; Town of Antlers; U. S. F. & G. Co.

For full biographical listings, see the Martindale-Hubbell Law Directory

*NORMAN,** Cleveland Co.

CROWE & DUNLEVY (AV)

A Professional Corporation
2500 South McGee, Suite 140, 73072-6705
Telephone: 405-321-7317
Fax: 405-360-4002
Email: marketing@crowedunlevy.com *URL:* http://www.crowedunlevy.com
Oklahoma City, Oklahoma Office: Crowe & Dunlevy, A Professional Corporation, 1800 Mid-America Tower, 20 North Broadway, 73102-8273.
Telephone: 405-235-7700.
Fax: 405-239-6651.
Tulsa, Oklahoma Office: Crowe & Dunlevy, A Professional Corporation, 500 Kennedy Building, 321 South Boston Avenue, 74103-3313.
Telephone: 918-592-9800.
Fax: 918-592-9801.

Mary Robertson

For Complete List of Firm Personnel, See General Section

For full biographical listings, see the Martindale-Hubbell Law Directory

*OKLAHOMA CITY,** Oklahoma Co.

ANDREWS DAVIS LEGG BIXLER MILSTEN & PRICE, A PROFESSIONAL CORPORATION (AV)

500 West Main, Suite 500, 73102
Telephone: 405-272-9241
FAX: 405-235-8786
Email: andrewsdavis@andrewsdavis.com *URL:* http://www.andrewsdavis.com

Shelia Darling Tims
R. Brown Wallace
Craig L. Cline

OF COUNSEL

Carolyn Gregg Hill
William D. Watts

For Complete List of Firm Personnel, See General Section

For full biographical listings, see the Martindale-Hubbell Law Directory

CONNER & WINTERS, A PROFESSIONAL CORPORATION (AV)

One Leadership Square, 211 North Robinson, Suite 1700, 73102-7101
Telephone: 405-272-5711
Facsimile: 405-232-2695
Email: postmaster@cwlaw.com
Tulsa, Oklahoma Office: 3700 First Place Tower, 15 East 5th Street, 74103-4344.
Telephone: 918-586-5711.
Facsimile: 918-586-8982.
Fayetteville, Arkansas Office: Conner & Winters, P.L.L.C., 100 West Center Street, Suite 200, 72701-6081.
Telephone: 501-582-5711.
Facsimile: 501-587-1426.
Washington, D.C. Office: 1050 Seventeenth Street, N.W., Suite 810, 20036-5503.
Telephone: 202-783-5711.
Facsimile: 202-783-5720.

Timothy J. Bomhoff

For Complete List of Firm Personnel, See General Section

For full biographical listings, see the Martindale-Hubbell Law Directory

CROWE & DUNLEVY, A PROFESSIONAL CORPORATION (AV)

1800 Mid-America Tower, 20 North Broadway, 73102-8273
Telephone: 405-235-7700
Fax: 405-239-6651
Email: marketing@crowedunlevy.com *URL:* http://www.crowedunlevy.com
Tulsa, Oklahoma Office: 500 Kennedy Building, 321 South Boston Avenue, 74103-3313.
Telephone: 918-592-9800.
Fax: 918-592-9801.
Norman, Oklahoma Office: Crowe & Dunlevy, 2500 South McGee, Suite 140, 73072-6705.
Telephone: 405-321-7317.
Fax: 405-360-4002.

(See Next Column)

Arlen E. Fielden
Leonard Court
Gayle L. Barrett
Dana M. Tacker

Jeremy Tubb
Courtney K. Warmington

OF COUNSEL

Ruth Gana Okediji (Not admitted in OK)

For Complete List of Firm Personnel, See General Section

For full biographical listings, see the Martindale-Hubbell Law Directory

DAY, EDWARDS, FEDERMAN, PROPESTER & CHRISTENSEN, P.C. (AV)

Suite 2900 Oklahoma Tower, 210 Park Avenue, 73102-5605
Telephone: 405-239-2121
Telecopier: 405-236-1012
URL: http://lawlinks.com/attys/ok/defpc.html

Bruce W. Day
Joe E. Edwards
Rodney J. Heggy

Ricki Valerie Sonders
Gary L. Farnum

Representative Clients: Bobby Joe Cudd Company; CD Warehouse, Inc.; The Frick Co.; Love's Country Stores, Inc.; Merrill Lynch, Pierce, Fenner & Smith, Inc.

For Complete List of Firm Personnel, See General Section

For full biographical listings, see the Martindale-Hubbell Law Directory

HARTZOG CONGER & CASON, A PROFESSIONAL CORPORATION (AV)

1600 Bank of Oklahoma Plaza 201 Robert S. Kerr, 73102
Telephone: 405-235-7000
Facsimile: 405-235-7329

Larry D. Hartzog
J. William Conger
Len Cason
James C. Prince
Steven C. Davis
Joseph P. Hogsett
John D. Robertson
Kurt M. Rupert
Laura Haag McConnell
Linda G. Scoggins
Susan B. Shields
Ryan S. Wilson
Amy J. Sine
Jon H. Trudgeon
Charles E. Geister, III
Phillip G. Whaley
Armand Paliotta

J. Christian Guzzy
Stacey D. Spivey
Melissa Beeson Heindselman
Christin V. Adkins
Byron K. Linkous

OF COUNSEL

Kent F. Frates
Kenneth R. Davis
Alan Newman

For full biographical listings, see the Martindale-Hubbell Law Directory

KERR, IRVINE, RHODES & ABLES, A PROFESSIONAL CORPORATION (AV)

201 Robert S. Kerr Avenue, Suite 600, 73102-4267
Telephone: 405-272-9221
Fax: 405-236-3121
Email: kira201@aol.com

Horace G. Rhodes
J. Angela Ables

Kevin R. Wisner

Representative Clients: Delta Dental Plan of Oklahoma; Life Assurance Co., Inc.; Midlands Management Corp.

For Complete List of Firm Personnel, See General Section

For full biographical listings, see the Martindale-Hubbell Law Directory

MCAFEE & TAFT, A PROFESSIONAL CORPORATION (AV)

Tenth Floor, Two Leadership Square, 73102
Telephone: 405-235-9621
Facsimile: (405) 235-0439 (405) 232-2404
Email: mcafee@ionet.net *URL:* http://www.mcafee-taft.com

Sam R. Fulkerson
Gary C. Pierson
Tony G. Puckett
Mark D. Spencer
Peter T. Van Dyke
Elizabeth Scott Wood

Representative Clients: Bank of Oklahoma, N.A.; Fleming Companies, Inc.; Paine Webber Group, Inc.; Arthur Andersen & Co.; Exxon Corp.; St. Paul Fire & Marine Insurance Co.; Columbia/HCA Healthcare Corp.

For Complete List of Firm Personnel, See General Section

For full biographical listings, see the Martindale-Hubbell Law Directory

Oklahoma City—Continued

McCaffrey & Tawwater (AV)

Suite 1950, One Leadership Square, 211 North Robinson, 73102-7124
Telephone: 405-235-2900
Fax: 405-231-2818
URL: http://www.mccaffreytawwater.com
Other Oklahoma City, Oklahoma Office: 3015 N.W. 59th, 73112.

MEMBERS OF FIRM

George J. McCaffrey
Larry A. Tawwater

ASSOCIATES

Jo Lynn Slama
Loren F. Gibson
Steven R. Davis
Piper E. John
David B. Custar

For full biographical listings, see the Martindale-Hubbell Law Directory

*TULSA,** Tulsa Co.

Boone, Smith, Davis, Hurst & Dickman, A Professional Corporation (AV)

500 Oneok Plaza, 100 West 5th Street, 74103
Telephone: 918-587-0000
Fax: 918-599-9317
URL: http://www.boonesmith.com

Byron V. Boone (1908-1988)
Teresa Meinders Burkett
John A. Burkhardt
Paul J. Cleary
Reuben Davis
J. Jerry Dickman
Monica Goodman
David J. Hyman
William C. Kellough
Donald A. Lepp
Mary Lohrke
Kimberly Lambert Love
Scott R. Rowland
Frederic N. (Nick) Schneider III
Jeffrey R. Schoborg
Stephen Schuller
L. K. Smith
Paul E. Swain III

OF COUNSEL

Edwin S. Hurst
Lloyd G. Minter

Representative Clients: American Airlines; BP Amoco Corp.; Chevron U.S.A., Inc.; Ford Motor Co.; Hillcrest Medical Center; PricewaterhouseCoopers; Phillips Petroleum Co.; The Boeing Company; Sears, Roebuck & Co.; World Publishing Co; Whirlpool Corp.

For full biographical listings, see the Martindale-Hubbell Law Directory

Conner & Winters, A Professional Corporation (AV)

3700 First Place Tower, 15 East 5th Street, 74103-4344
Telephone: 918-586-5711
Fax: 918-586-8982
Email: postmaster@cwlaw.com
Oklahoma City, Oklahoma Office: One Leadership Square, 211 North Robinson, Suite 1700, 73102-7101.
Telephone: 405-272-5711.
Facsimile: 405-232-2695.
Fayetteville, Arkansas Office: Conner & Winters, P.L.L.C., 100 West Center Street, Suite 200, 72701-6081.
Telephone: 501-582-5711.
Facsimile: 501-587-1426.
Washington, D.C. Office: 1050 Seventeenth Street, N.W., Suite 810, 20036-5503.
Telephone: 202-783-5711.
Facsimile: 202-783-5720.

J. Ronald Petrikin
Deirdre O'Neil E. Dexter
David R. Cordell
R. Mark Solano
John A. Bugg
Nancy E. Vaughn

Rebecca Sellers Woodward
Jacalyn W. Peter
Fern Holland

For Complete List of Firm Personnel, See General Section

For full biographical listings, see the Martindale-Hubbell Law Directory

Crowe & Dunlevy, A Professional Corporation (AV)

500 Kennedy Building, 321 South Boston Avenue, 74103-3313
Telephone: 918-592-9800
Fax: 918-592-9801
Email: marketing@crowedunlevy.com *URL:* http://www.crowedunlevy.com
Oklahoma City, Oklahoma Office: 1800 Mid-America Tower, 20 North Broadway, 73102-8273.
Telephone: 405-235-7700.
Fax: 405-239-6651.
Norman, Oklahoma Office: Crowe & Dunlevy, 2500 South McGee, Suite 140, 73072-6705.
Telephone: 405-321-7317.
Fax: 405-360-4002.

(See Next Column)

Craig W. Hoster
Michael J. Gibbens
Madalene A. B. Witterholt
Randall J. Snapp
Victor E. Morgan

Nancy Lynn Roberts

For Complete List of Firm Personnel, See General Section

For full biographical listings, see the Martindale-Hubbell Law Directory

Doerner, Saunders, Daniel & Anderson, L.L.P. (AV)

Suite 500, 320 South Boston Avenue, 74103-3725
Telephone: 918-582-1211
Fax: 918-591-5360
URL: http://www.dsda.com
Oklahoma City, Oklahoma Office: One Leadership Square, Suite 501.
Telephone: 405-319-3500.
Fax: 405-319-3509. URL: http://www.dsda.com.

MEMBERS OF FIRM

Erwin J. Doerner (1897-1980)
Samuel P. Daniel
William C. Anderson
Varley H. Taylor, Jr.
G. Michael Lewis
Lawrence T. Chambers, Jr.
Dallas E. Ferguson
Sam G. Bratton II
Gary M. McDonald
H. Wayne Cooper
Kevin C. Coutant
Richard P. Hix
Lynn Paul Mattson
William F. Riggs
Lewis N. Carter
Linda C. Martin
James Patrick McCann
Richard H. Foster
Charles S. Plumb
Leonard I. Pataki
S. Douglas Dodd
Elise Dunitz Brennan
Jon E. Brightmire
Tom Q. Ferguson
Richard J. Eagleton
Rebecca McCarthy Fowler
Kristen L. Brightmire
Michael C. Redman
Steven K. Metcalf

ASSOCIATES

Shelly L. Dalrymple
Russell W. Kroll
Robert A. Burk
Ronald W. Little
James C. Milton
Harry V. Rouse
Amy L. Osborn
Audra K. Hamilton
Angela M. Knight
James J. Robertson
R. Charles Wilkin

OF COUNSEL

Dickson M. Saunders
William B. Morgan
Kathy R. Neal

ATTORNEY IN OKLAHOMA CITY, OKLAHOMA

Jacque Brawner Lindsay

Gregory Frogge

Representative Clients: Public Service Company of Oklahoma; Kmart Corporation; City of Norman; City of Broken Arrow; City of Moore; City of McAlester.

For full biographical listings, see the Martindale-Hubbell Law Directory

Rhodes, Hieronymus, Jones, Tucker & Gable, P.L.L.C. (AV)

Oneok Plaza, 100 West 5th Street, Suite 400, P.O. Box 21100, 74121-1100
Telephone: 918-582-1173
Fax: 918-592-3390
URL: http://www.rhodesokla.com

MEMBERS OF FIRM

Kevin D. Berry
Jo Anne Deaton
Richard M. Eldridge
E. D. Hieronymus (1908 -1994)
Bert M. Jones
William S. Leach
Michael W. McGivern
William D. Perrine
Mary Quinn-Cooper
Robert P. Redemann
David P. Reid
Chris L. Rhodes, III
Thomas E. Steichen
Catherine C. Taylor
John H. Tucker
Wilson T. White
Harold C. Zuckerman

Ann E. Allison
Steven K. Bunting
Robert P. Coffey, Jr.
J. Christopher Davis
Andrew D. Downing
Dana L. Gish
Kerry R. Lewis
Andrew L. Richardson
Michael F. Smith
Leslie J. Southerland
Kimberly E. West
Keith A. Wilkes

OF COUNSEL

George W. Gable (Retired Partner)
Larry J. Fulton
Kelly M. Greenough

Representative Clients: American International Companies; Bechtel; Chubb Group of Insurance Companies; General Motors Corporation; Merrill, Lynch; Nissan Motor Corporation in U.S.A.; Pfizer, Inc.; Volkswagen of America, Volkswagen, A.G.; Zurich U.S.

For full biographical listings, see the Martindale-Hubbell Law Directory

Tulsa—Continued

STRECKER & ASSOCIATES, P.C. (AV)

15 West 6th Street, Suite 1600, 74119-5410
Telephone: 918-582-1716; 918-582-1734
Fax: 918-582-1780
Email: SandK@juno.com *URL:* http://www.lawyers.com/strecker&associates

David E. Strecker

James E. Erwin

For full biographical listings, see the Martindale-Hubbell Law Directory

LAW OFFICES OF MAYNARD I. UNGERMAN (AV)

Riverbridge Office Park, 1323 East 71st Street, Suite 300, 74136-5043
Telephone: 918-495-0550
Fax: 918-495-0561
Mailing Address: P.O. Box 701917, Tulsa, Oklahoma, 74170-1917

MEMBERS OF FIRM

Irvine E. Ungerman (1908-1980) Maynard I. Ungerman

Stephen J. Greubel

Representative Clients: Tulsa Paint; Norvell-Marcum Company; Tulsa Classroom Teachers Association; Oklahoma Education Association; Born Inc.

For full biographical listings, see the Martindale-Hubbell Law Directory

OREGON

LAKE OSWEGO, Clackamas Co.

WILLIAMS, ZOGRAFOS & PECK, A PROFESSIONAL CORPORATION (AV)

334 Third Street, P.O. Box 547, 97034
Telephone: 503-699-1300
Fax: 503-699-4111
Email: wzpattys@aol.com

Ronald J. Williams
Dean T. Zografos
Kathy A. Peck

Janice L. Holtorf Hirsch
Cynthia Halse Stutsman

For full biographical listings, see the Martindale-Hubbell Law Directory

*PORTLAND,** Multnomah Co.

BARRAN LIEBMAN LLP (AV)

601 SW Second Avenue, 23rd Floor, 97204-3159
Telephone: 503-228-0500
Fax: 503-274-1212
URL: http://www.barran.com

MEMBERS OF FIRM

Nelson D. Atkin II
Paula A. Barran
Robert L. Carey
Edwin A. Harnden
Richard C. Hunt
Richard F. Liebman
Bradley F. Tellam
Maryann Yelnosky

Caroline Marnock Carey
Allyson S. Krueger
Eve L. Logsdon
Kurt Nath Tandan

LEGAL SUPPORT PERSONNEL

Aaron Douglas (Client Services Director)

Representative Clients: Frito-Lay; Intel Corp.; Lloyds of London; Louisiana-Pacific Corporation; Pacific Maritime Association; RR Donnelley; The Oregonian; Tri-Met; United Parcel Service; Xerox Corporation.

For full biographical listings, see the Martindale-Hubbell Law Directory

BULLARD, KORSHOJ, SMITH & JERNSTEDT, A PROFESSIONAL CORPORATION (AV)

Suite 1900, 1000 S.W. Broadway, 97205
Telephone: 503-248-1134
Fax: 503-224-8851

Garry R. Bullard
Jim D. Korshoj (Retired)
Lester V. Smith, Jr.
Kenneth E. Jernstedt
Jonathan T. Harnish
John L. Zenor
David H. Wilson, Jr.
Richard J. Alli, Jr.
Robert J. Lee
Francis T. Barnwell
Alan M. Lee
David J. Riewald
Kathryn M. Hindman
Kenneth E. Bemis
Nancy J. King
Helle Rode
C. Akin Blitz

(See Next Column)

Barbara A. Flug
Kirk S. Peterson
Daniel R. Barnhart
Michael G. McClory
Adam S. Collier

Representative Corporate Labor Clients: Mid-Columbia Medical Center; Nike, Inc.; Portland General Electric Co.; Red Lion Inns; Schnitzer Industries; United Grocers, Inc.; Weyerhaeuser.
Representative Public Labor Clients: Mt. Hood Community College; Port of Portland.

For full biographical listings, see the Martindale-Hubbell Law Directory

CORBETT GORDON & ASSOCIATES, P.C. (AV)

1001 S.W. Fifth Avenue, Suite 1600, 97204
Telephone: 503-242-4262
Fax: 503-242-4263
Email: Gordon@aracnet.com *URL:* Http://www.gordon-law.com

Corbett Gordon

Heidi Guettler
Richard R. Meneghello
Kelliss Ann Collins
Russell S. Collins
Kenneth Piumarta

Representative Clients: Albertsons, Inc.; Taco Bell Corp.; NIKE, Inc.; Denny's, Inc.; Subway Development Corp.; Lenscrafters, Inc.; Advantica Restaurant Group, Inc.; Pameco Corp.

For full biographical listings, see the Martindale-Hubbell Law Directory

KELL, ALTERMAN & RUNSTEIN, LLP (AV)

1001 S.W. Fifth Avenue, Suite 1800, 97204
Telephone: 503-222-3531
Telecopier: 503-227-2980
Email: kell@teleport.com

MEMBERS OF FIRM

Raymond M. Kell (1911-1991)
Clifford B. Alterman (1925-1995)
Ted E. Runstein
Lee Davis Kell
Wayne D. Palmer
Lloyd R. Summers
William D. Dickas
Gary P. Compa
Charles R. Williamson
Mary Ellen Page Farr
Eric Sogge
Thomas J. Matsuda
Thomas R. Rask, III
Nicholas S. Fish

Dana L. Barnes
Cory Larvik
Robert E. Kabacy
Robin M. Runstein

References: Union Bank of California, N.A. (Portland Branch); The Bank of Tokyo-Mitsubishi, Ltd. (Portland Branch); Bank of America (5th S. Main Branch).

For full biographical listings, see the Martindale-Hubbell Law Directory

LANE POWELL SPEARS LUBERSKY LLP (AV)

Limited Liability Partnership composed of Individuals and Professional Service Corporations
601 S.W. Second Avenue, Suite 2100, 97204
Telephone: 503-778-2100
Facsimile: 503-778-2200
Email: information@lanepowell.com *URL:* http://www.lanepowell.com
Other Offices at: Seattle, Washington; Anchorage, Alaska; Olympia and Mount Vernon, Washington; London, England.

MEMBER OF FIRM

John C. Stevason

OF COUNSEL

William F. Lubersky Lewis K. Scott

For Complete List of Firm Personnel, See General Section

For full biographical listings, see the Martindale-Hubbell Law Directory

LINDSAY, HART, NEIL & WEIGLER, LLP (AV)

3400 Wells Fargo Center, 1300 S.W. Fifth Avenue, 97201-5696
Telephone: 503-226-7677
Telecopier: 503-226-7697
Email: LHNW@Europa.com
Washington, D.C. Office: 1201 Pennsylvania Avenue, N.W., Suite 821, 20004.
Telephone: 202-467-8383.
Fax: 202-467-8581.

MEMBERS OF FIRM

Dennis J. Lindsay
Glen P. McClendon
Lisa Rackner

ASSOCIATE

Steven M. Carpenter

Representative Clients: Merchants Exchange of Portland; Portland Grain Exchange; Wanke Cascade, Inc.; Walsh Construction Company; Columbia Grain, Inc.; United Grain Corporation.

(See Next Column)

LINDSAY, HART, NEIL & WEIGLER LLP, *Portland—Continued*

For full biographical listings, see the Martindale-Hubbell Law Directory

MILLER NASH LLP (AV)

A Limited Liability Partnership including Professional Corporations
111 S.W. Fifth Avenue, 97204-3699
Telephone: 503-224-5858
Telex: 364462, Kingmar PTL
Facsimile: 503-224-0155, 503-224-2450
Email: e-mail@millernash.com *URL:* http://www.millernash.com
Seattle, Washington Office: 4400 Two Union Square, 601 Union Street, 98101-2322.
Telephone: 206-622-8484.
Facsimile: 206-622-7485.

PORTLAND, OREGON PARTNERS

Donald A. Burns, P.C.
Donna M. Cameron, P.C.
Brian B. Doherty, P.C.
Louis B. Livingston, P.C.
Maureen R. Sloane, P.C.
Sharon L. Toncray, P.C.

SEATTLE, WASHINGTON PARTNERS

James R. Dickens, P.C.
Francis L. Van Dusen, Jr., P.C.

PORTLAND, OREGON SPECIAL COUNSEL

Robert J. Yanity

PORTLAND, OREGON ASSOCIATES

Craig R. Armstrong
Julia A. DeWitt
Heyke G. Nickerson

SEATTLE, WASHINGTON ASSOCIATES

Susan K. Stahlfeld
Michelle L. Valier

Representative Clients: Willamette Industries, Inc.; Portland Public Schools; Providence Health Systems; Merrill Lynch.

For Complete List of Firm Personnel, See General Section

For full biographical listings, see the Martindale-Hubbell Law Directory

SATHER, BYERLY & HOLLOWAY, LLP (AV)

621 Southwest Morrison Street, Suite 650, 97205
Telephone: 503-225-5858
Fax: 503-721-9272
Email: sbh@teleport.com *URL:* http://www.teleport.com/~sbh/sbh.htm

Deborah L. Sather
Bruce L. Byerly
Ronald C. Holloway
Krishna Balasubramani
Tracy J. White
Constance Lynn Wold

For full biographical listings, see the Martindale-Hubbell Law Directory

PENNSYLVANIA

BLUE BELL, Montgomery Co.

KELLEY & MURPHY (AV)

Union Meeting Corporate Center V, Suite 160 925 Harvest Drive, 19422
Telephone: 215-643-6500
Fax: 215-643-8356
Cable Address: "BIGTIME"
Email: kmlaw@counsel.com

Joseph T. Kelley, Jr.
Patrick G. Murphy
Joseph T. Kelley, III

LEGAL SUPPORT PERSONNEL

Marianne Rowen
Tanja M.Z. Barron

For full biographical listings, see the Martindale-Hubbell Law Directory

ELKINS PARK, Montgomery Co.

MONAGHAN & GOLD, P.C. (AV)

Manor Professional Building, 7837 Old York Road, 19027
Telephone: 215-782-1800
Fax: 215-782-1010
URL: http://www.MNG-LAW.com

Alan S. Gold
John F. X. Monaghan, Jr.

Murray R. Glickman
Tanya M. Sweet
Mitchell K. Brudno
Robert F. Fortin
Sean Robins
Kenneth W. Taylor
Francis D. Hennessy, Jr.

OF COUNSEL

Alan L. Butkovitz
Steven M. Zelitch
Barbara Malett Weitz

(See Next Column)

LEGAL SUPPORT PERSONNEL

Andrew Logan (Paralegal)
Carol Veach (Paralegal)
Janet McCrossen (Registered Nurse)

For full biographical listings, see the Martindale-Hubbell Law Directory

ROTHENBERG SILVERMAN & FURMAN, P.C. (AV)

333 Township Line Road, 19027-2260
Telephone: 215-663-9090
Fax: 215-663-8689
Email: laborlaw@home.com

I. Herbert Rothenberg (1910-1997)
Steven B. Silverman
Marc Furman

Thomas C. Zipfel

LEGAL SUPPORT PERSONNEL

Joseph T. Casey (Contract Administrator)

For full biographical listings, see the Martindale-Hubbell Law Directory

FORT WASHINGTON, Montgomery Co.

DALLER GREENBERG & DIETRICH, LLP (AV)

Valley Green Corporate Center, 7111 Valley Green Road, 19034
Telephone: 215-836-1100
Facsimile: 215-836-2845
URL: http://www.dallergreenberg.com
Haddon Heights, New Jersey Office: 2 White Horse Pike.
Telephone: 856-547-9068.
Facsimile: 856-547-2391.

PARTNERS

Morton F. Daller
Edward A. Greenberg
Gerhard P. Dietrich
Eileen M. Johnson
Dennis R. Callahan

ASSOCIATES

Tracy Canuso Nugent (Resident, Haddon Heights, New Jersey Office)
Catherine N. Walto
Mark S. Kirby
Marie Handrich Kramer
Alison R. Rohmer

For full biographical listings, see the Martindale-Hubbell Law Directory

HANOVER, York Co.

BARLEY, SNYDER, SENFT & COHEN, LLC (AV)

Formerly: Daniel M. Frey & Associates, P.C.
14 Center Square, 17331
Telephone: 717-637-6239
Fax: 717-637-5407
Email: barley@barley.com *URL:* http://www.barley.com
Lancaster, Pennsylvania Office: 126 East King Street.
Telephone: 717-299-5201.
Fax: 717-291-4660.
Harrisburg, Pennsylvania Office: 240 North Third Street.
Telephone: 717-238-8263.
Fax: 717-238-8278.
York, Pennsylvania Office: 100 East Market Street.
Telephone: 717-846-8888.
Fax: 717-843-8492.
Chambersburg, Pennsylvania Office: 247 Lincoln Way East.
Telephone: 717-264-6494.
Fax: 717-264-1662.
Reading, Pennsylvania Office: 501 Washington Street.
Telephone: 610-376-6651.
Fax: 610-376-5243.
Birdsboro, Pennsylvania Office: 115 E. Main Street.
Telephone: 610-582-2735.
Hamburg, Pennsylvania Office: 239 State Street.
Telephone: 610-562-3721.
Oley, Pennsylvania Office: Route 73 and Main Street.
Telephone: 610-987-6350.
Morgantown, Pennsylvania Office: Route 23.
Telephone: 610-286-5958.

MEMBERS OF FIRM

Daniel M. Frey
David R. Keller
Jeffrey D. Lobach
Paul G. Mattaini
Timothy P. Brown
Deborah A. Datte
Michael W. Davis

ASSOCIATES

Craig T. Trebilcock
John L. Senft
Kimberly J. Decker
Andrew T. Kravitz

Representative Clients: Bank of Hanover and Trust Co.; J.A. Myers Building and Development Inc.; Snyders of Hanover; Sheppard Enterprises; D.F. Stauffer Biscuit; Fulton Bank/Fulton Financial Corp.; Summit Health; South Central Community Health.

For Complete List of Firm Personnel, See General Section

For full biographical listings, see the Martindale-Hubbell Law Directory

*HARRISBURG,** Dauphin Co.

BECKLEY & MADDEN (AV)

Cranberry Court, 212 North Third Street, P.O. Box 11998, 17108
Telephone: 717-233-7691
Fax: 717-233-3740
Email: becks@pa.net

MEMBERS OF FIRM

Thomas A. Beckley
John G. Milakovic

ASSOCIATES

Charles O. Beckley, II
Elizabeth S. Beckley
Thomas S. Beckley

For Complete List of Firm Personnel, See General Section

For full biographical listings, see the Martindale-Hubbell Law Directory

JOHNSTON, ARONSON & DIAMOND, A PROFESSIONAL CORPORATION (AV)

150 Corporate Center Drive, Suite 100 (Camp Hill), 17011
Telephone: 717-975-5500
Telecopier: 717-975-5511

Charles W. Johnston
Irwin W. Aronson
James A. Diamond
John T. Kupchinsky

For full biographical listings, see the Martindale-Hubbell Law Directory

KILLIAN & GEPHART, LLP (AV)

218 Pine Street, P.O. Box 886, 17108
Telephone: 717-232-1851
Telecopier: 717-238-0592
Email: kg@killiangephart.com *URL:* http://www.killiangephart.com

MEMBERS OF FIRM

John D. Killian
Thomas W. Scott
Jane Gowen Penny
J. Paul Helvy

ASSOCIATE

Bradley A. Schutjer

Reference: Fulton Bank.

For full biographical listings, see the Martindale-Hubbell Law Directory

MCNEES, WALLACE & NURICK (AV)

100 Pine Street, P.O. Box 1166, 17108-1166
Telephone: 717-232-8000
Fax: 717-237-5300
Email: info@mwn.com *URL:* http://www.mwn.com
Columbus, Ohio Office: 21 East State Street, Suite 1700, 43215.
Telephone: 614-469-8000.
Fax: 614-469-4653.
Washington, D.C. Office: 1200 G Street, N.W., 20005.
Telephone: 202-434-8991.
Fax: 202-434-8707.
Hazleton, Pennsylvania Office: 1 South Church Street, Suite 302, 18201.
Telephone: 570-455-8300.
Fax: 570-455-8390.

MEMBERS OF THE FIRM

Bruce D. Bagley
Stephen R. Kern
Elizabeth A. Maguschak (Resident, Hazleton Office)
Norman I. White

ASSOCIATES

Jennifer LaPorta Baker
Thomas G. Collins
Schaun D. Henry
Brian F. Jackson
Jonathan Landesman
Andrew L. Levy

For Complete List of Firm Personnel, See General Section

For full biographical listings, see the Martindale-Hubbell Law Directory

REED SMITH SHAW & MCCLAY LLP (AV)

213 Market Street, 17101-2132
Telephone: 717-234-5988
FAX: 717-236-3777
Email: rssm@rssm.com *URL:* http://www.rssm.com
Pittsburgh, Pennsylvania Office: 435 Sixth Avenue, 15219-1886.
Telephone: 412-288-3131.
FAX: 412-288-3063.
Washington, D.C. Office: Suite 1100 - East Tower, 1301 K Street, N.W., 20005-3317.
Telephone: 202-414-9200.
FAX: 202-414-9299.
Philadelphia, Pennsylvania Office: 2500 One Liberty Place, 19103-7301.
Telephone: 215-851-8100.
FAX: 215-851-1420.
Princeton, New Jersey Office: 136 Main Street, Suite 250, 08540-5799.
Telephone: 609-987-0050.
FAX: 609-951-0824.

(See Next Column)

New York, N.Y. Office: 375 Park Avenue, 17th Floor, 10152.
Telephone: 212-521-5400.
FAX: 212-521-5450.
Newark, New Jersey Office: The Legal Center, One Riverfront Plaza, First Floor, 07102-5400.
Telephone: 973-621-3200.
FAX: 973-621-3199.
McLean, Virginia Office: Reed Smith Hazel & Thomas LLP, Suite 1100, 8251 Greensboro Drive, 22102-3844.
Telephone: 703-734-4600.
FAX: 703-734-4699.
Falls Church, Virginia Office: Reed Smith Hazel & Thomas, Suite 1400, 3110 Fairview Park Drive, P.O. Box 12001.
Telephone: 703-641-4200.
Fax: 703-641-4340.
Leesburg, Virginia Office: Reed Smith Hazel & Thomas LLP, 44084 Riverside Parkway, Suite 300.
Telephone: 703-729-8500. Metro: 703-478-1992.
Fax: 703-478-8003.
Richmond, Virginia Office: Reed Smith Hazel & Thomas LLP, Suite 600, 411 East Franklin Street, P.O. Box 788.
Telephone: 804-344-3400.
Fax: 804-344-3410.

MEMBER OF FIRM

Mark A. Fontana

For full biographical listings, see the Martindale-Hubbell Law Directory

THOMAS, THOMAS & HAFER, LLP (AV)

305 North Front Street, 6th Floor, P.O. Box 999, 17108
Telephone: 717-237-7100
Fax: 717-237-7105
Verify: 717-255-7642
Bethlehem, Pennsylvania Office: 12 East Market Street, P.O. Box 1172, 12016.
Telephone: 610-868-1675.
Fax: 610-868-1702.

MEMBERS OF FIRM

Joseph P. Hafer
James K. Thomas, II
Robertson B. Taylor
Jeffrey B. Rettig
Peter J. Curry
R. Burke McLemore, Jr.
Edward H. Jordan, Jr.
C. Kent Price
Randall G. Gale
David L. Schwalm
Peter J. Speaker
Douglas B. Marcello
Paul J. Dellasega

OF COUNSEL

James K. Thomas

Timothy I. Mark
Daniel J. Gallagher
Robert A. Taylor
Sarah W. Arosell
Eugene N. McHugh
Stephen E. Geduldig
Karen S. Coates
Gary T. Lathrop
Todd B. Narvol
James J. Dodd-o
Kenneth A. Rapp
Kevin C. McNamara
Brooks R. Foland
John Flounlacker
John M. Popilock
Michele J. Thorp

Representative Clients: Aetna Casualty & Surety Co.; Bethlehem Steel Corp.; Commercial Union Insurance Companies; Geisinger Medical Center; Hartford Insurance Group; Liberty Mutual Insurance Co.; Pennsylvania Hospital Insurance Co.; Roadway Services, Inc.; UGI Corp.; Weis Markets, Inc.;

For full biographical listings, see the Martindale-Hubbell Law Directory

HUNTINGDON VALLEY, Montgomery Co.

MICHAEL I. LEVIN AND ASSOCIATES, P.C. (AV)

1402 Masons Mill Business Park, 1800 Byberry Road, 19006
Telephone: 215-938-6378
Fax: 215-938-6375
Email: milevin@aol.com

Michael Ira Levin

Michael W. Jones
David W. Brown
Mark W. Voigt
Anne E. Hendricks

For full biographical listings, see the Martindale-Hubbell Law Directory

JENKINTOWN, Montgomery Co.

SEMANOFF, ORMSBY & GREENBERG, LLP (AV)

Suite 200 Jenkins Court, 610 Old York Road, 19046
Telephone: 215-887-0200
Fax: 215-884-3500
Email: info@soglaw.com *URL:* http://www.soglaw.com
Philadelphia, Pennsylvania Office: Suite 200, Two Penn Center Plaza.
Telephone: 215-887-2094.

Harold Semanoff
Charles W. Ormsby, Jr.
Howard N. Greenberg
Michael J. Torchia

(See Next Column)

SEMANOFF, ORMSBY & GREENBERG LLP, *Jenkintown—Continued*

Michael K. Yarnoff
Peter J. Smith
Claudia M. Becker
Michael B. Dubin
Beth S. Joseph
Joanne M. Murray

OF COUNSEL

David M. Seltzer
Frederick M. Savadove

For full biographical listings, see the Martindale-Hubbell Law Directory

*PHILADELPHIA,** Philadelphia Co.

BALLARD SPAHR ANDREWS & INGERSOLL, LLP (AV)

1735 Market Street, 51st Floor, 19103-7599
Telephone: 215-665-8500
Fax: 215-864-8999
URL: http://www.ballardspahr.com
Baltimore, Maryland Office: 300 East Lombard Street. 19th Floor.
Telephone: 410-528-5600.
Fax: 410-528-5650.
Camden, New Jersey Office: 800 Hudson Square, 5th Floor.
Telephone: 856-541-5577.
Fax: 856-541-8272.
Denver, Colorado Office: Seventeenth Street Plaza Building, Suite 2300, 1225 17th Street.
Telephone: 303-292-2400.
Fax: 303-296-3956.
Salt Lake City, Utah Office: One Utah Center, Suite 1200, 201 South Main Street.
Telephone: 801-531-3000.
Fax: 801-531-3001.
Voorhees, New Jersey Office: Suite 100, 1101 Laurel Oak Drive.
Telephone: 856-627-8555.
Fax: 856-627-1153.
Washington, D.C. Office: Suite 1000 South, 601 13th Street, N.W.
Telephone: 202-661-2200.
Fax: 202-661-2299.

David S. Fryman
Charisse R. Lillie
Maureen M. Rayborn
John B. Langel
Brian D. Pedrow
Richard L. Strouse
Suzanne E. Turner

Susan R. Becker
Shira Goodman
Daniel V. Johns
Gayle Baumgarten Stein
Abigail Lee Flitter
Matthew Moesel Gutt
Niza Maria Motola
Kelly A. Walenda

For Complete List of Firm Personnel, See General Section

For full biographical listings, see the Martindale-Hubbell Law Directory

GALFAND BERGER, LLP (AV)

1818 Market Street, 23rd Floor, 19103-3623
Telephone: 215-665-1600
Fax: 215-564-2262
Email: sdonaway@galfandberger.com *URL:* http://www.galfandberger.com

Debra A. Jensen
Joseph Lurie

Wayne A. Hamilton
Michael W. McGurrin

For full biographical listings, see the Martindale-Hubbell Law Directory

KITTREDGE, DONLEY, ELSON, FULLEM & EMBICK, LLP (AV)

Fifth Floor, The Bank Building, 421 Chestnut Street, 19106-2416
Telephone: 215-829-9900
Fax: 215-829-9888
Email: lawoffice@kdefe.com *URL:* http://www.kdefe.com

MEMBERS OF FIRM

Patrick W. Kittredge
Joseph M. Donley
Barry R. Elson
Joseph W. Fullem, Jr.
John R. Embick
Keith E. Johnston

ASSOCIATES

Glenn E. Davis
Michael S. Soule
Patricia Powers
Brendan P. McGlynn
Lisa G. Miller
Edward Bigham
Michael K. Smith (1963-1995)

OF COUNSEL

Richard B. Pearl

For full biographical listings, see the Martindale-Hubbell Law Directory

KLEINBARD, BELL & BRECKER LLP (AV)

Suite 700, 1900 Market Street, 19103
Telephone: 215-568-2000
Facsimile: 215-568-0140
Montclair, New Jersey Office: 240 Claremont Avenue, 07042.
Telephone: 973-233-0600.
Facsimile: 973-233-9390.

Joseph S. Kleinbard (1905-1994)
Robert John Brecker (1916-1996)

COUNSEL TO THE FIRM

Arthur S. Keyser

MEMBERS OF FIRM

Paul E. Bomze
Murray I. Blackman
Howard J. Davis
Steven R. Waxman
Steven J. Engelmyer (Resident, Montclair Office)
David L. Hyman (Resident, Montclair Office)
Imogene E. Hughes
John P. Hickey
Jay R. Goldstein
Ralph J. Mauro
Thomas H. Speranza
Lisa E. Brody

ASSOCIATES

Mary Beth H. Gray
Eric J. Rothschild
Mary Vassallo Slinkard
Michael A. Frattone
Benjamin C. Graff (Not admitted in PA)
Ralph F. Salgado

COUNSEL

Joseph Bell

For full biographical listings, see the Martindale-Hubbell Law Directory

LOVITZ AND GOLD, P.C. (AV)

Eleven Penn Center, 1835 Market Street Suite 515, 19103
Telephone: 215-569-1999
Fax: 215-569-3870

Hyman Lovitz
Sidney L. Gold
Kevin I. Lovitz

Jennifer L. Myers

OF COUNSEL

Baden Kramer Huffman & Brodsky, P.C., New York, New York

LEGAL SUPPORT PERSONNEL

Christine Johnson (Litigation Paralegal)

For full biographical listings, see the Martindale-Hubbell Law Directory

THE MAGER LAW FIRM, P.C. (AV)

One Liberty Place, 44th Floor, 1650 Market Street, 19103
Telephone: 215-569-6924
Fax: 215-569-6925
Email: mager@magerlaw.com *URL:* http://www.lawyers.com/themagerlaw
Delran, New Jersey Office: 5045 Route 130 South, Suite C, 08075.
Telephone: 609-461-5114.
Fax: 609-764-6532.
Haddonfield, New Jersey Office: 36 Tanner Street, 2nd Floor. 08033.
Telephone: 856-616-8840.
Fax: 856-427-0611.

Carol A. Mager
Claire Rocco (Resident, New Jersey Office)
Debora A. O'Neill
Deborah H. Simon
Yvonne R. Haddad
Denise K. Kontrack
Peter Ryan Rosenzweig

For full biographical listings, see the Martindale-Hubbell Law Directory

MANTA AND WELGE, A PROFESSIONAL CORPORATION (AV)

2000 Market Street, 6th Floor, 19103
Telephone: 215-851-6600
Telecopy: 215-851-6644
URL: http://www.mantalaw.com
Allentown, Pennsylvania Office: Suite 204, 5000 Tilghman Street.
Telephone: 610-395-7499.
Fax: 610-366-5096.
Harrisburg, Pennsylvania Office: Governors Row, 27 North Front Street.
Telephone: 717-236-8420.
West Trenton, New Jersey Office: 810 Bear Tavern Road, Suite 301.
Telephone: 609-883-6990.
Fax: 609-883-7730.
Wilmington, Delaware Office: Suite 1400, Mellon Bank Center, 919 Market Street.
Telephone: 302-655-7460.
Fax: 302-655-7004.

MEMBER OF FIRM

Mark J. Manta

(See Next Column)

MANTA AND WELGE A PROFESSIONAL CORPORATION—*Continued*

Daniel C. Moraglia
Yasmeen Sabina Khaleel
Jennifer M. Welding

For full biographical listings, see the Martindale-Hubbell Law Directory

McCoy & Associates, P.C. (AV)

The Windsor, Penthouse Suite, 1700 Benjamin Franklin Parkway, 19103
Telephone: 215-587-4322
Fax: 215-587-2110
Email: McCoylaw@msn.com *URL:* http://www.lawyers.com/mccoy&associates
Mount Laurel, New Jersey Office: 534 Charleston Court, 08054.
Telephone: 609-235-7676.
Fax: 609-234-4607.

Edwin F. McCoy

Steven J. Blumenthal
Laura J. Lifsey

For full biographical listings, see the Martindale-Hubbell Law Directory

McEldrew & Fullam, P.C. (AV)

Suite 5050 One Liberty Place, 19103
Telephone: 215-563-8300
800-223-3352
Fax: 215-563-6130
URL: http://www.lawyers.com/mceldrew&fullampc
New York, New York Office: McEldrew & Ressler, Suite 2101, 11 Pennsylvania Plaza, 10001.
Telephone: 212-695-6446.
Fax: 212-268-0287.

James J. McEldrew, III
Nancy H. Fullam

Marcella J. Schell
Sallie Updyke Mundy
Carol L. Vassallo
David Felderman

LEGAL SUPPORT PERSONNEL

Christine Doelp (Comptroller)

For full biographical listings, see the Martindale-Hubbell Law Directory

Neil A. Morris Associates, P.C. (AV)

The Widener Building, Suite 1700, One South Penn Square 1339 Chestnut Street, 19107
Telephone: 215-751-0600
Fax: 215-751-1425
URL: http://www.namapc.com
Marlton, New Jersey Office: Ten Lake Center Executive Park, 401 Route 73 North, Suite 204.
Telephone: 609-596-5656.
Telefax: 609-596-6164.

Neil A. Morris

Laurence L. Smith
Richard R. Morris
Daniel F. McLaughlin

OF COUNSEL

Jay H. Rosenfeld

LEGAL SUPPORT PERSONNEL

Jacqueline J. Ben

For full biographical listings, see the Martindale-Hubbell Law Directory

Reed Smith Shaw & McClay LLP (AV)

2500 One Liberty Place, 19103-7301
Telephone: 215-851-8100
FAX: 215-851-1420
Email: rssm@rssm.com *URL:* http://www.rssm.com
Pittsburgh, Pennsylvania Office: 435 Sixth Avenue, 15219-1886.
Telephone: 412-288-3131.
FAX: 412-288-3063.
Washington, D.C. Office: Suite 1100 - East Tower, 1301 K Street, N.W., 20005-3317.
Telephone: 202-414-9200.
FAX: 202-414-9299.
Harrisburg, Pennsylvania Office: 213 Market Street, 17101-2132.
Telephone: 717-234-5988.
FAX: 717-236-3777.
Princeton, New Jersey Office: 136 Main Street, Suite 250, 08540-5799.
Telephone: 609-987-0050.
FAX: 609-951-0824.
New York, N.Y. Office: 375 Park Avenue, 17th Floor, 10152.
Telephone: 212-521-5400.
FAX: 212-521-5450.
Newark, New Jersey Office: The Legal Center, One Riverfront Plaza, First Floor, 07102-5400.
Telephone: 973-621-3200.
FAX: 973-621-3199.

(See Next Column)

Falls Church, Virginia Office: Reed Smith Hazel & Thomas, Suite 1400, 3110 Fairview Park Drive, P.O. Box 12001.
Telephone: 703-641-4200.
Fax: 703-641-4340.
Leesburg, Virginia Office: Reed Smith Hazel & Thomas LLP, 44084 Riverside Parkway, Suite 300.
Telephone: 703-729-8500. Metro: 703-478-1992.
Fax: 703-478-8003.
McLean, Virginia Office: Reed Smith Hazel & Thomas LLP, Suite 1100, 8251 Greensboro Drive, 22102-3844.
Telephone: 703-734-4600.
FAX: 703-734-4699.
Richmond, Virginia Office: Reed Smith Hazel & Thomas LLP, Suite 600, 411 East Franklin Street, P.O. Box 788.
Telephone: 804-344-3400.
Fax: 804-344-3410.

MEMBERS OF FIRM

Sara A. Begley
John E. Quinn
Karl A. Fritton
Joseph C. Rudolf

For full biographical listings, see the Martindale-Hubbell Law Directory

*PITTSBURGH,** Allegheny Co.

Babst, Calland, Clements and Zomnir, A Professional Corporation (AV)

Two Gateway Center, 15222
Telephone: 412-394-5400
Fax: 412-394-6576
Email: BCCZ@BCCZ.com
Philadelphia, Pennsylvania Office: The Widener Building, Suite 1700, One South Penn Square.
Telephone: 215-567-1020.
Fax: 215-751-1425.

Sally Griffith Cimini
Maureen P. Kelly
Carl H. Hellerstedt, Jr.
David J. Laurent
John A. McCreary, Jr.

Pamela J. Castellani
Lisa G. Silverman

For full biographical listings, see the Martindale-Hubbell Law Directory

DeForest & Koscelnik (AV)

3000 Koppers Building, 436 Seventh Avenue, 15219
Telephone: 412-227-3100
Fax: 412-227-3130

Walter P. DeForest, III
Jacqueline A. Koscelnik

ASSOCIATES

David J. Berardinelli
Paul M. Thompson

Representative Clients: Carnegie Mellon University; Ohio Valley Medical Center; Cox Enterprises, Inc.; General Electric Co.; Chancellor Broadcasting; Shooting Star Broadcasting; Leybold Vacuum Products, Inc.; Demegen, Inc.; Emerson Electric Co.; Frank Bryan, Inc.; Rox Trucking, Inc.

For full biographical listings, see the Martindale-Hubbell Law Directory

Jones, Day, Reavis & Pogue (AV)

500 Grant Street 31st Floor, 15219
Telephone: 412-391-3939
Telecopier: 412-394-7959
Email: counsel@jonesday.com *URL:* http://www.jonesday.com
In Atlanta, Georgia: 3500 SunTrust Plaza, 303 Peachtree Street.
Telephone: 404-521-3939.
Telecopier: 404-581-8330.
In Brussels, Belgium: Avenue Louise 480, 7th Floor, B-1050 Brussels.
Telephone: 32-2-645-14-11.
Telecopier: 32-2-645-14-45.
In Chicago, Illinois: 77 West Wacker.
Telephone: 312-782-3939.
Telecopier: 312-782-8585.
In Cleveland, Ohio: North Point, 901 Lakeside Avenue.
Telephone: 216-586-3939.
Telecopier: 216-579-0212.
In Columbus, Ohio: 1900 Huntington Center.
Telephone: 614-469-3939.
Telecopier: 614-461-4198.
In Dallas, Texas: 2727 North Harwood Street.
Telephone: 214-220-3939.
Telecopier: 214-969-5100.
In Frankfurt, Germany: Hochhaus am Park, Grüneburgweg 102, 60323 Frankfurt am Main.
Telephone: 49-69-9726-3939.
Telecopier: 49-69-9726-3993.
In Geneva, Switzerland: 20, rue de Candolle.
Telephone: 41-22-320-2339.
Telecopier: 41-22-320-1232.
In Hong Kong: 29th Floor, Entertainment Building, 30 Queen's Road Central.
Telephone: 852-2526-6895.
Telecopier: 852-2868-5871 or 852-2868-5699.

(See Next Column)

JONES, DAY, REAVIS & POGUE, *Pittsburgh—Continued*

In Irvine, California: 5 Park Plaza, Suite 1100.
Telephone: 949-851-3939.
Telecopier: 949-553-7539.
In London, England: Bucklersbury House, 3 Queen Victoria Street.
Telephone: 44-171-236-3939.
Telecopier: 44-171-236-1113. 34000 Los Angeles, California: 555 West Fifth Street, Suite 4600.
Telephone: 213-489-3939.
Telecopier: 213-243-2539.
In New Delhi, India (Associate Office): Pathak & Associates (an associate firm of Jones, Day, Reavis & Pogue), 1st Floor, Dr. Gopal Das Bhaven, 28 Barakhamba Road.
Telephone: 91-11-373-8793; 91-11-335-7345.
Telecopier: 91-11-335-3761.
In New York, New York: 599 Lexington Avenue.
Telephone: 212-326-3939.
Telecopier: 212-755-7306.
In Paris, France: 120, rue du Faubourg Saint-Honoré.
Telephone: 33-1-56-59-39-39.
Telecopier: 33-1-56-59-39-38
In Riyadh, Saudi Arabia: The International Law Firm (In Association with Jones, Day, Reavis & Pogue), Sulaymaniyah, Prince Mishari IBN, Abdulaziz Street, P.O. Box 22166.
Telephone: (966-1) 462-8866.
Telecopier: (966-1) 462-9001.
In Shanghai, China: 2805 Kerry Centre, 1515 Nanjing Road West.
Telephone: 86-21-5298-6568.
Telecopier: 86-21-5298-6569.
In Sydney, Australia: Governor Phillip Tower, Level 38, 1 Farrer Place.
Telephone: 61-2-9210-6921.
Telecopier: 61-2-9210-6926.
In Taipei, Taiwan: 8th Floor, 2 Tun Hwa South Road, Section 2.
Telephone: (886-2) 2704-6808.
Telecopier: (886-2) 2704-6791.
In Tokyo, Japan: Toranomon MT Building, 4th Floor, 10-3, Toranomon 3-Chome, Minato-Ku, Tokyo 105, Japan.
Telephone: 81-3-3433-3939.
Telecopier: 81-3-5401-2725.
In Washington, D.C.: 51 Louisiana Avenue, N.W.
Telephone: 202-879-3939.
Telecopier: 202-626-1700.

MEMBER OF FIRM IN PITTSBURGH

Richard F. Shaw

For Complete List of Firm Personnel, See General Section

For full biographical listings, see the Martindale-Hubbell Law Directory

MARCUS & SHAPIRA LLP (AV)

35th Floor, One Oxford Centre, 301 Grant Street, 15219-6401
Telephone: 412-471-3490
Telecopier: 412-391-8758
Email: info@marcus-shapira.com *URL:* http://www.marcus-shapira.com

MEMBERS OF FIRM

Robert L. Allman, II
Susan Gromis Flynn
Elly Heller-Toig
James S. Larrimer
Bernard D. Marcus
Glenn M. Olcerst
Daniel H. Shapira
Stephen S. Zubrow

ASSOCIATES

Traci L. McDonald
Susan H. Snively

For Complete List of Firm Personnel, See General Section

For full biographical listings, see the Martindale-Hubbell Law Directory

REED SMITH SHAW & MCCLAY LLP (AV)

435 Sixth Avenue, 15219-1886
Telephone: 412-288-3131
FAX: 412-288-3063
Mailing Address: P.O. Box 2009, 15230-2009
Email: rssm@rssm.com *URL:* http://www.rssm.com
Washington, D.C. Office: Suite 1100 - East Tower, 1301 K Street, N.W., 20005-3317.
Telephone: 202-414-9200.
FAX: 202-414-9299.
Philadelphia, Pennsylvania Office: 2500 One Liberty Place, 19103-7301.
Telephone: 215-851-8100.
FAX: 215-851-1420.
Harrisburg, Pennsylvania Office: 213 Market Street, 17101-2132.
Telephone: 717-234-5988.
FAX: 717-236-3777.
Princeton, New Jersey Office: 136 Main Street, Suite 250, 08540-5799.
Telephone: 609-987-0050.
FAX: 609-951-0824.
New York, N.Y. Office: 375 Park Avenue, 17th Floor, 10152.
Telephone: 212-521-5400.
FAX: 212-521-5450.
Newark, New Jersey Office: The Legal Center, One Riverfront Plaza, First Floor, 07102-5400.
Telephone: 973-621-3200.
FAX: 973-621-3199.

(See Next Column)

Falls Church, Virginia Office: Reed Smith Hazel & Thomas, Suite 1400, 3110 Fairview Park Drive, P.O. Box 12001.
Telephone: 703-641-4200.
Fax: 703-641-4340.
Leesburg, Virginia Office: Reed Smith Hazel & Thomas LLP, 44084 Riverside Parkway, Suite 300.
Telephone: 703-729-8500. Metro: 703-478-1992.
Fax: 703-478-8003.
McLean, Virginia Office: Reed Smith Hazel & Thomas LLP, Suite 1100, 8251 Greensboro Drive, 22102-3844.
Telephone: 703-734-4600.
FAX: 703-734-4699.
Richmond, Virginia Office: Reed Smith Hazel & Thomas LLP, Suite 600, 411 East Franklin Street, P.O. Box 788.
Telephone: 804-344-3400.
Fax: 804-344-3410.

MEMBERS OF FIRM

William Bevan, III
Eugene K. Connors
Robert B. Cottington
James R. Haggerty
Robert W. Hartland
Carole S. Katz
David J. McAllister
Martha Hartle Munsch
Peter D. Post
Robert F. Prorok
Patrick W. Ritchey
Edward N. Stoner, II
John C. Unkovic
Scott F. Zimmerman

For full biographical listings, see the Martindale-Hubbell Law Directory

ROSE, SCHMIDT, HASLEY & DISALLE, P.C. (AV)

900 Oliver Building, 15222-2310
Telephone: 412-434-8600
Fax: 412-263-2829
Email: rshd@rshdlaw.com
Washington, Pennsylvania Office: 7th Floor, Millcraft Center.
Telephone: 724-228-8883.

Edmund M. Carney
R. Stanley Mitchel

For Complete List of Firm Personnel, See General Section

For full biographical listings, see the Martindale-Hubbell Law Directory

*READING,** Berks Co.

BARLEY, SNYDER, SENFT & COHEN, LLC (AV)

Formerly: Miller and Murray, LLP
501 Washington Street, P.O. Box 942, 19603-0942
Telephone: 610-376-6651
Fax: 610-376-5243
Email: barley@barley.com *URL:* http://www.barley.com
Harrisburg, Pennsylvania Office: 240 North Third Street.
Telephone: 717-238-8263.
Fax: 717-238-8278.
Lancaster, Pennsylvania Office: 126 East King Street.
Telephone: 717-299-5201.
Fax: 717-291-4660.
York, Pennsylvania Office: 100 East Market Street.
Telephone: 717-846-8888.
Fax: 717-843-8492.
Chambersburg, Pennsylvania Office: 247 Lincoln Way East.
Telephone: 717-264-6494.
Fax: 717-264-1662.
Hanover, Pennsylvania Office: 14 Center Square.
Telephone: 717-637-6239.
Fax: 717-637-5407.
Birdsboro, Pennsylvania Office: 115 E. Main Street.
Telephone: 610-582-2735.
Hamburg, Pennsylvania Office: 239 State Street.
Telephone: 610-562-3721.
Oley, Pennsylvania Office: Route 73 and Main Street.
Telephone: 610-987-6350.
Morgantown, Pennsylvania Office: Route 23.
Telephone: 610-286-5958.

MEMBERS OF FIRM

John S. Hibschman
Charles F. Fitzpatrick
Gregory R. Young
David R. Keller
Paul G. Mattaini
Elaine Pennington Stanko
William F. Colby, Jr.
Brian R. Ott
Melanie A. Zampini

ASSOCIATES

Michael P. Giles
Craig T. Trebilcock

COUNSEL

James H. Murray

Representative Clients: Associated Wholesalers, Inc.; Vlasic Farms; Bank of Pennsylvania; All American Plazas; Graham Packaging; D.F. Stauffer Biscuit; Fulton Bank/Fulton Financial Corp.; Summith Health; Lancaster General Hospital.

For Complete List of Firm Personnel, See General Section

For full biographical listings, see the Martindale-Hubbell Law Directory

SEWICKLEY, Allegheny Co.

THE VOLK LAW FIRM, P.C. (AV)

Blaymore I, Suite 301, 1606 Carmody Court, 15143
Telephone: 724-935-8888
Facsimile: 724-935-8811
Email: volklaw@sgi.net *URL:* http://www.lawyers.com/volklaw

Charles R. Volk
Jane Lewis Volk
Michael Jansen

Representative Clients: Koppers Industries, Inc.; Brownsville General Hospital; Constructors Association of Western Pennsylvania; Duquesne University; Weirton Steel Corp.; Scripps Howard, Inc.; Berry Metal Company.

For full biographical listings, see the Martindale-Hubbell Law Directory

*WILKES-BARRE,** Luzerne Co.

HOURIGAN, KLUGER & QUINN, A PROFESSIONAL CORPORATION (AV)

700 Mellon Bank Center, 8 West Market Street, 18701-1867
Telephone: 570-825-9401
FAX: 570-829-3460
Email: hkq@epix.net
Scranton, Pennsylvania Office: Suite 200, 434 Lackawanna Avenue.
Telephone: 570-346-8414.
Allentown, Pennsylvania Office: Sovereign Building, 609 Hamilton Mall.
Telephone: 610-437-1584.

Allan M. Kluger
Richard M. Goldberg
Alexia Kita Blake (Resident, Scranton Office)

Representative Client: Teamsters, Pope & Talbot Co., Inc.

For Complete List of Firm Personnel, See General Section

For full biographical listings, see the Martindale-Hubbell Law Directory

KOFF, WENDOLOWSKI, FERGUSON & MANGAN, P.C. (AV)

22 East Union Street, Suite 115, 18701-2721
Telephone: 570-822-5600
Telecopier: 570-825-1299
Email: kwfmlaw@compuserve.com
Scranton, Pennsylvania Office: 108 North Washington Avenue, Suite 1105, 18503.
Telephone: 570-961-2095.
Fax: 570-961-2990.

Richard M. Ferguson (1952-1996)
David E. Koff
Raymond P. Wendolowski
James F. Mangan
Cynthia R. Vullo
Scott C. Gartley
Janet H. Blaum

OF COUNSEL

Paula G. Bregman
William M. Blaum

LEGAL SUPPORT PERSONNEL

PARALEGALS

Judi Howe
Deborah A. Kapral
Lisa Soboleski
Sandra Kish

For full biographical listings, see the Martindale-Hubbell Law Directory

ROSENN, JENKINS & GREENWALD, L.L.P. (AV)

15 South Franklin Street, 18711-0075
Telephone: 570-826-5600
Fax: 570-826-5640
Email: rjg@rjglaw.com *URL:* http://www.rjglaw.com
Hazleton, Pennsylvania Office: P.O. Box 618, 18201-0618.
Telephone: 570-455-7112.
Fax: 570-455-8304.

MEMBERS OF FIRM

Donald H. Brobst
James P. Valentine
Mark A. Van Loon
James C. Oschal
Joseph G. Ferguson

ASSOCIATE

Elizabeth C. Leo

Representative Clients: C-TEC Corp.; Chicago Title Insurance Co.; Manufacturers & Traders Trust Company; Guard Insurance Group; May Department Stores Co.; Student Loan Marketing Assn. (Sallie Mae); Penn-State Geisinger Medical Center; Subaru of America, Inc.

For Complete List of Firm Personnel, See General Section

For full biographical listings, see the Martindale-Hubbell Law Directory

RHODE ISLAND

*PROVIDENCE,** Providence Co.

BLISH & CAVANAGH (AV)

Commerce Center, 30 Exchange Terrace, 02903
Telephone: 401-831-8900
Telecopier: 401-751-7542
Email: BLISHCAV@AOL.COM

MEMBERS OF FIRM

Joseph V. Cavanagh, Jr.
William R. Landry
Edmund L. Alves, Jr.
Stephen J. Reid, Jr.
Karen A. Pelczarski
Scott T. Spear
Raymond A. Marcaccio

Michael W. Carroll
Staci L. Sawyer
Kristin Rodgers Sullivan

OF COUNSEL

John H. Blish

Representative Clients: Providence Journal Co.; Rhode Island Hospital Trust National Bank; Fleet Bank; Metropolitan Insurance Co.; Allstate Insurance Co.; Delta Dental of Rhode Island; Colony Communications; Providence Housing Authority; Textron; A.T. Cross.

For full biographical listings, see the Martindale-Hubbell Law Directory

EDWARDS & ANGELL, LLP (AV)

A Partnership including Professional Corporations
2800 BankBoston Plaza, 02903
Telephone: 401-274-9200
Telecopier: 401-276-6611
Cable Address: "Edwangle Providence"
Telex: 952001 "E A PVD"
Email: postmaster@ealaw.com *URL:* http://www.ealaw.com
Boston, Massachusetts Office: 101 Federal Street, 02110-1800.
Telephone: 617-439-4444.
Telecopier: 617-439-4170.
New York, New York Office: 750 Lexington Avenue, 10022-1200.
Telephone: 212-308-4411.
Telecopier: 212-308-4844.
Palm Beach, Florida Office: 250 Royal Palm Way, Suite 300, 33480-4356.
Telephone: 561-833-7700.
Telecopier: 561-655-8719.
Short Hills, New Jersey Office: 51 John F. Kennedy Parkway, 07078.
Telephone: 973-376-7700.
Telecopier: 973-376-3380.
Hartford, Connecticut Office: 90 State House Square, 06103-2715.
Telephone: 860-525-5065.
Telecopier: 860-527-4198.
Newport, Rhode Island Office: 130 Bellevue Avenue, 02840.
Telephone: 401-849-7800.
Telecopier: 401-849-7887.

MEMBERS OF FIRM

Walter C. Hunter
Richard A. Perras (Not admitted in RI; Resident Boston, Massachusetts Office)
William E. Smith

COUNSEL

John B. Rosenquest III

OF COUNSEL

Alvin M. Glazerman (Not admitted in RI)

For Complete List of Firm Personnel, See General Section

For full biographical listings, see the Martindale-Hubbell Law Directory

HANSON, CURRAN, PARKS & WHITMAN (AV)

146 Westminster Street, 02903-2218
Telephone: 401-421-2154
Telecopier: 401-521-7040
URL: http://www.hcpw.com

Kirk Hanson (1948-1991)

MEMBERS OF FIRM

A. Lauriston Parks
David P. Whitman
Michael T. F. Wallor
Dennis J. McCarten
James T. Murphy
Seth E. Bowerman
Thomas R. Bender
Mark W. Dana

ASSOCIATES

Richard H. Burrows
Christopher J. Zangari (Resident)
Wendy J. Taylor

OF COUNSEL

William A. Curran

General Counsel for: Medical Malpractice Joint Underwriting Association of Rhode Island.

(See Next Column)

Greenville—Continued

HAYNSWORTH BALDWIN JOHNSON & GREAVES LLC (AV)

918 South Pleasantburg Drive, P.O. Box 10888, 29603
Telephone: 864-271-7410
Facsimile: 864-241-1861
Columbia, South Carolina Office: 1201 Main Street, Suite 1230.
Telephone: 803-799-5858.
Raleigh, North Carolina Office: 3605 Glenwood Avenue, Suite 210, P.O. Box 10035.
Telephone: 919-782-3340.
Greensboro, North Carolina Office: 2709 Henry Street, P.O. Box 13310.
Telephone: 336-375-9737.
Charlotte, North Carolina Office: 400 West Trade Street.
Telephone: 704-342-2588.
Jacksonville, Florida Office: 1301 Riverplace Boulevard, Suite 800, P.O. Box 40593.
Telephone: 904-396-3000.
Tampa, Florida Office: 600 North Westshore Boulevard, Suite 200.
Telephone: 813-289-1247.

Knox L. Haynsworth, Jr.
Bradley R. Johnson (Resident, Tampa, Florida Office)
Thomas G. Greaves III
John G. Creech
Bruce A. Petesch (Resident, Raleigh, North Carolina Office)
Wm. Ross McKibbon, Jr.
G. Thomas Harper (Resident, Jacksonville, Florida Office)
James B. Spears, Jr. (Resident, Charlotte, North Carolina Office)
J. Howard Daniel
Robert S. Phifer (Resident, Charlotte, North Carolina Office)
Joseph A. Rhodes, Jr.
David R. Wylie
James M. Powell (Resident, Greensboro, North Carolina Office)
Charles T. Speth II (Resident, Columbia, South Carolina Office)
Thomas A. Bright
Grant D. Petersen (Resident, Tampa, Florida Office)
Charles F. Henley, Jr. (Resident, Jacksonville, Florida Office)
Katherine Dudley Helms (Resident, Columbia, South Carolina Office)
M. Kristen Allman (Resident, Tampa, Florida Office)
Thomas T. Hodges
Gregory P. McGuire (Resident, Raleigh, North Carolina Office)
Leigh M. Nason (Resident, Columbia, South Carolina Office)
Rodolfo R. Agraz (Resident, Raleigh, North Carolina Office)
Andreas N. Satterfield, Jr.
Stephen D. Dellinger (Resident, Charlotte, North Carolina Office)
Brian M. Freedman (Resident, Greensboro, North Carolina Office)
Thomas M. Christina
Jacob J. Modla (Resident, Charlotte, North Carolina Office)
Lucretia D. Guia (Resident, Greensboro, North Carolina Office)
D. Christopher Lauderdale
John D. Cole (Resident, Charlotte, North Carolina Office)
Scott T. Justice (Resident, Columbia, South Carolina Office)

Donna M. Griffin (Resident, Tampa, Florida Office)
Kimberly T. Acuna (Resident, Jacksonville, Florida Office)
Elizabeth A. Maas (Resident, Jacksonville, Florida Office)
Vance E. Drawdy
Glenn L. Spencer
Patrick C. Fant, III
M. Brian Magargle (Resident, Columbia, South Carolina Office)
Ellison F. McCoy
D. Ross Hamilton, Jr. (Resident, Greensboro, North Carolina Office)
Joy Mandanas (Resident, Columbia, South Carolina Office)
J. Nathan Duggins III (Resident, Greensboro, North Carolina Office)
Charles E. McDonald III
Amy K. Reynolds (Resident, Charlotte, North Carolina Office)
Marc R. Edelman (Resident, Tampa, Florida Office)
D. Randle Moody II
Jerry H. Walters, Jr. (Resident, Charlotte, North Carolina Office)
Angela Rushton Miller
Linda M. Fox (Resident, Charlotte, North Carolina Office)
Ellis Reed-Hill Lesemann
Elizabeth J. M. Caldwell (Resident, Charlotte, North Carolina Office)
Lydia M. Nicosia (Resident, Tampa, Florida Office)
Linda B. Rogers (Resident, Greensboro, North Carolina Office)
Sarah Helen Berdahl (Resident, Raleigh, North Carolina Office)

OF COUNSEL

James J. Baldwin
John A. Hill (Resident, Columbia, South Carolina Office)
Preston R. Burch (Resident, Columbia, South Carolina Office)
Kelley M. Hall

Representative Clients: Greenville Hospital System; Harris Teeter, Inc.; Hoffmann-La Roche Inc.; Perdue, Inc.; Schneider National; Sears Merchandise Group; Springs Industries, Inc.; Timken Co.; Laboratory Corporation of America; Lockheed Martin.

For full biographical listings, see the Martindale-Hubbell Law Directory

OGLETREE, DEAKINS, NASH, SMOAK & STEWART, P.C. (AV)

The Ogletree Building, 300 North Main Street, P.O. Box 2757, 29602
Telephone: 864-271-1300
Facsimile: 864-235-8806
Email: Greenville@odnss.com *URL:* http://www.Ogletreedeakins.com
Atlanta, Georgia Office: 600 Peachtree Street, N.E., Suite 2100.
Telephone: 404-881-1300.
Washington, D.C. Office: Fifth Floor, 2400 N Street, N.W.
Telephone: 202-887-0855.
Houston, Texas Office: One Allen Center, 500 Dallas Street, Suite 3000.
Telephone: 713-655-0855.
Chicago, Illinois Office: Twenty-Fifth Floor, Two First National Plaza, 20 South Clark Street.
Telephone: 312-558-1220.
Nashville, Tennessee Office: SunTrust Center, Suite 800, 424 Church Street.
Telephone: 615-254-1900.
Birmingham, Alabama Office: 1900 SouthTrust Tower, 420 North 20th Street.
Telephone: 205-328-1900.
Charleston, South Carolina Office: 134 Meeting Street, Suite 500, P.O. Box 1808.
Telephone: 843-853-1300.
Columbia, South Carolina Office: 1501 Main Street, Suite 600, P.O. Box 11206.
Telephone: 803-252-1300.
Raleigh, North Carolina Office: 4101 Lake Boone Trail, Suite 511, P.O. Box 31608.
Telephone: 919-787-9700.
Winston-Salem, North Carolina Office: 150 South Stratford Road, Suite 350.
Telephone: 336-725-2110.

Homer L. Deakins, Jr.
Lewis Tyson Smoak
J. Hamilton Stewart, III
L. Gray Geddie, Jr.
Ralph M. Mellom
Robert Oliver King
Fred W. Suggs, Jr.
M. Baker Wyche III
Donald A. Cockrill
L. Franklin Elmore
John W. Hoag, III
Joel A. Daniel
Phillip A. Kilgore
Ronald E. Cardwell
Mary Lou Hill
Ingrid Blackwelder Erwin
Phillip Lee Conner
Glenn R. Goodwin
Kristofer K. Strasser
Kimila Lynn Wooten
Mark M. Stubley
Nancy Walker Monts
G. Scott Humphrey
E. Grantland Burns

Ellisa Huguley Culp
H. Bernard Tisdale III
Miles Lavan Green, Jr.
W.G. Griggs, III
Mason A. Goldsmith, Jr.
John F. Lomax, Jr.
Stephen R. Woods
Janet Quick Lewis

Representative Clients: Duke Energy Corp.; Eastman Kodak Company; Fluor Corporation; General Electric Co.; W.R. Grace & Co.; Hitachi Electronics Devices (USA), Inc.; Nissan Motor Manufacturing Corporation U.S.A.; VF Corporation; Wachovia Corporation; WestPoint Stevens, Inc.

For full biographical listings, see the Martindale-Hubbell Law Directory

LORIS, Horry Co.

STEVENS LAW FIRM, P.C. (AV)

3341 Broad Street P.O. Drawer 127, 29569-0127
Telephone: 843-756-7652
Fax: 843-756-3785
E-Mail: RUMMPOLE@AOL.COM
Email: JPKLAW@AOL.COM

James P. Stevens, Jr.
Jonathan P. Kresken

For full biographical listings, see the Martindale-Hubbell Law Directory

MYRTLE BEACH, Horry Co.

BELLAMY, RUTENBERG, COPELAND, EPPS, GRAVELY & BOWERS, P.A. (AV)

1000 29th Avenue North, P.O. Box 357, 29578
Telephone: 843-448-2400
Telecopier: 843-448-3022

Howell V. Bellamy, Jr.
John K. Rutenberg
John E. Copeland
Claude M. Epps, Jr.
David R. Gravely
Edward B. Bowers, Jr.
Bradley D. King
Henrietta U. Golding
M. Edwin Hinds, Jr.
Jill F. Griffith
Kathryn M. Cook
David B. Miller
C. Winfield Johnson, III
Sarah A. Johnson
Douglas M. Zayicek
Jeffrey W. King
Mary Anna Malpass
Martin Charles Dawsey

Representative Clients: Dargan Construction Co.; Coastal Federal Savings Bank; Sands Investments; Wachovia Bank of South Carolina; AVX Corp.; Bank of America; Parthenon Insurance Co.; Burroughs & Chapin Co.; International Paper Co.; Hospital Corporation of America.

For full biographical listings, see the Martindale-Hubbell Law Directory

*SPARTANBURG,** Spartanburg Co.

EDWARDS, BALLARD, BISHOP, STURM, CLARK & KEIM, P.A. (AV)

International Center, Suite 400, 101 North Pine Street, P.O. Box 5398, 29304-5398
Telephone: 864-542-8612
Fax: 864-542-8712
Email: lawfirm@ebbsck.com
Winston-Salem, North Carolina Office: Edwards, Ballard, Clark, Barrett and Carlson, P.A., 380 Knollwood, Suite 730, P.O. Box 1708. 27102-1708.
Telephone: 336-750-0707.
Fax: 336-750-0711.

James F. Edwards, Jr.
Wade E. Ballard
Michael W. Bishop
Kevin W. Sturm
Terry A. Clark (Resident Partner, Edwards, Ballard, Clark, Barrett and Carlson, P.A., Winston-Salem, North Carolina)
Thomas H. Keim, Jr.
Karen M. Tyner
Roger G. Chandler
Patrick L. Cont

S. Clay Keim
Krishna Y. McVey
W. Allen Myrick, Jr.
Penny Correll Wofford

Representative Clients: Texfi Industries, Inc.; Coca-Cola Bottling Co. Consolidated; Kobe Copper Products, Inc.; Van Waters & Rogers, Inc.; Spartanburg Steel Products, Inc.; Century Furniture Co.; Grimes Aerospace Corp.; Sulzer Ruti, Inc.; Comm/Scope, Inc.; South Carolina Insurance Reserve Fund.

For full biographical listings, see the Martindale-Hubbell Law Directory

SOUTH DAKOTA

*ABERDEEN,** Brown Co.

MALONEY & MALONEY (AV)

722 South Highway 281, P.O. Box 755, 57402-0755
Telephone: 605-229-2752
Fax: 605-226-0276
Email: maloney@nvc.net

MEMBERS OF FIRM

Dennis Maloney
Marilyn Marshall Maloney

For full biographical listings, see the Martindale-Hubbell Law Directory

*RAPID CITY,** Pennington Co.

BANGS, McCULLEN, BUTLER, FOYE & SIMMONS, L.L.P. (AV)

818 St. Joseph Street, P.O. Box 2670, 57709
Telephone: 605-343-1040
Telecopier: 605-343-1503
URL: http://www.bangsmccullen.com

MEMBERS OF FIRM

Thomas E. Simmons
Michael M. Hickey

ASSOCIATES

Veronica L. Bowen
Steven R. Nolan

Representative Clients: Norwest Bank South Dakota, N.A., Rapid City, S.D.; Pete Lien & Sons; The Travelers Insurance Co.; Rapid City Regional Hospital; Dakota Steel & Supply Co.; Great American Insurance Co.; Fireman's Fund Insurance; United States Automobile Association; Moyle Petroleum; Rapid City Area School District 51-4.

For Complete List of Firm Personnel, See General Section

For full biographical listings, see the Martindale-Hubbell Law Directory

TENNESSEE

*CHATTANOOGA,** Hamilton Co.

BAKER, DONELSON, BEARMAN & CALDWELL (AV)

1800 Republic Centre, 633 Chestnut Street, 37450-1800
Telephone: 423-756-2010
Telecopier: 423-756-3447
Email: info@bdbc.com *URL:* http://www.bakerdonelson.com
Memphis, Tennessee Office: 20th Floor, First Tennessee Building, 165 Madison, 38103.
Telephone: 901-526-2000.
Telecopier: 901-577-2303.

(See Next Column)

Nashville, Tennessee Office: 1700 Nashville City Center, 511 Union Street, 37219.
Telephone: 615-726-5600.
Telecopier: 615-726-0464.
Knoxville, Tennessee Office: 2200 Riverview Tower, 900 South Gay Street, 37901.
Telephone: 423-549-7000.
Telecopier: 423-525-8569.
Johnson City, Tennessee Office: SunTrust Bank Building, 207 Mockingbird Lane, P.O. Box 3038, 37602.
Telephone: 423-928-0181.
Telecopier: 423-928-5694; 423-928-3654; Kingsport: 423-246-6191.
Huntsville, Tennessee Office: 3 Courthouse Square, 37756.
Telephone: 423-663-2321.
Telecopier: 423-663-2111.
Washington, D.C. Office: Market Square, 801 Pennsylvania Avenue, N.W., 20004.
Telephone: 202-508-3400.
Telecopier: 202-508-3402.
Jackson, Mississippi Office: Suite 500, 700 North State Street, 39202.
Telephone: 601-351-2400.
Telecopier: 601-351-2424.

SHAREHOLDERS

Thomas O. Helton
Richard J. McAfee
John C. Harrison

ASSOCIATE

Russell W. Gray

For Complete List of Firm Personnel, See General Section

For full biographical listings, see the Martindale-Hubbell Law Directory

PHILLIP A. FLEISSNER, PLLC (AV)

600 Georgia Avenue, 37402
Telephone: 423-756-3591
Telecopier: 423-266-5455

Phillip A. Fleissner
David C. Nagle
Christopher Price Butler

For full biographical listings, see the Martindale-Hubbell Law Directory

FRANKLIN, COOPER & MARCUS, PLLC (AV)

837 Fort Wood Street, 37403
Telephone: 423-756-3596
Telecopier: 423-756-3597

David L. Franklin
Gary A. Cooper
H. Richard Marcus

For full biographical listings, see the Martindale-Hubbell Law Directory

SUMMERS & WYATT, P.C. (AV)

500 Lindsay Street, 37402
Telephone: 423-265-2385
Fax: 423-266-5211
Email: summers@voy.net

Jerry H. Summers
Thomas L. Wyatt
Jeffrey W. Rufolo

For Complete List of Firm Personnel, See General Section

For full biographical listings, see the Martindale-Hubbell Law Directory

WITT, GAITHER & WHITAKER, P.C. (AV)

1100 SunTrust Bank Building, 37402-2608
Telephone: 423-265-8881
Telefax: 423-266-4138; 423-756-5612

Philip B. Whitaker
Hugh J. Moore, Jr.
Frank P. Pinchak
K. Stephen Powers
Rosemarie Luise Bryan
Douglas E. Peck
Philip B. Whitaker, Jr.

Lisa M. Pate

Representative Clients: Associated General Agency, Inc.; Cannon Southeast; Kenco Group, Inc.; Lay Packing Co., Inc.; Plasti-Line, Inc.; Seaboard Corporation; Textile Printing Co.; Top Flight Paper Co.; Turnbull Bakeries; U.S. Xpress Enterprises, Inc.

For Complete List of Firm Personnel, See General Section

For full biographical listings, see the Martindale-Hubbell Law Directory

JOHNSON CITY, Washington Co.

BAKER, DONELSON, BEARMAN & CALDWELL (AV)

SunTrust Bank Building, 207 Mockingbird Lane, P.O. Box 3038, 37602
Telephone: 423-928-0181
Telecopier: 423-928-5694; 928-3654; Kingsport: 423-246-6191
Email: info@bdbc.com *URL:* http://www.bakerdonelson.com
Memphis, Tennessee Office: 20th Floor, First Tennessee Building, 165 Madison, 38103.
Telephone: 901-526-2000.
Telecopier: 901-577-2303.
Nashville, Tennessee Office: 1700 Nashville City Center, 511 Union Street, 37219.
Telephone: 615-726-5600.
Telecopier: 615-726-0464.
Chattanooga, Tennessee Office: 1800 Republic Centre, 633 Chestnut Street, 37450-1800.
Telephone: 423-756-2010.
Telecopier: 423-756-3447.
Knoxville, Tennessee Office: 2200 Riverview Tower, 900 South Gay Street, 37901.
Telephone: 423-549-7000.
Telecopier: 423-525-8569.
Huntsville, Tennessee Office: 3 Courthouse Square, 37756.
Telephone: 615-663-2321.
Telecopier: 615-663-2111.
Washington, D.C. Office: Market Square, 801 Pennsylvania Avenue, N.W., 20004.
Telephone: 202-508-3400.
Telecopier: 202-508-3402.
Jackson, Mississippi Office: Suite 500, 700 North State Street, 39202.
Telephone: 601-351-2400.
Telecopier: 601-351-2424.

ASSOCIATES

Steven H. Trent
Alice K. Corker
Jennifer P. Keller

For Complete List of Firm Personnel, See General Section

For full biographical listings, see the Martindale-Hubbell Law Directory

KINGSPORT, Sullivan Co.

HUNTER, SMITH & DAVIS, LLP (AV)

1212 North Eastman Road, P.O. Box 3740, 37664
Telephone: 423-378-8800
Telecopier: 423-378-8801
Email: info@hsdlaw.com *URL:* http://www.hsdlaw.com
Johnson City, Tennessee Office: Suite 500 First American Center, 208 Sunset Drive, 37604.
Telephone: 423-283-6300.
Telecopier: 423-283-6301.

MEMBERS OF FIRM

William C. Bovender
Michael L. Forrester
Stephen M. Darden

ASSOCIATE

Julie Poe Bennett

COUNSEL

Shelburne Ferguson, Jr.

Representative Clients: AFG Industries, Inc.; Sprint; Eastman Chemical Co.; Ball Corp.; Land-O-Sun Dairies, Inc.; American Greetings Corp.; Wellmont Health System (Bristol Regional Medical Center/Holston Valley Medical Center/Lonesome Pine Hospital); Quebecor Printing, Inc.; Willamette Industries, Inc.; First Tennessee Bank.

For Complete List of Firm Personnel, See General Section

For full biographical listings, see the Martindale-Hubbell Law Directory

SHINE & MASON LAW OFFICE (AV)

Suite 201, 433 East Center Street, 37660
Telephone: 423-246-8433
Fax: 423-246-7464
Email: shimas@mounet.com

MEMBERS OF FIRM

D. Bruce Shine
Donald F. Mason, Jr.

Reference: Citizens Bank, Kingsport, TN.

For full biographical listings, see the Martindale-Hubbell Law Directory

KNOXVILLE,* Knox Co.

ARNETT, DRAPER & HAGOOD (AV)

Suite 2300, First Tennessee Plaza, P.O. Box 300, 37901-0300
Telephone: 865-546-7000
Telecopier: 865-546-0423
Email: adandh@aol.com

(See Next Column)

MEMBERS OF FIRM

Lewis R. Hagood
Robert N. Townsend
Douglas Gerard Brehm

Representative Clients: Philips Consumer Electronics Co.; Consolidation Coal Co.; Shoney's of Knoxville, Inc.; England/Corsair, Inc.; Klote International; Vinylex Corp.; IT Corporation; Weigel's, Inc.; Vulcan Materials Co.; Nationwide Mutual Insurance Co.

For Complete List of Firm Personnel, See General Section

For full biographical listings, see the Martindale-Hubbell Law Directory

FRANTZ, MCCONNELL & SEYMOUR, LLP (AV)

550 Main Avenue, Suite 500, 37902
Telephone: 423-546-9321
Fax: 423-637-5249
Mailing Address: P.O. Box 39, Knoxville, TN, 37901
Email: Lwhitfield@fmsllp.com
Effective October 1, 1999, the Area Code will change to 865.

MEMBERS OF FIRM

Arthur G. Seymour, Jr.
Debra L. Fulton
John M. Lawhorn

References: ASARCO Incorporated; Aztex Enterprises; BellSouth Telecommunications, Inc.; Coca-Cola Enterprises, Inc.; Knoxville Transportation Authority; Maremont Exhaust Products, Inc.; NBC Bank, FSB; Norfolk Southern Railway Company; Racetrac Petroleum, Inc.; The Travelers Insurance Companies.

For Complete List of Firm Personnel, See General Section

For full biographical listings, see the Martindale-Hubbell Law Directory

LEIBOWITZ & COHEN (AV)

608 Gay Street, S.W., 37902
Telephone: 423-637-1809
FAX: 423-637-9276

MEMBERS OF FIRM

Arnold G. Cohen
Lawrence P. Leibowitz

ASSOCIATE

Melissa A. Ashburn

OF COUNSEL

Russell T. Greene

For full biographical listings, see the Martindale-Hubbell Law Directory

WATSON, HOLLOW & REEVES, P.L.C. (AV)

1700 First Tennessee Plaza, 800 South Gay Street, P.O. Box 131, 37901-0131
Telephone: 423-637-1700
Telecopier: 423-525-2514

MEMBERS OF FIRM

Robert Harmon Watson, Jr.
Jon Gilbert Roach
Richard L. Hollow
John Chapman Duffy
Pamela L. Reeves
John T. Batson, Jr.
Earl Jerome Melson

ASSOCIATES

Nathan D. Rowell
Beverley S. Cornett
Laura C. Webb
Jenny Coques Rogers

Representative Clients: Colonial Freight Systems, Inc.; Knoxville-Knox County Community Action Committee; City of Knoxville; Knox County, Tennessee; Minnewawa, Inc.; Atrix, Inc.; City of Morristown; Tennessee Municipal League Insurance Pool; Union County Board of Education.

For full biographical listings, see the Martindale-Hubbell Law Directory

WIMBERLY LAWSON & SEALE, PLLC (AV)

Suite 601, NationsBank Center, 550 Main Avenue, P.O. Box 2231, 37901-2231
Telephone: 423-546-1000
Telefax: 423-546-1001
Email: wls@wls-law.com
Cookeville, Tennessee Office: 524 Kentucky Road, P.O. Box 655.
Telephone: 931-372-9123.
Telefax: 931-372-9181.
Morristown, Tennessee Office: 929 West First North Street, P.O. Box 1066.
Telephone: 423-587-6870.
Telefax: 423-587-1479.
Nashville, Tennessee Office: 3200 West End Avenue, Suite 500.
Telephone: 615-783-2190.
Telefax: 615-783-1606.
Affiliated Firms:
Atlanta, Georgia Office: Wimberly, Lawson, Steckel, Nelson & Schneider, P.C., Suite 400, Lenox Towers, 3400 Peachtree Street, N.E.
Telephone: 404-365-0900.
Fax: 404-261-3707. E-Mail: wl@wimlaw.com.
Fernandina Beach, Florida Office: Wimberly, Lawson & Leggio, P.O. Box 1128.
Telephone: 904-277-2222.
Fax: 904-277-6598.

(See Next Column)

WIMBERLY LAWSON & SEALE PLLC—*Continued*

Greenville, South Carolina Office: Wimberly, Lawson Daniels & Brandon, Overlook Executive Park, 109 Laurens Road, Building 4, Suite A.
Telephone: 864-242-9484.
Fax: 864-242-6833. E-Mail: mldjr@aol.com.

Philip J. Lawson	Ronald G. Daves
William R. Seale	Mark C. Travis
Gary W. Wright	G. Gerard Jabaley

Jeffrey C. Taylor

ASSOCIATES

George R. Arrants, Jr.	J. Eric Harrison
Fredrick J. Bissinger	Mary Moffatt Helms
J. Timothy Bobo	Jeffrey G. Jones
Kelly A. Campbell	Robin M. King
Joseph J. Doherty	Jerome D. Pinn
Kevin M. Dorris	Scott M. Robbins
Robert Durham	Henry E. Sledge, Jr.
Robert S. Hahn	Lisa A. Temple
Stephanie J. Weber Hale	Patty K. Wheeler

For full biographical listings, see the Martindale-Hubbell Law Directory

*MEMPHIS,** Shelby Co.

ALLEN, SCRUGGS, SOSSAMAN & THOMPSON, P.C. (AV)

813 Ridge Lake Boulevard, Suite 300, 38120-9409
Telephone: 901-763-4200
Facsimile: 901-684-1768
Mailing Address: P.O. Box 17349, Memphis, TN, 38187-0349
Email: asstlaw@asstlaw.com

Richard H. Allen, Jr.	Shawn R. Lillie
John P. Scruggs	Heather C. Webb
William L. Sossaman	Kirk A. Caraway
Martin F. Thompson	Charles R. Keckler, III
James M. Simpson	M. Blake Barton

For full biographical listings, see the Martindale-Hubbell Law Directory

ARMSTRONG ALLEN PREWITT GENTRY JOHNSTON & HOLMES, PLLC (AV)

Brinkley Plaza, Suite 700, 80 Monroe Avenue, 38103-2467
Telephone: 901-523-8211
Facsimile: 901-524-4936
Little Rock, Arkansas Office: Suite 100, 100 Morgan Keegan Drive, 72202.
Telephone: 501-280-0100.
Facsimile: 501-280-0166.
Jackson, Mississippi Office: 2525 Lakeward Drive, Suite 200, 39216.
Telephone: 601-713-1192.
Facsimile: 601-713-2049.
Jackson, Tennessee Office: 464 North Parkway, Suite A, 38305.
Telephone: 901-660-2332.
Facsimile: 901-664-1109.

MEMBERS OF FIRM

Carl H. Langschmidt, Jr.	Prince C. Chambliss, Jr.
Ross B. Clark II	Thomas W. Lewis

Daniel W. Van Horn

For Complete List of Firm Personnel, See General Section

For full biographical listings, see the Martindale-Hubbell Law Directory

BAKER, DONELSON, BEARMAN & CALDWELL (AV)

20th Floor, First Tennessee Building, 165 Madison, 38103
Telephone: 901-526-2000
Telecopier: 901-577-2303
Email: info@bdbc.com *URL:* http://www.bakerdonelson.com
Nashville, Tennessee Office: 1700 Nashville City Center, 511 Union Street, 37219.
Telephone: 615-726-5600.
Telecopier: 615-726-0464.
Chattanooga, Tennessee Office: 1800 Republic Centre, 633 Chestnut Street, 37450-1800.
Telephone: 423-756-2010.
Telecopier: 423-756-3447.
Knoxville, Tennessee Office: 2200 Riverview Tower, 900 South Gay Street, 37901.
Telephone: 423-549-7000.
Telecopier: 423-525-8569.
Johnson City, Tennessee Office: SunTrust Bank Building, 207 Mockingbird Lane, P.O. Box 3038, 37602.
Telephone: 423-928-0181.
Telecopier: 423-928-5694; 423-928-3654; Kingsport: 423-246-6191.
Huntsville, Tennessee Office: 3 Courthouse Square, 37756.
Telephone: 423-663-2321.
Telecopier: 423-663-2111.
Washington, D.C. Office: Market Square, 801 Pennsylvania Avenue, N.W., 20004.
Telephone: 202-508-3400.
Telecopier: 202-508-3402.

(See Next Column)

Jackson, Mississippi Office: Suite 500, 700 North State Street, 39202.
Telephone: 601-351-2400.
Telecopier: 601-351-2424.

MANAGING PARTNER

Robert Mark Glover

SHAREHOLDERS

Lewis R. Donelson, III	Charles C. Harrell
Roy Keathley	Stephen D. Goodwin
David G. Williams	George T. Lewis, III
Leo Bearman, Jr.	Ben C. Adams, Jr.
Maurice Wexler	Eugene J. Podesta, Jr.
Frank L. Watson, Jr.	Sam B. Blair, Jr.
Robert Walker	Carla Peacher-Ryan
Boyd L. Rhodes, Jr.	Mary Aronov
W. Michael Richards	Jill M. Steinberg
John C. Speer	Matthew S. Heiter
Charles T. Tuggle, Jr.	Michael C. Patton
Larry E. Killebrew	Janis Wild Kesser
Jerry Stauffer	Stephen William Ragland
Robert C. Liddon	Monique A. Nassar
William H.D. Fones, Jr.	Bradley E. Trammell
William P. Kenworthy	M. Clay Bethell
Allan J. Wade	Desiree M. Franklin
Gregory G. Fletcher	R. Alan Pritchard, Jr.

Peter H. Kesser

OF COUNSEL

Frierson M. Graves, Jr.	Lynn Ackerman Landau
Donald A. Malmo	Paul E. Risner (Not admitted in TN)

ASSOCIATES

Paul R. O'Rourke	Jennifer R. Keown
Anne B. Mathes	Brett T. Parks
Elizabeth Einstman Chance	Cedric C.Y. Tan
Frank L. Watson, III	Lang Wiseman
W. Douglas Sweet	Diane Schratz Holitik
Wm. Scott Young	D. Benjamin Bullen
Mary Ann Jackson	Shannon M. Hernandez
Angela R. Merideth	Sylvia Monique Reed
Jackie G. Prester	Christopher G. Boling
David L. Bearman	Louise P. Gaerig
Clarissa M. Cissell	Lori Hackleman Patterson
Robert C. McConkey, III	Lea Hall Speed

For full biographical listings, see the Martindale-Hubbell Law Directory

FORD & HARRISON LLP (AV)

6750 Poplar Avenue, Suite 600, P.O. Box 171375, 38187-1375
Telephone: 901-756-1550
Telecopier: 901-756-1016
Email: firm@fordharrison.com *URL:* http://www.fordharrison.com
Atlanta, Georgia Office: 600 Peachtree at the Circle Building, 1275 Peachtree Street, N.E. 30309.
Telephone: 404-888-3800.
Fax: 404-888-3863.
Los Angeles, California Office: 333 South Grand Avenue, Suite 3680. 90071.
Telephone: 213-680-3410.
Fax: 213-680-4161.
Miami, Florida Office: 516 Ingraham Building, 25 S.E. 2nd Avenue. 33131.
Telephone: 305-379-3711.
Fax: 305-358-5933.
Tampa, Florida Office: 101 E. Kennedy Boulevard, Suite 900. 33602.
Telephone: 813-261-7800.
Fax: 813-261-7899.
Washington, D.C. Office: 1920 N Street, N.W., Suite 200. 20036.
Telephone: 202-463-6633.
Fax: 202-466-5705.

MEMBERS OF FIRM

Robert L. McKnight (1906-1976)	Louis P. Britt, III (Resident)
Fletcher L. Hudson (Resident)	Charles V. Holmes (Resident)
Herbert E. Gerson (Resident)	Robert M. Williams, Jr. (Resident)
Keith A. Warren (Resident)	Devon L. Gosnell (Resident)

SENIOR COUNSEL

Brian L. Kuhn (Resident)	Thomas J. Walsh, Jr. (Resident)

ASSOCIATES

Timothy S. Bland (Resident)	Michele L. Fowler (Resident)
Richard E. Circeo (Resident)	Michelle S. Harkavy (Resident)
Carrie L. Clark (Resident)	Carl Knox Morrison (Resident)
Blair Beavers Evans (Resident)	Ashley Swain Old (Resident)

Delaine R. Smith (Resident)

OF COUNSEL

Kenneth D. Henderson (Resident)

Representative Clients: Aetna Life & Annuity Company; City of Memphis; Clear Channel Broadcasting; Darden Restaurants, Inc.; Dobbs International Services, Inc.; General Electric; Georgia-Gulf Corporation; Hunter Fan Company; M.S. Carriers, Inc.; Union Planters National Bank.

For full biographical listings, see the Martindale-Hubbell Law Directory

Memphis—Continued

GLASSMAN, JETER, EDWARDS & WADE, P.C. (AV)

26 North Second Street Building, 38103
Telephone: 901-527-4673
Telecopier: 901-521-0940
Email: GJEWW@Memphisonline.com

Tim Edwards
John Barry Burgess
Rebecca Adelman
James F. Horner, Jr.

For full biographical listings, see the Martindale-Hubbell Law Directory

HARKAVY, SHAINBERG, KOSTEN, KAPLAN & DUNSTAN, PC (AV)

100 Peabody Place, Suite 1300, 38103
Telephone: 901-761-1263
Telecopier: 901-763-3340
Downtown Telecopier: 901-843-0864
Downtown Office: Memphis, Tennessee, 6060 Poplar Avenue, Suite 140, 38119.

MEMBERS AND ASSOCIATES

Ronald M. Harkavy
Raymond M. Shainberg
Alan L. Kosten
Michael D. Kaplan
Allen C. Dunstan
Neil Harkavy
Jerome A. Broadhurst
Alan M. Harkavy

OF COUNSEL

Ira D. Pruitt, Jr.
Laurie A. Cooper
G. Thomas McPherson

For full biographical listings, see the Martindale-Hubbell Law Directory

KIESEWETTER WISE KAPLAN SCHWIMMER & PRATHER, PLC (AV)

2650 Thousand Oaks Boulevard, Suite 2200, 38118
Telephone: 901-795-6695
Fax: 901-795-1646
URL: http://www.kiesewetterwise.com

Jonathan E. Kaplan
Jay W. Kiesewetter
Paul E. Prather
Cary Schwimmer
John W. Simmons
J. Edward Wise

ASSOCIATES

Sylvia R. Adams
Howard L. Cleveland IV
Karen W. Grochau
Lisa Lichterman Leach
Robert David Meyers
W. Terry Smith, Jr.
Todd E. Taylor
Tanja Lueck Thompson
Jason G. Wolfkill

LEGAL SUPPORT PERSONNEL

Patrick T. Fleming (Human Resources & Management Consultant)
Rachel Davis Spencer (Paralegal)
Michael A. Tenney (Human Resources & Management Consultant)
R. Bradley Mokros (Paralegal)

For full biographical listings, see the Martindale-Hubbell Law Directory

LEWIS, FISHER, HENDERSON & CLAXTON, LLP (AV)

5050 Poplar Avenue Suite 1717, 38157
Telephone: 901-767-6160
Fax: 901-767-7411
URL: http://www.lfhc.com
Los Angeles, California Office: 12100 Wilshire Boulevard, Suite 600, 90025.
Telephone: 310-820-3150.
Fax: 310-820-2830.

Frederick J. Lewis
Donna K. Fisher
Thomas L. Henderson
Linda K. Claxton (Not admitted in TN)

SENIOR COUNSEL

Conielyn Lowry Abernathy
Leslie E. Wallis (Not admitted in TN; Resident at Los Angeles, CA Office)

ASSOCIATES

Kelly S. Gooch
Nicole Marie Walthour
Thomas H. Lawrence
Keri Goldstein Unowsky (Not admitted in TN)
John M. Russell
Jeana M. Littrell
Oscar John Norris, III
Craig A. Cowart

For full biographical listings, see the Martindale-Hubbell Law Directory

SMITH, SABBATINI & MCLEARY, PLLC (AV)

100 Peabody Place Suite 1250, 38103
Telephone: 901-312-5555
Fax: 901-312-5667
Mailing Address: P.O. Box 3582, Memphis, TN, 38173
URL: http://www.smithlawetal.com

(See Next Column)

Gary K. Smith
Robert L. Sabbatini
Harold W. McLeary, Jr.
William D. Domico
James F. Kyle
James T. McColgan, III
G. Edward Coleman, III
Bryant C. Witt

Representative Clients: Premier RRG Insurance; Illinois Central Railroad; Medical Assurance; Albertson's, Inc.; Med. Marc (Chiro Co.); Medical Protective Co.; Methodist Health Systems; Hartford Insurance Co.; Sentry Insurance; State Farm Insurance.

For full biographical listings, see the Martindale-Hubbell Law Directory

WARING COX, PLC (AV)

Morgan Keegan Tower, 50 North Front Street, Suite 1300, 38103-1190
Telephone: 901-543-8000
Telecopy: 901-543-8030
Email: Desk@waringcox.com

Louis F. Allen
Charles W. Hill
Robert B.C. Hale

Howard Leo Beale, II
William F. Burns

Representative Clients: Federal Express Corp.; South Central Bell Telephone Co.; Flavorite Laboratories, Inc.; Fred's Inc.; Seabrook Wallcovering, Inc.; Health First Medical Group, P.C.

For Complete List of Firm Personnel, See General Section

For full biographical listings, see the Martindale-Hubbell Law Directory

WEINTRAUB, STOCK, BENNETT, GRISHAM & UNDERWOOD, P.C. (AV)

Suite 2560 One Commerce Square, 38103
Telephone: 901-526-0431
1-800-467-0435
Facsimile: 901-526-8183
Email: office@weintraubstock.com *URL:* http://www.weintraubstock.com
Jackson, Tennessee Office: Towering Oaks Office Park, 2815 North Highland Avenue, Suite B, 38305.
Telephone: 901-660-4747.
Fax: 901-668-2279.
Las Vegas, Nevada Office: 4270 Decatur Boulevard, Suite B-6, 89103.
Telephone: 702-968-8050.
Fax: 702-968-8077.

Jeff Weintraub
James H. Stock, Jr.
Richard D. Bennett
J. Gregory Grisham
Richard D. Underwood

Cecilia Suzette Barnes
James Francis Barna
Keith R. Thomas

OF COUNSEL

Jay R. Robinson

For Complete List of Firm Personnel, See General Section

For full biographical listings, see the Martindale-Hubbell Law Directory

*NASHVILLE,** Davidson Co.

BAKER, DONELSON, BEARMAN & CALDWELL (AV)

1700 Nashville City Center, 511 Union Street, 37219
Telephone: 615-726-5600
Telecopier: 615-726-0464
Email: info@bdbc.com *URL:* http://www.bakerdonelson.com
Memphis, Tennessee Office: 20th Floor, First Tennessee Building, 165 Madison, 38103.
Telephone: 901-526-2000.
Telecopier: 901-577-2303.
Chattanooga, Tennessee Office: 1800 Republic Centre, 633 Chestnut Street, 37450-1800.
Telephone: 423-756-2010.
Telecopier: 423-756-3447.
Knoxville, Tennessee Office: 2200 Riverview Tower, 900 South Gay Street, 37901.
Telephone: 423-549-7000.
Telecopier: 423-525-8569.
Johnson City, Tennessee Office: SunTrust Bank Building, 207 Mockingbird Lane, P.O. Box 3038, 37602.
Telephone: 423-928-0181.
Telecopier: 423-928-5694; 423-928-3654; Kingsport: 423-246-6191.
Huntsville, Tennessee Office: 3 Courthouse Square, 37756.
Telephone: 423-663-2321.
Telecopier: 423-663-2111.
Washington, D.C. Office: Market Square, 801 Pennsylvania Avenue, N.W., 20004.
Telephone: 202-508-3400.
Telecopier: 202-508-3402.
Jackson, Mississippi Office: Suite 500, 700 North State Street, 39202.
Telephone: 601-351-2400.
Telecopier: 601-351-2424.

(See Next Column)

BAKER, DONELSON, BEARMAN & CALDWELL—*Continued*

ASSOCIATES

Kenneth A. Weber
Lawrence S. Eastwood, Jr.

For Complete List of Firm Personnel, See General Section

For full biographical listings, see the Martindale-Hubbell Law Directory

BASS, BERRY & SIMS PLC (AV)

2700 First American Center, 37238-2700
Telephone: 615-742-6200
Telecopy: 615-742-6293
URL: http://www.bassberry.com
Knoxville, Tennessee Office: 1700 Riverview Tower, 900 S. Gay Street, 37902 and P.O. Box 1509, 37901-1509.
Telephone: 423-521-6200.
Telecopy: 423-521-6234.
Memphis, Tennessee Office: 119 S. Main Street, Suite 500, 38103.
Telephone: 901-312-9100.
Fax: 901-312-9101.

MEMBERS OF FIRM

Russell F. Morris, Jr.
William N. Ozier
Karen L.C. Ellis
Tim K. Garrett

ASSOCIATES

J. Davidson French
Robert W. Horton
Michael S. Moschel
Leslie B. Goff Sanders

Representative Clients: Vanderbilt University; Quebecor Printing, Inc.; GTE Mobile Communications; Leggett & Platt, Inc., Fiber & Textile Products Division; Toshiba America Consumer Products, Inc.; Oshkosh B'Gosh, Inc.; Goodyear Tire & Rubber Co.; Peterbilt Motors Co.; Cracker Barrel Old Country Stores, Inc.

For full biographical listings, see the Martindale-Hubbell Law Directory

BRANSTETTER, KILGORE, STRANCH & JENNINGS (AV)

227 Second Avenue, North Fourth Floor, 37201-1631
Telephone: 615-254-8801
Fax: 615-255-5419
Email: bksj@branstetterlaw.com

MEMBERS OF FIRM

Arthur Crownover, Jr. (1907-1965)
Cecil D. Branstetter
C. Dewey Branstetter, Jr.
Randall C. Ferguson
R. Jan Jennings
Carrol D. Kilgore
Donald L. Scholes
James G. Stranch, III
Jane Branstetter Stranch

LEGAL SUPPORT PERSONNEL

OFFICE MANAGER

Melissa Holloway

Counsel for: American Federation of Television and Radio Artists; Screen Actors Guild; International Alliance of Theatrical and Stage Employees; Nashville Building & Construction Trades Council; Tennessee Valley Trades & Labor Council; International Unions -- UFCW, IBEW, LIUNA, IAM and UA.

For full biographical listings, see the Martindale-Hubbell Law Directory

CHERNAU, CHAFFIN & BURNSED, PLLC (AV)

SunTrust Center, 424 Church Street, Suite 1750, 37219-2305
Telephone: 615-244-5480
Fax: 615-242-7951
Email: CCBABSMITH@AOL.COM

MEMBERS OF FIRM

Louis Leftwich, Jr. (1910-1960)
Stanley M. Chernau
R. Garry Chaffin
Linda F. Burnsed
Amy Bryson Smith

Representative Clients: Forklift Systems, Inc.; Edwin B. Raskins Co.; SouthTrust Bank National Association; B & G Wholesalers, Inc.; Continental Machinery Movers, Inc.

For full biographical listings, see the Martindale-Hubbell Law Directory

KING & BALLOW (AV)

Union Street Plaza, 315 Union Street, Suite 1100, 37201
Telephone: 615-259-3456
Fax: 615-254-7907
Email: lawfirm@king-ballow.com *URL:* http://www.king-ballow.com
San Diego, California Office: 2700 Symphony Towers, 750 B Street, 92101.
Telephone: 619-236-9401.
Fax: 619-236-9437.

MEMBERS OF FIRM

Frank S. King, Jr.
Robert L. Ballow
Richard C. Lowe
R. Eddie Wayland
Larry D. Crabtree
Paul H. Duvall (Resident, San Diego, California Office)
Steven C. Douse
Douglas R. Pierce
Howard M. Kastrinsky
Mark E. Hunt
John J. Matchulat
M. Kim Vance
R. Brent Ballow
Michael D. Oesterle
Richard S. Busch

(See Next Column)

ASSOCIATES

James P. Thompson
Darin E. Playle

Representative Clients: American Airlines, Nashville, Tennessee; Browning-Ferris Industries, Inc., Houston, TX; Cooper Industries, Inc., Houston, TX; Chubb Insurance Group, Dallas, TX; Ingram Micro, Inc., Santa Ana, CA; Opryland USA, Inc., Nashville, Tennessee; Pan American Electric, Nashville, TN; Pulitzer Publishing Company, St. Louis, Missouri; Roadway Express, Inc., Akron, OH; Tribune Company, Chicago, Illinois.

For Complete List of Firm Personnel, See General Section

For full biographical listings, see the Martindale-Hubbell Law Directory

ZINSER AND PATTERSON, P.L.L.C. (AV)

150 Second Avenue North, 37201
Telephone: 615-244-9700
Fax: 615-244-9734
URL: http://www.zinserpatterson.com

MEMBERS OF FIRM

L. Michael Zinser
James McMahan Patterson, Jr.

Representative Clients: Houston Chronicle; The Hearst Corporation; The Tennesseean; Donrey Media Group; Vista Metropolitan Media Co.; Stauffer Communications, Inc.; Eller Media Group, Inc.; Victorville Daily Press; American Publishing Co.; Southern Newspapers, Inc.

For full biographical listings, see the Martindale-Hubbell Law Directory

TEXAS

*AUSTIN,** Travis Co.

DAVIS & WILKERSON, P.C. (AV)

1801 South Mopac, Suite 300, P.O. Box 2283, 78768-2283
Telephone: 512-482-0614
Fax: 512-482-0342
Email: dwlaw@dwlaw.com *URL:* http://www.dwlaw.com
Alpine Office: 1110 East Holland, P.O. Box 777.
Telephone: 915-837-5547.

David M. Davis
Steven R. Welch
Glen Wilkerson
David A. Wright
Leonard W. Woods
Kevin A. Reed
J. Mark Holbrook
Brian E. Riewe
Brian McElroy
Robert L. Hargett
Michael Wilson
Frances W. Hamermesh
Fletcher H. Brown

Jennifer B. Claymon
David M. Coffey
Hollis Hudson Gaston
Steven C. Levatino
Diana Maldonado
Erin E. Matherne
Joel S. Pace
Stephen G. Wohleb
Michael P. Young

OF COUNSEL

Pete P. Gallego (Resident, Alpine Office)
Peter R. Meeker

For full biographical listings, see the Martindale-Hubbell Law Directory

JACKSON WALKER L.L.P. (AV)

100 Congress Avenue, Suite 1100, 78701-4099
Telephone: 512-236-2000
Fax: 512-236-2002
Email: hloftin@jw.com *URL:* http://www.jw.com
Dallas, Texas Office: 901 Main Street, Suite 6000.
Telephone: 214-953-6000.
Fax: 214-953-5822.
Fort Worth, Texas Office: 301 Commerce Street, Suite 2400.
Telephone: 817-334-7200.
Fax: 817-334-7290.
Houston, Texas Office: 1100 Louisiana, Suite 4200.
Telephone: 713-752-4200.
Fax: 713-752-4221.
Richardson, Texas Office: 2435 North Central Expressway, Suite 600.
Telephone: 972-671-2560.
Fax: 972-671-2566.
San Angelo, Texas Office: 225 West Beauregard Avenue.
Telephone: 915-481-2550.
Fax: 915-481-2552.
San Antonio, Texas Office: 112 E. Pecan Street, Suite 2100.
Telephone: 210-978-7700.
Fax: 210-978-7790.

MEMBERS OF FIRM

J. Matthew Dow
Louis K. Obdyke, IV
Peyton N. Smith
Gary A. Thornton

For Complete List of Firm Personnel, See General Section

For full biographical listings, see the Martindale-Hubbell Law Directory

Austin—Continued

SCHWARTZ & EICHELBAUM, P.C. (AV)

One Commodore Plaza, 800 Brazos, Suite 870, 78701
Telephone: 512-476-9944
Fax: 512-472-2599
Email: info@edlaw.com
San Antonio, Texas Office: 700 N. St. Mary's, Suite 1850, 78205.
Telephone: 210-228-9944.
Fax: 210-228-9950.
Plano, Texas Office, D/FW Metroplex: P.O. Box 250025, 75025.
Telephone: 972-377-7900.
Fax: 972-377-7277.

Leonard J. Schwartz
Dennis J. Eichelbaum (Resident, D/FW Metroplex, Texas)
Kelli Hamm Karczewski
Robert A. Schulman (Resident, San Antonio, Texas)
Cobby A. Caputo
Stacy C. Ferguson (Resident, San Antonio, Texas)

Holly Boyd Wardell
Cheryl Tremaine Mehl
Kaye Knox Feist
Suzanne Stephens Becker (Resident, San Antonio, Texas)
Deirdre Vasquez (Resident, San Antonio, Texas)

For full biographical listings, see the Martindale-Hubbell Law Directory

THOMPSON & KNIGHT L.L.P. (AV)

(Attorneys and Counselors)
1200 San Jacinto Center, 98 San Jacinto Boulevard, 78701
Telephone: 512-469-6100
Telecopy: 512-469-6180
URL: http://www.tklaw.com
Dallas, Texas Office: 1700 Pacific Avenue, Suite 3300, 75201.
Telephone: 214-969-1700.
Telecopy: 512-969-1751.
Telex: 732298.
Fort Worth, Texas Office: 801 Cherry Street, Suite 1600, 76102.
Telephone: 817-347-1700.
Telecopy: 817-347-1799.
Houston, Texas Office: Thompson Knight Brown Parker & Leahy L.L.P., 1200 Smith Street, Suite 3600, 77002-4595.
Telephone: 713-654-8111.
Telecopier: 713-654-1871.
San Pedro Garza Garcia, Nuevo León, Mexico Office: Edificio Losoles PD-4, Av. Lázaro Cárdenas No. 2400 Pte., C.P. 66220.
Telephone: (52-8) 363-0096.
Telecopy: (52-8) 363-3067.

PARTNERS

Holly Claghorn
Regina C. Williams

For Complete List of Firm Personnel, See General Section

For full biographical listings, see the Martindale-Hubbell Law Directory

BEDFORD, Tarrant Co.

ADAMS, LYNCH & LOFTIN, P.C. (AV)

1903 Central Drive, Suite 400, 76021
Telephone: 817-283-7742
Fax: 817-571-2947

Neal W. Adams
John T. Lynch, IV
Stacy B. Loftin
Jon A. McCormick

For full biographical listings, see the Martindale-Hubbell Law Directory

*DALLAS,** Dallas Co.

BAKER BOTTS L.L.P. (AV)

2001 Ross Avenue, 75201
Telephone: 214-953-6500
Fax: 214-953-6503
Email: postmaster@bakerbotts.com *URL:* http://www.bakerbotts.com
Houston, Texas Office: One Shell Plaza, 910 Louisiana.
Telephone: 713-229-1234.
Washington, D.C. Office: The Warner, 1299 Pennsylvania Avenue, N.W.
Telephone: 202-639-7700.
Austin, Texas Office: 1600 San Jacinto Center, 98 San Jacinto Boulevard.
Telephone: 512-322-2500.
New York, New York Office: 599 Lexington Avenue.
Telephone: 212-705-5000.
Moscow, Russia Office: 10 ul. Bolshaya Dimitrovka (formerly Pushkinskaya), 103031.
Telephone: 7095/921-5300 (Local); 7095/929-7070.
London, England Office: 45 Ludgate Hill.
Telephone: 0171-778-1400 (Local); 011-44-171-778-1400 (International).

(See Next Column)

Baku, Azerbaijan Office: 6-10 Vagif Mustafa-zadeh Street, Third Floor, Icheri Sheher, 370004.
Telephone: 994-12-97-63-88 (Local); 011-994-12-97-63-88 (International).

MEMBERS OF FIRM

Dan Hartsfield
Eric J. Senske

ASSOCIATES

Karen E. Griffin
Kelly D. Hine
Karen B. Peck
Pennie Peck
Katrin U. Schatz

For Complete List of Firm Personnel, See General Section

For full biographical listings, see the Martindale-Hubbell Law Directory

CALHOUN & STACY (AV)

Suite 5700 - Bank of America Plaza, 901 Main Street, 75202-3713
Telephone: 214-748-5000
Facsimile: 214-748-1421
Email: info@calhounstacy.com *URL:* http://www.calhounstacy.com

MEMBERS OF FIRM

Mark Alan Calhoun
LeAnn Wainscott Cross
David W. Elrod
Shannon B. Schuster
Roy L. Stacy
Michael C. Wright

ASSOCIATES

Scott S. Crocker
Sean P. Fitzgerald
Elizabeth Reding Gambrell
Jonathan G. Polak
Joel W. Reese
Barbara L. Wohlrabe

For Complete List of Firm Personnel, See General Section

For full biographical listings, see the Martindale-Hubbell Law Directory

CLARK, WEST, KELLER, BUTLER & ELLIS, L.L.P. (AV)

4800 Renaissance Tower, 1201 Elm Street, 75270-2146
Telephone: 214-741-1001
Telecopier: 214-760-9812

MEMBERS OF FIRM

William H. Clark (1861-1931)
William H. Clark, Jr. (1895-1943)
Robert L. Clark (1903-1963)
William L. Keller
Allen Butler
David M. Ellis
Melvyn L. Douglas
Mike M. Tabor
Mark A. Shank
Michael P. Maslanka
Kervyn B. Altaffer, Jr.
Kelly Gaffney McClure

ASSOCIATES

Veronica Cuadra
Melinda L. Eitzen
Wade A. Forsman
Theresa M. Gegen
M. Brenk Johnson
Christie A. Newkirk
Robert J. Wood, Jr.
John Peter Hagan
Sonja J. McGill

For full biographical listings, see the Martindale-Hubbell Law Directory

COHAN, SIMPSON, COWLISHAW & WULFF, L.L.P. (AV)

2700 One Dallas Centre, 350 North St. Paul Street, 75201-4283
Telephone: 214-754-0100
Telecopier: 214-754-0225

Linda S. Althoff
Michael Byrd
Robert M. Cohan
Patrick R. Cowlishaw
James A. Holmes (Resident)
Elizabeth Hawkins Hosch
John Martin Jackson
Kathleen M. LaValle
Ella J. Martinez
Scott M. McElhaney
Susan J. Sandidge
Kurt A. Schwarz
Lee M. Simpson
Mark R. Steiner
Shirley A. Stover
Bart Wulff

For full biographical listings, see the Martindale-Hubbell Law Directory

ERHARD, RUEBEL & JENNINGS, A PROFESSIONAL CORPORATION (AV)

1600 Pacific Avenue, 75201-3509
Telephone: 214-720-4001, 741-6201
Fax: 214-871-1655
Email: erjennings@compuserve.com *URL:* http://www.lawyers.com/erruje

James Albert Jennings
W. Christopher W. Haynes

OF COUNSEL

Susan Jane Stedman Jennings

Representative Client: Halliburton Co./Halliburton Energy Services.

For full biographical listings, see the Martindale-Hubbell Law Directory

FIGARI DAVENPORT & GRAVES, L.L.P. (AV)

A Partnership including a Professional Corporation
901 Main Street, LB 125, 4800 Bank of America Plaza, 75202-3796
Telephone: 214-939-2000
Fax: 214-939-2090

(See Next Column)

FIGARI DAVENPORT & GRAVES L.L.P.—*Continued*

MEMBERS OF FIRM

Ernest E. Figari, Jr., (P.C.)
Mark T. Davenport
Thomas A. Graves
Doug K. Butler
Donald Colleluori
Gary D. Eisenstat
Andrew G. Jubinsky
Parker D. Young
Michael G. Brown
Timothy A. Daniels
Keith R. Verges
Stephen D. Howen
Monica L. Luebker
Andrew C. Whitaker

Jill B. Davenport
Bill E. Davidoff
Amanda M. Inabnett
Dennis M. Lynch
Melissa A. Mitchell
Katherine S. Rabe
Lisa L. Traylor
Jennifer M. Trulock

For full biographical listings, see the Martindale-Hubbell Law Directory

GIBSON, McCLURE & WALLACE, L.L.P. (AV)

8080 North Central Expressway, Suite 1300, LB50, 75206
Telephone: 214-891-8040
Fax: 214-891-8010

MEMBERS OF FIRM

Dennis D. Gibson
Wade L. McClure
Jay M. Wallace
Gabrielle Honore Kickham
Ruth Ann Norton Daniels
James M. McCoy
Alan L. Rucker
Bryan D. Perkins

Evelyn A. Yeager
Connie Kay Wilhite

For full biographical listings, see the Martindale-Hubbell Law Directory

GILLESPIE, ROZEN & WATSKY, P.C. (AV)

3402 Oak Grove Avenue, Suite 200, 75204
Telephone: 214-720-2009
Metro: 972-988-3357
Fax: 214-720-2291

Hal K. Gillespie
Yona Rozen
David K. Watsky

Dale M. Rodriguez
Susan D. Motley
Edmond S. Moreland

OF COUNSEL

G. William Baab

For full biographical listings, see the Martindale-Hubbell Law Directory

GODWIN WHITE & GRUBER, A PROFESSIONAL CORPORATION (AV)

Suite 2500, 901 Main Street, 75202-3714
Telephone: 214-939-4400
Fax: 214-760-7332

James F. Bullock
Donald E. Godwin
Steven T. Polino
Harvey M. Shapan

ASSOCIATE

Debora Lynn Simon

For Complete List of Firm Personnel, See General Section

For full biographical listings, see the Martindale-Hubbell Law Directory

HUGHES & LUCE, L.L.P. (AV)

A Registered Limited Liability Partnership including Professional Corporations
1717 Main Street, Suite 2800, 75201
Telephone: 214-939-5500
Fax: 214-939-6100; 214-939-5849
Email: H&L@hughesluce.com *URL:* http://www.hughesluce.com
Austin, Texas Office: 111 Congress, Suite 900.
Telephone: 512-482-6800.
Fax: 512-482-6859.
Houston, Texas Office: 1600 Smith Street, Suite 3550.
Telephone: 713-754-5200.
Fax: 713-754-5270.

MEMBERS OF FIRM

Kim Juanita Askew
James Hunter Birch

ASSOCIATES

Kelly W. Milligan (Not admitted in TX)
Eric N. Roberson

For Complete List of Firm Personnel, See General Section

For full biographical listings, see the Martindale-Hubbell Law Directory

JACKSON WALKER L.L.P. (AV)

901 Main Street, Suite 6000, 75202-3797
Telephone: 214-953-6000
Fax: 214-953-5822
URL: http://www.jw.com
Austin, Texas Office: 100 Congress Avenue, Suite 1100.
Telephone: 512-236-2000.
Fax: 512-236-2002.
Fort Worth, Texas Office: 301 Commerce Street, Suite 2400.
Telephone: 817-334-7200.
Fax: 817-334-7290.
Houston, Texas Office: 1100 Louisiana, Suite 4200.
Telephone: 713-752-4200.
Fax: 713-752-4221.
Richardson, Texas Office: 2435 North Central Expressway, Suite 600.
Telephone: 972-671-2560.
Fax: 972-671-2566.
San Angelo, Texas Office: 225 West Beauregard Avenue.
Telephone: 915-481-2550.
Fax: 915-481-2552.
San Antonio, Texas Office: 112 E. Pecan Street, Suite 2100.
Telephone: 210-978-7700.
Fax: 210-978-7790.

MEMBERS OF FIRM

Bryan C. Collins
James R. Griffin
A. David Gross
Gary L. Ingram
Phillip Ray Jones
John A. Koepke

OF COUNSEL

George C. Dunlap

Representative Clients Furnished Upon Request.

For Complete List of Firm Personnel, See General Section

For full biographical listings, see the Martindale-Hubbell Law Directory

JONES, DAY, REAVIS & POGUE (AV)

2727 North Harwood Street, 75201-1515
Telephone: 214-220-3939
Telecopier: 214-969-5100
Email: counsel@jonesday.com *URL:* http://www.jonesday.com
In Atlanta, Georgia: 3500 SunTrust Plaza, 303 Peachtree Street.
Telephone: 404-521-3939.
Telecopier: 404-581-8330.
In Brussels, Belgium: Avenue Louise 480, 7th Floor, B-1050 Brussels.
Telephone: 32-2-645-14-11.
Telecopier: 32-2-645-14-45.
In Chicago, Illinois: 77 West Wacker.
Telephone: 312-782-3939.
Telecopier: 312-782-8585.
In Cleveland, Ohio: North Point, 901 Lakeside Avenue.
Telephone: 216-586-3939.
Telecopier: 216-579-0212.
In Columbus, Ohio: 1900 Huntington Center.
Telephone: 614-469-3939.
Telecopier: 614-461-4198.
In Frankfurt, Germany: Hochhaus am Park, Grüneburgweg 102, 60323 Frankfurt am Main.
Telephone: 49-69-9726-3939.
Telecopier: 49-69-9726-3993.
In Geneva, Switzerland: 20, rue de Candolle.
Telephone: 41-22-320-2339.
Telecopier: 41-22-320-1232.
In Hong Kong: 29th Floor, Entertainment Building, 30 Queen's Road Central.
Telephone: 852-2526-6895.
Telecopier: 852-2868-5871.
In Irvine, California: 5 Park Plaza, Suite 1100.
Telephone: 949-851-3939.
Telecopier: 949-553-7539.
In London, England: Bucklersbury House, 3 Queen Victoria Street.
Telephone: 44-20-7236-3939.
Telecopier: 44-20-7236-1113.
In Los Angeles, California: 555 West Fifth Street, Suite 4600.
Telephone: 213-489-3939.
Telecopier: 213-243-2539.
In New York, New York: 599 Lexington Avenue.
Telephone: 212-326-3939.
Telecopier: 212-755-7306.
In Paris, France: 120, rue du Faubourg Saint-Honoré.
Telephone: 33-1-56-59-39-39.
Telecopier: 33-1-56-59-39-38
In Pittsburgh, Pennsylvania: 500 Grant Street, 31st Floor.
Telephone: 412-391-3939.
Telecopier: 412-394-7959.
Riyadh, Saudi Arabia: The International Law Firm (In Association with Jones, Day, Reavis & Pogue), Sulaymaniyah, Prince Mishari IBN, Addulaziz Street, P.O. Box 22166.
Telephone: (966-1) 462-8866.
Telecopier: (966-1) 462-9001.
In Shanghai, China: 2805 Kerry Centre, 1515 Nanjing Road West.
Telephone: 86-21-5298-6568.
Telecopier: 86-21-5298-6569.

(See Next Column)

JONES, DAY, REAVIS & POGUE, *Dallas—Continued*

In Sydney, Australia: Governor Phillip Tower, Level 38, 1 Farrer Place.
Telephone: 61-2-9210-6921.
Telecopier: 61-2-9210-6926.
In Taipei, Taiwan: 8th Floor, 2 Tun Hwa South Road, Section 2.
Telephone: (886-2) 2704-6808.
Telecopier: (886-2) 2704-6791.
In Tokyo, Japan: Toranomon 45 Mori Building, 3rd Floor, 1-5, Toranomon, 5-Chome, Minato-ku, Tokyo 105, Japan.
Telephone: 81-3-3433-3939.
Telecopier: 81-3-5401-2725.
In Washington, D.C.: 51 Louisiana Avenue, N.W.
Telephone: 202-879-3939.
Telecopier: 202-626-1700.

MEMBER OF FIRM IN DALLAS

Stanley Weiner

For Complete List of Firm Personnel, See General Section

For full biographical listings, see the Martindale-Hubbell Law Directory

KILGORE & KILGORE, A PROFESSIONAL CORPORATION (AV)

700 McKinney Place, 3131 McKinney Avenue - LB 103, 75204-2471
Telephone: 214-969-9099
Fax: 214-953-0133; 214-953-0242; 214-953-0677

Wilmer D. Masterson, III
W. Stephen Swayze
Robert M. Thornton
Theodore C. Anderson, III
John H. Crouch, IV

D. Elizabeth Masterson

For full biographical listings, see the Martindale-Hubbell Law Directory

SMITH, UNDERWOOD & PERKINS, A PROFESSIONAL CORPORATION (AV)

600 Two Lincoln Centre, 5420 LBJ Freeway, 75240
Telephone: 972-661-5114
Telecopier: 972-661-5691
Email: firm@suandp.com *URL:* http://www.suplaw.com

Timothy S. Perkins
David W. Ralston
G. Lynn Smith
William J. Underwood, Jr.

Christine A. McGuire
Amy K. Ratzlaff
P. Theodore Stoinoff, II
Val C. Cronin
Ellen P. Stewart
Todd W. Shadle
Ruth C. Logan
Christina L. Betanzos
Kent D. Williamson

For full biographical listings, see the Martindale-Hubbell Law Directory

THOMPSON, COE, COUSINS & IRONS, L.L.P. (AV)

200 Crescent Court, Eleventh Floor, 75201-1853
Telephone: 214-871-8200
Fax: 214-871-8209
Austin, Texas Office: Suite 1500, Austin Centre, 701 Brazos, 78701.
Telephone: 512-708-8200.
Fax: 512-708-8777.

PARTNERS

John L. Ross
Sherry L. Travers

ASSOCIATES

Ryan E. Griffitts
Michelle E. Coburn

Representative Clients: Bridgestone, Inc.; Republic Parking Corp.; Dickens Data Systems, Inc.; United Stationers Supply Co.; Pizza Hut; Castrol North America; RaceTrac Petroleum; Nationwide Insurance Cos.; Holmes Protection Group, Inc.; Dallas County Schools.

For Complete List of Firm Personnel, See General Section

For full biographical listings, see the Martindale-Hubbell Law Directory

THOMPSON & KNIGHT L.L.P. (AV)

(Attorneys and Counselors)
1700 Pacific Avenue Suite 3300, 75201
Telephone: 214-969-1700
Telecopy: 214-969-1751
Telex: 732 298
URL: http://www.tklaw.com
Austin, Texas Office: 1200 San Jacinto Center, 98 San Jacinto Boulevard, 78701.
Telephone: 512-469-6100.
Telecopy: 512-469-6180.
Fort Worth, Texas Office: 801 Cherry Street, Suite 1600, 76102.
Telephone: 817-347-1700.
Telecopy: 817-347-1799.
Houston, Texas Office: Thompson Knight Brown Parker & Leahy L.L.P., 1200 Smith Street, Suite 3600, 77002-4595.
Telephone: 713-654-8111.
Telecopier: 713-654-1871.

(See Next Column)

San Pedro Garza Garcia, Nuevo León, Mexico Office: Edificio Losoles PD-4, Av. Lázaro Cárdenas No. 2400 Pte., C.P. 66220.
Telephone: (52-8) 363-0096.
Telecopy: (52-8) 363-3067.

PARTNERS

Bennett W. Cervin
Stephen F. Fink
Marc H. Klein
Mia M. Martin
Elizabeth A. Schartz
Steven W. Sloan
Arlene Switzer Steinfield

ASSOCIATES

Anthony J. Campiti
Andrea Hyatt
Jerry D. Mason
Bryan P. Neal
David M. Pryor
Carolyn Ritchie

STAFF ATTORNEY

Tracy B. Liden

For Complete List of Firm Personnel, See General Section

For full biographical listings, see the Martindale-Hubbell Law Directory

TOOLEY & VOSS (AV)

8214 Westchester Drive, Suite 420, 75225
Telephone: 214-368-2224
Fax: 214-368-8307
Email: JCToutfit@aol.com

Joe C. Tooley
Edwin P. Voss Jr.

For full biographical listings, see the Martindale-Hubbell Law Directory

*DENTON,** Denton Co.

ROBISON & ROBISON (AV)

120 North Austin, 76201
Telephone: 940-380-0911
Fax: 940-381-5024
Email: robison@iglobal.net *URL:* http://www.wld.com/firm/robison-robison/denton

Douglas M. Robison
Bonnie Jean Robison

For full biographical listings, see the Martindale-Hubbell Law Directory

WOOD, THACKER & WEATHERLY, P.C. (AV)

513 West Oak Street, 76201
Telephone: 817-565-6565
Fax: 817-566-6673

Grace A. Weatherly

For full biographical listings, see the Martindale-Hubbell Law Directory

*EL PASO,** El Paso Co.

KEMP, SMITH, DUNCAN & HAMMOND, A PROFESSIONAL CORPORATION (AV)

221 North Kansas, Suite 1700, 79901, P.O. Drawer 2800, 79999
Telephone: 915-533-4424
Fax: 915-546-5360
Email: ksdh@kempsmith.com *URL:* http://www.kempsmith.com
Austin, Texas Office: 816 Congress, Suite 1650.
Telephone: 512-320-5466.
Fax: 512-320-5431.

Charles C. High, Jr.
Michael D. McQueen
Clara B. Burns

R. Shawn Oller
Steven J. Blanco
Susan D. Zulkowski

Attorneys for: Asarco; Border Steel, Inc.; 3M Corporation.

For Complete List of Firm Personnel, See General Section

For full biographical listings, see the Martindale-Hubbell Law Directory

MOUNCE, GREEN, MYERS, SAFI & GALATZAN, A PROFESSIONAL CORPORATION (AV)

100 N. Stanton, Suite 1700, P.O. Box 1977, 79950-1977
Telephone: 915-532-2000
Fax: 915-541-1597
Email: mouncegreenmyers@worldnet.att.net

S. Anthony Safi
Carl H. Green
Steven L. Hughes
Mark D. Dore
Bruce A. Koehler

Carrie D. Helmcamp

Attorneys for: El Paso Independent School District; KDBC-TV Limited Partnership; Greater El Paso Association of Realtors; Farah Incorporated; El Paso Apparel Co., Inc.; Aii Technologies Inc. (Acer Computers); Snelling & Snelling, Inc.; U. Silver, Inc.; Southwest Convenience Stores, Inc.

(See Next Column)

MOUNCE, GREEN, MYERS, SAFI & GALATZAN A PROFESSIONAL CORPORATION—*Continued*

For Complete List of Firm Personnel, See General Section

For full biographical listings, see the Martindale-Hubbell Law Directory

RAY, MCCHRISTIAN & JEANS, A PROFESSIONAL CORPORATION (AV)

5822 Cromo Drive, Suite 400, 79912
Telephone: 915-832-7200
Fax: 915-832-7333
Email: rmj@rmjfirm.com

Jeff Ray
John W. McChristian, Jr.
David S. Jeans
James A. Mounts, III
Eduardo Miranda
Robin Collins
Leticia Nuñez

Daniel H. Hernandez
Michael K. Dean
Angelica B. Carreon
Todd E. Marshall
Stacy Bearden Zavala

Representative Clients: Wal-Mart Stores, Inc.; Sears Roebuck & Co.; State Farm Insurance Cos.; Union Pacific Railroad; Kemper Insurance Group; The Travelers Indemnity Co. and Aetna Casualty and Surety Co.; All Risk Claim Services, Inc.; Kessler Industries, Inc.; Texas Pizza Corporation; GTE Corporation.

For full biographical listings, see the Martindale-Hubbell Law Directory

*FORT WORTH,** Tarrant Co.

CANTEY & HANGER (AV)

A Registered Limited Liability Partnership
2100 Burnett Plaza, 801 Cherry Street, 76102-6899
Telephone: 817-877-2800, Metro Line: 429-3815
Telex: 758631 FAX: 877-2807
Dallas
Email: cantey@onramp.net
Dallas, Texas Office: 3330 Harwood Center, 1999 Bryan Street.
Telephone: 214-978-4100.
FAX: 214-978-4150. Email: chdallas@onramp.net
Austin, Texas Office: Cantey & Hanger Roan & Autrey L.L.P., 200 First State Bank Tower, 400 West Fifteenth Street.
Telephone: 512-474-4200.
FAX: 512-469-0470; 512-469-0474. Email: FIRM@ROAN-AUTREY.COM

MEMBERS OF FIRM

Donald K. Buckman
Clay Dean Humphries
Edward L. Kemble

ASSOCIATE

John B. Brown

Represent: General Motors Corp.; Miller Brewing Co.; The Medical Protective Co.; Texas Utilities Electric Co.; Bank of America, N.A.; Union Pacific Resources Company.

For Complete List of Firm Personnel, See General Section

For full biographical listings, see the Martindale-Hubbell Law Directory

JACKSON WALKER L.L.P. (AV)

301 Commerce Street, Suite 2400, 76102
Telephone: 817-334-7200
Fax: 817-334-7290
URL: http://www.jw.com
Austin, Texas Office: 100 Congress Avenue, Suite 1100.
Telephone: 512-236-2000.
Fax: 512-236-2002.
Dallas, Texas Office: 901 Main Street, Suite 6000.
Telephone: 214-953-6000.
Fax: 214-953-5822.
Houston, Texas Office: 1100 Louisiana, Suite 4200.
Telephone: 713-752-4200.
Fax: 713-752-4221.
Richardson, Texas Office: 2435 North Central Expressway, Suite 600.
Telephone: 972-671-2560.
Fax: 972-671-2566.
San Angelo, Texas Office: 225 West Beauregard Avenue.
Telephone: 915-481-2550.
Fax: 915-481-2552.
San Antonio, Texas Office: 112 E. Pecan Street, Suite 2100.
Telephone: 210-978-7700.
Fax: 210-978-7790.

MEMBERS OF FIRM

Gary L. Ingram
Jay K. Rutherford
Kent R. Smith

For Complete List of Firm Personnel, See General Section

For full biographical listings, see the Martindale-Hubbell Law Directory

ROD TANNER & ASSOCIATES, P.C. (AV)

1212 Bank One Tower, 500 Throckmorton Street, 76102-3790
Telephone: 817-870-1212
Metro: 817-429-3052
Fax: 817-870-1263

James Roddy (Rod) Tanner

Sherrie A. Schroder

OF COUNSEL

B. Craig Deats (Also Member of Jenkins & Deats, Austin)

Representative Clients: International Association of Machinists and Aerospace Workers, AFL-CIO; IAMAW District Lodge 776; Federated Independent Texas.
Reference: Allison Beck, General Counsel, International Association of Machinists and Aerospace Workers, AFL-CIO.

For full biographical listings, see the Martindale-Hubbell Law Directory

*HOUSTON,** Harris Co.

BAKER BOTTS L.L.P. (AV)

One Shell Plaza, 910 Louisiana, 77002
Telephone: 713-229-1234
Cable Address: "Boterlove"
Fax: 713-229-1522
Email: postmaster@bakerbotts.com *URL:* http://www.bakerbotts.com
Washington, D.C. Office: The Warner, 1299 Pennsylvania Avenue, N.W.
Telephone: 202-639-7700.
New York, New York Office: 599 Lexington Avenue.
Telephone: 212-705-5000.
Austin, Texas Office: 1600 San Jacinto Center, 98 San Jacinto Boulevard.
Telephone: 512-322-2500.
Dallas, Texas Office: 2001 Ross Avenue.
Telephone: 214-953-6500.
Moscow, Russia Office: 10 ul. Bolshaya Dimitrovka (formerly Pushkinskaya), 103031.
Telephone: 7095/921-5300 (Local); 7095/929-7070 (International).
London, England Office: 45 Ludgate Hill.
Telephone: 0171-778-1400 (Local); 011-44-171-778-1400 (International).
Baku, Azerbaijan Office: 6-10 Vagif Mustafa-zadeh Street, Third Floor, Icheri Sheher, 370004.
Telephone: 994-12-97-63-88 (Local); 011-994-12-97-63-88 (International).
Fax: 994-12-97-63-91 (Local); 011-994-12-97-63-91 (International)

MEMBERS OF FIRM

Maria Wyckoff Boyce
Richard R. Brann
Tony P. Rosenstein
L. Chapman Smith
Teresa S. Valderrama

ASSOCIATES

Mark G. Artlip
Alan F. Kansas
Sandra Thourot Krider
Claire Swift Kugler
Maryanne Lyons
Njeri I. Mathis
Laura B. Medina
Beth K. Neese
Teresa M. Potter
Cristina Espinosa Rodriguez
Kathryn Stegall Schueler
D'Andra Millsap Shu
Amy L. Snell
James R. Staley
Kathryn S. Vaughn
Shelley L. Ward
Shira R. Yoshor

For Complete List of Firm Personnel, See General Section

For full biographical listings, see the Martindale-Hubbell Law Directory

BAYKO GIBSON CARNEGIE HAGAN SCHOONMAKER & MEYER LLP (AV)

Chase Tower, 65th Floor, 77002-3008
Telephone: 713-223-0101
Facsimile: 713-223-0042
Email: baykogibson@nol.net

PARTNERS

Tom Bayko
Wendy K. B. Buskop
Jack G. Carnegie
Martin P. Detloff
Larry L. Evans
Michael W. Ford
Michael M. Gibson
John L. Hagan
Robert J. Leidich
M. Michael Meyer
Linda C. Schoonmaker
Leymon Solomon

OF COUNSEL

John T. S. Williams

David M. Bays
Julia Lynn Nye
Ruth E. Piller
Melissa Brook Romine
Lauri De Brie Thanheiser

For full biographical listings, see the Martindale-Hubbell Law Directory

BRUCKNER & SYKES, L.L.P. (AV)

5847 San Felipe, Suite 3900, 77057
Telephone: 713-877-8788
FAX: 713-877-8065

(See Next Column)

BRUCKNER & SYKES L.L.P., *Houston—Continued*

William H. Bruckner
Charles E. Sykes
Judith Batson Sadler
Richard J. (Rex) Burch
Jody Ray Mask

OF COUNSEL

Shelley L. Greene

For full biographical listings, see the Martindale-Hubbell Law Directory

DAVIS, ORETSKY & GUILFOYLE, P.C. (AV)

1415 Louisiana, Suite 4200, 77002
Telephone: 713-659-1010
Facsimile: 713-659-1122
Email: doglawfirm@dog.pc *URL:* http://www.dogpc.com
Affiliated Law Firm: Wommack Law Firm, P.C., 7 West Way Court, Suite A, P.O. Box 420, Lake Jackson, Texas 77566.
Telephone: 409-297-9755. Houston
Telephone: 713-355-5737.
Fax: 409-297-9761. Email: wdm-george@computron.net.

Tom M. Davis, Jr.
Andrew S. Oretsky
Matthew C. Guilfoyle
Juliann H. Panagos
Curt M. Langley
George T. Wommack, Jr.
David C. Redford

M. Lucille Anderson
Kristin Bauer
Robert M. Browning
Paige Black Larrabee
Norman W. Peters, Jr.
Jonathan L. Phillips
William R. Pilat

For full biographical listings, see the Martindale-Hubbell Law Directory

FISHER & PHILLIPS LLP (AV Ⓣ)

A Limited Liability Partnership including Professional Corporations and Professional Associations
6850 Chase Tower, 600 Travis, 77002
Telephone: 713-227-5410
Telecopier: 713-236-6949
URL: http://www.laborlawyers.com
Atlanta, Georgia Office: 1500 Resurgens Plaza, 945 East Paces Ferry Road, N.E., 30326.
Telephone: 404-231-1400.
Telecopier: 404-240-4249.
Fort Lauderdale, Florida Office: Suite 2300 NationsBank Tower, One Financial Plaza, 33394.
Telephone: 954-525-4800.
Telecopier: 954-525-8739.
Redwood City, California Office: Suite 345, Three Lagoon Drive, 94065.
Telephone: 650-592-6160.
Telecopier: 650-592-6385.
Newport Beach, California Office: 4675 MacArthur Court, Suite 550, 92660.
Telephone: 949-851-2424.
Telecopier: 949-851-0152.
New Orleans, Louisiana Office: 201 St. Charles Avenue, Suite 3710, 70170.
Telephone: 504-522-3303.
Telecopier: 504-529-3850.
Chicago, Illinois Office: 420 Marquette Building, 140 South Dearborn Street, 60603.
Telephone: 312-346-8061.
Telecopier: 312-346-3179.

RESIDENT MEMBER

Ralph J. Zatzkis

RESIDENT ASSOCIATE

Kristina M. Kerwin

For full biographical listings, see the Martindale-Hubbell Law Directory

DAVID T. LOPEZ & ASSOCIATES (AV)

3900 Montrose Boulevard, 77006-4959
Telephone: 713-523-3900
Telecopier: 713-523-3908
Email: david.lopez@lopezlawfirm.com *URL:* http://www.lawyers.com/davidlopezlaw

ASSOCIATE

Christopher D. Yokus

For full biographical listings, see the Martindale-Hubbell Law Directory

NEEL, HOOPER & KALMANS, P.C. (AV)

1700 West Loop South, Suite 1400, 77027-3008
Telephone: 713-629-1800
Fax: 713-629-1812
Email: lawinfo@neelhooper.com *URL:* http://www.neelhooper.com

James M. Neel
Samuel E. Hooper
Raymond L. Kalmans
Donna Smith Cude

(See Next Column)

Michael L. Brown
Kimberly McCluskey Green
Brian M. Steger

For full biographical listings, see the Martindale-Hubbell Law Directory

OGLETREE, DEAKINS, NASH, SMOAK & STEWART, P.C. (AV)

One Allen Center, 500 Dallas Street, Suite 3000, 77002
Telephone: 713-655-0855
Facsimile: 713-655-0020
Email: Houston@odnss.com *URL:* http://www.Ogletreedeakins.com
Atlanta, Georgia Office: 600 Peachtree Street, N.E., Suite 2100.
Telephone: 404-881-1300.
Washington, D.C. Office: Fifth Floor, 2400 N Street, N.W.
Telephone: 202-887-0855.
Chicago, Illinois Office: Twenty-Fifth Floor, Two First National Plaza, 20 South Clark Street.
Telephone: 312-558-1220.
Nashville, Tennessee Office: Office: SunTrust Center, Suite 800, 424 Church Street.
Telephone: 615-254-1900.
Birmingham, Alabama Office: 1900 SouthTrust Tower, 420 North 20th Street.
Telephone: 205-328-1900.
Greenville, South Carolina Office: The Ogletree Building, 300 North Main Street, P.O. Box 2757.
Telephone: 864-271-1300.
Charleston, South Carolina Office: 134 Meeting Street, Suite 500, P.O. Box 1808.
Telephone: 843-853-1300.
Columbia, South Carolina Office: 1501 Main Street, Suite 600, P.O. Box 11206.
Telephone: 803-252-1300.
Raleigh, North Carolina Office: 4101 Lake Boone Trail, Suite 511, P.O. Box 31608.
Telephone: 919-787-9700.
Winston-Salem, North Carolina Office: 150 South Stratford Road, Suite 350.
Telephone: 336-725-2110.
Dallas, Texas Office: 460 Preston Commons, 8117 Preston Road.
Telephone: 214-987-3800.
Fax: 214-987-3927.

Jeffrey C. Londa
James Alfred Southerland
F. Barham Lewis
Stephen H. Dimlich, Jr.

OF COUNSEL

Dennis C. Gardner

Anthony G. Stergio
Michael D. Mitchell
Kate McCormick
Matthew R. Pearson
Lara Cardin DeLeon

Representative Clients: Boise Cascade Corporation; Johnson Controls World Services, Inc.; Litwin Engineers & Constructors, Inc.; Lockheed Martin Engineering & Sciences Company; Mariner Post-Acute Network, Inc.; Metropolitan Transit Authority of Harris County, Texas; Occidental Petroleum Corporation; Reynolds Metals Company; S & B Engineers & Constructors, Inc.; Westin Hotels.

For full biographical listings, see the Martindale-Hubbell Law Directory

RAMSEY & MURRAY, A PROFESSIONAL CORPORATION (AV)

10000 Memorial Drive, Suite 700, 77024-3412
Telephone: 713-613-5400
Fax: 713-613-5414

Ben Ramsey
John A. Murray, Jr.
Russell J. Ramsey
Mark Ramsey
Curtis D. Collette
Michael Stout Wright
Rick McRory

Joseph W. Gagnon
R. Russell Hollenbeck
Adrian V. Villacorta
Brenda Renee Ferguson

Representative Clients: Great Central Insurance Co.; Republic Insurance Co.

For full biographical listings, see the Martindale-Hubbell Law Directory

SCHWARTZ JUNELL CAMPBELL & OATHOUT, L.L.P. (AV)

Two Houston Center, 909 Fannin, Suite 2000, 77010
Telephone: 713-752-0017
Telecopier: 713-752-0327
Email: dschwartz@schwartz-junell.com

Richard A. Schwartz
William Edward Junell, Jr.
Marshall S. Campbell
Monica F. Oathout
Steven R. Rech

Phillip W. Bechter
J. Parker Fauntleroy, Jr.

OF COUNSEL

Joe H. Reynolds
A. R. Schwartz

(See Next Column)

SCHWARTZ JUNELL CAMPBELL & OATHOUT L.L.P.—*Continued*

LEGAL SUPPORT PERSONNEL

PARALEGALS

Nannette Koger
Maria Woods
Shelly A. Savage, CLA

For full biographical listings, see the Martindale-Hubbell Law Directory

THOMPSON KNIGHT BROWN PARKER & LEAHY L.L.P. (AV)

A Registered Limited Liability Partnership including Professional Corporations
(Attorneys and Counselors)
1200 Smith Street, Suite 3600, 77002-4595
Telephone: 713-654-8111
Telecopier: 713-654-1871
URL: http://www.tklaw.com
Dallas, Texas Office: Thompson & Knight L.L.P., 1700 Pacific Avenue, Suite 3300, 75201.
Telephone: 214-969-1700.
Telecopy: 214-969-1751.
Telex: 732298.
Austin, Texas Office: Thompson & Knight L.L.P., 1200 San Jacinto Center, 98 San Jacinto Boulevard, 78701.
Telephone: 512-469-6100.
Telecopy: 512-469-6180.
Fort Worth, Texas Office: Thompson & Knight L.L.P., 801 Cherry Street, Suite 1600, 76102.
Telephone: 817-347-1700.
Telecopy: 817-347-1799.
San Pedro Garza Garcia, Nuevo León, Mexico Office: Thompson & Knight L.L.P., Edificio Losoles PD-4, Av. Lázaro Cárdenas No. 2400 PTE., C.P. 66220.
Telephone: (52-8) 363-0096.
Telecopy: (52-8) 363-3067.

PARTNER

Roxella T. Cavazos

For Complete List of Firm Personnel, See General Section

For full biographical listings, see the Martindale-Hubbell Law Directory

VINSON & ELKINS L.L.P. (AV)

2300 First City Tower, 1001 Fannin, 77002-6760
Telephone: 713-758-2222
Fax: 713-758-2346
Email: info@velaw.com *URL:* http://www.velaw.com
Austin, Texas Office: One American Center Suite 2700, 600 Congress Avenue, Austin, Texas, 78701-3200.
Telephone: 512-495-8400.
Fax: 512-495-8612.
Beijing, China Office: 20/F, Beijing Silver Tower, No. 2, Dong San Huan Bei Lu, Chaoyang District, 100027.
Telephone: +86-10-6410-6300.
Fax: +86-10-6410-6360.
Dallas, Texas Office: 3700 Trammell Crow Center, 2001 Ross Avenue, Dallas, Texas, 75201-2975.
Telephone: 214-220-7700.
Fax: 214-220-7716.
London, England Office: Regis House, 8th Floor, 45 King William Street, London, EC4R 9AN, England.
Telephone: (44-171) 618-6000.
Fax: (44-171) 618-6001.
Moscow, Russia Office: 16 Ulitsa Spiridonovka, Second Floor, 103001 Moscow, Russia.
Telephone: (7-095) 956-1995. Local
Fax: (7-095) 956-1996. U.S. Satellite
Fax: (212) 803-0142.
New York, N.Y. Office: 1325 Avenue of the Americas, 17th Floor, New York, N.Y., 10019.
Telephone: 917-206-8000.
Fax: 917-206-8100.
Singapore Office: 6 Battery Road, #39-01, Singapore, 049909.
Telephone: (65) 536-8300.
Fax: (65) 536-8311.
Washington, D.C. Office: The Willard Office Building, 1455 Pennsylvania Avenue, N.W., Washington, D.C., 20004-1008.
Telephone: 202-639-6500.
Fax: 202-639-6604.

MEMBERS OF FIRM

Douglas E. Hamel
Stuart Brooks Johnston, Jr. (Resident, Dallas, Texas Office)
W. Carl Jordan
Christopher A. Knepp (Resident, Austin, Texas Office)
Shadow Sloan
John H. Smither
Thomas H. Wilson

HOUSTON OF COUNSEL

Robert L. Ivey

(See Next Column)

ASSOCIATES

Anissa A. Allbritton (Resident, Austin, Texas Office)
Christopher V. Bacon
Jason S. Boulette (Resident, Austin, Texas Office)
Michael Curtis Brisch
Merritt B. Chastain III
Vanessa M. Clem
Dorene B. Cohen
Yvette Vanessa Gatling
Christopher H. Hahn (Resident, Austin, Texas Office)
Jack L. Johnson (Resident, New York, N.Y. Office)
Mary Michelle Mahony
Eric M. Ostermayer (Resident, Dallas, Texas Office)
Ann Abrams Price (Resident, Austin, Texas Office)
Ashley Ann Smith
Susanne K. Sullivan
Julie I. Ungerman (Resident, Dallas, Texas Office)

For Complete List of Firm Personnel, See General Section

For full biographical listings, see the Martindale-Hubbell Law Directory

*SAN ANTONIO,** Bexar Co.

COX & SMITH INCORPORATED (AV)

112 East Pecan Street, Suite 1800, 78205-1521
Telephone: 210-554-5500
Fax: 210-226-8395
Email: info@coxsmith.com *URL:* http://www.coxsmith.com

Donna K. McElroy
Ben F. Foster, Jr.
Robert D. Kilgore
Daniel R. Stern
Jeffery S. Darby
Ramon D. Bissmeyer
Larry E. Gee
E. Burke Huber, Jr.
Lauren R. Huckaby

Representative Clients: Abraxas Petroleum Corporation; Citicorp Bank N.A.; Fairchild Aircraft Incorporated; International Bank of Commerce, N.A.; L & H Packing Company; QVC Network, Inc.; South Texas Radiology Group; Tetco, Inc.; Trinity University; University of the Incarnate World.

For Complete List of Firm Personnel, See General Section

For full biographical listings, see the Martindale-Hubbell Law Directory

JACKSON WALKER L.L.P. (AV)

112 E. Pecan Street, Suite 2100, 78205-1521
Telephone: 210-978-7700
Fax: 210-978-7790
URL: http://www.jw.com
Austin, Texas Office: 100 Congress Avenue, Suite 1100.
Telephone: 512-236-2000.
Fax: 512-236-2002.
Dallas, Texas Office: 901 Main Street, Suite 6000.
Telephone: 214-953-6000.
Fax: 214-953-5822.
Fort Worth, Texas Office: 301 Commerce Street, Suite 2400.
Telephone: 817-334-7200.
Fax: 817-334-7290.
Houston, Texas Office: 1100 Louisiana, Suite 4200.
Telephone: 713-752-4200.
Fax: 713-752-4221.
Richardson, Texas Office: 2435 North Central Expressway, Suite 600.
Telephone: 972-671-2560.
Fax: 972-671-2566.
San Angelo, Texas Office: 225 West Beauregard Avenue.
Telephone: 915-481-2550.
Fax: 915-481-2552.

MEMBERS OF FIRM

Leo D. Figueroa
Dawn Bruner Finlayson
Richard G. Garza

For Complete List of Firm Personnel, See General Section

For full biographical listings, see the Martindale-Hubbell Law Directory

O'CONNELL, BENJAMIN & COGHLAN, L.L.P. (AV)

153 Treeline Park, Suite 200, 78209
Telephone: 210-824-0009
Fax: 210-824-9429
Email: obcllp@oconben.com

Keith B. O'Connell
David P. Benjamin
G. Thomas Coghlan
Ernest F. Avery
Les Katona, Jr.
Dan Vana

Gayla S. Corley
Cathrin J. Martinez

For full biographical listings, see the Martindale-Hubbell Law Directory

WEIR & ALVARADO, P.C. (AV)

115 Camaron Street, Suite 100, 78205
Telephone: 210-223-2685
Fax: 210-223-9464

(See Next Column)

WEIR & ALVARADO P.C., *San Antonio—Continued*

Warren Weir | Leo Alvarado, Jr.

For full biographical listings, see the Martindale-Hubbell Law Directory

*TYLER,** Smith Co.

RAMEY & FLOCK,. A PROFESSIONAL CORPORATION (AV)

500 First Place, P.O. Box 629, 75710
Telephone: 903-597-3301
Telecopier: 903-597-2413
Email: Ramey@Ramey-Flock.com *URL:* http://www.RameyFlock.com

Thomas B. Ramey (1892-1967)
Jack W. Flock
Tracy Crawford
Glenn Collins
Michael A. Hatchell
Tom Henson
Dennis G. Black
Paul H. Gilliam
R. Brian Craft
Gregory D. Smith
Michael T. Crawford
Mary H. Molly Hatchell
Rosemary Sage Jones
Ronald S. Vickery
John W. Ferguson, Jr.

Deron R. Dacus
Eric H. Findlay
Shannon Dacus
Maria Benecki Sowders
Jamy Mitchell Skaggs

Counsel for: Regions Bank; Exxon Co. U.S.A.; Kelly Springfield Tire Co.; Trinity-Mother Frances Health System; St. Paul Insurance Co.; The Travelers Cos.; Reliance Insurance Co.; Marshall Regional Medical Center.

For full biographical listings, see the Martindale-Hubbell Law Directory

*VICTORIA,** Victoria Co.

WALKER, KEELING & CARROLL, L.L.P. (AV)

210 East Constitution, P.O. Box 108, 77902
Telephone: 361-576-6800
Fax: 361-576-6196
Email: wkc@wkcfirm.com

Ronald B. Walker
Terry M. Carroll, Jr.
W. Lee Keeling
Patricia L. Hayden
Donna K. Grafe

LEGAL SUPPORT PERSONNEL

Sue A. Comstock (Legal Assistant)

For full biographical listings, see the Martindale-Hubbell Law Directory

UTAH

*SALT LAKE CITY,** Salt Lake Co.

CALLISTER NEBEKER & MCCULLOUGH, A PROFESSIONAL CORPORATION (AV)

Gateway Tower East, Suite 900, 10 East South Temple, 84133
Telephone: 801-530-7300
Telecopier: 801-364-9127
Email: mjeaston@cnmlaw.com *URL:* http://www.cnmlaw.com

Jeffrey N. Clayton | W. Waldan Lloyd

Representative Clients: Zions First National Bank; Sears Roebuck & Company; Utah Automobile Dealers Association; Sinclair Oil Corporation (Little America); Keystone Communications; Central Valley Water Reclamation Facility Board; Citicorp; Intermountain Health Care, Inc.; Children's Miracle Network (Osmond Foundation); Nu Skin International, Inc.

For Complete List of Firm Personnel, See General Section

For full biographical listings, see the Martindale-Hubbell Law Directory

PARR WADDOUPS BROWN GEE & LOVELESS, A PROFESSIONAL CORPORATION (AV)

Suite 1300, 185 South State Street, 84111-1537
Telephone: 801-532-7840
Fax: 801-532-7750
URL: http://www.pwlaw.com

Gary A. Dodge
Heidi E. C. Leithead
Terry E. Welch
Jonathan O. Hafen
Mark A. Wagner
Bentley J. Tolk

For Complete List of Firm Personnel, See General Section

For full biographical listings, see the Martindale-Hubbell Law Directory

PRINCE, YEATES & GELDZAHLER (AV)

City Centre I, Suite 900, 175 East 400 South, 84111
Telephone: 801-524-1000
Fax: 801-524-1099
Email: pyglaw.com
Park City, Utah Office: 614 Main Street.
Telephones: 801-524-1000; 649-7440.

MEMBERS OF FIRM

John S. Chindlund
James A. Boevers
Thomas J. Erbin
Roger J. McConkie

ASSOCIATE

Thomas R. Barton

Representative Clients: Labor Matters: Albertson's Inc.; Dan's Foods, Inc.; Geneva Rock Products, Inc.; Harmon City, Inc.; Intermountain Retail, Health & Welfare Pension; Salt Lake County; Smith's Food and Drug Centers, Inc.; United Concerts, Inc.; Utah-Idaho Teamsters Security Fund.

For Complete List of Firm Personnel, See General Section

For full biographical listings, see the Martindale-Hubbell Law Directory

RAY, QUINNEY & NEBEKER, A PROFESSIONAL CORPORATION (AV)

79 South Main Street, Suite 400, P.O. Box 45385, 84145-0385
Telephone: 801-532-1500
Fax: 801-532-7543
Email: rqn@rqn.com *URL:* http://www.rqn.com
Provo, Utah Office: 92 North University Avenue, Suite 210, 84601-4420.
Telephone: 801-342-2400.
Fax: 801-375-8379.
Albuquerque, New Mexico Office: Suite 620, 40 First Plaza, N.W.
Telephone: 505-243-6665.
Fax: 505-764-9890.

Janet Hugie Smith
Lisa A. Yerkovich
Michael E. Blue
Scott A. Hagen
Robert O. Rice

Frederick R. Thaler, Jr.
Paul C. Burke
D. Zachary Wiseman

Representative Clients: First Security Bank, N.A.; Borden, Inc.; Salt Lake Organizing Committee for the Winter Olympic Games of 2002; Southern Pacific Transportation; Utah Power & Light Co.; Travelers Insurance Co.; U.S. West.

For Complete List of Firm Personnel, See General Section

For full biographical listings, see the Martindale-Hubbell Law Directory

SNELL & WILMER L.L.P. (AV)

111 East Broadway, Suite 900, 84111-1004
Telephone: 801-237-1900
Fax: 801-237-1950
URL: http://www.swlaw.com
Phoenix, Arizona Office: One Arizona Center, 85004-2202.
Telephone: 602-382-6000.
Fax: 602-382-6070.
Tucson, Arizona Office: One South Church Avenue, Suite 1500, 85701-1612.
Telephone: 520-882-1200.
Fax: 520-884-1294.
Orange County Office: 1920 Main Street, Suite 1200, Irvine, California 92614-7230.
Telephone: 949-253-2700.
Fax: 949-955-2507.

MEMBER OF FIRM

Alan L. Sullivan

OF COUNSEL

Carol Clawson

ASSOCIATE

Julie A. Thomas

Representative Clients: For list of Representative Clients, see end of biographical listings in the Martindale-Hubbell Law Directory.

For Complete List of Firm Personnel, See General Section

For full biographical listings, see the Martindale-Hubbell Law Directory

STRONG & HANNI, A PROFESSIONAL CORPORATION (AV)

Sixth Floor Boston Building, 9 Exchange Place, 84111
Telephone: 801-532-7080
Fax: 801-596-1508
Email: pfishler@strongandhanni.com

Gordon R. Strong (1909-1969)
Glenn C. Hanni
Henry E. Heath
Philip R. Fishler
Roger H. Bullock
R. Scott Williams
Dennis M. Astill (Managing Partner)
Stuart H. Schultz
Paul M. Belnap

(See Next Column)

STRONG & HANNI A PROFESSIONAL CORPORATION—*Continued*

Stephen J. Trayner
Joseph J. Joyce
Bradley Wm. Bowen
Robert L. Janicki
Elizabeth L. Willey
H. Burt Ringwood
Peter H. Christensen
David R. Nielson

Kevin D. Swenson
Catherine M. Larson
Kristin Van Orman
Darren K. Nelson
Peter H. Barlow
Steven T. Densley
Jennifer C. Polley-Abramson
Shawn T. Welch

OF COUNSEL

Robert A. Burton

Representative Clients: State Farm Mutual Automobile Insurance Co.; Standard Accident Insurance Co.; United Services Automobile Assn.; Western Casualty & Surety Co.; Government Employees Insurance Co.; Guaranty Mutual Life Co.

For full biographical listings, see the Martindale-Hubbell Law Directory

VAN COTT, BAGLEY, CORNWALL & MCCARTHY, A PROFESSIONAL CORPORATION (AV)

50 South Main Street, Suite 1600, P.O. Box 45340, 84145-0340
Telephone: 801-532-3333
Telecopier: 801-534-0058
Email: info@vancott.com *URL:* http://www.vancott.com
Ogden, Utah Office: 2404 Washington Boulevard, Suite 900.
Telephone: 801-394-5783.
Park City, Utah Office: 2200 Park Avenue, Suite C200-A.
Telephone: 435-649-3889.

Jennifer K. Anderson
Sandra L. Crosland
Evan S. Strassberg

OF COUNSEL

Cecil R. Hedger

For Complete List of Firm Personnel, See General Section

For full biographical listings, see the Martindale-Hubbell Law Directory

WOOD CRAPO LLC (AV)

60 E. South Temple, Suite 500, 84111
Telephone: 801-366-6060
Fax: 801-366-6061

Mary Anne Q. Wood
David J. Crapo
Larry Stuart Jenkins
Darryl J. Lee

Susan J. Mueller
Eric T. Johnson
Richard J. Armstrong
Joi Gardner Pearson

OF COUNSEL

Kathryn Ogden Balmforth
James W. Stewart
Richard L. Evans
Pamela B. Hunsaker
Sheri Ann Mower
Stephen G. Wood

For full biographical listings, see the Martindale-Hubbell Law Directory

VERMONT

*BURLINGTON,** Chittenden Co.

DINSE, KNAPP & MCANDREW, P.C. (AV)

209 Battery Street, P.O. Box 988, 05402-0988
Telephone: 802-864-5751
Fax: 802-862-6409
URL: http://www.dinse.com

MEMBERS OF FIRM

Karen McAndrew
Robert R. McKearin
Pietro J. Lynn
Jeffrey J. Nolan

Representative Clients: Chittenden Trust Co.; Vermont Transit Co., Inc.; Sears, Roebuck & Co.; Ford Motor Co.; Inc.; Middlebury College; Vt. Teddy Bear Co., Inc.; Key Bank.

For Complete List of Firm Personnel, See General Section

For full biographical listings, see the Martindale-Hubbell Law Directory

MILLER, EGGLESTON & CRAMER, LTD. (AV)

150 South Champlain Street, P.O. Box 1489, 05402-1489
Telephone: 802-864-0880
Telecopier: 802-864-0328

Anne E. Cramer

(See Next Column)

OF COUNSEL

Patricia L. Rickard

For Complete List of Firm Personnel, See General Section

For full biographical listings, see the Martindale-Hubbell Law Directory

VIRGINIA

*ABINGDON,** Washington Co.

THE TATE LAW FIRM (AV)

Abingdon Professional Centre, 110 Abingdon Place, 24211
Telephone: 540-628-5185
Telecopier: 540-628-5045
Email: lynntate@naxs.com *URL:* http://www.tatelaw.com

Mary Lynn Tate

OF COUNSEL

Olen G. Haynes (Not admitted in VA)

LEGAL SUPPORT PERSONNEL

Rebecca A. Wyatt
Teresa L. Brown

For full biographical listings, see the Martindale-Hubbell Law Directory

ALEXANDRIA, (Independent City)

CARTER & COLEMAN (AV)

602 Cameron Street, 22314
Telephone: 703-739-4200
Fax: 703-739-4210
Email: rcarter@cartercoleman.com *URL:* http://www.lawyers.com/carter&coleman
Washington, D.C. Office: 900 Seventeenth Street, N.W., Suite 900, 20006.
Telephone: 202-326-8600.
Fax: 202-289-0184.

Richard D. Carter
Douglas M. Coleman
David C. Simmons
(Not admitted in VA)
James M. Loots
(Not admitted in VA)

ASSOCIATES

Juliane C. Miller
Mercedes Madole
(Not admitted in VA)
Paul A. Daniels

For full biographical listings, see the Martindale-Hubbell Law Directory

*ARLINGTON,** Arlington Co.

NILS GEORGE PETERSON (AV)

1001 North Highland Street Penthouse, 22201
Telephone: 703-524-0336
Fax: 703-243-6873
(Of Counsel to Edward F. Greco, Front Royal)

Elisabeth L. Roberts

For full biographical listings, see the Martindale-Hubbell Law Directory

*FAIRFAX,** (Ind. City; Seat of Fairfax Co.)

LEFFLER, HYLAND & THOMPSON, A PROFESSIONAL CORPORATION (AV)

Inns of Court, 4163 Chain Bridge Road, 22030-4102
Telephone: 703-293-9300
Facsimile: 703-293-9301
Email: mail@lefflerhyland.com *URL:* http://www.lefflerhyland.com

Rodney G. Leffler
Sharon E. Thompson

For full biographical listings, see the Martindale-Hubbell Law Directory

ODIN, FELDMAN & PITTLEMAN, P.C. (AV)

9302 Lee Highway, Suite 1100, 22031
Telephone: 703-218-2100
Facsimile: 703-218-2160
Email: OFP@OFPLAW.COM

Dexter S. Odin
John S. Wisiackas
Robert K. Richardson
F. Douglas Ross
Bruce M. Blanchard
Frances P. Dwornik
Edward W. Cameron

Matthew J. Britton
Misti Mukherjee
Matthew Anthony Rizzo

For Complete List of Firm Personnel, See General Section

For full biographical listings, see the Martindale-Hubbell Law Directory

*MANASSAS,** Prince William Co.

McCarthy & Massey, P.C. (AV)

9315 Center Street, Suite 104, 20110
Telephone: 703-330-2726; Metro: 703-551-2146
Fax: 703-330-2429

Tara M. McCarthy — Joyce A. Naumann Massey

Susan L. Mitchell — Marian L. Beckett

For full biographical listings, see the Martindale-Hubbell Law Directory

MCLEAN, Fairfax Co.

Kruchko & Fries (AV)

Suite 202, 7929 Westpark Drive, 22102
Telephone: 703-734-0554
Telecopier: 703-734-0876
Baltimore, Maryland Office: Suite 305, 600 Washington Avenue.
Telephone: 410-321-7310.
Washington, D.C. Office: 601 Pennsylvania Avenue, Suite 900.
Telephone: 202-347-6550.

MEMBERS OF FIRM

John G. Kruchko — Jay R. Fries

ASSOCIATE

Susan Tahernia (Resident, McLean, Virginia Office)

For full biographical listings, see the Martindale-Hubbell Law Directory

Reed Smith Hazel & Thomas LLP (AV)

Suite 1100, 8251 Greensboro Drive, 22102-3844
Telephone: 703-734-4600
FAX: 703-734-4699
Email: rssm@rssm.com *URL:* http://www.rssm.com
Fairfax County (Falls Church), Virginia Office: Suite 1400, 3110 Fairview Park Drive.
Telephone: 703-641-4200.
Fax: 703-641-4340.
Leesburg, Virginia Office: 44084 Riverside Parkway, Suite 300.
Telephone: 703-729-8500. Metro: 703-478-1992.
Fax: 703-478-8003.
Richmond, Virginia Office: 901 East Byrd Street, Suite 1700, 23219.
Telephone: 804-344-3400.
Fax: 804-344-3410.
Pittsburgh, Pennsylvania Office: Reed Smith Shaw & McClay LLP, 435 Sixth Avenue, 15219-1886.
Telephone: 412-288-3131.
FAX: 412-288-3063.
Philadelphia, Pennsylvania Office: Reed Smith Shaw & McClay LLP, 2500 One Liberty Place, 19103-7301.
Telephone: 215-851-8100.
FAX: 215-851-1420.
Harrisburg, Pennsylvania Office: Reed Smith Shaw & McClay LLP 213 Market Street, 17101-2132.
Telephone: 717-234-5988.
FAX: 717-236-3777.
Washington, D.C. Office: Reed Smith Shaw & McClay LLP, Suite 1100 - East Tower, 1301 K Street, N.W., 20005-3317.
Telephone: 202-414-9200.
FAX: 202-414-9299.
Princeton, New Jersey Office: Reed Smith Shaw & McClay LLP, 136 Main Street, Suite 250, 08540-5799.
Telephone: 609-987-0050.
FAX: 609-951-0824.
New York, N.Y. Office: 375 Park Avenue, 17th Floor, 10152.
Telephone: 212-521-5400.
FAX: 212-521-5450.
Newark, New Jersey Office: Reed Smith Shaw & McClay LLP, The Legal Center, One Riverfront Plaza, First Floor, 07102-5400.
Telephone: 973-621-3200.
FAX: 973-621-3199.

MEMBERS OF FIRM

John R. Erickson — W. Scott Railton

For full biographical listings, see the Martindale-Hubbell Law Directory

NORFOLK, (Independent City)

Payne, Gates, Farthing & Radd, P.C. (AV)

15th Floor, Dominion Tower, 999 Waterside Drive, Suite 1515, 23510-3309
Telephone: 757-640-1500
Facsimile: 757-627-6583
URL: http://www.paynegates.com

Ronald M. Gates — Glen M. Robertson
Philip R. Farthing — Brian R. Dinning
Anthony F. Radd — Todd J. Preti
Marshall A. Winslow, Jr.

(See Next Column)

C. Arthur Robinson, II — Stephen E. Heretick
Raymond L. Hogge, Jr.

OF COUNSEL

Charles E. Payne

For full biographical listings, see the Martindale-Hubbell Law Directory

Vandeventer Black LLP (AV)

500 World Trade Center, 23510-1699
Telephone: 757-446-8600
Cable Address: "Hughsvan"
Telecopier: 757-446-8670
URL: http://www.vanblk.com
Kitty Hawk, North Carolina Office: 6 Juniper Trail.
Telephone: 252-261-5055.
Fax: 252-261-8444. E-Mail: nshearin@pinn.net.
London, England Office: Mitre House, 4th Floor, 12-14 Mitre Street.
Telephone: (0171) 623-2081.
Facsimile: (0171) 929-0043.

PARTNERS OF FIRM

John M. Ryan — Dean T. Buckius
F. Nash Bilisoly — Valerie J. Brodsky
R. John Barrett — Arlene F. Klinedinst

For Complete List of Firm Personnel, See General Section

For full biographical listings, see the Martindale-Hubbell Law Directory

RESTON, Fairfax Co.

Charlson Bredehoft, P.C. (AV)

11260 Roger Bacon Drive, Suite 201, 20190
Telephone: 703-318-6800
Facsimile: 703-318-6808

Curtis L. Charlson (Not admitted in VA; Retired) — Elaine Charlson Bredehoft
John C. Cook

For full biographical listings, see the Martindale-Hubbell Law Directory

RICHMOND, (Independent City)

LeClair Ryan, A Professional Corporation (AV)

707 East Main Street, 11th Floor, 23219
Telephone: 804-783-2003
Facsmile: 804-783-2294
Email: email@leclairryan.com
Glen Allen, Virginia Office: 4201 Dominion Boulevard, Suite 200, 23060.
Telephone: 804-270-0070.
Facsimile: 804-270-4715.
Blacksburg, Virginia Office: 1872 Pratt Drive, Suite 1865, 24060.
Telephone: 540-961-2762.
Fax: 540-961-2781.
Norfolk, Virginia Office: 999 Waterside Drive, Suite 2025.
Telephone: 757-624-1454.
Facsimile: 757-624-3773.
Alexandria, Virginia Office: 225 Reinekers Lane, Suite 290, 22314.
Telephone: 703-684-8007.
Facsimile: 703-684-8075.
Charlottesville, Virginia Office: 108 S.E. Second Street, P.O. Box 2017, 22902.
Telephone: 804-971-7771.
Facsimile: 804-296-0905.

Deborah Swindells Donovan (Not admitted in VA) — Joseph D. McCluskey
Laura G. Fox — Sharon Maitland Moon
David E. Nagle

Kimberly G. Baldwin — Charles G. Meyer, III
Vijay Mago — Susan C. North
Ellen Duffy McKay (Not admitted in VA) — Andrea Lynn White

For full biographical listings, see the Martindale-Hubbell Law Directory

Levit, Mann & Halligan, P.C. (AV)

Hamilton Place, Suite 100, 1301 North Hamilton Street, 23230
Telephone: 804-355-7766
Fax: 804-355-8752
Email: levmanhal@mindspring.com *URL:* http://www.levmanhal.com
Ashland, Virginia Office: 127 Thompson Street.
Telephone: 804-798-3300.
Fax: 804-798-6744.

Jay J. Levit (Resident, Richmond Office) — Kelly A. Halligan (Resident, Ashland Office)
John B. Mann (Resident, Richmond Office) — Rosemary D. Halligan (Resident, Ashland Office)

Lisa A. Davis-Lee (Resident, Ashland Office)

For full biographical listings, see the Martindale-Hubbell Law Directory

Richmond—Continued

MALONEY, HUENNEKENS, PARKS, GECKER & PARSONS, A PROFESSIONAL CORPORATION (AV)

Bank of America Center, 1111 East Main Street, Suite 800, 23219-3103
Telephone: 804-644-0313
Telecopier: 804-783-6192

Yvonne Steenstra Wellford
Christopher A. Jones

Reference: First Union National Bank.

For Complete List of Firm Personnel, See General Section

For full biographical listings, see the Martindale-Hubbell Law Directory

PHILIP S. MARSTILLER, P.C. (AV)

16 South Second Street, 23219-3723
Telephone: 804-775-0169
Facsimile: 804-775-0653
Email: pmarstille@aol.com *URL:* http://www.lawyers.com/marstillerlaw

Philip S. Marstiller

For full biographical listings, see the Martindale-Hubbell Law Directory

MCGUIRE, WOODS, BATTLE & BOOTHE LLP (AV)

One James Center, 901 East Cary Street, 23219-4030
Telephone: 804-775-1000
Fax: 804-775-1061
Email: info@mwbb.com *URL:* http://www.mwbb.com
Atlanta, Georgia Office: 285 Peachtree Center Avenue, N.E., Suite 2200, Marquis Tower Two, 30303-1234.
Telephone: 404-443-5500.
Fax: 404-443-5599.
Baltimore, Maryland Office: 7 Saint Paul Street, Suite 1000, 21202-1671.
Telephone: 410-659-4400.
Fax: 410-659-4599.
Charlotte, North Carolina Offices: 3700 Bank of America Plaza, 101 South Tryon Street, 28280.
Telephone: 704-373-8999.
Fax: 704-373-8990 and Bank of America Corporate Center, Suite 2900, 100 North Tryon Street, 28202.
Telephone: 704-373-8999.
Fax: 704-373-8935.
Charlottesville, Virginia Office: Court Square Building, 310 Fourth Street, N.E., Suite 300, P.O. Box 1288, 22902-1288.
Telephone: 804-977-2500.
Fax: 804-980-2222.
Chicago, Illinois Office: R.R. Donnelly Building, 77 West Wacker Drive, Suite 4500, 60601-1635.
Telephone: 312-849-3699.
Fax: 312-849-3690.
Jacksonville, Florida Office: 50 North Laura Street, 32202-3635.
Telephone: 904-798-3200.
Fax: 904-798-3207.
McLean, (Tysons Corner) Virginia Office: 1750 Tysons Boulevard, Suite 1800, 22102-3892.
Telephone: 703-712-5000.
Fax: 703-712-5050.
Norfolk, Virginia Office: World Trade Center, 101 West Main Street, Suite 9000, 23510-1655.
Telephone: 757-640-3700.
Fax: 757-640-3701. 23219-4030.
Washington, D.C. Office: Washington Square, 1050 Connecticut Avenue, N.W., Suite 1200, 20036-5317.
Telephone: 202-857-1700.
Fax: 202-857-1737.
Almaty, Republic of Kazakhstan Office: Park Palace, 41 Kazibek Bi Street, 2nd Floor, 480100.
Telephone: 7-3272-608-300.
Fax: 7-3272-608-305.
Brussels, Belgium Office: 250 Avenue Louise, Bte. 64, 1050.
Telephone: 32-2-629-42-11.
Fax: 32-2-629-42-22.
Moscow, Russia Office: Paveltskaya Square, 1 Valovaya Street, 7th Floor, 13054.
Telephone: 7-502-937-0774.
Fax: 7-502-937-0776.

MEMBERS OF FIRM

John S. Barr
Gary S. Marshall
James P. McElligott Jr.
Dana L. Rust
Rodney A. Satterwhite
Eva S. Tashjian-Brown
William E. Twomey Jr.
W. Carter Younger

ASSOCIATES

David F. Dabbs
Theofilos G. Galoozis
Carol Rick Gibbons
Jonathan P. Harmon
Laura Clark McCoy
James A. Sonne

For Complete List of Firm Personnel, See General Section

For full biographical listings, see the Martindale-Hubbell Law Directory

WILLIAMS, MULLEN, CLARK & DOBBINS, A PROFESSIONAL CORPORATION (AV)

Two James Center, 1021 East Cary Street, P.O. Box 1320, 23218-1320
Telephone: 804-643-1991
Fax: 804-783-6507
URL: http://www.wmcd.com
Newport News Office: Harbor Bank Center, Suite 210, One Old Oyster Point Road, 23602-7119.
Telephone: 757-249-5100.
Fax: 757-249-5109.
Virginia Beach Office: One Columbus Center, 23462-6763.
Telephone: 757-499-8800.
Fax: 757-473-0395.
Vienna Office: 1593 Spring Hill Road, Suite 510, 22182.
Telephone: 703-760-5200.
Fax: 703-748-0244.
Washington, D.C. Office: The Farragut Building, 900 17th Street, N.W., Suite 700, 20006.
Telephone: 202-293-0213.
Fax: 804-783-6507. Fax Within D.C.: 202-293-5939.
London, England Office: Blake Lodge, Bridge Lane, SW11 3AD.
Telephone: (011-44-71) 223-2756.
Fax: (011-44-71) 350-0156.
Riyadh, Saudi Arabia Affiliate Office: Saudi-American Legal Consultants Commercial Building #2, Diplomatic Quarter, P.O. Box 57270, 11574.
Telephone: (011-966-1) 488-1563.
Fax: (011-966-1) 488-0542.

Steven D. Brown
Lynn F. Jacob
James V. Meath
Douglas M. Nabhan

Shannon P. Garbett
Sean M. Gibbons
G. William Norris, Jr.
King F. Tower

For Complete List of Firm Personnel, See General Section

For full biographical listings, see the Martindale-Hubbell Law Directory

SPRINGFIELD, Fairfax Co.

WILLIAM S. COLWELL (AV)

9112 Rockefeller Lane, 22153
Telephone: 703-451-9586
Fax: 703-451-5005
Email: leaderacc@aol.com *URL:* http://www.lawyers.com/wsclaw

For full biographical listings, see the Martindale-Hubbell Law Directory

WASHINGTON

*SEATTLE,** King Co.

LANE POWELL SPEARS LUBERSKY LLP (AV)

Limited Liability Partnership composed of Individuals and Professional Service Corporations
1420 Fifth Avenue, Suite 4100, 98101-2338
Telephone: 206-223-7000
Facsimile: 206-223-7107
Email: information@lanepowell.com *URL:* http://www.lanepowell.com
Other Offices at: Portland, Oregon; Anchorage, Alaska; Olympia and Mount Vernon, Washington; London, England.

MEMBERS OF FIRM

Clemens H. Barnes
Gail E. Mautner
Suzanne Kelly Michael
Paul M. Nordsletten
Ralph C. Pond
Clifford D. Sethness
Douglas E. Smith
Linda D. Walton

ASSOCIATES

Stephanie R. Alexander
Nancy Watkins Anderson

Representative Clients: Arco; AT&T Corp.; Eddie Bauer, Inc.; Enterprise Rent-A-Car; Fred Hutchinson Cancer Research Center; Georgia-Pacific Corp.; J. C. Penney Co.; Nordstrom; Pacific Maritime Assn.; Texaco Inc.

For Complete List of Firm Personnel, See General Section

For full biographical listings, see the Martindale-Hubbell Law Directory

PERKINS COIE LLP (AV)

Strategic Alliance with Russell & DuMoulin
1201 Third Avenue, Suite 4800, 98101-3099
Telephone: 206-583-8888
Facsimile: 206-583-8500
Email: perkins@perkinscoie.com *URL:* http://www.perkinscoie.com
Anchorage, Alaska: 1029 West Third Avenue, Suite 300, 99501-1970.
Telephone: 907-279-8561.
Facsimile: 907-276-3108.
Los Angeles, California: 1620 26th Street, 6th Floor, 90404.
Telephone: 310-788-9900.
Facsimile: 310-788-3399.

(See Next Column)

PERKINS COIE LLP, *Seattle—Continued*

Menlo Park, California: 135 Commonwealth Drive, Suite 250, 94025-1105.
Telephone: 650-752-6000.
Facsimile: 650-752-6050.
San Francisco, California: 180 Townsend Street, 94107-1909.
Telephone: 415-781-3200.
Facsimile: 415-781-2525.
Denver, Colorado: World Trade Center, 1675 Broadway, Suite 2800, 80202-062.
Telephone: 303-571-6100.
Facsimile: 303-571-6111.
Washington, D.C.: 607 Fourteenth Street, N.W., 20005-2011.
Telephone: 202-628-6600.
Telex: 44-0277 PCSO.
Facsimile: 202-434-1690.
Boise, Idaho: 714 West State Street, 83702.
Telephone: 208-343-3434.
Facsimile: 208-343-3232.
Portland, Oregon: Suite 1500, 1211 Southwest Fifth Avenue.
Telephone: 503-727-2000.
Facsimile: 503-727-2222.
Bellevue, Washington: Suite 1800, One Bellevue Center, 411 - 108th Avenue N.E., 98004-5584.
Telephone: 425-453-6980.
Facsimile: 425-453-7350.
Spokane, Washington: North 221 Wall Street, Suite 600, 99201-0826.
Telephone: 509-624-2212.
Facsimile: 509-458-3399.
Hong Kong: 17/F, Standard Charter Bank Building, 4 Des Voeux Road.
Telephone: 852-2878-1177.
Facsimile: 852-2524-9988.
Taipei, Taiwan, R.O.C.: 8/F Cathay United Bank Tower, 85 Jen Ai Rd., Section 5.
Telephone: 886-2-2778-1177.
Facsimile: 886-2-2777-9898.
Canada: Strategic Alliance with Russell & DuMoulin, 1700-1075 West Georgia Street. Vancouver, British Columbia, V6E 3G2.
Telephone: 604-631-3131.

PARTNERS

John F. Aslin
Bruce D. Corker
Bruce Michael Cross
Kevin J. Hamilton
Jeffrey A. Hollingsworth
Valerie L. Hughes
Philip S. Morse
Russell L. Perisho
Thomas E. Platt
Richard Ottesen Prentke
Michael T. Reynvaan
Bart Waldman
Nancy Williams

COUNSEL

J. David Andrews, P.S.

Counsel for: The Boeing Company; Puget Sound Energy; US West; Amazon.-com; Louisiana-Pacific; Lloyd's of London (Aviation); Weyerhauser.

For Complete List of Firm Personnel, See General Section

For full biographical listings, see the Martindale-Hubbell Law Directory

SCHWERIN CAMPBELL BARNARD LLP (AV)

18 West Mercer Street, Suite 400, 98119-3971
Telephone: 206-285-2828; Washington Toll Free: 1-800-238-4231
Fax: 206-378-4132
Email: scb@workerlaw.com

Lawrence R. Schwerin
David C. Campbell
Kathleen P Barnard
Elizabeth G. Ford
Melvin R. Kang

ASSOCIATES

Dmitri Iglitzin
Robert M. Lavitt
Nancy Maisano
Michelle L. Malkin
Stephanie Cogen
Sonja D. Fritts
Jason S. Kelly

For full biographical listings, see the Martindale-Hubbell Law Directory

SUMMIT LAW GROUP, PLLC (AV)

1505 Westlake Avenue North, Suite 300, 98109
Telephone: 206-281-9881
Fax: 206-281-9882
Email: info@summitlaw.com *URL:* http://www.summitlaw.com

Karen A. Andersen
Kristin D. Anger
Laura A. Bertin
Lynn M. Engel
Michael J. Erickson
Matthew R. Harris
David M. Heineck
Elizabeth Butler Kennar
Otto G. Klein, III
Lawrence C. Locker
Philip S. McCune
Polly L. McNeill
Ralph H. Palumbo
Bruce L. Schroeder
William R. Squires III
Monika Vasil
Mark F. Worthington
Rodney B. Younker

For full biographical listings, see the Martindale-Hubbell Law Directory

WINTERBAUER & DIAMOND, P.L.L.C. (AV)

1200 Fifth Avenue, Suite 1910, 98101
Telephone: 206-676-8440
Facsimile: 206-676-8441
Email: mail@winterbauer.com

MEMBERS OF FIRM

Steven H. Winterbauer
Felicia Latham
Kenneth J. Diamond
Adam G. Cuff
Ann Marie Lewis

For full biographical listings, see the Martindale-Hubbell Law Directory

WEST VIRGINIA

*CHARLESTON,** Kanawha Co.

GOODWIN & GOODWIN (AV)

1500 One Valley Square, 25301
Telephone: 304-346-7000
Fax: 304-344-9692
Email: g&glaw@goodwin.goodwin.com *URL:* http://www.goodwingoodwin.com
Ripley, West Virginia Office: 500 Church Street, P.O. Box 349.
Telephone: 304-372-2651.
Parkersburg, West Virginia Office: 201 Third Street, Town Square.
Telephone: 304-485-2345.
Fax: 304-485-3459.

Robert B. Goodwin (1909-1955)

OF COUNSEL

C. E. Goodwin

MEMBERS OF FIRM

Thomas R. Goodwin
Stephen P. Goodwin
Michael I. Spiker
Steven F. White
Richard E. Rowe
Leonard S. Coleman
Susan C. Wittemeier
Robert W. Full (Resident at Parkersburg Office)
Richard D. Owen
Tammy J. Owen
J. David Fenwick
Alexander Macia

ASSOCIATES

Suzanne Jett Trowbridge
William K. Bragg, Jr.
George M. Smith
John N. Ellem (Resident, Parkersburg Office)
Lisa A. Tackett
Robert (Booth) Goodwin, II
Carrie Goodwin Fenwick
Tiffany E. Davis

Representative Clients: Bucyrus-Erie Co.; CSX Corp.; Eastern American Energy Corp.; The Eureka Pipe Line Co.

For full biographical listings, see the Martindale-Hubbell Law Directory

JACKSON & KELLY (AV)

1600 Laidley Tower, P.O. Box 553, 25322
Telephone: 304-340-1000
Fax: 304-340-1130
Email: info@jacksonkelly.com *URL:* http://www.jacksonkelly.com
Martinsburg, West Virginia Office: 300 Foxcroft Avenue, P.O. Box 1068.
Telephone: 304-263-8800.
Fax: 304-263-7110.
Morgantown, West Virginia Office: 6000 Hampton Center, P.O. Box 619.
Telephone: 304-599-3000.
Fax: 304-285-2040.
New Martinsville, West Virginia Office: 256 Russell Avenue, P.O. Box 68.
Telephone: 304-455-1751.
Fax: 304-455-6314.
Parkersburg, West Virginia Office: 412 Market Street, Suite 202, P.O. Box 1144.
Telephone: 304-424-3490.
Fax: 304-424-3499.
Fairmont, West Virginia Office: 1000 Technology Drive, Suite 1310.
Telephone: 304-368-2000.
Fax: 304-368-2020.
Lexington, Kentucky Office: 175 East Main Street, Suite 500, P.O. Box 2150.
Telephone: 606-255-9500.
Fax: 606-281-6478.
Washington, D. C. Office: 2401 Pennsylvania Avenue, N.W., Suite 400.
Telephone: 202-973-0200.
Fax: 202-973-0232.
Denver, Colorado Office: Suite 2710, 1660 Lincoln Street.
Telephone: 303-390-0003.
Fax: 303-390-0040.
Wheeling, West Virginia Office: 1144 Market Street.
Telephone: 304-233-4000.
Fax: 304-233-4077.

(See Next Column)

JACKSON & KELLY—*Continued*

MEMBERS OF FIRM

Charles Q. Gage
Roger A. Wolfe
Michael D. Foster
Charles M. Surber, Jr.
Cheryl Harris Wolfe
Larry W. Blalock (Administrative Manager, New Martinsville and Wheeling, West Virginia Offices)
Daniel L. Stickler (Administrative Manager)
L. Anthony George (Resident, Denver, Colorado Office)
Albert F. Sebok
Julia M. Chico (Resident, Morgantown, West Virginia Office)

ASSOCIATES

Jacqueline Syers Duncan (Resident, Lexington, Kentucky Office)
Erin Magee Condaras
Kelley L. Mount
Victoria J. Sopranik (Resident, Lexington, Kentucky Office)

OF COUNSEL

David D. Johnson (Retired)
Katherine Shand Larkin (Resident, Denver, Colorado Office)

Representative Clients: A.T. Massey Coal Company, Inc.; CONSOL Inc.; Arch Coal, Inc.; One Valley Bancorp of West Virginia, Inc.; West Virginia-American Water Co.; Ramsay Health Care, Inc.; Charleston Newspapers; Union Carbide Corp.; K-Mart Corp.; Old Republic Insurance.

For Complete List of Firm Personnel, See General Section

For full biographical listings, see the Martindale-Hubbell Law Directory

*CLARKSBURG,** Harrison Co.

MCNEER, HIGHLAND, MCMUNN AND VARNER, L.C. (AV)

One Valley Bank Building, P.O. Drawer 2040, 26302-2040
Telephone: 304-626-1100
Facsimile: 304-623-3035
Martinsburg Office: 2520 Aikens Center, P.O. Box 2509.
Telephone: 304-264-4621.
Fax: 304-264-8623.
Parkersburg Office: 404 Market Street, Suite 204, P.O. Box 1507.
Telephone: 304-422-7193.
Facsimile: 304-422-7196.

C. David McMunn
J. Cecil Jarvis
James A. Varner
Robert W. Trumble (Resident, Martinsburg Office)
Catherine D. Munster
James N. Riley
Steven R. Bratke (Resident, Parkersburg Office)
Michael J. Novotny (Resident, Martinsburg Office)
Dennis M. Shreve
Geraldine S. Roberts
William F. Rohrbaugh (Resident, Martinsburg Office)
Gregory H. Schillace
Judy L. Shanholtz
Tiffany R. Durst
Gene W. Bailey, II

OF COUNSEL

James E. McNeer
Cecil B. Highland, Jr.
William L. Fury

Representative Clients: One Valley Bank of Clarksburg, National Assn.; Bruceton Bank; Harrison County Bank; Nationwide Mutual Insurance Cos.; Clarksburg Publishing Co.; C.I.T. Financial Services; State Automobile Mutual Insurance Co.; United Hospital Center, Inc.; West Virginia Coals, Inc.; Swanson Plating Co.

For full biographical listings, see the Martindale-Hubbell Law Directory

HUNTINGTON, Cabell & Wayne Cos.

BAKER, LANCIANESE, CAMPBELL & CONATY (AV)

The River Tower, 1108 Third Avenue, Suite 300, 25701-1578
Telephone: 304-522-6906
Facsimile: 304-522-6910
Email: BLCC@BLCCLAW.COM *URL:* http://www.BLCCLAW.COM
Washington, D.C. Office: 1090 Vermont Avenue, N.W. Suite 800.
Telephone: 202-966-1500.
Fax: 202-966-7075. E-Mail: BLCC@BLCCLAW.COM.
Lexington, Kentucky Office: 2265 Harrodsburg Road, Suite 200, 40504-3517.
Telephone: 606-278-0297.
Fax: 206-278-0334. E-Mail: BLCC@BLCCLAW.COM.

Roy D. Baker, Jr.
Richard L. Lancianese
David L. Campbell
Brian P. Conaty
Janice P. Epperly

OF COUNSEL

Margaret M. Brizzolara (Not admitted in WV)

For full biographical listings, see the Martindale-Hubbell Law Directory

*WHEELING,** Ohio Co.

CASSIDY, MYERS, COGAN, VOEGELIN & TENNANT, L.C. (AV)

The First State Capitol, 1413 Eoff Street, 26003-3582
Telephone: 304-232-8100
Fax: 304-232-8200
St. Clairsville, Ohio Office: 126 E. Main Street.
Telephone: 740-695-1350.
Fax: 740-695-1356.

Frank A. O'Brien, Jr.
Patrick S. Cassidy
William C. Gallagher
Thomas M. Myers (Resident at St. Clairsville, Ohio, Office)
Timothy F. Cogan
Wray V. Voegelin
Donald James Tennant, Jr.
Thomas M. Cunningham

Representative Clients: United Steel Workers of America AFL, CIO, CLC; District 6 United Mine Workers of America; District 23 United Food and Commercial Workers; Local 1149 Laborers National Union of North America; West Virginia Education Assn.; International Union of Oil, Chemical & Atomic Workers; International Union of Electrical, Radio & Machine Workers; Local 83 United Association of Plumbers and Steamfitters; Local 549, International Association of Bridge, Structural and Ornamental Iron Workers of Wheeling, WV.

For full biographical listings, see the Martindale-Hubbell Law Directory

SCHRADER BYRD & COMPANION, PLLC (AV)

(A Professional Limited Liability Company)
The Maxwell Centre, 32-20th Street, Suite 500, P.O. Box 6336, 26003
Telephone: 304-233-3390
Fax: 304-233-2769
URL: http://www.schraderlaw.com
Martins Ferry, Ohio Office: 205 North Fifth Street, P.O. Box 309, 43935.
Telephone: 740-633-9976.
Fax: 740-633-0400.
Weirton, West Virginia Office: 3205 Pennsylvania Avenue, Suite 103, Penn Place, P.O. Box 2785, 26062.
Telephone: 304-723-2674.
Fax: 304-723-2876.

MEMBERS

Ray A. Byrd
James F. Companion
Frank X. Duff
Teresa Rieman-Camilletti
Yolonda G. Lambert
Daniel P. Fry (Resident Partner, Martins Ferry, Ohio Office)
James P. Mazzone (Resident Member, Weirton, West Virginia Office)
Sandra K. Law
D. Kevin Coleman

SPECIAL COUNSEL

Thomas B. Miller

ASSOCIATES

Denise D. Klug
Michael A. Adams
John Porco
Aimee Morgan Stern
Kimberly R. Wilson
Christopher J. Adams

OF COUNSEL

James A. Byrum, Jr.

General Counsel: Reynolds Memorial Hospital; WesBanco Bank-Elm Grove.
Representative Clients: American Cyanamid Company; Bank One; Matlack Systems, Inc.; Moutaineer Gas Co.; Ohio County Board of Education; PHICO Insurance Co.; Wheeling Hospital; Wheeling-Pittsburg Steel Corp.

For full biographical listings, see the Martindale-Hubbell Law Directory

WISCONSIN

*MADISON,** Dane Co.

LAWTON & CATES, S.C. (AV)

10 East Doty Street Suite 400, P.O. Box 2965, 53701-2965
Telephone: 608-282-6200
Fax: 608-282-6252
Email: lawcat@madison.tds.net *URL:* http://www.lawtoncates.com

John C. Carlson
Bruce M. Davey
P. Scott Hassett
Steven J. Schooler
Victor M. Arellano

OF COUNSEL

Richard L. Cates

Reference: Bank One, Madison.

For full biographical listings, see the Martindale-Hubbell Law Directory

MELLI, WALKER, PEASE & RUHLY, S.C. (AV)

Suite 900, Ten East Doty, P.O. Box 1664, 53701-1664
Telephone: 608-257-4812
Telefax: 608-258-7470
URL: http://www.melliwalker.com

(See Next Column)

MELLI, WALKER, PEASE & RUHLY S.C., *Madison—Continued*

Jack D. Walker
James K. Pease, Jr.
James K. Ruhly
Thomas R. Crone
Philip J. Bradbury
JoAnn M. Hart
Susan C. Sheeran
Douglas E. Witte
Dana J. Erlandsen
Devon R. Baumbach
Daniel D. Barker
Jenifer L. Kraemer

OF COUNSEL

Joseph A. Melli

Representative Clients: Wisconsin Transportation Builders Assn.; Associated Builders & Contractors of Wisconsin, Inc.; Marshall Erdman & Associates, Inc.; Research Products Corp.; Kraemer Brothers, LLC.; Covance Laboratories; JJ Protective Services, Inc.; Racine Unified School District; Green Bay Area School District.

For full biographical listings, see the Martindale-Hubbell Law Directory

MILWAUKEE,* Milwaukee Co.

BECK, CHAET, MOLONY & BAMBERGER, S.C. (AV)

Two Plaza East, 330 East Kilbourn Avenue, Suite 1085, 53202
Telephone: 414-273-4200
Fax: 414-273-7786
Email: bcmb@execpc.com *URL:* http://www.bcmblaw.com
Madison, Wisconsin Office: 44 East Mifflin Street, Suite 304.
Telephone: 608-255-1140.
Fax: 608-255-0160.

Arthur E. Beck
Barry L. Chaet
Maureen A. Molony (Resident, Madison, Wisconsin Office)
Michael Bamberger
E. Vanessa Jones
Katherine L. Williams
Christopher J. Johnson
Kevin L. Keeler
Joshua B. Levy
LouAnn Koval
Daniel M. Lowndes
Edward B. Matkom

Drew J. Cochrane

OF COUNSEL

Robert P. Mandel

For full biographical listings, see the Martindale-Hubbell Law Directory

BRIGDEN & PETAJAN, S.C. (AV)

600 East Mason Street, 53202-3831
Telephone: 414-291-0666
Facsimile: 414-291-9204
Email: bp@employerslawyers.com *URL:* http://www.employerslawyers.com

Patrick H. Brigden (1931-1984)
Douglas A. Cairns (1944-1987)
Albert H. Petajan
John C. Patzke
Marna M. Tess-Mattner

Representative Clients: Appleton Mills; Europlast, Ltd.; Gold Cross Ambulance Services, Inc.; Mil-Mar Shoe Co., Inc.; Milwaukee Forge; The Mutual Group (U.S.); Penda Corp.; Safeguard Business Systems, Inc.; TriEnda Corp.; Vulcan Lead Products, Co.

For full biographical listings, see the Martindale-Hubbell Law Directory

DAVIS & KUELTHAU, S.C. (AV)

111 East Kilbourn Avenue, Suite 1400, 53202-6613
Telephone: 414-276-0200
Facsimile: 414-276-9369
Cable Address: "Shiplaw"
Email: info@daviskuelthau.com *URL:* http://www.daviskuelthau.com
Madison, Wisconsin Office: Ten East Doty Street, Suite 600, P.O. Box 1068, 53703.
Telephone: 608-280-8235.
Fax: 608-280-8231.
Sheboygan, Wisconsin Office: 605 North Eighth, Suite 610, P.O. Box 1287.
Telephone: 920-451-1461.
Fax: 920-451-1465.
Green Bay, Wisconsin Office: 414 East Walnut Street, Suite 240.
Telephone: 920-435-9378.
Fax: 920-435-9391.

James E. Braza
Clifford B. Buelow
Robert H. Buikema
Walter S. Davis
Richard J. Delacenserie (Resident at Madison Office)
Matthew J. Flanary
Paul C. Hemmer (Resident at Sheboygan Office)
Mary L. Hubacher
Jane M. Knasinski
Susan M. Love
Elizabeth A. McDuffie
Mark L. Olson
Robert J. Simandl
Mark F. Vetter
Daniel G. Vliet
Roger E. Walsh

Ellen K. Basting
Joy M. Burkholder
Shawn D. Guse
Gregory B. Ladewski
John E. Murray
Nancy L. Pirkey
Thomas R. Revnew
Timothy L. Stewart

(See Next Column)

Special Labor and Employment Counsel For: Chromalloy American Corp.; Grede Foundries; Mayline, Inc.; Leach Co.; Elmbrook, West Allis-West Milwaukee, Kenosha, Watertown, Wauwatosa and Whitefish Bay School Districts; Counties of Kenosha, Dodge and Washington; Schoeneck Containers Inc.; Pinkerton's.

For full biographical listings, see the Martindale-Hubbell Law Directory

KASDORF, LEWIS & SWIETLIK, S.C. (AV)

1551 South 108th Street, 53214
Telephone: 414-257-1055
Facsimile: 414-257-3759
Green Bay, Wisconsin Office: 727 East Walnut Street, 54301.
Telephone: 920-436-0304.
Wausau, Wisconsin Office: 2100 Stewart Avenue, Suite 230, 54401.
Telephone: 715-848-9250.
Facsimile: 715-849-2017.

James P. Reardon
Werner E. Scherr
Terrance E. Davczyk
Jeff Schmeckpeper
Gregory J. Cook
Michael J. Cieslewicz
Michael A. Mesirow
Joseph J. Ferris
James J. Kriva
David L. Styer
Robert J. Lauer
James M. Ryan
Robert P. Ochowicz

Michael C. Frohman
Charles G. Maris
Vicki L. Arrowood
Michael S. Murray
Peter J. Eckardt (Resident)
Christine D. Esser
Thomas A. Cabush
John K. Garofani
Bonni D. Fredrick
Christopher A. Duesing
Daniel W. Varline (Resident, Wausau Office)
Jerome A. Long (Resident, Wausau Office)

OF COUNSEL

Clifford C. Kasdorf
John M. Swietlik
Hugh E. Russell
Patti J. Kurth

Representative Clients: Allstate Insurance Co.; State Farm Mutual Automobile; Liberty Mutual Insurance Co.; Shelby Mutual Insurance Co.; Government Employees Insurance Co.
Reference: M & I Marshall & Ilsley Bank.

For full biographical listings, see the Martindale-Hubbell Law Directory

KRUKOWSKI & COSTELLO, S.C. (AV)

7111 West Edgerton Avenue, 53220
Telephone: 414-423-1330
Telefax: 414-423-1694
Email: tpk@kclegal.com *URL:* http://www.krukowski.com
Washington, D.C. Office: 1401 Eye Street, N.W., Suite 1210, 20005.
Telephone: 202-898-1031.
Fax: 202-898-1311.

Thomas P. Krukowski
Timothy G. Costello
Robert J. Bartel
Kevin J. Kinney
Marty R. Howard

David Loeffler
Elliot H. Shaller (Not admitted in WI; Resident, Washington, D.C. Office)
Erik C. J. Anderson (Not admitted in WI; Resident, Washington, D.C. Office)
Mark A. Johnson
Maria Pia Torretti Gekas (Not admitted in WI; Resident, Washington DC Office)
David A. McClurg
Joseph J. Perkoski (Not admitted in WI)
Bruce Frank Mills
Patrick M. Cooper
Gene Linkmeyer
Deborah A. Krukowski

Representative Clients: Briggs & Stratton Corporation; Firstar Corporation; Bemis Corporation; Roundy's, Inc.; Yellow Freight Systems, Inc.; Schreiber Foods, Inc.; Ryder System, Inc.; Kerry Ingredients; Lutheran Hospital, La Crosse; Roadmaster Corporation.

For full biographical listings, see the Martindale-Hubbell Law Directory

LINDNER & MARSACK, S.C. (AV)

411 East Wisconsin Avenue, Suite 1000, 53202
Telephone: 414-273-3910
FAX: 414-273-0522

Leon B. Lamfrom (1884-1970)
Egon W. Peck (1903-1979)
Dennis G. Lindner
Gary A. Marsack
Robert E. Schreiber, Jr.
Jonathan T. Swain
James R. Scott
Thomas W. Mackenzie
Douglas M. Feldman
Laurie A. Petersen

Donald J. Cairns
Lisa M. Bergersen
Alan M. Levy
John E. Drana
Oyvind Wistrom
John R. Jakubiak
Mark A. Schemmel
Timothy J. Schumann
Kirsten L. Hildebrand
Bethany C. McCurdy

(See Next Column)

LINDNER & MARSACK S.C.—*Continued*

Representative Corporate Labor Clients: Ansul Co.; Caterpillar Inc.; Roundy's Inc.; Strattec Security Corp.; Master Lock; McDonalds Corp.

For full biographical listings, see the Martindale-Hubbell Law Directory

MICHAEL BEST & FRIEDRICH LLP (AV)

100 East Wisconsin Avenue, 53202-4108
Telephone: 414-271-6560
Telecopier: 414-277-0656
Cable Address: "Mibef"
Email: info@mbf-law.com *URL:* http://www.mbf-law.com
Madison, Wisconsin Office: One South Pinckney Street, Firstar Plaza, P.O. Box 1806, 53701-1806.
Telephone: 608-257-3501.
Telecopier: 283-2275.
Manitowoc, Wisconsin Office: 1000 Maritime Drive, 54220.
Telephone: 920-686-2800.
Fax: 920-686-2810.
Chicago, Illinois Office: Michael Best & Friedrich LLC, 77 West Wacker Drive, Suite 4300, 60601-1635.
Telephone: 312-845-5800.
Telecopier: 312-845-5828.

PARTNERS

John R. Sapp
Thomas E. Obenberger
Marshall R. Berkoff
David W. Croysdale
Scott H. Engroff
Robert W. Mulcahy
Thomas W. Scrivner
Paul E. Prentiss
John C. Lapinski
Eric E. Hobbs
Robert D. Rothacker
José A. Olivieri
Jonathan O. Levine
Scott C. Beightol
Eric H. Rumbaugh
Mitchell W. Quick
Mark E. Toth
Paul R. Riegel

ASSOCIATES

Kathleen M. O'Toole
Stacie J. Andritsch
Amy Schmidt Jones
Brenda S. Kasper
Amy D. Katarincic
Jesús J. Villa

For Complete List of Firm Personnel, See General Section

For full biographical listings, see the Martindale-Hubbell Law Directory

PREVIANT, GOLDBERG, UELMEN, GRATZ, MILLER & BRUEGGEMAN, S.C. (AV)

1555 North RiverCenter Drive, Suite 202, 53212
Telephone: 414-271-4500
Fax: 414-271-6308
Green Bay, Wisconsin Office: 3257 Main Street, Suite A.
Telephone: 920-863-3500.
Fax: 920-863-6995.
Waukesha, Wisconsin Office: 2607 North Grandview Boulevard, Suite 102.
Telephone: 414-549-6300.
Fax: 414-549-6426.

David Previant (1910-1996)
David L. Uelmen
Richard M. Goldberg
Gerry M. Miller
Larry B. Brueggeman
Matthew R. Robbins
Marianne Goldstein Robbins
Scott D. Soldon
Thomas J. Flanagan
Dean M. Horwitz
Frederick Perillo
Hope K. Olson
Philip R. O'Brien
John J. Brennan
Michael D. Riegert
Shawn R. Crain
Frank G. Locante
Steven G. Kluender
Naomi E. Soldon
Steven D. Hitzeman

Ronald G. Tays
Lisa A. Bangert
Daniel L. Zitzer
Andrea F. Hoeschen
Jill M. Hartley
Jonathan M. Conti
Margaret A. Fischbach
Jackson T. Main, Jr.
Ryan J. Hetzel

Representative Clients: Wisconsin State AFL-CIO; Milwaukee Building and Construction Trades Council; Central Conference of Teamsters; Wisconsin Teamsters Joint Council 39; Machinists Dist. 10; United Paperworks International Union.

For full biographical listings, see the Martindale-Hubbell Law Directory

QUARLES & BRADY LLP (AV)

411 East Wisconsin Avenue, 53202-4497
Telephone: 414-277-5000
Fax: 414-271-3552
URL: http://www.quarles.com
Madison, Wisconsin Office: Firstar Plaza, One South Pinckney Street, P.O. Box 2113, 53701-2113.
Telephone: 608-251-5000.
Fax: 608-251-9166.
West Palm Beach, Florida Office: 222 Lakeview Avenue, 4th Floor, 33401.
Telephone: 561-653-5000.
Fax: 561-653-5333.

(See Next Column)

Naples, Florida Office: Barnett Center, 4501 Tamiami Trail North, Suite 300, 34103-3060.
Telephone: 941-262-5959.
Fax: 941-434-4999.
Phoenix, Arizona Office: One Camelback Building, One East Camelback Road, Suite 400, 85012-1649.
Telephone: 602-230-5500.
Fax: 602-230-5598.
Chicago, Illinois Office: Quarles & Brady LLC, Citicorp Center, 500 West Madison Street, Suite 3700.
Telephone: 312-715-5000.
Fax: 312-715-5155.

MEMBERS OF FIRM
(ALPHABETICALLY BY YEAR OF ADMISSION TO BAR)

Fred G. Groiss
Arthur B. Harris
Michael J. Spector
George K. Whyte, Jr.
Charles W. Herf (Resident, Phoenix, Arizona Office)
David E. Jarvis
Michael S. Weiden (Resident, Madison Office)
J. Paul Jacobson
John R. Maynard
William M. Shattuck (Resident, Phoenix, Arizona Office)
John W. Daniels, Jr.
Alyce C. Katayama
Patrick W. Schmidt
Fred Gants (Resident, Madison Office)
Mary Pat Ninneman
Jon E. Pettibone (Resident, Phoenix, Arizona Office)
Patricia K. Ballman
Michael S. McCauley
Waltraud A. Arts (Resident, Madison Office)
David B. Kern
Ely A. Leichtling
Jeffrey Morris
William H. Harbeck
Gary M. Ruesch
David A. Selden (Resident, Phoenix, Arizona Office)
Robert H. Duffy
Dana L. O'Brien
Michael D. Zeka
David P. Olson
Joseph E. Puchner
Colleen A. Scherkenbach (Resident, Phoenix, Arizona Office)

OF COUNSEL

Laurence E. Gooding, Jr.
James Urdan

ASSOCIATES

Lauri D. Morris (Resident, Madison Office)
Michael Aldana
Carmella A. Huser
David T. Barton (Resident, Phoenix, Arizona Office)
Julie A. Pace (Resident, Phoenix, Arizona Office)
Kurt T. Temple (Resident, Chicago, Illinois Office)
Pamela M. Ploor
Patricia A. Hintz
Shannon B. Farrell
Michael J. Fischer
Heidi B. Retzlaff
Gregory J. Stanton (Resident, Phoenix, Arizona Office)
C. Christine Burns (Resident, Phoenix, Arizona Office)
Thomas N. Shorter (Resident, Madison, Wisconsin Office)
Mireya Castillo Martin (Resident, Phoenix, Arizona Office)
Luis I. Arroyo
Keith A. Bruett

For Complete List of Firm Personnel, See General Section

For full biographical listings, see the Martindale-Hubbell Law Directory

SENECZKO LAW OFFICES, S.C. (AV)

Associated Bank Building, Suite 200, 10701 West National Avenue, 53227
Telephone: 414-321-5959
Fax: 414-321-1404
Email: seneczko@excepc.com

Alan E. Seneczko

For full biographical listings, see the Martindale-Hubbell Law Directory

WYOMING

*CASPER,** Natrona Co.

BROWN, DREW & MASSEY, LLP (AV)

Casper Business Center, Suite 800, 123 West First Street, 82601-2486
Telephone: 307-234-1000
800-877-6755
Telefax: 307-265-8025
Email: brwndrew@coffey.com

MEMBERS OF FIRM

Morris R. Massey
Thomas F. Reese
J. Kenneth Barbe
Jeffrey C. Brinkerhoff
P. Jaye Rippley
Courtney Robert Kepler

ASSOCIATES

Scott P. Klosterman
Timothy M. Stubson

Attorneys for: KMart; Walmart.

For Complete List of Firm Personnel, See General Section

For full biographical listings, see the Martindale-Hubbell Law Directory

PUERTO RICO

SAN JUAN, San Juan Dist.

FIDDLER GONZÁLEZ & RODRÍGUEZ, LLP

254 Muñoz Rivera Avenue (Hato Rey), P.O. Box 363507, 00936-3507
Telephone: 787-753-3113
Telecopier: 787-759-3123
Email: fiddler@fgrlaw.com *URL:* http://www.fgrlaw.com

MEMBERS OF FIRM

Pedro Pumarada
Juan Carlos Pérez-Otero
Tristán Reyes-Gilestra
José A. Silva-Cofresí
Arturo Bauermeister-Baldrich
José J. Santiago
Carlos V. J. Dávila
Lolita J. Semidey Garcia
Rosa M. Méndez-Santoni

Representative Clients: Banco Popular de Puerto Rico; Banco Santander-Puerto Rico; Citibank, N.A.; Pfizer, Inc.; Merck & Co., Inc.; Baxter Healthcare Corp.; American Cyanamid Co.; Telemundo Group, Inc.; El Nuevo Dia, Inc.; Triple S, Inc.

For Complete List of Firm Personnel, See General Section

For full biographical listings, see the Martindale-Hubbell Law Directory

GOLDMAN ANTONETTI & CÓRDOVA

American International Plaza Fourteenth & Fifteenth Floors, 250 Muñoz Rivera Avenue (Hato Rey), P.O. Box 70364, 00936-0364
Telephone: 787-759-8000
Telecopiers: 787-767-9333 (Main)
787-767-9177 (Litigation Department)
787-767-8660 (Labor & Corporate Law Departments)
787-767-9325 (Tax & Environmental Law Departments)
URL: http://www.gaclaw.com

MEMBERS OF FIRM

Vicente J. Antonetti
Luis F. Antonetti
Luis D. Ortiz-Abreu
Howard Pravda
Jorge R. Rodriguez-Micheo
Migdalia Davila-Garcia

OF COUNSEL

Heber E. Lugo-Rigau

ASSOCIATES

Vivian Nuñez
Hector Perez
Claribel Ortiz-Rodríguez
Frances R. Colon-Rivera
Aida Barrios-Castellanos
Nilsa Flores-Sola
Eugenia I. Orsini-Herencia
Yvette De Luna-Colon
Ricardo Pizarro
Ruben Rivera-Rosa
Angel Berberena

Representative Clients: American Airlines; Upjohn Manufacturing Corp.; Federal Express Corp.; Bumble Bee Puerto Rico, Inc.; Mayagüez Hilton International; Seven-Up Bottling Co.; Star Kist Caribe, Inc.; Abbott Laboratories.

For Complete List of Firm Personnel, See General Section

For full biographical listings, see the Martindale-Hubbell Law Directory

JIMÉNEZ, GRAFFAM & LAUSELL

Suite 505, Midtown Building, 421 Muñoz Rivera Avenue, Hato Rey, P.O. Box 366104, 00936-6104
Telephone: 787-767-1030; 767-1000; 767-1061; 767-1064
Telefax: 787-751-4068;
Cable: "Nezte"
RCA Telex: 325-2730
Email: manager@jgl.com *URL:* http://www.jgl.com

MEMBERS OF FIRM

William A. Graffam
Raquel M. Dulzaides

ASSOCIATES

Edgardo A. Vega-López
José Luis Suárez-Villafañe
Ruy V. Díaz-Díaz

Representative Clients: Sea-Land Service, Inc.; McAllister Brothers, Inc.; Crowley Maritime Corp.; Crowley Marine Services, Inc.; Crowley American Transport, Inc.; Insituform de Puerto Rico, Inc.

For Complete List of Firm Personnel, See General Section

For full biographical listings, see the Martindale-Hubbell Law Directory

MARTÍNEZ ODELL & CALABRIA

Banco Popular Center, 209 Muñoz Rivera Avenue, Suite 1600 (Hato Rey), P.O. Box 190998, 00919-0998
Telephone: 787-753-8914
Facsimile: 787-753-8402; 787-759-9075; 787-764-5664
Email: postmaster@mocpr.com

(See Next Column)

MEMBERS OF FIRM

Francisco M. Ramirez-Rivera
Graciela J. Belaval
Roberto E. Vega Pacheco
Francisco L. Acevedo-Nogueras
Manuel E. Lopez-Fernandez
Jose G. Fagot-Diaz

ASSOCIATES

Amelia Fortuño-Ruiz
Julio D. Vazquez-Rodriguez
Mildred L. Santana-Mejias
Roxana M. Viera-Canales

Representative Clients: Banco Popular de Puerto Rico; Daewoo Motor Corporation; Eckerd Corporation; Empresas Fonalledas; Hilton International; L'Aire Liquide, S.A.; Loctile Corporation; Lucent Technologies; Lutron Electronics Co., Inc.; Waste Management, Inc.

For Complete List of Firm Personnel, See General Section

For full biographical listings, see the Martindale-Hubbell Law Directory

CANADA
ALBERTA

*CALGARY,** Calgary Jud. Dist.

MCLENNAN ROSS (AV)

1801 Altius Centre, 500 - 4th Avenue S.W., T2P 2V6
Telephone: 403-543-9120
Fax: 403-543-9150
Email: calgary@mross.com *URL:* http://www.mross.com
Edmonton, Alberta Office: 600 West Chambers, 12220 Stony Plain Road.
Telephone: 780-482-9200.
Fax: 780-482-9100; 780-482-9101; 780-482-9102. Email: edmonton@mross.com
Yellowknife, Northwest Territories Office: 802 Precambrian Building, 4920-52nd Street, X1A 3T1.
Telephone: 867-873-5968.
Fax: 867-873-5972

Philip G. Ponting, Q.C.
Donald W. Dear
Damon S. Bailey
Thomas W. R. Ross

For full biographical listings, see the Martindale-Hubbell Law Directory

PARLEE MCLAWS (AV)

3400 Petro-Canada Centre, 150 - 6th Avenue, SW, T2P 3Y7
Telephone: 403-294-7000
Telecopier: 403-265-8263
Email: lawyers@parlee.com *URL:* http://www.parlee.com
Edmonton, Alberta Office: 15th Floor Manulife Place, 10180 101st Street.
Telephone: 403-423-8500.
Telecopier: 403-423-2870.

MEMBERS OF FIRM

Bruce Churchill-Smith
Gregory D. M. Stirling

ASSOCIATES

Paul J. Mason
Erin A. MacPherson
Tasha D. Backus

For Complete List of Firm Personnel, See General Section

For full biographical listings, see the Martindale-Hubbell Law Directory

*EDMONTON,** Edmonton Jud. Dist.

MCLENNAN ROSS (AV)

A Partnership including Professional Corporations
600 West Chambers, 12220 Stony Plain Road, T5N 3Y4
Telephone: 780-482-9200
Fax: 780-482-9100; 780-482-9101; 780-482-9102
Email: edmonton@mross.com *URL:* http://www.mross.com
Calgary, Alberta Office: 1801 Altius Centre, 500 - 4th Avenue S.W, T2P 2V6.
Telephone: 403-543-9120.
Fax: 403-543-9150. Email: calgary@mross.com
Yellowknife, Northwest Territory Office: 802 Precambrian Building, 4920-52nd Street, X1A 3T1.
Telephone: 867-873-5968.
Fax: 867-873-5972

David J. Ross, Q.C.
Frederick A. Day, Q.C. *
Hugh J. D. McPhail
Glenn D. Tait
Gerhard J. Seifner
Christopher J. Lane
Shawn W. McLeod
Vicki L. Giles

*Denotes Lawyer Whose Professional Corporation is a Member of the Partnership.

For Complete List of Firm Personnel, See General Section

For full biographical listings, see the Martindale-Hubbell Law Directory

Edmonton—Continued

PARLEE MCLAWS (AV)

15th Floor Manulife Place, 10180 101st Street, T5J 4K1
Telephone: 403-423-8500
Telecopier: 403-423-2870
Email: lawyers@parlee.com *URL:* http://www.parlee.com
Calgary, Alberta Office: 3400 Petro-Canada Centre, 150 - 6th Avenue, SW.
Telephone: 403-294-7000.
Telecopier: 403-265-8263.

MEMBERS OF FIRM

Robert P. James
Walter J. Pavlic

ASSOCIATES

Norah B. Ramsay
K. Colleen Verville

For Complete List of Firm Personnel, See General Section

For full biographical listings, see the Martindale-Hubbell Law Directory

CANADA
BRITISH COLUMBIA

*VANCOUVER,** Vancouver Co.

ALEXANDER, HOLBURN, BEAUDIN & LANG (AV)

P.O. Box 10057 2700 Toronto Dominion Bank Tower, 700 West Georgia Street, V7Y 1B8
Telephone: 604-688-1351
Fax: 604-669-7642
URL: http://www.ahbl.bc.ca
Hong Kong Office, In Association with Ong & Chung: Room 2101, 21/F Tower II, Admiralty Centre, No. 18 Harcourt Road.
Telephone: (852) 2526-1171.
Fax: (852) 2845-0686.

PARTNER

R. Patrick Saul

ASSOCIATE

Susan Sangha

A list of Representative Clients will be furnished on request.

For Complete List of Firm Personnel, See General Section

For full biographical listings, see the Martindale-Hubbell Law Directory

CANADA
NEW BRUNSWICK

*FREDERICTON,** York Co.

COX HANSON O'REILLY MATHESON (AV)

(Formerly Hanson Hashey)
Suite 400, Phoenix Square, P.O. Box 310, E3B 4Y9
Telephone: 506-453-7771
Fax: 506-453-9600
Email: fredericton@coxhanson.ca *URL:* http://www.coxhanson.ca
Halifax, Nova Scotia Office: Suite 1100, Purdy's Wharf Tower 1, P.O. Box 2380 Station Central RPO, B3J 3E5.
Telephone: 902-421-6262.
Fax: 902-421-3130. E-Mail: halifax@coxhanson.ca
Saint John, New Brunswick Office: 1212-One Brunswick Square, 1 Germain St. E2L 4V1.
Telephone: 506-652-7771.
Fax: 506-632-9600.
St. John's, Newfoundland Office: Scotia Centre, 401-235 Water Street, A1C 1B6.
Telephone: 709-726-3321.
Fax: 709-726-2992. E-Mail: stjohns@coxhanson.ca
Charlottetown, Prince Edward Island Office: Queen Square, Suite 202, 119 Queen Street, P.O. Box 875, Station Central, C1A 7L9.
Telephone: 902-894-7051.
Fax: 902-368-3762. E-Mail: charlottetown@coxhanson.ca

MEMBERS OF FIRM

H. A. Hanson, Q.C. (1909-1985)
David T. Hashey, Q.C.
David M. Norman, Q.C.
J. Ian M. Whitcomb, Q.C.
John M. Hanson, Q.C.
Walter D. Vail, Q.C.
Michael E. Bowlin
John D. Larlee, Q.C.
Bruce D. Hatfield, Q.C.
Julian A. G. Dickson, Q.C.
Anne D. Wooder
Terrence J. Morrison
Lucie Richard
Catherine M. Bowlen
J. Marc Richard

(See Next Column)

ASSOCIATES

Amanda J. Frenette
Monika M. L. Zauhar
Jade A. Spalding
William E. Gould
Christopher R. DeLong
Deborah M. Power
Corinne A. Godbout
Marc-Antoine Chiasson

For full biographical listings, see the Martindale-Hubbell Law Directory

MCINNES COOPER (AV)

Suite 600, 570 Queen Street, P.O. Box 610, E3B 5A6
Telephone: 506-458-8572
Fax: 506-458-9903
Email: mcrfton@mcrlaw.com *URL:* http://www.mcrlaw.com
Halifax, Nova Scotia Office: Summit Place, 1601 Lower Water Street, P.O. Box 730, B3J 2V1.
Telephone: 902-425-6500.
Fax: 902-425-6350. Email: mcrhfx@mcrlaw.com.
St. John's, Newfoundland Office: Baine Johnston Centre, 5th Floor, 10 Fort William Place, P.O. Box 5939, A1C 5X4.
Telephone: 709-722-8735.
Telecopier: 709-722-1763. Email: mcrsj@mcrlaw.com.
Moncton, New Brunswick Office: Place Moncton Place, 655 Main Street, P.O. Box 1368, E1C 8T6.
Telephone: 506-857-8970.
Fax: 506-857-4095. Email: mcrmctn@mcrlaw.com.
Charlottetown, Prince Edward Island Office: BDC Place, Suite 620, 119 Kent Street, C1A 1N3.
Telephone: 902-368-8473.
Fax: 902-368-8346. Email: mcrpei@mcrlaw.com.

PARTNER

David Duncan Young

ASSOCIATES

David D. Eidt
Patrick V. Windle
Lise C. Landry

For Complete List of Firm Personnel, See General Section

For full biographical listings, see the Martindale-Hubbell Law Directory

*SAINT JOHN,** Saint John Co.

CLARK DRUMMIE (AV)

40 Wellington Row, P.O. Box 6850, E2L 4S3
Telephone: 506-633-3800
Telecopier (Automatic): 506-633-3811
Email: cd@nbnet.nb.ca

MEMBERS OF FIRM

J. George Byrne
William B. Richards
Frederick A. Welsford

Reference: Royal Bank of Canada.

For Complete List of Firm Personnel, See General Section

For full biographical listings, see the Martindale-Hubbell Law Directory

CANADA
NEWFOUNDLAND

*ST. JOHN'S,**

MCINNES COOPER (AV)

Barristers, Solicitors & Trade Mark Agents
Baine Johnston Centre, 5th Floor, 10 Fort William Place, P.O. Box 5939, A1C 5X4
Telephone: 709-722-8735
Telecopier: 709-722-1763
Email: mcrsj@mcrlaw.com *URL:* http://www.mcrlaw.com
Halifax, Nova Scotia Office: Summit Place, 1601 Lower Water Street, P.O. Box 730, B3J 2V1.
Telephone: 902-425-6500.
Fax: 902-425-6350. Email: mcrhfx@mcrlaw.com.
Moncton, New Brunswick Office: Place Moncton Place, 655 Main Street, P.O. Box 1368, E1C 8T6.
Telephone: 506-857-8970.
Fax: 506-857-4095. Email: mcrmctn@mcrlaw.com.
Charlottetown, Prince Edward Island Office: BDC Place, Suite 620, 119 Kent Street, C1A 1N3.
Telephone: 902-368-8473.
Fax: 902-368-8346. Email: mcrpei@mcrlaw.com.
Fredericton, New Brunswick Office: Suite 600, 570 Queen Street, P.O. Box 610.
Telephone: 506-458-8572.
Fax: 506-458-9903. Email: mcrfton@mcrlaw.com.

PARTNERS

Thomas R. Kendell
Christine A. Fagan, Q.C.
Denis J. Mahoney

(See Next Column)

GAULEY & CO., *Saskatoon—Continued*

MEMBERS OF FIRM (Continued)

Peter Foley, Q.C.
William J. Shaw
David J. McKeague, Q.C.
Rex M. Beaton
Gary A. Zabos
Raymond Wiebe

ASSOCIATES

Dale G. Linn
Chris C. Boychuk
Leah A. Schatz
Eugene T. Harmel (Resident, Regina Office)
Neal W. Caldwell
Warren D. Martinson
Neil B. Fisher
Stephanie L. Tynan
William A. Nickel

Reference: Royal Bank of Canada.

For full biographical listings, see the Martindale-Hubbell Law Directory

LAND USE LAW

MINNESOTA

*MINNEAPOLIS,** Hennepin Co.

SIEGEL, BRILL, GREUPNER, DUFFY & FOSTER, P.A. (AV)

1300 Washington Square, 100 Washington Avenue South, 55401
Telephone: 612-339-7131
Telecopier: 612-339-6591

Josiah E. Brill, Jr.
Gerald S. Duffy
Thomas H. Goodman
Anthony J. Gleekel

Representative Clients: Holiday Companies, Inc.; Super America Stations, Inc.; Ashland Oil, Inc.; Mann Theaters; Homecraft Builders, Inc.; Fischer Sand and Aggregates Co.; Prior Lake Aggregates, Inc.; Bituminous Materials, Inc.; AVR, Inc.; River City Asphalt, Inc.

For Complete List of Firm Personnel, See General Section

For full biographical listings, see the Martindale-Hubbell Law Directory

MISSISSIPPI

*GULFPORT,** Harrison Co.

DUKES, DUKES, KEATING AND FANECA, P.A. (AV)

2909 13th Street, 6th Floor, P.O. Drawer W, 39501
Telephone: 228-868-1111
Fax: 228-863-2886
Email: ddkf@ddkf.com

Hugh D. Keating
Cy Faneca

Joan E. Lund
William W. Abbott, Jr.

For Complete List of Firm Personnel, See General Section
For full biographical listings, see the Martindale-Hubbell Law Directory

NEVADA

*CARSON CITY,** (Independent City)

THE LAW OFFICE OF DANIEL R. WALSH (AV)

Westwinds Professional Complex, 307 West Winnie Lane, Suite 3, 89703
Telephone: 775-882-8080
Fax: 775-882-6161

Daniel R. Walsh

ASSOCIATE

Kevin P. Walsh

For full biographical listings, see the Martindale-Hubbell Law Directory

*LAS VEGAS,** Clark Co.

LIONEL SAWYER & COLLINS (AV)

1700 Bank of America Plaza, 300 South Fourth Street, 89101
Telephone: 702-383-8888
Fax: 702-383-8845
Email: first initial last@lionelsawyer.com
Reno, Nevada Office: Suite 1100, Bank of America Plaza, 50 West Liberty Street.
Telephone: 702-788-8666.
Fax: 702-788-8682.

MEMBERS OF FIRM

Robert D. Faiss
Harvey Whittemore (Resident, Reno Office)
Gary Wayne Duhon (Resident, Reno Office)
Dan R. Reaser (Resident, Reno Office)
Carl D. Savely (Resident, Reno Office)
Paul E. Larsen

ASSOCIATES

Kevin D. Doty
Abbie Green Friedman
Scott A. Eaton

Representative Clients: Preferred Equities Corp.; ITT Sheraton Corporation; Amland Development; Pacific Properties; Las Vegas Sands, Inc.; Venetian Casino Resort, LLC; Triple Five Nevada Development Corporation.

For Complete List of Firm Personnel, See General Section

For full biographical listings, see the Martindale-Hubbell Law Directory

*RENO,** Washoe Co.

PREZANT & MOLLATH (AV)

6560 S.W. McCarran Boulevard, Suite A, 89509
Telephone: 775-786-3011
Telecopier: 775-786-1354

MEMBERS OF FIRM

William A. Prezant
Stephen C. Mollath

Reference: Small Business Banking, Bank of America, Nevada.
Representative Clients: CB-Richard Ellis; BHP Minerals; Eagle Hardware and Garden; Gordon Getty Family Trust; Home Depot; K Mart Corporation; PacifiCare Health Systems (HMO); ProLogis Trust; Sierra Pacific Power Company; Whittier Trust Company.

For full biographical listings, see the Martindale-Hubbell Law Directory

NEW JERSEY

ATLANTIC CITY, Atlantic Co.

PERSKIE NEHMAD & PERILLO, A PROFESSIONAL CORPORATION (AV)

Suite 711, 1125 Atlantic Avenue, 08401
Telephone: 609-348-1177
Telecopier: 609-348-4219

Stephen R. Nehmad
Philip J. Perskie
Salvatore Perillo
Steven J. Brog

Richard F. DeLucry
Richard S. Mairone
Christopher M. Baylinson

References: Fleet Bank, National Association.

For full biographical listings, see the Martindale-Hubbell Law Directory

CHERRY HILL, Camden Co.

FLASTER/GREENBERG, P.C. (AV)

Commerce Center, 1810 Chapel Avenue West, Third Floor, 08002-4609
Telephone: 856-661-1900
Telecopier: 856-661-1919
Email: FIRM@FLASTERGREENBERG.COM *URL:* http://www.flastergreenberg.com

Richard J. Flaster
Stephen M. Greenberg
Laura B. Wallenstein
Allen P. Fineberg
Markley S. Roderick
Peter R. Spirgel
Alan H. Zuckerman
William S. Skinner
J. Philip Kirchner
Paul J. Russoniello
Carl S. Bisgaier
Steven B. Sacharow
E. Richard Dressel
Kenneth S. Goodkind
Frank H. Wisniewski
Alma L. Saravia

OF COUNSEL

Peter M. Dolinger
James J. Binns

Elizabeth J. Hampton
Jeffrey Herskowitz
Christopher E. Kaltenbach
Steven J. Abrams
Julie A. Williamson
Donna T. Urban
Amelia Carolla
Matthew Azoulay
Elaine J. Petruzziello (Not admitted in NJ)
Ann Marie Iannone
Pasquale Guglietta

LEGAL SUPPORT PERSONNEL

PARALEGALS

Ann Gorman
Patricia D'Alessio
Theresa Cooke
Rosemary Dunaif

For full biographical listings, see the Martindale-Hubbell Law Directory

*HACKENSACK,** Bergen Co.

HERTEN, BURSTEIN, SHERIDAN, CEVASCO, BOTTINELLI & LITT, L.L.C. (AV)

Court Plaza North, 25 Main Street, 07601
Telephone: 201-342-6000
Telecopier: 201-342-6611

Thomas J. Herten
Albert Burstein
Philip F. Sheridan, Jr.
Andrew J. Cevasco
Terry Paul Bottinelli
Arnold D. Litt
Brian T. Campion
Menelaos W. Toskos
Mark P. Marotta
Susan M. Marra
John L. Molinelli
Kevin P. Kelly

(See Next Column)

HERTEN, BURSTEIN, SHERIDAN, CEVASCO, BOTTINELLI & LITT L.L.C., *Hackensack—Continued*

ASSOCIATES

Patrick Papalia
Anthony Ronald Suarez
Thomas S. McGuire
Donna T. Tamayne

For full biographical listings, see the Martindale-Hubbell Law Directory

STOLDT, HORAN AND KOWAL, A PROFESSIONAL CORPORATION (AV)

Continental Plaza I, 401 Hackensack Avenue, 07601
Telephone: 201-646-9200
Telecopier: 201-646-0167
Email: shlaw@bellatlantic.net *URL:* http://www.lawyers.com/stoldthoran&kowal

Sydney V. Stoldt, Jr.
John D. Horan
Dorothy A. Kowal
Heather A. Gallagher
Brian O'Reilly

OF COUNSEL

Judith R. Levinson

For full biographical listings, see the Martindale-Hubbell Law Directory

HADDONFIELD, Camden Co.

WILBRAHAM, LAWLER & BUBA, A PROFESSIONAL CORPORATION (AV Ⓣ)

24 Kings Highway West, 08033-2122
Telephone: 856-795-4422
Fax: 856-795-4699
Philadelphia, Pennsylvania Office: 1818 Market Street, Suite 3100.
Telephone: 215-564-4141.
Fax: 215-564-4385.
Wilmington, Delaware Office: Stoney Batter Office Building, 5301 Limestone Road, Suite 221.
Telephone: 302-234-8217.
Fax: 302-234-8218.

Edward J. Wilbraham
Michael J. Block
Mary S. Cook

For full biographical listings, see the Martindale-Hubbell Law Directory

LAWRENCEVILLE, Mercer Co.

SZAFERMAN, LAKIND, BLUMSTEIN, WATTER & BLADER, P.C. (AV)

Suite 104 Quakerbridge Executive Center, 101 Grovers Mill Road, 08648
Telephone: 609-275-0400
Telefax: 609-275-4511

Arnold C. Lakind
Barry D. Szaferman
Jeffrey P. Blumstein
Paul N. Watter
Steven Blader
Sidney H. Lehmann
Gerald B. Schenkman
David B. Beckett
Scott P. Borsack
Mary Lou Delahanty

Jennifer Weisberg Millner
Cathyanne A. Pisciotta
Jason N. Fruhschein
Demery J. Roberts
Stuart A. Tucker
Brian G. Paul
Victoria Rivera-Cruz
Thomas J. Burns III

LEGAL SUPPORT PERSONNEL

Paula M. Rossi (Office Administrator)
Patricia Hallstrum (Controller)

Representative Clients: Sun National Bank; First Washington Bank; Gilmore Securities & Co.; Communication Workers of America; The Eagle Group; Water's Edge Convalescent Center; Ronson Aviation, Inc.; Holmdel Township Board of Adjustment; Public Service Managers Association; Chemical Leaman Tank Lines.

For full biographical listings, see the Martindale-Hubbell Law Directory

MOORESTOWN, Burlington Co.

FREDERICK W. HARDT (AV)

Suite 101, 300 Chester Avenue, P.O. Box 840, 08057-2512
Telephone: 609-234-4141
Fax: 609-273-8617

ASSOCIATE

Pamela A. Moy

For full biographical listings, see the Martindale-Hubbell Law Directory

*NEWARK,** Essex Co.

MEYNER AND LANDIS (AV)

One Gateway Center, Suite 2500, 07102-5311
Telephone: 973-624-2800
Fax: 973-624-0356
Email: attys@meyner.com *URL:* http://www.meyner.com

Robert B. Meyner (1908-1990)
Edwin C. Landis, Jr.
John N. Malyska
William J. Fiore
Anthony F. Siliato
Francis R. Perkins
Howard O. Thompson
Scott T. McCleary
Linda Townley Snyder
William H. Schmidt, Jr.
David B. Grantz

For full biographical listings, see the Martindale-Hubbell Law Directory

SILLS CUMMIS RADIN TISCHMAN EPSTEIN & GROSS, A PROFESSIONAL CORPORATION (AV)

One Riverfront Plaza, 07102-5400
Telephone: 973-643-7000
Fax: 973-643-6500
Telex: 820630 Sillsbeck Nwk
Email: sillsmail@sillscummis.com *URL:* http://www.sillscummis.com
Atlantic City, New Jersey Office: 17 Gordon's Alley.
Telephone: 609-344-2800.
New York, N.Y. Office: 712 Fifth Avenue.
Telephone: 212-643-7000.
Washington, D.C. Office: 1800 K Street, N.W.
Telephone: 202-296-4750.

MEMBERS OF FIRM

Stephen J. Moses
Noah Bronkesh
Thomas Jay Hall
Ted Zangari

Paul P. Josephson

For Complete List of Firm Personnel, See General Section

For full biographical listings, see the Martindale-Hubbell Law Directory

ROSELAND, Essex Co.

BRACH, EICHLER, ROSENBERG, SILVER, BERNSTEIN, HAMMER & GLADSTONE, A PROFESSIONAL CORPORATION (AV)

101 Eisenhower Parkway, 07068
Telephone: 973-228-5700
Telecopier: 973-228-7852
Email: law@bracheichler.com *URL:* http://www.bracheichler.com

William L. Brach
Richard J. Driver

John P. Wyciskala, III
Christopher A. Erd

OF COUNSEL

George Y. Sodowick

Representative Clients: Advance Realty Group; Concept Engineering; Coastal Group, Inc.; Affiliated Management; Garden State Securities; Saint Barnabas Health System; Silverline Building Products; Wayne General Hospital; Eastman Construction; United Window & Door Manufacturing.

For Complete List of Firm Personnel, See General Section

For full biographical listings, see the Martindale-Hubbell Law Directory

RUTHERFORD, Bergen Co.

BRUINOOGE & ASSOCIATES (AV)

85 Orient Way, 07070
Telephone: 201-939-3303
Telefax: 201-939-4057
Email: bandalaw@bellatlantic.net *URL:* http://www.lawyers.com/bruinoogelaw

Thomas H. Bruinooge

Michael E. Patunas

OF COUNSEL

Gilbert W. Bowman
Brian D. Fuhro
Jean-Marc Zimmerman

For full biographical listings, see the Martindale-Hubbell Law Directory

*SOMERVILLE,** Somerset Co.

SCHACHTER, TROMBADORE, OFFEN, STANTON & PAVICS, A PROFESSIONAL CORPORATION (AV)

45 East High Street, P.O. Box 520, 08876-0520
Telephone: 908-722-5700
Fax: 908-722-8853

(See Next Column)

SCHACHTER, TROMBADORE, OFFEN, STANTON & PAVICS A PROFESSIONAL CORPORATION—*Continued*

Richard J. Schachter
John J. Trombadore
Stephen M. Offen
Michael J. Stanton
Thomas A. Pavics

Timothy P. McKeown
Jerry S. D'Aniello

For full biographical listings, see the Martindale-Hubbell Law Directory

*TRENTON,** Mercer Co.

SCHRAGGER, LAVINE & NAGY (AV)

Mountainview Office Park, 840 Bear Tavern Road, Suite 307, 08628
Telephone: 609-771-0700
Fax: 609-771-9535

Bruce M. Schragger

LEGAL SUPPORT PERSONNEL

Annemarie Saccani (Office Administrator)

Representative Clients: New Jersey Manufacturers Insurance Co.; Mercer County Community College; Mercer Mutual Insurance Co.; New Jersey Optometric Association; Allentown Caging; Dick Greenfield Dodge.

For Complete List of Firm Personnel, See General Section

For full biographical listings, see the Martindale-Hubbell Law Directory

WEST ORANGE, Essex Co.

RABINOWITZ, TRENK, LUBETKIN & TULLY, P.C. (AV)

200 Executive Drive Suite 225, 07052-3303
Telephone: 973-243-8600
Facsimile: 973-243-8677
URL: http://www.Rabinowitztrenk.com

Richard S. Schkolnick

Shoshana Schiff

For full biographical listings, see the Martindale-Hubbell Law Directory

NEW MEXICO

*ALBUQUERQUE,** Bernalillo Co.

MYERS, OLIVER & PRICE, P.C. (AV)

1401 Central Avenue NW, 87104
Telephone: 505-247-9080
Fax: 505-247-9109
Email: mop@moplaw.com

John A. Myers
Scott Oliver
Charles P. Price III
Kevin J. McCready
Hope Mead Wynn

For full biographical listings, see the Martindale-Hubbell Law Directory

RODEY, DICKASON, SLOAN, AKIN & ROBB, P.A. (AV)

Albuquerque Plaza, Suite 2200, 201 Third Street, N.W., P.O. Box 1888, 87103-1888
Telephone: 505-765-5900
Fax: 505-768-7395
Email: info@rodey.com *URL:* http://www.rodey.com
Santa Fe, New Mexico Office: Suite 101 Marcy Plaza, 123 East Marcy Street, P.O. Box 1357, 87504-1357.
Telephone: 505-984-0100.
Fax: 505-989-9542.

John P. Salazar
John P. Burton (Resident, Santa Fe Office)
Nancy J. Appleby
Joseph B. Rochelle
Susan K. Barger

For Complete List of Firm Personnel, See General Section

For full biographical listings, see the Martindale-Hubbell Law Directory

*SANTA FE,** Santa Fe Co.

HERRERA, LONG & POUND, P.A. (AV)

2200 Brothers Road, P.O. Box 5098, 87502-5098
Telephone: 505-982-8405
Fax: 505-982-8513
Email: hlplaw@aol.com

Judith C. Herrera
Nancy R. Long
John B. Pound

Mark E. Komer

(See Next Column)

LEGAL SUPPORT PERSONNEL

Shauna Allen Metzo

Reference: Bank of America.

For full biographical listings, see the Martindale-Hubbell Law Directory

NEW YORK

MELVILLE, Suffolk Co.

LAMB & BARNOSKY, LLP (AV)

534 Broadhollow Road-CS 9034, 11747-9034
Telephone: 631-694-2300
Telecopier: 631-694-2309
Email: thefirm@lambbarnosky.com *URL:* http://www.lambbarnosky.com

PARTNERS

Eugene R. Barnosky
Robert H. Cohen
Marcia Lyn Finkelstein
Michael J. Heller
Gary Holman
Scott M. Karson
P. L. Lamb
Arthur A. Lane
Joel M. Markowitz
Gerald P. Rosenberg
Patrice Dowd Shenn

OF COUNSEL

Louis E. Black
James F. Gesualdi
Howard W. Newman
Joseph J. Salvatore
Joseph H. Wishod

COUNSEL

Lloyd K. Chanin
Scott P. McBride

ASSOCIATES

Cathleen D. Allen
Catherine Healy Kanzler
Rita Fishman Sheena
Shari Lee Sugarman

For full biographical listings, see the Martindale-Hubbell Law Directory

STONY POINT, Rockland Co.

HURLEY, FOX, SELIG & KELLEHER (AV)

Liberty Building, Route 9 W, 10980
Telephone: 914-942-2222
Fax: 914-942-0378
Email: HFSKlaw@aol.com
New City, New York Office: 60 Pine Street.
Telephone: 614-634-2050.

MEMBERS OF FIRM

Benjamin E. Selig
Glenn W. Kelleher

ASSOCIATES

Steven L. Kahn
Dana Selig Kahn
Bob A. Kramer
Kenneth P. Silver

Representative Clients: Bradlees, Inc.; Stop & Shop Companies; CNA Insurance Cos.; Federal Insurance Co.; Chubb & Son; Commercial Union Group of Insurance Cos.; Empire Insurance Co.; Omaha, N.B.; Excelsior Insurance Co.; Fireman's Insurance Company of Washington, D.C.

For full biographical listings, see the Martindale-Hubbell Law Directory

*SYRACUSE,** Onondaga Co.

DEVORSETZ STINZIANO GILBERTI HEINTZ & SMITH, P.C. (AV)

555 East Genesee Street, 13202-2159
Telephone: 315-442-0100
Telecopier: 315-442-0106
Email: law@dsghs.com *URL:* http://www.devorsetzlaw.com
Albany, New York Office: 146 State Street.
Telephone: 518-476-2001.
Telecopier: 518-476-9646.
Harrisburg, Pennsylvania Office: 105 North Front Street, Suite 400.
Telephone: 717-232-5555.
Telecopier: 717-232-5515.

Tarky Lombardi, Jr.
Sidney Devorsetz
Francis D. Stinziano
William J. Gilberti, Jr.
Lynn H. Smith
Joshua H. Heintz
John F. Klucsik
Kevin C. Murphy
Michael J. Sarofeen
Mark T. Arbon
Adam J. Schultz

Karla M. Corpus
Laurel J. Eveleigh
Kevin G. Roe
Barry Martin Schreibman
Francis D. Stinziano, Jr.
Joseph Suich
Melanie Wlasuk
Joshua J. Yablonski

Reference: Fleet Bank.

For full biographical listings, see the Martindale-Hubbell Law Directory

*WHITE PLAINS,** Westchester Co.

DELBELLO DONNELLAN WEINGARTEN & TARTAGLIA, LLP (AV)

One North Lexington Avenue, 10601
Telephone: 914-681-0200
Telecopier: 914-684-0288
Email: general@ddwt.com

Alfred B. DelBello
Alfred E. Donnellan (Managing Partner)
Mark P. Weingarten
Daniel D. Tartaglia
Peter J. Wise
Lee S. Wiederkehr
Patrick M. Reilly
Robert A. Korren

ASSOCIATES

William E. Dumke
Christine Moccia
Suzanne Bogdanoff
Allyse B. Dunefsky
Jerry F. Kebrdle, II
Bradley D. Wank
Ann Farrissey Carlson
Janet J. Giris

OF COUNSEL

J. David Jutkowitz
Andrew J. Balint
Robert C. Epstein

For full biographical listings, see the Martindale-Hubbell Law Directory

OHIO

*CINCINNATI,** Hamilton Co.

MANLEY, BURKE, LIPTON & COOK A LEGAL PROFESSIONAL ASSOCIATION (AV)

225 West Court Street, 45202
Telephone: 513-721-5525
Fax: 513-721-4268
Email: mblc@mblclaw.com *URL:* http://www.mblclaw.com

Robert E. Manley
Timothy M. Burke
Gary E. Powell

Matthew W. Fellerhoff

OF COUNSEL

Richard C. Melfi

For full biographical listings, see the Martindale-Hubbell Law Directory

DUBLIN, Franklin Co.

BLAUGRUND, HERBERT & MARTIN, INCORPORATED (AV)

5455 Rings Road, Suite 500, 43017-7517
Telephone: 614-764-0681
Fax: 614-764-0774
Email: bhm@bhmlaw.net

Christopher T. Cline

For full biographical listings, see the Martindale-Hubbell Law Directory

OKLAHOMA

*OKLAHOMA CITY,** Oklahoma Co.

WILLIAMS, BOX, FORSHEE & BULLARD, P.C. (AV)

522 Colcord Drive, 73102-2202
Telephone: 405-232-0080
Telecopier: 405-236-5814

John Michael Williams
Dennis R. Box
Richard D. Forshee
William J. Bullard
Keith R. Gibson
Paul E. Lefebvre

Kimberly K. Brown

For full biographical listings, see the Martindale-Hubbell Law Directory

PENNSYLVANIA

*ALLENTOWN,** Lehigh Co.

RICHARD W. SHAFFER (AV)

740 Hamilton Mall, 18101
Telephone: 610-439-0800
Fax: 610-439-8852
Email: Rwspalaw@aol.com

LEGAL SUPPORT PERSONNEL

Barbara J. Nemes (Paralegal)

For full biographical listings, see the Martindale-Hubbell Law Directory

*CARLISLE,** Cumberland Co.

FISHMAN & MORGENTHAL (AV)

95 Alexander Spring Road, 17013
Telephone: 717-249-6333
Fax: 717-249-7334
Email: info@carlislelaw.com *URL:* http://www.carlislelaw.com

MEMBERS OF FIRM

Steven J. Fishman
Roger M. Morgenthal

For full biographical listings, see the Martindale-Hubbell Law Directory

*PHILADELPHIA,** Philadelphia Co.

WILBRAHAM, LAWLER & BUBA, A PROFESSIONAL CORPORATION (AV)

1818 Market Street, Suite 3100, 19103-3631
Telephone: 215-564-4141
Fax: 215-564-4385
Email: @wlbdeflaw.com
Haddonfield, New Jersey Office: 24 Kings Highway West.
Telephone: 856-795-4422.
Fax: 856-795-4699.
Wilmington, Delaware Office: Stoney Batter Office Building, 5301 Limestone Road, Suite 221.
Telephone: 302-234-8217.
Fax: 302-234-8218.

Edward J. Wilbraham
Robert B. Lawler
Barbara J. Buba
Michael J. Block

R. Erick Chizmar
Kevin J. Maginnis
InSook Kim
Sandra D. Terry-Crawford
John S. Howarth
David M. Maselli
Renee E. Berger
Edward T. Finch
Sean P. Buggy

OF COUNSEL

Walter J. Timby, Jr.
Daniel J. Allan

Representative Clients: GAF Corporation; Armstrong World Industries, Inc.; U.S. Gypsum Company; Georgia-Pacific Corporation; ARCO; Shell; Royal; AIG; Chubb; Keystone.

For full biographical listings, see the Martindale-Hubbell Law Directory

RHODE ISLAND

SMITHFIELD, Providence Co.

CHARLES S. SOKOLOFF INCORPORATED (AV)

Eleven Thurber Boulevard, 02917-1859
Telephone: 401-233-2800; Toll Free: 888-SOKOLAW
Fax: 401-233-2890
URL: http://www.sokolawyer.com
Email: sokolaw@sokolawyer.com *URL:* http://www.lawyers.com/sokolaw

Charles S. Sokoloff

Anne-Marie Krollman

For full biographical listings, see the Martindale-Hubbell Law Directory

SOUTH CAROLINA

*COLUMBIA,** Richland Co.

NEXSEN PRUET JACOBS & POLLARD, LLP (AV)

1441 Main Street, 15th Floor, P.O. Drawer 2426, 29202
Telephone: 803-771-8900
Facsimile: 803-253-8277
Email: NPJP@NPJP.COM *URL:* HTTP://WWW.NPJP.COM
Charleston, South Carolina Office: 200 Meeting Street, Suite 301. P.O. Box 486.
Telephone: 803-577-9440.
Facsimile: 803-720-1777.
Greenville, South Carolina Office: 201 West McBee Avenue, Fourth Floor, P.O. Box 10648.
Telephone: 864-370-2211.
Facsimile: 864-282-1177.
Myrtle Beach, South Carolina Office: 2411 Oak Street, Suite 105.
Telephone: 843-445-9688.
Facsimile: 843-445-9949.
Charlotte, North Carolina Office: 212 South Tryon Street, Suite 1700.
Telephone: 704-339-0304.
Facsimile: 704-338-5377.

MEMBERS OF FIRM

Brian F. Kernaghan (Charleston, SC and Myrtle Beach, SC Offices)
W. Leighton Lord III
Edward G. Menzie
Neil C. Robinson, Jr. (Resident, Charleston, SC Office)

For Complete List of Firm Personnel, See General Section

For full biographical listings, see the Martindale-Hubbell Law Directory

TENNESSEE

JOHNSON CITY, Washington Co.

LAW OFFICE OF EPPS AND EPPS (AV)

115 East Unaka Avenue, P.O. Drawer 2288, 37605-2288
Telephone: 423-928-7256
Fax: 423-928-0207

James H. Epps, III

For full biographical listings, see the Martindale-Hubbell Law Directory

*KNOXVILLE,** Knox Co.

LEIBOWITZ & COHEN (AV)

608 Gay Street, S.W., 37902
Telephone: 423-637-1809
FAX: 423-637-9276

MEMBERS OF FIRM

Arnold G. Cohen
Lawrence P. Leibowitz

ASSOCIATE

Melissa A. Ashburn

OF COUNSEL

Russell T. Greene

For full biographical listings, see the Martindale-Hubbell Law Directory

TEXAS

*DALLAS,** Dallas Co.

SMITH, UNDERWOOD & PERKINS, A PROFESSIONAL CORPORATION (AV)

600 Two Lincoln Centre, 5420 LBJ Freeway, 75240
Telephone: 972-661-5114
Telecopier: 972-661-5691
Email: firm@suandp.com *URL:* http://www.suplaw.com

Timothy S. Perkins
David W. Ralston
G. Lynn Smith
William J. Underwood, Jr.

Christine A. McGuire
Amy K. Ratzlaff
P. Theodore Stoinoff, II
Val C. Cronin
Ellen P. Stewart
Todd W. Shadle
Ruth C. Logan
Christina L. Betanzos
Kent D. Williamson

For full biographical listings, see the Martindale-Hubbell Law Directory

*EL PASO,** El Paso Co.

AINSA PARTNERS, LLP (AV)

5809 Acacia Circle, 79912
Telephone: 915-845-5300
Fax: 915-845-7800
Email: fain@acaciapark.com *URL:* http://www.ainsa.com

Francis S. Ainsa, Jr.
Michael F. Ainsa
David M. Driscoll

For full biographical listings, see the Martindale-Hubbell Law Directory

UTAH

*SALT LAKE CITY,** Salt Lake Co.

PARSONS, DAVIES, KINGHORN & PETERS, P.C. (AV)

185 South State Street, Suite 700, 84111
Telephone: 801-363-4300
Facsimile: 801-363-4378
Email: Attorneys@pdkplaw.com

Glen E. Davies
Gerald H. Kinghorn
Bill Thomas Peters
John N. Brems
Ken P. Jones

For Complete List of Firm Personnel, See General Section

For full biographical listings, see the Martindale-Hubbell Law Directory

VAN COTT, BAGLEY, CORNWALL & MCCARTHY, A PROFESSIONAL CORPORATION (AV)

50 South Main Street, Suite 1600, P.O. Box 45340, 84145-0340
Telephone: 801-532-3333
Telecopier: 801-534-0058
Email: info@vancott.com *URL:* http://www.vancott.com
Ogden, Utah Office: 2404 Washington Boulevard, Suite 900.
Telephone: 801-394-5783.
Park City, Utah Office: 2200 Park Avenue, Suite C200-A.
Telephone: 435-649-3889.

Thomas W. Clawson
Rand L. Cook
H. Michael Keller
David J. Smith
Stephen D. Swindle
Gregory P. Williams

Mara A. Brown
Kim S Colton
Tacy A. Hartman

OF COUNSEL

M. Scott Woodland

For Complete List of Firm Personnel, See General Section

For full biographical listings, see the Martindale-Hubbell Law Directory

VIRGINIA

*ARLINGTON,** Arlington Co.

WALSH, COLUCCI, STACKHOUSE, EMRICH & LUBELEY, P.C. (AV)

Courthouse Plaza, Thirteenth Floor, 2200 Clarendon Boulevard, 22201
Telephone: 703-528-4700
Facsimile: 703-525-3197
Email: mdwal@wcsel.com *URL:* http://www.wcsel.com
Woodbridge, Virginia Office: Village Square, 13663 Office Place, Suite 201.
Telephones: 703-680-4664; 690-4647.
Facsimile: 703-690-2412.
Leesburg, Virginia Office: One East Market Street, 3rd Floor, 20176.
Telephone: 703-737-3633.
Fax: 703-737-3632.

Martin D. ("Art") Walsh
Jerry K. Emrich
Michael D. Lubeley (Resident, Woodbridge Office)
Nan E. Terpak
Keith C. Martin
Jay du Von (Resident, Woodbridge Office)
J. Randall Minchew (Resident, Leesburg Office)
David J. Bomgardner (Resident, Woodbridge Office)
Lynne J. Strobel
John E. Rinaldi (Resident, Woodbridge Office)
Timothy S. Sampson
M. Catharine Puskar

For full biographical listings, see the Martindale-Hubbell Law Directory

*LEESBURG,** Loudoun Co.

Sevila, Saunders, Huddleston & White, A Professional Corporation (AV)

30 North King Street, 20176
Telephone: 703-777-5700
Metro: 471-9800; Fax: 703-771-4161

Robert E. Sevila
Richard R. Saunders, Jr.
Jon D. Huddleston
Craig E. White

Jeffrey A. Tuten
Jeanine M. Irving

LEGAL SUPPORT PERSONNEL

Joan Rust

For full biographical listings, see the Martindale-Hubbell Law Directory

WASHINGTON

*DAVENPORT,** Lincoln Co.

Brock, Carpenter & McGuire, P.S. (AV)

529 Morgan Street, P.O. Box 249, 99122
Telephone: 509-725-3101
Fax: 509-725-5854
Email: cbbcm@ior.com *URL:* http://www.lawyers.com/brockcarpenter
Spokane, Washington Office: 221 North Wall Street, Suite 424.
Telephone: 509-622-4707.
Fax: 509-622-4705.
Odessa, Washington Office: 9 East First Street, P.O. Box 65.
Telephone: 509-982-2672.
Fax: 509-982-2808.
St. John, Washington Office: White Building.
Telephone: 509-648-3683.
Fax: 509-648-3405.
Ritzville, Washington Office: 307 West Main, P.O. Box 496.
Telephone: 509-659-0425.
Fax: 509-659-0529.

Norman D. Brock (Davenport, Spokane and Ritzville Offices)
Kenneth D. Carpenter (Davenport, Spokane, Odessa and Ritzville Offices)
L. R. "Rusty" McGuire, Jr. (Davenport, Ritzville and St. John Offices)
Mark W. DeWulf (Resident, Odessa Office)
Corey F. Brock (Davenport and Spokane Offices)

For full biographical listings, see the Martindale-Hubbell Law Directory

*SEATTLE,** King Co.

Lane Powell Spears Lubersky LLP (AV)

Limited Liability Partnership composed of Individuals and Professional Service Corporations
1420 Fifth Avenue, Suite 4100, 98101-2338
Telephone: 206-223-7000
Facsimile: 206-223-7107
Email: information@lanepowell.com *URL:* http://www.lanepowell.com
Other Offices at: Portland, Oregon; Anchorage, Alaska; Olympia and Mount Vernon, Washington; London, England.

MEMBERS OF FIRM

Glenn J. Amster
Grant S. Degginger

Representative Clients: Battle Mountain Gold Co.; Home Depot U.S.A., Inc.; Huish Family Fun Centers; Lonview Fibre Co.; Madison Realty Partnership; Pep Boys; Pulte Home Corp.; Robert B. Aikens & Associates; Spieker Properties; Texaco Inc.

For Complete List of Firm Personnel, See General Section

For full biographical listings, see the Martindale-Hubbell Law Directory

WISCONSIN

*MILWAUKEE,** Milwaukee Co.

Quarles & Brady LLP (AV)

411 East Wisconsin Avenue, 53202-4497
Telephone: 414-277-5000
Fax: 414-271-3552
URL: http://www.quarles.com
Madison, Wisconsin Office: Firstar Plaza, One South Pinckney Street, P.O. Box 2113, 53701-2113.
Telephone: 608-251-5000.
Fax: 608-251-9166.
West Palm Beach, Florida Office: 222 Lakeview Avenue, 4th Floor, 33401.
Telephone: 561-653-5000.
Fax: 561-653-5333.
Naples, Florida Office: Barnett Center, 4501 Tamiami Trail North, Suite 300, 34103-3060.
Telephone: 941-262-5959.
Fax: 941-434-4999.
Phoenix, Arizona Office: One Camelback Building, One East Camelback Road, Suite 400, 85012-1649.
Telephone: 602-230-5500.
Fax: 602-230-5598.
Chicago, Illinois Office: Quarles & Brady LLC, Citicorp Center, 500 West Madison Street, Suite 3700.
Telephone: 312-715-5000.
Fax: 312-715-5155.

MEMBERS OF FIRM

(ALPHABETICALLY BY YEAR OF ADMISSION TO BAR)

Thomas E. Maloney (Resident, Naples, Florida Office)
David L. Petersen (Resident, Naples, Florida Office)
Lawrence J. Jost
Gerald E. Connolly
James H. Baxter III
F. Joseph McMackin, III (Resident, Naples, Florida Office)
Robert T. Bailes (Resident, Phoenix, Arizona Office)
John W. Daniels, Jr.
Timothy G. Hains (Resident, Naples, Florida Office)
Roger K. Spencer (Resident, Phoenix, Arizona Office)
Warren S. Blumenthal
Peter A. Terry (Resident, Phoenix, Arizona Office)
Ann M. Murphy
John A. Rothstein
Charles H. McMullen
Leo J. Salvatori (Resident, Naples, Florida Office)
David G. Beauchamp (Resident, Phoenix, Arizona Office)
Mary N. Fertl
Ann K. Comer
Michael D. Zeka
Kevin A. Delorey (Resident, Madison Office)
John D. Humphreville (Resident, Naples, Florida Office)
Scott L. Langlois
Joseph E. Puchner
Michael J. Ostermeyer

OF COUNSEL

Richard W. Cutler
John S. Sammond (Resident, West Palm Beach, Florida Office)
James Urdan
Roger P. Paulsen

ASSOCIATE

Lauri D. Morris (Resident, Madison Office)

For Complete List of Firm Personnel, See General Section

For full biographical listings, see the Martindale-Hubbell Law Directory

CANADA
NOVA SCOTIA

*HALIFAX,** Regional Munic. of Halifax

McInnes Cooper (AV)

Barristers, Solicitors & Trade Mark Agents
Summit Place, 1601 Lower Water Street, P.O. Box 730, B3J 2V1
Telephone: 902-425-6500
Fax: 902-425-6350
Email: mcrhfx@mcrlaw.com *URL:* http://www.mcrlaw.com
St. John's, Newfoundland Office: Baine Johnston Centre, 5th Floor, 10 Fort William Place, P.O. Box 5939, A1C 5X4.
Telephone: 709-722-8735.
Telecopier: 709-722-1763. Email: mcrsj@mcrlaw.com.
Moncton, New Brunswick Office: Place Moncton Place, 655 Main Street, P.O. Box 1368, E1C 8T6.
Telephone: 506-857-8970.
Fax: 506-857-4095. Email: mcrmctn@mcrlaw.com.
Charlottetown, Prince Edward Island Office: BDC Place, Suite 620, 119 Kent Street, C1A 1N3.
Telephone: 902-368-8473.
Fax: 902-368-8346. Email: mcrpei@mcrlaw.com.

(See Next Column)

McINNES COOPER—*Continued*

Fredericton, New Brunswick Office: Suite 600, 570 Queen Street, P.O. Box 610.
Telephone: 506-458-8572.
Fax: 506-458-9903. Email: mcrfton@mcrlaw.com.

PARTNERS

Peter J. E. McDonough, Q.C. Lawrence A. Freeman

For Complete List of Firm Personnel, See General Section

For full biographical listings, see the Martindale-Hubbell Law Directory

CANADA
PRINCE EDWARD ISLAND

*CHARLOTTETOWN,** Queen's Co.

McINNES COOPER (AV Ⓣ)

Barristers, Solicitors & Trade Mark Agents
BDC Place, Suite 620, 119 Kent Street, C1A 1N3
Telephone: 902-368-8473
Fax: 902-368-8346
Email: mcrpei@mcrlaw.com *URL:* http://www.mcrlaw.com
Halifax, Nova Scotia Office: Summit Place, 1601 Lower Water Street, P.O. Box 730, B3J 2V1.
Telephone: 902-425-6500.
Fax: 902-425-6350. Email: mcrhfx@mcrlaw.com.
St. John's, Newfoundland Office: Baine Johnston Centre, 5th Floor, 10 Fort William Place, P.O. Box 5939, A1C 5X4.
Telephone: 709-722-8735.
Telecopier: 709-722-1763. Email: mcrsj@mcrlaw.com.
Moncton, New Brunswick Office: Place Moncton Place, 655 Main Street, P.O. Box 1368, E1C 8T6.
Telephone: 506-857-8970.
Fax: 506-857-4095. Email: mcrmctn@mcrlaw.com.
Fredericton, New Brunswick Office: Suite 600, 570 Queen Street, P.O. Box 610.
Telephone: 506-458-8572.
Fax: 506-458-9903. Email: mcrfton@mcrlaw.com.

ASSOCIATE

L. Charles Keizer

For Complete List of Firm Personnel, See General Section

For full biographical listings, see the Martindale-Hubbell Law Directory

LEGAL MALPRACTICE

NEW JERSEY

MORRIS PLAINS, Morris Co.

VOORHEES & OUDA (AV)

Powder Mill Plaza, 51 Gibraltar Drive, 07950
Telephone: 201-267-6677
Fax: 201-267-9152
Mailing Address: P.O. Box 1236, Morristown, New Jersey, 07962-1236

MEMBERS OF FIRM

William Wolverton Voorhees, Jr. Peter A. Ouda

For full biographical listings, see the Martindale-Hubbell Law Directory

*NEWARK,** Essex Co.

MARAN & MARAN (AV)

The Legal Center, One Riverfront Plaza, Suite 315, 07102
Telephone: 973-622-5303
1-888-566-2726
Fax: 973-622-4352

MEMBERS OF FIRM

Joe Maran David Maran

For full biographical listings, see the Martindale-Hubbell Law Directory

RED BANK, Monmouth Co.

WHITE, FLEISCHNER & FINO (AV)

272 Broad Street, 07701
Telephone: 732-530-7787
Telecopier: 732-530-8552
New York, New York Office: 140 Broadway.
Telephone: 212-487-9700.
Telecopier: 212-487-9777.

Benjamin A. Fleischner

Representative Clients: Lloyd's Syndicates; Interstate Insurance Group; Chicago Insurance Group.

For full biographical listings, see the Martindale-Hubbell Law Directory

WAYNE, Passaic Co.

DEYOE HEISSENBUTTEL, L.L.C. (AV)

401 Hamburg Turnpike, P.O. Box 2449, 07474-2449
Telephone: 973-595-6300
Fax: 973-595-0146
Email: deyoelaw@ix.netcom.com *URL:* http://www.deyoe.com

MEMBERS OF FIRM

Charles P. DeYoe (1923-1973)
Wood M. DeYoe
Frederick C. Heissenbuttel
Scott B. Piekarsky

ASSOCIATES

Raymond F. Shenekji
Anne Hutton
Albert C. Buglione
Laureen A. Moloney

LEGAL SUPPORT PERSONNEL

Marilyn Moore (Office Manager)

Representative Clients: Hanover Insurance Inc.; Maryland Casualty Co.; Ohio Casualty Insurance Co.; Motor Club of America; Selective Insurance Co.; Prudential Property & Casualty; Reliance Ins. Co.

For full biographical listings, see the Martindale-Hubbell Law Directory

NEW YORK

*ALBANY,** Albany Co.

ROCHE CORRIGAN MCCOY & BUSH (AV)

The Wilem Van Zandt Building, 36 South Pearl Street, 12207
Telephone: 518-436-9370
Fax: 518-436-8233

MEMBERS OF FIRM

Robert P. Roche
Peter J. Corrigan
Joseph M. McCoy
Scott W. Bush

Local Counsel For: Home Insurance Co.; The Atlantic Companies; Travelers Insurance Co.; Preferred Mutual Insurance Co.; Chicago Insurance Co.

For full biographical listings, see the Martindale-Hubbell Law Directory

*BUFFALO,** Erie Co.

O'SHEA, REYNOLDS & CUMMINGS (AV)

237 Main Street, Suite 500, 14203
Telephone: 716-853-6341-2-3
Fax: 716-852-3880
Email: info@oshea-reynolds.com

MEMBERS OF FIRM

Frank Gibbons (1869-1953)
Henry W. Pottle (1872-1943)
Willard M. Pottle (1901-1967)
Philip J. O'Shea (1909-1984)
William S. Reynolds
C. DeForest Cummings, Jr.
David M. Stillwell
Gerard E. O'Connor
William A. Long, Jr.
Nelson E. Schule, Jr.

ASSOCIATES

Kevin D. Cox
Nicole A. Heary

Local Attorneys for: Amica Mutual Insurance Co.; Continental National American Group; Nationwide Mutual Insurance Co.; The Continental Insurance Cos.
Reference: Key Bank.

For full biographical listings, see the Martindale-Hubbell Law Directory

ROACH, BROWN, MCCARTHY & GRUBER, P.C. (AV)

1620 Liberty Building, 420 Main Street, 14202-3511
Telephone: 716-852-0400
Fax: 716-852-2535
Email: roachbrown@roachbrown.com

Daniel T. Roach
Edmund S. Brown, Jr.
T. Alan Brown
Joseph V. McCarthy
J. Mark Gruber
Mary J. Murray
John P. Danieu
Elizabeth G. Redmond
Gregory T. Miller
Teresa C. Brophy Bair
Jason A. Botticelli
Jennifer L. Noah
Joel J. Java, Jr.

OF COUNSEL

Arthur J. Maloney
John Y. Gallup

Local Attorneys for: American International Group; Chubb Group of Insurance Co.; Healthcare Underwriters Mutual Insurance Co.; Peter J. McBreen and Associates; Frontier Insurance Co.; Medical Liability Mutual Insurance Co.; Medical Malpractice Insurance Assn.; Merrill Dow; Reliance Insurance Group; Travelers Group.

For full biographical listings, see the Martindale-Hubbell Law Directory

*NEW YORK,** New York Co.

BELAIR & EVANS LLP (AV)

61 Broadway Suite 1320, 10006
Telephone: 212-344-3900
Facsimile: 212-514-6661
Cable Address: "Caduceus" New York
Telex: 226000
URL: http://www.belairevans.com
Mineola, New York Office: 136 Willis Avenue.
Telephone: 516-741-4800.

MEMBERS OF FIRM

Raymond W. Belair
John T. Evans
Lawrence W. Burnett
Brian P. Flynn

Jacqueline E. Sheehan-Hemmingson
Robert Radman
Andrew R. Leder
Michael J. Gudzy
Matthew J. Ross
James B. Reich
Robert L. Kerner, Jr.
Michael A. Swimmer
Randall M. Elfenbein
Brian T. Stapleton
Kevin E. Way

For full biographical listings, see the Martindale-Hubbell Law Directory

DE BLASIO, FIGMAN, EPSTEIN & LA ROCCA, P.C. (AV)

Woolworth Building, 233 Broadway, 10279
Telephone: 212-732-2620
Fax: 212-571-2045

Peter E. De Blasio
Alan H. Figman
Steven A. Epstein
Stephen S. La Rocca
John A. Orbon

For full biographical listings, see the Martindale-Hubbell Law Directory

WHITE, FLEISCHNER & FINO (AV)

140 Broadway, 10005
Telephone: 212-487-9700
Telecopier: 212-487-9777
Email: infor@wff-law.com
Red Bank, New Jersey Office: 272 Broad Street.
Telephone: 732-530-7787.
Telecopier: 732-530-8552.

(See Next Column)

WHITE, FLEISCHNER & FINO, *New York—Continued*

MEMBERS OF FIRM

Benjamin A. Fleischner
James A. Robbins

ASSOCIATE

Evan Asher Richman

Representative Clients: Interstate Insurance Group; Chicago Insurance Company; Lloyd's Syndicates.

For Complete List of Firm Personnel, See General Section

For full biographical listings, see the Martindale-Hubbell Law Directory

*SYRACUSE,** Onondaga Co.

SUGARMAN, WALLACE, MANHEIM & SCHOENWALD (AV)

HSBC Center, Fifth Floor, 360 South Warren Street, 13202-2680
Telephone: 315-474-2943
Fax: 315-474-0235
URL: http://www.sugarmanlaw.com
Buffalo Office: 1720 Rand Building, 14 Lafayette Square, 14203.
Telephone: 716-847-2523.
Fax: 716-847-2589.

MEMBERS OF FIRM

David B. Sugarman (1885-1968)
Milton Wallace (1917-1985)
George E. DeMore
James G. Stevens, Jr.
Samuel Vulcano
Robert P. Dwyer
Timothy J. Perry
Stephen G. Pesarchick
Charlene E. McGraw
Paul V. Mullin
David A. Kalabanka
Brian Sutter
Kevin T. Hunt
Sherry R. Bruce
Thomas J. Murphy
Sam A. Elbadawi

ASSOCIATES

Matthew D. Gumaer
Keith D. Miller
Brandon R. King
Kevin R. Van Duser
James E. Hanlon
James O. Taylor
Gina M. Panighetti
Gary H Collison
Tasha T. Dandridge

OF COUNSEL

Charles M. Manheim
Alan J. Goldberg
Donald L. Schoenwald

For full biographical listings, see the Martindale-Hubbell Law Directory

OHIO

*COLUMBUS,** Franklin Co.

NEMETH, CABORN & BUTAUSKI (AV)

21 East Frankfort Street, 43206-1069
Telephone: 614-443-4866
Fax: 614-443-4860
URL: http://www.lawyers.com/nemeth
Email: nemeth@nemethlaw.com *URL:* http://www.nemethlaw.com

John C. Nemeth
David A. Caborn
Joseph A. Butauski

ASSOCIATES

David A. Herd
Michael J. Collins

Representative Clients: Anheuser-Busch, Inc.; Central Ohio Transit Authority; Crawford & Co.; Erie Insurance Group; Home Insurance Co.; Safeco Insurance Co.; Mount Carmel Hospital; The Hartford Group; Citizens Insurance Co.; State Farm Insurance Co.

For full biographical listings, see the Martindale-Hubbell Law Directory

PENNSYLVANIA

*NORRISTOWN,** Montgomery Co.

MURPHY, OLIVER, CAIOLA & GOWEN, A PROFESSIONAL LAW CORPORATION (AV)

43 East Marshall Street, 19401-4828
Telephone: 610-272-4222; 610-279-3838
Fax: 610-272-2549; 610-275-0140
Email: molaw@injury-law.com *URL:* http://www.injury-law.com
Spring City, Pennsylvania Office: 500 S. Main Street, 19475.
Telephone: 610-948-3770.
Pottstown, Pennsylvania Office: 5 Sunnybrook Road, 19464.
Telephone: 610-323-3480.
West Chester, Pennsylvania Office: 1534 McDaniel Drive, Westtown Business Center, 19250.
Telephone: 610-272-4222.

(See Next Column)

James J. Oliver
Frank P. Murphy
Frank L. Caiola
Thomas L. Gowen, Jr.
Carla E. Connor
Barbara A. Barnes

John F. Haskins, Jr.
Cynthia Love Dengler
Carol A. Crisci

LEGAL SUPPORT PERSONNEL

Patricia A. Talese (Paralegal)
Kathleen Nicholson

For full biographical listings, see the Martindale-Hubbell Law Directory

RAYMOND M. VICTOR, P.C. (AV)

616 DeKalb Street, 19401
Telephone: 610-272-5253
Fax: 610-272-7422
Email: rdsquire@worldnet.att.net *URL:* http://www.lawyers.com/raymondmvictor

Raymond M. Victor
Christopher T. Moyer

For full biographical listings, see the Martindale-Hubbell Law Directory

*PITTSBURGH,** Allegheny Co.

EVANS, PORTNOY & QUINN (AV)

36th Floor, One Oxford Centre, 301 Grant Street, 15219-6401
Telephone: 412-765-3800
Fax: 412-765-3747

Charles E. Evans
Irving M. Portnoy
John E. Quinn

ASSOCIATES

Mark E. Milsop
Marc J. Reiter
Patricia L. Haas

For full biographical listings, see the Martindale-Hubbell Law Directory

SOUTH CAROLINA

*COLUMBIA,** Richland Co.

BARNES, ALFORD, STORK & JOHNSON, L.L.P. (AV)

1613 Main Street, P.O. Box 8448, 29202
Telephone: 803-799-1111
Telefax: 803-254-1335
Email: basj@basjlaw.com

Weldon R. Johnson
Curtis W. Dowling

For Complete List of Firm Personnel, See General Section

For full biographical listings, see the Martindale-Hubbell Law Directory

TEXAS

*AUSTIN,** Travis Co.

GARY F. DESHAZO & ASSOCIATES (AV)

823 Congress Avenue, Suite 1550, 78701
Telephone: 512-476-3800
Fax: 512-476-0435
Email: Deshazo@worldnet.att.net *URL:* http://www.lawyers.com/deshazolaw

OF COUNSEL

Jerome J. Schielfelbein (Not admitted in TX)

For full biographical listings, see the Martindale-Hubbell Law Directory

WINCKLER & HARVEY, L.L.P. (AV)

3101 Bee Caves Road, Suite 270, 78746
Telephone: 512-306-1800
Telecopier: 512-306-9442
Email: 2jayslaw@io.com *URL:* http://www.lawyers.com/winkler&harvey

MEMBERS OF FIRM

Jay L. Winckler
Jay Harvey

ASSOCIATE

Reed Teckenbrock

For full biographical listings, see the Martindale-Hubbell Law Directory

*CORPUS CHRISTI,** Nueces Co.

BROYLES & PRATT, A PROFESSIONAL CORPORATION (AV)

1001 Bank of America Center North, 500 North Shoreline Boulevard, 78471
Telephone: 361-886-6200
Fax: 361-886-6262
Austin, Texas Office: One Northpoint Centre, Suite 250, 6836 Austin Center Boulevard, 78731.
Telephone: 512-794-2100.
Fax: 512-794-2111.

Gaston M. Broyles, Jr.

For full biographical listings, see the Martindale-Hubbell Law Directory

*DALLAS,** Dallas Co.

BRUCE A. BUDNER & ASSOCIATES (AV)

2527 Fairmount Street, 75201
Telephone: 214-220-2111
Email: babudner@waymark.net *URL:* http://www.lawyers.com/bruceabudner

ASSOCIATE
Jill C. Adler

LEGAL SUPPORT PERSONNEL
Diane Smith (Paralegal)

For full biographical listings, see the Martindale-Hubbell Law Directory

JOHNSTON • TOBEY, P.C. (AV)

900 Jackson Street, Suite 710, 75202
Telephone: 214-741-6260
Facsimile: 214-741-6248

Coyt Randal Johnston
Robert L. Tobey

For full biographical listings, see the Martindale-Hubbell Law Directory

THOMPSON & KNIGHT L.L.P. (AV)

(Attorneys and Counselors)
1700 Pacific Avenue Suite 3300, 75201
Telephone: 214-969-1700
Telecopy: 214-969-1751
Telex: 732 298
URL: http://www.tklaw.com
Austin, Texas Office: 1200 San Jacinto Center, 98 San Jacinto Boulevard, 78701.
Telephone: 512-469-6100.
Telecopy: 512-469-6180.
Fort Worth, Texas Office: 801 Cherry Street, Suite 1600, 76102.
Telephone: 817-347-1700.
Telecopy: 817-347-1799.
Houston, Texas Office: Thompson Knight Brown Parker & Leahy L.L.P., 1200 Smith Street, Suite 3600, 77002-4595.
Telephone: 713-654-8111.
Telecopier: 713-654-1871.
San Pedro Garza Garcia, Nuevo León, Mexico Office: Edificio Losoles PD-4, Av. Lázaro Cárdenas No. 2400 Pte., C.P. 66220.
Telephone: (52-8) 363-0096.
Telecopy: (52-8) 363-3067.

PARTNERS
G. Luke Ashley
Beverly Ray Burlingame
F. Barrett Davis
Rachelle H. Glazer
Stephen C. Rasch

OF COUNSEL
Jerry P. Jones

For Complete List of Firm Personnel, See General Section

For full biographical listings, see the Martindale-Hubbell Law Directory

*FORT WORTH,** Tarrant Co.

LAW FIRM OF DARRELL KEITH, P.C. (AV)

The Keith Building, 1705 West Seventh Street, 76102
Telephone: 817-338-1400
Telefax: 817-870-2448

SHAREHOLDERS
Darrell L. Keith
Courtney S. Keith

Stephanie L. Merithew

For full biographical listings, see the Martindale-Hubbell Law Directory

*HOUSTON,** Harris Co.

CARPENTER & ASSOCIATES (AV)

Suite 604, River Oaks Bank Building, 2001 Kirby Drive, 77019
Telephone: 713-528-3118
Facsimile: 713-528-3198
Email: wscarpenter@juno.com

W. Scott Carpenter

For full biographical listings, see the Martindale-Hubbell Law Directory

THOMPSON KNIGHT BROWN PARKER & LEAHY L.L.P. (AV)

A Registered Limited Liability Partnership including Professional Corporations
(Attorneys and Counselors)
1200 Smith Street, Suite 3600, 77002-4595
Telephone: 713-654-8111
Telecopier: 713-654-1871
URL: http://www.tklaw.com
Dallas, Texas Office: Thompson & Knight L.L.P., 1700 Pacific Avenue, Suite 3300, 75201.
Telephone: 214-969-1700.
Telecopy: 214-969-1751.
Telex: 732298.
Austin, Texas Office: Thompson & Knight L.L.P., 1200 San Jacinto Center, 98 San Jacinto Boulevard, 78701.
Telephone: 512-469-6100.
Telecopy: 512-469-6180.
Fort Worth, Texas Office: Thompson & Knight L.L.P., 801 Cherry Street, Suite 1600, 76102.
Telephone: 817-347-1700.
Telecopy: 817-347-1799.
San Pedro Garza Garcia, Nuevo León, Mexico Office: Thompson & Knight L.L.P., Edificio Losoles PD-4, Av. Lázaro Cárdenas No. 2400 PTE., C.P. 66220.
Telephone: (52-8) 363-0096.
Telecopy: (52-8) 363-3067.

PARTNERS
J. Michael Bell
Grant Cook (P.C.)
E.F. Mano DeAyala
Robert L. Galloway
Robert S. MacIntyre, Jr.

For Complete List of Firm Personnel, See General Section

For full biographical listings, see the Martindale-Hubbell Law Directory

MEDICAL MALPRACTICE

MINNESOTA

*MINNEAPOLIS,** Hennepin Co.

BORKON, RAMSTEAD, MARIANI & LETOURNEAU, LTD. (AV)

485 Northstar East, 608 Second Avenue, South, 55402
Telephone: 612-333-7155
Fax: 612-333-5956

Edward H. Borkon
John H. Ramstead
John D. Mariani
Dennis R. Letourneau
William M. Fishman
Howard S. Carp
Howard S. Marker
Lewis H. Seltz
Lorrie L. Bescheinen
Martin T. Montilino
Howard L. Bolter
Michael C. Van Berkom

OF COUNSEL

William Seltz

Reference: Norwest Bank, Minneapolis.

For full biographical listings, see the Martindale-Hubbell Law Directory

HUNEGS, STONE, KOENIG, LENEAVE & KVAS, P.A. (AV)

1650 International Center Building, 900 Second Avenue South, 55402
Telephone: 612-339-4511; 800-328-4340
Fax: 612-339-5150
URL: http://hunegslaw.com

William H. DeParcq (1905-1988)
Richard Gene Hunegs
Robert N. Stone
Ralph E. Koenig
Randal W. LeNeave
Cortney S. LeNeave
William Kvas
Richard L. Carlson
Steven M. Hunegs
Kermit N. Fruechte

Reference: National City Bank of Minneapolis.

For full biographical listings, see the Martindale-Hubbell Law Directory

MESHBESHER & SPENCE (AV)

1616 Park Avenue, 55404
Telephone: 612-339-9121
Fax: 612-339-9188
URL: http://www.meshbesher.com
Woodbury, Minnesota Office: 8360 City Centre Drive, 55125.
Telephone: 651-578-8055.
St. Cloud, Minnesota Office: 510 Zapp Bank Plaza, 56301.
Telephone: 320-656-0484.
Rochester, Minnesota Office: 21 SW 2nd Street, 55902.
Telephone: 507-280-8090.
Maplewood, Minnesota Office: 2603 White Bear Avenue, 55109.
Telephone: 651-777-5858.
St. Louis Park, Minnesota Office: 9950 Wayzata Boulevard, 55426.
Telephone: 612-544-5959.

MEMBERS OF FIRM

Ronald I. Meshbesher
Russell M. Spence (Resident, Woodbury Office)
John P. Clifford
Dennis R. Johnson
Patrick K. Horan
Michael C. Snyder
John P. Sheehy
Mark D. Streed
Randall Spence
Katherine S. Flom
Jeffrey P. Oistad (Resident, St. Cloud Office)
Anthony J. Nemo
Colleen M. Christianson

For full biographical listings, see the Martindale-Hubbell Law Directory

SIEBEN, GROSE, VON HOLTUM & CAREY, LTD. (AV)

900 Midwest Plaza East, 800 Marquette Avenue, 55402
Telephone: 612-333-4500
Fax: 612-333-5970
URL: http://www.know-your-rights.com
Fairfax, Minnesota Office: 117 South Park Street.
Telephone: 507-426-8211.
Fax: 507-426-8213.
Duluth, Minnesota Office: 612 U.S. Bank Place, 130 Superior Street West.
Telephone: 218-722-6848. Toll Free (Minnesota): 800-422-0612.
Fax: 218-722-6841.
Lakeville, Minnesota Office: Southfork Office Centre, Suite 105, 17645 Juniper Path, 55044.
Telephone: 612-898-1894.
Fax: 612-898-4147.

Harry A. Sieben, Jr.
John W. Carey

Paul F. Schweiger (Resident, Duluth Office)

For full biographical listings, see the Martindale-Hubbell Law Directory

*ST. PAUL,** Ramsey Co.

GERAGHTY, O'LOUGHLIN & KENNEY, PROFESSIONAL ASSOCIATION (AV)

1400 Ecolab University Center, 386 North Wabasha Street, 55102-1308
Telephone: 651-291-1177
Fax: 651-291-9477
Email: gok@pclink.com

Terence J. O'Loughlin
Robert M. Mahoney
David C. Hutchinson
William H. Leary, III
Mary H. Alcorn
Ann D. Bray
Jean B. Hoppe
Kyle M. Thomas

OF COUNSEL

James H. Geraghty (Retired)
James W. Kenney (Retired)

Representative Clients: St. Paul Cos.; Allina Health System; Fairview Hospital and Healthcare Services; HealthEast; HealthPartners; MMI Cos.; Midwest Medical Insurance Co.; North Memorial Hospital; Aspen Medical Group.

For full biographical listings, see the Martindale-Hubbell Law Directory

MISSISSIPPI

BILOXI, Harrison Co.

JUDY M. GUICE A PROFESSIONAL ASSOCIATION (AV)

750 Dr. Martin Luther King Jr. Boulevard, P.O. Box 1919, 39533
Telephone: 228-374-9787
Fax: 228-374-9436
Email: judy@judyguice.com *URL:* http://www.judyguice.com

Judy Guice

For full biographical listings, see the Martindale-Hubbell Law Directory

MINOR AND ASSOCIATES (AV)

A Partnership including a Professional Association
160 Main Street, Drawer 1388, 39533-1388
Telephone: 228-374-5151
Fax: 228-374-6630
Email: pminoratty@aol.com

Paul S. Minor (P.A.)

Mark D. Lumpkin
James R. Reeves, Jr.
Christopher C. VanCleave

For full biographical listings, see the Martindale-Hubbell Law Directory

PAGE, MANNINO, PERESICH & McDERMOTT (AV)

A Professional Limited Liability Company
759 Vieux Marché Mall, P.O. Drawer 289, 39533
Telephone: 228-374-2100
Facsimile: 228-432-5539
Email: pmp@pmp.org

MEMBERS OF FIRM

Lyle M. Page (Resident)
Frederick J. Mannino (Resident)
Ronald G. Peresich (Resident)
Stephen G. Peresich (Resident)
Michael B. McDermott (Resident)
Tere Richardson Steel (Resident)
Michael E. Whitehead (Resident)
Mary Alexander Nichols (Resident)
David M. Allen (Resident)

ASSOCIATES

Henry N. Dick, III
Les W. Smith (Resident)
Emilie Whitehead
Kaara L. Liskow
Joel L. Blackledge

Representative Clients: United States Fidelity & Guaranty Co.; St. Paul Fire & Marine Insurance Co.; Crawford & Co.; Anheuser-Busch Corp.
General Counsel for: Peoples Bank of Biloxi, Mississippi; Biloxi Regional Medical Center; Bank of Mississippi (Gulf Coast Division).

For full biographical listings, see the Martindale-Hubbell Law Directory

*GULFPORT,** Harrison Co.

BOYCE HOLLEMAN A PROFESSIONAL CORPORATION (AV)

1913 15th Street, P.O. Drawer 1030, 39502
Telephone: 228-863-3142; 1-800-863-3140
Telecopier: 228-863-9829
Email: boyce1913@aol.com

Boyce Holleman

(See Next Column)

HARRISON, TUCKER & HYDE LLP, *Springfield—Continued*

MEMBERS OF FIRM

Jeffrey H. Harrison
James D. Tucker
Kent O. Hyde
William C. Love
Brian E. Hamburg
Aaron P. Lyons

For full biographical listings, see the Martindale-Hubbell Law Directory

MONTANA

*BILLINGS,** Yellowstone Co.

BROWN LAW FIRM, P.C. (AV)

315 North 24th Street, P.O. Drawer 849, 59103-0849
Telephone: 406-248-2611
FAX: 406-248-3128
URL: http://www.brownfirm.com
Bozeman, Montana Office: 510 South 23rd Street.
Telephone: 406-587-8486.
Fax: 406-587-4524.

Steven J. Harman
John J. Russell
Lisa A. Rodeghiero

For Complete List of Firm Personnel, See General Section

For full biographical listings, see the Martindale-Hubbell Law Directory

CROWLEY, HAUGHEY, HANSON, TOOLE & DIETRICH, P.L.L.P. (AV)

500 Transwestern II, 490 North 31st Street, P.O. Box 2529, 59103
Telephone: 406-252-3441
Fax: 406-259-4159
Email: crowley@crowleylaw.com
Helena, Montana Office: IBM Building, 100 North Park Avenue, Suite 300, 59601.
Telephone: 406-449-4165.
Fax: 406-449-5149.
Kalispell, Montana Office: 431 1st Avenue West, 59901.
Telephone: 406-752-6644.
Fax: 406-752-5108.
Williston, North Dakota Office: 113 East Broadway, 58801.
Telephone: 701-572-2200.
Fax: 701-572-7072.

MEMBERS OF FIRM

Herbert I. Pierce, III
Ronald R. Lodders
Joe C. Maynard, Jr.
Steven Robert Milch

Representative Clients: Montana Power Co.; First Interstate Bank of Commerce; MDU Resources Group, Inc.; Chevron U.S.A., Inc.; Noranda Minerals Corp.; United Parcel Service.
Insurance Clients: Farmers Insurance Group; New York Life Insurance Co.

For Complete List of Firm Personnel, See General Section

For full biographical listings, see the Martindale-Hubbell Law Directory

NEVADA

*LAS VEGAS,** Clark Co.

ALVERSON, TAYLOR, MORTENSEN, NELSON & SANDERS (AV)

7401 West Charleston Boulevard, 89117
Telephone: 702-384-7000
FAX: 702-385-7000
Email: alverson@intermind.net
Reno, Nevada Office: 245 East Liberty, Suite 520, 89505.
Telephone: 775-329-0473.
Fax: 775-329-3303.

MEMBERS OF FIRM

J. Bruce Alverson
Eric K. Taylor
David J. Mortensen
Erven T. Nelson
LeAnn Sanders

OF COUNSEL

Jack C. Cherry
Kurt D. Anderson
Philip C. Van Alstyne

ASSOCIATES

Rebecca Hopkins Miller
Sandra Smagac
Victoria L. Nelson
Aaron D. Lovaas
Diane Obritsch
Michael A. Olsen
Randal D. Shimon
Catherine A. Olendorff
Monica L. Pierce
Gabriel D. Lither
Kurt R. Bonds
Darius F. Rafie
Mark J. King, IV
Shell L. Mercer
Carrie S. Bourdeau
Jason Lane Earnest

(See Next Column)

ASSOCIATES (Continued)

Nathan R. Reinmiller
Donn C. Alexander
Afshin Tadayon
Eric O. Freeman
Lindsay L. Stadtlander
Julie M. Sueoka

Representative Clients: St. Paul Fire & Marine Insurance Company; The Doctors' Company; Medical Insurance Exchange of California (MIEC); MEDMARC; National Chiropractic Mutual Insurance Company; Lake Mead Hospital Medical Center; University Medical Center of Southern Nevada; American Healthcare Management; Ophthalmic Mutual Insurance Company; Osteopathic Mutual Insurance Company.

For full biographical listings, see the Martindale-Hubbell Law Directory

CROCKETT & MYERS, LTD. A PROFESSIONAL CORPORATION (AV)

700 South Third Street, 89101
Telephone: 702-382-6711
Fax: 702-384-8102
Email: cmlegal@wizard.com *URL:* http://www.lawyers.com/c&mlaw

J. R. Crockett, Jr.
Richard W. Myers
James V. Lavelle III

Reference: American Bank of Commerce.

For full biographical listings, see the Martindale-Hubbell Law Directory

GALATZ, EARL, & ASSOCIATES (AV)

710 South Fourth Street, 89101
Telephone: 702-386-0000
Fax: 702-384-0394
Email: neilgalatz@aol.com *URL:* http://www.lawyers.com/galatzlaw

Neil G. Galatz
Allan R. Earl

For full biographical listings, see the Martindale-Hubbell Law Directory

GILLOCK, MARKLEY & KILLEBREW (AV)

1640 West Alta, Suite 4, 89106
Telephone: 702-385-1482
Fax: 702-385-2604
Email: lawoffice@QUIK13.com *URL:* http://www.lawyers.com/gmklaw

MEMBERS OF FIRM

Gerald I. Gillock
Janet S. Markley
Antonia C. Killebrew
Julie A. Mersch

For full biographical listings, see the Martindale-Hubbell Law Directory

GARY LOGAN (AV)

Third Floor, 302 East Carson Avenue, 89101
Telephone: 702-385-9900
Telecopier: 702-382-4800
Email: GARYLOGAN@prodigy.net

OF COUNSEL

Richard I. Feinberg

References: Bank of America-Nevada; The Chase Manhattan Bank, N.A.

For full biographical listings, see the Martindale-Hubbell Law Directory

MAINOR & HARRIS (AV)

A Partnership of Professional Corporations
530 South Sixth Street, 89101
Telephone: 702-385-1400
Fax: 702-385-9408
Email: admin@mainorandharris.com *URL:* http://www.lawyers.com/mainorandharris

W. Randall Mainor (A Professional Corporation)
Richard A. Harris (A Professional Corporation)
Clark Seegmiller
Robert M. Adams
Nancy Quon
Robert W. Cottle

Reference: First Security Bank of Nevada, Las Vegas, Nevada.

For full biographical listings, see the Martindale-Hubbell Law Directory

MORSE & MOWBRAY, A PROFESSIONAL CORPORATION (AV)

Suite 1400 Bank of America Plaza, 300 South Fourth Street, 89101
Telephone: 702-384-6340
Telecopier: 702-384-4596
London, England Office: Lamb Building, Temple.
Telephone: 071-353-6701.

William R. Morse
Harold M. Morse
John H. Mowbray
Christopher H. Byrd
Kimberly A. Buchanan

For full biographical listings, see the Martindale-Hubbell Law Directory

Las Vegas—Continued

PICO & MITCHELL (AV)

2000 South Eastern Avenue, 89104
Telephone: 702-457-9099
FAX: 702-457-8451
Email: lawyers@picomitchell.com

MEMBERS OF FIRM

James F. Pico
Bert O. Mitchell
Christy Brad Escobar
James R. Rosenberger
E. Breen Arntz

ASSOCIATES

Michelle Schwarz
Rebecca L. Mastrangelo
Jill M. Chase
Daniel E. Carvalho
Stephen H. Rogers

Representative Clients: Home Insurance Co.; State Farm Mutual Insurance Co.; Industrial Indemnity Insurance Co.; Great American Insurance Co.; Argonaut Insurance Cos.; Clark County Medical Society; Rose de Lima Hospital; Fairway Chevrolet; American States Insurance Co.; The Hartford Insurance Co.

For full biographical listings, see the Martindale-Hubbell Law Directory

SMITH & WILLIAMS (AV)

1785 East Sahara, Suite 337, 89104
Telephone: 702-892-0000
Fax: 702-892-0788
Email: SWPIMAL@AOL.COM

MEMBERS OF FIRM

Roy E. Smith
Timothy C. Williams

For full biographical listings, see the Martindale-Hubbell Law Directory

VANNAH COSTELLO CANEPA RIEDY & RUBINO (AV)

A Partnership including a Professional Corporation
Greystone, 1850 East Flamingo, Suite 236, 89119
Telephone: 702-369-4161
Fax: 702-369-0104
Email: vannahnet@vannahnet.com

MEMBERS OF FIRM

Robert D. Vannah (Chartered)
Nathan M. Costello
Scott K. Canepa
Terry W. Riedy
Michael C. Rubino

ASSOCIATES

Connie J. Forsythe
Shawn D. Dorman
Adam Ganz
Denise M. Cooper
Jeffrey Ferguson
Matthew Vannah
Ronald J. Flinders
Russell M. Rowe
Jonathan G. Lattie (Not admitted in NV)

Representative Clients: Prudential Property and Casualty Insurance Co.; Continental Insurance Health Care; Chubb Group of Insurance; Reliance Insurance Co.; Transamerica Insurance Group; Foremost Insurance Co.; CNA Insurance Co.; Scottsdale Insurance Co.; The Maryland Insurance Group; Insurance Company of the West.

For full biographical listings, see the Martindale-Hubbell Law Directory

*RENO,** Washoe Co.

BRADLEY, DRENDEL & JEANNEY (AV)

401 Flint Street, P.O. Box 1987, 89505
Telephone: 775-329-2273
Fax: 775-329-6513
Email: bdandj@worldnet.att.net *URL:* http://www.lawyers.com/bd&jlaw

Bill Bradley
Joseph S. Bradley
Thomas E. Drendel
William C. Jeanney

OF COUNSEL

William O. "Bud" Bradley
John Squire Drendel

For full biographical listings, see the Martindale-Hubbell Law Directory

ERICKSON, THORPE & SWAINSTON, LTD. (AV)

99 West Arroyo Street, P.O. Box 3559, 89505
Telephone: 702-786-3930
Fax: 702-786-4160
Email: etsreno@aol.com

Roger L. Erickson
Donald A. Thorpe
George W. Swainston
William G. Cobb
Gary A. Cardinal
Thomas Peter Beko
John A. Aberasturi
Paul M. Bertone
Lisa E. Bruce
John C. Boyden

Representative Clients: CNA; St. Paul Insurance Cos.; National Chiropractic Mutual Insurance Company.

For full biographical listings, see the Martindale-Hubbell Law Directory

NEW HAMPSHIRE

*CONCORD,** Merrimack Co.

RATH, YOUNG AND PIGNATELLI, PROFESSIONAL ASSOCIATION (AV)

One Capital Plaza, P.O. Box 1500, 03302-1500
Telephone: 603-226-2600
Telecopier: 603-226-2700; 228-2294; 225-9774
Email: ryp@rathlaw.com *URL:* http://www.rathlaw.com
Nashua, New Hampshire Office: The Glass Tower, 20 Trafalgar Square.
Telephone: 603-889-9952.
Telecopier: 603-595-7489.

Thomas D. Rath
Michael A. Pignatelli

Claire W. Rouillard

For Complete List of Firm Personnel, See General Section

For full biographical listings, see the Martindale-Hubbell Law Directory

*DOVER,** Strafford Co.

BURNS, BRYANT, HINCHEY, COX & ROCKEFELLER, P.A. (AV)

Burns Building, 255 Washington Street, P.O. Box 608, 03820
Telephone: 603-742-2332
Fax: 603-749-4970
Email: bbhcr@concentric.net

George T. Hughes (1873-1943)
Stanley M. Burns (1902-1967)
Robert P. Shea (1936-1983)
Robert E. Hinchey (Retired)
Paul Richard Cox
Donald R. Bryant (Of Counsel)
Christine M. Rockefeller
Gregory J. Wenger

Matthew B. Cox
Carolyn F. Dickson

Representative Clients: Metropolitan Life Insurance Co.; Prudential Insurance Company of America; Concord Group Insurance Cos.

For full biographical listings, see the Martindale-Hubbell Law Directory

*MANCHESTER,** Hillsborough Co.

ABRAMSON, REIS, BROWN & DUGAN (AV)

1819 Elm Street, 03104
Telephone: 603-627-1819
Fax: 603-666-4227
URL: http://www.arbd.com
Nashua, New Hampshire Office: 20 Trafalgar Square, Suite 417.
Telephone: 603-886-0308.

MEMBERS OF FIRM

Stanley M. Brown (1916-1998)
Kenneth C. Brown
Randolph J. Reis
Mark A. Abramson
Kevin F. Dugan

ASSOCIATES

John P. Fagan
Jared R. Green

For full biographical listings, see the Martindale-Hubbell Law Directory

NASHUA, Hillsborough Co.

RATH, YOUNG AND PIGNATELLI, PROFESSIONAL ASSOCIATION (AV)

The Glass Tower, 20 Trafalgar Square, 03063
Telephone: 603-889-9952
Telecopier: 603-595-7489
Email: ryp@rathlaw.com *URL:* http://www.rathlaw.com
Concord, New Hampshire Office: One Capital Plaza, P.O. Box 1500.
Telephone: 603-226-2600.
Telecopier: 603-226-2700.

Thomas D. Rath
Michael A. Pignatelli

For full biographical listings, see the Martindale-Hubbell Law Directory

NEW JERSEY

BRICK, Ocean Co.

GROSSMAN, KRUTTSCHNITT, HEAVEY & JACOB, A PROFESSIONAL CORPORATION (AV)

Brick Professional Plaza, 1608 Highway 88 West, Suite 200, 08724
Telephone: 732-206-0200
Facsimile: 732-206-0205

(See Next Column)

GROSSMAN, KRUTTSCHNITT, HEAVEY & JACOB A PROFESSIONAL CORPORATION, *Brick—Continued*

Richard A. Grossman | Thomas J. Heavey
Herbert Kruttschnitt, III | Barbara Ann Jacob

Roberta Di Biase | Bradley F. Randell

References: First Fidelity Bank, N.A. New Jersey; The Bank of New York, National Community Division.

For full biographical listings, see the Martindale-Hubbell Law Directory

BURLINGTON, Burlington Co.

SMITH, GOLDSTEIN, MAGRAM & BERENATO, A PROFESSIONAL CORPORATION (AV)

415 High Street, P.O. Box 603, 08016-0603
Telephone: 609-386-2633
Fax: 609-386-8674

Louis A. Smith | Edward J. Magram
Jeffrey N. Goldstein | Elizabeth D. Berenato

David C. Michaud

Reference: First Union Bank, Burlington, New Jersey.

For full biographical listings, see the Martindale-Hubbell Law Directory

FLORHAM PARK, Morris Co.

D'ALESSANDRO, JACOVINO & GERSON (AV)

147 Columbia Turnpike, 07932
Telephone: 201-966-1910
Fax: 201-966-6774
URL: http://www.lawyers.com/djgattys
New York, N.Y. Office: 321 Broadway, 4th Floor.
Telephone: 212-608-7500.

MEMBERS OF FIRM

Edward G. D'Alessandro | Amedeo C. Jacovino
Frederick E. Gerson

ASSOCIATES

Edward G. D'Alessandro, Jr. | Anthony J. Bianciella

Reference: Midatlantic Bank.

For full biographical listings, see the Martindale-Hubbell Law Directory

*HACKENSACK,** Bergen Co.

HEIN, SMITH, BEREZIN, MALOOF & JACOBS, L.L.C. (AV)

Court Plaza East, 19 Main Street, 07601-7023
Telephone: 201-487-7400
Telecopier: 201-487-4228
Email: counsel@heinsmith.com

MEMBERS OF FIRM

Robert L. Baum | Ellen W. Smith
Lawrence H. Jacobs | Carla H. Madnick

ASSOCIATES

John L. Shanahan | Douglas V. Sanchez
Robert J. Logan

Representative Clients: Bergen County Joint Municipal Insurance Fund; Commercial General Union Insurance Cos. of New York; Crawford & Co.; Health Care Insurance Co.; Princeton Insurance Co.; St. Paul Fire & Marine Insurance Co.; Pro Mutual Insurance Company; NJ Cure.
Reference: Summit Bank.

For Complete List of Firm Personnel, See General Section

For full biographical listings, see the Martindale-Hubbell Law Directory

HADDONFIELD, Camden Co.

ANDRES & BERGER, A PROFESSIONAL CORPORATION (AV)

264 Kings Highway East, 08033
Telephone: 856-795-1444
Fax: 856-795-4464

Michael S. Berger | Kenneth G. Andres, Jr.
Kevin Haverty

For full biographical listings, see the Martindale-Hubbell Law Directory

LIVINGSTON, Essex Co.

PHILIP M. LUSTBADER & DAVID LUSTBADER A PROFESSIONAL CORPORATION (AV)

615 West Mount Pleasant Avenue, 07039
Telephone: 973-740-1000
Fax: 973-740-1520
URL: http://www.lawyers.com/lustbader,law

(See Next Column)

Philip M. Lustbader | David Lustbader

John L. Riordan, Jr. | James S. Colavito

For full biographical listings, see the Martindale-Hubbell Law Directory

MILLBURN, Essex Co.

MCDERMOTT & MCGEE (AV)

75 Main Street, P.O. Box 192, 07041-0192
Telephone: 973-467-8080
Fax: 973-376-8669

MEMBERS OF FIRM

John L. McDermott | Frank P. Leanza
John P. McGee | John L. McDermott, Jr.
Richard P. Maggi | David J. Dickinson
Thomas A. Wester | A. Charles Lorenzo
Richard M. Tango | Robert A. McDermott
Kevin John McGee

ASSOCIATES

Anthony John Verardi | Lindsay K. O'Shaughnessy
Andre L. McGuire

OF COUNSEL

Daniel K. Van Dorn

Representative Clients: Medical Inter-Insurance Exchange of New Jersey; The Maryland Insurance Group.

For full biographical listings, see the Martindale-Hubbell Law Directory

LAW OFFICES OF STEPHEN H. SCHECHNER (AV)

75 Main Street, 07041
Telephone: 973-376-6200
Fax: 973-376-5620

ASSOCIATE

Virginia T. Shea

For full biographical listings, see the Martindale-Hubbell Law Directory

MOORESTOWN, Burlington Co.

CHIERICI, CHIERICI & SMITH, A PROFESSIONAL CORPORATION (AV)

Blason Campus - III, 509 South Lenola Road Building Six, 08057-1561
Telephone: 856-234-6300
Fax: 856-234-9490

Donald R. Chierici, Jr. | Elizabeth Coleman Chierici
Julie C. Smith

Carolyn J. Kornas | Melvin McDowell
Mark G. Esposito | David J. Karbasian
Richard D. DiTomaso | Peter P. Sanchez
Donald R. Chierici, III

For full biographical listings, see the Martindale-Hubbell Law Directory

MORRIS PLAINS, Morris Co.

VOORHEES & OUDA (AV)

Powder Mill Plaza, 51 Gibraltar Drive, 07950
Telephone: 201-267-6677
Fax: 201-267-9152
Mailing Address: P.O. Box 1236, Morristown, New Jersey, 07962-1236

MEMBERS OF FIRM

William Wolverton Voorhees, Jr. | Peter A. Ouda

For full biographical listings, see the Martindale-Hubbell Law Directory

*MORRISTOWN,** Morris Co.

BAUMEISTER & SAMUELS, P.C. (AV Ⓣ)

1776 On The Green, P.O. Box 1116, 07962-1116
Telephone: 973-267-6666
Telecopier: 973-605-1812
Email: BAUMSAM@AOL.COM
New York, N.Y. Office: One Exchange Plaza, 10006-3008.
Telephone: 212-363-1200.
Telecopier: 212-363-1346.

Michel F. Baumeister | Dorothea M. Capone
Douglas A. Latto (Not admitted in NJ)

OF COUNSEL

Lynn F. Samuels | Marc Z. Edell
Robert S. Franklin (Not admitted in NJ)

For full biographical listings, see the Martindale-Hubbell Law Directory

Morristown—Continued

STEPHEN S. WEINSTEIN A PROFESSIONAL CORPORATION (AV)

20 Park Place, Suite 301, 07960
Telephone: 973-267-5200
Fax: 973-538-1779
Email: skippy@sswpa.com *URL:* http://www.sswpa.com

Stephen S. Weinstein

Gail S. Boertzel
William G. Johnson
Melissa H. Luce

For full biographical listings, see the Martindale-Hubbell Law Directory

*NEWARK,** Essex Co.

MARAN & MARAN (AV)

The Legal Center, One Riverfront Plaza, Suite 315, 07102
Telephone: 973-622-5303
1-888-566-2726
Fax: 973-622-4352

MEMBERS OF FIRM

Joe Maran
David Maran

For full biographical listings, see the Martindale-Hubbell Law Directory

SILLS CUMMIS RADIN TISCHMAN EPSTEIN & GROSS, A PROFESSIONAL CORPORATION (AV)

One Riverfront Plaza, 07102-5400
Telephone: 973-643-7000
Fax: 973-643-6500
Telex: 820630 Sillsbeck Nwk
Email: sillsmail@sillscummis.com *URL:* http://www.sillscummis.com
Atlantic City, New Jersey Office: 17 Gordon's Alley.
Telephone: 609-344-2800.
New York, N.Y. Office: 712 Fifth Avenue.
Telephone: 212-643-7000.
Washington, D.C. Office: 1800 K Street, N.W.
Telephone: 202-296-4750.

MEMBERS OF FIRM

Barry M. Epstein
Stuart M. Feinblatt

Representative Clients: Bristol-Myers Squibb Co.; Johnson & Johnson; Becton Dickinson and Company; Berlex Laboratories, Inc.; Gynopharma, Inc.; Bioengineering International (B.V.); Nova Pharmaceutical Corp.; Shering A.G.; Sorin Biomedica, S.p.A., Zambon Corp.

For Complete List of Firm Personnel, See General Section

For full biographical listings, see the Martindale-Hubbell Law Directory

NEW PROVIDENCE, Union Co.

TAFARO & FLYNN, P.A. (AV)

571 Central Avenue, Suite 119, 07974
Telephone: 908-508-0100
Fax: 908-508-0599
Email: tafaroflyn@aol.com

Stephen J. Tafaro
Catherine J. Flynn

Joan Bannan Harris
Eric L. Grogan
Fred J. Hughes
Cheryl M. DeKline
Suellen L. DeBlasio
Marisa R. Kussoy

For full biographical listings, see the Martindale-Hubbell Law Directory

PARSIPPANY, Morris Co.

REISEMAN SHARP KELSEY & BROWN LLP (AV)

4 Campus Drive, P.O. Box 431, 07054-0431
Telephone: 973-267-3600
Fax: 973-267-2332

MEMBERS OF FIRM

Neil Reiseman
James B. Sharp
Jane S. Kelsey
Kenneth M. Brown
Sam Rosenberg
Meghan E. Walsh

John C. Macce
Jayne E. Turner
Everett E. Gale, III
Robert T. Gunning
Gregory A. Bush

Representative Clients: Medical Inter-Insurance Exchange of New Jersey; Princeton Insurance Company; Health Care Insurance Company; Home Depot; United Capitol Insurance Company; New Jersey Property-Liability Insurance Guaranty Association; New Jersey Joint Underwriting Association; Franciscan Health Systems; Zurich American; Avis.

For full biographical listings, see the Martindale-Hubbell Law Directory

RED BANK, Monmouth Co.

PHILIP G. AUERBACH A PROFESSIONAL CORPORATION (AV)

231 Maple Avenue, P.O. Box Y, 07701
Telephone: 732-842-6660
Fax: 732-530-7925

Philip G. Auerbach

Edward A. Genz
John J. Ryan
John F. McLaughlin

For full biographical listings, see the Martindale-Hubbell Law Directory

WHITE, FLEISCHNER & FINO (AV)

272 Broad Street, 07701
Telephone: 732-530-7787
Telecopier: 732-530-8552
New York, New York Office: 140 Broadway.
Telephone: 212-487-9700.
Telecopier: 212-487-9777.

Benjamin A. Fleischner

ASSOCIATES

Virginia L. McGrane (Not admitted in NJ)
Elaine N. Chou

Representative Clients: Interstate Insurance Group; Hartford Insurance Group.

For full biographical listings, see the Martindale-Hubbell Law Directory

ROSELAND, Essex Co.

POST, POLAK, GOODSELL & MACNEILL, P.A. (AV)

75 Livingston Avenue, 07068-3701
Telephone: 973-994-1100
Telecopier: 973-994-1705
Email: administrator@ppgm.com
New York, New York Office: 575 Madison Avenue, Suite 1006.
Telephone: 212-486-1455.

Jay Scott MacNeill
Lauren Koffler O'Neill

Franca D. Maiorano
Joseph Tripodi
Thomas J. Pyle, Jr.

For Complete List of Firm Personnel, See General Section

For full biographical listings, see the Martindale-Hubbell Law Directory

SADDLE BROOK, Bergen Co.

COHN LIFLAND PEARLMAN HERRMANN & KNOPF LLP (AV)

Park 80 Plaza West-One, 07663
Telephone: 201-845-9600
Telecopier: 201-845-9423
Email: info@njlawfirm.com *URL:* http://www.njlawfirm.com

MEMBERS OF FIRM

Albert L. Cohn
Peter S. Pearlman
Barry A. Knopf
Daniel Crystal (Retired)
Jeffrey W. Herrmann
Robert D. Zatorski
Allen Susser
Mary Ann T. Stokes
Brian D. Zinn
Joshua P. Cohn

ASSOCIATES

Virginia A. Harper
Leonard Z. Kaufmann
Audra DePaolo
Robert Ricci, Jr.
Maurice W. McLaughlin
Andrew C. Abrams
Jessica V. Henry

OF COUNSEL

Sylvia J. Cohn
Jodi B. Scherl

For full biographical listings, see the Martindale-Hubbell Law Directory

SHIP BOTTOM, Ocean Co.

SHACKLETON, HAZELTINE AND BISHOP (AV)

22nd Street and Long Beach Boulevard, P.O. Box 410, 08008
Telephone: 609-494-2136
Telefax: 609-494-0870
Fairfield, New Jersey Office: One Passaic Avenue.
Telephone: 201-882-4646.
Telefax: 201-882-4620.

MEMBERS OF FIRM

Richard J. Shackleton
Colin R. Hazeltine
James E. Bishop

ASSOCIATES

Laura M. O'Regan
Marc Baden Powell
Robert Emmet Rue

(See Next Column)

SHACKLETON, HAZELTINE AND BISHOP, *Ship Bottom—Continued*

OF COUNSEL

Kenneth L. Leiby, Jr. (Resident, Fairfield Office)

References: Commerce Bank/Shore N/A; Summit Bank Corp.

For full biographical listings, see the Martindale-Hubbell Law Directory

SPRINGFIELD, Union Co.

HARDIN, KUNDLA, MCKEON, POLETTO & POLIFRONI, P.A., A PROFESSIONAL CORPORATION (AV)

673 Morris Avenue, P.O. Box 730, 07081
Telephone: 973-912-5222
Fax: 973-912-9212
Email: info@HKMPP.com
New York, New York Office: 55 John Street, 10038.
Telephone: 212-571-0111.
Fax: 212-571-1117.

George R. Hardin
Robert L. Polifroni
Janet L. Poletto
Mark S. Kundla
John F. McKeon
James R. Greene
Nicea J. D'Annunzio
John Samuel Favate
Patrick J. Clare
Anna Marie Strand

Jeffrey A. Oshin
Joseph R. Lowicky
Tracy C. Forsyth
Joseph A. DeFuria
John G. Kilbride
Jeffrey H. Goldsmith
Jeffrey Roth
Nora J. Grimbergen
William C. Sullivan, Jr.
Paul Daly
V. Christopher Hirsch
Richard S. Reig
Sam A. Dotro
Brian K. Kaiser
David M. Steiner
Lani M. D'Agostino
Sheila A. Glackin
Michael S. Schwartz
Kirsten L. McCaw
Sanjoy Mukherjee
Louisa B. Sargent
Michael A. Cifelli
James J. A. Mulhall
Kevin M. Regan
Lisa D. Chanel
Maria-Milagros Herrero
Brian A. King
Christina Fichera Dente
Andrea L. Strack
Roger J. Imhof
John P. Monaghan
Stephen J. Donahue
Cindy L. Thompson
Lisa A. Ganzhorn

Representative Clients: St. Paul Insurance Co.; CNA Insurance; Franciscan Health Systems; Care Insurance Exchange; Prineton Insurance Company; TIG.

For full biographical listings, see the Martindale-Hubbell Law Directory

JAVERBAUM WURGAFT HICKS & ZARIN, A PROFESSIONAL CORPORATION (AV)

Park Place Legal Center, 959 South Springfield Avenue, 07081-3555
Telephone: 973-379-4200
Fax: 973-379-7872
Email: javerbaumwurgafthicks@compuserve.com *URL:* http://www.lawyers.com/jwhz,law

Kenneth S. Javerbaum
Jack Wurgaft
Robert G. Hicks
Ira J. Zarin

Anthony P. Valenti
Eric G. Kahn
David L. Wikstrom

OF COUNSEL

Jeffrey E. Strauss

For full biographical listings, see the Martindale-Hubbell Law Directory

MCDONOUGH, KORN & EICHHORN, A PROFESSIONAL CORPORATION (AV)

Park Place Legal Center, 959 South Springfield Avenue, P.O. Box 712, 07081-0712
Telephone: 973-912-9099
Fax: 973-912-8604

Peter L. Korn
R. Scott Eichhorn
James R. Korn
William S. Mezzomo
Timothy J. Jaeger
Wilfred P. Coronato

Julia A. Klubenspies
Matthew S. Schorr
Danielle M. Verrastro
Jeffrey John Berezny

OF COUNSEL

Robert P. McDonough

Representative Clients: Chubb; Medical Inter-Insurance Exchange of New Jersey; Medical Liability Mutual Insurance Co.; Columbia Presbyterian Medical Center; Greater New York Blood Center; University of Medicine and Dentistry of New Jersey; Wausau Insurance Co.; New Jersey Property-Liability Ins. Guaranty Assoc.; Cigna Insurance.
Reference: First Union, Summit, N.J.

For full biographical listings, see the Martindale-Hubbell Law Directory

*TOMS RIVER,** Ocean Co.

NOVINS, YORK & PENTONY, A PROFESSIONAL CORPORATION (AV)

202 Main Street, 08753
Telephone: 732-349-7100
Email: info@nyplaw.com

Robert J. Novins (1910-1973)
Robert F. Novins
Harvey L. York
Kenneth R. Pentony
Ann K. Haskell
Robert M. McKeon

W. Mark Bayles
Robert J. Roth
Gregory S. Heizler
Anthony M. Pagano
Danziger Patricia Christoff
Michael A. Jacobus

OF COUNSEL

William E. O'Connor
Lorna S. Scanlon

Counsel for: Allstate Insurance Co.; Motor Club of America.

For full biographical listings, see the Martindale-Hubbell Law Directory

VINELAND, Cumberland Co.

JOSEPH D. O'NEILL A PROFESSIONAL CORPORATION (AV)

30 West Chestnut Avenue, P.O. Box 847, 08360
Telephone: 856-692-2400
Telecopier: 856-696-9036
URL: http://www.lawyers.com/josephoneill

Joseph D. O'Neill

Charles I. Coant
James T. Dugan
Amber Sharp Pallante

For full biographical listings, see the Martindale-Hubbell Law Directory

WEST ORANGE, Essex Co.

SACHS, MAITLIN, FLEMING, GREENE, WILSON & MAROTTE (AV)

80 Main Street, 3rd Floor, 07052
Telephone: 973-731-3400
Fax: 973-731-2896

Harold D. Feuerstein (1933-1967)
Marvin A. Sachs
Allan Maitlin
Raymond J. Fleming
Peter A. Greene
Bradley M. Wilson
Michael Marotte

ASSOCIATES

Steven L. Albertson
Philip B. Harrison
David Eric Maitlin
Theresa Mullen
Rosa Marques
Laura L. Milcsik

Reference: Fidelity Union Trust Co.

For full biographical listings, see the Martindale-Hubbell Law Directory

NEW MEXICO

*ALBUQUERQUE,** Bernalillo Co.

BRANCH LAW FIRM (AV)

Including a Professional Association
2025 Rio Grande Boulevard, N.W., 87104
Telephone: 505-243-3500
Fax: 505-243-3534
New Mexico Toll Free: 1-800-562-3456
Nationwide Toll Free: 1-800-828-4LAW
Email: reception@branchlawfirm.com *URL:* http://www.branchlawfirm.com
Durango, Colorado Office: Suite 205, 102 East Eighth Street.
Telephone: 303-385-7671.
Houston, Texas Office: 808 Travis Street, Suite 1303.
Telephone: 800-243-3545.
Fax: 713-224-1622.

Turner W. Branch (P.A.)
Margaret Moses Branch

Arthur M. Solon
Daniel R. Swiss
Rebecca C. Branch
Justin K. Hall
James P. Lyle
Rhett D. Klok
Suzanne Lafleur Klok
Clyde DeMersseman
Shari D. Thieman

(See Next Column)

BRANCH LAW FIRM—*Continued*

LEGAL SUPPORT PERSONNEL

Krisann Y. Matthes (Office Manager)
Jacqueline Adams
Amy Rigg
Shariesse McCannon
Judi Seff
Daphne Moore (Registered Nurse)
Yvette Rodarte
Shelly Hourani (Houston Office)

For full biographical listings, see the Martindale-Hubbell Law Directory

BUTKUS & REIMER, P.C. (AV)

500 Marquette N.W., Suite 720, 87102
Telephone: 505-246-2829
Fax: 505-246-2825

Carl J. Butkus
R. Galen Reimer

Gary J. Cade
Michael S. Jahner

LEGAL SUPPORT PERSONNEL

Vicki A. Haarhues
Bonita Werde

For full biographical listings, see the Martindale-Hubbell Law Directory

CARPENTER & CHÁVEZ, LTD. (AV)

1600 University Boulevard, N.E., Suite A, 87102-1711
Telephone: 505-243-1336
Facsimile: 505-243-1339
Email: carpchav@swcp.com *URL:* http://www.carpenter-law.com

William H. Carpenter
Edward L. Chávez
David J. Stout

Reference: Bank of America, Albuquerque, New Mexico.

For full biographical listings, see the Martindale-Hubbell Law Directory

EATON, MARTINEZ & HART, P.C. (AV)

3800 Osuna Road N.E., Suite 2, 87109
Telephone: 505-343-1776
Fax: 505-344-7709
URL: http://www.eatonmartinezhart.com
Email: rogeaton@aol.com *URL:* http://www.lawyers.com/eatonmartinez&hart

Roger V. Eaton
David B. Martinez
F. Michael Hart

Gabrielle M. Valdez
Wendy F. Jones

LEGAL SUPPORT PERSONNEL

Laura Paul (Legal Assistant)
Shaylin Buhrle (Legal Assistant)
Angela Stone (Legal Assistant)
Juan Loya (Legal Assistant)
Therse Quetone (Legal Assistant)

For full biographical listings, see the Martindale-Hubbell Law Directory

MADISON, HARBOUR, MROZ & BRENNAN, P.A. (AV)

Suite 1800 Albuquerque Plaza, 201 Third Street, N.W., P.O. Box 25467, 87102
Telephone: 505-242-2177
Fax: 505-242-7184
URL: http://www.madisonlaw.com
Santa Fe, New Mexico Office: Coronado Building, 2nd Floor, 141 East Palace Avenue, P.O. Box 1234.
Telephone: 505-992-8933.
Facsimile: 505-988-2987.

William C. Madison
Michael W. Brennan
Michael H. Harbour
Robert J. Mroz
Neils L. Thompson
M. Eliza Stewart
Lorri Krehbiel
Gregory D. Steinman

Michael Joseph Dekleva
Michele U. Estrada
Scott E. Turner
Shannon A. Parden
Corey A. Goldsand
Jude A. Cisneros

For full biographical listings, see the Martindale-Hubbell Law Directory

RODEY, DICKASON, SLOAN, AKIN & ROBB, P.A. (AV)

Albuquerque Plaza, Suite 2200, 201 Third Street, N.W., P.O. Box 1888, 87103-1888
Telephone: 505-765-5900
Fax: 505-768-7395
Email: info@rodey.com *URL:* http://www.rodey.com
Santa Fe, New Mexico Office: Suite 101 Marcy Plaza, 123 East Marcy Street, P.O. Box 1357, 87504-1357.
Telephone: 505-984-0100.
Fax: 505-989-9542.

(See Next Column)

Joseph J. Mullins
Robert G. McCorkle
Bruce Hall
W. Robert Lasater, Jr.
Mark C. Meiering
Travis R. Collier
W. Mark Mowery (Resident, Santa Fe Office)
Patrick M. Shay
Ellen T. Skrak
Tracy McGee Jenks
Charles K. Purcell
Andrew G. Schultz
Scott D. Gordon
Susan S. Throckmorton
Theresa W. Parrish
MacDonnell Gordon (Resident, Santa Fe Office)

Paul C. Collins
Deborah E. Mann
Lisa A. Chavez

For Complete List of Firm Personnel, See General Section

For full biographical listings, see the Martindale-Hubbell Law Directory

SIMONE, ROBERTS & WEISS, P.A. (AV)

8102 Menaul Boulevard N.E., 87110
Telephone: 505-298-9400
Fax: 505-298-7070

Stephen M. Simone
Randal W. Roberts
Norman F. Weiss
Michelle Lalley Blake
Thomas E. Perkins
Ashley Gauthier
Megan Day Hill

Representative Clients: Allstate Insurance Co.; Guaranty National Insurance Co.; State Farm Fire and Casualty Co.; State of New Mexico, Risk Management; Liberty Mutual Insurance Company; State Farm Mutual Auto.
Reference: Nationsbank.

For full biographical listings, see the Martindale-Hubbell Law Directory

*LAS CRUCES,** Dona Ana Co.

SANDENAW, CARRILLO & PIAZZA, P.C. (AV)

2951 Roadrunner Parkway, Suite A, 88011
Telephone: 505-522-7500
Fax: 505-522-5544
URL: http://www.lawyers.com/insurancedefenselaw

SHAREHOLDERS

Thomas A. Sandenaw, Jr.
Leonard J. Piazza
Raúl A. Carrillo, Jr.

Carlos M. Quiñones

OF COUNSEL

James T. Martin

For full biographical listings, see the Martindale-Hubbell Law Directory

*ROSWELL,** Chaves Co.

ATWOOD, MALONE, TURNER & SABIN, A PROFESSIONAL ASSOCIATION (AV)

400 North Pennsylvania Avenue Suite 1100, P.O. Drawer 700, 88202-0700
Telephone: 505-622-6221
Fax: 505-624-2883
Email: atwood@nm.net
Albuquerque, New Mexico Office: 500 Marquette N.W., Suite 750, P.O. Box 20.
Telephone: 505-842-5715.
Fax: 505-842-5713.

Jefferson Davis Atwood (1883-1960)
Ross L. Malone (1910-1974)
Robert E. Sabin (Resident)
Steven Lynn Bell (Resident)
Rod M. Schumacher (Resident)
John S. Nelson (Resident)
Lee M. Rogers, Jr. (Resident)
Timothy A. Lucas (Resident)
Victoria Davis Armstrong (Resident)
Remo E. Gay (Resident, Albuquerque Office)
Bryan Evans (Resident)
Timothy L. White (Resident, Albuquerque Office)
Barbara A. Reddy (Resident)

David J. Jaramillo (Resident, Albuquerque Office)
Bryon R. Hammer

OF COUNSEL

Charles F. Malone (1923-1999)
Bob F. Turner (Resident)

Representative Clients: Columbia Medical Center of Carlsbad (formerly Guadalupe Medical Center); Columbia Lea Regional Medical Center (formerly Lea Regional Hospital); American Continental Ins. Co. a subsidiary of MMI; Health Care Indemnity, Inc.; Medical Protection Company; Eastern New Mexico Medical Center; New Mexico Physicians Insurance Services; Mountain States Mutual Casualty Co.

For full biographical listings, see the Martindale-Hubbell Law Directory

NEW YORK

*ALBANY,** Albany Co.

FEATHERSTONHAUGH, CONWAY, WILEY & CLYNE, L.L.P. (AV)

99 Pine Street, Suite 207, 12207
Telephone: 518-436-0786
Fax: 518-427-0452
URL: http://www.fcwc-law.com

MEMBERS OF FIRM

James D. Featherstonhaugh
Thomas A. Conway
Stephen J. Wiley
Elizabeth K. Clyne

ASSOCIATES

Nadine Feiden Shadlock
Denis R. Hurley, Jr.
Andrew W. Kirby
William F. Conway, IV
Gerard L. Conway, Jr.
Steven M. Connolly

OF COUNSEL

William F. Conway
Jeffrey J. Conklin
David Weinraub
Randall J. Ezick

LEGAL SUPPORT PERSONNEL
GOVERNMENTAL RELATIONS

John L. Hardy
Daniel G. Plummer
John P. Griffin
David F. Fleming

For full biographical listings, see the Martindale-Hubbell Law Directory

HARVEY AND MUMFORD (AV)

20 Corporate Woods Boulevard, 12211-2396
Telephone: 518-463-4491
Telecopier: 518-463-5665
Email: thefirm@harveyandmumford.com

Arthur J. Harvey (1903-1986)

MEMBERS OF FIRM

Jonathan P. Harvey
Brian F. Mumford

ASSOCIATES

Eva Lynn M. Hayko
Karen Hendricks
Peter Baird Joslin, Jr.
Trudy L. Boulia
Keith J. Starlin

OF COUNSEL

Jack D. Harvey

For full biographical listings, see the Martindale-Hubbell Law Directory

MAYNARD, O'CONNOR, SMITH & CATALINOTTO, LLP (AV)

Seventh Floor, 80 State Street, 12207
Telephone: 518-465-3553
Fax: 518-465-5845
Saugerties, New York Office: Route 9W, P.O. Box 180.
Telephone: 914-246-3666.
Fax: 914-246-0390.

MEMBERS OF FIRM

William C. Maynard (1883-1972)
Gerald W. O'Connor (1896-1965)
J. Vincent Smith (1916-1991)
Michael E. Catalinotto
Stephen C. Prudente
Christopher K.H. Dressler
Thomas G. Daley
James R. Schultz
Bruce A. Bell
Concetta R. Lomanto
Edwin J. Tobin, Jr.

ASSOCIATES

Michael E. Catalinotto, Jr.
Robert A. Rausch
Teresa M. Morrisey
Aaron M. Baldwin
Laurel L. Bohl

OF COUNSEL

Earl S. Jones, Jr.

Local Counsel for: Utica Mutual Insurance Co.; General Motors; Medical Liability Mutual Insurance; Metropolitan Insurance Co.

For full biographical listings, see the Martindale-Hubbell Law Directory

O'CONNOR, O'CONNOR, MAYBERGER & FIRST, P.C. (AV)

20 Corporate Woods Boulevard, 12211-0400
Telephone: 518-465-0400
Facsimile: 518-465-0015
Email: info@1stlaw.com *URL:* http://www.1stlaw.com

Michael J. O'Connor
Terence P. O'Connor
Dianne Bresee Mayberger
Dennis A. First
Michele M. Monserrate
Cynthia Ann Platt

Justin O. Corcoran
Michael P. Cavanagh
Christopher D. Drake
Eugene N. Sarfoh
Francis J. Brennan
Colleen D. Galligan

For full biographical listings, see the Martindale-Hubbell Law Directory

POWERS & SANTOLA (AV)

39 N. Pearl Street, Suite 2, 12207-2785
Telephone: 518-465-5995; 1-800-540-8742
Fax: 518-426-4012
Email: jpowers@powers-santola.com *URL:* http://www.powers-santola.com

John K. Powers
Daniel R. Santola

ASSOCIATES

Timothy J. Higgins
John H. Fisher
Paul Berne Sherr

TABNER, RYAN AND KENIRY (AV)

26 Computer Drive West, P.O. Box 12605, 12212-2605
Telephone: 518-459-9000
Telecopier: 518-459-9165
Email: trk@tabnerryanandkeniry.com

MEMBERS OF FIRM

John W. Tabner
William F. Ryan, Jr.
William J. Keniry

OF COUNSEL

C. Theodore Carlson

ASSOCIATES

Eric N. Dratler
Jennifer K. Corona
Donald W. Biggs

Special Counsel for: Water and Sewer District for Towns of Colonie, Coxsackie, Guilderland, Johnstown, Queensbury, Rotterdam and Village Castleton.
References: FleetBank; Trustco Bank.

For full biographical listings, see the Martindale-Hubbell Law Directory

THORN AND GERSHON, LLP (AV)

5 Wembley Court, New Karner Road, P.O. Box 15054, 12212-5054
Telephone: 518-464-6770
Fax: 518-464-6778

MEMBERS OF FIRM

Richard M. Gershon
Arthur H. Thorn
Jeffrey J. Tymann
Maureen Sullivan Bonanni
Noreen J. Van Doren
Nancy Nicholson Bogan
Sheila Toborg

ASSOCIATES

Paul D. Jureller
Kristen H. Martin
William M. Hoblock
Kyle N. Kordich
Jennifer H. Goody

OF COUNSEL

Robert F. Doran

For full biographical listings, see the Martindale-Hubbell Law Directory

*BINGHAMTON,** Broome Co.

ASWAD & INGRAHAM (AV)

46 Front Street, 13905
Telephone: 607-722-3495
Fax: 607-722-2566; 607-722-7269
Email: office@AILAW.COM

MEMBERS OF FIRM

Richard N. Aswad
Charles O. Ingraham
Thomas A. Saitta
James F. Haley, Jr.
Angelina C. Cutrona
William M. Thomas

SPECIAL COUNSEL

James F. Moran

ASSOCIATE

Jeffrey Husisian

Reference: Charter One Bank.

For full biographical listings, see the Martindale-Hubbell Law Directory

O'CONNOR, GACIOCH, POPE & TAIT, L.L.P. (AV)

One Marine Midland Plaza, East Tower-Seventh Floor, P.O. Box 1964, 13902
Telephone: 607-772-9262
Fax: 607-724-6002
Email: ogplaw@compuserve.com

Thomas F. O'Connor
James C. Gacioch
Alan J. Pope
Jeffrey A. Tait
Hugh B. Leonard
Robert N. Nielsen, Jr.
Stephen B. Atkinson
Kurt D. Schrader
Richard M. Hill
Patricia A. Cummings
Robert C. Murphy

OF COUNSEL

Walter T. Gorman
Cheryl Insinga

For full biographical listings, see the Martindale-Hubbell Law Directory

*BRONX,** Bronx Co.

MAXWELL S. PFEIFER (AV)

714 East 241st Street, 10470
Telephone: 718-325-5000
Fax: 718-324-0333
Email: mspfeifer@aol.com
New York, New York Office: 18 East 50th Street, 7th Floor, 10022.
Telephone: 212-980-0777.
Fax: 718-324-0333.
Hallandale, Florida Office: 1920 East Hallandale Beach Boulevard, Suite 606.
Telephone: 954-454-1550.

ASSOCIATES

Steven E. Millon
Robert S. Summer

OF COUNSEL

Sandra Krevitsky Janin
Anthony J. Hatab
Hon. Alexander A. Delle Cese (1919-1997)

For full biographical listings, see the Martindale-Hubbell Law Directory

*BROOKLYN,** Kings Co.

BONINA & BONINA, P.C. (AV)

Suite 1608, 16 Court Street, 11241
Telephone: 718-522-1786
888-MEDLAW-1
Fax: 718-243-0414
URL: http://www.medlaw1.com

John Anthony Bonina
John Bonina, III
Elizabeth Bonina
Andrea E. Bonina

Deborah A. Trerotola
Tyrone Sergio
Amy L. Insler

LEGAL SUPPORT PERSONNEL

Pedro Cintron
Inez M. Diaz
Sandra Ferrari

Reference: Republic Bank of New York.

For full biographical listings, see the Martindale-Hubbell Law Directory

*BUFFALO,** Erie Co.

FELDMAN, KIEFFER & HERMAN, LLP (AV)

110 Pearl Street, Suite 400, 14202
Telephone: 716-852-5875
Fax: 716-852-4253
Email: info@fkhattys.com *URL:* http://www.fkhattys.com

PRINCIPALS OF THE FIRM

Andrew Feldman
James M. Kieffer
Ann W. Herman
Mark F. Scarcello
Gordon D. Tresch
Mary Jo Herrscher

For full biographical listings, see the Martindale-Hubbell Law Directory

O'SHEA, REYNOLDS & CUMMINGS (AV)

237 Main Street, Suite 500, 14203
Telephone: 716-853-6341-2-3
Fax: 716-852-3880
Email: info@oshea-reynolds.com

MEMBERS OF FIRM

Frank Gibbons (1869-1953)
Henry W. Pottle (1872-1943)
Willard M. Pottle (1901-1967)
Philip J. O'Shea (1909-1984)
William S. Reynolds
C. DeForest Cummings, Jr.
David M. Stillwell
Gerard E. O'Connor
William A. Long, Jr.
Nelson E. Schule, Jr.

ASSOCIATES

Kevin D. Cox
Nicole A. Heary

Local Attorneys for: Amica Mutual Insurance Co.; Continental National American Group; Nationwide Mutual Insurance Co.; The Continental Insurance Cos.
Reference: Key Bank.

For full biographical listings, see the Martindale-Hubbell Law Directory

ROACH, BROWN, McCARTHY & GRUBER, P.C. (AV)

1620 Liberty Building, 420 Main Street, 14202-3511
Telephone: 716-852-0400
Fax: 716-852-2535
Email: roachbrown@roachbrown.com

(See Next Column)

Daniel T. Roach
Edmund S. Brown, Jr.
T. Alan Brown
Joseph V. McCarthy
J. Mark Gruber
Mary J. Murray
John P. Danieu
Elizabeth G. Redmond
Gregory T. Miller
Teresa C. Brophy Bair
Jason A. Botticelli
Jennifer L. Noah
Joel J. Java, Jr.

OF COUNSEL

Arthur J. Maloney
John Y. Gallup

Local Attorneys for: American International Group; Chubb Group of Insurance Co.; Healthcare Underwriters Mutual Insurance Co.; Peter J. McBreen and Associates; Frontier Insurance Co.; Medical Liability Mutual Insurance Co.; Medical Malpractice Insurance Assn.; Merrill Dow; Reliance Insurance Group; Travelers Group.

For full biographical listings, see the Martindale-Hubbell Law Directory

ROSENTHAL, SIEGEL, MUENKEL & MALONEY, LLP (AV)

300 Main Street, 14202
Telephone: 716-854-1300
Fax: 716-842-6354
Email: rsm300@aol.com
Amherst, New York Office: Evanstown Plaza, 392 Evans Street.
Telephone: 716-634-8720.

MEMBERS OF FIRM

Jay N. Rosenthal
David Alan Siegel
Joseph P. Muenkel
Patrick J. Maloney

ASSOCIATES

Linda M. DiPasquale
David E. Rosenthal
Gina M. Guzman
Paul F. Murak

OF COUNSEL

J. Michael Wolf

LEGAL SUPPORT PERSONNEL

Patricia E. Lipka
Lois M. Cropp

For full biographical listings, see the Martindale-Hubbell Law Directory

GARDEN CITY, Nassau Co.

MONTFORT, HEALY, McGUIRE & SALLEY (AV)

1140 Franklin Avenue, 11530
Telephone: 516-747-4082
Telecopier: 516-746-0748

MEMBERS OF FIRM

E. Richard Rimmels, Jr. (1930-1999)
Frank J. Cafaro
Philip J. Catapano
Fredric C. Montfort
Donald S. Neumann, Jr.
James J. Keefe, Jr.
Michael A. Baranowicz
James Michael Murphy

OF COUNSEL

Fredric H. Montfort
Edward M. Salley, Jr.
David J. Fleming
Robert J. Mettalia

ASSOCIATES

Claudia C. Glacken
Marcie K. Glasser
Bruce A. Cook
Jeffrey D. Present
Joan E. Resnik
Susan H. Dempsey
Camille L. Hansen
Christopher T. Cafaro
Kathleen Dumont
Jeffrey B. Siler
Michael G. Kruzynski
Karen J. Cooper

For full biographical listings, see the Martindale-Hubbell Law Directory

SAWYER, DAVIS, HALPERN & DEMETRI (AV)

600 Old Country Road, 11530
Telephone: 516-222-4567
Telecopier: 516-222-4585
Email: litlaw@aol.com

MEMBER OF FIRM

James Sawyer

For full biographical listings, see the Martindale-Hubbell Law Directory

*ITHACA,** Tompkins Co.

WIGGINS AND MASSON, LLP (AV)

308 North Tioga Street, P.O. Box 399, 14851
Telephone: 607-272-0479
Telecopier: 607-273-0502
Email: law@wigginsandmasson.com *URL:* http://www.wigginsandmasson.com

MEMBERS OF FIRM

Walter J. Wiggins
Robin Abrahamson Masson
Erin E. McKinley

Approved Attorneys for: Ticor Title Guaranty Corp.
References: Tompkins County Trust Co.

(See Next Column)

WIGGINS AND MASSON LLP, *Ithaca—Continued*

For Complete List of Firm Personnel, See General Section

For full biographical listings, see the Martindale-Hubbell Law Directory

LAKE SUCCESS, Nassau Co.

IVONE, DEVINE & JENSEN, LLP (AV)

2001 Marcus Avenue, Suite N100, 11042
Telephone: 516-326-2400
Telecopier: 516-352-4952
Email: idjlaw@aol.com *URL:* http://www.lawyers.com/idjlaw

MEMBERS OF FIRM

Michael T. Ivone
Robert Devine
Richard C. Jensen
Brian E. Lee
Michael Ferguson

ASSOCIATES

Debora G. Nobel
Ellin M. Regis
Jonathan Rubin
Veronica Henry
Patrick G. Toner
Keith C. Jewell

For full biographical listings, see the Martindale-Hubbell Law Directory

MELVILLE, Suffolk Co.

ABBATE, LAWRENCE & WORDEN, P.C. (AV)

425 Broad Hollow Road, Suite 120, 11747
Telephone: 516-694-0033
Fax: 516-694-9331

John J. Abbate
Roger B. Lawrence
Robert P. Worden, Jr.

James L. Martell
Matthew Rainis
Kathleen Fugelsang
Margaret Herrmann
Jonathan F. Banks
Maria Zouros
MaryBeth Cameron

For full biographical listings, see the Martindale-Hubbell Law Directory

GANDIN, SCHOTSKY, RAPPAPORT, GLASS & GREENE, LLP (AV)

445 Broad Hollow Road, 11747
Telephone: 516-293-2300
Fax: 516-293-2918
Email: gsrmail@gsrlaw.com *URL:* http://www.gsrlaw.com
New York, N.Y. Office: 1212 Avenue of the Americas, 10036.
Telephone: 212-921-5200.
Fax: 212-921-5367.

PARTNERS

Charles J. Rappaport
Arnold M. Schotsky
Michael R. Greene
Michael G. Glass
Kevin E. Balfe
Michael S. Levine

ASSOCIATES

Margery Weinroth
Jonathan H. Freiberger
Brian Robert Gunn
Karen S. Bennett
Kenneth J. Lauri
Matthew J. Zullo
Diane G. Holland
James L. Forde

OF COUNSEL

Michael I. Gandin
Edward Kiley
Charles Krupin

For full biographical listings, see the Martindale-Hubbell Law Directory

MILLBROOK, Dutchess Co.

WILLIAM E. STANTON (AV)

Merritt Avenue and Elm Drive, P.O. Box 1252, 12545
Telephone: 914-677-9060
FAX: 914-677-9392
Stanfordville, New York Office: Bulls Head Road, 12581.
Telephone: 914-868-7514.
Fax: 914-868-7761.

Representative Clients: Dupont de Nemours & Co.; Millbrook School; New York Telephone Co.
Reference: Pawling Savings Bank.

For full biographical listings, see the Martindale-Hubbell Law Directory

*MINEOLA,** Nassau Co.

BARTLETT, MCDONOUGH, BASTONE & MONAGHAN, LLP (AV)

300 Old Country Road Suite 301, 11501
Telephone: 516-877-2900
Fax: 516-877-0732
Email: bmbmlaw@mail.idt.net
New York, New York Office: 237 Park Avenue, 10017.
Telephone: 212-983-2900.
Fax: 212-983-2901.
White Plains, New York Office: 81 Main Street, 4th Floor. 10601.
Telephone: 914-448-0200.
Fax: 914-448-0215.

(See Next Column)

MEMBERS OF FIRM

Clifford A. Bartlett, Jr.
Frank Bastone, Jr.
Peter G. Monaghan
Betty L. Atlas
Anthony F. Barbiero
Kenneth J. Burford
Richard W. Derry
Robert F. Elliott
Alan B. Friedberg
Edward J. Guardaro, Jr.
E. Gordon Haesloop
Sylvere M. Hyacinthe
Maureen C. Lavin
Garrett P. Lewis
Kenneth R. Reiser
F. Sean Rooney
Scott A. Singer
Alfred P. Vigorito
Janet C. Winter

OF COUNSEL

J. Edward McDonough

ASSOCIATES

John R. Aquaro
Peter E. Berman
Gina Bernardi
Robert J. Betz
Barbara A. Dalton
Deborah A. Dyckman
James C. Freeman
Jennine A. Gerrard
Steven S. Horowitz
Laura B. Jordan
John S. Kanzler
Belinda I. Katz
David G. Kelton
Peter A. Kolbert
Grace C. McCallen
Neil C. Mascolo, Jr.
Kevin R. Natale
Susan J. Onorato
John P. O'Sullivan
Warren J. Roth
Clare Salamida
Michael S. Sawaya
Tina Scognamillo
Milan P. Spisek
Christopher A. Terzian
Paul R. Varriale

For full biographical listings, see the Martindale-Hubbell Law Directory

DUBOIS BILLIG LOUGHLIN CONATY & WEISMAN (AV)

1501 Franklin Avenue, 11501
Telephone: 516-877-1808
Rock Hill, New York Office: 195 Lake Louise Marie Road, 12775.
Telephone: 914-796-2187.
Fax: 914-796-1506.
White Plains, New York Office: One North Lexington Avenue, 10601.
Telephone: 914-682-1700.

MEMBERS OF FIRM

Maribeth Slevin
Edward J. Arevalo
Debra A. Demarchena
Belinda Dawn Dodds-Marshall
Charles K. Faillace
Jeffrey C. Gerson
Paul S. Gruvman
Patricia Hart Nessler
Jane Holden
Rosemary E. Martinson
Harriet E. McDonnell
John Peter Reitano
Amy E. Strang
Richard J. Valent
Ellen F. Weisman

For full biographical listings, see the Martindale-Hubbell Law Directory

GALLAGHER, WALKER, BIANCO & PLASTARAS (AV)

98 Willis Avenue, 11501
Telephone: 516-248-2002
Fax: 516-248-2394

Gerard M. Gallagher
Robert J. Walker
Dominic P. Bianco
Thomas E. Plastaras

ASSOCIATES

Ann Willoughby
William P. Nolan

OF COUNSEL

Stephen P. Burke

For full biographical listings, see the Martindale-Hubbell Law Directory

SHAYNE, DACHS, STANISCI, CORKER & SAUER (AV)

250 Old Country Road, 11501
Telephone: 516-747-1100
Telecopier: 516-747-1185

MEMBERS OF FIRM

Moe Levine (1908-1974)
Neil T. Shayne (1932-1998)
Norman H. Dachs
W. Russell Corker
Brian J. Sauer
Kenneth J. Landau
Jonathan A. Dachs

Naomi R. Nathan

For full biographical listings, see the Martindale-Hubbell Law Directory

*NEW YORK,** New York Co.

WALTER G. ALTON, JR. & ASSOCIATES, P.C. (AV)

108 East 82nd Street, 10028
Telephone: 212-639-9646
Fax: 212-249-7482
URL: http://www.lawyers.com/walteralton
Email: walteralton@earthlink.net *URL:* http://home.earthlink.net/~walteralton/
Cherry Plain, New York Office: P.O. Box 60.
Telephone: 518-658-2060.
Fax: 518-658-2060.

(See Next Column)

WALTER G. ALTON, JR. & ASSOCIATES, P.C.—*Continued*

Walter G. Alton, Jr

For full biographical listings, see the Martindale-Hubbell Law Directory

BAUMEISTER & SAMUELS, P.C. (AV)

One Exchange Plaza, 10006-3008
Telephone: 212-363-1200
Telecopier: 212-363-1346
Email: BAUMSAM@AOL.COM
Morristown, New Jersey Office: 1776 On The Green, P.O. Box 1116, 07962-1116.
Telephone: 973-267-6666.
Telecopier: 973-605-1812.

Michel F. Baumeister
Douglas A. Latto
Dorothea M. Capone

OF COUNSEL

Lynn F. Samuels
Robert S. Franklin
Marc Z. Edell

For full biographical listings, see the Martindale-Hubbell Law Directory

BELAIR & EVANS LLP (AV)

61 Broadway Suite 1320, 10006
Telephone: 212-344-3900
Facsimile: 212-514-6661
Cable Address: "Caduceus" New York
Telex: 226000
URL: http://www.belairevans.com
Mineola, New York Office: 136 Willis Avenue.
Telephone: 516-741-4800.

MEMBERS OF FIRM

Raymond W. Belair
John T. Evans
Lawrence W. Burnett
Brian P. Flynn

Jacqueline E. Sheehan-Hemmingson
Robert Radman
Andrew R. Leder
Michael J. Gudzy
Matthew J. Ross
James B. Reich
Robert L. Kerner, Jr.
Michael A. Swimmer
Randall M. Elfenbein
Brian T. Stapleton
Kevin E. Way

For full biographical listings, see the Martindale-Hubbell Law Directory

CALLAN, REGENSTREICH, KOSTER & BRADY (AV)

One Whitehall Street 10th Floor, 10004
Telephone: 212-248-8800
Fax: 212-248-6815
Shrewsbury, New Jersey Office: 740 Broad Street.
Telephone: 732-345-9333.
Fax: 732-345-9444.
Garden City, New York Office: 1205 Franklin Avenue.
Telephone: 516-294-4383.
Fax: 516-294-4386.

MEMBERS OF FIRM

Paul F. Callan
Bruce N. Regenstreich
Warren S. Koster
Bruce M. Brady
William L. Brennan
Vincent A. Nagler
Scott W. Bermack

ASSOCIATES

Kenneth S. Merber
Michael P. Kandler
Vincent D. Finnegan
Stephanie Palermo
Walter Paterson Burrell
Beth S. Block
Meredith B. Borg
Pamela Patton Fynes
Mara J. Sibley
Eric A. Wasserfall
Amie Catherine Kalac (Resident, Shrewsbury, New Jersey Office)
Lisa B. Katz

For full biographical listings, see the Martindale-Hubbell Law Directory

BRUCE G. CLARK & ASSOCIATES (AV)

Room 3600 Woolworth Building, 233 Broadway, 10279
Telephone: 212-227-0020
Fax: 212-233-4247
URL: http://www.medicalmallaw.com
Email: brucegclark@compuserve.com *URL:* http://www.lawyers.com/medmal

Peter L. Gale
Valerie Ullman Taylor
Rhona A. Silverman
Beth Nancy Alson

For full biographical listings, see the Martindale-Hubbell Law Directory

DE BLASIO, FIGMAN, EPSTEIN & LA ROCCA, P.C. (AV)

Woolworth Building, 233 Broadway, 10279
Telephone: 212-732-2620
Fax: 212-571-2045

(See Next Column)

Peter E. De Blasio
Alan H. Figman
Steven A. Epstein
Stephen S. La Rocca
John A. Orbon

For full biographical listings, see the Martindale-Hubbell Law Directory

FRIEDMAN, LEVY & GOLDFARB, P.C. (AV)

250 West 57th Street Suite 1619, 10107
Telephone: 212-307-5800
Telefax: 212-262-6128
Email: info@flgpclaw.com

Robert A. Levy
Ira H. Goldfarb

Nora McCarthy
Jeffrey I. Weiner
Stephen A. Saltzman

OF COUNSEL

Michael A. Gallo
Stephen A. Geffner

For full biographical listings, see the Martindale-Hubbell Law Directory

FUCHSBERG & FUCHSBERG (AV)

100 Church Street, 18th Floor, 10007
Telephone: 212-962-2800
Fax: 212-385-2308

MEMBERS OF FIRM

Abraham Fuchsberg
Seymour Fuchsberg
Preston J. Douglas
Stephen M. Warner

Harvey Goldstein
Irwin M. Berg
Bruce H. Goldstone
Martin Diennor
Maurice Sieradzki
Mordecai T. Schwartz
Frank P. Nervo
Richard Cohen
Iris Claire Finder
Thomas A. Agoglia
Robert M. Futterman
Richard V. Zand
John C. Henninger
Roger N. Lavinsky
Joseph Campisi
Devin P. Cohen
David Jacobs
Alan D. Bernstein
Ari Michael Gross

For full biographical listings, see the Martindale-Hubbell Law Directory

THE JACOB D. FUCHSBERG LAW FIRM (AV)

500 Fifth Avenue, 10110-0393
Telephone: 212-869-3500
Fax: 212-398-1532
Email: Fuchsberg@aol.com *URL:* http://www.Fuchsberg.com

MEMBERS OF FIRM

Jacob D. Fuchsberg (1913-1995)
Rosalind Fuchsberg Kaufman
Alan L. Fuchsberg

OF COUNSEL

Melvin C. Hartman
Mark Glen Sokoloff
S. Stanley Kreutzer
Daniel M. Cohen

SPECIAL COUNSEL

Abraham Abramovsky

ASSOCIATES

Andrew J. Carboy
Bruce Robert Calderon

For full biographical listings, see the Martindale-Hubbell Law Directory

GARBARINI & SCHER, P.C. (AV)

1114 Avenue of the Americas, 10036-7790
Telephone: 212-764-4000
Tele-fax: 212-719-5018
Hackensack, New Jersey Office: 25 Main Street, Suite 600, 07601-7025.
Telephone: 201-343-2002.
Fax: 201-342-0612.

Stanley J. Scher
Leonard Weinstock
Myrna A. Levinson
George J. Kehayas
Michael Caliguiri
William G. Scher
Paul M. Paley
James W. Kachadoorian
Gregg D. Weinstock
Kurt Lee Weinmann

Barry M. Ruderman
Barry Rothman
Nancy Breslow
Mary Ann Candelario
Marilyn C. Daignault
Yuval D. Bar-Kokhba
Lori E. Katz
Thomas M. Cooper
Michael Milchan
Christine E. Fernandez
Karen Nourizadeh
Michael Young

Representative Clients: American Home Assurance Co.; The Archdiocese of New York; Chubb & Son, Inc; Crum & Forster; Marriott Corp.; St. Barnabas Hospital; Travelers Insurance Co.; Lloyds of London and British Cos.; McDonald's Corp.; Allstate Insurance Co.

For full biographical listings, see the Martindale-Hubbell Law Directory

New York—Continued

GARSON GERSPACH DECORATO & COHEN, LLP (AV)

One Whitehall Street, Tenth Floor, 10004
Telephone: 212-742-8700
Fax: 212-742-1471
Email: ASGGGDC@aol.com *URL:* http://www.MEDILAW@aol.com

Andrew S. Garson — Linda J. DeCorato
Thomas J. Gerspach — Joshua R. Cohen

For full biographical listings, see the Martindale-Hubbell Law Directory

GINSBERG & BROOME (AV)

225 Broadway, Suite 3105, 10007
Telephone: 212-227-4225
Fax: 212-227-4228

Robert M. Ginsberg — Alvin H. Broome

ASSOCIATE

Christopher Jon Longman

OF COUNSEL

Jody H. Brackman — Anna Lewis
Simon Ginsberg

For full biographical listings, see the Martindale-Hubbell Law Directory

LAW OFFICES OF DAVID B. GOLOMB (AV)

Suite 527, 230 Park Avenue, 10169
Telephone: 212-661-9000
Telecopier: 212-661-6181
Email: golomblaw@aol.com

ASSOCIATE

Frank A. Longo

For full biographical listings, see the Martindale-Hubbell Law Directory

HARLEY & BROWNE (AV)

18 East 41st Street, 10017
Telephone: 212-545-7900
Email: harleybrowne@worldnet.att.net

MEMBERS OF FIRM

J. Austin Browne — Robert G. Harley

ASSOCIATES

Bradley S. Zimmerman — Enid O-Donnell Joseph
Danielle George

OF COUNSEL

Emily K. Harley — Bridget Asaro

Reference: Citibank.

For full biographical listings, see the Martindale-Hubbell Law Directory

HEIDELL, PITTONI, MURPHY & BACH, LLP (AV)

99 Park Avenue, 10016
Telephone: 212-286-8585
Telecopier: 212-490-8966
Email: hpmb@hpmb.com
Stamford, Connecticut Office: 24 Richmond Hill Avenue.
Telephone: 203-327-1800. Email: hpmb@hpbm.com

Luke M. Pittoni — Michael D. Shalhoub
Raymond W. Murphy — Stephen R. Marshall
Charles L. Bach, Jr. — Louise A. Derevlany
Rosary A. Morelli — John F. Costa
Bruce F. Gilpatrick — E. Marc Hyman
Robin R. Dolsky — Cheryl A. Harris
Elizabeth Cornacchio — John J. Murphy, Jr.
Austa S. Devlin — Terrence P. St. John
Daniel S. Ratner

OF COUNSEL

Robert C. Heidell

Linda M. Ruma — Paul Sean Curtin
Janice Kirsten Lunde — Lori Wallace-Fischler
Geraldine Koeneke Russell — Ronit Rubin
Carol L. Morris-Fox — Joseph A. Sack
Raphael J. Berman — Karen T. Grottalio
Michael S. Coulston — Tonya M Lindsey
Daniel Newman — Harold Clement Baker, III
Sandra Erica Ann Dwyer — Suzanne R. Byrne
Matthew S. Hirsch — Daryl Paxson
Elizabeth D. Stuart — Ellen Griffel
Holly Anne Brown — Fern H Block
Anne Margaret Bracken — Andrea L. Crawford
Stacey L. Mahdavian — William A. Elder
Robert W. Finke — Arthur J. Robb
Tracey J. Knuckles — Leah J. Terranova
Theresann J. Potter — (Not admitted in NY)

(See Next Column)

Bill P. Chimos — David N. Esterman
Amgad Michael Sabongui — Danielle L. Sullivan
Russell S. Jamison

For full biographical listings, see the Martindale-Hubbell Law Directory

JULIEN & SCHLESINGER, P.C. (AV)

150 William Street, 19th Floor, 10038
Telephone: 212-962-8020

Alfred S. Julien (1910-1989) — Stuart A. Schlesinger

Mary Elizabeth Burns — Marla L. Stein
Richard A. Robbins — Adam Schlesinger
Michael J. Taub — Michael S. Schlesinger

For full biographical listings, see the Martindale-Hubbell Law Directory

KRAMER, DILLOF, TESSEL, DUFFY & MOORE (AV)

233 Broadway, 45th Floor, 10279-0137
Telephone: 212-267-4177
Fax: 212-233-8525
Email: kdtdm@compuserve.com

Charles Kramer (1916-1988) — Judith A. Livingston
Thomas A. Moore — Thomas J. Principe
James R. Duffy — Matthew Gaier

ASSOCIATES

Andrew S. Targum — Carmine Rubino
William T. Burdo — Anthony DiPietro

OF COUNSEL

Norman Bard — Stanley Tessel
Henry H. Dillof — William R. Dillof

For full biographical listings, see the Martindale-Hubbell Law Directory

KREINDLER & KREINDLER (AV)

100 Park Avenue, 10017
Telephone: 212-687-8181
Telecopier: 212-972-9432
Email: legal@kreindler.com *URL:* http://www.kreindler.com

MEMBERS OF FIRM

Harry E. Kreindler (1896-1983) — James P. Kreindler
Lee S. Kreindler — David C. Cook
Marc S. Moller — David Beekman
Francis G. Fleming, Jr. — Blanca I. Rodriguez
Steven R. Pounian — Noah H. Kushlefsky
Robert J. Spragg

OF COUNSEL

Paul S. Edelman — Milton G. Sincoff
Henry A. Gluckstern

ASSOCIATES

Lori B. Lasson — David G. Nanz
Susan Friery (Not admitted in NY) — Justin Timothy Green
Daniel O. Rose
Andrew J. Maloney, III — Jacqueline M. James
Brian J. Alexander — Victoria J. Maniatis

For full biographical listings, see the Martindale-Hubbell Law Directory

LEAHEY & JOHNSON, P.C. (AV)

Suite 2220, 120 Wall Street, 10005
Telephone: 212-269-7308
Facsimile: 212-422-4751
Email: Leaheylaw@Aol.com

Peter James Johnson — William G. Murphy
Peter James Johnson, Jr. — Kevin Brian Lynch

James P. Tenney — Nadine M. Duhamel
Steven Martin — Sharon A. Toussaint
William J. Gordon — Melissa Ann Weinberg
Christopher Delamere Clarke — Edward J. White
Vincent L. Gallo, Jr. — Daniel Michael Sullivan
Joseph Francis Ferrette — Lennon C. Edwards
Gregory Wilson — Carmen M. Vasquez
Michael Cannella — Eric L. Horn
James Gerard Mcgovern — Sean T. O'Leary (Not admitted in NY)

For full biographical listings, see the Martindale-Hubbell Law Directory

MCALOON & FRIEDMAN, P.C. (AV)

116 John Street, 10038
Telephone: 212-732-8700
Fax: 212-227-2903

(See Next Column)

McALOON & FRIEDMAN P.C.—*Continued*

Edward H. McAloon (1908-1986)
Stanley D. Friedman
Gunther H. Kilsch
Theodore B. Rosenzweig
Gary A. Greenfield
Brendan J. Lantier
Lawrence W. Mumm
Laura R. Shapiro
Lisa B. Goldstein
Thomas Medardo Oliva
Adam R. Goldsmith
Wayne M. Roth
Kenneth S. Oliver
Stephen S. York

Jennifer D. Correale
Mark Gregory Duncan
Kenneth Gordon Ellison
Ilene R. Fish
Gillian Fisher
Kenneth Fox
Evette E. Harrison
Alex Johnson
Ross Katz
Sherry Levin
Robin P. Lorell
Carolan Magnoli
Linda P. McMillan
Douglas M. Nadjari
Timothy O'Shaugnessy
Matthew Luke Prisco
Caryn Rosen
Corey Lee Wishner

LEGAL SUPPORT PERSONNEL

Robyn L. Reyes (Firm Administrator)

For full biographical listings, see the Martindale-Hubbell Law Directory

STEVEN E. NORTH, P.C. (AV)

148 East 74th Street, 10021
Telephone: 212-861-5000
Telecopier: 212-861-4055
Email: buzsen@aol.com

Steven E. North

For full biographical listings, see the Martindale-Hubbell Law Directory

PARKER & WAICHMAN (AV)

38th Floor, 233 Broadway, 10279
Telephone: 212-267-6700
URL: http://www.lawyers.com/800lawinfo
Email: INFO@800LAWINFO.COM *URL:* http://www.800lawinfo.com
Long Island Office: 111 Great Neck Road, Great Neck, N.Y. 11021-5042.
Telephone: 516-466-6500.
Newark, New Jersey Office: One Gateway Center, Suite 2500, 07102.
Telephone: 973-297-1020.

PARTNERS

Jerrold S. Parker
Herbert L. Waichman

MANAGING ATTORNEY

Fred R. Rosenthal

ASSOCIATES

Lauren J. Gould
Andres F. Alonso
David J. Broderick
John Andrew Mullan
David B. Krangle

OF COUNSEL

Bruce David Katz
Charles Silverstein
Marc Jay Bern
Benjamin Levine

For full biographical listings, see the Martindale-Hubbell Law Directory

PELTZ & WALKER (AV)

222 Broadway - 25th Floor, 10038
Telephone: 212-349-6775
Cable Address: "Dypelaw New York"
Telex: 230199 SWIFTUR ATTDPW
Telefax: (212) 227-4002
Email: Pelzwalker@aol.com

MEMBERS OF FIRM

Alexander Peltz
Paul E. Walker
Edward M. Schoenman
Miles S. Reiner
Bhalinder L. Rikhye
Jaymie L. Einhorn
Robert A. Rosenfeld

ASSOCIATES

Steven M. Silverman
L. Ruby Rey
Patrice R. McKenna
Sharon Elmaleh
Mitchel Lidowsky

OF COUNSEL

John J. O'Donnell
Edward V. Schwendemann
Jane Himelfarb

LEGAL SUPPORT PERSONNEL

PARALEGALS

Joseph Lipari
Melissa Jamison
H. Steven Ortiz
Maria D. Corvaia

For full biographical listings, see the Martindale-Hubbell Law Directory

RHEINGOLD, VALET, RHEINGOLD & SHKOLNIK, P.C. (AV)

113 East 37th Street, 10016-3042
Telephone: 212-684-1880
Fax: 212-689-8156
Email: info@rheingoldlaw.com *URL:* http://www.rheingoldlaw.com

Paul D. Rheingold
Thomas P. Valet
David B. Rheingold
Hunter J. Shkolnik
Terrence E. McCartney
Thomas P. Giuffra

Ryan S. Goldstein

For full biographical listings, see the Martindale-Hubbell Law Directory

ROSENBLUM & FILAN, L.L.C. (AV)

400 Madison Avenue, 10017
Telephone: 212-888-8001
Fax: 212-888-3331
Email: JBR@Counsel.Com
Stamford, Connecticut Office: One Landmark Square.
Telephone: 203-358-9200.
Fax: 203-358-0687.
White Plains Office: 50 Main Street.
Telephone: 914-686-6100.
Fax: 914-686-6140.

MEMBERS OF FIRM

Patrick J. Filan
James B. Rosenblum
James S. Newfield

James F. Biondo

OF COUNSEL

Theodore J. Greene

For full biographical listings, see the Martindale-Hubbell Law Directory

SCHNEIDER, KLEINICK, WEITZ, DAMASHEK & SHOOT (AV)

233 Broadway, Fifth Floor, 10279-0003
Telephone: 212-553-9000
Fax: 212-804-0820
Email: mail@lawyer1.com *URL:* http://www.lawyer1.com

Ivan S. Schneider
Arnold L. Kleinick
Harvey Weitz
Philip M. Damashek
Brian J. Shoot
Robert B. Jackson
Clifford J. Stern
Gregory J. Cannata
Keith A. Kleinick
Richard B. Ancowitz
Charles J. Nolet, Jr.
Leslie Debra Kelmachter
Louis J. Mitchell

John Kieran Daly
Jonathan S. Damashek
Thomas V. Deffina
Dawn S. DeWeil
David W. Druker
Steven Gold
Keith H. Gross
Erin K. Hurley
Judy Keenan
Paul A. Marber
Lloyd M. Roberts
Joseph S. Rosato
Derek S. Sells
Lawrence A. Wilson, II
James M. Lane
Donald D. Casale

For full biographical listings, see the Martindale-Hubbell Law Directory

SHANDELL, BLITZ, BLITZ, GLASS, BOOKSON & KERN, LLP (AV)

150 Broadway, 10038-4498
Telephone: 212-513-1300
Fax: 212-385-1916
Email: SBBGBK@aol.com

MEMBERS OF FIRM

Herman B. Glaser (1915-1994)
Richard E. Shandell
Bert A. Blitz
Arthur Blitz
Shoshana T. Bookson
Chet W. Kern

Mitchel H. Ashley
Fredrick A. Schulman

For full biographical listings, see the Martindale-Hubbell Law Directory

WHITE, FLEISCHNER & FINO (AV)

140 Broadway, 10005
Telephone: 212-487-9700
Telecopier: 212-487-9777
Email: infor@wff-law.com
Red Bank, New Jersey Office: 272 Broad Street.
Telephone: 732-530-7787.
Telecopier: 732-530-8552.

MEMBERS OF FIRM

Benjamin A. Fleischner
Paul A. Fino, Jr.

(See Next Column)

WHITE, FLEISCHNER & FINO, *New York—Continued*

ASSOCIATES

Virginia L. McGrane
Elaine N. Chou

Representative Clients: Interstate Insurance Group; Hartford Insurance Group.

For Complete List of Firm Personnel, See General Section

For full biographical listings, see the Martindale-Hubbell Law Directory

PALMYRA, Wayne Co.

FOLEY & FOLEY (AV)

235 East Main Street, P.O. Box 211, 14522
Telephone: 315-597-6611
Fax: 315-597-8920
Email: JFOLEY12@MSN.COM

MEMBERS OF FIRM

James F. Foley
Ann Firestine Foley

Reference: Marine Midland Bank (Palmyra Office).

For full biographical listings, see the Martindale-Hubbell Law Directory

PORT WASHINGTON, Nassau Co.

DAVID S. POLLACK (AV)

151 Haven Avenue, 11050
Telephone: 516-767-8888; 800-747-4940
Fax: 516-767-5194
Email: dspollack@aol.com *URL:* http://www.lawyers.com/medical_malpractice

Patricia S. Holden

For full biographical listings, see the Martindale-Hubbell Law Directory

*ROCHESTER,** Monroe Co.

FARACI & LANGE, LLP (AV)

400 Crossroads Building, Two State Street, 14614
Telephone: 716-325-5150
Toll Free: 888-325-5150
Fax: 716-325-3285
Satellite Office, Rochester, New York: IUE Local 509 Building, 1515 Lyell Avenue, 14606.
Telephone: 716-458-2800. Union Toll Free Number: 800-483-4882.
Fax: 716-458-3015.

John A. Bryant (1943-1995)
Angelo G. Faraci
Paul K. Lange
Joseph A. Regan
Stephen G. Schwarz
Vincent M. Moyer
Brian M. Zorn
Anthony A. Di Nitto
Matthew F. Belanger

ASSOCIATES

Michelle L. Callan
Carol A. Mckenna
James L. Bradley
Bradley P. Kammholz
John A. Falk
Patrick K. Russi

OF COUNSEL

Joseph S. Guadagnino

For full biographical listings, see the Martindale-Hubbell Law Directory

HALLENBECK, LASCELL, NORRIS & HELLER (AV)

A Limited Liability Partnership
One Exchange Street, 14614
Telephone: 716-423-5900
Fax: 716-423-5910
Email: HLNZ@hlnz.com

MEMBERS OF FIRM

Alfred M. Hallenbeck
David M. Lascell
Michael D. Norris
Cheryl A. Heller

COUNSEL

Robert A. Feldman
David A. Wier

Daniel P. Purcell
Meghan Mc Manus Di Pasquale
Suzanne E. Ouellette
Andrea F. Basso
Robert S. Attardo

For full biographical listings, see the Martindale-Hubbell Law Directory

*SYRACUSE,** Onondaga Co.

SMITH, SOVIK, KENDRICK & SUGNET, P.C. (AV)

250 South Clinton Street, Suite 600, 13202-1252
Telephone: 315-474-2911
Fax: 315-474-6015
URL: http://www.smithsovik.com

(See Next Column)

John Timothy Smith (1902-1964)
Nelson J. Smith (1923-1967)
Martin F. Kendrick (1917-1983)
Laurence Sovik (1904-1998)
Laurence F. Sovik
William E. Sugnet (Retired)
James A. O'Shea
James D. Lantier
Michael P. Ringwood
Peter J. Cambs
Kevin E. Hulslander
Thomas N. Kaufmann
Daniel A. Bronk
Steven W. Williams
Mary Kendrick-Gaffney
James W. Cunningham

Thomas P. Roerden
Robert P Cahalan
Denis J. Bastible
G. John Flemma
Theresa N. C. McCorry

OF COUNSEL

Gary A. Hall

For full biographical listings, see the Martindale-Hubbell Law Directory

*TROY,** Rensselaer Co.

E. STEWART JONES (AV)

28 Second Street, 12181
Telephone: 518-274-5820
Fax: 518-274-5875
Email: info@esjlaw.com

E. Stewart Jones, Jr.
W. Farley Jones
Jeffrey K. Anderson
David J. Taffany
Peter J. Moschetti, Jr.

OF COUNSEL

E. Stewart Jones
Arthur L. Rosen
Abbott H. Jones (1873-1939)
Charles W. Marshall (1882-1945)

References: Key Bank and On Bank; Troy Savings Bank.

For full biographical listings, see the Martindale-Hubbell Law Directory

*UTICA,** Oneida Co.

JULIAN & PERTZ, P.C. (AV)

1629 Oneida Street, 13501-4701
Telephone: 315-797-5610
Fax: 315-797-7403

Robert F. Julian
Richard Pertz

LEGAL SUPPORT PERSONNEL

Tracey A. Mills (Paralegal)
Barbara A. Clark (Paralegal)
Nadine J. McIntyre (Paralegal)

For full biographical listings, see the Martindale-Hubbell Law Directory

*WHITE PLAINS,** Westchester Co.

BOEGGEMAN, GEORGE, HODGES & CORDE, P.C. (AV)

11 Martine Avenue, 10606
Telephone: 914-761-2252
Telecopier: 914-761-5211
Email: boeggeman@bghc-law.com *URL:* http://www.bghc-law.com
Albany, New York Office: 46 Columbia Street, 12207-2716.
Telephone: 518-465-1100.
Fax: 518-465-1800.

George S. Hodges
Richard G. Corde
John J. Walsh, II
Harold L. Moroknek
Robert S. Ondrovic
Thomas A. Sica (Resident Managing Attorney, Albany Office)

Karen A.D. Jockimo
William M. Wingertzahn
Elizabeth C. Mirisola
Cynthia Dolan
Marcella M. Green
Paul A. Hurley
Leslie K. Arfine
John T. Holden
James J. Lofrese
Jeanne M. Hurley
Ira H. Lapp
Matt Randolph Belkin
Cynthia K. Messemer

OF COUNSEL

Joseph H. George
John E. Boeggeman (1919-1993)

Representative Clients: American Telephone & Telegraph; Anheuser-Busch Companies, Inc.; Lowe's Home Centers; Great Atlantic & Pacific Tea Company; Reliance National Insurance Company; Metropolitan Property & Casualty Insurance Company; Fisher Price, Inc.; CGU Insurance Company; United Services Automobile Association; New York Central Mutual Fire Insurance Company.

For full biographical listings, see the Martindale-Hubbell Law Directory

ROSENBLUM & FILAN, L.L.C. (AV)

50 Main Street, 10606
Telephone: 914-686-6100
Fax: 914-686-6140
Stamford, Connecticut Office: One Landmark Square.
Telephone: 203-358-9200.
Fax: 203-358-0687.

(See Next Column)

ROSENBLUM & FILAN L.L.C.—*Continued*

New York City Office: 400 Madison Avenue.
Telephone: 212-888-8001.
Fax: 212-888-3331.

MEMBERS OF FIRM

Patrick J. Filan
James B. Rosenblum
James S. Newfield

James F. Biondo

OF COUNSEL

Theodore J. Greene

For full biographical listings, see the Martindale-Hubbell Law Directory

VOUTÉ, LOHRFINK, MAGRO & COLLINS, LLP (AV)

170 Hamilton Avenue, 10601-1789
Telephone: 914-946-1400
Facsimile: 914-946-8024

Arthur J. Vouté, Jr.
Richard L. Magro
Charles D. Lohrfink, Jr.
Charles A. Collins, Jr.

Elliot A. Cristantello
Stephen F. Fischer
Ralph F. Schoene
Kevin P. Fitzpatrick
Catherine F. Gale
Hal Roberts
Stephen J. Riebling, Jr.
John A. Howard
Michael A. Sonkin
Kelly E. Cardany

Representative Clients: Aetna Casualty & Surety Co.; Allstate Insurance Co.; Chubb Group; CNA Companies; Medical Liability Mutual Insurance Co.; National Car Rental System, Inc.; Physicians Reciprocal Insurance Co.; Preferred Physicians Medical Insurance Co.; Risk Enterprise Management; St. Josephs Medical Center.

For full biographical listings, see the Martindale-Hubbell Law Directory

WILSON, BAVE, CONBOY, COZZA & COUZENS, P.C. (AV)

Two William Street, 10601
Telephone: 914-686-9010
Telecopier: 914-686-0873
Email: wbcc@aol.com

William H. Bave (1919-1991)
Donald C. Wilson (1917-1994)
R. Kevin Conboy
William H. Bave, Jr.
Michael J. Cozza
John C. Couzens, Jr.
Patricia Bave-Planell
Kevin D. Odell
Leo T. McGrath
Alexandra C. Karamitsos
Joel A. Hirshfield
Megan J. Conboy
Teresa A. Gruber

LEGAL SUPPORT PERSONNEL

PARALEGAL

John R. Pearsall

Representative Clients: State Farm Mutual Automobile Insurance Co.; Continental National American Group; Medical Liability Mutual Insurance Co.; General Accident Insurance Co.; Metropolitan Property and Liability; Royal Insurance; County of Westchester; City of Yonkers.

For full biographical listings, see the Martindale-Hubbell Law Directory

NORTH CAROLINA

*ASHEVILLE,** Buncombe Co.

ELMORE, ELMORE & WILLIAMS, P.A. (AV)

53 North Market Street, 28801
Telephone: 828-253-1492
Fax: 828-253-9648
Email: eewlaw@wnc.com *URL:* http://www.lawyers.com/elmore-elmore-williams

Bruce A. Elmore
Bruce A. Elmore, Jr.
Reed G. Williams

For full biographical listings, see the Martindale-Hubbell Law Directory

VAN WINKLE, BUCK, WALL, STARNES AND DAVIS, P.A. (AV)

11 North Market Street, P.O. Box 7376, 28801
Telephone: 828-258-2991
FAX: 828-255-0255; 257-2767
Hendersonville, North Carolina Office: 422 South Main Street.
Telephone: 828-697-6196.
Fax: 828-693-3999.

Kingsland Van Winkle (1879-1972)
Charles G. Buck (Retired)
Robertson Wall (1913-1996)
O. E. Starnes
Roy W. Davis, Jr.
Brian F. D. Lavelle
Larry S. McDevitt

(See Next Column)

Philip J. Smith
Barry B. Kempson
Albert L. Sneed, Jr.
Robert H. Haggard (Resident, Hendersonville)
Marla Tugwell Adams
Jones Pharr Byrd
Allan R. Tarleton
Larry C. Harris, Jr.
Michelle Rippon
William Perry Fisher, II
Michael M. Thompson (Resident, Hendersonville, North Carolina Office)
Mark A. Pinkston
Stephen J. Grabenstein
Craig D. Justus
Cynthia W. Eller
Stephen B. Williamson
Adam Langdon Shealy
John G. Kelso
Dale A. Curriden
W. Carleton Metcalf
David G. Redding
W. Kevin McLaughlin, Jr.
Jennifer Wayland Moore
Robert J. Fedder
Juliet M. Sarkessian
Carolyn Lloyd Coward

Western Region General Counsel for: Wachovia Bank & Trust Co.
Attorneys for: Carolina Power & Light Co.; Charles D. Owen Manufacturing Co.; Clyde Savings and Loan Assn.; Continental Telephone Company of N.C.; Gerber Products Co.; Liberty Mutual Insurance Co.; Reliance Insurance Co.; State Farm Mutual Automobile Insurance Co.; United States Fidelity & Guaranty Co.

For full biographical listings, see the Martindale-Hubbell Law Directory

*CHARLOTTE,** Mecklenburg Co.

FERGUSON, STEIN, WALLAS, ADKINS, GRESHAM & SUMTER, P.A. (AV)

741 Kenilworth Avenue, Suite 300, 28204-2828
Telephone: 704-375-8461
Fax: 704-334-5654
Mailing Address: P.O. Box 36486, 28236-6486
Email: FSWAGS@aol.com
Chapel Hill, North Carolina Office: Suite 2, 312 West Franklin Street.
Telephone: 919-933-5300.
Fax: 919-967-4953.

James E. Ferguson, II
Adam Stein (Resident, Chapel Hill Office)
Jonathan Wallas
Karl Adkins
John W. Gresham
Geraldine Sumter
Henderson Hill
Thomas M. Stern (Resident, Chapel Hill Office)
C. Margaret Errington
Stephen Luke Largess

Rebecca Ann Thorne
James E. Ferguson, III
Corie Diane Pauling
Ann C. Todd

For full biographical listings, see the Martindale-Hubbell Law Directory

TIM L. HARRIS AND ASSOCIATES (AV)

4000 Tuckaseegee Road, 28208
Telephone: 704-392-4111
Fax: 704-391-1905
URL: http://www.timharris.com
Gastonia, North Carolina Office: 616 Cox Road. P.O. Box 249.
Telephone: 704-864-3409.
Fax: 704-853-1040.
Monroe, North Carolina Office: 3513 Highway 74 West, Suite E.
Telephone: 704-283-9200.
Fax: 704-392-9695.
Concord, North Carolina Office: 435 Church Street.
Telephone: 704-795-9317.
Fax: 704-795-5738

MEMBERS OF FIRM

Tim L. Harris
Jerry Neil Ragan (Resident, Gastonia Office)
Brent A. Patterson (Resident, Gastonia Office)

For full biographical listings, see the Martindale-Hubbell Law Directory

*GASTONIA,** Gaston Co.

TIM L. HARRIS AND ASSOCIATES (AV)

616 Cox Road, P.O. Box 249, 28053-0249
Telephone: 704-864-3409
Fax: 704-853-1040
Charlotte, North Carolina Office: 4000 Tuckaseegee Road.
Telephone: 704-392-4111.
Monroe, North Carolina Office: 3513 Highway 74 West, Suite E.
Telephone: 704-283-9200.
Fax: 704-392-9695.
Concord, North Carolina Office: 435 Church Street North.
Telephone: 704-795-4317.
Fax: 704-795-5738.

MEMBERS OF FIRM

Tim L. Harris
Jerry Neil Ragan (Resident)
Brent A. Patterson (Resident)

For full biographical listings, see the Martindale-Hubbell Law Directory

*GREENSBORO,** Guilford Co.

ALEXANDER RALSTON, SPECKHARD & SPECKHARD, L.L.P. (AV)

218 West Friendly Avenue, 27401
Telephone: 336-379-9302
Fax: 336-370-1232
URL: http://www.lawyers.com/aralston,speckhard

Donald K. Speckhard
Stanley E. Speckhard

Representative Clients: Preferred Furniture Components, Inc.; Spring Financial Services, Inc.; Blazer Financial Services; Omega Sports, Inc.; Power & Heat Systems, Inc.; Branch & Company, P.A.; Acme Florist Supply, Inc.

For full biographical listings, see the Martindale-Hubbell Law Directory

BARRON & BERRY, L.L.P. (AV)

301 South Greene Street, Suite 310, 27401
Telephone: 336-274-4782
Fax: 336-379-8592
Mailing Address: P.O. Box 2370, Greensboro, North Carolina, 27402-2370
Email: vbarron@worldnet.att.net *URL:* http://www.lawyers.com/barronberrylaw

Vance Barron, Jr.
Frederick L. Berry

For full biographical listings, see the Martindale-Hubbell Law Directory

CLARK BLOSS & MCIVER, PLLC (AV)

600 Dixie Building, 125 South Elm Street, P.O. Box 1349, 27402
Telephone: 336-275-7275
Fax: 336-275-1401
Email: cbm@cbm-law.com

David M. Clark
John F. Bloss
Robert G. McIver
Jonathan Wall

Representative Clients: The Prudential Insurance Company of America (litigation); Johnson Controls, Inc.
Approved Attorneys for: Jefferson-Pilot Insurance Co.

For full biographical listings, see the Martindale-Hubbell Law Directory

GREESON & ASSOCIATES (AV)

408 Battleground Avenue, P.O. Box 2460, 27402
Telephone: 336-370-4800
Fax: 336-370-0305
Email: Greeson-Legal@worldnet.att.net

Harold F. Greeson

OF COUNSEL

Mark F. Griffin

George Podgorny, Jr.

For full biographical listings, see the Martindale-Hubbell Law Directory

LAWING SHARPLESS & STAVOLA, P.A. (AV)

826 North Elm Street, P.O. Box 22106, 27420
Telephone: 336-333-6400
Facsimile: 336-333-6399
URL: http://www.elsfirm.com

Sally A. Lawing
Brenda S. McClearn
Pamela A. Robertson
Frederick K. Sharpless
Joseph M. Stavola

Joseph P. Booth, III
Eugene E. Lester, III
Marylynn E. Skaggs

Representative Clients: American Continental Insurance Company; High Point Regional Hospital; Medical Mutual Insurance Co.; The Medical Protective Insurance Co.; The Moses H. Cone Memorial Hospital; Wesley Long Community Hospital.

For full biographical listings, see the Martindale-Hubbell Law Directory

*RALEIGH,** Wake Co.

FULLER, BECTON, SLIFKIN & BELL, P.A. (AV)

4020 Westchase Boulevard Suite 375, 27607
Telephone: 919-755-1068
Fax: 919-828-7543

James C. Fuller, Jr.
Charles L. Becton
Anne R. Slifkin
Asa L. Bell, Jr.
Sally Greene
(Not admitted in NC)

For full biographical listings, see the Martindale-Hubbell Law Directory

KIRBY & HOLT, L.L.P. (AV)

Suite 100 3201 Glenwood Avenue, P.O. Box 31665, 27622
Telephone: 919-881-2111
Fax: 919-781-8630
URL: http://www.kirby-holt.com

David F. Kirby
C. Mark Holt
William B. Bystrynski
Isaac L. Thorp

For full biographical listings, see the Martindale-Hubbell Law Directory

ELIZABETH F. KUNIHOLM (AV)

4101 Lake Boone Trail, Suite 504, P.O. Box 30303, 27622
Telephone: 919-782-4494
Telecopier: 919-782-4517
Email: efk@efkuniholm.com

Toni M. Benham

For full biographical listings, see the Martindale-Hubbell Law Directory

MICHAELS, JONES, MARTIN, PARRIS & TESSENER LAW OFFICES, PLLC (AV)

Suite 200, 410 Glenwood Avenue, 27603
Telephone: 919-821-0005
Fax: 919-832-7426
URL: http://www.michaelsandjones.com
Durham, North Carolina Office: University Tower, Suite 526, 27707.
Telephone: 919-544-3000.
Wilmington, North Carolina Office: 1213 Culbreth Drive, Suite 104, 28405.
Telephone: 910-256-4005.
Charlotte, North Carolina Office: 301 South McDowell Street, Suite 400.
Telephone: 1-800-662-1234.

Paul J. Michaels
John Alan Jones
Gregory M. Martin
E. Spencer Parris
Hoyt G. Tessener
Kenneth B. Oettinger
H. Forest Horne, Jr.
Gary W. Jackson
Tamara R. Nance
John Michael Riley
Monique M. Peebles
Sandra W. Mitterling
Gabriel F. Jiménez
(Not admitted in NC)
Ronald L. Pressley

For full biographical listings, see the Martindale-Hubbell Law Directory

PATTERSON, DILTHEY, CLAY & BRYSON, L.L.P. (AV)

4020 Westchase Boulevard, Suite 550, 27607
Telephone: 919-821-4020
Fax: 919-829-0055
URL: HTTP://WWW.PDCB.COM
Wilmington, North Carolina Office: 2214-C Wrightsville Avenue.
Telephone: 910-762-6544.
Fax: 910-762-4241.

MEMBERS OF FIRM

Grady S. Patterson, Jr. (Retired)
Ronald C. Dilthey
Robert M. Clay
E. C. Bryson, Jr.
Reid Russell
Stuart L. Egerton
(Resident, Wilmington Office)
Mark E. Anderson
Donna Renfrow Rutala
Phillip J. Anthony
G. Lawrence Reeves, Jr.
Jonathan E. Hall

ASSOCIATES

Charles George
Mary McHugh Webb
Charles A. Madison
Claire A. Modlin
Scott B. Goodson
Sean A.B. Cole
Christian Michael Kennedy
Christopher J. Derrenbacher
J. Scott Lewis
Christopher M. Hinnant
(Resident, Wilmington Office)
Patrick M. Meacham
Daniel M. Gaylord

Representative Clients: American Casualty Insurance Co.; Medical Protective Co.; CNA HealthPro; The Virginia Insurance Reciprocal; University of North Carolina Liability Insurance Trust Fund; Duke University Medical Center - Private Diagnostic Clinic; The Doctor's Company.

For full biographical listings, see the Martindale-Hubbell Law Directory

TWIGGS, ABRAMS, STRICKLAND & TREHY, P.A. (AV)

First Union Capitol Center, 150 Fayetteville Street Mall, Suite 1100, P.O. Drawer 30, 27602
Telephone: 919-828-4357
Fax: 919-833-7924
Email: tastlaw@tast.com

Howard F. Twiggs
Douglas B. Abrams
Donald R. Strickland
Jerome P. Trehy, Jr.
Karen M. Rabenau

OF COUNSEL

Donald H. Beskind
Margaret Smith Abrams
Jeff Erick Essen

For full biographical listings, see the Martindale-Hubbell Law Directory

Raleigh—Continued

YATES, MCLAMB & WEYHER, L.L.P. (AV)

One Hannover Square, 421 Fayetteville Street Mall, Suite 1200, 27601
Telephone: 919-835-0900
Fax: 919-835-0910
Mailing Address: P.O. Box 2889, 27602-2889

MEMBERS OF FIRM

R. Scott Brown
Derek M. Crump
Dan J. McLamb
John W. Minier
Rodney E. Pettey
O. Craig Tierney, Jr.
Andrew A. Vanore, III
Kirk G. Warner
Barbara B. Weyher
Joseph W. Yates, III (Retired)

ASSOCIATES

Virginia Green Adams
Michael J. Byrne
Hunt K. Choi
Barry S. Cobb
Renee Billings Crawford
Susan T. Fountain
Gwenda L. Laws
Michael E. McDaniel
Travis K. Morton
Shirley Maring Pruitt
Beth Y. Smoot
Diane S. Tilley
Michael W. Washburn

OF COUNSEL

Michael C. Hurley

Representative Clients: Medical Mutual Insurance Co.; Medical Protective Co.; MMI Companies, Inc.; Spectrum Emergency Care; St. Paul Insurance Cos.; University of North Carolina Hospitals.

For full biographical listings, see the Martindale-Hubbell Law Directory

---

ROCKY MOUNT, Edgecombe & Nash Cos.

HENSON AND FUERST, P.A. (AV)

2317 Sunset Avenue, 27804
Telephone: 252-443-2111
Fax: 252-443-9429
Email: henson-fuerst@lawmed.com

Thomas W. Henson
Robert L. Fuerst
Ronald D. Manasco
Thomas W. Henson, Jr.

David S. Henson

For full biographical listings, see the Martindale-Hubbell Law Directory

---

*SMITHFIELD,** Johnston Co.

ARMSTRONG & ARMSTRONG, P.A. (AV)

602 South Third Street, P.O. Box 27, 27577
Telephone: 919-934-1575
Fax: 919-934-1846

L. Lamar Armstrong, Jr.
Marcia H. Armstrong

For full biographical listings, see the Martindale-Hubbell Law Directory

---

*WILMINGTON,** New Hanover Co.

SHIPMAN & ASSOCIATES, L.L.P. (AV)

11 South Fifth Avenue, 28401
Telephone: 910-762-1990
Fax: 910-762-6752
Email: shipman-associates@orotech.com

MEMBER OF FIRM

Gary K. Shipman

ASSOCIATES

Carl W. Thurman, III
C. Wes Hodges, II
Jennifer Jernigan Slusser

For full biographical listings, see the Martindale-Hubbell Law Directory

---

*WINSTON-SALEM,** Forsyth Co.

BENNETT & GUTHRIE, P.L.L.C. (AV)

3334 Healy Drive, Suite 203, 27103-1476
Telephone: 336-765-3121
Fax: 336-765-8622

Richard V. Bennett
Rodney A. Guthrie
Stanley P. Dean

Kevin J. Williams

Representative Clients: American Continental Insurance Company; Commercial Union Insurance Company; Integon Insurance; Kentucky Medical Insurance Company; Medtronic, Inc.; Montgomery Mutual Insurance Company; Novant Health, Inc.; Pennsylvania Lumberman's Mutual Insurance Company; St. Paul Fire & Marine Insurance Company; Zurich Insurance Company.

For full biographical listings, see the Martindale-Hubbell Law Directory

COMERFORD & BRITT, L.L.P. (AV)

250 West First Street Suite 300, 27101
Telephone: 336-631-8510
Fax: 336-631-8228
Email: @comerfordbritt.com *URL:* http://www.comerfordbritt.com

MEMBERS OF FIRM

W. Thompson Comerford, Jr.
Clifford Britt

ASSOCIATE

Martha Marie Eastman

For full biographical listings, see the Martindale-Hubbell Law Directory

---

WOMBLE CARLYLE SANDRIDGE & RICE (AV)

A Professional Limited Liability Company
200 West Second Street, P.O. Drawer 84, 27102
Telephone: 336-721-3600
Fax: 336-721-3660
Email: lawyers@wcsr.com *URL:* http://www.wcsr.com
Charlotte, North Carolina Office: 3300 One First Union Center, 301 South College Street.
Telephone: 704-331-4900.
Fax: 704-331-4955.
Raleigh, North Carolina Office: 2100 First Union Capitol Center, 150 Fayetteville Street Mall, P.O. Box 831.
Telephone: 919-755-2100.
Fax: 919-755-2150.
Research Triangle Park, North Carolina Office: 2505 Meridian Parkway, Suite 300 (Durham), 27713.
Telephone: 919-484-2300.
Fax: 919-484-2340.
Atlanta, Georgia Office: One Atlantic Center, 1201 West Peachtree Street, Suite 3500.
Telephone: 404-872-7000.
Fax: 404-888-7490.
Other Atlanta, Georgia Office: Suite 404, 2296 Henderson Mill Road, N.E.
Telephone: 770-492-9030.
Fax: 770-492-9609.
Washington, D.C. Office: 1120 Nineteenth Street, N.W., Eighth Floor.
Telephone: 202-857-4400.
Fax: 202-467-6910.
Greenville, South Carolina Office: 15 South Main Street, Suite 601, P.O. Box 10208.
Telephone: 864-255-5400.
Fax: 864-255-5440.

RESIDENT MEMBERS

Allan R. Gitter
William F. Womble, Jr.

Representative Clients: Brad Ragan, Inc.; Brenner Companies; Food Lion, Inc.; Hanes Companies, Inc.; North Carolina Baptist Hospitals, Inc.; R.J. Reynolds Tobacco Co.; Thomasville Furniture Industries, Inc.; Wachovia Corp.; Wake Forest University.

For Complete List of Firm Personnel, See General Section

For full biographical listings, see the Martindale-Hubbell Law Directory

OHIO

*AKRON,** Summit Co.

MICHAEL M. DJORDJEVIC CO. LPA (AV)

17 South Main Street at Maiden Lane Suite 201, 44308
Telephone: 330-376-6766
Fax: 330-376-7344
Email: mickdlaw@aol.com *URL:* http://www.lawyers.com/michaeldjordjevic

Michael M. Djordjevic

For full biographical listings, see the Martindale-Hubbell Law Directory

PERANTINIDES & NOLAN CO., L.P.A. (AV)

300 Courtyard Square, 80 South Summit Street, 44308-1736
Telephone: 330-253-5454
Telecopier: 330-253-6524
Email: pn@perantinides.com

Paul G. Perantinides
Chris T. Nolan

James J. Gutbrod
Christopher L. Parker
Peter D. Janos
Antonios P. Tsarouhas
Christina Simoudis
Sophie Mitsopoulos

References: First National Bank of Akron; National City Bank, Akron; Society Bank; Charter One Bank.

For full biographical listings, see the Martindale-Hubbell Law Directory

Akron—Continued

SCANLON & GEARINGER CO., L.P.A. (AV)

1100 First National Tower, 106 South Main Street, 44308-1463
Telephone: 330-376-4558
Telecopier: 330-376-3550

Timothy F. Scanlon
Bradford M. Gearinger
Michael J. Del Medico
Mark Hilkert
Patrick J. Hart
Robert A. Royer
Kevin P. Hardman
Maura E. Scanlon
John F. Hill

John T. Scanlon

For full biographical listings, see the Martindale-Hubbell Law Directory

A. RUSSELL SMITH (AV)

503 Key Building, 159 South Main Street, 44308
Telephone: 330-434-7167; 877-434-7167
Fax: 330-434-7195
Email: smithar@bright.net

A. Russell Smith

R. Bryan Nace

For full biographical listings, see the Martindale-Hubbell Law Directory

A. WILLIAM ZAVARELLO CO., L.P.A. (AV)

313 South High Street, Corner South High and Buchtel, 44308-1532
Telephone: 330-762-9700
Fax: 330-762-1680
Email: RhDavis3205@msn.com
Email: wzavarello@aol.com

A. William Zavarello
Rhonda Gail Davis

References: First National Bank of Ohio; National City Bank, Akron.

For full biographical listings, see the Martindale-Hubbell Law Directory

*CINCINNATI,** Hamilton Co.

KEATING, MUETHING & KLEKAMP, P.L.L. (AV)

1400 Provident Tower, One East Fourth Street, 45202
Telephone: 513-579-6400
Facsimile: 513-579-6457
URL: http://www.kmklaw.com

MEMBERS OF FIRM

Louis F. Gilligan
William A. Posey
Gregory M. Utter
James R. Matthews

ASSOCIATE

Joseph M. Callow Jr.

Representative Clients: American Financial Group; BP America Inc.; Chiquita Brands International, Inc.; Cintas Corporation; Comair Holdings, Inc.; Duke Realty Limited Partnership; LSI Industries Inc.; Mosler Inc.; Provident Financial Group Inc.

For Complete List of Firm Personnel, See General Section

For full biographical listings, see the Martindale-Hubbell Law Directory

THE LAWRENCE FIRM, L.P.A. (AV)

2100 Firstar Center at Fountain Square, 425 Walnut Street, 45202
Telephone: 513-651-4130
Fax: Available upon request
Email: lawyers@lawrencefirm.com *URL:* http://www.lawrencefirm.com

Richard D. Lawrence

David A. Johns
Richard Lanahan Goodman
Thomas C. Korbee
Roger N. Braden
Jennifer L. Lawrence
Patrick J. Beirne
Donna M. Bloemer
Virginia M. Baker
Rick J. Sommer

For full biographical listings, see the Martindale-Hubbell Law Directory

LINDHORST & DREIDAME CO., L.P.A. (AV)

312 Walnut Street, Suite 2300, 45202-4091
Telephone: 513-421-6630
Telecopier: 513-421-0212

SENIOR COUNSEL

Leo J. Breslin
John A. Goldberg
Michael F. Lyon

Representative Clients: Medical Protective Co.; Fireman's Fund-American Group; CNA; U.S.F.&G.; Ohio Hospital Insurance Co.; Middletown Hospital; Scottsdale Insurance Co.

(See Next Column)

For Complete List of Firm Personnel, See General Section

For full biographical listings, see the Martindale-Hubbell Law Directory

SHEA & ASSOCIATES (AV)

600 Flatiron Building, 401 East Court Street, 45202-1355
Telephone: 513-621-8333
Telecopier: 513-651-3272
Email: SheaLawFrm@aol.com *URL:* http://www.attyfind.com/jwshea

Joseph W. Shea III

ASSOCIATE

Shirley A. Coffey

LEGAL SUPPORT PERSONNEL

Connie DeFillippo

For full biographical listings, see the Martindale-Hubbell Law Directory

STRAUSS & TROY A LEGAL PROFESSIONAL ASSOCIATION (AV)

The Federal Reserve Building, 150 East Fourth Street, 45202-4018
Telephone: 513-621-2120
Telecopier: 513-241-8259
URL: http://www.strauss-troy.com
Northern Kentucky Office: Suite 1400, 50 East Rivercenter Boulevard, Covington, Kentucky, 41011.
Telephone: 513-621-8900; 513-621-2120.
Telecopier: 513-629-9444.

Thomas L. Stachler

OF COUNSEL

Charles G. Atkins

Representative Clients: PNC Bank, N.A. (Ohio and Kentucky); Corporex Companies, Inc.; Mercantile Stores Co., Inc.; Star Bank, N.A. (Ohio and Kentucky).

For Complete List of Firm Personnel, See General Section

For full biographical listings, see the Martindale-Hubbell Law Directory

*CLEVELAND,** Cuyahoga Co.

APICELLA AND TRAPP (AV)

1200 Bond Court Building, 1300 East Ninth Street, 44114-1503
Telephone: 216-696-3550
Fax: 216-696-3830
Email: aptrapp@msn.com

MEMBERS OF FIRM

F. M. Apicella
Mary Jane Trapp

Reference: Key Bank.

For full biographical listings, see the Martindale-Hubbell Law Directory

BONEZZI SWITZER MURPHY & POLITO CO. L.P.A. (AV)

Leader Building, Suite 1400, 526 Superior Avenue, 44114-1491
Telephone: 216-875-2767
Telecopier: 216-875-1570
Email: bsmp@bsmplaw.com

William D. Bonezzi
Donald H. Switzer
Patrick Joseph Murphy
John S. Polito
Steven J. Hupp

Susan M. Reinker
Kevin O. Kadlec
Edward E. Taber

Representative Clients: The Cleveland Clinic Foundation; Southwest General Health Center; Ashtabula County Medical Center; Mutual Assurance Company; The Doctors' Company; Kentucky Medical Insurance Company; Liberty Mutual Insurance Company; Kaiser Engineering; MMI Companies; Medical Inter-Insurance Exchange.

For full biographical listings, see the Martindale-Hubbell Law Directory

DAVIS & YOUNG (AV)

A Legal Professional Association
1700 Midland Building, 44115
Telephone: 216-348-1700
Fax: 216-621-0602
Cable: DANDY CLE
Email: atty@davisyoung.com *URL:* http://www.davisyoung.com
Akron, Ohio Office: 1015 Society Building, 159 South Main Street.
Telephone 216-376-1717.
Fax: 216-376-1797.
Youngstown, Ohio Office: 406 Wick Building, 34 Federal Plaza West, 44503.
Telephone: 330-743-1717.

(See Next Column)

DAVIS & YOUNG—*Continued*

George W. Lutjen
Martin J. Murphy
C. Richard McDonald
Paul D. Eklund
Jan L. Roller
Thomas W. Wright
David J. Fagnilli
Gregory H. Collins
William Vance
Patrick F. Roche

David G. Utley
Timothy L. Kerwin
Marc A. Sanchez
Ann Marie O'Brien
Susan L. Fricker
Michele Y. Wharton
Larry D. Wilkes
Timothy G. Welsh

OF COUNSEL

R. Emmett Moran

Counsel for: Westfield Companies; Cincinnati Insurance Company; University Hospitals of Cleveland; Medical Protective Company; Ohio Insurance Guaranty Association; Alliance Insurance Co.; Amerisure Companies; Avis Rent-A-Car Systems Inc.; Black & Decker; Dana Corp.; Central Mutual Insurance Co.; Eagle Picher Industries Inc.; TOPS Friendly Markets; U.S. Fidelty & Guaranty Co.

For Complete List of Firm Personnel, See General Section

For full biographical listings, see the Martindale-Hubbell Law Directory

---

FRIEDMAN, DOMIANO & SMITH CO., L.P.A. (AV)

Sixth Floor, Standard Building, 1370 Ontario Street, 44113-1701
Telephone: 216-621-0070; 1-800-280-0070
Fax: 216-621-4008
Email: fds.atty@worldnet.att.net *URL:* http://www.fds@advpages.com
Marco Island, Florida Office: 881 Panama Court, Suite 305, 33937.
Telephone: 941-642-0252.

Jeffrey H. Friedman
Joseph C. Domiano
M. David Smith
Lisa M. Gerlack

Stephen S. Vanek
Michael L. Eisner
Kevin L. Lenson
Tracey S. McGurk

For full biographical listings, see the Martindale-Hubbell Law Directory

---

GALLAGHER, SHARP, FULTON & NORMAN (AV)

(Formerly Hauxhurst, Sharp, Mollison & Gallagher)
Bulkley Building, Seventh Floor, 1501 Euclid Avenue, 44115
Telephone: 216-241-5310
Telecopier: 216-241-1608
Email: gsfn.com *URL:* http://www.gsfn.com

MEMBERS OF FIRM

H. Austin Hauxhurst (1881-1962)
Frank X. Cull (1887-1965)
I. Walter Sharp (1884-1966)
Clarence L. Mollison (1906-1981)
Robert C. Horrigan (1916-1993)
Forrest A. Norman
Edward J. Cass
John B. Robertson
Thomas E. Betz
Alan M. Petrov
Alton L. Stephens, Jr.
Virginia L. Heidloff
Jay Clinton Rice
Joseph W. Pappalardo
Thomas E. Dover
James F. Koehler
Robert H. Eddy
Thomas J. Kaiser
D John Travis
Paul J. Schumacher, Jr.
William F. Gibson
Gary L. Nicholson
Lynn L. Moore
Ernest W. Auciello, Jr.
Patrick M. Foy
Kevin C. Alexandersen
Stanley M. Dub
Timothy T. Brick
Sheila A. McKeon
Thomas J. Cabral
Timothy J. Fitzgerald
Mark A. Greer

OF COUNSEL

Michael R. Gallagher
Robert W. Sharp
George W. Stuhldreher
Burt J. Fulton
James F. Sweeney
James G. Gowan
James L. Ryhal, Jr.

Edward G. Kagels
John T. Murphy
M. Terence Cawley
Todd M. Haemmerle
Brian R. McGraw
Timothy P. Whitford
Daniel J. Michalec
Alexander E. Goetsch
Joseph J. Santoro
Monica A. Sansalone
John A. Simon
Dennis G. Rehor
Beth A. Nagel
Timothy Patrick Roth
Gregory K. Boop
Janice Aitken
Gary F. Werner
Mark Joseph Savage
Catherine A. Davis
Charles Allston Bowers
Pamela S. Schremp
James T. Tyminski, Jr.
Matthew J. Hatchadorian

STAFF ATTORNEY

Daniel L. Herak

Counsel for: Associated Aviation Underwriters; Conrail; The Continental Insurance Cos.; Continental National American Group; Fireman's Fund Insurance Cos.; The Home Insurance Co.; Motorist Ins. Co.; Norfolk Southern Corp.; Royal Insurance Co.; United States Aviation Underwriters.

(See Next Column)

For full biographical listings, see the Martindale-Hubbell Law Directory

---

KREMBS & ALKIRE LLP (AV)

750 Courthouse Square, 310 West Lakeside Avenue, 44113-1021
Telephone: 216-875-7500
Fax: 216-875-7501
URL: http://www.krembs-alkire.com

Andrew P. Krembs
Richard C. Alkire
Dean C. Nieding

For full biographical listings, see the Martindale-Hubbell Law Directory

---

LEVIN, MARMAROS & CHARMS CO., L.P.A. (AV)

2970 BP Tower, 200 Public Square, 44114
Telephone: 216-781-4900
Fax: 216-787-0330
URL: http://www.lawyers.com/lmc

Joel Levin
Peter W. Marmaros
Stephen J. Charms

Anthony R. Brighton

For full biographical listings, see the Martindale-Hubbell Law Directory

---

LOWE • EKLUND • WAKEFIELD CO., L.P.A. (AV)

Tower City Center 610 Skylight Office Tower, 1660 West Second Street, 44113-1454
Telephone: 216-781-2600
Fax: 216-781-2610
Email: lew@lewlaw.com *URL:* http://www.lewlaw.com

James A. Lowe
Claudia Rieth Eklund
Mark L. Wakefield
Dennis P. Mulvihill

Gregory S. Scott
Andrew S. Goldwasser

OF COUNSEL

Donald Cybulski

For full biographical listings, see the Martindale-Hubbell Law Directory

---

NURENBERG, PLEVIN, HELLER & MCCARTHY CO., L.P.A. (AV)

1370 Ontario Street First Floor, 44113-1792
Telephone: 216-621-2300; Toll Free: 1-800-562-7438
Fax: 216-771-2242
Email: nphm@nphm.com *URL:* http://www.nphm.com

A. H. Dudnik (1905-1963)
S. F. Komito (1902-1984)
Marshall I. Nurenberg
Leon M. Plevin
Maurice L. Heller
John J. McCarthy
Thomas Mester
Harlan M. Gordon
David M. Paris
Richard L. Demsey
Jamie R. Lebovitz
William S. Jacobson
Jeffrey A. Leikin

Robin J. Peterson
Robert S. Zeller
Ellen M. McCarthy
J. Charles Ruiz-Bueno
Kathleen J. St. John
Jonathan D. Mester
Brenda M. Johnson

Reference: Society Key Corp.

For full biographical listings, see the Martindale-Hubbell Law Directory

---

TIMOTHY A. SHIMKO & ASSOCIATES A LEGAL PROFESSIONAL ASSOCIATION (AV)

2010 Huntington Building, 925 Euclid Avenue, 44115
Telephone: 216-241-8300
Fax: 216-241-2702
Email: taslaw@ix.netcom.com *URL:* http://www.netcom.com/~taslaw

Timothy A. Shimko

Frank E. Piscitelli, Jr.

Reference: National City Bank, Cleveland.

For full biographical listings, see the Martindale-Hubbell Law Directory

---

SPANGENBERG, SHIBLEY & LIBER LLP (AV)

2400 National City Center, 1900 East Ninth Street, 44114-3400
Telephone: 216-696-3232
Fax: 216-696-3924
Email: ssl@Spanglaw.com *URL:* http://www.Spanglaw.com

MEMBERS OF FIRM

Craig Spangenberg (1914-1998)
Norman W. Shibley (1921-1992)
Donald P. Traci (Retired)
John D. Liber
Robert A. Marcis
Peter H. Weinberger
William Hawal
Peter J. Brodhead
Dennis R. Lansdowne

(See Next Column)

SPANGENBERG, SHIBLEY & LIBER LLP, *Cleveland—Continued*

ASSOCIATES

Justin F. Madden
Mary A. Cavanaugh
Stuart E. Scott
Rhonda Baker Debevec

For full biographical listings, see the Martindale-Hubbell Law Directory

STEWART AND DE CHANT CO., L.P.A. (AV)

The Atrium Office Plaza-Suite 850, 668 Euclid Avenue, 44114-3060
Telephone: 216-781-2258
Fax: 216-781-8210
Email: INFO@STEWARTDECHANT.COM *URL:* http://www.STEWARTdeChant.COM

Lawrence E. Stewart
Thomas H. De Chant
Fred Wendel III
Scott E. Stewart
Samuel V. Butcher
Lawrence C. Davison
Matthew T. Brady

Reference: Keybank (Main Office).

For full biographical listings, see the Martindale-Hubbell Law Directory

TRACI & MARX CO., L.P.A. (AV)

55 Public Square, Suite 1550, 44113
Telephone: 216-623-8010
Fax: 216-623-8012
Email: lawyers@tracimarx.com

Robert V. Traci
James A. Marx

For full biographical listings, see the Martindale-Hubbell Law Directory

*COLUMBUS,** Franklin Co.

HAMMOND & SEWARDS (AV)

22 East Gay Street - Suite 700, 43215
Telephone: 614-461-5300
Telephone: 1-800-842-5475
Fax: 614-461-8285
Email: pmartz@hammondsewards.com *URL:* http://www.lawyers.com/hammondlawoffice

MEMBERS OF FIRM

Gary W. Hammond
Frederick A. Sewards

ASSOCIATE

Scott E. Williams

LEGAL SUPPORT PERSONNEL

Heather Vekasy (Secretary to Attorney Williams and Attorney Sewards)
Heather Rodgers (Secretary to Attorney Hammond)
Prindall H. Martz (Office Manager)

For full biographical listings, see the Martindale-Hubbell Law Directory

LAMKIN, VAN EMAN, TRIMBLE, BEALS & ROURKE (AV)

Suite 200, 500 South Front Street, 43215-5671
Telephone: 614-224-8187
Fax: 614-224-4943
URL: http://www.lawyers.com/lvtb&rlaw

MEMBERS OF FIRM

William W. Lamkin
Timothy L. Van Eman
Thomas W. Trimble
David A. Beals
Michael J. Rourke
Kathy A. Dougherty
Kenneth S. Blumenthal

Reference: Huntington National Bank.

For full biographical listings, see the Martindale-Hubbell Law Directory

JERRY L. MALOON CO., L.P.A. (AV)

1335 Dublin Road, Suite 100-A, 43215-7007
Telephone: 614-488-9621
Fax: 614-488-9687
Email: JMaloon@aol.com *URL:* http://www.lawyers.com/jmaloonlaw

Jerry L. Maloon

For full biographical listings, see the Martindale-Hubbell Law Directory

MCCARTHY, PALMER, VOLKEMA & THOMAS A LEGAL PROFESSIONAL ASSOCIATION (AV)

140 East Town Street, Suite 1100, 43215
Telephone: Telephone: 614-221-4400
Telecopier: 614-221-6010
URL: http://www.mccarthypalmer.com
Email: attorneys@mccarthypalmer.com *URL:* http://www.lawyers.com/attorneysmccarthy

(See Next Column)

Dennis M. McCarthy
Robert Gray Palmer
Daniel R. Volkema
Warner M. Thomas, Jr.
Michael S. Miller
Elizabeth Schorpp Burkett
Craig P. Scott
Tony C. Merry

Jennifer K. Thivener

Reference: Huntington National Bank.

For full biographical listings, see the Martindale-Hubbell Law Directory

SCHERNER, HANSON & CORNWELL, LLC (AV)

130 Northwoods Boulevard, 43235-4725
Telephone: 614-431-7200
Fax: 614-431-7262
Delaware, Ohio Office: 5300 David Road.
Telephone: 614-595-3366.
Lima, Ohio Office: 2100 Lost Creek Boulevard.
Telephone: 419-222-1155.
Fax: 419-227-3131.

Hans Scherner
Robert E. Hanson
Ted E. Cornwell

For full biographical listings, see the Martindale-Hubbell Law Directory

WOLSKE & BLUE A LEGAL PROFESSIONAL ASSOCIATION (AV)

580 South High Street, 43215-5672
Telephone: 614-228-6969
Fax: 614-228-4367
URL: http://www.lawyers.com/wolske&blue
Cincinnati, Ohio Office: The Grand Baldwin Building, 655 Eden Park Drive, Suite 770, 45202.
Telephone: 513-579-1181.
Fax: 513-579-0320.

Jason A. Blue
Walter J. Wolske, Jr.

Reference: Bank One of Columbus, N.A.

For full biographical listings, see the Martindale-Hubbell Law Directory

*DAYTON,** Montgomery Co.

DAVID M. DEUTSCH CO., L.P.A. (AV)

The Pollack House, 208 West Monument Avenue, 45402
Telephone: 937-223-7170
Facsimile: 937-223-7180
Email: ddeutsch@erinet.com *URL:* ddeutsch@hotmail.com

David M. Deutsch

For full biographical listings, see the Martindale-Hubbell Law Directory

FREUND, FREEZE & ARNOLD A LEGAL PROFESSIONAL ASSOCIATION (AV)

Suite 1800 One Dayton Centre, One South Main Street, 45402-2017
Telephone: 937-222-2424
Telecopier: 937-222-5369
Email: ffalawda@ffalaw.com *URL:* http://www.ffalaw.com
Cincinnati, Ohio Office: 8805 Governor's Hill Drive, Suite 300, 45249-3313.
Telephone: 513-583-3700.
FAX: 513-583-3703. Email: ffalawci@ffalaw.com.

Neil F. Freund
Stephen V. Freeze
Robert N. Snyder
Susan Blasik-Miller
Scott F. McDaniel
Wayne E. Waite
Thomas B. Bruns
Mark L. Schumacher
Jennifer L. Kirkpatrick
Lynnette Pisone Ballato
Julie M. Olson

Local Counsel For: CNA Insurance Co.; Childrens Medical Center; Grandview/Southview Hospital; Miami Valley Hospital; OHIC Insurance Co.; Frontier Ins. Co.; Kentucky Medical Ins. Co.; Physicians Ins. Co. of Mich.; Mutual Assurance; Monroe Guaranty.

For full biographical listings, see the Martindale-Hubbell Law Directory

*ELYRIA,** Lorain Co.

ZAGRANS LAW FIRM A LEGAL PROFESSIONAL ASSOCIATION (AV)

5338 Meadow Lane Court, 44035-1469
Telephone: 440-934-7000
Facsimile: 440-934-7001
Email: eric@zagrans.com *URL:* http://www.zagrans.com

Eric H. Zagrans

Joshua M. Marks

LEGAL SUPPORT PERSONNEL

Jeannette M. Wolff (Legal Assistant)

For full biographical listings, see the Martindale-Hubbell Law Directory

*WARREN,** Trumbull Co.

Charles L. Richards (AV)

159 East Market Street, Suite 300, 44481-1122
Telephone: 330-373-1000
Fax: 330-394-5291

ASSOCIATES

Robert C. Maynard
Maureen E. Richards
Vincent E. Cononico

For full biographical listings, see the Martindale-Hubbell Law Directory

*ZANESVILLE,** Muskingum Co.

Micheli, Baldwin, Bopeley & Northrup Co., L.P.A. (AV)

2806 Bell Street, P.O. Box 788, 43702-0788
Telephone: 614-454-2545
Fax: 614-454-6372

Frank J. Micheli
Michael J. Micheli
James C. Micheli (1956-1992)
Steven R. Baldwin
Thomas R. Bopeley
Michael A. Northrup

Eric D. Martin

Representative Clients: Bank One Cambridge, N.A.; Consolidated Rail Corp.; Medical Protective Co.; Nationwide Insurance Cos.; Continental Insurance Cos.; Motorists Mutual Insurance Co.; Frontier Insurance Co.
Reference: Mutual Federal Savings Bank

For full biographical listings, see the Martindale-Hubbell Law Directory

OKLAHOMA

*OKLAHOMA CITY,** Oklahoma Co.

Gary L. Brooks and Associates (AV)

7100 North Classen Boulevard, Suite 300, 73116-7101
Telephone: 405-840-1066
Fax: 405-843-8446
Email: GLB@medlaws.com *URL:* http://www.medlaws.com

Ann Brooks
Christopher J. Bergin

For full biographical listings, see the Martindale-Hubbell Law Directory

Lee, Durocher, Kisner, Walker & Reid (AV)

An Association of Professional Associations
5532 North Western, 73118
Telephone: 405-848-5532
Facsimile: 405-848-5502

Jim W. Lee
Daniel L. Durocher
David W. Kisner
David A. Walker
James M. Reid

For full biographical listings, see the Martindale-Hubbell Law Directory

McCaffrey & Tawwater (AV)

Suite 1950, One Leadership Square, 211 North Robinson, 73102-7124
Telephone: 405-235-2900
Fax: 405-231-2818
URL: http://www.mccaffreytawwater.com
Other Oklahoma City, Oklahoma Office: 3015 N.W. 59th, 73112.

MEMBERS OF FIRM

George J. McCaffrey
Larry A. Tawwater

ASSOCIATES

Jo Lynn Slama
Loren F. Gibson
Steven R. Davis
Piper E. John
David B. Custar

For full biographical listings, see the Martindale-Hubbell Law Directory

Merritt & Associates, P.C. (AV)

917 North Robinson, P.O. Box 1377, 73101
Telephone: 405-236-2222
Nationwide Toll Free: 1-800-690-2277
Fax: 405-232-8630

John M. Merritt

Michael M. Blue

For full biographical listings, see the Martindale-Hubbell Law Directory

The Mills Law Firm, P.C. (AV)

500 One Leadership Square, 211 North Robinson, 73102
Telephone: 405-239-2501
Fax: 405-239-2575
Email: millsfirm@attymail.com

Earl D. Mills
Robert B. Mills
W. Wayne Mills
Barbara K. Buratti

Margaret K. Myers
Daniel K. Jones
J. Drew Houghton
Carole L. Dulisse

For full biographical listings, see the Martindale-Hubbell Law Directory

Pierce Couch Hendrickson Baysinger & Green, L.L.P. (AV)

1109 North Francis, P.O. Box 26350, 73126
Telephone: 405-235-1611
Fax: 405-235-2904
Tulsa, Oklahoma Office: Suite 707, 100 W. 5th, ONEOK Plaza, 74103.
Telephone: 918-583-8100.
Fax: 918-583-8107.

MEMBERS OF FIRM

Calvin W. Hendrickson
Inona Jane Harness
Russell L. Hendrickson
John Roger Hurt
John Christopher Condren
G. Calvin Sharpe

ASSOCIATES

E. Marissa Lane
Edwin J. Carlton

Representative Clients: Physicians Liability Insurance Company; CNA Insurance Cos.; Continental Insurance Healthcare; Texas Medical Liability Trust; Sterling Medical Associates; PHICO Insurance Co.; The Doctors' Company; Western Indemnity Insurance Co.; American Continental Insurance Co.; American International Cos.

For Complete List of Firm Personnel, See General Section

For full biographical listings, see the Martindale-Hubbell Law Directory

Whitten, McGuire, Wood, Terry, Roselius & Dittrich A Professional Limited Liability Company (AV)

Suite 400, One Leadership Square, 211 North Robinson, 73102
Telephone: 405-239-2522
Fax: 405-239-2573
Email: whitten@whitten-mcguire.com
Tulsa, Oklahoma Office: 3600 First Place Tower, 15 East Fifth Street.
Telephone: 918-582-9903.

Reggie N. Whitten
Kent R. McGuire
Douglas A. Terry
Jason E. Roselius

Simone Gosnell Fulmer
Philip W. Anderson
R. Gregory Kirby
Derrick T. Dewitt

Representative Client: The St. Paul Insurance Cos; Biomet, Inc.; OML Municipal Assurance Group; Progressive Casualty; Shelter Ins. Co.; Fireman's Fund Ins. Co.; Pharmacists Mutual Ins. Co.

For full biographical listings, see the Martindale-Hubbell Law Directory

*TULSA,** Tulsa Co.

Atkinson, Haskins, Nellis, Boudreaux, Holeman, Phipps & Brittingham, A Professional Corporation (AV)

1500 ParkCentre, 525 South Main Street, 74103
Telephone: 918-582-8877
Fax: 918-585-8096
Email: ahnmail@ahn-law.com

Michael P. Atkinson, P.C.
Walter D. Haskins, P.C.
Gregory D. Nellis, P.C.
Daniel E. Holeman, P.C.
K. Clark Phipps
Martha J. Phillips
William A. Fiasco

OF COUNSEL

Joseph F. Glass

LEGAL SUPPORT PERSONNEL

Beverly J. Rubino, M.D. (Medical Counsel)

Representative Clients: Allstate Insurance Co.; Bayer Corp.; Crum & Forster Insurance Co.; Hartford Insurance Company; National American Insurance Co.; Federated Insurance Co.; Liberty Mutual Insurance Co.; Physicians Liability Insurance Co.; State Farm Mutual Automobile Insurance Co.; United States Aviation Underwriters.

For full biographical listings, see the Martindale-Hubbell Law Directory

Best & Sharp, A Professional Corporation (AV)

Oneok Plaza, 100 W. 5th, Suite 808, 74103-4225
Telephone: 918-582-1234
Fax: 918-585-9447
Email: Webmaster@BestSharp.com *URL:* http://www.BestSharp.com

(See Next Column)

BEST & SHARP A PROFESSIONAL CORPORATION, *Tulsa—Continued*

Joseph A. Sharp
Timothy G. Best
Daniel S. Sullivan
Amy E. Kempfert
Karen M. Grundy
Terry S. O'Donnell

Jeffrey W. Swanson
Dan W. Ernst
Thomas A. Le Blanc
Matthew B. Free

For full biographical listings, see the Martindale-Hubbell Law Directory

BREWSTER, SHALLCROSS AND DEANGELIS (AV)

2021 South Lewis Avenue, Suite 675, 74104
Telephone: 918-742-2021
Fax: 918-742-2197
Email: ADVOCATUS@AOL.COM

MEMBERS OF FIRM

Clark O. Brewster
Richard A. Shallcross
Jennifer L. DeAngelis

ASSOCIATES

Guy A. Fortney
Montgomery Loyd Lair
Daniel B. Graves

For full biographical listings, see the Martindale-Hubbell Law Directory

FELDMAN, FRANDEN, WOODARD & FARRIS (AV)

1000 Park Centre, 525 South Main, 74103-4514
Telephone: 918-583-7129
Telecopier: 918-584-3814
Email: feldman@tulsalawyer.com *URL:* http://www.tulsalawyer.com

MEMBERS OF FIRM

W. E. Green (1889-1977)
William S. Hall (1930-1991)
Raymond G. Feldman
Robert A. Franden
John R. Woodard, III
Joseph R. Farris
Victor R. Seagle
Tony M. Graham
J. David Mustain
Jody R. Nathan
R. Jack Freeman
R. Jay McAtee
Paula J. Quillin

ASSOCIATES

Timothy E. Tipton
Kristin Blue Fisher
Cheryl S. Gan
Leah P. Keele
R. Bryan Morrison
Thayla Painter Bohn

Representative Clients: CIGNA; The Equitable Life Assurance Society of the United States; Browning-Ferris Industries, Inc.; American Cyanamid Co.; American Home Assurance Co.; Oklahoma Bar Professional Liability Insurance Co.; American Motors Corp.; Sunbeam Corp.; Aviation Underwriters Inc.; Progressive Casualty Insurance Co.

For full biographical listings, see the Martindale-Hubbell Law Directory

RHODES, HIERONYMUS, JONES, TUCKER & GABLE, P.L.L.C. (AV)

Oneok Plaza, 100 West 5th Street, Suite 400, P.O. Box 21100, 74121-1100
Telephone: 918-582-1173
Fax: 918-592-3390
URL: http://www.rhodesokla.com

MEMBERS OF FIRM

Kevin D. Berry
Jo Anne Deaton
Richard M. Eldridge
E. D. Hieronymus (1908 -1994)
Bert M. Jones
William S. Leach
Michael W. McGivern
William D. Perrine
Mary Quinn-Cooper
Robert P. Redemann
David P. Reid
Chris L. Rhodes, III
Thomas E. Steichen
Catherine C. Taylor
John H. Tucker
Wilson T. White
Harold C. Zuckerman

Ann E. Allison
Steven K. Bunting
Robert P. Coffey, Jr.
J. Christopher Davis
Andrew D. Downing
Dana L. Gish
Kerry R. Lewis
Andrew L. Richardson
Michael F. Smith
Leslie J. Southerland
Kimberly E. West
Keith A. Wilkes

OF COUNSEL

George W. Gable (Retired Partner)
Larry J. Fulton
Kelly M. Greenough

Representative Clients: American International Companies; Bechtel; Chubb Group of Insurance Companies; General Motors Corporation; Merrill, Lynch; Nissan Motor Corporation in U.S.A.; Pfizer, Inc.; Volkswagen of America, Volkswagen, A.G.; Zurich U.S.

For full biographical listings, see the Martindale-Hubbell Law Directory

RICHARDS & CONNOR (AV)

9 East 4th Street, Suite 910, 74103-5103
Telephone: 918-585-2394
Fax: 918-585-1449

(See Next Column)

MEMBERS OF FIRM

Phil R. Richards
James W. Connor, Jr.

ASSOCIATES

Rachel Carver Mathis
Malinda S. Matlock
Thomas D. Hird
Jan L. Heister
Jason Lee Glass
John A.L. Campbell

For full biographical listings, see the Martindale-Hubbell Law Directory

SECREST, HILL & FOLLUO (AV)

7134 South Yale, Suite 900, 74136-6342
Telephone: 918-494-5905
Fax: 918-494-2847
Email: jksecrest@webzone.net

MEMBERS OF FIRM

James K. Secrest, II
W. Michael Hill
Dan S. Folluo

Richard C. Honn
Edward John Main
Roger N. Butler, Jr.
Nathan E. Clark
David A. Russell
John Jay Bowling
J. Derek Ingle
Brian J. Goree
Bradley A. Jackson

Representative Clients: AAOMS Mutual Insurance Co.; CNA Insurance Cos.; Hospital Casualty Co.; Physicians Liability Insurance Co.; State Volunteer Mutual Insurance Co.; North American Physicians Insurance Risk Retention Group; Podiatry Insurance Co. of America; Shand Morahan & Company, Inc.; American Continental Insurance Co.

For full biographical listings, see the Martindale-Hubbell Law Directory

WILBURN, MASTERSON & SMILING (AV)

Executive Center II, 7134 South Yale, Suite 560, 74136-6337
Telephone: 918-494-0414
Fax: 918-493-3455
Email: wmslaw@ionet.net

Ray H. Wilburn
Michael J. Masterson
A. Mark Smiling

ASSOCIATES

Rhett Henry Wilburn
Scott R. Taylor
Jane R. Cowdery
Thomas J. Sullivent, Jr.
Elizabeth A. Ballard

For full biographical listings, see the Martindale-Hubbell Law Directory

OREGON

*PORTLAND,** Multnomah Co.

SWANSON, THOMAS & COON (AV)

American Bank Building, 621 S.W. Morrison, Suite 900, 97205-3892
Telephone: 503-228-5222
Fax: 503-273-9175
URL: http://www.stc-law.com

MEMBERS OF FIRM

Douglas A. Swanson
Raymond F. Thomas
James S. Coon

ASSOCIATES

Megan E. Glor
Alan Stuart Graf
Margaret F. Weddell

For full biographical listings, see the Martindale-Hubbell Law Directory

PENNSYLVANIA

BENSALEM, Bucks Co.

RUDOLPH, DORIAN, GOLDSTEIN, ROCHESTIE, WISNIEWSKI & TAYLOR, P.C. (AV)

Neshaminy Valley Commons, 2410 Bristol Road, 19020
Telephone: 215-750-7200
Fax: 215-750-9294
Email: admin@rudolphdorian.com *URL:* http://www.palaw.lawoffice.com
Philadelphia, Pennsylvania Office: 1818 Market Street, Suite 2300, 19103.
Telephone: 215-299-9900.
Fax: 215-299-9910.

(See Next Column)

RUDOLPH, DORIAN, GOLDSTEIN, ROCHESTIE, WISNIEWSKI & TAYLOR P.C.—*Continued*

Edward Rudolph
Harry A. Dorian, Jr.
Stephan H. Goldstein
Gary A. Rochestie
Mark A. Wisniewski
John J. Taylor
Jeffrey S. Orchinik
Kim A. Piermattei
Michael Parlow
Lawrence P. Kempner
Nancy M. Bonner

For full biographical listings, see the Martindale-Hubbell Law Directory

BLUE BELL, Montgomery Co.

DAVID W. SUMNER (AV)

Building 18, Suite One, 1787 Sentry Parkway West, 19422
Telephone: 215-619-3017
Fax: 215-619-3045
Email: david.sumner@worldnet.att.net *URL:* http://www.lawyers.com/davidwsumner-medmal

For full biographical listings, see the Martindale-Hubbell Law Directory

CONWAY, Beaver Co.

CONTE, MELTON & D'ANTONIO (AV)

300 Ninth Street, 15027-1696
Telephone: 724-869-2164; 775-1850; 412-766-5112
Fax: 724-869-2246
Email: CMDlaw@acba.org

MEMBERS OF FIRM

John Alan Conte
Scott L. Melton
Daniel M. D'Antonio

Joseph M. Spratt
Robert A. Krebs
Elisabeth A. McIntyre

For full biographical listings, see the Martindale-Hubbell Law Directory

DOWNINGTOWN, Chester Co.

WUSINICH AND BROGAN (AV)

537 West Uwchlan Avenue, Suite 200, P.O. Box 478, 19335-0478
Telephone: 610-594-1600
Fax: 610-594-6518
Email: info@wusinichbrogan.com *URL:* http://www.wusinichbrogan.com
Reading, Pennsylvania Office: 522 Washington Street.
Telephone: 610-373-8550.
West Chester, Pennsylvania Office: Nineteen South High Street.
Telephone: 610-436-6280.

MEMBERS OF FIRM

Joseph F. Wusinich, III
Dennis D. Brogan
John J. Stanzione

Louis Aurely, III
David V. Grow
Edward C. Sweeney

For full biographical listings, see the Martindale-Hubbell Law Directory

*EASTON,** Northampton Co.

COHEN & FEELEY, P.C. (AV)

2940 William Penn Highway, 18045
Telephone: 610-258-0111
Fax: 610-258-8095
Email: cohenfeeley@enter.net *URL:* http://www.seriouslyinjured.com
Allentown, Pennsylvania Office: 1405 North Cedar Crest Boulevard, Suite 205, 18104.
Telephone: 610-821-7702.
Fax: 610-821-9067.

Martin D. Cohen
Dennis F. Feeley

For full biographical listings, see the Martindale-Hubbell Law Directory

GUS MILIDES (AV)

654 Wolf Avenue, 18042
Telephone: 610-258-0433
Fax: 610-258-4875

For full biographical listings, see the Martindale-Hubbell Law Directory

ELKINS PARK, Montgomery Co.

MONAGHAN & GOLD, P.C. (AV)

Manor Professional Building, 7837 Old York Road, 19027
Telephone: 215-782-1800
Fax: 215-782-1010
URL: http://www.MNG-LAW.com

Alan S. Gold
John F. X. Monaghan, Jr.

(See Next Column)

Murray R. Glickman
Tanya M. Sweet
Mitchell K. Brudno
Robert F. Fortin
Sean Robins
Kenneth W. Taylor
Francis D. Hennessy, Jr.

OF COUNSEL

Alan L. Butkovitz
Steven M. Zelitch
Barbara Malett Weitz

LEGAL SUPPORT PERSONNEL

Andrew Logan (Paralegal)
Carol Veach (Paralegal)
Janet McCrossen (Registered Nurse)

For full biographical listings, see the Martindale-Hubbell Law Directory

*HARRISBURG,** Dauphin Co.

ANGINO & ROVNER, P.C. (AV)

4503 North Front Street, 17110
Telephone: 717-238-6791
Fax: 717-238-5610
Email: lawfirm@angino-rovner.com *URL:* http://www.angino-rovner.com
Carlisle, Pennsylvania Office: 28 South Pitt Street, 17013.
Telephone: 717-241-2661.

Richard C. Angino
Neil J. Rovner

References: Credit Bureau of Greater Harrisburg; CoreStates.

For full biographical listings, see the Martindale-Hubbell Law Directory

GOLDBERG, KATZMAN & SHIPMAN, P.C. (AV)

320 Market Street - Strawberry Square, P.O. Box 1268, 17108-1268
Telephone: 717-234-4161
Telecopier: 717-234-6808; 717-234-6810
Email: gks@gkslaw.com

F. Lee Shipman
April L. Strang-Kutay
Guy H. Brooks

John R. Ninosky

Representative Client: Fulton Bank.

For Complete List of Firm Personnel, See General Section

For full biographical listings, see the Martindale-Hubbell Law Directory

METZGER, WICKERSHAM, KNAUSS & ERB, P.C. (AV)

3211 North Front Street, P.O. Box 5300, 17110-0300
Telephone: 717-238-8187
Telefax: 717-234-9478
Other Harrisburg, Pennsylvania Office: 4813 Jonestown Road, P.O. Box 5300, 17110-0300.
Telephone: 717-652-7020.

Maurice R. Metzger (1918-1980)
F. Brewster Wickersham (1918-1974)
Edward E. Knauss, III (Retired)
Christian S. Erb, Jr.
Robert E. Yetter
James F. Carl
Edward E. Knauss, IV
Jered L. Hock
Karl R. Hildabrand
Richard B. Druby
Steven P. Miner

Clark DeVere
Carrie L. Carroll

Representative Clients: Allstate Insurance Co.; Chubb Group of Insurance Companies; Fireman's Fund American Insurance Group; Liberty Mutual Insurance Co.; Crum & Forster; CNA Insurance; Prudential Insurance Co.

For full biographical listings, see the Martindale-Hubbell Law Directory

PETERS & WASILEFSKI (AV)

2931 North Front Street, 17110
Telephone: 717-238-7555
Fax: 717-238-7750
Email: pwlaw@redrose.net

MEMBERS OF FIRM

William J. Peters
Charles E. Wasilefski
Dennis J. Bonetti
Joseph C. Phillips
Michael R. Bonshock
Thomas A. Lang

ASSOCIATES

Pamela S. Parascandola
Stephen F. Moore
Cindy J. Murphy
James A. Garver

Reference: Commonwealth National Bank.

For full biographical listings, see the Martindale-Hubbell Law Directory

Harrisburg—Continued

THOMAS, THOMAS & HAFER, LLP (AV)

305 North Front Street, 6th Floor, P.O. Box 999, 17108
Telephone: 717-237-7100
Fax: 717-237-7105
Verify: 717-255-7642
Bethlehem, Pennsylvania Office: 12 East Market Street, P.O. Box 1172, 12016.
Telephone: 610-868-1675.
Fax: 610-868-1702.

MEMBERS OF FIRM

Joseph P. Hafer
James K. Thomas, II
Robertson B. Taylor
Jeffrey B. Rettig
Peter J. Curry
R. Burke McLemore, Jr.
Edward H. Jordan, Jr.
C. Kent Price
Randall G. Gale
David L. Schwalm
Peter J. Speaker
Douglas B. Marcello
Paul J. Dellasega

OF COUNSEL

James K. Thomas

Timothy I. Mark
Daniel J. Gallagher
Robert A. Taylor
Sarah W. Arosell
Eugene N. McHugh
Stephen E. Geduldig
Karen S. Coates
Gary T. Lathrop
Todd B. Narvol
James J. Dodd-o
Kenneth A. Rapp
Kevin C. McNamara
Brooks R. Foland
John Flounlacker
John M. Popilock
Michele J. Thorp

Representative Clients: Aetna Casualty & Surety Co.; Commercial Union Insurance Companies; Geisinger Medical Center; Hartford Insurance Group; Liberty Mutual Insurance Co.; Medical Inter-Insurance Exchange; Medical Protective Co.; Pennsylvania Hospital Insurance Co.; Pennsylvania Medical Society Liability Insurance Co.

For full biographical listings, see the Martindale-Hubbell Law Directory

*LANCASTER,** Lancaster Co.

ATLEE, HALL & BROOKHART, L.L.P. (AV)

8 North Queen Street, P.O. Box 449, 17608-0449
Telephone: 717-393-9596
Fax: 717-393-2138
Email: law@atleehall.com

MEMBERS OF FIRM

William A. Atlee, Jr.
Thomas W. Hall
Dan M. Brookhart

ASSOCIATES

Edward R. Kennett
Jaime D. Jackson
Robin A. Jabour

For full biographical listings, see the Martindale-Hubbell Law Directory

*MEDIA,** Delaware Co.

BEATTY, CRAMP, KAUFFMAN & LINCKE (AV)

215 North Olive Street, P.O. Box 901, 19063
Telephone: 610-565-8800
Fax: 610-565-8127
Email: BCKLLaw@aol.com

MEMBERS OF FIRM

Lewis B. Beatty, Jr.
Joseph W. Kauffman
David J. Otis
David G. Blake
William P. Lincke
Natalie M. Habert
Peter W. Dicce

ASSOCIATES

Regina M. MacKenzie
Bereth K. Graeff
Daniel J. McCusker
Kelly A. Barnes

OF COUNSEL

John F. Cramp
Ralph B. D'Iorio
Robert C. Grasberger

Joseph R. Young (1921-1993)

Representative Clients: Medical Professional Liability Catastrophe Loss Fund.

For full biographical listings, see the Martindale-Hubbell Law Directory

*NORRISTOWN,** Montgomery Co.

CREEDON & FELICIANI, P.C. (AV)

29 East Marshall Street, 19401
Telephone: 610-239-9630
Fax: 610-239-1599
Email: creedon_feliciani@compuserve.com *URL:* http://www.lawyers.com/creedonfeliciani

(See Next Column)

Michael P. Creedon
Joseph L. Feliciani

For full biographical listings, see the Martindale-Hubbell Law Directory

MURPHY, OLIVER, CAIOLA & GOWEN, A PROFESSIONAL LAW CORPORATION (AV)

43 East Marshall Street, 19401-4828
Telephone: 610-272-4222; 610-279-3838
Fax: 610-272-2549; 610-275-0140
Email: molaw@injury-law.com *URL:* http://www.injury-law.com
Spring City, Pennsylvania Office: 500 S. Main Street, 19475.
Telephone: 610-948-3770.
Pottstown, Pennsylvania Office: 5 Sunnybrook Road, 19464.
Telephone: 610-323-3480.
West Chester, Pennsylvania Office: 1534 McDaniel Drive, Westtown Business Center, 19250.
Telephone: 610-272-4222.

James J. Oliver
Frank P. Murphy
Frank L. Caiola
Thomas L. Gowen, Jr.
Carla E. Connor
Barbara A. Barnes

John F. Haskins, Jr.
Cynthia Love Dengler
Carol A. Crisci

LEGAL SUPPORT PERSONNEL

Patricia A. Talese (Paralegal)
Kathleen Nicholson

For full biographical listings, see the Martindale-Hubbell Law Directory

RAYMOND M. VICTOR, P.C. (AV)

616 DeKalb Street, 19401
Telephone: 610-272-5253
Fax: 610-272-7422
Email: rdsquire@worldnet.att.net *URL:* http://www.lawyers.com/raymondmvictor

Raymond M. Victor
Christopher T. Moyer

For full biographical listings, see the Martindale-Hubbell Law Directory

*PHILADELPHIA,** Philadelphia Co.

ANAPOL, SCHWARTZ, WEISS, COHAN, FELDMAN AND SMALLEY, P.C. (AV)

1900 Delancey Place, 19103
Telephone: 215-735-1130
Fax: 215-735-2024
URL: http://www.aswc.net
Other Philadelphia, Pennsylvania Office: 1710 Spruce Street.
Fax: 215-735-2211.
Cherry Hill, New Jersey Office: 402 Park Boulevard, 08002.
Telephone: 1-609-427-9229.
Fax: 609-488-1396.
Fairless Hills, Pennsylvania Office: 920 Trenton Road.
Telephone: 215-945-6799.
Reading, Pennsylvania Office: 146 North 6th Street.
Telephone: 610-375-7488.
Media, Pennsylvania Office: 334 W. Front Street, 19063.
Telephone: 610-892-3714.

Alan Schwartz
Sol H. Weiss
Lawrence R. Cohan
Joel D. Feldman
Howard J. Levin
Bernard W. Smalley
Stanton Dubin
Margaret A. Barry
Stephen J. Pokiniewski, Jr.
Sidney M. Grobman
Nelson Levin

Nathaniel E.P. Ehrlich
Thomas R. Anapol
Miriam Benton Barish
Patrice A. Gillotti
Michele Lee Reed
Heather J. Lipson
Michelle L. Altenpohl
Lisa R. Schwartz
Kevin R. Marciano
Brian J. Taylor
Tobias L. Millrood
Tracy A. Finken

OF COUNSEL

Paul R. Anapol
Richard B. Schwartz (Resident, Other Philadelphia Office)
Mark F. Seltzer

Reference: Meridian Bank, Philadelphia, Pennsylvania.

For full biographical listings, see the Martindale-Hubbell Law Directory

MARVIN I. BARISH LAW OFFICES A PROFESSIONAL CORPORATION (AV)

6th and Walnut Streets, Suite 801E, 19106-3308
Telephone: 215-923-8900; 800-233-7101
Email: mbarish@aol.com *URL:* http://www.lawyers.com/barishlawoffices
Cherry Hill, New Jersey Office: 1930 East Marlton Pike, Suite Q-38.
Telephone: 609-338-0550.

(See Next Column)

MARVIN I. BARISH LAW OFFICES A PROFESSIONAL CORPORATION—*Continued*

Marvin I. Barish

Gregory L. Nester

For full biographical listings, see the Martindale-Hubbell Law Directory

MICHAEL D. BENJAMIN, P.C. (AV)

1831 Chestnut Street, Tenth Floor South, 19103
Telephone: 215-567-2723
Fax: 215-567-2759
Email: mdbpc@aol.com *URL:* http://www.lawyers.com/mdbpclaw

Michael D. Benjamin

LEGAL SUPPORT PERSONNEL

Fay Martin

For full biographical listings, see the Martindale-Hubbell Law Directory

CHRISTIE, PABARUE, MORTENSEN AND YOUNG, A PROFESSIONAL CORPORATION (AV)

1880 JFK Boulevard - Tenth Floor, 19103
Telephone: 215-587-1600
Fax: 215-587-1699
Email: cpmy@cpmy.com *URL:* http://www.cpmy.com
Cherry Hill, New Jersey Office: Woodland Falls Corporate Park, 200 Lake Drive East.
Telephone: 609-482-7887.
Fax: 609-482-7438.
New York, N.Y. Office: 20 Exchange Place, 31st Floor.
Telephone: 212-366-1310.
Fax: 212-797-3545.
Boston, Massachusetts, Office: One State Street, Fifteenth Floor.
Telephone: 617-854-8315.
Fax: 617-854-8311.
Radnor, Pennsylvania Office: Radnor Station Building No. 2, Suite 222, 290 King of Prussia Road.
Telephone: 610-688-5778.
Fax: 610-688-5788.

James W. Christie
Bradley J. Mortensen
James A. A. Pabarue, Jr.
James A. Young
Jerome E. Bogutz
Marc L. Bogutz
John D. Frumer (Resident, Boston, Massachusetts Office)
Ralph J. Luongo
Peter J. Lynch
Stella M. Tsai
Brian C. Vance

Anthony J. Arena
Carolyn Bates
Rex F. Brien
K. Tia Burke
Michael J. Burns
Michael E. DiFebbo, Jr.
John C. Falls (Resident, Cherry Hill, New Jersey Office)
Christie L. Gamble
Nadine M. Hunt
Elaine Whiteman Klinger
Randy J. Maniloff
Richard S. Margulies
Christopher M. Martin
Etienne C. Maumus
William F. McDevitt
Catherine O. Raymond
Heather A. Salko
Marie T. Sarkees
Barbara L. Schmuck
Paul V. Shehadi
Randee Lynn Strair
June A. Taima
Christina G. Tershakovec
Thaddeus J. Weaver
Marybeth Smith Werb
Lisa B. Zucker

For full biographical listings, see the Martindale-Hubbell Law Directory

LAW OFFICES OF JAMES E. COLLERAN (AV)

1525 Locust Street 18th Floor, 19102
Telephone: 215-790-5500
FAX: 215-790-5509
Email: colleran@colleran.com

James E. Colleran, Jr.
Francis T. Colleran
Teresa Colleran Quinn
Mary T. Colleran
James I. Devine
David C. Devine

For full biographical listings, see the Martindale-Hubbell Law Directory

FARAGE, MCBRIDE & RUGGIERI (AV)

836 Suburban Station Building, 1617 John F. Kennedy Boulevard, 19103
Telephone: 215-563-3973
Fax: 215-563-3094
URL: http://www.lawyers.com/fmrlaw
Woodbury, New Jersey Office: 9 South Broad Street, 08096.
Telephone: 609-845-9448.
Fax: 606-845-4888.

MEMBERS OF FIRM

Donald J. Farage (1909-1998)
James F. McBride
Thomas J. Ruggieri

For full biographical listings, see the Martindale-Hubbell Law Directory

FURIA AND TURNER (AV)

1717 Rittenhouse Square, 19103-6109
Telephone: 215-985-4500
Telecopier: 215-985-2824
Email: rfuria1717@aol.com *URL:* http://www.lawyers.com/furiaandturner

ASSOCIATE

Gina R. Furia

For full biographical listings, see the Martindale-Hubbell Law Directory

GALFAND BERGER, LLP (AV)

1818 Market Street, 23rd Floor, 19103-3623
Telephone: 215-665-1600
Fax: 215-564-2262
Email: sdonaway@galfandberger.com *URL:* http://www.galfandberger.com

Robert G. Mangold
Eric J. Swan

For full biographical listings, see the Martindale-Hubbell Law Directory

GOLDFEIN & JOSEPH, A PROFESSIONAL CORPORATION (AV)

1600 Market Street 33rd Floor, 19103-7288
Telephone: 215-979-8200
Fax: 215-979-8201
URL: http://www.goldfeinlaw.com
Princeton, New Jersey Office: Princeton Metro Center, Suite 115, 5 Vaughn Drive.
Telephone: 609-520-0400.
Fax: 609-520-1450.
Wilmington, Delaware Office: PNC Bank Center, Suite 1110, P.O. Box 2206, 222 Delaware Avenue.
Telephone: 302-656-3301.
Fax: 302-656-0643.
New York, New York Office: 150 Broadway, Suite 1212, 10038.
Telephone: 212-791-0340.
Fax: 212-791-0347.

Edward B. Joseph
Fredric L. Goldfein
E. Chandler Hosmer, III
David C. Weinberg
Bernard L. Levinthal
Roseann Lynn Brenner
Gary H. Kaplan
John A. Turlik

Michael A. Billotti
Medford J. Brown, III
Robert P. Coleman
Robert T. Connor
Charles D. Cooper
Kelly A. Costello
Lawrence E. Currier
Janet E. Golup
Christine Renee Guiliano
David M. Katzenstein
Matthew A Kelly, III
Deborah M. Knight
Pamela A. Post
Thomas M. Savon
Julie M. Sebring (Not admitted in PA)
Robert M. Stroh
Marc R. Wilner
Anthony F. Zabicki, Jr.

For full biographical listings, see the Martindale-Hubbell Law Directory

KANE & SILVERMAN, PROFESSIONAL CORPORATION (AV)

The Philadelphian Suite 1C-44, 2401 Pennsylvania Avenue, 19130
Telephone: 215-232-1000
Fax: 215-232-0181
Email: HGS@palegaladvice.com *URL:* http://www.palegaladvice.com

Michael C. Kane
Howard G. Silverman

For full biographical listings, see the Martindale-Hubbell Law Directory

KESSLER, COHEN & ROTH, A PROFESSIONAL CORPORATION (AV)

Two Penn Center Plaza, Suite 1705, 19102
Telephone: 215-567-3500
Fax: 215-567-6019
Email: lawyers@kesslercohen.com

Arnold M. Kessler
Stewart L. Cohen
Harry M. Roth
Karen R. Bramblett
Stephen R. Kurens
David L. Gordon
William D. Marvin

For full biographical listings, see the Martindale-Hubbell Law Directory

LEVIN, FISHBEIN, SEDRAN & BERMAN (AV)

Suite 500, 510 Walnut Street, 19106-3697
Telephone: 215-592-1500
Fax: 215-592-4663
Email: lfsb@psinet.com

MEMBERS OF FIRM

Arnold Levin
Michael D. Fishbein
Howard J. Sedran
Laurence S. Berman
Frederick S. Longer

(See Next Column)

LEVIN, FISHBEIN, SEDRAN & BERMAN, *Philadelphia—Continued*

Craig D. Ginsburg
Cheryl R. Brown Hill
Donald E. Haviland, Jr.
Daniel C. Levin
Terrianne Benedetto
Charles E. Schaffer
Austin B. Cohen

LEGAL SUPPORT PERSONNEL

Lee Ann Fitzpatrick
Cheryl Hesson

For full biographical listings, see the Martindale-Hubbell Law Directory

MARKS, O'NEILL, REILLY, O'BRIEN & COURTNEY, P.C. (AV)

1880 John F. Kennedy Boulevard Suite 1200, 19103
Telephone: 215-564-6688
Fax: 215-564-2526
Email: moro1@morocpa.com
Norristown, Pennsylvania Office: 411 Cherry Street.
Telephone: 215-277-7601.
Pittsburgh, Pennsylvania Office: 707 Grant Street, Gulf Tower, Suite 3200.
Telephone: 412-391-6171.
Fax: 412-391-8804.
Westmont, New Jersey Office: 216 Haddon Avenue, Suite 500.
Telephone: 856-858-6110.
Fax: 856-858-3687. E-Mail: moro1@morocnj.com
Wilmington, Delaware Office: 2004 Foulk Road, Suite 7.
Telephone: 302-475-5500.
Fax: 302-475-5584.

Jerome E. Marks
Joseph M. O'Neill
Vincent F. Reilly
Kevin J. O'Brien
Dawn R. Courtney
Sean Xavier Kelly
Gino P. Mecoli
John J. Repcheck (Resident, Pittsburgh Office)

David P. Helwig (Resident, Pittsburgh Office)
Maureen Murray-O'Toole
Patrick C. Lamb
Christine G. Boyle
Nancy E. Mancheski
Michael T. Hamilton
Kelly L. Bracken
Tracey Marie McDevitt
Sharon A. Connors (Resident, Westmont, New Jersey Office)
Malissa A. Richetti
Patricia M. Henrich
Judith H. Ring
Gary Weinberg (Resident, Westmont, New Jersey Office)
Lee J. Janiczek
Wendy D. Testa (Resident, Westmont, New Jersey Office)
Gary F. Sharlock (Resident, Pittsburgh Office)
Robert Dale Leidigh (Resident, Pittsburgh Office)
Joseph L. Orszulak, II (Resident, Pittsburgh Office)
Diane Beckman Carvell
Karen J. Stanzione
Michael A. Kosar
Susan D. Grant (Resident, Westmont, New Jersey Office)
Frances Wang-Deveney (Resident, Westmont, New Jersey)
Courtney E. Passin
Stephanie Victoria Shreibman
Megan Kochell D'Iorio (Resident, Wilmington, Delaware Office)
Megan Trocki Mantzavinos (Resident, Wilmington, Delaware Office)
Toni Anderson Moore
Natalie M. Nugent
Frank Gattuso
Michael A. Ring (Resident, Westmont, New Jersey Office)
Ann M. Madden (Not admitted in PA)
Matthew J. Zamites
Salvatore A. Clemente

LEGAL SUPPORT PERSONNEL

PARALEGALS

Gregory P. Sabo
Elisa LaRosa
Frances P. Rossi
Heather Feenan
Jerry Ezekiel
Steven Randisi
Sharon Williams
Melanie Gaskins

For full biographical listings, see the Martindale-Hubbell Law Directory

MCCORMICK & PRIORE, P.C. (AV)

One Penn Square West, 30 S. 15th Street, Suite 1500, 19102
Telephone: 215-972-0161
Fax: 215-972-5580
Email: mccormick5@aol.com
Marlton, New Jersey Office: One Greentree Centre, Suite 201, 08053.
Telephone: 609-988-5452.
Fax: 609-596-8359.

David M. McCormick
Philip D. Priore
Stephen M. McManus

OF COUNSEL

Harry A. Short, Jr.

Wendy L. Schmidt-Levin
H. Joseph Byron
Michelle Nick Rossi
Christina A. Toriello
Jill Schneider
John P. Lock

LEGAL SUPPORT PERSONNEL

Deborah Stefan
Jane Coley

For full biographical listings, see the Martindale-Hubbell Law Directory

MCELDREW & FULLAM, P.C. (AV)

Suite 5050 One Liberty Place, 19103
Telephone: 215-563-8300
800-223-3352
Fax: 215-563-6130
URL: http://www.lawyers.com/mceldrew&fullampc
New York, New York Office: McEldrew & Ressler, Suite 2101, 11 Pennsylvania Plaza, 10001.
Telephone: 212-695-6446.
Fax: 212-268-0287.

James J. McEldrew, III
Nancy H. Fullam

Marcella J. Schell
Carol L. Vassallo
Sallie Updyke Mundy
David Felderman

LEGAL SUPPORT PERSONNEL

Christine Doelp (Comptroller)

Representative Clients: TWU, Local 2001 and 2013; TWU, Railroad Division.

For full biographical listings, see the Martindale-Hubbell Law Directory

MCKISSOCK & HOFFMAN, P.C. (AV)

1700 Market Street, Suite 3000, 19103
Telephone: 215-246-2100
Fax: 215-246-2144
Westmont, New Jersey Office: 216 Haddon Avenue, Suite 603.
Telephone: 609-858-1650.
Fax: 609-858-1466.
Doylestown, Pennsylvania Office: 16 North Franklin Street, Suite 300.
Telephone: 215-345-4501.
Fax: 215-246-4503.
Harrisburg, Pennsylvania Office: 105 North Front Street, Suite 205.
Telephone: 717-234-0103.
Fax: 717-234-1350.
West Chester, Pennsylvania Office: 31 South High Street, P.O. Box 3086.
Telephone: 610-738-8850.
Fax: 610-738-9121.

J. Bruce McKissock
Peter J. Hoffman
Leslie Anne Miller
Jeffrey B. Albert
Jill Baratz Clarke
John J. McGrath (Resident, Westmont, New Jersey Office)
Donald J. Brooks, Jr.
William J. Mundy
Bryan Craig Black (Resident, Harrisburg Office)
Eileen Lampe
Christopher Thomson (Resident Shareholder, West Chester Office)
K. Reed Haywood
Maureen P. Fitzgerald

For full biographical listings, see the Martindale-Hubbell Law Directory

PERRY, FIALKOWSKI & PERRY (AV)

Suite 1600 One Penn Square West, 30 South 15th Street, 19102
Telephone: 215-561-4110
Fax: 215-561-4177
Email: pfp@pfplaw.com *URL:* http://www.pfplaw.com
Clementon, New Jersey Office: 180 White Horse Pike.
Telephone: 609-627-1005.

MEMBERS OF FIRM

David Perry
Anne E. Fialkowski
Sherryl R. Perry
Marcia F. Rosenbaum

LEGAL SUPPORT PERSONNEL

Lisa Garrett

For full biographical listings, see the Martindale-Hubbell Law Directory

ROSENTHAL AND WEISBERG, P.C. (AV)

Two Logan Square Suite 1565, 18th & Arch Streets, 19103
Telephone: 215-656-4100
Fax: 215-656-4119

Brian D. Rosenthal
Michael Stuart Weisberg

Neil T. Murray
Margaret M. Foley

LEGAL SUPPORT PERSONNEL

Wendy Frost (Paralegal)
Lynn Gibbs (Paralegal)

For full biographical listings, see the Martindale-Hubbell Law Directory

RALPH D. SAMUEL & CO. A PROFESSIONAL CORPORATION (AV)

225 South 15th Street, Suite 1776, 19102
Telephone: 215-893-9992
Fax: 215-893-9996
Email: RalphSamuel@lawmine.com *URL:* http://www.lawyers.com/ralphdsamuellaw

Ralph David Samuel
Lynn Malmgren

For full biographical listings, see the Martindale-Hubbell Law Directory

Philadelphia—Continued

SHRAGER, MCDAID, LOFTUS, FLUM & SPIVEY (AV)

32nd Floor, Two Commerce Square, 2001 Market Street, 19103
Telephone: 215-568-7771
Fax: 215-568-7495
Email: shragerone@aol.com
Voorhees, New Jersey Office: 502 Haddonfield-Berlin Road.
Telephone: 609-354-9116.

MEMBERS OF FIRM

David S. Shrager
Edward B. McDaid
William A. Loftus (1929-1998)
Joanna Hamill Flum
Wayne R. Spivey
Michael S. Bloom
Robert L. Sachs, Jr.
Daniel S. Weinstock

LEGAL SUPPORT PERSONNEL

Roberta Sawyer
Catherine Collins (Paralegal)
Elizabeth A. Thayer

For full biographical listings, see the Martindale-Hubbell Law Directory

*PITTSBURGH,** Allegheny Co.

JOHN A. CAPUTO & ASSOCIATES (AV)

Fifth Floor, Three Gateway Center, 15222
Telephone: 412-391-4990
Fax: 412-391-3121

John A. Caputo

Allan Meyers Cox
Bernard C. Caputo
David L. Conn

For full biographical listings, see the Martindale-Hubbell Law Directory

DAVIES MCFARLAND & CARROLL, P.C. (AV)

One Gateway Center, Tenth Floor, 15222
Telephone: 412-281-0737
Email: firm@dmcpc.com

Daniel P. Carroll
Francis Garger
Lynn E. Bell
M.J. (Jeff) Tindall

Kristin L. Pieseski
Mary Kathleen Coleman
Julie L. Nord
Andrew G. Thiros

Representative Clients: Pennsylvania Medical Society Liability Insurance Co.; Medical Protective Co.; Medical Inter-Insurance Exchange; Cincinatti Frontier Inurance Co.; PHICO Insurance Co.; Professional Claims Management; West Penn Hospital; Mercy Hospital of Pittsburgh.

For Complete List of Firm Personnel, See General Section

For full biographical listings, see the Martindale-Hubbell Law Directory

EVANS, PORTNOY & QUINN (AV)

36th Floor, One Oxford Centre, 301 Grant Street, 15219-6401
Telephone: 412-765-3800
Fax: 412-765-3747

Charles E. Evans
Irving M. Portnoy
John E. Quinn

ASSOCIATES

Mark E. Milsop
Marc J. Reiter
Patricia L. Haas

For full biographical listings, see the Martindale-Hubbell Law Directory

HEINTZMAN, WARREN, WISE & FORNELLA, P.C. (AV)

The 35th Floor, Gulf Tower, 707 Grant Street, 15219
Telephone: 412-394-7810
Fax: 412-263-5222
Email: hww@hwwlaw.com *URL:* http://www.hwwlaw.com

Michael D. Heintzman
Charles S. Warren

Jeanne Welch Sopher

For full biographical listings, see the Martindale-Hubbell Law Directory

KAPETAN MEYERS ROSEN & LOUIK, P.C. (AV)

Suite 200 The Frick Building, 15219-6003
Telephone: 412-281-4200
Fax: 412-281-2997
URL: http://www.lawyers.com/kmr&llaw
Email: law@malpractice-lawyers.net *URL:* http://www.malpractice-lawyers.net

Jerry I. Meyers
Neil R. Rosen
Jon R. Perry

For full biographical listings, see the Martindale-Hubbell Law Directory

KIGER & ALPERN (AV)

1404 Grant Building, 15219
Telephone: 412-765-1811
Fax: 412-765-0440

MEMBERS OF FIRM

Jerome W. Kiger
Charles H. Alpern

ASSOCIATE

Amy B. Kubisiak

For full biographical listings, see the Martindale-Hubbell Law Directory

HOWARD F. MESSER, P.C. (AV)

1404 Grant Building, 15219
Telephone: 412-281-7200
FAX: 412-765-0440
URL: http://www.lawyers.com/messerlaw

Howard F. Messer

Philip A. Fabiano

For full biographical listings, see the Martindale-Hubbell Law Directory

RAIZMAN & FRISCHMAN, P.C. (AV)

The Grant Building, Suite 3400, 310 Grant Street, 15219
Telephone: 412-281-3633; 888-281-3632
Fax: 412-281-3306
Email: raizman@law.pgh.com *URL:* http://www.lawyers.com/raizman&frischman

Dorothy L. Raizman
Craig E. Frischman

Jason M. Lichtenstein

OF COUNSEL

Steven Chernus

For full biographical listings, see the Martindale-Hubbell Law Directory

SWENSEN PERER & KONTOS (AV)

Two PNC Plaza, Suite 2710, 15222
Telephone: 412-281-1970
Fax: 412-281-2808
Email: general2@swensenperer.com
Erie, Pennsylvania Office: Swensen Perer & McCandless. 209 Court House Commons.
Telephone: 814-456-0489. Email: erie@swensenperer.com.

MEMBERS OF FIRM

Jan C. Swensen
Alan H. Perer
John W. McCandless (Resident Partner, Erie Office)
George M. Kontos

ASSOCIATES

Anthony C. Mengine
Daniel J. Sinclair

OF COUNSEL

Diane W. Perer
David A. Schroeder
Anthony J. Sciarrino

For full biographical listings, see the Martindale-Hubbell Law Directory

THE TARASI LAW FIRM, P.C. (AV)

510 Third Avenue, 15219
Telephone: 412-391-7135
Fax: 412-471-2673
Email: tarasilaw@aol.com *URL:* http://www.lawyers.com/tarasilaw

Louis M. Tarasi, Jr.

Craig L. Fishman

For Complete List of Firm Personnel, See General Section

For full biographical listings, see the Martindale-Hubbell Law Directory

*SCRANTON,** Lackawanna Co.

FOLEY, MCLANE, FOLEY, MCDONALD & MACGREGOR (AV)

Linden Plaza, 600 Linden Street, P.O. Box 1108, 18501-1108
Telephone: 570-342-8194
Fax: 570-342-4658
Email: foleylawfirm@worldnet.att.net
Stroudsburg Office: 26 North Sixth Street.
Telephone: 570-424-1757.
Fax: 570-424-2764.

Thomas J. Foley, Jr.
John T. McLane
Michael J. Foley
Michael J. McDonald
Thomas J. Foley, III
Kevin P. Foley
Malcolm L. MacGregor
Michael J. Eagen, Jr. (Resident, Stroudsburg Office)

(See Next Column)

FOLEY, MCLANE, FOLEY, MCDONALD & MACGREGOR, *Scranton—Continued*

NURSE PARALEGALS

Marsia Konanski | Debra Halvorsen

For full biographical listings, see the Martindale-Hubbell Law Directory

MUNLEY, MUNLEY & CARTWRIGHT, P.C. (AV)

205 Madison Avenue, 18503
Telephone: 570-346-7401
Fax: 570-346-3452
URL: http://www.lawyers.com/mmclaw
Email: lawyers@munley.com *URL:* http://www.munley.com

Robert W. Munley | Marion Munley

Reference: First National Bank of Jermyn.

For full biographical listings, see the Martindale-Hubbell Law Directory

O'MALLEY & HARRIS, P.C. (AV)

345 Wyoming Avenue, 18503
Telephone: 570-348-3711
Fax: 570-348-4092
Email: ohpc@epix.net *URL:* http://www.ohpclaw.com
Stroudsburg, Pennsylvania Office: 111 North Seventh Street.
Telephone: 570-421-2252; 570-422-1280.
FAX: 570-422-1281. Email: cerato@ptdprolog.net.
Wilkes-Barre, Pennsylvania Office: 61 North Washington Street.
Telephone: 570-829-3232.
FAX: 570-829-4418. Email: ohpcwb@epix.net.
Williamsport, Pennsylvania Office: 321 Pine Street, Suite 308.
Telephone: 570-323-4380.

Eugene Nogi (1905-1975)
Henry Nogi (1900-1976)
Russell J. O'Malley, Sr. (1904-1993)
Norman Harris (1907-1998)
William H. Amesbury (Resident, Wilkes-Barre Office)
Paul A. Barrett
Matthew P. Barrett
J. Scott Brady (Resident, Wilkes-Barre Office)
Lori J. Cerato (Resident, Stroudsburg Office)
Bruce L. Coyer
John Q. Durkin
Gerald J. Hanchulak
Richard K. Hodges
Timothy J. Holland (Resident, Wilkes-Barre Office)
John F. Kennedy (Resident, Wilkes-Barre Office)
Daniel Morgan
Michael Perry
James M. Tressler
Joseph Timothy Healey
A. Ruth Whalen (Resident, Wilkes-Barre Office)

Representative Clients: Pennsylvania Hospital Insurance Co.; MMI Systems Agency, Inc.; State Farm Insurance Company; ITT Specialty Risk Services; St. Paul Fire & Marine Insurance Co.; Chubb Group of Insurance Companies; Geisingen System Services; Princeton Insurance Company; Northeastern Pennsylvania Physicians Organization; Catholic Healthcare Partners.

For full biographical listings, see the Martindale-Hubbell Law Directory

SCANLON, HOWLEY, SCANLON & DOHERTY (AV)

321 Spruce Street, 10th Floor, 18503
Telephone: 570-346-7651
Fax: 570-344-1542

MEMBERS OF FIRM

James M. Howley
James M. Scanlon
James A. Doherty, Jr.
Thomas R. Nealon
Thomas B. Helbig
Patrick R. Casey

Counsel for: CNA Insurance Company; The Medical Protective Co.; Harleysville Insurance Co.; The Procter & Gamble Co.; Prudential-Bach Securities, Inc.; Zurich-American Insurance Co.; The Keystone Coca-Cola Bottling Co.; The Home Insurance Co.; The Travelers Insurance Co.; Utica First Ins. Co.

For full biographical listings, see the Martindale-Hubbell Law Directory

*WILKES-BARRE,** Luzerne Co.

HOURIGAN, KLUGER & QUINN, A PROFESSIONAL CORPORATION (AV)

700 Mellon Bank Center, 8 West Market Street, 18701-1867
Telephone: 570-825-9401
FAX: 570-829-3460
Email: hkq@epix.net
Scranton, Pennsylvania Office: Suite 200, 434 Lackawanna Avenue.
Telephone: 570-346-8414.
Allentown, Pennsylvania Office: Sovereign Building, 609 Hamilton Mall.
Telephone: 610-437-1584.

Joseph A. Lach (Managing Principal)
Neil E. Wenner (Resident, Allentown Office)
John R. Hill (Resident, Allentown Office)

Representative Client: The Medical Protective Co.

For Complete List of Firm Personnel, See General Section

For full biographical listings, see the Martindale-Hubbell Law Directory

*WILLIAMSPORT,** Lycoming Co.

MITCHELL, MITCHELL, GRAY & GALLAGHER, A PROFESSIONAL CORPORATION (AV)

10 West Third Street, 17701-6513
Telephone: 570-323-8404
Fax: 570-323-8585
Email: mmggpc@csrlink.net

Jacob Neafie Mitchell (1919-1996)
C. Edward S. Mitchell
Richard A. Gray
Robert A. Gallagher
Gary L. Weber
Bret J. Southard

Darryl R. Wishard

For full biographical listings, see the Martindale-Hubbell Law Directory

RHODE ISLAND

*PROVIDENCE,** Providence Co.

BLISH & CAVANAGH (AV)

Commerce Center, 30 Exchange Terrace, 02903
Telephone: 401-831-8900
Telecopier: 401-751-7542
Email: BLISHCAV@AOL.COM

MEMBERS OF FIRM

Joseph V. Cavanagh, Jr.
William R. Landry
Edmund L. Alves, Jr.
Stephen J. Reid, Jr.
Karen A. Pelczarski
Scott T. Spear
Raymond A. Marcaccio

Michael W. Carroll
Staci L. Sawyer
Kristin Rodgers Sullivan

OF COUNSEL

John H. Blish

Representative Clients: Providence Journal Co.; Rhode Island Hospital Trust National Bank; Fleet Bank; Metropolitan Insurance Co.; Allstate Insurance Co.; Delta Dental of Rhode Island; Colony Communications; Providence Housing Authority; Textron; A.T. Cross.

For full biographical listings, see the Martindale-Hubbell Law Directory

SOUTH CAROLINA

*BEAUFORT,** Beaufort Co.

DAVIS, TUPPER & GRIMSLEY, L.L.P. (AV)

611 Bay Street, P.O. Box 2055, 29901-2055
Telephone: 843-524-1116
Facsimile: 843-524-1463
Email: DTGS@Hargray.com

MEMBERS OF FIRM

Hutson S. Davis, Jr.
Ralph E. Tupper
James A. Grimsley, III
Erin D. Dean
R. Gerald Chambers, Jr.
Virginia D. Meeks

For full biographical listings, see the Martindale-Hubbell Law Directory

*CHARLESTON,** Charleston Co.

HAYNSWORTH, MARION, MCKAY & GUÉRARD, L.L.P. (AV)

134 Meeting Street, P.O. Box 1119, 29402
Telephone: 843-722-7606
Facsimile: 843-724-8016
Columbia, South Carolina Office: Suite 2400 Affinity Building, 1201 Main Street, P.O. Drawer 7157, 29202.
Telephone: 803-765-1818. Facsimile 803-765-2399.
Greenville, South Carolina Office: 75 Beattie Place, Eleventh Floor, P.O. Box 2048, 29602.
Telephone: 864-240-3200.
Facsimile: 864-240-3300.

MEMBERS OF FIRM

James J. Hinchey, Jr. | Thomas S. White

Counsel for: Baker Hospital; Healthsource of South Carolina; Allstate Insurance Co.; CSX Corporation; Lloyd's Underwriters; Byerly Hospital.

For Complete List of Firm Personnel, See General Section

For full biographical listings, see the Martindale-Hubbell Law Directory

Charleston—Continued

HOOD LAW FIRM (AV)

172 Meeting Street, P.O. Box 1508, 29402
Telephone: 843-577-4435
Fax: 843-722-1630
Email: hlf@hoodlaw.com *URL:* http://www.hoodlaw.com

MEMBERS OF FIRM

Robert H. Hood
Louis P. Herns
G. Mark Phillips
Carl Everette Pierce, II
John K. Blincow, Jr.
James G. Kennedy
Barbara Wynne Showers
Joseph C. Wilson, IV
James Dowell Gandy, III

Dixon F. Pearce, II
Hugh Willcox Buyck
Allan Poe Sloan, III
Mary Agnes Hood Craig
Allison Snead Patrick
P. Gunnar Nistad
Robert H. Hood, Jr.
William Mullins McLeod, Jr.

For full biographical listings, see the Martindale-Hubbell Law Directory

*COLUMBIA,** Richland Co.

BARNES, ALFORD, STORK & JOHNSON, L.L.P. (AV)

1613 Main Street, P.O. Box 8448, 29202
Telephone: 803-799-1111
Telefax: 803-254-1335
Email: basj@basjlaw.com

Weldon R. Johnson
Kay Gaffney Crowe

Representative Clients: St. Paul Ins. Cos.; MMI; S.C. Insurance Reserve Fund; Zurich.

For Complete List of Firm Personnel, See General Section

For full biographical listings, see the Martindale-Hubbell Law Directory

HAYNSWORTH, MARION, MCKAY & GUÉRARD, L.L.P. (AV)

Suite 2400 Affinity Building, 1201 Main Street, P.O. Drawer 7157, 29202
Telephone: 803-765-1818
Facsimile: 803-765-2399
Greenville, South Carolina Office: 75 Beattie Place, Eleventh Floor, P.O. Box 2048, 29602.
Telephone: 864-240-3200.
Facsimile: 864-240-3300.
Charleston, South Carolina Office: 134 Meeting Street, P.O. Box 1119, 29402.
Telephone: 843-722-7606.
Facsimile: 843-724-8016.

MEMBERS OF FIRM

William P. Simpson
Steven Todd Moon

Counsel for: St. Paul Insurance Group; Allstate Insurance Co.; Fluor-Daniel Corp.; South Carolina Jobs - Economic Development Authority; Anheuser Busch Company; CSX Transportation; Ernst & Young, LLP; Willis Corroon of South Carolina, Inc.; Westinghouse Savannah River Co.; Wachovia Bank of South Carolina, N.A.

For Complete List of Firm Personnel, See General Section

For full biographical listings, see the Martindale-Hubbell Law Directory

LEE, EADON, ISGETT AND POPWELL, P.A. (AV)

1314 Lincoln Street, P.O. Box 1505, 29202
Telephone: 803-799-9811; 1-800-882-0742
Telecopier: 803-779-8572
URL: http://www.lawyers.com/leeeadonisgett&popwell

Luther M. Lee (1923-1996)
Sherod H. Eadon, Jr.
Christopher C. Isgett
Gary W. Popwell, Jr.

Gerald E. Reardon

For full biographical listings, see the Martindale-Hubbell Law Directory

MCKAY & MCKAY, P.A. (AV)

1325 Laurel Street, P.O. Box 7217, 29202
Telephone: 803-256-4645
FAX: 803-765-1839

Douglas McKay, Jr.
Julius W. McKay, II

Representative Clients: South Carolina Division of General Services-Insurance Reserve Fund (IRF); South Carolina Medical Malpractice Joint Underwriting Assn. (JUA).

For Complete List of Firm Personnel, See General Section

For full biographical listings, see the Martindale-Hubbell Law Directory

ERNEST J. NAUFUL, JR., P.C. (AV)

1321 Lady Street Suite 670, P.O. Box 11866, 29211
Telephone: 803-256-4045
Facsimile: 803-256-7044
Email: nauful@aol.com

Ernest J. Nauful, Jr.

For full biographical listings, see the Martindale-Hubbell Law Directory

RICHARDSON, PLOWDEN, CARPENTER & ROBINSON, P.A. (AV)

1600 Marion Street, P.O. Drawer 7788, 29202
Telephone: 803-771-4400
Telecopy: 803-779-0016
Email: atty@rpcrlaw.com *URL:* http://www.rpcrlaw.com
Myrtle Beach, South Carolina Office: 2103 B Farlow Street, P.O. Box 3646, 29578.
Telephone: 843-448-1008.
FAX: 843-448-1533.

George C. Beighley

Marian Williams Scalise
William C. McDow

OF COUNSEL

Donald V. Richardson, III

Representative Clients: St. Paul Insurance Co.; S.C. Medical Malpractice Joint Underwriting Assn.; S.C. Division of General Services Insurance Reserve; Continental Insurance Co.

For Complete List of Firm Personnel, See General Section

For full biographical listings, see the Martindale-Hubbell Law Directory

TURNER, PADGET, GRAHAM & LANEY, P.A. (AV)

Seventeenth Floor, 1901 Main Street, P.O. Box 1473, 29202
Telephone: 803-254-2200
Telecopy: 803-799-3957
Florence, South Carolina Office: Fourth Floor, 1831 West Evans Street, P.O. Box 5478, 29502.
Telephone: 843-662-9008.
Fax: 843-667-0828.
Charleston, South Carolina Office: 21 Broad Street, 1st Floor, P.O. Box 836, 29402.
Telephone: 843-723-1622.
Fax: 843-577-3369.

Charles E. Hill
John S. Wilkerson, III (Resident, Florence, SC, Office)
Teresa A. Arnold

OF COUNSEL

Laura Chandler Rublee (Resident, Florence, SC, Office)

Michael C. Abbott (Resident, Florence, SC, Office)
William C. Barnes, Jr. (Resident, Florence, SC, Office)
Richard C. Burke (Resident, Florence, SC, Office)
Tiffni Drawdy Shealy (Resident, Florence, SC, Office)

For Complete List of Firm Personnel, See General Section

For full biographical listings, see the Martindale-Hubbell Law Directory

*CONWAY,** Horry Co.

MCCUTCHEON, MCCUTCHEON & BAXTER, P.A. (AV)

McCutcheon Building, 208 Elm Street, P.O. Box 1003, 29528
Telephone: 843-248-7225
Telecopier: 843-248-3568
Email: mmb4@gte.net

John Betts McCutcheon (1915-1997)
John Betts McCutcheon, Jr.
Mary Ruth M. Baxter

Lisa A. Thomas
Arrigo P. Carotti

Representative Clients: State of South Carolina, Division of General Services, Insurance Reserve Fund; South Carolina Medical Malpractice Joint Underwriters Assn.; Virginia Professional Underwriters, Inc.; Companion Property and Casualty Co.; Blue Cross and Blue Shield of South Carolina, Inc.; National Indemnity Co.; American Continental Insurance Co.; The Travelers Insurance Group.

For full biographical listings, see the Martindale-Hubbell Law Directory

*GREENVILLE,** Greenville Co.

HAYNSWORTH, MARION, MCKAY & GUÉRARD, L.L.P. (AV)

75 Beattie Place, Eleventh Floor, P.O. Box 2048, 29602
Telephone: 864-240-3200
Facsimile: 864-240-3300
Columbia, South Carolina Office: Suite 2400 Affinity Building, 1201 Main Street, P.O. Drawer 7157, 29202
Telephone: 803-765-1818.
Facsimile: 803-765-2399.

(See Next Column)

HAYNSWORTH, MARION, MCKAY & GUÉRARD L.L.P., *Greenville—Continued*

Charleston, South Carolina Office: 134 Meeting Street, P.O. Box 1119, 29402.
Telephone: 843-722-7606.
Facsimile: 843-724-8016.

MEMBERS OF FIRM

G. Dewey Oxner, Jr. | Edwin Brown Parkinson, Jr.
W. Francis Marion, Jr. | Sarah M. (Sally) Purnell

ASSOCIATE

J. Ben Alexander

Counsel for: St. Paul Insurance Group; Greenville Hospital System; Oconee Hospital; Carolinas Medical Center; South Carolina Medical Malpractice Joint Underwriting Association; Wallace Thompson Hospital.

For Complete List of Firm Personnel, See General Section

For full biographical listings, see the Martindale-Hubbell Law Directory

LOVE, THORNTON, ARNOLD & THOMASON, P.A. (AV)

410 East Washington Street, P.O. Box 10045, 29603
Telephone: 864-242-6360
Telefax: 864-271-7972
Email: lovelaw@globalvision.net *URL:* http://www.ltatlaw.com
Greer, South Carolina Office: 1115 West Poinsett Street, P.O. Box 449, 29652-0449.
Telephone: 864-879-0144.
Telefax: 864-879-0149.

William M. Hagood, III | V. Clark Price

Counsel for: South Carolina Joint Underwriters Association; St. Paul Fire and Marine Insurance; South Carolina Insurance Reserve Fund; Aetna Life and Casualty Insurance Co.; American Continental Insurance Company; The Doctors' Company.

For Complete List of Firm Personnel, See General Section

For full biographical listings, see the Martindale-Hubbell Law Directory

PARHAM & SMITH, L.L.C. (AV)

Smith Barney Building-Second Floor, 501 River Street, P.O. Box 2800, 29601
Telephone: 864-242-9008
1-800-849-7777
Fax: 864-271-6155
Mailing Address: P.O. Box 2800, Greenville, SC, 29602
Email: mparham@parhamlaw.com *URL:* http://www.lawyers.com/parham&smithlaw

MEMBERS OF FIRM

Michael Parham | Barney O. Smith, Jr. (1952-1996)

Steven Blakely Smith

For full biographical listings, see the Martindale-Hubbell Law Directory

MYRTLE BEACH, Horry Co.

FURR AND HENSHAW (AV)

A Partnership of Professional Corporations
1900 Oak Street, P.O. Box 2909, 29578
Telephone: 843-626-7621
Fax: 843-448-6445
Email: f&h@sccoast.net *URL:* http://www.lawyers.com/f&hlaw
Columbia, South Carolina Office: 1534 Blanding Street.
Telephone: 803-252-4050.
FAX: 803-254-7513.

O. Fayrell Furr, Jr. (P.C.)

Karolan F. Ohanesian (Resident)

Reference: Anchor Bank, Myrtle Beach, S.C.

For full biographical listings, see the Martindale-Hubbell Law Directory

*SPARTANBURG,** Spartanburg Co.

HOLCOMBE, BOMAR, GUNN AND BRADFORD, P.A. (AV)

Advantica Plaza, 203 East Main Street, P.O. Drawer 1897, 29304-1897
Telephone: 864-585-4273
Telecopier: 864-585-3844
Email: hbgb@teleplex.net

William U. Gunn | Perry D. Boulier

Representative Clients: Advantica Restaurant Group, Inc.; Denny's, Inc.; Wachovia Bank of South Carolina, N.A.; Community Cash Stores; Liberty Mutual Insurance Cos.; Mary Black Memorial Hospital, Inc.; Metromont Materials Corp.; S.C. Insurance Reserve Fund (State Budget and Control Board).

(See Next Column)

For Complete List of Firm Personnel, See General Section

For full biographical listings, see the Martindale-Hubbell Law Directory

MICHAEL E. SPEARS, P.A. (AV)

215 Magnolia Street, P.O. Box 5806, 29304-5806
Telephone: 864-582-5472
FAX: 864-582-7280

Michael E. Spears

For full biographical listings, see the Martindale-Hubbell Law Directory

*WALHALLA,** Oconee Co.

LARRY C. BRANDT, P.A. (AV)

205 West Main Street, P.O. Drawer 738, 29691
Telephone: 864-638-5406
864-638-7873
Email: lbrandt@innova.net

Larry C. Brandt

LEGAL SUPPORT PERSONNEL

Debra C. Miller

For full biographical listings, see the Martindale-Hubbell Law Directory

SOUTH DAKOTA

*BELLE FOURCHE,** Butte Co.

QUINN, DAY & BARKER, P.L.L.C. (AV)

117 Fifth Avenue, P.O. Box 370, 57717-0370
Telephone: 605-892-2743
Fax: 605-892-4273
Email: bfqedb@dtgcom.net
Rapid City, South Dakota Office: 4200 Beach Drive, P.O. Box 9335.
Telephone: 605-343-6400.
Telecopier: 605-343-4841.

Terence R. Quinn | Bradley A. Schreiber
Michael W. Day | Michael A. Wilson (Resident, Rapid City Office)
Kenneth E. Barker | Michael P. Reynolds (Resident, Rapid City Office)
Robert L. Morris, II

ASSOCIATE

Michael C. Loos (Resident, Rapid City Office)

OF COUNSEL

R. E. Brandenburg

Representative Clients: Pioneer Bank & Trust, Belle Fourche, Spearfish and Rapid City Offices; Belle Fourche Irrigation District; Butte-Meade Sanitary Water District; Igloo-Provo Water User Project; Strawberry Hill Mining Co.; American Family Insurance Group.

For full biographical listings, see the Martindale-Hubbell Law Directory

*RAPID CITY,** Pennington Co.

JOHNSON EIESLAND HUFFMAN & CLAYBORNE LAW FIRM, LLP (AV)

2201 Jackson Boulevard, Suite 200, P.O. Box 6900, 57709-6900
Telephone: 605-348-7300; 800-998-3998
FAX: 605-348-4757
Email: jehc22@aol.com *URL:* http://www.jehc-law.com

Glen H. Johnson | Richard E. Huffman
Gregory A. Eiesland | Courtney R. Clayborne

Kristi K. Wammen

For full biographical listings, see the Martindale-Hubbell Law Directory

TENNESSEE

*CHATTANOOGA,** Hamilton Co.

FOSTER, FOSTER, ALLEN & DURRENCE, P.C. (AV)

Formerly Hall, Haynes, Lusk & Foster
801 Broad Street - Suite 515, 37402
Telephone: 423-266-1141
Telecopier: 423-266-4618
Email: dward@ffadlaw.com

(See Next Column)

FOSTER, FOSTER, ALLEN & DURRENCE P.C.—*Continued*

George Lane Foster
William M. Foster
Craig R. Allen
Phillip M. Durrence, Jr.
David J. Ward
Clayton M. Whittaker
John M. Hull

LEGAL SUPPORT PERSONNEL

Peggy Sue Bates

Division Counsel For: Norfolk Southern Corp.
Attorneys For: CNA/Insurance; United States Fidelity & Guaranty Co. (USF&G); Bridgestone-Firestone, Inc.; State Volunteer Mutual Insurance Co. (SVMIC); Exxon Corp.; Murphy Oil Corp.; Chicago Title Insurance Co.; Jim Walter Homes; Mid-State Homes, Inc.

For full biographical listings, see the Martindale-Hubbell Law Directory

SUMMERS & WYATT, P.C. (AV)

500 Lindsay Street, 37402
Telephone: 423-265-2385
Fax: 423-266-5211
Email: summers@voy.net

Jerry H. Summers

For Complete List of Firm Personnel, See General Section

For full biographical listings, see the Martindale-Hubbell Law Directory

*CLEVELAND,** Bradley Co.

JENNE, SCOTT & JENNE (AV)

260 Ocoee Street, P.O. Box 161, 37364-0161
Telephone: 423-476-5506
Fax: 423-476-5058
Email: MichaelJenne@mindspring.com

MEMBERS OF FIRM

Roger E. Jenne
Robert A. Scott (1940-1984)
Michael E. Jenne

For full biographical listings, see the Martindale-Hubbell Law Directory

KINGSPORT, Sullivan Co.

HAWKINS, MOODY, BINGHAM, MILLER & ASSOCIATES, P.C. (AV)

1397 East Center Street, 37664
Telephone: 423-246-9100
Fax: 423-246-9282

William W. Hawkins (1929-1997)
Edgar G. Moody
John S. Bingham
J. David Miller

For full biographical listings, see the Martindale-Hubbell Law Directory

WEST & ROSE (AV)

537 East Center Street, P.O. Box 1404, 37660
Telephone: 423-246-8176
Fax: 423-246-4028

MEMBERS OF FIRM

M. Lacy West
Steven C. Rose
Julia C. West

For full biographical listings, see the Martindale-Hubbell Law Directory

*KNOXVILLE,** Knox Co.

GILREATH & ASSOCIATES (AV)

550 Main Avenue, Suite 600, P.O. Box 1270, 37901-1270
Telephone: 423-637-2442
Fax: 423-971-4116
Email: gilknox@sidgilreath.com *URL:* http://www.sidgilreath.com
Nashville, Tennessee Office: 2828 Renaissance Tower, 611 Commerce Street.
Telephone: 615-256-3388.
Memphis, Tennessee Office: 44 North Second Street, Suite 200.
Telephone: 901-527-8288.

MEMBER OF FIRM

Sidney W. Gilreath

ASSOCIATES

Meridith C. Bond
Paul Kaufman
Richard L. Duncan
Dianne E. Lashmit
R. Christopher Gilreath
Patricia Taylor Bruner (Not admitted in TN)

LEGAL SUPPORT PERSONNEL

Tammy Ailshie (Legal Assistant to Senior Partner)
Janie Howerton (Legal Assistant)
Darla R. Johnson (Legal Assistant)
Janet L. Tucker (Legal Assistant to Senior Partner)
Pamela Smith Wise (Senior Legal Assistant)
Susan Stogner (Legal Assistant to Senior Partner)

(See Next Column)

LEGAL SUPPORT PERSONNEL (Continued)

Bryan L. Capps (Legal Administrator)
Danielle E. Barto (Firm Administrator)

Representative Client: Transportation Communications International Union; Brotherhood of Locomotive Engineers Union.
Reference: Suntrust Bank.

For full biographical listings, see the Martindale-Hubbell Law Directory

LEIBOWITZ & COHEN (AV)

608 Gay Street, S.W., 37902
Telephone: 423-637-1809
FAX: 423-637-9276

MEMBERS OF FIRM

Arnold G. Cohen
Lawrence P. Leibowitz

ASSOCIATE

Melissa A. Ashburn

OF COUNSEL

Russell T. Greene

For full biographical listings, see the Martindale-Hubbell Law Directory

PRYOR, FLYNN, PRIEST & HARBER (AV)

Suite 600 Two Centre Square, 625 Gay Street, P.O. Box 870, 37901
Telephone: 423-522-4191
Telecopier: 423-522-0910

Robert E. Pryor
Frank L. Flynn, Jr.
Timothy A. Priest
John K. Harber

ASSOCIATES

Mark E. Floyd
Donald R. Coffey
M. Christopher Coffey
Robert E. Pryor, Jr.

References: First Vantage Bank; Sun Trust Bank.

For full biographical listings, see the Martindale-Hubbell Law Directory

WATSON, HOLLOW & REEVES, P.L.C. (AV)

1700 First Tennessee Plaza, 800 South Gay Street, P.O. Box 131, 37901-0131
Telephone: 423-637-1700
Telecopier: 423-525-2514

MEMBERS OF FIRM

Robert Harmon Watson, Jr.
Richard L. Hollow
Pamela L. Reeves
Jon Gilbert Roach
John Chapman Duffy
John T. Batson, Jr.
Earl Jerome Melson

ASSOCIATES

Nathan D. Rowell
Laura C. Webb
Beverley S. Cornett
Jenny Coques Rogers

Representative Client: State Volunteer Mutual Insurance Co.

For full biographical listings, see the Martindale-Hubbell Law Directory

*MEMPHIS,** Shelby Co.

ARMSTRONG ALLEN PREWITT GENTRY JOHNSTON & HOLMES, PLLC (AV)

Brinkley Plaza, Suite 700, 80 Monroe Avenue, 38103-2467
Telephone: 901-523-8211
Facsimile: 901-524-4936
Little Rock, Arkansas Office: Suite 100, 100 Morgan Keegan Drive, 72202.
Telephone: 501-280-0100.
Facsimile: 501-280-0166.
Jackson, Mississippi Office: 2525 Lakeward Drive, Suite 200, 39216.
Telephone: 601-713-1192.
Facsimile: 601-713-2049.
Jackson, Tennessee Office: 464 North Parkway, Suite A, 38305.
Telephone: 901-660-2332.
Facsimile: 901-664-1109.

MEMBERS OF FIRM

Thomas R. Prewitt, Jr.
Robert V. Redding (Resident, Jackson, Tennessee Office)
Randall D. Noel
Mark S. Norris
Lucian T. Pera
Robertson M. Leatherman, Jr.
Cannon F. Allen
Heber S. Simmons III (Resident, Jackson, Mississippi Office)
Richard R. Roberts
Thomas W. Lewis

OF COUNSEL

Gavin M. Gentry

Kimberly Brown

For Complete List of Firm Personnel, See General Section

For full biographical listings, see the Martindale-Hubbell Law Directory

Memphis—Continued

HALE HEADRICK DEWEY & WOLF, PLLC (AV)

One Memphis Place, 200 Jefferson Avenue Suite 1450, 38103
Telephone: 901-523-1123
Fax: 901-523-7472
Nashville, Tennessee Office: Suntrust Bank Building, 201 Fourth Avenue North, Suite 1450, 37219.
Telephone: 615-843-5160.
Fax: 615-843-5165

Stephen P. Hale
S. Russell Headrick
H. Tucker Dewey
Herbert B. Wolf, Jr.
John S. Golwen

OF COUNSEL

Steven L. Gill

Jennifer Ziegenhorn
Wendy A. Geurin
John W. Campbell
Joseph M. Koury
Holly N. Knight
Charles S. Blatteis
Jennifer S. Kiesewetter
J. William Williams

For full biographical listings, see the Martindale-Hubbell Law Directory

SMITH, SABBATINI & MCLEARY, PLLC (AV)

100 Peabody Place Suite 1250, 38103
Telephone: 901-312-5555
Fax: 901-312-5667
Mailing Address: P.O. Box 3582, Memphis, TN, 38173
URL: http://www.smithlawetal.com

Gary K. Smith
Robert L. Sabbatini
Harold W. McLeary, Jr.
William D. Domico
James F. Kyle
James T. McColgan, III
G. Edward Coleman, III
Bryant C. Witt

Representative Clients: Premier RRG Insurance; Illinois Central Railroad; Medical Assurance; Albertson's, Inc.; Med. Marc (Chiro Co.); Medical Protective Co.; Methodist Health Systems; Hartford Insurance Co.; Sentry Insurance; State Farm Insurance.

For full biographical listings, see the Martindale-Hubbell Law Directory

*NASHVILLE,** Davidson Co.

DAVIES & HUMPHREYS (AV)

150 Second Avenue North, Suite 225, P.O. Box 190609, 37219-0609
Telephone: 615-256-8125
Fax: 615-242-7853
Email: davies__h@bellsouth.net

MEMBERS OF FIRM

Ed Reynolds Davies
Robert R. Davies
E. Reynolds Davies, Jr.

ASSOCIATE

John T. Horton

Representative Clients: The Doctor's Company; Opthalmic Mutual Insurance Co.; State Volunteer Mutual Insurance Company; Shand Morhan.

For full biographical listings, see the Martindale-Hubbell Law Directory

KINNARD, CLAYTON & BEVERIDGE (AV)

The Woodlawn, 127 Woodmont Boulevard, 37205
Telephone: 615-297-1007
Facsimile: 615-297-1505
Email: general@kcbattys.com

MEMBERS OF FIRM

Randall L. Kinnard
Daniel L. Clayton
Mark S. Beveridge

ASSOCIATES

Cherry D. Williams
Jonathan L. Griffith

LEGAL SUPPORT PERSONNEL

PARALEGALS

Tracie S. Carter
N. Jayne Taylor
Debbie M. Lightfoot
Mary V. West (Certified Legal Assistant)
Cynthia S. Purkey (Certified Legal Assistant)
Jennifer D. Kirkham

For full biographical listings, see the Martindale-Hubbell Law Directory

DAVID RANDOLPH SMITH & ASSOCIATES (AV)

611 Commerce Street, 3121 Renaissance Tower, 37203
Telephone: 615-742-1775; 800-394-2119
Fax: 615-742-1223
URL: http://www.lawyers.com/drs&associates
Email: info@drslawfirm.com *URL:* http://www.drslawfirm.com

For full biographical listings, see the Martindale-Hubbell Law Directory

WILLIAMS & ASSOCIATES, P.C. (AV)

First American Center Suite 1425, 315 Deaderick Street, 37238
Telephone: 615-242-2800
Fax: 615-256-6618
Email: wmsassoc@isdn.net *URL:* http://www.wmsandassociates.com

Charles J. Williams

Kenneth M. Switzer
Wade B. Cowan
John B. Carlson
Anna B. Williams
Francis M. (Trey) Hamilton, III

For full biographical listings, see the Martindale-Hubbell Law Directory

TEXAS

*AUSTIN,** Travis Co.

KARL BAYER (AV)

900 Norwood Tower, 114 West Seventh Street, 78701
Telephone: 512-476-1226
Fax: 512-476-1280
Email: karl@karlbayer.com

Karl Bayer

For full biographical listings, see the Martindale-Hubbell Law Directory

BYRD, DAVIS AND EISENBERG, L.L.P. (AV)

A Partnership including Professional Corporations
707 West 34th Street, 78705
Telephone: 512-454-3751
Fax: 512-451-5857
Email: 70720.3104@compuserve.com

MEMBERS OF FIRM

L. Tonnett Byrd (P.C.)
Don L. Davis
David H. Walter
James H. Furman
Daniel W. Andrews

ASSOCIATE

Derek L. Davis

OF COUNSEL

Jack C. Eisenberg (P.C.)

For full biographical listings, see the Martindale-Hubbell Law Directory

COLBERT, FREEMAN & STRIBLING (AV)

400 West 14th Street, Suite 120, 78701
Telephone: 512-477-6111

MEMBERS OF FIRM

Joe Colbert
Rick Freeman
Tom Stribling

General Counsel for: Austin Police Association and Travis County Sheriff's Officers Association; Austin Emergency Medical Services Personnel Association.

For full biographical listings, see the Martindale-Hubbell Law Directory

DAVIS & WILKERSON, P.C. (AV)

1801 South Mopac, Suite 300, P.O. Box 2283, 78768-2283
Telephone: 512-482-0614
Fax: 512-482-0342
Email: dwlaw@dwlaw.com *URL:* http://www.dwlaw.com
Alpine Office: 1110 East Holland, P.O. Box 777.
Telephone: 915-837-5547.

David M. Davis
Steven R. Welch
Glen Wilkerson
David A. Wright
Leonard W. Woods
Kevin A. Reed
J. Mark Holbrook
Brian E. Riewe
Brian McElroy
Robert L. Hargett
Michael Wilson
Frances W. Hamermesh
Fletcher H. Brown

Jennifer B. Claymon
David M. Coffey
Hollis Hudson Gaston
Steven C. Levatino
Diana Maldonado
Erin E. Matherne
Joel S. Pace
Stephen G. Wohleb
Michael P. Young

OF COUNSEL

Pete P. Gallego (Resident, Alpine Office)
Peter R. Meeker

For full biographical listings, see the Martindale-Hubbell Law Directory

Austin—Continued

The Onstad Law Firm (AV)

907 Ranch Road 620 South, Suite 302, 78734-5609
Telephone: 512-263-7600
Facimile: 512-263-7800
Email: rockonstad@ispchannel.com

Rockne W. Onstad
Blake C. Erskine, Jr.
James Francis Twombly

For full biographical listings, see the Martindale-Hubbell Law Directory

Thompson & Knight L.L.P. (AV)

(Attorneys and Counselors)
1200 San Jacinto Center, 98 San Jacinto Boulevard, 78701
Telephone: 512-469-6100
Telecopy: 512-469-6180
URL: http://www.tklaw.com
Dallas, Texas Office: 1700 Pacific Avenue, Suite 3300, 75201.
Telephone: 214-969-1700.
Telecopy: 512-969-1751.
Telex: 732298.
Fort Worth, Texas Office: 801 Cherry Street, Suite 1600, 76102.
Telephone: 817-347-1700.
Telecopy: 817-347-1799.
Houston, Texas Office: Thompson Knight Brown Parker & Leahy L.L.P., 1200 Smith Street, Suite 3600, 77002-4595.
Telephone: 713-654-8111.
Telecopier: 713-654-1871.
San Pedro Garza Garcia, Nuevo León, Mexico Office: Edificio Losoles PD-4, Av. Lázaro Cárdenas No. 2400 Pte., C.P. 66220.
Telephone: (52-8) 363-0096.
Telecopy: (52-8) 363-3067.

PARTNERS

Jeffrey S. Boyd
Eugene W. Brees, II

For Complete List of Firm Personnel, See General Section

For full biographical listings, see the Martindale-Hubbell Law Directory

Whitehurst, Harkness, Ozmun & Archuleta, A Professional Corporation (AV)

24th Floor, Westgate Building, P.O. Box 1802, 78767
Telephone: 512-476-4346
Fax: 512-476-4400

William O. Whitehurst, Jr.
Thomas R. Harkness
Scott A. Ozmun
Michael E.J. Archuleta
Cynthia K. Stewart
Sally S. Metcalfe
Michelle M. Cheng
Sylvia H. Imhoff

For full biographical listings, see the Martindale-Hubbell Law Directory

Winckler & Harvey, L.L.P. (AV)

3101 Bee Caves Road, Suite 270, 78746
Telephone: 512-306-1800
Telecopier: 512-306-9442
Email: 2jayslaw@io.com *URL:* http://www.lawyers.com/winkler&harvey

MEMBERS OF FIRM

Jay L. Winckler
Jay Harvey

ASSOCIATE

Reed Teckenbrock

For full biographical listings, see the Martindale-Hubbell Law Directory

*BEAUMONT,** Jefferson Co.

Mehaffy & Weber, A Professional Corporation (AV)

2615 Calder Avenue, Suite 800, P.O. Box 16, 77704
Telephone: 409-835-5011
Fax: 409-835-5729; 835-5177
Email: MehaffyWeber.com
Orange, Texas Office: 1006 Green Avenue, P.O. Drawer 189.
Telephone: 409-886-7766.
Houston, Texas Office: One Allen Center, 500 Dallas, Suite 1200.
Telephone: 713-655-1200.

James W. Mehaffy (1914-1985)
Patricia Chamblin
John E. Haught

Bridget M. Fuselier
Chris H. Booth
Sean Stotsky

Representative Clients: E.I. du Pont de Nemours and Co.; Eli Lilly & Co.; Merrell Dow; Jefferson County Tax Appraisal District; W.R. Grace & Co.-Conn.; Bank of America; Christus Health; Christus St. Elizabeth; Christus St. Mary; Burlington Northern Santa Fe Railway.
Approved Attorneys for: Stewart Title Guaranty Co.

For Complete List of Firm Personnel, See General Section

For full biographical listings, see the Martindale-Hubbell Law Directory

*BROWNSVILLE,** Cameron Co.

Riley & Harris, L.L.P. (AV)

845 E. Harrison, Suite A, 78520-7120
Telephone: 956-550-8825
Fax: 956-550-8854
Email: txlaw@riley-harris.com *URL:* http://www.riley-harris.com
Houston, Texas Office: One Houston Center, 1221 Mckinney, Suite 3000, 77010-2023.
Telephone: 713-646-1000.
Fax: 713-646-1036. Email: txlaw@riley-harris.com.

MEMBER OF FIRM

Timothy D. Riley

For full biographical listings, see the Martindale-Hubbell Law Directory

*CENTER,** Shelby Co.

Fairchild, Price, Thomas, Haley & Willingham, L.L.P. (AV)

413 Shelbyville Street, P.O. Drawer 1719, 75935
Telephone: 409-598-2981
Fax: 409-598-7712
Email: wmthomas@fpthw.com
Nacogdoches, Texas Office: 1801 North Street, P. O. Box 631668, 75963-1668.
Telephone: 409-569-2327.
Fax: 409-569-7932. E-Mail: chaley@fpthw.com
Houston, Texas Office: 440 Louisiana Street, Suite 2110, 77002-4205.
Telephone: 713-426-1700.
Fax: 713-426-1717. E-Mail: mwillingham@fpthw.com

MEMBERS OF FIRM

John L. Price
W. Miller Thomas
C. Victor Haley
R. Mark Willingham
Ryan A. Beason (Resident at Houston Office)
Travis P. Clardy
David J. Fisher
Clayton H. Haley
Russell R. Smith
James A. Payne, Jr.

OF COUNSEL

Robert L. Fairchild

ASSOCIATES

David Edward Ash
Campbell Cox
Jefferson B. Davis
Thomas L. Cougill
Jeffrey Pierce Fultz
Matthew D. Mettauer

Representative Clients: Continental National American Group (CNA); St. Paul Insurance Company; Texas Medical Liability Trust (TMLT).

For full biographical listings, see the Martindale-Hubbell Law Directory

*DALLAS,** Dallas Co.

Law Offices of James C. Barber (AV)

4310 Gaston Avenue, 75246
Telephone: 214-821-8840
Metro: 972-263-6866
Fax: 214-821-3834
URL: http://www.gtesupersite.com/lojcbarber
Email: jcbarber@gte.net *URL:* http://www.lawyers.com/jamescbarber

ASSOCIATE

Larry Chad Kluever

For full biographical listings, see the Martindale-Hubbell Law Directory

Law Offices of Frank L. Branson, P.C. (AV)

18th Floor, Highland Park Place, 4514 Cole Avenue, 75205-4185
Telephone: 214-522-0200
Metro: 972-263-7452
Fax: 214-521-5485
URL: http://www.lawyers.com/frankbranson

Frank L. Branson
Debbie D. Branson
George A. Quesada, Jr.
Jerry M. White
Thomas J. Farmer
William B. Curtis
Robert D. Crain
Charles E. Moody

OF COUNSEL

Ted Z. Robertson
J. Hadley Edgar, Jr.

For full biographical listings, see the Martindale-Hubbell Law Directory

Calhoun & Stacy (AV)

Suite 5700 - Bank of America Plaza, 901 Main Street, 75202-3713
Telephone: 214-748-5000
Facsimile: 214-748-1421
Email: info@calhounstacy.com *URL:* http://www.calhounstacy.com

MEMBERS OF FIRM

Mark Alan Calhoun
Dennis D. Conder
LeAnn Wainscott Cross
Roy L. Stacy
Michael C. Wright

(See Next Column)

CALHOUN & STACY, *Dallas—Continued*

For Complete List of Firm Personnel, See General Section

For full biographical listings, see the Martindale-Hubbell Law Directory

CRACKEN, HARKEY & PAYNE, LLP (AV)

5956 Sherry Lane, Suite 1401, 75225
Telephone: 214-750-1855
Fax: 214-750-7086
Email: info@cracken-harkey.com *URL:* http://www.cracken-harkey.com

John R. W. Cracken
Christopher A. Payne
John D. Harkey, Jr.
James R. Snell

For full biographical listings, see the Martindale-Hubbell Law Directory

FRALEY & FRALEY, L.L.P. (AV)

901 Main Street, Suite 6510, 75202
Telephone: 214-761-6460
Fax: 214-761-6469
Email: info@fraleyandfraley.com *URL:* http://www.fraleyandfraley.com

R. Scott Fraley
Elizabeth Masters Fraley
J. Patrick Bredehoft

J. David Criss

For full biographical listings, see the Martindale-Hubbell Law Directory

HOWIE & SWEENEY, L.L.P. (AV)

14th Floor, Park Place on Turtle Creek, 2911 Turtle Creek Boulevard, 75219
Telephone: 214-523-8800; 800-523-2339
Telecopier: 214-523-8888
Email: email@howie-sweeney.com *URL:* http://www.howie-sweeney.com

MEMBERS OF FIRM

John R. Howie
Paula Sweeney

Al Ellis
Valerie A. Mosman
Jon Kettles
Ladd Sanger
Andrew L. Payne
Elizabeth A. Florence

For full biographical listings, see the Martindale-Hubbell Law Directory

JOHNSON & SYLVAN, P.C. (AV)

4440 Renaissance Tower, P.O. Box 50189, 75250
Telephone: 214-748-4747
Telecopier: 214-748-3191

Stephen W. Johnson
Stephen D. McKimmey
W. Coleman Sylvan
Benjamin H. Read
Charles W. Arnold

Charles B. Mitchell, Jr.
Shelly S. Jock
James K. Campbell
Susan C. Austin
James E. Johnson
Ruben Rios
Robert C. Brown
Travis B. Hulka
Heather A Hohmann

For full biographical listings, see the Martindale-Hubbell Law Directory

LAW OFFICES OF ALAN K. LAUFMAN, J.D., M.D. A PROFESSIONAL CORPORATION (AV)

Suite 1000 Turtle Creek Centre, 3811 Turtle Creek Boulevard, 75219
Telephone: 214-559-3300
Fax: 214-526-1150
Email: medlaw@texas.net *URL:* http://www.lawyers.com/medlaw

Alan K. Laufman

For full biographical listings, see the Martindale-Hubbell Law Directory

MORGAN & WEISBROD, L.L.P. (AV)

10260 North Central Expressway, Suite 100N, P.O. Box 821329, 75382
Telephone: 214-373-3761; 800-800-6353
Fax: 214-739-4732
Email: info@morganweisbrod.com *URL:* http://www.morganweisbrod.com
Houston, Texas Office: 6800 West Loop South, Suite 450, 77401.
Telephone: 713-838-0003.
Fax: 713-838-0066.

Carl M. Weisbrod
Jennifer L. Fry
Les Weisbrod
William A. Newman
David R. Norton
Paul B. Burkhalter
Paul N. Gold
David R. Deary
Larry F. Smith
Leanna Marchand
David V. Marchand

(See Next Column)

ASSOCIATES

Wiebke Breuer
Gal Lahat
John M. Driskill
Robbie S. Partida-Kipness
Kevin Robinowitz

OF COUNSEL

Melvin D. Morgan
Lynn C. Absher
James M. Rauer

For full biographical listings, see the Martindale-Hubbell Law Directory

NEEDHAM JOHNSON, A PROFESSIONAL CORPORATION (AV)

Four Forest Plaza, Suite 1050, 12222 Merit Drive, 75251
Telephone: 972-980-1782
Watts: 1-800-545-8188
Fax: 972-980-0583

Tom Needham
Joe Johnson, Jr.
Barry Johnson

For full biographical listings, see the Martindale-Hubbell Law Directory

THE SCHMIDT FIRM (AV)

3102 Oak Lawn, Suite 730, LB 158, 75219
Telephone: 214-521-4898
Toll Free No. 1-800-745-1372, x4898
Fax: 214-521-9995
Email: schmidt@schmidtlaw.com *URL:* http://www.schmidtlaw.com

C. L. Mike Schmidt

For full biographical listings, see the Martindale-Hubbell Law Directory

SMITH, UNDERWOOD & PERKINS, A PROFESSIONAL CORPORATION (AV)

600 Two Lincoln Centre, 5420 LBJ Freeway, 75240
Telephone: 972-661-5114
Telecopier: 972-661-5691
Email: firm@suandp.com *URL:* http://www.suplaw.com

Timothy S. Perkins
G. Lynn Smith
David W. Ralston
William J. Underwood, Jr.

Christine A. McGuire
Ellen P. Stewart
Amy K. Ratzlaff
Todd W. Shadle
P. Theodore Stoinoff, II
Ruth C. Logan
Val C. Cronin
Christina L. Betanzos
Kent D. Williamson

For full biographical listings, see the Martindale-Hubbell Law Directory

THOMPSON & KNIGHT L.L.P. (AV)

(Attorneys and Counselors)
1700 Pacific Avenue Suite 3300, 75201
Telephone: 214-969-1700
Telecopy: 214-969-1751
Telex: 732 298
URL: http://www.tklaw.com
Austin, Texas Office: 1200 San Jacinto Center, 98 San Jacinto Boulevard, 78701.
Telephone: 512-469-6100.
Telecopy: 512-469-6180.
Fort Worth, Texas Office: 801 Cherry Street, Suite 1600, 76102.
Telephone: 817-347-1700.
Telecopy: 817-347-1799.
Houston, Texas Office: Thompson Knight Brown Parker & Leahy L.L.P., 1200 Smith Street, Suite 3600, 77002-4595.
Telephone: 713-654-8111.
Telecopier: 713-654-1871.
San Pedro Garza Garcia, Nuevo León, Mexico Office: Edificio Losoles PD-4, Av. Lázaro Cárdenas No. 2400 Pte., C.P. 66220.
Telephone: (52-8) 363-0096.
Telecopy: (52-8) 363-3067.

PARTNERS

L. James Berglund, II
Cheryl E. Diaz
Michael R. Berry
John A. Mackintosh, Jr.
Jane Politz Brandt
Maureen A. Murry
Beverly Ray Burlingame
Stephen C. Rasch
Lori L. Dalton
Michael E. Schonberg
Dawn Marie Wright

ASSOCIATE

Julia Elizabeth Jones

For Complete List of Firm Personnel, See General Section

For full biographical listings, see the Martindale-Hubbell Law Directory

TURLEY & STUTZ, P.C. (AV)

610 University Tower, 6440 N. Central Expressway, 75206
Telephone: 214-691-1880
Fax: 214-691-1955
Email: tstutz@quantumdata.net

(See Next Column)

TURLEY & STUTZ P.C.—*Continued*

Linda Turley
Thomas J. Stutz

For full biographical listings, see the Martindale-Hubbell Law Directory

*EL PASO,** El Paso Co.

HICKS & LUCKY, A PROFESSIONAL CORPORATION (AV)

5812 Cromo Drive, 79912-5502
Telephone: 915-834-8400
Fax: 915-587-8401
Toll Free: 888-738-8401
Email: info@hicksandlucky.com *URL:* http://www.hicksandlucky.com

Larry W. Hicks
Jeffrey T. Lucky
Hadley A. Huchton

John Scott Mann
Cynthia C. Llamas
Jennifer F. Callan
Melissa A. Dorman
Laura Montalvo

For full biographical listings, see the Martindale-Hubbell Law Directory

MOUNCE, GREEN, MYERS, SAFI & GALATZAN, A PROFESSIONAL CORPORATION (AV)

100 N. Stanton, Suite 1700, P.O. Box 1977, 79950-1977
Telephone: 915-532-2000
Fax: 915-541-1597
Email: mouncegreenmyers@worldnet.att.net

H. Keith Myers
Barbara Wiederstein

Attorneys for: R.E. Thomason General Hospital; Texas Property and Casualty Ins. Guaranty Assoc.; Zurich-US; Century American Insurance Group; Professional Liability Insurance Co.; Shand Morahan & Company; St. Paul Insurance Companies; Texas Medical Liability Trust; The Medical Protective Company; Western Indemnity.

For Complete List of Firm Personnel, See General Section

For full biographical listings, see the Martindale-Hubbell Law Directory

RAY, MCCHRISTIAN & JEANS, A PROFESSIONAL CORPORATION (AV)

5822 Cromo Drive, Suite 400, 79912
Telephone: 915-832-7200
Fax: 915-832-7333
Email: rmj@rmjfirm.com

Jeff Ray
John W. McChristian, Jr.
David S. Jeans
James A. Mounts, III
Eduardo Miranda
Robin Collins
Leticia Nuñez

Daniel H. Hernandez
Michael K. Dean
Angelica B. Carreon
Todd E. Marshall
Stacy Bearden Zavala

Representative Clients: Texas Medical Liability Trust; Texas Medical Liability Insurance Underwriters Association (JUA); American Physicians Insurance Exchange; Medical Claims Management Group; The Medical Protective Insurance Co.; Professional Liability Insurance Co.; Walgreen Co.; St. Paul Insurance Cos.; Kemper Insurance Group.

For full biographical listings, see the Martindale-Hubbell Law Directory

*FORT WORTH,** Tarrant Co.

LAW OFFICES OF DANIEL R. BARRETT (AV)

500 Throckmorton, Suite 3400, 76102-3821
Telephone: 817-332-2580
Fax: 817-332-4740
Email: dan@danbarrett.com *URL:* http://www.danbarrett.com

For full biographical listings, see the Martindale-Hubbell Law Directory

DECKER, JONES, MCMACKIN, MCCLANE, HALL & BATES, A PROFESSIONAL CORPORATION (AV)

2500 Bank One Tower, 500 Throckmorton Street, 76102-3812
Telephone: 817-336-2400; Metro: 817-429-5260
Fax: 817-332-3043; 336-2181
Email: email@deckerjones.com *URL:* http://www.deckerjones.com

Daniel L. Bates
Robert W. Decker
Mark S. Dugan
Janet L. Hahn
Randy J. Hall
Raymond B. Kelly, III
John B. McClane
John W. McMackin
Charles B. Milliken
Gary M. Moates
Bradley H. Rice
Jeffrey W. Storie
James L. Stripling
Brian K. Yost
Tamera H. Bennett
Arthur F. Zobal
Geoffrey A. Mantooth

(See Next Column)

Representative Clients: Medical Protective Co.; Texas Medical Liability Trust; MIIX Group; Employers Insurance of Texas; American International Group; Redman Homes, Inc.; Liberty Mutual Insurance; The St. Paul Insurance Cos.; Ohio Casualty.

For full biographical listings, see the Martindale-Hubbell Law Directory

JOSE, HENRY, BRANTLEY & KELTNER, L.L.P. (AV)

675 North Henderson Street, 76107-8495
Telephone: 817-877-3303
Fax: 817-338-9109

John S. Jose
Michael J. Henry
Rickey J. Brantley
David E. Keltner

Karen S. Precella
Scotty MacLean
Anna L. Kingsley
Sara K. Turman-Vedral

For full biographical listings, see the Martindale-Hubbell Law Directory

LAW FIRM OF DARRELL KEITH, P.C. (AV)

The Keith Building, 1705 West Seventh Street, 76102
Telephone: 817-338-1400
Telefax: 817-870-2448

SHAREHOLDERS

Darrell L. Keith
Courtney S. Keith

Stephanie L. Merithew

For full biographical listings, see the Martindale-Hubbell Law Directory

LAW OFFICES OF PATRICK H. O'NEILL (AV)

110 West 7th Street, Suite 1100, 76102
Telephone: 817-878-3333
Fax: 817-878-3672

Patrick H. O'Neill

James L. Jackson, Jr.
Glenn T. Lupo

For full biographical listings, see the Martindale-Hubbell Law Directory

RUSSELL, TURNER, LAIRD & JONES, L.L.P. (AV)

One Colonial Place, 2400 Scott Avenue, 76103-2200
Telephone: 817-531-3000; 1-800-448-2889
Fax: 817-535-3046
Irving, Texas Office: Williams Square, Central Tower, Suite 700, 5215 North O'Connor Boulevard, Las Colinas Urban Center.
Telephone: 972-444-0444; 1-800-448-2889.

Wm. Greg Russell
Randall E. Turner
Steven C. Laird
Gregory G. Jones

For full biographical listings, see the Martindale-Hubbell Law Directory

THOMPSON & KNIGHT L.L.P. (AV)

(Attorneys and Counselors)
801 Cherry Street, Suite 1600, 76102
Telephone: 817-347-1700
Telecopy: 817-347-1799
URL: http://www.tklaw.com
Dallas, Texas Office: 1700 Pacific Avenue, Suite 3300, 75201.
Telephone: 214-969-1700.
Telecopy: 214-969-1751.
Telex: 732298.
Austin, Texas Office: 1200 San Jacinto Center, 98 San Jacinto Boulevard, 78701.
Telephone: 512-469-6100.
Telecopy: 512-469-6180.
Houston, Texas Office: Thompson Knight Brown Parker & Leahy L.L.P., 1200 Smith Street, Suite 3600, 77002-4595.
Telephone: 713-654-8111.
Telecopier: 713-654-1871.
San Pedro Garza Garcia, Nuevo León, Mexico Office: Edificio Losoles PD-4, Av. Lázaro Cárdenas No. 2400 Pte., C.P. 66220.
Telephone: (52-8) 363-0096.
Telecopy: (52-8) 363-3067.

PARTNER

E. Michael Sheehan

For Complete List of Firm Personnel, See General Section

For full biographical listings, see the Martindale-Hubbell Law Directory

HARLINGEN, Cameron Co.

ADAMS & GRAHAM, L.L.P. (AV)

222 East Van Buren, West Tower, 78550
Telephone: 956-428-7495
Fax: 956-428-2954
Email: office@adamsgraham.com *URL:* http://www.adamsgraham.com
Affiliate Austin, Texas Office: Hill Gilstrap Adams & Graham, L.L.P., 1005 Congress Avenue, Suite 880, 78701.
Telephone: 512-457-9806.
Fax: 512-457-9066.

John Q. Adams (1900-1968)
Marshall W. Graham (1924-1988)
James S. Graham, Jr. (1922-1990)
Ferriel C. Hamby, Jr.
Tom A. Lockhart
Jim Denison
Leo C. Salzman
Roger W. Hughes
Craig H. Vittitoe
William L. Pope
Patricia Kelly
Jaime Balli
Gina M. Benavides
Charlie J. Cilfone
Juan A. Gonzalez
Barry Ray
Wilbert (Will) Hughes
Trinidad P. Galdean

Representative Clients: The Travelers Insurance Cos.; State Farm Insurance Co.; Valley Baptist Medical Center; Continental Loss Adjusting Services; McAllen Medical Center; Brownsville Medical Center; American International Companies; American Health Choice, Inc.; Gallagher-Bassett; CIGNA.

For full biographical listings, see the Martindale-Hubbell Law Directory

*HOUSTON,** Harris Co.

BERG & ANDROPHY (AV)

3704 Travis, 77002-9550
Telephone: 713-529-5622
Fax: 713-529-3785
URL: http://www.lawyers.com/b&alaw
Email: mail@bahou.com *URL:* http://www.bafirm.com
New York, New York Office: 230 Park Avenue, Suite 1000, 10169-1099.
Telephone: 212-808-6580.
Fax: 212-808-3020.

David H. Berg (P.C.)
Joel M. Androphy
Cynthia R. Levin Moulton

Wade T. Howard
Geoffrey A. Berg
Gabriel A. Berg (Not admitted in TX)

For full biographical listings, see the Martindale-Hubbell Law Directory

JAMES R. BOSTON & ASSOCIATES, P.C. (AV)

1360 Post Oak Boulevard Suite 1650, 77056
Telephone: 713-961-1122
Fax: 713-965-0883
Email: admin@boston-associates.com

James R. Boston, Jr.

Matthew B.E. Hughes
Virginia Barry
Gary A. Sommer

For full biographical listings, see the Martindale-Hubbell Law Directory

CRUSE, SCOTT, HENDERSON & ALLEN, L.L.P. (AV)

Chase Tower, 600 Travis, Suite 3900, 77002-2910
Telephone: 713-650-6600
Fax: 713-650-1720

Sam W. Cruse, Jr.
John P. Scott
Jay H. Henderson
T. Scott Allen, Jr.
Samuel A. Houston
George W. (Billy) Shepherd, III
John R. Strawn, Jr.
Stephen R. Bailey
John D. Vogel
Wayne Clawater

ASSOCIATES

Debra L. Elmore
Merritt McReynolds Marinelli
David J. McTaggart
Matthew M. Prewett

For full biographical listings, see the Martindale-Hubbell Law Directory

DUNN, KACAL, ADAMS, PAPPAS & LAW, A PROFESSIONAL CORPORATION (AV)

2600 America Tower, 2929 Allen Parkway at Waugh, 77019-2151
Telephone: 713-529-3992
Telefax: 713-529-8161
Email: DKAPL@worldnet.att.net

(See Next Column)

Charles R. Dunn
Jerry Kacal
Robert L. Adams
Christopher C. Pappas
Richard M. Law
Gordon M. Carver, III
Michael C. Feehan
Daniel D. King
Kenneth D. Rhodes
Frances Moore
A.M. "Andy" Landry, III
Robert Scherrer
James D. Smith

Karen M. Alvarado
Darrell R. Greer
Lucille Anderson Reiter
Andrew J. Sarne
J. Christopher Dean
Daniel F. Crowder
Laurel A. Agris
Tamara L. Sheffield
M. Laura Lopez
Karen R. Dow
Kevin Douglas Bowie
Melanie A. Rubinsky

For full biographical listings, see the Martindale-Hubbell Law Directory

FAIRCHILD, PRICE, THOMAS, HALEY & WILLINGHAM, L.L.P. (AV)

440 Louisiana Street, Suite 2110, 77002-4205
Telephone: 713-426-1700
Fax: 713-426-1717.
Email: mwillingham@fpthw.com
Center, Texas Office: 413 Shelbyville Street, P.O. Drawer 1719, 75935.
Telephone: 409-598-2981.
Fax: 409-598-7712. E-Mail: wmthomas@fpthw.com
Nacogdoches, Texas Office: 1801 North Street, P.O. Box 631668, 75963-1668.
Telephone: 409-569-2327.
Fax: 409-569-7932. E-Mail: chaley@fpthw.com

John L. Price
W. Miller Thomas
C. Victor Haley
R. Mark Willingham
Travis P. Clardy
David J. Fisher
Clayton H. Haley
Russell R. Smith
Ryan A. Beason

OF COUNSEL

Robert L. Fairchild

James A. Payne, Jr.
David Edward Ash
Campbell Cox
Jefferson B. Davis
Thomas L. Cougill
Jeffrey Pierce Fultz
Matthew D. Mettauer

Representative Clients: Continental National American Group (CNA); St. Paul Insurance Company; Texas Medical Liability Trust (TMLT).

For full biographical listings, see the Martindale-Hubbell Law Directory

FRANKLIN, CARDWELL & JONES (AV)

Chase Tower, 24th Floor, 600 Travis Street, 77002-2910
Telephone: 713-222-6025
Fax: 713-222-0938
Email: attorneys@fcj.com *URL:* http://www.fcj.com

Suzan K. Cardwell
A. Scott Alford
Mary Angela Meyer
Jeffrey D. Meyer
Sheila Wollam

For full biographical listings, see the Martindale-Hubbell Law Directory

FRIEND & ASSOCIATES, L.L.P. (AV)

1301 McKinney Street, Suite 2900, 77010
Telephone: 713-650-0024
Fax: 713-650-7100

Gail N. Friend

Alicia K. Dowdy
Staci Reeves Bouthillette
Susanne Witt Langlais

For full biographical listings, see the Martindale-Hubbell Law Directory

GALLAGHER, YOUNG, LEWIS, HAMPTON & DOWNEY, L.L.P. (AV)

NationsBank Building, 700 Louisiana, 40th Floor, 77002
Telephone: 713-222-8080
Fax: 713-222-0066

Michael T. Gallagher
William H. Young
Craig Lewis
Hartley Hampton
Daniel M. Downey

Martin John de la Torre
Andrew Sher
Candace Kaiser Eindorf
Scott H. Mclemore
John J. Klevenhagen, III
Araceli E. Flores

OF COUNSEL

Rosemary Conlon McCarthy

For full biographical listings, see the Martindale-Hubbell Law Directory

Houston—Continued

HANEN, ALEXANDER, JOHNSON & SPALDING, L.L.P. (AV)

910 Travis, Suite 1700, 77002
Telephone: 713-222-2323
Fax: 713-222-2226

Andrew S. Hanen
John E. Spalding
Joseph R. Alexander, Jr.
Frank A. Doyle
Brian P. Johnson
Lawrence J. West
T. Christopher Trent

Geoffrey C. Guill
Lisa M. Moran
Tamara M. Madden
Shashi Patel
Richard Todd Marshall
Annette Sepulveda Kenefick
Raphael (Rafe) Taylor
Craig A. Choate

For full biographical listings, see the Martindale-Hubbell Law Directory

HOUSSIERE, DURANT & HOUSSIERE, LLP (AV)

Three Post Oak Central, 1990 Post Oak Boulevard, Suite 800, 77056-3812
Telephone: 713-626-3700
Fax: 713-626-3709
Email: lhoussi@hdhtex.com *URL:* http://www.hdhtex.com

Charles R. Houssiere, III
Linda D. Houssiere
Harry L. Durant (Retired)
Randal A. Kauffman
Monica C. Vaughan

Chad D. Points

For full biographical listings, see the Martindale-Hubbell Law Directory

LANIER, PARKER & SULLIVAN, P.C. (AV)

Four Houston Center, Suite 1550 1331 Lamar Street, 77010
Telephone: 713-659-5200
FAX: 713-659-2204

W. Mark Lanier
Kevin P. Parker
Kent C. Sullivan

Becky J. Lanier
Edward W. Fudge
Leslie M. Stewart
Patrick N. Haines
Robert E. Leone
Dara Grisbee Hegar
Eugene R. Egdorf

For full biographical listings, see the Martindale-Hubbell Law Directory

MARKLE, RAMOS & ZITO, A PROFESSIONAL CORPORATION (AV)

777 Post Oak Boulevard, Suite 350, 77056
Telephone: 713-861-9595
Facsimile: 713-861-8368
Email: mrz@marzpc.com

Spencer G. Markle
Dion Ramos
Nicholas E. Zito

Nathan A. Hardee
Andrea Frey Lopes
Shelley V. Hutson
Heather L. Nistler
Angela Nolan

For full biographical listings, see the Martindale-Hubbell Law Directory

THE PERDUE LAW FIRM, L.L.P. (AV)

2727 Allen Parkway, Suite 800, 77019
Telephone: 713-520-2500
Fax: 713-520-2525
Email: firm@perduelaw.com *URL:* http://www.perduelaw.com

MEMBERS OF FIRM

Jim M. Perdue
Jim M. Perdue, Jr.

ASSOCIATES

Tracy Kesler
Christopher L. Thetford
Parker Bond Binion

For full biographical listings, see the Martindale-Hubbell Law Directory

RILEY & HARRIS, L.L.P. (AV)

One Houston Center, 1221 McKinney, Suite 3000, 77010-2023
Telephone: 713-646-1000
Fax: 713-646-1036
Email: txlaw@riley-harris.com *URL:* http://www.riley-harris.com
Brownsville, Texas Office: 845 E. Harrison, Suite A, 78520-7120.
Telephone: 956-550-8825.
Fax: 956-550-8854.

MEMBERS OF FIRM

Timothy D. Riley
Britton B. Harris
Patrick W. O'Briant

(See Next Column)

Brett J. Sileo
Matthew T. Heffner
Jill Ellen Ferguson

For full biographical listings, see the Martindale-Hubbell Law Directory

THOMPSON KNIGHT BROWN PARKER & LEAHY L.L.P. (AV)

A Registered Limited Liability Partnership including Professional Corporations
(Attorneys and Counselors)
1200 Smith Street, Suite 3600, 77002-4595
Telephone: 713-654-8111
Telecopier: 713-654-1871
URL: http://www.tklaw.com
Dallas, Texas Office: Thompson & Knight L.L.P., 1700 Pacific Avenue, Suite 3300, 75201.
Telephone: 214-969-1700.
Telecopy: 214-969-1751.
Telex: 732298.
Austin, Texas Office: Thompson & Knight L.L.P., 1200 San Jacinto Center, 98 San Jacinto Boulevard, 78701.
Telephone: 512-469-6100.
Telecopy: 512-469-6180.
Fort Worth, Texas Office: Thompson & Knight L.L.P., 801 Cherry Street, Suite 1600, 76102.
Telephone: 817-347-1700.
Telecopy: 817-347-1799.
San Pedro Garza Garcia, Nuevo León, Mexico Office: Thompson & Knight L.L.P., Edificio Losoles PD-4, Av. Lázaro Cárdenas No. 2400 PTE., C.P. 66220.
Telephone: (52-8) 363-0096.
Telecopy: (52-8) 363-3067.

PARTNER

Gregory S. Meece

ASSOCIATES

Mary-Olga Ferguson
Peter M. Roossien

For Complete List of Firm Personnel, See General Section

For full biographical listings, see the Martindale-Hubbell Law Directory

*LUBBOCK,** Lubbock Co.

CRENSHAW, DUPREE & MILAM, L.L.P. (AV)

Norwest Center, 1500 Broadway, 10th Floor, P.O. Box 1499, 79408-1499
Telephone: 806-762-5281
Fax: 806-762-3510
Email: attorney@cdmlaw.com

Chas. C. Crenshaw (1886-1964)
Geo. W. Dupree (1890-1973)
James H. Milam (1911-1994)

MEMBERS OF FIRM

Cecil C. Kuhne
David R. Cobb
John Crews
Robert L. Duncan
William J. Wade
W. Chris Boyer
Jack McCutchin, Jr.
Robert L. Jones
W C Bratcher
Mark W. Harmon
Layton Z. Woodul
Mark O. Blankenship
Charlotte D. Bingham

ASSOCIATES

Sheila M. Kidwell
Jeff R. Lashaway
Matt D. Matzner
Taylor L. Pope

OF COUNSEL

Tom S. Milam
William R. Moss

For full biographical listings, see the Martindale-Hubbell Law Directory

MIKE MILLSAP (AV)

1116A Broadway, 79401
Telephone: 806-747-0264
Fax: 806-747-0292
Email: mikemillsap@msn.com

Reference: Norwest Bank.

For full biographical listings, see the Martindale-Hubbell Law Directory

*MIDLAND,** Midland Co.

MAX E. WRIGHT A PROFESSIONAL CORPORATION (AV)

505 North Big Spring, Suite 300, 79701
Telephone: 915-686-0080
Fax: 915-686-8247
Email: mwright@iglobal.net *URL:* http://www.lawyers.com/maxlaw

Max E. Wright

Scott M. Kidwell
Julian L. Rivera

(See Next Column)

MAX E. WRIGHT A PROFESSIONAL CORPORATION, *Midland—Continued*

LEGAL SUPPORT PERSONNEL

Kathleen Dory (Legal Assistant)
Evelyn McKown, R.N. (Medical Legal Assistant)

For full biographical listings, see the Martindale-Hubbell Law Directory

*NACOGDOCHES,** Nacogdoches Co.

FAIRCHILD, PRICE, THOMAS, HALEY & WILLINGHAM, L.L.P. (AV)

1801 North Street, P.O. Box 631668, 75963-1668
Telephone: 409-569-2327
Fax: 409-569-7932.
Email: chaley@fpthw.com
Center, Texas Office: 413 Shelbyville Street, P.O. Drawer 1719, 75935.
Telephone: 409-598-2981.
Fax: 409-598-7712. E-Mail: wmthomas@fpthw.com
Houston, Texas Office: 440 Louisiana Street, Suite 2110, 77002-4205.
Telephone: 713-426-1700.
Fax: 713-426-1717. E-Mail: mwillingham@fpthw.com

John L. Price
W. Miller Thomas
C. Victor Haley
R. Mark Willingham
Travis P. Clardy
David J. Fisher
Clayton H. Haley
Russell R. Smith
Ryan A. Beason

OF COUNSEL

Robert L. Fairchild

James A. Payne, Jr.
David Edward Ash
Campbell Cox
Jefferson B. Davis
Thomas L. Cougill
Jeffrey Pierce Fultz
Matthew D. Mettauer

Representative Clients: Continental National American Group (CNA); St. Paul Insurance Company; Texas Medical Liability Trust (TMLT).

For full biographical listings, see the Martindale-Hubbell Law Directory

*SAN ANTONIO,** Bexar Co.

ADKISSON & JACKSON, L.L.P. (AV)

Suite 850, Alamo National Bank Building, 105 South St. Mary's Street, 78205
Telephone: 210-472-0500
Fax: 210-472-0515
Email: adkisson@satexlaw.com

MEMBERS OF FIRM

Randall C. Jackson
David M. Adkisson

For full biographical listings, see the Martindale-Hubbell Law Directory

LAW OFFICES OF JEFFREY C. ANDERSON (AV)

9601 McAllister Freeway, Suite 1250, 78216
Telephone: 210-340-8880 (1-800-980-8880)
Fax: 210-340-8885
Email: jca@texaslawfirm.com *URL:* http://www.texaslawfirm.com

For full biographical listings, see the Martindale-Hubbell Law Directory

LYONS & RHODES, P.C. (AV)

126 Villita Street, 78205
Telephone: 210-225-5251
Fax: 210-225-6545
Email: lyonrhod@txdirect.net *URL:* http://www.lyonsandrhodes.com
Brownsville, Texas Office: 1325 Palm Boulevard, Suite B.
Telephone: 956-544-1932.

Clem Lyons
J. Thomas Rhodes, III
Mary Wilson
Robert E. Brzezinski

Sean M. Lyons

For full biographical listings, see the Martindale-Hubbell Law Directory

O'CONNELL, BENJAMIN & COGHLAN, L.L.P. (AV)

153 Treeline Park, Suite 200, 78209
Telephone: 210-824-0009
Fax: 210-824-9429
Email: obcllp@oconben.com

Keith B. O'Connell
David P. Benjamin
G. Thomas Coghlan
Ernest F. Avery
Les Katona, Jr.
Dan Vana

Gayla S. Corley
Cathrin J. Martinez

For full biographical listings, see the Martindale-Hubbell Law Directory

TINSMAN & HOUSER, INC. (AV)

One Riverwalk Place, 14th Floor, 700 North St. Mary's Street, 78205
Telephone: 210-225-3121
U.S. Wats: 1-800-292-9999
Fax: 210-225-6235
Email: info@thlaw.com *URL:* http://www.thlaw.com

Richard Tinsman
Franklin D. Houser
Margaret M. Maisel
David G. Jayne
Robert C. Scott
Daniel J. T. Sciano
Rey Perez
Bernard Wm. Fischman
Sharon L. Savage
Ronald J. Salazar
Sue Dodson
Dennis P. Bujnoch

For full biographical listings, see the Martindale-Hubbell Law Directory

TEXARKANA, Bowie Co.

PATTON, TIDWELL & SANDEFUR, L.L.P. (AV)

4605 Texas Boulevard, P.O. Box 5398, 75505-5398
Telephone: 903-792-7080; 903-792-5859
Fax: 903-792-8233
Email: KTIDW87157@aol.com

Nicholas H. Patton
Kelly B. Tidwell
Gregory C. Sandefur

For Complete List of Firm Personnel, See General Section

For full biographical listings, see the Martindale-Hubbell Law Directory

*TYLER,** Smith Co.

HOWARD, DAVIS & BUNT, P.C. (AV)

216 West Erwin, Suite 200, 75702
Telephone: 903-533-9997
Fax: 903-533-0260
Mailing Address: P.O. Box P.O.Drawer 1050, Tyler, TX, 75710
Email: bhoward@ballistic.com

Brent C. Howard
Dick Davis
Robert C. Bunt

For full biographical listings, see the Martindale-Hubbell Law Directory

RAMEY & FLOCK, A PROFESSIONAL CORPORATION (AV)

500 First Place, P.O. Box 629, 75710
Telephone: 903-597-3301
Telecopier: 903-597-2413
Email: Ramey@Ramey-Flock.com *URL:* http://www.RameyFlock.com

Thomas B. Ramey (1892-1967)
Jack W. Flock
Tracy Crawford
Glenn Collins
Michael A. Hatchell
Tom Henson
Dennis G. Black
Paul H. Gilliam
R. Brian Craft
Gregory D. Smith
Michael T. Crawford
Mary H. Molly Hatchell
Rosemary Sage Jones
Ronald S. Vickery
John W. Ferguson, Jr.

Deron R. Dacus
Eric H. Findlay
Shannon Dacus
Maria Benecki Sowders
Jamy Mitchell Skaggs

Counsel for: Regions Bank; Exxon Co. U.S.A.; Kelly Springfield Tire Co.; Trinity-Mother Frances Health System; St. Paul Insurance Co.; The Travelers Cos.; Reliance Insurance Co.; Marshall Regional Medical Center.

For full biographical listings, see the Martindale-Hubbell Law Directory

UTAH

*SALT LAKE CITY,** Salt Lake Co.

JOEL M. ALLRED, P.C. (AV)

Suite 800, McIntyre Building, 68 South Main Street, 84101
Telephone: 801-531-8300 (Downtown Office)
801-582-2309 (Home Office)
Fax: 801-533-2463 (Office Hours)
801-363-2420 (After Office Hours)
Email: jallred@vii.com

Joel M. Allred

Amy Allred Dolce

For full biographical listings, see the Martindale-Hubbell Law Directory

Salt Lake City—Continued

EPPERSON & RENCHER, A PROFESSIONAL CORPORATION (AV)

Established in 1895 as Stewart & Stewart
Crandall Building, Suite 500, 10 West 100 South, 84101-1566
Telephone: 801-983-9800
Fax: 801-983-9808
Email: erlaw@aros.net

David H. Epperson
Jaryl L. Rencher

Stephen W. Owens
R. Scott Wood

For full biographical listings, see the Martindale-Hubbell Law Directory

PLANT, WALLACE, CHRISTENSEN & KANELL, A PROFESSIONAL CORPORATION (AV)

136 East South Temple Suite 1700, 84110-2970
Telephone: 801-363-7611
Fax: 801-531-9747
URL: http://www.pwcklaw.com

Robert R. Wallace
Scott W. Christensen
Terry M. Plant
Theodore E. Kanell
John N. Braithwaite
Mark J. Williams

Lisa Watts Baskin
Jason Max Kerr
Robert C. Olsen
Mollio L. McDonald

Representative Clients: PHICO Group, Inc.; Travelers Group; Interstate Insurance Group.

For full biographical listings, see the Martindale-Hubbell Law Directory

STRONG & HANNI, A PROFESSIONAL CORPORATION (AV)

Sixth Floor Boston Building, 9 Exchange Place, 84111
Telephone: 801-532-7080
Fax: 801-596-1508
Email: pfishler@strongandhanni.com

Gordon R. Strong (1909-1969)
Glenn C. Hanni
Henry E. Heath
Philip R. Fishler
Roger H. Bullock
R. Scott Williams
Dennis M. Astill (Managing Partner)
Stuart H. Schultz
Paul M. Belnap
Stephen J. Trayner
Joseph J. Joyce
Bradley Wm. Bowen
Robert L. Janicki
Elizabeth L. Willey
H. Burt Ringwood
Peter H. Christensen
David R. Nielson

Kevin D. Swenson
Catherine M. Larson
Kristin Van Orman
Darren K. Nelson
Peter H. Barlow
Steven T. Densley
Jennifer C. Polley-Abramson
Shawn T. Welch

OF COUNSEL

Robert A. Burton

Representative Clients: State Farm Mutual Automobile Insurance Co.; Standard Accident Insurance Co.; United Services Automobile Assn.; Western Casualty & Surety Co.; Government Employees Insurance Co.; Guaranty Mutual Life Co.

For full biographical listings, see the Martindale-Hubbell Law Directory

VAN COTT, BAGLEY, CORNWALL & McCARTHY, A PROFESSIONAL CORPORATION (AV)

50 South Main Street, Suite 1600, P.O. Box 45340, 84145-0340
Telephone: 801-532-3333
Telecopier: 801-534-0058
Email: info@vancott.com *URL:* http://www.vancott.com
Ogden, Utah Office: 2404 Washington Boulevard, Suite 900.
Telephone: 801-394-5783.
Park City, Utah Office: 2200 Park Avenue, Suite C200-A.
Telephone: 435-649-3889.

Jeremy M. Hoffman
Kenneth W. Yeates

For Complete List of Firm Personnel, See General Section

For full biographical listings, see the Martindale-Hubbell Law Directory

VERMONT

*BURLINGTON,** Chittenden Co.

MANCHESTER LAW OFFICES, PROFESSIONAL CORPORATION (AV)

One Lawson Lane, P.O. Box 1459, 05402-1459
Telephone: 802-658-7444
Fax: 802-658-2078
Email: mlo@together.net *URL:* http://www.lawyers.com/manchesterlaw

(See Next Column)

Robert E. Manchester

Tina L. Shoup
George N. Collias

LEGAL SUPPORT PERSONNEL

Maureen P. Neacy (Legal Nurse Consultant)

For full biographical listings, see the Martindale-Hubbell Law Directory

SYLVESTER & MALEY, INC. (AV)

78 Pine Street, P.O. Box 1053, 05402-1053
Telephone: 802-864-5722
Fax: 802-658-6124
Email: sylvester-maley@worldnet.att.net

Alan F. Sylvester
John P. Maley
Michael S. Brow
Amy E. Sylvester

For full biographical listings, see the Martindale-Hubbell Law Directory

*MONTPELIER,** Washington Co.

THERIAULT & JOSLIN, P.C. (AV)

141 Main Street, P.O. Box 249, 05601-0249
Telephone: 802-223-2381
Fax: 802-223-1461
Email: LAWYERS@TJOSLIN.COM

Peter B. Joslin
Fletcher Brian (Ted) Joslin

Representative Clients: American International Group; Doctors' Company, The; Atlantic Risk Management Co.; AAO Insurance Company; AAOMS Mutual Insurance Company; Kaiser Permanent/CHP; Health Care Underwriters Mutual Ins. Co.; Medical Mutual Insurance Co.; PHICO Insurance Co.; St. Paul Insurance Co.

For Complete List of Firm Personnel, See General Section

For full biographical listings, see the Martindale-Hubbell Law Directory

*RUTLAND,** Rutland Co.

MILLER FAIGNANT & BEHRENS, P.C. (AV)

36 Merchants Row, P.O. Box 6688, 05702-6688
Telephone: 802-775-2521
Fax: 802-775-8274
Email: lhblaw@aol.com *URL:* http://www.lawyers.com/millerfaignantbehrenslaw

Lawrence Miller
John Paul Faignant
Lawrence H. Behrens

OF COUNSEL

Lisa L. Chalidze

LEGAL SUPPORT PERSONNEL

Marie Peck Fabian
Kim J. Miller

Representative Clients: Travelers Insurance Co.; Government Employees Insurance Co.; Utica Mutual Insurance Co.; Universal Underwriters Insurance Co.; Zurich American Acadia Insurance.
References: Travelers Insurance Co.; Universal Underwriters Insurance Co.

For full biographical listings, see the Martindale-Hubbell Law Directory

VIRGINIA

*ABINGDON,** Washington Co.

THE TATE LAW FIRM (AV)

Abingdon Professional Centre, 110 Abingdon Place, 24211
Telephone: 540-628-5185
Telecopier: 540-628-5045
Email: lynntate@naxs.com *URL:* http://www.tatelaw.com

Mary Lynn Tate

OF COUNSEL

Olen G. Haynes (Not admitted in VA)

LEGAL SUPPORT PERSONNEL

Rebecca A. Wyatt
Teresa L. Brown

For full biographical listings, see the Martindale-Hubbell Law Directory

*ARLINGTON,** Arlington Co.

WILLIAM E. ARTZ A PROFESSIONAL CORPORATION (AV)

1010 Rosslyn Metro Center, 1700 North Moore Street, 22209
Telephone: 703-243-3500
Facsimile: 703-524-8770
Email: wartzpc@erols.com *URL:* http://www.the-a-team.com

William E. Artz

(See Next Column)

WILLIAM E. ARTZ A PROFESSIONAL CORPORATION, *Arlington—Continued*

Dominique D. Michel

For full biographical listings, see the Martindale-Hubbell Law Directory

SCHWARTZ AND ELLIS, LTD. (AV)

6950 North Fairfax Drive, 22213
Telephone: 703-532-9300
Telex: 892320
Facsimile: 703-534-0329
Email: schwellis@aol.com *URL:* http://www.lawyers.com/schwartzandellis

John P. Ellis

John S. Petrillo

References: First Virginia Bank; Bank of America; First Union National Bank.

For full biographical listings, see the Martindale-Hubbell Law Directory

*FAIRFAX,** (Ind. City; Seat of Fairfax Co.)

CREMINS & ASSOCIATES, P.C. (AV)

Suite 310, 10777 Main Street, 22030-6903
Telephone: 703-352-4800
Fax: 703-352-4805
Email: cremins@bellatlantic.net

William D. Cremins

Jennifer Eileen Cremins
Anisa P. Kelley

For full biographical listings, see the Martindale-Hubbell Law Directory

MCCANDLISH & LILLARD, A PROFESSIONAL CORPORATION (AV)

Fair Oaks Plaza, 11350 Random Hills Road, Suite 500, 22030-7429
Telephone: 703-273-2288
Fax: 703-352-4300
Email: mccand@patriot.net *URL:* http://www.mccandlaw.com
Leesburg, Virginia Office: 305 Harrison Street, S.E., Third Floor.
Telephone: 703-737-0200.
Fax: 703-737-0165.

Robert J. McCandlish, Jr. (1909-1996)
Rothwell J. Lillard (1910-1989)
Jesse B. Wilson, III
Peter A. Arntson
Gary W. Brown
Randolph A. Sutliff
Robert H. J. Loftus
William McCauley Arnold
Stephen C. Price
Stephen K. Fox
Douglas J. Sanderson
R. Peyton Mahaffey
William L. Carey
John W. Farrell
Eric J. Berghold
Ralph M. Tener
Vicki L. Layman
Adam W. Smith

Daniel P. Lyon
Lawrence J. McClafferty
Brian R. Sanderson

For full biographical listings, see the Martindale-Hubbell Law Directory

*MANASSAS,** Prince William Co.

MCCARTHY & MASSEY, P.C. (AV)

9315 Center Street, Suite 104, 20110
Telephone: 703-330-2726; Metro: 703-551-2146
Fax: 703-330-2429

Tara M. McCarthy
Joyce A. Naumann Massey

Susan L. Mitchell
Marian L. Beckett

For full biographical listings, see the Martindale-Hubbell Law Directory

MCLEAN, Fairfax Co.

PLEDGER & FEORD P.L.C. (AV)

Suite 204, 1489 Chain Bridge Road, 22101
Telephone: 703-821-1250
Fax: 703-790-7250
Email: Pledger@his.com *URL:* http://www.lawyers.com/pledgerlaw

R. Harrison Pledger, Jr.
Bernard G. Feord, Jr.

Kevin D. Pledger

For full biographical listings, see the Martindale-Hubbell Law Directory

NORFOLK, (Independent City)

BREIT, DRESCHER & BREIT, P.C. (AV)

1000 Dominion Tower, 999 Waterside Drive, 23510
Telephone: 757-670-3888
Fax: 757-670-3895
Email: jbreit@livenet.net

John W. Drescher
Jeffrey A. Breit
George T. Albiston
Michael F. Imprevento
Latane' Ware Brown
John L. Watts

For full biographical listings, see the Martindale-Hubbell Law Directory

HARLAN & FLORA, P.C. (AV)

Dominion Tower, 999 Waterside Drive, Suite 1200, 23510
Telephone: 757-625-8300
Fax: 757-625-3714
Email: lawyers@harlan-flora.com *URL:* http://www.harlan-flora.com

Thomas J. Harlan, Jr.
John M. Flora

For full biographical listings, see the Martindale-Hubbell Law Directory

RESTON, Fairfax Co.

GARVER LAW OFFICES, P.C. (AV)

11702 Bowman Green Drive, P.O. Box 2430, 20195
Telephone: 703-471-1090; 800-440-8605
Fax: 703-471-1095
Email: GLAW@Erols.com *URL:* http://www.lawyers.com/stevengarver

Steven M. Garver
Cheryl Gilley Rice

For full biographical listings, see the Martindale-Hubbell Law Directory

RICHMOND, (Independent City)

BRENNER, DOHNAL, EVANS & YOFFY, P.C. (AV)

411 East Franklin Street, Suite 200, P.O. Box 470, 23218-0470
Telephone: 804-644-1300
Facsimile: 804-644-1354
Email: bdeyp@erols.com

Theodore I. Brenner
Dennis W. Dohnal
Ronald S. Evans
James S. Yoffy

Jay O. Millman
Gregory S. Hooe
Kathryn Spruill Lingle
Mary J. Bennett
Thomas D. Stokes, III

For full biographical listings, see the Martindale-Hubbell Law Directory

CREWS & HANCOCK, P.L.C. (AV)

Suite 1015, 700 Building, 700 East Main Street, 23219-2693
Telephone: 804-649-9333
Telecopier: 804-783-1759
Email: admin@crewshancock.com
Fairfax, Virginia Office: Flint Hill Centre, Suite 300, 3050 Chain Bridge Road.
Telephone: 703-591-3440.
Telecopier: 703-591-7646.
Roanoke, Virginia Office: P.O. Box 21187.
Telephone: 540-774-6655.
Telecopier: 540-774-7947.
Virginia Beach, Virginia Office: One Columbus Center, Suite 619.
Telephone: 757-490-7802.
Fax: 757-490-7820.

John William Crews
Thomas F. Hancock, III
Martin A. Donlan, Jr.
Karen A. Gould
John A. Blazer (Resident, Fairfax, Virginia Office)
John E. McIntosh, Jr. (Resident, Fairfax, Virginia Office)
Richard W. E. Bland
Judith B. Henry
Peter M. Mellette
Thomas T. Palmer (Resident, Roanoke, Virginia Office)
John R. Redmond
James M. Daniel, Jr.
W. Scott Johnson
B. Page Gravely, Jr.
Thomas L. Appler (Resident, Fairfax, Virginia Office)

Richard L. Nagle (Resident, Fairfax, Virginia Office)
Mary C. Malone (Resident, Virginia Beach, Virginia Office)
Christina S. Yehle (Resident, Fairfax, Virginia Office)
Scott J. Sorkin
Jeannie A. Adams
Elizabeth V. Syer
Martha L. Steele
Andrea L. Bailey
Katherine R. McMillen (Resident, Fairfax, Virginia Office)
Wesley G. Russell, Jr.
William O. Quirey, Jr.
Peter J. Haggerty (Resident, Fairfax, Virginia Office)
Robin M. Vogel
Wirt P. Marks, IV
W. Christopher Shea
Matthew A. Haddad
John B. Mumford, Jr.

(See Next Column)

CREWS & HANCOCK P.L.C.—*Continued*

William H. Hall, Jr.
Stephanie Lindsey Hiss
Amy M.E. Edwards
Sean P. Byrne
Michael E. Olszewski (Resident, Fairfax, Virginia Office)
Frank J. Russo, III
Maura Jane Brown (Resident, Fairfax, Virginia Office)
Mark D. Epley
Mark Henry Schmidt

For full biographical listings, see the Martindale-Hubbell Law Directory

ROANOKE, Roanoke City Co.

MUNDY, ROGERS & FRITH, LLP (AV)

Third Street and Woods Avenue, S.W., P.O. Box 2240, 24009
Telephone: 540-982-2900
FAX: 540-982-1362
Email: info@mrf-law.com *URL:* http://www.mrf-law.com

MEMBERS OF FIRM

G. Marshall Mundy
Frank W. Rogers, III
T. Daniel Frith, III
Cheryl Watson Smith
Edward B. Walker

Reference: First Union.

For full biographical listings, see the Martindale-Hubbell Law Directory

WOOTEN & HART, A PROFESSIONAL CORPORATION (AV)

707 Building, Suite 300, P.O. Box 12247, 24024-2247
Telephone: 540-343-2451; 540-342-9672
Telecopier: 540-345-6417
URL: http://www.wootenhart.com

George W. Wooten
David B. Hart
L. Thompson Hanes
Susan A. Waddell
Bradley D. McGraw
John L. Cooley
Thomas W. Farrell
Paul C. Kuhnel
Peter D. Vieth

David W. Hearn
John Mark Cooley
Christopher W. Stevens
Elizabeth D. Guilbert
Eunice Park Austin

OF COUNSEL

M. Lanier Woodrum

Representative Clients: Wachovia Bank; St. Paul Insurance Cos.
Approved Attorneys for: Lawyers Title Insurance Corp.
Reference: First Union National Bank.

For full biographical listings, see the Martindale-Hubbell Law Directory

VIRGINIA BEACH, (Independent City)

BRYDGES, MAHAN, O'BRIEN & FRUCCI, P.C. (AV)

Professional Building, 1369 Laskin Road, 23451
Telephone: 757-428-6021
Fax: 757-491-7634

Richard G. Brydges
Stephen C. Mahan
William R. "Buster" O'Brien
Steven C. Frucci

Approved Mediators/Arbitrators for: United States Arbitration and Mediation, Inc.; Arbitration Associates, Inc.- Jams/Endispute.
Reference: The Bank of Tidewater.

For full biographical listings, see the Martindale-Hubbell Law Directory

SHUTTLEWORTH RULOFF & GIORDANO, P.C. (AV)

4525 South Boulevard, Suite 300, 23452
Telephone: 757-671-6000
Fax: 757-671-6004
Email: srg@visi.net *URL:* http://www.srgpclaw.com
Newport News, Virginia Office: Historic Hilton Village, 10234 Warwick Boulevard, 23605.
Telephone: 757-873-9999.
Facsimile: 757-873-8758.

Robert J. Haddad
Robert G. Morecock
Lisa Palmer O'Donnell
Thomas B. Shuttleworth, II
Lawrence H. Woodward, Jr.

Reference: Central Fidelity Bank.

For full biographical listings, see the Martindale-Hubbell Law Directory

WASHINGTON

BAINBRIDGE ISLAND, Kitsap Co.

MORROW & OTOROWSKI (AV)

298 Winslow Way West, 98110
Telephone: 206-842-1000
Facsimile: 206-842-0797
URL: http://www.medilaw.com
Email: m-o@medilaw.com *URL:* http://www.lawyers.com/medilaw

MEMBERS OF FIRM

Albert Morrow
Christopher L. Otorowski

ASSOCIATE

Carol N. Johnston

For full biographical listings, see the Martindale-Hubbell Law Directory

*SEATTLE,** King Co.

THE DAVIS FIRM (AV)

5301 Ballard Avenue N.W., 98107
Telephone: 206-789-1056
Fax: 206-789-9690
Email: thedavisfirm@seanet.com *URL:* http://www.lawyers.com/thedavisfirm

MEMBERS OF FIRM

Susan R. Davis
Donald K. Davis

For full biographical listings, see the Martindale-Hubbell Law Directory

LAW OFFICE OF RON PEREY (AV)

2025 First Avenue, Suite 250, 98121-2147
Telephone: 206-443-7600
Fax: 206-443-4785

LEGAL SUPPORT PERSONNEL

MEDICAL DIRECTOR

Alexandra Finney McCafferty (Medical Doctor)

CASE MANAGERS

P.J. Anderson (Registered Nurse)
David Ubaldi

For full biographical listings, see the Martindale-Hubbell Law Directory

SCHROETER, GOLDMARK & BENDER, P.S. (AV)

500 Central Building, 810 Third Avenue, 98104
Telephone: 206-622-8000; 1-800-809-2234
FAX: 206-682-2305
Email: lastname@schroeter-goldmark.com

Croil J. Anderson
Adam J. Berger
James D. Hailey
Kristin Houser
Amanda E. Lee
Mark Leemon
Douglas D. McBroom
Janet L. Rice
Jeffery P. Robinson
Rebecca J. Roe
Sidney Stillerman Royer
William Rutzick
Sandra E. Widlan
Corrie Johnson Yackulic
John Goldmark (1917-1979)
Dean Bender (1933-1988)

OF COUNSEL

Jenny A. Durkan

For full biographical listings, see the Martindale-Hubbell Law Directory

*SPOKANE,** Spokane Co.

BACKMAN & BLUMEL, P.S. (AV)

900 Northtown Office Building, North 4407 Division, 99207
Telephone: 509-487-1651
FAX: 509-483-5016
Email: joeb@omnicast.net *URL:* http://www.lawyers.com/backblumlaw

Stephen F. Backman
Joseph A. Blumel, III

For full biographical listings, see the Martindale-Hubbell Law Directory

WEST VIRGINIA

*CHARLESTON,** Kanawha Co.

BERTHOLD, TIANO & O'DELL (AV)

208 Capitol Street, P.O. Box 3508, 25335
Telephone: 304-345-5700
Fax: 304-345-5703

(See Next Column)

BERTHOLD, TIANO & O'DELL, *Charleston—Continued*

Robert V. Berthold, Jr.
William M. Tiano
Tony L. O'Dell

References: Huntington Banks; Bank One; United National Bank.

For full biographical listings, see the Martindale-Hubbell Law Directory

BUCCI, BAILEY & JAVINS, L.C. (AV)

Bank One Center Suite 910, 707 Virginia Street, East, P.O. Box 3712, 25337
Telephone: 304-345-0346
Fax: 304-345-0375
Email: kpaxton@citynet.net

Guy R. Bucci
Timothy C. Bailey
L. Lee Javins, II

J. Mark Adkins
Jon K. Cormany
V. Paul Bucci, II

For full biographical listings, see the Martindale-Hubbell Law Directory

SALSBERY & DRUCKMAN (AV)

606 Virginia Street East, Suite 100, 25305
Telephone: 304-343-0075
Fax: 304-343-0099
Email: salsdruck@citynet.net

H. F. Salsbery
William S. Druckman
Madonna C. Estep

OF COUNSEL

Anne E. Shaffer

For full biographical listings, see the Martindale-Hubbell Law Directory

SHUMAN ANNAND BAILEY WYANT & EARLES (AV)

Suite 1007, 405 Capitol Street, P.O. Box 3953, 25339
Telephone: 304-345-1400
Telecopier: 304-343-1826
Email: shuman@newwave.net
Wheeling, West Virginia Office: Suite 3002, 1233 Main Street, 26003.
Telephone: 304-233-3100.
Telecopier: 304-233-0201.

MEMBERS OF FIRM

David L. Shuman
Stephen Darley Annand
Charles R. Bailey
Richard L. Earles
David L. Wyant (Resident, Wheeling, West Virginia Office)
Mark William Browning
William R. Slicer
George J. Joseph
Thomas E. Buck (Resident at Wheeling, West Virginia Office)

ASSOCIATES

DesireéHalkias Divita
Roberta F. Green
Paul Kipling Reese
Heidi A. Kossuth (Resident, Wheeling, West Virginia Office)
Lou Ann S. Cassell
Dwayne E. Cyrus
Eric W. Santos (Not admitted in WV; Resident, Wheeling, West Virginia Office)
John T. Molleur
Mark A. Kepple (Resident, Wheeling, West Virginia Office)
David J. Mincer
Karen M. Tracy
Virginia Ann Grottendieck
Arden J. Cogar
Melissa A. Morris
Stacie L. Price (Resident, Wheeling, West Virginia Office)
J. Parker Bazzle
Lisa Bray
Darin C. James
Brian D. Morrison

OF COUNSEL

John F. McCuskey

Representative Clients: American International/Companies (AIG); CNA Insurance Companies; Insurance Corporation of America; Metropolitan Property & Liability Insurance Co.; MMI Companies, Inc.; Motorists Insurance Cos.; Travelers Insurance Cos.; Westfield Companies.
Reference: One Valley Bank.

For full biographical listings, see the Martindale-Hubbell Law Directory

*CLARKSBURG,** Harrison Co.

JOHNSON, SIMMERMAN & BROUGHTON, L.C. (AV)

Ogden Building, 203 West Main Street, 26301
Telephone: 304-624-6555; 304-623-4900
Telecopier: 304-623-4933
Mailing Address: P.O. Box 150, Clarksburg, West Virginia, 26302-0150

(See Next Column)

Charles G. Johnson
Frank E. Simmerman, Jr.
Marcia Allen Broughton
Bridget D. Furbee
Robin Queen Triplett

For full biographical listings, see the Martindale-Hubbell Law Directory

MCNEER, HIGHLAND, MCMUNN AND VARNER, L.C. (AV)

One Valley Bank Building, P.O. Drawer 2040, 26302-2040
Telephone: 304-626-1100
Facsimile: 304-623-3035
Martinsburg Office: 2520 Aikens Center, P.O. Box 2509.
Telephone: 304-264-4621.
Fax: 304-264-8623.
Parkersburg Office: 404 Market Street, Suite 204, P.O. Box 1507.
Telephone: 304-422-7193.
Facsimile: 304-422-7196.

C. David McMunn
J. Cecil Jarvis
James A. Varner
Robert W. Trumble (Resident, Martinsburg Office)
Catherine D. Munster
James N. Riley
Steven R. Bratke (Resident, Parkersburg Office)
Michael J. Novotny (Resident, Martinsburg Office)
Dennis M. Shreve
Geraldine S. Roberts
William F. Rohrbaugh (Resident, Martinsburg Office)
Gregory H. Schillace
Judy L. Shanholtz
Tiffany R. Durst
Gene W. Bailey, II

OF COUNSEL

James E. McNeer
Cecil B. Highland, Jr.
William L. Fury

Representative Clients: One Valley Bank of Clarksburg, National Assn.; Bruceton Bank; Harrison County Bank; Nationwide Mutual Insurance Cos.; Clarksburg Publishing Co.; C.I.T. Financial Services; State Automobile Mutual Insurance Co.; United Hospital Center, Inc.; West Virginia Coals, Inc.; Swanson Plating Co.

For full biographical listings, see the Martindale-Hubbell Law Directory

HUNTINGTON, Cabell & Wayne Cos.

BAKER, LANCIANESE, CAMPBELL & CONATY (AV)

The River Tower, 1108 Third Avenue, Suite 300, 25701-1578
Telephone: 304-522-6906
Facsimile: 304-522-6910
Email: BLCC@BLCCLAW.COM *URL:* http://www.BLCCLAW.COM
Washington, D.C. Office: 1090 Vermont Avenue, N.W. Suite 800.
Telephone: 202-966-1500.
Fax: 202-966-7075. E-Mail: BLCC@BLCCLAW.COM.
Lexington, Kentucky Office: 2265 Harrodsburg Road, Suite 200, 40504-3517.
Telephone: 606-278-0297.
Fax: 206-278-0334. E-Mail: BLCC@BLCCLAW.COM.

Roy D. Baker, Jr.
Richard L. Lancianese
David L. Campbell
Brian P. Conaty
Janice P. Epperly

OF COUNSEL

Margaret M. Brizzolara (Not admitted in WV)

For full biographical listings, see the Martindale-Hubbell Law Directory

OFFUTT, FISHER & NORD (AV)

949 Third Avenue, Suite 300, P.O. Box 2868, 25728-2868
Telephone: 304-529-2868; Toll Free: 1-800-529-2868
Fax: 304-529-2999
Charleston
Email: oefn@earthlink.net
Charleston, West Virginia Office: 208 Capitol Street, Suite 400, 25530.
Telephone: 304-343-2869.
Fax: 304-343-3053.

MEMBERS OF FIRM

D. C. Offutt, Jr.
Michael M. Fisher
Steven K. Nord

ASSOCIATES

Scott W. Andrews
Sonja L. Carpenter
Perry W. Oxley
Tammy R. Harvey
Monica L. Robinson

Representative Clients: St. Paul Insurance Co.; Home Insurance Co.; Federal Kemper Insurance Co.; Insurance Corporation of America; Erie Insurance Co.; Continental Insurance Co.; Liberty Mutual Insurance Co.; Colonial Insurance Company of California; CIGNA Insurance Cos.; Westfield Insurance Co.

For full biographical listings, see the Martindale-Hubbell Law Directory

*PRINCETON,** Mercer Co.

GIBSON, LEFLER & ASSOCIATES (AV)

1345 Mercer Street, 24740
Telephone: 304-425-8276
800-742-3545

(See Next Column)

GIBSON, LEFLER & ASSOCIATES—*Continued*

MEMBERS OF FIRM

Michael F. Gibson
Derrick W. Lefler

LEGAL SUPPORT PERSONNEL

NURSE PARALEGAL

Melody Lambert, RN-RLNC

SOCIAL SECURITY PARALEGAL

Nancy Belcher

PERSONAL INJURY PARALEGAL

Kathy Richards

WORKERS COMPENSATION PARALEGAL

Carol Hylton

MEDICAL NEGLIGENCE PARALEGAL

Deborah Frye

For full biographical listings, see the Martindale-Hubbell Law Directory

*WHEELING,** Ohio Co.

SCHRADER BYRD & COMPANION, PLLC (AV)

(A Professional Limited Liability Company)
The Maxwell Centre, 32-20th Street, Suite 500, P.O. Box 6336, 26003
Telephone: 304-233-3390
Fax: 304-233-2769
URL: http://www.schraderlaw.com
Martins Ferry, Ohio Office: 205 North Fifth Street, P.O. Box 309, 43935.
Telephone: 740-633-9976.
Fax: 740-633-0400.
Weirton, West Virginia Office: 3205 Pennsylvania Avenue, Suite 103, Penn Place, P.O. Box 2785, 26062.
Telephone: 304-723-2674.
Fax: 304-723-2876.

MEMBERS

Ray A. Byrd
James F. Companion
Frank X. Duff
Teresa Rieman-Camilletti
Yolonda G. Lambert
Daniel P. Fry (Resident Partner, Martins Ferry, Ohio Office)
James P. Mazzone (Resident Member, Weirton, West Virginia Office)
Sandra K. Law
D. Kevin Coleman

SPECIAL COUNSEL

Thomas B. Miller

ASSOCIATES

Denise D. Klug
Michael A. Adams
John Porco
Aimee Morgan Stern
Kimberly R. Wilson
Christopher J. Adams

OF COUNSEL

James A. Byrum, Jr.

General Counsel: Reynolds Memorial Hospital; WesBanco Bank-Elm Grove.
Representative Clients: American Cyanamid Company; Bank One; Matlack Systems, Inc.; Moutaineer Gas Co.; Ohio County Board of Education; PHICO Insurance Co.; Wheeling Hospital; Wheeling-Pittsburg Steel Corp.

For full biographical listings, see the Martindale-Hubbell Law Directory

WISCONSIN

*APPLETON,** Outagamie Co.

HABUSH, HABUSH, DAVIS & ROTTIER, S.C. (AV)

4100 Boardwalk Court, 54915
Telephone: 920-738-0900
Fax: 920-738-5850
Email: info@habush.com *URL:* http://www.habush.com/
Milwaukee, Wisconsin Office: Suite 2300, First Wisconsin Center, 777 East Wisconsin Avenue.
Telephone: 414-271-0900.
FAX: 414-271-6854.
Madison, Wisconsin Office: 150 East Gilman Street, Suite 2000.
Telephone: 608-255-6663.
FAX: 608-255-0745.
Wausau, Wisconsin Office: 3100 Eagle Avenue.
Telephone: 715-842-4444.
FAX: 715-845-8898.
Racine, Wisconsin Office: Durand Place, 5439 Durand Avenue, Suite 220.
Telephone: 262-554-6200.
FAX: 262-554-7166.
Waukesha, Wisconsin Office: Stone Ridge I, N14 W23755 Stone Ridge Drive, Suite 225.
Telephone: 262-523-4700.
FAX: 262-523-4545.
Rhinelander, Wisconsin Office: 26 South Brown Street.
Telephone: 715-365-1900.
FAX: 715-365-1910.

(See Next Column)

Green Bay, Wisconsin Office: P.O. Box 22545, 314 South Madison Street.
Telephone: 920-437-0900.
FAX: 920-437-0910.
Stevens Point, Wisconsin Office: 5370 East Highway 10.
Telephone: 715-345-0004.
FAX: 715-343-2207.
Lake Geneva, Wisconsin Office: First Banking Center Plaza, Suite 120, 569 Broad Street.
Telephone: 262-248-5200.
FAX: 262-248-5222.

John D. Murray
Craig A. Christensen

For full biographical listings, see the Martindale-Hubbell Law Directory

*GREEN BAY,** Brown Co.

EVERSON, WHITNEY, EVERSON & BREHM, S.C. (AV)

Suite 106, 125 South Jefferson Street, P.O. Box 22248, 54305-2248
Telephone: 920-435-3734
Fax: 920-435-0126
Email: eweb@execpc.com

John C. Whitney (1915-1994)
Philip R. Brehm
John E. Herald
Rodney A. Charnholm
George F. Savage
Peter J. Hickey
Susan J. Reigel
John M. Thompson, IV
Jeffrey T. DeMeuse
John H. Heide

OF COUNSEL

James L. Everson

Peter C. Brehm
Katherine L. Pleger
Erik J. Pless

LEGAL SUPPORT PERSONNEL

PARALEGAL

Cheryl Lynn Morin

Counsel for: American Family Insurance; Bank One; Rural Mutual Medical Protective; U.S. Fidelity & Guaranty Co.; Employers Insurance of Wausau; State Farm Mutual Cos.; Travelers Insurance Co.; Farmers Insurance Group; Liberty Mutual Insurance Co.

For full biographical listings, see the Martindale-Hubbell Law Directory

HABUSH, HABUSH, DAVIS & ROTTIER, S.C. (AV)

314 South Madison Street, P.O. Box 22545, 54305-2545
Telephone: 920-437-0900
Fax: 920-437-0910
Email: info@habush.com *URL:* http://www.habush.com/
Milwaukee, Wisconsin Office: Suite 2300. First Wisconsin Center, 777 East Wisconsin Avenue.
Telephone: 414-271-0900.
FAX: 414-271-6854.
Madison, Wisconsin Office: 150 East Gilman Street, Suite 2000.
Telephone: 608-255-6663.
FAX: 608-255-0745.
Appleton, Wisconsin Office: 4100 Boardwalk Court.
Telephone: 920-738-0900.
FAX: 920-738-5850.
Wausau, Wisconsin Office: 3100 Eagle Avenue.
Telephone: 715-842-4444.
FAX: 715-845-8898.
Racine, Wisconsin Office: Durand Place, 5439 Durand Avenue, Suite 220.
Telephone: 262-554-6200.
FAX: 262-554-7166.
Waukesha, Wisconsin Office: Stone Ridge I, N14 W23755 Stone Ridge Drive, Suite 225.
Telephone: 262-523-4700.
FAX: 262-523-4545.
Rhinelander, Wisconsin Office: 26 South Brown Street.
Telephone: 715-365-1900.
FAX: 715-365-1910.
Stevens Point, Wisconsin Office: 5370 East Highway 10.
Telephone: 715-345-0004.
FAX: 715-343-2207.
Lake Geneva, Wisconsin Office: First Banking Center Plaza, Suite 120, 569 Broad Street.
Telephone: 262-248-5200.
FAX: 262-248-5222.

Ralph J. Tease, Jr.
Edward J. Vopal

For full biographical listings, see the Martindale-Hubbell Law Directory

LAKE GENEVA, Walworth Co.

Habush, Habush, Davis & Rottier, S.C. (AV)

First Banking Center Plaza, Suite 120, 569 Broad Street, 53147
Telephone: 262-248-5200
Fax: 262-248-5222
Email: info@habush.com *URL:* http://www.habush.com/
Milwaukee, Wisconsin Office: Suite 2300, First Wisconsin Center, 777 East Wisconsin Avenue.
Telephone: 414-271-0900.
FAX: 414-271-6854.
Madison, Wisconsin Office: 150 East Gilman Street, Suite 2000.
Telephone: 608-255-6663.
FAX: 608-255-0745.
Appleton, Wisconsin Office: 4100 Boardwalk Court.
Telephone: 920-738-0900.
FAX: 920-738-5850.
Wausau, Wisconsin Office: 3100 Eagle Avenue.
Telephone: 715-842-4444.
FAX: 715-845-8898.
Racine, Wisconsin Office: Durand Place, 5439 Durand Avenue, Suite 220.
Telephone: 262-554-6200.
FAX: 262-554-7166.
Waukesha, Wisconsin Office: Stone Ridge I, N14 W23755 Stone Ridge Drive, Suite 225.
Telephone: 262-523-4700.
FAX: 262-523-4545.
Rhinelander, Wisconsin Office: 26 South Brown Street.
Telephone: 715-365-1900.
FAX: 715-365-1910.
Green Bay, Wisconsin Office: P.O. Box 22545, 314 South Madison Street.
Telephone: 920-437-0900.
FAX: 920-437-0910.
Stevens Point, Wisconsin Office: 5370 East Highway 10.
Telephone: 715-345-0004.
FAX: 715-343-2207.

Michael J. Jassak

For full biographical listings, see the Martindale-Hubbell Law Directory

*MADISON,** Dane Co.

Atterbury & Riley, S.C. (AV)

7001 Old Sauk Road, P.O. Box 45020, 53744-5020
Telephone: 608-821-4600
Fax: 608-821-4610
Email: arlaw@chorus.net *URL:* http://WWW.EXECPC.COM/~ARL

Lee R. Atterbury · Michael Riley
Rebecca M. Orvick · Alexander S. Kammer

OF COUNSEL

Eldred M. Swingen

A list of Representative Clients will be furnished upon request.
Reference: M & I Bank of Madison.

For full biographical listings, see the Martindale-Hubbell Law Directory

Axley Brynelson, LLP (AV)

(Formerly Brynelson, Herrick, Bucaida, Dorschel & Armstrong Including the former Easton & Assoc., S.C.)
2 East Mifflin Street, P.O. Box 1767, 53701-1767
Telephone: 608-257-5661
Fax: 608-257-5444
Email: law@axley.com *URL:* http://www.axley.com

MEMBERS OF FIRM

John C. Mitby · Curtis C. Swanson
Joy L. O'Grosky

ASSOCIATE

Nicholas S. Harned

For Complete List of Firm Personnel, See General Section

For full biographical listings, see the Martindale-Hubbell Law Directory

Habush, Habush, Davis & Rottier, S.C. (AV)

150 East Gilman Street, Suite 2000, 53703
Telephone: 608-255-6663
Fax: 608-255-0745
Email: info@habush.com *URL:* http://www.habush.com/
Milwaukee, Wisconsin Office: Suite 2300, First Wisconsin Center, 777 East Wisconsin Avenue.
Telephone: 414-271-0900.
FAX: 414-271-6854.
Appleton, Wisconsin Office: 4100 Boardwalk Court.
Telephone: 920-738-0900.
FAX: 920-738-5850.
Wausau, Wisconsin Office: 3100 Eagle Avenue.
Telephone: 715-842-4444.
FAX: 715-845-8898.

(See Next Column)

Racine, Wisconsin Office: Durand Place, 5439 Durand Avenue, Suite 220.
Telephone: 262-554-6200.
FAX: 262-554-7166.
Waukesha, Wisconsin Office: Stone Ridge I, N14 W23755 Stone Ridge Drive, Suite 225.
Telephone: 262-523-4700.
FAX: 262-523-4545.
Rhinelander, Wisconsin Office: 26 South Brown Street.
Telephone: 715-365-1900.
FAX: 715-365-1910.
Green Bay, Wisconsin Office: P.O. Box 22545, 314 South Madison Street.
Telephone: 920-437-0900.
FAX: 920-437-0910.
Stevens Point, Wisconsin Office: 5370 East Highway 10.
Telephone: 715-345-0004.
FAX: 715-343-2207.
Lake Geneva, Wisconsin Office: First Banking Center Plaza, Suite 120, 569 Broad Street.
Telephone: 262-248-5200.
FAX: 262-248-5222.

Daniel A. Rottier · Nicholas J. McNamara
James R. Jansen · Stefanie A. O'Shea
Susan R. Steingass · Rhonda L. Lanford

For full biographical listings, see the Martindale-Hubbell Law Directory

*MILWAUKEE,** Milwaukee Co.

Habush, Habush, Davis & Rottier, S.C. (AV)

Suite 2300 First Wisconsin Center, 777 East Wisconsin Avenue, 53202
Telephone: 414-271-0900
Fax: 414-271-6854
Email: info@habush.com *URL:* http://www.habush.com/
Madison, Wisconsin Office: 150 East Gilman Street, Suite 2000.
Telephone: 608-255-6663.
FAX: 608-255-0745.
Appleton, Wisconsin Office: 4100 Boardwalk Court.
Telephone: 920-738-0900.
FAX: 920-738-5850.
Wausau, Wisconsin Office: 3100 Eagle Avenue.
Telephone: 715-842-4444.
FAX: 715-845-8898.
Racine, Wisconsin Office: Durand Place, 5439 Durand Avenue, Suite 220.
Telephone: 262-554-6200.
FAX: 262-554-7166.
Waukesha, Wisconsin Office: Stone Ridge I, N14 W23755 Stone Ridge Drive, Suite 225.
Telephone: 262-523-4700.
FAX: 262-523-4545.
Rhinelander, Wisconsin Office: 26 South Brown Street.
Telephone: 715-365-1900.
FAX: 715-365-1910.
Green Bay, Wisconsin Office: P.O. Box 22545, 314 South Madison Street.
Telephone: 920-437-0900.
FAX: 920-437-0910.
Stevens Point, Wisconsin Office: 5370 East Highway 10.
Telephone: 715-345-0004.
FAX: 715-343-2207.
Lake Geneva, Wisconsin Office: First Banking Center Plaza, Suite 120, 569 Broad Street.
Telephone: 262-248-5200.
FAX: 262-248-5222.

Michael D. Egelhoff

For full biographical listings, see the Martindale-Hubbell Law Directory

*RACINE,** Racine Co.

Habush, Habush, Davis & Rottier, S.C. (AV)

Durand Place, 5439 Durand Avenue, Suite 220, 53406
Telephone: 262-554-6200
Fax: 262-554-7166
Email: info@habush.com *URL:* http://www.habush.com/
Milwaukee Wisconsin Office: Suite 2300, First Wisconsin Center, 777 East Wisconsin Avenue. Telephone 414-271-0900.
FAX: 414-271-6854.
Madison, Wisconsin Office: 150 East Gilman Street, Suite 2000.
Telephone: 608-255-6663.
FAX: 608-255-0745.
Appleton, Wisconsin Office: 4100 Boardwalk Court.
Telephone: 920-738-0900.
FAX: 920-738-5850.
Wausau, Wisconsin Office: 3100 Eagle Avenue.
Telephone: 715-842-4444.
FAX: 715-845-8898.
Waukesha, Wisconsin Office: Stone Ridge I, N14 W23755 Stone Ridge Drive, Suite 225.
Telephone: 262-523-4700.
FAX: 262-523-4545.
Rhinelander, Wisconsin Office: 26 South Brown Street.
Telephone: 715-365-1900.
FAX: 715-365-1910.

(See Next Column)

HABUSH, HABUSH, DAVIS & ROTTIER S.C.—*Continued*

Green Bay, Wisconsin Office: P.O. Box 22545, 314 South Madison Street.
Telephone: 920-437-0900.
FAX: 920-437-0910.
Stevens Point, Wisconsin Office: 5370 East Highway 10.
Telephone: 715-345-0004.
FAX: 715-343-2207.
Lake Geneva, Wisconsin Office: First Banking Center Plaza, Suite 120, 569 Broad Street.
Telephone: 262-248-5200.
FAX: 262-248-5222.

Michael J. Jassak Steven T. Botzau

For full biographical listings, see the Martindale-Hubbell Law Directory

*RHINELANDER,** Oneida Co.

HABUSH, HABUSH, DAVIS & ROTTIER, S.C. (AV)

26 South Brown Street, 54501
Telephone: 715-365-1900
Fax: 715-365-1910
Email: habush@newnorth.net *URL:* http://www.habush.com/
Milwaukee, Wisconsin Office: Suite 2300 First Wisconsin Center, 777 East Wisconsin Avenue.
Telephone: 414-271-0900.
FAX: 414-271-6854.
Madison, Wisconsin Office: 150 East Gilman Street, Suite 2000.
Telephone: 608-255-6663.
FAX: 608-255-0745.
Appleton, Wisconsin Office: 4100 Boardwalk Court.
Telephone: 920-738-0900.
FAX: 920-738-5850.
Wausau, Wisconsin Office: 3100 Eagle Avenue.
Telephone: 715-842-4444.
FAX: 715-845-8898.
Racine, Wisconsin Office: Durand Place, 5439 Durand Avenue, Suite 220.
Telephone: 262-554-6200.
FAX: 262-554-7166.
Waukesha, Wisconsin Office: Stone Ridge I, N14 W23755 Stone Ridge Drive, Suite 225.
Telephone: 262-523-4700.
FAX: 262-523-4545.
Green Bay, Wisconsin Office: P.O. Box 22545, 314 South Madison Street.
Telephone: 920-437-0900.
FAX: 920-437-0910.
Stevens Point, Wisconsin Office: 5370 East Highway 10.
Telephone: 715-345-0004.
FAX: 715-343-2207.
Lake Geneva, Wisconsin Office: First Banking Center Plaza, Suite 120, 569 Broad Street.
Telephone: 262-248-5200.
FAX: 262-248-5222.

Dana James Weis

For full biographical listings, see the Martindale-Hubbell Law Directory

*WAUKESHA,** Waukesha Co.

HABUSH, HABUSH, DAVIS & ROTTIER, S.C. (AV)

Stone Ridge I, N14 W23755 Stone Ridge Drive, Suite 225, 53186
Telephone: 262-523-4700
Fax: 262-523-4545
Email: info@habush.com *URL:* http://www.habush.com/
Milwaukee Wisconsin Office: Suite 2300, First Wisconsin Center, 777 East Wisconsin Avenue.
Telephone: 414-271-0900.
FAX: 414-271-6854.
Madison, Wisconsin Office: 150 East Gilman Street, Suite 2000.
Telephone: 608-255-6663.
FAX: 608-255-0745.
Appleton, Wisconsin Office: 4100 Boardwalk Court.
Telephone: 920-738-0900.
FAX: 920-738-5850.
Wausau, Wisconsin Office: 3100 Eagle Avenue.
Telephone: 715-842-4444.
FAX: 715-845-8898.
Racine, Wisconsin Office: Durand Place, 5439 Durand Avenue, Suite 220.
Telephone: 262-554-6200.
FAX: 262-554-7166.
Rhinelander, Wisconsin Office: 26 South Brown Street.
Telephone: 715-365-1900.
FAX: 715-365-1910.
Green Bay, Wisconsin Office: P.O. Box 22545, 314 South Madison Street.
Telephone: 920-437-0900.
FAX: 920-437-0910.
Stevens Point, Wisconsin Office: 5370 East Highway 10.
Telephone: 715-345-0004.
FAX: 715-343-2207.
Lake Geneva, Wisconsin Office: First Banking Center Plaza, Suite 120, 569 Broad Street.
Telephone: 262-248-5200.
FAX: 262-248-5222.

(See Next Column)

Gary R. Kuphall Douglas E. Swanson

For full biographical listings, see the Martindale-Hubbell Law Directory

*WAUSAU,** Marathon Co.

HABUSH, HABUSH, DAVIS & ROTTIER, S.C. (AV)

3100 Eagle Avenue, 54402-1987
Telephone: 715-842-4444
Fax: 715-845-8898
Email: info@habush.com *URL:* http://www.habush.com/
Milwaukee, Wisconsin Office: Suite 2300, First Wisconsin Center, 777 East Wisconsin Avenue.
Telephone: 414-271-0900.
FAX: 414-271-6854.
Madison, Wisconsin Office: 150 East Gilman Street, Suite 2000.
Telephone: 608-255-6663.
FAX: 608-255-0745.
Appleton, Wisconsin Office: 4100 Boardwalk Court.
Telephone: 920-738-0900.
FAX: 920-738-5850.
Racine, Wisconsin Office: Durand Place, 5439 Durand Avenue, Suite 220.
Telephone: 262-554-6200.
FAX: 262-554-7166.
Waukesha, Wisconsin Office: Stone Ridge I, N14 W23755 Stone Ridge Drive, Suite 225.
Telephone: 262-523-4700.
FAX: 262-523-4545.
Rhinelander, Wisconsin Office: 26 South Brown Street.
Telephone: 715-365-1900.
FAX: 715-365-1910.
Green Bay, Wisconsin Office: P.O. Box 22545, 314 South Madison Street.
Telephone: 920-437-0900.
FAX: 920-437-0910.
Stevens Point, Wisconsin Office: 5370 East Highway 10.
Telephone: 715-345-0004.
FAX: 715-343-2207.
Lake Geneva, Wisconsin Office: First Banking Center Plaza, Suite 120, 569 Broad Street.
Telephone: 262-248-5200.
FAX: 262-248-5222.

Dana James Weis David E. Sunby
Marlene F. Wahlstrom

For full biographical listings, see the Martindale-Hubbell Law Directory

JEROME A. MAEDER LAW OFFICES, S.C. (AV)

602 Jackson Street, P.O. Box 1626, 54401
Telephone: 715-842-2281
Fax: 715-842-1046

Jerome A. Maeder

Vincent A. Maeder Robert J. Gray

For full biographical listings, see the Martindale-Hubbell Law Directory

WYOMING

*CHEYENNE,** Laramie Co.

THE FITZGERALD LAW FIRM (AV)

A Partnership of Professional Corporations
2108 Warren Avenue, 82001-3740
Telephone: 307-634-4000
Telecopier: 307-635-2391
Email: lawyers@fitzgeraldlaw.com *URL:* http://www.fitzgeraldlaw.com

MEMBERS OF FIRM

James E. Fitzgerald (P.C.) Sharon A. Fitzgerald (P.C.)

OF COUNSEL

A. G. McClintock

For full biographical listings, see the Martindale-Hubbell Law Directory

WOLF & TIEDEKEN (AV)

Suite 300 Equality State Bank Building, P.O. Box 491, 82001
Telephone: 307-635-2876
Fax: 307-632-4902
Email: lawyers@cheyenneweb.com

MEMBERS OF FIRM

Richard C. Wolf Robert W. Tiedeken

For full biographical listings, see the Martindale-Hubbell Law Directory

*JACKSON,** Teton Co.

SPENCE, MORIARITY & SCHUSTER, LLC (AV)

15 South Jackson Street, P.O. Box 548, 83001
Telephone: 307-733-7290
Fax: 307-733-5248
Salt Lake City, Utah Office: 39 Exchange Place, Suite 101, 84111.
Telephone: 801-521-0811.
Fax: 801-521-0437.

MEMBERS OF FIRM

Gerry L. Spence, P.C.
J. Douglas McCalla
Edward P. Moriarity
Roy A. Jacobson, Jr.
Robert P. Schuster
Kent W. Spence
Gary L. Shockey
Robert A. Krause

ASSOCIATES

Glen G. Debroder
David M. Gosar
R. Daniel Fleck
Gerard R. Bosch
G. Bryan Ulmer, III
Jeffrey Gooch
Laura N. MacPherson (Not admitted in WY)

Reference: First Interstate Bank, Casper, Wyoming.

For full biographical listings, see the Martindale-Hubbell Law Directory

PUERTO RICO

SAN JUAN, San Juan Dist.

JIMÉNEZ, GRAFFAM & LAUSELL

Suite 505, Midtown Building, 421 Muñoz Rivera Avenue, Hato Rey, P.O. Box 366104, 00936-6104
Telephone: 787-767-1030; 767-1000; 767-1061; 767-1064
Telefax: 787-751-4068;
Cable: "Nezte"
RCA Telex: 325-2730
Email: manager@jgl.com *URL:* http://www.jgl.com

MEMBER OF FIRM

José Juan Torres-Escalera

ASSOCIATES

Isabel J. Vélez-Serrano
Edgardo A. Vega-López
Ruy V. Díaz-Díaz

Representative Clients: Shand Morahan & Company, Inc.; Global Insurance Co.; University of Puerto Rico Hospital; Auxilio Mutuo Hospital.

For Complete List of Firm Personnel, See General Section

For full biographical listings, see the Martindale-Hubbell Law Directory

CANADA ALBERTA

*CALGARY,** Calgary Jud. Dist.

BENNETT JONES (AV)

4500 Bankers Hall East, 855-2nd Street S.W., T2P 4K7
Telephone: 403-298-3100
Facsimile: 403-265-7219
Email: firmwatch@bennettjones.ca *URL:* http://www.bennettjones.ca
Edmonton, Alberta Office: 1000, 10035-105 Street.
Telephone: 780-421-8133.
Facsimile: 780-421-7951.
Toronto, Ontario Office: 3400 1 First Canadian Place, P.O. Box 130.
Telephone: 416-863-1200.
Facsimile: 416-863-1716.

MEMBER OF FIRM

John G. Martland, Q.C.

For Complete List of Firm Personnel, See General Section

For full biographical listings, see the Martindale-Hubbell Law Directory

CANADA NEW BRUNSWICK

*FREDERICTON,** York Co.

MCINNES COOPER (AV)

Suite 600, 570 Queen Street, P.O. Box 610, E3B 5A6
Telephone: 506-458-8572
Fax: 506-458-9903
Email: mcrfton@mcrlaw.com *URL:* http://www.mcrlaw.com
Halifax, Nova Scotia Office: Summit Place, 1601 Lower Water Street, P.O. Box 730, B3J 2V1.
Telephone: 902-425-6500.
Fax: 902-425-6350. Email: mcrhfx@mcrlaw.com.
St. John's, Newfoundland Office: Baine Johnston Centre, 5th Floor, 10 Fort William Place, P.O. Box 5939, A1C 5X4.
Telephone: 709-722-8735.
Telecopier: 709-722-1763. Email: mcrsj@mcrlaw.com.
Moncton, New Brunswick Office: Place Moncton Place, 655 Main Street, P.O. Box 1368, E1C 8T6.
Telephone: 506-857-8970.
Fax: 506-857-4095. Email: mcrmctn@mcrlaw.com.
Charlottetown, Prince Edward Island Office: BDC Place, Suite 620, 119 Kent Street, C1A 1N3.
Telephone: 902-368-8473.
Fax: 902-368-8346. Email: mcrpei@mcrlaw.com.

PARTNER

David Duncan Young

ASSOCIATES

David D. Eidt
Patrick V. Windle

For Complete List of Firm Personnel, See General Section

For full biographical listings, see the Martindale-Hubbell Law Directory

*MONCTON,** Westmorland Co.

MCINNES COOPER (AV)

Barristers, Solicitors & Trade Mark Agents
Place Moncton Place, 655 Main Street, P.O. Box 1368, E1C 8T6
Telephone: 506-857-8970
Fax: 506-857-4095
Email: mcrmctn@mcrlaw.com *URL:* http://www.mcrlaw.com
Halifax, Nova Scotia Office: Summit Place, 1601 Lower Water Street, P.O. Box 730, B3J 2V1.
Telephone: 902-425-6500.
Fax: 902-425-6350. Email: mcrhfx@mcrlaw.com.
St. John's, Newfoundland Office: Baine Johnston Centre, 5th Floor, 10 Fort William Place, P.O. Box 5939, A1C 5X4.
Telephone: 709-722-8735.
Telecopier: 709-722-1763. Email: mcrsj@mcrlaw.com.
Charlottetown, Prince Edward Island Office: BDC Place, Suite 620, 119 Kent Street, C1A 1N3.
Telephone: 902-368-8473.
Fax: 902-368-8346. Email: mcrpei@mcrlaw.com.
Fredericton, New Brunswick Office: Suite 600, 570 Queen Street, P.O. Box 610.
Telephone: 506-458-8572.
Fax: 506-458-9903. Email: mcrfton@mcrlaw.com.

ASSOCIATE

John C. Friel, Q.C.

For Complete List of Firm Personnel, See General Section

For full biographical listings, see the Martindale-Hubbell Law Directory

CANADA NEWFOUNDLAND

*ST. JOHN'S,**

MCINNES COOPER (AV)

Barristers, Solicitors & Trade Mark Agents
Baine Johnston Centre, 5th Floor, 10 Fort William Place, P.O. Box 5939, A1C 5X4
Telephone: 709-722-8735
Telecopier: 709-722-1763
Email: mcrsj@mcrlaw.com *URL:* http://www.mcrlaw.com
Halifax, Nova Scotia Office: Summit Place, 1601 Lower Water Street, P.O. Box 730, B3J 2V1.
Telephone: 902-425-6500.
Fax: 902-425-6350. Email: mcrhfx@mcrlaw.com.
Moncton, New Brunswick Office: Place Moncton Place, 655 Main Street, P.O. Box 1368, E1C 8T6.
Telephone: 506-857-8970.
Fax: 506-857-4095. Email: mcrmctn@mcrlaw.com.

(See Next Column)

MCINNES COOPER—*Continued*

Charlottetown, Prince Edward Island Office: BDC Place, Suite 620, 119 Kent Street, C1A 1N3.
Telephone: 902-368-8473.
Fax: 902-368-8346. Email: mcrpei@mcrlaw.com.
Fredericton, New Brunswick Office: Suite 600, 570 Queen Street, P.O. Box 610.
Telephone: 506-458-8572.
Fax: 506-458-9903. Email: mcrfton@mcrlaw.com.

PARTNER

Deborah L. J. Hutchings

For Complete List of Firm Personnel, See General Section

For full biographical listings, see the Martindale-Hubbell Law Directory

CANADA NOVA SCOTIA

*HALIFAX,** Regional Munic. of Halifax

MCINNES COOPER (AV)

Barristers, Solicitors & Trade Mark Agents
Summit Place, 1601 Lower Water Street, P.O. Box 730, B3J 2V1
Telephone: 902-425-6500
Fax: 902-425-6350
Email: mcrhfx@mcrlaw.com *URL:* http://www.mcrlaw.com
St. John's, Newfoundland Office: Baine Johnston Centre, 5th Floor, 10 Fort William Place, P.O. Box 5939, A1C 5X4.
Telephone: 709-722-8735.
Telecopier: 709-722-1763. Email: mcrsj@mcrlaw.com.
Moncton, New Brunswick Office: Place Moncton Place, 655 Main Street, P.O. Box 1368, E1C 8T6.
Telephone: 506-857-8970.
Fax: 506-857-4095. Email: mcrmctn@mcrlaw.com.
Charlottetown, Prince Edward Island Office: BDC Place, Suite 620, 119 Kent Street, C1A 1N3.
Telephone: 902-368-8473.
Fax: 902-368-8346. Email: mcrpei@mcrlaw.com.
Fredericton, New Brunswick Office: Suite 600, 570 Queen Street, P.O. Box 610.
Telephone: 506-458-8572.
Fax: 506-458-9903. Email: mcrfton@mcrlaw.com.

PARTNERS

Stewart McInnes, P.C., Q.C.
Christopher C. Robinson, Q.C.
Peter M. S. Bryson
George W. MacDonald, Q.C.
David A. Graves
Deborah K. Smith
Michelle C. Awad

ASSOCIATE

Tara A. Miller

For Complete List of Firm Personnel, See General Section

For full biographical listings, see the Martindale-Hubbell Law Directory

CANADA ONTARIO

*TORONTO,** Regional Munic. of Toronto

BORDEN & ELLIOT (AV)

Barristers & Solicitors
Scotia Plaza, 40 King Street West, M5H 3Y4
Telephone: 416-367-6000
Telecopier: 416-367-6749
Email: info@borden.com *URL:* http://www.borden.com
Ottawa, Ontario Office: Borden Elliot Scott & Aylen, 1000-60 Rue Queen Street.
Telephone: 613-237-5160; 800-661-4237. General
Facsimile: 613-230-8842. IP Dept.
Facsimile: 613-787-3558. Email: ottinfo@scottaylen.com. URL: http://www.borden.com.

William A. McClelland

For Complete List of Firm Personnel, See General Section

For full biographical listings, see the Martindale-Hubbell Law Directory

KELLY AFFLECK GREENE (AV)

One First Canadian Place, Suite 840, P.O. Box 489, M5X 1E5
Telephone: 416-360-2800
Fax: 416-360-5960
Email: info@kag.net *URL:* http://www.kag.net

(See Next Column)

MEMBERS OF FIRM

W. Anthony Kelly, Q.C.
Donald S. Affleck, Q.C.
Peter R. Greene
Donald B. Houston
James C. Orr
Peter C. Wardle
Helen A. Daley
Melissa J. Kennedy

ASSOCIATES

Kenneth A. Dekker
W. Michael G. Osborne
Jason C. Markwell
Patrice F. Band

For full biographical listings, see the Martindale-Hubbell Law Directory

*WINDSOR,** Essex Co.

SUTTS, STROSBERG LLP (AV)

600 Westcourt Place, 251 Goyeau Street, P.O. Box 670, N9A 6V4
Telephone: 519-258-9333
Detroit Michigan: 313-962-0137
Facsimile: Windsor 519-258-9527
Detroit 313-962-0139

MEMBERS OF FIRM

Achille F. Gignac, Q.C. (1902-1984)
Robert E. Barnes, Q.C.
Clifford N. Sutts, Q.C.
Harvey T. Strosberg, Q.C.
Gary V. Wortley
James K. Ball
John C. Holland
Mary M. S. Fox
William C. Chapman
Donald M. Gordon
Paul C. Nesseth
Heather Rumble Peterson
Patricia A. Speight
Edward W. Ducharme
Michelle A. Gagnon
Craig J. Allen
Werner H. Keller
Francine A. Herlehy
Paul Simard
Jasminka Kalajdzic

COUNSEL FOR CRIMINAL MATTERS

Patrick J. Ducharme

For full biographical listings, see the Martindale-Hubbell Law Directory

CANADA PRINCE EDWARD ISLAND

*CHARLOTTETOWN,** Queen's Co.

MCINNES COOPER (AV Ⓣ)

Barristers, Solicitors & Trade Mark Agents
BDC Place, Suite 620, 119 Kent Street, C1A 1N3
Telephone: 902-368-8473
Fax: 902-368-8346
Email: mcrpei@mcrlaw.com *URL:* http://www.mcrlaw.com
Halifax, Nova Scotia Office: Summit Place, 1601 Lower Water Street, P.O. Box 730, B3J 2V1.
Telephone: 902-425-6500.
Fax: 902-425-6350. Email: mcrhfx@mcrlaw.com.
St. John's, Newfoundland Office: Baine Johnston Centre, 5th Floor, 10 Fort William Place, P.O. Box 5939, A1C 5X4.
Telephone: 709-722-8735.
Telecopier: 709-722-1763. Email: mcrsj@mcrlaw.com.
Moncton, New Brunswick Office: Place Moncton Place, 655 Main Street, P.O. Box 1368, E1C 8T6.
Telephone: 506-857-8970.
Fax: 506-857-4095. Email: mcrmctn@mcrlaw.com.
Fredericton, New Brunswick Office: Suite 600, 570 Queen Street, P.O. Box 610.
Telephone: 506-458-8572.
Fax: 506-458-9903. Email: mcrfton@mcrlaw.com.

ASSOCIATE

Murray L. Murphy

For Complete List of Firm Personnel, See General Section

For full biographical listings, see the Martindale-Hubbell Law Directory

CANADA QUEBEC

*MONTREAL,** Montreal Dist.

MCMASTER GERVAIS (AV)

A General Partnership
1000 de La Gauchetière Street West, Suite 900, H3B 5H4
Telephone: 514-879-1212
Fax: 514-954-1905
Email: info@mcmastergervais.com *URL:* http://www.mcmastergervais.com

(See Next Column)

McMASTER GERVAIS, *Montreal—Continued*

MEMBERS OF FIRM

Alex K. Paterson, O.C., O.Q., Q.C.
Jacques Gauthier
John G. Murphy
Stéphanie Moffatt

COUNSEL

Bartha M. Knoppers

For Complete List of Firm Personnel, See General Section

For full biographical listings, see the Martindale-Hubbell Law Directory

CANADA SASKATCHEWAN

*REGINA,** Regina Jud. Centre

MacPHERSON LESLIE & TYERMAN (AV)

1500-1874 Scarth Street, S4P 4E9
Telephone: 306-347-8000
Telecopier: 306-352-5250
Email: mltreg@mlt.com
Saskatoon, Saskatchewan Office: 1500-410 22nd Street East, S7K 5T6.
Telephone: 306-975-7100.
Telecopier: 306-975-7145.

ASSOCIATE

Jeffrey D. Scott

For Complete List of Firm Personnel, See General Section

For full biographical listings, see the Martindale-Hubbell Law Directory

MERGERS AND ACQUISITIONS

MISSOURI

ST. LOUIS, (Independent City)

HELFREY, SIMON & JONES, P.C. (AV)

120 South Central Avenue Suite 1500, 63105
Telephone: 314-725-9100
Facsimile: 314-725-5754

David L. Jones
David F. Neiers

Jeffrey M. Igou
Michael C. Seamands

For full biographical listings, see the Martindale-Hubbell Law Directory

THE KOHN PARTNERSHIP, L.P. (AV)

7820 Maryland Avenue, 63105
Telephone: 314-721-8888
Fax: 314-721-6609
Tucson, Arizona Office: 1200 North El Dorado Place, Suite H-810, 85715.
Telephone: 520-721-4921.
Fax: 520-722-5767.

Michael E. Kohn
Sidney Y. Kohn (Resident, Tucson, Arizona Office)
Thomas C. Piccioli (Not admitted in MO)

Jeff D. Figge

OF COUNSEL

Catherine Kriegshauser Kohn

For full biographical listings, see the Martindale-Hubbell Law Directory

THE STOLAR PARTNERSHIP (AV)

7th Floor, 911 Washington Avenue, 63101
Telephone: 314-231-2800
Telex: 880984
Telecopier: 314-436-8400
Belleville, Illinois Office: 7 North High Street.
Telephone: 618-277-1030.

MEMBERS OF FIRM

Marc W. Braun
Harvey A. Harris
Thomas E. Lowther
Randall A. Martin
John A. Niemoeller
Jeffrey H. Pass
Geetha R. Sant
Lewis E. Striebeck Jr.

For full biographical listings, see the Martindale-Hubbell Law Directory

NEBRASKA

*LINCOLN,** Lancaster Co.

CLINE, WILLIAMS, WRIGHT, JOHNSON & OLDFATHER (AV)

1900 U.S. Bank Building, 233 South 13th Street, 68508
Telephone: 402-474-6900
Fax: 402-474-5393
Email: postmaster@cline-law.com *URL:* http://www.cline-law.com
Omaha, Nebraska Office: Suite 720, One Pacific Place, 1125 South 103rd Street, 68124.
Telephone: 402-397-1700.
Fax: 402-397-1806.

ATTORNEYS

Allen L. Graves
Charles M. Pallesen, Jr.
Fredric H. Kauffman
Donald F. Burt
Alan E. Peterson
Stephen E. Gehring
Robert J. Routh
Kevin Colleran
L. Bruce Wright
James M. Bausch
Larry A. Holle
David R. Buntain
Stephen H. Nelsen
Michael C. Mueller
Lauren W. Wismer
Daniel R. Stogsdill
Scott D. Kelly
Terry R. Wittler
Pamela Hastings Carrier
Mark A. Christensen
Richard P. Garden, Jr.
Shawn D. Renner
John C. Miles
Mary Kay Frank
Thomas C. Huston
Sonya S. Ekart
Don R. Janssen
Susan Kubert Sapp
Kevin J. Schneider
Andrew D. Strotman
Jill Gossin Jensen
Rochelle A. Mullen
John L. Horan
Bryan S. Hatch
Steven C. Likes
Tracy A. Oldemeyer

(See Next Column)

ATTORNEYS (Continued)

Jolene M. Papa
Timothy G. Aschoff
Eric N. Bergquist
Janis J. Winterhof
Andrea Dylan Snowden

OF COUNSEL

Charles E. Wright
Richard P. Jeffries
Mary M. Campbell

RETIRED PARTNERS

Flavel A. Wright (Retired)
Warren C. Johnson (Retired)
Charles E. Oldfather (1927-1998)

Representative Clients: U.S. Bank National Association; University of Nebraska; Nebraska Medical Assn.; Saint Elizabeth Regional Medical Center; Media of Nebraska; Cargill Inc.; State Farm Insurance Cos.; Wal-Mart Stores, Inc.; Textron/Cushman; Isco, Inc.

For full biographical listings, see the Martindale-Hubbell Law Directory

SCUDDER LAW FIRM, P.C. (AV)

Second Floor, 411 South 13th Street, P.O. Box 81277, 68508
Telephone: 402-435-3223
Fax: 402-435-4239
Email: firm@scudderlaw.com *URL:* http://www.scudderlaw.com

Earl H. Scudder
Christine C. Schwartzkopf Schroff
Mark A. Scudder
Michael O. Dunn
Heidi Hornung Scherr
William J. Strait

PROFESSIONAL ASSISTANTS

Annette Elston (Firm Administrator)
Lynn K. Hilger (Legal Assistant)
Tisha Gilreath Mullen (Legal Assistant)
Kristin Ann Brown
Marleen M. Kelley
Heather Ropes-Gale (Director of Communications)

For full biographical listings, see the Martindale-Hubbell Law Directory

*OMAHA,** Douglas Co.

MCGILL, GOTSDINER, WORKMAN & LEPP, P.C. (AV)

Suite 500 - First National Plaza, 11404 West Dodge Road, 68154
Telephone: 402-492-9200
Telecopier: 402-492-9222
Email: mgwl@mgwl.com

Stephen T. McGill (1932-1997)
R. Thomas Workman
Gary M. Gotsdiner
Robert J. Kmiecik
Keith A. Green

Representative Clients: Behlen Mfg. Co.; Metz Baking Company; Service Data Corporation.

For Complete List of Firm Personnel, See General Section

For full biographical listings, see the Martindale-Hubbell Law Directory

NEVADA

HENDERSON, Clark Co.

ROOKER & GIBSON (AV)

Suite 105, 701 North Green Valley Parkway, 89014
Telephone: 702-990-8100
Telecopier: 702-932-5266

C. Keith Rooker
James B. Gibson

Reference: BankWest of Nevada.

For full biographical listings, see the Martindale-Hubbell Law Directory

NEW JERSEY

LIBERTY CORNER, Somerset Co.

KALISON, MCBRIDE & JACKSON, P.A. (AV)

Liberty Corner Executive Center, 645 Martinsville Road, P.O. Box 814, 07938
Telephone: 908-647-4600
Telecopier: 908-647-6226

Michael J. Kalison
Andrew F. McBride III
Paul R. Murphy
John Zen Jackson
James V. Hetzel
James Acre Robertson, IV

(See Next Column)

KALISON, MCBRIDE & JACKSON P.A., *Liberty Corner—Continued*

Barry Liss	Daniel R. Esposito
Sloane S. Belitz	Alison Wholey Mynick
Todd Schaper	Jennifer Candace Weissman

OF COUNSEL

Wendy C. Tomey

LEGAL SUPPORT PERSONNEL

Susan R. Buchanan	Roman Bohoslawec

For full biographical listings, see the Martindale-Hubbell Law Directory

NEW YORK

MELVILLE, Suffolk Co.

LAMB & BARNOSKY, LLP (AV)

534 Broadhollow Road-CS 9034, 11747-9034
Telephone: 631-694-2300
Telecopier: 631-694-2309
Email: thefirm@lambbarnosky.com *URL:* http://www.lambbarnosky.com

PARTNERS

Eugene R. Barnosky	Scott M. Karson
Robert H. Cohen	P. L. Lamb
Marcia Lyn Finkelstein	Arthur A. Lane
Michael J. Heller	Joel M. Markowitz
Gary Holman	Gerald P. Rosenberg

Patrice Dowd Shenn

OF COUNSEL

Louis E. Black	Howard W. Newman
James F. Gesualdi	Joseph J. Salvatore

Joseph H. Wishod

COUNSEL

Lloyd K. Chanin	Scott P. McBride

ASSOCIATES

Cathleen D. Allen	Rita Fishman Sheena
Catherine Healy Kanzler	Shari Lee Sugarman

For full biographical listings, see the Martindale-Hubbell Law Directory

*NEW YORK,** New York Co.

PARKER CHAPIN LLP (AV)

Chrysler Building, 405 Lexington Avenue, 10017
Telephone: 212-704-6000
Telecopier: 212-704-6288
URL: http://www.parkerchapin.com
Great Neck, New York Office: 175 Great Neck Road.
Telephone: 516-482-4422.
Telecopier: 516-482-4469.
Hackensack, New Jersey: 190 Morre Street, Suite 307.
Telephone: 210-883-6400.
Telecopier: 210-883-6404.
Beverly Hills, California: 9454 Wilshire Boulevard.
Telephone: 310-288-8367.
Telecopier: 310-288-8365.

MEMBERS OF FIRM

James Alterbaum	Henry I. Rothman
Christopher Stewart Auguste	Richard A. Rubin
Lloyd Frank	Michael J. Shef
Mark S. Hirsch	Gary J. Simon
Jordan A. Horvath	Alvin M. Stein
Timothy I. Kahler	Melvin Weinberg
Edward R. Mandell	Michael Weinsier

Martin Eric Weisberg

For Complete List of Firm Personnel, See General Section

For full biographical listings, see the Martindale-Hubbell Law Directory

PILIERO GOLDSTEIN JENKINS & SULLIVAN, LLP (AV)

292 Madison Avenue, 10017
Telephone: 212-213-8200
Fax: 212-685-2028
Email: lawyers@pgjhlaw.com *URL:* http://www.pgjhlaw.com
Carlstadt, New Jersey Office: One Palmer Terrace.
Telephone: 201-507-5157.
FAX: 201-507-5221.
Washington, D.C. Office: 888 17th Street, N.W., Suite 1100.
Telephone: 202-467-6991.
FAX: 202-467-6703.
San Francisco, California Office: 507 Howard Street, Suite 200.
Telephone: 415-281-3631.
Fax: 415-281-3630.

(See Next Column)

MEMBERS OF FIRM

Kimberlee S. Bogen	Marc A. Lebowitz
Edward J. Goldstein	Robert D. Piliero
Jon Mark Jenkins	George O. Richardson, III

Michael T. Sullivan

ASSOCIATES

Craig Avedisian	Eric M. Kogan
Rosemary G. Feit	Mariano Schwed

OF COUNSEL

Kenneth D. Arbeeny	Christopher P. Hall

For full biographical listings, see the Martindale-Hubbell Law Directory

NORTH CAROLINA

*GREENSBORO,** Guilford Co.

SCHELL BRAY AYCOCK ABEL & LIVINGSTON P.L.L.C. (AV)

1500 Renaissance Plaza, 230 North Elm Street, P.O. Box 21847, 27420
Telephone: 336-370-8800
Fax: 336-370-8830
Email: Info@sbaal.com *URL:* http://www.sbaal.com

MEMBERS OF FIRM

Braxton Schell	Paul H. Livingston, Jr.
Doris R. Bray	Thomas C. Watkins
William P. Aycock, II	Dan T. Barker, Jr.
Michael R. Abel	Barbara R. Christy

John A. McLendon, Jr.

ASSOCIATES

Kathleen A. Kingsbury	Gregory M. Chabon
Jacqueline E. Camp	Jennifer Johnson
A. Nicholas Purrington	Eric M. Braun

Garland V. Gibbes

Representative Clients: The Breakers Palm Beach, Inc.; CBP Resources, Inc. (Carolina By-Products); Cone Mills Corp.; Cornwallis Development Co.; Kenan Transport Co.; Klaussner Furniture Industries, Inc.; North Carolina Trust Co.; Texfi Industries, Inc.; University of North Carolina at Chapel Hill Foundation, Inc.; Vanguard Cellular Systems, Inc.

For full biographical listings, see the Martindale-Hubbell Law Directory

OHIO

*CLEVELAND,** Cuyahoga Co.

CONWAY, MARKEN, WYNER, KURANT & KERN CO., L.P.A. (AV)

30195 Chagrin Boulevard, Pepper Pike Place, Suite 300, 44124
Telephone: 216-292-3300
Telecopier: 216-292-3340

James J. Conway	Kevin R. Keogh
Howard A. Marken	Peter D. Brosse
Jeffrey G. Wyner	Mark Leskovec
Jack Kurant	Michael R. Stavnicky
Keith W. Kern	Michele R. Yeh
Peter Turner	Jennifer A. Corso

For full biographical listings, see the Martindale-Hubbell Law Directory

WALTER & HAVERFIELD, P.L.L. (AV)

1300 Terminal Tower, 44113-2253
Telephone: 216-781-1212
Telecopier: 216-575-0911
Email: law@walterhav.com *URL:* http://www.walterhav.com
Columbus, Ohio Office: 88 East Broad Street.
Telephone: 614-898-1096.

MEMBERS OF FIRM

Robert J. Crump	David W. Welty
Charles R. Schaefer	Gary A. Zwick
James P. Conroy	Carl E. Anderson

David P.N. Silk

ASSOCIATES

Teresa M. Beasley	Mary E. Zeit
Amy Leopard Woodhall	Mia M. Mounts

OF COUNSEL

Ricky Lee Bertram

Representative Clients: AGA Gas, Inc.; Braden Sutphin Ink Company; Chemix, Inc.; Multi-Care Management; Edgepark Surgical; Hytree Pharmacy, Inc.; Allen Medical Systems, Inc.

(See Next Column)

WALTER & HAVERFIELD P.L.L.—*Continued*

For Complete List of Firm Personnel, See General Section

For full biographical listings, see the Martindale-Hubbell Law Directory

*COLUMBUS,** Franklin Co.

BRICKER & ECKLER LLP (AV)

100 South Third Street, 43215-4291
Telephone: 614-227-2300
Telecopy: 614-227-2390
Email: info@be.bricker.com *URL:* http://www.bricker.com

Richard D. Rogovin
Michael F. Sullivan
John P. Beavers (Managing Partner)
Steven R. Kerber
James A. Rutledge
John W. Cook, III
Michael E. Flowers
Gordon F. Litt
Mark C. Pomeroy
Thomas R. Brownlee, Jr.

Laurie A. Briggs
Juliana M. Faris

Representative Clients: Westfield Insurance Companies; Mill's Pride; State Auto Insurance Companies.

For Complete List of Firm Personnel, See General Section

For full biographical listings, see the Martindale-Hubbell Law Directory

SWEDLOW, BUTLER, LEVINE, LEWIS & DYE CO., L.P.A. (AV)

10 West Broad Street, Suite 2400, 43215-3469
Telephone: 614-461-1100
Telecopier: 614-461-8178
Email: SBILLlaw@aol.com

Gerald H. Swedlow
Jack C. Butler
Richard L. Levine
Jeffrey M. Lewis
David A. Dye
Steven A. Baenen
Todd H. Neuman
Sean M. Gouhin

Reference: National City Bank; Fifth Third Bank.

For full biographical listings, see the Martindale-Hubbell Law Directory

*DAYTON,** Montgomery Co.

PICKREL, SCHAEFFER & EBELING (AV)

2700 Kettering Tower, 45423-2700
Telephone: 937-223-1130
Facsimile: 937-223-0339
URL: http://www.pselaw.com

Paul E. Zimmer
Jon M. Rosemeyer

Jeffrey S. Senney
Cara W. Powers

Representative Clients: STC Broadcasting (WDTN-TV2); Roberds Inc.; AcuSport Corp.; Ameritech; Dayton Foods dba Cub Foods; Provident Bank; Sears Roebuck.

For full biographical listings, see the Martindale-Hubbell Law Directory

SEBALY, SHILLITO & DYER A LEGAL PROFESSIONAL ASSOCIATION (AV)

1300 Courthouse Plaza, NE, P.O. Box 220, 45402-0220
Telephone: 937-222-2500
Telefax: 937-222-6554; 222-8279
URL: http://www.ssdlaw.com

Martin A. Beyer
Daniel A. Brown
James A. Dyer
Gale S. Finley
John R. Glankler
Deborah D. Hunt
Michael P. Moloney
Jon M. Sebaly
Beverly F. Shillito
Jeffrey B. Shulman
Karl R. Ulrich
Lawrence S. Walter
Nita S. Yates

OF COUNSEL

William W. Lambert

Michael A. Booth
Robert E. Goff, Jr.
Leslie Blair Graden
Joseph V. Hatala
J. David Ruffner, II
Kendra F. Thompson

For full biographical listings, see the Martindale-Hubbell Law Directory

OKLAHOMA

*OKLAHOMA CITY,** Oklahoma Co.

PRINGLE & PRINGLE, A PROFESSIONAL CORPORATION (AV)

4101 North Classen Boulevard Suite A, 73118-2432
Telephone: 405-848-4810
Fax: 405-848-4819
Email: pringle@pringleandpringle.com *URL:* http://www.pringleandpringle.com

Lynn A. Pringle
Laura Nan Smith Pringle
Conni L. Allen

OF COUNSEL

Alvin C. Harrell
Michael P. Sullivan

Representative Clients: Bankers Systems, Inc.; Bank of Western Oklahoma, Elk City; The First National Bank and Trust Co., Chickasha; The Farmers Bank, Carnegie; Bank of the Panhandle, Guymon; FirstPlus Financial; Citizens State Bank, Roma, Texas; The Daniluk Corporation; Bank of Union; Pringle Publications Corporation.

For full biographical listings, see the Martindale-Hubbell Law Directory

*TULSA,** Tulsa Co.

BOESCHE, MCDERMOTT & ESKRIDGE (AV)

Suite 800 Oneok Plaza, 100 West Fifth Street, 74103
Telephone: 918-583-1777
Fax: 918-592-5809
Email: bme@intellex.com
Muskogee, Oklahoma Office: 1111 West Broadway, P.O. Box 2669, 74402.
Telephone: 918-683-6100.
Fax: 918-683-2303.

MEMBERS OF FIRM

R. Casey Cooper
David B. McKinney
Bradley K. Beasley
David A. Johnson

OF COUNSEL

Clifford K. Cate, Jr. (Resident at Muskogee)

Representative Clients: Tulsa Regional Medical Center; Helmerich & Payne, Inc.

For Complete List of Firm Personnel, See General Section

For full biographical listings, see the Martindale-Hubbell Law Directory

OREGON

*PORTLAND,** Multnomah Co.

ROBERT G. BURT, P.C. (AV)

The 1515 Building, Suite 600, 1515 S.W. Fifth Avenue, 97201-5449
Telephone: 503-223-3600
Fax: 503-274-0778

Robert G. Burt

For full biographical listings, see the Martindale-Hubbell Law Directory

JAMES, DENECKE, URRUTIA, MARMADUKE & LAWSON, P.C. (AV)

1150 Pioneer Tower, 888 S.W. Fifth Avenue, 97204-2025
Telephone: 503-228-7967
Fax: 503-222-7261
Email: jdum@jdum.com *URL:* http://www.jdum.com

Christopher James
David R. Denecke
Jerry L. Lawson, Jr.
Amy J. Carlton

CeeAnn Callahan
Jill D. Laney

For full biographical listings, see the Martindale-Hubbell Law Directory

KELL, ALTERMAN & RUNSTEIN, LLP (AV)

1001 S.W. Fifth Avenue, Suite 1800, 97204
Telephone: 503-222-3531
Telecopier: 503-227-2980
Email: kell@teleport.com

(See Next Column)

KELL, ALTERMAN & RUNSTEIN LLP, *Portland—Continued*

MEMBERS OF FIRM

Raymond M. Kell (1911-1991)
Clifford B. Alterman (1925-1995)
Ted E. Runstein
Lee Davis Kell
Wayne D. Palmer
Lloyd R. Summers
William D. Dickas
Gary P. Compa
Charles R. Williamson
Mary Ellen Page Farr
Eric Sogge
Thomas J. Matsuda
Thomas R. Rask, III
Nicholas S. Fish

Dana L. Barnes
Cory Larvik
Robert E. Kabacy
Robin M. Runstein

References: Union Bank of California, N.A. (Portland Branch); The Bank of Tokyo-Mitsubishi, Ltd. (Portland Branch); Bank of America (5th S. Main Branch).

For full biographical listings, see the Martindale-Hubbell Law Directory

PENNSYLVANIA

BALA CYNWYD, Montgomery Co.

KANIA, LINDNER, LASAK AND FEENEY (AV)

Suite 525, Two Bala Plaza, 19004
Telephone: 610-667-3240
Fax: 610-668-9676
Email: kllf@aol.com

Arthur J. Kania
Albert A. Lindner
John Lasak
Thomas J. Feeney, III
Robert A. Griffiths

A list of Representative Clients for which the firm serves as General Counsel or Local Counsel will be supplied upon request.

For full biographical listings, see the Martindale-Hubbell Law Directory

*PHILADELPHIA,** Philadelphia Co.

KLEINBARD, BELL & BRECKER LLP (AV)

Suite 700, 1900 Market Street, 19103
Telephone: 215-568-2000
Facsimile: 215-568-0140
Montclair, New Jersey Office: 240 Claremont Avenue, 07042.
Telephone: 973-233-0600.
Facsimile: 973-233-9390.

Joseph S. Kleinbard (1905-1994)
Robert John Brecker (1916-1996)

COUNSEL TO THE FIRM

Arthur S. Keyser

MEMBERS OF FIRM

Paul E. Bomze
Murray I. Blackman
Howard J. Davis
Steven R. Waxman
Steven J. Engelmyer (Resident, Montclair Office)
David L. Hyman (Resident, Montclair Office)
Imogene E. Hughes
John P. Hickey
Jay R. Goldstein
Ralph J. Mauro
Thomas H. Speranza
Lisa E. Brody

ASSOCIATES

Mary Beth H. Gray
Eric J. Rothschild
Mary Vassallo Slinkard
Michael A. Frattone
Benjamin C. Graff (Not admitted in PA)
Ralph F. Salgado

COUNSEL

Joseph Bell

For full biographical listings, see the Martindale-Hubbell Law Directory

WYOMISSING, Berks Co.

LEISAWITZ HELLER ABRAMOWITCH PHILLIPS, P.C. (AV)

2201 Ridgewood Road Suite 400, 19610
Telephone: 610-372-3500
Fax: 610-372-8671
Email: lhap@lhaplaw.com
Reading, Pennsylvania Office: 138 North Fifth Street.
Telephone: 610-372-3500.
Hamburg, Pennsylvania Office: 178 North Third Street.
Telephone: 610-562-4145.

Alan G. Leisawitz
Mervin A. Heller, Jr.
Jay N. Abramowitch
Charles J. Phillips
William R. Blumer
Allen R. Shollenberger

Robert J. Kirwan, II
Kevin A. Moore
Kathleen A. B. Kovach
Douglas Paul Rauch
Kenneth Millman

For full biographical listings, see the Martindale-Hubbell Law Directory

RHODE ISLAND

*PROVIDENCE,** Providence Co.

HINCKLEY, ALLEN & SNYDER LLP (AV)

1500 Fleet Center, 02903-2393
Telephone: 401-274-2000
Fax: 401-277-9600
Email: firm@haslaw.com *URL:* http://www.haslaw.com
Boston, Massachusetts Office: 28 State Street, 30th Floor.
Telephone: 617-345-9000.
Fax: 617-345-9020. URL: http://www.haslaw.com.

MEMBERS OF FIRM

Paula K. Andrews (Not admitted in RI)
David D. Barricelli
E. Jerome Batty
Jonathan Bell
Paul Bork (Not admitted in RI)
Stephen J. Carlotti
David Barry Connolly (Not admitted in RI)
Joseph P. Curran
Michael P. DeFanti
Eric F. Eisenberg (Not admitted in RI)
Malcolm Farmer, III
Margaret D. Farrell
Hugh J. Gorman, III (Not admitted in RI)
Alan P. Gottlieb (Not admitted in RI)
William R. Grimm
Paul A. Hedstrom (Not admitted in RI)
Richard L. E. Jocelyn
Joel Lewin (Not admitted in RI)
Sandra Matrone Mack
Matthew T. Marcello, III
Frederick P. McClure
Elizabeth Murdock Myers
Paul F. O'Donnell, III (Not admitted in RI)
H. Peter Olsen
Julianne Palumbo (Not admitted in RI)
John J. Pendergast, III
Gerald J. Petros
James O. Reavis
Jeremy Ritzenberg (Not admitted in RI)
Ralph J. Rivkind (Not admitted in RI)
David J. Rubin
Charles E. Schaub, Jr. (Not admitted in RI)
Douglas F. Seaver (Not admitted in RI)
Herman Snyder (Not admitted in RI)
David R. Sullivan (Not admitted in RI)
Robert F. Sylvia (Not admitted in RI)
Howard E. Walker
Richard D. Wayne (Not admitted in RI)

ASSOCIATES

Jessica M. Bettencourt
Mark Bianchi
Alyssa V. Boss
Alexandra K. Callam
Jane E. Cohen (Not admitted in RI)
Andrew D. Cummings (Not admitted in RI)
June E. Daniel
Kim Herman Goslant (Not admitted in RI)
Gloria Maria Gutierrez (Not admitted in RI)
Kelley Jordan-Price
Catherine S. Kim (Not admitted in RI)
Christopher W. Morog (Not admitted in RI)
Elena B. Olson (Not admitted in RI)
Joseph D. Whelan

OF COUNSEL

Willard Krasnow (Not admitted in RI)
Willard R. Pope (Not admitted in RI)
Bentley Tobin
Joachim A. Weissfeld

For Complete List of Firm Personnel, See General Section

For full biographical listings, see the Martindale-Hubbell Law Directory

SOUTH CAROLINA

*GREENVILLE,** Greenville Co.

MERLINE & THOMAS, P.A. (AV)

812 East North Street, P.O. Box 10796, 29603
Telephone: 864-242-4080
Fax: 864-242-5758

David A. Merline
John R. Thomas
David A. Merline, Jr.
Keith G. Meacham
Randy E. Fisher
Robert E. August
Tommy D. Permenter, Jr.

LEGAL SUPPORT PERSONNEL

Mary S. Rose (Legal Administrator)

For full biographical listings, see the Martindale-Hubbell Law Directory

TENNESSEE

*MEMPHIS,** Shelby Co.

HALE HEADRICK DEWEY & WOLF, PLLC (AV)

One Memphis Place, 200 Jefferson Avenue Suite 1450, 38103
Telephone: 901-523-1123
Fax: 901-523-7472
Nashville, Tennessee Office: Suntrust Bank Building, 201 Fourth Avenue North, Suite 1450, 37219.
Telephone: 615-843-5160.
Fax: 615-843-5165

Stephen P. Hale
S. Russell Headrick
H. Tucker Dewey
Herbert B. Wolf, Jr.
John S. Golwen

OF COUNSEL

Steven L. Gill

Jennifer Ziegenhorn
Wendy A. Geurin
John W. Campbell
Joseph M. Koury
Holly N. Knight
Charles S. Blatteis
Jennifer S. Kiesewetter
J. William Williams

For full biographical listings, see the Martindale-Hubbell Law Directory

HARRIS, SHELTON, DUNLAP AND COBB, P.L.L.C. (AV)

Suite 2700, One Commerce Square, 38103-2555
Telephone: 901-525-1455
Telecopier: 901-526-4084
Email: hsdclaw@hsdclaw.com
Other Memphis Office: 6363 Poplar, Suite 430.
Telephone: 901-682-1455.
Fax: 901-682-4446.
Oxford, Mississippi Office: 428 North Lamar Boulevard, Suite 2.
Telephone: 662-238-2855.
Fax: 662-238-2895.

MEMBERS OF FIRM

Walter Chandler (1887-1967)
John H. Harris, Jr.
Max Shelton
William W. Dunlap, Jr.
M. Anderson Cobb, Jr.
James L. Kirby
James R. Garts, Jr.
George T. Wheeler, Jr.
James D. Wilson
Charles C. Drennon, III (Resident, Poplar Avenue Office)
Michael F. Rafferty
A. Neal Graham
G. Rice Byars, Jr.
Jonathan E. Scharff

ASSOCIATES

Tabitha Francisco McNabb
Brett A. Hughes
Chesney Falk McAfee
Christopher S. Campbell
Estelle C. Gaerig
Donrua Barnes-Hulsey
Shawn L. Verner

For full biographical listings, see the Martindale-Hubbell Law Directory

*NASHVILLE,** Davidson Co.

BAKER, DONELSON, BEARMAN & CALDWELL (AV)

1700 Nashville City Center, 511 Union Street, 37219
Telephone: 615-726-5600
Telecopier: 615-726-0464
Email: info@bdbc.com *URL:* http://www.bakerdonelson.com
Memphis, Tennessee Office: 20th Floor, First Tennessee Building, 165 Madison, 38103.
Telephone: 901-526-2000.
Telecopier: 901-577-2303.
Chattanooga, Tennessee Office: 1800 Republic Centre, 633 Chestnut Street, 37450-1800.
Telephone: 423-756-2010.
Telecopier: 423-756-3447.

(See Next Column)

Knoxville, Tennessee Office: 2200 Riverview Tower, 900 South Gay Street, 37901.
Telephone: 423-549-7000.
Telecopier: 423-525-8569.
Johnson City, Tennessee Office: SunTrust Bank Building, 207 Mockingbird Lane, P.O. Box 3038, 37602.
Telephone: 423-928-0181.
Telecopier: 423-928-5694; 423-928-3654; Kingsport: 423-246-6191.
Huntsville, Tennessee Office: 3 Courthouse Square, 37756.
Telephone: 423-663-2321.
Telecopier: 423-663-2111.
Washington, D.C. Office: Market Square, 801 Pennsylvania Avenue, N.W., 20004.
Telephone: 202-508-3400.
Telecopier: 202-508-3402.
Jackson, Mississippi Office: Suite 500, 700 North State Street, 39202.
Telephone: 601-351-2400.
Telecopier: 601-351-2424.

SHAREHOLDERS

James L. McElroy
Philip Stuart McSween

For Complete List of Firm Personnel, See General Section

For full biographical listings, see the Martindale-Hubbell Law Directory

TUKE YOPP & SWEENEY, PLC (AV)

NationsBank Plaza Suite 1100, 414 Union Street, 37219
Telephone: 615-313-3300
Fax: 615-313-3310

MEMBERS OF FIRM

Robert D. Tuke
G. Michael Yopp
Matthew J. Sweeney, III
Lawrence C. Maxwell
Peter H. Curry
Barrett B. Sutton, Jr.
John W. Stone, III
Gary M. Brown
David J. White
Robert P. Felber, Jr.
Robb S. Harvey
Gerald F. Mace
Kathryn A. Stephenson
John C. Tishler

ASSOCIATES

W. Edward Ramage
Lisa L. Collins
Theresa M. Costonis
E. Blaine Sprouse
Warren A. Jasper
Mark W. Miller
Elizabeth A. Carnahan
Richard L. Pensinger

OF COUNSEL

Kenneth E. Douthat
William B. Drescher
Michael T. Folks (Not admitted in TN)
Larry D. Soderquist
Charles K. Grant

For full biographical listings, see the Martindale-Hubbell Law Directory

TEXAS

*DALLAS,** Dallas Co.

MEADOWS, OWENS, COLLIER, REED, COUSINS & BLAU, L.L.P. (AV)

901 Main Street, Suite 3700, 75202-3725
Telephone: 214-744-3700; 800-451-0093
Fax: 214-747-3732
URL: http://www.meadowsowens.com

MEMBERS OF FIRM

Charles M. Meadows, Jr.
Rodney J. Owens
Robert Don Collier
David N. Reed
Thomas G. Hineman
William R. Cousins, III
Charles W. Blau
George R. Bedell
Michael E. McCue
Fielder F. Nelms
Joel N. Crouch
Alan K. Davis
Charles D. Pulman

ASSOCIATES

Patricia King Dorey
Robert M. Bolton
M. Todd Welty
Josh O. Ungerman
Robyn A. Frohlin
Gregory A. Cardenas
Sara E. Lankford
Sarah Q. Qureshi
Bradley G. Korell
Todd A. Kraft
Alan L. Stroud
Matthew D. Richards

For full biographical listings, see the Martindale-Hubbell Law Directory

SMITH, UNDERWOOD & PERKINS, A PROFESSIONAL CORPORATION (AV)

600 Two Lincoln Centre, 5420 LBJ Freeway, 75240
Telephone: 972-661-5114
Telecopier: 972-661-5691
Email: firm@suandp.com *URL:* http://www.suplaw.com

(See Next Column)

SMITH, UNDERWOOD & PERKINS A PROFESSIONAL CORPORATION, *Dallas—Continued*

Timothy S. Perkins
David W. Ralston
G. Lynn Smith
William J. Underwood, Jr.

Christine A. McGuire
Amy K. Ratzlaff
P. Theodore Stoinoff, II
Val C. Cronin
Ellen P. Stewart
Todd W. Shadle
Ruth C. Logan
Christina L. Betanzos
Kent D. Williamson

For full biographical listings, see the Martindale-Hubbell Law Directory

THOMPSON & KNIGHT L.L.P. (AV)

(Attorneys and Counselors)
1700 Pacific Avenue Suite 3300, 75201
Telephone: 214-969-1700
Telecopy: 214-969-1751
Telex: 732 298
URL: http://www.tklaw.com
Austin, Texas Office: 1200 San Jacinto Center, 98 San Jacinto Boulevard, 78701.
Telephone: 512-469-6100.
Telecopy: 512-469-6180.
Fort Worth, Texas Office: 801 Cherry Street, Suite 1600, 76102.
Telephone: 817-347-1700.
Telecopy: 817-347-1799.
Houston, Texas Office: Thompson Knight Brown Parker & Leahy L.L.P., 1200 Smith Street, Suite 3600, 77002-4595.
Telephone: 713-654-8111.
Telecopier: 713-654-1871.
San Pedro Garza Garcia, Nuevo León, Mexico Office: Edificio Losoles PD-4, Av. Lázaro Cárdenas No. 2400 Pte., C.P. 66220.
Telephone: (52-8) 363-0096.
Telecopy: (52-8) 363-3067.

PARTNERS

Kenn W. Webb
Bill R. Womble

For Complete List of Firm Personnel, See General Section

For full biographical listings, see the Martindale-Hubbell Law Directory

*FORT WORTH,** Tarrant Co.

DECKER, JONES, MCMACKIN, MCCLANE, HALL & BATES, A PROFESSIONAL CORPORATION (AV)

2500 Bank One Tower, 500 Throckmorton Street, 76102-3812
Telephone: 817-336-2400; Metro: 817-429-5260
Fax: 817-332-3043; 336-2181
Email: email@deckerjones.com *URL:* http://www.deckerjones.com

Daniel L. Bates
Robert W. Decker
Mark S. Dugan
Janet L. Hahn
Randy J. Hall
Raymond B. Kelly, III
John B. McClane
John W. McMackin
Charles B. Milliken
Gary M. Moates
Bradley H. Rice
Jeffrey W. Storie
James L. Stripling
Brian K. Yost
Tamera H. Bennett
Arthur F. Zobal
Geoffrey A. Mantooth

Representative Clients: Martin-Sprocket and Gear, Inc.; Williamson-Dickie Manufacturing Co.; MICA Corp.; Ibertech, Inc.; Harbison-Fischer Manufacturing Co.; Employers Insurance of Texas; American International Group; Medical Protective Co.; Redman Homes, Inc.; Liberty Mutual Insurance.

For full biographical listings, see the Martindale-Hubbell Law Directory

*HOUSTON,** Harris Co.

CORDRAY & GOODRICH, PROFESSIONAL CORPORATION (AV)

3306 Sul Ross, 77098-1808
Telephone: 713-630-0600
Facsimile: 713-630-0017

Howard F. Cordray, Jr.
Christopher M. Goodrich
Richard Alan Tomlin
Gregory A. Goodrich
Glynn D. Nance, Jr.

OF COUNSEL

Ellen M. Lang
Van A. Cates
Robert G. Bailey

For full biographical listings, see the Martindale-Hubbell Law Directory

UTAH

*SALT LAKE CITY,** Salt Lake Co.

VAN COTT, BAGLEY, CORNWALL & MCCARTHY, A PROFESSIONAL CORPORATION (AV)

50 South Main Street, Suite 1600, P.O. Box 45340, 84145-0340
Telephone: 801-532-3333
Telecopier: 801-534-0058
Email: info@vancott.com *URL:* http://www.vancott.com
Ogden, Utah Office: 2404 Washington Boulevard, Suite 900.
Telephone: 801-394-5783.
Park City, Utah Office: 2200 Park Avenue, Suite C200-A.
Telephone: 435-649-3889.

Rand L. Cook
Arthur B. Ralph
David J. Smith
Stephen D. Swindle
Gregory P. Williams

Kim S Colton
Tacy A. Hartman

OF COUNSEL

M. Scott Woodland

For Complete List of Firm Personnel, See General Section

For full biographical listings, see the Martindale-Hubbell Law Directory

VIRGINIA

MCLEAN, Fairfax Co.

THOMAS M. DAVIDSON (AV®)

1750 Tysons Boulevard Suite 240, 22102
Telephone: 703-556-8887
Email: TMD@DAVIDSONCAPITAL.com *URL:* http://www.lawyers.com/davidsonlaw
(Not admitted in VA)

ASSOCIATE

Amy Davidson Bryant (Not admitted in VA)

For full biographical listings, see the Martindale-Hubbell Law Directory

NORFOLK, (Independent City)

PAYNE, GATES, FARTHING & RADD, P.C. (AV)

15th Floor, Dominion Tower, 999 Waterside Drive, Suite 1515, 23510-3309
Telephone: 757-640-1500
Facsimile: 757-627-6583
URL: http://www.paynegates.com

Ronald M. Gates
Philip R. Farthing
Anthony F. Radd
Glen M. Robertson
Brian R. Dinning
Todd J. Preti
Marshall A. Winslow, Jr.

C. Arthur Robinson, II
Stephen E. Heretick
Raymond L. Hogge, Jr.

OF COUNSEL

Charles E. Payne

For full biographical listings, see the Martindale-Hubbell Law Directory

VIENNA, Fairfax Co.

GARY & GOODMAN LIMITED (AV)

8500 Leesburg Pike, Suite 7000 (Tysons Corner), 22182
Telephone: 703-848-2828
Facsimile: 703-893-9276
Email: garygoodman@ggllaw.com

Stuart H. Gary

OF COUNSEL

George B. Delta

For full biographical listings, see the Martindale-Hubbell Law Directory

WASHINGTON

BELLEVUE, King Co.

PETERSON RUSSELL COFANO PLLC (AV)

870 Skyline Tower, 10900 N.E. Fourth Street, 98004-5873
Telephone: 425-462-4700
Fax: 425-451-0714
Email: grussell@prclegal.com *URL:* http://www.prclegal.com

Peter E. Peterson
Gregory L. Russell
Russell G. Cofano
Patrick M. Moran

ASSOCIATES

David M. Paltzik
John F. Sherwood, Jr.

OF COUNSEL

John F. Sherwood
Michael T. Callan

For full biographical listings, see the Martindale-Hubbell Law Directory

WEST VIRGINIA

*CLARKSBURG,** Harrison Co.

MCNEER, HIGHLAND, MCMUNN AND VARNER, L.C. (AV)

One Valley Bank Building, P.O. Drawer 2040, 26302-2040
Telephone: 304-626-1100
Facsimile: 304-623-3035
Martinsburg Office: 2520 Aikens Center, P.O. Box 2509.
Telephone: 304-264-4621.
Fax: 304-264-8623.
Parkersburg Office: 404 Market Street, Suite 204, P.O. Box 1507.
Telephone: 304-422-7193.
Facsimile: 304-422-7196.

C. David McMunn
J. Cecil Jarvis
James A. Varner
Robert W. Trumble (Resident, Martinsburg Office)
Catherine D. Munster
James N. Riley
Steven R. Bratke (Resident, Parkersburg Office)
Michael J. Novotny (Resident, Martinsburg Office)
Dennis M. Shreve
Geraldine S. Roberts
William F. Rohrbaugh (Resident, Martinsburg Office)
Gregory H. Schillace
Judy L. Shanholtz
Tiffany R. Durst
Gene W. Bailey, II

OF COUNSEL

James E. McNeer
Cecil B. Highland, Jr.
William L. Fury

Representative Clients: One Valley Bank of Clarksburg, National Assn.; Bruceton Bank; Harrison County Bank; Nationwide Mutual Insurance Cos.; Clarksburg Publishing Co.; C.I.T. Financial Services; State Automobile Mutual Insurance Co.; United Hospital Center, Inc.; West Virginia Coals, Inc.; Swanson Plating Co.

For full biographical listings, see the Martindale-Hubbell Law Directory

WATERS, WARNER & HARRIS, PLLC (AV)

Formerly Stathers & Cantrall
701 Goff Building, P.O. Box 1716, 26301
Telephone: 304-624-5571
Fax: 304-624-7228
Email: wwh.atty@northnap.citynet.net

Birk S. Stathers (1884-1945)
W. G. Stathers (1889-1970)
Arch M. Cantrall (1896-1967)
Stuart R. Waters
Boyd L. Warner
James A. Harris
Scott E. Wilson
James C. Turner
G. Thomas Smith

ASSOCIATES

D. Andrew McMunn
David C. Glover

Representative Clients: Bethlehem Steel Corp.; Grafton Coal Co.; Harry Green Chevrolet, Inc.; Emax Oil Co.; Southern Steel Products Co.; The Houston Exploration Co.; Seneca-Upshur Petroleum, Inc.; Union Drilling, Inc.; Electrical Systems, Inc.

For full biographical listings, see the Martindale-Hubbell Law Directory

*MORGANTOWN,** Monongalia Co.

THE FUSCO LEGAL GROUP, L.C. (AV)

2400 Cranberry Square, 26505-9209
Telephone: 304-594-1000
Telecopier: 304-594-1181
URL: http://www.fuscolegalgroup.com
Email: fnlaw@wvlaw.com *URL:* http://www.wvlaw.com

Andrew G. Fusco

(See Next Column)

William J. Leon, Jr.
Jeffrey A. Ray

For Complete List of Firm Personnel, See General Section

For full biographical listings, see the Martindale-Hubbell Law Directory

WISCONSIN

*MILWAUKEE,** Milwaukee Co.

D. WINTHROP HASS, S.C. (AV)

205 East Wisconsin Avenue, Suite 405, 53202
Telephone: 414-276-1776
Fax: 414-276-4850
Email: david@imericana.com *URL:* http://www.lawyers.com/dhass

D. Winthrop Hass

OF COUNSEL

Hal Harlowe

For full biographical listings, see the Martindale-Hubbell Law Directory

CANADA NEW BRUNSWICK

*FREDERICTON,** York Co.

MCINNES COOPER (AV)

Suite 600, 570 Queen Street, P.O. Box 610, E3B 5A6
Telephone: 506-458-8572
Fax: 506-458-9903
Email: mcrfton@mcrlaw.com *URL:* http://www.mcrlaw.com
Halifax, Nova Scotia Office: Summit Place, 1601 Lower Water Street, P.O. Box 730, B3J 2V1.
Telephone: 902-425-6500.
Fax: 902-425-6350. Email: mcrhfx@mcrlaw.com.
St. John's, Newfoundland Office: Baine Johnston Centre, 5th Floor, 10 Fort William Place, P.O. Box 5939, A1C 5X4.
Telephone: 709-722-8735.
Telecopier: 709-722-1763. Email: mcrsj@mcrlaw.com.
Moncton, New Brunswick Office: Place Moncton Place, 655 Main Street, P.O. Box 1368, E1C 8T6.
Telephone: 506-857-8970.
Fax: 506-857-4095. Email: mcrmctn@mcrlaw.com.
Charlottetown, Prince Edward Island Office: BDC Place, Suite 620, 119 Kent Street, C1A 1N3.
Telephone: 902-368-8473.
Fax: 902-368-8346. Email: mcrpei@mcrlaw.com.

PARTNER

Carol J. Downs

For Complete List of Firm Personnel, See General Section

For full biographical listings, see the Martindale-Hubbell Law Directory

CANADA NEWFOUNDLAND

*ST. JOHN'S,**

MCINNES COOPER (AV)

Barristers, Solicitors & Trade Mark Agents
Baine Johnston Centre, 5th Floor, 10 Fort William Place, P.O. Box 5939, A1C 5X4
Telephone: 709-722-8735
Telecopier: 709-722-1763
Email: mcrsj@mcrlaw.com *URL:* http://www.mcrlaw.com
Halifax, Nova Scotia Office: Summit Place, 1601 Lower Water Street, P.O. Box 730, B3J 2V1.
Telephone: 902-425-6500.
Fax: 902-425-6350. Email: mcrhfx@mcrlaw.com.
Moncton, New Brunswick Office: Place Moncton Place, 655 Main Street, P.O. Box 1368, E1C 8T6.
Telephone: 506-857-8970.
Fax: 506-857-4095. Email: mcrmctn@mcrlaw.com.
Charlottetown, Prince Edward Island Office: BDC Place, Suite 620, 119 Kent Street, C1A 1N3.
Telephone: 902-368-8473.
Fax: 902-368-8346. Email: mcrpei@mcrlaw.com.

(See Next Column)

McINNES COOPER, *St. John's—Continued*

Fredericton, New Brunswick Office: Suite 600, 570 Queen Street, P.O. Box 610.
Telephone: 506-458-8572.
Fax: 506-458-9903. Email: mcrfton@mcrlaw.com.

PARTNERS

John M. Green, Q.C. Caroline C. Watton

For Complete List of Firm Personnel, See General Section

For full biographical listings, see the Martindale-Hubbell Law Directory

CANADA
NOVA SCOTIA

*HALIFAX,** Regional Munic. of Halifax

McINNES COOPER (AV)

Barristers, Solicitors & Trade Mark Agents
Summit Place, 1601 Lower Water Street, P.O. Box 730, B3J 2V1
Telephone: 902-425-6500
Fax: 902-425-6350
Email: mcrhfx@mcrlaw.com *URL:* http://www.mcrlaw.com
St. John's, Newfoundland Office: Baine Johnston Centre, 5th Floor, 10 Fort William Place, P.O. Box 5939, A1C 5X4.
Telephone: 709-722-8735.
Telecopier: 709-722-1763. Email: mcrsj@mcrlaw.com.
Moncton, New Brunswick Office: Place Moncton Place, 655 Main Street, P.O. Box 1368, E1C 8T6.
Telephone: 506-857-8970.
Fax: 506-857-4095. Email: mcrmctn@mcrlaw.com.
Charlottetown, Prince Edward Island Office: BDC Place, Suite 620, 119 Kent Street, C1A 1N3.
Telephone: 902-368-8473.
Fax: 902-368-8346. Email: mcrpei@mcrlaw.com.
Fredericton, New Brunswick Office: Suite 600, 570 Queen Street, P.O. Box 610.
Telephone: 506-458-8572.
Fax: 506-458-9903. Email: mcrfton@mcrlaw.com.

PARTNERS

Lawrence J. Hayes, Q.C. Joseph A. F. Macdonald, Q.C.
Lawrence A. Freeman Marcia L. Brennan
Malcolm D. Boyle

For Complete List of Firm Personnel, See General Section

For full biographical listings, see the Martindale-Hubbell Law Directory

CANADA
PRINCE EDWARD ISLAND

*CHARLOTTETOWN,** Queen's Co.

McINNES COOPER (AV Ⓣ)

Barristers, Solicitors & Trade Mark Agents
BDC Place, Suite 620, 119 Kent Street, C1A 1N3
Telephone: 902-368-8473
Fax: 902-368-8346
Email: mcrpei@mcrlaw.com *URL:* http://www.mcrlaw.com
Halifax, Nova Scotia Office: Summit Place, 1601 Lower Water Street, P.O. Box 730, B3J 2V1.
Telephone: 902-425-6500.
Fax: 902-425-6350. Email: mcrhfx@mcrlaw.com.
St. John's, Newfoundland Office: Baine Johnston Centre, 5th Floor, 10 Fort William Place, P.O. Box 5939, A1C 5X4.
Telephone: 709-722-8735.
Telecopier: 709-722-1763. Email: mcrsj@mcrlaw.com.
Moncton, New Brunswick Office: Place Moncton Place, 655 Main Street, P.O. Box 1368, E1C 8T6.
Telephone: 506-857-8970.
Fax: 506-857-4095. Email: mcrmctn@mcrlaw.com.
Fredericton, New Brunswick Office: Suite 600, 570 Queen Street, P.O. Box 610.
Telephone: 506-458-8572.
Fax: 506-458-9903. Email: mcrfton@mcrlaw.com.

PARTNER

Mark Ledwell

For Complete List of Firm Personnel, See General Section

For full biographical listings, see the Martindale-Hubbell Law Directory

CANADA
QUEBEC

*MONTREAL,** Montreal Dist.

POULIOT, MERCURE (AV)

CIBC Tower, 31st Floor, 1155 René-Lévesque Boulevard, West, H3B 3S6
Telephone: 514-875-5210
Telecopier: 514-875-4308
Email: POUMER@CEDEP.COM
Genève, Suisse Office: 8, Rue de la Rôtisserie, 1204 Geneva, Switzerland.
Telephone: +41 22-28 79 40.
Telecopier: +41 22-21 23 67.

MEMBERS OF FIRM

Georges A. Pouliot, Q.C. Gilles Bertrand
Gilles Brunelle Jean Larivière
Luc Gratton Louis-Michel Tremblay
Brian Riordan David I. Johnston
Pierre Paquet Stéphane Hébert
Anne-Marie Gauthier Jacques LeBel, Q.C.
Yvon Brizard Joel A. Silcoff
Robert Tessier Ronald M. Auclair
Daniel Gagné Philippe Roy
Lilia Pouliot Maxime B. Rhéaume
Marco Veilleux Serge Desrochers
Alain Nadon C. Keenan LaPierre
Jean H. Gagnon Alain Bond
Richard Fontaine Louis Coallier
Normand Royal Nicole Chouinard
Stéphane Teasdale

ASSOCIATES

Micheline Perrault Brent J. Muir
Caroline Lemoine Louise Tremblay
Béatrice Arronis Chantal Joubert
Yvan Nantel Normand D'Amour
Sylvie Boulanger Pascale Cloutier
Vincent Frenette Eric Couture
Robert Cardin Frédéric Chatel
Alexandre Henri Mary-Lynn Breton
Alexandre Ajami

For full biographical listings, see the Martindale-Hubbell Law Directory

MUNICIPAL AND ZONING LAW

MINNESOTA

*MINNEAPOLIS,** Hennepin Co.

HESSIAN & McKASY, P.A. (AV)

4700 IDS Center, 80 South Eighth Street, 55402-2228
Telephone: 612-330-3000
Telecopier: 612-371-0653
St. Paul, Minnesota Offices: 2050 Piper Jaffray Plaza, 444 Cedar Street, 55101.
Telephone: 612-330-3071.
Fax: 651-228-9161.

Jaymes D. Littlejohn

SHAREHOLDERS

David W. Larson

For full biographical listings, see the Martindale-Hubbell Law Directory

*ST. PAUL,** Ramsey Co.

BANNIGAN & KELLY, P.A. (AV)

Suite 1750, North Central Life Tower, 445 Minnesota Street, 55101
Telephone: 651-224-3781
Fax: 651-223-8019

John F. Bannigan, Jr.
Patrick J. Kelly

Song Lo Fawcett
Stephen Kelly
Sia Lo

MISSISSIPPI

*CLARKSDALE,** Coahoma Co.

HUNT & ROSS, A PROFESSIONAL ASSOCIATION (AV)

123 Court Street, P.O. Box 1196, 38614
Telephone: 601-627-5251
Telecopier No.: 601-627-5254
Email: huntross@clarksdale.com *URL:* http://www.lawyers.com/h&rlaw

Tom T. Ross (1903-1993)
David R. Hunt
Tom T. Ross, Jr.

Thomas W. Allen
Katherine Blackwell Parker

Representative Clients: Coahoma County, MS.

For full biographical listings, see the Martindale-Hubbell Law Directory

*GULFPORT,** Harrison Co.

DUKES, DUKES, KEATING AND FANECA, P.A. (AV)

2909 13th Street, 6th Floor, P.O. Drawer W, 39501
Telephone: 228-868-1111
Fax: 228-863-2886
Email: ddkf@ddkf.com

Hugh D. Keating
Phillip W. Jarrell

For Complete List of Firm Personnel, See General Section

For full biographical listings, see the Martindale-Hubbell Law Directory

MONTANA

*BOZEMAN,** Gallatin Co.

KIRWAN & BARRETT, P.C. (AV)

215 West Mendenhall, P.O. Box 1348, 59771-1348
Telephone: 406-586-1553
Fax: 406-586-8971

Stephen M. Barrett

For full biographical listings, see the Martindale-Hubbell Law Directory

NEBRASKA

*LINCOLN,** Lancaster Co.

ERICKSON & SEDERSTROM, P.C. (AV)

Suite 400, Cornhusker Plaza, 301 South 13th Street, 68508
Telephone: 402-476-1000
Fax: 402-476-6167
Omaha, Nebraska Office: Regency Westpointe, 10330 Regency Parkway Drive, Suite 100, 68114-3761.
Telephone: 402-397-2200.
Fax: 402-390-7137.

Charles D. Humble
Alan M. Wood

Representative Clients: Lincoln Electric System; Village Of Eagle; Village of Douglas; Village of Palmyra; McDonalds Corp.; Shopko, Inc.; Best Buy, Inc.; Broadmoor Development Co.; Nebraska Municipal Power Pool; Municipal Energy Agency of Nebraska.

For Complete List of Firm Personnel, See General Section

For full biographical listings, see the Martindale-Hubbell Law Directory

NEVADA

HENDERSON, Clark Co.

ROOKER & GIBSON (AV)

Suite 105, 701 North Green Valley Parkway, 89014
Telephone: 702-990-8100
Telecopier: 702-932-5266

C. Keith Rooker
James B. Gibson

Reference: BankWest of Nevada.

For full biographical listings, see the Martindale-Hubbell Law Directory

*LAS VEGAS,** Clark Co.

CURRAN & PARRY (AV)

Quail Park II, Suite C-23, 601 South Rancho Drive, 89106
Telephone: 702-471-7000
Fax: 702-471-7070

MEMBERS OF FIRM

William P. Curran
Stanley W. Parry
Lynn Kirsch
John W. Burge
J. Lynn Johnson
Joshua H. Reisman (Not admitted in NV)

LEGAL SUPPORT PERSONNEL

Diane Loew (Paralegal)
Samara Johnston (Not admitted in NV; Law Clerk)

For full biographical listings, see the Martindale-Hubbell Law Directory

JOLLEY, URGA, WIRTH & WOODBURY (AV)

3800 Howard Hughes Parkway Suite 1600, 89109
Telephone: 702-699-7500
Facsimile: 702-699-7555
URL: http://www.juww.com
Boulder City, Nevada Office: Suite 105, 1000 Nevada Highway, 89005.
Telephone: 702-293-3674.

MEMBERS OF FIRM

William R. Urga
Allen D. Emmel

Representative Clients: Wells Fargo Bank and its predecessor, First Interstate Bank of Nevada; Nevada State Bank; Chicago Title Insurance Co.; Melvin Simon & Associates, Inc.; General Motors Acceptance Corp.; Toyota Motor Credit Corporation; Champion Home Builders Co.; Circus Circus Casinos, Inc.

For Complete List of Firm Personnel, See General Section

For full biographical listings, see the Martindale-Hubbell Law Directory

McDONALD CARANO WILSON McCUNE BERGIN FRANKOVICH & HICKS LLP (AV)

Suite 1000, 2300 West Sahara Avenue, 89102
Telephone: 702-873-4100
Telecopier: 702-873-9966
URL: http://www.mcdonaldcarano.com
Reno, Nevada Office: 241 Ridge Street.
Telephone: 775-788-2000.
Telecopier: 775-788-2020.

MEMBER OF FIRM

Andrew P. Gordon

Representative Clients: AT&T Communications of Nevada; Boyd Gaming Corp.; Jackpot Enterprises, Inc.; Shaver Construction.

(See Next Column)

McDonald Carano Wilson McCune Bergin Frankovich & Hicks LLP, *Las Vegas—Continued*

For Complete List of Firm Personnel, See General Section

For full biographical listings, see the Martindale-Hubbell Law Directory

*RENO,** Washoe Co.

McDonald Carano Wilson McCune Bergin Frankovich & Hicks LLP (AV)

241 Ridge Street, 89501
Telephone: 775-788-2000
Telecopier: 775-788-2020
URL: http://www.mcdonaldcarano.com
Las Vegas, Nevada Office: Suite 1000, 2300 West Sahara Avenue.
Telephone: 702-873-4100.
Telecopier: 702-873-9966.

MEMBERS OF FIRM

Leo P. Bergin, III
John J. Frankovich
Andrew P. Gordon

ASSOCIATE

David F. Grove

Representative Clients: Associated General Contractors of America; AT & T; Eldorado Hotel & Casino; Scolari's Warehouse Markets, Inc.

For Complete List of Firm Personnel, See General Section

For full biographical listings, see the Martindale-Hubbell Law Directory

NEW JERSEY

*HACKENSACK,** Bergen Co.

Contant, Scherby & Atkins (AV)

33 Hudson Street, 07601
Telephone: 201-342-1070
Fax: 201-342-5213
Email: LawfirmCSA@aol.com *URL:* http://www.lawyers.com/csalaw

MEMBERS OF THE FIRM

John M. Contant (1907-1988)
Richard J. Contant
Michael L. Scherby
Bruce L. Atkins
Matthew S. Rogers
Andrew T. Fede
Brian T. Keane
Robert B. Hille

ASSOCIATES

Geraldine E. Beers
Suzanne J. Ryderman
Lisa R. Aljian
Christina A. Stoneburner
Sheila O'Shea

OF COUNSEL

Fenster & Weiss, New City, New York

For full biographical listings, see the Martindale-Hubbell Law Directory

Stoldt, Horan and Kowal, A Professional Corporation (AV)

Continental Plaza I, 401 Hackensack Avenue, 07601
Telephone: 201-646-9200
Telecopier: 201-646-0167
Email: shlaw@bellatlantic.net *URL:* http://www.lawyers.com/stoldthoran&kowal

Sydney V. Stoldt, Jr.
John D. Horan
Dorothy A. Kowal
Heather A. Gallagher
Brian O'Reilly

OF COUNSEL

Judith R. Levinson

For full biographical listings, see the Martindale-Hubbell Law Directory

HAWTHORNE, Passaic Co.

Jeffer, Hopkinson & Vogel (AV)

(Formerly Jeffer, Walter, Tierney, DeKorte, Hopkinson & Vogel)
Law Building, 1600 Route 208N, P.O. Box 507, 07507
Telephone: 973-423-0100
Fax: 973-423-5614
Tequesta, Florida Office: Jeffer, Cioffi & Cicalese. 250 Tequesta Drive, 33469.
Telephone: 561-747-6000.
Fax: 561-575-9167.

MEMBERS OF FIRM

Herman M. Jeffer
Reginald F. Hopkinson
Jerome A. Vogel

(See Next Column)

ASSOCIATES

Melinda B. Maidens
E. David Becker
David H. Altman

Counsel for: Brioschi, Inc.; Opici Wine Co.; Gas Pumpers of America Corp.; The Paterson Market Growers Assn.; Dowling Fuel Oil Co.; Becton, Dickinson; JFC International, Inc.; Loews Theaters; Christian Health Care Center.

For Complete List of Firm Personnel, See General Section

For full biographical listings, see the Martindale-Hubbell Law Directory

LIVINGSTON, Essex Co.

Skoloff & Wolfe, P.C. (AV)

293 Eisenhower Parkway, 07039
Telephone: 973-992-0900
Fax: 973-992-0301
Morristown, New Jersey Office: 10 Park Place.
Telephone: 973-267-3511.

Saul A. Wolfe
Gary N. Skoloff
Richard H. Singer, Jr. (Resident at Morristown Office)
Stephen P. Haller
Robert F. Giancaterino
Edward J. O'Donnell
Beatrice E. Kandell
Heather A. Turnbull

Garry J. Roettger
Nancy C. Richmond
Gigi Hanna

OF COUNSEL

Bertram Polow

For full biographical listings, see the Martindale-Hubbell Law Directory

MOORESTOWN, Burlington Co.

Frederick W. Hardt (AV)

Suite 101, 300 Chester Avenue, P.O. Box 840, 08057-2512
Telephone: 609-234-4141
Fax: 609-273-8617

ASSOCIATE

Pamela A. Moy

For full biographical listings, see the Martindale-Hubbell Law Directory

*NEWARK,** Essex Co.

Sills Cummis Radin Tischman Epstein & Gross, A Professional Corporation (AV)

One Riverfront Plaza, 07102-5400
Telephone: 973-643-7000
Fax: 973-643-6500
Telex: 820630 Sillsbeck Nwk
Email: sillsmail@sillscummis.com *URL:* http://www.sillscummis.com
Atlantic City, New Jersey Office: 17 Gordon's Alley.
Telephone: 609-344-2800.
New York, N.Y. Office: 712 Fifth Avenue.
Telephone: 212-643-7000.
Washington, D.C. Office: 1800 K Street, N.W.
Telephone: 202-296-4750.

MEMBER OF FIRM

Stephen J. Moses

For Complete List of Firm Personnel, See General Section

For full biographical listings, see the Martindale-Hubbell Law Directory

NORTH BRUNSWICK, Middlesex Co.

Borrus, Goldin, Foley, Vignuolo, Hyman, Stahl & Clarkin, A Professional Corporation (AV)

2875 U.S. Highway 1, Route 1 & Finnigans Lane, P.O. Box 7463, 08902
Telephone: 732-422-1000
Fax: 732-422-1016
Email: attys@borrus.com *URL:* http://www.borrus.com

Jack Borrus
Martin S. Goldin
David M. Foley
Anthony B. Vignuolo
Jeffrey M. Hyman
James E. Stahl
James F. Clarkin III
Eileen Mary Foley

Robert C. Nisenson
Rosalind Westlake
Lisa M. Vignuolo
Steven L. Fox
Peter A. Vignuolo
Gerald T. Foley (1903-1976)

Representative Clients: Summit Bank; R. J. Reynolds Tobacco Co.; K. Hovnanian Enterprises, Inc.; Johnson and Johnson; Foster Wheeler, Inc.; Hartz Mountain Industries; Middlesex County Vocational Services Commission; Borough of South Plainfield Board of Adjustment; U-Haul of Northern NJ.

For full biographical listings, see the Martindale-Hubbell Law Directory

North Brunswick—Continued

BUSCH AND BUSCH, LLP (AV)

215 North Center Drive, Commerce Center - U.S. #1 South, P.O. Box 7448, 08902-7448
Telephone: 732-821-2300
Telecopier: 732-821-5588
Email: busch@ifu.net

MEMBERS OF FIRM

Lewis D. Busch (1901-1986)
Henry Busch (Retired)
Malcolm R. Busch
Ronald J. Busch
Bertram E. Busch
Mark N. Busch
Leonard R. Busch
Steven F. Satz
Donald J. Sears

ASSOCIATE

Paul Alan VanBuskirk

Representative Clients: Utica Mutual Insurance Co.; New Brunswick Tomorrow; Township of South Brunswick; Township of Monroe, Board of Education; Township of East Brunswick; Minnesota Mutual Life Insurance Co.

For full biographical listings, see the Martindale-Hubbell Law Directory

PRINCETON, Mercer Co.

MCCARTHY AND SCHATZMAN, P.A. (AV)

228 Alexander Street, P.O. Box 2329, 08543-2329
Telephone: 609-924-1199
Fax: 609-683-5251

John F. McCarthy, Jr.
Richard Schatzman
G. Christopher Baker
John F. McCarthy, III
Michael A. Spero
Barbara Strapp Nelson
W. Scott Stoner
James J. Britt, Jr.

Charly Gayden

Representative Clients: Trustees of Princeton University; Carnegie Center Associates; Merrill Lynch Pierce Fenner & Smith, Inc.; Calton Homes, Inc.

For full biographical listings, see the Martindale-Hubbell Law Directory

SHORT HILLS, Essex Co.

EDWIN R. MATTHEWS, P.C. (AV)

150 John F. Kennedy Parkway CN 5008, 07078-2707
Telephone: 973-912-9500
Telecopier: 973-912-9411
Email: mwgf@mail.att.net

Edwin R. Matthews

Robert J. Pansulla
Daniel J. Bonner
Drew D. Krause
Lisa A. Grattan

For full biographical listings, see the Martindale-Hubbell Law Directory

*SOMERVILLE,** Somerset Co.

SCHACHTER, TROMBADORE, OFFEN, STANTON & PAVICS, A PROFESSIONAL CORPORATION (AV)

45 East High Street, P.O. Box 520, 08876-0520
Telephone: 908-722-5700
Fax: 908-722-8853

Richard J. Schachter
John J. Trombadore
Stephen M. Offen
Michael J. Stanton
Thomas A. Pavics

Timothy P. McKeown
Jerry S. D'Aniello

For full biographical listings, see the Martindale-Hubbell Law Directory

*TOMS RIVER,** Ocean Co.

LOMELL, MUCCIFORI, ADLER, RAVASCHIERE, AMABILE & PEHLIVANIAN, A PROFESSIONAL CORPORATION (AV)

250 Washington Street, P.O. Box 787, 08754
Telephone: 732-349-2443
Fax: 732-349-6917
Email: thefirm@lomell.com *URL:* http://www.lomell.com

Herman A. Adler
Dominic Ravaschiere
John S. Pehlivanian
Ronald E. Prusek
Jeffrey R. Surenian
James M. McKenna
Teresa K. Gierla
Arthur F. Leyden, III

Marc S. Galella
Robyn A. Belluardo
Janet Zaorski Kalapos
James S. Braaten
Regina M. Butler
Paul J Capotorto

Representative Clients: Homdel Township; Howell Township; Wall Township; Middletown Township (Monmouth County); Barnegat Township; Brick Township; Berkeley Township; Jackson Township (Ocean County); Randolph Township (Morris County).

(See Next Column)

For Complete List of Firm Personnel, See General Section

For full biographical listings, see the Martindale-Hubbell Law Directory

*TRENTON,** Mercer Co.

SCHRAGGER, LAVINE & NAGY (AV)

Mountainview Office Park, 840 Bear Tavern Road, Suite 307, 08628
Telephone: 609-771-0700
Fax: 609-771-9535

Bruce M. Schragger
Raymond L. Nagy
James A. Schragger
Jonathan S. Robinson
Michael E. Sullivan

OF COUNSEL

Henry C. Schragger
Alan S. Lavine
Frank P. Reiche
A. Jerome Moore

LEGAL SUPPORT PERSONNEL

Annemarie Saccani (Office Administrator)

Representative Clients: New Jersey Manufacturers Insurance Co.; Mercer County Community College; Mercer Mutual Insurance Co.; New Jersey Optometric Association; Allentown Caging; Dick Greenfield Dodge.

For full biographical listings, see the Martindale-Hubbell Law Directory

VINELAND, Cumberland Co.

GRUCCIO, PEPPER GIOVINAZZI, DESANTO & FARNOLY, P.A. (AV)

817 Landis Avenue, P.O. Box 1501, 08362
Telephone: 856-691-0100
Fax: 856-692-4095
Email: Gruccio1@eticomm.net
Woodbury, New Jersey Office: 21 Delaware Street.
Telephone: 856-848-5558.
Fax: 856-384-1181.
Bridgeton, New Jersey Office: 120 West Broad Street.
Telephone: 856-459-3334.
Fax: 856-692-4095.

James J. Gruccio, Sr.
Lawrence Pepper, Jr.
Cosmo A. Giovinazzi, III
Robert A. DeSanto
E. Edward Bowman

Gerald R. Spall

Representative Clients: State Farm Mutual Automobile Insurance Cos.; United States Fidelity & Guaranty Co.; South Jersey Transportation Authority; County of Salem; County of Cape May; Cumberland Mutual Fire Insurance Co.; Farmers and Merchants National Bank of Bridgeton; Vineland Board of Education; Southern Intercounty Medical Association; Sun National Bank of N.J.

For Complete List of Firm Personnel, See General Section

For full biographical listings, see the Martindale-Hubbell Law Directory

WALL TOWNSHIP, Monmouth Co.

MAGEE AND ISHERWOOD, L.L.P. (AV)

Mirne & Simmill
Mirne, Nowels, Fundler Magee & Kirschner
1937 Route 35 at Allaire Road, P.O. Box 1200, 07719
Telephone: 732-449-2500
Telecopier: 732-449-4005

MEMBERS OF FIRM

Granville D. Magee
Thomas Isherwood

ASSOCIATE

Granville M. Magee

OF COUNSEL

Michael B. Kirschner

Representative Clients: Royal Insurance Cos.; Township of Upper Freehold.
References: Central Jersey Bank & Trust Co.; Commerce Bank Shore N.A.

For full biographical listings, see the Martindale-Hubbell Law Directory

WAYNE, Passaic Co.

GERBER & SAMSON, L.L.C. (AV)

155 Willowbrook Boulevard, 07470
Telephone: 973-256-9000
Fax: 973-256-9001
Email: njlaw@gerberlaw.com *URL:* http://www.gerberlaw.com

MEMBERS OF FIRM

Steven Gerber
Linda H. Samson
Mary Patricia Gallagher

ASSOCIATES

Mark J. Semeraro
Patti A. Scott
Keith A. Bregman
N. Noelle Letcher

(See Next Column)

GERBER & SAMSON L.L.C., *Wayne—Continued*

OF COUNSEL
Richard P. Weiss

For full biographical listings, see the Martindale-Hubbell Law Directory

WEST ORANGE, Essex Co.

RABINOWITZ, TRENK, LUBETKIN & TULLY, P.C. (AV)

200 Executive Drive Suite 225, 07052-3303
Telephone: 973-243-8600
Facsimile: 973-243-8677
URL: http://www.Rabinowitztrenk.com

Richard D. Trenk
Richard S. Schkolnick

Joshua H. Raymond
Shoshana Schiff

For full biographical listings, see the Martindale-Hubbell Law Directory

NEW MEXICO

*SANTA FE,** Santa Fe Co.

HERRERA, LONG & POUND, P.A. (AV)

2200 Brothers Road, P.O. Box 5098, 87502-5098
Telephone: 505-982-8405
Fax: 505-982-8513
Email: hlplaw@aol.com

Judith C. Herrera
Nancy R. Long
John B. Pound

Mark E. Komer

LEGAL SUPPORT PERSONNEL
Shauna Allen Metzo

Reference: Bank of America.

For full biographical listings, see the Martindale-Hubbell Law Directory

NEW YORK

*ALBANY,** Albany Co.

SHANLEY, SWEENEY, REILLY & ALLEN, P.C. (AV)

The Castle at Ten Thurlow Terrace, 12203
Telephone: 518-463-1415
Fax: 518-463-3210
Email: lawyers@shanleysweeney.com *URL:* http://www.shanleysweeney.com

Michael P. Shanley, Jr.
Robert L. Sweeney
J. Stephen Reilly
John L. Allen
Gregory D. Faucher
J. Michael Naughton
Steven S. Heyman
Scott P. Olson
David C. Kuracina
Thomas A. Shepardson
Melissa M. Beskid
Mark T. Sweeney

Christopher E. Buckey
Stacey Weisenfeld

For full biographical listings, see the Martindale-Hubbell Law Directory

TABNER, RYAN AND KENIRY (AV)

26 Computer Drive West, P.O. Box 12605, 12212-2605
Telephone: 518-459-9000
Telecopier: 518-459-9165
Email: trk@tabnerryanandkeniry.com

MEMBERS OF FIRM
John W. Tabner
William F. Ryan, Jr.
William J. Keniry

OF COUNSEL
C. Theodore Carlson

ASSOCIATES
Eric N. Dratler
Jennifer K. Corona
Donald W. Biggs

Special Counsel for: Water and Sewer District for Towns of Colonie, Coxsackie, Guilderland, Johnstown, Queensbury, Rotterdam and Village Castleton.
References: FleetBank; Trustco Bank.

For full biographical listings, see the Martindale-Hubbell Law Directory

*BINGHAMTON,** Broome Co.

HOGAN & SARZYNSKI, L.L.P. (AV)

20 Hawley Street, P.O. Box 660, 13902-0660
Telephone: 607-723-7413
Fax: 607-723-0129
Email: hsatty@pronetisp.net

MEMBERS OF FIRM
John B. Hogan
Edward J. Sarzynski
John P. Lynch
Michael G. Surowka

Wendy K. DeWind

For full biographical listings, see the Martindale-Hubbell Law Directory

EAST MEADOW, Nassau Co.

CERTILMAN BALIN ADLER & HYMAN, LLP (AV)

90 Merrick Avenue, 11554
Telephone: 516-296-7000
Telecopier: 516-296-7111
URL: http://www.cbah.com

MEMBERS OF FIRM
Ira J. Adler
Dale Allinson
Michael C. Axelrod
Herbert M. Balin
Bruce J. Bergman
Eileen O'Boyle Bitetto
Michael D. Brofman
Lewis J. Campanella
Morton L. Certilman
Robert J. Ciovacco
Brian J. Davis
Wayne G. Edwards
Joseph P. Famighetti
Howard R. Gladstone
Murray Greenberg
Gavin C. Grusd
David Z. Herman
Richard Herzbach
M. Allan Hyman
Bernard Hyman
Donna-Marie Korth
Steven J. Kuperschmid
Jeffrey S. Lisabeth
Jaspreet S. Mayall
Richard J. McCord
Thomas J. McNamara
Michael F. O'Shea
Marilyn Price
Fred S. Skolnik
Louis Soloway
Harold Somer
Howard M. Stein
Brian K. Ziegler

OF COUNSEL
Daniel S. Cohan
Joseph N. Mondello

ASSOCIATES
Lawrence A. Altholtz
Meredith W. Ayres
Daniel J. Baker
Kimberly I. Berson
Scott B. Black
Brendan J. DeRiggi
Thomas M. Farrell
Mary C. Florentz
Candace Reid Gladstone
Harry P. Greenbaum
David E. Herold
Jodi S. Hoffman
James G. Kapralos
Linda P. Manfredi
Edward G. McCabe
Patrick McCormick
Susan L. McWalters
Jothy Narendran
James A. Rose
Wayne J. Schaefer
Leslie H. Scharf
Afsheen Ashley Shah
Victor Spinnelli
Russell H. Stern
Robert G. Wilk

For full biographical listings, see the Martindale-Hubbell Law Directory

GARDEN CITY, Nassau Co.

LAW OFFICES OF JACK L. LIBERT (AV)

377 Oak Street, 11530
Telephone: 516-745-0160
Fax: 516-745-0213
Email: jacklibert@msn.com

ASSOCIATE
Jay Simens

For full biographical listings, see the Martindale-Hubbell Law Directory

ISLIP, Suffolk Co.

SHLIMBAUM, SHLIMBAUM AND JABLONSKI (AV)

265 Main Street, P.O. Box 8, 11751-0008
Telephone: 516-277-4300
Telecopier: 516-277-4350

MEMBERS OF FIRM
C. Donald Shlimbaum
Lark J. Shlimbaum
Edward C. Jablonski

ASSOCIATES
Laura Mc Kenna
Joseph R. Mercurio

For full biographical listings, see the Martindale-Hubbell Law Directory

MELVILLE, Suffolk Co.

CAHN WISHOD & KNAUER, LLP (AV)

425 Broadhollow Road Suite 315, 11747
Telephone: 631-752-1600
Fax: 631-752-1555
URL: http://www.cahnwishod.com
URL: http://www.lawyers.com/cahnwishod&knauer

MEMBERS OF FIRM

Richard C. Cahn
Eugene L. Wishod
Todd A. Knauer

ASSOCIATES

Brian T. Egan
Patricia A. Rooney

LEGAL SUPPORT PERSONNEL

Susan M. Stonelli (Paralegal)

For full biographical listings, see the Martindale-Hubbell Law Directory

LAMB & BARNOSKY, LLP (AV)

534 Broadhollow Road-CS 9034, 11747-9034
Telephone: 631-694-2300
Telecopier: 631-694-2309
Email: thefirm@lambbarnosky.com *URL:* http://www.lambbarnosky.com

PARTNERS

Eugene R. Barnosky
Robert H. Cohen
Marcia Lyn Finkelstein
Michael J. Heller
Gary Holman
Scott M. Karson
P. L. Lamb
Arthur A. Lane
Joel M. Markowitz
Gerald P. Rosenberg
Patrice Dowd Shenn

OF COUNSEL

Louis E. Black
James F. Gesualdi
Howard W. Newman
Joseph J. Salvatore
Joseph H. Wishod

COUNSEL

Lloyd K. Chanin
Scott P. McBride

ASSOCIATES

Cathleen D. Allen
Catherine Healy Kanzler
Rita Fishman Sheena
Shari Lee Sugarman

For full biographical listings, see the Martindale-Hubbell Law Directory

*MINEOLA,** Nassau Co.

KOEPPEL MARTONE LEISTMAN & HERMAN, L.L.P. (AV)

155 First Street, 11501
Telephone: 516-747-6300
Telecopier: 516-741-5065
URL: HTTP://WWW.TAXCERT.COM

Bernard Sommer (1922-1992)
Adolph Koeppel
Michael R. Martone
Donald F. Leistman
Jay M. Herman

Jamie P. Alpern
Risë E. Rosen
Lisa M. LaValle Russ
Carol Rizzo

OF COUNSEL

Joel P. Koeppel
Gerald C. Limone

Reference: European American Bank.

For full biographical listings, see the Martindale-Hubbell Law Directory

MOUNT KISCO, Westchester Co.

SHAMBERG MARWELL HOCHERMAN DAVIS & HOLLIS, P.C. (AV)

55 Smith Avenue, 10549
Telephone: 914-666-5600
Telecopier: 914-666-6267
Email: smhdh@ix.netcom.com

Stuart R. Shamberg
John S. Marwell
Henry M. Hocherman
Robert F. Davis
P. Daniel Hollis, III
Adam L. Wekstein
Geraldine N. Tortorella
Frederick J. Koelsch
Catherine B. Andreycak

Donald W. Macaulay
Anne A. Colucci

OF COUNSEL

Stanley E. Anderson, Jr.

For full biographical listings, see the Martindale-Hubbell Law Directory

SINGLETON & SINGLETON (AV)

50 Main Street, 10549
Telephone: 914-666-4400
Telecopier: 914-666-6442

(See Next Column)

Thomas J. Singleton
Whitney Singleton

For full biographical listings, see the Martindale-Hubbell Law Directory

*PLATTSBURGH,** Clinton Co.

LEWIS, ROGERS & KUDRLE, P.C. (AV)

53 Court Street, 12901-2834
Telephone: 518-561-3700
Fax: 518-561-2080
Email: lrk@westelcom.com *URL:* http://www.lawyers.com/lrklaw

Clyde A. Lewis
Mark J. Rogers
Larry A. Kudrle
Harold A. Jerry (1893-1990)
Robert A. Lyon (1924-1982)

Attorneys for: Graystone Materials, Inc.; Plattsburgh Motor Service Inc.; The Development Corporation, Clinton County, New York.

For full biographical listings, see the Martindale-Hubbell Law Directory

*POUGHKEEPSIE,** Dutchess Co.

LEWIS & GREER, P.C. (AV)

11 Raymond Avenue, P.O. Box 2990, 12603
Telephone: 914-454-1200
Telecopier: 914-454-3315
Email: info@lewisgreer.com *URL:* http://www.lewisgreer.com

Lou Lewis
J. Scott Greer
Michael J. Englert

Daniel P. Adams
Veronica A. McMillan

For full biographical listings, see the Martindale-Hubbell Law Directory

*ROCHESTER,** Monroe Co.

LAWRENCE, WERNER, KESSELRING, SWARTOUT & BROWN, LLP (AV)

Formerly Suter Doyle Kesselring Lawrence & Werner
700 First Federal Plaza, 14614-1909
Telephone: 716-325-6446
Fax: 716-262-5185
Email: rochester@lwksb.com *URL:* http://www.lwksb.com
Canandaigua, New York Office: 23 Sly Street, 14424.
Telephone: 716-396-4000.
Fax: 716-396-1210. Email: canandaigua@lwksb.com.
Clifton Springs, New York: 26 East Main Street, P.O. Box 604, 14432.
Telephone: 315-462-3010.
Fax: 315-462-5039. Email: clifton_springs@lwksb.com

Paul J. Suter (1918-1989)

MEMBERS OF FIRM

Leo J. Kesselring
C. Bruce Lawrence
Christopher K. Werner
Colleen A. Brown
Steven H. Swartout
Mary Jo S. Korona

OF COUNSEL

James B. Doyle
Craig J. Doran
John F. Riley

ASSOCIATE

Jeffrey D. Graff

Representative Clients: Canandaigua National Bank; Hadlock Paint Company, Inc.; F.F. Thompson Health Systems, Inc.; Keuka College; Towns of Farmington and Gorham, NY; Toyota Motor Credit Corp.
References: Canandaigua National Bank; Fleet Bank, Rochester; National Association of Credit Manager, Rochester.

For full biographical listings, see the Martindale-Hubbell Law Directory

STONY POINT, Rockland Co.

HURLEY, FOX, SELIG & KELLEHER (AV)

Liberty Building, Route 9 W, 10980
Telephone: 914-942-2222
Fax: 914-942-0378
Email: HFSKlaw@aol.com
New City, New York Office: 60 Pine Street.
Telephone: 614-634-2050.

MEMBERS OF FIRM

Benjamin E. Selig
Glenn W. Kelleher

ASSOCIATES

Steven L. Kahn
Dana Selig Kahn
Bob A. Kramer
Kenneth P. Silver

Representative Clients: Bradlees, Inc.; Stop & Shop Companies; CNA Insurance Cos.; Federal Insurance Co.; Chubb & Son; Commercial Union Group of Insurance Cos.; Empire Insurance Co.; Omaha, N.B.; Excelsior Insurance Co.; Fireman's Insurance Company of Washington, D.C.

For full biographical listings, see the Martindale-Hubbell Law Directory

*SYRACUSE,** Onondaga Co.

SHULMAN, CURTIN, GRUNDNER, REGAN & SNYDER, P.C. (AV)

250 South Clinton Street, Suite 502, 13202-1262
Telephone: 315-424-8944
Fax: 315-424-8205
Email: reception@scgrslaw.com

C. Daniel Shulman
Charles H. Grundner
Paul J. Curtin, Jr.
Paul M. Regan
Joseph M. Snyder

Stephen G. Etoll
Christian J. Danaher

For full biographical listings, see the Martindale-Hubbell Law Directory

VALATIE, Columbia Co.

BURNS F. BARFORD, JR. (AV)

1019 Kinderhook Street, 12184
Telephone: 518-758-7161
Facsimile: 518-758-9885
Counsel for: National Union Bank of Kinderhook.

For full biographical listings, see the Martindale-Hubbell Law Directory

*WHITE PLAINS,** Westchester Co.

HOFFMAN, WACHTELL, KOSTER & MAIER (AV)

399 Knollwood Road, 10603
Telephone: 914-682-8000
FAX: 914-682-1512
URL: http://www.lawyers.com/hwk&mlaw

MEMBERS OF FIRM

Lee A. Hoffman, Jr.
Eric D. Koster
Marc J. Wachtell
Lynn J. Maier

Representative Clients: Ginsburg Development Corp.; The Chiselhurst Company, Inc.; Mount Hope Mines, Inc.; Eastern Educational Consortium; Westchester Community College; Prime Office Systems, Inc.; Purchase Environmental Protection Association, Inc.; The Jay Coalition; The Town of Greenburgh; The Town of Mamaroneck; The City of Mt. Vernon; The Village of Port Chester.
Reference: Citibank, N.A. (White Plains Branch).

For full biographical listings, see the Martindale-Hubbell Law Directory

KEANE & BEANE, P.C. (AV)

One North Broadway, 10601
Telephone: 914-946-4777
Telecopier: 914-946-6868
Rye, New York Office: 15 Elm Place.
Telephone: 914-967-3936.

Thomas F. Keane, Jr. (1932-1991)
Edward F. Beane
Donna E. Frosco
David Glasser
Lance H. Klein
Ronald A. Longo
Richard L. O'Rourke
Lawrence Praga
Joel H. Sachs
Steven A. Schurkman
Judson K. Siebert

Stephanie L. Burns
Eric L. Gordon
Jonathan Kornblatt
Stephanie M. Orefice
Patrick J. O'Sullivan
Frances M. Pantaleo
Nicholas M. Ward-Willis

OF COUNSEL

Peter A. Borrok
John F. Burkhardt
Eric F. Jensen

LEGAL SUPPORT PERSONNEL

Lenny Amodeo (Legal Assistant)
Barbara S. Durkin (Office Manager)
Sylvia J. Zuckerman (Legal Assistant)

For full biographical listings, see the Martindale-Hubbell Law Directory

STEPHENS, BARONI, REILLY & LEWIS LLP (AV)

Northcourt Building, 175 Main Street, 10601
Telephone: 914-761-0300; 683-5185
Telecopier: 914-761-0995; 683-1323
URL: http://www.lawyers.com/sbrl
Cross River, New York Office: Northern Westchester Office, Old Post Road Professional Building, 10518.
Telephone: 914-763-3232.

MEMBERS OF FIRM

Gerald D. Reilly
Roland A. Baroni, Jr.
Stephen R. Lewis

ASSOCIATE

Roland T. Koke

(See Next Column)

OF COUNSEL

James R. Caruso (1906-1994)

For full biographical listings, see the Martindale-Hubbell Law Directory

JOHN E. WATKINS, JR. (AV)

175 Main Street, 10601
Telephone: 914-428-1292
Telecopier: 914-428-4104
Local 800 Service: 1-800-33WATKINS
Email: wat2kins@netcom.com *URL:* http://www.lawyers.com/johnewatkinsjr
New York, New York Office: 29 Broadway.
Telephone: 212-968-1500.

ASSOCIATE

Ira S. Levy

For full biographical listings, see the Martindale-Hubbell Law Directory

NORTH CAROLINA

*GREENSBORO,** Guilford Co.

ISAACSON & ISAACSON (AV)

Suite 400 Bank of America Building, 101 West Friendly Avenue, P.O. Box 1888, 27402
Telephone: 336-275-7626
Fax: 336-273-7293
Email: ikeandike@aol.com *URL:* http://www.lawyers.com/isaacson

MEMBERS OF FIRM

Henry H. Isaacson
Marc L. Isaacson

ASSOCIATES

Jennifer N. Fountain
Anna Gregory Wagoner

Representative Clients: Alliance Properties; Auto Zone; BP Oil Co.; Burger King Restaurants; Carmike Theaters; Faison Companies; McDonald's Corporation; Target Stores.

For full biographical listings, see the Martindale-Hubbell Law Directory

*RALEIGH,** Wake Co.

HOLT YORK MCDARRIS, LLP (AV)

The Landmark Center, 4601 Six Forks Road, Suite 207, P.O. Box 17105, 27619
Telephone: 919-420-7826; Toll Free: 888-285-7634
Fax: 919-420-7838
Email: HOLTYORK@IX.NETCOM.COM

PARTNERS

Clyde Holt, III
David L. York
Charles F. McDarris

Barbara A. Jackson
Elizabeth Carr Trahos
Jeffrey P. Gray

For full biographical listings, see the Martindale-Hubbell Law Directory

*WINSTON-SALEM,** Forsyth Co.

WOMBLE CARLYLE SANDRIDGE & RICE (AV)

A Professional Limited Liability Company
200 West Second Street, P.O. Drawer 84, 27102
Telephone: 336-721-3600
Fax: 336-721-3660
Email: lawyers@wcsr.com *URL:* http://www.wcsr.com
Charlotte, North Carolina Office: 3300 One First Union Center, 301 South College Street.
Telephone: 704-331-4900.
Fax: 704-331-4955.
Raleigh, North Carolina Office: 2100 First Union Capitol Center, 150 Fayetteville Street Mall, P.O. Box 831.
Telephone: 919-755-2100.
Fax: 919-755-2150.
Research Triangle Park, North Carolina Office: 2505 Meridian Parkway, Suite 300 (Durham), 27713.
Telephone: 919-484-2300.
Fax: 919-484-2340.
Atlanta, Georgia Office: One Atlantic Center, 1201 West Peachtree Street, Suite 3500.
Telephone: 404-872-7000.
Fax: 404-888-7490.
Other Atlanta, Georgia Office: Suite 404, 2296 Henderson Mill Road, N.E.
Telephone: 770-492-9030.
Fax: 770-492-9609.
Washington, D.C. Office: 1120 Nineteenth Street, N.W., Eighth Floor.
Telephone: 202-857-4400.
Fax: 202-467-6910.

(See Next Column)

WOMBLE CARLYLE SANDRIDGE & RICE—*Continued*

Greenville, South Carolina Office: 15 South Main Street, Suite 601, P.O. Box 10208.
Telephone: 864-255-5400.
Fax: 864-255-5440.

RESIDENT MEMBERS

Anthony H. Brett | Roddey M. Ligon, Jr.

RESIDENT ASSOCIATE

Joel M. Leander

Representative Clients: Brad Ragan, Inc.; Brenner Companies; Food Lion, Inc.; Hanes Companies, Inc.; North Carolina Baptist Hospitals, Inc.; R.J. Reynolds Tobacco Co.; Thomasville Furniture Industries, Inc.; Wachovia Corp.; Wake Forest University.

For Complete List of Firm Personnel, See General Section

For full biographical listings, see the Martindale-Hubbell Law Directory

OHIO

*CINCINNATI,** Hamilton Co.

BARRETT & WEBER A LEGAL PROFESSIONAL ASSOCIATION (AV)

500 Fourth & Walnut Centre, 105 East Fourth Street, 45202
Telephone: 513-721-2120
Facsimile: 513-721-2139

C. Francis Barrett

For full biographical listings, see the Martindale-Hubbell Law Directory

KATZ, TELLER, BRANT & HILD A LEGAL PROFESSIONAL ASSOCIATION (AV)

2400 Chemed Center, 255 East Fifth Street, 45202-4724
Telephone: 513-721-4532
Telecopier: 513-721-7120
Email: corp@ktbh.com

Ronald J. Goret | James F. McCarthy, III

For Complete List of Firm Personnel, See General Section

For full biographical listings, see the Martindale-Hubbell Law Directory

MANLEY, BURKE, LIPTON & COOK A LEGAL PROFESSIONAL ASSOCIATION (AV)

225 West Court Street, 45202
Telephone: 513-721-5525
Fax: 513-721-4268
Email: mblc@mblclaw.com *URL:* http://www.mblclaw.com

Robert E. Manley
Timothy M. Burke
Andrew S. Lipton
Gary E. Powell

Bernice L. Walker | Matthew W. Fellerhoff

OF COUNSEL

William A. McClain | Richard C. Melfi

For full biographical listings, see the Martindale-Hubbell Law Directory

*CLEVELAND,** Cuyahoga Co.

KELLEY, McCANN & LIVINGSTONE, LLP (AV)

3500 BP Tower, 200 Public Square, 44114-2302
Telephone: 216-241-3141
Fax: 216-241-3707
Email: Attorneys@kmlegal.com

MEMBERS OF FIRM

Fred J. Livingstone
Stephen M. O'Bryan
John D. Brown
Margaret Anne Cannon
Mark J. Valponi
Thomas J. Lee
Mary Grace Balazs
Robert A. Brindza II

ASSOCIATES

Corinne Katz Moore
Gregory J. O'Brien
Charles D. Price
Joshua D. Goldstein

For Complete List of Firm Personnel, See General Section

For full biographical listings, see the Martindale-Hubbell Law Directory

SEELEY, SAVIDGE AND EBERT A LEGAL PROFESSIONAL ASSOCIATION (AV)

800 Bank One Center, 600 Superior Avenue, East, 44114-2655
Telephone: 216-566-8200
Fax-Telecopier: 216-566-0213
URL: http://www.sse-law.com

(See Next Column)

Gary A. Ebert

Andrew D. Bemer | Marc N. Silberman

Reference: KeyBank.

For Complete List of Firm Personnel, See General Section

For full biographical listings, see the Martindale-Hubbell Law Directory

WALTER & HAVERFIELD, P.L.L. (AV)

1300 Terminal Tower, 44113-2253
Telephone: 216-781-1212
Telecopier: 216-575-0911
Email: law@walterhav.com *URL:* http://www.walterhav.com
Columbus, Ohio Office: 88 East Broad Street.
Telephone: 614-898-1096.

MEMBERS OF FIRM

Charles T. Riehl, III
John H. Gibbon
Christopher L. Gibbon
Carl E. Anderson
Frederick W. Whatley
Jonathan D. Greenberg
R. Todd Hunt

ASSOCIATES

Barbara Rhodes Marburger
Janet Alter
Susan M. Zidek

OF COUNSEL

James E. Betts

Representative Clients: Cities of Bedford Heights, Cleveland, Cleveland Heights, Cuyahoga Heights, Gates Mills, Hudson, Moreland Hills, Pepper Pike, Richfield and Richmond Heights.

For Complete List of Firm Personnel, See General Section

For full biographical listings, see the Martindale-Hubbell Law Directory

*COLUMBUS,** Franklin Co.

KEGLER, BROWN, HILL & RITTER (AV)

Capitol Square Suite 1800, 65 East State Street, 43215-4294
Telephone: 614-462-5400
Telecopier: 614-464-2634
Cable Address: "Law KBHR"
Telex: 246671
Email: info@kbhr.com *URL:* http://www.kbhr.com
Marion, Ohio Office: 250 Executive Drive, Suite B, P.O. Box 919.
Telephone: 614-387-3501.
Facsimile: 614-387-3630.

William J. Brown
R. Kevin Kerns
Robert G. Schuler
Michael E. Zatezalo

T.A. Ward, II

Representative Clients: AT&T Wireless; Diocese of Columbus; Medco Containment Services, Inc.; Ohio Manufactured Housing Association.

For Complete List of Firm Personnel, See General Section

For full biographical listings, see the Martindale-Hubbell Law Directory

DUBLIN, Franklin Co.

BLAUGRUND, HERBERT & MARTIN, INCORPORATED (AV)

5455 Rings Road, Suite 500, 43017-7517
Telephone: 614-764-0681
Fax: 614-764-0774
Email: bhm@bhmlaw.net

David S. Blaugrund | Christopher T. Cline

John W. Herbert

For full biographical listings, see the Martindale-Hubbell Law Directory

*TOLEDO,** Lucas Co.

RITTER, ROBINSON, McCREADY & JAMES (AV)

1850 National City Bank Building, 405 Madison Avenue, 43624
Telephone: 419-241-3213
FAX: 419-241-4925

MEMBER OF FIRM

William S. McCready

Counsel for: Chrysler Corp.; Rubini Motors, Inc.; Ohio Casualty Insurance Co.; National Mutual Insurance Co.; Celina Mutual Insurance Co.; Westfield Insurance Co.; Northwestern National Insurance Co.; Midwestern Insurance Co.; United Ohio Insurance Co.; Toledo Auto Electric Co.

For Complete List of Firm Personnel, See General Section

For full biographical listings, see the Martindale-Hubbell Law Directory

OKLAHOMA

*OKLAHOMA CITY,** Oklahoma Co.

WILLIAMS, BOX, FORSHEE & BULLARD, P.C. (AV)
522 Colcord Drive, 73102-2202
Telephone: 405-232-0080
Telecopier: 405-236-5814

John Michael Williams
Dennis R. Box
Richard D. Forshee
William J. Bullard
Keith R. Gibson
Paul E. Lefebvre

Kimberly K. Brown

For full biographical listings, see the Martindale-Hubbell Law Directory

*TULSA,** Tulsa Co.

BOONE, SMITH, DAVIS, HURST & DICKMAN, A PROFESSIONAL CORPORATION (AV)
500 Oneok Plaza, 100 West 5th Street, 74103
Telephone: 918-587-0000
Fax: 918-599-9317
URL: http://www.boonesmith.com

Byron V. Boone (1908-1988)
Teresa Meinders Burkett
John A. Burkhardt
Paul J. Cleary
Reuben Davis
J. Jerry Dickman
Monica Goodman
David J. Hyman
William C. Kellough
Donald A. Lepp
Mary Lohrke
Kimberly Lambert Love
Scott R. Rowland
Frederic N. (Nick) Schneider III
Jeffrey R. Schoborg
Stephen Schuller
L. K. Smith
Paul E. Swain III

OF COUNSEL

Edwin S. Hurst
Lloyd G. Minter

Representative Clients: American Airlines; BP Amoco Corp.; Chevron U.S.A., Inc.; Ford Motor Co.; Hillcrest Medical Center; PricewaterhouseCoopers; Phillips Petroleum Co.; The Boeing Company; Sears, Roebuck & Co.; World Publishing Co; Whirlpool Corp.

For full biographical listings, see the Martindale-Hubbell Law Directory

PENNSYLVANIA

*ALLENTOWN,** Lehigh Co.

FONZONE & ASHLEY (AV)
33 South Seventh Street, P.O. Box 4180, 18105-4180
Telephone: 610-433-0121
Fax: 610-434-8440
Email: fonzlaw@aol.com

MEMBERS OF FIRM

Charles J. Fonzone
John W. Ashley

OF COUNSEL

James L. Weirbach

ASSOCIATES

Christopher W. Gittinger
Brian R. Longenhagen
Frances Ann Fruhwirth
Maryann E. Higgins
Frank G. Procyk

Representative Clients: Borough of Quakertown; Borough of Coopersburg; Fountain Hill Zoning Hearing Board and Planning Commission; Upper Saucon Zoning Hearing Board; Borough of Alburtis Zoning Hearing Board; Borough of Emmaus General Authority; East Allen Township; East Allen Township Planning Commission; Washington Township Zoning Hearing Board; Lehigh-Northampton Airport Authority.

For full biographical listings, see the Martindale-Hubbell Law Directory

CAMP HILL, Cumberland Co.

REAGER & ADLER, P.C. (AV)
2331 Market Street, 17011
Telephone: 717-763-1383
Fax: 717-730-7366
Email: reagerpc@epix.net *URL:* http://www.ReagerAdlerPC.com

Theodore A. Adler
David W. Reager
Linus E. Fenicle
Debra Denison Cantor

Thomas O. Williams
Susan H. Confair
Julie A. McConahy

(See Next Column)

LEGAL SUPPORT PERSONNEL

Monica D. Zercher (Paralegal)

Representative Clients: The Homestead Group, Inc.

For full biographical listings, see the Martindale-Hubbell Law Directory

*CARLISLE,** Cumberland Co.

FISHMAN & MORGENTHAL (AV)
95 Alexander Spring Road, 17013
Telephone: 717-249-6333
Fax: 717-249-7334
Email: info@carlislelaw.com *URL:* http://www.carlislelaw.com

MEMBERS OF FIRM

Steven J. Fishman
Roger M. Morgenthal

For full biographical listings, see the Martindale-Hubbell Law Directory

*HARRISBURG,** Dauphin Co.

GOLDBERG, KATZMAN & SHIPMAN, P.C. (AV)
320 Market Street - Strawberry Square, P.O. Box 1268, 17108-1268
Telephone: 717-234-4161
Telecopier: 717-234-6808; 717-234-6810
Email: gks@gkslaw.com

Ronald M. Katzman
Neil Hendershot
Jesse Jay Cooper

Arnold B. Kogan

Representative Clients: Dauphin County General Authority; Hampden Township Sewer Authority.
References: Fulton Bank; Dauphin Deposit Bank and Trust.

For Complete List of Firm Personnel, See General Section

For full biographical listings, see the Martindale-Hubbell Law Directory

MECHANICSBURG, Cumberland Co.

SNELBAKER, BRENNEMAN & SPARE, P.C. (AV)
44 West Main Street, P.O. Box 318, 17055-6249
Telephone: 717-697-8528
Fax: 717-697-7681

Richard C. Snelbaker
Keith O. Brenneman
Philip H. Spare

Representative Clients: Big Spring School District; Borough of Mount Holly Springs; Cumberland Valley School District; East Pennsboro Area School District; Mechanicsburg Area School District; Middlesex Township Municipal Authority; Silver Spring Township Authority; Township of Hampden; Township of Middlesex; Township of Silver Spring.

For full biographical listings, see the Martindale-Hubbell Law Directory

*MEDIA,** Delaware Co.

BEATTY, CRAMP, KAUFFMAN & LINCKE (AV)
215 North Olive Street, P.O. Box 901, 19063
Telephone: 610-565-8800
Fax: 610-565-8127
Email: BCKLLaw@aol.com

MEMBERS OF FIRM

Lewis B. Beatty, Jr.
Joseph W. Kauffman
David J. Otis
David G. Blake
William P. Lincke
Natalie M. Habert
Peter W. Dicce

ASSOCIATES

Regina M. MacKenzie
Bereth K. Graeff
Daniel J. McCusker
Kelly A. Barnes

OF COUNSEL

John F. Cramp
Ralph B. D'Iorio
Robert C. Grasberger

Joseph R. Young (1921-1993)

Representative Clients: Brookhaven Borough; City of Chester; Garnet Valley School District; Delaware County Vocational Technical School Authority.

For full biographical listings, see the Martindale-Hubbell Law Directory

*PHILADELPHIA,** Philadelphia Co.

DIDONATO & WINTERHALTER, P.C. (AV)
1818 Market Street, Suite 3520, 19103-3629
Telephone: 215-564-5050
Telecopier: 215-564-5597
URL: http://www.lawyers.com/didonato
Marlton, New Jersey Office: One Greentree Centre, Route 73 & Greenfield Road, Suite 201, 08053.
Telephone: 609-263-2700.
Telecopier: 609-263-9192.

(See Next Column)

DIDONATO & WINTERHALTER P.C.—*Continued*

Edward J. DiDonato | Paul J. Winterhalter
Eugene Camposano

For full biographical listings, see the Martindale-Hubbell Law Directory

KLEINBARD, BELL & BRECKER LLP (AV)

Suite 700, 1900 Market Street, 19103
Telephone: 215-568-2000
Facsimile: 215-568-0140
Montclair, New Jersey Office: 240 Claremont Avenue, 07042.
Telephone: 973-233-0600.
Facsimile: 973-233-9390.

Joseph S. Kleinbard (1905-1994)
Robert John Brecker (1916-1996)

COUNSEL TO THE FIRM

Arthur S. Keyser

MEMBERS OF FIRM

Paul E. Bomze
Murray I. Blackman
Howard J. Davis
Steven R. Waxman
Steven J. Engelmyer (Resident, Montclair Office)
David L. Hyman (Resident, Montclair Office)
Imogene E. Hughes
John P. Hickey
Jay R. Goldstein
Ralph J. Mauro
Thomas H. Speranza
Lisa E. Brody

ASSOCIATES

Mary Beth H. Gray
Eric J. Rothschild
Mary Vassallo Slinkard
Michael A. Frattone
Benjamin C. Graff (Not admitted in PA)
Ralph F. Salgado

COUNSEL

Joseph Bell

For full biographical listings, see the Martindale-Hubbell Law Directory

*PITTSBURGH,** Allegheny Co.

BABST, CALLAND, CLEMENTS AND ZOMNIR, A PROFESSIONAL CORPORATION (AV)

Two Gateway Center, 15222
Telephone: 412-394-5400
Fax: 412-394-6576
Email: BCCZ@BCCZ.com
Philadelphia, Pennsylvania Office: The Widener Building, Suite 1700, One South Penn Square.
Telephone: 215-567-1020.
Fax: 215-751-1425.

Patricia L. McGrail

Jeffrey T. Jochims

For full biographical listings, see the Martindale-Hubbell Law Directory

MOLLICA & MURRAY (AV)

450 Trimont Plaza, 1305 Grandview Avenue, 15211
Telephone: 412-381-7000
Fax: 412-381-7111
Email: firm@mollicamurray.com *URL:* http://www.mollicamurray.com

MEMBERS OF FIRM

James A. Mollica, Jr.
Dr. John E. Murray, Jr.
Cathy Ann Chromulak
Timothy Murray
William J. Moorhead, Jr.

Michael E. Flaherty | Michelle D. Smith

For full biographical listings, see the Martindale-Hubbell Law Directory

PLOWMAN, SPIEGEL & LEWIS, P.C. (AV)

Second Floor, The Grant Building, 310 Grant Street, 15219-2201
Telephone: 412-471-8521
Fax: 412-471-4481

Jack W. Plowman | James A. Lewis

Mark A. Griffith | Frank J. Kernan

Reference: Pittsburgh National Bank.

For Complete List of Firm Personnel, See General Section

For full biographical listings, see the Martindale-Hubbell Law Directory

WARRINGTON, Bucks Co.

HARRIS AND HARRIS, A PROFESSIONAL CORPORATION (AV)

1760 Bristol Road, P.O. Box 160, 18976
Telephone: 215-343-9000
Fax: 215-343-9012
Email: firmmail@harris-palaw.com

Arthur R. Harris
Stephen B. Harris
Gregory L. Sturn
David J. Sander

For full biographical listings, see the Martindale-Hubbell Law Directory

*WEST CHESTER,** Chester Co.

BUCKLEY, NAGLE, GENTRY, BRION, MCGUIRE & MORRIS (AV)

304 North High Street, 19380
Telephone: 610-436-4400
Telecopier: 610-436-8305
URL: http://www.buckleynagle.com

MEMBERS OF FIRM

C. Barry Buckley
Ronald C. Nagle
W. Richard Gentry
Joseph E. Brion
Stephen P. McGuire
Anthony Morris
Jeffrey R. Sommer

ASSOCIATES

John T. Mannato
Kristin S. Camp
Donald F. Kohler, Jr.

For full biographical listings, see the Martindale-Hubbell Law Directory

GAWTHROP, GREENWOOD & HALSTED, A PROFESSIONAL CORPORATION (AV)

119 North High Street, P.O. Box 562, 19381-0562
Telephone: 610-696-8225
Fax: 610-344-0922
Email: gghlaw@gawthrop.com *URL:* http://www.gawthrop.com

John S. Halsted
Robert F. Adams
Kevin Holleran
George C. Zumbano
Mark L. Tunnell
Roger N. Huggins
Walter P. Eells

Andrew D.H. Rau
Jeffrey T. Baker
Miguel D. Pena

Counsel for: Tredyffrin Township Municipal Authority; Tredyffrin Township Zoning Hearing Board; Easttown Township; Coatesville Area School District; Oxford Borough; Kennett Square Borough; Wooldridge Construction of Pa; The Rouse Group; Pulte Home Corporation; National Fairways, Inc.

For full biographical listings, see the Martindale-Hubbell Law Directory

RHODE ISLAND

*PROVIDENCE,** Providence Co.

HINCKLEY, ALLEN & SNYDER LLP (AV)

1500 Fleet Center, 02903-2393
Telephone: 401-274-2000
Fax: 401-277-9600
Email: firm@haslaw.com *URL:* http://www.haslaw.com
Boston, Massachusetts Office: 28 State Street, 30th Floor.
Telephone: 617-345-9000.
Fax: 617-345-9020. URL: http://www.haslaw.com.

MEMBERS OF FIRM

David D. Barricelli
E. Jerome Batty
Jonathan Bell
Paul Bork (Not admitted in RI)
Stephen J. Carlotti
David Barry Connolly (Not admitted in RI)
Eric F. Eisenberg (Not admitted in RI)
Malcolm Farmer, III
Hugh J. Gorman, III (Not admitted in RI)
Alan P. Gottlieb (Not admitted in RI)
William R. Grimm
Paul A. Hedstrom (Not admitted in RI)
Richard L. E. Jocelyn
Joel Lewin (Not admitted in RI)
Sandra Matrone Mack
Frederick P. McClure
Elizabeth Murdock Myers
Paul F. O'Donnell, III (Not admitted in RI)
H. Peter Olsen
Julianne Palumbo (Not admitted in RI)
John J. Pendergast, III
Gerald J. Petros
James O. Reavis
Jeremy Ritzenberg (Not admitted in RI)
Ralph J. Rivkind (Not admitted in RI)
David J. Rubin
Charles E. Schaub, Jr. (Not admitted in RI)
Douglas F. Seaver (Not admitted in RI)
Herman Snyder (Not admitted in RI)
David R. Sullivan (Not admitted in RI)

(See Next Column)

HINCKLEY, ALLEN & SNYDER LLP, *Providence—Continued*

MEMBERS OF FIRM (Continued)

Robert F. Sylvia (Not admitted in RI)
Howard E. Walker
Richard D. Wayne (Not admitted in RI)

ASSOCIATES

Jessica M. Bettencourt
Mark Bianchi
Alyssa V. Boss
Alexandra K. Callam
Jane E. Cohen (Not admitted in RI)
Andrew D. Cummings (Not admitted in RI)
June E. Daniel
Kim Herman Goslant (Not admitted in RI)
Gloria Maria Gutierrez (Not admitted in RI)
Kelley Jordan-Price
Catherine S. Kim (Not admitted in RI)
Christopher W. Morog (Not admitted in RI)
Elena B. Olson (Not admitted in RI)
Joseph D. Whelan

OF COUNSEL

Willard Krasnow (Not admitted in RI)
Willard R. Pope (Not admitted in RI)
Bentley Tobin
Joachim A. Weissfeld

For Complete List of Firm Personnel, See General Section

For full biographical listings, see the Martindale-Hubbell Law Directory

SOUTH CAROLINA

*BEAUFORT,** Beaufort Co.

HARVEY & BATTEY, P.A. (AV)

1001 Craven Street, P.O. Drawer 1107, 29902
Telephone: 843-524-3109
Telefax: 843-524-6973

W. Brantley Harvey, Jr.
William B. Harvey, III

Approved Attorneys for: Lawyers Title Insurance Corp.; Chicago Title Insurance Corp.
Representative Clients: Nations Bank; First Bank, F.S.B.; Pleasant Point Plantation Associates; Century 21-Carolina Realty, Inc.; Lobeco Products, Inc.; Beaufort County Association of Realtors; The Fripp Company.

For Complete List of Firm Personnel, See General Section

For full biographical listings, see the Martindale-Hubbell Law Directory

*CHARLESTON,** Charleston Co.

REGAN & CANTWELL (AV)

104 Church Street, P.O. Box 1001, 29402
Telephone: 843-722-4064
Fax: 843-722-3320
Email: regncant@bellsouth.net

William B. Regan
Frances I. Cantwell

Reference: NationsBank of South Carolina.

For full biographical listings, see the Martindale-Hubbell Law Directory

*COLUMBIA,** Richland Co.

TURNER, PADGET, GRAHAM & LANEY, P.A. (AV)

Seventeenth Floor, 1901 Main Street, P.O. Box 1473, 29202
Telephone: 803-254-2200
Telecopy: 803-799-3957
Florence, South Carolina Office: Fourth Floor, 1831 West Evans Street, P.O. Box 5478, 29502.
Telephone: 843-662-9008.
Fax: 843-667-0828.
Charleston, South Carolina Office: 21 Broad Street, 1st Floor, P.O. Box 836, 29402.
Telephone: 843-723-1622.
Fax: 843-577-3369.

Thomas C. Salane
Danny C. Crowe
Donnell G. Jennings

For Complete List of Firm Personnel, See General Section

For full biographical listings, see the Martindale-Hubbell Law Directory

SOUTH DAKOTA

*SIOUX FALLS,** Minnehaha Co.

HUGHES LAW OFFICES (AV)

412 West Ninth Street, 57104-3602
Telephone: 605-339-3939
Fax: 605-339-3940

John R. Hughes

LeeAnn Larson LaFave

For full biographical listings, see the Martindale-Hubbell Law Directory

TENNESSEE

*CHATTANOOGA,** Hamilton Co.

NELSON, MCMAHAN & NOBLETT (AV)

(An Association of Attorneys)
400 Pioneer Bank Building, 37402
Telephone: 423-756-2291
Fax: 423-756-0737

Randall L. Nelson
Michael A. McMahan
Phillip A. Noblett
Douglas M. Cox
Kenneth O. Fritz
Lawrence W. Kelly

For full biographical listings, see the Martindale-Hubbell Law Directory

JOHNSON CITY, Washington Co.

LAW OFFICE OF EPPS AND EPPS (AV)

115 East Unaka Avenue, P.O. Drawer 2288, 37605-2288
Telephone: 423-928-7256
Fax: 423-928-0207

James H. Epps, III

For full biographical listings, see the Martindale-Hubbell Law Directory

*MEMPHIS,** Shelby Co.

FARRIS, MATHEWS, BRANAN & HELLEN, P.L.C. (AV)

One Commerce Square, Suite 2000, 38103
Telephone: 901-259-7100
Fax: 901-259-7150
Email: firm@farris-law.com
East Memphis, Tennessee Office: Suite 400. First Commercial Bank Building. 5384 Poplar Avenue.
Telephone: 901-763-4000.
Fax: 901-763-4095.
Nashville, Tennessee Office: Nashville City Center, 511 Union Street, Suite 2400.
Telephone: 615-726-1200.
Fax: 615-726-1776.

MEMBERS OF FIRM

Homer B. Branan, III
John M. Farris
Dedrick Brittenum, Jr.

ASSOCIATES

Harold W. Fonville, II
Fred D. Thompson, Jr. (Resident, Nashville Office)

For Complete List of Firm Personnel, See General Section

For full biographical listings, see the Martindale-Hubbell Law Directory

HARKAVY, SHAINBERG, KOSTEN, KAPLAN & DUNSTAN, PC (AV)

100 Peabody Place, Suite 1300, 38103
Telephone: 901-761-1263
Telecopier: 901-763-3340
Downtown Telecopier: 901-843-0864
Downtown Office: Memphis, Tennessee, 6060 Poplar Avenue, Suite 140, 38119.

MEMBERS AND ASSOCIATES

Ronald M. Harkavy
Raymond M. Shainberg
Alan L. Kosten
Michael D. Kaplan
Allen C. Dunstan
Neil Harkavy
Jerome A. Broadhurst
Alan M. Harkavy

OF COUNSEL

Ira D. Pruitt, Jr.
Laurie A. Cooper
G. Thomas McPherson

For full biographical listings, see the Martindale-Hubbell Law Directory

TEXAS

*AUSTIN,** Travis Co.

THOMPSON & KNIGHT L.L.P. (AV)

(Attorneys and Counselors)
1200 San Jacinto Center, 98 San Jacinto Boulevard, 78701
Telephone: 512-469-6100
Telecopy: 512-469-6180
URL: http://www.tklaw.com
Dallas, Texas Office: 1700 Pacific Avenue, Suite 3300, 75201.
Telephone: 214-969-1700.
Telecopy: 512-969-1751.
Telex: 732298.
Fort Worth, Texas Office: 801 Cherry Street, Suite 1600, 76102.
Telephone: 817-347-1700.
Telecopy: 817-347-1799.
Houston, Texas Office: Thompson Knight Brown Parker & Leahy L.L.P., 1200 Smith Street, Suite 3600, 77002-4595.
Telephone: 713-654-8111.
Telecopier: 713-654-1871.
San Pedro Garza Garcia, Nuevo León, Mexico Office: Edificio Losoles PD-4, Av. Lázaro Cárdenas No. 2400 Pte., C.P. 66220.
Telephone: (52-8) 363-0096.
Telecopy: (52-8) 363-3067.

PARTNER

James E. Cousar

For Complete List of Firm Personnel, See General Section

For full biographical listings, see the Martindale-Hubbell Law Directory

*DALLAS,** Dallas Co.

CALHOUN & STACY (AV)

Suite 5700 - Bank of America Plaza, 901 Main Street, 75202-3713
Telephone: 214-748-5000
Facsimile: 214-748-1421
Email: info@calhounstacy.com *URL:* http://www.calhounstacy.com

MEMBERS OF FIRM

Mark Alan Calhoun
Parker Nelson

For Complete List of Firm Personnel, See General Section

For full biographical listings, see the Martindale-Hubbell Law Directory

COWLES & THOMPSON, A PROFESSIONAL CORPORATION (AV)

901 Main Street Suite 4000, 75202
Telephone: 214-672-2000
Metro: 972-263-0005
Fax: 214-672-2020
URL: http://www.cowlesthompson.com
McKinney, Texas Office: 307 S. McDonald St., 75069-5659.
Telephone: 972-542-5000. Metro: 972-562-2270.
Fax: 972-542-5040.
Tyler, Texas Office: 1103 First Place, P.O. Box 239, 75710-0239.
Telephone: 903-593-7508.
Fax: 903-593-4057.

Hardy E. Thompson, III
Pete Eckert
John M. Hill
Angela K. Washington

OF COUNSEL

Kenneth C. Dippel

For Complete List of Firm Personnel, See General Section

For full biographical listings, see the Martindale-Hubbell Law Directory

NICHOLS, JACKSON, DILLARD, HAGER & SMITH, L.L.P. (AV)

(formerly Nichols, Jackson, Kirk & Dillard)
1800 Lincoln Plaza, 75201
Telephone: 214-965-9900
Telecopier: 214-965-0010
Email: NJDHS@NJDHS.COM

MEMBERS OF FIRM

R. E. L. Saner (1871-1938)
John C. Saner (1874-1948)
W. Harry Jack (1899-1984)
Robert L. Dillard, III
Robert E. Hager
Peter G. Smith
David M. Berman

ASSOCIATES

Bruce A. Stockard
John F. Roehm, III
Jason C. Marshall
John David Dodd, III

(See Next Column)

OF COUNSEL

R. L. Dillard, Jr.
H. Louis Nichols
Lawrence W. Jackson

Representative Clients: City of Richardson; City of Duncanville; City of University Park; City of Lancaster; Dallas Central Appraisal District; City of Coppell; Gallagher-Bassett; Texas Municipal League Intergovernmental Risk; City of DeSoto Pool.

For full biographical listings, see the Martindale-Hubbell Law Directory

THOMPSON & KNIGHT L.L.P. (AV)

(Attorneys and Counselors)
1700 Pacific Avenue Suite 3300, 75201
Telephone: 214-969-1700
Telecopy: 214-969-1751
Telex: 732 298
URL: http://www.tklaw.com
Austin, Texas Office: 1200 San Jacinto Center, 98 San Jacinto Boulevard, 78701.
Telephone: 512-469-6100.
Telecopy: 512-469-6180.
Fort Worth, Texas Office: 801 Cherry Street, Suite 1600, 76102.
Telephone: 817-347-1700.
Telecopy: 817-347-1799.
Houston, Texas Office: Thompson Knight Brown Parker & Leahy L.L.P., 1200 Smith Street, Suite 3600, 77002-4595.
Telephone: 713-654-8111.
Telecopier: 713-654-1871.
San Pedro Garza Garcia, Nuevo León, Mexico Office: Edificio Losoles PD-4, Av. Lázaro Cárdenas No. 2400 Pte., C.P. 66220.
Telephone: (52-8) 363-0096.
Telecopy: (52-8) 363-3067.

PARTNERS

James B. Harris
Geoffrey D. Osborn
Clint Shouse

For Complete List of Firm Personnel, See General Section

For full biographical listings, see the Martindale-Hubbell Law Directory

TOOLEY & VOSS (AV)

8214 Westchester Drive, Suite 420, 75225
Telephone: 214-368-2224
Fax: 214-368-8307
Email: JCToutfit@aol.com

Joe C. Tooley
Edwin P. Voss Jr.

For full biographical listings, see the Martindale-Hubbell Law Directory

*EL PASO,** El Paso Co.

AINSA PARTNERS, LLP (AV)

5809 Acacia Circle, 79912
Telephone: 915-845-5300
Fax: 915-845-7800
Email: fain@acaciapark.com *URL:* http://www.ainsa.com

Francis S. Ainsa, Jr.
Michael F. Ainsa
David M. Driscoll

For full biographical listings, see the Martindale-Hubbell Law Directory

*FORT WORTH,** Tarrant Co.

TAYLOR, OLSON, ADKINS, SRALLA & ELAM, L.L.P. (AV)

3400 Bank One Tower, 500 Throckmorton Street, 76102-3821
Telephone: 817-332-2580
Fax: 817-332-4740
Email: TOASE.COM

Carvan E. Adkins
Robert M. Allibon
D'Ann Nichols Drennan
Elizabeth A. Elam
Cara F. Leahy White
Analeslie Muncy
Wayne K. Olson
Kuruvilla Oommen
Tim G. Sralla
E. Allen Taylor, Jr.
Trey Harlin

OF COUNSEL

Debra Adami Drayovitch
George A. Staples, Jr.

Representative Clients: City of Alvarado; City of Annetta South; City of Azle; City of Benbrook; City of Blue Mound; City of Boyd; City of Burleson; City of Everman; City of Haltom City; City of Kennedale.

For full biographical listings, see the Martindale-Hubbell Law Directory

*HOUSTON,** Harris Co.

GREGG & GREGG, P.C. (AV)

16055 Space Center Boulevard Suite 150, 77062
Telephone: 281-480-1211
Fax: 281-480-1210
Email: dhgregg3@flash.net

(See Next Column)

GREGG & GREGG P.C., *Houston—Continued*

Dick H. Gregg, Jr. Dick H. Gregg, III

For full biographical listings, see the Martindale-Hubbell Law Directory

UTAH

*SALT LAKE CITY,** Salt Lake Co.

DART ADAMSON DONOVAN & HANSON (AV)

A Partnership of Professional Corporations
370 E. South Temple, Suite 400, 84111
Telephone: 801-521-6383
Telefax: 801-355-2513

Craig G. Adamson (P.C.)

ASSOCIATE

Eric P. Lee (P.C.)

A list of References will be furnished upon request.

For full biographical listings, see the Martindale-Hubbell Law Directory

PARR WADDOUPS BROWN GEE & LOVELESS, A PROFESSIONAL CORPORATION (AV)

Suite 1300, 185 South State Street, 84111-1537
Telephone: 801-532-7840
Fax: 801-532-7750
URL: http://www.pwlaw.com

David E. Gee
Roger D. Henriksen
Brian J. Romriell
Stephen E. W. Hale
Robert A. McConnell
Brett J. Swanson

For Complete List of Firm Personnel, See General Section

For full biographical listings, see the Martindale-Hubbell Law Directory

PARSONS, DAVIES, KINGHORN & PETERS, P.C. (AV)

185 South State Street, Suite 700, 84111
Telephone: 801-363-4300
Facsimile: 801-363-4378
Email: Attorneys@pdkplaw.com

Glen E. Davies
Gerald H. Kinghorn
Bill Thomas Peters
John N. Brems
Ken P. Jones

For Complete List of Firm Personnel, See General Section

For full biographical listings, see the Martindale-Hubbell Law Directory

VAN COTT, BAGLEY, CORNWALL & MCCARTHY, A PROFESSIONAL CORPORATION (AV)

50 South Main Street, Suite 1600, P.O. Box 45340, 84145-0340
Telephone: 801-532-3333
Telecopier: 801-534-0058
Email: info@vancott.com *URL:* http://www.vancott.com
Ogden, Utah Office: 2404 Washington Boulevard, Suite 900.
Telephone: 801-394-5783.
Park City, Utah Office: 2200 Park Avenue, Suite C200-A.
Telephone: 435-649-3889.

Rand L. Cook
David J. Smith
Gregory P. Williams

Mara A. Brown
Kim S Colton
Kevin M. Sheff

For Complete List of Firm Personnel, See General Section

For full biographical listings, see the Martindale-Hubbell Law Directory

VERMONT

*BURLINGTON,** Chittenden Co.

GRAVEL AND SHEA, A PROFESSIONAL CORPORATION (AV)

Corporate Plaza, 76 St. Paul Street, P.O. Box 369, 05402-0369
Telephone: 802-658-0220
Fax: 802-658-1456

(See Next Column)

Stephen R. Crampton
John R. Ponsetto
Dennis R. Pearson

For Complete List of Firm Personnel, See General Section

For full biographical listings, see the Martindale-Hubbell Law Directory

VIRGINIA

ALEXANDRIA, (Independent City)

HART & CALLEY, P.C. (AV)

307 North Washington Street, 22314
Telephone: 703-836-5757
Fax: 703-548-5443
Email: hcpc@erols.com

Harry P. Hart
Cyril D. Calley

For full biographical listings, see the Martindale-Hubbell Law Directory

*ARLINGTON,** Arlington Co.

WALSH, COLUCCI, STACKHOUSE, EMRICH & LUBELEY, P.C. (AV)

Courthouse Plaza, Thirteenth Floor, 2200 Clarendon Boulevard, 22201
Telephone: 703-528-4700
Facsimile: 703-525-3197
Email: mdwal@wcsel.com *URL:* http://www.wcsel.com
Woodbridge, Virginia Office: Village Square, 13663 Office Place, Suite 201.
Telephones: 703-680-4664; 690-4647.
Facsimile: 703-690-2412.
Leesburg, Virginia Office: One East Market Street, 3rd Floor, 20176.
Telephone: 703-737-3633.
Fax: 703-737-3632.

Martin D. ("Art") Walsh
Jerry K. Emrich
Michael D. Lubeley (Resident, Woodbridge Office)
Nan E. Terpak
Keith C. Martin
Jay du Von (Resident, Woodbridge Office)
J. Randall Minchew (Resident, Leesburg Office)
David J. Bomgardner (Resident, Woodbridge Office)
Lynne J. Strobel
John E. Rinaldi (Resident, Woodbridge Office)
Timothy S. Sampson
M. Catharine Puskar

For full biographical listings, see the Martindale-Hubbell Law Directory

RICHMOND, (Independent City)

WILLIAMS, MULLEN, CLARK & DOBBINS, A PROFESSIONAL CORPORATION (AV)

Two James Center, 1021 East Cary Street, P.O. Box 1320, 23218-1320
Telephone: 804-643-1991
Fax: 804-783-6507
URL: http://www.wmcd.com
Newport News Office: Harbor Bank Center, Suite 210, One Old Oyster Point Road, 23602-7119.
Telephone: 757-249-5100.
Fax: 757-249-5109.
Virginia Beach Office: One Columbus Center, 23462-6763.
Telephone: 757-499-8800.
Fax: 757-473-0395.
Vienna Office: 1593 Spring Hill Road, Suite 510, 22182.
Telephone: 703-760-5200.
Fax: 703-748-0244.
Washington, D.C. Office: The Farragut Building, 900 17th Street, N.W., Suite 700, 20006.
Telephone: 202-293-0213.
Fax: 804-783-6507. Fax Within D.C.: 202-293-5939.
London, England Office: Blake Lodge, Bridge Lane, SW11 3AD.
Telephone: (011-44-71) 223-2756.
Fax: (011-44-71) 350-0156.
Riyadh, Saudi Arabia Affiliate Office: Saudi-American Legal Consultants Commercial Building #2, Diplomatic Quarter, P.O. Box 57270, 11574.
Telephone: (011-966-1) 488-1563.
Fax: (011-966-1) 488-0542.

Ralph L. Axselle, Jr.
Charles L. Cabell
Howard W. Dobbins
Sarah Hopkins Finley
A. Brooks Hock
Philip deB. Rome

For Complete List of Firm Personnel, See General Section

For full biographical listings, see the Martindale-Hubbell Law Directory

WASHINGTON

*SEATTLE,** King Co.

Buck & Gordon LLP (AV)

902 Waterfront Place, 1011 Western Avenue, 98104-1097
Telephone: 206-382-9540
Telecopier: 206-626-0675
Email: BG@buckgordon.com

Alison D. Birmingham
William H. Block
Peter L. Buck
Brent Carson
Jay P. Derr
Joel M. Gordon
Amy L. Kosterlitz
Keith E. Moxon
Samuel W. Plauché, IV

Susan M. Ridgley

OF COUNSEL

Aliza C. Allen
Kitteridge Oldham

LEGAL SUPPORT PERSONNEL

PROJECT MANAGER

Bradley J. S. Liljequist

COMMUNITY RELATIONS

Margaret E. Potter

PARALEGAL

Patricia J. Wolfson

Reference: Seafirst Bank, Seattle, Washington (Metropolitan Branch).

For full biographical listings, see the Martindale-Hubbell Law Directory

WISCONSIN

*MILWAUKEE,** Milwaukee Co.

Quarles & Brady LLP (AV)

411 East Wisconsin Avenue, 53202-4497
Telephone: 414-277-5000
Fax: 414-271-3552
URL: http://www.quarles.com
Madison, Wisconsin Office: Firstar Plaza, One South Pinckney Street, P.O. Box 2113, 53701-2113.
Telephone: 608-251-5000.
Fax: 608-251-9166.
West Palm Beach, Florida Office: 222 Lakeview Avenue, 4th Floor, 33401.
Telephone: 561-653-5000.
Fax: 561-653-5333.
Naples, Florida Office: Barnett Center, 4501 Tamiami Trail North, Suite 300, 34103-3060.
Telephone: 941-262-5959.
Fax: 941-434-4999.
Phoenix, Arizona Office: One Camelback Building, One East Camelback Road, Suite 400, 85012-1649.
Telephone: 602-230-5500.
Fax: 602-230-5598.
Chicago, Illinois Office: Quarles & Brady LLC, Citicorp Center, 500 West Madison Street, Suite 3700.
Telephone: 312-715-5000.
Fax: 312-715-5155.

MEMBERS OF FIRM

(ALPHABETICALLY BY YEAR OF ADMISSION TO BAR)

James H. Baxter III
Julianna Ebert
Brian G. Lanser
Kevin A. Delorey (Resident, Madison Office)
Rebecca A. Speckhard

OF COUNSEL

Richard W. Cutler

For Complete List of Firm Personnel, See General Section

For full biographical listings, see the Martindale-Hubbell Law Directory

CANADA ALBERTA

*EDMONTON,** Edmonton Jud. Dist.

Parlee McLaws (AV)

15th Floor Manulife Place, 10180 101st Street, T5J 4K1
Telephone: 403-423-8500
Telecopier: 403-423-2870
Email: lawyers@parlee.com *URL:* http://www.parlee.com
Calgary, Alberta Office: 3400 Petro-Canada Centre, 150 - 6th Avenue, SW.
Telephone: 403-294-7000.
Telecopier: 403-265-8263.

MEMBERS OF FIRM

Michael D. MacDonald
F. Richard Haldane, Q.C.
Brian J. Curial

For Complete List of Firm Personnel, See General Section

For full biographical listings, see the Martindale-Hubbell Law Directory

CANADA NEW BRUNSWICK

*MONCTON,** Westmorland Co.

McInnes Cooper (AV)

Barristers, Solicitors & Trade Mark Agents
Place Moncton Place, 655 Main Street, P.O. Box 1368, E1C 8T6
Telephone: 506-857-8970
Fax: 506-857-4095
Email: mcrmctn@mcrlaw.com *URL:* http://www.mcrlaw.com
Halifax, Nova Scotia Office: Summit Place, 1601 Lower Water Street, P.O. Box 730, B3J 2V1.
Telephone: 902-425-6500.
Fax: 902-425-6350. Email: mcrhfx@mcrlaw.com.
St. John's, Newfoundland Office: Baine Johnston Centre, 5th Floor, 10 Fort William Place, P.O. Box 5939, A1C 5X4.
Telephone: 709-722-8735.
Telecopier: 709-722-1763. Email: mcrsj@mcrlaw.com.
Charlottetown, Prince Edward Island Office: BDC Place, Suite 620, 119 Kent Street, C1A 1N3.
Telephone: 902-368-8473.
Fax: 902-368-8346. Email: mcrpei@mcrlaw.com.
Fredericton, New Brunswick Office: Suite 600, 570 Queen Street, P.O. Box 610.
Telephone: 506-458-8572.
Fax: 506-458-9903. Email: mcrfton@mcrlaw.com.

ASSOCIATED ATTORNEY

Robert E. Radford, Q.C.

For Complete List of Firm Personnel, See General Section

For full biographical listings, see the Martindale-Hubbell Law Directory

*SAINT JOHN,** Saint John Co.

Clark Drummie (AV)

40 Wellington Row, P.O. Box 6850, E2L 4S3
Telephone: 506-633-3800
Telecopier (Automatic): 506-633-3811
Email: cd@nbnet.nb.ca

MEMBERS OF FIRM

Deno P. Pappas, Q.C.
Donald F. MacGowan, Q.C.

Reference: Royal Bank of Canada.

For Complete List of Firm Personnel, See General Section

For full biographical listings, see the Martindale-Hubbell Law Directory

CANADA
NOVA SCOTIA

*HALIFAX,** Regional Munic. of Halifax

McInnes Cooper (AV)

Barristers, Solicitors & Trade Mark Agents
Summit Place, 1601 Lower Water Street, P.O. Box 730, B3J 2V1
Telephone: 902-425-6500
Fax: 902-425-6350
Email: mcrhfx@mcrlaw.com *URL:* http://www.mcrlaw.com
St. John's, Newfoundland Office: Baine Johnston Centre, 5th Floor, 10 Fort William Place, P.O. Box 5939, A1C 5X4.
Telephone: 709-722-8735.
Telecopier: 709-722-1763. Email: mcrsj@mcrlaw.com.
Moncton, New Brunswick Office: Place Moncton Place, 655 Main Street, P.O. Box 1368, E1C 8T6.
Telephone: 506-857-8970.
Fax: 506-857-4095. Email: mcrmctn@mcrlaw.com.
Charlottetown, Prince Edward Island Office: BDC Place, Suite 620, 119 Kent Street, C1A 1N3.
Telephone: 902-368-8473.
Fax: 902-368-8346. Email: mcrpei@mcrlaw.com.
Fredericton, New Brunswick Office: Suite 600, 570 Queen Street, P.O. Box 610.
Telephone: 506-458-8572.
Fax: 506-458-9903. Email: mcrfton@mcrlaw.com.

PARTNER

Peter J. E. McDonough, Q.C.

For Complete List of Firm Personnel, See General Section

For full biographical listings, see the Martindale-Hubbell Law Directory

CANADA
ONTARIO

*TORONTO,** Regional Munic. of Toronto

Borden & Elliot (AV)

Barristers & Solicitors
Scotia Plaza, 40 King Street West, M5H 3Y4
Telephone: 416-367-6000
Telecopier: 416-367-6749
Email: info@borden.com *URL:* http://www.borden.com
Ottawa, Ontario Office: Borden Elliot Scott & Aylen, 1000-60 Rue Queen Street.
Telephone: 613-237-5160; 800-661-4237. General
Facsimile: 613-230-8842. IP Dept.
Facsimile: 613-787-3558. Email: ottinfo@scottaylen.com. URL: http://www.borden.com.

F.F. (Rick) Coburn

For Complete List of Firm Personnel, See General Section

For full biographical listings, see the Martindale-Hubbell Law Directory

Kelly Affleck Greene (AV)

One First Canadian Place, Suite 840, P.O. Box 489, M5X 1E5
Telephone: 416-360-2800
Fax: 416-360-5960
Email: info@kag.net *URL:* http://www.kag.net

MEMBERS OF FIRM

W. Anthony Kelly, Q.C.
Donald S. Affleck, Q.C.
Peter R. Greene
Donald B. Houston
James C. Orr
Peter C. Wardle
Helen A. Daley
Melissa J. Kennedy

ASSOCIATES

Kenneth A. Dekker
W. Michael G. Osborne
Jason C. Markwell
Patrice F. Band

For full biographical listings, see the Martindale-Hubbell Law Directory

CANADA
QUEBEC

*MONTREAL,** Montreal Dist.

McMaster Gervais (AV)

A General Partnership
1000 de La Gauchetière Street West, Suite 900, H3B 5H4
Telephone: 514-879-1212
Fax: 514-954-1905
Email: info@mcmastergervais.com *URL:* http://www.mcmastergervais.com

MEMBER OF FIRM

Yves A. Dubois

COUNSEL

Marc Laperrière

For Complete List of Firm Personnel, See General Section

For full biographical listings, see the Martindale-Hubbell Law Directory

MUNICIPAL BOND/PUBLIC AUTHORITY FINANCING

MISSISSIPPI

*GULFPORT,** Harrison Co.

BLACKWELL & WHITE (AV)

1613 Twenty-Third Avenue, 39501
Telephone: 228-864-1484
FAX: 228-868-6484
Mailing Address: P.O. Box 430, 39502-0430,

MEMBERS OF FIRM

Leonard A. Blackwell, II
Gary White

ASSOCIATES

James B. Wright, Jr.
Patricia S. Tisdale

References: Merchants Bank & Trust Co.; Hancock Bank.

For full biographical listings, see the Martindale-Hubbell Law Directory

MISSOURI

KANSAS CITY, Jackson, Clay, Platte & Cass Cos.

GILMORE & BELL, A PROFESSIONAL CORPORATION (AV)

2405 Grand Boulevard Suite 1100, 64108
Telephone: 816-221-1000
Telecopier: 816-221-1018
Email: mail@gilmorebell.com
Wichita, Kansas Office: One Main Place, Suite 800.
Telephone: 316-267-2091.
St. Louis, Missouri Office: One Metropolitan Square, Suite 2350.
Telephone: 314-436-1000.

Webb R. Gilmore
Kim B. Wells
James W. Winn
Christopher D. Ahrens
David W. Queen
Lynd K. Mische
Clark R. Irey, II
Alvin D. Wilken
E. Sid Douglas, III
Nancy N.C. Lear
Richard M. Wright, Jr.
Gary A. Anderson
Michael D. McRobbie
Kay E. Thornton
James G. Caldwell
Tracy E. Coates
Thomas B. Becker
B. Lynn Jackson

Elizabeth S. Brown

OF COUNSEL

Richard E. Petrie

For full biographical listings, see the Martindale-Hubbell Law Directory

ST. LOUIS, (Independent City)

LEWIS, RICE & FINGERSH (AV)

A Limited Liability Company
500 North Broadway, Suite 2000, 63102-2147
Telephone: 314-444-7600
Telecopier: 314-241-6056
URL: http://www.lrf.com
Belleville, Illinois Office: 325 South High Street.
Telephone: 618-234-8636.
Leawood, Kansas Office: Suite 375, 8900 State Line Road.
Telephone: 913-381-8898.
Creve Coeur, Missouri Office: 700 Office Parkway, Suite 15.
Telephone: 314-569-2262.
Kansas City, Missouri Office: 1010 Walnut, Suite 500.
Telephone: 816-421-2500.
Washington, Missouri Office: 216 West Main, P.O. Box 1040.
Telephone: 636-239-7747.

RESIDENT MEMBERS

Henry F. Luepke, Jr.
Joseph H. Weyhrich

For Complete List of Firm Personnel, See General Section

For full biographical listings, see the Martindale-Hubbell Law Directory

MONTANA

*BILLINGS,** Yellowstone Co.

CROWLEY, HAUGHEY, HANSON, TOOLE & DIETRICH, P.L.L.P. (AV)

500 Transwestern II, 490 North 31st Street, P.O. Box 2529, 59103
Telephone: 406-252-3441
Fax: 406-259-4159
Email: crowley@crowleylaw.com
Helena, Montana Office: IBM Building, 100 North Park Avenue, Suite 300, 59601.
Telephone: 406-449-4165.
Fax: 406-449-5149.
Kalispell, Montana Office: 431 1st Avenue West, 59901.
Telephone: 406-752-6644.
Fax: 406-752-5108.
Williston, North Dakota Office: 113 East Broadway, 58801.
Telephone: 701-572-2200.
Fax: 701-572-7072.

OF COUNSEL

Gareld F. Krieg

MEMBERS OF FIRM

Terry B. Cosgrove (Resident, Helena, Montana Office)
Michael S. Dockery

Representative Clients: Montana Power Co.; First Interstate Bank of Commerce; MDU Resources Group, Inc.; Chevron U.S.A., Inc.; Noranda Minerals Corp.; United Parcel Service.
Insurance Clients: Farmers Insurance Group; New York Life Insurance Co.

For Complete List of Firm Personnel, See General Section

For full biographical listings, see the Martindale-Hubbell Law Directory

NEBRASKA

*LINCOLN,** Lancaster Co.

CLINE, WILLIAMS, WRIGHT, JOHNSON & OLDFATHER (AV)

1900 U.S. Bank Building, 233 South 13th Street, 68508
Telephone: 402-474-6900
Fax: 402-474-5393
Email: postmaster@cline-law.com *URL:* http://www.cline-law.com
Omaha, Nebraska Office: Suite 720, One Pacific Place, 1125 South 103rd Street, 68124.
Telephone: 402-397-1700.
Fax: 402-397-1806.

ATTORNEYS

Allen L. Graves
Charles M. Pallesen, Jr.
Fredric H. Kauffman
Donald F. Burt
Alan E. Peterson
Stephen E. Gehring
Robert J. Routh
Kevin Colleran
L. Bruce Wright
James M. Bausch
Larry A. Holle
David R. Buntain
Stephen H. Nelsen
Michael C. Mueller
Lauren W. Wismer
Daniel R. Stogsdill
Scott D. Kelly
Terry R. Wittler
Pamela Hastings Carrier
Mark A. Christensen
Richard P. Garden, Jr.
Shawn D. Renner
John C. Miles
Mary Kay Frank
Thomas C. Huston
Sonya S. Ekart
Don R. Janssen
Susan Kubert Sapp
Kevin J. Schneider
Andrew D. Strotman
Jill Gossin Jensen
Rochelle A. Mullen
John L. Horan
Bryan S. Hatch
Steven C. Likes
Tracy A. Oldemeyer
Jolene M. Papa
Timothy G. Aschoff
Eric N. Bergquist
Janis J. Winterhof
Andrea Dylan Snowden

OF COUNSEL

Charles E. Wright
Richard P. Jeffries
Mary M. Campbell

RETIRED PARTNERS

Flavel A. Wright (Retired)
Warren C. Johnson (Retired)
Charles E. Oldfather (1927-1998)

Representative Clients: U.S. Bank National Association; University of Nebraska; Nebraska Medical Assn.; Saint Elizabeth Regional Medical Center; Media of Nebraska; Cargill Inc.; State Farm Insurance Cos.; Wal-Mart Stores, Inc.; Textron/Cushman; Isco, Inc.

For full biographical listings, see the Martindale-Hubbell Law Directory

NEVADA

*LAS VEGAS,** Clark Co.

ALVERSON, TAYLOR, MORTENSEN, NELSON & SANDERS (AV)

7401 West Charleston Boulevard, 89117
Telephone: 702-384-7000
FAX: 702-385-7000
Email: alverson@intermind.net
Reno, Nevada Office: 245 East Liberty, Suite 520, 89505.
Telephone: 775-329-0473.
Fax: 775-329-3303.

MEMBERS OF FIRM

J. Bruce Alverson
David J. Mortensen
Eric K. Taylor
Erven T. Nelson
LeAnn Sanders

OF COUNSEL

Jack C. Cherry
Kurt D. Anderson
Philip C. Van Alstyne

ASSOCIATES

Rebecca Hopkins Miller
Darius F. Rafie
Sandra Smagac
Mark J. King, IV
Victoria L. Nelson
Shell L. Mercer
Aaron D. Lovaas
Carrie S. Bourdeau
Diane Obritsch
Jason Lane Earnest
Michael A. Olsen
Nathan R. Reinmiller
Randal D. Shimon
Donn C. Alexander
Catherine A. Olendorff
Afshin Tadayon
Monica L. Pierce
Eric O. Freeman
Gabriel D. Lither
Lindsay L. Stadtlander
Kurt R. Bonds
Julie M. Sueoka

Representative Clients: The City of Las Vegas, Nevada; The County of Clark, Nevada; Clark County McCarran International Airport.

For full biographical listings, see the Martindale-Hubbell Law Directory

SWENDSEID & STERN (AV)

A member in Sherman & Howard L.L.C.
317 Sixth Street, 89101
Telephone: 702-387-6073
Telecopier: 702-382-9370
Reno, Nevada Office: 50 West Liberty Street, Suite 660, 89501.
Telephone: 702-323-1980.
Denver, Colorado Office: Sherman & Howard L.L.C., 633 Seventeenth Street, Suite 3000, 80202.
Telephone: 303-297-2900.
Colorado Springs, Colorado Office: Sherman & Howard L.L.C., Suite 1500, 90 South Cascade Avenue, 80903.
Telephone: 719-475-2440.

John O. Swendseid
Jennifer Stern
Kendra S. Follett

Representative Clients: State of Nevada; Clark County; Clark County School District; Washoe County School District, University of Nevada System; Las Vegas Valley Water District; Clark County Sanitation District; Washoe County; Carson City; Douglas County; City of Las Vegas; City of Reno.

For full biographical listings, see the Martindale-Hubbell Law Directory

*RENO,** Washoe Co.

SWENDSEID & STERN (AV)

A member in Sherman & Howard L.L.C.
50 West Liberty Street Suite 660, 89501
Telephone: 702-323-1980
Telecopier: 702-323-2339
Email: jswendse@sah.com
Las Vegas, Nevada Office: 317 Sixth Street, 89101.
Telephone: 702-387-6073.
Denver, Colorado Office: Sherman & Howard L.L.C., 633 17th Street, Suite 3000, 80202.
Telephone: 303-297-2900.
Colorado Springs, Colorado Office: Sherman & Howard L.L.C., Suite 1500, 90 South Cascade Avenue, 80903.
Telephone: 719-475-2440.

John O. Swendseid
Jennifer Stern
Kendra S. Follett

Representative Clients: State of Nevada; Clark County; Clark County School District; Washoe County School District, University of Nevada System; Las Vegas Valley Water District; Clark County Sanitation District; Washoe County; Carson City; Douglas County, City of Las Vegas; City of Reno.

For full biographical listings, see the Martindale-Hubbell Law Directory

NEW JERSEY

BAYONNE, Hudson Co.

FITZPATRICK & WATERMAN (AV)

90 West 40th Street, P.O. Box 1227, 07002
Telephone: 201-339-4000
800 BOND LAW
Secaucus, New Jersey Office: 400 Plaza Drive, P.O. Box 3159, 07096-3159.
Telephone: 201-865-9100.
Facsimile: 201-865-4805.

Harold F. Fitzpatrick

For full biographical listings, see the Martindale-Hubbell Law Directory

HAWTHORNE, Passaic Co.

JEFFER, HOPKINSON & VOGEL (AV)

(Formerly Jeffer, Walter, Tierney, DeKorte, Hopkinson & Vogel)
Law Building, 1600 Route 208N, P.O. Box 507, 07507
Telephone: 973-423-0100
Fax: 973-423-5614
Tequesta, Florida Office: Jeffer, Cioffi & Cicalese. 250 Tequesta Drive, 33469.
Telephone: 561-747-6000.
Fax: 561-575-9167.

MEMBERS OF FIRM

Herman M. Jeffer
Reginald F. Hopkinson
Jerome A. Vogel

ASSOCIATES

Melinda B. Maidens
E. David Becker
David H. Altman

Counsel for: Brioschi, Inc.; Opici Wine Co.; Gas Pumpers of America Corp.; John Royle & Sons; Christian Health Care Center; Valley Hospital.

For Complete List of Firm Personnel, See General Section

For full biographical listings, see the Martindale-Hubbell Law Directory

LAKEWOOD, Ocean Co.

BATHGATE, WEGENER & WOLF, P.C. (AV)

One Airport Road, P.O. Box 2043, 08701
Telephone: 732-363-0666
Telecopier: 732-363-9864
Email: bathweg@idt.net

Lawrence E. Bathgate, II
Ross D. Gertner
Peter H. Wegener
Edward B. Kasselman
William J. Wolf
Dominic J. Aprile
Jan L. Wouters
Nancy G. Wright
Michael M. DiCicco

COUNSEL

Neil Brodsky
Peter A. Valenti

Jonathan S. Fabricant
Peter G. Licata
Robert J. Gillispie, Jr.
Steven E Robertson

For full biographical listings, see the Martindale-Hubbell Law Directory

*NEWARK,** Essex Co.

MCCARTER & ENGLISH, LLP (AV)

Four Gateway Center, 100 Mulberry Street, P.O. Box 652, 07101-0652
Telephone: 973-622-4444
Telecopier: 973-624-7070
URL: http://www.mccarter.com
Cherry Hill, New Jersey Office: 1820 Chapel Avenue West, Suite 380.
Telephone: 609-662-8444.
Telecopier: 609-662-6203.
New York, New York Office: Suite 2247, One World Trade Center.
Telephone: 212-466-9018.
Telecopier: 212-432-6568.
Boca Raton, Florida Office: 2255 Glades Road, Suite 319-A.
Telephone: 561-994-6262.
Telecopier: 561-241-0798.
Wilmington, Delaware Office: Mellon Bank Center, 919 Market Street.
Telephone: 302-654-8010.
Telecopier: 302-654-0795.
Philadelphia, Pennsylvania Office: One Commerce Square, 2005 Market Street, Suite 3600.
Telephone: 215-557-7700.
Telecopier: 215-557-6544.

MEMBERS OF FIRM

John J. Scally, Jr.
Stephen B. Pearlman
Scott A. Kobler
Jacqueline P. Shanes
Gary Duescher

SPECIAL COUNSEL

Jeannette M. Bond

(See Next Column)

McCarter & English LLP—*Continued*

ASSOCIATES

Deborah S. Verderame
Richard T. Nolan, Jr.
Nicholas A. Concilio, III
Kevin J. Quinn
Mark E. Hopkins

For Complete List of Firm Personnel, See General Section

For full biographical listings, see the Martindale-Hubbell Law Directory

McManimon & Scotland, L.L.C. (AV)

One Riverfront Plaza, 4th Floor, 07102-5311
Telephone: 973-622-1800
Fax: 973-622-7333; 973-622-3744

MEMBERS OF FIRM

Joseph P. Baumann, Jr.
John V. Cavaliere
John B. Hall
Glenn F. Scotland
Ronald J. Ianoale
Andrea L. Kahn
Jeffrey G. Kramer
Leslie G. London
Edward J. McManimon, III

OF COUNSEL

Norman M. Robertson
Carla J. Brundage

ASSOCIATES

Peter S. Crisafi
Sheila Newsome Maddox
M. Frances Ciesla
Kristin Dwyer Ganley
Joseph C. Jasaitis
Stephen N. Severud
Thomas J. Hastie, Jr.

LEGAL SUPPORT PERSONNEL

Helen Lysaght

PARALEGALS

Sandra Simoes

For full biographical listings, see the Martindale-Hubbell Law Directory

St. John & Wayne, L.L.C. (AV)

Two Penn Plaza East, 07105-2249
Telephone: 973-491-3600
Fax: 973-491-3555
Email: firm@nwk.stjohn-law.com *URL:* http://www.stjohn-law.com
Rochester, New York Office: St. John & Curtin, L.L.C., First Federal Plaza.
Telephone: 716-262-6780.
Fax: 716-262-6755.
New York, New York Office: Heron Tower, 70 East 55th. Street.
Telephone: 212-446-5000.
Fax: 212-446-5055.

Lee A. Albanese
Timothy R. Curtin (Resident at Rochester, New York Office)
Bernard S. Davis
Timothy R. McGill (Resident at Rochester, New York Office)
Bryan G. Petkanics (Resident at New York, New York Office)

For Complete List of Firm Personnel, See General Section

For full biographical listings, see the Martindale-Hubbell Law Directory

Sills Cummis Radin Tischman Epstein & Gross, A Professional Corporation (AV)

One Riverfront Plaza, 07102-5400
Telephone: 973-643-7000
Fax: 973-643-6500
Telex: 820630 Sillsbeck Nwk
Email: sillsmail@sillscummis.com *URL:* http://www.sillscummis.com
Atlantic City, New Jersey Office: 17 Gordon's Alley.
Telephone: 609-344-2800.
New York, N.Y. Office: 712 Fifth Avenue.
Telephone: 212-643-7000.
Washington, D.C. Office: 1800 K Street, N.W.
Telephone: 202-296-4750.

MEMBERS OF FIRM

Clive S. Cummis
Stephen J. Moses
Gerald Span
Alan E. Sherman
Jerry Genberg

OF COUNSEL

Diane M. Lavenda

Representative Clients: County of Essex; Hudson County Improvement Authority; GAF Corp.; Jersey City Medical Center; U.S. Generating Co.; Six Flags Great Adventure; The Lefrak Organization; New Jersey Economic Development Authority; City of Newark; J.P. Morgan Securities, Inc.

For Complete List of Firm Personnel, See General Section

For full biographical listings, see the Martindale-Hubbell Law Directory

PRINCETON, Mercer Co.

Reed Smith Shaw & McClay LLP (AV)

136 Main Street, Suite 250, 08540-5799
Telephone: 609-987-0050
FAX: 609-951-0824
Email: rssm@rssm.com *URL:* http://www.rssm.com
Pittsburgh, Pennsylvania Office: 435 Sixth Avenue, 15219-1886.
Telephone: 412-288-3131.
FAX: 412-288-3063.
Washington, D.C. Office: Suite 1100 - East Tower, 1301 K Street, N.W., 20005-3317.
Telephone: 202-414-9200.
FAX: 202-414-9299.
Philadelphia, Pennsylvania Office: 2500 One Liberty Place, 19103-7301.
Telephone: 215-851-8100.
FAX: 215-851-1420.
Harrisburg, Pennsylvania Office: 213 Market Street, 17101-2132.
Telephone: 717-234-5988.
FAX: 717-236-3777.
New York, N.Y. Office: 375 Park Avenue, 17th Floor, 10152.
Telephone: 212-521-5400.
FAX: 212-521-5450.
Newark, New Jersey Office: The Legal Center, One Riverfront Plaza, First Floor, 07102-5400.
Telephone: 973-621-3200.
FAX: 973-621-3199.
McLean, Virginia Office: Reed Smith Hazel & Thomas LLP, Suite 1100, 8251 Greensboro Drive, 22102-3844.
Telephone: 703-734-4600.
FAX: 703-734-4699.
Falls Church, Virginia Office: Reed Smith Hazel & Thomas, Suite 1400, 3110 Fairview Park Drive, P.O. Box 12001.
Telephone: 703-641-4200.
Fax: 703-641-4340.
Leesburg, Virginia Office: Reed Smith Hazel & Thomas LLP, 44084 Riverside Parkway, Suite 300.
Telephone: 703-729-8500. Metro: 703-478-1992.
Fax: 703-478-8003.
Richmond, Virginia Office: Reed Smith Hazel & Thomas LLP, Suite 600, 411 East Franklin Street, P.O. Box 788.
Telephone: 804-344-3400.
Fax: 804-344-3410.

MEMBER OF FIRM

Daniel F. Peck, Jr.

For full biographical listings, see the Martindale-Hubbell Law Directory

ROSELAND, Essex Co.

Carella, Byrne, Bain, Gilfillan, Cecchi, Stewart & Olstein, A Professional Corporation (AV)

Six Becker Farm Road, 07068-1739
Telephone: 973-994-1700
Telecopier: 973-994-1744

Peter G. Stewart
Elliot M. Olstein
Arthur T. Vanderbilt, II
James T. Byers

Jo Anne C. Gerber

OF COUNSEL

Herbert M. Rinaldi

Representative Clients: NJ Higher Educational Student Assistance Authority, Trenton, N.J.; NJ Economic Development Authority, Trenton, N.J.; Passaic County, N.J.

For Complete List of Firm Personnel, See General Section

For full biographical listings, see the Martindale-Hubbell Law Directory

SECAUCUS, Hudson Co.

Fitzpatrick & Waterman (AV)

400 Plaza Drive, P.O. Box 3159, 07096-3159
Telephone: 201-865-9100
800 BOND LAW
Facsimile: 201-865-4805
Bayonne, New Jersey Office: 90 West 40th Street, P.O. Box 1227, 07002.
Telephone: 201-339-4000; 1-800 BOND LAW.

Harold F. Fitzpatrick
Stephen P. Waterman

ASSOCIATES

Glenn C. Merritt
Jeanette M. Samra

OF COUNSEL

Michael J. Israels
Andre Shramenko

For full biographical listings, see the Martindale-Hubbell Law Directory

WESTFIELD, Union Co.

LINDABURY, MCCORMICK & ESTABROOK, P.A. (AV)

53 Cardinal Drive, P.O. Box 2369, 07091
Telephone: 908-233-6800
Fax: 908-233-5078
New York, N.Y. Office: 26 Broadway, Suite 2300.
Telephone: 212-742-3390.
Fax: 212-269-5016.

Richard R. Width — Robert S. Burney

Representative Clients: A list of representative clients will be furnished upon request.

For Complete List of Firm Personnel, See General Section

For full biographical listings, see the Martindale-Hubbell Law Directory

WOODBRIDGE, Middlesex Co.

WILENTZ, GOLDMAN & SPITZER, A PROFESSIONAL CORPORATION (AV)

90 Woodbridge Center Drive Suite 900, Box 10, 07095
Telephone: 732-636-8000
Telecopier: 732-855-6117
URL: http://www.newjerseylaw.com
Eatontown, New Jersey Office: Meridian Center I, Two Industrial Way West, 07724.
Telephone: 732-542-4500.
Telecopier: 732-493-8387.
New York, New York Office: Wall Street Plaza, 88 Pine Street, 9th Floor, 10005.
Telephone: 212-267-3091.
Telecopier: 212-267-3828.

Anthony J. Pannella, Jr.
John T. Kelly
C. Kenneth Shank
Robert C. Kautz
Cheryl J. Oberdorf
Lisa A. Gorab

Representative Clients: Middlesex County Utilities Authority; City of New Brunswick; Middlesex County Improvement Authority; Borough of Lodi; Perth Amboy Board of Education; Southeast Morris County Municipal Utilities Authority; New Brunswick Housing Authority; City of South Amboy; New Brunswick Parking Authority.

For Complete List of Firm Personnel, See General Section

For full biographical listings, see the Martindale-Hubbell Law Directory

NEW MEXICO

*ALBUQUERQUE,** Bernalillo Co.

HUGHES & STRUMOR, LTD. CO. (AV)

320 Gold Avenue SW, Suite 1000, 87102
Telephone: 505-842-6700
Fax: 505-764-0012
Email: hsltdco@aol.com
Santa Fe, New Mexico Office: 142 West Palace Avenue, 87501.
Telephone: 505-986-1033.

Tommy D. Hughes — Robert M. Strumor

For full biographical listings, see the Martindale-Hubbell Law Directory

NEW YORK

*ALBANY,** Albany Co.

SHANLEY, SWEENEY, REILLY & ALLEN, P.C. (AV)

The Castle at Ten Thurlow Terrace, 12203
Telephone: 518-463-1415
Fax: 518-463-3210
Email: lawyers@shanleysweeney.com *URL:* http://www.shanleysweeney.com

Michael P. Shanley, Jr.
Robert L. Sweeney
John L. Allen

For Complete List of Firm Personnel, See General Section

For full biographical listings, see the Martindale-Hubbell Law Directory

*BINGHAMTON,** Broome Co.

HINMAN, HOWARD & KATTELL, LLP (AV)

700 Security Mutual Building, 80 Exchange Street, P.O. Box 5250, 13902-5250
Telephone: 607-723-5341
Fax: 607-723-6605
Email: jworband@hhk.com *URL:* http://www.hhk.com
Norwich, New York Office: 48 Hale Street, 13815-2039.
Telephone: 607-334-5896.
Fax: 607-336-1628.
Oneonta, New York Office: 12 South Main Street, 13820-2542.
Telephone: 607-432-5331.
Fax: 607-432-2683.
New York, N.Y. Office: 500 5th Avenue, Suite 1725, 10110.
Telephone: 212-840-3017.
Fax: 212-840-2345.

COUNSEL

A. Edward Hill

Representative Clients: The Chase Manhattan Bank; BSB Bank & Trust Co.; International Business Machines Corp.; Universal Instruments Corp.; Security Mutual Life Insurance Company of New York; Bell Atlantic; Preferred Mutual Insurance Company; New York State Electric & Gas Corp.; Exxon Corp.

For Complete List of Firm Personnel, See General Section

For full biographical listings, see the Martindale-Hubbell Law Directory

*NEW YORK,** New York Co.

CAHILL GORDON & REINDEL (AV)

A Partnership including a Professional Corporation
80 Pine Street, 10005-1702
Telephone: 212-701-3000
Facsimile: 212-269-5420
Confirmation: 212-701-3557
European Office: 19 rue Francois 1er, 75008, Paris, France.
Telephone: 33.1-47.20.10.50.
Facsimile: 33.1-47.23.06.38.
District of Columbia Office: 1990 K Street, N.W., Washington, D.C., 20006-1103.
Telephone: 202-862-8900.
Facsimile: 202-862-8958.

MEMBERS OF FIRM

Roger Andrus
Helene R. Banks
Michael A. Becker
James J. Clark
Walter C. Cliff (P.C.)
Benjamin J. Cohen
W. Leslie Duffy
Bart Friedman
Ciro A. Gamboni
William B. Gannett
Stephen A. Greene
Robert M. Hallman
William M. Hartnett
Craig M. Horowitz
Lawrence A. Kobrin
Immanuel Kohn
Geoffrey E. Liebmann
Jonathan I. Mark
Gerard M. Meistrell
Roger Meltzer
Clifford L. Michel
Michael E. Michetti
John P. Mitchell
Kenneth W. Orce
James C. Robinson
Jonathan A. Schaffzin
John J. Schuster
Gerald S. Tanenbaum
John A. Tripodoro
Robert Usadi
Gary W. Wolf
Daniel J. Zubkoff

SENIOR COUNSEL

Joseph P. Conway

For Complete List of Firm Personnel, See General Section

For full biographical listings, see the Martindale-Hubbell Law Directory

DEWEY BALLANTINE LLP (AV)

1301 Avenue of the Americas, 10019-6092
Telephone: 212-259-8000
Cable Address: "Dewbalaw"
Telex: 12-6825
Facsimile: 212-259-6333
URL: http://www.deweyballantine.com
Washington, D.C. Office: 1775 Pennsylvania Avenue, N.W., 20006-4605.
Telephone: 202-862-1000.
Fax: 202-862-1093.
Los Angeles, California Office: 333 South Hope Street, 90071-1406.
Telephone: 213-626-3399.
Fax: 213-625-0562.
London, England Office: Dewey Ballantine, 1 Undershaft, London EC3A 8LP, England.
Telephone: 011 44 171 456-6000.
Fax: 011 44 171 456-6001.
Hong Kong Office: Asia Pacific Finance Tower, Suite 3907, Citibank Plaza, 3 Garden Road, Central, Hong Kong.
Telephone: 011-852-2509-7000.
Fax: 011-852-2509-7088.

(See Next Column)

DEWEY BALLANTINE LLP—*Continued*

Budapest, Hungary Office: Dewey Ballantine, Andrássy út 60, H-1062 Budapest, Hungary.
Telephone: 36 1 374-2660.
Fax: 36 1 374-2661.
Prague, Czech Republic Office: Dewey Ballantine, Adria Palace, Jungmannova 31, 5th Floor, 110 00 Prague 1, Czech Republic.
Telephone: 420 2 2494-9005.
Fax: 420 2 2494-9010.
Warsaw, Poland Office: Dewey Ballantine Sp. z.o.o., Warsaw Towers, ul. Sienna 39, 00-121 Warsaw, Poland.
Telephone: 48-22-526-9999.
Fax: 48-22-526-9988.

MEMBERS OF FIRM

Christopher J. DiAngelo
E.N. Ellis, IV
John G. Fritzinger, Jr.
E. Ann Gill
David M. Irwin
Frederick W. Kanner
Bernard E. Kury
Steven R. Loeshelle
Richard B. Romney
Richard Shutran
Richard A. Stenberg

For Complete List of Firm Personnel, See General Section

For full biographical listings, see the Martindale-Hubbell Law Directory

JONES, DAY, REAVIS & POGUE (AV)

599 Lexington Avenue, 10022
Telephone: 212-326-3939
Telecopier: 212-755-7306
Email: counsel@jonesday.com *URL:* http://www.jonesday.com
In Atlanta, Georgia: 3500 SunTrust Plaza, 303 Peachtree Street.
Telephone: 404-521-3939.
Telecopier: 404-581-8330.
In Brussels, Belgium: Avenue Louise 480, 7th Floor, B-1050 Brussels.
Telephone: 32-2-645-14-11.
Telecopier: 32-2-645-14-45.
In Chicago, Illinois: 77 West Wacker.
Telephone: 312-782-3939.
Telecopier: 312-782-8585.
In Cleveland, Ohio: North Point, 901 Lakeside Avenue.
Telephone: 216-586-3939.
Telecopier: 216-579-0212.
In Columbus, Ohio: 1900 Huntington Center.
Telephone: 614-469-3939.
Telecopier: 614-461-4198.
In Dallas, Texas: 2727 North Harwood Street.
Telephone: 214-220-3939.
Telecopier: 214-969-5100.
In Frankfurt, Germany: Hochhaus am Park, Grüneburgweg 102, 60323 Frankfurt am Main.
Telephone: 49-69-9726-3939.
Telecopier: 49-69-9726-3993.
In Geneva, Switzerland: 20, rue de Candolle.
Telephone: 41-22-320-2339.
Telecopier: 41-22-320-1232.
In Hong Kong: 29th Floor, Entertainment Building, 30 Queen's Road Central.
Telephone: 852-2526-6895.
Telecopier: 852-2868-5871.
In Irvine, California: 5 Park Plaza, Suite 1100.
Telephone: 949-851-3939.
Telecopier: 949-553-7539.
In London, England: Bucklersbury House, 3 Queen Victoria Street.
Telephone: 44-20-7236-3939
Telecopier: 44-20-7236-1113.
In Los Angeles, California: 555 West Fifth Street, Suite 4600.
Telephone: 213-489-3939.
Telecopier: 213-243-2539.
In Paris, France: 120, rue du Faubourg Saint-Honoré.
Telephone: 33-1-56-59-39-39.
Telecopier: 33-1-56-59-39-38
In Pittsburgh, Pennsylvania: 500 Grant Street, 31st Floor.
Telephone: 412-391-3939.
Telecopier: 412-394-7959.
In Riyadh, Saudi Arabia: The International Law Firm (In Association with Jones, Day, Reavis & Pogue), Sulaymaniyah, Prince Mishari IBN, Abdulaziz Street, P.O. Box 22166.
Telephone: (966-1) 462-8866.
Telecopier: (966-1) 462-9001.
In Shanghai, China: 2805 Kerry Centre, 1515 Nanjing Road West.
Telephone: 86-21-5298-6568.
Telecopier: 86-21-5298-6569.
In Sydney, Australia: Governor Phillip Tower, Level 38, 1 Farrer Place.
Telephone: 61-2-9210-6921.
Telecopier: 61-2-9210-6926.
In Taipei, Taiwan: 8th Floor, 2 Tun Hwa South Road, Section 2.
Telephone: (886-2) 2704-6808.
Telecopier: (886-2) 2704-6791.
In Tokyo, Japan: Toranomon 45 Mori Building, 3rd Floor, 1-5, Toranomon 5-Chome, Minato-Ku, Tokyo 105, Japan.
Telephone: 81-3-3433-3939.
Telecopier: 81-3-5401-2725.

(See Next Column)

In Washington, D.C.: 51 Louisiana Avenue, N.W.
Telephone: 202-879-3939.
Telecopier: 202-626-1700.

MEMBERS OF FIRM IN NEW YORK

David M. Mahle
Donald F. Devine
William F. Henze, II
Wanda N. Goodloe

For Complete List of Firm Personnel, See General Section

For full biographical listings, see the Martindale-Hubbell Law Directory

WILLKIE FARR & GALLAGHER (AV)

The Equitable Center, 787 Seventh Avenue, 10019-6099
Telephone: 212-728-8000
Fax: 212-728-8111
Washington, D.C. Office: Three Lafayette Centre, 1155 21st Street, N.W., 20036-3384.
Telephone: 202-328-8000.
Fax: 202-887-8979; 202-331-8187.
Paris, France Office: 21-23 rue de la Ville l'Evêque, 75008.
Telephone: 011-33-1-53-43-45-00.
Fax: 011-33-1-40-06-96-06.
London, England Office: 35 Wilson Street, EC2M 2SJ.
Telephone: 011-44-171-696-9060.
Fax: 011-44-171-417-9191.

MEMBERS OF FIRM

Dennis R. Deveney
Alexander T. Galloway II
William E. Hiller
Peter J. Kenny
Leslie M. Mazza
Thomas M. Rothman
Richard C. Sammis
Brent W. White

For Complete List of Firm Personnel, See General Section

For full biographical listings, see the Martindale-Hubbell Law Directory

*SYRACUSE,** Onondaga Co.

HANCOCK & ESTABROOK, LLP (AV)

MONY Tower 1, P.O. Box 4976, 13221-4976
Telephone: 315-471-3151
Telecopier: 315-471-3167
Email: DBYRNE@HANCOCKLAW.COM
Albany, New York Office: Suite 505, 125 Wolf Road.
Telephone: 518-458-7660.
Telecopier: 518-458-7731.

MEMBERS OF FIRM

Richard W. Cook
Gerald F. Stack
Jeffrey B. Andrus

Representative Clients: HSBC; Crucible Materials Corp.; Mobil Oil Corp.; Syracuse City School District; Metropolitan Development Assoc.; Metropolitan Life Insurance Co.; Amerada Hess Corp.; Cooper Industries, Inc.; Carrier Corp.; LeMoyne College; Conmed; Crouse Hospital; Chrysler Corporation; Ryder Transportation Services, Inc.

For Complete List of Firm Personnel, See General Section

For full biographical listings, see the Martindale-Hubbell Law Directory

NORTH CAROLINA

*CHARLOTTE,** Mecklenburg Co.

WOMBLE CARLYLE SANDRIDGE & RICE (AV)

A Professional Limited Liability Company
3300 One First Union Center, 301 South College Street, 28202-6025
Telephone: 704-331-4900
Fax: 704-331-4955
Email: lawyers@wcsr.com *URL:* http://www.wcsr.com
Winston-Salem, North Carolina Office: 200 West Second Street, P.O. Drawer 84.
Telephone: 336-721-3600.
Fax: 336-721-3660.
Raleigh, North Carolina Office: 2100 First Union Capitol Center, 150 Fayetteville Street Mall, P.O. Box 831.
Telephone: 919-755-2100.
Fax: 919-755-2150.
Research Triangle Park, North Carolina Office: 2505 Meridian Parkway, Suite 300 (Durham), 27713.
Telephone: 919-484-2300.
Fax: 919-484-2340.
Atlanta, Georgia Office: One Atlantic Center, 1201 West Peachtree Street, Suite 3500.
Telephone: 404-872-7000.
Fax: 404-888-7490.
Other Atlanta, Georgia Office: Suite 404, 2296 Henderson Mill Road, N.E.
Telephone: 770-492-9030.
Fax: 770-492-9609.

(See Next Column)

WOMBLE CARLYLE SANDRIDGE & RICE, *Charlotte—Continued*

Washington, D.C. Office: 1120 Nineteenth Street, N.W., Eighth Floor.
Telephone: 202-857-4400.
Fax: 202-467-6910.
Greenville, South Carolina Office: 15 South Main Street, Suite 601, P.O. Box 10208.
Telephone: 864-255-5400.
Fax: 864-255-5440.

RESIDENT MEMBERS

Gary D. Chamblee
Joe B. Cogdell, Jr.
Bobby D. Hinson
William P. McMillan

Representative Clients: Childress Klein Properties, Inc.; Food Lion, Inc.; J.A. Jones Construction Co.; Parkdale Mills, Inc.; Pillowtex; Duke Power Co.; Bowles Hollowell Conner & Co.; ALLTEL Carolina, Inc.; Belk Store Services, Inc.; Philip Holzmann A.G.

For Complete List of Firm Personnel, See General Section

For full biographical listings, see the Martindale-Hubbell Law Directory

*RALEIGH,** Wake Co.

WOMBLE CARLYLE SANDRIDGE & RICE (AV)

A Professional Limited Liability Company
2100 First Union Capitol Center, 150 Fayetteville Street Mall, P.O. Box 831, 27602
Telephone: 919-755-2100
Fax: 919-755-2150
Email: lawyers@wcsr.com *URL:* http://www.wcsr.com
Charlotte, North Carolina Office: 3300 One First Union Center, 301 South College Street.
Telephone: 704-331-4900.
Fax: 704-331-4955.
Winston-Salem, North Carolina Office: 200 West Second Street, P.O. Drawer 84.
Telephone: 336-721-3600.
Fax: 336-721-3660.
Research Triangle Park, North Carolina Office: 2505 Meridian Parkway, Suite 300 (Durham), 27713.
Telephone: 919-484-2300.
Fax: 919-484-2340.
Atlanta, Georgia Office: One Atlantic Center, 1201 West Peachtree Street, Suite 3500.
Telephone: 404-872-7000.
Fax: 404-888-7490.
Other Atlanta, Georgia Office: Suite 404, 2296 Henderson Mill Road, N.E.
Telephone: 770-492-9030.
Fax: 770-492-9609.
Washington, D.C. Office: 1120 Nineteenth Street, N.W., Eighth Floor.
Telephone: 202-857-4400.
Fax: 202-467-6910.
Greenville, South Carolina Office: 15 South Main Street, Suite 601, P.O. Box 10208.
Telephone: 864-255-5400.
Fax: 864-255-5440.

RESIDENT MEMBERS

Donald A. Donadio
William C. Matthews, Jr.
Stephen A. Yeagy

RESIDENT ASSOCIATE

Nellie Shipley Tomlinson

Representative Clients: Aetna Casualty and Surety Co., Inc.; ALSCO/AmeriMark Building Products, Inc.; Aoki Corporation America, Inc.; Hackney Brothers, Inc.; Lawyers Mutual Liability Insurance Company of North Carolina; Meredith College; Regency Park Corp.; Wachovia Bank, N.A.

For Complete List of Firm Personnel, See General Section

For full biographical listings, see the Martindale-Hubbell Law Directory

*WINSTON-SALEM,** Forsyth Co.

WOMBLE CARLYLE SANDRIDGE & RICE (AV)

A Professional Limited Liability Company
200 West Second Street, P.O. Drawer 84, 27102
Telephone: 336-721-3600
Fax: 336-721-3660
Email: lawyers@wcsr.com *URL:* http://www.wcsr.com
Charlotte, North Carolina Office: 3300 One First Union Center, 301 South College Street.
Telephone: 704-331-4900.
Fax: 704-331-4955.
Raleigh, North Carolina Office: 2100 First Union Capitol Center, 150 Fayetteville Street Mall, P.O. Box 831.
Telephone: 919-755-2100.
Fax: 919-755-2150.
Research Triangle Park, North Carolina Office: 2505 Meridian Parkway, Suite 300 (Durham), 27713.
Telephone: 919-484-2300.
Fax: 919-484-2340.

(See Next Column)

Atlanta, Georgia Office: One Atlantic Center, 1201 West Peachtree Street, Suite 3500.
Telephone: 404-872-7000.
Fax: 404-888-7490.
Other Atlanta, Georgia Office: Suite 404, 2296 Henderson Mill Road, N.E.
Telephone: 770-492-9030.
Fax: 770-492-9609.
Washington, D.C. Office: 1120 Nineteenth Street, N.W., Eighth Floor.
Telephone: 202-857-4400.
Fax: 202-467-6910.
Greenville, South Carolina Office: 15 South Main Street, Suite 601, P.O. Box 10208.
Telephone: 864-255-5400.
Fax: 864-255-5440.

RESIDENT MEMBERS

Anthony H. Brett
Leslie E. Browder
W. Andrew Copenhaver
Hardin G. Halsey
Roddey M. Ligon, Jr.
Kim Kelly Mann
Dennis W. McNames
Kenneth A. Moser
Robert L. Quick
W. P. Sandridge, Jr.
David A. Shirlen
Ashley O. Thrift

RESIDENT ASSOCIATE

Joel M. Leander

Representative Clients: Brad Ragan, Inc.; Brenner Companies; Food Lion, Inc.; Hanes Companies, Inc.; North Carolina Baptist Hospitals, Inc.; R.J. Reynolds Tobacco Co.; Thomasville Furniture Industries, Inc.; Wachovia Corp.; Wake Forest University.

For Complete List of Firm Personnel, See General Section

For full biographical listings, see the Martindale-Hubbell Law Directory

NORTH DAKOTA

*FARGO,** Cass Co.

OHNSTAD TWICHELL, P.C. (AV)

15 Broadway, Suite 206, 58102
Telephone: 701-280-5801
Fax: 701-280-5803
West Fargo, North Dakota Office: 901 13th Avenue East, P.O. Box 458.
Telephone 701-282-3249.
Fax: 701-282-0825.
Hillsboro, North Dakota Office: West Caledonia Avenue, P.O. Box 220.
Telephone 701-436-5700.
Fax: 701-436-4025.
Mayville, North Dakota Office: 12 Third Street S.E., P.O. Box 547.
Telephone: 701-786-3251.
Fax: 701-786-4243.

Daniel R. Twichell (Resident, West Fargo Office)
Duane R. Breitling
Brian D. Neugebauer (Resident, West Fargo Office)

Bond Counsel For: City of Fargo; City of West Fargo; City of Jamestown; City of Valley City; City of Enderlin; City of Gwinner; SE Cass Water Resource District; Minot Public School District.

For Complete List of Firm Personnel, See General Section

For full biographical listings, see the Martindale-Hubbell Law Directory

OHIO

*CLEVELAND,** Cuyahoga Co.

BAKER & HOSTETLER LLP (AV)

3200 National City Center, 1900 East Ninth Street, 44114-3485
Telephone: 216-621-0200
Telecopier: 216-696-0740
TWX: 810 421 8375
RCA Telex: 215032
To contact an attorney on the Internet use first initial and surname followed by @baker-hostetler.com
URL: http://www.bakerlaw.com
In Cincinnati, Ohio: 312 Walnut Street, Suite 2650.
Telephone: 513-929-3400.
In Columbus, Ohio: Capitol Square, Suite 2100, 65 East State Street.
Telephone: 614-228-1541.
In Denver, Colorado: 303 East 17th Avenue, Suite 1100.
Telephone: 303-861-0600.
In Houston, Texas: 1000 Louisiana, Suite 2000.
Telephone: 713-751-1600.
In Beverly Hills, California: 9150 Wilshire Boulevard, Suite 205.
Telephone: 310-385-7500.
In Long Beach, California: 300 Oceangate, Suite 620.
Telephone: 562-432-2827.

(See Next Column)

BAKER & HOSTETLER LLP—*Continued*

In Los Angeles, California: 600 Wilshire Boulevard.
Telephone: 213-624-2400.
In Orlando, Florida: SunBank Center, Suite 2300, 200 South Orange Avenue.
Telephone: 407-649-4000.
In Washington, D.C.: Washington Square, Suite 1100, 1050 Connecticut Avenue, N.W.
Telephone: 202-861-1500.

PARTNERS

Albert T. Adams
Edward S. Ginsburg
Richard R. Hollington, Jr.

For Complete List of Firm Personnel, See General Section

For full biographical listings, see the Martindale-Hubbell Law Directory

JONES, DAY, REAVIS & POGUE (AV)

North Point, 901 Lakeside Avenue, 44114
Telephone: 216-586-3939
Telecopier: 216-579-0212
Email: counsel@jonesday.com *URL:* http://www.jonesday.com
In Columbus, Ohio: 1900 Huntington Center.
Telephone: 614-469-3939.
Telecopier: 614-461-4198.
In Atlanta, Georgia: 3500 SunTrust Plaza, 303 Peachtree Street.
Telephone: 404-521-3939.
Telecopier: 404-581-8330.
In Brussels, Belgium: Avenue Louise 480, 7th Floor. B-1050 Brussels.
Telephone: 32-2-645-14-11.
Telecopier: 32-2-645-14-45.
In Chicago, Illinois: 77 West Wacker.
Telephone: 312-782-3939.
Telecopier: 312-782-8585.
In Dallas, Texas: 2727 North Harwood Street.
Telephone: 214-220-3939.
Telecopier: 214-969-5100.
In Frankfurt, Germany: Hochhaus am Park, Grüneburgweg 102, 60323 Frankfurt am Main.
Telephone: 49-69-9726-3939.
Telecopier: 49-69-9726-3993.
In Geneva, Switzerland: 20, rue de Candolle.
Telephone: 41-22-320-2339.
Telecopier: 41-22-320-1232.
In Hong Kong, China: 29th Floor, Entertainment Building, 30 Queen's Road Central.
Telephone: 852-2526-6895.
Telecopier: 852-2868-5871 or 852-2868-5699.
In Irvine, California: 5 Park Plaza, Suite 1100.
Telephone: 949-851-3939.
Telecopier: 949-553-7539.
In London, England: Bucklersbury House, 3 Queen Victoria Street.
Telephone: 44-171-236-3939.
Telecopier: 44-171-236-1113.
In Los Angeles, California: 555 West Fifth Street, Suite 4600.
Telephone: 213-489-3939.
Telecopier: 213-243-2539.
In New Delhi, India (Associate Office): Pathak & Associates (an associate firm of Jones, Day, Reavis & Pogue), 1st Floor, Dr. Gopal Das Bhaven, 28 Barakhamba Road.
Telephone: 91-11-373-8793; 91-11-335-7345.
Telecopier: 91-11-335-3761.
In New York, N.Y.: 599 Lexington Avenue.
Telephone: 212-326-3939.
Telecopier: 212-755-7306.
In Paris, France: 120, rue du Faubourg Saint-Honoré.
Telephone: 33-1-56-59-39-39.
Telecopier: 33-1-56-59-39-38
In Pittsburgh, Pennsylvania: 500 Grant Street, 31st Floor.
Telephone: 412-391-3939.
Telecopier: 412-394-7959.
In Riyadh, Saudi Arabia: The International Law Firm (In Association with Jones, Day, Reavis & Pogue), Sulaymaniyah, Prince Mishari IBN, Abdulaziz Street, P.O. Box 22166.
Telephone: (966-1) 462-8866.
Telecopier: (966-1) 462-9001.
In Shanghai, China: 2805 Kerry Centre, 1515 Nanjing Road West.
Telephone: 86-21-5298-6568.
Telecopier: 86-21-5298-6569.
In Sydney, Australia: Governor Phillip Tower, Level 38, 1 Farrer Place.
Telephone: 61-2-9210-6921.
Telecopier: 61-2-9210-6926.
In Taipei, Taiwan: 8th Floor, Tun Hwa South Road, Section 2.
Telephone: (886-2) 2704-6808.
Telecopier: (886-2) 2704-6791.
In Tokyo, Japan: Toranomon MT Building, 4th Floor, 10-3, Toranomon 3-Chome, Minato-ku, Tokyo 105, Japan.
Telephone: 81-3-3433-3939.
Telecopier: 81-3-5401-2725.
In Washington, D.C.: 51 Louisiana Avenue, N.W.
Telephone: 202-879-3939.
Telecopier: 202-626-1700.

(See Next Column)

MEMBERS OF FIRM IN CLEVELAND

John W. Sager
Zachary T. Paris
Anthony R. Moore
Louis Rorimer
John D. Currivan
David P. Porter

For Complete List of Firm Personnel, See General Section

For full biographical listings, see the Martindale-Hubbell Law Directory

KAUFMAN & CUMBERLAND CO., L.P.A. (AV)

1500 Republic Building, 25 Prospect Avenue, West, 44115-1000
Telephone: 216-861-0707
Telefax: 216-694-6883
TDD: 216-694-6891

Steven S. Kaufman
Frank J. Cumberland, Jr. (Retired)
Frank R. DeSantis
Robert A. Blattner

Representative Client: CertainTeed Corp.

For full biographical listings, see the Martindale-Hubbell Law Directory

*COLUMBUS,** Franklin Co.

BRICKER & ECKLER LLP (AV)

100 South Third Street, 43215-4291
Telephone: 614-227-2300
Telecopy: 614-227-2390
Email: info@be.bricker.com *URL:* http://www.bricker.com

Richard F. Kane
Richard C. Simpson
David A. Rogers
David C. Spialter
Randall Edwin Moore
Michael E. Flowers
Rebecca Coleman Princehorn
Luther L. Liggett, Jr.
William T. Conard, II
Price D. Finley

Anne DeVoe

Representative Clients: City of Columbus; Cleveland Tomorrow; Rickenbacker Port Authority; Ohio Building Authority; The Ohio State University; Banc One Capital Markets, Inc.; Seasongood & Mayer; A.G. Edwards Sons, Inc.; McDonald Investments, Inc.; Medina City School District.

For Complete List of Firm Personnel, See General Section

For full biographical listings, see the Martindale-Hubbell Law Directory

JONES, DAY, REAVIS & POGUE (AV)

1900 Huntington Center, 43215
Telephone: 614-469-3939
Telecopier: 614-461-4198
Email: counsel@jonesday.com *URL:* http://www.jonesday.com
In Cleveland, Ohio: North Point, 901 Lakeside Avenue.
Telephone: 216-586-3939.
Telecopier: 216-579-0212.
In Atlanta, Georgia: 3500 SunTrust Plaza, 303 Peachtree Street.
Telephone: 404-521-3939.
Telecopier: 404-581-8330.
In Brussels, Belgium: Avenue Louise 480, 7th Floor, B-1050 Brussels.
Telephone: 32-2-645-14-11.
Telecopier: 32-2-645-14-45.
In Chicago, Illinois: 77 West Wacker.
Telephone: 312-782-3939.
Telecopier: 312-782-8585.
In Dallas, Texas: 2727 North Harwood Street.
Telephone: 214-220-3939.
Telecopier: 214-969-5100.
In Frankfurt, Germany: Hochhaus am Park, Grüneburgweg 102, 60323 Frankfurt am Main.
Telephone: 49-69-9726-3939.
Telecopier: 49-69-9726-3993.
In Geneva, Switzerland: 20, rue de Candolle.
Telephone: 41-22-320-2339.
Telecopier: 41-22-320-1232.
In Hong Kong: 29th Floor, Entertainment Building, 30 Queen's Road Central.
Telephone: 852-2526-6895.
Telecopier: 852-2868-5871 or 852-2868-5699.
In Irvine, California: 5 Park Plaza, Suite 1100.
Telephone: 949-851-3939.
Telecopier: 949-553-7539.
In London, England: Bucklersbury House, 3 Queen Victoria Street.
Telephone: 44-171-236-3939.
Telecopier: 44-171-236-1113.
In Los Angeles, California: 555 West Fifth Street, Suite 4600.
Telephone: 213-489-3939.
Telecopier: 213-243-2539.
In New Delhi, India (Associate Office): Pathak & Associates (an associate firm of Jones, Day, Reavis & Pogue), 1st Floor, Dr. Gopal Das Bhaven, 28 Barakhamba Road.
Telephone: 91-11-373-8793; 91-11-335-7345.
Telecopier: 91-11-335-3761.

(See Next Column)

JONES, DAY, REAVIS & POGUE, *Columbus—Continued*

In New York, New York: 599 Lexington Avenue.
Telephone: 212-326-3939.
Telecopier: 212-755-7306.
In Paris, France: 120, rue du Faubourg Saint-Honoré.
Telephone: 33-1-56-59-39-39.
Telecopier: 33-1-56-59-39-38
In Pittsburgh, Pennsylvania: 500 Grant Street, 31st Floor.
Telephone: 412-391-3939.
Telecopier: 412-394-7959.
In Riyadh, Saudi Arabia: The International Law Firm (In Association with Jones, Day, Reavis & Pogue), Sulaymaniyah, Prince Mishari IBN, Abdulaziz Street, P.O. Box 22166.
Telephone: (966-1) 462-8866.
Telecopier: (966-1) 462-9001.
In Shanghai, China: 2805 Kerry Centre, 1515 Nanjing Road West.
Telephone: 86-21-5298-6568.
Telecopier: 86-21-5298-6569.
In Sydney, Australia: Governor Phillip Tower, Level 38, 1 Farrer Place.
Telephone: 61-2-9210-6921.
Telecopier: 61-2-9210-6926.
In Taipei, Taiwan: 8th Floor, 2 Tun Hwa South Road, Section 2.
Telephone: (886-2) 2704-6808.
Telecopier: (886-2) 2704-6791.
In Tokyo, Japan: Toranomon MT Building, 4th Floor, 10-3, Toranomon 3-Chome, Minato-ku, Tokyo 105, Japan.
Telephone: 81-3-3433-3939.
Telecopier: 81-3-5401-2725.
In Washington, D.C.: 51 Louisiana Avenue, N.W.
Telephone: 202-879-3939.
Telecopier: 202-626-1700.

MEMBER OF FIRM IN COLUMBUS

Roger R. Stinehart

For Complete List of Firm Personnel, See General Section

For full biographical listings, see the Martindale-Hubbell Law Directory

PORTER WRIGHT MORRIS & ARTHUR LLP (AV)

41 South High Street, 43215-6194
Telephone: 614-227-2000; (800-533-2794)
Fax: 614-227-2100
Email: cmh@porterwright.com *URL:* http://www.porterwright.com
Cincinnati, Ohio Office: 250 E. Fifth Street, Suite 2200, 45202-4199.
Telephones: 513-381-4700; (800-582-5813).
Fax: 513-421-0991. Internet: cvg@porterwright.com.
Cleveland, Ohio Office: 925 Euclid Avenue, Suite 1700, 44115-1483.
Telephones: 216-443-9000; (800-824-1980).
Fax: 216-443-9011. Internet: cle@porterwright.com.
Dayton, Ohio Office: One Dayton Centre, One South Main Street, Suite 1600, 45402-2028.
Telephones: 937-449-6810; (800-533-4434).
Fax: 937-449-6820. Internet: day@porterwright.com.
Naples, Florida Office: 5801 Pelican Bay Boulevard, Suite 300, 34108-2709.
Telephones: 941-593-2900; (800-876-7962).
Fax: 941-593-2990. Internet: apf@porterwright.com.
Washington, D.C. Office: 1667 K Street, N.W., Suite 1100, 20006-1605.
Telephones: 202-778-3000; (800-456-7962).
Fax: 202-778-3063. Internet: dca@porterwright.com.

MEMBERS OF FIRM
COLUMBUS, OHIO OFFICE

Thomas C. Coady
Amy D. Klaben
Nancy B. Young

OF COUNSEL
COLUMBUS, OHIO OFFICE

Ronald W. Gabriel

DAYTON, OHIO OFFICE
RESIDENT MEMBERS

Thomas A. Holton
Charles Y. Kidwell, Jr.

CLEVELAND, OHIO OFFICE
RESIDENT MEMBERS

Ralph Streza
David C. Tryon

For Complete List of Firm Personnel, See General Section

For full biographical listings, see the Martindale-Hubbell Law Directory

SMITH & HALE (AV)

(Formerly Wilson & Rector)
37 West Broad Street, 43215
Telephone: 614-221-4255

MEMBERS OF FIRM

Harrison W. Smith (1900-1978)
Harrison W. Smith, Jr.
Ben W. Hale, Jr.
Jeffrey L. Brown
Glen A. Dugger
Jackson B. Reynolds, III

For full biographical listings, see the Martindale-Hubbell Law Directory

VORYS, SATER, SEYMOUR AND PEASE LLP (AV)

52 East Gay Street, P.O. Box 1008, 43216-1008
Telephone: 614-464-6400
Telecopier: 614-464-6350
URL: http://www.vssp.com
Washington, D.C. Office: 1828 L Street, N.W., 20036-5109.
Telephone: 202-467-8800.
Telex: 440693.
Telecopier: 202-467-8900.
Cleveland, Ohio Office: 2100 One Cleveland Center, 1375 East Ninth Street, 44114-1724.
Telephone: 216-479-6100.
Telecopier: 216-479-6060.
Cincinnati, Ohio Office: Suite 2100, 221 East Fourth Street, P.O. Box 0236, 45201-0236.
Telephone: 513-723-4000.
Telecopier: 513-723-4056.
Alexandria, Virginia Office: 277 South Washington St., Suite 310, 22314.
Telephone: 703-549-4282.
Telecopier: 703-549-4492.

MEMBERS OF FIRM

George L. Jenkins
Philip C. Johnston
Daniel H. Schoedinger
Phillip L. Nunnally
George N. Corey
Bruce R. Henke
Douglas L. Rogers
Carole A. Mitchell
Russell R. Rosler

Local Counsel: Abbott Laboratories; Connecticut General Life Insurance Co.; The Children's Hospital; General Motors Corp.; The Kroger Co.; Navistar International Trans.; Wendy's International, Inc.; Honda of America Mfg., Inc.; Worthington Industries, Inc.; Worthington Foods.

For Complete List of Firm Personnel, See General Section

For full biographical listings, see the Martindale-Hubbell Law Directory

OKLAHOMA

*NORMAN,** Cleveland Co.

CROWE & DUNLEVY (AV)

A Professional Corporation
2500 South McGee, Suite 140, 73072-6705
Telephone: 405-321-7317
Fax: 405-360-4002
Email: marketing@crowedunlevy.com *URL:* http://www.crowedunlevy.com
Oklahoma City, Oklahoma Office: Crowe & Dunlevy, A Professional Corporation, 1800 Mid-America Tower, 20 North Broadway, 73102-8273.
Telephone: 405-235-7700.
Fax: 405-239-6651.
Tulsa, Oklahoma Office: Crowe & Dunlevy, A Professional Corporation, 500 Kennedy Building, 321 South Boston Avenue, 74103-3313.
Telephone: 918-592-9800.
Fax: 918-592-9801.

Robert L. Pendarvis

For Complete List of Firm Personnel, See General Section

For full biographical listings, see the Martindale-Hubbell Law Directory

FLOYD LAW FIRM, P.C. (AV)

118 East Main Street, P.O. Box 396, 73070
Telephone: 405-364-6660
Fax: 405-360-5076
Email: floydpc@swbell.net

Glenn E. Floyd
B. Lynne Lam
J. Brent Clark

OF COUNSEL

Philip R. Russ

Representative Client: Bank One, Oklahoma City, Oklahoma.

For full biographical listings, see the Martindale-Hubbell Law Directory

*OKLAHOMA CITY,** Oklahoma Co.

CROWE & DUNLEVY, A PROFESSIONAL CORPORATION (AV)

1800 Mid-America Tower, 20 North Broadway, 73102-8273
Telephone: 405-235-7700
Fax: 405-239-6651
Email: marketing@crowedunlevy.com *URL:* http://www.crowedunlevy.com
Tulsa, Oklahoma Office: 500 Kennedy Building, 321 South Boston Avenue, 74103-3313.
Telephone: 918-592-9800.
Fax: 918-592-9801.

(See Next Column)

CROWE & DUNLEVY A PROFESSIONAL CORPORATION—*Continued*

Norman, Oklahoma Office: Crowe & Dunlevy, 2500 South McGee, Suite 140, 73072-6705.
Telephone: 405-321-7317.
Fax: 405-360-4002.

Earl A. Skarky

Eric S. Fisher
OF COUNSEL
James C. Gibbens

For Complete List of Firm Personnel, See General Section

For full biographical listings, see the Martindale-Hubbell Law Directory

---

WILLIAMS, BOX, FORSHEE & BULLARD, P.C. (AV)

522 Colcord Drive, 73102-2202
Telephone: 405-232-0080
Telecopier: 405-236-5814

John Michael Williams
Dennis R. Box
Richard D. Forshee
William J. Bullard
Keith R. Gibson
Paul E. Lefebvre

Kimberly K. Brown

For full biographical listings, see the Martindale-Hubbell Law Directory

---

*TULSA,** Tulsa Co.

CROWE & DUNLEVY, A PROFESSIONAL CORPORATION (AV)

500 Kennedy Building, 321 South Boston Avenue, 74103-3313
Telephone: 918-592-9800
Fax: 918-592-9801
Email: marketing@crowedunlevy.com *URL:* http://www.crowedunlevy.com
Oklahoma City, Oklahoma Office: 1800 Mid-America Tower, 20 North Broadway, 73102-8273.
Telephone: 405-235-7700.
Fax: 405-239-6651.
Norman, Oklahoma Office: Crowe & Dunlevy, 2500 South McGee, Suite 140, 73072-6705.
Telephone: 405-321-7317.
Fax: 405-360-4002.

Lon Foster, III

For Complete List of Firm Personnel, See General Section

For full biographical listings, see the Martindale-Hubbell Law Directory

---

STONE JESSUP, P.C. (AV)

320 South Boston, 74103-4736
Telephone: 918-583-1178
Fax: 918-583-0277

Samuel C. Stone
James R. Jessup (1936-1991)

For full biographical listings, see the Martindale-Hubbell Law Directory

---

PENNSYLVANIA

*HARRISBURG,** Dauphin Co.

GOLDBERG, KATZMAN & SHIPMAN, P.C. (AV)

320 Market Street - Strawberry Square, P.O. Box 1268, 17108-1268
Telephone: 717-234-4161
Telecopier: 717-234-6808; 717-234-6810
Email: gks@gkslaw.com

Ronald M. Katzman
Neil Hendershot
Jesse Jay Cooper

Arnold B. Kogan
Steven E. Grubb

Representative Client: Dauphin County General Authority.
Reference: Fulton Bank.

For Complete List of Firm Personnel, See General Section

For full biographical listings, see the Martindale-Hubbell Law Directory

---

METTE, EVANS & WOODSIDE, A PROFESSIONAL CORPORATION (AV)

3401 North Front Street, P.O. Box 5950, 17110-0950
Telephone: 717-232-5000
Fax: 717-236-1816
Email: MEW@Mette.com *URL:* HTTP://WWW.METTE.COM

(See Next Column)

Howell C. Mette
Robert Moore
Charles B. Zwally
James A. Ulsh
Thomas F. Smida

Counsel for: Dauphin County General Authority; Mifflin County Hospital Authority; Central Dauphin School District; Northern York School District; Bloomsburg Area School District; Mercersburg Borough Authority; West Shore School District; York County Industrial Development Authority; Township of Lower Makefield.

For Complete List of Firm Personnel, See General Section

For full biographical listings, see the Martindale-Hubbell Law Directory

---

RHOADS & SINON LLP (AV)

One South Market Square, 12th Floor, P.O. Box 1146, 17108-1146
Telephone: 717-233-5731
Fax: 717-232-1459
Boca Raton, Florida Affiliated Office: Charles L. Sieck, 1700 South Dixie Highway, Suite 2-C.
Telephone: 561-395-5595.
Fax: 561-395-9497.
York, Pennsylvania Office: 15 North Cherry Lane, Suite 21.
Telephone: 717-843-1718.
Fax: 717-232-1459.

OF COUNSEL
Nathan H. Waters, Jr.

MEMBERS OF FIRM

Robert H. Long, Jr.
Richard B. Wood
Frank J. Leber
Paul A. Lundeen
David O. Twaddell
Jens H. Damgaard

ASSOCIATE
Robert J. Tribeck

For Complete List of Firm Personnel, See General Section

For full biographical listings, see the Martindale-Hubbell Law Directory

---

*PHILADELPHIA,** Philadelphia Co.

BALLARD SPAHR ANDREWS & INGERSOLL, LLP (AV)

1735 Market Street, 51st Floor, 19103-7599
Telephone: 215-665-8500
Fax: 215-864-8999
URL: http://www.ballardspahr.com
Baltimore, Maryland Office: 300 East Lombard Street. 19th Floor.
Telephone: 410-528-5600.
Fax: 410-528-5650.
Camden, New Jersey Office: 800 Hudson Square, 5th Floor.
Telephone: 856-541-5577.
Fax: 856-541-8272.
Denver, Colorado Office: Seventeenth Street Plaza Building, Suite 2300, 1225 17th Street.
Telephone: 303-292-2400.
Fax: 303-296-3956.
Salt Lake City, Utah Office: One Utah Center, Suite 1200, 201 South Main Street.
Telephone: 801-531-3000.
Fax: 801-531-3001.
Voorhees, New Jersey Office: Suite 100, 1101 Laurel Oak Drive.
Telephone: 856-627-8555.
Fax: 856-627-1153.
Washington, D.C. Office: Suite 1000 South, 601 13th Street, N.W.
Telephone: 202-661-2200.
Fax: 202-661-2299.

Frederic L. Ballard, Jr.
Kevin R. Cunningham
H. David Prior
Jere G. Thompson
Jeffrey T. Chappelle
Thomas Jay Ellis
William P. Scott
J. Brian Walsh

COUNSEL
Barbara R. Beckman

Richard F. Booker
William C. Rhodes
Mara Williams

For Complete List of Firm Personnel, See General Section

For full biographical listings, see the Martindale-Hubbell Law Directory

---

ROTAN E. LEE (AV)

6333 Woodbine Avenue, 19151
Telephone: 215-790-2450

For full biographical listings, see the Martindale-Hubbell Law Directory

Philadelphia—Continued

REED SMITH SHAW & MCCLAY LLP (AV)

2500 One Liberty Place, 19103-7301
Telephone: 215-851-8100
FAX: 215-851-1420
Email: rssm@rssm.com *URL:* http://www.rssm.com
Pittsburgh, Pennsylvania Office: 435 Sixth Avenue, 15219-1886.
Telephone: 412-288-3131.
FAX: 412-288-3063.
Washington, D.C. Office: Suite 1100 - East Tower, 1301 K Street, N.W., 20005-3317.
Telephone: 202-414-9200.
FAX: 202-414-9299.
Harrisburg, Pennsylvania Office: 213 Market Street, 17101-2132.
Telephone: 717-234-5988.
FAX: 717-236-3777.
Princeton, New Jersey Office: 136 Main Street, Suite 250, 08540-5799.
Telephone: 609-987-0050.
FAX: 609-951-0824.
New York, N.Y. Office: 375 Park Avenue, 17th Floor, 10152.
Telephone: 212-521-5400.
FAX: 212-521-5450.
Newark, New Jersey Office: The Legal Center, One Riverfront Plaza, First Floor, 07102-5400.
Telephone: 973-621-3200.
FAX: 973-621-3199.
Falls Church, Virginia Office: Reed Smith Hazel & Thomas, Suite 1400, 3110 Fairview Park Drive, P.O. Box 12001.
Telephone: 703-641-4200.
Fax: 703-641-4340.
Leesburg, Virginia Office: Reed Smith Hazel & Thomas LLP, 44084 Riverside Parkway, Suite 300.
Telephone: 703-729-8500. Metro: 703-478-1992.
Fax: 703-478-8003.
McLean, Virginia Office: Reed Smith Hazel & Thomas LLP, Suite 1100, 8251 Greensboro Drive, 22102-3844.
Telephone: 703-734-4600.
FAX: 703-734-4699.
Richmond, Virginia Office: Reed Smith Hazel & Thomas LLP, Suite 600, 411 East Franklin Street, P.O. Box 788.
Telephone: 804-344-3400.
Fax: 804-344-3410.

MEMBERS OF FIRM

Carl E. Esser
Stephen M. Lyons, III
S. William Richter

For full biographical listings, see the Martindale-Hubbell Law Directory

*PITTSBURGH,** Allegheny Co.

REED SMITH SHAW & MCCLAY LLP (AV)

435 Sixth Avenue, 15219-1886
Telephone: 412-288-3131
FAX: 412-288-3063
Mailing Address: P.O. Box 2009, 15230-2009
Email: rssm@rssm.com *URL:* http://www.rssm.com
Washington, D.C. Office: Suite 1100 - East Tower, 1301 K Street, N.W., 20005-3317.
Telephone: 202-414-9200.
FAX: 202-414-9299.
Philadelphia, Pennsylvania Office: 2500 One Liberty Place, 19103-7301.
Telephone: 215-851-8100.
FAX: 215-851-1420.
Harrisburg, Pennsylvania Office: 213 Market Street, 17101-2132.
Telephone: 717-234-5988.
FAX: 717-236-3777.
Princeton, New Jersey Office: 136 Main Street, Suite 250, 08540-5799.
Telephone: 609-987-0050.
FAX: 609-951-0824.
New York, N.Y. Office: 375 Park Avenue, 17th Floor, 10152.
Telephone: 212-521-5400.
FAX: 212-521-5450.
Newark, New Jersey Office: The Legal Center, One Riverfront Plaza, First Floor, 07102-5400.
Telephone: 973-621-3200.
FAX: 973-621-3199.
Falls Church, Virginia Office: Reed Smith Hazel & Thomas, Suite 1400, 3110 Fairview Park Drive, P.O. Box 12001.
Telephone: 703-641-4200.
Fax: 703-641-4340.
Leesburg, Virginia Office: Reed Smith Hazel & Thomas LLP, 44084 Riverside Parkway, Suite 300.
Telephone: 703-729-8500. Metro: 703-478-1992.
Fax: 703-478-8003.
McLean, Virginia Office: Reed Smith Hazel & Thomas LLP, Suite 1100, 8251 Greensboro Drive, 22102-3844.
Telephone: 703-734-4600.
FAX: 703-734-4699.
Richmond, Virginia Office: Reed Smith Hazel & Thomas LLP, Suite 600, 411 East Franklin Street, P.O. Box 788.
Telephone: 804-344-3400.
Fax: 804-344-3410.

(See Next Column)

MEMBERS OF FIRM

David L. DeNinno
Frank T. Guadagnino
Glenn R. Mahone
Kimberly L. Sachse
William J. Smith
Leonard L. Stewart
Thomas Todd

For full biographical listings, see the Martindale-Hubbell Law Directory

RHODE ISLAND

*PROVIDENCE,** Providence Co.

BLISH & CAVANAGH (AV)

Commerce Center, 30 Exchange Terrace, 02903
Telephone: 401-831-8900
Telecopier: 401-751-7542
Email: BLISHCAV@AOL.COM

MEMBERS OF FIRM

Joseph V. Cavanagh, Jr.
William R. Landry
Edmund L. Alves, Jr.
Stephen J. Reid, Jr.
Karen A. Pelczarski
Scott T. Spear
Raymond A. Marcaccio

Michael W. Carroll
Staci L. Sawyer
Kristin Rodgers Sullivan

OF COUNSEL

John H. Blish

Representative Clients: Providence Journal Co.; Rhode Island Hospital Trust National Bank; Fleet Bank; Metropolitan Insurance Co.; Allstate Insurance Co.; Delta Dental of Rhode Island; Colony Communications; Providence Housing Authority; Textron; A.T. Cross.

For full biographical listings, see the Martindale-Hubbell Law Directory

EDWARDS & ANGELL, LLP (AV)

A Partnership including Professional Corporations
2800 BankBoston Plaza, 02903
Telephone: 401-274-9200
Telecopier: 401-276-6611
Cable Address: "Edwangle Providence"
Telex: 952001 "E A PVD"
Email: postmaster@ealaw.com *URL:* http://www.ealaw.com
Boston, Massachusetts Office: 101 Federal Street, 02110-1800.
Telephone: 617-439-4444.
Telecopier: 617-439-4170.
New York, New York Office: 750 Lexington Avenue, 10022-1200.
Telephone: 212-308-4411.
Telecopier: 212-308-4844.
Palm Beach, Florida Office: 250 Royal Palm Way, Suite 300, 33480-4356.
Telephone: 561-833-7700.
Telecopier: 561-655-8719.
Short Hills, New Jersey Office: 51 John F. Kennedy Parkway, 07078.
Telephone: 973-376-7700.
Telecopier: 973-376-3380.
Hartford, Connecticut Office: 90 State House Square, 06103-2715.
Telephone: 860-525-5065.
Telecopier: 860-527-4198.
Newport, Rhode Island Office: 130 Bellevue Avenue, 02840.
Telephone: 401-849-7800.
Telecopier: 401-849-7887.

MEMBERS OF FIRM

James R. McGuirk
James J. Skeffington
Kurt J. von Boeselager

OF COUNSEL

Alvin M. Glazerman (Not admitted in RI)

For Complete List of Firm Personnel, See General Section

For full biographical listings, see the Martindale-Hubbell Law Directory

HINCKLEY, ALLEN & SNYDER LLP (AV)

1500 Fleet Center, 02903-2393
Telephone: 401-274-2000
Fax: 401-277-9600
Email: firm@haslaw.com *URL:* http://www.haslaw.com
Boston, Massachusetts Office: 28 State Street, 30th Floor.
Telephone: 617-345-9000.
Fax: 617-345-9020. URL: http://www.haslaw.com.

MEMBERS OF FIRM

Paula K. Andrews (Not admitted in RI)
David D. Barricelli
E. Jerome Batty
Jonathan Bell
Paul Bork (Not admitted in RI)
Stephen J. Carlotti
David Barry Connolly (Not admitted in RI)
Joseph P. Curran
Michael P. DeFanti
Eric F. Eisenberg (Not admitted in RI)
Malcolm Farmer, III

(See Next Column)

HINCKLEY, ALLEN & SNYDER LLP—*Continued*

MEMBERS OF FIRM (Continued)

Margaret D. Farrell
Hugh J. Gorman, III (Not admitted in RI)
Alan P. Gottlieb (Not admitted in RI)
Gerard R. Goulet
William R. Grimm
Paul A. Hedstrom (Not admitted in RI)
Richard L. E. Jocelyn
Joel Lewin (Not admitted in RI)
Sandra Matrone Mack
Matthew T. Marcello, III
Frederick P. McClure
Elizabeth Murdock Myers
Paul F. O'Donnell, III (Not admitted in RI)
H. Peter Olsen
Julianne Palumbo (Not admitted in RI)
John J. Pendergast, III
Gerald J. Petros
James O. Reavis
Jeremy Ritzenberg (Not admitted in RI)
Ralph J. Rivkind (Not admitted in RI)
David J. Rubin
Charles E. Schaub, Jr. (Not admitted in RI)
Douglas F. Seaver (Not admitted in RI)
Herman Snyder (Not admitted in RI)
David R. Sullivan (Not admitted in RI)
Robert F. Sylvia (Not admitted in RI)
Howard E. Walker
Richard D. Wayne (Not admitted in RI)

ASSOCIATES

Jessica M. Bettencourt
Mark Bianchi
Alyssa V. Boss
Jane E. Cohen (Not admitted in RI)
Andrew D. Cummings (Not admitted in RI)
June E. Daniel
Kim Herman Goslant (Not admitted in RI)
Gloria Maria Gutierrez (Not admitted in RI)
Kelley Jordan-Price
Catherine S. Kim (Not admitted in RI)
Christopher W. Morog (Not admitted in RI)
Elena B. Olson (Not admitted in RI)
Joseph D. Whelan

OF COUNSEL

Willard Krasnow (Not admitted in RI)
Willard R. Pope (Not admitted in RI)
Bentley Tobin
Joachim A. Weissfeld

For Complete List of Firm Personnel, See General Section

For full biographical listings, see the Martindale-Hubbell Law Directory

SOUTH CAROLINA

*CHARLESTON,** Charleston Co.

HAYNSWORTH, MARION, McKAY & GUÉRARD, L.L.P. (AV)

134 Meeting Street, P.O. Box 1119, 29402
Telephone: 843-722-7606
Facsimile: 843-724-8016
Columbia, South Carolina Office: Suite 2400 Affinity Building, 1201 Main Street, P.O. Drawer 7157, 29202.
Telephone: 803-765-1818. Facsimile 803-765-2399.
Greenville, South Carolina Office: 75 Beattie Place, Eleventh Floor, P.O. Box 2048, 29602.
Telephone: 864-240-3200.
Facsimile: 864-240-3300.

MEMBERS OF FIRM

J. Paul Trouche
Samuel W. Howell, IV
Carol L. Clark

ASSOCIATE

Jeremy L. Cook

Counsel for: State of South Carolina; South Carolina Public Service Authority; South Carolina Jobs - Economic Development Authority; Charleston County; Dorchester County; City of North Charleston; City of Beaufort; Town of Mt. Pleasant; Colleton County.

For Complete List of Firm Personnel, See General Section

For full biographical listings, see the Martindale-Hubbell Law Directory

SINKLER & BOYD, P.A. (AV)

160 East Bay Street, P.O. Box 340, 29402-0340
Telephone: 843-722-3366
FAX: 843-722-2266
Email: firm@sinklerboyd.com *URL:* http://www.sinklerboyd.com
Columbia, South Carolina Office: Suite 1200 The Palmetto Center, 1426 Main Street, P.O. Box 11889.
Telephone: 803-779-3080.
FAX: 803-765-1243.
Greenville, South Carolina Office: 15 South Main Street, Insignia Financial Center on Main, Suite 500, P.O. Box 275.
Telephone: 864-467-1100.
FAX: 864-467-1521.

(See Next Column)

George S. King, Jr. (Resident, Columbia Office)
Thomas A. Hutcheson
Margaret Christian Pope (Resident, Columbia Office)
Charlton deSaussure, Jr.
F. Mitchell Johnson, Jr.
Robert S. Galloway, III (Resident, Greenville Office)
Steve A. Matthews (Resident, Columbia Office)
Theodore B. DuBose (Resident, Columbia Office)
John K. Van Duys (Resident, Columbia Office)

OF COUNSEL

Martin C. McWilliams, Jr. (Resident, Columbia Office)

Attorneys for: Wachovia Bank, N.A.; Westvaco Corp.; The City of Charleston, S.C., The South Carolina State Housing Finance and Development Authority.

For Complete List of Firm Personnel, See General Section

For full biographical listings, see the Martindale-Hubbell Law Directory

*COLUMBIA,** Richland Co.

HAYNSWORTH, MARION, McKAY & GUÉRARD, L.L.P. (AV)

Suite 2400 Affinity Building, 1201 Main Street, P.O. Drawer 7157, 29202
Telephone: 803-765-1818
Facsimile: 803-765-2399
Greenville, South Carolina Office: 75 Beattie Place, Eleventh Floor, P.O. Box 2048, 29602.
Telephone: 864-240-3200.
Facsimile: 864-240-3300.
Charleston, South Carolina Office: 134 Meeting Street, P.O. Box 1119, 29402.
Telephone: 843-722-7606.
Facsimile: 843-724-8016.

MEMBER OF FIRM

Edward G. Kluiters

ASSOCIATE

Shiryl R. Ballard

Counsel for: South Carolina Jobs-Economic Development Authority; South Carolina Public Service Authority; Richland County; Town of Lexington; Town of Winnsboro; The State of South Carolina; Business Development Corp. of South Carolina; Santee Cooper Electric Cooperative; Cooper River Park and Playground Commission; John Deere Industrial Development, Inc.; School District of Richland County.

For Complete List of Firm Personnel, See General Section

For full biographical listings, see the Martindale-Hubbell Law Directory

NEXSEN PRUET JACOBS & POLLARD, LLP (AV)

1441 Main Street, 15th Floor, P.O. Drawer 2426, 29202
Telephone: 803-771-8900
Facsimile: 803-253-8277
Email: NPJP@NPJP.COM *URL:* HTTP://WWW.NPJP.COM
Charleston, South Carolina Office: 200 Meeting Street, Suite 301. P.O. Box 486.
Telephone: 803-577-9440.
Facsimile: 803-720-1777.
Greenville, South Carolina Office: 201 West McBee Avenue, Fourth Floor, P.O. Box 10648.
Telephone: 864-370-2211.
Facsimile: 864-282-1177.
Myrtle Beach, South Carolina Office: 2411 Oak Street, Suite 105.
Telephone: 843-445-9688.
Facsimile: 843-445-9949.
Charlotte, North Carolina Office: 212 South Tryon Street, Suite 1700.
Telephone: 704-339-0304.
Facsimile: 704-338-5377.

MEMBERS OF FIRM

Patrick F. Brown (Resident, Charlotte, NC Office)
David W. Gossett (Resident, Greenville, SC Office)
Alan M. Lipsitz
April C. Lucas

For Complete List of Firm Personnel, See General Section

For full biographical listings, see the Martindale-Hubbell Law Directory

SINKLER & BOYD, P.A. (AV)

Suite 1200 The Palmetto Center, 1426 Main Street, P.O. Box 11889, 29211-1889
Telephone: 803-779-3080
FAX: 803-765-1243
Email: firm@sinklerboyd.com *URL:* http://www.sinklerboyd.com
Charleston, South Carolina Office: 160 East Bay Street, P.O. Box 340.
Telephone: 843-722-3366.
FAX: 843-722-2266.
Greenville, South Carolina Office: 15 South Main Street, Insignia Financial Center on Main, Suite 500, P.O. Box 275.
Telephone: 864-467-1100.
FAX: 864-467-1521.

(See Next Column)

SINKLER & BOYD P.A., *Columbia—Continued*

George S. King, Jr.
Thomas A. Hutcheson (Resident, Charleston Office)
Margaret Christian Pope
Charlton deSaussure, Jr. (Resident, Charleston Office)
F. Mitchell Johnson, Jr. (Resident, Charleston Office)
Robert S. Galloway, III (Resident, Greenville Office)
Steve A. Matthews
Theodore B. DuBose
John K. Van Duys

OF COUNSEL

Martin C. McWilliams, Jr.

Counsel For: South Carolina State Housing Finance and Development Authority; City of Charleston, S.C.; Clemson University; Western Carolina Regional Sewer Authority.

For Complete List of Firm Personnel, See General Section

For full biographical listings, see the Martindale-Hubbell Law Directory

*GREENVILLE,** Greenville Co.

HAYNSWORTH, MARION, MCKAY & GUÉRARD, L.L.P. (AV)

75 Beattie Place, Eleventh Floor, P.O. Box 2048, 29602
Telephone: 864-240-3200
Facsimile: 864-240-3300
Columbia, South Carolina Office: Suite 2400 Affinity Building, 1201 Main Street, P.O. Drawer 7157, 29202
Telephone: 803-765-1818.
Facsimile: 803-765-2399.
Charleston, South Carolina Office: 134 Meeting Street, P.O. Box 1119, 29402.
Telephone: 843-722-7606.
Facsimile: 843-724-8016.

MEMBERS OF FIRM

J. Wesley Crum III
Kathleen Crum McKinney
Frank T. Davis, III

ASSOCIATE

E. Tyler Smith

Counsel for: Greenville County; City of Greenville; City of Greer; Oconee County; Greenville Memorial Auditorium District.

For Complete List of Firm Personnel, See General Section

For full biographical listings, see the Martindale-Hubbell Law Directory

SINKLER & BOYD, P.A. (AV)

15 South Main Street, Insignia Financial Center on Main, Suite 500, P.O. Box 275, 29602-0275
Telephone: 864-467-1100
FAX: 864-467-1521
Email: firm@sinklerboyd.com *URL:* http://www.sinklerboyd.com
Columbia, South Carolina Office: Suite 1200 The Palmetto Center, 1426 Main Street, P.O. Box 11889.
Telephone: 803-779-3080.
FAX: 803-765-1243.
Charleston, South Carolina Office: 160 East Bay Street, P.O. Box 340.
Telephone: 843-722-3366.
FAX: 843-722-2266.

Robert S. Galloway, III
George S. King, Jr. (Resident, Columbia Office)
Thomas A. Hutcheson (Resident, Charleston Office)
Margaret Christian Pope (Resident, Columbia Office)
Charlton deSaussure, Jr. (Resident, Charleston Office)
F. Mitchell Johnson, Jr. (Resident, Charleston Office)
Steve A. Matthews (Resident, Columbia Office)
Theodore B. DuBose (Resident, Columbia Office)
John K. Van Duys (Resident, Columbia Office)

OF COUNSEL

Martin C. McWilliams, Jr. (Resident, Columbia Office)

Attorneys for: Wachovia Bank, N.A.; Westvaco Corp.; The City of Charleston, S.C.; The South Carolina State Housing Finance and Development Authority.

For full biographical listings, see the Martindale-Hubbell Law Directory

TENNESSEE

KINGSPORT, Sullivan Co.

HUNTER, SMITH & DAVIS, LLP (AV)

1212 North Eastman Road, P.O. Box 3740, 37664
Telephone: 423-378-8800
Telecopier: 423-378-8801
Email: info@hsdlaw.com *URL:* http://www.hsdlaw.com
Johnson City, Tennessee Office: Suite 500 First American Center, 208 Sunset Drive, 37604.
Telephone: 423-283-6300.
Telecopier: 423-283-6301.

MEMBERS OF FIRM

T. Arthur Scott, Jr.
William C. Argabrite
Cynthia S. Kessler

Representative Clients: The Industrial Development Board of the City of Kingsport, Tennessee; The Industrial Development Board of the City of Bristol, Tennessee; The Industrial Development Board of the County of Sullivan, Tennessee; The Industrial Development Board of Washington County, Tennessee; The Health and Educational Facilities Board of Sullivan County, Tennessee; The Health and Educational Facilities Board of the City of Bristol, Tennessee; The Industrial Development Board of Johnson City, Tennessee; The Industrial Development Authority of the City of Bristol, Virginia; Tri-Cities Regional Airport Tennessee-Virginia.

For Complete List of Firm Personnel, See General Section

For full biographical listings, see the Martindale-Hubbell Law Directory

*MEMPHIS,** Shelby Co.

ARMSTRONG ALLEN PREWITT GENTRY JOHNSTON & HOLMES, PLLC (AV)

Brinkley Plaza, Suite 700, 80 Monroe Avenue, 38103-2467
Telephone: 901-523-8211
Facsimile: 901-524-4936
Little Rock, Arkansas Office: Suite 100, 100 Morgan Keegan Drive, 72202.
Telephone: 501-280-0100.
Facsimile: 501-280-0166.
Jackson, Mississippi Office: 2525 Lakeward Drive, Suite 200, 39216.
Telephone: 601-713-1192.
Facsimile: 601-713-2049.
Jackson, Tennessee Office: 464 North Parkway, Suite A, 38305.
Telephone: 901-660-2332.
Facsimile: 901-664-1109.

MEMBERS OF FIRM

Elmore Holmes, III
B. Douglas Earthman
James B. McLaren, Jr.

For Complete List of Firm Personnel, See General Section

For full biographical listings, see the Martindale-Hubbell Law Directory

BAKER, DONELSON, BEARMAN & CALDWELL (AV)

20th Floor, First Tennessee Building, 165 Madison, 38103
Telephone: 901-526-2000
Telecopier: 901-577-2303
Email: info@bdbc.com *URL:* http://www.bakerdonelson.com
Nashville, Tennessee Office: 1700 Nashville City Center, 511 Union Street, 37219.
Telephone: 615-726-5600.
Telecopier: 615-726-0464.
Chattanooga, Tennessee Office: 1800 Republic Centre, 633 Chestnut Street, 37450-1800.
Telephone: 423-756-2010.
Telecopier: 423-756-3447.
Knoxville, Tennessee Office: 2200 Riverview Tower, 900 South Gay Street, 37901.
Telephone: 423-549-7000.
Telecopier: 423-525-8569.
Johnson City, Tennessee Office: SunTrust Bank Building, 207 Mockingbird Lane, P.O. Box 3038, 37602.
Telephone: 423-928-0181.
Telecopier: 423-928-5694; 423-928-3654; Kingsport: 423-246-6191.
Huntsville, Tennessee Office: 3 Courthouse Square, 37756.
Telephone: 423-663-2321.
Telecopier: 423-663-2111.
Washington, D.C. Office: Market Square, 801 Pennsylvania Avenue, N.W., 20004.
Telephone: 202-508-3400.
Telecopier: 202-508-3402.
Jackson, Mississippi Office: Suite 500, 700 North State Street, 39202.
Telephone: 601-351-2400.
Telecopier: 601-351-2424.

MANAGING PARTNER

Robert Mark Glover

(See Next Column)

BAKER, DONELSON, BEARMAN & CALDWELL—*Continued*

SHAREHOLDERS

Lewis R. Donelson, III
Roy Keathley
David G. Williams
Leo Bearman, Jr.
Maurice Wexler
Frank L. Watson, Jr.
Robert Walker
Boyd L. Rhodes, Jr.
W. Michael Richards
John C. Speer
Charles T. Tuggle, Jr.
Larry E. Killebrew
Jerry Stauffer
Robert C. Liddon
William H.D. Fones, Jr.
William P. Kenworthy
Allan J. Wade
Gregory G. Fletcher
Charles C. Harrell
Stephen D. Goodwin
George T. Lewis, III
Ben C. Adams, Jr.
Eugene J. Podesta, Jr.
Sam B. Blair, Jr.
Carla Peacher-Ryan
Mary Aronov
Jill M. Steinberg
Matthew S. Heiter
Michael C. Patton
Janis Wild Kesser
Stephen William Ragland
Monique A. Nassar
Bradley E. Trammell
M. Clay Bethell
Desiree M. Franklin
R. Alan Pritchard, Jr.
Peter H. Kesser

OF COUNSEL

Frierson M. Graves, Jr.
Donald A. Malmo
Lynn Ackerman Landau
Paul E. Risner (Not admitted in TN)

ASSOCIATES

Paul R. O'Rourke
Anne B. Mathes
Elizabeth Einstman Chance
Frank L. Watson, III
W. Douglas Sweet
Wm. Scott Young
Mary Ann Jackson
Angela R. Merideth
Jackie G. Prester
David L. Bearman
Clarissa M. Cissell
Robert C. McConkey, III
Jennifer R. Keown
Brett T. Parks
Cedric C.Y. Tan
Lang Wiseman
Diane Schratz Holitik
D. Benjamin Bullen
Shannon M. Hernandez
Sylvia Monique Reed
Christopher G. Boling
Louise P. Gaerig
Lori Hackleman Patterson
Lea Hall Speed

For full biographical listings, see the Martindale-Hubbell Law Directory

WARING COX, PLC (AV)

Morgan Keegan Tower, 50 North Front Street, Suite 1300, 38103-1190
Telephone: 901-543-8000
Telecopy: 901-543-8030
Email: Desk@waringcox.com

Robert L. Cox
Jerald H. Sklar

For Complete List of Firm Personnel, See General Section

For full biographical listings, see the Martindale-Hubbell Law Directory

*NASHVILLE,** Davidson Co.

BASS, BERRY & SIMS PLC (AV)

2700 First American Center, 37238-2700
Telephone: 615-742-6200
Telecopy: 615-742-6293
URL: http://www.bassberry.com
Knoxville, Tennessee Office: 1700 Riverview Tower, 900 S. Gay Street, 37902 and P.O. Box 1509, 37901-1509.
Telephone: 423-521-6200.
Telecopy: 423-521-6234.
Memphis, Tennessee Office: 119 S. Main Street, Suite 500, 38103.
Telephone: 901-312-9100.
Fax: 901-312-9101.

MEMBERS OF FIRM

Charles K. Wray
Keith B. Simmons
George H. Masterson
G. Mark Mamantov (Resident, Knoxville, Tennessee Office)
Karen Scott Neal

ASSOCIATE

Jeffrey A. Oldham

Representative Clients: Blount County; City of Jackson; City of Knoxville; Knoxville Utilities Board; Madison County; Metropolitan Government of Nashville and Davidson County; Public Building Authority of Sevier County; Rutherford County; Washington County; Wiliiamson County.

For full biographical listings, see the Martindale-Hubbell Law Directory

TEXAS

*AUSTIN,** Travis Co.

FISHER & NEWSOM, P.C. (AV)

111 Congress Avenue, Suite 820, 78701-4043
Telephone: 512-477-4121
Fax: 512-477-2860
Email: fishnew@swbell.net *URL:* http://www.lawyers.com/fisher&newsom
Irving, Texas Office: 4201 Wingren, Suite 106.
Telephone: 972-281-5820.
Fax: 972-650-1057.

Rick P. Fisher
Bernard D. (Skip) Newsom, Jr.

Leroy Grawunder, Jr. (Resident, Irving, Texas Office)

For full biographical listings, see the Martindale-Hubbell Law Directory

*DALLAS,** Dallas Co.

JONES, DAY, REAVIS & POGUE (AV)

2727 North Harwood Street, 75201-1515
Telephone: 214-220-3939
Telecopier: 214-969-5100
Email: counsel@jonesday.com *URL:* http://www.jonesday.com
In Atlanta, Georgia: 3500 SunTrust Plaza, 303 Peachtree Street.
Telephone: 404-521-3939.
Telecopier: 404-581-8330.
In Brussels, Belgium: Avenue Louise 480, 7th Floor, B-1050 Brussels.
Telephone: 32-2-645-14-11.
Telecopier: 32-2-645-14-45.
In Chicago, Illinois: 77 West Wacker.
Telephone: 312-782-3939.
Telecopier: 312-782-8585.
In Cleveland, Ohio: North Point, 901 Lakeside Avenue.
Telephone: 216-586-3939.
Telecopier: 216-579-0212.
In Columbus, Ohio: 1900 Huntington Center.
Telephone: 614-469-3939.
Telecopier: 614-461-4198.
In Frankfurt, Germany: Hochhaus am Park, Grüneburgweg 102, 60323 Frankfurt am Main.
Telephone: 49-69-9726-3939.
Telecopier: 49-69-9726-3993.
In Geneva, Switzerland: 20, rue de Candolle.
Telephone: 41-22-320-2339.
Telecopier: 41-22-320-1232.
In Hong Kong: 29th Floor, Entertainment Building, 30 Queen's Road Central.
Telephone: 852-2526-6895.
Telecopier: 852-2868-5871.
In Irvine, California: 5 Park Plaza, Suite 1100.
Telephone: 949-851-3939.
Telecopier: 949-553-7539.
In London, England: Bucklersbury House, 3 Queen Victoria Street.
Telephone: 44-20-7236-3939.
Telecopier: 44-20-7236-1113.
In Los Angeles, California: 555 West Fifth Street, Suite 4600.
Telephone: 213-489-3939.
Telecopier: 213-243-2539.
In New York, New York: 599 Lexington Avenue.
Telephone: 212-326-3939.
Telecopier: 212-755-7306.
In Paris, France: 120, rue du Faubourg Saint-Honoré.
Telephone: 33-1-56-59-39-39.
Telecopier: 33-1-56-59-39-38
In Pittsburgh, Pennsylvania: 500 Grant Street, 31st Floor.
Telephone: 412-391-3939.
Telecopier: 412-394-7959.
Riyadh, Saudi Arabia: The International Law Firm (In Association with Jones, Day, Reavis & Pogue), Sulaymaniyah, Prince Mishari IBN, Addulaziz Street, P.O. Box 22166.
Telephone: (966-1) 462-8866.
Telecopier: (966-1) 462-9001.
In Shanghai, China: 2805 Kerry Centre, 1515 Nanjing Road West.
Telephone: 86-21-5298-6568.
Telecopier: 86-21-5298-6569.
In Sydney, Australia: Governor Phillip Tower, Level 38, 1 Farrer Place.
Telephone: 61-2-9210-6921.
Telecopier: 61-2-9210-6926.
In Taipei, Taiwan: 8th Floor, 2 Tun Hwa South Road, Section 2.
Telephone: (886-2) 2704-6808.
Telecopier: (886-2) 2704-6791.
In Tokyo, Japan: Toranomon 45 Mori Building, 3rd Floor, 1-5, Toranomon, 5-Chome, Minato-ku, Tokyo 105, Japan.
Telephone: 81-3-3433-3939.
Telecopier: 81-3-5401-2725.
In Washington, D.C.: 51 Louisiana Avenue, N.W.
Telephone: 202-879-3939.
Telecopier: 202-626-1700.

(See Next Column)

WEST VIRGINIA

*CHARLESTON,** Kanawha Co.

GOODWIN & GOODWIN (AV)

1500 One Valley Square, 25301
Telephone: 304-346-7000
Fax: 304-344-9692
Email: g&glaw@goodwin.goodwin.com *URL:* http://www.goodwingoodwin.com
Ripley, West Virginia Office: 500 Church Street, P.O. Box 349.
Telephone: 304-372-2651.
Parkersburg, West Virginia Office: 201 Third Street, Town Square.
Telephone: 304-485-2345.
Fax: 304-485-3459.

MEMBERS OF FIRM

Thomas R. Goodwin
Steven F. White
Michael I. Spiker
Leonard S. Coleman
Susan C. Wittemeier

Representative Clients: Pennzoil Co.; CSX Corp.; The Eureka Pipe Line Company.

For Complete List of Firm Personnel, See General Section

For full biographical listings, see the Martindale-Hubbell Law Directory

JACKSON & KELLY (AV)

1600 Laidley Tower, P.O. Box 553, 25322
Telephone: 304-340-1000
Fax: 304-340-1130
Email: info@jacksonkelly.com *URL:* http://www.jacksonkelly.com
Martinsburg, West Virginia Office: 300 Foxcroft Avenue, P.O. Box 1068.
Telephone: 304-263-8800.
Fax: 304-263-7110.
Morgantown, West Virginia Office: 6000 Hampton Center, P.O. Box 619.
Telephone: 304-599-3000.
Fax: 304-285-2040.
New Martinsville, West Virginia Office: 256 Russell Avenue, P.O. Box 68.
Telephone: 304-455-1751.
Fax: 304-455-6314.
Parkersburg, West Virginia Office: 412 Market Street, Suite 202, P.O. Box 1144.
Telephone: 304-424-3490.
Fax: 304-424-3499.
Fairmont, West Virginia Office: 1000 Technology Drive, Suite 1310.
Telephone: 304-368-2000.
Fax: 304-368-2020.
Lexington, Kentucky Office: 175 East Main Street, Suite 500, P.O. Box 2150.
Telephone: 606-255-9500.
Fax: 606-281-6478.
Washington, D. C. Office: 2401 Pennsylvania Avenue, N.W., Suite 400.
Telephone: 202-973-0200.
Fax: 202-973-0232.
Denver, Colorado Office: Suite 2710, 1660 Lincoln Street.
Telephone: 303-390-0003.
Fax: 303-390-0040.
Wheeling, West Virginia Office: 1144 Market Street.
Telephone: 304-233-4000.
Fax: 304-233-4077.

MEMBERS OF FIRM

James Knight Brown
Taunja Willis Miller
Lee O. Hill
Samme L. Gee

Representative Clients: West Virginia Water Development Authority; City of Charleston; West Virginia Regional Jail & Correctional Facility Authority; West Virginia University; Charleston Area Medical Center; Davis Memorial Hospital; One Valley Bank, N.A.

For Complete List of Firm Personnel, See General Section

For full biographical listings, see the Martindale-Hubbell Law Directory

WISCONSIN

*MADISON,** Dane Co.

QUARLES & BRADY LLP (AV)

Firstar Plaza, One South Pinckney Street, P.O. Box 2113, 53701-2113
Telephone: 608-251-5000
Fax: 608-251-9166
URL: http://www.quarles.com
Milwaukee, Wisconsin Office: 411 East Wisconsin Avenue, 53202-4497.
Telephone: 414-277-5000.
Fax: 414-271-3552.
West Palm Beach, Florida Office: 222 Lakeview Avenue, 4th Floor, 33401.
Telephone: 561-653-5000.
Fax: 561-653-5333.

(See Next Column)

Naples, Florida Office: Barnett Center, 4501 Tamiami Trail North, Suite 300, 34103-3060.
Telephone: 941-262-5959.
Fax: 941-434-4999.
Phoenix, Arizona Office: One Camelback Building, One East Camelback Road, Suite 400, 85012-1649.
Telephone: 602-230-5500.
Fax: 602-230-5598.
Chicago, Illinois Office: Quarles & Brady LLC, Citicorp Center, 500 West Madison Street, Suite 3700.
Telephone: 312-715-5000.
Fax: 312-715-5155.

PARTNERS

John S. Holbrook, Jr.
John T. Whiting
Jennifer V. Powers

For Complete List of Firm Personnel, See General Section

For full biographical listings, see the Martindale-Hubbell Law Directory

*MILWAUKEE,** Milwaukee Co.

DAVIS & KUELTHAU, S.C. (AV)

111 East Kilbourn Avenue, Suite 1400, 53202-6613
Telephone: 414-276-0200
Facsimile: 414-276-9369
Cable Address: "Shiplaw"
Email: info@daviskuelthau.com *URL:* http://www.daviskuelthau.com
Madison, Wisconsin Office: Ten East Doty Street, Suite 600, P.O. Box 1068, 53703.
Telephone: 608-280-8235.
Fax: 608-280-8231.
Sheboygan, Wisconsin Office: 605 North Eighth, Suite 610, P.O. Box 1287.
Telephone: 920-451-1461.
Fax: 920-451-1465.
Green Bay, Wisconsin Office: 414 East Walnut Street, Suite 240.
Telephone: 920-435-9378.
Fax: 920-435-9391.

John E. Rothschild (Resident at Madison Office)

For full biographical listings, see the Martindale-Hubbell Law Directory

MICHAEL BEST & FRIEDRICH LLP (AV)

100 East Wisconsin Avenue, 53202-4108
Telephone: 414-271-6560
Telecopier: 414-277-0656
Cable Address: "Mibef"
Email: info@mbf-law.com *URL:* http://www.mbf-law.com
Madison, Wisconsin Office: One South Pinckney Street, Firstar Plaza, P.O. Box 1806, 53701-1806.
Telephone: 608-257-3501.
Telecopier: 283-2275.
Manitowoc, Wisconsin Office: 1000 Maritime Drive, 54220.
Telephone: 920-686-2800.
Fax: 920-686-2810.
Chicago, Illinois Office: Michael Best & Friedrich LLC, 77 West Wacker Drive, Suite 4300, 60601-1635.
Telephone: 312-845-5800.
Telecopier: 312-845-5828.

PARTNERS

Frank J. Pelisek
Peggy E. Brever

For Complete List of Firm Personnel, See General Section

For full biographical listings, see the Martindale-Hubbell Law Directory

QUARLES & BRADY LLP (AV)

411 East Wisconsin Avenue, 53202-4497
Telephone: 414-277-5000
Fax: 414-271-3552
URL: http://www.quarles.com
Madison, Wisconsin Office: Firstar Plaza, One South Pinckney Street, P.O. Box 2113, 53701-2113.
Telephone: 608-251-5000.
Fax: 608-251-9166.
West Palm Beach, Florida Office: 222 Lakeview Avenue, 4th Floor, 33401.
Telephone: 561-653-5000.
Fax: 561-653-5333.
Naples, Florida Office: Barnett Center, 4501 Tamiami Trail North, Suite 300, 34103-3060.
Telephone: 941-262-5959.
Fax: 941-434-4999.
Phoenix, Arizona Office: One Camelback Building, One East Camelback Road, Suite 400, 85012-1649.
Telephone: 602-230-5500.
Fax: 602-230-5598.
Chicago, Illinois Office: Quarles & Brady LLC, Citicorp Center, 500 West Madison Street, Suite 3700.
Telephone: 312-715-5000.
Fax: 312-715-5155.

(See Next Column)

QUARLES & BRADY LLP—*Continued*

MEMBERS OF FIRM

(ALPHABETICALLY BY YEAR OF ADMISSION TO BAR)

John S. Holbrook, Jr. (Resident, Madison Office)
Stephen E. Richman
Michael L. Roshar
John T. Whiting (Resident, Madison Office)
Ann M. Murphy
Julianna Ebert
Brian G. Lanser
Rebecca A. Speckhard

OF COUNSEL

Laurence C. Hammond, Jr.

For Complete List of Firm Personnel, See General Section

For full biographical listings, see the Martindale-Hubbell Law Directory

PUERTO RICO

SAN JUAN, San Juan Dist.

FIDDLER GONZÁLEZ & RODRÍGUEZ, LLP

254 Muñoz Rivera Avenue (Hato Rey), P.O. Box 363507, 00936-3507
Telephone: 787-753-3113
Telecopier: 787-759-3123
Email: fiddler@fgrlaw.com *URL:* http://www.fgrlaw.com

MEMBERS OF FIRM

Julio L. Aguirre
José Julián Alvarez-Maldonado

Representative Clients: Chase Securities; Shearson, Lehman, Hutton; Banco Santander; Government Development Bank for Puerto Rico.

For Complete List of Firm Personnel, See General Section

For full biographical listings, see the Martindale-Hubbell Law Directory

GOLDMAN ANTONETTI & CÓRDOVA

American International Plaza Fourteenth & Fifteenth Floors, 250 Muñoz Rivera Avenue (Hato Rey), P.O. Box 70364, 00936-0364
Telephone: 787-759-8000
Telecopiers: 787-767-9333 (Main)
787-767-9177 (Litigation Department)
787-767-8660 (Labor & Corporate Law Departments)
787-767-9325 (Tax & Environmental Law Departments)
URL: http://www.gaclaw.com

MEMBERS OF FIRM

Jorge Souss
Pedro Morell Losada
Thelma Rivera-Miranda
Georgiana S. Colón

SPECIAL COUNSEL

Jaime Morgan-Stubbe

ASSOCIATES

María Patricia Lake
Vanessa Bayonet-Tartak
Maura Santiago-Ducos

Representative Clients: Banque Paribas; Scotiabank de Puerto Rico.

For Complete List of Firm Personnel, See General Section

For full biographical listings, see the Martindale-Hubbell Law Directory

MARTÍNEZ ODELL & CALABRIA

Banco Popular Center, 209 Muñoz Rivera Avenue, Suite 1600 (Hato Rey), P.O. Box 190998, 00919-0998
Telephone: 787-753-8914
Facsimile: 787-753-8402; 787-759-9075; 787-764-5664
Email: postmaster@mocpr.com

MEMBERS OF FIRM

Juan Ramón Cancio-Ortiz
Carlos P. Santiago-Sarkis

ASSOCIATES

Jorge L. Covas-Mendoza
Gustavo J. Umpierre-Ponton
Brigitte S. Krumhansl
Mario Loyola

Representative Clients: Banco Popular de Puerto Rico; Daewoo Motor Corporation; Eckerd Corporation; Empresas Fonalledas; Hilton International; L'Aire Liquide, S.A.; Loctile Corporation; Lucent Technologies; Lutron Electronics Co., Inc.; Waste Management, Inc.

For Complete List of Firm Personnel, See General Section

For full biographical listings, see the Martindale-Hubbell Law Directory

CANADA NOVA SCOTIA

*HALIFAX,** Regional Munic. of Halifax

McINNES COOPER (AV)

Barristers, Solicitors & Trade Mark Agents
Summit Place, 1601 Lower Water Street, P.O. Box 730, B3J 2V1
Telephone: 902-425-6500
Fax: 902-425-6350
Email: mcrhfx@mcrlaw.com *URL:* http://www.mcrlaw.com
St. John's, Newfoundland Office: Baine Johnston Centre, 5th Floor, 10 Fort William Place, P.O. Box 5939, A1C 5X4.
Telephone: 709-722-8735.
Telecopier: 709-722-1763. Email: mcrsj@mcrlaw.com.
Moncton, New Brunswick Office: Place Moncton Place, 655 Main Street, P.O. Box 1368, E1C 8T6.
Telephone: 506-857-8970.
Fax: 506-857-4095. Email: mcrmctn@mcrlaw.com.
Charlottetown, Prince Edward Island Office: BDC Place, Suite 620, 119 Kent Street, C1A 1N3.
Telephone: 902-368-8473.
Fax: 902-368-8346. Email: mcrpei@mcrlaw.com.
Fredericton, New Brunswick Office: Suite 600, 570 Queen Street, P.O. Box 610.
Telephone: 506-458-8572.
Fax: 506-458-9903. Email: mcrfton@mcrlaw.com.

PARTNER

Joseph A. F. Macdonald, Q.C.

For Complete List of Firm Personnel, See General Section

For full biographical listings, see the Martindale-Hubbell Law Directory

CANADA QUEBEC

*MONTREAL,** Montreal Dist.

McMASTER GERVAIS (AV)

A General Partnership
1000 de La Gauchetière Street West, Suite 900, H3B 5H4
Telephone: 514-879-1212
Fax: 514-954-1905
Email: info@mcmastergervais.com *URL:* http://www.mcmastergervais.com

MEMBERS OF FIRM

Richard W. Shannon
H. John Godber

COUNSEL

Thomas C. Camp, Q.C.

For Complete List of Firm Personnel, See General Section

For full biographical listings, see the Martindale-Hubbell Law Directory

POULIOT, MERCURE (AV)

CIBC Tower, 31st Floor, 1155 René-Lévesque Boulevard, West, H3B 3S6
Telephone: 514-875-5210
Telecopier: 514-875-4308
Email: POUMER@CEDEP.COM
Genève, Suisse Office: 8, Rue de la Rôtisserie, 1204 Geneva, Switzerland.
Telephone: +41 22-28 79 40.
Telecopier: +41 22-21 23 67.

MEMBERS OF FIRM

Georges A. Pouliot, Q.C.
Gilles Brunelle
Luc Gratton
Brian Riordan
Pierre Paquet
Anne-Marie Gauthier
Yvon Brizard
Robert Tessier
Daniel Gagné
Lilia Pouliot
Marco Veilleux
Alain Nadon
Jean H. Gagnon
Richard Fontaine
Normand Royal
Gilles Bertrand
Jean Larivière
Louis-Michel Tremblay
David I. Johnston
Stéphane Hébert
Jacques LeBel, Q.C.
Joel A. Silcoff
Ronald M. Auclair
Philippe Roy
Maxime B. Rhéaume
Serge Desrochers
C. Keenan LaPierre
Alain Bond
Louis Coallier
Nicole Chouinard
Stéphane Teasdale

ASSOCIATES

Micheline Perrault
Caroline Lemoine
Béatrice Arronis
Yvan Nantel
Brent J. Muir
Louise Tremblay
Chantal Joubert
Normand D'Amour

(See Next Column)

POULIOT, MERCURE, *Montreal—Continued*

ASSOCIATES (Continued)

Sylvie Boulanger
Vincent Frenette
Robert Cardin
Alexandre Henri
Pascale Cloutier
Eric Couture
Frédéric Chatel
Mary-Lynn Breton
Alexandre Ajami

For full biographical listings, see the Martindale-Hubbell Law Directory

NATURAL RESOURCES LAW

MISSISSIPPI

*ABERDEEN,** Monroe Co.

PATTERSON & PATTERSON (AV)

304 East Jefferson Street, P.O. Box 663, 39730
Telephone: 662-369-2476
Fax: 662-369-9806
Email: JPP@ebicom.net

MEMBERS OF FIRM

Robert D. Patterson
Jan P. Patterson
Peter T. Martin

Local Counsel for: National Bank of Commerce of Mississippi; American Colloid Company; Condea Vista Company; Pruet Production Co.; Arco Oil & Gas Co.; Chemical Corporation; Unimin Corporation; Hughes Eastern Corporation.
Approved Title Attorneys for: First American Title Insurance Co.; Mississippi Valley Title Insurance Co.

For full biographical listings, see the Martindale-Hubbell Law Directory

*CLARKSDALE,** Coahoma Co.

HUNT & ROSS, A PROFESSIONAL ASSOCIATION (AV)

123 Court Street, P.O. Box 1196, 38614
Telephone: 601-627-5251
Telecopier No.: 601-627-5254
Email: huntross@clarksdale.com *URL:* http://www.lawyers.com/h&rlaw

Tom T. Ross (1903-1993)
David R. Hunt
Tom T. Ross, Jr.

Thomas W. Allen
Katherine Blackwell Parker

Representative Client: North Delta Joint Municipal Water Management District, Clarksdale, Mississippi.

For full biographical listings, see the Martindale-Hubbell Law Directory

*CLEVELAND,** Bolivar Co.

GRIFFITH & GRIFFITH (AV)

123 South Court Street, Post Office Drawer 1680, 38732
Telephone: 662-843-6100
Telecopier: 662-843-8153
Email: griffith@tecinfo.com *URL:* http://www.vralitigator.com

MEMBERS OF FIRM

L. Ellis Griffith (1926-1987)
Benjamin E. Griffith
Daniel J. Griffith

Reference: The Cleveland State Bank.

For full biographical listings, see the Martindale-Hubbell Law Directory

*JACKSON,** Hinds Co.

ALSTON & JONES (AV)

A Professional Limited Liability Company
121 North State Street, P.O. Drawer 1532, 39215-1532
Telephone: 601-948-6882
Fax: 601-948-6902
Email: ARVS@Teclink.net

MEMBER OF FIRM

Alex A. Alston, Jr.

Counsel for: Southland Oil Co.; Georgia-Pacific Corp.; Forest Oil Corp.; Conoco, Inc.; Transcontinental Gas Pipeline, Inc.; Chemrich, Inc.; E. I. du Pont de Nemours & Co.; The Dow Chemical Co.; Hunt Energy Corp.; The Travelers Ins. Cos.

For Complete List of Firm Personnel, See General Section

For full biographical listings, see the Martindale-Hubbell Law Directory

COPELAND COOK TAYLOR & BUSH, A PROFESSIONAL ASSOCIATION (AV)

200 Concourse, Suite 200, 1062 Highland Colony Parkway, P.O. Box 2132, 39225-2132
Telephone: 601-856-7200
Facsimile: 601-856-7626
Email: mail@cctb.com *URL:* http://www.cctb.com
Ridgeland, Mississippi Office: Post Office Box 6020, 39158.
Telephone: 601-856-7200.
Facsimile: 601-856-7626.

(See Next Column)

Charles G. Copeland
Thomas A. Cook
Glenn Gates Taylor
C. Glen Bush
Thomas C. Gerity
James T. Knight
James R. Moore, Jr.
J. Tucker Mitchell
Robert P. Thompson
Thomas R. Hudson
R. Nash Neyland
Michael W. Baxter
C. Ted Sanderson, Jr.
Monte L. Barton, Jr.
W. Shan Thompson
C. Dale Shearer
Robert C. Richardson
Lee Howell, III
John M. Breland
Jefferson P.W. Skelton
Patricia H. Cottingham
Samuel S. Goza
Amanda L. Baham
Samuel O. Morris, IV
Michelle C. Partridge
John E. Gough, Jr.
Victor Donald Hunt
Donald J. Blackwood, Jr.
Rhonda Lea McCullough

OF COUNSEL

James P. Knight, Jr.
Robert L. Goza

For full biographical listings, see the Martindale-Hubbell Law Directory

RUSSELL P. GRANT, JR. (AV)

1818 Aztec Drive, 39211-6503
Telephone: 601-362-4222
FAX: 601-366-6381
Email: grantjr@unidial.com

For full biographical listings, see the Martindale-Hubbell Law Directory

WATKINS & EAGER (AV)

A Professional Limited Liability Company
Suite 300 The Emporium Building, 400 East Capitol Street, P.O. Box 650, 39205
Telephone: 601-948-6470
Facsimile: 601-354-3623

MEMBERS OF FIRM

William F. Goodman, Jr.
Thomas R. Crews
P. Nicholas Harkins, III
John G. Corlew
Paul H. Stephenson, III

Representative Clients: Ashland Inc.; Blossman Gas, Inc.; Chevron U.S.A. Inc.; Chesley Pruet Drillng Co.; Jetta Production Co., Inc.; International Paper Co.; Plantation Pipeline Co.; Shell Oil Co.; Texaco Inc.; Union Oil Company of California.

For Complete List of Firm Personnel, See General Section

For full biographical listings, see the Martindale-Hubbell Law Directory

MONTANA

*BILLINGS,** Yellowstone Co.

CROWLEY, HAUGHEY, HANSON, TOOLE & DIETRICH, P.L.L.P. (AV)

500 Transwestern II, 490 North 31st Street, P.O. Box 2529, 59103
Telephone: 406-252-3441
Fax: 406-259-4159
Email: crowley@crowleylaw.com
Helena, Montana Office: IBM Building, 100 North Park Avenue, Suite 300, 59601.
Telephone: 406-449-4165.
Fax: 406-449-5149.
Kalispell, Montana Office: 431 1st Avenue West, 59901.
Telephone: 406-752-6644.
Fax: 406-752-5108.
Williston, North Dakota Office: 113 East Broadway, 58801.
Telephone: 701-572-2200.
Fax: 701-572-7072.

OF COUNSEL

Bruce R. Toole
Louis R. Moore

MEMBERS OF FIRM

Arthur F. Lamey, Jr.
Kemp J. Wilson
Steven P. Ruffatto
Carolyn S. Ostby
Christopher Mangen, Jr.
Michael E. Webster
Janice L. Rehberg
Michael S. Lahr (Resident, Helena, Montana Office)

Representative Clients: Noranda Minerals Corp.; Chevron U.S.A., Inc.; Kennecott Corporation; Conoco, Inc.; Pegasus Gold Corp.; Norfolk Energy, Inc.; Sinclair Oil Corp.; Peabody Coal Co.; Decker Coal Co.; Montana Power Company.

For Complete List of Firm Personnel, See General Section

For full biographical listings, see the Martindale-Hubbell Law Directory

*HELENA,** Lewis and Clark Co.

BROWNING, KALECZYC, BERRY & HOVEN, P.C. (AV)

139 North Last Chance Gulch, P.O. Box 1697, 59624
Telephone: 406-443-6820
Telefax: 406-443-6882
Email: BKBH@BKBH.COM *URL:* http://www.BKBH.com

R. Stephen Browning
Catherine A. Laughner
Leo Berry
Mark D. Etchart

Steven T. Wade
Mark R. Taylor

Representative Clients: The Burlington Northern and Santa Fe Railway Co.; Columbia Falls Aluminum Company; Cyprus AMAX Minerals; Burlington Resources Oil and Gas Company; R-Y Timber Company.

For full biographical listings, see the Martindale-Hubbell Law Directory

NEVADA

*LAS VEGAS,** Clark Co.

JOLLEY, URGA, WIRTH & WOODBURY (AV)

3800 Howard Hughes Parkway Suite 1600, 89109
Telephone: 702-699-7500
Facsimile: 702-699-7555
URL: http://www.juww.com
Boulder City, Nevada Office: Suite 105, 1000 Nevada Highway, 89005.
Telephone: 702-293-3674.

MEMBERS OF FIRM

R. Gardner Jolley
Allen D. Emmel

Representative Clients: Wells Fargo Bank and its predecessor, First Interstate Bank of Nevada; Nevada State Bank; Melvin Simon & Associates, Inc.; Nevada Mobilehome Park Owners Association; First Security Bank of Nevada; First Nationwide Bank; Wells Cargo, Inc.; Dean Roofing Co.; Lincoln Property Co.

For Complete List of Firm Personnel, See General Section

For full biographical listings, see the Martindale-Hubbell Law Directory

*RENO,** Washoe Co.

ERWIN THOMPSON & HASCHEFF (AV)

A Partnership including Professional Corporations
Suite 424, One East Liberty Street, P.O. Box 40817, 89501-2123
Telephone: 775-786-9494
Facsimile: 775-786-1180
Email: erwin@renolaw.com *URL:* http://www.renolaw.com

Pierre A. Hascheff
Frank W. Thompson
Thomas P. Erwin

Reference: U.S. Bank (Reno, Nevada, Main Office).

For full biographical listings, see the Martindale-Hubbell Law Directory

HALE LANE PEEK DENNISON HOWARD AND ANDERSON (AV)

100 West Liberty Street, Tenth Floor, P.O. Box 3237, 89505
Telephone: 775-327-3000
Telefax: 775-786-6179
Email: info@halelane.com
Las Vegas, Nevada Office: Nevada Financial Center, 2300 West Sahara Avenue, Eighth Floor, Box 8.
Telephone: 702-222-2500.
Fax: 702-365-6940.
Carson City, Nevada Office: 777 East William Street, Suite 200, P.O. Box 2620.
Telephone: 775-684-6000.
Telefax: 775-684-6001.

MEMBERS OF FIRM

R. Craig Howard
Alex J. Flangas
Roger W. Jeppson

Representative Clients: Caughlin Ranch; Primm South Real Estate Company.

For Complete List of Firm Personnel, See General Section

For full biographical listings, see the Martindale-Hubbell Law Directory

HARRIS, TRIMMER & THOMPSON (AV)

An Association of Attorneys
6121 Lakeside Drive, Suite 260, P.O. Box 70250, 89570-0250
Telephone: 702-825-4300
Fax: 702-825-4829

(See Next Column)

Richard W. Harris
Kathleen S. Trimmer
Richard Kent Thompson

Representative Clients: Cameco Corp.; Magma Copper Co.; Uranerz U.S.A, Inc.; Viceroy Gold Corp.

For full biographical listings, see the Martindale-Hubbell Law Directory

MARSHALL HILL CASSAS & DE LIPKAU (AV)

Suite 300 Holcomb Professional Building, 333 Holcomb Avenue, P.O. Box 2790, 89505-2790
Telephone: 775-323-1601
Telecopier: 775-348-7250
Email: general@MHCL-law.com

MEMBERS OF FIRM

Robert W. Marshall
John P. Fowler
Earl M. Hill
Rew R. Goodenow
Frank Cassas
Michael R. Kealy
Ross E. de Lipkau
A. Stanyan Peck

For full biographical listings, see the Martindale-Hubbell Law Directory

WOODBURN AND WEDGE (AV)

One East First Street, Suite 1600, P.O. Box 2311, 89505
Telephone: 775-688-3000
Telecopier: 775-688-3088
Email: postmaster@woodburnlaw.com *URL:* http://www.woodburnlaw.com
Las Vegas, Nevada Office: Suite 700 Bank of America Plaza, 300 South Fourth Street.
Telephone: 702-387-1000.
Telecopier: 702-387-0024.

MEMBERS OF FIRM

Casey Woodburn Vlautin
W. Chris Wicker
Gordon H. DePaoli
R. Blain Andrus

ASSOCIATE

Dale E. Ferguson

Representative Clients: Atlantic Richfield Co.; Sierra Pacific Power Co.; The Union Pacific Railroad Co.; Western Union Telegraph Co.; Bank of America; Cyprus Minerals Corp.; The Roman Catholic Bishop of Reno, A Corporation Sole; Placer Dome, U.S., Inc.; Amax Gold, Inc.; Glamis Gold, Inc.

For full biographical listings, see the Martindale-Hubbell Law Directory

NEW JERSEY

CHERRY HILL, Camden Co.

TOMAR, SIMONOFF, ADOURIAN, O'BRIEN, KAPLAN, JACOBY & GRAZIANO, A PROFESSIONAL CORPORATION (AV)

20 Brace Road, 08034
Telephone: 609-429-1100
Telecopier: 609-429-8164
Email: TOMAR@TOMARLAW.COM *URL:* http://www.tomarlaw.com
Atlantic City, New Jersey Office: Commerce Building, Suite 220, 1200 Atlantic Avenue.
Telephone: 609-348-5900.
Camden, New Jersey Office: 200 North Fifth Street.
Telephone: 609-338-0553.
Northfield, New Jersey Office: The Executive Plaza, Suite 101, 2111 New Road.
Telephone: 609-485-0800.
Telecopier: 609-484-9388.
Wilmington, Delaware Office: Tomar, Simonoff, Adourian, O'Brien, Kaplan, Jacoby & Graziano, The Mellon Bank Center, Suite 1701, 919 Market Street.
Telephone: 302-655-0500.
Telecopier: 302-428-0963.
Media, Pennsylvania Office: 334 West Front Street.
Telephone: 215-574-0635.

William Tomar
Alan H. Sklarsky
David Jacoby
Joshua M. Spielberg

For full biographical listings, see the Martindale-Hubbell Law Directory

*NEWARK,** Essex Co.

HELLRING LINDEMAN GOLDSTEIN & SIEGAL LLP (AV)

One Gateway Center, 07102-5386
Telephone: 973-621-9020
Fax: 973-621-7406
Englewood, New Jersey Office: 32-40 North Dean Street.
Telephone: 201-871-3060.

(See Next Column)

HELLRING LINDEMAN GOLDSTEIN & SIEGAL LLP—*Continued*

Philip Lindeman, II
Joel D. Siegal
Jonathan L. Goldstein
Margaret Dee Hellring
Richard D. Shapiro
Charles Oransky
Richard B. Honig
Richard K. Coplon
Robert S. Raymar
Ronny Jo Greenwald Siegal
Stephen L. Dreyfuss
John A. Adler
Judah I. Elstein
Bruce S. Etterman
Matthew E. Moloshok
Rachel N. Davidson
David N. Narciso
Ronnie F. Liebowitz
Sheryl E. Koomer

For Complete List of Firm Personnel, See General Section

For full biographical listings, see the Martindale-Hubbell Law Directory

MCCARTER & ENGLISH, LLP (AV)

Four Gateway Center, 100 Mulberry Street, P.O. Box 652, 07101-0652
Telephone: 973-622-4444
Telecopier: 973-624-7070
URL: http://www.mccarter.com
Cherry Hill, New Jersey Office: 1820 Chapel Avenue West, Suite 380.
Telephone: 609-662-8444.
Telecopier: 609-662-6203.
New York, New York Office: Suite 2247, One World Trade Center.
Telephone: 212-466-9018.
Telecopier: 212-432-6568.
Boca Raton, Florida Office: 2255 Glades Road, Suite 319-A.
Telephone: 561-994-6262.
Telecopier: 561-241-0798.
Wilmington, Delaware Office: Mellon Bank Center, 919 Market Street.
Telephone: 302-654-8010.
Telecopier: 302-654-0795.
Philadelphia, Pennsylvania Office: One Commerce Square, 2005 Market Street, Suite 3600.
Telephone: 215-557-7700.
Telecopier: 215-557-6544.

MEMBERS OF FIRM

Alfred L. Ferguson
John A. McKinney, Jr.
Lanny S. Kurzweil
Frank E. Ferruggia
Keith E. Lynott
David C. Apy

COUNSEL

Gary T. Hall
J. Forrest Jones
Paul C. Dritsas

ASSOCIATES

Brenda C. Liss
Vito A. Pinto
J. Wylie Donald
John Carl Mills
Meredith L. Bryant

For Complete List of Firm Personnel, See General Section

For full biographical listings, see the Martindale-Hubbell Law Directory

SILLS CUMMIS RADIN TISCHMAN EPSTEIN & GROSS, A PROFESSIONAL CORPORATION (AV)

One Riverfront Plaza, 07102-5400
Telephone: 973-643-7000
Fax: 973-643-6500
Telex: 820630 Sillsbeck Nwk
Email: sillsmail@sillscummis.com *URL:* http://www.sillscummis.com
Atlantic City, New Jersey Office: 17 Gordon's Alley.
Telephone: 609-344-2800.
New York, N.Y. Office: 712 Fifth Avenue.
Telephone: 212-643-7000.
Washington, D.C. Office: 1800 K Street, N.W.
Telephone: 202-296-4750.

MEMBERS OF FIRM

Philip R. Sellinger
Lori G. Singer
Jeffrey M. Pollock

For Complete List of Firm Personnel, See General Section

For full biographical listings, see the Martindale-Hubbell Law Directory

NEW MEXICO

*ALBUQUERQUE,** Bernalillo Co.

KREHBIEL, BANNERMAN & HORN, P.A. (AV)

6400 Uptown Boulevard, N.E., Suite 310 East, 87110
Telephone: 505-837-1900
Fax: 505-837-1800
Email: kbh@kbh-lawfirm.com *URL:* http://www.kbh-lawfirm.com

Phil Krehbiel
John A. Bannerman
Barry D. Williams

(See Next Column)

Rikki L. Quintana
Carol Lisa Smith
David H. Johnson
Lucinda R. Bovee

OF COUNSEL

Ronald F. Horn

For full biographical listings, see the Martindale-Hubbell Law Directory

MILLER, STRATVERT & TORGERSON, P.A. (AV)

500 Marquette Avenue, N.W., Suite 1100, P.O. Box 25687, 87102
Telephone: 505-842-1950
Facsimile: 505-243-4408
Email: info@mstLAW.com *URL:* http://www.mstLAW.com
Farmington, New Mexico Office: 300 West Arrington, Suite 300, P.O. Box 869.
Telephone: 505-326-4521.
Facsimile: 505-325-5474.
Las Cruces, New Mexico Office: 500 South Main, Suite 800, P.O. Box 1209.
Telephone: 505-523-2481.
Facsimile: 505-526-2215.
Santa Fe, New Mexico Office: 150 Washington Avenue, Suite 300, P.O. Box 1986.
Telephone: 505-989-9614.
Facsimile: 505-989-9857.

Ranne B. Miller
Lyman G. Sandy
Seth V. Bingham (Resident at Farmington Office)
James B. Collins (Resident at Farmington Office)
Marte D. Lightstone
J. Scott Hall (Resident at Santa Fe Office)
Henry Brook Laskey
Michael C. Ross
Katherine N. Blackett

Representative Clients: BP Amoco Corp.; Energen Resources Corp.; Pendragon Energy Partners, Inc.; Pittsburg Midway Coal Mining; Texaco, Inc.; Ultramar Diamond Shamrock.

For Complete List of Firm Personnel, See General Section

For full biographical listings, see the Martindale-Hubbell Law Directory

RODEY, DICKASON, SLOAN, AKIN & ROBB, P.A. (AV)

Albuquerque Plaza, Suite 2200, 201 Third Street, N.W., P.O. Box 1888, 87103-1888
Telephone: 505-765-5900
Fax: 505-768-7395
Email: info@rodey.com *URL:* http://www.rodey.com
Santa Fe, New Mexico Office: Suite 101 Marcy Plaza, 123 East Marcy Street, P.O. Box 1357, 87504-1357.
Telephone: 505-984-0100.
Fax: 505-989-9542.

John P. Salazar
Joseph B. Rochelle
Mary Keleher Castle

OF COUNSEL

John D. Robb

For Complete List of Firm Personnel, See General Section

For full biographical listings, see the Martindale-Hubbell Law Directory

*SANTA FE,** Santa Fe Co.

CARPENTER & NIXON, LLP (AV)

315 Paseo De Peralta, P.O. Box 1837, 87504-1837
Telephone: 505-989-8690
Fax: 505-989-9457
Email: rncoffice@aol.com *URL:* http://www.lawyers.com/carpenter&nixon

MEMBERS OF FIRM

Richard N. Carpenter
Sunny J. Nixon

For full biographical listings, see the Martindale-Hubbell Law Directory

COMEAU, MALDEGEN, TEMPLEMAN & INDALL, L.L.P. (AV)

Coronado Building, 141 East Palace Avenue, P.O. Box 669, 87504-0669
Telephone: 505-982-4611
Telecopier: 505-988-2987
Email: cmtilaw@earthlink.net

MEMBERS OF FIRM

Michael R. Comeau
Larry D. Maldegen
William P. Templeman
Jon J. Indall
Stephen J. Lauer
Paula Ann Cook
Grey Handy
Joseph E. Manges

Michael C. Smith
Christian A. Hatfield

OF COUNSEL

Jeffrey R. Brannen

Representative Clients: Homestake Mining Co.; United Nuclear Corp.; Uranium Producers of America; Kerr-McGee Corp.

For full biographical listings, see the Martindale-Hubbell Law Directory

Santa Fe—Continued

HUFFAKER & CONWAY, A PROFESSIONAL CORPORATION (AV)

155 Grant Avenue, P.O. Box 1868, 87504-1868
Telephone: 505-988-8921
Fax: 505-983-3927
Email: sfstaff@sisna.com
Albuquerque, New Mexico Office: 201 Third Street, N.W., Suite 1910.
Telephone: 505-244-0021.
Facsimile: 505-244-1372.

Gregory D. Huffaker, Jr.
Ann Maloney Conway
Lisa A. Joynes
Seth L. Sparks
Edward C. Bagley

Representative Clients: Chevron Products Co.

For full biographical listings, see the Martindale-Hubbell Law Directory

MONTGOMERY & ANDREWS, PROFESSIONAL ASSOCIATION (AV)

325 Paseo de Peralta, P.O. Box 2307, 87504-2307
Telephone: 505-982-3873
Fax: 505-982-4289
Email: montand@montand.com

Gary Kilpatric
John B. Draper
Nancy M. Anderson King
Sarah Michael Singleton
Galen M. Buller
Edmund H. Kendrick
Louis W. Rose
Andrew S. Montgomery

Representative Clients: Burlington Resources Oil and Gas Co.; Conoco, Inc.; Copar Pumice Co.; C.R. Minerals Co.; El Paso Corp.; Franklin Industries Inc.; Giant Industries Arizona, Inc.; Idaho Timber Co.; LAC Minerals (USA) Inc.; Mobil Exploration and Producing U.S. Inc.; Phelps Dodge Mining Co.; Phillips Petroleum Co.; State of Kansas.

For Complete List of Firm Personnel, See General Section

For full biographical listings, see the Martindale-Hubbell Law Directory

WHITE, KOCH, KELLY & McCARTHY, A PROFESSIONAL ASSOCIATION (AV)

433 Paseo De Peralta, P.O. Box 787, 87504-0787
Telephone: 505-982-4374
ABA/NET: 1154
Fax: 505-982-0350; 984-8631
Email: WKKM@NM.NET

Benjamin J. Phillips
Rebecca A. Dempsey

SPECIAL COUNSEL

Paul L. Bloom

Representative Clients: City of El Paso, Texas; City of Las Vegas, New Mexico; Bluewater Toltec Irrigation District.

For Complete List of Firm Personnel, See General Section

For full biographical listings, see the Martindale-Hubbell Law Directory

NEW YORK

*BINGHAMTON,** Broome Co.

HINMAN, HOWARD & KATTELL, LLP (AV)

700 Security Mutual Building, 80 Exchange Street, P.O. Box 5250, 13902-5250
Telephone: 607-723-5341
Fax: 607-723-6605
Email: jworband@hhk.com *URL:* http://www.hhk.com
Norwich, New York Office: 48 Hale Street, 13815-2039.
Telephone: 607-334-5896.
Fax: 607-336-1628.
Oneonta, New York Office: 12 South Main Street, 13820-2542.
Telephone: 607-432-5331.
Fax: 607-432-2683.
New York, N.Y. Office: 500 5th Avenue, Suite 1725, 10110.
Telephone: 212-840-3017.
Fax: 212-840-2345.

MEMBERS OF FIRM

N. Theodore Sommer
James F. Lee
Katherine A. Fitzgerald
Albert J. Millus, Jr.

Representative Clients: The Chase Manhattan Bank; BSB Bank & Trust Co.; International Business Machines Corp.; Universal Instruments Corp.; Security Mutual Life Insurance Company of New York; Bell Atlantic; Preferred Mutual Insurance Company; New York State Electric & Gas Corp.; Exxon Corp.

For Complete List of Firm Personnel, See General Section

For full biographical listings, see the Martindale-Hubbell Law Directory

NORTH CAROLINA

*CHARLOTTE,** Mecklenburg Co.

WOMBLE CARLYLE SANDRIDGE & RICE (AV)

A Professional Limited Liability Company
3300 One First Union Center, 301 South College Street, 28202-6025
Telephone: 704-331-4900
Fax: 704-331-4955
Email: lawyers@wcsr.com *URL:* http://www.wcsr.com
Winston-Salem, North Carolina Office: 200 West Second Street, P.O. Drawer 84.
Telephone: 336-721-3600.
Fax: 336-721-3660.
Raleigh, North Carolina Office: 2100 First Union Capitol Center, 150 Fayetteville Street Mall, P.O. Box 831.
Telephone: 919-755-2100.
Fax: 919-755-2150.
Research Triangle Park, North Carolina Office: 2505 Meridian Parkway, Suite 300 (Durham), 27713.
Telephone: 919-484-2300.
Fax: 919-484-2340.
Atlanta, Georgia Office: One Atlantic Center, 1201 West Peachtree Street, Suite 3500.
Telephone: 404-872-7000.
Fax: 404-888-7490.
Other Atlanta, Georgia Office: Suite 404, 2296 Henderson Mill Road, N.E.
Telephone: 770-492-9030.
Fax: 770-492-9609.
Washington, D.C. Office: 1120 Nineteenth Street, N.W., Eighth Floor.
Telephone: 202-857-4400.
Fax: 202-467-6910.
Greenville, South Carolina Office: 15 South Main Street, Suite 601, P.O. Box 10208.
Telephone: 864-255-5400.
Fax: 864-255-5440.

RESIDENT MEMBER

Bradford A. DeVore

Representative Clients: Childress Klein Properties, Inc.; Food Lion, Inc.; J.A. Jones Construction Co.; Parkdale Mills, Inc.; Pillowtex; Duke Power Co.; Bowles Hollowell Conner & Co.; ALLTEL Carolina, Inc.; Belk Store Services, Inc.; Philip Holzmann A.G.

For Complete List of Firm Personnel, See General Section

For full biographical listings, see the Martindale-Hubbell Law Directory

*RALEIGH,** Wake Co.

WOMBLE CARLYLE SANDRIDGE & RICE (AV)

A Professional Limited Liability Company
2100 First Union Capitol Center, 150 Fayetteville Street Mall, P.O. Box 831, 27602
Telephone: 919-755-2100
Fax: 919-755-2150
Email: lawyers@wcsr.com *URL:* http://www.wcsr.com
Charlotte, North Carolina Office: 3300 One First Union Center, 301 South College Street.
Telephone: 704-331-4900.
Fax: 704-331-4955.
Winston-Salem, North Carolina Office: 200 West Second Street, P.O. Drawer 84.
Telephone: 336-721-3600.
Fax: 336-721-3660.
Research Triangle Park, North Carolina Office: 2505 Meridian Parkway, Suite 300 (Durham), 27713.
Telephone: 919-484-2300.
Fax: 919-484-2340.
Atlanta, Georgia Office: One Atlantic Center, 1201 West Peachtree Street, Suite 3500.
Telephone: 404-872-7000.
Fax: 404-888-7490.
Other Atlanta, Georgia Office: Suite 404, 2296 Henderson Mill Road, N.E.
Telephone: 770-492-9030.
Fax: 770-492-9609.
Washington, D.C. Office: 1120 Nineteenth Street, N.W., Eighth Floor.
Telephone: 202-857-4400.
Fax: 202-467-6910.
Greenville, South Carolina Office: 15 South Main Street, Suite 601, P.O. Box 10208.
Telephone: 864-255-5400.
Fax: 864-255-5440.

RESIDENT MEMBER

Marilyn R. Forbes

(See Next Column)

WOMBLE CARLYLE SANDRIDGE & RICE—*Continued*

RESIDENT OF COUNSEL

Kurt D. Weaver (Not admitted in NC)

Representative Clients: Aetna Casualty and Surety Co., Inc.; ALSCO/AmeriMark Building Products, Inc.; Aoki Corporation America, Inc.; Hackney Brothers, Inc.; Lawyers Mutual Liability Insurance Company of North Carolina; Meredith College; Regency Park Corp.; Wachovia Bank, N.A.

For Complete List of Firm Personnel, See General Section

For full biographical listings, see the Martindale-Hubbell Law Directory

*WINSTON-SALEM,** Forsyth Co.

WOMBLE CARLYLE SANDRIDGE & RICE (AV)

A Professional Limited Liability Company
200 West Second Street, P.O. Drawer 84, 27102
Telephone: 336-721-3600
Fax: 336-721-3660
Email: lawyers@wcsr.com *URL:* http://www.wcsr.com
Charlotte, North Carolina Office: 3300 One First Union Center, 301 South College Street.
Telephone: 704-331-4900.
Fax: 704-331-4955.
Raleigh, North Carolina Office: 2100 First Union Capitol Center, 150 Fayetteville Street Mall, P.O. Box 831.
Telephone: 919-755-2100.
Fax: 919-755-2150.
Research Triangle Park, North Carolina Office: 2505 Meridian Parkway, Suite 300 (Durham), 27713.
Telephone: 919-484-2300.
Fax: 919-484-2340.
Atlanta, Georgia Office: One Atlantic Center, 1201 West Peachtree Street, Suite 3500.
Telephone: 404-872-7000.
Fax: 404-888-7490.
Other Atlanta, Georgia Office: Suite 404, 2296 Henderson Mill Road, N.E.
Telephone: 770-492-9030.
Fax: 770-492-9609.
Washington, D.C. Office: 1120 Nineteenth Street, N.W., Eighth Floor.
Telephone: 202-857-4400.
Fax: 202-467-6910.
Greenville, South Carolina Office: 15 South Main Street, Suite 601, P.O. Box 10208.
Telephone: 864-255-5400.
Fax: 864-255-5440.

RESIDENT MEMBERS

Jeffrey L. Furr
Ellen M. Gregg
R. Howard Grubbs
Lori Privette Hinnant
Martin L. Holton, III
Keith W. Vaughan
G. Criston Windham

RESIDENT ASSOCIATES

Amy L. Bircher
Brandy K. Gillenwater
Murray C. Greason (Not admitted in NC)
Stanley B. Green
Ursula M. Henninger
Neil D. Kodsi
Christopher A. Kreiner
William E. Latham II
G. Wriston Marshburn, Jr
Stephanie U. Roberts
Patricia G. Scales
Lawrence B. Somers
Theresa M. Sprain
John R. Still
Allison L. Thompson (Not admitted in NC)

MEMBER OF COUNSEL

W. David Edwards

STAFF ATTORNEY

Daniel Patrick Foley (Not admitted in NC)

Representative Clients: Brad Ragan, Inc.; Brenner Companies; Food Lion, Inc.; Hanes Companies, Inc.; North Carolina Baptist Hospitals, Inc.; R.J. Reynolds Tobacco Co.; Thomasville Furniture Industries, Inc.; Wachovia Corp.; Wake Forest University.

For Complete List of Firm Personnel, See General Section

For full biographical listings, see the Martindale-Hubbell Law Directory

NORTH DAKOTA

*BISMARCK,** Burleigh Co.

PEARCE AND DURICK, PLLP (AV)

314 East Thayer Avenue, P.O. Box 400, 58502
Telephone: 701-223-2890
Fax: 701-223-7865
Email: law.office@pearce-durick.com *URL:* http://www.pearce-durick.com

(See Next Column)

MEMBERS OF FIRM

William P. Pearce
Lawrence Bender

Representative Clients: Amoco Oil Co.; Chevron U.S.A., Inc.; Conoco, Inc.; Continental Resources, Inc.; MDU Resources Group, Inc.; Phillips Petroleum Co.; Texaco, Inc.

For Complete List of Firm Personnel, See General Section

For full biographical listings, see the Martindale-Hubbell Law Directory

OHIO

*COLUMBUS,** Franklin Co.

KEGLER, BROWN, HILL & RITTER (AV)

Capitol Square Suite 1800, 65 East State Street, 43215-4294
Telephone: 614-462-5400
Telecopier: 614-464-2634
Cable Address: "Law KBHR"
Telex: 246671
Email: info@kbhr.com *URL:* http://www.kbhr.com
Marion, Ohio Office: 250 Executive Drive, Suite B, P.O. Box 919.
Telephone: 614-387-3501.
Facsimile: 614-387-3630.

Allen L. Handlan
Paul D. Ritter, Jr.
Kevin L. Sykes

Representative Clients: The Benatty Corp.

For Complete List of Firm Personnel, See General Section

For full biographical listings, see the Martindale-Hubbell Law Directory

VORYS, SATER, SEYMOUR AND PEASE LLP (AV)

52 East Gay Street, P.O. Box 1008, 43216-1008
Telephone: 614-464-6400
Telecopier: 614-464-6350
URL: http://www.vssp.com
Washington, D.C. Office: 1828 L Street, N.W., 20036-5109.
Telephone: 202-467-8800.
Telex: 440693.
Telecopier: 202-467-8900.
Cleveland, Ohio Office: 2100 One Cleveland Center, 1375 East Ninth Street, 44114-1724.
Telephone: 216-479-6100.
Telecopier: 216-479-6060.
Cincinnati, Ohio Office: Suite 2100, 221 East Fourth Street, P.O. Box 0236, 45201-0236.
Telephone: 513-723-4000.
Telecopier: 513-723-4056.
Alexandria, Virginia Office: 277 South Washington St., Suite 310, 22314.
Telephone: 703-549-4282.
Telecopier: 703-549-4492.

MEMBERS OF FIRM

Sheldon A. Taft
Joseph D. Lonardo (Resident, Washington, D.C. Office)
W. Jonathan Airey
John K. Keller
William S. Newcomb, Jr.
M. Howard Petricoff
Benita A. Kahn
Robert H. Maynard
Robert J. Styduhar
Elizabeth E. Tulman
Scott M. Doran
Paul J. Coval
Anthony J. Giuliani
Kristin L. Watt

OF COUNSEL

Martyn T. Brodnik
Stephen M. Howard
Theodore A. Boggs
John W. Hoberg

Local Counsel: General Motors Corp.; Viking Resources Corp.; Clinton Gas Systems, Inc.; Access Energy Corporation; The Ohio Manufacturers Association; Honda of America Mfg., Inc.; Stone Container Corporation; Chemical Waste Management; Stanley Steemer International, Inc.; Worthington Industries, Inc.

For Complete List of Firm Personnel, See General Section

For full biographical listings, see the Martindale-Hubbell Law Directory

OKLAHOMA

*OKLAHOMA CITY,** Oklahoma Co.

CONNER & WINTERS, A PROFESSIONAL CORPORATION (AV)

One Leadership Square, 211 North Robinson, Suite 1700, 73102-7101
Telephone: 405-272-5711
Facsimile: 405-232-2695
Email: postmaster@cwlaw.com
Tulsa, Oklahoma Office: 3700 First Place Tower, 15 East 5th Street, 74103-4344.
Telephone: 918-586-5711.
Facsimile: 918-586-8982.
Fayetteville, Arkansas Office: Conner & Winters, P.L.L.C., 100 West Center Street, Suite 200, 72701-6081.
Telephone: 501-582-5711.
Facsimile: 501-587-1426.
Washington, D.C. Office: 1050 Seventeenth Street, N.W., Suite 810, 20036-5503.
Telephone: 202-783-5711.
Facsimile: 202-783-5720.

Irwin H. Steinhorn
Mitchell D. Blackburn

For Complete List of Firm Personnel, See General Section

For full biographical listings, see the Martindale-Hubbell Law Directory

DAY, EDWARDS, FEDERMAN, PROPESTER & CHRISTENSEN, P.C. (AV)

Suite 2900 Oklahoma Tower, 210 Park Avenue, 73102-5605
Telephone: 405-239-2121
Telecopier: 405-236-1012
URL: http://lawlinks.com/attys/ok/defpc.html

Joe E. Edwards
J. Clay Christensen
William B. Federman
Kent A. Gilliland
Ricki Valerie Sonders

Representative Clients: Bobby Joe Cudd Company; Delta Western Drilling Funds; Fluid Technologies; Scientic Drilling International, Inc.; Wild West Control, Inc.; Worldwide Well Control, Inc.

For Complete List of Firm Personnel, See General Section

For full biographical listings, see the Martindale-Hubbell Law Directory

MCAFEE & TAFT, A PROFESSIONAL CORPORATION (AV)

Tenth Floor, Two Leadership Square, 73102
Telephone: 405-235-9621
Facsimile: (405) 235-0439 (405) 232-2404
Email: mcafee@ionet.net *URL:* http://www.mcafee-taft.com

Stewart W. Mark (1915-1993)
Judson S. Woodruff (1925-1997)
Terry R. Barrett
Gary W. Catron
Stanley L. Cunningham
Robert W. Dace
Philip D. Hart
Laurence M. Huffman
Myrna Schack Latham
C. David Stinson
Drew D. Webb
Steven R. Welch

Representative Clients: Bank of Oklahoma, N.A.; Fleming Companies, Inc.; Paine Webber Group, Inc.; Arthur Andersen & Co.; Exxon Corp.; St. Paul Fire & Marine Insurance Co.; Columbia/HCA Healthcare Corp.

For Complete List of Firm Personnel, See General Section

For full biographical listings, see the Martindale-Hubbell Law Directory

MONNET, HAYES, BULLIS, THOMPSON & EDWARDS (AV)

Suite 1719 First National Center West, 120 North Robinson, 73102
Telephone: 405-232-5481
Fax: 405-235-9159
Email: MHBullis@AOL.COM

MEMBERS OF FIRM

John T. Edwards
James M. Peters
James S. Drennan
Sarah H. Stuhr
Gayle Freeman Cook
Robert C. Smith, Jr.
Steven K. McKinney

Representative Clients: Natural Gas Pipeline Company of America; Chevron, U.S.A.; Mid-Con Corp.; Enron Oil & Gas Co.; Oryx Energy Co.; OXY USA, Inc.; Apache Corp.; Cross Timbers Oil Company; Citation Oil and Gas Corporation; H&L Operating Company.

For Complete List of Firm Personnel, See General Section

For full biographical listings, see the Martindale-Hubbell Law Directory

SELF, GIDDENS & LEES, INC. (AV)

2725 Oklahoma Tower, 210 Park Avenue, 73102-5643
Telephone: 405-232-3001
Telecopier: 405-232-5553

(See Next Column)

Thomas J. Blalock
Jared D. Giddens
C. Ray Lees
Shannon T. Self
Bryan J. Wells

Michael D. Meleen
John E. Gatliff II

For full biographical listings, see the Martindale-Hubbell Law Directory

*TULSA,** Tulsa Co.

BOESCHE, MCDERMOTT & ESKRIDGE (AV)

Suite 800 Oneok Plaza, 100 West Fifth Street, 74103
Telephone: 918-583-1777
Fax: 918-592-5809
Email: bme@intellex.com
Muskogee, Oklahoma Office: 1111 West Broadway, P.O. Box 2669, 74402.
Telephone: 918-683-6100.
Fax: 918-683-2303.

MEMBERS OF FIRM

R. Casey Cooper
Bradley K. Beasley
David A. Johnson
Nik Jones
R. Kevin Layton
Sheila M. Powers

ASSOCIATES

Byron E. (Rusty) Brown
Christopher K. Woosley

OF COUNSEL

Clifford K. Cate, Jr. (Resident at Muskogee)
Linda McQuillen Kulp

Representative Clients: Amax Oil & Gas, Inc.; Apache Corp.; Atlantic Richfield; Elf Atochem North America, Inc.; Enogex Corp.; Enron Corp.; Oxy USA, Inc.; Helmerich & Payne, Inc.; Sequa; Unit Corp.

For Complete List of Firm Personnel, See General Section

For full biographical listings, see the Martindale-Hubbell Law Directory

CONNER & WINTERS, A PROFESSIONAL CORPORATION (AV)

3700 First Place Tower, 15 East 5th Street, 74103-4344
Telephone: 918-586-5711
Fax: 918-586-8982
Email: postmaster@cwlaw.com
Oklahoma City, Oklahoma Office: One Leadership Square, 211 North Robinson, Suite 1700, 73102-7101.
Telephone: 405-272-5711.
Facsimile: 405-232-2695.
Fayetteville, Arkansas Office: Conner & Winters, P.L.L.C., 100 West Center Street, Suite 200, 72701-6081.
Telephone: 501-582-5711.
Facsimile: 501-587-1426.
Washington, D.C. Office: 1050 Seventeenth Street, N.W., Suite 810, 20036-5503.
Telephone: 202-783-5711.
Facsimile: 202-783-5720.

John E. Barry
Joseph J. McCain, Jr.
Lynnwood R. Moore, Jr.
Randolph L. Jones, Jr.
R. Kevin Redwine
David R. Cordell
Lawrence A. Hall

For Complete List of Firm Personnel, See General Section

For full biographical listings, see the Martindale-Hubbell Law Directory

DOERNER, SAUNDERS, DANIEL & ANDERSON, L.L.P. (AV)

Suite 500, 320 South Boston Avenue, 74103-3725
Telephone: 918-582-1211
Fax: 918-591-5360
URL: http://www.dsda.com
Oklahoma City, Oklahoma Office: One Leadership Square, Suite 501.
Telephone: 405-319-3500.
Fax: 405-319-3509. URL: http://www.dsda.com.

MEMBERS OF FIRM

Erwin J. Doerner (1897-1980)
Samuel P. Daniel
William C. Anderson
Varley H. Taylor, Jr.
G. Michael Lewis
Lawrence T. Chambers, Jr.
Dallas E. Ferguson
Sam G. Bratton II
Gary M. McDonald
H. Wayne Cooper
Kevin C. Coutant
Richard P. Hix
Lynn Paul Mattson
William F. Riggs
Lewis N. Carter
Linda C. Martin
James Patrick McCann
Richard H. Foster
Charles S. Plumb
Leonard I. Pataki
S. Douglas Dodd
Elise Dunitz Brennan
Jon E. Brightmire
Tom Q. Ferguson
Richard J. Eagleton
Rebecca McCarthy Fowler
Kristen L. Brightmire
Michael C. Redman
Steven K. Metcalf

(See Next Column)

DOERNER, SAUNDERS, DANIEL & ANDERSON L.L.P.—*Continued*

ASSOCIATES

Shelly L. Dalrymple
Harry V. Rouse
Russell W. Kroll
Amy L. Osborn
Robert A. Burk
Audra K. Hamilton
Ronald W. Little
Angela M. Knight
James C. Milton
James J. Robertson
R. Charles Wilkin

OF COUNSEL

Dickson M. Saunders
William B. Morgan
Kathy R. Neal

ATTORNEY IN OKLAHOMA CITY, OKLAHOMA

Jacque Brawner Lindsay

Gregory Frogge

Representative Clients: Public Service Company of Oklahoma.

For full biographical listings, see the Martindale-Hubbell Law Directory

FREDERIC DORWART (AV)

Old City Hall, 124 East Fourth Street, 74103-5010
Telephone: 918-583-9922
Fax: 918-583-8251
Email: fdorwart@fdlaw.kfoc.net

J. Michael Medina
Matthew James Browne, III
Richard J. Cipolla, Jr.
Paul DeMuro
Tamara R. Wagman

OF COUNSEL

John D. Clayman

Representative Clients: BOK Financial Corp.; Bank of Oklahoma, N.A.; Bank of Texas, N.A.; Bank of Albuquerque, N.A.; Kaiser-Francis Oil Co.; The Williford Companies; Williford Energy Co.; Williford Building Corp.; Safety Training Systems, Inc.; Sooner Southwest Bancshares, Inc.

For full biographical listings, see the Martindale-Hubbell Law Directory

HOLLIMAN LANGHOLZ RUNNELS FORSMAN & SELLERS, A PROFESSIONAL CORPORATION (AV)

Ten East Third Street, Suite 500, 74103-3695
Telephone: 918-584-1471
Fax: 918-587-9652,
Telex: 251773 GRC UR
Email: lawfirm@tulsaokla.com

Robert W. Langholz
Michael S. Forsman
Gail R. Runnels
Keith F. Sellers
James D. Bryant

OF COUNSEL

Joe M. Holliman

Representative Clients: The F & M Bank and Trust Company, Tulsa, Ok.; Transportation Leasing Co., Inc.; Kaiser-Francis Oil Co.

For full biographical listings, see the Martindale-Hubbell Law Directory

SNEED LANG, P.C. (AV)

2300 Williams Center Tower II, Two West Second Street, 74103
Telephone: 918-583-3145
Telecopier: 918-582-0410

James C. Lang
Robbie Emery Burke
D. Faith Orlowski
Patrick O. Waddel
Brian S. Gaskill
Randolph P. Stainer
G. Steven Stidham
Steven K. Balman
Stephen R. McNamara
Brian T. Inbody
Thomas E. Black, Jr.
D. Michael McBride III

OF COUNSEL

James L. Sneed

Representative Clients: Amoco Production Co.; Bank One, Texas; Enron Corp.; Halliburton Energy Services; Helmerich & Payne, Inc.; Shell Oil Co.; State Farm Mutual Automobile Insurance Co.; The Williams Companies.

For full biographical listings, see the Martindale-Hubbell Law Directory

OREGON

*PORTLAND,** Multnomah Co.

BLACK HELTERLINE LLP (AV)

1200 Union Bank of California Tower, 707 S.W. Washington Street, 97205
Telephone: 503-224-5560
Telecopier: 503-224-6148
URL: http://www.bhlaw.com

(See Next Column)

MEMBERS OF FIRM

Stark Ackerman
Paul R. Hribernick
Steven R. Schell

ASSOCIATE

Eric J. TenBrook

Representative Clients: Ataka Lumber America, Inc.; Bayview Transit Mix, Inc.; C.C. Meisel, Inc.; Eagle-Picher Minerals, Inc.; Morse Bros., Inc.; Oregon Concrete and Aggregate Producers Association, Inc.; Quartz Hill Mining Co.; R-DMAC, Inc.; Windsor Rock Products, Inc.

For Complete List of Firm Personnel, See General Section

For full biographical listings, see the Martindale-Hubbell Law Directory

RHODE ISLAND

*PROVIDENCE,** Providence Co.

EDWARDS & ANGELL, LLP (AV)

A Partnership including Professional Corporations
2800 BankBoston Plaza, 02903
Telephone: 401-274-9200
Telecopier: 401-276-6611
Cable Address: "Edwangle Providence"
Telex: 952001 "E A PVD"
Email: postmaster@ealaw.com *URL:* http://www.ealaw.com
Boston, Massachusetts Office: 101 Federal Street, 02110-1800.
Telephone: 617-439-4444.
Telecopier: 617-439-4170.
New York, New York Office: 750 Lexington Avenue, 10022-1200.
Telephone: 212-308-4411.
Telecopier: 212-308-4844.
Palm Beach, Florida Office: 250 Royal Palm Way, Suite 300, 33480-4356.
Telephone: 561-833-7700.
Telecopier: 561-655-8719.
Short Hills, New Jersey Office: 51 John F. Kennedy Parkway, 07078.
Telephone: 973-376-7700.
Telecopier: 973-376-3380.
Hartford, Connecticut Office: 90 State House Square, 06103-2715.
Telephone: 860-525-5065.
Telecopier: 860-527-4198.
Newport, Rhode Island Office: 130 Bellevue Avenue, 02840.
Telephone: 401-849-7800.
Telecopier: 401-849-7887.

MEMBERS OF FIRM

Gail E. McCann
Lorne W. McDougall
Mark A. Pogue
Deming E. Sherman
Lynn Wright (Not admitted in RI; New York, New York and Newark, New Jersey Office)

For Complete List of Firm Personnel, See General Section

For full biographical listings, see the Martindale-Hubbell Law Directory

TENNESSEE

*KNOXVILLE,** Knox Co.

WAGNER, MYERS & SANGER, A PROFESSIONAL CORPORATION (AV)

1801 First Tennessee Plaza, P.O. Box 1308, 37901-1308
Telephone: 423-525-4600
Fax: 423-524-5731
Email: wms1801@usit.net

Herbert S. Sanger, Jr.
Charles A. Wagner III

Representative Clients: Beazer East, Inc.; Costain Coal Co.; Colquest Energy, Inc.; Cullman Electric Membership Corp.; Facts About Coal in Tennessee; Gatliff Coal Co., Inc.; Kopper-Glo Fuels, Inc.; A. B. Long Cos.; Nerco Coal Co.; Skyline Coal Company.

For Complete List of Firm Personnel, See General Section

For full biographical listings, see the Martindale-Hubbell Law Directory

TEXAS

*AUSTIN,** Travis Co.

HARRISON & RIAL, L.L.P. (AV)

100 Congress Avenue, Suite 1550, 78701
Telephone: 512-472-6900
Facsimile: 512-477-8480

Richard W. Harrison — J. Hamilton Rial, III

Kelli A. N. Carlton

Representative Clients: General Motors Corporation; Union Pacific Resources Company; Eaton Corporation; U.S. TeleCoin Corp.; Bay Maintenance Company, Inc.

For full biographical listings, see the Martindale-Hubbell Law Directory

THOMPSON & KNIGHT L.L.P. (AV)

(Attorneys and Counselors)
1200 San Jacinto Center, 98 San Jacinto Boulevard, 78701
Telephone: 512-469-6100
Telecopy: 512-469-6180
URL: http://www.tklaw.com
Dallas, Texas Office: 1700 Pacific Avenue, Suite 3300, 75201.
Telephone: 214-969-1700.
Telecopy: 512-969-1751.
Telex: 732298.
Fort Worth, Texas Office: 801 Cherry Street, Suite 1600, 76102.
Telephone: 817-347-1700.
Telecopy: 817-347-1799.
Houston, Texas Office: Thompson Knight Brown Parker & Leahy L.L.P., 1200 Smith Street, Suite 3600, 77002-4595.
Telephone: 713-654-8111.
Telecopier: 713-654-1871.
San Pedro Garza Garcia, Nuevo León, Mexico Office: Edificio Losoles PD-4, Av. Lázaro Cárdenas No. 2400 Pte., C.P. 66220.
Telephone: (52-8) 363-0096.
Telecopy: (52-8) 363-3067.

PARTNER

James E. Cousar

ASSOCIATE

Peter A. Vermillion

For Complete List of Firm Personnel, See General Section

For full biographical listings, see the Martindale-Hubbell Law Directory

*BEAUMONT,** Jefferson Co.

BENCKENSTEIN & OXFORD, L.L.P. (AV)

Community Bank Building, P.O. Box 150, 77704
Telephone: 409-833-9182
Cable Address: "Bmor"
Telex: 779485
Telefax: 409-833-8819
Email: lawfirm@benoxford.com
Houston, Texas Office: Two Post Oak Central, 1980 Post Oak Boulevard, Suite 1600, 77056.
Telephone: 713-629-0345.
Fax: 713-629-0614.

MEMBERS OF FIRM

L. J. Benckenstein (1894-1966)
F. L. Benckenstein (1918-1987)
Hubert Oxford, III
Alan G. Sampson
Frank D. Calvert
Dana Timaeus
Frances Blair Bethea
Robert J. Rose, Sr.

ASSOCIATES

F. Blair Clarke
Michael K. Eaves
Alex J. Stelly, Jr.
Robert W. Craft
Lauren Miller Robbins (Resident, Houston Office)

Representative Clients: Marine Office of American Corp. (MOAC); Moran Towing and Transportation Co., Inc.

For full biographical listings, see the Martindale-Hubbell Law Directory

*DALLAS,** Dallas Co.

KILGORE & KILGORE, A PROFESSIONAL CORPORATION (AV)

700 McKinney Place, 3131 McKinney Avenue - LB 103, 75204-2471
Telephone: 214-969-9099
Fax: 214-953-0133; 214-953-0242; 214-953-0677

Wilmer D. Masterson, III
W. Stephen Swayze
Robert M. Thornton
Theodore C. Anderson, III

For Complete List of Firm Personnel, See General Section

For full biographical listings, see the Martindale-Hubbell Law Directory

THOMPSON & KNIGHT L.L.P. (AV)

(Attorneys and Counselors)
1700 Pacific Avenue Suite 3300, 75201
Telephone: 214-969-1700
Telecopy: 214-969-1751
Telex: 732 298
URL: http://www.tklaw.com
Austin, Texas Office: 1200 San Jacinto Center, 98 San Jacinto Boulevard, 78701.
Telephone: 512-469-6100.
Telecopy: 512-469-6180.
Fort Worth, Texas Office: 801 Cherry Street, Suite 1600, 76102.
Telephone: 817-347-1700.
Telecopy: 817-347-1799.
Houston, Texas Office: Thompson Knight Brown Parker & Leahy L.L.P., 1200 Smith Street, Suite 3600, 77002-4595.
Telephone: 713-654-8111.
Telecopier: 713-654-1871.
San Pedro Garza Garcia, Nuevo León, Mexico Office: Edificio Losoles PD-4, Av. Lázaro Cárdenas No. 2400 Pte., C.P. 66220.
Telephone: (52-8) 363-0096.
Telecopy: (52-8) 363-3067.

PARTNERS

Dorothy H. Bjorck
Andrew B. Derman
Timothy W. Dowdy
Dennis J. Grindinger
Thornton Hardie III
James L. Irish, III
James W. McKellar
John W. Rain
Debra J. Villarreal
Bill R. Womble
William R. Wright
Jeffrey A. Zlotky

SENIOR ATTORNEY

Ron W. Fry

For Complete List of Firm Personnel, See General Section

For full biographical listings, see the Martindale-Hubbell Law Directory

*GEORGE WEST,** Live Oak Co.

SCHNEIDER & MCWILLIAMS, P.C. (AV)

301 Bowie Street, P.O. Box 550, 78022
Telephone: 361-449-1501
Fax: 361-449-2042
Email: schneidr@speccom.net

R. E. Schneider, Jr. (1906-1976)
J. R. Schneider
Dwayne L. McWilliams

Joseph Robert Schneider, Jr. — Thomas Rex Forehand

Counsel for: First National Bank in George West; San Patricio Electric Cooperative, Inc.

For full biographical listings, see the Martindale-Hubbell Law Directory

*HOUSTON,** Harris Co.

FARNSWORTH & VONBERG (AV)

A Limited Liability Partnership
333 North Sam Houston Parkway, Suite 300, 77060
Telephone: 281-931-8902
Telecopy: 281-931-6032

T Brooke Farnsworth — Mary Frances vonBerg

ASSOCIATE

Bennett S. Bartlett

For full biographical listings, see the Martindale-Hubbell Law Directory

THOMPSON KNIGHT BROWN PARKER & LEAHY L.L.P. (AV)

A Registered Limited Liability Partnership including Professional Corporations
(Attorneys and Counselors)
1200 Smith Street, Suite 3600, 77002-4595
Telephone: 713-654-8111
Telecopier: 713-654-1871
URL: http://www.tklaw.com
Dallas, Texas Office: Thompson & Knight L.L.P., 1700 Pacific Avenue, Suite 3300, 75201.
Telephone: 214-969-1700.
Telecopy: 214-969-1751.
Telex: 732298.
Austin, Texas Office: Thompson & Knight L.L.P., 1200 San Jacinto Center, 98 San Jacinto Boulevard, 78701.
Telephone: 512-469-6100.
Telecopy: 512-469-6180.
Fort Worth, Texas Office: Thompson & Knight L.L.P., 801 Cherry Street, Suite 1600, 76102.
Telephone: 817-347-1700.
Telecopy: 817-347-1799.

(See Next Column)

THOMPSON KNIGHT BROWN PARKER & LEAHY L.L.P.—*Continued*

San Pedro Garza Garcia, Nuevo León, Mexico Office: Thompson & Knight L.L.P., Edificio Losoles PD-4, Av. Lázaro Cárdenas No. 2400 PTE., C.P. 66220.
Telephone: (52-8) 363-0096.
Telecopy: (52-8) 363-3067.

PARTNERS

Michael K. Pierce
Christopher D. Thompson

OF COUNSEL

James B. Barnes

For Complete List of Firm Personnel, See General Section

For full biographical listings, see the Martindale-Hubbell Law Directory

VINSON & ELKINS L.L.P. (AV)

2300 First City Tower, 1001 Fannin, 77002-6760
Telephone: 713-758-2222
Fax: 713-758-2346
Email: info@velaw.com *URL:* http://www.velaw.com
Austin, Texas Office: One American Center Suite 2700, 600 Congress Avenue, Austin, Texas, 78701-3200.
Telephone: 512-495-8400.
Fax: 512-495-8612.
Beijing, China Office: 20/F, Beijing Silver Tower, No. 2, Dong San Huan Bei Lu, Chaoyang District, 100027.
Telephone: +86-10-6410-6300.
Fax: +86-10-6410-6360.
Dallas, Texas Office: 3700 Trammell Crow Center, 2001 Ross Avenue, Dallas, Texas, 75201-2975.
Telephone: 214-220-7700.
Fax: 214-220-7716.
London, England Office: Regis House, 8th Floor, 45 King William Street, London, EC4R 9AN, England.
Telephone: (44-171) 618-6000.
Fax: (44-171) 618-6001.
Moscow, Russia Office: 16 Ulitsa Spiridonovka, Second Floor, 103001 Moscow, Russia.
Telephone: (7-095) 956-1995. Local
Fax: (7-095) 956-1996. U.S. Satellite
Fax: (212) 803-0142.
New York, N.Y. Office: 1325 Avenue of the Americas, 17th Floor, New York, N.Y., 10019.
Telephone: 917-206-8000.
Fax: 917-206-8100.
Singapore Office: 6 Battery Road, #39-01, Singapore, 049909.
Telephone: (65) 536-8300.
Fax: (65) 536-8311.
Washington, D.C. Office: The Willard Office Building, 1455 Pennsylvania Avenue, N.W., Washington, D.C., 20004-1008.
Telephone: 202-639-6500.
Fax: 202-639-6604.

MEMBER OF FIRM

William H. Drushel, Jr. (Administrative Partner)

MEMBERS OF FIRM

Christopher B. Amandes
Charles L. Berry
John C. Brannan, Jr. (Resident, Dallas, Texas Office)
Molly Cagle (Resident, Austin, Texas Office)
Fielding B. Cochran, III
Susan G. Conway (Resident, Austin, Texas Office)
James L. Cuclis
Stephen D. Davis (Resident, Singapore Office)
Paul C. Deemer (Resident, London, England Office)
Carol E. Dinkins
Kevin A. Gaynor (Resident, Washington, D.C. Office)
Douglas B. Glass (Resident, London, England Office)
George C. Hopkins (Resident, Washington, D.C. Office)
John C. LaMaster (Resident, London, England Office)
Sharon M. Mattox
Thomas V. McMahan
Larry W. Nettles
Benjamin H. Powell, III
Patrick Ford Thompson (Resident, Austin, Texas Office)
Michael J. Tomsu (Resident, Austin, Texas Office)
David J. Tuckfield (Resident, Austin, Texas Office)

HOUSTON OF COUNSEL

Larry J. Pechacek

ASSOCIATES

Kacy S. Burnsed (Not admitted in TX)
Christopher K. Carr (Resident, Washington, D.C. Office)
David T. Cindric
James P. Dyer (Resident, Austin, Texas Office)
Murray A. Greene
Keith W. Lapeze
Benjamin S. Lippard (Resident, Washington, D.C. Office)
Dennis W. Moore, Jr. (Resident, Austin, Texas Office)
Aric K. Short (Resident, Austin, Texas Office)
Lewis C. Sutherland
Kristie M. Tice
George O. Wilkinson, Jr.

For Complete List of Firm Personnel, See General Section

For full biographical listings, see the Martindale-Hubbell Law Directory

*LAREDO,** Webb Co.

PERSON, WHITWORTH, RAMOS, BORCHERS & MORALES, L.L.P. (AV)

602 East Calton Road, P.O. Box 6668, 78042-6668
Telephone: 956-727-4441
Fax: 956-727-2696

MEMBERS OF FIRM

George J. Person
Stephen A. Whitworth
Donato D. Ramos
Charles R. Borchers (1943-1997)
Richard G. Morales, Jr.
Alejandro E. Villarreal, III
William E. Casey
Mark D. Willett
Martha Cigarroa Dellano
Maria Cristina Gonzalez
Baldemar Garcia, Jr.
Richard E. Morales
Katrina Borchers Mohrer

For full biographical listings, see the Martindale-Hubbell Law Directory

*MIDLAND,** Midland Co.

KERR & WARD, L.L.P. (AV)

500 W. Texas, Suite 1310, Drawer 2858, 79702
Telephone: 915-684-9990
Fax: 915-684-9997
Email: info@kerr-ward.com *URL:* http://www.kerr-ward.com

OF COUNSEL

Wm. Monroe Kerr
Theodore M. Kerr

PARTNERS

Harris E. Kerr
William E. Ward
William M. Kerr, Jr.
Brian T. McLaughlin
James Devin Alsup

For full biographical listings, see the Martindale-Hubbell Law Directory

LYNCH, CHAPPELL & ALSUP, A PROFESSIONAL CORPORATION (AV)

The Summit, Suite 700, 300 North Marienfeld, 79701
Telephone: 915-683-3351
Fax: 915-683-2587

Robert A. Spears
Jeffrey D. Hewett

OF COUNSEL

Clovis G. Chappell

Representative Clients: Tom Brown, Inc.; NationsBank of Texas, N.A.; Pioneer Natural Resources; Chevron U.S.A. Inc.; Norwest Bank Texas, Midland, N.A.; Wagner & Brown, Ltd.

For Complete List of Firm Personnel, See General Section

For full biographical listings, see the Martindale-Hubbell Law Directory

TURNER & DAVIS, A PROFESSIONAL CORPORATION (AV)

400 West Illinois, Suite 1400, P.O. Box 2796, 79701
Telephone: 915-687-0011
Fax: 915-687-1735
Email: turdavpc@iglobal.net

J. Randy Turner
John Allen "Jad" Davis, Jr.
Frank N. Cremer, Jr.
James R. "Rusty" Fuller
Patrick S. Gerald
Holly B. Williams

Robert P. Crumpler, Jr.
David H. Smith

For full biographical listings, see the Martindale-Hubbell Law Directory

*PERRYTON,** Ochiltree Co.

LEMON, SHEARER, EHRLICH, PHILLIPS & GOOD, A PROFESSIONAL CORPORATION (AV)

311 South Main Street, P.O. Box 1066, 79070
Telephone: 806-435-6544
FAX: 806-435-4377
Email: lsepglaw@ren.net
Booker, Texas Office: 122 South Main Street, P.O. Box 348.
Telephone: 806-658-4545.
FAX: 806-658-4524.

Robert D. Lemon
Otis C. Shearer
Mitchell Ehrlich
Randall M. Phillips
F. Keith Good

Representative Clients: The Perryton National Bank; The Perryton Equity Exchange; The North Plains Ground Water Conservation District; Natural Gas Anadarko Co.; Courson Oil & Gas, Inc.; The City of Perryton; The Booker Equity Exchange; The Follett National Bank; Unit Petroleum Co.

For full biographical listings, see the Martindale-Hubbell Law Directory

*SAN ANTONIO,** Bexar Co.

COX & SMITH INCORPORATED (AV)

112 East Pecan Street, Suite 1800, 78205-1521
Telephone: 210-554-5500
Fax: 210-226-8395
Email: info@coxsmith.com *URL:* http://www.coxsmith.com

Paul H. Smith	Raymond E. Gallaway, Jr.
Richard T. Brady	Margaret Pedrick Sullivan
Jon R. Ray	David H.O. Roth
Kevin M. Beiter	Scott B. Bankler

Representative Clients: Abraxas Petroleum Corporation; Bergstein Oil & Gas Partnership; Clayton Williams Energy, Inc.; Conoco Inc.; Forest Oil Corporation; International Bank of Commerce; Maguire Oil Company; Sage Energy Company; Tesoro Petroleum Corporation; Tri-C Resources, Inc.

For Complete List of Firm Personnel, See General Section

For full biographical listings, see the Martindale-Hubbell Law Directory

UTAH

*SALT LAKE CITY,** Salt Lake Co.

CALLISTER NEBEKER & McCULLOUGH, A PROFESSIONAL CORPORATION (AV)

Gateway Tower East, Suite 900, 10 East South Temple, 84133
Telephone: 801-530-7300
Telecopier: 801-364-9127
Email: mjeaston@cnmlaw.com *URL:* http://www.cnmlaw.com

Fred W. Finlinson	James R. Holbrook

Brian W. Burnett

Representative Clients: Central Valley Water Reclamation Facility Board; Washington County Conservancy District; Sinclair Oil (Little America).

For Complete List of Firm Personnel, See General Section

For full biographical listings, see the Martindale-Hubbell Law Directory

PARR WADDOUPS BROWN GEE & LOVELESS, A PROFESSIONAL CORPORATION (AV)

Suite 1300, 185 South State Street, 84111-1537
Telephone: 801-532-7840
Fax: 801-532-7750
URL: http://www.pwlaw.com

Clayton J. Parr	Daniel A. Jensen

For Complete List of Firm Personnel, See General Section

For full biographical listings, see the Martindale-Hubbell Law Directory

PARSONS BEHLE & LATIMER, A PROFESSIONAL CORPORATION (AV)

One Utah Center, 201 South Main Street, Suite 1800, P.O. Box 45898, 84145-0898
Telephone: 801-532-1234
Telecopy: 801-536-6111
Email: pbl@pblutah.com *URL:* http://www.pblutah.com

James B. Lee	David L. Deisley
Gordon L. Roberts	Hal J. Pos
F. Robert Reeder	J. Michael Bailey
Lawrence E. Stevens	M. Lindsay Ford
Daniel M. Allred	Jim Butler
Dallin W. Jensen	Craig D. Galli
Kent W. Winterholler	James E. Karkut
David R. Bird	Michael J. Malmquist
David W. Tundermann	Lisa A. Kirschner
Neil Orloff	Elizabeth Kitchens
Lee Kapaloski	Michael J. Tomko
Stephen Hull	Edward B. Grandy
Patricia J. Winmill	Richard J. Angell
Maxwell A. Miller	Anne E. Rice
R. Craig Johnson	Vicki M. Baldwin
Lucy B. Jenkins	Jared G. Parkinson (Not admitted in UT)

OF COUNSEL

Keith E. Taylor

Representative Clients: Alliant Techsystems, Inc.; Barrick Gold Corp.; Battle Mountain Gold Co.; Coastal States Energy Co.; Kennecott Corp.; Questar Corp.

For Complete List of Firm Personnel, See General Section

For full biographical listings, see the Martindale-Hubbell Law Directory

PARSONS, DAVIES, KINGHORN & PETERS, P.C. (AV)

185 South State Street, Suite 700, 84111
Telephone: 801-363-4300
Facsimile: 801-363-4378
Email: Attorneys@pdkplaw.com

Glen E. Davies	Gerald H. Kinghorn

For Complete List of Firm Personnel, See General Section

For full biographical listings, see the Martindale-Hubbell Law Directory

PRUITT, GUSHEE & BACHTELL (AV)

Suite 1850 Beneficial Life Tower, 36 South State Street, 84111
Telephone: 801-531-8446
Fax: 801-531-8468; 533-9223
Email: pgb.law@cwix.com

MEMBERS OF FIRM

Robert G. Pruitt, Jr.	John F. Waldo
Oliver W. Gushee, Jr.	Angela L. Franklin
Thomas W. Bachtell	John S. Flitton
A. John Davis, III	Michael S. Johnson
John W. Anderson	George S. Young
Frederick M. MacDonald	William E. Ward

OF COUNSEL

Robert G. Pruitt, III	Brent A. Bohman

Representative Clients: The State of Utah; BHP Minerals International Inc.; Pennzoil Co.; Enron Oil & Gas Co.; Marathon Oil Co.; City of Midway; Brush Wellman, Inc.; Texasgulf, Inc.; Shoshone Irrigation District.

For full biographical listings, see the Martindale-Hubbell Law Directory

RAY, QUINNEY & NEBEKER, A PROFESSIONAL CORPORATION (AV)

79 South Main Street, Suite 400, P.O. Box 45385, 84145-0385
Telephone: 801-532-1500
Fax: 801-532-7543
Email: rqn@rqn.com *URL:* http://www.rqn.com
Provo, Utah Office: 92 North University Avenue, Suite 210, 84601-4420.
Telephone: 801-342-2400.
Fax: 801-375-8379.
Albuquerque, New Mexico Office: Suite 620, 40 First Plaza, N.W.
Telephone: 505-243-6665.
Fax: 505-764-9890.

Alan A. Enke	John P. Harrington
Robert P. Hill	John A. Adams

Representative Clients: First Security Bank, N.A.; Borden, Inc.; Salt Lake Organizing Committee for the Winter Olympic Games of 2002; Southern Pacific Transportation; Utah Power & Light Co.; Travelers Insurance Co.; U.S. West.

For Complete List of Firm Personnel, See General Section

For full biographical listings, see the Martindale-Hubbell Law Directory

SNELL & WILMER L.L.P. (AV)

111 East Broadway, Suite 900, 84111-1004
Telephone: 801-237-1900
Fax: 801-237-1950
URL: http://www.swlaw.com
Phoenix, Arizona Office: One Arizona Center, 85004-2202.
Telephone: 602-382-6000.
Fax: 602-382-6070.
Tucson, Arizona Office: One South Church Avenue, Suite 1500, 85701-1612.
Telephone: 520-882-1200.
Fax: 520-884-1294.
Orange County Office: 1920 Main Street, Suite 1200, Irvine, California 92614-7230.
Telephone: 949-253-2700.
Fax: 949-955-2507.

MEMBERS OF FIRM

Greg R. Nielsen	Alan L. Sullivan
Phillip Wm. Lear	Denise A. Dragoo

Bradley R. Cahoon

ASSOCIATE

Chris D. Jones

Representative Clients: For list of Representative Clients, see end of biographical listings in the Martindale-Hubbell Law Directory.

For Complete List of Firm Personnel, See General Section

For full biographical listings, see the Martindale-Hubbell Law Directory

Salt Lake City—Continued

VAN COTT, BAGLEY, CORNWALL & McCARTHY, A PROFESSIONAL CORPORATION (AV)

50 South Main Street, Suite 1600, P.O. Box 45340, 84145-0340
Telephone: 801-532-3333
Telecopier: 801-534-0058
Email: info@vancott.com *URL:* http://www.vancott.com
Ogden, Utah Office: 2404 Washington Boulevard, Suite 900.
Telephone: 801-394-5783.
Park City, Utah Office: 2200 Park Avenue, Suite C200-A.
Telephone: 435-649-3889.

Thomas W. Clawson
H. Michael Keller
Matthew F. McNulty, III

Mara A. Brown
Mary E. Westby (On Leave)

OF COUNSEL

Franklin N. Smith

For Complete List of Firm Personnel, See General Section

For full biographical listings, see the Martindale-Hubbell Law Directory

WEST VIRGINIA

*CHARLESTON,** Kanawha Co.

JACKSON & KELLY (AV)

1600 Laidley Tower, P.O. Box 553, 25322
Telephone: 304-340-1000
Fax: 304-340-1130
Email: info@jacksonkelly.com *URL:* http://www.jacksonkelly.com
Martinsburg, West Virginia Office: 300 Foxcroft Avenue, P.O. Box 1068.
Telephone: 304-263-8800.
Fax: 304-263-7110.
Morgantown, West Virginia Office: 6000 Hampton Center, P.O. Box 619.
Telephone: 304-599-3000.
Fax: 304-285-2040.
New Martinsville, West Virginia Office: 256 Russell Avenue, P.O. Box 68.
Telephone: 304-455-1751.
Fax: 304-455-6314.
Parkersburg, West Virginia Office: 412 Market Street, Suite 202, P.O. Box 1144.
Telephone: 304-424-3490.
Fax: 304-424-3499.
Fairmont, West Virginia Office: 1000 Technology Drive, Suite 1310.
Telephone: 304-368-2000.
Fax: 304-368-2020.
Lexington, Kentucky Office: 175 East Main Street, Suite 500, P.O. Box 2150.
Telephone: 606-255-9500.
Fax: 606-281-6478.
Washington, D. C. Office: 2401 Pennsylvania Avenue, N.W., Suite 400.
Telephone: 202-973-0200.
Fax: 202-973-0232.
Denver, Colorado Office: Suite 2710, 1660 Lincoln Street.
Telephone: 303-390-0003.
Fax: 303-390-0040.
Wheeling, West Virginia Office: 1144 Market Street.
Telephone: 304-233-4000.
Fax: 304-233-4077.

MEMBERS OF FIRM

James Knight Brown
John L. McClaugherty
Thomas E. Potter
Charles Q. Gage
James R. Snyder
Thomas N. McJunkin
Laura E. Beverage (Administrative Manager, Denver, Colorado Office)
Robert G. McLusky
Thad S. Huffman (Administrative Manager, Washington, D.C. Office)
Kevin M. McGuire (Resident, Lexington, Kentucky Office)
Wendel B. Turner
David M. Flannery
Robert D. Fluharty
Kathy G. Beckett

ASSOCIATES

Brooks K. Barkwill (Resident, New Martinsville, West Virginia Office)
William C. Miller, II

OF COUNSEL

Katherine Shand Larkin (Resident, Denver, Colorado Office)

Representative Clients: A.T. Massey Coal Company, Inc.; ANR Coal Co.; Arch Coal, Inc.; Cabot Corp.; Carbon Industries, Inc.; CONSOL, Inc.; Cyprus AMAX Minerals Co.; Pittston Coal Management Co.; West Virginia Coal Assn.; Westvaco Corp.

For Complete List of Firm Personnel, See General Section

For full biographical listings, see the Martindale-Hubbell Law Directory

*CLARKSBURG,** Harrison Co.

McNEER, HIGHLAND, McMUNN AND VARNER, L.C. (AV)

One Valley Bank Building, P.O. Drawer 2040, 26302-2040
Telephone: 304-626-1100
Facsimile: 304-623-3035
Martinsburg Office: 2520 Aikens Center, P.O. Box 2509.
Telephone: 304-264-4621.
Fax: 304-264-8623.
Parkersburg Office: 404 Market Street, Suite 204, P.O. Box 1507.
Telephone: 304-422-7193.
Facsimile: 304-422-7196.

C. David McMunn
J. Cecil Jarvis
James A. Varner
Robert W. Trumble (Resident, Martinsburg Office)
Catherine D. Munster
James N. Riley
Steven R. Bratke (Resident, Parkersburg Office)
Michael J. Novotny (Resident, Martinsburg Office)
Dennis M. Shreve
Geraldine S. Roberts
William F. Rohrbaugh (Resident, Martinsburg Office)
Gregory H. Schillace
Judy L. Shanholtz
Tiffany R. Durst
Gene W. Bailey, II

OF COUNSEL

James E. McNeer
Cecil B. Highland, Jr.
William L. Fury

Representative Clients: One Valley Bank of Clarksburg, National Assn.; Bruceton Bank; Harrison County Bank; Nationwide Mutual Insurance Cos.; Clarksburg Publishing Co.; C.I.T. Financial Services; State Automobile Mutual Insurance Co.; United Hospital Center, Inc.; West Virginia Coals, Inc.; Swanson Plating Co.

For full biographical listings, see the Martindale-Hubbell Law Directory

WATERS, WARNER & HARRIS, PLLC (AV)

Formerly Stathers & Cantrall
701 Goff Building, P.O. Box 1716, 26301
Telephone: 304-624-5571
Fax: 304-624-7228
Email: wwh.atty@northnap.citynet.net

Birk S. Stathers (1884-1945)
W. G. Stathers (1889-1970)
Arch M. Cantrall (1896-1967)
Stuart R. Waters
Boyd L. Warner
James A. Harris
Scott E. Wilson
James C. Turner
G. Thomas Smith

ASSOCIATES

D. Andrew McMunn
David C. Glover

Representative Clients: Bethlehem Steel Corp.; Dowell Schlumberger, Inc.; FIVE-J Energy, Inc.; Grafton Coal Co.; Emax Oil Company; Tygart Coal Co.; The Houston Exploration Company; Seneca-Upshur Petroleum, Inc.; EnerVest Operating, L.L.C.

For full biographical listings, see the Martindale-Hubbell Law Directory

WISCONSIN

*MILWAUKEE,** Milwaukee Co.

MICHAEL BEST & FRIEDRICH LLP (AV)

100 East Wisconsin Avenue, 53202-4108
Telephone: 414-271-6560
Telecopier: 414-277-0656
Cable Address: "Mibef"
Email: info@mbf-law.com *URL:* http://www.mbf-law.com
Madison, Wisconsin Office: One South Pinckney Street, Firstar Plaza, P.O. Box 1806, 53701-1806.
Telephone: 608-257-3501.
Telecopier: 283-2275.
Manitowoc, Wisconsin Office: 1000 Maritime Drive, 54220.
Telephone: 920-686-2800.
Fax: 920-686-2810.
Chicago, Illinois Office: Michael Best & Friedrich LLC, 77 West Wacker Drive, Suite 4300, 60601-1635.
Telephone: 312-845-5800.
Telecopier: 312-845-5828.

PARTNERS

Raymond R. Krueger
Jeffrey L. Abraham
David V. Meany
Paul E. Prentiss
Gary A. Ahrens
Donald P. Gallo
Michael P. Dunn
Donald F. Kiesling
Grant C. Killoran

(See Next Column)

MICHAEL BEST & FRIEDRICH LLP, *Milwaukee—Continued*

ASSOCIATES

Cynthia E. Smith
Mark C. Treter
Pamela L. Gergens

For Complete List of Firm Personnel, See General Section

For full biographical listings, see the Martindale-Hubbell Law Directory

WYOMING

*CASPER,** Natrona Co.

BROWN, DREW & MASSEY, LLP (AV)

Casper Business Center, Suite 800, 123 West First Street, 82601-2486
Telephone: 307-234-1000
800-877-6755
Telefax: 307-265-8025
Email: brwndrew@coffey.com

MEMBERS OF FIRM

Morris R. Massey
Harry B. Durham, III
Donn J. McCall
Thomas F. Reese
P. Jaye Rippley
Courtney Robert Kepler

ASSOCIATE

Timothy M. Stubson

Attorneys for: Chevron USA Inc.; Santa Fe Industries Co.; Citation Oil & Gas Corp.; Cross Timbers Oil Co.; Enron Group of Energy Cos.; North American Resources Co.; Wold Companies; KN Energy Corp.

For Complete List of Firm Personnel, See General Section

For full biographical listings, see the Martindale-Hubbell Law Directory

CRAIG NEWMAN (AV)

242 South Park Street, P.O. Box 530, 82602
Telephone: 307-265-3843
Fax: 307-235-0243
Email: cmannew@aol.com

For full biographical listings, see the Martindale-Hubbell Law Directory

PUERTO RICO

SAN JUAN, San Juan Dist.

GOLDMAN ANTONETTI & CÓRDOVA

American International Plaza Fourteenth & Fifteenth Floors, 250 Muñoz Rivera Avenue (Hato Rey), P.O. Box 70364, 00936-0364
Telephone: 787-759-8000
Telecopiers: 787-767-9333 (Main)
787-767-9177 (Litigation Department)
787-767-8660 (Labor & Corporate Law Departments)
787-767-9325 (Tax & Environmental Law Departments)
URL: http://www.gaclaw.com

MEMBERS OF FIRM

Francis Torres-Fernández
Braulio García Jiménez
Karín G. Díaz-Toro

ASSOCIATES

Gretchen M. Mendez-Vilella
Mayra Del C. Doble-Ruiz
Raul Negron Casasnovas
Guillermo J. Silva-Wiscovich
Alicia Lamboy

Representative Clients: Baxter Health Care Corp.; Chevron U.S.A.; Owen-Illinois; Puerto Rico Manufacturers Association; Britol Myers Squibb.

For Complete List of Firm Personnel, See General Section

For full biographical listings, see the Martindale-Hubbell Law Directory

CANADA
ALBERTA

*CALGARY,** Calgary Jud. Dist.

BENNETT JONES (AV)

4500 Bankers Hall East, 855-2nd Street S.W., T2P 4K7
Telephone: 403-298-3100
Facsimile: 403-265-7219
Email: firmwatch@bennettjones.ca *URL:* http://www.bennettjones.ca
Edmonton, Alberta Office: 1000, 10035-105 Street.
Telephone: 780-421-8133.
Facsimile: 780-421-7951.
Toronto, Ontario Office: 3400 1 First Canadian Place, P.O. Box 130.
Telephone: 416-863-1200.
Facsimile: 416-863-1716.

MEMBER OF FIRM

Robert P. Desbarats

For Complete List of Firm Personnel, See General Section

For full biographical listings, see the Martindale-Hubbell Law Directory

PARLEE MCLAWS (AV)

3400 Petro-Canada Centre, 150 - 6th Avenue, SW, T2P 3Y7
Telephone: 403-294-7000
Telecopier: 403-265-8263
Email: lawyers@parlee.com *URL:* http://www.parlee.com
Edmonton, Alberta Office: 15th Floor Manulife Place, 10180 101st Street.
Telephone: 403-423-8500.
Telecopier: 403-423-2870.

MEMBERS OF FIRM

Everett L. Bunnell, Q.C.
Gordon M. Adams
Nancy M. Penner
William R. Pieschel, Q.C.
Bruce A. Lawrence
Terry R. Davis

ASSOCIATES

Ariane E. Young
Anne Marie Godin
Barbara E. Janzen
Angela M. Tripathy

For Complete List of Firm Personnel, See General Section

For full biographical listings, see the Martindale-Hubbell Law Directory

CANADA
NEW BRUNSWICK

*MONCTON,** Westmorland Co.

MCINNES COOPER (AV)

Barristers, Solicitors & Trade Mark Agents
Place Moncton Place, 655 Main Street, P.O. Box 1368, E1C 8T6
Telephone: 506-857-8970
Fax: 506-857-4095
Email: mcrmctn@mcrlaw.com *URL:* http://www.mcrlaw.com
Halifax, Nova Scotia Office: Summit Place, 1601 Lower Water Street, P.O. Box 730, B3J 2V1.
Telephone: 902-425-6500.
Fax: 902-425-6350. Email: mcrhfx@mcrlaw.com.
St. John's, Newfoundland Office: Baine Johnston Centre, 5th Floor, 10 Fort William Place, P.O. Box 5939, A1C 5X4.
Telephone: 709-722-8735.
Telecopier: 709-722-1763. Email: mcrsj@mcrlaw.com.
Charlottetown, Prince Edward Island Office: BDC Place, Suite 620, 119 Kent Street, C1A 1N3.
Telephone: 902-368-8473.
Fax: 902-368-8346. Email: mcrpei@mcrlaw.com.
Fredericton, New Brunswick Office: Suite 600, 570 Queen Street, P.O. Box 610.
Telephone: 506-458-8572.
Fax: 506-458-9903. Email: mcrfton@mcrlaw.com.

PARTNER

Bernard F. Miller

For Complete List of Firm Personnel, See General Section

For full biographical listings, see the Martindale-Hubbell Law Directory

CANADA NEWFOUNDLAND

*ST. JOHN'S,**

McInnes Cooper (AV)

Barristers, Solicitors & Trade Mark Agents
Baine Johnston Centre, 5th Floor, 10 Fort William Place, P.O. Box 5939, A1C 5X4
Telephone: 709-722-8735
Telecopier: 709-722-1763
Email: mcrsj@mcrlaw.com *URL:* http://www.mcrlaw.com
Halifax, Nova Scotia Office: Summit Place, 1601 Lower Water Street, P.O. Box 730, B3J 2V1.
Telephone: 902-425-6500.
Fax: 902-425-6350. Email: mcrhfx@mcrlaw.com.
Moncton, New Brunswick Office: Place Moncton Place, 655 Main Street, P.O. Box 1368, E1C 8T6.
Telephone: 506-857-8970.
Fax: 506-857-4095. Email: mcrmctn@mcrlaw.com.
Charlottetown, Prince Edward Island Office: BDC Place, Suite 620, 119 Kent Street, C1A 1N3.
Telephone: 902-368-8473.
Fax: 902-368-8346. Email: mcrpei@mcrlaw.com.
Fredericton, New Brunswick Office: Suite 600, 570 Queen Street, P.O. Box 610.
Telephone: 506-458-8572.
Fax: 506-458-9903. Email: mcrfton@mcrlaw.com.

PARTNERS

Christine A. Fagan, Q.C.
Caroline C. Watton

ASSOCIATE

Dennis N. Clarke

For Complete List of Firm Personnel, See General Section

For full biographical listings, see the Martindale-Hubbell Law Directory

CANADA NOVA SCOTIA

*HALIFAX,** Regional Munic. of Halifax

McInnes Cooper (AV)

Barristers, Solicitors & Trade Mark Agents
Summit Place, 1601 Lower Water Street, P.O. Box 730, B3J 2V1
Telephone: 902-425-6500
Fax: 902-425-6350
Email: mcrhfx@mcrlaw.com *URL:* http://www.mcrlaw.com
St. John's, Newfoundland Office: Baine Johnston Centre, 5th Floor, 10 Fort William Place, P.O. Box 5939, A1C 5X4.
Telephone: 709-722-8735.
Telecopier: 709-722-1763. Email: mcrsj@mcrlaw.com.
Moncton, New Brunswick Office: Place Moncton Place, 655 Main Street, P.O. Box 1368, E1C 8T6.
Telephone: 506-857-8970.
Fax: 506-857-4095. Email: mcrmctn@mcrlaw.com.
Charlottetown, Prince Edward Island Office: BDC Place, Suite 620, 119 Kent Street, C1A 1N3.
Telephone: 902-368-8473.
Fax: 902-368-8346. Email: mcrpei@mcrlaw.com.
Fredericton, New Brunswick Office: Suite 600, 570 Queen Street, P.O. Box 610.
Telephone: 506-458-8572.
Fax: 506-458-9903. Email: mcrfton@mcrlaw.com.

PARTNERS

George T. H. Cooper, Q.C.
Thomas E. Hart
F. Van W. Penick
Aidan J. Meade

ASSOCIATE

Kristi Sebalj

For Complete List of Firm Personnel, See General Section

For full biographical listings, see the Martindale-Hubbell Law Directory

CANADA ONTARIO

*TORONTO,** Regional Munic. of Toronto

Borden & Elliot (AV)

Barristers & Solicitors
Scotia Plaza, 40 King Street West, M5H 3Y4
Telephone: 416-367-6000
Telecopier: 416-367-6749
Email: info@borden.com *URL:* http://www.borden.com
Ottawa, Ontario Office: Borden Elliot Scott & Aylen, 1000-60 Rue Queen Street.
Telephone: 613-237-5160; 800-661-4237. General
Facsimile: 613-230-8842. IP Dept.
Facsimile: 613-787-3558. Email: ottinfo@scottaylen.com. URL: http://www.borden.com.

Edmund F. Merringer

For Complete List of Firm Personnel, See General Section

For full biographical listings, see the Martindale-Hubbell Law Directory

CANADA SASKATCHEWAN

*REGINA,** Regina Jud. Centre

MacPherson Leslie & Tyerman (AV)

1500-1874 Scarth Street, S4P 4E9
Telephone: 306-347-8000
Telecopier: 306-352-5250
Email: mltreg@mlt.com
Saskatoon, Saskatchewan Office: 1500-410 22nd Street East, S7K 5T6.
Telephone: 306-975-7100.
Telecopier: 306-975-7145.

MEMBERS OF FIRM

Harold H. MacKay, Q.C.
A. Robson Garden, Q.C. (Resident, Saskatoon Office)
Danny R. Anderson (Resident, Saskatoon Office)
Robert B. Pletch, Q.C.
R. Neil MacKay (Resident, Saskatoon Office)
Randy U. Brunet
John A. Dipple

ASSOCIATES

Scott D. Whitby
Barclay A. Laughland (Resident, Saskatoon Office)

For Complete List of Firm Personnel, See General Section

For full biographical listings, see the Martindale-Hubbell Law Directory

NONPROFIT AND TAX EXEMPT ORGANIZATIONS

MINNESOTA

*MINNEAPOLIS,** Hennepin Co.

MARTIN & ASSOCIATES, P.A. (AV)
1650 West 82nd Street, Suite 1460, 55431
Telephone: 612-885-5665
Fax: 612-885-5664
Email: mail@martinandassociates.com

Judith Martin Ventres

Michael J. Zitta
Richard William Van Sickle

For full biographical listings, see the Martindale-Hubbell Law Directory

NEW JERSEY

*NEWARK,** Essex Co.

MEYNER AND LANDIS (AV)
One Gateway Center, Suite 2500, 07102-5311
Telephone: 973-624-2800
Fax: 973-624-0356
Email: attys@meyner.com *URL:* http://www.meyner.com

Robert B. Meyner (1908-1990)
Edwin C. Landis, Jr.
John N. Malyska
William J. Fiore
Anthony F. Siliato
Francis R. Perkins
Howard O. Thompson
Scott T. McCleary
Linda Townley Snyder
William H. Schmidt, Jr.
David B. Grantz

For full biographical listings, see the Martindale-Hubbell Law Directory

NEW YORK

*ALBANY,** Albany Co.

ISEMAN, CUNNINGHAM, RIESTER & HYDE, LLP (AV)
9 Thurlow Terrace, 12203
Telephone: 518-462-3000
Telecopier: 518-462-4199
Email: lawfirm@icrh.com *URL:* http://www.icrh.com
Canandaigua, New York Office: 37 East Gibson Street, P.O. Box 179, 14424.
Telephone: 716-394-1450.
Fax: 716-394-5121.

MEMBERS OF FIRM

Frederick C. Riester
Michael J. Cunningham
Robert Hall Iseman
Carol Ann Hyde
Linda J. Clark

Brian M. Culnan
Kihyun S. Kim
Richard A. Frankel
Stephanie E. Moriarty
Valerie R. Lape Handy
Marcia B. Smith
Ellen Gillerman Cox
Jennifer A. Grego
Cara E. Johnson

OF COUNSEL

Michael J. McNeil
Deborah A. Kirby

For full biographical listings, see the Martindale-Hubbell Law Directory

*NEW YORK,** New York Co.

GRAHAM, CAMPAIGN P.C. (AV)
The Bar Building, 36 West 44th Street, 10036-8178
Telephone: 212-354-5650
Cable Address: "Forbland"
Telex: 6502048313 MCI UW
MCI Mail: 204-8313
Telecopier: 212-354-6354
Email: gracam@aol.com *URL:* http://www.lawyers.com/trademarks

(See Next Column)

Andrew J. Graham (1911-1986)
William L. McGuire, Sr. (1926-1992)
H. John Campaign
John M. Keene
Charles H. Knull
Gail E. Nickols
William C. Wright

OF COUNSEL

Gerard H. Davis

For full biographical listings, see the Martindale-Hubbell Law Directory

NORTH CAROLINA

*RALEIGH,** Wake Co.

LAW OFFICES OF STEVEN D. SIMPSON, P.A. (AV)
Landmark Center II, 4601 Six Forks Road, Suite 530, 27609
Telephone: 919-788-9677
Telefax: 919-788-0775
Email: simpsonl@gte.net *URL:* http://www.ssimpsonlaw.com

Steven D. Simpson

For full biographical listings, see the Martindale-Hubbell Law Directory

OHIO

*COLUMBUS,** Franklin Co.

BRICKER & ECKLER LLP (AV)
100 South Third Street, 43215-4291
Telephone: 614-227-2300
Telecopy: 614-227-2390
Email: info@be.bricker.com *URL:* http://www.bricker.com

Mark A. Engel
Jerry O. Allen
Gordon F. Litt

Mary Leslie Robins
Christine M. Poth

Representative Clients: Ohio Health Corp.; OHA: The Association for Hospitals and Health Systems; National Groundwater Association; Kenyon College.

For Complete List of Firm Personnel, See General Section

For full biographical listings, see the Martindale-Hubbell Law Directory

DUBLIN, Franklin Co.

BLAUGRUND, HERBERT & MARTIN, INCORPORATED (AV)
5455 Rings Road, Suite 500, 43017-7517
Telephone: 614-764-0681
Fax: 614-764-0774
Email: bhm@bhmlaw.net

David S. Blaugrund
Sharon Cason-Adams
Christopher T. Cline
Lawrence H. Cohen
David J. Demers
Beverly J. Farlow
John W. Herbert
John S. Jones
David S. Kessler
Emily J. Lewis
Steven A. Martin
Sharon L. R. Miller
Marc E. Myers
Stephen P. Postalakis
Teri G. Rasmussen

Jerry T. Burditt
Steven E. Hillman
Roxi Ann Liming
Michael C. Mentel
William Scott Simon
Carole D. Weiss

For full biographical listings, see the Martindale-Hubbell Law Directory

OKLAHOMA

*TULSA,** Tulsa Co.

PHILIP S. HANEY ASSOCIATES (AV)
Boulder Towers, 1437 South Boulder, Suite 1050, 74119
Telephone: 918-744-1023
Facsimile: 918-744-1043
Email: philhaney@juno.com *URL:* http://www.lawyers.com/churchlaw

Philip S. Haney

For full biographical listings, see the Martindale-Hubbell Law Directory

RHODE ISLAND

SMITHFIELD, Providence Co.

Charles S. Sokoloff Incorporated (AV)

Eleven Thurber Boulevard, 02917-1859
Telephone: 401-233-2800; Toll Free: 888-SOKOLAW
Fax: 401-233-2890
URL: http://www.sokolawyer.com
Email: sokolaw@sokolawyer.com *URL:* http://www.lawyers.com/sokolaw

Charles S. Sokoloff

Anne-Marie Krollman

For full biographical listings, see the Martindale-Hubbell Law Directory

TEXAS

IRVING, Dallas Co.

Brewer, Brewer, Anthony & Middlebrook (AV)

A Professional Legal Corporation
1159 Cottonwood Lane, Suite 150, 75038
Telephone: 972-870-9898; Metro: 972-953-0533
FAX: 972-870-9053
Email: brewer10@airmail.net

MEMBERS OF FIRM

Dennis G. Brewer, Sr.
Dennis G. Brewer, Jr. (P.C.)
John Matthew Anthony
David O. Middlebrook

ASSOCIATES

Cynthia Bullock Dunn
Monika L. Manor
David R. Joe
Jenny L. Womack

OF COUNSEL

Cary Jay Cross

For full biographical listings, see the Martindale-Hubbell Law Directory

UTAH

*SALT LAKE CITY,** Salt Lake Co.

Callister Nebeker & McCullough, A Professional Corporation (AV)

Gateway Tower East, Suite 900, 10 East South Temple, 84133
Telephone: 801-530-7300
Telecopier: 801-364-9127
Email: mjeaston@cnmlaw.com *URL:* http://www.cnmlaw.com

Leland S. McCullough
Craig F. McCullough
Laurie S. Hart

David R. York
Lee S. McCullough, III

Representative Clients: Zions First National Bank; Sears Roebuck & Company; Utah Automobile Dealers Association; Sinclair Oil Corporation (Little America); Keystone Communications; Central Valley Water Reclamation Facility Board; Citicorp; Intermountain Health Care, Inc.; Children's Miracle Network (Osmond Foundation); Nu Skin International, Inc.

For Complete List of Firm Personnel, See General Section

For full biographical listings, see the Martindale-Hubbell Law Directory

Holme Roberts & Owen LLP (AV)

Suite 1100, 111 East Broadway, 84111
Telephone: 801-521-5800
Telecopier: 801-521-9639
Email: hro@hro.com *URL:* http://www.hro.com
Denver, Colorado Office: Suite 4100, 1700 Lincoln.
Telephone: 303-861-7000.
Telecopier: 303-866-0200.
Boulder, Colorado Office: Suite 400, 1401 Pearl Street.
Telephone: 303-444-5955.
Telecopier: 303-444-1063.
Colorado Springs, Colorado Office: Suite 1300, 90 South Cascade Avenue.
Telephone: 719-473-3800.
Telecopier: 719-633-1518.
London, England Office: Heathcoat House 3rd Floor, 20 Savile Row.
Telephone: 011-44-171-494-5600.
Telecopier: 011-44-171-287-9344.

PARTNER OF FIRM

Gary R. Thorup

For Complete List of Firm Personnel, See General Section

For full biographical listings, see the Martindale-Hubbell Law Directory

WISCONSIN

*MILWAUKEE,** Milwaukee Co.

Meissner Tierney Fisher & Nichols S.C. (AV)

The Milwaukee Center, 111 East Kilbourn Avenue, 19th Floor, 53202-6622
Telephone: 414-273-1300
Facsimile: 414-273-5840
URL: http://www.mtfn.com

Joseph E. Tierney III
Dennis L. Fisher
Thomas J. Nichols
Randal J. Brotherhood
Michael J. Cohen

Michael A. Kallas
Christopher L. Rexroat
Justin B. Nelsen
William T. Stuart
Jeffrey A. Ellis
Adam J. Tutaj

OF COUNSEL

Paul F. Meissner

For full biographical listings, see the Martindale-Hubbell Law Directory

OIL AND GAS LAW

NEW MEXICO

*ALBUQUERQUE,** Bernalillo Co.

EAVES, BARDACKE, BAUGH KIERST & KIERNAN, P.A. (AV)

6400 Uptown Boulevard, N.E., Suite 110-W, P.O. Box 35670, 87176
Telephone: 505-888-4300
Facsimile: 505-883-4406
Email: LGLEAVES@EB-B.com

John M. Eaves
Paul Bardacke
John G. Baugh
Peter S. Kierst
Kerry Kiernan

Derek V. Larson
Karen S. Mendenhall
C. Shannon Bacon

OF COUNSEL

Jennifer J. Pruett

For full biographical listings, see the Martindale-Hubbell Law Directory

KENNETH C. LEACH, P.C. (AV)

1110 Pennsylvania N.E., Suite A, 87110
Telephone: 505-243-3322
Fax: 505-242-1268
URL: http://www.lawyers.com/leachlaw

Kenneth C. Leach

Jonathan Reid Mowrer

LEGAL SUPPORT PERSONNEL

Wayne C. Edwards (CEO)
Marilyn Alires Marsh (Paralegal)
Virginia Bosworth (Paralegal)

For full biographical listings, see the Martindale-Hubbell Law Directory

*SANTA FE,** Santa Fe Co.

WHITE, KOCH, KELLY & McCARTHY, A PROFESSIONAL ASSOCIATION (AV)

433 Paseo De Peralta, P.O. Box 787, 87504-0787
Telephone: 505-982-4374
ABA/NET: 1154
Fax: 505-982-0350; 984-8631
Email: WKKM@NM.NET

Mary E. Walta

Representative Clients: Northern Trust Bank of Texas; Shell Energy.

For Complete List of Firm Personnel, See General Section

For full biographical listings, see the Martindale-Hubbell Law Directory

NEW YORK

*BINGHAMTON,** Broome Co.

HINMAN, HOWARD & KATTELL, LLP (AV)

700 Security Mutual Building, 80 Exchange Street, P.O. Box 5250, 13902-5250
Telephone: 607-723-5341
Fax: 607-723-6605
Email: jworband@hhk.com *URL:* http://www.hhk.com
Norwich, New York Office: 48 Hale Street, 13815-2039.
Telephone: 607-334-5896.
Fax: 607-336-1628.
Oneonta, New York Office: 12 South Main Street, 13820-2542.
Telephone: 607-432-5331.
Fax: 607-432-2683.
New York, N.Y. Office: 500 5th Avenue, Suite 1725, 10110.
Telephone: 212-840-3017.
Fax: 212-840-2345.

MEMBERS OF FIRM

Harvey D. Hinman (1864-1954)
Archibald Howard (1872-1962)
Thomas B. Kattell (1875-1947)
Dana B. Hinman (1874-1970)
Roger P. Clark (1869-1934)
C. Addison Keeler (1897-1979)
Thomas H. Fogarty (1902-1966)
Prescott D. Perkins (1902-1969)
Morris Gitlitz (1902-1984)
Charles F. Fish (1910-1987)
William L. Ransom, Jr. (1918-1967)
Edward L. Tirrell, Jr. (1917-1993)
John M. Keane (1914-1994)

(See Next Column)

A. Lawrence Abrams (1906-1996)
George Lyon Hinman (1905-1997)
Lee R. Cirba (1954-1999)
James W. Orband
Lawrence C. Anderson
James S. Gleason
Clayton M. Axtell, Jr.
Warren M. Anderson
Keith E. Osber
Colin T. Naylor, III
Richard H. Pille
N. Theodore Sommer
Eugene E. Peckham
John C. Fish
James L. Chivers
James M. Hayes
Peter J. Vivona
Clayton M. Axtell, III
James F. Lee
John G. Dowd
Katherine A. Fitzgerald
James R. Franz
Albert J. Millus, Jr.
Lillian L. Levy
Wilbur D. Dahlgren
Kenneth F. Tomko
Paul T. Sheppard
Harvey D. Mervis
Leslie Prechtl Guy
Thomas W. Cusimano, Jr.
John E. Jones
Eugene D. Faughnan
Allen J. Hall
Thomas A. Conlon, Jr.
John M. Keeler
C. Addison Keeler, Jr.

COUNSEL

A. Edward Hill
Joseph P. Minnich, Jr.
Darwin R. Wales
Erik Edward Joh
Paul J. Sternberg

RESIDENT COUNSEL

Bernard I. Flateman (Resident, New York Office)

SPECIAL COUNSEL

Donald R. Campbell
Richard S. Ringwood
Brian R. Wright
Robert H. Wedlake
Catherine M. Berthel (Resident, Oneonta Office)
Kurt D. Schulte (Resident, Oneonta Office)
Amy Shapiro
Frederick A. Griffen
Scott J. Clippinger (Resident, Norwich Office)
Lori Grumet Schapiro
Martin J. Kane
Richard C. Lewis
William C. Burtis, Jr.

ASSOCIATES

Michael S. Sinicki
John D. Denmon
Alyssa M. Barreiro
Alex C. Dell
Eric D. Farrell
Dianne Oakes
Ronald Louis Greene
Anne Hillis
Kathleen S. Campbell
Laurie M. Ceparano
Dominic S. DePersis
Erik T. Koons
Jeffrey LaBarge
Anthony J. D'Elia
Stacey M. Gates

Representative Clients: The Chase Manhattan Bank; BSB Bank & Trust Co.; International Business Machines Corp.; Universal Instruments Corp.; Security Mutual Life Insurance Company of New York; Bell Atlantic; Preferred Mutual Insurance Company; New York State Electric & Gas Corp.; Exxon Corp.

For full biographical listings, see the Martindale-Hubbell Law Directory

OKLAHOMA

*OKLAHOMA CITY,** Oklahoma Co.

CROWE & DUNLEVY, A PROFESSIONAL CORPORATION (AV)

1800 Mid-America Tower, 20 North Broadway, 73102-8273
Telephone: 405-235-7700
Fax: 405-239-6651
Email: marketing@crowedunlevy.com *URL:* http://www.crowedunlevy.com
Tulsa, Oklahoma Office: 500 Kennedy Building, 321 South Boston Avenue, 74103-3313.
Telephone: 918-592-9800.
Fax: 918-592-9801.
Norman, Oklahoma Office: Crowe & Dunlevy, 2500 South McGee, Suite 140, 73072-6705.
Telephone: 405-321-7317.
Fax: 405-360-4002.

Gary W. Davis
John J. Griffin, Jr.
Mark D. Christiansen
L. Mark Walker
Stephen L. DeGiusti
Paul D. Trimble

C. Robert Stell
Brian C. Henderson

OF COUNSEL

Val R. Miller
James A. Peabody
James W. George

For Complete List of Firm Personnel, See General Section

For full biographical listings, see the Martindale-Hubbell Law Directory

Oklahoma City—Continued

DAY, EDWARDS, FEDERMAN, PROPESTER & CHRISTENSEN, P.C. (AV)

Suite 2900 Oklahoma Tower, 210 Park Avenue, 73102-5605
Telephone: 405-239-2121
Telecopier: 405-236-1012
URL: http://lawlinks.com/attys/ok/defpc.html

Joe E. Edwards
William B. Federman
J. Clay Christensen

Ricki Valerie Sonders

Representative Clients: Bobby Joe Cudd Company; Delta Western Drilling Funds; Fluid Technologies; Scientific Drilling International, Inc.; Wild Well Control, Inc.; Worldwide Well Control, Inc.

For Complete List of Firm Personnel, See General Section

For full biographical listings, see the Martindale-Hubbell Law Directory

ROBERT A. MILLER (AV)

2850 Bank One Tower, 100 North Broadway, 73102
Telephone: 405-272-0881
Fax: 405-272-0884
Email: rob73120@aol.com

For full biographical listings, see the Martindale-Hubbell Law Directory

*TULSA,** Tulsa Co.

BOESCHE, McDERMOTT & ESKRIDGE (AV)

Suite 800 Oneok Plaza, 100 West Fifth Street, 74103
Telephone: 918-583-1777
Fax: 918-592-5809
Email: bme@intellex.com
Muskogee, Oklahoma Office: 1111 West Broadway, P.O. Box 2669, 74402.
Telephone: 918-683-6100.
Fax: 918-683-2303.

MEMBERS OF FIRM

R. Casey Cooper
Bradley K. Beasley
David A. Johnson
Nik Jones
R. Kevin Layton
Sheila M. Powers

ASSOCIATES

Byron E. (Rusty) Brown
Christopher K. Woosley

OF COUNSEL

Clifford K. Cate, Jr. (Resident at Muskogee)
Linda McQuillen Kulp

Representative Clients: Apache Corporation; Helmerich & Payne; Shell Oil Company; Williford Energy.

For Complete List of Firm Personnel, See General Section

For full biographical listings, see the Martindale-Hubbell Law Directory

CROWE & DUNLEVY, A PROFESSIONAL CORPORATION (AV)

500 Kennedy Building, 321 South Boston Avenue, 74103-3313
Telephone: 918-592-9800
Fax: 918-592-9801
Email: marketing@crowedunlevy.com *URL:* http://www.crowedunlevy.com
Oklahoma City, Oklahoma Office: 1800 Mid-America Tower, 20 North Broadway, 73102-8273.
Telephone: 405-235-7700.
Fax: 405-239-6651.
Norman, Oklahoma Office: Crowe & Dunlevy, 2500 South McGee, Suite 140, 73072-6705.
Telephone: 405-321-7317.
Fax: 405-360-4002.

Gary C. Clark
Malcolm E. Rosser IV
Jeffrey T. Hills

For Complete List of Firm Personnel, See General Section

For full biographical listings, see the Martindale-Hubbell Law Directory

FREDERIC DORWART (AV)

Old City Hall, 124 East Fourth Street, 74103-5010
Telephone: 918-583-9922
Fax: 918-583-8251
Email: fdorwart@fdlaw.kfoc.net

J. Michael Medina
Richard J. Cipolla, Jr.
Matthew James Browne, III
Paul DeMuro
Tamara R. Wagman

OF COUNSEL

John D. Clayman

Representative Clients: BOK Financial Corp.; Bank of Oklahoma, N.A.; Bank of Texas, N.A.; Bank of Albuquerque, N.A.; Kaiser-Francis Oil Co.; The Williford Companies; Williford Energy Co.; Williford Building Corp.; Safety Training Systems, Inc.; Sooner Southwest Bancshares, Inc.

For full biographical listings, see the Martindale-Hubbell Law Directory

PENNSYLVANIA

*GREENSBURG,** Westmoreland Co.

SEAN CASSIDY (AV)

118 North Main Street, 15601
Telephone: 724-836-4900
Fax: 724-836-2090
URL: http://www.lawyers.com/cassidy

Representative Clients: CNG Producing Co.; CNG Transmission Corp.; Consolidation Coal Co.; Cabot Oil and Gas Corp.; Equitrans, Inc.; Amerikohl Mining, Inc.; North Coast Energy, Inc.; Range Resources Corp.

For full biographical listings, see the Martindale-Hubbell Law Directory

*PITTSBURGH,** Allegheny Co.

YUKEVICH, MARCHETTI, LIEKAR & ZANGRILLI, P.C. (AV)

Sixth Floor, One Gateway Center, 15222-1424
Telephone: 412-261-6777
Fax: 412-261-6789
URL: http://www.ymlz.com

Michael Yukevich, Jr.
Christopher J. Marchetti
John P. Liekar, Jr.
Albert J. Zangrilli, Jr.
Mark Fischer
Michael I. Frachioni
Lori Nolan Lindey
Keith J. Rothfus

For full biographical listings, see the Martindale-Hubbell Law Directory

SOUTH DAKOTA

*RAPID CITY,** Pennington Co.

DELANEY & SUMNER (AV)

623 Quincy Street Suite 103, 57701
Telephone: 605-388-3153
Fax: 605-388-3155
Mailing Address: P.O. Box 8305, Rapid City, SD, 57709-8305
Email: toogoodoo1@aol.com

MEMBERS OF FIRM

John J. Delaney
Scott Sumner

For full biographical listings, see the Martindale-Hubbell Law Directory

TEXAS

*AUSTIN,** Travis Co.

McCALL & RITCHIE, LLP (AV)

2700 Via Fortuna, Suite 150, 78746
Telephone: 512-477-4242
Facsimile: 512-477-2271
Email: McRitch4@aol.com

Tom C. McCall
David B. McCall
Wesley G. Ritchie
Mark K. Leaverton
John M. Kyser
Robert F. Johnson, III

OF COUNSEL

Brook, Pizza & van Loon, L.L.P., New Orleans, Louisiana

For full biographical listings, see the Martindale-Hubbell Law Directory

*FORT WORTH,** Tarrant Co.

DECKER, JONES, McMACKIN, McCLANE, HALL & BATES, A PROFESSIONAL CORPORATION (AV)

2500 Bank One Tower, 500 Throckmorton Street, 76102-3812
Telephone: 817-336-2400; Metro: 817-429-5260
Fax: 817-332-3043; 336-2181
Email: email@deckerjones.com *URL:* http://www.deckerjones.com

(See Next Column)

DECKER, JONES, MCMACKIN, MCCLANE, HALL & BATES A PROFESSIONAL CORPORATION—*Continued*

Daniel L. Bates
Robert W. Decker
Mark S. Dugan
Janet L. Hahn
Randy J. Hall
Raymond B. Kelly, III
John B. McClane
John W. McMackin
Charles B. Milliken
Gary M. Moates
Bradley H. Rice
Jeffrey W. Storie
James L. Stripling
Brian K. Yost
Tamera H. Bennett
Arthur F. Zobal
Geoffrey A. Mantooth

Representative Clients: Wheeler Oil Co.; Kimball Oil Co. of Texas; Martin-Sprocket and Gear, Inc.; Williamson-Dickie Manufacturing Co.; Harbison-Fischer Manufacturing Co.; Employers Insurance of Texas; American International Group; Medical Protective Co.; Redman Homes, Inc.; Liberty Mutual Insurance.

For full biographical listings, see the Martindale-Hubbell Law Directory

*HOUSTON,** Harris Co.

KILBURN, JONES, GILL & CAMPBELL, L.L.P. (AV)

1100 Louisiana, Suite 3400, 77002-5234
Telephone: 713-652-4068
Fax: 713-652-4078
Email: info@kjgc.com *URL:* http://www.kjgc.com

Kerry A. Kilburn
Michael D. Jones
Lee S. Gill
K. Ray Campbell

David A. Birchall
K. Anne Bullen
Jeffery Robin Koch
Debra D. Sandefer

OF COUNSEL

Lynn C. Woods, Jr.

For full biographical listings, see the Martindale-Hubbell Law Directory

*SWEETWATER,** Nolan Co.

STEAKLEY & WETSEL (AV)

207 Oak Street, P.O. Box 78, 79556
Telephone: 915-235-4944
Fax: 915-235-3526
Email: swlaw@camalott.com

MEMBERS OF FIRM

Zollie C. Steakley
Roderick E. Wetsel

Reference: First National Bank, Sweetwater, Texas; Texas National Bank, Sweetwater, Texas.

For full biographical listings, see the Martindale-Hubbell Law Directory

*TYLER,** Smith Co.

LAW OFFICES OF M. DEWAYNE VARNADORE, P.C. (AV)

6101 South Broadway, Suite 590, 75703
Telephone: 903-561-6614
Fax: 903-561-4915

M. DeWayne Varnadore

LEGAL SUPPORT PERSONNEL

Renda Spencer (Office Administrator/Legal Assistant)

For full biographical listings, see the Martindale-Hubbell Law Directory

UTAH

*SALT LAKE CITY,** Salt Lake Co.

VAN COTT, BAGLEY, CORNWALL & MCCARTHY, A PROFESSIONAL CORPORATION (AV)

50 South Main Street, Suite 1600, P.O. Box 45340, 84145-0340
Telephone: 801-532-3333
Telecopier: 801-534-0058
Email: info@vancott.com *URL:* http://www.vancott.com
Ogden, Utah Office: 2404 Washington Boulevard, Suite 900.
Telephone: 801-394-5783.
Park City, Utah Office: 2200 Park Avenue, Suite C200-A.
Telephone: 435-649-3889.

Thomas W. Clawson
H. Michael Keller
Gregory P. Williams

Mara A. Brown
Mary E. Westby (On Leave)

For Complete List of Firm Personnel, See General Section

For full biographical listings, see the Martindale-Hubbell Law Directory

CANADA NEW BRUNSWICK

*MONCTON,** Westmorland Co.

MCINNES COOPER (AV)

Barristers, Solicitors & Trade Mark Agents
Place Moncton Place, 655 Main Street, P.O. Box 1368, E1C 8T6
Telephone: 506-857-8970
Fax: 506-857-4095
Email: mcrmctn@mcrlaw.com *URL:* http://www.mcrlaw.com
Halifax, Nova Scotia Office: Summit Place, 1601 Lower Water Street, P.O. Box 730, B3J 2V1.
Telephone: 902-425-6500.
Fax: 902-425-6350. Email: mcrhfx@mcrlaw.com.
St. John's, Newfoundland Office: Baine Johnston Centre, 5th Floor, 10 Fort William Place, P.O. Box 5939, A1C 5X4.
Telephone: 709-722-8735.
Telecopier: 709-722-1763. Email: mcrsj@mcrlaw.com.
Charlottetown, Prince Edward Island Office: BDC Place, Suite 620, 119 Kent Street, C1A 1N3.
Telephone: 902-368-8473.
Fax: 902-368-8346. Email: mcrpei@mcrlaw.com.
Fredericton, New Brunswick Office: Suite 600, 570 Queen Street, P.O. Box 610.
Telephone: 506-458-8572.
Fax: 506-458-9903. Email: mcrfton@mcrlaw.com.

COUNSEL

Frank J. McKenna

For Complete List of Firm Personnel, See General Section

For full biographical listings, see the Martindale-Hubbell Law Directory

CANADA NEWFOUNDLAND

*ST. JOHN'S,**

MCINNES COOPER (AV)

Barristers, Solicitors & Trade Mark Agents
Baine Johnston Centre, 5th Floor, 10 Fort William Place, P.O. Box 5939, A1C 5X4
Telephone: 709-722-8735
Telecopier: 709-722-1763
Email: mcrsj@mcrlaw.com *URL:* http://www.mcrlaw.com
Halifax, Nova Scotia Office: Summit Place, 1601 Lower Water Street, P.O. Box 730, B3J 2V1.
Telephone: 902-425-6500.
Fax: 902-425-6350. Email: mcrhfx@mcrlaw.com.
Moncton, New Brunswick Office: Place Moncton Place, 655 Main Street, P.O. Box 1368, E1C 8T6.
Telephone: 506-857-8970.
Fax: 506-857-4095. Email: mcrmctn@mcrlaw.com.
Charlottetown, Prince Edward Island Office: BDC Place, Suite 620, 119 Kent Street, C1A 1N3.
Telephone: 902-368-8473.
Fax: 902-368-8346. Email: mcrpei@mcrlaw.com.
Fredericton, New Brunswick Office: Suite 600, 570 Queen Street, P.O. Box 610.
Telephone: 506-458-8572.
Fax: 506-458-9903. Email: mcrfton@mcrlaw.com.

PARTNERS

Thomas R. Kendell
Christine A. Fagan, Q.C.

ASSOCIATE

William James O'Keefe

For Complete List of Firm Personnel, See General Section

For full biographical listings, see the Martindale-Hubbell Law Directory

CANADA
NOVA SCOTIA

*HALIFAX,** Regional Munic. of Halifax

McINNES COOPER (AV)

Barristers, Solicitors & Trade Mark Agents
Summit Place, 1601 Lower Water Street, P.O. Box 730, B3J 2V1
Telephone: 902-425-6500
Fax: 902-425-6350
Email: mcrhfx@mcrlaw.com *URL:* http://www.mcrlaw.com
St. John's, Newfoundland Office: Baine Johnston Centre, 5th Floor, 10 Fort William Place, P.O. Box 5939, A1C 5X4.
Telephone: 709-722-8735.
Telecopier: 709-722-1763. Email: mcrsj@mcrlaw.com.
Moncton, New Brunswick Office: Place Moncton Place, 655 Main Street, P.O. Box 1368, E1C 8T6.
Telephone: 506-857-8970.
Fax: 506-857-4095. Email: mcrmctn@mcrlaw.com.
Charlottetown, Prince Edward Island Office: BDC Place, Suite 620, 119 Kent Street, C1A 1N3.
Telephone: 902-368-8473.
Fax: 902-368-8346. Email: mcrpei@mcrlaw.com.
Fredericton, New Brunswick Office: Suite 600, 570 Queen Street, P.O. Box 610.
Telephone: 506-458-8572.
Fax: 506-458-9903. Email: mcrfton@mcrlaw.com.

PARTNERS

George T. H. Cooper, Q.C.
F. Van W. Penick
Aidan J. Meade

ASSOCIATE

Kristi Sebalj

For Complete List of Firm Personnel, See General Section

For full biographical listings, see the Martindale-Hubbell Law Directory

CANADA
PRINCE EDWARD ISLAND

*CHARLOTTETOWN,** Queen's Co.

McINNES COOPER (AV Ⓣ)

Barristers, Solicitors & Trade Mark Agents
BDC Place, Suite 620, 119 Kent Street, C1A 1N3
Telephone: 902-368-8473
Fax: 902-368-8346
Email: mcrpei@mcrlaw.com *URL:* http://www.mcrlaw.com
Halifax, Nova Scotia Office: Summit Place, 1601 Lower Water Street, P.O. Box 730, B3J 2V1.
Telephone: 902-425-6500.
Fax: 902-425-6350. Email: mcrhfx@mcrlaw.com.
St. John's, Newfoundland Office: Baine Johnston Centre, 5th Floor, 10 Fort William Place, P.O. Box 5939, A1C 5X4.
Telephone: 709-722-8735.
Telecopier: 709-722-1763. Email: mcrsj@mcrlaw.com.
Moncton, New Brunswick Office: Place Moncton Place, 655 Main Street, P.O. Box 1368, E1C 8T6.
Telephone: 506-857-8970.
Fax: 506-857-4095. Email: mcrmctn@mcrlaw.com.
Fredericton, New Brunswick Office: Suite 600, 570 Queen Street, P.O. Box 610.
Telephone: 506-458-8572.
Fax: 506-458-9903. Email: mcrfton@mcrlaw.com.

PARTNER

Mark Ledwell

ASSOCIATE

L. Charles Keizer

For Complete List of Firm Personnel, See General Section

For full biographical listings, see the Martindale-Hubbell Law Directory

PATENT, TRADEMARK, COPYRIGHT AND UNFAIR COMPETITION

(See also listings under Trademark, Copyright and Unfair Competition)

MINNESOTA

*MINNEAPOLIS,** Hennepin Co.

ARNOLD WHITE & DURKEE, A PROFESSIONAL CORPORATION (AV Ⓣ)

4850 U.S. Bank Place, 601 Second Avenue South, 55402-4320
Telephone: 612-321-2800
Facsimile: 612-321-9600
Email: info@awd.com *URL:* http://www.awd.com
Houston, Texas Office: 750 Bering Drive, 77057-2198.
Telephone: 713-787-1400.
Facsimile: 713-787-1440.
Austin, Texas Office: 1900 One American Center, 600 Congress Avenue, 78701-3248.
Telephone: 512-418-3000.
Facsimile: 512-474-7577.
Washington, D.C. Office: One Franklin Square, 1301 K Street, N.W., Suite 350, East Tower, 20005.
Telephone: 202-289-0229.
Facsimile: 202-289-7535.
Chicago, Illinois Office: 800 Quaker Tower, 321 North Clark Street, 60610-4714.
Telephone: 312-744-0090.
Facsimile: 312-755-4489.
Menlo Park, California Office: 155 Linfield Drive, 94025-3741.
Telephone: 650-614-4500.
Facsimile: 650-614-4599.

Charles H. De La Garza
Stephen R. Baird
Mark L. Gleason
Timothy M. Kenny
Marsha Stolt
Michael L. Gannon
Tong Wu

OF COUNSEL

Jana L. France

For full biographical listings, see the Martindale-Hubbell Law Directory

HAUGEN LAW FIRM, PLLP (AV)

121 South Eighth Street, Suite 1130, 55402
Telephone: 612-339-8300
Fax: 612-339-8200
Email: ohaugen@haugenlaw.com *URL:* http://www.haugenlaw.com

Orrin M. Haugen
Eric O. Haugen

OF COUNSEL

Douglas E. Mackenzie

For full biographical listings, see the Martindale-Hubbell Law Directory

MACKALL, CROUNSE & MOORE, PLC (AV)

1400 AT&T Tower, 901 Marquette Avenue, 55402-2859
Telephone: 612-305-1400
Fax: 612-305-1414
URL: http://www.mcmlaw.com

MEMBERS OF FIRM

G. Thomas MacIntosh, II
Gerald E. Helget
James A. Wahl
Nelson R. Capes

For Complete List of Firm Personnel, See General Section

For full biographical listings, see the Martindale-Hubbell Law Directory

MOORE & HANSEN (AV)

2900 Norwest Center, 90 South 7th Street, 55402
Telephone: 612-332-8200
Toll-free WATS: 1-888-667-2066
Fax: 612-332-1780
Email: MOOREHANSN@AOL.COM

Malcolm L. Moore
Conrad A. Hansen

OF COUNSEL

Robert C. Freed

ASSOCIATES

Christopher J. McLaughlin (Not admitted in MN)
John D. Kramm

(See Next Column)

PATENT AGENT

David John McKinley

Representative Clients: Liberty Diversified Industries; MedAmicus, Inc.; Stratasys, Inc.; Regis Corp.; Service Ideas, Inc.; Domain, Inc., New Richmond, Wis.; Dodger Industries, Inc., Eldora, Iowa; Slidell, Inc., Owatonna, Mn.

For full biographical listings, see the Martindale-Hubbell Law Directory

NIKOLAI, MERSEREAU & DIETZ, P.A. (AV)

820 International Centre, 900 Second Avenue South, 55402
Telephone: 612-339-7461
Telecopier: 612-349-6556
Email: tnikolai@prodigy.net

Thomas J. Nikolai
James T. Nikolai
Charles G. Mersereau
Paul T. Dietz

Reference: Norwest Bank.

For full biographical listings, see the Martindale-Hubbell Law Directory

OPPENHEIMER WOLFF & DONNELLY LLP (AV)

3400 Plaza VII, 45 South Seventh Street, 55402
Telephone: 612-607-7000
FAX: 612-607-7100
URL: http://www.owdlaw.com
Amsterdam, The Netherlands Office: Keizergracht 241.
Telephone: 31-20-423-4555.
FAX: 31-20-423-4545.
Brussels, Belgium Office: Avenue Louise 240, Box 5, 1050.
Telephone: 32-2-626-0500.
FAX: 32-2-626-0510.
Geneva, Switzerland Office: Rue Gabriel Eynard, 6, 1205.
Telephone: (41/22) 311-7410.
FAX: (41/22) 311-7407.
New York, N.Y. Office: Citicorp Center, 153 East 53rd Street, 10022.
Telephone: 212-826-5000.
FAX: 212-486-0708.
Newport Beach, California Office: 500 Newport Center Drive, Suite 700, 92660.
Telephone: 949-719-6000.
FAX: 949-719-6020.
Paris, France Office: 53 Avenue Montaigne, 75008.
Telephone: (33/1) 44 95 03 50.
FAX: (33/1) 44 95 03 40.
St. Paul, Minnesota Office: 1700 First National Bank Building, 55101.
Telephone: 651-605-2000.
FAX: 651-605-2100.
Washington, D.C. Office: Oppenheimer Wolff Donnelly & Bayh LLP, 1350 Eye Street, N.W., Suite 200, 20005.
Telephone: 202-312-8000.
FAX: 202-312-8100.
Los Angeles, California Office: 2029 Century Park East, 38th Floor, 90067.
Telephone: 310-788-5000.
FAX: 310-277-1297.
San Jose, California Office: 101 Park Center Plaza, Suite 300, 95113.
Telephone: 408-795-3000.
FAX: 408-795-3100.
Chicago, Illinois Office: Oppenheimer Wolff & Donnelly (Illinois), Two Prudential Plaza, 45th Floor, 180 North Stetson Avenue, 60601.
Telephone: 312-616-1800.
Fax: 312-616-5800.

RESIDENT PARTNERS

Harold D. Jastram
James E. Schatz
Edward M. Laine
Barbara J. Grahn
Jake M. Holdreith
Craig J. Lervick

RESIDENT ASSOCIATES

Alan D. Kamrath
Chad A. Klingbeil
Erika S. Koster
Ernest W. Grumbles, III
Bridget A. Sullivan
Daniel G. Chapik
Cyrus A. Morton

For Complete List of Firm Personnel, See General Section

For full biographical listings, see the Martindale-Hubbell Law Directory

MISSOURI

KANSAS CITY, Jackson, Clay, Platte & Cass Cos.

LITMAN, KRAAI AND BROWN, L.L.C. (AV)

Formerly Fishburn, Gold and Litman
4700 Belleview, Suite 200, 64112
Telephone: 816-931-1800
Fax: 816-931-8820
Email: dac@lmblaw.com *URL:* http://www.lmblaw.com

(See Next Column)

LITMAN, KRAAI AND BROWN L.L.C., *Kansas City—Continued*

MEMBERS OF FIRM

Orville O. Gold (1908-1980)
Claude A. Fishburn (1896-1982)
Malcolm A. Litman
Gerald M. Kraai
Mark E. Brown
Michael Elbein
Kent R. Erickson
Gerald L. Brigance

ASSOCIATES

Marcia J. Rodgers
Brian Richard McGinley

PATENT AGENT

Dennis A. Crawford

OF COUNSEL

John C. McMahon

For full biographical listings, see the Martindale-Hubbell Law Directory

ST. LOUIS, (Independent City)

COHN, POWELL AND HIND, P.C. (AV)

7700 Clayton Road, 63117
Telephone: 314-645-2442
Telecopier: 314-645-0913
Email: cphpc@swbell.net

Lawrence H. Cohn (1905-1976)
Frank B. Powell (1925-1983)
Ronald W. Hind

Timothy Keith Klintworth
Mary Lu Sanders-Zinser

For full biographical listings, see the Martindale-Hubbell Law Directory

GRACE J. FISHEL (AV)

11970 Borman Drive, Suite 220, 63146
Telephone: 314-878-0440
Fax: 314-275-7693
Email: 70121.121@compuserve.com

For full biographical listings, see the Martindale-Hubbell Law Directory

HAVERSTOCK, GARRETT AND ROBERTS (AV)

611 Olive Street, Suite 1610, 63101
Telephone: 314-241-4427
Telefax: 314-241-3317
Email: hgr@inlink.com

MEMBERS OF FIRM

Charles B. Haverstock
Robert M. Garrett
Herbert B. Roberts
Samuel Digirolamo
Veo Peoples, Jr.
David H. Chervitz
Stephen R. Matthews

ASSOCIATE

Holly M. Amjad

For full biographical listings, see the Martindale-Hubbell Law Directory

HOWELL & HAFERKAMP, L.C. (AV)

Suite 1400, Pierre Laclede Building, 7733 Forsyth Boulevard, 63105-1783
Telephone: 314-727-5188
Telecopier: 314-727-6092
Email: law@howellhafer.com *URL:* http://www.howellhafer.com

Lawrence C. Kingsland (1884-1969)
Estill E. Ezell (1906-1971)
Edmund C. Rogers (1908-1996)
John M. Howell
Richard E. Haferkamp
Kenneth Solomon
Joseph M. Rolnicki
Joseph E. Walsh, Jr.
Alan H. Norman
Donald R. Holland
Bryan K. Wheelock
Anthony G. Simon

Charles E. Dunlap
Michael Joseph Thomas
Thomas A. Polcyn
Melodie W. Henderson
David B. Jinkins
Evan R. Sotiriou
Jeffery H. Urian

For full biographical listings, see the Martindale-Hubbell Law Directory

POLSTER, LIEDER, WOODRUFF & LUCCHESI, L.C. (AV)

763 South New Ballas Road, 63141-8750
Telephone: 314-872-8118
Fax: 314-991-2178
Email: PLWL@PATPRO.COM
Louisville, Kentucky Office: 2303 Tuckaho Road.
Telephone: 505-895-4672.
Belleville, Illinois Office: 2 Park Place Professional Centre, 62223.
Telephone: 618-257-8340.

(See Next Column)

Roy Lieder (1924-1991)
Philip B. Polster
Frederick M. Woodruff
J. Philip Polster
Lionel L. Lucchesi
William B. Cunningham, Jr.
William G. Bruns
Edward A. Boeschenstein
Michael Kovac
J. Joseph Muller
McPherson D. Moore
Jonathan P. Soifer
Ned W. Randle

Catherine Wynne Wall
Philip B. Polster II
Mark E. Books

OF COUNSEL

Ralph B. Brick (Resident, Louisville, Kentucky Office)
Martha A. Michaels
Richard J. Sher
Rose N. Perotti

For full biographical listings, see the Martindale-Hubbell Law Directory

SENNIGER, POWERS, LEAVITT & ROEDEL (AV)

Formerly Koenig, Senniger, Powers and Leavitt
One Metropolitan Square, 16th Floor, 63102
Telephone: 314-231-5400
Cable Address: "Patent"
Fax: 314-231-4342
URL: http://www.senniger.com

Delos G. Haynes (1887-1950)
Lloyd R. Koenig (1900-1986)
Stuart N. Senniger (1921-1997)

MEMBERS OF FIRM

Frank R. Agovino
Robert M. Bain
G. Harley Blosser
James Bennett Clark
Robert M. Evans, Jr.
Paul I. J. Fleischut
Michael E. Godar
Edward J. Hejlek
Kurt F. James
Vincent M. Keil
William E. Lahey
Donald G. Leavitt
Kathleen M. Petrillo
John K. Roedel, Jr.

ASSOCIATES

Derick E. Allen
Richard L. Bridge
James E. Butler (Not admitted in MO)
Sarah Janette Chickos
Charles E. Cohen
David E. Crawford, Jr.
Matthew Lawrence Cutler
Patrick S. Eagleman
Elie H. Gendloff
Christopher M. Goff
David M. Gryte
Karen Y. Hui
Anthony R. Kinney
Paul A. Maddock
Michael G. Munsell
Laura R. Polcyn
Steven M. Ritchey
Joseph A. Schaper
Meg Marshall Thomas
Donald W. Tuegel
Scott Alan Williams

OF COUNSEL

Irving Powers
Richard G. Heywood
Robert J. Lewis

For full biographical listings, see the Martindale-Hubbell Law Directory

*SPRINGFIELD,** Greene Co.

WILLIAM H. McDONALD & ASSOCIATES, P.C. (AV)

300 South Jefferson, Suite 600, P.O. Box 1245, 65801
Telephone: 417-869-0581
Facsimile: 417-831-7852
Email: mcdassoc@dialnet.net *URL:* http://www.mcdonaldassoc.com

William H. McDonald

Dana A. Chamblee

For Complete List of Firm Personnel, See General Section

For full biographical listings, see the Martindale-Hubbell Law Directory

MONTANA

*BOZEMAN,** Gallatin Co.

PAUL R. WYLIE A PROFESSIONAL CORPORATION (AV㊉)

1805 West Dickerson #2, Suite 3, 59715
Telephone: 406-585-7344
Telecopier: 406-585-7358
Email: PWLAW@AOL.COM

Paul R. Wylie

Reference: First Security Bank, Bozeman, Montana.

For full biographical listings, see the Martindale-Hubbell Law Directory

NEBRASKA

*OMAHA,** Douglas Co.

SUITER & ASSOCIATES P.C. (AV)

11516 Nicholas Street, Suite 205, 68154-4409
Telephone: 402-496-0300
Facsimile: 402-496-0333
URL: http://www.suiter.com

Sean Patrick Suiter

Kenneth J. Cool
Scott C. Rand
Kevin E. West
William J. Breen, III

LEGAL SUPPORT PERSONNEL

Nancy S. Husarik (Patent Agent)

For full biographical listings, see the Martindale-Hubbell Law Directory

NEW HAMPSHIRE

*MANCHESTER,** Hillsborough Co.

DAVIS AND BUJOLD (AV)

500 North Commercial Street, 03101
Telephone: 603-624-9220
Telecopier: 603-624-9229
Email: patent@tiac.net

Anthony G. M. Davis (Not admitted in NH)
Michael J. Bujold
Scott A. Daniels
Gary D. Clapp (Not admitted in NH)

For full biographical listings, see the Martindale-Hubbell Law Directory

NEW JERSEY

*HACKENSACK,** Bergen Co.

LAW OFFICES OF ARTHUR JACOB (AV)

25 East Salem Street, P.O. Box 686, 07602
Telephone: 201-488-8700
Fax: 201-487-9393

For full biographical listings, see the Martindale-Hubbell Law Directory

KLAUBER & JACKSON (AV)

Continental Plaza, 411 Hackensack Avenue, 07601
Telephone: 201-487-5800
Telex: 133521
Fax: 201-343-1684; 343-7544
Email: kjiplaw@webspan.net
Email: 6261210@mcimail.com

MEMBER OF FIRM

David A. Jackson

ASSOCIATES

Michael D. Davis (Not admitted in NJ)
Donald J. Cox, Jr. (Not admitted in NJ)

OF COUNSEL

Stefan J. Klauber
Jack Matalon
Roger M. Rathbun

LEGAL SUPPORT PERSONNEL

Christine E. Dietzel (Patent Agent)
Michael A. Yamin (Patent Agent)

For full biographical listings, see the Martindale-Hubbell Law Directory

*NEWARK,** Essex Co.

SILLS CUMMIS RADIN TISCHMAN EPSTEIN & GROSS, A PROFESSIONAL CORPORATION (AV)

One Riverfront Plaza, 07102-5400
Telephone: 973-643-7000
Fax: 973-643-6500
Telex: 820630 Sillsbeck Nwk
Email: sillsmail@sillscummis.com *URL:* http://www.sillscummis.com
Atlantic City, New Jersey Office: 17 Gordon's Alley.
Telephone: 609-344-2800.
New York, N.Y. Office: 712 Fifth Avenue.
Telephone: 212-643-7000.
Washington, D.C. Office: 1800 K Street, N.W.
Telephone: 202-296-4750.

(See Next Column)

MEMBERS OF FIRM

Clive S. Cummis
Jeffrey J. Greenbaum
Jeffrey Barton Cahn
Ira A. Rosenberg
James M. Hirschhorn

Noel D. Humphreys

Representative Clients: Dominos Pizza, Inc.; Alpine Lace Brands; Bally entertainment Corp.; Trophix Pharmaceuticals, Inc.; Lane Laboratories, Inc.; Swan International Optical, Inc.; Big M, Inc.; Trecom Business Systems, Inc.

For Complete List of Firm Personnel, See General Section

For full biographical listings, see the Martindale-Hubbell Law Directory

NEW PROVIDENCE, Union Co.

COOPER & STIELER (AV)

A Partnership including a Professional Corporation
(Formerly Smith & Stieler)
27 Murray Hill Square, 07974
Telephone: 908-665-2828
Fax: 908-771-7792
Cable Address: "Cooper Stieler"
Email: info@cooperstieler.com
Mailing Address: 41 Mountain Avenue, P.O. Box Box 125, New Providence, New Jersey, 07974
Email: cooperstieler@lawyers.com *URL:* http://www.lawyers.com/cooperstieler
Summit, New Jersey Office: Harper Plaza, Suite 100, 34 River Road, P.O. Box 361.
Telephone: 908-467-0900.
Fax: 908-467-0911.

MEMBER OF FIRM

Scott R. Stieler III (Not admitted in NJ; Resident, Summit Office)

LEGAL SUPPORT PERSONNEL

Paul G. Rispoli, Jr. (Patent Agent)

For full biographical listings, see the Martindale-Hubbell Law Directory

PARSIPPANY, Morris Co.

HOFFMANN & BARON, LLP (AV)

1055 Parsippany Boulevard, 07054
Telephone: 973-331-1700
Fax: 973-331-1717
Syosset, New York Office: 6900 Jericho Turnpike, 11791.
Telephone: 516-822-3550.
Telecopier: 516-822-3582.

MEMBER OF FIRM

Daniel A. Scola, Jr.
Salvatore J. Abbruzzese

ASSOCIATES

Kirk M. Miles
Robert F. Chisholm (Not admitted in NJ)
Mark E. Baron
Kellyanne Merkel
John S. Sopko
Barry H. Jacobsen

LEGAL SUPPORT PERSONNEL
PATENT AGENTS

Keith R. Lange
Gloria K. Szakiel

For full biographical listings, see the Martindale-Hubbell Law Directory

ROSELAND, Essex Co.

CARELLA, BYRNE, BAIN, GILFILLAN, CECCHI, STEWART & OLSTEIN, A PROFESSIONAL CORPORATION (AV)

Six Becker Farm Road, 07068-1739
Telephone: 973-994-1700
Telecopier: 973-994-1744

John N. Bain
John G. Gilfillan, III
Elliot M. Olstein

Raymond J. Lillie
William Squire
Alan J. Grant (Not admitted in NJ)

OF COUNSEL

Donald S. Brooks

Representative Clients: FL Industries, Inc., Livingston, N.J.; Werner and Pfeiderer Corp., Ramsey, N.J.; Russ Berrie and Co., Inc., Oakland, N.J.; Fortex Industries; Genetic Therapy, Gaithersburg, Md.; Biotransplant Inc., Charlestown, Ma.; Med Immune, Inc., Gaithersburg, Md.

For Complete List of Firm Personnel, See General Section

For full biographical listings, see the Martindale-Hubbell Law Directory

WESTFIELD, Union Co.

LERNER, DAVID, LITTENBERG, KRUMHOLZ & MENTLIK (AV)

600 South Avenue West, 07090-1497
Telephone: 908-654-5000
Facsimile: 908-654-7866
Email: law@ldlkm.com *URL:* http://www.ldlkm.com

MEMBERS OF FIRM

Sidney David
Joseph S. Littenberg
Arnold H. Krumholz
William L. Mentlik
John R. Nelson
Roy H. Wepner
Stephen B. Goldman
Charles P. Kennedy
Paul H. Kochanski
Marcus J. Millet
Bruce H. Sales
Arnold B. Dompieri
Keith E. Gilman
Robert B. Cohen

Michael H. Teschner
Gregory S. Gewirtz
Jonathan A. David
Shawn P. Foley (Not admitted in NJ)
John P. Maldjian
Stephen F. Roth
Thomas M. Palisi
Kimberly V. Perry
Jason Garbell
Renée M. Robeson
Brian K. Johnson
Lynne A. Borchers (Not admitted in NJ)
Peter A. Cicala
Michael J. Doherty
Michael J. Wallace, Jr (Not admitted in NJ)

OF COUNSEL

Lawrence I. Lerner
Daniel H. Bobis
Raymond W. Augustin (Not admitted in NJ)
Harvey L. Cohen
Jeffrey S. Dickey

For full biographical listings, see the Martindale-Hubbell Law Directory

NEW YORK

*ALBANY,** Albany Co.

HESLIN & ROTHENBERG, P.C. (AV)

5 Columbia Circle, 12203
Telephone: 518-452-5600
Facsimile: 518-452-5579
Email: hesroth@hriplaw.com

Robert E. Heslin
Jeff Rothenberg
Kevin P. Radigan
Susan E. Farley
Nicholas Mesiti
Blanche E. Schiller
Wayne F. Reinke

Jeffrey R. Klembczyk
Martha L. Boden
Candice J. Clement
Kathy Smith Dias
Mary Louise Gioeni
Michael J. Bendel (Not admitted in NY)
David A. Pascarella
Leo M. Loughlin
Daniel H. Beaty
Victor A. Cardona

PATENT AGENT

Philip E. Hansen

For full biographical listings, see the Martindale-Hubbell Law Directory

*BUFFALO,** Erie Co.

HODGSON, RUSS, ANDREWS, WOODS & GOODYEAR, LLP (AV)

A Registered Limited Liability Partnership including Professional Associations
One M & T Plaza, Suite 2000, 14203
Telephone: 716-856-4000
Fax: 716-849-0349
Email: info@hodgsonruss.com *URL:* www.hodgsonruss.com
Albany, New York Office: Three City Square, 12207.
Telephone: 518-465-2333.
Fax: 518-465-1567.
Boca Raton, Florida Office: Suite 400, 2000 Glades Road, 33431.
Telephone: 561-394-0500.
Fax: 561-394-3862.
Toronto, Ontario, Canada Office: 150 King Street West, Suite 2309, M5H 1J9, P.O. Box 30.
Telephone: 416-595-5100.
Fax: 416-595-5021.
New York, New York Office: 65 East 55th Street, 10th Floor, 10022.
Telephone: 212-751-4300.
Fax: 212-751-0928.
Gloversville, New York Office: 6 Fremont Street, 12078.
Telephone: 518-725-6347.
Fax: 518-773-7350.
Newark, New Jersey Office: One Gateway Center, Suite 2600, 07102.
Telephone: 973-645-0577.
Fax: 973-645-0551.

(See Next Column)

MEMBERS OF FIRM

(ALPHABETICALLY BY YEAR OF ADMISSION TO BAR)

Edwin T. Bean, Jr.
Martin G. Linihan
Tricia Thomas Semmelhack
Paul I. Perlman
Daniel C. Oliverio

ASSOCIATES

(ALPHABETICALLY BY YEAR OF ADMISSION TO BAR)

Michael F. Scalise
David L. Principe
R. Kent Roberts (Not admitted in NY)
Kevin D. McCarthy
Ranjana Kadle

For Complete List of Firm Personnel, See General Section

For full biographical listings, see the Martindale-Hubbell Law Directory

MCGEE & GELMAN (AV)

200 Summer Street, 14222-2271
Telephone: 716-883-7272
Fax: 716-883-7084
Email: counsel@mcgee-gelman.com

MEMBERS OF FIRM

Michael R. McGee
Warren B. Gelman
F. Brendan Burke, Jr.
Laura A. Colca
Jennifer L. Friedman

David S. Widenor

For full biographical listings, see the Martindale-Hubbell Law Directory

GARDEN CITY, Nassau Co.

SCULLY, SCOTT, MURPHY & PRESSER, A PROFESSIONAL CORPORATION (AV)

400 Garden City Plaza, 11530
Telephone: 516-742-4343
Facsimile: 516-742-4366
Email: intprop@ssmp.com

John F. Scully (Retired)
Anthony C. Scott (1931-1994)
William E. McNulty (1927-1993)
Stephen D. Murphy
Leopold Presser
Kenneth L. King
Frank S. DiGiglio
Paul J. Esatto, Jr.
John S. Sensny
Mark J. Cohen
Richard L. Catania
Edward W. Grolz
William C. Roch

Peter I. Bernstein
Marvin Bressler
Steven Fischman
Ann R. Pokalsky
Thomas Spinelli, Sr.
John F. Vodopia
Patricia A. Wilczynski

COUNSEL

Allen R. Morganstern
Stephen A. Young

LEGAL SUPPORT PERSONNEL

PROFESSIONAL TECHNICAL ASSOCIATE

Leslie S. Szivos, Ph.D.
Alexander G. Vodovozov
Xiaochun Zhu, Ph.D.

For full biographical listings, see the Martindale-Hubbell Law Directory

*NEW YORK,** New York Co.

AMSTER, ROTHSTEIN & EBENSTEIN (AV)

90 Park Avenue, 10016
Telephone: 212-697-5995
Facsimile: 212-286-0854

MEMBERS OF FIRM

Morton Amster
Jesse Rothstein (Retired)
Daniel S. Ebenstein
Philip H. Gottfried (Patent Attorney)
Michael J. Berger
Neil M. Zipkin
Anthony F. Lo Cicero
Joel E. Lutzker
Karen Artz Ash
Kenneth P. George
Abraham Kasdan
Leonard S. Sorgi
Ira E. Silfin

ASSOCIATES

Neal L. Rosenberg
Chester Rothstein
David H. Kagan
Denise A. Lindenauer
Craig J. Arnold
Nancy Meredith Dodderidge
Patrick E. Boland (Not admitted in NY)
Charles R. Macedo
Trebor Lloyd
Joseph M. Casino
Jane Ungaro
Donna L. Angotti
Neal S. Greenfield
Simon Bock
John C. Garces
Mark J. Rosenberg
Beth Kotran
Michael V. Solomita
Holly Pekowsky
John S. Economou
Daniel Basov
Ian R. Blum
Michael P. Kenney

(See Next Column)

AMSTER, ROTHSTEIN & EBENSTEIN—*Continued*

ASSOCIATES (Continued)

Kenneth M. Bernstein
Barbara Anne Parvis
(Not admitted in NY)
Marion Peter Metelski
(Not admitted in NY)
Monique L. Ribando
Jan Tamulewicz
Alison R. Kelly
Kevin J. Stein
Catherine S. Reynolds

For full biographical listings, see the Martindale-Hubbell Law Directory

BAKER BOTTS L.L.P. (AV)

599 Lexington Avenue, 10022-6030 and 30 Rockefeller Plaza, 10112-0228
Telephone: 212-705-5000
Fax: 212-705-5125 (599 Lexington Ave.)
Fax: 212-705-5020 (30 Rockeffeller Plaza)
Email: postmaster@bakerbotts.com *URL:* http://www.bakerbotts.com
Washington, D.C. Office: The Warner, 1299 Pennsylvania Avenue, N.W.
Telephone: 202-639-7700.
Austin, Texas Office: 1600 San Jacinto Center, 98 San Jacinto Boulevard.
Telephone: 512-322-2500.
Dallas, Texas Office: 2001 Ross Avenue.
Telephone: 214-953-6500.
Houston, Texas Office: One Shell Plaza, 910 Louisiana.
Telephone: 713-229-1234.
Moscow, Russia Office: 10 ul. Bolshaya Dimitrovka (formerly ul. Pushkinskaya), 103031.
Telephone: 7095/921-5300 (Local); 7095/929-7070 (International).
London, England Office: 45 Ludgate Hill.
Telephone: 0171-778-1400 (Local); 011-44-171-778-1400.
Baku, Azerbaijan Office: 6-10 Vagif Mustafa-zadeh Street, Third Floor, Icheri Sheher, 370004.
Telephone: 994-12-97-63-88 (Local); 011-994-12-97-63-88 (International).
Fax: 994-12-97-63-91 (Local); 011-994-12-97-63-61 (International).

MEMBERS OF FIRM

Richard G. Berkley
Gary M. Butter
Richard S. Clark
Doreen Leavens Costa
Marta E. Delsignore
Russell H. Falconer
John A. Fogarty, Jr.
Bradley B. Geist
Lisa B. Kole
James J. Maune
John D. Murnane
Thomas R. Nesbitt, Jr.
Robert Neuner
Robert C. Scheinfeld
Rochelle K. Seide
Louis S. Sorell
Henry Tang

RETIRED FIRM MEMBERS

Frederick C. Carver
Dana M. Raymond
Arthur S. Tenser

OF COUNSEL

Joseph D. Garon
Ronald B. Hildreth
Francis J. Hone

ASSOCIATES

Paul D. Ackerman
Lindsay S. Adams
Richard L. Blaylock
Anthony Giaccio
Robert L. Greenfeld
Steven R. Gustavson
Jeanne M. Hamburg
Samuel SungMok Lee
(Not admitted in NY)
Dr. Janet M. MacLeod
Paul A. Ragusa
Paul J. Reilly
Anne W. Salisbury
Neil P. Sirota
David W. Whealan
Karen Wuertz

For Complete List of Firm Personnel, See General Section

For full biographical listings, see the Martindale-Hubbell Law Directory

COBRIN & GITTES (AV)

750 Lexington Avenue, 10022
Telephone: 212-486-4000
Telecopier: 212-486-4007
Email: cgpats@ix.netcom.com

Peter T. Cobrin
Marvin S. Gittes
Richard M. Lehrer
David W. Denenberg

Robert J. Hess
Michael A. Adler
Gerald J. Cechony
(Not admitted in NY)
Oren J. Warshavsky
Clyde Alvin Shuman
Lawrence E. Russ

Representative Clients: Northern Telecom, Inc.; DataPoint Corporation; Magnivision, Inc.; Atico; Global Direct Mail Corporation; MW; Oxigene, Inc.; Horphag Research, LTD.

For full biographical listings, see the Martindale-Hubbell Law Directory

COLUCCI & UMANS (AV)

Manhattan Tower, 101 East 52nd Street, 10022
Telephone: 212-935-5700
Facsimile: 212-935-5728
Telex: 661503 WUI
Email: emial@colucci-umans.com
Westchester County, Scarsdale, New York Office: 670 White Plains Road, Scarsdale.
Telephone: 914-472-1500.
Facsimile: 914-472-1551.

MEMBERS OF FIRM

Frank J. Colucci
Courtney Wilson Monahan

Thomas A. Kain
Raymond J. Glynn
W. Brant Mossop
Susan B. Jacobson
Gregory J. Colucci
(Resident, Scarsdale Office)
Richard P. Jacobson
David M. Dahan
Katherine Beecher Carlburg
Kathleen M. McGann
Renée L. Duff
(Resident, Scarsdale Office)

OF COUNSEL

Angelo Notaro

For full biographical listings, see the Martindale-Hubbell Law Directory

COOPER & DUNHAM LLP (AV)

1185 Avenue of the Americas, 10036
Telephone: 212-278-0400
Fax: 212-391-0525
Email: counsel@cooperdunham.com *URL:* http://www.cooperdunham.com

MEMBERS OF FIRM

Christopher C. Dunham
Norman H. Zivin
John P. White
William E. Pelton
Robert D. Katz
Peter J. Phillips
Wendy E. Miller
Ivan S. Kavrukov
Peter D. Murray
Jay H. Maioli
Robert B. G. Horowitz
Donald S. Dowden
Donna A. Tobin
Richard S. Milner
Albert Wai-Kit Chan

ASSOCIATES

Robert T. Maldonado
Elizabeth M. Wieckowski
Pedro C. Fernandez
Todd W. Evans
Michael F. Morano
Spencer H. Schneider
Paul Teng
Richard F. Jaworski
Gary J. Gershik
William Y. Lee
(Not admitted in NY)
Raymond A. DiPerna

OF COUNSEL

Gerald W. Griffin
John R. Garber

LEGAL SUPPORT PERSONNEL

SCIENTIFIC ADVISORS

Jane M. Love
Alan D. Miller

For full biographical listings, see the Martindale-Hubbell Law Directory

DAVIDSON, DAVIDSON & KAPPEL, LLC (AV)

1140 Avenue of the Americas, 15th Floor, 10036
Telephone: 212-997-1028
Fax: 212-997-1037
URL: http://www.lawyers.com/dd&klaw

Clifford M. Davidson
Leslye B. Davidson
Cary S. Kappel
William C. Gehris
Julie L. Bowker

ASSOCIATES

Robert J. Paradiso
Scott L. Appelbaum
Jane E. Alexander
(Not admitted in NY)
Marc D. Baker
Cynthia Moore

For full biographical listings, see the Martindale-Hubbell Law Directory

FABRICANT & YESKOO, LLP (AV)

535 Fifth Avenue, 10017
Telephone: 212-983-0900
Telecopier: 212-983-0907
Hoboken, New Jersey Office: Hudson Legal Center, 86 Hudson Street.
Telephone: 201-420-8650.

Alfred R. Fabricant
Richard C. Yeskoo

Thomas T. Tamlyn, Jr.
Elénee Argentinis

For full biographical listings, see the Martindale-Hubbell Law Directory

New York—Continued

FISH & NEAVE (AV)

Fish, Richardson & Neave, New York (1916-1969)
1251 Avenue of the Americas, 10020
Telephone: 212-596-9000
Telex: 14-8367
Cable Address: Fishneave
Telecopier: 212-596-9090
URL: http://www.fishneave.com
Palo Alto, California Office: 525 University Avenue, Suite 300, 94301.
Telephone: 650-617-4000.
Telecopier: 650-617-4090.

Frederick P. Fish (1855-1930) Charles Neave (1867-1937)

PARTNERS

Albert E. Fey
John O. Tramontine
Herbert F. Schwartz
Lars I. Kulleseid
Eric C. Woglom
John E. Nathan
Robert C. Morgan
Kenneth B. Herman
Edward F. Mullowney (Resident, Palo Alto, California Office)
Robert R. Jackson
Jesse J. Jenner
W. Edward Bailey
Patricia A. Martone
James F. Haley, Jr.
Richard M. Barnes
Laurence S. Rogers
Thomas L. Giannetti
Vincent N. Palladino
Robert J. Goldman (Resident, Palo Alto, California Office)
Thomas L. Secrest
Daniel M. Gantt
Norman H. Beamer (Resident, Palo Alto, California Office)
Kevin J. Culligan
Glenn A. Ousterhout
Susan Progoff
Margaret A. Pierri
Douglas J. Gilbert
Denise L. Loring
Jeffrey H. Ingerman
Mark H. Bloomberg
Jane A. Massaro
Duane-David Hough
Mark D. Rowland (Resident, Palo Alto, California Office)
Edward J. DeFranco
Eric R. Hubbard
Kelsey I. Nix
William J. McCabe
Marta E. Gross
John M. Hintz
Vicki S. Veenker (Resident, Palo Alto, California Office)
Richard A. Inz
Nicola A. Pisano (Resident, Palo Alto, California Office)
Frances M. Lynch
Christopher J. Harnett

RETIRED PARTNERS

Harry R. Pugh, Jr.
William K. Kerr
Rynn Berry
Henry J. Zafian
Donald E. Degling
Charles B. Smith
David W. Plant

SENIOR ATTORNEYS

A. Peter Adler
Thomas J. Vetter
Charles Quinn
Lisa E. Cristal
Gabrielle E. Higgins (Resident, Palo Alto, California Office)

ASSOCIATES

Hope H. Liebke
Lianna L. Cleland
Richard G. Gervase, Jr.
Louis H. Weinstein
Alison Joy Arnold
William H. Steinmetz (Resident, Palo Alto, California Office)
Steven C. Cherny
Lewis V. Popovski
Eric D. Kirsch
Jeanne C. Curtis
Terrence J. P. Kearney (Resident, Palo Alto, California Office)
Joseph M. Guiliano
Gerald J. Flattmann, Jr.
Gene W. Lee
Kevin P.B. Johnson (Resident, Palo Alto, California Office)
James E. Hopenfeld (Resident, Palo Alto, California Office)
William L. Leschensky (Resident, Palo Alto, California Office)
Robert W. Morris
Avinash S. Lele
Jane Tower Gunnison
Petrina S. Hsi (Resident, Palo Alto, California Office)
James Trosino (Resident, Palo Alto, California Office)
Joseph C. Kirincich
Regan L. Trumper
G. Victor Treyz
Armando Irizarry
Martin A. Leroy
Thomas P. Burke
Pablo Daniel Hendler
Theresa A. Moehlman
Keith A. Zullow
James P. Doyle, Jr.
Peter J. Knudsen
Karen J. Jacobs
Brian C. Cannon (Resident, Palo Alto, California Office)
Glenn F. Frankenberger
John Frank Beninati
Maria C. Walsh
Andrew J. Hollander
Victor F. DeFrancis
Walter M. Egbert, III
Daniel M. Becker (Resident, Palo Alto, California Office)
Hallie Kostrinsky
Kurtis D. MacFerrin (Resident, Palo Alto, California Office)
Jennifer T. Weissman
Daniel S. Hulme
David A. Makman (Resident, Palo Alto, California Office)
Charles E. Phipps
Nicholas J. Shaw
Jennifer D. Choe
Michelle Waites (Not admitted in NY)
Barbara A. Ruskin
Brett G. Alten
Art C. Cody
Catherine Nyarady
Sasha G. Rao
Robert B. Wilson
David Young
Michelle L. Finneran (Resident, Palo Alto, California)
Keith D. Agisim
Chad Yohn

(See Next Column)

ASSOCIATES (Continued)

Martin F. Noonan
Gerard Bilotto
Nicholas A. Tyacke
Arpan Bob Ghosh
Matthew T. Byrne
Ching-Lee Shen
Lowell Dashefsky
Lisa M. Knight
Bryan Moore
Sona De (Not admitted in NY)
Eric Huang
Joel Weiss
Diana J. Diasparra
Paul B. Keller
Tina S. Patel (Resident, Palo Alto, California Office)
Steven Pepe
H. John Rizvi
Steven John Cahill (Resident, Palo Alto, California Office)
Charles A. Krauss (Not admitted in NY)
Joseph A. Cilluffo
Richard M. Feustel, Jr.
John P. Hanish
Eugene T. Lee
P. Anthony Sammi
Rebecca Gibbs
Adam P. Noah (Resident, Palo Alto, California Office)

For full biographical listings, see the Martindale-Hubbell Law Directory

FITZPATRICK, CELLA, HARPER & SCINTO (AV)

30 Rockefeller Plaza, 10112-3801
Telephone: 212-218-2100
Cable Address: "Fitzcel New York"
International-Telex: FCHS 236262
Facsimile: 212-218-2200
Washington, D.C. Office: 1900 K Street, N.W.
Telephone: 202-530-1010.
Facsimile: 202-530-1055.
Orange County, California Office: 650 Town Center Drive, Suite 1800, Costa Mesa.
Telephone: 714-540-8700.
Facsimile: 714-540-9823.

MEMBERS OF FIRM

Joseph M. Fitzpatrick
Lawrence F. Scinto
William J. Brunet
Robert L. Baechtold
John A. O'Brien
John A. Krause
Henry J. Renk
David F. Ryan
Peter Saxon
Anthony M. Zupcic
Charles P. Baker
Stevan J. Bosses
Edward E. Vassallo
Ronald A. Clayton
Nicholas M. Cannella
Hugh C. Barrett
Pasquale A. Razzano
John W. Behringer (Washington, D.C. Office)
Lawrence A. Stahl (Washington, D.C. Office)
Leonard P. Diana
William M. Wannisky (Washington, D.C. Office)
Nina Shreve
Robert H. Fischer
Donald J. Curry
Warren E. Olsen (Washington, D.C. Office)
Nicholas N. Kallas
Bruce C. Haas
Thomas H. Beck
Lawrence S. Perry
Michael K. O'Neill (Orange County, California Office)
Richard P. Bauer (Washington, D.C. Office)
Errol B. Taylor
Nicholas Groombridge
Leslie K. Mitchell
Scott K. Reed
Fredrick M. Zullow
Scott D. Malpede (Washington, D.C. Office)
Thomas J. O'Connell (Washington, D.C. Office)
Steven E. Warner (Washington, D.C. Office)
Raymond R. Mandra
Leonard J. Santisi
Steven C. Kline
Dominick A. Conde
Brian V. Slater
Joseph M. O'Malley, Jr.
Mark A. Williamson (Washington, D.C. Office)
Mark J. Itri (Orange County, California Office)
Diego Scambia
Timothy J. Kelly
Michael P. Sandonato
Bruce M. Wexler
Gregory B. Sephton
Anne M. Maher (Limited to matters and proceedings before federal courts and agencies) (Washington, D.C. Office)
John D. Carlin
Lisa Barons Baeurle

COUNSEL

Robert C. Kline (Washington, D.C. Office)

ASSOCIATES

Laura A. Bauer
Christopher Philip Wrist (Washington, D.C. Office)
Gary M. Jacobs (Washington, D.C. Office)
David L. Schaeffer
Jack S. Cubert (Limited to matters and proceedings before federal courts and agencies) (Washington, D.C. Office)
Jean K. Dudek (Washington, D.C. Office)
Jack M. Arnold (Not admitted in NY)
Joseph W. Ragusa
Daniel S. Glueck (Washington, D.C. Office)
Brian L. Klock (Washington, D.C. Office)
Dolores Moro-Grossman
Douglas Sharrott
T Tom C. Gellenthien (Washington, D.C. Office)
Sean W. O'Brien (Limited to matters and proceedings before federal courts and agencies) (Washington, D.C. Office)
Matthew J. Golden
William E. Solander
Lee A. Goldberg
Leisa M. Smith
Jennifer A. Reda
Amr O. Aly
Kathryn Lutomski Sieburth

(See Next Column)

FITZPATRICK, CELLA, HARPER & SCINTO—*Continued*

ASSOCIATES (Continued)

Flora W. Feng
Lee B. Shelton
Jennifer A. Gilleece
Victoria J.B. Doyle
Tara A. Byrne
Shawn W. Fraser (Limited to matters and proceedings before federal courts and agencies) (Washington, D.C. Office)
Shogo Asaji
Elizabeth F. Holowacz
Brian P. Hopkins
Edmund J. Haughey, III (Limited to matters and proceedings before federal courts and agencies) (Washington, D.C. Office)
Justin J. Oliver (Limited to matters and proceedings before federal courts and agencies) (Washington, D.C. Office)
David P. Dalke (Orange County, California Office)
Erica Rayburn Halstead
Frank A. DeLucia, Jr. (Not admitted in NY)
Dennis A. Duchene (Orange County, California Office)
Marc J. Pensabene
Bonny B. Rozzo
Thomas F. Presson
Colleen Tracy
Nicole E. Miller
Steven Wayne Stewart (Limited to matters and proceedings before federal courts and agencies) (Washington, D.C. Office)
Gavin T. Bogle
Daniel R. Cahoy
David Greenbaum
Albert R. Ubieta
Wendy H. Lei
Lock See Yu-Jahnes
Joshua I. Rothman
Herbert William Rea
James M. Gibson
Aaron S. Haleva
Michael R. Brew

For full biographical listings, see the Martindale-Hubbell Law Directory

FROMMER LAWRENCE & HAUG LLP (AV)

745 Fifth Avenue, 10151
Telephone: 212-588-0800
Fax: 212-588-0500
Email: firm@FLHlaw.com

MEMBERS OF FIRM

William S. Frommer
William F. Lawrence
Edgar H. Haug
Matthew K. Ryan
Barry S. White
Thomas J. Kowalski
John R. Lane
Dennis M. Smid (Not admitted in NY)
Daniel G. Brown
Barbara Z. Morrissey
Steven M. Amundson
Marilyn Matthes Brogan
James K. Stronski

COUNSEL

A. Thomas S. Safford
Jerome Rosenstock
Raymond R. Wittekind

ASSOCIATES

Gordon M. Kessler
Mark W. Russell (Not admitted in NY)
Bruno Polito
Grace L. Pan (Not admitted in NY)
Jeffrey A. Hovden
Joe H. Shallenburger
Christian M. Smolizza
Glenn F. Savit
Robert E. Colletti
Dexter T. Chang
Lindsey A. Möhle
Deena P. Levy

For full biographical listings, see the Martindale-Hubbell Law Directory

HOPGOOD, CALIMAFDE, KALIL & JUDLOWE LLP (AV)

A Partnership including Professional Corporations
Lincoln Building, 60 East 42nd Street, 10165
Telephone: 212-551-5000
Telecopier: 212-949-2795; 212-949-9623

MEMBERS OF FIRM

Roy C. Hopgood
John M. Calimafde (P.C.)
Eugene J. Kalil
Stephen B. Judlowe (P.C.)
Dennis J. Mondolino
Ira B. Winkler
James M. Bollinger
Brian P. Murphy
Janet B. Linn
Bradley N. Ruben (Not admitted in NY)
Robert G. Gibbons
Lisa M. Ferri

ASSOCIATES

Eve Kunen
Michael F. Hurley
Edward M. Reisner
Jason A. Lief
Richard C. Pettus
Gordon F. Belcher
Keith T. Takeda
John F. Gallagher III
Steven R. Bartholomew (Not admitted in NY)
G. Michael Bryner
Jeffrey M. Gold
Dennis C. Hopkins
Vivek S. Suri
Michael H. Imbacuan
David J. Garrod
Frank Chesky (Not admitted in NY)
Douglas R. Weider (Not admitted in NY)
Vincent A. Sireci
Anthony L. Meola, Jr.
Richard McCormick (Not admitted in NY)
Esther H. Steinhauer
Philip L. Hirschhorn

For full biographical listings, see the Martindale-Hubbell Law Directory

JONES, DAY, REAVIS & POGUE (AV)

599 Lexington Avenue, 10022
Telephone: 212-326-3939
Telecopier: 212-755-7306
Email: counsel@jonesday.com *URL:* http://www.jonesday.com
In Atlanta, Georgia: 3500 SunTrust Plaza, 303 Peachtree Street.
Telephone: 404-521-3939.
Telecopier: 404-581-8330.
In Brussels, Belgium: Avenue Louise 480, 7th Floor, B-1050 Brussels.
Telephone: 32-2-645-14-11.
Telecopier: 32-2-645-14-45.
In Chicago, Illinois: 77 West Wacker.
Telephone: 312-782-3939.
Telecopier: 312-782-8585.
In Cleveland, Ohio: North Point, 901 Lakeside Avenue.
Telephone: 216-586-3939.
Telecopier: 216-579-0212.
In Columbus, Ohio: 1900 Huntington Center.
Telephone: 614-469-3939.
Telecopier: 614-461-4198.
In Dallas, Texas: 2727 North Harwood Street.
Telephone: 214-220-3939.
Telecopier: 214-969-5100.
In Frankfurt, Germany: Hochhaus am Park, Grüneburgweg 102, 60323 Frankfurt am Main.
Telephone: 49-69-9726-3939.
Telecopier: 49-69-9726-3993.
In Geneva, Switzerland: 20, rue de Candolle.
Telephone: 41-22-320-2339.
Telecopier: 41-22-320-1232.
In Hong Kong: 29th Floor, Entertainment Building, 30 Queen's Road Central.
Telephone: 852-2526-6895.
Telecopier: 852-2868-5871.
In Irvine, California: 5 Park Plaza, Suite 1100.
Telephone: 949-851-3939.
Telecopier: 949-553-7539.
In London, England: Bucklersbury House, 3 Queen Victoria Street.
Telephone: 44-20-7236-3939
Telecopier: 44-20-7236-1113.
In Los Angeles, California: 555 West Fifth Street, Suite 4600.
Telephone: 213-489-3939.
Telecopier: 213-243-2539.
In Paris, France: 120, rue du Faubourg Saint-Honoré.
Telephone: 33-1-56-59-39-39.
Telecopier: 33-1-56-59-39-38.
In Pittsburgh, Pennsylvania: 500 Grant Street, 31st Floor.
Telephone: 412-391-3939.
Telecopier: 412-394-7959.
In Riyadh, Saudi Arabia: The International Law Firm (In Association with Jones, Day, Reavis & Pogue), Sulaymaniyah, Prince Mishari IBN, Abdulaziz Street, P.O. Box 22166.
Telephone: (966-1) 462-8866.
Telecopier: (966-1) 462-9001.
In Shanghai, China: 2805 Kerry Centre, 1515 Nanjing Road West.
Telephone: 86-21-5298-6568.
Telecopier: 86-21-5298-6569.
In Sydney, Australia: Governor Phillip Tower, Level 38, 1 Farrer Place.
Telephone: 61-2-9210-6921.
Telecopier: 61-2-9210-6926.
In Taipei, Taiwan: 8th Floor, 2 Tun Hwa South Road, Section 2.
Telephone: (886-2) 2704-6808.
Telecopier: (886-2) 2704-6791.
In Tokyo, Japan: Toranomon 45 Mori Building, 3rd Floor, 1-5, Toranomon 5-Chome, Minato-Ku, Tokyo 105, Japan.
Telephone: 81-3-3433-3939.
Telecopier: 81-3-5401-2725.
In Washington, D.C.: 51 Louisiana Avenue, N.W.
Telephone: 202-879-3939.
Telecopier: 202-626-1700.

MEMBER OF FIRM IN NEW YORK

Thomas V. Heyman

For Complete List of Firm Personnel, See General Section

For full biographical listings, see the Martindale-Hubbell Law Directory

JORDAN AND HAMBURG (AV)

122 East 42nd Street, 10168
Telephone: 212-986-2340
Cable Address: "Patentmark"
Telex: 237057 JAH UR
Telecopier: 212-953-7733
Email: jandh@ipattorneys.com *URL:* http://www.iplaw-worldwide.com
Washington, D.C. Area Office: Suite 520, 2361 Jefferson Davis Highway, Arlington, Virginia.

C. Bruce Hamburg
Frank J. Jordan

ASSOCIATES

Herbert F. Ruschmann
Marvin Turken
Alfred A. D'Andrea, Jr. (Not admitted in NY)
Hoang Steve Ngo (Not admitted in NY)

(See Next Column)

JORDAN AND HAMBURG, *New York—Continued*

OF COUNSEL

Thomas M. Furth
Lawrence I. Wechsler
Martin P. Hoffman
(Resident, Arlington, Virginia)

Representative Clients: Consac Industries, Inc.; Andersen Products, Inc.; Accurate Surgical & Scientific Instruments Corp.; Accurate Chemical & Scientific Corp.; Atomergic Chemical Corp.; American Roland Chemical Corp.; Burlington Bio-Medical & Scientific Corp.; Emigrant Savings Bank.

For full biographical listings, see the Martindale-Hubbell Law Directory

KENYON & KENYON (AV)

One Broadway, 10004
Telephone: 212-425-7200
Fax: Dex (212) 425-5288
Washington, D.C. Office: 1500 K Street, N.W.
Telephone: 202-220-4200.
Fax: (202) 220-4201.
Frankfurt, Germany Office: Schillerstrasse 19-25, 60313 Frankfurt am Main.
Telephone: (69) 97-58-05-0.
Fax: (69) 97-58-05-99.
San Jose, California Office: 333 West San Carlos Street.
Telephone: 408-975-7500.
Fax: (408) 975-7501.

MEMBERS OF FIRM

Edward W. Greason
Charles R. Brainard
Richard L. Mayer
Edward J. Handler, III
Robert T. Tobin
Paul H. Heller
Albert J. Breneisen
Stuart J. Sinder
George E. Badenoch
John C. Altmiller (Resident, Washington, D.C. Office)
Michael J. Lennon
Philip J. McCabe (Resident, San Jose, California Office)
James Galbraith
Walter E. Hanley, Jr.
Richard L. DeLucia
James E. Rosini
Edward T. Colbert (Resident, Washington, D.C. Office)
William K. Wells, Jr. (Resident, Washington, D.C. Office)
Jonathan D. Reichman
Patrick J. Birde (Resident, Frankfurt, Germany Office)
Howard J. Shire
Richard S. Gresalfi
Michael D. Loughnane
Steven J. Lee
John Flock
Estelle J. Tsevdos (Not admitted in NY)
Richard M. Rosati
Frank Pietrantonio (Resident, Washington, D.C. Office)
Allen J. Baden (Resident, San Jose, California Office)
Thomas F. Meagher
Robert F. Perry
Donna M. Praiss
Thomas J. Meloro
Frederick H. Rein
Jeffrey M. Butler
Joseph F. Nicholson
Gerard A. Messina
Suzanne M. Parker (Resident, Washington, D.C. Office)
Brian S. Mudge (Resident, Washington, D.C. Office)
Maria L. Palmese
Deborah A. Somerville
Elizabeth Gardner

OF COUNSEL

Arthur D. Gray
Felix L. D'Arienzo, Jr.

COUNSEL

John J. Kelly, Jr.
Lynne Darcy
John E. Tsavaris, II
James Prizant (Not admitted in NY)
Elizabeth J. Holland
Patrick J. Fay
John R. Kenny (Resident, San Jose, California Office)

ASSOCIATES

Andrea Harris Scheidt
Paul M. Richter, Jr.
Douglas E. Ringel
Mark M. Supko (Resident, Washington, D.C. Office)
Benjamin Hershkowitz
Maria Anita Pamintuan Fusco
Shawn W. O'Dowd (Resident, San Jose, California Office)
Alexas D. Skucas
Linda D. Mettes
Michelle M. Carniaux
Jong H. Lee
Judith L. Toffenetti (Resident, Washington, D.C. Office)
Paul A. Bondor
Reem F. Jishi
C. Kyle Musgrove (Resident, Washington, D.C. Office)
Joseph R. Palmieri (Resident, San Jose Office)
Gary Abelev
Dana Renee Kaplan
Dervis Magistre
Gary S. Morris (Resident, Washington, D.C. Office)
William M. Merone (Resident, Washington, D.C. Office)
M. Lisa Wilson (Not admitted in NY)
Charles A. Weiss
John W. Bateman (Resident, Washington, D.C. Office)
John McGroarty (Resident, Washington, D.C. Office)
Thomas P. Canty (Resident, Frankfurt, Germany Office)
Robin A. Chadwick
Timothy M. Devlin (Resident, Washington, D.C. Office)
David E. Foster (Resident, San Jose Office)
Winston Henderson
William G. James II
Gregg A. Paradise
Azeen H. Roohi
Mark W. Rueh
John R. Hutchins (Resident, Washington, D.C. Office)
Christopher R. Hutter (Resident, Washington, D.C. Office)
Mark Hannemann

(See Next Column)

ASSOCIATES (Continued)

John J. Skinner, Jr.
Robert L. Grabarek, Jr. (Resident, Washington, D.C. Office)
Robert L. Hails, Jr. (Resident, Washington, D.C. Office)
Sterlon Mason (Resident, Washington, D.C. Office)
Earl D. Brown, Jr. (Not admitted in NY)
Karen L. Feisthamel (Resident, Washington, D.C. Office)
Pamela G. Salkeld
Stuart D. Smolen (Resident, Washington, D.C. Office)
Mark I. Koffsky
Robert V. Cerwinski
Michael J. Cummings
Oleg F. Kaplun
Brian M. Koide (Resident, Washington, D.C. Office)
Michael J. Marcin
A. Antony Pfeffer
Marian Underweiser
George O. Winborne
Linda M. Shudy (Resident, Frankfurt, Germany Office)
Erik R. Swanson (Resident, Frankfurt, Germany Office)
Lawrence B. Ebert
Yvonne K. Tran
Joseph P. Aiena (Not admitted in NY)
Jonathan L. Lederman
Clark P. Russell
Selene H. Costello (Not admitted in NY)
Teresa A. Lavenue (Resident, Washington, D.C. Office)
Diane P. Tso
Christine M. Wilkes
James M. Ross (Resident, Washington, D.C. Office)
Mitul I. Desai
Thomas George (San Jose, California Office)
Kevin T. Godlewski
Angie M. Hankins
Dalia S. Grimberg
Bradley J. Meier
Michael Stimson
Adam Albrett (Resident, San Jose, California Office)
Michael T. Cruz (Not admitted in NY)
Kevin G. Daley (Resident, San Jose, California Office)
Stefan C. Grant
Michael N. Haynes (Resident, Washington, D.C. Office)
Kristina M. Jahns (Resident, Washington. D.C. Office)
Mark H. Neblett (Resident, Washington, D.C. Office)
David R. Schaffer (Resident, Washington, D.C. Office)
Susan A. Smith (Resident, Washington, D.C. Office)
Laurie S. Mintzer (Resident, Washington, D.C. Office)
Jeffrey A. Glazer (Not admitted in NY)
Bradley S. Corsello
Sinan Utku (Resident, Washington, D.C. Office)
Neil M. McCarthy (Resident, Washington, D.C. Office)
Christopher E. Loh
Paolo M. Trevisan (Resident, Washington, D.C. Office)
Nicholas J. DuBois
Alan A. Pollack
Jerry Haynes
Aaron C. Deditch
Fred Grasso (Resident, Washington, D.C. Office)
Clint A. Gerdine (Resident, Washington, D.C. Office)
Kenneth R. Corsello (Resident, Washington, D.C. Office)
David Lammey (Not admitted in NY)
Dan Salehi (Resident, Washington, D.C. Office)
Jeffrey S. Ginsberg
R. Paul Zeineddin (Resident, Washington, D.C. Office)
Michael M. Shen (Resident, Washington, D.C. Office)
James F. Feeney (Resident, San Jose, California Office)
Anthony Dreux (Resident, Washington, D.C. Office)
Paul Johnson (Not admitted in NY)
John B. Starr Jr.

For full biographical listings, see the Martindale-Hubbell Law Directory

LIEBERMAN & NOWAK, LLP (AV)

805 Third Avenue, 21st Floor, 10022
Telephone: 212-532-4447
Telefax: 212-481-0543
Email: ip@lieberman-nowak.com

MEMBERS OF FIRM

Arthur M. Lieberman
Keith D. Nowak
James P. Lynn

For full biographical listings, see the Martindale-Hubbell Law Directory

MORGAN & FINNEGAN, L.L.P. (AV)

A Registered Liability Partnership
345 Park Avenue, 10154
Telephone: 212-758-4800
Cable Address: "Findurpine"
Telecopier: (212) 751-6849
Telex: ITT 421792
Email: info@morganfinnegan.com *URL:* http://www.morganfinnegan.com
Washington, D.C. Office: 1775 Eye Street, N.W., 4th Floor, 20006.
Telephone: 202-857-7887.
Facsimile: 202-857-7929.

PARTNERS

John D. Morgan (1893-1939)
Hobart N. Durham (1930-1969)
Granville M. Pine (1939-1994)
George B. Finnegan, Jr.
John A. Diaz
John C. Vassil
Alfred P. Ewert
David H. Pfeffer
Harry C. Marcus
Robert E. Paulson
Stephen R. Smith
Kurt E. Richter
J. Robert Dailey
Eugene Moroz
John F. Sweeney
Arnold I. Rady
Christopher A. Hughes
William S. Feiler
Janet Dore
Joseph A. Calvaruso
James W. Gould
Richard C. Komson
Israel Blum
Christopher K. Hu

(See Next Column)

MORGAN & FINNEGAN L.L.P.—*Continued*

Bartholomew Verdirame
Dickerson M. Downing
Maria C. H. Lin
Joseph A. DeGirolamo
Michael P. Dougherty
Seth J. Atlas
Andrew M. Riddles
Bruce D. DeRenzi
Michael M. Murray
Mark J. Abate
Edward A. Pennington (Resident, Washington, D.C. Office)
John T. Gallagher
Steven F. Meyer
Kenneth H. Sonnenfeld
Alfred L. Haffner, Jr.
Harold Haidt
David H. T. Kane
Siegrun D. Kane
Tony V. Pezzano
Andrea L. Wayda
Walter G. Hanchuk

COUNSEL

Jerome G. Lee
John D. Foley
Thomas P. Dowling
Warren H. Rotert
Roger S. Smith
John P. Sinnott
David A. Loewenstein

OF COUNSEL

Kathleen E. McCarthy

ASSOCIATES

Thomas M. Hammond (Not admitted in NY)
Scott D. Greenberg
Bruce D. Radin
Mary J. Morry
Robert K. Goethals
John W. Osborne
Cindy M. Zelson
Laurence J. Bromberg
Peter N. Fill
Kenneth S. Weitzman
Richard Straussman
Dorothy R. Auth
David V. Rossi
Brenda Pomerance
Kathryn E. Diaz
Gerard A. Haddad
Richard W. Erwine
Michael O. Cummings
Richard W. Bork
Kimber L. Wilson
Christopher J. Horgan
John T. Moehringer
Mark J. Schildkraut
Christopher J. Gaspar (Not admitted in NY)
Christine K. Garcia
Chris L. Holm
Sybil A. Lombillo (Not admitted in NY)
Matthew K. Blackburn (Not admitted in NY)
James Hwa
Brandon N. Sklar
Brendan P. McFeely
Amy L. Nelkin
Tod Melgar
Brett M. Hutton
Claudio Buttitta
Jon T. Hohenthaner

For full biographical listings, see the Martindale-Hubbell Law Directory

OPPENHEIMER WOLFF & DONNELLY LLP (AV)

The Chrysler East Building 19th Floor, 666 Third Avenue, 10017
Telephone: 212-826-5000
FAX: 212-486-0708
URL: http://www.oppenheimer.com
Minneapolis, Minnesota Office: 3300 Plaza VII, 45 South Seventh Street. 55402.
Telephone: 612-607-7000.
FAX: 612-607-7100.
Amsterdam, The Netherlands Office: Keizergracht 241.
Telephone: 31-20-423-4555.
FAX: 312-20-423-4545.
Brussels, Belgium Office: Avenue Louise 240, Box 5, 1050.
Telephone: 32-2-626-0500.
FAX: 32-2-626-0510.
Geneva, Switzerland Office: Rue Gabriel Eynard, 6, 1205.
Telephone: (41/22) 311-7410.
FAX: (41/22) 311-4707.
Newport Beach, California Office: 500 Newport Center Drive, Suite 700, 92660.
Telephone: 949-823-6000.
FAX: 949-823-6100.
Paris, France Office: 35 Boulevard des Capucines, 75002.
Telephone: (33/1) 53 45 40 00.
FAX: (33/1) 53 45 40 10.
St. Paul, Minnesota Office: 1700 First National Bank Building, 55101.
Telephone: 651-605-2000.
FAX: 651-605-2100.
Washington, D.C. Office: Oppenheimer Wolff Donnelly & Bayh LLP, 1350 Eye Street, N.W., Suite 200, 20005.
Telephone: 202-312-8000.
FAX: 202-312-8100.
Los Angeles, California Office: 2029 Century Park East, 38th Floor, 90067.
Telephone: 310-788-5000.
FAX: 310-277-1297.
Palo Alto, California Office: 3373 Hillview Avenue, Suite 200, 94304.
Telephone: 650-320-4000.
FAX: 650-320-4100.
Chicago, Illinois Office: Oppenheimer Wolff & Donnelly (Illinois), Two Prudential Plaza, 45th Floor, 180 North Stetson Avenue, 60601.
Telephone: 312-616-1800.
Fax: 312-616-5800.

RESIDENT PARTNERS

Joseph J. Vicinanza (Resident Managing Partner)
Herbert C. Ross, Jr.

(See Next Column)

RESIDENT ASSOCIATES

Teresa J. Olson
Kimberley K. Adams
Joseph E. Petersen

For full biographical listings, see the Martindale-Hubbell Law Directory

OSTROLENK, FABER, GERB & SOFFEN, LLP (AV)

1180 Avenue of the Americas, 10036
Telephone: 212-382-0700
Cable Address: "Ostrofaber"
Facsimile: 212-382-0888
Email: email@ostrolenk.com *URL:* http://www.forman.com/ostrolenk
Washington, DC Office: 1725 K Street, NW. 20006.
Telephone: 202-457-7785.
Fax: 202-429-8919.

MEMBERS OF THE FIRM

Samuel Ostrolenk (1898-1968)
Sidney G. Faber (1912-1992)
Bernard Gerb (Retired)
Marvin C. Soffen (Retired)
Samuel H. Weiner
Robert C. Faber
Edward A. Meilman
Stanley H. Lieberstein
Steven I. Weisburd
Max Moskowitz
Stephen A. Soffen
James A. Finder
William O. Gray, III
Louis C. Dujmich
Charles P. LaPolla
Douglas A. Miro
Harold Einhorn

ASSOCIATES

Peter McGee (Not admitted in NY)
Marc A. Lieberstein
Matthew Brooke Dernier
Michael J. Scheer
Allison B. Hoch
Ellen S. Tao (Not admitted in NY)
Alan Michael Weisberg
Larissa A. Rippa
Peter S. Sloane
Daniel E. Tierney

OF COUNSEL

Jerome M. Berliner
Martin Pfeffer
Leon Zitver (Not admitted in NY)
J. David Dainow

For full biographical listings, see the Martindale-Hubbell Law Directory

PENNIE & EDMONDS LLP (AV)

1155 Avenue of the Americas, 10036
Telephone: 212-790-9090
Facsimile: GI/GII/GIII (212) 869-9741
GIII (212) 869-8864
Email: pennie.com *URL:* http://www.pennie.com
Washington, D.C. Office: 1667 K Street, N.W.
Telephone: 202-496-4400.
Facsimile: 202-496-4444.
Palo Alto, California Office: 3300 Hillview Avenue.
Telephone: 650-493-4935.
Facsimile: 650-493-5556.

John C. Pennie (1858-1921)
Dean S. Edmonds (1879-1972)

MEMBERS OF FIRM

S. Leslie Misrock
Harry C. Jones, III
Berj A. Terzian
David Weild, III
Jonathan A. Marshall
Barry D. Rein
Stanton T. Lawrence, III
Charles E. Miller
Francis E. Morris
Gidon D. Stern
John J. Lauter
Brian M. Poissant
Brian D. Coggio
Charles E. McKenney
Philip T. Shannon
John M. Richardson
Rory J. Radding
Stephen J. Harbulak
Donald J. Goodell
James N. Palik
William G. Pecau
Joseph Diamante
Thomas E. Friebel
Laura A. Coruzzi
Jennifer Gordon
Jon R. Stark (Resident, Palo Alto, California Office)
James W. Dabney
Paul R. De Stefano (Resident, Palo Alto, California Office)
Allan A. Fanucci
Geraldine F. Baldwin
Victor N. Balancia
Peter D. Vogl
John J. Normile, Jr.
Catherine H. Stockell
Samuel B. Abrams
Thomas A. Canova
Steven I. Wallach
Jonathan E. Moskin
Adriane M. Antler
Paul J. Zegger (Resident, Washington, D.C. Office)
Edmond R. Bannon
Marcia H. Sundeen (Resident, Washington, D.C. Office)
Bruce J. Barker
Thomas G. Rowan
James G. Markey
Darren W. Saunders
Thomas D. Kohler (Resident, Palo Alto, California Office)
Scott D. Stimpson
William S. Galliani (Resident, Palo Alto, California Office)
Gary S. Williams (Resident, Palo Alto, California Office)
Ann L. Gisolfi
Scott B. Familant
Todd A. Wagner
Kelly D. Talcott

COUNSEL

Constance Golden
Ilene B. Tannen
Nancy A. Zoubek

(See Next Column)

PENNIE & EDMONDS LLP, *New York—Continued*

ASSOCIATES

Wilma F. Triebwasser (Resident, Washington, D.C. Office)
Hailing Zhang
Mikhail Lotvin
Brian M. Rothery
Brian D. Siff
William J. Sipio
Alan Tenenbaum
F. Dominic Cerrito
Ronald M. Daignault
Jacqueline M. Lesser
Edward R. Gomez
Anthony M. Insogna
Joyce M. Ferraro
Garland T. Stephens
Michael J. Lyons (Resident, Palo Alto, California Office)
Maria E. Pasquale
Susan C. Shin
Troy R. Lester (Resident, Washington, D.C. Office)
Katharine E. Smith
Wendy A. Haller
Andrew J. Gray, IV (Resident, Palo Alto, California Office)
Carol M. Wilhelm
H.T. Than (Resident, Washington, D.C. Office)
Lester L. Levy (Resident, Palo Alto, California Office)
Bryan W. Butler (Resident, Palo Alto, California Office)
Gianni P. Servodidio
Kenneth L. Stein
John D. Garretson
Alan P. Force
Maria S. Kratzer
Karen G. Horowitz
Ognjan V. Shentov
Nongfan Zhu
Daniel Hansburg
Catharina Chin Eng
Stephen S. Rabinowitz
Nanda K. Alapati (Resident, Washington, D.C. Office)
Nathan P. Letts
Timothy E. DeMasi
Nikolaos Charles George
Carl P. Bretscher (Resident, Washington, D.C. Office)
Pablo Perhacs (Not admitted in NY)
Eric J. Fues (Resident, Washington, D.C. Office)
Jonathan L. Klein-Evans (Resident, Washington, D.C. Office)
Matthew E. Langer
Greg P. Roggin (Resident, Washington, D.C. Office)
Leo Merken
Kathleen Fowler (Resident, Palo Alto, California Office)
Lorri W. Jones (Resident, Washington, D.C. Office)
Nancy H. Lutz (Resident, Washington, D.C. Office)
Jeffrey A. Wolfson (Resident, Washington, D.C. Office)
Anne M. Coughlin
Caroline R. Clark
Margaret Bolce Brivanlou
Henry C. Lebowitz
Granetta M. Coleman (Resident, Washington, D.C. Office)
David R. Owens (Resident, Palo Alto, California Office)
Michèle A. Moser
Lavatus V. Powell
Steven D. Chin
Emil Bradley Gould (Resident, Washington, D.C. Office)
James S. McDonald (Resident, Palo Alto, California Office)
Andrew Sanders
George A. Senich
Scott Jacobson
John P. Mulgrew (Resident, Washington, D.C. Office)
Daniel L. Malone (Not admitted in NY)
Todd L. Krause
Philip H. Lee (Resident, Palo Alto, California Office)
Alexandra Haner
Brian T. Clarke (Resident, Palo Alto, California Office)
Peter L. Herridge (Not admitted in NY)
Claudia D.P. Zumbro
Ian Scott
Janet M. Skafar (Resident, Palo Alto, California Office)
Elizabeth S. Langston (Not admitted in NY)
Atulya Agarwal (Resident, Washington, D.C. Office)
Vivian S. Kuo (Resident, Washington, D.C. Office)
C. Edward Polk, Jr. (Resident, Washington, D.C. Office)
Anthony H. Kahng (Resident, Washington, D.C. Office)
Patrick M. Boucher
James A. DeFelice (Resident, Washington, D.C. Office)
Paul E. Dietze (Resident, Washington, D.C. Office)
Colleen M. Keegan (Not admitted in NY)
Lewis E. Hudnell III
Charles R. Richard (Resident, Washington, D.C. Office)
Steven D. Underwood
Keith A. Walter, Jr.
Gail H. Zarick
Julie M. Holloway (Resident, Palo Alto, California Office)
Serge Sira (Resident, Washington, D.C. Office)
Matthew J. Engle (Resident, Palo Alto, California Office)
Dion M. Bregman (Resident, Palo Alto, California Office)
Gary Zhang (Resident, Washington, D.C. Office)
Deborah J. Barnett
Margaret A. Pepper
Susie S. Cheng
Lawrence S. Graham
Youngtack Shim (Resident, Palo Alto, California Office)
Seth Alain Watkins (Resident, Washington, D.C. Office)
David Chan Lee (Resident, Washington, D.C. Office)
Ann M. Caviani Pease (Resident, Palo Alto, California Office)
Tracy L. Hurt (Resident, Palo Alto, California Office)
Birgit Millauer (Resident, Palo Alto, California Office)

For full biographical listings, see the Martindale-Hubbell Law Directory

STEINBERG & RASKIN, P.C. (AV)

1140 Avenue of the Americas 15th Floor, 10036
Telephone: 212-768-3800
Fax: 212-382-2124
URL: http://www.srpat.com
Email: sr@srpat.com *URL:* http://www.lawyers.com/steinbergraskin

Martin G. Raskin

(See Next Column)

Amy F. Divino
Joshua L. Raskin
Judith L. Smulow
Jason E. Hardiman
Paul J. Higgins

OF COUNSEL

Harold D. Steinberg

For full biographical listings, see the Martindale-Hubbell Law Directory

SCARSDALE, Westchester Co.

COLUCCI & UMANS (AV)

670 White Plains Road, 10583
Telephone: 914-472-1500
Facsimile: 914-472-1551
New York, New York Office: Manhattan Tower, 101 East 52nd Street.
Telephone: 212-935-5700.
Facsimile: 212-935-5728.

MEMBERS OF FIRM

Frank J. Colucci
Courtney Wilson Monahan
Gregory J. Colucci (Resident)
Nathaniel H. Weisel
Renée L. Duff

For full biographical listings, see the Martindale-Hubbell Law Directory

SYOSSET, Nassau Co.

HOFFMANN & BARON, LLP (AV)

6900 Jericho Turnpike, 11791
Telephone: 516-822-3550
Telecopier: 516-822-3582
Parsippany, New Jersey Office: 1055 Parsippany Blvd., 07054.
Telephone: 973-331-1700.
Telecopier: 973-331-1717.

ASSOCIATES

R. Glenn Schroeder
Glenn T. Henneberger
Kirk M. Miles (Resident, Parsippany, New Jersey Office)
Anthony E. Bennett
Robert Francis Chisholm (Not admitted in NY; Resident, Parsippany, New Jersey Office)
Gregory W. Bachmann
Mark E. Baron (Resident, Parsippany, New Jersey Office)
Steven T. Zuschlag
Kellyanne Merkel (Resident, Parsippany, New Jersey Office)
Susan A. Sipos
Samir R. Patel
James F. Harrington
Kevin E. McDermott
Robert C. Morriss
Roderick S.W. Turner
John S. Sopko (Resident, Parsippany, New Jersey Office)
Barry H. Jacobsen (Resident, Parsippany, New Jersey Office)
Richard LaCava
Robert L. Bernstein
Justin K. Holmes

For full biographical listings, see the Martindale-Hubbell Law Directory

UNIONDALE, Nassau Co.

DILWORTH & BARRESE (AV)

333 Earle Ovington Boulevard, 11553
Telephone: 516-228-8484
Telecopier: 516-228-8516
Email: iplaw@dilworthbarrese.com

MEMBERS OF FIRM

Peter G. Dilworth
Rocco S. Barrese
David M. Carter
Paul J. Farrell
Peter DeLuca
Jeffrey S. Steen

ASSOCIATES

Adrian Thomas Calderone
George M. Kaplan
Joseph W. Schmidt
Raymond E. Farrell
Russell R. Kassner
Christopher G. Trainor (Not admitted in NY)
George Likourezos
James M. Loeffler
Edward C. Meagher
Peter B. Sorell
Michael P. Dilworth
Michael Scaturro
Glenn D. Smith (Not admitted in NY)

OF COUNSEL

Frederick W. Pepper

For full biographical listings, see the Martindale-Hubbell Law Directory

*WHITE PLAINS,** Westchester Co.

MILDE, HOFFBERG & MACKLIN, LLP (AV)

10 Bank Street, Suite 460, 10606
Telephone: 914-949-3100
Fax: 914-949-3416
Email: INTPROP@aol.com *URL:* http://www.milde.com

(See Next Column)

MILDE, HOFFBERG & MACKLIN LLP—*Continued*

Karl F. Milde, Jr. Steven M. Hoffberg

OF COUNSEL

Kenneth E. Macklin

For full biographical listings, see the Martindale-Hubbell Law Directory

NORTH CAROLINA

*CHARLOTTE,** Mecklenburg Co.

MINEO & WHITTAKER (AV)

5950 Fairview Road Suite 622, P.O. Box 10615, 28212
Telephone: 704-571-4022
Email: IPlitigate@aol.com
Raleigh, North Carolina Office: 150 Fayetteville Street, Suite 1700.
Telephone: 919-831-8728.
Telecopier: 919-782-5244.

MEMBERS OF FIRM

Robert A. Mineo (Resident, Raleigh Office)
Malcolm E. Whittaker

For full biographical listings, see the Martindale-Hubbell Law Directory

*DURHAM,** Durham Co.

JENKINS & WILSON, P.A. (AV)

Suite 1400 University Tower, 3100 Tower Boulevard, 27707-6226
Telephone: 919-493-8000
Fax: 919-419-0383
URL: http://www.jenkinsandwilson.com

Richard E. Jenkins
Jeffrey L. Wilson

Jennifer L. Skord
Arles A. Taylor, Jr.
David P. Gloekler (Not admitted in NC)
Gregory A. Hunt

Representative Clients: Bell and Howell Mail Processing Systems; Duke University; Freudenberg Spunweb Co. (The Lutravil Co.); Glaxo Wellcome, Inc.; Huesker, Inc.; North Carolina State University; Rhone-Poulenc AG Co.; Sumitomo Electric Lightwave Corp.; The University of North Carolina at Chapel Hill; Vanderbilt University.

For full biographical listings, see the Martindale-Hubbell Law Directory

MOORE & VAN ALLEN, PLLC (AV)

Suite 800, 2200 West Main Street, 27705
Telephone: 919-286-8000
Fax: 919-286-8199
URL: http://www.mvalaw.com
Charleston, South Carolina Office: 40 Calhoun Street, Suite 300.
Telephone: 843-579-7000.
Fax: 843-579-7099.
Charlotte, North Carolina Office: 100 North Tryon Street, Floor 47.
Telephone: 704-331-1000.
Fax: 704-331-1159.
Raleigh, North Carolina Office: One Hannover Square, Suite 1700, P.O. Box 26507.
Telephone: 919-821-6200.
Fax: 919-821-6500.

Dominic J. Chiantera
David A. Harlow

OF COUNSEL

William G. Dossé
William L. London, III

COUNSEL

Rita M.K. Purut

ASSOCIATES

Arlene D. Hanks
Michael G. Johnston
Laura Keohane
Scott W. Reid
Mark H. Webbink

For full biographical listings, see the Martindale-Hubbell Law Directory

OLIVE AND OLIVE, P.A. (AV)

500 Memorial Street, P.O. Box 2049, 27702-2049
Telephone: 919-683-5514
Fax: 919-688-3781
Email: iplaw@oliveandolive.com *URL:* http://oliveandolive.com

B. B. Olive
Susan Freya Olive

Michael R. Philips
Tara J. Williams
Bruce Vrana
Vedia Jones-Richardson

(See Next Column)

LEGAL SUPPORT PERSONNEL

Barbara Porterfield (Administrator)

Reference: North Carolina Bar Assn.

For full biographical listings, see the Martindale-Hubbell Law Directory

*GREENSBORO,** Guilford Co.

RHODES & MASON, P.L.L.C. (AV)

1600 First Union Tower, 300 North Greene Street, P.O. Box 2974, 27402
Telephone: 336-273-4422
Fax: 336-271-2830
Email: @rhodesmason.com *URL:* http://www.rhodesmason.com
Wilmington, North Carolina Office: 201 N. Front Street, Suite 604.
Telephone: 910-763-2382.
Fax: 910-763-2386.

MEMBERS OF FIRM

Charles Robert Rhodes
Edward W. Rilee
Howard A. MacCord, Jr.
William J. Mason (Resident, Wilmington Office)
Jack B. Hicks
James L. Lester

OF COUNSEL

Jeffrey R. McFadden

ASSOCIATES

Clinton H. Hallman, Jr.
Gilbert J. Andia, Jr.
Amy Fix
Lewis S. Rowell

For full biographical listings, see the Martindale-Hubbell Law Directory

*RALEIGH,** Wake Co.

MINEO & WHITTAKER (AV)

First Union Capitol Center, 150 Fayetteville Street, Suite 1700, 27601
Telephone: 919-831-8728
Telecopier: 919-782-5244
Email: NCAIRLAW@AOL.COM
Charlotte, North Carolina Office: 5950 Fairview Road, Suite 622. P.O. Box 10615.
Telephone: 704-571-4022.

MEMBERS OF FIRM

Robert A. Mineo
Malcolm E. Whittaker (Resident, Charlotte Office)
Athena R. Mineo

For full biographical listings, see the Martindale-Hubbell Law Directory

WOMBLE CARLYLE SANDRIDGE & RICE (AV)

A Professional Limited Liability Company
2100 First Union Capitol Center, 150 Fayetteville Street Mall, P.O. Box 831, 27602
Telephone: 919-755-2100
Fax: 919-755-2150
Email: lawyers@wcsr.com *URL:* http://www.wcsr.com
Charlotte, North Carolina Office: 3300 One First Union Center, 301 South College Street.
Telephone: 704-331-4900.
Fax: 704-331-4955.
Winston-Salem, North Carolina Office: 200 West Second Street, P.O. Drawer 84.
Telephone: 336-721-3600.
Fax: 336-721-3660.
Research Triangle Park, North Carolina Office: 2505 Meridian Parkway, Suite 300 (Durham), 27713.
Telephone: 919-484-2300.
Fax: 919-484-2340.
Atlanta, Georgia Office: One Atlantic Center, 1201 West Peachtree Street, Suite 3500.
Telephone: 404-872-7000.
Fax: 404-888-7490.
Other Atlanta, Georgia Office: Suite 404, 2296 Henderson Mill Road, N.E.
Telephone: 770-492-9030.
Fax: 770-492-9609.
Washington, D.C. Office: 1120 Nineteenth Street, N.W., Eighth Floor.
Telephone: 202-857-4400.
Fax: 202-467-6910.
Greenville, South Carolina Office: 15 South Main Street, Suite 601, P.O. Box 10208.
Telephone: 864-255-5400.
Fax: 864-255-5440.

RESIDENT MEMBER

M. Christopher Bolen

RESIDENT ASSOCIATE

Jennifer Long Collins

Representative Clients: Aetna Casualty and Surety Co., Inc.; ALSCO/AmeriMark Building Products, Inc.; Aoki Corporation America, Inc.; Hackney Brothers, Inc.; Lawyers Mutual Liability Insurance Company of North Carolina; Meredith College; Regency Park Corp.; Wachovia Bank, N.A.

(See Next Column)

WOMBLE CARLYLE SANDRIDGE & RICE, *Raleigh—Continued*

For Complete List of Firm Personnel, See General Section

For full biographical listings, see the Martindale-Hubbell Law Directory

*WILMINGTON,** New Hanover Co.

RHODES & MASON, P.L.L.C. (AV)

201 North Front Street, Suite 604, 28401
Telephone: 910-763-2382
Fax: 910-763-2386
Email: wmason@bellsouth.net *URL:* http://www.rhodesmason.com
Greensboro, North Carolina Office: 1600 First Union Tower, 300 North Greene Street, P.O. Box 2974.
Telephone: 336-273-4422.
FAX: 336-271-2830.

William J. Mason (Resident)

For full biographical listings, see the Martindale-Hubbell Law Directory

OHIO

*AKRON,** Summit Co.

RENNER, KENNER, GREIVE, BOBAK, TAYLOR & WEBER A LEGAL PROFESSIONAL ASSOCIATION (AV)

Sixteenth Floor, First National Tower, 44308-1456
Telephone: 330-376-1242; 330-376-1034
Facsimile: 330-376-9646
Email: patlaw@rennerkenner.com *URL:* http://www.rennerkenner.com
Westlake, Ohio Office: 24500 Center Ridge Road, Suite 280, 44145.
Telephone: 440-808-0011.
Fax: 440-808-0657.

Reese Taylor
Phillip L. Kenner
Edward G. Greive
Donald J. Bobak
Ray L. Weber
Joseph G. Curatolo (Resident, Westlake, Ohio Office)
Rodney Lee Skoglund

Andrew B. Morton
Arthur M. Reginelli
Laura J. Gentilcore
Shannon V. McCue

OF COUNSEL

Jack L. Renner
Sylvia A. Petrosky

LEGAL SUPPORT PERSONNEL

Michael F. Morgan (Patent Agent)
Salvatore A. Sidoti (Patent Agent) (Resident, Westlake Office)

Reference: Key Bank.

For full biographical listings, see the Martindale-Hubbell Law Directory

*CANTON,** Stark Co.

RENNER, KENNER, GREIVE, BOBAK, TAYLOR & WEBER A LEGAL PROFESSIONAL ASSOCIATION

(See Akron)

*CINCINNATI,** Hamilton Co.

FROST & JACOBS LLP (AV)

2500 PNC Center, 201 East Fifth Street, 45202
Telephone: 513-651-6800
Telecopier: 513-651-6981
URL: http://www.frojac.com
Columbus, Ohio Office: One Columbus, 10 West Broad Street, 43215.
Telephone: 614-464-1211.
Telecopier: 614-464-1737.
Lexington, Kentucky Office: 1100 Vine Center Tower, 333 West Vine Street, 40507.
Telephone: 606-254-1100.
Telecopier: 606-253-2990.
Middletown, Ohio Office: 400 First National Bank Building, 2 North Main Street, 45042.
Telephone: 513-422-2001.
Telecopier: 513-422-3010.
Frankfort, Kentucky Office: 201 W. Main Street, 40601.
Telephone: 502-223-1400.
Telecopier: 502-223-1410.

PATENT, TRADEMARK AND COPYRIGHT ATTORNEYS
MEMBERS OF FIRM

David E. Schmit
Steven J. Goldstein
Kenneth B. Germain
Edwin R. Acheson, Jr.
Louis K. Ebling

(See Next Column)

ASSOCIATES

Ann Gallagher Robinson
Kevin S. Sprecher
Sean P. Hodge
Karen E. Kreider
Katherine F. Horvath

OF COUNSEL

Stephen E. Gillen
Gretchen R. Blum
Glenn D. Bellamy

Representative Clients: AK Steel Corporation; Chiquita; Cincinnati Bell Inc.; Cincinnati Machine; B.F. Goodrich-Hilton Davis Inc.; Hillenbrand Industries; Lexmark International; Senco Products, Inc.; Standard Textile Company, Inc.; University of Cincinnati.

For Complete List of Firm Personnel, See General Section

For full biographical listings, see the Martindale-Hubbell Law Directory

*CLEVELAND,** Cuyahoga Co.

DAVID A. BURGE CO., L.P.A. (AV)

2901 South Park Boulevard, 44120-1842
Telephone: 216-921-8900
Fax: 216-921-0209
Email: daburge@daburge.com *URL:* http://www.daburge.com

David A. Burge

For full biographical listings, see the Martindale-Hubbell Law Directory

FAY, SHARPE, FAGAN, MINNICH & MCKEE, LLP (AV)

1100 Superior Avenue, Seventh Floor, 44114
Telephone: 216-861-5582
FAX: 216-241-1666
Email: fs@faysharpe.com *URL:* http://www.faysharpe.com

MEMBERS OF FIRM

Albert P. Sharpe, III
Christopher B. Fagan
Richard J. Minnich
James W. McKee
Patrick R. Roche
Thomas E. Kocovsky, Jr.
Timothy E. Nauman
Richard M. Klein
Jay F. Moldovanyi
Philip J. Moy, Jr.
Mark S. Svat
Joseph D. Dreher
Scott Andrew McCollister
Mark E. Bandy
Michael E. Hudzinski

ASSOCIATES

Sandra M. Koenig
Jude A. Fry
Colleen Flynn Goss
Brian E. Kondas
Steven M. Auvil
R. Scott Speroff
Steven M. Haas
John P. Cornely
Ann M. Skerry
James E. Scarbrough
W. Scott Harders
Brian G. Bembenick
Christopher P. Harris

OF COUNSEL

Sue Ellen Phillips

For full biographical listings, see the Martindale-Hubbell Law Directory

JONES, DAY, REAVIS & POGUE (AV)

North Point, 901 Lakeside Avenue, 44114
Telephone: 216-586-3939
Telecopier: 216-579-0212
Email: counsel@jonesday.com *URL:* http://www.jonesday.com
In Columbus, Ohio: 1900 Huntington Center.
Telephone: 614-469-3939.
Telecopier: 614-461-4198.
In Atlanta, Georgia: 3500 SunTrust Plaza, 303 Peachtree Street.
Telephone: 404-521-3939.
Telecopier: 404-581-8330.
In Brussels, Belgium: Avenue Louise 480, 7th Floor. B-1050 Brussels.
Telephone: 32-2-645-14-11.
Telecopier: 32-2-645-14-45.
In Chicago, Illinois: 77 West Wacker.
Telephone: 312-782-3939.
Telecopier: 312-782-8585.
In Dallas, Texas: 2727 North Harwood Street.
Telephone: 214-220-3939.
Telecopier: 214-969-5100.
In Frankfurt, Germany: Hochhaus am Park, Grüneburgweg 102, 60323 Frankfurt am Main.
Telephone: 49-69-9726-3939.
Telecopier: 49-69-9726-3993.
In Geneva, Switzerland: 20, rue de Candolle.
Telephone: 41-22-320-2339.
Telecopier: 41-22-320-1232.
In Hong Kong, China: 29th Floor, Entertainment Building, 30 Queen's Road Central.
Telephone: 852-2526-6895.
Telecopier: 852-2868-5871 or 852-2868-5699.
In Irvine, California: 5 Park Plaza, Suite 1100.
Telephone: 949-851-3939.
Telecopier: 949-553-7539.

(See Next Column)

JONES, DAY, REAVIS & POGUE—*Continued*

In London, England: Bucklersbury House, 3 Queen Victoria Street.
Telephone: 44-171-236-3939.
Telecopier: 44-171-236-1113.
In Los Angeles, California: 555 West Fifth Street, Suite 4600.
Telephone: 213-489-3939.
Telecopier: 213-243-2539.
In New Delhi, India (Associate Office): Pathak & Associates (an associate firm of Jones, Day, Reavis & Pogue), 1st Floor, Dr. Gopal Das Bhaven, 28 Barakhamba Road.
Telephone: 91-11-373-8793; 91-11-335-7345.
Telecopier: 91-11-335-3761.
In New York, N.Y.: 599 Lexington Avenue.
Telephone: 212-326-3939.
Telecopier: 212-755-7306.
In Paris, France: 120, rue du Faubourg Saint-Honoré.
Telephone: 33-1-56-59-39-39.
Telecopier: 33-1-56-59-39-38
In Pittsburgh, Pennsylvania: 500 Grant Street, 31st Floor.
Telephone: 412-391-3939.
Telecopier: 412-394-7959.
In Riyadh, Saudi Arabia: The International Law Firm (In Association with Jones, Day, Reavis & Pogue), Sulaymaniyah, Prince Mishari IBN, Abdulaziz Street, P.O. Box 22166.
Telephone: (966-1) 462-8866.
Telecopier: (966-1) 462-9001.
In Shanghai, China: 2805 Kerry Centre, 1515 Nanjing Road West.
Telephone: 86-21-5298-6568.
Telecopier: 86-21-5298-6569.
In Sydney, Australia: Governor Phillip Tower, Level 38, 1 Farrer Place.
Telephone: 61-2-9210-6921.
Telecopier: 61-2-9210-6926.
In Taipei, Taiwan: 8th Floor, Tun Hwa South Road, Section 2.
Telephone: (886-2) 2704-6808.
Telecopier: (886-2) 2704-6791.
In Tokyo, Japan: Toranomon MT Building, 4th Floor, 10-3, Toranomon 3-Chome, Minato-ku, Tokyo 105, Japan.
Telephone: 81-3-3433-3939.
Telecopier: 81-3-5401-2725.
In Washington, D.C.: 51 Louisiana Avenue, N.W.
Telephone: 202-879-3939.
Telecopier: 202-626-1700.

MEMBERS OF FIRM IN CLEVELAND

Regan J. Fay
Robert Conley Kahrl
Kenneth R. Adamo
Robert P. Ducatman
Timothy J. O'Hearn

For Complete List of Firm Personnel, See General Section

For full biographical listings, see the Martindale-Hubbell Law Directory

RANKIN, HILL, PORTER & CLARK LLP (AV)

700 Huntington Building, 925 Euclid Avenue, 44115-1405
Telephone: 216-566-9700
Fax: 216-566-9711
Email: rankin@rhpc.com

Carl A. Rankin
Wayne D. Porter, Jr.
Stephen A. Hill
Kenneth A. Clark
Randolph E. Digges, III

For full biographical listings, see the Martindale-Hubbell Law Directory

*COLUMBUS,** Franklin Co.

MUELLER AND SMITH A LEGAL PROFESSIONAL ASSOCIATION (AV)

Mueller-Smith Building, 7700 Rivers Edge Drive, 43235-1131
Telephone: 614-436-0600
Telecopier: 614-436-0057
Email: patents@infinet.com *URL:* http://www.lawyers.com/muellerandsmith

Jerry K. Mueller, Jr.
Gerald L. Smith

Representative Clients: Ashland Chemical Co.; Battelle Columbus Laboratories; General Electric Co.; Liebert Corp.; OCLC Online Computer Library Center, Inc.; Neoprobe Corporation; The Edward Orton, Jr. Ceramic Foundation; The Ohio State University Research Foundation.

For full biographical listings, see the Martindale-Hubbell Law Directory

PORTER WRIGHT MORRIS & ARTHUR LLP (AV)

41 South High Street, 43215-6194
Telephone: 614-227-2000; (800-533-2794)
Fax: 614-227-2100
Email: cmh@porterwright.com *URL:* http://www.porterwright.com
Cincinnati, Ohio Office: 250 E. Fifth Street, Suite 2200, 45202-4199.
Telephones: 513-381-4700; (800-582-5813).
Fax: 513-421-0991. Internet: cvg@porterwright.com.
Cleveland, Ohio Office: 925 Euclid Avenue, Suite 1700, 44115-1483.
Telephones: 216-443-9000; (800-824-1980).
Fax: 216-443-9011. Internet: cle@porterwright.com.

(See Next Column)

Dayton, Ohio Office: One Dayton Centre, One South Main Street, Suite 1600, 45402-2028.
Telephones: 937-449-6810; (800-533-4434).
Fax: 937-449-6820. Internet: day@porterwright.com.
Naples, Florida Office: 5801 Pelican Bay Boulevard, Suite 300, 34108-2709.
Telephones: 941-593-2900; (800-876-7962).
Fax: 941-593-2990. Internet: apf@porterwright.com.
Washington, D.C. Office: 1667 K Street, N.W., Suite 1100, 20006-1605.
Telephones: 202-778-3000; (800-456-7962).
Fax: 202-778-3063. Internet: dca@porterwright.com.

MEMBERS OF FIRM
COLUMBUS, OHIO OFFICE

Edwin M. Baranowski
Deborah S. Winkler

ASSOCIATES
COLUMBUS, OHIO OFFICE

Mark E. Duell
Karen K. Hammond
Laurie N. Jacques

CINCINNATI, OHIO OFFICE
RESIDENT MEMBER

Wm. Cates Rambo

For Complete List of Firm Personnel, See General Section

For full biographical listings, see the Martindale-Hubbell Law Directory

*DAYTON,** Montgomery Co.

BIEBEL & FRENCH A LEGAL PROFESSIONAL ASSOCIATION (AV)

35 East First Street, 45402
Telephone: 937-461-4543
Fax: 937-443-0861
Email: biebel@erinet.com

Lawrence B. Biebel (1906-1989)
Thomas W. Flynn
Nathaniel R. French (1913-1994)
Bruce E. Peacock
Michael D. Folkerts

Steven D. A. McCarthy
Douglas Alan Yerkeson
Nicole D. Vickroy
Mark E. Rose

COUNSEL

Gilbert N. Henderson
John Bostjancich (Not admitted in OH)
Patricia S. Smart (Not admitted in OH)

For full biographical listings, see the Martindale-Hubbell Law Directory

KILLWORTH, GOTTMAN, HAGAN & SCHAEFF, L.L.P. (AV)

One Dayton Centre, One South Main Street, Suite 500, 45402-2023
Telephone: 937-223-2050
Fax: 937-223-0724
Email: kghs@kghs.com

MEMBERS OF FIRM

Richard A. Killworth
Richard C. Stevens
James F. Gottman
Robert L. Showalter
Timothy W. Hagan
Kimberly Gambrel
B. Joseph Schaeff
James E. Beyer

ASSOCIATES

Jody H. Armstrong
Michael G. Frey
Daniel C. Stelter

OF COUNSEL

David A. Shough
Patricia L. Prior

LEGAL SUPPORT PERSONNEL

Susan M. Luna
Carolyn M. Sloane

For full biographical listings, see the Martindale-Hubbell Law Directory

*TOLEDO,** Lucas Co.

EMCH, SCHAFFER, SCHAUB & PORCELLO CO., L.P.A. (AV)

One Seagate, Suite 1980, P.O. Box 916, 43697-0916
Telephone: 419-243-1294
Fax: 419-243-8502
Email: EMCHETAL@COMPUSERVE.COM

Mark C. Schaffer
Catherine B. Martineau
Charles R. Schaub
Gregg W. Emch
James F. Porcello, Jr.
Philip M. Rice
Patrick P. Pacella

OF COUNSEL

Richard D. Emch

For full biographical listings, see the Martindale-Hubbell Law Directory

OKLAHOMA

*OKLAHOMA CITY,** Oklahoma Co.

CROWE & DUNLEVY, A PROFESSIONAL CORPORATION (AV)

1800 Mid-America Tower, 20 North Broadway, 73102-8273
Telephone: 405-235-7700
Fax: 405-239-6651
Email: marketing@crowedunlevy.com *URL:* http://www.crowedunlevy.com
Tulsa, Oklahoma Office: 500 Kennedy Building, 321 South Boston Avenue, 74103-3313.
Telephone: 918-592-9800.
Fax: 918-592-9801.
Norman, Oklahoma Office: Crowe & Dunlevy, 2500 South McGee, Suite 140, 73072-6705.
Telephone: 405-321-7317.
Fax: 405-360-4002.

Bill D. McCarthy
Daniel S. Hodgins

Phillip L. Free, Jr.
Randall K. McCarthy
Paige S. Bass

For Complete List of Firm Personnel, See General Section

For full biographical listings, see the Martindale-Hubbell Law Directory

DUNLAP, CODDING & ROGERS, P.C. (AV)

Suite 420, 9400 North Broadway, 73114
Telephone: 405-478-5344
Fax: 405-478-5349; 475-9815
Email: PATENTS@IONET.NET

Jerry J. Dunlap
Charles A. Codding
G. Neal Rogers

Glen M. Burdick
Sue Corbett
Joseph P. Titterington
Nicholas D. Rouse
Douglas J. Sorocco
Marc A. Brockhaus
Carl Michael Smith
Mitchell K. McCarthy (North Oklahoma City Office)

PATENT AGENT

Christopher W. Corbett, Ph.D.

Reference: Banc First, Oklahoma City.

For full biographical listings, see the Martindale-Hubbell Law Directory

MCAFEE & TAFT, A PROFESSIONAL CORPORATION (AV)

Tenth Floor, Two Leadership Square, 73102
Telephone: 405-235-9621
Facsimile: (405) 235-0439 (405) 232-2404
Email: mcafee@ionet.net *URL:* http://www.mcafee-taft.com

Sheryl N. Barr
Robert W. Dace
C. Clark Dougherty, Jr.
Clifford Clark Dougherty, III
E. Harry Gilbert, III
Henry D. Hoss
John A. Kenney
John R. Morris
Anthony L. Rahhal
Reid E. Robison

OF COUNSEL

Neal R. Kennedy
James C. McMillin

Representative Clients: Bank of Oklahoma, N.A.; Fleming Companies, Inc.; Paine Webber Group, Inc.; Arthur Andersen & Co.; Exxon Corp.; St. Paul Fire & Marine Insurance Co.; Columbia/HCA Healthcare Corp.

For Complete List of Firm Personnel, See General Section

For full biographical listings, see the Martindale-Hubbell Law Directory

OREGON

*PORTLAND,** Multnomah Co.

BANNER & WITCOFF, LTD. (AV㊦)

Established In 1920 - Predecessor Parent
601 SW Second Avenue Suite 1900, 97204
Telephone: 503-279-6330
Fax: 503-279-6328
Email: cooperman@bannerwitcoff.com *URL:* http://www.bannerwitcoff.com
Chicago, Illinois Office: Ten South Wacker Drive.
Telephone: 312-715-1000.
Facsimile: 312-715-1234.
Washington, D.C. Office: 1001 G Street, N.W.
Telephone: 202-508-9100.
Facsimile: 202-508-9299.

(See Next Column)

Boston, Massachusetts Office: 28 State Street, 28th Floor.
Telephone: 617-227-7111.
Fax: 617-227-4399.

James A. Niegowski

John R. Dawson
Thomas L. Evans (Not admitted in OR)

For full biographical listings, see the Martindale-Hubbell Law Directory

BIRDWELL, JANKE & DURANDO, LLP (AV)

Suite 1925 900 S.W. Fifth Avenue, 97204-1221
Telephone: 503-228-1841
Facsimile: 503-228-2635
Email: wab@birdwelljanke.com
Tucson, Arizona Office: Durando, Birdwell & Janke, LLP, 2929 East Broadway Boulevard, 85716.
Telephone: 520-881-9442.
Fax: 520-881-9448.

William A. Birdwell
Garth Janke
Antonio R. Durando (Not admitted in OR)

Allen W. Field
Janeanne Peterson

Representative Clients: Audio Precision, Inc.; Ideas For Medicine, Inc.; II Morrow, Inc.; Key Knife, Inc.; Oersted Technology Corporation; Prototype Solutions, Inc.; Olympia Cheese Co.

For full biographical listings, see the Martindale-Hubbell Law Directory

CHERNOFF, VILHAUER, MCCLUNG & STENZEL, LLP (AV)

600 Benj. Franklin Plaza, One S.W. Columbia, 97258
Telephone: 503-227-5631
Facsimile: 503-228-4373
Email: postmaster@chernofflaw.com

MEMBERS OF FIRM

Daniel P. Chernoff (1935-1995)
Jacob E. Vilhauer, Jr.
Dennis E. Stenzel
Charles D. McClung
Donald B. Haslett
J. Peter Staples
William O. Geny
Nancy J. Moriarty
Julianne R. Davis
Bruce W. DeKock
Robert K. Lau
Tim A. Long

Kevin L. Russell
Timothy E. Siegel

OF COUNSEL

Howard Eisenberg (Not admitted in OR)

LEGAL SUPPORT PERSONNEL

David Sylvan Fine

Representative Clients: Bend Research, Inc.; Cascade Corp.; Cascade Microtech, Inc.; Columbia Sportswear Co.; Gunderson, Inc.; Jeld-Wen, Inc.; Leatherman Tool Group, Inc.; Longview Fibre Co.; Planar Systems, Inc.; Soloflex, Inc.
Reference: U.S. National Bank of Oregon.

For full biographical listings, see the Martindale-Hubbell Law Directory

MARGER, JOHNSON & MCCOLLOM, P.C. (AV)

1030 S.W. Morrison Street, 97205
Telephone: 503-222-3613
FAX: 503-274-4622
Email: inquiry@techlaw.com *URL:* http://www.techlaw.com
Bend, Oregon Office: 777 N.W. Wall, Suite 308, 97702.
Telephone: 541-312-2500.
Fax: 541-312-8900.

Alexander C. Johnson, Jr.
Alan T. McCollom
Glenn C. Brown
Stephen S. Ford

Scott A. Schaffer
Joseph S. Makuch
Graciela G. Cowger
Hosoon Lee
Ariel S. Rogson
Gregory T. Kavounas
James E. Harris
James G. Stewart
Craig R. Rogers

LEGAL SUPPORT PERSONNEL

PARALEGAL

Kimberly A. Hubbell

OF COUNSEL

Jerome S. Marger

Representative Clients: Adidas; Advanced Power Technology; Analog Devices; Baker Hughes Inc.; Battelle Pacific Northwest Laboratories; Cisco Systems; Columbia Machine, Inc.; Elmers Restaurants, Inc.; Hanson Natural Resources Co.; Hewlett-Packard Co.

For full biographical listings, see the Martindale-Hubbell Law Directory

Portland—Continued

MILLER NASH LLP (AV)

A Limited Liability Partnership including Professional Corporations
111 S.W. Fifth Avenue, 97204-3699
Telephone: 503-224-5858
Telex: 364462, Kingmar PTL
Facsimile: 503-224-0155, 503-224-2450
Email: e-mail@millernash.com *URL:* http://www.millernash.com
Seattle, Washington Office: 4400 Two Union Square, 601 Union Street, 98101-2322.
Telephone: 206-622-8484.
Facsimile: 206-622-7485.

PORTLAND, OREGON PARTNERS

Erich W. Merrill, Jr., P.C.
John F. Neupert, P.C.
Dennis P. Rawlinson, P.C.

SEATTLE, WASHINGTON PARTNER

Bruce A. Kaser, P.C.

PORTLAND, OREGON ASSOCIATE

Matthew D. Rabdau

Representative Clients: U. S. Bancorp; Louisiana-Pacific Corp.; Willamette Industries, Inc.; Portland Public Schools; St. Vincent Hospital and Medical Center; Merrill Lynch, Pierce, Fenner & Smith, Inc.; Epitope, Inc.

For Complete List of Firm Personnel, See General Section

For full biographical listings, see the Martindale-Hubbell Law Directory

PENNSYLVANIA

*MEDIA,** Delaware Co.

ELMAN & ASSOCIATES, A PROFESSIONAL CORPORATION (AV)

20 West Third Street, Suite 200, P.O. Box 1969, 19063
Telephone: 610-892-9580
Fax: 610-892-9577
Email: info@elman.com *URL:* http://www.elman.com

Gerry J. Elman

Brian P. Canniff
Loretta F. Smith (Not admitted in PA)

SPECIAL COUNSEL

William Adair Bonner

OF COUNSEL

Allan J. Jacobson

TECHNICAL ADVISOR

I.J. (Illy) Sobel, P.E.

SCIENTIFIC ADVISOR

Jahan Ara, Ph.D.

For full biographical listings, see the Martindale-Hubbell Law Directory

*PHILADELPHIA,** Philadelphia Co.

CAESAR, RIVISE, BERNSTEIN, COHEN & POKOTILOW, LTD. (AV)

12th Floor, 1635 Market Street, 19103-2212
Telephone: 215-567-2010
Telecopier: 215-751-1142
Email: gatekeeper@Caesarrivise.com

Alan H. Bernstein
Stanley H. Cohen
Manny D. Pokotilow
Barry A. Stein
Martin L. Faigus
Eric S. Marzluf
Robert S. Silver
Michael J. Berkowitz
Scott M. Slomowitz
Mona Gupta
David M. Tener
James J. Kozuch
Salvatore Guerriero (Not admitted in PA)
William J. Castillo (Not admitted in PA)
Francis M. Linguiti

OF COUNSEL

Max Goldman

For full biographical listings, see the Martindale-Hubbell Law Directory

DANN, DORFMAN, HERRELL AND SKILLMAN, A PROFESSIONAL CORPORATION (AV)

Suite 720, 1601 Market Street, 19103-2307
Telephone: 215-563-4100
Fax: 215-563-4044
Email: internet:email@ddhs.com

(See Next Column)

John C. Dorfman
Henry H. Skillman
Roger W. Herrell
Patrick J. Hagan
Donald R. Piper, Jr.
Vincent T. Pace
Janet E. Reed
Stephen H. Eland
Craig M. Bell
Clement A. Berard (Not admitted in PA)
Alfred W. Zaher

OF COUNSEL

C. Marshall Dann
John S. Child, Jr.
Charles N. Quinn

LEGAL SUPPORT PERSONNEL

PATENT AGENTS

John B. Berryhill
Kathleen D. Rigaut

TECHNICAL ADVISOR

Ellen Klann
Niels Haun (Technical Advisor)

For full biographical listings, see the Martindale-Hubbell Law Directory

PAUL & PAUL (AV)

2900 Two Thousand Market Street, 19103
Telephone: 215-568-4900
Cable Address: "Caveat"
Telex: 710-670-1352 Dex
Telecopier: 215-567-5057
Email: paulandpaul@compuserve.com

MEMBERS OF FIRM

James C. McConnon
John F. McNulty
Alex R. Sluzas

ASSOCIATES

Frank J. Bonini, Jr.
Paul A. Taufer
Gary A. Greene

For full biographical listings, see the Martindale-Hubbell Law Directory

SYNNESTVEDT & LECHNER LLP (AV)

2600 Aramark Tower, 1101 Market Street, 19107-2950
Telephone: 215-923-4466
Facsimile: 215-923-2189
Email: synnlech@synnlech.com *URL:* http://www.synnlech.com

Paul Synnestvedt (1870-1950)
Harvey L. Lechner (1885-1954)
Raymond H. Synnestvedt (1902-1986)
Andrew R. Klein (1928-1987)
Albert L. Free (1922-1996)
William H. Elliott, Jr. (1918-1997)

MEMBERS OF FIRM

John T. Synnestvedt
Charles H. Lindrooth
Alexis Barron
Joseph F. Posillico
Bryna S. Silver
Gary A. Hecht
Theodore Naccarella

SENIOR COUNSEL

Irving Newman (Not admitted in PA)

ASSOCIATES

Lisa B. Lane
Stephen J. Driscoll
Joshua R. Slavitt
Mark D. Simpson
Patrick John Kelly
John A. Chionchio
Gregory S. Bernabeo
Stephen James Weed (Not admitted in PA)
Peter J. Butch III (Not admitted in PA)

OF COUNSEL

Richard D. Weber

LEGAL SUPPORT PERSONNEL

SCIENTIFIC ADVISORS

Brett T. Freeman
Gene J. Yao

For full biographical listings, see the Martindale-Hubbell Law Directory

WOODCOCK WASHBURN KURTZ MACKIEWICZ & NORRIS LLP (AV)

One Liberty Place - 46th Floor, 17th & Market Streets, 19103
Telephone: 215-568-3100
Fax: 215-568-3439
URL: http://www.woodcock.com

Virgil E. Woodcock (1905-1974)
Lawrence T. Phelan (1900-1969)
Robert B. Washburn
Richard E. Kurtz
John J. Mackiewicz
Norman L. Norris
Dale M. Heist
Philip S. Johnson
John W. Caldwell
Gary H. Levin
Steven J. Rocci
Dianne B. Elderkin
Francis A. Paintin
John P. Donohue, Jr.
Henrik D. Parker
Suzanne E. Miller
Lynn Bavaro Morreale
Mark DeLuca
Laura Genovese Miller
Joseph Lucci
Michael P. Dunnam
Michael D. Stein
Albert J. Marcellino
David R. Bailey
Doreen Y. Trujillo

(See Next Column)

WOODCOCK WASHBURN KURTZ MACKIEWICZ & NORRIS LLP, *Philadelphia—Continued*

ASSOCIATES

Barbara Lynn Mullin
Kevin M. Flannery
Lynn A. Malinoski
Michael P. Straher
David A. Cherry
Michael J. Swope
Michael J. Bonella
Harold H. Fullmer
William R. Richter
John E. McGlynn
Kimberly R. Hild
Lawrence A. Aaronson
Jonathan M. Waldman
Chad E. Ziegler
Gwilym J.O. Attwell
David N. Farsiou
Paul K. Legaard
Maureen S. Gibbons
Steven H. Meyer
Thomas D. Smith
Paul B. Milcetic
Joseph R. Condo
Michael K. Jones
Frank T. Carroll
Hans J. Crosby
Mark J. Rosen
Camille M. Miller
Rena Patel
Mitchell R. Brustein
Thomas E. Watson (Not admitted in PA)
Eric H. Vance
Peter M. Ullman
Richard B. LeBlanc (Not admitted in PA)
Vincent J. Roccia
Denise Incorvaia Mroz (Not admitted in PA)

COUNSEL

Albert W. Preston, Jr.

OF COUNSEL

Anthony J. Rossi
Kathleen A. Milsark

LEGAL SUPPORT PERSONNEL

Christine A. Goddard (Scientific Advisor)

For full biographical listings, see the Martindale-Hubbell Law Directory

*PITTSBURGH,** Allegheny Co.

PAUL A. BECK & ASSOCIATES (AV)

1106 Frick Building, 437 Grant Street, 15219-6101
Telephone: 412-261-4599
Fax: 412-471-6068
Email: pbeck46571@aol.com

OF COUNSEL

Floyd B. Carothers
William L. Krayer
George Raynovich, Jr.

LEGAL SUPPORT PERSONNEL

Amanda M. Dunyak (Legal Assistant)
John C. Thomas (Law Clerk)

For full biographical listings, see the Martindale-Hubbell Law Directory

ECKERT SEAMANS CHERIN & MELLOTT, LLC (AV)

600 Grant Street, 44th Floor, 15219
Telephone: 412-566-6000
Facsimile: 412-566-6099
Email: escm.pit.pit2.@escm.com *URL:* http://www.escm.com
Harrisburg, Pennsylvania Office: 213 Market Street, Eighth Floor.
Telephone: 717-237-6000.
Facsimile: 717-237-6019.
Philadelphia, Pennsylvania Office: 1515 Market Street, Ninth Floor.
Telephone: 215-851-8400.
Facsimile: 215-851-8383.
Boston, Massachusetts Office: One International Place, 18th Floor.
Telephone: 617-342-6800.
Facsimile: 617-342-6899.
Fort Lauderdale, Florida Office: Las Olas Centre, Suite 800, 450 East Las Olas Boulevard.
Telephone: 954-523-0400.
Facsimile: 954-523-7002.
Haddonfield, New Jersey Office: 36 Tanner Street, Second Floor.
Telephone: 609-427-6240.
Facsimile: 609-427-0611.
Washington, D.C. Office: 1250 24th Street, N.W., Suite 700.
Telephone: 202-659-6600.
Facsimile: 202-659-6699.

PATENT AND TRADEMARK MEMBERS

Daniel C. Abeles
David W. Brownlee
Robert P. Lenart
David V. Radack
Arnold B. Silverman
Alan G. Towner
Richard V. Westerhoff

SPECIAL COUNSEL

Daniel P. Cillo

COUNSEL

Walter J. Blenko, Jr.

ASSOCIATES

Kirk D. Houser
David C. Jenkins
Michael D. Lazzara
Diane R. Meyers
Benjamin T. Queen, II

For Complete List of Firm Personnel, See General Section

For full biographical listings, see the Martindale-Hubbell Law Directory

WEBB ZIESENHEIM LOGSDON ORKIN & HANSON, P.C. (AV)

700 Koppers Building, 436 Seventh Avenue, 15219-1818
Telephone: 412-471-8815
Cable Address: "Webblaw"
Fax: 412-471-4094
Email: webblaw@webblaw.com
Harrisburg, Pennsylvania Office: 100 Pine Street. 17106-1166.
Telephone: 717-238-1555.
Fax: 717-238-1755.

William Hess Webb (1905-1997)
David C. Bruening (1936-1997)
William H. Logsdon
Russell D. Orkin
David C. Hanson
Richard L. Byrne
Frederick B. Ziesenheim
Kent E. Baldauf
Barbara E. Johnson
Paul M. Reznick
John W. McIlvaine, III

Blynn L. Shideler
Julie W. Meder
Lester N. Fortney
Randall A. Notzen
Jesse A. Hirshman
James G. Porcelli
Kent E. Baldauf, Jr.
Christian E. Schuster
Deborah M. Altman
Thomas J. Clinton

OF COUNSEL

Michael I. Shamos

PATENT AGENTS

Dean E. Geibel
Nathan J. Prepelka

For full biographical listings, see the Martindale-Hubbell Law Directory

SPRING HOUSE, Montgomery Co.

HOWSON & HOWSON (AV)

One Spring House Corporate Center, 321 Norristown Road, P.O. Box 457, 19477
Telephone: 215-540-9200
Telecopier: 215-540-5818

Stanley B. Kita
George A. Smith, Jr.
Mary E. Bak
Cathy Ann Kodroff
Charles M. Allen
Henry Hansen
William Bak
Irene J. Frangos
Wilson Oberdorfer (Retired)

LEGAL SUPPORT PERSONNEL

Sandra L. Weiss

For full biographical listings, see the Martindale-Hubbell Law Directory

VALLEY FORGE, Chester Co.

MICHAEL F. PETOCK (AV)

46 The Commons at Valley Forge, 1220 Valley Forge Road, P.O. Box 856, 19482-0856
Telephone: 610-935-8600; 215-922-5550
Fax: 610-933-9300
Email: MFP@iplaw-petock.com *URL:* http://www.IPLaw-petock.com

For full biographical listings, see the Martindale-Hubbell Law Directory

ZACHARY T. WOBENSMITH, III (AV)

86 The Commons at Valley Forge East, 1288 Valley Forge Road, P.O. Box 750, 19482-0750
Telephone: 610-935-9750
Telecopier: 610-935-0600
URL: http://www.lawyers.com/zachary&wobensmith

For full biographical listings, see the Martindale-Hubbell Law Directory

RHODE ISLAND

*PROVIDENCE,** Providence Co.

HINCKLEY, ALLEN & SNYDER LLP (AV)

1500 Fleet Center, 02903-2393
Telephone: 401-274-2000
Fax: 401-277-9600
Email: firm@haslaw.com *URL:* http://www.haslaw.com
Boston, Massachusetts Office: 28 State Street, 30th Floor.
Telephone: 617-345-9000.
Fax: 617-345-9020. URL: http://www.haslaw.com.

MEMBERS OF FIRM

Paula K. Andrews (Not admitted in RI)
David D. Barricelli
E. Jerome Batty
Jonathan Bell
Deborah L. Benson (Not admitted in RI)
Paul Bork (Not admitted in RI)
Stephen J. Carlotti
David Barry Connolly (Not admitted in RI)
Joseph P. Curran
Michael P. DeFanti
Eric F. Eisenberg (Not admitted in RI)
Malcolm Farmer, III

(See Next Column)

HINCKLEY, ALLEN & SNYDER LLP—*Continued*

MEMBERS OF FIRM (Continued)

Margaret D. Farrell
Hugh J. Gorman, III (Not admitted in RI)
Alan P. Gottlieb (Not admitted in RI)
William R. Grimm
Paul A. Hedstrom (Not admitted in RI)
Joel Lewin (Not admitted in RI)
Sandra Matrone Mack
Matthew T. Marcello, III
Elizabeth Murdock Myers
Paul F. O'Donnell, III (Not admitted in RI)
H. Peter Olsen
Gerald J. Petros
James O. Reavis
Jeremy Ritzenberg (Not admitted in RI)
Ralph J. Rivkind (Not admitted in RI)
Lawrence R. Robins (Not admitted in RI)
David J. Rubin
Charles E. Schaub, Jr. (Not admitted in RI)
Herman Snyder (Not admitted in RI)
David R. Sullivan (Not admitted in RI)
Robert F. Sylvia (Not admitted in RI)
Howard E. Walker

ASSOCIATES

Jessica M. Bettencourt
Mark Bianchi
Alyssa V. Boss
Alexandra K. Callam
Jane E. Cohen (Not admitted in RI)
Andrew D. Cummings (Not admitted in RI)
June E. Daniel
Kim Herman Goslant (Not admitted in RI)
Gloria Maria Gutierrez (Not admitted in RI)
Kelley Jordan-Price
Catherine S. Kim (Not admitted in RI)
Christopher W. Morog (Not admitted in RI)
Elena B. Olson (Not admitted in RI)
Joseph D. Whelan

OF COUNSEL

Willard R. Pope (Not admitted in RI)
Bentley Tobin
Joachim A. Weissfeld

For Complete List of Firm Personnel, See General Section

For full biographical listings, see the Martindale-Hubbell Law Directory

WM. W. RYMER (AV)

400 South Main Street, 02903
Telephone: 401-331-0181
Telecopier: 401-274-5070

For full biographical listings, see the Martindale-Hubbell Law Directory

SOUTH CAROLINA

*GREENVILLE,** Greenville Co.

RALPH BAILEY, P.A. (AV)

125 Broadus Avenue, 29601
Telephone: 864-242-5454
Fax: 864-242-3040
Email: RBailey107@aol.com

Ralph Bailey

For full biographical listings, see the Martindale-Hubbell Law Directory

DORITY & MANNING, P.A. (AV)

700 East North Street, 29602
Telephone: 864-271-1592
Facsimile: 864-233-7342
Mailing Address: P.O. Box 1449, Greenville, S.C., 29602-1449
URL: http://www.dority-manning.com
Columbia, South Carolina Office: NBSC Building, 1122 Lady Street, Suite 810, 29201, P.O. Box 2200, 29202.
Telephone: 803-256-2005.
Fax: 803-933-0066.

Julian W. Dority
Wellington M. Manning, Jr.
James M. Bagarazzi
Richard M. Moose
Mark C. Dukes (Resident, Columbia Office)
Stephen E. Bondura
Neil C. Jones
Craig N. Killen (Resident, Columbia Office)
Timothy A. Cassidy
Lloyd G. Farr (Also at Columbia, South Carolina Office)

Jeffrey M. Karmilovich
Frances Barnes Elliott
John Bennett Mullinax
Tim F. Williams
John E. Vick, Jr. (Not admitted in SC)
Judy Jarecki-Black
Wesley Dodgen Few

Representative Clients: Rieter Ingolstadt Spinnereimaschinenbau Aktiengesellschaft; Maschinenfabrik Rieter (Swiss); Steel Heddle Manufacturing Co.; Beverage Air Co.; Meyn B.V.; Clemson University; Kimberly-Clark Corporation; Policy Management Systems Corporation; Riverwood International; Rockwell Automation.

(See Next Column)

For full biographical listings, see the Martindale-Hubbell Law Directory

HAYNSWORTH, MARION, MCKAY & GUÉRARD, L.L.P. (AV)

75 Beattie Place, Eleventh Floor, P.O. Box 2048, 29602
Telephone: 864-240-3200
Facsimile: 864-240-3300
Columbia, South Carolina Office: Suite 2400 Affinity Building, 1201 Main Street, P.O. Drawer 7157, 29202
Telephone: 803-765-1818.
Facsimile: 803-765-2399.
Charleston, South Carolina Office: 134 Meeting Street, P.O. Box 1119, 29402.
Telephone: 843-722-7606.
Facsimile: 843-724-8016.

MEMBERS OF FIRM

Ellis M. Johnston, II
John B. McLeod
Bryan Francis Hickey

ASSOCIATE

William David Conner

OF COUNSEL

O. G. Calhoun, Jr.

Counsel for: Duke Power Co.; Liberty Mutual Insurance Co.; Equitable Life Assurance Society of the United States; St. Paul Insurance Group; Allstate Insurance Co.; Fluor-Daniel Corp.; Synalloy Corp.; Greenville Hospital System; Peeler Jersey Farms, Inc.

For Complete List of Firm Personnel, See General Section

For full biographical listings, see the Martindale-Hubbell Law Directory

LEATHERWOOD WALKER TODD & MANN, P.C. (AV)

100 East Coffee Street, P.O. Box 87, 29602
Telephone: 864-242-6440
FAX: 864-240-2477
Email: leatherwood@lwtm.com *URL:* http://www.lwtm.com
Spartanburg, South Carolina Office: 1451 East Main Street, P.O. Box 3188.
Telephone: 864-582-4365.
Telefax: 864-583-8961.

Natalma M. McKnew
Steven E. Farrar
Eugene C. McCall, Jr.
Thomas W. Epting

COUNSEL

J. Brantley Phillips, Jr.

For Complete List of Firm Personnel, See General Section

For full biographical listings, see the Martindale-Hubbell Law Directory

TENNESSEE

*KNOXVILLE,** Knox Co.

LUEDEKA, NEELY & GRAHAM, P.C. (AV)

Suite 1871, Riverview Tower, 900 South Gay Street, P.O. Box 1871, 37901-1871
Telephone: 423-546-4305
Fax: 423-523-4478
Email: firm@lng-patent.com *URL:* http://www.LNG-patent.com

Edwin M. Luedeka (1920-1999)
Andrew S. Neely
Mark S. Graham
Robert O. Fox
David E. LaRose
Michael E. Sellers
Richard W. Barnes, Jr.

Jason L. Hornkohl
Mark P. Crockett

OF COUNSEL

J. Frederick Thomsen

For full biographical listings, see the Martindale-Hubbell Law Directory

TEXAS

*AUSTIN,** Travis Co.

ARNOLD WHITE & DURKEE, A PROFESSIONAL CORPORATION (AV)

1900 One American Center, 600 Congress Avenue, 78701-3248
Telephone: 512-418-3000
Facsimile: 512-474-7577
Email: info@awd.com *URL:* http://www.awd.com
Houston, Texas Office: 750 Bering Drive, 77057-2198.
Telephone: 713-787-1400.
Facsimile: 713-787-1440.
Washington, D.C. Office: One Franklin Square, 1301 K Street, N.W., Suite 350, East Tower, 20005.
Telephone: 202-289-0229.
Facsimile: 202-289-7535.
Chicago, Illinois Office: 800 Quaker Tower, 321 North Clark Street, 60610-4714.
Telephone: 312-744-0090.
Facsimile: 312-755-4489.
Minneapolis, Minnesota Office: 4850 U.S. Bank Place, 601 Second Avenue South, 55402-4320.
Telephone: 612-321-2800.
Facsimile: 612-321-9600.
Menlo Park, California Office: 155 Linfield Drive, 94025-3741.
Telephone: 650-614-4500.
Facsimile: 650-614-4599.

Louis T. Pirkey
William D. Raman
Richard J. Groos
David L. Parker
David D. Bahler
Stephen D. Dellett
William G. Barber
Michael S. Metteauer
Shannon Timothy Vale
Amber L. Hatfield
Roderick B. Williams

Mark B. Wilson
Mark A. Thurmon
Rose A. Hagan
Steven L. Highlander
Teresa J. Bowles
Mark J. Rozman
Stephen P. Meleen
G. Scott Thomas
Richard A. Nakashima
Debra L. Dennett
Betty Chang
Nicole W. Stafford
Sharon L. Williamson
Christopher L. Graff
Randolph B. Houston, Jr.
Michael C. Barrett
Gina N. Shishima
Chad R. Anson
Mark T. Garrett
H. Melissa Mather
Dori F. Moses
Stephen M. Hash
Alicia Morris Groos

OF COUNSEL

Neil W. Netanel (Not admitted in TX)
Henry W. Jones, III
Charles D. Huston

SCIENTIFIC ADVISORS

Jonathan D. Hurt
Bill T. Brazil
Priya D. Subramony
Karl D. Normington

For full biographical listings, see the Martindale-Hubbell Law Directory

BAKER BOTTS L.L.P. (AV)

1600 San Jacinto Center, 98 San Jacinto Boulevard, 78701
Telephone: 512-322-2500
Fax: 512-322-2501
Email: postmaster@bakerbotts.com *URL:* http://www.bakerbotts.com
Houston, Texas Office: One Shell Plaza, 910 Louisiana.
Telephone: 713-229-1234.
Dallas, Texas Office: 2001 Ross Avenue.
Telephone: 214-953-6500.
Washington, D.C. Office: The Warner, 1299 Pennsylvania Avenue, N.W.
Telephone: 202-639-7700.
New York, New York Office: 599 Lexington Avenue.
Telephone: 212-705-5000.
Moscow, Russia Office: 10 ul. Bolshaya Dimitrovka (formerly Pushkinskaya), 103031.
Telephone: 7095/921-5300 (Local); 7501/929-7070 (International).
London, England Office: 45 Ludgate Hill.
Telephone: 0171-778-1400 (Local); 011-44-171-778-1400 (International).
Baku, Azerbaijan Office: 6-10 Vagif Mustafa-zadeh Street, Third Floor, Icheri Sheher, 370004.
Telephone: 994-12-97-63-88 (Local); 011-994-12-97-63-88 (International).
Fax: 994-12-97-63-61 (Local); 011-994-12-97-63-91 (International).

SPECIAL COUNSEL

Thomas R. Felger

ASSOCIATES

Robert W. Holland
Anna Conyers Kuhn
Ann Livingston
Scott T. Morris

For Complete List of Firm Personnel, See General Section

For full biographical listings, see the Martindale-Hubbell Law Directory

KARL BAYER (AV)

900 Norwood Tower, 114 West Seventh Street, 78701
Telephone: 512-476-1226
Fax: 512-476-1280
Email: karl@karlbayer.com

Karl Bayer

For full biographical listings, see the Martindale-Hubbell Law Directory

*DALLAS,** Dallas Co.

BAKER BOTTS L.L.P. (AV)

2001 Ross Avenue, 75201
Telephone: 214-953-6500
Fax: 214-953-6503
Email: postmaster@bakerbotts.com *URL:* http://www.bakerbotts.com
Houston, Texas Office: One Shell Plaza, 910 Louisiana.
Telephone: 713-229-1234.
Washington, D.C. Office: The Warner, 1299 Pennsylvania Avenue, N.W.
Telephone: 202-639-7700.
Austin, Texas Office: 1600 San Jacinto Center, 98 San Jacinto Boulevard.
Telephone: 512-322-2500.
New York, New York Office: 599 Lexington Avenue.
Telephone: 212-705-5000.
Moscow, Russia Office: 10 ul. Bolshaya Dimitrovka (formerly Pushkinskaya), 103031.
Telephone: 7095/921-5300 (Local); 7095/929-7070.
London, England Office: 45 Ludgate Hill.
Telephone: 0171-778-1400 (Local); 011-44-171-778-1400 (International).
Baku, Azerbaijan Office: 6-10 Vagif Mustafa-zadeh Street, Third Floor, Icheri Sheher, 370004.
Telephone: 994-12-97-63-88 (Local); 011-994-12-97-63-88 (International).

MEMBERS OF FIRM

Robert M. Chiaviello, Jr.
Charles S. Fish
Robert W. Jordan
Robert W. Kantner
Kevin J. Meek
Jerry W. Mills

SPECIAL COUNSEL

T. Murray Smith (Not admitted in TX)

OF COUNSEL

Harold E. Meier

ASSOCIATES

James L. Baudino
Jeffery D. Baxter
Samir A. Bhavsar
William R. Borchers
Robin Annette Brooks
Darren W. Collins
Keiko Ichiye
Wei Wei Jeang
Jay B. Johnson (Not admitted in TX)
Christopher W. Kennerly
Tara D. Knapp
Douglas M. Kubehl
Randall W. Mishler (Not admitted in TX)
Brian W. Oaks
Luke K. Pedersen
Steven G. Schortgen
Barton Earl Showalter
Alexandra L. Siegel
Terry J. Stalford
Alfred Steiner
Matthew B. Talpis
David G. Wille
Bradley P. Williams

For Complete List of Firm Personnel, See General Section

For full biographical listings, see the Martindale-Hubbell Law Directory

CALHOUN & STACY (AV)

Suite 5700 - Bank of America Plaza, 901 Main Street, 75202-3713
Telephone: 214-748-5000
Facsimile: 214-748-1421
Email: info@calhounstacy.com *URL:* http://www.calhounstacy.com

MEMBERS OF FIRM

Rees T. Bowen, III
Mark Alan Calhoun
David W. Elrod
Thomas E. Rosen
Roy L. Stacy

For Complete List of Firm Personnel, See General Section

For full biographical listings, see the Martindale-Hubbell Law Directory

CRUTSINGER & BOOTH (AV)

Thanksgiving Tower, 1601 Elm Street, Suite 1950, 75201-4744
Telephone: 214-220-0444
Facsimile: 214-220-0445
Email: cblaw@flash.net *URL:* http://www.lawyers.com/cblawfirm

MEMBERS OF FIRM

Gerald G. Crutsinger
John F. Booth
Todd E. Albanesi

ASSOCIATES

David L. Joers
Peter V. Schroeder

OF COUNSEL

James O. Dixon

For full biographical listings, see the Martindale-Hubbell Law Directory

Dallas—Continued

JACKSON WALKER L.L.P. (AV)

901 Main Street, Suite 6000, 75202-3797
Telephone: 214-953-6000
Fax: 214-953-5822
URL: http://www.jw.com
Austin, Texas Office: 100 Congress Avenue, Suite 1100.
Telephone: 512-236-2000.
Fax: 512-236-2002.
Fort Worth, Texas Office: 301 Commerce Street, Suite 2400.
Telephone: 817-334-7200.
Fax: 817-334-7290.
Houston, Texas Office: 1100 Louisiana, Suite 4200.
Telephone: 713-752-4200.
Fax: 713-752-4221.
Richardson, Texas Office: 2435 North Central Expressway, Suite 600.
Telephone: 972-671-2560.
Fax: 972-671-2566.
San Angelo, Texas Office: 225 West Beauregard Avenue.
Telephone: 915-481-2550.
Fax: 915-481-2552.
San Antonio, Texas Office: 112 E. Pecan Street, Suite 2100.
Telephone: 210-978-7700.
Fax: 210-978-7790.

MEMBERS OF FIRM

Carl C. Butzer
Alan N. Greenspan
Robert P. Latham
Frank C. Vecella
Bradley L. Whitlock

Representative Clients Furnished Upon Request.

For Complete List of Firm Personnel, See General Section

For full biographical listings, see the Martindale-Hubbell Law Directory

THOMPSON & KNIGHT L.L.P. (AV)

(Attorneys and Counselors)
1700 Pacific Avenue Suite 3300, 75201
Telephone: 214-969-1700
Telecopy: 214-969-1751
Telex: 732 298
URL: http://www.tklaw.com
Austin, Texas Office: 1200 San Jacinto Center, 98 San Jacinto Boulevard, 78701.
Telephone: 512-469-6100.
Telecopy: 512-469-6180.
Fort Worth, Texas Office: 801 Cherry Street, Suite 1600, 76102.
Telephone: 817-347-1700.
Telecopy: 817-347-1799.
Houston, Texas Office: Thompson Knight Brown Parker & Leahy L.L.P., 1200 Smith Street, Suite 3600, 77002-4595.
Telephone: 713-654-8111.
Telecopier: 713-654-1871.
San Pedro Garza Garcia, Nuevo León, Mexico Office: Edificio Losoles PD-4, Av. Lázaro Cárdenas No. 2400 Pte., C.P. 66220.
Telephone: (52-8) 363-0096.
Telecopy: (52-8) 363-3067.

PARTNERS

Jane Politz Brandt
Beverly Ray Burlingame
Frank Finn
Herbert J. Hammond
Bruce S. Sostek
Peter J. Thoma

ASSOCIATES

Priscilla Lynn Dunckel
Anna E. Marple
Richard L. Wynne, Jr.

For Complete List of Firm Personnel, See General Section

For full biographical listings, see the Martindale-Hubbell Law Directory

TIMMONS & KELLY (AV)

The White House on Turtle Creek, 2401 Turtle Creek Boulevard, 75219-4760
Telephone: 214-528-1881 Fax: 214-528-1882
URL: http://www.ippractice.com

MEMBERS OF FIRM

W. Thomas Timmons
H. Dennis Kelly

ASSOCIATES

Jeffrey T. Hubbard
John S. Torkelson

OF COUNSEL

Daniel Rubin

For full biographical listings, see the Martindale-Hubbell Law Directory

*FORT WORTH,** Tarrant Co.

FELSMAN, BRADLEY, GUNTER & DILLON, LLP (AV)

A Registered Limited Liability Partnership
201 Main Street, Suite 1600, 76102
Telephone: 817-332-8143
Telecopier: 817-332-8409
Email: ftworth@fbgd.com
Austin, Texas Office: Suite 350, Lakewood On The Park, 7600 B North Capital of Texas Highway, 78731.
Telephone: 512-343-6116.
Fax: 512-343-6002. Email: austin@fbgd.com
Houston, Texas Office: 3900 Essex Lane, Suite 1120, 77027.
Telephone: 713-840-8143.
Fax: 713-840-8149. Email: houston@fbgd.com

OF COUNSEL

Robert A. Felsman

MEMBERS OF FIRM

James E. Bradley
Charles D. Gunter, Jr.
Massimo "Max" Ciccarelli

Daniel F. Venglarik
Sidney L. Weatherford
Matthew S. Anderson

For full biographical listings, see the Martindale-Hubbell Law Directory

*HOUSTON,** Harris Co.

ARNOLD WHITE & DURKEE, A PROFESSIONAL CORPORATION (AV)

750 Bering Drive, 77057-2198
Telephone: 713-787-1400
Facsimile: 713-787-1440
Email: info@awd.com *URL:* http://www.awd.com
Austin, Texas Office: 1900 One American Center, 600 Congress Avenue, 78701-3248.
Telephone: 512-418-3000.
Facsimile: 512-474-7577.
Washington, D.C. Office: One Franklin Square, 1301 K Street, N.W., Suite 350, East Tower, 20005.
Telephone: 202-289-0229.
Facsimile: 202-289-7535.
Chicago, Illinois Office: 800 Quaker Tower, 321 North Clark Street, 60610-4714.
Telephone: 312-744-0090.
Facsimile: 312-755-4489.
Minneapolis, Minnesota Office: 4850 U.S. Bank Place, 601 Second Avenue South, 55402-4320.
Telephone: 612-321-2800.
Facsimile: 612-321-9600.
Menlo Park, California Office: 155 Linfield Drive, 94025-3741.
Telephone: 650-614-4500.
Facsimile: 650-614-4599.

Tom Arnold
Robert A. White (1929-1977)
Bill Durkee
Louis T. Pirkey (Resident, Austin, Texas Office)
John F. Lynch (Resident, Menlo Park, California Office)
Rodney K. Caldwell
Stephen G. Rudisill (Resident, Chicago, Illinois Office)
Floyd R. Nation
Charles H. De La Garza (Resident, Minneapolis, Minnesota Office)
J. Paul Williamson (Resident, Washington, D.C. Office)
Travis Gordon White
John D. Norris
William D. Raman (Resident, Austin, Texas Office)
Patricia A. Kammerer
Peter J. Shurn III
Stephen H. Cagle
Thomas A. Miller
Craig M. Lundell
Ronald B. Coolley (Resident, Chicago, Illinois Office)
Richard C. Auchterlonie
Christopher R. Benson
Richard J. Groos (Resident, Austin, Texas Office)
Glenn W. Rhodes (Resident, Menlo Park, California Office)
David L. Parker (Resident, Austin, Texas Office)
David D. Bahler (Resident, Austin, Texas Office)
Stephen D. Dellett (Resident, Austin, Texas Office)
Melinda L. Patterson
William G. Barber (Resident, Austin, Texas Office)
Richard L. Stanley
Robert N. Phillips (Resident, Menlo Park, California Office)
Henry A. Petri, Jr.
Susan K. Knoll
Michael S. Metteauer (Resident, Austin, Texas Office)
Joseph D. Lechtenberger
Shannon Timothy Vale (Resident, Austin, Texas Office)
Mark K. Dickson (Resident, Menlo Park, California Office)
Amber L. Hatfield (Resident, Austin, Texas Office)
Robert J. McAughan, Jr.
David L. Bilsker (Resident, Menlo Park, California Office)
James F. Valentine (Resident, Menlo Park, California Office)
Albert B. Deaver, Jr.
L. Gene Spears, Jr.
Michael E. Lee
Robert B. Lytle
Slawomir (Steve) Z. Szczepanski (Resident, Chicago, Illinois Office)
Roderick B. Williams (Resident, Austin, Texas Office)

(See Next Column)

ARNOLD WHITE & DURKEE A PROFESSIONAL CORPORATION, *Houston—Continued*

Michael J. Blankstein (Resident, Chicago, Illinois Office)
John C. Cain
Michael S. Dowler
Stephen E. Edwards
Mark B. Wilson (Resident, Austin, Texas Office)
Nicolas G. Barzoukas
Paul R. Kitch (Resident, Chicago, Illinois Office)
Hugh R. Kress
Peter J. Chassman
Richard J. Lutton, Jr. (Resident, Menlo Park, California Office)
Mark A. Thurmon (Resident, Austin, Texas Office)
Rose A. Hagan (Resident, Austin, Texas Office)
Michael J. Collins
Steven L. Highlander (Resident, Austin, Texas Office)
Janelle D. Waack
Mary Jo Boldingh (Resident, Chicago, Illinois Office)
Daniel J. Burnham (Resident, Chicago, Illinois Office)
C. Gerard Harrison
Timothy R. Baumann (Resident, Chicago, Illinois Office)
Teresa J. Bowles (Resident, Austin, Texas Office)
Mark J. Rozman (Resident, Austin, Texas Office)
Connie Flores Jones
James A. Jorgensen
Brian L. Jackson
John R. Keville
Thomas V. Miller (Resident, Chicago, Illinois Office)
Terril G. Lewis
Stephen P. Meleen (Resident, Austin, Texas Office)
Jon D. Shutter (Resident, Chicago, Illinois Office)
G. Scott Thomas (Resident, Austin, Texas Office)
John C. Gatz (Resident, Chicago, Illinois Office)
Richard A. Nakashima (Resident, Austin, Texas Office)
James C. Pistorino
Daniel T. Shvodian (Resident, Menlo Park, California Office)
Debra L. Dennett (Resident, Austin, Texas Office)
Mark L. Gleason (Resident, Minneapolis, Minnesota Office)
Natalie J. Spahr
Betty Chang (Resident, Austin, Texas Office)
Timothy M. Kenny (Resident, Minneapolis, Minnesota Office)
Steven G. Spears
Lisa M. Martens (Resident, Menlo Park, California Office)
H.H. (Shashi) Kewalramani
Mark V. Campagna (Resident, Chicago, Illinois Office)
Janet M. Garetto (Resident, Chicago, Illinois Office)
Jose C. Villarreal
Nicole W. Stafford (Resident, Austin, Texas Office)
Scott J. Garber
Michael S. Perez
Darrell G. Dotson
Gerard M. Devlin, Jr.
Sharon L. Williamson (Resident, Austin, Texas Office)
Christopher L. Graff (Resident, Austin, Texas Office)
Randolph B. Houston, Jr. (Resident, Austin, Texas Office)
Brian E. Simmons
Gregg A. Duffey
Ari O. Pramudji
Tong Wu (Resident, Minneapolis, Minnesota Office)
Matthew O. Brady (Resident, Chicago, Illinois Office)
Russell J. Genet (Resident, Chicago, Illinois Office)
Rimas (Ray) T. Lukas (Resident, Chicago, Illinois Office)
Scott W. Clark
Tracy S. Parris
Ira D. Finkelstein
Michael C. Barrett (Resident, Austin, Texas Office)
Gina N. Shishima (Resident, Austin, Texas Office)
Chad R. Anson (Resident, Austin, Texas Office)
Mark T. Garrett (Resident, Austin, Texas Office)
Henry M. Pogorzelski
Mary G. Manley (Resident, Menlo Park, California Office)
Bobby A. Ghajar (Resident, Menlo Park, California Office)
Marina N. Saito (Resident, Chicago, Illinois Office)
Mark A. Seka (Resident, Menlo Park, California Office)
H. Melissa Mather (Resident, Austin, Texas Office)
Marianna Burris
Meredith M. McKenzie (Resident, Menlo Park, California Office)
Patrick J. Gallagher (Resident, Minneapolis, Minnesota Office)
Zachary J. Smolinski (Resident, Chicago, Illinois Office)
Timothy M. Kowalski (Resident, Chicago, Illinois Office)
Dori F. Moses (Resident, Austin, Texas Office)
M. Suzy Strickland
Stephen M. Hash (Resident, Austin, Texas Office)
Billy C. Allen
Yoo-Sun Park
Collin A. Rose
Tod T. Tumey
Michael D. Braunstein
Alicia Morris Groos (Resident, Austin, Texas Office)
Ann K. Burns

OF COUNSEL

Paul M. Janicke
Neil W. Netanel (Resident, Austin, Texas Office)
Keith B. Willhelm (Not admitted in TX)
Harold N. Wells (Resident, Chicago, Illinois Office)
Carla C. Calcagno (Resident, Washington, D.C. Office)
Roger J. French (Resident, Chicago, Illinois Office)
Lisa A. Garono (Resident, Menlo Park, California Office)
Thomas L. Casagrande
Scott D. Eads (Not admitted in TX)
Henry W. Jones, III (Resident, Austin, Texas Office)
Charles D. Huston (Resident, Austin, Texas Office)

(See Next Column)

SCIENTIFIC ADVISORS

Christopher J. Buntel
Carter J. White
Raymund F. Eich
Jonathan D. Hurt (Resident, Austin, Texas Office)
Bill T. Brazil (Resident, Austin, Texas Office)
Priya D. Subramony (Resident, Austin, Texas Office)
Karl D. Normington (Resident, Austin, Texas Office)
Matthew L. Madsen
M. Todd Rands

For full biographical listings, see the Martindale-Hubbell Law Directory

BAKER BOTTS L.L.P. (AV)

One Shell Plaza, 910 Louisiana, 77002
Telephone: 713-229-1234
Cable Address: "Boterlove"
Fax: 713-229-1522
Email: postmaster@bakerbotts.com *URL:* http://www.bakerbotts.com
Washington, D.C. Office: The Warner, 1299 Pennsylvania Avenue, N.W.
Telephone: 202-639-7700.
New York, New York Office: 599 Lexington Avenue.
Telephone: 212-705-5000.
Austin, Texas Office: 1600 San Jacinto Center, 98 San Jacinto Boulevard.
Telephone: 512-322-2500.
Dallas, Texas Office: 2001 Ross Avenue.
Telephone: 214-953-6500.
Moscow, Russia Office: 10 ul. Bolshaya Dimitrovka (formerly Pushkinskaya), 103031.
Telephone: 7095/921-5300 (Local); 7095/929-7070 (International).
London, England Office: 45 Ludgate Hill.
Telephone: 0171-778-1400 (Local); 011-44-171-778-1400 (International).
Baku, Azerbaijan Office: 6-10 Vagif Mustafa-zadeh Street, Third Floor, Icheri Sheher, 370004.
Telephone: 994-12-97-63-88 (Local); 011-994-12-97-63-88 (International).
Fax: 994-12-97-63-91 (Local); 011-994-12-97-63-91 (International)

MEMBERS OF FIRM

Thomas H. Adolph
Mitchell D. Lukin
Scott F. Partridge
Michael E. Wilson

OF COUNSEL

Claude E. Cooke, Jr.

ASSOCIATES

Anita Sani Damian
Nellie Agah Fisher
Roger J. Fulghum
Carey Jordan Hetherington
Michael G. Locklar
Robin Lightner Maisashvili (Not admitted in TX)
Lori D. Stiffler
Khannan Suntharam
Melissa J. Szanto
Gerard Alan Witte

For Complete List of Firm Personnel, See General Section

For full biographical listings, see the Martindale-Hubbell Law Directory

BROWNING BUSHMAN, A PROFESSIONAL CORPORATION (AV)

5718 Westheimer, Suite 1800, 77057
Telephone: 713-266-5593
Facsimile: 713-266-5169
Email: iplaw@echonet.com *URL:* http://www.lawyers.com/browningbushman

Ralph R. Browning (1905-1979)
C. James Bushman
Walter R. Brookhart
Loren G. Helmreich

OF COUNSEL

Carlos A. Torres
Marvin B. Eickenroht
Eugene N. Riddle

Representative Clients: Keystone International, Inc.; CONDEA Vista Chemical Co.; Dresser Industries, Inc.; Baroid Corp.; Coastal Corp.; Varco/-Shaffer, Inc.; Hydro-Chem Industrial Services, Inc.; Baker-Hughes, Inc.; J.M. Huber Corp.; American Oilfield Divers, Inc.

For full biographical listings, see the Martindale-Hubbell Law Directory

PAYNE, LUNDEEN, D'AMBROSIO & ARISMENDI, L.L.P. (AV)

A Limited Liability Partnership of Professional Corporations
1700 West Loop South, Suite 1230, 77027
Telephone: 713-840-8008
Facsimile: 713-840-8088
Email: alpayne@netropolis.net

Alton W. Payne, Jr., (P.C.)
Daniel N. Lundeen (P.C.)
Jo Katherine D'Ambrosio (P.C.)
Andres M. Arismendi, Jr. (P.C.)
Delmar L. Sroufe (P.C.) (Retired)

For full biographical listings, see the Martindale-Hubbell Law Directory

ROSENTHAL & OSHA, L.L.P. (AV®)

700 Louisiana Street, Suite 4550, 77002
Telephone: 713-228-8600
Fax: 713-228-8778

Alan D. Rosenthal
Jonathan P. Osha

(See Next Column)

ROSENTHAL & OSHA L.L.P.—*Continued*

ASSOCIATES

Richard A. Fagin
K. Karan Reed
David E. Mixon

OF COUNSEL

L. Wayne White

LEGAL SUPPORT PERSONNEL

Adenike A. Adewuya (Patent Agent)
Daniel G. Nguyen (Patent Agent)
Thomas K. Scherer (Patent Agent)
Y. Renee Alsandor (Patent Engineer)
Jeffrey S. Bergman (Patent Engineer)
Scott W. Hejny (Patent Engineer)
W. Thomas Morrow (Patent Engineer)
Daniel H. Watanabe, Ph.D. (Japan Practice Specialist)

For full biographical listings, see the Martindale-Hubbell Law Directory

VINSON & ELKINS L.L.P. (AV)

2300 First City Tower, 1001 Fannin, 77002-6760
Telephone: 713-758-2222
Fax: 713-758-2346
Email: info@velaw.com *URL:* http://www.velaw.com
Austin, Texas Office: One American Center Suite 2700, 600 Congress Avenue, Austin, Texas, 78701-3200.
Telephone: 512-495-8400.
Fax: 512-495-8612.
Beijing, China Office: 20/F, Beijing Silver Tower, No. 2, Dong San Huan Bei Lu, Chaoyang District, 100027.
Telephone: +86-10-6410-6300.
Fax: +86-10-6410-6360.
Dallas, Texas Office: 3700 Trammell Crow Center, 2001 Ross Avenue, Dallas, Texas, 75201-2975.
Telephone: 214-220-7700.
Fax: 214-220-7716.
London, England Office: Regis House, 8th Floor, 45 King William Street, London, EC4R 9AN, England.
Telephone: (44-171) 618-6000.
Fax: (44-171) 618-6001.
Moscow, Russia Office: 16 Ulitsa Spiridonovka, Second Floor, 103001 Moscow, Russia.
Telephone: (7-095) 956-1995. Local
Fax: (7-095) 956-1996. U.S. Satellite
Fax: (212) 803-0142.
New York, N.Y. Office: 1325 Avenue of the Americas, 17th Floor, New York, N.Y., 10019.
Telephone: 917-206-8000.
Fax: 917-206-8100.
Singapore Office: 6 Battery Road, #39-01, Singapore, 049909.
Telephone: (65) 536-8300.
Fax: (65) 536-8311.
Washington, D.C. Office: The Willard Office Building, 1455 Pennsylvania Avenue, N.W., Washington, D.C., 20004-1008.
Telephone: 202-639-6500.
Fax: 202-639-6604.

MEMBERS OF FIRM

Steven R. Borgman
George Harvey Dunn, III (Resident, Dallas, Texas Office)
William L. LaFuze
J. Clark Martin
Peter E. Mims
W. Ronald Robins
Willem G. Schuurman (Resident, Austin, Texas Office)
Karen Tucker White

HOUSTON OF COUNSEL

W. Scott Brown

ASSOCIATES

Barry Bumgardner (Resident, Dallas, Texas Office)
Brian K. Buss (Resident, Austin, Texas Office)
Tracey B. Davies (Resident, Austin, Texas Office)
Andrew DiNovo (Resident, Austin, Texas Office)
Barry E. Engel
Adam V. Floyd (Resident, Austin, Texas Office)
Stuart J. Ford
Sunil Kalara
Gerald D. Malpass, Jr.
Stephen J. Moloney (Resident, Austin, Texas Office)
Minh-Hien Nguyen (Resident, Austin, Texas Office)
Gregory Lawrence Porter (Resident, Austin, Texas Office)
Michael A. Sanzo (Resident, Washington, D.C. Office)
John F. Woodson, II

For Complete List of Firm Personnel, See General Section

For full biographical listings, see the Martindale-Hubbell Law Directory

WILLIAMS, MORGAN & AMERSON, P.C. (AV)

7676 Hillmont, Suite 250, 77040
Telephone: 713-934-7000
Fax: 713-934-7011

(See Next Column)

Danny L. Williams (Shareholder)
Terry D. Morgan (Shareholder)
J. Mike Amerson (Shareholder)
Kenneth D. Goodman (Shareholder)
Alexandra Barbara Kitchell (Shareholder)
Jeffrey A. Pyle (Shareholder)

Ruben S. Bains
Jaison C. John
Randall C. Furlong, Ph.D.

LEGAL SUPPORT PERSONNEL

Scott F. Diring (Patent Agent)
Jeffrey E. Hundley, Ph.D (Patent Agent)
George J. Oehling (Patent Agent)
Chris Cravey (Patent Law Clerk)
Shelley P. M. Fussey, Ph.D. (Patent Agent)
David W. Hibler, Ph.D. (Patent Agent)
Mark D. Moore, Ph.D. (Patent Agent)

For full biographical listings, see the Martindale-Hubbell Law Directory

*SAN ANTONIO,** Bexar Co.

COX & SMITH INCORPORATED (AV)

112 East Pecan Street, Suite 1800, 78205-1521
Telephone: 210-554-5500
Fax: 210-226-8395
Email: info@coxsmith.com *URL:* http://www.coxsmith.com

Gale R. Peterson
J. Daniel Harkins
James M. Truss
W. Bradley Barnes
Courtenay B. Allen

Representative Clients: Clarke-American Checks, Inc.; Southwest Foundation for Biomedical Research; Texas Tech University.

For Complete List of Firm Personnel, See General Section

For full biographical listings, see the Martindale-Hubbell Law Directory

JACKSON WALKER L.L.P. (AV)

112 E. Pecan Street, Suite 2100, 78205-1521
Telephone: 210-978-7700
Fax: 210-978-7790
URL: http://www.jw.com
Austin, Texas Office: 100 Congress Avenue, Suite 1100.
Telephone: 512-236-2000.
Fax: 512-236-2002.
Dallas, Texas Office: 901 Main Street, Suite 6000.
Telephone: 214-953-6000.
Fax: 214-953-5822.
Fort Worth, Texas Office: 301 Commerce Street, Suite 2400.
Telephone: 817-334-7200.
Fax: 817-334-7290.
Houston, Texas Office: 1100 Louisiana, Suite 4200.
Telephone: 713-752-4200.
Fax: 713-752-4221.
Richardson, Texas Office: 2435 North Central Expressway, Suite 600.
Telephone: 972-671-2560.
Fax: 972-671-2566.
San Angelo, Texas Office: 225 West Beauregard Avenue.
Telephone: 915-481-2550.
Fax: 915-481-2552.

MEMBERS OF FIRM

William B. Nash
Mark H. Miller
Thomas E. Sisson
Daniel D. Chapman

For Complete List of Firm Personnel, See General Section

For full biographical listings, see the Martindale-Hubbell Law Directory

UTAH

*SALT LAKE CITY,** Salt Lake Co.

MADSON & METCALF, A PROFESSIONAL CORPORATION (AV)

900 Gateway Tower West, 15 West South Temple, 84101
Telephone: 801-537-1700
Facsimile: 801-537-1799
Email: info@mmlaw.com *URL:* http://www.mmlaw.com

Craig J. Madson
L. Craig Metcalf
Evan R. Witt
A. John (Jack) Pate
Gary D.E. Pierce
David B. Fonda

John R. Thompson
Brian C. Kunzler
Barton W. Giddings
Hal D. Baird
Eric M. Barzee
Kory Christensen

For full biographical listings, see the Martindale-Hubbell Law Directory

Salt Lake City—Continued

MALLINCKRODT & MALLINCKRODT (AV)

Suite 510 Newhouse Building, 10 Exchange Place, 84111
Telephone: 801-328-1624
FAX: 801-328-1627
URL: http://www.lawyers.com/mallinckrodt
Kansas City, Missouri Office: Peer Mallinckrodt & Mallinckrodt. 2931 Holmes Street.
Telephone: 816-561-9426.

MEMBERS OF FIRM

Philip A. Mallinckrodt
Robert R. Mallinckrodt

ASSOCIATE

Brian Richard Rayve

OF COUNSEL

Peter M. Peer, II

Representative Clients: BSD Medical Corp.; Christensen Mining Products; Mountain Fuel Supply Co.; Wescor, Inc.

For full biographical listings, see the Martindale-Hubbell Law Directory

TRASK, BRITT & ROSSA, A PROFESSIONAL CORPORATION (AV)

230 South 500 East, Suite 300, P.O. Box 2550, 84110-2550
Telephone: 801-532-1922
Toll Free: 800-900-2001
Telecopier: 801-531-9168
URL: http://www.tbrlaw.com

David V. Trask
William S. Britt
Thomas J. Rossa
Laurence B. Bond
Joseph A. Walkowski
James R. Duzan
H. Dickson Burton
Allen C. Turner
Kent S. Burningham
Edgar R. Cataxinos
Brick Power
Paul C. Oestreich

Reference: Key Bank.

For full biographical listings, see the Martindale-Hubbell Law Directory

SANDY, Salt Lake Co.

CLAYTON, HOWARTH & CANNON, P.C. (AV)

10150 South Centennial Parkway, Suite 400, P.O. Box 1909, 84091
Telephone: 801-255-5335
Fax: 801-256-2043
Email: patlaw@chcpat.com

Grant R. Clayton
Alan J. Howarth
Karl R. Cannon

For full biographical listings, see the Martindale-Hubbell Law Directory

THORPE, NORTH & WESTERN, L.L.P. (AV)

A Partnership including a Professional Corporation
8180 South 700 East, Suite 200, 84070
Telephone: 801-566-6633
Fax: 801-566-0750
Mailing Address: P.O. Box 1219, Sandy, Utah, 84091
Email: patlaw@tnw.com *URL:* http://www.tnw.com
Las Vegas, Nevada Office: 2345 Red Rock Street, Suite 310. Telephone 702-368-7767.

Calvin E. Thorpe (1938-1999)
Vaughn W. North
M. Wayne Western

ASSOCIATES

Michael W. Starkweather (Not admitted in UT)
Clifton W. Thompson (Not admitted in UT)
Garron M. Hobson
Peter M. deJonge
Weili Cheng, PhD.
David R. McKinney
Steve M. Perry
Gary P. Oakeson
David W. Osborne

TECHNICAL CONSULTANT

Loren Hulse

OF COUNSEL

Neil J. Beller (Resident, Las Vegas, Nevada Office)

For full biographical listings, see the Martindale-Hubbell Law Directory

VIRGINIA

ALEXANDRIA, (Independent City)

BURNS, DOANE, SWECKER & MATHIS, L.L.P. (AV)

Suite 500, 1737 King Street, 22314
Telephone: 703-836-6620
Facsimile: 703-836-2021; 703-836-7356; 703-836-3503; Group 4: 703-836-0028
Mailing Address: P.O. Box 1404, 22313-1404
Email: info@burnsdoane.com *URL:* http://www.burnsdoane.com
Redwood Shores, California Office: Suite 700, 333 Twin Dolphin Drive, Redwood Shores, 94065-1418.
Telephone: 650-622-2300.
Fax: 650-631-7600.
Research Triangle Park, North Carolina Office: P.O. Box 14846, Research Triangle Park, 27709-4846, 1009 Slater Road, Suite 210, Durham, 27703.
Telephone: 919-941-9240.
Facsimile: 919-941-1515.

J. Preston Swecker (1904-1996)

MEMBERS OF FIRM

Robert S. Swecker
Platon N. Mandros
Benton S. Duffett, Jr.
Norman H. Stepno
Ronald L. Grudziecki (Admitted in District of Columbia; limited admission in Virginia)
Frederick G. Michaud, Jr.
Alan E. Kopecki
Regis E. Slutter
Samuel C. Miller, III
Robert G. Mukai
George A. Hovanec, Jr.
James A. LaBarre
E. Joseph Gess
R. Danny Huntington
Eric H. Weisblatt
Teresa Stanek Rea (Not admitted in VA)
Robert E. Krebs (Redwood Shores, California Office)
Adrienne L. White
William C. Rowland
T. Gene Dillahunty (Redwood Shores, California Office)
Patrick C. Keane (Not admitted in VA)
B. Jefferson Boggs, Jr.
William H. Benz (Redwood Shores, California Office)
Peter K. Skiff
Richard J. McGrath
Matthew L. Schneider
Michael G. Savage (Research Triangle Park, North Carolina Office)
Gerald F. Swiss (Redwood Shores, California Office)
David M. Schlitz
Robert DeVos
B. Parker Livingston, Jr.
Bassam N. Ibrahim
Michael J. Ure (Redwood Shores, California Office)
Charles F. Wieland III
Bruce T. Wieder
Todd Ray Walters
Ronni S. Jillions
Harold R. Brown, III
Allen R. Baum (Research Triangle Park, North Carolina Office)
Steven M. DuBois

OF COUNSEL

William L. Mathis
Peter H. Smolka
Roy H. Massengill
William A. Knoeller

ASSOCIATES

Kenneth B. Leffler
Leslie A. Mooi (Redwood Shores, California Office)
Donna M. Meuth
Charles H. Jew (Redwood Shores, California Office)
Robin L. Teskin
Richard C. Ekstrom
Fred W. Hathaway
Allan M. Soobert
Jonathan D. Baskin
Nhat D. Phan
Mark R. Kresloff (Not admitted in VA)
Matthew P. Blischak
Leslie J. Boley (Redwood Shores, California Office)
Barbara Webb Walker (Not admitted in VA)
Michael A. Wrenn
Jeffrey A. Hagenah (Redwood Shores, California Office)
Robert S. Babayi (Not admitted in VA)
Rel S. Ambrozy (Not admitted in VA)
Wendi L. Weinstein (Not admitted in VA)
Susan M. Dadio
Adam Jason Cermak
M. David Ream (Not admitted in VA)
Mary Ann Dillahunty (Redwood Shores, California Office)
Krishna Kalidindi (Not admitted in VA)
Cindy A. Lynch (Redwood Shores, California Office)
Curtis A. Evans (Not admitted in VA)
Kathleen Neuner Manne
Alan L. Whitehurst
S. Lloyd Smith (Not admitted in VA)
Scott W. Cummings
Khaled Shami (Redwood Shores, California Office)
Jennifer Pearson Wright (Research Triangle Park, North Carolina Office)
John J.G. Kim (Not admitted in VA)

For full biographical listings, see the Martindale-Hubbell Law Directory

DONALD C. CASEY (AV)

Suite 100 311 North Washington Street, 22314
Telephone: 703-548-2131
Facsimile: 703-548-8961
Email: dcclaw@aol.com

For full biographical listings, see the Martindale-Hubbell Law Directory

Alexandria—Continued

LARSON & TAYLOR (AV)

Transpotomac Plaza, 1199 North Fairfax Street, Suite 900, 22314
Telephone: 703-739-4900
Facsimile: 703-739-9577
Email: iplaw@larsontaylor.com *URL:* http://www.larsontaylor.com

MEMBERS OF FIRM

Roberts B. Larson (1904-1985)
Andrew E. Taylor (Retired)
Walter C. Gillis
Marvin Petry *
Thomas P. Sarro
Ross F. Hunt, Jr.
William E. Jackson (Not admitted in VA)
Douglas E. Jackson (Not admitted in VA)
Brewster B. Taylor (Not admitted in VA)
B. Aaron Schulman (Not admitted in VA)
Linda R. Poteate

ASSOCIATE

Kevin R. Klein

OF COUNSEL

E. Fulton Brylawski (P.C.) (Not admitted in VA)

*Admission in Virginia limited to Patent, Trademark, Copyright and Unfair Competition Causes only.

For full biographical listings, see the Martindale-Hubbell Law Directory

OLIFF & BERRIDGE, PLC (AV)

277 South Washington Street, Suite 500, 22314
Telephone: 703-836-6400
Facsimile: 703-836-2787
Email: commcenter@oliff.com *URL:* http://www.oliff.com

MEMBERS OF FIRM

James A. Oliff
William P. Berridge
Kirk M. Hudson
Thomas J. Pardini
Edward P. Walker
Robert A. Miller
Mario A. Costantino
Michael S. Culver
Caroline D. Dennison (Not admitted in VA)

OF COUNSEL

Darle M. Short (Not admitted in VA)
Richard E. Rice (Not admitted in VA)
William J. Utermohlen
George A. Montanye

ASSOCIATES

Stephen J. Roe
David J. Zibelli
Joel S. Armstrong
Christopher W. Brown
Melanie L. Mealy
Paul T. Bowen
Paul Tsou
Robert E. Hunt
Eric D. Morehouse (Not admitted in VA)
John W. O'Meara (Not admitted in VA)
Ronald E. Prass, Jr. (Not admitted in VA)
Thu A. Dang
Edward A. Brown (Not admitted in VA)
Jason H. Vick (Not admitted in VA)
Christine M. Hoeft
Robert K. Carpenter (Not admitted in VA)
John S. Kern
Blair M. Jacobs
Jennifer Fraser (Not admitted in VA)
Carolyn T. Baumgardner (Not admitted in VA)
John P. Darling

For full biographical listings, see the Martindale-Hubbell Law Directory

PARKHURST & WENDEL, L.L.P. (AV)

Suite 210, 1421 Prince Street, 22314-2805
Telephone: 703-739-0220
Facsimile: 703-739-0229
Email: 701-4718@mcimail.com

MEMBERS OF FIRM

Roger W. Parkhurst
Charles A. Wendel

ASSOCIATES

Janet G. Ricciuti
Bradley Dale Goldizen

OF COUNSEL

Gerald E. Battist

For full biographical listings, see the Martindale-Hubbell Law Directory

ROGERS & KILLEEN (AV)

Suite 400, 510 King Street, 22314
Telephone: 703-836-0400
Telex: 283843 LAWR UR
Cable Address: "LAWROGERS"
Facsimile: 703-836-1539
Email: ideas@randk.com

MEMBERS OF FIRM

Joseph M. Killeen (1947-1998)
L. Lawton Rogers, III
Mark Charles Comtois
D. Joseph English
Patrick Dennis McPherson (Not admitted in VA)

(See Next Column)

ASSOCIATES

Howard N. Shipley
Patrick J. Wells (Not admitted in VA)
Donna D. King (Not admitted in VA)

For full biographical listings, see the Martindale-Hubbell Law Directory

SHERMAN & SHALLOWAY (AV)

413 North Washington Street, P.O. Box 788, 22314
Telephone: 703-549-2282
Fax: (G3) 703-836-0106
(G4) 703-271-3080
Email: shermshall@worldnet.att.net

MEMBERS OF FIRM

Leonard W. Sherman (Not admitted in VA)
Edwin A. Shalloway
Richard A. Steinberg

ASSOCIATES

Robert L. Haines
Perry Carvellas
Alan Holler

For full biographical listings, see the Martindale-Hubbell Law Directory

*ARLINGTON,** Arlington Co.

ANTONELLI, TERRY, STOUT & KRAUS, LLP (AV)

1300 North Seventeenth Street, Suite 1800, 22209
Telephone: 703-312-6600
Telefacsimile: 703-312-6666
Email: email@antonelli.com

Donald R. Antonelli
David T. Terry
Melvin Kraus
William I. Solomon (Not admitted in VA)
Gregory E. Montone
Ronald J. Shore
Donald E. Stout
Alan E. Schiavelli
James N. Dresser
Carl I. Brundidge (Not admitted in VA)
Paul J. Skwierawski (Not admitted in VA)

Randall S. Svihla
David S. Lee (Not admitted in VA)
Robert M. Bauer
Demetra J. Mills
Hung H. Bui (Not admitted in VA)
R. Edward Brake (Not admitted in VA)
George N. Stevens (Not admitted in VA)
Frederick D. Bailey
Henry M. Zykorie (Not admitted in VA)

OF COUNSEL

Dale Curtis Hogue, Sr.
James H. Laughlin, Jr.

LEGAL SUPPORT PERSONNEL

PATENT AGENT

Larry N. Anagnos

For full biographical listings, see the Martindale-Hubbell Law Directory

BERGERT & BERGERT (AV)

Suite 706, 2121 Crystal Drive, 22202
Telephone: 703-521-6590
Facsimile: 703-521-8928
Email: bertlaw1@aol.com

MEMBERS OF FIRM

Frederick L. Bergert *
Thomas F. Bergert

*Admission in Virginia limited to Patent, Trademark, Copyright and Unfair Competition Causes only.

For full biographical listings, see the Martindale-Hubbell Law Directory

LITMAN LAW OFFICES, LTD. (AV)

Patent Law Building, 3717 Columbia Pike, 22204
Telephone: 1-800-4-PATENT; 703-486-1000
Facsimile: 1-888-4-PATENT; 703-486-7000
Mailing Address: P.O. Box 15035, Arlington (Crystal City), Virginia, 22215-0035
Email: litman@4patent.com *URL:* http://www.4patent.com

Richard C. Litman

Charles K. Friedman (Not admitted in VA)
William S. Goldman (Not admitted in VA)
Mary-Jacq Holroyd
Walter E. Kubitz
Stephen J. Kushnir
Robert B. Lyons (Not admitted in VA)
Ourmazd S. Ojan (Not admitted in VA)
Dana F. Richard (Not admitted in VA)
Patrick F. Roughen (Not admitted in VA)
John R. Wenzel

(See Next Column)

LITMAN LAW OFFICES LTD., *Arlington—Continued*

PATENT AGENTS

Warren S. Edmonds
Edward G. Favors
George T. Ozaki
Thomas C. Schoeffler
Dolph H. Torrence
Donald E. Watkins

For full biographical listings, see the Martindale-Hubbell Law Directory

MILLEN, WHITE, ZELANO & BRANIGAN, P.C. (AV)

2200 Clarendon Boulevard Suite 1400, 22201
Telephone: 703-243-6333
FAX: 703-243-6410
Email: mail@mwzb.com
Richmond, Virginia Office: 1561 East Main Street, 23219.
Telephone: 804-344-8130.
Fax: 804-644-3643.

I. William Millen
John Leslie White
Anthony J. Zelano
Alan E. J. Branigan
John R. Moses
Harry Benjamin Shubin
Brion P. Heaney
Richard J. Traverso
John A. Sopp
John H. Thomas
Cecelia Oneathia-Lucenda Davis (Not admitted in VA)
Catherine M. Joyce (Not admitted in VA)

OF COUNSEL

Richard M. Lebovitz

For full biographical listings, see the Martindale-Hubbell Law Directory

NIXON & VANDERHYE P.C. (AV)

8th Floor, 1100 North Glebe Road, 22201
Telephone: 703-816-4000
Facsimile: 703-816-4100
URL: http://www.nixon-vanderhye.com

Larry S. Nixon
Robert A. Vanderhye
Arthur R. Crawford
James T. Hosmer
Robert W. Faris
Michael J. Keenan
Mark E. Nusbaum
Richard G. Besha
Robert W. Adams
Bryan H. Davidson
Stanley C. Spooner
Leonard C. Mitchard
Robert A. Rowan
Duane M. Byers
Jeffry H. Nelson
Donna J. Bunton
John R. Lastova
H. Warren Burnam, Jr.
Thomas E. Byrne (Not admitted in VA)
Mary J. Wilson (Not admitted in VA)
J. Scott Davidson
Alan M. Kagen
Michael E. Crawford
Robert A. Molan
James D. Berquist
B.J. Sadoff (Not admitted in VA)
U.S. Mickey Gill
Michael J. Shea (Not admitted in VA)
Jonathon T. Reavill
Donald L. Jackson
Sheryl L. Scharmach
Michelle N. Lester (Not admitted in VA)
Frank P. Presta
Joseph S. Presta

For full biographical listings, see the Martindale-Hubbell Law Directory

OBLON, SPIVAK, MCCLELLAND, MAIER & NEUSTADT, P.C. (AV)

Fourth Floor, 1755 Jefferson Davis Highway, 22202
Telephone: 703-413-3000
Cable Address: "Oblonpat Washington, D.C."
Telex: 248855
Facsimile: 703-413-2220
Email: oblonpat@oblon.com *URL:* http://www.oblon.com

Norman F. Oblon
Marvin J. Spivak
C. Irvin McClelland
Gregory J. Maier
Arthur I. Neustadt
Richard D. Kelly
James D. Hamilton
Eckhard H. Kuesters
Robert T. Pous
David J. Kera
Charles L. Gholz
William E. Beaumont
Robert F. Gnuse
Jean-Paul P.M. Lavalleye
Jeffrey H. Kaufman
Brian D. Anderson
Roberta S. Bren
Stephen G. Baxter
Richard L. Treanor
Steven P. Weihrouch
John T. Goolkasian (Not admitted in VA)
Richard L. Chinn
Steven E. Lipman
Carl E. Schlier
Patrick Jay Hines
James J. Kulbaski
Richard A. Neifeld
J. Derek Mason
Surinder Sachar
Jonathan Hudis
Christina M. Gadiano
Jeffrey Bayne McIntyre (Not admitted in VA)
William T. Enos (Not admitted in VA)
Michael E. McCabe, Jr. (Not admitted in VA)
Steven C. Tabackman
Jordan S. Weinstein
Bradley D. Lytle
Michael R. Casey

(See Next Column)

Frank J. West (Not admitted in VA)
Kathleen Cooney-Porter (Not admitted in VA)
Andrew M. Ollis
Margo Livesay (Not admitted in VA)
Corwin P. Umbach
Ron Myers (Not admitted in VA)
W. Todd Baker (Not admitted in VA)
David D'Zurilla
Joseph Scafetta, Jr.
Mandy M. Petrocelli
Edwin Donnell Garlepp
Alexander E. Gasser (Not admitted in VA)
Christopher D. Ward
Thomas M. Cunningham
Clayton W. Thompson, II

JAPANESE PATENT ATTORNEY

Masayasu Mori (Not admitted in VA)

OF COUNSEL

Gerald J. Mossinghoff
Milton Sterman (Not admitted in VA)
Samuel H. Blech (Not admitted in VA)
John O. Tresansky (Not admitted in VA)
Alton D. Rollins
James R. Boler (Not admitted in VA)
Raymond F. Cardillo, Jr.
Harris A. Pitlick (Not admitted in VA)
Robert W. Hahl
Neal Goldfarb

LEGAL SUPPORT PERSONNEL

Frederick D. Vastine (Patent Agent)
John K. Pike (Patent Agent)
George F. Lesmes (Patent Agent)
James J. Kelly (Patent Agent)
David A. Bilodeau (Patent Agent)
Stamatios G. Mylonakis (Patent Agent)
Philippe J.C. Signore (Patent Agent)
Kevin A. Nordberg (Patent Agent)

Reference: First Union.

For full biographical listings, see the Martindale-Hubbell Law Directory

ROPER & QUIGG (AV)

Three Crystal Park, 2231 Crystal Drive, Suite 410, 22202
Telephone: 703-920-8910
Facsimile: 703-979-5227
URL: http://www.roperandquigg.com
Chicago, Illinois Office: 200 South Michigan Avenue, Suite 1000.
Telephone: 312-408-0855.
Facsimile: 312-408-0865.

MEMBERS OF FIRM

Harry J. Roper (Not admitted in VA)
Donald J. Quigg
Archie W. Umphlett (Not admitted in VA)

For full biographical listings, see the Martindale-Hubbell Law Directory

YOUNG & THOMPSON (AV)

745 South 23rd Street, Suite 200, 22202
Telephone: 703-521-2297
Fax: 703-685-0573; 979-4709
Email: embon@pipeline.com

MEMBERS OF FIRM

Robert John Patch
Andrew John Patch
Robert F. Hargest
Benoit Castel
Thomas W. Perkins

ASSOCIATES

Eric Jensen
Roland E. Long, Jr.

OF COUNSEL

Douglas V. Rigler (Not admitted in VA)
Thomas R. Kline (Not admitted in VA)

REGISTERED PATENT AGENT

Larry J. Hume

For full biographical listings, see the Martindale-Hubbell Law Directory

FALLS CHURCH, (Independent City)

BIRCH, STEWART, KOLASCH & BIRCH, LLP (AV)

8110 Gatehouse Road, Suite 500 East, P.O. Box 747, 22040-0747
Telephone: 703-205-8000
Telecopier Facsimile: 703-205-8050; 703-698-8590 (G IV)
Email: mailroom@bskb.com *URL:* http://www.bskb.com/
Costa Mesa, California Office: Suite 1120, 650 Town Center Drive.
Telephone: 714-708-8555.
Fax: 714-708-8565.

MEMBERS OF FIRM

Terrell C. Birch *
Raymond C. Stewart
Joseph A. Kolasch
James M. Slattery
Bernard L. Sweeney (Not admitted in VA)
Michael K. Mutter
Charles Gorenstein *
Gerald M. Murphy, Jr.
Terry L. Clark *
Andrew D. Meikle
Marc S. Weiner

(See Next Column)

BIRCH, STEWART, KOLASCH & BIRCH LLP—*Continued*

MEMBERS OF FIRM (Continued)

Joe McKinney Muncy
Robert J. Kenney
Donald J. Daley
John W. Bailey
John A. Castellano, III

ASSOCIATES

Gary D. Yacura
Thomas S. Auchterlonie
Michael R. Cammarata
James T. Eller, Jr.
Scott L. Lowe
Mary Ann Capria
Mark J. Nuell
Darin E. Bartholomew (Not admitted in VA)
D. Richard Anderson, Jr.
Paul C. Lewis
W. Karl Renner
Mark W. Milstead (Not admitted in VA)
John Campa (Not admitted in VA)

OF COUNSEL

Elliot A. Goldberg (Not admitted in VA)
William L. Gates (Not admitted in VA)
Edward H. Valance
Rupert J. Brady (Not admitted in VA; Retired)

LEGAL SUPPORT PERSONNEL

REGISTERED PATENT AGENTS

Frederick R. Handren
Andrew J. Telesz, Jr.
Maryanne Liotta
Maki Hatsumi
Mike S. Ryu
Craig A. McRobbie
Garth M. Dahlen
Laura Lutz
Robert E. Goozner
Hyung Sohn
Alan Pederson-Giles

TECHNICAL-LEGAL ADVISORS

Keum Seop Chin
Binli Guan
Matthew J. Lattig
Timothy R. Wyckoff
Hermes M. Soyez
C. Keith Montgomery
Eve L. Hunovice
Kristi L. Rupert

*Admission in Virginia limited to Patent, Trademark, Copyright and Unfair Competition Causes only

For full biographical listings, see the Martindale-Hubbell Law Directory

KERKAM, STOWELL, KONDRACKI & CLARKE, P.C. (AV)

Formerly Cameron, Kerkam, Sutton, Stowell & Stowell, P.C.
Two Skyline Place, 5203 Leesburg Pike Suite 600, 22041
Telephone: 703-998-3302
Facsimile Groups I, II and III: 703-998-5634
Email: patmark@patmarklaw.com *URL:* http://www.patmarklaw.com

Gordon W. Daisley (1902-1979)
Harold L. Stowell (1921-1996)
Edward J. Kondracki
Dennis P. Clarke *
William L. Feeney
John C. Kerins
Robert N. Wieland (Not admitted in VA)

OF COUNSEL

James L. Bean

*Admission in Virginia limited to Patent, Trademark, Copyright and Unfair Competition Causes only

For full biographical listings, see the Martindale-Hubbell Law Directory

MCLEAN, Fairfax Co.

SIXBEY, FRIEDMAN, LEEDOM & FERGUSON, P.C. (AV)

Suite 800, 8180 Greensboro Drive, 22102
Telephone: 703-790-9110
Telecopier: 703-883-0370
Email: INFO@sixbey.com *URL:* http://www.sixbey.com
Arlington, Virginia Office: 2001 Jefferson Davis Highway.
Telephone: 703-415-0416.
Telecopier: 703-415-0417.

Daniel W. Sixbey (Not admitted in VA)
Stuart J. Friedman (Not admitted in VA)
Charles M. Leedom, Jr. *
Gerald J. Ferguson, Jr. *
David S. Safran
Thomas W. Cole *
Donald R. Studebaker (Not admitted in VA)
Jeffrey L. Costellia
Tim Leonard Brackett, Jr.
Eric J. Robinson
Robert M. Schulman (Not admitted in VA)
Thomas M. Blasey (Not admitted in VA)

Lawrence D. Eisen

OF COUNSEL

Joan Kux Lawrence

*Admission in Virginia limited to Patent, Trademark, Copyright and Unfair Competition Causes only.

For full biographical listings, see the Martindale-Hubbell Law Directory

NORFOLK, (Independent City)

PAYNE, GATES, FARTHING & RADD, P.C. (AV)

15th Floor, Dominion Tower, 999 Waterside Drive, Suite 1515, 23510-3309
Telephone: 757-640-1500
Facsimile: 757-627-6583
URL: http://www.paynegates.com

Ronald M. Gates
Philip R. Farthing
Anthony F. Radd
Glen M. Robertson
Brian R. Dinning
Todd J. Preti
Marshall A. Winslow, Jr.

C. Arthur Robinson, II
Stephen E. Heretick
Raymond L. Hogge, Jr.

OF COUNSEL

Charles E. Payne

For full biographical listings, see the Martindale-Hubbell Law Directory

RICHMOND, (Independent City)

LECLAIR RYAN, A PROFESSIONAL CORPORATION (AV)

707 East Main Street, 11th Floor, 23219
Telephone: 804-783-2003
Facsmile: 804-783-2294
Email: email@leclairryan.com
Glen Allen, Virginia Office: 4201 Dominion Boulevard, Suite 200, 23060.
Telephone: 804-270-0070.
Facsimile: 804-270-4715.
Blacksburg, Virginia Office: 1872 Pratt Drive, Suite 1865, 24060.
Telephone: 540-961-2762.
Fax: 540-961-2781.
Norfolk, Virginia Office: 999 Waterside Drive, Suite 2025.
Telephone: 757-624-1454.
Facsimile: 757-624-3773.
Alexandria, Virginia Office: 225 Reinekers Lane, Suite 290, 22314.
Telephone: 703-684-8007.
Facsimile: 703-684-8075.
Charlottesville, Virginia Office: 108 S.E. Second Street, P.O. Box 2017, 22902.
Telephone: 804-971-7771.
Facsimile: 804-296-0905.

Lawrence B. Cann, III
Christopher J. Mugel
David G. Shuford
Charles M. Sims

Carol Jeanne Anderson

For full biographical listings, see the Martindale-Hubbell Law Directory

MILLEN, WHITE, ZELANO & BRANIGAN, P.C. (AV)

1561 East Main Street, 23219
Telephone: 804-344-8130
FAX: 804-644-3643
Email: mail@mwzb.com
Arlington, Virginia Office: 2200 Clarendon Boulevard, Suite 1400, 22201.
Telephone: 703-243-6333.
Fax: 703-243-6410.

Alan E. J. Branigan
John H. Thomas

For full biographical listings, see the Martindale-Hubbell Law Directory

WASHINGTON

*BELLINGHAM,** Whatcom Co.

HUGHES & SCHACHT, P.S. (AV)

2801 Meridian Street, Suite 1, 98225-2412
Telephone: 360-647-1296
Telecopier: 360-671-2489
URL: http://www.lawyers.com/hm&sps
Email: mschacht@inventionlaw.com *URL:* http://www.inventionlaw.com

Robert B. Hughes (Resident)
Michael R. Schacht (Resident)

Michael F. Hughes

For full biographical listings, see the Martindale-Hubbell Law Directory

*SEATTLE,** King Co.

CHRISTENSEN, O'CONNOR, JOHNSON & KINDNESS, PLLC (AV)

1420 Fifth Avenue, Suite 2800, 98101-2347
Telephone: 206-682-8100
Telecopier: 206-224-0779
URL: http://www.cojk.com

(See Next Column)

CHRISTENSEN, O'CONNOR, JOHNSON & KINDNESS PLLC, *Seattle—Continued*

MEMBERS OF FIRM

Orland M. Christensen (1920-1984)
Michael G. Toner (1943-1992)
Bruce E. O'Connor
Lee E. Johnson
Gary S. Kindness
James W. Anable
James R. Uhlir
Jerald E. Nagae
Dennis K. Shelton
Frederick Ross Boundy
KiSong Kim Lang-Caditz
Jeffrey M. Sakoi
Ward Brown
Robert J. Carlson
Marcia S. Kelbon
Rodney C. Tullett
Daiva K. Tautvydas

OF COUNSEL

Thomas D. Theisen
Faye L. Tomlinson
Philip P. Mann

ASSOCIATES

Maria L. Culic
Julie C. Vanderzanden
George E. Renzoni
George S. Farber
Kevan L. Morgan
John D. Denkenberger
Barry Francis McGurl
Melanie J. Seelig
Brooke W. Quist
Shoko I. Leek
Mark I. Crohn
Lawrence E. Lycke
Lorraine Linford
John W. Branch
Marcia Ann Tunheim
R. Douglas Bradley
John E. Whitaker
Steven P. Fricke
Timothy P. Sullivan (Not admitted in WA)

LEGAL SUPPORT PERSONNEL

Gary Tomlinson (Executive Director)

Representative Clients: The Boeing Company; Fred Hutchinson Cancer Research Center; Icicle Seafoods, Inc.; K-2 Corporation; Microsoft Corporation; Nalley's Fine Foods; Nintendo of America, Inc.; University of Washington; Westin Hotel Company; Weyerhaeuser Company.

For full biographical listings, see the Martindale-Hubbell Law Directory

SEED AND BERRY LLP (AV)

6300 Columbia Center, 98104-7092
Telephone: 206-622-4900
Facsimile: 206-682-6031
URL: http://www.seed-berry.com

MEMBERS OF FIRM

Richard W. Seed
Robert J. Baynham
Edward W. Bulchis
George C. Rondeau, Jr.
David H. Deits
William O. Ferron, Jr.
Paul T. Meiklejohn
David J. Maki
David V. Carlson
Richard G. Sharkey
Karl R. Hermanns
David D. McMasters (Managing Partner)
Michael J. Donohue

OF COUNSEL

Ellen M. Bierman
Jane E. R. Potter

ASSOCIATES

David W. Parker
Frank Abramonte
E. Russell Tarleton
Stephen J. Rosenman
Thomas E. Loop
Dale C. Barr
Kevin S. Costanza
Brian L. Johnson
Susan D. Betcher
Mark Roberts
Dennis M. de Guzman
Kimton N. Eng
Andrew F. Pratt
William T. Christiansen II
Timothy L. Boller
Robert Iannucci
Gary M. Myles
Brian C. Park
Kenneth H. Tarbet (Not admitted in WA)

For full biographical listings, see the Martindale-Hubbell Law Directory

WISCONSIN

BROOKFIELD, Waukesha Co.

RYAN KROMHOLZ & MANION, S.C. (AV)

3360 Gateway Road, 53045
Telephone: 262-797-6700
Facsimile: 262-797-9600
Toll No: 800-686-9333
URL: http://www.rkmiplaw.com

Daniel D. Ryan
Joseph A. Kromholz
John M. Manion

Patricia Gollhardt Jones
Laura A. Dable
Daniel R. Johnson

SENIOR COUNSEL

Allan O. Maki
Paul R. Puerner

(See Next Column)

OF COUNSEL

Arnold J. Ericsen
Henry C. Fuller, Jr.
Ralph G. Hohenfeldt (Emeritus)
Allan B. Wheeler (Emeritus)

For full biographical listings, see the Martindale-Hubbell Law Directory

*MADISON,** Dane Co.

DEWITT ROSS & STEVENS S.C. (AV)

2 East Mifflin Street, Suite 600, 53703
Telephone: 608-255-8891
Facsimile: 608-252-9243
West Madison Office: 8000 Excelsior Drive, Suite 401, Madison, WI 53717.
Telephone: 608-831-2100.
Telecopier: 608-831-2106.

Charles S. Sara
Joseph T. Leone
Craig A. Fieschko

Representative Clients: Wisconsin Alumni Research Foundation; Promega Corporation; Wisconsin Milk Marketing Board; Cancer Immuno-Biology Laboratory; Marshfield Clinic; DMV USA, Inc.; PDQ Food Stores, Inc.; PostalSoft, Inc.; Strandex Corporation; Larex, Inc.

For Complete List of Firm Personnel, See General Section

For full biographical listings, see the Martindale-Hubbell Law Directory

LATHROP & CLARK, LLP (AV)

Suite 400, 740 Regent Street, P.O. Box 1507, 53701-1507
Telephone: 608-257-7766
FAX: 608-257-1507
URL: http://www.lathropclark.com
Poynette, Wisconsin Office: 111 North Main Street, P.O. Box 128.
Telephone: 608-635-4324.
FAX: 608-635-4690.
Lodi, Wisconsin Office: 108 Lodi Street, P.O. Box 256.
Telephone: 608-592-3877.
FAX: 608-592-5844.
Belleville, Wisconsin Office: 27 West Main.
Telephone: 608-424-3404.

MEMBERS OF FIRM

Theodore J. Long
Jeffrey S. Ward
David R. J. Stiennon
Jeffry W. Smith
Patrick J. G. Stiennon

Representative Clients: Westfalia-Surge, LLC; Beloit Corp.; Breed Technologies; Novopharm Ltd.; TriEnda Corp.; Placon Corp.; Highsmith Inc.; Auto Glass Specialists, Inc.; Springs Window Fashions Division, Inc.; Penda Corporation.

For Complete List of Firm Personnel, See General Section

For full biographical listings, see the Martindale-Hubbell Law Directory

NEIDER & BOUCHER, S.C. (AV)

440 Science Drive, P.O. Box 5510, 53705-0510
Telephone: 608-661-4500
Facsimile: 608-661-4510
URL: http://www.neiderboucher.com
URL: http://www.lawyers.com/neider&boucher-sc

Ronald C. Berman
Joseph W. Boucher
Charles E. Neider
Steven C. Underwood

Susan M. De Groot
Erik W. Ibele
Rana Kang
Cynthia L. Richson
Matthew L. Schemmel
Kent L. Schlienger
Dean T. Stange

OF COUNSEL

Ralph M. Cagle
Ronald R. Smith

For full biographical listings, see the Martindale-Hubbell Law Directory

QUARLES & BRADY LLP (AV)

Firstar Plaza, One South Pinckney Street, P.O. Box 2113, 53701-2113
Telephone: 608-251-5000
Fax: 608-251-9166
URL: http://www.quarles.com
Milwaukee, Wisconsin Office: 411 East Wisconsin Avenue, 53202-4497.
Telephone: 414-277-5000.
Fax: 414-271-3552.
West Palm Beach, Florida Office: 222 Lakeview Avenue, 4th Floor, 33401.
Telephone: 561-653-5000.
Fax: 561-653-5333.
Naples, Florida Office: Barnett Center, 4501 Tamiami Trail North, Suite 300, 34103-3060.
Telephone: 941-262-5959.
Fax: 941-434-4999.
Phoenix, Arizona Office: One Camelback Building, One East Camelback Road, Suite 400, 85012-1649.
Telephone: 602-230-5500.
Fax: 602-230-5598.

(See Next Column)

QUARLES & BRADY LLP—*Continued*

Chicago, Illinois Office: Quarles & Brady LLC, Citicorp Center, 500 West Madison Street, Suite 3700.
Telephone: 312-715-5000.
Fax: 312-715-5155.

PARTNERS

James R. Cole
Nicholas J. Seay
Kenneth J. Hansen
Anthony A. Tomaselli
Jean C. Baker

ASSOCIATES

Gregory T. Everts
Bennett J. Berson
Sarah Edelman Coyne
Jill A. Fahrlander
David M. Kettner

For Complete List of Firm Personnel, See General Section

For full biographical listings, see the Martindale-Hubbell Law Directory

*MILWAUKEE,** Milwaukee Co.

ANDRUS, SCEALES, STARKE & SAWALL, LLP (AV)

100 East Wisconsin Avenue, Suite 1100, 53202-4178
Telephone: 414-271-7590
Toll Free: 1-800-448-6302
E-Mail: office@andruslaw.com
Telefax: 414-271-5770
URL: http://www.andruslaw.com

MEMBERS OF FIRM

Elwin A. Andrus (1939-1982)
Merl E. Sceales (1941-1987)
Glenn O. Starke
Eugene R. Sawall
Daniel D. Fetterley
George H. Solveson
Gary A. Essmann
Thomas M. Wozny
Michael E. Taken
Joseph J. Jochman, Jr.
Andrew S. McConnell
Edward R. Williams, Jr.

ASSOCIATES

Joseph D. Kuborn
Denise L. Stoker
Mathew E. Corr

LEGAL SUPPORT PERSONNEL

William L. Falk (Patent Agent)

Patent Counsel for: Briggs & Stratton Corp.; Johnson Controls, Inc.; Kolmar Laboratories, Inc.; Research Products Corp., Madison, Wis.; Overly Inc., Neenah, Wis.; Kelly Co.; Nelson Industries, Stoughton, Wis.; Green Bay Packaging, Inc., Green Bay; Mercury Marine Division of Brunswick Corp.; Wisconsin Alumni Research Foundation; Wisconsin Electric Power Co.

For full biographical listings, see the Martindale-Hubbell Law Directory

MICHAEL BEST & FRIEDRICH LLP (AV)

100 East Wisconsin Avenue, 53202-4108
Telephone: 414-271-6560
Telecopier: 414-277-0656
Cable Address: "Mibef"
Email: info@mbf-law.com *URL:* http://www.mbf-law.com
Madison, Wisconsin Office: One South Pinckney Street, Firstar Plaza, P.O. Box 1806, 53701-1806.
Telephone: 608-257-3501.
Telecopier: 283-2275.
Manitowoc, Wisconsin Office: 1000 Maritime Drive, 54220.
Telephone: 920-686-2800.
Fax: 920-686-2810.
Chicago, Illinois Office: Michael Best & Friedrich LLC, 77 West Wacker Drive, Suite 4300, 60601-1635.
Telephone: 312-845-5800.
Telecopier: 312-845-5828.

PARTNERS

David B. Smith
Joseph A. Gemignani
Michael E. Husmann
David R. Price
Toni Lee Bonney
Casimir F. Laska
David L. De Bruin
Timothy M. Kelley
Dyann L. Kostello
Thomas A. Miller
Kevin P. Moran
Billie Jean Strandt

OF COUNSEL

Bayard H. Michael
Robert E. Clemency

ASSOCIATES

Edward R. Lawson, Jr.
Andrew R. Peret
Daniel S. Jones

For Complete List of Firm Personnel, See General Section

For full biographical listings, see the Martindale-Hubbell Law Directory

QUARLES & BRADY LLP (AV)

411 East Wisconsin Avenue, 53202-4497
Telephone: 414-277-5000
Fax: 414-271-3552
URL: http://www.quarles.com
Madison, Wisconsin Office: Firstar Plaza, One South Pinckney Street, P.O. Box 2113, 53701-2113.
Telephone: 608-251-5000.
Fax: 608-251-9166.
West Palm Beach, Florida Office: 222 Lakeview Avenue, 4th Floor, 33401.
Telephone: 561-653-5000.
Fax: 561-653-5333.
Naples, Florida Office: Barnett Center, 4501 Tamiami Trail North, Suite 300, 34103-3060.
Telephone: 941-262-5959.
Fax: 941-434-4999.
Phoenix, Arizona Office: One Camelback Building, One East Camelback Road, Suite 400, 85012-1649.
Telephone: 602-230-5500.
Fax: 602-230-5598.
Chicago, Illinois Office: Quarles & Brady LLC, Citicorp Center, 500 West Madison Street, Suite 3700.
Telephone: 312-715-5000.
Fax: 312-715-5155.

MEMBERS OF FIRM

(ALPHABETICALLY BY YEAR OF ADMISSION TO BAR)

Thomas W. Ehrmann
Richard L. Horn (Resident, Chicago, Illinois Office)
J. Rodman Steele, Jr. (Resident, West Palm Beach, Florida Office)
Wayne E. Babler, Jr.
James R. Cole (Resident, Madison Office)
Barry E. Sammons
Michael J. McGovern
Robert L. Titley
George E. Haas
Timothy G. Hains (Resident, Naples, Florida Office)
Nicholas J. Seay (Resident, Madison Office)
Carl R. Schwartz
David R. Cross
Glenn Spencer Bacal (Resident, Phoenix, Arizona Office)
John D. Franzini
Marta S. Levine
Gregory A. Nelson (Resident, West Palm Beach, Florida Office)
Keith M. Baxter
Jeffrey O. Davis
Kenneth J. Hansen (Resident, Madison, Wisconsin Office)
Anthony A. Tomaselli (Resident, Madison Office)
Joseph W. Bain (Resident, West Palm Beach, Florida Office)
Jean C. Baker
Robert J. Sacco (Resident, West Palm Beach, Florida Office)

OF COUNSEL

Thad F. Kryshak
Thomas O. Kloehn

ASSOCIATES

Neil E. Hamilton
Gregory T. Everts (Resident, Madison Office)
Bennett J. Berson (Resident, Madison, Wisconsin Office)
Sean D. Garrison (Resident, Phoenix, Arizona Office)
Michael A. Jaskolski
David G. Ryser
Jennifer A. Lazewski
Sarah Edelman Coyne (Resident, Madison, Wisconsin Office)
Jill A. Fahrlander (Resident, Madison, Wisconsin Office)
Allen J. Moss (Resident, Phoenix, Arizona Office)
Daniel G. Radler
David M. Kettner (Resident, Madison, Wisconsin Office)
Stanley A. Kim (Resident, West Palm Beach, Florida Office)
Steven J. Wietrzny

For Complete List of Firm Personnel, See General Section

For full biographical listings, see the Martindale-Hubbell Law Directory

CANADA
ALBERTA

*EDMONTON,** Edmonton Jud. Dist.

EMERY JAMIESON (AV)

1700 Oxford Tower, 10235 - 101 Street, T5J 3G1
Telephone: 780-426-5220
Fax: 780-420-6277
Email: general@emeryjamieson.com *URL:* http://www.emeryjamieson.com
Calgary, Alberta Office: 206 Kensington House, 1167 Kensington Crescent, N.W., T2N 1X7.
Telephone: 403-543-6010.
Fax: 403-270-8080. E-mail: ejcalg@emeryjamieson.com

MEMBERS OF FIRM

Howard T. Emery, Q.C. (1899-1990)
John H. Jamieson, Q.C. (Retired)
Sydney A. Bercov, Q.C.
Henry B. Martin, Q.C.
Richard B. Drewry
W. Paul Sharek, Q.C.
Robert W. Thompson
Phyllis A. Smith, Q.C.
Gordon D. Sustrik
Shirley A. McNeilly
Michael J. Penny
G. Bruce Comba

(See Next Column)

EMERY JAMIESON, *Edmonton—Continued*

MEMBERS OF FIRM (Continued)

Rex M. Nielsen
Donna Carson Read
Susan L. Bercov
Bruce F. Hughson
Murray F. Tait
Robert D. McDonald
Jeffrey K. Friesen
Blair E. Maxston
Frederica L. Schutz
Janet N. Alexander-Smith
Claire M. Klassen
Earl J. Evaniew

ASSOCIATES

Regina M. Corrigan (Resident, Calgary Office)
Stuart J. Weatherill
Scott H. Chen
Michael D. Cooper (Resident at Calgary Office)
Patrick G. Nugent
Heidi K. Robinson
Christopher R. Ontkean

Reference: Canadian Imperial Bank of Commerce.

For full biographical listings, see the Martindale-Hubbell Law Directory

CANADA BRITISH COLUMBIA

*VANCOUVER,** Vancouver Co.

SMART & BIGGAR (AV)

Box 11560, Vancouver Centre, 2200 - 650 West Georgia Street, V6B 4N8
Telephone: 604-682-7295
Facsimile: 604-682-0274
Email: vancouver@smart-biggar.ca *URL:* http://www.smart-biggar.ca
Ottawa, Ontario Office: Suite 900, 55 Metcalfe Street, P.O. Box 2999, Station D, K1P 5Y6.
Telephone: 613-232-2486.
Facsimile: 613-232-8440. Email: ottawa@smart-biggar.ca.
Toronto, Ontario Office: Box 111, The First Century Tower, 1500-438 University Avenue, M5G 2K8.
Telephone: 416-593-5514.
Facsimile: 416-591-1690. Email: toronto@smart-biggar.ca.
Montreal, Quebec Office: 1000 De La Gauchetière Street West, Suite 3400, H3B 4W5.
Telephone: 514-954-1500.
Facsimile: 514-954-1396. Email: montreal@smart-biggar.ca.

MEMBERS OF FIRM

Michael D. Manson (Resident)
Brian G. Kingwell (Resident)
J. Christopher Robinson (Resident)

ASSOCIATES

Otto Zsigmond
Theodore W. Sum (Resident)
Timothy P. Lo (Resident)
Stephen J. Ferance (Resident)

PATENT & TRADEMARK AGENTS

Brian J. Wood (Resident)
John W. Knox (Resident)
Neil S. Clark (Resident)

For full biographical listings, see the Martindale-Hubbell Law Directory

CANADA NEWFOUNDLAND

*ST. JOHN'S,**

McINNES COOPER (AV)

Barristers, Solicitors & Trade Mark Agents
Baine Johnston Centre, 5th Floor, 10 Fort William Place, P.O. Box 5939, A1C 5X4
Telephone: 709-722-8735
Telecopier: 709-722-1763
Email: mcrsj@mcrlaw.com *URL:* http://www.mcrlaw.com
Halifax, Nova Scotia Office: Summit Place, 1601 Lower Water Street, P.O. Box 730, B3J 2V1.
Telephone: 902-425-6500.
Fax: 902-425-6350. Email: mcrhfx@mcrlaw.com.
Moncton, New Brunswick Office: Place Moncton Place, 655 Main Street, P.O. Box 1368, E1C 8T6.
Telephone: 506-857-8970.
Fax: 506-857-4095. Email: mcrmctn@mcrlaw.com.
Charlottetown, Prince Edward Island Office: BDC Place, Suite 620, 119 Kent Street, C1A 1N3.
Telephone: 902-368-8473.
Fax: 902-368-8346. Email: mcrpei@mcrlaw.com.
Fredericton, New Brunswick Office: Suite 600, 570 Queen Street, P.O. Box 610.
Telephone: 506-458-8572.
Fax: 506-458-9903. Email: mcrfton@mcrlaw.com.

(See Next Column)

ASSOCIATE

Jacqueline S. Bartlett

For Complete List of Firm Personnel, See General Section

For full biographical listings, see the Martindale-Hubbell Law Directory

CANADA ONTARIO

*OTTAWA,** Regional Munic. of Ottawa-Carleton

BORDEN ELLIOT SCOTT & AYLEN (AV)

1000-60 Rue Queen Street, K1P 5Y7
Telephone: 613-237-5160; 800-661-4237
General Facsimile: 613-230-8842
IP Dept. Facsimile: 613-787-3558
Email: ottinfo@scottaylen.com *URL:* http://www.borden.com
Toronto, Ontario Office: Borden & Elliot: Scotia Plaza, 40 King Street West.
Telephone: 416-367-6000.
Telecopier: 416-367-6749. Email: info @borden.com. URL: http://www.borden.com.

David W. Scott, Q.C.
Kevin LaRoche
Johanne M. Asselin

PATENT AND TRADEMARK AGENTS

Anthony J. Graham
L. Brooke Keneford
Tracey L. Mosley
Joachim T. Fritz
Christine J. Collard
Edward B. O'Connor
Sohrab Sabet
Mary Jane Lemenchick
Andrew Hicks
Michael D. Crinson

For full biographical listings, see the Martindale-Hubbell Law Directory

RIDOUT & MAYBEE (AV)

Barristers & Solicitors
Patent and Trademark Agents
19th Floor, 150 Metcalfe Street, K2P 1P1
Telephone: 613-236-1995
Facsimile: 613-236-2485; 613-563-9185
Email: ipinfo@ridoutmaybee.com *URL:* http://www.ridoutmaybee.com
Toronto, Ontario Office: One Queen Street East, Suite 2400, M5C 3B1.
Telephone: 416-868-1482.
Fax: 416-362-0823, 416-362-8865. Email: ridbee@ridoutmaybee.com

W. Charles Kent
William R. Edgar
James R. Lake
Randall S. Mitchell
P. Scott Maclean
Lynn S. Cassan
Janet M. Fuhrer
Marcus T. Gallie
William B. Vass

Roland H. Joachim
James E. Longwell
Mitchell B. Charness
Ian C. McMillan
David J. Heller

PATENT AND TRADEMARK AGENTS

P. Ewan McArdle
Richard A.R. Parsons
Philip K. Holland
Robert G. Hirons
Kimberley A. Brulé
Lynda E.E. Doxsee
Mary L. Malvaso

OF COUNSEL

Malcolm Johnston, Q.C.

CONSULTANTS

William L. Hayhurst (Resident, Toronto Office)
Godfrey P. Orleans (Resident, Toronto Office)
Kenneth M. Garrett (Resident, Toronto Office)
I. Jane Parsons (Resident, Toronto Office)

For full biographical listings, see the Martindale-Hubbell Law Directory

SHAPIRO, COHEN (AV)

112 Kent Street, P.O. Box 3440, Station D, K1P 6P1
Telephone: 613-232-5300
Telecopier: 613-563-9231
Email: info@shapirocohen.com *URL:* http://www.shapirocohen.com

MEMBERS OF FIRM

Jonathan C. Cohen
Adele Finlayson
Susan D. Beaubien
Chantal Bertoša

ASSOCIATES

Dr. Victoria E. Carrington
Hollie E. Elder (1964-1999)

OF COUNSEL

Howard F. Knopf

LEGAL SUPPORT PERSONNEL

PATENT AGENTS

Robert A. Wilkes
Robert G. Hendry

(See Next Column)

SHAPIRO, COHEN—*Continued*

TRADEMARK AGENTS

Mary H. Cardillo
Christine St. Denis
Gladys A. Tibbo Witt

TECHNICAL CONSULTANTS

Edward Pascal
Harry Baker
Art Brion

For full biographical listings, see the Martindale-Hubbell Law Directory

SMART & BIGGAR (AV)

Suite 900, 55 Metcalfe Street, P.O. Box 2999, Station D, K1P 5Y6
Telephone: 613-232-2486
Facsimile: 613-232-8440
Email: ottawa@smart-biggar.ca *URL:* http://www.smart-biggar.ca
Toronto, Ontario Office: Box 111, The First Century Tower, 1500-438 University Avenue, M5G 2K8.
Telephone: 416-593-5514.
Facsimile: 416-591-1690. Email: toronto@smart-biggar.ca.
Montreal, Quebec Office: 1000 De La Gauchetière Street West, Suite 3400, H3B 4W5.
Telephone: 514-954-1500.
Facsimile: 514-954-1396. Email: montreal@smart-biggar.ca.
Vancouver, British Columbia Office: Box 11560, Vancouver Centre, 2200 - 650 West Georgia Street, V6B 4N8.
Telephone: 604-682-7295.
Facsimile: 604-682-0274. Email: vancouver@smart-biggar.ca.

MEMBERS OF FIRM

James D. Kokonis, Q.C.
Alan R. Campbell
Robert D. Gould
Raymond Trudeau
**(Not admitted in ON)
Joy D. Morrow
Gunars A. Gaikis *
Michael D. Manson ***
Ronald D. Faggetter *
Mark K. Evans *
Alistair G. Simpson *
Steven B. Garland
Nicholas H. Fyfe, Q.C.
A. David Morrow
John R. Morrissey *
Thomas R. Kelly
John Bochnovic
François Guay
**(Not admitted in ON)
Keltie R. Sim *
Glen B. Tremblay
J. Christopher Robinson ***
Brian P. Isaac
J. Sheldon Hamilton *
Brian G. Kingwell ***

ASSOCIATES

Donald F. Phenix
Yoon Kang *
Matthew Zischka *
Christian Bolduc
**(Not admitted in ON)
Elliott S. Simcoe
Theodore W. Sum ***
Grant W. Lynds
Shonagh L. McVean *
Kohji Suzuki
Kevin K. Graham
Marc-André Huot
**(Not admitted in ON)
Daphne L. Maravei
Stephen J. Ferance ***
Peter R. Wilcox *
Philip Lapin
Otto Zsigmond ***
Dennis S.K. Leung
Ywe J. Looper
Timothy P. Lo ***
Marc Gagnon
**(Not admitted in ON)
Nancy P. Pei *
Christine N. Genge
Geneviève M. Prévost *
Mark G. Biernacki *
Robert Guay
Kevin A. O'Neil *
Jean-Sébastien Brière **
Ekaterina K. Tsimberis **

COUNSEL

Immanuel Goldsmith, Q.C. *

PATENT & TRADEMARK AGENTS

Hugh O'Gorman
James McGraw
Michael E. Wheeler
Tokuo Hirama
John W. Knox ***
Brian J. Wood ***
A. Dennis Armstrong
R. John Haley
Stephan P. Georgiev **
Neil S. Clark ***
R. Allan Brett

*Toronto Office
**Montreal Office
***Vancouver Office

For full biographical listings, see the Martindale-Hubbell Law Directory

*TORONTO,** Regional Munic. of Toronto

BERESKIN & PARR (AV)

Box 401, 40 King Street West, M5H 3Y2
Telephone: 416-364-7311
Telecopier: 416-361-1398
URL: http://www.bereskinparr.com

MEMBERS AND ASSOCIATES

Daniel R. Bereskin, Q.C.
Richard J. Parr
H. Roger Hart
C. Lloyd Sarginson
Robert H. C. MacFarlane
Cynthia Rowden
Timothy J. Sinnott
Robert B. Storey
Philip C. Mendes da Costa
Jill Diane Jarvis-Tonus
Michael E. Charles
Robin L. Coster
Amalia Trister
Jonathan G. Colombo
Jill M. Holmes
John R. Rudolph

(See Next Column)

MEMBERS AND ASSOCIATES (Continued)

Mark L. Robbins
Justine Wiebe
Andrew I. McIntosh
Shawn D. Jacka
Anita Nador
Todd D. Bailey
Isis E. Caulder
Scott R. Pundsack
Christine M. Pallotta
Tai W. Nahm
Bhupinder S. Randhawa
Lillian Sversky

PATENT AND TRADEMARK AGENTS

David W. R. Langton
H. Samuel Frost
Marie E. Manza
Terry Edwards
Jane Sarjeant
Micheline Gravelle
Stephen M. Beney
Janice M. Bereskin
Mark Schisler

For full biographical listings, see the Martindale-Hubbell Law Directory

BORDEN & ELLIOT (AV)

Barristers & Solicitors
Scotia Plaza, 40 King Street West, M5H 3Y4
Telephone: 416-367-6000
Telecopier: 416-367-6749
Email: info@borden.com *URL:* http://www.borden.com
Ottawa, Ontario Office: Borden Elliot Scott & Aylen, 1000-60 Rue Queen Street.
Telephone: 613-237-5160; 800-661-4237. General
Facsimile: 613-230-8842. IP Dept.
Facsimile: 613-787-3558. Email: ottinfo@scottaylen.com. URL: http://www.borden.com.

Gordon J. Zimmerman

For Complete List of Firm Personnel, See General Section

For full biographical listings, see the Martindale-Hubbell Law Directory

DEETH WILLIAMS WALL, LLP (AV)

National Bank Building, 150 York Street, Suite 400, M5H 3S5
Telephone: 416-941-9440
Facsimile: 416-941-9443
Email: info@dww.com *URL:* http://www.dww.com

MEMBERS OF FIRM

Douglas N. Deeth
Amy-Lynne Williams
Gervas W. Wall
A. Marijo Coates
Victor V. Butsky
Michael Erdle

ASSOCIATES

Gordon S. Jepson
Diane M. LaCalamita
Noel A. Courage
Shereen Hamdy
Ailbe C. Flynn

For full biographical listings, see the Martindale-Hubbell Law Directory

DIMOCK STRATTON CLARIZIO (AV)

20 Queen Street West, Suite 3202, P.O. Box 102, M5H 3R3
Telephone: 416-971-7202
Fax: 416-971-6638
Email: firm@dimock.com *URL:* http://www.dimock.com

PARTNERS

Ronald E. Dimock
Bruce W. Stratton
Dino P. Clarizio
Michelle L. Wassenaar
Mark B. Eisen
David M. Reive
Henry Lue

ASSOCIATES

Cynthia J. Ledgley
Andrew Mark Shaughnessy
C. Michelle Nelles
Angela Furlanetto

For full biographical listings, see the Martindale-Hubbell Law Directory

KELLY AFFLECK GREENE (AV)

One First Canadian Place, Suite 840, P.O. Box 489, M5X 1E5
Telephone: 416-360-2800
Fax: 416-360-5960
Email: info@kag.net *URL:* http://www.kag.net

MEMBERS OF FIRM

W. Anthony Kelly, Q.C.
Donald S. Affleck, Q.C.
Peter R. Greene
Donald B. Houston
James C. Orr
Peter C. Wardle
Helen A. Daley
Melissa J. Kennedy

ASSOCIATES

Kenneth A. Dekker
W. Michael G. Osborne
Jason C. Markwell
Patrice F. Band

For full biographical listings, see the Martindale-Hubbell Law Directory

Toronto—Continued

RIDOUT & MAYBEE (AV)

Barristers and Solicitors
Patent and Trademark Agents
One Queen Street East, Suite 2400, M5C 3B1
Telephone: 416-868-1482
Fax: 416-362-0823, 416-362-8865
Email: ridbee@ridoutmaybee.com *URL:* http://www.ridoutmaybee.com
Ottawa, Ontario Office: 19th Floor, 150 Metcalfe Street, K2P 1P1.
Telephone: 613-236-1995.
Facsimile: 613-236-2485; 613-563-9185. Email: ipinfo@ridoutmaybee.com

P. Ewan McArdle (Patent and Trademark Agent)
W. Charles Kent
William R. Edgar
Richard A.R. Parsons (Patent and Trademark Agent)
Philip K. Holland (Patent and Trademark Agent)
James R. Lake
Randall S. Mitchell
P. Scott Maclean
Lynn S. Cassan
Janet M. Fuhrer
Marcus T. Gallie
William B. Vass

Robert G. Hirons (Patent and Trademark Agent)
Kimberley A. Brulé (Trademark Agent)
Mary L. Malvaso (Trademark Agent)
Lynda E.E. Doxsee (Trademark Agent)
Roland H. Joachim
James E. Longwell
Mitchell B. Charness
Ian C. McMillan
David J. Heller

OF COUNSEL

Malcolm Johnston, Q.C.

CONSULTANTS

Kenneth M. Garrett
Godfrey P. Orleans
William L. Hayhurst
I. Jane Parsons (Resident, Toronto Office)

For full biographical listings, see the Martindale-Hubbell Law Directory

ROGERS LAW OFFICE (AV)

Suite 1004, 357 Bay Street, M5H 2T7
Telephone: 416-363-6626
Fax: 416-363-6628
Email: patents@rogersiplaw.com *URL:* http://www.rogersiplaw.com

David Rogers, Q.C.

For full biographical listings, see the Martindale-Hubbell Law Directory

SIM, HUGHES, ASHTON & MCKAY (AV)

Sixth Floor, 330 University Avenue, M5G 1R7
Telephone: 416-595-1155
Cable Address: "Simbas" Toronto
Telex: 065-24567
Telecopier: 416-595-1163
Email: mailsim@sim-mcburney.com *URL:* http://www.sim-mcburney.com

Donald F. Sim, Q.C. (1927-1986)
Roger T. Hughes, Q.C.
Toni B. Polson Ashton
Kenneth D. McKay
Timothy M. Lowman
Stephen M. Lane
Arthur B. Renaud
Patricia A. Rae
Barbara J. Murchie

ASSOCIATES

John N. Allport
Steven L. Nemetz
Robert C. T. Liang
Kamleh J. Nicola
Gillian M. Smith
L. E. Trent Horne

PATENT AND TRADEMARK AGENTS

Peter W. McBurney
Michael I. Stewart
John H. Woodley
Brenda L. Boardman
Stephen J. Perry
David A. Ruston
Thomas T. Rieder
Warren J. Galloway
Lola A. Bartoszewicz
Jeffrey W. Wong

TECHNICAL ASSISTANTS

Ursula M. McGuinness
Kimberly A. McManus

For full biographical listings, see the Martindale-Hubbell Law Directory

SMART & BIGGAR (AV)

Box 111, The First Century Tower, 1500-438 University Avenue, M5G 2K8
Telephone: 416-593-5514
Facsimile: 416-591-1690
Email: toronto@smart-biggar.ca *URL:* http://www.smart-biggar.ca
Ottawa, Ontario Office: Suite 900, 55 Metcalfe Street, P.O. Box 2999, Station D, K1P 5Y6.
Telephone: 613-232-2486.
Facsimile: 613-232-8440. Email: ottawa@smart-biggar.ca.
Montreal, Quebec Office: 1000 De La Gauchetière Street West, Suite 3400, H3B 4W5.
Telephone: 514-954-1500.
Facsimile: 514-954-1396. Email: montreal@smart-biggar.ca.
Vancouver, British Columbia Office: Box 11560, Vancouver Centre, 2200 - 650 West Georgia Street, V6B 4N8.
Telephone: 604-682-7295.
Facsimile: 604-682-0274. Email: vancouver@smart-biggar.ca.

MEMBERS OF FIRM

John R. Morrissey (Resident)
Keltie R. Sim (Resident)
Mark K. Evans (Resident)
Gunars A. Gaikis (Resident)
Ronald D. Faggetter (Resident)
Alistair G. Simpson (Resident)
J. Sheldon Hamilton (Resident)

ASSOCIATES

Peter R. Wilcox (Resident)
Matthew Zischka (Resident)
Nancy P. Pei (Resident)
Mark G. Biernacki (Resident)
Yoon Kang (Resident)
Shonagh L. McVean (Resident)
Geneviève M. Prévost (Resident)
Kevin A. O'Neil (Resident)

COUNSEL

Immanuel Goldsmith, Q.C. (Resident)

For full biographical listings, see the Martindale-Hubbell Law Directory

CANADA QUEBEC

*MONTREAL,** Montreal Dist.

MENDELSOHN ROSENTZVEIG SHACTER (AV)

1000 Sherbrooke Street West, 27th Floor, H3A 3G4
Telephone: 514-987-5000
Telex: 05-27284 Colorlaw
Telecopier: 514-987-1213
Email: mrs@mrslaw.com *URL:* http://www.mrslaw.com

PARTNERS

S. Leon Mendelsohn, Q.C. (1902-1996)
Leo Rosentzveig, Q.C.
Manuel Shacter, Q.C.
Jack C. Shayne
William Levitt
Arthur A. Garvis
Edward E. Aronoff
L. Michael Blumenstein
Max Mendelsohn
Earl S. Cohen
Michael Garonce
Donald M. Devine
Richard S. Uditsky
Joel Weitzman
Ian R. Rudnikoff
Marc I. Leiter
L. B. Erdle
Fredric L. Carsley
Frank Zylberberg
Jules Brossard
David L. Rosentzveig
Judie K. Jokinen
Gilles Seguin
Martin Desrosiers
Andrew Etcovitch
Alain Breault
Jean Carrière
Henri M. Bybelezer
Louis Frédérick Côté
Sandra Abitan

ASSOCIATES

Carl M. Ravinsky
Catherine Muraz
Francine Wiseman
Joelle Sebag
Maria R. Battaglia
Keyvan Nassiry
Linda Schachter
Emmanuelle Saucier
Arnold Cohen
Aaron Makovka
Michel Rochefort
Céline Tessier
Sophie Crevier
Annick Joyal
Francis Desmarais
Nicolas J. Beugnot
Jean-François Brière
Marc-Antoine Deschamps
Philipp F. Duffy
Fred Purkey
Martin Sills
David Tardif-Latourelle

For full biographical listings, see the Martindale-Hubbell Law Directory

PENSION AND PROFIT SHARING

MINNESOTA

*FERGUS FALLS,** Otter Tail Co.

DAVID F. LUNDEEN (AV)
107 Court Street, 56537
Telephone: 218-736-4866
FAX: 218-736-7747
Email: dlundlaw@prtel.com

For full biographical listings, see the Martindale-Hubbell Law Directory

NEBRASKA

*LINCOLN,** Lancaster Co.

CLINE, WILLIAMS, WRIGHT, JOHNSON & OLDFATHER (AV)
1900 U.S. Bank Building, 233 South 13th Street, 68508
Telephone: 402-474-6900
Fax: 402-474-5393
Email: postmaster@cline-law.com *URL:* http://www.cline-law.com
Omaha, Nebraska Office: Suite 720, One Pacific Place, 1125 South 103rd Street, 68124.
Telephone: 402-397-1700.
Fax: 402-397-1806.

ATTORNEYS

Allen L. Graves
Charles M. Pallesen, Jr.
Fredric H. Kauffman
Donald F. Burt
Alan E. Peterson
Stephen E. Gehring
Robert J. Routh
Kevin Colleran
L. Bruce Wright
James M. Bausch
Larry A. Holle
David R. Buntain
Stephen H. Nelsen
Michael C. Mueller
Lauren W. Wismer
Daniel R. Stogsdill
Scott D. Kelly
Terry R. Wittler
Pamela Hastings Carrier
Mark A. Christensen
Richard P. Garden, Jr.
Shawn D. Renner
John C. Miles
Mary Kay Frank
Thomas C. Huston
Sonya S. Ekart
Don R. Janssen
Susan Kubert Sapp
Kevin J. Schneider
Andrew D. Strotman
Jill Gossin Jensen
Rochelle A. Mullen
John L. Horan
Bryan S. Hatch
Steven C. Likes
Tracy A. Oldemeyer
Jolene M. Papa
Timothy G. Aschoff
Eric N. Bergquist
Janis J. Winterhof
Andrea Dylan Snowden

OF COUNSEL

Charles E. Wright
Richard P. Jeffries
Mary M. Campbell

RETIRED PARTNERS

Flavel A. Wright (Retired)
Warren C. Johnson (Retired)
Charles E. Oldfather (1927-1998)

Representative Clients: U.S. Bank National Association; University of Nebraska; Nebraska Medical Assn.; Saint Elizabeth Regional Medical Center; Media of Nebraska; Cargill Inc.; State Farm Insurance Cos.; Wal-Mart Stores, Inc.; Textron/Cushman; Isco, Inc.

For full biographical listings, see the Martindale-Hubbell Law Directory

NEVADA

*RENO,** Washoe Co.

WALTHER, KEY, MAUPIN, OATS, COX & LEGOY, A PROFESSIONAL CORPORATION (AV)
Lakeside Professional Plaza, 3500 Lakeside Court, 89509
Telephone: 775-827-2000
Facsimile: 775-827-2185
Mailing Address: P.O. Box 30000, Reno, Nevada, 89520

L. Robert LeGoy, Jr.
Michael E. Malloy
Kim G. Rowe
Donald A. Lattin
Gustave J. Rossi
Kurt O. Hunsberger

(See Next Column)

Michaelle D. Rafferty

Representative Clients: Associated Anesthesiologists of Reno; Bi-State Petroleum; Model Dairy, Inc.; Radiation Oncology; Regional Ambulance Services; Reno Radiological; Sierra Anesthesiologists; Sparks Nugget, Inc.; Washoe Health System; Western Nevada Supply Co.

For full biographical listings, see the Martindale-Hubbell Law Directory

NEW JERSEY

CHERRY HILL, Camden Co.

FLASTER/GREENBERG, P.C. (AV)
Commerce Center, 1810 Chapel Avenue West, Third Floor, 08002-4609
Telephone: 856-661-1900
Telecopier: 856-661-1919
Email: FIRM@FLASTERGREENBERG.COM *URL:* http://www.flastergreenberg.com

Richard J. Flaster
Stephen M. Greenberg
Laura B. Wallenstein
Allen P. Fineberg
Markley S. Roderick
Peter R. Spirgel
Alan H. Zuckerman
William S. Skinner
J. Philip Kirchner
Paul J. Russoniello
Carl S. Bisgaier
Steven B. Sacharow
E. Richard Dressel
Kenneth S. Goodkind
Frank H. Wisniewski
Alma L. Saravia

OF COUNSEL

Peter M. Dolinger
James J. Binns

Elizabeth J. Hampton
Jeffrey Herskowitz
Christopher E. Kaltenbach
Steven J. Abrams
Julie A. Williamson
Donna T. Urban
Amelia Carolla
Matthew Azoulay
Elaine J. Petruzziello (Not admitted in NJ)
Ann Marie Iannone
Pasquale Guglietta

LEGAL SUPPORT PERSONNEL

PARALEGALS

Ann Gorman
Patricia D'Alessio
Theresa Cooke
Rosemary Dunaif

For full biographical listings, see the Martindale-Hubbell Law Directory

PENNSAUKEN, Camden Co.

SHERMAN, SILVERSTEIN, KOHL, ROSE & PODOLSKY, A PROFESSIONAL CORPORATION (AV)
Fairway Corporate Center, 4300 Haddonfield Road, Suite 311, 08109
Telephone: 856-662-0700
Fax: 856-662-0165
URL: http://www.sskrplaw.com
Bala Cynwyd, Pennsylvania Office: 11 Bala Avenue.
Telephone: 215-923-2513.

Lee S. Sherman
Lee Silverstein
John W. Kohl
M. Zev Rose
Steven M. Podolsky
Alan C. Milstein
Andrew J. Karcich
Nan S. Famular
John R. Lolio, Jr.
Robert W. Lynch
Phyllis Z. Sherman
Daniel J. Barrison
Thomas J. Tamburelli
Rhonda R. Feld
Leon H. Rose
Leonard R. Rossetti
Robert E. Schwartz
Charles Bender
Harris L. Pogust
Nancy L. Wasch (Not admitted in NJ)
John M. Hanamirian
David C. Silverman
Matthew Podolnick
Jeffrey Resnick
Derek T. Braslow

OF COUNSEL

Robert M. Washburn

For full biographical listings, see the Martindale-Hubbell Law Directory

NEW YORK

*WHITE PLAINS,** Westchester Co.

DANZIGER & MARKHOFF LLP (AV)
A Limited Liability Partnership including a Professional Corporation
Centroplex-123 Main Street, 10601
Telephone: 914-948-1556
Telecopier: 914-948-1706
Email: danziger-markhoff@worldnet.att.net

(See Next Column)

DANZIGER & MARKHOFF LLP, *White Plains—Continued*

Joel Danziger
Harris Markhoff
Ira Langer (P.C.)
Scott M. Sherman
Joshua S. Levine
Robert B. Danziger
Michael Markhoff
Edward A. Berlin
Gregory R. Tapfar

Susan I. Porter
Stephen C.F. Diamond

LEGAL SUPPORT PERSONNEL

ENROLLED ACTUARIES

William Martin Miller
Aileen T. Palazzo

COUNSEL

Irwin N. Rubin

References: Chase Manhattan Bank, White Plains, N.Y. (Trust Dept.); Bank of New York County Trust Region; Lazard Freres & Co.

For full biographical listings, see the Martindale-Hubbell Law Directory

OHIO

*CLEVELAND,** Cuyahoga Co.

McDONALD, HOPKINS, BURKE & HABER CO., L.P.A. (AV)

2100 Bank One Center, 600 Superior Avenue, E., 44114-2653
Telephone: 216-348-5400
Telecopier: 216-348-5474
Email: attorney@mhbh.com *URL:* http://www.mhbh.com

Patrick J. Berry
Jeffrey P. Consolo
Jerome W. Cook
Richard S. Cooper
Anthony J. DiVenere
Paul N. Edwards
Theodore J. Esborn
Steven L. Gardner
Carl J. Grassi
James A. Griffith
Jeffrey R. Huntsberger
Brian J. Jereb
Bernard L. Karr
Thomas W. Keen
Roger L. Kleinman
Joseph J. LoPresti, Jr.
Dan L. Makee
George L. McGaughey, Jr.
John T. Mulligan
Brian M. O'Neill
William J. O'Neill
Stephen T. Parisi
R. Jeffrey Pollock
Michael G. Riley
Shawn M. Riley
Albert N. Salvatore
Thomas C. Schrader
Roger L. Shumaker
Barbara J. Smith
James M. Stone
Dale R. Vlasek
Kenneth J. Walsh
John M. Wirtshafter
Jane Marie Pine Wood
Charles B. Zellmer

OF COUNSEL

John J. Monroe

Julie A. Callsen
Anne T. Corrigan
Steven A. Eisenberg
G. Andrew Gardner
Anuj Goswami
Donald E. Kacmar
David M. Kall
Jeffrey B. Keiper
Kevin J. Kessinger
Mark D. Klimek
Alan M. Koschik
Deviani M. Kuhar
Paul W. Linehan
Tyler L. Mathews
Jennifer A. Mills
Antoinette K. Palmer
Ketan K. Patel
Sharon Szolosi Regas
Douglas B. Schnee
Michele Smolin
Glenn D. Southworth
Michael R. Spreng

For full biographical listings, see the Martindale-Hubbell Law Directory

WALTER & HAVERFIELD, P.L.L. (AV)

1300 Terminal Tower, 44113-2253
Telephone: 216-781-1212
Telecopier: 216-575-0911
Email: law@walterhav.com *URL:* http://www.walterhav.com
Columbus, Ohio Office: 88 East Broad Street.
Telephone: 614-898-1096.

MEMBERS OF FIRM

Russell C. Shaw
David P.N. Silk

OF COUNSEL

Sheldon M. Young
Ricky Lee Bertram

Representative Clients: AGA Gas, Inc.; Andrews Moving & Storage, Inc.; Bellevue Manufacturing; Louis Berkman Company; Braden Sutphin Ink Company; Flair Corporation; International Metal Hose Co.; Key Trust Company of Ohio, N.A.; Sea-Land Chemical Company.

For Complete List of Firm Personnel, See General Section

For full biographical listings, see the Martindale-Hubbell Law Directory

OKLAHOMA

*TULSA,** Tulsa Co.

BOESCHE, McDERMOTT & ESKRIDGE (AV)

Suite 800 Oneok Plaza, 100 West Fifth Street, 74103
Telephone: 918-583-1777
Fax: 918-592-5809
Email: bme@intellex.com
Muskogee, Oklahoma Office: 1111 West Broadway, P.O. Box 2669, 74402.
Telephone: 918-683-6100.
Fax: 918-683-2303.

MEMBER OF FIRM

David B. McKinney

Representative Clients: University of Tulsa; Phillips Petroleum; Springer Clinic; Elf Atochem North America.

For Complete List of Firm Personnel, See General Section

For full biographical listings, see the Martindale-Hubbell Law Directory

EAGLETON, EAGLETON AND HARRISON, INC. (AV)

Suite 1700, 320 South Boston Avenue, 74103-4706
Telephone: 918-584-0462
Fax: 918-584-3724
Email: eagleton@worldnet.att.net

E. John Eagleton
James R. Eagleton
Charles D. Harrison

OF COUNSEL

Norma Eagleton

For full biographical listings, see the Martindale-Hubbell Law Directory

PENNSYLVANIA

*HARRISBURG,** Dauphin Co.

JOHNSTON, ARONSON & DIAMOND, A PROFESSIONAL CORPORATION (AV)

150 Corporate Center Drive, Suite 100 (Camp Hill), 17011
Telephone: 717-975-5500
Telecopier: 717-975-5511

Charles W. Johnston
Irwin W. Aronson
James A. Diamond
John T. Kupchinsky

For full biographical listings, see the Martindale-Hubbell Law Directory

*PHILADELPHIA,** Philadelphia Co.

KLEINBARD, BELL & BRECKER LLP (AV)

Suite 700, 1900 Market Street, 19103
Telephone: 215-568-2000
Facsimile: 215-568-0140
Montclair, New Jersey Office: 240 Claremont Avenue, 07042.
Telephone: 973-233-0600.
Facsimile: 973-233-9390.

Joseph S. Kleinbard (1905-1994)
Robert John Brecker (1916-1996)

COUNSEL TO THE FIRM

Arthur S. Keyser

MEMBERS OF FIRM

Paul E. Bomze
Murray I. Blackman
Howard J. Davis
Steven R. Waxman
Steven J. Engelmyer (Resident, Montclair Office)
David L. Hyman (Resident, Montclair Office)
Imogene E. Hughes
John P. Hickey
Jay R. Goldstein
Ralph J. Mauro
Thomas H. Speranza
Lisa E. Brody

ASSOCIATES

Mary Beth H. Gray
Eric J. Rothschild
Mary Vassallo Slinkard
Michael A. Frattone
Benjamin C. Graff (Not admitted in PA)
Ralph F. Salgado

COUNSEL

Joseph Bell

For full biographical listings, see the Martindale-Hubbell Law Directory

Philadelphia—Continued

MERVIN M. WILF, LTD. (AV)

3901 Mellon Bank Center, 1735 Market Street, 19103
Telephone: 215-994-1430; 215-568-4842
Facsimile: 215-994-1432
Email: mwilf@erols.com
Cambridge, Massachusetts Office: 2 Berkeley Place, 02138.
Telephone: 617-876-5200.

Mervin M. Wilf

A list of Representative Clients and References will be furnished upon request.

For full biographical listings, see the Martindale-Hubbell Law Directory

RHODE ISLAND

*PROVIDENCE,** Providence Co.

HINCKLEY, ALLEN & SNYDER LLP (AV)

1500 Fleet Center, 02903-2393
Telephone: 401-274-2000
Fax: 401-277-9600
Email: firm@haslaw.com *URL:* http://www.haslaw.com
Boston, Massachusetts Office: 28 State Street, 30th Floor.
Telephone: 617-345-9000.
Fax: 617-345-9020. URL: http://www.haslaw.com.

MEMBERS OF FIRM

Paula K. Andrews (Not admitted in RI)
David D. Barricelli
E. Jerome Batty
Jonathan Bell
Leon C. Boghossian III
Paul Bork (Not admitted in RI)
Stephen J. Carlotti
Eric F. Eisenberg (Not admitted in RI)
Malcolm Farmer, III
Margaret D. Farrell
Noel M. Field, Jr.
Pasco Gasbarro Jr.
Hugh J. Gorman, III (Not admitted in RI)
Gerard R. Goulet
William R. Grimm
Richard L. E. Jocelyn
Michael J. Kelly (Not admitted in RI)
Joel Lewin (Not admitted in RI)
Doris Jami Licht
Sandra Matrone Mack
Matthew T. Marcello, III
Frederick P. McClure
Elizabeth Murdock Myers
Paul F. O'Donnell, III (Not admitted in RI)
H. Peter Olsen
Julianne Palumbo (Not admitted in RI)
John J. Pendergast, III
Gerald J. Petros
Richard H. Pierce
James O. Reavis
Jeremy Ritzenberg (Not admitted in RI)
Ralph J. Rivkind (Not admitted in RI)
Charles E. Schaub, Jr. (Not admitted in RI)
Douglas F. Seaver (Not admitted in RI)
Paul A. Silver
Herman Snyder (Not admitted in RI)
David R. Sullivan (Not admitted in RI)
Robert F. Sylvia (Not admitted in RI)
Howard E. Walker
Richard D. Wayne (Not admitted in RI)

ASSOCIATES

Jessica M. Bettencourt
Mark Bianchi
Alyssa V. Boss
Alexandra K. Callam
Clifford R. Cohen (Not admitted in RI)
Jane E. Cohen (Not admitted in RI)
Andrew D. Cummings (Not admitted in RI)
June E. Daniel
Kelley Jordan-Price
Catherine S. Kim (Not admitted in RI)
Christopher W. Morog (Not admitted in RI)
Elena B. Olson (Not admitted in RI)
Joseph D. Whelan

OF COUNSEL

Willard Krasnow (Not admitted in RI)
Bentley Tobin
Joachim A. Weissfeld

For Complete List of Firm Personnel, See General Section

For full biographical listings, see the Martindale-Hubbell Law Directory

SOUTH CAROLINA

*GREENVILLE,** Greenville Co.

MERLINE & THOMAS, P.A. (AV)

812 East North Street, P.O. Box 10796, 29603
Telephone: 864-242-4080
Fax: 864-242-5758

(See Next Column)

David A. Merline
John R. Thomas
David A. Merline, Jr.
Keith G. Meacham
Randy E. Fisher
Robert E. August
Tommy D. Permenter, Jr.

LEGAL SUPPORT PERSONNEL

Mary S. Rose (Legal Administrator)

For full biographical listings, see the Martindale-Hubbell Law Directory

TEXAS

*DALLAS,** Dallas Co.

SMITH, UNDERWOOD & PERKINS, A PROFESSIONAL CORPORATION (AV)

600 Two Lincoln Centre, 5420 LBJ Freeway, 75240
Telephone: 972-661-5114
Telecopier: 972-661-5691
Email: firm@suandp.com *URL:* http://www.suplaw.com

Timothy S. Perkins
David W. Ralston
G. Lynn Smith
William J. Underwood, Jr.

Christine A. McGuire
Amy K. Ratzlaff
P. Theodore Stoinoff, II
Val C. Cronin
Ellen P. Stewart
Todd W. Shadle
Ruth C. Logan
Christina L. Betanzos
Kent D. Williamson

For full biographical listings, see the Martindale-Hubbell Law Directory

UTAH

*SALT LAKE CITY,** Salt Lake Co.

CALLISTER NEBEKER & McCULLOUGH, A PROFESSIONAL CORPORATION (AV)

Gateway Tower East, Suite 900, 10 East South Temple, 84133
Telephone: 801-530-7300
Telecopier: 801-364-9127
Email: mjeaston@cnmlaw.com *URL:* http://www.cnmlaw.com

Jeffrey N. Clayton
W. Waldan Lloyd

Representative Clients: Zions First National Bank; Sears Roebuck & Company; Utah Automobile Dealers Association; Sinclair Oil Corporation (Little America); Keystone Communications; Central Valley Water Reclamation Facility Board; Citicorp; Intermountain Health Care, Inc.; Children's Miracle Network (Osmond Foundation); Nu Skin International, Inc.

For Complete List of Firm Personnel, See General Section

For full biographical listings, see the Martindale-Hubbell Law Directory

PARSONS, DAVIES, KINGHORN & PETERS, P.C. (AV)

185 South State Street, Suite 700, 84111
Telephone: 801-363-4300
Facsimile: 801-363-4378
Email: Attorneys@pdkplaw.com

Langdon T. Owen, Jr.
John S. Bradley

For Complete List of Firm Personnel, See General Section

For full biographical listings, see the Martindale-Hubbell Law Directory

VAN COTT, BAGLEY, CORNWALL & McCARTHY, A PROFESSIONAL CORPORATION (AV)

50 South Main Street, Suite 1600, P.O. Box 45340, 84145-0340
Telephone: 801-532-3333
Telecopier: 801-534-0058
Email: info@vancott.com *URL:* http://www.vancott.com
Ogden, Utah Office: 2404 Washington Boulevard, Suite 900.
Telephone: 801-394-5783.
Park City, Utah Office: 2200 Park Avenue, Suite C200-A.
Telephone: 435-649-3889.

David E. Sloan
Stephen D. Swindle

Stephen R. Sloan

OF COUNSEL

David E. Salisbury

For Complete List of Firm Personnel, See General Section

For full biographical listings, see the Martindale-Hubbell Law Directory

VIRGINIA

*CHARLOTTESVILLE,** Charlottesville City Co.

ROBERT M. MUSSELMAN & ASSOCIATES (AV)

413 7th Street, N.E., P.O. Box 254, 22902
Telephone: 804-977-4500
Fax: 804-293-5727
Email: rmmesquire@aol.com

ASSOCIATES

Carolyn C. Musselman
Douglas E. Little
Jonathan B. Burns

LEGAL SUPPORT PERSONNEL

Eleanor P. Carter (Legal Secretary and Real Estate Paralegal)
Faye M. McBurney (Legal Secretary and Bankruptcy Paralegal)

For full biographical listings, see the Martindale-Hubbell Law Directory

CANADA
NOVA SCOTIA

*HALIFAX,** Regional Munic. of Halifax

McINNES COOPER (AV)

Barristers, Solicitors & Trade Mark Agents
Summit Place, 1601 Lower Water Street, P.O. Box 730, B3J 2V1
Telephone: 902-425-6500
Fax: 902-425-6350
Email: mcrhfx@mcrlaw.com *URL:* http://www.mcrlaw.com
St. John's, Newfoundland Office: Baine Johnston Centre, 5th Floor, 10 Fort William Place, P.O. Box 5939, A1C 5X4.
Telephone: 709-722-8735.
Telecopier: 709-722-1763. Email: mcrsj@mcrlaw.com.
Moncton, New Brunswick Office: Place Moncton Place, 655 Main Street, P.O. Box 1368, E1C 8T6.
Telephone: 506-857-8970.
Fax: 506-857-4095. Email: mcrmctn@mcrlaw.com.
Charlottetown, Prince Edward Island Office: BDC Place, Suite 620, 119 Kent Street, C1A 1N3.
Telephone: 902-368-8473.
Fax: 902-368-8346. Email: mcrpei@mcrlaw.com.
Fredericton, New Brunswick Office: Suite 600, 570 Queen Street, P.O. Box 610.
Telephone: 506-458-8572.
Fax: 506-458-9903. Email: mcrfton@mcrlaw.com.

PARTNERS

Peter McLellan, Q.C.
Malcolm D. Boyle

ASSOCIATE

Hugh Wright

For Complete List of Firm Personnel, See General Section

For full biographical listings, see the Martindale-Hubbell Law Directory

PERSONAL INJURY

MINNESOTA

*HALLOCK,** Kittson Co.

BRINK, SOBOLIK, SEVERSON, MALM & ALBRECHT, P.A. (AV)

217 South Birch Avenue, P.O. Box 790, 56728
Telephone: 218-843-3686
FAX: 218-843-2724
Email: brink@rural-access.com

Lyman A. Brink (1909-1972)
Dennis M. Sobolik
Robert K. Severson
Roger C. Malm
Robert M. Albrecht
Blake S. Sobolik
Jeffrey W. Hane

Representative Clients: Northwestern State Bank, Hallock, Minn.; Prime Security Bank, Karlstad, Minn.; Argyle State Bank, Argyle, Minn.; City of Hallock; American Federal Savings & Loan Assn.; State Farm Insurance Co.; Minnesota Rice Growers, Inc.

For full biographical listings, see the Martindale-Hubbell Law Directory

*HASTINGS,** Dakota Co.

SIEBEN, POLK, LAVERDIERE, JONES & HAWN, A PROFESSIONAL ASSOCIATION (AV)

999 Westview Drive, 55033
Telephone: 651-437-3148
Fax: 651-437-2732
St. Paul, Minnesota Office: Galtier Plaza, Suite 550, Box 45, 175 Fifth Street East.
Telephone: 651-222-4146.
Fax: 651-223-8279.

Michael R. Sieben
Michael S. Polk
Harvey N. Jones
Richard A. LaVerdiere
Steven D. Hawn (Resident, St. Paul Office)

Thomas R. Longfellow (Resident, St. Paul Office)
Bernie M. Dusich
Michael R. Strom
John P. Sieben
Scott J. Hertogs
Brian T. Mak (Resident, St. Paul Office)
Lynn A. O'Leary

For full biographical listings, see the Martindale-Hubbell Law Directory

*MINNEAPOLIS,** Hennepin Co.

ABRAMS & SMITH, A PROFESSIONAL ASSOCIATION (AV)

700 Northstar West, 55402
Telephone: 612-332-4273; 800-659-2679
Fax: 612-342-2107
Email: abrams@pclink.com

Harold J. Carroll (1901-1978)
Frank X. Cronan (1912-1975)
Jerome B. Abrams
Paul R. Smith
Lauris Heyerdahl
Bradford J. Roegge

Representative Clients: Hawkeye Security Insurance Co.; CNA Insurance; Employer's Mutual Insurance Co.

For full biographical listings, see the Martindale-Hubbell Law Directory

ARNOLD, ANDERSON & DOVE, P.L.L.P. (AV)

5881 Cedar Lake Road, 55416-1492
Telephone: 612-545-9000
Wats Line: 800-343-4545
Fax: 612-545-1793; 612-542-9210
Email: aad@aadlaw.com
Princeton, Minnesota Office: 501 South Fourth Street.
Telephone: 612-389-2214.
Hutchinson, Minnesota Office: 101 Park Place.
Telephone: 320-587-7575.
Red Wing, Minnesota Office: 481 Fridell Crescent, 55066.
Telephone: 651-388-3454.

MEMBER OF FIRM
David B. Arnold

ASSOCIATE
Richard G. McGee

For Complete List of Firm Personnel, See General Section

For full biographical listings, see the Martindale-Hubbell Law Directory

BASS & CARLSON, P.A. (AV)

Centre Village Offices, Suite 2525, 431 South Seventh Street, 55415
Telephone: 612-344-1555
Fax: 612-344-1315
Email: bass@isd.net
Buffalo, Minnesota Office: 7 First Street, N.E. P.O. Box 548. 55313.
Telephone: 612-682-2220.
Fax: 612-682-3330.

Louis D. Bass
John J. Carlson
Robert Victor Jones

For full biographical listings, see the Martindale-Hubbell Law Directory

BASSFORD, LOCKHART, TRUESDELL & BRIGGS, P.A. (AV)

(Formerly Richards, Montgomery, Cobb & Bassford, P.A.)
3550 Multifoods Tower, 55402-3787
Telephone: 612-333-3000
Telecopier: 612-333-8829

Greer E. Lockhart
Frederick E. Finch
John M. Degnan
Lewis A. Remele, Jr.
Kevin P. Keenan
James O. Redman
Rebecca Egge Moos
John M. Anderson
Charles E. Lundberg
Gregory P. Bulinski
Dale M. Wagner
Louis J. Speltz
Laura J. McKnight
Mark P. Hodkinson
Thomas J. Niemiec
Andrew L. Marshall
Michael A. Klutho
Gregory W. Deckert
Kevin P. Hickey
Stanford P. Hill
Mark R. Whitmore
Fred B. Snyder (1859-1951)
Edward C. Gale (1862-1943)
Frank A. Janes (1908-1959)
Nathan A. Cobb, Sr. (1905-1976)
Bergmann Richards (1888-1978)
Edmund T. Montgomery (1904-1987)
Charles A. Bassford (1914-1990)
Jerome C. Briggs (Retired)
Lynn G. Truesdell (Retired)

Dani M. Shimon
Christopher R. Morris
Kelly A. Putney
Jennifer L. Hill
Robin Ann Williams
Michael A. Switzer
Shalanda Denise Ballard

Representative Clients: Chubb/Pacific Indemnity Group; John Hancock Mutual Life Insurance Co.; Medical Protective Co.; The Travelers Insurance Cos.; The St. Paul Insurance Cos.

For full biographical listings, see the Martindale-Hubbell Law Directory

BORKON, RAMSTEAD, MARIANI & LETOURNEAU, LTD. (AV)

485 Northstar East, 608 Second Avenue, South, 55402
Telephone: 612-333-7155
Fax: 612-333-5956

Edward H. Borkon
John H. Ramstead
John D. Mariani
Dennis R. Letourneau
William M. Fishman
Howard S. Carp
Howard S. Marker
Lewis H. Seltz
Lorrie L. Bescheinen
Martin T. Montilino
Howard L. Bolter
Michael C. Van Berkom

OF COUNSEL
William Seltz

Reference: Norwest Bank, Minneapolis.

For full biographical listings, see the Martindale-Hubbell Law Directory

COX, GOUDY, MCNULTY & WALLACE, P.L.L.P. (AV)

100 North Sixth Street, #676A, 55403
Telephone: 612-338-1414
Fax: 612-338-6754
Email: mcwall@bitstream.net
St. Paul Office: 1300 Minnesota Building, 46 East 4th Street.
Telephone: 651-293-9194.

MEMBERS OF FIRM
Charles A. Cox
Craig A. Goudy
Marcy S. Wallace
Charles A. Cox, III

OF COUNSEL
John C. McNulty

For full biographical listings, see the Martindale-Hubbell Law Directory

FETTERLY & GORDON, P.A. (AV)

1800 U.S. Bank Place, 650 Third Avenue South, 55402
Telephone: 612-288-2501
800-288-2501
Fax: 612-288-2551
Email: mail@Fetterly.com *URL:* http://www.fetterly.com

James L. Fetterly
Gary J. Gordon
Keith A. Hanson

(See Next Column)

FETTERLY & GORDON P.A., *Minneapolis—Continued*

Stephen G. Lickteig
Diane B. Bratvold
Timothy J. Fetterly
Thomas J. Basting, Jr.
Katherine A. Killen Hall
Christopher J. Sorenson
Stephen M. Warner

Reference: National City Bank.

For full biographical listings, see the Martindale-Hubbell Law Directory

GARTNER, BENNETT & SCHUPP, P.C. (AV)

One Financial Plaza, Suite 2200, 120 South Sixth Street, 55402-1824
Telephone: 612 333-3839
Telecopier: 612-333-3129

Ludwig B. Gartner, Jr.
Robert Bennett
Timothy R. Schupp
William J. Tipping
Heidi A. Schneider
Eric William Hageman

Matthew McBride

For full biographical listings, see the Martindale-Hubbell Law Directory

HUNEGS, STONE, KOENIG, LENEAVE & KVAS, P.A. (AV)

1650 International Center Building, 900 Second Avenue South, 55402
Telephone: 612-339-4511; 800-328-4340
Fax: 612-339-5150
URL: http://hunegslaw.com

William H. DeParcq (1905-1988)
Richard Gene Hunegs
Robert N. Stone
Ralph E. Koenig
Randal W. LeNeave
Cortney S. LeNeave
William Kvas
Richard L. Carlson
Steven M. Hunegs
Kermit N. Fruechte

Reference: National City Bank of Minneapolis.

For full biographical listings, see the Martindale-Hubbell Law Directory

MESHBESHER & SPENCE (AV)

1616 Park Avenue, 55404
Telephone: 612-339-9121
Fax: 612-339-9188
URL: http://www.meshbesher.com
Woodbury, Minnesota Office: 8360 City Centre Drive, 55125.
Telephone: 651-578-8055.
St. Cloud, Minnesota Office: 510 Zapp Bank Plaza, 56301.
Telephone: 320-656-0484.
Rochester, Minnesota Office: 21 SW 2nd Street, 55902.
Telephone: 507-280-8090.
Maplewood, Minnesota Office: 2603 White Bear Avenue, 55109.
Telephone: 651-777-5858.
St. Louis Park, Minnesota Office: 9950 Wayzata Boulevard, 55426.
Telephone: 612-544-5959.

MEMBERS OF FIRM

Kenneth Meshbesher
Ronald I. Meshbesher
Russell M. Spence (Resident, Woodbury Office)
John P. Clifford
Dennis R. Johnson
Patrick K. Horan
Michael C. Snyder
John P. Sheehy
Mark D. Streed
Randall Spence
Katherine S. Flom
Jeffrey P. Oistad (Resident, St. Cloud Office)
Anthony J. Nemo
Colleen M. Christianson
Paul Dahlberg (Resident, Rochester Office)

For full biographical listings, see the Martindale-Hubbell Law Directory

SIEBEN, GROSE, VON HOLTUM & CAREY, LTD. (AV)

900 Midwest Plaza East, 800 Marquette Avenue, 55402
Telephone: 612-333-4500
Fax: 612-333-5970
URL: http://www.know-your-rights.com
Fairfax, Minnesota Office: 117 South Park Street.
Telephone: 507-426-8211.
Fax: 507-426-8213.
Duluth, Minnesota Office: 612 U.S. Bank Place, 130 Superior Street West.
Telephone: 218-722-6848. Toll Free (Minnesota): 800-422-0612.
Fax: 218-722-6841.
Lakeville, Minnesota Office: Southfork Office Centre, Suite 105, 17645 Juniper Path, 55044.
Telephone: 612-898-1894.
Fax: 612-898-4147.

Harry A. Sieben, Jr.
John W. Carey
James P. Carey
William O. Bongard
Arthur C. Kosieradzki
Susan M. Holden

Steven D. Emmings
Paul F. Schweiger (Resident, Duluth Office)
Judy L. Emmings
Robert W. Schaumann

For full biographical listings, see the Martindale-Hubbell Law Directory

*ROCHESTER,** Olmsted Co.

GEORGE F. RESTOVICH & ASSOCIATES (AV)

117 East Center Street, 55904
Telephone: 507-288-4840
Fax: 507-288-4908
Email: gfrlaw@infonet.isl.net

ASSOCIATES

Bruce K. Piotrowski
Richard W. Kimlinger
Gary A. Gittus

For full biographical listings, see the Martindale-Hubbell Law Directory

*ST. PAUL,** Ramsey Co.

R. A. AWSUMB & ASSOCIATES, PLC (AV)

1525 Landmark Towers, 345 Saint Peter Street, 55102
Telephone: 651-225-9255
Fax: 651-848-0011
Toll Free: 1-888-225-9566
Email: raawsumb@medrate.com

Robert A. Awsumb

For full biographical listings, see the Martindale-Hubbell Law Directory

COLLINS, BUCKLEY, SAUNTRY AND HAUGH, P.L.L.P. (AV)

West 1100 First National Bank Building, 332 Minnesota Street, 55101
Telephone: 651-227-0611
Telecopier: 651-227-0758
Email: info@cbsh.net *URL:* http://www.cbsh.net

MEMBERS OF FIRM

Eugene D. Buckley (Retired)
Michael J. Sauntry
William E. Haugh, Jr.
Mark W. Gehan, Jr.
Patrick T. Tierney
Thomas J. Germscheid
John R. Schulz
Thomas R. O'Connell
Dan C. O'Connell
Christine L. Stroemer
Thomas E. McEllistrem

OF COUNSEL

Theodore J. Collins

For Complete List of Firm Personnel, See General Section

For full biographical listings, see the Martindale-Hubbell Law Directory

MCCULLOUGH, SMITH, WRIGHT & KEMPE, P.A. (AV)

Maple Hills Office Center, 905 Parkway Drive, 55106
Telephone: 612-772-3446
Fax: 612-772-2177

D. Patrick McCullough
Jeffrey M. Smith

For full biographical listings, see the Martindale-Hubbell Law Directory

*WILLMAR,** Kandiyohi Co.

SCHNEIDER LAW FIRM (AV)

706 South First Street, P.O. Box 776, 56201
Telephone: 320-235-1902
WATS: 800-242-1902
Fax: 320-235-3611
Email: JSJSJamin@aol.com
St. Cloud, Minnesota Office: 925 South First Street, 56302.
Telephone: 320-253-2007.

Ronald H. Schneider (P.A.)

David W. Schneider
Steven C. Wang

Reference: US Bank Willmar.

For full biographical listings, see the Martindale-Hubbell Law Directory

*WINONA,** Winona Co.

STREATER & MURPHY, P.A. (AV)

64 East Fourth Street, 55987-0310
Telephone: 507-454-2925
Fax: 507-454-2929
Email: kentg@luminet.net

John Borman

Representative Clients: Winona Banc Holding Co.; Winona National and Savings Bank; Town & Country State Bank; Winona Daily News; Winona School District; Badger Construction Equipment Co.; Winona General Hospital Assn.; EMD Associates, Inc.; Fastenal Co.; Hiawatha Education Foundation.

For Complete List of Firm Personnel, See General Section

For full biographical listings, see the Martindale-Hubbell Law Directory

MISSISSIPPI

*BATESVILLE,** Panola Co.

SMITH, PHILLIPS, MITCHELL, SCOTT & RUTHERFORD (AV)

103 Bates Street, P.O. Drawer 1586, 38606
Telephone: 601-563-4613
Fax: 601-563-1546
URL: http://www.smithphillips.com
Hernando, Mississippi Office: 2545 Caffey Street.
Telephone: 601-429-5041.

MEMBERS OF FIRM

D. Briggs Smith, Jr.
Richard T. Phillips
Colmon S. Mitchell
Paul R. Scott
Leigh A. Rutherford
Wallace A. Welshans, III
Rebecca S. Thompson
David L. Calder

Robert R. Morris, III

References: First Security Bank; United Planters Bank; Bank of Mississippi.

For full biographical listings, see the Martindale-Hubbell Law Directory

BILOXI, Harrison Co.

JUDY M. GUICE A PROFESSIONAL ASSOCIATION (AV)

750 Dr. Martin Luther King Jr. Boulevard, P.O. Box 1919, 39533
Telephone: 228-374-9787
Fax: 228-374-9436
Email: judy@judyguice.com *URL:* http://www.judyguice.com

Judy Guice

For full biographical listings, see the Martindale-Hubbell Law Directory

MINOR AND ASSOCIATES (AV)

A Partnership including a Professional Association
160 Main Street, Drawer 1388, 39533-1388
Telephone: 228-374-5151
Fax: 228-374-6630
Email: pminoratty@aol.com

Paul S. Minor (P.A.)

Mark D. Lumpkin
James R. Reeves, Jr.
Christopher C. VanCleave

For full biographical listings, see the Martindale-Hubbell Law Directory

PAGE, MANNINO, PERESICH & McDERMOTT (AV)

A Professional Limited Liability Company
759 Vieux Marché Mall, P.O. Drawer 289, 39533
Telephone: 228-374-2100
Facsimile: 228-432-5539
Email: pmp@pmp.org

MEMBERS OF FIRM

Lyle M. Page (Resident)
Frederick J. Mannino (Resident)
Ronald G. Peresich (Resident)
Stephen G. Peresich (Resident)
Michael B. McDermott (Resident)
Tere Richardson Steel (Resident)
Michael E. Whitehead (Resident)
Mary Alexander Nichols (Resident)
David M. Allen (Resident)

ASSOCIATES

Henry N. Dick, III
Les W. Smith (Resident)
Emilie Whitehead
Kaara L. Liskow
Joel L. Blackledge

Representative Clients: United States Fidelity & Guaranty Co.; St. Paul Fire & Marine Insurance Co.; Crawford & Co.; Anheuser-Busch Corp.
General Counsel for: Peoples Bank of Biloxi, Mississippi; Biloxi Regional Medical Center; Bank of Mississippi (Gulf Coast Division).

For full biographical listings, see the Martindale-Hubbell Law Directory

*BROOKHAVEN,** Lincoln Co.

ALLEN, ALLEN, BOERNER & BREELAND (AV)

214 Justice Street, P.O. Box 751, 39602-0751
Telephone: 601-833-4361
Fax: 601-833-6647
Email: aabblaw@tislink.com

Emmette P. Allen (1915-1999)
Robert O. Allen
William D. Boerner
Durwood J. Breeland

ASSOCIATE

Sally Burchfield Doty

For full biographical listings, see the Martindale-Hubbell Law Directory

*CLARKSDALE,** Coahoma Co.

CHAPMAN, LEWIS & SWAN (AV)

501 First Street, P.O. Box 428, 38614
Telephone: 601-627-4105
FAX: 601-627-4171
Email: cls@gminet *URL:* http://www.lawyers.com/clslaw

Ralph E. Chapman
Richard B. Lewis
Dana J. Swan

ASSOCIATE

Sherry S. Fernandez

For full biographical listings, see the Martindale-Hubbell Law Directory

*GULFPORT,** Harrison Co.

ALLEN, VAUGHN, COBB & HOOD, P.A. (AV)

One Hancock Plaza, Suite 1209, P.O. Drawer 4108, 39502-4108
Telephone: 601-864-4011
Fax: 601-864-4852
Email: avchlaw@sunherald.infinet.com

Harry R. Allen
Thomas E. Vaughn
David L. Cobb
Billy W. Hood
Joy Lambert Phillips
Robert W. Atkinson
Benjamin U. Bowden
Richard B. Tubertini
Rodney Douglas Robinson
E. Colette Towles
David W. Crane
John A. Foxworth, Jr.

J. Adrian Smith
Michael J. Casano

OF COUNSEL

D. Knox White

LEGAL SUPPORT PERSONNEL

Kevin C. Stachowski (Paralegal)

For full biographical listings, see the Martindale-Hubbell Law Directory

DUKES, DUKES, KEATING AND FANECA, P.A. (AV)

2909 13th Street, 6th Floor, P.O. Drawer W, 39501
Telephone: 228-868-1111
Fax: 228-863-2886
Email: ddkf@ddkf.com

William F. Dukes
Walter W. Dukes
Hugh D. Keating
Cy Faneca
Phillip W. Jarrell

Joan E. Lund
W. Edward Hatten, Jr.
Thomas William Busby
William W. Abbott, Jr.
Trace D. McRaney
Stephen M. Cozart
Derek R. Cusick

For full biographical listings, see the Martindale-Hubbell Law Directory

BOYCE HOLLEMAN A PROFESSIONAL CORPORATION (AV)

1913 15th Street, P.O. Drawer 1030, 39502
Telephone: 228-863-3142; 1-800-863-3140
Telecopier: 228-863-9829
Email: boyce1913@aol.com

Boyce Holleman

Timothy C. Holleman
Leslie Dean Holleman
David J. "Jeff" White

References: Hancock Bank, Gulfport; Merchants Bank & Trust Co., Gulfport; Bank of Wiggins, Wiggins, Mississippi.

For full biographical listings, see the Martindale-Hubbell Law Directory

HOPKINS, CRAWLEY, BAGWELL & UPSHAW, P.L.L.C. (AV)

2701 24th Avenue, P.O. Box 1510, 39501-4941
Telephone: 228-864-2200
Mississippi and USA Wats: 1-800-421-3629
Fax: 228-868-9358; 228-863-4227
Email: Hopkins@MSLawyer.com
Jackson, Mississippi Office: 499 South President Street, Second Floor, Suite 1.
Telephone: 601-355-6510.
Fax: 601-355-6503. Email: TCrawley@MSLawyer.com.

MEMBERS OF FIRM

Alben N. Hopkins
Timothy D. Crawley
Douglas Bagwell
Jessica Sibley Upshaw
Thomas Alan Waller

ASSOCIATES

Raymond D. Carter
Kenneth S. Womack
Mary Benton-Shaw
Pat Sharkey Burke, Jr.
David E. Wilson
Laura Faye Paulk
Ronald C. Small (Not admitted in MS)

(See Next Column)

HOPKINS, CRAWLEY, BAGWELL & UPSHAW P.L.L.C., *Gulfport—Continued*

Representative Clients: Coregis Group; General Cable Corp.; Insurance Company of North America; Liberty Mutual Insurance Group; Reliance Insurance Co.; USX Corp.; Employers Insurance of Wausau; American International Group (AIG); Quaker Chemical Corp.

For full biographical listings, see the Martindale-Hubbell Law Directory

OWEN & GALLOWAY (AV)

Markham Building, 2301 14th Street, 39502
Telephone: 601-868-2821
Telecopier: 601-864-6421
Email: ogc@digiscape.com

MEMBERS OF FIRM

Joe Sam Owen
Ben F. Galloway, III

Robert P. Myers, Jr.
Steven J. Irwin

References: Merchants Bank & Trust Co.; Hancock Bank.

For full biographical listings, see the Martindale-Hubbell Law Directory

PERRY & MURR (AV)

2409 14th Street, P.O. Box 359, 39502
Telephone: 228-863-0092
Fax: 228-865-9657

MEMBERS OF FIRM

Lee N. Perry
Timothy L. Murr
George E. Morse
Owen T. Palmer, Jr. (1920-1999)

Approved Attorneys for: Mississippi Valley Title Insurance Co.; First American Title Insurance Co.

For full biographical listings, see the Martindale-Hubbell Law Directory

*JACKSON,** Hinds Co.

SULLIVAN AND SULLIVAN (AV)

Suite 200, 5448 I-55 North, 39211
Telephone: 601-952-0799
Facsimile: 601-952-0599;
Cable Address: "Sullaw"

MEMBERS OF FIRM

John C. Sullivan, Sr. (1910-1993)
John C. Sullivan, Jr.

ASSOCIATE

Patricia Alexander Killgore

For full biographical listings, see the Martindale-Hubbell Law Directory

WATKINS & EAGER (AV)

A Professional Limited Liability Company
Suite 300 The Emporium Building, 400 East Capitol Street, P.O. Box 650, 39205
Telephone: 601-948-6470
Facsimile: 601-354-3623

MEMBERS OF FIRM

James A. Becker, Jr.
Michael W. Ulmer
David L. Ayers
Lewis W. Bell
Susan Latham Steffey
Lynn Plimpton Risley

Representative Clients: Bayer Corp.; Caterpillar Inc.; Mazda (North America), Inc.; Goodyear Tire & Rubber; R.J. Reynolds Tobacco Co.; Toyota Motor Sales, U.S.A., Inc.; Sturm Ruger & Co.; Nissan North America, Inc.; Bristol Myers Squibb Co.; New Holland North American, Inc.

For Complete List of Firm Personnel, See General Section

For full biographical listings, see the Martindale-Hubbell Law Directory

*LAUREL,** Jones Co.

MELVIN & MELVIN (AV)

Sawmill Road, P.O. Box 142, 39441-0142
Telephone: 601-426-6306; 426-6307
Telecopier: 601-649-7571

MEMBERS OF FIRM

Leonard B. Melvin (1896-1972)
Leonard B. Melvin, Jr.

For full biographical listings, see the Martindale-Hubbell Law Directory

MADISON, Madison Co.

BELL & ASSOCIATES, P.A. (AV)

967 Madison Avenue, 39110
Telephone: 601-898-1111
Toll Free: 1-888-898-1600
Fax: 601-898-1102
Mailing Address: P.O. Box 890, Madison, Mississippi, 39130-0890
Email: JamesDBell@aol.com *URL:* http://www.lawyers.com/bell&associates

(See Next Column)

James D. Bell

Eduardo Alberto Flechas

For full biographical listings, see the Martindale-Hubbell Law Directory

*MERIDIAN,** Lauderdale Co.

HAMILTON & LINDER (AV)

2713 Seventh Street, P.O. Box 1511, 39302-1511
Telephone: 601-693-5548
Fax: 601-693-2949
URL: http://www.lawyers.com/handllaw

MEMBERS OF FIRM

Joe Clay Hamilton
David H. Linder

ASSOCIATES

Will Parker
G. Richard Baker

For full biographical listings, see the Martindale-Hubbell Law Directory

*NATCHEZ,** Adams Co.

MULHEARN & MULHEARN (AV)

202 South Wall Street, P.O. Box 967, 39120
Telephone: 601-442-4808
Fax: 601-446-6224
Email: woodland@bkbank.com *URL:* http:/www.lawyers.com/mulhearnlaw

MEMBERS OF FIRM

John E. Mulhearn (1910-1981)
John E. Mulhearn, Jr.

LEGAL SUPPORT PERSONNEL

Eva Ruth Seale
Judith A. Strickland

Representative Clients: Ashland Plantation; Exxon Corporation; Belle Oil, Inc.; Supermarket Operations, Inc.; Petron, Inc.; Concordia Bank & Trust Co.; Dunleith; J.M. Jones Lumber Co., Inc.; Southwest Mississippi Anesthesia P.A.; Paradise Foods, Inc.

For full biographical listings, see the Martindale-Hubbell Law Directory

OCEAN SPRINGS, Jackson Co.

DENHAM & KING, PLLC (AV)

424 Washington Avenue, P.O. Box P.O.Drawer 580, 39566-0580
Telephone: 228-875-1234
Fax: 228-875-4553
URL: http://www.lawyers.com/denham&king

Earl Lamar Denham
Ralph Preston King, II
Olen L. Anderson
Ben L. Saucier

Wendy Hollingsworth

LEGAL SUPPORT PERSONNEL

Karen Kosztur (Paralegal)
Connie Bradley (Paralegal)

For full biographical listings, see the Martindale-Hubbell Law Directory

*OXFORD,** Lafayette Co.

TOLLISON LAW FIRM, P.A. (AV)

100 Courthouse Square, P.O. Box 1216, 38655
Telephone: Telephone: 601-234-7070
Fax: 601-234-7095
Email: tollison@watervalley.net

Grady F. Tollison, Jr.
Nina Stubblefield Tollison
William K. Duke
Gray Tollison
E. Farish Percy
Barbara Miller Dollarhide
J. Rhea Tannehill, Jr.

OF COUNSEL

Edward J. Bogen, Jr.

References: Merchants & Farmers Bank; Pike County National Bank.

For full biographical listings, see the Martindale-Hubbell Law Directory

*PASCAGOULA,** Jackson Co.

COLINGO, WILLIAMS, HEIDELBERG, STEINBERGER & MCELHANEY, P.A. (AV)

711 Delmas Avenue, P.O. Box 1407, 39568-1407
Telephone: 228-762-8021
FAX: 228-762-7589
Email: info@colingowilliams.com *URL:* http://www.ColingoWilliams.com

Joe R. Colingo
James H. Heidelberg
James H. Colmer, Jr.

Representative Clients: International Paper Co.; R.J. Reynolds; CBS Corp.; Kemper Group; Singing River Hospital System; Mississippi Gulf Coast Regional Wastewater Authority; Medical Assurance Company of Mississippi; Mutual Assurance of Alabama; Dole Food Co.

(See Next Column)

COLINGO, WILLIAMS, HEIDELBERG, STEINBERGER & MCELHANEY P.A.—*Continued*

For full biographical listings, see the Martindale-Hubbell Law Directory

OSWALD AND REED (AV)

Markland Building, 3106 Canty Street, P.O. Box 1428, 39568-1428
Telephone: 228-769-1027
Telecopier: 228-769-9019

Robert H. Oswald
William Townsend Reed

For full biographical listings, see the Martindale-Hubbell Law Directory

ROBERT A. PRITCHARD (AV)

934 Jackson Avenue, P.O. Drawer 1707, 39567-1707
Telephone: 228-769-2211; 1-800-340-2240
Fax: 228-762-6005
Email: rap@datasyc.com
Harriston, Mississippi Office: General, Asb/Sil. 100 Old Harriston Road.
Telephone: 601-786-6200; 888-786-6200.
Fax: 601-786-6211.

ASSOCIATE

Christopher E. Fitzgerald

For full biographical listings, see the Martindale-Hubbell Law Directory

*POPLARVILLE,** Pearl River Co.

WILLIAMS, WILLIAMS AND MONTGOMERY, P.A. (AV)

109 Erlanger Street, P.O. Box 113, 39470
Telephone: 601-795-4572
Fax: 601-795-8382

E. B. Williams (1890-1976)
E. B. Williams, Jr. (1917-1990)
Lampton O'Neal Williams
Joseph H. Montgomery
E. Bragg Williams, III
L. O'Neal Williams, Jr.

Michael E. Patten
Anne M. Parker

Representative Clients: Hancock Bank, Bank of Commerce Branch; Lumberton Linne School District; Garrett Industries, Inc.; Bass Pecan Co., Lumberton, Miss.; Joe N. Miles & Sons Lumber Co., Inc., Lumberton and Silver Creek, Miss. and Bogalusa, La.
Reference: Hancock Bank, Bank of Commerce Branch, Poplarville, Mississippi.

For full biographical listings, see the Martindale-Hubbell Law Directory

MISSOURI

*COLUMBIA,** Boone Co.

RICHARD C. THOMAS (AV)

609 East Broadway, 65201
Telephone: 573-442-3000
Fax: 573-449-1094

References: Boone County National Bank; Mercantile Bank.

For full biographical listings, see the Martindale-Hubbell Law Directory

GLADSTONE, Clay Co.

LAW OFFICES OF G. SPENCER MILLER, L.L.C. (AV)

207 N.E. 72nd Street Suite A, 64118
Telephone: 816-468-1010
Fax: 816-468-1112
URL: http://www.lawyers.com/gmillerlaw

MEMBER OF FIRM

G. Spencer Miller

ASSOCIATES

Christopher L. Heigele
Tracy B. Weiner

LEGAL SUPPORT PERSONNEL

Maureen Lobdell, Legal Administrator

For full biographical listings, see the Martindale-Hubbell Law Directory

*INDEPENDENCE,** Jackson Co.

WHITE, ALLINDER & GRAHAM, L.L.C. (AV)

Hidden Creek Office Park, 14801 East 42nd Street, 64055
Telephone: 816-373-9080
Fax: 816-373-9319

MEMBERS OF FIRM

Steven W. White
John K. Allinder
Gene P. Graham, Jr.

(See Next Column)

ASSOCIATE

Mary Beth Clune

For full biographical listings, see the Martindale-Hubbell Law Directory

*JEFFERSON CITY,** Cole Co.

CARSON & COIL, P.C. (AV)

515 East High, P.O. Box 28, 65102
Telephone: 573-636-2177
Telecopier: 573-636-7119
Email: general@carsoncoil.com

Forrest P. Carson (1910-1981)
Cullen Coil (1907-1989)
Michael P. Riley
Ronald R. McMillin
Eugene G. Bushmann
James W. Gallaher
Lori J. Levine
Rudolph L. Veit
Michael Madsen
R. Max Humphreys
Mark A. Ludwig
Dana L. Frese
Edward C. Clausen
Carla G. Holste
Kent L. Brown
Douglas W. Hennon
Charles J. McPheeters
Paul T. Graham

Charles A. "Chip" Gentry
James W. "Jamie" Gallaher, Jr.

General Counsel for: Capital Reserve Life Insurance Co.; Missouri Farm Bureau; Healthcare Services Group.
Reference: Central Trust Bank.

For full biographical listings, see the Martindale-Hubbell Law Directory

JOPLIN, Jasper Co.

HERSHEWE & GULICK, P.C. (AV)

431 Virginia, 64801-2399
Telephone: 417-782-3790
Fax: 417-782-8482

Edward J. Hershewe
Glenn R. Gulick, Jr.

Alison R. Bunch
William Scott Gallagher
Roger A. Johnson

References: First State Bank of Joplin; Commerce Bank of Joplin.

For full biographical listings, see the Martindale-Hubbell Law Directory

KANSAS CITY, Jackson, Clay, Platte & Cass Cos.

BARTIMUS, FRICKLETON & PRESLEY, A PROFESSIONAL CORPORATION (AV)

23rd Floor City Center Square, 1100 Main Street, 64196
Telephone: 816-842-2300
Fax: 816-421-2111
Email: bfplaw@bfplaw.com *URL:* http://www.bfplaw.com
Jefferson City, Missouri Office: 122 East High, Suite 200, 65101.
Telephone: 573-659-4454.

James R. Bartimus
James P. Frickleton
Kirk R. Presley
Peter S. Obetz

Stephen M. Gorny
Christopher A. Wright

OF COUNSEL

Edward D. Robertson, Jr. (Resident, Jefferson City Office)
Julie C. Frickleton

LEGAL SUPPORT PERSONNEL

LEGAL ASSISTANTS

Tammy J. Gilliams
Laura M. Burbach
Patricia E. Cook
Martha C. Fann

For full biographical listings, see the Martindale-Hubbell Law Directory

FRANKE & SCHULTZ, A PROFESSIONAL CORPORATION (AV)

1312 Commerce Tower, 911 Main Street, 64105
Telephone: 816-421-7100
Telecopier: 816-421-7915
Email: Franke.Schultz@Micro.com
Springfield, Missouri Office: 300 John Q. Hammons Pkwy., Suite 701, 65806.
Telephone: 417-863-0040.
Fax: 417-863-6286.
Overland Park, Kansas Office: 5340 College, 66211.
Telephone: 913-327-7661.
Fax: 913-327-7669.

John E. Franke
John G. Schultz
John L. Mullen
Bradley C. Nielsen
Ryan E. Karaim
Jill Frost
Keith A. Cary
Wendell E. Koerner, Jr.

(See Next Column)

FRANKE & SCHULTZ A PROFESSIONAL CORPORATION, *Kansas City—Continued*

Cari F. Walsh — Laurel Stevenson
Michael J. Tubbesing — Shawn G. Foster
Andrew D. Hennier — John H. Kizer
Edward J. Barbosa

For full biographical listings, see the Martindale-Hubbell Law Directory

REDFEARN & BROWN, A PROFESSIONAL CORPORATION (AV)

Suite 814, 1125 Grand Boulevard, 64106
Telephone: 816-421-5301
FAX: 816-421-3785
Stockton Office: 12 Public Square, P.O. BOX 299.
Telephone: 417-276-6250.

Paul L. Redfearn — Daniel R. Brown

OF COUNSEL

Michael D. Holzknecht, P.C.

LEGAL SUPPORT PERSONNEL

Denise J. Davis (Senior Legal Assistant)

For full biographical listings, see the Martindale-Hubbell Law Directory

STITES, HOPKINS & FAIR (AV)

A Partnership including Professional Corporations and Associations
1101 Walnut, Suite 1400, 64106-2215
Telephone: 816-842-8889
Fax: 816-842-3088
1-800-899-8874

Ronald J. Stites (P.C.) — William C. Hopkins, II

Diane L. Fair — Carol A. Lindgren-Bron

OF COUNSEL

Sandra C. Midkiff — Elizabeth Diane Baker
John B. Meyer

For full biographical listings, see the Martindale-Hubbell Law Directory

ARTHUR H. STOUP & ASSOCIATES, P.C. (AV)

1710 Mercantile Tower, 1101 Walnut Street, 64106
Telephone: 816-474-0707; 417-887-3600
Fax: 816-474-0714; 417-887-3600
Email: Stoup@msn.com
Springfield, Missouri Office: 1949 East Sunshine, Suite 1-108.
Telephone: 417-887-3600.

Arthur H. Stoup

Stephen W. Nichols

For full biographical listings, see the Martindale-Hubbell Law Directory

RAYMORE, Cass Co.

HENSLEY & HENSLEY (AV)

401 West 58 Highway, P.O. Box 620, 64083
Telephone: 816-322-4466
Email: hensley8.@worldnet.att.net

MEMBERS OF FIRM

Kenneth C. Hensley — Teresa Hensley

Representative Clients: Farmers Bank of Northern Missouri; Corporate Dental Care, Inc.; Cole & Myers Oil Co.

For full biographical listings, see the Martindale-Hubbell Law Directory

*ST. CHARLES,** St. Charles Co.

KELL & FLACH (AV)

A Partnership of Professional Corporations
1148 South Benton, 63301-2430
Telephone: 636-949-8111
Fax: 636-949-8880
Email: kellflach@aol.com *URL:* http://www.lawyers.com/bodilyinjurylaw.com

John Mark Kell — Thomas M. Flach

For full biographical listings, see the Martindale-Hubbell Law Directory

ST. LOUIS, (Independent City)

ABELE & SANDERSON, L.L.C. (AV)

Suite 1024, 1015 Locust, 63101-1323
Telephone: 314-241-3123; 1-800-886-3123
Fax: 314-241-4361
Email: abelesand@aol.com *URL:* http://www.lawyers.com/abele&sanderson

(See Next Column)

Charles R. Abele — M. Melinda Sanderson

For full biographical listings, see the Martindale-Hubbell Law Directory

BRASHER LAW FIRM, L.C. (AV)

One Metropolitan Square, 211 North Broadway, Suite 2300, 63102
Telephone: 314-621-7700
Telecopier: 314-621-1088
Email: BRASHERLAW@AOL.COM

William A. Brasher — Patricia Daly Brasher
Thomas J. Prebil — Terry (Mary Therese) Buescher
Richard F. Nash — Peter J. Barkofske
Gerard F. Hempstead — Gary K. Burger, Jr.
Paul R. Ferber — Paul E. Petruska
Paul E. Littleton — Paul T. Slocomb

OF COUNSEL

Richard L. Daly

Representative Clients: Burlington Northern and Santa Fe Railway Company; Burlington Motor Carriers; Canadian National Ry. Co.; CSX Transportation, Inc.; Fidelity and Deposit Company of Maryland; Frozen Food Express Industries, Inc.; Norfolk Southern Corporation; Rollins, Inc.; Terminal Railroad Association of St. Louis; Triple Crown Services, Inc.

For full biographical listings, see the Martindale-Hubbell Law Directory

LAW OFFICES THOMAS M. BURKE, P.C. (AV)

Gateway One Building, 701 Market Street, Suite 1075, 63101
Telephone: 314-241-8200
Telecopier: 314-241-5890

Thomas M. Burke

Scott L. Kolker

For full biographical listings, see the Martindale-Hubbell Law Directory

CERVANTES & ASSOCIATES (AV)

1007 Olive, Fourth Floor, 63101
Telephone: 314-621-6558
Fax: 314-621-6705

Leonard P. Cervantes

ASSOCIATES

Francisco J. Carretero — Phillip A. Cervantes

For full biographical listings, see the Martindale-Hubbell Law Directory

COFFEY & GRIESBACH (AV)

6202 Columbia Avenue, 63139
Telephone: 314-647-0033
Fax: 314-647-8231
Email: candg@I1.net *URL:* http://www.lawyers.com/c&g

Mary Coffey — Toni Griesbach

For full biographical listings, see the Martindale-Hubbell Law Directory

DANIEL P. FINNEY, JR. (AV)

1015 Locust Street, Suite 820, 63101
Telephone: 314-436-0600
Fax: 314-436-6992
Email: DPF@aol.com *URL:* http://www.lawyers.com/finneylaw

For full biographical listings, see the Martindale-Hubbell Law Directory

THE FLOYD LAW FIRM, P.C. (AV)

8151 Clayton Road #202, 63117-1103
Telephone: 314-863-4114
Telecopier: 314-863-4150
URL: http://www.lawyers.com/injurylaw

Walter L. Floyd — Mark L. Floyd
Richard Mixson

For full biographical listings, see the Martindale-Hubbell Law Directory

THE FRANK LAW FIRM, L.L.P. (AV)

Suite 1500 Equitable Building, 10 South Broadway, 63102
Telephone: 314-421-2811
Fax: 314-421-3121

John J. Frank — Joseph A. Frank

ASSOCIATES

Jennifer J. Finley — David T. Dolan
Theodore G. Pashos — Gregory T. Mueller

For full biographical listings, see the Martindale-Hubbell Law Directory

St. Louis—Continued

Greenberg & Pleban (AV)

100 South Fourth Street, Suite 600, 63102
Telephone: 314-241-4141
Telecopier: 314-241-1038

Burton M. Greenberg
C. John Pleban

ASSOCIATES

Karen A. Greenberg
Michael J. Schaller
Richard P. Hereford

OF COUNSEL

Sarah Shelledy Pleban

Reference: Boatmen's National Bank.

For full biographical listings, see the Martindale-Hubbell Law Directory

Growe & Buchholz (AV)

Suite 410, 230 South Bemiston (Clayton), 63105
Telephone: 314-863-7033
Fax: 314-863-7521
URL: http://www.lawyers.com/growbuc

Gary A. Growe
William G. Buchholz, II

For full biographical listings, see the Martindale-Hubbell Law Directory

The Holloran Law Firm, P.C. (AV)

906 Olive Street, Suite 1200, 63101
Telephone: 314-621-2121
FAX: 314-621-8512

James P. Holloran
Thomas Lee Stewart
Jan Adams
Andrew A. O'Brien
Thomas E. Schwartz

COUNSEL

Charles V. Marshall

For full biographical listings, see the Martindale-Hubbell Law Directory

Hullverson & Hullverson, L.L.C. (AV)

7777 Bonhomme Avenue, Suite 1616 (Clayton), 63105
Telephone: 314-725-1616
Fax: 314-212-5601
Email: jrgr8db8@aol.com

James E. Hullverson, Jr.
James E. Hullverson

For full biographical listings, see the Martindale-Hubbell Law Directory

The Hullverson Law Firm (AV)

Suite 1550, 1010 Market Street, 63101-2091
Telephone: 314-421-2313
Fax: 314-421-2341
URL: http://www.hullverson.com

Everett Hullverson (1897-1975)
Thomas C. Hullverson
Stephen H. Ringkamp
Philip C. Denton
Spencer E. Farris
Mark J. Becker
John E. Hullverson
Theresa A. Appelbaum

For full biographical listings, see the Martindale-Hubbell Law Directory

McGlynn & McGlynn (AV Ⓣ)

222 South Central, Suite 1101, 63105
Telephone: 314-727-1000
Fax: 314-862-4484

Joseph B. McGlynn, Jr.
Maureen A. McGlynn

For full biographical listings, see the Martindale-Hubbell Law Directory

David J. Rauscher, P.C. (AV)

8112 Maryland Avenue Suite 205, 63105-3700
Telephone: 314-721-2220
Fax: 314-721-2746
Email: rauscherdj@aol.com *URL:* http://www.attorneyfind.com/homepage/rauscher.html

David J. Rauscher

Kathleen L. Rauscher

For full biographical listings, see the Martindale-Hubbell Law Directory

Donald L. Schlapprizzi, P.C. (AV)

Gateway One on The Mall, 701 Market Street, Suite 1550, 63101
Telephone: 314-241-0763
Fax: 314-241-0787
Email: dschlapprizzi@compuserve.com

Donald L. Schlapprizzi

(See Next Column)

Patricia Lynne Brownlee
Michael R. Swafford

OF COUNSEL

Albert Lebowitz

For full biographical listings, see the Martindale-Hubbell Law Directory

Schlichter, Bogard & Denton (AV)

Suite 900, 100 South Fourth Street, 63102
Telephone: 314-621-6115
Fax: 314-621-7151
Swansea, Illinois Office: 2661 N. Illinois, Suite 187, 62226.
Telephone: 618-632-3329.

MEMBERS OF FIRM

Jerome J. Schlichter
Robert S. Bogard
Roger C. Denton
Steven L. Groves

ASSOCIATES

Nannette A. Baker
Nelson G. Wolff
Jay B. White

For full biographical listings, see the Martindale-Hubbell Law Directory

Sindel & Sindel, P.C. (AV)

Suite 301, 8008 Carondelet, 63105
Telephone: 314-721-6040
Telecopier: 314-721-8545
Email: CSindel@sindellaw.cnchost.com *URL:* http://www.sindellaw.com

Charles D. Sindel

For full biographical listings, see the Martindale-Hubbell Law Directory

*SPRINGFIELD,** Greene Co.

Harrison, Tucker & Hyde, LLP (AV)

1121 South Glenstone, 65804
Telephone: 417-831-4046
Fax: 417-831-4989
Email: 100576.2300@compuserve.com

MEMBERS OF FIRM

Jeffrey H. Harrison
James D. Tucker
Kent O. Hyde
William C. Love
Brian E. Hamburg
Aaron P. Lyons

For full biographical listings, see the Martindale-Hubbell Law Directory

The Strong Law Firm A Professional Corporation (AV)

901 East Battlefield, 65807
Telephone: 417-887-4300
Fax: 417-887-4385
Email: slf@stronglaw.com *URL:* http://www.stronglaw.com

Thomas Strong
Steve Garner
Steven D. Harrell
James A. Burt
Clifton M. Smart, III
A. Allan Gordus, Jr.
Neil Chanter

Michael L. Johnson

For full biographical listings, see the Martindale-Hubbell Law Directory

Taylor, Stafford, Woody, Clithero & Fitzgerald, LLP (AV)

Ridgeview Business Center, 3315 East Ridgeview, Suite 1000, 65804
Telephone: 417-887-2020; 800-749-0004
Facsimile: 417-887-8431
Email: taylorstafford@atlascomm.net

MEMBERS OF FIRM

O. J. Taylor
Warren S. Stafford
Donald E. Woody
Monte P. Clithero
Kevin M. FitzGerald
Warren E. Harris

For full biographical listings, see the Martindale-Hubbell Law Directory

MONTANA

*BILLINGS,** Yellowstone Co.

CROWLEY, HAUGHEY, HANSON, TOOLE & DIETRICH, P.L.L.P. (AV)
500 Transwestern II, 490 North 31st Street, P.O. Box 2529, 59103
Telephone: 406-252-3441
Fax: 406-259-4159
Email: crowley@crowleylaw.com
Helena, Montana Office: IBM Building, 100 North Park Avenue, Suite 300, 59601.
Telephone: 406-449-4165.
Fax: 406-449-5149.
Kalispell, Montana Office: 431 1st Avenue West, 59901.
Telephone: 406-752-6644.
Fax: 406-752-5108.
Williston, North Dakota Office: 113 East Broadway, 58801.
Telephone: 701-572-2200.
Fax: 701-572-7072.

OF COUNSEL

Bruce R. Toole
Neil S. Keefer
George C. Dalthorp

MEMBERS OF FIRM

Herbert I. Pierce, III
Ronald R. Lodders
Lawrence B. Cozzens
Carolyn S. Ostby
Steven J. Lehman
Donald L. Harris
William J. Mattix
Peter F. Habein
Jon T. Dyre (Resident, Kalispell, Montana Office)
Bruce A. Fredrickson
Janice L. Rehberg
Joe C. Maynard, Jr.
Steven Robert Milch
Leonard H. Smith
Neil G. Westesen

Representative Clients: Crawford & Co.; Farmers Insurance Group; St. Paul Insurance Cos.; The Doctor's Co.; The Home Insurance Cos.; Montana State Compensation Insurance Fund.

For Complete List of Firm Personnel, See General Section

For full biographical listings, see the Martindale-Hubbell Law Directory

EDWARDS, TOLSTEDT & FRICKLE (AV)
1601 Lewis Avenue, Suite 206, P.O. Box 20039, 59104
Telephone: 406-256-8155
Fax: 406-256-8159
Toll Free: 1-800-556-8155
Email: edwardslaw@mcn.net

A. Clifford Edwards
Michael W. Tolstedt
Roger W. Frickle

Elizabeth A. Halverson
Roberta Anner-Hughes

For full biographical listings, see the Martindale-Hubbell Law Directory

*BOZEMAN,** Gallatin Co.

KIRWAN & BARRETT, P.C. (AV)
215 West Mendenhall, P.O. Box 1348, 59771-1348
Telephone: 406-586-1553
Fax: 406-586-8971

Peter M. Kirwan
Stephen M. Barrett

For full biographical listings, see the Martindale-Hubbell Law Directory

NEBRASKA

*LINCOLN,** Lancaster Co.

CLINE, WILLIAMS, WRIGHT, JOHNSON & OLDFATHER (AV)
1900 U.S. Bank Building, 233 South 13th Street, 68508
Telephone: 402-474-6900
Fax: 402-474-5393
Email: postmaster@cline-law.com *URL:* http://www.cline-law.com
Omaha, Nebraska Office: Suite 720, One Pacific Place, 1125 South 103rd Street, 68124.
Telephone: 402-397-1700.
Fax: 402-397-1806.

ATTORNEYS

Allen L. Graves
Charles M. Pallesen, Jr.
Fredric H. Kauffman
Donald F. Burt
Alan E. Peterson
Stephen E. Gehring
Robert J. Routh
Kevin Colleran
L. Bruce Wright
James M. Bausch
Larry A. Holle
David R. Buntain
Stephen H. Nelsen
Michael C. Mueller
Lauren W. Wismer
Daniel R. Stogsdill

(See Next Column)

ATTORNEYS (Continued)

Scott D. Kelly
Terry R. Wittler
Pamela Hastings Carrier
Mark A. Christensen
Richard P. Garden, Jr.
Shawn D. Renner
John C. Miles
Mary Kay Frank
Thomas C. Huston
Sonya S. Ekart
Don R. Janssen
Susan Kubert Sapp
Kevin J. Schneider
Andrew D. Strotman
Jill Gossin Jensen
Rochelle A. Mullen
John L. Horan
Bryan S. Hatch
Steven C. Likes
Tracy A. Oldemeyer
Jolene M. Papa
Timothy G. Aschoff
Eric N. Bergquist
Janis J. Winterhof
Andrea Dylan Snowden

OF COUNSEL

Charles E. Wright
Richard P. Jeffries
Mary M. Campbell

RETIRED PARTNERS

Flavel A. Wright (Retired)
Warren C. Johnson (Retired)
Charles E. Oldfather (1927-1998)

Representative Clients: U.S. Bank National Association; University of Nebraska; Nebraska Medical Assn.; Saint Elizabeth Regional Medical Center; Media of Nebraska; Cargill Inc.; State Farm Insurance Cos.; Wal-Mart Stores, Inc.; Textron/Cushman; Isco, Inc.

For full biographical listings, see the Martindale-Hubbell Law Directory

ERICKSON & SEDERSTROM, P.C. (AV)
Suite 400, Cornhusker Plaza, 301 South 13th Street, 68508
Telephone: 402-476-1000
Fax: 402-476-6167
Omaha, Nebraska Office: Regency Westpointe, 10330 Regency Parkway Drive, Suite 100, 68114-3761.
Telephone: 402-397-2200.
Fax: 402-390-7137.

Charles D. Humble
David C. Mussman

Representative Clients: Lincoln Electric System; Lincoln General Hospital; Nash Finch Co.; LinWeld, Inc.; Bryant Air Conditioning & Heating; Osco Drug; Citadel Communication; Douglas Theatres; Sioux City Foundry; American Honda.

For Complete List of Firm Personnel, See General Section

For full biographical listings, see the Martindale-Hubbell Law Directory

REHM LAW FIRM, A PROFESSIONAL CORPORATION (AV)
1327 "H" Street, Suite 200, 68508
Telephone: 402-474-2300
Fax: 402-474-4716
Email: RR33224@navix.net *URL:* http://www.rehmlawfirm.com

Rod Rehm

Todd D. Bennett
Daniel A. Fix

OF COUNSEL

William R. Hoppner

For full biographical listings, see the Martindale-Hubbell Law Directory

*OMAHA,** Douglas Co.

JAMES MARTIN DAVIS (AV)
Suite 500, Farnam Plaza, 1623 Farnam Street, 68102
Telephone: 402-341-9900
Fax: 402-341-8144

For full biographical listings, see the Martindale-Hubbell Law Directory

DOMINA LAW PC (AV)
1065 North 115th Street, 68154-4423
Telephone: 402-493-4100
Fax: 402-493-9782
Email: law@dominalaw.com

David A. Domina
Cletus W. Blakeman
Jerold V. Fennell

W. Craig Howell
Pamela J. Dahlquist
Nora M. Kane
James F. Cann

For full biographical listings, see the Martindale-Hubbell Law Directory

DWYER, SMITH, GARDNER, LAZER, POHREN, ROGERS & FORREST (AV)
Suite 400, 8712 West Dodge Road, 68114
Telephone: 402-392-0101
Telefax: 402-392-1011
Email: dwyerlaw@dwyer-smith.com *URL:* http://www.dwyer-smith.com

(See Next Column)

DWYER, SMITH, GARDNER, LAZER, POHREN, ROGERS & FORREST—*Continued*

MEMBERS OF FIRM

Michael L. Lazer
Bruce H. Abrahamson
H. Daniel Smith
Edward F. Pohren

ASSOCIATE

Patrick Edward Griffin, Jr.

For Complete List of Firm Personnel, See General Section

For full biographical listings, see the Martindale-Hubbell Law Directory

ERICKSON & SEDERSTROM, P.C. (AV)

Regency Westpointe, 10330 Regency Parkway Drive, Suite 100, 68114-3761
Telephone: 402-397-2200
Fax: 402-390-7137
Lincoln, Nebraska Office: Suite 400, Cornhusker Plaza, 301 South 13th Street, 68508-2571.
Telephone: 402-476-1000.
Fax: 402-476-6167.

Donald H. Erickson
Daniel D. Koukol
Wm. E. Morrow, Jr.
Soren S. Jensen
Daniel B. Kinnamon
Virgil K. Johnson
Charles V. Sederstrom, Jr.
Michael C. Washburn
John C. Brownrigg
Thomas J. Culhane
Richard J. Gilloon
Samuel Earle Clark
Gary L. Hoffman
J Russell Derr
Jerald L. Rauterkus
William T. Foley
David C. Mussman

Andrea M. Jahn
Kevin R. McManaman
Michelle B. Miller

OF COUNSEL

Lewis R. Leigh
Leo Eisenstatt
Roland J. Santoni

Representative Clients: Nebraska State Bank of Omaha; Berkshire Hathaway, Inc.; Bozell, Inc.; IBP, Inc. Quaker Oats Co.; United A-G Cooperative, Inc.; Immanuel Medical Center; Cornhusker Casualty Co.; Hartford Accident & Indemnity Co.; Mortgage Guaranty Insurance Corp. (MGIC).

For Complete List of Firm Personnel, See General Section

For full biographical listings, see the Martindale-Hubbell Law Directory

RASMUSSEN & MITCHELL (AV)

11605 Miracle Hills Drive, Suite 205, 68154
Telephone: 402-493-3300
Fax: 402-496-0766
Email: lawman000@aol.com *URL:* http://www.lawyers.com/rasmussen&mitchell

MEMBERS OF FIRM

Wayne S. Rasmussen
James S. Mitchell
Kathryn J. Derr
Shane M. Niebergall

For full biographical listings, see the Martindale-Hubbell Law Directory

NEVADA

*LAS VEGAS,** Clark Co.

KENNETH C. CORY A PROFESSIONAL CORPORATION (AV)

626 South Third Street, 89101
Telephone: 702-384-0111
Fax: 702-384-0763
Email: kcory@accessnv.com *URL:* http://www.lawyers.com/kennethcory

Kenneth C. Cory

For full biographical listings, see the Martindale-Hubbell Law Directory

CROCKETT & MYERS, LTD. A PROFESSIONAL CORPORATION (AV)

700 South Third Street, 89101
Telephone: 702-382-6711
Fax: 702-384-8102
Email: cmlegal@wizard.com *URL:* http://www.lawyers.com/c&mlaw

J. R. Crockett, Jr.
Richard W. Myers
James V. Lavelle III

Reference: American Bank of Commerce.

For full biographical listings, see the Martindale-Hubbell Law Directory

DICKERSON, DICKERSON, CONSUL & POCKER (AV)

Suite 1130, 330 South Third Street, 89101
Telephone: 702-388-8600
Fax: 702-388-0210

MEMBERS OF FIRM

George M. Dickerson
Robert P. Dickerson
Vincent A. Consul
Richard J. Pocker
Douglass A. Mitchell
Paul J. Lal
Bryce C. Duckworth

ASSOCIATES

Stacie L. Brown
Shann D. Winesett
David F. Sampson

Reference: Citibank.

For full biographical listings, see the Martindale-Hubbell Law Directory

FOLEY & JONES (AV)

850 East Bonneville Avenue, 89101
Telephone: 702-383-9852
Fax: 702-383-8154
Email: FoleyJones@worldnet.att.net *URL:* http://www.lawyers.com/f&jlaw

Joseph M. Foley
Daniel T. Foley
Diana J. Foley
Mark M. Jones

For full biographical listings, see the Martindale-Hubbell Law Directory

GALATZ, EARL, & ASSOCIATES (AV)

710 South Fourth Street, 89101
Telephone: 702-386-0000
Fax: 702-384-0394
Email: neilgalatz@aol.com *URL:* http://www.lawyers.com/galatzlaw

Neil G. Galatz
Allan R. Earl

For full biographical listings, see the Martindale-Hubbell Law Directory

KEITH E. GALLIHER, JR. CHARTERED (AV)

Suite 107, 1850 East Sahara, 89104
Telephone: 702-735-0049
Fax: 702-735-0204

Keith E. Galliher, Jr.

For full biographical listings, see the Martindale-Hubbell Law Directory

GILLOCK, MARKLEY & KILLEBREW (AV)

1640 West Alta, Suite 4, 89106
Telephone: 702-385-1482
Fax: 702-385-2604
Email: lawoffice@QUIK13.com *URL:* http://www.lawyers.com/gmklaw

MEMBERS OF FIRM

Gerald I. Gillock
Janet S. Markley
Antonia C. Killebrew
Julie A. Mersch

For full biographical listings, see the Martindale-Hubbell Law Directory

GOODMAN CHESNOFF & KEACH, A PROFESSIONAL CORPORATION (AV)

520 South Fourth Street, 89101-6593
Telephone: 702-384-5563
Fax: 702-598-1425

Oscar B. Goodman
David Z. Chesnoff
Eckley M. Keach

For full biographical listings, see the Martindale-Hubbell Law Directory

GREENMAN, GOLDBERG, RABY & MARTINEZ, PROFESSIONAL CORPORATION (AV)

601 South Ninth Street, 89101-7012
Telephone: 702-384-1616
FAX: 702-384-2990

John A. Greenman
Aubrey Goldberg
Paul E. Raby
Gabriel A. Martinez

Michael J. Ryan
Lisa M. Anderson
John R. Gordon

For full biographical listings, see the Martindale-Hubbell Law Directory

HILBRECHT & ASSOCIATES, CHARTERED (AV)

723 South Casino Center Boulevard, 89101-6716
Telephone: 702-384-1036
Facsimile: 702-384-2LAW
URL: http://www.lawyers.com/hilbrecht&associates
Email: hilbrcht@skylink.net *URL:* http://1stpage.sharednet.com/1/hilbrecht

(See Next Column)

HILBRECHT & ASSOCIATES CHARTERED, *Las Vegas—Continued*

Norman Ty Hilbrecht

Representative Clients: Bristol-Myers Squibb; Calzona Tankways; City Wide Enterprises; Coldwell Banker; Desert Chrysler-Plymouth; Enstrom Helicopter Co.; Las Vegas Congeneration; New England Life; Paul Revere Insurance;
Reference: First Security Bank of Nevada.

For full biographical listings, see the Martindale-Hubbell Law Directory

JOLLEY, URGA, WIRTH & WOODBURY (AV)

3800 Howard Hughes Parkway Suite 1600, 89109
Telephone: 702-699-7500
Facsimile: 702-699-7555
URL: http://www.juww.com
Boulder City, Nevada Office: Suite 105, 1000 Nevada Highway, 89005.
Telephone: 702-293-3674.

MEMBERS OF FIRM

R. Gardner Jolley
Bruce L. Woodbury
Brian E. Holthus

ASSOCIATE

Scott Day Freeman

For Complete List of Firm Personnel, See General Section

For full biographical listings, see the Martindale-Hubbell Law Directory

LEFEBVRE, BARRON & VIVONE, CHTD. (AV)

1404 South Jones Boulevard, 89146-1231
Telephone: 702-383-8668
Facsimile: 702-383-6828
Email: lb@coam.net

Alan J. Lefebvre
David L. Barron
Thomas J. Vivone
Raymond W. Holland
Michelle O. Tobler
William Howard Pruitt
Bradley V. Gibbons
Jared Casper (Not admitted in NV)
Kevin S. Smith

LEGAL SUPPORT PERSONNEL

Jennifer L. Hageman

For full biographical listings, see the Martindale-Hubbell Law Directory

GARY LOGAN (AV)

Third Floor, 302 East Carson Avenue, 89101
Telephone: 702-385-9900
Telecopier: 702-382-4800
Email: GARYLOGAN@prodigy.net

OF COUNSEL

Richard I. Feinberg

References: Bank of America-Nevada; The Chase Manhattan Bank, N.A.

For full biographical listings, see the Martindale-Hubbell Law Directory

MAINOR & HARRIS (AV)

A Partnership of Professional Corporations
530 South Sixth Street, 89101
Telephone: 702-385-1400
Fax: 702-385-9408
Email: admin@mainorandharris.com *URL:* http://www.lawyers.com/mainorandharris

W. Randall Mainor (A Professional Corporation)
Richard A. Harris (A Professional Corporation)
Clark Seegmiller
Robert M. Adams
Nancy Quon
Robert W. Cottle

Reference: First Security Bank of Nevada, Las Vegas, Nevada.

For full biographical listings, see the Martindale-Hubbell Law Directory

PICO & MITCHELL (AV)

2000 South Eastern Avenue, 89104
Telephone: 702-457-9099
FAX: 702-457-8451
Email: lawyers@picomitchell.com

MEMBERS OF FIRM

James F. Pico
Bert O. Mitchell
Christy Brad Escobar
James R. Rosenberger
E. Breen Arntz

ASSOCIATES

Michelle Schwarz
Rebecca L. Mastrangelo
Jill M. Chase
Daniel E. Carvalho
Stephen H. Rogers

Representative Clients: Home Insurance Co.; State Farm Mutual Insurance Co.; Industrial Indemnity Insurance Co.; Great American Insurance Co.; Argonaut Insurance Cos.; Clark County Medical Society; Rose de Lima Hospital; Fairway Chevrolet; American States Insurance Co.; The Hartford Insurance Co.

(See Next Column)

For full biographical listings, see the Martindale-Hubbell Law Directory

SMITH & WILLIAMS (AV)

1785 East Sahara, Suite 337, 89104
Telephone: 702-892-0000
Fax: 702-892-0788
Email: SWPIMAL@AOL.COM

MEMBERS OF FIRM

Roy E. Smith
Timothy C. Williams

For full biographical listings, see the Martindale-Hubbell Law Directory

VANNAH COSTELLO CANEPA RIEDY & RUBINO (AV)

A Partnership including a Professional Corporation
Greystone, 1850 East Flamingo, Suite 236, 89119
Telephone: 702-369-4161
Fax: 702-369-0104
Email: vannahnet@vannahnet.com

MEMBERS OF FIRM

Robert D. Vannah (Chartered)
Nathan M. Costello
Scott K. Canepa
Terry W. Riedy
Michael C. Rubino

ASSOCIATES

Connie J. Forsythe
Shawn D. Dorman
Adam Ganz
Denise M. Cooper
Jeffrey Ferguson
Matthew Vannah
Ronald J. Flinders
Russell M. Rowe
Jonathan G. Lattie (Not admitted in NV)

Representative Clients: Prudential Property and Casualty Insurance Co.; Continental Insurance Health Care; Chubb Group of Insurance; Reliance Insurance Co.; Transamerica Insurance Group; Foremost Insurance Co.; CNA Insurance Co.; Scottsdale Insurance Co.; The Maryland Insurance Group; Insurance Company of the West.

For full biographical listings, see the Martindale-Hubbell Law Directory

*LOVELOCK,** Pershing Co.

BELANGER & PLIMPTON (AV)

1135 Central Avenue, P.O. Box 59, 89419
Telephone: 702-273-2631
Fax: 702-273-2649
Email: todd@todd.lovelock.nv.us

MEMBERS OF FIRM

Roland W. Belanger
Todd A. Plimpton

Representative Clients: Sturgeon's Log Cabin, Inc.; Burns Bros., Inc.; Humboldt River Ranch Homeowner's Association.
Reference: Burns Bros., Inc.

For full biographical listings, see the Martindale-Hubbell Law Directory

*RENO,** Washoe Co.

BRADLEY, DRENDEL & JEANNEY (AV)

401 Flint Street, P.O. Box 1987, 89505
Telephone: 775-329-2273
Fax: 775-329-6513
Email: bdandj@worldnet.att.net *URL:* http://www.lawyers.com/bd&jlaw

Bill Bradley
Joseph S. Bradley
Thomas E. Drendel
William C. Jeanney

OF COUNSEL

William O. "Bud" Bradley
John Squire Drendel

For full biographical listings, see the Martindale-Hubbell Law Directory

WALTHER, KEY, MAUPIN, OATS, COX & LEGOY, A PROFESSIONAL CORPORATION (AV)

Lakeside Professional Plaza, 3500 Lakeside Court, 89509
Telephone: 775-827-2000
Facsimile: 775-827-2185
Mailing Address: P.O. Box 30000, Reno, Nevada, 89520

Steven T. Walther
Jon J. Key
Ernest J. Maupin
C. Robert Cox
L. Robert LeGoy, Jr.
Michael E. Malloy
G. Barton Mowry
Procter J. Hug
Donald A. Lattin
Paul J. Anderson
Gustave J. Rossi
Robert A. Winkel
Kurt O. Hunsberger
Michael A. Nivinskus
Christopher D. Jaime

Rick R. Hsu
Michaelle D. Rafferty

Representative Clients: Bank America of Nevada (Trust Dept.); Bechtel Corporations; Bill Pearce Olds, BMW, Volvo; Wells Fargo, N.A. (Trust Dept.); General Motors Acceptance Corp.; Nevada Realtors; Radiation Oncology Associates; The Ralph M. Parsons Corporation; Parsons Corporation; Reno Air, Inc.

(See Next Column)

Walther, Key, Maupin, Oats, Cox & LeGoy A Professional Corporation—*Continued*

For full biographical listings, see the Martindale-Hubbell Law Directory

NEW HAMPSHIRE

*CONCORD,** Merrimack Co.

Douglas, Robinson, Leonard & Garvey, P.C. (AV)

6 Loudon Road Suite 502, 03301
Telephone: 603-224-1988
Fax: 603-229-1988
Email: drlg@grolen.com *URL:* http://www.lawyers.com/drl&glaw

Charles G. Douglas, III
C. Kevin Leonard
Timothy I. Robinson
Carolyn S. Garvey
Susanna G. Robinson

For full biographical listings, see the Martindale-Hubbell Law Directory

Rath, Young and Pignatelli, Professional Association (AV)

One Capital Plaza, P.O. Box 1500, 03302-1500
Telephone: 603-226-2600
Telecopier: 603-226-2700; 228-2294; 225-9774
Email: ryp@rathlaw.com *URL:* http://www.rathlaw.com
Nashua, New Hampshire Office: The Glass Tower, 20 Trafalgar Square.
Telephone: 603-889-9952.
Telecopier: 603-595-7489.

Thomas D. Rath
Andrew W. Serell
Michael A. Pignatelli
Brian T. Tucker

For Complete List of Firm Personnel, See General Section

For full biographical listings, see the Martindale-Hubbell Law Directory

*DOVER,** Strafford Co.

Burns, Bryant, Hinchey, Cox & Rockefeller, P.A. (AV)

Burns Building, 255 Washington Street, P.O. Box 608, 03820
Telephone: 603-742-2332
Fax: 603-749-4970
Email: bbhcr@concentric.net

George T. Hughes (1873-1943)
Paul Richard Cox
Stanley M. Burns (1902-1967)
Donald R. Bryant (Of Counsel)
Robert P. Shea (1936-1983)
Christine M. Rockefeller
Robert E. Hinchey (Retired)
Gregory J. Wenger

Matthew B. Cox
Carolyn F. Dickson

Representative Clients: Metropolitan Life Insurance Co.; Prudential Insurance Company of America; Concord Group Insurance Cos.

For full biographical listings, see the Martindale-Hubbell Law Directory

*LACONIA,** Belknap Co.

Normandin, Cheney & O'Neil (AV)

Normandin Square, 213 Union Avenue, P.O. Box 575, 03247-0575
Telephone: 603-524-4380
Fax: 603-528-6831
Email: nco@lr.net

MEMBERS OF FIRM

A. Gerard O'Neil
A.G. O'Neil, Jr.
James F. LaFrance

ASSOCIATES

Philip P. Bonafide
Anne Marshall Rice

Counsel for: Laconia Savings Bank; Lakes Region Mental Health Center; Laconia Airport Authority; Central New Hampshire Realty, Inc.; All Metals Industries, Inc.; Lakes Region Anesthesiology, P.A.; Cormier Corp.; Scotia Technology; Vemaline Products.

For Complete List of Firm Personnel, See General Section

For full biographical listings, see the Martindale-Hubbell Law Directory

*MANCHESTER,** Hillsborough Co.

Abramson, Reis, Brown & Dugan (AV)

1819 Elm Street, 03104
Telephone: 603-627-1819
Fax: 603-666-4227
URL: http://www.arbd.com
Nashua, New Hampshire Office: 20 Trafalgar Square, Suite 417.
Telephone: 603-886-0308.

(See Next Column)

MEMBERS OF FIRM

Stanley M. Brown (1916-1998)
Randolph J. Reis
Kenneth C. Brown
Mark A. Abramson
Kevin F. Dugan

ASSOCIATES

John P. Fagan
Jared R. Green

For full biographical listings, see the Martindale-Hubbell Law Directory

Sheehan Phinney Bass + Green, Professional Association (AV)

Hampshire Plaza, 1000 Elm Street, P.O. Box 3701, 03105-3701
Telephone: 603-668-0300
800-625-SPBG
Fax: 603-627-8121
Email: postmaster@sheehan.com *URL:* http://www.sheehan.com
Portsmouth, New Hampshire Office: Old City Hall, 126 Daniel Street.
Telephone: 603-433-2111.
Fax: 603-433-3126.
Concord, New Hampshire Office: 143 North Main Street.
Telephone: 603-223-2020.
Fax: 603-224-8899.

James E. Higgins
Claudia Cords Damon
W. Michael Dunn
Peter S. Cowan
James Q. Shirley
Douglas G. Verge
Robert R. Lucic

Representative Clients: Anheuser-Busch, Inc.; Bank of New Hampshire Corp.; The Elliot Hospital of Manchester; Granite State Packing Co.; Moore Business Forms, Inc.; New Hampshire College; New Hampshire Dental Service Corp.; New Hampshire Yankee Electric Corp.; Numerica Financial Corp.

For Complete List of Firm Personnel, See General Section

For full biographical listings, see the Martindale-Hubbell Law Directory

NEW JERSEY

ATLANTIC CITY, Atlantic Co.

Westmoreland, Vesper & Schwartz, A Professional Corporation (AV)

Bayport One, Yacht Club Drive Suite 500, 08232-0034
Telephone: 609-645-1111
Fax: 609-646-2781
URL: http://www.westmorelandvesper.com

Rudolph C. Westmoreland
Mark G. Schwartz
Thomas J. Vesper
Dara A. Quattrone

David I. Sinderbrand
Katherine M. Morris
Carmelo Tony Torraca

Representative Clients: Cape May Foods; The Bank of New York; Title Company of Jersey; Money Store; Re/Max of New Jersey; AT&T Capital; Unitel Cellular; Yank Boat Works; Tomasello Winery.
Reference: Sun National Bank.

For full biographical listings, see the Martindale-Hubbell Law Directory

*BRIDGETON,** Cumberland Co.

John P. Morris (AV)

200 West Commerce Street, P.O. Box 299, 08302
Telephone: 609-453-1000
Fax: 609-453-0200
URL: http://www.lawyers.com/johnpmorris

LEGAL SUPPORT PERSONNEL

Tara Dickson (Paralegal)

For full biographical listings, see the Martindale-Hubbell Law Directory

BURLINGTON, Burlington Co.

Smith, Goldstein, Magram & Berenato, A Professional Corporation (AV)

415 High Street, P.O. Box 603, 08016-0603
Telephone: 609-386-2633
Fax: 609-386-8674

Louis A. Smith
Edward J. Magram
Jeffrey N. Goldstein
Elizabeth D. Berenato

David C. Michaud

Reference: First Union Bank, Burlington, New Jersey.

For full biographical listings, see the Martindale-Hubbell Law Directory

CHATHAM, Morris Co.

O'CONNOR & DEMAS, P.C. (AV)

383 Main Street, 07928
Telephone: 973-635-2210
Fax: 973-635-2622
URL: http://www.lawyers.com/geraldoconnor
Brick, New Jersey Office: 1480 Route 88 West. 08724.
Telephone: 732-836-0770.

Gerald B. O'Connor | Vivian Demas
Paul A. O'Connor, III

Thomas J. Demarest

OF COUNSEL

Patricia J. Cooney

For full biographical listings, see the Martindale-Hubbell Law Directory

CHERRY HILL, Camden Co.

TOMAR, SIMONOFF, ADOURIAN, O'BRIEN, KAPLAN, JACOBY & GRAZIANO, A PROFESSIONAL CORPORATION (AV)

20 Brace Road, 08034
Telephone: 609-429-1100
Telecopier: 609-429-8164
Email: TOMAR@TOMARLAW.COM *URL:* http://www.tomarlaw.com
Atlantic City, New Jersey Office: Commerce Building, Suite 220, 1200 Atlantic Avenue.
Telephone: 609-348-5900.
Camden, New Jersey Office: 200 North Fifth Street.
Telephone: 609-338-0553.
Northfield, New Jersey Office: The Executive Plaza, Suite 101, 2111 New Road.
Telephone: 609-485-0800.
Telecopier: 609-484-9388.
Wilmington, Delaware Office: Tomar, Simonoff, Adourian, O'Brien, Kaplan, Jacoby & Graziano, The Mellon Bank Center, Suite 1701, 919 Market Street.
Telephone: 302-655-0500.
Telecopier: 302-428-0963.
Media, Pennsylvania Office: 334 West Front Street.
Telephone: 215-574-0635.

William Tomar | Ronald A. Graziano
Edward N. Adourian, Jr. | Charles N. Riley
Michael Alan Kaplan | Alan H. Sklarsky
David Jacoby | Jaffa F. Stein

For full biographical listings, see the Martindale-Hubbell Law Directory

FLORHAM PARK, Morris Co.

HACK, PIRO, O'DAY, MERKLINGER, WALLACE & MCKENNA, P.A. (AV)

30 Columbia Turnpike, P.O. Box 941, 07932-0941
Telephone: 973-301-6500
Fax: 973-301-0094
Email: hpom@ix.netcom.com

Peter A. Piro | Patrick M. Sages
William J. O'Day | Bonny G. Rafel
M. Richard Merklinger | Robert G. Alencewicz
Joseph V. Wallace | John T. West
Peter T. Melnyk | Thomas M. Madden

Michael J. Leegan | Peter Nastasi
Joanne Vos | Carol A. Rankin

For Complete List of Firm Personnel, See General Section

For full biographical listings, see the Martindale-Hubbell Law Directory

*FREEHOLD,** Monmouth Co.

CERRATO, DAWES, COLLINS, SAKER & BROWN, A PROFESSIONAL CORPORATION (AV)

Wemrock Professional Mall, 509 Stillwells Corner Road, P.O. Box 6009, 07728
Telephone: 732-431-5000; 462-0480
Fax: 732-462-0483

Dominick A. Cerrato | James E. Collins
John I. Dawes | Mark F. Saker
Sanford D. Brown

Helen M. Wilder

OF COUNSEL

Barry William Messinger (Not admitted in NJ)

Representative Clients: Nat West; Freehold Regional High School; New Jersey Conservation Foundation; United Methodist Homes of New Jersey; Southern New Jersey Conference, United Methodist Church; Presbytery of Monmouth; Monmouth Council, Boy Scouts of America; Bayliner Marine Corp.

(See Next Column)

For full biographical listings, see the Martindale-Hubbell Law Directory

*HACKENSACK,** Bergen Co.

HEIN, SMITH, BEREZIN, MALOOF & JACOBS, L.L.C. (AV)

Court Plaza East, 19 Main Street, 07601-7023
Telephone: 201-487-7400
Telecopier: 201-487-4228
Email: counsel@heinsmith.com

MEMBERS OF FIRM

Robert J. Maloof | Lawrence H. Jacobs
Robert L. Baum | Ellen W. Smith
Carla H. Madnick

ASSOCIATES

John L. Shanahan | Douglas V. Sanchez
Robert J. Logan

Representative Clients: Bergen County Joint Municipal Insurance Fund; Commercial General Union Insurance Cos. of New York; Crawford & Co.; Health Care Insurance Co.; Princeton Insurance Co.; St. Paul Fire & Marine Insurance Co.; Pro Mutual Insurance Company; NJ Cure.
Reference: Summit Bank.

For Complete List of Firm Personnel, See General Section

For full biographical listings, see the Martindale-Hubbell Law Directory

LAWRENCEVILLE, Mercer Co.

SZAFERMAN, LAKIND, BLUMSTEIN, WATTER & BLADER, P.C. (AV)

Suite 104 Quakerbridge Executive Center, 101 Grovers Mill Road, 08648
Telephone: 609-275-0400
Telefax: 609-275-4511

Arnold C. Lakind | Sidney H. Lehmann
Barry D. Szaferman | Gerald B. Schenkman
Jeffrey P. Blumstein | David B. Beckett
Paul N. Watter | Scott P. Borsack
Steven Blader | Mary Lou Delahanty

Jennifer Weisberg Millner | Stuart A. Tucker
Cathyanne A. Pisciotta | Brian G. Paul
Jason N. Fruhschein | Victoria Rivera-Cruz
Demery J. Roberts | Thomas J. Burns III

LEGAL SUPPORT PERSONNEL

Paula M. Rossi (Office Administrator) | Patricia Hallstrum (Controller)

Representative Clients: Sun National Bank; First Washington Bank; Gilmore Securities & Co.; Communication Workers of America; The Eagle Group; Water's Edge Convalescent Center; Ronson Aviation, Inc.; Holmdel Township Board of Adjustment; Public Service Managers Association; Chemical Leaman Tank Lines.

For full biographical listings, see the Martindale-Hubbell Law Directory

LIVINGSTON, Essex Co.

PHILIP M. LUSTBADER & DAVID LUSTBADER A PROFESSIONAL CORPORATION (AV)

615 West Mount Pleasant Avenue, 07039
Telephone: 973-740-1000
Fax: 973-740-1520
URL: http://www.lawyers.com/lustbader,law

Philip M. Lustbader | David Lustbader

John L. Riordan, Jr. | James S. Colavito

For full biographical listings, see the Martindale-Hubbell Law Directory

MAPLEWOOD, Essex Co.

LAW OFFICES OF EMANUEL S. FISH (AV)

2040 Millburn Avenue, 07040
Telephone: 973-763-2001
Fax: 973-763-2832
Email: Afishl@aol.com *URL:* http://www.lawyers.com/esflaw

ASSOCIATE

Thomas J. O'Grady

OF COUNSEL

John D. Kovac

For full biographical listings, see the Martindale-Hubbell Law Directory

MILLBURN, Essex Co.

McDermott & McGee (AV)

75 Main Street, P.O. Box 192, 07041-0192
Telephone: 973-467-8080
Fax: 973-376-8669

MEMBERS OF FIRM

John L. McDermott
John P. McGee
Richard P. Maggi
Thomas A. Wester
Richard M. Tango
Frank P. Leanza
John L. McDermott, Jr.
David J. Dickinson
A. Charles Lorenzo
Robert A. McDermott
Kevin John McGee

ASSOCIATES

Anthony John Verardi
Lindsay K. O'Shaughnessy
Andre L. McGuire

OF COUNSEL

Daniel K. Van Dorn

Representative Clients: Affiliated Building Service, Inc.; Allstate Insurance Co.; General Agents Insurance Company of America; Greater New York Mutual; General Accident Group; ISS International Service System, Inc.; Zurich-American Insurance Co.; Penn National Insurance Co.; Tokio Marine & Fire Insurance Co.; Medical Inter-Insurance Exchange of New Jersey.

For full biographical listings, see the Martindale-Hubbell Law Directory

MOORESTOWN, Burlington Co.

Chierici, Chierici & Smith, A Professional Corporation (AV)

Blason Campus - III, 509 South Lenola Road Building Six, 08057-1561
Telephone: 856-234-6300
Fax: 856-234-9490

Donald R. Chierici, Jr.
Elizabeth Coleman Chierici
Julie C. Smith

Carolyn J. Kornas
Mark G. Esposito
Richard D. DiTomaso
Melvin McDowell
David J. Karbasian
Peter P. Sanchez
Donald R. Chierici, III

For full biographical listings, see the Martindale-Hubbell Law Directory

*MORRISTOWN,** Morris Co.

Baumeister & Samuels, P.C. (AV Ⓣ)

1776 On The Green, P.O. Box 1116, 07962-1116
Telephone: 973-267-6666
Telecopier: 973-605-1812
Email: BAUMSAM@AOL.COM
New York, N.Y. Office: One Exchange Plaza, 10006-3008.
Telephone: 212-363-1200.
Telecopier: 212-363-1346.

Michel F. Baumeister
Douglas A. Latto
(Not admitted in NJ)
Dorothea M. Capone

OF COUNSEL

Lynn F. Samuels
Robert S. Franklin
(Not admitted in NJ)
Marc Z. Edell

For full biographical listings, see the Martindale-Hubbell Law Directory

Rand, Algeier, Tosti & Woodruff, A Professional Corporation (AV)

60 Washington Street, 07960
Telephone: 973-539-2600
Telecopier: 973-984-0430
Email: randlaw@bellatlantic.net

Gary C. Algeier
David B. Rand
Robert M. Tosti
Robert B. Woodruff
John F. McDonnell
John E. Croot, Jr.

Kathryn J. Kingree
Deborah A. White

OF COUNSEL

Ronald M. Pflug
Ellen S. Bass
Tamara Krikorian

For full biographical listings, see the Martindale-Hubbell Law Directory

Stephen S. Weinstein A Professional Corporation (AV)

20 Park Place, Suite 301, 07960
Telephone: 973-267-5200
Fax: 973-538-1779
Email: skippy@sswpa.com *URL:* http://www.sswpa.com

Stephen S. Weinstein

(See Next Column)

Gail S. Boertzel
William G. Johnson
Melissa H. Luce

For full biographical listings, see the Martindale-Hubbell Law Directory

*NEWARK,** Essex Co.

Carpenter, Bennett & Morrissey (AV)

Three Gateway Center, 17th Floor, 100 Mulberry Street, 07102-4079
Telephone: 973-622-7711
New York City: 212-943-6530
Telex: 139405
Telecopier: 973-622-5314
Email: cbm@carpben.com

MEMBERS OF FIRM

John E. Keale
John P. Dwyer
Rosemary J. Bruno
William A. Carpenter, Jr.
Thomas F. McGuane
Joseph D. Rasnek
Robert M. Goodman
Thomas M. Moore
Jane A. Rigby

OF COUNSEL

John C. Heavey

ASSOCIATES

Michelle S. Hydrusko
C. Brian Kornbrek
John M. O'Connor
Robert P. McGovern
Claire C. Cecchi
Kenneth B. Rotter
Elizabeth A. Kenny
Deborah A. Young

Representative Clients: General Motors Corp.; E. I. du Pont de Nemours and Co.; Texaco Inc.; AT&T; Litton Industries; ITT Industries, Inc.; International Flavors & Fragrances Inc.; New Jersey Manufacturers Insurance Co.; Hartford Insurance Co.; Caterpillar, Inc.

For Complete List of Firm Personnel, See General Section

For full biographical listings, see the Martindale-Hubbell Law Directory

Fitzsimmons Ringle & Jacobs, P.C. (AV)

50 Park Place, 07102
Telephone: 973-623-5350
Fax: 973-623-5927
New York, New York: 130 E. 35th Street, 10016.
Telephone: 212-343-0677.

Frank J. Fitzsimmons
Richard Ringle
Andrew R. Jacobs

COUNSEL

Ronald Leibman

Michael E. Coslit
Lisa M. Papp
Martin Trevor Hughes Lyons

For full biographical listings, see the Martindale-Hubbell Law Directory

McCarter & English, LLP (AV)

Four Gateway Center, 100 Mulberry Street, P.O. Box 652, 07101-0652
Telephone: 973-622-4444
Telecopier: 973-624-7070
URL: http://www.mccarter.com
Cherry Hill, New Jersey Office: 1820 Chapel Avenue West, Suite 380.
Telephone: 609-662-8444.
Telecopier: 609-662-6203.
New York, New York Office: Suite 2247, One World Trade Center.
Telephone: 212-466-9018.
Telecopier: 212-432-6568.
Boca Raton, Florida Office: 2255 Glades Road, Suite 319-A.
Telephone: 561-994-6262.
Telecopier: 561-241-0798.
Wilmington, Delaware Office: Mellon Bank Center, 919 Market Street.
Telephone: 302-654-8010.
Telecopier: 302-654-0795.
Philadelphia, Pennsylvania Office: One Commerce Square, 2005 Market Street, Suite 3600.
Telephone: 215-557-7700.
Telecopier: 215-557-6544.

MEMBERS OF FIRM

John E. Flaherty
James H. Keale

COUNSEL

Joseph F. Falgiani

For Complete List of Firm Personnel, See General Section

For full biographical listings, see the Martindale-Hubbell Law Directory

Newark—Continued

SILLS CUMMIS RADIN TISCHMAN EPSTEIN & GROSS, A PROFESSIONAL CORPORATION (AV)

One Riverfront Plaza, 07102-5400
Telephone: 973-643-7000
Fax: 973-643-6500
Telex: 820630 Sillsbeck Nwk
Email: sillsmail@sillscummis.com *URL:* http://www.sillscummis.com
Atlantic City, New Jersey Office: 17 Gordon's Alley.
Telephone: 609-344-2800.
New York, N.Y. Office: 712 Fifth Avenue.
Telephone: 212-643-7000.
Washington, D.C. Office: 1800 K Street, N.W.
Telephone: 202-296-4750.

MEMBERS OF FIRM

Barry M. Epstein
Jeffrey Barton Cahn
Stuart M. Feinblatt
James D. Toll (Resident at Atlantic City, N.J. Office)
Alan J. Cohen (Resident at Atlantic City, N.J. Office)
Beth S. Rose

OF COUNSEL

Steven R. Rowland

Eric D. Mann (Resident at Atlantic City, N.J. Office)

For Complete List of Firm Personnel, See General Section

For full biographical listings, see the Martindale-Hubbell Law Directory

NEW PROVIDENCE, Union Co.

TAFARO & FLYNN, P.A. (AV)

571 Central Avenue, Suite 119, 07974
Telephone: 908-508-0100
Fax: 908-508-0599
Email: tafaroflyn@aol.com

Stephen J. Tafaro
Catherine J. Flynn

Joan Bannan Harris
Eric L. Grogan
Fred J. Hughes
Cheryl M. DeKline
Suellen L. DeBlasio
Marisa R. Kussoy

For full biographical listings, see the Martindale-Hubbell Law Directory

NORTH BRUNSWICK, Middlesex Co.

BORRUS, GOLDIN, FOLEY, VIGNUOLO, HYMAN, STAHL & CLARKIN, A PROFESSIONAL CORPORATION (AV)

2875 U.S. Highway 1, Route 1 & Finnigans Lane, P.O. Box 7463, 08902
Telephone: 732-422-1000
Fax: 732-422-1016
Email: attys@borrus.com *URL:* http://www.borrus.com

Jack Borrus
Martin S. Goldin
David M. Foley
Anthony B. Vignuolo
Jeffrey M. Hyman
James E. Stahl
James F. Clarkin III
Eileen Mary Foley

Robert C. Nisenson
Rosalind Westlake
Lisa M. Vignuolo
Steven L. Fox
Peter A. Vignuolo
Gerald T. Foley (1903-1976)

Representative Clients: Summit Bank; R. J. Reynolds Tobacco Co.; K. Hovnanian Enterprises, Inc.; Johnson and Johnson; Foster Wheeler, Inc.; Hartz Mountain Industries; Middlesex County Vocational Services Commission; Borough of South Plainfield Board of Adjustment; U-Haul of Northern NJ.

For full biographical listings, see the Martindale-Hubbell Law Directory

BUSCH AND BUSCH, LLP (AV)

215 North Center Drive, Commerce Center - U.S. #1 South, P.O. Box 7448, 08902-7448
Telephone: 732-821-2300
Telecopier: 732-821-5588
Email: busch@ifu.net

MEMBERS OF FIRM

Lewis D. Busch (1901-1986)
Henry Busch (Retired)
Malcolm R. Busch
Ronald J. Busch
Bertram E. Busch
Mark N. Busch
Leonard R. Busch
Steven F. Satz
Donald J. Sears

ASSOCIATE

Paul Alan VanBuskirk

Representative Clients: Utica Mutual Insurance Co.; New Brunswick Tomorrow; Township of South Brunswick; Township of Monroe, Board of Education; Township of East Brunswick; Minnesota Mutual Life Insurance Co.

For full biographical listings, see the Martindale-Hubbell Law Directory

LYNCH, MARTIN, KANE, KUPER, KEEFE & BARTELS, LLC (AV)

1368 How Lane, P.O. Box 6022, 08902-6022
Telephone: 732-545-0745
Fax: 732-545-4780
Email: LYNCHMRTN@aol.com

John A. Lynch, Sr. (1908-1978)
John A. Lynch
James D. Martin, Jr.
John J. Kane
Eric Kuper
John E. Keefe, Jr.
Patrick J. Bartels
Carl W. Swanson
James Den Uyl
John W. Harding
Lori A. Dvorak
Bernard P. Hvozdovic, Jr.
Joseph J. LaCosta
Timothy E. Annin

Laura M. Shea
Robyn M. Mitchell
Christine Klimczuk

OF COUNSEL

Robert T. Quackenboss (Retired Superior Court Judge)

LEGAL SUPPORT PERSONNEL

Sharon Stewart (Administrator)

For full biographical listings, see the Martindale-Hubbell Law Directory

NORTHFIELD, Atlantic Co.

MCALLISTER, HYBERG & WHITE (AV)

Executive Plaza, 2111 New Road, Suite 105, 08225
Telephone: 609-407-1000
Fax: 609-407-1010
Email: McAllister-Hyberg@prodigy.net

Robert N. McAllister
Lars S. Hyberg
Joseph B. White

ASSOCIATE

Keith T. Smith

For full biographical listings, see the Martindale-Hubbell Law Directory

PARSIPPANY, Morris Co.

CUYLER BURK (AV)

Parsippany Corporate Center, Four Century Drive, 07054-4663
Telephone: 973-734-3200
Telex: 429071
Telecopier: 973-734-3201
Email: Main@Cuyler.com *URL:* http://www.cuyler.com
New York, New York Office: 350 Fifth Avenue, Suite 3304. 10018.
Telephone: 212-645-4039.

MEMBERS OF FIRM

Stephen D. Cuyler
Jo Ann Burk
Stefano Calogero
David L. Menzel
Peter Petrou
Richard A. Crooker
Michael J. Jones

COUNSEL

Anne M. Mohan
Frank J. Miele

ASSOCIATES

Jan C. Walker
Kathleen Jane Olear
Claudia L. Marchese
Mark G. Eliades
Kimberly A. Joel
Christy A. Ramunno
Catherine E. Youngman
Andrew K. Craig
Mark S. Winter
Thomas J. Castano
Hugo A. Hilgendorff, IV

LEGAL SUPPORT PERSONNEL

Frederick M. H. Currie, Jr.

For full biographical listings, see the Martindale-Hubbell Law Directory

GENNET, KALLMANN, ANTIN & ROBINSON, A PROFESSIONAL CORPORATION (AV)

6 Campus Drive, 07054-4406
Telephone: 973-285-1919
Fax: 973-285-1177
Email: gkar@nac.net
New York, New York Office: Litman Suite, 45 Broadway Atrium, 10006.
Telephone: 212-406-1919.

Stanley W. Kallmann
Mark L. Antin
Harry Robinson, III
Richard S. Nichols

William Gary Hanft
Thomas J. Olsen, IV
Francie E. Joseph
Paul A. Tumbleson

LEGAL SUPPORT PERSONNEL

Eleanor Dawalt (Administrator)

Representative Clients: Aetna Insurance Co.; Hartford Fire; Lloyds of London; New England Mutuals.
Reference: United Jersey Bank.

For full biographical listings, see the Martindale-Hubbell Law Directory

Parsippany—Continued

REISEMAN SHARP KELSEY & BROWN LLP (AV)

4 Campus Drive, P.O. Box 431, 07054-0431
Telephone: 973-267-3600
Fax: 973-267-2332

MEMBERS OF FIRM

Neil Reiseman
James B. Sharp
Jane S. Kelsey
Kenneth M. Brown
Sam Rosenberg
Meghan E. Walsh

John C. Macce
Jayne E. Turner
Everett E. Gale, III
Robert T. Gunning
Gregory A. Bush

Representative Clients: Medical Inter-Insurance Exchange of New Jersey; Princeton Insurance Company; Health Care Insurance Company; Home Depot; United Capitol Insurance Company; New Jersey Property-Liability Insurance Guaranty Association; New Jersey Joint Underwriting Association; Franciscan Health Systems; Zurich American; Avis.

For full biographical listings, see the Martindale-Hubbell Law Directory

PRINCETON, Mercer Co.

BERGMAN & BARRETT (AV)

9 Tamarack Circle, Montgomery Knoll, U.S. Highway 206 North, P.O. Box 1273, 08542
Telephone: 609-921-1502
Fax: 609-683-0288

Edward J. Bergman
Michael T. Barrett

LEGAL SUPPORT PERSONNEL

Kelli E. Murphy (Paralegal)

For full biographical listings, see the Martindale-Hubbell Law Directory

STARK & STARK, A PROFESSIONAL CORPORATION (AV)

Princeton Pike Corporate Center, P.O. Box 5315, 08543-5315
Telephone: 609-896-9060
Fax: 609-896-0629
Email: info@stark-stark.com *URL:* http://www.stark-stark.com

David M. Botwinick
J. Robert Bratman
David R. Cohen
Paul N. Daly
Godfrey W. Harper, III
Arthur H. Kravitz
Eric J. Ludwig
Christopher M. Pyne
John A. Sakson
Albert M. Stark
Bruce H. Stern

OF COUNSEL

Timothy J. Mc Namara
Frank Orbach

Vicki W. Beyer
Mark W. Davis
Michael G. Donahue
Denise Mariani Forrester
Michael H. Foster
Samuel M. Gaylord
Lorena Haumann Miller
Jason G. Steinhart

For full biographical listings, see the Martindale-Hubbell Law Directory

RED BANK, Monmouth Co.

PHILIP G. AUERBACH A PROFESSIONAL CORPORATION (AV)

231 Maple Avenue, P.O. Box Y, 07701
Telephone: 732-842-6660
Fax: 732-530-7925

Philip G. Auerbach

Edward A. Genz
John J. Ryan
John F. McLaughlin

For full biographical listings, see the Martindale-Hubbell Law Directory

ROSELAND, Essex Co.

BRACH, EICHLER, ROSENBERG, SILVER, BERNSTEIN, HAMMER & GLADSTONE, A PROFESSIONAL CORPORATION (AV)

101 Eisenhower Parkway, 07068
Telephone: 973-228-5700
Telecopier: 973-228-7852
Email: law@bracheichler.com *URL:* http://www.bracheichler.com

Alan H. Bernstein
Charles X. Gormally
Alan S. Pralgever

Stuart Jeffrey Polkowitz
Carl J. Soranno
Jonathan E. Levitt

OF COUNSEL

Lance A. Posner

(See Next Column)

COUNSEL

David J. Klein
David S. Bernstein

Representative Clients: Great American American Insurance Co.; Ohio Casualty Insurance Group.

For Complete List of Firm Personnel, See General Section

For full biographical listings, see the Martindale-Hubbell Law Directory

SADDLE BROOK, Bergen Co.

COHN LIFLAND PEARLMAN HERRMANN & KNOPF LLP (AV)

Park 80 Plaza West-One, 07663
Telephone: 201-845-9600
Telecopier: 201-845-9423
Email: info@njlawfirm.com *URL:* http://www.njlawfirm.com

MEMBERS OF FIRM

Albert L. Cohn
Peter S. Pearlman
Barry A. Knopf
Daniel Crystal (Retired)
Jeffrey W. Herrmann
Robert D. Zatorski
Allen Susser
Mary Ann T. Stokes
Brian D. Zinn
Joshua P. Cohn

ASSOCIATES

Virginia A. Harper
Leonard Z. Kaufmann
Audra DePaolo
Robert Ricci, Jr.
Maurice W. McLaughlin
Andrew C. Abrams
Jessica V. Henry

OF COUNSEL

Sylvia J. Cohn
Jodi B. Scherl

For full biographical listings, see the Martindale-Hubbell Law Directory

SCOTCH PLAINS, Union Co.

JON M. BRAMNICK (AV)

1827 East Second Street, 07076
Telephone: 908-322-7000
Fax: 908-322-6997
URL: http://www.lawyers.com/jonbramnick

ASSOCIATES

John C. Rodriguez
Stephanie Ann Mitterhoff

OF COUNSEL

Clarence A. Abramson

For full biographical listings, see the Martindale-Hubbell Law Directory

SHIP BOTTOM, Ocean Co.

SHACKLETON, HAZELTINE AND BISHOP (AV)

22nd Street and Long Beach Boulevard, P.O. Box 410, 08008
Telephone: 609-494-2136
Telefax: 609-494-0870
Fairfield, New Jersey Office: One Passaic Avenue.
Telephone: 201-882-4646.
Telefax: 201-882-4620.

MEMBERS OF FIRM

Richard J. Shackleton
Colin R. Hazeltine
James E. Bishop

ASSOCIATES

Laura M. O'Regan
Marc Baden Powell
Robert Emmet Rue

OF COUNSEL

Kenneth L. Leiby, Jr. (Resident, Fairfield Office)

References: Commerce Bank/Shore N/A; Summit Bank Corp.

For full biographical listings, see the Martindale-Hubbell Law Directory

*SOMERVILLE,** Somerset Co.

SCHACHTER, TROMBADORE, OFFEN, STANTON & PAVICS, A PROFESSIONAL CORPORATION (AV)

45 East High Street, P.O. Box 520, 08876-0520
Telephone: 908-722-5700
Fax: 908-722-8853

Richard J. Schachter
Stephen M. Offen
Thomas A. Pavics

Timothy P. McKeown

For full biographical listings, see the Martindale-Hubbell Law Directory

SPRINGFIELD, Union Co.

JAVERBAUM WURGAFT HICKS & ZARIN, A PROFESSIONAL CORPORATION (AV)

Park Place Legal Center, 959 South Springfield Avenue, 07081-3555
Telephone: 973-379-4200
Fax: 973-379-7872
Email: javerbaumwurgafthicks@compuserve.com *URL:* http://www.lawyers.com/jwhz,law

Kenneth S. Javerbaum
Robert G. Hicks
Jack Wurgaft
Ira J. Zarin

Anthony P. Valenti
Eric G. Kahn
David L. Wikstrom

OF COUNSEL

Jeffrey E. Strauss

For full biographical listings, see the Martindale-Hubbell Law Directory

MCDONOUGH, KORN & EICHHORN, A PROFESSIONAL CORPORATION (AV)

Park Place Legal Center, 959 South Springfield Avenue, P.O. Box 712, 07081-0712
Telephone: 973-912-9099
Fax: 973-912-8604

Peter L. Korn
William S. Mezzomo
R. Scott Eichhorn
Timothy J. Jaeger
James R. Korn
Wilfred P. Coronato

Julia A. Klubenspies
Danielle M. Verrastro
Matthew S. Schorr
Jeffrey John Berezny

OF COUNSEL

Robert P. McDonough

Representative Client: Meeker Sharkey & MacBean.
Reference: First Union, Summit, N.J.

For full biographical listings, see the Martindale-Hubbell Law Directory

*TOMS RIVER,** Ocean Co.

LOMELL, MUCCIFORI, ADLER, RAVASCHIERE, AMABILE & PEHLIVANIAN, A PROFESSIONAL CORPORATION (AV)

250 Washington Street, P.O. Box 787, 08754
Telephone: 732-349-2443
Fax: 732-349-6917
Email: thefirm@lomell.com *URL:* http://www.lomell.com

Herman A. Adler
Jeffrey R. Surenian
Dominic Ravaschiere
James M. McKenna
John S. Pehlivanian
Teresa K. Gierla
Ronald E. Prusek
Arthur F. Leyden, III

Marc S. Galella
James S. Braaten
Robyn A. Belluardo
Regina M. Butler
Janet Zaorski Kalapos
Paul J Capotorto

For Complete List of Firm Personnel, See General Section

For full biographical listings, see the Martindale-Hubbell Law Directory

NOVINS, YORK & PENTONY, A PROFESSIONAL CORPORATION (AV)

202 Main Street, 08753
Telephone: 732-349-7100
Email: info@nyplaw.com

Kenneth R. Pentony
Ann K. Haskell

W. Mark Bayles
Gregory S. Heizler
Robert J. Roth
Anthony M. Pagano

Counsel for: Allstate Insurance Co.; Motor Club of America.

For Complete List of Firm Personnel, See General Section

For full biographical listings, see the Martindale-Hubbell Law Directory

STARKEY, KELLY, BLANEY & WHITE (AV)

2 Hooper Avenue, 08753
Telephone: 732-240-3600
Fax: 732-240-3777
Brick, New Jersey Office: 459 Jack Martin Boulevard, 08724.
Telephone: 732-840-5900.
Fax: 732-840-5901.
Manasquan, New Jersey Office: 23 Route 71, 08736.
Telephone: 732-223-7328.
Fax: 732-240-3777.

(See Next Column)

MEMBERS OF FIRM

Charles E. Starkey
William V. Kelly
James M. Blaney

ASSOCIATES

Natalie Pouch
Scott W. Kenneally
Anthony Mancuso
Susan K. White
Robert A. Bauer
Brent D. Miller

Representative Clients: Hartford Insurance Co.; New Jersey Education Assn.; New Jersey Psychiatric Assn.; Ocean County Utilities Authority; Brick Township Municipal Utilities Authority; Manasquan River Regional Sewerage Authority; Hanover Insurance Co.; John Hancock Insurance Co.; Rider Inc. Co.

For full biographical listings, see the Martindale-Hubbell Law Directory

VINELAND, Cumberland Co.

JAY H. GREENBLATT & ASSOCIATES A PROFESSIONAL CORPORATION (AV)

200 North Eighth Street, P.O. Box 883, 08360-0883
Telephone: 609-691-0424
Facsimile: 609-696-1010
Email: jhg@algorithms.com *URL:* http://home.earthlink.net/~greenblatt/

M. Joseph Greenblatt (1896-1992)
Jay H. Greenblatt

Bonnie L. Laube
Nicholas Kiernieskу

Counsel for: Ware's Van & Storage Co., Inc.; Consolidated Motor Oils, Inc.; Joffe Lumber & Supply Co., Inc.
Local Counsel for: A. O. Smith Corp.; Chance Industries, Inc.; Coca Cola Bottlers' Association; Fireman's Fund Insurance Co.; Ford Motor Co.; Thermadyne Industries; The West Bend Company.

For full biographical listings, see the Martindale-Hubbell Law Directory

GRUCCIO, PEPPER GIOVINAZZI, DESANTO & FARNOLY, P.A. (AV)

817 Landis Avenue, P.O. Box 1501, 08362
Telephone: 856-691-0100
Fax: 856-692-4095
Email: Gruccio1@eticomm.net
Woodbury, New Jersey Office: 21 Delaware Street.
Telephone: 856-848-5558.
Fax: 856-384-1181.
Bridgeton, New Jersey Office: 120 West Broad Street.
Telephone: 856-459-3334.
Fax: 856-692-4095.

James J. Gruccio, Sr.
Cosmo A. Giovinazzi, III
Robert A. DeSanto

Representative Clients: State Farm Mutual Automobile Insurance Cos.; United States Fidelity & Guaranty Co.; South Jersey Transportation Authority; County of Salem; County of Cape May; Cumberland Mutual Fire Insurance Co.; Farmers and Merchants National Bank of Bridgeton; Vineland Board of Education; Southern Intercounty Medical Association; Sun National Bank of N.J.

For Complete List of Firm Personnel, See General Section

For full biographical listings, see the Martindale-Hubbell Law Directory

JOSEPH D. O'NEILL A PROFESSIONAL CORPORATION (AV)

30 West Chestnut Avenue, P.O. Box 847, 08360
Telephone: 856-692-2400
Telecopier: 856-696-9036
URL: http://www.lawyers.com/josephoneill

Joseph D. O'Neill

Charles I. Coant
James T. Dugan
Amber Sharp Pallante

For full biographical listings, see the Martindale-Hubbell Law Directory

WALL TOWNSHIP, Monmouth Co.

MAGEE AND ISHERWOOD, L.L.P. (AV)

Mirne & Simmill
Mirne, Nowels, Fundler Magee & Kirschner
1937 Route 35 at Allaire Road, P.O. Box 1200, 07719
Telephone: 732-449-2500
Telecopier: 732-449-4005

MEMBERS OF FIRM

Granville D. Magee
Thomas Isherwood

ASSOCIATE

Granville M. Magee

(See Next Column)

MAGEE AND ISHERWOOD L.L.P.—*Continued*

OF COUNSEL

Michael B. Kirschner

Representative Clients: Royal Insurance Cos.; Township of Upper Freehold.
References: Central Jersey Bank & Trust Co.; Commerce Bank Shore N.A.

For full biographical listings, see the Martindale-Hubbell Law Directory

WAYNE, Passaic Co.

DEYOE HEISSENBUTTEL, L.L.C. (AV)

401 Hamburg Turnpike, P.O. Box 2449, 07474-2449
Telephone: 973-595-6300
Fax: 973-595-0146
Email: deyoelaw@ix.netcom.com *URL:* http://www.deyoe.com

MEMBERS OF FIRM

Charles P. DeYoe (1923-1973)
Wood M. DeYoe
Frederick C. Heissenbuttel
Scott B. Piekarsky

ASSOCIATES

Raymond F. Shenekji
Anne Hutton
Albert C. Buglione
Laureen A. Moloney

LEGAL SUPPORT PERSONNEL

Marilyn Moore (Office Manager)

Representative Clients: Hanover Insurance Inc.; Maryland Casualty Co.; Ohio Casualty Insurance Co.; Motor Club of America; Selective Insurance Co.; Prudential Property & Casualty; Reliance Ins. Co.

For full biographical listings, see the Martindale-Hubbell Law Directory

NEW MEXICO

*ALBUQUERQUE,** Bernalillo Co.

BRANCH LAW FIRM (AV)

Including a Professional Association
2025 Rio Grande Boulevard, N.W., 87104
Telephone: 505-243-3500
Fax: 505-243-3534
New Mexico Toll Free: 1-800-562-3456
Nationwide Toll Free: 1-800-828-4LAW
Email: reception@branchlawfirm.com *URL:* http://www.branchlawfirm.com
Durango, Colorado Office: Suite 205, 102 East Eighth Street.
Telephone: 303-385-7671.
Houston, Texas Office: 808 Travis Street, Suite 1303.
Telephone: 800-243-3545.
Fax: 713-224-1622.

Turner W. Branch (P.A.)
Margaret Moses Branch

Arthur M. Solon
Daniel R. Swiss
Rebecca C. Branch
Justin K. Hall
James P. Lyle
Rhett D. Klok
Suzanne Lafleur Klok
Clyde DeMersseman
Shari D. Thieman

LEGAL SUPPORT PERSONNEL

Krisann Y. Matthes (Office Manager)
Jacqueline Adams
Amy Rigg
Shariesse McCannon
Judi Seff
Daphne Moore (Registered Nurse)
Yvette Rodarte
Shelly Hourani (Houston Office)

For full biographical listings, see the Martindale-Hubbell Law Directory

CARPENTER & CHÁVEZ, LTD. (AV)

1600 University Boulevard, N.E., Suite A, 87102-1711
Telephone: 505-243-1336
Facsimile: 505-243-1339
Email: carpchav@swcp.com *URL:* http://www.carpenter-law.com

William H. Carpenter
Edward L. Chávez
David J. Stout

Reference: Bank of America, Albuquerque, New Mexico.

For full biographical listings, see the Martindale-Hubbell Law Directory

EATON, MARTINEZ & HART, P.C. (AV)

3800 Osuna Road N.E., Suite 2, 87109
Telephone: 505-343-1776
Fax: 505-344-7709
URL: http://www.eatonmartinezhart.com
Email: rogeaton@aol.com *URL:* http://www.lawyers.com/eatonmartinez&hart

(See Next Column)

Roger V. Eaton
David B. Martinez
F. Michael Hart

Gabrielle M. Valdez
Wendy F. Jones

LEGAL SUPPORT PERSONNEL

Laura Paul (Legal Assistant)
Shaylin Buhrle (Legal Assistant)
Angela Stone (Legal Assistant)
Juan Loya (Legal Assistant)
Therse Quetone (Legal Assistant)

For full biographical listings, see the Martindale-Hubbell Law Directory

FINE & FAURE (AV)

A Partnership including Professional Associations
220 Ninth Street, N.W., 87102
Telephone: 505-243-4541
Fax: 505-242-2716
Santa Fe, New Mexico Office: 1421 Luisa Street, Suite L.
Telephone: 505-988-9566.
Fax: 505-983-1543.

MEMBERS OF FIRM

Joseph M. Fine (P.A.)
John P. Faure (P.A.) (Resident, Santa Fe Office)

ASSOCIATES

Jalynn M. Clayton
Edward F. Snow
Donald E. Martinez
Bradford K. Goodwin
Robynn Sena

For full biographical listings, see the Martindale-Hubbell Law Directory

WILLIAM G. GILSTRAP (AV)

301 Edith, N.E., P.O. Drawer H, 87103
Telephone: 505-842-8600

For full biographical listings, see the Martindale-Hubbell Law Directory

GUEBERT & YEOMANS, P.C. (AV)

6743 Academy Road NE, Suite A, P.O. Box 93880, 87199-3880
Telephone: 505-823-2300
Fax: 505-823-9600

Terry R. Guebert
Richard D. Yeomans
Don Bruckner
RaMona G. Bootes
Timothy L. Hartley
Alysan Boothe Collins
Richard F. Rowley, III
Patricia M. Monaghan

For full biographical listings, see the Martindale-Hubbell Law Directory

JAMES T. ROACH (AV)

Third Central Plaza, Suite 1500 West, 300 Central, S.W., 87102
Telephone: 505-243-4419
Fax: 505-243-4169

For full biographical listings, see the Martindale-Hubbell Law Directory

RODEY, DICKASON, SLOAN, AKIN & ROBB, P.A. (AV)

Albuquerque Plaza, Suite 2200, 201 Third Street, N.W., P.O. Box 1888, 87103-1888
Telephone: 505-765-5900
Fax: 505-768-7395
Email: info@rodey.com *URL:* http://www.rodey.com
Santa Fe, New Mexico Office: Suite 101 Marcy Plaza, 123 East Marcy Street, P.O. Box 1357, 87504-1357.
Telephone: 505-984-0100.
Fax: 505-989-9542.

James C. Ritchie
Joseph J. Mullins
Robert G. McCorkle
Mark C. Meiering
Travis R. Collier
W. Mark Mowery (Resident, Santa Fe Office)
Patrick M. Shay
Tracy McGee Jenks
Charles K. Purcell
Andrew G. Schultz
Susan S. Throckmorton
R. Nelson Franse
Paul R. Koller

For Complete List of Firm Personnel, See General Section

For full biographical listings, see the Martindale-Hubbell Law Directory

SIMONE, ROBERTS & WEISS, P.A. (AV)

8102 Menaul Boulevard N.E., 87110
Telephone: 505-298-9400
Fax: 505-298-7070

Stephen M. Simone
Randal W. Roberts
Norman F. Weiss
Michelle Lalley Blake
Thomas E. Perkins
Ashley Gauthier
Megan Day Hill

Representative Clients: Allstate Insurance Co.; Guaranty National Insurance Co.; State Farm Fire and Casualty Co.; State of New Mexico, Risk Management; Liberty Mutual Insurance Company; State Farm Mutual Auto.

(See Next Column)

SIMONE, ROBERTS & WEISS P.A., *Albuquerque—Continued*

Reference: Nationsbank.

For full biographical listings, see the Martindale-Hubbell Law Directory

*ROSWELL,** Chaves Co.

LAW OFFICES OF MICHAEL L. STOUT (AV)

215 West 6th Street, 88201
Telephone: 505-624-1471
Fax: 505-622-1086
Email: mlstout@nm.net

For full biographical listings, see the Martindale-Hubbell Law Directory

*SANTA FE,** Santa Fe Co.

STEVEN G. FARBER (AV)

306 Catron Street, P.O. Box 2473, 87504-2473
Telephone: 505-988-9725
Fax: 505-988-9250
Email: sgfsaf@aol.com

For full biographical listings, see the Martindale-Hubbell Law Directory

NEW YORK

*ALBANY,** Albany Co.

FEATHERSTONHAUGH, CONWAY, WILEY & CLYNE, L.L.P. (AV)

99 Pine Street, Suite 207, 12207
Telephone: 518-436-0786
Fax: 518-427-0452
URL: http://www.fcwc-law.com

MEMBERS OF FIRM

James D. Featherstonhaugh
Thomas A. Conway
Stephen J. Wiley
Elizabeth K. Clyne

ASSOCIATES

Nadine Feiden Shadlock
Denis R. Hurley, Jr.
Andrew W. Kirby
William F. Conway, IV
Gerard L. Conway, Jr.
Steven M. Connolly

OF COUNSEL

William F. Conway
Jeffrey J. Conklin
David Weinraub
Randall J. Ezick

LEGAL SUPPORT PERSONNEL
GOVERNMENTAL RELATIONS

John L. Hardy
Daniel G. Plummer
John P. Griffin
David F. Fleming

For full biographical listings, see the Martindale-Hubbell Law Directory

HARVEY AND MUMFORD (AV)

20 Corporate Woods Boulevard, 12211-2396
Telephone: 518-463-4491
Telecopier: 518-463-5665
Email: thefirm@harveyandmumford.com

Arthur J. Harvey (1903-1986)

MEMBERS OF FIRM

Jonathan P. Harvey
Brian F. Mumford

ASSOCIATES

Eva Lynn M. Hayko
Karen Hendricks
Peter Baird Joslin, Jr.
Trudy L. Boulia
Keith J. Starlin

OF COUNSEL

Jack D. Harvey

For full biographical listings, see the Martindale-Hubbell Law Directory

ISEMAN, CUNNINGHAM, RIESTER & HYDE, LLP (AV)

9 Thurlow Terrace, 12203
Telephone: 518-462-3000
Telecopier: 518-462-4199
Email: lawfirm@icrh.com *URL:* http://www.icrh.com
Canandaigua, New York Office: 37 East Gibson Street, P.O. Box 179, 14424.
Telephone: 716-394-1450.
Fax: 716-394-5121.

MEMBERS OF FIRM

Frederick C. Riester
Michael J. Cunningham
Robert Hall Iseman
Carol Ann Hyde
Linda J. Clark

(See Next Column)

Brian M. Culnan
Kihyun S. Kim
Richard A. Frankel
Stephanie E. Moriarty
Valerie R. Lape Handy
Marcia B. Smith
Ellen Gillerman Cox
Jennifer A. Grego
Cara E. Johnson

OF COUNSEL

Michael J. McNeil
Deborah A. Kirby

For full biographical listings, see the Martindale-Hubbell Law Directory

MAYNARD, O'CONNOR, SMITH & CATALINOTTO, LLP (AV)

Seventh Floor, 80 State Street, 12207
Telephone: 518-465-3553
Fax: 518-465-5845
Saugerties, New York Office: Route 9W, P.O. Box 180.
Telephone: 914-246-3666.
Fax: 914-246-0390.

MEMBERS OF FIRM

William C. Maynard (1883-1972)
Gerald W. O'Connor (1896-1965)
J. Vincent Smith (1916-1991)
Michael E. Catalinotto
Stephen C. Prudente
Christopher K.H. Dressler
Thomas G. Daley
James R. Schultz
Bruce A. Bell
Concetta R. Lomanto
Edwin J. Tobin, Jr.

ASSOCIATES

Michael E. Catalinotto, Jr.
Robert A. Rausch
Teresa M. Morrisey
Aaron M. Baldwin
Laurel L. Bohl

OF COUNSEL

Earl S. Jones, Jr.

Local Counsel for: Utica Mutual Insurance Co.; General Motors; Medical Liability Mutual Insurance; Metropolitan Insurance Co.

For full biographical listings, see the Martindale-Hubbell Law Directory

POWERS & SANTOLA (AV)

39 N. Pearl Street, Suite 2, 12207-2785
Telephone: 518-465-5995; 1-800-540-8742
Fax: 518-426-4012
Email: jpowers@powers-santola.com *URL:* http://www.powers-santola.com

John K. Powers
Daniel R. Santola

ASSOCIATES

Timothy J. Higgins
John H. Fisher
Paul Berne Sherr

ROCHE CORRIGAN MCCOY & BUSH (AV)

The Wilem Van Zandt Building, 36 South Pearl Street, 12207
Telephone: 518-436-9370
Fax: 518-436-8233

MEMBERS OF FIRM

Robert P. Roche
Peter J. Corrigan
Joseph M. McCoy
Scott W. Bush

For full biographical listings, see the Martindale-Hubbell Law Directory

RUBERTI, GIRVIN & FERLAZZO, P.C. (AV)

120 State Street, 2nd Floor, 12207-2829
Telephone: 518-462-0300
Fax: 518-462-5037
Email: attorneys@rgflaw.com

PARTNERS

E. Michael Ruberti
James E. Girvin
Salvatore D. Ferlazzo
Kristine Amodeo Lanchantin
Jeffrey D. Honeywell
M. Cornelia Cahill
Gregg Tyler Johnson

ASSOCIATES

Patrick J. McKenna
Kathy Ann Wolverton
Christopher P. Langlois
Bruce I. Kopf
Maureen Finnegan Harris

SPECIAL COUNSEL

Mary Helen Moses
James A. P. McCarthy
Elaine M. Pers
Karen S. Norlander

For full biographical listings, see the Martindale-Hubbell Law Directory

TABNER, RYAN AND KENIRY (AV)

26 Computer Drive West, P.O. Box 12605, 12212-2605
Telephone: 518-459-9000
Telecopier: 518-459-9165
Email: trk@tabnerryanandkeniry.com

MEMBERS OF FIRM

John W. Tabner
William F. Ryan, Jr.
William J. Keniry

(See Next Column)

TABNER, RYAN AND KENIRY—*Continued*

OF COUNSEL

C. Theodore Carlson

ASSOCIATES

Eric N. Dratler
Jennifer K. Corona
Donald W. Biggs

Special Counsel for: Water and Sewer District for Towns of Colonie, Coxsackie, Guilderland, Johnstown, Queensbury, Rotterdam and Village Castleton.
References: FleetBank; Trustco Bank.

For full biographical listings, see the Martindale-Hubbell Law Directory

AMHERST, Erie Co.

ROSENTHAL, SIEGEL, MUENKEL & MALONEY, LLP (AV)

Evanstown Plaza, 392 Evans Street, 14221
Telephone: 716-634-8720
Fax: 716-634-3435
Email: rsm300@aol.com
Buffalo, New York Office: 300 Main Street.
Telephone: 716-854-1300.
Fax: 716-842-6354.

MEMBERS OF FIRM

Jay N. Rosenthal
David Alan Siegel
Joseph P. Muenkel
Patrick J. Maloney

ASSOCIATES

Linda M. DiPasquale
Gina M. Guzman
Paul F. Murak

OF COUNSEL

J. Michael Wolf

For full biographical listings, see the Martindale-Hubbell Law Directory

BAY SHORE, Suffolk Co.

LONG, TUMINELLO, BESSO, SELIGMAN, QUINLAN & WERNER (AV)

120 Fourth Avenue, P.O. Box 591 P, 11706
Telephone: 516-666-5766; 516-666-2500
Fax: 516-666-8401
Email: bob_quinlan_ltbsqw@msn.com
Naples, Florida Office: 1300 Third Street South, Suite 302 B.
Telephone: 813-262-3377.
Fax: 813-262-0313.

MEMBERS OF FIRM

John E. Long, Jr. (Resident, Naples, Florida Office)
Barry M. Tuminello
David H. Besso
Harold Seligman
Robert F. Quinlan
Kevin J. Werner

ASSOCIATE

Kevin R. Johnston

OF COUNSEL

Hon. Arthur M. Cromarty
Thomas J. Lavallee

For full biographical listings, see the Martindale-Hubbell Law Directory

*BINGHAMTON,** Broome Co.

BALL, MCDONOUGH & ARTZ, P.C. (AV)

The Professional Building, 117 Hawley Street, P.O. Box 1740, 13902-1740
Telephone: 607-772-6070
Fax: 607-772-0173

Dwight R. Ball
Kevin F. McDonough
Philip J. Artz

For full biographical listings, see the Martindale-Hubbell Law Directory

O'CONNOR, GACIOCH, POPE & TAIT, L.L.P. (AV)

One Marine Midland Plaza, East Tower-Seventh Floor, P.O. Box 1964, 13902
Telephone: 607-772-9262
Fax: 607-724-6002
Email: ogplaw@compuserve.com

Thomas F. O'Connor
James C. Gacioch
Alan J. Pope
Jeffrey A. Tait
Hugh B. Leonard
Robert N. Nielsen, Jr.
Stephen B. Atkinson
Kurt D. Schrader
Richard M. Hill
Patricia A. Cummings
Robert C. Murphy

OF COUNSEL

Walter T. Gorman
Cheryl Insinga

For full biographical listings, see the Martindale-Hubbell Law Directory

*BRONX,** Bronx Co.

MAXWELL S. PFEIFER (AV)

714 East 241st Street, 10470
Telephone: 718-325-5000
Fax: 718-324-0333
Email: mspfeifer@aol.com
New York, New York Office: 18 East 50th Street, 7th Floor, 10022.
Telephone: 212-980-0777.
Fax: 718-324-0333.
Hallandale, Florida Office: 1920 East Hallandale Beach Boulevard, Suite 606.
Telephone: 954-454-1550.

ASSOCIATES

Steven E. Millon
Robert S. Summer

OF COUNSEL

Sandra Krevitsky Janin
Anthony J. Hatab
Hon. Alexander A. Delle Cese (1919-1997)

For full biographical listings, see the Martindale-Hubbell Law Directory

*BROOKLYN,** Kings Co.

BONINA & BONINA, P.C. (AV)

Suite 1608, 16 Court Street, 11241
Telephone: 718-522-1786
888-MEDLAW-1
Fax: 718-243-0414
URL: http://www.medlaw1.com

John Anthony Bonina
John Bonina, III
Elizabeth Bonina
Andrea E. Bonina

Deborah A. Trerotola
Tyrone Sergio
Amy L. Insler

LEGAL SUPPORT PERSONNEL

Pedro Cintron
Inez M. Diaz
Sandra Ferrari

Reference: Republic Bank of New York.

For full biographical listings, see the Martindale-Hubbell Law Directory

*BUFFALO,** Erie Co.

BROWN & KELLY, L.L.P. (AV)

1500 Liberty Building, 14202-3663
Telephone: 716-854-2620
Fax: 716-854-0082
Email: mail@brownkelly.com *URL:* http://www.brownkelly.com

MEMBERS OF FIRM

Thomas J. Kelly
Rodney O. Personius
Frederick D. Turner
Paul Michael Hassett
Peter E. Klaasesz
Donald B. Eppers
Andrew D. Merrick
William P. Wiles
William D. Harrington
Joseph M. Schnitter
Paula L. Feroleto
Daniel J. Marren
Lisa T. Sofferin

OF COUNSEL

Ogden R. Brown
Charles F. Harrington
James T. Duggan
Karen Cook Serotte
Roland R. Benzow
Philip B. Abramowitz
Elizabeth R. O'Connor
Catherine E. Marra

ASSOCIATES

David S. Zygaj
Olney H. Clowe
Brian M. Melber
David O. Teach
Patricia S. Ciccarelli
Susan J. Schmidt

For full biographical listings, see the Martindale-Hubbell Law Directory

J. MICHAEL HAYES (AV)

69 Delaware Avenue, Suite 1111, 14202
Telephone: 716-852-2707
Fax: 716-852-0711
Email: JMHAYES@pcem.net *URL:* http://www.lawyers.com/jmichaelhayes

ASSOCIATES

R. Colin Campbell
Michael A. Riehler
David C. Caywood

For full biographical listings, see the Martindale-Hubbell Law Directory

QUINN, MCGARRY & CAFFERY, P.C. (AV)

1600 Statler Towers, 14202
Telephone: 716-856-6066
Fax: 716-856-2914

(See Next Column)

QUINN, MCGARRY & CAFFERY P.C., *Buffalo—Continued*

David C. Quinn
Francis P. McGarry
Michael P. Caffery
John P. Quinn, Jr.
Kenneth A. Patricia
Thomas J. DeBoy

Reference: Key Bank.

For full biographical listings, see the Martindale-Hubbell Law Directory

RENALDO, MYERS & PALUMBO, P.C. (AV)
350 Essjay Road, Suite 200 (Williamsville), 14221
Telephone: 716-631-5157
Fax: 716-631 0476

Anthony J. Renaldo
James I. Myers
Jeffery D. Palumbo

John C. Garas
Kelly C. Fitzgerald
Sean W. Hopkins

References: Manufacturers & Traders Trust Co. (Main Office); Marine Midland Bank.

For full biographical listings, see the Martindale-Hubbell Law Directory

ROSENTHAL, SIEGEL, MUENKEL & MALONEY, LLP (AV)
300 Main Street, 14202
Telephone: 716-854-1300
Fax: 716-842-6354
Email: rsm300@aol.com
Amherst, New York Office: Evanstown Plaza, 392 Evans Street.
Telephone: 716-634-8720.

MEMBERS OF FIRM

Jay N. Rosenthal
David Alan Siegel
Joseph P. Muenkel
Patrick J. Maloney

ASSOCIATES

Linda M. DiPasquale
David E. Rosenthal
Gina M. Guzman
Paul F. Murak

OF COUNSEL

J. Michael Wolf

LEGAL SUPPORT PERSONNEL

Patricia E. Lipka
Lois M. Cropp

For full biographical listings, see the Martindale-Hubbell Law Directory

*COOPERSTOWN,** Otsego Co.

GOZIGIAN, WASHBURN & CLINTON (AV)
Orange L. Van Horne (1907-1946)
Van Horne & Feury (1946-1970)
Van Horne, Feury & Gozigian (1970-1979)
Feury, Gozigian & Washburn (1979-1992)
201-204 Key Bank Building, P.O. Box 431, 13326
Telephone: 607-547-2522
Fax: 607-547-2845
Email: GozigianWC@aol.com

MEMBERS OF FIRM

Edward Gozigian
Philip L. Washburn
David J. Clinton

ASSOCIATE

E.W. Garo Gozigan

Counsel for: New York Central Mutual Insurance Co.
Local Counsel for: Key Bank, N.A.; Empire Farm Credit ACA.

For full biographical listings, see the Martindale-Hubbell Law Directory

FISHKILL, Dutchess Co.

FELDMAN, KLEIDMAN & COFFEY, L.L.P. (AV)
153 Main Street, P.O. Box A, 12524
Telephone: 914-897-5199
Fax: 914-897-5945
URL: http://www.fkc-law.com

MEMBERS OF FIRM

Jeffrey M. Feldman
Paul S. Kleidman
Richard J. Coffey
Robert F. Rich, Jr.

Reference: Bank of New York.

For full biographical listings, see the Martindale-Hubbell Law Directory

GARDEN CITY, Nassau Co.

GALLAGHER GOSSEEN FALLER KAPLAN & CROWLEY (AV)
1010 Franklin Avenue, Suite 400, 11530-2927
Telephone: 516-742-2500
Fax: 516-742-2516
Email: GGFKC__Postmaster@GGFKC.com
New York, New York Office: 350 Fifth Avenue, Suite 603.
Telephone: 212-947-5800.
Fax: 212-967-4965.

MEMBERS OF FIRM

James A. Gallagher, Jr.
Robert I. Gosseen (Resident, New York City Office)
Robert A. Faller
Alan D. Kaplan
Michael J. Crowley
William E. Vita
Brian P. Morrissey

ASSOCIATES

David H. Arntsen
Joseph A. Latasso
Amy L. Ruina
Gerald A. Corallo, Jr.

OF COUNSEL

John P. Coogan
Peter F. Vetro
William A. Bales, Jr.

For full biographical listings, see the Martindale-Hubbell Law Directory

SAWYER, DAVIS, HALPERN & DEMETRI (AV)
600 Old Country Road, 11530
Telephone: 516-222-4567
Telecopier: 516-222-4585
Email: litlaw@aol.com

MEMBER OF FIRM

James Sawyer

For full biographical listings, see the Martindale-Hubbell Law Directory

ISLIP, Suffolk Co.

SHLIMBAUM, SHLIMBAUM AND JABLONSKI (AV)
265 Main Street, P.O. Box 8, 11751-0008
Telephone: 516-277-4300
Telecopier: 516-277-4350

MEMBERS OF FIRM

C. Donald Shlimbaum
Lark J. Shlimbaum
Edward C. Jablonski

ASSOCIATES

Laura Mc Kenna
Joseph R. Mercurio

For full biographical listings, see the Martindale-Hubbell Law Directory

*ITHACA,** Tompkins Co.

WIGGINS AND MASSON, LLP (AV)
308 North Tioga Street, P.O. Box 399, 14851
Telephone: 607-272-0479
Telecopier: 607-273-0502
Email: law@wigginsandmasson.com *URL:* http://www.wigginsandmasson.com

MEMBERS OF FIRM

Walter J. Wiggins
Robin Abrahamson Masson
Erin E. McKinley
Lorraine Moynihan

Approved Attorneys for: Ticor Title Guaranty Corp.
References: Tompkins County Trust Co.

For full biographical listings, see the Martindale-Hubbell Law Directory

JAMESTOWN, Chautauqua Co.

BURGETT & ROBBINS (AV)
15 East Fifth Street, P.O. Box 3090, 14702-3090
Telephone: 716-488-3090
Fax: 716-483-3765
1-800-832-6582
Email: help@burgettandrobbins.com *URL:* http://www.burgettandrobbins.com

Dalton J. Burgett
Dale C. Robbins
Kenneth M. Lasker
Mary Speedy Hajdu
Robert A. Liebers
Andrew T. Radack

References: Fleet Bank, Jamestown, New York; Marine Midland Bank, Jamestown, New York; Lake Shore Savings and Loan Association, Jamestown, New York.

For full biographical listings, see the Martindale-Hubbell Law Directory

ERICKSON, WEBB & SCOLTON (AV)
111 West Second Street, 14701
Telephone: 716-488-1178
Fax: 716-488-1448
Email: ews@netsync.net

(See Next Column)

ERICKSON, WEBB & SCOLTON—*Continued*

MEMBERS OF FIRM

Alton R. Erickson (1904-1968)
Philip A. Erickson
Paul V. Webb, Jr.
Bruce S. Scolton
Lyle T. Hajdu

References: Marine Midland Bank, N.A.; Chase Manhattan Bank.

For full biographical listings, see the Martindale-Hubbell Law Directory

JERICHO, Nassau Co.

MARTIN, VAN DE WALLE, DONOHUE, MCGAHAN, CATALANO & FAIRGRIEVE (AV)

555 North Broadway, P.O. Box 350, 11753
Telephone: 516-681-3100
Telecopier: 516-681-5357

MEMBERS OF FIRM

Jules Martin (1928-1995)
Charles R. Van de Walle
Joseph A. Guarino (1946-1991)
Nicholas J. Donohue
James M. McGahan
Thomas C. Catalano, Jr.
Scott Fairgrieve
Michael Belitsis

ASSOCIATES

Randi M. Seidner
Laurie Ann Corallo

Representative Clients: Fidelity National Title Insurance Company of New York; Bancker Construction Corp.; Biener Pontiac-Nissan, Inc.; Festo Corp.; Chaminade High School; New York State Land Title Association, Inc.; Liberty-Mutual Insurance Company; Long Island Community Newspapers; Leaseway Transportation Corp.; Jones Fund; Northeast Adjustment Co., Inc.; Carolina Mirror Co.; Genesis Mirror Co.; New York Schools Insurance Reciprocal; New York Municipal Insurance Reciprocal; Leo and Arnstein Agency.

For full biographical listings, see the Martindale-Hubbell Law Directory

LAKE SUCCESS, Nassau Co.

DIKMAN AND DIKMAN (AV)

5 Dakota Drive, Suite 208, 11042
Telephone: 516-354-2526
Fax: 516-354-2528
Jamaica, New York Office: 161-10 Jamaica Avenue,
Telephone: 718-739-4830.

MEMBERS OF FIRM

Michael Dikman
David S. Dikman

Reference: Chase Manhattan Bank.

For full biographical listings, see the Martindale-Hubbell Law Directory

*MALONE,** Franklin Co.

FISCHER, BESSETTE & MULDOWNEY, L.L.P. (AV)

Country Club Road, P.O. Box 420, 12953
Telephone: 518-481-5000
Fax: 518-481-5203
Email: fbm@northnet.org *URL:* http://www.lawyers.com/fb&mlaw

William J. Herron (1905-1993)

OF COUNSEL

Henry A. Fischer

MEMBERS OF FIRM

James P. Bessette
John J. Muldowney
Richard F. Hunter

For full biographical listings, see the Martindale-Hubbell Law Directory

MELVILLE, Suffolk Co.

GANDIN, SCHOTSKY, RAPPAPORT, GLASS & GREENE, LLP (AV)

445 Broad Hollow Road, 11747
Telephone: 516-293-2300
Fax: 516-293-2918
Email: gsrmail@gsrlaw.com *URL:* http://www.gsrlaw.com
New York, N.Y. Office: 1212 Avenue of the Americas, 10036.
Telephone: 212-921-5200.
Fax: 212-921-5367.

PARTNERS

Charles J. Rappaport
Arnold M. Schotsky
Michael R. Greene
Michael G. Glass
Kevin E. Balfe
Michael S. Levine

ASSOCIATES

Margery Weinroth
Jonathan H. Freiberger
Brian Robert Gunn
Karen S. Bennett
Kenneth J. Lauri
Matthew J. Zullo
Diane G. Holland
James L. Forde

OF COUNSEL

Michael I. Gandin
Edward Kiley
Charles Krupin

For full biographical listings, see the Martindale-Hubbell Law Directory

MIDDLETOWN, Orange Co.

MACVEAN, LEWIS, SHERWIN & MCDERMOTT, P.C. (AV)

34 Grove Street, P.O. Box 310, 10940
Telephone: 914-343-3000
Fax: 914-343-3866

Kenneth A. MacVean (1926-1999)
Kermit W. Lewis
Louis H. Sherwin
Paul T. McDermott
Jeffrey D. Sherwin
Thomas P. Clarke, Jr.
John M. Clancy

SENIOR TRIAL COUNSEL

George F. Roesch, III

Kevin F. Preston
Ferol Reed McDermott
Anthony R. LoBiondo
James V. Galvin

OF COUNSEL

Samuel W. Eager, Jr.

Counsel for: Orange County Trust Co.; Middletown Savings Bank; First Federal Savings & Loan Association of Middletown; Goshen Savings Bank; Advest Bank.

For full biographical listings, see the Martindale-Hubbell Law Directory

*MINEOLA,** Nassau Co.

BARTLETT, MCDONOUGH, BASTONE & MONAGHAN, LLP (AV)

300 Old Country Road Suite 301, 11501
Telephone: 516-877-2900
Fax: 516-877-0732
Email: bmbmlaw@mail.idt.net
New York, New York Office: 237 Park Avenue, 10017.
Telephone: 212-983-2900.
Fax: 212-983-2901.
White Plains, New York Office: 81 Main Street, 4th Floor. 10601.
Telephone: 914-448-0200.
Fax: 914-448-0215.

MEMBERS OF FIRM

Clifford A. Bartlett, Jr.
Frank Bastone, Jr.
Peter G. Monaghan
Betty L. Atlas
Anthony F. Barbiero
Kenneth J. Burford
Richard W. Derry
Robert F. Elliott
Alan B. Friedberg
Edward J. Guardaro, Jr.
E. Gordon Haesloop
Sylvere M. Hyacinthe
Maureen C. Lavin
Garrett P. Lewis
Kenneth R. Reiser
F. Sean Rooney
Scott A. Singer
Alfred P. Vigorito
Janet C. Winter

OF COUNSEL

J. Edward McDonough

ASSOCIATES

John R. Aquaro
Peter E. Berman
Gina Bernardi
Robert J. Betz
Barbara A. Dalton
Deborah A. Dyckman
James C. Freeman
Jennine A. Gerrard
Steven S. Horowitz
Laura B. Jordan
John S. Kanzler
Belinda I. Katz
David G. Kelton
Peter A. Kolbert
Grace C. McCallen
Neil C. Mascolo, Jr.
Kevin R. Natale
Susan J. Onorato
John P. O'Sullivan
Warren J. Roth
Clare Salamida
Michael S. Sawaya
Tina Scognamillo
Milan P. Spisek
Christopher A. Terzian
Paul R. Varriale

For full biographical listings, see the Martindale-Hubbell Law Directory

HATTER, DONOVAN & MCFAUL, LLP (AV)

47 Mineola Boulevard, 11501
Telephone: 516-873-8800
Fax: 516-873-1418
Email: law@hdmlaw.com
URL: http://www.hdmlaw.com

MEMBERS OF FIRM

James R. Hatter
Thomas J. Donovan
John M. McFaul

Lawrence J. Freeze, III

For full biographical listings, see the Martindale-Hubbell Law Directory

HESSION & BEKOFF (AV)

29 Roslyn Road, 11501
Telephone: 516-746-2900
Telecopier: 516-877-0789

MEMBERS OF FIRM

Ronald Jay Bekoff
Thomas R. Hession

(See Next Column)

HESSION & BEKOFF, *Mineola—Continued*

ASSOCIATE

William Scott Petrillo

For full biographical listings, see the Martindale-Hubbell Law Directory

SHAYNE, DACHS, STANISCI, CORKER & SAUER (AV)

250 Old Country Road, 11501
Telephone: 516-747-1100
Telecopier: 516-747-1185

MEMBERS OF FIRM

Moe Levine (1908-1974)
Neil T. Shayne (1932-1998)
Norman H. Dachs
W. Russell Corker
Brian J. Sauer
Kenneth J. Landau
Jonathan A. Dachs

Naomi R. Nathan

For full biographical listings, see the Martindale-Hubbell Law Directory

*NEW YORK,** New York Co.

WALTER G. ALTON, JR. & ASSOCIATES, P.C. (AV)

108 East 82nd Street, 10028
Telephone: 212-639-9646
Fax: 212-249-7482
URL: http://www.lawyers.com/walteralton
Email: walteralton@earthlink.net *URL:* http://home.earthlink.net/~walteralton/
Cherry Plain, New York Office: P.O. Box 60.
Telephone: 518-658-2060.
Fax: 518-658-2060.

Walter G. Alton, Jr

For full biographical listings, see the Martindale-Hubbell Law Directory

BAUMEISTER & SAMUELS, P.C. (AV)

One Exchange Plaza, 10006-3008
Telephone: 212-363-1200
Telecopier: 212-363-1346
Email: BAUMSAM@AOL.COM
Morristown, New Jersey Office: 1776 On The Green, P.O. Box 1116, 07962-1116.
Telephone: 973-267-6666.
Telecopier: 973-605-1812.

Michel F. Baumeister
Douglas A. Latto
Dorothea M. Capone

OF COUNSEL

Lynn F. Samuels
Robert S. Franklin
Marc Z. Edell

For full biographical listings, see the Martindale-Hubbell Law Directory

CALLAN, REGENSTREICH, KOSTER & BRADY (AV)

One Whitehall Street 10th Floor, 10004
Telephone: 212-248-8800
Fax: 212-248-6815
Shrewsbury, New Jersey Office: 740 Broad Street.
Telephone: 732-345-9333.
Fax: 732-345-9444.
Garden City, New York Office: 1205 Franklin Avenue.
Telephone: 516-294-4383.
Fax: 516-294-4386.

MEMBERS OF FIRM

Paul F. Callan
Bruce N. Regenstreich
Warren S. Koster
Bruce M. Brady
William L. Brennan
Vincent A. Nagler
Scott W. Bermack

ASSOCIATES

Kenneth S. Merber
Michael P. Kandler
Vincent D. Finnegan
Stephanie Palermo
Walter Paterson Burrell
Beth S. Block
Meredith B. Borg
Pamela Patton Fynes
Mara J. Sibley
Eric A. Wasserfall
Amie Catherine Kalac (Resident, Shrewsbury, New Jersey Office)
Lisa B. Katz

For full biographical listings, see the Martindale-Hubbell Law Directory

THE LAW OFFICES OF MICHAEL E. CURAN, P.C. (AV)

59 John Street, Third Floor, 10038
Telephone: 212-513-1578
Fax: 212-513-1592

Michael E. Curan

Anthony Van Zwaren
Robert J. Callahan
Steven R. Mitlitzky

(See Next Column)

OF COUNSEL

William H. Maloney, Jr.

For full biographical listings, see the Martindale-Hubbell Law Directory

DE BLASIO, FIGMAN, EPSTEIN & LA ROCCA, P.C. (AV)

Woolworth Building, 233 Broadway, 10279
Telephone: 212-732-2620
Fax: 212-571-2045

Peter E. De Blasio
Alan H. Figman
Steven A. Epstein
Stephen S. La Rocca
John A. Orbon

For full biographical listings, see the Martindale-Hubbell Law Directory

FRIEDMAN, LEVY & GOLDFARB, P.C. (AV)

250 West 57th Street Suite 1619, 10107
Telephone: 212-307-5800
Telefax: 212-262-6128
Email: info@flgpclaw.com

Robert A. Levy
Ira H. Goldfarb

Nora McCarthy
Jeffrey I. Weiner
Stephen A. Saltzman

OF COUNSEL

Michael A. Gallo
Stephen A. Geffner

For full biographical listings, see the Martindale-Hubbell Law Directory

FUCHSBERG & FUCHSBERG (AV)

100 Church Street, 18th Floor, 10007
Telephone: 212-962-2800
Fax: 212-385-2308

MEMBERS OF FIRM

Abraham Fuchsberg
Seymour Fuchsberg
Preston J. Douglas
Stephen M. Warner

Harvey Goldstein
Irwin M. Berg
Bruce H. Goldstone
Martin Diennor
Maurice Sieradzki
Mordecai T. Schwartz
Frank P. Nervo
Richard Cohen
Iris Claire Finder
Thomas A. Agoglia
Robert M. Futterman
Richard V. Zand
John C. Henninger
Roger N. Lavinsky
Joseph Campisi
Devin P. Cohen
David Jacobs
Alan D. Bernstein
Ari Michael Gross

For full biographical listings, see the Martindale-Hubbell Law Directory

THE JACOB D. FUCHSBERG LAW FIRM (AV)

500 Fifth Avenue, 10110-0393
Telephone: 212-869-3500
Fax: 212-398-1532
Email: Fuchsberg@aol.com *URL:* http://www.Fuchsberg.com

MEMBERS OF FIRM

Jacob D. Fuchsberg (1913-1995)
Rosalind Fuchsberg Kaufman
Alan L. Fuchsberg

OF COUNSEL

Melvin C. Hartman
Mark Glen Sokoloff
S. Stanley Kreutzer
Daniel M. Cohen

SPECIAL COUNSEL

Abraham Abramovsky

ASSOCIATES

Andrew J. Carboy
Bruce Robert Calderon

For full biographical listings, see the Martindale-Hubbell Law Directory

GAIR, GAIR, CONASON, STEIGMAN & MACKAUF (AV)

80 Pine Street, 10005
Telephone: 212-943-1090
Fax: 212-425-7513
Email: mail@gairgair.com *URL:* http://www.gairgair.com

MEMBERS OF FIRM

Harry A. Gair (1894-1975)
Robert L. Conason
Seymour Boyers
Ernest R. Steigman
Stephen H. Mackauf
Jerome I. Katz
David G. Miller
Candice Singer Ram
Jeffrey B. Bloom
Anthony H. Gair
Ben B. Rubinowitz
Howard S. Hershenhorn
Mary Nicholls
Rhonda E. Kay

APPELLATE COUNSEL

Herman Schmertz

(See Next Column)

GAIR, GAIR, CONASON, STEIGMAN & MACKAUF—*Continued*

ASSOCIATES

Herbert H. Hirschhorn
Warren J. Willinger
Ronald Berson
Vincent F. Maher
Daniel A. Gair
Richard M. Steigman
Diana M.A. Carnemolla

COUNSEL

Harriet E. Gair

For full biographical listings, see the Martindale-Hubbell Law Directory

GINSBERG & BROOME (AV)

225 Broadway, Suite 3105, 10007
Telephone: 212-227-4225
Fax: 212-227-4228

Robert M. Ginsberg
Alvin H. Broome

ASSOCIATE

Christopher Jon Longman

OF COUNSEL

Jody H. Brackman
Anna Lewis
Simon Ginsberg

For full biographical listings, see the Martindale-Hubbell Law Directory

LAW OFFICES OF DAVID B. GOLOMB (AV)

Suite 527, 230 Park Avenue, 10169
Telephone: 212-661-9000
Telecopier: 212-661-6181
Email: golomblaw@aol.com

ASSOCIATE

Frank A. Longo

For full biographical listings, see the Martindale-Hubbell Law Directory

JULIEN & SCHLESINGER, P.C. (AV)

150 William Street, 19th Floor, 10038
Telephone: 212-962-8020

Alfred S. Julien (1910-1989)
Stuart A. Schlesinger

Mary Elizabeth Burns
Richard A. Robbins
Michael J. Taub
Marla L. Stein
Adam Schlesinger
Michael S. Schlesinger

For full biographical listings, see the Martindale-Hubbell Law Directory

KRAMER, DILLOF, TESSEL, DUFFY & MOORE (AV)

233 Broadway, 45th Floor, 10279-0137
Telephone: 212-267-4177
Fax: 212-233-8525
Email: kdtdm@compuserve.com

Charles Kramer (1916-1988)
Thomas A. Moore
James R. Duffy
Judith A. Livingston
Thomas J. Principe
Matthew Gaier

ASSOCIATES

Andrew S. Targum
William T. Burdo
Carmine Rubino
Anthony DiPietro

OF COUNSEL

Norman Bard
Henry H. Dillof
Stanley Tessel
William R. Dillof

For full biographical listings, see the Martindale-Hubbell Law Directory

KREINDLER & KREINDLER (AV)

100 Park Avenue, 10017
Telephone: 212-687-8181
Telecopier: 212-972-9432
Email: legal@kreindler.com *URL:* http://www.kreindler.com

MEMBERS OF FIRM

Harry E. Kreindler (1896-1983)
Lee S. Kreindler
Marc S. Moller
Francis G. Fleming, Jr.
Steven R. Pounian
James P. Kreindler
David C. Cook
David Beekman
Blanca I. Rodriguez
Noah H. Kushlefsky
Robert J. Spragg

OF COUNSEL

Paul S. Edelman
Milton G. Sincoff
Henry A. Gluckstern

ASSOCIATES

Lori B. Lasson
Susan Friery
(Not admitted in NY)
Andrew J. Maloney, III
Brian J. Alexander
David G. Nanz
Justin Timothy Green
Daniel O. Rose
Jacqueline M. James
Victoria J. Maniatis

For full biographical listings, see the Martindale-Hubbell Law Directory

LIPSIG, SHAPEY, MANUS & MOVERMAN, P.C. (AV)

40 Fulton Street, 10038-1850
Telephone: 212-285-3300
Fax: 212-406-4544

Harry H. Lipsig (1901-1995)
Mark J. Manus
Thomas J. Moverman
Alan M. Shapey
Marc R. Mauser

Josefina A. Belmonte
Glenn P. Dolan
Kent L. Benziger
Rene G. Garcia

OF COUNSEL

Henry R. Simon

For full biographical listings, see the Martindale-Hubbell Law Directory

LITMAN, ASCHE & GIOIELLA, LLP (AV)

45 Broadway Atrium, 10006
Telephone: 212-809-4500
Telecopier: GP II, III (212) 509-8403

MEMBERS OF FIRM

Richard M. Asche
Jack T. Litman
Russell M. Gioiella

ASSOCIATES

Thomas H. Burt
Howard Weiner

OF COUNSEL

Stephen Hogan

For full biographical listings, see the Martindale-Hubbell Law Directory

MCALOON & FRIEDMAN, P.C. (AV)

116 John Street, 10038
Telephone: 212-732-8700
Fax: 212-227-2903

Edward H. McAloon (1908-1986)
Stanley D. Friedman
Gunther H. Kilsch
Theodore B. Rosenzweig
Gary A. Greenfield
Brendan J. Lantier
Lawrence W. Mumm
Laura R. Shapiro
Lisa B. Goldstein
Thomas Medardo Oliva
Adam R. Goldsmith
Wayne M. Roth
Kenneth S. Oliver
Stephen S. York

Jennifer D. Correale
Mark Gregory Duncan
Kenneth Gordon Ellison
Ilene R. Fish
Gillian Fisher
Kenneth Fox
Evette E. Harrison
Alex Johnson
Ross Katz
Sherry Levin
Robin P. Lorell
Carolan Magnoli
Linda P. McMillan
Douglas M. Nadjari
Timothy O'Shaugnessy
Matthew Luke Prisco
Caryn Rosen
Corey Lee Wishner

LEGAL SUPPORT PERSONNEL

Robyn L. Reyes (Firm Administrator)

For full biographical listings, see the Martindale-Hubbell Law Directory

STEVEN E. NORTH, P.C. (AV)

148 East 74th Street, 10021
Telephone: 212-861-5000
Telecopier: 212-861-4055
Email: buzsen@aol.com

Steven E. North

For full biographical listings, see the Martindale-Hubbell Law Directory

PELTZ & WALKER (AV)

222 Broadway - 25th Floor, 10038
Telephone: 212-349-6775
Cable Address: "Dypelaw New York"
Telex: 230199 SWIFTUR ATTDPW
Telefax: (212) 227-4002
Email: Pelzwalker@aol.com

MEMBERS OF FIRM

Alexander Peltz
Paul E. Walker
Edward M. Schoenman
Miles S. Reiner
Bhalinder L. Rikhye
Jaymie L. Einhorn
Robert A. Rosenfeld

ASSOCIATES

Steven M. Silverman
L. Ruby Rey
Patrice R. McKenna
Sharon Elmaleh
Mitchel Lidowsky

OF COUNSEL

John J. O'Donnell
Edward V. Schwendemann
Jane Himelfarb

(See Next Column)

PELTZ & WALKER, *New York—Continued*

LEGAL SUPPORT PERSONNEL

PARALEGALS

Joseph Lipari
H. Steven Ortiz
Melissa Jamison
Maria D. Corvaia

For full biographical listings, see the Martindale-Hubbell Law Directory

RHEINGOLD, VALET, RHEINGOLD & SHKOLNIK, P.C. (AV)

113 East 37th Street, 10016-3042
Telephone: 212-684-1880
Fax: 212-689-8156
Email: info@rheingoldlaw.com *URL:* http://www.rheingoldlaw.com

Paul D. Rheingold
Hunter J. Shkolnik
Thomas P. Valet
Terrence E. McCartney
David B. Rheingold
Thomas P. Giuffra

Ryan S. Goldstein

For full biographical listings, see the Martindale-Hubbell Law Directory

JEFFREY SAMEL & PARTNERS (AV)

150 Broadway, 20th Floor, 10038
Telephone: 212-587-9690
Fax: 212-587-9673

Jeffrey Samel
David S. Gary
Dorothy Samel

ASSOCIATES

Robert G. Spevack
David M. Samel
Stacey L. Schwartz

OF COUNSEL

Richard A. Soberman

Representative Clients: New York City Transit Authority; New York City Housing Authority; Empire Insurance Co.; National General Insurance Co.; Federal Express Corp.; Shell Oil Corp.; American Building Maintenance Corp; United Fidelity & Guaranty Corp.; Little Caesar Enterprises, Inc.; Showbiz Pizza Time, Inc.

For full biographical listings, see the Martindale-Hubbell Law Directory

SCHNEIDER, KLEINICK, WEITZ, DAMASHEK & SHOOT (AV)

233 Broadway, Fifth Floor, 10279-0003
Telephone: 212-553-9000
Fax: 212-804-0820
Email: mail@lawyer1.com *URL:* http://www.lawyer1.com

Ivan S. Schneider
Clifford J. Stern
Arnold L. Kleinick
Gregory J. Cannata
Harvey Weitz
Keith A. Kleinick
Philip M. Damashek
Richard B. Ancowitz
Brian J. Shoot
Charles J. Nolet, Jr.
Robert B. Jackson
Leslie Debra Kelmachter
Louis J. Mitchell

John Kieran Daly
Judy Keenan
Jonathan S. Damashek
Paul A. Marber
Thomas V. Deffina
Lloyd M. Roberts
Dawn S. DeWeil
Joseph S. Rosato
David W. Druker
Derek S. Sells
Steven Gold
Lawrence A. Wilson, II
Keith H. Gross
James M. Lane
Erin K. Hurley
Donald D. Casale

For full biographical listings, see the Martindale-Hubbell Law Directory

PAUL A. SCRUDATO (AV)

150 E. 52nd Street, Suite 2700, 10022
Telephone: 212-371-1153
Fax: 212-753-5044
Email: paulscrudato@ibm.net

For full biographical listings, see the Martindale-Hubbell Law Directory

MARK E. SEITELMAN LAW OFFICES (AV)

Woolworth Building, 233 Broadway, 9th Floor, 10279
Telephone: 212-962-2626
Fax: 212-962-5050

For full biographical listings, see the Martindale-Hubbell Law Directory

SHANDELL, BLITZ, BLITZ, GLASS, BOOKSON & KERN, LLP (AV)

150 Broadway, 10038-4498
Telephone: 212-513-1300
Fax: 212-385-1916
Email: SBBGBK@aol.com

(See Next Column)

MEMBERS OF FIRM

Herman B. Glaser (1915-1994)
Arthur Blitz
Richard E. Shandell
Shoshana T. Bookson
Bert A. Blitz
Chet W. Kern

Mitchel H. Ashley
Fredrick A. Schulman

For full biographical listings, see the Martindale-Hubbell Law Directory

THE GERALD NEAL SWARTZ LAW OFFICES (AV)

767 Third Avenue, 26th Floor, 10017
Telephone: 212-421-9292
Fax: 212-421-9351
Email: gnswartz@aol.com *URL:* http://members.aol.com/gnswartz/index.html

For full biographical listings, see the Martindale-Hubbell Law Directory

WEISFUSE & WEISFUSE (AV)

300 East 42nd Street, 10017
Telephone: 212-983-3000
URL: http://www.lawyers.com/weisfuse&weisfuse

MEMBERS OF FIRM

Martin H. Weisfuse
Doreen K. Weisfuse

ASSOCIATE

Maureen Ann Sockett

For full biographical listings, see the Martindale-Hubbell Law Directory

WHITE, FLEISCHNER & FINO (AV)

140 Broadway, 10005
Telephone: 212-487-9700
Telecopier: 212-487-9777
Email: infor@wff-law.com
Red Bank, New Jersey Office: 272 Broad Street.
Telephone: 732-530-7787.
Telecopier: 732-530-8552.

MEMBER OF FIRM

Paul A. Fino, Jr.

For Complete List of Firm Personnel, See General Section

For full biographical listings, see the Martindale-Hubbell Law Directory

OLEAN, Cattaraugus Co.

DWYER & BLACK, P.C. (AV)

1616 West State Street, P.O. Box 648, 14760
Telephone: 716-373-1920
Fax: 716-373-3110
Email: dwyerblk@eznet.net

Joseph C. Dwyer
Jeffrey A. Black

References: First Tier Bank and Trust; Key Bank of New York.

For full biographical listings, see the Martindale-Hubbell Law Directory

ONEONTA, Otsego Co.

THE SCARZAFAVA LAW OFFICE (AV)

48 Dietz Street, Suite C, 13820-5107
Telephone: 607-432-9341
Fax: 607-432-1986
Email: eelittle@telegram.infi.net

John F. Scarzafava

ASSOCIATES

Elizabeth E. Little
Theodoros Basdekis

Reference: Key Bank.

For full biographical listings, see the Martindale-Hubbell Law Directory

PALMYRA, Wayne Co.

FOLEY & FOLEY (AV)

235 East Main Street, P.O. Box 211, 14522
Telephone: 315-597-6611
Fax: 315-597-8920
Email: JFOLEY12@MSN.COM

MEMBERS OF FIRM

James F. Foley
Ann Firestine Foley

Reference: Marine Midland Bank (Palmyra Office).

For full biographical listings, see the Martindale-Hubbell Law Directory

*POUGHKEEPSIE,** Dutchess Co.

HANKIN, HANIG, STALL, CAPLICKI, REDL & CURTIN, LLP (AV)

319 Main Mall Rear, P.O. Box 911, 12602-0911
Telephone: 914-471-7177
FAX: 914-471-0105
Email: hhscrc@aol.com *URL:* http://www.hvlaw.com
Newburgh, New York Office: 6 Jeanne Drive, P.O. Box 7229, 12550.
Telephone: 914-566-8888.
Fax: 914-566-3886.
LaGrangeville, New York Office: Lexington Park, Route 55, P.O. Box 15, LaGrangeville, New York.
Telephone: 914-473-1200.

MEMBERS OF FIRM

Jerard S. Hankin
Joel D. Hanig
Todd S. Stall
Edmund V. Caplicki, Jr.
Frank E. Redl
Daniel F. Curtin

Lynn M. Smookler
David V. Hasin

For full biographical listings, see the Martindale-Hubbell Law Directory

RHINEBECK, Dutchess Co.

STEVEN M. MELLEY (AV)

22 East Market Street, 12572
Telephone: 914-876-4057
Fax: 914-876-5745
Email: maizefield@aol.com *URL:* http://www.lawyers.com/stevenmmelley

For full biographical listings, see the Martindale-Hubbell Law Directory

*ROCHESTER,** Monroe Co.

FARACI & LANGE, LLP (AV)

400 Crossroads Building, Two State Street, 14614
Telephone: 716-325-5150
Toll Free: 888-325-5150
Fax: 716-325-3285
Satellite Office, Rochester, New York: IUE Local 509 Building, 1515 Lyell Avenue, 14606.
Telephone: 716-458-2800. Union Toll Free Number: 800-483-4882.
Fax: 716-458-3015.

John A. Bryant (1943-1995)
Angelo G. Faraci
Paul K. Lange
Joseph A. Regan
Stephen G. Schwarz
Vincent M. Moyer
Brian M. Zorn
Anthony A. Di Nitto
Matthew F. Belanger

ASSOCIATES

Michelle L. Callan
Carol A. Mckenna
James L. Bradley
Bradley P. Kammholz
John A. Falk
Patrick K. Russi

OF COUNSEL

Joseph S. Guadagnino

For full biographical listings, see the Martindale-Hubbell Law Directory

HALLENBECK, LASCELL, NORRIS & HELLER (AV)

A Limited Liability Partnership
One Exchange Street, 14614
Telephone: 716-423-5900
Fax: 716-423-5910
Email: HLNZ@hlnz.com

MEMBERS OF FIRM

Alfred M. Hallenbeck
David M. Lascell
Michael D. Norris
Cheryl A. Heller

COUNSEL

Robert A. Feldman
David A. Wier

Daniel P. Purcell
Meghan Mc Manus Di Pasquale
Suzanne E. Ouellette
Andrea F. Basso
Robert S. Attardo

For full biographical listings, see the Martindale-Hubbell Law Directory

LACY, KATZEN, RYEN & MITTLEMAN, LLP (AV)

The Granite Building, 130 East Main Street, 14604
Telephone: 716-454-5650
FAX: 716-454-6525
Email: MSS@Frontiernet.net
Charlotte, New York Office: 4292 Lake Avenue.
Telephone: 716-663-4543.
Hilton, New York Office: 20 Main Street.
Telephone: 716-392-2990.
Canandaigua, New York Office: 23 North Main Street.
Telephone: 716-394-5220.

(See Next Column)

Greece, New York Office: County Village Center, 110 Long Pond Road, Suite 214.
Telephone: 716-225-2470.
Fax: 716-225-5620.
Bergen, New York Office: 16 North Lake Street.
Telephone: 716-494-1382.
Ontario, New York Office: 1276 Ridge Road.
Telephone: 315-524-5000.
Roseland, New Jersey Office: 103 Eisenhower Parkway.
Telephone: 201-403-8001.
Penn Yan, New York Office: 116 Main Street, 2nd Floor, P.O. Box 439.
Telephone: 315-536-6281.

MEMBERS OF FIRM

Louis A. Ryen
Ronald A. Mittleman
Michael S. Schnittman
Peter T. Rodgers
Sally A. Smith
Karen Schaefer
Richard G. Curtis
Lawrence J. Schwind
David H. Walsh IV
David E. Anderson
Craig R. Welch
Christopher B. Mumford
Leslie W. Kernan, Jr.

COUNSEL

Leon Katzen
George F. Frey, Jr.
John J. Keigher
Paul A. Sandars, III

ASSOCIATES

David D. MacKnight
Nia J. Nichols
Terrance W. Emmens
Mark H. Stein
Denine K. Carr
Jacqueline M. Thomas
Stephen M. O'Neill
Jennifer Lynn Chadwick
William H. Drumm
Matthew A. Ryen
Roxanne A. Marvasti
Julie E. Meyer

General Counsel for: Village of Bergen, Bergen, New York; Village of Hilton, Hilton, New York; Byron-Bergen Central School District No. 1, Bergen, New York; Ferris Industries, Inc.; L. Woerner, Inc.d/b/a HCR.
Reference: The Chase Manhattan Bank, Rochester, N.Y.

For full biographical listings, see the Martindale-Hubbell Law Directory

ROBERT J. MICHAEL (AV)

39 State Street, Suite 420, 14614
Telephone: 716-232-3460
Fax: 716-232-4583

OF COUNSEL

Mark H. Tiernan

Reference: The Chase Manhattan Bank.

For full biographical listings, see the Martindale-Hubbell Law Directory

TREVETT, LENWEAVER & SALZER, P.C. (AV)

700 Reynolds Arcade, 16 East Main Street, 14614
Telephone: 716-454-2181
Telecopier: 716-454-4026

Oscar J. Brown (1884-1958)
Melvin H. Zurett (1905-1967)
Eric P. Smith (1900-1967)
Thomas W. Sullivan (1916-1981)
William V. Gough (1922-1985)
Walter C. Eves (Retired)
Robert T. Skipworth (Retired)
Ronald James Summers (Retired)
Thomas N. Trevett
Bohdan Wenglowskyj
Thomas E. Lenweaver
Kenneth Bersani
Richard M. Doyle
James A. Valenti
Karl F. Salzer
Peter A. Jacobson
Louis B. Cristo
Cynthia A. Constantino
Henry L. Jesserer, III
Lawrence J. Andolina
James C. Gocker

John C. Palermo
Jon Paul Getz
Nicole L. Black

Representative Clients: American Motorists Insurance Co.; Lumbermens Mutual Casualty Co.; Nationwide Mutual Insurance Co.; Interboro Mutual Indemnity Insurance Co.; Michigan Mutual Liability Insurance Co.; Virginia Surety Co.; Allstate Insurance Co.; American Hardware Insurance Co.; Pearl Assurance Co., Ltd.

For full biographical listings, see the Martindale-Hubbell Law Directory

ROME, Oneida Co.

PAUL L. PILECKAS (AV)

Professional Building, 217 North Washington Street, 13440
Telephone: 315-339-3020
Utica: 315-724-6381
Fax: 315-337-3876

Representative Clients: Don Davidson Motors, Inc.; Rome Rental, Inc.; West Electric, Inc.

For full biographical listings, see the Martindale-Hubbell Law Directory

ROSLYN HEIGHTS, Nassau Co.

NATISS, NATISS & GORDON, P.C. (AV)
277 Willis Avenue, 11577
Telephone: 516-621-0900
Telecopier: 516-621-1304
Email: MNatisslaw@aol.com

Marvin Natiss | Gary M. Natiss
Stacey Natiss Gordon

Sharon G. Haut

For full biographical listings, see the Martindale-Hubbell Law Directory

SALAMANCA, Cattaraugus Co.

BRADY, BROOKS & O'CONNELL, LLP (AV)
41 Main Street, P.O. Box 227, 14779
Telephone: 716-945-2000
Telecopier: 716-945-3566
Email: bbolaw@aol.com *URL:* http://www.lawyers.com/bbolaw
Randolph, New York Office: 165 Main Street.
Telephone: 716-358-6800.
Ellicottville, New York Office: 1887 Building, 1 Washington Street, P.O. Box 550.
Telephone: 716-699-8010.

MEMBERS OF FIRM

Thomas C. Brady | Kameron K. G. Brooks
Brian E. O'Connell, Jr.

Lori Pettit Rieman

For full biographical listings, see the Martindale-Hubbell Law Directory

*STATEN ISLAND,** Richmond Co.

MYRON G. LASSER, P.C. (AV)
60 Bay Street, 10301
Telephone: 718-727-8900
Telecopier: 718-727-9837

Myron G. Lasser

Reference: Citibank.

For full biographical listings, see the Martindale-Hubbell Law Directory

STONY POINT, Rockland Co.

HURLEY, FOX, SELIG & KELLEHER (AV)
Liberty Building, Route 9 W, 10980
Telephone: 914-942-2222
Fax: 914-942-0378
Email: HFSKlaw@aol.com
New City, New York Office: 60 Pine Street.
Telephone: 614-634-2050.

MEMBERS OF FIRM

Benjamin E. Selig | Glenn W. Kelleher

ASSOCIATES

Steven L. Kahn | Bob A. Kramer
Dana Selig Kahn | Kenneth P. Silver

Representative Clients: Bradlees, Inc.; Stop & Shop Companies; CNA Insurance Cos.; Federal Insurance Co.; Chubb & Son; Commercial Union Group of Insurance Cos.; Empire Insurance Co.; Omaha, N.B.; Excelsior Insurance Co.; Fireman's Insurance Company of Washington, D.C.

For full biographical listings, see the Martindale-Hubbell Law Directory

*SYRACUSE,** Onondaga Co.

CARROLL, CARROLL, DAVIDSON & YOUNG, P.C. (AV)
The Galleries of Syracuse, Second Floor, 441 South Salina Street, 13202-0352
Telephone: 315-474-5356
Fax: 315-474-5451

Lee Carroll | Eugene B. Young
John Benjamin Carroll (P.C.) | J. Alexander Davidson

Woodruff L. Carroll | Sarkis L. Harootunian

For full biographical listings, see the Martindale-Hubbell Law Directory

GREENE AND REID (AV)
Brighton Hill, 892 East Brighton Avenue, 13205
Telephone: 315-492-9665
FAX: 315-492-9741
Toll Free: 1-800-886-9665
Email: cajansen@worldnet.att.net *URL:* http://www.nofaultlawyer.com
Newark, New York Office: 330 East Avenue.
Telephone: 315-331-5633.

(See Next Column)

Sackets Harbor, New York Office: 101 East Main Street.
Telephone: 315-646-2500.
Fax: 315-646-1732.

MEMBERS OF FIRM

Arthur M. Greene | James E. Reid

LEGAL SUPPORT PERSONNEL

John F. Hogan | Polly Spring

Reference: M&T Bank.

For full biographical listings, see the Martindale-Hubbell Law Directory

LYNN LAW OFFICE (AV)
802 M & T Bank Building, 101 S. Salina Street, 13202
Telephone: 315-474-1267
Fax: 315-474-4514
Skaneateles, New York Office: 88 East Genesee Street.
Telephone: 315-685-1207.
Fax: 315-685-1047.

MEMBERS OF FIRM

William F. Lynn | Patricia A. Lynn-Ford
Thomas F. Shannon

For full biographical listings, see the Martindale-Hubbell Law Directory

MARTIN, MARTIN & WOODARD, LLP (AV)
Suite 300, One Lincoln Center, 13202-3010
Telephone: 315-478-2222
Fax: 315-478-4318

MEMBERS OF FIRM

Donald J. Martin | Lee E. Woodard
David P. Martin | Harold P. Goldberg
David M. Capriotti

ASSOCIATES

Wendy A. Kinsella | James T. Snyder
Daniel E. Dyer

For full biographical listings, see the Martindale-Hubbell Law Directory

SUGARMAN, WALLACE, MANHEIM & SCHOENWALD (AV)
HSBC Center, Fifth Floor, 360 South Warren Street, 13202-2680
Telephone: 315-474-2943
Fax: 315-474-0235
URL: http://www.sugarmanlaw.com
Buffalo Office: 1720 Rand Building, 14 Lafayette Square, 14203.
Telephone: 716-847-2523.
Fax: 716-847-2589.

MEMBERS OF FIRM

George E. DeMore | Stephen G. Pesarchick
Robert P. Dwyer | Sam A. Elbadawi

Representative Clients: Allstate Insurance Co.; CNA Insurance Companies; Chubb & Son; Liberty Mutual Insurance Co.; Carpenter Manufacturing Co., Inc.; General Accident Group; Hartford Accident & Indemnity Co.; Firemans Fund; New York Central Mutual; Progressive Insurance Co.
Reference: HSBC.

For full biographical listings, see the Martindale-Hubbell Law Directory

*TROY,** Rensselaer Co.

E. STEWART JONES (AV)
28 Second Street, 12181
Telephone: 518-274-5820
Fax: 518-274-5875
Email: info@esjlaw.com

E. Stewart Jones, Jr. | Jeffrey K. Anderson
W. Farley Jones | David J. Taffany
Peter J. Moschetti, Jr.

OF COUNSEL

E. Stewart Jones | Abbott H. Jones (1873-1939)
Arthur L. Rosen | Charles W. Marshall (1882-1945)

References: Key Bank and On Bank; Troy Savings Bank.

For full biographical listings, see the Martindale-Hubbell Law Directory

*UTICA,** Oneida Co.

JULIAN & PERTZ, P.C. (AV)
1629 Oneida Street, 13501-4701
Telephone: 315-797-5610
Fax: 315-797-7403

Robert F. Julian | Richard Pertz

LEGAL SUPPORT PERSONNEL

Tracey A. Mills (Paralegal) | Barbara A. Clark (Paralegal)
Nadine J. McIntyre (Paralegal)

For full biographical listings, see the Martindale-Hubbell Law Directory

*WHITE PLAINS,** Westchester Co.

MARVIN A. COOPER, P.C. (AV)

Suite 706, Northcourt Building, 175 Main Street, 10601
Telephone: 914-428-9200; 718-405-9700
Telecopier: 914-428-4126

Marvin A. Cooper — William H. Cooper

Reference: Chase Bank.

For full biographical listings, see the Martindale-Hubbell Law Directory

JAMES F. DONOHUE (AV)

81 Main Street, Suite 505, 10601
Telephone: 914-949-7766
Fax: 914-949-0324

ASSOCIATE

Thomas M. Roach, Jr.

Representative Clients: Nova Casualty Co.
Reference: Chase Bank/NBW Division, White Plains Branch.

For full biographical listings, see the Martindale-Hubbell Law Directory

KEANE & BEANE, P.C. (AV)

One North Broadway, 10601
Telephone: 914-946-4777
Telecopier: 914-946-6868
Rye, New York Office: 15 Elm Place.
Telephone: 914-967-3936.

Thomas F. Keane, Jr. (1932-1991)
Edward F. Beane
Donna E. Frosco
David Glasser
Lance H. Klein
Ronald A. Longo
Richard L. O'Rourke
Lawrence Praga
Joel H. Sachs
Steven A. Schurkman
Judson K. Siebert

Stephanie L. Burns
Eric L. Gordon
Jonathan Kornblatt
Stephanie M. Orefice
Patrick J. O'Sullivan
Frances M. Pantaleo
Nicholas M. Ward-Willis

OF COUNSEL

Peter A. Borrok
John F. Burkhardt
Eric F. Jensen

LEGAL SUPPORT PERSONNEL

Lenny Amodeo (Legal Assistant)
Barbara S. Durkin (Office Manager)
Sylvia J. Zuckerman (Legal Assistant)

For full biographical listings, see the Martindale-Hubbell Law Directory

RAYMOND J. KEEGAN & ASSOC., LLP (AV)

180 East Post Road, 10601
Telephone: 914-683-1100; Toll Free: 800-224-4878
Fax: 914-683-7363
Email: keegan@bestweb.net *URL:* http://www.keegan-law.com

Raymond J. Keegan — Jeffrey J. Keegan

For full biographical listings, see the Martindale-Hubbell Law Directory

O'KEEFFE & LINDGREN, LLP (AV)

707 Westchester Avenue, 10604
Telephone: 914-948-5300
Fax: 914-948-5399
URL: http://www.lawyers.com/okeeffe&lindgrenlaw

MEMBERS OF FIRM

Richard J. O'Keeffe
Thomas K. Lindgren
Joseph J. Staropoli, Jr.

OF COUNSEL

Robert L. Conkling

LEGAL SUPPORT PERSONNEL

PARALEGAL

Elizabeth M. Cleary

Reference: Chase Bank/NBW.

For full biographical listings, see the Martindale-Hubbell Law Directory

ROGAN GUIDA & ORENSTEIN (AV)

235 Mamaroneck Avenue, 10605
Telephone: 1-888-WIN-WITH-US; 914-328-4480
Fax: 914-328-4479
URL: http://www.NYlawyers.com
Email: RoganGO@aol.com *URL:* http://www.lawyers.com/personalinjury

(See Next Column)

Jeffrey P. Rogan
Toni M. Guida
David L. Orenstein

Representative Clients: Recore One Mortgage Corp.; LEASCO; Pappas Enterprises Inc.; Steelcase, Inc.; Printing Center of Westchester Inc.; Corporate Imaging, Inc.; King Jolo's Flowers, Inc.; Systems Exchange, Inc.; Domus Realty.
Reference: Fleet Bank.

For full biographical listings, see the Martindale-Hubbell Law Directory

VOUTÉ, LOHRFINK, MAGRO & COLLINS, LLP (AV)

170 Hamilton Avenue, 10601-1789
Telephone: 914-946-1400
Facsimile: 914-946-8024

Arthur J. Vouté, Jr.
Richard L. Magro
Charles D. Lohrfink, Jr.
Charles A. Collins, Jr.

Elliot A. Cristantello
Stephen F. Fischer
Ralph F. Schoene
Kevin P. Fitzpatrick
Catherine F. Gale
Hal Roberts
Stephen J. Riebling, Jr.
John A. Howard
Michael A. Sonkin
Kelly E. Cardany

Representative Clients: Aetna Casualty & Surety Co.; Allstate Insurance Co.; Chubb Group; CNA Companies; Medical Liability Mutual Insurance Co.; National Car Rental System, Inc.; Physicians Reciprocal Insurance Co.; Preferred Physicians Medical Insurance Co.; Risk Enterprise Management; St. Josephs Medical Center.

For full biographical listings, see the Martindale-Hubbell Law Directory

WILSON, BAVE, CONBOY, COZZA & COUZENS, P.C. (AV)

Two William Street, 10601
Telephone: 914-686-9010
Telecopier: 914-686-0873
Email: wbcc@aol.com

William H. Bave (1919-1991)
Donald C. Wilson (1917-1994)
R. Kevin Conboy
William H. Bave, Jr.
Michael J. Cozza
John C. Couzens, Jr.
Patricia Bave-Planell
Kevin D. Odell
Leo T. McGrath
Alexandra C. Karamitsos
Joel A. Hirshfield
Megan J. Conboy
Teresa A. Gruber

LEGAL SUPPORT PERSONNEL

PARALEGAL

John R. Pearsall

Representative Clients: State Farm Mutual Automobile Insurance Co.; Continental National American Group; Medical Liability Mutual Insurance Co.; General Accident Insurance Co.; Metropolitan Property and Liability; Royal Insurance; County of Westchester; City of Yonkers.

For full biographical listings, see the Martindale-Hubbell Law Directory

FRANCIS X. YOUNG (AV)

81 Main Street, 10601
Telephone: 914-285-1500
Fax: 914-285-0055
Email: leighyoung@mindspring.com *URL:* http://www.lawyers.com/fxyounglaw
New York City Office: 67 Wall Street, 24th Floor, 10005.
Telephone: 212-323-8040.
Fax: 212-943-2300.

For full biographical listings, see the Martindale-Hubbell Law Directory

YONKERS, Westchester Co.

ECKER, LOEHR, ECKER & ECKER, L.L.P. (AV)

One Executive Boulevard, 10701
Telephone: 914-968-0500; 914-965-4288
FAX: 914-968-0918
Email: eleellp@aol.com
New York, New York Office: 521 Fifth Avenue, 27th Floor, 10175.
Telephone: 914-965-4288;
Fax: 914-968-0918.

MEMBERS OF FIRM

Gerald E. Loehr
Louis A. Ecker
Lawrence H. Ecker
Robert L. Ecker

OF COUNSEL

Jock Thornton
Iris J. Iler
Tammi L. Blank-Ecker

LEGAL SUPPORT PERSONNEL

Carolyn Caruso

Reference: Hudson Valley National Bank.

For full biographical listings, see the Martindale-Hubbell Law Directory

NORTH CAROLINA

*ASHEVILLE,** Buncombe Co.

ELMORE, ELMORE & WILLIAMS, P.A. (AV)

53 North Market Street, 28801
Telephone: 828-253-1492
Fax: 828-253-9648
Email: eewlaw@wnc.com *URL:* http://www.lawyers.com/elmore-elmore-williams

Bruce A. Elmore
Bruce A. Elmore, Jr.
Reed G. Williams

For full biographical listings, see the Martindale-Hubbell Law Directory

*BEAUFORT,** Carteret Co.

DAVIS, MURRELLE & LUMSDEN, P.A. (AV)

412 Front Street, P.O. Box 819, 28516
Telephone: 252-728-4080
Fax: 252-728-3235
URL: http://www.lawyers.com/dmtlaw

Edward L. Murrelle
Treve B. Lumsden

Janet M. Lyles

OF COUNSEL

Warren J. Davis

Representative Clients: Cooperative Bank for Savings; Roman Catholic Diocese of Raleigh for Carteret County; International Longshoreman's Association Local 1807; Town of Cedar Point; John Yancey Corp.; Morehead City Export Terminal, Inc.; Crow Hill Farms, Inc.; Phoenix Foods, Inc.; Core Sound Waterfowl Museum, Inc.; Northland Ins. Co.

For full biographical listings, see the Martindale-Hubbell Law Directory

CHAPEL HILL, Orange Co.

EPTING & HACKNEY (AV)

410 Airport Road, P.O. Box 1329, 27514
Telephone: 919-929-0323
Fax: 919-929-3960

MEMBERS OF FIRM

Robert Epting
Elizabeth Lackey Jacobs
Joe Hackney
Karen P. Davidson
Steve Lackey

For full biographical listings, see the Martindale-Hubbell Law Directory

J. KIRK OSBORN (AV)

100 Europa Drive, Suite 421, 27514
Telephone: 919-929-0987
Fax: 919-942-1822
Email: kirkosborn@aol.com

For full biographical listings, see the Martindale-Hubbell Law Directory

*CHARLOTTE,** Mecklenburg Co.

BAILEY, PATTERSON, CADDELL, HART, MILLIKEN & BAILEY, P.A. (AV)

Suite 502, Cameron Brown Building, 301 South McDowell Street, 28204
Telephone: 704-333-8612
FAX: 704-333-5279
Email: BaileyPA8@aol.com

Allen A. Bailey
Walter L. Hart, IV
Michael A. Bailey
Emery E. Milliken
William J. Patterson
Martha L. Ramsay
H. Morris Caddell, Jr.
Helen Ruth Harwell

For full biographical listings, see the Martindale-Hubbell Law Directory

CAUDLE & SPEARS, P.A. (AV)

2600 Interstate Tower, 121 West Trade Street, 28202
Telephone: 704-377-1200
Telecopier: 704-338-5858
Email: caudlespears@caudlespears.com

Harold C. Spears
L. Cameron Caudle, Jr.
Timothy T. Leach

Counsel for: Bituminous Casualty Corp.; Baumann Springs A.G.; The A. G. Boone Co.; Capitol Funds, Inc.; Consolidated Freightways; Employers Mutual Casualty Co.; Mark Oil Company, Inc.; Metromont Materials; Otis Elevator Co.; N.C. Farm Bureau Mutual Insurance Co.

For Complete List of Firm Personnel, See General Section

For full biographical listings, see the Martindale-Hubbell Law Directory

DOZIER, MILLER, POLLARD & MURPHY (AV)

Cameron Brown Building, 301 South McDowell Street, Suite 700, 28204
Telephone: 704-372-6373
Fax: 704-347-0674
URL: http://www.dmpm.com

MEMBERS OF FIRM

W. Joseph Dozier, Jr.
Timothy H. Graham
R. Craig Miller, Jr.
George N. Miller
Scott T. Pollard
Richard S. Gordon
Gary L. Murphy
Thomas J. Falish
William Patrick Hobson
Kristin L. Smith

For full biographical listings, see the Martindale-Hubbell Law Directory

FERGUSON, STEIN, WALLAS, ADKINS, GRESHAM & SUMTER, P.A. (AV)

741 Kenilworth Avenue, Suite 300, 28204-2828
Telephone: 704-375-8461
Fax: 704-334-5654
Mailing Address: P.O. Box 36486, 28236-6486
Email: FSWAGS@aol.com
Chapel Hill, North Carolina Office: Suite 2, 312 West Franklin Street.
Telephone: 919-933-5300.
Fax: 919-967-4953.

James E. Ferguson, II
Geraldine Sumter
Adam Stein (Resident, Chapel Hill Office)
Henderson Hill
Jonathan Wallas
Thomas M. Stern (Resident, Chapel Hill Office)
Karl Adkins
C. Margaret Errington
John W. Gresham
Stephen Luke Largess

Rebecca Ann Thorne
Corie Diane Pauling
James E. Ferguson, III
Ann C. Todd

For full biographical listings, see the Martindale-Hubbell Law Directory

TIM L. HARRIS AND ASSOCIATES (AV)

4000 Tuckaseegee Road, 28208
Telephone: 704-392-4111
Fax: 704-391-1905
URL: http://www.timharris.com
Gastonia, North Carolina Office: 616 Cox Road. P.O. Box 249.
Telephone: 704-864-3409.
Fax: 704-853-1040.
Monroe, North Carolina Office: 3513 Highway 74 West, Suite E.
Telephone: 704-283-9200.
Fax: 704-392-9695.
Concord, North Carolina Office: 435 Church Street.
Telephone: 704-795-9317.
Fax: 704-795-5738

MEMBERS OF FIRM

Tim L. Harris
Brent A. Patterson (Resident, Gastonia Office)
Jerry Neil Ragan (Resident, Gastonia Office)

ASSOCIATES

Rebecca L. Thomas (Resident)
J. Neal Rodgers (Resident)
James W. Ragan (Resident)
Scott M. Adams (Resident, Concord Office)
Kathryn E. Rubi (Resident, Monroe Office)
Thomas H. Ainsworth, III (Resident)

For full biographical listings, see the Martindale-Hubbell Law Directory

PRICE, SMITH, HARGETT, PETHO & ANDERSON (AV)

A Partnership including a Professional Corporation
1430 Elizabeth Avenue, 28204
Telephone: 704-372-2160
800-737-2160
Facsimile: 704-372-6516
Email: priceatty@aol.com
Forest City, North Carolina Office: 552 Oak Street, 28043.
Telephone: 828-248-1448.
Fax: 828-248-4405.

Larry E. Price (P.A.)
Jeffrey B. Hargett
Wm. Benjamin Smith
Douglas A. Petho
Richard Lee Anderson

For full biographical listings, see the Martindale-Hubbell Law Directory

RAWLS & DICKINSON, P.A. (AV)

The Carillon Building, 227 West Trade Street Suite 2140, 28202
Telephone: 704-376-3200
Facsimile: 704-332-2716
URL: http://www.lawyers.com/rawls&dickinson

Thomas W. Dickinson

References: NationsBank of North Carolina; First Union National Bank of North Carolina.

(See Next Column)

RAWLS & DICKINSON P.A.—*Continued*

For full biographical listings, see the Martindale-Hubbell Law Directory

*DURHAM,** Durham Co.

GLENN, MILLS & FISHER, P.A. (AV)

Suite 709, South Bank Building, 400 West Main Street, P.O. Drawer 3865, 27702-3865
Telephone: 919-683-2135
Fax: 919-688-9339

Robert B. Glenn, Jr. William S. Mills
Stewart W. Fisher

Caitlyn T. Fulghum

For full biographical listings, see the Martindale-Hubbell Law Directory

HAYES HOFLER & ASSOCIATES, P.A. (AV)

1007 Vickers Avenue, 27707-1355
Telephone: 919-682-9663
Fax: 919-682-2016

R. Hayes Hofler

OF COUNSEL

Daniel B. Hill

For full biographical listings, see the Martindale-Hubbell Law Directory

*GASTONIA,** Gaston Co.

TIM L. HARRIS AND ASSOCIATES (AV)

616 Cox Road, P.O. Box 249, 28053-0249
Telephone: 704-864-3409
Fax: 704-853-1040
Charlotte, North Carolina Office: 4000 Tuckaseegee Road.
Telephone: 704-392-4111.
Monroe, North Carolina Office: 3513 Highway 74 West, Suite E.
Telephone: 704-283-9200.
Fax: 704-392-9695.
Concord, North Carolina Office: 435 Church Street North.
Telephone: 704-795-4317.
Fax: 704-795-5738.

MEMBERS OF FIRM

Tim L. Harris Jerry Neil Ragan (Resident)
Brent A. Patterson (Resident)

For full biographical listings, see the Martindale-Hubbell Law Directory

*GREENSBORO,** Guilford Co.

ALEXANDER RALSTON, SPECKHARD & SPECKHARD, L.L.P. (AV)

218 West Friendly Avenue, 27401
Telephone: 336-379-9302
Fax: 336-370-1232
URL: http://www.lawyers.com/aralston,speckhard

Donald K. Speckhard Stanley E. Speckhard

Representative Clients: Preferred Furniture Components, Inc.; Spring Financial Services, Inc.; Blazer Financial Services; Omega Sports, Inc.; Power & Heat Systems, Inc.; Branch & Company, P.A.; Acme Florist Supply, Inc.

For full biographical listings, see the Martindale-Hubbell Law Directory

BARRON & BERRY, L.L.P. (AV)

301 South Greene Street, Suite 310, 27401
Telephone: 336-274-4782
Fax: 336-379-8592
Mailing Address: P.O. Box 2370, Greensboro, North Carolina, 27402-2370
Email: vbarron@worldnet.att.net *URL:* http://www.lawyers.com/barronberrylaw

Vance Barron, Jr. Frederick L. Berry

For full biographical listings, see the Martindale-Hubbell Law Directory

BURTON & SUE, L.L.P. (AV)

419 North Elm Street, P.O. Box 20083, 27420
Telephone: 336-275-0512
Facsimile: 336-378-1390

MEMBERS OF FIRM

Gary K. Sue Walter K. Burton

ASSOCIATES

James D Secor, III William L. Hill
William T. Corbett, Jr. Kurt A. Seeber

For full biographical listings, see the Martindale-Hubbell Law Directory

CLARK BLOSS & MCIVER, PLLC (AV)

600 Dixie Building, 125 South Elm Street, P.O. Box 1349, 27402
Telephone: 336-275-7275
Fax: 336-275-1401
Email: cbm@cbm-law.com

David M. Clark Robert G. McIver
John F. Bloss Jonathan Wall

Representative Clients: The Prudential Insurance Company of America (litigation); Johnson Controls, Inc.
Approved Attorneys for: Jefferson-Pilot Insurance Co.

For full biographical listings, see the Martindale-Hubbell Law Directory

CLIFFORD CLENDENIN O'HALE & JONES, L.L.P. (AV)

415 West Friendly Avenue, 27401
Telephone: 336-378-1212
Fax: 336-333-9820
Email: ccojcd@nr.infi.net

MEMBERS OF FIRM

Harry H. Clendenin, III Robert O'Hale

For full biographical listings, see the Martindale-Hubbell Law Directory

GREESON & ASSOCIATES (AV)

408 Battleground Avenue, P.O. Box 2460, 27402
Telephone: 336-370-4800
Fax: 336-370-0305
Email: Greeson-Legal@worldnet.att.net

Harold F. Greeson

OF COUNSEL

Mark F. Griffin

George Podgorny, Jr.

For full biographical listings, see the Martindale-Hubbell Law Directory

HENSON & HENSON, L.L.P. (AV)

Suite 600, The Piedmont Building, 114 North Elm Street, 27401
Telephone: 336-275-0587
Facsimile: 336-273-2585
Mailing Address: P.O. Box 3525, 27402,
Email: hensnlaw@bellsouth.net

MEMBERS OF FIRM

Perry C. Henson Perry C. Henson, Jr.

ASSOCIATE

Clayton B. Krohn

For full biographical listings, see the Martindale-Hubbell Law Directory

PINTO COATES KYRE & BROWN, PLLC (AV)

3203 Brassfield Road, 27410
Telephone: 336-282-8848
Facsimile: 336-282-8409
Mailing Address: P.O. Box 4848, Greensboro, N.C., 27404
Email: PCKB@Interpath.com

Richard L. Pinto Martha P. Brown
Paul D. Coates Nancy R. Meyers
Kenneth Kyre, Jr. John I. Malone, Jr.
David L. Brown Deborah J. Bowers

Representative Clients: Travelers; Grain Dealers Mutual Insurance Co.; N.C. Farm Bureau Insurance Co.; Southern Pilot Insurance Co.; Peerless Insurance Co.; Penn National Insurance Co.; Virginia Mutual Insurance Co.; GAB Business Services; Harleysville Mutual Insurance Co.; Selective Insurance.

For full biographical listings, see the Martindale-Hubbell Law Directory

*GREENVILLE,** Pitt Co.

GAYLORD, MCNALLY, STRICKLAND & SNYDER, L.L.P. (AV)

498 Red Banks Road, P.O. Drawer 545, 27835-0545
Telephone: 252-321-7111
Fax: 252-321-7112

MEMBERS OF FIRM

Louis W. Gaylord, Jr. (Retired) D. Michael Strickland
Danny D. McNally Vernon G. Snyder, III

ASSOCIATE

Emma Stallings Holscher

Representative Clients: Wachovia Bank, N.A.; Nationsbank, N.A.; Garris Evans Lumber Co., Inc.; United States Fidelity and Guaranty Co.; The Daily Reflector, Inc.; Hastings Ford, Inc.; Nationwide Mutual Insurance Co.; U.S. Cellular; Ironwood Development, Inc.

For full biographical listings, see the Martindale-Hubbell Law Directory

HIGH POINT, Guilford Co.

SCHOCH & WOODRUFF, L.L.P. (AV)

500 East Green Drive, P.O. Box 1893, 27261
Telephone: 336-884-4151
Telecopier: 336-883-7151
Email: swlawgbo@bellsouth.net
Greensboro, North Carolina Office: 420 West Market Street, 27401.
Telephone: 336-272-9122.
Telecopier: 336-272-7991.

MEMBERS OF FIRM

Arch K. Schoch (1909-1980)
Louise Rodes Schoch (1909-1995)
Arch K. Schoch IV

ASSOCIATE

Arch K. Schoch V

Representative Clients: Archdale Oil Co.; Classic Gallery, Inc.; Cramer Wood Products, Inc.; The High Point Enterprise, Inc.; Jones & Peacock Insurance, Inc.; Phillips Industries, Inc.; Piedmont Chemical Industries, Inc.

For full biographical listings, see the Martindale-Hubbell Law Directory

*MONROE,** Union Co.

TIM L. HARRIS AND ASSOCIATES (AV)

Suite E., 3513 Highway 74, West, 28110
Telephone: 704-283-9200
Fax: 704-283-9200
Gastonia, North Carolina Office: 616 Cox Road. P.O. Box 249.
Telephone: 704-864-3409.
Fax: 704-853-1040.
Charlotte, North Carolina Office: 4000 Tuckaseegee Road.
Telephone: 704-392-4111.
Fax: 704-391-1905.
Concord, North Carolina Office: 435 Church Street.
Telephone: 704-795-9317.
Fax: 704-795-5738

MEMBER OF FIRM

Tim L. Harris

ASSOCIATE

Kathryn E. Rubi (Resident)

*MORGANTON,** Burke Co.

BYRD, BYRD, ERVIN, WHISNANT, McMAHON & ERVIN, P.A. (AV)

One Northsquare, Post Office Drawer 1269, 28680
Telephone: 828-437-4220
Fax: 828-438-4517
Email: info@byrdlaw.com

Joe K. Byrd (Retired)
Robert B. Byrd
John W. Ervin, Jr.
C. Scott Whisnant
Lawrence D. McMahon, Jr.
Robert C. Ervin
Peggy McDaniel Saunders

Michelle C. Pritchard

For full biographical listings, see the Martindale-Hubbell Law Directory

*NEW BERN,** Craven Co.

KELLUM & JONES, P.A. (AV)

219 Broad Street, P.O. Box 866, 28563
Telephone: 919-633-2550
Fax: 919-633-4623
Jacksonville, North Carolina Office: 445-L Western Boulevard.
Telephone: 910-455-4546.
Fax: 910-455-2422.

John W. Beaman (1911-1984)
Norman B. Kellum, Jr.
Douglas M. Jones

Michael E. Garland
John T. Briggs
T. Russell Peterman, Jr.
Russell L. Needell
J. Kevin Jones

For full biographical listings, see the Martindale-Hubbell Law Directory

*RALEIGH,** Wake Co.

BAILEY & DIXON, L.L.P. (AV)

2500 Two Hannover Square, 434 Fayetteville Street Mall, P.O. Box 1351, 27602
Telephone: 919-828-0731
Facsimile: 919-828-6592
Email: info@bdixon.com *URL:* http://www.bdixon.com

(See Next Column)

MEMBERS OF FIRM

Ralph McDonald
Gary S. Parsons
Carson Carmichael, III
Alan J. Miles
Patricia P. Kerner
Cathleen M. Plaut
David S. Coats
M. Denise Stanford
Kenyann Brown Stanford

OF COUNSEL

J. Ruffin Bailey
Wright T. Dixon, Jr. (Retired)
James H. Walker (1920-1994)
David M. Britt

ASSOCIATES

David Scott Wisz
Warren Tobin Savage, IV
Rita Lane Hanshumaker
Dayatra T. King
Philip Todd Gray
Ali John Hoomani

Representative Clients: Employers Casualty Co.; North Carolina League of Municipalities Risk Management Services; Lawyers Mutual Liability Insurance Company of North Carolina; Interlocal Risk Financing Fund of North Carolina; Nationwide Insurance Company; Liberty Mutual Insurance Co.; Erie Insurance Company; Southern Pilot Insurance Co.; Hartford Insurance Group; Scottsdale Insurance Co.; State Auto Insurance Co.

For full biographical listings, see the Martindale-Hubbell Law Directory

CRANFILL, SUMNER & HARTZOG, L.L.P. (AV)

Hillsborough Place, 225 Hillsborough Street, Suite 300, P.O. Box 27808, 27611-7808
Telephone: 919-828-5100
Fax: 919-828-2277
Charlotte, North Carolina Office: 301 South McDowell Street, Suite 1100.
Telephone: 704-332-8300.
Fax: 704-332-9994.

MEMBERS OF FIRM

Paul L. Cranfill
Robert W. Sumner
Dan M. Hartzog, Managing Partner
Alene M. Mercer
Richard T. Boyette
David D. Ward
Patricia L. Holland
David H. Batten
H. Lee Evans, Jr.
C. D. Taylor Pace
Samuel H. Poole, Jr. (Resident, Charlotte Office)
Susan K. Burkhart
Buxton S. Copeland
Robert H. Griffin
Kari Russwurm Johnson
Stephanie Hutchins Autry
Gregory M. Kash
Joseph B. Chambliss, Jr.
Anthony T. Lathrop (Resident, Charlotte Office)
William W. Pollock
Patrick H Flanagan
Emerson M. Thompson III
W. Scott Fuller

ASSOCIATES

Nicholas Peter Valaoras (Resident, Charlotte Office)
William J. Garrity (Resident, Charlotte Office)
Edward C. Lecarpentier III
Leigh Ann G. Smith
Jeffrey C. Thompson (Resident, Charlotte Office)

Representative Clients: American International Group; CNA Insurance Cos.; Great American Insurance Group; ITT Hartford; The Kemper Group; Liberty Mutual Insurance Co.; The Medical Protective Co.; The PMA Group; Safeco Insurance Co.; St. Paul Insurance Co.

For full biographical listings, see the Martindale-Hubbell Law Directory

FULLER, BECTON, SLIFKIN & BELL, P.A. (AV)

4020 Westchase Boulevard Suite 375, 27607
Telephone: 919-755-1068
Fax: 919-828-7543

James C. Fuller, Jr.
Charles L. Becton
Anne R. Slifkin
Asa L. Bell, Jr.
Sally Greene (Not admitted in NC)

For full biographical listings, see the Martindale-Hubbell Law Directory

RICHARD S. HUNTER, JR. (AV)

First Union Capitol Center, 150 Fayetteville Street Mall, Suite 1700 P.O. Drawer 470, 27602-0470
Telephone: 919-831-8722
Fax: 919-831-8734
Email: hunteratty@aol.com *URL:* http://www.lawyers.com/rshunter

For full biographical listings, see the Martindale-Hubbell Law Directory

KIRBY & HOLT, L.L.P. (AV)

Suite 100 3201 Glenwood Avenue, P.O. Box 31665, 27622
Telephone: 919-881-2111
Fax: 919-781-8630
URL: http://www.kirby-holt.com

David F. Kirby
C. Mark Holt
William B. Bystrynski
Isaac L. Thorp

For full biographical listings, see the Martindale-Hubbell Law Directory

Raleigh—Continued

MICHAELS, JONES, MARTIN, PARRIS & TESSENER LAW OFFICES, PLLC (AV)

Suite 200, 410 Glenwood Avenue, 27603
Telephone: 919-821-0005
Fax: 919-832-7426
URL: http://www.michaelsandjones.com
Durham, North Carolina Office: University Tower, Suite 526, 27707.
Telephone: 919-544-3000.
Wilmington, North Carolina Office: 1213 Culbreth Drive, Suite 104, 28405.
Telephone: 910-256-4005.
Charlotte, North Carolina Office: 301 South McDowell Street, Suite 400.
Telephone: 1-800-662-1234.

Paul J. Michaels
John Alan Jones
Gregory M. Martin
E. Spencer Parris
Hoyt G. Tessener
Kenneth B. Oettinger
H. Forest Horne, Jr.
Gary W. Jackson
Tamara R. Nance
John Michael Riley
Monique M. Peebles
Sandra W. Mitterling
Gabriel F. Jiménez (Not admitted in NC)
Ronald L. Pressley

For full biographical listings, see the Martindale-Hubbell Law Directory

PATTERSON, DILTHEY, CLAY & BRYSON, L.L.P. (AV)

4020 Westchase Boulevard, Suite 550, 27607
Telephone: 919-821-4020
Fax: 919-829-0055
URL: HTTP://WWW.PDCB.COM
Wilmington, North Carolina Office: 2214-C Wrightsville Avenue.
Telephone: 910-762-6544.
Fax: 910-762-4241.

MEMBERS OF FIRM

Grady S. Patterson, Jr. (Retired)
Ronald C. Dilthey
Robert M. Clay
E. C. Bryson, Jr.
Reid Russell
Stuart L. Egerton (Resident, Wilmington Office)
Mark E. Anderson
Donna Renfrow Rutala
Phillip J. Anthony
G. Lawrence Reeves, Jr.
Jonathan E. Hall

ASSOCIATES

Charles George
Mary McHugh Webb
Charles A. Madison
Claire A. Modlin
Scott B. Goodson
Sean A.B. Cole
Christian Michael Kennedy
Christopher J. Derrenbacher
J. Scott Lewis
Christopher M. Hinnant (Resident, Wilmington Office)
Patrick M. Meacham
Daniel M. Gaylord

Representative Clients: Amica Mutual Insurance Co.; Great American Insurance Group; Kemper Insurance Group; Medical Protective Insurance Co.

For full biographical listings, see the Martindale-Hubbell Law Directory

PIPKIN, KNOTT, CLARK & BERGER, L.L.P. (AV)

3101 Glenwood Avenue, Suite 250, 27612-5096
Telephone: 919-783-5900
Telecopier: 919-783-9650

MEMBERS OF FIRM

Ashmead P. Pipkin
Joe Thomas Knott, III
Michael Wood Clark
Bruce W. Berger

For full biographical listings, see the Martindale-Hubbell Law Directory

TWIGGS, ABRAMS, STRICKLAND & TREHY, P.A. (AV)

First Union Capitol Center, 150 Fayetteville Street Mall, Suite 1100, P.O. Drawer 30, 27602
Telephone: 919-828-4357
Fax: 919-833-7924
Email: tastlaw@tast.com

Howard F. Twiggs
Douglas B. Abrams
Donald R. Strickland
Jerome P. Trehy, Jr.
Karen M. Rabenau

OF COUNSEL

Donald H. Beskind
Margaret Smith Abrams
Jeff Erick Essen

For full biographical listings, see the Martindale-Hubbell Law Directory

*ROCKINGHAM,** Richmond Co.

HENRY B. WANSKER (AV)

316 East Washington Street, P.O. Drawer 220, 28380-3644
Telephone: 910-997-2522
Fax: 910-895-0511
WATS IN: 800-552-9587

For full biographical listings, see the Martindale-Hubbell Law Directory

ROCKY MOUNT, Edgecombe & Nash Cos.

HENSON AND FUERST, P.A. (AV)

2317 Sunset Avenue, 27804
Telephone: 252-443-2111
Fax: 252-443-9429
Email: henson-fuerst@lawmed.com

Thomas W. Henson
Robert L. Fuerst
Ronald D. Manasco
Thomas W. Henson, Jr.

David S. Henson

For full biographical listings, see the Martindale-Hubbell Law Directory

*SMITHFIELD,** Johnston Co.

ARMSTRONG & ARMSTRONG, P.A. (AV)

602 South Third Street, P.O. Box 27, 27577
Telephone: 919-934-1575
Fax: 919-934-1846

L. Lamar Armstrong, Jr.

For full biographical listings, see the Martindale-Hubbell Law Directory

*WILMINGTON,** New Hanover Co.

STEPHEN E. CULBRETH (AV)

514 Chestnut Street, P.O. Box 446, 28402
Telephone: 910-763-3416
Facsimile: 910-763-9975
Email: culbreth@wilmington.net *URL:* http://www.lawyers.com/culbrethlaw

For full biographical listings, see the Martindale-Hubbell Law Directory

HALL, CASHWELL & SULLIVAN, L.L.P. (AV)

718 Market Street, 28401
Telephone: 910-343-8433
Fax: 910-343-8165
Email: alex@hcslaw.com

Alexander M. Hall
Roseanna C. Cashwell
Dennis H. Sullivan, Jr.
John Green, II

For full biographical listings, see the Martindale-Hubbell Law Directory

SHIPMAN & ASSOCIATES, L.L.P. (AV)

11 South Fifth Avenue, 28401
Telephone: 910-762-1990
Fax: 910-762-6752
Email: shipman-associates@orotech.com

MEMBER OF FIRM

Gary K. Shipman

ASSOCIATES

Carl W. Thurman, III
C. Wes Hodges, II
Jennifer Jernigan Slusser

For full biographical listings, see the Martindale-Hubbell Law Directory

ZIMMER AND ZIMMER, L.L.P. (AV)

111 Princess Street, P.O. Box 2628, 28402
Telephone: 910-763-4669
Telecopier: 910-762-1999

MEMBERS OF FIRM

Herbert J. Zimmer
Jeffrey Lee Zimmer

Miriam M. Thompson
Susan E. Sutton
Jay S. Neisen

Reference: Wachovia Bank of North Carolina, N.A.; Centura Bank.

For full biographical listings, see the Martindale-Hubbell Law Directory

*WINSTON-SALEM,** Forsyth Co.

COMERFORD & BRITT, L.L.P. (AV)

250 West First Street Suite 300, 27101
Telephone: 336-631-8510
Fax: 336-631-8228
Email: @comerfordbritt.com *URL:* http://www.comerfordbritt.com

MEMBERS OF FIRM

W. Thompson Comerford, Jr.
Clifford Britt

ASSOCIATE

Martha Marie Eastman

For full biographical listings, see the Martindale-Hubbell Law Directory

Winston-Salem—Continued

WHITE AND CRUMPLER (AV)

11 West Fourth Street, 27101
Telephone: 336-725-1304
Fax: 336-761-8845

MEMBERS OF FIRM

James G. White (1924-1974)
Frank M. Armstrong (1900-1979)
Clyde C. Randolph, Jr. (1928-1995)
Fred G. Crumpler, Jr.
G. Edgar Parker
David B. Freedman
Dudley A. Witt

ASSOCIATES

Laurie A. Schlossberg
F. Kevin Mauney

OF COUNSEL

Barbara C. Westmoreland
Fred S. Hutchins, Jr.

Reference: Wachovia Bank and Trust Co., N.A., Winston-Salem, North Carolina.

For full biographical listings, see the Martindale-Hubbell Law Directory

NORTH DAKOTA

*FARGO,** Cass Co.

CONMY, FESTE, HUBBARD, CORWIN & BRUST, LTD. (AV)

200 Norwest Center, 406 Main Avenue, 58126
Telephone: 701-293-9911
Fax: 701-293-3133
URL: http://www.conmylaw.com

Charles A. Feste
Paul M. Hubbard
Wickham Corwin
Kim E. Brust
Michael M. Thomas
Robert J. Schultz
Nancy J. Morris

OF COUNSEL

Lauris N. Molbert
E. T. Conmy, Jr.

For full biographical listings, see the Martindale-Hubbell Law Directory

NILLES, HANSEN & DAVIES, LTD. (AV)

1800 Radisson Tower, P.O. Box 2626, 58108
Telephone: 701-237-5544
Facsimile: 701-280-0762
Williston, North Dakota Office: Energy Resource Building, 504 East Broadway, Suite 101, P.O. Box 1525.
Telephone: 701-572-5544.
Fax: 701-572-5561.

Stephen W. Plambeck
Leo F. J. Wilking

For Complete List of Firm Personnel, See General Section

For full biographical listings, see the Martindale-Hubbell Law Directory

VOGEL, WEIR, BYE, HUNKE & MCCORMICK, LTD. (AV)

502 First Avenue North, P.O. Box 1389, 58107
Telephone: 701-237-6983
Facsimile: 701-237-0847
Email: vogellaw@vogellaw.com *URL:* http://www.vogellaw.com

Carlton J. Hunke
Mart Daniel Vogel
W. Todd Haggart
Bruce Douglas Quick
Wayne W. Carlson

Representative Clients: American Family Insurance Group; CIGNA Companies; CNA Insurance Company; Dakota Fire Insurance Company; Midwest Medical Insurance Company; Milbank State Automobile Insurance Company; National Farmers Union Insurance Company; Phico Insurance Company; St. Paul Insurance Companies.

For Complete List of Firm Personnel, See General Section

For full biographical listings, see the Martindale-Hubbell Law Directory

OHIO

*AKRON,** Summit Co.

GRISI & RIEGLER (AV)

159 South Main Street, Suite 1030, 44308
Telephone: 216-535-8171
Fax: 216-535-0106
Email: grisi@nls.net

(See Next Column)

Charles E. Grisi
Edward J. Riegler

For full biographical listings, see the Martindale-Hubbell Law Directory

PERANTINIDES & NOLAN CO., L.P.A. (AV)

300 Courtyard Square, 80 South Summit Street, 44308-1736
Telephone: 330-253-5454
Telecopier: 330-253-6524
Email: pn@perantinides.com

Paul G. Perantinides
Chris T. Nolan

James J. Gutbrod
Christopher L. Parker
Peter D. Janos
Antonios P. Tsarouhas
Christina Simoudis
Sophie Mitsopoulos

References: First National Bank of Akron; National City Bank, Akron; Society Bank; Charter One Bank.

For full biographical listings, see the Martindale-Hubbell Law Directory

SCANLON & GEARINGER CO., L.P.A. (AV)

1100 First National Tower, 106 South Main Street, 44308-1463
Telephone: 330-376-4558
Telecopier: 330-376-3550

Timothy F. Scanlon
Bradford M. Gearinger
Michael J. Del Medico
Mark Hilkert
Patrick J. Hart
Robert A. Royer
Kevin P. Hardman
Maura E. Scanlon
John F. Hill

John T. Scanlon

For full biographical listings, see the Martindale-Hubbell Law Directory

A. RUSSELL SMITH (AV)

503 Key Building, 159 South Main Street, 44308
Telephone: 330-434-7167; 877-434-7167
Fax: 330-434-7195
Email: smithar@bright.net

A. Russell Smith

R. Bryan Nace

For full biographical listings, see the Martindale-Hubbell Law Directory

*BOWLING GREEN,** Wood Co.

SPITLER, VOGTSBERGER & HUFFMAN, LLP (AV)

131 East Court Street, 43402-2495
Telephone: 419-352-2535
Fax: 419-353-8728
Email: svh@svhlaw.com
Rossford, Ohio Office: 932 Dixie Highway.
Telephone: 419-666-7130.

Emmett V. Spitler (1911-1995)

MEMBERS OF FIRM

Daniel T. Spitler
Robert E. Spitler
Thomas H. Vogtsberger
Rex H. Huffman
Diane Rausch Huffman
Steven L. Spitler

Mimi S. Yoon
Megan E. Newlove

Representative Clients: First Federal Bank; Prudential Insurance Company of America; The Mutual Benefit Life Insurance Co.; John Hancock Mutual Life Insurance Co.; Equitable Life Assurance Society of the U.S.; Minnesota Mutual Life Insurance Co.; Wood County Regional Water and Sewer District.

For full biographical listings, see the Martindale-Hubbell Law Directory

*CINCINNATI,** Hamilton Co.

CLEMENTS, MAHIN & COHEN (AV)

708 Walnut Street, Suite 600, 45202-4009
Telephone: 513-721-6500
Facsimile: 513-763-6415

MEMBERS OF FIRM

William E. Clements
John E. Mahin
Edward Cohen

For full biographical listings, see the Martindale-Hubbell Law Directory

ROBERT J. GEHRING CO., L.P.A. (AV)

4th Floor, 105 East Fourth Street, 45202
Telephone: 513-721-2758
Fax: 513-621-9285

Robert J. Gehring

For full biographical listings, see the Martindale-Hubbell Law Directory

Cincinnati—Continued

GOODMAN & GOODMAN A LEGAL PROFESSIONAL ASSOCIATION (AV)

123 East Fourth Street, 45202
Telephone: 513-621-1505; 1-800-494-4529
Fax: 513-621-6900
URL: http://www.goodlaw.com

Sol Goodman (1906-1971) — Stanley Goodman
Ronald J. Goodman

Donald P. Morrisroe — Reneé S. Frankel
John E. Stillpass — Jeffrey S. Goodman

For full biographical listings, see the Martindale-Hubbell Law Directory

KEPLEY, GILLIGAN & EYRICH A LEGAL PROFESSIONAL ASSOCIATION (AV)

525 Vine Street, Suite 2200, 45202
Telephone: 513-241-5540; 621-1045
Fax: 513-241-8111; 621-0038

Augustine Giglio

Representative Clients and References furnished upon request.

For full biographical listings, see the Martindale-Hubbell Law Directory

THE LAWRENCE FIRM, L.P.A. (AV)

2100 Firstar Center at Fountain Square, 425 Walnut Street, 45202
Telephone: 513-651-4130
Fax: Available upon request
Email: lawyers@lawrencefirm.com *URL:* http://www.lawrencefirm.com

Richard D. Lawrence

David A. Johns — Jennifer L. Lawrence
Richard Lanahan Goodman — Patrick J. Beirne
Thomas C. Korbee — Donna M. Bloemer
Roger N. Braden — Virginia M. Baker
Rick J. Sommer

For full biographical listings, see the Martindale-Hubbell Law Directory

SHEA & ASSOCIATES (AV)

600 Flatiron Building, 401 East Court Street, 45202-1355
Telephone: 513-621-8333
Telecopier: 513-651-3272
Email: SheaLawFrm@aol.com *URL:* http://www.attyfind.com/jwshea

Joseph W. Shea III

ASSOCIATE

Shirley A. Coffey

LEGAL SUPPORT PERSONNEL

Connie DeFillippo

For full biographical listings, see the Martindale-Hubbell Law Directory

WAITE, SCHNEIDER, BAYLESS & CHESLEY CO., L.P.A. (AV)

1513 Central Trust Tower, Fourth and Vine Streets, 45202
Telephone: 513-621-0267
Fax: 513-381-2375; 621-0262

Stanley M. Chesley

Thomas F. Rehme — Jerome L. Skinner
Robert A. Steinberg — Janet G. Abaray
Fay E. Stilz — Paul M. De Marco
Louise M. Roselle — Terrence L. Goodman
D. Arthur Rabourn — Colleen M. Hegge

For full biographical listings, see the Martindale-Hubbell Law Directory

*CLEVELAND,** Cuyahoga Co.

APICELLA AND TRAPP (AV)

1200 Bond Court Building, 1300 East Ninth Street, 44114-1503
Telephone: 216-696-3550
Fax: 216-696-3830
Email: aptrapp@msn.com

MEMBERS OF FIRM

F. M. Apicella — Mary Jane Trapp

Reference: Key Bank.

For full biographical listings, see the Martindale-Hubbell Law Directory

BERGER & ZAVESKY CO., L.P.A. (AV)

Rockefeller Building, Suite 1425, 614 Superior Avenue, N.W., 44113
Telephone: 216-830-9000
Toll Free in Ohio: 1-877-515-5677
Fax: 216-830-4200
Email: bergzav@oh.verio.com *URL:* http://www.lawyers.com/bzlaw

I. Joseph Berger — Robert J. Zavesky

Jeffrey D. Lojewski — Anthony R. Petruzzi
Marc D. Stone

OF COUNSEL

George W. White

For full biographical listings, see the Martindale-Hubbell Law Directory

FRIEDMAN, DOMIANO & SMITH CO., L.P.A. (AV)

Sixth Floor, Standard Building, 1370 Ontario Street, 44113-1701
Telephone: 216-621-0070; 1-800-280-0070
Fax: 216-621-4008
Email: fds.atty@worldnet.att.net *URL:* http://www.fds@advpages.com
Marco Island, Florida Office: 881 Panama Court, Suite 305, 33937.
Telephone: 941-642-0252.

Jeffrey H. Friedman — M. David Smith
Joseph C. Domiano — Lisa M. Gerlack

Stephen S. Vanek — Kevin L. Lenson
Michael L. Eisner — Tracey S. McGurk

For full biographical listings, see the Martindale-Hubbell Law Directory

HERMANN, CAHN & SCHNEIDER (AV)

Suite 500, 1301 East Ninth Street, 44114
Telephone: 216-781-5515
Facsimile: 216-781-1030
Email: hcs@en.com

MEMBER OF FIRM

Kent B. Schneider

For full biographical listings, see the Martindale-Hubbell Law Directory

JANIK & FORBES (AV)

Building Two, 8223 Brecksville Road, 44141-1371
Telephone: 440-838-7600
Fax: 440-838-7601

MEMBERS OF FIRM

Steven G. Janik — Steven Forbes

For Complete List of Firm Personnel, See General Section

For full biographical listings, see the Martindale-Hubbell Law Directory

KREMBS & ALKIRE LLP (AV)

750 Courthouse Square, 310 West Lakeside Avenue, 44113-1021
Telephone: 216-875-7500
Fax: 216-875-7501
URL: http://www.krembs-alkire.com

Andrew P. Krembs — Richard C. Alkire
Dean C. Nieding

For full biographical listings, see the Martindale-Hubbell Law Directory

LEVIN, MARMAROS & CHARMS CO., L.P.A. (AV)

2970 BP Tower, 200 Public Square, 44114
Telephone: 216-781-4900
Fax: 216-787-0330
URL: http://www.lawyers.com/lmc

Joel Levin — Peter W. Marmaros
Stephen J. Charms

Anthony R. Brighton

For full biographical listings, see the Martindale-Hubbell Law Directory

LOWE • EKLUND • WAKEFIELD CO., L.P.A. (AV)

Tower City Center 610 Skylight Office Tower, 1660 West Second Street, 44113-1454
Telephone: 216-781-2600
Fax: 216-781-2610
Email: lew@lewlaw.com *URL:* http://www.lewlaw.com

James A. Lowe — Mark L. Wakefield
Claudia Rieth Eklund — Dennis P. Mulvihill

Gregory S. Scott — Andrew S. Goldwasser

(See Next Column)

LOWE • EKLUND • WAKEFIELD CO. L.P.A., *Cleveland—Continued*

OF COUNSEL

Donald Cybulski

For full biographical listings, see the Martindale-Hubbell Law Directory

NURENBERG, PLEVIN, HELLER & MCCARTHY CO., L.P.A. (AV)

1370 Ontario Street First Floor, 44113-1792
Telephone: 216-621-2300; Toll Free: 1-800-562-7438
Fax: 216-771-2242
Email: nphm@nphm.com *URL:* http://www.nphm.com

A. H. Dudnik (1905-1963)
S. F. Komito (1902-1984)
Marshall I. Nurenberg
Leon M. Plevin
Maurice L. Heller
John J. McCarthy
Thomas Mester
Harlan M. Gordon
David M. Paris
Richard L. Demsey
Jamie R. Lebovitz
William S. Jacobson
Jeffrey A. Leikin

Robin J. Peterson
Robert S. Zeller
Ellen M. McCarthy
J. Charles Ruiz-Bueno
Kathleen J. St. John
Jonathan D. Mester
Brenda M. Johnson

Reference: Society Key Corp.

For full biographical listings, see the Martindale-Hubbell Law Directory

ROBERT P. RUTTER (AV)

One Summit Office Park, 4700 Rockside Road Suite 650, 44131
Telephone: 216-642-1425
Fax: 216-642-0613
URL: http://www.rocklaw.com

For full biographical listings, see the Martindale-Hubbell Law Directory

TIMOTHY A. SHIMKO & ASSOCIATES A LEGAL PROFESSIONAL ASSOCIATION (AV)

2010 Huntington Building, 925 Euclid Avenue, 44115
Telephone: 216-241-8300
Fax: 216-241-2702
Email: taslaw@ix.netcom.com *URL:* http://www.netcom.com/~taslaw

Timothy A. Shimko

Frank E. Piscitelli, Jr.

Reference: National City Bank, Cleveland.

For full biographical listings, see the Martindale-Hubbell Law Directory

SPANGENBERG, SHIBLEY & LIBER LLP (AV)

2400 National City Center, 1900 East Ninth Street, 44114-3400
Telephone: 216-696-3232
Fax: 216-696-3924
Email: ssl@Spanglaw.com *URL:* http://www.Spanglaw.com

MEMBERS OF FIRM

Craig Spangenberg (1914-1998)
Norman W. Shibley (1921-1992)
Donald P. Traci (Retired)
John D. Liber
Robert A. Marcis
Peter H. Weinberger
William Hawal
Peter J. Brodhead
Dennis R. Lansdowne

ASSOCIATES

Justin F. Madden
Mary A. Cavanaugh
Stuart E. Scott
Rhonda Baker Debevec

For full biographical listings, see the Martindale-Hubbell Law Directory

STEWART AND DE CHANT CO., L.P.A. (AV)

The Atrium Office Plaza-Suite 850, 668 Euclid Avenue, 44114-3060
Telephone: 216-781-2258
Fax: 216-781-8210
Email: INFO@STEWARTDECHANT.COM *URL:* http://www.STEWARTdeChant.COM

Lawrence E. Stewart
Thomas H. De Chant
Fred Wendel III
Scott E. Stewart
Samuel V. Butcher
Lawrence C. Davison
Matthew T. Brady

Reference: Keybank (Main Office).

For full biographical listings, see the Martindale-Hubbell Law Directory

TRACI & MARX CO., L.P.A. (AV)

55 Public Square, Suite 1550, 44113
Telephone: 216-623-8010
Fax: 216-623-8012
Email: lawyers@tracimarx.com

(See Next Column)

Robert V. Traci
James A. Marx

For full biographical listings, see the Martindale-Hubbell Law Directory

*COLUMBUS,** Franklin Co.

J. BOYD BINNING (AV)

592 South Third Street, 43215
Telephone: 614-224-1979
Facsimile: 614-224-1984

For full biographical listings, see the Martindale-Hubbell Law Directory

DENMEAD & MALONEY (AV)

37 West Broad Street, Suite 1150, 43215-4189
Telephone: 614-228-5271
Telecopier: 614-228-7624
Email: cdkmlaw@infinet.com

Craig Denmead
Kevin M. Maloney

For full biographical listings, see the Martindale-Hubbell Law Directory

GERRITY AND BURRIER (AV)

50 West Broad Street, 43215
Telephone: 614-464-2211
Fax: 614-464-0110
URL: http://www.lawyers.com/gerrity&associates

Timothy D. Gerrity
Brian C. Burrier

For full biographical listings, see the Martindale-Hubbell Law Directory

GERTNER & GERTNER (AV)

Suite 1780, 88 East Broad Street, 43215
Telephone: 614-463-9393
Fax: 614-463-9669
URL: http://www.lawyers.com/gertner&gertner

MEMBERS OF FIRM

Abraham Gertner (1909-1996)
Michael H. Gertner

For full biographical listings, see the Martindale-Hubbell Law Directory

KEENER DOUCHER CURLEY & PATTERSON A LEGAL PROFESSIONAL ASSOCIATION (AV)

88 East Broad Street, Suite 1750, 43215
Telephone: 614-280-1100
Fax: 614-280-9503
Email: KDCP@IWAYNET.NET

Thomas J. Keener
Paul M. Doucher
W. Charles Curley
David T. Patterson
Kevin R. Bush

Michael J. Kelley
Kimberley A. Doucher
Amy K. Schermer

For full biographical listings, see the Martindale-Hubbell Law Directory

MARK KITRICK CO., L.P.A. (AV)

First Avenue Office Center, 929 Harrison Avenue, Suite 102-103, 43215-6501
Telephone: 614-297-7711
Fax: 614-297-8985
URL: http://www.kitricklaw.com
Email: mkitrick@ljextra.com *URL:* http://www.lawyers.com/markkitrick
Cincinnati, Ohio Office: 6912 Silverton Avenue, P.O. Box 36213, 45236.
Telephone: 513-984-9584

Mark M. Kitrick

Mark D. Lewis

For full biographical listings, see the Martindale-Hubbell Law Directory

LAMKIN, VAN EMAN, TRIMBLE, BEALS & ROURKE (AV)

Suite 200, 500 South Front Street, 43215-5671
Telephone: 614-224-8187
Fax: 614-224-4943
URL: http://www.lawyers.com/lvtb&rlaw

MEMBERS OF FIRM

William W. Lamkin
Timothy L. Van Eman
Thomas W. Trimble
David A. Beals
Michael J. Rourke
Kathy A. Dougherty
Kenneth S. Blumenthal

Reference: Huntington National Bank.

For full biographical listings, see the Martindale-Hubbell Law Directory

Columbus—Continued

McCarthy, Palmer, Volkema & Thomas A Legal Professional Association (AV)

140 East Town Street, Suite 1100, 43215
Telephone: Telephone: 614-221-4400
Telecopier: 614-221-6010
URL: http://www.mccarthypalmer.com
Email: attorneys@mccarthypalmer.com *URL:* http://www.lawyers.com/attorneysmccarthy

Dennis M. McCarthy
Robert Gray Palmer
Daniel R. Volkema
Warner M. Thomas, Jr.
Michael S. Miller
Elizabeth Schorpp Burkett
Craig P. Scott
Tony C. Merry

Jennifer K. Thivener

Reference: Huntington National Bank.

For full biographical listings, see the Martindale-Hubbell Law Directory

Nemeth, Caborn & Butauski (AV)

21 East Frankfort Street, 43206-1069
Telephone: 614-443-4866
Fax: 614-443-4860
URL: http://www.lawyers.com/nemeth
Email: nemeth@nemethlaw.com *URL:* http://www.nemethlaw.com

John C. Nemeth
David A. Caborn
Joseph A. Butauski

ASSOCIATES

David A. Herd
Michael J. Collins

Representative Clients: Anheuser-Busch, Inc.; Central Ohio Transit Authority; Crawford & Co.; Erie Insurance Group; Home Insurance Co.; Safeco Insurance Co.; Mount Carmel Hospital; The Hartford Group; Citizens Insurance Co.; State Farm Insurance Co.

For full biographical listings, see the Martindale-Hubbell Law Directory

Walter W. Reckless (AV)

Suite 702, 33 North High Street, 43215-7315
Telephone: 614-221-4740
Fax: Available
Email: wwrlawofc@aol.com *URL:* http://www.lawyers.com/recklesslawoffice

References: Huntington National Bank; National City Bank.

For full biographical listings, see the Martindale-Hubbell Law Directory

Scherner, Hanson & Cornwell, LLC (AV)

130 Northwoods Boulevard, 43235-4725
Telephone: 614-431-7200
Fax: 614-431-7262
Delaware, Ohio Office: 5300 David Road.
Telephone: 614-595-3366.
Lima, Ohio Office: 2100 Lost Creek Boulevard.
Telephone: 419-222-1155.
Fax: 419-227-3131.

Hans Scherner
Robert E. Hanson
Ted E. Cornwell

For full biographical listings, see the Martindale-Hubbell Law Directory

Teaford, Rich, Crites & Wesp (AV)

Twenty East Broad Street, 43215-3682
Telephone: 614-228-5822
Telecopier: 614-228-2725
Email: TeaRich@aol.com

Jeffrey A. Rich
D. Michael Crites
E. Joel Wesp (Resident)

ASSOCIATES

Jeffrey A. Dittmer
Mark H. Gillis
James L Ervin, Jr

OF COUNSEL

Robert E. Teaford
Rosemary Sova
Murray R. Teaford
James R. Gorry

References: Huntington National Bank, N.A.; Fifth Third Bank.

For full biographical listings, see the Martindale-Hubbell Law Directory

White & Fish, L.P.A., Inc. (AV)

1335 Dublin Road Suite 201 (C), 43215
Telephone: 614-485-9300
Fax: 614-485-9462
Email: WFLPA@AOL.COM *URL:* http://www.lawyers.com/white&fish

(See Next Column)

Arnold S. White
Jeffrey D. Fish

For full biographical listings, see the Martindale-Hubbell Law Directory

Wolske & Blue A Legal Professional Association (AV)

580 South High Street, 43215-5672
Telephone: 614-228-6969
Fax: 614-228-4367
URL: http://www.lawyers.com/wolske&blue
Cincinnati, Ohio Office: The Grand Baldwin Building, 655 Eden Park Drive, Suite 770, 45202.
Telephone: 513-579-1181.
Fax: 513-579-0320.

Jason A. Blue
Walter J. Wolske, Jr.

Reference: Bank One of Columbus, N.A.

For full biographical listings, see the Martindale-Hubbell Law Directory

*DAYTON,** Montgomery Co.

David M. Deutsch Co., L.P.A. (AV)

The Pollack House, 208 West Monument Avenue, 45402
Telephone: 937-223-7170
Facsimile: 937-223-7180
Email: ddeutsch@erinet.com *URL:* ddeutsch@hotmail.com

David M. Deutsch

For full biographical listings, see the Martindale-Hubbell Law Directory

Dyer, Garofalo, Mann & Schultz A Legal Professional Association (AV)

The Barclay Building at 1st and Main Street, 137 North Main Street, 45402
Telephone: 937-223-8888
Fax: 937-223-0127
URL: http://www.dcmslaw.com
Email: jane.pearl@worldnet.att.net *URL:* http://www.lawyers.com/dgmslaw
Springfield, Ohio Office: 1714 Valley Loop Road, 45504.
Telephone: 513-324-9794.

Michael E. Dyer
Carmine M. Garofalo
Douglas A. Mann
Ronald E. Schultz
John A. Smalley

Kenneth J. Ignozzi
R. Casey Daganhardt
Diane E. Hanson
Douglas A. Hess
Henry Hyde, III
Anthony R. Kidd
Robert J. Janes
David W. Marquis
Ronald J. Maurer
Joseph P. McDonald

For full biographical listings, see the Martindale-Hubbell Law Directory

E. S. Gallon & Associates (AV)

40 West Fourth Street Centre Suite 2200, 45402
Telephone: 937-586-3100; 800-998-4374
Fax: 937-586-3200
URL: http://www.esgallon.com

MEMBERS OF FIRM

Jack A. Cervay
David A. Saphire
Joseph R. Ebenger
Joan B. Brenner
James D. Dennis
James R. Piercy
Richard M. Malone
Kyle D. Martin
Natalie J. Tackett

ASSOCIATE

David R. Salyer

For full biographical listings, see the Martindale-Hubbell Law Directory

DUBLIN, Franklin Co.

Blaugrund, Herbert & Martin, Incorporated (AV)

5455 Rings Road, Suite 500, 43017-7517
Telephone: 614-764-0681
Fax: 614-764-0774
Email: bhm@bhmlaw.net

Christopher T. Cline
David J. Demers

Steven E. Hillman

For full biographical listings, see the Martindale-Hubbell Law Directory

*FINDLAY,** Hancock Co.

Bernard K. Bauer Co., L.P.A. (AV)

410 West Sandusky Street, Suite One, P.O. Box 932, 45839
Telephone: 419-423-2673
FAX: 419-423-2127
Email: bauertrial@turbosurf.net

(See Next Column)

BERNARD K. BAUER CO., L.P.A., *Findlay—Continued*

Bernard K. Bauer

For full biographical listings, see the Martindale-Hubbell Law Directory

MIDDLETOWN, Butler Co.

CASPER AND CASPER (AV)

615 Gas & Electric Building, One North Main Street, P.O. Box 510, 45042
Telephone: 513-424-2401;
Cincinnati: 513-381-7096;
Dayton: 937-224-1222;
Hamilton: 513-892-2560
Fax: 513-424-0622

I. A. Casper (1910-1981)
Jack A. Casper (1912-1996)
Arthur Brandeis Casper
E. Jeffrey Casper
Douglas W. Casper
Sanford I. Casper
Ronald M. Kabakoff
Rebecca L. Wilkinson
Patrick W. Allen
Barbara L. Strady
Margaret Halnon McCollum
Mark A. Summers
Megan Richards
Nicole C. Allbritain
William P. Allen

For full biographical listings, see the Martindale-Hubbell Law Directory

SWANTON, Fulton Co.

THE MCQUADES CO., L.P.A. (AV)

Lincoln at Broadway, P.O. Box 237, 43558
Telephone: 419-826-0055
Fax: 419-825-3871
Email: mcquadelaw@cs.com *URL:* http://www.lawyers.com/mcquadelaw
Archbold, Ohio Office: 200 N. Defiance Street.
Telephone: 419-445-3755.
Whitehouse, Ohio Office: 6632 Providence Street.
Telephone: 419-877-0746.

Richard B. McQuade, Sr. (1912-1996)
Daniel P. McQuade
Colin J. McQuade

Alan J. Lehenbauer

For full biographical listings, see the Martindale-Hubbell Law Directory

*TOLEDO,** Lucas Co.

CARUSO & GEORGETTI (AV)

405 Madison Avenue, Suite 2300, 43604-1207
Telephone: 419-248-2300
Fax: 419-242-1605
Email: JCarusoEsq@aol.com

James D. Caruso
Anthony P. Georgetti

ASSOCIATE

Julie A. Jensen

For full biographical listings, see the Martindale-Hubbell Law Directory

CONTRADA & ASSOCIATES (AV)

6641 Sylvania Avenue, Suite 8, 43560-3921
Telephone: 419-841-4400
Fax: 419-841-4463

Carol A. Contrada
Charles V. Contrada

ASSOCIATE

Russell W. Jones

For full biographical listings, see the Martindale-Hubbell Law Directory

LACKEY, NUSBAUM, HARRIS, RENY & TORZEWSKI A LEGAL PROFESSIONAL ASSOCIATION (AV)

Two Maritime Plaza Third Floor, 43604
Telephone: 419-243-1105
Fax: 419-243-8953

D. Michael Reny

References: Fifth Third Bank; Society Bank.

For full biographical listings, see the Martindale-Hubbell Law Directory

MORAN & MORAN (AV)

626 Madison Avenue, Suite 300, 43604
Telephone: 419-241-8171
Fax: Available Upon Request

Wayne R. Peppers (1894-1978)
Peter L. Moran
Mary Beth Moran

Representative Clients: The Exchange Bank; Payak Insurance Agency; Monroe Pharmacy, Inc.

(See Next Column)

References: Society Bank; The Fifth Third Bank, Toledo, Ohio.

For full biographical listings, see the Martindale-Hubbell Law Directory

RITTER, ROBINSON, MCCREADY & JAMES (AV)

1850 National City Bank Building, 405 Madison Avenue, 43624
Telephone: 419-241-3213
FAX: 419-241-4925

MEMBERS OF FIRM

William S. McCready
Timothy C. James

Counsel for: Chrysler Corp.; Rubini Motors, Inc.; Ohio Casualty Insurance Co.; National Mutual Insurance Co.; Celina Mutual Insurance Co.; Westfield Insurance Co.; Northwestern National Insurance Co.; Midwestern Insurance Co.; United Ohio Insurance Co.; Toledo Auto Electric Co.

For Complete List of Firm Personnel, See General Section

For full biographical listings, see the Martindale-Hubbell Law Directory

SCHNORF & SCHNORF CO., L.P.A. A PROFESSIONAL CORPORATION (AV)

1400 National City Bank Building, 405 Madison Avenue, 43604
Telephone: 419-248-2646
Facsimile: 419-248-2889

David M. Schnorf
Christopher F. Parker

Local Counsel for: Universal Underwriters Group; Medical Mutual of Ohio; Bankers Multiple Line Insurance Company; National City Bank, Northwest
Representative Clients: American Federation of Teachers, AFL-CIO; Ohio Federation of Teachers, AFL-CIO; Toledo Federation of Teachers, AFL-CIO; Hart Associates, Inc.

For Complete List of Firm Personnel, See General Section

For full biographical listings, see the Martindale-Hubbell Law Directory

OKLAHOMA

*OKLAHOMA CITY,** Oklahoma Co.

ABEL, MUSSER, SOKOLOSKY, MARES & KOURI (AV)

Suite 600, One Leadership Square, 211 North Robinson, 73102
Telephone: 405-239-7046
Fax: 405-272-1090
Email: lynnmares@abelmusser.com *URL:* http://www.abellawfirm.com

Ed Abel
Sidney A. Musser, Jr.
Jerry D. Sokolosky
Lynn B. Mares
Harry J. (Trey) Kouri, III
Barry R. Davis
Steven T. Horton

OF COUNSEL

John A. Alberts
Arthur R. Angel
Warner E. Lovell, Jr.
Aletia Haynes Timmons
Leo H. Whinery

For full biographical listings, see the Martindale-Hubbell Law Directory

ABOWITZ, RHODES & DAHNKE, P.C. (AV)

Tenth Floor 15 North Robinson, P.O. Box 1937, 73101
Telephone: 405-236-4645
Telecopier: 405-239-2843

Murray E. Abowitz
Sarah Jackson Rhodes
George W. Dahnke

Lisa Luschen Dietrich
Janice M. Dansby
Kayce L. Gisinger
Stephen S. Parker
Andrew D. Schwartz
Blake A. Bittel

For full biographical listings, see the Martindale-Hubbell Law Directory

ADAMS & ASSOCIATES (AV)

City Place Building, 204 North Robinson Twenty-Fifth Floor, 73102
Telephone: 405-232-9100
Fax: 405-232-9114
Email: Adams1@IAmerica.net

R. Scott Adams

ASSOCIATES

Josh T. Welch
Joe Brett Reynolds

OF COUNSEL

O. Clifton Gooding

For full biographical listings, see the Martindale-Hubbell Law Directory

Oklahoma City—Continued

GARY L. BROOKS AND ASSOCIATES (AV)

7100 North Classen Boulevard, Suite 300, 73116-7101
Telephone: 405-840-1066
Fax: 405-843-8446
Email: GLB@medlaws.com *URL:* http://www.medlaws.com

Ann Brooks
Christopher J. Bergin

For full biographical listings, see the Martindale-Hubbell Law Directory

LEE, DUROCHER, KISNER, WALKER & REID (AV)

An Association of Professional Associations
5532 North Western, 73118
Telephone: 405-848-5532
Facsimile: 405-848-5502

Jim W. Lee
Daniel L. Durocher
David W. Kisner
David A. Walker
James M. Reid

For full biographical listings, see the Martindale-Hubbell Law Directory

McCAFFREY & TAWWATER (AV)

Suite 1950, One Leadership Square, 211 North Robinson, 73102-7124
Telephone: 405-235-2900
Fax: 405-231-2818
URL: http://www.mccaffreytawwater.com
Other Oklahoma City, Oklahoma Office: 3015 N.W. 59th, 73112.

MEMBERS OF FIRM

George J. McCaffrey
Larry A. Tawwater

ASSOCIATES

Jo Lynn Slama
Loren F. Gibson
Steven R. Davis
Piper E. John
David B. Custar

For full biographical listings, see the Martindale-Hubbell Law Directory

MERRITT & ASSOCIATES, P.C. (AV)

917 North Robinson, P.O. Box 1377, 73101
Telephone: 405-236-2222
Nationwide Toll Free: 1-800-690-2277
Fax: 405-232-8630

John M. Merritt

Michael M. Blue

For full biographical listings, see the Martindale-Hubbell Law Directory

THE MILLS LAW FIRM, P.C. (AV)

500 One Leadership Square, 211 North Robinson, 73102
Telephone: 405-239-2501
Fax: 405-239-2575
Email: millsfirm@attymail.com

Earl D. Mills
Robert B. Mills
W. Wayne Mills
Barbara K. Buratti

Margaret K. Myers
Daniel K. Jones
J. Drew Houghton
Carole L. Dulisse

For full biographical listings, see the Martindale-Hubbell Law Directory

WHITE LAW FIRM (AV)

900 N.E. 63rd Street, P.O. Box 18427, 73154
Telephone: 405-858-8899
Fax: 405-858-8844
Email: whitelawok@aol.com

Joe E. White, Jr.

ASSOCIATES

Greg S. Wilson
Derek B. Smith

For full biographical listings, see the Martindale-Hubbell Law Directory

WHITTEN, McGUIRE, WOOD, TERRY, ROSELIUS & DITTRICH A PROFESSIONAL LIMITED LIABILITY COMPANY (AV)

Suite 400, One Leadership Square, 211 North Robinson, 73102
Telephone: 405-239-2522
Fax: 405-239-2573
Email: whitten@whitten-mcguire.com
Tulsa, Oklahoma Office: 3600 First Place Tower, 15 East Fifth Street.
Telephone: 918-582-9903.

Reggie N. Whitten
Kent R. McGuire
Douglas A. Terry
Jason E. Roselius

(See Next Column)

Simone Gosnell Fulmer
Philip W. Anderson
R. Gregory Kirby
Derrick T. Dewitt

Representative Clients: The St. Paul Insurance Cos.; Crim & Forster Commercial Insurance Co.; OML Municipal Assurance Group; Progressive Casualty.

For full biographical listings, see the Martindale-Hubbell Law Directory

*TULSA,** Tulsa Co.

ATKINSON, HASKINS, NELLIS, BOUDREAUX, HOLEMAN, PHIPPS & BRITTINGHAM, A PROFESSIONAL CORPORATION (AV)

1500 ParkCentre, 525 South Main Street, 74103
Telephone: 918-582-8877
Fax: 918-585-8096
Email: ahnmail@ahn-law.com

Michael P. Atkinson, P.C.
Walter D. Haskins, P.C.
Gregory D. Nellis, P.C.
Paul T. Boudreaux, P.C.
Daniel E. Holeman, P.C.
K. Clark Phipps
Galen Lee Brittingham, P.C.
John S. Gladd
John J. Carwile
Martha J. Phillips
William A. Fiasco
Jon D. Starr
Mark W. Maguire
Marthanda J. Beckworth
James N. Edmonds

Kirsten E. Pace
Scott R. Hall
Jeffrey L. Wilson
Whitney M. Eschenheimer
Margaret M. Clarke
Margaret A. Nunnery
Jeffrey A. Risch
Jennifer Annis
Eric J. Begin
Roni S. Rierson
Christine M. Benson
Bret A. Sanders

OF COUNSEL

Joseph F. Glass

LEGAL SUPPORT PERSONNEL

Beverly J. Rubino, M.D. (Medical Counsel)

Representative Clients: Allstate Insurance Co.; Bayer Corp.; Crum & Forster Insurance Co.; Hartford Insurance Company; National American Insurance Co.; Federated Insurance Co.; Liberty Mutual Insurance Co.; Physicians Liability Insurance Co.; State Farm Mutual Automobile Insurance Co.; United States Aviation Underwriters.

For full biographical listings, see the Martindale-Hubbell Law Directory

BEST & SHARP, A PROFESSIONAL CORPORATION (AV)

Oneok Plaza, 100 W. 5th, Suite 808, 74103-4225
Telephone: 918-582-1234
Fax: 918-585-9447
Email: Webmaster@BestSharp.com *URL:* http://www.BestSharp.com

Joseph M. Best
Joseph A. Sharp
Timothy G. Best
Daniel S. Sullivan
Amy E. Kempfert
Karen M. Grundy
Terry S. O'Donnell

Catherine L. Campbell
Malcom D. Smith, Jr.
Jeffrey W. Swanson
Dan W. Ernst
Thomas A. Le Blanc

For full biographical listings, see the Martindale-Hubbell Law Directory

FRASIER, FRASIER & HICKMAN (AV)

1700 Southwest Boulevard, 74107
Telephone: 918-584-4724
Fax: 918-583-5637
Email: frasier@tulsa.com *URL:* http://www.frasierlaw.com

MEMBERS OF FIRM

Thomas Dee Frasier
James E. Frasier
Steven R. Hickman
John W. Flippo
Everett R. Bennett, Jr.
Jerry L. Franks, Jr.
Robert A. Flynn
Frank Frasier, III

ASSOCIATE

Gary G. Brasel
George M. Miles

References: Community State Bank, Tulsa, Oklahoma; American Exchange Bank, Tulsa, Oklahoma; The Bank of Oklahoma, Tulsa, Oklahoma.

For full biographical listings, see the Martindale-Hubbell Law Directory

RHODES, HIERONYMUS, JONES, TUCKER & GABLE, P.L.L.C. (AV)

Oneok Plaza, 100 West 5th Street, Suite 400, P.O. Box 21100, 74121-1100
Telephone: 918-582-1173
Fax: 918-592-3390
URL: http://www.rhodesokla.com

(See Next Column)

RHODES, HIERONYMUS, JONES, TUCKER & GABLE P.L.L.C., *Tulsa—Continued*

MEMBERS OF FIRM

Kevin D. Berry
Jo Anne Deaton
Richard M. Eldridge
E. D. Hieronymus (1908 -1994)
Bert M. Jones
William S. Leach
Michael W. McGivern
William D. Perrine
Mary Quinn-Cooper
Robert P. Redemann
David P. Reid
Chris L. Rhodes, III
Thomas E. Steichen
Catherine C. Taylor
John H. Tucker
Wilson T. White
Harold C. Zuckerman

Ann E. Allison
Steven K. Bunting
Robert P. Coffey, Jr.
J. Christopher Davis
Andrew D. Downing
Dana L. Gish
Kerry R. Lewis
Andrew L. Richardson
Michael F. Smith
Leslie J. Southerland
Kimberly E. West
Keith A. Wilkes

OF COUNSEL

George W. Gable (Retired Partner)
Larry J. Fulton
Kelly M. Greenough

Representative Clients: American International Companies; Bechtel; Chubb Group of Insurance Companies; General Motors Corporation; Merrill, Lynch; Nissan Motor Corporation in U.S.A.; Pfizer, Inc.; Volkswagen of America, Volkswagen, A.G.; Zurich U.S.

For full biographical listings, see the Martindale-Hubbell Law Directory

THE ROACH LAW FIRM, P.C. (AV)

Park Centre, Suite 660, 525 South Main Street, 74103-4521
Telephone: 918-587-2544
Fax: 918-582-0551

Loyal J. Roach, III

Reference: Nations Bank, Tulsa.

For full biographical listings, see the Martindale-Hubbell Law Directory

SNEED LANG, P.C. (AV)

2300 Williams Center Tower II, Two West Second Street, 74103
Telephone: 918-583-3145
Telecopier: 918-582-0410

James C. Lang
D. Faith Orlowski
Brian S. Gaskill
G. Steven Stidham
Stephen R. McNamara
Thomas E. Black, Jr.
Robbie Emery Burke
Patrick O. Waddel
Randolph P. Stainer
Steven K. Balman
Brian T. Inbody
D. Michael McBride III

OF COUNSEL

James L. Sneed

Representative Clients: Amoco Production Co.; Bank One, Texas; Enron Corp.; Halliburton Energy Services; Helmerich & Payne, Inc.; Shell Oil Co.; State Farm Mutual Automobile Insurance Co.; The Williams Companies.

For full biographical listings, see the Martindale-Hubbell Law Directory

LAW OFFICES OF MAYNARD I. UNGERMAN (AV)

Riverbridge Office Park, 1323 East 71st Street, Suite 300, 74136-5043
Telephone: 918-495-0550
Fax: 918-495-0561
Mailing Address: P.O. Box 701917, Tulsa, Oklahoma, 74170-1917

MEMBERS OF FIRM

Irvine E. Ungerman (1908-1980)
Maynard I. Ungerman

Stephen J. Greubel

Representative Clients: Tulsa Paint; Norvell-Marcum Company; Tulsa Classroom Teachers Association; Oklahoma Education Association; Born Inc.

For full biographical listings, see the Martindale-Hubbell Law Directory

OREGON

*CORVALLIS,** Benton Co.

RINGO, STUBER, ENSOR & HADLOCK, P.C. (AV)

605 S.W. Jefferson Avenue, P.O. Box 1108, 97339
Telephone: 541-757-1414
FAX: 541-753-0884
Email: ringoseh@peak.org

(See Next Column)

Robert G. Ringo
Larry W. Stuber
Stephen R. Ensor
Patrick L. Hadlock

Reference: Citizens Bank of Corvallis; Wells Fargo Bank.

For full biographical listings, see the Martindale-Hubbell Law Directory

*EUGENE,** Lane Co.

JOHNSON, CLIFTON, LARSON & CORSON, P.C. (AV)

10th Floor, Citizens Building, 975 Oak Street, 97401-3124
Telephone: 541-484-2434
Fax: 541-484-0882
Email: jclc@jclc.com

Arthur C. Johnson
Jacob K. Clifton, Jr.
Richard L. Larson
Don Corson
Douglas G. Schaller
Derek C. Johnson
Dennis M. Gerl
Lara Christine Johnson
Marilyn Heiken
Scott C. Lucas

For full biographical listings, see the Martindale-Hubbell Law Directory

*NEWPORT,** Lincoln Co.

BARTON AND STREVER, P.C. (AV)

214 South West Coast Highway, P.O. Box 870, 97365
Telephone: 541-265-5377
Fax: 541-265-5614
Email: bartstreve@netridge.net *URL:* http://www.lawyers.com/barton&strever

William A. Barton
Kevin K. Strever

LEGAL SUPPORT PERSONNEL

Greg A. Estep

Reference: West One Bank, Newport, Oregon.

For full biographical listings, see the Martindale-Hubbell Law Directory

*PORTLAND,** Multnomah Co.

KELL, ALTERMAN & RUNSTEIN, LLP (AV)

1001 S.W. Fifth Avenue, Suite 1800, 97204
Telephone: 503-222-3531
Telecopier: 503-227-2980
Email: kell@teleport.com

MEMBERS OF FIRM

Raymond M. Kell (1911-1991)
Clifford B. Alterman (1925-1995)
Ted E. Runstein
Lee Davis Kell
Wayne D. Palmer
Lloyd R. Summers
William D. Dickas
Gary P. Compa
Charles R. Williamson
Mary Ellen Page Farr
Eric Sogge
Thomas J. Matsuda
Thomas R. Rask, III
Nicholas S. Fish

Dana L. Barnes
Cory Larvik
Robert E. Kabacy
Robin M. Runstein

References: Union Bank of California, N.A. (Portland Branch); The Bank of Tokyo-Mitsubishi, Ltd. (Portland Branch); Bank of America (5th S. Main Branch).

For full biographical listings, see the Martindale-Hubbell Law Directory

RIEKE & SAVAGE, P.C. (AV)

Thomas Mann Building, 140 S.W. Yamhill Street, 97204-3090
Telephone: 503-222-0200
Fax: 503-243-1820

Forrest N. Rieke
John William Savage

H. Scott Raivio
Paul G. Ellis
Cheryl Albrecht
Christopher A. Larsen
Robert L. Salisbury
Paul Hart
Angela J. Hart
Lisa J. Ludwig
Alan R. Scott

For full biographical listings, see the Martindale-Hubbell Law Directory

SWANSON, THOMAS & COON (AV)

American Bank Building, 621 S.W. Morrison, Suite 900, 97205-3892
Telephone: 503-228-5222
Fax: 503-273-9175
URL: http://www.stc-law.com

MEMBERS OF FIRM

Douglas A. Swanson
Raymond F. Thomas
James S. Coon

(See Next Column)

SWANSON, THOMAS & COON—*Continued*

ASSOCIATES

Megan E. Glor
Alan Stuart Graf
Margaret F. Weddell

For full biographical listings, see the Martindale-Hubbell Law Directory

PENNSYLVANIA

*ALLENTOWN,** Lehigh Co.

HUBER AND WALDRON (AV)

535 Hamilton Mall, Suite 301, 18101
Telephone: 610-435-9790
FAX: 610-435-1238

MEMBERS OF FIRM

James T. Huber
John J. Waldron

For full biographical listings, see the Martindale-Hubbell Law Directory

BENSALEM, Bucks Co.

RUDOLPH, DORIAN, GOLDSTEIN, ROCHESTIE, WISNIEWSKI & TAYLOR, P.C. (AV)

Neshaminy Valley Commons, 2410 Bristol Road, 19020
Telephone: 215-750-7200
Fax: 215-750-9294
Email: admin@rudolphdorian.com *URL:* http://www.palaw.lawoffice.com
Philadelphia, Pennsylvania Office: 1818 Market Street, Suite 2300, 19103.
Telephone: 215-299-9900.
Fax: 215-299-9910.

Edward Rudolph
Harry A. Dorian, Jr.
Stephan H. Goldstein
Gary A. Rochestie
Mark A. Wisniewski
John J. Taylor
Jeffrey S. Orchinik
Kim A. Piermattei
Michael Parlow
Lawrence P. Kempner
Nancy M. Bonner

For full biographical listings, see the Martindale-Hubbell Law Directory

BLUE BELL, Montgomery Co.

GERBER & GERBER (AV)

790 Penllyn-Blue Bell Pike, Suite 100, 19422
Telephone: 610-279-6700; 215-540-9100
Fax: 215-540-9424
Email: grbrlaw@dynanet.com *URL:* http://www.lawyers.com/gerber&gerber

Morris Gerber (1908-1995)

MEMBER OF FIRM

A. Richard Gerber

For full biographical listings, see the Martindale-Hubbell Law Directory

KELLEY & MURPHY (AV)

Union Meeting Corporate Center V, Suite 160 925 Harvest Drive, 19422
Telephone: 215-643-6500
Fax: 215-643-8356
Cable Address: "BIGTIME"
Email: kmlaw@counsel.com

Joseph T. Kelley, Jr.
Patrick G. Murphy
Joseph T. Kelley, III

LEGAL SUPPORT PERSONNEL

Marianne Rowen
Tanja M.Z. Barron

For full biographical listings, see the Martindale-Hubbell Law Directory

SHINGLES & CAPPELLI (AV)

794 Penllyn Blue Bell Pike, Suite 101, 19422
Telephone: 610-941-4444
Fax: 610-941-9880
800-974-9444
URL: http://www.lawyers.com/shingles&cappelli

MEMBERS OF FIRM

Stanley M. Shingles
Joseph J. Cappelli

ASSOCIATES

Elizabeth L. Schmidt
Shawn M. Sassaman

OF COUNSEL

Robert J. F. Brobyn

SPECIAL COUNSEL

Joseph S. Ziccardi

For full biographical listings, see the Martindale-Hubbell Law Directory

CONWAY, Beaver Co.

CONTE, MELTON & D'ANTONIO (AV)

300 Ninth Street, 15027-1696
Telephone: 724-869-2164; 775-1850; 412-766-5112
Fax: 724-869-2246
Email: CMDlaw@acba.org

MEMBERS OF FIRM

John Alan Conte
Scott L. Melton
Daniel M. D'Antonio

Joseph M. Spratt
Robert A. Krebs
Elisabeth A. McIntyre

For full biographical listings, see the Martindale-Hubbell Law Directory

DOWNINGTOWN, Chester Co.

WUSINICH AND BROGAN (AV)

537 West Uwchlan Avenue, Suite 200, P.O. Box 478, 19335-0478
Telephone: 610-594-1600
Fax: 610-594-6518
Email: info@wusinichbrogon.com *URL:* http://www.wusinichbrogan.com
Reading, Pennsylvania Office: 522 Washington Street.
Telephone: 610-373-8550.
West Chester, Pennsylvania Office: Nineteen South High Street.
Telephone: 610-436-6280.

MEMBERS OF FIRM

Joseph F. Wusinich, III
Dennis D. Brogan
John J. Stanzione

Louis Aurely, III
David V. Grow
Edward C. Sweeney

For full biographical listings, see the Martindale-Hubbell Law Directory

*DOYLESTOWN,** Bucks Co.

THE LAW OFFICES OF MELLON, WEBSTER & MELLON A PROFESSIONAL CORPORATION (AV)

87 North Broad Street, 18901
Telephone: 215-348-7700
Fax: 215-348-0171

Thomas E. Mellon, Jr.
Robert J. Mellon
Sara M. Webster
Deborah A. Romanski
Carol A. Shelly
Elliot Alan Kolodny
Joseph A. Cullen, Jr.

OF COUNSEL

Jonathan A. Briskin

For full biographical listings, see the Martindale-Hubbell Law Directory

*EASTON,** Northampton Co.

COHEN & FEELEY, P.C. (AV)

2940 William Penn Highway, 18045
Telephone: 610-258-0111
Fax: 610-258-8095
Email: cohenfeeley@enter.net *URL:* http://www.seriouslyinjured.com
Allentown, Pennsylvania Office: 1405 North Cedar Crest Boulevard, Suite 205, 18104.
Telephone: 610-821-7702.
Fax: 610-821-9067.

Martin D. Cohen
Dennis F. Feeley

For full biographical listings, see the Martindale-Hubbell Law Directory

FOX, OLDT & BROWN (AV)

Suite 508, First Union Bank Building, Six South Third Street, Center Square, 18042
Telephone: 610-258-6111
Fax: 610-253-4532
URL: http://www.lawyers.com/foxoldt&brown

MEMBERS OF FIRM

Charles L. Oldt
Robert C. Brown, Jr.

Counsel for: First Union National Bank; Easton Cemetery; Travelers Insurance Co.

For full biographical listings, see the Martindale-Hubbell Law Directory

GUS MILIDES (AV)

654 Wolf Avenue, 18042
Telephone: 610-258-0433
Fax: 610-258-4875

For full biographical listings, see the Martindale-Hubbell Law Directory

*ERIE,** Erie Co.

CONNER & RILEY (AV)

The Bell Telephone Building, 17 West 10th Street, 16501-1401
Telephone: 814-453-3343
Fax: 814-454-6713
URL: http://www.lawyers.com/connerlaw

MEMBERS OF FIRM

Andrew J. Conner
Steven E. "Tim" Riley, Jr.

For full biographical listings, see the Martindale-Hubbell Law Directory

*HARRISBURG,** Dauphin Co.

ANGINO & ROVNER, P.C. (AV)

4503 North Front Street, 17110
Telephone: 717-238-6791
Fax: 717-238-5610
Email: lawfirm@angino-rovner.com *URL:* http://www.angino-rovner.com
Carlisle, Pennsylvania Office: 28 South Pitt Street, 17013.
Telephone: 717-241-2661.

Richard C. Angino
Neil J. Rovner

References: Credit Bureau of Greater Harrisburg; CoreStates.

For full biographical listings, see the Martindale-Hubbell Law Directory

GOLDBERG, KATZMAN & SHIPMAN, P.C. (AV)

320 Market Street - Strawberry Square, P.O. Box 1268, 17108-1268
Telephone: 717-234-4161
Telecopier: 717-234-6808; 717-234-6810
Email: gks@gkslaw.com

F. Lee Shipman
Thomas E. Brenner
John A. Statler
April L. Strang-Kutay
Guy H. Brooks
Jefferson J. Shipman
Thomas J. Weber

John R. Ninosky

Reference: Fulton Bank.

For Complete List of Firm Personnel, See General Section

For full biographical listings, see the Martindale-Hubbell Law Directory

THE LAW OFFICES OF SPERO T. LAPPAS (AV)

205 State Street, P.O. Box 808, 17108-0808
Telephone: 717-238-4286
Fax: 717-238-4826
Email: Lawyers@Lawyers1.com *URL:* http://www.Lawyer1.com

ASSOCIATE

Ann Economou Ariano

For full biographical listings, see the Martindale-Hubbell Law Directory

MANCKE, WAGNER, HERSHEY AND TULLY (AV)

2233 North Front Street, 17110
Telephone: 717-234-7051

MEMBERS OF FIRM

John B. Mancke
P. Richard Wagner
David E. Hershey
William T. Tully

For full biographical listings, see the Martindale-Hubbell Law Directory

METZGER, WICKERSHAM, KNAUSS & ERB, P.C. (AV)

3211 North Front Street, P.O. Box 5300, 17110-0300
Telephone: 717-238-8187
Telefax: 717-234-9478
Other Harrisburg, Pennsylvania Office: 4813 Jonestown Road, P.O. Box 5300, 17110-0300.
Telephone: 717-652-7020.

Maurice R. Metzger (1918-1980)
F. Brewster Wickersham (1918-1974)
Edward E. Knauss, III (Retired)
Christian S. Erb, Jr.
Robert E. Yetter
James F. Carl
Edward E. Knauss, IV
Jered L. Hock
Karl R. Hildabrand
Richard B. Druby
Steven P. Miner

Clark DeVere
Carrie L. Carroll

Representative Clients: Allstate Insurance Co.; Chubb Group of Insurance Companies; Fireman's Fund American Insurance Group; Liberty Mutual Insurance Co.; Crum & Forster; CNA Insurance; Prudential Insurance Co.

For full biographical listings, see the Martindale-Hubbell Law Directory

SCHMIDT, RONCA AND KRAMER, P.C. (AV)

209 State Street, 17101
Telephone: 717-232-6300
Fax: 717-232-6467
URL: http://www.schmidtandronca.com

Charles E. Schmidt, Jr.
James R. Ronca
Gerard C. Kramer
Scott B. Cooper
Todd Dale Getgen

For full biographical listings, see the Martindale-Hubbell Law Directory

*LANCASTER,** Lancaster Co.

ATLEE, HALL & BROOKHART, L.L.P. (AV)

8 North Queen Street, P.O. Box 449, 17608-0449
Telephone: 717-393-9596
Fax: 717-393-2138
Email: law@atleehall.com

MEMBERS OF FIRM

William A. Atlee, Jr.
Thomas W. Hall
Dan M. Brookhart

ASSOCIATES

Edward R. Kennett
Jaime D. Jackson
Robin A. Jabour

For full biographical listings, see the Martindale-Hubbell Law Directory

MIKUS LAW ASSOCIATES (AV)

408 West Chestnut Street, 17603
Telephone: 717-299-4840; 299-4575
Fax: 717-299-6869
Email: mikuslaw@redrose.net *URL:* http://www.mikuslaw.com

Kent D. Mikus

Michael P. McDonald
David B. Diffenbach
Loura A. Selfe

LEGAL SUPPORT PERSONNEL

LITIGATION PARALEGALS

Donna L. Simpson
C. Andrea Gadd
Sherry L. Amspacher
Olga F. Karel

For full biographical listings, see the Martindale-Hubbell Law Directory

*MEDIA,** Delaware Co.

MICHAEL G. DEFINO (AV)

200 East State Street, Suite 108, 19063-3434
Telephone: 610-566-3131
Fax: 610-566-3232
Email: mgdlaw@dca.net *URL:* http://www.definolaw.com

OF COUNSEL

Dorothy S. Langton
Henry J. Lunardi
Jody T. Curcillo

For full biographical listings, see the Martindale-Hubbell Law Directory

DIORIO & SERENI, LLP (AV)

Front and Plum Streets, P.O. Box 1789, 19063
Telephone: 610-565-5700
Fax: 610-891-0652
Email: info@dioriosereni.com

Robert M. DiOrio
Mark A. Sereni

ASSOCIATES

Kenneth J. D. Boyden
Christopher R. Mattox

For full biographical listings, see the Martindale-Hubbell Law Directory

HUGHEY, FLICK & CATANIA (AV)

Monroe Professional Building, 117 North Monroe Street, P.O. Box 87, 19063-0087
Telephone: 610-565-9050; 565-9060
Fax: 610-891-7960
Email: hfcesq@erols.com *URL:* http://www.lawyers.com/hfcesq

Richard L. Hughey
James R. Flick
Joseph V. Catania
Stephen J. Schukraft

For full biographical listings, see the Martindale-Hubbell Law Directory

*NEW CASTLE,** Lawrence Co.

LUXENBERG, GARBETT, KELLY & SAPIENZA, P.C. (AV)

303 Central Building, 16101-3763
Telephone: 724-658-8535
Fax: 724-658-8013
Ellwood City, Pennsylvania Office: 317 Seventh Street.
Telephone: 412-758-7581.
Fax: 412-758-0690.

(See Next Column)

LUXENBERG, GARBETT, KELLY & SAPIENZA P.C.—*Continued*

Charles W. Garbett
Lawrence M. Kelly
Charles P. Sapienza, Jr.

Representative Clients: Erie Insurance Exchange; ESB Bank, F.S.B. (formerly Ellwood Federal Savings Bank); Ohio Casualty Insurance Co.; Beneficial Consumer Discount Co.; Keystone Insurance Co.; Ellwood City Hospital; Lititz Mutual Insurance Co.

For full biographical listings, see the Martindale-Hubbell Law Directory

*NORRISTOWN,** Montgomery Co.

CREEDON & FELICIANI, P.C. (AV)

29 East Marshall Street, 19401
Telephone: 610-239-9630
Fax: 610-239-1599
Email: creedon_feliciani@compuserve.com *URL:* http://www.lawyers.com/creedonfeliciani

Michael P. Creedon
Joseph L. Feliciani

For full biographical listings, see the Martindale-Hubbell Law Directory

MURPHY, OLIVER, CAIOLA & GOWEN, A PROFESSIONAL LAW CORPORATION (AV)

43 East Marshall Street, 19401-4828
Telephone: 610-272-4222; 610-279-3838
Fax: 610-272-2549; 610-275-0140
Email: molaw@injury-law.com *URL:* http://www.injury-law.com
Spring City, Pennsylvania Office: 500 S. Main Street, 19475.
Telephone: 610-948-3770.
Pottstown, Pennsylvania Office: 5 Sunnybrook Road, 19464.
Telephone: 610-323-3480.
West Chester, Pennsylvania Office: 1534 McDaniel Drive, Westtown Business Center, 19250.
Telephone: 610-272-4222.

James J. Oliver
Frank P. Murphy
Frank L. Caiola
Thomas L. Gowen, Jr.
Carla E. Connor
Barbara A. Barnes

John F. Haskins, Jr.
Cynthia Love Dengler
Carol A. Crisci

LEGAL SUPPORT PERSONNEL

Patricia A. Talese (Paralegal)
Kathleen Nicholson

For full biographical listings, see the Martindale-Hubbell Law Directory

RAYMOND M. VICTOR, P.C. (AV)

616 DeKalb Street, 19401
Telephone: 610-272-5253
Fax: 610-272-7422
Email: rdsquire@worldnet.att.net *URL:* http://www.lawyers.com/raymondmvictor

Raymond M. Victor
Christopher T. Moyer

For full biographical listings, see the Martindale-Hubbell Law Directory

*PHILADELPHIA,** Philadelphia Co.

AGINS HAAZ & SEIDEL, L.L.P. (AV)

1604 Locust Street Third Floor, 19103
Telephone: 215-985-9699
Fax: 215-985-0912
URL: http://www.lawyers.com/aginshaaz&seidel

Stuart J. Agins
Richard P. Haaz
Richard S. Seidel

For full biographical listings, see the Martindale-Hubbell Law Directory

ANAPOL, SCHWARTZ, WEISS, COHAN, FELDMAN AND SMALLEY, P.C. (AV)

1900 Delancey Place, 19103
Telephone: 215-735-1130
Fax: 215-735-2024
URL: http://www.aswc.net
Other Philadelphia, Pennsylvania Office: 1710 Spruce Street.
Fax: 215-735-2211.
Cherry Hill, New Jersey Office: 402 Park Boulevard, 08002.
Telephone: 1-609-427-9229.
Fax: 609-488-1396.
Fairless Hills, Pennsylvania Office: 920 Trenton Road.
Telephone: 215-945-6799.
Reading, Pennsylvania Office: 146 North 6th Street.
Telephone: 610-375-7488.
Media, Pennsylvania Office: 334 W. Front Street, 19063.
Telephone: 610-892-3714.

(See Next Column)

Alan Schwartz
Sol H. Weiss
Lawrence R. Cohan
Joel D. Feldman
Howard J. Levin
Bernard W. Smalley
Stanton Dubin
Margaret A. Barry
Stephen J. Pokiniewski, Jr.
Sidney M. Grobman
Nelson Levin

Nathaniel E.P. Ehrlich
Thomas R. Anapol
Miriam Benton Barish
Patrice A. Gillotti
Michele Lee Reed
Heather J. Lipson
Michelle L. Altenpohl
Lisa R. Schwartz
Kevin R. Marciano
Brian J. Taylor
Tobias L. Millrood
Tracy A. Finken

OF COUNSEL

Paul R. Anapol
Richard B. Schwartz (Resident, Other Philadelphia Office)
Mark F. Seltzer

Reference: Meridian Bank, Philadelphia, Pennsylvania.

For full biographical listings, see the Martindale-Hubbell Law Directory

ASTOR WEISS KAPLAN & ROSENBLUM, LLP (AV)

The Bellevue, 6th Floor, 200 South Broad Street, 19102
Telephone: 215-790-0100
Fax: 215-790-0509
Email: lawyers@astorweiss.com
Bala Cynwyd, Pennsylvania Office: 401 City Avenue, Suite 500.
Telephone: 610-667-8660.
Fax: 610-667-2783.

MEMBERS OF FIRM

Alvin M. Weiss (1936-1976)
Paul C. Astor
G. David Rosenblum
Arthur H. Kaplan
Barbara Oaks Silver
David S. Workman
David Gutin
David S. Mandel
Gerald J. Schorr

ASSOCIATES

Christopher P. Flannery
Janet G. Felgoise
Elizabeth F. Warner
Daniel A. Shabel
Frances F. Freedman

SPECIAL COUNSEL

Neil Hurowitz
Jerrold V. Moss
Robert P. Style

OF COUNSEL

Edward W. Silver

For full biographical listings, see the Martindale-Hubbell Law Directory

MARVIN I. BARISH LAW OFFICES A PROFESSIONAL CORPORATION (AV)

6th and Walnut Streets, Suite 801E, 19106-3308
Telephone: 215-923-8900; 800-233-7101
Email: mbarish@aol.com *URL:* http://www.lawyers.com/barishlawoffices
Cherry Hill, New Jersey Office: 1930 East Marlton Pike, Suite Q-38.
Telephone: 609-338-0550.

Marvin I. Barish

Gregory L. Nester

For full biographical listings, see the Martindale-Hubbell Law Directory

BRUCE G. CASSIDY & ASSOCIATES, P.A. (AV)

Suite 1040, 21 South 12th Street, 19107
Telephone: 215-568-6700
Fax: 215-568-4077
Email: bgclaw@aol.com
Princeton, New Jersey Office: 345 Witherspoon Street, 08542.
Telephone: 609-252-9800.
Fax: 609-252-9111.

Bruce G. Cassidy

David E. Breslau

OF COUNSEL

Dr. Peter H. Feuerstein (Not admitted United States)
Halina Pilarska (Not Admitted in United States)

For full biographical listings, see the Martindale-Hubbell Law Directory

LAW OFFICES OF JAMES E. COLLERAN (AV)

1525 Locust Street 18th Floor, 19102
Telephone: 215-790-5500
FAX: 215-790-5509
Email: colleran@colleran.com

(See Next Column)

LAW OFFICES OF JAMES E. COLLERAN, *Philadelphia—Continued*

James E. Colleran, Jr. | Mary T. Colleran
Francis T. Colleran | James I. Devine
Teresa Colleran Quinn | David C. Devine

For full biographical listings, see the Martindale-Hubbell Law Directory

COZEN AND O'CONNOR, A PROFESSIONAL CORPORATION (AV)

1900 Market Street, 19103
Telephone: 215-665-2000
800-523-2900
Fax: 215-665-2013
Email: postmaster@cozen.com *URL:* http://www.cozen.com
Charlotte, North Carolina Office: One First Union Center, Suite 2100, 301 S. College Street, 28202.
Telephones: 704-376-3400; 800-762-3575.
Fax: 704-334-3351.
Dallas, Texas Office: 2300 BankOne Center, 1717 Main Street, 75201.
Telephones: 214-462-3000; 800-448-1207.
Fax: 214-462-3299.
New York, N.Y. Office: 45 Broadway Atrium, 16th Floor, 10006.
Telephones: 212-509-9400; 800-437-7040.
Fax: 212-509-9492.
West Conshohocken, Pennsylvania Office: 200 Four Falls Corporate Center, Suite 400, P.O. Box 800, 19428.
Telephone: 610-941-5400.
Fax: 610-941-0711.
San Diego, California Office: Suite 1610, 501 West Broadway, 92101.
Telephones: 619-234-1700; 800-782-3366.
Fax: 619-234-7831.
Los Angeles, California Office: 777 Tower, 777 South Figueroa Street, Suite 2850, 90017.
Telephones: 213-892-7900; 800-563-1027.
Fax: 213-892-7999.
Seattle, Washington Office: Suite 5200, Washington Mutual Tower, 1201 Third Avenue, 98101.
Telephones: 206-340-1000; 800-423-1950.
Fax: 206-621-8783.
Westmont, New Jersey Office: 316 Haddon Avenue, 08108.
Telephones: 609-854-4900; 800-523-2900.
Fax: 609-854-1782.
Newark, New Jersey Office: One Newark Center, Suite 1900, 1085 Raymond Boulevard, 07102.
Telephone: 973-286-1200; 888-200-9521.
Fax: 973-242-2121.
Atlanta, Georgia Office: Suite 2200, SunTrust Plaza, 303 Peachtree Street, N.E., 30308.
Telephones: 404-572-2000; 800-890-1393.
Fax: 404-572-2199.
London, England Office: Cozen and O'Connor at Radcliffes, 5 Great College Street, Westminster, SW1P 3SJ.
Telephone: 011-44-207-654-7600.
Fax: 011-44-207-654-7613.
Wilmington, Delaware Office: Chase Manhattan Centre, 1201 North Market Street, Suite 1400, 19801.
Telephone: 302-295-2000; 888-207-2440.
Fax: 302-295-2013.
Mt. Laurel, New Jersey Office: 10,000 Midlantic Drive, Suite 301, 08054.

A. Richard Bailey | Christopher C. Fallon, Jr.

Representative Clients: Available upon request.

For Complete List of Firm Personnel, See General Section
For full biographical listings, see the Martindale-Hubbell Law Directory

FURIA AND TURNER (AV)

1717 Rittenhouse Square, 19103-6109
Telephone: 215-985-4500
Telecopier: 215-985-2824
Email: rfuria1717@aol.com *URL:* http://www.lawyers.com/furiaandturner

MEMBERS OF FIRM

Richard F. Furia | James M. Turner, Jr.

ASSOCIATES

Gina R. Furia | Donna DiPietro-Gerace

For full biographical listings, see the Martindale-Hubbell Law Directory

GALFAND BERGER, LLP (AV)

1818 Market Street, 23rd Floor, 19103-3623
Telephone: 215-665-1600
Fax: 215-564-2262
Email: sdonaway@galfandberger.com *URL:* http://www.galfandberger.com

Richard M. Jurewicz | Robert G. Mangold
Joseph Lurie | Peter M. Patton
Eric J. Swan

(See Next Column)

Arthur L. Bugay | Joseph Z. Traub

For full biographical listings, see the Martindale-Hubbell Law Directory

LAW OFFICES OF JOHN J. GALLAGHER, P.C. (AV)

Suite 1100, 1760 Market Street, 19103
Telephone: 215-963-1555
Fax: 215-963-9104
Email: jjgall@ix.netcom.com *URL:* http://www.lawyers.com/johngallagher

John J. Gallagher

Michael S. Henry | Joseph H. Meltzer
Laura Carberry Muldowney | Larisa Tenberg

LEGAL SUPPORT PERSONNEL

Ronald Winkelvoss | Helene Schramm

For full biographical listings, see the Martindale-Hubbell Law Directory

GAY & CHACKER, A PROFESSIONAL CORPORATION (AV)

1731 Spring Garden Street, 19130-3893
Telephone: 215-567-7955
Fax: 215-567-6809
Email: gc@cyberenet.net *URL:* http://www.gay-chacker.com
Northeast Philadelphia Office: 12018 Bustleton Avenue.
Telephone: 215-698-9300.
Marlton, New Jersey Office: 10000 Sagemore Drive, Suite 10202.
Telephone: 609-988-3100.
Fax: 609-988-0194.

Andrew G. Gay | Neil I. Mittin
Edward F. Chacker | Daniel J. Siegel

Lee David Rosenfeld

LEGAL SUPPORT PERSONNEL

Flora Jean Herbert Ruben

For full biographical listings, see the Martindale-Hubbell Law Directory

KANE & SILVERMAN, PROFESSIONAL CORPORATION (AV)

The Philadelphian Suite 1C-44, 2401 Pennsylvania Avenue, 19130
Telephone: 215-232-1000
Fax: 215-232-0181
Email: HGS@palegaladvice.com *URL:* http://www.palegaladvice.com

Michael C. Kane | Howard G. Silverman

For full biographical listings, see the Martindale-Hubbell Law Directory

KELLEY, JASONS, MCGUIRE & SPINELLI, L.L.P. (AV)

One Penn Center, Suite 1400, 1617 JFK Boulevard, 19103
Telephone: 215-854-0658
Fax: 215-854-8434; 215-854-0777
Marlton, New Jersey Office: One Greentree Centre, Suite 201, 08053.
Telephone: 609-988-5543.
Fax: 609-988-9165.
Wilmington, Delaware Office: 800 Delaware Avenue, P.O. Box 194, 19899.
Telephone: 302-652-8560.
Fax: 302-652-8405.

MEMBERS OF FIRM

John Patrick Kelley | Robert N. Spinelli
Catherine N. Jasons | Thomas P. Hanna
Joseph W. McGuire | Thomas J. Johanson
Armand J. Della Porta, Jr. | Michael L. Turner
Christopher N. Santoro | Richard L. Walker, II
Timothy McGowan

ASSOCIATES

Neal C. Glenn | Ann C. Lebowitz
W. Matthew Reber | Anthony J. Ryan

OF COUNSEL

Matthew D. Blum

For full biographical listings, see the Martindale-Hubbell Law Directory

KESSLER, COHEN & ROTH, A PROFESSIONAL CORPORATION (AV)

Two Penn Center Plaza, Suite 1705, 19102
Telephone: 215-567-3500
Fax: 215-567-6019
Email: lawyers@kesslercohen.com

Arnold M. Kessler | Karen R. Bramblett
Stewart L. Cohen | Stephen R. Kurens
Harry M. Roth | David L. Gordon
William D. Marvin

For full biographical listings, see the Martindale-Hubbell Law Directory

Philadelphia—Continued

MARKS, O'NEILL, REILLY, O'BRIEN & COURTNEY, P.C. (AV)

1880 John F. Kennedy Boulevard Suite 1200, 19103
Telephone: 215-564-6688
Fax: 215-564-2526
Email: morol@morocpa.com
Norristown, Pennsylvania Office: 411 Cherry Street.
Telephone: 215-277-7601.
Pittsburgh, Pennsylvania Office: 707 Grant Street, Gulf Tower, Suite 3200.
Telephone: 412-391-6171.
Fax: 412-391-8804.
Westmont, New Jersey Office: 216 Haddon Avenue, Suite 500.
Telephone: 856-858-6110.
Fax: 856-858-3687. E-Mail: morol@morocnj.com
Wilmington, Delaware Office: 2004 Foulk Road, Suite 7.
Telephone: 302-475-5500.
Fax: 302-475-5584.

Jerome E. Marks
Joseph M. O'Neill
Vincent F. Reilly
Kevin J. O'Brien
Dawn R. Courtney
Sean Xavier Kelly
Gino P. Mecoli
John J. Repcheck (Resident, Pittsburgh Office)

David P. Helwig (Resident, Pittsburgh Office)
Maureen Murray-O'Toole
Patrick C. Lamb
Christine G. Boyle
Nancy E. Mancheski
Michael T. Hamilton
Kelly L. Bracken
Tracey Marie McDevitt
Sharon A. Connors (Resident, Westmont, New Jersey Office)
Malissa A. Richetti
Patricia M. Henrich
Judith H. Ring
Gary Weinberg (Resident, Westmont, New Jersey Office)
Lee J. Janiczek
Wendy D. Testa (Resident, Westmont, New Jersey Office)
Gary F. Sharlock (Resident, Pittsburgh Office)
Robert Dale Leidigh (Resident, Pittsburgh Office)
Joseph L. Orszulak, II (Resident, Pittsburgh Office)
Diane Beckman Carvell
Karen J. Stanzione
Michael A. Kosar
Susan D. Grant (Resident, Westmont, New Jersey Office)
Frances Wang-Deveney (Resident, Westmont, New Jersey)
Courtney E. Passin
Stephanie Victoria Shreibman
Megan Kochell D'Iorio (Resident, Wilmington, Delaware Office)
Megan Trocki Mantzavinos (Resident, Wilmington, Delaware Office)
Toni Anderson Moore
Natalie M. Nugent
Frank Gattuso
Michael A. Ring (Resident, Westmont, New Jersey Office)
Ann M. Madden (Not admitted in PA)
Matthew J. Zamites
Salvatore A. Clemente

LEGAL SUPPORT PERSONNEL

PARALEGALS

Gregory P. Sabo
Elisa LaRosa
Frances P. Rossi
Heather Feenan
Jerry Ezekiel
Steven Randisi
Sharon Williams
Melanie Gaskins

For full biographical listings, see the Martindale-Hubbell Law Directory

MCELDREW & FULLAM, P.C. (AV)

Suite 5050 One Liberty Place, 19103
Telephone: 215-563-8300
800-223-3352
Fax: 215-563-6130
URL: http://www.lawyers.com/mceldrew&fullampc
New York, New York Office: McEldrew & Ressler, Suite 2101, 11 Pennsylvania Plaza, 10001.
Telephone: 212-695-6446.
Fax: 212-268-0287.

James J. McEldrew, III
Nancy H. Fullam

Marcella J. Schell
Carol L. Vassallo
Sallie Updyke Mundy
David Felderman

LEGAL SUPPORT PERSONNEL

Christine Doelp (Comptroller)

For full biographical listings, see the Martindale-Hubbell Law Directory

MULVEY & FLANAGAN, P.C. (AV)

1520 Locust Street, 10th Floor, 19102
Telephone: 215-731-0100
Fax: 215-731-0180
Email: mulvey@ix.netcom.com *URL:* http://www.lawyers.com/mflaw

W. Michael Mulvey
Michael J. Flanagan

Maureen Hope Flanagan
Michael G. Dryden
Richard R. Budney, Jr.

For full biographical listings, see the Martindale-Hubbell Law Directory

WILLIAM D. PARRY (AV)

Suite 900, 1608 Walnut Street, 19103
Telephone: 215-735-3500
Fax: 215-735-1858
Email: WDPARRY@AOL.COM

For full biographical listings, see the Martindale-Hubbell Law Directory

PERRY, FIALKOWSKI & PERRY (AV)

Suite 1600 One Penn Square West, 30 South 15th Street, 19102
Telephone: 215-561-4110
Fax: 215-561-4177
Email: pfp@pfplaw.com *URL:* http://www.pfplaw.com
Clementon, New Jersey Office: 180 White Horse Pike.
Telephone: 609-627-1005.

MEMBERS OF FIRM

David Perry
Anne E. Fialkowski
Sherryl R. Perry
Marcia F. Rosenbaum

LEGAL SUPPORT PERSONNEL

Lisa Garrett

For full biographical listings, see the Martindale-Hubbell Law Directory

DANIEL M. PREMINGER, P.C. (AV)

Suite 1050, Robinson Building, 42 South 15th Street, 19102
Telephone: 215-564-1227
Fax: 215-564-0396
Cape May, New Jersey Office: 811 Columbia Avenue, P.O. Box 908, 08204.
Telephone: 609-463-9091.
Fax: 609-465-4061.

Daniel M. Preminger

For full biographical listings, see the Martindale-Hubbell Law Directory

RAYNES, MCCARTY, BINDER, ROSS & MUNDY (AV)

1845 Walnut Street, 20th Floor, 19103
Telephone: 215-568-6190
Fax: 215-988-0618
Cable Address: "RAYMAC"
Haddon Heights, New Jersey Office: 116 White Horse Pike, 08035.
Telephone: 856-546-5454.
Fax: 856-546-9746.

MEMBERS OF FIRM

Arthur G. Raynes
David F. Binder
James F. Mundy
Eugene D. McGurk, Jr.
A. Roy DeCaro
Harold I. Goodman
Nathan B. Ploener
Frank C. DePasquale, Jr.
Nancy R. Dubow
Stephen E. Raynes
James C. King
Kimberly C. Sheinen

OF COUNSEL

John J. McCarty
Robert M. Ross

For full biographical listings, see the Martindale-Hubbell Law Directory

ROSENTHAL AND WEISBERG, P.C. (AV)

Two Logan Square Suite 1565, 18th & Arch Streets, 19103
Telephone: 215-656-4100
Fax: 215-656-4119

Brian D. Rosenthal
Michael Stuart Weisberg

Neil T. Murray
Margaret M. Foley

LEGAL SUPPORT PERSONNEL

Wendy Frost (Paralegal)
Lynn Gibbs (Paralegal)

For full biographical listings, see the Martindale-Hubbell Law Directory

LAW FIRM OF ALLEN L. ROTHENBERG (AV)

Rothenberg Tower, 1518 Walnut Street, 19102
Telephone: 215-732-7000
1-800-624-8888; 1-800-ROTHENBERG
Fax: 215-732-2758
Email: allen@injurylawyer.com *URL:* http://www.injurylawyer.com
New York, N.Y. Office: 450 Seventh Avenue, Corner of 34th Street.
Telephone: 212-563-0100; 1-800-257-4878.
Fax: 212-629-6813.

MEMBERS OF FIRM

Allen L. Rothenberg
Barbara Rothenberg
William R. Solvibile
Joseph C. Murray
Harry Rothenberg

For full biographical listings, see the Martindale-Hubbell Law Directory

Philadelphia—Continued

RUTHRAUFF & ARMBRUST, P.C. (AV)

1601 Market Street, 16th Floor, 19103
Telephone: 215-567-3700
Fax: 215-587-0409
Email: rutharm@erols.com
Cherry Hill, New Jersey Office: 200 Lake Drive East, Suite 206, 08002.
Telephone: 609-482-7856.
Fax: 609-482-8099.

Wilbur Bourne Ruthrauff R. Mark Armbrust

David Ira Rosenbaum

LEGAL SUPPORT PERSONNEL

Charlane Sutton

For full biographical listings, see the Martindale-Hubbell Law Directory

RYAN, BROWN, McDONNELL, BERGER GIBBONS & LaROCCA, LLP (AV)

1600 Market Street, Suite 2500, 19103-7240
Telephone: 215-564-3800
Facsimile: 215-564-1301
Email: lawfirm@ryanbrown.com
Cherry Hill, New Jersey Office: 500 Kings Highway South, 08034.
Telephone: 609-216-8155.
Facsimile: 609-429-7726.

Daniel J. Ryan
John R. Brown
Michael T. McDonnell, III
Mitchell S. Berger
Patrick J. Gibbons
Robert J. LaRocca

For full biographical listings, see the Martindale-Hubbell Law Directory

RALPH D. SAMUEL & CO. A PROFESSIONAL CORPORATION (AV)

225 South 15th Street, Suite 1776, 19102
Telephone: 215-893-9992
Fax: 215-893-9996
Email: RalphSamuel@lawmine.com *URL:* http://www.lawyers.com/ralphdsamuellaw

Ralph David Samuel Lynn Malmgren

For full biographical listings, see the Martindale-Hubbell Law Directory

SCHWARTZ & BLACKMAN (AV)

Washington West Building, 235 South 8th Street, 19106-3593
Telephone: 215-925-5800
Fax: 215-925-1590
Cherry Hill, New Jersey Office: 411 East Route 70, Suite 200 A, 08034.
Telephone: 609-427-0614.

Stacey L. Schwartz Philip L. Blackman

For full biographical listings, see the Martindale-Hubbell Law Directory

SHRAGER, McDAID, LOFTUS, FLUM & SPIVEY (AV)

32nd Floor, Two Commerce Square, 2001 Market Street, 19103
Telephone: 215-568-7771
Fax: 215-568-7495
Email: shragerone@aol.com
Voorhees, New Jersey Office: 502 Haddonfield-Berlin Road.
Telephone: 609-354-9116.

MEMBERS OF FIRM

David S. Shrager
Edward B. McDaid
William A. Loftus (1929-1998)
Joanna Hamill Flum
Wayne R. Spivey
Michael S. Bloom
Robert L. Sachs, Jr.
Daniel S. Weinstock

LEGAL SUPPORT PERSONNEL

Roberta Sawyer
Catherine Collins (Paralegal)
Elizabeth A. Thayer

For full biographical listings, see the Martindale-Hubbell Law Directory

JOHN M. WILLIS (AV)

1845 Walnut Street, Suite 1600, 19103
Telephone: 215-567-5555
Fax: 215-567-2559
Email: willislaw@msn.com *URL:* http://www.lawyers.com/willislaw

For full biographical listings, see the Martindale-Hubbell Law Directory

*PITTSBURGH,** Allegheny Co.

JOHN A. CAPUTO & ASSOCIATES (AV)

Fifth Floor, Three Gateway Center, 15222
Telephone: 412-391-4990
Fax: 412-391-3121

John A. Caputo

(See Next Column)

Allan Meyers Cox
Bernard C. Caputo
David L. Conn

For full biographical listings, see the Martindale-Hubbell Law Directory

CAROSELLI, BEACHLER, McTIERNAN & CONBOY, LLC (AV)

312 Boulevard of Allies, 8th Floor, 15222
Telephone: 412-391-9860
Pennsylvania Only: 1-800-222-8816
Nationally: 1-800-554-5864
Fax: 412-391-7453
URL: http://www.cbmclaw.com

ASSOCIATE

Kelly L. Enders

For full biographical listings, see the Martindale-Hubbell Law Directory

EVANS, PORTNOY & QUINN (AV)

36th Floor, One Oxford Centre, 301 Grant Street, 15219-6401
Telephone: 412-765-3800
Fax: 412-765-3747

Charles E. Evans
Irving M. Portnoy
John E. Quinn

ASSOCIATES

Mark E. Milsop
Marc J. Reiter
Patricia L. Haas

For full biographical listings, see the Martindale-Hubbell Law Directory

FECZKO AND SEYMOUR (AV)

520 Grant Building, 15219
Telephone: 412-261-4970
Fax: Available upon Request
Bethel Park, Pennsylvania Office: 3400 South Park Road.
Telephone: 412-833-5554.

MEMBERS OF FIRM

Albert G. Feczko, Jr. Michael J. Seymour

ASSOCIATE

Michael D. Seymour

Reference: Pittsburgh National Bank.

For full biographical listings, see the Martindale-Hubbell Law Directory

FELDSTEIN GRINBERG STEIN & McKEE, A PROFESSIONAL CORPORATION (AV)

428 Boulevard of the Allies, 15219
Telephone: 412-471-0677
Fax: 412-263-6129
URL: http://www.fgsmlaw.com
Elizabeth, Pennsylvania Office: 400 Second Street.
Telephone: 412-384-6111.

Jay H. Feldstein Gary M. Lang

James C. Heneghan

For full biographical listings, see the Martindale-Hubbell Law Directory

KAPETAN MEYERS ROSEN & LOUIK, P.C. (AV)

Suite 200 The Frick Building, 15219-6003
Telephone: 412-281-4200
Fax: 412-281-2997
URL: http://www.lawyers.com/kmr&llaw
Email: law@malpractice-lawyers.net *URL:* http://www.malpractice-lawyers.net

Jerry I. Meyers
Neil R. Rosen
Michael Louik
Jon R. Perry

For full biographical listings, see the Martindale-Hubbell Law Directory

KIGER & ALPERN (AV)

1404 Grant Building, 15219
Telephone: 412-765-1811
Fax: 412-765-0440

MEMBERS OF FIRM

Jerome W. Kiger Charles H. Alpern

For full biographical listings, see the Martindale-Hubbell Law Directory

MARCUS & SHAPIRA LLP (AV)

35th Floor, One Oxford Centre, 301 Grant Street, 15219-6401
Telephone: 412-471-3490
Telecopier: 412-391-8758
Email: info@marcus-shapira.com *URL:* http://www.marcus-shapira.com

(See Next Column)

MARCUS & SHAPIRA LLP—*Continued*

MEMBERS OF FIRM

Robert L. Allman, II
Robert M. Barnes
James S. Larrimer
Scott D. Livingston
Bernard D. Marcus
James F. Rosenberg
Daniel H. Shapira
Stephen S. Zubrow

ASSOCIATES

Moira E. Cain
Susan H. Snively

For Complete List of Firm Personnel, See General Section

For full biographical listings, see the Martindale-Hubbell Law Directory

WILLIAM W. MCVAY (AV)

Suite 530, 2559 Washington Road, 15241
Telephone: 412-854-3250
Fax: 412-854-5791

ASSOCIATE

James M. McVay, II

Legal Counsel for: United Transportation Union.

For full biographical listings, see the Martindale-Hubbell Law Directory

MERCER & MERCER (AV)

Three Gateway Center 20th Floor, East Wing, 15222
Telephone: 412-281-2728
Fax: 412-281-2248
Email: FredMercerIII@MartindaleMail.com

H. Fred Mercer (1904-1939)
H. Fred Mercer, III

Gina M. Campisano

OF COUNSEL

H. Fred Mercer

For full biographical listings, see the Martindale-Hubbell Law Directory

HOWARD F. MESSER, P.C. (AV)

1404 Grant Building, 15219
Telephone: 412-281-7200
FAX: 412-765-0440
URL: http://www.lawyers.com/messerlaw

Howard F. Messer

Philip A. Fabiano

For full biographical listings, see the Martindale-Hubbell Law Directory

SWENSEN PERER & KONTOS (AV)

Two PNC Plaza, Suite 2710, 15222
Telephone: 412-281-1970
Fax: 412-281-2808
Email: general2@swensenperer.com
Erie, Pennsylvania Office: Swensen Perer & McCandless. 209 Court House Commons.
Telephone: 814-456-0489. Email: erie@swensenperer.com.

MEMBERS OF FIRM

Jan C. Swensen
Alan H. Perer
John W. McCandless (Resident Partner, Erie Office)
George M. Kontos

ASSOCIATES

Anthony C. Mengine
Daniel J. Sinclair

OF COUNSEL

Diane W. Perer
David A. Schroeder
Anthony J. Sciarrino

For full biographical listings, see the Martindale-Hubbell Law Directory

THE TARASI LAW FIRM, P.C. (AV)

510 Third Avenue, 15219
Telephone: 412-391-7135
Fax: 412-471-2673
Email: tarasilaw@aol.com *URL:* http://www.lawyers.com/tarasilaw

Louis M. Tarasi, Jr.

Elizabeth M. Tarasi
Craig L. Fishman
Christina K. Hurnyak

For Complete List of Firm Personnel, See General Section

For full biographical listings, see the Martindale-Hubbell Law Directory

VOLLMER RULONG & KEATING, P.C. (AV)

Suite 1212 Grant Building, 310 Grant Street, 15219
Telephone: 412-391-2121
Telecopier: 412-391-3578
Email: vollmer@vollmerlaw.com *URL:* http://www.vollmerlaw.com

Charles J. Vollmer
Roger G. Rulong, Jr.
John R. Keating

Pamela J. Royesky

For full biographical listings, see the Martindale-Hubbell Law Directory

PUNXSUTAWNEY, Jefferson Co.

LORENZO & GIANVITO, P.C. (AV)

410 West Mahoning Street, P.O. Box 495, 15767-1908
Telephone: 814-938-6390
Fax: 814-938-6412
Email: LGPC@Penn.com

Nicholas F. Lorenzo, Jr.
Nicholas A. Gianvito

For full biographical listings, see the Martindale-Hubbell Law Directory

*SCRANTON,** Lackawanna Co.

FOLEY, MCLANE, FOLEY, MCDONALD & MACGREGOR (AV)

Linden Plaza, 600 Linden Street, P.O. Box 1108, 18501-1108
Telephone: 570-342-8194
Fax: 570-342-4658
Email: foleylawfirm@worldnet.att.net
Stroudsburg Office: 26 North Sixth Street.
Telephone: 570-424-1757.
Fax: 570-424-2764.

Thomas J. Foley, Jr.
John T. McLane
Michael J. Foley
Michael J. McDonald
Thomas J. Foley, III
Kevin P. Foley
Malcolm L. MacGregor
Michael J. Eagen, Jr. (Resident, Stroudsburg Office)

NURSE PARALEGALS

Marsia Konanski
Debra Halvorsen

For full biographical listings, see the Martindale-Hubbell Law Directory

KREDER, BROOKS, HAILSTONE & LUDWIG (AV)

Suite 200, 220 Penn Avenue, 18503
Telephone: 570-346-7922
Telecopier: 570-346-3715

Cody H. Brooks
Andrew Hailstone
Lawrence M. Ludwig
Lucille Marsh
Michael J. Donohue

Counsel For: U.S. Fidelity & Guaranty Co.; Nationwide Insurance Co.; Liberty Mutual Insurance Co.; United States Automobile Assn.; Maryland Casualty Insurance Co.

For Complete List of Firm Personnel, See General Section

For full biographical listings, see the Martindale-Hubbell Law Directory

LENAHAN & DEMPSEY, A PROFESSIONAL CORPORATION (AV)

116 North Washington Avenue, 18503-0234
Telephone: 717-346-2097; 1-888-LENAHAN
Fax: 717-346-1174
Mailing Address: P.O. Box 234, Scranton, Pennsylvania, 18501-0234

John R. Lenahan, Sr. (1915-1998)
William J. Dempsey (Of Counsel)
John R. Lenahan, Jr.
Joseph P. Lenahan
Kathleen A. Lenahan
David E. Heisler
Timothy G. Lenahan
Matthew D. Dempsey

Alan P. Schoen
Brian J. Lenahan
Diane Hepford Lenahan
George E. Mehalchick
Brian Yeager
Thomas R. Daniels
Terrence E. Dempsey
Christine S. Mayernick-Lezinski
John M. Mulcahey
Margaret M. Dempsey
Lisa G. Wilson

Representative Insurance Clients: Allstate Insurance Co.; America Security Insurance Co.; Metropolitan Casualty Insurance Co.; Aetna Insurance Co.; Pennsylvania National Insurance Group; Kemper Insurance Group; American Mutual Insurance Cos.; American States Insurance, Co.

For full biographical listings, see the Martindale-Hubbell Law Directory

MUNLEY, MUNLEY & CARTWRIGHT, P.C. (AV)

205 Madison Avenue, 18503
Telephone: 570-346-7401
Fax: 570-346-3452
URL: http://www.lawyers.com/mmclaw
Email: lawyers@munley.com *URL:* http://www.munley.com

(See Next Column)

MUNLEY, MUNLEY & CARTWRIGHT P.C., *Scranton—Continued*

Robert W. Munley
Marion Munley
Matthew A. Cartwright
James Christopher Munley
Daniel W. Munley
Robert W. Munley, III

Reference: First National Bank of Jermyn.

For full biographical listings, see the Martindale-Hubbell Law Directory

O'MALLEY & HARRIS, P.C. (AV)

345 Wyoming Avenue, 18503
Telephone: 570-348-3711
Fax: 570-348-4092
Email: ohpc@epix.net *URL:* http://www.ohpclaw.com
Stroudsburg, Pennsylvania Office: 111 North Seventh Street.
Telephone: 570-421-2252; 570-422-1280.
FAX: 570-422-1281. Email: cerato@ptdprolog.net.
Wilkes-Barre, Pennsylvania Office: 61 North Washington Street.
Telephone: 570-829-3232.
FAX: 570-829-4418. Email: ohpcwb@epix.net.
Williamsport, Pennsylvania Office: 321 Pine Street, Suite 308.
Telephone: 570-323-4380.

Eugene Nogi (1905-1975)
Henry Nogi (1900-1976)
Russell J. O'Malley, Sr. (1904-1993)
Norman Harris (1907-1998)
William H. Amesbury (Resident, Wilkes-Barre Office)
Paul A. Barrett
Matthew P. Barrett
J. Scott Brady (Resident, Wilkes-Barre Office)
Lori J. Cerato (Resident, Stroudsburg Office)
Bruce L. Coyer
John Q. Durkin
Gerald J. Hanchulak
Richard K. Hodges
Timothy J. Holland (Resident, Wilkes-Barre Office)
John F. Kennedy (Resident, Wilkes-Barre Office)
Daniel Morgan
Michael Perry
James M. Tressler
Joseph Timothy Healey
A. Ruth Whalen (Resident, Wilkes-Barre Office)

Representative Clients: Pennsylvania Hospital Insurance Co.; MMI Systems Agency, Inc.; State Farm Insurance Company; ITT Specialty Risk Services; St. Paul Fire & Marine Insurance Co.; Chubb Group of Insurance Companies; Geisingen System Services; Princeton Insurance Company; Northeastern Pennsylvania Physicians Organization; Catholic Healthcare Partners.

For full biographical listings, see the Martindale-Hubbell Law Directory

SCANLON, HOWLEY, SCANLON & DOHERTY (AV)

321 Spruce Street, 10th Floor, 18503
Telephone: 570-346-7651
Fax: 570-344-1542

MEMBERS OF FIRM

James M. Howley
James M. Scanlon
James A. Doherty, Jr.
Thomas R. Nealon
Thomas B. Helbig
Patrick R. Casey

Counsel for: CNA Insurance Company; The Medical Protective Co.; Harleysville Insurance Co.; The Procter & Gamble Co.; Prudential-Bach Securities, Inc.; Zurich-American Insurance Co.; The Keystone Coca-Cola Bottling Co.; The Home Insurance Co.; The Travelers Insurance Co.; Utica First Ins. Co.

For full biographical listings, see the Martindale-Hubbell Law Directory

*WEST CHESTER,** Chester Co.

DUFFY & GREEN (AV)

10 North Church Street, Suite 307, 19380
Telephone: 610-692-0500
Fax: 610-430-6668

MEMBERS OF FIRM

John J. Duffy
Joseph P. Green, Jr.

ASSOCIATE

P.J. Redmond

For full biographical listings, see the Martindale-Hubbell Law Directory

MACELREE, HARVEY, GALLAGHER, FEATHERMAN & SEBASTIAN, LTD. (AV)

17 West Miner Street, P.O. Box 660, 19381-0660
Telephone: 610-436-0100
Fax: 610-430-7885
Kennett Square, Pennsylvania Office: 211 E. State Street, P. O. Box 363.
Telephone 610-444-3180.
Fax: 610-444-3270.
Exton, Pennsylvania Office: 740 Springdale Drive, Suite 110.
Telephone: 610-524-7575.
Fax: 610-524-9857.

Randy L. Sebastian (1946-1997)
Joseph F. Harvey (1921-1985)

For full biographical listings, see the Martindale-Hubbell Law Directory

*WILKES-BARRE,** Luzerne Co.

ANZALONE LAW OFFICES (AV)

Suite 200, Phoenix Building, 22 East Union Street, 18701
Telephone: 570-825-2719; 570-654-4810
Fax: 570-826-9820
Scranton, Pennsylvania Office: 538 Spruce Street, Suite 712.
Telephone: 570-207-8154.
Stroudsburg, Pennsylvania Office: 930 N. 9th Street, 18360.
Telephone: 570-421-7110.

William F. Anzalone

For full biographical listings, see the Martindale-Hubbell Law Directory

HOURIGAN, KLUGER & QUINN, A PROFESSIONAL CORPORATION (AV)

700 Mellon Bank Center, 8 West Market Street, 18701-1867
Telephone: 570-825-9401
FAX: 570-829-3460
Email: hkq@epix.net
Scranton, Pennsylvania Office: Suite 200, 434 Lackawanna Avenue.
Telephone: 570-346-8414.
Allentown, Pennsylvania Office: Sovereign Building, 609 Hamilton Mall.
Telephone: 610-437-1584.

Joseph A. Quinn, Jr.
Joseph A. Lach (Managing Principal)
Eugene D. Sperazza
Melissa A. Scartelli
Daniel J. Distasio, Jr.
Michelle Quinn

For Complete List of Firm Personnel, See General Section

For full biographical listings, see the Martindale-Hubbell Law Directory

LARRY S. KEISER (AV)

138 South Main Street, P.O. Box 220, 18703-0220
Telephone: 570-822-2929
Fax: 570-822-2931
Email: keiser@tl.infi.net

For full biographical listings, see the Martindale-Hubbell Law Directory

*WILLIAMSPORT,** Lycoming Co.

MITCHELL, MITCHELL, GRAY & GALLAGHER, A PROFESSIONAL CORPORATION (AV)

10 West Third Street, 17701-6513
Telephone: 570-323-8404
Fax: 570-323-8585
Email: mmggpc@csrlink.net

Jacob Neafie Mitchell (1919-1996)
C. Edward S. Mitchell
Richard A. Gray
Robert A. Gallagher
Gary L. Weber
Bret J. Southard

Darryl R. Wishard

For full biographical listings, see the Martindale-Hubbell Law Directory

WYOMISSING, Berks Co.

LEISAWITZ HELLER ABRAMOWITCH PHILLIPS, P.C. (AV)

2201 Ridgewood Road Suite 400, 19610
Telephone: 610-372-3500
Fax: 610-372-8671
Email: lhap@lhaplaw.com
Reading, Pennsylvania Office: 138 North Fifth Street.
Telephone: 610-372-3500.
Hamburg, Pennsylvania Office: 178 North Third Street.
Telephone: 610-562-4145.

Alan G. Leisawitz
Mervin A. Heller, Jr.
Jay N. Abramowitch
Charles J. Phillips
William R. Blumer
Allen R. Shollenberger

Robert J. Kirwan, II
Kevin A. Moore
Kathleen A. B. Kovach
Douglas Paul Rauch
Kenneth Millman

For full biographical listings, see the Martindale-Hubbell Law Directory

RHODE ISLAND

*PROVIDENCE,** Providence Co.

BLISH & CAVANAGH (AV)

Commerce Center, 30 Exchange Terrace, 02903
Telephone: 401-831-8900
Telecopier: 401-751-7542
Email: BLISHCAV@AOL.COM

MEMBERS OF FIRM

Joseph V. Cavanagh, Jr.
Stephen J. Reid, Jr.
William R. Landry
Karen A. Pelczarski
Edmund L. Alves, Jr.
Scott T. Spear
Raymond A. Marcaccio

Michael W. Carroll
Staci L. Sawyer
Kristin Rodgers Sullivan

OF COUNSEL

John H. Blish

Representative Clients: Providence Journal Co.; Rhode Island Hospital Trust National Bank; Fleet Bank; Metropolitan Insurance Co.; Allstate Insurance Co.; Delta Dental of Rhode Island; Colony Communications; Providence Housing Authority; Textron; A.T. Cross.

For full biographical listings, see the Martindale-Hubbell Law Directory

MARTIN K. DONOVAN (AV)

One Park Row, 02903-1235
Telephone: 401-831-2500
Facsimile: 401-751-7830

Reference: Fleet National Bank.

For full biographical listings, see the Martindale-Hubbell Law Directory

WARWICK, Kent Co.

KIRSHENBAUM LAW ASSOCIATES (AV)

67 Jefferson Boulevard, 02888-1053
Telephone: 401-467-5300
Fax: 401-461-4464

MEMBERS OF FIRM

Allen M. Kirshenbaum
Carolyn R. Barone

Lauri Medwin Fine
Evan M. Kirshenbaum

For full biographical listings, see the Martindale-Hubbell Law Directory

WESTERLY, Washington Co.

ADAMO AND NEWMAN (AV)

42 Granite Street, 02891
Telephone: 401-596-7795
Telecopier: 401-596-9000
URL: http://www.lawyers.com/adamonewmanlaw

MEMBERS OF FIRM

John Joseph Adamo
Edward H. Newman

For full biographical listings, see the Martindale-Hubbell Law Directory

SOUTH CAROLINA

*ANDERSON,** Anderson Co.

CHAPMAN, BYRHOLDT & YON (AV)

117 West Benson Street, P.O. Box 2506, 29622
Telephone: 864-225-1411
Fax: 864-231-9131

MEMBER OF FIRM

W. Patrick Yon

For full biographical listings, see the Martindale-Hubbell Law Directory

*BEAUFORT,** Beaufort Co.

HARVEY & BATTEY, P.A. (AV)

1001 Craven Street, P.O. Drawer 1107, 29902
Telephone: 843-524-3109
Telefax: 843-524-6973

W. Brantley Harvey, Jr.
William B. Harvey, III
Colden R. Battey, Jr.
John M. Tatum, III
Thomas A. Holloway

Approved Attorneys for: Lawyers Title Insurance Corp.; Chicago Title Insurance Corp.

(See Next Column)

Representative Clients: Nations Bank; First Bank, F.S.B.; Pleasant Point Plantation Associates; Century 21-Carolina Realty, Inc.; Lobeco Products, Inc.; Beaufort County Association of Realtors; The Fripp Company.

For Complete List of Firm Personnel, See General Section

For full biographical listings, see the Martindale-Hubbell Law Directory

*CHARLESTON,** Charleston Co.

HOOD LAW FIRM (AV)

172 Meeting Street, P.O. Box 1508, 29402
Telephone: 843-577-4435
Fax: 843-722-1630
Email: hlf@hoodlaw.com *URL:* http://www.hoodlaw.com

MEMBERS OF FIRM

Robert H. Hood
John K. Blincow, Jr.
Louis P. Herns
James G. Kennedy
G. Mark Phillips
Barbara Wynne Showers
Carl Everette Pierce, II
Joseph C. Wilson, IV
James Dowell Gandy, III

Dixon F. Pearce, II
Allison Snead Patrick
Hugh Willcox Buyck
P. Gunnar Nistad
Allan Poe Sloan, III
Robert H. Hood, Jr.
Mary Agnes Hood Craig
William Mullins McLeod, Jr.

For full biographical listings, see the Martindale-Hubbell Law Directory

GEDNEY M. HOWE, III, P.A. (AV)

8 Chalmers Street, P.O. Box 1034, 29402
Telephone: 843-722-8048
FAX: 843-722-2140

Gedney M. Howe, Jr. (1914-1981)
Gedney M. Howe, III
Alvin J. Hammer

Caroline M.W. Dillon

For full biographical listings, see the Martindale-Hubbell Law Directory

RAY P. MCCLAIN, ATTORNEY, P.A. (AV)

38 Broad Street, Third Floor, P.O. Box 608, 29402-0608
Telephone: 843-577-3170
Telefax: 843-577-3097
Email: rpmcclain@worldnet.att.net

Ray P. McClain

For full biographical listings, see the Martindale-Hubbell Law Directory

SAVAGE & SAVAGE, P.A. (AV)

15 Prioleau Street, P.O. Box 1002, 29402-1002
Telephone: 843-720-7470
Fax: 843-720-7478
Email: savage@savlaw.com *URL:* http://savlaw.com

Andrew J. Savage, III
David L. Savage

For full biographical listings, see the Martindale-Hubbell Law Directory

SOLOMON, BUDMAN, STRICKER & SCHWARTZ, L.L.P. (AV)

Parkshore Centre, 1 Poston Road, Suite 395, P.O. Box 30280, 29417-0280
Telephone: 843-763-1118
Telecopier: 843-763-7518

A. Bernard Solomon
Michael A. Stricker
Donald J. Budman
Lester S. Schwartz

Local Counsel for: Lawyers Title Insurance Corp.

For full biographical listings, see the Martindale-Hubbell Law Directory

MARK C. TANENBAUM, P.A. (AV)

241-243 East Bay Street, P.O. Box 20757, 29413
Telephone: 843-577-5100
Telecopy: 843-722-4688
Email: mark@tanenbaumlaw.com

Mark C. Tanenbaum

Stephen A. Butaitis

For full biographical listings, see the Martindale-Hubbell Law Directory

*COLUMBIA,** Richland Co.

FINKEL & ALTMAN, L.L.C. (AV)

Suite 1800, 1201 Main Street, P.O. Box 1799, 29202
Telephone: 803-765-2935
Fax: 803-252-0786
Email: webmaster@finkellaw.com *URL:* http://www.finkellaw.com
Charleston, South Carolina Office: 12 Exchange Street, P.O. Box 225.
Telephone: 843-577-5460.
Fax: 843-577-5135.

Gerald M. Finkel
Harry L. Goldberg
Howard S. Sheftman

Representative Clients: First Union National Bank; Banc One Mortgage Co.; Motorola Communications & Electronics Corp.

For full biographical listings, see the Martindale-Hubbell Law Directory

GLENN MURPHY GRAY & STEPP, L.L.P. (AV)

B B & T Bank Building, Suite 390, 1901 Assembly Street, P.O. Box 1550, 29202-1550
Telephone: 803-765-1100
Telecopy: 803-765-0755

Terrell L. Glenn (1930-1993)

MEMBERS OF FIRM

Peter L. Murphy
Robert E. Stepp
Elizabeth Van Doren Gray
Elizabeth G. Howard

Robert C. Rhodes
Roland M. Franklin
Laura W. Robinson
C. Shawn Dryer

Reference: BB&T.

For full biographical listings, see the Martindale-Hubbell Law Directory

LEE, EADON, ISGETT AND POPWELL, P.A. (AV)

1314 Lincoln Street, P.O. Box 1505, 29202
Telephone: 803-799-9811; 1-800-882-0742
Telecopier: 803-779-8572
URL: http://www.lawyers.com/leeeadonisgett&popwell

Luther M. Lee (1923-1996)
Christopher C. Isgett
Sherod H. Eadon, Jr.
Gary W. Popwell, Jr.

Gerald E. Reardon

For full biographical listings, see the Martindale-Hubbell Law Directory

RICHARDSON, PLOWDEN, CARPENTER & ROBINSON, P.A. (AV)

1600 Marion Street, P.O. Drawer 7788, 29202
Telephone: 803-771-4400
Telecopy: 803-779-0016
Email: atty@rpcrlaw.com *URL:* http://www.rpcrlaw.com
Myrtle Beach, South Carolina Office: 2103 B Farlow Street, P.O. Box 3646, 29578.
Telephone: 843-448-1008.
FAX: 843-448-1533.

Charles E. Carpenter, Jr.
Leslie A. Cotter, Jr.
George C. Beighley
Douglas C. Baxter
Mary Sowell League

OF COUNSEL

Donald V. Richardson, III
Michael A. Pulliam

Representative Clients: Insurance: CNA Insurance Co.; The Hartford; Kemper Insurance Co.; Pennsylvania National Mutual Casualty Insurance Co.; Wausau Insurance Cos.; The Reudlinger Cos.

For Complete List of Firm Personnel, See General Section

For full biographical listings, see the Martindale-Hubbell Law Directory

TURNER, PADGET, GRAHAM & LANEY, P.A. (AV)

Seventeenth Floor, 1901 Main Street, P.O. Box 1473, 29202
Telephone: 803-254-2200
Telecopy: 803-799-3957
Florence, South Carolina Office: Fourth Floor, 1831 West Evans Street, P.O. Box 5478, 29502.
Telephone: 843-662-9008.
Fax: 843-667-0828.
Charleston, South Carolina Office: 21 Broad Street, 1st Floor, P.O. Box 836, 29402.
Telephone: 843-723-1622.
Fax: 843-577-3369.

Ronald E. Boston
John E. Cuttino
Charles E. Hill
Arthur E. Justice, Jr. (Resident, Florence, SC, Office)
Thomas C. Salane
Danny C. Crowe
Edward W. Laney, IV
John S. Wilkerson, III (Resident, Florence, SC, Office)
Elbert S. Dorn

(See Next Column)

Hugh M. Claytor (Resident, Florence, SC, Office)
O. Carlisle Edwards, Jr.
Vernon F. Dunbar
Richard L. Hinson (Resident, Florence, SC, Office)
J. Kenneth Carter, Jr.
Wilson S. Sheldon (Resident, Florence, SC, Office)

OF COUNSEL

Laura Chandler Rublee (Resident, Florence, SC, Office)

David W. Keller, Jr. (Resident, Florence, SC Office)
William C. Barnes, Jr. (Resident, Florence, SC, Office)
Jessica C. Moe (Resident, Charleston, SC, Office)
Cynthia C. Dooley
Richard C. Burke (Resident, Florence, SC, Office)
Curtis L. Ott
Michael C. Abbott (Resident, Florence, SC, Office)
Steven R. LeBlanc
David S. Cobb (Resident, Charleston, SC, Office)
Patrick W. Carr (Resident, Florence, SC, Office)
Donnell G. Jennings
James David Smith, Jr. (Resident, Florence, SC, Office)
D. Andrew Williams

For Complete List of Firm Personnel, See General Section

For full biographical listings, see the Martindale-Hubbell Law Directory

WOODWARD COTHRAN & HERNDON (AV)

1200 Main Street, Suite 600, 29201
Telephone: 803-799-9772
Fax: 803-799-3256
Mailing Address: P.O. Box 12399, Columbia, South Carolina, 29211
Email: wch1@usit.net

OF COUNSEL

Edward M. Woodward, Sr.

General Counsel for: The Columbia College; Sandhills Bank; Heater Utilities.

For full biographical listings, see the Martindale-Hubbell Law Directory

*CONWAY,** Horry Co.

HEARN, BRITTAIN & MARTIN, P.A. (AV)

1206 Third Avenue, 29526
Telephone: 843-248-3172
Fax: 843-248-4911
Myrtle Beach, South Carolina Office: 4614 Oleander Drive.
Telephone: 843-449-8562.
Fax: 843-497-6124.

George M. Hearn, Jr.
L. Morgan Martin
Thomas C. Brittain
Scott B. Umstead
G. Scott Bellamy

Peter Lee Hearn, Sr.

For full biographical listings, see the Martindale-Hubbell Law Directory

*GREENVILLE,** Greenville Co.

PARHAM & SMITH, L.L.C. (AV)

Smith Barney Building-Second Floor, 501 River Street, P.O. Box 2800, 29601
Telephone: 864-242-9008
1-800-849-7777
Fax: 864-271-6155
Mailing Address: P.O. Box 2800, Greenville, SC, 29602
Email: mparham@parhamlaw.com *URL:* http://www.lawyers.com/parham&smithlaw

MEMBERS OF FIRM

Michael Parham
Barney O. Smith, Jr. (1952-1996)

Steven Blakely Smith

For full biographical listings, see the Martindale-Hubbell Law Directory

HILTON HEAD ISLAND, Beaufort Co.

BARRY L. JOHNSON, P.A. (AV)

35-A Bow Circle, Palmetto Bay Offices (Suite 35-A), P.O. Box 7261, 29938
Telephone: 843-341-3777
Fax: 843-341-3007
Beaufort, South Carolina Office: 1611 North Street.
Telephone: 843-982-0089.
Fax: 986-9203.

Barry L. Johnson

For full biographical listings, see the Martindale-Hubbell Law Directory

LORIS, Horry Co.

STEVENS LAW FIRM, P.C. (AV)

3341 Broad Street P.O. Drawer 127, 29569-0127
Telephone: 843-756-7652
Fax: 843-756-3785
E-Mail: RUMMPOLE@AOL.COM
Email: JPKLAW@AOL.COM

James P. Stevens, Jr. Jonathan P. Kresken

For full biographical listings, see the Martindale-Hubbell Law Directory

MYRTLE BEACH, Horry Co.

BELLAMY, RUTENBERG, COPELAND, EPPS, GRAVELY & BOWERS, P.A. (AV)

1000 29th Avenue North, P.O. Box 357, 29578
Telephone: 843-448-2400
Telecopier: 843-448-3022

Howell V. Bellamy, Jr.
John K. Rutenberg
John E. Copeland
Claude M. Epps, Jr.
David R. Gravely
Edward B. Bowers, Jr.
Bradley D. King
Henrietta U. Golding
M. Edwin Hinds, Jr.
Jill F. Griffith
Kathryn M. Cook
David B. Miller
C. Winfield Johnson, III
Sarah A. Johnson
Douglas M. Zayicek
Jeffrey W. King
Mary Anna Malpass
Martin Charles Dawsey

Representative Clients: Dargan Construction Co.; Coastal Federal Savings Bank; Sands Investments; Wachovia Bank of South Carolina; AVX Corp.; Bank of America; Parthenon Insurance Co.; Burroughs & Chapin Co.; International Paper Co.; Hospital Corporation of America.

For full biographical listings, see the Martindale-Hubbell Law Directory

FURR AND HENSHAW (AV)

A Partnership of Professional Corporations
1900 Oak Street, P.O. Box 2909, 29578
Telephone: 843-626-7621
Fax: 843-448-6445
Email: f&h@sccoast.net *URL:* http://www.lawyers.com/f&hlaw
Columbia, South Carolina Office: 1534 Blanding Street.
Telephone: 803-252-4050.
FAX: 803-254-7513.

O. Fayrell Furr, Jr. (P.C.)

Karolan F. Ohanesian (Resident)

Reference: Anchor Bank, Myrtle Beach, S.C.

For full biographical listings, see the Martindale-Hubbell Law Directory

NORTH CHARLESTON, Charleston Co.

RIESEN LAW FIRM, L.L.P. (AV)

3660 West Montague Avenue, P.O. Box 40997, 29423-0997
Telephone: 843-760-2450
FAX: 843-767-3282

MEMBERS OF FIRM

John D. Bradley, III (1946-1998)
Fred W. Riesen, Jr.
Gary Alan Ling
E. Paul Gibson
Timothy Clay Kulp
Philip A. Berlinsky
Allison A. Stover
Jody V. McKnight

Ellen Howard

For full biographical listings, see the Martindale-Hubbell Law Directory

PAWLEYS ISLAND, Georgetown Co.

DANIEL & DANIEL (AV)

10 B Pawleys Station, 10080 Ocean Highway (US 17 S), P.O. Box 857, 29585
Telephone: 843-237-4792
Email: reesedaniel@email.msn.com

MEMBERS OF FIRM

J. Reese Daniel Michael R. Daniel

For full biographical listings, see the Martindale-Hubbell Law Directory

*SPARTANBURG,** Spartanburg Co.

HARRISON, WHITE, SMITH, HAYES & COGGINS, P.A. (AV)

178 West Main Street, 29306
Telephone: 864-542-2990
Fax: 864-542-2994

(See Next Column)

Benjamin C. Harrison
John B. White, Jr.
J. Mark Hayes, II
Danny R. Smith
Donald C. Coggins, Jr.

For full biographical listings, see the Martindale-Hubbell Law Directory

SURFSIDE BEACH, Horry Co.

KELAHER, CONNELL & CONNOR, P.C. (AV)

Suite 209, The Courtyard, 1500 U.S. Highway 17 North, P.O. Drawer 14547, 29587
Telephone: 843-238-5648
Fax: 843-238-5050

Edward T. Kelaher
Gene M. Connell, Jr.
L. Sidney Connor, IV

Lisa Poe Davis

Representative Clients and References furnished upon request.

For full biographical listings, see the Martindale-Hubbell Law Directory

*WALHALLA,** Oconee Co.

LARRY C. BRANDT, P.A. (AV)

205 West Main Street, P.O. Drawer 738, 29691
Telephone: 864-638-5406
864-638-7873
Email: lbrandt@innova.net

Larry C. Brandt

LEGAL SUPPORT PERSONNEL

Debra C. Miller

For full biographical listings, see the Martindale-Hubbell Law Directory

SOUTH DAKOTA

*ABERDEEN,** Brown Co.

MALONEY & MALONEY (AV)

722 South Highway 281, P.O. Box 755, 57402-0755
Telephone: 605-229-2752
Fax: 605-226-0276
Email: maloney@nvc.net

MEMBERS OF FIRM

Dennis Maloney Marilyn Marshall Maloney

For full biographical listings, see the Martindale-Hubbell Law Directory

*BELLE FOURCHE,** Butte Co.

QUINN, DAY & BARKER, P.L.L.C. (AV)

117 Fifth Avenue, P.O. Box 370, 57717-0370
Telephone: 605-892-2743
Fax: 605-892-4273
Email: bfqedb@dtgcom.net
Rapid City, South Dakota Office: 4200 Beach Drive, P.O. Box 9335.
Telephone: 605-343-6400.
Telecopier: 605-343-4841.

Terence R. Quinn
Michael W. Day
Kenneth E. Barker
Robert L. Morris, II
Bradley A. Schreiber
Michael A. Wilson (Resident, Rapid City Office)
Michael P. Reynolds (Resident, Rapid City Office)

ASSOCIATE

Michael C. Loos (Resident, Rapid City Office)

OF COUNSEL

R. E. Brandenburg

Representative Clients: Pioneer Bank & Trust, Belle Fourche, Spearfish and Rapid City Offices; Belle Fourche Irrigation District; Butte-Meade Sanitary Water District; Igloo-Provo Water User Project; Strawberry Hill Mining Co.; American Family Insurance Group.

For full biographical listings, see the Martindale-Hubbell Law Directory

LEAD, Lawrence Co.

FULLER, TELLINGHUISEN, GORDON & PERCY, P.C. (AV)

203 West Main Street, P.O. Box 898, 57754
Telephone: 605-584-2440
Fax: 605-584-1979
Email: leadlaw@mato.com
Spearfish, South Dakota Office: 132 East Illinois, 57783.
Telephone: 605-642-8080.
Fax: 605-642-1756. E-mail: spflaw@mato.com

(See Next Column)

FULLER, TELLINGHUISEN, GORDON & PERCY P.C., *Lead—Continued*

A. P. Fuller
Roger A. Tellinghuisen
Bradley P. Gordon
Michelle Palmer Percy

Representative Clients: Homestake Mining Co.; Hotel Franklin & Gaming; Black Hills Novelty/Automatic Vending, Inc.; Northern Hills General Hospital; Lantis Enterprises, Inc.; Norwest Bank South Dakota N.A.; Lead-Deadwood Independent School District # 40-1; City of Lead.

For full biographical listings, see the Martindale-Hubbell Law Directory

*RAPID CITY,** Pennington Co.

BANGS, MCCULLEN, BUTLER, FOYE & SIMMONS, L.L.P. (AV)

818 St. Joseph Street, P.O. Box 2670, 57709
Telephone: 605-343-1040
Telecopier: 605-343-1503
URL: http://www.bangsmccullen.com

MEMBERS OF FIRM

George A. Bangs (1915-1995)
W. A. McCullen (1907-1987)
Joseph M. Butler
Thomas E. Simmons
Allen G. Nelson
James P. Hurley
Michael M. Hickey
Terry L. Hofer
Rod Schlauger
Daniel F. Duffy
Jeffrey G. Hurd

ASSOCIATES

Veronica L. Bowen
Terry G. Westergaard

Representative Clients: Norwest Bank South Dakota, N.A., Rapid City, S.D.; Pete Lien & Sons; The Travelers Insurance Co.; Rapid City Regional Hospital; Dakota Steel & Supply Co.; Great American Insurance Co.; Fireman's Fund Insurance; United States Automobile Association; Moyle Petroleum; Rapid City Area School District 51-4.

For Complete List of Firm Personnel, See General Section

For full biographical listings, see the Martindale-Hubbell Law Directory

DELANEY & SUMNER (AV)

623 Quincy Street Suite 103, 57701
Telephone: 605-388-3153
Fax: 605-388-3155
Mailing Address: P.O. Box 8305, Rapid City, SD, 57709-8305
Email: toogoodoo1@aol.com

MEMBERS OF FIRM

John J. Delaney
Scott Sumner

For full biographical listings, see the Martindale-Hubbell Law Directory

LYNN, JACKSON, SHULTZ & LEBRUN, P.C. (AV)

First National Bank Building Eighth Floor, 909 Saint Joseph Street, P.O. Box 8250, 57709
Telephone: 605-342-2592
Telecopier: 605-342-5185
Email: ljlawrc@lynnjackson.com *URL:* http://www.lynnjackson.com
Sioux Falls, South Dakota Office: U.S. Bank Building, Eighth Floor, P.O. Box 1920.
Telephone: 605-332-5999.
Telecopier: 605-332-4249.

Thomas G. Fritz
Jay C. Shultz
Jon C. Sogn (Resident, Sioux Falls Office)
R. Alan Peterson (Resident, Sioux Falls Office)

Representative Clients: U.S. Bank of South Dakota; Employers Mutual of Wausau; South Dakota School of Mines & Technology; CIGNA Insurance Co.; E.D. Jones & Co.
General Counsel for: Rushmore Electric Power Cooperative; Black Hills Regional Eye Institute.

For Complete List of Firm Personnel, See General Section

For full biographical listings, see the Martindale-Hubbell Law Directory

WHITING, HAGG & HAGG (AV)

1220 Mt. Rushmore Road, Suite Two, P.O. Box 8008, 57701
Telephone: 605-348-1125
Fax: 605-348-9744
URL: http://www.amatteroflaw.com

MEMBERS OF FIRM

Brian D. Hagg
Rexford A. Hagg
John Stanton Dorsey

ASSOCIATES

Kent R. Hagg
Robert J. Hollan
Kevin W. Klapprodt

LEGAL SUPPORT PERSONNEL

Beverly J. McCracken
Becky J. Buhmann

For full biographical listings, see the Martindale-Hubbell Law Directory

*SIOUX FALLS,** Minnehaha Co.

DAVENPORT, EVANS, HURWITZ & SMITH, L.L.P. (AV)

513 South Main Avenue, P.O. Box 1030, 57101-1030
Telephone: 605-336-2880
Telecopier: 605-335-3639
Email: lawyers@dehs.com

MEMBERS OF FIRM

Edwin E. Evans
Michael L. Luce
Michael J. Schaffer
Thomas M. Frankman
Rick W. Orr
Susan Brunick Simons
Roberto A. Lange
Cheryle Wiedmeier Gering
Lori Purcell Fossen
Mark W. Haigh
Sandra K. Hoglund

Counsel for: American Society of Composers, Authors and Publishers (A.S.C.A.P.); Continental Insurance Cos.; The First National Bank in Sioux Falls; Ford Motor Credit Co.; General Motors Corp.; The St. Paul Cos.; The Travelers.

For Complete List of Firm Personnel, See General Section

For full biographical listings, see the Martindale-Hubbell Law Directory

HUGHES LAW OFFICES (AV)

412 West Ninth Street, 57104-3602
Telephone: 605-339-3939
Fax: 605-339-3940

John R. Hughes

LeeAnn Larson LaFave

For full biographical listings, see the Martindale-Hubbell Law Directory

TENNESSEE

*CHATTANOOGA,** Hamilton Co.

FOSTER, FOSTER, ALLEN & DURRENCE, P.C. (AV)

Formerly Hall, Haynes, Lusk & Foster
801 Broad Street - Suite 515, 37402
Telephone: 423-266-1141
Telecopier: 423-266-4618
Email: dward@ffadlaw.com

George Lane Foster
William M. Foster
Craig R. Allen
Phillip M. Durrence, Jr.
David J. Ward
Clayton M. Whittaker
John M. Hull

LEGAL SUPPORT PERSONNEL

Peggy Sue Bates

Division Counsel For: Norfolk Southern Corp.
Attorneys For: CNA/Insurance; United States Fidelity & Guaranty Co. (USF&G); Bridgestone-Firestone, Inc.; State Volunteer Mutual Insurance Co. (SVMIC); Exxon Corp.; Murphy Oil Corp.; Chicago Title Insurance Co.; Jim Walter Homes; Mid-State Homes, Inc.

For full biographical listings, see the Martindale-Hubbell Law Directory

FRANKLIN, COOPER & MARCUS, PLLC (AV)

837 Fort Wood Street, 37403
Telephone: 423-756-3596
Telecopier: 423-756-3597

David L. Franklin
Gary A. Cooper
H. Richard Marcus

For full biographical listings, see the Martindale-Hubbell Law Directory

NELSON, MCMAHAN & NOBLETT (AV)

(An Association of Attorneys)
400 Pioneer Bank Building, 37402
Telephone: 423-756-2291
Fax: 423-756-0737

Randall L. Nelson
Michael A. McMahan
Phillip A. Noblett
Douglas M. Cox
Kenneth O. Fritz
Lawrence W. Kelly

For full biographical listings, see the Martindale-Hubbell Law Directory

O'NEAL, WALKER & BOEHM (AV)

An Association including a Professional Corporation
808 Maclellan Building, 721 Broad Street, 37402
Telephone: 423-756-5111
Fax: 423-756-7945

(See Next Column)

O'NEAL, WALKER & BOEHM—*Continued*

Thomas H. O'Neal (P.C.) | J. Taylor Walker | Jeffrey D. Boehm

Counsel for: American Consumers, Inc. (Shop-Rite).

For full biographical listings, see the Martindale-Hubbell Law Directory

SUMMERS & WYATT, P.C. (AV)

500 Lindsay Street, 37402
Telephone: 423-265-2385
Fax: 423-266-5211
Email: summers@voy.net

Jerry H. Summers | Thomas L. Wyatt | Jeffrey W. Rufolo

For Complete List of Firm Personnel, See General Section

For full biographical listings, see the Martindale-Hubbell Law Directory

*CLARKSVILLE,** Montgomery Co.

RUNYON AND RUNYON, PLLC (AV)

301 Main Street, P.O. Box 1023, 37041-1023
Telephone: 931-647-3377
Fax: 931-551-3561
URL: http://www.lawyers.com/runyonandrunyon
Erin Office: 143 East Main.
Telephone: 931-289-5900.

MEMBERS OF FIRM

Charles V. Runyon (1886-1973) | Markley Runyon Gill
Frank J. Runyon | Frank J. Runyon, III
Raymond F. Runyon

Representative Clients: Clarksville Department of Electricity; St. Paul Insurance Co.; The Trane Co.; Aetna Life & Casualty Co.; Houston County; Union Planters Bank, National Association; Prudential Professional Realty.
Reference: First Union Bank, Clarksville.

For full biographical listings, see the Martindale-Hubbell Law Directory

PAUL WELKER (AV)

First Union Bank Building, One Public Square Fourth Floor, Suite 400, 37040
Telephone: 931-552-9163
Facsimile: 931-552-9164
Email: pwelker@midwest.net

For full biographical listings, see the Martindale-Hubbell Law Directory

*CLEVELAND,** Bradley Co.

JENNE, SCOTT & JENNE (AV)

260 Ocoee Street, P.O. Box 161, 37364-0161
Telephone: 423-476-5506
Fax: 423-476-5058
Email: MichaelJenne@mindspring.com

MEMBERS OF FIRM

Roger E. Jenne | Robert A. Scott (1940-1984)
Michael E. Jenne

For full biographical listings, see the Martindale-Hubbell Law Directory

*CLINTON,** Anderson Co.

RIDENOUR, RIDENOUR & FOX (AV)

108 South Main Street, 37716
Telephone: 423-457-0755
Fax: 423-457-4878
1-800-810-3476

MEMBERS OF FIRM

Roger L. Ridenour | Ronald H. Ridenour
Bruce D. Fox

ASSOCIATES

Michael S. Farley | April Dawn Carroll
Lea Ellen Ridenour Agee | Jason E. Legg

For full biographical listings, see the Martindale-Hubbell Law Directory

*DYERSBURG,** Dyer Co.

PALMER LAW FIRM (AV)

116 West Court Street, P.O. Box 746, 38024
Telephone: 901-285-7382
Fax: 901-286-6537

MEMBERS OF FIRM

E. T. "Rocky" Palmer (1907-1986) | John W. Palmer

(See Next Column)

ASSOCIATE

Earl F. Johnson

For full biographical listings, see the Martindale-Hubbell Law Directory

KINGSPORT, Sullivan Co.

HAWKINS, MOODY, BINGHAM, MILLER & ASSOCIATES, P.C. (AV)

1397 East Center Street, 37664
Telephone: 423-246-9100
Fax: 423-246-9282

William W. Hawkins (1929-1997) | Edgar G. Moody
John S. Bingham
J. David Miller

For full biographical listings, see the Martindale-Hubbell Law Directory

*KNOXVILLE,** Knox Co.

GILREATH & ASSOCIATES (AV)

550 Main Avenue, Suite 600, P.O. Box 1270, 37901-1270
Telephone: 423-637-2442
Fax: 423-971-4116
Email: gilknox@sidgilreath.com *URL:* http://www.sidgilreath.com
Nashville, Tennessee Office: 2828 Renaissance Tower, 611 Commerce Street.
Telephone: 615-256-3388.
Memphis, Tennessee Office: 44 North Second Street, Suite 200.
Telephone: 901-527-8288.

MEMBER OF FIRM

Sidney W. Gilreath

ASSOCIATES

Meridith C. Bond | Dianne E. Lashmit
Paul Kaufman | R. Christopher Gilreath
Richard L. Duncan | Patricia Taylor Bruner (Not admitted in TN)

LEGAL SUPPORT PERSONNEL

Tammy Ailshie (Legal Assistant to Senior Partner) | Pamela Smith Wise (Senior Legal Assistant)
Janie Howerton (Legal Assistant) | Susan Stogner (Legal Assistant to Senior Partner)
Darla R. Johnson (Legal Assistant) | Bryan L. Capps (Legal Administrator)
Janet L. Tucker (Legal Assistant to Senior Partner) | Danielle E. Barto (Firm Administrator)

Representative Client: Transportation Communications International Union; Brotherhood of Locomotive Engineers Union.
Reference: Suntrust Bank.

For full biographical listings, see the Martindale-Hubbell Law Directory

LEIBOWITZ & COHEN (AV)

608 Gay Street, S.W., 37902
Telephone: 423-637-1809
FAX: 423-637-9276

MEMBERS OF FIRM

Arnold G. Cohen | Lawrence P. Leibowitz

ASSOCIATE

Melissa A. Ashburn

OF COUNSEL

Russell T. Greene

For full biographical listings, see the Martindale-Hubbell Law Directory

PRYOR, FLYNN, PRIEST & HARBER (AV)

Suite 600 Two Centre Square, 625 Gay Street, P.O. Box 870, 37901
Telephone: 423-522-4191
Telecopier: 423-522-0910

Robert E. Pryor | Timothy A. Priest
Frank L. Flynn, Jr. | John K. Harber

ASSOCIATES

Mark E. Floyd | M. Christopher Coffey
Donald R. Coffey | Robert E. Pryor, Jr.

References: First Vantage Bank; Sun Trust Bank.

For full biographical listings, see the Martindale-Hubbell Law Directory

*MARYVILLE,** Blount Co.

NICHOLSON, GARNER & DUGGAN (AV)

250 High Street, P.O. Box 5059, 37802-5059
Telephone: 423-984-1460
Knoxville: 423-637-1970
Telecopier: 423-982-2595
Real Estate Fax: 423-982-2595
Litigation Fax: 423-984-9275
Email: jnicholson@earthlink.net *URL:* http://www.lawyers.com/ngdlaw

(See Next Column)

NICHOLSON, GARNER & DUGGAN, *Maryville—Continued*

MEMBERS OF FIRM

Joe Nicholson
J. Michael Garner
David R. Duggan

ASSOCIATES

Angelia D. Morie
Daphne H. Cornwell

Representative Clients: Will be furnished by request.

For full biographical listings, see the Martindale-Hubbell Law Directory

*MEMPHIS,** Shelby Co.

ARMSTRONG ALLEN PREWITT GENTRY JOHNSTON & HOLMES, PLLC (AV)

Brinkley Plaza, Suite 700, 80 Monroe Avenue, 38103-2467
Telephone: 901-523-8211
Facsimile: 901-524-4936
Little Rock, Arkansas Office: Suite 100, 100 Morgan Keegan Drive, 72202.
Telephone: 501-280-0100.
Facsimile: 501-280-0166.
Jackson, Mississippi Office: 2525 Lakeward Drive, Suite 200, 39216.
Telephone: 601-713-1192.
Facsimile: 601-713-2049.
Jackson, Tennessee Office: 464 North Parkway, Suite A, 38305.
Telephone: 901-660-2332.
Facsimile: 901-664-1109.

MEMBERS OF FIRM

Thomas R. Prewitt
Charles A. Banks (Resident, Little Rock, Arkansas Office)
Robert V. Redding (Resident, Jackson, Tennessee Office)
Robertson M. Leatherman, Jr.
Cannon F. Allen
Thomas W. Lewis

For Complete List of Firm Personnel, See General Section

For full biographical listings, see the Martindale-Hubbell Law Directory

GLASSMAN, JETER, EDWARDS & WADE, P.C. (AV)

26 North Second Street Building, 38103
Telephone: 901-527-4673
Telecopier: 901-521-0940
Email: GJEWW@Memphisonline.com

Richard Glassman
William M. Jeter
Tim Edwards
B. J. Wade
Carl K. Wyatt, Jr.
Dale H. Tuttle
John Barry Burgess
Robert A. Cox
Rebecca Adelman
Lori J. Keen
James F. Horner, Jr.
Richard E. Sorin

Todd Britton Murrah
Heather Walters Thompson

For full biographical listings, see the Martindale-Hubbell Law Directory

HALE HEADRICK DEWEY & WOLF, PLLC (AV)

One Memphis Place, 200 Jefferson Avenue Suite 1450, 38103
Telephone: 901-523-1123
Fax: 901-523-7472
Nashville, Tennessee Office: Suntrust Bank Building, 201 Fourth Avenue North, Suite 1450, 37219.
Telephone: 615-843-5160.
Fax: 615-843-5165

Stephen P. Hale
S. Russell Headrick
H. Tucker Dewey
Herbert B. Wolf, Jr.
John S. Golwen

OF COUNSEL

Steven L. Gill

Jennifer Ziegenhorn
Wendy A. Geurin
John W. Campbell
Joseph M. Koury
Holly N. Knight
Charles S. Blatteis
Jennifer S. Kiesewetter
J. William Williams

For full biographical listings, see the Martindale-Hubbell Law Directory

SMITH, SABBATINI & MCLEARY, PLLC (AV)

100 Peabody Place Suite 1250, 38103
Telephone: 901-312-5555
Fax: 901-312-5667
Mailing Address: P.O. Box 3582, Memphis, TN, 38173
URL: http://www.smithlawetal.com

Gary K. Smith
Robert L. Sabbatini
Harold W. McLeary, Jr.
William D. Domico
James F. Kyle
James T. McColgan, III
G. Edward Coleman, III
Bryant C. Witt

(See Next Column)

Representative Clients: Premier RRG Insurance; Illinois Central Railroad; Medical Assurance; Albertson's, Inc.; Med. Marc (Chiro Co.); Medical Protective Co.; Methodist Health Systems; Hartford Insurance Co.; Sentry Insurance; State Farm Insurance.

For full biographical listings, see the Martindale-Hubbell Law Directory

*MURFREESBORO,** Rutherford Co.

WALDRON AND FANN (AV)

202 West Main Street, 37130
Telephone: 615-890-7365
Telecopier: 615-848-1658
Email: tfann@bellsouth.net

MEMBERS OF FIRM

R. Steven Waldron
Terry A. Fann

For full biographical listings, see the Martindale-Hubbell Law Directory

*NASHVILLE,** Davidson Co.

MICHAEL W. BINKLEY, P.C. (AV)

150 Second Avenue North, Suite 300, 37201
Telephone: 615-244-8630
Fax: 615-244-8644
Email: Mwbpc@aol.com *URL:* http://www.lawyers.com/binkleylaw

Michael W. Binkley

For full biographical listings, see the Martindale-Hubbell Law Directory

LAW OFFICES OF JACK A. BUTLER (AV)

Suite 2395, 315 Deaderick Street, 37238-0083
Telephone: 615-244-3300
Facsimile: 615-244-8625

Tony L. Maples
Leslie A. Bruce
Jeffrey R. Kohl
Karen M. Weimar

For full biographical listings, see the Martindale-Hubbell Law Directory

GARFINKLE, MCLEMORE & WALKER, PLLC (AV)

2000 Richard Jones Road, P.O. Box 158249, 37215-8249
Telephone: 615-383-9495
Telecopier: 615-292-9848
Email: gmwpllc@sprynet.com *URL:* http://www.citysearch.com/nas/gmwpllc

Robert M. Garfinkle

For full biographical listings, see the Martindale-Hubbell Law Directory

THE LAW OFFICE OF GARY R. GOBER (AV)

2505 21st Avenue South, Suite 301, 37212
Telephone: 615-297-8300; 1-800-634-6237
Fax: 615-297-2886
Mailing Address: P.O. Box 121497, Nashville, Tennessee, 37212
Email: garygoberlaw@mindspring.com

For full biographical listings, see the Martindale-Hubbell Law Directory

LAW OFFICES OF TOM NEBEL A PROFESSIONAL CORPORATION (AV)

501 Union Street, Suite 504, 37219
Telephone: 615-244-4700
Facsimile: 615-244-9555
Email: info@tomnebelpc.com *URL:* http://www.tomnebelpc.com

G. Thomas Nebel
John I. Harris, III

Cynthia W. Fitzgerald
Jeffrey Todd Loy

OF COUNSEL

Bobby Lee Cook (Not admitted in TN)

For full biographical listings, see the Martindale-Hubbell Law Directory

JAMES R. OMER & ASSOCIATES (AV)

An Association of Attorneys
Suite 200 Trial Lawyers Building, 430 Third Avenue North, 37201
Telephone: 615-244-7271
FAX: 615-255-7660
Email: mailto:jromerlaw@aol.com *URL:* http://www.tennlaw-omer.com

James R. Omer
Terrance E. McNabb
James R. Omer, Jr.

Douglas B. Omer

OF COUNSEL

Robert J. Shockey

For full biographical listings, see the Martindale-Hubbell Law Directory

Nashville—Continued

DAVID RANDOLPH SMITH & ASSOCIATES (AV)

611 Commerce Street, 3121 Renaissance Tower, 37203
Telephone: 615-742-1775; 800-394-2119
Fax: 615-742-1223
URL: http://www.lawyers.com/drs&associates
Email: info@drslawfirm.com *URL:* http://www.drslawfirm.com

For full biographical listings, see the Martindale-Hubbell Law Directory

WILLIAMS & ASSOCIATES, P.C. (AV)

First American Center Suite 1425, 315 Deaderick Street, 37238
Telephone: 615-242-2800
Fax: 615-256-6618
Email: wmsassoc@isdn.net *URL:* http://www.wmsandassociates.com

Charles J. Williams

Kenneth M. Switzer
John B. Carlson
Wade B. Cowan
Anna B. Williams
Francis M. (Trey) Hamilton, III

For full biographical listings, see the Martindale-Hubbell Law Directory

*TRENTON,** Gibson Co.

HARRELL AND HARRELL (AV)

110 NW Court Square, 38382
Telephone: 901-855-1351; 855-1352
Fax: 901-855-1212
Email: harrell@usit.net

MEMBER OF FIRM

Limmie Lee Harrell, Jr.

ASSOCIATE

Jerald M. Campbell, Jr.

Representative Clients: Trenton Gin Co., Trenton, Tenn.; Bank of Commerce, Trenton, Tenn.; Toshiba America; Chuck Graves Chevrolet, Olsmobile, Cadillac, GMC Trucks; Donnie Hatcher Chevrolet, Buick, Oldsmobile; Wade Electric Co.; Tecumseh, Inc., New Pacific Machinery, Inc.; Kellwood.
Reference: The Bank of Commerce, Trenton.

For full biographical listings, see the Martindale-Hubbell Law Directory

TEXAS

*AMARILLO,** Potter Co.

GARNER & STEIN, LLP (AV)

777 Amarillo National Plaza/Two, 500 South Taylor, LB #233, 79101-2446
Telephone: 806-373-0505
Telecopier: 806-379-8056
Email: regarner@tcac.net

MEMBERS OF FIRM

Robert E. Garner
Sam L. Stein

ASSOCIATE

Ana E. Estevez

LEGAL SUPPORT PERSONNEL

PARALEGALS

Michele Kindle
Roxann Sillivent

Representative Clients: Panhandle Capitol Corp.; Friona Industries, L.P.; Page and Associates, Contractors; Hereford Bi-Products, Inc.; Amarillo National Bank.

For full biographical listings, see the Martindale-Hubbell Law Directory

NANCY J. STONE (AV)

Maxor Building, Suite 820, 320 South Polk Street, Lobby Box 32, 79101
Telephone: 806-374-9300
Fax: 806-373-3008
Email: nstone@arn.net *URL:* http://www.nancyjstone.com/806-374-9300/2-1.html

For full biographical listings, see the Martindale-Hubbell Law Directory

*AUSTIN,** Travis Co.

KARL BAYER (AV)

900 Norwood Tower, 114 West Seventh Street, 78701
Telephone: 512-476-1226
Fax: 512-476-1280
Email: karl@karlbayer.com

(See Next Column)

Karl Bayer

For full biographical listings, see the Martindale-Hubbell Law Directory

BYRD, DAVIS AND EISENBERG, L.L.P. (AV)

A Partnership including Professional Corporations
707 West 34th Street, 78705
Telephone: 512-454-3751
Fax: 512-451-5857
Email: 70720.3104@compuserve.com

MEMBERS OF FIRM

L. Tonnett Byrd (P.C.)
David H. Walter
Don L. Davis
James H. Furman
Daniel W. Andrews

ASSOCIATE

Derek L. Davis

OF COUNSEL

Jack C. Eisenberg (P.C.)

For full biographical listings, see the Martindale-Hubbell Law Directory

COLBERT, FREEMAN & STRIBLING (AV)

400 West 14th Street, Suite 120, 78701
Telephone: 512-477-6111

MEMBERS OF FIRM

Joe Colbert
Rick Freeman
Tom Stribling

General Counsel for: Austin Police Association and Travis County Sheriff's Officers Association; Austin Emergency Medical Services Personnel Association.

For full biographical listings, see the Martindale-Hubbell Law Directory

MITHOFF & JACKS, L.L.P. (AV)

Suite 1010, Franklin Plaza, 111 Congress Avenue, 78701
Telephone: 512-478-4422
Telecopier: 512-478-5015
Houston, Texas Office: Penthouse, 3450 One Allen Center.
Telephone: 713-654-1122.
Fax: 713-739-8085.

Richard Warren Mithoff
Tommy Jacks

James L. Wright
Mark George Einfalt
Belinda Manning Howell
Greig W. Coates
David Drew Wright

For full biographical listings, see the Martindale-Hubbell Law Directory

THE ONSTAD LAW FIRM (AV)

907 Ranch Road 620 South, Suite 302, 78734-5609
Telephone: 512-263-7600
Facimile: 512-263-7800
Email: rockonstad@ispchannel.com

Rockne W. Onstad
Blake C. Erskine, Jr.
James Francis Twombly

For full biographical listings, see the Martindale-Hubbell Law Directory

SLACK & DAVIS, L.L.P. (AV)

A Partnership including a Professional Corporation
8911 Capital of Texas Highway Suite 2110, 78759
Telephone: 512-795-8686
Fax: 512-795-8787

MEMBERS OF FIRM

Steven E. Aldous
Mike Davis
Michael L. Slack

ASSOCIATE

Donna J. Bowen

OF COUNSEL

Tom H. Davis, P.C.

For full biographical listings, see the Martindale-Hubbell Law Directory

WATSON, BISHOP, LONDON, GALOW, P.C. (AV)

The Littlefield Building, 106 East Sixth Street, Suite 700, 78701
Telephone: 512-479-5900
Telefax: 512-479-5934

Kirk P. Watson
Alice London
Daniel W. Bishop, II
Jerry Galow

Christina Carlson Dodds
Joseph F. Brophy
Phillip H. Schmandt
Cory W. Smith

For full biographical listings, see the Martindale-Hubbell Law Directory

Austin—Continued

WHITEHURST, HARKNESS, OZMUN & ARCHULETA, A PROFESSIONAL CORPORATION (AV)

24th Floor, Westgate Building, P.O. Box 1802, 78767
Telephone: 512-476-4346
Fax: 512-476-4400

William O. Whitehurst, Jr.
Thomas R. Harkness
Scott A. Ozmun
Michael E.J. Archuleta
Cynthia K. Stewart
Sally S. Metcalfe
Michelle M. Cheng
Sylvia H. Imhoff

For full biographical listings, see the Martindale-Hubbell Law Directory

WINCKLER & HARVEY, L.L.P. (AV)

3101 Bee Caves Road, Suite 270, 78746
Telephone: 512-306-1800
Telecopier: 512-306-9442
Email: 2jayslaw@io.com *URL:* http://www.lawyers.com/winkler&harvey

MEMBERS OF FIRM

Jay L. Winckler
Jay Harvey

ASSOCIATE

Reed Teckenbrock

For full biographical listings, see the Martindale-Hubbell Law Directory

*BEAUMONT,** Jefferson Co.

BENCKENSTEIN, NORVELL & NATHAN, L.L.P. (AV)

550 Fannin, Suite 200, P.O. Box 551, 77704
Telephone: 409-833-4309
Telecopier: 409-833-9558
Email: bmtlaw@aol.com
Houston, Texas Office: One Riverway, Suite 100
Telephone: 713-871-8081.
Fax: 713-871-1509.

MEMBERS OF FIRM

Lipscomb Norvell, Jr.
Gerald W. Riedmueller
Michael J. Reviere (Resident, Houston Office)
Paul A. Scheurich
Craig H. Clendenin (Resident, Houston Office)

ASSOCIATES

Floyd F. McSpadden, Jr.
Dennis S. Dresden (Resident, Houston Office)
David A. Oubre (Resident, Houston Office)
J. Keith Stanley

OF COUNSEL

Jerry J. Nathan

Representative Clients: Chubb/Pacific Indemnity Group; Mobil Oil Corp.; Travelers; Wausau; American International Group; CNA; Kemper Insurance Group; E.I. DuPont; Zurich American; Fina Oil & Chemical Co.

For full biographical listings, see the Martindale-Hubbell Law Directory

MICHAEL R. MCGOWN (AV)

2615 Calder Street, Suite 300, P.O. Box 5876, 77726-5876
Telephone: 409-839-8389
Fax: 409-839-8387
Email: mcgown@ih2000.net *URL:* http://www.mcgown@ih2000.net

For full biographical listings, see the Martindale-Hubbell Law Directory

MEHAFFY & WEBER, A PROFESSIONAL CORPORATION (AV)

2615 Calder Avenue, Suite 800, P.O. Box 16, 77704
Telephone: 409-835-5011
Fax: 409-835-5729; 835-5177
Email: MehaffyWeber.com
Orange, Texas Office: 1006 Green Avenue, P.O. Drawer 189.
Telephone: 409-886-7766.
Houston, Texas Office: One Allen Center, 500 Dallas, Suite 1200.
Telephone: 713-655-1200.

James W. Mehaffy (1914-1985)
Roger S. McCabe
Jim I. Graves
John Cash Smith
Arthur R. Almquist
Louis M. Scofield
Patricia Chamblin
Gene M. Williams
David B. Gaultney
Robert A. Black
Sandra F. Clark
M. C. Carrington
Barbara J. Barron
Elizabeth Brandes Pratt
John E. Haught
Keith W. Foley
Charles Stanton Perry
Ernest W. Boyd
Michele Y. Smith

(See Next Column)

Vickie R. Thompson
Paul R. Heyburn
James G. Martingano
Debra N. Bigler
Elizabeth C. Turley
Peter T. Gregg
E. Wade Carpenter
Nikkee E. Rutherford
Bridget M. Fuselier
Jonathan C. Allen
Chris H. Booth
Maryalyce W. Cox
Timothy A. Gasaway
Elna Nguyen Griggs
Sean Stotsky

OF COUNSEL

Otto J. Weber, Jr.
Dewey J. Gonsoulin
John J. Durkay

Representative Clients: E.I. du Pont de Nemours and Co.; Eli Lilly & Co.; Merrell Dow; Jefferson County Tax Appraisal District; W.R. Grace & Co.-Conn.; Bank of America; Christus Health; Christus St. Elizabeth; Christus St. Mary; Burlington Northern Santa Fe Railway.
Approved Attorneys for: Stewart Title Guaranty Co.

For Complete List of Firm Personnel, See General Section

For full biographical listings, see the Martindale-Hubbell Law Directory

REAUD, MORGAN & QUINN (AV)

801 Laurel, 77701
Telephone: 409-838-1000
Fax: 409-833-8236

MEMBERS OF FIRM

Wayne A. Reaud
Glen W. Morgan
Cris Quinn
Richard J. Clarkson
Bob Wortham
Curtis W. Leister
Gary T. Cornwell

ASSOCIATES

Mary Ferguson Bradford
John Werner
David W. Ferrell
J. Trenton Bond
Sally A. Gary

For full biographical listings, see the Martindale-Hubbell Law Directory

WELLER, GREEN, TOUPS & TERRELL, L.L.P. (AV)

2615 Calder Street, Suite 400, P.O. Box 350, 77704
Telephone: 409-838-0101
Telecopy: 409-838-6780
Houston, Texas Office: 4265 San Felipe, Suite 1045.
Telephone: 713-626-1126.
Fax: 713-626-1363.
Tallahassee, Florida Office: 2937 A-2 Kerry Forest Parkway, 32308.
Telephone: 850-906-9880.
Fax: 850-906-9878.

George A. Weller (1911-1986)
Edward H. Green
Mitchell A. Toups
B. Adam Terrell
William H. Garvin III (Not admitted in TX)
E. Hart Green
Steven C. Toups

Giles R. Kibbe
Paul T. Warner

For full biographical listings, see the Martindale-Hubbell Law Directory

*BROWNSVILLE,** Cameron Co.

FRANK COSTILLA, JR., P.L.L.C. (AV)

5 East Elizabeth Street, P.O. Box 4417, 78520
Telephone: 956-541-4982
Fax: 956-544-3152
Email: cano@hiline.net *URL:* http://www.costilla.com

Frank Costilla, Jr.

For full biographical listings, see the Martindale-Hubbell Law Directory

RILEY & HARRIS, L.L.P. (AV)

845 E. Harrison, Suite A, 78520-7120
Telephone: 956-550-8825
Fax: 956-550-8854
Email: txlaw@riley-harris.com *URL:* http://www.riley-harris.com
Houston, Texas Office: One Houston Center, 1221 Mckinney, Suite 3000, 77010-2023.
Telephone: 713-646-1000.
Fax: 713-646-1036. Email: txlaw@riley-harris.com.

MEMBER OF FIRM

Timothy D. Riley

For full biographical listings, see the Martindale-Hubbell Law Directory

RODRIGUEZ, COLVIN & CHANEY, L.L.P. (AV)

1201 East Van Buren, P.O. Box 2155, 78520
Telephone: 956-542-7441
Fax: 956-541-2170
McAllen, Texas Office: 4900 North 10th.
Telephone: 956-686-1287.
Telecopier: 956-686-6197.

(See Next Column)

RODRIGUEZ, COLVIN & CHANEY L.L.P.—*Continued*

Harlingen, Texas Office: 402 East Van Buren.
Telephone: 956-423-0216.
Telecopier: 956-423-2035.

MEMBERS OF FIRM

Eduardo R. Rodriguez
Norton A. Colvin, Jr.
Mitchell C. Chaney
Marjory Colvin Batsell
Jaime A. Saenz
Joseph A. (Tony) Rodriguez
Alison D. Kennamer

ASSOCIATES

Laura J. Urbis
Lecia L. Chaney
Daniel D. Herink
Robert Patrick Rodriguez
Rosa Maria Villagomez
Vanessa Garza
Teri L. Danish

OF COUNSEL

Orrin W. Johnson (Resident, Harlingen Office)
Benjamin S. Hardy (1912-1993)
Neil E. Norquest (Resident, McAllen Office)
Chris A. Brisack (Resident, McAllen Office)
Raymond A. Cowley

Division Attorneys for: Union Pacific Railroad.
Counsel for: Texas Commerce Bank-Rio Grande Valley, N.A.; Texas Commerce Bancshares, Inc.

For full biographical listings, see the Martindale-Hubbell Law Directory

*CORPUS CHRISTI,** Nueces Co.

LAW OFFICES OF WILLIAM J. CHRISS, P.C. (AV)

719 South Shoreline, Suite 100, P.O. Box 2946, 78403
Telephone: 361-884-3330
Facsimile: 361-883-9187

William J. Chriss

Michael Nored

For full biographical listings, see the Martindale-Hubbell Law Directory

PATTERSON & ASSOCIATES (AV)

101 North Shoreline, Suite 210, 78403
Telephone: 361-887-1881
Fax: 361-887-6761
Email: bob@pattersonassoc.com

Robert J. Patterson

Raymond C. Alexander

For full biographical listings, see the Martindale-Hubbell Law Directory

KATHRYN SNAPKA (AV)

Suite 800, 545 North Broadway, P.O. Drawer 23017, 78403
Telephone: 512-888-7676
Fax: 512-884-8545
Email: Snapkaofc@aol.com

ASSOCIATE

Gregory W. Turman

LEGAL SUPPORT PERSONNEL

Holly G. Peterson (Legal Assistant)
Ann R. Giddens

For full biographical listings, see the Martindale-Hubbell Law Directory

JAMES M. WHITTEN (AV)

540 Frost Bank Plaza, 802 North Carancahua Street, 78470
Telephone: 361-881-8000
FAX: 361-887-9103
Sinton, Texas Office: 401 West Fulton St., P.O. Box 760.
Telephone: 361-364-3000.
Fax: 361-364-5911.

For full biographical listings, see the Martindale-Hubbell Law Directory

*DALLAS,** Dallas Co.

BAKER BOTTS L.L.P. (AV)

2001 Ross Avenue, 75201
Telephone: 214-953-6500
Fax: 214-953-6503
Email: postmaster@bakerbotts.com *URL:* http://www.bakerbotts.com
Houston, Texas Office: One Shell Plaza, 910 Louisiana.
Telephone: 713-229-1234.
Washington, D.C. Office: The Warner, 1299 Pennsylvania Avenue, N.W.
Telephone: 202-639-7700.
Austin, Texas Office: 1600 San Jacinto Center, 98 San Jacinto Boulevard.
Telephone: 512-322-2500.
New York, New York Office: 599 Lexington Avenue.
Telephone: 212-705-5000.

(See Next Column)

Moscow, Russia Office: 10 ul. Bolshaya Dimitrovka (formerly Pushkinskaya), 103031.
Telephone: 7095/921-5300 (Local); 7095/929-7070.
London, England Office: 45 Ludgate Hill.
Telephone: 0171-778-1400 (Local); 011-44-171-778-1400 (International).
Baku, Azerbaijan Office: 6-10 Vagif Mustafa-zadeh Street, Third Floor, Icheri Sheher, 370004.
Telephone: 994-12-97-63-88 (Local); 011-994-12-97-63-88 (International).

MEMBERS OF FIRM

Earl B. Austin
Peter A. Moir

ASSOCIATES

David M. Genender
Jose M. Luzarraga
J. Kemp Sawers

For Complete List of Firm Personnel, See General Section

For full biographical listings, see the Martindale-Hubbell Law Directory

LAW OFFICES OF JAMES C. BARBER (AV)

4310 Gaston Avenue, 75246
Telephone: 214-821-8840
Metro: 972-263-6866
Fax: 214-821-3834
URL: http://www.gtesupersite.com/lojcbarber
Email: jcbarber@gte.net *URL:* http://www.lawyers.com/jamescbarber

ASSOCIATE

Larry Chad Kluever

For full biographical listings, see the Martindale-Hubbell Law Directory

LAW OFFICES OF FRANK L. BRANSON, P.C. (AV)

18th Floor, Highland Park Place, 4514 Cole Avenue, 75205-4185
Telephone: 214-522-0200
Metro: 972-263-7452
Fax: 214-521-5485
URL: http://www.lawyers.com/frankbranson

Frank L. Branson
Debbie D. Branson
George A. Quesada, Jr.
Jerry M. White
Thomas J. Farmer
William B. Curtis
Robert D. Crain
Charles E. Moody

OF COUNSEL

Ted Z. Robertson
J. Hadley Edgar, Jr.

For full biographical listings, see the Martindale-Hubbell Law Directory

BRUCE A. BUDNER & ASSOCIATES (AV)

2527 Fairmount Street, 75201
Telephone: 214-220-2111
Email: babudner@waymark.net *URL:* http://www.lawyers.com/bruceabudner

ASSOCIATE

Jill C. Adler

LEGAL SUPPORT PERSONNEL

Diane Smith (Paralegal)

For full biographical listings, see the Martindale-Hubbell Law Directory

BUSH CRADDOCK & RENEKER, L.L.P. (AV)

Chase Bank Building, 6517 Hillcrest Avenue, Suite 110, 75205-1857
Telephone: 214-750-3550
Fax: 214-750-3551
Email: info@bcrlaw.com *URL:* http://www.bcrlaw.com
Marshall, Texas Office: 201 W. Grand.
Telephone: 903-935-9700.
Fax: 903-935-9743.

MEMBERS OF FIRM

Don D. Bush
Michael J. Craddock
D. Ronald Reneker
Douglas J. Buncher
Craig M. Patrick
Katherine Kolenberg Miracle
Kevin T. White

OF COUNSEL

Richard K. Berger

Representative Clients: CSX Transportation, Inc.; Fresenius Medical Care-North America; Palm Harbor Homes, Inc.; Union Pacific Railroad Co.

For full biographical listings, see the Martindale-Hubbell Law Directory

CALHOUN & STACY (AV)

Suite 5700 - Bank of America Plaza, 901 Main Street, 75202-3713
Telephone: 214-748-5000
Facsimile: 214-748-1421
Email: info@calhounstacy.com *URL:* http://www.calhounstacy.com

(See Next Column)

CALHOUN & STACY, *Dallas—Continued*

MEMBERS OF FIRM

Mark Alan Calhoun
Dennis D. Conder
LeAnn Wainscott Cross
Shannon B. Schuster
Roy L. Stacy
Michael C. Wright

ASSOCIATES

David G. Allen
Joseph G. Barkate, Jr.
Scott S. Crocker
Sean P. Fitzgerald
Elizabeth Reding Gambrell
Leanne Capps Medford
Joel W. Reese
Barbara L. Wohlrabe

For Complete List of Firm Personnel, See General Section

For full biographical listings, see the Martindale-Hubbell Law Directory

CANTEY & HANGER (AV)

A Registered Limited Liability Partnership
3330 Harwood Center, 1999 Bryan Street, 75201
Telephone: 214-978-4100; Metro 972-263-7729
FAX: 214-978-4150
Email: cantey@onramp.net
Fort Worth, Texas Office: 2100 Burnett Plaza, 801 Cherry Street.
Telephone: 817-877-2800, Metro Line: 429-3815.
Telex: 758631.
FAX: 877-2807. Email: cantey@onramp.net
Austin, Texas Office: Cantey & Hanger Roan & Autrey L.L.P., 200 First State Bank Tower, 400 West Fifteenth Street.
Telephone: 512-474-4200.
FAX: 512-469-0470; 512-469-0474. Email: FIRM@ROAN-AUTREY.COM

MEMBERS OF FIRM

Thomas L. Kelly, Jr.
Ashley Ty Parrish

Represent: CNA; Houston General Insurance Company; Winn Dixie Stores; Insurance Company of the West; Ohio Casualty Group; Inspire Insurance Solutions; Underwriters at Lloyds.

For Complete List of Firm Personnel, See General Section

For full biographical listings, see the Martindale-Hubbell Law Directory

CRACKEN, HARKEY & PAYNE, LLP (AV)

5956 Sherry Lane, Suite 1401, 75225
Telephone: 214-750-1855
Fax: 214-750-7086
Email: info@cracken-harkey.com *URL:* http://www.cracken-harkey.com

John R. W. Cracken
John D. Harkey, Jr.
Christopher A. Payne
James R. Snell

For full biographical listings, see the Martindale-Hubbell Law Directory

DEHAY & ELLISTON, L.L.P. (AV)

3500 NationsBank Plaza, 901 Main Street, 75202-3736
Telephone: 214-210-2400
Facsimile: 214-210-2500
Beaumont, Texas Office: 215 Orleans Street, 77701.
Telephone: 409-833-0900.
Facsimile: 409-833-0964.

J. Carlisle DeHay, Jr. (1922-1991)

PARTNERS

Gary D. Elliston
David W. Crowe
Mel D. Bailey
Eric D. Wewers
Christopher P. Manning
Paul E. Hamilton
Laura E. Kugler
Melinda S. Huff
Charlene R. Echols

OF COUNSEL

W. Scott Berry
Kathryn O. Hermes

Brent M. Karren
Stuart G. Brooks
Anthony S. Miller
Todd D. Ogden
William C. Arnold
Todd J. Suddleson (Not admitted in TX)
Kyle Christophen Steele
Lily Chang Myers
Kirsten L. Alessio
Russell J. DePalma
Tandy V. Jouret
M. Lauren Mathews
Jill G. Adams
John W. Arnold
William A. Fynes
Jeffrey M. Marosz
Kenneth D. Morris
Todd H. Ramsey
Mitzi S. Wallace
Susan Chapman

For full biographical listings, see the Martindale-Hubbell Law Directory

FOREMAN, BOUDREAUX, SMITH & JOHNSON (AV)

Walnut Glen Tower, Suite 1150, 8144 Walnut Hill Lane, Lock Box 62, 75231-4316
Telephone: 214-750-7661
Fax: 214-739-2715

(See Next Column)

OF COUNSEL

Jim Foreman

MEMBERS OF FIRM

Joe N. Boudreaux
Joseph F. Smith
Gary L. Johnson

ASSOCIATE

Shawn Thompson

LEGAL SUPPORT PERSONNEL

Charlene Illingworth

For full biographical listings, see the Martindale-Hubbell Law Directory

FRALEY & FRALEY, L.L.P. (AV)

901 Main Street, Suite 6510, 75202
Telephone: 214-761-6460
Fax: 214-761-6469
Email: info@fraleyandfraley.com *URL:* http://www.fraleyandfraley.com

R. Scott Fraley
Elizabeth Masters Fraley
J. Patrick Bredehoft

J. David Criss

For full biographical listings, see the Martindale-Hubbell Law Directory

HOWIE & SWEENEY, L.L.P. (AV)

14th Floor, Park Place on Turtle Creek, 2911 Turtle Creek Boulevard, 75219
Telephone: 214-523-8800; 800-523-2339
Telecopier: 214-523-8888
Email: email@howie-sweeney.com *URL:* http://www.howie-sweeney.com

MEMBERS OF FIRM

John R. Howie
Paula Sweeney

Al Ellis
Jon Kettles
Andrew L. Payne
Valerie A. Mosman
Ladd Sanger
Elizabeth A. Florence

For full biographical listings, see the Martindale-Hubbell Law Directory

JACKSON WALKER L.L.P. (AV)

901 Main Street, Suite 6000, 75202-3797
Telephone: 214-953-6000
Fax: 214-953-5822
URL: http://www.jw.com
Austin, Texas Office: 100 Congress Avenue, Suite 1100.
Telephone: 512-236-2000.
Fax: 512-236-2002.
Fort Worth, Texas Office: 301 Commerce Street, Suite 2400.
Telephone: 817-334-7200.
Fax: 817-334-7290.
Houston, Texas Office: 1100 Louisiana, Suite 4200.
Telephone: 713-752-4200.
Fax: 713-752-4221.
Richardson, Texas Office: 2435 North Central Expressway, Suite 600.
Telephone: 972-671-2560.
Fax: 972-671-2566.
San Angelo, Texas Office: 225 West Beauregard Avenue.
Telephone: 915-481-2550.
Fax: 915-481-2552.
San Antonio, Texas Office: 112 E. Pecan Street, Suite 2100.
Telephone: 210-978-7700.
Fax: 210-978-7790.

MEMBERS OF FIRM

E. Leon Carter
H. Dudley Chambers
Alan N. Greenspan
Michael L. Knapek
John L. Lancaster, III
Robert P. Latham
Billy R. McGill
Retta A. Miller
David T. Moran
David C. Myers
Robert F. Ruckman
Frank C. Vecella
Troy Michael Wilson

Representative Clients Furnished Upon Request.

For Complete List of Firm Personnel, See General Section

For full biographical listings, see the Martindale-Hubbell Law Directory

LAW OFFICES OF ALAN K. LAUFMAN, J.D., M.D. A PROFESSIONAL CORPORATION (AV)

Suite 1000 Turtle Creek Centre, 3811 Turtle Creek Boulevard, 75219
Telephone: 214-559-3300
Fax: 214-526-1150
Email: medlaw@texas.net *URL:* http://www.lawyers.com/medlaw

Alan K. Laufman

For full biographical listings, see the Martindale-Hubbell Law Directory

Dallas—Continued

MORGAN & WEISBROD, L.L.P. (AV)

10260 North Central Expressway, Suite 100N, P.O. Box 821329, 75382
Telephone: 214-373-3761; 800-800-6353
Fax: 214-739-4732
Email: info@morganweisbrod.com *URL:* http://www.morganweisbrod.com
Houston, Texas Office: 6800 West Loop South, Suite 450, 77401.
Telephone: 713-838-0003.
Fax: 713-838-0066.

Carl M. Weisbrod
Les Weisbrod
David R. Norton
Paul N. Gold
Larry F. Smith
Jennifer L. Fry
William A. Newman
Paul B. Burkhalter
David R. Deary
Leanna Marchand
David V. Marchand

ASSOCIATES

Wiebke Breuer
John M. Driskill
Gal Lahat
Robbie S. Partida-Kipness
Kevin Robinowitz

OF COUNSEL

Melvin D. Morgan
Lynn C. Absher
James M. Rauer

For full biographical listings, see the Martindale-Hubbell Law Directory

LAW OFFICES OF WILLIAM W. PARISH (AV)

Suite One, 2214 Main Street, 75201
Telephone: 214-741-3154
Fax: 214-741-4624
Email: parish@worldnet.att.net *URL:* http://www.lawyers.com/parish

For full biographical listings, see the Martindale-Hubbell Law Directory

THE SCHMIDT FIRM (AV)

3102 Oak Lawn, Suite 730, LB 158, 75219
Telephone: 214-521-4898
Toll Free No. 1-800-745-1372, x4898
Fax: 214-521-9995
Email: schmidt@schmidtlaw.com *URL:* http://www.schmidtlaw.com

C. L. Mike Schmidt

Michael E. Schmidt

LEGAL SUPPORT PERSONNEL

Carol S. Stimson (Litigation Administrator)
Paula Thomas (Legal Assistant)
Camilia Beth Walker (Legal Assistant)
Anita Kelley
Shannon Smith (Legal Assistant)

For full biographical listings, see the Martindale-Hubbell Law Directory

ATTORNEYS' OFFICES OF JAMES W. SHOECRAFT, P.C. (AV)

Highland Park Place, Suite 1000, North Central at Knox-Henderson 4514 Cole Avenue - LB14, 75205
Telephone: 214-528-8800; 1-800-552-5774
Fax: 214-528-3349

James W. Shoecraft

For full biographical listings, see the Martindale-Hubbell Law Directory

SIFFORD & ANDERSON, L.L.P. (AV)

A Partnership including Professional Corporations
6300 NationsBank Plaza, 901 Main Street, 75202-3771
Telephone: 214-742-1200
Fax: 214-220-0206

MEMBERS OF FIRM

Lewis R. Sifford (P.C.)
L. W. Anderson
John L. Ratcliffe (P.C.)

Michele A. Ratcliffe
Kevin W. Vice
Ron G. MacFarlane, Jr.

For full biographical listings, see the Martindale-Hubbell Law Directory

TOOLEY & VOSS (AV)

8214 Westchester Drive, Suite 420, 75225
Telephone: 214-368-2224
Fax: 214-368-8307
Email: JCToutfit@aol.com

Joe C. Tooley
Edwin P. Voss Jr.

For full biographical listings, see the Martindale-Hubbell Law Directory

TURLEY & STUTZ, P.C. (AV)

610 University Tower, 6440 N. Central Expressway, 75206
Telephone: 214-691-1880
Fax: 214-691-1955
Email: tstutz@quantumdata.net

Linda Turley
Thomas J. Stutz

For full biographical listings, see the Martindale-Hubbell Law Directory

LAW OFFICES OF WINDLE TURLEY, P.C. (AV)

1000 University Tower, 6440 North Central Expressway, 75206
Telephone: 214-691-4025
Telefax: 214-361-5802
Telex: 734049
Email: htpillturley@wturley.com *URL:* http://www.wturley.com

Windle Turley
Michael G. Sawicki
R. Christopher Cowan
William J. Dunleavy
Phillip L. Brown

Dale R. Rose
Deana Tunnell
Lori A. Watson
Patrick C. Patterson
Brent Stewart Freefield
Jeffrey T. Embry

For full biographical listings, see the Martindale-Hubbell Law Directory

LAW OFFICES OF EDDIE VASSALLO, P.C. (AV)

Regency Plaza, 3710 Rawlins, Suite 1200, 75219-4217
Telephone: 214-559-7200
Fax: 214-559-7209
Email: mikkiwes@aol.com *URL:* http://www.lawyers.com/vassallolaw

Edward DiMare Vassallo, Jr.

Charles A. Salazar
Christene Jones
Scott T. Doggett

For full biographical listings, see the Martindale-Hubbell Law Directory

*DENTON,** Denton Co.

PHILIPS, HOPKINS, EAMES & COBB, P.C. (AV)

525 North Locust, P.O. Box 2027, 76202-2027
Telephone: 940-566-7010; Metro 940-243-0946
Facsimile: 940-898-0502
Email: dentonlaw.com

Brian T. Cartwright
Gerald W. Cobb

Representative Clients: First Federal Bank of North Texas; First State Bank of Texas, Denton, Texas; Sanger Bank, Sanger, Texas; BankOne, Texas, N.A.; Provident Bank, Denton, Texas; Dentex Title Co., Denton, Texas.

For full biographical listings, see the Martindale-Hubbell Law Directory

ROBISON & ROBISON (AV)

120 North Austin, 76201
Telephone: 940-380-0911
Fax: 940-381-5024
Email: robison@iglobal.net *URL:* http://www.wld.com/firm/robison-robison/denton

Douglas M. Robison
Bonnie Jean Robison

For full biographical listings, see the Martindale-Hubbell Law Directory

SPRINGER, LYLE & WATT L.L.P. (AV)

Limited Liability Partnership
1807 Westminster, 76205
Telephone: 940-387-0404
Fax: 940-383-7656
URL: http://www.springer-lyle.com

J. Jeffrey Springer
Frank G. Lyle
Howard E. Watt

For full biographical listings, see the Martindale-Hubbell Law Directory

WOOD, THACKER & WEATHERLY, P.C. (AV)

513 West Oak Street, 76201
Telephone: 817-565-6565
Fax: 817-566-6673

R. William Wood
C. Jane Thacker
Grace A. Weatherly

For full biographical listings, see the Martindale-Hubbell Law Directory

*EDINBURG,** Hidalgo Co.

HOCKEMA, TIPPIT & ESCOBEDO, L.L.P. (AV)
Building 101, 1 Paseo del Prado, 78539-9672
Telephone: 956-631-9112; 800-966-9112
Fax: 956-630-9472
Mailing Address: P.O. Box 720540, McAllen, Texas, 78504-0540
Email: htelaw@ibm.net

David H. Hockema
John L. Tippit, III
Jose Escobedo, Jr.

ASSOCIATE

Michael L. Young

For full biographical listings, see the Martindale-Hubbell Law Directory

*EL PASO,** El Paso Co.

CHARLES A. DEASON, JR. (AV)
1141 East Rio Grande, 79902-1371
Telephone: 915-544-1371
Fax: 915-544-2013
Email: charliedeason@prodigy.net

For full biographical listings, see the Martindale-Hubbell Law Directory

DUDLEY, DUDLEY & WINDLE (AV)
310 North Mesa, Suite 823, 79901
Telephone: 915-544-3090
Fax: 915-542-2651

MEMBER OF FIRM

Wayne Windle

OF COUNSEL

William C. (Pat) Dudley
Paul W. Dudley

ASSOCIATES

Troy C. Brown
Bobbie Marie Guerra

Representative Clients: A.I.G. Group; The Charter Group; Chubb Group of Insurance Companies; CNA Insurance Co.; Crawford & Co.

For full biographical listings, see the Martindale-Hubbell Law Directory

HICKS & LUCKY, A PROFESSIONAL CORPORATION (AV)
5812 Cromo Drive, 79912-5502
Telephone: 915-834-8400
Fax: 915-587-8401
Toll Free: 888-738-8401
Email: info@hicksandlucky.com *URL:* http://www.hicksandlucky.com

Larry W. Hicks
Jeffrey T. Lucky
Hadley A. Huchton

John Scott Mann
Jennifer F. Callan
Cynthia C. Llamas
Melissa A. Dorman
Laura Montalvo

For full biographical listings, see the Martindale-Hubbell Law Directory

*FORT WORTH,** Tarrant Co.

CANTEY & HANGER (AV)
A Registered Limited Liability Partnership
2100 Burnett Plaza, 801 Cherry Street, 76102-6899
Telephone: 817-877-2800, Metro Line: 429-3815
Telex: 758631 FAX: 877-2807
Dallas
Email: cantey@onramp.net
Dallas, Texas Office: 3330 Harwood Center, 1999 Bryan Street.
Telephone: 214-978-4100.
FAX: 214-978-4150. Email: chdallas@onramp.net
Austin, Texas Office: Cantey & Hanger Roan & Autrey L.L.P., 200 First State Bank Tower, 400 West Fifteenth Street.
Telephone: 512-474-4200.
FAX: 512-469-0470; 512-469-0474. Email: FIRM@ROAN-AUTREY.COM

MEMBERS OF FIRM

Mark D. Beatty
D. Mark Daniel
David Bradley Dowell
Thomas Patrick Gordon III
John F. Gray
Tolbert L. Greenwood
William L. Hughes, Jr.
Stephen A. Madsen
Bradley C. Poulos
John C. Stewart

ASSOCIATE

Andrew D. Keetch

Represent: CNA; Houston General Insurance; Winn Dixie Stores; Insurance Company of the West; Ohio Casualty Group; Inspire Insurance Solutions.

For Complete List of Firm Personnel, See General Section

For full biographical listings, see the Martindale-Hubbell Law Directory

HANDY & ROBINSON, P.C. (AV)
3650 City Center, Tower II, 301 Commerce Street, 76102-4118
Telephone: 817-336-4700
Fax: 817-332-5505
Email: firm@mikehandy.com *URL:* http://www.mikehandy.com

Michael Handy
David B. Robinson

Cynthia A. Cook
Christian Ellis

For full biographical listings, see the Martindale-Hubbell Law Directory

THE HASLAM FIRM (AV)
555 South Summit Avenue, 76104-2004
Telephone: 817-332-3115
Fax: 817-332-3148
Email: rhaslam@flash.net

Robert E. Haslam

For full biographical listings, see the Martindale-Hubbell Law Directory

JOSE, HENRY, BRANTLEY & KELTNER, L.L.P. (AV)
675 North Henderson Street, 76107-8495
Telephone: 817-877-3303
Fax: 817-338-9109

John S. Jose
Rickey J. Brantley
Michael J. Henry
David E. Keltner

Karen S. Precella
Anna L. Kingsley
Scotty MacLean
Sara K. Turman-Vedral

For full biographical listings, see the Martindale-Hubbell Law Directory

McMULLEN LAW FIRM (AV)
6300 Ridglea Place Suite 509, 76116-5731
Telephone: 817-731-4163
Fax: 817-731-4340
Email: wademcmullen@msn.com

Wade H. McMullen

For full biographical listings, see the Martindale-Hubbell Law Directory

LAW OFFICES OF PATRICK H. O'NEILL (AV)
110 West 7th Street, Suite 1100, 76102
Telephone: 817-878-3333
Fax: 817-878-3672

Patrick H. O'Neill

James L. Jackson, Jr.
Glenn T. Lupo

For full biographical listings, see the Martindale-Hubbell Law Directory

RUSSELL, TURNER, LAIRD & JONES, L.L.P. (AV)
One Colonial Place, 2400 Scott Avenue, 76103-2200
Telephone: 817-531-3000; 1-800-448-2889
Fax: 817-535-3046
Irving, Texas Office: Williams Square, Central Tower, Suite 700, 5215 North O'Connor Boulevard, Las Colinas Urban Center.
Telephone: 972-444-0444; 1-800-448-2889.

Wm. Greg Russell
Steven C. Laird
Randall E. Turner
Gregory G. Jones

For full biographical listings, see the Martindale-Hubbell Law Directory

THE WAGNER LAW FIRM (AV)
2702 Bank One Tower, 500 Throckmorton, 76102
Telephone: 817-882-9422
Fax: 817-338-0830
Email: jpwagner@concentric.net *URL:* http://www.lawyers.com/wagnerlawfirm

James P. Wagner

For full biographical listings, see the Martindale-Hubbell Law Directory

WELLS, PURCELL & KRAATZ (AV)
500 Main Street, Suite 1200, 76102
Telephone: 817-335-5525
Fax: 817-335-6208
Email: wpk@flash.net *URL:* http://www.4law.com

Davis Purcell
Ken Kraatz

OF COUNSEL

H. G. Wells

(See Next Column)

WELLS, PURCELL & KRAATZ—*Continued*

LEGAL SUPPORT PERSONNEL

Jack Dineen (Licensed Adjuster)

For full biographical listings, see the Martindale-Hubbell Law Directory

*HALLETTSVILLE,** Lavaca Co.

SCHWARTZ & SCHWARTZ (AV)

North LaGrange Street, P.O. Box 385, 77964
Telephone: 361-798-3668
Fax: 361-798-3660

MEMBERS OF FIRM

Armond G. Schwartz
Marcus F. Schwartz

For full biographical listings, see the Martindale-Hubbell Law Directory

*HENDERSON,** Rusk Co.

WELLBORN, HOUSTON, ADKISON, MANN, SADLER & HILL, L.L.P. (AV)

300 West Main Street, P.O. Box 1109, 75653-1109
Telephone: 903-657-8544; 903-657-7227
Fax: 903-657-6108
Email: FD@whamsh.com *URL:* http://www.whamsh.com

MEMBERS OF FIRM

Rex Houston
Ron Adkison
J. Mark Mann
Paul L. Sadler
David Hill
J. Mitchell Beard
James Andrew Holmes

For full biographical listings, see the Martindale-Hubbell Law Directory

*HOUSTON,** Harris Co.

BAKER BOTTS L.L.P. (AV)

One Shell Plaza, 910 Louisiana, 77002
Telephone: 713-229-1234
Cable Address: "Boterlove"
Fax: 713-229-1522
Email: postmaster@bakerbotts.com *URL:* http://www.bakerbotts.com
Washington, D.C. Office: The Warner, 1299 Pennsylvania Avenue, N.W.
Telephone: 202-639-7700.
New York, New York Office: 599 Lexington Avenue.
Telephone: 212-705-5000.
Austin, Texas Office: 1600 San Jacinto Center, 98 San Jacinto Boulevard.
Telephone: 512-322-2500.
Dallas, Texas Office: 2001 Ross Avenue.
Telephone: 214-953-6500.
Moscow, Russia Office: 10 ul. Bolshaya Dimitrovka (formerly Pushkinskaya), 103031.
Telephone: 7095/921-5300 (Local); 7095/929-7070 (International).
London, England Office: 45 Ludgate Hill.
Telephone: 0171-778-1400 (Local); 011-44-171-778-1400 (International).
Baku, Azerbaijan Office: 6-10 Vagif Mustafa-zadeh Street, Third Floor, Icheri Sheher, 370004.
Telephone: 994-12-97-63-88 (Local); 011-994-12-97-63-88 (International).
Fax: 994-12-97-63-91 (Local); 011-994-12-97-63-91 (International)

MEMBERS OF FIRM

Maria Wyckoff Boyce
Charles Tynan Buthod
F. Walter Conrad, Jr.
Michael S. Goldberg
Richard L. Josephson
William Karl Kroger
Ronald C. Lewis
Karen Kay Maston
David R. Poage
Travis James Sales
George T. Shipley
Stephen Gillham Tipps
Allister M. Waldrop, Jr.

ASSOCIATES

John Anaipakos
Kay M. Peterson

For Complete List of Firm Personnel, See General Section

For full biographical listings, see the Martindale-Hubbell Law Directory

BERG & ANDROPHY (AV)

3704 Travis, 77002-9550
Telephone: 713-529-5622
Fax: 713-529-3785
URL: http://www.lawyers.com/b&alaw
Email: mail@bahou.com *URL:* http://www.bafirm.com
New York, New York Office: 230 Park Avenue, Suite 1000, 10169-1099.
Telephone: 212-808-6580.
Fax: 212-808-3020.

David H. Berg (P.C.)
Joel M. Androphy
Cynthia R. Levin Moulton

Wade T. Howard
Geoffrey A. Berg
Gabriel A. Berg (Not admitted in TX)

For full biographical listings, see the Martindale-Hubbell Law Directory

BURROW & PARROTT, L.L.P. (AV)

A Registered Limited Liability Partnership
3500 Chevron Tower, 1301 McKinney, 77010-3092
Telephone: 713-222-6333
Fax: 713-650-6333
Email: bpfirm@bpcd.com *URL:* http://www.lawyers.com/burrowlaw

David H. Burrow
Alice Oliver-Parrott

Philip Brashier
Randall R. Smidt

OF COUNSEL

Robert H. Walker

For full biographical listings, see the Martindale-Hubbell Law Directory

CRAWFORD & MCKINNEY (AV)

550 Westcott, Suite 590, 77007-5096
Telephone: 713-869-1500
Fax: 713-880-4638
URL: http://www.piattorney.com

R. L. Pete McKinney
Patrice McKinney

OF COUNSEL

Stanley W. Crawford

For full biographical listings, see the Martindale-Hubbell Law Directory

DAVIS, ORETSKY & GUILFOYLE, P.C. (AV)

1415 Louisiana, Suite 4200, 77002
Telephone: 713-659-1010
Facsimile: 713-659-1122
Email: doglawfirm@dog.pc *URL:* http://www.dogpc.com
Affiliated Law Firm: Wommack Law Firm, P.C., 7 West Way Court, Suite A, P.O. Box 420, Lake Jackson, Texas 77566.
Telephone: 409-297-9755. Houston
Telephone: 713-355-5737.
Fax: 409-297-9761. Email: wdm-george@computron.net.

Tom M. Davis, Jr.
Andrew S. Oretsky
Matthew C. Guilfoyle
Juliann H. Panagos
Curt M. Langley
George T. Wommack, Jr.
David C. Redford

M. Lucille Anderson
Kristin Bauer
Robert M. Browning
Paige Black Larrabee
Norman W. Peters, Jr.
Jonathan L. Phillips
William R. Pilat

For full biographical listings, see the Martindale-Hubbell Law Directory

FISHER, BOYD, BROWN, BOUDREAUX & HUGUENARD, L.L.P. (AV)

70th Floor Wells Fargo Plaza, 1000 Louisiana, 77002
Telephone: 713-400-4000
Telefax: 713-400-4050

Wayne Fisher
Larry P. Boyd
Thomas K. Brown
Olan J. Boudreaux
James A. Huguenard

Bernard G. Johnson, III
Kay K. (Daniel) Morgan

For full biographical listings, see the Martindale-Hubbell Law Directory

FLEMING & ASSOCIATES, L.L.P. (AV)

1330 Post Oak Boulevard, Suite 3030, 77056
Telephone: 713-621-7944
Fax: 713-621-9638
URL: http://www.fleming-law.com

George M. Fleming
Robert R. Herring, Jr.
Sylvia Davidow
Bruce B. Kemp
Jim Doyle
Russell T. Abney
D'Lisa R. Simmons
Katrina Von Hedemann
Rand P. Nolen
Christopher A. Kesler
Andres C. Pereira
G. Sean Jez
Anthony E. Farah

For full biographical listings, see the Martindale-Hubbell Law Directory

FRANKLIN, CARDWELL & JONES (AV)

Chase Tower, 24th Floor, 600 Travis Street, 77002-2910
Telephone: 713-222-6025
Fax: 713-222-0938
Email: attorneys@fcj.com *URL:* http://www.fcj.com

(See Next Column)

FRANKLIN, CARDWELL & JONES, *Houston—Continued*

Ronald G. Franklin
Scott G. Burdine
Gregory N. Jones
Jeffrey D. Meyer
Joseph A. Fischer, III

For full biographical listings, see the Martindale-Hubbell Law Directory

GALLAGHER, YOUNG, LEWIS, HAMPTON & DOWNEY, L.L.P. (AV)

NationsBank Building, 700 Louisiana, 40th Floor, 77002
Telephone: 713-222-8080
Fax: 713-222-0066

Michael T. Gallagher
Craig Lewis
William H. Young
Hartley Hampton
Daniel M. Downey

Martin John de la Torre
Scott H. Mclemore
Andrew Sher
John J. Klevenhagen, III
Candace Kaiser Eindorf
Araceli E. Flores

OF COUNSEL

Rosemary Conlon McCarthy

For full biographical listings, see the Martindale-Hubbell Law Directory

GILPIN, PAXSON & BERSCH (AV)

A Registered Limited Liability Partnership
Attorney at Law
1900 West Loop South, Suite 2000, 77027-3259
Telephone: 713-623-8800
Telecopier: 713-993-8451
Email: gpb@gpblaw.com *URL:* http://www.texinslaw.com

PARTNERS

Gary M. Alletag
Darryl W. Malone
Timothy R. Bersch
Michael J. Pappert
John D. Gilpin
Stephen Paxson
Kevin F. Risley

OF COUNSEL

Harless R. Benthul
David F. Webb

ASSOCIATES

Joseph D. Batson
Jeri Pharis Wechsler

Representative Clients: BMW of North America, Inc.; Federal Deposit Insurance Corporation; Greater Houston Builders Association; Owens Corning Fiberglas Corporation; Shaw Industries, Inc.; Southwest Guaranty Trust Company, N.A.; Sprint Communications Company L.P.; Volkswagen of America, Inc.; Volvo North America Corporation; Wells Fargo Bank (Texas), N.A.

For full biographical listings, see the Martindale-Hubbell Law Directory

GLOVER, ANDERSON, LEWIS & PREBEG P.C., PROFESSIONAL CORPORATION (AV)

5599 San Felipe, Suite 1600, 77056
Telephone: 713-621-3306
Facsimile: 713-621-2259

Arthur M. Glover, Jr.
James B. Lewis
Paul E. Anderson, Jr.
Matthew J.M. Prebeg

Scott J. Davenport

For full biographical listings, see the Martindale-Hubbell Law Directory

GROSSMAN & WALDMAN, L.L.P. (AV)

Wedge International Tower, 1415 Louisiana, Suite 3555, 77002
Telephone: 713-655-9999; 1-800-655-9939
Facsimile: 713-752-0311
Email: lawyers@grossmanandwaldman.com *URL:* http://www.grossmanandwaldman.com
Beaumont, Texas Office: Kyle Building, 281 Orleans at Liberty.
Telephone: 409-833-9121.

Joel M. Grossman
Steve Waldman
Robert Grossman
Jonathan C. Juhan

For full biographical listings, see the Martindale-Hubbell Law Directory

G.P. HARDY III, P.C. (AV)

500 Two Houston Center, 909 Fannin at McKinney, 77010
Telephone: 713-222-0381
Fax: 713-759-9650
Bay City, Texas Office: 2042 Avenue F.
Telephone: 409-245-3797.
Fax: 409-245-4713.

G. P. Hardy, Jr. (1913-1988)
G. P. Hardy, III
Gail Johns

(See Next Column)

Timothy M. Purcell
Mark G. Cypert
Patricia Haylon

References: Southwest Bank of Texas; International Bank of Commerce.

For full biographical listings, see the Martindale-Hubbell Law Directory

HAYS, MCCONN, RICE & PICKERING (AV)

400 Two Allen Center, 1200 Smith Street, 77002
Telephone: 713-654-1111
Fax: 713-650-0027
Email: HMRP@HaysMcConn.com *URL:* http://www.haysmcconn.com

MEMBERS OF FIRM

Michael S. Hays
Margaret Twomey Brenner
James J. McConn, Jr.
W. Michael Scott
B. Stephen Rice
Jeffery Allen Addicks
Michael R. Pickering
J. Philip Griffis
Mark A. Padon
A. Scott Kidd
Bruce Gaible
Robert E. Purgatorio
Susan Crowley Stevenson
Brian Tew
Allen Till
Steven M. Duble
Craig S. Wolcott
Lance K. Thomas
Naomi S. Ostfeld
Michael W. Magee

ASSOCIATES

Troy A. Williams
William Jason Walker
Shannon D. Robbie
Michael A. Durr
Staton M. Childers
Leslie M. Henry
Timothy R. Hightower
Amanda F. Bell
David Wilson, II

OF COUNSEL

John T. Golden

For full biographical listings, see the Martindale-Hubbell Law Directory

HILL & PARKER, A PROFESSIONAL CORPORATION (AV)

5300 Memorial, Suite 700, 77007-8292
Telephone: 713-868-5581
Telefax: 713-868-1275
Email: hillparker@compuserve.com *URL:* http://www.hillparker.com

John Graham Hill
Brian Q. Carmichael
Charles R. Parker
John Roberson
Hector A. Canales

Reference: Chase Texas Bank, N.A.

For full biographical listings, see the Martindale-Hubbell Law Directory

IRESON & WEIZEL, P.C. (AV)

Chase Bank Building, 711 Travis, Suite 3000, 77002
Telephone: 713-216-1160
Fax: 713-216-1161
Email: law@iresonweizel.com

Lansford O. Ireson, Jr.
Ira D. Weizel

Charlotte J. Fischer
Margot M. Ireson
Frederick J. Wagner
Lionel J. Castro
Gina L. Miller

For full biographical listings, see the Martindale-Hubbell Law Directory

JACKSON WALKER L.L.P. (AV)

1100 Louisiana, Suite 4200, P.O. Box 4771, 77002
Telephone: 713-752-4200
Fax: 713-752-4221
URL: http://www.jw.com
Austin, Texas Office: 100 Congress Avenue, Suite 1100.
Telephone: 512-236-2000.
Fax: 512-236-2002.
Dallas, Texas Office: 901 Main Street, Suite 6000.
Telephone: 214-953-6000.
Fax: 214-953-5822.
Fort Worth, Texas Office: 301 Commerce Street, Suite 2400.
Telephone: 817-334-7200.
Fax: 817-334-7290.
Richardson, Texas Office: 2435 North Central Expressway, Suite 600.
Telephone: 972-671-2560.
Fax: 972-671-2566.
San Angelo, Texas Office: 225 West Beauregard Avenue.
Telephone: 915-481-2550.
Fax: 915-481-2552.
San Antonio, Texas Office: 112 E. Pecan Street, Suite 2100.
Telephone: 210-978-7700.
Fax: 210-978-7790.

MEMBERS OF FIRM

W. Todd Barnett
Richard Earl Griffin
Janet Douvas Chafin
Nancy Wells Hamilton
John R. Clayton
Mollie Cohn Lambert
Linda J. Cole
Lisa A. Powell
Anne Marie Finch
Fred A. Simpson

(See Next Column)

JACKSON WALKER L.L.P.—*Continued*

OF COUNSEL

Laurie B. Easter
Mary Lou Flynn-DuPart
Randall L. Smith

For Complete List of Firm Personnel, See General Section

For full biographical listings, see the Martindale-Hubbell Law Directory

JOHNSON, FERGUSON & PIPKIN (AV)

4900 Woodway, Suite 1100, 77056
Telephone: 713-961-3730
Facsimile: 713-961-5438
Email: Johnsoned@johnsonassoc.com

Ned W. Johnson
Richard Y. Ferguson
John E. Pipkin
Clinton E. Phillips
William C. Nantz
Elizabeth Barnes Phillips
Catherine A. Dickerson

OF COUNSEL

James E. Brown, Jr.
Annelie Menke

For full biographical listings, see the Martindale-Hubbell Law Directory

THE KRIST LAW FIRM, P.C. (AV)

17555 El Camino Real (Clear Lake City), 77058
Telephone: 281-283-8500
Fax: 281-488-3489
URL: http://www.lawyers.com/kristlaw

Ronald D. Krist
Kevin D. Krist
Scott C. Krist
Perry O. Barber Jr. (1938-1992)

Reference: Horizon Capital Bank, Webster, Texas.

For full biographical listings, see the Martindale-Hubbell Law Directory

LANIER, PARKER & SULLIVAN, P.C. (AV)

Four Houston Center, Suite 1550 1331 Lamar Street, 77010
Telephone: 713-659-5200
FAX: 713-659-2204

W. Mark Lanier
Kevin P. Parker
Kent C. Sullivan

Becky J. Lanier
Leslie M. Stewart
Robert E. Leone
Edward W. Fudge
Patrick N. Haines
Dara Grisbee Hegar
Eugene R. Egdorf

For full biographical listings, see the Martindale-Hubbell Law Directory

MARKLE, RAMOS & ZITO, A PROFESSIONAL CORPORATION (AV)

777 Post Oak Boulevard, Suite 350, 77056
Telephone: 713-861-9595
Facsimile: 713-861-8368
Email: mrz@marzpc.com

Spencer G. Markle
Dion Ramos
Nicholas E. Zito

Nathan A. Hardee
Shelley V. Hutson
Andrea Frey Lopes
Heather L. Nistler
Angela Nolan

For full biographical listings, see the Martindale-Hubbell Law Directory

MEHAFFY & WEBER, A PROFESSIONAL CORPORATION (AV)

One Allen Center, 500 Dallas, Suite 1200, 77002
Telephone: 713-655-1200
Fax: 713-655-0222
Email: MehaffyWeber.com
Beaumont, Texas Office: 2615 Calder Avenue, Suite 800, P.O. Box 16.
Telephone: 409-835-5011.
Orange, Texas Office: 1006 Green Avenue, P.O. Drawer 189.
Telephone: 409-886-7766.

Jim I. Graves
Arthur R. Almquist
Charles Stanton Perry

Paul R. Heyburn
James G. Martingano
Debra N. Bigler
Peter T. Gregg
Elna Nguyen Griggs

Representative Clients: E.I. duPont de Nemours and Co.; W.R. Grace & Co.-Conn.; Merrill Dow; Eli Lilly & Company; Burlington, Northen, Santa Fe Railway Company; Christus Health.

For full biographical listings, see the Martindale-Hubbell Law Directory

THE PERDUE LAW FIRM, L.L.P. (AV)

2727 Allen Parkway, Suite 800, 77019
Telephone: 713-520-2500
Fax: 713-520-2525
Email: firm@perduelaw.com *URL:* http://www.perduelaw.com

MEMBERS OF FIRM

Jim M. Perdue
Jim M. Perdue, Jr.

ASSOCIATES

Tracy Kesler
Christopher L. Thetford
Parker Bond Binion

For full biographical listings, see the Martindale-Hubbell Law Directory

RAMSEY & MURRAY, A PROFESSIONAL CORPORATION (AV)

10000 Memorial Drive, Suite 700, 77024-3412
Telephone: 713-613-5400
Fax: 713-613-5414

Ben Ramsey
John A. Murray, Jr.
Russell J. Ramsey
Mark Ramsey
Curtis D. Collette
Michael Stout Wright
Rick McRory

Joseph W. Gagnon
R. Russell Hollenbeck
Adrian V. Villacorta
Brenda Renee Ferguson

Representative Clients: Great Central Insurance Co.; Republic Insurance Co.

For full biographical listings, see the Martindale-Hubbell Law Directory

RIDDLE & BAUMGARTNER (AV)

A Registered Limited Liability Partnership
6810 FM 1960 West, Suite 200, 77069
Telephone: 281-893-4567
FAX: 281-893-1827

Don R. Riddle
Gregory S. Baumgartner
Todd A. Riddle

For full biographical listings, see the Martindale-Hubbell Law Directory

RILEY & HARRIS, L.L.P. (AV)

One Houston Center, 1221 McKinney, Suite 3000, 77010-2023
Telephone: 713-646-1000
Fax: 713-646-1036
Email: txlaw@riley-harris.com *URL:* http://www.riley-harris.com
Brownsville, Texas Office: 845 E. Harrison, Suite A, 78520-7120.
Telephone: 956-550-8825.
Fax: 956-550-8854.

MEMBERS OF FIRM

Timothy D. Riley
Britton B. Harris
Patrick W. O'Briant

Brett J. Sileo
Matthew T. Heffner
Jill Ellen Ferguson

For full biographical listings, see the Martindale-Hubbell Law Directory

STEINBURG, CARWILE, HERZIK & PRIETO (AV)

1001 Fannin, Suite 200, 77002-6708
Telephone: 713-654-7800
Fax: 713-652-0110
Email: MuciaP@aol.com

MEMBERS OF FIRM

Rodney V. Steinburg
John A. Carwile
Michael L. Herzik
M. Lucia Prieto

For full biographical listings, see the Martindale-Hubbell Law Directory

TEKELL, BOOK, MATTHEWS & LIMMER, L.L.P. (AV)

4300 One Houston Center, 1221 McKinney, 77010
Telephone: 713-222-9542
Fax: 713-655-7727
Email: tbml@tbml.com
Corpus Christi, Texas Office: 711 North Carancahua, Suite 902, 78475.
Telephone: 361-883-6100.
Fax: 361-883-6103. Email: cctbml@swbell.net.

Kenneth Tekell
William Book
Raymond T. Matthews
James H. Limmer
Mark K. Allen
Michael P. Morris
Todd A. Kissner
Matt W. Childs
Jeff Murphrey

Michele E. Taylor
David W. Burns
Kevin D. Didway
Kathleen Carney
WC "Trey" Book
Kenneth L. Tekell, Jr.
J. Gregory McEldowney
Robin T. Balette

(See Next Column)

UTAH

CEDAR CITY, Iron Co.

HIGBEE, JENSEN & MACFARLANE, P.C. (AV)

250 South Main Street, P.O. Box 726, 84720
Telephone: 435-586-4404
Fax: 435-586-1002
Email: mtgraff@go.com *URL:* http://www.southernutahlaw.com

Thomas M. Higbee
James W. Jensen
R. Todd MacFarlane

Justin W. Wayment
Matthew T. Graff

Representative Clients: Carter Enterprises, Inc.; Cedar Land Title, Inc.; First Security Bank of Utah, N.A.; Iron County School District; New Castle Water Co.; Quality Ready Mix Concrete, Inc.; Security Title Co.; State Bank of Southern Utah; Southern Utah Title Company of Cedar City, Inc.; Elk Meadows Resort.

For full biographical listings, see the Martindale-Hubbell Law Directory

*SALT LAKE CITY,** Salt Lake Co.

JOEL M. ALLRED, P.C. (AV)

Suite 800, McIntyre Building, 68 South Main Street, 84101
Telephone: 801-531-8300 (Downtown Office)
801-582-2309 (Home Office)
Fax: 801-533-2463 (Office Hours)
801-363-2420 (After Office Hours)
Email: jallred@vii.com

Joel M. Allred

Amy Allred Dolce

For full biographical listings, see the Martindale-Hubbell Law Directory

BURBIDGE AND MITCHELL (AV)

Suite 2001, 139 East South Temple, 84111
Telephone: 801-355-6677
Fax: 801-355-2341
Email: Burbidge@xmission.com

Richard D. Burbidge
Stephen B. Mitchell

ASSOCIATES

Jefferson W. Gross
Jason D. Boren

For full biographical listings, see the Martindale-Hubbell Law Directory

CALLISTER NEBEKER & MCCULLOUGH, A PROFESSIONAL CORPORATION (AV)

Gateway Tower East, Suite 900, 10 East South Temple, 84133
Telephone: 801-530-7300
Telecopier: 801-364-9127
Email: mjeaston@cnmlaw.com *URL:* http://www.cnmlaw.com

Gary R. Howe
P. Bryan Fishburn

Representative Client: Workers Compensation Fund of Utah.

For Complete List of Firm Personnel, See General Section

For full biographical listings, see the Martindale-Hubbell Law Directory

DART ADAMSON DONOVAN & HANSON (AV)

A Partnership of Professional Corporations
370 E. South Temple, Suite 400, 84111
Telephone: 801-521-6383
Telefax: 801-355-2513

Craig G. Adamson (P.C.)

ASSOCIATES

Eric P. Lee (P.C.)
Cameron S. Denning

A list of References will be furnished upon request.

For full biographical listings, see the Martindale-Hubbell Law Directory

KIPP AND CHRISTIAN, P.C. (AV)

10 Exchange Place, Fourth Floor, 84111
Telephone: 801-521-3773
Fax: 801-359-9004
Email: kc1gsb@inquo.net

Carman E. Kipp
J. Anthony Eyre
Gregory J. Sanders
Heinz J. Mahler
Michael F. Skolnick
Shawn McGarry
Kirk G. Gibbs

(See Next Column)

OF COUNSEL

D. Gary Christian

Representative Clients: CNA Insurance Co; Coregis; Utah State Bar; Reliance Insurance Co.; National Farmers Union Insurance Co.; Utah Medical Insurance Association (UMIA); Utah Paper Box; Skivations, Condominium & Land Developers; Montgomery Elevators; Tim Dahle Imports/Nissan.

For Complete List of Firm Personnel, See General Section

For full biographical listings, see the Martindale-Hubbell Law Directory

KIRTON & MCCONKIE, A PROFESSIONAL CORPORATION (AV)

1800 Eagle Gate Tower, 60 East South Temple, 84111
Telephone: 801-328-3600
Telecopier: 801-321-4893

Randy T. Austin
Lorin C. Barker
Anthony I. Bentley, Jr.
Rolf H. Berger
Berne S. Broadbent
Charles W. Dahlquist, II
Jerry W. Dearinger
Robert W. Edwards
James E. Ellsworth
Fred D. Essig
Wallace O. Felsted
Clark B. Fetzer
R. Bruce Findlay
David J. Hardy
Keith L. Hargrove
Read R. Hellewell
Dale E. Hulse
Lee Ford Hunter
Richard G. Johnson, Jr.
Von G. Keetch
Raeburn G. Kennard
Wilford W. Kirton, Jr.
Michael F. Krieger
Paul H. Matthews
Daniel S. McConkie
David M. McConkie
Oscar W. McConkie, III
Oscar W. McConkie, Jr.
Samuel D. McVey
William A. Meaders, Jr.
Thomas L. Monson
Denis Roy Morrill
Merrill F. Nelson
Richard R. Neslen
Eric C. Olson
R. Willis Orton
B. Lloyd Poelman
Robert S. Prince
Gregory M. Simonsen
Robert T. Smith (Not admitted in UT)
Myron L. Sorensen
Jon E. Waddoups
David M. Wahlquist
Thomas D. Walk
Stuart F. Weed
David A. Westerby
Todd E. Zenger

Randall C. Allen
Bryan H. Booth
Michael M. Conger
David S. Doty
Alexander Dushku
Scott C. Krieger
Melinda R. Porter
Matthew K. Richards
Dorany Rodriguez-Baltazar (Not admitted in UT)
Jeffrey Dean Stevens
Amy S. Thomas
Steven L. Whitehead

For full biographical listings, see the Martindale-Hubbell Law Directory

MORGAN, MEYER & RICE, L.C. (AV)

Kearns Building, Eighth Floor, 136 South Main Street, 84101
Telephone: 801-531-7888
Telefax: 801-531-9732
Email: morgan@inquo.net

MEMBERS OF FIRM

Stephen G. Morgan
Cynthia K.C. Meyer
Mitchel T. Rice
Joseph E. Minnock
Jeffrey C. Miner

Representative Clients: Albertson's Inc.; Smith Food and Drug Centers, Inc.; Colorado Casualty; Farmers Insurance Group; SCL Airport Authority; St. Paul Fire and Marine Insurance Co.; State Farm Fire and Casualty; State Farm Mutual Automobile Insurance Co.; Utah Farm Bureau Insurance Co.; Utah Local Government's Insurance Trust.

For full biographical listings, see the Martindale-Hubbell Law Directory

VAN COTT, BAGLEY, CORNWALL & MCCARTHY, A PROFESSIONAL CORPORATION (AV)

50 South Main Street, Suite 1600, P.O. Box 45340, 84145-0340
Telephone: 801-532-3333
Telecopier: 801-534-0058
Email: info@vancott.com *URL:* http://www.vancott.com
Ogden, Utah Office: 2404 Washington Boulevard, Suite 900.
Telephone: 801-394-5783.
Park City, Utah Office: 2200 Park Avenue, Suite C200-A.
Telephone: 435-649-3889.

Jeremy M. Hoffman
Kenneth W. Yeates

For Complete List of Firm Personnel, See General Section

For full biographical listings, see the Martindale-Hubbell Law Directory

VERMONT

*BURLINGTON,** Chittenden Co.

BERGERON, PARADIS & FITZPATRICK, LLP (AV)

27 Main Street, P.O. Box 925, 05402
Telephone: 802-863-1191
FAX: 802-863-5798
Email: bpf@essex.bpflegal.com *URL:* http://www.BPFlegal.com
Essex Junction, Vermont Office: 34 Pearl Street, P.O. Box 174.
Telephone: 802-879-6304.
Fax: 802-879-6533.

John J. Bergeron
Vincent A. Paradis (Resident, Essex Junction, Vermont Office)
Edward D. Fitzpatrick (Resident, Essex Junction, Vermont Office)
Priscilla Bondy Dubé
Douglas G. Kallen
Daniel P. O'Rourke (Resident, Essex Junction, Vermont Office)

Michael D. Danley

OF COUNSEL

John W. O'Donnell

For full biographical listings, see the Martindale-Hubbell Law Directory

MANCHESTER LAW OFFICES, PROFESSIONAL CORPORATION (AV)

One Lawson Lane, P.O. Box 1459, 05402-1459
Telephone: 802-658-7444
Fax: 802-658-2078
Email: mlo@together.net *URL:* http://www.lawyers.com/manchesterlaw

Robert E. Manchester

Tina L. Shoup
George N. Collias

LEGAL SUPPORT PERSONNEL

Maureen P. Neacy (Legal Nurse Consultant)

For full biographical listings, see the Martindale-Hubbell Law Directory

O'NEILL CRAWFORD & GREEN, P.C. (AV)

159 Bank Street, P.O. Box 5359, 05402-5359
Telephone: 802-865-4700
Fax: 802-865-4778

Jerome F. O'Neill
Geoffrey W. Crawford
Michael I. Green

Samantha W. Foxen

For full biographical listings, see the Martindale-Hubbell Law Directory

SYLVESTER & MALEY, INC. (AV)

78 Pine Street, P.O. Box 1053, 05402-1053
Telephone: 802-864-5722
Fax: 802-658-6124
Email: sylvester-maley@worldnet.att.net

Alan F. Sylvester
John P. Maley
Michael S. Brow
Amy E. Sylvester

For full biographical listings, see the Martindale-Hubbell Law Directory

*RUTLAND,** Rutland Co.

MILLER FAIGNANT & BEHRENS, P.C. (AV)

36 Merchants Row, P.O. Box 6688, 05702-6688
Telephone: 802-775-2521
Fax: 802-775-8274
Email: lhblaw@aol.com *URL:*
http://www.lawyers.com/millerfaignantbehrenslaw

Lawrence Miller
John Paul Faignant
Lawrence H. Behrens

OF COUNSEL

Lisa L. Chalidze

LEGAL SUPPORT PERSONNEL

Marie Peck Fabian
Kim J. Miller

Representative Clients: Travelers Insurance Co.; Government Employees Insurance Co.; Utica Mutual Insurance Co.; Universal Underwriters Insurance Co.; Zurich American Acadia Insurance.
References: Travelers Insurance Co.; Universal Underwriters Insurance Co.

For full biographical listings, see the Martindale-Hubbell Law Directory

*ST. ALBANS,** Franklin Co.

JAMES L. LEVY, P.C. (AV)

79 North Main Street, 05478
Telephone: 802-524-2108
Fax: Number available upon request

James L. Levy

For full biographical listings, see the Martindale-Hubbell Law Directory

VIRGINIA

*ABINGDON,** Washington Co.

THE TATE LAW FIRM (AV)

Abingdon Professional Centre, 110 Abingdon Place, 24211
Telephone: 540-628-5185
Telecopier: 540-628-5045
Email: lynntate@naxs.com *URL:* http://www.tatelaw.com

Mary Lynn Tate

OF COUNSEL

Olen G. Haynes (Not admitted in VA)

LEGAL SUPPORT PERSONNEL

Rebecca A. Wyatt
Teresa L. Brown

For full biographical listings, see the Martindale-Hubbell Law Directory

*ACCOMAC,** Accomack Co.

JON C. POULSON (AV)

23349 Cross Street, P.O. Box 478, 23301-0478
Telephone: 757-787-2620
Facsimile: 757-787-2749

For full biographical listings, see the Martindale-Hubbell Law Directory

ALEXANDRIA, (Independent City)

ROSENBLUM & ROSENBLUM, L.L.C. (AV)

228 South Washington Street, Suite 300, P.O. Box 19110, 22320
Telephone: 703-548-9002
Fax: 703-548-8774
Email: rrlawllc@clark.net *URL:*
http://www.lawyers.com/rosenblum&rosenblum

Alan Rosenblum
David Rosenblum

For full biographical listings, see the Martindale-Hubbell Law Directory

*ARLINGTON,** Arlington Co.

WILLIAM E. ARTZ A PROFESSIONAL CORPORATION (AV)

1010 Rosslyn Metro Center, 1700 North Moore Street, 22209
Telephone: 703-243-3500
Facsimile: 703-524-8770
Email: wartzpc@erols.com *URL:* http://www.the-a-team.com

William E. Artz

Dominique D. Michel

For full biographical listings, see the Martindale-Hubbell Law Directory

BEAN, KINNEY & KORMAN, A PROFESSIONAL CORPORATION (AV)

2000 North 14th Street, Suite 100, 22201
Telephone: 703-525-4000
Facsimile: 703-525-2207
Email: bkk@beankinney.com

L. Lee Bean (1916-1989)
David B. Kinney (Emeritus)
James W. Korman
Jonathan C. Kinney
Frederick R. Taylor
Leo S. Fisher
James Bruce Davis
James R. Schroll
Carol Schrier-Polak
Joseph P. Corish
Jennifer A. Brust
David C. Canfield
C. Erik Gustafson

OF COUNSEL

John Morland

Marbeth M. Spreyer
Thomas W. Repczynski
Daryl S. Taylor
Christie L. Dowling
Timothy J. McEvoy
William E. Buchanan
Jennifer C. Bier
Leslie J. Long
Lisa J. Tomasseti

(See Next Column)

BEAN, KINNEY & KORMAN A PROFESSIONAL CORPORATION, *Arlington—Continued*

Counsel for: First Union National Banks of Virginia; Bank of America.

For full biographical listings, see the Martindale-Hubbell Law Directory

SCHWARTZ AND ELLIS, LTD. (AV)

6950 North Fairfax Drive, 22213
Telephone: 703-532-9300
Telex: 892320
Facsimile: 703-534-0329
Email: schwellis@aol.com *URL:* http://www.lawyers.com/schwartzandellis

John P. Ellis

John S. Petrillo

References: First Virginia Bank; Bank of America; First Union National Bank.

For full biographical listings, see the Martindale-Hubbell Law Directory

BLACKSBURG, Montgomery Co.

GILMER, SADLER, INGRAM, SUTHERLAND & HUTTON (AV)

201 West Roanoke Street, P.O. Box 908, 24063-0908
Telephone: 540-552-1061; 888-887-9997
Telecopier: 540-552-8227
Pulaski, Virginia Office: Midtown Professional Building, 65 East Main Street, P.O. Box 878.
Telephone: 540-980-1360; 540-639-0027; 800-330-3344.
Telecopier: 540-980-5264.

MEMBERS OF FIRM

James L. Hutton
Howard C. Gilmer, Jr. (1906-1975)
Roby K. Sutherland (1909-1975)
Philip M. Sadler (1915-1994)
Robert J. Ingram
Thomas J. McCarthy, Jr.
John J. Gill
Gary C. Hancock
Jackson M. Bruce
Michael J. Barbour
Deborah Wood Dobbins
Timothy Edmond Kirtner
Robin J. Kegley

Representative Clients: Appalachian Power Co.; Magnox, Inc.; Norfolk Southern Railway Co.; Pulaski Furniture Corp.; NationsBank; Charles Lunsford Sons & Associates; First National Bank; Corning Glass Works.

For full biographical listings, see the Martindale-Hubbell Law Directory

DANVILLE, (Independent City)

GARDNER, BARROW & SHARPE, A PROFESSIONAL CORPORATION (AV)

494 Piney Forest Road, 25441
Telephone: 804-799-1111
Fax: 804-799-1422
Martinsville, Virginia Office: First Citizens Bank Building, 4th Floor, Church and Clay Streets, 24112.
Telephone: 540-638-2455.
Fax: 540-638-2458.

Philip G. Gardner (Resident)

For full biographical listings, see the Martindale-Hubbell Law Directory

*FAIRFAX,** (Ind. City; Seat of Fairfax Co.)

PETER D. GREENSPUN & ASSOCIATES, P.C. (AV)

Building A-5, 10605 Judicial Drive, 22030-5167
Telephone: 703-352-0100
Fax: 703-591-7268
Email: G&A@Greenspunlaw.com

Peter D. Greenspun

Thomas Peter Mann
Cynthia Ann Bailey
Vladimir I. Arezina

Representative Client: Moore Cadillac Co.

For full biographical listings, see the Martindale-Hubbell Law Directory

WILLIAM O. P. SNEAD, III (AV)

Fairfax Commons, 3923 Old Lee Highway, Suite 62-B, 22030
Telephone: 703-359-8111
Fax: 703-359-0897

Mark A. Towery
Ann Lacroix Jones

For full biographical listings, see the Martindale-Hubbell Law Directory

*LEESBURG,** Loudoun Co.

SEVILA, SAUNDERS, HUDDLESTON & WHITE, A PROFESSIONAL CORPORATION (AV)

30 North King Street, 20176
Telephone: 703-777-5700
Metro: 471-9800; Fax: 703-771-4161

Robert E. Sevila
Richard R. Saunders, Jr.
Jon D. Huddleston
Craig E. White

Jeffrey A. Tuten
Jeanine M. Irving

LEGAL SUPPORT PERSONNEL

Joan Rust

For full biographical listings, see the Martindale-Hubbell Law Directory

*MARTINSVILLE,** (Ind. City; Seat of Henry Co.)

GARDNER, GARDNER, BARROW & SHARPE, A PROFESSIONAL CORPORATION (AV)

First Citizens Bank Building, 4th Floor, Church and Clay Streets, 24112
Telephone: 540-638-2455
Fax: 540-638-2458
Danville, Virginia Office: 494 Piney Forest Road, 24541.
Telephone: 804-799-1111.
Fax: 804-799-1422.

Benjamin R. Gardner
Philip G. Gardner (Resident, Danville Office)
Hoyett L. Barrow, Jr.
B. Patrick Sharpe
George Lyle

Representative Clients: Furnished upon request.

For full biographical listings, see the Martindale-Hubbell Law Directory

MCLEAN, Fairfax Co.

JOHNSON & ROCHE (AV)

8355 Greensboro Drive, Tysons Corner, 22102
Telephone: 703-821-3740
Fax: 703-790-9462

MEMBERS OF FIRM

Robert A. Johnson
Brien A. Roche

References: Nations Bank; First Virginia Bank; Signet Bank.

For full biographical listings, see the Martindale-Hubbell Law Directory

NORFOLK, (Independent City)

BREIT, DRESCHER & BREIT, P.C. (AV)

1000 Dominion Tower, 999 Waterside Drive, 23510
Telephone: 757-670-3888
Fax: 757-670-3895
Email: jbreit@livenet.net

John W. Drescher
Jeffrey A. Breit
George T. Albiston
Michael F. Imprevento
Latane' Ware Brown
John L. Watts

For full biographical listings, see the Martindale-Hubbell Law Directory

GOLDBLATT, LIPKIN & COHEN, P.C. (AV)

Suite 300, 415 St. Paul's Boulevard, P.O. Box 3505, 23514
Telephone: 757-627-6225
Telefax: 757-622-3698

Robert S. Cohen
Steven M. Legum
Mary G. Commander
Neal C. Schulwolf

For full biographical listings, see the Martindale-Hubbell Law Directory

HARLAN & FLORA, P.C. (AV)

Dominion Tower, 999 Waterside Drive, Suite 1200, 23510
Telephone: 757-625-8300
Fax: 757-625-3714
Email: lawyers@harlan-flora.com *URL:* http://www.harlan-flora.com

Thomas J. Harlan, Jr.
John M. Flora

For full biographical listings, see the Martindale-Hubbell Law Directory

PAYNE, GATES, FARTHING & RADD, P.C. (AV)

15th Floor, Dominion Tower, 999 Waterside Drive, Suite 1515, 23510-3309
Telephone: 757-640-1500
Facsimile: 757-627-6583
URL: http://www.paynegates.com

Ronald M. Gates
Philip R. Farthing
Anthony F. Radd
Todd J. Preti
Marshall A. Winslow, Jr.

(See Next Column)

PAYNE, GATES, FARTHING & RADD P.C.—*Continued*

Stephen E. Heretick | Raymond L. Hogge, Jr.

OF COUNSEL

Charles E. Payne

For full biographical listings, see the Martindale-Hubbell Law Directory

SACKS & SACKS, A PROFESSIONAL CORPORATION (AV)

Suite 501 Town Point Center, 150 Boush Street, 23510-1615
Telephone: 757-623-2753
FAX: 757-640-7170
Email: sacks@series2000.com *URL:* http://www.lawyers.com/sacks&sacks-com

Herman A. Sacks (1886-1983) | Stanley E. Sacks
Andrew M. Sacks

LEGAL SUPPORT PERSONNEL

James S. McMahan (Litigation Manager) | Thomas L. Gilchrist (Legal Assistant)
Virginia S. McCann (Paralegal) | Marshall T. Walker, Jr. (Investigator)
Maryjane Evans (Paralegal)

For full biographical listings, see the Martindale-Hubbell Law Directory

TAVSS, FLETCHER, MAIDEN & KING, P.C. (AV)

Fourteenth Floor, 555 Main Street, 23510
Telephone: 757-625-1214
Fax: 757-622-7295
Mailing Address: P.O. Box 3747, 23514
Email: tavss@pilot.infi.net

Richard J. Tavss | Besianne Tavss Maiden
John R. Fletcher | Michael B. Hamar
Ray W. King | Kevin J. O'Leary

LEGAL SUPPORT PERSONNEL

Maurice J. O'Connor | Retha Rish (Paralegal)

Reference: Bank of the Commonwealth.

For full biographical listings, see the Martindale-Hubbell Law Directory

*ORANGE,** Orange Co.

SHACKELFORD, HONENBERGER, THOMAS, WILLIS & GREGG, P.L.C. (AV)

149 West Main Street, P.O. Box 871, 22960
Telephone: 540-672-2711
Fax: 540-672-2714
Email: shtwg1@ns.gemlink.com
Culpeper, Virginia Office: 147 West Davis Street, P.O. Box 1002.
Telephone: 540-825-0305.

OF COUNSEL

Virginius R. Shackelford, Jr.

MEMBERS OF FIRM

Virginius R. Shackelford, III | Jere M. H. Willis, III (Resident, Culpeper, Virginia Office)
Christopher J. Honenberger | Sarah Collins Honenberger
Frank A. Thomas, III
Sean D. Gregg

For full biographical listings, see the Martindale-Hubbell Law Directory

PETERSBURG, (Independent City)

CUTHBERT LAW OFFICES, A PROFESSIONAL CORPORATION (AV)

220 North Sycamore Street, 23803
Telephone: 804-733-3100
Fax: 804-732-4658
Email: mail@cuthbertlaw.com

Charles H. Cuthbert, Jr.

Margaret Cuthbert Broaddus

For full biographical listings, see the Martindale-Hubbell Law Directory

PORTSMOUTH, (Independent City)

BANGEL, BANGEL & BANGEL, L.L.P. (AV)

505 Court Street, P.O. Box 760, 23705-0760
Telephone: 757-397-3471
Telecopier: 757-393-3736

MEMBERS OF FIRM

A. A. Bangel (1893-1978) | Michael J. Blachman
Stanley J. Bangel (1925-1992) | John W. Eppler
Herbert K. Bangel | J. Darrell Foster
Keith H. Bangel | Edward H. McNew, Jr.
Burle U. Stromberg

(See Next Column)

ASSOCIATE

Lawrence W. I'Anson, III

For full biographical listings, see the Martindale-Hubbell Law Directory

KASS LAW FIRM (AV)

364 Crawford Street, P.O. Box 938, 23705
Telephone: 757-397-7777
Fax: 757-397-3607
Email: KASSLAW777@AOL.COM

William E. Kass

LEGAL SUPPORT PERSONNEL

Beverly L. Turner

For full biographical listings, see the Martindale-Hubbell Law Directory

MOODY, STROPLE & KLOEPPEL, INC. (AV)

500 Crawford Street, Suite 300, P.O. Box 1138, 23705-1138
Telephone: 757-393-4093
Fax: 757-397-7257
URL: http://www.moodyrrlaw.com
Tampa, Florida Office: 9280 Bay Plaza Boulevard, Suite 714, 33619.
Telephone 813-627-9202.
Fax: 813-627-9423.

Willard J. Moody, Sr.

Willard J. Moody, Jr. | John C. Henry
Raymond H. Strople | Steven S. Nelson
Robert A. Small | Andrew K. Chafin
John E. Basilone | Claude W. Anderson, Jr.
Joseph J. Perez | John W. Hall
Thomas F. Burris, III | Kenneth C. Whalen (Resident, Tampa, Florida Office)
E. Stanley Murphy

OF COUNSEL

Byron P. Kloeppel, Retired

Reference: BB&T Bank.

For full biographical listings, see the Martindale-Hubbell Law Directory

*PULASKI,** Pulaski Co.

GILMER, SADLER, INGRAM, SUTHERLAND & HUTTON (AV)

Midtown Professional Building, 65 East Main Street, P.O. Box 878, 24301-0878
Telephone: 540-980-1360; 540-639-0027; 888-330-3344
Telecopier: 540-980-5264
Blacksburg (Montgomery County), Virginia Office: 201 West Roanoke Street, P.O. Box 908.
Telephone: 540-552-1061.
Telecopier: 540-552-8227.

MEMBERS OF FIRM

Howard C. Gilmer, Jr. (1906-1975) | Thomas J. McCarthy, Jr.
Roby K. Sutherland (1909-1975) | John J. Gill
Philip M. Sadler (1915-1994) | Gary C. Hancock
Robert J. Ingram | Jackson M. Bruce
James L. Hutton (Resident, Blacksburg Office) | Michael J. Barbour
| Deborah Wood Dobbins
| Timothy Edmond Kirtner
Robin J. Kegley

Representative Clients: Appalachian Power Co.; Norfolk Southern Railway Co.; NationsBank; Travelers Insurance Group; Volvo-GM Heavy Truck Corp.; Pulaski Furniture Corp.; Renfro Corp.

For full biographical listings, see the Martindale-Hubbell Law Directory

RESTON, Fairfax Co.

GARVER LAW OFFICES, P.C. (AV)

11702 Bowman Green Drive, P.O. Box 2430, 20195
Telephone: 703-471-1090; 800-440-8605
Fax: 703-471-1095
Email: GLAW@Erols.com *URL:* http://www.lawyers.com/stevengarver

Steven M. Garver | Cheryl Gilley Rice

For full biographical listings, see the Martindale-Hubbell Law Directory

HALL AND SICKELS, P.C. (AV)

Reston Executive Center, 12120 Sunset Hills Road, Suite 150, 20190
Telephone: 703-925-0500
Telecopier: 703-925-0501
URL: http://www.hallandsickels.com

Robert T. Hall | Charles W. Sickels

Holly Parkhurst Lear | Steven M. Frei
Donna Miller-Rostant

For full biographical listings, see the Martindale-Hubbell Law Directory

RICHMOND, (Independent City)

ALLEN, ALLEN, ALLEN & ALLEN, A PROFESSIONAL CORPORATION (AV)

1809 Staples Mill Road, P.O. Box 6855, 23230
Telephone: 804-257-7500; 800-768-2222
FAX: 804-257-7599
Petersburg, Virginia Office: 106 South Market Street.
Telephone: 804-733-8753.
Chesterfield, Virginia Office: 9509 Hull Street Road.
Telephone: 804-745-1200.
Fredericksburg, Virginia Office: 3405 Plank Road, 22407.
Telephone: 703-786-4100.
Mechanicsville, Virginia Office: 7255 Mechanicsville Turnpike.
Telephone: 804-746-4900.

George E. Allen, Sr. (1885-1972)
Cary L. Branch (1918-1989)
George E. Allen, Jr. (1914-1990)
Ashby B. Allen
Wilbur C. Allen
Boyd F. Collier
George E. Allen, III
Christopher Allen Meyer
W. Coleman Allen, Jr.
Charles L. Allen
R. Clayton Allen (Resident, Chesterfield Office)
Elizabeth M. Allen (Resident, Petersburg Office)
P. Christopher Guedri
Edward L. Allen (Resident, Fredericksburg Office)
Courtney A. Van Winkle
Tammy Stafford Ruble
Melinda H. South
Trent S. Kerns
Douglas A. Barry
Pamela Heflin Sellers

References: Signet Bank; Crestar Bank.

For full biographical listings, see the Martindale-Hubbell Law Directory

BOONE, BEALE, COSBY & LONG (AV)

A Partnership including Professional Law Corporations
27 North 17th Street, 23219
Telephone: 804-780-1729
Fax: 804-648-6211
Woodbridge, Virginia Office: 4391 Ridgewood Center Drive, Suite H.
Telephone: 703-690-1222.
Fax: 703-680-0559.

David E. Boone
J. Burkhardt Beale (Resident, Woodbridge Office)
Charles C. Cosby, Jr.
Andrea C. Long
Stacy F. Garrett, III
W. Edward Riley, IV

Reference: Nations Bank, Richmond, Virginia.

For full biographical listings, see the Martindale-Hubbell Law Directory

BRENNER, DOHNAL, EVANS & YOFFY, P.C. (AV)

411 East Franklin Street, Suite 200, P.O. Box 470, 23218-0470
Telephone: 804-644-1300
Facsimile: 804-644-1354
Email: bdeyp@erols.com

Theodore I. Brenner
Dennis W. Dohnal
Ronald S. Evans
James S. Yoffy

Jay O. Millman
Gregory S. Hooe
Kathryn Spruill Lingle
Mary J. Bennett
Thomas D. Stokes, III

For full biographical listings, see the Martindale-Hubbell Law Directory

MALONEY, HUENNEKENS, PARKS, GECKER & PARSONS, A PROFESSIONAL CORPORATION (AV)

Bank of America Center, 1111 East Main Street, Suite 800, 23219-3103
Telephone: 804-644-0313
Telecopier: 804-783-6192

Malcolm Parks
Joel G. Clarke

Ruth E. Nathanson

OF COUNSEL

Frank C. Maloney III

Reference: First Union National Bank.

For Complete List of Firm Personnel, See General Section

For full biographical listings, see the Martindale-Hubbell Law Directory

MORCHOWER, LUXTON AND WHALEY (AV)

An Affiliation of Attorneys
9 East Franklin Street, 23219
Telephone: 804-643-0147
FAX: 804-648-5514

Michael Morchower
John W. Luxton
C. David Whaley

(See Next Column)

ASSOCIATES

S. Michael Glass
Sharon Gregory Jacobs
Joseph J. Pecoraro
Lauren A. Caudill
Anthony G. Spencer
Lee White Kilduff
Sherry L. Gill

For full biographical listings, see the Martindale-Hubbell Law Directory

ROANOKE, Roanoke City Co.

MUNDY, ROGERS & FRITH, LLP (AV)

Third Street and Woods Avenue, S.W., P.O. Box 2240, 24009
Telephone: 540-982-2900
FAX: 540-982-1362
Email: info@mrf-law.com *URL:* http://www.mrf-law.com

MEMBERS OF FIRM

G. Marshall Mundy
Frank W. Rogers, III
T. Daniel Frith, III
Cheryl Watson Smith
Edward B. Walker

Reference: First Union.

For full biographical listings, see the Martindale-Hubbell Law Directory

*RUSTBURG,** Campbell Co.

OVERBEY, HAWKINS & SELZ (AV)

Court House Square, P.O. Box 38, 24588
Telephone: 804-332-5155
FAX: 804-332-5143

W. Hutchings Overbey (1906-1991)
A. David Hawkins
Bryan K. Selz

ASSOCIATE

Frank A. Wright, Jr.

OF COUNSEL

W. Hutchings Overbey, Jr.

Local Counsel for: First Virginia Bank, Piedmont; Colonial Farm Credit, ACA; Browning-Ferris Industries; WESTVACO; Truck Body Corp.; Falwell Aviation, Inc.; Campbell County School Board; Bedford County School Board; Industrial Development Authority of the County of Campbell; Modern Home Construction, Inc.

For full biographical listings, see the Martindale-Hubbell Law Directory

*TAZEWELL,** Tazewell Co.

DUDLEY, GALUMBECK & NECESSARY (AV)

104 West Main Street, P.O. Box 626, 24651
Telephone: 540-988-9436; 988-6561
Telecopier: 540-988-2921
Bluefield, Virginia Office: 728 Virginia Avenue, P.O. Box 468, 24605.
Telephone: 540-322-3454; 540-988-6590; 1-800-580-6590.
Telecopier: 540-322-4420.
Wytheville, Virginia Office: 100 West Main Street, Suite 201, 24382.
Telephone: 540-228-6060.
Fax: 540-228-7573.

MEMBERS OF FIRM

James W. Dudley (Resident, Bluefield Office)
Robert M. Galumbeck (Resident)
Kelly Combs Necessary (Resident)
Charles A. Stacy (Resident, Bluefield Office)
Clinton Sherwood Kegley (Resident, Wytheville Office)

References: Lawyers Title Insurance; Bank of Tazewell County.

For full biographical listings, see the Martindale-Hubbell Law Directory

VIRGINIA BEACH, (Independent City)

BRYDGES, MAHAN, O'BRIEN & FRUCCI, P.C. (AV)

Professional Building, 1369 Laskin Road, 23451
Telephone: 757-428-6021
Fax: 757-491-7634

Richard G. Brydges
Stephen C. Mahan
William R. "Buster" O'Brien
Steven C. Frucci

Approved Mediators/Arbitrators for: United States Arbitration and Mediation, Inc.; Arbitration Associates, Inc.- Jams/Endispute.
Reference: The Bank of Tidewater.

For full biographical listings, see the Martindale-Hubbell Law Directory

SHUTTLEWORTH RULOFF & GIORDANO, P.C. (AV)

4525 South Boulevard, Suite 300, 23452
Telephone: 757-671-6000
Fax: 757-671-6004
Email: srg@visi.net *URL:* http://www.srgpclaw.com
Newport News, Virginia Office: Historic Hilton Village, 10234 Warwick Boulevard, 23605.
Telephone: 757-873-9999.
Facsimile: 757-873-8758.

(See Next Column)

SHUTTLEWORTH RULOFF & GIORDANO P.C.—*Continued*

Robert J. Haddad
Robert G. Morecock
Lisa Palmer O'Donnell
Thomas B. Shuttleworth, II
Lawrence H. Woodward, Jr.

For full biographical listings, see the Martindale-Hubbell Law Directory

WOLCOTT, RIVERS, WHEARY, BASNIGHT & KELLY, P.C. (AV)

One Columbus Center, Suite 1100, 23462-6765
Telephone: 757-497-6633
FAX: 757-497-7267
Email: wolriv@series2000.com

Wilson L. Rivers
William A. Wheary, III
W. Brantley Basnight, III
Monroe Kelly, III
Carl A. Eason
Joseph R. Mayes
Samuel W. Meekins, Jr.
Edward W. Wolcott, Jr.
Barry Dorans
Leslie R. Watson
David N. Reda
Richard E. Biemiller
Cheshire I'Anson Eveleigh
M. Powell Peters
Neil L. Rose
Robert D. Marotta

David M. Bastiaans
Deborah Kirkpatrick

Counsel for: Metropolitan Life Insurance Co.; Ford Motor Co.
Approved Attorneys for: Lawyers Title Insurance Corp.

For full biographical listings, see the Martindale-Hubbell Law Directory

WASHINGTON

BAINBRIDGE ISLAND, Kitsap Co.

MORROW & OTOROWSKI (AV)

298 Winslow Way West, 98110
Telephone: 206-842-1000
Facsimile: 206-842-0797
URL: http://www.medilaw.com
Email: m-o@medilaw.com *URL:* http://www.lawyers.com/medilaw

MEMBERS OF FIRM

Albert Morrow
Christopher L. Otorowski

ASSOCIATE

Carol N. Johnston

For full biographical listings, see the Martindale-Hubbell Law Directory

BELLEVUE, King Co.

PATRICK H. LEPLEY (AV)

4122 Factoria Boulevard, S.E., Suite 301, 98006
Telephone: 425-641-5353
Fax: 425-747-0611
Email: phllaw@msn.com

Karen K. Greig

Reference: Sea-First (Factoria).

For full biographical listings, see the Martindale-Hubbell Law Directory

MOSES LAKE, Grant Co.

CALBOM & SCHWAB, P.S.C. (AV)

1240 South Pioneer Way, P.O. Drawer 1429, 98837
Telephone: 509-765-1851
Toll Free: 1-800-497-1755
Fax: 509-766-2727
Wenatchee, Kennewick, Chelan, Brewster, Ellensburg
URL: http://www.calbomschwab.com
Wenatchee, Washington Office: 819 N. Miller.
Telephone: 509-662-5677.
Kennewick, Washington Office: 118 Vista Way.
Telephone: 509-736-0866.
Chelan, Washington Office: 127 E. Woodin Avenue.
Telephone: 509-682-4364.
Brewster, Washington Office: 102 S. Bridge Street.
Telephone: 509-689-2615.
Ellensburg, Washington Office: 1633 Vantage Highway.
Telephone: 509-962-6080.

G. Joe Schwab
John E. Calbom (1925-1995)
David L. Lybbert
Kathleen G. Kilcullen

Jeffrey Schwab

(See Next Column)

LEGAL SUPPORT PERSONNEL

PARALEGALS

Jeff Parkinson
Jane V. King
Gracie Ortiz

Reference: Seattle-First National Bank, Moses Lake Branch.

For full biographical listings, see the Martindale-Hubbell Law Directory

RENTON, King Co.

HARDWICK LAW FIRM (AV)

15 South Grady Way, Suite 300, 98055
Telephone: 425-228-3860
Fax: 425-226-4988
URL: http://www.lawyers.com/hardwicklawfirm

Morton T. Hardwick
Joseph E. Pendergast, III

For full biographical listings, see the Martindale-Hubbell Law Directory

*SEATTLE,** King Co.

THE DAVIS FIRM (AV)

5301 Ballard Avenue N.W., 98107
Telephone: 206-789-1056
Fax: 206-789-9690
Email: thedavisfirm@seanet.com *URL:* http://www.lawyers.com/thedavisfirm

MEMBERS OF FIRM

Susan R. Davis
Donald K. Davis

For full biographical listings, see the Martindale-Hubbell Law Directory

WILLIAM H. FLIGELTAUB (AV)

4100 First Interstate Center, 999 Third Avenue, 98104
Telephone: 206-343-9490
Fax: 206-464-9559

For full biographical listings, see the Martindale-Hubbell Law Directory

LAW OFFICES OF LEMBHARD G. HOWELL, P.S. (AV)

Pacific Building, Suite 2105, 720 Third Avenue, 98104
Telephone: 206-623-5296
Fax: 206-628-6474
Cable Address: "Old Seattle"

Lembhard G. Howell

Mark E. Koontz

For full biographical listings, see the Martindale-Hubbell Law Directory

KARGIANIS WATKINS WERNER, L.L.P., P.S. (AV)

Market Place Tower, Penthouse Suite A, 2025 First Avenue, 98121-2157
Telephone: 206-448-7969; Toll Free: 800-424-3352
Fax: 206-448-7950

George Kargianis
Michael T. Watkins
Joanne R. Werner

For full biographical listings, see the Martindale-Hubbell Law Directory

OSBORN SMITH, P.L.L.C. (AV)

1111 Third Avenue, Suite 2650, 98101
Telephone: 206-386-5505
Facsimile: 206-652-2516
Email: flyonsmith@msn.com *URL:* http://www.lawyers.com/stevenrobinson

Simeon J. Osborn
Franklin L. Smith

Theodore R. Parry
Susan Machler

For full biographical listings, see the Martindale-Hubbell Law Directory

LAW OFFICE OF RON PEREY (AV)

2025 First Avenue, Suite 250, 98121-2147
Telephone: 206-443-7600
Fax: 206-443-4785

LEGAL SUPPORT PERSONNEL

MEDICAL DIRECTOR

Alexandra Finney McCafferty (Medical Doctor)

CASE MANAGERS

P.J. Anderson (Registered Nurse)
David Ubaldi

For full biographical listings, see the Martindale-Hubbell Law Directory

Seattle—Continued

SCHROETER, GOLDMARK & BENDER, P.S. (AV)

500 Central Building, 810 Third Avenue, 98104
Telephone: 206-622-8000; 1-800-809-2234
FAX: 206-682-2305
Email: lastname@schroeter-goldmark.com

Croil J. Anderson
Adam J. Berger
James D. Hailey
Kristin Houser
Amanda E. Lee
Mark Leemon
Douglas D. McBroom
Janet L. Rice
Jeffery P. Robinson
Rebecca J. Roe
Sidney Stillerman Royer
William Rutzick
Sandra E. Widlan
Corrie Johnson Yackulic
John Goldmark (1917-1979)
Dean Bender (1933-1988)

OF COUNSEL

Jenny A. Durkan

For full biographical listings, see the Martindale-Hubbell Law Directory

*SPOKANE,** Spokane Co.

BACKMAN & BLUMEL, P.S. (AV)

900 Northtown Office Building, North 4407 Division, 99207
Telephone: 509-487-1651
FAX: 509-483-5016
Email: joeb@omnicast.net *URL:* http://www.lawyers.com/backblumlaw

Stephen F. Backman
Joseph A. Blumel, III

For full biographical listings, see the Martindale-Hubbell Law Directory

*TACOMA,** Pierce Co.

DAVID A. BUFALINI, P.S., INC. (AV)

2915 N. McCarver, Suite 100, 98403-3336
Telephone: 253-272-2100
Fax: 253-272-9988
Email: dab2915@aol.com *URL:* http://www.lawyers.com/buflaw

David A. Bufalini

For full biographical listings, see the Martindale-Hubbell Law Directory

MESSINA BULZOMI (AV)

Attorneys at Law
5316 Orchard Street West, 98467
Telephone: 253-472-6000; 1-800-992-9LAW
Fax: 253-475-7886
Email: messinalaw@aol.com

John L. Messina
Stephen L. Bulzomi
John R. Christensen
Cynthia M. Morgan
Jeffrey H. Sadler

For full biographical listings, see the Martindale-Hubbell Law Directory

*YAKIMA,** Yakima Co.

ABEYTA-NELSON P.C. (AV)

1102 West Yakima Avenue, 98902-3029
Telephone: 509-575-1588
Fax: 509-457-8426
Email: injurylaw@abeytanelson.com *URL:* http://www.abeytanelson.com

Terry P. Abeyta
Rodney K. Nelson
Derek L. Sutton

John S. Kapuza

Reference: Central Valley Bank.

For full biographical listings, see the Martindale-Hubbell Law Directory

WEST VIRGINIA

*CHARLESTON,** Kanawha Co.

BUCCI, BAILEY & JAVINS, L.C. (AV)

Bank One Center Suite 910, 707 Virginia Street, East, P.O. Box 3712, 25337
Telephone: 304-345-0346
Fax: 304-345-0375
Email: kpaxton@citynet.net

Guy R. Bucci
Timothy C. Bailey
L. Lee Javins, II

(See Next Column)

J. Mark Adkins
Jon K. Cormany
V. Paul Bucci, II

For full biographical listings, see the Martindale-Hubbell Law Directory

GOODWIN & GOODWIN (AV)

1500 One Valley Square, 25301
Telephone: 304-346-7000
Fax: 304-344-9692
Email: g&glaw@goodwin.goodwin.com *URL:* http://www.goodwingoodwin.com
Ripley, West Virginia Office: 500 Church Street, P.O. Box 349. *Telephone:* 304-372-2651.
Parkersburg, West Virginia Office: 201 Third Street, Town Square. *Telephone:* 304-485-2345. *Fax:* 304-485-3459.

MEMBERS OF FIRM

Thomas R. Goodwin
Richard E. Rowe
Richard D. Owen

Representative Clients: Bucyrus-Erie Co.; CSX Corp.; Eastern American Energy Corp.; The Eureka Pipe Line Co.

For Complete List of Firm Personnel, See General Section

For full biographical listings, see the Martindale-Hubbell Law Directory

MASTERS & TAYLOR, L.C. (AV)

181 Summers Street, 25301
Telephone: 304-342-3106
Fax: 304-342-3189
Email: masters-taylor@iname.com

Marvin W. Masters
Robert A. Taylor
David L. Stuart
Janet Gerwig Masters
Laurie Garrigan McKowen
David L. White
Anthony J. Majestro
Kathleen T. Pettigrew
Richard A. Monahan
Paula L. Wilson
Rachael A. Stickler
Charles M. Love IV

References: One Valley Bank; Parkersburg Inn (Holiday Inn, Parkersburg).

For full biographical listings, see the Martindale-Hubbell Law Directory

SALSBERY & DRUCKMAN (AV)

606 Virginia Street East, Suite 100, 25305
Telephone: 304-343-0075
Fax: 304-343-0099
Email: salsdruck@citynet.net

H. F. Salsbery
William S. Druckman
Madonna C. Estep

OF COUNSEL

Anne E. Shaffer

For full biographical listings, see the Martindale-Hubbell Law Directory

*CLARKSBURG,** Harrison Co.

JOHNSON, SIMMERMAN & BROUGHTON, L.C. (AV)

Ogden Building, 203 West Main Street, 26301
Telephone: 304-624-6555; 304-623-4900
Telecopier: 304-623-4933
Mailing Address: P.O. Box 150, Clarksburg, West Virginia, 26302-0150

Charles G. Johnson
Frank E. Simmerman, Jr.
Marcia Allen Broughton
Bridget D. Furbee
Robin Queen Triplett

For full biographical listings, see the Martindale-Hubbell Law Directory

MCNEER, HIGHLAND, MCMUNN AND VARNER, L.C. (AV)

One Valley Bank Building, P.O. Drawer 2040, 26302-2040
Telephone: 304-626-1100
Facsimile: 304-623-3035
Martinsburg Office: 2520 Aikens Center, P.O. Box 2509. *Telephone:* 304-264-4621. *Fax:* 304-264-8623.
Parkersburg Office: 404 Market Street, Suite 204, P.O. Box 1507. *Telephone:* 304-422-7193. *Facsimile:* 304-422-7196.

C. David McMunn
J. Cecil Jarvis
James A. Varner
Robert W. Trumble (Resident, Martinsburg Office)
Catherine D. Munster
James N. Riley
Steven R. Bratke (Resident, Parkersburg Office)
Michael J. Novotny (Resident, Martinsburg Office)
Dennis M. Shreve
Geraldine S. Roberts
William F. Rohrbaugh (Resident, Martinsburg Office)
Gregory H. Schillace
Judy L. Shanholtz
Tiffany R. Durst
Gene W. Bailey, II

(See Next Column)

McNeer, Highland, McMunn and Varner L.C.—*Continued*

OF COUNSEL

James E. McNeer
Cecil B. Highland, Jr.
William L. Fury

Representative Clients: One Valley Bank of Clarksburg, National Assn.; Bruceton Bank; Harrison County Bank; Nationwide Mutual Insurance Cos.; Clarksburg Publishing Co.; C.I.T. Financial Services; State Automobile Mutual Insurance Co.; United Hospital Center, Inc.; West Virginia Coals, Inc.; Swanson Plating Co.

For full biographical listings, see the Martindale-Hubbell Law Directory

*PRINCETON,** Mercer Co.

Gibson, Lefler & Associates (AV)

1345 Mercer Street, 24740
Telephone: 304-425-8276
800-742-3545

MEMBERS OF FIRM

Michael F. Gibson
Derrick W. Lefler

LEGAL SUPPORT PERSONNEL

NURSE PARALEGAL

Melody Lambert, RN-RLNC

SOCIAL SECURITY PARALEGAL

Nancy Belcher

PERSONAL INJURY PARALEGAL

Kathy Richards

WORKERS COMPENSATION PARALEGAL

Carol Hylton

MEDICAL NEGLIGENCE PARALEGAL

Deborah Frye

For full biographical listings, see the Martindale-Hubbell Law Directory

Johnston, Holroyd & Associates (AV)

1438 Main Street, 24740
Telephone: 304-425-2103
Fax: 304-425-5385
Email: mlawdog@inet1.net

MEMBERS OF FIRM

W. Broughton Johnston (1905-1978)
Robert E. Holroyd
Anthony Bisaha
Michael A. Lawrence
Scott A. Ash

Representative Clients: McDowell-Pocahontas Coal Co.; One Valley Bank; Princeton Community Hospital.

For full biographical listings, see the Martindale-Hubbell Law Directory

Sanders, Austin, Swope & Flanigan (AV)

Hunter Park, 320 Courthouse Road, 24740-2421
Telephone: 304-425-8125
FAX: 304-425-4155
Email: sasf@inetone.net

MEMBERS OF FIRM

Hartley Sanders (1879-1952)
Lane O. Austin
Derek C. Swope
William H. Sanders, III
William B. Flanigan
Gregory S. Prudich

ASSOCIATES

S. Paige Burress
Omar J. Aboulhosn

OF COUNSEL

William H. Sanders, II

References: First Community Bank-Princeton; One Valley Bank-Princeton.

For full biographical listings, see the Martindale-Hubbell Law Directory

WEIRTON, Hancock & Brooke Cos.

Frankovitch, Anetakis, Colantonio & Simon (AV)

337 Penco Road, 26062
Telephone: 304-723-4400
Fax: 304-723-5892
Email: fanda@1stnet
Wheeling, West Virginia Office: United National Bank Building, Suite 504, 21 Twelfth Street.
Telephone: 304-233-1212.
Fax: 304-233-1251.
Chester, West Virginia Office: 529 Carolina Avenue, 26034.
Telephone: 304-387-4400.
Fax: 304-387-4412.

MEMBERS OF FIRM

George J. Anetakis
Carl N. Frankovitch
John J. Anetakis
M. Eric Frankovitch
Mark A. Colantonio
Michael G. Simon

(See Next Column)

ASSOCIATES

Bryan S. Neft
Thomas J. Decapio
J. George (Jack) Anetakis

For Complete List of Firm Personnel, See General Section

For full biographical listings, see the Martindale-Hubbell Law Directory

*WHEELING,** Ohio Co.

Bachmann, Hess, Bachmann & Garden, P.L.L.C. (AV)

1226 Chapline Street, P.O. Box 351, 26003-0046
Telephone: 304-233-3511
Fax: 304-233-3199
Email: info@bhbglaw.com *URL:* http://www.bhbglaw.com

MEMBERS OF FIRM

Carl G. Bachmann (1890-1980)
Lester C. Hess (1903-1971)
John B. Garden (1925-1994)
Gilbert S. Bachmann
Lester C. Hess, Jr.
John L. Allen
Paul T. Tucker
George E. McLaughlin
Jeffrey R. Miller
Anthony Ira Werner
Jeffrey A. Grove
Elizabeth Abraham Delk

ASSOCIATE

David L. Delk, Jr.

Representative Clients: American Electric Power; Ohio Power Co.; United National Bank; Wheeling Housing Authority; Windsor Coal Co.

For full biographical listings, see the Martindale-Hubbell Law Directory

Cassidy, Myers, Cogan, Voegelin & Tennant, L.C. (AV)

The First State Capitol, 1413 Eoff Street, 26003-3582
Telephone: 304-232-8100
Fax: 304-232-8200
St. Clairsville, Ohio Office: 126 E. Main Street.
Telephone: 740-695-1350.
Fax: 740-695-1356.

Frank A. O'Brien, Jr.
Patrick S. Cassidy
William C. Gallagher
Thomas M. Myers (Resident at St. Clairsville, Ohio, Office)
Timothy F. Cogan
Wray V. Voegelin
Donald James Tennant, Jr.
Thomas M. Cunningham

Representative Clients: United Steel Workers of America AFL, CIO, CLC; District 6 United Mine Workers of America; District 23 United Food and Commercial Workers; Local 1149 Laborers National Union of North America; West Virginia Education Assn.; International Union of Oil, Chemical & Atomic Workers; International Union of Electrical, Radio & Machine Workers; Local 83 United Association of Plumbers and Steamfitters; Local 549, International Association of Bridge, Structural and Ornamental Iron Workers of Wheeling, WV.

For full biographical listings, see the Martindale-Hubbell Law Directory

Schrader Byrd & Companion, PLLC (AV)

(A Professional Limited Liability Company)
The Maxwell Centre, 32-20th Street, Suite 500, P.O. Box 6336, 26003
Telephone: 304-233-3390
Fax: 304-233-2769
URL: http://www.schraderlaw.com
Martins Ferry, Ohio Office: 205 North Fifth Street, P.O. Box 309, 43935.
Telephone: 740-633-9976.
Fax: 740-633-0400.
Weirton, West Virginia Office: 3205 Pennsylvania Avenue, Suite 103, Penn Place, P.O. Box 2785, 26062.
Telephone: 304-723-2674.
Fax: 304-723-2876.

MEMBERS

Ray A. Byrd
James F. Companion
Frank X. Duff
Teresa Rieman-Camilletti
Yolonda G. Lambert
Daniel P. Fry (Resident Partner, Martins Ferry, Ohio Office)
James P. Mazzone (Resident Member, Weirton, West Virginia Office)
Sandra K. Law
D. Kevin Coleman

SPECIAL COUNSEL

Thomas B. Miller

ASSOCIATES

Denise D. Klug
Michael A. Adams
John Porco
Aimee Morgan Stern
Kimberly R. Wilson
Christopher J. Adams

OF COUNSEL

James A. Byrum, Jr.

General Counsel: Reynolds Memorial Hospital; WesBanco Bank-Elm Grove.
Representative Clients: American Cyanamid Company; Bank One; Matlack Systems, Inc.; Moutaineer Gas Co.; Ohio County Board of Education; PHICO Insurance Co.; Wheeling Hospital; Wheeling-Pittsburg Steel Corp.

For full biographical listings, see the Martindale-Hubbell Law Directory

WISCONSIN

*APPLETON,** Outagamie Co.

HABUSH, HABUSH, DAVIS & ROTTIER, S.C. (AV)

4100 Boardwalk Court, 54915
Telephone: 920-738-0900
Fax: 920-738-5850
Email: info@habush.com *URL:* http://www.habush.com/
Milwaukee, Wisconsin Office: Suite 2300, First Wisconsin Center, 777 East Wisconsin Avenue.
Telephone: 414-271-0900.
FAX: 414-271-6854.
Madison, Wisconsin Office: 150 East Gilman Street, Suite 2000.
Telephone: 608-255-6663.
FAX: 608-255-0745.
Wausau, Wisconsin Office: 3100 Eagle Avenue.
Telephone: 715-842-4444.
FAX: 715-845-8898.
Racine, Wisconsin Office: Durand Place, 5439 Durand Avenue, Suite 220.
Telephone: 262-554-6200.
FAX: 262-554-7166.
Waukesha, Wisconsin Office: Stone Ridge I, N14 W23755 Stone Ridge Drive, Suite 225.
Telephone: 262-523-4700.
FAX: 262-523-4545.
Rhinelander, Wisconsin Office: 26 South Brown Street.
Telephone: 715-365-1900.
FAX: 715-365-1910.
Green Bay, Wisconsin Office: P.O. Box 22545, 314 South Madison Street.
Telephone: 920-437-0900.
FAX: 920-437-0910.
Stevens Point, Wisconsin Office: 5370 East Highway 10.
Telephone: 715-345-0004.
FAX: 715-343-2207.
Lake Geneva, Wisconsin Office: First Banking Center Plaza, Suite 120, 569 Broad Street.
Telephone: 262-248-5200.
FAX: 262-248-5222.

John D. Murray — Craig A. Christensen

For full biographical listings, see the Martindale-Hubbell Law Directory

BROOKFIELD, Waukesha Co.

CANNON & DUNPHY, S.C. (AV)

595 North Barker Road, P.O. Box 1750, 53008-1750
Telephone: 414-782-2700
Facsimile: 414-796-5800
URL: http://www.cannon-dunphy.com

William M. Cannon — Lynn R. Laufenberg
Patrick O. Dunphy — Mark L. Thomsen
M. Angela Dentice

Sarah E. Frink — Ellen L. Wiesner
Edward E. Robinson

For full biographical listings, see the Martindale-Hubbell Law Directory

*GREEN BAY,** Brown Co.

HABUSH, HABUSH, DAVIS & ROTTIER, S.C. (AV)

314 South Madison Street, P.O. Box 22545, 54305-2545
Telephone: 920-437-0900
Fax: 920-437-0910
Email: info@habush.com *URL:* http://www.habush.com/
Milwaukee, Wisconsin Office: Suite 2300. First Wisconsin Center, 777 East Wisconsin Avenue.
Telephone: 414-271-0900.
FAX: 414-271-6854.
Madison, Wisconsin Office: 150 East Gilman Street, Suite 2000.
Telephone: 608-255-6663.
FAX: 608-255-0745.
Appleton, Wisconsin Office: 4100 Boardwalk Court.
Telephone: 920-738-0900.
FAX: 920-738-5850.
Wausau, Wisconsin Office: 3100 Eagle Avenue.
Telephone: 715-842-4444.
FAX: 715-845-8898.
Racine, Wisconsin Office: Durand Place, 5439 Durand Avenue, Suite 220.
Telephone: 262-554-6200.
FAX: 262-554-7166.
Waukesha, Wisconsin Office: Stone Ridge I, N14 W23755 Stone Ridge Drive, Suite 225.
Telephone: 262-523-4700.
FAX: 262-523-4545.
Rhinelander, Wisconsin Office: 26 South Brown Street.
Telephone: 715-365-1900.
FAX: 715-365-1910.

(See Next Column)

Stevens Point, Wisconsin Office: 5370 East Highway 10.
Telephone: 715-345-0004.
FAX: 715-343-2207.
Lake Geneva, Wisconsin Office: First Banking Center Plaza, Suite 120, 569 Broad Street.
Telephone: 262-248-5200.
FAX: 262-248-5222.

Ralph J. Tease, Jr. — Edward J. Vopal

For full biographical listings, see the Martindale-Hubbell Law Directory

LAKE GENEVA, Walworth Co.

BRADEN & OLSON (AV)

716 Wisconsin Street, P.O. Box 940, 53147
Telephone: 414-248-6636
Fax: 414-248-2901
Email: bando@genevaonline.com

MEMBERS OF FIRM

Berwyn B. Braden — John O. Olson

ASSOCIATES

Christine Tomas — Daniel S. Draper

For full biographical listings, see the Martindale-Hubbell Law Directory

HABUSH, HABUSH, DAVIS & ROTTIER, S.C. (AV)

First Banking Center Plaza, Suite 120, 569 Broad Street, 53147
Telephone: 262-248-5200
Fax: 262-248-5222
Email: info@habush.com *URL:* http://www.habush.com/
Milwaukee, Wisconsin Office: Suite 2300, First Wisconsin Center, 777 East Wisconsin Avenue.
Telephone: 414-271-0900.
FAX: 414-271-6854.
Madison, Wisconsin Office: 150 East Gilman Street, Suite 2000.
Telephone: 608-255-6663.
FAX: 608-255-0745.
Appleton, Wisconsin Office: 4100 Boardwalk Court.
Telephone: 920-738-0900.
FAX: 920-738-5850.
Wausau, Wisconsin Office: 3100 Eagle Avenue.
Telephone: 715-842-4444.
FAX: 715-845-8898.
Racine, Wisconsin Office: Durand Place, 5439 Durand Avenue, Suite 220.
Telephone: 262-554-6200.
FAX: 262-554-7166.
Waukesha, Wisconsin Office: Stone Ridge I, N14 W23755 Stone Ridge Drive, Suite 225.
Telephone: 262-523-4700.
FAX: 262-523-4545.
Rhinelander, Wisconsin Office: 26 South Brown Street.
Telephone: 715-365-1900.
FAX: 715-365-1910.
Green Bay, Wisconsin Office: P.O. Box 22545, 314 South Madison Street.
Telephone: 920-437-0900.
FAX: 920-437-0910.
Stevens Point, Wisconsin Office: 5370 East Highway 10.
Telephone: 715-345-0004.
FAX: 715-343-2207.

Michael J. Jassak

For full biographical listings, see the Martindale-Hubbell Law Directory

*MADISON,** Dane Co.

ATTERBURY & RILEY, S.C. (AV)

7001 Old Sauk Road, P.O. Box 45020, 53744-5020
Telephone: 608-821-4600
Fax: 608-821-4610
Email: arlaw@chorus.net *URL:* http://WWW.EXECPC.COM/~ARL

Lee R. Atterbury — Michael Riley

Rebecca M. Orvick — Alexander S. Kammer

OF COUNSEL

Eldred M. Swingen

A list of Representative Clients will be furnished upon request.
Reference: M & I Bank of Madison.

For full biographical listings, see the Martindale-Hubbell Law Directory

AXLEY BRYNELSON, LLP (AV)

(Formerly Brynelson, Herrick, Bucaida, Dorschel & Armstrong Including the former Easton & Assoc., S.C.)
2 East Mifflin Street, P.O. Box 1767, 53701-1767
Telephone: 608-257-5661
Fax: 608-257-5444
Email: law@axley.com *URL:* http://www.axley.com

(See Next Column)

AXLEY BRYNELSON LLP—*Continued*

MEMBERS OF FIRM

Bradley D. Armstrong
John H. Schmid, Jr.
Timothy D. Fenner
John C. Mitby
Daniel T. Hardy
John Walsh
Bruce L. Harms
David Easton
Curtis C. Swanson
Michael S. Anderson
Patricia M. Gibeault
Michael J. Westcott
Larry K. Libman
Richard E. Petershack
Steven A. Brezinski
Steven M. Streck
Joy L. O'Grosky
Arthur E. Kurtz
Edith F. Merila
Michael J. Modl

OF COUNSEL

Ralph E. Axley (1902-1995)
Floyd A. Brynelson (1914-1998)
James C. Herrick
Frank J. Bucaida
Griffin G. Dorschel

For Complete List of Firm Personnel, See General Section

For full biographical listings, see the Martindale-Hubbell Law Directory

HABUSH, HABUSH, DAVIS & ROTTIER, S.C. (AV)

150 East Gilman Street, Suite 2000, 53703
Telephone: 608-255-6663
Fax: 608-255-0745
Email: info@habush.com *URL:* http://www.habush.com/
Milwaukee, Wisconsin Office: Suite 2300, First Wisconsin Center, 777 East Wisconsin Avenue.
Telephone: 414-271-0900.
FAX: 414-271-6854.
Appleton, Wisconsin Office: 4100 Boardwalk Court.
Telephone: 920-738-0900.
FAX: 920-738-5850.
Wausau, Wisconsin Office: 3100 Eagle Avenue.
Telephone: 715-842-4444.
FAX: 715-845-8898.
Racine, Wisconsin Office: Durand Place, 5439 Durand Avenue, Suite 220.
Telephone: 262-554-6200.
FAX: 262-554-7166.
Waukesha, Wisconsin Office: Stone Ridge I, N14 W23755 Stone Ridge Drive, Suite 225.
Telephone: 262-523-4700.
FAX: 262-523-4545.
Rhinelander, Wisconsin Office: 26 South Brown Street.
Telephone: 715-365-1900.
FAX: 715-365-1910.
Green Bay, Wisconsin Office: P.O. Box 22545, 314 South Madison Street.
Telephone: 920-437-0900.
FAX: 920-437-0910.
Stevens Point, Wisconsin Office: 5370 East Highway 10.
Telephone: 715-345-0004.
FAX: 715-343-2207.
Lake Geneva, Wisconsin Office: First Banking Center Plaza, Suite 120, 569 Broad Street.
Telephone: 262-248-5200.
FAX: 262-248-5222.

Daniel A. Rottier
James R. Jansen
Susan R. Steingass
Nicholas J. McNamara
Stefanie A. O'Shea
Rhonda L. Lanford

For full biographical listings, see the Martindale-Hubbell Law Directory

LAWTON & CATES, S.C. (AV)

10 East Doty Street Suite 400, P.O. Box 2965, 53701-2965
Telephone: 608-282-6200
Fax: 608-282-6252
Email: lawcat@madison.tds.net *URL:* http://www.lawtoncates.com

John C. Carlson
James A. Olson
James W. Gardner
Kent I. Carnell
Victor M. Arellano

Reference: Bank One, Madison.

For full biographical listings, see the Martindale-Hubbell Law Directory

*MILWAUKEE,** Milwaukee Co.

HABUSH, HABUSH, DAVIS & ROTTIER, S.C. (AV)

Suite 2300 First Wisconsin Center, 777 East Wisconsin Avenue, 53202
Telephone: 414-271-0900
Fax: 414-271-6854
Email: info@habush.com *URL:* http://www.habush.com/
Madison, Wisconsin Office: 150 East Gilman Street, Suite 2000.
Telephone: 608-255-6663.
FAX: 608-255-0745.
Appleton, Wisconsin Office: 4100 Boardwalk Court.
Telephone: 920-738-0900.
FAX: 920-738-5850.
Wausau, Wisconsin Office: 3100 Eagle Avenue.
Telephone: 715-842-4444.
FAX: 715-845-8898.

(See Next Column)

Racine, Wisconsin Office: Durand Place, 5439 Durand Avenue, Suite 220.
Telephone: 262-554-6200.
FAX: 262-554-7166.
Waukesha, Wisconsin Office: Stone Ridge I, N14 W23755 Stone Ridge Drive, Suite 225.
Telephone: 262-523-4700.
FAX: 262-523-4545.
Rhinelander, Wisconsin Office: 26 South Brown Street.
Telephone: 715-365-1900.
FAX: 715-365-1910.
Green Bay, Wisconsin Office: P.O. Box 22545, 314 South Madison Street.
Telephone: 920-437-0900.
FAX: 920-437-0910.
Stevens Point, Wisconsin Office: 5370 East Highway 10.
Telephone: 715-345-0004.
FAX: 715-343-2207.
Lake Geneva, Wisconsin Office: First Banking Center Plaza, Suite 120, 569 Broad Street.
Telephone: 262-248-5200.
FAX: 262-248-5222.

Michael D. Egelhoff

For full biographical listings, see the Martindale-Hubbell Law Directory

MICHAEL F. HUPY & ASSOCIATES, S.C. (AV)

100 East Wisconsin Avenue Suite 1110, 53202
Telephone: 414-223-4800
Fax: 414-271-3374
URL: http://www.lawyers.com/hupyassociates

Michael F. Hupy
Jason F. Abraham
Thomas K. Houck
Teena M. Abraham
Michael T. Savaglio

For full biographical listings, see the Martindale-Hubbell Law Directory

KERSTEN & MCKINNON, S.C. (AV)

231 West Wisconsin Avenue, Suite 1200, 53203
Telephone: 414-271-0054
Fax: 414-271-7131
Email: Kersten3@ExecPc.com

Charles J. Kersten (1929-1972)
Arlo McKinnon (1929-1999)
J. P. McKinnon (1943-1973)
E. Campion Kersten
George P. Kersten
Kenan J. Kersten
Leslie Van Buskirk
Matthew T. Fricker

For full biographical listings, see the Martindale-Hubbell Law Directory

MURPHY, GILLICK, WICHT & PRACHTHAUSER (AV)

Suite 1200, 330 East Kilbourn Avenue, 53202
Telephone: 414-271-1011
Milwaukee: 800-942-2880
Fax: 414-271-9987
Email: mail@murphygillick.com *URL:* http://www.murphygillick.com
South Office: State Financial Bank Building, 4811 South 76th Street.
Telephone: 414-281-5700.
North Office: M&I Bank Building, 9001 North 76th Street.
Telephone: 414-354-5051.
Brookfield, Wisconsin Office: Brookfield Lakes Corporate Center, Suite 260, 300 North Corporate Drive (180th Street and Blue Mound Road).
Telephone: 414-792-0888.
Racine, Wisconsin Office: 4701 Washington Avenue.
Telephone: 414-635-8967.
Mequon, Wisconsin Office: 1496 West Mequon Road.
Telephone: 414-240-1138.

MEMBERS OF FIRM

Lawrence D. Gillick (1914-1984)
James J. Murphy
Michael H. Gillick
Dennis H. Wicht
Don C. Prachthauser
George F. Graf (Resident, Brookfield and Racine Offices)
Patrick J. Gillick
Melita M. Biese
Kevin J. Kukor

ASSOCIATES

Keith R. Stachowiak
Thadd J. Llaurado
Mark D. Baus
Sandra K. Graf
Frank T. Pasternak
Charles J. Graf

OF COUNSEL

M. Josef Zimmermann

For full biographical listings, see the Martindale-Hubbell Law Directory

TECHMEIER & VAN GRUNSVEN, S.C. (AV)

411 East Wisconsin Avenue, Suite 1100, 53202
Telephone: 414-223-1050
Telefax: 414-223-4355
Email: tvlaw@msn.com

Willard P. Techmeier
Paul R. Van Grunsven
David J. McCormick

For full biographical listings, see the Martindale-Hubbell Law Directory

*OSHKOSH,** Winnebago Co.

CURTIS LAW OFFICE (AV)

2905 Universal Street, P.O. Box 2845, 54903-2845
Telephone: 920-233-1010
Fax: 920-233-8053
Email: osowski@execpc.com

George W. Curtis

Scott C. Woldt Beth Driscoll Osowski

Reference: M & I Bank.

For full biographical listings, see the Martindale-Hubbell Law Directory

*RACINE,** Racine Co.

HABUSH, HABUSH, DAVIS & ROTTIER, S.C. (AV)

Durand Place, 5439 Durand Avenue, Suite 220, 53406
Telephone: 262-554-6200
Fax: 262-554-7166
Email: info@habush.com *URL:* http://www.habush.com/
Milwaukee Wisconsin Office: Suite 2300, First Wisconsin Center, 777 East Wisconsin Avenue. Telephone 414-271-0900.
FAX: 414-271-6854.
Madison, Wisconsin Office: 150 East Gilman Street, Suite 2000.
Telephone: 608-255-6663.
FAX: 608-255-0745.
Appleton, Wisconsin Office: 4100 Boardwalk Court.
Telephone: 920-738-0900.
FAX: 920-738-5850.
Wausau, Wisconsin Office: 3100 Eagle Avenue.
Telephone: 715-842-4444.
FAX: 715-845-8898.
Waukesha, Wisconsin Office: Stone Ridge I, N14 W23755 Stone Ridge Drive, Suite 225.
Telephone: 262-523-4700.
FAX: 262-523-4545.
Rhinelander, Wisconsin Office: 26 South Brown Street.
Telephone: 715-365-1900.
FAX: 715-365-1910.
Green Bay, Wisconsin Office: P.O. Box 22545, 314 South Madison Street.
Telephone: 920-437-0900.
FAX: 920-437-0910.
Stevens Point, Wisconsin Office: 5370 East Highway 10.
Telephone: 715-345-0004.
FAX: 715-343-2207.
Lake Geneva, Wisconsin Office: First Banking Center Plaza, Suite 120, 569 Broad Street.
Telephone: 262-248-5200.
FAX: 262-248-5222.

Michael J. Jassak Steven T. Botzau

For full biographical listings, see the Martindale-Hubbell Law Directory

*RHINELANDER,** Oneida Co.

HABUSH, HABUSH, DAVIS & ROTTIER, S.C. (AV)

26 South Brown Street, 54501
Telephone: 715-365-1900
Fax: 715-365-1910
Email: habush@newnorth.net *URL:* http://www.habush.com/
Milwaukee, Wisconsin Office: Suite 2300 First Wisconsin Center, 777 East Wisconsin Avenue.
Telephone: 414-271-0900.
FAX: 414-271-6854.
Madison, Wisconsin Office: 150 East Gilman Street, Suite 2000.
Telephone: 608-255-6663.
FAX: 608-255-0745.
Appleton, Wisconsin Office: 4100 Boardwalk Court.
Telephone: 920-738-0900.
FAX: 920-738-5850.
Wausau, Wisconsin Office: 3100 Eagle Avenue.
Telephone: 715-842-4444.
FAX: 715-845-8898.
Racine, Wisconsin Office: Durand Place, 5439 Durand Avenue, Suite 220.
Telephone: 262-554-6200.
FAX: 262-554-7166.
Waukesha, Wisconsin Office: Stone Ridge I, N14 W23755 Stone Ridge Drive, Suite 225.
Telephone: 262-523-4700.
FAX: 262-523-4545.
Green Bay, Wisconsin Office: P.O. Box 22545, 314 South Madison Street.
Telephone: 920-437-0900.
FAX: 920-437-0910.
Stevens Point, Wisconsin Office: 5370 East Highway 10.
Telephone: 715-345-0004.
FAX: 715-343-2207.
Lake Geneva, Wisconsin Office: First Banking Center Plaza, Suite 120, 569 Broad Street.
Telephone: 262-248-5200.
FAX: 262-248-5222.

(See Next Column)

Dana James Weis

For full biographical listings, see the Martindale-Hubbell Law Directory

RIVER FALLS, Pierce Co.

BYE, GOFF & ROHDE, LTD. (AV)

P.O. Box 167, 54022
Telephone: 715-425-8161; 1-800-607-3030
FAX: 715-425-7413
URL: http://www.byegoff.com

Chuck Bye Steven B. Goff
Dean R. Rohde

Stephen C. Nick Susanne M. Glasser

For full biographical listings, see the Martindale-Hubbell Law Directory

*WAUKESHA,** Waukesha Co.

HABUSH, HABUSH, DAVIS & ROTTIER, S.C. (AV)

Stone Ridge I, N14 W23755 Stone Ridge Drive, Suite 225, 53186
Telephone: 262-523-4700
Fax: 262-523-4545
Email: info@habush.com *URL:* http://www.habush.com/
Milwaukee Wisconsin Office: Suite 2300, First Wisconsin Center, 777 East Wisconsin Avenue.
Telephone: 414-271-0900.
FAX: 414-271-6854.
Madison, Wisconsin Office: 150 East Gilman Street, Suite 2000.
Telephone: 608-255-6663.
FAX: 608-255-0745.
Appleton, Wisconsin Office: 4100 Boardwalk Court.
Telephone: 920-738-0900.
FAX: 920-738-5850.
Wausau, Wisconsin Office: 3100 Eagle Avenue.
Telephone: 715-842-4444.
FAX: 715-845-8898.
Racine, Wisconsin Office: Durand Place, 5439 Durand Avenue, Suite 220.
Telephone: 262-554-6200.
FAX: 262-554-7166.
Rhinelander, Wisconsin Office: 26 South Brown Street.
Telephone: 715-365-1900.
FAX: 715-365-1910.
Green Bay, Wisconsin Office: P.O. Box 22545, 314 South Madison Street.
Telephone: 920-437-0900.
FAX: 920-437-0910.
Stevens Point, Wisconsin Office: 5370 East Highway 10.
Telephone: 715-345-0004.
FAX: 715-343-2207.
Lake Geneva, Wisconsin Office: First Banking Center Plaza, Suite 120, 569 Broad Street.
Telephone: 262-248-5200.
FAX: 262-248-5222.

Gary R. Kuphall Douglas E. Swanson

For full biographical listings, see the Martindale-Hubbell Law Directory

*WAUSAU,** Marathon Co.

HABUSH, HABUSH, DAVIS & ROTTIER, S.C. (AV)

3100 Eagle Avenue, 54402-1987
Telephone: 715-842-4444
Fax: 715-845-8898
Email: info@habush.com *URL:* http://www.habush.com/
Milwaukee, Wisconsin Office: Suite 2300, First Wisconsin Center, 777 East Wisconsin Avenue.
Telephone: 414-271-0900.
FAX: 414-271-6854.
Madison, Wisconsin Office: 150 East Gilman Street, Suite 2000.
Telephone: 608-255-6663.
FAX: 608-255-0745.
Appleton, Wisconsin Office: 4100 Boardwalk Court.
Telephone: 920-738-0900.
FAX: 920-738-5850.
Racine, Wisconsin Office: Durand Place, 5439 Durand Avenue, Suite 220.
Telephone: 262-554-6200.
FAX: 262-554-7166.
Waukesha, Wisconsin Office: Stone Ridge I, N14 W23755 Stone Ridge Drive, Suite 225.
Telephone: 262-523-4700.
FAX: 262-523-4545.
Rhinelander, Wisconsin Office: 26 South Brown Street.
Telephone: 715-365-1900.
FAX: 715-365-1910.
Green Bay, Wisconsin Office: P.O. Box 22545, 314 South Madison Street.
Telephone: 920-437-0900.
FAX: 920-437-0910.
Stevens Point, Wisconsin Office: 5370 East Highway 10.
Telephone: 715-345-0004.
FAX: 715-343-2207.

(See Next Column)

HABUSH, HABUSH, DAVIS & ROTTIER S.C.—*Continued*

Lake Geneva, Wisconsin Office: First Banking Center Plaza, Suite 120, 569 Broad Street.
Telephone: 262-248-5200.
FAX: 262-248-5222.

Dana James Weis | David E. Sunby | Marlene F. Wahlstrom

For full biographical listings, see the Martindale-Hubbell Law Directory

JEROME A. MAEDER LAW OFFICES, S.C. (AV)

602 Jackson Street, P.O. Box 1626, 54401
Telephone: 715-842-2281
Fax: 715-842-1046

Jerome A. Maeder

Vincent A. Maeder | Robert J. Gray

For full biographical listings, see the Martindale-Hubbell Law Directory

WYOMING

*CHEYENNE,** Laramie Co.

THE FITZGERALD LAW FIRM (AV)

A Partnership of Professional Corporations
2108 Warren Avenue, 82001-3740
Telephone: 307-634-4000
Telecopier: 307-635-2391
Email: lawyers@fitzgeraldlaw.com *URL:* http://www.fitzgeraldlaw.com

MEMBERS OF FIRM

James E. Fitzgerald (P.C.) | Sharon A. Fitzgerald (P.C.)

OF COUNSEL

A. G. McClintock

For full biographical listings, see the Martindale-Hubbell Law Directory

HICKEY, MACKEY, EVANS & WALKER (AV)

1800 Carey Avenue, Suite 700, P.O. Drawer 467, 82003
Telephone: 307-634-1525
Telecopier: 307-638-7335
URL: http://www.hickeymackey.com

MEMBERS OF FIRM

Paul J. Hickey
Terry W. Mackey
David F. Evans
John M. Walker
Roger C. Fransen
Richard D. Tim Bush
Mary A. Throne

A List of Representative Clients will be furnished upon request.
Reference: Norwest Bank, Cheyenne, N.A.

For full biographical listings, see the Martindale-Hubbell Law Directory

WOLF & TIEDEKEN (AV)

Suite 300 Equality State Bank Building, P.O. Box 491, 82001
Telephone: 307-635-2876
Fax: 307-632-4902
Email: lawyers@cheyenneweb.com

MEMBERS OF FIRM

Richard C. Wolf | Robert W. Tiedeken

For full biographical listings, see the Martindale-Hubbell Law Directory

*JACKSON,** Teton Co.

W. KEITH GOODY (AV)

155 E. Pearl, P.O. Box 2488, 83001
Telephone: 307-733-4446
Fax: 307-733-2774
Email: goodylaw@blissnet.com

LEGAL SUPPORT PERSONNEL

Mary C. Goody

For full biographical listings, see the Martindale-Hubbell Law Directory

KING AND KING, L.L.C. (AV)

Suite 201 Centennial Building, 610 West Broadway, P.O. Box 40, 83001
Telephone: 307-733-2904
Fax: 307-733-1058
Email: kinglaw@blissnet.com *URL:* http://www.lawyers.com/kingandking

Floyd R. King | Bret F. King

(See Next Column)

Kyra Knapp

Reference: Community First Bank, Jackson, Wyoming.

For full biographical listings, see the Martindale-Hubbell Law Directory

SPENCE, MORIARITY & SCHUSTER, LLC (AV)

15 South Jackson Street, P.O. Box 548, 83001
Telephone: 307-733-7290
Fax: 307-733-5248
Salt Lake City, Utah Office: 39 Exchange Place, Suite 101, 84111.
Telephone: 801-521-0811.
Fax: 801-521-0437.

MEMBERS OF FIRM

Gerry L. Spence, P.C.
Edward P. Moriarity
Robert P. Schuster
Gary L. Shockey
J. Douglas McCalla
Roy A. Jacobson, Jr.
Kent W. Spence
Robert A. Krause

ASSOCIATES

Glen G. Debroder
R. Daniel Fleck
G. Bryan Ulmer, III
Laura N. MacPherson (Not admitted in WY)
David M. Gosar
Gerard R. Bosch
Jeffrey Gooch

Reference: First Interstate Bank, Casper, Wyoming.

For full biographical listings, see the Martindale-Hubbell Law Directory

PUERTO RICO

SAN JUAN, San Juan Dist.

INDIANO, WILLIAMS & WEINSTEIN-BACAL

Hato Rey Tower, 21st Floor, 268 Muñoz Rivera Avenue (Hato Rey), 00918
Telephone: 787-754-2323; 763-0485
Fax: 787-766-3366
Email: iww@microjuris.com

MEMBERS OF FIRM

Stuart A. Weinstein-Bacal
David C. Indiano
Jeffrey M. Williams

ASSOCIATES

Peter W. Miller
Edgar A. Lee-Navas
Edward W. Hill Tollinche
Alexander H. Bopp (Not admitted in PR)

For full biographical listings, see the Martindale-Hubbell Law Directory

JIMÉNEZ, GRAFFAM & LAUSELL

Suite 505, Midtown Building, 421 Muñoz Rivera Avenue, Hato Rey, P.O. Box 366104, 00936-6104
Telephone: 787-767-1030; 767-1000; 767-1061; 767-1064
Telefax: 787-751-4068;
Cable: "Nezte"
RCA Telex: 325-2730
Email: manager@jgl.com *URL:* http://www.jgl.com

MEMBERS OF FIRM

William A. Graffam
Steven C. Lausell
J. Ramón Rivera-Morales
José Juan Torres-Escalera
Raquel M. Dulzaides
Manolo T. Rodríguez-Bird

ASSOCIATES

Patricia A. Garrity
Isabel J. Vélez-Serrano
Edgardo A. Vega-López
José Luis Suárez-Villafañe
Jorge F. Blasini
Ruy V. Díaz-Díaz
Rafael A. Rosado-Marrero

Representative Clients: McAllister Brothers, Inc.; The United Kingdom Steamship P & I Association; The Britannia Steamship Insurance Association; The West of England Ship Owners Mutual Insurance Association; Assurance Foreningen Skuld; The Standard Steamship Owners' P & I Association.

For Complete List of Firm Personnel, See General Section

For full biographical listings, see the Martindale-Hubbell Law Directory

VIRGIN ISLANDS

*CHRISTIANSTED, ST. CROIX,** St. Croix

ALKON, RHEA & HART (AV)

2115 Queen Street, 00820
Telephone: 340-773-3305
Fax: 340-773-4491
URL: http://www.lawyers.com/ar&hlaw

Gordon C. Rhea
Thomas H. Hart, III

ASSOCIATES

Maxwell D. McIntosh
James A. Meaney

OF COUNSEL

Thomas Alkon

For full biographical listings, see the Martindale-Hubbell Law Directory

*CHARLOTTE AMALIE, ST. THOMAS,** St. Thomas

GRUNERT STOUT & BRUCH

24-25 Kongensgade, P.O. Box 1030, 00804
Telephone: 340-774-1320
Fax: 340-774-7839
Email: gsbusvi@viaccess.net
Affiliated with: Solomon Pearl Blum & Quinn LLP, New York, New York and Denver, Colorado.

MEMBERS OF FIRM

John E. Stout
Susan Bruch Moorehead

ASSOCIATE

Gabriel J. Villegas

OF COUNSEL

William L. Blum

For full biographical listings, see the Martindale-Hubbell Law Directory

CANADA ALBERTA

*CALGARY,** Calgary Jud. Dist.

PARLEE McLAWS (AV)

3400 Petro-Canada Centre, 150 - 6th Avenue, SW, T2P 3Y7
Telephone: 403-294-7000
Telecopier: 403-265-8263
Email: lawyers@parlee.com *URL:* http://www.parlee.com
Edmonton, Alberta Office: 15th Floor Manulife Place, 10180 101st Street.
Telephone: 403-423-8500.
Telecopier: 403-423-2870.

MEMBERS OF FIRM

Patrick J. McGovern
Nancy M. Carruthers

ASSOCIATES

Alec N. Silenzi
Morey D. Sair

For Complete List of Firm Personnel, See General Section

For full biographical listings, see the Martindale-Hubbell Law Directory

*EDMONTON,** Edmonton Jud. Dist.

PARLEE McLAWS (AV)

15th Floor Manulife Place, 10180 101st Street, T5J 4K1
Telephone: 403-423-8500
Telecopier: 403-423-2870
Email: lawyers@parlee.com *URL:* http://www.parlee.com
Calgary, Alberta Office: 3400 Petro-Canada Centre, 150 - 6th Avenue, SW.
Telephone: 403-294-7000.
Telecopier: 403-265-8263.

MEMBER OF FIRM

Robert G. McBean

For Complete List of Firm Personnel, See General Section

For full biographical listings, see the Martindale-Hubbell Law Directory

CANADA MANITOBA

*WINNIPEG,** Eastern Jud. Dist.

AIKINS, MACAULAY & THORVALDSON (AV)

Thirtieth Floor, Commodity Exchange Tower, 360 Main Street, R3C 4G1
Telephone: 204-957-0050
Fax: 204-957-0840
Email: amt@aikins.com *URL:* http://www.aikins.com

MEMBERS OF FIRM

Michael J. Mercury, Q.C.
Colin R. MacArthur, Q.C.
Knox B. Foster, Q.C.
Rod E. Stephenson, Q.C.
Cyril G. Labman
Thor J. Hansell
Barbara S. MacDonald

Counsel for: Air Canada; Bank of Montreal; Boeing of Canada; Canada Safeway Limited; Canadian Medical Protective Assn.; The Great West Life Assurance Co.; John Labatt Limited; Russel Metals Inc.; Winnipeg Free Press.

For Complete List of Firm Personnel, See General Section

For full biographical listings, see the Martindale-Hubbell Law Directory

CANADA NEW BRUNSWICK

*FREDERICTON,** York Co.

McINNES COOPER (AV)

Suite 600, 570 Queen Street, P.O. Box 610, E3B 5A6
Telephone: 506-458-8572
Fax: 506-458-9903
Email: mcrfton@mcrlaw.com *URL:* http://www.mcrlaw.com
Halifax, Nova Scotia Office: Summit Place, 1601 Lower Water Street, P.O. Box 730, B3J 2V1.
Telephone: 902-425-6500.
Fax: 902-425-6350. Email: mcrhfx@mcrlaw.com.
St. John's, Newfoundland Office: Baine Johnston Centre, 5th Floor, 10 Fort William Place, P.O. Box 5939, A1C 5X4.
Telephone: 709-722-8735.
Telecopier: 709-722-1763. Email: mcrsj@mcrlaw.com.
Moncton, New Brunswick Office: Place Moncton Place, 655 Main Street, P.O. Box 1368, E1C 8T6.
Telephone: 506-857-8970.
Fax: 506-857-4095. Email: mcrmctn@mcrlaw.com.
Charlottetown, Prince Edward Island Office: BDC Place, Suite 620, 119 Kent Street, C1A 1N3.
Telephone: 902-368-8473.
Fax: 902-368-8346. Email: mcrpei@mcrlaw.com.

PARTNER

David Duncan Young

ASSOCIATES

David D. Eidt
Patrick V. Windle

For Complete List of Firm Personnel, See General Section

For full biographical listings, see the Martindale-Hubbell Law Directory

*MONCTON,** Westmorland Co.

McINNES COOPER (AV)

Barristers, Solicitors & Trade Mark Agents
Place Moncton Place, 655 Main Street, P.O. Box 1368, E1C 8T6
Telephone: 506-857-8970
Fax: 506-857-4095
Email: mcrmctn@mcrlaw.com *URL:* http://www.mcrlaw.com
Halifax, Nova Scotia Office: Summit Place, 1601 Lower Water Street, P.O. Box 730, B3J 2V1.
Telephone: 902-425-6500.
Fax: 902-425-6350. Email: mcrhfx@mcrlaw.com.
St. John's, Newfoundland Office: Baine Johnston Centre, 5th Floor, 10 Fort William Place, P.O. Box 5939, A1C 5X4.
Telephone: 709-722-8735.
Telecopier: 709-722-1763. Email: mcrsj@mcrlaw.com.
Charlottetown, Prince Edward Island Office: BDC Place, Suite 620, 119 Kent Street, C1A 1N3.
Telephone: 902-368-8473.
Fax: 902-368-8346. Email: mcrpei@mcrlaw.com.
Fredericton, New Brunswick Office: Suite 600, 570 Queen Street, P.O. Box 610.
Telephone: 506-458-8572.
Fax: 506-458-9903. Email: mcrfton@mcrlaw.com.

(See Next Column)

McInnes Cooper—Continued

ASSOCIATES

John C. Friel, Q.C. — Christa A. Bourque

For Complete List of Firm Personnel, See General Section

For full biographical listings, see the Martindale-Hubbell Law Directory

*SAINT JOHN,** Saint John Co.

Clark Drummie (AV)

40 Wellington Row, P.O. Box 6850, E2L 4S3
Telephone: 506-633-3800
Telecopier (Automatic): 506-633-3811
Email: cd@nbnet.nb.ca

MEMBERS OF FIRM

Barry R. Morrison, Q.C. — Norman J. Bossé
W. Andrew LeMesurier — J. George Byrne
William B. Richards — Ewan W. Clark

Reference: Royal Bank of Canada.

For Complete List of Firm Personnel, See General Section

For full biographical listings, see the Martindale-Hubbell Law Directory

CANADA NEWFOUNDLAND

*ST. JOHN'S,**

McInnes Cooper (AV)

Barristers, Solicitors & Trade Mark Agents
Baine Johnston Centre, 5th Floor, 10 Fort William Place, P.O. Box 5939, A1C 5X4
Telephone: 709-722-8735
Telecopier: 709-722-1763
Email: mcrsj@mcrlaw.com *URL:* http://www.mcrlaw.com
Halifax, Nova Scotia Office: Summit Place, 1601 Lower Water Street, P.O. Box 730, B3J 2V1.
Telephone: 902-425-6500.
Fax: 902-425-6350. Email: mcrhfx@mcrlaw.com.
Moncton, New Brunswick Office: Place Moncton Place, 655 Main Street, P.O. Box 1368, E1C 8T6.
Telephone: 506-857-8970.
Fax: 506-857-4095. Email: mcrmctn@mcrlaw.com.
Charlottetown, Prince Edward Island Office: BDC Place, Suite 620, 119 Kent Street, C1A 1N3.
Telephone: 902-368-8473.
Fax: 902-368-8346. Email: mcrpei@mcrlaw.com.
Fredericton, New Brunswick Office: Suite 600, 570 Queen Street, P.O. Box 610.
Telephone: 506-458-8572.
Fax: 506-458-9903. Email: mcrfton@mcrlaw.com.

PARTNERS

Thomas R. Kendell — Deborah L. J. Hutchings
Philip J. Buckingham

ASSOCIATE

Genevieve M. Dawson

For Complete List of Firm Personnel, See General Section

For full biographical listings, see the Martindale-Hubbell Law Directory

CANADA NOVA SCOTIA

*HALIFAX,** Regional Munic. of Halifax

McInnes Cooper (AV)

Barristers, Solicitors & Trade Mark Agents
Summit Place, 1601 Lower Water Street, P.O. Box 730, B3J 2V1
Telephone: 902-425-6500
Fax: 902-425-6350
Email: mcrhfx@mcrlaw.com *URL:* http://www.mcrlaw.com
St. John's, Newfoundland Office: Baine Johnston Centre, 5th Floor, 10 Fort William Place, P.O. Box 5939, A1C 5X4.
Telephone: 709-722-8735.
Telecopier: 709-722-1763. Email: mcrsj@mcrlaw.com.
Moncton, New Brunswick Office: Place Moncton Place, 655 Main Street, P.O. Box 1368, E1C 8T6.
Telephone: 506-857-8970.
Fax: 506-857-4095. Email: mcrmctn@mcrlaw.com.

(See Next Column)

Charlottetown, Prince Edward Island Office: BDC Place, Suite 620, 119 Kent Street, C1A 1N3.
Telephone: 902-368-8473.
Fax: 902-368-8346. Email: mcrpei@mcrlaw.com.
Fredericton, New Brunswick Office: Suite 600, 570 Queen Street, P.O. Box 610.
Telephone: 506-458-8572.
Fax: 506-458-9903. Email: mcrfton@mcrlaw.com.

PARTNERS

Stewart McInnes, P.C., Q.C. — Alan J. Stern, Q.C.
Robert G. Belliveau, Q.C. — Christopher C. Robinson, Q.C.
David A. Graves — Deborah K. Smith
Stephen Kingston — John Kulik
Aidan J. Meade — G. Grant Machum
Michelle C. Awad

ASSOCIATES

Tara A. Miller — Janet Clark

For Complete List of Firm Personnel, See General Section

For full biographical listings, see the Martindale-Hubbell Law Directory

CANADA ONTARIO

*HAMILTON,** Regional Munic. of Hamilton-Wentworth

William Morris Law Offices (AV)

151 John Street South, L8N 2C3
Telephone: 905-526-8080
Telecopier: 905-521-1927
Email: wmorris@netinc.ca

William Morris, Q.C. — Robert J. Hooper
Michael J. Kemeny — Allen J. Wynperle

LEGAL SUPPORT PERSONNEL

Jill Trites — Kathy Gaudun

For full biographical listings, see the Martindale-Hubbell Law Directory

KITCHENER, Regional Munic. of Waterloo

Giffen Lee (AV)

50 Queen Street North, P.O. Box 2396, N2H 6M3
Telephone: 519-578-4150
Fax: 519-578-8740
Email: info@GiffenLeeLaw.com *URL:* http://www.GiffenLeeLaw.com

MEMBERS OF FIRM

J. Peter Giffen, Q.C. — Brian R. Wagner
Bruce L. Lee — Philip A. Garbutt
J. Scott Morley — Daniel J. Fife

ASSOCIATES

(Ms.) Milena Protich — Graham M. Bennett
Cindy L. Dickinson — Mitra Golnaraghi
Edward J. Vanderkloet — Donald C. Olson

For full biographical listings, see the Martindale-Hubbell Law Directory

*TORONTO,** Regional Munic. of Toronto

Borden & Elliot (AV)

Barristers & Solicitors
Scotia Plaza, 40 King Street West, M5H 3Y4
Telephone: 416-367-6000
Telecopier: 416-367-6749
Email: info@borden.com *URL:* http://www.borden.com
Ottawa, Ontario Office: Borden Elliot Scott & Aylen, 1000-60 Rue Queen Street.
Telephone: 613-237-5160; 800-661-4237. General
Facsimile: 613-230-8842. IP Dept.
Facsimile: 613-787-3558. Email: ottinfo@scottaylen.com. URL: http://www.borden.com.

Edward A. Ayers, Q.C.

For Complete List of Firm Personnel, See General Section

For full biographical listings, see the Martindale-Hubbell Law Directory

Kelly Affleck Greene (AV)

One First Canadian Place, Suite 840, P.O. Box 489, M5X 1E5
Telephone: 416-360-2800
Fax: 416-360-5960
Email: info@kag.net *URL:* http://www.kag.net

(See Next Column)

OPPENHEIMER WOLFF & DONNELLY LLP, *Minneapolis—Continued*

St. Paul, Minnesota Office: 1700 First National Bank Building, 55101.
Telephone: 651-605-2000.
FAX: 651-605-2100.
Washington, D.C. Office: Oppenheimer Wolff Donnelly & Bayh LLP, 1350 Eye Street, N.W., Suite 200, 20005.
Telephone: 202-312-8000.
FAX: 202-312-8100.
Los Angeles, California Office: 2029 Century Park East, 38th Floor, 90067.
Telephone: 310-788-5000.
FAX: 310-277-1297.
San Jose, California Office: 101 Park Center Plaza, Suite 300, 95113.
Telephone: 408-795-3000.
FAX: 408-795-3100.
Chicago, Illinois Office: Oppenheimer Wolff & Donnelly (Illinois), Two Prudential Plaza, 45th Floor, 180 North Stetson Avenue, 60601.
Telephone: 312-616-1800.
Fax: 312-616-5800.

RESIDENT PARTNERS

William P. Studer
Mark S. Olson
Paula D. Osborn
Cynthia J. Atsatt
David P. Graham

RESIDENT ASSOCIATE

Jacqueline M. Moen

For Complete List of Firm Personnel, See General Section

For full biographical listings, see the Martindale-Hubbell Law Directory

*ST. PAUL,** Ramsey Co.

R. A. AWSUMB & ASSOCIATES, PLC (AV)

1525 Landmark Towers, 345 Saint Peter Street, 55102
Telephone: 651-225-9255
Fax: 651-848-0011
Toll Free: 1-888-225-9566
Email: raawsumb@medrate.com

Robert A. Awsumb

For full biographical listings, see the Martindale-Hubbell Law Directory

*WILLMAR,** Kandiyohi Co.

SCHNEIDER LAW FIRM (AV)

706 South First Street, P.O. Box 776, 56201
Telephone: 320-235-1902
WATS: 800-242-1902
Fax: 320-235-3611
Email: JSJSJamin@aol.com
St. Cloud, Minnesota Office: 925 South First Street, 56302.
Telephone: 320-253-2007.

Ronald H. Schneider (P.A.)

David W. Schneider
Steven C. Wang

Reference: US Bank Willmar.

For full biographical listings, see the Martindale-Hubbell Law Directory

*WINONA,** Winona Co.

STREATER & MURPHY, P.A. (AV)

64 East Fourth Street, 55987-0310
Telephone: 507-454-2925
Fax: 507-454-2929
Email: kentg@luminet.net

John Borman

Representative Clients: Winona Banc Holding Co.; Winona National and Savings Bank; Town & Country State Bank; Winona Daily News; Winona School District; Badger Construction Equipment Co.; Winona General Hospital Assn.; EMD Associates, Inc.; Fastenal Co.; Hiawatha Education Foundation.

For Complete List of Firm Personnel, See General Section

For full biographical listings, see the Martindale-Hubbell Law Directory

MISSISSIPPI

BILOXI, Harrison Co.

BROWN, WATT & BUCHANAN, P.A. (AV)

115 Main Street, P.O. Box 1377, 39533-1377
Telephone: 228-374-2999
Telecopier: 228-435-7090
Email: mail@bwblaw.com *URL:* http://www.bwblaw.com
Pascagoula, Mississippi Office: 3112 Canty Street, P.O. Box 2220.
Telephone: 228-762-0035.
Fax: 228-762-0299.

Raymond L. Brown
W. Lee Watt
Patrick R. Buchanan
W. Mark Edwards
A. Kelly Sessoms, III
Alan K. Sudduth

Representative Clients: Beaird-Poulan-Weedeater; Black & Decker; Brown & Williamson Corp.; Chicago Pneumatic; Deere & Co.; Emerson Electric; Honda North America; 3M; Olin Winchester.

For full biographical listings, see the Martindale-Hubbell Law Directory

JUDY M. GUICE A PROFESSIONAL ASSOCIATION (AV)

750 Dr. Martin Luther King Jr. Boulevard, P.O. Box 1919, 39533
Telephone: 228-374-9787
Fax: 228-374-9436
Email: judy@judyguice.com *URL:* http://www.judyguice.com

Judy Guice

For full biographical listings, see the Martindale-Hubbell Law Directory

MINOR AND ASSOCIATES (AV)

A Partnership including a Professional Association
160 Main Street, Drawer 1388, 39533-1388
Telephone: 228-374-5151
Fax: 228-374-6630
Email: pminoratty@aol.com

Paul S. Minor (P.A.)

Mark D. Lumpkin
James R. Reeves, Jr.
Christopher C. VanCleave

For full biographical listings, see the Martindale-Hubbell Law Directory

PAGE, MANNINO, PERESICH & MCDERMOTT (AV)

A Professional Limited Liability Company
759 Vieux Marché Mall, P.O. Drawer 289, 39533
Telephone: 228-374-2100
Facsimile: 228-432-5539
Email: pmp@pmp.org

MEMBERS OF FIRM

Lyle M. Page (Resident)
Frederick J. Mannino (Resident)
Ronald G. Peresich (Resident)
Stephen G. Peresich (Resident)
Michael B. McDermott (Resident)
Tere Richardson Steel (Resident)
Michael E. Whitehead (Resident)
Mary Alexander Nichols (Resident)
David M. Allen (Resident)

ASSOCIATES

Henry N. Dick, III
Les W. Smith (Resident)
Emilie Whitehead
Kaara L. Liskow
Joel L. Blackledge

Representative Clients: United States Fidelity & Guaranty Co.; St. Paul Fire & Marine Insurance Co.; Crawford & Co.; Anheuser-Busch Corp.
General Counsel for: Peoples Bank of Biloxi, Mississippi; Biloxi Regional Medical Center; Bank of Mississippi (Gulf Coast Division).

For full biographical listings, see the Martindale-Hubbell Law Directory

RUSHING & GUICE (AV)

683 Water Street, P.O. Box 1925, 39533-1925
Telephone: 228-374-2313
Telecopier: 228-374-8155
Email: rushguice@rushing-guice.com *URL:* http://www.rushing-guice.com

MEMBERS OF FIRM

Charles L. Rushing (1881-1923)
William L. Guice (1887-1971)
William Lee Guice III

OF COUNSEL

Jacob D. Guice

ASSOCIATES

R. Scott Wells
Maria M. Cobb

LEGAL SUPPORT PERSONNEL

Antonia Strong

For full biographical listings, see the Martindale-Hubbell Law Directory

*CLARKSDALE,** Coahoma Co.

HENKE-BUFKIN, A PROFESSIONAL ASSOCIATION (AV)

408 Hopson Street, P.O. Box 39, 38614
Telephone: 601-624-8500
Telecopier: 601-624-8040

W. Kurt Henke
Elizabeth T. Bufkin
Michael D. Stevens
Jeffrey S. Dilley
Roy Jefferson Allen

OF COUNSEL

William Cliff Heaton

Reference: United Southern Bank, Clarksdale, Mississippi.

For full biographical listings, see the Martindale-Hubbell Law Directory

*CLEVELAND,** Bolivar Co.

JACKS, ADAMS & WESTERFIELD, P.A. (AV)

106 South Pearman Avenue, P.O. Box 1209, 38732
Telephone: 662-843-6171
FAX: 662-843-6176
Email: jaws@tecinfo.com

Gerald H. Jacks
William S. Adams, Jr.
Andrew M. W. Westerfield
S. David Norquist
Thomas B. Janoush

General Counsel for: The Valley Bank; Cleveland School District 4; Commonwealth National Life Insurance Co.
Area Counsel for: Commercial Union; United States Fidelity & Guaranty Co.; Baxter International, Inc.; New Hampshire Insurance Co.; American International Adjustment Co.; Imperial Casualty Co.; Self Insurers Service, Inc.

For full biographical listings, see the Martindale-Hubbell Law Directory

*GULFPORT,** Harrison Co.

ALLEN, VAUGHN, COBB & HOOD, P.A. (AV)

One Hancock Plaza, Suite 1209, P.O. Drawer 4108, 39502-4108
Telephone: 601-864-4011
Fax: 601-864-4852
Email: avchlaw@sunherald.infinet.com

Harry R. Allen
Thomas E. Vaughn
David L. Cobb
Billy W. Hood
Joy Lambert Phillips
Robert W. Atkinson
Benjamin U. Bowden
Richard B. Tubertini
Rodney Douglas Robinson
E. Colette Towles
David W. Crane
John A. Foxworth, Jr.

J. Adrian Smith
Michael J. Casano

OF COUNSEL

D. Knox White

LEGAL SUPPORT PERSONNEL

Kevin C. Stachowski (Paralegal)

For full biographical listings, see the Martindale-Hubbell Law Directory

DUKES, DUKES, KEATING AND FANECA, P.A. (AV)

2909 13th Street, 6th Floor, P.O. Drawer W, 39501
Telephone: 228-868-1111
Fax: 228-863-2886
Email: ddkf@ddkf.com

William F. Dukes
Walter W. Dukes
Cy Faneca
Phillip W. Jarrell

Thomas William Busby

For Complete List of Firm Personnel, See General Section

For full biographical listings, see the Martindale-Hubbell Law Directory

BOYCE HOLLEMAN A PROFESSIONAL CORPORATION (AV)

1913 15th Street, P.O. Drawer 1030, 39502
Telephone: 228-863-3142; 1-800-863-3140
Telecopier: 228-863-9829
Email: boyce1913@aol.com

Boyce Holleman

Timothy C. Holleman
Leslie Dean Holleman
David J. "Jeff" White

References: Hancock Bank, Gulfport; Merchants Bank & Trust Co., Gulfport; Bank of Wiggins, Wiggins, Mississippi.

For full biographical listings, see the Martindale-Hubbell Law Directory

HOPKINS, CRAWLEY, BAGWELL & UPSHAW, P.L.L.C. (AV)

2701 24th Avenue, P.O. Box 1510, 39501-4941
Telephone: 228-864-2200
Mississippi and USA Wats: 1-800-421-3629
Fax: 228-868-9358; 228-863-4227
Email: Hopkins@MSLawyer.com
Jackson, Mississippi Office: 499 South President Street, Second Floor, Suite 1.
Telephone: 601-355-6510.
Fax: 601-355-6503. Email: TCrawley@MSLawyer.com.

MEMBERS OF FIRM

Alben N. Hopkins
Timothy D. Crawley
Douglas Bagwell
Jessica Sibley Upshaw
Thomas Alan Waller

ASSOCIATES

Raymond D. Carter
Kenneth S. Womack
Mary Benton-Shaw
Pat Sharkey Burke, Jr.
David E. Wilson
Laura Faye Paulk
Ronald C. Small
(Not admitted in MS)

Representative Clients: Coregis Group; General Cable Corp.; Insurance Company of North America; Liberty Mutual Insurance Group; Reliance Insurance Co.; USX Corp.; Employers Insurance of Wausau; American International Group (AIG); Quaker Chemical Corp.

For full biographical listings, see the Martindale-Hubbell Law Directory

*JACKSON,** Hinds Co.

SULLIVAN AND SULLIVAN (AV)

Suite 200, 5448 I-55 North, 39211
Telephone: 601-952-0799
Facsimile: 601-952-0599;
Cable Address: "Sullaw"

MEMBERS OF FIRM

John C. Sullivan, Sr. (1910-1993)
John C. Sullivan, Jr.

ASSOCIATE

Patricia Alexander Killgore

For full biographical listings, see the Martindale-Hubbell Law Directory

*LAUREL,** Jones Co.

MELVIN & MELVIN (AV)

Sawmill Road, P.O. Box 142, 39441-0142
Telephone: 601-426-6306; 426-6307
Telecopier: 601-649-7571

MEMBERS OF FIRM

Leonard B. Melvin (1896-1972)
Leonard B. Melvin, Jr.

For full biographical listings, see the Martindale-Hubbell Law Directory

*OXFORD,** Lafayette Co.

FREELAND & FREELAND (AV)

1013 Jackson Avenue, P.O. Box 269, 38655
Telephone: 662-234-3414
Telecopier: 662-234-0604
Email: thf4@watervalley.net

MEMBERS OF FIRM

T. H. Freeland, III
T. H. Freeland, IV

Representative Clients: The Ohio Casualty Group; Crum & Forester.

For full biographical listings, see the Martindale-Hubbell Law Directory

*PASCAGOULA,** Jackson Co.

BROWN, WATT & BUCHANAN, P.A. (AV)

3112 Canty Street, P.O. Box 2220, 39569-2220
Telephone: 228-762-0035
Telecopier: 228-762-0299
Email: mail@bwblaw.com *URL:* http://www.bwblaw.com
Biloxi, Mississippi Office: 115 Main Street, P.O. Box 1377.
Telephone: 228-374-2999.
Fax: 228-435-7090.

Raymond L. Brown
W. Lee Watt
Patrick R. Buchanan
W. Mark Edwards
A. Kelly Sessoms, III
Alan K. Sudduth

Representative Clients: Beaird-Poulan-Weedeater; Black & Decker; Brown & Williamson Corp.; Chicago Pneumatic; Deere & Co.; Emerson Electric; Honda North America; 3M; Olin Winchester.

For full biographical listings, see the Martindale-Hubbell Law Directory

COLINGO, WILLIAMS, HEIDELBERG, STEINBERGER & McELHANEY, P.A. (AV)

711 Delmas Avenue, P.O. Box 1407, 39568-1407
Telephone: 228-762-8021
FAX: 228-762-7589
Email: info@colingowilliams.com *URL:* http://www.ColingoWilliams.com

(See Next Column)

COLINGO, WILLIAMS, HEIDELBERG, STEINBERGER & MCELHANEY P.A., *Pascagoula—Continued*

Roy C. Williams
James H. Heidelberg
James H. Colmer, Jr.

Robert Michael Cunningham, II

Representative Clients: International Paper Co.; R.J. Reynolds; CBS Corp.; Kemper Group; Singing River Hospital System; Mississippi Gulf Coast Regional Wastewater Authority; Medical Assurance Company of Mississippi; Mutual Assurance of Alabama; Dole Food Co.

For full biographical listings, see the Martindale-Hubbell Law Directory

ROBERT A. PRITCHARD (AV)

934 Jackson Avenue, P.O. Drawer 1707, 39567-1707
Telephone: 228-769-2211; 1-800-340-2240
Fax: 228-762-6005
Email: rap@datasyc.com
Harriston, Mississippi Office: General, Asb/Sil. 100 Old Harriston Road.
Telephone: 601-786-6200; 888-786-6200.
Fax: 601-786-6211.

ASSOCIATE

Christopher E. Fitzgerald

For full biographical listings, see the Martindale-Hubbell Law Directory

MISSOURI

*COLUMBIA,** Boone Co.

RICHARD C. THOMAS (AV)

609 East Broadway, 65201
Telephone: 573-442-3000
Fax: 573-449-1094

References: Boone County National Bank; Mercantile Bank.

For full biographical listings, see the Martindale-Hubbell Law Directory

KANSAS CITY, Jackson, Clay, Platte & Cass Cos.

BARTIMUS, FRICKLETON & PRESLEY, A PROFESSIONAL CORPORATION (AV)

23rd Floor City Center Square, 1100 Main Street, 64196
Telephone: 816-842-2300
Fax: 816-421-2111
Email: bfplaw@bfplaw.com *URL:* http://www.bfplaw.com
Jefferson City, Missouri Office: 122 East High, Suite 200, 65101.
Telephone: 573-659-4454.

James R. Bartimus
Kirk R. Presley
James P. Frickleton
Peter S. Obetz

Stephen M. Gorny
Christopher A. Wright

OF COUNSEL

Edward D. Robertson, Jr. (Resident, Jefferson City Office)
Julie C. Frickleton

LEGAL SUPPORT PERSONNEL

LEGAL ASSISTANTS

Tammy J. Gilliams
Patricia E. Cook
Laura M. Burbach
Martha C. Fann

For full biographical listings, see the Martindale-Hubbell Law Directory

FRANKE & SCHULTZ, A PROFESSIONAL CORPORATION (AV)

1312 Commerce Tower, 911 Main Street, 64105
Telephone: 816-421-7100
Telecopier: 816-421-7915
Email: Franke.Schultz@Micro.com
Springfield, Missouri Office: 300 John Q. Hammons Pkwy., Suite 701, 65806.
Telephone: 417-863-0040.
Fax: 417-863-6286.
Overland Park, Kansas Office: 5340 College, 66211.
Telephone: 913-327-7661.
Fax: 913-327-7669.

John E. Franke
Ryan E. Karaim
John G. Schultz
Jill Frost
John L. Mullen
Keith A. Cary
Bradley C. Nielsen
Wendell E. Koerner, Jr.

(See Next Column)

Cari F. Walsh
Laurel Stevenson
Michael J. Tubbesing
Shawn G. Foster
Andrew D. Hennier
John H. Kizer
Edward J. Barbosa

For full biographical listings, see the Martindale-Hubbell Law Directory

REDFEARN & BROWN, A PROFESSIONAL CORPORATION (AV)

Suite 814, 1125 Grand Boulevard, 64106
Telephone: 816-421-5301
FAX: 816-421-3785
Stockton Office: 12 Public Square, P.O. BOX 299.
Telephone: 417-276-6250.

Paul L. Redfearn
Daniel R. Brown

OF COUNSEL

Michael D. Holzknecht, P.C.

LEGAL SUPPORT PERSONNEL

Denise J. Davis (Senior Legal Assistant)

For full biographical listings, see the Martindale-Hubbell Law Directory

STITES, HOPKINS & FAIR (AV)

A Partnership including Professional Corporations and Associations
1101 Walnut, Suite 1400, 64106-2215
Telephone: 816-842-8889
Fax: 816-842-3088
1-800-899-8874

Ronald J. Stites (P.C.)
William C. Hopkins, II

Diane L. Fair
Carol A. Lindgren-Bron

OF COUNSEL

Sandra C. Midkiff
Elizabeth Diane Baker
John B. Meyer

For full biographical listings, see the Martindale-Hubbell Law Directory

WAGSTAFF & CARTMELL, LLP (AV)

Suite 1240, 4520 Main Street, 64111
Telephone: 816-701-1100
Fax: 816-531-2372

Thomas W. Wagstaff
Robert G. Rooney
Thomas P. Cartmell
Jonathan P. Kieffer

Marc K. Erickson
Thomas L. Wagstaff

For full biographical listings, see the Martindale-Hubbell Law Directory

ST. LOUIS, (Independent City)

ABELE & SANDERSON, L.L.C. (AV)

Suite 1024, 1015 Locust, 63101-1323
Telephone: 314-241-3123; 1-800-886-3123
Fax: 314-241-4361
Email: abelesand@aol.com *URL:* http://www.lawyers.com/abele&sanderson

Charles R. Abele
M. Melinda Sanderson

For full biographical listings, see the Martindale-Hubbell Law Directory

COFFEY & GRIESBACH (AV)

6202 Columbia Avenue, 63139
Telephone: 314-647-0033
Fax: 314-647-8231
Email: candg@I1.net *URL:* http://www.lawyers.com/c&g

Mary Coffey
Toni Griesbach

For full biographical listings, see the Martindale-Hubbell Law Directory

THE FLOYD LAW FIRM, P.C. (AV)

8151 Clayton Road #202, 63117-1103
Telephone: 314-863-4114
Telecopier: 314-863-4150
URL: http://www.lawyers.com/injurylaw

Walter L. Floyd
Mark L. Floyd
Richard Mixson

For full biographical listings, see the Martindale-Hubbell Law Directory

GREENBERG & PLEBAN (AV)

100 South Fourth Street, Suite 600, 63102
Telephone: 314-241-4141
Telecopier: 314-241-1038

Burton M. Greenberg
C. John Pleban

(See Next Column)

GREENBERG & PLEBAN—*Continued*

ASSOCIATES

Karen A. Greenberg Michael J. Schaller
Richard P. Hereford

OF COUNSEL

Sarah Shelledy Pleban

Reference: Boatmen's National Bank.

For full biographical listings, see the Martindale-Hubbell Law Directory

THE HOLLORAN LAW FIRM, P.C. (AV)

906 Olive Street, Suite 1200, 63101
Telephone: 314-621-2121
FAX: 314-621-8512

James P. Holloran
Thomas Lee Stewart
Jan Adams
Andrew A. O'Brien
Thomas E. Schwartz

COUNSEL

Charles V. Marshall

For full biographical listings, see the Martindale-Hubbell Law Directory

THE HULLVERSON LAW FIRM (AV)

Suite 1550, 1010 Market Street, 63101-2091
Telephone: 314-421-2313
Fax: 314-421-2341
URL: http://www.hullverson.com

Everett Hullverson (1897-1975)
Thomas C. Hullverson
Stephen H. Ringkamp
Philip C. Denton
Spencer E. Farris
Mark J. Becker
John E. Hullverson
Theresa A. Appelbaum

For full biographical listings, see the Martindale-Hubbell Law Directory

ROBERTS, PERRYMAN, BOMKAMP & MEIVES, P.C. (AV)

Suite 2300, One Mercantile Center, 63101
Telephone: 314-421-1850
Cable Address: "Henrogo"
Telecopier: 314-421-4346
Email: rpbm@istnet.net
Belleville, Illinois Office: 23 Public Square, Suite 402.
Telephone: 618-277-9955.

Ted L. Perryman
Gary W. Bomkamp
John I. Schaberg
John L. Walker
Thomas J. Kernell
Michael P. McDonald, Jr.

Reference: Boatmen's National Bank.

For full biographical listings, see the Martindale-Hubbell Law Directory

*SPRINGFIELD,** Greene Co.

HARRISON, TUCKER & HYDE, LLP (AV)

1121 South Glenstone, 65804
Telephone: 417-831-4046
Fax: 417-831-4989
Email: 100576.2300@compuserve.com

MEMBERS OF FIRM

Jeffrey H. Harrison
James D. Tucker
Kent O. Hyde
William C. Love
Brian E. Hamburg
Aaron P. Lyons

For full biographical listings, see the Martindale-Hubbell Law Directory

WILLIAM H. MCDONALD & ASSOCIATES, P.C. (AV)

300 South Jefferson, Suite 600, P.O. Box 1245, 65801
Telephone: 417-869-0581
Facsimile: 417-831-7852
Email: mcdassoc@dialnet.net *URL:* http://www.mcdonaldassoc.com

William H. McDonald

William Craig Hosmer
Stuart H. King
James Richard Royce
James A. Endicott
David Andrew Collins
Dana A. Chamblee
Joseph S. Dressner
Eric O. Nau
Venus V. Harry

For full biographical listings, see the Martindale-Hubbell Law Directory

LAW OFFICES OF ROBERT M. N. PALMER, P.C. (AV)

The Holland Building, 205 Park Central East, Suite 511, P.O. Box 5720, 65801-5720
Telephone: 417-865-3234
Fax: 417-865-1698
Email: info@palmerlaw.com *URL:* http://www.palmerlaw.com

Robert M. N. Palmer William G. Petrus, Jr.

(See Next Column)

Chantel L. Kelly

OF COUNSEL

Waco Carter

LEGAL SUPPORT PERSONNEL

LEGAL ASSISTANTS

A. Lee Worman Cliff Carter

For full biographical listings, see the Martindale-Hubbell Law Directory

MONTANA

*BILLINGS,** Yellowstone Co.

CROWLEY, HAUGHEY, HANSON, TOOLE & DIETRICH, P.L.L.P. (AV)

500 Transwestern II, 490 North 31st Street, P.O. Box 2529, 59103
Telephone: 406-252-3441
Fax: 406-259-4159
Email: crowley@crowleylaw.com
Helena, Montana Office: IBM Building, 100 North Park Avenue, Suite 300, 59601.
Telephone: 406-449-4165.
Fax: 406-449-5149.
Kalispell, Montana Office: 431 1st Avenue West, 59901.
Telephone: 406-752-6644.
Fax: 406-752-5108.
Williston, North Dakota Office: 113 East Broadway, 58801.
Telephone: 701-572-2200.
Fax: 701-572-7072.

OF COUNSEL

Bruce R. Toole George C. Dalthorp

MEMBERS OF FIRM

Ronald R. Lodders
Christopher Mangen, Jr.
Bruce A. Fredrickson
Leonard H. Smith

Representative Clients: Montana Power Co.; First Interstate Bank of Commerce; MDU Resources Group, Inc.; Chevron U.S.A., Inc.; Noranda Minerals Corp.; United Parcel Service.
Insurance Clients: Farmers Insurance Group; New York Life Insurance Co.

For Complete List of Firm Personnel, See General Section

For full biographical listings, see the Martindale-Hubbell Law Directory

*MISSOULA,** Missoula Co.

PHILLIPS & BOHYER, P.C. (AV)

Suite 301 River Front Place, 283 W. Front Street, P.O. Box 8569, 59807-8569
Telephone: 406-721-7880
Telecopier: 406-549-2253
Email: phillips@montana.com

Robert J. Phillips
John E. Bohyer
Tammy Wyatt-Shaw
Fred Simpson, Jr.
John F. Jenks

LEGAL SUPPORT PERSONNEL

Mary J. Maynard
Elaine LaPointe-Vetter
Martin Suda

For full biographical listings, see the Martindale-Hubbell Law Directory

NEBRASKA

*LINCOLN,** Lancaster Co.

CLINE, WILLIAMS, WRIGHT, JOHNSON & OLDFATHER (AV)

1900 U.S. Bank Building, 233 South 13th Street, 68508
Telephone: 402-474-6900
Fax: 402-474-5393
Email: postmaster@cline-law.com *URL:* http://www.cline-law.com
Omaha, Nebraska Office: Suite 720, One Pacific Place, 1125 South 103rd Street, 68124.
Telephone: 402-397-1700.
Fax: 402-397-1806.

ATTORNEYS

Allen L. Graves
Charles M. Pallesen, Jr.
Fredric H. Kauffman
Donald F. Burt
Alan E. Peterson
Stephen E. Gehring
Robert J. Routh
Kevin Colleran
L. Bruce Wright
James M. Bausch
Larry A. Holle
David R. Buntain
Stephen H. Nelsen
Michael C. Mueller

(See Next Column)

CLINE, WILLIAMS, WRIGHT, JOHNSON & OLDFATHER, *Lincoln—Continued*

ATTORNEYS (Continued)

Lauren W. Wismer
Daniel R. Stogsdill
Scott D. Kelly
Terry R. Wittler
Pamela Hastings Carrier
Mark A. Christensen
Richard P. Garden, Jr.
Shawn D. Renner
John C. Miles
Mary Kay Frank
Thomas C. Huston
Sonya S. Ekart
Don R. Janssen
Susan Kubert Sapp
Kevin J. Schneider
Andrew D. Strotman
Jill Gossin Jensen
Rochelle A. Mullen
John L. Horan
Bryan S. Hatch
Steven C. Likes
Tracy A. Oldemeyer
Jolene M. Papa
Timothy G. Aschoff
Eric N. Bergquist
Janis J. Winterhof
Andrea Dylan Snowden

OF COUNSEL

Charles E. Wright
Richard P. Jeffries
Mary M. Campbell

RETIRED PARTNERS

Flavel A. Wright (Retired)
Warren C. Johnson (Retired)
Charles E. Oldfather (1927-1998)

Representative Clients: U.S. Bank National Association; University of Nebraska; Nebraska Medical Assn.; Saint Elizabeth Regional Medical Center; Media of Nebraska; Cargill Inc.; State Farm Insurance Cos.; Wal-Mart Stores, Inc.; Textron/Cushman; Isco, Inc.

For full biographical listings, see the Martindale-Hubbell Law Directory

*OMAHA,** Douglas Co.

CLINE, WILLIAMS, WRIGHT, JOHNSON & OLDFATHER (AV)

One Pacific Place, 1125 South 103rd Street, Suite 720, 68124
Telephone: 402-397-1700
Fax: 402-397-1806
Email: postmaster@cline-law.com *URL:* http://www.cline-law.com
Lincoln, Nebraska Office: 1900 U.S. Bank Building, 233 South 13th Street, 68508.
Telephone: 402-474-6900.
Fax: 402-474-5393.

ATTORNEYS

Donald F. Burt
Stephen E. Gehring
James M. Bausch
Michael C. Mueller
Daniel R. Stogsdill
Scott D. Kelly
John C. Miles
Mary Kay Frank
Andrew D. Strotman
Rochelle A. Mullen
Steven C. Likes
Tracy A. Oldemeyer
Timothy G. Aschoff

OF COUNSEL

Richard P. Jeffries

Representative Clients: U.S. Bank National Association; University of Nebraska; Nebraska Medical Assn.; Saint Elizabeth Regional Medical Center; Media of Nebraska; Cargill Inc.; State Farm Insurance Cos.; Wal-Mart Stores, Inc.; Textron/Cushman; ISCO, Inc.

For full biographical listings, see the Martindale-Hubbell Law Directory

NEVADA

*LAS VEGAS,** Clark Co.

EDWARDS, SOOY & BYRON, A PROFESSIONAL CORPORATION (AV(T))

3960 Howard Hughes Parkway Fifth Floor, 89109
Telephone: 702-474-0861
Fax: 702-474-4538
Email: esb-legal.com *URL:* http://www.esb-legal.com
San Diego, California Office: 101 West Broadway, Ninth Floor, 92101.
Telephone: 619-231-1500.
Fax: 619-231-1588.

Michael M. Edwards (Not admitted in NV)
Richard R. Sooy
Thomas W. Byron

Alfred Paul Centofanti, III
Bart M. Blechschmidt
Michael M. Edwards, Jr.

For full biographical listings, see the Martindale-Hubbell Law Directory

GALATZ, EARL, & ASSOCIATES (AV)

710 South Fourth Street, 89101
Telephone: 702-386-0000
Fax: 702-384-0394
Email: neilgalatz@aol.com *URL:* http://www.lawyers.com/galatzlaw

(See Next Column)

Neil G. Galatz
Allan R. Earl

For full biographical listings, see the Martindale-Hubbell Law Directory

LEFEBVRE, BARRON & VIVONE, CHTD. (AV)

1404 South Jones Boulevard, 89146-1231
Telephone: 702-383-8668
Facsimile: 702-383-6828
Email: lb@coam.net

Alan J. Lefebvre
David L. Barron
Thomas J. Vivone
Raymond W. Holland
Michelle O. Tobler
William Howard Pruitt
Bradley V. Gibbons
Jared Casper (Not admitted in NV)
Kevin S. Smith

LEGAL SUPPORT PERSONNEL

Jennifer L. Hageman

For full biographical listings, see the Martindale-Hubbell Law Directory

MAINOR & HARRIS (AV)

A Partnership of Professional Corporations
530 South Sixth Street, 89101
Telephone: 702-385-1400
Fax: 702-385-9408
Email: admin@mainorandharris.com *URL:* http://www.lawyers.com/mainorandharris

W. Randall Mainor (A Professional Corporation)
Richard A. Harris (A Professional Corporation)
Clark Seegmiller
Robert M. Adams
Nancy Quon
Robert W. Cottle

Reference: First Security Bank of Nevada, Las Vegas, Nevada.

For full biographical listings, see the Martindale-Hubbell Law Directory

PICO & MITCHELL (AV)

2000 South Eastern Avenue, 89104
Telephone: 702-457-9099
FAX: 702-457-8451
Email: lawyers@picomitchell.com

MEMBERS OF FIRM

James F. Pico
Bert O. Mitchell
Christy Brad Escobar
James R. Rosenberger
E. Breen Arntz

ASSOCIATES

Michelle Schwarz
Rebecca L. Mastrangelo
Jill M. Chase
Daniel E. Carvalho
Stephen H. Rogers

Representative Clients: Home Insurance Co.; State Farm Mutual Insurance Co.; Industrial Indemnity Insurance Co.; Great American Insurance Co.; Argonaut Insurance Cos.; Clark County Medical Society; Rose de Lima Hospital; Fairway Chevrolet; American States Insurance Co.; The Hartford Insurance Co.

For full biographical listings, see the Martindale-Hubbell Law Directory

SCHRECK MORRIS (AV)

1200 Bank of America Plaza, 300 South Fourth Street, 89101
Telephone: 702-382-2101
Fax: 702-382-8135; 702-474-9422
URL: http://www.schreckmorris.com
Reno, Nevada Office: 100 West Liberty, Suite 940, 89501.
Telephone: 775-322-7777.
Facsimile: 775-322-7791.

MEMBERS OF FIRM

Frank A. Schreck
Steve Morris
Andrew S. Brignone
Leslie Terry Jones
Mary Kristina Pickering
John A. Godfrey
Ann Morgan
Sean T. McGowan
Ellen Schulhofer
James J. Pisanelli
Clark V. Vellis
Todd L. Bice

ASSOCIATES

James R. Chamberlain
Dennis V. Gallagher
Margaret L. Sanner
F. Edward Mulholland, II
Elizabeth M. Fielder
Elayna Youchah
Sonia C. Vermeys
Denise Michaelides
Mary J. Drury
John P. Desmond
Adam P. Segal
Matthew McCaughey
Amelia R. De Los Santos
Wendy Medura
Robert J. Grasso
Shawn G. Pearson
David Dornak
Matthew L. Heinhold
Paul D. Colton

For full biographical listings, see the Martindale-Hubbell Law Directory

Las Vegas—Continued

VANNAH COSTELLO CANEPA RIEDY & RUBINO (AV)

A Partnership including a Professional Corporation
Greystone, 1850 East Flamingo, Suite 236, 89119
Telephone: 702-369-4161
Fax: 702-369-0104
Email: vannahnet@vannahnet.com

MEMBERS OF FIRM

Robert D. Vannah (Chartered)
Nathan M. Costello
Scott K. Canepa
Terry W. Riedy
Michael C. Rubino

ASSOCIATES

Connie J. Forsythe
Shawn D. Dorman
Adam Ganz
Denise M. Cooper
Jeffrey Ferguson
Matthew Vannah
Ronald J. Flinders
Russell M. Rowe
Jonathan G. Lattie (Not admitted in NV)

Representative Clients: Prudential Property and Casualty Insurance Co.; Continental Insurance Health Care; Chubb Group of Insurance; Reliance Insurance Co.; Transamerica Insurance Group; Foremost Insurance Co.; CNA Insurance Co.; Scottsdale Insurance Co.; The Maryland Insurance Group; Insurance Company of the West.

For full biographical listings, see the Martindale-Hubbell Law Directory

*RENO,** Washoe Co.

BRADLEY, DRENDEL & JEANNEY (AV)

401 Flint Street, P.O. Box 1987, 89505
Telephone: 775-329-2273
Fax: 775-329-6513
Email: bdandj@worldnet.att.net *URL:* http://www.lawyers.com/bd&jlaw

Bill Bradley
Joseph S. Bradley
Thomas E. Drendel
William C. Jeanney

OF COUNSEL

William O. "Bud" Bradley
John Squire Drendel

For full biographical listings, see the Martindale-Hubbell Law Directory

ERICKSON, THORPE & SWAINSTON, LTD. (AV)

99 West Arroyo Street, P.O. Box 3559, 89505
Telephone: 702-786-3930
Fax: 702-786-4160
Email: etsreno@aol.com

Roger L. Erickson
Donald A. Thorpe
George W. Swainston
William G. Cobb
Gary A. Cardinal
Thomas Peter Beko
John A. Aberasturi
Paul M. Bertone
Lisa E. Bruce
John C. Boyden

Representative Clients: Bridgestone/Firestone, Inc.; Brown and Williamson Tobacco Corp.; Chrysler Motors Corp.; Dow Corning; Reno Toyota/Lexus; Supply One, Inc.; U.S. Rentals, Inc.; Toys R US; Owens Corning.

For full biographical listings, see the Martindale-Hubbell Law Directory

NEW HAMPSHIRE

*LACONIA,** Belknap Co.

NORMANDIN, CHENEY & O'NEIL (AV)

Normandin Square, 213 Union Avenue, P.O. Box 575, 03247-0575
Telephone: 603-524-4380
Fax: 603-528-6831
Email: nco@lr.net

MEMBERS OF FIRM

A. Gerard O'Neil
A.G. O'Neil, Jr.

ASSOCIATE

Anne Marshall Rice

OF COUNSEL

Duncan J. Farmer

Counsel for: Laconia Savings Bank; Lakes Region Mental Health Center; Laconia Airport Authority; Central New Hampshire Realty, Inc.; All Metals Industries, Inc.; Lakes Region Anesthesiology, P.A.; Cormier Corp.; Scotia Technology; Vemaline Products.

For Complete List of Firm Personnel, See General Section

For full biographical listings, see the Martindale-Hubbell Law Directory

*MANCHESTER,** Hillsborough Co.

SHEEHAN PHINNEY BASS + GREEN, PROFESSIONAL ASSOCIATION (AV)

Hampshire Plaza, 1000 Elm Street, P.O. Box 3701, 03105-3701
Telephone: 603-668-0300
800-625-SPBG
Fax: 603-627-8121
Email: postmaster@sheehan.com *URL:* http://www.sheehan.com
Portsmouth, New Hampshire Office: Old City Hall, 126 Daniel Street.
Telephone: 603-433-2111.
Fax: 603-433-3126.
Concord, New Hampshire Office: 143 North Main Street.
Telephone: 603-223-2020.
Fax: 603-224-8899.

James E. Higgins
Peter F. Kearns
James Q. Shirley
William J. Donovan
Edward A. Haffer
Michael C. Harvell
Stephen E. Weyl
Peter S. Cowan
Katherine M. Hanna
Douglas G. Verge
Christopher Cole
Robert R. Lucic
David W. McGrath
James F. Ogorchock

Representative Clients: Anheuser-Busch, Inc.; Bank of New Hampshire Corp.; The Elliot Hospital of Manchester; Granite State Packing Co.; Moore Business Forms, Inc.; New Hampshire College; New Hampshire Dental Service Corp.; New Hampshire Yankee Electric Corp.; Numerica Financial Corp.

For Complete List of Firm Personnel, See General Section

For full biographical listings, see the Martindale-Hubbell Law Directory

NEW JERSEY

BEDMINSTER, Somerset Co.

PURCELL, RIES, SHANNON, MULCAHY & O'NEILL (AV)

One Pluckemin Way, P.O. Box 754, 07921
Telephone: 908-658-3800
Fax: 908-658-4659
Email: general@prsmo.com *URL:* http://www.prsmo.com
Philadelphia, Pennsylvania Office: 12th Floor, East Tower, Centre Square, 1500 Market Square.
Telephone: 215-665-5602.
Fax: 215-569-8228.

MEMBERS OF FIRM

Eugene M. Purcell
William P. Ries
John J. Shannon
Thomas M. Mulcahy
Michael F. O'Neill
David M. Hawkins
Joseph R. Purcell
Kevin R. Brotz
John M. Bowens
Kevin Kovacs
Kenneth D. Merin
Valerie K. Bollheimer
Andrew L. Indeck
Joseph M. Donegan
Mark Mattia

ASSOCIATES

Rita F. Barone
Kathleen J. Devlin
Paul L. Gallagher
Gary Grabas
John R. Haggerty
William T. Hilliard
Eric J. Konecke
Susan Lawless
Michael J. McCaffrey
Kathleen M. Quinn
Thomas Charles Savoth
Donna M. Stephan-Nolan
Barbara C. Zimmerman

OF COUNSEL

David D. Furman
C. Judson Hamlin

LEGAL SUPPORT PERSONNEL

Gary Molloy

Reference: Somerset Trust Co.

For full biographical listings, see the Martindale-Hubbell Law Directory

BURLINGTON, Burlington Co.

SMITH, GOLDSTEIN, MAGRAM & BERENATO, A PROFESSIONAL CORPORATION (AV)

415 High Street, P.O. Box 603, 08016-0603
Telephone: 609-386-2633
Fax: 609-386-8674

Louis A. Smith
Jeffrey N. Goldstein
Edward J. Magram
Elizabeth D. Berenato

David C. Michaud

Reference: First Union Bank, Burlington, New Jersey.

For full biographical listings, see the Martindale-Hubbell Law Directory

CEDAR KNOLLS, Morris Co.

LEARY, BRIDE, TINKER & MORAN, A PROFESSIONAL CORPORATION (AV)

7 Ridgedale Avenue, 07927
Telephone: 973-539-2090
Fax: 973-539-0806

W. Stephen Leary
James D. Bride
John G. Tinker, Jr.
Glenn R. Moran
James T. Gill
William H. Mergner, Jr.
Mark Bongiovanni

Tracey L. VanWiemokly
James P. McHugh III
Brian Peoples
Marguerite Anne Leary
Mark J. Brancato
Wendy Allyson Reek
David J. Dering
Peter M. Bouton
Christopher H. Frick
Mark A. Trudeau

For full biographical listings, see the Martindale-Hubbell Law Directory

EDISON, Middlesex Co.

HANLON & LAVIGNE, A PROFESSIONAL CORPORATION (AV)

Suite 200, Executive Plaza, 10 Parsonage Road, 08837
Telephone: 732-549-9880
North Jersey Number: 973-808-0186
Fax: 732-549-3068
Email: larry@hlt-law.com *URL:* http://HanlonLavigne.com
New York, New York Office: One Word Trade Center, Suite 7967, 10048.
Telephone: 212-775-7142 and 212-775-7187.
Marysville, Pennsylvania Office: 505 Maple Avenue, P.O. Box 149, 17053-0149.
Telephone: 717-957-4292.
Fax: 717-957-4293.

William F. Hanlon (1901-1972)
Robert M. Hanlon
Lawrence N. Lavigne
Bonnie H. Hanlon

Richard P. Grossman, Jr.
Robert Michael Hanlon, Jr.
Robert M. Cook
Christine Giordano Hanlon

For full biographical listings, see the Martindale-Hubbell Law Directory

FLORHAM PARK, Morris Co.

CARLIN, MADDOCK, FAY & CERBONE, P.C. (AV)

25 Vreeland Road, P.O. Box 751, 07932
Telephone: 201-377-3350
Fax: 201-377-5626
URL: http://www.lawyers.com/cmfclaw

John J. Carlin, Jr.
Laurence R. Maddock
Donald J. Fay
Richard R. Cerbone

Arthur G. Warden, III

For full biographical listings, see the Martindale-Hubbell Law Directory

HACK, PIRO, O'DAY, MERKLINGER, WALLACE & MCKENNA, P.A. (AV)

30 Columbia Turnpike, P.O. Box 941, 07932-0941
Telephone: 973-301-6500
Fax: 973-301-0094
Email: hpom@ix.netcom.com

Peter A. Piro
William J. O'Day
M. Richard Merklinger
Peter T. Melnyk
Patrick M. Sages
Bonny G. Rafel
Robert G. Alencewicz

For Complete List of Firm Personnel, See General Section

For full biographical listings, see the Martindale-Hubbell Law Directory

*HACKENSACK,** Bergen Co.

HEIN, SMITH, BEREZIN, MALOOF & JACOBS, L.L.C. (AV)

Court Plaza East, 19 Main Street, 07601-7023
Telephone: 201-487-7400
Telecopier: 201-487-4228
Email: counsel@heinsmith.com

MEMBER OF FIRM

Robert J. Maloof

ASSOCIATE

John L. Shanahan

Representative Clients: Bergen County Joint Municipal Insurance Fund; Commercial General Union Insurance Cos. of New York; Crawford & Co.; Health Care Insurance Co.; Princeton Insurance Co.; St. Paul Fire & Marine Insurance Co.; Pro Mutual Insurance Company; NJ Cure.
Reference: Summit Bank.

(See Next Column)

For Complete List of Firm Personnel, See General Section

For full biographical listings, see the Martindale-Hubbell Law Directory

HERTEN, BURSTEIN, SHERIDAN, CEVASCO, BOTTINELLI & LITT, L.L.C. (AV)

Court Plaza North, 25 Main Street, 07601
Telephone: 201-342-6000
Telecopier: 201-342-6611

Thomas J. Herten
Albert Burstein
Philip F. Sheridan, Jr.
Andrew J. Cevasco
Terry Paul Bottinelli
Arnold D. Litt
Brian T. Campion
Menelaos W. Toskos
Mark P. Marotta
Susan M. Marra
John L. Molinelli
Kevin P. Kelly

ASSOCIATES

Patrick Papalia
Anthony Ronald Suarez
Thomas S. McGuire
Donna T. Tamayne

For full biographical listings, see the Martindale-Hubbell Law Directory

NOWELL AMOROSO KLEIN BIERMAN, P.A. (AV)

155 Polifly Road, 07601
Telephone: 201-343-5001
Facsimile: 201-343-5181
Email: nakb@erols.com
New York, New York Office: 140 Broadway.
Telephone: 212-858-7710.
Facsimile: 212-858-7750.

Daniel C. Nowell
Henry J. Amoroso
Herbert C. Klein
William D. Bierman
Jeanne M. Damgen
Linda Dunne
William R. DeLorenzo, Jr.
Richard J. Kapner
David Edelberg

Craig E. Parles
Andrew A. Elman
Christopher M. McGarry
William T. Curran
Lisa M. Parles
Daniel S. Eichhorn
Brian M. Doyno
Samer E. Khalaf

OF COUNSEL

John J. Cariddi
Barbara L. de Mare
Karen A. Passaro

For full biographical listings, see the Martindale-Hubbell Law Directory

HADDONFIELD, Camden Co.

WILBRAHAM, LAWLER & BUBA, A PROFESSIONAL CORPORATION (AV㊀)

24 Kings Highway West, 08033-2122
Telephone: 856-795-4422
Fax: 856-795-4699
Philadelphia, Pennsylvania Office: 1818 Market Street, Suite 3100.
Telephone: 215-564-4141.
Fax: 215-564-4385.
Wilmington, Delaware Office: Stoney Batter Office Building, 5301 Limestone Road, Suite 221.
Telephone: 302-234-8217.
Fax: 302-234-8218.

Edward J. Wilbraham
Michael J. Block
Mary S. Cook

For full biographical listings, see the Martindale-Hubbell Law Directory

LIVINGSTON, Essex Co.

PHILIP M. LUSTBADER & DAVID LUSTBADER A PROFESSIONAL CORPORATION (AV)

615 West Mount Pleasant Avenue, 07039
Telephone: 973-740-1000
Fax: 973-740-1520
URL: http://www.lawyers.com/lustbader,law

Philip M. Lustbader
David Lustbader

John L. Riordan, Jr.
James S. Colavito

For full biographical listings, see the Martindale-Hubbell Law Directory

MAPLEWOOD, Essex Co.

LAW OFFICES OF EMANUEL S. FISH (AV)

2040 Millburn Avenue, 07040
Telephone: 973-763-2001
Fax: 973-763-2832
Email: Afishl@aol.com *URL:* http://www.lawyers.com/esflaw

ASSOCIATE

Thomas J. O'Grady

(See Next Column)

LAW OFFICES OF EMANUEL S. FISH—*Continued*

OF COUNSEL

John D. Kovac

For full biographical listings, see the Martindale-Hubbell Law Directory

MOORESTOWN, Burlington Co.

CHIERICI, CHIERICI & SMITH, A PROFESSIONAL CORPORATION (AV)

Blason Campus - III, 509 South Lenola Road Building Six, 08057-1561
Telephone: 856-234-6300
Fax: 856-234-9490

Donald R. Chierici, Jr.
Elizabeth Coleman Chierici
Julie C. Smith

Carolyn J. Kornas
Mark G. Esposito
Richard D. DiTomaso
Melvin McDowell
David J. Karbasian
Peter P. Sanchez
Donald R. Chierici, III

For full biographical listings, see the Martindale-Hubbell Law Directory

*MORRISTOWN,** Morris Co.

BAUMEISTER & SAMUELS, P.C. (AV⊕)

1776 On The Green, P.O. Box 1116, 07962-1116
Telephone: 973-267-6666
Telecopier: 973-605-1812
Email: BAUMSAM@AOL.COM
New York, N.Y. Office: One Exchange Plaza, 10006-3008.
Telephone: 212-363-1200.
Telecopier: 212-363-1346.

Michel F. Baumeister
Douglas A. Latto (Not admitted in NJ)
Dorothea M. Capone

OF COUNSEL

Lynn F. Samuels
Robert S. Franklin (Not admitted in NJ)
Marc Z. Edell

For full biographical listings, see the Martindale-Hubbell Law Directory

STEPHEN S. WEINSTEIN A PROFESSIONAL CORPORATION (AV)

20 Park Place, Suite 301, 07960
Telephone: 973-267-5200
Fax: 973-538-1779
Email: skippy@sswpa.com *URL:* http://www.sswpa.com

Stephen S. Weinstein

Gail S. Boertzel
William G. Johnson
Melissa H. Luce

For full biographical listings, see the Martindale-Hubbell Law Directory

*NEWARK,** Essex Co.

FITZSIMMONS RINGLE & JACOBS, P.C. (AV)

50 Park Place, 07102
Telephone: 973-623-5350
Fax: 973-623-5927
New York, New York: 130 E. 35th Street, 10016.
Telephone: 212-343-0677.

Frank J. Fitzsimmons
Richard Ringle
Andrew R. Jacobs

COUNSEL

Ronald Leibman

Michael E. Coslit
Lisa M. Papp
Martin Trevor Hughes Lyons

For full biographical listings, see the Martindale-Hubbell Law Directory

MARAN & MARAN (AV)

The Legal Center, One Riverfront Plaza, Suite 315, 07102
Telephone: 973-622-5303
1-888-566-2726
Fax: 973-622-4352

MEMBERS OF FIRM

Joe Maran
David Maran

For full biographical listings, see the Martindale-Hubbell Law Directory

SILLS CUMMIS RADIN TISCHMAN EPSTEIN & GROSS, A PROFESSIONAL CORPORATION (AV)

One Riverfront Plaza, 07102-5400
Telephone: 973-643-7000
Fax: 973-643-6500
Telex: 820630 Sillsbeck Nwk
Email: sillsmail@sillscummis.com *URL:* http://www.sillscummis.com
Atlantic City, New Jersey Office: 17 Gordon's Alley.
Telephone: 609-344-2800.
New York, N.Y. Office: 712 Fifth Avenue.
Telephone: 212-643-7000.
Washington, D.C. Office: 1800 K Street, N.W.
Telephone: 202-296-4750.

MEMBERS OF FIRM

Barry M. Epstein
Steven E. Gross
Jeffrey Barton Cahn
Stuart M. Feinblatt
Trent S. Dickey
Beth S. Rose

OF COUNSEL

Kenneth R. Weiner (Not admitted in NJ)
Steven R. Rowland

Bennet Susser
Rhonda Sobral O'Toole
William R. Stuart III
Andrew W. Schwartz
Gwen L. Coleman
Eric I. Abraham
Derrick R. Freijomil
Vincent R. Lodato

Representative Clients: Bristol-Myers Squibb Co.; Johnson & Johnson; Becton Dickinson and Company; Berlex Laboratories, Inc.; Gynopharma, Inc.; Bioengineering International (B.V.); Nova Pharmaceutical Corp.; Shering A.G.; Sorin Biomedica, S.p.A., Zambon Corp.

For Complete List of Firm Personnel, See General Section

For full biographical listings, see the Martindale-Hubbell Law Directory

NORTH BRUNSWICK, Middlesex Co.

BORRUS, GOLDIN, FOLEY, VIGNUOLO, HYMAN, STAHL & CLARKIN, A PROFESSIONAL CORPORATION (AV)

2875 U.S. Highway 1, Route 1 & Finnigans Lane, P.O. Box 7463, 08902
Telephone: 732-422-1000
Fax: 732-422-1016
Email: attys@borrus.com *URL:* http://www.borrus.com

Jack Borrus
Martin S. Goldin
David M. Foley
Anthony B. Vignuolo
Jeffrey M. Hyman
James E. Stahl
James F. Clarkin III
Eileen Mary Foley

Robert C. Nisenson
Rosalind Westlake
Lisa M. Vignuolo
Steven L. Fox
Peter A. Vignuolo
Gerald T. Foley (1903-1976)

Representative Clients: Summit Bank; R. J. Reynolds Tobacco Co.; K. Hovnanian Enterprises, Inc.; Johnson and Johnson; Foster Wheeler, Inc.; Hartz Mountain Industries; Middlesex County Vocational Services Commission; Borough of South Plainfield Board of Adjustment; U-Haul of Northern NJ.

For full biographical listings, see the Martindale-Hubbell Law Directory

LYNCH, MARTIN, KANE, KUPER, KEEFE & BARTELS, LLC (AV)

1368 How Lane, P.O. Box 6022, 08902-6022
Telephone: 732-545-0745
Fax: 732-545-4780
Email: LYNCHMRTN@aol.com

John A. Lynch, Sr. (1908-1978)
John A. Lynch
James D. Martin, Jr.
John J. Kane
Eric Kuper
John E. Keefe, Jr.
Patrick J. Bartels
Carl W. Swanson
James Den Uyl
John W. Harding
Lori A. Dvorak
Bernard P. Hvozdovic, Jr.
Joseph J. LaCosta
Timothy E. Annin

Laura M. Shea
Robyn M. Mitchell
Christine Klimczuk

OF COUNSEL

Robert T. Quackenboss (Retired Superior Court Judge)

LEGAL SUPPORT PERSONNEL

Sharon Stewart (Administrator)

For full biographical listings, see the Martindale-Hubbell Law Directory

NORTHFIELD, Atlantic Co.

MCALLISTER, HYBERG & WHITE (AV)

Executive Plaza, 2111 New Road, Suite 105, 08225
Telephone: 609-407-1000
Fax: 609-407-1010
Email: McAllister-Hyberg@prodigy.net

(See Next Column)

McALLISTER, HYBERG & WHITE, *Northfield—Continued*

Robert N. McAllister
Lars S. Hyberg
Joseph B. White

ASSOCIATE

Keith T. Smith

For full biographical listings, see the Martindale-Hubbell Law Directory

PARSIPPANY, Morris Co.

REISEMAN SHARP KELSEY & BROWN LLP (AV)

4 Campus Drive, P.O. Box 431, 07054-0431
Telephone: 973-267-3600
Fax: 973-267-2332

MEMBERS OF FIRM

Neil Reiseman
James B. Sharp
Jane S. Kelsey
Kenneth M. Brown
Sam Rosenberg
Meghan E. Walsh

John C. Macce
Jayne E. Turner
Everett E. Gale, III
Robert T. Gunning
Gregory A. Bush

Representative Clients: Medical Inter-Insurance Exchange of New Jersey; Princeton Insurance Company; Health Care Insurance Company; Home Depot; United Capitol Insurance Company; New Jersey Property-Liability Insurance Guaranty Association; New Jersey Joint Underwriting Association; Franciscan Health Systems; Zurich American; Avis.

For full biographical listings, see the Martindale-Hubbell Law Directory

PRINCETON, Mercer Co.

STARK & STARK, A PROFESSIONAL CORPORATION (AV)

Princeton Pike Corporate Center, P.O. Box 5315, 08543-5315
Telephone: 609-896-9060
Fax: 609-896-0629
Email: info@stark-stark.com *URL:* http://www.stark-stark.com

Paul N. Daly
Eric J. Ludwig
John A. Sakson

Michael G. Donahue
Michael H. Foster
Lorena Haumann Miller
Jason G. Steinhart

For full biographical listings, see the Martindale-Hubbell Law Directory

RARITAN, Somerset Co.

LAW OFFICES OF LAUB & FRANCHINO, L.L.C. (AV)

901 U.S. Highway 202, 08869-1419
Telephone: 908-725-1411
Fax: 908-725-9303
URL: http://www.lawyers.com/laub&franchino

Salvatore L. Franchino
Peter N. Laub

James J. Pieper
Peter J. O'Connor

OF COUNSEL

Daniel A. Lime, II
William J. Salmond

For full biographical listings, see the Martindale-Hubbell Law Directory

RED BANK, Monmouth Co.

PHILIP G. AUERBACH A PROFESSIONAL CORPORATION (AV)

231 Maple Avenue, P.O. Box Y, 07701
Telephone: 732-842-6660
Fax: 732-530-7925

Philip G. Auerbach

Edward A. Genz
John J. Ryan
John F. McLaughlin

For full biographical listings, see the Martindale-Hubbell Law Directory

WHITE, FLEISCHNER & FINO (AV)

272 Broad Street, 07701
Telephone: 732-530-7787
Telecopier: 732-530-8552
New York, New York Office: 140 Broadway.
Telephone: 212-487-9700.
Telecopier: 212-487-9777.

Benjamin A. Fleischner
Sheri E. Holland

Representative Clients: Interstate Insurance Group; Lloyd's Syndicates.

For full biographical listings, see the Martindale-Hubbell Law Directory

ROSELAND, Essex Co.

SELLAR RICHARDSON, P.C. (AV)

Six Becker Farm Road, 07068-1735
Telephone: 973-535-1400
Fax: 973-535-6522
Email: info@sellarrichardson.com

James P. Richardson
Wendy H. Smith
John M. Kearney
Denise M. Luckenbach
Shawn R. Stowell

Patricia R. Carley
Julia C. Talarick
Deborah M. Taub
Albert N. Montano
Jennifer R. Sentivan
Victoria F. Pratt

OF COUNSEL

Alastair J. Sellar
E. Scott Garrett
Anthony C. Stuart

For full biographical listings, see the Martindale-Hubbell Law Directory

SADDLE BROOK, Bergen Co.

COHN LIFLAND PEARLMAN HERRMANN & KNOPF LLP (AV)

Park 80 Plaza West-One, 07663
Telephone: 201-845-9600
Telecopier: 201-845-9423
Email: info@njlawfirm.com *URL:* http://www.njlawfirm.com

MEMBERS OF FIRM

Albert L. Cohn
Peter S. Pearlman
Barry A. Knopf
Daniel Crystal (Retired)
Jeffrey W. Herrmann
Robert D. Zatorski
Allen Susser
Mary Ann T. Stokes
Brian D. Zinn
Joshua P. Cohn

ASSOCIATES

Virginia A. Harper
Leonard Z. Kaufmann
Audra DePaolo
Robert Ricci, Jr.
Maurice W. McLaughlin
Andrew C. Abrams
Jessica V. Henry

OF COUNSEL

Sylvia J. Cohn
Jodi B. Scherl

For full biographical listings, see the Martindale-Hubbell Law Directory

SHIP BOTTOM, Ocean Co.

SHACKLETON, HAZELTINE AND BISHOP (AV)

22nd Street and Long Beach Boulevard, P.O. Box 410, 08008
Telephone: 609-494-2136
Telefax: 609-494-0870
Fairfield, New Jersey Office: One Passaic Avenue.
Telephone: 201-882-4646.
Telefax: 201-882-4620.

MEMBERS OF FIRM

Richard J. Shackleton
Colin R. Hazeltine
James E. Bishop

ASSOCIATES

Laura M. O'Regan
Marc Baden Powell
Robert Emmet Rue

OF COUNSEL

Kenneth L. Leiby, Jr. (Resident, Fairfield Office)

References: Commerce Bank/Shore N/A; Summit Bank Corp.

For full biographical listings, see the Martindale-Hubbell Law Directory

SHORT HILLS, Essex Co.

EDWIN R. MATTHEWS, P.C. (AV)

150 John F. Kennedy Parkway CN 5008, 07078-2707
Telephone: 973-912-9500
Telecopier: 973-912-9411
Email: mwgf@mail.att.net

Edwin R. Matthews

Robert J. Pansulla
Daniel J. Bonner
Drew D. Krause
Lisa A. Grattan

For full biographical listings, see the Martindale-Hubbell Law Directory

SPRINGFIELD, Union Co.

HARDIN, KUNDLA, MCKEON, POLETTO & POLIFRONI, P.A., A PROFESSIONAL CORPORATION (AV)

673 Morris Avenue, P.O. Box 730, 07081
Telephone: 973-912-5222
Fax: 973-912-9212
Email: info@HKMPP.com
New York, New York Office: 55 John Street, 10038.
Telephone: 212-571-0111.
Fax: 212-571-1117.

George R. Hardin
Robert L. Polifroni
Janet L. Poletto
Mark S. Kundla
John F. McKeon
James R. Greene
Nicea J. D'Annunzio
John Samuel Favate
Patrick J. Clare
Anna Marie Strand

Jeffrey A. Oshin
Joseph R. Lowicky
Tracy C. Forsyth
Joseph A. DeFuria
John G. Kilbride
Jeffrey H. Goldsmith
Jeffrey Roth
Nora J. Grimbergen
William C. Sullivan, Jr.
Paul Daly
V. Christopher Hirsch
Richard S. Reig
Sam A. Dotro
Brian K. Kaiser
David M. Steiner
Lani M. D'Agostino
Sheila A. Glackin
Michael S. Schwartz
Kirsten L. McCaw
Sanjoy Mukherjee
Louisa B. Sargent
Michael A. Cifelli
James J. A. Mulhall
Kevin M. Regan
Lisa D. Chanel
Maria-Milagros Herrero
Brian A. King
Christina Fichera Dente
Andrea L. Strack
Roger J. Imhof
John P. Monaghan
Stephen J. Donahue
Cindy L. Thompson
Lisa A. Ganzhorn

Representative Clients: Volvo North America Corp.; BOC; Lincoln Electric Co.; Sea Ray Boats, Inc.; Suburban Propane Co.; Chrysler Corp.; United Chair.

For full biographical listings, see the Martindale-Hubbell Law Directory

JAVERBAUM WURGAFT HICKS & ZARIN, A PROFESSIONAL CORPORATION (AV)

Park Place Legal Center, 959 South Springfield Avenue, 07081-3555
Telephone: 973-379-4200
Fax: 973-379-7872
Email: javerbaumwurgafthicks@compuserve.com *URL:* http://www.lawyers.com/jwhz,law

Kenneth S. Javerbaum
Jack Wurgaft
Robert G. Hicks
Ira J. Zarin

Anthony P. Valenti
Eric G. Kahn
David L. Wikstrom

OF COUNSEL

Jeffrey E. Strauss

For full biographical listings, see the Martindale-Hubbell Law Directory

MCDONOUGH, KORN & EICHHORN, A PROFESSIONAL CORPORATION (AV)

Park Place Legal Center, 959 South Springfield Avenue, P.O. Box 712, 07081-0712
Telephone: 973-912-9099
Fax: 973-912-8604

Peter L. Korn
R. Scott Eichhorn
James R. Korn
William S. Mezzomo
Timothy J. Jaeger
Wilfred P. Coronato

Julia A. Klubenspies
Matthew S. Schorr
Danielle M. Verrastro
Jeffrey John Berezny

OF COUNSEL

Robert P. McDonough

Representative Client: Meeker Sharkey & MacBean.
Reference: First Union, Summit, N.J.

For full biographical listings, see the Martindale-Hubbell Law Directory

*TOMS RIVER,** Ocean Co.

LOMELL, MUCCIFORI, ADLER, RAVASCHIERE, AMABILE & PEHLIVANIAN, A PROFESSIONAL CORPORATION (AV)

250 Washington Street, P.O. Box 787, 08754
Telephone: 732-349-2443
Fax: 732-349-6917
Email: thefirm@lomell.com *URL:* http://www.lomell.com

(See Next Column)

Herman A. Adler
Dominic Ravaschiere
John S. Pehlivanian
Ronald E. Prusek
Jeffrey R. Surenian
James M. McKenna
Teresa K. Gierla
Arthur F. Leyden, III

Marc S. Galella
Robyn A. Belluardo
Janet Zaorski Kalapos
James S. Braaten
Regina M. Butler
Paul J Capotorto

Representative Clients: Ingersoll-Rand Company; Cooper Industries; Industrial Welding Supply, Inc.; Georgia Pacific Corp.; Montgomery Elevator Company; John Deere & Company.

For Complete List of Firm Personnel, See General Section

For full biographical listings, see the Martindale-Hubbell Law Directory

*TRENTON,** Mercer Co.

NEEDELL, SIEKERKA & CASTELLANI, A PROFESSIONAL CORPORATION (AV)

Quakerbridge Commons, 2681 Quakerbridge Road, 08619-1625
Telephone: 609-584-7700
Fax: 609-584-0123
Email: nsclaw@aol.com

Stanley H. Needell
Michele N. Siekerka
Anthony P. Castellani

John M. Cinti
Dean C. Gresek

LEGAL SUPPORT PERSONNEL

PARALEGALS

Marlene Griesbach
Carolyn D. Shaw
Veronica A. Mitchell

For full biographical listings, see the Martindale-Hubbell Law Directory

VINELAND, Cumberland Co.

JAY H. GREENBLATT & ASSOCIATES A PROFESSIONAL CORPORATION (AV)

200 North Eighth Street, P.O. Box 883, 08360-0883
Telephone: 609-691-0424
Facsimile: 609-696-1010
Email: jhg@algorithms.com *URL:* http://home.earthlink.net/~greenblatt/

M. Joseph Greenblatt (1896-1992)
Jay H. Greenblatt

Bonnie L. Laube
Nicholas Kiernіesky

Counsel for: Consolidated Motor Oils, Inc.; Joffe Lumber & Supply Co., Inc.
Local Counsel for: A.O. Smith Corp.; Chance Industries; Great American Insurance Companies; Highlands Insurance Group; The MacDonald Companies, Inc.; Pennsylvania Lumbermans Mutual Insurance Co.; Sky Clumber, Inc.; Thermadyne Industries.

For full biographical listings, see the Martindale-Hubbell Law Directory

WAYNE, Passaic Co.

DEYOE HEISSENBUTTEL, L.L.C. (AV)

401 Hamburg Turnpike, P.O. Box 2449, 07474-2449
Telephone: 973-595-6300
Fax: 973-595-0146
Email: deyoelaw@ix.netcom.com *URL:* http://www.deyoe.com

MEMBERS OF FIRM

Charles P. DeYoe (1923-1973)
Wood M. DeYoe
Frederick C. Heissenbuttel
Scott B. Piekarsky

ASSOCIATES

Raymond F. Shenekji
Anne Hutton
Albert C. Buglione
Laureen A. Moloney

LEGAL SUPPORT PERSONNEL

Marilyn Moore (Office Manager)

Representative Clients: Hanover Insurance Inc.; Maryland Casualty Co.; Ohio Casualty Insurance Co.; Motor Club of America; Selective Insurance Co.; Prudential Property & Casualty; Reliance Ins. Co.

For full biographical listings, see the Martindale-Hubbell Law Directory

WEST ORANGE, Essex Co.

SACHS, MAITLIN, FLEMING, GREENE, WILSON & MAROTTE (AV)

80 Main Street, 3rd Floor, 07052
Telephone: 973-731-3400
Fax: 973-731-2896

(See Next Column)

SACHS, MAITLIN, FLEMING, GREENE, WILSON & MAROTTE, *West Orange—Continued*

Harold D. Feuerstein (1933-1967)
Raymond J. Fleming
Marvin A. Sachs
Peter A. Greene
Allan Maitlin
Bradley M. Wilson
Michael Marotte

ASSOCIATES

Steven L. Albertson
Theresa Mullen
Philip B. Harrison
Rosa Marques
David Eric Maitlin
Laura L. Milcsik

Reference: Fidelity Union Trust Co.

For full biographical listings, see the Martindale-Hubbell Law Directory

NEW MEXICO

*ALBUQUERQUE,** Bernalillo Co.

BRANCH LAW FIRM (AV)

Including a Professional Association
2025 Rio Grande Boulevard, N.W., 87104
Telephone: 505-243-3500
Fax: 505-243-3534
New Mexico Toll Free: 1-800-562-3456
Nationwide Toll Free: 1-800-828-4LAW
Email: reception@branchlawfirm.com *URL:* http://www.branchlawfirm.com
Durango, Colorado Office: Suite 205, 102 East Eighth Street.
Telephone: 303-385-7671.
Houston, Texas Office: 808 Travis Street, Suite 1303.
Telephone: 800-243-3545.
Fax: 713-224-1622.

Turner W. Branch (P.A.)
Margaret Moses Branch

Arthur M. Solon
James P. Lyle
Daniel R. Swiss
Rhett D. Klok
Rebecca C. Branch
Suzanne Lafleur Klok
Justin K. Hall
Clyde DeMersseman
Shari D. Thieman

LEGAL SUPPORT PERSONNEL

Krisann Y. Matthes (Office Manager)
Judi Seff
Jacqueline Adams
Daphne Moore (Registered Nurse)
Amy Rigg
Yvette Rodarte
Shariesse McCannon
Shelly Hourani (Houston Office)

For full biographical listings, see the Martindale-Hubbell Law Directory

BUTT, THORNTON & BAEHR, P.C. (AV)

4101 Indian School Road N.E., Suite 300S, P.O. Box 3170, 87190
Telephone: 505-884-0777
Fax: 505-889-8870

J. Duke Thornton
J. Douglas Compton
Carlos G. Martinez
David N. Whitham
Norman L. Gagne
Emily A. Franke
Alfred L. Green, Jr.
Jane A. Laflin
James H. Johansen
Paul T. Yarbrough
Rodney L. Schlagel
Glenna Hayes Long
Martin Diamond
Michael P. Clemens

Sherrill K. Filter
Monica R. Garcia
Agnes Fuentevilla Padilla
Laura J. Ramos
Gregory P. Williams
Robert Tabor Booms
Louis N. Colón
J. Scott Steinberger

OF COUNSEL

Paul L. Butt
Raymond A. Baehr
John A. Klecan

Representative Clients: Alamo Rent-A-Car; American Honda Motor Company; ARA Correctional Medical Systems; ARA Spectrum Emergency Care Services, Inc.; Armco Insurance Group; Circle K Corp.; City of Albuquerque; Colonial Penn Insurance Group; Federal Express Corp.; F.M.C. Corp.

For full biographical listings, see the Martindale-Hubbell Law Directory

CARPENTER & CHÁVEZ, LTD. (AV)

1600 University Boulevard, N.E., Suite A, 87102-1711
Telephone: 505-243-1336
Facsimile: 505-243-1339
Email: carpchav@swcp.com *URL:* http://www.carpenter-law.com

(See Next Column)

William H. Carpenter
Edward L. Chávez
David J. Stout

Reference: Bank of America, Albuquerque, New Mexico.

For full biographical listings, see the Martindale-Hubbell Law Directory

EATON, MARTINEZ & HART, P.C. (AV)

3800 Osuna Road N.E., Suite 2, 87109
Telephone: 505-343-1776
Fax: 505-344-7709
URL: http://www.eatonmartinezhart.com
Email: rogeaton@aol.com *URL:* http://www.lawyers.com/eatonmartinez&hart

Roger V. Eaton
David B. Martinez
F. Michael Hart

Gabrielle M. Valdez
Wendy F. Jones

LEGAL SUPPORT PERSONNEL

Laura Paul (Legal Assistant)
Juan Loya (Legal Assistant)
Shaylin Buhrle (Legal Assistant)
Therse Quetone (Legal Assistant)
Angela Stone (Legal Assistant)

For full biographical listings, see the Martindale-Hubbell Law Directory

GUEBERT & YEOMANS, P.C. (AV)

6743 Academy Road NE, Suite A, P.O. Box 93880, 87199-3880
Telephone: 505-823-2300
Fax: 505-823-9600

Terry R. Guebert
Timothy L. Hartley
Richard D. Yeomans
Alysan Boothe Collins
Don Bruckner
Richard F. Rowley, III
RaMona G. Bootes
Patricia M. Monaghan

For full biographical listings, see the Martindale-Hubbell Law Directory

MADISON, HARBOUR, MROZ & BRENNAN, P.A. (AV)

Suite 1800 Albuquerque Plaza, 201 Third Street, N.W., P.O. Box 25467, 87102
Telephone: 505-242-2177
Fax: 505-242-7184
URL: http://www.madisonlaw.com
Santa Fe, New Mexico Office: Coronado Building, 2nd Floor, 141 East Palace Avenue, P.O. Box 1234.
Telephone: 505-992-8933.
Facsimile: 505-988-2987.

William C. Madison
Neils L. Thompson
Michael W. Brennan
M. Eliza Stewart
Michael H. Harbour
Lorri Krehbiel
Robert J. Mroz
Gregory D. Steinman

Michael Joseph Dekleva
Shannon A. Parden
Michele U. Estrada
Corey A. Goldsand
Scott E. Turner
Jude A. Cisneros

For full biographical listings, see the Martindale-Hubbell Law Directory

JAMES T. ROACH (AV)

Third Central Plaza, Suite 1500 West, 300 Central, S.W., 87102
Telephone: 505-243-4419
Fax: 505-243-4169

For full biographical listings, see the Martindale-Hubbell Law Directory

RODEY, DICKASON, SLOAN, AKIN & ROBB, P.A. (AV)

Albuquerque Plaza, Suite 2200, 201 Third Street, N.W., P.O. Box 1888, 87103-1888
Telephone: 505-765-5900
Fax: 505-768-7395
Email: info@rodey.com *URL:* http://www.rodey.com
Santa Fe, New Mexico Office: Suite 101 Marcy Plaza, 123 East Marcy Street, P.O. Box 1357, 87504-1357.
Telephone: 505-984-0100.
Fax: 505-989-9542.

James C. Ritchie
Patrick M. Shay
Joseph J. Mullins
Tracy McGee Jenks
Robert G. McCorkle
Charles K. Purcell
Bruce Hall
Susan S. Throckmorton
Jonathan W. Hewes
R. Nelson Franse
W. Robert Lasater, Jr.
Theresa W. Parrish
Mark C. Meiering
Paul R. Koller
Travis R. Collier
Susan K. Barger
W. Mark Mowery (Resident, Santa Fe Office)

Jeffrey M. Croasdell
Glenn A. Beard
Thomas A. Outler
Lisa A. Chavez
Jocelyn C. Drennan

(See Next Column)

RODEY, DICKASON, SLOAN, AKIN & ROBB P.A.—*Continued*

For Complete List of Firm Personnel, See General Section

For full biographical listings, see the Martindale-Hubbell Law Directory

SIMONE, ROBERTS & WEISS, P.A. (AV)

8102 Menaul Boulevard N.E., 87110
Telephone: 505-298-9400
Fax: 505-298-7070

Stephen M. Simone
Randal W. Roberts
Norman F. Weiss
Michelle Lalley Blake
Thomas E. Perkins
Ashley Gauthier
Megan Day Hill

Representative Clients: Allstate Insurance Co.; Guaranty National Insurance Co.; State Farm Fire and Casualty Co.; State of New Mexico, Risk Management; Liberty Mutual Insurance Company; State Farm Mutual Auto.
Reference: Nationsbank.

For full biographical listings, see the Martindale-Hubbell Law Directory

*SANTA FE,** Santa Fe Co.

HERRERA, LONG & POUND, P.A. (AV)

2200 Brothers Road, P.O. Box 5098, 87502-5098
Telephone: 505-982-8405
Fax: 505-982-8513
Email: hlplaw@aol.com

Judith C. Herrera
Nancy R. Long
John B. Pound

Mark E. Komer

LEGAL SUPPORT PERSONNEL

Shauna Allen Metzo

Reference: Bank of America.

For full biographical listings, see the Martindale-Hubbell Law Directory

NEW YORK

*ALBANY,** Albany Co.

AINSWORTH, SULLIVAN, TRACY, KNAUF, WARNER & RUSLANDER, P.C. (AV)

Brandon Place, 403 New Karner Road, P.O. Box 12849, 12212-2849
Telephone: 518-464-0600
Fax: 518-464-0679
Email: foc@brokerlaw.com *URL:* http://www.brokerlaw.com

Danforth E. Ainsworth (1908-1927)
Charles B. Sullivan (1881-1975)
Thomas F. Tracy (1914-1994)
John E. Knauf (1914-1996)
Frank J. Warner, Jr.
Robert K. Ruslander
James E. McHenry
John W. Bailey
Frank M. Pell
Elizabeth M. Dumas
Margaret Comard Lynch
Michael J. Murphy
Timothy J. O'Connor
Dennis W. Habel
Maria C. Tebano

Colleen M. O'Connell
Anthony V. Cardona, Jr.
Rebecca A. Slezak
Scott R. Almas

OF COUNSEL

Bruce R. Sullivan

Local Counsel for: Liberty Insurance Co.; United Service Auto Assn.; Continental Insurance Cos.; American International Insurance Co.; Aetna Insurance Co.; Kemper Insurance Co.; Sears Roebuck & Co.; Yamaha Motor Corp.; Chubb & Sons, Inc.; Grand Union Co.

For full biographical listings, see the Martindale-Hubbell Law Directory

FEATHERSTONHAUGH, CONWAY, WILEY & CLYNE, L.L.P. (AV)

99 Pine Street, Suite 207, 12207
Telephone: 518-436-0786
Fax: 518-427-0452
URL: http://www.fcwc-law.com

MEMBERS OF FIRM

James D. Featherstonhaugh
Thomas A. Conway
Stephen J. Wiley
Elizabeth K. Clyne

ASSOCIATES

Nadine Feiden Shadlock
Denis R. Hurley, Jr.
Andrew W. Kirby
William F. Conway, IV
Gerard L. Conway, Jr.
Steven M. Connolly

OF COUNSEL

William F. Conway
Jeffrey J. Conklin
David Weinraub
Randall J. Ezick

(See Next Column)

LEGAL SUPPORT PERSONNEL

GOVERNMENTAL RELATIONS

John L. Hardy
Daniel G. Plummer
John P. Griffin
David F. Fleming

For full biographical listings, see the Martindale-Hubbell Law Directory

HARVEY AND MUMFORD (AV)

20 Corporate Woods Boulevard, 12211-2396
Telephone: 518-463-4491
Telecopier: 518-463-5665
Email: thefirm@harveyandmumford.com

Arthur J. Harvey (1903-1986)

MEMBERS OF FIRM

Jonathan P. Harvey
Brian F. Mumford

ASSOCIATES

Eva Lynn M. Hayko
Karen Hendricks
Peter Baird Joslin, Jr.
Trudy L. Boulia
Keith J. Starlin

OF COUNSEL

Jack D. Harvey

For full biographical listings, see the Martindale-Hubbell Law Directory

O'CONNOR, O'CONNOR, MAYBERGER & FIRST, P.C. (AV)

20 Corporate Woods Boulevard, 12211-0400
Telephone: 518-465-0400
Facsimile: 518-465-0015
Email: info@1stlaw.com *URL:* http://www.1stlaw.com

Michael J. O'Connor
Terence P. O'Connor
Dianne Bresee Mayberger
Dennis A. First
Michele M. Monserrate
Cynthia Ann Platt

Justin O. Corcoran
Michael P. Cavanagh
Christopher D. Drake
Eugene N. Sarfoh
Francis J. Brennan
Colleen D. Galligan

For full biographical listings, see the Martindale-Hubbell Law Directory

POWERS & SANTOLA (AV)

39 N. Pearl Street, Suite 2, 12207-2785
Telephone: 518-465-5995; 1-800-540-8742
Fax: 518-426-4012
Email: jpowers@powers-santola.com *URL:* http://www.powers-santola.com

John K. Powers
Daniel R. Santola

ASSOCIATES

Timothy J. Higgins
John H. Fisher
Paul Berne Sherr

THORN AND GERSHON, LLP (AV)

5 Wembley Court, New Karner Road, P.O. Box 15054, 12212-5054
Telephone: 518-464-6770
Fax: 518-464-6778

MEMBERS OF FIRM

Richard M. Gershon
Arthur H. Thorn
Jeffrey J. Tymann
Maureen Sullivan Bonanni
Noreen J. Van Doren
Nancy Nicholson Bogan
Sheila Toborg

ASSOCIATES

Paul D. Jureller
Kristen H. Martin
William M. Hoblock
Kyle N. Kordich
Jennifer H. Goody

OF COUNSEL

Robert F. Doran

For full biographical listings, see the Martindale-Hubbell Law Directory

*BRONX,** Bronx Co.

MAXWELL S. PFEIFER (AV)

714 East 241st Street, 10470
Telephone: 718-325-5000
Fax: 718-324-0333
Email: mspfeifer@aol.com
New York, New York Office: 18 East 50th Street, 7th Floor, 10022.
Telephone: 212-980-0777.
Fax: 718-324-0333.
Hallandale, Florida Office: 1920 East Hallandale Beach Boulevard, Suite 606.
Telephone: 954-454-1550.

ASSOCIATES

Steven E. Millon
Robert S. Summer

(See Next Column)

MAXWELL S. PFEIFER, *Bronx—Continued*

OF COUNSEL

Sandra Krevitsky Janin
Anthony J. Hatab
Hon. Alexander A. Delle Cese (1919-1997)

For full biographical listings, see the Martindale-Hubbell Law Directory

*BROOKLYN,** Kings Co.

BONINA & BONINA, P.C. (AV)

Suite 1608, 16 Court Street, 11241
Telephone: 718-522-1786
888-MEDLAW-1
Fax: 718-243-0414
URL: http://www.medlaw1.com

John Anthony Bonina
John Bonina, III
Elizabeth Bonina
Andrea E. Bonina

Deborah A. Trerotola
Tyrone Sergio
Amy L. Insler

LEGAL SUPPORT PERSONNEL

Pedro Cintron
Inez M. Diaz
Sandra Ferrari

Reference: Republic Bank of New York.

For full biographical listings, see the Martindale-Hubbell Law Directory

*BUFFALO,** Erie Co.

FELDMAN, KIEFFER & HERMAN, LLP (AV)

110 Pearl Street, Suite 400, 14202
Telephone: 716-852-5875
Fax: 716-852-4253
Email: info@fkhattys.com *URL:* http://www.fkhattys.com

PRINCIPALS OF THE FIRM

Andrew Feldman
James M. Kieffer
Ann W. Herman
Mark F. Scarcello
Gordon D. Tresch
Mary Jo Herrscher

For full biographical listings, see the Martindale-Hubbell Law Directory

O'SHEA, REYNOLDS & CUMMINGS (AV)

237 Main Street, Suite 500, 14203
Telephone: 716-853-6341-2-3
Fax: 716-852-3880
Email: info@oshea-reynolds.com

MEMBERS OF FIRM

Frank Gibbons (1869-1953)
Henry W. Pottle (1872-1943)
Willard M. Pottle (1901-1967)
Philip J. O'Shea (1909-1984)
William S. Reynolds
C. DeForest Cummings, Jr.
David M. Stillwell
Gerard E. O'Connor
William A. Long, Jr.
Nelson E. Schule, Jr.

ASSOCIATES

Kevin D. Cox
Nicole A. Heary

Local Attorneys for: Amica Mutual Insurance Co.; Continental National American Group; Nationwide Mutual Insurance Co.; The Continental Insurance Cos.
Reference: Key Bank.

For full biographical listings, see the Martindale-Hubbell Law Directory

ROACH, BROWN, MCCARTHY & GRUBER, P.C. (AV)

1620 Liberty Building, 420 Main Street, 14202-3511
Telephone: 716-852-0400
Fax: 716-852-2535
Email: roachbrown@roachbrown.com

Daniel T. Roach
Edmund S. Brown, Jr.
T. Alan Brown
Joseph V. McCarthy
J. Mark Gruber
Mary J. Murray
John P. Danieu
Elizabeth G. Redmond
Gregory T. Miller
Teresa C. Brophy Bair
Jason A. Botticelli
Jennifer L. Noah
Joel J. Java, Jr.

OF COUNSEL

Arthur J. Maloney
John Y. Gallup

Local Attorneys for: American International Group; Chubb Group of Insurance Co.; Healthcare Underwriters Mutual Insurance Co.; Peter J. McBreen and Associates; Frontier Insurance Co.; Medical Liability Mutual Insurance Co.; Medical Malpractice Insurance Assn.; Merrill Dow; Reliance Insurance Group; Travelers Group.

For full biographical listings, see the Martindale-Hubbell Law Directory

GARDEN CITY, Nassau Co.

GALLAGHER GOSSEEN FALLER KAPLAN & CROWLEY (AV)

1010 Franklin Avenue, Suite 400, 11530-2927
Telephone: 516-742-2500
Fax: 516-742-2516
Email: GGFKC_Postmaster@GGFKC.com
New York, New York Office: 350 Fifth Avenue, Suite 603.
Telephone: 212-947-5800.
Fax: 212-967-4965.

MEMBERS OF FIRM

James A. Gallagher, Jr.
Robert I. Gosseen (Resident, New York City Office)
Robert A. Faller
Alan D. Kaplan
Michael J. Crowley
William E. Vita
Brian P. Morrissey

ASSOCIATES

David H. Arntsen
Joseph A. Latasso
Amy L. Ruina
Gerald A. Corallo, Jr.

OF COUNSEL

John P. Coogan
Peter F. Vetro
William A. Bales, Jr.

For full biographical listings, see the Martindale-Hubbell Law Directory

L'ABBATE, BALKAN, COLAVITA & CONTINI, L.L.P. (AV)

1050 Franklin Avenue, 11530
Telephone: 516-294-8844
Telecopier: 516-294-8202; 742-6563
Email: law@labbatebalkan.com *URL:* http://www.labbatebalkan.com
Livingston, New Jersey Office: 7 Regent Street, Suite 711, 07039.
Telephone: 973-422-0422.
Telecopier: 973-422-0420.

MEMBERS OF FIRM

Donald R. L'Abbate
Anthony P. Colavita
Peter L. Contini
Monte E. Sokol
Douglas L. Pintauro
Richard P. Byrne
Jane M. Myers
Paula M. Gart
Anna M. DiLonardo
David B. Kosakoff
Lewis A. Bartell
Marian C. Rice
Ralph A. Catalano
Douglas R. Halstrom
Steven R. Goldstein
Gary Petropoulos
Domingo R. Gallardo
Mercedes Colwin

COUNSEL TO THE FIRM

Kenneth J. Balkan

SPECIAL COUNSEL

Arthur D. Bromberg (Resident, Livingston, New Jersey Office)
Jonathan M. Kuller (Resident, Livingston, New Jersey Office)

OF COUNSEL

Marianne S. Conklin
Joanne C. Watson
Marie Ann Hoenings

ASSOCIATES

Colleen M. Cronin
Wendy S. Van Dorn
Nicholas Toumbekis
Andrew Marc Warshauer
Michelle J. Simon
Annalee J. Cataldo-Barile
Martin A. Schwartzberg
Louis M. Goldberg
Scott Evan Kossove
Peter D. Rigelhaupt
Orin J. Ketyer
Anthony T. Battaglia
Christopher B. Block (Resident, Livingston, New Jersey Office)
James S. Montano (Resident, Livingston, New Jersey Office)
Maureen E. Scott
John D. McKenna
Michael B. Curan
Jeffrey E. Edelman (Resident, Livingston, New Jersey Office)
Matthew K. Flanagan
Claudia M. Kessler

A list of References and Representative Clients will be furnished upon request.

For full biographical listings, see the Martindale-Hubbell Law Directory

MONTFORT, HEALY, MCGUIRE & SALLEY (AV)

1140 Franklin Avenue, 11530
Telephone: 516-747-4082
Telecopier: 516-746-0748

MEMBERS OF FIRM

E. Richard Rimmels, Jr. (1930-1999)
Frank J. Cafaro
Philip J. Catapano
Fredric C. Montfort
Donald S. Neumann, Jr.
James J. Keefe, Jr.
Michael A. Baranowicz
James Michael Murphy

OF COUNSEL

Fredric H. Montfort
Edward M. Salley, Jr.
David J. Fleming
Robert J. Mettalia

(See Next Column)

MONTFORT, HEALY, MCGUIRE & SALLEY—*Continued*

ASSOCIATES

Claudia C. Glacken
Marcie K. Glasser
Bruce A. Cook
Jeffrey D. Present
Joan E. Resnik
Susan H. Dempsey
Camille L. Hansen
Christopher T. Cafaro
Kathleen Dumont
Jeffrey B. Siler
Michael G. Kruzynski
Karen J. Cooper

For full biographical listings, see the Martindale-Hubbell Law Directory

HAUPPAUGE, Suffolk Co.

ERIC H. HOLTZMAN (AV)

330 Vanderbilt Motor Parkway, P.O. Box 11005, 11788-0903
Telephone: 631-435-8800
Fax: 631-435-8832

Richard E. Trachtenberg
David H. Eisenberg

Reference: European-American Bank & Trust Co.

For full biographical listings, see the Martindale-Hubbell Law Directory

JAMESTOWN, Chautauqua Co.

BURGETT & ROBBINS (AV)

15 East Fifth Street, P.O. Box 3090, 14702-3090
Telephone: 716-488-3090
Fax: 716-483-3765
1-800-832-6582
Email: help@burgettandrobbins.com *URL:* http://www.burgettandrobbins.com

Dalton J. Burgett
Dale C. Robbins
Kenneth M. Lasker
Mary Speedy Hajdu
Robert A. Liebers
Andrew T. Radack

References: Fleet Bank, Jamestown, New York; Marine Midland Bank, Jamestown, New York; Lake Shore Savings and Loan Association, Jamestown, New York.

For full biographical listings, see the Martindale-Hubbell Law Directory

MELVILLE, Suffolk Co.

ABBATE, LAWRENCE & WORDEN, P.C. (AV)

425 Broad Hollow Road, Suite 120, 11747
Telephone: 516-694-0033
Fax: 516-694-9331

John J. Abbate
Roger B. Lawrence
Robert P. Worden, Jr.

James L. Martell
Matthew Rainis
Kathleen Fugelsang
Margaret Herrmann
Jonathan F. Banks
Maria Zouros
MaryBeth Cameron

For full biographical listings, see the Martindale-Hubbell Law Directory

GANDIN, SCHOTSKY, RAPPAPORT, GLASS & GREENE, LLP (AV)

445 Broad Hollow Road, 11747
Telephone: 516-293-2300
Fax: 516-293-2918
Email: gsrmail@gsrlaw.com *URL:* http://www.gsrlaw.com
New York, N.Y. Office: 1212 Avenue of the Americas, 10036.
Telephone: 212-921-5200.
Fax: 212-921-5367.

PARTNERS

Charles J. Rappaport
Arnold M. Schotsky
Michael R. Greene
Michael G. Glass
Kevin E. Balfe
Michael S. Levine

ASSOCIATES

Margery Weinroth
Jonathan H. Freiberger
Brian Robert Gunn
Karen S. Bennett
Kenneth J. Lauri
Matthew J. Zullo
Diane G. Holland
James L. Forde

OF COUNSEL

Michael I. Gandin
Edward Kiley
Charles Krupin

For full biographical listings, see the Martindale-Hubbell Law Directory

*MINEOLA,** Nassau Co.

GALLAGHER, WALKER, BIANCO & PLASTARAS (AV)

98 Willis Avenue, 11501
Telephone: 516-248-2002
Fax: 516-248-2394

(See Next Column)

Gerard M. Gallagher
Robert J. Walker
Dominic P. Bianco
Thomas E. Plastaras

ASSOCIATES

Ann Willoughby
William P. Nolan

OF COUNSEL

Stephen P. Burke

For full biographical listings, see the Martindale-Hubbell Law Directory

*NEW YORK,** New York Co.

BAUMEISTER & SAMUELS, P.C. (AV)

One Exchange Plaza, 10006-3008
Telephone: 212-363-1200
Telecopier: 212-363-1346
Email: BAUMSAM@AOL.COM
Morristown, New Jersey Office: 1776 On The Green, P.O. Box 1116, 07962-1116.
Telephone: 973-267-6666.
Telecopier: 973-605-1812.

Michel F. Baumeister
Douglas A. Latto
Dorothea M. Capone

OF COUNSEL

Lynn F. Samuels
Robert S. Franklin
Marc Z. Edell

For full biographical listings, see the Martindale-Hubbell Law Directory

BEATIE AND OSBORN LLP (AV)

599 Lexington Avenue, 42nd Floor, 10022
Telephone: 212-888-9000
Fax: 212-888-9664
Email: bandolaw@aol.com *URL:* http://www.bandolaw@aol.com

Russel H. Beatie, Jr.
Daniel A. Osborn

ASSOCIATES

Curt D. Marshall
Eduard Korsinsky

OF COUNSEL

Richard M. Cummings

For full biographical listings, see the Martindale-Hubbell Law Directory

CALLAN, REGENSTREICH, KOSTER & BRADY (AV)

One Whitehall Street 10th Floor, 10004
Telephone: 212-248-8800
Fax: 212-248-6815
Shrewsbury, New Jersey Office: 740 Broad Street.
Telephone: 732-345-9333.
Fax: 732-345-9444.
Garden City, New York Office: 1205 Franklin Avenue.
Telephone: 516-294-4383.
Fax: 516-294-4386.

MEMBERS OF FIRM

Paul F. Callan
Bruce N. Regenstreich
Warren S. Koster
Bruce M. Brady
William L. Brennan
Vincent A. Nagler
Scott W. Bermack

ASSOCIATES

Kenneth S. Merber
Michael P. Kandler
Vincent D. Finnegan
Stephanie Palermo
Walter Paterson Burrell
Beth S. Block
Meredith B. Borg
Pamela Patton Fynes
Mara J. Sibley
Eric A. Wasserfall
Amie Catherine Kalac (Resident, Shrewsbury, New Jersey Office)
Lisa B. Katz

For full biographical listings, see the Martindale-Hubbell Law Directory

DE BLASIO, FIGMAN, EPSTEIN & LA ROCCA, P.C. (AV)

Woolworth Building, 233 Broadway, 10279
Telephone: 212-732-2620
Fax: 212-571-2045

Peter E. De Blasio
Alan H. Figman
Steven A. Epstein
Stephen S. La Rocca
John A. Orbon

For full biographical listings, see the Martindale-Hubbell Law Directory

DE ORCHIS, WALKER & CORSA, LLP (AV)

One Battery Park Plaza, Second Floor, 10004-1480
Telephone: 212-344-4700
MCI Telex: 673-4608
Telefax: 212-509-7886
Email: DW&C@MCIMAIL.COM *URL:* http://www.marinelex.com
Union, New Jersey Office: 1495 Morris Avenue, P.O. Box 1718.
Telephone: 973-467-4740.
Telefax: 908-687-0255.

(See Next Column)

DE ORCHIS, WALKER & CORSA LLP, *New York—Continued*

Stamford, Connecticut Office: 999 Summer Street.
Telephone: 203-323-9120.
Telefax: 203-323-9015.
Boston, Massachusetts Office: One Boston Place, 5th Floor, 02180.
Telephone: 617-619-3610.
Telefax: 617-619-3924.
Miami, Florida Office: De Orchis, Corsa & Hillerbrand, LLP, 2650 Biscayne Boulevard, 33137.
Telephone: 305-571-9200.
Telefax: 305-571-9250.

PARTNERS

LeRoy S. Corsa
Vincent M. De Orchis
Christopher H. Mansuy
Alexander V. Sansone
John A. Orzel
Michael E. Unger
Cary R. Wiener

ASSOCIATES

R. Brett Kelly
William E. Lakis
Marc I. Kunkin
Francesco A. Di Pietro

RESIDENT COUNSEL

M. E. De Orchis

OF COUNSEL

Ara A. Shimshidian
Bruce H. Neuman

For full biographical listings, see the Martindale-Hubbell Law Directory

FUCHSBERG & FUCHSBERG (AV)

100 Church Street, 18th Floor, 10007
Telephone: 212-962-2800
Fax: 212-385-2308

MEMBERS OF FIRM

Abraham Fuchsberg
Seymour Fuchsberg
Preston J. Douglas
Stephen M. Warner

Harvey Goldstein
Irwin M. Berg
Bruce H. Goldstone
Martin Diennor
Maurice Sieradzki
Mordecai T. Schwartz
Frank P. Nervo
Richard Cohen
Iris Claire Finder
Thomas A. Agoglia
Robert M. Futterman
Richard V. Zand
John C. Henninger
Roger N. Lavinsky
Joseph Campisi
Devin P. Cohen
David Jacobs
Alan D. Bernstein
Ari Michael Gross

For full biographical listings, see the Martindale-Hubbell Law Directory

GARBARINI & SCHER, P.C. (AV)

1114 Avenue of the Americas, 10036-7790
Telephone: 212-764-4000
Tele-fax: 212-719-5018
Hackensack, New Jersey Office: 25 Main Street, Suite 600, 07601-7025.
Telephone: 201-343-2002.
Fax: 201-342-0612.

Stanley J. Scher
Leonard Weinstock
Myrna A. Levinson
George J. Kehayas
Michael Caliguiri
William G. Scher
Paul M. Paley
James W. Kachadoorian
Gregg D. Weinstock
Kurt Lee Weinmann

Barry M. Ruderman
Barry Rothman
Nancy Breslow
Mary Ann Candelario
Marilyn C. Daignault
Yuval D. Bar-Kokhba
Lori E. Katz
Thomas M. Cooper
Michael Milchan
Christine E. Fernandez
Karen Nourizadeh
Michael Young

Representative Clients: American Home Assurance Co.; The Archdiocese of New York; Chubb & Son, Inc; Crum & Forster; Marriott Corp.; St. Barnabas Hospital; Travelers Insurance Co.; Lloyds of London and British Cos.; McDonald's Corp.; Allstate Insurance Co.

For full biographical listings, see the Martindale-Hubbell Law Directory

GINSBERG & BROOME (AV)

225 Broadway, Suite 3105, 10007
Telephone: 212-227-4225
Fax: 212-227-4228

Robert M. Ginsberg
Alvin H. Broome

ASSOCIATE

Christopher Jon Longman

OF COUNSEL

Jody H. Brackman
Anna Lewis
Simon Ginsberg

For full biographical listings, see the Martindale-Hubbell Law Directory

LAW OFFICES OF DAVID B. GOLOMB (AV)

Suite 527, 230 Park Avenue, 10169
Telephone: 212-661-9000
Telecopier: 212-661-6181
Email: golomblaw@aol.com

ASSOCIATE

Frank A. Longo

For full biographical listings, see the Martindale-Hubbell Law Directory

JULIEN & SCHLESINGER, P.C. (AV)

150 William Street, 19th Floor, 10038
Telephone: 212-962-8020

Alfred S. Julien (1910-1989)
Stuart A. Schlesinger

Mary Elizabeth Burns
Richard A. Robbins
Michael J. Taub
Marla L. Stein
Adam Schlesinger
Michael S. Schlesinger

For full biographical listings, see the Martindale-Hubbell Law Directory

KREINDLER & KREINDLER (AV)

100 Park Avenue, 10017
Telephone: 212-687-8181
Telecopier: 212-972-9432
Email: legal@kreindler.com *URL:* http://www.kreindler.com

MEMBERS OF FIRM

Harry E. Kreindler (1896-1983)
Lee S. Kreindler
Marc S. Moller
Francis G. Fleming, Jr.
Steven R. Pounian
James P. Kreindler
David C. Cook
David Beekman
Blanca I. Rodriguez
Noah H. Kushlefsky
Robert J. Spragg

OF COUNSEL

Paul S. Edelman
Milton G. Sincoff
Henry A. Gluckstern

ASSOCIATES

Lori B. Lasson
Susan Friery (Not admitted in NY)
Andrew J. Maloney, III
Brian J. Alexander
David G. Nanz
Justin Timothy Green
Daniel O. Rose
Jacqueline M. James
Victoria J. Maniatis

For full biographical listings, see the Martindale-Hubbell Law Directory

LAVIN, COLEMAN, O'NEIL, RICCI, FINARELLI & GRAY (AV)

7th Floor, 767 Third Avenue, 10017
Telephone: 212-319-6898
Fax: 212-319-6932
Philadelphia, Pennsylvania Office: Suite 1000, 510 Walnut Street.
Telephone: 215-627-0303.
Fax: 215-627-2551.
Mount Laurel, New Jersey Office: 8000 Midlantic Drive, Suite 201 South.
Telephone: 609-778-5544.
Fax: 609-778-3383.

Francis F. Quinn
William J. Ricci
Edward A. Gray
Joseph A. McGinley
Michael D. Brophy

Jessica Faden (Resident, Mount Laurel, New Jersey Office)
Margot L. Ludlam
Leona C. McFadden
Timothy J. McHugh
Michelle S. Regan
Elizabeth A. Weill
Christopher P. Yodice

For full biographical listings, see the Martindale-Hubbell Law Directory

LEAHEY & JOHNSON, P.C. (AV)

Suite 2220, 120 Wall Street, 10005
Telephone: 212-269-7308
Facsimile: 212-422-4751
Email: Leaheylaw@Aol.com

Peter James Johnson
Peter James Johnson, Jr.
William G. Murphy
Kevin Brian Lynch

James P. Tenney
Steven Martin
William J. Gordon
Christopher Delamere Clarke
Vincent L. Gallo, Jr.
Joseph Francis Ferrette
Gregory Wilson
Michael Cannella
James Gerard Mcgovern
Nadine M. Duhamel
Sharon A. Toussaint
Melissa Ann Weinberg
Edward J. White
Daniel Michael Sullivan
Lennon C. Edwards
Carmen M. Vasquez
Eric L. Horn
Sean T. O'Leary (Not admitted in NY)

For full biographical listings, see the Martindale-Hubbell Law Directory

New York—Continued

LEDY-GURREN & BLUMENSTOCK, L.L.P. (AV)

150 East 52nd Street-30th Floor, 10022
Telephone: 212-753-4444
Fax: 212-753-1003
Email: ledygurren@aol.com

Nancy Ledy-Gurren
John U. H. Blumenstock
Deborah Bass
Daniel E. Siff

Elissa L. Shechter

OF COUNSEL

Elizabeth Marion Young

For full biographical listings, see the Martindale-Hubbell Law Directory

LIEBER & LIEBER (AV)

111 John Street, 10038
Telephone: 212-608-5844
Fax: 212-608-5848

MEMBERS OF FIRM

Joel M. Lieber (1953-1992)
Eugene H. Lieber

Representative Clients: Johnson Controls, Inc.; The Manitowoc Co., Inc.; Bucyrus-Erie Co.; Wausau Insurance Cos.; General Accident Group; The Heil Co.; Manitowoc-Forsythe Corp.; Kemper Group; Lexington Insurance Co.

For full biographical listings, see the Martindale-Hubbell Law Directory

LIPSIG, SHAPEY, MANUS & MOVERMAN, P.C. (AV)

40 Fulton Street, 10038-1850
Telephone: 212-285-3300
Fax: 212-406-4544

Harry H. Lipsig (1901-1995)
Mark J. Manus
Thomas J. Moverman
Alan M. Shapey
Marc R. Mauser

Josefina A. Belmonte
Glenn P. Dolan
Kent L. Benziger
Rene G. Garcia

OF COUNSEL

Henry R. Simon

For full biographical listings, see the Martindale-Hubbell Law Directory

LONDON FISCHER LLP (AV)

59 Maiden Lane, 10038
Telephone: 212-972-1000
Facsimile: 212-972-1030
Email: Law@LondonFischer.com

MEMBERS OF FIRM

Bernard London
James L. Fischer
Daniel Zemann, Jr.
John E. Sparling
Richard S. Endres
Leah Campbell
Marvin B. Segal
James Walsh
Anthony F. Tagliagambe

For full biographical listings, see the Martindale-Hubbell Law Directory

PARKER CHAPIN LLP (AV)

Chrysler Building, 405 Lexington Avenue, 10017
Telephone: 212-704-6000
Telecopier: 212-704-6288
URL: http://www.parkerchapin.com
Great Neck, New York Office: 175 Great Neck Road.
Telephone: 516-482-4422.
Telecopier: 516-482-4469.
Hackensack, New Jersey: 190 Morre Street, Suite 307.
Telephone: 210-883-6400.
Telecopier: 210-883-6404.
Beverly Hills, California: 9454 Wilshire Boulevard.
Telephone: 310-288-8367.
Telecopier: 310-288-8365.

MEMBERS OF FIRM

Charles P. Greenman
Angela D. Vitali

OF COUNSEL

M. Jane Kronenberger

For Complete List of Firm Personnel, See General Section

For full biographical listings, see the Martindale-Hubbell Law Directory

PILIERO GOLDSTEIN JENKINS & SULLIVAN, LLP (AV)

292 Madison Avenue, 10017
Telephone: 212-213-8200
Fax: 212-685-2028
Email: lawyers@pgjhlaw.com *URL:* http://www.pgjhlaw.com
Carlstadt, New Jersey Office: One Palmer Terrace.
Telephone: 201-507-5157.
FAX: 201-507-5221.
Washington, D.C. Office: 888 17th Street, N.W., Suite 1100.
Telephone: 202-467-6991.
FAX: 202-467-6703.
San Francisco, California Office: 507 Howard Street, Suite 200.
Telephone: 415-281-3631.
Fax: 415-281-3630.

MEMBERS OF FIRM

Kimberlee S. Bogen
Edward J. Goldstein
Jon Mark Jenkins
Marc A. Lebowitz
Robert D. Piliero
George O. Richardson, III
Michael T. Sullivan

ASSOCIATES

Craig Avedisian
Rosemary G. Feit
Eric M. Kogan
Mariano Schwed

OF COUNSEL

Kenneth D. Arbeeny
Christopher P. Hall

For full biographical listings, see the Martindale-Hubbell Law Directory

RHEINGOLD, VALET, RHEINGOLD & SHKOLNIK, P.C. (AV)

113 East 37th Street, 10016-3042
Telephone: 212-684-1880
Fax: 212-689-8156
Email: info@rheingoldlaw.com *URL:* http://www.rheingoldlaw.com

Paul D. Rheingold
Thomas P. Valet
David B. Rheingold
Hunter J. Shkolnik
Terrence E. McCartney
Thomas P. Giuffra

Ryan S. Goldstein

For full biographical listings, see the Martindale-Hubbell Law Directory

JEFFREY SAMEL & PARTNERS (AV)

150 Broadway, 20th Floor, 10038
Telephone: 212-587-9690
Fax: 212-587-9673

Jeffrey Samel
David S. Gary
Dorothy Samel

ASSOCIATES

Robert G. Spevack
David M. Samel
Stacey L. Schwartz

OF COUNSEL

Richard A. Soberman

Representative Clients: New York City Transit Authority; New York City Housing Authority; Empire Insurance Co.; National General Insurance Co.; Federal Express Corp.; Shell Oil Corp.; American Building Maintenance Corp.; Morbark Industries; United States Fidelity and Guaranty Corp.; Little Caesar Enterprises, Inc.

For full biographical listings, see the Martindale-Hubbell Law Directory

SCHNEIDER, KLEINICK, WEITZ, DAMASHEK & SHOOT (AV)

233 Broadway, Fifth Floor, 10279-0003
Telephone: 212-553-9000
Fax: 212-804-0820
Email: mail@lawyer1.com *URL:* http://www.lawyer1.com

Ivan S. Schneider
Arnold L. Kleinick
Harvey Weitz
Philip M. Damashek
Brian J. Shoot
Robert B. Jackson
Clifford J. Stern
Gregory J. Cannata
Keith A. Kleinick
Richard B. Ancowitz
Charles J. Nolet, Jr.
Leslie Debra Kelmachter
Louis J. Mitchell

John Kieran Daly
Jonathan S. Damashek
Thomas V. Deffina
Dawn S. DeWeil
David W. Druker
Steven Gold
Keith H. Gross
Erin K. Hurley
Judy Keenan
Paul A. Marber
Lloyd M. Roberts
Joseph S. Rosato
Derek S. Sells
Lawrence A. Wilson, II
James M. Lane
Donald D. Casale

For full biographical listings, see the Martindale-Hubbell Law Directory

New York—Continued

PAUL A. SCRUDATO (AV)

150 E. 52nd Street, Suite 2700, 10022
Telephone: 212-371-1153
Fax: 212-753-5044
Email: paulscrudato@ibm.net

For full biographical listings, see the Martindale-Hubbell Law Directory

SHANDELL, BLITZ, BLITZ, GLASS, BOOKSON & KERN, LLP (AV)

150 Broadway, 10038-4498
Telephone: 212-513-1300
Fax: 212-385-1916
Email: SBBGBK@aol.com

MEMBERS OF FIRM

Herman B. Glaser (1915-1994)
Richard E. Shandell
Bert A. Blitz
Arthur Blitz
Shoshana T. Bookson
Chet W. Kern

Mitchel H. Ashley
Fredrick A. Schulman

For full biographical listings, see the Martindale-Hubbell Law Directory

THE GERALD NEAL SWARTZ LAW OFFICES (AV)

767 Third Avenue, 26th Floor, 10017
Telephone: 212-421-9292
Fax: 212-421-9351
Email: gnswartz@aol.com *URL:* http://members.aol.com/gnswartz/index.html

For full biographical listings, see the Martindale-Hubbell Law Directory

WADE CLARK MULCAHY (AV)

111 Broadway, 10006
Telephone: 212-267-1900
Fax: 212-267-9470
Email: info@wcmlaw.com *URL:* http://www.wcmlaw.com
Westfield, New Jersey Office: 211 North Avenue East, 07090.
Telephone: 908-789-1681.
Fax: 908-789-0984.

PARTNERS

Dennis M. Wade
Paul F. Clark
John Mulcahy
Owen B. Carragher, Jr.

ASSOCIATES

Kathleen M. Mulholland
Rose M. McGrinder
Andrea E. Sacco
Christopher C. Mauro
Linda D. Werbel
Nicole Y. Brown
Suzanne M. O'Keefe

For full biographical listings, see the Martindale-Hubbell Law Directory

WHITE, FLEISCHNER & FINO (AV)

140 Broadway, 10005
Telephone: 212-487-9700
Telecopier: 212-487-9777
Email: infor@wff-law.com
Red Bank, New Jersey Office: 272 Broad Street.
Telephone: 732-530-7787.
Telecopier: 732-530-8552.

MEMBERS OF FIRM

Allan P. White
Benjamin A. Fleischner
Patti F. Potash
Wendy K. Carrano
Stephanie M. Holzback
Sheri E. Holland
James A. Robbins

Representative Clients: Interstate Insurance Group; Lloyd's Syndicates.

For Complete List of Firm Personnel, See General Section

For full biographical listings, see the Martindale-Hubbell Law Directory

ONEONTA, Otsego Co.

THE SCARZAFAVA LAW OFFICE (AV)

48 Dietz Street, Suite C, 13820-5107
Telephone: 607-432-9341
Fax: 607-432-1986
Email: eelittle@telegram.infi.net

John F. Scarzafava

ASSOCIATES

Elizabeth E. Little
Theodoros Basdekis

Reference: Key Bank.

For full biographical listings, see the Martindale-Hubbell Law Directory

PALMYRA, Wayne Co.

FOLEY & FOLEY (AV)

235 East Main Street, P.O. Box 211, 14522
Telephone: 315-597-6611
Fax: 315-597-8920
Email: JFOLEY12@MSN.COM

MEMBERS OF FIRM

James F. Foley
Ann Firestine Foley

Reference: Marine Midland Bank (Palmyra Office).

For full biographical listings, see the Martindale-Hubbell Law Directory

*ROCHESTER,** Monroe Co.

CONNORS & CORCORAN, L.L.P. (AV)

Suite 250, 45 Exchange Street, 14614-2002
Telephone: 716-232-5885
Fax: 716-546-3631
Email: buholtz@frontiernet.net *URL:* http://www.connorscorcoran.com

MEMBERS OF FIRM

Herbert J. LePage
Roger W. Avery
Joseph G. Fritsch, Jr.
James E. Maslyn
Eileen E. Buholtz
Cheryl Loria-Dinolfo
Gregory T. Phillips

Attorneys for: Allstate Insurance Co.; Continental National American Group; Criterion Insurance Co.; General Accident Group; Ideal Mutual Insurance Co.; Prudential Property & Casualty Co.; SAFECO; Sentry Insurance; Travelers Property Casualty.
Reference: Marine Midland Bank.

For full biographical listings, see the Martindale-Hubbell Law Directory

FARACI & LANGE, LLP (AV)

400 Crossroads Building, Two State Street, 14614
Telephone: 716-325-5150
Toll Free: 888-325-5150
Fax: 716-325-3285
Satellite Office, Rochester, New York: IUE Local 509 Building, 1515 Lyell Avenue, 14606.
Telephone: 716-458-2800. Union Toll Free Number: 800-483-4882.
Fax: 716-458-3015.

John A. Bryant (1943-1995)
Angelo G. Faraci
Paul K. Lange
Joseph A. Regan
Stephen G. Schwarz
Vincent M. Moyer
Brian M. Zorn
Anthony A. Di Nitto
Matthew F. Belanger

ASSOCIATES

Michelle L. Callan
Carol A. Mckenna
James L. Bradley
Bradley P. Kammholz
John A. Falk
Patrick K. Russi

OF COUNSEL

Joseph S. Guadagnino

For full biographical listings, see the Martindale-Hubbell Law Directory

HALLENBECK, LASCELL, NORRIS & HELLER (AV)

A Limited Liability Partnership
One Exchange Street, 14614
Telephone: 716-423-5900
Fax: 716-423-5910
Email: HLNZ@hlnz.com

MEMBERS OF FIRM

Alfred M. Hallenbeck
David M. Lascell
Michael D. Norris
Cheryl A. Heller

COUNSEL

Robert A. Feldman
David A. Wier

Daniel P. Purcell
Meghan Mc Manus Di Pasquale
Suzanne E. Ouellette
Andrea F. Basso
Robert S. Attardo

For full biographical listings, see the Martindale-Hubbell Law Directory

ROBERT J. MICHAEL (AV)

39 State Street, Suite 420, 14614
Telephone: 716-232-3460
Fax: 716-232-4583

OF COUNSEL

Mark H. Tiernan

Reference: The Chase Manhattan Bank.

For full biographical listings, see the Martindale-Hubbell Law Directory

Rochester—Continued

LAW OFFICES OF PEARL & SMITH (AV)

16 Main Street West, Suite 141, 14614-1601
Telephone: 716-454-7550
Fax: 716-454-4602
Email: pearlaw@frontiernet.net *URL:* http://www.lawyers.com/pearl&smith

Robert J. Pearl — Donald A. W. Smith

For full biographical listings, see the Martindale-Hubbell Law Directory

ROCKVILLE CENTRE, Nassau Co.

JACOBSON & SCHWARTZ (AV)

510 Merrick Road, P.O. Box 46, 11571
Telephone: 516-536-0900
Telecopier: 516-536-2371

Jacob N. Schwartz
Ronald A. Jacobson (1935-1993)
Gary R. Schwartz
Robert M. Bridges

Paul Goodovitch
Eric P. Tosca
Jeffrey D. Kadushin
Walter P. Wagner
Rhonda Hammer Barry
Susan B. Mandiberg
Anthony Eugene Graziani
Marc G. Schultz

OF COUNSEL

Bernard Adler

For full biographical listings, see the Martindale-Hubbell Law Directory

STONY POINT, Rockland Co.

HURLEY, FOX, SELIG & KELLEHER (AV)

Liberty Building, Route 9 W, 10980
Telephone: 914-942-2222
Fax: 914-942-0378
Email: HFSKlaw@aol.com
New City, New York Office: 60 Pine Street.
Telephone: 614-634-2050.

MEMBERS OF FIRM

Benjamin E. Selig — Glenn W. Kelleher

ASSOCIATES

Steven L. Kahn
Dana Selig Kahn
Bob A. Kramer
Kenneth P. Silver

Representative Clients: Bradlees, Inc.; Stop & Shop Companies; CNA Insurance Cos.; Federal Insurance Co.; Chubb & Son; Commercial Union Group of Insurance Cos.; Empire Insurance Co.; Omaha, N.B.; Excelsior Insurance Co.; Fireman's Insurance Company of Washington, D.C.

For full biographical listings, see the Martindale-Hubbell Law Directory

*SYRACUSE,** Onondaga Co.

ANDREWS LAW OFFICES (AV)

217 South Salina Street, Sixth Floor, 13202
Telephone: 315-471-2413
Telecopier: 315-471-7849
Email: andrews@servtech.com

William S. Andrews

For full biographical listings, see the Martindale-Hubbell Law Directory

*TROY,** Rensselaer Co.

E. STEWART JONES (AV)

28 Second Street, 12181
Telephone: 518-274-5820
Fax: 518-274-5875
Email: info@esjlaw.com

E. Stewart Jones, Jr.
W. Farley Jones
Jeffrey K. Anderson
David J. Taffany
Peter J. Moschetti, Jr.

OF COUNSEL

E. Stewart Jones
Arthur L. Rosen
Abbott H. Jones (1873-1939)
Charles W. Marshall (1882-1945)

References: Key Bank and On Bank; Troy Savings Bank.

For full biographical listings, see the Martindale-Hubbell Law Directory

*UTICA,** Oneida Co.

JULIAN & PERTZ, P.C. (AV)

1629 Oneida Street, 13501-4701
Telephone: 315-797-5610
Fax: 315-797-7403

Robert F. Julian — Richard Pertz

(See Next Column)

LEGAL SUPPORT PERSONNEL

Tracey A. Mills (Paralegal)
Barbara A. Clark (Paralegal)
Nadine J. McIntyre (Paralegal)

For full biographical listings, see the Martindale-Hubbell Law Directory

*WHITE PLAINS,** Westchester Co.

BOEGGEMAN, GEORGE, HODGES & CORDE, P.C. (AV)

11 Martine Avenue, 10606
Telephone: 914-761-2252
Telecopier: 914-761-5211
Email: boeggeman@bghc-law.com *URL:* http://www.bghc-law.com
Albany, New York Office: 46 Columbia Street, 12207-2716.
Telephone: 518-465-1100.
Fax: 518-465-1800.

George S. Hodges
Richard G. Corde
John J. Walsh, II
Harold L. Moroknek
Robert S. Ondrovic
Thomas A. Sica (Resident Managing Attorney, Albany Office)

Karen A.D. Jockimo
William M. Wingertzahn
Elizabeth C. Mirisola
Cynthia Dolan
Marcella M. Green
Paul A. Hurley
Leslie K. Arfine
John T. Holden
James J. Lofrese
Jeanne M. Hurley
Ira H. Lapp
Matt Randolph Belkin
Cynthia K. Messemer

OF COUNSEL

Joseph H. George — John E. Boeggeman (1919-1993)

Representative Clients: American Telephone & Telegraph; Anheuser-Busch Companies, Inc.; Lowe's Home Centers; Great Atlantic & Pacific Tea Company; Reliance National Insurance Company; Metropolitan Property & Casualty Insurance Company; Fisher Price, Inc.; CGU Insurance Company; United Services Automobile Association; New York Central Mutual Fire Insurance Company.

For full biographical listings, see the Martindale-Hubbell Law Directory

MARVIN A. COOPER, P.C. (AV)

Suite 706, Northcourt Building, 175 Main Street, 10601
Telephone: 914-428-9200; 718-405-9700
Telecopier: 914-428-4126

Marvin A. Cooper — William H. Cooper

Reference: Chase Bank.

For full biographical listings, see the Martindale-Hubbell Law Directory

O'CONNOR, MCGUINNESS, CONTE, DOYLE & OLESON (AV)

One Barker Avenue, 10601
Telephone: 914-948-4500
Telecopier: 914-948-0645
Email: attys@omcdoc.com

MEMBERS OF FIRM

Dennis L. O'Connor (1913-1989)
Rocco Conte
Dennis T. Doyle
William S. Oleson
Richard C. Oleson
Dennis L. O'Connor, Jr.
William R. Watson
Kevin M. Loftus

ASSOCIATES

Louis K. Szarka
Montgomery Lee Effinger
Philomena Basuk
Debora J. Dillon
Daniel M. Miller
Peter Hyun Kim
James R. Callan
Dawn T. McConnell
George M. Lesnett
Robert Wolf

OF COUNSEL

Eugene J. McGuinness — Russell J. Hauck

Attorneys for: Allstate Insurance Co.; Continental Insurance Group; Government Employers Insurance Co.; Merchants Mutual Insurance Co.; Prudential Insurance Co.; Medical Liability Mutual Insurance Co.; Colonial Penn Insurance Co.; G&W Electric Co.; CIGNA; Alexis.

For full biographical listings, see the Martindale-Hubbell Law Directory

ROGAN GUIDA & ORENSTEIN (AV)

235 Mamaroneck Avenue, 10605
Telephone: 1-888-WIN-WITH-US; 914-328-4480
Fax: 914-328-4479
URL: http://www.NYlawyers.com
Email: RoganGO@aol.com *URL:* http://www.lawyers.com/personalinjury

Jeffrey P. Rogan
Toni M. Guida
David L. Orenstein

Representative Clients: Recore One Mortgage Corp.; LEASCO; Pappas Enterprises Inc.; Steelcase, Inc.; Printing Center of Westchester Inc.; Corporate Imaging, Inc.; King Jolo's Flowers, Inc.; Systems Exchange, Inc.; Domus Realty.

(See Next Column)

ROGAN GUIDA & ORENSTEIN, *White Plains—Continued*

Reference: Fleet Bank.

For full biographical listings, see the Martindale-Hubbell Law Directory

VOUTÉ, LOHRFINK, MAGRO & COLLINS, LLP (AV)

170 Hamilton Avenue, 10601-1789
Telephone: 914-946-1400
Facsimile: 914-946-8024

Arthur J. Vouté, Jr.
Richard L. Magro
Charles D. Lohrfink, Jr.
Charles A. Collins, Jr.

Elliot A. Cristantello
Stephen F. Fischer
Ralph F. Schoene
Kevin P. Fitzpatrick
Catherine F. Gale
Hal Roberts
Stephen J. Riebling, Jr.
John A. Howard
Michael A. Sonkin
Kelly E. Cardany

Representative Clients: Aetna Casualty & Surety Co.; Allstate Insurance Co.; Chubb Group; CNA Companies; Medical Liability Mutual Insurance Co.; National Car Rental System, Inc.; Physicians Reciprocal Insurance Co.; Preferred Physicians Medical Insurance Co.; Risk Enterprise Management; St. Josephs Medical Center.

For full biographical listings, see the Martindale-Hubbell Law Directory

NORTH CAROLINA

*RALEIGH,** Wake Co.

BAILEY & DIXON, L.L.P. (AV)

2500 Two Hannover Square, 434 Fayetteville Street Mall, P.O. Box 1351, 27602
Telephone: 919-828-0731
Facsimile: 919-828-6592
Email: info@bdixon.com *URL:* http://www.bdixon.com

MEMBERS OF FIRM

Ralph McDonald
Gary S. Parsons
Carson Carmichael, III
Alan J. Miles
Patricia P. Kerner
Cathleen M. Plaut
David S. Coats
M. Denise Stanford
Kenyann Brown Stanford

OF COUNSEL

J. Ruffin Bailey
Wright T. Dixon, Jr. (Retired)
James H. Walker (1920-1994)
David M. Britt

ASSOCIATES

David Scott Wisz
Warren Tobin Savage, IV
Rita Lane Hanshumaker
Dayatra T. King
Philip Todd Gray
Ali John Hoomani

Representative Clients: Nationwide Insurance Co.; Aetna Life and Casualty Insurance Company; Santee Carriers; Abbott Laboratories, Inc.; GAB Business Services, Inc.; Sta-Rite Industries, Inc.; Hartford Insurance Group; Erie Insurance Co.; Southern Pilot Insurance Co.

For full biographical listings, see the Martindale-Hubbell Law Directory

MICHAELS, JONES, MARTIN, PARRIS & TESSENER LAW OFFICES, PLLC (AV)

Suite 200, 410 Glenwood Avenue, 27603
Telephone: 919-821-0005
Fax: 919-832-7426
URL: http://www.michaelsandjones.com
Durham, North Carolina Office: University Tower, Suite 526, 27707.
Telephone: 919-544-3000.
Wilmington, North Carolina Office: 1213 Culbreth Drive, Suite 104, 28405.
Telephone: 910-256-4005.
Charlotte, North Carolina Office: 301 South McDowell Street, Suite 400.
Telephone: 1-800-662-1234.

Paul J. Michaels
John Alan Jones
Gregory M. Martin
E. Spencer Parris
Hoyt G. Tessener
Kenneth B. Oettinger
H. Forest Horne, Jr.
Gary W. Jackson
Tamara R. Nance
John Michael Riley
Monique M. Peebles
Sandra W. Mitterling
Gabriel F. Jiménez (Not admitted in NC)
Ronald L. Pressley

For full biographical listings, see the Martindale-Hubbell Law Directory

TWIGGS, ABRAMS, STRICKLAND & TREHY, P.A. (AV)

First Union Capitol Center, 150 Fayetteville Street Mall, Suite 1100, P.O. Drawer 30, 27602
Telephone: 919-828-4357
Fax: 919-833-7924
Email: tastlaw@tast.com

(See Next Column)

Howard F. Twiggs
Douglas B. Abrams
Donald R. Strickland
Jerome P. Trehy, Jr.
Karen M. Rabenau

OF COUNSEL

Donald H. Beskind
Margaret Smith Abrams
Jeff Erick Essen

For full biographical listings, see the Martindale-Hubbell Law Directory

WOMBLE CARLYLE SANDRIDGE & RICE (AV)

A Professional Limited Liability Company
2100 First Union Capitol Center, 150 Fayetteville Street Mall, P.O. Box 831, 27602
Telephone: 919-755-2100
Fax: 919-755-2150
Email: lawyers@wcsr.com *URL:* http://www.wcsr.com
Charlotte, North Carolina Office: 3300 One First Union Center, 301 South College Street.
Telephone: 704-331-4900.
Fax: 704-331-4955.
Winston-Salem, North Carolina Office: 200 West Second Street, P.O. Drawer 84.
Telephone: 336-721-3600.
Fax: 336-721-3660.
Research Triangle Park, North Carolina Office: 2505 Meridian Parkway, Suite 300 (Durham), 27713.
Telephone: 919-484-2300.
Fax: 919-484-2340.
Atlanta, Georgia Office: One Atlantic Center, 1201 West Peachtree Street, Suite 3500.
Telephone: 404-872-7000.
Fax: 404-888-7490.
Other Atlanta, Georgia Office: Suite 404, 2296 Henderson Mill Road, N.E.
Telephone: 770-492-9030.
Fax: 770-492-9609.
Washington, D.C. Office: 1120 Nineteenth Street, N.W., Eighth Floor.
Telephone: 202-857-4400.
Fax: 202-467-6910.
Greenville, South Carolina Office: 15 South Main Street, Suite 601, P.O. Box 10208.
Telephone: 864-255-5400.
Fax: 864-255-5440.

RESIDENT MEMBERS

Robert E. Fields III
Frederick W. Rom

RESIDENT ASSOCIATES

Charles L. Becker
Mary Sheehan Pollard

Representative Clients: Aetna Casualty and Surety Co., Inc.; ALSCO/AmeriMark Building Products, Inc.; Aoki Corporation America, Inc.; Hackney Brothers, Inc.; Lawyers Mutual Liability Insurance Company of North Carolina; Meredith College; Regency Park Corp.; Wachovia Bank, N.A.

For Complete List of Firm Personnel, See General Section

For full biographical listings, see the Martindale-Hubbell Law Directory

YATES, MCLAMB & WEYHER, L.L.P. (AV)

One Hannover Square, 421 Fayetteville Street Mall, Suite 1200, 27601
Telephone: 919-835-0900
Fax: 919-835-0910
Mailing Address: P.O. Box 2889, 27602-2889

MEMBERS OF FIRM

R. Scott Brown
Derek M. Crump
Dan J. McLamb
John W. Minier
Rodney E. Pettey
O. Craig Tierney, Jr.
Andrew A. Vanore, III
Kirk G. Warner
Barbara B. Weyher
Joseph W. Yates, III (Retired)

ASSOCIATES

Virginia Green Adams
Michael J. Byrne
Hunt K. Choi
Barry S. Cobb
Renee Billings Crawford
Susan T. Fountain
Gwenda L. Laws
Michael E. McDaniel
Travis K. Morton
Shirley Maring Pruitt
Beth Y. Smoot
Diane S. Tilley
Michael W. Washburn

OF COUNSEL

Michael C. Hurley

Representative Clients: Chrysler Corp.; Ford Motor Corp.; General Electric Co.; Honda North America, Inc.; Kawasaki Motors Corp., USA; Mitsubishi Motors Corp.; Nissan Motor Corp.; Sears Roebuck & Co.; Upjohn Co.; Sandoz Pharmaceuticals Corp.

For full biographical listings, see the Martindale-Hubbell Law Directory

*WINSTON-SALEM,** Forsyth Co.

THE LAW OFFICES OF WILLIAM F. MAREADY (AV)

1076 West Fourth Street, Suite 100, 27101-2411
Telephone: 336-722-1027
Fax: 336-722-1028
Email: info@mareadylaw.com *URL:* http://www.mareadylaw.com

ASSOCIATE

Celie Benton Richardson

For full biographical listings, see the Martindale-Hubbell Law Directory

WOMBLE CARLYLE SANDRIDGE & RICE (AV)

A Professional Limited Liability Company
200 West Second Street, P.O. Drawer 84, 27102
Telephone: 336-721-3600
Fax: 336-721-3660
Email: lawyers@wcsr.com *URL:* http://www.wcsr.com
Charlotte, North Carolina Office: 3300 One First Union Center, 301 South College Street.
Telephone: 704-331-4900.
Fax: 704-331-4955.
Raleigh, North Carolina Office: 2100 First Union Capitol Center, 150 Fayetteville Street Mall, P.O. Box 831.
Telephone: 919-755-2100.
Fax: 919-755-2150.
Research Triangle Park, North Carolina Office: 2505 Meridian Parkway, Suite 300 (Durham), 27713.
Telephone: 919-484-2300.
Fax: 919-484-2340.
Atlanta, Georgia Office: One Atlantic Center, 1201 West Peachtree Street, Suite 3500.
Telephone: 404-872-7000.
Fax: 404-888-7490.
Other Atlanta, Georgia Office: Suite 404, 2296 Henderson Mill Road, N.E.
Telephone: 770-492-9030.
Fax: 770-492-9609.
Washington, D.C. Office: 1120 Nineteenth Street, N.W., Eighth Floor.
Telephone: 202-857-4400.
Fax: 202-467-6910.
Greenville, South Carolina Office: 15 South Main Street, Suite 601, P.O. Box 10208.
Telephone: 864-255-5400.
Fax: 864-255-5440.

RESIDENT MEMBERS

Reid C. Adams, Jr.
Conrad C. Baldwin, Jr.
S. Fraley Bost
Keith A. Clinard
Jonathan M. Engram
Hada V. Haulsee
R. Michael Leonard
Alexander S. Nicholas
Robert S. Pierce
Thomas D. Schroeder
J. Keith Tart
Erna A. P. Womble
William F. Womble, Jr.

RESIDENT ASSOCIATES

Kenneth R. Ashford
Christina U. Douglas
Elizabeth A. Flagg
Jacqueline M. Goble
Kimberly S. Herring
D. Christopher Howard (Not admitted in NC)
Christopher A. Kreiner
Michael Montecalvo
Patricia F. Poole
Donald J. Scales
Lisa M. Sheppard (Not admitted in NC)
Cynthia G. Spivey
John R. Still
Brent L. Thompson (Not admitted in NC)
C. Andrew Wattleworth
William G. Winter
Laura M. Wolfe

Representative Clients: Brad Ragan, Inc.; Brenner Companies; Food Lion, Inc.; Hanes Companies, Inc.; North Carolina Baptist Hospitals, Inc.; R.J. Reynolds Tobacco Co.; Thomasville Furniture Industries, Inc.; Wachovia Corp.; Wake Forest University.

For Complete List of Firm Personnel, See General Section

For full biographical listings, see the Martindale-Hubbell Law Directory

NORTH DAKOTA

*BISMARCK,** Burleigh Co.

PEARCE AND DURICK, PLLP (AV)

314 East Thayer Avenue, P.O. Box 400, 58502
Telephone: 701-223-2890
Fax: 701-223-7865
Email: law.office@pearce-durick.com *URL:* http://www.pearce-durick.com

MEMBERS OF FIRM

Patrick W. Durick
B. Timothy Durick
Jerome C. Kettleson
Larry L. Boschee

(See Next Column)

ASSOCIATE

Jonathan P. Sanstead

Representative Clients: AGCO Corporation; American Insurance Assn.; Case Corp.; Cigna-INA Insurance Co.; Deere & Co.; Emerson Electric Co.; Ford Motor Co.; General Motors Corp.; Navistar International Transportation; Travelers Insurance Co.

For Complete List of Firm Personnel, See General Section

For full biographical listings, see the Martindale-Hubbell Law Directory

OHIO

*AKRON,** Summit Co.

PERANTINIDES & NOLAN CO., L.P.A. (AV)

300 Courtyard Square, 80 South Summit Street, 44308-1736
Telephone: 330-253-5454
Telecopier: 330-253-6524
Email: pn@perantinides.com

Paul G. Perantinides
Chris T. Nolan

James J. Gutbrod
Christopher L. Parker
Peter D. Janos
Antonios P. Tsarouhas
Christina Simoudis
Sophie Mitsopoulos

References: First National Bank of Akron; National City Bank, Akron; Society Bank; Charter One Bank.

For full biographical listings, see the Martindale-Hubbell Law Directory

SCANLON & GEARINGER CO., L.P.A. (AV)

1100 First National Tower, 106 South Main Street, 44308-1463
Telephone: 330-376-4558
Telecopier: 330-376-3550

Timothy F. Scanlon
Bradford M. Gearinger
Michael J. Del Medico
Mark Hilkert
Patrick J. Hart
Robert A. Royer
Kevin P. Hardman
Maura E. Scanlon
John F. Hill

John T. Scanlon

For full biographical listings, see the Martindale-Hubbell Law Directory

*CINCINNATI,** Hamilton Co.

ROBERT J. GEHRING CO., L.P.A. (AV)

4th Floor, 105 East Fourth Street, 45202
Telephone: 513-721-2758
Fax: 513-621-9285

Robert J. Gehring

For full biographical listings, see the Martindale-Hubbell Law Directory

THE LAWRENCE FIRM, L.P.A. (AV)

2100 Firstar Center at Fountain Square, 425 Walnut Street, 45202
Telephone: 513-651-4130
Fax: Available upon request
Email: lawyers@lawrencefirm.com *URL:* http://www.lawrencefirm.com

Richard D. Lawrence

David A. Johns
Richard Lanahan Goodman
Thomas C. Korbee
Roger N. Braden
Jennifer L. Lawrence
Patrick J. Beirne
Donna M. Bloemer
Virginia M. Baker
Rick J. Sommer

For full biographical listings, see the Martindale-Hubbell Law Directory

SHEA & ASSOCIATES (AV)

600 Flatiron Building, 401 East Court Street, 45202-1355
Telephone: 513-621-8333
Telecopier: 513-651-3272
Email: SheaLawFrm@aol.com *URL:* http://www.attyfind.com/jwshea

Joseph W. Shea III

ASSOCIATE

Shirley A. Coffey

LEGAL SUPPORT PERSONNEL

Connie DeFillippo

For full biographical listings, see the Martindale-Hubbell Law Directory

Cincinnati—Continued

WAITE, SCHNEIDER, BAYLESS & CHESLEY CO., L.P.A. (AV)

1513 Central Trust Tower, Fourth and Vine Streets, 45202
Telephone: 513-621-0267
Fax: 513-381-2375; 621-0262

Stanley M. Chesley

Thomas F. Rehme
Robert A. Steinberg
Fay E. Stilz
Louise M. Roselle
D. Arthur Rabourn
Jerome L. Skinner
Janet G. Abaray
Paul M. De Marco
Terrence L. Goodman
Colleen M. Hegge
Jane H. Walker
Renée Infante
James F. Keller
Jean M. Geoppinger
Robert Heuck II

For full biographical listings, see the Martindale-Hubbell Law Directory

*CLEVELAND,** Cuyahoga Co.

DAVIS & YOUNG (AV)

A Legal Professional Association
1700 Midland Building, 44115
Telephone: 216-348-1700
Fax: 216-621-0602
Cable: DANDY CLE
Email: atty@davisyoung.com *URL:* http://www.davisyoung.com
Akron, Ohio Office: 1015 Society Building, 159 South Main Street. Telephone 216-376-1717.
Fax: 216-376-1797.
Youngstown, Ohio Office: 406 Wick Building, 34 Federal Plaza West, 44503.
Telephone: 330-743-1717.

George W. Lutjen
Martin J. Murphy
C. Richard McDonald
Paul D. Eklund
Jan L. Roller
Thomas W. Wright
David J. Fagnilli
Gregory H. Collins
William Vance
Patrick F. Roche

David G. Utley
Timothy L. Kerwin
Marc A. Sanchez
Ann Marie O'Brien
Susan L. Fricker
Michele Y. Wharton
Larry D. Wilkes
Timothy G. Welsh

OF COUNSEL

R. Emmett Moran

Counsel for: Westfield Companies; Cincinnati Insurance Company; University Hospitals of Cleveland; Medical Protective Company; Ohio Insurance Guaranty Association; Alliance Insurance Co.; Amerisure Companies; Avis Rent-A-Car Systems Inc.; Black & Decker; Dana Corp.; Central Mutual Insurance Co.; Eagle Picher Industries Inc.; TOPS Friendly Markets; U.S. Fidelity & Guaranty Co.

For Complete List of Firm Personnel, See General Section

For full biographical listings, see the Martindale-Hubbell Law Directory

FRIEDMAN, DOMIANO & SMITH CO., L.P.A. (AV)

Sixth Floor, Standard Building, 1370 Ontario Street, 44113-1701
Telephone: 216-621-0070; 1-800-280-0070
Fax: 216-621-4008
Email: fds.atty@worldnet.att.net *URL:* http://www.fds@advpages.com
Marco Island, Florida Office: 881 Panama Court, Suite 305, 33937.
Telephone: 941-642-0252.

Jeffrey H. Friedman
Joseph C. Domiano
M. David Smith
Lisa M. Gerlack

Stephen S. Vanek
Michael L. Eisner
Kevin L. Lenson
Tracey S. McGurk

For full biographical listings, see the Martindale-Hubbell Law Directory

GALLAGHER, SHARP, FULTON & NORMAN (AV)

(Formerly Hauxhurst, Sharp, Mollison & Gallagher)
Bulkley Building, Seventh Floor, 1501 Euclid Avenue, 44115
Telephone: 216-241-5310
Telecopier: 216-241-1608
Email: gsfn.com *URL:* http://www.gsfn.com

MEMBERS OF FIRM

H. Austin Hauxhurst (1881-1962)
Frank X. Cull (1887-1965)
I. Walter Sharp (1884-1966)
Clarence L. Mollison (1906-1981)
Robert C. Horrigan (1916-1993)
Forrest A. Norman
Edward J. Cass
John B. Robertson
Thomas E. Betz
Alan M. Petrov
Alton L. Stephens, Jr.
Virginia L. Heidloff
Jay Clinton Rice
Joseph W. Pappalardo
Thomas E. Dover
James F. Koehler

(See Next Column)

MEMBERS OF FIRM (Continued)

Robert H. Eddy
Thomas J. Kaiser
D John Travis
Paul J. Schumacher, Jr.
William F. Gibson
Gary L. Nicholson
Lynn L. Moore
Ernest W. Auciello, Jr.
Patrick M. Foy
Kevin C. Alexandersen
Stanley M. Dub
Timothy T. Brick
Sheila A. McKeon
Thomas J. Cabral
Timothy J. Fitzgerald
Mark A. Greer

OF COUNSEL

Michael R. Gallagher
Robert W. Sharp
George W. Stuhldreher
Burt J. Fulton
James F. Sweeney
James G. Gowan
James L. Ryhal, Jr.

Edward G. Kagels
John T. Murphy
M. Terence Cawley
Todd M. Haemmerle
Brian R. McGraw
Timothy P. Whitford
Daniel J. Michalec
Alexander E. Goetsch
Joseph J. Santoro
Monica A. Sansalone
John A. Simon
Dennis G. Rehor
Beth A. Nagel
Timothy Patrick Roth
Gregory K. Boop
Janice Aitken
Gary F. Werner
Mark Joseph Savage
Catherine A. Davis
Charles Allston Bowers
Pamela S. Schremp
James T. Tyminski, Jr.
Matthew J. Hatchadorian

STAFF ATTORNEY

Daniel L. Herak

Counsel for: Associated Aviation Underwriters; Conrail; The Continental Insurance Cos.; Continental National American Group; Fireman's Fund Insurance Cos.; The Home Insurance Co.; Motorist Ins. Co.; Norfolk Southern Corp.; Royal Insurance Co.; United States Aviation Underwriters.

For full biographical listings, see the Martindale-Hubbell Law Directory

HERMANN, CAHN & SCHNEIDER (AV)

Suite 500, 1301 East Ninth Street, 44114
Telephone: 216-781-5515
Facsimile: 216-781-1030
Email: hcs@en.com

MEMBERS OF FIRM

Gary D. Hermann
James S. Cahn
Kent B. Schneider
Anthony J. Hartman
Robert Warren, Jr.
Kerry S. Volsky
Peter J. Krembs

ASSOCIATES

Jay H. Salamon
Thomas P. Marotta
Romney B. Cullers

For full biographical listings, see the Martindale-Hubbell Law Directory

JANIK & FORBES (AV)

Building Two, 8223 Brecksville Road, 44141-1371
Telephone: 440-838-7600
Fax: 440-838-7601

MEMBERS OF FIRM

Steven G. Janik
Steven Forbes

For Complete List of Firm Personnel, See General Section

For full biographical listings, see the Martindale-Hubbell Law Directory

KAUFMAN & CUMBERLAND CO., L.P.A. (AV)

1500 Republic Building, 25 Prospect Avenue, West, 44115-1000
Telephone: 216-861-0707
Telefax: 216-694-6883
TDD: 216-694-6891

Steven S. Kaufman
Frank J. Cumberland, Jr. (Retired)
Frank R. DeSantis
Gail E. Sindell
William W. Jacobs
Thomas L. Feher
Mitchell Ehrenberg
Douglas P. Whipple

Susan L. Belman
Charles P. Royer
Craig P. Kvale
Robin M. Wilson

OF COUNSEL

Edda Sara Post

Representative Client: CertainTeed Corp.

For full biographical listings, see the Martindale-Hubbell Law Directory

Cleveland—Continued

KELLER AND CURTIN CO., L.P.A. (AV)

Suite 330 The Hanna Building, 44115-1901
Telephone: 216-566-7100
Fax: 216-566-5430
Email: keller@en.com
Akron, Ohio Office: 920 Key Building, 159 South Main Street, 44308-1318.
Telephone: 330-376-7245.
Fax: 330-376-8128. Email: kcakron@en.com.
Elyria, Ohio Office: 120 East Avenue, 44035-5228.
Telephone: 440-323-8662.
Fax: 440-323-6610.

Stanley S. Keller
G. Michael Curtin
Walter H. Krohngold
James M. Johnson
Joseph G. Ritzler
Thomas M. Coughlin, Jr.
John Swansinger
Camille D. Kuri
Franklin C. Malemud
Brian D. Spitz
Deena Charisse Miller

Reference: Bank One, Cleveland.

For full biographical listings, see the Martindale-Hubbell Law Directory

KREMBS & ALKIRE LLP (AV)

750 Courthouse Square, 310 West Lakeside Avenue, 44113-1021
Telephone: 216-875-7500
Fax: 216-875-7501
URL: http://www.krembs-alkire.com

Andrew P. Krembs
Richard C. Alkire
Dean C. Nieding

For full biographical listings, see the Martindale-Hubbell Law Directory

LEVIN, MARMAROS & CHARMS CO., L.P.A. (AV)

2970 BP Tower, 200 Public Square, 44114
Telephone: 216-781-4900
Fax: 216-787-0330
URL: http://www.lawyers.com/lmc

Joel Levin
Peter W. Marmaros
Stephen J. Charms

Anthony R. Brighton

For full biographical listings, see the Martindale-Hubbell Law Directory

LOWE • EKLUND • WAKEFIELD CO., L.P.A. (AV)

Tower City Center 610 Skylight Office Tower, 1660 West Second Street, 44113-1454
Telephone: 216-781-2600
Fax: 216-781-2610
Email: lew@lewlaw.com *URL:* http://www.lewlaw.com

James A. Lowe
Claudia Rieth Eklund
Mark L. Wakefield
Dennis P. Mulvihill

Gregory S. Scott
Andrew S. Goldwasser

OF COUNSEL
Donald Cybulski

For full biographical listings, see the Martindale-Hubbell Law Directory

MEYERS, HENTEMANN & REA CO., L.P.A. (AV)

21st Floor, Superior Building, 815 Superior Avenue, N.E., 44114
Telephone: 216-241-3435
Telecopier: 216-241-6568
Elyria, Ohio Office: 301 Fifth Street, 44035.
Telephone: 216-323-6920.

John S. Rea
Henry A. Hentemann

OF COUNSEL
Richard C. Talbert

Representative Clients: State Farm Mutual Insurance Co.; Travelers Insurance Co.; Lloyds Underwriters, London, England; Preferred Risk Mutual Insurance Co.; Detroit Automobile Inter-Insurance Exchange; Electrical Mutual.

For Complete List of Firm Personnel, See General Section

For full biographical listings, see the Martindale-Hubbell Law Directory

NURENBERG, PLEVIN, HELLER & MCCARTHY CO., L.P.A. (AV)

1370 Ontario Street First Floor, 44113-1792
Telephone: 216-621-2300; Toll Free: 1-800-562-7438
Fax: 216-771-2242
Email: nphm@nphm.com *URL:* http://www.nphm.com

(See Next Column)

A. H. Dudnik (1905-1963)
S. F. Komito (1902-1984)
Marshall I. Nurenberg
Leon M. Plevin
Maurice L. Heller
John J. McCarthy
Thomas Mester
Harlan M. Gordon
David M. Paris
Richard L. Demsey
Jamie R. Lebovitz
William S. Jacobson
Jeffrey A. Leikin

Robin J. Peterson
Robert S. Zeller
Ellen M. McCarthy
J. Charles Ruiz-Bueno
Kathleen J. St. John
Jonathan D. Mester
Brenda M. Johnson

Reference: Society Key Corp.

For full biographical listings, see the Martindale-Hubbell Law Directory

RODGERS AND CO., L.P.A. (AV)

1750 Guildhall, Landmark Office Towers, 45 Prospect Avenue, West, 44115
Telephone: 216-861-6191
Fax: 216-861-4699
Email: attys@rodgers-lpa.com

Walter A. Rodgers

Jeffrey M. Elzeer
Shawn A. Cormier

For full biographical listings, see the Martindale-Hubbell Law Directory

TIMOTHY A. SHIMKO & ASSOCIATES A LEGAL PROFESSIONAL ASSOCIATION (AV)

2010 Huntington Building, 925 Euclid Avenue, 44115
Telephone: 216-241-8300
Fax: 216-241-2702
Email: taslaw@ix.netcom.com *URL:* http://www.netcom.com/~taslaw

Timothy A. Shimko

Frank E. Piscitelli, Jr.

Reference: National City Bank, Cleveland.

For full biographical listings, see the Martindale-Hubbell Law Directory

SMITH, MARSHALL, WEAVER AND VERGON (AV)

500 National City East Sixth Building, 1965 East Sixth Street, 44114
Telephone: 216-781-4994
Telecopier: 216-781-9448
Email: smw@multiverse.com.

MEMBERS OF FIRM

Philip J. Weaver, Jr.
Frederick P. Vergon, Jr.

Representative Clients: American States Insurance Co.; Federated Mutual Group; Hartford Insurance Group; State Automobile Mutual Insurance Co.

For full biographical listings, see the Martindale-Hubbell Law Directory

SPANGENBERG, SHIBLEY & LIBER LLP (AV)

2400 National City Center, 1900 East Ninth Street, 44114-3400
Telephone: 216-696-3232
Fax: 216-696-3924
Email: ssl@Spanglaw.com *URL:* http://www.Spanglaw.com

MEMBERS OF FIRM

Craig Spangenberg (1914-1998)
Norman W. Shibley (1921-1992)
Donald P. Traci (Retired)
John D. Liber
Robert A. Marcis
Peter H. Weinberger
William Hawal
Peter J. Brodhead
Dennis R. Lansdowne

ASSOCIATES

Justin F. Madden
Mary A. Cavanaugh
Stuart E. Scott
Rhonda Baker Debevec

For full biographical listings, see the Martindale-Hubbell Law Directory

STEWART AND DE CHANT CO., L.P.A. (AV)

The Atrium Office Plaza-Suite 850, 668 Euclid Avenue, 44114-3060
Telephone: 216-781-2258
Fax: 216-781-8210
Email: INFO@STEWARTDECHANT.COM *URL:* http://www.STEWARTdeChant.COM

Lawrence E. Stewart
Thomas H. De Chant
Fred Wendel III
Scott E. Stewart
Samuel V. Butcher
Lawrence C. Davison
Matthew T. Brady

Reference: Keybank (Main Office).

For full biographical listings, see the Martindale-Hubbell Law Directory

Cleveland—Continued

TRACI & MARX CO., L.P.A. (AV)

55 Public Square, Suite 1550, 44113
Telephone: 216-623-8010
Fax: 216-623-8012
Email: lawyers@tracimarx.com

Robert V. Traci
James A. Marx

For full biographical listings, see the Martindale-Hubbell Law Directory

*COLUMBUS,** Franklin Co.

KEENER DOUCHER CURLEY & PATTERSON A LEGAL PROFESSIONAL ASSOCIATION (AV)

88 East Broad Street, Suite 1750, 43215
Telephone: 614-280-1100
Fax: 614-280-9503
Email: KDCP@IWAYNET.NET

Thomas J. Keener
Paul M. Doucher
W. Charles Curley
David T. Patterson
Kevin R. Bush

Michael J. Kelley
Kimberley A. Doucher
Amy K. Schermer

For full biographical listings, see the Martindale-Hubbell Law Directory

LAMKIN, VAN EMAN, TRIMBLE, BEALS & ROURKE (AV)

Suite 200, 500 South Front Street, 43215-5671
Telephone: 614-224-8187
Fax: 614-224-4943
URL: http://www.lawyers.com/lvtb&rlaw

MEMBERS OF FIRM

William W. Lamkin
Timothy L. Van Eman
Thomas W. Trimble
David A. Beals
Michael J. Rourke
Kathy A. Dougherty
Kenneth S. Blumenthal

Reference: Huntington National Bank.

For full biographical listings, see the Martindale-Hubbell Law Directory

MCCARTHY, PALMER, VOLKEMA & THOMAS A LEGAL PROFESSIONAL ASSOCIATION (AV)

140 East Town Street, Suite 1100, 43215
Telephone: Telephone: 614-221-4400
Telecopier: 614-221-6010
URL: http://www.mccarthypalmer.com
Email: attorneys@mccarthypalmer.com *URL:* http://www.lawyers.com/attorneysmccarthy

Dennis M. McCarthy
Robert Gray Palmer
Daniel R. Volkema
Warner M. Thomas, Jr.
Michael S. Miller
Elizabeth Schorpp Burkett
Craig P. Scott
Tony C. Merry

Jennifer K. Thivener

Reference: Huntington National Bank.

For full biographical listings, see the Martindale-Hubbell Law Directory

WALTER W. RECKLESS (AV)

Suite 702, 33 North High Street, 43215-7315
Telephone: 614-221-4740
Fax: Available
Email: wwrlawofc@aol.com *URL:* http://www.lawyers.com/recklesslawoffice

References: Huntington National Bank; National City Bank.

For full biographical listings, see the Martindale-Hubbell Law Directory

SCHERNER, HANSON & CORNWELL, LLC (AV)

130 Northwoods Boulevard, 43235-4725
Telephone: 614-431-7200
Fax: 614-431-7262
Delaware, Ohio Office: 5300 David Road.
Telephone: 614-595-3366.
Lima, Ohio Office: 2100 Lost Creek Boulevard.
Telephone: 419-222-1155.
Fax: 419-227-3131.

Hans Scherner
Robert E. Hanson
Ted E. Cornwell

For full biographical listings, see the Martindale-Hubbell Law Directory

ZEIGER & CARPENTER (AV)

1600 Huntington Center, 41 South High Street, 43215
Telephone: 614-365-4100
Facsimile: 614-365-9145

MEMBERS OF FIRM

John W. Zeiger
Michael H. Carpenter
Jeffrey A. Lipps
Steven W. Tigges
David A. Wallace
Marion H. Little, Jr.
Michael Romanello

ASSOCIATES

Timothy R. Bricker
Daniel R. Mordarski
Joseph T. Olecki
Michael N. Beekhuizen
Ronald E. Laymon
Angela Paul
Craig Calcaterra
John J. Todor

OF COUNSEL

Daniel R. Freytag
Mary R. True
Douglas R. Cole (Not admitted in OH)
Stuart G. Parsell

For full biographical listings, see the Martindale-Hubbell Law Directory

*DAYTON,** Montgomery Co.

DAVID M. DEUTSCH CO., L.P.A. (AV)

The Pollack House, 208 West Monument Avenue, 45402
Telephone: 937-223-7170
Facsimile: 937-223-7180
Email: ddeutsch@erinet.com *URL:* ddeutsch@hotmail.com

David M. Deutsch

For full biographical listings, see the Martindale-Hubbell Law Directory

FREUND, FREEZE & ARNOLD A LEGAL PROFESSIONAL ASSOCIATION (AV)

Suite 1800 One Dayton Centre, One South Main Street, 45402-2017
Telephone: 937-222-2424
Telecopier: 937-222-5369
Email: ffalawda@ffalaw.com *URL:* http://www.ffalaw.com
Cincinnati, Ohio Office: 8805 Governor's Hill Drive, Suite 300, 45249-3313.
Telephone: 513-583-3700.
FAX: 513-583-3703. Email: ffalawci@ffalaw.com.

Neil F. Freund
Stephen V. Freeze
Gordon D. Arnold
Stephen C. Findley
Christopher W. Carrigg
John G. Witherspoon, Jr.
Ray C. Freudiger
Kevin C. Connell
Margaret R. Young
Jennifer L. Kirkpatrick
Timothy B. Schenkel
Daniel D. Ernst
John J. Garvey, III
David J. Cusack
Marc G. Pera
T. Andrew Vollmar
Robert W. Young

Local Counsel for: Auto-Owners Insurance Co.; CNA Insurance Co.; Employers Reinsurance Corp.; Farmers Insurance Group; General Accident Ins. Co.; Medical Protective; Midwestern Group; Motorists Mutual Ins.

For full biographical listings, see the Martindale-Hubbell Law Directory

E. S. GALLON & ASSOCIATES (AV)

40 West Fourth Street Centre Suite 2200, 45402
Telephone: 937-586-3100; 800-998-4374
Fax: 937-586-3200
URL: http://www.esgallon.com

MEMBERS OF FIRM

Jack A. Cervay
David A. Saphire
Joseph R. Ebenger
Joan B. Brenner
James D. Dennis
James R. Piercy
Richard M. Malone
Kyle D. Martin
Natalie J. Tackett

ASSOCIATE

David R. Salyer

For full biographical listings, see the Martindale-Hubbell Law Directory

*ELYRIA,** Lorain Co.

ZAGRANS LAW FIRM A LEGAL PROFESSIONAL ASSOCIATION (AV)

5338 Meadow Lane Court, 44035-1469
Telephone: 440-934-7000
Facsimile: 440-934-7001
Email: eric@zagrans.com *URL:* http://www.zagrans.com

Eric H. Zagrans

Joshua M. Marks

(See Next Column)

ZAGRANS LAW FIRM A LEGAL PROFESSIONAL ASSOCIATION—*Continued*

LEGAL SUPPORT PERSONNEL

Jeannette M. Wolff (Legal Assistant)

For full biographical listings, see the Martindale-Hubbell Law Directory

*TOLEDO,** Lucas Co.

LACKEY, NUSBAUM, HARRIS, RENY & TORZEWSKI A LEGAL PROFESSIONAL ASSOCIATION (AV)

Two Maritime Plaza Third Floor, 43604
Telephone: 419-243-1105
Fax: 419-243-8953

Melvin G. Nusbaum
D. Michael Reny
Jay Harris
Joan Torzewski

Kenneth E. Boyd
John D. Franklin
P. Chris McGowan
Michael S. Jones

OF COUNSEL

Gerald B. Lackey
Dean A. Robb (Not admitted in OH)

References: Fifth Third Bank; Society Bank.

For full biographical listings, see the Martindale-Hubbell Law Directory

ROHRBACHERS, LIGHT, CRON, ZMUDA & TRIMBLE CO., L.P.A. (AV)

National City Bank Building 8th Floor, 405 Madison Avenue, 43604-1243
Telephone: 419-248-2600
Telecopier: 419-248-2614
URL: http://www.rlczt.com
URL: http://www.lawyers.com/rlcztcom

Vernon E. Rohrbacher (1920-1978)
C. Randolph Light
Nicholas J. Cron
David J. Rohrbacher
Gene A. Zmuda
Matthew J. Rohrbacher
J. Mark Trimble

Beverly J. St. Clair
Diane J. Knoblauch
Todd M. Zimmerman

OF COUNSEL

Brent B. Nicholson

LEGAL SUPPORT PERSONNEL

PARALEGAL

Anne E. Scott

For full biographical listings, see the Martindale-Hubbell Law Directory

OKLAHOMA

*OKLAHOMA CITY,** Oklahoma Co.

GARY L. BROOKS AND ASSOCIATES (AV)

7100 North Classen Boulevard, Suite 300, 73116-7101
Telephone: 405-840-1066
Fax: 405-843-8446
Email: GLB@medlaws.com *URL:* http://www.medlaws.com

Ann Brooks
Christopher J. Bergin

For full biographical listings, see the Martindale-Hubbell Law Directory

DAY, EDWARDS, FEDERMAN, PROPESTER & CHRISTENSEN, P.C. (AV)

Suite 2900 Oklahoma Tower, 210 Park Avenue, 73102-5605
Telephone: 405-239-2121
Telecopier: 405-236-1012
URL: http://lawlinks.com/attys/ok/defpc.html

Rodney J. Heggy

Kenneth A. Brokaw
Stuart W. Emmons
Gary L. Farnum

Representative Clients: BASF Corporation; Conair Corporation; DeLonghi America, Inc.; General Star Indemnity Corporation.

For Complete List of Firm Personnel, See General Section

For full biographical listings, see the Martindale-Hubbell Law Directory

KING LAW FIRM (AV)

15 North Robinson, Suite 1100, 73102
Telephone: 405-239-6143
Fax: 405-236-3934
Email: kinglaw@flash.net

(See Next Column)

Tom L. King

ASSOCIATES

Richard M. Glasgow
Scott K. Suchy
Scott F. McKinney
John J. Foley

OF COUNSEL

Donald E. DeSpain

References: BankOne; BancFirst.

For full biographical listings, see the Martindale-Hubbell Law Directory

LEE, DUROCHER, KISNER, WALKER & REID (AV)

An Association of Professional Associations
5532 North Western, 73118
Telephone: 405-848-5532
Facsimile: 405-848-5502

Jim W. Lee
David W. Kisner
Daniel L. Durocher
David A. Walker
James M. Reid

For full biographical listings, see the Martindale-Hubbell Law Directory

MERRITT & ASSOCIATES, P.C. (AV)

917 North Robinson, P.O. Box 1377, 73101
Telephone: 405-236-2222
Nationwide Toll Free: 1-800-690-2277
Fax: 405-232-8630

John M. Merritt

Michael M. Blue

For full biographical listings, see the Martindale-Hubbell Law Directory

THE MILLS LAW FIRM, P.C. (AV)

500 One Leadership Square, 211 North Robinson, 73102
Telephone: 405-239-2501
Fax: 405-239-2575
Email: millsfirm@attymail.com

Earl D. Mills
W. Wayne Mills
Robert B. Mills
Barbara K. Buratti

Margaret K. Myers
J. Drew Houghton
Daniel K. Jones
Carole L. Dulisse

For full biographical listings, see the Martindale-Hubbell Law Directory

PIERCE COUCH HENDRICKSON BAYSINGER & GREEN, L.L.P. (AV)

1109 North Francis, P.O. Box 26350, 73126
Telephone: 405-235-1611
Fax: 405-235-2904
Tulsa, Oklahoma Office: Suite 707, 100 W. 5th, ONEOK Plaza, 74103.
Telephone: 918-583-8100.
Fax: 918-583-8107.

MEMBERS OF FIRM

Gerald P. Green
John Roger Hurt
Stephen L. Olson
John Christopher Condren
D. Lynn Babb
G. Calvin Sharpe

OF COUNSEL

Kathleen J. Adler

Representative Clients: Brown & Root; Cessna Aircraft Corp.; Halliburton Cos.; Oklahoma Natural Gas; Overhead Door Corp.; Sears, Roebuck & Company; U.S. Aviation Underwriters; Van Waters & Rogers; Well-Tech Corp.; White Consolidated Industries.

For Complete List of Firm Personnel, See General Section

For full biographical listings, see the Martindale-Hubbell Law Directory

WHITTEN, MCGUIRE, WOOD, TERRY, ROSELIUS & DITTRICH A PROFESSIONAL LIMITED LIABILITY COMPANY (AV)

Suite 400, One Leadership Square, 211 North Robinson, 73102
Telephone: 405-239-2522
Fax: 405-239-2573
Email: whitten@whitten-mcguire.com
Tulsa, Oklahoma Office: 3600 First Place Tower, 15 East Fifth Street.
Telephone: 918-582-9903.

Reggie N. Whitten
Douglas A. Terry
Kent R. McGuire
Jason E. Roselius

Simone Gosnell Fulmer
R. Gregory Kirby
Philip W. Anderson
Derrick T. Dewitt

Representative Clients: The St. Paul Insurance Cos.; Crum & Forster Commercial Insurance Co.; Weyerhaeuser Co.; Biomet, Inc.; Pharmacists Mutual Insurance Co.; Ferno Manufacturing, Inc.; Eagle Manufacturing Co.; The

(See Next Column)

WHITTEN, MCGUIRE, WOOD, TERRY, ROSELIUS & DITTRICH A PROFESSIONAL LIMITED LIABILITY COMPANY, *Oklahoma City—Continued*

Rival Co.; S.C. Johnson & Sons; LWP Services, Inc.; Atlantic Mutual Insurance Co.

For full biographical listings, see the Martindale-Hubbell Law Directory

*TULSA,** Tulsa Co.

ATKINSON, HASKINS, NELLIS, BOUDREAUX, HOLEMAN, PHIPPS & BRITTINGHAM, A PROFESSIONAL CORPORATION (AV)

1500 ParkCentre, 525 South Main Street, 74103
Telephone: 918-582-8877
Fax: 918-585-8096
Email: ahnmail@ahn-law.com

Michael P. Atkinson, P.C.
Walter D. Haskins, P.C.
Gregory D. Nellis, P.C.
Paul T. Boudreaux, P.C.
Daniel E. Holeman, P.C.
K. Clark Phipps
Galen Lee Brittingham, P.C.
John S. Gladd
John J. Carwile
Martha J. Phillips
William A. Fiasco
Jon D. Starr
Mark W. Maguire
Marthanda J. Beckworth
James N. Edmonds

Kirsten E. Pace
Scott R. Hall
Jeffrey L. Wilson
Whitney M. Eschenheimer
Margaret M. Clarke
Margaret A. Nunnery
Jeffrey A. Risch
Jennifer Annis
Eric J. Begin
Roni S. Rierson
Christine M. Benson
Bret A. Sanders

OF COUNSEL

Joseph F. Glass

LEGAL SUPPORT PERSONNEL

Beverly J. Rubino, M.D. (Medical Counsel)

Representative Clients: Allstate Insurance Co.; Bayer Corp.; Crum & Forster Insurance Co.; Hartford Insurance Company; National American Insurance Co.; Federated Insurance Co.; Liberty Mutual Insurance Co.; Physicians Liability Insurance Co.; State Farm Mutual Automobile Insurance Co.; United States Aviation Underwriters.

For full biographical listings, see the Martindale-Hubbell Law Directory

FRASIER, FRASIER & HICKMAN (AV)

1700 Southwest Boulevard, 74107
Telephone: 918-584-4724
Fax: 918-583-5637
Email: frasier@tulsa.com *URL:* http://www.frasierlaw.com

MEMBERS OF FIRM

Thomas Dee Frasier
James E. Frasier
Steven R. Hickman
John W. Flippo
Everett R. Bennett, Jr.
Jerry L. Franks, Jr.
Robert A. Flynn
Frank Frasier, III

ASSOCIATE

Gary G. Brasel
George M. Miles

References: Community State Bank, Tulsa, Oklahoma; American Exchange Bank, Tulsa, Oklahoma; The Bank of Oklahoma, Tulsa, Oklahoma.

For full biographical listings, see the Martindale-Hubbell Law Directory

RHODES, HIERONYMUS, JONES, TUCKER & GABLE, P.L.L.C. (AV)

Oneok Plaza, 100 West 5th Street, Suite 400, P.O. Box 21100, 74121-1100
Telephone: 918-582-1173
Fax: 918-592-3390
URL: http://www.rhodesokla.com

MEMBERS OF FIRM

Kevin D. Berry
Jo Anne Deaton
Richard M. Eldridge
E. D. Hieronymus (1908 -1994)
Bert M. Jones
William S. Leach
Michael W. McGivern
William D. Perrine
Mary Quinn-Cooper
Robert P. Redemann
David P. Reid
Chris L. Rhodes, III
Thomas E. Steichen
Catherine C. Taylor
John H. Tucker
Wilson T. White
Harold C. Zuckerman

Ann E. Allison
Steven K. Bunting
Robert P. Coffey, Jr.
J. Christopher Davis
Andrew D. Downing
Dana L. Gish
Kerry R. Lewis
Andrew L. Richardson
Michael F. Smith
Leslie J. Southerland
Kimberly E. West
Keith A. Wilkes

(See Next Column)

OF COUNSEL

George W. Gable (Retired Partner)
Larry J. Fulton
Kelly M. Greenough

Representative Clients: American International Companies; Bechtel; Chubb Group of Insurance Companies; General Motors Corporation; Merrill, Lynch; Nissan Motor Corporation in U.S.A.; Pfizer, Inc.; Volkswagen of America, Volkswagen, A.G.; Zurich U.S.

For full biographical listings, see the Martindale-Hubbell Law Directory

THE ROACH LAW FIRM, P.C. (AV)

Park Centre, Suite 660, 525 South Main Street, 74103-4521
Telephone: 918-587-2544
Fax: 918-582-0551

Loyal J. Roach, III

Reference: Nations Bank, Tulsa.

For full biographical listings, see the Martindale-Hubbell Law Directory

SECREST, HILL & FOLLUO (AV)

7134 South Yale, Suite 900, 74136-6342
Telephone: 918-494-5905
Fax: 918-494-2847
Email: jksecrest@webzone.net

MEMBERS OF FIRM

James K. Secrest, II
W. Michael Hill
Dan S. Folluo

Richard C. Honn
Edward John Main
Roger N. Butler, Jr.
Nathan E. Clark
David A. Russell
John Jay Bowling
J. Derek Ingle
Brian J. Goree
Bradley A. Jackson

Representative Clients: Avis Rent-A-Car; Contract Freighters, Inc.; Cooper Tire and Rubber Co.; Park, Davis & Company; Sears, Roebuck and Company; Warner Lambert Co.; Cessna Aircraft Company; Freightliner Corp.; Speed Queen Co.; Waste Management Co.

For full biographical listings, see the Martindale-Hubbell Law Directory

OREGON

BEAVERTON, Washington Co.

CASE & DUSTERHOFF, LLP (AV)

9800 SW Beaverton Hillsdale Highway, Suite 200, 97005
Telephone: 503-641-7222
Facsimile: 503-643-5522
Email: jcase@case-dusterhoff.com

James D. Case
R. Bruce Dusterhoff
Leo A. Reinikka

For full biographical listings, see the Martindale-Hubbell Law Directory

*EUGENE,** Lane Co.

JOHNSON, CLIFTON, LARSON & CORSON, P.C. (AV)

10th Floor, Citizens Building, 975 Oak Street, 97401-3124
Telephone: 541-484-2434
Fax: 541-484-0882
Email: jclc@jclc.com

Arthur C. Johnson
Jacob K. Clifton, Jr.
Richard L. Larson
Don Corson
Douglas G. Schaller
Derek C. Johnson
Dennis M. Gerl
Lara Christine Johnson
Marilyn Heiken
Scott C. Lucas

For full biographical listings, see the Martindale-Hubbell Law Directory

*PORTLAND,** Multnomah Co.

SWANSON, THOMAS & COON (AV)

American Bank Building, 621 S.W. Morrison, Suite 900, 97205-3892
Telephone: 503-228-5222
Fax: 503-273-9175
URL: http://www.stc-law.com

MEMBERS OF FIRM

Douglas A. Swanson
Raymond F. Thomas
James S. Coon

(See Next Column)

SWANSON, THOMAS & COON—*Continued*

ASSOCIATES

Megan E. Glor
Alan Stuart Graf
Margaret F. Weddell

For full biographical listings, see the Martindale-Hubbell Law Directory

PENNSYLVANIA

BENSALEM, Bucks Co.

RUDOLPH, DORIAN, GOLDSTEIN, ROCHESTIE, WISNIEWSKI & TAYLOR, P.C. (AV)

Neshaminy Valley Commons, 2410 Bristol Road, 19020
Telephone: 215-750-7200
Fax: 215-750-9294
Email: admin@rudolphdorian.com *URL:* http://www.palaw.lawoffice.com
Philadelphia, Pennsylvania Office: 1818 Market Street, Suite 2300, 19103.
Telephone: 215-299-9900.
Fax: 215-299-9910.

Edward Rudolph
Harry A. Dorian, Jr.
Stephan H. Goldstein
Gary A. Rochestie
Mark A. Wisniewski
John J. Taylor
Jeffrey S. Orchinik
Kim A. Piermattei
Michael Parlow
Lawrence P. Kempner
Nancy M. Bonner

For full biographical listings, see the Martindale-Hubbell Law Directory

*EASTON,** Northampton Co.

COHEN & FEELEY, P.C. (AV)

2940 William Penn Highway, 18045
Telephone: 610-258-0111
Fax: 610-258-8095
Email: cohenfeeley@enter.net *URL:* http://www.seriouslyinjured.com
Allentown, Pennsylvania Office: 1405 North Cedar Crest Boulevard, Suite 205, 18104.
Telephone: 610-821-7702.
Fax: 610-821-9067.

Martin D. Cohen
Dennis F. Feeley

For full biographical listings, see the Martindale-Hubbell Law Directory

GUS MILIDES (AV)

654 Wolf Avenue, 18042
Telephone: 610-258-0433
Fax: 610-258-4875

For full biographical listings, see the Martindale-Hubbell Law Directory

ELKINS PARK, Montgomery Co.

MONAGHAN & GOLD, P.C. (AV)

Manor Professional Building, 7837 Old York Road, 19027
Telephone: 215-782-1800
Fax: 215-782-1010
URL: http://www.MNG-LAW.com

Alan S. Gold
John F. X. Monaghan, Jr.

Murray R. Glickman
Tanya M. Sweet
Mitchell K. Brudno
Robert F. Fortin
Sean Robins
Kenneth W. Taylor
Francis D. Hennessy, Jr.

OF COUNSEL

Alan L. Butkovitz
Steven M. Zelitch
Barbara Malett Weitz

LEGAL SUPPORT PERSONNEL

Andrew Logan (Paralegal)
Carol Veach (Paralegal)
Janet McCrossen (Registered Nurse)

For full biographical listings, see the Martindale-Hubbell Law Directory

FORT WASHINGTON, Montgomery Co.

DALLER GREENBERG & DIETRICH, LLP (AV)

Valley Green Corporate Center, 7111 Valley Green Road, 19034
Telephone: 215-836-1100
Facsimile: 215-836-2845
URL: http://www.dallergreenberg.com
Haddon Heights, New Jersey Office: 2 White Horse Pike.
Telephone: 856-547-9068.
Facsimile: 856-547-2391.

(See Next Column)

PARTNERS

Morton F. Daller
Edward A. Greenberg
Gerhard P. Dietrich
Eileen M. Johnson
Dennis R. Callahan

ASSOCIATES

Tracy Canuso Nugent (Resident, Haddon Heights, New Jersey Office)
Catherine N. Walto
Mark S. Kirby
Marie Handrich Kramer
Alison R. Rohmer

For full biographical listings, see the Martindale-Hubbell Law Directory

*HARRISBURG,** Dauphin Co.

ANGINO & ROVNER, P.C. (AV)

4503 North Front Street, 17110
Telephone: 717-238-6791
Fax: 717-238-5610
Email: lawfirm@angino-rovner.com *URL:* http://www.angino-rovner.com
Carlisle, Pennsylvania Office: 28 South Pitt Street, 17013.
Telephone: 717-241-2661.

Richard C. Angino
Neil J. Rovner

References: Credit Bureau of Greater Harrisburg; CoreStates.

For full biographical listings, see the Martindale-Hubbell Law Directory

GOLDBERG, KATZMAN & SHIPMAN, P.C. (AV)

320 Market Street - Strawberry Square, P.O. Box 1268, 17108-1268
Telephone: 717-234-4161
Telecopier: 717-234-6808; 717-234-6810
Email: gks@gkslaw.com

F. Lee Shipman
Thomas E. Brenner
John A. Statler
April L. Strang-Kutay
Guy H. Brooks
Jefferson J. Shipman

John R. Ninosky

Representative Clients: Atlantic Mutual Companies; Cincinnati Insurance Co.; Eric Insurance Group; Maryland Commercial Insurance Group; Fulton Bank.

For Complete List of Firm Personnel, See General Section

For full biographical listings, see the Martindale-Hubbell Law Directory

METZGER, WICKERSHAM, KNAUSS & ERB, P.C. (AV)

3211 North Front Street, P.O. Box 5300, 17110-0300
Telephone: 717-238-8187
Telefax: 717-234-9478
Other Harrisburg, Pennsylvania Office: 4813 Jonestown Road, P.O. Box 5300, 17110-0300.
Telephone: 717-652-7020.

Maurice R. Metzger (1918-1980)
F. Brewster Wickersham (1918-1974)
Edward E. Knauss, III (Retired)
Christian S. Erb, Jr.
Robert E. Yetter
James F. Carl
Edward E. Knauss, IV
Jered L. Hock
Karl R. Hildabrand
Richard B. Druby
Steven P. Miner

Clark DeVere
Carrie L. Carroll

Representative Clients: Allstate Insurance Co.; Chubb Group of Insurance Companies; Fireman's Fund American Insurance Group; Liberty Mutual Insurance Co.; Crum & Forster; CNA Insurance; Prudential Insurance Co.

For full biographical listings, see the Martindale-Hubbell Law Directory

PETERS & WASILEFSKI (AV)

2931 North Front Street, 17110
Telephone: 717-238-7555
Fax: 717-238-7750
Email: pwlaw@redrose.net

MEMBERS OF FIRM

William J. Peters
Charles E. Wasilefski
Dennis J. Bonetti
Joseph C. Phillips
Michael R. Bonshock
Thomas A. Lang

ASSOCIATES

Pamela S. Parascandola
Stephen F. Moore
Cindy J. Murphy
James A. Garver

Reference: Commonwealth National Bank.

For full biographical listings, see the Martindale-Hubbell Law Directory

*LANCASTER,** Lancaster Co.

ATLEE, HALL & BROOKHART, L.L.P. (AV)

8 North Queen Street, P.O. Box 449, 17608-0449
Telephone: 717-393-9596
Fax: 717-393-2138
Email: law@atleehall.com

(See Next Column)

ATLEE, HALL & BROOKHART L.L.P., *Lancaster—Continued*

MEMBERS OF FIRM

William A. Atlee, Jr. | Thomas W. Hall
Dan M. Brookhart

ASSOCIATES

Edward R. Kennett | Jaime D. Jackson
Robin A. Jabour

For full biographical listings, see the Martindale-Hubbell Law Directory

MIKUS LAW ASSOCIATES (AV)

408 West Chestnut Street, 17603
Telephone: 717-299-4840; 299-4575
Fax: 717-299-6869
Email: mikuslaw@redrose.net *URL:* http://www.mikuslaw.com

Kent D. Mikus

Michael P. McDonald | David B. Diffenbach
Loura A. Selfe

LEGAL SUPPORT PERSONNEL
LITIGATION PARALEGALS

Donna L. Simpson | Sherry L. Amspacher
C. Andrea Gadd | Olga F. Karel

For full biographical listings, see the Martindale-Hubbell Law Directory

*NORRISTOWN,** Montgomery Co.

CREEDON & FELICIANI, P.C. (AV)

29 East Marshall Street, 19401
Telephone: 610-239-9630
Fax: 610-239-1599
Email: creedon_feliciani@compuserve.com *URL:* http://www.lawyers.com/creedonfeliciani

Michael P. Creedon | Joseph L. Feliciani

For full biographical listings, see the Martindale-Hubbell Law Directory

MURPHY, OLIVER, CAIOLA & GOWEN, A PROFESSIONAL LAW CORPORATION (AV)

43 East Marshall Street, 19401-4828
Telephone: 610-272-4222; 610-279-3838
Fax: 610-272-2549; 610-275-0140
Email: molaw@injury-law.com *URL:* http://www.injury-law.com
Spring City, Pennsylvania Office: 500 S. Main Street, 19475.
Telephone: 610-948-3770.
Pottstown, Pennsylvania Office: 5 Sunnybrook Road, 19464.
Telephone: 610-323-3480.
West Chester, Pennsylvania Office: 1534 McDaniel Drive, Westtown Business Center, 19250.
Telephone: 610-272-4222.

James J. Oliver | Thomas L. Gowen, Jr.
Frank P. Murphy | Carla E. Connor
Frank L. Caiola | Barbara A. Barnes

John F. Haskins, Jr. | Cynthia Love Dengler
Carol A. Crisci

LEGAL SUPPORT PERSONNEL

Patricia A. Talese (Paralegal) | Kathleen Nicholson

For full biographical listings, see the Martindale-Hubbell Law Directory

RAYMOND M. VICTOR, P.C. (AV)

616 DeKalb Street, 19401
Telephone: 610-272-5253
Fax: 610-272-7422
Email: rdsquire@worldnet.att.net *URL:* http://www.lawyers.com/raymondmvictor

Raymond M. Victor | Christopher T. Moyer

For full biographical listings, see the Martindale-Hubbell Law Directory

*PHILADELPHIA,** Philadelphia Co.

BRIGHAM AND TREVOR, P.C. (AV)

1818 Market Street, Suite 3535, 19103
Telephone: 215-640-0500
Fax: 215-981-0801
URL: http://www.lawyers.com/brighamandtrevor

Martin K. Brigham | Eunice Trevor

Noreen C. O'Grady | Daniel Bencivenga

For full biographical listings, see the Martindale-Hubbell Law Directory

LAW OFFICES OF JAMES E. COLLERAN (AV)

1525 Locust Street 18th Floor, 19102
Telephone: 215-790-5500
FAX: 215-790-5509
Email: colleran@colleran.com

James E. Colleran, Jr. | Mary T. Colleran
Francis T. Colleran | James I. Devine
Teresa Colleran Quinn | David C. Devine

For full biographical listings, see the Martindale-Hubbell Law Directory

JOHN GERARD DEVLIN & ASSOCIATES, P.C. (AV)

1515 Market Street Suite 2010, 19102
Telephone: 215-564-6740
Telefax: 215-564-6732
Email: devlinlaw@aol.com
Allentown, Pennsylvania Office: The Sovereign Building, Executive Suite 103, 609 Hamilton Mall.
Telephone: 215-820-6422.
Westmont, New Jersey Office: 216 Haddon Avenue, Suite 103.
Telephone: 609-858-1690.
Fax: 609-858-8998.
East Brunswick, New Jersey Office: 190 Route 18, Suite 3000.
Telephone: 908-214-2621.
Fax: 908-246-2917.
Wilkes-Barre, Pennsylvania Office: Cross Creek Pointe, 1065 Hwy 315, Suite H.
Telephone: 610-820-6422.

John Gerard Devlin | Michael Malarick
James B. Corrigan, Jr. | Suzanne Curran Murphy
Joseph T. Murphy, Jr. | Arthur F. Wheeler
Thomas Paschos | Paul A. Lawless, Jr.

Representative Clients: Lloyds of London; Commercial Union; John Hancock Property and Casualty Insurance Co.; Wausau Insurance Co.; Hanseco Insurance Co.; American Family Insurance Co.; Liberty Mutual Insurance Co.; Linberg Adjustment Co.

For full biographical listings, see the Martindale-Hubbell Law Directory

FARAGE, MCBRIDE & RUGGIERI (AV)

836 Suburban Station Building, 1617 John F. Kennedy Boulevard, 19103
Telephone: 215-563-3973
Fax: 215-563-3094
URL: http://www.lawyers.com/fmrlaw
Woodbury, New Jersey Office: 9 South Broad Street, 08096.
Telephone: 609-845-9448.
Fax: 606-845-4888.

MEMBERS OF FIRM

Donald J. Farage (1909-1998) | James F. McBride
Thomas J. Ruggieri

For full biographical listings, see the Martindale-Hubbell Law Directory

FURIA AND TURNER (AV)

1717 Rittenhouse Square, 19103-6109
Telephone: 215-985-4500
Telecopier: 215-985-2824
Email: rfuria1717@aol.com *URL:* http://www.lawyers.com/furiaandturner

MEMBERS OF FIRM

Richard F. Furia | James M. Turner, Jr.

ASSOCIATES

Gina R. Furia | Donna DiPietro-Gerace

For full biographical listings, see the Martindale-Hubbell Law Directory

GALFAND BERGER, LLP (AV)

1818 Market Street, 23rd Floor, 19103-3623
Telephone: 215-665-1600
Fax: 215-564-2262
Email: sdonaway@galfandberger.com *URL:* http://www.galfandberger.com

Richard M. Jurewicz | Robert G. Mangold
Joseph Lurie | Peter M. Patton
Eric J. Swan

Arthur L. Bugay | Joseph Z. Traub

For full biographical listings, see the Martindale-Hubbell Law Directory

Philadelphia—Continued

GOLDFEIN & JOSEPH, A PROFESSIONAL CORPORATION (AV)

1600 Market Street 33rd Floor, 19103-7288
Telephone: 215-979-8200
Fax: 215-979-8201
URL: http://www.goldfeinlaw.com
Princeton, New Jersey Office: Princeton Metro Center, Suite 115, 5 Vaughn Drive.
Telephone: 609-520-0400.
Fax: 609-520-1450.
Wilmington, Delaware Office: PNC Bank Center, Suite 1110, P.O. Box 2206, 222 Delaware Avenue.
Telephone: 302-656-3301.
Fax: 302-656-0643.
New York, New York Office: 150 Broadway, Suite 1212, 10038.
Telephone: 212-791-0340.
Fax: 212-791-0347.

Edward B. Joseph
Fredric L. Goldfein
E. Chandler Hosmer, III
David C. Weinberg
Bernard L. Levinthal
Roseann Lynn Brenner
Gary H. Kaplan
John A. Turlik

Michael A. Billotti
Medford J. Brown, III
Robert P. Coleman
Robert T. Connor
Charles D. Cooper
Kelly A. Costello
Lawrence E. Currier
Janet E. Golup
Christine Renee Guiliano
David M. Katzenstein
Matthew A Kelly, III
Deborah M. Knight
Pamela A. Post
Thomas M. Savon
Julie M. Sebring (Not admitted in PA)
Robert M. Stroh
Marc R. Wilner
Anthony F. Zabicki, Jr.

For full biographical listings, see the Martindale-Hubbell Law Directory

HOLLSTEIN KEATING CATTELL JOHNSON & GOLDSTEIN, P.C. (AV)

Suite 1602 1608 Walnut Street, 19103
Telephone: 215-893-9488
Fax: 215-893-9480
Email: JFJ@HKCJG.com
Voorhees, New Jersey Office: 1016 Laurel Oak Road, Suite 2, 08043.
Telephone: 609-309-9000.
Fax: 609-309-0337.
Wilmington, Delaware Office: One Commerce Center, Suite 730, 12th and Orange Streets, 19801.
Telephone: 302-884-6700.
Fax: 302-573-2507.

Richard W. Hollstein
E. Michael Keating, III
Edward V. Cattell, Jr.
James W. Johnson
Stuart M. Goldstein (Resident, Voorhees, New Jersey Office)
Mark G. Lionetti
John E. Tyrrell
Lynne M. Parker (at Voorhees, New Jersey and Wilmington, Delaware Offices)
Paul F. Weisbein
James D. Lloyd
Nancy D. Wagman
Margaret M. Grasso

LEGAL SUPPORT PERSONNEL

Nancy Hevener (Paralegal)
Libby Carrol (Paralegal)

For full biographical listings, see the Martindale-Hubbell Law Directory

KANE & SILVERMAN, PROFESSIONAL CORPORATION (AV)

The Philadelphian Suite 1C-44, 2401 Pennsylvania Avenue, 19130
Telephone: 215-232-1000
Fax: 215-232-0181
Email: HGS@palegaladvice.com *URL:* http://www.palegaladvice.com

Michael C. Kane
Howard G. Silverman

For full biographical listings, see the Martindale-Hubbell Law Directory

KELLEY, JASONS, MCGUIRE & SPINELLI, L.L.P. (AV)

One Penn Center, Suite 1400, 1617 JFK Boulevard, 19103
Telephone: 215-854-0658
Fax: 215-854-8434; 215-854-0777
Marlton, New Jersey Office: One Greentree Centre, Suite 201, 08053.
Telephone: 609-988-5543.
Fax: 609-988-9165.
Wilmington, Delaware Office: 800 Delaware Avenue, P.O. Box 194, 19899.
Telephone: 302-652-8560.
Fax: 302-652-8405.

MEMBERS OF FIRM

John Patrick Kelley
Catherine N. Jasons
Joseph W. McGuire
Armand J. Della Porta, Jr.
Christopher N. Santoro
Robert N. Spinelli
Thomas P. Hanna
Thomas J. Johanson
Michael L. Turner
Richard L. Walker, II
Timothy McGowan

(See Next Column)

ASSOCIATES

Neal C. Glenn
W. Matthew Reber
Ann C. Lebowitz
Anthony J. Ryan

OF COUNSEL

Matthew D. Blum

For full biographical listings, see the Martindale-Hubbell Law Directory

KESSLER, COHEN & ROTH, A PROFESSIONAL CORPORATION (AV)

Two Penn Center Plaza, Suite 1705, 19102
Telephone: 215-567-3500
Fax: 215-567-6019
Email: lawyers@kesslercohen.com

Arnold M. Kessler
Stewart L. Cohen
Harry M. Roth
Karen R. Bramblett
Stephen R. Kurens
David L. Gordon
William D. Marvin

For full biographical listings, see the Martindale-Hubbell Law Directory

LAVIN, COLEMAN, O'NEIL, RICCI, FINARELLI & GRAY (AV)

Suite 1000, 510 Walnut Street, 19106
Telephone: 215-627-0303
Fax: 215-627-2551
Mount Laurel, New Jersey Office: 8000 Midlantic Drive, Suite 201 South.
Telephone: 609-778-5544.
Fax: 609-778-3383.
New York, New York Office: 7th Floor, 767 Third Avenue.
Telephone: 212-319-6898.
Fax: 212-319-6932.

George J. Lavin, Jr.
Thomas Finarelli
William V. Coleman
Francis F. Quinn
Joseph E. O'Neil
Francis P. Burns, III
William J. Ricci
Edward A. Gray
Basil A. DiSipio
Wayne A. Graver
Gerard Cedrone
Mary Grace Maley
Christine O. Boyd
Michael D. Brophy
Joseph A. McGinley
Robert J. Hafner
Robert J. Martin
Susan Ellyn Satkowski
Henry Michael Clinton
Francis J. Grey, Jr.
Richard B. Wickersham, Jr.
John J. Bateman
Ronald W. Boak
Michael T. Droogan, Jr.
Eugene Hamill
Michael P. Kinkopf
Stephen E. Moore
Michael J. Quinn
William E. Staas, III
Denise Carroll Chaplin
Marsha E. Flora
Peter M. Newman
John J. O'Donnell
Jo E. Peifer

Valerie Aabdollah
Lee R. Allman
Jennifer M. Brooks
Jessica Faden (Resident, Mount Laurel, New Jersey Office)
Frank C. B. Friestedt
Julie M. Holland
Leland I. Kellner
George J. Lavin, III
Margot L. Ludlam (Resident, New York, New York Office)
Daniel P. Lynch
Leona C. McFadden
Lorraine B. McGlynn
Henry James Noye
Michael J. O'Neill
Monica Tamar Proffitt
Sheila Marie Raftery
Michelle S. Regan (Resident, New York, New York Office)
Robert L. Sanzo
William E. Schaefer
Richard J. Sexton
Gregory Steven Spizer
Susan L. Troxell
Fiona J. Van Dyck
Anne E. Walters
Dennis P. Ziemba

For full biographical listings, see the Martindale-Hubbell Law Directory

LEVIN, FISHBEIN, SEDRAN & BERMAN (AV)

Suite 500, 510 Walnut Street, 19106-3697
Telephone: 215-592-1500
Fax: 215-592-4663
Email: lfsb@psinet.com

MEMBERS OF FIRM

Arnold Levin
Michael D. Fishbein
Howard J. Sedran
Laurence S. Berman
Frederick S. Longer

Craig D. Ginsburg
Cheryl R. Brown Hill
Donald E. Haviland, Jr.
Daniel C. Levin
Terrianne Benedetto
Charles E. Schaffer
Austin B. Cohen

LEGAL SUPPORT PERSONNEL

Lee Ann Fitzpatrick
Cheryl Hesson

For full biographical listings, see the Martindale-Hubbell Law Directory

Philadelphia—Continued

MANTA AND WELGE, A PROFESSIONAL CORPORATION (AV)

2000 Market Street, 6th Floor, 19103
Telephone: 215-851-6600
Telecopy: 215-851-6644
URL: http://www.mantalaw.com
Allentown, Pennsylvania Office: Suite 204, 5000 Tilghman Street.
Telephone: 610-395-7499.
Fax: 610-366-5096.
Harrisburg, Pennsylvania Office: Governors Row, 27 North Front Street.
Telephone: 717-236-8420.
West Trenton, New Jersey Office: 810 Bear Tavern Road, Suite 301.
Telephone: 609-883-6990.
Fax: 609-883-7730.
Wilmington, Delaware Office: Suite 1400, Mellon Bank Center, 919 Market Street.
Telephone: 302-655-7460.
Fax: 302-655-7004.

MEMBERS OF FIRM

Joseph G. Manta
Mark A. Welge
William R. Hourican
Albert L. Piccerilli
Margaret E. Wenke
Mark J. Manta
Stephen W. Miller
Thomas B. O'Brien, Jr.
Kim Hollaender
Albert M. Saltz

Joseph B. Silverstein
Ellen R. Tarrington
Robert M. Cavalier
Janelle E. Fulton
Denise Adamucci
Robert S. Stickley

For full biographical listings, see the Martindale-Hubbell Law Directory

MARKS, O'NEILL, REILLY, O'BRIEN & COURTNEY, P.C. (AV)

1880 John F. Kennedy Boulevard Suite 1200, 19103
Telephone: 215-564-6688
Fax: 215-564-2526
Email: moro1@morocpa.com
Norristown, Pennsylvania Office: 411 Cherry Street.
Telephone: 215-277-7601.
Pittsburgh, Pennsylvania Office: 707 Grant Street, Gulf Tower, Suite 3200.
Telephone: 412-391-6171.
Fax: 412-391-8804.
Westmont, New Jersey Office: 216 Haddon Avenue, Suite 500.
Telephone: 856-858-6110.
Fax: 856-858-3687. E-Mail: moro1@morocnj.com
Wilmington, Delaware Office: 2004 Foulk Road, Suite 7.
Telephone: 302-475-5500.
Fax: 302-475-5584.

Jerome E. Marks
Joseph M. O'Neill
Vincent F. Reilly
Kevin J. O'Brien
Dawn R. Courtney
Sean Xavier Kelly
Gino P. Mecoli
John J. Repcheck (Resident, Pittsburgh Office)

David P. Helwig (Resident, Pittsburgh Office)
Maureen Murray-O'Toole
Patrick C. Lamb
Christine G. Boyle
Nancy E. Mancheski
Michael T. Hamilton
Kelly L. Bracken
Tracey Marie McDevitt
Sharon A. Connors (Resident, Westmont, New Jersey Office)
Malissa A. Richetti
Patricia M. Henrich
Judith H. Ring
Gary Weinberg (Resident, Westmont, New Jersey Office)
Lee J. Janiczek
Wendy D. Testa (Resident, Westmont, New Jersey Office)
Gary F. Sharlock (Resident, Pittsburgh Office)
Robert Dale Leidigh (Resident, Pittsburgh Office)
Joseph L. Orszulak, II (Resident, Pittsburgh Office)
Diane Beckman Carvell
Karen J. Stanzione
Michael A. Kosar
Susan D. Grant (Resident, Westmont, New Jersey Office)
Frances Wang-Deveney (Resident, Westmont, New Jersey)
Courtney E. Passin
Stephanie Victoria Shreibman
Megan Kochell D'Iorio (Resident, Wilmington, Delaware Office)
Megan Trocki Mantzavinos (Resident, Wilmington, Delaware Office)
Toni Anderson Moore
Natalie M. Nugent
Frank Gattuso
Michael A. Ring (Resident, Westmont, New Jersey Office)
Ann M. Madden (Not admitted in PA)
Matthew J. Zamites
Salvatore A. Clemente

LEGAL SUPPORT PERSONNEL

PARALEGALS

Gregory P. Sabo
Elisa LaRosa
Frances P. Rossi
Heather Feenan
Jerry Ezekiel
Steven Randisi
Sharon Williams
Melanie Gaskins

For full biographical listings, see the Martindale-Hubbell Law Directory

MCCORMICK & PRIORE, P.C. (AV)

One Penn Square West, 30 S. 15th Street, Suite 1500, 19102
Telephone: 215-972-0161
Fax: 215-972-5580
Email: mccormick5@aol.com
Marlton, New Jersey Office: One Greentree Centre, Suite 201, 08053.
Telephone: 609-988-5452.
Fax: 609-596-8359.

David M. McCormick
Philip D. Priore
Stephen M. McManus

OF COUNSEL

Harry A. Short, Jr.

Wendy L. Schmidt-Levin
H. Joseph Byron
Michelle Nick Rossi
Christina A. Toriello
Jill Schneider
John P. Lock

LEGAL SUPPORT PERSONNEL

Deborah Stefan
Jane Coley

For full biographical listings, see the Martindale-Hubbell Law Directory

MCELDREW & FULLAM, P.C. (AV)

Suite 5050 One Liberty Place, 19103
Telephone: 215-563-8300
800-223-3352
Fax: 215-563-6130
URL: http://www.lawyers.com/mceldrew&fullampc
New York, New York Office: McEldrew & Ressler, Suite 2101, 11 Pennsylvania Plaza, 10001.
Telephone: 212-695-6446.
Fax: 212-268-0287.

James J. McEldrew, III
Nancy H. Fullam

Marcella J. Schell
Carol L. Vassallo
Sallie Updyke Mundy
David Felderman

LEGAL SUPPORT PERSONNEL

Christine Doelp (Comptroller)

For full biographical listings, see the Martindale-Hubbell Law Directory

MCKISSOCK & HOFFMAN, P.C. (AV)

1700 Market Street, Suite 3000, 19103
Telephone: 215-246-2100
Fax: 215-246-2144
Westmont, New Jersey Office: 216 Haddon Avenue, Suite 603.
Telephone: 609-858-1650.
Fax: 609-858-1466.
Doylestown, Pennsylvania Office: 16 North Franklin Street, Suite 300.
Telephone: 215-345-4501.
Fax: 215-246-4503.
Harrisburg, Pennsylvania Office: 105 North Front Street, Suite 205.
Telephone: 717-234-0103.
Fax: 717-234-1350.
West Chester, Pennsylvania Office: 31 South High Street, P.O. Box 3086.
Telephone: 610-738-8850.
Fax: 610-738-9121.

J. Bruce McKissock
Peter J. Hoffman
Leslie Anne Miller
Jeffrey B. Albert
Jill Baratz Clarke
John J. McGrath (Resident, Westmont, New Jersey Office)
Donald J. Brooks, Jr.
William J. Mundy
Bryan Craig Black (Resident, Harrisburg Office)
Eileen Lampe
Christopher Thomson (Resident Shareholder, West Chester Office)
K. Reed Haywood
Maureen P. Fitzgerald

For full biographical listings, see the Martindale-Hubbell Law Directory

PERRY, FIALKOWSKI & PERRY (AV)

Suite 1600 One Penn Square West, 30 South 15th Street, 19102
Telephone: 215-561-4110
Fax: 215-561-4177
Email: pfp@pfplaw.com *URL:* http://www.pfplaw.com
Clementon, New Jersey Office: 180 White Horse Pike.
Telephone: 609-627-1005.

MEMBERS OF FIRM

David Perry
Anne E. Fialkowski
Sherryl R. Perry
Marcia F. Rosenbaum

LEGAL SUPPORT PERSONNEL

Lisa Garrett

For full biographical listings, see the Martindale-Hubbell Law Directory

Philadelphia—Continued

RAWLE & HENDERSON LLP (AV)

(Rawle Law Offices Founded 1783)
The Widener Building, One South Penn Square, 19107
Telephone: 215-575-4200
Telecopier: 215-563-2583
Email: info@rawle.com *URL:* http://www.rawle.com
Marlton, New Jersey Office: Suite 204, Ten Lake Center Executive Park, 401 Route 73 North.
Telephone: 609-596-4800.
Telecopier: 609-596-6164.
New York, N.Y. Office: 140 Broadway, Forty-Sixth Floor.
Telephone: 212-858-7570. Fax 212-858-7750.

Carl D. Buchholz, III
Fred B. Buck
Joseph J. Hamill, Jr.
Thomas A. Kuzmick
Peter A. Lentini
John H. McCarthy
John E. Salmon
Thomas P. Wagner
Michael P. Zipfel

Joshua Bachrach
Mark J. Dianno
John T. Donovan
Cari N. Kohn
Matthew J. McLees
John Christie McMeekin, II
Michael A. Meehan
Phillip J. Meyer
Stewart R. Singer

For full biographical listings, see the Martindale-Hubbell Law Directory

---

ROSENTHAL AND WEISBERG, P.C. (AV)

Two Logan Square Suite 1565, 18th & Arch Streets, 19103
Telephone: 215-656-4100
Fax: 215-656-4119

Brian D. Rosenthal
Michael Stuart Weisberg

Neil T. Murray
Margaret M. Foley

LEGAL SUPPORT PERSONNEL

Wendy Frost (Paralegal)
Lynn Gibbs (Paralegal)

For full biographical listings, see the Martindale-Hubbell Law Directory

---

RUTHRAUFF & ARMBRUST, P.C. (AV)

1601 Market Street, 16th Floor, 19103
Telephone: 215-567-3700
Fax: 215-587-0409
Email: rutharm@erols.com
Cherry Hill, New Jersey Office: 200 Lake Drive East, Suite 206, 08002.
Telephone: 609-482-7856.
Fax: 609-482-8099.

Wilbur Bourne Ruthrauff
R. Mark Armbrust

David Ira Rosenbaum

LEGAL SUPPORT PERSONNEL

Charlane Sutton

For full biographical listings, see the Martindale-Hubbell Law Directory

---

RALPH D. SAMUEL & CO. A PROFESSIONAL CORPORATION (AV)

225 South 15th Street, Suite 1776, 19102
Telephone: 215-893-9992
Fax: 215-893-9996
Email: RalphSamuel@lawmine.com *URL:* http://www.lawyers.com/ralphdsamuellaw

Ralph David Samuel
Lynn Malmgren

For full biographical listings, see the Martindale-Hubbell Law Directory

---

CLAYTON H. THOMAS, JR. (AV)

37th Floor, Bell Atlantic Tower Building, 1717 Arch Street, 19103-2793
Telephone: 215-994-5290
Fax: 215-994-5296

Benjamin Rose

For full biographical listings, see the Martindale-Hubbell Law Directory

---

WILBRAHAM, LAWLER & BUBA, A PROFESSIONAL CORPORATION (AV)

1818 Market Street, Suite 3100, 19103-3631
Telephone: 215-564-4141
Fax: 215-564-4385
Email: @wlbdeflaw.com
Haddonfield, New Jersey Office: 24 Kings Highway West.
Telephone: 856-795-4422.
Fax: 856-795-4699.

(See Next Column)

Wilmington, Delaware Office: Stoney Batter Office Building, 5301 Limestone Road, Suite 221.
Telephone: 302-234-8217.
Fax: 302-234-8218.

Edward J. Wilbraham
Robert B. Lawler
Barbara J. Buba
Michael J. Block

R. Erick Chizmar
Kevin J. Maginnis
InSook Kim
Sandra D. Terry-Crawford
John S. Howarth
David M. Maselli
Renee E. Berger
Edward T. Finch
Sean P. Buggy

OF COUNSEL

Walter J. Timby, Jr.
Daniel J. Allan

Representative Clients: GAF Corporation; Armstrong World Industries, Inc.; U.S. Gypsum Company; Georgia-Pacific Corporation; ARCO; Shell; Royal; AIG; Chubb; Keystone.

For full biographical listings, see the Martindale-Hubbell Law Directory

---

*PITTSBURGH,** Allegheny Co.

JOHN A. CAPUTO & ASSOCIATES (AV)

Fifth Floor, Three Gateway Center, 15222
Telephone: 412-391-4990
Fax: 412-391-3121

John A. Caputo

Allan Meyers Cox
Bernard C. Caputo
David L. Conn

For full biographical listings, see the Martindale-Hubbell Law Directory

---

DAVIES MCFARLAND & CARROLL, P.C. (AV)

One Gateway Center, Tenth Floor, 15222
Telephone: 412-281-0737
Email: firm@dmcpc.com

Ralph A. Davies
William D. Geiger
M.J. (Jeff) Tindall
Eric K. Falk
David E. Lamm

Howard K. Hilner
Kristin L. Pieseski
Mary Kathleen Coleman
Julie L. Nord

Representative Clients: The BOC Group; The Goodyear Tire & Rubber Co.; Hobart Brothers Co.; The Travelers Insurance Co.; The Lincoln Electric Company; Allegheny-Teledyne, Inc.; USF&G; Allied Signal, Inc.; Mine Safety Appliance Co.; General Motors Corp.

For Complete List of Firm Personnel, See General Section

For full biographical listings, see the Martindale-Hubbell Law Directory

---

EVANS, PORTNOY & QUINN (AV)

36th Floor, One Oxford Centre, 301 Grant Street, 15219-6401
Telephone: 412-765-3800
Fax: 412-765-3747

Charles E. Evans
Irving M. Portnoy
John E. Quinn

ASSOCIATES

Mark E. Milsop
Marc J. Reiter
Patricia L. Haas

For full biographical listings, see the Martindale-Hubbell Law Directory

---

HEINTZMAN, WARREN, WISE & FORNELLA, P.C. (AV)

The 35th Floor, Gulf Tower, 707 Grant Street, 15219
Telephone: 412-394-7810
Fax: 412-263-5222
Email: hww@hwwlaw.com *URL:* http://www.hwwlaw.com

Michael D. Heintzman
Charles S. Warren
Roger L. Wise
Joseph R. Schaper
Kenneth F. Klanica

Jeanine L. Fonner

For full biographical listings, see the Martindale-Hubbell Law Directory

---

KAPETAN MEYERS ROSEN & LOUIK, P.C. (AV)

Suite 200 The Frick Building, 15219-6003
Telephone: 412-281-4200
Fax: 412-281-2997
URL: http://www.lawyers.com/kmr&llaw
Email: law@malpractice-lawyers.net *URL:* http://www.malpractice-lawyers.net

(See Next Column)

KAPETAN MEYERS ROSEN & LOUIK P.C., *Pittsburgh—Continued*

Jerry I. Meyers | Michael Louik
Neil R. Rosen | Jon R. Perry

For full biographical listings, see the Martindale-Hubbell Law Directory

KIGER & ALPERN (AV)

1404 Grant Building, 15219
Telephone: 412-765-1811
Fax: 412-765-0440

MEMBERS OF FIRM

Jerome W. Kiger | Charles H. Alpern

For full biographical listings, see the Martindale-Hubbell Law Directory

HOWARD F. MESSER, P.C. (AV)

1404 Grant Building, 15219
Telephone: 412-281-7200
FAX: 412-765-0440
URL: http://www.lawyers.com/messerlaw

Howard F. Messer

Philip A. Fabiano

For full biographical listings, see the Martindale-Hubbell Law Directory

SWENSEN PERER & KONTOS (AV)

Two PNC Plaza, Suite 2710, 15222
Telephone: 412-281-1970
Fax: 412-281-2808
Email: general2@swensenperer.com
Erie, Pennsylvania Office: Swensen Perer & McCandless. 209 Court House Commons.
Telephone: 814-456-0489. Email: erie@swensenperer.com.

MEMBERS OF FIRM

Jan C. Swensen | John W. McCandless (Resident Partner, Erie Office)
Alan H. Perer

George M. Kontos

ASSOCIATES

Anthony C. Mengine | Daniel J. Sinclair

OF COUNSEL

Diane W. Perer | David A. Schroeder

Anthony J. Sciarrino

For full biographical listings, see the Martindale-Hubbell Law Directory

*SCRANTON,** Lackawanna Co.

FOLEY, MCLANE, FOLEY, MCDONALD & MACGREGOR (AV)

Linden Plaza, 600 Linden Street, P.O. Box 1108, 18501-1108
Telephone: 570-342-8194
Fax: 570-342-4658
Email: foleylawfirm@worldnet.att.net
Stroudsburg Office: 26 North Sixth Street.
Telephone: 570-424-1757.
Fax: 570-424-2764.

Thomas J. Foley, Jr. | Thomas J. Foley, III
John T. McLane | Kevin P. Foley
Michael J. Foley | Malcolm L. MacGregor
Michael J. McDonald | Michael J. Eagen, Jr. (Resident, Stroudsburg Office)

NURSE PARALEGALS

Marsia Konanski | Debra Halvorsen

For full biographical listings, see the Martindale-Hubbell Law Directory

KREDER, BROOKS, HAILSTONE & LUDWIG (AV)

Suite 200, 220 Penn Avenue, 18503
Telephone: 570-346-7922
Telecopier: 570-346-3715

Cody H. Brooks | Lucille Marsh
Lawrence M. Ludwig | Michael J. Donohue

Counsel For: U.S. Fidelity & Guaranty Co.; Nationwide Insurance Co.; Liberty Mutual Insurance Co.

For Complete List of Firm Personnel, See General Section
For full biographical listings, see the Martindale-Hubbell Law Directory

MUNLEY, MUNLEY & CARTWRIGHT, P.C. (AV)

205 Madison Avenue, 18503
Telephone: 570-346-7401
Fax: 570-346-3452
URL: http://www.lawyers.com/mmclaw
Email: lawyers@munley.com *URL:* http://www.munley.com

(See Next Column)

Robert W. Munley | James Christopher Munley
Marion Munley | Daniel W. Munley
Matthew A. Cartwright | Robert W. Munley, III

Reference: First National Bank of Jermyn.

For full biographical listings, see the Martindale-Hubbell Law Directory

O'MALLEY & HARRIS, P.C. (AV)

345 Wyoming Avenue, 18503
Telephone: 570-348-3711
Fax: 570-348-4092
Email: ohpc@epix.net *URL:* http://www.ohpclaw.com
Stroudsburg, Pennsylvania Office: 111 North Seventh Street.
Telephone: 570-421-2252; 570-422-1280.
FAX: 570-422-1281. Email: cerato@ptdprolog.net.
Wilkes-Barre, Pennsylvania Office: 61 North Washington Street.
Telephone: 570-829-3232.
FAX: 570-829-4418. Email: ohpcwb@epix.net.
Williamsport, Pennsylvania Office: 321 Pine Street, Suite 308.
Telephone: 570-323-4380.

Eugene Nogi (1905-1975) | Bruce L. Coyer
Henry Nogi (1900-1976) | John Q. Durkin
Russell J. O'Malley, Sr. (1904-1993) | Gerald J. Hanchulak
Norman Harris (1907-1998) | Richard K. Hodges
William H. Amesbury (Resident, Wilkes-Barre Office) | Timothy J. Holland (Resident, Wilkes-Barre Office)
Paul A. Barrett | John F. Kennedy (Resident, Wilkes-Barre Office)
Matthew P. Barrett | Daniel Morgan
J. Scott Brady (Resident, Wilkes-Barre Office) | Michael Perry
Lori J. Cerato (Resident, Stroudsburg Office) | James M. Tressler
Joseph Timothy Healey
A. Ruth Whalen (Resident, Wilkes-Barre Office)

Representative Clients: Pennsylvania Hospital Insurance Co.; MMI Systems Agency, Inc.; State Farm Insurance Company; ITT Specialty Risk Services; St. Paul Fire & Marine Insurance Co.; Chubb Group of Insurance Companies; Geisingen System Services; Princeton Insurance Company; Northeastern Pennsylvania Physicians Organization; Catholic Healthcare Partners.

For full biographical listings, see the Martindale-Hubbell Law Directory

SCANLON, HOWLEY, SCANLON & DOHERTY (AV)

321 Spruce Street, 10th Floor, 18503
Telephone: 570-346-7651
Fax: 570-344-1542

MEMBERS OF FIRM

James M. Howley | Thomas R. Nealon
James M. Scanlon | Thomas B. Helbig
James A. Doherty, Jr. | Patrick R. Casey

Counsel for: CNA Insurance Company; The Medical Protective Co.; Harleysville Insurance Co.; The Procter & Gamble Co.; Prudential-Bach Securities, Inc.; Zurich-American Insurance Co.; The Keystone Coca-Cola Bottling Co.; The Home Insurance Co.; The Travelers Insurance Co.; Utica First Ins. Co.

For full biographical listings, see the Martindale-Hubbell Law Directory

*WILLIAMSPORT,** Lycoming Co.

MITCHELL, MITCHELL, GRAY & GALLAGHER, A PROFESSIONAL CORPORATION (AV)

10 West Third Street, 17701-6513
Telephone: 570-323-8404
Fax: 570-323-8585
Email: mmggpc@csrlink.net

Jacob Neafie Mitchell (1919-1996) | Richard A. Gray
C. Edward S. Mitchell | Robert A. Gallagher
Gary L. Weber

Bret J. Southard

Darryl R. Wishard

For full biographical listings, see the Martindale-Hubbell Law Directory

RHODE ISLAND

*PROVIDENCE,** Providence Co.

HINCKLEY, ALLEN & SNYDER LLP (AV)

1500 Fleet Center, 02903-2393
Telephone: 401-274-2000
Fax: 401-277-9600
Email: firm@haslaw.com *URL:* http://www.haslaw.com
Boston, Massachusetts Office: 28 State Street, 30th Floor.
Telephone: 617-345-9000.
Fax: 617-345-9020. URL: http://www.haslaw.com.

(See Next Column)

HINCKLEY, ALLEN & SNYDER LLP—*Continued*

MEMBERS OF FIRM

David D. Barricelli
Eric F. Eisenberg (Not admitted in RI)
Malcolm Farmer, III
Hugh J. Gorman, III (Not admitted in RI)
William R. Grimm
Joel Lewin (Not admitted in RI)
Gerald J. Petros
Jeremy Ritzenberg (Not admitted in RI)
Charles E. Schaub, Jr. (Not admitted in RI)
Herman Snyder (Not admitted in RI)
Robert F. Sylvia (Not admitted in RI)
Howard E. Walker

ASSOCIATES

Mark Bianchi
Alexandra K. Callam
Kelley Jordan-Price
Catherine S. Kim (Not admitted in RI)
Christopher W. Morog (Not admitted in RI)
Elena B. Olson (Not admitted in RI)
Joseph D. Whelan

For Complete List of Firm Personnel, See General Section

For full biographical listings, see the Martindale-Hubbell Law Directory

VETTER & WHITE, INCORPORATED (AV)

20 Washington Place, 02903
Telephone: 401-421-3060
Telecopier: 401-272-6803
Email: vetlit@aol.com

Benjamin V. White, III
Gordon P. Cleary
Howard A. Merten, Jr.
Brooks R. Magratten

OF COUNSEL

George Vetter

Kimberly A. Simpson
Michael W. Long

For full biographical listings, see the Martindale-Hubbell Law Directory

SOUTH CAROLINA

*BEAUFORT,** Beaufort Co.

DAVIS, TUPPER & GRIMSLEY, L.L.P. (AV)

611 Bay Street, P.O. Box 2055, 29901-2055
Telephone: 843-524-1116
Facsimile: 843-524-1463
Email: DTGS@Hargray.com

MEMBERS OF FIRM

Hutson S. Davis, Jr.
Ralph E. Tupper
James A. Grimsley, III
Erin D. Dean
R. Gerald Chambers, Jr.
Virginia D. Meeks

For full biographical listings, see the Martindale-Hubbell Law Directory

*CHARLESTON,** Charleston Co.

BARNWELL WHALEY PATTERSON & HELMS, LLC (AV)

134 Meeting Street, Suite 300, P.O. Drawer H, 29402
Telephone: 843-577-7700
Telecopier: 843-577-7708
Email: bwph@barnwell-whaley.com *URL:* http://barnwell-whaley.com

MEMBERS OF FIRM

Robert A. Patterson
William C. Helms, III
M. Dawes Cooke, Jr.
Bruce E. Miller
B. C. Killough
Matthew H. Henrikson
Frank E. Grimball
James E. Reeves

ASSOCIATES

J. Matthew Dillon
James H. Elliott, Jr.
Lucinda Gardner Wichmann
Deborah C. Lacombe (Not admitted in SC)
William E. McIntosh
Wendy Johnson Keefer

SPECIAL COUNSEL

J. Gail Rahn

Representative Clients: The Citadel, The Military College of South Carolina; S.C. Insurance Reserve Fund; Brown & Root, Inc.; Continental Insurance; Medical University of South Carolina; Liberty Mutual Insurance Co.; Tiffin Motor Homes; United States Aviation Underwriters.

For full biographical listings, see the Martindale-Hubbell Law Directory

BUIST, MOORE, SMYTHE & MCGEE, P.A. (AV)

Successors to Buist, Buist, Smythe and Smythe and Moore, Mouzon and McGee.
Five Exchange Street, P.O. Box 999, 29402
Telephone: 843-722-3400
Cable Address: "Conferees"
Telex: 57-6488
Telecopier: 843-723-7398
Email: bmsm@lawyer-sc.com *URL:* http://www.lawyer-sc.com

Joseph H. McGee
Gordon D. Schreck
Henry B. Smythe, Jr.
Henry E. Grimball
James D. Myrick
Elizabeth Henry Warner
David S. Yandle

David S. Cox
Gregory Horton

OF COUNSEL

Charles J. Baker, III

Representative Clients: Bridgestone/Firestone, Inc.; Caterpillar, Inc.; Dillards; Dupont; Foster-Wheeler; General Electric Company; Otis Elevator Company; Philip Morris; Viking Yachts; Wal-Mart.

For Complete List of Firm Personnel, See General Section

For full biographical listings, see the Martindale-Hubbell Law Directory

HAYNSWORTH, MARION, MCKAY & GUÉRARD, L.L.P. (AV)

134 Meeting Street, P.O. Box 1119, 29402
Telephone: 843-722-7606
Facsimile: 843-724-8016
Columbia, South Carolina Office: Suite 2400 Affinity Building, 1201 Main Street, P.O. Drawer 7157, 29202.
Telephone: 803-765-1818. Facsimile 803-765-2399.
Greenville, South Carolina Office: 75 Beattie Place, Eleventh Floor, P.O. Box 2048, 29602.
Telephone: 864-240-3200.
Facsimile: 864-240-3300.

MEMBERS OF FIRM

William C. Cleveland
Thomas S. White

Counsel for: Baker Hospital; Healthsource of South Carolina; Allstate Insurance Co.; CSX Corporation; Lloyd's Underwriters; Coward-Hund Construction Co.; South Carolina Public Service Authority; City of Hanahan.

For Complete List of Firm Personnel, See General Section

For full biographical listings, see the Martindale-Hubbell Law Directory

HOOD LAW FIRM (AV)

172 Meeting Street, P.O. Box 1508, 29402
Telephone: 843-577-4435
Fax: 843-722-1630
Email: hlf@hoodlaw.com *URL:* http://www.hoodlaw.com

MEMBERS OF FIRM

Robert H. Hood
Louis P. Herns
G. Mark Phillips
Carl Everette Pierce, II
John K. Blincow, Jr.
James G. Kennedy
Barbara Wynne Showers
Joseph C. Wilson, IV
James Dowell Gandy, III

Dixon F. Pearce, II
Hugh Willcox Buyck
Allan Poe Sloan, III
Mary Agnes Hood Craig
Allison Snead Patrick
P. Gunnar Nistad
Robert H. Hood, Jr.
William Mullins McLeod, Jr.

For full biographical listings, see the Martindale-Hubbell Law Directory

GEDNEY M. HOWE, III, P.A. (AV)

8 Chalmers Street, P.O. Box 1034, 29402
Telephone: 843-722-8048
FAX: 843-722-2140

Gedney M. Howe, Jr. (1914-1981)
Gedney M. Howe, III
Alvin J. Hammer

Caroline M.W. Dillon

For full biographical listings, see the Martindale-Hubbell Law Directory

MARK C. TANENBAUM, P.A. (AV)

241-243 East Bay Street, P.O. Box 20757, 29413
Telephone: 843-577-5100
Telecopy: 843-722-4688
Email: mark@tanenbaumlaw.com

Mark C. Tanenbaum

Stephen A. Butaitis

For full biographical listings, see the Martindale-Hubbell Law Directory

*COLUMBIA,** Richland Co.

BARNES, ALFORD, STORK & JOHNSON, L.L.P. (AV)

1613 Main Street, P.O. Box 8448, 29202
Telephone: 803-799-1111
Telefax: 803-254-1335
Email: basj@basjlaw.com

Richard C. Thomas

For Complete List of Firm Personnel, See General Section

For full biographical listings, see the Martindale-Hubbell Law Directory

GLENN MURPHY GRAY & STEPP, L.L.P. (AV)

B B & T Bank Building, Suite 390, 1901 Assembly Street, P.O. Box 1550, 29202-1550
Telephone: 803-765-1100
Telecopy: 803-765-0755

Terrell L. Glenn (1930-1993)

MEMBERS OF FIRM

Peter L. Murphy
Elizabeth Van Doren Gray
Robert E. Stepp
Elizabeth G. Howard

Robert C. Rhodes
Laura W. Robinson
Roland M. Franklin
C. Shawn Dryer

Reference: BB&T.

For full biographical listings, see the Martindale-Hubbell Law Directory

HAYNSWORTH, MARION, MCKAY & GUÉRARD, L.L.P. (AV)

Suite 2400 Affinity Building, 1201 Main Street, P.O. Drawer 7157, 29202
Telephone: 803-765-1818
Facsimile: 803-765-2399
Greenville, South Carolina Office: 75 Beattie Place, Eleventh Floor, P.O. Box 2048, 29602.
Telephone: 864-240-3200.
Facsimile: 864-240-3300.
Charleston, South Carolina Office: 134 Meeting Street, P.O. Box 1119, 29402.
Telephone: 843-722-7606.
Facsimile: 843-724-8016.

MEMBERS OF FIRM

William P. Simpson
Steven Todd Moon
Stephen F. McKinney

Counsel for: The B. F. Goodrich Company; Bausch & Lomb, Inc.; General Motors; Ford Motor Company; Stone Manufacturing Co.; Dunlop Slazenger Corp.; Caterpillar Corporation; E. I. DuPont Corp.; Gerber Childrenswear, Inc.; Steel Heddle Mfg. Co.

For Complete List of Firm Personnel, See General Section

For full biographical listings, see the Martindale-Hubbell Law Directory

HOWSER, NEWMAN & BESLEY, L.L.C. (AV)

1508 Washington Street, P.O. Box 12009, 29211
Telephone: 803-758-6000
Fax: 803-758-4445
Email: rdhowser@hnblaw.com

R. Davis Howser
James P. Newman, Jr.
William G. Besley
Benjamin D. McCoy

Kelley S. Shull
Andrew E. Haselden
Janet Brooks

Representative Clients: American Modern Home Company; Clayton Homes; CNA Risk Management Group; DPIC Companies, Inc.; Horace Mann Insurance Company; Zurich Companies; Selective Insurance Company; South Carolina School Boards Insurance Trust; State Auto Insurance Company; Utica National Insurance Group.

For full biographical listings, see the Martindale-Hubbell Law Directory

LEE, EADON, ISGETT AND POPWELL, P.A. (AV)

1314 Lincoln Street, P.O. Box 1505, 29202
Telephone: 803-799-9811; 1-800-882-0742
Telecopier: 803-779-8572
URL: http://www.lawyers.com/leeeadonisgett&popwell

Luther M. Lee (1923-1996)
Sherod H. Eadon, Jr.
Christopher C. Isgett
Gary W. Popwell, Jr.

Gerald E. Reardon

For full biographical listings, see the Martindale-Hubbell Law Directory

MCKAY & MCKAY, P.A. (AV)

1325 Laurel Street, P.O. Box 7217, 29202
Telephone: 803-256-4645
FAX: 803-765-1839

Douglas McKay, Jr.
Julius W. McKay, II

Representative Clients: Americlaim Adjustment Corp.; Britanco Underwriters, Inc.; Pennsylvania Manufacturers' Association Ins. Co. (PMA); South Carolina Medical Malpractice Joint Underwriting Assn. (JUA); Underwriters Laboratories, Inc.

For Complete List of Firm Personnel, See General Section

For full biographical listings, see the Martindale-Hubbell Law Directory

ERNEST J. NAUFUL, JR., P.C. (AV)

1321 Lady Street Suite 670, P.O. Box 11866, 29211
Telephone: 803-256-4045
Facsimile: 803-256-7044
Email: nauful@aol.com

Ernest J. Nauful, Jr.

For full biographical listings, see the Martindale-Hubbell Law Directory

RICHARDSON, PLOWDEN, CARPENTER & ROBINSON, P.A. (AV)

1600 Marion Street, P.O. Drawer 7788, 29202
Telephone: 803-771-4400
Telecopy: 803-779-0016
Email: atty@rpcrlaw.com *URL:* http://www.rpcrlaw.com
Myrtle Beach, South Carolina Office: 2103 B Farlow Street, P.O. Box 3646, 29578.
Telephone: 843-448-1008.
FAX: 843-448-1533.

Leslie A. Cotter, Jr.
Douglas C. Baxter

David C. Slough

OF COUNSEL

Michael A. Pulliam

Representative Clients: Insurance: CNA Insurance Co.; The Hartford; Kemper Insurance Co.; Pennsylvania National Mutual Casualty Insurance Co.; Wausau Insurance Cos.; The Reudlinger Cos.; Sumitomo Marine Claims Services (USA); Honda North America, Inc.; Yamaha Motor Corp. (USA).

For Complete List of Firm Personnel, See General Section

For full biographical listings, see the Martindale-Hubbell Law Directory

TURNER, PADGET, GRAHAM & LANEY, P.A. (AV)

Seventeenth Floor, 1901 Main Street, P.O. Box 1473, 29202
Telephone: 803-254-2200
Telecopy: 803-799-3957
Florence, South Carolina Office: Fourth Floor, 1831 West Evans Street, P.O. Box 5478, 29502.
Telephone: 843-662-9008.
Fax: 843-667-0828.
Charleston, South Carolina Office: 21 Broad Street, 1st Floor, P.O. Box 836, 29402.
Telephone: 843-723-1622.
Fax: 843-577-3369.

Ronald E. Boston
John S. Wilkerson, III (Resident, Florence, SC, Office)
Steven W. Ouzts
John E. Cuttino
Elbert S. Dorn
Hugh M. Claytor (Resident, Florence, SC, Office)
J. Kenneth Carter, Jr.
Richard L. Hinson (Resident, Florence, SC, Office)

Curtis L. Ott
Mark B. Tinsley

For Complete List of Firm Personnel, See General Section

For full biographical listings, see the Martindale-Hubbell Law Directory

*GREENVILLE,** Greenville Co.

COVINGTON, PATRICK, HAGINS, STERN & LEWIS, P.A. (AV)

211 Pettigru Street, 29601
Telephone: 864-242-9000
Fax: 864-233-9777
Mailing Address: P.O. Box 2343, 29602
Email: cphsl@mindspring.com

John A. Hagins, Jr.
Douglas F. Patrick
Eugene C. Covington, Jr.
T. S. Stern, Jr.
Stephen R. H. Lewis
Thomas E. Dudley, III

Karen W. Creech

For full biographical listings, see the Martindale-Hubbell Law Directory

Greenville—Continued

GRANT, LEATHERWOOD & PITTS, P.A. (AV)

Palmetto Bank Building, 306 East North Street, 2nd Floor, P.O. Box 10367, 29603-0367
Telephone: 864-242-2300
Facsimile: 864-242-2280
Email: attorneys@grantleatherwood.com

William M. Grant, Jr. — Judith A. Leatherwood
Michael S. Pitts

Langdon Cheves, III — Paul C. Rathke

LEGAL SUPPORT PERSONNEL

Jackie L. Carver (Litigation Paralegal) — Sarah A. Carmichael (Paralegal)
Mary A. Fuller (Paralegal)

For full biographical listings, see the Martindale-Hubbell Law Directory

HAYNSWORTH, MARION, MCKAY & GUÉRARD, L.L.P. (AV)

75 Beattie Place, Eleventh Floor, P.O. Box 2048, 29602
Telephone: 864-240-3200
Facsimile: 864-240-3300
Columbia, South Carolina Office: Suite 2400 Affinity Building, 1201 Main Street, P.O. Drawer 7157, 29202
Telephone: 803-765-1818.
Facsimile: 803-765-2399.
Charleston, South Carolina Office: 134 Meeting Street, P.O. Box 1119, 29402.
Telephone: 843-722-7606.
Facsimile: 843-724-8016.

MEMBERS OF FIRM

G. Dewey Oxner, Jr. — Edwin Brown Parkinson, Jr.
James B. Pressly, Jr. — H. Sam Mabry, III
H. Donald Sellers — F. Matlock Elliott
Ellis M. Johnston, II — Moffatt Grier McDonald
W. Francis Marion, Jr. — Amy Miller Snyder
John B. McLeod — Eric Keith Englebardt
J. Derrick Quattlebaum

ASSOCIATES

Boyd B. Nicholson, Jr. — William David Conner
Sherry L. Boswell

OF COUNSEL

Donald L. Ferguson

Representative Clients: State Industries; Wausau Insurance Co.; Fireman's Fund Insurance Co.; Prudential Property & Casualty; Owens Corning Fiberglas; Anheuser Bush; 3M; Traveler's Insurance Co.; McGahn Medical Corp.; Allstate Insurance.

For Complete List of Firm Personnel, See General Section

For full biographical listings, see the Martindale-Hubbell Law Directory

LOVE, THORNTON, ARNOLD & THOMASON, P.A. (AV)

410 East Washington Street, P.O. Box 10045, 29603
Telephone: 864-242-6360
Telefax: 864-271-7972
Email: lovelaw@globalvision.net *URL:* http://www.ltatlaw.com
Greer, South Carolina Office: 1115 West Poinsett Street, P.O. Box 449, 29652-0449.
Telephone: 864-879-0144.
Telefax: 864-879-0149.

Theron G. Cochran — David L. Moore, Jr.
V. Clark Price

Counsel for: Aetna Life and Casualty Insurance Co.; Selective Insurance Co.; Risk Enterprise Management (Formerly The Home Insurance Co.); Kemper Insurance Group; State Farm Fire and Casualty; Reliance Insurance Companies Group; Chrysler Corp.; The Trane Company.

For Complete List of Firm Personnel, See General Section

For full biographical listings, see the Martindale-Hubbell Law Directory

PARHAM & SMITH, L.L.C. (AV)

Smith Barney Building-Second Floor, 501 River Street, P.O. Box 2800, 29601
Telephone: 864-242-9008
1-800-849-7777
Fax: 864-271-6155
Mailing Address: P.O. Box 2800, Greenville, SC, 29602
Email: mparham@parhamlaw.com *URL:* http://www.lawyers.com/parham&smithlaw

MEMBERS OF FIRM

Michael Parham — Barney O. Smith, Jr. (1952-1996)

Steven Blakely Smith

For full biographical listings, see the Martindale-Hubbell Law Directory

LORIS, Horry Co.

STEVENS LAW FIRM, P.C. (AV)

3341 Broad Street P.O. Drawer 127, 29569-0127
Telephone: 843-756-7652
Fax: 843-756-3785
E-Mail: RUMMPOLE@AOL.COM
Email: JPKLAW@AOL.COM

James P. Stevens, Jr. — Jonathan P. Kresken

For full biographical listings, see the Martindale-Hubbell Law Directory

MYRTLE BEACH, Horry Co.

BELLAMY, RUTENBERG, COPELAND, EPPS, GRAVELY & BOWERS, P.A. (AV)

1000 29th Avenue North, P.O. Box 357, 29578
Telephone: 843-448-2400
Telecopier: 843-448-3022

Howell V. Bellamy, Jr. — Jill F. Griffith
John K. Rutenberg — Kathryn M. Cook
John E. Copeland — David B. Miller
Claude M. Epps, Jr. — C. Winfield Johnson, III
David R. Gravely — Sarah A. Johnson
Edward B. Bowers, Jr. — Douglas M. Zayicek
Bradley D. King — Jeffrey W. King
Henrietta U. Golding — Mary Anna Malpass
M. Edwin Hinds, Jr. — Martin Charles Dawsey

Representative Clients: Dargan Construction Co.; Coastal Federal Savings Bank; Sands Investments; Wachovia Bank of South Carolina; AVX Corp.; Bank of America; Parthenon Insurance Co.; Burroughs & Chapin Co.; International Paper Co.; Hospital Corporation of America.

For full biographical listings, see the Martindale-Hubbell Law Directory

*SPARTANBURG,** Spartanburg Co.

HOLCOMBE, BOMAR, GUNN AND BRADFORD, P.A. (AV)

Advantica Plaza, 203 East Main Street, P.O. Drawer 1897, 29304-1897
Telephone: 864-585-4273
Telecopier: 864-585-3844
Email: hbgb@teleplex.net

William U. Gunn

Representative Clients: Advantica Restaurant Group, Inc.; Denny's, Inc.; Wachovia Bank of South Carolina, N.A.; Community Cash Stores; Liberty Mutual Insurance Cos.; Mary Black Memorial Hospital, Inc.; Metromont Materials Corp.; CNA Insurance Companies.

For Complete List of Firm Personnel, See General Section

For full biographical listings, see the Martindale-Hubbell Law Directory

*WALHALLA,** Oconee Co.

LARRY C. BRANDT, P.A. (AV)

205 West Main Street, P.O. Drawer 738, 29691
Telephone: 864-638-5406
864-638-7873
Email: lbrandt@innova.net

Larry C. Brandt

LEGAL SUPPORT PERSONNEL

Debra C. Miller

For full biographical listings, see the Martindale-Hubbell Law Directory

TENNESSEE

*CHATTANOOGA,** Hamilton Co.

PHILLIP A. FLEISSNER, PLLC (AV)

600 Georgia Avenue, 37402
Telephone: 423-756-3591
Telecopier: 423-266-5455

Phillip A. Fleissner — David C. Nagle
Christopher Price Butler

For full biographical listings, see the Martindale-Hubbell Law Directory

FRANKLIN, COOPER & MARCUS, PLLC (AV)

837 Fort Wood Street, 37403
Telephone: 423-756-3596
Telecopier: 423-756-3597

(See Next Column)

FRANKLIN, COOPER & MARCUS PLLC, *Chattanooga—Continued*

David L. Franklin
Gary A. Cooper
H. Richard Marcus

For full biographical listings, see the Martindale-Hubbell Law Directory

*CLEVELAND,** Bradley Co.

JENNE, SCOTT & JENNE (AV)

260 Ocoee Street, P.O. Box 161, 37364-0161
Telephone: 423-476-5506
Fax: 423-476-5058
Email: MichaelJenne@mindspring.com

MEMBERS OF FIRM

Roger E. Jenne
Robert A. Scott (1940-1984)
Michael E. Jenne

For full biographical listings, see the Martindale-Hubbell Law Directory

KINGSPORT, Sullivan Co.

HAWKINS, MOODY, BINGHAM, MILLER & ASSOCIATES, P.C. (AV)

1397 East Center Street, 37664
Telephone: 423-246-9100
Fax: 423-246-9282

William W. Hawkins (1929-1997)
Edgar G. Moody
John S. Bingham
J. David Miller

For full biographical listings, see the Martindale-Hubbell Law Directory

*KNOXVILLE,** Knox Co.

BERNSTEIN, STAIR & MCADAMS LLP (AV)

Suite 600, 530 South Gay Street, 37902
Telephone: 423-546-8030
Telecopier: 423-522-8879
Effective October 1, 1999 Area Code will change to 865.

MEMBERS OF FIRM

Bernard E. Bernstein
L. Caesar Stair III
Thomas N. McAdams
Doris C. Allen
Celeste H. Herbert
James W. Parris

ASSOCIATES

W. Tyler Chastain
Lauren G. Strange-Boston
Margo J. Maxwell

Representative Clients: ABB Flakt, Inc.; Camel Manufacturing Company; Clayton Homes, Inc.; Modern Supply Co.; Nova, Inc.; Plasti-Line, Inc.; Post and Company, Inc.; Rafferty's Restaurants; Saks, Inc.; Vanderbilt Mortgage and Finance, Inc.; West Town Mall.

For full biographical listings, see the Martindale-Hubbell Law Directory

GILREATH & ASSOCIATES (AV)

550 Main Avenue, Suite 600, P.O. Box 1270, 37901-1270
Telephone: 423-637-2442
Fax: 423-971-4116
Email: gilknox@sidgilreath.com *URL:* http://www.sidgilreath.com
Nashville, Tennessee Office: 2828 Renaissance Tower, 611 Commerce Street.
Telephone: 615-256-3388.
Memphis, Tennessee Office: 44 North Second Street, Suite 200.
Telephone: 901-527-8288.

MEMBER OF FIRM

Sidney W. Gilreath

ASSOCIATES

Meridith C. Bond
Paul Kaufman
Richard L. Duncan
Dianne E. Lashmit
R. Christopher Gilreath
Patricia Taylor Bruner (Not admitted in TN)

LEGAL SUPPORT PERSONNEL

Tammy Ailshie (Legal Assistant to Senior Partner)
Janie Howerton (Legal Assistant)
Darla R. Johnson (Legal Assistant)
Janet L. Tucker (Legal Assistant to Senior Partner)
Pamela Smith Wise (Senior Legal Assistant)
Susan Stogner (Legal Assistant to Senior Partner)
Bryan L. Capps (Legal Administrator)
Danielle E. Barto (Firm Administrator)

Representative Client: Transportation Communications International Union; Brotherhood of Locomotive Engineers Union.
Reference: Suntrust Bank.

For full biographical listings, see the Martindale-Hubbell Law Directory

PRYOR, FLYNN, PRIEST & HARBER (AV)

Suite 600 Two Centre Square, 625 Gay Street, P.O. Box 870, 37901
Telephone: 423-522-4191
Telecopier: 423-522-0910

Robert E. Pryor
Frank L. Flynn, Jr.
Timothy A. Priest
John K. Harber

ASSOCIATES

Mark E. Floyd
Donald R. Coffey
M. Christopher Coffey
Robert E. Pryor, Jr.

References: First Vantage Bank; Sun Trust Bank.

For full biographical listings, see the Martindale-Hubbell Law Directory

WATSON, HOLLOW & REEVES, P.L.C. (AV)

1700 First Tennessee Plaza, 800 South Gay Street, P.O. Box 131, 37901-0131
Telephone: 423-637-1700
Telecopier: 423-525-2514

MEMBERS OF FIRM

Robert Harmon Watson, Jr.
Richard L. Hollow
Pamela L. Reeves
Jon Gilbert Roach
John Chapman Duffy
John T. Batson, Jr.
Earl Jerome Melson

ASSOCIATES

Nathan D. Rowell
Laura C. Webb
Beverley S. Cornett
Jenny Coques Rogers

Representative Clients: Sherwin-Williams; Rhone-Poulenc Rorer; American Cyanamid; Atlantic Mutual Insurance Company.

For full biographical listings, see the Martindale-Hubbell Law Directory

*MARYVILLE,** Blount Co.

NICHOLSON, GARNER & DUGGAN (AV)

250 High Street, P.O. Box 5059, 37802-5059
Telephone: 423-984-1460
Knoxville: 423-637-1970
Telecopier: 423-982-2595
Real Estate Fax: 423-982-2595
Litigation Fax: 423-984-9275
Email: jnicholson@earthlink.net *URL:* http://www.lawyers.com/ngdlaw

MEMBERS OF FIRM

Joe Nicholson
J. Michael Garner
David R. Duggan

ASSOCIATES

Angelia D. Morie
Daphne H. Cornwell

Representative Clients: Will furnished upon request.

For full biographical listings, see the Martindale-Hubbell Law Directory

*MEMPHIS,** Shelby Co.

ARMSTRONG ALLEN PREWITT GENTRY JOHNSTON & HOLMES, PLLC (AV)

Brinkley Plaza, Suite 700, 80 Monroe Avenue, 38103-2467
Telephone: 901-523-8211
Facsimile: 901-524-4936
Little Rock, Arkansas Office: Suite 100, 100 Morgan Keegan Drive, 72202.
Telephone: 501-280-0100.
Facsimile: 501-280-0166.
Jackson, Mississippi Office: 2525 Lakeward Drive, Suite 200, 39216.
Telephone: 601-713-1192.
Facsimile: 601-713-2049.
Jackson, Tennessee Office: 464 North Parkway, Suite A, 38305.
Telephone: 901-660-2332.
Facsimile: 901-664-1109.

MEMBERS OF FIRM

Thomas F. Johnston
Paul A. Matthews
Randall D. Noel
Mark S. Norris
Robertson M. Leatherman, Jr.
Cannon F. Allen
Richard R. Roberts
Thomas W. Lewis

OF COUNSEL

Gavin M. Gentry

For Complete List of Firm Personnel, See General Section

For full biographical listings, see the Martindale-Hubbell Law Directory

GLASSMAN, JETER, EDWARDS & WADE, P.C. (AV)

26 North Second Street Building, 38103
Telephone: 901-527-4673
Telecopier: 901-521-0940
Email: GJEWW@Memphisonline.com

(See Next Column)

GLASSMAN, JETER, EDWARDS & WADE P.C.—*Continued*

Richard Glassman
William M. Jeter
Tim Edwards
B. J. Wade
Carl K. Wyatt, Jr.
Dale H. Tuttle
John Barry Burgess
Robert A. Cox
Rebecca Adelman
Lori J. Keen
James F. Horner, Jr.
Richard E. Sorin

Todd Britton Murrah
Heather Walters Thompson

For full biographical listings, see the Martindale-Hubbell Law Directory

HALE HEADRICK DEWEY & WOLF, PLLC (AV)

One Memphis Place, 200 Jefferson Avenue Suite 1450, 38103
Telephone: 901-523-1123
Fax: 901-523-7472
Nashville, Tennessee Office: Suntrust Bank Building, 201 Fourth Avenue North, Suite 1450, 37219.
Telephone: 615-843-5160.
Fax: 615-843-5165

Stephen P. Hale
S. Russell Headrick
H. Tucker Dewey
Herbert B. Wolf, Jr.
John S. Golwen

OF COUNSEL

Steven L. Gill

Jennifer Ziegenhorn
Wendy A. Geurin
John W. Campbell
Joseph M. Koury
Holly N. Knight
Charles S. Blatteis
Jennifer S. Kiesewetter
J. William Williams

For full biographical listings, see the Martindale-Hubbell Law Directory

McDONALD KUHN (AV)

80 Monroe Avenue, Suite 550, P.O. Box 3160, 38173-0160
Telephone: 901-526-0606
Fax: 901-521-8397

MEMBERS OF FIRM

W. Percy McDonald (1890-1969)
W. Percy McDonald, Jr. (1921-1967)
Braxton C. Gandy (1915-1979)
Edward W. Kuhn (1904-1983)
Henry T. V. Miller
William A. Lucchesi
Carol Mills Hayden

ASSOCIATES

Loys A. "Trey" Jordan, III
Stephen P. Miller
June Kinney
Evan Nahmias

For full biographical listings, see the Martindale-Hubbell Law Directory

SMITH, SABBATINI & McLEARY, PLLC (AV)

100 Peabody Place Suite 1250, 38103
Telephone: 901-312-5555
Fax: 901-312-5667
Mailing Address: P.O. Box 3582, Memphis, TN, 38173
URL: http://www.smithlawetal.com

Gary K. Smith
Robert L. Sabbatini
Harold W. McLeary, Jr.
William D. Domico
James F. Kyle
James T. McColgan, III
G. Edward Coleman, III
Bryant C. Witt

Representative Clients: Premier RRG Insurance; Illinois Central Railroad; Medical Assurance; Albertson's, Inc.; Med. Marc (Chiro Co.); Medical Protective Co.; Methodist Health Systems; Hartford Insurance Co.; Sentry Insurance; State Farm Insurance.

For full biographical listings, see the Martindale-Hubbell Law Directory

*NASHVILLE,** Davidson Co.

DAVIES & HUMPHREYS (AV)

150 Second Avenue North, Suite 225, P.O. Box 190609, 37219-0609
Telephone: 615-256-8125
Fax: 615-242-7853
Email: davies_h@bellsouth.net

MEMBERS OF FIRM

Ed Reynolds Davies
Robert R. Davies
E. Reynolds Davies, Jr.

ASSOCIATE

John T. Horton

Representative Clients: Bituminous Insurance Companies; Carrier Corporation; E.B.I. Companies (Orion Group); Liberty Mutual Insurance Company; Ohio Casualty Insurance Group; Otis Elevator Company; St. Paul/United States Fidelity & Guaranty Company; State Volunteer Mutual Insurance Company; United HealthCare Corporation; Wausau Insurance Companies.

For full biographical listings, see the Martindale-Hubbell Law Directory

DAVID RANDOLPH SMITH & ASSOCIATES (AV)

611 Commerce Street, 3121 Renaissance Tower, 37203
Telephone: 615-742-1775; 800-394-2119
Fax: 615-742-1223
URL: http://www.lawyers.com/drs&associates
Email: info@drslawfirm.com *URL:* http://www.drslawfirm.com

For full biographical listings, see the Martindale-Hubbell Law Directory

TEXAS

*AUSTIN,** Travis Co.

KARL BAYER (AV)

900 Norwood Tower, 114 West Seventh Street, 78701
Telephone: 512-476-1226
Fax: 512-476-1280
Email: karl@karlbayer.com

Karl Bayer

For full biographical listings, see the Martindale-Hubbell Law Directory

BYRD, DAVIS AND EISENBERG, L.L.P. (AV)

A Partnership including Professional Corporations
707 West 34th Street, 78705
Telephone: 512-454-3751
Fax: 512-451-5857
Email: 70720.3104@compuserve.com

MEMBERS OF FIRM

L. Tonnett Byrd (P.C.)
Don L. Davis
David H. Walter
James H. Furman
Daniel W. Andrews

ASSOCIATE

Derek L. Davis

OF COUNSEL

Jack C. Eisenberg (P.C.)

For full biographical listings, see the Martindale-Hubbell Law Directory

HARRISON & RIAL, L.L.P. (AV)

100 Congress Avenue, Suite 1550, 78701
Telephone: 512-472-6900
Facsimile: 512-477-8480

Richard W. Harrison
J. Hamilton Rial, III

Kelli A. N. Carlton

Representative Clients: General Motors Corporation; Union Pacific Resources Company; Eaton Corporation; U.S. TeleCoin Corp.; Bay Maintenance Company, Inc.

For full biographical listings, see the Martindale-Hubbell Law Directory

SLACK & DAVIS, L.L.P. (AV)

A Partnership including a Professional Corporation
8911 Capital of Texas Highway Suite 2110, 78759
Telephone: 512-795-8686
Fax: 512-795-8787

MEMBERS OF FIRM

Steven E. Aldous
Mike Davis
Michael L. Slack

ASSOCIATE

Donna J. Bowen

OF COUNSEL

Tom H. Davis, P.C.

For full biographical listings, see the Martindale-Hubbell Law Directory

THOMPSON & KNIGHT L.L.P. (AV)

(Attorneys and Counselors)
1200 San Jacinto Center, 98 San Jacinto Boulevard, 78701
Telephone: 512-469-6100
Telecopy: 512-469-6180
URL: http://www.tklaw.com
Dallas, Texas Office: 1700 Pacific Avenue, Suite 3300, 75201.
Telephone: 214-969-1700.
Telecopy: 512-969-1751.
Telex: 732298.
Fort Worth, Texas Office: 801 Cherry Street, Suite 1600, 76102.
Telephone: 817-347-1700.
Telecopy: 817-347-1799.

(See Next Column)

THOMPSON & KNIGHT L.L.P., *Austin—Continued*

Houston, Texas Office: Thompson Knight Brown Parker & Leahy L.L.P., 1200 Smith Street, Suite 3600, 77002-4595.
Telephone: 713-654-8111.
Telecopier: 713-654-1871.
San Pedro Garza Garcia, Nuevo León, Mexico Office: Edificio Losoles PD-4, Av. Lázaro Cárdenas No. 2400 Pte., C.P. 66220.
Telephone: (52-8) 363-0096.
Telecopy: (52-8) 363-3067.

PARTNERS

Jeffrey S. Boyd
Eugene W. Brees, II
Frank L. Hill

For Complete List of Firm Personnel, See General Section

For full biographical listings, see the Martindale-Hubbell Law Directory

WHITEHURST, HARKNESS, OZMUN & ARCHULETA, A PROFESSIONAL CORPORATION (AV)

24th Floor, Westgate Building, P.O. Box 1802, 78767
Telephone: 512-476-4346
Fax: 512-476-4400

William O. Whitehurst, Jr.
Thomas R. Harkness
Scott A. Ozmun
Michael E.J. Archuleta
Cynthia K. Stewart
Sally S. Metcalfe
Michelle M. Cheng
Sylvia H. Imhoff

For full biographical listings, see the Martindale-Hubbell Law Directory

*BEAUMONT,** Jefferson Co.

MICHAEL R. MCGOWN (AV)

2615 Calder Street, Suite 300, P.O. Box 5876, 77726-5876
Telephone: 409-839-8389
Fax: 409-839-8387
Email: mcgown@ih2000.net *URL:* http://www.mcgown@ih2000.net

For full biographical listings, see the Martindale-Hubbell Law Directory

MEHAFFY & WEBER, A PROFESSIONAL CORPORATION (AV)

2615 Calder Avenue, Suite 800, P.O. Box 16, 77704
Telephone: 409-835-5011
Fax: 409-835-5729; 835-5177
Email: MehaffyWeber.com
Orange, Texas Office: 1006 Green Avenue, P.O. Drawer 189.
Telephone: 409-886-7766.
Houston, Texas Office: One Allen Center, 500 Dallas, Suite 1200.
Telephone: 713-655-1200.

James W. Mehaffy (1914-1985)
Roger S. McCabe
Jim I. Graves
John Cash Smith
Arthur R. Almquist
Louis M. Scofield
Patricia Chamblin
Gene M. Williams
David B. Gaultney
Robert A. Black
Sandra F. Clark
M. C. Carrington
Barbara J. Barron
Elizabeth Brandes Pratt
John E. Haught
Keith W. Foley
Charles Stanton Perry
Ernest W. Boyd
Michele Y. Smith

Vickie R. Thompson
Paul R. Heyburn
James G. Martingano
Debra N. Bigler
Elizabeth C. Turley
Peter T. Gregg
E. Wade Carpenter
Nikkee E. Rutherford
Bridget M. Fuselier
Jonathan C. Allen
Chris H. Booth
Maryalyce W. Cox
Timothy A. Gasaway
Elna Nguyen Griggs
Sean Stotsky

OF COUNSEL

Otto J. Weber, Jr.
Dewey J. Gonsoulin

Representative Clients: E.I. du Pont de Nemours and Co.; Eli Lilly & Co.; Merrell Dow; Jefferson County Tax Appraisal District; W.R. Grace & Co.-Conn.; Bank of America; Christus Health; Christus St. Elizabeth; Christus St. Mary; Burlington Northern Santa Fe Railway.
Approved Attorneys for: Stewart Title Guaranty Co.

For Complete List of Firm Personnel, See General Section

For full biographical listings, see the Martindale-Hubbell Law Directory

PATE & DODSON (AV)

470 Orleans Building, Suite 1201, 77701
Telephone: 409-838-6578
Fax: 409-838-6922

MEMBERS OF FIRM

Gordon R. Pate
Joe Michael Dodson
Karen L. Spivey
Christy Amuny

(See Next Column)

ASSOCIATE

Mark William Frasher

Representative Clients: The Travelers Insurance Co.; Universal Underwriters Insurance Co.; Allstate Insurance Co.; City Coach Lines, Inc.; Commercial Union Insurance Co.; Scottsdale Insurance Co.; GAINSCO; Hartford Insurance Co.; American International Adjustment Co., Inc.; Fidelity and Deposit Company of Maryland.

For full biographical listings, see the Martindale-Hubbell Law Directory

REAUD, MORGAN & QUINN (AV)

801 Laurel, 77701
Telephone: 409-838-1000
Fax: 409-833-8236

MEMBERS OF FIRM

Wayne A. Reaud
Glen W. Morgan
Cris Quinn
Richard J. Clarkson
Bob Wortham
Curtis W. Leister
Gary T. Cornwell

ASSOCIATES

Mary Ferguson Bradford
John Werner
David W. Ferrell
J. Trenton Bond
Sally A. Gary

For full biographical listings, see the Martindale-Hubbell Law Directory

*BROWNSVILLE,** Cameron Co.

RODRIGUEZ, COLVIN & CHANEY, L.L.P. (AV)

1201 East Van Buren, P.O. Box 2155, 78520
Telephone: 956-542-7441
Fax: 956-541-2170
McAllen, Texas Office: 4900 North 10th.
Telephone: 956-686-1287.
Telecopier: 956-686-6197.
Harlingen, Texas Office: 402 East Van Buren.
Telephone: 956-423-0216.
Telecopier: 956-423-2035.

MEMBERS OF FIRM

Eduardo R. Rodriguez
Norton A. Colvin, Jr.
Mitchell C. Chaney
Marjory Colvin Batsell
Jaime A. Saenz
Joseph A. (Tony) Rodriguez
Alison D. Kennamer

ASSOCIATES

Laura J. Urbis
Lecia L. Chaney
Daniel D. Herink
Robert Patrick Rodriguez
Rosa Maria Villagomez
Vanessa Garza
Teri L. Danish

OF COUNSEL

Orrin W. Johnson (Resident, Harlingen Office)
Benjamin S. Hardy (1912-1993)
Neil E. Norquest (Resident, McAllen Office)
Chris A. Brisack (Resident, McAllen Office)
Raymond A. Cowley

Division Attorneys for: Union Pacific Railroad.
Counsel for: Texas Commerce Bank-Rio Grande Valley, N.A.; Texas Commerce Bancshares, Inc.

For full biographical listings, see the Martindale-Hubbell Law Directory

*CENTER,** Shelby Co.

FAIRCHILD, PRICE, THOMAS, HALEY & WILLINGHAM, L.L.P. (AV)

413 Shelbyville Street, P.O. Drawer 1719, 75935
Telephone: 409-598-2981
Fax: 409-598-7712
Email: wmthomas@fpthw.com
Nacogdoches, Texas Office: 1801 North Street, P. O. Box 631668, 75963-1668.
Telephone: 409-569-2327.
Fax: 409-569-7932. E-Mail: chaley@fpthw.com
Houston, Texas Office: 440 Louisiana Street, Suite 2110, 77002-4205.
Telephone: 713-426-1700.
Fax: 713-426-1717. E-Mail: mwillingham@fpthw.com

MEMBERS OF FIRM

John L. Price
W. Miller Thomas
C. Victor Haley
R. Mark Willingham
Ryan A. Beason (Resident at Houston Office)
Travis P. Clardy
David J. Fisher
Clayton H. Haley
Russell R. Smith
James A. Payne, Jr.

OF COUNSEL

Robert L. Fairchild

ASSOCIATES

David Edward Ash
Campbell Cox
Jefferson B. Davis
Thomas L. Cougill
Jeffrey Pierce Fultz
Matthew D. Mettauer

(See Next Column)

FAIRCHILD, PRICE, THOMAS, HALEY & WILLINGHAM L.L.P.—*Continued*

Representative Clients: AIG; Chubb Group of Insurance Companies; Continental National American Group (CNA); Fireman's Fund Insurance Company; Kemper Insurance Companies; Liberty Mutual Insurance Company; St. Paul Insurance Company; State Farm Insurance Company.

For full biographical listings, see the Martindale-Hubbell Law Directory

*CORPUS CHRISTI,** Nueces Co.

PATTERSON & ASSOCIATES (AV)

101 North Shoreline, Suite 210, 78403
Telephone: 361-887-1881
Fax: 361-887-6761
Email: bob@pattersonassoc.com

Robert J. Patterson

Raymond C. Alexander

For full biographical listings, see the Martindale-Hubbell Law Directory

*DALLAS,** Dallas Co.

CALHOUN & STACY (AV)

Suite 5700 - Bank of America Plaza, 901 Main Street, 75202-3713
Telephone: 214-748-5000
Facsimile: 214-748-1421
Email: info@calhounstacy.com *URL:* http://www.calhounstacy.com

MEMBERS OF FIRM

Mark Alan Calhoun
Dennis D. Conder
LeAnn Wainscott Cross
Roy L. Stacy
Michael C. Wright

ASSOCIATES

Scott S. Crocker
Sean P. Fitzgerald
Elizabeth Reding Gambrell
Jonathan G. Polak
Joel W. Reese
Barbara L. Wohlrabe

For Complete List of Firm Personnel, See General Section

For full biographical listings, see the Martindale-Hubbell Law Directory

CLARK, WEST, KELLER, BUTLER & ELLIS, L.L.P. (AV)

4800 Renaissance Tower, 1201 Elm Street, 75270-2146
Telephone: 214-741-1001
Telecopier: 214-760-9812

MEMBERS OF FIRM

William H. Clark (1861-1931)
William H. Clark, Jr. (1895-1943)
Robert L. Clark (1903-1963)
William L. Keller
Allen Butler
David M. Ellis
Melvyn L. Douglas
Mike M. Tabor
Mark A. Shank
Michael P. Maslanka
Kervyn B. Altaffer, Jr.
Kelly Gaffney McClure

ASSOCIATES

Veronica Cuadra
Melinda L. Eitzen
Wade A. Forsman
Theresa M. Gegen
M. Brenk Johnson
Christie A. Newkirk
Robert J. Wood, Jr.
John Peter Hagan
Sonja J. McGill

For full biographical listings, see the Martindale-Hubbell Law Directory

CRACKEN, HARKEY & PAYNE, LLP (AV)

5956 Sherry Lane, Suite 1401, 75225
Telephone: 214-750-1855
Fax: 214-750-7086
Email: info@cracken-harkey.com *URL:* http://www.cracken-harkey.com

John R. W. Cracken
John D. Harkey, Jr.
Christopher A. Payne
James R. Snell

For full biographical listings, see the Martindale-Hubbell Law Directory

DEHAY & ELLISTON, L.L.P. (AV)

3500 NationsBank Plaza, 901 Main Street, 75202-3736
Telephone: 214-210-2400
Facsimile: 214-210-2500
Beaumont, Texas Office: 215 Orleans Street, 77701.
Telephone: 409-833-0900.
Facsimile: 409-833-0964.

J. Carlisle DeHay, Jr. (1922-1991)

PARTNERS

Gary D. Elliston
David W. Crowe
Mel D. Bailey
Eric D. Wewers
Christopher P. Manning
Paul E. Hamilton
Laura E. Kugler
Melinda S. Huff
Charlene R. Echols

(See Next Column)

OF COUNSEL

W. Scott Berry
Kathryn O. Hermes

Brent M. Karren
Stuart G. Brooks
Anthony S. Miller
Todd D. Ogden
William C. Arnold
Todd J. Suddleson (Not admitted in TX)
Kyle Christophen Steele
Lily Chang Myers
Kirsten L. Alessio
Russell J. DePalma
Tandy V. Jouret
M. Lauren Mathews
Jill G. Adams
John W. Arnold
William A. Fynes
Jeffrey M. Marosz
Kenneth D. Morris
Todd H. Ramsey
Mitzi S. Wallace
Susan Chapman

For full biographical listings, see the Martindale-Hubbell Law Directory

FOREMAN, BOUDREAUX, SMITH & JOHNSON (AV)

Walnut Glen Tower, Suite 1150, 8144 Walnut Hill Lane, Lock Box 62, 75231-4316
Telephone: 214-750-7661
Fax: 214-739-2715

OF COUNSEL

Jim Foreman

MEMBERS OF FIRM

Joe N. Boudreaux
Joseph F. Smith
Gary L. Johnson

ASSOCIATE

Shawn Thompson

LEGAL SUPPORT PERSONNEL

Charlene Illingworth

For full biographical listings, see the Martindale-Hubbell Law Directory

HOWIE & SWEENEY, L.L.P. (AV)

14th Floor, Park Place on Turtle Creek, 2911 Turtle Creek Boulevard, 75219
Telephone: 214-523-8800; 800-523-2339
Telecopier: 214-523-8888
Email: email@howie-sweeney.com *URL:* http://www.howie-sweeney.com

MEMBERS OF FIRM

John R. Howie
Paula Sweeney

Al Ellis
Jon Kettles
Andrew L. Payne
Valerie A. Mosman
Ladd Sanger
Elizabeth A. Florence

For full biographical listings, see the Martindale-Hubbell Law Directory

JACKSON WALKER L.L.P. (AV)

901 Main Street, Suite 6000, 75202-3797
Telephone: 214-953-6000
Fax: 214-953-5822
URL: http://www.jw.com
Austin, Texas Office: 100 Congress Avenue, Suite 1100.
Telephone: 512-236-2000.
Fax: 512-236-2002.
Fort Worth, Texas Office: 301 Commerce Street, Suite 2400.
Telephone: 817-334-7200.
Fax: 817-334-7290.
Houston, Texas Office: 1100 Louisiana, Suite 4200.
Telephone: 713-752-4200.
Fax: 713-752-4221.
Richardson, Texas Office: 2435 North Central Expressway, Suite 600.
Telephone: 972-671-2560.
Fax: 972-671-2566.
San Angelo, Texas Office: 225 West Beauregard Avenue.
Telephone: 915-481-2550.
Fax: 915-481-2552.
San Antonio, Texas Office: 112 E. Pecan Street, Suite 2100.
Telephone: 210-978-7700.
Fax: 210-978-7790.

MEMBERS OF FIRM

E. Leon Carter
H. Dudley Chambers
Michael L. Knapek
John L. Lancaster, III
Robert P. Latham
Billy R. McGill
Retta A. Miller
David T. Moran
David C. Myers
Robert F. Ruckman
Frank C. Vecella
Troy Michael Wilson

Representative Clients Furnished Upon Request.

For Complete List of Firm Personnel, See General Section

For full biographical listings, see the Martindale-Hubbell Law Directory

Dallas—Continued

LAW OFFICES OF ALAN K. LAUFMAN, J.D., M.D. A PROFESSIONAL CORPORATION (AV)

Suite 1000 Turtle Creek Centre, 3811 Turtle Creek Boulevard, 75219
Telephone: 214-559-3300
Fax: 214-526-1150
Email: medlaw@texas.net *URL:* http://www.lawyers.com/medlaw

Alan K. Laufman

For full biographical listings, see the Martindale-Hubbell Law Directory

MORGAN & WEISBROD, L.L.P. (AV)

10260 North Central Expressway, Suite 100N, P.O. Box 821329, 75382
Telephone: 214-373-3761; 800-800-6353
Fax: 214-739-4732
Email: info@morganweisbrod.com *URL:* http://www.morganweisbrod.com
Houston, Texas Office: 6800 West Loop South, Suite 450, 77401.
Telephone: 713-838-0003.
Fax: 713-838-0066.

Carl M. Weisbrod
Les Weisbrod
David R. Norton
Paul N. Gold
Larry F. Smith
Jennifer L. Fry
William A. Newman
Paul B. Burkhalter
David R. Deary
Leanna Marchand
David V. Marchand

ASSOCIATES

Wiebke Breuer
John M. Driskill
Gal Lahat
Robbie S. Partida-Kipness
Kevin Robinowitz

OF COUNSEL

Melvin D. Morgan
Lynn C. Absher
James M. Rauer

For full biographical listings, see the Martindale-Hubbell Law Directory

SIFFORD & ANDERSON, L.L.P. (AV)

A Partnership including Professional Corporations
6300 NationsBank Plaza, 901 Main Street, 75202-3771
Telephone: 214-742-1200
Fax: 214-220-0206

MEMBERS OF FIRM

Lewis R. Sifford (P.C.)
L. W. Anderson
John L. Ratcliffe (P.C.)

Michele A. Ratcliffe
Kevin W. Vice
Ron G. MacFarlane, Jr.

For full biographical listings, see the Martindale-Hubbell Law Directory

THOMPSON & KNIGHT L.L.P. (AV)

(Attorneys and Counselors)
1700 Pacific Avenue Suite 3300, 75201
Telephone: 214-969-1700
Telecopy: 214-969-1751
Telex: 732 298
URL: http://www.tklaw.com
Austin, Texas Office: 1200 San Jacinto Center, 98 San Jacinto Boulevard, 78701.
Telephone: 512-469-6100.
Telecopy: 512-469-6180.
Fort Worth, Texas Office: 801 Cherry Street, Suite 1600, 76102.
Telephone: 817-347-1700.
Telecopy: 817-347-1799.
Houston, Texas Office: Thompson Knight Brown Parker & Leahy L.L.P., 1200 Smith Street, Suite 3600, 77002-4595.
Telephone: 713-654-8111.
Telecopier: 713-654-1871.
San Pedro Garza Garcia, Nuevo León, Mexico Office: Edificio Losoles PD-4, Av. Lázaro Cárdenas No. 2400 Pte., C.P. 66220.
Telephone: (52-8) 363-0096.
Telecopy: (52-8) 363-3067.

PARTNERS

P. Jefferson Ballew
F. Barrett Davis
Cheryl E. Diaz
Stephen S. Livingston
John A. Mackintosh, Jr.
Maureen A. Murry
Joseph S. Pevsner
Stephen C. Schoettmer
Michael E. Schonberg
Molly Steele
Dawn Marie Wright

ASSOCIATES

Julia Elizabeth Jones
Anna E. Marple

For Complete List of Firm Personnel, See General Section

For full biographical listings, see the Martindale-Hubbell Law Directory

TOOLEY & VOSS (AV)

8214 Westchester Drive, Suite 420, 75225
Telephone: 214-368-2224
Fax: 214-368-8307
Email: JCToutfit@aol.com

Joe C. Tooley
Edwin P. Voss Jr.

For full biographical listings, see the Martindale-Hubbell Law Directory

TURLEY & STUTZ, P.C. (AV)

610 University Tower, 6440 N. Central Expressway, 75206
Telephone: 214-691-1880
Fax: 214-691-1955
Email: tstutz@quantumdata.net

Linda Turley
Thomas J. Stutz

For full biographical listings, see the Martindale-Hubbell Law Directory

*DECATUR,** Wise Co.

SIMPSON & BOYD, P.L.L.C. (AV)

105 North State Street, Suite B, P.O. Box 957, 76234
Telephone: 940-627-8308
Fax: 940-627-8092
Email: Derrick@wf.net
Email: sbblo@wf.net *URL:* http://www.lawyers.com/simpson&boydpllc
Bridgeport, Texas Office: 1119 Halsell Street, P.O. Box 685, 76426.
Telephone: 940-683-4098.
Fax: 940-683-3122.

Michael A. Simpson
Ross M. Simpson
Derrick S. Boyd

G. Alan Powers
J. Michael Carrillo

For full biographical listings, see the Martindale-Hubbell Law Directory

*EL PASO,** El Paso Co.

CHARLES A. DEASON, JR. (AV)

1141 East Rio Grande, 79902-1371
Telephone: 915-544-1371
Fax: 915-544-2013
Email: charliedeason@prodigy.net

For full biographical listings, see the Martindale-Hubbell Law Directory

MOUNCE, GREEN, MYERS, SAFI & GALATZAN, A PROFESSIONAL CORPORATION (AV)

100 N. Stanton, Suite 1700, P.O. Box 1977, 79950-1977
Telephone: 915-532-2000
Fax: 915-541-1597
Email: mouncegreenmyers@worldnet.att.net

S. Anthony Safi
H. Keith Myers
Carl H. Green
Barbara Wiederstein
Kurt G. Paxson
Mark C. Walker
Steven L. Hughes
Bruce A. Koehler
Darryl S. Vereen

Carrie D. Helmcamp
James A. Martinez

Attorneys for: CIGNA Cos.; Safeco Insurance Company; St. Paul Fire and Marine Insurance Company; State Farm Mutual Automobile Insurance Co.; Farmers Insurance Group; Furr's Supermarkets, Inc.; Reliance Insurance Co.; Scottsdale Insurance Company; Montgomery Kone; Zurich-US.

For Complete List of Firm Personnel, See General Section

For full biographical listings, see the Martindale-Hubbell Law Directory

RAY, McCHRISTIAN & JEANS, A PROFESSIONAL CORPORATION (AV)

5822 Cromo Drive, Suite 400, 79912
Telephone: 915-832-7200
Fax: 915-832-7333
Email: rmj@rmjfirm.com

Jeff Ray
John W. McChristian, Jr.
David S. Jeans
James A. Mounts, III
Eduardo Miranda
Robin Collins
Leticia Nuñez

Daniel H. Hernandez
Michael K. Dean
Angelica B. Carreon
Todd E. Marshall
Stacy Bearden Zavala

Representative Clients: Kemper Insurance Group; St. Paul Cos.; Kawasaki Motors Corp., U.S.A.; Georgia-Pacific Corp.; Reliance Insurance Co,; Commercial Union Insurance Cos.; General Motors Corp.; The Travelers Indemnity Co. and Aetna Casualty & Surety Co.; Royal Insurance Co.

(See Next Column)

RAY, MCCHRISTIAN & JEANS A PROFESSIONAL CORPORATION—*Continued*

For full biographical listings, see the Martindale-Hubbell Law Directory

*FORT WORTH,** Tarrant Co.

JOSE, HENRY, BRANTLEY & KELTNER, L.L.P. (AV)

675 North Henderson Street, 76107-8495
Telephone: 817-877-3303
Fax: 817-338-9109

John S. Jose
Michael J. Henry
Rickey J. Brantley
David E. Keltner

Karen S. Precella
Scotty MacLean
Anna L. Kingsley
Sara K. Turman-Vedral

For full biographical listings, see the Martindale-Hubbell Law Directory

LAW OFFICES OF PATRICK H. O'NEILL (AV)

110 West 7th Street, Suite 1100, 76102
Telephone: 817-878-3333
Fax: 817-878-3672

Patrick H. O'Neill

James L. Jackson, Jr.
Glenn T. Lupo

For full biographical listings, see the Martindale-Hubbell Law Directory

RUSSELL, TURNER, LAIRD & JONES, L.L.P. (AV)

One Colonial Place, 2400 Scott Avenue, 76103-2200
Telephone: 817-531-3000; 1-800-448-2889
Fax: 817-535-3046
Irving, Texas Office: Williams Square, Central Tower, Suite 700, 5215 North O'Connor Boulevard, Las Colinas Urban Center.
Telephone: 972-444-0444; 1-800-448-2889.

Wm. Greg Russell
Randall E. Turner
Steven C. Laird
Gregory G. Jones

For full biographical listings, see the Martindale-Hubbell Law Directory

THOMPSON & KNIGHT L.L.P. (AV)

(Attorneys and Counselors)
801 Cherry Street, Suite 1600, 76102
Telephone: 817-347-1700
Telecopy: 817-347-1799
URL: http://www.tklaw.com
Dallas, Texas Office: 1700 Pacific Avenue, Suite 3300, 75201.
Telephone: 214-969-1700.
Telecopy: 214-969-1751.
Telex: 732298.
Austin, Texas Office: 1200 San Jacinto Center, 98 San Jacinto Boulevard, 78701.
Telephone: 512-469-6100.
Telecopy: 512-469-6180.
Houston, Texas Office: Thompson Knight Brown Parker & Leahy L.L.P., 1200 Smith Street, Suite 3600, 77002-4595.
Telephone: 713-654-8111.
Telecopier: 713-654-1871.
San Pedro Garza Garcia, Nuevo León, Mexico Office: Edificio Losoles PD-4, Av. Lázaro Cárdenas No. 2400 Pte., C.P. 66220.
Telephone: (52-8) 363-0096.
Telecopy: (52-8) 363-3067.

PARTNERS

Lonnie J. Copps
Jennifer Pettijohn Henry
E. Michael Sheehan

For Complete List of Firm Personnel, See General Section

For full biographical listings, see the Martindale-Hubbell Law Directory

HARLINGEN, Cameron Co.

ADAMS & GRAHAM, L.L.P. (AV)

222 East Van Buren, West Tower, 78550
Telephone: 956-428-7495
Fax: 956-428-2954
Email: office@adamsgraham.com *URL:* http://www.adamsgraham.com
Affiliate Austin, Texas Office: Hill Gilstrap Adams & Graham, L.L.P., 1005 Congress Avenue, Suite 880, 78701.
Telephone: 512-457-9806.
Fax: 512-457-9066.

John Q. Adams (1900-1968)
Marshall W. Graham (1924-1988)
James S. Graham, Jr. (1922-1990)
Ferriel C. Hamby, Jr.
Tom A. Lockhart
Jim Denison
Leo C. Salzman
Roger W. Hughes
Craig H. Vittitoe
William L. Pope

(See Next Column)

Patricia Kelly
Jaime Balli
Gina M. Benavides
Charlie J. Cilfone
Juan A. Gonzalez
Barry Ray
Wilbert (Will) Hughes
Trinidad P. Galdean

Representative Clients: The Travelers Insurance Cos.; CIGNA; State Farm Insurance Co.; Valley Baptist Medical Center; Continental Loss Adjusting Services; McAllen Medical Center; Brownsville Medical Center; W.R. Grace; Pittsburg Corning; Bristol-Myers Squibb Co.

For full biographical listings, see the Martindale-Hubbell Law Directory

*HENDERSON,** Rusk Co.

WELLBORN, HOUSTON, ADKISON, MANN, SADLER & HILL, L.L.P. (AV)

300 West Main Street, P.O. Box 1109, 75653-1109
Telephone: 903-657-8544; 903-657-7227
Fax: 903-657-6108
Email: FD@whamsh.com *URL:* http://www.whamsh.com

MEMBERS OF FIRM

Rex Houston
Ron Adkison
J. Mark Mann
David Hill

For full biographical listings, see the Martindale-Hubbell Law Directory

*HOUSTON,** Harris Co.

BERG & ANDROPHY (AV)

3704 Travis, 77002-9550
Telephone: 713-529-5622
Fax: 713-529-3785
URL: http://www.lawyers.com/b&alaw
Email: mail@bahou.com *URL:* http://www.bafirm.com
New York, New York Office: 230 Park Avenue, Suite 1000, 10169-1099.
Telephone: 212-808-6580.
Fax: 212-808-3020.

David H. Berg (P.C.)
Joel M. Androphy
Cynthia R. Levin Moulton

Wade T. Howard
Geoffrey A. Berg
Gabriel A. Berg (Not admitted in TX)

For full biographical listings, see the Martindale-Hubbell Law Directory

PATRICIA KAY DUBE, P.C. (AV)

4140 Bank of America Center, 700 Louisiana Street, 77002
Telephone: 713-225-2297
Facsimile: 713-225-2298
Email: pkdube@wt.net *URL:* http://www.lawyers.com/dubelaw

Patricia Kay Dube
Clare I. Vetters
Lee Broze

OF COUNSEL

Alan J. Winters
Harold J. Eisenman

For full biographical listings, see the Martindale-Hubbell Law Directory

FAIRCHILD, PRICE, THOMAS, HALEY & WILLINGHAM, L.L.P. (AV)

440 Louisiana Street, Suite 2110, 77002-4205
Telephone: 713-426-1700
Fax: 713-426-1717.
Email: mwillingham@fpthw.com
Center, Texas Office: 413 Shelbyville Street, P.O. Drawer 1719, 75935.
Telephone: 409-598-2981.
Fax: 409-598-7712. E-Mail: wmthomas@fpthw.com
Nacogdoches, Texas Office: 1801 North Street, P.O. Box 631668, 75963-1668.
Telephone: 409-569-2327.
Fax: 409-569-7932. E-Mail: chaley@fpthw.com

John L. Price
W. Miller Thomas
C. Victor Haley
R. Mark Willingham
Travis P. Clardy
David J. Fisher
Clayton H. Haley
Russell R. Smith
Ryan A. Beason

OF COUNSEL

Robert L. Fairchild

James A. Payne, Jr.
David Edward Ash
Campbell Cox
Jefferson B. Davis
Thomas L. Cougill
Jeffrey Pierce Fultz
Matthew D. Mettauer

Representative Clients: AIG; Chubb Group of Insurance Companies; Continental National American Group (CNA); Fireman's Fund Insurance Company; Kemper Insurance Companies; Liberty Mutual Insurance Company; St. Paul Insurance Company; State Farm Insurance Company.

For full biographical listings, see the Martindale-Hubbell Law Directory

Houston—Continued

FISHER, BOYD, BROWN, BOUDREAUX & HUGUENARD, L.L.P. (AV)
70th Floor Wells Fargo Plaza, 1000 Louisiana, 77002
Telephone: 713-400-4000
Telefax: 713-400-4050

Wayne Fisher
Larry P. Boyd
Thomas K. Brown
Olan J. Boudreaux
James A. Huguenard

Bernard G. Johnson, III
Kay K. (Daniel) Morgan

For full biographical listings, see the Martindale-Hubbell Law Directory

FLEMING & ASSOCIATES, L.L.P. (AV)
1330 Post Oak Boulevard, Suite 3030, 77056
Telephone: 713-621-7944
Fax: 713-621-9638
URL: http://www.fleming-law.com

George M. Fleming
Robert R. Herring, Jr.
Sylvia Davidow
Bruce B. Kemp
Jim Doyle
Russell T. Abney
D'Lisa R. Simmons
Katrina Von Hedemann
Rand P. Nolen
Christopher A. Kesler
Andres C. Pereira
G. Sean Jez
Anthony E. Farah

For full biographical listings, see the Martindale-Hubbell Law Directory

GALLAGHER, YOUNG, LEWIS, HAMPTON & DOWNEY, L.L.P. (AV)
NationsBank Building, 700 Louisiana, 40th Floor, 77002
Telephone: 713-222-8080
Fax: 713-222-0066

Michael T. Gallagher
William H. Young
Craig Lewis
Hartley Hampton
Daniel M. Downey

Martin John de la Torre
Andrew Sher
Candace Kaiser Eindorf
Scott H. Mclemore
John J. Klevenhagen, III
Araceli E. Flores

OF COUNSEL
Rosemary Conlon McCarthy

For full biographical listings, see the Martindale-Hubbell Law Directory

GILPIN, PAXSON & BERSCH (AV)
A Registered Limited Liability Partnership
Attorney at Law
1900 West Loop South, Suite 2000, 77027-3259
Telephone: 713-623-8800
Telecopier: 713-993-8451
Email: gpb@gpblaw.com *URL:* http://www.texinslaw.com

PARTNERS

Gary M. Alletag
Timothy R. Bersch
John D. Gilpin
Darryl W. Malone
Michael J. Pappert
Stephen Paxson
Kevin F. Risley

OF COUNSEL

Harless R. Benthul
David F. Webb

ASSOCIATES

Joseph D. Batson
Jeri Pharis Wechsler

Representative Clients: BMW of North America, Inc.; Federal Deposit Insurance Corporation; Greater Houston Builders Association; Owens Corning Fiberglas Corporation; Shaw Industries, Inc.; Southwest Guaranty Trust Company, N.A.; Sprint Communications Company L.P.; Volkswagen of America, Inc.; Volvo North America Corporation; Wells Fargo Bank (Texas), N.A.

For full biographical listings, see the Martindale-Hubbell Law Directory

GLOVER, ANDERSON, LEWIS & PREBEG P.C., PROFESSIONAL CORPORATION (AV)
5599 San Felipe, Suite 1600, 77056
Telephone: 713-621-3306
Facsimile: 713-621-2259

Arthur M. Glover, Jr.
Paul E. Anderson, Jr.
James B. Lewis
Matthew J.M. Prebeg

Scott J. Davenport

For full biographical listings, see the Martindale-Hubbell Law Directory

HANEN, ALEXANDER, JOHNSON & SPALDING, L.L.P. (AV)
910 Travis, Suite 1700, 77002
Telephone: 713-222-2323
Fax: 713-222-2226

Andrew S. Hanen
Joseph R. Alexander, Jr.
Brian P. Johnson
John E. Spalding
Frank A. Doyle
Lawrence J. West
T. Christopher Trent

Geoffrey C. Guill
Tamara M. Madden
Richard Todd Marshall
Raphael (Rafe) Taylor
Lisa M. Moran
Shashi Patel
Annette Sepulveda Kenefick
Craig A. Choate

For full biographical listings, see the Martindale-Hubbell Law Directory

HOUSSIERE, DURANT & HOUSSIERE, LLP (AV)
Three Post Oak Central, 1990 Post Oak Boulevard, Suite 800, 77056-3812
Telephone: 713-626-3700
Fax: 713-626-3709
Email: lhoussi@hdhtex.com *URL:* http://www.hdhtex.com

Charles R. Houssiere, III
Harry L. Durant (Retired)
Linda D. Houssiere
Randal A. Kauffman
Monica C. Vaughan

Chad D. Points

For full biographical listings, see the Martindale-Hubbell Law Directory

IRESON & WEIZEL, P.C. (AV)
Chase Bank Building, 711 Travis, Suite 3000, 77002
Telephone: 713-216-1160
Fax: 713-216-1161
Email: law@iresonweizel.com

Lansford O. Ireson, Jr.
Ira D. Weizel

Charlotte J. Fischer
Frederick J. Wagner
Margot M. Ireson
Lionel J. Castro
Gina L. Miller

For full biographical listings, see the Martindale-Hubbell Law Directory

LANIER, PARKER & SULLIVAN, P.C. (AV)
Four Houston Center, Suite 1550 1331 Lamar Street, 77010
Telephone: 713-659-5200
FAX: 713-659-2204

W. Mark Lanier
Kevin P. Parker
Kent C. Sullivan

Becky J. Lanier
Leslie M. Stewart
Robert E. Leone
Edward W. Fudge
Patrick N. Haines
Dara Grisbee Hegar
Eugene R. Egdorf

For full biographical listings, see the Martindale-Hubbell Law Directory

MEHAFFY & WEBER, A PROFESSIONAL CORPORATION (AV)
One Allen Center, 500 Dallas, Suite 1200, 77002
Telephone: 713-655-1200
Fax: 713-655-0222
Email: MehaffyWeber.com
Beaumont, Texas Office: 2615 Calder Avenue, Suite 800, P.O. Box 16.
Telephone: 409-835-5011.
Orange, Texas Office: 1006 Green Avenue, P.O. Drawer 189.
Telephone: 409-886-7766.

Jim I. Graves
Arthur R. Almquist
Charles Stanton Perry

Paul R. Heyburn
James G. Martingano
Debra N. Bigler
Peter T. Gregg
Elna Nguyen Griggs

Representative Clients: E.I. duPont de Nemours and Co.; W.R. Grace & Co.-Conn.; Merrill Dow; Eli Lilly & Company; Burlington, Northen, Santa Fe Railway Company; Christus Health.

For full biographical listings, see the Martindale-Hubbell Law Directory

RAMSEY & MURRAY, A PROFESSIONAL CORPORATION (AV)
10000 Memorial Drive, Suite 700, 77024-3412
Telephone: 713-613-5400
Fax: 713-613-5414

(See Next Column)

RAMSEY & MURRAY A PROFESSIONAL CORPORATION—*Continued*

Ben Ramsey
John A. Murray, Jr.
Russell J. Ramsey
Mark Ramsey
Curtis D. Collette
Michael Stout Wright
Rick McRory

Joseph W. Gagnon
R. Russell Hollenbeck
Adrian V. Villacorta
Brenda Renee Ferguson

Representative Clients: Great Central Insurance Co.; Republic Insurance Co.

For full biographical listings, see the Martindale-Hubbell Law Directory

THOMPSON KNIGHT BROWN PARKER & LEAHY L.L.P. (AV)

A Registered Limited Liability Partnership including Professional Corporations
(Attorneys and Counselors)
1200 Smith Street, Suite 3600, 77002-4595
Telephone: 713-654-8111
Telecopier: 713-654-1871
URL: http://www.tklaw.com
Dallas, Texas Office: Thompson & Knight L.L.P., 1700 Pacific Avenue, Suite 3300, 75201.
Telephone: 214-969-1700.
Telecopy: 214-969-1751.
Telex: 732298.
Austin, Texas Office: Thompson & Knight L.L.P., 1200 San Jacinto Center, 98 San Jacinto Boulevard, 78701.
Telephone: 512-469-6100.
Telecopy: 512-469-6180.
Fort Worth, Texas Office: Thompson & Knight L.L.P., 801 Cherry Street, Suite 1600, 76102.
Telephone: 817-347-1700.
Telecopy: 817-347-1799.
San Pedro Garza Garcia, Nuevo León, Mexico Office: Thompson & Knight L.L.P., Edificio Losoles PD-4, Av. Lázaro Cárdenas No. 2400 PTE., C.P. 66220.
Telephone: (52-8) 363-0096.
Telecopy: (52-8) 363-3067.

PARTNERS

Gregory S. Meece
Robert L. Pittsford

For Complete List of Firm Personnel, See General Section

For full biographical listings, see the Martindale-Hubbell Law Directory

*LONGVIEW,** Gregg Co.

ERSKINE & MCMAHON, L.L.P. (AV)

426 North Center Street, P.O. Box 3485, 75606
Telephone: 903-757-8435
1-800-544-5479
Fax: 903-757-9429
Email: brucek@erskine-mcmahon.com *URL:* http://www.lawyers.com/erskine-mcmahon

MEMBERS OF FIRM

Blake C. Erskine
Mark P. McMahon

Kathy D. Colvin
Dennis M. McKinney

For full biographical listings, see the Martindale-Hubbell Law Directory

STROUP & JONES, L.L.P. (AV)

420 North Green Street Suite C, 75601
Telephone: 903-236-4878
Fax: 903-236-6210
Email: stroupjones@stroup-jones.com *URL:* http://www.stroup-jones.com

Danny M. Stroup
Christopher D. Jones

For full biographical listings, see the Martindale-Hubbell Law Directory

*LUBBOCK,** Lubbock Co.

MIKE MILLSAP (AV)

1116A Broadway, 79401
Telephone: 806-747-0264
Fax: 806-747-0292
Email: mikemillsap@msn.com

Reference: Norwest Bank.

For full biographical listings, see the Martindale-Hubbell Law Directory

MCALLEN, Hidalgo Co.

FLORES, CASSO & PETTITT, L.L.P. (AV)

321 South 12th Street, P.O. Box 2128, 78505
Telephone: 956-686-9591
Telecopy: 956-686-9478
Email: office@f-c-p.com *URL:* http://www.f-f-p.com

(See Next Column)

Rafael H. Flores
David Casso
B. Buck Pettitt

LEGAL SUPPORT PERSONNEL

LITIGATION ADMINISTRATORS

Edmundo Martinez
Mario Garza

For full biographical listings, see the Martindale-Hubbell Law Directory

RODRIGUEZ, COLVIN & CHANEY, L.L.P. (AV)

4900 North 10th Street, 78504
Telephone: 956-686-1287
Telecopier: 956-686-6197
Brownsville, Texas Office: 1201 East Van Buren Street.
Telephone: 956-542-7441.
Telecopier: 956-541-2170.
Harlingen, Texas Office: 402 East Van Buren.
Telephone: 956-423-0216.
Telecopier: 956-423-2035.

OF COUNSEL

Neil E. Norquest
Chris A. Brisack
Raymond A. Cowley

Division Attorneys for: Union Pacific Railroad.
Counsel for: Texas Commerce Bank-Rio Grande Valley, N.A.; Texas Commerce Bancshares, Inc.

For full biographical listings, see the Martindale-Hubbell Law Directory

*NACOGDOCHES,** Nacogdoches Co.

FAIRCHILD, PRICE, THOMAS, HALEY & WILLINGHAM, L.L.P. (AV)

1801 North Street, P.O. Box 631668, 75963-1668
Telephone: 409-569-2327
Fax: 409-569-7932.
Email: chaley@fpthw.com
Center, Texas Office: 413 Shelbyville Street, P.O. Drawer 1719, 75935.
Telephone: 409-598-2981.
Fax: 409-598-7712. E-Mail: wmthomas@fpthw.com
Houston, Texas Office: 440 Louisiana Street, Suite 2110, 77002-4205.
Telephone: 713-426-1700.
Fax: 713-426-1717. E-Mail: mwillingham@fpthw.com

John L. Price
W. Miller Thomas
C. Victor Haley
R. Mark Willingham
Travis P. Clardy
David J. Fisher
Clayton H. Haley
Russell R. Smith
Ryan A. Beason

OF COUNSEL

Robert L. Fairchild

James A. Payne, Jr.
David Edward Ash
Campbell Cox
Jefferson B. Davis
Thomas L. Cougill
Jeffrey Pierce Fultz
Matthew D. Mettauer

Representative Clients: AIG; Chubb Group of Insurance Companies; Continental National American Group (CNA); Fireman's Fund Insurance Company; Kemper Insurance Companies; Liberty Mutual Insurance Company; St. Paul Insurance Company; State Farm Insurance Company.

For full biographical listings, see the Martindale-Hubbell Law Directory

*SAN ANTONIO,** Bexar Co.

ADKISSON & JACKSON, L.L.P. (AV)

Suite 850, Alamo National Bank Building, 105 South St. Mary's Street, 78205
Telephone: 210-472-0500
Fax: 210-472-0515
Email: adkisson@satexlaw.com

MEMBERS OF FIRM

Randall C. Jackson
David M. Adkisson

For full biographical listings, see the Martindale-Hubbell Law Directory

BROCK & PERSON, A PROFESSIONAL CORPORATION (AV)

Union Square Building, 10101 Reunion Place, Suite 1000, 78216-4157
Telephone: 210-979-0100
Fax: 210-979-7810

Roy C. Brock
Stephen L. Dittlinger
John A. Guerra
Audrey A. Haake
David B. Person
Ricardo R. Reyna

O. Rene Diaz
A.J. Dimaline, IV
Julie K. Hogenauer
Mark R. Strandmo
Jorge Albert Tuckler

For full biographical listings, see the Martindale-Hubbell Law Directory

San Antonio—Continued

LANE, GANNON & TALIAFERRO, L.L.P. (AV)

8620 North New Braunfels, Suite 310, 78217
Telephone: 210-829-1545
Telecopier: 210-829-1633
Email: gannon@lgtlaw.com
Austin, Texas Office: 816 Congress Avenue, Suite 1100, 78701.
Telephone: 512-485-4595.
Fax: 512-485-4594.

MEMBERS OF FIRM

Gregory Gannon
John R. Lane, Jr.
William Craig Taliaferro

ASSOCIATES

Sharon Denise Hobbs
Frederick D. Schraub
Georganne G. Leonard
John R. Resendez
Brent Austin Biggs
Alfred Michael Casillas
Christia M. Antolik
Hella V. Caldera

OF COUNSEL

C. Gilbert House
James B. House

For full biographical listings, see the Martindale-Hubbell Law Directory

O'CONNELL, BENJAMIN & COGHLAN, L.L.P. (AV)

153 Treeline Park, Suite 200, 78209
Telephone: 210-824-0009
Fax: 210-824-9429
Email: obcllp@oconben.com

Keith B. O'Connell
David P. Benjamin
G. Thomas Coghlan
Ernest F. Avery
Les Katona, Jr.
Dan Vana

Gayla S. Corley
Cathrin J. Martinez

For full biographical listings, see the Martindale-Hubbell Law Directory

TINSMAN & HOUSER, INC. (AV)

One Riverwalk Place, 14th Floor, 700 North St. Mary's Street, 78205
Telephone: 210-225-3121
U.S. Wats: 1-800-292-9999
Fax: 210-225-6235
Email: info@thlaw.com *URL:* http://www.thlaw.com

Richard Tinsman
Franklin D. Houser
Margaret M. Maisel
David G. Jayne
Robert C. Scott
Daniel J. T. Sciano
Rey Perez
Bernard Wm. Fischman
Sharon L. Savage
Ronald J. Salazar
Sue Dodson
Dennis P. Bujnoch

For full biographical listings, see the Martindale-Hubbell Law Directory

TEXARKANA, Bowie Co.

PATTON, TIDWELL & SANDEFUR, L.L.P. (AV)

4605 Texas Boulevard, P.O. Box 5398, 75505-5398
Telephone: 903-792-7080; 903-792-5859
Fax: 903-792-8233
Email: KTIDW87157@aol.com

Nicholas H. Patton
Kelly B. Tidwell
Gregory C. Sandefur

For Complete List of Firm Personnel, See General Section

For full biographical listings, see the Martindale-Hubbell Law Directory

*TYLER,** Smith Co.

RAMEY & FLOCK, A PROFESSIONAL CORPORATION (AV)

500 First Place, P.O. Box 629, 75710
Telephone: 903-597-3301
Telecopier: 903-597-2413
Email: Ramey@Ramey-Flock.com *URL:* http://www.RameyFlock.com

Thomas B. Ramey (1892-1967)
Jack W. Flock
Tracy Crawford
Glenn Collins
Michael A. Hatchell
Tom Henson
Dennis G. Black
Paul H. Gilliam
R. Brian Craft
Gregory D. Smith
Michael T. Crawford
Mary H. Molly Hatchell
Rosemary Sage Jones
Ronald S. Vickery
John W. Ferguson, Jr.

Deron R. Dacus
Eric H. Findlay
Shannon Dacus
Maria Benecki Sowders
Jamy Mitchell Skaggs

Counsel for: Regions Bank; Exxon Co. U.S.A.; Kelly Springfield Tire Co.; Trinity-Mother Frances Health System; St. Paul Insurance Co.; The Travelers Cos.; Reliance Insurance Co.; Marshall Regional Medical Center.

For full biographical listings, see the Martindale-Hubbell Law Directory

UTAH

*SALT LAKE CITY,** Salt Lake Co.

JOEL M. ALLRED, P.C. (AV)

Suite 800, McIntyre Building, 68 South Main Street, 84101
Telephone: 801-531-8300 (Downtown Office)
801-582-2309 (Home Office)
Fax: 801-533-2463 (Office Hours)
801-363-2420 (After Office Hours)
Email: jallred@vii.com

Joel M. Allred

Amy Allred Dolce

For full biographical listings, see the Martindale-Hubbell Law Directory

MORGAN, MEYER & RICE, L.C. (AV)

Kearns Building, Eighth Floor, 136 South Main Street, 84101
Telephone: 801-531-7888
Telefax: 801-531-9732
Email: morgan@inquo.net

MEMBERS OF FIRM

Stephen G. Morgan
Cynthia K.C. Meyer
Mitchel T. Rice
Joseph E. Minnock
Jeffrey C. Miner

For full biographical listings, see the Martindale-Hubbell Law Directory

PARR WADDOUPS BROWN GEE & LOVELESS, A PROFESSIONAL CORPORATION (AV)

Suite 1300, 185 South State Street, 84111-1537
Telephone: 801-532-7840
Fax: 801-532-7750
URL: http://www.pwlaw.com

Patricia W. Christensen
Terry E. Welch
Jonathan O. Hafen

For Complete List of Firm Personnel, See General Section

For full biographical listings, see the Martindale-Hubbell Law Directory

SNELL & WILMER L.L.P. (AV)

111 East Broadway, Suite 900, 84111-1004
Telephone: 801-237-1900
Fax: 801-237-1950
URL: http://www.swlaw.com
Phoenix, Arizona Office: One Arizona Center, 85004-2202.
Telephone: 602-382-6000.
Fax: 602-382-6070.
Tucson, Arizona Office: One South Church Avenue, Suite 1500, 85701-1612.
Telephone: 520-882-1200.
Fax: 520-884-1294.
Orange County Office: 1920 Main Street, Suite 1200, Irvine, California 92614-7230.
Telephone: 949-253-2700.
Fax: 949-955-2507.

MEMBERS OF FIRM

Bryon J. Benevento
Tracy H. Fowler
Curtis J. Drake

ASSOCIATES

Todd M. Shaughnessy
David N. Wolf

Representative Clients: For list of Representative Clients, see end of biographical listings in the Martindale-Hubbell Law Directory.

For Complete List of Firm Personnel, See General Section

For full biographical listings, see the Martindale-Hubbell Law Directory

STRONG & HANNI, A PROFESSIONAL CORPORATION (AV)

Sixth Floor Boston Building, 9 Exchange Place, 84111
Telephone: 801-532-7080
Fax: 801-596-1508
Email: pfishler@strongandhanni.com

Gordon R. Strong (1909-1969)
Glenn C. Hanni
Henry E. Heath
Philip R. Fishler
Roger H. Bullock
R. Scott Williams
Dennis M. Astill (Managing Partner)
Stuart H. Schultz
Paul M. Belnap
Stephen J. Trayner
Joseph J. Joyce

(See Next Column)

STRONG & HANNI A PROFESSIONAL CORPORATION—*Continued*

Bradley Wm. Bowen
Robert L. Janicki
Elizabeth L. Willey
H. Burt Ringwood
Peter H. Christensen
David R. Nielson

Kevin D. Swenson
Catherine M. Larson
Kristin Van Orman
Darren K. Nelson
Peter H. Barlow
Steven T. Densley
Jennifer C. Polley-Abramson
Shawn T. Welch

OF COUNSEL

Robert A. Burton

Representative Clients: State Farm Mutual Automobile Insurance Co.; Standard Accident Insurance Co.; United Services Automobile Assn.; Western Casualty & Surety Co.; Government Employees Insurance Co.; Guaranty Mutual Life Co.

For full biographical listings, see the Martindale-Hubbell Law Directory

VAN COTT, BAGLEY, CORNWALL & MCCARTHY, A PROFESSIONAL CORPORATION (AV)

50 South Main Street, Suite 1600, P.O. Box 45340, 84145-0340
Telephone: 801-532-3333
Telecopier: 801-534-0058
Email: info@vancott.com *URL:* http://www.vancott.com
Ogden, Utah Office: 2404 Washington Boulevard, Suite 900.
Telephone: 801-394-5783.
Park City, Utah Office: 2200 Park Avenue, Suite C200-A.
Telephone: 435-649-3889.

David A. Greenwood
Kenneth W. Yeates

Justin Toth (Not admitted in UT)

For Complete List of Firm Personnel, See General Section

For full biographical listings, see the Martindale-Hubbell Law Directory

VERMONT

*MONTPELIER,** Washington Co.

THERIAULT & JOSLIN, P.C. (AV)

141 Main Street, P.O. Box 249, 05601-0249
Telephone: 802-223-2381
Fax: 802-223-1461
Email: LAWYERS@TJOSLIN.COM

William N. Theriault (1877-1961)
Peter B. Joslin
Fletcher Brian (Ted) Joslin

John Davis Buckley
Barbara R. Blackman

OF COUNSEL

Fletcher B. Joslin
Jeffry W. White

For full biographical listings, see the Martindale-Hubbell Law Directory

*RUTLAND,** Rutland Co.

CLEARY SHAHI ASSOCIATES, A PROFESSIONAL CORPORATION (AV)

110 Merchants Row, P.O. Box 6740, 05702-6740
Telephone: 802-775-8800
Telefax: 802-775-8809
URL: http://www.lawyers.com/vermonttriallaw

David L. Cleary
Kaveh S. Shahi

Thomas P. Aicher
Karen S. Heald
John R. Dean

For full biographical listings, see the Martindale-Hubbell Law Directory

MILLER FAIGNANT & BEHRENS, P.C. (AV)

36 Merchants Row, P.O. Box 6688, 05702-6688
Telephone: 802-775-2521
Fax: 802-775-8274
Email: lhblaw@aol.com *URL:* http://www.lawyers.com/millerfaignantbehrenslaw

Lawrence Miller
John Paul Faignant
Lawrence H. Behrens

OF COUNSEL

Lisa L. Chalidze

(See Next Column)

LEGAL SUPPORT PERSONNEL

Marie Peck Fabian
Kim J. Miller

Representative Clients: Travelers Insurance Co.; Government Employees Insurance Co.; Utica Mutual Insurance Co.; Universal Underwriters Insurance Co.; Zurich American Acadia Insurance.
References: Travelers Insurance Co.; Universal Underwriters Insurance Co.

For full biographical listings, see the Martindale-Hubbell Law Directory

VIRGINIA

*ABINGDON,** Washington Co.

THE TATE LAW FIRM (AV)

Abingdon Professional Centre, 110 Abingdon Place, 24211
Telephone: 540-628-5185
Telecopier: 540-628-5045
Email: lynntate@naxs.com *URL:* http://www.tatelaw.com

Mary Lynn Tate

OF COUNSEL

Olen G. Haynes (Not admitted in VA)

LEGAL SUPPORT PERSONNEL

Rebecca A. Wyatt
Teresa L. Brown

For full biographical listings, see the Martindale-Hubbell Law Directory

*FAIRFAX,** (Ind. City; Seat of Fairfax Co.)

BRAULT, PALMER, GROVE, ZIMMERMAN, WHITE & STEINHILBER (AV)

10533 Main Street, P.O. Box 1010, 22030-1010
Telephone: 703-273-6400
Fax: 703-273-3514
Manassas, Virginia Office: 8567-D Sudley Road, 20110. Mailing Address: P.O. Box 534, Manassas, VA 20108.
Telephone: 703-369-7500; 631-9727.
Fax: 703-369-2285.

MEMBERS OF FIRM

Adelard L. Brault (Emeritus)
Thomas C. Palmer, Jr. (Resident, Manassas Office)
Edward H. Grove, III
Michael L. Zimmerman
Bruce D. White
August W. Steinhilber, III

ASSOCIATES

Jack A. Robbins, Jr. (Resident, Manassas Office)
C. Mark Whittington
Craig J. Franco
Bobby Puri (Resident, Manassas Office)

Representative Clients: Alamo Rent-A-Car, Inc.; CNA Insurance Companies; E.I. du Pont de Nemours and Company; Erie Insurance Group; Fidelity & Deposit Company of Maryland; Hanover Insurance Company; Harleysville Insurance Companies; Home Insurance Company; J.B. Hunt Transport, Inc.; Kemper Insurance Group.

For full biographical listings, see the Martindale-Hubbell Law Directory

NORFOLK, (Independent City)

BREIT, DRESCHER & BREIT, P.C. (AV)

1000 Dominion Tower, 999 Waterside Drive, 23510
Telephone: 757-670-3888
Fax: 757-670-3895
Email: jbreit@livenet.net

John W. Drescher
Jeffrey A. Breit
George T. Albiston
Michael F. Imprevento
Latane' Ware Brown
John L. Watts

For full biographical listings, see the Martindale-Hubbell Law Directory

HARLAN & FLORA, P.C. (AV)

Dominion Tower, 999 Waterside Drive, Suite 1200, 23510
Telephone: 757-625-8300
Fax: 757-625-3714
Email: lawyers@harlan-flora.com *URL:* http://www.harlan-flora.com

Thomas J. Harlan, Jr.
John M. Flora

For full biographical listings, see the Martindale-Hubbell Law Directory

SACKS & SACKS, A PROFESSIONAL CORPORATION (AV)

Suite 501 Town Point Center, 150 Boush Street, 23510-1615
Telephone: 757-623-2753
FAX: 757-640-7170
Email: sacks@series2000.com *URL:* http://www.lawyers.com/sacks&sacks-com

(See Next Column)

SACKS & SACKS A PROFESSIONAL CORPORATION, *Norfolk—Continued*

Herman A. Sacks (1886-1983)
Stanley E. Sacks
Andrew M. Sacks

LEGAL SUPPORT PERSONNEL

James S. McMahan (Litigation Manager)
Thomas L. Gilchrist (Legal Assistant)
Virginia S. McCann (Paralegal)
Marshall T. Walker, Jr. (Investigator)
Maryjane Evans (Paralegal)

For full biographical listings, see the Martindale-Hubbell Law Directory

RICHMOND, (Independent City)

ALLEN, ALLEN, ALLEN & ALLEN, A PROFESSIONAL CORPORATION (AV)

1809 Staples Mill Road, P.O. Box 6855, 23230
Telephone: 804-257-7500; 800-768-2222
FAX: 804-257-7599
Petersburg, Virginia Office: 106 South Market Street.
Telephone: 804-733-8753.
Chesterfield, Virginia Office: 9509 Hull Street Road.
Telephone: 804-745-1200.
Fredericksburg, Virginia Office: 3405 Plank Road, 22407.
Telephone: 703-786-4100.
Mechanicsville, Virginia Office: 7255 Mechanicsville Turnpike.
Telephone: 804-746-4900.

George E. Allen, Sr. (1885-1972)
Cary L. Branch (1918-1989)
George E. Allen, Jr. (1914-1990)
Ashby B. Allen
Wilbur C. Allen
Boyd F. Collier
George E. Allen, III
Christopher Allen Meyer
W. Coleman Allen, Jr.
Charles L. Allen
R. Clayton Allen (Resident, Chesterfield Office)
Elizabeth M. Allen (Resident, Petersburg Office)
P. Christopher Guedri
Edward L. Allen (Resident, Fredericksburg Office)
Courtney A. Van Winkle
Tammy Stafford Ruble
Melinda H. South
Trent S. Kerns
Douglas A. Barry
Pamela Heflin Sellers

References: Signet Bank; Crestar Bank.

For full biographical listings, see the Martindale-Hubbell Law Directory

BRENNER, DOHNAL, EVANS & YOFFY, P.C. (AV)

411 East Franklin Street, Suite 200, P.O. Box 470, 23218-0470
Telephone: 804-644-1300
Facsimile: 804-644-1354
Email: bdeyp@erols.com

Theodore I. Brenner
Dennis W. Dohnal
Ronald S. Evans
James S. Yoffy

Jay O. Millman
Gregory S. Hooe
Kathryn Spruill Lingle
Mary J. Bennett
Thomas D. Stokes, III

For full biographical listings, see the Martindale-Hubbell Law Directory

LECLAIR RYAN, A PROFESSIONAL CORPORATION (AV)

707 East Main Street, 11th Floor, 23219
Telephone: 804-783-2003
Facsmile: 804-783-2294
Email: email@leclairryan.com
Glen Allen, Virginia Office: 4201 Dominion Boulevard, Suite 200, 23060.
Telephone: 804-270-0070.
Facsimile: 804-270-4715.
Blacksburg, Virginia Office: 1872 Pratt Drive, Suite 1865, 24060.
Telephone: 540-961-2762.
Fax: 540-961-2781.
Norfolk, Virginia Office: 999 Waterside Drive, Suite 2025.
Telephone: 757-624-1454.
Facsimile: 757-624-3773.
Alexandria, Virginia Office: 225 Reinekers Lane, Suite 290, 22314.
Telephone: 703-684-8007.
Facsimile: 703-684-8075.
Charlottesville, Virginia Office: 108 S.E. Second Street, P.O. Box 2017, 22902.
Telephone: 804-971-7771.
Facsimile: 804-296-0905.

William W. Belt, Jr.
John M. Fitzpatrick
Sharon J. Glover
Ronald P. Herbert
Kelvin L. Newsome
Robert F. Redmond, Jr.
Anne G. Scher
Charles M. Sims

Michael J. Hudak
Charles G. Meyer, III
Patricia M. Powis

For full biographical listings, see the Martindale-Hubbell Law Directory

PHILIP S. MARSTILLER, P.C. (AV)

16 South Second Street, 23219-3723
Telephone: 804-775-0169
Facsimile: 804-775-0653
Email: pmarstille@aol.com *URL:* http://www.lawyers.com/marstillerlaw

Philip S. Marstiller

For full biographical listings, see the Martindale-Hubbell Law Directory

SMITH & JENSEN, P.C. A PROFESSIONAL CORPORATION (AV)

The Campbell Building, Suite 415, 8002 Discovery Drive, 23229
Telephone: 804-285-2742
Fax: 282-8738
Email: sonofyens@aol.com

Nathan H. Smith
Eric S. Jensen

Mark S. Paullin

For full biographical listings, see the Martindale-Hubbell Law Directory

ROANOKE, Roanoke City Co.

WOOTEN & HART, A PROFESSIONAL CORPORATION (AV)

707 Building, Suite 300, P.O. Box 12247, 24024-2247
Telephone: 540-343-2451; 540-342-9672
Telecopier: 540-345-6417
URL: http://www.wootenhart.com

George W. Wooten
David B. Hart
L. Thompson Hanes
Susan A. Waddell
Bradley D. McGraw
John L. Cooley
Thomas W. Farrell
Paul C. Kuhnel
Peter D. Vieth

David W. Hearn
John Mark Cooley
Christopher W. Stevens
Elizabeth D. Guilbert
Eunice Park Austin

OF COUNSEL

M. Lanier Woodrum

Representative Clients: Wachovia Bank; St. Paul Insurance Cos.
Approved Attorneys for: Lawyers Title Insurance Corp.
Reference: First Union National Bank.

For full biographical listings, see the Martindale-Hubbell Law Directory

VIRGINIA BEACH, (Independent City)

BRYDGES, MAHAN, O'BRIEN & FRUCCI, P.C. (AV)

Professional Building, 1369 Laskin Road, 23451
Telephone: 757-428-6021
Fax: 757-491-7634

Richard G. Brydges
Stephen C. Mahan
William R. "Buster" O'Brien
Steven C. Frucci

Approved Mediators/Arbitrators for: United States Arbitration and Mediation, Inc.; Arbitration Associates, Inc.- Jams/Endispute.
Reference: The Bank of Tidewater.

For full biographical listings, see the Martindale-Hubbell Law Directory

SHUTTLEWORTH RULOFF & GIORDANO, P.C. (AV)

4525 South Boulevard, Suite 300, 23452
Telephone: 757-671-6000
Fax: 757-671-6004
Email: srg@visi.net *URL:* http://www.srgpclaw.com
Newport News, Virginia Office: Historic Hilton Village, 10234 Warwick Boulevard, 23605.
Telephone: 757-873-9999.
Facsimile: 757-873-8758.

Robert J. Haddad
Robert G. Morecock
Lisa Palmer O'Donnell
Thomas B. Shuttleworth, II
Lawrence H. Woodward, Jr.

For full biographical listings, see the Martindale-Hubbell Law Directory

WASHINGTON

*SEATTLE,** King Co.

THE DAVIS FIRM (AV)

5301 Ballard Avenue N.W., 98107
Telephone: 206-789-1056
Fax: 206-789-9690
Email: thedavisfirm@seanet.com *URL:* http://www.lawyers.com/thedavisfirm

(See Next Column)

THE DAVIS FIRM—*Continued*

MEMBERS OF FIRM

Susan R. Davis
Donald K. Davis

For full biographical listings, see the Martindale-Hubbell Law Directory

KARGIANIS WATKINS WERNER, L.L.P., P.S. (AV)

Market Place Tower, Penthouse Suite A, 2025 First Avenue, 98121-2157
Telephone: 206-448-7969; Toll Free: 800-424-3352
Fax: 206-448-7950

George Kargianis
Michael T. Watkins
Joanne R. Werner

For full biographical listings, see the Martindale-Hubbell Law Directory

LAW OFFICE OF RON PEREY (AV)

2025 First Avenue, Suite 250, 98121-2147
Telephone: 206-443-7600
Fax: 206-443-4785

LEGAL SUPPORT PERSONNEL

MEDICAL DIRECTOR

Alexandra Finney McCafferty (Medical Doctor)

CASE MANAGERS

P.J. Anderson (Registered Nurse)
David Ubaldi

For full biographical listings, see the Martindale-Hubbell Law Directory

SCHROETER, GOLDMARK & BENDER, P.S. (AV)

500 Central Building, 810 Third Avenue, 98104
Telephone: 206-622-8000; 1-800-809-2234
FAX: 206-682-2305
Email: lastname@schroeter-goldmark.com

Croil J. Anderson
Adam J. Berger
James D. Hailey
Kristin Houser
Amanda E. Lee
Mark Leemon
Douglas D. McBroom
Janet L. Rice
Jeffery P. Robinson
Rebecca J. Roe
Sidney Stillerman Royer
William Rutzick
Sandra E. Widlan
Corrie Johnson Yackulic
John Goldmark (1917-1979)
Dean Bender (1933-1988)

OF COUNSEL

Jenny A. Durkan

For full biographical listings, see the Martindale-Hubbell Law Directory

WEINSTEIN & BERGMAN A PROFESSIONAL SERVICES CORPORATION (AV)

1201 Third Avenue, Suite 5300, 98101-3000
Telephone: 206-583-2190
Fax: 206-583-2191
URL: http://www.weinstein-law.com

Brian Weinstein
Matthew P. Bergman

Meg Pageler

For full biographical listings, see the Martindale-Hubbell Law Directory

*YAKIMA,** Yakima Co.

ABEYTA-NELSON P.C. (AV)

1102 West Yakima Avenue, 98902-3029
Telephone: 509-575-1588
Fax: 509-457-8426
Email: injurylaw@abeytanelson.com *URL:* http://www.abeytanelson.com

Terry P. Abeyta
Rodney K. Nelson
Derek L. Sutton

John S. Kapuza

Reference: Central Valley Bank.

For full biographical listings, see the Martindale-Hubbell Law Directory

WEST VIRGINIA

*CHARLESTON,** Kanawha Co.

BERTHOLD, TIANO & O'DELL (AV)

208 Capitol Street, P.O. Box 3508, 25335
Telephone: 304-345-5700
Fax: 304-345-5703

(See Next Column)

Robert V. Berthold, Jr.
William M. Tiano
Tony L. O'Dell

References: Huntington Banks; Bank One; United National Bank.

For full biographical listings, see the Martindale-Hubbell Law Directory

BUCCI, BAILEY & JAVINS, L.C. (AV)

Bank One Center Suite 910, 707 Virginia Street, East, P.O. Box 3712, 25337
Telephone: 304-345-0346
Fax: 304-345-0375
Email: kpaxton@citynet.net

Guy R. Bucci
Timothy C. Bailey
L. Lee Javins, II

J. Mark Adkins
Jon K. Cormany
V. Paul Bucci, II

For full biographical listings, see the Martindale-Hubbell Law Directory

FLAHERTY, SENSABAUGH & BONASSO, P.L.L.C. (AV)

200 Capitol Street, P.O. Box 3843, 25301
Telephone: 304-345-0200
Telecopier: 304-345-0260
Email: ralphj@fsbwv.com *URL:* http://www.fsbwv.com
Morgantown, West Virginia Office: 7000 Hampton Center, Suite I.
Telephone: 304-598-0788.
Fax: 304-598-0790.
Wheeling, West Virginia Office: 1031 National Road, P.O. Box 6545.
Telephone: 304-242-3941.
Fax: 304-242-3944.

MEMBERS

Thomas V. Flaherty
Michael Bonasso
William J. Hanna
Pamela Dawn Tarr

ASSOCIATES

Andrew B. Cooke
Amberly A. Warner
Keith M. Kodosky
Robert P. Lorea
Christopher A. Brumley
Scott H. Kaminski

For full biographical listings, see the Martindale-Hubbell Law Directory

MACCORKLE LAVENDER & CASEY PLLC (AV)

800 One Valley Square, P.O. Box 3283, 25332
Telephone: 304-344-5600
Fax: 304-344-8141

EQUITY MEMBERS

John L. MacCorkle
George William Lavender, III
Anita R. Casey
Thomas S. Sweeney

NON-EQUITY MEMBERS

Renatha S. Garner
Cynthia A. Majestro
Albert C. Dunn, Jr
Monica N. Haddad

ASSOCIATES

Christopher J. Pyles
Erin R. Brewster
Macel E. Rhodes
Rhonda L. Miller

For full biographical listings, see the Martindale-Hubbell Law Directory

SALSBERY & DRUCKMAN (AV)

606 Virginia Street East, Suite 100, 25305
Telephone: 304-343-0075
Fax: 304-343-0099
Email: salsdruck@citynet.net

H. F. Salsbery
William S. Druckman
Madonna C. Estep

OF COUNSEL

Anne E. Shaffer

For full biographical listings, see the Martindale-Hubbell Law Directory

SHUMAN ANNAND BAILEY WYANT & EARLES (AV)

Suite 1007, 405 Capitol Street, P.O. Box 3953, 25339
Telephone: 304-345-1400
Telecopier: 304-343-1826
Email: shuman@newwave.net
Wheeling, West Virginia Office: Suite 3002, 1233 Main Street, 26003.
Telephone: 304-233-3100.
Telecopier: 304-233-0201.

MEMBERS OF FIRM

David L. Shuman
Stephen Darley Annand
Charles R. Bailey
Richard L. Earles
David L. Wyant (Resident, Wheeling, West Virginia Office)
Mark William Browning
William R. Slicer
George J. Joseph
Thomas E. Buck (Resident at Wheeling, West Virginia Office)

(See Next Column)

Madison—Continued

QUARLES & BRADY LLP (AV)

Firstar Plaza, One South Pinckney Street, P.O. Box 2113, 53701-2113
Telephone: 608-251-5000
Fax: 608-251-9166
URL: http://www.quarles.com
Milwaukee, Wisconsin Office: 411 East Wisconsin Avenue, 53202-4497.
Telephone: 414-277-5000.
Fax: 414-271-3552.
West Palm Beach, Florida Office: 222 Lakeview Avenue, 4th Floor, 33401.
Telephone: 561-653-5000.
Fax: 561-653-5333.
Naples, Florida Office: Barnett Center, 4501 Tamiami Trail North, Suite 300, 34103-3060.
Telephone: 941-262-5959.
Fax: 941-434-4999.
Phoenix, Arizona Office: One Camelback Building, One East Camelback Road, Suite 400, 85012-1649.
Telephone: 602-230-5500.
Fax: 602-230-5598.
Chicago, Illinois Office: Quarles & Brady LLC, Citicorp Center, 500 West Madison Street, Suite 3700.
Telephone: 312-715-5000.
Fax: 312-715-5155.

PARTNER

Michael L. Zaleski

For Complete List of Firm Personnel, See General Section

For full biographical listings, see the Martindale-Hubbell Law Directory

*MILWAUKEE,** Milwaukee Co.

CHERNOV, STERN & KRINGS, S.C. (AV)

Suite 1275, Two Plaza East, 330 East Kilbourn Avenue, 53202
Telephone: 414-276-4080
Fax: 414-276-4152
Email: mail@chernovlaw.com *URL:* http://www.lawyers.com/chernovlaw

John M. Filachek

For full biographical listings, see the Martindale-Hubbell Law Directory

HABUSH, HABUSH, DAVIS & ROTTIER, S.C. (AV)

Suite 2300 First Wisconsin Center, 777 East Wisconsin Avenue, 53202
Telephone: 414-271-0900
Fax: 414-271-6854
Email: info@habush.com *URL:* http://www.habush.com/
Madison, Wisconsin Office: 150 East Gilman Street, Suite 2000.
Telephone: 608-255-6663.
FAX: 608-255-0745.
Appleton, Wisconsin Office: 4100 Boardwalk Court.
Telephone: 920-738-0900.
FAX: 920-738-5850.
Wausau, Wisconsin Office: 3100 Eagle Avenue.
Telephone: 715-842-4444.
FAX: 715-845-8898.
Racine, Wisconsin Office: Durand Place, 5439 Durand Avenue, Suite 220.
Telephone: 262-554-6200.
FAX: 262-554-7166.
Waukesha, Wisconsin Office: Stone Ridge I, N14 W23755 Stone Ridge Drive, Suite 225.
Telephone: 262-523-4700.
FAX: 262-523-4545.
Rhinelander, Wisconsin Office: 26 South Brown Street.
Telephone: 715-365-1900.
FAX: 715-365-1910.
Green Bay, Wisconsin Office: P.O. Box 22545, 314 South Madison Street.
Telephone: 920-437-0900.
FAX: 920-437-0910.
Stevens Point, Wisconsin Office: 5370 East Highway 10.
Telephone: 715-345-0004.
FAX: 715-343-2207.
Lake Geneva, Wisconsin Office: First Banking Center Plaza, Suite 120, 569 Broad Street.
Telephone: 262-248-5200.
FAX: 262-248-5222.

Michael D. Egelhoff

For full biographical listings, see the Martindale-Hubbell Law Directory

KASDORF, LEWIS & SWIETLIK, S.C. (AV)

1551 South 108th Street, 53214
Telephone: 414-257-1055
Facsimile: 414-257-3759
Green Bay, Wisconsin Office: 727 East Walnut Street, 54301.
Telephone: 920-436-0304.
Wausau, Wisconsin Office: 2100 Stewart Avenue, Suite 230, 54401.
Telephone: 715-848-9250.
Facsimile: 715-849-2017.

(See Next Column)

James P. Reardon
Werner E. Scherr
Terrance E. Davczyk
Jeff Schmeckpeper
Gregory J. Cook
Michael J. Cieslewicz
Michael A. Mesirow
Joseph J. Ferris
James J. Kriva
David L. Styer
Robert J. Lauer
James M. Ryan
Robert P. Ochowicz

Michael C. Frohman
Charles G. Maris
Vicki L. Arrowood
Michael S. Murray
Peter J. Eckardt (Resident)
Christine D. Esser
Thomas A. Cabush
John K. Garofani
Bonni D. Fredrick
Christopher A. Duesing
Daniel W. Varline (Resident, Wausau Office)
Jerome A. Long (Resident, Wausau Office)

OF COUNSEL

Clifford C. Kasdorf
John M. Swietlik
Hugh E. Russell
Patti J. Kurth

Representative Clients: Allstate Insurance Co.; State Farm Mutual Automobile; Liberty Mutual Insurance Co.; Shelby Mutual Insurance Co.; Government Employees Insurance Co.
Reference: M & I Marshall & Ilsley Bank.

For full biographical listings, see the Martindale-Hubbell Law Directory

QUALE, FELDBRUEGGE, CALVELLI, THOM & CROKE, S.C. (AV)

(Formerly Prosser, Wiedabach & Quale, S.C.)
710 North Plankinton Avenue, 9th Floor, 53203-2404
Telephone: 414-271-2266
FAX: 414-276-0417
Email: qfctc@execpc.com

Frederick H. Prosser (1901-1981)
David M. Quale (1932-1997)
John E. Feldbruegge
Rocke A. Calvelli
Terrence C. Thom
William P. Croke
Dorothy H. Dey

Bradley S. Foley

OF COUNSEL

Jack R. Wiedabach

For full biographical listings, see the Martindale-Hubbell Law Directory

QUARLES & BRADY LLP (AV)

411 East Wisconsin Avenue, 53202-4497
Telephone: 414-277-5000
Fax: 414-271-3552
URL: http://www.quarles.com
Madison, Wisconsin Office: Firstar Plaza, One South Pinckney Street, P.O. Box 2113, 53701-2113.
Telephone: 608-251-5000.
Fax: 608-251-9166.
West Palm Beach, Florida Office: 222 Lakeview Avenue, 4th Floor, 33401.
Telephone: 561-653-5000.
Fax: 561-653-5333.
Naples, Florida Office: Barnett Center, 4501 Tamiami Trail North, Suite 300, 34103-3060.
Telephone: 941-262-5959.
Fax: 941-434-4999.
Phoenix, Arizona Office: One Camelback Building, One East Camelback Road, Suite 400, 85012-1649.
Telephone: 602-230-5500.
Fax: 602-230-5598.
Chicago, Illinois Office: Quarles & Brady LLC, Citicorp Center, 500 West Madison Street, Suite 3700.
Telephone: 312-715-5000.
Fax: 312-715-5155.

MEMBERS OF FIRM

(ALPHABETICALLY BY YEAR OF ADMISSION TO BAR)

Michael L. Zaleski (Resident, Madison Office)
Frank J. Daily
Patrick W. Schmidt
Eric J. Van Vugt
John A. Rothstein
David B. Bartel
Nancy Meissner Kennedy
Michael J. Gonring
Mark A. Kircher
Francis H. LoCoco
Margaret C. Kelsey
Colleen A. Scherkenbach (Resident, Phoenix, Arizona Office)
Jeffrey K. Spoerk

ASSOCIATES

Mitchell S. Moser
Daniel J. La Fave
Nora M. Platt
C. Christine Burns (Resident, Phoenix, Arizona Office)
Richard G. Frohling
Cory L. Nettles
Janice L. Tucker

For Complete List of Firm Personnel, See General Section

For full biographical listings, see the Martindale-Hubbell Law Directory

*RACINE,** Racine Co.

HABUSH, HABUSH, DAVIS & ROTTIER, S.C. (AV)

Durand Place, 5439 Durand Avenue, Suite 220, 53406
Telephone: 262-554-6200
Fax: 262-554-7166
Email: info@habush.com *URL:* http://www.habush.com/
Milwaukee Wisconsin Office: Suite 2300, First Wisconsin Center, 777 East Wisconsin Avenue. Telephone 414-271-0900.
FAX: 414-271-6854.
Madison, Wisconsin Office: 150 East Gilman Street, Suite 2000.
Telephone: 608-255-6663.
FAX: 608-255-0745.
Appleton, Wisconsin Office: 4100 Boardwalk Court.
Telephone: 920-738-0900.
FAX: 920-738-5850.
Wausau, Wisconsin Office: 3100 Eagle Avenue.
Telephone: 715-842-4444.
FAX: 715-845-8898.
Waukesha, Wisconsin Office: Stone Ridge I, N14 W23755 Stone Ridge Drive, Suite 225.
Telephone: 262-523-4700.
FAX: 262-523-4545.
Rhinelander, Wisconsin Office: 26 South Brown Street.
Telephone: 715-365-1900.
FAX: 715-365-1910.
Green Bay, Wisconsin Office: P.O. Box 22545, 314 South Madison Street.
Telephone: 920-437-0900.
FAX: 920-437-0910.
Stevens Point, Wisconsin Office: 5370 East Highway 10.
Telephone: 715-345-0004.
FAX: 715-343-2207.
Lake Geneva, Wisconsin Office: First Banking Center Plaza, Suite 120, 569 Broad Street.
Telephone: 262-248-5200.
FAX: 262-248-5222.

Michael J. Jassak Steven T. Botzau

For full biographical listings, see the Martindale-Hubbell Law Directory

*RHINELANDER,** Oneida Co.

HABUSH, HABUSH, DAVIS & ROTTIER, S.C. (AV)

26 South Brown Street, 54501
Telephone: 715-365-1900
Fax: 715-365-1910
Email: habush@newnorth.net *URL:* http://www.habush.com/
Milwaukee, Wisconsin Office: Suite 2300 First Wisconsin Center, 777 East Wisconsin Avenue.
Telephone: 414-271-0900.
FAX: 414-271-6854.
Madison, Wisconsin Office: 150 East Gilman Street, Suite 2000.
Telephone: 608-255-6663.
FAX: 608-255-0745.
Appleton, Wisconsin Office: 4100 Boardwalk Court.
Telephone: 920-738-0900.
FAX: 920-738-5850.
Wausau, Wisconsin Office: 3100 Eagle Avenue.
Telephone: 715-842-4444.
FAX: 715-845-8898.
Racine, Wisconsin Office: Durand Place, 5439 Durand Avenue, Suite 220.
Telephone: 262-554-6200.
FAX: 262-554-7166.
Waukesha, Wisconsin Office: Stone Ridge I, N14 W23755 Stone Ridge Drive, Suite 225.
Telephone: 262-523-4700.
FAX: 262-523-4545.
Green Bay, Wisconsin Office: P.O. Box 22545, 314 South Madison Street.
Telephone: 920-437-0900.
FAX: 920-437-0910.
Stevens Point, Wisconsin Office: 5370 East Highway 10.
Telephone: 715-345-0004.
FAX: 715-343-2207.
Lake Geneva, Wisconsin Office: First Banking Center Plaza, Suite 120, 569 Broad Street.
Telephone: 262-248-5200.
FAX: 262-248-5222.

Dana James Weis

For full biographical listings, see the Martindale-Hubbell Law Directory

*WAUKESHA,** Waukesha Co.

HABUSH, HABUSH, DAVIS & ROTTIER, S.C. (AV)

Stone Ridge I, N14 W23755 Stone Ridge Drive, Suite 225, 53186
Telephone: 262-523-4700
Fax: 262-523-4545
Email: info@habush.com *URL:* http://www.habush.com/
Milwaukee Wisconsin Office: Suite 2300, First Wisconsin Center, 777 East Wisconsin Avenue.
Telephone: 414-271-0900.
FAX: 414-271-6854.

(See Next Column)

Madison, Wisconsin Office: 150 East Gilman Street, Suite 2000.
Telephone: 608-255-6663.
FAX: 608-255-0745.
Appleton, Wisconsin Office: 4100 Boardwalk Court.
Telephone: 920-738-0900.
FAX: 920-738-5850.
Wausau, Wisconsin Office: 3100 Eagle Avenue.
Telephone: 715-842-4444.
FAX: 715-845-8898.
Racine, Wisconsin Office: Durand Place, 5439 Durand Avenue, Suite 220.
Telephone: 262-554-6200.
FAX: 262-554-7166.
Rhinelander, Wisconsin Office: 26 South Brown Street.
Telephone: 715-365-1900.
FAX: 715-365-1910.
Green Bay, Wisconsin Office: P.O. Box 22545, 314 South Madison Street.
Telephone: 920-437-0900.
FAX: 920-437-0910.
Stevens Point, Wisconsin Office: 5370 East Highway 10.
Telephone: 715-345-0004.
FAX: 715-343-2207.
Lake Geneva, Wisconsin Office: First Banking Center Plaza, Suite 120, 569 Broad Street.
Telephone: 262-248-5200.
FAX: 262-248-5222.

Gary R. Kuphall Douglas E. Swanson

For full biographical listings, see the Martindale-Hubbell Law Directory

*WAUSAU,** Marathon Co.

HABUSH, HABUSH, DAVIS & ROTTIER, S.C. (AV)

3100 Eagle Avenue, 54402-1987
Telephone: 715-842-4444
Fax: 715-845-8898
Email: info@habush.com *URL:* http://www.habush.com/
Milwaukee, Wisconsin Office: Suite 2300, First Wisconsin Center, 777 East Wisconsin Avenue.
Telephone: 414-271-0900.
FAX: 414-271-6854.
Madison, Wisconsin Office: 150 East Gilman Street, Suite 2000.
Telephone: 608-255-6663.
FAX: 608-255-0745.
Appleton, Wisconsin Office: 4100 Boardwalk Court.
Telephone: 920-738-0900.
FAX: 920-738-5850.
Racine, Wisconsin Office: Durand Place, 5439 Durand Avenue, Suite 220.
Telephone: 262-554-6200.
FAX: 262-554-7166.
Waukesha, Wisconsin Office: Stone Ridge I, N14 W23755 Stone Ridge Drive, Suite 225.
Telephone: 262-523-4700.
FAX: 262-523-4545.
Rhinelander, Wisconsin Office: 26 South Brown Street.
Telephone: 715-365-1900.
FAX: 715-365-1910.
Green Bay, Wisconsin Office: P.O. Box 22545, 314 South Madison Street.
Telephone: 920-437-0900.
FAX: 920-437-0910.
Stevens Point, Wisconsin Office: 5370 East Highway 10.
Telephone: 715-345-0004.
FAX: 715-343-2207.
Lake Geneva, Wisconsin Office: First Banking Center Plaza, Suite 120, 569 Broad Street.
Telephone: 262-248-5200.
FAX: 262-248-5222.

Dana James Weis David E. Sunby
Marlene F. Wahlstrom

For full biographical listings, see the Martindale-Hubbell Law Directory

WYOMING

*CHEYENNE,** Laramie Co.

THE FITZGERALD LAW FIRM (AV)

A Partnership of Professional Corporations
2108 Warren Avenue, 82001-3740
Telephone: 307-634-4000
Telecopier: 307-635-2391
Email: lawyers@fitzgeraldlaw.com *URL:* http://www.fitzgeraldlaw.com

MEMBERS OF FIRM

James E. Fitzgerald (P.C.) Sharon A. Fitzgerald (P.C.)

OF COUNSEL

A. G. McClintock

For full biographical listings, see the Martindale-Hubbell Law Directory

*JACKSON,** Teton Co.

SPENCE, MORIARTY & SCHUSTER, LLC (AV)

15 South Jackson Street, P.O. Box 548, 83001
Telephone: 307-733-7290
Fax: 307-733-5248
Salt Lake City, Utah Office: 39 Exchange Place, Suite 101, 84111.
Telephone: 801-521-0811.
Fax: 801-521-0437.

MEMBERS OF FIRM

Gerry L. Spence, P.C.
Edward P. Moriarty
Robert P. Schuster
Gary L. Shockey
J. Douglas McCalla
Roy A. Jacobson, Jr.
Kent W. Spence
Robert A. Krause

ASSOCIATES

Glen G. Debroder
R. Daniel Fleck
G. Bryan Ulmer, III
Laura N. MacPherson (Not admitted in WY)
David M. Gosar
Gerard R. Bosch
Jeffrey Gooch

Reference: First Interstate Bank, Casper, Wyoming.

For full biographical listings, see the Martindale-Hubbell Law Directory

PUERTO RICO

SAN JUAN, San Juan Dist.

JIMÉNEZ, GRAFFAM & LAUSELL

Suite 505, Midtown Building, 421 Muñoz Rivera Avenue, Hato Rey, P.O. Box 366104, 00936-6104
Telephone: 787-767-1030; 767-1000; 767-1061; 767-1064
Telefax: 787-751-4068;
Cable: "Nezte"
RCA Telex: 325-2730
Email: manager@jgl.com *URL:* http://www.jgl.com

OF COUNSEL

Nicolás Jiménez

MEMBERS OF FIRM

William A. Graffam
Steven C. Lausell
J. Ramón Rivera-Morales
José Juan Torres-Escalera
Manolo T. Rodríguez-Bird

ASSOCIATES

Patricia A. Garrity
Isabel J. Vélez-Serrano
Edgardo A. Vega-López
Jorge F. Blasini
Ruy V. Díaz-Díaz
Rafael A. Rosado-Marrero

Representative Clients: Sea-Land Service, Inc.; McAllister Brothers, Inc.; Crowley Maritime Corp.; General Motors Overseas Distribution Corp.; University of Puerto Rico; Chubb Insurance Group.

For Complete List of Firm Personnel, See General Section

For full biographical listings, see the Martindale-Hubbell Law Directory

VIRGIN ISLANDS

*CHRISTIANSTED, ST. CROIX,** St. Croix

R. ERIC MOORE (AV)

2108 Company Street, P.O. Box 3086, 00822
Telephone: 340-773-4150
Fax: 340-778-7168
Email: rericmoore@worldnet.att.net

ASSOCIATES

Edgar A. Christensen
Ivan A. Guzman
Odis Simpson Mingus, II
Franklin G. Quow

For full biographical listings, see the Martindale-Hubbell Law Directory

CANADA BRITISH COLUMBIA

*VANCOUVER,** Vancouver Co.

SINGLETON URQUHART (AV)

1200 - 1125 Howe Street, V6Z 2K8
Telephone: 604-682-7474
Fax: 604-682-1283
Email: reception@singleton.com *URL:* http://www.singleton.com

John R. Singleton, Q.C.
Derek A. Brindle
Jeffery A. Hand
C. L. (Kate) Mclean

Representative Clients: ENCON Insurance Managers Inc.; Commonwealth Insurance Company; Allianz Canada; Municipal Insurance Association.

For Complete List of Firm Personnel, See General Section

For full biographical listings, see the Martindale-Hubbell Law Directory

CANADA NEW BRUNSWICK

*FREDERICTON,** York Co.

MCINNES COOPER (AV)

Suite 600, 570 Queen Street, P.O. Box 610, E3B 5A6
Telephone: 506-458-8572
Fax: 506-458-9903
Email: mcrfton@mcrlaw.com *URL:* http://www.mcrlaw.com
Halifax, Nova Scotia Office: Summit Place, 1601 Lower Water Street, P.O. Box 730, B3J 2V1.
Telephone: 902-425-6500.
Fax: 902-425-6350. Email: mcrhfx@mcrlaw.com.
St. John's, Newfoundland Office: Baine Johnston Centre, 5th Floor, 10 Fort William Place, P.O. Box 5939, A1C 5X4.
Telephone: 709-722-8735.
Telecopier: 709-722-1763. Email: mcrsj@mcrlaw.com.
Moncton, New Brunswick Office: Place Moncton Place, 655 Main Street, P.O. Box 1368, E1C 8T6.
Telephone: 506-857-8970.
Fax: 506-857-4095. Email: mcrmctn@mcrlaw.com.
Charlottetown, Prince Edward Island Office: BDC Place, Suite 620, 119 Kent Street, C1A 1N3.
Telephone: 902-368-8473.
Fax: 902-368-8346. Email: mcrpei@mcrlaw.com.

ASSOCIATE

David D. Eidt

For Complete List of Firm Personnel, See General Section

For full biographical listings, see the Martindale-Hubbell Law Directory

*MONCTON,** Westmorland Co.

MCINNES COOPER (AV)

Barristers, Solicitors & Trade Mark Agents
Place Moncton Place, 655 Main Street, P.O. Box 1368, E1C 8T6
Telephone: 506-857-8970
Fax: 506-857-4095
Email: mcrmctn@mcrlaw.com *URL:* http://www.mcrlaw.com
Halifax, Nova Scotia Office: Summit Place, 1601 Lower Water Street, P.O. Box 730, B3J 2V1.
Telephone: 902-425-6500.
Fax: 902-425-6350. Email: mcrhfx@mcrlaw.com.
St. John's, Newfoundland Office: Baine Johnston Centre, 5th Floor, 10 Fort William Place, P.O. Box 5939, A1C 5X4.
Telephone: 709-722-8735.
Telecopier: 709-722-1763. Email: mcrsj@mcrlaw.com.
Charlottetown, Prince Edward Island Office: BDC Place, Suite 620, 119 Kent Street, C1A 1N3.
Telephone: 902-368-8473.
Fax: 902-368-8346. Email: mcrpei@mcrlaw.com.
Fredericton, New Brunswick Office: Suite 600, 570 Queen Street, P.O. Box 610.
Telephone: 506-458-8572.
Fax: 506-458-9903. Email: mcrfton@mcrlaw.com.

PARTNER

Eric LeDrew

ASSOCIATE

John C. Friel, Q.C.

For Complete List of Firm Personnel, See General Section

For full biographical listings, see the Martindale-Hubbell Law Directory

CANADA NEWFOUNDLAND

*ST. JOHN'S,**

McInnes Cooper (AV)

Barristers, Solicitors & Trade Mark Agents
Baine Johnston Centre, 5th Floor, 10 Fort William Place, P.O. Box 5939, A1C 5X4
Telephone: 709-722-8735
Telecopier: 709-722-1763
Email: mcrsj@mcrlaw.com *URL:* http://www.mcrlaw.com
Halifax, Nova Scotia Office: Summit Place, 1601 Lower Water Street, P.O. Box 730, B3J 2V1.
Telephone: 902-425-6500.
Fax: 902-425-6350. Email: mcrhfx@mcrlaw.com.
Moncton, New Brunswick Office: Place Moncton Place, 655 Main Street, P.O. Box 1368, E1C 8T6.
Telephone: 506-857-8970.
Fax: 506-857-4095. Email: mcrmctn@mcrlaw.com.
Charlottetown, Prince Edward Island Office: BDC Place, Suite 620, 119 Kent Street, C1A 1N3.
Telephone: 902-368-8473.
Fax: 902-368-8346. Email: mcrpei@mcrlaw.com.
Fredericton, New Brunswick Office: Suite 600, 570 Queen Street, P.O. Box 610.
Telephone: 506-458-8572.
Fax: 506-458-9903. Email: mcrfton@mcrlaw.com.

PARTNER

Deborah L. J. Hutchings

For Complete List of Firm Personnel, See General Section

For full biographical listings, see the Martindale-Hubbell Law Directory

CANADA NOVA SCOTIA

*HALIFAX,** Regional Munic. of Halifax

McInnes Cooper (AV)

Barristers, Solicitors & Trade Mark Agents
Summit Place, 1601 Lower Water Street, P.O. Box 730, B3J 2V1
Telephone: 902-425-6500
Fax: 902-425-6350
Email: mcrhfx@mcrlaw.com *URL:* http://www.mcrlaw.com
St. John's, Newfoundland Office: Baine Johnston Centre, 5th Floor, 10 Fort William Place, P.O. Box 5939, A1C 5X4.
Telephone: 709-722-8735.
Telecopier: 709-722-1763. Email: mcrsj@mcrlaw.com.
Moncton, New Brunswick Office: Place Moncton Place, 655 Main Street, P.O. Box 1368, E1C 8T6.
Telephone: 506-857-8970.
Fax: 506-857-4095. Email: mcrmctn@mcrlaw.com.
Charlottetown, Prince Edward Island Office: BDC Place, Suite 620, 119 Kent Street, C1A 1N3.
Telephone: 902-368-8473.
Fax: 902-368-8346. Email: mcrpei@mcrlaw.com.
Fredericton, New Brunswick Office: Suite 600, 570 Queen Street, P.O. Box 610.
Telephone: 506-458-8572.
Fax: 506-458-9903. Email: mcrfton@mcrlaw.com.

PARTNERS

Harry E. Wrathall, Q.C.
George W. MacDonald, Q.C.
G. Grant Machum
Stewart McInnes, P.C., Q.C.
Aidan J. Meade
Michelle C. Awad

ASSOCIATES

Tara A. Miller
Janet Clark

For Complete List of Firm Personnel, See General Section

For full biographical listings, see the Martindale-Hubbell Law Directory

CANADA ONTARIO

*HAMILTON,** Regional Munic. of Hamilton-Wentworth

Thoman Soule Gage (AV)

46 Jackson Street East, P.O. Box 187, L8N 3C5
Telephone: 905-529-8195
Fax: 905-529-7906

J. Douglas Thoman, Q.C.
John A. Soule
George S. Gage
J. Neil Smith
S. Stuart Aird
David J. Sherman
Lesley G. Matthewson
William F. Bastien
James Scott Greve
Catherine A. Korte

For full biographical listings, see the Martindale-Hubbell Law Directory

*TORONTO,** Regional Munic. of Toronto

Kelly Affleck Greene (AV)

One First Canadian Place, Suite 840, P.O. Box 489, M5X 1E5
Telephone: 416-360-2800
Fax: 416-360-5960
Email: info@kag.net *URL:* http://www.kag.net

MEMBERS OF FIRM

W. Anthony Kelly, Q.C.
Donald S. Affleck, Q.C.
Peter R. Greene
Donald B. Houston
James C. Orr
Peter C. Wardle
Helen A. Daley
Melissa J. Kennedy

ASSOCIATES

Kenneth A. Dekker
W. Michael G. Osborne
Jason C. Markwell
Patrice F. Band

For full biographical listings, see the Martindale-Hubbell Law Directory

*WINDSOR,** Essex Co.

Sutts, Strosberg LLP (AV)

600 Westcourt Place, 251 Goyeau Street, P.O. Box 670, N9A 6V4
Telephone: 519-258-9333
Detroit Michigan: 313-962-0137
Facsimile: Windsor 519-258-9527
Detroit 313-962-0139

MEMBERS OF FIRM

Achille F. Gignac, Q.C. (1902-1984)
Robert E. Barnes, Q.C.
Clifford N. Sutts, Q.C.
Harvey T. Strosberg, Q.C.
Gary V. Wortley
James K. Ball
John C. Holland
Mary M. S. Fox
William C. Chapman
Donald M. Gordon
Paul C. Nesseth
Heather Rumble Peterson
Patricia A. Speight
Edward W. Ducharme
Michelle A. Gagnon
Craig J. Allen
Werner H. Keller
Francine A. Herlehy
Paul Simard
Jasminka Kalajdzic

COUNSEL FOR CRIMINAL MATTERS

Patrick J. Ducharme

For full biographical listings, see the Martindale-Hubbell Law Directory

CANADA QUEBEC

*MONTREAL,** Montreal Dist.

McMaster Gervais (AV)

A General Partnership
1000 de La Gauchetière Street West, Suite 900, H3B 5H4
Telephone: 514-879-1212
Fax: 514-954-1905
Email: info@mcmastergervais.com *URL:* http://www.mcmastergervais.com

MEMBERS OF FIRM

Alex K. Paterson, O.C., O.Q., Q.C.
Robert E. Charbonneau
Daniel Ayotte
Peter Richardson
John G. Murphy

COUNSEL

Jacques Brien

For Complete List of Firm Personnel, See General Section

For full biographical listings, see the Martindale-Hubbell Law Directory

Montreal—Continued

WOODS & PARTNERS (AV)

2000 McGill College Avenue, Suite 1100, H3A 3H3
Telephone: 514-982-4545
Telecopier: 514-284-2046
Email: general@woods.qc.ca

MEMBERS OF FIRM

James A. Woods
Christian Immer
Julien Cools-Lartigue
Nathalie Chalifour
Christopher Lund Richter
Annie Galarneau
Sébastien Richemont
Kathleen Beaugé
Marjorie Delagrave

For full biographical listings, see the Martindale-Hubbell Law Directory

PROFESSIONAL LIABILITY

MISSOURI

GLADSTONE, Clay Co.

LAW OFFICES OF G. SPENCER MILLER, L.L.C. (AV)

207 N.E. 72nd Street Suite A, 64118
Telephone: 816-468-1010
Fax: 816-468-1112
URL: http://www.lawyers.com/gmillerlaw

MEMBER OF FIRM

G. Spencer Miller

ASSOCIATES

Christopher L. Heigele
Tracy B. Weiner

LEGAL SUPPORT PERSONNEL

Maureen Lobdell, Legal Administrator

For full biographical listings, see the Martindale-Hubbell Law Directory

KANSAS CITY, Jackson, Clay, Platte & Cass Cos.

WAGSTAFF & CARTMELL, LLP (AV)

Suite 1240, 4520 Main Street, 64111
Telephone: 816-701-1100
Fax: 816-531-2372

Thomas W. Wagstaff
Thomas P. Cartmell
Robert G. Rooney
Jonathan P. Kieffer

Marc K. Erickson
Thomas L. Wagstaff

For full biographical listings, see the Martindale-Hubbell Law Directory

ST. LOUIS, (Independent City)

WUESTLING & JAMES, L.C. (AV)

Suite 730, The Locust Building, 1015 Locust Street, 63101
Telephone: 314-421-6565
FAX: 314-421-4724

MEMBERS OF FIRM

Richard C. Wuestling, III (1928-1984)
William F. James
R. C. Wuestling
James G. Onder

ASSOCIATES

Lindsay A. Dibler
Michael W. Shelton
Elizabeth G. Roper
Heejun "Jay" Kim

Reference: Mercantile Trust Co.

For full biographical listings, see the Martindale-Hubbell Law Directory

NEBRASKA

*LINCOLN,** Lancaster Co.

CLINE, WILLIAMS, WRIGHT, JOHNSON & OLDFATHER (AV)

1900 U.S. Bank Building, 233 South 13th Street, 68508
Telephone: 402-474-6900
Fax: 402-474-5393
Email: postmaster@cline-law.com *URL:* http://www.cline-law.com
Omaha, Nebraska Office: Suite 720, One Pacific Place, 1125 South 103rd Street, 68124.
Telephone: 402-397-1700.
Fax: 402-397-1806.

ATTORNEYS

Allen L. Graves
Charles M. Pallesen, Jr.
Fredric H. Kauffman
Donald F. Burt
Alan E. Peterson
Stephen E. Gehring
Robert J. Routh
Kevin Colleran
L. Bruce Wright
James M. Bausch
Larry A. Holle
David R. Buntain
Stephen H. Nelsen
Michael C. Mueller
Lauren W. Wismer
Daniel R. Stogsdill
Scott D. Kelly
Terry R. Wittler
Pamela Hastings Carrier
Mark A. Christensen
Richard P. Garden, Jr.
Shawn D. Renner
John C. Miles
Mary Kay Frank
Thomas C. Huston
Sonya S. Ekart
Don R. Janssen
Susan Kubert Sapp
Kevin J. Schneider
Andrew D. Strotman
Jill Gossin Jensen
Rochelle A. Mullen
John L. Horan
Bryan S. Hatch
Steven C. Likes
Tracy A. Oldemeyer

(See Next Column)

ATTORNEYS (Continued)

Jolene M. Papa
Timothy G. Aschoff
Eric N. Bergquist
Janis J. Winterhof
Andrea Dylan Snowden

OF COUNSEL

Charles E. Wright
Richard P. Jeffries
Mary M. Campbell

RETIRED PARTNERS

Flavel A. Wright (Retired)
Warren C. Johnson (Retired)
Charles E. Oldfather (1927-1998)

Representative Clients: U.S. Bank National Association; University of Nebraska; Nebraska Medical Assn.; Saint Elizabeth Regional Medical Center; Media of Nebraska; Cargill Inc.; State Farm Insurance Cos.; Wal-Mart Stores, Inc.; Textron/Cushman; Isco, Inc.

For full biographical listings, see the Martindale-Hubbell Law Directory

*OMAHA,** Douglas Co.

KATSKEE, HENATSCH & SUING (AV)

10404 Essex Court, Suite 100, 68114
Telephone: 402-391-1697
Fax: 402-391-8932
Email: katskee@uswest.net

MEMBERS OF FIRM

Milton A. Katskee
Dean F. Suing
Jerry W. Katskee

ASSOCIATES

Francis T. Belsky
David A. Castello
John B. Henley
Todd W. Weidemann

OF COUNSEL

Harry R. Henatsch

Reference: Mid-City Bank.

For full biographical listings, see the Martindale-Hubbell Law Directory

NEW JERSEY

*BRIDGETON,** Cumberland Co.

JOHN P. MORRIS (AV)

200 West Commerce Street, P.O. Box 299, 08302
Telephone: 609-453-1000
Fax: 609-453-0200
URL: http://www.lawyers.com/johnpmorris

LEGAL SUPPORT PERSONNEL

Tara Dickson (Paralegal)

For full biographical listings, see the Martindale-Hubbell Law Directory

FLORHAM PARK, Morris Co.

HACK, PIRO, O'DAY, MERKLINGER, WALLACE & MCKENNA, P.A. (AV)

30 Columbia Turnpike, P.O. Box 941, 07932-0941
Telephone: 973-301-6500
Fax: 973-301-0094
Email: hpom@ix.netcom.com

Peter A. Piro
William J. O'Day
M. Richard Merklinger
Joseph V. Wallace
John M. McKenna
Peter T. Melnyk
Patrick M. Sages
Bonny G. Rafel
Robert G. Alencewicz
John T. West
Thomas M. Madden

Robert P. Morgan
Angela J. Mendelsohn
Michael J. Leegan
Stephen DeNaro
Joanne Vos
Peter Nastasi
Carol A. Rankin

OF COUNSEL

David L. Hack
William D. Dougherty
George A. West

For full biographical listings, see the Martindale-Hubbell Law Directory

LAWRENCEVILLE, Mercer Co.

SZAFERMAN, LAKIND, BLUMSTEIN, WATTER & BLADER, P.C. (AV)

Suite 104 Quakerbridge Executive Center, 101 Grovers Mill Road, 08648
Telephone: 609-275-0400
Telefax: 609-275-4511

(See Next Column)

SZAFERMAN, LAKIND, BLUMSTEIN, WATTER & BLADER P.C., *Lawrenceville—Continued*

Arnold C. Lakind
Barry D. Szaferman
Jeffrey P. Blumstein
Paul N. Watter
Steven Blader
Sidney H. Lehmann
Gerald B. Schenkman
David B. Beckett
Scott P. Borsack
Mary Lou Delahanty

Jennifer Weisberg Millner
Cathyanne A. Pisciotta
Jason N. Fruhschein
Demery J. Roberts
Stuart A. Tucker
Brian G. Paul
Victoria Rivera-Cruz
Thomas J. Burns III

LEGAL SUPPORT PERSONNEL

Paula M. Rossi (Office Administrator)
Patricia Hallstrum (Controller)

Representative Clients: Sun National Bank; First Washington Bank; Gilmore Securities & Co.; Communication Workers of America; The Eagle Group; Water's Edge Convalescent Center; Ronson Aviation, Inc.; Holmdel Township Board of Adjustment; Public Service Managers Association; Chemical Leaman Tank Lines.

For full biographical listings, see the Martindale-Hubbell Law Directory

MILLBURN, Essex Co.

MCDERMOTT & MCGEE (AV)

75 Main Street, P.O. Box 192, 07041-0192
Telephone: 973-467-8080
Fax: 973-376-8669

MEMBERS OF FIRM

John L. McDermott
John P. McGee
Richard P. Maggi
Thomas A. Wester
Richard M. Tango
Frank P. Leanza
John L. McDermott, Jr.
David J. Dickinson
A. Charles Lorenzo
Robert A. McDermott
Kevin John McGee

ASSOCIATES

Anthony John Verardi
Lindsay K. O'Shaughnessy
Andre L. McGuire

OF COUNSEL

Daniel K. Van Dorn

Representative Clients: Affiliated Building Service, Inc.; Allstate Insurance Co.; General Agents Insurance Company of America; Greater New York Mutual; General Accident Group; ISS International Service System, Inc.; Zurich-American Insurance Co.; Penn National Insurance Co.; Tokio Marine & Fire Insurance Co.; Medical Inter-Insurance Exchange of New Jersey.

For full biographical listings, see the Martindale-Hubbell Law Directory

LAW OFFICES OF STEPHEN H. SCHECHNER (AV)

75 Main Street, 07041
Telephone: 973-376-6200
Fax: 973-376-5620

ASSOCIATE

Virginia T. Shea

For full biographical listings, see the Martindale-Hubbell Law Directory

MORRIS PLAINS, Morris Co.

VOORHEES & OUDA (AV)

Powder Mill Plaza, 51 Gibraltar Drive, 07950
Telephone: 201-267-6677
Fax: 201-267-9152
Mailing Address: P.O. Box 1236, Morristown, New Jersey, 07962-1236

MEMBERS OF FIRM

William Wolverton Voorhees, Jr.
Peter A. Ouda

For full biographical listings, see the Martindale-Hubbell Law Directory

*MORRISTOWN,** Morris Co.

STEPHEN S. WEINSTEIN A PROFESSIONAL CORPORATION (AV)

20 Park Place, Suite 301, 07960
Telephone: 973-267-5200
Fax: 973-538-1779
Email: skippy@sswpa.com *URL:* http://www.sswpa.com

Stephen S. Weinstein

Gail S. Boertzel
William G. Johnson
Melissa H. Luce

For full biographical listings, see the Martindale-Hubbell Law Directory

*NEWARK,** Essex Co.

MARAN & MARAN (AV)

The Legal Center, One Riverfront Plaza, Suite 315, 07102
Telephone: 973-622-5303
1-888-566-2726
Fax: 973-622-4352

MEMBERS OF FIRM

Joe Maran
David Maran

For full biographical listings, see the Martindale-Hubbell Law Directory

RED BANK, Monmouth Co.

WHITE, FLEISCHNER & FINO (AV)

272 Broad Street, 07701
Telephone: 732-530-7787
Telecopier: 732-530-8552
New York, New York Office: 140 Broadway.
Telephone: 212-487-9700.
Telecopier: 212-487-9777.

Benjamin A. Fleischner

ASSOCIATE

Virginia L. McGrane (Not admitted in NJ)

Representative Clients: Hartford Insurance Group; Interstate Insurance Group; Chicago Insurance Group; Lloyd's Syndicates.

For full biographical listings, see the Martindale-Hubbell Law Directory

SPRINGFIELD, Union Co.

JAVERBAUM WURGAFT HICKS & ZARIN, A PROFESSIONAL CORPORATION (AV)

Park Place Legal Center, 959 South Springfield Avenue, 07081-3555
Telephone: 973-379-4200
Fax: 973-379-7872
Email: javerbaumwurgafthicks@compuserve.com *URL:* http://www.lawyers.com/jwhz,law

Kenneth S. Javerbaum
Jack Wurgaft
Robert G. Hicks
Ira J. Zarin

Anthony P. Valenti
Eric G. Kahn
David L. Wikstrom

OF COUNSEL

Jeffrey E. Strauss

For full biographical listings, see the Martindale-Hubbell Law Directory

MCDONOUGH, KORN & EICHHORN, A PROFESSIONAL CORPORATION (AV)

Park Place Legal Center, 959 South Springfield Avenue, P.O. Box 712, 07081-0712
Telephone: 973-912-9099
Fax: 973-912-8604

Peter L. Korn
R. Scott Eichhorn
James R. Korn
William S. Mezzomo
Timothy J. Jaeger
Wilfred P. Coronato

Julia A. Klubenspies
Matthew S. Schorr
Danielle M. Verrastro
Jeffrey John Berezny

OF COUNSEL

Robert P. McDonough

Representative Client: Meeker Sharkey & MacBean.
Reference: First Union, Summit, N.J.

For full biographical listings, see the Martindale-Hubbell Law Directory

VINELAND, Cumberland Co.

JAY H. GREENBLATT & ASSOCIATES A PROFESSIONAL CORPORATION (AV)

200 North Eighth Street, P.O. Box 883, 08360-0883
Telephone: 609-691-0424
Facsimile: 609-696-1010
Email: jhg@algorithms.com *URL:* http://home.earthlink.net/~greenblatt/

M. Joseph Greenblatt (1896-1992)
Jay H. Greenblatt

Bonnie L. Laube
Nicholas Kierniesky

For full biographical listings, see the Martindale-Hubbell Law Directory

WAYNE, Passaic Co.

DeYoe Heissenbuttel, L.L.C. (AV)

401 Hamburg Turnpike, P.O. Box 2449, 07474-2449
Telephone: 973-595-6300
Fax: 973-595-0146
Email: deyoelaw@ix.netcom.com *URL:* http://www.deyoe.com

MEMBERS OF FIRM

Charles P. DeYoe (1923-1973)
Wood M. DeYoe
Frederick C. Heissenbuttel
Scott B. Piekarsky

ASSOCIATES

Raymond F. Shenekji
Anne Hutton
Albert C. Buglione
Laureen A. Moloney

LEGAL SUPPORT PERSONNEL

Marilyn Moore (Office Manager)

Representative Clients: Hanover Insurance Inc.; Maryland Casualty Co.; Ohio Casualty Insurance Co.; Motor Club of America; Selective Insurance Co.; Prudential Property & Casualty; Reliance Ins. Co.

For full biographical listings, see the Martindale-Hubbell Law Directory

NEW MEXICO

*ALBUQUERQUE,** Bernalillo Co.

Dines, Gross & Esquivel, P.C. (AV)

6301 Indian School Road, N.E., Suite 900, 87110
Telephone: 505-889-4050
Fax: 505-889-4049
Email: law@dge.psemail.com *URL:* http://www.lawyers.com/dgelaw

James M. Dines
Michael A. Gross

Peter H. Pierotti

For full biographical listings, see the Martindale-Hubbell Law Directory

NEW YORK

*ALBANY,** Albany Co.

Harvey and Mumford (AV)

20 Corporate Woods Boulevard, 12211-2396
Telephone: 518-463-4491
Telecopier: 518-463-5665
Email: thefirm@harveyandmumford.com

Arthur J. Harvey (1903-1986)

MEMBERS OF FIRM

Jonathan P. Harvey
Brian F. Mumford

ASSOCIATES

Eva Lynn M. Hayko
Karen Hendricks
Peter Baird Joslin, Jr.
Trudy L. Boulia
Keith J. Starlin

OF COUNSEL

Jack D. Harvey

For full biographical listings, see the Martindale-Hubbell Law Directory

Roche Corrigan McCoy & Bush (AV)

The Wilem Van Zandt Building, 36 South Pearl Street, 12207
Telephone: 518-436-9370
Fax: 518-436-8233

MEMBERS OF FIRM

Robert P. Roche
Peter J. Corrigan
Joseph M. McCoy
Scott W. Bush

For full biographical listings, see the Martindale-Hubbell Law Directory

GARDEN CITY, Nassau Co.

Montfort, Healy, McGuire & Salley (AV)

1140 Franklin Avenue, 11530
Telephone: 516-747-4082
Telecopier: 516-746-0748

MEMBERS OF FIRM

E. Richard Rimmels, Jr. (1930-1999)
Frank J. Cafaro
Philip J. Catapano
Fredric C. Montfort
Donald S. Neumann, Jr.
James J. Keefe, Jr.
Michael A. Baranowicz
James Michael Murphy

(See Next Column)

OF COUNSEL

Fredric H. Montfort
Edward M. Salley, Jr.
David J. Fleming
Robert J. Mettalia

ASSOCIATES

Claudia C. Glacken
Marcie K. Glasser
Bruce A. Cook
Jeffrey D. Present
Joan E. Resnik
Susan H. Dempsey
Camille L. Hansen
Christopher T. Cafaro
Kathleen Dumont
Jeffrey B. Siler
Michael G. Kruzynski
Karen J. Cooper

For full biographical listings, see the Martindale-Hubbell Law Directory

HEMPSTEAD, Nassau Co.

Deegan & Deegan, L.L.P. (AV)

550 Front Street, 11550
Telephone: 516-486-9400
Telecopier: 516-486-8680
Email: deegan550@aol.com

MEMBERS OF FIRM

Donald E. Deegan
James V. Deegan

ASSOCIATES

Michael A. Wolf
James M. Hayes
Robert H. Doud
Mary E. Hayes
Gregg M. McGrath

OF COUNSEL

Diane Klaum Farrell
Thomas G. Nolan
John S. White
George Planos
Donald F. McCarthy
Gregory M. Maurer
George A. Boehling
Theresa Rho

For full biographical listings, see the Martindale-Hubbell Law Directory

*MINEOLA,** Nassau Co.

Shayne, Dachs, Stanisci, Corker & Sauer (AV)

250 Old Country Road, 11501
Telephone: 516-747-1100
Telecopier: 516-747-1185

MEMBERS OF FIRM

Moe Levine (1908-1974)
Neil T. Shayne (1932-1998)
Norman H. Dachs
W. Russell Corker
Brian J. Sauer
Kenneth J. Landau
Jonathan A. Dachs

Naomi R. Nathan

For full biographical listings, see the Martindale-Hubbell Law Directory

*NEW YORK,** New York Co.

Conway, Farrell, Curtin & Kelly, P.C. (AV)

63 Wall Street, 10005
Telephone: 212-785-2929
Fax: 212-785-7229

Patrick E. Curtin, Jr.
Kevin J. Kelly
John A. McManus
Anne P. Richter
Jonathan T. Uejio

Debora A. Pitman
Susan M. Johnson
Peter D. Suglia
Ann Marie Forte

Representative Clients: Chicago Insurance Company; CNA Insurance Company; Risk Enterprise Management.

For full biographical listings, see the Martindale-Hubbell Law Directory

Law Offices of David B. Golomb (AV)

Suite 527, 230 Park Avenue, 10169
Telephone: 212-661-9000
Telecopier: 212-661-6181
Email: golomblaw@aol.com

ASSOCIATE

Frank A. Longo

For full biographical listings, see the Martindale-Hubbell Law Directory

Postner & Rubin (AV)

17 Battery Place, 10004
Telephone: 212-269-2510
Fax: 212-425-0968
Email: postner@aol.com
Holmdel, New Jersey Office: 42 West Main Street,
Telephone: 732-946-9001.
Fax: 732-946-9005.

Robert A. Rubin
William J. Postner
Robert J. MacPherson
Jeffrey R. Cruz

(See Next Column)

POSTNER & RUBIN, *New York—Continued*

ASSOCIATES

Patricia M. Caplicki
Dana Wordes
Michael W. Bautz

NEW JERSEY RESIDENT COUNSEL

Sarah B. Biser

For full biographical listings, see the Martindale-Hubbell Law Directory

WHITE, FLEISCHNER & FINO (AV)

140 Broadway, 10005
Telephone: 212-487-9700
Telecopier: 212-487-9777
Email: infor@wff-law.com
Red Bank, New Jersey Office: 272 Broad Street.
Telephone: 732-530-7787.
Telecopier: 732-530-8552.

MEMBERS OF FIRM

Allan P. White
Benjamin A. Fleischner
Paul A. Fino, Jr.
James A. Robbins

ASSOCIATES

Virginia L. McGrane
Evan Asher Richman

Representative Clients: Hartford Insurance Group; Interstate Insurance Group; Chicago Insurance Company; Lloyd's Syndicates.

For Complete List of Firm Personnel, See General Section

For full biographical listings, see the Martindale-Hubbell Law Directory

*SYRACUSE,** Onondaga Co.

SUGARMAN, WALLACE, MANHEIM & SCHOENWALD (AV)

HSBC Center, Fifth Floor, 360 South Warren Street, 13202-2680
Telephone: 315-474-2943
Fax: 315-474-0235
URL: http://www.sugarmanlaw.com
Buffalo Office: 1720 Rand Building, 14 Lafayette Square, 14203.
Telephone: 716-847-2523.
Fax: 716-847-2589.

MEMBERS OF FIRM

George E. DeMore
Samuel Vulcano

Representative Clients: Allstate Insurance Co.; CNA Insurance Companies; Chubb & Son; Liberty Mutual Insurance Co.; Carpenter Manufacturing Co., Inc.; General Accident Group; Hartford Accident & Indemnity Co.; Firemans Fund; New York Central Mutual; Progressive Insurance Co.
Reference: HSBC.

For full biographical listings, see the Martindale-Hubbell Law Directory

*WHITE PLAINS,** Westchester Co.

O'CONNOR, MCGUINNESS, CONTE, DOYLE & OLESON (AV)

One Barker Avenue, 10601
Telephone: 914-948-4500
Telecopier: 914-948-0645
Email: attys@omcdoc.com

MEMBERS OF FIRM

Dennis L. O'Connor (1913-1989)
Rocco Conte
Dennis T. Doyle
William S. Oleson
Richard C. Oleson
Dennis L. O'Connor, Jr.
William R. Watson
Kevin M. Loftus

ASSOCIATES

Louis K. Szarka
Montgomery Lee Effinger
Philomena Basuk
Debora J. Dillon
Daniel M. Miller
Peter Hyun Kim
James R. Callan
Dawn T. McConnell
George M. Lesnett
Robert Wolf

OF COUNSEL

Eugene J. McGuinness
Russell J. Hauck

For full biographical listings, see the Martindale-Hubbell Law Directory

OHIO

*AKRON,** Summit Co.

MICHAEL M. DJORDJEVIC CO. LPA (AV)

17 South Main Street at Maiden Lane Suite 201, 44308
Telephone: 330-376-6766
Fax: 330-376-7344
Email: mickdlaw@aol.com *URL:* http://www.lawyers.com/michaeldjordjevic

Michael M. Djordjevic

For full biographical listings, see the Martindale-Hubbell Law Directory

*CINCINNATI,** Hamilton Co.

ROBERT J. GEHRING CO., L.P.A. (AV)

4th Floor, 105 East Fourth Street, 45202
Telephone: 513-721-2758
Fax: 513-621-9285

Robert J. Gehring

For full biographical listings, see the Martindale-Hubbell Law Directory

*CLEVELAND,** Cuyahoga Co.

GALLAGHER, SHARP, FULTON & NORMAN (AV)

(Formerly Hauxhurst, Sharp, Mollison & Gallagher)
Bulkley Building, Seventh Floor, 1501 Euclid Avenue, 44115
Telephone: 216-241-5310
Telecopier: 216-241-1608
Email: gsfn.com *URL:* http://www.gsfn.com

MEMBERS OF FIRM

H. Austin Hauxhurst (1881-1962)
Frank X. Cull (1887-1965)
I. Walter Sharp (1884-1966)
Clarence L. Mollison (1906-1981)
Robert C. Horrigan (1916-1993)
Forrest A. Norman
Edward J. Cass
John B. Robertson
Thomas E. Betz
Alan M. Petrov
Alton L. Stephens, Jr.
Virginia L. Heidloff
Jay Clinton Rice
Joseph W. Pappalardo
Thomas E. Dover
James F. Koehler
Robert H. Eddy
Thomas J. Kaiser
D John Travis
Paul J. Schumacher, Jr.
William F. Gibson
Gary L. Nicholson
Lynn L. Moore
Ernest W. Auciello, Jr.
Patrick M. Foy
Kevin C. Alexandersen
Stanley M. Dub
Timothy T. Brick
Sheila A. McKeon
Thomas J. Cabral
Timothy J. Fitzgerald
Mark A. Greer

OF COUNSEL

Michael R. Gallagher
Robert W. Sharp
George W. Stuhldreher
Burt J. Fulton
James F. Sweeney
James G. Gowan
James L. Ryhal, Jr.

Edward G. Kagels
John T. Murphy
M. Terence Cawley
Todd M. Haemmerle
Brian R. McGraw
Timothy P. Whitford
Daniel J. Michalec
Alexander E. Goetsch
Joseph J. Santoro
Monica A. Sansalone
John A. Simon
Dennis G. Rehor
Beth A. Nagel
Timothy Patrick Roth
Gregory K. Boop
Janice Aitken
Gary F. Werner
Mark Joseph Savage
Catherine A. Davis
Charles Allston Bowers
Pamela S. Schremp
James T. Tyminski, Jr.
Matthew J. Hatchadorian

STAFF ATTORNEY

Daniel L. Herak

Counsel for: Associated Aviation Underwriters; Conrail; The Continental Insurance Cos.; Continental National American Group; Fireman's Fund Insurance Cos.; The Home Insurance Co.; Motorist Ins. Co.; Norfolk Southern Corp.; Royal Insurance Co.; United States Aviation Underwriters.

For full biographical listings, see the Martindale-Hubbell Law Directory

OKLAHOMA

*OKLAHOMA CITY,** Oklahoma Co.

LEE, DUROCHER, KISNER, WALKER & REID (AV)

An Association of Professional Associations
5532 North Western, 73118
Telephone: 405-848-5532
Facsimile: 405-848-5502

Jim W. Lee
Daniel L. Durocher
David W. Kisner
David A. Walker
James M. Reid

For full biographical listings, see the Martindale-Hubbell Law Directory

*TULSA,** Tulsa Co.

BEST & SHARP, A PROFESSIONAL CORPORATION (AV)

Oneok Plaza, 100 W. 5th, Suite 808, 74103-4225
Telephone: 918-582-1234
Fax: 918-585-9447
Email: Webmaster@BestSharp.com *URL:* http://www.BestSharp.com

(See Next Column)

BEST & SHARP A PROFESSIONAL CORPORATION—*Continued*

Joseph M. Best
Daniel S. Sullivan
Amy E. Kempfert
Karen M. Grundy
Terry S. O'Donnell

Catherine L. Campbell
Malcom D. Smith, Jr.
Jeffrey W. Swanson
Dan W. Ernst
Thomas A. Le Blanc

For full biographical listings, see the Martindale-Hubbell Law Directory

RHODES, HIERONYMUS, JONES, TUCKER & GABLE, P.L.L.C. (AV)

Oneok Plaza, 100 West 5th Street, Suite 400, P.O. Box 21100, 74121-1100
Telephone: 918-582-1173
Fax: 918-592-3390
URL: http://www.rhodesokla.com

MEMBERS OF FIRM

Kevin D. Berry
Jo Anne Deaton
Richard M. Eldridge
E. D. Hieronymus (1908-1994)
Bert M. Jones
William S. Leach
Michael W. McGivern
William D. Perrine
Mary Quinn-Cooper
Robert P. Redemann
David P. Reid
Chris L. Rhodes, III
Thomas E. Steichen
Catherine C. Taylor
John H. Tucker
Wilson T. White
Harold C. Zuckerman

Ann E. Allison
Steven K. Bunting
Robert P. Coffey, Jr.
J. Christopher Davis
Andrew D. Downing
Dana L. Gish
Kerry R. Lewis
Andrew L. Richardson
Michael F. Smith
Leslie J. Southerland
Kimberly E. West
Keith A. Wilkes

OF COUNSEL

George W. Gable (Retired Partner)
Larry J. Fulton
Kelly M. Greenough

Representative Clients: American International Companies; Bechtel; Chubb Group of Insurance Companies; General Motors Corporation; Merrill, Lynch; Nissan Motor Corporation in U.S.A.; Pfizer, Inc.; Volkswagen of America, Volkswagen, A.G.; Zurich U.S.

For full biographical listings, see the Martindale-Hubbell Law Directory

OREGON

*PORTLAND,** Multnomah Co.

BANKS & UNDERHILL, P.C. (AV)

KOIN Center, Suite 1200, 222 S.W. Columbia Street, 97201
Telephone: 503-222-7475
Telecopier: 503-222-7288
URL: http://www.banksunderhill.com
URL: http://www.lawyers.com/banks&underhill

Robert S. Banks, Jr.
Dayna E. Underhill

Reference: Bank of America.

For full biographical listings, see the Martindale-Hubbell Law Directory

RIEKE & SAVAGE, P.C. (AV)

Thomas Mann Building, 140 S.W. Yamhill Street, 97204-3090
Telephone: 503-222-0200
Fax: 503-243-1820

Forrest N. Rieke
John William Savage

H. Scott Raivio
Paul G. Ellis
Cheryl Albrecht
Christopher A. Larsen
Robert L. Salisbury
Paul Hart
Angela J. Hart
Lisa J. Ludwig
Alan R. Scott

For full biographical listings, see the Martindale-Hubbell Law Directory

SATHER, BYERLY & HOLLOWAY, LLP (AV)

621 Southwest Morrison Street, Suite 650, 97205
Telephone: 503-225-5858
Fax: 503-721-9272
Email: sbh@teleport.com *URL:* http://www.teleport.com/~sbh/sbh.htm

(See Next Column)

Deborah L. Sather
Bruce L. Byerly
Ronald C. Holloway
Krishna Balasubramani
Tracy J. White
Constance Lynn Wold

For full biographical listings, see the Martindale-Hubbell Law Directory

PENNSYLVANIA

*HARRISBURG,** Dauphin Co.

ANGINO & ROVNER, P.C. (AV)

4503 North Front Street, 17110
Telephone: 717-238-6791
Fax: 717-238-5610
Email: lawfirm@angino-rovner.com *URL:* http://www.angino-rovner.com
Carlisle, Pennsylvania Office: 28 South Pitt Street, 17013.
Telephone: 717-241-2661.

Richard C. Angino
Neil J. Rovner

References: Credit Bureau of Greater Harrisburg; CoreStates.

For full biographical listings, see the Martindale-Hubbell Law Directory

*PHILADELPHIA,** Philadelphia Co.

ANAPOL, SCHWARTZ, WEISS, COHAN, FELDMAN AND SMALLEY, P.C. (AV)

1900 Delancey Place, 19103
Telephone: 215-735-1130
Fax: 215-735-2024
URL: http://www.aswc.net
Other Philadelphia, Pennsylvania Office: 1710 Spruce Street.
Fax: 215-735-2211.
Cherry Hill, New Jersey Office: 402 Park Boulevard, 08002.
Telephone: 1-609-427-9229.
Fax: 609-488-1396.
Fairless Hills, Pennsylvania Office: 920 Trenton Road.
Telephone: 215-945-6799.
Reading, Pennsylvania Office: 146 North 6th Street.
Telephone: 610-375-7488.
Media, Pennsylvania Office: 334 W. Front Street, 19063.
Telephone: 610-892-3714.

Alan Schwartz
Sol H. Weiss
Lawrence R. Cohan
Joel D. Feldman
Howard J. Levin
Bernard W. Smalley
Stanton Dubin
Margaret A. Barry
Stephen J. Pokiniewski, Jr.
Sidney M. Grobman
Nelson Levin

Nathaniel E.P. Ehrlich
Thomas R. Anapol
Miriam Benton Barish
Patrice A. Gillotti
Michele Lee Reed
Heather J. Lipson
Michelle L. Altenpohl
Lisa R. Schwartz
Kevin R. Marciano
Brian J. Taylor
Tobias L. Millrood
Tracy A. Finken

OF COUNSEL

Paul R. Anapol
Richard B. Schwartz (Resident, Other Philadelphia Office)
Mark F. Seltzer

Reference: Meridian Bank, Philadelphia, Pennsylvania.

For full biographical listings, see the Martindale-Hubbell Law Directory

CHRISTIE, PABARUE, MORTENSEN AND YOUNG, A PROFESSIONAL CORPORATION (AV)

1880 JFK Boulevard - Tenth Floor, 19103
Telephone: 215-587-1600
Fax: 215-587-1699
Email: cpmy@cpmy.com *URL:* http://www.cpmy.com
Cherry Hill, New Jersey Office: Woodland Falls Corporate Park, 200 Lake Drive East.
Telephone: 609-482-7887.
Fax: 609-482-7438.
New York, N.Y. Office: 20 Exchange Place, 31st Floor.
Telephone: 212-366-1310.
Fax: 212-797-3545.
Boston, Massachusetts, Office: One State Street, Fifteenth Floor.
Telephone: 617-854-8315.
Fax: 617-854-8311.
Radnor, Pennsylvania Office: Radnor Station Building No. 2, Suite 222, 290 King of Prussia Road.
Telephone: 610-688-5778.
Fax: 610-688-5788.

(See Next Column)

CHRISTIE, PABARUE, MORTENSEN AND YOUNG A PROFESSIONAL CORPORATION, *Philadelphia—Continued*

James W. Christie
Bradley J. Mortensen
James A. A. Pabarue, Jr.
James A. Young
Jerome E. Bogutz
Marc L. Bogutz
John D. Frumer (Resident, Boston, Massachusetts Office)
Ralph J. Luongo
Peter J. Lynch
Stella M. Tsai
Brian C. Vance

Anthony J. Arena
Carolyn Bates
Rex F. Brien
K. Tia Burke
Michael J. Burns
Michael E. DiFebbo, Jr.
John C. Falls (Resident, Cherry Hill, New Jersey Office)
Christie L. Gamble
Nadine M. Hunt
Elaine Whiteman Klinger
Randy J. Maniloff
Richard S. Margulies
Christopher M. Martin
Etienne C. Maumus
William F. McDevitt
Catherine O. Raymond
Heather A. Salko
Marie T. Sarkees
Barbara L. Schmuck
Paul V. Shehadi
Randee Lynn Strair
June A. Taima
Christina G. Tershakovec
Thaddeus J. Weaver
Marybeth Smith Werb
Lisa B. Zucker

For full biographical listings, see the Martindale-Hubbell Law Directory

GOLDFEIN & JOSEPH, A PROFESSIONAL CORPORATION (AV)

1600 Market Street 33rd Floor, 19103-7288
Telephone: 215-979-8200
Fax: 215-979-8201
URL: http://www.goldfeinlaw.com
Princeton, New Jersey Office: Princeton Metro Center, Suite 115, 5 Vaughn Drive.
Telephone: 609-520-0400.
Fax: 609-520-1450.
Wilmington, Delaware Office: PNC Bank Center, Suite 1110, P.O. Box 2206, 222 Delaware Avenue.
Telephone: 302-656-3301.
Fax: 302-656-0643.
New York, New York Office: 150 Broadway, Suite 1212, 10038.
Telephone: 212-791-0340.
Fax: 212-791-0347.

Edward B. Joseph
Fredric L. Goldfein
E. Chandler Hosmer, III
David C. Weinberg
Bernard L. Levinthal
Roseann Lynn Brenner
Gary H. Kaplan
John A. Turlik

Michael A. Billotti
Medford J. Brown, III
Robert P. Coleman
Robert T. Connor
Charles D. Cooper
Kelly A. Costello
Lawrence E. Currier
Janet E. Golup
Christine Renee Guiliano
David M. Katzenstein
Matthew A Kelly, III
Deborah M. Knight
Pamela A. Post
Thomas M. Savon
Julie M. Sebring (Not admitted in PA)
Robert M. Stroh
Marc R. Wilner
Anthony F. Zabicki, Jr.

For full biographical listings, see the Martindale-Hubbell Law Directory

MCELDREW & FULLAM, P.C. (AV)

Suite 5050 One Liberty Place, 19103
Telephone: 215-563-8300
800-223-3352
Fax: 215-563-6130
URL: http://www.lawyers.com/mceldrew&fullampc
New York, New York Office: McEldrew & Ressler, Suite 2101, 11 Pennsylvania Plaza, 10001.
Telephone: 212-695-6446.
Fax: 212-268-0287.

James J. McEldrew, III
Nancy H. Fullam

Marcella J. Schell
Carol L. Vassallo
Sallie Updyke Mundy
David Felderman

LEGAL SUPPORT PERSONNEL

Christine Doelp (Comptroller)

For full biographical listings, see the Martindale-Hubbell Law Directory

RUTHRAUFF & ARMBRUST, P.C. (AV)

1601 Market Street, 16th Floor, 19103
Telephone: 215-567-3700
Fax: 215-587-0409
Email: rutharm@erols.com
Cherry Hill, New Jersey Office: 200 Lake Drive East, Suite 206, 08002.
Telephone: 609-482-7856.
Fax: 609-482-8099.

(See Next Column)

Wilbur Bourne Ruthrauff
R. Mark Armbrust

David Ira Rosenbaum

LEGAL SUPPORT PERSONNEL

Charlane Sutton

For full biographical listings, see the Martindale-Hubbell Law Directory

SOUTH CAROLINA

*CHARLESTON,** Charleston Co.

HOOD LAW FIRM (AV)

172 Meeting Street, P.O. Box 1508, 29402
Telephone: 843-577-4435
Fax: 843-722-1630
Email: hlf@hoodlaw.com *URL:* http://www.hoodlaw.com

MEMBERS OF FIRM

Robert H. Hood
Louis P. Herns
G. Mark Phillips
Carl Everette Pierce, II
John K. Blincow, Jr.
James G. Kennedy
Barbara Wynne Showers
Joseph C. Wilson, IV
James Dowell Gandy, III

Dixon F. Pearce, II
Hugh Willcox Buyck
Allan Poe Sloan, III
Mary Agnes Hood Craig
Allison Snead Patrick
P. Gunnar Nistad
Robert H. Hood, Jr.
William Mullins McLeod, Jr.

For full biographical listings, see the Martindale-Hubbell Law Directory

*COLUMBIA,** Richland Co.

HOWSER, NEWMAN & BESLEY, L.L.C. (AV)

1508 Washington Street, P.O. Box 12009, 29211
Telephone: 803-758-6000
Fax: 803-758-4445
Email: rdhowser@hnblaw.com

R. Davis Howser
James P. Newman, Jr.
William G. Besley
Benjamin D. McCoy

Kelley S. Shull
Andrew E. Haselden
Janet Brooks

Representative Clients: American Modern Home Company; Clayton Homes; CNA Risk Management Group; DPIC Companies, Inc.; Horace Mann Insurance Company; Zurich Companies; Selective Insurance Company; South Carolina School Boards Insurance Trust; State Auto Insurance Company; Utica National Insurance Group.

For full biographical listings, see the Martindale-Hubbell Law Directory

TENNESSEE

*MEMPHIS,** Shelby Co.

SMITH, SABBATINI & MCLEARY, PLLC (AV)

100 Peabody Place Suite 1250, 38103
Telephone: 901-312-5555
Fax: 901-312-5667
Mailing Address: P.O. Box 3582, Memphis, TN, 38173
URL: http://www.smithlawetal.com

Gary K. Smith
Robert L. Sabbatini
Harold W. McLeary, Jr.
William D. Domico
James F. Kyle
James T. McColgan, III
G. Edward Coleman, III
Bryant C. Witt

Representative Clients: Premier RRG Insurance; Illinois Central Railroad; Medical Assurance; Albertson's, Inc.; Med. Marc (Chiro Co.); Medical Protective Co.; Methodist Health Systems; Hartford Insurance Co.; Sentry Insurance; State Farm Insurance.

For full biographical listings, see the Martindale-Hubbell Law Directory

TEXAS

*AMARILLO,** Potter Co.

WHITTENBURG WHITTENBURG & SCHACHTER, P.C. (AV)

1010 South Harrison, P.O. Box 31718, 79120
Telephone: 806-372-5700
Facsimile: 806-372-5757
Dallas, Texas Office: 2300 Plaza of the Americas, 600 North Pearl, LB 133.
Telephone: 214-999-5700.
Facsimile: 214-999-5747.

Deborah Ashmore Harris

For Complete List of Firm Personnel, See General Section

For full biographical listings, see the Martindale-Hubbell Law Directory

*CENTER,** Shelby Co.

FAIRCHILD, PRICE, THOMAS, HALEY & WILLINGHAM, L.L.P. (AV)

413 Shelbyville Street, P.O. Drawer 1719, 75935
Telephone: 409-598-2981
Fax: 409-598-7712
Email: wmthomas@fpthw.com
Nacogdoches, Texas Office: 1801 North Street, P. O. Box 631668, 75963-1668.
Telephone: 409-569-2327.
Fax: 409-569-7932. E-Mail: chaley@fpthw.com
Houston, Texas Office: 440 Louisiana Street, Suite 2110, 77002-4205.
Telephone: 713-426-1700.
Fax: 713-426-1717. E-Mail: mwillingham@fpthw.com

MEMBERS OF FIRM

John L. Price
W. Miller Thomas
C. Victor Haley
R. Mark Willingham
Ryan A. Beason (Resident at Houston Office)
Travis P. Clardy
David J. Fisher
Clayton H. Haley
Russell R. Smith
James A. Payne, Jr.

OF COUNSEL

Robert L. Fairchild

ASSOCIATES

David Edward Ash
Campbell Cox
Jefferson B. Davis
Thomas L. Cougill
Jeffrey Pierce Fultz
Matthew D. Mettauer

Representative Clients: AIG; Chubb Group of Insurance Companies; Continental National American Group (CNA); Fireman's Fund Insurance Company; Kemper Insurance Companies; Liberty Mutual Insurance Company; St. Paul Insurance Company.

For full biographical listings, see the Martindale-Hubbell Law Directory

*DALLAS,** Dallas Co.

CONANT FRENCH & CHANEY, LLP (AV)

3880 Bank One Center, 1717 Main Street, 75201
Telephone: 214-915-0620
Fasimile: 214-915-0634
Email: cfc@cfc-law.com *URL:* http://www.cfc-law.com

A. B. Conant, Jr.
William J. French
William B. Chaney
Linda A. Hale
Glen E. Lavy
Shawn W. Phelan
James D. MacIntyre

For full biographical listings, see the Martindale-Hubbell Law Directory

FRALEY & FRALEY, L.L.P. (AV)

901 Main Street, Suite 6510, 75202
Telephone: 214-761-6460
Fax: 214-761-6469
Email: info@fraleyandfraley.com *URL:* http://www.fraleyandfraley.com

R. Scott Fraley
Elizabeth Masters Fraley
J. Patrick Bredehoft

J. David Criss

For full biographical listings, see the Martindale-Hubbell Law Directory

JOHNSTON • TOBEY, P.C. (AV)

900 Jackson Street, Suite 710, 75202
Telephone: 214-741-6260
Facsimile: 214-741-6248

Coyt Randal Johnston
Robert L. Tobey

For full biographical listings, see the Martindale-Hubbell Law Directory

MORGAN & WEISBROD, L.L.P. (AV)

10260 North Central Expressway, Suite 100N, P.O. Box 821329, 75382
Telephone: 214-373-3761; 800-800-6353
Fax: 214-739-4732
Email: info@morganweisbrod.com *URL:* http://www.morganweisbrod.com
Houston, Texas Office: 6800 West Loop South, Suite 450, 77401.
Telephone: 713-838-0003.
Fax: 713-838-0066.

Carl M. Weisbrod
Les Weisbrod
David R. Norton
Paul N. Gold
Larry F. Smith
Jennifer L. Fry
William A. Newman
Paul B. Burkhalter
David R. Deary
Leanna Marchand
David V. Marchand

ASSOCIATES

Wiebke Breuer
John M. Driskill
Gal Lahat
Robbie S. Partida-Kipness
Kevin Robinowitz

OF COUNSEL

Melvin D. Morgan
Lynn C. Absher
James M. Rauer

For full biographical listings, see the Martindale-Hubbell Law Directory

SMITH, UNDERWOOD & PERKINS, A PROFESSIONAL CORPORATION (AV)

600 Two Lincoln Centre, 5420 LBJ Freeway, 75240
Telephone: 972-661-5114
Telecopier: 972-661-5691
Email: firm@suandp.com *URL:* http://www.suplaw.com

Timothy S. Perkins
David W. Ralston
G. Lynn Smith
William J. Underwood, Jr.

Christine A. McGuire
Amy K. Ratzlaff
P. Theodore Stoinoff, II
Val C. Cronin
Ellen P. Stewart
Todd W. Shadle
Ruth C. Logan
Christina L. Betanzos
Kent D. Williamson

For full biographical listings, see the Martindale-Hubbell Law Directory

WHITTENBURG WHITTENBURG & SCHACHTER, P.C. (AV)

2300 Plaza of the Americas, 600 North Pearl, LB 133, 75201
Telephone: 214-999-5700
Facsimile: 214-999-5747
Amarillo, Texas Office: 1010 South Harrison.
Telephone: 806-372-5700.
Facsimile: 806-372-5757.

Deborah Ashmore Harris

For Complete List of Firm Personnel, See General Section

For full biographical listings, see the Martindale-Hubbell Law Directory

*EL PASO,** El Paso Co.

RAY, MCCHRISTIAN & JEANS, A PROFESSIONAL CORPORATION (AV)

5822 Cromo Drive, Suite 400, 79912
Telephone: 915-832-7200
Fax: 915-832-7333
Email: rmj@rmjfirm.com

Jeff Ray
John W. McChristian, Jr.
David S. Jeans
James A. Mounts, III
Eduardo Miranda
Robin Collins
Leticia Nuñez

Daniel H. Hernandez
Michael K. Dean
Angelica B. Carreon
Todd E. Marshall
Stacy Bearden Zavala

Representative Clients: Texas Medical Liability Trust; Texas Medical Liability Insurance Underwriters Association (JUA); American Physicians Insurance Exchange; Medical Claims Management Group; The Medical Protective Insurance Co.; Professional Liability Insurance Co.; Walgreen Co.; St. Paul Insurance Cos.; Kemper Insurance Group.

For full biographical listings, see the Martindale-Hubbell Law Directory

HARLINGEN, Cameron Co.

ADAMS & GRAHAM, L.L.P. (AV)

222 East Van Buren, West Tower, 78550
Telephone: 956-428-7495
Fax: 956-428-2954
Email: office@adamsgraham.com *URL:* http://www.adamsgraham.com
Affiliate Austin, Texas Office: Hill Gilstrap Adams & Graham, L.L.P., 1005 Congress Avenue, Suite 880, 78701.
Telephone: 512-457-9806.
Fax: 512-457-9066.

John Q. Adams (1900-1968)
Marshall W. Graham (1924-1988)
James S. Graham, Jr. (1922-1990)
Ferriel C. Hamby, Jr.
Tom A. Lockhart
Jim Denison
Leo C. Salzman
Roger W. Hughes
Craig H. Vittitoe
William L. Pope
Patricia Kelly
Jaime Balli
Gina M. Benavides
Charlie J. Cilfone
Juan A. Gonzalez
Barry Ray
Wilbert (Will) Hughes
Trinidad P. Galdean

Representative Clients: The Travelers Insurance Cos.; CIGNA; AIAC; GAB; State Farm Insurance Co.; Valley Baptist Medical Center; Continental Loss Adjusting Services; McAllen Medical Center; Brownsville Medical Center; Trinity Insurance Companies.

For full biographical listings, see the Martindale-Hubbell Law Directory

*HOUSTON,** Harris Co.

CRAWFORD & MCKINNEY (AV)

550 Westcott, Suite 590, 77007-5096
Telephone: 713-869-1500
Fax: 713-880-4638
URL: http://www.piattorney.com

R. L. Pete McKinney
Patrice McKinney

OF COUNSEL

Stanley W. Crawford

For full biographical listings, see the Martindale-Hubbell Law Directory

CRUSE, SCOTT, HENDERSON & ALLEN, L.L.P. (AV)

Chase Tower, 600 Travis, Suite 3900, 77002-2910
Telephone: 713-650-6600
Fax: 713-650-1720

Sam W. Cruse, Jr.
John P. Scott
Jay H. Henderson
T. Scott Allen, Jr.
Samuel A. Houston
George W. (Billy) Shepherd, III
John R. Strawn, Jr.
Stephen R. Bailey
John D. Vogel
Wayne Clawater

ASSOCIATES

Debra L. Elmore
Merritt McReynolds Marinelli
David J. McTaggart
Matthew M. Prewett

For full biographical listings, see the Martindale-Hubbell Law Directory

DAVIS, ORETSKY & GUILFOYLE, P.C. (AV)

1415 Louisiana, Suite 4200, 77002
Telephone: 713-659-1010
Facsimile: 713-659-1122
Email: doglawfirm@dog.pc *URL:* http://www.dogpc.com
Affiliated Law Firm: Wommack Law Firm, P.C., 7 West Way Court, Suite A, P.O. Box 420, Lake Jackson, Texas 77566.
Telephone: 409-297-9755. Houston
Telephone: 713-355-5737.
Fax: 409-297-9761. Email: wdm-george@computron.net.

Tom M. Davis, Jr.
Andrew S. Oretsky
Matthew C. Guilfoyle
Juliann H. Panagos
Curt M. Langley
George T. Wommack, Jr.
David C. Redford

M. Lucille Anderson
Kristin Bauer
Robert M. Browning
Paige Black Larrabee
Norman W. Peters, Jr.
Jonathan L. Phillips
William R. Pilat

For full biographical listings, see the Martindale-Hubbell Law Directory

FAIRCHILD, PRICE, THOMAS, HALEY & WILLINGHAM, L.L.P. (AV)

440 Louisiana Street, Suite 2110, 77002-4205
Telephone: 713-426-1700
Fax: 713-426-1717.
Email: mwillingham@fpthw.com
Center, Texas Office: 413 Shelbyville Street, P.O. Drawer 1719, 75935.
Telephone: 409-598-2981.
Fax: 409-598-7712. E-Mail: wmthomas@fpthw.com

(See Next Column)

Nacogdoches, Texas Office: 1801 North Street, P.O. Box 631668, 75963-1668.
Telephone: 409-569-2327.
Fax: 409-569-7932. E-Mail: chaley@fpthw.com

John L. Price
W. Miller Thomas
C. Victor Haley
R. Mark Willingham
Travis P. Clardy
David J. Fisher
Clayton H. Haley
Russell R. Smith
Ryan A. Beason

OF COUNSEL

Robert L. Fairchild

James A. Payne, Jr.
David Edward Ash
Campbell Cox
Jefferson B. Davis
Thomas L. Cougill
Jeffrey Pierce Fultz
Matthew D. Mettauer

Representative Clients: AIG; Chubb Group of Insurance Companies; Continental National American Group (CNA); Fireman's Fund Insurance Company; Kemper Insurance Companies; Liberty Mutual Insurance Company; St. Paul Insurance Company.

For full biographical listings, see the Martindale-Hubbell Law Directory

*NACOGDOCHES,** Nacogdoches Co.

FAIRCHILD, PRICE, THOMAS, HALEY & WILLINGHAM, L.L.P. (AV)

1801 North Street, P.O. Box 631668, 75963-1668
Telephone: 409-569-2327
Fax: 409-569-7932.
Email: chaley@fpthw.com
Center, Texas Office: 413 Shelbyville Street, P.O. Drawer 1719, 75935.
Telephone: 409-598-2981.
Fax: 409-598-7712. E-Mail: wmthomas@fpthw.com
Houston, Texas Office: 440 Louisiana Street, Suite 2110, 77002-4205.
Telephone: 713-426-1700.
Fax: 713-426-1717. E-Mail: mwillingham@fpthw.com

John L. Price
W. Miller Thomas
C. Victor Haley
R. Mark Willingham
Travis P. Clardy
David J. Fisher
Clayton H. Haley
Russell R. Smith
Ryan A. Beason

OF COUNSEL

Robert L. Fairchild

James A. Payne, Jr.
David Edward Ash
Campbell Cox
Jefferson B. Davis
Thomas L. Cougill
Jeffrey Pierce Fultz
Matthew D. Mettauer

Representative Clients: AIG; Chubb Group of Insurance Companies; Continental National American Group (CNA); Fireman's Fund Insurance Company; Kemper Insurance Companies; Liberty Mutual Insurance Company; St. Paul Insurance Company.

For full biographical listings, see the Martindale-Hubbell Law Directory

*SAN ANTONIO,** Bexar Co.

O'CONNELL, BENJAMIN & COGHLAN, L.L.P. (AV)

153 Treeline Park, Suite 200, 78209
Telephone: 210-824-0009
Fax: 210-824-9429
Email: obcllp@oconben.com

Keith B. O'Connell
David P. Benjamin
G. Thomas Coghlan
Ernest F. Avery
Les Katona, Jr.
Dan Vana

Gayla S. Corley
Cathrin J. Martinez

For full biographical listings, see the Martindale-Hubbell Law Directory

UTAH

*SALT LAKE CITY,** Salt Lake Co.

VAN COTT, BAGLEY, CORNWALL & MCCARTHY, A PROFESSIONAL CORPORATION (AV)

50 South Main Street, Suite 1600, P.O. Box 45340, 84145-0340
Telephone: 801-532-3333
Telecopier: 801-534-0058
Email: info@vancott.com *URL:* http://www.vancott.com
Ogden, Utah Office: 2404 Washington Boulevard, Suite 900.
Telephone: 801-394-5783.
Park City, Utah Office: 2200 Park Avenue, Suite C200-A.
Telephone: 435-649-3889.

(See Next Column)

VAN COTT, BAGLEY, CORNWALL & MCCARTHY A PROFESSIONAL CORPORATION—*Continued*

Robert M. Anderson (President of Firm)
Kenneth W. Yeates

For Complete List of Firm Personnel, See General Section

For full biographical listings, see the Martindale-Hubbell Law Directory

VERMONT

*MONTPELIER,** Washington Co.

THERIAULT & JOSLIN, P.C. (AV)

141 Main Street, P.O. Box 249, 05601-0249
Telephone: 802-223-2381
Fax: 802-223-1461
Email: LAWYERS@TJOSLIN.COM

William N. Theriault (1877-1961)
Peter B. Joslin
Fletcher Brian (Ted) Joslin

John Davis Buckley
Barbara R. Blackman

OF COUNSEL

Fletcher B. Joslin
Jeffry W. White

Representative Clients: Allstate Insurance Co.; American International Group; Hartford Insurance Group; St. Paul Insurance Cos.; Nationwide Insurance Cos.; Commercial Union Insurance Cos.; Prudential Insurance Cos.; PHICO Insurance Co.; Maryland Insurance Group.

For full biographical listings, see the Martindale-Hubbell Law Directory

*RUTLAND,** Rutland Co.

MILLER FAIGNANT & BEHRENS, P.C. (AV)

36 Merchants Row, P.O. Box 6688, 05702-6688
Telephone: 802-775-2521
Fax: 802-775-8274
Email: lhblaw@aol.com *URL:* http://www.lawyers.com/millerfaignantbehrenslaw

Lawrence Miller
John Paul Faignant
Lawrence H. Behrens

OF COUNSEL

Lisa L. Chalidze

LEGAL SUPPORT PERSONNEL

Marie Peck Fabian
Kim J. Miller

Representative Clients: Travelers Insurance Co.; Government Employees Insurance Co.; Utica Mutual Insurance Co.; Universal Underwriters Insurance Co.; Zurich American Acadia Insurance.
References: Travelers Insurance Co.; Universal Underwriters Insurance Co.

For full biographical listings, see the Martindale-Hubbell Law Directory

VIRGINIA

ROANOKE, Roanoke City Co.

WOOTEN & HART, A PROFESSIONAL CORPORATION (AV)

707 Building, Suite 300, P.O. Box 12247, 24024-2247
Telephone: 540-343-2451; 540-342-9672
Telecopier: 540-345-6417
URL: http://www.wootenhart.com

George W. Wooten
David B. Hart
L. Thompson Hanes
Susan A. Waddell
Bradley D. McGraw
John L. Cooley
Thomas W. Farrell
Paul C. Kuhnel
Peter D. Vieth

David W. Hearn
John Mark Cooley
Christopher W. Stevens
Elizabeth D. Guilbert
Eunice Park Austin

OF COUNSEL

M. Lanier Woodrum

Representative Clients: Wachovia Bank; St. Paul Insurance Cos.
Approved Attorneys for: Lawyers Title Insurance Corp.
Reference: First Union National Bank.

For full biographical listings, see the Martindale-Hubbell Law Directory

WEST VIRGINIA

*CHARLESTON,** Kanawha Co.

FLAHERTY, SENSABAUGH & BONASSO, P.L.L.C. (AV)

200 Capitol Street, P.O. Box 3843, 25301
Telephone: 304-345-0200
Telecopier: 304-345-0260
Email: ralphj@fsbwv.com *URL:* http://www.fsbwv.com
Morgantown, West Virginia Office: 7000 Hampton Center, Suite I.
Telephone: 304-598-0788.
Fax: 304-598-0790.
Wheeling, West Virginia Office: 1031 National Road, P.O. Box 6545.
Telephone: 304-242-3941.
Fax: 304-242-3944.

MEMBER

Thomas V. Flaherty

ASSOCIATES

Keith M. Kodosky
Christopher A. Brumley
Scott H. Kaminski

For full biographical listings, see the Martindale-Hubbell Law Directory

HUNTINGTON, Cabell & Wayne Cos.

BAKER, LANCIANESE, CAMPBELL & CONATY (AV)

The River Tower, 1108 Third Avenue, Suite 300, 25701-1578
Telephone: 304-522-6906
Facsimile: 304-522-6910
Email: BLCC@BLCCLAW.COM *URL:* http://www.BLCCLAW.COM
Washington, D.C. Office: 1090 Vermont Avenue, N.W. Suite 800.
Telephone: 202-966-1500.
Fax: 202-966-7075. E-Mail: BLCC@BLCCLAW.COM.
Lexington, Kentucky Office: 2265 Harrodsburg Road, Suite 200, 40504-3517.
Telephone: 606-278-0297.
Fax: 206-278-0334. E-Mail: BLCC@BLCCLAW.COM.

Roy D. Baker, Jr.
Richard L. Lancianese
David L. Campbell
Brian P. Conaty
Janice P. Epperly

OF COUNSEL

Margaret M. Brizzolara (Not admitted in WV)

For full biographical listings, see the Martindale-Hubbell Law Directory

WISCONSIN

BROOKFIELD, Waukesha Co.

CANNON & DUNPHY, S.C. (AV)

595 North Barker Road, P.O. Box 1750, 53008-1750
Telephone: 414-782-2700
Facsimile: 414-796-5800
URL: http://www.cannon-dunphy.com

William M. Cannon
Patrick O. Dunphy
Lynn R. Laufenberg
Mark L. Thomsen
M. Angela Dentice

Sarah E. Frink
Ellen L. Wiesner
Edward E. Robinson

For full biographical listings, see the Martindale-Hubbell Law Directory

*MILWAUKEE,** Milwaukee Co.

KASDORF, LEWIS & SWIETLIK, S.C. (AV)

1551 South 108th Street, 53214
Telephone: 414-257-1055
Facsimile: 414-257-3759
Green Bay, Wisconsin Office: 727 East Walnut Street, 54301.
Telephone: 920-436-0304.
Wausau, Wisconsin Office: 2100 Stewart Avenue, Suite 230, 54401.
Telephone: 715-848-9250.
Facsimile: 715-849-2017.

James P. Reardon
Werner E. Scherr
Terrance E. Davczyk
Jeff Schmeckpeper
Gregory J. Cook
Michael J. Cieslewicz
Michael A. Mesirow
Joseph J. Ferris
James J. Kriva
David L. Styer
Robert J. Lauer
James M. Ryan
Robert P. Ochowicz

(See Next Column)

[illegible] & Swietlik S.C., Milwaukee—Continued

Michael C. Frohman	John K. [illegible]
Charles G. Maris	Bonn[illegible]
Vicki L. Arrowood	[illegible]her A. Duesing
Michael [illegible]	Daniel W. Va[illegible]
Peter J. Eckardt [illegible]	(Resident, W[illegible])
Christine [illegible]	Jerome A[illegible]
Thomas A. C[illegible]	(Resident, [illegible])

OF COUNSEL

[illegible]	Hugh [illegible] Russell
John M. Swietlik	Patti J. Kurth

Representative Clients: Allstate Insurance Co.; State Farm Mutual Automobile; Liberty Mutual Insurance Co.; [illegible] Insurance Co.; Government Employees Insurance Co.
Reference: M & I Marshall [illegible]

For full biographical listings, see the Martindale-Hubbell Law Directory

CANADA
NEW BRUNSWICK

FREDERICTON,* York Co.

McInnes Cooper (AV)

[illegible]

ASSOCIATE

David [illegible]

For Complete List of Firm Personnel, See General Section

For full biographical listings, see the Martindale-Hubbell Law Directory

MONCTON,* Westmorland Co.

McInnes Cooper (AV)

Barristers, Solicitors & Trade Mark Agents
[illegible] Place, 655 Main Street, P.O. Box [illegible]
Telephone: [illegible]
Fax: [illegible]
Email: [illegible]
Halifax, Nova Scotia Office: Summit Place, 1601 Lower Water Street, P.O. Box 730, B3J 2V1.
Telephone: 902-425-6500.
Fax: 902-425-6350. *Email:* mcrhfx@mcrlaw.com.
St. John's, Newfoundland Office: Baine Johnston Centre, 5th Floor, 10 Fort William Place, P.O. Box 5939, A1C 5X4.
Telephone: [illegible]
Telecopier: [illegible] *Email:* [illegible]
Charlottetown, Prince Edward Island Office: BDC Place, Suite 620, 119 Kent Street, C1A 1N3.
Telephone: 902-368-8473.
Fax: 902-368-8346. *Email:* [illegible]@mcrlaw.com.
Fredericton, New Brunswick Office: Suite 600, 570 Queen Street, P.O. Box 610.
Telephone: 506-458-8572.
Fax: 506-458-9903. *Email:* mcrfton@mcrlaw.com.

ASSOCIATE

John C. [illegible], Q.C.

For Complete List of Firm Personnel, See General Section

For full biographical listings, see the Martindale-Hubbell Law Directory

CANADA
NEWFOUNDLAND

ST. JOHN'S,* [illegible]

McInnes Cooper (AV)

Barristers, Solicitors & Trade Mark Agents
Baine Johnston Centre, 5th Floor, 10 Fort William Place, P.O. Box 5939, A1C 5X4
Telephone: 709-722-8735
Telecopier: 709-722-1763
Email: mcrsj@mcrlaw.com *URL:* http://www.mcrlaw.com
Halifax, Nova Scotia Office: Summit Place, 1601 Lower Water Street, P.O. Box 730, B3J 2V1.
Telephone: 902-425-6500.
Fax: 902-425-6350. *Email:* [illegible]
Moncton, New Brunswick Office: Place Moncton Place, [illegible]
[illegible]
Telephone: [illegible]
Fax: [illegible]
Charlottetown, Prince Edward Island Office: BDC Place, Suite 620, 119 Kent Street, C1A 1N3.
Telephone: 902-368-8473.
Fax: 902-368-8346. *Email:* [illegible]
Fredericton, New Brunswick Office: [illegible]
[illegible]
Telephone: 506-458-8572.
Fax: 506-458-9903. *Email:* [illegible]

PARTNERS

[illegible]

For Complete List of Firm Personnel, See General Section

For full biographical listings, see the Martindale-Hubbell Law Directory

CANADA
[illegible]

[illegible]

McInnes Cooper (AV)

[illegible]
Summit Place, 1601 Lower Water Street, P.O. Box 730, B3J 2V1
Telephone: 902-425-6500
Fax: 902-425-6350
Email: [illegible] *URL:* http://www.mcrlaw.com
St. John's, Newfoundland Office: Baine Johnston Centre, 5th Floor, 10 Fort William Place, P.O. Box 5939, A1C 5X4.
Telephone: 709-722-8735.
Telecopier: 709-722-1763. *Email:* mcrsj@mcrlaw.com.
Moncton, New Brunswick Office: [illegible]
P.O. Box 1368, E1C 8T6.
Telephone: [illegible]
Fax: [illegible] *Email:* [illegible]@mcrlaw.com.
Charlottetown, Prince Edward Island Office: BDC Place, Suite 620, 119 Kent Street, C1A 1N3.
Telephone: 902-368-8473.
Fax: 902-368-8346. *Email:* [illegible]
Fredericton, New Brunswick Office: [illegible]
[illegible]
Telephone: 506-458-8572.
Fax: 506-458-9903. *Email:* mcrfton@mcrlaw.com.

PARTNERS

Reginald A. Cluney, Q.C.	Harry [illegible]
Stewart McInnes, P.C., Q.C.	James L. [illegible]
George W. MacDonald, Q.C.	[illegible]
Peter M. S. Bryson	[illegible]
Stephen Kingston	[illegible]
Aidan J. Meade	Michelle C. A[illegible]

For full biographical listings, see the Martindale-Hubbell Law Directory

PUBLIC UTILITIES LAW

MISSISSIPPI

*CLARKSDALE,** Coahoma Co.

HUNT & ROSS, A PROFESSIONAL ASSOCIATION (AV)

123 Court Street, P.O. Box 1196, 38614
Telephone: 601-627-5251
Telecopier No.: 601-627-5254
Email: huntross@clarksdale.com *URL:* http://www.lawyers.com/h&rlaw

Tom T. Ross (1903-1993)
David R. Hunt
Tom T. Ross, Jr.

Thomas W. Allen
Katherine Blackwell Parker

Representative Clients: Clarksdale Public Utilities, Clarksdale, MS; Hollywood Water Assn., Robinsonville, MS.

For full biographical listings, see the Martindale-Hubbell Law Directory

MONTANA

*BILLINGS,** Yellowstone Co.

CROWLEY, HAUGHEY, HANSON, TOOLE & DIETRICH, P.L.L.P. (AV)

500 Transwestern II, 490 North 31st Street, P.O. Box 2529, 59103
Telephone: 406-252-3441
Fax: 406-259-4159
Email: crowley@crowleylaw.com
Helena, Montana Office: IBM Building, 100 North Park Avenue, Suite 300, 59601.
Telephone: 406-449-4165.
Fax: 406-449-5149.
Kalispell, Montana Office: 431 1st Avenue West, 59901.
Telephone: 406-752-6644.
Fax: 406-752-5108.
Williston, North Dakota Office: 113 East Broadway, 58801.
Telephone: 701-572-2200.
Fax: 701-572-7072.

OF COUNSEL

Bruce R. Toole
Louis R. Moore

MEMBERS OF FIRM

Carolyn S. Ostby
Michael E. Webster
Jon T. Dyre (Resident, Kalispell, Montana Office)

Representative Clients: Montana Power Co.; First Interstate Bank of Commerce; MDU Resources Group, Inc.; Chevron U.S.A., Inc.; Noranda Minerals Corp.; United Parcel Service.
Insurance Clients: Farmers Insurance Group; New York Life Insurance Co.

For Complete List of Firm Personnel, See General Section

For full biographical listings, see the Martindale-Hubbell Law Directory

NEW HAMPSHIRE

*CONCORD,** Merrimack Co.

RATH, YOUNG AND PIGNATELLI, PROFESSIONAL ASSOCIATION (AV)

One Capital Plaza, P.O. Box 1500, 03302-1500
Telephone: 603-226-2600
Telecopier: 603-226-2700; 228-2294; 225-9774
Email: ryp@rathlaw.com *URL:* http://www.rathlaw.com
Nashua, New Hampshire Office: The Glass Tower, 20 Trafalgar Square.
Telephone: 603-889-9952.
Telecopier: 603-595-7489.

Thomas D. Rath
William F. J. Ardinger
M. Curtis Whittaker
Charles G. Willing, Jr.

For Complete List of Firm Personnel, See General Section

For full biographical listings, see the Martindale-Hubbell Law Directory

NEW JERSEY

*NEWARK,** Essex Co.

MEYNER AND LANDIS (AV)

One Gateway Center, Suite 2500, 07102-5311
Telephone: 973-624-2800
Fax: 973-624-0356
Email: attys@meyner.com *URL:* http://www.meyner.com

Robert B. Meyner (1908-1990)
Edwin C. Landis, Jr.
John N. Malyska
William J. Fiore
Anthony F. Siliato
Francis R. Perkins
Howard O. Thompson
Scott T. McCleary
Linda Townley Snyder
William H. Schmidt, Jr.
David B. Grantz

For full biographical listings, see the Martindale-Hubbell Law Directory

SILLS CUMMIS RADIN TISCHMAN EPSTEIN & GROSS, A PROFESSIONAL CORPORATION (AV)

One Riverfront Plaza, 07102-5400
Telephone: 973-643-7000
Fax: 973-643-6500
Telex: 820630 Sillsbeck Nwk
Email: sillsmail@sillscummis.com *URL:* http://www.sillscummis.com
Atlantic City, New Jersey Office: 17 Gordon's Alley.
Telephone: 609-344-2800.
New York, N.Y. Office: 712 Fifth Avenue.
Telephone: 212-643-7000.
Washington, D.C. Office: 1800 K Street, N.W.
Telephone: 202-296-4750.

MEMBER OF FIRM

James M. Hirschhorn

Representative Clients: Blue Cross/Blue Shield of New Jersey; Bristol-Myers Squibb Co.; Circuit City Stores; Eastman Kodak; New Jersey Performing Arts Center; Six Flags Corporation; WWOR-TV, Inc.; PNC Bank Corp.

For Complete List of Firm Personnel, See General Section

For full biographical listings, see the Martindale-Hubbell Law Directory

WESTFIELD, Union Co.

LINDABURY, McCORMICK & ESTABROOK, P.A. (AV)

53 Cardinal Drive, P.O. Box 2369, 07091
Telephone: 908-233-6800
Fax: 908-233-5078
New York, N.Y. Office: 26 Broadway, Suite 2300.
Telephone: 212-742-3390.
Fax: 212-269-5016.

William R. Watkins

Representative Clients: Allied Signal, Inc.; Chevron U.S.A.; General Motors Corporation; New Jersey Industrial Energy Users.

For Complete List of Firm Personnel, See General Section

For full biographical listings, see the Martindale-Hubbell Law Directory

THE ROTHFELDER LAW OFFICES (AV)

625 Central Avenue, 07090
Telephone: 908-301-1211
Fax: 908-301-1212
URL: http://www.lawyers.com/rothfelder,law
Email: mail@rlo-law.com *URL:* http://www.rlo-law.com

Martin C. Rothfelder
Maureen Rothfelder
Nathan T. Foose (Not admitted in NJ)

For full biographical listings, see the Martindale-Hubbell Law Directory

NEW MEXICO

*ALBUQUERQUE,** Bernalillo Co.

RODEY, DICKASON, SLOAN, AKIN & ROBB, P.A. (AV)

Albuquerque Plaza, Suite 2200, 201 Third Street, N.W., P.O. Box 1888, 87103-1888
Telephone: 505-765-5900
Fax: 505-768-7395
Email: info@rodey.com *URL:* http://www.rodey.com
Santa Fe, New Mexico Office: Suite 101 Marcy Plaza, 123 East Marcy Street, P.O. Box 1357, 87504-1357.
Telephone: 505-984-0100.
Fax: 505-989-9542.

(See Next Column)

RODEY, DICKASON, SLOAN, AKIN & ROBB P.A., *Albuquerque—Continued*

Mark K. Adams
MacDonnell Gordon (Resident, Santa Fe Office)

OF COUNSEL

John D. Robb

For Complete List of Firm Personnel, See General Section

For full biographical listings, see the Martindale-Hubbell Law Directory

*SANTA FE,** Santa Fe Co.

CARPENTER & NIXON, LLP (AV)

315 Paseo De Peralta, P.O. Box 1837, 87504-1837
Telephone: 505-989-8690
Fax: 505-989-9457
Email: rncoffice@aol.com *URL:* http://www.lawyers.com/carpenter&nixon

MEMBERS OF FIRM

Richard N. Carpenter
Sunny J. Nixon

For full biographical listings, see the Martindale-Hubbell Law Directory

WHITE, KOCH, KELLY & MCCARTHY, A PROFESSIONAL ASSOCIATION (AV)

433 Paseo De Peralta, P.O. Box 787, 87504-0787
Telephone: 505-982-4374
ABA/NET: 1154
Fax: 505-982-0350; 984-8631
Email: WKKM@NM.NET

John F. McCarthy, Jr.
Benjamin J. Phillips
Kevin V. Reilly
M. Karen Kilgore
Rebecca A. Dempsey

Representative Clients: Public Service Company of New Mexico; Kit Carson Electric Cooperative, Inc.; Central New Mexico Electric Cooperative, Inc.; Sprint Communications.

For Complete List of Firm Personnel, See General Section

For full biographical listings, see the Martindale-Hubbell Law Directory

NEW YORK

*ALBANY,** Albany Co.

COUCH WHITE, LLP (AV)

540 Broadway, P.O. Box 22222, 12201
Telephone: 518-426-4600
Telecopier: 518-426-0376
Email: CouchWhiteBrenn@Global2000.net *URL:* http://www.couchwhite.com
Washington, D.C. Office: 700 Thirteenth Street, N.W., Suite 950.
Telephone: 202-434-4503.
Fax: 202-434-4562.

MEMBERS OF FIRM

Leslie F. Couch
Algird F. White, Jr.
Barbara S. Brenner
Joel M. Howard, III
Paul A. Feigenbaum
Robert M. Loughney
Harold N. Iselin
Leonard H. Singer
Keith B. Rose
Christopher A. Cernik
Michael B. Mager
Mark F. Glaser
Pamela A. Madeiros
James J. Barriere
Doreen Unis Saia

SENIOR COUNSEL

Lawrence H. Cooke

ASSOCIATES

David G. Anderson
Tricia A. Asaro
James S. King
Marc A. Madia

For full biographical listings, see the Martindale-Hubbell Law Directory

*NEW YORK,** New York Co.

BERLACK, ISRAELS & LIBERMAN LLP (AV)

120 West 45th Street, 10036
Telephone: 212-704-0100
Cable Address: "Berilib"
Telecopier: 212-704-0196
Email: info@berlack.com
Morristown, New Jersey Office: 65 Madison Avenue.
Telephone: 201-644-3400.
Telecopier: 201-644-3159.

(See Next Column)

MEMBERS OF FIRM

Harris Berlack (1946-1968)
Carlos L. Israels (1946-1969)
Kenneth R. Asher
Claude A. Baum
Scott M. Berman
Wade M. Boswell
Douglas E. Davidson
Alan N. Forman
Steven E. Greenbaum
Harvey M. Katz
James B. Liberman
Stuart Neuhauser
Robert D. Schmicker
Martin S. Siegel
Steven F. Wasserman
Edward S. Weisfelner

SENIOR ATTORNEYS

Andrew S. Dash
Erica M. Ryland

ASSOCIATES

John P. Biedermann
Anne M. Cunningham
Pauline Foley (Resident, Morristown, New Jersey Office)
Julie L. Friedberg (Resident, Morristown, New Jersey Office)
Emilio A. Galván
Linda B. Goebel
Louis Lombardo
Rachel F. Mayerson (Not admitted in NY)
Amy P. K. Motzenbecker (Resident, Morristown, New Jersey Office)
Antonio Peguero, Jr.
Elizabeth Quirk (Resident, Morristown, New Jersey Office)
Marcela M. Sanchez
Melissa Sarubbi

OF COUNSEL

Gerald W. Conway (Not admitted in NY; Resident, Morristown, New Jersey Office)
Marc B. Lasky (Resident, Morristown, New Jersey Office)

For full biographical listings, see the Martindale-Hubbell Law Directory

SEHAM SEHAM MELTZ & PETERSEN, LLP (AV)

380 Madison Avenue, Suite 17, 10017-2513
Telephone: 212-557-9577
Email: ssmpls@aol.com

Martin C. Seham
Scott C. Petersen

For full biographical listings, see the Martindale-Hubbell Law Directory

*POUGHKEEPSIE,** Dutchess Co.

LEWIS & GREER, P.C. (AV)

11 Raymond Avenue, P.O. Box 2990, 12603
Telephone: 914-454-1200
Telecopier: 914-454-3315
Email: info@lewisgreer.com *URL:* http://www.lewisgreer.com

Lou Lewis
J. Scott Greer
Michael J. Englert

Daniel P. Adams
Veronica A. McMillan

For full biographical listings, see the Martindale-Hubbell Law Directory

NORTH CAROLINA

*RALEIGH,** Wake Co.

BAILEY & DIXON, L.L.P. (AV)

2500 Two Hannover Square, 434 Fayetteville Street Mall, P.O. Box 1351, 27602
Telephone: 919-828-0731
Facsimile: 919-828-6592
Email: info@bdixon.com *URL:* http://www.bdixon.com

MEMBERS OF FIRM

Ralph McDonald
Gary S. Parsons
Carson Carmichael, III
Alan J. Miles
Patricia P. Kerner
Cathleen M. Plaut
David S. Coats
M. Denise Stanford
Kenyann Brown Stanford

OF COUNSEL

J. Ruffin Bailey
Wright T. Dixon, Jr. (Retired)
James H. Walker (1920-1994)
David M. Britt

ASSOCIATES

David Scott Wisz
Warren Tobin Savage, IV
Rita Lane Hanshumaker
Dayatra T. King
Philip Todd Gray
Ali John Hoomani

Representative Clients: MCI World Com; Carolina Industrial Groups for Fair Utility Rates.

For full biographical listings, see the Martindale-Hubbell Law Directory

Raleigh—Continued

ROBERT W. KAYLOR, P.A. (AV)

225 Hillsborough Street, Suite 480, 27603
Telephone: 919-828-5250
Fax: 919-828-5240
Email: RWKaylor@duke-energy.com

Robert W. Kaylor

For full biographical listings, see the Martindale-Hubbell Law Directory

OHIO

*COLUMBUS,** Franklin Co.

BRICKER & ECKLER LLP (AV)

100 South Third Street, 43215-4291
Telephone: 614-227-2300
Telecopy: 614-227-2390
Email: info@be.bricker.com *URL:* http://www.bricker.com

Sally W. Bloomfield
Mark A. Engel
Kurtis A. Tunnell

Julia L. Dorrian

Representative Clients: Columbia Energy Services; Teligent, Inc.; Telecommunications Resellers Association; Mobile Media Communiations, Inc.; Frontier Communications Services.

For Complete List of Firm Personnel, See General Section

For full biographical listings, see the Martindale-Hubbell Law Directory

CHESTER, WILLCOX AND SAXBE LLP (AV)

17 South High Street, Suite 900, 43215-3413
Telephone: 614-221-4000
Fax: 614-221-4012
Email: cwslaw.com

PARTNER

John W. Bentine

ASSOCIATE

Jeffrey L. Small

Representative Client: American Municipal Power-Ohio, Inc.

For full biographical listings, see the Martindale-Hubbell Law Directory

KEGLER, BROWN, HILL & RITTER (AV)

Capitol Square Suite 1800, 65 East State Street, 43215-4294
Telephone: 614-462-5400
Telecopier: 614-464-2634
Cable Address: "Law KBHR"
Telex: 246671
Email: info@kbhr.com *URL:* http://www.kbhr.com
Marion, Ohio Office: 250 Executive Drive, Suite B, P.O. Box 919.
Telephone: 614-387-3501.
Facsimile: 614-387-3630.

Roger P. Sugarman

COUNSEL

Leigh Anne Reardon

Representative Clients: Time Warner Communications.

For Complete List of Firm Personnel, See General Section

For full biographical listings, see the Martindale-Hubbell Law Directory

OKLAHOMA

*OKLAHOMA CITY,** Oklahoma Co.

WILLIAMS, BOX, FORSHEE & BULLARD, P.C. (AV)

522 Colcord Drive, 73102-2202
Telephone: 405-232-0080
Telecopier: 405-236-5814

John Michael Williams
Dennis R. Box
Richard D. Forshee
William J. Bullard
Keith R. Gibson
Paul E. Lefebvre

Kimberly K. Brown

For full biographical listings, see the Martindale-Hubbell Law Directory

PENNSYLVANIA

*PHILADELPHIA,** Philadelphia Co.

LAW OFFICES OF JOHN J. GALLAGHER, P.C. (AV)

Suite 1100, 1760 Market Street, 19103
Telephone: 215-963-1555
Fax: 215-963-9104
Email: jjgall@ix.netcom.com *URL:* http://www.lawyers.com/johngallagher

John J. Gallagher

Michael S. Henry
Laura Carberry Muldowney
Joseph H. Meltzer
Larisa Tenberg

LEGAL SUPPORT PERSONNEL

Ronald Winkelvoss
Helene Schramm

For full biographical listings, see the Martindale-Hubbell Law Directory

SCHUBERT, BELLWOAR, CAHILL & QUINN, A PROFESSIONAL CORPORATION (AV)

Two Penn Center, Suite 1400, 1500 John F. Kennedy Boulevard, 19102-1890
Telephone: 215-569-3535
Fax: 215-557-7426
Email: attorneys@sbcq.com
Haddon Township, New Jersey Office: 311 West Cuthbert Boulevard, 08108.
Telephone: 856-854-5757.

Thomas M. Schubert (1924-1989)
William E. Schubert, Jr. (1921-1998)
Harry J. J. Bellwoar, III
John P. Quinn
John J. Cahill, Jr.
Robert T. Lynch
Robert G. Bellwoar
John P. Gallagher
James O. Hausch
Deborah E. Kolodner
Richard T. Mulcahey, Jr.
James M. Tyler
Jan M. Ritchie

Joseph W. Cunningham
Michael S. Piotrowicz
Patricia Farrell Kerelo
Christopher B. Hogan
Kathleen M. O'Connell
Mark Pfeiffer
Eric A. Feldhake

OF COUNSEL

John D. Lucey, Jr.
Robert F. Blanck

For full biographical listings, see the Martindale-Hubbell Law Directory

RHODE ISLAND

*PROVIDENCE,** Providence Co.

HINCKLEY, ALLEN & SNYDER LLP (AV)

1500 Fleet Center, 02903-2393
Telephone: 401-274-2000
Fax: 401-277-9600
Email: firm@haslaw.com *URL:* http://www.haslaw.com
Boston, Massachusetts Office: 28 State Street, 30th Floor.
Telephone: 617-345-9000.
Fax: 617-345-9020. URL: http://www.haslaw.com.

MEMBERS OF FIRM

Paula K. Andrews (Not admitted in RI)
David D. Barricelli
E. Jerome Batty
Jonathan Bell
Paul Bork (Not admitted in RI)
Stephen J. Carlotti
David Barry Connolly (Not admitted in RI)
Joseph P. Curran
Michael P. DeFanti
Eric F. Eisenberg (Not admitted in RI)
Malcolm Farmer, III
Margaret D. Farrell
Hugh J. Gorman, III (Not admitted in RI)
Alan P. Gottlieb (Not admitted in RI)
William R. Grimm
Paul A. Hedstrom (Not admitted in RI)
Richard L. E. Jocelyn
Joel Lewin (Not admitted in RI)
Sandra Matrone Mack
Matthew T. Marcello, III
Frederick P. McClure
Elizabeth Murdock Myers
Paul F. O'Donnell, III (Not admitted in RI)
H. Peter Olsen
Julianne Palumbo (Not admitted in RI)
John J. Pendergast, III
Gerald J. Petros
James O. Reavis
Jeremy Ritzenberg (Not admitted in RI)
Ralph J. Rivkind (Not admitted in RI)
David J. Rubin
Charles E. Schaub, Jr. (Not admitted in RI)
Douglas F. Seaver (Not admitted in RI)

(See Next Column)

HINCKLEY, ALLEN & SNYDER LLP, *Providence—Continued*

MEMBERS OF FIRM (Continued)

Herman Snyder (Not admitted in RI)
David R. Sullivan (Not admitted in RI)
Robert F. Sylvia (Not admitted in RI)
Howard E. Walker
Richard D. Wayne (Not admitted in RI)

ASSOCIATES

Jessica M. Bettencourt
Mark Bianchi
Alyssa V. Boss
Alexandra K. Callam
Jane E. Cohen (Not admitted in RI)
Andrew D. Cummings (Not admitted in RI)
June E. Daniel
Kim Herman Goslant (Not admitted in RI)
Gloria Maria Gutierrez (Not admitted in RI)
Kelley Jordan-Price
Catherine S. Kim (Not admitted in RI)
Christopher W. Morog (Not admitted in RI)
Elena B. Olson (Not admitted in RI)
Joseph D. Whelan

OF COUNSEL

Willard Krasnow (Not admitted in RI)
Willard R. Pope (Not admitted in RI)
Bentley Tobin
Joachim A. Weissfeld

For Complete List of Firm Personnel, See General Section

For full biographical listings, see the Martindale-Hubbell Law Directory

SOUTH CAROLINA

*COLUMBIA,** Richland Co.

BEACH LAW FIRM, P.A. (AV)

1321 Lady Street, Suite 310, 29211-1547
Telephone: 803-779-0066
Fax: 803-799-8479
Mailing Address: P.O. Box 11547, Columbia, South Carolina, 29211-1547
Email: firm@beachlaw.net

John F. Beach

John J. Pringle, Jr.

For full biographical listings, see the Martindale-Hubbell Law Directory

HAYNSWORTH, MARION, MCKAY & GUÉRARD, L.L.P. (AV)

Suite 2400 Affinity Building, 1201 Main Street, P.O. Drawer 7157, 29202
Telephone: 803-765-1818
Facsimile: 803-765-2399
Greenville, South Carolina Office: 75 Beattie Place, Eleventh Floor, P.O. Box 2048, 29602.
Telephone: 864-240-3200.
Facsimile: 864-240-3300.
Charleston, South Carolina Office: 134 Meeting Street, P.O. Box 1119, 29402.
Telephone: 843-722-7606.
Facsimile: 843-724-8016.

MEMBERS OF FIRM

William P. Simpson
Russell B. Shetterly

Counsel for: Duke Power Co.; South Carolina Jobs - Economic Development Authority; The State of South Carolina; Business Development Corp. of South Carolina; Santee Cooper Electric Cooperative; Cooper River Park and Playground Commission; John Deer Industrial Development, Inc.; School District of Richland County.

For Complete List of Firm Personnel, See General Section

For full biographical listings, see the Martindale-Hubbell Law Directory

SHERRILL & ROOF, L.L.P. (AV)

1122 Lady Street, Suite 1100, P.O. Box 11497, 29211-1497
Telephone: 803-733-3433
Fax: 803-733-2990
Email: info@sherrillandroof.com

Henry F. Sherrill
Daniel B. Lott, Jr.

Representative Clients: South Carolina Energy Users Committee.

For full biographical listings, see the Martindale-Hubbell Law Directory

WILLOUGHBY & HOEFER, P.A. (AV)

1022 Calhoun Street, Suite 302, P.O. Box 8416, 29202-8416
Telephone: 803-252-3300
Telecopier: 803-256-8062
Email: willhoef@sc-online.net

(See Next Column)

Mitchell M. Willoughby
John M. S. Hoefer
Alvis J. Bynum, Jr.
B. Craig Collins

Elizabeth Zeck

Representative Clients: South Carolina Electric & Gas Co.; S.C. Pipeline; SCANA Communications, Inc.; Bell Atlantic Mobile; Melrose Utilities, Inc.; Palmetto Utilities, Inc.; ITC DeltaCommunications, Inc.; Carolina Water Service, Inc., a Subsidiary of Utilities, Inc.

For full biographical listings, see the Martindale-Hubbell Law Directory

TENNESSEE

*KNOXVILLE,** Knox Co.

WAGNER, MYERS & SANGER, A PROFESSIONAL CORPORATION (AV)

1801 First Tennessee Plaza, P.O. Box 1308, 37901-1308
Telephone: 423-525-4600
Fax: 423-524-5731
Email: wms1801@usit.net

Sam F. Fowler, Jr.
Herbert S. Sanger, Jr.
Charles W. Van Beke
Charles A. Wagner III
William C. Myers, Jr.
M. Douglas Campbell, Jr.

Nicholas A. Della Volpe
Ronald D. Garland
Barbara D. Boulton
Robert G. Crane
John G. Brock
Kenneth C. Tucker

Representative Clients: Carolina Power & Light Co.; Cullman Electric Cooperative; Diversified Energy, Inc.; Fort Sanders Health Systems; Gatliff Coal Co.; Lockheed Martin Energy Systems, Inc.; North American Rayon Corp.; Regal Cinemas, Inc.; Roddy Vending; Sigmon Coal Company, Inc.; Skyline Coal Co.

For full biographical listings, see the Martindale-Hubbell Law Directory

TEXAS

*AUSTIN,** Travis Co.

BROYLES & PRATT, A PROFESSIONAL CORPORATION (AV)

One Northpoint Centre, Suite 250, 6836 Austin Center Boulevard, 78731
Telephone: 361-886 6200
Fax: 361-886 6262
Corpus Christi, Texas Office: 1001 Bank of America Center North. 500 North Shoreline Boulevard, 78471.
Telephone: 361-886-6200.
Fax: 361-886-6262.

R. Michael Anderson
Larry W. Brewer
Mark Held
Joe N. Pratt
Davison W. Grant
Mason L. Terry

Dudley McClellan

OF COUNSEL

Richard H. Cory

For full biographical listings, see the Martindale-Hubbell Law Directory

MCCOLLOUGH & ASSOCIATES, P.C. (AV)

1801 North Lamar, Suite 104, 78701
Telephone: 512-485-7920
Fax: 512-485-7921
Email: wsmc@smccollough.com *URL:* http://www.smccollough.com

W. Scott McCollough

David Bolduc

LEGAL SUPPORT PERSONNEL

Carrie L. Keese (Paralegal)
Debbie Vera (Paralegal)

For full biographical listings, see the Martindale-Hubbell Law Directory

*CORPUS CHRISTI,** Nueces Co.

BROYLES & PRATT, A PROFESSIONAL CORPORATION (AV)

1001 Bank of America Center North, 500 North Shoreline Boulevard, 78471
Telephone: 361-886-6200
Fax: 361-886-6262
Austin, Texas Office: One Northpoint Centre, Suite 250, 6836 Austin Center Boulevard, 78731.
Telephone: 512-794-2100.
Fax: 512-794-2111.

Gaston M. Broyles, Jr.
Hal George
Milton E. Lorenz, Jr.
Richard A. Houston

For full biographical listings, see the Martindale-Hubbell Law Directory

UTAH

*SALT LAKE CITY,** Salt Lake Co.

PARR WADDOUPS BROWN GEE & LOVELESS, A PROFESSIONAL CORPORATION (AV)

Suite 1300, 185 South State Street, 84111-1537
Telephone: 801-532-7840
Fax: 801-532-7750
URL: http://www.pwlaw.com

Gary A. Dodge
Mark A. Wagner

For Complete List of Firm Personnel, See General Section

For full biographical listings, see the Martindale-Hubbell Law Directory

VAN COTT, BAGLEY, CORNWALL & McCARTHY, A PROFESSIONAL CORPORATION (AV)

50 South Main Street, Suite 1600, P.O. Box 45340, 84145-0340
Telephone: 801-532-3333
Telecopier: 801-534-0058
Email: info@vancott.com *URL:* http://www.vancott.com
Ogden, Utah Office: 2404 Washington Boulevard, Suite 900.
Telephone: 801-394-5783.
Park City, Utah Office: 2200 Park Avenue, Suite C200-A.
Telephone: 435-649-3889.

Matthew F. McNulty, III
Arthur B. Ralph
David J. Smith

Kim S Colton
Stephen R. Sloan

For Complete List of Firm Personnel, See General Section

For full biographical listings, see the Martindale-Hubbell Law Directory

VERMONT

*BURLINGTON,** Chittenden Co.

MILLER, EGGLESTON & CRAMER, LTD. (AV)

150 South Champlain Street, P.O. Box 1489, 05402-1489
Telephone: 802-864-0880
Telecopier: 802-864-0328

Martin K. Miller
Victoria J. Brown

For Complete List of Firm Personnel, See General Section

For full biographical listings, see the Martindale-Hubbell Law Directory

WEST VIRGINIA

*CHARLESTON,** Kanawha Co.

JACKSON & KELLY (AV)

1600 Laidley Tower, P.O. Box 553, 25322
Telephone: 304-340-1000
Fax: 304-340-1130
Email: info@jacksonkelly.com *URL:* http://www.jacksonkelly.com
Martinsburg, West Virginia Office: 300 Foxcroft Avenue, P.O. Box 1068.
Telephone: 304-263-8800.
Fax: 304-263-7110.

(See Next Column)

Morgantown, West Virginia Office: 6000 Hampton Center, P.O. Box 619.
Telephone: 304-599-3000.
Fax: 304-285-2040.
New Martinsville, West Virginia Office: 256 Russell Avenue, P.O. Box 68.
Telephone: 304-455-1751.
Fax: 304-455-6314.
Parkersburg, West Virginia Office: 412 Market Street, Suite 202, P.O. Box 1144.
Telephone: 304-424-3490.
Fax: 304-424-3499.
Fairmont, West Virginia Office: 1000 Technology Drive, Suite 1310.
Telephone: 304-368-2000.
Fax: 304-368-2020.
Lexington, Kentucky Office: 175 East Main Street, Suite 500, P.O. Box 2150.
Telephone: 606-255-9500.
Fax: 606-281-6478.
Washington, D. C. Office: 2401 Pennsylvania Avenue, N.W., Suite 400.
Telephone: 202-973-0200.
Fax: 202-973-0232.
Denver, Colorado Office: Suite 2710, 1660 Lincoln Street.
Telephone: 303-390-0003.
Fax: 303-390-0040.
Wheeling, West Virginia Office: 1144 Market Street.
Telephone: 304-233-4000.
Fax: 304-233-4077.

MEMBERS OF FIRM

James Knight Brown
Michael A. Albert
Jeffrey J. Yost (Resident, Lexington, Kentucky Office)
Samme L. Gee
John Philip Melick

Representative Clients: West Virginia-American Water Co.; Citizens Utilities Co.; Cabot Oil and Gas Corporation; S & S Grading, Inc. (Eastern Environmental Sucs Inc.); Monongahela Power Co.; West Virginia Power & Gas Service; GTE South Incorporated; Southwestern Bell Mobile Systems, Inc.; Virginia Electric & Power Co.; Contel Cellular, Inc.

For Complete List of Firm Personnel, See General Section

For full biographical listings, see the Martindale-Hubbell Law Directory

E. DANDRIDGE McDONALD (AV)

1001 United Center, 500 Virginia Street, East, P.O. Box 2189, 25328
Telephone: 304-344-5113
Telecopier: 304-345-7368
Email: dmcdonald1@compuserve.com

For full biographical listings, see the Martindale-Hubbell Law Directory

WISCONSIN

*MILWAUKEE,** Milwaukee Co.

QUARLES & BRADY LLP (AV)

411 East Wisconsin Avenue, 53202-4497
Telephone: 414-277-5000
Fax: 414-271-3552
URL: http://www.quarles.com
Madison, Wisconsin Office: Firstar Plaza, One South Pinckney Street, P.O. Box 2113, 53701-2113.
Telephone: 608-251-5000.
Fax: 608-251-9166.
West Palm Beach, Florida Office: 222 Lakeview Avenue, 4th Floor, 33401.
Telephone: 561-653-5000.
Fax: 561-653-5333.
Naples, Florida Office: Barnett Center, 4501 Tamiami Trail North, Suite 300, 34103-3060.
Telephone: 941-262-5959.
Fax: 941-434-4999.
Phoenix, Arizona Office: One Camelback Building, One East Camelback Road, Suite 400, 85012-1649.
Telephone: 602-230-5500.
Fax: 602-230-5598.
Chicago, Illinois Office: Quarles & Brady LLC, Citicorp Center, 500 West Madison Street, Suite 3700.
Telephone: 312-715-5000.
Fax: 312-715-5155.

MEMBERS OF FIRM
(ALPHABETICALLY BY YEAR OF ADMISSION TO BAR)

Robert H. Diaz, Jr.
Larry J. Martin
Jane F. Clokey (Resident, Madison Office)
Anthony A. Tomaselli (Resident, Madison Office)

ASSOCIATE

Brian D. Winters

For Complete List of Firm Personnel, See General Section

For full biographical listings, see the Martindale-Hubbell Law Directory

WYOMING

*CASPER,** Natrona Co.

BROWN, DREW & MASSEY, LLP (AV)

Casper Business Center, Suite 800, 123 West First Street, 82601-2486
Telephone: 307-234-1000
800-877-6755
Telefax: 307-265-8025
Email: brwndrew@coffey.com

MEMBERS OF FIRM

Morris R. Massey
Thomas F. Reese
Donn J. McCall
Courtney Robert Kepler

ASSOCIATE

Timothy M. Stubson

For Complete List of Firm Personnel, See General Section

For full biographical listings, see the Martindale-Hubbell Law Directory

*CHEYENNE,** Laramie Co.

HICKEY, MACKEY, EVANS & WALKER (AV)

1800 Carey Avenue, Suite 700, P.O. Drawer 467, 82003
Telephone: 307-634-1525
Telecopier: 307-638-7335
URL: http://www.hickeymackey.com

MEMBERS OF FIRM

Paul J. Hickey
John M. Walker
Terry W. Mackey
Roger C. Fransen
David F. Evans
Richard D. Tim Bush
Mary A. Throne

A List of Representative Clients will be furnished upon request.
Reference: Norwest Bank, Cheyenne, N.A.

For full biographical listings, see the Martindale-Hubbell Law Directory

CANADA ALBERTA

*CALGARY,** Calgary Jud. Dist.

BENNETT JONES (AV)

4500 Bankers Hall East, 855-2nd Street S.W., T2P 4K7
Telephone: 403-298-3100
Facsimile: 403-265-7219
Email: firmwatch@bennettjones.ca *URL:* http://www.bennettjones.ca
Edmonton, Alberta Office: 1000, 10035-105 Street.
Telephone: 780-421-8133.
Facsimile: 780-421-7951.
Toronto, Ontario Office: 3400 1 First Canadian Place, P.O. Box 130.
Telephone: 416-863-1200.
Facsimile: 416-863-1716.

MEMBER OF FIRM

William L. Britton, Q.C.

For Complete List of Firm Personnel, See General Section

For full biographical listings, see the Martindale-Hubbell Law Directory

*EDMONTON,** Edmonton Jud. Dist.

PARLEE MCLAWS (AV)

15th Floor Manulife Place, 10180 101st Street, T5J 4K1
Telephone: 403-423-8500
Telecopier: 403-423-2870
Email: lawyers@parlee.com *URL:* http://www.parlee.com
Calgary, Alberta Office: 3400 Petro-Canada Centre, 150 - 6th Avenue, SW.
Telephone: 403-294-7000.
Telecopier: 403-265-8263.

MEMBER OF FIRM

Ian L. MacLachlan

For Complete List of Firm Personnel, See General Section

For full biographical listings, see the Martindale-Hubbell Law Directory

CANADA NEWFOUNDLAND

*ST. JOHN'S,**

MCINNES COOPER (AV)

Barristers, Solicitors & Trade Mark Agents
Baine Johnston Centre, 5th Floor, 10 Fort William Place, P.O. Box 5939, A1C 5X4
Telephone: 709-722-8735
Telecopier: 709-722-1763
Email: mcrsj@mcrlaw.com *URL:* http://www.mcrlaw.com
Halifax, Nova Scotia Office: Summit Place, 1601 Lower Water Street, P.O. Box 730, B3J 2V1.
Telephone: 902-425-6500.
Fax: 902-425-6350. Email: mcrhfx@mcrlaw.com.
Moncton, New Brunswick Office: Place Moncton Place, 655 Main Street, P.O. Box 1368, E1C 8T6.
Telephone: 506-857-8970.
Fax: 506-857-4095. Email: mcrmctn@mcrlaw.com.
Charlottetown, Prince Edward Island Office: BDC Place, Suite 620, 119 Kent Street, C1A 1N3.
Telephone: 902-368-8473.
Fax: 902-368-8346. Email: mcrpei@mcrlaw.com.
Fredericton, New Brunswick Office: Suite 600, 570 Queen Street, P.O. Box 610.
Telephone: 506-458-8572.
Fax: 506-458-9903. Email: mcrfton@mcrlaw.com.

PARTNER

James R. Chalker, Q.C.

For Complete List of Firm Personnel, See General Section

For full biographical listings, see the Martindale-Hubbell Law Directory

CANADA NOVA SCOTIA

*HALIFAX,** Regional Munic. of Halifax

MCINNES COOPER (AV)

Barristers, Solicitors & Trade Mark Agents
Summit Place, 1601 Lower Water Street, P.O. Box 730, B3J 2V1
Telephone: 902-425-6500
Fax: 902-425-6350
Email: mcrhfx@mcrlaw.com *URL:* http://www.mcrlaw.com
St. John's, Newfoundland Office: Baine Johnston Centre, 5th Floor, 10 Fort William Place, P.O. Box 5939, A1C 5X4.
Telephone: 709-722-8735.
Telecopier: 709-722-1763. Email: mcrsj@mcrlaw.com.
Moncton, New Brunswick Office: Place Moncton Place, 655 Main Street, P.O. Box 1368, E1C 8T6.
Telephone: 506-857-8970.
Fax: 506-857-4095. Email: mcrmctn@mcrlaw.com.
Charlottetown, Prince Edward Island Office: BDC Place, Suite 620, 119 Kent Street, C1A 1N3.
Telephone: 902-368-8473.
Fax: 902-368-8346. Email: mcrpei@mcrlaw.com.
Fredericton, New Brunswick Office: Suite 600, 570 Queen Street, P.O. Box 610.
Telephone: 506-458-8572.
Fax: 506-458-9903. Email: mcrfton@mcrlaw.com.

PARTNERS

George T. H. Cooper, Q.C.
John D. Stringer, Q.C.

For Complete List of Firm Personnel, See General Section

For full biographical listings, see the Martindale-Hubbell Law Directory

CANADA
PRINCE EDWARD ISLAND

*CHARLOTTETOWN,** Queen's Co.

McInnes Cooper (AV Ⓣ)

Barristers, Solicitors & Trade Mark Agents
BDC Place, Suite 620, 119 Kent Street, C1A 1N3
Telephone: 902-368-8473
Fax: 902-368-8346
Email: mcrpei@mcrlaw.com *URL:* http://www.mcrlaw.com
Halifax, Nova Scotia Office: Summit Place, 1601 Lower Water Street, P.O. Box 730, B3J 2V1.
Telephone: 902-425-6500.
Fax: 902-425-6350. Email: mcrhfx@mcrlaw.com.
St. John's, Newfoundland Office: Baine Johnston Centre, 5th Floor, 10 Fort William Place, P.O. Box 5939, A1C 5X4.
Telephone: 709-722-8735.
Telecopier: 709-722-1763. Email: mcrsj@mcrlaw.com.
Moncton, New Brunswick Office: Place Moncton Place, 655 Main Street, P.O. Box 1368, E1C 8T6.
Telephone: 506-857-8970.
Fax: 506-857-4095. Email: mcrmctn@mcrlaw.com.
Fredericton, New Brunswick Office: Suite 600, 570 Queen Street, P.O. Box 610.
Telephone: 506-458-8572.
Fax: 506-458-9903. Email: mcrfton@mcrlaw.com.

ASSOCIATE

L. Charles Keizer

For Complete List of Firm Personnel, See General Section

For full biographical listings, see the Martindale-Hubbell Law Directory

CANADA
QUEBEC

*MONTREAL,** Montreal Dist.

McMaster Gervais (AV)

A General Partnership
1000 de La Gauchetière Street West, Suite 900, H3B 5H4
Telephone: 514-879-1212
Fax: 514-954-1905
Email: info@mcmastergervais.com *URL:* http://www.mcmastergervais.com

MEMBERS OF FIRM

Yves A. Dubois
Sylvie Bouvette
Lise Fortier

For Complete List of Firm Personnel, See General Section

For full biographical listings, see the Martindale-Hubbell Law Directory

REAL ESTATE LAW

MINNESOTA

*DULUTH,** St. Louis Co.

MAGIE, ANDRESEN, HAAG, PACIOTTI, BUTTERWORTH & McCARTHY, P.A. (AV)

1000 Alworth Building, P.O. Box 745, 55801
Telephone: 218-722-1411
Telecopier: 218-720-6817
Email: lawduluth@aol.com

Charles H. Andresen
Sandra E. Butterworth
Bryan N. Anderson

Representative Clients: Inland Steel Mining Company; Abstract & Title Services of Carlton, Inc.; Lakehead Pipe Line Company; Great Lakes Gas Transmission Limited Partnership; National Steel; Cleveland-Cliffs, Inc.; Blackwoods Companies, Murphy Oil USA; National Steel Pellet Company; Housing & Redevelopment Authority of Duluth, Minnesota; Oneida Realty; London Development Corp.

For Complete List of Firm Personnel, See General Section

For full biographical listings, see the Martindale-Hubbell Law Directory

*FERGUS FALLS,** Otter Tail Co.

DAVID F. LUNDEEN (AV)

107 Court Street, 56537
Telephone: 218-736-4866
FAX: 218-736-7747
Email: dlundlaw@prtel.com

For full biographical listings, see the Martindale-Hubbell Law Directory

*HASTINGS,** Dakota Co.

LANGLAIS & SCHUMACHER, P.A. (AV)

Suite 13, 1303 South Frontage Road, 55033
Telephone: 651-438-3789
Fax: 651-438-3936
Email: langlais@minn.net *URL:* http://www.lawyers.com/langlais&schumacher

Richard J. Langlais
Jean M. Langlais
Leo F. Schumacher
Susan T. Steveken
Christopher W. Brownell

For full biographical listings, see the Martindale-Hubbell Law Directory

*MINNEAPOLIS,** Hennepin Co.

ABDO AND ABDO, P.A. (AV)

710 Northstar West 625 Marquette Avenue, 55402
Telephone: 612-333-1526
Fax: 612-342-2608
Email: abdoabdo@aol.com *URL:* http://www.abdo.com.br

E. John Abdo (1912-1993)
Robert P. Abdo
Steven R. Hedges
Keith J. Broady
Kenneth J. Abdo
Timothy C. Matson

For Complete List of Firm Personnel, See General Section

For full biographical listings, see the Martindale-Hubbell Law Directory

ARNOLD, ANDERSON & DOVE, P.L.L.P. (AV)

5881 Cedar Lake Road, 55416-1492
Telephone: 612-545-9000
Wats Line: 800-343-4545
Fax: 612-545-1793; 612-542-9210
Email: aad@aadlaw.com
Princeton, Minnesota Office: 501 South Fourth Street.
Telephone: 612-389-2214.
Hutchinson, Minnesota Office: 101 Park Place.
Telephone: 320-587-7575.
Red Wing, Minnesota Office: 481 Fridell Crescent, 55066.
Telephone: 651-388-3454.

MEMBERS OF FIRM

David B. Arnold
Steven A. Anderson
Paul D. Dove

For Complete List of Firm Personnel, See General Section

For full biographical listings, see the Martindale-Hubbell Law Directory

STEPHEN J. DAVIS (AV)

4601 Excelsior Boulevard, Suite 500, 55416-4960
Telephone: 612-285-9200
Fax: 612-285-9985

LEGAL SUPPORT PERSONNEL

Margaret M. Boisvert

For full biographical listings, see the Martindale-Hubbell Law Directory

HAGERTY, JOHNSON, ALBRIGHTSON & BEITZ, P.A. (AV)

Suite 901, 701 Fourth Avenue South, 55415
Telephone: 612-349-9000
Telecopier: 612-332-3751
Email: hjab@hjab.com

Jon B. Albrightson

Representative Clients: Augustana Care Foundation; Data-Metalcraft,Inc.; Distribution Alternatives, Inc.; Fidelity National Title Insurance Company of New York; Independent Fire Protection, Inc.; PaR Systems Corportion; Universal Hospital Services, Inc.; Nott Co.; Zinpro Corp.
Reference: Norwest Bank of Minnesota, N.A.

For full biographical listings, see the Martindale-Hubbell Law Directory

HESSIAN & McKASY, P.A. (AV)

4700 IDS Center, 80 South Eighth Street, 55402-2228
Telephone: 612-330-3000
Telecopier: 612-371-0653
St. Paul, Minnesota Offices: 2050 Piper Jaffray Plaza, 444 Cedar Street, 55101.
Telephone: 612-330-3071.
Fax: 651-228-9161.

Glen E. Schumann
Jaymes D. Littlejohn

OF COUNSEL

Darrell B. Johnson

For full biographical listings, see the Martindale-Hubbell Law Directory

HOLPER, WELSH & MITCHELL, LTD. (AV)

10 South Fifth Street, Suite 300, 55402
Telephone: 612-317-1012
Fax: 612-317-0947
Email: rholper@aol.com *URL:* http://www.lawyers.com/holperwelsh&mitchell
Phoenix, Arizona Office: 2415 East Camelback Road, Suite 700, 85016.
Telephone: 602-508-6033.
Fax: 480-483-0269.

Richard D. Holper
Mary Ann Welsh
Ralph V. Mitchell, Jr.

For full biographical listings, see the Martindale-Hubbell Law Directory

LOMMEN, NELSON, COLE & STAGEBERG, P.A. (AV)

1800 IDS Center, 80 South 8th Street, 55402
Telephone: 612-339-8131
Fax: 612-339-8064
Email: postmaster@email.lommen.com *URL:* http://www.lommen.com
Hudson, Wisconsin Office: Grandview Professional Building, 400 South Second Street, Suite 210.
Telephones: 715-386-8217 and 612-436-8085.

W. Wyman Smith (1914-1994)
Henry H. Feikema (1926-1996)
V. Owen Nelson (1928-1998)
John P. Lommen (1927-1988)
Michael P. Shroyer (1953-1993)
Leonard T. Juster
Alvin S. Malmon
Ronald L. Haskvitz
Phillip A. Cole
Roger V. Stageberg
Glenn R. Kessel
Thomas R. Jacobson (Resident, Hudson, Wisconsin Office)
John M. Giblin
John R. McBride
J. Christopher Cuneo
Thomas F. Dougherty
Stacey A. DeKalb
Kay N. Hunt
Richard L. Plagens
Ehrich L. Koch
Margie R. Bodas
James M. Lockhart
Stephen C. Rathke
James C. Searls
Paul L. Dinger
Sherri D. Ulland
Reid R. Lindquist
James R. Johnson (Resident, Hudson, Wisconsin Office)
Marc A. Johannsen
Barry A. O'Neil

Scott M. Nelson
Scott N. Ross
Mary I. King
David M. Hudson
Sheila A. Bjorklund
David S. Ezrilov
Susan Hayes Stephan
Geraint D. Powell
Brent R. Johnson (Resident, Hudson, Wisconsin Office)
Laura L. Enga
Christopher R. Grote

OF COUNSEL

Thomas F. Miller

Representative Clients: James Corrigan/Corrigan Homes; Elk River Development Company; Bruce Bren Homes, Inc.

(See Next Column)

LOMMEN, NELSON, COLE & STAGEBERG P.A., *Minneapolis—Continued*

For full biographical listings, see the Martindale-Hubbell Law Directory

MARTIN & ASSOCIATES, P.A. (AV)

1650 West 82nd Street, Suite 1460, 55431
Telephone: 612-885-5665
Fax: 612-885-5664
Email: mail@martinandassociates.com

Judith Martin Ventres

Michael J. Zitta
Richard William Van Sickle

For full biographical listings, see the Martindale-Hubbell Law Directory

PARSINEN KAPLAN LEVY ROSBERG & GOTLIEB P.A. (AV)

100 South 5th Street Suite 1100, 55402-1298
Telephone: 612-333-2111
Fax: 612-333-6798

John Parsinen
Robert A. Levy
Sidney Kaplan
Jack A. Rosberg
David Gotlieb
Karen A. Ciegler Hansen
Joseph M. Sokolowski
Howard J. Rubin
David A. Orenstein
John C. Levy
Steven R. Katz
Kathleen Doar
Brian R. Martens
Rebecca J. McDaniel
Stephen M. Hickok
Ann Marks Sanford
Jude Anne Carluccio
Pamela A. Curran
David B. Gollin

Theresa M. Kowalski
Joan P. Kurlander
Bryan D. Biesterfeld
Daniel W. Eck
Nels E. Carlson
John Scott De Lanoy
Ann S. Grayson
Kimberley Ste. Marie Becker
Heidi E. Pergament

For full biographical listings, see the Martindale-Hubbell Law Directory

ROBERT MERRILL ROSENBERG, P.A. (AV)

520 Marquette Avenue South, Suite 900, 55402-1105
Telephone: 612-349-5290
Facsimile: 612-349-9962
Email: RMR@Rosenberg-Law.com

Robert Merrill Rosenberg

For full biographical listings, see the Martindale-Hubbell Law Directory

SMITH, GENDLER, SHIELL, SHEFF & FORD, P.A. (AV)

3350 U.S. Bank Place, 601 Second Avenue South, 55402
Telephone: 612-332-1000
Facsimile: 612-332-3836

John M. Gendler
Douglas J. Shiell
Harold H. Sheff
Margaret A. Ford

OF COUNSEL

Benjamin J. Smith

For full biographical listings, see the Martindale-Hubbell Law Directory

ZAMANSKY PROFESSIONAL ASSOCIATION (AV)

3901 IDS Tower, 55402
Telephone: 612-340-9720
Fax: 612-340-9662
Email: ZPA4924@aol.com
St. Paul, Minnesota Office: 6 West 5th Street.
Telephone: 612-297-6400.

Ronald A. Zamansky

Matthew B. Cohen

OF COUNSEL

Stephen B. Solomon

Reference: Norwest Bank Minneapolis, N.A.

For full biographical listings, see the Martindale-Hubbell Law Directory

*ROCHESTER,** Olmsted Co.

O'BRIEN, EHRICK, WOLF, DEANER & MAUS, L.L.P. (AV)

206 South Broadway, Suite 611, P.O. Box 968, 55903-0968
Telephone: 507-289-4041
Fax: 507-281-4778

MEMBER OF FIRM

Ted E. Deaner

Representative Clients: County of Olmsted; Eastwood Bank; AgSTAR Farm Credit Services; U.S. Bank National Association; F & M Community Bank; Jordan Realty Corporation.

(See Next Column)

For Complete List of Firm Personnel, See General Section

For full biographical listings, see the Martindale-Hubbell Law Directory

*ST. PAUL,** Ramsey Co.

JOHN MURRAY & ASSOCIATES, LTD. (AV)

Suite 920 Piper Jaffray Plaza, 444 Cedar Street, 55101
Telephone: 651-227-8820
Telecopier: 651-223-5332
Email: jmurray@abanet.org

John A. Murray

Reference: American National (Firstar) Bank, St. Paul.

For full biographical listings, see the Martindale-Hubbell Law Directory

STEIN, MOORE & FAY, P.A. (AV)

1010 Minnesota Building, 55101
Telephone: 651-224-9683
Telecopier: 651-223-5212
URL: http://www.steinmoorefay.com

Peter B. Stein
Ralph L. Moore
Jonathan (Jack) R. Fay

Reference: Firstar Bank of Minnesota, N.A.

For full biographical listings, see the Martindale-Hubbell Law Directory

MISSISSIPPI

*BROOKHAVEN,** Lincoln Co.

ALLEN, ALLEN, BOERNER & BREELAND (AV)

214 Justice Street, P.O. Box 751, 39602-0751
Telephone: 601-833-4361
Fax: 601-833-6647
Email: aabblaw@tislink.com

Emmette P. Allen (1915-1999)
Robert O. Allen
William D. Boerner
Durwood J. Breeland

ASSOCIATE

Sally Burchfield Doty

For full biographical listings, see the Martindale-Hubbell Law Directory

*CLARKSDALE,** Coahoma Co.

HUNT & ROSS, A PROFESSIONAL ASSOCIATION (AV)

123 Court Street, P.O. Box 1196, 38614
Telephone: 601-627-5251
Telecopier No.: 601-627-5254
Email: huntross@clarksdale.com *URL:* http://www.lawyers.com/h&rlaw

Tom T. Ross (1903-1993)
David R. Hunt
Tom T. Ross, Jr.

Thomas W. Allen
Katherine Blackwell Parker

Representative Client: The Prudential Realty Group, Agricultural Investments, Lisle, Illinois; Delta Ag, LTD.; West Memphis, AR.

For full biographical listings, see the Martindale-Hubbell Law Directory

*GULFPORT,** Harrison Co.

ALLEN, VAUGHN, COBB & HOOD, P.A. (AV)

One Hancock Plaza, Suite 1209, P.O. Drawer 4108, 39502-4108
Telephone: 601-864-4011
Fax: 601-864-4852
Email: avchlaw@sunherald.infinet.com

Harry R. Allen
Thomas E. Vaughn
David L. Cobb
Billy W. Hood
Joy Lambert Phillips
Robert W. Atkinson
Benjamin U. Bowden
Richard B. Tubertini
Rodney Douglas Robinson
E. Colette Towles
David W. Crane
John A. Foxworth, Jr.

J. Adrian Smith
Michael J. Casano

OF COUNSEL

D. Knox White

LEGAL SUPPORT PERSONNEL

Kevin C. Stachowski (Paralegal)

For full biographical listings, see the Martindale-Hubbell Law Directory

Gulfport—Continued

Dukes, Dukes, Keating and Faneca, P.A. (AV)
2909 13th Street, 6th Floor, P.O. Drawer W, 39501
Telephone: 228-868-1111
Fax: 228-863-2886
Email: ddkf@ddkf.com

Hugh D. Keating — Cy Faneca

Joan E. Lund — William W. Abbott, Jr.

For Complete List of Firm Personnel, See General Section

For full biographical listings, see the Martindale-Hubbell Law Directory

Franke, Rainey & Salloum, PLLC (AV)
2605 14th Street, P.O. Drawer 460, 39502
Telephone: 228-868-7070
Telecopier: 228-868-7090
Email: frs@diversicomm.com

Paul M. Franke, Jr. — Paul B. Howell
William M. Rainey — Fredrick B. Feeney, II
Richard P. Salloum — Traci M. Castille
Donald P. Moore

Kaleel G. Salloum, Jr. — Brandi C. Schwartz
James C. Simpson, Jr.

For full biographical listings, see the Martindale-Hubbell Law Directory

Meadows Riley Law Firm (AV)
1720 23rd Avenue, P.O. Box 550, 39502
Telephone: 601-864-4511
Telecopier: 601-868-2178

Joseph R. Meadows — Jerry D. Riley
Donnie D. Riley — Karen J. Young

Representative Clients: Bubba Oustalat Lincoln Mercury, Inc.; Lee Tractor Co. of Mississippi.
Reference: Hancock Bank.

For full biographical listings, see the Martindale-Hubbell Law Directory

Newton and Hoff, L.L.P. (AV)
2019 23rd Avenue, P.O. Box 910, 39502-0910
Telephone: 228-863-8827
Fax: 228-868-6007
Email: newtonhoff@aol.com *URL:* http://www.newtonhoff.com

Paul M. Newton (Resident) — Frederick T. Hoff, Jr. (Resident)
Paul M. Newton, Jr. (Resident)

For full biographical listings, see the Martindale-Hubbell Law Directory

*JACKSON,** Hinds Co.

Rhoden, Lacy, Downey & Colbert (AV)
111 Park Circle Drive, P.O. Box 13762, 39236
Telephone: 601-932-1155
Telecopier: 601-936-2515
Email: rldclaw@netdoor.com *URL:* http://www.Thrhoden-law.com

MEMBERS OF FIRM

Thomas H. Rhoden — Don P. Lacy

For full biographical listings, see the Martindale-Hubbell Law Directory

Underwood Law Firm (AV)
340 Edgewood Terrace Drive, P.O. Box 16852, 37206
Telephone: 601-981-7773
Telecopier: 601-362-5673
Email: ulfm@aol.com *URL:* http://www.lawyers.com/underwoodlawfirm

John C. Underwood, Jr.

ASSOCIATES

Catherine W. Underwood — Robert E Moorehead

For full biographical listings, see the Martindale-Hubbell Law Directory

Watkins & Eager (AV)

A Professional Limited Liability Company
Suite 300 The Emporium Building, 400 East Capitol Street, P.O. Box 650, 39205
Telephone: 601-948-6470
Facsimile: 601-354-3623

MEMBERS OF FIRM

Thomas R. Crews — Frank J. Hammond, III
George R. Fair — M. Binford Williams, Jr.
Jamie G. Houston, III — J. Fred Spencer, Jr.
J. Grant Sellers

(See Next Column)

Representative Clients: Freide Goldman International, Inc.; Blossman Gas, Inc.; Chevron U.S.A. Inc.; SouthTrust Bank, National Association; Deposit Guaranty National Bank; Dollar General Corp.; Chrysler Capital Corp.; Goldman Sachs & Co.; Millsaps College; Whitney National Bank.

For Complete List of Firm Personnel, See General Section

For full biographical listings, see the Martindale-Hubbell Law Directory

*LAUREL,** Jones Co.

Gibbes Graves Mullins Hortman Harlow Martindale & Jones, PLLC (AV)
414 West Oak Street, P.O. Drawer 1409, 39441-1409
Telephone: 601-649-8611
FAX: 601-649-6062

MEMBERS OF FIRM

William S. Mullins, III — Eugene M. Harlow
Norman Gene Hortman, Jr. — David L. Martindale
Deidra D. Jones

ASSOCIATES

Brett W. Robinson — Leslie P. Barry

Representative Clients: Texaco Inc.; Masonite Corp., a Division of International Paper Co.; St. Paul Insurance; Chevron U.S.A., Inc.; BellSouth; Shell Oil; Deposit Guaranty National Bank; Dixie Electric Power Assn.; Denbury Management, Inc.; U.S. Outdoor Advertising Co.

For full biographical listings, see the Martindale-Hubbell Law Directory

*MERIDIAN,** Lauderdale Co.

Glover, Young, Walton, Phillips & Tucker, PLLC (AV)
Jefferson Square Office Plaza, 1724-A 23rd Avenue, P.O. Box 5514, 39302-5514
Telephone: 601-693-1301
Telecopy: 601-693-1363
Email: gywptpsp@hotmail.com

H. Wingfield Glover, Jr. — Ronnie L. Walton
Ralph E. Young, Jr. — P. Scott Phillips
Judson T. Tucker

Representative Clients: Alfa Insurance Companies; American States Insurance Co.; Deposit Guaranty National Bank; General Agents Insurance Company of America, Inc.; Great River Insurance; Jeff Anderson Regional Medical Center; Liberty National Life Insurance Co.; Mississippi Power Co.; State Auto Insurance Companies; Universal Underwriters.

For Complete List of Firm Personnel, See General Section

For full biographical listings, see the Martindale-Hubbell Law Directory

*NATCHEZ,** Adams Co.

Mulhearn & Mulhearn (AV)
202 South Wall Street, P.O. Box 967, 39120
Telephone: 601-442-4808
Fax: 601-446-6224
Email: woodland@bkbank.com *URL:* http://www.lawyers.com/mulhearnlaw

MEMBERS OF FIRM

John E. Mulhearn (1910-1981) — John E. Mulhearn, Jr.

LEGAL SUPPORT PERSONNEL

Eva Ruth Seale — Judith A. Strickland

Representative Clients: Ashland Plantation; Exxon Corporation; Belle Oil, Inc.; Supermarket Operations, Inc.; Petron, Inc.; Concordia Bank & Trust Co.; Dunleith; J.M. Jones Lumber Co., Inc.; Southwest Mississippi Anesthesia P.A.; Paradise Foods, Inc.

For full biographical listings, see the Martindale-Hubbell Law Directory

Truly, Smith & Latham (AV)
100 South Pearl Street, P.O. Box 1307, 39121-1307
Telephone: 601-442-6495
Telecopier: 601-442-8874
URL: http://www.lawyers.com/trulysmith&latham

George Lawrence Adams (1913-1994) — R. Brent Forman (1917-1994)
E. C. Ward (1928-1994)

MEMBERS OF FIRM

William Marion Smith — Robert C. Latham

OF COUNSEL

Everette Truly

Representative Clients: Deposit Guaranty National Bank; Exxon U.S.A.; Mississippi Power & Light Co.; Southwest Mississippi Electric Power Assn.; South Central Bell Telephone Co.; Sears, Roebuck & Co.; American International Group; Kemper Insurance Co.

For full biographical listings, see the Martindale-Hubbell Law Directory

*OXFORD,** Lafayette Co.

FREELAND & FREELAND (AV)

1013 Jackson Avenue, P.O. Box 269, 38655
Telephone: 662-234-3414
Telecopier: 662-234-0604
Email: thf4@watervalley.net

MEMBERS OF FIRM

T. H. Freeland, III
T. H. Freeland, IV

Representative Clients: The Ohio Casualty Group; Crum & Forester.

For full biographical listings, see the Martindale-Hubbell Law Directory

*PASCAGOULA,** Jackson Co.

COLINGO, WILLIAMS, HEIDELBERG, STEINBERGER & McELHANEY, P.A. (AV)

711 Delmas Avenue, P.O. Box 1407, 39568-1407
Telephone: 228-762-8021
FAX: 228-762-7589
Email: info@colingowilliams.com *URL:* http://www.ColingoWilliams.com

John M. Kinard

Representative Clients: International Paper Co.; R.J. Reynolds; CBS Corp.; Kemper Group; Singing River Hospital System; Mississippi Gulf Coast Regional Wastewater Authority; Medical Assurance Company of Mississippi; Mutual Assurance of Alabama; Dole Food Co.

For full biographical listings, see the Martindale-Hubbell Law Directory

SOUTHAVEN, De Soto Co.

BRIDGFORTH & BUNTIN (AV)

1607 State Line Road, P.O. Box 241, 38671
Telephone: 601-393-4450
Fax: 601-342-5646

MEMBERS OF FIRM

Dudley B. Bridgforth, Jr.
Taylor D. Buntin, III
Barry W. Bridgforth, Jr.

For full biographical listings, see the Martindale-Hubbell Law Directory

MISSOURI

*JEFFERSON CITY,** Cole Co.

CARSON & COIL, P.C. (AV)

515 East High, P.O. Box 28, 65102
Telephone: 573-636-2177
Telecopier: 573-636-7119
Email: general@carsoncoil.com

Forrest P. Carson (1910-1981)
Cullen Coil (1907-1989)
Michael P. Riley
Ronald R. McMillin
Eugene G. Bushmann
James W. Gallaher
Lori J. Levine
Rudolph L. Veit
Michael Madsen
R. Max Humphreys
Mark A. Ludwig
Dana L. Frese
Edward C. Clausen
Carla G. Holste
Kent L. Brown
Douglas W. Hennon
Charles J. McPheeters

Charles A. "Chip" Gentry
James W. "Jamie" Gallaher, Jr.

General Counsel for: Capital Reserve Life Insurance Co.; Missouri Farm Bureau; Healthcare Services Group.
Reference: Central Trust Bank.

For full biographical listings, see the Martindale-Hubbell Law Directory

KANSAS CITY, Jackson, Clay, Platte & Cass Cos.

SWANSON MIDGLEY, LLC (AV)

Crown Center, 2420 Pershing Road, Suite 400, 64108
Telephone: 816-842-6100
Fax: 816-842-0013
Email: mail@swansonmidgley.com *URL:* http://www.swansonmidgley.com
Overland Park, Kansas Office: Commerce Plaza I, 7th Floor, 7300 W. 110th Street.
Telephone: 913-317-2717.
FAX: 913-317-1505.

(See Next Column)

Robert R. Bartunek
George H. Gangwere, Jr.
James H. McLarney
Charles F. Zarter

Counsel For: Certified Master Builders; BSC Holding, Inc.; Home Builders Association of Greater K.C.; First Horizon Corp. (United Country); S.T. Carter, Inc.; Morana Enterprises; American Home Shield; Prospect Group, Inc.; Lawrence Home Builders Assn.

For Complete List of Firm Personnel, See General Section

For full biographical listings, see the Martindale-Hubbell Law Directory

LEE'S SUMMIT, Jackson Co.

CARL CHINNERY & ASSOCIATES, P.C. (AV)

200 S.E. Douglas Street, Suite 200, 64063-2375
Telephone: 816-525-2050

Carl L. Chinnery

Nancy E. Blackwell

OF COUNSEL

Elizabeth Unger Carlyle

LEGAL SUPPORT PERSONNEL

PARALEGALS

Jean Wehner Chinnery
Elaine K. Hanrahan
Alicia Hodges
Susan Breitenbach
Pam Kane
Virginia Galate
Alice Mistler

For full biographical listings, see the Martindale-Hubbell Law Directory

ST. LOUIS, (Independent City)

DANKENBRING GREIMAN OSTERHOLT & HOFFMANN, P.C. (AV)

Clayton Centre, Fifth Floor, 120 S. Central Avenue, 63105
Telephone: 314-863-7733
Fax: 314-862-4656
URL: http://www.dgohlaw.com

James R. Dankenbring
Thomas E. Osterholt, Jr.

Thomas W. Jerry
James R. Loranger

OF COUNSEL

Timothy R. Wolf

For full biographical listings, see the Martindale-Hubbell Law Directory

DEVEREUX, MURPHY, STRILER, BRICKEY & SHER, L.L.C. (AV)

10 South Brentwood Boulevard (Clayton), 63105
Telephone: 314-721-1516
FAX: 314-721-4434

Stephen C. Murphy
Robert L. Striler
Robert L. Devereux

For full biographical listings, see the Martindale-Hubbell Law Directory

HELFREY, SIMON & JONES, P.C. (AV)

120 South Central Avenue Suite 1500, 63105
Telephone: 314-725-9100
Facsimile: 314-725-5754

David L. Jones
David F. Neiers
Paul Simon, Jr.
Philip C. Graham

Jeffrey M. Igou
Gregory M. Power
Michael C. Seamands

OF COUNSEL

Clifford L. Goetz

For full biographical listings, see the Martindale-Hubbell Law Directory

JENKINS & KLING, P.C. (AV)

10 South Brentwood, Suite 200, 63105
Telephone: 314-721-2525
Telecopier: 314-721-5525
Email: jklaw@swbell.net

Stephen L. Kling, Jr.
Jason M. Rugo
Rebecca A. Kling
Michael P. Stephens

For full biographical listings, see the Martindale-Hubbell Law Directory

JEROME R. MANDELSTAMM (AV)

Suite 1600, 1010 Market Street, 63101-2082
Telephone: 314-621-2261
Fax: 314-436-2303

For full biographical listings, see the Martindale-Hubbell Law Directory

St. Louis—Continued

MILLSAP & SINGER, P.C. (AV)

Suite 2300, 7777 Bonhomme Avenue (Clayton), 63105
Telephone: 314-726-6545
Fax: 314-726-6483

Wayne L. Millsap
Vernon D. Singer

Kip J. Bilderback
Cynthia M. Woolverton

For full biographical listings, see the Martindale-Hubbell Law Directory

ROSENBLUM, GOLDENHERSH, SILVERSTEIN & ZAFFT, P.C. (AV)

Fourth Floor, 7733 Forsyth Boulevard, 63105
Telephone: 314-726-6868
Telecopier: 314-726-6786
Belleville, Illinois Office: 2 Park Place Professional Centre, 62221.
Telephone: 618-234-9900.
Columbia, Missouri Office: 3201 South Providence, Suite 101, 65205-4000.
Telephone: 573-441-8686.

Stanley M. Rosenblum
Robert S. Goldenhersh
Merle L. Silverstein
Gene M. Zafft
Carl C. Lang
Richard S. Bender
Michael A. Markenson
David V. Capes
Mark E. Goodman
Jay A. Nathanson
Richard Greenberg
Bennett S. Keller
Leonard D. Vines
Roger M. Herman
Thomas A. Duda
Paul G. Klug
Ira L. Blank
Ellen Levy Siwak
Joshua M. Schindler
Sanford J. Boxerman
Carl R. Desenberg
Scott H. Malin

Jeffrey Alan Cohen
Kristen L. Maly
Todd C. Brockmann
Marilyn Eichler Nathanson
Shelley H. Koren
Jared M. Minkoff

For full biographical listings, see the Martindale-Hubbell Law Directory

STONE, LEYTON & GERSHMAN, A PROFESSIONAL CORPORATION (AV)

7733 Forsyth Boulevard, Suite 500, 63105
Telephone: 314-721-7011
Telefax: 314-721-8660

Steven M. Stone
Steven H. Leyton
Jeffrey S. Gershman
Lynn G. Carey

Phyllis R. Williamson
Catherine L. Kolb

OF COUNSEL

Sidney L. Stone

For full biographical listings, see the Martindale-Hubbell Law Directory

MONTANA

*BIG TIMBER,** Sweet Grass Co.

JOSEPHSON, LOVELL & DRINGMAN (AV)

115 West Second Avenue, P.O. Box 1047, 59011
Telephone: 406-932-5440
Fax: 406-932-5752
Email: josephsonlaw@mcn.net

Richard W. Josephson
R. Mark Josephson
Lance Lovell
Patrick N. Dringman
Page C. Dringman

LEGAL SUPPORT PERSONNEL

Dawn M. Curry (Legal Assistant)
Barbara W. Cutchin (Legal Assistant)
Colleen A. Ellis (Legal Secretary)
Carmen Hodges (Legal Assistant)
Shirle Norquist (Legal Assistant)
Esther S. Pearce (Legal Assistant)
Lauren M. Rudd (Legal Secretary and Administrative Assistant)

OTHER STAFF

Bev Josephson (Accounting)
Gail Burmeister (Receptionist and Office Administrator)

For full biographical listings, see the Martindale-Hubbell Law Directory

*BILLINGS,** Yellowstone Co.

CROWLEY, HAUGHEY, HANSON, TOOLE & DIETRICH, P.L.L.P. (AV)

500 Transwestern II, 490 North 31st Street, P.O. Box 2529, 59103
Telephone: 406-252-3441
Fax: 406-259-4159
Email: crowley@crowleylaw.com
Helena, Montana Office: IBM Building, 100 North Park Avenue, Suite 300, 59601.
Telephone: 406-449-4165.
Fax: 406-449-5149.
Kalispell, Montana Office: 431 1st Avenue West, 59901.
Telephone: 406-752-6644.
Fax: 406-752-5108.
Williston, North Dakota Office: 113 East Broadway, 58801.
Telephone: 701-572-2200.
Fax: 701-572-7072.

OF COUNSEL

John M. Dietrich
Gareld F. Krieg
Myles J. Thomas

MEMBERS OF FIRM

Arthur F. Lamey, Jr.
Terry B. Cosgrove (Resident, Helena, Montana Office)
Allan L. Karell
Daniel N. McLean (Resident, Helena, Montana Office)
Robert G. Michelotti, Jr.
John R. Alexander
William D. Lamdin, III
Michael S. Dockery
Malcolm H. Goodrich
Mary Scrim Dyre (Resident, Kalispell, Montana Office)
Eric K. Anderson
Renee L. Coppock
John R. Lee (Resident, Williston, North Dakota Office)
Scott M. Heard
Michael S. Lahr (Resident, Helena, Montana Office)

Representative Clients: Aetna; Metropolitan Life Insurance Co.; Mutual Life Insurance Co., N.Y.; Equitable Life Assurance Society of the United States; Turner Enterprises, Inc.

For Complete List of Firm Personnel, See General Section

For full biographical listings, see the Martindale-Hubbell Law Directory

MURPHY, KIRKPATRICK & FAIN, P.L.L.P. (AV)

Suite 300, Western Security Bank Building, 2929 Third Avenue North, 59101
Telephone: 406-256-9700
Fax: 406-256-9755
Email: mailbox@murphkirk.com *URL:* http://www.murphkirk.com

James P. Murphy
Stewart R. Kirkpatrick
Bruce F. Fain

LEGAL SUPPORT PERSONNEL

Michelle A. Kennedy (Paralegal)

For full biographical listings, see the Martindale-Hubbell Law Directory

*BOZEMAN,** Gallatin Co.

KIRWAN & BARRETT, P.C. (AV)

215 West Mendenhall, P.O. Box 1348, 59771-1348
Telephone: 406-586-1553
Fax: 406-586-8971

Peter M. Kirwan
Stephen M. Barrett

For full biographical listings, see the Martindale-Hubbell Law Directory

*KALISPELL,** Flathead Co.

HASH & O'BRIEN, PLLP (AV)

Plaza West, 136 First Avenue, West, P.O. Box 1178, 59901
Telephone: 406-755-6919
Fax: 406-755-6911
Email: cmhash@digisys.net

MEMBERS OF FIRM

Charles L. Hash
Kenneth E. O'Brien
C. Mark Hash

General Counsel for: Glacier Bancorp, Inc; Glacier Bank, Eureka and Whitefish; First National Bank of Eureka; Vortex Fishing Systems.
Representative Clients: Western Surety Co.; Liberty Mutual Insurance Co.; Allstate Insurance Co.; Lincoln Electric Cooperative; Read Enterprises.
Reference: Glacier Bancorp, Inc.

For full biographical listings, see the Martindale-Hubbell Law Directory

HALE LANE PEEK DENNISON HOWARD AND ANDERSON, *Las Vegas—Continued*

MEMBERS OF FIRM

Steve Lane
J. Stephen Peek
Karen D. Dennison (Resident, Reno, Nevada)
R. Craig Howard (Resident, Reno, Nevada)
Stephen V. Novacek (Resident, Reno, Nevada)
William C. Davis, Jr.
Patricia J. Curtis

Representative Clients: Lenders: Bank of America, N.A.; Allstate Life Insurance Company. Title Companies: Chicago Title Insurance Co. Construction and Development: Peccole Nevada Corporation; Lake at Las Vegas Joint Venture; Juliett Corporation.

For Complete List of Firm Personnel, See General Section

For full biographical listings, see the Martindale-Hubbell Law Directory

BILL C. HAMMER & ASSOCIATES (AV)

BankWest Building, 4270 South Decatur Boulevard, Suite B-10, 89103
Telephone: 702-387-0530
Fax: 702-387-0928
Email: bchlawoff@aol.com *URL:* http://www.lawyers.com/billchammer

Bill C. Hammer

For full biographical listings, see the Martindale-Hubbell Law Directory

JOLLEY, URGA, WIRTH & WOODBURY (AV)

3800 Howard Hughes Parkway Suite 1600, 89109
Telephone: 702-699-7500
Facsimile: 702-699-7555
URL: http://www.juww.com
Boulder City, Nevada Office: Suite 105, 1000 Nevada Highway, 89005.
Telephone: 702-293-3674.

MEMBERS OF FIRM

R. Gardner Jolley
William R. Urga
Roger A. Wirth
Allen D. Emmel

Representative Clients: Wells Fargo Bank and its predecessor, First Interstate Bank of Nevada; Nevada State Bank; Citicorp National Services, Inc.; Chicago Title Insurance Co.; National Title Company; Fidelity National Title; Melvin Simon & Associates, Inc.; Continental National Bank; First Nationwide Bank; Citizens Bank.

For Complete List of Firm Personnel, See General Section

For full biographical listings, see the Martindale-Hubbell Law Directory

KOLESAR & LEATHAM, CHARTERED (AV)

Norwest Bank Center, 3320 West Sahara Avenue, Suite 380, 89102
Telephone: 702-362-7800
Telecopier: 702-362-9472

Robert J. Kolesar
Nile Leatham
Elliott R. Eisner
Howard Goldstein
Charles H. Miles, Jr.
Craig S. Newman

Mark W. Patterson
Matthew D. Saltzman

Representative Clients: Agassi Enterprises, Inc.; American Nevada, Inc.; Champion Homes; Coca-Cola Company; Commonwealth Land Title Insurance Company; Credit Suisse First Boston Mortgage Capital; Enterprise Auto Leasing; Forest City Enterprises; Lawyers Title Insurance Company; Weingarten Realty Investments/Management Co.

For full biographical listings, see the Martindale-Hubbell Law Directory

KRAVITZ, SCHNITZER & SLOANE, CHARTERED, A PROFESSIONAL CORPORATION (AV)

2300 West Sahara Avenue, Suite 500, 89102
Telephone: 702-362-6666
Fax: 702-362-2203
Email: KRAVSCHNIT@AOL.COM

Martin J. Kravitz
Gary E. Schnitzer
Jeffrey G. Sloane
Michael Bradley Johnson
Jane Eberhardy
Marisa C. Guarino

David J. Feldman
Jerry R. Graf

LEGAL SUPPORT PERSONNEL

Sandye Smith (Legal Administrator)

Representative Clients: Realty Executives; Shearson Lehman Mortgage Co.; Prudential Mortgage; Baushman & Turner Civil Engineers; Makena Development; Galaxy Mall; Dunmore Homes, Inc.; Green Hills Homes, Inc.; Chase Manhattan Mortgage; U.S. Home Corp.; Allstate Insurance Company.

For full biographical listings, see the Martindale-Hubbell Law Directory

JOHN PETER LEE, LTD. (AV)

830 Las Vegas Boulevard South, 89101
Telephone: 702-382-4044
Telecopier: 702-383-9950

John Peter Lee

Paul C. Ray
Timothy P. Thomas

For Complete List of Firm Personnel, See General Section

For full biographical listings, see the Martindale-Hubbell Law Directory

LIONEL SAWYER & COLLINS (AV)

1700 Bank of America Plaza, 300 South Fourth Street, 89101
Telephone: 702-383-8888
Fax: 702-383-8845
Email: first initial last@lionelsawyer.com
Reno, Nevada Office: Suite 1100, Bank of America Plaza, 50 West Liberty Street.
Telephone: 702-788-8666.
Fax: 702-788-8682.

MEMBERS OF FIRM

Jeffrey P. Zucker
David C. Whittemore
Mark H. Goldstein
Colleen A. Dolan (Resident, Reno Office)
Gary Wayne Duhon (Resident, Reno Office)
Carl D. Savely (Resident, Reno Office)
Layne J. Butt
Mark Lemmons

ASSOCIATES

Mark A. McIntire
Lynn S. Fulstone
Christopher R. Coley (Resident, Reno Office)
Craig E. Etem (Resident, Reno Office)
Deidre J. Call
Abbie Green Friedman
Broady R. Hodder
Emilia K. Cargill
Kirk Douglas Johnson (Not admitted in NV)
Matthew E. Watson

Representative Clients: Dermody Properties; Howard Hughes Properties; Starwood Hotels & Resorts; Lake at Las Vegas; Lewis Homes of Nevada; MGM Grand, Inc.; Pacific Properties & Development Corporation; Bank of America; Preferred Equities Corp.; Lakes Gaming, Inc.

For Complete List of Firm Personnel, See General Section

For full biographical listings, see the Martindale-Hubbell Law Directory

BRYAN A LOWE & ASSOCIATES A PROFESSIONAL LAW CORPORATION (AV)

4011 Meadows Lane, Suite 102, 89107
Telephone: 702-259-0002
Fax: 702-259-7774
Email: LoweAssoc@aol.com *URL:* http://www.lawyers.com/lowelaw
Boulder City, Nevada Office: 916 Nevada highway, Suite 6, 89005.
Telephone: 702-293-6888.

Bryan A. Lowe

Robert Winn
S. Craig Stone, II

Representative Client: Clark County Housing Authority.
References: Wells Fargo Bank, Trust Department; Bank of America, Trust Department; Clark County, Nevada, Public Administrator.

For full biographical listings, see the Martindale-Hubbell Law Directory

McDONALD CARANO WILSON McCUNE BERGIN FRANKOVICH & HICKS LLP (AV)

Suite 1000, 2300 West Sahara Avenue, 89102
Telephone: 702-873-4100
Telecopier: 702-873-9966
URL: http://www.mcdonaldcarano.com
Reno, Nevada Office: 241 Ridge Street.
Telephone: 775-788-2000.
Telecopier: 775-788-2020.

MEMBERS OF FIRM

Andrew P. Gordon
Bryan R. Clark

ASSOCIATES

Andrew S. Gabriel
Donald G. Martin

Representative Clients: AT&T Communications of Nevada; Boyd Gaming Corp.; Jackpot Enterprises, Inc.; Nevada State Bank; Shaver Construction.

For Complete List of Firm Personnel, See General Section

For full biographical listings, see the Martindale-Hubbell Law Directory

MORSE & MOWBRAY, A PROFESSIONAL CORPORATION (AV)

Suite 1400 Bank of America Plaza, 300 South Fourth Street, 89101
Telephone: 702-384-6340
Telecopier: 702-384-4596
London, England Office: Lamb Building, Temple.
Telephone: 071-353-6701.

(See Next Column)

MORSE & MOWBRAY A PROFESSIONAL CORPORATION—*Continued*

William R. Morse | John H. Mowbray
Harold M. Morse | Christopher H. Byrd
Kimberly A. Buchanan

For full biographical listings, see the Martindale-Hubbell Law Directory

PICO & MITCHELL (AV)

2000 South Eastern Avenue, 89104
Telephone: 702-457-9099
FAX: 702-457-8451
Email: lawyers@picomitchell.com

MEMBERS OF FIRM

James F. Pico
Christy Brad Escobar
Bert O. Mitchell
James R. Rosenberger
E. Breen Arntz

ASSOCIATES

Michelle Schwarz
Jill M. Chase
Rebecca L. Mastrangelo
Daniel E. Carvalho
Stephen H. Rogers

Representative Clients: Home Insurance Co.; State Farm Mutual Insurance Co.; Industrial Indemnity Insurance Co.; Great American Insurance Co.; Argonaut Insurance Cos.; Clark County Medical Society; Rose de Lima Hospital; Fairway Chevrolet; American States Insurance Co.; The Hartford Insurance Co.

For full biographical listings, see the Martindale-Hubbell Law Directory

SCHRECK MORRIS (AV)

1200 Bank of America Plaza, 300 South Fourth Street, 89101
Telephone: 702-382-2101
Fax: 702-382-8135; 702-474-9422
URL: http://www.schreckmorris.com
Reno, Nevada Office: 100 West Liberty, Suite 940, 89501.
Telephone: 775-322-7777.
Facsimile: 775-322-7791.

MEMBERS OF FIRM

Frank A. Schreck
Ann Morgan
Steve Morris
Sean T. McGowan
Andrew S. Brignone
Ellen Schulhofer
Leslie Terry Jones
James J. Pisanelli
Mary Kristina Pickering
Clark V. Vellis
John A. Godfrey
Todd L. Bice

ASSOCIATES

James R. Chamberlain
John P. Desmond
Dennis V. Gallagher
Adam P. Segal
Margaret L. Sanner
Matthew McCaughey
F. Edward Mulholland, II
Amelia R. De Los Santos
Elizabeth M. Fielder
Wendy Medura
Elayna Youchah
Robert J. Grasso
Sonia C. Vermeys
Shawn G. Pearson
Denise Michaelides
David Dornak
Mary J. Drury
Matthew L. Heinhold
Paul D. Colton

For full biographical listings, see the Martindale-Hubbell Law Directory

SMITH LARSEN & WIXOM, CHARTERED (AV)

3360 West Sahara Avenue, Suite 175, 89102
Telephone: 702-252-5002
Fax: 702-252-5006
Email: slwlaw@slwlaw.com

Jay Earl Smith
Kent F. Larsen
Michael B. Wixom

Stewart C. Fitts

Representative Clients: City of Las Vegas Redevelopment Agency; Norwest Bank Nevada, N.A.; Wells Fargo Bank; Pioneer Citizens Bank; Commercial Bank of Nevada; Long Beach Mortgage Company; American Fidelity Assurance Company; AMRESCO Capital Corporation; Toyota Motor Credit Corporation; Archon Group.

For full biographical listings, see the Martindale-Hubbell Law Directory

*RENO,** Washoe Co.

ERWIN THOMPSON & HASCHEFF (AV)

A Partnership including Professional Corporations
Suite 424, One East Liberty Street, P.O. Box 40817, 89501-2123
Telephone: 775-786-9494
Facsimile: 775-786-1180
Email: erwin@renolaw.com *URL:* http://www.renolaw.com

Pierre A. Hascheff
Frank W. Thompson
Thomas P. Erwin

Reference: U.S. Bank (Reno, Nevada, Main Office).

For full biographical listings, see the Martindale-Hubbell Law Directory

HALE LANE PEEK DENNISON HOWARD AND ANDERSON (AV)

100 West Liberty Street, Tenth Floor, P.O. Box 3237, 89505
Telephone: 775-327-3000
Telefax: 775-786-6179
Email: info@halelane.com
Las Vegas, Nevada Office: Nevada Financial Center, 2300 West Sahara Avenue, Eighth Floor, Box 8.
Telephone: 702-222-2500.
Fax: 702-365-6940.
Carson City, Nevada Office: 777 East William Street, Suite 200, P.O. Box 2620.
Telephone: 775-684-6000.
Telefax: 775-684-6001.

MEMBERS OF FIRM

Karen D. Dennison
Stephen V. Novacek
R. Craig Howard
Marilyn L. Skender
William C. Davis, Jr.

ASSOCIATE

Kevin M. Crosby

OF COUNSEL

Linda E. Johnson (Resident, Carson City, Nevada)

Representative Clients: Lenders: Bank of America, N.A. Title Companies: Chicago Title Insurance Co. Construction and Development: Caughlin Ranch; Centex Homes.

For Complete List of Firm Personnel, See General Section

For full biographical listings, see the Martindale-Hubbell Law Directory

THOMAS J. HALL (AV)

305 South Arlington Avenue, P.O. Box 3948, 89505
Telephone: 775-348-7011
Telecopier: 775-348-7211
Email: tjhlaw@aol.com

ASSOCIATE

Michael C. Radmilovich

For full biographical listings, see the Martindale-Hubbell Law Directory

MCDONALD CARANO WILSON MCCUNE BERGIN FRANKOVICH & HICKS LLP (AV)

241 Ridge Street, 89501
Telephone: 775-788-2000
Telecopier: 775-788-2020
URL: http://www.mcdonaldcarano.com
Las Vegas, Nevada Office: Suite 1000, 2300 West Sahara Avenue.
Telephone: 702-873-4100.
Telecopier: 702-873-9966.

MEMBERS OF FIRM

John J. McCune
Larry R. Hicks
Leo P. Bergin, III
Andrew P. Gordon
John J. Frankovich
Valerie P. Cooke

ASSOCIATES

Bonnie Fleischer Drinkwater
Jane M. Long (Not admitted in NV)
Andrew S. Gabriel

Representative Clients: Boomtown, Inc.; Eldorado Hotel & Casino; Intermountain Federal Land Bank Association (Nevada Counsel); Jackpot Enterprises, Inc.; James Hardie (USA), Inc.; Pioneer Citizens Bank of Nevada.

For Complete List of Firm Personnel, See General Section

For full biographical listings, see the Martindale-Hubbell Law Directory

WALTHER, KEY, MAUPIN, OATS, COX & LEGOY, A PROFESSIONAL CORPORATION (AV)

Lakeside Professional Plaza, 3500 Lakeside Court, 89509
Telephone: 775-827-2000
Facsimile: 775-827-2185
Mailing Address: P.O. Box 30000, Reno, Nevada, 89520

Steven T. Walther
G. Barton Mowry
Jon J. Key
Procter J. Hug
Ernest J. Maupin
Donald A. Lattin
C. Robert Cox
Gustave J. Rossi
L. Robert LeGoy, Jr.
Robert A. Winkel
Michael E. Malloy
Kurt O. Hunsberger
W. Douglass Maupin
Michael A. Nivinskus
Christopher D. Jaime

Rick R. Hsu
Michaelle D. Rafferty
Debra O. Waggoner

Representative Clients: Bank America of Nevada (Trust Dept.); Bechtel Corporations; Bill Pearce Olds, BMW, Volvo; Wells Fargo, N.A. (Trust Dept.); General Motors Acceptance Corp.; Nevada Realtors; Radiation Oncology Associates; The Ralph M. Parsons Corporation; Parsons Corporation; Reno Air, Inc.

For full biographical listings, see the Martindale-Hubbell Law Directory

Reno—Continued

WOODBURN AND WEDGE (AV)

One East First Street, Suite 1600, P.O. Box 2311, 89505
Telephone: 775-688-3000
Telecopier: 775-688-3088
Email: postmaster@woodburnlaw.com *URL:* http://www.woodburnlaw.com
Las Vegas, Nevada Office: Suite 700 Bank of America Plaza, 300 South Fourth Street.
Telephone: 702-387-1000.
Telecopier: 702-387-0024.

MEMBERS OF FIRM

Casey Woodburn Vlautin
Gordon H. DePaoli
Kirk S. Schumacher
Gregg P. Barnard

ASSOCIATE

Dale E. Ferguson

Representative Clients: Atlantic Richfield Co.; Sierra Pacific Power Co.; The Union Pacific Railroad Co.; Western Union Telegraph Co.; Bank of America; Cyprus Minerals Corp.; The Roman Catholic Bishop of Reno, A Corporation Sole; Shell Oil Co.

For full biographical listings, see the Martindale-Hubbell Law Directory

NEW HAMPSHIRE

HAMPTON, Rockingham Co.

CASASSA AND RYAN (AV)

459 Lafayette Road, 03842
Telephone: 603-926-6336
Fax: 603-926-4127
Email: casassa@concentric.net

MEMBERS OF FIRM

H. Alfred Casassa
John J. Ryan
Peter J. Saari
Robert A. Casassa
Faye R. Goldberg

ASSOCIATE

Daniel R. Hartley

General Counsel: Foss Manufacturing Company.
Representative Clients: Town of Hampton Falls; Town of North Hampton; Rye Beach Village District; Hampton School District; Susan Conway Enterprises; Wal-Mart Inc.

For full biographical listings, see the Martindale-Hubbell Law Directory

*LACONIA,** Belknap Co.

NORMANDIN, CHENEY & O'NEIL (AV)

Normandin Square, 213 Union Avenue, P.O. Box 575, 03247-0575
Telephone: 603-524-4380
Fax: 603-528-6831
Email: nco@lr.net

MEMBERS OF FIRM

Paul L. Normandin
John D. O'Shea, Jr.
Robert A. Dietz

ASSOCIATE

Regina A. Nadeau

Counsel for: Laconia Savings Bank; Lakes Region Mental Health Center; Laconia Airport Authority; Central New Hampshire Realty, Inc.; All Metals Industries, Inc.; Lakes Region Anesthesiology, P.A.; Cormier Corp.; Scotia Technology; Vemaline Products; FEN RealtyTrust.

For Complete List of Firm Personnel, See General Section

For full biographical listings, see the Martindale-Hubbell Law Directory

NEW JERSEY

ATLANTIC CITY, Atlantic Co.

WESTMORELAND, VESPER & SCHWARTZ, A PROFESSIONAL CORPORATION (AV)

Bayport One, Yacht Club Drive Suite 500, 08232-0034
Telephone: 609-645-1111
Fax: 609-646-2781
URL: http://www.westmorelandvesper.com

Rudolph C. Westmoreland
Thomas J. Vesper
Mark G. Schwartz
Dara A. Quattrone

(See Next Column)

David I. Sinderbrand
Katherine M. Morris
Carmelo Tony Torraca

Representative Clients: Cape May Foods; The Bank of New York; Title Company of Jersey; Money Store; Re/Max of New Jersey; AT&T Capital; Unitel Cellular; Yank Boat Works; Tomasello Winery.
Reference: Sun National Bank.

For full biographical listings, see the Martindale-Hubbell Law Directory

BEDMINSTER, Somerset Co.

PURCELL, RIES, SHANNON, MULCAHY & O'NEILL (AV)

One Pluckemin Way, P.O. Box 754, 07921
Telephone: 908-658-3800
Fax: 908-658-4659
Email: general@prsmo.com *URL:* http://www.prsmo.com
Philadelphia, Pennsylvania Office: 12th Floor, East Tower, Centre Square, 1500 Market Square.
Telephone: 215-665-5602.
Fax: 215-569-8228.

MEMBERS OF FIRM

Eugene M. Purcell
William P. Ries
John J. Shannon
Thomas M. Mulcahy
Michael F. O'Neill
David M. Hawkins
Joseph R. Purcell
Kevin R. Brotz
John M. Bowens
Kevin Kovacs
Kenneth D. Merin
Valerie K. Bollheimer
Andrew L. Indeck
Joseph M. Donegan
Mark Mattia

ASSOCIATES

Rita F. Barone
Kathleen J. Devlin
Paul L. Gallagher
Gary Grabas
John R. Haggerty
William T. Hilliard
Eric J. Konecke
Susan Lawless
Michael J. McCaffrey
Kathleen M. Quinn
Thomas Charles Savoth
Donna M. Stephan-Nolan
Barbara C. Zimmerman

OF COUNSEL

David D. Furman
C. Judson Hamlin

LEGAL SUPPORT PERSONNEL

Gary Molloy

Reference: Somerset Trust Co.

For full biographical listings, see the Martindale-Hubbell Law Directory

BERNARDSVILLE, Somerset Co.

SHAIN, SCHAFFER & RAFANELLO, A PROFESSIONAL CORPORATION (AV)

Plaza 202, 150 Morristown Road, Suite 105, 07924
Telephone: 908-953-9300
Fax: 908-953-2969
Email: ssrpc@aol.com

Joel L. Shain
Marguerite M. Schaffer
Richard A. Rafanello
Gary L. Maher
Robert A. Pinel
Phedra R. Rudell (Not admitted in NJ)

OF COUNSEL

Elliott L. Katz

LEGAL SUPPORT PERSONNEL

Tracy DeWitt (Legal Researcher)

For full biographical listings, see the Martindale-Hubbell Law Directory

CHERRY HILL, Camden Co.

FLASTER/GREENBERG, P.C. (AV)

Commerce Center, 1810 Chapel Avenue West, Third Floor, 08002-4609
Telephone: 856-661-1900
Telecopier: 856-661-1919
Email: FIRM@FLASTERGREENBERG.COM *URL:* http://www.flastergreenberg.com

Richard J. Flaster
Stephen M. Greenberg
Laura B. Wallenstein
Allen P. Fineberg
Markley S. Roderick
Peter R. Spirgel
Alan H. Zuckerman
William S. Skinner
J. Philip Kirchner
Paul J. Russoniello
Carl S. Bisgaier
Steven B. Sacharow
E. Richard Dressel
Kenneth S. Goodkind
Frank H. Wisniewski
Alma L. Saravia

OF COUNSEL

Peter M. Dolinger
James J. Binns

(See Next Column)

FLASTER/GREENBERG P.C.—*Continued*

Elizabeth J. Hampton
Jeffrey Herskowitz
Christopher E. Kaltenbach
Steven J. Abrams
Julie A. Williamson
Donna T. Urban
Amelia Carolla
Matthew Azoulay
Elaine J. Petruzziello (Not admitted in NJ)
Ann Marie Iannone
Pasquale Guglietta

LEGAL SUPPORT PERSONNEL

PARALEGALS

Ann Gorman
Patricia D'Alessio
Theresa Cooke
Rosemary Dunaif

For full biographical listings, see the Martindale-Hubbell Law Directory

FLORHAM PARK, Morris Co.

DRINKER BIDDLE & SHANLEY LLP (AV)

A Pennsylvania Limited Liability Partnership
500 Campus Drive, 07932-1047
Telephone: 973-360-1100
Fax: 973-285-1625; 360-9831
URL: http://www.dbr.com
Philadelphia, Pennsylvania Office: Drinker Biddle & Reath LLP, One Logan Square, 18th & Cherry Streets.
Telephone: 215-988-2700.
Telefax: 215-988-2757.
Cable Address: "Debemac."
Washington, D.C. Office: Drinker Biddle & Reath LLP, 1500 K Street, N.W., Suite 1100.
Telephone: 202-842-8800.
Telefax: 202-842-8465.
Princeton, New Jersey Office: Suite 300, 105 College Road East.
Telephone: 609-716-6500.
Telefax: 609-799-7000.
Berwyn, Pennsylvania Office: Drinker Biddle & Reath LLP, Suite 300, 1000 Westlakes Drive.
Telephone: 610-993-2200.
Telefax: 610-993-8585.
New York, New York Office: Drinker Biddle & Reath LLP, 89th Floor, One World Trade Center.
Telephone: 212-321-1812.
Telecopier: 1-212-466-0569.

Gerald W. Hull, Jr.
Glenn S. Pantel
Richard D. Prentice
Robert A. Klausner

COUNSEL

Robert A. Del Vecchio
Stephen A. Urban

Michael E. Rothpletz, Jr.
Dean J. Donatelli
Lisa Ann DeMarzo
Paul C. Pawlowski
Thomas P. Rohan, III
David K. Richter

For Complete List of Firm Personnel, See General Section

For full biographical listings, see the Martindale-Hubbell Law Directory

HACK, PIRO, O'DAY, MERKLINGER, WALLACE & MCKENNA, P.A. (AV)

30 Columbia Turnpike, P.O. Box 941, 07932-0941
Telephone: 973-301-6500
Fax: 973-301-0094
Email: hpom@ix.netcom.com

John M. McKenna

Angela J. Mendelsohn
Peter Nastasi

Representative Clients: Cenlar Federal Savings Bank; County Mortgage Company, Inc.; First Fidelity Bank, N.A., N.J.; Citicorp Mortgage, Inc.; Travelers Insurance Co.; State Farm Insurance Companies; Aetna Life & Casualty Co.

For Complete List of Firm Personnel, See General Section

For full biographical listings, see the Martindale-Hubbell Law Directory

*HACKENSACK,** Bergen Co.

CONTANT, SCHERBY & ATKINS (AV)

33 Hudson Street, 07601
Telephone: 201-342-1070
Fax: 201-342-5213
Email: LawfirmCSA@aol.com *URL:* http://www.lawyers.com/csalaw

MEMBERS OF THE FIRM

John M. Contant (1907-1988)
Richard J. Contant
Michael L. Scherby
Bruce L. Atkins
Matthew S. Rogers
Andrew T. Fede
Brian T. Keane
Robert B. Hille

ASSOCIATES

Geraldine E. Beers
Suzanne J. Ryderman
Lisa R. Aljian
Christina A. Stoneburner
Sheila O'Shea

(See Next Column)

OF COUNSEL

Fenster & Weiss, New City, New York

For full biographical listings, see the Martindale-Hubbell Law Directory

FERRO LABELLA LOGERFO & ZUCKER, A PROFESSIONAL CORPORATION (AV)

The Landmark Building, 27 Warren Street, 07601
Telephone: 201-489-9110
Fax: 201-489-5653

Michael J. Ferro, Jr.
Rocco J. Labella
Michael F. Logerfo
Arthur P. Zucker
Sean M. Aylward
Christopher L. Weiss

Rocio T. Aliaga
Melanie J. Scroble
E. Vicki Arians

Representative Clients: Summit Bank; CoreStates New Jersey National Bank; Bio Medic Corp.; Lab Products, Inc.; COSCO North Americas, Inc.; Thomas J. Lipton Co.

For full biographical listings, see the Martindale-Hubbell Law Directory

HEIN, SMITH, BEREZIN, MALOOF & JACOBS, L.L.C. (AV)

Court Plaza East, 19 Main Street, 07601-7023
Telephone: 201-487-7400
Telecopier: 201-487-4228
Email: counsel@heinsmith.com

MEMBERS OF FIRM

Robert J. Maloof
Robert L. Baum

OF COUNSEL

Seymour A. Smith

For Complete List of Firm Personnel, See General Section

For full biographical listings, see the Martindale-Hubbell Law Directory

HOGAN, PALACE & SCULLY (AV)

20 Court Street, 07601
Telephone: 201-342-4422
Fax: 201-342-2554
Email: hpsnj@bellatlantic.net *URL:* http://www.lawyers.com/hogan&palace

MEMBERS OF FIRM

Thomas A. Hogan
Thomas W. Palace
Michael R. Scully

LEGAL SUPPORT PERSONNEL

Shannon S. Casey (Real Estate Paralegal)

Reference: Bergen Commercial Bank, New Jersey.

For full biographical listings, see the Martindale-Hubbell Law Directory

STEPHEN H. ROTH (AV)

62 Summit Avenue, 07601
Telephone: 201-489-3737
Fax: 201-489-0557

ASSOCIATE

Michele M. De Santis

For full biographical listings, see the Martindale-Hubbell Law Directory

SHAPIRO & CROLAND (AV)

A Partnership including Professional Corporations
Continental Plaza II, 411 Hackensack Avenue, 07601
Telephone: 201-488-3900
Fax: 201-488-9481

Barry I. Croland, P.C.
Robert P. Shapiro, P.C.
Barry L. Baime
Jay Rubenstein
Kenneth S. Apfel
Kenneth S. Goldrich, P.C.
Bruce J. Ackerman
Stuart Reiser, P.C.
Meridith J. Bronson
John P. Di Iorio
David O. Marcus
Robert F. Green
Lizabeth Sarakin
David Torchin
Robin C. Bogan
Craig D. Spector

OF COUNSEL

Harvey R. Sorkow

Donald R. Sorkow (1930-1985)

Reference: Bank of New York-National Community Division.

For full biographical listings, see the Martindale-Hubbell Law Directory

SOKOL, BEHOT AND FIORENZO (AV)

433 Hackensack Avenue, 07601
Telephone: 201-488-1300
Fax: 201-488-6541

(See Next Column)

SOKOL, BEHOT AND FIORENZO, *Hackensack—Continued*

MEMBERS OF FIRM

Leon J. Sokol
Joseph F. Behot, Jr.
Joseph B. Fiorenzo
Jeffrey A. Zenn
Arthur Bergman
Michael P. Feltman

ASSOCIATES

Siobhan Spillane Bailey
Mitchell B. Levine
Steven Seigel
Andrew S. Bosin

COUNSEL

Alan Prigal

For full biographical listings, see the Martindale-Hubbell Law Directory

STOLDT, HORAN AND KOWAL, A PROFESSIONAL CORPORATION (AV)

Continental Plaza I, 401 Hackensack Avenue, 07601
Telephone: 201-646-9200
Telecopier: 201-646-0167
Email: shlaw@bellatlantic.net *URL:* http://www.lawyers.com/stoldthoran&kowal

Sydney V. Stoldt, Jr.
John D. Horan
Dorothy A. Kowal
Heather A. Gallagher
Brian O'Reilly

OF COUNSEL

Judith R. Levinson

For full biographical listings, see the Martindale-Hubbell Law Directory

HAWTHORNE, Passaic Co.

JEFFER, HOPKINSON & VOGEL (AV)

(Formerly Jeffer, Walter, Tierney, DeKorte, Hopkinson & Vogel)
Law Building, 1600 Route 208N, P.O. Box 507, 07507
Telephone: 973-423-0100
Fax: 973-423-5614
Tequesta, Florida Office: Jeffer, Cioffi & Cicalese. 250 Tequesta Drive, 33469.
Telephone: 561-747-6000.
Fax: 561-575-9167.

MEMBERS OF FIRM

Herman M. Jeffer
Reginald F. Hopkinson
Jerome A. Vogel

ASSOCIATES

Melinda B. Maidens
E. David Becker
David H. Altman

Counsel for: Brioschi, Inc.; Opici Wine Co.; Gas Pumpers of America Corp.; Burroughs Development Corp.; Cedar Hill Developers; McBride Enterprises; Thomas Construction Co.

For Complete List of Firm Personnel, See General Section

For full biographical listings, see the Martindale-Hubbell Law Directory

LINDEN, Union Co.

WINETSKY AND WINETSKY (AV)

401 North Wood Avenue, P.O. Box 1053, 07036
Telephone: 908-486-2761; 908-486-2762
Fax: 908-486-2661

MEMBERS OF FIRM

Lewis Winetsky (1929-1986)
Charles N. Winetsky

Reference: First Union Bank, Linden, New Jersey.

For full biographical listings, see the Martindale-Hubbell Law Directory

LIVINGSTON, Essex Co.

SKOLOFF & WOLFE, P.C. (AV)

293 Eisenhower Parkway, 07039
Telephone: 973-992-0900
Fax: 973-992-0301
Morristown, New Jersey Office: 10 Park Place.
Telephone: 973-267-3511.

Saul A. Wolfe

For Complete List of Firm Personnel, See General Section

For full biographical listings, see the Martindale-Hubbell Law Directory

MANASQUAN, Monmouth Co.

RICHARD W. WIGHT (AV)

Mallard Park Professional Building, 200 Atlantic Avenue, 08736
Telephone: 732-528-3700
Fax: 732-528-3833
Email: wihgt@monmouth.com *URL:* http://www.lawyers.com/wight

For full biographical listings, see the Martindale-Hubbell Law Directory

MONTCLAIR, Essex Co.

GARIPPA AND DAVENPORT, A PROFESSIONAL CORPORATION (AV)

66 Park Street, 07042
Telephone: 201-744-1688
Telecopier: 201-744-1641
Email: gd@taxappeal.com *URL:* http://www.taxappeal.com

John E. Garippa
Seth I. Davenport
Philip J. Giannuario
Gregory G. Lotz

Daniel J. Mulligan

For full biographical listings, see the Martindale-Hubbell Law Directory

MEISLIK & LEVAVY (AV)

66 Park Street, 07042
Telephone: 973-783-3000
Fax: 973-744-5757
Email: meislik@meislik.com *URL:* http://www.meislik.com

MEMBERS OF FIRM

Ira Meislik
Bardin Levavy

For full biographical listings, see the Martindale-Hubbell Law Directory

MOORESTOWN, Burlington Co.

FREDERICK W. HARDT (AV)

Suite 101, 300 Chester Avenue, P.O. Box 840, 08057-2512
Telephone: 609-234-4141
Fax: 609-273-8617

ASSOCIATE

Pamela A. Moy

For full biographical listings, see the Martindale-Hubbell Law Directory

*MORRISTOWN,** Morris Co.

McKIRDY AND RISKIN, A PROFESSIONAL CORPORATION (AV)

136 South Street, 07962-2379
Telephone: 973-539-8900
Fax: 973-984-5529
URL: http://www.lawyers.com/m&rlaw

Edward D. McKirdy
Harry J. Riskin
John H. Buonocore, Jr.
Thomas M. Olson
Anthony F. Della Pelle

Debra L. Kudriavetz

For full biographical listings, see the Martindale-Hubbell Law Directory

PITNEY, HARDIN, KIPP & SZUCH LLP (AV)

P.O. Box 1945, 07962-1945
Telephone: 973-966-6300
New York City: 212-687-6000
Telex: 642014
Telecopier: 973-966-1550
URL: http://www.phks.com
New York, New York Office: 711 Third Avenue, 10017-4014.
Telephone: 212-687-6000.
Fax: 212-682-3485.

MEMBERS OF FIRM

David J. Connolly, Jr.
Lawrence F. Reilly
Roger R. Gottilla
Glenn C. Geiger
Joel M. Rosen
Thomas J. Malman
Colleen R. Donovan
Deirdre E. Moore

COUNSEL

Paul E. Flanagan

ASSOCIATES

Michael T. Lavigne
Grace J. Shin
Susan Yeu
Michael J. Vitiello

Representative Clients: American Home Products Corporation; AT&T Corp.; HFS,Incorporated; Ford Motor Credit.

For Complete List of Firm Personnel, See General Section

For full biographical listings, see the Martindale-Hubbell Law Directory

*NEWARK,** Essex Co.

CARPENTER, BENNETT & MORRISSEY (AV)

Three Gateway Center, 17th Floor, 100 Mulberry Street, 07102-4079
Telephone: 973-622-7711
New York City: 212-943-6530
Telex: 139405
Telecopier: 973-622-5314
Email: cbm@carpben.com

(See Next Column)

CARPENTER, BENNETT & MORRISSEY—*Continued*

MEMBERS OF FIRM

Francis X. O'Brien
John D. Goldsmith

OF COUNSEL

Edward F. Day, Jr.

ASSOCIATES

Hans G. Polak
Mary B. Goldhirsch
Marny Lundy Solazzo

Representative Clients: General Motors Corp.; E. I. du Pont de Nemours and Co.; Texaco Inc.; AT&T; Litton Industries; ITT Industries, Inc.; International Flavors & Fragrances Inc.; Johnson & Johnson; Prudential Insurance Company of America; Hartford Insurance Co.

For Complete List of Firm Personnel, See General Section

For full biographical listings, see the Martindale-Hubbell Law Directory

HELLRING LINDEMAN GOLDSTEIN & SIEGAL LLP (AV)

One Gateway Center, 07102-5386
Telephone: 973-621-9020
Fax: 973-621-7406
Englewood, New Jersey Office: 32-40 North Dean Street.
Telephone: 201-871-3060.

Philip Lindeman, II
Michael Edelson
Charles Oransky
Robert S. Raymar
John A. Adler
Judah I. Elstein
David N. Narciso

For Complete List of Firm Personnel, See General Section

For full biographical listings, see the Martindale-Hubbell Law Directory

MCCARTER & ENGLISH, LLP (AV)

Four Gateway Center, 100 Mulberry Street, P.O. Box 652, 07101-0652
Telephone: 973-622-4444
Telecopier: 973-624-7070
URL: http://www.mccarter.com
Cherry Hill, New Jersey Office: 1820 Chapel Avenue West, Suite 380.
Telephone: 609-662-8444.
Telecopier: 609-662-6203.
New York, New York Office: Suite 2247, One World Trade Center.
Telephone: 212-466-9018.
Telecopier: 212-432-6568.
Boca Raton, Florida Office: 2255 Glades Road, Suite 319-A.
Telephone: 561-994-6262.
Telecopier: 561-241-0798.
Wilmington, Delaware Office: Mellon Bank Center, 919 Market Street.
Telephone: 302-654-8010.
Telecopier: 302-654-0795.
Philadelphia, Pennsylvania Office: One Commerce Square, 2005 Market Street, Suite 3600.
Telephone: 215-557-7700.
Telecopier: 215-557-6544.

MEMBERS OF FIRM

Lois M. Van Deusen
Frank E. Ferruggia
Carol C. Stern
Martin F. Dowd

For Complete List of Firm Personnel, See General Section

For full biographical listings, see the Martindale-Hubbell Law Directory

MCMANIMON & SCOTLAND, L.L.C. (AV)

One Riverfront Plaza, 4th Floor, 07102-5311
Telephone: 973-622-1800
Fax: 973-622-7333; 973-622-3744

MEMBERS OF FIRM

Joseph P. Baumann, Jr.
John V. Cavaliere
John B. Hall
Glenn F. Scotland
Ronald J. Ianoale
Andrea L. Kahn
Jeffrey G. Kramer
Leslie G. London
Edward J. McManimon, III

OF COUNSEL

Norman M. Robertson
Carla J. Brundage

ASSOCIATES

Peter S. Crisafi
Sheila Newsome Maddox
M. Frances Ciesla
Kristin Dwyer Ganley
Joseph C. Jasaitis
Stephen N. Severud
Thomas J. Hastie, Jr.

LEGAL SUPPORT PERSONNEL

Helen Lysaght

PARALEGALS

Sandra Simoes

For full biographical listings, see the Martindale-Hubbell Law Directory

MEYNER AND LANDIS (AV)

One Gateway Center, Suite 2500, 07102-5311
Telephone: 973-624-2800
Fax: 973-624-0356
Email: attys@meyner.com *URL:* http://www.meyner.com

Robert B. Meyner (1908-1990)
Edwin C. Landis, Jr.
John N. Malyska
William J. Fiore
Anthony F. Siliato
Francis R. Perkins
Howard O. Thompson
Scott T. McCleary
Linda Townley Snyder
William H. Schmidt, Jr.
David B. Grantz

For full biographical listings, see the Martindale-Hubbell Law Directory

SILLS CUMMIS RADIN TISCHMAN EPSTEIN & GROSS, A PROFESSIONAL CORPORATION (AV)

One Riverfront Plaza, 07102-5400
Telephone: 973-643-7000
Fax: 973-643-6500
Telex: 820630 Sillsbeck Nwk
Email: sillsmail@sillscummis.com *URL:* http://www.sillscummis.com
Atlantic City, New Jersey Office: 17 Gordon's Alley.
Telephone: 609-344-2800.
New York, N.Y. Office: 712 Fifth Avenue.
Telephone: 212-643-7000.
Washington, D.C. Office: 1800 K Street, N.W.
Telephone: 202-296-4750.

MEMBERS OF FIRM

Michael B. Tischman
Jeffrey Hugh Newman
Morris Yamner
Gerald Span
Margaret F. Black
David J. Rabinowitz
Thomas Jay Hall
Ted Zangari
Robert R. DiVita

Noel D. Humphreys
Katherine Sloss (Not admitted in NJ)
Harry B. Noretsky
Karen Levine
Robert R. Hempstead
Ben-Tzion H. Zur
Richard T. Cadigan
Kathleen A. Crocco
Naomi I. Cohen

Representative Clients: Ann Taylor; B. Moss; Christian Bernard; Circuit City Stores; Edison Brothers Stores; J.C. Penny; Mandee Shops; Office Depot; Payless Shoe Source; Philips International Holding Co.

For Complete List of Firm Personnel, See General Section

For full biographical listings, see the Martindale-Hubbell Law Directory

*NEWTON,** Sussex Co.

TRAPASSO, DOLAN & HOLLANDER (AV)

40 Park Place, P.O. Box 99, 07860
Telephone: 973-383-3233
Fax: 973-383-4922
Email: TDH@nac.net

MEMBERS OF FIRM

Albert P. Trapasso (1923-1990)
Frank A. Dolan (Retired)
Sanford Lloyd Hollander
Paul L. Abramo
David J. Weaver
William E. Hinkes

ASSOCIATE

John D. Williams

OF COUNSEL

Chester Kosarek

Representative Clients: Town of Newton; Green Township; Fredon Township; Borough of Ogdensburg; Hopatcong Board of Education; Newton Memorial Hospital; The Nature Conservancy; Sussex County Farm and Horse Show Association, Inc.; Andover Nursing Home; Newton Medical Building.
Reference: Newton Trust Company; Sussex County State Bank.

For full biographical listings, see the Martindale-Hubbell Law Directory

NORTH BRUNSWICK, Middlesex Co.

BORRUS, GOLDIN, FOLEY, VIGNUOLO, HYMAN, STAHL & CLARKIN, A PROFESSIONAL CORPORATION (AV)

2875 U.S. Highway 1, Route 1 & Finnigans Lane, P.O. Box 7463, 08902
Telephone: 732-422-1000
Fax: 732-422-1016
Email: attys@borrus.com *URL:* http://www.borrus.com

Jack Borrus
Martin S. Goldin
David M. Foley
Anthony B. Vignuolo
Jeffrey M. Hyman
James E. Stahl
James F. Clarkin III
Eileen Mary Foley

Robert C. Nisenson
Rosalind Westlake
Lisa M. Vignuolo
Steven L. Fox
Peter A. Vignuolo
Gerald T. Foley (1903-1976)

(See Next Column)

BORRUS, GOLDIN, FOLEY, VIGNUOLO, HYMAN, STAHL & CLARKIN A PROFESSIONAL CORPORATION, *North Brunswick—Continued*

Representative Clients: Summit Bank; R. J. Reynolds Tobacco Co.; K. Hovnanian Enterprises, Inc.; Johnson and Johnson; Foster Wheeler, Inc.; Hartz Mountain Industries; Middlesex County Vocational Services Commission; Borough of South Plainfield Board of Adjustment; U-Haul of Northern NJ.

For full biographical listings, see the Martindale-Hubbell Law Directory

BUSCH AND BUSCH, LLP (AV)

215 North Center Drive, Commerce Center - U.S. #1 South, P.O. Box 7448, 08902-7448
Telephone: 732-821-2300
Telecopier: 732-821-5588
Email: busch@ifu.net

MEMBERS OF FIRM

Lewis D. Busch (1901-1986)
Henry Busch (Retired)
Malcolm R. Busch
Ronald J. Busch
Bertram E. Busch
Mark N. Busch
Leonard R. Busch
Steven F. Satz
Donald J. Sears

ASSOCIATE

Paul Alan VanBuskirk

Representative Clients: Utica Mutual Insurance Co.; New Brunswick Tomorrow; Township of South Brunswick; Township of Monroe, Board of Education; Township of East Brunswick; Minnesota Mutual Life Insurance Co.

For full biographical listings, see the Martindale-Hubbell Law Directory

NUTLEY, Essex Co.

ARTHUR S. HORN, P.A. (AV)

247 Franklin Avenue, 07110
Telephone: 973-235-1550
Fax: 973-235-1582

Arthur S. Horn

Reference: First Union Bank.

For full biographical listings, see the Martindale-Hubbell Law Directory

PARAMUS, Bergen Co.

STRASSER & ASSOCIATES, A PROFESSIONAL CORPORATION (AV)

Paramus Plaza I, 140 Route 17 North, Suite 265, 07652-2816
Telephone: 201-262-7177
Fax: 201-262-3113

William I. Strasser

Conrad M. Olear
Constantinos J. Ballas

Representative Clients: Consumer Value Stores (CVS); Melville Corp.; Melville Realty Corp.; Linens 'N Things, Inc.; This End Up Furniture Co., Inc.; Universal Foods Corp.; Essex Computers, Inc.; Polevoy Associates; Footstar, Inc.; Bob's Stores.

For full biographical listings, see the Martindale-Hubbell Law Directory

PARSIPPANY, Morris Co.

CUYLER BURK (AV)

Parsippany Corporate Center, Four Century Drive, 07054-4663
Telephone: 973-734-3200
Telex: 429071
Telecopier: 973-734-3201
Email: Main@Cuyler.com *URL:* http://www.cuyler.com
New York, New York Office: 350 Fifth Avenue, Suite 3304. 10018.
Telephone: 212-645-4039.

MEMBERS OF FIRM

Stephen D. Cuyler
Jo Ann Burk
Stefano Calogero
David L. Menzel
Peter Petrou
Richard A. Crooker
Michael J. Jones

COUNSEL

Anne M. Mohan
Frank J. Miele

ASSOCIATES

Jan C. Walker
Kathleen Jane Olear
Claudia L. Marchese
Mark G. Eliades
Kimberly A. Joel
Christy A. Ramunno
Catherine E. Youngman
Andrew K. Craig
Mark S. Winter
Thomas J. Castano
Hugo A. Hilgendorff, IV

LEGAL SUPPORT PERSONNEL

Frederick M. H. Currie, Jr.

For full biographical listings, see the Martindale-Hubbell Law Directory

PRINCETON, Mercer Co.

MASON, GRIFFIN & PIERSON, A PROFESSIONAL CORPORATION (AV)

101 Poor Farm Road, 08540
Telephone: 609-921-6543
Fax: 609-683-7978
Email: mgp@mgplaw.com *URL:* http://www.mgplaw.com
Flemington, New Jersey, Office: P.O. Box 2420, 151 Main Street, 08822.
Telephone: 908-782-2900.
Fax: 908-782-2428. Email: denilaw@erols.com.

Ralph S. Mason (1913-1988)
Craig H. Davis (1947-1997)
Gordon D. Griffin
Kester R. Pierson
Edwin W. Schmierer
Kristina Pike Hadinger
Donald B. Veix, Jr.
Charles F. Harris
Edmond M. Konin
Shawn M. Neufeld
Valerie L. Howe

Barbara J. Morgan
Christopher H. DeGrezia
F. Clifford Gibbons
Carleen M. Steward
Georgia M. Fraser

OF COUNSEL

William P. Deni, Sr.
Jules Farkas

Representative Clients: Connecticut Indemnity Company; Griffith Electric Supply Company, Inc.; Johnson Controls World Services, Inc.; The Pennington School; Township of Montgomery; Township of Princeton; Management Planning, Inc.

For full biographical listings, see the Martindale-Hubbell Law Directory

MCCARTHY AND SCHATZMAN, P.A. (AV)

228 Alexander Street, P.O. Box 2329, 08543-2329
Telephone: 609-924-1199
Fax: 609-683-5251

John F. McCarthy, Jr.
Richard Schatzman
G. Christopher Baker
John F. McCarthy, III
Michael A. Spero
Barbara Strapp Nelson
W. Scott Stoner
James J. Britt, Jr.

Charly Gayden

Representative Clients: Trustees of Princeton University; Carnegie Center Associates; Merrill Lynch Pierce Fenner & Smith, Inc.; Calton Homes, Inc.

For full biographical listings, see the Martindale-Hubbell Law Directory

STARK & STARK, A PROFESSIONAL CORPORATION (AV)

Princeton Pike Corporate Center, P.O. Box 5315, 08543-5315
Telephone: 609-896-9060
Fax: 609-896-0629
Email: info@stark-stark.com *URL:* http://www.stark-stark.com

Timothy P. Duggan
A. Christopher Florio
Daniel L. Haggerty, III
Richard F. Hamilton

OF COUNSEL

Sharon L. Wynn

Mary W. Barrett
David J. Byrne
Francis J. McGovern, Jr.
Christopher J. Preate
Rachel L. Stark

For full biographical listings, see the Martindale-Hubbell Law Directory

ROCHELLE PARK, Bergen Co.

FORMAN HOLT & ELIADES LLC (AV)

218 Route 17 North, 07662
Telephone: 201-845-1000
Fax: 201-845-9112
Email: firm@formanlaw.com

Charles M. Forman
Michael E. Holt
Daniel M. Eliades, Jr.
Joseph M. Cerra
Julie L. Singer
Kim R. Lynch

OF COUNSEL

Erin J. Kennedy

For full biographical listings, see the Martindale-Hubbell Law Directory

ROSELAND, Essex Co.

BRACH, EICHLER, ROSENBERG, SILVER, BERNSTEIN, HAMMER & GLADSTONE, A PROFESSIONAL CORPORATION (AV)

101 Eisenhower Parkway, 07068
Telephone: 973-228-5700
Telecopier: 973-228-7852
Email: law@bracheichler.com *URL:* http://www.bracheichler.com

(See Next Column)

BRACH, EICHLER, ROSENBERG, SILVER, BERNSTEIN, HAMMER & GLADSTONE A PROFESSIONAL CORPORATION—*Continued*

Thomas E. Cohn
Burton L. Eichler
Alan R. Hammer
Bruce Kleinman
Paul F. Rosenberg
Michael I. Schneck

Jeffrey H. Itzkowitz
Joseph M. Davis
John P. Inglesino
Allen J. Popowitz
Evan S. Glanz
Jill H. Blumberg

OF COUNSEL

Harris R. Silver
George Y. Sodowick

COUNSEL

Alois V. Habjan

Representative Clients: ARC Properties, Inc.; Bocina Development; Cali Associates; Cirkus Real Estate, Inc.; Eastman Construction Co.; Gebroe-Hammer Associates; Growth & Income, Inc.; I. Heller Construction Co. Inc.; The Kushner Companies; Tibor Pivko + Company.

For Complete List of Firm Personnel, See General Section

For full biographical listings, see the Martindale-Hubbell Law Directory

POST, POLAK, GOODSELL & MACNEILL, P.A. (AV)

75 Livingston Avenue, 07068-3701
Telephone: 973-994-1100
Telecopier: 973-994-1705
Email: administrator@ppgm.com
New York, New York Office: 575 Madison Avenue, Suite 1006.
Telephone: 212-486-1455.

John N. Post
Robert A. Goodsell
Paul D. Strauchler

Nilufer O. DeScherer

PARALEGALS

Susan B. Cobb
Nancy G. Barrett

For Complete List of Firm Personnel, See General Section

For full biographical listings, see the Martindale-Hubbell Law Directory

RUTHERFORD, Bergen Co.

BRUINOOGE & ASSOCIATES (AV)

85 Orient Way, 07070
Telephone: 201-939-3303
Telefax: 201-939-4057
Email: bandalaw@bellatlantic.net *URL:* http://www.lawyers.com/bruinoogelaw

Thomas H. Bruinooge

Michael E. Patunas

OF COUNSEL

Gilbert W. Bowman
Brian D. Fuhro
Jean-Marc Zimmerman

For full biographical listings, see the Martindale-Hubbell Law Directory

SHIP BOTTOM, Ocean Co.

SHACKLETON, HAZELTINE AND BISHOP (AV)

22nd Street and Long Beach Boulevard, P.O. Box 410, 08008
Telephone: 609-494-2136
Telefax: 609-494-0870
Fairfield, New Jersey Office: One Passaic Avenue.
Telephone: 201-882-4646.
Telefax: 201-882-4620.

MEMBERS OF FIRM

Richard J. Shackleton
Colin R. Hazeltine
James E. Bishop

ASSOCIATES

Laura M. O'Regan
Marc Baden Powell
Robert Emmet Rue

OF COUNSEL

Kenneth L. Leiby, Jr. (Resident, Fairfield Office)

References: Commerce Bank/Shore N/A; Summit Bank Corp.

For full biographical listings, see the Martindale-Hubbell Law Directory

*SOMERVILLE,** Somerset Co.

SCHACHTER, TROMBADORE, OFFEN, STANTON & PAVICS, A PROFESSIONAL CORPORATION (AV)

45 East High Street, P.O. Box 520, 08876-0520
Telephone: 908-722-5700
Fax: 908-722-8853

Thomas A. Pavics

(See Next Column)

Timothy P. McKeown

For full biographical listings, see the Martindale-Hubbell Law Directory

RAYMOND R. & DAVID W. TROMBADORE, P.C. A PROFESSIONAL CORPORATION (AV)

33 East High Street, 08876
Telephone: 908-722-7555
Fax: 908-722-6269
URL: http://www.trombadorelaw.com

Raymond R. Trombadore
David W. Trombadore

OF COUNSEL

Ann W. Trombadore

References: Summit Bank; Somerset Savings & Loan Assn.

For full biographical listings, see the Martindale-Hubbell Law Directory

SUMMIT, Union Co.

BOURNE, NOLL & KENYON, A PROFESSIONAL CORPORATION (AV)

382 Springfield Avenue, P.O. Box 690, 07902-0690
Telephone: 908-277-2200
Facsimile: 908-277-6808

Cary R. Hardy
Charles R. Berman
Martin Rubashkin
Roger Mehner
James R. Ottobre
Lawrence A. Rudnick
John F. Kuntz

OF COUNSEL

Edward T. Kenyon
Robert B. Bourne

COUNSEL

Ellyn A. Draikiwicz

Jaime A. O'Brien
Timothy A. Kalas
Alan F. Schwarz
Ross W. Smith

For full biographical listings, see the Martindale-Hubbell Law Directory

TEANECK, Bergen Co.

ROSENBLUM, WOLF & LLOYD, A PROFESSIONAL CORPORATION (AV)

Glenpointe Centre East, 300 Frank W. Burr Boulevard, 07666
Telephone: 201-836-0400
Fax: 201-836-8365
Email: rwlnj@cs.com

Leo Rosenblum (1906-1990)
Edward G. Rosenblum
Nathan P. Wolf
John R. Lloyd

Reference: The Bank of New York, formerly National Community Bank.

For full biographical listings, see the Martindale-Hubbell Law Directory

*TOMS RIVER,** Ocean Co.

NOVINS, YORK & PENTONY, A PROFESSIONAL CORPORATION (AV)

202 Main Street, 08753
Telephone: 732-349-7100
Email: info@nyplaw.com

Robert J. Novins (1910-1973)
Robert F. Novins
Harvey L. York
Kenneth R. Pentony
Ann K. Haskell
Robert M. McKeon

W. Mark Bayles
Robert J. Roth
Gregory S. Heizler
Anthony M. Pagano
Danziger Patricia Christoff
Michael A. Jacobus

OF COUNSEL

William E. O'Connor
Lorna S. Scanlon

Counsel for: Allstate Insurance Co.; Motor Club of America.

For full biographical listings, see the Martindale-Hubbell Law Directory

STARKEY, KELLY, BLANEY & WHITE (AV)

2 Hooper Avenue, 08753
Telephone: 732-240-3600
Fax: 732-240-3777
Brick, New Jersey Office: 459 Jack Martin Boulevard, 08724.
Telephone: 732-840-5900.
Fax: 732-840-5901.
Manasquan, New Jersey Office: 23 Route 71, 08736.
Telephone: 732-223-7328.
Fax: 732-240-3777.

(See Next Column)

STARKEY, KELLY, BLANEY & WHITE, *Toms River—Continued*

MEMBERS OF FIRM

Charles E. Starkey
William V. Kelly
James M. Blaney

ASSOCIATES

Natalie Pouch
Scott W. Kenneally
Anthony Mancuso
Susan K. White
Robert A. Bauer
Brent D. Miller

Representative Clients: Hartford Insurance Co.; New Jersey Education Assn.; New Jersey Psychiatric Assn.; Ocean County Utilities Authority; Brick Township Municipal Utilities Authority; Manasquan River Regional Sewerage Authority; Hanover Insurance Co.; John Hancock Insurance Co.; Rider Inc. Co.

For full biographical listings, see the Martindale-Hubbell Law Directory

*TRENTON,** Mercer Co.

SCHRAGGER, LAVINE & NAGY (AV)

Mountainview Office Park, 840 Bear Tavern Road, Suite 307, 08628
Telephone: 609-771-0700
Fax: 609-771-9535

Bruce M. Schragger
Raymond L. Nagy
James A. Schragger

OF COUNSEL

Henry C. Schragger
Alan S. Lavine
A. Jerome Moore

LEGAL SUPPORT PERSONNEL

Annemarie Saccani (Office Administrator)

Representative Clients: New Jersey Manufacturers Insurance Co.; Mercer County Community College; Mercer Mutual Insurance Co.; New Jersey Optometric Association; Allentown Caging; Dick Greenfield Dodge.

For Complete List of Firm Personnel, See General Section

For full biographical listings, see the Martindale-Hubbell Law Directory

VINELAND, Cumberland Co.

RIESENBURGER & KIZNER, P.C. (AV)

190 South Main Road, P.O. Box 640, 08362-0640
Telephone: 856-691-6200
Telecopier: 856-696-8150
Email: rieskizn@eticomm.net *URL:* http://www.rklawyers.com
Cherry Hill Office: 413 Route 70 East.
Telephone: 609-354-7500.

Franklin J. Riesenburger
Mitchell H. Kizner

Vivian R. Salmon
Robert P. Merenich

For full biographical listings, see the Martindale-Hubbell Law Directory

WESTFIELD, Union Co.

LINDABURY, MCCORMICK & ESTABROOK, P.A. (AV)

53 Cardinal Drive, P.O. Box 2369, 07091
Telephone: 908-233-6800
Fax: 908-233-5078
New York, N.Y. Office: 26 Broadway, Suite 2300.
Telephone: 212-742-3390.
Fax: 212-269-5016.

William R. Watkins
James K. Estabrook
John R. Blasi
Robert S. Burney
John H. Schmidt, Jr.
David R. Pierce
Jay Lavroff

OF COUNSEL

Kenneth L. Estabrook

Representative Clients: Elberon Development Co.; E'Town Corp.; Kingwood Township Board of Adjustment; Kingwood Township Planning Board; T. Rowe Price-Renaissance Fund, Ltd.

For Complete List of Firm Personnel, See General Section

For full biographical listings, see the Martindale-Hubbell Law Directory

WESTMONT, Camden Co.

EARP COHN P.C. (AV)

222 Haddon Avenue, 08108
Telephone: 856-854-7100
Fax: 856-854-6434
Email: administrator@earpcohn.com *URL:* http://www.earpcohn.com
Philadelphia, Pennsylvania Office: 2 Penn Center Plaza, Suite 200. 19102-1706.
Telephone: 215-963-9520.
Fax: 215-963-9620.

(See Next Column)

Thomas L. Earp
Kathryn R. Renahan
Richard B. Cohn
Carol Schuler Harding
Irving Koffler
Samantha P. Zazzo
Douglas F. Johnson
Jeff Schwartz

For full biographical listings, see the Martindale-Hubbell Law Directory

WOODBRIDGE, Middlesex Co.

GREENBAUM, ROWE, SMITH, RAVIN, DAVIS AND HIMMEL LLP (AV)

Metro Corporate Campus I, P.O. Box 5600, 07095-0988
Telephone: 732-549-5600
Fax: 732-549-1881 529
Email: info@greenbaumlaw.com *URL:* http://www.greenbaumlaw.com
Roseland, New Jersey Office: 6 Becker Farm Road.
Telephone: 973-535-1600.
Fax: 973-535-1698.

MEMBERS OF FIRM

Robert S. Greenbaum
Peter A. Buchsbaum
Arthur M. Greenbaum
Thomas J. Denitzio, Jr.
Wendell A. Smith
Kenneth T. Bills
Dean A. Gaver
Christine F. Li
Robert C. Schachter
Meryl Ann Greenhause Gonchar
Benjamin D. Lambert, Jr.
Lloyd H. Tubman

ASSOCIATES

Steven Firkser
Rosemary Culcasi
Marc D. Policastro
Arren S. Goldman

For Complete List of Firm Personnel, See General Section

For full biographical listings, see the Martindale-Hubbell Law Directory

WILENTZ, GOLDMAN & SPITZER, A PROFESSIONAL CORPORATION (AV)

90 Woodbridge Center Drive Suite 900, Box 10, 07095
Telephone: 732-636-8000
Telecopier: 732-855-6117
URL: http://www.newjerseylaw.com
Eatontown, New Jersey Office: Meridian Center I, Two Industrial Way West, 07724.
Telephone: 732-542-4500.
Telecopier: 732-493-8387.
New York, New York Office: Wall Street Plaza, 88 Pine Street, 9th Floor, 10005.
Telephone: 212-267-3091.
Telecopier: 212-267-3828.

Robert A. Petito
Joseph J. Jankowski
Nicholas L. Santowasso
Roy H. Tanzman
Vincent P. Maltese
Jeffrey R. Rich
Sheldon E. Jaffe
Myron Rosner

Susanne Salzer O'Donohue
Lori Ann Buza
Elizabeth W. Eaton

Representative Clients: Bankers Savings; Amerada Hess Corp.; First Union National Bank.

For Complete List of Firm Personnel, See General Section

For full biographical listings, see the Martindale-Hubbell Law Directory

NEW MEXICO

*ALBUQUERQUE,** Bernalillo Co.

FAIRFIELD, FARROW, FLOWERS, PIERSON & STROTZ, P.C. (AV)

2400 Louisiana N.E., AFC 3, Suite 100, P.O. Box 35400, 87176-5400
Telephone: 505-881-8300
Fax: 505-889-0553
Email: fairlaw@nm.net

John Edwin Farrow
Raymond R. (Dick) Flowers, Jr.
Bruce H. Strotz

OF COUNSEL

Steven R. Fairfield

Representative Clients: Albuquerque Title Co.; First American Title Co.

For full biographical listings, see the Martindale-Hubbell Law Directory

KENNETH C. LEACH, P.C. (AV)

1110 Pennsylvania N.E., Suite A, 87110
Telephone: 505-243-3322
Fax: 505-242-1268
URL: http://www.lawyers.com/leachlaw

Kenneth C. Leach

(See Next Column)

KENNETH C. LEACH, P.C.—*Continued*

Jonathan Reid Mowrer

LEGAL SUPPORT PERSONNEL

Wayne C. Edwards (CEO)
Marilyn Alires Marsh (Paralegal)
Virginia Bosworth (Paralegal)

For full biographical listings, see the Martindale-Hubbell Law Directory

MILLER, STRATVERT & TORGERSON, P.A. (AV)

500 Marquette Avenue, N.W., Suite 1100, P.O. Box 25687, 87102
Telephone: 505-842-1950
Facsimile: 505-243-4408
Email: info@mstLAW.com *URL:* http://www.mstLAW.com
Farmington, New Mexico Office: 300 West Arrington, Suite 300, P.O. Box 869.
Telephone: 505-326-4521.
Facsimile: 505-325-5474.
Las Cruces, New Mexico Office: 500 South Main, Suite 800, P.O. Box 1209.
Telephone: 505-523-2481.
Facsimile: 505-526-2215.
Santa Fe, New Mexico Office: 150 Washington Avenue, Suite 300, P.O. Box 1986.
Telephone: 505-989-9614.
Facsimile: 505-989-9857.

Lyman G. Sandy
Seth V. Bingham (Resident at Farmington Office)
Sharon P. Gross
J. Scott Hall (Resident at Santa Fe Office)
Joel T. Newton (Resident at Las Cruces Office)
Thomas M. Domme
Dana M. Kyle (Resident at Las Cruces Office)

COUNSEL

Paul W. Robinson
Ralph Wm. Richards (Resident at Las Cruces Office)
Ross B. Perkal
James J. Widland
Bradley D. Tepper

For Complete List of Firm Personnel, See General Section

For full biographical listings, see the Martindale-Hubbell Law Directory

MYERS, OLIVER & PRICE, P.C. (AV)

1401 Central Avenue NW, 87104
Telephone: 505-247-9080
Fax: 505-247-9109
Email: mop@moplaw.com

John A. Myers
Scott Oliver
Charles P. Price III
Kevin J. McCready
Hope Mead Wynn

For full biographical listings, see the Martindale-Hubbell Law Directory

OMAN, GENTRY & YNTEMA, P.A. (AV)

Suite 201, 215 Gold Avenue, S.W., P.O. Box 1748, 87103
Telephone: 505-843-9565
Fax: 505-242-2879

Kester L. Oman
Hessel E. Yntema, III
Christopher B. Behling

Representative Clients: S & J Enterprises, Inc.; E. T. Consultants, Inc.
Reference: Norwest Bank.

For full biographical listings, see the Martindale-Hubbell Law Directory

RODEY, DICKASON, SLOAN, AKIN & ROBB, P.A. (AV)

Albuquerque Plaza, Suite 2200, 201 Third Street, N.W., P.O. Box 1888, 87103-1888
Telephone: 505-765-5900
Fax: 505-768-7395
Email: info@rodey.com *URL:* http://www.rodey.com
Santa Fe, New Mexico Office: Suite 101 Marcy Plaza, 123 East Marcy Street, P.O. Box 1357, 87504-1357.
Telephone: 505-984-0100.
Fax: 505-989-9542.

Robert M. St. John
Mark K. Adams
John P. Salazar
John P. Burton (Resident, Santa Fe Office)
Catherine T. Goldberg
Jo Saxton Brayer
Nancy J. Appleby
David C. Davenport, Jr. (Resident, Santa Fe Office)
Joseph B. Rochelle
Mark A. Smith
Jay D. Hill
Susan K. Barger

OF COUNSEL

John D. Robb

For Complete List of Firm Personnel, See General Section

For full biographical listings, see the Martindale-Hubbell Law Directory

USSERY & PARRISH, P.A. (AV)

200 Rio Grande Valley Building, 501 Tijeras Avenue, N.W., P.O. Box 487, 87103-0487
Telephone: 505-247-0145
Fax: 505-843-6912

Albert T. Ussery
David C. Mielke
L. Lamar Parrish (1936-1998)

Jennifer L. Bradley
Kathleen Baca

Counsel for: Isleta Pueblo; Sandia Pueblo; San Juan Pueblo; Zia Pueblo.
Representative Client: Auerbach Financial, Inc.
Reference: Wells Fargo Bank New Mexico, N.A.

For full biographical listings, see the Martindale-Hubbell Law Directory

WATROUS & REARDON (AV)

A Partnership of Professional Associations
3733 Eubank Boulevard, N.E., 87111-3536
Telephone: 505-293-7000
Fax: 505-293-0831

MEMBERS OF FIRM

Thomas S. Watrous (P.A.)
Walter L. Reardon, Jr., (P.A.)

Representative Clients: U.S. West, Inc.; State Street Bank and Trust Co.; Angel Fire Ski Area and Resort; Air Touch Cellular; American Linen; Rio Pecos Oil Company; First Health Plan (FHP); Albuquerque Title Co.; Furrow Building materials; Melloy Nissan.

For full biographical listings, see the Martindale-Hubbell Law Directory

*LAS CRUCES,** Dona Ana Co.

REEVES, CHAVEZ, GREENFIELD & WALKER, P.A. (AV)

300 South Water Street, P.O. Box 2769, 88004-2769
Telephone: 505-524-9617
Fax: 505-524-1954
Email: rcgw@zianet.com

B. James Reeves
Frank N. Chavez
Charlotte Greenfield
William A. Walker, Jr.
Kelly P. Albers
Joyce A. Montes
William R. Anderson
Carolyn J. Baca

Glenn D. Hall
CaraLyn Banks

For full biographical listings, see the Martindale-Hubbell Law Directory

*SANTA FE,** Santa Fe Co.

CATRON, CATRON & SAWTELL, A PROFESSIONAL ASSOCIATION (AV)

2006 Botulph Road, P.O. Box 788, 87504-0788
Telephone: 505-982-1947
Telecopier: 505-986-1013
Email: catronlaw@aol.com

Thomas B. Catron III
John S. Catron
Fletcher R. Catron
W. Anthony Sawtell

LEGAL SUPPORT PERSONNEL

Peggy L. Feldt (Certified Public Accountant)

For Complete List of Firm Personnel, See General Section

For full biographical listings, see the Martindale-Hubbell Law Directory

HERRERA, LONG & POUND, P.A. (AV)

2200 Brothers Road, P.O. Box 5098, 87502-5098
Telephone: 505-982-8405
Fax: 505-982-8513
Email: hlplaw@aol.com

Judith C. Herrera
Nancy R. Long
John B. Pound

Mark E. Komer

LEGAL SUPPORT PERSONNEL

Shauna Allen Metzo

Reference: Bank of America.

For full biographical listings, see the Martindale-Hubbell Law Directory

SCHEUER, YOST & PATTERSON, A PROFESSIONAL CORPORATION (AV)

125 Lincoln Avenue, Suite 223, P.O. Drawer 9570, 87504
Telephone: 505-982-9911
505-989-7500
Fax: 505-982-1621
Email: firm@santafelawyers.com

(See Next Column)

SCHEUER, YOST & PATTERSON, A PROFESSIONAL CORPORATION, *Santa Fe—Continued*

Melvin T. Yost (Retired)
Ralph H. Scheuer
Mel E. Yost
John N. Patterson
Byron L. Treaster
Donald A. Walcott
Christopher M. Grimmer
Daniel J. Monte

OF COUNSEL

Reverdy Johnson

Representative Clients: Century Bank, FSB; Chama Title Co.; Los Alamos National Bank; Santa Fe Abstract, Ltd.; St. John's College; Santa Fe Housing Authority; Sun Loan Companies; Territorial Abstract & Title Co.; Texas Commerce Bank; Ticor Title Insurance Co.

For full biographical listings, see the Martindale-Hubbell Law Directory

WHITE, KOCH, KELLY & MCCARTHY, A PROFESSIONAL ASSOCIATION (AV)

433 Paseo De Peralta, P.O. Box 787, 87504-0787
Telephone: 505-982-4374
ABA/NET: 1154
Fax: 505-982-0350; 984-8631
Email: WKKM@NM.NET

John F. McCarthy, Jr.
Charles W. N. Thompson, Jr.
Sandra J. Brinck
Mary E. Walta

Representative Clients: First American Title Insurance Co.; Chicago Title Insurance Co.; Title Resources Insurance Co.; Lawyers Title Insurance Company; Santa Fe Association of Realtors; Santa Fe Estates, Inc.

For Complete List of Firm Personnel, See General Section

For full biographical listings, see the Martindale-Hubbell Law Directory

NEW YORK

*ALBANY,** Albany Co.

ISEMAN, CUNNINGHAM, RIESTER & HYDE, LLP (AV)

9 Thurlow Terrace, 12203
Telephone: 518-462-3000
Telecopier: 518-462-4199
Email: lawfirm@icrh.com *URL:* http://www.icrh.com
Canandaigua, New York Office: 37 East Gibson Street, P.O. Box 179, 14424.
Telephone: 716-394-1450.
Fax: 716-394-5121.

MEMBERS OF FIRM

Frederick C. Riester
Michael J. Cunningham
Robert Hall Iseman
Carol Ann Hyde
Linda J. Clark

Brian M. Culnan
Kihyun S. Kim
Richard A. Frankel
Stephanie E. Moriarty
Valerie R. Lape Handy
Marcia B. Smith
Ellen Gillerman Cox
Jennifer A. Grego
Cara E. Johnson

OF COUNSEL

Michael J. McNeil
Deborah A. Kirby

For full biographical listings, see the Martindale-Hubbell Law Directory

SEGEL, GOLDMAN & MAZZOTTA, P.C. (AV)

5 Washington Square Washington Avenue Extension, 12205
Telephone: 518-452-0941
Telecopier: 518-452-0417
Email: mazzotta@capital.net

Kenneth B. Segel
Thomas G. Mazzotta
Paul J. Goldman
Jeffrey A. Siegel

Robert J. Koshgarian
Polly J. Feigenbaum
Debra J. Lambek

OF COUNSEL

Peter Bishko
Richard J. Sherwood

For full biographical listings, see the Martindale-Hubbell Law Directory

SHANLEY, SWEENEY, REILLY & ALLEN, P.C. (AV)

The Castle at Ten Thurlow Terrace, 12203
Telephone: 518-463-1415
Fax: 518-463-3210
Email: lawyers@shanleysweeney.com *URL:* http://www.shanleysweeney.com

(See Next Column)

Michael P. Shanley, Jr.
Robert L. Sweeney
J. Stephen Reilly
John L. Allen
Gregory D. Faucher
J. Michael Naughton
Steven S. Heyman
Scott P. Olson
David C. Kuracina
Thomas A. Shepardson
Melissa M. Beskid
Mark T. Sweeney

Christopher E. Buckey
Stacey Weisenfeld

For full biographical listings, see the Martindale-Hubbell Law Directory

EUGENE M. SNEERINGER, JR. (AV)

50 Chapel Street, 12207
Telephone: 518-434-0127
Fax: 518-434-9997
Email: emsjr@sprtitle.com *URL:* http://www.sprtitle.com
Troy, New York Office: 52 Second Street.
Telephone: 518-434-0127.
Fax: 518-434-9997.
Ballston Spa, New York Office: 36 Remsen Street.
Telephone: 518-885-8700.
Fax: 518-884-2564.

ASSOCIATES

Stephen W. Easton
Robert J. Sneeringer
William A. Kuchinski

OF COUNSEL

Eugene M. Sneeringer

Reference: Key Bank of New York.

For full biographical listings, see the Martindale-Hubbell Law Directory

SULLIVAN, CUNNINGHAM, KEENAN, MRAZ & LEMIRE (AV)

152 Central Avenue, 12206
Telephone: 518-434-1022
Fax: 518-434-2304
Email: complaw@empireone.net

William J. Sullivan (1904-1980)

MEMBERS OF FIRM

John J. Cunningham
Michael J. Keenan
Mary J. Mraz
Christopher R. Lemire

ASSOCIATES

Michael D. Violando
Nannette R. Kelleher
Michael Rosenblum

Reference: Trustco Bank.

For full biographical listings, see the Martindale-Hubbell Law Directory

TABNER, RYAN AND KENIRY (AV)

26 Computer Drive West, P.O. Box 12605, 12212-2605
Telephone: 518-459-9000
Telecopier: 518-459-9165
Email: trk@tabnerryanandkeniry.com

MEMBERS OF FIRM

John W. Tabner
William F. Ryan, Jr.
William J. Keniry

OF COUNSEL

C. Theodore Carlson

ASSOCIATES

Eric N. Dratler
Jennifer K. Corona
Donald W. Biggs

Special Counsel for: Water and Sewer District for Towns of Colonie, Coxsackie, Guilderland, Johnstown, Queensbury, Rotterdam and Village Castleton.
References: FleetBank; Trustco Bank.

For full biographical listings, see the Martindale-Hubbell Law Directory

*AUBURN,** Cayuga Co.

CONTIGUGLIA & GIACONA (AV)

The Federal House, 7 William Street, 13021
Telephone: 315-253-9746
Fax: 315-253-0880

MEMBERS OF FIRM

Anthony J. Contiguglia (1897-1986)
Louis P. Contiguglia
Samuel P. Giacona

David A. Contiguglia

Representative Clients: Cayuga Bank; Cayuga Homesite Development Corp.; Homested Funding Corp.; Statewide Funding Corp.; American Residential Mortgage Corp.; GE Capital Home Equity Services; Commonwealth Mortgage Co., Inc.
References: Marine Midland Bank (Auburn Office); Cayuga Savings Bank; The Key Bank of Central New York.

For full biographical listings, see the Martindale-Hubbell Law Directory

*BATH,** Steuben Co.

Cole Law Offices, P.C. (AV)

7 East Steuben Street, P.O. Box 232, 14810
Telephone: 607-776-3306
Fax: 607-776-4189
Email: RCole@LinkNY.Com
Hammondsport, New York Office: Railroad Station Depot, Water Street, P.O. Box 396, 14840.
Telephone: 607-569-2213.
Fax: 607-569-2214,

Robert H. Cole

Christine Valkenburgh
James H. Burns
William H. Reed

General Counsel for: Bath National Bank; Mercury Aircraft, Inc.
Local Counsel for: Equitable Life Assurance Society of the United States.
Reference: Bath National Bank.

For full biographical listings, see the Martindale-Hubbell Law Directory

*BINGHAMTON,** Broome Co.

Aswad & Ingraham (AV)

46 Front Street, 13905
Telephone: 607-722-3495
Fax: 607-722-2566; 607-722-7269
Email: office@AILAW.COM

MEMBERS OF FIRM

Richard N. Aswad
Charles O. Ingraham
Thomas A. Saitta
James F. Haley, Jr.
Angelina C. Cutrona
William M. Thomas

SPECIAL COUNSEL

James F. Moran

ASSOCIATE

Jeffrey Husisian

Reference: Charter One Bank.

For full biographical listings, see the Martindale-Hubbell Law Directory

Ball, McDonough & Artz, P.C. (AV)

The Professional Building, 117 Hawley Street, P.O. Box 1740, 13902-1740
Telephone: 607-772-6070
Fax: 607-772-0173

Dwight R. Ball
Kevin F. McDonough
Philip J. Artz

For full biographical listings, see the Martindale-Hubbell Law Directory

BRIDGEHAMPTON, Suffolk Co.

Payne, Wood & Littlejohn (AV)

1936 Montauk Highway, P.O. Box 1980, 11932-1980
Telephone: 516-537-3100
Telefax: 516-537-0560
Email: mail@paynewood.com
Melville, New York Office: 290 Broad Hollow Road.
Telephone: 516-547-8400.
Telefax: 516-547-0501.
Locust Valley, New York Office: 83 Birch Hill Road.
Telephone: 516-676-0700.
Telefax: 516-676-0703.

MEMBER OF FIRM

Alan C. Polacek (Managing Partner)

For full biographical listings, see the Martindale-Hubbell Law Directory

BRONXVILLE, Westchester Co.

Griffin, Coogan & Veneruso, P.C. (AV)

51 Pondfield Road, 10708
Telephone: 914-961-1300
Telecopier: 914-961-1476; 914-961-9385

William E. Griffin
James M. Coogan
James J. Veneruso

Daniel J. Griffin
Paul R. Herrick
Thomas G. Marzullo
William E. Sulzer (Not admitted in NY)

Approved Closing Attorneys: Hudson Valley Bank.

For full biographical listings, see the Martindale-Hubbell Law Directory

*BUFFALO,** Erie Co.

Block & Colucci, P.C. (AV)

1250 Statler Towers, 14202-3695
Telephone: 716-854-4080; 1-800-388-2595
Fax: 716-854-0059
Litigation Telephone: 716-853-4080
Jupiter, Florida Office: 1001 N. U.S. Highway One, Suite 400.
Telephone: 561-747-0110.
Fax: 561-743-0046.
Clifton Park, New York Office: 9 Executive Park Drive, P.O. Box 5018.
Telephone: 518-348-1000.
Fax: 518-348-2000.
Rochester, New York Office: 311 Alexander Street, Suite 415.
Telephone: 716-454-1660.
Fax: 716-454-7461.

Lester H. Block (1906-1997)
Ernest L. Colucci (1909-1989)
Anthony J. Colucci, Jr.

Elpiniki M. Bechakas
Brandi Burns (Resident, Clifton Park Office)
Heather A. Corey-Mongue (Resident, Clifton Park Office)
Dennis M. Hyatt
Scott J. Leitten (Not admitted in NY)
Mark J. Longo
Melanie C. Marotto
Joel P. Peller
Michael W. Schafer
Debra A. Spellman
Jennifer L. Stoeckl (Resident, Rochester Office)
Kevin P. Wheatley (Resident, Clifton Park Office)

References: Manufacturers & Traders Trust Co.; Palm Beach National Bank & Trust Co.

For full biographical listings, see the Martindale-Hubbell Law Directory

Brown & Kelly, L.L.P. (AV)

1500 Liberty Building, 14202-3663
Telephone: 716-854-2620
Fax: 716-854-0082
Email: mail@brownkelly.com *URL:* http://www.brownkelly.com

MEMBERS OF FIRM

Thomas J. Kelly
Rodney O. Personius
Frederick D. Turner
Paul Michael Hassett
Peter E. Klaasesz
Donald B. Eppers
Andrew D. Merrick
William P. Wiles
William D. Harrington
Joseph M. Schnitter
Paula L. Feroleto
Daniel J. Marren
Lisa T. Sofferin

OF COUNSEL

Ogden R. Brown
Charles F. Harrington
James T. Duggan
Karen Cook Serotte
Roland R. Benzow
Philip B. Abramowitz
Elizabeth R. O'Connor
Catherine E. Marra

ASSOCIATES

David S. Zygaj
Olney H. Clowe
Brian M. Melber
David O. Teach
Patricia S. Ciccarelli
Susan J. Schmidt

For full biographical listings, see the Martindale-Hubbell Law Directory

Rolls Kohn & Associates, LLP (AV)

Twenty Court Street, 14202-3201
Telephone: 716-856-2700
Fax: 716-856-2777

MEMBERS OF FIRM

James E. Rolls
Gerald L. Kohn

Robert M. Goldstein

For full biographical listings, see the Martindale-Hubbell Law Directory

Sullivan & Oliverio (AV)

600 Main Place Tower, 14202-3706
Telephone: 716-854-5300
Telecopier: 716-854-5299
Email: sulliolaw@aol.com

MEMBERS OF FIRM

Richard T. Sullivan
B. P. Oliverio
Bruce W. Hoover

Thomas M. Moll
Michael E. Appelbaum
Kevin M. Carter

OF COUNSEL

Paul D. Pearson

For full biographical listings, see the Martindale-Hubbell Law Directory

CARLE PLACE, Nassau Co.

DOLLINGER, GONSKI & GROSSMAN (AV)

One Old Country Road, 11514
Telephone: 516-747-1010
Telecopier: 516-747-2494
Fairfield, New Jersey Office: 710 Route 46 East, Suite 212, 07004.
Telephone: 973-276-0530.
Fax: 973-276-0533.

MEMBERS OF FIRM

Matthew Dollinger
Dennis M. Gonski
Floyd G. Grossman

ASSOCIATES

Leslie Ann Foodim
Bruce N. Roberts
Michael J. Spithogiannis
Alicia B. Devins
Jessica M. Seidman
Mindy Anne Wallach
Joshua N. Krellen

OF COUNSEL

Joseph Goldstein

Reference: Marine Midland National Bank, Carle Place, New York.

For full biographical listings, see the Martindale-Hubbell Law Directory

*COOPERSTOWN,** Otsego Co.

GOZIGIAN, WASHBURN & CLINTON (AV)

Orange L. Van Horne (1907-1946)
Van Horne & Feury (1946-1970)
Van Horne, Feury & Gozigian (1970-1979)
Feury, Gozigian & Washburn (1979-1992)
201-204 Key Bank Building, P.O. Box 431, 13326
Telephone: 607-547-2522
Fax: 607-547-2845
Email: GozigianWC@aol.com

MEMBERS OF FIRM

Edward Gozigian
Philip L. Washburn
David J. Clinton

ASSOCIATE

E.W. Garo Gozigan

Counsel for: New York Central Mutual Insurance Co.
Local Counsel for: Key Bank, N.A.; Empire Farm Credit ACA.

For full biographical listings, see the Martindale-Hubbell Law Directory

EAST MEADOW, Nassau Co.

CERTILMAN BALIN ADLER & HYMAN, LLP (AV)

90 Merrick Avenue, 11554
Telephone: 516-296-7000
Telecopier: 516-296-7111
URL: http://www.cbah.com

MEMBERS OF FIRM

Ira J. Adler
David Z. Herman
Dale Allinson
Richard Herzbach
Michael C. Axelrod
M. Allan Hyman
Herbert M. Balin
Bernard Hyman
Bruce J. Bergman
Donna-Marie Korth
Eileen O'Boyle Bitetto
Steven J. Kuperschmid
Michael D. Brofman
Jeffrey S. Lisabeth
Lewis J. Campanella
Jaspreet S. Mayall
Morton L. Certilman
Richard J. McCord
Robert J. Ciovacco
Thomas J. McNamara
Brian J. Davis
Michael F. O'Shea
Wayne G. Edwards
Marilyn Price
Joseph P. Famighetti
Fred S. Skolnik
Howard R. Gladston
Louis Soloway
Murray Greenberg
Harold Somer
Gavin C. Grusd
Howard M. Stein
Brian K. Ziegler

OF COUNSEL

Daniel S. Cohan
Joseph N. Mondello

ASSOCIATES

Lawrence A. Altholtz
James G. Kapralos
Meredith W. Ayres
Linda P. Manfredi
Daniel J. Baker
Edward G. McCabe
Kimberly I. Berson
Patrick McCormick
Scott B. Black
Susan L. McWalters
Brendan J. DeRiggi
Jothy Narendran
Thomas M. Farrell
James A. Rose
Mary C. Florentz
Wayne J. Schaefer
Candace Reid Gladston
Leslie H. Scharf
Harry P. Greenbaum
Afsheen Ashley Shah
David E. Herold
Victor Spinnelli
Jodi S. Hoffman
Russell H. Stern
Robert G. Wilk

For full biographical listings, see the Martindale-Hubbell Law Directory

GARDEN CITY, Nassau Co.

COLLERAN, O'HARA & MILLS (AV)

1225 Franklin Avenue, Suite 450, 11530
Telephone: 516-248-5757; 212-614-9119
Telecopier: 516-742-1765

Walter M. Colleran (1912-1998)
Edward J. Groarke
Richard L. O'Hara
Christopher P. O'Hara
John F. Mills
Carol L. O'Rourke

ASSOCIATES

Scott P. Shelkin
Michael D. Jew
Jennifer Berlingieri
Stephanie Suarez
Denis A. Engel
Robin A. Young

COUNSEL

Glenn A. Krebs
Elizabeth Pollina Donlon
Patricia Ann Harold

LEGAL SUPPORT PERSONNEL

Ann Carolan
Jack Groarke
Laura Harrington
Madeleine B. Solarchik

For full biographical listings, see the Martindale-Hubbell Law Directory

EUGENE S. GINSBERG (AV)

300 Garden City Plaza, 11530-3324
Telephone: 516-746-9307
Fax: 516-393-8282

For full biographical listings, see the Martindale-Hubbell Law Directory

MORITT, HOCK & HAMROFF, LLP (AV)

400 Garden City Plaza, Suite 202, 11530
Telephone: 516-873-2000
Fax: 516-873-2010
Email: lawyers@mhhlaw.com *URL:* http://www.mhhlaw.com

PARTNERS

Neil J. Moritt
David H. Cohen
Alan S. Hock
Robert M. Tils
Marc L. Hamroff
Gary C. Hisiger

ASSOCIATES

William P. Laino
David A. Loglisci
Robert S. Cohen
David Z. Ottensoser
Terese L. Arenth
Ellen R. Leibowitz
Leslie A. Berkoff
Amy J. Zamir
Michael S. Re
Michael Cardello, III
Gary E. Ostroff

For full biographical listings, see the Martindale-Hubbell Law Directory

GREAT NECK, Nassau Co.

STEVEN WIMPFHEIMER (AV)

8 Bond Street, Suite 203, 11021
Telephone: 516-504-8585
Telecopier: 516-504-1003
Email: WIMPF@WORLDNET.ATT.NET *URL:* http://www.lawyers.com/wimpfheimer

For full biographical listings, see the Martindale-Hubbell Law Directory

HAUPPAUGE, Suffolk Co.

LAW OFFICES OF HARVEY B. BESUNDER (AV)

The Woodlands, 700 Veterans Memorial Highway, Suite 310, 11788
Telephone: 516-361-5131
Fax: 516-361-5134

For full biographical listings, see the Martindale-Hubbell Law Directory

HUNTINGTON, Suffolk Co.

SMYTH & LACK (AV)

143 Main Street, 11743
Telephone: 516-271-7500
Telecopier: 516-271-7504
URL: http://www.lawyers.com/smyth&lacklaw

MEMBERS OF FIRM

Vincent A. Smyth
James J. Lack

ASSOCIATES

Dana M. Barberis
Edmund J.M. Smyth
Karen E. Nora

Reference: Chemical Bank.

For full biographical listings, see the Martindale-Hubbell Law Directory

ISLANDIA, Suffolk Co.

LAW OFFICES OF ANDREW D. PRESBERG, P.C. (AV)

100 Corporate Plaza, 11722
Telephone: 516-232-4444
Fax: 516-232-2603
Email: preslaw@erols.com *URL:* http://www.presberg.com

Andrew D. Presberg

For full biographical listings, see the Martindale-Hubbell Law Directory

JAMESTOWN, Chautauqua Co.

ERICKSON, WEBB & SCOLTON (AV)

111 West Second Street, 14701
Telephone: 716-488-1178
Fax: 716-488-1448
Email: ews@netsync.net

MEMBERS OF FIRM

Alton R. Erickson (1904-1968)
Philip A. Erickson
Paul V. Webb, Jr.
Bruce S. Scolton
Lyle T. Hajdu

References: Marine Midland Bank, N.A.; Chase Manhattan Bank.

For full biographical listings, see the Martindale-Hubbell Law Directory

JERICHO, Nassau Co.

BLAU, KRAMER, WACTLAR & LIEBERMAN, P.C. (AV)

100 Jericho Quadrangle, 11753
Telephone: 516-822-4820
Telecopier: 516-822-4824
Email: BKWLLAW@aol.com

Harvey R. Blau
Edward I. Kramer
David H. Lieberman, P.C.
Edward S. Wactlar
Lonnie Coleman
Nancy D. Lieberman

Reference: Fleet Bank.

For full biographical listings, see the Martindale-Hubbell Law Directory

MARTIN, VAN DE WALLE, DONOHUE, McGAHAN, CATALANO & FAIRGRIEVE (AV)

555 North Broadway, P.O. Box 350, 11753
Telephone: 516-681-3100
Telecopier: 516-681-5357

MEMBERS OF FIRM

Jules Martin (1928-1995)
Charles R. Van de Walle
Joseph A. Guarino (1946-1991)
Nicholas J. Donohue
James M. McGahan
Thomas C. Catalano, Jr.
Scott Fairgrieve
Michael Belitsis

ASSOCIATES

Randi M. Seidner
Laurie Ann Corallo

Representative Clients: Fidelity National Title Insurance Company of New York; Bancker Construction Corp.; Festo Corp.; First Investors Corp.; First Financial Savings Bank, S.L.A.; Oppenheimer Funds, Inc.; Old Republic National Title Insurance Company; New York State Land Title Association, Inc.; Chase Manhattan Mortgage Corp.; First Investors Corp.; Leaseway Transportation Corp.; Jones Fund; Northeast Adjustment Co., Inc.; Chase Manhattan Bank, N.A.; Capital Trading Corp.; New York Schools Insurance Reciprocal; New York Municipal Insurance Reciprocal.

For full biographical listings, see the Martindale-Hubbell Law Directory

*KINGSTON,** Ulster Co.

HOWARD C. ST. JOHN AND ASSOCIATES (AV)

P.O. Box 4380, 12402
Telephone: 914-338-4500
Fax: 914-338-0638

ASSOCIATES

Richard A. Anthony
Joseph L. Canino
John J. Cook
Michael Francis Jordan
J. Michael Bruhn, Jr.

General Counsel for: Ulster Savings Bank.
Representative Clients: Government Employees Insurance Co.; National Grange Insurance Co.; New York Central Mutual Fire Insurance Co.; AT&T (local counsel); Volkswagen of America, Inc. (local counsel); Inland Steel (local counsel).

For full biographical listings, see the Martindale-Hubbell Law Directory

LAKE SUCCESS, Nassau Co.

DIKMAN AND DIKMAN (AV)

5 Dakota Drive, Suite 208, 11042
Telephone: 516-354-2526
Fax: 516-354-2528
Jamaica, New York Office: 161-10 Jamaica Avenue,
Telephone: 718-739-4830.

MEMBERS OF FIRM

Leo Dikman
David S. Dikman

Reference: Chase Manhattan Bank.

For full biographical listings, see the Martindale-Hubbell Law Directory

MELVILLE, Suffolk Co.

LAMB & BARNOSKY, LLP (AV)

534 Broadhollow Road-CS 9034, 11747-9034
Telephone: 631-694-2300
Telecopier: 631-694-2309
Email: thefirm@lambbarnosky.com *URL:* http://www.lambbarnosky.com

PARTNERS

Eugene R. Barnosky
Robert H. Cohen
Marcia Lyn Finkelstein
Michael J. Heller
Gary Holman
Scott M. Karson
P. L. Lamb
Arthur A. Lane
Joel M. Markowitz
Gerald P. Rosenberg
Patrice Dowd Shenn

OF COUNSEL

Louis E. Black
James F. Gesualdi
Howard W. Newman
Joseph J. Salvatore
Joseph H. Wishod

COUNSEL

Lloyd K. Chanin
Scott P. McBride

ASSOCIATES

Cathleen D. Allen
Catherine Healy Kanzler
Rita Fishman Sheena
Shari Lee Sugarman

For full biographical listings, see the Martindale-Hubbell Law Directory

PAYNE, WOOD & LITTLEJOHN (AV)

290 Broad Hollow Road, 11747-4805
Telephone: 516-547-8400
Telefax: 516-547-0501
Email: mail@paynewood.com
Bridgehampton, New York Office: 1936 Montauk Highway. P.O. Box 1980, 11932.
Telephone: 516-537-3100.
Telefax: 516-537-0560.
Locust Valley, New York Office: 83 Birch Hill Road, 11560.
Telephone: 516-676-0700.
Fax: 516-676-0703.

MEMBERS OF FIRM

Philip C. Kilian
Beverly J. Bell
Alan C. Polacek (Managing Partner)
Jed C. Albert
Peter B. Colgrove
Theresa K. Quigley
Janet Ganio
John P. McEntee

OF COUNSEL

Daren A. Rathkopf
Victor C. McCuaig, Jr.
Warren I. Titus, Jr.
Edwin F. Hendrickson
James A. Eisenman

COUNSEL

Kevin J. Barry
Mark A. Cuthbertson

ASSOCIATES

Susan H. Jannace
Ilene S. Kreitzer
Joseph L. Hunsberger
Carol King
Kevin M. Knab
Walter J. Johnson

For full biographical listings, see the Martindale-Hubbell Law Directory

MERRICK, Nassau Co.

JACK A. BENNARDO (AV)

2163 Merrick Avenue, P.O. Box 360, 11566
Telephone: 516-378-1110
Fax: 516-378-1252
Email: jablaw1@aol.com *URL:* http://www.lawyers.com/bennardolaw

For full biographical listings, see the Martindale-Hubbell Law Directory

MIDDLETOWN, Orange Co.

MACVEAN, LEWIS, SHERWIN & McDERMOTT, P.C. (AV)

34 Grove Street, P.O. Box 310, 10940
Telephone: 914-343-3000
Fax: 914-343-3866

(See Next Column)

New York—Continued

LOEB & LOEB LLP (AV)

A Limited Liability Partnership including Professional Corporations
345 Park Avenue, 10154-0037
Telephone: 212-407-4000
Facsimile: 212-407-4990
Email: info@loeb.com *URL:* http://www.loeb.com
Los Angeles, California Office: Suite 1800, 1000 Wilshire Boulevard, 90017-2475.
Telephone: 213-688-3400.
Facsimile: 213-688-3460.
Century City (Los Angeles), California Office: Suite 2200, 10100 Santa Monica Boulevard, Los Angeles, 90067-4164.
Telephone: 310-282-2000.
Facsimile: 310-282-2192.
Nashville, Tennessee Office: 45 Music Square West, 37203-3205.
Telephone: 615-749-8300.
Facsimile: 615-749-8308.
Rome, Italy Office: Piazza Digione 1, 00197.
Telephone: 011-3906-808-8456.
Facsimile: 011-3906-808-8288.

MEMBERS OF FIRM

Michael D. Beck (A.P.C.)
Kenneth D. Freeman
Michael Bryce Kinney
Andrew E. Lippmann
Scott I. Schneider

OF COUNSEL

Frank E. Feder (A P.C.)

ASSOCIATES

Nina B. Luban
Samuel Mark Mizrahi

For Complete List of Firm Personnel, See General Section

For full biographical listings, see the Martindale-Hubbell Law Directory

MCALOON & FRIEDMAN, P.C. (AV)

116 John Street, 10038
Telephone: 212-732-8700
Fax: 212-227-2903

Edward H. McAloon (1908-1986)
Stanley D. Friedman
Gunther H. Kilsch
Theodore B. Rosenzweig
Gary A. Greenfield
Brendan J. Lantier
Lawrence W. Mumm
Laura R. Shapiro
Lisa B. Goldstein
Thomas Medardo Oliva
Adam R. Goldsmith
Wayne M. Roth
Kenneth S. Oliver
Stephen S. York

Jennifer D. Correale
Mark Gregory Duncan
Kenneth Gordon Ellison
Ilene R. Fish
Gillian Fisher
Kenneth Fox
Evette E. Harrison
Alex Johnson
Ross Katz
Sherry Levin
Robin P. Lorell
Carolan Magnoli
Linda P. McMillan
Douglas M. Nadjari
Timothy O'Shaugnessy
Matthew Luke Prisco
Caryn Rosen
Corey Lee Wishner

LEGAL SUPPORT PERSONNEL

Robyn L. Reyes (Firm Administrator)

For full biographical listings, see the Martindale-Hubbell Law Directory

MORGANROTH & MORGANROTH (AV)

156 W. 56th Street, Suite 1101, 10019
Telephone: 212-586-5905
URL: http://www.lawyers.com/morganroth&morganrothlaw
Southfield, Michigan Office: 3000 Town Center, Suite 1500, 48075.
Telephone: 248-355-3084.
Fax: 248-355-3017.

Mayer Morganroth
Jeffrey B. Morganroth

For full biographical listings, see the Martindale-Hubbell Law Directory

OTTERBOURG, STEINDLER, HOUSTON & ROSEN, P.C. (AV)

230 Park Avenue, 29th Floor, 10169
Telephone: 212-661-9100
Telecopier: 212-682-6104

Donald N. Gellert
William M. Silverman
Daniel Wallen
Anthony M. Piccione
Alan Kardon

GENERAL COUNSEL

Kurt J. Wolff

Stephen H. Alpert
Susan A. Joyce

For Complete List of Firm Personnel, See General Section

For full biographical listings, see the Martindale-Hubbell Law Directory

PARKER CHAPIN LLP (AV)

Chrysler Building, 405 Lexington Avenue, 10017
Telephone: 212-704-6000
Telecopier: 212-704-6288
URL: http://www.parkerchapin.com
Great Neck, New York Office: 175 Great Neck Road.
Telephone: 516-482-4422.
Telecopier: 516-482-4469.
Hackensack, New Jersey: 190 Morre Street, Suite 307.
Telephone: 210-883-6400.
Telecopier: 210-883-6404.
Beverly Hills, California: 9454 Wilshire Boulevard.
Telephone: 310-288-8367.
Telecopier: 310-288-8365.

MEMBERS OF FIRM

Miles M. Borden
Aurora Cassirer
Will Burt Sandler

OF COUNSEL

Harvey M. Boneparth
Flora Schnall

For Complete List of Firm Personnel, See General Section

For full biographical listings, see the Martindale-Hubbell Law Directory

PILIERO GOLDSTEIN JENKINS & SULLIVAN, LLP (AV)

292 Madison Avenue, 10017
Telephone: 212-213-8200
Fax: 212-685-2028
Email: lawyers@pgjhlaw.com *URL:* http://www.pgjhlaw.com
Carlstadt, New Jersey Office: One Palmer Terrace.
Telephone: 201-507-5157.
FAX: 201-507-5221.
Washington, D.C. Office: 888 17th Street, N.W., Suite 1100.
Telephone: 202-467-6991.
FAX: 202-467-6703.
San Francisco, California Office: 507 Howard Street, Suite 200.
Telephone: 415-281-3631.
Fax: 415-281-3630.

MEMBERS OF FIRM

Kimberlee S. Bogen
Edward J. Goldstein
Jon Mark Jenkins
Marc A. Lebowitz
Robert D. Piliero
George O. Richardson, III
Michael T. Sullivan

ASSOCIATES

Craig Avedisian
Rosemary G. Feit
Eric M. Kogan
Mariano Schwed

OF COUNSEL

Kenneth D. Arbeeny
Christopher P. Hall

For full biographical listings, see the Martindale-Hubbell Law Directory

RICK, STEINER, P.C. (AV)

Three New York Plaza, 10004
Telephone: 212-422-0488
Facsimile: 212-422-0158

Jay H. Rick
Jacob Steiner
Jack Segal
Alan Fell

Ariane C. Economon

OF COUNSEL

Joel A. Drucker

For full biographical listings, see the Martindale-Hubbell Law Directory

ROSEN, EINBINDER & DUNN, P.C. (AV)

641 Lexington Avenue, 10022
Telephone: 212-888-7717
FAX: 212-980-1444
Email: info@redlawfirm.com *URL:* http://www.redlawfirm.com

Richard L. Rosen
Michael Einbinder
Terrence M. Dunn

Leonardo D'Alessandro

For full biographical listings, see the Martindale-Hubbell Law Directory

ROSS & COHEN, LLP (AV)

711 Third Avenue, 10017
Telephone: 212-370-1200
Telecopier: 212-370-0334
Email: law@rosscohen.com

(See Next Column)

ROSS & COHEN LLP—*Continued*

MEMBERS OF FIRM

Allen Ross, Michael A. Mulqueen, Frederick S. Cohen, Mark Canizio, Dennis A. Konner, Michael L. Chartan, Charles Fastenberg, John S. Wojak, Jr., Gerard J. Romski

ASSOCIATES

Midge J. Nutman, Frank X. Acocella, Andrew L. Richards, David A. Etkind, Lawrence Chiarelli, Lori Marks, Jose A. Aquino, Gregory J. Colao (Not admitted in NY)

OF COUNSEL

Irwin M. Echtman, Kenneth H. Lazaruk

For full biographical listings, see the Martindale-Hubbell Law Directory

SCHILLER & ASSOCIATES, P.C. (AV)

598 Madison Avenue, 15th Floor, 10022
Telephone: 212-688-4100
Telecopier: 212-753-8940

Craig Schiller

OF COUNSEL

Paul K. Landau, Richard J. Weiss

For full biographical listings, see the Martindale-Hubbell Law Directory

SOLOVAY, EDLIN & EISEMAN (AV)

845 Third Avenue, Eighth Floor, 10022
Telephone: 212-752-1000
Facsimile: 212-355-4608

Richard A. Edlin, Jonathan Eiseman, Norman Solovay, Wayne R. Lehrhaupt, Michael B. Solovay, Eric R. Levine

OF COUNSEL

Daniel James Cooper, Stephen L. Weinstein, Joseph M. Harary, Peter Kakoyiannis, Sam Schwartz

ASSOCIATES

Murray D. Schneier, Howard S. Roitman

For full biographical listings, see the Martindale-Hubbell Law Directory

STADTMAUER BAILKIN, LLP (AV)

850 Third Avenue, 19th Floor, 10022
Telephone: 212-751-8600
Telecopier: 212-980-9578

Michael D. Bailkin, Kenneth Gordon, David I. Stadtmauer, Howard Alan Zipser, Marshall J. Cohen, Louis A. Perfetto, Steven P. Polivy, Jerry D. Reichelscheimer

David J. Fernandez, Jennifer C. Padnick

COUNSEL

Steven Barshov, Richard N. Bowers

For full biographical listings, see the Martindale-Hubbell Law Directory

WAGNER, DAVIS & GOLD, P.C. (AV)

99 Madison Avenue, 10016
Telephone: 212-481-9600
Telefax: 212-481-8245

Steven R. Wagner, John R. Wagner, Ronald Jay Gold, Bonnie Reid Berkow, William R. Fried

OF COUNSEL

Deborah Lynn Davis

Adam D. Finkelstein, Glen C. Rosenberg, Keith L. Woodside, Mikelle V. Lipsius (Not admitted in NY), Robert J. Patchen

LEGAL SUPPORT PERSONNEL

Nicole J. Ottley (Paralegal), Tracey A. Lewis (Paralegal), Steven Henderson (Paralegal), Karen Chin (Paralegal), Daniel E. Glatter (Law Clerk)

For full biographical listings, see the Martindale-Hubbell Law Directory

WALLMAN, GREENBERG, GASMAN & MCKNIGHT, LLP (AV)

350 Fifth Avenue, Suite 3000, 10118
Telephone: 212-695-6000
Fax: 212-695-6007

(See Next Column)

MEMBERS OF FIRM

Lester Wallman, Gerald B. Gasman, Philip A. Greenberg, Elaine McKnight, Donald R. Wall

OF COUNSEL

Clement Segal, Roy L. Jacobs, Daniel E. Clement, Frank J. Hariton

LEGAL SUPPORT PERSONNEL

Lisa Chiodi (Office Administrator)

For full biographical listings, see the Martindale-Hubbell Law Directory

ONEONTA, Otsego Co.

GETMAN LAW FIRM (AV)

16 Dietz Street, P.O. Box 613, 13820
Telephone: 607-432-3530
Fax: 607-432-3571
Email: getmanlw@wpe.com

Frank W. Getman, Michael F. Getman

References: Key Bank of New York; Wilber National Bank Oneonta, N.Y.

For full biographical listings, see the Martindale-Hubbell Law Directory

*POUGHKEEPSIE,** Dutchess Co.

HANKIN, HANIG, STALL, CAPLICKI, REDL & CURTIN, LLP (AV)

319 Main Mall Rear, P.O. Box 911, 12602-0911
Telephone: 914-471-7177
FAX: 914-471-0105
Email: hhscrc@aol.com *URL:* http://www.hvlaw.com
Newburgh, New York Office: 6 Jeanne Drive, P.O. Box 7229, 12550.
Telephone: 914-566-8888.
Fax: 914-566-3886.
LaGrangeville, New York Office: Lexington Park, Route 55, P.O. Box 15, LaGrangeville, New York.
Telephone: 914-473-1200.

MEMBERS OF FIRM

Jerard S. Hankin, Edmund V. Caplicki, Jr., Joel D. Hanig, Frank E. Redl, Todd S. Stall, Daniel F. Curtin

Lynn M. Smookler, David V. Hasin

For full biographical listings, see the Martindale-Hubbell Law Directory

LEWIS & GREER, P.C. (AV)

11 Raymond Avenue, P.O. Box 2990, 12603
Telephone: 914-454-1200
Telecopier: 914-454-3315
Email: info@lewisgreer.com *URL:* http://www.lewisgreer.com

Lou Lewis, J. Scott Greer, Michael J. Englert

Daniel P. Adams, Veronica A. McMillan

For full biographical listings, see the Martindale-Hubbell Law Directory

VAN DEWATER & VAN DEWATER (AV)

40 Garden Street, P.O. Box 112, 12602
Telephone: 914-452-5900
Fax: 914-452-5848
Pawling, New York Office: 243 Route 22, P.O. Box 668.
Telephone: 914-855-5900.
Fax: 914-855-5945.

MEMBERS OF FIRM

John B. Van DeWater (1892-1968), John K. Gifford, James E. Nelson, Robert B. Van DeWater (1920-1990), Craig T. Digilio, Gerard J. Comatos, David D. Hagstrom, Ronald C. Blass, Jr.

OF COUNSEL

Noel deCordova, Jr., James D. Benson, Edward VK. Cunningham, Jr., Susanna E. Bedell

ASSOCIATES

Rebecca Supple Mensch, Michael G. Hayes

Counsel for: J. D. Johnson Co., Inc.; The Fishkill National Bank; The Bank of the Hudson; Vassar Brothers Hospital.
Local Counsel for: Vassar College; Chemprene Div. of Witco Chemical Corp.; Gannett Satellite Information Network, Inc.

For full biographical listings, see the Martindale-Hubbell Law Directory

PURCHASE, Westchester Co.

GIOFFRE & GIOFFRE, PROFESSIONAL CORPORATION (AV)

2900 Westchester Avenue Suite 206, 10577
Telephone: 914-696-3800
Fax: 914-696-3833

Bruno J. Gioffre
Lisa Gioffre Baird

Anthony B. Gioffre, III
Russell A. Giorno

Representative Clients: Sound Federal Savings & Loan Assn.; Port Chester Public Library; Rye Town Hilton Inn; Westchester Business Institute.

For full biographical listings, see the Martindale-Hubbell Law Directory

*ROCHESTER,** Monroe Co.

FARACI & LANGE, LLP (AV)

400 Crossroads Building, Two State Street, 14614
Telephone: 716-325-5150
Toll Free: 888-325-5150
Fax: 716-325-3285
Satellite Office, Rochester, New York: IUE Local 509 Building, 1515 Lyell Avenue, 14606.
Telephone: 716-458-2800. Union Toll Free Number: 800-483-4882.
Fax: 716-458-3015.

John A. Bryant (1943-1995)
Angelo G. Faraci
Paul K. Lange
Joseph A. Regan
Stephen G. Schwarz
Vincent M. Moyer
Brian M. Zorn
Anthony A. Di Nitto
Matthew F. Belanger

ASSOCIATES

Michelle L. Callan
Carol A. Mckenna
James L. Bradley
Bradley P. Kammholz
John A. Falk
Patrick K. Russi

OF COUNSEL

Joseph S. Guadagnino

For full biographical listings, see the Martindale-Hubbell Law Directory

FORSYTH, HOWE, O'DWYER, KALB & MURPHY, P.C. (AV)

Suite 1600, Midtown Tower, 14604
Telephone: 716-325-7515
Fax: 716-325-6407
URL: http://www.forsythhowe.com

Charles B. Forsyth (1890-1968)
C. Benn Forsyth
Gordon A. Howe, II
Duncan W. O'Dwyer
Robert J. Kalb
Gerald N. Murphy

Nancy A. Pappal

OF COUNSEL

John F. Forsyth (Retired)
Allan Wolk
Hoffman Stone
Debra A. Martin
Janice M. Iati
Cathleen W. Smith
Thad F. Sondej

References: The Chase Manhattan Bank; Fleet Bank.

For full biographical listings, see the Martindale-Hubbell Law Directory

ROME, Oneida Co.

GRIFFITH LAW OFFICES (AV)

225 North Washington Street, 13440
Telephone: 315-336-6500
Fax: 315-336-6628
Email: griffi@aiusa.com *URL:* http://www.lawyers.com/griffith

MEMBER OF FIRM

Emlyn I. Griffith

Representative Clients: Alcan Aluminum Corporation; Camroden Associates, Inc.; C & H Plastics, Inc.; Covewood Mobile Park; D & H Asphalt Co., Inc.; Legendary Corp.; Statewide Funding Corp; Stonehedge Nursing Home.
Approved Attorneys for: The Title Guarantee Co.

For full biographical listings, see the Martindale-Hubbell Law Directory

ROSLYN HEIGHTS, Nassau Co.

NATISS, NATISS & GORDON, P.C. (AV)

277 Willis Avenue, 11577
Telephone: 516-621-0900
Telecopier: 516-621-1304
Email: MNatisslaw@aol.com

Marvin Natiss
Gary M. Natiss
Stacey Natiss Gordon

(See Next Column)

Sharon G. Haut

For full biographical listings, see the Martindale-Hubbell Law Directory

STONY POINT, Rockland Co.

HURLEY, FOX, SELIG & KELLEHER (AV)

Liberty Building, Route 9 W, 10980
Telephone: 914-942-2222
Fax: 914-942-0378
Email: HFSKlaw@aol.com
New City, New York Office: 60 Pine Street.
Telephone: 614-634-2050.

MEMBERS OF FIRM

Benjamin E. Selig
Glenn W. Kelleher

ASSOCIATES

Steven L. Kahn
Dana Selig Kahn
Bob A. Kramer
Kenneth P. Silver

Representative Clients: Bradlees, Inc.; Stop & Shop Companies; CNA Insurance Cos.; Federal Insurance Co.; Chubb & Son; Commercial Union Group of Insurance Cos.; Empire Insurance Co.; Omaha, N.B.; Excelsior Insurance Co.; Fireman's Insurance Company of Washington, D.C.

For full biographical listings, see the Martindale-Hubbell Law Directory

*SYRACUSE,** Onondaga Co.

ALDERMAN AND ALDERMAN (AV)

Suite 555 Empire Building, 472 South Salina Street, 13202
Telephone: 315-422-8131
Fax: 315-474-7507
Email: aldermanoffice@worldnet.att.net *URL:* http://www.lawyers.com/aldermanlaw

MEMBERS OF FIRM

Saul H. Alderman (1901-1985)
Bernard Samuels (1907-1985)
Edward B. Alderman
Richard B. Alderman

ASSOCIATE

Janet Jule Dougherty

LEGAL SUPPORT PERSONNEL

Judy M. Conger
Leticia A. Wicks
Tracy A. Esposito

Reference: First National of Rochester.

For full biographical listings, see the Martindale-Hubbell Law Directory

ALI, PAPPAS & COX, P.C. (AV)

Syracuse Building, 224 Harrison Street, 13202
Telephone: 315-472-4481
FAX: 315-472-8299
Email: alpaco@dreamscape.com

Lucien Ali
C. Andrew Pappas
Robert B. Cox
Thomas P. Givas
P. Douglas Dodd
David P. Doherty

OF COUNSEL

Edward F. Gerber

LEGAL SUPPORT PERSONNEL

Brenda M. Barch

Representative Clients: Agway, Inc.; Agway Petroleum Corp.; Arcom Labs; Countryside Federal Credit Union; PineCone Federal Credit Union; Oswego City Savings Bank; Telmark, Inc.; Syracuse Executive Air Services, Inc.; Fairbanks Capital Corp.
References: M&T Bank; 1st National Bank of Rochester.

For full biographical listings, see the Martindale-Hubbell Law Directory

COSTELLO COONEY & FEARON, LLP (AV)

Salina Place, 205 South Salina Street, 13202
Telephone: 315-422-1152
Fax: 315-422-1139
Email: ccf-law.com *URL:* http://www.ccf-law.com

MEMBERS OF FIRM

Warren W. Bader
Robert D. Essig
Michael A. Tremont
Alicia S. Calagiovanni
Timothy J. Conan

ASSOCIATES

David S. Grasso
Samuel C. Young

OF COUNSEL

Richard D. Hillman

General Counsel for: Auburn Memorial Hospital; Crouse Hospital; Health Services Association of Central New York; St. Joseph's Hospital Health Center.
Local Counsel for: Deere & Co.; New York Telephone Co.; Crum & Forster Insurance Co.; The Travelers Insurance Companies; Caterpillar, Inc.; Otis Elevator.

(See Next Column)

COSTELLO COONEY & FEARON LLP—*Continued*

For Complete List of Firm Personnel, See General Section

For full biographical listings, see the Martindale-Hubbell Law Directory

SHULMAN, CURTIN, GRUNDNER, REGAN & SNYDER, P.C. (AV)

250 South Clinton Street, Suite 502, 13202-1262
Telephone: 315-424-8944
Fax: 315-424-8205
Email: reception@scgrslaw.com

C. Daniel Shulman
Paul J. Curtin, Jr.
Charles H. Grundner
Paul M. Regan
Joseph M. Snyder

Stephen G. Etoll
Christian J. Danaher

For full biographical listings, see the Martindale-Hubbell Law Directory

*TROY,** Rensselaer Co.

MARTIN, SHUDT, WALLACE, DILORENZO & JOHNSON (AV)

The Dauchy Building, 279 River Street, P.O. Box 1530, 12181
Telephone: 518-272-6565
Fax: 518-272-5573
URL: http://www.estateplanning.com/martinlawfirm

Carl E. Martin (1902-1988)
Edwyn L. Shudt
Richard P. Wallace
Kirby W. DiLorenzo
Robert Wm. Johnson, III
James E. Prout
Frank C. Sarratori
Paul M. Macari

ASSOCIATES

Jennifer A. Cusack
Jaime B. Thomas
Matthew L. Hosford
Ronald J. Moss

OF COUNSEL

Thomas B. Hunt (Not admitted in NY)

For full biographical listings, see the Martindale-Hubbell Law Directory

VALATIE, Columbia Co.

BURNS F. BARFORD, JR. (AV)

1019 Kinderhook Street, 12184
Telephone: 518-758-7161
Facsimile: 518-758-9885

Counsel for: National Union Bank of Kinderhook.

For full biographical listings, see the Martindale-Hubbell Law Directory

*WARSAW,** Wyoming Co.

SMALLWOOD-COOK & SCHMIEDER (AV)

140 North Main Street, 14569-1103
Telephone: 716-786-2274
FAX: 716-786-2138
Email: smallwood@wycol.com

MEMBERS OF FIRM

Charlotte Smallwood-Cook
Jane A.C. Schmieder

Reference: Wyoming County Bank.

For full biographical listings, see the Martindale-Hubbell Law Directory

*WHITE PLAINS,** Westchester Co.

DELBELLO DONNELLAN WEINGARTEN & TARTAGLIA, LLP (AV)

One North Lexington Avenue, 10601
Telephone: 914-681-0200
Telecopier: 914-684-0288
Email: general@ddwt.com

Alfred B. DelBello
Alfred E. Donnellan (Managing Partner)
Mark P. Weingarten
Daniel D. Tartaglia
Peter J. Wise
Lee S. Wiederkehr
Patrick M. Reilly
Robert A. Korren

ASSOCIATES

William E. Dumke
Christine Moccia
Suzanne Bogdanoff
Allyse B. Dunefsky
Jerry F. Kebrdle, II
Bradley D. Wank
Ann Farrissey Carlson
Janet J. Giris

OF COUNSEL

J. David Jutkowitz
Andrew J. Balint
Robert C. Epstein

For full biographical listings, see the Martindale-Hubbell Law Directory

HOFFMAN, WACHTELL, KOSTER & MAIER (AV)

399 Knollwood Road, 10603
Telephone: 914-682-8000
FAX: 914-682-1512
URL: http://www.lawyers.com/hwk&mlaw

(See Next Column)

MEMBERS OF FIRM

Lee A. Hoffman, Jr.
Marc J. Wachtell
Eric D. Koster
Lynn J. Maier

Representative Clients: Ginsburg Development Corp.; The Chiselhurst Company, Inc.; Mount Hope Mines, Inc.; Eastern Educational Consortium; Westchester Community College; Prime Offices Systems, Inc.; Gateway Management Corp.; The City of Mt. Vernon; The Town of Greenburgh; The Town of Mamaroneck; The Village of Port Chester.
Reference: Citibank, N.A. (White Plains Branch).

For full biographical listings, see the Martindale-Hubbell Law Directory

KEANE & BEANE, P.C. (AV)

One North Broadway, 10601
Telephone: 914-946-4777
Telecopier: 914-946-6868
Rye, New York Office: 15 Elm Place.
Telephone: 914-967-3936.

Thomas F. Keane, Jr. (1932-1991)
Edward F. Beane
Donna E. Frosco
David Glasser
Lance H. Klein
Ronald A. Longo
Richard L. O'Rourke
Lawrence Praga
Joel H. Sachs
Steven A. Schurkman
Judson K. Siebert

Stephanie L. Burns
Eric L. Gordon
Jonathan Kornblatt
Stephanie M. Orefice
Patrick J. O'Sullivan
Frances M. Pantaleo
Nicholas M. Ward-Willis

OF COUNSEL

Peter A. Borrok
John F. Burkhardt
Eric F. Jensen

LEGAL SUPPORT PERSONNEL

Lenny Amodeo (Legal Assistant)
Barbara S. Durkin (Office Manager)
Sylvia J. Zuckerman (Legal Assistant)

For full biographical listings, see the Martindale-Hubbell Law Directory

KENT, HAZZARD, JAEGER, GREER, WILSON & FAY (AV)

50 Main Street, 10606
Telephone: 914-948-4700
Telecopier: 914-948-4721
Email: KentHazz@aol.com

MEMBERS OF FIRM

Ralph S. Kent (1878-1949)
Lawrence S. Hazzard (1900-1958)
William J. Greer (1920-1994)
Mizell Wilson, Jr. (1927-1995)
Lawrence F. Fay
Robert D. Hazzard
Katharine Wilson Conroy

ASSOCIATE

John A. Verni

OF COUNSEL

Malcolm Wilson
Otto C. Jaeger
John R. Dinin
Harold L. Wood

Representative Client: The Bank of New York.
References: Bank of New York.

For full biographical listings, see the Martindale-Hubbell Law Directory

MARCUS, GOULD & SUSSMAN, LLP (AV)

222 Bloomingdale Road, 10605
Telephone: 914-683-0090
Telecopier: 914-683-0098
Email: firm@marcus-gould-sussman.com *URL:* http://www.lawyers.com/marcusgould&sussman

MEMBERS OF FIRM

Myron Marcus
Kenneth J. Gould
Marianne L. Sussman

References: Bennett, Kielson & Co.; Citibank, N.A.; Chemical Bank.

For full biographical listings, see the Martindale-Hubbell Law Directory

POSNER, POSNER & ASSOCIATES, PC (AV)

399 Knollwood Road, 10603
Telephone: 914-948-6620
Telecopier: 914-948-0864
Email: relawyer@aol.com *URL:* http://www.lawyers.com/posner_posner&assoc

Henry A. Greenburg
Martin Louis Posner
Jane Y. Posner

Peter J. McCarthy
Karen Olson

References: Chemical Bank; Citibank.

For full biographical listings, see the Martindale-Hubbell Law Directory

White Plains—Continued

ROGAN GUIDA & ORENSTEIN (AV)

235 Mamaroneck Avenue, 10605
Telephone: 1-888-WIN-WITH-US; 914-328-4480
Fax: 914-328-4479
URL: http://www.NYlawyers.com
Email: RoganGO@aol.com *URL:* http://www.lawyers.com/personalinjury

Jeffrey P. Rogan — Toni M. Guida
David L. Orenstein

Representative Clients: Recore One Mortgage Corp.; LEASCO; Pappas Enterprises Inc.; Steelcase, Inc.; Printing Center of Westchester Inc.; Corporate Imaging, Inc.; King Jolo's Flowers, Inc.; Systems Exchange, Inc.; Domus Realty.
Reference: Fleet Bank.

For full biographical listings, see the Martindale-Hubbell Law Directory

SMITH, RANSCHT, CONNORS, MUTINO, NORDELL & SIRIGNANO, P.C. (AV)

235 Main Street, 10601
Telephone: 914-946-8800
Telecopier: 914-946-8861
Cable Address: "Smiran" White Plains, New York

James P. Connors, Jr. — Michael Nordell
Peter J. Mutino — George A. Sirignano, Jr.

Counsel for: Universal Builders Supply, Inc.; The Walter Karl Cos.; Hartsdale Canine Cemetery; Wise Components, Inc.; Facsimile Communications Industries, Inc.; Carlcraft Knit Sales, Inc.
Closing Attorneys for: First Union Mortgage Corp.
Representative Client: United Airlines, Corporate Express, Inc.

For full biographical listings, see the Martindale-Hubbell Law Directory

JOHN E. WATKINS, JR. (AV)

175 Main Street, 10601
Telephone: 914-428-1292
Telecopier: 914-428-4104
Local 800 Service: 1-800-33WATKINS
Email: wat2kins@netcom.com *URL:* http://www.lawyers.com/johnewatkinsjr
New York, New York Office: 29 Broadway.
Telephone: 212-968-1500.

ASSOCIATE

Ira S. Levy

For full biographical listings, see the Martindale-Hubbell Law Directory

YONKERS, Westchester Co.

ECKER, LOEHR, ECKER & ECKER, L.L.P. (AV)

One Executive Boulevard, 10701
Telephone: 914-968-0500; 914-965-4288
FAX: 914-968-0918
Email: eleellp@aol.com
New York, New York Office: 521 Fifth Avenue, 27th Floor, 10175.
Telephone: 914-965-4288;
Fax: 914-968-0918.

MEMBERS OF FIRM

Gerald E. Loehr — Lawrence H. Ecker
Louis A. Ecker — Robert L. Ecker

OF COUNSEL

Jock Thornton — Iris J. Iler
Tammi L. Blank-Ecker

LEGAL SUPPORT PERSONNEL

Carolyn Caruso

Reference: Hudson Valley National Bank.

For full biographical listings, see the Martindale-Hubbell Law Directory

NORTH CAROLINA

*ASHEVILLE,** Buncombe Co.

THE FRUE LAW FIRM, L.L.P. (AV)

16 Church Street, P.O. Box 7627, 28802
Telephone: 704-258-0570
Fax: 704-258-0591

MEMBERS OF FIRM

William C. Frue, Jr. — Michael Calhoun Frue

Reference: First Union National Bank.

For full biographical listings, see the Martindale-Hubbell Law Directory

CHAPEL HILL, Orange Co.

EPTING & HACKNEY (AV)

410 Airport Road, P.O. Box 1329, 27514
Telephone: 919-929-0323
Fax: 919-929-3960

MEMBERS OF FIRM

Robert Epting — Elizabeth Lackey Jacobs
Steve Lackey

For Complete List of Firm Personnel, See General Section

For full biographical listings, see the Martindale-Hubbell Law Directory

*CHARLOTTE,** Mecklenburg Co.

BLEDSOE & BLEDSOE, P.L.L.C. (AV)

1057 East Morehead Street, P.O. Box 36779, 28236-6779
Telephone: 704-372-1676
Fax: 704-372-1677
Email: labjrbled@aol.com

Louis A. Bledsoe, Jr.

Margaret M. Bledsoe (1966-1996)

General Counsel for: Milner Airco, Inc.; Grace Christian Center, Inc.; Rasberry Agency, Ltd.; McEwen Indusries, Inc.; The Charlotte Montessori School, Inc.; Charlotte Country Day School; JOAL Realty, LLC; Fabrictex, Inc.

For full biographical listings, see the Martindale-Hubbell Law Directory

BURRIS, MACMILLAN, PEARCE & MAYER, L.L.P. (AV)

6857 Fairview Road, 28210
Telephone: 704-365-2600
Fax: 704-364-2637

Robert N. Burris — Hugo A. Pearce, III
Douglas P. MacMillan — Gregory P. Mayer
Margery A. Burris

For full biographical listings, see the Martindale-Hubbell Law Directory

PARHAM, HELMS, HARRIS, BLYTHE & MORTON (AV)

6310 Fairview Road, Suite 200, 28210
Telephone: 704-366-6607
Fax: 704-366-6973
Email: lmbatty@mindspring.com

MEMBERS OF FIRM

Lewis H. Parham, Jr. — Ralph C. Harris, Jr.
Neal G. Helms — Robert B. Blythe
James H. Morton

ASSOCIATE

Lyn Morton Batty

OF COUNSEL

John L. Hazlehurst

Representative Clients: Marsh Associates, Inc.; Home Federal Savings and Loan.
Reference: Nationsbank of North Carolina.

For full biographical listings, see the Martindale-Hubbell Law Directory

PERRY, PATRICK, FARMER & MICHAUX, P.A. (AV)

2200 The Carillon, 227 West Trade Street, 28202
Telephone: 704-372-1120
Fax: 704-372-9635
Other Charlotte, North Carolina Office: South Park, 1901 Roxborough Road, Suite 100.
Telephone: 704-364-9695.
Fax: 704-364-9698.
Raleigh, North Carolina Office: 3716 National Drive, Suite 100.
Telephone: 919-787-8812.
Fax: 919-787-3312.

Robert E. Perry, Jr. — Bryan W. Pittman
Bailey Patrick, Jr. — Laura L. Yaeger
B. D. Farmer, III — Richard W. Moore
Roy H. Michaux, Jr. — (Resident, Raleigh Office)
James G. Wallace — Leslie Miller Webb
Carolyn Gilmer Hisley — John H. Carmichael

Representative Clients: The Bissell Cos.; Centex Real Estate Corp.; Charlotte Pipe and Foundry Co.; The Crosland Group, Inc.; Crown Life Insurance Co.; C.D. Spangler Construction Co.; International Construction Equipment, Inc.; The Manufacturers Life Insurance Co.; M/I Schottenstein Cos., Inc.; The Ryland Group, Inc.

For Complete List of Firm Personnel, See General Section

For full biographical listings, see the Martindale-Hubbell Law Directory

Charlotte—Continued

WOMBLE CARLYLE SANDRIDGE & RICE (AV)

A Professional Limited Liability Company
3300 One First Union Center, 301 South College Street, 28202-6025
Telephone: 704-331-4900
Fax: 704-331-4955
Email: lawyers@wcsr.com *URL:* http://www.wcsr.com
Winston-Salem, North Carolina Office: 200 West Second Street, P.O. Drawer 84.
Telephone: 336-721-3600.
Fax: 336-721-3660.
Raleigh, North Carolina Office: 2100 First Union Capitol Center, 150 Fayetteville Street Mall, P.O. Box 831.
Telephone: 919-755-2100.
Fax: 919-755-2150.
Research Triangle Park, North Carolina Office: 2505 Meridian Parkway, Suite 300 (Durham), 27713.
Telephone: 919-484-2300.
Fax: 919-484-2340.
Atlanta, Georgia Office: One Atlantic Center, 1201 West Peachtree Street, Suite 3500.
Telephone: 404-872-7000.
Fax: 404-888-7490.
Other Atlanta, Georgia Office: Suite 404, 2296 Henderson Mill Road, N.E.
Telephone: 770-492-9030.
Fax: 770-492-9609.
Washington, D.C. Office: 1120 Nineteenth Street, N.W., Eighth Floor.
Telephone: 202-857-4400.
Fax: 202-467-6910.
Greenville, South Carolina Office: 15 South Main Street, Suite 601, P.O. Box 10208.
Telephone: 864-255-5400.
Fax: 864-255-5440.

RESIDENT MEMBERS

Gary D. Chamblee | Bobby D. Hinson
William P. McMillan

RESIDENT ASSOCIATE

A. Britten Canady

Representative Clients: Childress Klein Properties, Inc.; Food Lion, Inc.; J.A. Jones Construction Co.; Parkdale Mills, Inc.; Pillowtex; Duke Power Co.; Bowles Hollowell Conner & Co.; ALLTEL Carolina, Inc.; Belk Store Services, Inc.; Philip Holzmann A.G.

For Complete List of Firm Personnel, See General Section

For full biographical listings, see the Martindale-Hubbell Law Directory

*GREENSBORO,** Guilford Co.

ALEXANDER RALSTON, SPECKHARD & SPECKHARD, L.L.P. (AV)

218 West Friendly Avenue, 27401
Telephone: 336-379-9302
Fax: 336-370-1232
URL: http://www.lawyers.com/aralston,speckhard

Donald K. Speckhard | Stanley E. Speckhard

Representative Clients: Preferred Furniture Components, Inc.; Spring Financial Services, Inc.; Blazer Financial Services; Omega Sports, Inc.; Power & Heat Systems, Inc.; Branch & Company, P.A.; Acme Florist Supply, Inc.

For full biographical listings, see the Martindale-Hubbell Law Directory

ISAACSON & ISAACSON (AV)

Suite 400 Bank of America Building, 101 West Friendly Avenue, P.O. Box 1888, 27402
Telephone: 336-275-7626
Fax: 336-273-7293
Email: ikeandike@aol.com *URL:* http://www.lawyers.com/isaacson

MEMBERS OF FIRM

Henry H. Isaacson | Marc L. Isaacson

ASSOCIATES

Jennifer N. Fountain | Anna Gregory Wagoner

For full biographical listings, see the Martindale-Hubbell Law Directory

SCHELL BRAY AYCOCK ABEL & LIVINGSTON P.L.L.C. (AV)

1500 Renaissance Plaza, 230 North Elm Street, P.O. Box 21847, 27420
Telephone: 336-370-8800
Fax: 336-370-8830
Email: Info@sbaal.com *URL:* http://www.sbaal.com

MEMBERS OF FIRM

Braxton Schell | Paul H. Livingston, Jr.
Doris R. Bray | Thomas C. Watkins
William P. Aycock, II | Dan T. Barker, Jr.
Michael R. Abel | Barbara R. Christy
John A. McLendon, Jr.

(See Next Column)

ASSOCIATES

Kathleen A. Kingsbury | Gregory M. Chabon
Jacqueline E. Camp | Jennifer Johnson
A. Nicholas Purrington | Eric M. Braun
Garland V. Gibbes

Representative Clients: The Breakers Palm Beach, Inc.; Steven D. Bell & Company; Cone Mills Corp.; Cornwalls Development Co.; Vanguard Cellular Systems, Inc.; Ellison Properties Group; Graham Associates, Inc.; John Smith & Son; Landfall Associates; The Osborne Company of North Carolina, Inc.; Homer E. Wright Jr., Inc. (St. James Plantation).

For full biographical listings, see the Martindale-Hubbell Law Directory

STERN & KLEPFER, L.L.P. (AV)

600 NationsBank Building, P.O. Box 3112, 27402
Telephone: 336-373-1500
Fax: 336-272-8258

Sidney J. Stern, Jr. (1914-1991) | John L. Rendleman (1932-1983)

MEMBERS OF FIRM

Robert O. Klepfer, Jr. | James W. Miles, Jr.
John T. Higgins, Jr. | Brinton D. Wright
William A. Eagles

ASSOCIATES

Melanie H. Rodenbough | Ronda Leigh Lowe
Maureen Breen Gerhardt | Douglas M. Heberle

Representative Clients: Bankers Trust of North Carolina; NationsBank of North Carolina, N.A.; Tannenbaum-Sternberger Foundation; Bennett College; Endura Products, Inc.; Carlyle & Co. Jewelers.

For full biographical listings, see the Martindale-Hubbell Law Directory

*GREENVILLE,** Pitt Co.

GAYLORD, MCNALLY, STRICKLAND & SNYDER, L.L.P. (AV)

498 Red Banks Road, P.O. Drawer 545, 27835-0545
Telephone: 252-321-7111
Fax: 252-321-7112

MEMBERS OF FIRM

Louis W. Gaylord, Jr. (Retired) | D. Michael Strickland
Danny D. McNally | Vernon G. Snyder, III

ASSOCIATE

Emma Stallings Holscher

Representative Clients: Wachovia Bank, N.A.; Nationsbank, N.A.; Garris Evans Lumber Co., Inc.; United States Fidelity and Guaranty Co.; The Daily Reflector, Inc.; Hastings Ford, Inc.; Nationwide Mutual Insurance Co.; U.S. Cellular; Ironwood Development, Inc.

For full biographical listings, see the Martindale-Hubbell Law Directory

*HENDERSONVILLE,** Henderson Co.

HOWE, WATERS & CARPENTER, P.A. (AV)

134 South Main Street, P.O. Box 586, 28793
Telephone: 828-692-9636
Telefax: 828-692-2643

William B. W. Howe | Walter C. Carpenter
R. Charles Waters | Linda A. Moxley

General Counsel for: Hendersonville Housing Authority.
Approved Attorneys for: Lawyers Title Insurance Corp.; Chicago Title Insurance Co.; Investors Title Insurance Co.
References: Wachovia Bank and Trust Co.; First Union National Bank of North Carolina; First Citizens Bank & Trust Co.; Centura Bank.

For full biographical listings, see the Martindale-Hubbell Law Directory

HICKORY, Catawba Co.

SIGMON, CLARK, MACKIE, HUTTON & HANVEY, P.A. (AV)

420 Third Avenue, N.W., P.O. Drawer 1470, 28603
Telephone: 828-328-2596
FAX: 828-328-6876

William R. Sigmon | Warren A. Hutton
E. Fielding Clark, II | J. Scott Hanvey
Jeffrey T. Mackie | Forrest A. Ferrell

Stephen L. Palmer

OF COUNSEL

Marshall V. Yount

Representative Clients: First Union National Bank; Cox Manufacturing Co.
Local Counsel for: The Ohio Casualty Group of Insurance Cos.; United States Fidelity and Guaranty Insurance Co.

For full biographical listings, see the Martindale-Hubbell Law Directory

*RALEIGH,** Wake Co.

PERRY, PATRICK, FARMER & MICHAUX, P.A. (AV)

3716 National Drive, Suite 100, 27612
Telephone: 919-787-8812
Fax: 919-787-3312
Charlotte, North Carolina Office: 2200 The Carillon, 227 West Trade Street.
Telephone: 704-372-1120.
Fax: 704-372-9635.
Other Charlotte, North Carolina Office: South Park, 1901 Roxborough Road, Suite 100.
Telephone: 704-364-9695.
Fax: 704-364-9698.

Richard W. Moore

G. Mark Teague
Virginia G. Dockery
Katherine M. Lewis

Representative Clients: The Bissell Cos.; Centex Real Estate Corp.; Charlotte Pipe and Foundry Co.; The Crosland Group, Inc.; Crown Life Insurance Co.; C.D. Spangler Construction Co.; International Construction Equipment, Inc.; The Manufacturers Life Insurance Co.; M/I Schottenstein Cos., Inc.; The Ryland Group, Inc.

For full biographical listings, see the Martindale-Hubbell Law Directory

RAGSDALE LIGGETT, PLLC (AV)

A Professional Limited Liability Company
Suite 400 Crosspointe Plaza, 2840 Plaza Place, P.O. Box 31507, 27612
Telephone: 919-787-5200
Fax: 919-783-8991; 881-2045

MEMBERS OF FIRM

George R. Ragsdale
Frank R. Liggett III
William A. Mann
Steven I. Reinhard
William S. Bost, III
Dorothy Bass Burch
James Allen Hoffman (Not admitted in NC)

OF COUNSEL

Joseph E. Johnson

ASSOCIATES

Kathleen Pepi Southern
Walter L. Tippett, Jr.
David K. Liggett
Kathleen C. Mcconnell

For full biographical listings, see the Martindale-Hubbell Law Directory

WOMBLE CARLYLE SANDRIDGE & RICE (AV)

A Professional Limited Liability Company
2100 First Union Capitol Center, 150 Fayetteville Street Mall, P.O. Box 831, 27602
Telephone: 919-755-2100
Fax: 919-755-2150
Email: lawyers@wcsr.com *URL:* http://www.wcsr.com
Charlotte, North Carolina Office: 3300 One First Union Center, 301 South College Street.
Telephone: 704-331-4900.
Fax: 704-331-4955.
Winston-Salem, North Carolina Office: 200 West Second Street, P.O. Drawer 84.
Telephone: 336-721-3600.
Fax: 336-721-3660.
Research Triangle Park, North Carolina Office: 2505 Meridian Parkway, Suite 300 (Durham), 27713.
Telephone: 919-484-2300.
Fax: 919-484-2340.
Atlanta, Georgia Office: One Atlantic Center, 1201 West Peachtree Street, Suite 3500.
Telephone: 404-872-7000.
Fax: 404-888-7490.
Other Atlanta, Georgia Office: Suite 404, 2296 Henderson Mill Road, N.E.
Telephone: 770-492-9030.
Fax: 770-492-9609.
Washington, D.C. Office: 1120 Nineteenth Street, N.W., Eighth Floor.
Telephone: 202-857-4400.
Fax: 202-467-6910.
Greenville, South Carolina Office: 15 South Main Street, Suite 601, P.O. Box 10208.
Telephone: 864-255-5400.
Fax: 864-255-5440.

RESIDENT MEMBERS

Donald A. Donadio
William C. Matthews, Jr.
Stephen A. Yeagy

RESIDENT ASSOCIATE

Nellie Shipley Tomlinson

Representative Clients: Aetna Casualty and Surety Co., Inc.; ALSCO/AmeriMark Building Products, Inc.; Aoki Corporation America, Inc.; Hackney Brothers, Inc.; Lawyers Mutual Liability Insurance Company of North Carolina; Meredith College; Regency Park Corp.; Wachovia Bank, N.A.

(See Next Column)

For Complete List of Firm Personnel, See General Section

For full biographical listings, see the Martindale-Hubbell Law Directory

REIDSVILLE, Rockingham Co.

HOLT & WATT (AV)

211 Gilmer Street, P.O. Box 728, 27320
Telephone: 336-342-2997
Fax: 336-342-9158

Clark M. Holt
Robert L. Watt, III

Representative Clients: Branch Banking & Trust Co. (BB&T); NationsBank; First National Bank Southeast; Rentz Oil Co.
Approved Attorneys for: Lawyers Title Insurance Corp.; Chicago Title Insurance Co.; First American Title Insurance Co.

For full biographical listings, see the Martindale-Hubbell Law Directory

*SYLVA,** Jackson Co.

COWARD, HICKS & SILER, P.A. (AV)

705 West Main Street, 28779
Telephone: 828-586-2147
Fax: 828-586-2605
Franklin, North Carolina Office: 43 West Main Street, 28734.
Telephone: 828-524-6475.
Fax: 828-524-9833.
Cashiers, North Carolina Office: P.O. Box 1918, 28717.
Telephone: 828-743-2401.
Fax: 828-743-2403.

James Kent Coward (1929-1989)
Orville D. Coward
Ralph L. Hicks (Resident, Cashiers Office)
Robert F. Siler (Resident, Franklin Office)
Orville D. Coward, Jr. (Resident, Franklin Office)
J. K. Coward, Jr.
William H. Coward (Resident, Franklin Office)
Kimberly R. Coward (Resident, Cashiers Office)
Monty C. Beck (Resident, Franklin Office)
Richard K. Walker (Resident at Franklin Office)

Representative Clients: First Union National Bank; Wachovia Bank and Trust Co.; Haywood Savings and Loan Association; NationsBank of North Carolina; Cotton States Mutual Insurance Co.

For full biographical listings, see the Martindale-Hubbell Law Directory

*WILMINGTON,** New Hanover Co.

DAVID E. HUFFINE, P.A. (AV)

508 Market Street, P.O. Box 2154, 28402-2154
Telephone: 910-251-1954
Fax: 910-251-8590
Email: huffine@wilmington.net

David E. Huffine

Lawrence S. Craige

For full biographical listings, see the Martindale-Hubbell Law Directory

KAUFMAN & GREEN, L.L.P. (AV)

Landfall Park North, 1985 Eastwood Road, Suite 200, 28403
Telephone: 910-256-5135
Fax: 910-256-6451

James J. Kaufman
Michael A. Green

Owen D. Lewis, Jr.

Approved Attorney For: The Title Company of NC, Inc.; Lawyers Title of North Carolina, Inc.; Chicago Title Insurance Co.; Security Union Title Insurance Co.; Investors Title; Commonwealth Title; Ticor Title Guarantee Co.; FMHA; Citizens Federal Bank; Hometown Funding, Inc.

For full biographical listings, see the Martindale-Hubbell Law Directory

MURCHISON, TAYLOR & GIBSON, L.L.P. (AV)

16 North Fifth Avenue, 28401-4593
Telephone: 910-763-2426
Fax: 910-763-6561

MEMBERS OF FIRM

Wallace C. Murchison (Retired)
Joseph O. Taylor, Jr.
Frank B. Gibson, Jr.
Michael Murchison
Nancy M. Guyton
W. Berry Trice
G. Stephen Diab
James W. Latshaw

ASSOCIATE

Frances Youngblood Trask

Representative Clients: Bell South; Branch Banking & Trust Co.; DR Horton, Inc.; First National Bank, Southeast; General Electric Co.; LaDane Williamson, LLC; Landfall Assn.; Landmark Organization, Inc.; Ocean Ridge Farms, Inc.; Telechron, Inc.; Worsley Cos., Inc.

(See Next Column)

MURCHISON, TAYLOR & GIBSON L.L.P.—*Continued*

For full biographical listings, see the Martindale-Hubbell Law Directory

SHANKLIN & MCDANIEL, L.L.P. (AV)

214 Market Street, P.O. Box 1347, 28402-1347
Telephone: 910-762-9400
Fax: 910-251-1773
Email: shanklaw@wilmington.net

Kenneth A. Shanklin Susan J. McDaniel

ASSOCIATE

G. Grady Richardson, Jr.

For full biographical listings, see the Martindale-Hubbell Law Directory

*WINSTON-SALEM,** Forsyth Co.

STEPHEN G. CALAWAY (AV)

Ashley Square, 1330 Ashley Brook Lane, 27103
Telephone: 336-760-6420
Fax: 336-760-8811

References: Nations Bank of North Carolina; Branch Bank and Trust Co.

For full biographical listings, see the Martindale-Hubbell Law Directory

JOHN R. SURRATT, P.A. (AV)

102 West Third Street Suite 700, 27101
Telephone: 336-725-8323
Facsimile: 336-722-5218
Email: surrattpa@aol.com

John R. Surratt Anita M. Conrad

For full biographical listings, see the Martindale-Hubbell Law Directory

WOMBLE CARLYLE SANDRIDGE & RICE (AV)

A Professional Limited Liability Company
200 West Second Street, P.O. Drawer 84, 27102
Telephone: 336-721-3600
Fax: 336-721-3660
Email: lawyers@wcsr.com *URL:* http://www.wcsr.com
Charlotte, North Carolina Office: 3300 One First Union Center, 301 South College Street.
Telephone: 704-331-4900.
Fax: 704-331-4955.
Raleigh, North Carolina Office: 2100 First Union Capitol Center, 150 Fayetteville Street Mall, P.O. Box 831.
Telephone: 919-755-2100.
Fax: 919-755-2150.
Research Triangle Park, North Carolina Office: 2505 Meridian Parkway, Suite 300 (Durham), 27713.
Telephone: 919-484-2300.
Fax: 919-484-2340.
Atlanta, Georgia Office: One Atlantic Center, 1201 West Peachtree Street, Suite 3500.
Telephone: 404-872-7000.
Fax: 404-888-7490.
Other Atlanta, Georgia Office: Suite 404, 2296 Henderson Mill Road, N.E.
Telephone: 770-492-9030.
Fax: 770-492-9609.
Washington, D.C. Office: 1120 Nineteenth Street, N.W., Eighth Floor.
Telephone: 202-857-4400.
Fax: 202-467-6910.
Greenville, South Carolina Office: 15 South Main Street, Suite 601, P.O. Box 10208.
Telephone: 864-255-5400.
Fax: 864-255-5440.

RESIDENT MEMBERS

Leslie E. Browder
Hardin G. Halsey
Christopher E. Leon
Kim Kelly Mann
Dennis W. McNames
Kenneth A. Moser
Robert L. Quick
W. P. Sandridge, Jr.

RESIDENT ASSOCIATE

F. Scott Thomas

Representative Clients: Brad Ragan, Inc.; Brenner Companies; Food Lion, Inc.; Hanes Companies, Inc.; North Carolina Baptist Hospitals, Inc.; R.J. Reynolds Tobacco Co.; Thomasville Furniture Industries, Inc.; Wachovia Corp.; Wake Forest University.

For Complete List of Firm Personnel, See General Section

For full biographical listings, see the Martindale-Hubbell Law Directory

NORTH DAKOTA

*BISMARCK,** Burleigh Co.

PEARCE AND DURICK, PLLP (AV)

314 East Thayer Avenue, P.O. Box 400, 58502
Telephone: 701-223-2890
Fax: 701-223-7865
Email: law.office@pearce-durick.com *URL:* http://www.pearce-durick.com

MEMBERS OF FIRM

William P. Pearce Lawrence Bender

Representative Clients: Amoco Oil Co.; Conoco Inc.; Continental Resources, Inc.; Lakehead Pipeline Co.; MDU Resources Group, Inc.; Texaco Inc.

For Complete List of Firm Personnel, See General Section

For full biographical listings, see the Martindale-Hubbell Law Directory

*FARGO,** Cass Co.

CONMY, FESTE, HUBBARD, CORWIN & BRUST, LTD. (AV)

200 Norwest Center, 406 Main Avenue, 58126
Telephone: 701-293-9911
Fax: 701-293-3133
URL: http://www.conmylaw.com

Charles A. Feste
Paul M. Hubbard
Wickham Corwin
Kim E. Brust
Michael M. Thomas
Robert J. Schultz
Nancy J. Morris

OF COUNSEL

Lauris N. Molbert E. T. Conmy, Jr.

State Counsel for: Metropolitan Life Insurance Company.
Representative Clients: Ford Motor Credit Co.; Norwest Bank, North Dakota, N.A.; Norwest Bank Minnesota West, N.A.; U.S. Gypsum Co.; Bremer Bank, N.A.

For full biographical listings, see the Martindale-Hubbell Law Directory

NILLES, HANSEN & DAVIES, LTD. (AV)

1800 Radisson Tower, P.O. Box 2626, 58108
Telephone: 701-237-5544
Facsimile: 701-280-0762
Williston, North Dakota Office: Energy Resource Building, 504 East Broadway, Suite 101, P.O. Box 1525.
Telephone: 701-572-5544.
Fax: 701-572-5561.

Timothy Q. Davies
Robert L. Stroup, II
Gregory B. Selbo
Andrew L. B. Noah

Representative Clients: U.S. Bank National Association; Chicago Title Insurance Company.

For Complete List of Firm Personnel, See General Section

For full biographical listings, see the Martindale-Hubbell Law Directory

VOGEL, WEIR, BYE, HUNKE & MCCORMICK, LTD. (AV)

502 First Avenue North, P.O. Box 1389, 58107
Telephone: 701-237-6983
Facsimile: 701-237-0847
Email: vogellaw@vogellaw.com *URL:* http://www.vogellaw.com

C. Nicholas Vogel

Daniel A. Bueide

Representative Clients: Associated General Contractors of North Dakota; Blue Shield of North Dakota; Cass County Electric Cooperative, Inc.; Clark Equipment Co.; Forum Communications Company; Merit Care Medical Group; Northern Improvement Co.; Dakota Clinic Ltd.; United Parcel Service; Gateway Chevrolet, Inc.

For Complete List of Firm Personnel, See General Section

For full biographical listings, see the Martindale-Hubbell Law Directory

OHIO

*CHILLICOTHE,** Ross Co.

CUTRIGHT & CUTRIGHT (AV)

76 West Second Street, 45601
Telephone: 740-772-5595
Fax: 740-773-9261
Email: atlaw@bright.net

(See Next Column)

CUTRIGHT & CUTRIGHT, *Chillicothe—Continued*

MEMBERS OF FIRM

James M. Cutright | James K. Cutright

Representative Clients: Citizens National Bank; Chivaho Federal Credit Union; Rockhold, Brown & Co. Bank; Litter Industries; Scioto Valley Mental Health Center; Paint Valley A.D.A.M.H.S. Board.
Approved Attorneys for: Lawyers Title Insurance Co.; Ohio Bar Title Insurance Co.; Chicago Title Insurance Co., Inc.

For full biographical listings, see the Martindale-Hubbell Law Directory

*CINCINNATI,** Hamilton Co.

BARRETT & WEBER A LEGAL PROFESSIONAL ASSOCIATION (AV)

500 Fourth & Walnut Centre, 105 East Fourth Street, 45202
Telephone: 513-721-2120
Facsimile: 513-721-2139

C. Francis Barrett

For full biographical listings, see the Martindale-Hubbell Law Directory

FROST & JACOBS LLP (AV)

2500 PNC Center, 201 East Fifth Street, 45202
Telephone: 513-651-6800
Telecopier: 513-651-6981
URL: http://www.frojac.com
Columbus, Ohio Office: One Columbus, 10 West Broad Street, 43215.
Telephone: 614-464-1211.
Telecopier: 614-464-1737.
Lexington, Kentucky Office: 1100 Vine Center Tower, 333 West Vine Street, 40507.
Telephone: 606-254-1100.
Telecopier: 606-253-2990.
Middletown, Ohio Office: 400 First National Bank Building, 2 North Main Street, 45042.
Telephone: 513-422-2001.
Telecopier: 513-422-3010.
Frankfort, Kentucky Office: 201 W. Main Street, 40601.
Telephone: 502-223-1400.
Telecopier: 502-223-1410.

MEMBERS OF FIRM

Lawrence H. Kyte, Jr. | Charles E. Schroer
Samuel M. Scoggins | Frederick W. Kindel
Jeffery R. Rush | W. Russell Wilson
E. Richard Oberschmidt | John C. Krug
P. Reid Lemasters | David S. Bence

ASSOCIATES

Bryan S. Blade | Rita M. Stolper
Sandra L. Nunn | Colleen M. Haas
Michael J. O'Grady | Jan R. Wenning
Christina M. Sprecher | Suzanne Wentzel

OF COUNSEL

Kimberly K. Mauer | Mary Ann Schenk

COLUMBUS, OHIO OFFICE
MEMBER OF FIRM
John I. Cadwallader

COLUMBUS, OHIO OFFICE
ASSOCIATE
Cara E. Gunder

LEXINGTON, KENTUCKY OFFICE
MEMBER OF FIRM
Greg E. Mitchell

MIDDLETOWN, OHIO OFFICE
SENIOR ATTORNEY
Daniel J. Picard

Representative Clients: Bank One, N.A.; Cincinnati Bell, Inc.; Cincinnati Machine; Federated Department Stores; First National Bank of Southwestern Ohio; KeyBank, National Association; PNC Bank, National Association; Firstar, National Association; Turner Construction Co.

For Complete List of Firm Personnel, See General Section

For full biographical listings, see the Martindale-Hubbell Law Directory

GOODMAN & GOODMAN A LEGAL PROFESSIONAL ASSOCIATION (AV)

123 East Fourth Street, 45202
Telephone: 513-621-1505; 1-800-494-4529
Fax: 513-621-6900
URL: http://www.goodlaw.com

Sol Goodman (1906-1971) | Stanley Goodman
Ronald J. Goodman

(See Next Column)

Donald P. Morrisroe | Reneé S. Frankel
John E. Stillpass | Jeffrey S. Goodman

For full biographical listings, see the Martindale-Hubbell Law Directory

GRIFFIN & FLETCHER (AV)

125 East Ninth Street, P.O. Box 926, 45201
Telephone: 513-421-1313
Fax: 513-421-1118

Earl W. Griffin (1890-1970) | Edward P. Hackett (1922-1989)

OF COUNSEL

John R. Fletcher | Dale W. Griffin

MEMBER OF FIRM
Michael C. Fletcher

ASSOCIATES

James C. Bodley | Linda G. Gilmore
Karen L Mastruserio, L.P.A.

Representative Clients: Lawyers Title Insurance Corp.; Aegon USA Realty Advisors, Inc.; The Equitable Life Assurance Society; Fifth Third Bank; Star Bank.

For full biographical listings, see the Martindale-Hubbell Law Directory

KATZ, TELLER, BRANT & HILD A LEGAL PROFESSIONAL ASSOCIATION (AV)

2400 Chemed Center, 255 East Fifth Street, 45202-4724
Telephone: 513-721-4532
Telecopier: 513-721-7120
Email: corp@ktbh.com

Ronald J. Goret | Daniel P. Utt

For Complete List of Firm Personnel, See General Section

For full biographical listings, see the Martindale-Hubbell Law Directory

KEATING, MUETHING & KLEKAMP, P.L.L. (AV)

1400 Provident Tower, One East Fourth Street, 45202
Telephone: 513-579-6400
Facsimile: 513-579-6457
URL: http://www.kmklaw.com

MEMBERS OF FIRM

Don R. Gardner | Vivian M. Raby
Herbert B. Weiss | Kenneth P. Kreider
Joseph L. Trauth, Jr. | Gail Glassmeyer Pryse
Mark J. Weber | Jody T. Klekamp

ASSOCIATE
Michael A. Brown

OF COUNSEL
William J. Keating

Representative Clients: American Financial Group; BP America Inc.; Chiquita Brands International, Inc.; Cintas Corporation; Comair Holdings, Inc.; Duke Realty Limited Partnership; LSI Industries Inc.; Mosler Inc.; Provident Financial Group Inc.

For Complete List of Firm Personnel, See General Section

For full biographical listings, see the Martindale-Hubbell Law Directory

KEPLEY, GILLIGAN & EYRICH A LEGAL PROFESSIONAL ASSOCIATION (AV)

525 Vine Street, Suite 2200, 45202
Telephone: 513-241-5540; 621-1045
Fax: 513-241-8111; 621-0038

David J. Eyrich | Paul D. Rattermann
Robert H. Siegel

Representative Clients and References furnished upon request.

For full biographical listings, see the Martindale-Hubbell Law Directory

STRAUSS & TROY A LEGAL PROFESSIONAL ASSOCIATION (AV)

The Federal Reserve Building, 150 East Fourth Street, 45202-4018
Telephone: 513-621-2120
Telecopier: 513-241-8259
URL: http://www.strauss-troy.com
Northern Kentucky Office: Suite 1400, 50 East Rivercenter Boulevard, Covington, Kentucky, 41011.
Telephone: 513-621-8900; 513-621-2120.
Telecopier: 513-629-9444.

Mark H. Berliant | Martin C. Butler (Resident, Covington, Kentucky Office)
William V. Strauss | Andrew M. Shott
Daniel H. Demmerle, II | Anthony M. Barlow
James G. Heldman |

Michael A. Ruh, Jr.

(See Next Column)

STRAUSS & TROY A LEGAL PROFESSIONAL ASSOCIATION—*Continued*

OF COUNSEL

John G. Parnell

Representative Clients: CSX Realty, Inc.; B.P. Oil Company; Standard Textile; Winegardner & Hammons, Inc.; Star Bank, N.A., (Ohio and Kentucky); National Amusements, Inc.; Corporex Properties, Inc.

For Complete List of Firm Personnel, See General Section

For full biographical listings, see the Martindale-Hubbell Law Directory

WAITE, SCHNEIDER, BAYLESS & CHESLEY CO., L.P.A. (AV)

1513 Central Trust Tower, Fourth and Vine Streets, 45202
Telephone: 513-621-0267
Fax: 513-381-2375; 621-0262

Stanley M. Chesley

Thomas F. Rehme	Paul M. De Marco
Robert A. Steinberg	Terrence L. Goodman
Fay E. Stilz	Colleen M. Hegge
Louise M. Roselle	Jane H. Walker
D. Arthur Rabourn	Renée Infante
Jerome L. Skinner	James F. Keller
Janet G. Abaray	Jean M. Geoppinger

Robert Heuck II

For full biographical listings, see the Martindale-Hubbell Law Directory

*CLEVELAND,** Cuyahoga Co.

BAKER & HOSTETLER LLP (AV)

3200 National City Center, 1900 East Ninth Street, 44114-3485
Telephone: 216-621-0200
Telecopier: 216-696-0740
TWX: 810 421 8375
RCA Telex: 215032
To contact an attorney on the Internet use first initial and surname followed by @baker-hostetler.com
URL: http://www.bakerlaw.com
In Cincinnati, Ohio: 312 Walnut Street, Suite 2650.
Telephone: 513-929-3400.
In Columbus, Ohio: Capitol Square, Suite 2100, 65 East State Street.
Telephone: 614-228-1541.
In Denver, Colorado: 303 East 17th Avenue, Suite 1100.
Telephone: 303-861-0600.
In Houston, Texas: 1000 Louisiana, Suite 2000.
Telephone: 713-751-1600.
In Beverly Hills, California: 9150 Wilshire Boulevard, Suite 205.
Telephone: 310-385-7500.
In Long Beach, California: 300 Oceangate, Suite 620.
Telephone: 562-432-2827.
In Los Angeles, California: 600 Wilshire Boulevard.
Telephone: 213-624-2400.
In Orlando, Florida: SunBank Center, Suite 2300, 200 South Orange Avenue.
Telephone: 407-649-4000.
In Washington, D.C.: Washington Square, Suite 1100, 1050 Connecticut Avenue, N.W.
Telephone: 202-861-1500.

PARTNERS

Paul E. Bennett	Elaine A. Chotlos
Dale A. Bradford	Lawrence V. Lindberg
Arthur V.N. Brooks	Patricia J. O'Donnell

For Complete List of Firm Personnel, See General Section

For full biographical listings, see the Martindale-Hubbell Law Directory

CONWAY, MARKEN, WYNER, KURANT & KERN CO., L.P.A. (AV)

30195 Chagrin Boulevard, Pepper Pike Place, Suite 300, 44124
Telephone: 216-292-3300
Telecopier: 216-292-3340

James J. Conway	Kevin R. Keogh
Howard A. Marken	Peter D. Brosse
Jeffrey G. Wyner	Mark Leskovec
Jack Kurant	Michael R. Stavnicky
Keith W. Kern	Michele R. Yeh
Peter Turner	Jennifer A. Corso

For full biographical listings, see the Martindale-Hubbell Law Directory

HENNENBERG & ASSOCIATES (AV)

30100 Chagrin Boulevard, Suite 301, 44124-5704
Telephone: 216-765-9600
Fax: 216-765-8292
Email: Hennenberg@aol.com

Michael C. Hennenberg

(See Next Column)

ASSOCIATE

John A. Fatica

For full biographical listings, see the Martindale-Hubbell Law Directory

HURTUK & DAROFF CO., L.P.A. (AV)

One Corporate Exchange, 25825 Science Park Drive, Suite 210, 44122
Telephone: 216-464-4001
Facsimile: 216-464-4007
Email: HDCOLPA@aol.com

Edward A. Hurtuk	Charles Daroff, II

Robert C. Ondak, Jr.	Eric C. Cotton

OF COUNSEL

Edward Small

For full biographical listings, see the Martindale-Hubbell Law Directory

JONES, DAY, REAVIS & POGUE (AV)

North Point, 901 Lakeside Avenue, 44114
Telephone: 216-586-3939
Telecopier: 216-579-0212
Email: counsel@jonesday.com *URL:* http://www.jonesday.com
In Columbus, Ohio: 1900 Huntington Center.
Telephone: 614-469-3939.
Telecopier: 614-461-4198.
In Atlanta, Georgia: 3500 SunTrust Plaza, 303 Peachtree Street.
Telephone: 404-521-3939.
Telecopier: 404-581-8330.
In Brussels, Belgium: Avenue Louise 480, 7th Floor. B-1050 Brussels.
Telephone: 32-2-645-14-11.
Telecopier: 32-2-645-14-45.
In Chicago, Illinois: 77 West Wacker.
Telephone: 312-782-3939.
Telecopier: 312-782-8585.
In Dallas, Texas: 2727 North Harwood Street.
Telephone: 214-220-3939.
Telecopier: 214-969-5100.
In Frankfurt, Germany: Hochhaus am Park, Grüneburgweg 102, 60323 Frankfurt am Main.
Telephone: 49-69-9726-3939.
Telecopier: 49-69-9726-3993.
In Geneva, Switzerland: 20, rue de Candolle.
Telephone: 41-22-320-2339.
Telecopier: 41-22-320-1232.
In Hong Kong, China: 29th Floor, Entertainment Building, 30 Queen's Road Central.
Telephone: 852-2526-6895.
Telecopier: 852-2868-5871 or 852-2868-5699.
In Irvine, California: 5 Park Plaza, Suite 1100.
Telephone: 949-851-3939.
Telecopier: 949-553-7539.
In London, England: Bucklersbury House, 3 Queen Victoria Street.
Telephone: 44-171-236-3939.
Telecopier: 44-171-236-1113.
In Los Angeles, California: 555 West Fifth Street, Suite 4600.
Telephone: 213-489-3939.
Telecopier: 213-243-2539.
In New Delhi, India (Associate Office): Pathak & Associates (an associate firm of Jones, Day, Reavis & Pogue), 1st Floor, Dr. Gopal Das Bhaven, 28 Barakhamba Road.
Telephone: 91-11-373-8793; 91-11-335-7345.
Telecopier: 91-11-335-3761.
In New York, N.Y.: 599 Lexington Avenue.
Telephone: 212-326-3939.
Telecopier: 212-755-7306.
In Paris, France: 120, rue du Faubourg Saint-Honoré.
Telephone: 33-1-56-59-39-39.
Telecopier: 33-1-56-59-39-38
In Pittsburgh, Pennsylvania: 500 Grant Street, 31st Floor.
Telephone: 412-391-3939.
Telecopier: 412-394-7959.
In Riyadh, Saudi Arabia: The International Law Firm (In Association with Jones, Day, Reavis & Pogue), Sulaymaniyah, Prince Mishari IBN, Abdulaziz Street, P.O. Box 22166.
Telephone: (966-1) 462-8866.
Telecopier: (966-1) 462-9001.
In Shanghai, China: 2805 Kerry Centre, 1515 Nanjing Road West.
Telephone: 86-21-5298-6568.
Telecopier: 86-21-5298-6569.
In Sydney, Australia: Governor Phillip Tower, Level 38, 1 Farrer Place.
Telephone: 61-2-9210-6921.
Telecopier: 61-2-9210-6926.
In Taipei, Taiwan: 8th Floor, Tun Hwa South Road, Section 2.
Telephone: (886-2) 2704-6808.
Telecopier: (886-2) 2704-6791.
In Tokyo, Japan: Toranomon MT Building, 4th Floor, 10-3, Toranomon 3-Chome, Minato-ku, Tokyo 105, Japan.
Telephone: 81-3-3433-3939.
Telecopier: 81-3-5401-2725.

(See Next Column)

JONES, DAY, REAVIS & POGUE, *Cleveland—Continued*

In Washington, D.C.: 51 Louisiana Avenue, N.W.
Telephone: 202-879-3939.
Telecopier: 202-626-1700.

MEMBERS OF FIRM IN CLEVELAND

Gary W. Melsher
Irvin A. Leonard
Zachary T. Paris
Richard L. Reppert
Stephen C. Mixter
William A. Herzberger

COUNSEL

Randall A. Cole
Marc Alan Silverstein

ASSOCIATE

Bernadette Mihalic Mast

For Complete List of Firm Personnel, See General Section

For full biographical listings, see the Martindale-Hubbell Law Directory

KAUFMAN & CUMBERLAND CO., L.P.A. (AV)

1500 Republic Building, 25 Prospect Avenue, West, 44115-1000
Telephone: 216-861-0707
Telefax: 216-694-6883
TDD: 216-694-6891

Steven S. Kaufman
Frank J. Cumberland, Jr. (Retired)
Robert A. Blattner

Susan L. Belman

OF COUNSEL

Anthony R. Troia
Edda Sara Post

Representative Clients: CertainTeed Corp.; Jaylin Development Corp.; Perl Building Corp.

For full biographical listings, see the Martindale-Hubbell Law Directory

KELLEY, MCCANN & LIVINGSTONE, LLP (AV)

3500 BP Tower, 200 Public Square, 44114-2302
Telephone: 216-241-3141
Fax: 216-241-3707
Email: Attorneys@kmlegal.com

MEMBERS OF FIRM

Fred J. Livingstone
John D. Brown
Margaret Anne Cannon
Donna M. Flammang
Bruce L. Waterhouse, Jr.

OF COUNSEL

David E. Burke

ASSOCIATE

Christine A. Allport

For Complete List of Firm Personnel, See General Section

For full biographical listings, see the Martindale-Hubbell Law Directory

MAYS, KARBERG & WACHTER (AV)

Suite 250, Corporate Circle, 30100 Chagrin Boulevard, 44124-5705
Telephone: 216-464-3030
Fax: 216-765-1258
Email: mkw@lawmkw.com

A. R. (Bud) Mays
Bruce K. Karberg
Mark I. Wachter

For full biographical listings, see the Martindale-Hubbell Law Directory

MCDONALD, HOPKINS, BURKE & HABER CO., L.P.A. (AV)

2100 Bank One Center, 600 Superior Avenue, E., 44114-2653
Telephone: 216-348-5400
Telecopier: 216-348-5474
Email: attorney@mhbh.com *URL:* http://www.mhbh.com

Patrick J. Berry
Jeffrey P. Consolo
Jerome W. Cook
Richard S. Cooper
Anthony J. DiVenere
Paul N. Edwards
Theodore J. Esborn
Steven L. Gardner
Carl J. Grassi
James A. Griffith
Jeffrey R. Huntsberger
Brian J. Jereb
Bernard L. Karr
Thomas W. Keen
Roger L. Kleinman
Joseph J. LoPresti, Jr.
Dan L. Makee
George L. McGaughey, Jr.
John T. Mulligan
Brian M. O'Neill
William J. O'Neill
Stephen T. Parisi
R. Jeffrey Pollock
Michael G. Riley
Shawn M. Riley
Albert N. Salvatore
Thomas C. Schrader
Roger L. Shumaker
Barbara J. Smith
James M. Stone
Dale R. Vlasek
Kenneth J. Walsh
John M. Wirtshafter
Jane Marie Pine Wood
Charles B. Zellmer

(See Next Column)

OF COUNSEL

John J. Monroe

Julie A. Callsen
Anne T. Corrigan
Steven A. Eisenberg
G. Andrew Gardner
Anuj Goswami
Donald E. Kacmar
David M. Kall
Jeffrey B. Keiper
Kevin J. Kessinger
Mark D. Klimek
Alan M. Koschik
Deviani M. Kuhar
Paul W. Linehan
Tyler L. Mathews
Jennifer A. Mills
Antoinette K. Palmer
Ketan K. Patel
Sharon Szolosi Regas
Douglas B. Schnee
Michele Smolin
Glenn D. Southworth
Michael R. Spreng

For full biographical listings, see the Martindale-Hubbell Law Directory

RODGERS AND CO., L.P.A. (AV)

1750 Guildhall, Landmark Office Towers, 45 Prospect Avenue, West, 44115
Telephone: 216-861-6191
Fax: 216-861-4699
Email: attys@rodgers-lpa.com

Walter A. Rodgers

Jeffrey M. Elzeer
Shawn A. Cormier

For full biographical listings, see the Martindale-Hubbell Law Directory

SPIETH, BELL, MCCURDY & NEWELL CO., L.P.A. (AV)

2000 Huntington Building, 925 Euclid Avenue, 44115-1496
Telephone: 216-696-4700
Fax: 216-696-2706
Email: law@spiethbell.com

Clyde E. Williams, Jr.
Henry E. Seibert, IV
Frederick I. Taft
James M. Havach
Benjamin Calkins
Kristin L. Ubersax

Representative Clients: Cleveland Cavaliers; Gund Arena; Nationwide Advertising Services, Inc.; Independent Steel Co.; Baldwin Wallace College; The Tool-Die Engineering Co.

For Complete List of Firm Personnel, See General Section

For full biographical listings, see the Martindale-Hubbell Law Directory

WALTER & HAVERFIELD, P.L.L. (AV)

1300 Terminal Tower, 44113-2253
Telephone: 216-781-1212
Telecopier: 216-575-0911
Email: law@walterhav.com *URL:* http://www.walterhav.com
Columbus, Ohio Office: 88 East Broad Street.
Telephone: 614-898-1096.

MEMBERS OF FIRM

Anthony J. Viola
John W. Waldeck, Jr.
Mark P. McGrievy

ASSOCIATES

Christopher W. Siemen
Debora S. Lasch
Teresa M. Beasley
Mary E. Zeit

OF COUNSEL

Daniel N. Steiger

For Complete List of Firm Personnel, See General Section

For full biographical listings, see the Martindale-Hubbell Law Directory

---

*COLUMBUS,** Franklin Co.

BRICKER & ECKLER LLP (AV)

100 South Third Street, 43215-4291
Telephone: 614-227-2300
Telecopy: 614-227-2390
Email: info@be.bricker.com *URL:* http://www.bricker.com

David G. Baker
Charles H. McCreary, III
David K. Conrad
Craig A. Haddox
L. Brent Miller
Andrew A. Folkerth
Frank L. Merrill
Thomas R. Brownlee, Jr.

Stephen Intihar
Christine A. Bricker

OF COUNSEL

John C. Rosenberger

Representative Clients: Banc One Corporation; Capitol South Community Urban Redevelopment Corporation; Discover Financial Services, Inc. (Morgan Stanley/Dean Witter/Novus); Firstar Bank, N.A.; The Huntington National Bank; KeyBank; The McGraw-Hill Companies, Inc.; National City Bank; New Par/AirTouch Cellular; Opus North Corporation.

(See Next Column)

BRICKER & ECKLER LLP—*Continued*

For Complete List of Firm Personnel, See General Section

For full biographical listings, see the Martindale-Hubbell Law Directory

CHESTER, WILLCOX AND SAXBE LLP (AV)

17 South High Street, Suite 900, 43215-3413
Telephone: 614-221-4000
Fax: 614-221-4012
Email: cwslaw.com

PARTNERS

James J. Chester
John J. Chester
John J. Chester, Jr.
J. Richard Emens
J. Anthony Kington
Roderick H. Willcox
Beatrice E. Wolper

ASSOCIATE

Thomas H. Mallory, Jr.

Representative Clients: American Municipal Power-Ohio, Inc.; The Limited; Scioto Downs, Inc.; R.J. Solove & Associates; Tee Jaye's Country Place Restaurants.

For full biographical listings, see the Martindale-Hubbell Law Directory

JOSEPH & JOSEPH (AV)

931 South Front Street, 43206
Telephone: 614-449-8282
FAX: 614-449-8287
Email: jandjoseph@aol.com *URL:* http://www.lawyers.com/joseph&joseph

MEMBER OF FIRM

John J. Joseph

For full biographical listings, see the Martindale-Hubbell Law Directory

KEGLER, BROWN, HILL & RITTER (AV)

Capitol Square Suite 1800, 65 East State Street, 43215-4294
Telephone: 614-462-5400
Telecopier: 614-464-2634
Cable Address: "Law KBHR"
Telex: 246671
Email: info@kbhr.com *URL:* http://www.kbhr.com
Marion, Ohio Office: 250 Executive Drive, Suite B, P.O. Box 919.
Telephone: 614-387-3501.
Facsimile: 614-387-3630.

Allen L. Handlan
Larry J. McClatchey
Richard W. Schuermann, Jr.
Kevin L. Sykes
Michael E. Zatezalo

COUNSEL

John C. Deal
Robert D. Marotta
Ted M. McKinniss (Resident, Marion Office)

T.A. Ward, II

Representative Clients: National City Bank.

For Complete List of Firm Personnel, See General Section

For full biographical listings, see the Martindale-Hubbell Law Directory

HARVEY S. MINTON & ASSOCIATES (AV)

6641 North High Street, 43085-4038
Telephone: 614-848-9600
Telecopier: 614-848-9818
URL: http://www.lawyers.com/mintonlaw

OF COUNSEL

Richard E. Gombert
Rainer E. Steinhoff

For full biographical listings, see the Martindale-Hubbell Law Directory

SCHOTTENSTEIN, ZOX & DUNN A LEGAL PROFESSIONAL ASSOCIATION (AV)

The Huntington Center, 41 South High Street, 43215
Telephone: 614-462-2700
Telecopier: 614-462-5135
Telex: 650 24 444 365
URL: http://www.szd.com
Cincinnati, Ohio Office: Bank One Towers, 8044 Montgomery Road, Suite 700, 45236-2926.
Telephone: 513-792-2730.
Cleveland, Ohio Office: One Cleveland Center, 1375 East 9th Street, Suite 950.
Telephone: 216-621-6501.
Fax: 216-621-6502.

Benjamin L. Zox
Herbert R. Godby
Randall S. Arndt
Daniel J. Kayne
William F. Simpson
Joanne I. Goldhand

(See Next Column)

Michelle K. Robinson
Dennis J. Rasor
Colin A. Mathews
Darrel R. Davison
Neil K. Sethi (Not admitted in OH)

Reference: Bank One of Columbus, N.A.

For Complete List of Firm Personnel, See General Section

For full biographical listings, see the Martindale-Hubbell Law Directory

SMITH & HALE (AV)

(Formerly Wilson & Rector)
37 West Broad Street, 43215
Telephone: 614-221-4255

MEMBERS OF FIRM

Harrison W. Smith (1900-1978)
Harrison W. Smith, Jr.
Ben W. Hale, Jr.
Jeffrey L. Brown
Glen A. Dugger
Jackson B. Reynolds, III

For full biographical listings, see the Martindale-Hubbell Law Directory

SWEDLOW, BUTLER, LEVINE, LEWIS & DYE CO., L.P.A. (AV)

10 West Broad Street, Suite 2400, 43215-3469
Telephone: 614-461-1100
Telecopier: 614-461-8178
Email: SBILLlaw@aol.com

Gerald H. Swedlow
Jack C. Butler
Richard L. Levine
Jeffrey M. Lewis
David A. Dye
Steven A. Baenen
Todd H. Neuman
Sean M. Gouhin

Reference: National City Bank; Fifth Third Bank.

For full biographical listings, see the Martindale-Hubbell Law Directory

TEAFORD, RICH, CRITES & WESP (AV)

Twenty East Broad Street, 43215-3682
Telephone: 614-228-5822
Telecopier: 614-228-2725
Email: TeaRich@aol.com

Jeffrey A. Rich
D. Michael Crites
E. Joel Wesp (Resident)

ASSOCIATES

Jeffrey A. Dittmer
Mark H. Gillis
James L Ervin, Jr

OF COUNSEL

Robert E. Teaford
Rosemary Sova
Murray R. Teaford
James R. Gorry

References: Huntington National Bank, N.A.; Fifth Third Bank.

For full biographical listings, see the Martindale-Hubbell Law Directory

VORYS, SATER, SEYMOUR AND PEASE LLP (AV)

52 East Gay Street, P.O. Box 1008, 43216-1008
Telephone: 614-464-6400
Telecopier: 614-464-6350
URL: http://www.vssp.com
Washington, D.C. Office: 1828 L Street, N.W., 20036-5109.
Telephone: 202-467-8800.
Telex: 440693.
Telecopier: 202-467-8900.
Cleveland, Ohio Office: 2100 One Cleveland Center, 1375 East Ninth Street, 44114-1724.
Telephone: 216-479-6100.
Telecopier: 216-479-6060.
Cincinnati, Ohio Office: Suite 2100, 221 East Fourth Street, P.O. Box 0236, 45201-0236.
Telephone: 513-723-4000.
Telecopier: 513-723-4056.
Alexandria, Virginia Office: 277 South Washington St., Suite 310, 22314.
Telephone: 703-549-4282.
Telecopier: 703-549-4492.

MEMBERS OF FIRM

Daniel H. Schoedinger
Stephen R. Buchenroth
James M. Ball
Gary E. Davis
John P. Wellner
J. Thomas Mason
Daniel J. Minor
Webb I. Vorys
Kenneth A. Golonka, Jr.
John B. Weimer

Representative Client: Honda of America Mfg., Inc.
Local Counsel: Abbott Laboratories; Anheuser-Busch, Inc.; Connecticut General Life Insurance Co.; General Motors Corp.; Navistar International Trans.; Ohio Manufacturers' Assn.; Ranco Inc.; The Limited, Inc.; Wendy's International, Inc.

For Complete List of Firm Personnel, See General Section

For full biographical listings, see the Martindale-Hubbell Law Directory

*DAYTON,** Montgomery Co.

FROELICH & WEPRIN CO. LPA (AV)

1812 Kettering Tower, 45423-1812
Telephone: 937-226-1776
Fax: 937-226-1945
Email: froelich4g@aol.com *URL:* http://www.lawyers.com/froelich&weprin

Gary L. Froelich | James I. Weprin

James P. Langendorf

Reference: Key Bank, N.A. of Dayton, Ohio.

For full biographical listings, see the Martindale-Hubbell Law Directory

DOVER, Tuscarawas Co.

MARIO D. CORSI (AV)

117 East Third Street, 44622
Telephone: 330-364-4414
Fax: 330-364-4472

References: The Huntington National Bank; Bank One of Dover.

For full biographical listings, see the Martindale-Hubbell Law Directory

DUBLIN, Franklin Co.

BLAUGRUND, HERBERT & MARTIN, INCORPORATED (AV)

5455 Rings Road, Suite 500, 43017-7517
Telephone: 614-764-0681
Fax: 614-764-0774
Email: bhm@bhmlaw.net

Christopher T. Cline

For full biographical listings, see the Martindale-Hubbell Law Directory

*PAINESVILLE,** Lake Co.

DWORKEN & BERNSTEIN CO., L.P.A. A PROFESSIONAL CORPORATION (AV)

153 East Erie, 44077
Telephone: 440-946-7656
Fax: 440-352-3469
Mailing Address: 55 Public Square, Suite 950, Cleveland, Ohio, 44113

Howard W. Bernstein
Marvin P. Dworken
Melvyn E. Resnick
David J. Richards, Jr.
Patrick J. Perotti
Irving Rosner
Alec Berezin
Howard S. Rabb

Patrick T. Murphy
Gary S. Okin
Dean M. Rooney
Geoffrey H. Turoff
Lisa M. Spano-Harting

SENIOR COUNSEL

David M. Dworken (Retired)

For full biographical listings, see the Martindale-Hubbell Law Directory

*TOLEDO,** Lucas Co.

DOYLE, LEWIS & WARNER (AV)

202 North Erie Street, P.O. Box 2168, 43603
Telephone: 419-248-1500
Fax: 419-248-2002
Email: dlw1@primenet.com

MEMBERS OF FIRM

Steven Timonere
Richard F. Ellenberger
Michael E. Hyrne
Michael A. Bruno
David W. Doerner

ASSOCIATES

Kevin A. Pituch | Maureen O. Atkins

Counsel for: Consolidated Rail Corp.; The Lakefront Dock & Railroad Terminal Co.; Prudential Insurance Co. of America; Equitable Life Assurance Society of the U.S.; Metropolitan Life Insurance Co.; Greyhound Lines; Fireman's Fund Insurance Cos.

For Complete List of Firm Personnel, See General Section

For full biographical listings, see the Martindale-Hubbell Law Directory

EASTMAN & SMITH LTD. (AV)

One Seagate, Twenty-Fourth Floor, P.O. Box 10032, 43699-0032
Telephone: 419-241-6000
Telecopier: 419-247-1777
Columbus, Ohio Office: 65 East State Street, Suite 1000, 43215.
Telephone: 614-460-3556.
Telecopier: 614-228-5371.

(See Next Column)

MEMBERS OF FIRM

David L. Kuhl | Steven D. Reinbolt

Counsel for: Chrysler Corp.; Marathon Oil; Envirosafe Service of Ohio, Inc.; Glasstech, Inc.; Toledo-Lucas County Port Authority; Huntington National Bank; Capital Bank, N.A.; Riverside Hospital; The Travelers Group; The Hartford Insurance Group.

For Complete List of Firm Personnel, See General Section

For full biographical listings, see the Martindale-Hubbell Law Directory

MORAN & MORAN (AV)

626 Madison Avenue, Suite 300, 43604
Telephone: 419-241-8171
Fax: Available Upon Request

Wayne R. Peppers (1894-1978)
Peter L. Moran
Mary Beth Moran

Representative Clients: The Exchange Bank; Payak Insurance Agency; Monroe Pharmacy, Inc.
References: Society Bank; The Fifth Third Bank, Toledo, Ohio.

For full biographical listings, see the Martindale-Hubbell Law Directory

RITTER, ROBINSON, MCCREADY & JAMES (AV)

1850 National City Bank Building, 405 Madison Avenue, 43624
Telephone: 419-241-3213
FAX: 419-241-4925

MEMBER OF FIRM

William S. McCready

Counsel For: Chrysler Corp.; Rubini Motors, Inc.; Ohio Casualty Insurance Co.; National Mutual Insurance Co.; Celina Mutual Insurance Co.; Westfield Insurance Co.; Northwestern National Insurance Co.; Midwestern Insurance Co.; United Ohio Insurance Co.; Toledo Auto Electric Co.

For Complete List of Firm Personnel, See General Section

For full biographical listings, see the Martindale-Hubbell Law Directory

OKLAHOMA

*NORMAN,** Cleveland Co.

CROWE & DUNLEVY (AV)

A Professional Corporation
2500 South McGee, Suite 140, 73072-6705
Telephone: 405-321-7317
Fax: 405-360-4002
Email: marketing@crowedunlevy.com *URL:* http://www.crowedunlevy.com
Oklahoma City, Oklahoma Office: Crowe & Dunlevy, A Professional Corporation, 1800 Mid-America Tower, 20 North Broadway, 73102-8273.
Telephone: 405-235-7700.
Fax: 405-239-6651.
Tulsa, Oklahoma Office: Crowe & Dunlevy, A Professional Corporation, 500 Kennedy Building, 321 South Boston Avenue, 74103-3313.
Telephone: 918-592-9800.
Fax: 918-592-9801.

Gary C. Rawlinson

Christopher R. Graves

For Complete List of Firm Personnel, See General Section

For full biographical listings, see the Martindale-Hubbell Law Directory

*OKLAHOMA CITY,** Oklahoma Co.

ANDREWS DAVIS LEGG BIXLER MILSTEN & PRICE, A PROFESSIONAL CORPORATION (AV)

500 West Main, Suite 500, 73102
Telephone: 405-272-9241
FAX: 405-235-8786
Email: andrewsdavis@andrewsdavis.com *URL:* http://www.andrewsdavis.com

J. Edward Barth
C. Temple Bixler
Charles C. Callaway, Jr.
Alan C. Durbin
Lloyd T. Hardin, Jr.
Sally A. Hasenfratz
John D. Hastie

OF COUNSEL

John P. Roberts

For Complete List of Firm Personnel, See General Section

For full biographical listings, see the Martindale-Hubbell Law Directory

Oklahoma City—Continued

CONNER & WINTERS, A PROFESSIONAL CORPORATION (AV)

One Leadership Square, 211 North Robinson, Suite 1700, 73102-7101
Telephone: 405-272-5711
Facsimile: 405-232-2695
Email: postmaster@cwlaw.com
Tulsa, Oklahoma Office: 3700 First Place Tower, 15 East 5th Street, 74103-4344.
Telephone: 918-586-5711.
Facsimile: 918-586-8982.
Fayetteville, Arkansas Office: Conner & Winters, P.L.L.C., 100 West Center Street, Suite 200, 72701-6081.
Telephone: 501-582-5711.
Facsimile: 501-587-1426.
Washington, D.C. Office: 1050 Seventeenth Street, N.W., Suite 810, 20036-5503.
Telephone: 202-783-5711.
Facsimile: 202-783-5720.

John W. Funk
Kiran A. Phansalkar

For Complete List of Firm Personnel, See General Section

For full biographical listings, see the Martindale-Hubbell Law Directory

---

CROWE & DUNLEVY, A PROFESSIONAL CORPORATION (AV)

1800 Mid-America Tower, 20 North Broadway, 73102-8273
Telephone: 405-235-7700
Fax: 405-239-6651
Email: marketing@crowedunlevy.com *URL:* http://www.crowedunlevy.com
Tulsa, Oklahoma Office: 500 Kennedy Building, 321 South Boston Avenue, 74103-3313.
Telephone: 918-592-9800.
Fax: 918-592-9801.
Norman, Oklahoma Office: Crowe & Dunlevy, 2500 South McGee, Suite 140, 73072-6705.
Telephone: 405-321-7317.
Fax: 405-360-4002.

Henry Rheinberger
Robert M. Johnson
James F. Hartmann, Jr.
Michael S. Laird

For Complete List of Firm Personnel, See General Section

For full biographical listings, see the Martindale-Hubbell Law Directory

---

DAY, EDWARDS, FEDERMAN, PROPESTER & CHRISTENSEN, P.C. (AV)

Suite 2900 Oklahoma Tower, 210 Park Avenue, 73102-5605
Telephone: 405-239-2121
Telecopier: 405-236-1012
URL: http://lawlinks.com/attys/ok/defpc.html

Joe E. Edwards
J. Clay Christensen
Richard P. Propester
Kent A. Gilliland

Thomas Pitchlynn Howell, IV
Joel Warren Harmon

Representative Clients: BancFirst; Bank One, Oklahoma City; Bank of America, N.A.; Federal Deposit Insurance Corp.; First Community Bank, Binger; First National Bank and Trust Company of Weatherford; First State Bank & Trust Co., Hollis; Harris Developments, Inc.; Local Oklahoma Bank.

For Complete List of Firm Personnel, See General Section

For full biographical listings, see the Martindale-Hubbell Law Directory

---

DURBIN, LARIMORE & BIALICK, P.C. (AV)

920 North Harvey, 73102-2610
Telephone: 405-235-9584
Fax: 405-235-0551
Email: DLB@Telepath.com

Gerald E. Durbin, II
James K. Larimore
Mark E. Bialick
Jerry John Hager, Jr.
David B. Donchin
Micheal L. Darrah

Rodney D. Stewart
Bill M. Roberts
Katherine Taylor Loy
J. Logan Johnson
Hilary S. Allen
Frances J. Stanton
Amy L. Alden
R. Brad Miller
Susanna M. Gattoni

For full biographical listings, see the Martindale-Hubbell Law Directory

---

HARTZOG CONGER & CASON, A PROFESSIONAL CORPORATION (AV)

1600 Bank of Oklahoma Plaza 201 Robert S. Kerr, 73102
Telephone: 405-235-7000
Facsimile: 405-235-7329

(See Next Column)

Larry D. Hartzog
J. William Conger
Len Cason
James C. Prince
Steven C. Davis
Joseph P. Hogsett
John D. Robertson
Kurt M. Rupert
Laura Haag McConnell
Linda G. Scoggins
Susan B. Shields
Ryan S. Wilson
Amy J. Sine
Jon H. Trudgeon
Charles E. Geister, III
Phillip G. Whaley
Armand Paliotta

J. Christian Guzzy
Stacey D. Spivey
Melissa Beeson Heindselman
Christin V. Adkins
Byron K. Linkous

OF COUNSEL

Kent F. Frates
Kenneth R. Davis
Alan Newman

For full biographical listings, see the Martindale-Hubbell Law Directory

---

SELF, GIDDENS & LEES, INC. (AV)

2725 Oklahoma Tower, 210 Park Avenue, 73102-5643
Telephone: 405-232-3001
Telecopier: 405-232-5553

Thomas J. Blalock
Jared D. Giddens
C. Ray Lees
Shannon T. Self
Bryan J. Wells

Michael D. Meleen
John E. Gatliff II

For full biographical listings, see the Martindale-Hubbell Law Directory

---

STEPHEN A. SHERMAN & ASSOCIATES (AV)

117 Park Avenue Building, Fourth Floor, 73102
Telephone: 405-235-0707
Fax: 405-235-0712
Email: ssherman@shermanfirm.com

Stephen A. Sherman

Representative Clients: Insignia Commercial Investments Group, Inc.; Kaiser-Francis Oil Co.; U.S. Foodservice, Inc.; B.F. Saul Co.; Irish Realty Corp.; Hogan Property Corp.; Western Industries, Inc.; ISC Telecom, Inc.; Rockcity.com, L.L.C.

For full biographical listings, see the Martindale-Hubbell Law Directory

---

WILLIAMS, BOX, FORSHEE & BULLARD, P.C. (AV)

522 Colcord Drive, 73102-2202
Telephone: 405-232-0080
Telecopier: 405-236-5814

John Michael Williams
Dennis R. Box
Richard D. Forshee
William J. Bullard
Keith R. Gibson
Paul E. Lefebvre

Kimberly K. Brown

For full biographical listings, see the Martindale-Hubbell Law Directory

---

*TULSA,** Tulsa Co.

BOONE, SMITH, DAVIS, HURST & DICKMAN, A PROFESSIONAL CORPORATION (AV)

500 Oneok Plaza, 100 West 5th Street, 74103
Telephone: 918-587-0000
Fax: 918-599-9317
URL: http://www.boonesmith.com

Byron V. Boone (1908-1988)
Teresa Meinders Burkett
John A. Burkhardt
Paul J. Cleary
Reuben Davis
J. Jerry Dickman
Monica Goodman
David J. Hyman
William C. Kellough
Donald A. Lepp
Mary Lohrke
Kimberly Lambert Love
Scott R. Rowland
Frederic N. (Nick) Schneider III
Jeffrey R. Schoborg
Stephen Schuller
L. K. Smith
Paul E. Swain III

OF COUNSEL

Edwin S. Hurst
Lloyd G. Minter

Representative Clients: American Airlines; BP Amoco Corp.; Chevron U.S.A., Inc.; Ford Motor Co.; Hillcrest Medical Center; PricewaterhouseCoopers; Phillips Petroleum Co.; The Boeing Company; Sears, Roebuck & Co.; World Publishing Co; Whirlpool Corp.

For full biographical listings, see the Martindale-Hubbell Law Directory

Blue Bell—Continued

KAPLIN STEWART MELOFF REITER & STEIN, PROFESSIONAL CORPORATION (AV)

350 Sentry Parkway, Building 640, P.O. Box 3037, 19422-0765
Telephone: 610-260-6000
Telecopier: 610-260-1240
Cherry Hill, New Jersey Office: 900 Dudley Avenue, #250, 08002-4426.
Telephone: 856-486-1044.
Fax: 856-486-1074.

MEMBERS OF FIRM

Marc B. Kaplin
William K. Stewart, Jr.
Bruce J. Meloff
Neil A. Stein
L. Leonard Lundy
Patricia L. Talcott

ASSOCIATES

Jeffrey L. Silberman
Stephen Marshall
William T. Dion

For full biographical listings, see the Martindale-Hubbell Law Directory

KELLEY & MURPHY (AV)

Union Meeting Corporate Center V, Suite 160 925 Harvest Drive, 19422
Telephone: 215-643-6500
Fax: 215-643-8356
Cable Address: "BIGTIME"
Email: kmlaw@counsel.com

Joseph T. Kelley, Jr.
Patrick G. Murphy
Joseph T. Kelley, III

LEGAL SUPPORT PERSONNEL

Marianne Rowen
Tanja M.Z. Barron

For full biographical listings, see the Martindale-Hubbell Law Directory

CAMP HILL, Cumberland Co.

REAGER & ADLER, P.C. (AV)

2331 Market Street, 17011
Telephone: 717-763-1383
Fax: 717-730-7366
Email: reagerpc@epix.net *URL:* http://www.ReagerAdlerPC.com

Theodore A. Adler
David W. Reager
Linus E. Fenicle
Debra Denison Cantor

Susan H. Confair

Representative Clients: The Homestead Group, Inc.; Dauphin Plaza Associates; First United Mortgage Services; First American Title Insurance Co.; Rothman, Schubert & Reed; Legg Mason Real Estate Services, Inc.; Standard Mortgage Investors, LLC.

For full biographical listings, see the Martindale-Hubbell Law Directory

*EASTON,** Northampton Co.

LITTNER, DESCHLER & LITTNER

(See Bethlehem)

FORT WASHINGTON, Montgomery Co.

MAX L. LIEBERMAN & ASSOCIATES (AV)

512 Bethlehem Pike, Second Floor, 19034
Telephone: 215-542-9150
Fax: 215-542-9397
Email: liebermn@lslaw.com *URL:* http://www.lawyers.com/lieberman

For full biographical listings, see the Martindale-Hubbell Law Directory

*HARRISBURG,** Dauphin Co.

GOLDBERG, KATZMAN & SHIPMAN, P.C. (AV)

320 Market Street - Strawberry Square, P.O. Box 1268, 17108-1268
Telephone: 717-234-4161
Telecopier: 717-234-6808; 717-234-6810
Email: gks@gkslaw.com

Ronald M. Katzman
Jesse Jay Cooper

Arnold B. Kogan

References: Fulton Bank; RVG Management & Development Co., Inc.

For Complete List of Firm Personnel, See General Section

For full biographical listings, see the Martindale-Hubbell Law Directory

MCNEES, WALLACE & NURICK (AV)

100 Pine Street, P.O. Box 1166, 17108-1166
Telephone: 717-232-8000
Fax: 717-237-5300
Email: info@mwn.com *URL:* http://www.mwn.com
Columbus, Ohio Office: 21 East State Street, Suite 1700, 43215.
Telephone: 614-469-8000.
Fax: 614-469-4653.
Washington, D.C. Office: 1200 G Street, N.W., 20005.
Telephone: 202-434-8991.
Fax: 202-434-8707.
Hazleton, Pennsylvania Office: 1 South Church Street, Suite 302, 18201.
Telephone: 570-455-8300.
Fax: 570-455-8390.

MEMBERS OF THE FIRM

Robert M. Cherry
David B. Disney
Steven J. Weingarten

ASSOCIATES

Charles M. Courtney
Rhonda Markle Weaver

For Complete List of Firm Personnel, See General Section

For full biographical listings, see the Martindale-Hubbell Law Directory

METTE, EVANS & WOODSIDE, A PROFESSIONAL CORPORATION (AV)

3401 North Front Street, P.O. Box 5950, 17110-0950
Telephone: 717-232-5000
Fax: 717-236-1816
Email: MEW@Mette.com *URL:* HTTP://WWW.METTE.COM

Charles B. Zwally
Peter J. Ressler
Jeffrey A. Ernico
P. Daniel Altland
Paula J. Leicht
Guy P. Beneventano

Bradley A. Walker
James M. Strong, VI
Bryan Scott Megary
John M. Hartzell

Counsel for: The B. F. Goodrich Co.; Juniata Valley Financial Corp.; MCI Telecommunications Corp.; Monongahela Power Co.; Community Banks; GTE Products Corp.; Commerce Bank; 360 Communications.

For Complete List of Firm Personnel, See General Section

For full biographical listings, see the Martindale-Hubbell Law Directory

JENKINTOWN, Montgomery Co.

VIRGINIA M. DUFFY (AV)

Noble Plaza, Suite 201, 801 Old York Road, 19046-1611
Telephone: 215-885-7540
Fax: 215-885-7543

For full biographical listings, see the Martindale-Hubbell Law Directory

SEMANOFF, ORMSBY & GREENBERG, LLP (AV)

Suite 200 Jenkins Court, 610 Old York Road, 19046
Telephone: 215-887-0200
Fax: 215-884-3500
Email: info@soglaw.com *URL:* http://www.soglaw.com
Philadelphia, Pennsylvania Office: Suite 200, Two Penn Center Plaza.
Telephone: 215-887-2094.

Harold Semanoff
Charles W. Ormsby, Jr.
Howard N. Greenberg
Michael J. Torchia

Michael K. Yarnoff
Peter J. Smith
Claudia M. Becker
Michael B. Dubin
Beth S. Joseph
Joanne M. Murray

OF COUNSEL

David M. Seltzer
Frederick M. Savadove

For full biographical listings, see the Martindale-Hubbell Law Directory

*PHILADELPHIA,** Philadelphia Co.

ADELMAN LAVINE GOLD AND LEVIN, A PROFESSIONAL CORPORATION (AV)

Suite 1900, Two Penn Center Plaza, 19102-1799
Telephone: 215-568-7515
Facsimile: 215-557-7922
Wayne Office: 1101 West DeKalb Pike, 2nd Floor, 19087.
Telephone: 610-992-0400.
Facsimile: 610-992-1005.

Lewis H. Gold
Robert H. Levin
Gary M. Schildhorn
Barry D. Kleban
Gary D. Bressler
Steven D. Usdin
Kevin W. Walsh
Raymond H. Lemisch

(See Next Column)

ADELMAN LAVINE GOLD AND LEVIN A PROFESSIONAL CORPORATION—*Continued*

Kathleen E. Torbit
Leon R. Barson
Matthew J. Swett
Bradford J. Sandler
William R. Hinchman
Victoria M. Endriss
Sebastian Ferrer

LEGAL SUPPORT PERSONNEL

Jacqueline Parsio (Paralegal)
Diana J. Papalini (Paralegal)
Wendy A. Raskas (Paralegal)

For full biographical listings, see the Martindale-Hubbell Law Directory

ASTOR WEISS KAPLAN & ROSENBLUM, LLP (AV)

The Bellevue, 6th Floor, 200 South Broad Street, 19102
Telephone: 215-790-0100
Fax: 215-790-0509
Email: lawyers@astorweiss.com
Bala Cynwyd, Pennsylvania Office: 401 City Avenue, Suite 500.
Telephone: 610-667-8660.
Fax: 610-667-2783.

MEMBERS OF FIRM

Alvin M. Weiss (1936-1976)
Paul C. Astor
G. David Rosenblum
Arthur H. Kaplan
Barbara Oaks Silver
David S. Workman
David Gutin
David S. Mandel
Gerald J. Schorr

ASSOCIATES

Christopher P. Flannery
Janet G. Felgoise
Elizabeth F. Warner
Daniel A. Shabel
Frances F. Freedman

SPECIAL COUNSEL

Neil Hurowitz
Jerrold V. Moss
Robert P. Style

OF COUNSEL

Edward W. Silver

For full biographical listings, see the Martindale-Hubbell Law Directory

BALLARD SPAHR ANDREWS & INGERSOLL, LLP (AV)

1735 Market Street, 51st Floor, 19103-7599
Telephone: 215-665-8500
Fax: 215-864-8999
URL: http://www.ballardspahr.com
Baltimore, Maryland Office: 300 East Lombard Street. 19th Floor.
Telephone: 410-528-5600.
Fax: 410-528-5650.
Camden, New Jersey Office: 800 Hudson Square, 5th Floor.
Telephone: 856-541-5577.
Fax: 856-541-8272.
Denver, Colorado Office: Seventeenth Street Plaza Building, Suite 2300, 1225 17th Street.
Telephone: 303-292-2400.
Fax: 303-296-3956.
Salt Lake City, Utah Office: One Utah Center, Suite 1200, 201 South Main Street.
Telephone: 801-531-3000.
Fax: 801-531-3001.
Voorhees, New Jersey Office: Suite 100, 1101 Laurel Oak Drive.
Telephone: 856-627-8555.
Fax: 856-627-1153.
Washington, D.C. Office: Suite 1000 South, 601 13th Street, N.W.
Telephone: 202-661-2200.
Fax: 202-661-2299.

Lynn R. Axelroth
Frederic W. Clark
Thomas R. Eshelman
David B. Gifford
Howard I. Grossman
Bart I. Mellits
David L. Pollack
Michael Sklaroff
Richard J. Braemer
Mark S. DePillis
Carl H. Fridy
Richard R. Goldberg
Philip B. Korb
Joanne Phillips
Alan S. Ritterband
William Y. Webb

OF COUNSEL

Gardner A. Evans
Lisa Fair Pliskin
Marcy Newman Hart
David K. Roscher

Alicia B. Clark (Not admitted in PA)
Ira A. Kauderer
Kathleen M. Sandone
Michael D. Silbert
Dominic J. De Simone
Austin S. Faberman
Tina R. Makoulian
Caroline Mouallem Schultz
Sharon Suleta
Elizabeth Farrelly Sur

For Complete List of Firm Personnel, See General Section

For full biographical listings, see the Martindale-Hubbell Law Directory

F. EMMETT FITZPATRICK, P.C. (AV)

926 Public Ledger Building, 19106
Telephone: 215-925-5200
Fax: 215-925-5991
Email: info@toplaw.com *URL:* http://www.toplaw.com

F. Emmett Fitzpatrick
F. Emmett Fitzpatrick, III

NiaLena Caravasos

LEGAL SUPPORT PERSONNEL

Doreen Howley (Paralegal)

For full biographical listings, see the Martindale-Hubbell Law Directory

FOX, ROTHSCHILD, O'BRIEN & FRANKEL, LLP (AV)

2000 Market Street, Tenth Floor, 19103-3291
Telephone: 215-299-2000
Cable Address: FROF
Fax: 215-299-2150
Email: frof@frof.com *URL:* http://www.frof.com
Atlantic City, New Jersey Office: CitiCenter Building, Suite 500, 1300 Atlantic Avenue, 08401.
Telephone: 609-348-4515.
Fax: 609-348-6834.
Doylestown, Pennsylvania Office: 102 North Main Street, P.O. Box 1589, 18901-0700.
Telephone: 215-345-7500.
Fax: 215-345-7507.
Exton, Pennsylvania Office: Eagleview Corporate Center, 760 Constitution Drive, Suite 104, P.O. Box 673, 19341-0673.
Telephone: 610-458-7500.
Fax: 610-458-7337.
Lansdale, Pennsylvania Office: 1250 South Broad Street, Suite 1000, P.O. Box 431, 19446.
Telephone: 215-699-6000.
Fax: 215-699-0231.
Sellersville, Pennsylvania Office: 64 North Main Street, 18960-0580.
Telephone: 215-257-3661.
Fax: 215-257-7999.
Trenton (Lawrenceville), New Jersey Office: Princeton Pike Corporate Center, 997 Lenox Drive, Building 3, 08648-2311.
Telephone: 609-896-3600.
Fax: 609-896-1469.
Voorhees, New Jersey Office: Laurelwood, Suite 103, 1103 Laurel Oak Road, 08043.
Telephone: 856-782-6000.
Fax: 856-346-9866.

MEMBERS OF FIRM

Herbert Bass
Stanley S. Cohen
John D. Trainer (Resident, Doylestown, Pennsylvania Office)
Mary Ann Rossi (Resident, Exton, Pennsylvania Office)
Elaine N. Moranz
Mark L. Morris
Gregory Kleiber
Marc E. Needles
Robert W. Gundlach, Jr.

ASSOCIATES

Craig L. Finger
Michael J. Kornacki (Not admitted in PA)

SPECIAL COUNSEL

Marjorie Stern Jacobs
Herbert K. Sudfeld, Jr. (Resident, Doylestown, Pennsylvania Office)

For Complete List of Firm Personnel, See General Section

For full biographical listings, see the Martindale-Hubbell Law Directory

FURIA AND TURNER (AV)

1717 Rittenhouse Square, 19103-6109
Telephone: 215-985-4500
Telecopier: 215-985-2824
Email: rfuria1717@aol.com *URL:* http://www.lawyers.com/furiaandturner

MEMBER OF FIRM

Richard F. Furia

ASSOCIATE

Gina R. Furia

OF COUNSEL

Robert S. Esposito

For full biographical listings, see the Martindale-Hubbell Law Directory

Philadelphia—Continued

WEIR & PARTNERS LLP (AV)

A Pennsylvania Limited Liability Partnership
Suite 500, The Widener Building, 1339 Chestnut Street, 19107
Telephone: 215-665-8181
Telefax: 215-665-8464
Email: info@weirpartners.com
Turnersville, New Jersey Office: 215 Fries Mill Road, 08012.
Telephone: 609-740-1490.
Telefax: 609-740-1491.

MEMBERS OF FIRM

Walter Weir, Jr.
Leonard S. Goodman
Susan Verbonitz
Jeffrey L. Rudnick
Robert D. Sayre
Stephen M. Giroux
Richard P. Coe, Jr.
Brett A. Datto
John B. York
Joseph C. Hare

ASSOCIATES

Bonnie R. Golub
Debra N. Nathanson
Tina L. Colman
Andrew K. Stutzman
Jeffrey A. Guth
Jason M Reiser
Madeline Flanagan

For full biographical listings, see the Martindale-Hubbell Law Directory

ROBERT H. ZIMMERMAN (AV)

The Ninth Floor, 1608 Walnut Street, 19103
Telephone: 215-546-8825
Fax: 215-735-1858
Email: RHZIM@AOL.COM

For full biographical listings, see the Martindale-Hubbell Law Directory

*PITTSBURGH,** Allegheny Co.

GLOSSER & SHREVE (AV)

Suite 200, 213 Smithfield Street, 15222-2224
Telephone: 412-281-6555
FAX: 412-281-6597
Email: mark.glosser@commersel.com *URL:* http://www.lawyers.com/debtorcreditlaw

Mark L. Glosser
Steven T. Shreve

Representative Clients: Crawford Construction Company, Inc.; Franklin & Locust Realty, Inc.; Digital Equipment Corporation, Inc.; Household Financial Corporation; First Union Bank; C.J. Betters Co.

For full biographical listings, see the Martindale-Hubbell Law Directory

MARCUS & SHAPIRA LLP (AV)

35th Floor, One Oxford Centre, 301 Grant Street, 15219-6401
Telephone: 412-471-3490
Telecopier: 412-391-8758
Email: info@marcus-shapira.com *URL:* http://www.marcus-shapira.com

MEMBERS OF FIRM

Robert L. Allman, II
Joseph J. Barnes
Estelle F. Comay
Charles G. Knox
Carrie Kochenbach
James F. Rosenberg

For Complete List of Firm Personnel, See General Section

For full biographical listings, see the Martindale-Hubbell Law Directory

MOLLICA & MURRAY (AV)

450 Trimont Plaza, 1305 Grandview Avenue, 15211
Telephone: 412-381-7000
Fax: 412-381-7111
Email: firm@mollicamurray.com *URL:* http://www.mollicamurray.com

MEMBERS OF FIRM

James A. Mollica, Jr.
Dr. John E. Murray, Jr.
Cathy Ann Chromulak
Timothy Murray
William J. Moorhead, Jr.

Michael E. Flaherty
Michelle D. Smith

For full biographical listings, see the Martindale-Hubbell Law Directory

PAPERNICK & GEFSKY, A PROFESSIONAL CORPORATION (AV)

34th Floor, One Oxford Centre, 15219
Telephone: 412-765-2212
Fax: 412-765-3319
URL: http://www.papernick-gefsky.com
Additional Pittsburgh Office: Suite 235, 5700 Corporate Drive.
Telephone: 412-366-5322.
Pittsburgh Suburban Offices: Northern Pike Pavilion, Monroeville.
Telephone: 412-373-2212.

(See Next Column)

Alan Papernick
Martyn I. Gefsky
William G. Merchant
Robert L. Murphy
Stephen M. Papernick
Melissa S. Lobos

Brenda J. Yurick
Diane K. Wohlfarth
Howard F. Murphy, IV
Jennifer K. Hughes

Representative Clients: Amore Companies, Inc.; Confederation Life Insurance Co.; Dollar Bank; ESB Bank; National City Bank of Pennsylvania; Lawyers Title Insurance Corp.; First American Title Insurance Co.; Mellon Bank, N.A.; PNC Bank.

For full biographical listings, see the Martindale-Hubbell Law Directory

PLOWMAN, SPIEGEL & LEWIS, P.C. (AV)

Second Floor, The Grant Building, 310 Grant Street, 15219-2201
Telephone: 412-471-8521
Fax: 412-471-4481

Jack W. Plowman
John L. Spiegel
James A. Lewis

Mark A. Griffith
Frank J. Kernan

Reference: Pittsburgh National Bank.

For Complete List of Firm Personnel, See General Section

For full biographical listings, see the Martindale-Hubbell Law Directory

WEISMAN GOLDMAN BOWEN & GROSS LLP (AV)

310 Grant Street, Suite 420, 15219
Telephone: 412-566-2520
Fax: 412-566-1088

James L. Weisman
S. James Goldman
Alden Earl Bowen
Sanford P. Gross
Barry J. Lipson
Howard J. Schulberg
Christopher J. Klein
Samuel F. Reynolds, Jr.
Frank J. Grzywinski
David J. Brosky
Robert L. Monks

Reference: Pittsburgh National Bank.

For full biographical listings, see the Martindale-Hubbell Law Directory

*READING,** Berks Co.

MOGEL, SPEIDEL, BOBB & KERSHNER, A PROFESSIONAL CORPORATION (AV)

520 Walnut Street, P.O. Box 8581, 19603-8581
Telephone: 610-376-1515
Telecopier: 610-372-8710

George B. Balmer (1902-1969)
George A. Kershner (1907-1969)
Carl F. Mogel (1919-1994)
Edwin H. Kershner
Frederick R. Mogel
Michael L. Mixell
George M. Lutz
Paul M. Yatron
Stephen H. Price
Kathryn K. Harenza

Sean J. O'Brien
Matthew Earl Glinn

OF COUNSEL

Harry W. Speidel
Donald K. Bobb
Henry A. Gass

Representative Clients: Great Valley Bank; Union Township, Berks County, Pennsylvania.

For full biographical listings, see the Martindale-Hubbell Law Directory

*SCRANTON,** Lackawanna Co.

O'MALLEY & HARRIS, P.C. (AV)

345 Wyoming Avenue, 18503
Telephone: 570-348-3711
Fax: 570-348-4092
Email: ohpc@epix.net *URL:* http://www.ohpclaw.com
Stroudsburg, Pennsylvania Office: 111 North Seventh Street.
Telephone: 570-421-2252; 570-422-1280.
FAX: 570-422-1281. Email: cerato@ptdprolog.net.
Wilkes-Barre, Pennsylvania Office: 61 North Washington Street.
Telephone: 570-829-3232.
FAX: 570-829-4418. Email: ohpcwb@epix.net.
Williamsport, Pennsylvania Office: 321 Pine Street, Suite 308.
Telephone: 570-323-4380.

(See Next Column)

O'MALLEY & HARRIS P.C.—*Continued*

Eugene Nogi (1905-1975)
Henry Nogi (1900-1976)
Russell J. O'Malley, Sr. (1904-1993)
Norman Harris (1907-1998)
William H. Amesbury (Resident, Wilkes-Barre Office)
Paul A. Barrett
Matthew P. Barrett
J. Scott Brady (Resident, Wilkes-Barre Office)
Michael Perry
James M. Tressler
Lori J. Cerato (Resident, Stroudsburg Office)
Bruce L. Coyer
John Q. Durkin
Gerald J. Hanchulak
Richard K. Hodges
Timothy J. Holland (Resident, Wilkes-Barre Office)
John F. Kennedy (Resident, Wilkes-Barre Office)
Daniel Morgan
Joseph Timothy Healey
A. Ruth Whalen (Resident, Wilkes-Barre Office)

Representative Clients: Pennsylvania Hospital Insurance Co.; MMI Systems Agency, Inc.; State Farm Insurance Company; ITT Specialty Risk Services; St. Paul Fire & Marine Insurance Co.; Chubb Group of Insurance Companies; Geisingen System Services; Princeton Insurance Company; Northeastern Pennsylvania Physicians Organization; Catholic Healthcare Partners.

For full biographical listings, see the Martindale-Hubbell Law Directory

WELLES & MCGRATH (AV)

1117 Bank Towers, 321 Spruce Street, 18503
Telephone: 570-348-4951
Fax: 570-348-4954

MEMBERS OF FIRM

Charles H. Welles, Jr. (1876-1962)
Matthew D. Mackie (1897-1965)
Charles H. Welles (1907-1997)
Henry C. McGrath
Charles H. Welles, IV

Counsel For: Grange National Bank; Scranton Industrial Development Co.; Bear Creek Nursing Home; Northeastern Ob-Gyn Associates, P.C.; Metropolitan Life Insurance Co.; New Health Management Systems, Inc.; Chamberlin Insurance Inc.

For full biographical listings, see the Martindale-Hubbell Law Directory

*TUNKHANNOCK,** Wyoming Co.

FARR, DAVIS & FITZE (AV)

7 Marion Street, P.O. Box H, 18657
Telephone: 570-836-3185
Facsimile: 570-836-4991

MEMBERS OF FIRM

John B. Farr (1907-1995)
James E. Davis
Judd B. Fitze

Representative Clients: Community Bank & Trust Co.; Proctor & Gamble Paper Products Co.
Title Agents for: Commonwealth Land Title Insurance Co.
References: Mellon Bank, Tunkhannock, PA Office; First Union Bank (Tunkhannock, PA Office); Community Bank and Trust Co.; Grange National Bank of Wyoming County.

For full biographical listings, see the Martindale-Hubbell Law Directory

*WILKES-BARRE,** Luzerne Co.

HOURIGAN, KLUGER & QUINN, A PROFESSIONAL CORPORATION (AV)

700 Mellon Bank Center, 8 West Market Street, 18701-1867
Telephone: 570-825-9401
FAX: 570-829-3460
Email: hkq@epix.net
Scranton, Pennsylvania Office: Suite 200, 434 Lackawanna Avenue.
Telephone: 570-346-8414.
Allentown, Pennsylvania Office: Sovereign Building, 609 Hamilton Mall.
Telephone: 610-437-1584.

Allan M. Kluger
Richard S. Bishop (Resident, Scranton Office)
Joseph E. Kluger

For Complete List of Firm Personnel, See General Section

For full biographical listings, see the Martindale-Hubbell Law Directory

ROSENN, JENKINS & GREENWALD, L.L.P. (AV)

15 South Franklin Street, 18711-0075
Telephone: 570-826-5600
Fax: 570-826-5640
Email: rjg@rjglaw.com *URL:* http://www.rjglaw.com
Hazleton, Pennsylvania Office: P.O. Box 618, 18201-0618.
Telephone: 570-455-7112.
Fax: 570-455-8304.

MEMBERS OF FIRM

Murray Ufberg
Joseph L. Persico
Garry S. Taroli
Mark A. Van Loon
Lee S. Piatt
Patricia Ermel Lakhia

ASSOCIATES

Thomas J. MacNeely
Ernest A. Sposto

Representative Clients: C-TEC Corp.; Chicago Title Insurance Co.; Manufacturers & Traders Trust Company; Guard Insurance Group; May Department Stores Co.; Student Loan Marketing Assn. (Sallie Mae); Penn-State Geisinger Medical Center; Subaru of America, Inc.

For Complete List of Firm Personnel, See General Section

For full biographical listings, see the Martindale-Hubbell Law Directory

WYOMISSING, Berks Co.

LEISAWITZ HELLER ABRAMOWITCH PHILLIPS, P.C. (AV)

2201 Ridgewood Road Suite 400, 19610
Telephone: 610-372-3500
Fax: 610-372-8671
Email: lhap@lhaplaw.com
Reading, Pennsylvania Office: 138 North Fifth Street.
Telephone: 610-372-3500.
Hamburg, Pennsylvania Office: 178 North Third Street.
Telephone: 610-562-4145.

Alan G. Leisawitz
Mervin A. Heller, Jr.
Jay N. Abramowitch
Charles J. Phillips
William R. Blumer
Allen R. Shollenberger

Robert J. Kirwan, II
Kevin A. Moore
Kathleen A. B. Kovach
Douglas Paul Rauch
Kenneth Millman

For full biographical listings, see the Martindale-Hubbell Law Directory

YOUNGWOOD, Westmoreland Co.

MILLSTEIN & KNUPP (AV)

Cherry Creek Commons Armbrust Road, P.O. Box 467, 15697-0467
Telephone: 724-837-3333
Fax: 724-837-8344

David J. Millstein

For Complete List of Firm Personnel, See General Section

For full biographical listings, see the Martindale-Hubbell Law Directory

RHODE ISLAND

*PROVIDENCE,** Providence Co.

HINCKLEY, ALLEN & SNYDER LLP (AV)

1500 Fleet Center, 02903-2393
Telephone: 401-274-2000
Fax: 401-277-9600
Email: firm@haslaw.com *URL:* http://www.haslaw.com
Boston, Massachusetts Office: 28 State Street, 30th Floor.
Telephone: 617-345-9000.
Fax: 617-345-9020. URL: http://www.haslaw.com.

MEMBERS OF FIRM

Paula K. Andrews (Not admitted in RI)
David D. Barricelli
E. Jerome Batty
Jonathan Bell
Paul Bork (Not admitted in RI)
Stephen J. Carlotti
David Barry Connolly (Not admitted in RI)
Joseph P. Curran
Michael P. DeFanti
Eric F. Eisenberg (Not admitted in RI)
Malcolm Farmer, III
Margaret D. Farrell
Hugh J. Gorman, III (Not admitted in RI)
Alan P. Gottlieb (Not admitted in RI)
William R. Grimm
Paul A. Hedstrom (Not admitted in RI)
Joel Lewin (Not admitted in RI)
Sandra Matrone Mack
Matthew T. Marcello, III
Elizabeth Murdock Myers
Paul F. O'Donnell, III (Not admitted in RI)
H. Peter Olsen
Gerald J. Petros
James O. Reavis
Jeremy Ritzenberg (Not admitted in RI)

(See Next Column)

HINCKLEY, ALLEN & SNYDER LLP, *Providence—Continued*

MEMBERS OF FIRM (Continued)

Ralph J. Rivkind (Not admitted in RI)
David J. Rubin
Charles E. Schaub, Jr. (Not admitted in RI)
Scott E. Sheridan (Not admitted in RI)
Herman Snyder (Not admitted in RI)
David R. Sullivan (Not admitted in RI)
Robert F. Sylvia (Not admitted in RI)
Christopher C. Tsouros (Not admitted in RI)
Howard E. Walker

ASSOCIATES

Jessica M. Bettencourt
Mark Bianchi
Alyssa V. Boss
Alexandra K. Callam
Jane E. Cohen (Not admitted in RI)
Andrew D. Cummings (Not admitted in RI)
June E. Daniel
Kristine L. Donabedian
Kim Herman Goslant (Not admitted in RI)
Gloria Maria Gutierrez (Not admitted in RI)
Kelley Jordan-Price
Catherine S. Kim (Not admitted in RI)
Christopher W. Morog (Not admitted in RI)
Katharine Carter Noble
Elena B. Olson (Not admitted in RI)
Andrew F. Shure (Not admitted in RI)
Joseph D. Whelan

OF COUNSEL

Willard R. Pope (Not admitted in RI)
Bentley Tobin
Joachim A. Weissfeld

For Complete List of Firm Personnel, See General Section

For full biographical listings, see the Martindale-Hubbell Law Directory

SMITHFIELD, Providence Co.

CHARLES S. SOKOLOFF INCORPORATED (AV)

Eleven Thurber Boulevard, 02917-1859
Telephone: 401-233-2800; Toll Free: 888-SOKOLAW
Fax: 401-233-2890
URL: http://www.sokolawyer.com
Email: sokolaw@sokolawyer.com *URL:* http://www.lawyers.com/sokolaw

Charles S. Sokoloff

Anne-Marie Krollman

For full biographical listings, see the Martindale-Hubbell Law Directory

WESTERLY, Washington Co.

ORSINGER & NARDONE (AV)

Narragansett Building, 53 High Street, P.O. Box 558, 02891-0558
Telephone: 401-596-2094
Telecopier: 401-596-4555

MEMBERS OF FIRM

Victor J. Orsinger
William A. Nardone

ASSOCIATE

Jon D. Lallo

References: The Washington Trust Co.; Fleet National Bank.

For full biographical listings, see the Martindale-Hubbell Law Directory

SOUTH CAROLINA

*BEAUFORT,** Beaufort Co.

DAVIS, TUPPER & GRIMSLEY, L.L.P. (AV)

611 Bay Street, P.O. Box 2055, 29901-2055
Telephone: 843-524-1116
Facsimile: 843-524-1463
Email: DTGS@Hargray.com

MEMBERS OF FIRM

Hutson S. Davis, Jr.
Ralph E. Tupper
James A. Grimsley, III
Erin D. Dean
R. Gerald Chambers, Jr.
Virginia D. Meeks

For full biographical listings, see the Martindale-Hubbell Law Directory

HARVEY & BATTEY, P.A. (AV)

1001 Craven Street, P.O. Drawer 1107, 29902
Telephone: 843-524-3109
Telefax: 843-524-6973

W. Brantley Harvey, Jr.
Thomas C. Davis
Thomas A. Holloway
Derek C. Gilbert

Approved Attorneys for: Lawyers Title Insurance Corp.; Chicago Title Insurance Corp.

(See Next Column)

Representative Clients: Nations Bank; First Bank, F.S.B.; Pleasant Point Plantation Associates; Century 21-Carolina Realty, Inc.; Lobeco Products, Inc.; Beaufort County Association of Realtors; The Fripp Company.

For Complete List of Firm Personnel, See General Section

For full biographical listings, see the Martindale-Hubbell Law Directory

LEVIN & GILLEY (AV)

811 Craven Street, P.O. Box 2358, 29901-2358
Telephone: 843-522-9000
Fax: 843-524-8248
Email: dcg@hargray.com *URL:* http://www.lawyers.com/levinandgilley

Julian S. Levin
Dewey C. Gilley, Jr.

Approved Attorneys for: Old Republic National Title Insurance Company.

For full biographical listings, see the Martindale-Hubbell Law Directory

*CHARLESTON,** Charleston Co.

BUIST, MOORE, SMYTHE & MCGEE, P.A. (AV)

Successors to Buist, Buist, Smythe and Smythe and Moore, Mouzon and McGee.
Five Exchange Street, P.O. Box 999, 29402
Telephone: 843-722-3400
Cable Address: "Conferees"
Telex: 57-6488
Telecopier: 843-723-7398
Email: bmsm@lawyer-sc.com *URL:* http://www.lawyer-sc.com

Susan M. Smythe
W. Foster Gaillard
Morris A. Ellison
David H. Crawford

Representative Clients: The Harry Frank Guggenheim Foundation; Daniel Island Development Co., Inc.; The Bennett-Hofford Company; Historic Charleston Foundation; Metropolitan Life Insurance Co.; E.I. duPont deNemours & Co.; General Dynamics Corp.; Independent Life & Accident Co.; Georgia-Pacific Corporation.

For Complete List of Firm Personnel, See General Section

For full biographical listings, see the Martindale-Hubbell Law Directory

HAYNSWORTH, MARION, MCKAY & GUÉRARD, L.L.P. (AV)

134 Meeting Street, P.O. Box 1119, 29402
Telephone: 843-722-7606
Facsimile: 843-724-8016
Columbia, South Carolina Office: Suite 2400 Affinity Building, 1201 Main Street, P.O. Drawer 7157, 29202.
Telephone: 803-765-1818. Facsimile 803-765-2399.
Greenville, South Carolina Office: 75 Beattie Place, Eleventh Floor, P.O. Box 2048, 29602.
Telephone: 864-240-3200.
Facsimile: 864-240-3300.

ASSOCIATE

Jeremy L. Cook

Counsel for: Baker Hospital; Healthsource of South Carolina; Allstate Insurance Co.; CSX Corporation; Lloyd's Underwriters; Coward-Hund Construction Co.; South Carolina Public Service Authority; City of Hanahan.

For Complete List of Firm Personnel, See General Section

For full biographical listings, see the Martindale-Hubbell Law Directory

OBERMAN & OBERMAN (AV)

38 Broad Street, 29401
Telephone: 843-577-7010
Fax: 843-722-7359

MEMBERS OF FIRM

Marvin I. Oberman
Harold A. Oberman

For full biographical listings, see the Martindale-Hubbell Law Directory

SOLOMON, BUDMAN, STRICKER & SCHWARTZ, L.L.P. (AV)

Parkshore Centre, 1 Poston Road, Suite 395, P.O. Box 30280, 29417-0280
Telephone: 843-763-1118
Telecopier: 843-763-7518

A. Bernard Solomon
Donald J. Budman
Michael A. Stricker
Lester S. Schwartz

Local Counsel for: Lawyers Title Insurance Corp.

For full biographical listings, see the Martindale-Hubbell Law Directory

WARREN & SINKLER, L.L.P. (AV)

Suite 340 171 Church Street, P.O. Box 1254, 29402
Telephone: 843-577-0660
Fax: 843-577-6843
Email: law@warren-sinkler.com

(See Next Column)

WARREN & SINKLER L.L.P.—*Continued*

MEMBERS OF FIRM

G. Dana Sinkler
John H. Warren, III
Henry B. Fishburne, Jr.
Scott Y. Barnes
Mark S. Sharpe
Elizabeth W. Settle
Andrea Hall Duenas
William O. Hanahan, III
Holly R. Jensen

For full biographical listings, see the Martindale-Hubbell Law Directory

*COLUMBIA,** Richland Co.

BARNES, ALFORD, STORK & JOHNSON, L.L.P. (AV)

1613 Main Street, P.O. Box 8448, 29202
Telephone: 803-799-1111
Telefax: 803-254-1335
Email: basj@basjlaw.com

William C. Stork
David G. Wolff

For Complete List of Firm Personnel, See General Section

For full biographical listings, see the Martindale-Hubbell Law Directory

FINKEL & ALTMAN, L.L.C. (AV)

Suite 1800, 1201 Main Street, P.O. Box 1799, 29202
Telephone: 803-765-2935
Fax: 803-252-0786
Email: webmaster@finkellaw.com *URL:* http://www.finkellaw.com
Charleston, South Carolina Office: 12 Exchange Street, P.O. Box 225.
Telephone: 843-577-5460.
Fax: 843-577-5135.

Charles S. Altman (Resident, Charleston South Carolina Office)
Howard S. Sheftman
Beverly J. Finkel

Representative Clients: Hewitt-Robins; 1st Union National Bank; Banc One Mortgage Co.; Motorola Communications & Electronics Corp.

For full biographical listings, see the Martindale-Hubbell Law Directory

HAYNSWORTH, MARION, MCKAY & GUÉRARD, L.L.P. (AV)

Suite 2400 Affinity Building, 1201 Main Street, P.O. Drawer 7157, 29202
Telephone: 803-765-1818
Facsimile: 803-765-2399
Greenville, South Carolina Office: 75 Beattie Place, Eleventh Floor, P.O. Box 2048, 29602.
Telephone: 864-240-3200.
Facsimile: 864-240-3300.
Charleston, South Carolina Office: 134 Meeting Street, P.O. Box 1119, 29402.
Telephone: 843-722-7606.
Facsimile: 843-724-8016.

MEMBERS OF FIRM

Gary W. Morris
Edward G. Kluiters

Counsel for: St. Paul Insurance Group; Allstate Insurance Co.; Fluor-Daniel Corp.; South Carolina Jobs - Economic Development Authority; Anheuser Busch Company; CSX Transportation; Ernst & Young, LLP; Willis Corroon of South Carolina, Inc.; Westinghouse Savannah River Co.; Wachovia Bank of South Carolina, N.A.

For Complete List of Firm Personnel, See General Section

For full biographical listings, see the Martindale-Hubbell Law Directory

QUINN, PATTERSON & WILLARD (AV)

2019 Park Street, P.O. Box 73, 29202
Telephone: 803-779-6365
Telefax: 803-779-6372
Email: qpw@bellsouth.net

MEMBERS OF FIRM

Michael H. Quinn
Grady L. Patterson, III
Theodore DuBose Willard, Jr.

Representative Clients: Miller Development, LLC; McTeer Real Estate Co.; Dial, Dunlap, McRacken & Smith Real Estate; McDonalds Corporation; South Carolina Electric & Gas Co.

For full biographical listings, see the Martindale-Hubbell Law Directory

RICHARDSON, PLOWDEN, CARPENTER & ROBINSON, P.A. (AV)

1600 Marion Street, P.O. Drawer 7788, 29202
Telephone: 803-771-4400
Telecopy: 803-779-0016
Email: atty@rpcrlaw.com *URL:* http://www.rpcrlaw.com
Myrtle Beach, South Carolina Office: 2103 B Farlow Street, P.O. Box 3646, 29578.
Telephone: 843-448-1008.
FAX: 843-448-1533.

(See Next Column)

Frank E. Robinson, II
Frederick A. Crawford
S. Nelson Weston Jr.

Representative Clients: Metropolitan Life Insurance Co.; Life Insurance Company of Georgia; Ohio National Life Insurance Co.; Connecticut General Life Insurance Co.; John Alden Life Insurance Co.; Carolina First Bank; Farmers & Merchants Bank of South Carolina; Baita Company International; Hancock Development Co.; Alec H. Chaplin Co.

For Complete List of Firm Personnel, See General Section

For full biographical listings, see the Martindale-Hubbell Law Directory

ROGERS TOWNSEND & THOMAS, PC (AV)

1441 Main Street, 10th Floor, P.O. Box 100200, 29202-3200
Telephone: 803-771-7900
Fax: 803-254-6305; 343-7017; 343-7019
URL: http://www.rtt-law.com

Robert Bryan Barnes
B. Michael Brackett
Sherwood M. Cleveland
Harry B. Gregory, Jr.
Clifford O. Koon, Jr.
Albert L. Moses
Eugene F. Rogers
Robert J. Thomas
Joe W. Underwood
Samuel C. Waters
W. Alex Weatherly, Jr.
Robert P. Wood
James C. Leventis
Richard M. Unger
Cheryl H. Fisher
D. Randolph Whitt
Stacey Lynch Hewson
Kendall R. Walker
Wm. Bert Brannon

Glen Paul Caulk
Thomas McRoy Shelley, III
Denis A. Brosnan, Jr.
Paul D. de Holczer

OF COUNSEL

James S. Guignard
Gwendelyn Geidel

LEGAL SUPPORT PERSONNEL

Carol A. Cummings

For full biographical listings, see the Martindale-Hubbell Law Directory

TURNER, PADGET, GRAHAM & LANEY, P.A. (AV)

Seventeenth Floor, 1901 Main Street, P.O. Box 1473, 29202
Telephone: 803-254-2200
Telecopy: 803-799-3957
Florence, South Carolina Office: Fourth Floor, 1831 West Evans Street, P.O. Box 5478, 29502.
Telephone: 843-662-9008.
Fax: 843-667-0828.
Charleston, South Carolina Office: 21 Broad Street, 1st Floor, P.O. Box 836, 29402.
Telephone: 843-723-1622.
Fax: 843-577-3369.

W. Duvall Spruill
Lanneau William Lambert, Jr.
Jeffrey L. Payne (Resident, Florence, SC, Office)
Michael S. Hopewell (Resident, Florence, SC, Office)

David W. Keller, Jr. (Resident, Florence, SC Office)
William O. Higgins

For Complete List of Firm Personnel, See General Section

For full biographical listings, see the Martindale-Hubbell Law Directory

TYLER, CASSELL, JACKSON, PEACE & SILVER, L.L.P. (AV)

1331 Elmwood Avenue, Suite 300, P.O. Box 11656, 29211-1656
Telephone: 803-779-4997
Telecopier: 803-765-2468

MEMBERS OF FIRM

Donald W. Tyler
Herbert C. Cassell, Jr.
Thomas B. Jackson, III
M. Alan Peace
Jeffrey L. Silver

References: Branch Banking and Trust Company; SouthTrust Bank; Centex Real Estate Corporation; McDonald's Corp.; CTX Mortgage; Chicago Title Ins. Co.; First American Title.

For full biographical listings, see the Martindale-Hubbell Law Directory

WHITENER & WHARTON, P.A. (AV)

2001 Park Street Park at Calhoun, 29201-2006
Telephone: 803-779-7830
Facsimile: 803-765-4649
Email: wwlaw@bellsouth.net

H. Dave Whitener, Jr.
L. Patricia Wharton

Representative Clients: Mortgage Lenders Network; D.R. Horton, Inc.; Torrey Homes; Investors Title Insurance Company of South Carolina; Better Business Bureau of South Carolina; Coastal Federal Savings Bank; Newberry Federal Savings Bank; SouthTrust Bank, N.A., Boyd & Company; Boyd Management Company.

(See Next Column)

*MARYVILLE,** Blount Co.

NICHOLSON, GARNER & DUGGAN (AV)
250 High Street, P.O. Box 5059, 37802-5059
Telephone: 423-984-1460
Knoxville: 423-637-1970
Telecopier: 423-982-2595
Real Estate Fax: 423-982-2595
Litigation Fax: 423-984-9275
Email: jnicholson@earthlink.net *URL:* http://www.lawyers.com/ngdlaw

MEMBERS OF FIRM
Joe Nicholson
J. Michael Garner
David R. Duggan

ASSOCIATES
Angelia D. Morie
Daphne H. Cornwell

Representative Clients: Lawyers Title Insurance Corporation; Fidelity National Title Insurance Company.

For full biographical listings, see the Martindale-Hubbell Law Directory

*MEMPHIS,** Shelby Co.

ARMSTRONG ALLEN PREWITT GENTRY JOHNSTON & HOLMES, PLLC (AV)
Brinkley Plaza, Suite 700, 80 Monroe Avenue, 38103-2467
Telephone: 901-523-8211
Facsimile: 901-524-4936
Little Rock, Arkansas Office: Suite 100, 100 Morgan Keegan Drive, 72202.
Telephone: 501-280-0100.
Facsimile: 501-280-0166.
Jackson, Mississippi Office: 2525 Lakeward Drive, Suite 200, 39216.
Telephone: 601-713-1192.
Facsimile: 601-713-2049.
Jackson, Tennessee Office: 464 North Parkway, Suite A, 38305.
Telephone: 901-660-2332.
Facsimile: 901-664-1109.

MEMBERS OF FIRM
Wm. Rowlett Scott
Paul A. Matthews
Sidney W. Farnsworth, III

Eugene E. Tibbs, Jr.

For Complete List of Firm Personnel, See General Section

For full biographical listings, see the Martindale-Hubbell Law Directory

FARRIS, MATHEWS, BRANAN & HELLEN, P.L.C. (AV)
One Commerce Square, Suite 2000, 38103
Telephone: 901-259-7100
Fax: 901-259-7150
Email: firm@farris-law.com
East Memphis, Tennessee Office: Suite 400. First Commercial Bank Building. 5384 Poplar Avenue.
Telephone: 901-763-4000.
Fax: 901-763-4095.
Nashville, Tennessee Office: Nashville City Center, 511 Union Street, Suite 2400.
Telephone: 615-726-1200.
Fax: 615-726-1776.

MEMBERS OF FIRM
Barry F. White
Robert A. McLean
Anita I. Lotz

ASSOCIATE
Harold W. Fonville, II

For Complete List of Firm Personnel, See General Section

For full biographical listings, see the Martindale-Hubbell Law Directory

HARKAVY, SHAINBERG, KOSTEN, KAPLAN & DUNSTAN, PC (AV)
100 Peabody Place, Suite 1300, 38103
Telephone: 901-761-1263
Telecopier: 901-763-3340
Downtown Telecopier: 901-843-0864
Downtown Office: Memphis, Tennessee, 6060 Poplar Avenue, Suite 140, 38119.

MEMBERS AND ASSOCIATES
Ronald M. Harkavy
Allen C. Dunstan
Raymond M. Shainberg
Neil Harkavy
Alan L. Kosten
Jerome A. Broadhurst
Michael D. Kaplan
Alan M. Harkavy

OF COUNSEL
Ira D. Pruitt, Jr.
Laurie A. Cooper
G. Thomas McPherson

For full biographical listings, see the Martindale-Hubbell Law Directory

JOHNSON, GRUSIN, KEE & SURPRISE, P.C. (AV)
An Association of Attorneys at Law
780 Ridge Lake Boulevard, Suite 202, 38120
Telephone: 901-682-3450
Fax: 901-682-3590

David J. Johnson

For Complete List of Firm Personnel, See General Section

For full biographical listings, see the Martindale-Hubbell Law Directory

KRIVCHER MAGIDS PLC (AV)
International Place II, 6410 Poplar Avenue, Suite 300, 38119-4839
Telephone: 901-682-6431
Facsimile: 901-682-6453
Email: lawfirm@kmplc.com

L. Don Campbell, Jr.
Charles C. Cottam
Jack Steven Magids

ASSOCIATES
Shawn A. Tidwell
Geoffrey M. Hirsch

For Complete List of Firm Personnel, See General Section

For full biographical listings, see the Martindale-Hubbell Law Directory

ROSSIE, LUCKETT, PARKER & RIDDER, P.C. (AV)
675 Oakleaf Office Lane, Suite 200, 38117-4863
Telephone: 901-763-1800
Telecopier: 901-767-6514
Email: rlpr@rlpr.com

J. Richard Rossie

For Complete List of Firm Personnel, See General Section

For full biographical listings, see the Martindale-Hubbell Law Directory

WARING COX, PLC (AV)
Morgan Keegan Tower, 50 North Front Street, Suite 1300, 38103-1190
Telephone: 901-543-8000
Telecopy: 901-543-8030
Email: Desk@waringcox.com

Robert S. Kirk, Jr.

Douglas R. Pyne
Joel B. Sklar
Joshua B. Lawhead

Representative Clients: Fred's, Inc.; Catherine's Stores Corp.; Boyle Investment Co.; Vining-Sparks IBG.

For Complete List of Firm Personnel, See General Section

For full biographical listings, see the Martindale-Hubbell Law Directory

*NASHVILLE,** Davidson Co.

BAKER, DONELSON, BEARMAN & CALDWELL (AV)
1700 Nashville City Center, 511 Union Street, 37219
Telephone: 615-726-5600
Telecopier: 615-726-0464
Email: info@bdbc.com *URL:* http://www.bakerdonelson.com
Memphis, Tennessee Office: 20th Floor, First Tennessee Building, 165 Madison, 38103.
Telephone: 901-526-2000.
Telecopier: 901-577-2303.
Chattanooga, Tennessee Office: 1800 Republic Centre, 633 Chestnut Street, 37450-1800.
Telephone: 423-756-2010.
Telecopier: 423-756-3447.
Knoxville, Tennessee Office: 2200 Riverview Tower, 900 South Gay Street, 37901.
Telephone: 423-549-7000.
Telecopier: 423-525-8569.
Johnson City, Tennessee Office: SunTrust Bank Building, 207 Mockingbird Lane, P.O. Box 3038, 37602.
Telephone: 423-928-0181.
Telecopier: 423-928-5694; 423-928-3654; Kingsport: 423-246-6191.
Huntsville, Tennessee Office: 3 Courthouse Square, 37756.
Telephone: 423-663-2321.
Telecopier: 423-663-2111.
Washington, D.C. Office: Market Square, 801 Pennsylvania Avenue, N.W., 20004.
Telephone: 202-508-3400.
Telecopier: 202-508-3402.
Jackson, Mississippi Office: Suite 500, 700 North State Street, 39202.
Telephone: 601-351-2400.
Telecopier: 601-351-2424.

MANAGING PARTNER
Laurence M. Papel

SHAREHOLDERS
John A. Gupton, III
J. Steven Kirkham

(See Next Column)

BAKER, DONELSON, BEARMAN & CALDWELL—*Continued*

ASSOCIATE

John M. Bryant, Jr.

For Complete List of Firm Personnel, See General Section

For full biographical listings, see the Martindale-Hubbell Law Directory

CHERNAU, CHAFFIN & BURNSED, PLLC (AV)

SunTrust Center, 424 Church Street, Suite 1750, 37219-2305
Telephone: 615-244-5480
Fax: 615-242-7951
Email: CCBABSMITH@AOL.COM

MEMBERS OF FIRM

Louis Leftwich, Jr. (1910-1960) | R. Garry Chaffin
Stanley M. Chernau | Linda F. Burnsed
Amy Bryson Smith

Representative Clients: SouthTrust Mortgage Corp.; Edwin B. Raskins Co.; Belz Enterprises; Chemical Residential Mortgage Corp.; NationsBanc Mortgage Corp.; SouthTrust Bank National Association.

For full biographical listings, see the Martindale-Hubbell Law Directory

CORBETT CROCKETT & LECKRONE (AV)

An Association of Attorneys including a Professional Corporation
Suite 1050, American Center, 3100 West End Avenue, 37203
Telephone: 615-383-0500
Facsimile: 615-383-5556
Email: counsel@ccllaw.com *URL:* http://www.lawyers.com/ccl

W. Lee Corbett (P.C.) | Joe Vaulx Crockett, III

For full biographical listings, see the Martindale-Hubbell Law Directory

GRISSIM & HODGES (AV)

323 Union Street, 37201
Telephone: 615-255-7496
Telecopier: 615-726-3014

MEMBERS OF FIRM

Sam D. Hodges, III | Mark E. Morrison

RETIRED

John M. Grissim

Representative Clients: John Alden Life Insurance Co. - Mortgage Loan Department; First Tennessee National Bank; T. W. Frierson Contractor, Inc.

For full biographical listings, see the Martindale-Hubbell Law Directory

GAIL P. PIGG (AV)

219 Second Avenue North, 37201
Telephone: 615-244-0001
Fax: 615-244-0003
References: Nations Bank.

For full biographical listings, see the Martindale-Hubbell Law Directory

TEXAS

ADDISON, Dallas Co.

BARRETT BURKE WILSON CASTLE DAFFIN & FRAPPIER, L.L.P. (AV)

A Limited Liability Partnership including Professional Corporations
15000 Surveyor Boulevard, Suite 100, 75001
Telephone: 972-386-5040
Fax: 972-386-7673
Houston, Texas Office: 24 Greenway Plaza, Suite 2001.
Telephone: 713-621-8673.
Denver, Colorado Affiliated Office: Castle Barrett Daffin & Frappier, 1099 Eighteenth Street, Suite 2200.
Telephone: 303-299-1800.
Fax: 303-299-1808.
Little Rock, Arkansas Affiliated Office: Wilson & Associates, P.A. 1521 Merrill Drive, Suite D220.
Telephone: 501-219-9388.

Michael C. Barrett

For full biographical listings, see the Martindale-Hubbell Law Directory

BRUCE E. TURNER (AV)

16901 N. Dallas Parkway Suite 204, 75001
Telephone: 972-818-6716
Fax: 972-818-6719
Email: bturner@cdg-inc.com

For full biographical listings, see the Martindale-Hubbell Law Directory

*AUSTIN,** Travis Co.

BAKER BOTTS L.L.P. (AV)

1600 San Jacinto Center, 98 San Jacinto Boulevard, 78701
Telephone: 512-322-2500
Fax: 512-322-2501
Email: postmaster@bakerbotts.com *URL:* http://www.bakerbotts.com
Houston, Texas Office: One Shell Plaza, 910 Louisiana.
Telephone: 713-229-1234.
Dallas, Texas Office: 2001 Ross Avenue.
Telephone: 214-953-6500.
Washington, D.C. Office: The Warner, 1299 Pennsylvania Avenue, N.W.
Telephone: 202-639-7700.
New York, New York Office: 599 Lexington Avenue.
Telephone: 212-705-5000.
Moscow, Russia Office: 10 ul. Bolshaya Dimitrovka (formerly Pushkinskaya), 103031.
Telephone: 7095/921-5300 (Local); 7501/929-7070 (International).
London, England Office: 45 Ludgate Hill.
Telephone: 0171-778-1400 (Local); 011-44-171-778-1400 (International).
Baku, Azerbaijan Office: 6-10 Vagif Mustafa-zadeh Street, Third Floor, Icheri Sheher, 370004.
Telephone: 994-12-97-63-88 (Local); 011-994-12-97-63-88 (International).
Fax: 994-12-97-63-61 (Local); 011-994-12-97-63-91 (International).

MEMBERS OF FIRM

Aileen M. Hooks | William F. Stutts, Jr.

SPECIAL COUNSEL

Shelley W. Austin

ASSOCIATE

Derek R. McDonald

For Complete List of Firm Personnel, See General Section

For full biographical listings, see the Martindale-Hubbell Law Directory

DRENNER & STUART, L.L.P. (AV)

301 Congress Avenue Suite 2100, 78701
Telephone: 512-404-2200
Telecopier: 512-404-2244
Email: legal@drenner-stuart.com

Stephen O. Drenner | Donald L. Stuart
John W. Elliott | David A. Wolff
R. Kemp Kasling | Steven C. Metcalfe
Michael L. Robertson | Alexander Nicolai von Kreisler
Wallace M. Smith | Alan M. Glen

Christopher K. Bell | M. Daniel Guerra
James A. Bastien | Thomas Edward Rodman, Jr.
Craig McKinney Douglas

OF COUNSEL

J.B. Ruhl

For full biographical listings, see the Martindale-Hubbell Law Directory

H. GLENN HALL, JR. (AV)

301 Congress Avenue, Suite 2025, 78701
Telephone: 512-236-8955
Fax: 512-320-4162

For full biographical listings, see the Martindale-Hubbell Law Directory

SAEGERT, ANGENEND & AUGUSTINE, P.C. (AV)

1145 West Fifth Street, Suite 300, 78703-5341
Telephone: 512-474-6521
Fax: 512-477-4512

Jerry C. Saegert

Walter C. Guebert

Representative Clients: Del Valle Independent School District; Leander Independent School District; U-First, L.L.C.; Legend Homebuilders, Inc.; Texas District Luthern Church-Missouri Synod.

For full biographical listings, see the Martindale-Hubbell Law Directory

BEDFORD, Tarrant Co.

ADAMS, LYNCH & LOFTIN, P.C. (AV)

1903 Central Drive, Suite 400, 76021
Telephone: 817-283-7742
Fax: 817-571-2947

Neal W. Adams
John T. Lynch, IV
Stacy B. Loftin

Jon A. McCormick

For full biographical listings, see the Martindale-Hubbell Law Directory

*CENTER,** Shelby Co.

FAIRCHILD, PRICE, THOMAS, HALEY & WILLINGHAM, L.L.P. (AV)

413 Shelbyville Street, P.O. Drawer 1719, 75935
Telephone: 409-598-2981
Fax: 409-598-7712
Email: wmthomas@fpthw.com
Nacogdoches, Texas Office: 1801 North Street, P. O. Box 631668, 75963-1668.
Telephone: 409-569-2327.
Fax: 409-569-7932. E-Mail: chaley@fpthw.com
Houston, Texas Office: 440 Louisiana Street, Suite 2110, 77002-4205.
Telephone: 713-426-1700.
Fax: 713-426-1717. E-Mail: mwillingham@fpthw.com

MEMBERS OF FIRM

John L. Price
W. Miller Thomas
C. Victor Haley
R. Mark Willingham
Ryan A. Beason (Resident at Houston Office)
Travis P. Clardy
David J. Fisher
Clayton H. Haley
Russell R. Smith
James A. Payne, Jr.

OF COUNSEL

Robert L. Fairchild

ASSOCIATES

David Edward Ash
Campbell Cox
Jefferson B. Davis
Thomas L. Cougill
Jeffrey Pierce Fultz
Matthew D. Mettauer

For full biographical listings, see the Martindale-Hubbell Law Directory

*CORPUS CHRISTI,** Nueces Co.

DAVID Z. CONOLY, P.C. (AV)

1100 Wilson Plaza West, 78476
Telephone: 361-887-0707
Fax: 361-887-7329
Email: dzc@aol.com

David Z. Conoly

For full biographical listings, see the Martindale-Hubbell Law Directory

*DALLAS,** Dallas Co.

BAKER BOTTS L.L.P. (AV)

2001 Ross Avenue, 75201
Telephone: 214-953-6500
Fax: 214-953-6503
Email: postmaster@bakerbotts.com *URL:* http://www.bakerbotts.com
Houston, Texas Office: One Shell Plaza, 910 Louisiana.
Telephone: 713-229-1234.
Washington, D.C. Office: The Warner, 1299 Pennsylvania Avenue, N.W.
Telephone: 202-639-7700.
Austin, Texas Office: 1600 San Jacinto Center, 98 San Jacinto Boulevard.
Telephone: 512-322-2500.
New York, New York Office: 599 Lexington Avenue.
Telephone: 212-705-5000.
Moscow, Russia Office: 10 ul. Bolshaya Dimitrovka (formerly Pushkinskaya), 103031.
Telephone: 7095/921-5300 (Local); 7095/929-7070.
London, England Office: 45 Ludgate Hill.
Telephone: 0171-778-1400 (Local); 011-44-171-778-1400 (International).
Baku, Azerbaijan Office: 6-10 Vagif Mustafa-zadeh Street, Third Floor, Icheri Sheher, 370004.
Telephone: 994-12-97-63-88 (Local); 011-994-12-97-63-88 (International).

MEMBERS OF FIRM

Jonathan W. Dunlay
Patricia M. Stanton

ASSOCIATES

David C. Druffner
J. Atwood Jeter
Joel M. Overton, Jr.
Anita J. Smith

For Complete List of Firm Personnel, See General Section

For full biographical listings, see the Martindale-Hubbell Law Directory

CALHOUN & STACY (AV)

Suite 5700 - Bank of America Plaza, 901 Main Street, 75202-3713
Telephone: 214-748-5000
Facsimile: 214-748-1421
Email: info@calhounstacy.com *URL:* http://www.calhounstacy.com

MEMBERS OF FIRM

Rees T. Bowen, III
Mark Alan Calhoun
David W. Elrod
Parker Nelson
Thomas E. Rosen

For Complete List of Firm Personnel, See General Section

For full biographical listings, see the Martindale-Hubbell Law Directory

CLARK, WEST, KELLER, BUTLER & ELLIS, L.L.P. (AV)

4800 Renaissance Tower, 1201 Elm Street, 75270-2146
Telephone: 214-741-1001
Telecopier: 214-760-9812

MEMBERS OF FIRM

William H. Clark (1861-1931)
William H. Clark, Jr. (1895-1943)
Robert L. Clark (1903-1963)
William L. Keller
Allen Butler
David M. Ellis
Melvyn L. Douglas
Mike M. Tabor
Mark A. Shank
Michael P. Maslanka
Kervyn B. Altaffer, Jr.
Kelly Gaffney McClure

ASSOCIATES

Veronica Cuadra
Melinda L. Eitzen
Wade A. Forsman
Theresa M. Gegen
M. Brenk Johnson
Christie A. Newkirk
Robert J. Wood, Jr.
John Peter Hagan
Sonja J. McGill

For full biographical listings, see the Martindale-Hubbell Law Directory

GWEN M. EISENSTEIN (AV)

5025 North Central Expressway, 75205
Telephone: 214-520-3366
Fax: 214-520-3729

For full biographical listings, see the Martindale-Hubbell Law Directory

FERNANDEZ & KNEBEL, A PROFESSIONAL CORPORATION (AV)

Bank One Center, 1717 Main Street, Suite 2100, 75201
Telephone: 214-747-2100
Fax: 214-747-2144

Bennett I. Abramowitz
Clint A. Corrie
Raymond R. Fernandez, Jr.
Delbert L. Gibbs
Robert L. Knebel, Jr.
Mary Jo Vida

Barbara F. Blaylock
Herbert J. Gilles
Maria Isabel Roman
Jon M. Payne
Joseph L. Mira

For full biographical listings, see the Martindale-Hubbell Law Directory

GEARY, PORTER & DONOVAN, P.C. (AV)

One Bent Tree Tower, 16475 Dallas Parkway, Suite 500, 75001-6837
Telephone: 972-931-9901
Facsimile: 972-931-9208
Mailing Address: P.O. Box 700248, Dallas, Texas, 75370-0248
Email: firm@gpd.com *URL:* http://www.gpd.com

Emmett W. Berryman
Laura M. Keith
Jeffrey T. Libby
Gregory L. Miller
James T. Porter
Kim Alan Roberts
Thomas L. Staley
David M. Tatum

For full biographical listings, see the Martindale-Hubbell Law Directory

GRIFFITH & NIXON, P.C. (AV)

One Lincoln Center, 5400 LBJ Freeway, Suite 1025, 75240
Telephone: 972-386-8988
Fax: 972-386-8985
Email: griffnix@flash.net

Scott Griffith
Michael S. Nixon

Kimberly A. Davison
Benjamin D. Halpern
L. Christopher Harris
Anthony P. Jach
Jeffery Harold Rusthoven
Scott V. Siddons

For full biographical listings, see the Martindale-Hubbell Law Directory

Dallas—Continued

The Holmes Firm A Professional Corporation (AV)

250 Park Place, 2911 Turtle Creek Boulevard, 75219-6242
Telephone: 214-559-2299
Facsimile: 214-559-3115
Email: theholmesfirm@earthlink.net *URL:* http://www.lawyers.com/holmeslaw

Ronald L. Holmes

S. Elizabeth Lamar Bruni

Representative Clients: Centre Development Co., Inc.; Bradford Putnam Realty, Inc.; Clubhouse Inns; Corplan Corrections, LL.C.; HCB Enterprises, Inc. (d/b/a/ Bibbentucker's); Kurz Group, Inc.; L&N Commercial, Inc.; International Capital, Inc.; Limestone Group, Inc.; Hunt Capital, L.L.C.; Rainbow Trading Corporation.

For full biographical listings, see the Martindale-Hubbell Law Directory

Hughes & Luce, L.L.P. (AV)

A Registered Limited Liability Partnership including Professional Corporations
1717 Main Street, Suite 2800, 75201
Telephone: 214-939-5500
Fax: 214-939-6100; 214-939-5849
Email: H&L@hughesluce.com *URL:* http://www.hughesluce.com
Austin, Texas Office: 111 Congress, Suite 900.
Telephone: 512-482-6800.
Fax: 512-482-6859.
Houston, Texas Office: 1600 Smith Street, Suite 3550.
Telephone: 713-754-5200.
Fax: 713-754-5270.

MEMBERS OF FIRM

Michael J. Dalton
Deborah J. Eichner
Zammurad Hyatt Feroze
David Lee Fields
Daniel K. Hennessy
James A. Moomaw
Dwight A. Shupe

ASSOCIATES

Stefanie L. Cooper
Clifton M. Dugas, III
Allison L. Elko
Martin E. Garza
Christopher C. Lewis (Not admitted in TX)
Lynne A. Messina
Anthony Gorham Soards
Misty M. Ventura

For Complete List of Firm Personnel, See General Section

For full biographical listings, see the Martindale-Hubbell Law Directory

Jackson Walker L.L.P. (AV)

901 Main Street, Suite 6000, 75202-3797
Telephone: 214-953-6000
Fax: 214-953-5822
URL: http://www.jw.com
Austin, Texas Office: 100 Congress Avenue, Suite 1100.
Telephone: 512-236-2000.
Fax: 512-236-2002.
Fort Worth, Texas Office: 301 Commerce Street, Suite 2400.
Telephone: 817-334-7200.
Fax: 817-334-7290.
Houston, Texas Office: 1100 Louisiana, Suite 4200.
Telephone: 713-752-4200.
Fax: 713-752-4221.
Richardson, Texas Office: 2435 North Central Expressway, Suite 600.
Telephone: 972-671-2560.
Fax: 972-671-2566.
San Angelo, Texas Office: 225 West Beauregard Avenue.
Telephone: 915-481-2550.
Fax: 915-481-2552.
San Antonio, Texas Office: 112 E. Pecan Street, Suite 2100.
Telephone: 210-978-7700.
Fax: 210-978-7790.

MEMBERS OF FIRM

Bryan C. Birkeland
Michael Patrick Haggerty

OF COUNSEL

Roy Howard Baskin, III

Representative Clients Furnished Upon Request.

For Complete List of Firm Personnel, See General Section

For full biographical listings, see the Martindale-Hubbell Law Directory

Kane, Russell, Coleman & Logan, A Professional Corporation (AV)

3700 Thanksgiving Tower, 1601 Elm Street, 75201-7207
Telephone: 214-777-4200
Fax: 214-777-4299
Email: krcl@krcl.com

(See Next Column)

Raymond J. Kane
Gordon B. Russell
Joseph M. Coleman
Michael A. Logan
Patrick V. Stark
Kenneth W. Biermacher
David N. Condon
Karen A. Cox
William D. Elliott
Joseph A. Friedman
Robert N. LeMay
Michael L. Atchley, II
Margaret M. McLeod Jordan

Terry Flett Barakis
Harold R. Busch
Priscilla K. Davenport
Deborah A. DiMarco
Evangelos J. Gegas (Not admitted in TX)
Shelli R. Inmon
Kenneth C. Johnston
Jaqluin M. Bickmore Lloyd
Robert L. Manteuffel
David D. Ritter
Holly J. Roman
Jeffrey S. Seeburger
Jeffrey Charles Tasker
Steven M. Thornton
Karin M. Zaner

For full biographical listings, see the Martindale-Hubbell Law Directory

Krage & Janvey, L.L.P. (AV)

2001 Bryan Tower, Suite 2700, 75201-3059
Telephone: 214-969-7500
Telecopier: 214-220-0230

Ben L. Krage

Representative Client: Regal Capital Co.

For full biographical listings, see the Martindale-Hubbell Law Directory

Meadows, Owens, Collier, Reed, Cousins & Blau, L.L.P. (AV)

901 Main Street, Suite 3700, 75202-3725
Telephone: 214-744-3700; 800-451-0093
Fax: 214-747-3732
URL: http://www.meadowsowens.com

MEMBERS OF FIRM

Charles M. Meadows, Jr.
Rodney J. Owens
Robert Don Collier
David N. Reed
Thomas G. Hineman
William R. Cousins, III
Charles W. Blau
George R. Bedell
Michael E. McCue
Fielder F. Nelms
Joel N. Crouch
Alan K. Davis
Charles D. Pulman

ASSOCIATES

Patricia King Dorey
Robert M. Bolton
M. Todd Welty
Josh O. Ungerman
Robyn A. Frohlin
Gregory A. Cardenas
Sara E. Lankford
Sarah Q. Qureshi
Bradley G. Korell
Todd A. Kraft
Alan L. Stroud
Matthew D. Richards

For full biographical listings, see the Martindale-Hubbell Law Directory

Middleberg, Riddle & Gianna (AV)

2323 Bryan Street, Suite 1600, 75201
Telephone: 214-220-6300
Telecopier: 214-220-2785
New Orleans, Louisiana Office: 201 St. Charles Avenue, Suite 3100.
Telephone: 504-525-7200.
Telecopier: 504-581-5983.
Austin, Texas Office: 1300 South Mopac Expressway, First Floor.
Telephone: 512-434-8334.
Houston, Texas Office: 7676 Woodway, Suite 325.
Telephone: 713-430-5000.
Telecopier: 713-430-5090.

Ira Joel Middleberg (Not admitted in TX)
Michael Lee Riddle
Dominic J. Gianna (Not admitted in TX)

Kay A. King
Laura C. LaRaia
Angela R. Maverick
Lisa E. Minkoff
Carol J. Riddle
Robert A. Schlanger
Alexandra Smith
Marsha L. Williams
Christina R. Wommack

OF COUNSEL

Richard S. Wilensky
Robert M. Duval

For full biographical listings, see the Martindale-Hubbell Law Directory

Owens, Clary & Aiken, L.L.P. (AV)

1717 Main Street, Suite 2400, 75201
Telephone: 214-698-2100
Facsimile: 214-698-2121

MEMBERS OF FIRM

Leighton Aiken
Dana Mark Campbell
Robert J. Clary
Charles R. Haworth
Robert L. Owens
Leon G. Scroggins, II

(See Next Column)

OWENS, CLARY & AIKEN L.L.P., *Dallas—Continued*

ASSOCIATES

Jamie King Harrison
Mary T. Ritter

For full biographical listings, see the Martindale-Hubbell Law Directory

PEIRSON & PATTERSON, L.L.P. (AV)

4400 Alpha Road, 75244-4505
Telephone: 972-392-7770
800-899-9027
Fax: 972-490-9338
Email: lawyers@loan-docs.com
Arlington, Texas Office: 1111 West Arkansas, 76013-6325.
Telephone: 817-461-5500.
Fax: 817-856-6060.

Chris A. Peirson
William H. Peirson
Michael H. Patterson (Resident, Arlington, Texas Office)

ASSOCIATES

Gaylan Goodnight
Victoria A. Saulnier

For full biographical listings, see the Martindale-Hubbell Law Directory

CHRISTOPHER G. SHARP, P.C. (AV)

6116 North Central Expressway, Suite 520, 75206
Telephone: 214-368-3600
Fax: 214-368-3632
Email: CGSPC@Prodigy.com *URL:* http://www.lawyers.com/christophergsharplaw

Christopher G. Sharp

For full biographical listings, see the Martindale-Hubbell Law Directory

SMITH, UNDERWOOD & PERKINS, A PROFESSIONAL CORPORATION (AV)

600 Two Lincoln Centre, 5420 LBJ Freeway, 75240
Telephone: 972-661-5114
Telecopier: 972-661-5691
Email: firm@suandp.com *URL:* http://www.suplaw.com

Timothy S. Perkins
G. Lynn Smith
David W. Ralston
William J. Underwood, Jr.

Christine A. McGuire
Ellen P. Stewart
Amy K. Ratzlaff
Todd W. Shadle
P. Theodore Stoinoff, II
Ruth C. Logan
Val C. Cronin
Christina L. Betanzos
Kent D. Williamson

For full biographical listings, see the Martindale-Hubbell Law Directory

THOMPSON & KNIGHT L.L.P. (AV)

(Attorneys and Counselors)
1700 Pacific Avenue Suite 3300, 75201
Telephone: 214-969-1700
Telecopy: 214-969-1751
Telex: 732 298
URL: http://www.tklaw.com
Austin, Texas Office: 1200 San Jacinto Center, 98 San Jacinto Boulevard, 78701.
Telephone: 512-469-6100.
Telecopy: 512-469-6180.
Fort Worth, Texas Office: 801 Cherry Street, Suite 1600, 76102.
Telephone: 817-347-1700.
Telecopy: 817-347-1799.
Houston, Texas Office: Thompson Knight Brown Parker & Leahy L.L.P., 1200 Smith Street, Suite 3600, 77002-4595.
Telephone: 713-654-8111.
Telecopier: 713-654-1871.
San Pedro Garza Garcia, Nuevo León, Mexico Office: Edificio Losoles PD-4, Av. Lázaro Cárdenas No. 2400 Pte., C.P. 66220.
Telephone: (52-8) 363-0096.
Telecopy: (52-8) 363-3067.

PARTNERS

Steven R. Baggett
Michael E. Schonberg
George C. Chapman
Molly Steele

OF COUNSEL

Julia Patterson Forrester

For Complete List of Firm Personnel, See General Section

For full biographical listings, see the Martindale-Hubbell Law Directory

*DENTON,** Denton Co.

PHILIPS, HOPKINS, EAMES & COBB, P.C. (AV)

525 North Locust, P.O. Box 2027, 76202-2027
Telephone: 940-566-7010; Metro 940-243-0946
Facsimile: 940-898-0502
Email: dentonlaw.com

Lawrence C. Collister
William P. Philips, Jr.

Representative Clients: First Federal Bank of North Texas; First State Bank of Texas, Denton, Texas; Sanger Bank, Sanger, Texas; BankOne, Texas, N.A.; Provident Bank, Denton, Texas; Dentex Title Co., Denton, Texas.

For full biographical listings, see the Martindale-Hubbell Law Directory

*EL PASO,** El Paso Co.

AINSA PARTNERS, LLP (AV)

5809 Acacia Circle, 79912
Telephone: 915-845-5300
Fax: 915-845-7800
Email: fain@acaciapark.com *URL:* http://www.ainsa.com

Francis S. Ainsa, Jr.
Michael F. Ainsa
David M. Driscoll

For full biographical listings, see the Martindale-Hubbell Law Directory

CROWSON & INGRAM (AV)

Suite 706, The Cortez, 310 North Mesa, P.O. Box 862, 79945
Telephone: 915-533-7717
Telefax: 915-533-1495
Email: crowsing@huntleigh.net

MEMBERS OF FIRM

Harold E. Crowson, Jr.
Temple B. Ingram, Jr.

Reference: Bank of America, N.A.; Norwest Bank, El Paso, N.A.; Bank of the West, El Paso, Texas.

For full biographical listings, see the Martindale-Hubbell Law Directory

*FORT WORTH,** Tarrant Co.

BISHOP, PAYNE, HARVARD & KAITCER, L.L.P. (AV)

Eighteenth Floor, 500 West Seventh Street, 76102
Telephone: 817-335-4911
Telecopier: 817-870-2631
Email: BishopPayne@BishopPayne.com

Philip R. Bishop
Timothy J. Harvard
Hershel R. Payne
Michael D. Kaitcer

Andrew S. Jones
Jonathan S. Hyman

OF COUNSEL

Richard L. Brown

For full biographical listings, see the Martindale-Hubbell Law Directory

BROUDE, SMITH & JENNINGS, P.C. (AV)

309 West Seventh Street Suite 1100, 76102
Telephone: 817-335-1615
Metro: 817-654-3505
Fax: 817-335-1603

John S. Broude
Cary L. Jennings
Steven M. Smith
Kathryn Durham McGlinchey
Jerry Betsill

OF COUNSEL

Janna Ward Clarke

LEGAL SUPPORT PERSONNEL

Laura deLagerheim (Paralegal).

For full biographical listings, see the Martindale-Hubbell Law Directory

DECKER, JONES, MCMACKIN, MCCLANE, HALL & BATES, A PROFESSIONAL CORPORATION (AV)

2500 Bank One Tower, 500 Throckmorton Street, 76102-3812
Telephone: 817-336-2400; *Metro:* 817-429-5260
Fax: 817-332-3043; 336-2181
Email: email@deckerjones.com *URL:* http://www.deckerjones.com

Daniel L. Bates
Charles B. Milliken
Robert W. Decker
Gary M. Moates
Mark S. Dugan
Bradley H. Rice
Janet L. Hahn
Jeffrey W. Storie
Randy J. Hall
James L. Stripling
Raymond B. Kelly, III
Brian K. Yost
John B. McClane
Tamera H. Bennett
John W. McMackin
Arthur F. Zobal
Geoffrey A. Mantooth

(See Next Column)

DECKER, JONES, MCMACKIN, MCCLANE, HALL & BATES A PROFESSIONAL CORPORATION—*Continued*

Representative Clients: Frost National Bank; Summit National Bank; Alamo Title Co.; Martin-Sprocket and Gear, Inc.; Williamson-Dickie Manufacturing Co.; Harbison-Fischer Manufacturing Co.; Employers Insurance of Texas; American International Group; Medical Protective Co.; Redman Homes, Inc.

For full biographical listings, see the Martindale-Hubbell Law Directory

JACKSON WALKER L.L.P. (AV)

301 Commerce Street, Suite 2400, 76102
Telephone: 817-334-7200
Fax: 817-334-7290
URL: http://www.jw.com
Austin, Texas Office: 100 Congress Avenue, Suite 1100.
Telephone: 512-236-2000.
Fax: 512-236-2002.
Dallas, Texas Office: 901 Main Street, Suite 6000.
Telephone: 214-953-6000.
Fax: 214-953-5822.
Houston, Texas Office: 1100 Louisiana, Suite 4200.
Telephone: 713-752-4200.
Fax: 713-752-4221.
Richardson, Texas Office: 2435 North Central Expressway, Suite 600.
Telephone: 972-671-2560.
Fax: 972-671-2566.
San Angelo, Texas Office: 225 West Beauregard Avenue.
Telephone: 915-481-2550.
Fax: 915-481-2552.
San Antonio, Texas Office: 112 E. Pecan Street, Suite 2100.
Telephone: 210-978-7700.
Fax: 210-978-7790.

MEMBERS OF FIRM

Sheldon Anisman
Susan A. Halsey
Wayne F. Malecha
Walter E. Tate

For Complete List of Firm Personnel, See General Section

For full biographical listings, see the Martindale-Hubbell Law Directory

THOMPSON & KNIGHT L.L.P. (AV)

(Attorneys and Counselors)
801 Cherry Street, Suite 1600, 76102
Telephone: 817-347-1700
Telecopy: 817-347-1799
URL: http://www.tklaw.com
Dallas, Texas Office: 1700 Pacific Avenue, Suite 3300, 75201.
Telephone: 214-969-1700.
Telecopy: 214-969-1751.
Telex: 732298.
Austin, Texas Office: 1200 San Jacinto Center, 98 San Jacinto Boulevard, 78701.
Telephone: 512-469-6100.
Telecopy: 512-469-6180.
Houston, Texas Office: Thompson Knight Brown Parker & Leahy L.L.P., 1200 Smith Street, Suite 3600, 77002-4595.
Telephone: 713-654-8111.
Telecopier: 713-654-1871.
San Pedro Garza García, Nuevo León, Mexico Office: Edificio Losoles PD-4, Av. Lázaro Cárdenas No. 2400 Pte., C.P. 66220.
Telephone: (52-8) 363-0096.
Telecopy: (52-8) 363-3067.

PARTNER

Susan E. Coleman

For Complete List of Firm Personnel, See General Section

For full biographical listings, see the Martindale-Hubbell Law Directory

*HOUSTON,** Harris Co.

BAKER BOTTS L.L.P. (AV)

One Shell Plaza, 910 Louisiana, 77002
Telephone: 713-229-1234
Cable Address: "Boterlove"
Fax: 713-229-1522
Email: postmaster@bakerbotts.com *URL:* http://www.bakerbotts.com
Washington, D.C. Office: The Warner, 1299 Pennsylvania Avenue, N.W.
Telephone: 202-639-7700.
New York, New York Office: 599 Lexington Avenue.
Telephone: 212-705-5000.
Austin, Texas Office: 1600 San Jacinto Center, 98 San Jacinto Boulevard.
Telephone: 512-322-2500.
Dallas, Texas Office: 2001 Ross Avenue.
Telephone: 214-953-6500.
Moscow, Russia Office: 10 ul. Bolshaya Dimitrovka (formerly Pushkinskaya), 103031.
Telephone: 7095/921-5300 (Local); 7095/929-7070 (International).
London, England Office: 45 Ludgate Hill.
Telephone: 0171-778-1400 (Local); 011-44-171-778-1400 (International).

(See Next Column)

Baku, Azerbaijan Office: 6-10 Vagif Mustafa-zadeh Street, Third Floor, Icheri Sheher, 370004.
Telephone: 994-12-97-63-88 (Local); 011-994-12-97-63-88 (International).
Fax: 994-12-97-63-91 (Local); 011-994-12-97-63-91 (International)

MEMBERS OF FIRM

Fred H. Dunlop
Paul B. Landen
Marley Lott
Peter M. Oxman
Hugh Tucker
Wade H. Whilden
Robert P. Wright

SPECIAL COUNSEL

LeAnn Vaughn

OF COUNSEL

Greg N. Martin
James LeGrand Read

ASSOCIATES

Amy Spear Hampton
Michelle A. Neumann
Consuella D. Simmons
Stacey F. Tilley

For Complete List of Firm Personnel, See General Section

For full biographical listings, see the Martindale-Hubbell Law Directory

CASH JONES, L.L.P. (AV)

Chase Tower, 600 Travis, Suite 6710, 77002
Telephone: 713-224-6767
Telecopier: 713-227-6222

MEMBERS OF FIRM

Michael P. Cash
Bill Jones

ASSOCIATES

Susan E. Kinkaid
John D. Walker
Robert J. Montoya
Eleanor H. Hodges
R. Bryant Siddoway

OF COUNSEL

David A. Springhetti
Denice Smith

For full biographical listings, see the Martindale-Hubbell Law Directory

CORDRAY & GOODRICH, PROFESSIONAL CORPORATION (AV)

3306 Sul Ross, 77098-1808
Telephone: 713-630-0600
Facsimile: 713-630-0017

Howard F. Cordray, Jr.
Christopher M. Goodrich
Richard Alan Tomlin
Gregory A. Goodrich
Glynn D. Nance, Jr.

OF COUNSEL

Ellen M. Lang
Van A. Cates
Robert G. Bailey

For full biographical listings, see the Martindale-Hubbell Law Directory

BILL DE LA GARZA & ASSOCIATES, P.C. (AV)

17050 El Camino Real, 77058-2610
Telephone: 281-486-7007
Fax: 281-486-0229
Email: bdlg@priorityx.net

Bill De La Garza

David M. Oualline

For full biographical listings, see the Martindale-Hubbell Law Directory

DOW, COGBURN & FRIEDMAN, P.C. (AV)

Nine Greenway Plaza, Suite 2300, 77046
Telephone: 713-940-6000
Telecopier: 713-940-6099
Email: dcf@dcf.com *URL:* http://www.dcf.com

Harry Dow (1899-1985)
Melvin A. Dow
Bernard O. Dow
Abraham P. Friedman
Vincent L. Marino
Paul Easterwood
George A. Rustay
B. Edward Williamson
K. Gregory Erwin
Bruce W. Merwin
Kenneth H. Kates
Warren A. Hoffman
Barry E. Putterman
Jeff D. Lefkowitz
Irene Kopelman Cruden
Michael J. Mazzone
Thomas J. McCaffrey
David L. Pybus
Derek J. Lisk
P. Randall Crump
David J. Owens
Joseph A. Michels
Scott J. Thomas
Kevin P. Hanratty

Lauren G. Friedman
J. W. Beverly
E. Scot Dixon
Sanford L. Dow
Henry A. Schwaeble
Earl W. Spencer
Justin V. Switzer
Peggy S. McClard
Boyd S. Hoekel

(See Next Column)

DOW, COGBURN & FRIEDMAN P.C., *Houston—Continued*

OF COUNSEL

Edmund L. Cogburn | Clarence A. West

Representative Clients: Weingarten Realty Investors (Shopping Center Developers); Weiner's Stores, Inc. (Department Store); Transamerica Realty Services; Belin Developers (Residential Subdivisions); Sugarland Properties Incorporated (Mixed Use Community Developer); Moody-Rambin Interests (Real Estate Development, Leasing and Management).

For full biographical listings, see the Martindale-Hubbell Law Directory

FAIRCHILD, PRICE, THOMAS, HALEY & WILLINGHAM, L.L.P. (AV)

440 Louisiana Street, Suite 2110, 77002-4205
Telephone: 713-426-1700
Fax: 713-426-1717.
Email: mwillingham@fpthw.com
Center, Texas Office: 413 Shelbyville Street, P.O. Drawer 1719, 75935.
Telephone: 409-598-2981.
Fax: 409-598-7712. E-Mail: wmthomas@fpthw.com
Nacogdoches, Texas Office: 1801 North Street, P.O. Box 631668, 75963-1668.
Telephone: 409-569-2327.
Fax: 409-569-7932. E-Mail: chaley@fpthw.com

John L. Price
W. Miller Thomas
C. Victor Haley
R. Mark Willingham
Travis P. Clardy
David J. Fisher
Clayton H. Haley
Russell R. Smith
Ryan A. Beason

OF COUNSEL

Robert L. Fairchild

James A. Payne, Jr.
David Edward Ash
Campbell Cox
Jefferson B. Davis
Thomas L. Cougill
Jeffrey Pierce Fultz
Matthew D. Mettauer

For full biographical listings, see the Martindale-Hubbell Law Directory

GILLIS & SLOGAR (AV)

6905 Wells Fargo Plaza, 1000 Louisiana, 77002
Telephone: 713-951-9100
Telecopier: 713-951-9718
Email: gillisslogar@worldnet.att.net

Charles Michael Gillis
John Michael Slogar

OF COUNSEL

Randall W. Heinrich

For full biographical listings, see the Martindale-Hubbell Law Directory

GILPIN, PAXSON & BERSCH (AV)

A Registered Limited Liability Partnership
Attorney at Law
1900 West Loop South, Suite 2000, 77027-3259
Telephone: 713-623-8800
Telecopier: 713-993-8451
Email: gpb@gpblaw.com *URL:* http://www.texinslaw.com

PARTNERS

Gary M. Alletag
Timothy R. Bersch
John D. Gilpin
Darryl W. Malone
Michael J. Pappert
Stephen Paxson
Kevin F. Risley

OF COUNSEL

Harless R. Benthul
David F. Webb

ASSOCIATES

Joseph D. Batson
Jeri Pharis Wechsler

Representative Clients: BMW of North America, Inc.; Federal Deposit Insurance Corporation; Greater Houston Builders Association; Owens Corning Fiberglas Corporation; Shaw Industries, Inc.; Southwest Guaranty Trust Company, N.A.; Sprint Communications Company L.P.; Volkswagen of America, Inc.; Volvo North America Corporation; Wells Fargo Bank (Texas), N.A.

For full biographical listings, see the Martindale-Hubbell Law Directory

GREGG & GREGG, P.C. (AV)

16055 Space Center Boulevard Suite 150, 77062
Telephone: 281-480-1211
Fax: 281-480-1210
Email: dhgregg3@flash.net

Dick H. Gregg, Jr.
Dick H. Gregg, III

For full biographical listings, see the Martindale-Hubbell Law Directory

ROBERTS, MARKEL & FOLGER, L.L.P. (AV)

A Limited Liability Partnership of Professional Corporations
Weslayan Tower, Suite 2000, 24 Greenway Plaza, 77046
Telephone: 713-840-1666
Telecopier: 713-840-9404

MEMBER OF FIRM

Marc D. Markel

ASSOCIATES

Stephanie Lee Quade
Clayton Hearn

For full biographical listings, see the Martindale-Hubbell Law Directory

SCHLANGER, MILLS, MAYER & SILVER, L.L.P. (AV)

A Limited Liability Partnership including Professional Corporations
109 North Post Oak Lane, 77024
Telephone: 713-785-1700
Facsimile: 713-785-2091
Email: info@smmg-law.com

Daniel Schlanger (1902-1973)
Joel W. Cook (1910-1986)
Lee D. Schlanger (P.C.)
Stephen C. Paine (P.C.)
Irwin M. Barg (P.C.)
Louis E. Silver (P.C.)
Marcy Higbie (P.C.)
Jon D. Totz
Kyle Longhofer
Marc L. Ellison
Gary Rachlin
Jack A. Lapin (P.C.)
Julia A. Cook

Lydia Kale
Sherri R. Wagner
Michael D. Stein
John Schneller IV
James R. Mustard, Jr.
Michele E. Marquit
Andrew B. Totz

OF COUNSEL

David R. Toomim
Michael A. Mills (P.C.)
Clarence Mayer (P.C.)
Steven D. Lerner (P.C.)

For full biographical listings, see the Martindale-Hubbell Law Directory

STUMPF CRADDOCK MASSEY & PULMAN, A PROFESSIONAL CORPORATION (AV)

1400 Post Oak Boulevard Suite 400, 77056
Telephone: 713-871-0919
Fax: 713-871-0408
URL: http://www.sfcm.com
San Antonio, Texas Office: One Riverwalk Place, 700 North St. Mary's, Suite 1150, 78205.
Telephone: 210-231-0919.
Fax: 210-231-0004.
Beaumont, Texas Office: 550 Fannin, Suite 230, 77701.
Telephone: 409-813-1761.
Fax: 409-813-1786.

Frederick W. Stumpf
Daniel K. Craddock
Michael B. Massey
Clayton C. Cannon
John M. Castillo (Resident, San Antonio Office)
Scott A. Farrimond (Resident, San Antonio Office)
Henry J. Fasthoff, IV (Resident, San Antonio Office)
Lawrence J. Fontana
Robert F. Maher (P.C.)
Randall A. Pulman (Resident, San Antonio Office)
Shari Pullen Pulman (Resident, San Antonio Office)
Douglas S. Sandage (P.C.)
Ray B. Jeffrey

OF COUNSEL

Tilman J. Falgout, III
John H. Marshall

For full biographical listings, see the Martindale-Hubbell Law Directory

THOMPSON KNIGHT BROWN PARKER & LEAHY L.L.P. (AV)

A Registered Limited Liability Partnership including Professional Corporations
(Attorneys and Counselors)
1200 Smith Street, Suite 3600, 77002-4595
Telephone: 713-654-8111
Telecopier: 713-654-1871
URL: http://www.tklaw.com
Dallas, Texas Office: Thompson & Knight L.L.P., 1700 Pacific Avenue, Suite 3300, 75201.
Telephone: 214-969-1700.
Telecopy: 214-969-1751.
Telex: 732298.
Austin, Texas Office: Thompson & Knight L.L.P., 1200 San Jacinto Center, 98 San Jacinto Boulevard, 78701.
Telephone: 512-469-6100.
Telecopy: 512-469-6180.
Fort Worth, Texas Office: Thompson & Knight L.L.P., 801 Cherry Street, Suite 1600, 76102.
Telephone: 817-347-1700.
Telecopy: 817-347-1799.

(See Next Column)

THOMPSON KNIGHT BROWN PARKER & LEAHY L.L.P.—*Continued*

San Pedro Garza Garcia, Nuevo León, Mexico Office: Thompson & Knight L.L.P., Edificio Losoles PD-4, Av. Lázaro Cárdenas No. 2400 PTE., C.P. 66220.
Telephone: (52-8) 363-0096.
Telecopy: (52-8) 363-3067.

PARTNERS

J. Michael Bell
E.F. Mano DeAyala
Nancy Wilson Hargrove
Boris A. Hidalgo

For Complete List of Firm Personnel, See General Section

For full biographical listings, see the Martindale-Hubbell Law Directory

JOE F. WHEAT (AV)

2600 Citadel Plaza Drive, Suite 105, 77008
Telephone: 713-869-5911
Telecopier: 713-869-4511
Email: jfwheat@iapc.net

For full biographical listings, see the Martindale-Hubbell Law Directory

*NACOGDOCHES,** Nacogdoches Co.

FAIRCHILD, PRICE, THOMAS, HALEY & WILLINGHAM, L.L.P. (AV)

1801 North Street, P.O. Box 631668, 75963-1668
Telephone: 409-569-2327
Fax: 409-569-7932.
Email: chaley@fpthw.com
Center, Texas Office: 413 Shelbyville Street, P.O. Drawer 1719, 75935.
Telephone: 409-598-2981.
Fax: 409-598-7712. *E-Mail:* wmthomas@fpthw.com
Houston, Texas Office: 440 Louisiana Street, Suite 2110, 77002-4205.
Telephone: 713-426-1700.
Fax: 713-426-1717. *E-Mail:* mwillingham@fpthw.com

John L. Price
W. Miller Thomas
C. Victor Haley
R. Mark Willingham
Travis P. Clardy
David J. Fisher
Clayton H. Haley
Russell R. Smith
Ryan A. Beason

OF COUNSEL

Robert L. Fairchild

James A. Payne, Jr.
David Edward Ash
Campbell Cox
Jefferson B. Davis
Thomas L. Cougill
Jeffrey Pierce Fultz
Matthew D. Mettauer

For full biographical listings, see the Martindale-Hubbell Law Directory

*SAN ANTONIO,** Bexar Co.

BARTON & SCHNEIDER, L.L.P. (AV)

Suite 1825, One Riverwalk Place, 700 North St. Marys, 78205
Telephone: 210-225-1655
Fax: 210-225-8999

J. Cary Barton
Raymond J. Schneider
M. Frank Russell
Robert J. Birnbaum
Rosemary B. Jackson

ASSOCIATES

Martha Vanek Hardy
Larry B. Oxford

For full biographical listings, see the Martindale-Hubbell Law Directory

BENTON CLARK & TAYLOR, P.C. (AV)

105 South St. Marys Street, Suite 905, 78205
Telephone: 210-472-1800
Fax: 210-472-1872

Barry G. Benton
R. Christopher Clark
Richard M. Taylor, III

Phillip R. Hall

For full biographical listings, see the Martindale-Hubbell Law Directory

COX & SMITH INCORPORATED (AV)

112 East Pecan Street, Suite 1800, 78205-1521
Telephone: 210-554-5500
Fax: 210-226-8395
Email: info@coxsmith.com *URL:* http://www.coxsmith.com

James M. McDonough
Michael A. Morell
Kerry T. Benedict
Jonathan A. Nixon
Brian N. Jaeckle
Courtney C. Solcher
Peter R. Broderick

(See Next Column)

OF COUNSEL

Teresa Ereon Giltner

Representative Clients: Barshop & Oles Company, Inc.; Chase Bank of Texas, N.A.; Del Rio National Bank; Hixon Properties Incorporated; International Bank of Commerce; Jefferson State Bank; NationsBank of Texas, N.A.; Principal Mutual Life Insurance Company; San Antonio Federal Credit Union; TETCO, Inc.

For Complete List of Firm Personnel, See General Section

For full biographical listings, see the Martindale-Hubbell Law Directory

SCHOENBAUM, CURPHY & SCANLAN, P.C. (AV)

NationsBank Plaza, Suite 1775, 300 Convent Street, 78205-3744
Telephone: 210-224-4491
Fax: 210-224-7983

Stanley Schoenbaum
R. James Curphy
William Scanlan, Jr.
Alfred G. Holcomb
Banks M. Smith
Darin N. Digby
Patricia Flora Sitchler
Emily Harrison Liljenwall

Stacey Alison Warnix

For full biographical listings, see the Martindale-Hubbell Law Directory

TEXARKANA, Bowie Co.

PATTON, HALTOM, ROBERTS, MCWILLIAMS & GREER, L.L.P. (AV)

A Registered Limited Liability Partnership including Professional Corporations
700 Hibernia National Bank Building, P.O. Box 1928, 75504-1928
Telephone: 903-794-3341
Fax: 903-792-6542; 903-792-0448
URL: http://www.pattonhaltom.com

Kirk Patton (P.C.)
William B. Roberts
Donald W. Capshaw

For Complete List of Firm Personnel, See General Section

For full biographical listings, see the Martindale-Hubbell Law Directory

*TYLER,** Smith Co.

SAMMONS & PARKER, A PROFESSIONAL CORPORATION (AV)

218 North College, 75702
Telephone: 903-595-4541
FAX: 903-595-2864

Martin Z. Sammons, Jr.
Jerry C. Parker
Clay M. White
Jeffery J. Shaver
Reid Wm. Martin
J. Chad Parker

W. Todd Parker
Alan D. Wharton
John F. (Jack) Walker, III
Vanessa L. Vance

Representative Clients: A list of Representative Clients will be furnished upon request.

For full biographical listings, see the Martindale-Hubbell Law Directory

*WACO,** McLennan Co.

DUNNAM & DUNNAM, L.L.P. (AV)

4125 West Waco Drive, P.O. Box 8418, 76714-8418
Telephone: 254-753-6437
Fax: 254-753-7434

MEMBERS OF FIRM

W. V. Dunnam (1891-1974)
W. V. Dunnam, Jr.
Vance Dunnam
Vance Dunnam, Jr.
James R. Dunnam

ASSOCIATES

Alan Stucky
John Porter Mabry, Jr.
James Robert Angel

For full biographical listings, see the Martindale-Hubbell Law Directory

UTAH

*SALT LAKE CITY,** Salt Lake Co.

BALLARD SPAHR ANDREWS & INGERSOLL, LLP (AV)
201 South Main Street, Suite 1200, 84111-2215
Telephone: 801-531-3000
Fax: 801-531-3001
URL: http://www.ballardspahr.com
Baltimore, Maryland Office: 300 East Lombard Street, 19th Floor.
Telephone: 410-528-5600.
Fax: 410-528-5650.
Camden, New Jersey Office: 800 Hudson Square, 5th Floor.
Telephone: 856-541-5577.
Fax: 856-541-8272.
Denver, Colorado Office: Seventeenth Street Plaza Building, Suite 2300, 1225 17th Street.
Telephone: 303-292-2400.
Fax: 303-296-3956.
Philadelphia, Pennsylvania Office: 1735 Market Street, 51st Floor.
Telephone: 215-665-8500.
Fax: 215-864-8999.
Voorhees, New Jersey Office: Suite 100, 1101 Laurel Oak Drive.
Telephone: 856-627-8555.
Fax: 856-627-1153.
Washington, D.C. Office: Suite 1000 South, 601 13th Street, N.W.
Telephone: 202-661-2200.
Fax: 202-661-2299.

Harry E. McCoy II
Steven D. Peterson

COUNSEL

Thomas G. Bennett

For full biographical listings, see the Martindale-Hubbell Law Directory

CALLISTER NEBEKER & McCULLOUGH, A PROFESSIONAL CORPORATION (AV)
Gateway Tower East, Suite 900, 10 East South Temple, 84133
Telephone: 801-530-7300
Telecopier: 801-364-9127
Email: mjeaston@cnmlaw.com *URL:* http://www.cnmlaw.com

Louis H. Callister
Dorothy C. Pleshe
John A. Beckstead
Steven E. Tyler
Randall D Benson
T. Richard Davis
John H. Rees

Representative Clients: Zions First National Bank; Federal Land Bank Association of Utah; Aetna Insurance Company; Home Builders Association of Utah; Zions Mortgage Company.

For Complete List of Firm Personnel, See General Section

For full biographical listings, see the Martindale-Hubbell Law Directory

DART ADAMSON DONOVAN & HANSON (AV)
A Partnership of Professional Corporations
370 E. South Temple, Suite 400, 84111
Telephone: 801-521-6383
Telefax: 801-355-2513

Craig G. Adamson (P.C.)

ASSOCIATES

Eric P. Lee (P.C.)
Cameron S. Denning

A list of References will be furnished upon request.

For full biographical listings, see the Martindale-Hubbell Law Directory

DURHAM JONES & PINEGAR, A PROFESSIONAL CORPORATION (AV)
Key Bank Tower 50 South Main, Suite 800, 84144
Telephone: 801-538-2424
Fax: 801-538-2425
Email: djp@djplaw.com
Ogden Utah Office: The Aerospace Center, Suite 710, 1104 Country Hills Drive, 84403.
Telephone: 801-395-2424.
Fax: 801-395-2430.

Paul M. Durham
David F. Klomp
Douglas A. Taggart (Resident, Ogden Office)

Jennifer Thompson Lessie
Kyle C. Jones

For full biographical listings, see the Martindale-Hubbell Law Directory

KIRTON & McCONKIE, A PROFESSIONAL CORPORATION (AV)
1800 Eagle Gate Tower, 60 East South Temple, 84111
Telephone: 801-328-3600
Telecopier: 801-321-4893

(See Next Column)

Randy T. Austin
Lorin C. Barker
Anthony I. Bentley, Jr.
Rolf H. Berger
Berne S. Broadbent
Charles W. Dahlquist, II
Jerry W. Dearinger
Robert W. Edwards
James E. Ellsworth
Fred D. Essig
Wallace O. Felsted
Clark B. Fetzer
R. Bruce Findlay
David J. Hardy
Keith L. Hargrove
Read R. Hellewell
Dale E. Hulse
Lee Ford Hunter
Richard G. Johnson, Jr.
Von G. Keetch
Raeburn G. Kennard
Wilford W. Kirton, Jr.
Michael F. Krieger
Paul H. Matthews
Daniel S. McConkie
David M. McConkie
Oscar W. McConkie, III
Oscar W. McConkie, Jr.
Samuel D. McVey
William A. Meaders, Jr.
Thomas L. Monson
Denis Roy Morrill
Merrill F. Nelson
Richard R. Neslen
Eric C. Olson
R. Willis Orton
B. Lloyd Poelman
Robert S. Prince
Gregory M. Simonsen
Robert T. Smith (Not admitted in UT)
Myron L. Sorensen
Jon E. Waddoups
David M. Wahlquist
Thomas D. Walk
Stuart F. Weed
David A. Westerby
Todd E. Zenger

Randall C. Allen
Bryan H. Booth
Michael M. Conger
David S. Doty
Alexander Dushku
Scott C. Krieger
Melinda R. Porter
Matthew K. Richards
Dorany Rodriguez-Baltazar (Not admitted in UT)
Jeffrey Dean Stevens
Amy S. Thomas
Steven L. Whitehead

For full biographical listings, see the Martindale-Hubbell Law Directory

PARR WADDOUPS BROWN GEE & LOVELESS, A PROFESSIONAL CORPORATION (AV)
Suite 1300, 185 South State Street, 84111-1537
Telephone: 801-532-7840
Fax: 801-532-7750
URL: http://www.pwlaw.com

David E. Gee
Scott W. Loveless
Victor A. Taylor
Ronald G. Russell
Roger D. Henriksen
Daniel A. Jensen
Mark A. Wagner
Robert A. McConnell
Eric D. Bawden
Brett J. Swanson
R. Eric Smith

OF COUNSEL

Charles L. Maak
Bruce A. Maak

For Complete List of Firm Personnel, See General Section

For full biographical listings, see the Martindale-Hubbell Law Directory

PARSONS, DAVIES, KINGHORN & PETERS, P.C. (AV)
185 South State Street, Suite 700, 84111
Telephone: 801-363-4300
Facsimile: 801-363-4378
Email: Attorneys@pdkplaw.com

John M. Parsons
Glen E. Davies
Gerald H. Kinghorn
Bill Thomas Peters
Langdon T. Owen, Jr.
R. Kimball Mosier
John N. Brems
Ken P. Jones
David W. Scofield
Stuart W. Hinckley
John S. Bradley
Harold L. Reiser
Wm. Shane Topham
J. Scott Brown
Katherine S. Gregory
Paige Bigelow

For full biographical listings, see the Martindale-Hubbell Law Directory

PRINCE, YEATES & GELDZAHLER (AV)
City Centre I, Suite 900, 175 East 400 South, 84111
Telephone: 801-524-1000
Fax: 801-524-1099
Email: pyglaw.com
Park City, Utah Office: 614 Main Street.
Telephones: 801-524-1000; 649-7440.

MEMBERS OF FIRM

Jon C. Heaton
Richard L. Blanck
J. Randall Call
David K. Broadbent
Carl W. Barton
Richard H. Thornton

Representative Clients: Cirque Properties, L.C.; CrossLand Mortgage; Sundance Ski Resort; Trizac Hahn Centers; Zions First National Bank.

For Complete List of Firm Personnel, See General Section

For full biographical listings, see the Martindale-Hubbell Law Directory

Salt Lake City—Continued

RAY, QUINNEY & NEBEKER, A PROFESSIONAL CORPORATION (AV)

79 South Main Street, Suite 400, P.O. Box 45385, 84145-0385
Telephone: 801-532-1500
Fax: 801-532-7543
Email: rqn@rqn.com *URL:* http://www.rqn.com
Provo, Utah Office: 92 North University Avenue, Suite 210, 84601-4420.
Telephone: 801-342-2400.
Fax: 801-375-8379.
Albuquerque, New Mexico Office: Suite 620, 40 First Plaza, N.W.
Telephone: 505-243-6665.
Fax: 505-764-9890.

Alan A. Enke
Scott Hancock Clark
Douglas Matsumori
Larry G. Moore
Ira B. Rubinfeld
Cameron M. Hancock

Representative Clients: First Security Bank, N.A.; Borden, Inc.; Salt Lake Organizing Committee for the Winter Olympic Games of 2002; Southern Pacific Transportation; Utah Power & Light Co.; Travelers Insurance Co.; U.S. West.

For Complete List of Firm Personnel, See General Section

For full biographical listings, see the Martindale-Hubbell Law Directory

SCALLEY & READING, A PROFESSIONAL CORPORATION (AV)

261 East 300 South, Second Floor, 84111
Telephone: 801-531-7870
Fax: 801-531-7968
Email: law@scalleyreading.com

Ford G. Scalley
Marlon L. Bates
Steven B. Smith

For full biographical listings, see the Martindale-Hubbell Law Directory

VAN COTT, BAGLEY, CORNWALL & MCCARTHY, A PROFESSIONAL CORPORATION (AV)

50 South Main Street, Suite 1600, P.O. Box 45340, 84145-0340
Telephone: 801-532-3333
Telecopier: 801-534-0058
Email: info@vancott.com *URL:* http://www.vancott.com
Ogden, Utah Office: 2404 Washington Boulevard, Suite 900.
Telephone: 801-394-5783.
Park City, Utah Office: 2200 Park Avenue, Suite C200-A.
Telephone: 435-649-3889.

Robert M. Anderson (President of Firm)
Thomas T. Billings
Timothy W. Blackburn (Resident, Ogden, Utah Office)
Thomas W. Clawson
Rand L. Cook
David J. Smith
Gerald H. Suniville
Stephen D. Swindle
Gregory P. Williams

Kim S Colton
Tacy A. Hartman

OF COUNSEL

Franklin N. Smith
M. Scott Woodland

For Complete List of Firm Personnel, See General Section

For full biographical listings, see the Martindale-Hubbell Law Directory

VERMONT

*BURLINGTON,** Chittenden Co.

GRAVEL AND SHEA, A PROFESSIONAL CORPORATION (AV)

Corporate Plaza, 76 St. Paul Street, P.O. Box 369, 05402-0369
Telephone: 802-658-0220
Fax: 802-658-1456

Stephen R. Crampton
James E. Knapp
John R. Ponsetto

Robert H. Rushford

OF COUNSEL

Charles T. Shea

For Complete List of Firm Personnel, See General Section

For full biographical listings, see the Martindale-Hubbell Law Directory

VIRGINIA

*ACCOMAC,** Accomack Co.

JON C. POULSON (AV)

23349 Cross Street, P.O. Box 478, 23301-0478
Telephone: 757-787-2620
Facsimile: 757-787-2749

For full biographical listings, see the Martindale-Hubbell Law Directory

ALEXANDRIA, (Independent City)

YOUNG, GOLDMAN & VAN BEEK, A PROFESSIONAL CORPORATION (AV)

510 King Street, Suite 416, 22314
Telephone: 703-684-3260
Facsimile: 703-548-4742
Email: YGVB@Erols.com
Washington, D.C. Office: 2000 L Street, N.W. Suite 800.
Telephone: 703-684-3260.

H. Alan Young
Neil D. Goldman
John P. Van Beek

OF COUNSEL

Garrett C. Burke

For full biographical listings, see the Martindale-Hubbell Law Directory

*ARLINGTON,** Arlington Co.

WALSH, COLUCCI, STACKHOUSE, EMRICH & LUBELEY, P.C. (AV)

Courthouse Plaza, Thirteenth Floor, 2200 Clarendon Boulevard, 22201
Telephone: 703-528-4700
Facsimile: 703-525-3197
Email: mdwal@wcsel.com *URL:* http://www.wcsel.com
Woodbridge, Virginia Office: Village Square, 13663 Office Place, Suite 201.
Telephones: 703-680-4664; 690-4647.
Facsimile: 703-690-2412.
Leesburg, Virginia Office: One East Market Street, 3rd Floor, 20176.
Telephone: 703-737-3633.
Fax: 703-737-3632.

Martin D. ("Art") Walsh
Thomas J. Colucci
Peter K. Stackhouse
Jerry K. Emrich
Michael D. Lubeley (Resident, Woodbridge Office)
Nan E. Terpak
Keith C. Martin
Jay du Von (Resident, Woodbridge Office)
J. Randall Minchew (Resident, Leesburg Office)
William A. Fogarty
David J. Bomgardner (Resident, Woodbridge Office)
Lynne J. Strobel
H. Mark Goetzman
John E. Rinaldi (Resident, Woodbridge Office)
Michael L. Murray
Timothy S. Sampson
M. Catharine Puskar

For full biographical listings, see the Martindale-Hubbell Law Directory

*FAIRFAX,** (Ind. City; Seat of Fairfax Co.)

LEFFLER, HYLAND & THOMPSON, A PROFESSIONAL CORPORATION (AV)

Inns of Court, 4163 Chain Bridge Road, 22030-4102
Telephone: 703-293-9300
Facsimile: 703-293-9301
Email: mail@lefflerhyland.com *URL:* http://www.lefflerhyland.com

Rodney G. Leffler
Timothy B. Hyland

For full biographical listings, see the Martindale-Hubbell Law Directory

MACKALL, MACKALL & GIBB, A PROFESSIONAL CORPORATION (AV)

4031 Chain Bridge Road, 22030
Telephone: 703-273-0320
Fax: 703-273-0267
Email: mackall@wizard.net

Henry C. Mackall
Douglass S. Mackall, III
Nancy E. Gibb
Mary D. Wagaman
Laura L. Ratchford

For full biographical listings, see the Martindale-Hubbell Law Directory

Fairfax—Continued

McCandlish & Lillard, A Professional Corporation (AV)

Fair Oaks Plaza, 11350 Random Hills Road, Suite 500, 22030-7429
Telephone: 703-273-2288
Fax: 703-352-4300
Email: mccand@patriot.net *URL:* http://www.mccandlaw.com
Leesburg, Virginia Office: 305 Harrison Street, S.E., Third Floor.
Telephone: 703-737-0200.
Fax: 703-737-0165.

Robert J. McCandlish, Jr. (1909-1996)
Rothwell J. Lillard (1910-1989)
Jesse B. Wilson, III
Peter A. Arntson
Gary W. Brown
Randolph A. Sutliff
Robert H. J. Loftus
William McCauley Arnold
Stephen C. Price
Stephen K. Fox
Douglas J. Sanderson
R. Peyton Mahaffey
William L. Carey
John W. Farrell
Eric J. Berghold
Ralph M. Tener
Vicki L. Layman
Adam W. Smith

Daniel P. Lyon
Lawrence J. McClafferty
Brian R. Sanderson

For full biographical listings, see the Martindale-Hubbell Law Directory

Odin, Feldman & Pittleman, P.C. (AV)

9302 Lee Highway, Suite 1100, 22031
Telephone: 703-218-2100
Facsimile: 703-218-2160
Email: OFP@OFPLAW.COM

David E. Feldman
Leslye S. Fenton

Caeli A. Keddie

OF COUNSEL

Douglas Wyatt Bethel

For Complete List of Firm Personnel, See General Section

For full biographical listings, see the Martindale-Hubbell Law Directory

*LEESBURG,** Loudoun Co.

Walsh, Colucci, Stackhouse, Emrich & Lubeley, P.C. (AV)

One East Market Street, 3rd Floor, 20176
Telephone: 703-737-3633
Fax: 703-737-3632
Email: jrmin@wcsel.com *URL:* http://www.wcsel.com
Arlington, Virginia Office: Courthouse Plaza, Thirteenth Floor. 2200 Clarendon Boulevard.
Telephone: 703-528-4700.
Facsimile: 703-525-3197.
Woodbridge, Virginia Office: Village Square, 13663 Office Place, Suite 201.
Telephones: 703-680-4664; 690-4647.
Facsimile: 703-690-2412.

J. Randall Minchew

For full biographical listings, see the Martindale-Hubbell Law Directory

MCLEAN, Fairfax Co.

Michael Horwatt & Associates P.C. (AV)

8280 Greensboro Drive, Suite 601, 22102
Telephone: 703-749-6060
Fax: 703-749-6063
Email: msh@horwattassoc.com

Michael S. Horwatt

For full biographical listings, see the Martindale-Hubbell Law Directory

Roeder and Associates, P.C. (AV)

8280 Greensboro Drive, Suite 601, 22102
Telephone: 703-749-6050
Fax: 703-749-6027
Email: wfroeder@erols.com

William F. Roeder, Jr.

Brian J. Lubkeman

For full biographical listings, see the Martindale-Hubbell Law Directory

Talbott and Gallagher, A Professional Corporation (AV)

6824 Elm Street, Suite 350, 22101
Telephone: 703-893-6361
Facsimile: 703-893-6825
Email: jct@talbottgallagher.com *URL:* http://www.lawyers.com/talbottgallagher

John C. Talbott
Kathleen G. Gallagher

For full biographical listings, see the Martindale-Hubbell Law Directory

Venable Attorneys At Law Venable, Baetjer and Howard, LLP (AV)

A Partnership including Professional Corporations
Suite 400, 2010 Corporate Ridge, 22102
Telephone: 703-760-1600
Fax: 703-821-8949
URL: http://www.venable.com
Baltimore, Maryland Office: 1800 Mercantile Bank & Trust Building, 2 Hopkins Plaza.
Telephone: 410-244-7400.
Fax: 410-244-7742.
Washington, D.C. Office: Venable, Baetjer, Howard & Civiletti LLP, Suite 1000, 1201 New York Avenue, N.W.
Telephone: 202-962-4800.
Fax: 202-962-8300.
Rockville, Maryland Office: Suite 500, One Church Street, P.O. Box 1906.
Telephone: 301-217-5600.
Fax: 301-217-5617.
Towson, Maryland Office: 210 Allegheny Avenue, P. O. Box 5517.
Telephone: 410-494-6200.
Fax: 410-821-0147.

MEMBERS OF FIRM

Ellen F. Dyke
David G. Lane
John G. Milliken
Michael W. Robinson
Elizabeth Corr Smedley
M. Jay Yurow

For Complete List of Firm Personnel, See General Section

For full biographical listings, see the Martindale-Hubbell Law Directory

Watt, Tieder, Hoffar & Fitzgerald, L.L.P. (AV)

7929 Westpark Drive, Suite 400, 22102
Telephone: 703-749-1000
Telecopier: 703-893-8029
Email: contactus@wthf.com *URL:* http://www.wthf.com
Washington, D.C. Office: 601 Pennsylvania Ave, N.W., Suite 900.
Telephone: 703-749-1000.
Irvine, California Office: 3 Park Plaza, Suite 1500.
Telephone: 949-852-6700.

MEMBERS OF FIRM

John B. Tieder, Jr.
Robert G. Watt
Julian F. Hoffar
Robert M. Fitzgerald
Robert K. Cox
Charles E. Raley
Lewis J. Baker
Benjamin T. Riddles, II
Wayne G. Tatusko
Richard G. Mann, Jr.
Henry D. Danforth
Carter B. Reid
Mark A. Sgarlata
Michael G. Long (Resident, Irvine, California Office)
Thomas J. Powell
Edward Parrott
Steven J. Weber
Paul A. Varela
Vivian Katsantonis
Kathleen Olden Barnes
Christopher P. Pappas (Resident, Irvine, California Office)
Shelly L. Ewald
Christopher J. Brasco
John G. Lavoie
Robert C. Niesley (Resident, Irvine, California Office)
Colin J. Smith
Fred A. Mendicino
Timothy E. Heffernan (Not admitted in VA)

OF COUNSEL

Avv. Roberto Tassi

ASSOCIATES

Robert G. Barbour
Keith C. Phillips
Marybeth Z. Gaul
William Drew Mallender
Joseph W. Rasnic
Heidi B. Hering
James M. Donahue
Bennett J. Lee (Not admitted in VA)
Todd R. Metz (Not admitted in VA)
Joseph S. Guarino
Lewis I. Askew, Jr.
Erica S. Beardsley
Robert James Lloyd, III
Harish C. Mirchandani (Not admitted in VA)
William Kennedy
Michael J. Kirwin (Not admitted in VA)
Peter L. Vanderloo
Scott W. Kowalski
Carol Kelly Skrabak
J. Brian Cashmere
Michele Mintz
David A. Leib (Not admitted in VA)
Denis W. Kohl
Elizabeth A. Hall

For full biographical listings, see the Martindale-Hubbell Law Directory

NORFOLK, (Independent City)

Tavss, Fletcher, Maiden & King, P.C. (AV)

Fourteenth Floor, 555 Main Street, 23510
Telephone: 757-625-1214
Fax: 757-622-7295
Mailing Address: P.O. Box 3747, 23514
Email: tavss@pilot.infi.net

Richard J. Tavss
John R. Fletcher
Ray W. King
Besianne Tavss Maiden
Michael B. Hamar
Kevin J. O'Leary

Reference: Bank of the Commonwealth.

For Complete List of Firm Personnel, See General Section

For full biographical listings, see the Martindale-Hubbell Law Directory

Vandeventer Black LLP (AV)

500 World Trade Center, 23510-1699
Telephone: 757-446-8600
Cable Address: "Hughsvan"
Telecopier: 757-446-8670
URL: http://www.vanblk.com
Kitty Hawk, North Carolina Office: 6 Juniper Trail.
Telephone: 252-261-5055.
Fax: 252-261-8444. E-Mail: nshearin@pinn.net.
London, England Office: Mitre House, 4th Floor, 12-14 Mitre Street.
Telephone: (0171) 623-2081.
Facsimile: (0171) 929-0043.

PARTNERS OF FIRM

Geoffrey F. Birkhead
Norman W. Shearin, Jr. (Not admitted in VA; Resident Partner, Kitty Hawk, North Carolina Office)
Bryant C. McGann

For Complete List of Firm Personnel, See General Section

For full biographical listings, see the Martindale-Hubbell Law Directory

*ORANGE,** Orange Co.

Shackelford, Honenberger, Thomas, Willis & Gregg, P.L.C. (AV)

149 West Main Street, P.O. Box 871, 22960
Telephone: 540-672-2711
Fax: 540-672-2714
Email: shtwg1@ns.gemlink.com
Culpeper, Virginia Office: 147 West Davis Street, P.O. Box 1002.
Telephone: 540-825-0305.

OF COUNSEL

Virginius R. Shackelford, Jr.

MEMBERS OF FIRM

Virginius R. Shackelford, III
Christopher J. Honenberger
Frank A. Thomas, III
Jere M. H. Willis, III (Resident, Culpeper, Virginia Office)
Sarah Collins Honenberger
Sean D. Gregg

For full biographical listings, see the Martindale-Hubbell Law Directory

RICHMOND, (Independent City)

LeClair Ryan, A Professional Corporation (AV)

707 East Main Street, 11th Floor, 23219
Telephone: 804-783-2003
Facsmile: 804-783-2294
Email: email@leclairryan.com
Glen Allen, Virginia Office: 4201 Dominion Boulevard, Suite 200, 23060.
Telephone: 804-270-0070.
Facsimile: 804-270-4715.
Blacksburg, Virginia Office: 1872 Pratt Drive, Suite 1865, 24060.
Telephone: 540-961-2762.
Fax: 540-961-2781.
Norfolk, Virginia Office: 999 Waterside Drive, Suite 2025.
Telephone: 757-624-1454.
Facsimile: 757-624-3773.
Alexandria, Virginia Office: 225 Reinekers Lane, Suite 290, 22314.
Telephone: 703-684-8007.
Facsimile: 703-684-8075.
Charlottesville, Virginia Office: 108 S.E. Second Street, P.O. Box 2017, 22902.
Telephone: 804-971-7771.
Facsimile: 804-296-0905.

Steven D. Delaney
Richard W. Gregory
Otto W. Konrad
Lawrence E. Marshall, II
E. Duffy Myrtetus

Karen S. French

For full biographical listings, see the Martindale-Hubbell Law Directory

Little, Parsley & Cluverius, P.C. (AV)

1300 Federal Reserve Bank Building, P.O. Box 555, 23218
Telephone: 804-644-4100
Facsimile: 804-644-0800
Email: admin@lpc-va.com

George B. Little
J. Terry Parsley
James K. Cluverius

Nathan McAdams Lord
Andrew M. Lohmann

Reference: Crestar Bank.

For full biographical listings, see the Martindale-Hubbell Law Directory

Williams, Mullen, Clark & Dobbins, A Professional Corporation (AV)

Two James Center, 1021 East Cary Street, P.O. Box 1320, 23218-1320
Telephone: 804-643-1991
Fax: 804-783-6507
URL: http://www.wmcd.com
Newport News Office: Harbor Bank Center, Suite 210, One Old Oyster Point Road, 23602-7119.
Telephone: 757-249-5100.
Fax: 757-249-5109.
Virginia Beach Office: One Columbus Center, 23462-6763.
Telephone: 757-499-8800.
Fax: 757-473-0395.
Vienna Office: 1593 Spring Hill Road, Suite 510, 22182.
Telephone: 703-760-5200.
Fax: 703-748-0244.
Washington, D.C. Office: The Farragut Building, 900 17th Street, N.W., Suite 700, 20006.
Telephone: 202-293-0213.
Fax: 804-783-6507. Fax Within D.C.: 202-293-5939.
London, England Office: Blake Lodge, Bridge Lane, SW11 3AD.
Telephone: (011-44-71) 223-2756.
Fax: (011-44-71) 350-0156.
Riyadh, Saudi Arabia Affiliate Office: Saudi-American Legal Consultants Commercial Building #2, Diplomatic Quarter, P.O. Box 57270, 11574.
Telephone: (011-966-1) 488-1563.
Fax: (011-966-1) 488-0542.

Ralph L. Axselle, Jr.
Lawrence H. Bryant (Resident, Virginia Beach Office)
Michael C. Buseck
Charles L. Cabell
Robert E. Eicher
Eric A. Hauser (Resident, Virginia Beach Office)
A. Brooks Hock
Samuel M. Kroll (Resident, Virginia Beach Office)
John M. Mercer
Warren E. Nowlin (Resident, Washington, D.C. Office)
Philip deB. Rome
Robert D. Roseman (Resident, Washington, D.C. Office)
C. Grigsby Scifres (Resident, Virginia Beach Office)
Lawrence R. Siegel (Resident, Virginia Beach Office)
Thomas E. Snyder (Resident, Virginia Beach Office)
W. Scott Street, III
Russell Alton Wright

Bradford D. Bimson (Resident, Virginia Beach Office)
Andrew M. Condlin
David V. DuVal
Tasos A. Galiotos (Resident, Virginia Beach Office)
Brian C. Purcell (Resident, Virginia Beach Office)
Patrick J. Sanderson

For Complete List of Firm Personnel, See General Section

For full biographical listings, see the Martindale-Hubbell Law Directory

SPRINGFIELD, Fairfax Co.

Madigan & Scott, Inc. (AV)

7880 Backlick Road, 22150-2288
Telephone: 703-455-1800; 451-2080
Fax: 703-451-4121
Email: MADSCOTT@EROLS.COM
Manassas, Virginia Office: 9100 Church Street, Suite 107.
Telephone: 703-361-0185. Metro: 631-9193.
Fax: 703-631-9633.

Robert J. Madigan
Paul A. Scott

Mark J. Madigan

OF COUNSEL

Mitchell Komaroff

Richard G. Hornig (1958-1994)

For full biographical listings, see the Martindale-Hubbell Law Directory

UPPERVILLE, Fauquier Co.

MILDRED FLETCHER SLATER (AV)

9005 John Mosby Highway, P.O. Box 238, 20185-0238
Telephone: 540-592-3600
Fax: 540-592-3833
Email: mfslater@crosslink.net

For full biographical listings, see the Martindale-Hubbell Law Directory

VIENNA, Fairfax Co.

GARY & GOODMAN LIMITED (AV)

8500 Leesburg Pike, Suite 7000 (Tysons Corner), 22182
Telephone: 703-848-2828
Facsimile: 703-893-9276
Email: garygoodman@ggllaw.com

Bernard E. Goodman
Stuart H. Gary

Nancy D. Greene

For full biographical listings, see the Martindale-Hubbell Law Directory

VIRGINIA BEACH, (Independent City)

WOLCOTT, RIVERS, WHEARY, BASNIGHT & KELLY, P.C. (AV)

One Columbus Center, Suite 1100, 23462-6765
Telephone: 757-497-6633
FAX: 757-497-7267
Email: wolriv@series2000.com

Wilson L. Rivers
William A. Wheary, III
W. Brantley Basnight, III
Monroe Kelly, III
Carl A. Eason
Joseph R. Mayes
Samuel W. Meekins, Jr.
Edward W. Wolcott, Jr.
Barry Dorans
Leslie R. Watson
David N. Reda
Richard E. Biemiller
Cheshire I'Anson Eveleigh
M. Powell Peters
Neil L. Rose
Robert D. Marotta

David M. Bastiaans
Deborah Kirkpatrick

Counsel for: Metropolitan Life Insurance Co.; Ford Motor Co.
Approved Attorneys for: Lawyers Title Insurance Corp.

For full biographical listings, see the Martindale-Hubbell Law Directory

WOODBRIDGE, Prince William Co.

WALSH, COLUCCI, STACKHOUSE, EMRICH & LUBELEY, P.C. (AV)

Village Square, 13663 Office Place, Suite 201, 22192
Telephone: 703-680-4664; 690-4647
Facsimile: 703-690-2412
Email: mdlub@wcsel.com *URL:* http://www.wcsel.com
Arlington, Virginia Office: Courthouse Plaza, Thirteenth Floor. 2200 Clarendon Boulevard.
Telephone: 703-528-4700.
Facsimile: 703-525-3197.
Leesburg, Virginia Office: One East Market Street, 3rd Floor, 20176.
Telephone: 703-737-3633.
Fax: 703-737-3632.

Michael D. Lubeley
Jay du Von
David J. Bomgardner
John E. Rinaldi

For full biographical listings, see the Martindale-Hubbell Law Directory

WASHINGTON

*SEATTLE,** King Co.

BUCK & GORDON LLP (AV)

902 Waterfront Place, 1011 Western Avenue, 98104-1097
Telephone: 206-382-9540
Telecopier: 206-626-0675
Email: BG@buckgordon.com

Alison D. Birmingham
William H. Block
Peter L. Buck
Brent Carson
Jay P. Derr
Joel M. Gordon
Amy L. Kosterlitz
Keith E. Moxon
Samuel W. Plauché, IV

Susan M. Ridgley

OF COUNSEL

Aliza C. Allen
Kitteridge Oldham

(See Next Column)

LEGAL SUPPORT PERSONNEL

PROJECT MANAGER

Bradley J. S. Liljequist

COMMUNITY RELATIONS

Margaret E. Potter

PARALEGAL

Patricia J. Wolfson

Reference: Seafirst Bank, Seattle, Washington (Metropolitan Branch).

For full biographical listings, see the Martindale-Hubbell Law Directory

LANE POWELL SPEARS LUBERSKY LLP (AV)

Limited Liability Partnership composed of Individuals and Professional Service Corporations
1420 Fifth Avenue, Suite 4100, 98101-2338
Telephone: 206-223-7000
Facsimile: 206-223-7107
Email: information@lanepowell.com *URL:* http://www.lanepowell.com
Other Offices at: Portland, Oregon; Anchorage, Alaska; Olympia and Mount Vernon, Washington; London, England.

MANAGING PARTNER

Michael D. Dwyer

MEMBERS OF FIRM

Glenn J. Amster
Scott F. Campbell
Michael L. Cohen
Charles R. Ekberg (P.S.)
Thomas F. Grohman
David G. Johansen
Kenyon P. Kellogg
Jeffrey D. Laveson
Gail E. Mautner
Jane Rakay Nelson
Hartley Paul
Douglas E. Wheeler

COUNSEL

Paul McCarthy
Joan E. Robinson

Representative Clients: C.D. Stimson, Co.; The Home Depot; Lincoln National Life Insurance Co.; The Manufacturers Life Insurance Co.; Nordstrom, Inc.; The Ohio National Life Insurance Co.; Resolution Trust Corp.; Seattle Mortgage Co.; Sentinel Real Estate Group; Union Pacific Railroad Co.

For Complete List of Firm Personnel, See General Section

For full biographical listings, see the Martindale-Hubbell Law Directory

JON G. SCHNEIDLER (AV)

4100 Wells Fargo Center, 999 Third Avenue, 98104
Telephone: 206-624-9400
Telecopier: 206-464-9559
Email: jonandbeth@budsters.com

Reference: Key Bank of Washington.

For full biographical listings, see the Martindale-Hubbell Law Directory

WEST VIRGINIA

*BECKLEY,** Raleigh Co.

FILE, PAYNE, SCHERER & FILE (AV)

Law Building, 130 Main Street, P.O. Drawer L, 25802
Telephone: 304-253-3358
Fax: 304-255-5136
Email: filepayne@mtneer.net

MEMBERS OF FIRM

Edward M. Payne, III
John Payne Scherer
Robert N. File
William H. File, III

ASSOCIATE

Floyd M. Sayre, III

OF COUNSEL

William Henry File, Jr.

Representative Clients: City National Bank; City Holding Co.; Norfolk and Western Railway Co.; A. T. Massey Coal Co.; State Automobile Mutual Insurance Co.; Continental Insurance Group; Professional Medical Insurance Co.; Natiowide Insurance Company.

For full biographical listings, see the Martindale-Hubbell Law Directory

*CHARLESTON,** Kanawha Co.

JACKSON & KELLY (AV)

1600 Laidley Tower, P.O. Box 553, 25322
Telephone: 304-340-1000
Fax: 304-340-1130
Email: info@jacksonkelly.com *URL:* http://www.jacksonkelly.com
Martinsburg, West Virginia Office: 300 Foxcroft Avenue, P.O. Box 1068.
Telephone: 304-263-8800.
Fax: 304-263-7110.

(See Next Column)

JACKSON & KELLY—*Continued*

Morgantown, West Virginia Office: 6000 Hampton Center, P.O. Box 619.
Telephone: 304-599-3000.
Fax: 304-285-2040.
New Martinsville, West Virginia Office: 256 Russell Avenue, P.O. Box 68.
Telephone: 304-455-1751.
Fax: 304-455-6314.
Parkersburg, West Virginia Office: 412 Market Street, Suite 202, P.O. Box 1144.
Telephone: 304-424-3490.
Fax: 304-424-3499.
Fairmont, West Virginia Office: 1000 Technology Drive, Suite 1310.
Telephone: 304-368-2000.
Fax: 304-368-2020.
Lexington, Kentucky Office: 175 East Main Street, Suite 500, P.O. Box 2150.
Telephone: 606-255-9500.
Fax: 606-281-6478.
Washington, D. C. Office: 2401 Pennsylvania Avenue, N.W., Suite 400.
Telephone: 202-973-0200.
Fax: 202-973-0232.
Denver, Colorado Office: Suite 2710, 1660 Lincoln Street.
Telephone: 303-390-0003.
Fax: 303-390-0040.
Wheeling, West Virginia Office: 1144 Market Street.
Telephone: 304-233-4000.
Fax: 304-233-4077.

MEMBERS OF FIRM

Thomas E. Potter
Lee O. Hill
John R. Lukens
Charles Q. Gage
Harvey Alan Siler
Mary Clare Eros (Administrative Manager, Martinsburg and Charles Town, West Virginia Offices)
James I. Manion (Resident, Martinsburg and Charles Town, West Virginia Offices)
W. Rodes Brown (Resident, Lexington, Kentucky Office)
Wendel B. Turner
Eric H. London (Morgantown, West Virginia Office)
William Prentice Young (Martinsburg and Charles Town, West Virginia Offices)
Robert D. Fluharty

ASSOCIATES

Brooks K. Barkwill (Resident, New Martinsville, West Virginia Office)
Dennis N. Broglio
James Eric Whytsell (Resident, Fairmont Office)
Steven M. Condaras

Representative Clients: Lawyers Title Insurance Corporation; Go-Mart, Inc.; Pittston Coal Management Co.; The Travelers Insurance Co.; Westvaco Corporation; Carbon Fuel Co.; Haddad & Associates; Pocahontas Land Corp.; McDonalds Corporation; One Valley Bancorp of West Virginia, Inc.;

For Complete List of Firm Personnel, See General Section

For full biographical listings, see the Martindale-Hubbell Law Directory

*CLARKSBURG,** Harrison Co.

McNEER, HIGHLAND, McMUNN AND VARNER, L.C. (AV)

One Valley Bank Building, P.O. Drawer 2040, 26302-2040
Telephone: 304-626-1100
Facsimile: 304-623-3035
Martinsburg Office: 2520 Aikens Center, P.O. Box 2509.
Telephone: 304-264-4621.
Fax: 304-264-8623.
Parkersburg Office: 404 Market Street, Suite 204, P.O. Box 1507.
Telephone: 304-422-7193.
Facsimile: 304-422-7196.

C. David McMunn
J. Cecil Jarvis
James A. Varner
Robert W. Trumble (Resident, Martinsburg Office)
Catherine D. Munster
James N. Riley
Steven R. Bratke (Resident, Parkersburg Office)
Michael J. Novotny (Resident, Martinsburg Office)
Dennis M. Shreve
Geraldine S. Roberts
William F. Rohrbaugh (Resident, Martinsburg Office)
Gregory H. Schillace
Judy L. Shanholtz
Tiffany R. Durst
Gene W. Bailey, II

OF COUNSEL

James E. McNeer
Cecil B. Highland, Jr.
William L. Fury

Representative Clients: One Valley Bank of Clarksburg, National Assn.; Bruceton Bank; Harrison County Bank; Nationwide Mutual Insurance Cos.; Clarksburg Publishing Co.; C.I.T. Financial Services; State Automobile Mutual Insurance Co.; United Hospital Center, Inc.; West Virginia Coals, Inc.; Swanson Plating Co.

For full biographical listings, see the Martindale-Hubbell Law Directory

WATERS, WARNER & HARRIS, PLLC (AV)

Formerly Stathers & Cantrall
701 Goff Building, P.O. Box 1716, 26301
Telephone: 304-624-5571
Fax: 304-624-7228
Email: wwh.atty@northnap.citynet.net

Birk S. Stathers (1884-1945)
W. G. Stathers (1889-1970)
Arch M. Cantrall (1896-1967)
Stuart R. Waters
Boyd L. Warner
James A. Harris
Scott E. Wilson
James C. Turner
G. Thomas Smith

ASSOCIATES

D. Andrew McMunn
David C. Glover

Representative Clients: Bethlehem Steel Corp.; Grafton Coal Co.; Emax Oil Co.; Hartland Planing Mill Co.; Gas Flame Federal Credit Union; City of Clarksburg Federal Credit Union; The Houston Exploration Company; Seneca-Upshur Petroleum, Inc.; EnerVest Operating, L.L.C.; Clarksburg Urban Renewal Authority; Huntington National Bank West Virginia.

For full biographical listings, see the Martindale-Hubbell Law Directory

*FAIRMONT,** Marion Co.

FURBEE, AMOS, WEBB & CRITCHFIELD (AV)

132 Adams Street, P.O. Box 1189, 26555
Telephone: 304-363-8800
Telecopier: 304-366-3783
Morgantown, West Virginia Office: 5000 Hampton Center, Suite 4.
Telephone: 304-598-0900.
Telecopier: 304-598-2712.

MEMBERS OF FIRM

Russell L. Furbee (1898-1978)
John D. Amos
Benjamin Hays Webb
Charles Vincent Critchfield
Alfred J. Lemley
Billy Atkins
Kenneth R. Miller
Stephen R. Brooks
William T. Holmes
Debra Hodges Scudiere (Resident at Morgantown Office)
Rebecca J. Zuleski
Tamara J. DeFazio

ASSOCIATE

Peter T. DeMasters

Attorneys for: Consolidation Coal Co.; Westinghouse Electric Co.; Monongahela Power Co.; Eastern Associated Coal Corp.; West Virginia Community Television Association; Continental Casualty Co.; State Farm Insurance Co.; Nationwide Insurance Co.

For full biographical listings, see the Martindale-Hubbell Law Directory

HUNTINGTON, Cabell & Wayne Cos.

BAKER, LANCIANESE, CAMPBELL & CONATY (AV)

The River Tower, 1108 Third Avenue, Suite 300, 25701-1578
Telephone: 304-522-6906
Facsimile: 304-522-6910
Email: BLCC@BLCCLAW.COM *URL:* http://www.BLCCLAW.COM
Washington, D.C. Office: 1090 Vermont Avenue, N.W. Suite 800.
Telephone: 202-966-1500.
Fax: 202-966-7075. E-Mail: BLCC@BLCCLAW.COM.
Lexington, Kentucky Office: 2265 Harrodsburg Road, Suite 200, 40504-3517.
Telephone: 606-278-0297.
Fax: 206-278-0334. E-Mail: BLCC@BLCCLAW.COM.

Roy D. Baker, Jr.
Richard L. Lancianese
David L. Campbell
Brian P. Conaty
Janice P. Epperly

OF COUNSEL

Margaret M. Brizzolara (Not admitted in WV)

For full biographical listings, see the Martindale-Hubbell Law Directory

*WESTON,** Lewis Co.

WEBER & WEBER (AV)

208 Main Avenue, P.O. Box 270, 26452
Telephone: 304-269-2228
Fax: 304-269-7938
URL: http://www.lawyers.com/webercom

W. T. Weber, Jr.
W. T. Weber, III

LEGAL SUPPORT PERSONNEL

Greta Wade
Carla Kemper
Stephanie Frazier

Reference: The Citizens Bank Of Weston, Inc.

For full biographical listings, see the Martindale-Hubbell Law Directory

*WHEELING,** Ohio Co.

SCHRADER BYRD & COMPANION, PLLC (AV)

(A Professional Limited Liability Company)
The Maxwell Centre, 32-20th Street, Suite 500, P.O. Box 6336, 26003
Telephone: 304-233-3390
Fax: 304-233-2769
URL: http://www.schraderlaw.com
Martins Ferry, Ohio Office: 205 North Fifth Street, P.O. Box 309, 43935.
Telephone: 740-633-9976.
Fax: 740-633-0400.
Weirton, West Virginia Office: 3205 Pennsylvania Avenue, Suite 103, Penn Place, P.O. Box 2785, 26062.
Telephone: 304-723-2674.
Fax: 304-723-2876.

MEMBERS

Ray A. Byrd
James F. Companion
Frank X. Duff
Teresa Rieman-Camilletti
Yolonda G. Lambert
Daniel P. Fry (Resident Partner, Martins Ferry, Ohio Office)
James P. Mazzone (Resident Member, Weirton, West Virginia Office)
Sandra K. Law
D. Kevin Coleman

SPECIAL COUNSEL

Thomas B. Miller

ASSOCIATES

Denise D. Klug
Michael A. Adams
John Porco
Aimee Morgan Stern
Kimberly R. Wilson
Christopher J. Adams

OF COUNSEL

James A. Byrum, Jr.

General Counsel: Reynolds Memorial Hospital; WesBanco Bank-Elm Grove.
Representative Clients: American Cyanamid Company; Bank One; Matlack Systems, Inc.; Moutaineer Gas Co.; Ohio County Board of Education; PHICO Insurance Co.; Wheeling Hospital; Wheeling-Pittsburg Steel Corp.

For full biographical listings, see the Martindale-Hubbell Law Directory

WISCONSIN

*EAU CLAIRE,** Eau Claire Co.

WILCOX, WILCOX, ENRIGHT, HALLSTEIN, McMAHON & ADLER, LLC (AV)

Limited Liability Company
1030 Regis Court, P.O. Box 128, 54701
Telephone: 715-832-6645
Fax: 715-832-8438
Email: willaw@win.bright.net

MEMBERS OF FIRM

Roy P. Wilcox (1873-1946)
Francis J. Wilcox
Roy S. Wilcox
Daniel A. Enright
John F. Wilcox
Howard G. McMahon
George W. Hallstein
Timothy J. Adler

Attorneys for: Aetna Insurance Group; Medical Protective Assn.; American Surety Co.; Viking Insurance Co.; American Mutual Liability Ins. Co.; Continental Cas. Co.; Farmers Insurance Group.

For full biographical listings, see the Martindale-Hubbell Law Directory

LAKE GENEVA, Walworth Co.

BRADEN & OLSON (AV)

716 Wisconsin Street, P.O. Box 940, 53147
Telephone: 414-248-6636
Fax: 414-248-2901
Email: bando@genevaonline.com

MEMBERS OF FIRM

Berwyn B. Braden
John O. Olson

ASSOCIATES

Christine Tomas
Daniel S. Draper

For full biographical listings, see the Martindale-Hubbell Law Directory

*MADISON,** Dane Co.

NEIDER & BOUCHER, S.C. (AV)

440 Science Drive, P.O. Box 5510, 53705-0510
Telephone: 608-661-4500
Facsimile: 608-661-4510
URL: http://www.neiderboucher.com
URL: http://www.lawyers.com/neider&boucher-sc

(See Next Column)

Ronald C. Berman
Joseph W. Boucher
Charles E. Neider
Steven C. Underwood

Susan M. De Groot
Erik W. Ibele
Rana Kang
Cynthia L. Richson
Matthew L. Schemmel
Kent L. Schlienger
Dean T. Stange

OF COUNSEL

Ralph M. Cagle
Ronald R. Smith

For full biographical listings, see the Martindale-Hubbell Law Directory

STROUD, WILLINK & HOWARD, LLC (AV)

25 West Main Street, Suite 300, P.O. Box 2236, 53701
Telephone: 608-257-2281
Fax: 608-257-7643
Email: email@stroudlaw.com

MEMBERS OF FIRM

C. Vernon Howard
Ronald W. Todd
Robert R. Stroud
H. Dale Peterson
Robert J. Schwab
Carolyn A. Hegge
James F. Gebhart
Joseph P. Bartol

OF COUNSEL

Seward Ritchey Stroud
Donald R. Stroud
Donald D. Willink
Dale R. Thompson

ASSOCIATES

Sverre David Roang
Peter J. Richter
Norman D. Farnam

General Counsel for: Temperature Systems, Inc.; Wisconsin Farm Bureau Federation; Anchor Bank, SSB; The Wisconsin Cheeseman, Inc.; J.H. Findorff & Son, Inc.; Edward Kraemer & Sons, Inc.; Hilldale Shopping Center; American T.V. & Appliance of Madison, Inc.; Demco, Inc.; Schoep's Ice Cream Co., Inc.

For full biographical listings, see the Martindale-Hubbell Law Directory

*MILWAUKEE,** Milwaukee Co.

CHERNOV, STERN & KRINGS, S.C. (AV)

Suite 1275, Two Plaza East, 330 East Kilbourn Avenue, 53202
Telephone: 414-276-4080
Fax: 414-276-4152
Email: mail@chernovlaw.com *URL:* http://www.lawyers.com/chernovlaw

Benjamin S. Stern
Jerome D. Krings

OF COUNSEL

Ben L. Chernov

For full biographical listings, see the Martindale-Hubbell Law Directory

DAVIS & KUELTHAU, S.C. (AV)

111 East Kilbourn Avenue, Suite 1400, 53202-6613
Telephone: 414-276-0200
Facsimile: 414-276-9369
Cable Address: "Shiplaw"
Email: info@daviskuelthau.com *URL:* http://www.daviskuelthau.com
Madison, Wisconsin Office: Ten East Doty Street, Suite 600, P.O. Box 1068, 53703.
Telephone: 608-280-8235.
Fax: 608-280-8231.
Sheboygan, Wisconsin Office: 605 North Eighth, Suite 610, P.O. Box 1287.
Telephone: 920-451-1461.
Fax: 920-451-1465.
Green Bay, Wisconsin Office: 414 East Walnut Street, Suite 240.
Telephone: 920-435-9378.
Fax: 920-435-9391.

James A. Brindley
Robert E. Kuelthau
Brett K. Miller
Bradley D. Page
Amy Klemm Verbos

Stacy Alvarez Delzer
Steven R. Glaser
Eric L. Robinson

For full biographical listings, see the Martindale-Hubbell Law Directory

DRINKA, LEVINE & MASSON, S.C. (AV)

2000 Milwaukee Center, 111 East Kilbourn Avenue, 53202-6618
Telephone: 414-291-6080
Fax: 414-291-6090
URL: http://www.lawyers.com/drinkalevine&masson

Judith A. Drinka
Micaela H. Levine
Grace M. Masson

For full biographical listings, see the Martindale-Hubbell Law Directory

Milwaukee—Continued

MEISSNER TIERNEY FISHER & NICHOLS S.C. (AV)

The Milwaukee Center, 111 East Kilbourn Avenue, 19th Floor, 53202-6622
Telephone: 414-273-1300
Facsimile: 414-273-5840
URL: http://www.mtfn.com

Joseph E. Tierney III
Thomas J. Nichols
Dennis L. Fisher
Randal J. Brotherhood
Michael J. Cohen

William T. Stuart

OF COUNSEL

Paul F. Meissner

For full biographical listings, see the Martindale-Hubbell Law Directory

QUARLES & BRADY LLP (AV)

411 East Wisconsin Avenue, 53202-4497
Telephone: 414-277-5000
Fax: 414-271-3552
URL: http://www.quarles.com
Madison, Wisconsin Office: Firstar Plaza, One South Pinckney Street, P.O. Box 2113, 53701-2113.
Telephone: 608-251-5000.
Fax: 608-251-9166.
West Palm Beach, Florida Office: 222 Lakeview Avenue, 4th Floor, 33401.
Telephone: 561-653-5000.
Fax: 561-653-5333.
Naples, Florida Office: Barnett Center, 4501 Tamiami Trail North, Suite 300, 34103-3060.
Telephone: 941-262-5959.
Fax: 941-434-4999.
Phoenix, Arizona Office: One Camelback Building, One East Camelback Road, Suite 400, 85012-1649.
Telephone: 602-230-5500.
Fax: 602-230-5598.
Chicago, Illinois Office: Quarles & Brady LLC, Citicorp Center, 500 West Madison Street, Suite 3700.
Telephone: 312-715-5000.
Fax: 312-715-5155.

MEMBERS OF FIRM
(ALPHABETICALLY BY YEAR OF ADMISSION TO BAR)

Samuel J. Recht
Jeremy C. Shea (Resident, Madison Office)
Hugh S. McManus
Thomas E. Maloney (Resident, Naples, Florida Office)
David L. Petersen (Resident, Naples, Florida Office)
Lawrence J. Jost
Gerald E. Connolly
James H. Baxter III
F. Joseph McMackin, III (Resident, Naples, Florida Office)
Robert T. Bailes (Resident, Phoenix, Arizona Office)
John W. Daniels, Jr.
Timothy G. Hains (Resident, Naples, Florida Office)
John H. Lhost
Roger K. Spencer (Resident, Phoenix, Arizona Office)
Warren S. Blumenthal
Peter A. Terry (Resident, Phoenix, Arizona Office)
Ann M. Murphy
John A. Rothstein
Charles H. McMullen
Elizabeth A. Orelup
Leo J. Salvatori (Resident, Naples, Florida Office)
David G. Beauchamp (Resident, Phoenix, Arizona Office)
Mary N. Fertl
Elizabeth G. Nowakowski
Ann K. Comer
Michael D. Zeka
Kevin A. Delorey (Resident, Madison Office)
John D. Humphreville (Resident, Naples, Florida Office)
Scott L. Langlois
Joseph E. Puchner
Michael J. Ostermeyer
George J. Marek

OF COUNSEL

Richard W. Cutler
John S. Sammond (Resident, West Palm Beach, Florida Office)
James Urdan
Roger P. Paulsen

ASSOCIATES

Susan A. Cerbins
Brenda J. Stugelmeyer
Jessamyn L. Bagley (Resident, Chicago, Illinois Office)
Marcia E. Facey

For Complete List of Firm Personnel, See General Section

For full biographical listings, see the Martindale-Hubbell Law Directory

WALSH & KEATING, S.C. (AV)

1505 Wawatosa Avenue, 53213
Telephone: 414-257-9929
Fax: 414-257-9959
URL: http://www.lawyers.com/walshandkeating

Gerald S. Walsh
David C. Keating

(See Next Column)

ASSOCIATE

Peter J. Walsh

Representative Clients: Immtech International, Inc.; Howard Precision Metals Inc.; James L. Callan Inc.; Milwaukee Chaplet & Mfg. Co., Inc.; Milwaukee Envelope, Inc.; Stearns Foundation, Inc.; Wausau Tile, Inc.; August Urbanek Investments, Inc.; Germantown Market Place, Inc.; Precision Metrology, Inc.

For full biographical listings, see the Martindale-Hubbell Law Directory

WYOMING

*BUFFALO,** Johnson Co.

KIRVEN & KIRVEN, P.C. (AV)

104 Fort Street, P.O. Box 640, 82834
Telephone: 307-684-2248
Fax: 307-684-2242
Email: tkirven@wyo.com

William J. Kirven (Retired)
Dennis M. Kirven
Timothy J. Kirven

Representative Clients: Texaco Inc.; Wyoming Bank and Trust Co.; Buffalo Federal Savings & Loan Assn.; Reeves Concrete Products; Gordon Ranch; Powder River Corporation Reservoir; TR Ranch; School District Coalition; City of Buffalo.

For full biographical listings, see the Martindale-Hubbell Law Directory

*CASPER,** Natrona Co.

BROWN, DREW & MASSEY, LLP (AV)

Casper Business Center, Suite 800, 123 West First Street, 82601-2486
Telephone: 307-234-1000
800-877-6755
Telefax: 307-265-8025
Email: brwndrew@coffey.com

MEMBERS OF FIRM

Morris R. Massey
Harry B. Durham, III
Donn J. McCall
Thomas F. Reese
J. Kenneth Barbe
P. Jaye Rippley
Courtney Robert Kepler

ASSOCIATE

Timothy M. Stubson

OF COUNSEL

B. J. Baker

For Complete List of Firm Personnel, See General Section

For full biographical listings, see the Martindale-Hubbell Law Directory

*CHEYENNE,** Laramie Co.

HIRST & APPLEGATE, A PROFESSIONAL CORPORATION (AV)

1720 Carey Avenue, Suite 200, P.O. Box 1083, 82003-1083
Telephone: 307-632-0541
Telefax: 307-632-4999
Email: attorneys@hirstapplegate.com *URL:* http://hirstapplegate.com

James L. Applegate
Thomas G. Gorman
Thomas A. Nicholas III
Gary R. Scott
John J. Metzke
Dale W. Cottam

Richard A. Mincer
Misha E. Westby
Boyd M. McMaster
Ryan T. Schelhaas

Representative Clients: American Insurance Group; ARCO; Ford Motor Company; Scottsdale Insurance Co.; The Doctors Company; Copley Pharmaceutical, Inc.; Royal Insurance Co.; Wyoming Stock Growers Assn.; General Motors Corp.; Fassett-Nickel, Inc.
Reference: Norwest Bank Wyoming Cheyenne, N.A.

For full biographical listings, see the Martindale-Hubbell Law Directory

PUERTO RICO

SAN JUAN, San Juan Dist.

FIDDLER GONZÁLEZ & RODRÍGUEZ, LLP

254 Muñoz Rivera Avenue (Hato Rey), P.O. Box 363507, 00936-3507
Telephone: 787-753-3113
Telecopier: 787-759-3123
Email: fiddler@fgrlaw.com *URL:* http://www.fgrlaw.com

(See Next Column)

FIDDLER GONZÁLEZ & RODRÍGUEZ LLP, *San Juan—Continued*

MEMBERS OF FIRM

Leopoldo J. Cabassa-Sauri
Raúl J. Vilá-Sellés
Pedro A. Cantero-Frau

Representative Clients: The Chase Manhattan Bank; The Equitable Life Assurance Society of the U.S.; Pfizer, Inc.; Merck & Co., Inc.; American Cyanamid Co.; Metropolitan Life Insurance Co.; Bacardi Corp.; Pep Boys, McDonald's Corp.; General Electric Company, Real Estate and Construction Operation; Interstate General.

For Complete List of Firm Personnel, See General Section

For full biographical listings, see the Martindale-Hubbell Law Directory

GOLDMAN ANTONETTI & CÓRDOVA

American International Plaza Fourteenth & Fifteenth Floors, 250 Muñoz Rivera Avenue (Hato Rey), P.O. Box 70364, 00936-0364
Telephone: 787-759-8000
Telecopiers: 787-767-9333 (Main)
787-767-9177 (Litigation Department)
787-767-8660 (Labor & Corporate Law Departments)
787-767-9325 (Tax & Environmental Law Departments)
URL: http://www.gaclaw.com

MEMBERS OF FIRM

Francisco de Jesús-Schuck
Pedro Morell Losada
Thelma Rivera-Miranda

ASSOCIATES

Maria Patricia Lake
Vanessa Bayonet-Tartak

Representative Clients: Banque Paribas; Matsushita Electric of Puerto Rico, Inc.; AIG Condado Hotel Partnership; Normandie Limited Partnership; Cadillac Uniforms and Linen Supply.

For Complete List of Firm Personnel, See General Section

For full biographical listings, see the Martindale-Hubbell Law Directory

JORGE R. JIMENEZ LAW OFFICES

Suite 807 IBM Building, 654 Muñoz Rivera Avenue (Hato Rey), 00918
Telephone: 787-763-0106
Fax: 787-763-0574

MEMBERS OF FIRM

Jorge R. Jimenez
Juan F. Doval

For full biographical listings, see the Martindale-Hubbell Law Directory

MARTÍNEZ ODELL & CALABRIA

Banco Popular Center, 209 Muñoz Rivera Avenue, Suite 1600 (Hato Rey), P.O. Box 190998, 00919-0998
Telephone: 787-753-8914
Facsimile: 787-753-8402; 787-759-9075; 787-764-5664
Email: postmaster@mocpr.com

MEMBERS OF FIRM

Luis E. Lopez Correa
Arnaldo Villamil
Luis Morales-Steinmann
Jose Antonio Fernandez-Jaquete
Jose David Medina-Rivera

OF COUNSEL

Jose B. Diaz Asencio
Hernan R. Franco

ASSOCIATES

Carmen J. Rocafort
Mariela Garcia-Colberg
Brunilda R. Santiago-Acevedo
Luis A. Hernandez-Vivoni

Representative Clients: Banco Popular de Puerto Rico; Daewoo Motor Corporation; Eckerd Corporation; Empresas Fonalledas; Hilton International; L'Aire Liquide, S.A.; Loctile Corporation; Lucent Technologies; Lutron Electronics Co., Inc.; Waste Management, Inc.

For Complete List of Firm Personnel, See General Section

For full biographical listings, see the Martindale-Hubbell Law Directory

VIRGIN ISLANDS

*CHARLOTTE AMALIE, ST. THOMAS,** St. Thomas

GRUNERT STOUT & BRUCH

24-25 Kongensgade, P.O. Box 1030, 00804
Telephone: 340-774-1320
Fax: 340-774-7839
Email: gsbusvi@viaccess.net
Affiliated with: Solomon Pearl Blum & Quinn LLP, New York, New York and Denver, Colorado.

MEMBERS OF FIRM

John E. Stout
Susan Bruch Moorehead

ASSOCIATE

Gabriel J. Villegas

(See Next Column)

OF COUNSEL

William L. Blum

For full biographical listings, see the Martindale-Hubbell Law Directory

CANADA ALBERTA

*CALGARY,** Calgary Jud. Dist.

BENNETT JONES (AV)

4500 Bankers Hall East, 855-2nd Street S.W., T2P 4K7
Telephone: 403-298-3100
Facsimile: 403-265-7219
Email: firmwatch@bennettjones.ca *URL:* http://www.bennettjones.ca
Edmonton, Alberta Office: 1000, 10035-105 Street.
Telephone: 780-421-8133.
Facsimile: 780-421-7951.
Toronto, Ontario Office: 3400 1 First Canadian Place, P.O. Box 130.
Telephone: 416-863-1200.
Facsimile: 416-863-1716.

MEMBER OF FIRM

Wayne R. Whitlock

For Complete List of Firm Personnel, See General Section

For full biographical listings, see the Martindale-Hubbell Law Directory

PARLEE MCLAWS (AV)

3400 Petro-Canada Centre, 150 - 6th Avenue, SW, T2P 3Y7
Telephone: 403-294-7000
Telecopier: 403-265-8263
Email: lawyers@parlee.com *URL:* http://www.parlee.com
Edmonton, Alberta Office: 15th Floor Manulife Place, 10180 101st Street.
Telephone: 403-423-8500.
Telecopier: 403-423-2870.

MEMBERS OF FIRM

Richard B. Mask
Andrew P. Bedford

COUNSEL

Jeffrey H. Selby

For Complete List of Firm Personnel, See General Section

For full biographical listings, see the Martindale-Hubbell Law Directory

*EDMONTON,** Edmonton Jud. Dist.

PARLEE MCLAWS (AV)

15th Floor Manulife Place, 10180 101st Street, T5J 4K1
Telephone: 403-423-8500
Telecopier: 403-423-2870
Email: lawyers@parlee.com *URL:* http://www.parlee.com
Calgary, Alberta Office: 3400 Petro-Canada Centre, 150 - 6th Avenue, SW.
Telephone: 403-294-7000.
Telecopier: 403-265-8263.

MEMBERS OF FIRM

Robert A. Newton, Q.C.
Frank J. Niziol
H. Douglas Montemurro
F. Richard Haldane, Q.C.
David G. Finlay
Ian L. MacLachlan
Kevin L. Lynch
David S. Tam

ASSOCIATES

George E. Flemming
Deborah J. Polny

For Complete List of Firm Personnel, See General Section

For full biographical listings, see the Martindale-Hubbell Law Directory

CANADA BRITISH COLUMBIA

*VANCOUVER,** Vancouver Co.

JENKINS MARZBAN LOGAN (AV)

A Partnership of Law Corporations
Suite 1414, Nelson Square, 808 Nelson Street, P.O. Box 12144, V6Z 2H2
Telephone: 604-681-6564
Facsimile: 604-681-0766
URL: http://www.JML.CA

Dinyar Marzban
Robert W. Jenkins
John S. Logan

(See Next Column)

JENKINS MARZBAN LOGAN—*Continued*

William S. McLean
Donald A. Thompson
Brent D. Jordan
Scott Booth

For full biographical listings, see the Martindale-Hubbell Law Directory

LADNER DOWNS (AV)

1200 Waterfront Centre, 200 Burrard Street, P.O. Box 48600, V7X 1T2
Telephone: 604-687-5744
Fax: 604-687-1415
Email: ldmaster@ladner-downs.com *URL:* http://www.ladner-downs.com

FIRM MEMBERS

David K. Camp
Barry D. Chase
Sandy Lloyd
David P. L. Mydske
Larry R. Sandrin
Mary Jo E. Campbell
Mark V. Lewis
David C.S. Longcroft
John L. Sampson
Jann M. Winters

Representative Clients: Marathon Developments Inc./Canadian Pacific Properties Inc.; Grosvenor International Holdings Ltd.; Sun Life Assurance Company of Canada; The Manufacturers Life Insurance Company; Canadian National Railway Company/Canada Lands Company Limited; BC Rail Ltd./BCR Properties Ltd.; Omers (Ontario Municipal Employees Retirement Board); GWL Realty Advisors Inc.; Oxford Properties Group Inc.; Morguard Investments Limited; The Molson Companies Limited; British Columbia Assets and Land Corporation; Home Depot of Canada; Edgecombe Group.

For Complete List of Firm Personnel, See General Section

For full biographical listings, see the Martindale-Hubbell Law Directory

CANADA
NEW BRUNSWICK

*FREDERICTON,** York Co.

COX HANSON O'REILLY MATHESON (AV)

(Formerly Hanson Hashey)
Suite 400, Phoenix Square, P.O. Box 310, E3B 4Y9
Telephone: 506-453-7771
Fax: 506-453-9600
Email: fredericton@coxhanson.ca *URL:* http://www.coxhanson.ca
Halifax, Nova Scotia Office: Suite 1100, Purdy's Wharf Tower 1, P.O. Box 2380 Station Central RPO, B3J 3E5.
Telephone: 902-421-6262.
Fax: 902-421-3130. E-Mail: halifax@coxhanson.ca
Saint John, New Brunswick Office: 1212-One Brunswick Square, 1 Germain St. E2L 4V1.
Telephone: 506-652-7771.
Fax: 506-632-9600.
St. John's, Newfoundland Office: Scotia Centre, 401-235 Water Street, A1C 1B6.
Telephone: 709-726-3321.
Fax: 709-726-2992. E-Mail: stjohns@coxhanson.ca
Charlottetown, Prince Edward Island Office: Queen Square, Suite 202, 119 Queen Street, P.O. Box 875, Station Central, C1A 7L9.
Telephone: 902-894-7051.
Fax: 902-368-3762. E-Mail: charlottetown@coxhanson.ca

MEMBERS OF FIRM

H. A. Hanson, Q.C. (1909-1985)
David T. Hashey, Q.C.
David M. Norman, Q.C.
J. Ian M. Whitcomb, Q.C.
John M. Hanson, Q.C.
Walter D. Vail, Q.C.
Michael E. Bowlin
John D. Larlee, Q.C.
Bruce D. Hatfield, Q.C.
Julian A. G. Dickson, Q.C.
Anne D. Wooder
Terrence J. Morrison
Lucie Richard
Catherine M. Bowlen
J. Marc Richard

ASSOCIATES

Amanda J. Frenette
Monika M. L. Zauhar
Jade A. Spalding
William E. Gould
Christopher R. DeLong
Deborah M. Power
Corinne A. Godbout
Marc-Antoine Chiasson

For full biographical listings, see the Martindale-Hubbell Law Directory

McINNES COOPER (AV)

Suite 600, 570 Queen Street, P.O. Box 610, E3B 5A6
Telephone: 506-458-8572
Fax: 506-458-9903
Email: mcrfton@mcrlaw.com *URL:* http://www.mcrlaw.com
Halifax, Nova Scotia Office: Summit Place, 1601 Lower Water Street, P.O. Box 730, B3J 2V1.
Telephone: 902-425-6500.
Fax: 902-425-6350. Email: mcrhfx@mcrlaw.com.

(See Next Column)

St. John's, Newfoundland Office: Baine Johnston Centre, 5th Floor, 10 Fort William Place, P.O. Box 5939, A1C 5X4.
Telephone: 709-722-8735.
Telecopier: 709-722-1763. Email: mcrsj@mcrlaw.com.
Moncton, New Brunswick Office: Place Moncton Place, 655 Main Street, P.O. Box 1368, E1C 8T6.
Telephone: 506-857-8970.
Fax: 506-857-4095. Email: mcrmctn@mcrlaw.com.
Charlottetown, Prince Edward Island Office: BDC Place, Suite 620, 119 Kent Street, C1A 1N3.
Telephone: 902-368-8473.
Fax: 902-368-8346. Email: mcrpei@mcrlaw.com.

PARTNERS

Leonard T. Hoyt
Carol J. Downs

For Complete List of Firm Personnel, See General Section

For full biographical listings, see the Martindale-Hubbell Law Directory

*MONCTON,** Westmorland Co.

McINNES COOPER (AV)

Barristers, Solicitors & Trade Mark Agents
Place Moncton Place, 655 Main Street, P.O. Box 1368, E1C 8T6
Telephone: 506-857-8970
Fax: 506-857-4095
Email: mcrmctn@mcrlaw.com *URL:* http://www.mcrlaw.com
Halifax, Nova Scotia Office: Summit Place, 1601 Lower Water Street, P.O. Box 730, B3J 2V1.
Telephone: 902-425-6500.
Fax: 902-425-6350. Email: mcrhfx@mcrlaw.com.
St. John's, Newfoundland Office: Baine Johnston Centre, 5th Floor, 10 Fort William Place, P.O. Box 5939, A1C 5X4.
Telephone: 709-722-8735.
Telecopier: 709-722-1763. Email: mcrsj@mcrlaw.com.
Charlottetown, Prince Edward Island Office: BDC Place, Suite 620, 119 Kent Street, C1A 1N3.
Telephone: 902-368-8473.
Fax: 902-368-8346. Email: mcrpei@mcrlaw.com.
Fredericton, New Brunswick Office: Suite 600, 570 Queen Street, P.O. Box 610.
Telephone: 506-458-8572.
Fax: 506-458-9903. Email: mcrfton@mcrlaw.com.

ASSOCIATES

Christopher A. Borden
Sylvie C. Roussel

ASSOCIATED ATTORNEY

Robert E. Radford, Q.C.

For Complete List of Firm Personnel, See General Section

For full biographical listings, see the Martindale-Hubbell Law Directory

*SAINT JOHN,** Saint John Co.

CLARK DRUMMIE (AV)

40 Wellington Row, P.O. Box 6850, E2L 4S3
Telephone: 506-633-3800
Telecopier (Automatic): 506-633-3811
Email: cd@nbnet.nb.ca

MEMBERS OF FIRM

Donald F. MacGowan, Q.C.
Willard M. Jenkins

Reference: Royal Bank of Canada.

For Complete List of Firm Personnel, See General Section

For full biographical listings, see the Martindale-Hubbell Law Directory

CANADA
NEWFOUNDLAND

*ST. JOHN'S,**

McINNES COOPER (AV)

Barristers, Solicitors & Trade Mark Agents
Baine Johnston Centre, 5th Floor, 10 Fort William Place, P.O. Box 5939, A1C 5X4
Telephone: 709-722-8735
Telecopier: 709-722-1763
Email: mcrsj@mcrlaw.com *URL:* http://www.mcrlaw.com
Halifax, Nova Scotia Office: Summit Place, 1601 Lower Water Street, P.O. Box 730, B3J 2V1.
Telephone: 902-425-6500.
Fax: 902-425-6350. Email: mcrhfx@mcrlaw.com.
Moncton, New Brunswick Office: Place Moncton Place, 655 Main Street, P.O. Box 1368, E1C 8T6.
Telephone: 506-857-8970.
Fax: 506-857-4095. Email: mcrmctn@mcrlaw.com.

(See Next Column)

MCINNES COOPER, *St. John's—Continued*

Charlottetown, Prince Edward Island Office: BDC Place, Suite 620, 119 Kent Street, C1A 1N3.
Telephone: 902-368-8473.
Fax: 902-368-8346. Email: mcrpei@mcrlaw.com.
Fredericton, New Brunswick Office: Suite 600, 570 Queen Street, P.O. Box 610.
Telephone: 506-458-8572.
Fax: 506-458-9903. Email: mcrfton@mcrlaw.com.

PARTNERS

W. Gary Rowe, Q.C.
Thomas R. Kendell
Michael J. Crosbie

ASSOCIATES

Genevieve M. Dawson
Dennis N. Clarke

For Complete List of Firm Personnel, See General Section

For full biographical listings, see the Martindale-Hubbell Law Directory

CANADA NOVA SCOTIA

*HALIFAX,** Regional Munic. of Halifax

MCINNES COOPER (AV)

Barristers, Solicitors & Trade Mark Agents
Summit Place, 1601 Lower Water Street, P.O. Box 730, B3J 2V1
Telephone: 902-425-6500
Fax: 902-425-6350
Email: mcrhfx@mcrlaw.com *URL:* http://www.mcrlaw.com
St. John's, Newfoundland Office: Baine Johnston Centre, 5th Floor, 10 Fort William Place, P.O. Box 5939, A1C 5X4.
Telephone: 709-722-8735.
Telecopier: 709-722-1763. Email: mcrsj@mcrlaw.com.
Moncton, New Brunswick Office: Place Moncton Place, 655 Main Street, P.O. Box 1368, E1C 8T6.
Telephone: 506-857-8970.
Fax: 506-857-4095. Email: mcrmctn@mcrlaw.com.
Charlottetown, Prince Edward Island Office: BDC Place, Suite 620, 119 Kent Street, C1A 1N3.
Telephone: 902-368-8473.
Fax: 902-368-8346. Email: mcrpei@mcrlaw.com.
Fredericton, New Brunswick Office: Suite 600, 570 Queen Street, P.O. Box 610.
Telephone: 506-458-8572.
Fax: 506-458-9903. Email: mcrfton@mcrlaw.com.

PARTNERS

Stewart McInnes, P.C., Q.C.
Peter J. E. McDonough, Q.C.
David H. Reardon, Q.C.
Lawrence A. Freeman

ASSOCIATES

Brenda L. Rice-Thomson
Frank E. Hughes
Jeffrey R. Blucher

For Complete List of Firm Personnel, See General Section

For full biographical listings, see the Martindale-Hubbell Law Directory

CANADA ONTARIO

*OTTAWA,** Regional Munic. of Ottawa-Carleton

BORDEN ELLIOT SCOTT & AYLEN (AV)

1000-60 Rue Queen Street, K1P 5Y7
Telephone: 613-237-5160; 800-661-4237
General Facsimile: 613-230-8842
IP Dept. Facsimile: 613-787-3558
Email: ottinfo@scottaylen.com *URL:* http://www.borden.com
Toronto, Ontario Office: Borden & Elliot: Scotia Plaza, 40 King Street West.
Telephone: 416-367-6000.
Telecopier: 416-367-6749. Email: info @borden.com. URL: http://www.borden.com.

John G. Aylen, Q.C.
Laird J. Rasmussen
Walter V. Di Cesare
Yves J. Ménard
Paule Desjardins-Hageltorn

For full biographical listings, see the Martindale-Hubbell Law Directory

*TORONTO,** Regional Munic. of Toronto

BORDEN & ELLIOT (AV)

Barristers & Solicitors
Scotia Plaza, 40 King Street West, M5H 3Y4
Telephone: 416-367-6000
Telecopier: 416-367-6749
Email: info@borden.com *URL:* http://www.borden.com
Ottawa, Ontario Office: Borden Elliot Scott & Aylen, 1000-60 Rue Queen Street.
Telephone: 613-237-5160; 800-661-4237. General
Facsimile: 613-230-8842. IP Dept.
Facsimile: 613-787-3558. Email: ottinfo@scottaylen.com. URL: http://www.borden.com.

Morton G. Gross, Q.C.

For Complete List of Firm Personnel, See General Section

For full biographical listings, see the Martindale-Hubbell Law Directory

DAVIES, WARD & BECK (AV)

1 First Canadian Place, M5X 1B1
Telephone: 416-863-0900
Fax: 416-863-0871
Email: info@dwb.com *URL:* http://www.dwb.com

PARTNERS AND ASSOCIATES

Donald C. Stanbury
Gregory J. Howard
James J. Lawson
Kent F. Beattie
Sabrina Gherbaz
Robert T. Bauer
Paul M. Kennedy
David A. Dell
Gabriella Lombardi
Gregory G. Southam

For Complete List of Firm Personnel, See General Section

For full biographical listings, see the Martindale-Hubbell Law Directory

MCDONALD & HAYDEN (AV)

One Queen Street East Suite 1500, M5C 2Y3
Telephone: 416-364-3100
Telecopier: 416-601-4100
Email: ddouglas@mchayden.on.ca *URL:* http://www.mchayden.on.ca

MEMBERS OF FIRM

John G. McDonald, Q.C. (1922-1993)
Peter Reginald Hayden, Q.C.
David C. Nathanson, Q.C.
Marvin D. Demone
D. H. Jack
David R. Street
Clifford M. Goldlist
Wendy C. Posluns
Warren S. Rapoport
David H. Goldman
A. Richard Rodier
Mark Adilman
John D. Brunt
Kevin Cai
Jane Southren
Shea T. Small

ASSOCIATE

Bram J. Green

For full biographical listings, see the Martindale-Hubbell Law Directory

*WINDSOR,** Essex Co.

MCTAGUE LAW FIRM (AV)

455 Pelissier Street, N9A 6Z9
Telephone: 519-255-4300
Detroit, Michigan Telephone: 313-965-1332
Fax: 519-255-4360(Corporate/Labor)
Fax: 519-255-4384 (Litigation/Real Estate)

MEMBERS OF FIRM

J. Douglas Lawson, Q.C.
Alexander R. Szalkai, Q.C.
Peter J. Kuker
George W. King
Josephine Stark
Tom Serafimovski
Roger A. Skinner
Daniel K. Moorhouse
Jerry B. Udell
Michael K. Coughlin
John D. Leslie
Marilee Marcotte

ASSOCIATES

Kevin G. Fanick
Michael A. Wills
Dana J. Young
Jeffrey W. MacKinnon
Brian L. Chillman

For Complete List of Firm Personnel, See General Section

For full biographical listings, see the Martindale-Hubbell Law Directory

CANADA
PRINCE EDWARD ISLAND

*CHARLOTTETOWN,** Queen's Co.

McINNES COOPER (AV⓪)

Barristers, Solicitors & Trade Mark Agents
BDC Place, Suite 620, 119 Kent Street, C1A 1N3
Telephone: 902-368-8473
Fax: 902-368-8346
Email: mcrpei@mcrlaw.com *URL:* http://www.mcrlaw.com
Halifax, Nova Scotia Office: Summit Place, 1601 Lower Water Street, P.O. Box 730, B3J 2V1.
Telephone: 902-425-6500.
Fax: 902-425-6350. Email: mcrhfx@mcrlaw.com.
St. John's, Newfoundland Office: Baine Johnston Centre, 5th Floor, 10 Fort William Place, P.O. Box 5939, A1C 5X4.
Telephone: 709-722-8735.
Telecopier: 709-722-1763. Email: mcrsj@mcrlaw.com.
Moncton, New Brunswick Office: Place Moncton Place, 655 Main Street, P.O. Box 1368, E1C 8T6.
Telephone: 506-857-8970.
Fax: 506-857-4095. Email: mcrmctn@mcrlaw.com.
Fredericton, New Brunswick Office: Suite 600, 570 Queen Street, P.O. Box 610.
Telephone: 506-458-8572.
Fax: 506-458-9903. Email: mcrfton@mcrlaw.com.

PARTNERS

Horace B. Carver, Q.C.
Michele M. Murphy

ASSOCIATES

Kevin J. Kiley
Paul Kiley

For Complete List of Firm Personnel, See General Section

For full biographical listings, see the Martindale-Hubbell Law Directory

CANADA
QUEBEC

*MONTREAL,** Montreal Dist.

de GRANDPRÉ CHAIT (AV)

1000, De La Gauchetière Street West, Suite 2900, H3B 4W5
Telephone: 514-878-4311
Fax: 514-878-4333
Email: info@degrandpre-chait.com

PARTNER OF FIRM

Founding Partner Samuel Chait, Q.C. (1904-1982)

Christiane Alary
Normand Amyot
Jacques L. Archambault
André P. Asselin
François Beauchamp
Marc Beauchemin
Jean Benoît
Jacques Bourque
Arthur I. Bronstein
Pierre Brossoit
J. Brian Cornish
Louis Demers
Jean-Pierre Desmarais
Gilles Fafard
Jean-Jacques Gagnon
Guy Gilain
Jean François Giroux
Gilles Godin, Q.C.
Andrée Gosselin
Frederica Jacobs
David H. Kauffman
Sandor J. Klein
Gabriel Kordovi
Pierre Labelle
Diane Lajeunesse
Eric Lalanne
Virginia K. H. Lam
Benoît Larose
Philippe Leclercq
Daniel Lessard
Ronald H. Levy
C. Ralph Lipper
Jean-François Ménard
Pierre Mercille
Benoît Pelchat
Yves Poirier
Olivier Prat, Q.C.
Alain Robichaud
Marc J. Rubin
Louis Samuel
Ronald L. Stein
Mark E. Turcot

For full biographical listings, see the Martindale-Hubbell Law Directory

GOLDSTEIN, FLANZ & FISHMAN (AV)

Suite 4100, 1250 René-Lévesque Boulevard West, H3B 4W8
Telephone: 514-932-4100
Cable Address: "Meybat"
Telex: 05-24593
Telecopier: 514-932-4170
Email: counsel@gff.qc.ca

(See Next Column)

MEMBERS OF FIRM

Yoine Goldstein
Leonard W. Flanz
Avram Fishman
Mark Schrager
Gilles Paquin
Mark E. Meland
Ellen Amdursky
Alain Daigle
Cathy Noseworthy
Suzanne Villeneuve

For full biographical listings, see the Martindale-Hubbell Law Directory

McMASTER GERVAIS (AV)

A General Partnership
1000 de La Gauchetière Street West, Suite 900, H3B 5H4
Telephone: 514-879-1212
Fax: 514-954-1905
Email: info@mcmastergervais.com *URL:* http://www.mcmastergervais.com

MEMBERS OF FIRM

Timothy R. Carsley
Norman A. Saibil
Yves A. Dubois
Sylvie Bouvette
P. Vivian Cyriacopoulos
Patricia Galella
David Torralbo
Peter C. Casey
Ian B. Taylor
Pierre Trudeau
D. James Papadimitriou
Lise Fortier
Catherine Guertin
Sébastien Berthelet
Daniel Ferreira

For Complete List of Firm Personnel, See General Section

For full biographical listings, see the Martindale-Hubbell Law Directory

MENDELSOHN ROSENTZVEIG SHACTER (AV)

1000 Sherbrooke Street West, 27th Floor, H3A 3G4
Telephone: 514-987-5000
Telex: 05-27284 Colorlaw
Telecopier: 514-987-1213
Email: mrs@mrslaw.com *URL:* http://www.mrslaw.com

PARTNERS

S. Leon Mendelsohn, Q.C. (1902-1996)
Leo Rosentzveig, Q.C.
Manuel Shacter, Q.C.
Jack C. Shayne
William Levitt
Arthur A. Garvis
Edward E. Aronoff
L. Michael Blumenstein
Max Mendelsohn
Earl S. Cohen
Michael Garonce
Donald M. Devine
Richard S. Uditsky
Joel Weitzman
Ian R. Rudnikoff
Marc I. Leiter
L. B. Erdle
Fredric L. Carsley
Frank Zylberberg
Jules Brossard
David L. Rosentzveig
Judie K. Jokinen
Gilles Seguin
Martin Desrosiers
Andrew Etcovitch
Alain Breault
Jean Carrière
Henri M. Bybelezer
Louis Frédérick Côté
Sandra Abitan

ASSOCIATES

Carl M. Ravinsky
Catherine Muraz
Francine Wiseman
Joelle Sebag
Maria R. Battaglia
Keyvan Nassiry
Linda Schachter
Emmanuelle Saucier
Arnold Cohen
Aaron Makovka
Michel Rochefort
Céline Tessier
Sophie Crevier
Annick Joyal
Francis Desmarais
Nicolas J. Beugnot
Jean-François Brière
Marc-Antoine Deschamps
Philipp F. Duffy
Fred Purkey
Martin Sills
David Tardif-Latourelle

For full biographical listings, see the Martindale-Hubbell Law Directory

POULIOT, MERCURE (AV)

CIBC Tower, 31st Floor, 1155 René-Lévesque Boulevard, West, H3B 3S6
Telephone: 514-875-5210
Telecopier: 514-875-4308
Email: POUMER@CEDEP.COM
Genève, Suisse Office: 8, Rue de la Rôtisserie, 1204 Geneva, Switzerland.
Telephone: +41 22-28 79 40.
Telecopier: +41 22-21 23 67.

MEMBERS OF FIRM

Georges A. Pouliot, Q.C.
Gilles Brunelle
Luc Gratton
Brian Riordan
Pierre Paquet
Anne-Marie Gauthier
Yvon Brizard
Robert Tessier
Daniel Gagné
Lilia Pouliot
Marco Veilleux
Alain Nadon
Jean H. Gagnon
Gilles Bertrand
Jean Larivière
Louis-Michel Tremblay
David I. Johnston
Stéphane Hébert
Jacques LeBel, Q.C.
Joel A. Silcoff
Ronald M. Auclair
Philippe Roy
Maxime B. Rhéaume
Serge Desrochers
C. Keenan LaPierre
Alain Bond

(See Next Column)

POULIOT, MERCURE, *Montreal—Continued*

MEMBERS OF FIRM (Continued)

Richard Fontaine
Normand Royal
Louis Coallier
Nicole Chouinard
Stéphane Teasdale

ASSOCIATES

Micheline Perrault
Caroline Lemoine
Béatrice Arronis
Yvan Nantel
Sylvie Boulanger
Vincent Frenette
Robert Cardin
Alexandre Henri
Brent J. Muir
Louise Tremblay
Chantal Joubert
Normand D'Amour
Pascale Cloutier
Eric Couture
Frédéric Chatel
Mary-Lynn Breton
Alexandre Ajami

For full biographical listings, see the Martindale-Hubbell Law Directory

CANADA
SASKATCHEWAN

*REGINA,** Regina Jud. Centre

MACPHERSON LESLIE & TYERMAN (AV)

1500-1874 Scarth Street, S4P 4E9
Telephone: 306-347-8000
Telecopier: 306-352-5250
Email: mltreg@mlt.com
Saskatoon, Saskatchewan Office: 1500-410 22nd Street East, S7K 5T6.
Telephone: 306-975-7100.
Telecopier: 306-975-7145.

MEMBERS OF FIRM

R. Neil MacKay (Resident, Saskatoon Office)
John A. Dipple
Garret J. Oledzki
James S. Kerby (Resident, Saskatoon Office)
Scott A. Exner

ASSOCIATES

David B. Jahnke (Resident, Saskatoon Office)
Michele T. Klebuc-Simes
Kevin D. Trumpour (Resident, Saskatoon Office)

For Complete List of Firm Personnel, See General Section

For full biographical listings, see the Martindale-Hubbell Law Directory

SECURITIES LAW

MINNESOTA

*MINNEAPOLIS,** Hennepin Co.

ABDO AND ABDO, P.A. (AV)

710 Northstar West 625 Marquette Avenue, 55402
Telephone: 612-333-1526
Fax: 612-342-2608
Email: abdoabdo@aol.com *URL:* http://www.abdo.com.br

E. John Abdo (1912-1993)
Robert P. Abdo
Steven R. Hedges
Keith J. Broady

Representative Client: Global Financial Group, Inc.; Drummer Boy Films; Bison Instruments, Inc.

For Complete List of Firm Personnel, See General Section

For full biographical listings, see the Martindale-Hubbell Law Directory

BRIOL & ASSOCIATES (AV)

3905 IDS Center, 80 South Eighth Street, 55402
Telephone: 612-337-8410
Fax: 612-337-5151
Email: briol@mm.com

Mark J. Briol

ASSOCIATES

Amy J. Ihlan
Scott A. Benson
Mary E. Briol
Ellen R. Brostrom

For full biographical listings, see the Martindale-Hubbell Law Directory

HEAD, SEIFERT & VANDER WEIDE, A PROFESSIONAL ASSOCIATION (AV)

One Financial Plaza, Suite 2400, 120 South Sixth Street, 55402
Telephone: 612-339-1601
Fax: 612-339-3372
Email: hsvw@wavefront.com

Jerome Truhn (1940-1982)
Douglas M. Head
Thomas V. Seifert
Vernon J. Vander Weide
Howard J. Kauffman
Kenneth A. Larson
Marianne E. Durkin
Charles H. Clay
Aaron F. Biber

For full biographical listings, see the Martindale-Hubbell Law Directory

HENSON & EFRON, P.A. (AV)

400 Second Avenue South, Suite 1200, 55401-2496
Telephone: 612-339-2500
Fax: 612-339-6364
Email: firm@hensonefron.com

Stanley Efron
Alan C. Eidsness
Susan E. Vandenberg
Clark D. Opdahl
Jennie A. Clarke

Angela D. Lageson

Representative Clients: Pentair, Inc.; Hawkins Chemical, Inc.

For Complete List of Firm Personnel, See General Section

For full biographical listings, see the Martindale-Hubbell Law Directory

SALITERMAN & SIEFFERMAN, P.C. (AV)

Suite 1000 Northstar Center East, 608 Second Avenue South, 55402
Telephone: 612-339-1400
Fax: 612-349-2908
URL: http://www.saliterman.com

Richard A. Saliterman
Floyd E. Siefferman, Jr.
Nicholas M. Wenner
Thomas J. Seymour
Paul A. Ledford

For full biographical listings, see the Martindale-Hubbell Law Directory

MISSOURI

ST. LOUIS, (Independent City)

GREEN, SCHAAF & JACOBSON, P.C. (AV)

Suite 700 Pierre Laclede Center, 7733 Forsyth Boulevard (Clayton), 63105
Telephone: 314-862-6800
Telecopier: 314-862-1606
Email: info@stlouislaw.com *URL:* http://www.stlouislaw.com

George E. Schaaf (1930-1995)
Martin M. Green
Joe D. Jacobson
David T. Butsch

Jonathan F. Andres
Allen P. Press
Daniel S. Peters

OF COUNSEL

Howard L. Kanefield

For full biographical listings, see the Martindale-Hubbell Law Directory

KODNER, WATKINS, MUCHNICK & DUNNE, L.C. (AV)

Suite 200, 168 North Meramec Avenue (Clayton), 63105-3578
Telephone: 314-727-9111
Facsimile: 314-727-9110
Email: KWMD@primary.net

Mark C. Kodner
Albert S. Watkins
Todd I. Muchnick
Gerald M. Dunne
L. Steven Goldblatt

James N. Fendelman
D. Andrew Weigley
Nancy O. Bodet
Richard B. Hein
Kenneth Mack Brison
Richard M. Stewart
William M. Green
J. Christopher Wehrle
David A. Reed
M. Zane Yates
Nancy M. Watkins
Joseph B. Kloecker, Jr.

OF COUNSEL

Gerald T. Dunne
Carl A. Wattenberg, Jr.

For full biographical listings, see the Martindale-Hubbell Law Directory

THE LOWENBAUM PARTNERSHIP, L.L.C. (AV)

222 South Central Avenue, Suite 901 (Clayton), 63105
Telephone: 314-863-0092
Facsimile: 314-746-4848
Email: rml@lowenbaumlaw.com

Timothy L. Elliott
J. Timothy Gorman

Representative Clients: LaserSight Incorporated.

For full biographical listings, see the Martindale-Hubbell Law Directory

MONTANA

*BILLINGS,** Yellowstone Co.

CROWLEY, HAUGHEY, HANSON, TOOLE & DIETRICH, P.L.L.P. (AV)

500 Transwestern II, 490 North 31st Street, P.O. Box 2529, 59103
Telephone: 406-252-3441
Fax: 406-259-4159
Email: crowley@crowleylaw.com
Helena, Montana Office: IBM Building, 100 North Park Avenue, Suite 300, 59601.
Telephone: 406-449-4165.
Fax: 406-449-5149.
Kalispell, Montana Office: 431 1st Avenue West, 59901.
Telephone: 406-752-6644.
Fax: 406-752-5108.
Williston, North Dakota Office: 113 East Broadway, 58801.
Telephone: 701-572-2200.
Fax: 701-572-7072.

OF COUNSEL

John M. Dietrich

MEMBER OF FIRM

Allan L. Karell

Representative Clients: Montana Power Co.; First Interstate Bank of Commerce; MDU Resources Group, Inc.; Chevron U.S.A., Inc.; Noranda Minerals Corp.; United Parcel Service.
Insurance Clients: Farmers Insurance Group; New York Life Insurance Co.

For Complete List of Firm Personnel, See General Section

For full biographical listings, see the Martindale-Hubbell Law Directory

NEBRASKA

*LINCOLN,** Lancaster Co.

CLINE, WILLIAMS, WRIGHT, JOHNSON & OLDFATHER (AV)

1900 U.S. Bank Building, 233 South 13th Street, 68508
Telephone: 402-474-6900
Fax: 402-474-5393
Email: postmaster@cline-law.com *URL:* http://www.cline-law.com
Omaha, Nebraska Office: Suite 720, One Pacific Place, 1125 South 103rd Street, 68124.
Telephone: 402-397-1700.
Fax: 402-397-1806.

ATTORNEYS

Allen L. Graves
Charles M. Pallesen, Jr.
Fredric H. Kauffman
Donald F. Burt
Alan E. Peterson
Stephen E. Gehring
Robert J. Routh
Kevin Colleran
L. Bruce Wright
James M. Bausch
Larry A. Holle
David R. Buntain
Stephen H. Nelsen
Michael C. Mueller
Lauren W. Wismer
Daniel R. Stogsdill
Scott D. Kelly
Terry R. Wittler
Pamela Hastings Carrier
Mark A. Christensen
Richard P. Garden, Jr.
Shawn D. Renner
John C. Miles
Mary Kay Frank
Thomas C. Huston
Sonya S. Ekart
Don R. Janssen
Susan Kubert Sapp
Kevin J. Schneider
Andrew D. Strotman
Jill Gossin Jensen
Rochelle A. Mullen
John L. Horan
Bryan S. Hatch
Steven C. Likes
Tracy A. Oldemeyer
Jolene M. Papa
Timothy G. Aschoff
Eric N. Bergquist
Janis J. Winterhof
Andrea Dylan Snowden

OF COUNSEL

Charles E. Wright
Richard P. Jeffries
Mary M. Campbell

RETIRED PARTNERS

Flavel A. Wright (Retired)
Warren C. Johnson (Retired)
Charles E. Oldfather (1927-1998)

Representative Clients: U.S. Bank National Association; University of Nebraska; Nebraska Medical Assn.; Saint Elizabeth Regional Medical Center; Media of Nebraska; Cargill Inc.; State Farm Insurance Cos.; Wal-Mart Stores, Inc.; Textron/Cushman; Isco, Inc.

For full biographical listings, see the Martindale-Hubbell Law Directory

SCUDDER LAW FIRM, P.C. (AV)

Second Floor, 411 South 13th Street, P.O. Box 81277, 68508
Telephone: 402-435-3223
Fax: 402-435-4239
Email: firm@scudderlaw.com *URL:* http://www.scudderlaw.com

Earl H. Scudder
Christine C. Schwartzkopf Schroff
Mark A. Scudder
Michael O. Dunn
Heidi Hornung Scherr
William J. Strait

PROFESSIONAL ASSISTANTS

Annette Elston (Firm Administrator)
Lynn K. Hilger (Legal Assistant)
Tisha Gilreath Mullen (Legal Assistant)
Kristin Ann Brown
Marleen M. Kelley
Heather Ropes-Gale (Director of Communications)

For full biographical listings, see the Martindale-Hubbell Law Directory

*OMAHA,** Douglas Co.

CLINE, WILLIAMS, WRIGHT, JOHNSON & OLDFATHER (AV)

One Pacific Place, 1125 South 103rd Street, Suite 720, 68124
Telephone: 402-397-1700
Fax: 402-397-1806
Email: postmaster@cline-law.com *URL:* http://www.cline-law.com
Lincoln, Nebraska Office: 1900 U.S. Bank Building, 233 South 13th Street, 68508.
Telephone: 402-474-6900.
Fax: 402-474-5393.

ATTORNEYS

Donald F. Burt
Stephen E. Gehring
James M. Bausch
Michael C. Mueller
Daniel R. Stogsdill
Scott D. Kelly
John C. Miles
Mary Kay Frank
Andrew D. Strotman
Rochelle A. Mullen
Steven C. Likes
Tracy A. Oldemeyer
Timothy G. Aschoff

(See Next Column)

OF COUNSEL

Richard P. Jeffries

Representative Clients: U.S. Bank National Association; University of Nebraska; Nebraska Medical Assn.; Saint Elizabeth Regional Medical Center; Media of Nebraska; Cargill Inc.; State Farm Insurance Cos.; Wal-Mart Stores, Inc.; Textron/Cushman; ISCO, Inc.

For full biographical listings, see the Martindale-Hubbell Law Directory

ERICKSON & SEDERSTROM, P.C. (AV)

Regency Westpointe, 10330 Regency Parkway Drive, Suite 100, 68114-3761
Telephone: 402-397-2200
Fax: 402-390-7137
Lincoln, Nebraska Office: Suite 400, Cornhusker Plaza, 301 South 13th Street, 68508-2571.
Telephone: 402-476-1000.
Fax: 402-476-6167.

Donald H. Erickson
Gary L. Hoffman

Representative Clients: Nebraska State Bank of Omaha; Berkshire Hathaway, Inc.; Bozell, Inc.; IBP, Inc. Quaker Oats Co.; United A-G Cooperative, Inc.; Immanuel Medical Center; Cornhusker Casualty Co.; Hartford Accident & Indemnity Co.; Mortgage Guaranty Insurance Corp. (MGIC).

For Complete List of Firm Personnel, See General Section

For full biographical listings, see the Martindale-Hubbell Law Directory

NEVADA

HENDERSON, Clark Co.

ROOKER & GIBSON (AV)

Suite 105, 701 North Green Valley Parkway, 89014
Telephone: 702-990-8100
Telecopier: 702-932-5266

C. Keith Rooker
James B. Gibson

Reference: BankWest of Nevada.

For full biographical listings, see the Martindale-Hubbell Law Directory

*LAS VEGAS,** Clark Co.

KUMMER KAEMPFER BONNER & RENSHAW (AV)

Seventh Floor, 3800 Howard Hughes Parkway, 89109-0907
Telephone: 702-792-7000
Fax: 702-796-7181
Email: nvlaw@kkbr.com

MEMBERS OF FIRM

John C. Renshaw
Thomas F. Kummer
Christopher L. Kaempfer
Michael J. Bonner
Kathleen Jane England
John N. Brewer
Gerald D. Waite
Sherwood N. Cook
Shari Cassin Patterson
John C. Jeppsen
Mark H. Fiorentino
John A. Curtas

OF COUNSEL

H. Gregory Nasky
James H. Bilbray
Michael W. Brimley

ASSOCIATES

Thomas D. Amick
Sean L. Anderson (Not admitted in NV)
Nikki L. Baker
George J. Claseman
L. Joe Coppedge
Gregory S. Gilbert
Robert J. Gronauer
Robert C. Kim
Kurt C. Lambeth
Angela Turriciano Otto
Elizabeth A. Savage
Lyssa M. Simonelli
James E. Smyth II
Gregg R. Vermeys
Anthony A. Zmaila

For full biographical listings, see the Martindale-Hubbell Law Directory

*RENO,** Washoe Co.

HALE LANE PEEK DENNISON HOWARD AND ANDERSON (AV)

100 West Liberty Street, Tenth Floor, P.O. Box 3237, 89505
Telephone: 775-327-3000
Telefax: 775-786-6179
Email: info@halelane.com
Las Vegas, Nevada Office: Nevada Financial Center, 2300 West Sahara Avenue, Eighth Floor, Box 8.
Telephone: 702-222-2500.
Fax: 702-365-6940.
Carson City, Nevada Office: 777 East William Street, Suite 200, P.O. Box 2620.
Telephone: 775-684-6000.
Telefax: 775-684-6001.

(See Next Column)

HALE LANE PEEK DENNISON HOWARD AND ANDERSON—*Continued*

MEMBERS OF FIRM

Robert C. Anderson
David A. Garcia

OF COUNSEL

Roy L. Farrow (Resident, Carson City, Nevada)

For Complete List of Firm Personnel, See General Section

For full biographical listings, see the Martindale-Hubbell Law Directory

NEW HAMPSHIRE

*MANCHESTER,** Hillsborough Co.

SHEEHAN PHINNEY BASS + GREEN, PROFESSIONAL ASSOCIATION (AV)

Hampshire Plaza, 1000 Elm Street, P.O. Box 3701, 03105-3701
Telephone: 603-668-0300
800-625-SPBG
Fax: 603-627-8121
Email: postmaster@sheehan.com *URL:* http://www.sheehan.com
Portsmouth, New Hampshire Office: Old City Hall, 126 Daniel Street.
Telephone: 603-433-2111.
Fax: 603-433-3126.
Concord, New Hampshire Office: 143 North Main Street.
Telephone: 603-223-2020.
Fax: 603-224-8899.

Alan L. Reische
James E. Higgins
Robert B. Field, Jr.
Stephen E. Weyl
Daniel N. Gregoire
Michael Jeffrey Drooff
Robert R. Lucic

Representative Clients: Anheuser-Busch, Inc.; Bank of New Hampshire Corp.; The Elliot Hospital of Manchester; Granite State Packing Co.; Moore Business Forms, Inc.; New Hampshire College; New Hampshire Dental Service Corp.; New Hampshire Yankee Electric Corp.; Numerica Financial Corp.

For Complete List of Firm Personnel, See General Section

For full biographical listings, see the Martindale-Hubbell Law Directory

NEW JERSEY

LAWRENCEVILLE, Mercer Co.

SZAFERMAN, LAKIND, BLUMSTEIN, WATTER & BLADER, P.C. (AV)

Suite 104 Quakerbridge Executive Center, 101 Grovers Mill Road, 08648
Telephone: 609-275-0400
Telefax: 609-275-4511

Arnold C. Lakind
Barry D. Szaferman
Jeffrey P. Blumstein
Paul N. Watter
Steven Blader
Sidney H. Lehmann
Gerald B. Schenkman
David B. Beckett
Scott P. Borsack
Mary Lou Delahanty

Jennifer Weisberg Millner
Cathyanne A. Pisciotta
Jason N. Fruhschein
Demery J. Roberts
Stuart A. Tucker
Brian G. Paul
Victoria Rivera-Cruz
Thomas J. Burns III

LEGAL SUPPORT PERSONNEL

Paula M. Rossi (Office Administrator)
Patricia Hallstrum (Controller)

Representative Clients: Sun National Bank; First Washington Bank; Gilmore Securities & Co.; Communication Workers of America; The Eagle Group; Water's Edge Convalescent Center; Ronson Aviation, Inc.; Holmdel Township Board of Adjustment; Public Service Managers Association; Chemical Leaman Tank Lines.

For full biographical listings, see the Martindale-Hubbell Law Directory

*NEWARK,** Essex Co.

HELLRING LINDEMAN GOLDSTEIN & SIEGAL LLP (AV)

One Gateway Center, 07102-5386
Telephone: 973-621-9020
Fax: 973-621-7406
Englewood, New Jersey Office: 32-40 North Dean Street.
Telephone: 201-871-3060.

(See Next Column)

Joel D. Siegal
Jonathan L. Goldstein
James A. Scarpone
Michael Edelson
Richard D. Shapiro
Richard K. Coplon
Robert S. Raymar
Stephen L. Dreyfuss
Matthew E. Moloshok
Rachel N. Davidson

For Complete List of Firm Personnel, See General Section

For full biographical listings, see the Martindale-Hubbell Law Directory

MCCARTER & ENGLISH, LLP (AV)

Four Gateway Center, 100 Mulberry Street, P.O. Box 652, 07101-0652
Telephone: 973-622-4444
Telecopier: 973-624-7070
URL: http://www.mccarter.com
Cherry Hill, New Jersey Office: 1820 Chapel Avenue West, Suite 380.
Telephone: 609-662-8444.
Telecopier: 609-662-6203.
New York, New York Office: Suite 2247, One World Trade Center.
Telephone: 212-466-9018.
Telecopier: 212-432-6568.
Boca Raton, Florida Office: 2255 Glades Road, Suite 319-A.
Telephone: 561-994-6262.
Telecopier: 561-241-0798.
Wilmington, Delaware Office: Mellon Bank Center, 919 Market Street.
Telephone: 302-654-8010.
Telecopier: 302-654-0795.
Philadelphia, Pennsylvania Office: One Commerce Square, 2005 Market Street, Suite 3600.
Telephone: 215-557-7700.
Telecopier: 215-557-6544.

MEMBERS OF FIRM

William H. Horton
Bart J. Colli
Theodore D. Moskowitz
Seth T. Taube
Peter S. Twombly
David F. Broderick

For Complete List of Firm Personnel, See General Section

For full biographical listings, see the Martindale-Hubbell Law Directory

MCMANIMON & SCOTLAND, L.L.C. (AV)

One Riverfront Plaza, 4th Floor, 07102-5311
Telephone: 973-622-1800
Fax: 973-622-7333; 973-622-3744

MEMBERS OF FIRM

Joseph P. Baumann, Jr.
John V. Cavaliere
John B. Hall
Glenn F. Scotland
Ronald J. Ianoale
Andrea L. Kahn
Jeffrey G. Kramer
Leslie G. London
Edward J. McManimon, III

OF COUNSEL

Norman M. Robertson
Carla J. Brundage

ASSOCIATES

Peter S. Crisafi
Sheila Newsome Maddox
M. Frances Ciesla
Kristin Dwyer Ganley
Joseph C. Jasaitis
Stephen N. Severud
Thomas J. Hastie, Jr.

LEGAL SUPPORT PERSONNEL

Helen Lysaght

PARALEGALS

Sandra Simoes

For full biographical listings, see the Martindale-Hubbell Law Directory

SILLS CUMMIS RADIN TISCHMAN EPSTEIN & GROSS, A PROFESSIONAL CORPORATION (AV)

One Riverfront Plaza, 07102-5400
Telephone: 973-643-7000
Fax: 973-643-6500
Telex: 820630 Sillsbeck Nwk
Email: sillsmail@sillscummis.com *URL:* http://www.sillscummis.com
Atlantic City, New Jersey Office: 17 Gordon's Alley.
Telephone: 609-344-2800.
New York, N.Y. Office: 712 Fifth Avenue.
Telephone: 212-643-7000.
Washington, D.C. Office: 1800 K Street, N.W.
Telephone: 202-296-4750.

MEMBERS OF FIRM

Michael B. Tischman
Steven E. Gross
Steven M. Goldman
Ira A. Rosenberg
Robert Max Crane
Arlene Elgart Mirsky
Jerry Genberg
Brian S. Coven
Stanley U. North, III
Victor H. Boyajian
Frederic M. Tudor
Steven R. Kamen

OF COUNSEL

Diane M. Lavenda

(See Next Column)

SILLS CUMMIS RADIN TISCHMAN EPSTEIN & GROSS A PROFESSIONAL CORPORATION, *Newark—Continued*

Noel D. Humphreys
Gary W. Herschman
Lori M. Waldron
Christian Peter Johnson (Not admitted in NJ)
Jonathan N. Marcus
Joseph A. Becht, Jr.

Representative Clients: Blue Cross/Blue Shield of New Jersey; Bristol-Myers Squibb Co.; Circuit City Stores; Eastman Kodak; New Jersey Performing Arts Center; Six Flags Corporation; WWOR-TV, Inc.; PNC Bank Corp.

For Complete List of Firm Personnel, See General Section

For full biographical listings, see the Martindale-Hubbell Law Directory

PRINCETON, Mercer Co.

STARK & STARK, A PROFESSIONAL CORPORATION (AV)

Princeton Pike Corporate Center, P.O. Box 5315, 08543-5315
Telephone: 609-896-9060
Fax: 609-896-0629
Email: info@stark-stark.com *URL:* http://www.stark-stark.com

Brian A. Carlis
Thomas D. Giachetti
Kevin M. Hart
Craig S. Hilliard
Thomas B. Lewis

Daniel A. Bernstein
Brian S. Hamburger
John E. MacDonald
Rachel L. Stark

For full biographical listings, see the Martindale-Hubbell Law Directory

SADDLE BROOK, Bergen Co.

COHN LIFLAND PEARLMAN HERRMANN & KNOPF LLP (AV)

Park 80 Plaza West-One, 07663
Telephone: 201-845-9600
Telecopier: 201-845-9423
Email: info@njlawfirm.com *URL:* http://www.njlawfirm.com

MEMBERS OF FIRM

Albert L. Cohn
Peter S. Pearlman
Barry A. Knopf
Daniel Crystal (Retired)
Jeffrey W. Herrmann
Robert D. Zatorski
Allen Susser
Mary Ann T. Stokes
Brian D. Zinn
Joshua P. Cohn

ASSOCIATES

Virginia A. Harper
Leonard Z. Kaufmann
Audra DePaolo
Robert Ricci, Jr.
Maurice W. McLaughlin
Andrew C. Abrams
Jessica V. Henry

OF COUNSEL

Sylvia J. Cohn
Jodi B. Scherl

For full biographical listings, see the Martindale-Hubbell Law Directory

KRUGMAN & KAILES LLP (AV)

Park 80 West-Plaza Two, 07663-5835
Telephone: 201-845-3434; 212-695-3262
Telecopier: 201-845-9627
Email: counsel@krugmankailes.com
New York, New York Office: 99 Park Avenue, Suite 2200.
Telephone: 212-599-1060.
Telecopier: 212-599-6282.
London, England Office: 90 Fetter Lane, London EC4A-1PT.
Telephone: 011 (44) 171-421-7918.
Telecopier: 011 (44) 171-831-6407.

MEMBERS OF FIRM

Martin Krugman (1916-1994)
Howard Kailes
Thomas J. Goodwin
Ward C. Laracy
Robert I. Wexler
Alan H. Fox
Joy M. Mercer
Kerry B. Flowers

OF COUNSEL

James D. Krugman

COUNSEL

Judith S. Musicant

ASSOCIATES

Anne M. Wallace (Not admitted in NJ)
April A. Savoye
Lisa Ann Miller
Patrizia E. DeBari
David J. Hanley, Jr.
Anjana D. Patel
W. Mark O'Brien

For full biographical listings, see the Martindale-Hubbell Law Directory

WOODBRIDGE, Middlesex Co.

DEUTCH & FALK, A PROFESSIONAL CORPORATION (AV)

843 Rahway Avenue, 07095-3699
Telephone: 732-636-4200
Fax: 732-636-3575
URL: http://www.deutchfalk.com
URL: http://www.lawyers.com/dflaw
Linden, New Jersey Office: 924 North Wood Avenue, Second Floor, 07036.
Telephone: 908-486-2422.
New York, N.Y. Office: 2 Pennsylvania Plaza, Suite 1910, 10121.
Telephone: 212-319-7332.

Victor A. Deutch
Kenneth B. Falk

John F. Kwasnik
Monica Kowalski

OF COUNSEL

Kenneth A. Wallach

Representative Clients: C.M.M. Funding, LLC; Educational Compliance Management; TheNet Digital Seravices, Inc.; San Clemente Financial Group Securities, Inc.; SecurFone New York, Inc.

For full biographical listings, see the Martindale-Hubbell Law Directory

NEW MEXICO

*ALBUQUERQUE,** Bernalillo Co.

FREEDMAN BOYD DANIELS HOLLANDER GOLDBERG & CLINE P.A. (AV)

20 First Plaza, Suite 700, 87102
Telephone: 505-842-9960
Fax: 505-842-0761

David A. Freedman

For full biographical listings, see the Martindale-Hubbell Law Directory

HUGHES & STRUMOR, LTD. CO. (AV)

320 Gold Avenue SW, Suite 1000, 87102
Telephone: 505-842-6700
Fax: 505-764-0012
Email: hsltdco@aol.com
Santa Fe, New Mexico Office: 142 West Palace Avenue, 87501.
Telephone: 505-986-1033.

Tommy D. Hughes
Robert M. Strumor

For full biographical listings, see the Martindale-Hubbell Law Directory

RODEY, DICKASON, SLOAN, AKIN & ROBB, P.A. (AV)

Albuquerque Plaza, Suite 2200, 201 Third Street, N.W., P.O. Box 1888, 87103-1888
Telephone: 505-765-5900
Fax: 505-768-7395
Email: info@rodey.com *URL:* http://www.rodey.com
Santa Fe, New Mexico Office: Suite 101 Marcy Plaza, 123 East Marcy Street, P.O. Box 1357, 87504-1357.
Telephone: 505-984-0100.
Fax: 505-989-9542.

Robert G. McCorkle
Rex D. Throckmorton

COUNSEL

S. I. Betzer, Jr.

For Complete List of Firm Personnel, See General Section

For full biographical listings, see the Martindale-Hubbell Law Directory

NEW YORK

EAST MEADOW, Nassau Co.

CERTILMAN BALIN ADLER & HYMAN, LLP (AV)

90 Merrick Avenue, 11554
Telephone: 516-296-7000
Telecopier: 516-296-7111
URL: http://www.cbah.com

MEMBERS OF FIRM

Ira J. Adler
Dale Allinson
Michael C. Axelrod
Herbert M. Balin
Bruce J. Bergman
Eileen O'Boyle Bitetto
Michael D. Brofman
Lewis J. Campanella

(See Next Column)

CERTILMAN BALIN ADLER & HYMAN LLP—*Continued*

MEMBERS OF FIRM (Continued)

Morton L. Certilman
Robert J. Ciovacco
Brian J. Davis
Wayne G. Edwards
Joseph P. Famighetti
Howard R. Gladstone
Murray Greenberg
Gavin C. Grusd
David Z. Herman
Richard Herzbach
M. Allan Hyman
Bernard Hyman
Donna-Marie Korth
Steven J. Kuperschmid
Jeffrey S. Lisabeth
Jaspreet S. Mayall
Richard J. McCord
Thomas J. McNamara
Michael F. O'Shea
Marilyn Price
Fred S. Skolnik
Louis Soloway
Harold Somer
Howard M. Stein
Brian K. Ziegler

OF COUNSEL

Daniel S. Cohan
Joseph N. Mondello

ASSOCIATES

Lawrence A. Altholtz
Meredith W. Ayres
Daniel J. Baker
Kimberly I. Berson
Scott B. Black
Brendan J. DeRiggi
Thomas M. Farrell
Mary C. Florentz
Candace Reid Gladston
Harry P. Greenbaum
David E. Herold
Jodi S. Hoffman
James G. Kapralos
Linda P. Manfredi
Edward G. McCabe
Patrick McCormick
Susan L. McWalters
Jothy Narendran
James A. Rose
Wayne J. Schaefer
Leslie H. Scharf
Afsheen Ashley Shah
Victor Spinnelli
Russell H. Stern
Robert G. Wilk

For full biographical listings, see the Martindale-Hubbell Law Directory

JERICHO, Nassau Co.

BLAU, KRAMER, WACTLAR & LIEBERMAN, P.C. (AV)

100 Jericho Quadrangle, 11753
Telephone: 516-822-4820
Telecopier: 516-822-4824
Email: BKWLLAW@aol.com

Harvey R. Blau
Edward I. Kramer
David H. Lieberman, P.C.
Edward S. Wactlar
Lonnie Coleman
Nancy D. Lieberman

Reference: Fleet Bank.

For full biographical listings, see the Martindale-Hubbell Law Directory

MELVILLE, Suffolk Co.

LAMB & BARNOSKY, LLP (AV)

534 Broadhollow Road-CS 9034, 11747-9034
Telephone: 631-694-2300
Telecopier: 631-694-2309
Email: thefirm@lambbarnosky.com *URL:* http://www.lambbarnosky.com

PARTNERS

Eugene R. Barnosky
Robert H. Cohen
Marcia Lyn Finkelstein
Michael J. Heller
Gary Holman
Scott M. Karson
P. L. Lamb
Arthur A. Lane
Joel M. Markowitz
Gerald P. Rosenberg
Patrice Dowd Shenn

OF COUNSEL

Louis E. Black
James F. Gesualdi
Howard W. Newman
Joseph J. Salvatore
Joseph H. Wishod

COUNSEL

Lloyd K. Chanin
Scott P. McBride

ASSOCIATES

Cathleen D. Allen
Catherine Healy Kanzler
Rita Fishman Sheena
Shari Lee Sugarman

For full biographical listings, see the Martindale-Hubbell Law Directory

*NEW YORK,** New York Co.

ARKIN SCHAFFER & KAPLAN LLP (AV)

590 Madison Avenue, 10022
Telephone: 212-333-0200
Fax: 212-333-2350
Email: info@ARKIN-LAW.com

Stanley S. Arkin
Hyman L. Schaffer
Jeffrey M. Kaplan
Mark S. Cohen
Howard J. Kaplan

ASSOCIATES

Harry B. Feder
Sean R. O'Brien
Robert Pfeffer

(See Next Column)

OF COUNSEL

Michelle A. Rice

For full biographical listings, see the Martindale-Hubbell Law Directory

BEATIE AND OSBORN LLP (AV)

599 Lexington Avenue, 42nd Floor, 10022
Telephone: 212-888-9000
Fax: 212-888-9664
Email: bandolaw@aol.com *URL:* http://www.bandolaw@aol.com

Russel H. Beatie, Jr.
Daniel A. Osborn

ASSOCIATES

Curt D. Marshall
Eduard Korsinsky

OF COUNSEL

Richard M. Cummings

For full biographical listings, see the Martindale-Hubbell Law Directory

BERLACK, ISRAELS & LIBERMAN LLP (AV)

120 West 45th Street, 10036
Telephone: 212-704-0100
Cable Address: "Berilib"
Telecopier: 212-704-0196
Email: info@berlack.com
Morristown, New Jersey Office: 65 Madison Avenue.
Telephone: 201-644-3400.
Telecopier: 201-644-3159.

MEMBERS OF FIRM

Harris Berlack (1946-1968)
Carlos L. Israels (1946-1969)
Kenneth R. Asher
Claude A. Baum
Scott M. Berman
Wade M. Boswell
Douglas E. Davidson
Alan N. Forman
Steven E. Greenbaum
Harvey M. Katz
James B. Liberman
Stuart Neuhauser
Robert D. Schmicker
Martin S. Siegel
Steven F. Wasserman
Edward S. Weisfelner

SENIOR ATTORNEYS

Andrew S. Dash
Erica M. Ryland

ASSOCIATES

John P. Biedermann
Anne M. Cunningham
Pauline Foley (Resident, Morristown, New Jersey Office)
Julie L. Friedberg (Resident, Morristown, New Jersey Office)
Emilio A. Galván
Linda B. Goebel
Louis Lombardo
Rachel F. Mayerson (Not admitted in NY)
Amy P. K. Motzenbecker (Resident, Morristown, New Jersey Office)
Antonio Peguero, Jr.
Elizabeth Quirk (Resident, Morristown, New Jersey Office)
Marcela M. Sanchez
Melissa Sarubbi

OF COUNSEL

Gerald W. Conway (Not admitted in NY; Resident, Morristown, New Jersey Office)
Marc B. Lasky (Resident, Morristown, New Jersey Office)

For full biographical listings, see the Martindale-Hubbell Law Directory

BERNSTEIN LITOWITZ BERGER & GROSSMANN LLP (AV)

1285 Avenue of the Americas, 10019
Telephone: 212-554-1400
Telecopier: 212-554-1444
Email: blbg@blbglaw.com *URL:* http://www.blbglaw.com

MEMBERS OF FIRM

Paul M. Bernstein (1929-1990)
Max W. Berger
Edward A. Grossmann
Jeffrey A. Klafter
Daniel L. Berger
Douglas M. McKeige
Seth R. Lesser
John P. Coffey
Robert S. Gans
Darnley Dickinson Stewart

ASSOCIATES

Lisa K. Buckser
Thomas E. Chase
Patricia S. Gillane
Leah Beth Guggenheimer
Rochelle Feder Hansen
Jeffrey N. Leibell
Nancy Bea Lipin
Louis C. Paul
Ryan D. Poliakoff
Robert W. Rodriguez (Not admitted in NY)
Gerald H. Silk
Steven B. Singer

OF COUNSEL

Ronald Litowitz

For full biographical listings, see the Martindale-Hubbell Law Directory

New York—Continued

BRESLOW & WALKER, LLP (AV)
767 Third Avenue, 10017
Telephone: 212-832-1930
Fax: 212-888-4955
Email: breslow767@aol.com
Jericho, New York Office: 100 Jericho Quadrangle, 11753.
Telephone: 516-822-6505.
Fax: 516-822-6544.

Joel M. Walker
Howard S. Breslow
Leonard J. Breslow

Kevin W. Waite

OF COUNSEL

Roy H. Carlin

For full biographical listings, see the Martindale-Hubbell Law Directory

CORBIN SILVERMAN & SANSEVERINO LLP (AV)
805 Third Avenue, 10022-7513
Telephone: 212-308-5000
Telecopier: 212-308-7189

MEMBERS OF FIRM

Stephen B. Silverman
Raymond A. Sanseverino
Joseph W. Muccia
Richard A. Nardi
Kenneth W. Sold
Marc J. Gottridge
John J. Gallagher, Jr.
James T. Sandnes
Garry C. Berman
Adam H. Schuman
Mary B. Templeton

SENIOR COUNSEL

Sol Neil Corbin

OF COUNSEL

Joseph L. Broadwin

ASSOCIATES

Mark A. Shapiro
Joseph J. Macchiarola
Theodora L. Hunter

For full biographical listings, see the Martindale-Hubbell Law Directory

TIMOTHY J. DENNIN, P.C. (AV)
415 Madison Avenue, 22nd Floor, 10017
Telephone: 212-826-1500
Telecopier: 212-688-6457
Email: timden@ix.netcom.com

Timothy J. Dennin

For full biographical listings, see the Martindale-Hubbell Law Directory

ENTWISTLE & CAPPUCCI LLP (AV)
400 Park Avenue, 16th Floor, 10022
Telephone: 212-894-7200
Facsimile: 212-894-7272
URL: http://www.entwistle-law.com
Princeton, New Jersey Office: 791 Alexander Road.
Telephone: 609-520-9455.
Facsimile: 609-520-1298.

Andrew J. Entwistle
Vincent R. Cappucci
William S. Gyves
Gary Mailman (Resident, Princeton, New Jersey Office)

ASSOCIATES

Robert N. Cappucci
Edward L. Doherty

OF COUNSEL

Thomas W. Alfano
David Garfield Roland
William B. Horton, II

For full biographical listings, see the Martindale-Hubbell Law Directory

FOX HORAN & CAMERINI LLP (AV)
One Broadway, 10004
Telephone: 212-480-4800
Telecopier: 212-269-2383; 212-709-0248
Email: webmaster@foxhoran.com *URL:* http://www.foxhoran.com

MEMBERS OF FIRM

Donald T. Fox
John R. Horan
Ezequiel A. Camerini
Patrick L. Ferriere
Rafael A. Ginebra
Alan R. Johnson
Michael F. Johnston
Kathleen M. Kundar
Robert Courtney Mangone
Edward C. Marschner
Clifford A. Rathkopf, Jr.
Oleg Rivkin
Christopher H. Seymour
Eduardo L. Tabio

OF COUNSEL

Rafael Urquia II

(See Next Column)

ASSOCIATES

David C. Camerini
Drew G.L. Chapman
William S. Kogan
Eric Lindquist
V. David Rivkin

For full biographical listings, see the Martindale-Hubbell Law Directory

FRIEDMAN KAPLAN & SEILER LLP (AV)
875 Third Avenue, 10022-6225
Telephone: 212-833-1100
Facsimile: 212-355-6401
Email: info@fkslaw.com
Newark, New Jersey Office: One Gateway Center, 25th Floor, 07102-5311.
Telephone: 973-297-4700.
Facsimile: 973-297-4701.

MEMBERS OF FIRM

Bruce S. Kaplan
Edward A. Friedman
Barry A. Adelman
Eric Seiler
Robert D. Kaplan
Gary D. Friedman
Andrew W. Goldwater
Robert J. Lack
Gregg S. Lerner
Hal Neier
Philippe Adler
Matthew S. Haiken
Paul J. Fishman
Richard M. Hoffman
Lance J. Gotko

COUNSEL

Robert D. Wurwarg
Ira A. Freedman

ASSOCIATES

Craig J. Codlin
Michael B. Dorff
Andrew R. Greengrass
Ellen A. Harnick
Sophia S. Hartch
Mishell B. Kneeland
Robert S. Loigman
Craig Nemiroff
Joshua M. Olshin
Katherine L. Pringle
Daniel B. Rapport
Meryl S. Rosenblatt
Robert C. Scherer
Donna Segal
Jonathan M. Silver
Lee D. Sossen
David I. Tanenbaum
Marla J. Wasserman
Sian E. Zelbo

For full biographical listings, see the Martindale-Hubbell Law Directory

GOLENBOCK, EISEMAN, ASSOR & BELL (AV)
437 Madison Avenue, 10022
Telephone: 212-907-7300
Telecopier: 212-754-0330
Email: postmaster@golenbock.com

MEMBERS OF FIRM

Nathan E. Assor
Lawrence M. Bell
David J. Eiseman
Jeffrey T. Golenbock
Andrew C. Peskoe
Richard S. Taffet
Robert B. Goebel
Leonard Eisenberg
Martin S. Hyman
Steven G. Chill
Donald A. Hamburg
Charles D. Schmerler
Jeffrey S. Berger
Lawrence R. Haut
Andrew M. Singer
Janice B. Grubin
Jacqueline G. Veit

OF COUNSEL

William G. Pearlstein
Jonathan S. Hacker

ASSOCIATES

Debra S. Schachtel
Charles B. Rich
Thomas J. Wilson
Elizabeth A. Jaffe
Adam C. Silverstein
Alvin R. Chin
Joel S. Tennenberg
Ruth G. Hirshfeld
Leslie J. Sherman
Hilda B. Gilfillan
David A. Collins
David K. Leitner
Richard S. Kaplan
Aielleen P. Fajardo (Not admitted in NY)
Gioia M. Ligos (Not admitted in NY)
Elaine S. Moshe

For full biographical listings, see the Martindale-Hubbell Law Directory

GUSRAE, KAPLAN & BRUNO (AV)
120 Wall Street, 10005-3977
Telephone: 212-269-1400
Fax: 212-809-5449
URL: http://www.seclaw.com/gkb1.htm

MEMBERS OF FIRM

Mark J. Astarita
Cirino M. Bruno
Melvyn J. Falis
Martin H. Kaplan
Lawrence G. Nusbaum, III
Robert Perez

SENIOR ATTORNEYS

James J. D'Esposito
Shirley Kaplan
Brian D. Graifman
Stuart Meissner

ASSOCIATES

Scott L. Silver
Meredith S. Katz

OF COUNSEL

Bert L. Gusrae
Robert L. Blessey

For full biographical listings, see the Martindale-Hubbell Law Directory

New York—Continued

Hoffinger Friedland Dobrish & Stern, P.C. (AV)

A Professional Corporation including Professional Corporations
110 East 59th Street, 10022-1392
Telephone: 212-421-4000
Telecopier: 212-223-3857

Jack S. Hoffinger
Lawrence N. Friedland
Robert Z. Dobrish (P.C.)
Stephen R. Stern (P.C.)
Samuel P. Ross
Warren R. Gleicher
Philip S. Ross

Michael J. Sherman
Fran Hoffinger
John H. Friedland
Lydia A. Milone
Devorah S. Weinschneider
Eric I. Wrubel
Nina S. Gross
Scott Lawrence D'Aloise

For full biographical listings, see the Martindale-Hubbell Law Directory

Hoffman Pollok & Pickholz LLP (AV)

260 Madison Avenue, 10016
Telephone: 212-679-2900
FAX: 212-679-1844
Email: hppdefen@WEBSPAN.NET

MEMBERS OF FIRM

Jeffrey C. Hoffman
John L. Pollok
Marvin G. Pickholz
Susan C. Wolfe

ASSOCIATE

Francine Miller

OF COUNSEL

Michael S. Pollok

For full biographical listings, see the Martindale-Hubbell Law Directory

Kostelanetz & Fink, LLP (AV)

530 Fifth Avenue, 22nd Floor, 10036
Telephone: 212-808-8100
Fax: 212-808-8108
Email: mail@kostelanetzfink.com

SENIOR COUNSEL

Boris Kostelanetz

MEMBERS OF FIRM

Robert S. Fink
Kevin M. Flynn
Bryan C. Skarlatos

COUNSEL

Norman Sinrich
Theodore F. Dickson
Caroline Rule
Brian C. Wille
William F. Cuozzi, III
Dawn Ngo

For full biographical listings, see the Martindale-Hubbell Law Directory

Lovell & Stewart, LLP (AV)

A Limited Liability Partnership including a Professional Corporation
500 Fifth Avenue, 10110
Telephone: 212-608-1900
Telefax: 212-719-4677
Email: sklovell@aol.com

Christopher Lovell, P.C.
Victor E. Stewart
Gary S. Jacobson

Peggy J. Wedgworth
Geoffrey M. Horn
William W. Foshay, III
Ian T. Stoll

For full biographical listings, see the Martindale-Hubbell Law Directory

Milbank, Tweed, Hadley & McCloy LLP (AV)

1 Chase Manhattan Plaza, 10005-1413
Telephone: 212-530-5000
Fax: 212-530-5219
Email: postmaster@milbank.com *URL:* http://www.milbank.com
Midtown Office: 375 Park Avenue, Suite 3601, 10152.
Telephone: 212-530-5800.
Fax: 212-530-0158.
Los Angeles, California Office: 601 South Figueroa Street, 30th Floor, 90017.
Telephone: 213-892-4000.
Fax: 213-629-5063.
Washington, D.C. Office: International Square Building, Suite 1100, 1825 Eye Street, N.W., 20006.
Telephone: 202-835-7500.
Fax: 202-835-7586.
Tokyo, Japan Office: Fukoku Seimei Building, 2-2, Uchisaiwai-cho 2-Chome, Chiyoda-ku, Tokyo 100-0011, Japan.
Telephone: 011-81-3-3504-1050.
Fax: 011-81-3-3595-2790, 011-81-3-3595-2840.

(See Next Column)

London, England Office: Dashwood House, 69 Old Broad Street, London EC2M 1QS.
Telephone: 011-44-207-448-3000.
Fax: 011-44-207-448-3029.
Hong Kong Office: 3007 Alexandra House, 16 Chater Road.
Telephone: 011-852-2971-4888.
Fax: 011-852-2840-0792; 011-852-2845-9046.
Singapore Office: 14-00 Caltex House, 30 Raffles Place, 048622.
Telephone: 011-65-428-2400.
Fax: 011-65-428-2500.
Moscow, Russia Office: 24/27 Sadovaya-Samotyochnya, Moscow, 103051.
Telephone: 011-7-501-258-5015.
Fax: 011-7-501-258-5014.

MEMBERS OF FIRM

Oren B. Azar (Resident, Singapore Office)
Michael C. Banks
Kenneth J. Baronsky (Resident, Los Angeles, California Office)
Deborah Baumgart (Resident, Los Angeles, California Office)
Elizabeth Besio
Donald B. Brant, Jr.
Linda Dakin-Grimm (Resident, Los Angeles, California Office)
Trayton M. Davis
Raymond J. Fisher
Joy K. Gallup
Guilford W. Gaylord
Jay D. Grushkin
Joris M. Hogan
Douglas W. Jones
Marcelo A. Mottesi
Robert W. Mullen, Jr.
Robert S. O'Hara, Jr.
Arnold B. Peinado, III
Anthony Root (Resident, Hong Kong Office)
Eric H. Schunk (Resident, Los Angeles, California Office)
Thomas B. Siebens (Resident, London, England Office)
Robert E. Spring
Douglas A. Tanner (Resident, Hong Kong Office)
Neil J Wertlieb (Resident, Los Angeles, California Office)
Robert B. Williams

ASSOCIATES

Steven J. Abrams
James H. Ball, Jr.
Charles D. Bethill
Steven L. Chan
Brett D. Goldblatt (Resident, Los Angeles, California Office)
Quang J. Ha
Edward V. Kayukov (Resident, Los Angeles, California Office)
Deborah P. Kubiak
Jacqueline Leung (Resident, Hong Kong Office)
Evelyn Lim
Tobin D. Lippert (Resident, Los Angeles, California Office)
Melainie K. Mansfield (Resident, Los Angeles, California Office)
Yeshim O'Donnell
Albert A. Pisa
Dayan R. Rosen
Kendrick F. Royer (Resident, Los Angeles, California Office)
Tracey L. Schell (Resident, Hong Kong Office)
Hiral H. Shah
Harry Sherman
Lalenya W. Siegel
Robert Sternthal
Adam E. Vital
Melanie J. Wilson (Resident, London, England Office)

For Complete List of Firm Personnel, See General Section

For full biographical listings, see the Martindale-Hubbell Law Directory

Otterbourg, Steindler, Houston & Rosen, P.C. (AV)

230 Park Avenue, 29th Floor, 10169
Telephone: 212-661-9100
Telecopier: 212-682-6104

Donald N. Gellert
Daniel Wallen

Lloyd M. Green
John J. Kenny

For Complete List of Firm Personnel, See General Section

For full biographical listings, see the Martindale-Hubbell Law Directory

Parker Chapin LLP (AV)

Chrysler Building, 405 Lexington Avenue, 10017
Telephone: 212-704-6000
Telecopier: 212-704-6288
URL: http://www.parkerchapin.com
Great Neck, New York Office: 175 Great Neck Road.
Telephone: 516-482-4422.
Telecopier: 516-482-4469.
Hackensack, New Jersey: 190 Morre Street, Suite 307.
Telephone: 210-883-6400.
Telecopier: 210-883-6404.
Beverly Hills, California: 9454 Wilshire Boulevard.
Telephone: 310-288-8367.
Telecopier: 310-288-8365.

MEMBERS OF FIRM

Mark Abramowitz
James Alterbaum
Christopher Stewart Auguste
Aurora Cassirer
Elliot Cohen
Lloyd Frank
William D. Freedman
Mark S. Hirsch
Jordan A. Horvath
Timothy I. Kahler
Edward R. Mandell
Stephen G. Rinehart
Henry I. Rothman
Richard A. Rubin
Michael J. Shef
Gary J. Simon
Alvin M. Stein
Melvin Weinberg
Michael Weinsier
Martin Eric Weisberg

(See Next Column)

PARKER CHAPIN LLP, *New York—Continued*

OF COUNSEL

Katherine Cooney Ash
Philip J. Hoblin, Jr.
Herbert L. Rosedale

For Complete List of Firm Personnel, See General Section

For full biographical listings, see the Martindale-Hubbell Law Directory

PILIERO GOLDSTEIN JENKINS & SULLIVAN, LLP (AV)

292 Madison Avenue, 10017
Telephone: 212-213-8200
Fax: 212-685-2028
Email: lawyers@pgjhlaw.com *URL:* http://www.pgjhlaw.com
Carlstadt, New Jersey Office: One Palmer Terrace.
Telephone: 201-507-5157.
FAX: 201-507-5221.
Washington, D.C. Office: 888 17th Street, N.W., Suite 1100.
Telephone: 202-467-6991.
FAX: 202-467-6703.
San Francisco, California Office: 507 Howard Street, Suite 200.
Telephone: 415-281-3631.
Fax: 415-281-3630.

MEMBERS OF FIRM

Kimberlee S. Bogen
Edward J. Goldstein
Jon Mark Jenkins
Marc A. Lebowitz
Robert D. Piliero
George O. Richardson, III
Michael T. Sullivan

ASSOCIATES

Craig Avedisian
Rosemary G. Feit
Eric M. Kogan
Mariano Schwed

OF COUNSEL

Kenneth D. Arbeeny
Christopher P. Hall

For full biographical listings, see the Martindale-Hubbell Law Directory

RABIN & PECKEL LLP (AV)

275 Madison Avenue, 10016
Telephone: 212-682-1818
Telecopier: 212-682-1892
Email: email@rabinlaw.com *URL:* http://www.rabinlaw.com

I. Stephen Rabin
Allan K. Peckel
Brian P. Murray
Marvin L. Frank

Jacqueline Sailer
Joseph V. McBride
Donald J. Wallace
Shaye J. Fuchs
(Not admitted in NY)

For full biographical listings, see the Martindale-Hubbell Law Directory

RICHARDS SPEARS KIBBE & ORBE (AV)

One Chase Manhattan Plaza 57th Floor, 10005-3102
Telephone: 212-530-1800
Fax: 212-530-1801
Email: info@rsko.com
Washington, D.C. Office: 1775 Eye Street, N.W., 20006-2401.
Telephone: 202-261-2960.
Fax: 202-291-2999.

MEMBERS OF FIRM

MaryJeanette Dee
Donna I. Dennis
Brian S. Fraser
Arthur S. Greenspan
Larry G. Halperin
Paul B. Haskel
Linda Imes
Jonathan Kibbe
Michael D. Mann
Adam D. Mitzner
William Q. Orbe
Lee S. Richards III
David Spears
James Q. Walker
Andrew M. Weinfeld

ASSOCIATES

James M. Aquilina
Eva Marie Carney
(Not admitted in NY)
Lauren E. Fischer
Michael Friedman
Shanah D. Glick
(Not admitted in NY)
Kenneth P. Held
James J. Ohlig
Eric M. O'Meara
Jahan Sharifi
Susan J. Steinthal
Kimberly M. Versace
Daniel C. Zinman

OF COUNSEL

Paul A. Leder
(Not admitted in NY)
Lucinda O. McConathy
(Not admitted in NY)

For full biographical listings, see the Martindale-Hubbell Law Directory

SINGER FRUMENTO LLP (AV)

40 Exchange Place, 20th Floor, 10005
Telephone: 212-809-8550
Fax: 212-344-0394
Email: info@singerfru.com *URL:* http://www.singerfru.com

(See Next Column)

Bill T. Singer
Linda Lerner
Aegis J. Frumento

ASSOCIATES

Corey S. Marell
Stephanie Rosenblatt

OF COUNSEL

Aimee E. Goldstein
Thomas A. Rigilano

For full biographical listings, see the Martindale-Hubbell Law Directory

SIROTA & SIROTA, LLP (AV)

110 Wall Street, 21st Floor, 10005
Telephone: 212-425-9055
Fax: 212-425-9093
Email: info@sirotalaw.com *URL:* http://www.sirotalaw.com

MEMBERS OF FIRM

Howard B. Sirota
Rachell Roffé Sirota
Saul Roffé

OF COUNSEL

Mark B. Brenner
Howard Schickler
(Not admitted in NY)

For full biographical listings, see the Martindale-Hubbell Law Directory

SOLOVAY, EDLIN & EISEMAN (AV)

845 Third Avenue, Eighth Floor, 10022
Telephone: 212-752-1000
Facsimile: 212-355-4608

Richard A. Edlin
Norman Solovay
Michael B. Solovay
Jonathan Eiseman
Wayne R. Lehrhaupt
Eric R. Levine

OF COUNSEL

Daniel James Cooper
Joseph M. Harary
Stephen L. Weinstein
Peter Kakoyiannis
Sam Schwartz

ASSOCIATES

Murray D. Schneier
Howard S. Roitman

For full biographical listings, see the Martindale-Hubbell Law Directory

UNIONDALE, Nassau Co.

LEHMAN & EILEN LLP (AV)

50 Charles Lindbergh Boulevard, Suite 505, 11553-3600
Telephone: 516-222-0888
Fax: 516-222-0948
Email: info@lehmaneilen.com *URL:* http://www.securitiesattys.com

MEMBERS OF FIRM

Bob E. Lehman
Howard S. Eilen

OF COUNSEL

Hank Gracin
Timothy P. Kebbe

ASSOCIATES

Stephanie G. Senzer
Maureen Ann Porette
Eva M. Possavino
Audrey Blain
Scott D. Stechman
Steven J. Pappas

For full biographical listings, see the Martindale-Hubbell Law Directory

*WHITE PLAINS,** Westchester Co.

GREENSPAN & GREENSPAN (AV)

34 South Broadway, Suite 605, 10601-4400
Telephone: 914-946-2500
Cable Address: "Gadlex"
Telecopier: 914-946-1432
Email: GandGEsqs@aol.com
Boca Raton, Florida Office: Greenspan & Kane, 301 Yamato Road, Suite 3160.
Telephone: 561-995-8140.
Oradell, New Jersey Office: 690 Kinderkamack Rd., 07649.
Telephone: 201-599-2849; 800-553-6009.

MEMBERS OF FIRM

Leon J. Greenspan
Michael E. Greenspan

For full biographical listings, see the Martindale-Hubbell Law Directory

NORTH CAROLINA

*CHARLOTTE,** Mecklenburg Co.

RAYBURN, MOON & SMITH, P.A. (AV)

The Carillon, 227 West Trade Street, Suite 1200, 28202-1675
Telephone: 704-334-0891
Fax: 704-377-1897; 704-377-0395
Email: rmslaw@aol.com

(See Next Column)

RAYBURN, MOON & SMITH P.A.—*Continued*

Albert F. Durham
Travis W. Moon
C. Richard Rayburn, Jr.
James C. Smith
W. Scott Cooper
Paul R. Baynard
James B. Gatehouse
G. Kirkland Hardymon
James L. Bagwell
Patricia B. Edmondson
Natalie R. Denton
Robert Aubrey Cox, Jr.
Tricia L. Rolewicz

For full biographical listings, see the Martindale-Hubbell Law Directory

WOMBLE CARLYLE SANDRIDGE & RICE (AV)

A Professional Limited Liability Company
3300 One First Union Center, 301 South College Street, 28202-6025
Telephone: 704-331-4900
Fax: 704-331-4955
Email: lawyers@wcsr.com *URL:* http://www.wcsr.com
Winston-Salem, North Carolina Office: 200 West Second Street, P.O. Drawer 84.
Telephone: 336-721-3600.
Fax: 336-721-3660.
Raleigh, North Carolina Office: 2100 First Union Capitol Center, 150 Fayetteville Street Mall, P.O. Box 831.
Telephone: 919-755-2100.
Fax: 919-755-2150.
Research Triangle Park, North Carolina Office: 2505 Meridian Parkway, Suite 300 (Durham), 27713.
Telephone: 919-484-2300.
Fax: 919-484-2340.
Atlanta, Georgia Office: One Atlantic Center, 1201 West Peachtree Street, Suite 3500.
Telephone: 404-872-7000.
Fax: 404-888-7490.
Other Atlanta, Georgia Office: Suite 404, 2296 Henderson Mill Road, N.E.
Telephone: 770-492-9030.
Fax: 770-492-9609.
Washington, D.C. Office: 1120 Nineteenth Street, N.W., Eighth Floor.
Telephone: 202-857-4400.
Fax: 202-467-6910.
Greenville, South Carolina Office: 15 South Main Street, Suite 601, P.O. Box 10208.
Telephone: 864-255-5400.
Fax: 864-255-5440.

RESIDENT MEMBERS

Joe B. Cogdell, Jr.
Cyrus M. Johnson, Jr.
J. Alexander Salisbury

RESIDENT ASSOCIATES

Douglas A. Mays
Ellen A. Perrin
Daniel G. Schmedlen, Jr.
Todd C. Taylor

RESIDENT OF COUNSEL

Jane Jeffries Jones

Representative Clients: Childress Klein Properties, Inc.; Food Lion, Inc.; J.A. Jones Construction Co.; Parkdale Mills, Inc.; Pillowtex; Duke Power Co.; Bowles Hollowell Conner & Co.; ALLTEL Carolina, Inc.; Belk Store Services, Inc.; Philip Holzmann A.G.

For Complete List of Firm Personnel, See General Section

For full biographical listings, see the Martindale-Hubbell Law Directory

*GREENSBORO,** Guilford Co.

CLARK BLOSS & MCIVER, PLLC (AV)

600 Dixie Building, 125 South Elm Street, P.O. Box 1349, 27402
Telephone: 336-275-7275
Fax: 336-275-1401
Email: cbm@cbm-law.com

David M. Clark
John F. Bloss
Robert G. McIver
Jonathan Wall

Representative Clients: The Prudential Insurance Company of America (litigation); Johnson Controls, Inc.
Approved Attorneys for: Jefferson-Pilot Insurance Co.

For full biographical listings, see the Martindale-Hubbell Law Directory

SCHELL BRAY AYCOCK ABEL & LIVINGSTON P.L.L.C. (AV)

1500 Renaissance Plaza, 230 North Elm Street, P.O. Box 21847, 27420
Telephone: 336-370-8800
Fax: 336-370-8830
Email: Info@sbaal.com *URL:* http://www.sbaal.com

MEMBERS OF FIRM

Braxton Schell
Doris R. Bray
William P. Aycock, II
Michael R. Abel
Paul H. Livingston, Jr.
Thomas C. Watkins
Dan T. Barker, Jr.
Barbara R. Christy
John A. McLendon, Jr.

(See Next Column)

ASSOCIATES

Kathleen A. Kingsbury
Jacqueline E. Camp
A. Nicholas Purrington
Gregory M. Chabon
Jennifer Johnson
Eric M. Braun
Garland V. Gibbes

Representative Clients: The Breakers Palm Beach, Inc.; CBP Resources, Inc. (Carolina By-Products); Cone Mills Corp.; Cornwallis Development Co.; Kenan Transport Co.; Klaussner Furniture Industries, Inc.; North Carolina Trust Co.; Texfi Industries, Inc.; University of North Carolina at Chapel Hill Foundation, Inc.; Vanguard Cellular Systems, Inc.

For full biographical listings, see the Martindale-Hubbell Law Directory

*RALEIGH,** Wake Co.

MARVIN SCHILLER (AV)

Two Hannover Square, Suite 1250, 434 Fayetteville Street Mall, 27601
Telephone: 919-836-8800
Fax: 919-836-8838
URL: http://www.lawyers.com/marvinschiller

For full biographical listings, see the Martindale-Hubbell Law Directory

WOMBLE CARLYLE SANDRIDGE & RICE (AV)

A Professional Limited Liability Company
2100 First Union Capitol Center, 150 Fayetteville Street Mall, P.O. Box 831, 27602
Telephone: 919-755-2100
Fax: 919-755-2150
Email: lawyers@wcsr.com *URL:* http://www.wcsr.com
Charlotte, North Carolina Office: 3300 One First Union Center, 301 South College Street.
Telephone: 704-331-4900.
Fax: 704-331-4955.
Winston-Salem, North Carolina Office: 200 West Second Street, P.O. Drawer 84.
Telephone: 336-721-3600.
Fax: 336-721-3660.
Research Triangle Park, North Carolina Office: 2505 Meridian Parkway, Suite 300 (Durham), 27713.
Telephone: 919-484-2300.
Fax: 919-484-2340.
Atlanta, Georgia Office: One Atlantic Center, 1201 West Peachtree Street, Suite 3500.
Telephone: 404-872-7000.
Fax: 404-888-7490.
Other Atlanta, Georgia Office: Suite 404, 2296 Henderson Mill Road, N.E.
Telephone: 770-492-9030.
Fax: 770-492-9609.
Washington, D.C. Office: 1120 Nineteenth Street, N.W., Eighth Floor.
Telephone: 202-857-4400.
Fax: 202-467-6910.
Greenville, South Carolina Office: 15 South Main Street, Suite 601, P.O. Box 10208.
Telephone: 864-255-5400.
Fax: 864-255-5440.

RESIDENT MEMBER

Heather K. Mallard

Representative Clients: Aetna Casualty and Surety Co., Inc.; ALSCO/AmeriMark Building Products, Inc.; Aoki Corporation America, Inc.; Hackney Brothers, Inc.; Lawyers Mutual Liability Insurance Company of North Carolina; Meredith College; Regency Park Corp.; Wachovia Bank, N.A.

For Complete List of Firm Personnel, See General Section

For full biographical listings, see the Martindale-Hubbell Law Directory

*WINSTON-SALEM,** Forsyth Co.

WOMBLE CARLYLE SANDRIDGE & RICE (AV)

A Professional Limited Liability Company
200 West Second Street, P.O. Drawer 84, 27102
Telephone: 336-721-3600
Fax: 336-721-3660
Email: lawyers@wcsr.com *URL:* http://www.wcsr.com
Charlotte, North Carolina Office: 3300 One First Union Center, 301 South College Street.
Telephone: 704-331-4900.
Fax: 704-331-4955.
Raleigh, North Carolina Office: 2100 First Union Capitol Center, 150 Fayetteville Street Mall, P.O. Box 831.
Telephone: 919-755-2100.
Fax: 919-755-2150.
Research Triangle Park, North Carolina Office: 2505 Meridian Parkway, Suite 300 (Durham), 27713.
Telephone: 919-484-2300.
Fax: 919-484-2340.
Atlanta, Georgia Office: One Atlantic Center, 1201 West Peachtree Street, Suite 3500.
Telephone: 404-872-7000.
Fax: 404-888-7490.

(See Next Column)

WOMBLE CARLYLE SANDRIDGE & RICE, *Winston-Salem—Continued*

Other Atlanta, Georgia Office: Suite 404, 2296 Henderson Mill Road, N.E.
Telephone: 770-492-9030.
Fax: 770-492-9609.
Washington, D.C. Office: 1120 Nineteenth Street, N.W., Eighth Floor.
Telephone: 202-857-4400.
Fax: 202-467-6910.
Greenville, South Carolina Office: 15 South Main Street, Suite 601, P.O. Box 10208.
Telephone: 864-255-5400.
Fax: 864-255-5440.

RESIDENT MEMBERS

Linwood L. Davis
William A. Davis, II
John L. W. Garrou
Murray C. Greason, Jr.
Jeffrey C. Howland
Robert A. West
Calder W. Womble
William F. Womble

RESIDENT ASSOCIATES

Roger E. Cole
Adam B. Hirschfeld
Robert F. Pomper

Representative Clients: Brad Ragan, Inc.; Brenner Companies; Food Lion, Inc.; Hanes Companies, Inc.; North Carolina Baptist Hospitals, Inc.; R.J. Reynolds Tobacco Co.; Thomasville Furniture Industries, Inc.; Wachovia Corp.; Wake Forest University.

For Complete List of Firm Personnel, See General Section

For full biographical listings, see the Martindale-Hubbell Law Directory

OHIO

*CINCINNATI,** Hamilton Co.

BROWN, CUMMINS & BROWN CO., L.P.A. (AV)

3500 Carew Tower, 441 Vine Street, 45202
Telephone: 513-381-2121
Fax: 513-381-2125

James R. Cummins
Donald S. Mendelsohn
Amy G. Applegate
Melanie S. Corwin

JoAnn M. Strasser

Counsel for: Midwest Group of Funds; The Fairmont Fund Trust; Bartlett Funds; PC&J Funds; Analysts Investment Trust; The Jhaveri Trust; Johnson Mutual Funds; AmeriPrime Funds.
Reference: Star Bank of Cincinnati.

For full biographical listings, see the Martindale-Hubbell Law Directory

LAW OFFICES OF JACK A. DONENFELD A LEGAL PROFESSIONAL ASSOCIATION (AV)

119 East Court Street, 45202
Telephone: 513-632-5311
Fax: 513-721-1213

Jack A. Donenfeld

OF COUNSEL

Robert W. Edler (Not admitted in OH)
Bruce S. Fenton (Not admitted in OH)
David A. Fisher (Not admitted in OH)
Michael A. Shapiro (Not admitted in OH)

For full biographical listings, see the Martindale-Hubbell Law Directory

KATZ, TELLER, BRANT & HILD A LEGAL PROFESSIONAL ASSOCIATION (AV)

2400 Chemed Center, 255 East Fifth Street, 45202-4724
Telephone: 513-721-4532
Telecopier: 513-721-7120
Email: corp@ktbh.com

Andrew R. Berger
John R. Gierl

For Complete List of Firm Personnel, See General Section

For full biographical listings, see the Martindale-Hubbell Law Directory

KEATING, MUETHING & KLEKAMP, P.L.L. (AV)

1400 Provident Tower, One East Fourth Street, 45202
Telephone: 513-579-6400
Facsimile: 513-579-6457
URL: http://www.kmklaw.com

MEMBERS OF FIRM

Paul V. Muething
Robert E. Coletti
Edward E. Steiner
Kenneth P. Kreider
Mark A. Weiss

(See Next Column)

ASSOCIATES

Thomas E. Frooman
F. Mark Reuter
Joshua D. Goldberg (Not admitted in OH)

Representative Clients: American Financial Group; BP America Inc.; Chiquita Brands International, Inc.; Cintas Corporation; Comair Holdings, Inc.; Duke Realty Limited Partnership; LSI Industries Inc.; Mosler Inc.; Provident Financial Group Inc.

For Complete List of Firm Personnel, See General Section

For full biographical listings, see the Martindale-Hubbell Law Directory

GENE MESH & ASSOCIATES (AV)

2605 Burnet Avenue, 45219-2502
Telephone: 513-221-8800
Fax: 513-221-1097
Email: GeneMesh@aol.com

ASSOCIATES

R. Michael Phebus
Michael G. Brautigam (Not admitted in OH)

LEGAL SUPPORT PERSONNEL

Charles H. Short

For full biographical listings, see the Martindale-Hubbell Law Directory

STRAUSS & TROY A LEGAL PROFESSIONAL ASSOCIATION (AV)

The Federal Reserve Building, 150 East Fourth Street, 45202-4018
Telephone: 513-621-2120
Telecopier: 513-241-8259
URL: http://www.strauss-troy.com
Northern Kentucky Office: Suite 1400, 50 East Rivercenter Boulevard, Covington, Kentucky, 41011.
Telephone: 513-621-8900; 513-621-2120.
Telecopier: 513-629-9444.

Alan Comstock Rosser
Thomas C. Rink
James G. Heldman
Ann W. Gerwin
Richard S. Wayne
William K. Flynn
Shawn M. Young

Representative Clients: PNC Bank, N.A. (Ohio and Kentucky); Corporex Companies, Inc.; Mercantile Stores Co., Inc.; Star Bank, N.A. (Ohio and Kentucky).

For Complete List of Firm Personnel, See General Section

For full biographical listings, see the Martindale-Hubbell Law Directory

WAITE, SCHNEIDER, BAYLESS & CHESLEY CO., L.P.A. (AV)

1513 Central Trust Tower, Fourth and Vine Streets, 45202
Telephone: 513-621-0267
Fax: 513-381-2375; 621-0262

Stanley M. Chesley

Thomas F. Rehme
Robert A. Steinberg
Fay E. Stilz
Louise M. Roselle
D. Arthur Rabourn
Jerome L. Skinner
Janet G. Abaray
Paul M. De Marco
Terrence L. Goodman
Colleen M. Hegge
Jane H. Walker
Renée Infante
James F. Keller
Jean M. Geoppinger
Robert Heuck II

For full biographical listings, see the Martindale-Hubbell Law Directory

*CLEVELAND,** Cuyahoga Co.

GOODMAN WEISS MILLER LLP (AV)

100 Erieview Plaza, 27th Floor, 44114-1824
Telephone: 216-696-3366
Telecopier: 216-363-5835

Deborah J. Michelson

For full biographical listings, see the Martindale-Hubbell Law Directory

JANIK & FORBES (AV)

Building Two, 8223 Brecksville Road, 44141-1371
Telephone: 440-838-7600
Fax: 440-838-7601

MEMBERS OF FIRM

Steven G. Janik
Steven Forbes

For Complete List of Firm Personnel, See General Section

For full biographical listings, see the Martindale-Hubbell Law Directory

Cleveland—Continued

Seeley, Savidge and Ebert A Legal Professional Association (AV)

800 Bank One Center, 600 Superior Avenue, East, 44114-2655
Telephone: 216-566-8200
Fax-Telecopier: 216-566-0213
URL: http://www.sse-law.com

Gregory D. Seeley

Connie S. Carr
David T. Reed

Reference: KeyBank.

For Complete List of Firm Personnel, See General Section

For full biographical listings, see the Martindale-Hubbell Law Directory

*COLUMBUS,** Franklin Co.

Bricker & Eckler LLP (AV)

100 South Third Street, 43215-4291
Telephone: 614-227-2300
Telecopy: 614-227-2390
Email: info@be.bricker.com *URL:* http://www.bricker.com

Michael F. Sullivan
Richard F. Kane
John P. Beavers (Managing Partner)
Steven R. Kerber
David A. Rogers
John W. Cook, III
David K. Conrad
Price D. Finley

Lloyd Pierre-Louis

Representative Clients: McDonald Investments, Inc.; Banc One Capital Markets, Inc.; A.G. Edwards & Sons, Inc.; Seasongood & Mayer; Paine Webber, Inc.; Bear, Stearns & Co., Inc.; Merrill Lynch & Co.; Fifth Third Securities.

For Complete List of Firm Personnel, See General Section

For full biographical listings, see the Martindale-Hubbell Law Directory

Chester, Willcox and Saxbe LLP (AV)

17 South High Street, Suite 900, 43215-3413
Telephone: 614-221-4000
Fax: 614-221-4012
Email: cwslaw.com

PARTNERS

Andrew J. Art
John W. Bentine
Donald C. Brey
James J. Chester
John J. Chester
John J. Chester, Jr.
J. Richard Emens
Stephen C. Fitch
Richard A. Frye
Guy R. Humphrey
J. Anthony Kington
Eugene B. Lewis
Charles Rockwell Saxbe
Frank A. Titus
Elizabeth Jean Watters
Roderick H. Willcox
Beatrice E. Wolper

ASSOCIATES

David J. Butler
Maryellen Corna
Karen S. Hockstad
Karen A. Hoffman
Thomas H. Mallory, Jr.
Sarah D Morrison
George D. Schreibeis
Jeffrey L. Small

OF COUNSEL

Bruce E. Johnson
William B. Saxbe
J. Craig R. Wright

Representative Clients: American Municipal Power-Ohio, Inc.; The Limited; Scioto Downs, Inc.; Tee Jaye's Country Place Restaurants.

For full biographical listings, see the Martindale-Hubbell Law Directory

*DAYTON,** Montgomery Co.

Sebaly, Shillito & Dyer A Legal Professional Association (AV)

1300 Courthouse Plaza, NE, P.O. Box 220, 45402-0220
Telephone: 937-222-2500
Telefax: 937-222-6554; 222-8279
URL: http://www.ssdlaw.com

Martin A. Beyer
Daniel A. Brown
James A. Dyer
Gale S. Finley
John R. Glankler
Deborah D. Hunt
Michael P. Moloney
Jon M. Sebaly
Beverly F. Shillito
Jeffrey B. Shulman
Karl R. Ulrich
Lawrence S. Walter
Nita S. Yates

OF COUNSEL

William W. Lambert

Michael A. Booth
Robert E. Goff, Jr.
Leslie Blair Graden
Joseph V. Hatala
J. David Ruffner, II
Kendra F. Thompson

(See Next Column)

For full biographical listings, see the Martindale-Hubbell Law Directory

*ELYRIA,** Lorain Co.

Zagrans Law Firm A Legal Professional Association (AV)

5338 Meadow Lane Court, 44035-1469
Telephone: 440-934-7000
Facsimile: 440-934-7001
Email: eric@zagrans.com *URL:* http://www.zagrans.com

Eric H. Zagrans

Joshua M. Marks

LEGAL SUPPORT PERSONNEL

Jeannette M. Wolff (Legal Assistant)

For full biographical listings, see the Martindale-Hubbell Law Directory

OKLAHOMA

*OKLAHOMA CITY,** Oklahoma Co.

Abowitz, Rhodes & Dahnke, P.C. (AV)

Tenth Floor 15 North Robinson, P.O. Box 1937, 73101
Telephone: 405-236-4645
Telecopier: 405-239-2843

Murray E. Abowitz
Sarah Jackson Rhodes
George W. Dahnke

Lisa Luschen Dietrich
Janice M. Dansby
Kayce L. Gisinger
Stephen S. Parker
Andrew D. Schwartz
Blake A. Bittel

For full biographical listings, see the Martindale-Hubbell Law Directory

Andrews Davis Legg Bixler Milsten & Price, A Professional Corporation (AV)

500 West Main, Suite 500, 73102
Telephone: 405-272-9241
FAX: 405-235-8786
Email: andrewsdavis@andrewsdavis.com *URL:* http://www.andrewsdavis.com

D. Joe Rockett
N. Janine Wheeler

For Complete List of Firm Personnel, See General Section

For full biographical listings, see the Martindale-Hubbell Law Directory

Conner & Winters, A Professional Corporation (AV)

One Leadership Square, 211 North Robinson, Suite 1700, 73102-7101
Telephone: 405-272-5711
Facsimile: 405-232-2695
Email: postmaster@cwlaw.com
Tulsa, Oklahoma Office: 3700 First Place Tower, 15 East 5th Street, 74103-4344.
Telephone: 918-586-5711.
Facsimile: 918-586-8982.
Fayetteville, Arkansas Office: Conner & Winters, P.L.L.C., 100 West Center Street, Suite 200, 72701-6081.
Telephone: 501-582-5711.
Facsimile: 501-587-1426.
Washington, D.C. Office: 1050 Seventeenth Street, N.W., Suite 810, 20036-5503.
Telephone: 202-783-5711.
Facsimile: 202-783-5720.

Irwin H. Steinhorn
P. Blake Allen
Mark H. Bennett

Cecily H. Murray

For Complete List of Firm Personnel, See General Section

For full biographical listings, see the Martindale-Hubbell Law Directory

Crowe & Dunlevy, A Professional Corporation (AV)

1800 Mid-America Tower, 20 North Broadway, 73102-8273
Telephone: 405-235-7700
Fax: 405-239-6651
Email: marketing@crowedunlevy.com *URL:* http://www.crowedunlevy.com
Tulsa, Oklahoma Office: 500 Kennedy Building, 321 South Boston Avenue, 74103-3313.
Telephone: 918-592-9800.
Fax: 918-592-9801.

(See Next Column)

KLEINBARD, BELL & BRECKER LLP, *Philadelphia—Continued*

Joseph S. Kleinbard (1905-1994)
Robert John Brecker (1916-1996)

COUNSEL TO THE FIRM

Arthur S. Keyser

MEMBERS OF FIRM

Paul E. Bomze
Murray I. Blackman
Howard J. Davis
Steven R. Waxman
Steven J. Engelmyer (Resident, Montclair Office)
David L. Hyman (Resident, Montclair Office)
Imogene E. Hughes
John P. Hickey
Jay R. Goldstein
Ralph J. Mauro
Thomas H. Speranza
Lisa E. Brody

ASSOCIATES

Mary Beth H. Gray
Eric J. Rothschild
Mary Vassallo Slinkard
Michael A. Frattone
Benjamin C. Graff (Not admitted in PA)
Ralph F. Salgado

COUNSEL

Joseph Bell

For full biographical listings, see the Martindale-Hubbell Law Directory

LEVIN, FISHBEIN, SEDRAN & BERMAN (AV)

Suite 500, 510 Walnut Street, 19106-3697
Telephone: 215-592-1500
Fax: 215-592-4663
Email: lfsb@psinet.com

MEMBERS OF FIRM

Arnold Levin
Michael D. Fishbein
Howard J. Sedran
Laurence S. Berman
Frederick S. Longer

Craig D. Ginsburg
Cheryl R. Brown Hill
Donald E. Haviland, Jr.
Daniel C. Levin
Terrianne Benedetto
Charles E. Schaffer
Austin B. Cohen

LEGAL SUPPORT PERSONNEL

Lee Ann Fitzpatrick
Cheryl Hesson

For full biographical listings, see the Martindale-Hubbell Law Directory

SAVETT FRUTKIN PODELL & RYAN, P.C. (AV)

Suite 700, 325 Chestnut Street, 19106
Telephone: 215-923-5400
FAX: 923-9353
Email: SFPRPC@OP.NET

Stuart H. Savett
Robert P. Frutkin
Barbara A. Podell
Katharine M. Ryan

For full biographical listings, see the Martindale-Hubbell Law Directory

SPECTOR & ROSEMAN, A PROFESSIONAL CORPORATION (AV)

1818 Market Street, Suite 2500, 19103
Telephone: 215-496-0300
Telecopier: 215-496-6611
Email: espector@spectorandroseman.com *URL:* http://www.spectorandroseman.com
San Diego, California Office: 600 West Broadway, 1600 One American Plaza, 92101.
Telephone: 619-338-4514.
Telecopier: 619-231-7423.

Eugene A. Spector
Robert M. Roseman
Jeffrey L. Kodroff
Ellen Gusikoff Stewart (Not admitted in PA)

Ronnie D. Seidel
Diane Doherty (Not admitted in PA)
Anthony Chu
Andrew D. Abramowitz (Not admitted in PA)
Joshua H. Grabar
Howard C. Gottlieb
Michael P. Nachman
Beth Mandel Rosenthal

OF COUNSEL

Anthony J. Bolognese

LEGAL SUPPORT PERSONNEL

PARALEGALS

Joseph Morrison
Michelle Adams
Carole Staiger

For full biographical listings, see the Martindale-Hubbell Law Directory

*PITTSBURGH,** Allegheny Co.

KATARINCIC & SALMON (AV)

2600 CNG Tower, 625 Liberty Avenue, 15222
Telephone: 412-338-2900
Facsimile: 412-261-2212
URL: http://www.kandslaw.com
Wheeling, West Virginia Office: 900 Mull Center, 1025 Main Street.
Telephone: 304-234-6600.
Fax: 304-234-6601.

Joseph A. Katarincic

For full biographical listings, see the Martindale-Hubbell Law Directory

MARCUS & SHAPIRA LLP (AV)

35th Floor, One Oxford Centre, 301 Grant Street, 15219-6401
Telephone: 412-471-3490
Telecopier: 412-391-8758
Email: info@marcus-shapira.com *URL:* http://www.marcus-shapira.com

MEMBERS OF FIRM

Robert L. Allman, II
Robert M. Barnes
Estelle F. Comay
James S. Larrimer
Scott D. Livingston
Bernard D. Marcus
Daniel H. Shapira

For Complete List of Firm Personnel, See General Section

For full biographical listings, see the Martindale-Hubbell Law Directory

PLOWMAN, SPIEGEL & LEWIS, P.C. (AV)

Second Floor, The Grant Building, 310 Grant Street, 15219-2201
Telephone: 412-471-8521
Fax: 412-471-4481

Jack W. Plowman
James A. Lewis

Charles B. Jarrett, Jr.

Reference: Pittsburgh National Bank.

For Complete List of Firm Personnel, See General Section

For full biographical listings, see the Martindale-Hubbell Law Directory

*SCRANTON,** Lackawanna Co.

LENAHAN & DEMPSEY, A PROFESSIONAL CORPORATION (AV)

116 North Washington Avenue, 18503-0234
Telephone: 717-346-2097; 1-888-LENAHAN
Fax: 717-346-1174
Mailing Address: P.O. Box 234, Scranton, Pennsylvania, 18501-0234

John R. Lenahan, Sr. (1915-1998)
William J. Dempsey (Of Counsel)
John R. Lenahan, Jr.
Joseph P. Lenahan
Kathleen A. Lenahan
David E. Heisler
Timothy G. Lenahan
Matthew D. Dempsey

Alan P. Schoen
Brian J. Lenahan
Diane Hepford Lenahan
George E. Mehalchick
Brian Yeager
Thomas R. Daniels
Terrence E. Dempsey
Christine S. Mayernick-Lezinski
John M. Mulcahey
Margaret M. Dempsey
Lisa G. Wilson

Representative Insurance Clients: Allstate Insurance Co.; America Security Insurance Co.; Metropolitan Casualty Insurance Co.; Aetna Insurance Co.; Pennsylvania National Insurance Group; Kemper Insurance Group; American Mutual Insurance Cos.; American States Insurance, Co.

For full biographical listings, see the Martindale-Hubbell Law Directory

RHODE ISLAND

*PROVIDENCE,** Providence Co.

HINCKLEY, ALLEN & SNYDER LLP (AV)

1500 Fleet Center, 02903-2393
Telephone: 401-274-2000
Fax: 401-277-9600
Email: firm@haslaw.com *URL:* http://www.haslaw.com
Boston, Massachusetts Office: 28 State Street, 30th Floor.
Telephone: 617-345-9000.
Fax: 617-345-9020. URL: http://www.haslaw.com.

MEMBERS OF FIRM

Paula K. Andrews (Not admitted in RI)
David D. Barricelli
Jonathan Bell
Paul Bork (Not admitted in RI)
Stephen J. Carlotti
Joseph P. Curran
Michael P. DeFanti
Eric F. Eisenberg (Not admitted in RI)
Malcolm Farmer, III
Margaret D. Farrell
Hugh J. Gorman, III (Not admitted in RI)
William R. Grimm
Joel Lewin (Not admitted in RI)
Sandra Matrone Mack
Matthew T. Marcello, III
Elizabeth Murdock Myers
Paul F. O'Donnell, III (Not admitted in RI)
H. Peter Olsen
Gerald J. Petros
James O. Reavis
Jeremy Ritzenberg (Not admitted in RI)
Ralph J. Rivkind (Not admitted in RI)
Charles E. Schaub, Jr. (Not admitted in RI)
Herman Snyder (Not admitted in RI)
David R. Sullivan (Not admitted in RI)
Robert F. Sylvia (Not admitted in RI)
Howard E. Walker

ASSOCIATES

Jessica M. Bettencourt
Mark Bianchi
Alexandra K. Callam
Jane E. Cohen (Not admitted in RI)
Andrew D. Cummings (Not admitted in RI)
June E. Daniel
Kelley Jordan-Price
Catherine S. Kim (Not admitted in RI)
Christopher W. Morog (Not admitted in RI)
Elena B. Olson (Not admitted in RI)
Joseph D. Whelan

OF COUNSEL

Bentley Tobin
Joachim A. Weissfeld

For Complete List of Firm Personnel, See General Section

For full biographical listings, see the Martindale-Hubbell Law Directory

MEDEIROS + SANFORD INC. (AV)

One Turks Head Place, Suite 700, 02903-2215
Telephone: 401-831-0700
Fax: 401-274-2752 or 401-861-7249

Matthew F. Medeiros
Paul M. Sanford
Stacey P. Nakasian

Jane E. Brockmann

For full biographical listings, see the Martindale-Hubbell Law Directory

SOUTH CAROLINA

*CHARLESTON,** Charleston Co.

HAYNSWORTH, MARION, MCKAY & GUÉRARD, L.L.P. (AV)

134 Meeting Street, P.O. Box 1119, 29402
Telephone: 843-722-7606
Facsimile: 843-724-8016
Columbia, South Carolina Office: Suite 2400 Affinity Building, 1201 Main Street, P.O. Drawer 7157, 29202.
Telephone: 803-765-1818. Facsimile 803-765-2399.
Greenville, South Carolina Office: 75 Beattie Place, Eleventh Floor, P.O. Box 2048, 29602.
Telephone: 864-240-3200.
Facsimile: 864-240-3300.

MEMBERS OF FIRM

Samuel W. Howell, IV
Carol L. Clark

Representative Clients: Ernst & Young, LLP; AT&T Capital Corporation; Synalloy Corporation; Equitable Life Assurance Society of the United States; St. Paul Insurance Group; Columbia Capital Markets; Southern Financial Group.

(See Next Column)

For Complete List of Firm Personnel, See General Section

For full biographical listings, see the Martindale-Hubbell Law Directory

WARREN & SINKLER, L.L.P. (AV)

Suite 340 171 Church Street, P.O. Box 1254, 29402
Telephone: 843-577-0660
Fax: 843-577-6843
Email: law@warren-sinkler.com

MEMBERS OF FIRM

G. Dana Sinkler
John H. Warren, III
Henry B. Fishburne, Jr.
Scott Y. Barnes
Mark S. Sharpe
Elizabeth W. Settle
Andrea Hall Duenas
William O. Hanahan, III
Holly R. Jensen

For full biographical listings, see the Martindale-Hubbell Law Directory

*COLUMBIA,** Richland Co.

BEACH LAW FIRM, P.A. (AV)

1321 Lady Street, Suite 310, 29211-1547
Telephone: 803-779-0066
Fax: 803-799-8479
Mailing Address: P.O. Box 11547, Columbia, South Carolina, 29211-1547
Email: firm@beachlaw.net

John F. Beach

John J. Pringle, Jr.

For full biographical listings, see the Martindale-Hubbell Law Directory

HAYNSWORTH, MARION, MCKAY & GUÉRARD, L.L.P. (AV)

Suite 2400 Affinity Building, 1201 Main Street, P.O. Drawer 7157, 29202
Telephone: 803-765-1818
Facsimile: 803-765-2399
Greenville, South Carolina Office: 75 Beattie Place, Eleventh Floor, P.O. Box 2048, 29602.
Telephone: 864-240-3200.
Facsimile: 864-240-3300.
Charleston, South Carolina Office: 134 Meeting Street, P.O. Box 1119, 29402.
Telephone: 843-722-7606.
Facsimile: 843-724-8016.

MEMBERS OF FIRM

Gary W. Morris
Edward G. Kluiters

Counsel For: Ernst & Young, LLP; AT&T Capital Corporation; Synalloy Corporation; Equitable Life Assurance Society of the United States; St. Paul Insurance Group; The Bank of South Carolina.

For Complete List of Firm Personnel, See General Section

For full biographical listings, see the Martindale-Hubbell Law Directory

TURNER, PADGET, GRAHAM & LANEY, P.A. (AV)

Seventeenth Floor, 1901 Main Street, P.O. Box 1473, 29202
Telephone: 803-254-2200
Telecopy: 803-799-3957
Florence, South Carolina Office: Fourth Floor, 1831 West Evans Street, P.O. Box 5478, 29502.
Telephone: 843-662-9008.
Fax: 843-667-0828.
Charleston, South Carolina Office: 21 Broad Street, 1st Floor, P.O. Box 836, 29402.
Telephone: 843-723-1622.
Fax: 843-577-3369.

Julie Jeffords Moose (Resident, Florence, SC, Office)

For Complete List of Firm Personnel, See General Section

For full biographical listings, see the Martindale-Hubbell Law Directory

WILLOUGHBY & HOEFER, P.A. (AV)

1022 Calhoun Street, Suite 302, P.O. Box 8416, 29202-8416
Telephone: 803-252-3300
Telecopier: 803-256-8062
Email: willhoef@sc-online.net

Mitchell M. Willoughby

Robin M. Johnson

Representative Clients: Bell Atlantic Mobile; National Educational Communications Association; SCANA Communications; ITC DeltaCommunications, Inc.

For full biographical listings, see the Martindale-Hubbell Law Directory

TENNESSEE

*CHATTANOOGA,** Hamilton Co.

BAKER, DONELSON, BEARMAN & CALDWELL (AV)

1800 Republic Centre, 633 Chestnut Street, 37450-1800
Telephone: 423-756-2010
Telecopier: 423-756-3447
Email: info@bdbc.com *URL:* http://www.bakerdonelson.com
Memphis, Tennessee Office: 20th Floor, First Tennessee Building, 165 Madison, 38103.
Telephone: 901-526-2000.
Telecopier: 901-577-2303.
Nashville, Tennessee Office: 1700 Nashville City Center, 511 Union Street, 37219.
Telephone: 615-726-5600.
Telecopier: 615-726-0464.
Knoxville, Tennessee Office: 2200 Riverview Tower, 900 South Gay Street, 37901.
Telephone: 423-549-7000.
Telecopier: 423-525-8569.
Johnson City, Tennessee Office: SunTrust Bank Building, 207 Mockingbird Lane, P.O. Box 3038, 37602.
Telephone: 423-928-0181.
Telecopier: 423-928-5694; 423-928-3654; Kingsport: 423-246-6191.
Huntsville, Tennessee Office: 3 Courthouse Square, 37756.
Telephone: 423-663-2321.
Telecopier: 423-663-2111.
Washington, D.C. Office: Market Square, 801 Pennsylvania Avenue, N.W., 20004.
Telephone: 202-508-3400.
Telecopier: 202-508-3402.
Jackson, Mississippi Office: Suite 500, 700 North State Street, 39202.
Telephone: 601-351-2400.
Telecopier: 601-351-2424.

SHAREHOLDERS

Kenneth C. Beckman
J. Porter Durham, Jr.

ASSOCIATES

Victoria S. Childres
Roddy Bailey (Not admitted in TN)

For Complete List of Firm Personnel, See General Section

For full biographical listings, see the Martindale-Hubbell Law Directory

FOSTER, FOSTER, ALLEN & DURRENCE, P.C. (AV)

Formerly Hall, Haynes, Lusk & Foster
801 Broad Street - Suite 515, 37402
Telephone: 423-266-1141
Telecopier: 423-266-4618
Email: dward@ffadlaw.com

George Lane Foster
William M. Foster
Craig R. Allen
Phillip M. Durrence, Jr.
David J. Ward
Clayton M. Whittaker
John M. Hull

LEGAL SUPPORT PERSONNEL

Peggy Sue Bates

Division Counsel for: Norfolk Southern Railway Co.
Attorneys for: CNA/Insurance; United States Fidelity & Guaranty Co. (USF&G); Bridgestone-Firestone, Inc.; Exxon Corp.; Murphy Oil Corp.; Chicago Title Insurance Co.; Jim Walter Homes; Mid-State Homes, Inc.

For full biographical listings, see the Martindale-Hubbell Law Directory

WITT, GAITHER & WHITAKER, P.C. (AV)

1100 SunTrust Bank Building, 37402-2608
Telephone: 423-265-8881
Telefax: 423-266-4138; 423-756-5612

John W. Murrey, III
John F. Henry, Jr.
Geoffrey G. Young
Ralph M. Killebrew, Jr.
Steven R. Barrett

Representative Clients: American Consumers, Inc.; Chattanooga Bakery, Inc.; Carriage Industries, Inc.; Coca-Cola Bottling Co. Consolidated; The Dixie Group, Inc.; Masland Carpets, Inc.; Signal Apparel Company, Inc.; Transcommunications, Incorporated; U.S. Xpress Enterprises, Inc.

For Complete List of Firm Personnel, See General Section

For full biographical listings, see the Martindale-Hubbell Law Directory

JOHNSON CITY, Washington Co.

BAKER, DONELSON, BEARMAN & CALDWELL (AV)

SunTrust Bank Building, 207 Mockingbird Lane, P.O. Box 3038, 37602
Telephone: 423-928-0181
Telecopier: 423-928-5694; 928-3654; Kingsport: 423-246-6191
Email: info@bdbc.com *URL:* http://www.bakerdonelson.com
Memphis, Tennessee Office: 20th Floor, First Tennessee Building, 165 Madison, 38103.
Telephone: 901-526-2000.
Telecopier: 901-577-2303.
Nashville, Tennessee Office: 1700 Nashville City Center, 511 Union Street, 37219.
Telephone: 615-726-5600.
Telecopier: 615-726-0464.
Chattanooga, Tennessee Office: 1800 Republic Centre, 633 Chestnut Street, 37450-1800.
Telephone: 423-756-2010.
Telecopier: 423-756-3447.
Knoxville, Tennessee Office: 2200 Riverview Tower, 900 South Gay Street, 37901.
Telephone: 423-549-7000.
Telecopier: 423-525-8569.
Huntsville, Tennessee Office: 3 Courthouse Square, 37756.
Telephone: 615-663-2321.
Telecopier: 615-663-2111.
Washington, D.C. Office: Market Square, 801 Pennsylvania Avenue, N.W., 20004.
Telephone: 202-508-3400.
Telecopier: 202-508-3402.
Jackson, Mississippi Office: Suite 500, 700 North State Street, 39202.
Telephone: 601-351-2400.
Telecopier: 601-351-2424.

PARTNER

Linda M. Crouch

ASSOCIATE

William L. Phillips, III

For Complete List of Firm Personnel, See General Section

For full biographical listings, see the Martindale-Hubbell Law Directory

*KNOXVILLE,** Knox Co.

BAKER, DONELSON, BEARMAN & CALDWELL (AV)

2200 Riverview Tower, 900 South Gay Street, 37901
Telephone: 423-549-7000
Telecopier: 423-525-8569
Email: info@bdbc.com *URL:* http://www.bakerdonelson.com
Memphis, Tennessee Office: 20th Floor, First Tennessee Building, 165 Madison, 38103.
Telephone: 901-526-2000.
Telecopier: 901-577-2303.
Nashville, Tennessee Office: 1700 Nashville City Center, 511 Union Street, 37219.
Telephone: 615-726-5600.
Telecopier: 615-726-0464.
Chattanooga, Tennessee Office: 1800 Republic Centre, 633 Chestnut Street, 37450-1800.
Telephone: 423-756-2010.
Telecopier: 423-756-3447.
Johnson City, Tennessee Office: SunTrust Bank Building, 207 Mockingbird Lane, P.O. Box 3038, 37602.
Telephone: 423-928-0181.
Telecopier: 423-928-5694; 423-928-3654; Kingsport: 423-246-6191.
Huntsville, Tennessee Office: 3 Courthouse Square, 37756.
Telephone: 423-663-2321.
Telecopier: 423-663-2111.
Washington, D.C. Office: Market Square, 801 Pennsylvania Avenue, N.W., 20004.
Telephone: 202-508-3400.
Telecopier: 202-508-3402.
Jackson, Mississippi Office: Suite 500, 700 North State Street, 39202.
Telephone: 601-351-2400.
Telecopier: 601-351-2424.

PARTNER

Bruce C. Doeg

ASSOCIATES

Wm. Gregory Hall, Jr.
David L. Morehous (Not admitted in TN)

For Complete List of Firm Personnel, See General Section

For full biographical listings, see the Martindale-Hubbell Law Directory

*MEMPHIS,** Shelby Co.

ARMSTRONG ALLEN PREWITT GENTRY JOHNSTON & HOLMES, PLLC (AV)

Brinkley Plaza, Suite 700, 80 Monroe Avenue, 38103-2467
Telephone: 901-523-8211
Facsimile: 901-524-4936
Little Rock, Arkansas Office: Suite 100, 100 Morgan Keegan Drive, 72202.
Telephone: 501-280-0100.
Facsimile: 501-280-0166.
Jackson, Mississippi Office: 2525 Lakeward Drive, Suite 200, 39216.
Telephone: 601-713-1192.
Facsimile: 601-713-2049.
Jackson, Tennessee Office: 464 North Parkway, Suite A, 38305.
Telephone: 901-660-2332.
Facsimile: 901-664-1109.

MEMBERS OF FIRM

Elmore Holmes, III
Paul A. Matthews
Charles R. Crawford

OF COUNSEL

Edward M. Kaplan

For Complete List of Firm Personnel, See General Section

For full biographical listings, see the Martindale-Hubbell Law Directory

BAKER, DONELSON, BEARMAN & CALDWELL (AV)

20th Floor, First Tennessee Building, 165 Madison, 38103
Telephone: 901-526-2000
Telecopier: 901-577-2303
Email: info@bdbc.com *URL:* http://www.bakerdonelson.com
Nashville, Tennessee Office: 1700 Nashville City Center, 511 Union Street, 37219.
Telephone: 615-726-5600.
Telecopier: 615-726-0464.
Chattanooga, Tennessee Office: 1800 Republic Centre, 633 Chestnut Street, 37450-1800.
Telephone: 423-756-2010.
Telecopier: 423-756-3447.
Knoxville, Tennessee Office: 2200 Riverview Tower, 900 South Gay Street, 37901.
Telephone: 423-549-7000.
Telecopier: 423-525-8569.
Johnson City, Tennessee Office: SunTrust Bank Building, 207 Mockingbird Lane, P.O. Box 3038, 37602.
Telephone: 423-928-0181.
Telecopier: 423-928-5694; 423-928-3654; Kingsport: 423-246-6191.
Huntsville, Tennessee Office: 3 Courthouse Square, 37756.
Telephone: 423-663-2321.
Telecopier: 423-663-2111.
Washington, D.C. Office: Market Square, 801 Pennsylvania Avenue, N.W., 20004.
Telephone: 202-508-3400.
Telecopier: 202-508-3402.
Jackson, Mississippi Office: Suite 500, 700 North State Street, 39202.
Telephone: 601-351-2400.
Telecopier: 601-351-2424.

SHAREHOLDERS

Robert Walker
Matthew S. Heiter
Janis Wild Kesser
Desiree M. Franklin

ASSOCIATES

Mary Ann Jackson
Jackie G. Prester
D. Benjamin Bullen
Shannon M. Hernandez
Sylvia Monique Reed
Louise P. Gaerig

For Complete List of Firm Personnel, See General Section

For full biographical listings, see the Martindale-Hubbell Law Directory

BOROD & KRAMER, P.C. (AV)

Beale Street Landing, 245 Wagner Place, Suite 350, 38103
Telephone: 901-524-0200
Telecopier: 901-523-0043
Email: administrator@borodankramer.com *URL:* http://www.borodandkramer.com

Bruce S. Kramer

Jeffrey C. Smith
Jeffery D. Parrish

For Complete List of Firm Personnel, See General Section

For full biographical listings, see the Martindale-Hubbell Law Directory

THE BUHLER LAW FIRM (AV)

Morgan Keegan Tower, 50 North Front Street, Suite 610, 38103
Telephone: 901-527-9007
Fax: 901-527-9067
Email: lbuhler@worldnet.att.net

(See Next Column)

Lynn Buhler

For full biographical listings, see the Martindale-Hubbell Law Directory

WARING COX, PLC (AV)

Morgan Keegan Tower, 50 North Front Street, Suite 1300, 38103-1190
Telephone: 901-543-8000
Telecopy: 901-543-8030
Email: Desk@waringcox.com

Jerald H. Sklar
Samuel D. Chafetz
John E. Kruger
Douglas P. Quay
Paul D. Amos
William T. Mays, Jr.
Robert C. Starnes

Representative Clients: Memphis Gastroenterology Group; Delta and Pine Land Company; Bayer Corporation; Lewis Supply Company, Inc.; Hancock Fabrics; Hilliard Lyons, Inc.; Osceola Foods, Inc.; Mid-South Milling Company, Inc.; Mitsui & Co. (U.S.A.), Inc.; Helm Fertilizer Corp.

For Complete List of Firm Personnel, See General Section

For full biographical listings, see the Martindale-Hubbell Law Directory

*NASHVILLE,** Davidson Co.

BAKER, DONELSON, BEARMAN & CALDWELL (AV)

1700 Nashville City Center, 511 Union Street, 37219
Telephone: 615-726-5600
Telecopier: 615-726-0464
Email: info@bdbc.com *URL:* http://www.bakerdonelson.com
Memphis, Tennessee Office: 20th Floor, First Tennessee Building, 165 Madison, 38103.
Telephone: 901-526-2000.
Telecopier: 901-577-2303.
Chattanooga, Tennessee Office: 1800 Republic Centre, 633 Chestnut Street, 37450-1800.
Telephone: 423-756-2010.
Telecopier: 423-756-3447.
Knoxville, Tennessee Office: 2200 Riverview Tower, 900 South Gay Street, 37901.
Telephone: 423-549-7000.
Telecopier: 423-525-8569.
Johnson City, Tennessee Office: SunTrust Bank Building, 207 Mockingbird Lane, P.O. Box 3038, 37602.
Telephone: 423-928-0181.
Telecopier: 423-928-5694; 423-928-3654; Kingsport: 423-246-6191.
Huntsville, Tennessee Office: 3 Courthouse Square, 37756.
Telephone: 423-663-2321.
Telecopier: 423-663-2111.
Washington, D.C. Office: Market Square, 801 Pennsylvania Avenue, N.W., 20004.
Telephone: 202-508-3400.
Telecopier: 202-508-3402.
Jackson, Mississippi Office: Suite 500, 700 North State Street, 39202.
Telephone: 601-351-2400.
Telecopier: 601-351-2424.

SHAREHOLDERS

Robert G. McCullough
James L. McElroy
J. Porter Durham, Jr.

For Complete List of Firm Personnel, See General Section

For full biographical listings, see the Martindale-Hubbell Law Directory

BASS, BERRY & SIMS PLC (AV)

2700 First American Center, 37238-2700
Telephone: 615-742-6200
Telecopy: 615-742-6293
URL: http://www.bassberry.com
Knoxville, Tennessee Office: 1700 Riverview Tower, 900 S. Gay Street, 37902 and P.O. Box 1509, 37901-1509.
Telephone: 423-521-6200.
Telecopy: 423-521-6234.
Memphis, Tennessee Office: 119 S. Main Street, Suite 500, 38103.
Telephone: 901-312-9100.
Fax: 901-312-9101.

MEMBERS OF FIRM

J. Bradbury Reed
James H. Cheek, III
Robins H. Ledyard
Bob F. Thompson
George H. Masterson
Leigh Walton
Samuel E. Stumpf, Jr.
F. Mitchell Walker, Jr.
J. Page Davidson
T. Andrew Smith
Cynthia Y. Reisz
John A. Good (Resident, Memphis, Tennessee Office)
Howard H. Lamar, III

OF COUNSEL

Barbara Mendel Mayden

ASSOCIATES

J. Allen Overby
Caldwell D. Lowrance, Jr. (Resident, Memphis, Tennessee Office)
Carolyn L. Taylor
Robert J. DelPriore (Resident, Memphis, Tennessee Office)
J. James Jenkins, Jr.
Lori Bryant Morgan
Todd J. Rolapp

(See Next Column)

BASS, BERRY & SIMS PLC, *Nashville—Continued*

ASSOCIATES (Continued)

Kelvin D. Jones, III
Jennifer Horn Noonan
Oscar L. Thomas (Resident, Memphis, Tennessee Office)
Kevin P. O'Hara
Laura E. Rakow
Judith S. Blade
Valerie A. Dormady
Derek S. Hughey
Timothy P. Manning
Gary John Meise
Anna S. Mills
Martin F. Shea, Jr. (Resident, Memphis, Tennessee Office)
Matthew K. White (Resident, Memphis, Tennessee Office)
Daniel E. Cortez
Sheldon M. Francis
D. Scott Holley
Shannon Evans Pinkston
Herbert Warren Sanger (Resident, Knoxville, Tennessee Office)

Representative Clients: American Healthcorp.; J.C. Bradford & Co.; Coventry Corp.; Dollar General Corp.; ENVOY Corp.; Gaylord Entertainment Co.; Ingram Industries, Inc.; Merrill Lynch & Co.; Service Merchandise Company, Inc.; Shoney's.

For full biographical listings, see the Martindale-Hubbell Law Directory

TEXAS

*AUSTIN,** Travis Co.

THOMPSON & KNIGHT L.L.P. (AV)

(Attorneys and Counselors)
1200 San Jacinto Center, 98 San Jacinto Boulevard, 78701
Telephone: 512-469-6100
Telecopy: 512-469-6180
URL: http://www.tklaw.com
Dallas, Texas Office: 1700 Pacific Avenue, Suite 3300, 75201.
Telephone: 214-969-1700.
Telecopy: 512-969-1751.
Telex: 732298.
Fort Worth, Texas Office: 801 Cherry Street, Suite 1600, 76102.
Telephone: 817-347-1700.
Telecopy: 817-347-1799.
Houston, Texas Office: Thompson Knight Brown Parker & Leahy L.L.P., 1200 Smith Street, Suite 3600, 77002-4595.
Telephone: 713-654-8111.
Telecopier: 713-654-1871.
San Pedro Garza Garcia, Nuevo León, Mexico Office: Edificio Losoles PD-4, Av. Lázaro Cárdenas No. 2400 Pte., C.P. 66220.
Telephone: (52-8) 363-0096.
Telecopy: (52-8) 363-3067.

PARTNER

James E. Cousar

For Complete List of Firm Personnel, See General Section

For full biographical listings, see the Martindale-Hubbell Law Directory

*DALLAS,** Dallas Co.

CALHOUN & STACY (AV)

Suite 5700 - Bank of America Plaza, 901 Main Street, 75202-3713
Telephone: 214-748-5000
Facsimile: 214-748-1421
Email: info@calhounstacy.com *URL:* http://www.calhounstacy.com

MEMBERS OF FIRM

Rees T. Bowen, III
Mark Alan Calhoun
LeAnn Wainscott Cross
David W. Elrod
Parker Nelson
Roy L. Stacy
Pamela J. Touchstone
Michael C. Wright

ASSOCIATES

David G. Allen
Joseph G. Barkate, Jr.
Scott S. Crocker
Sean P. Fitzgerald
Leanne Capps Medford
Jonathan G. Polak
Joel W. Reese
Barbara L. Wohlrabe

For Complete List of Firm Personnel, See General Section

For full biographical listings, see the Martindale-Hubbell Law Directory

CONANT FRENCH & CHANEY, LLP (AV)

3880 Bank One Center, 1717 Main Street, 75201
Telephone: 214-915-0620
Fasimile: 214-915-0634
Email: cfc@cfc-law.com *URL:* http://www.cfc-law.com

A. B. Conant, Jr.
William J. French
William B. Chaney
Linda A. Hale
Glen E. Lavy
Shawn W. Phelan
James D. MacIntyre

For full biographical listings, see the Martindale-Hubbell Law Directory

HUGHES & LUCE, L.L.P. (AV)

A Registered Limited Liability Partnership including Professional Corporations
1717 Main Street, Suite 2800, 75201
Telephone: 214-939-5500
Fax: 214-939-6100; 214-939-5849
Email: H&L@hughesluce.com *URL:* http://www.hughesluce.com
Austin, Texas Office: 111 Congress, Suite 900.
Telephone: 512-482-6800.
Fax: 512-482-6859.
Houston, Texas Office: 1600 Smith Street, Suite 3550.
Telephone: 713-754-5200.
Fax: 713-754-5270.

MEMBERS OF FIRM

Alan J. Bogdanow
Kenneth G. Hawari
Glen J. Hettinger
John B. Holden, Jr., (P.C.)
Mont P. Hoyt
David G. Luther, Jr.
William A. McCormack
Ross Clayton Mulford
Dudley W. Murrey

ASSOCIATES

Joanna H. Buck
James E. Cahill, III
Robert B. Hale
Gary W. Hays
Laura M. Kalesnik
Michael S.J. Lozich
Richard H. Mains
Bliss Burdett Pak
Anne-Marie Roy
Morgan A. Ryder
John Sepehri
John R. Wilcox III
Scott M. Wilson

OF COUNSEL

Nancy Figg Duessel

For Complete List of Firm Personnel, See General Section

For full biographical listings, see the Martindale-Hubbell Law Directory

KRAGE & JANVEY, L.L.P. (AV)

2001 Bryan Tower, Suite 2700, 75201-3059
Telephone: 214-969-7500
Telecopier: 214-220-0230

Ralph Janvey
Kristie L. Garrison

Representative Client: Regal Capital Co.

For full biographical listings, see the Martindale-Hubbell Law Directory

MEADOWS, OWENS, COLLIER, REED, COUSINS & BLAU, L.L.P. (AV)

901 Main Street, Suite 3700, 75202-3725
Telephone: 214-744-3700; 800-451-0093
Fax: 214-747-3732
URL: http://www.meadowsowens.com

MEMBERS OF FIRM

Charles M. Meadows, Jr.
Rodney J. Owens
Robert Don Collier
David N. Reed
Thomas G. Hineman
William R. Cousins, III
Charles W. Blau
George R. Bedell
Michael E. McCue
Fielder F. Nelms
Joel N. Crouch
Alan K. Davis
Charles D. Pulman

ASSOCIATES

Patricia King Dorey
Robert M. Bolton
M. Todd Welty
Josh O. Ungerman
Robyn A. Frohlin
Gregory A. Cardenas
Sara E. Lankford
Sarah Q. Qureshi
Bradley G. Korell
Todd A. Kraft
Alan L. Stroud
Matthew D. Richards

For full biographical listings, see the Martindale-Hubbell Law Directory

SMITH, UNDERWOOD & PERKINS, A PROFESSIONAL CORPORATION (AV)

600 Two Lincoln Centre, 5420 LBJ Freeway, 75240
Telephone: 972-661-5114
Telecopier: 972-661-5691
Email: firm@suandp.com *URL:* http://www.suplaw.com

Timothy S. Perkins
David W. Ralston
G. Lynn Smith
William J. Underwood, Jr.

Christine A. McGuire
Amy K. Ratzlaff
P. Theodore Stoinoff, II
Val C. Cronin
Ellen P. Stewart
Todd W. Shadle
Ruth C. Logan
Christina L. Betanzos
Kent D. Williamson

For full biographical listings, see the Martindale-Hubbell Law Directory

Dallas—Continued

THOMPSON & KNIGHT L.L.P. (AV)

(Attorneys and Counselors)
1700 Pacific Avenue Suite 3300, 75201
Telephone: 214-969-1700
Telecopy: 214-969-1751
Telex: 732 298
URL: http://www.tklaw.com
Austin, Texas Office: 1200 San Jacinto Center, 98 San Jacinto Boulevard, 78701.
Telephone: 512-469-6100.
Telecopy: 512-469-6180.
Fort Worth, Texas Office: 801 Cherry Street, Suite 1600, 76102.
Telephone: 817-347-1700.
Telecopy: 817-347-1799.
Houston, Texas Office: Thompson Knight Brown Parker & Leahy L.L.P., 1200 Smith Street, Suite 3600, 77002-4595.
Telephone: 713-654-8111.
Telecopier: 713-654-1871.
San Pedro Garza Garcia, Nuevo León, Mexico Office: Edificio Losoles PD-4, Av. Lázaro Cárdenas No. 2400 Pte., C.P. 66220.
Telephone: (52-8) 363-0096.
Telecopy: (52-8) 363-3067.

PARTNERS

William L. Banowsky
L. James Berglund, II
Michael R. Berry
Jane Politz Brandt
George C. Chapman
Steven K. Cochran
Greg W. Curry
Lori L. Dalton
Cheryl E. Diaz
Veronica Smith Lewis
Timothy R. McCormick
Stephen C. Rasch
Michael E. Schonberg
Bruce S. Sostek
Molly Steele
Peter J. Thoma

ASSOCIATES

Julia Elizabeth Jones
William M. Katz, Jr.

OF COUNSEL

Laura Peterson Elkind
Jerry P. Jones

For Complete List of Firm Personnel, See General Section

For full biographical listings, see the Martindale-Hubbell Law Directory

WHITTENBURG WHITTENBURG & SCHACHTER, P.C. (AV)

2300 Plaza of the Americas, 600 North Pearl, LB 133, 75201
Telephone: 214-999-5700
Facsimile: 214-999-5747
Amarillo, Texas Office: 1010 South Harrison.
Telephone: 806-372-5700.
Facsimile: 806-372-5757.

Deborah Ashmore Harris

For Complete List of Firm Personnel, See General Section

For full biographical listings, see the Martindale-Hubbell Law Directory

*FORT WORTH,** Tarrant Co.

THOMPSON & KNIGHT L.L.P. (AV)

(Attorneys and Counselors)
801 Cherry Street, Suite 1600, 76102
Telephone: 817-347-1700
Telecopy: 817-347-1799
URL: http://www.tklaw.com
Dallas, Texas Office: 1700 Pacific Avenue, Suite 3300, 75201.
Telephone: 214-969-1700.
Telecopy: 214-969-1751.
Telex: 732298.
Austin, Texas Office: 1200 San Jacinto Center, 98 San Jacinto Boulevard, 78701.
Telephone: 512-469-6100.
Telecopy: 512-469-6180.
Houston, Texas Office: Thompson Knight Brown Parker & Leahy L.L.P., 1200 Smith Street, Suite 3600, 77002-4595.
Telephone: 713-654-8111.
Telecopier: 713-654-1871.
San Pedro Garza Garcia, Nuevo León, Mexico Office: Edificio Losoles PD-4, Av. Lázaro Cárdenas No. 2400 Pte., C.P. 66220.
Telephone: (52-8) 363-0096.
Telecopy: (52-8) 363-3067.

PARTNER

Jennifer Pettijohn Henry

For Complete List of Firm Personnel, See General Section

For full biographical listings, see the Martindale-Hubbell Law Directory

*HOUSTON,** Harris Co.

BREWER & PRITCHARD, A PROFESSIONAL CORPORATION (AV)

24th Floor, Heritage Plaza, 1111 Bagby, 77002
Telephone: 713-209-2950
Facsimile: 713-659-5302
Email: info@bplaw.com *URL:* http://www.bplaw.com

Thomas C. Pritchard
Margaret C. Fitzgerald

Cavas Pavri

For full biographical listings, see the Martindale-Hubbell Law Directory

CUNNINGHAM, DARLOW, ZOOK & CHAPOTON, LLP (AV)

1000 Louisiana, Suite 6900, 77002
Telephone: 713-659-5522
Fax: 713-659-4466
Email: sgosslee@cdzc.com

Tom Alan Cunningham
Debbie Crupain Darlow
Richard J. Zook
John E. Chapoton, Jr.

ASSOCIATES

Kelley M. Keller
Jon T. Powell

For full biographical listings, see the Martindale-Hubbell Law Directory

HOUSSIERE, DURANT & HOUSSIERE, LLP (AV)

Three Post Oak Central, 1990 Post Oak Boulevard, Suite 800, 77056-3812
Telephone: 713-626-3700
Fax: 713-626-3709
Email: lhoussi@hdhtex.com *URL:* http://www.hdhtex.com

Charles R. Houssiere, III
Harry L. Durant (Retired)
Linda D. Houssiere
Randal A. Kauffman
Monica C. Vaughan

Chad D. Points

For full biographical listings, see the Martindale-Hubbell Law Directory

THOMPSON KNIGHT BROWN PARKER & LEAHY L.L.P. (AV)

A Registered Limited Liability Partnership including Professional Corporations
(Attorneys and Counselors)
1200 Smith Street, Suite 3600, 77002-4595
Telephone: 713-654-8111
Telecopier: 713-654-1871
URL: http://www.tklaw.com
Dallas, Texas Office: Thompson & Knight L.L.P., 1700 Pacific Avenue, Suite 3300, 75201.
Telephone: 214-969-1700.
Telecopy: 214-969-1751.
Telex: 732298.
Austin, Texas Office: Thompson & Knight L.L.P., 1200 San Jacinto Center, 98 San Jacinto Boulevard, 78701.
Telephone: 512-469-6100.
Telecopy: 512-469-6180.
Fort Worth, Texas Office: Thompson & Knight L.L.P., 801 Cherry Street, Suite 1600, 76102.
Telephone: 817-347-1700.
Telecopy: 817-347-1799.
San Pedro Garza Garcia, Nuevo León, Mexico Office: Thompson & Knight L.L.P., Edificio Losoles PD-4, Av. Lázaro Cárdenas No. 2400 PTE., C.P. 66220.
Telephone: (52-8) 363-0096.
Telecopy: (52-8) 363-3067.

PARTNERS

J. Michael Bell
Nancy Wilson Hargrove
Jon L. Tankersley

For Complete List of Firm Personnel, See General Section

For full biographical listings, see the Martindale-Hubbell Law Directory

*SAN ANTONIO,** Bexar Co.

COX & SMITH INCORPORATED (AV)

112 East Pecan Street, Suite 1800, 78205-1521
Telephone: 210-554-5500
Fax: 210-226-8395
Email: info@coxsmith.com *URL:* http://www.coxsmith.com

Dan G. Webster, III
James B. Smith, Jr.
Cary Plotkin Kavy
Stephen D. Seidel
Steven R. Jacobs
William J. McDonough, Jr.
Steven A. Elder
Elizabeth Johnson Keig
Tobin E. Olson
Lauren M. Sheinberg
Angie D. Patrick

(See Next Column)

COX & SMITH INCORPORATED, *San Antonio—Continued*

Representative Clients: Abraxas Petroleum Corporation; Eye Care Centers of America, Inc.; First Victoria National Bank; International Bancshares Corp.; Kinetic Concepts, Inc.; Merrill Lynch, Pierce, Fenner & Smith, Inc.; Rio Grande, Inc.

For Complete List of Firm Personnel, See General Section

For full biographical listings, see the Martindale-Hubbell Law Directory

UTAH

*SALT LAKE CITY,** Salt Lake Co.

CALLISTER NEBEKER & MCCULLOUGH, A PROFESSIONAL CORPORATION (AV)

Gateway Tower East, Suite 900, 10 East South Temple, 84133
Telephone: 801-530-7300
Telecopier: 801-364-9127
Email: mjeaston@cnmlaw.com *URL:* http://www.cnmlaw.com

Louis H. Callister
Damon E. Coombs
Craig F. McCullough
Laurie S. Hart

Representative Clients: Zions Bancorporation; Alpnet, Inc.; Covol Technologies, Inc.; Field Aircraft.

For Complete List of Firm Personnel, See General Section

For full biographical listings, see the Martindale-Hubbell Law Directory

DURHAM JONES & PINEGAR, A PROFESSIONAL CORPORATION (AV)

Key Bank Tower 50 South Main, Suite 800, 84144
Telephone: 801-538-2424
Fax: 801-538-2425
Email: djp@djplaw.com
Ogden Utah Office: The Aerospace Center, Suite 710, 1104 Country Hills Drive, 84403.
Telephone: 801-395-2424.
Fax: 801-395-2430.

Jeffrey M. Jones
Wayne D. Swan
Kevin R. Pinegar
N. Todd Leishman

C. Parkinson Lloyd
Alan W. Bell

For full biographical listings, see the Martindale-Hubbell Law Directory

PARR WADDOUPS BROWN GEE & LOVELESS, A PROFESSIONAL CORPORATION (AV)

Suite 1300, 185 South State Street, 84111-1537
Telephone: 801-532-7840
Fax: 801-532-7750
URL: http://www.pwlaw.com

Richard G. Brown
Bryan T. Allen
Robert S. Clark
Eric D. Bawden
Brian G. Lloyd
Brett J. Swanson
Jonathan O. Hafen
Douglas C. Waddoups

For Complete List of Firm Personnel, See General Section

For full biographical listings, see the Martindale-Hubbell Law Directory

VAN COTT, BAGLEY, CORNWALL & MCCARTHY, A PROFESSIONAL CORPORATION (AV)

50 South Main Street, Suite 1600, P.O. Box 45340, 84145-0340
Telephone: 801-532-3333
Telecopier: 801-534-0058
Email: info@vancott.com *URL:* http://www.vancott.com
Ogden, Utah Office: 2404 Washington Boulevard, Suite 900.
Telephone: 801-394-5783.
Park City, Utah Office: 2200 Park Avenue, Suite C200-A.
Telephone: 435-649-3889.

Arthur B. Ralph
David J. Smith

Tacy A. Hartman

OF COUNSEL

M. Scott Woodland

For Complete List of Firm Personnel, See General Section

For full biographical listings, see the Martindale-Hubbell Law Directory

VERMONT

*BURLINGTON,** Chittenden Co.

MILLER, EGGLESTON & CRAMER, LTD. (AV)

150 South Champlain Street, P.O. Box 1489, 05402-1489
Telephone: 802-864-0880
Telecopier: 802-864-0328

Jon R. Eggleston
Mark A. Saunders

For Complete List of Firm Personnel, See General Section

For full biographical listings, see the Martindale-Hubbell Law Directory

VIRGINIA

MCLEAN, Fairfax Co.

TALBOTT AND GALLAGHER, A PROFESSIONAL CORPORATION (AV)

6824 Elm Street, Suite 350, 22101
Telephone: 703-893-6361
Facsimile: 703-893-6825
Email: jct@talbottgallagher.com *URL:* http://www.lawyers.com/talbottgallagher

John C. Talbott
Kathleen G. Gallagher

For full biographical listings, see the Martindale-Hubbell Law Directory

NORFOLK, (Independent City)

PAYNE, GATES, FARTHING & RADD, P.C. (AV)

15th Floor, Dominion Tower, 999 Waterside Drive, Suite 1515, 23510-3309
Telephone: 757-640-1500
Facsimile: 757-627-6583
URL: http://www.paynegates.com

Ronald M. Gates
Glen M. Robertson
Philip R. Farthing
Brian R. Dinning
Anthony F. Radd
Todd J. Preti
Marshall A. Winslow, Jr.

C. Arthur Robinson, II
Stephen E. Heretick
Raymond L. Hogge, Jr.

OF COUNSEL

Charles E. Payne

For full biographical listings, see the Martindale-Hubbell Law Directory

RICHMOND, (Independent City)

LECLAIR RYAN, A PROFESSIONAL CORPORATION (AV)

707 East Main Street, 11th Floor, 23219
Telephone: 804-783-2003
Facsmile: 804-783-2294
Email: email@leclairryan.com
Glen Allen, Virginia Office: 4201 Dominion Boulevard, Suite 200, 23060.
Telephone: 804-270-0070.
Facsimile: 804-270-4715.
Blacksburg, Virginia Office: 1872 Pratt Drive, Suite 1865, 24060.
Telephone: 540-961-2762.
Fax: 540-961-2781.
Norfolk, Virginia Office: 999 Waterside Drive, Suite 2025.
Telephone: 757-624-1454.
Facsimile: 757-624-3773.
Alexandria, Virginia Office: 225 Reinekers Lane, Suite 290, 22314.
Telephone: 703-684-8007.
Facsimile: 703-684-8075.
Charlottesville, Virginia Office: 108 S.E. Second Street, P.O. Box 2017, 22902.
Telephone: 804-971-7771.
Facsimile: 804-296-0905.

Alfred J. T. Byrne
Richard L. Hurlbert, Jr.
Debra J.C. Dowd
Gary D. LeClair
Michael P. Drzal
James A. Murphy
J. Benjamin English
Dennis M. Ryan
Stephen T. Gannon
Douglas L. Sbertoli
Robert J. Grey, Jr.
Andrew W. White
Bradley A. Haneberg
George P. Whitley
Jonathan M. Harris
(Not admitted in VA)

(See Next Column)

LECLAIR RYAN A PROFESSIONAL CORPORATION—*Continued*

Pamela Catania	Scott H. Richter
Scott W. Fancher	Jeffrey A. Sanborn
Karen S. French	Saundra R. Schmidt
Michael Liberman	Russell J. Singer
Todd Manley Lynn	Wendy Elizabeth Warren

For full biographical listings, see the Martindale-Hubbell Law Directory

MALONEY, HUENNEKENS, PARKS, GECKER & PARSONS, A PROFESSIONAL CORPORATION (AV)

Bank of America Center, 1111 East Main Street, Suite 800, 23219-3103
Telephone: 804-644-0313
Telecopier: 804-783-6192

James M. Wilson

Reference: First Union National Bank.

For Complete List of Firm Personnel, See General Section

For full biographical listings, see the Martindale-Hubbell Law Directory

WILLIAMS, MULLEN, CLARK & DOBBINS, A PROFESSIONAL CORPORATION (AV)

Two James Center, 1021 East Cary Street, P.O. Box 1320, 23218-1320
Telephone: 804-643-1991
Fax: 804-783-6507
URL: http://www.wmcd.com
Newport News Office: Harbor Bank Center, Suite 210, One Old Oyster Point Road, 23602-7119.
Telephone: 757-249-5100.
Fax: 757-249-5109.
Virginia Beach Office: One Columbus Center, 23462-6763.
Telephone: 757-499-8800.
Fax: 757-473-0395.
Vienna Office: 1593 Spring Hill Road, Suite 510, 22182.
Telephone: 703-760-5200.
Fax: 703-748-0244.
Washington, D.C. Office: The Farragut Building, 900 17th Street, N.W., Suite 700, 20006.
Telephone: 202-293-0213.
Fax: 804-783-6507. Fax Within D.C.: 202-293-5939.
London, England Office: Blake Lodge, Bridge Lane, SW11 3AD.
Telephone: (011-44-71) 223-2756.
Fax: (011-44-71) 350-0156.
Riyadh, Saudi Arabia Affiliate Office: Saudi-American Legal Consultants Commercial Building #2, Diplomatic Quarter, P.O. Box 57270, 11574.
Telephone: (011-966-1) 488-1563.
Fax: (011-966-1) 488-0542.

R. Brian Ball	Warren E. Nowlin (Resident, Washington, D.C. Office)
Theodore L. Chandler, Jr.	William L. Pitman
David R. Johnson	Robert E. Spicer, Jr.
R. Hart Lee	

Wayne A. Whitham, Jr.

John M. Oakey, III	Kathryn W. Sanborn

Aisha J. Sykes

For Complete List of Firm Personnel, See General Section

For full biographical listings, see the Martindale-Hubbell Law Directory

WASHINGTON

*SEATTLE,** King Co.

SUMMIT LAW GROUP, PLLC (AV)

1505 Westlake Avenue North, Suite 300, 98109
Telephone: 206-281-9881
Fax: 206-281-9882
Email: info@summitlaw.com *URL:* http://www.summitlaw.com

Karen A. Andersen	Lawrence C. Locker
Kristin D. Anger	Philip S. McCune
Laura A. Bertin	Polly L. McNeill
Lynn M. Engel	Ralph H. Palumbo
Michael J. Erickson	Bruce L. Schroeder
Matthew R. Harris	William R. Squires III
David M. Heineck	Monika Vasil
Elizabeth Butler Kennar	Mark F. Worthington
Otto G. Klein, III	Rodney B. Younker

For full biographical listings, see the Martindale-Hubbell Law Directory

WEST VIRGINIA

*CHARLESTON,** Kanawha Co.

JACKSON & KELLY (AV)

1600 Laidley Tower, P.O. Box 553, 25322
Telephone: 304-340-1000
Fax: 304-340-1130
Email: info@jacksonkelly.com *URL:* http://www.jacksonkelly.com
Martinsburg, West Virginia Office: 300 Foxcroft Avenue, P.O. Box 1068.
Telephone: 304-263-8800.
Fax: 304-263-7110.
Morgantown, West Virginia Office: 6000 Hampton Center, P.O. Box 619.
Telephone: 304-599-3000.
Fax: 304-285-2040.
New Martinsville, West Virginia Office: 256 Russell Avenue, P.O. Box 68.
Telephone: 304-455-1751.
Fax: 304-455-6314.
Parkersburg, West Virginia Office: 412 Market Street, Suite 202, P.O. Box 1144.
Telephone: 304-424-3490.
Fax: 304-424-3499.
Fairmont, West Virginia Office: 1000 Technology Drive, Suite 1310.
Telephone: 304-368-2000.
Fax: 304-368-2020.
Lexington, Kentucky Office: 175 East Main Street, Suite 500, P.O. Box 2150.
Telephone: 606-255-9500.
Fax: 606-281-6478.
Washington, D. C. Office: 2401 Pennsylvania Avenue, N.W., Suite 400.
Telephone: 202-973-0200.
Fax: 202-973-0232.
Denver, Colorado Office: Suite 2710, 1660 Lincoln Street.
Telephone: 303-390-0003.
Fax: 303-390-0040.
Wheeling, West Virginia Office: 1144 Market Street.
Telephone: 304-233-4000.
Fax: 304-233-4077.

MEMBERS OF FIRM

James Knight Brown	Charles D. Dunbar
Louis S. Southworth, II	Charles W. Loeb, Jr.
Michael A. Albert	Elizabeth Osenton Lord

Representative Clients: One Valley Bancorp of West Virginia, Inc.; Horizon Bancorp, Inc.; Virginia Inn Management, Inc.

For Complete List of Firm Personnel, See General Section

For full biographical listings, see the Martindale-Hubbell Law Directory

WISCONSIN

*MADISON,** Dane Co.

NEIDER & BOUCHER, S.C. (AV)

440 Science Drive, P.O. Box 5510, 53705-0510
Telephone: 608-661-4500
Facsimile: 608-661-4510
URL: http://www.neiderboucher.com
URL: http://www.lawyers.com/neider&boucher-sc

Ronald C. Berman	Charles E. Neider
Joseph W. Boucher	Steven C. Underwood

Susan M. De Groot	Cynthia L. Richson
Erik W. Ibele	Matthew L. Schemmel
Rana Kang	Kent L. Schlienger

Dean T. Stange

OF COUNSEL

Ralph M. Cagle	Ronald R. Smith

For full biographical listings, see the Martindale-Hubbell Law Directory

QUARLES & BRADY LLP (AV)

Firstar Plaza, One South Pinckney Street, P.O. Box 2113, 53701-2113
Telephone: 608-251-5000
Fax: 608-251-9166
URL: http://www.quarles.com
Milwaukee, Wisconsin Office: 411 East Wisconsin Avenue, 53202-4497.
Telephone: 414-277-5000.
Fax: 414-271-3552.
West Palm Beach, Florida Office: 222 Lakeview Avenue, 4th Floor, 33401.
Telephone: 561-653-5000.
Fax: 561-653-5333.
Naples, Florida Office: Barnett Center, 4501 Tamiami Trail North, Suite 300, 34103-3060.
Telephone: 941-262-5959.
Fax: 941-434-4999.

(See Next Column)

QUARLES & BRADY LLP, *Madison—Continued*

Phoenix, Arizona Office: One Camelback Building, One East Camelback Road, Suite 400, 85012-1649.
Telephone: 602-230-5500.
Fax: 602-230-5598.
Chicago, Illinois Office: Quarles & Brady LLC, Citicorp Center, 500 West Madison Street, Suite 3700.
Telephone: 312-715-5000.
Fax: 312-715-5155.

PARTNER
Roy L. Prange, Jr.

ASSOCIATE
Valerie L. Bailey-Rihn

For Complete List of Firm Personnel, See General Section

For full biographical listings, see the Martindale-Hubbell Law Directory

*MILWAUKEE,** Milwaukee Co.

MEISSNER TIERNEY FISHER & NICHOLS S.C. (AV)

The Milwaukee Center, 111 East Kilbourn Avenue, 19th Floor, 53202-6622
Telephone: 414-273-1300
Facsimile: 414-273-5840
URL: http://www.mtfn.com

Joseph E. Tierney III
Thomas J. Nichols
Randal J. Brotherhood

Adam J. Tutaj

OF COUNSEL
Paul F. Meissner

For full biographical listings, see the Martindale-Hubbell Law Directory

QUARLES & BRADY LLP (AV)

411 East Wisconsin Avenue, 53202-4497
Telephone: 414-277-5000
Fax: 414-271-3552
URL: http://www.quarles.com
Madison, Wisconsin Office: Firstar Plaza, One South Pinckney Street, P.O. Box 2113, 53701-2113.
Telephone: 608-251-5000.
Fax: 608-251-9166.
West Palm Beach, Florida Office: 222 Lakeview Avenue, 4th Floor, 33401.
Telephone: 561-653-5000.
Fax: 561-653-5333.
Naples, Florida Office: Barnett Center, 4501 Tamiami Trail North, Suite 300, 34103-3060.
Telephone: 941-262-5959.
Fax: 941-434-4999.
Phoenix, Arizona Office: One Camelback Building, One East Camelback Road, Suite 400, 85012-1649.
Telephone: 602-230-5500.
Fax: 602-230-5598.
Chicago, Illinois Office: Quarles & Brady LLC, Citicorp Center, 500 West Madison Street, Suite 3700.
Telephone: 312-715-5000.
Fax: 312-715-5155.

MEMBERS OF FIRM
(ALPHABETICALLY BY YEAR OF ADMISSION TO BAR)

John S. Holbrook, Jr. (Resident, Madison Office)
Jeffrey B. Bartell (Resident, Madison Office)
Charles W. Herf (Resident, Phoenix, Arizona Office)
Conrad G. Goodkind
Bruce C. Davidson
P. Robert Moya (Resident, Phoenix, Arizona Office)
Peter C. Karegeannes
Michael H. Schaalman
Phillip E. Recht
Joseph D. Masterson
Kenneth V. Hallett
Fredrick G. Lautz
Kathryn M. Buono
Charles M. Weber
Walter J. Skipper

OF COUNSEL
Neal E. Madisen

ASSOCIATES
Cheryl A. Johnson
Mark K. Briggs (Resident, Phoenix, Arizona Office)

For Complete List of Firm Personnel, See General Section

For full biographical listings, see the Martindale-Hubbell Law Directory

CANADA
ALBERTA

*CALGARY,** Calgary Jud. Dist.

BENNETT JONES (AV)

4500 Bankers Hall East, 855-2nd Street S.W., T2P 4K7
Telephone: 403-298-3100
Facsimile: 403-265-7219
Email: firmwatch@bennettjones.ca *URL:* http://www.bennettjones.ca
Edmonton, Alberta Office: 1000, 10035-105 Street.
Telephone: 780-421-8133.
Facsimile: 780-421-7951.
Toronto, Ontario Office: 3400 1 First Canadian Place, P.O. Box 130.
Telephone: 416-863-1200.
Facsimile: 416-863-1716.

MEMBER OF FIRM
William S. Rice

For Complete List of Firm Personnel, See General Section

For full biographical listings, see the Martindale-Hubbell Law Directory

PARLEE MCLAWS (AV)

3400 Petro-Canada Centre, 150 - 6th Avenue, SW, T2P 3Y7
Telephone: 403-294-7000
Telecopier: 403-265-8263
Email: lawyers@parlee.com *URL:* http://www.parlee.com
Edmonton, Alberta Office: 15th Floor Manulife Place, 10180 101st Street.
Telephone: 403-423-8500.
Telecopier: 403-423-2870.

MEMBERS OF FIRM
Bruce A. Lawrence
Nancy M. Penner

ASSOCIATES
Ariane E. Young
Anne Marie Godin
Seema S. Johal

For Complete List of Firm Personnel, See General Section

For full biographical listings, see the Martindale-Hubbell Law Directory

*EDMONTON,** Edmonton Jud. Dist.

PARLEE MCLAWS (AV)

15th Floor Manulife Place, 10180 101st Street, T5J 4K1
Telephone: 403-423-8500
Telecopier: 403-423-2870
Email: lawyers@parlee.com *URL:* http://www.parlee.com
Calgary, Alberta Office: 3400 Petro-Canada Centre, 150 - 6th Avenue, SW.
Telephone: 403-294-7000.
Telecopier: 403-265-8263.

MEMBERS OF FIRM
Bruce D. Hirsche, Q.C.
David G. Finlay
Kevin L. Lynch
David S. Tam

ASSOCIATES
Lorne J. Ruzicka
George E. Flemming

For Complete List of Firm Personnel, See General Section

For full biographical listings, see the Martindale-Hubbell Law Directory

CANADA
NEW BRUNSWICK

*FREDERICTON,** York Co.

MCINNES COOPER (AV)

Suite 600, 570 Queen Street, P.O. Box 610, E3B 5A6
Telephone: 506-458-8572
Fax: 506-458-9903
Email: mcrfton@mcrlaw.com *URL:* http://www.mcrlaw.com
Halifax, Nova Scotia Office: Summit Place, 1601 Lower Water Street, P.O. Box 730, B3J 2V1.
Telephone: 902-425-6500.
Fax: 902-425-6350. Email: mcrhfx@mcrlaw.com.
St. John's, Newfoundland Office: Baine Johnston Centre, 5th Floor, 10 Fort William Place, P.O. Box 5939, A1C 5X4.
Telephone: 709-722-8735.
Telecopier: 709-722-1763. Email: mcrsj@mcrlaw.com.
Moncton, New Brunswick Office: Place Moncton Place, 655 Main Street, P.O. Box 1368, E1C 8T6.
Telephone: 506-857-8970.
Fax: 506-857-4095. Email: mcrmctn@mcrlaw.com.

(See Next Column)

McInnes Cooper—*Continued*

Charlottetown, Prince Edward Island Office: BDC Place, Suite 620, 119 Kent Street, C1A 1N3.
Telephone: 902-368-8473.
Fax: 902-368-8346. Email: mcrpei@mcrlaw.com.

PARTNER

Carol J. Downs

For Complete List of Firm Personnel, See General Section

For full biographical listings, see the Martindale-Hubbell Law Directory

*MONCTON,** Westmorland Co.

McInnes Cooper (AV)

Barristers, Solicitors & Trade Mark Agents
Place Moncton Place, 655 Main Street, P.O. Box 1368, E1C 8T6
Telephone: 506-857-8970
Fax: 506-857-4095
Email: mcrmctn@mcrlaw.com *URL:* http://www.mcrlaw.com
Halifax, Nova Scotia Office: Summit Place, 1601 Lower Water Street, P.O. Box 730, B3J 2V1.
Telephone: 902-425-6500.
Fax: 902-425-6350. Email: mcrhfx@mcrlaw.com.
St. John's, Newfoundland Office: Baine Johnston Centre, 5th Floor, 10 Fort William Place, P.O. Box 5939, A1C 5X4.
Telephone: 709-722-8735.
Telecopier: 709-722-1763. Email: mcrsj@mcrlaw.com.
Charlottetown, Prince Edward Island Office: BDC Place, Suite 620, 119 Kent Street, C1A 1N3.
Telephone: 902-368-8473.
Fax: 902-368-8346. Email: mcrpei@mcrlaw.com.
Fredericton, New Brunswick Office: Suite 600, 570 Queen Street, P.O. Box 610.
Telephone: 506-458-8572.
Fax: 506-458-9903. Email: mcrfton@mcrlaw.com.

ASSOCIATE

Sylvie C. Roussel

For Complete List of Firm Personnel, See General Section

For full biographical listings, see the Martindale-Hubbell Law Directory

CANADA NEWFOUNDLAND

*ST. JOHN'S,**

McInnes Cooper (AV)

Barristers, Solicitors & Trade Mark Agents
Baine Johnston Centre, 5th Floor, 10 Fort William Place, P.O. Box 5939, A1C 5X4
Telephone: 709-722-8735
Telecopier: 709-722-1763
Email: mcrsj@mcrlaw.com *URL:* http://www.mcrlaw.com
Halifax, Nova Scotia Office: Summit Place, 1601 Lower Water Street, P.O. Box 730, B3J 2V1.
Telephone: 902-425-6500.
Fax: 902-425-6350. Email: mcrhfx@mcrlaw.com.
Moncton, New Brunswick Office: Place Moncton Place, 655 Main Street, P.O. Box 1368, E1C 8T6.
Telephone: 506-857-8970.
Fax: 506-857-4095. Email: mcrmctn@mcrlaw.com.
Charlottetown, Prince Edward Island Office: BDC Place, Suite 620, 119 Kent Street, C1A 1N3.
Telephone: 902-368-8473.
Fax: 902-368-8346. Email: mcrpei@mcrlaw.com.
Fredericton, New Brunswick Office: Suite 600, 570 Queen Street, P.O. Box 610.
Telephone: 506-458-8572.
Fax: 506-458-9903. Email: mcrfton@mcrlaw.com.

PARTNERS

John M. Green, Q.C. Thomas R. Kendell
Caroline C. Watton

ASSOCIATE

Jacqueline S. Bartlett

For Complete List of Firm Personnel, See General Section

For full biographical listings, see the Martindale-Hubbell Law Directory

CANADA NOVA SCOTIA

*HALIFAX,** Regional Munic. of Halifax

McInnes Cooper (AV)

Barristers, Solicitors & Trade Mark Agents
Summit Place, 1601 Lower Water Street, P.O. Box 730, B3J 2V1
Telephone: 902-425-6500
Fax: 902-425-6350
Email: mcrhfx@mcrlaw.com *URL:* http://www.mcrlaw.com
St. John's, Newfoundland Office: Baine Johnston Centre, 5th Floor, 10 Fort William Place, P.O. Box 5939, A1C 5X4.
Telephone: 709-722-8735.
Telecopier: 709-722-1763. Email: mcrsj@mcrlaw.com.
Moncton, New Brunswick Office: Place Moncton Place, 655 Main Street, P.O. Box 1368, E1C 8T6.
Telephone: 506-857-8970.
Fax: 506-857-4095. Email: mcrmctn@mcrlaw.com.
Charlottetown, Prince Edward Island Office: BDC Place, Suite 620, 119 Kent Street, C1A 1N3.
Telephone: 902-368-8473.
Fax: 902-368-8346. Email: mcrpei@mcrlaw.com.
Fredericton, New Brunswick Office: Suite 600, 570 Queen Street, P.O. Box 610.
Telephone: 506-458-8572.
Fax: 506-458-9903. Email: mcrfton@mcrlaw.com.

PARTNERS

Joseph A. F. Macdonald, Q.C. Fae J. Shaw

ASSOCIATE

Jennifer A. Healy

For Complete List of Firm Personnel, See General Section

For full biographical listings, see the Martindale-Hubbell Law Directory

CANADA ONTARIO

*OTTAWA,** Regional Munic. of Ottawa-Carleton

Borden Elliot Scott & Aylen (AV)

1000-60 Rue Queen Street, K1P 5Y7
Telephone: 613-237-5160; 800-661-4237
General Facsimile: 613-230-8842
IP Dept. Facsimile: 613-787-3558
Email: ottinfo@scottaylen.com *URL:* http://www.borden.com
Toronto, Ontario Office: Borden & Elliot: Scotia Plaza, 40 King Street West.
Telephone: 416-367-6000.
Telecopier: 416-367-6749. Email: info @borden.com. URL: http://www.borden.com.

Laird J. Rasmussen Jeremy Stuart T. Farr
Timothy J. McCunn Patricia John
Douglas R. Hewson

For full biographical listings, see the Martindale-Hubbell Law Directory

*TORONTO,** Regional Munic. of Toronto

Borden & Elliot (AV)

Barristers & Solicitors
Scotia Plaza, 40 King Street West, M5H 3Y4
Telephone: 416-367-6000
Telecopier: 416-367-6749
Email: info@borden.com *URL:* http://www.borden.com
Ottawa, Ontario Office: Borden Elliot Scott & Aylen, 1000-60 Rue Queen Street.
Telephone: 613-237-5160; 800-661-4237. General *Facsimile:* 613-230-8842. IP Dept. *Facsimile:* 613-787-3558. Email: ottinfo@scottaylen.com. URL: http://www.borden.com.

Paul G. Findlay

For Complete List of Firm Personnel, See General Section

For full biographical listings, see the Martindale-Hubbell Law Directory

Davies, Ward & Beck (AV)

1 First Canadian Place, M5X 1B1
Telephone: 416-863-0900
Fax: 416-863-0871
Email: info@dwb.com *URL:* http://www.dwb.com

(See Next Column)

DAVIES, WARD & BECK, *Toronto—Continued*

PARTNERS AND ASSOCIATES

Mark Q. Connelly	Nicholas J. Leblovic
William M. O'Reilly	Jay A. Swartz
I. Berl Nadler	Arthur S. Shiff
Jean-Paul Bisnaire	Patricia L. Olasker
Gray E. Taylor	Michael Disney
Gregory J. Howard	William M. Ainley
Carol D. Pennycook	Neil Finkelstein
A. Gerold Goldlist	Edward C. Hannah
Jeffrey O. Palmer	Catherine G. Ross
Paul M. Kennedy	D. Shawn McReynolds
Kevin J. Thomson	Michael Creery
Ian D. Johnson	Thomas A. Smee
Carol Hansell	Ian R. McBride
Vincent A. Mercier	Cameron M. Rusaw
Timothy H. Moran	Michael W. Clifford
Patrick G. Barry	Sarbjit S. Basra
Gillian R. Stacey	Andrew L. Welsh
Paolo Boni	Julianna S. Ahn
Delphine Brooker	Andrea E. Daly
Sabrina Gherbaz	Terrance J. Ritchie
Mitchell P. Finkelstein	Warren M. Katz
Paul W. Golding	Steven M. Harris
Christopher H. Jones	Jennifer L. Toone
Alana G. McPhee	Patrick E. Moyer
Rosemary A. Newman	James R. Reid
Robin G. Tessier	Derek R. G. Vesey
Tarne P. Whiteley	Paul A. Beauregard
Andrée M. Blais	R. Michael Brisson
Michael S. Brown	Donald S. Harrison
Erinn E. Somerville	Lori K. Sullivan

For Complete List of Firm Personnel, See General Section

For full biographical listings, see the Martindale-Hubbell Law Directory

MCDONALD & HAYDEN (AV)

One Queen Street East Suite 1500, M5C 2Y3
Telephone: 416-364-3100
Telecopier: 416-601-4100
Email: ddouglas@mchayden.on.ca *URL:* http://www.mchayden.on.ca

MEMBERS OF FIRM

John G. McDonald, Q.C. (1922-1993)	Wendy C. Posluns
Peter Reginald Hayden, Q.C.	Warren S. Rapoport
David C. Nathanson, Q.C.	David H. Goldman
Marvin D. Demone	A. Richard Rodier
D. H. Jack	Mark Adilman
David R. Street	John D. Brunt
Clifford M. Goldlist	Kevin Cai
	Jane Southren

Shea T. Small

ASSOCIATE

Bram J. Green

For full biographical listings, see the Martindale-Hubbell Law Directory

CANADA QUEBEC

*MONTREAL,** Montreal Dist.

MCMASTER GERVAIS (AV)

A General Partnership
1000 de La Gauchetière Street West, Suite 900, H3B 5H4
Telephone: 514-879-1212
Fax: 514-954-1905
Email: info@mcmastergervais.com *URL:* http://www.mcmastergervais.com

MEMBERS OF FIRM

Peter C. Casey	Richard W. Shannon
Johanne Thomas	H. John Godber
Michael Bantey	David Torralbo

COUNSEL

Thomas C. Camp, Q.C.

For Complete List of Firm Personnel, See General Section

For full biographical listings, see the Martindale-Hubbell Law Directory

MENDELSOHN ROSENTZVEIG SHACTER (AV)

1000 Sherbrooke Street West, 27th Floor, H3A 3G4
Telephone: 514-987-5000
Telex: 05-27284 Colorlaw
Telecopier: 514-987-1213
Email: mrs@mrslaw.com *URL:* http://www.mrslaw.com

(See Next Column)

PARTNERS

S. Leon Mendelsohn, Q.C. (1902-1996)	Ian R. Rudnikoff
	Marc I. Leiter
Leo Rosentzveig, Q.C.	L. B. Erdle
Manuel Shacter, Q.C.	Fredric L. Carsley
Jack C. Shayne	Frank Zylberberg
William Levitt	Jules Brossard
Arthur A. Garvis	David L. Rosentzveig
Edward E. Aronoff	Judie K. Jokinen
L. Michael Blumenstein	Gilles Seguin
Max Mendelsohn	Martin Desrosiers
Earl S. Cohen	Andrew Etcovitch
Michael Garonce	Alain Breault
Donald M. Devine	Jean Carrière
Richard S. Uditsky	Henri M. Bybelezer
Joel Weitzman	Louis Frédérick Côté

Sandra Abitan

ASSOCIATES

Carl M. Ravinsky	Céline Tessier
Catherine Muraz	Sophie Crevier
Francine Wiseman	Annick Joyal
Joelle Sebag	Francis Desmarais
Maria R. Battaglia	Nicolas J. Beugnot
Keyvan Nassiry	Jean-François Brière
Linda Schachter	Marc-Antoine Deschamps
Emmanuelle Saucier	Philipp F. Duffy
Arnold Cohen	Fred Purkey
Aaron Makovka	Martin Sills
Michel Rochefort	David Tardif-Latourelle

For full biographical listings, see the Martindale-Hubbell Law Directory

CANADA SASKATCHEWAN

*REGINA,** Regina Jud. Centre

MACPHERSON LESLIE & TYERMAN (AV)

1500-1874 Scarth Street, S4P 4E9
Telephone: 306-347-8000
Telecopier: 306-352-5250
Email: mltreg@mlt.com
Saskatoon, Saskatchewan Office: 1500-410 22nd Street East, S7K 5T6.
Telephone: 306-975-7100.
Telecopier: 306-975-7145.

MEMBERS OF FIRM

Robert B. Pletch, Q.C.	Douglas A. Ballou
Danny R. Anderson (Resident, Saskatoon Office)	Randy U. Brunet
	Scott A. Exner

ASSOCIATES

Barclay A. Laughland (Resident, Saskatoon Office)	Aaron D. Runge
	Bradley N. Vance

For Complete List of Firm Personnel, See General Section

For full biographical listings, see the Martindale-Hubbell Law Directory

CHINA

HONG KONG,

American Lawyers In Hong Kong

MILBANK, TWEED, HADLEY & MCCLOY LLP

3007 Alexandra House, 16 Chater Road, Hong Kong
Telephone: 852-2971-4888
Fax: 852-2840-0792, 852-2845-9046
Email: postmaster@milbank.com *URL:* http://www.milbank.com
New York, New York Office: 1 Chase Manhattan Plaza, 10005-1413.
Telephone: 212-530-5000.
Fax: 212- 530-5219.
Midtown Office: 375 Park Avenue, Suite 3601, 10152.
Telephone: 212-530-5800.
Fax: 212-530-0158.
Los Angeles, California Office: 601 South Figueroa Street, 90017.
Telephone: 213-892-4000.
Fax: 213-629-5063.
Washington, D.C. Office: International Square Building, Suite 1100, 1825 Eye Street, N.W., 20006.
Telephone: 202-835-7500.
Fax: 202-835-7586.
Tokyo, Japan Office: Fukoku Seimei Building, 2-2, Uchisaiwai-cho 2-Chome, Chiyoda-ku, Tokyo 100-0011, Japan.
Telephone: 81-3-3504-1050.
Fax: 81-3-3595-2790, 81-3-3595-2840.

(See Next Column)

MILBANK, TWEED, HADLEY & MCCLOY LLP—*Continued*

London, England Office: Dashwood House, 69 Old Broad Street, London, EC2M 1QS.
Telephone: 44-207-448-3000.
Fax: 44-207-448-3029.
Singapore Office: 14-00 Caltex House, 30 Raffles Place, 048622.
Telephone: 65-428-2400.
Fax: 65-428-2500.
Moscow, Russia Office: 24/27 Sadovaya-Samotyochnaya, Moscow, 103051.
Telephone: 7-501-258-5015.
Fax: 7-501-258-5014.

PARTNERS

Caroline G. Angoorly (Not admitted in China)
Anthony Root (Not admitted in China)
Douglas A. Tanner (Not admitted in China)

ASSOCIATES

Jacqueline S. Leung (Not admitted in China)
Tracey L. Schell
Bing Song (Not admitted in China)
Desiree Woo (Not admitted in China)

(Not admitted to practice in Hong Kong courts)

For Complete List of Firm Personnel, See General Section

For full biographical listings, see the Martindale-Hubbell Law Directory

ENGLAND

*LONDON,**

American Lawyers In London

MILBANK, TWEED, HADLEY & MCCLOY LLP

Dashwood House, 69 Old Broad Street, London EC2M 1QS
Telephone: 44-207-448-3000
Fax: 44-207-448-3029
Email: postmaster@milbank.com *URL:* http://www.milbank.com
Offices of an Affiliated Partnership:
New York, New York Office: 1 Chase Manhattan Plaza, 10005-1413.
Telephone: 212-530-5000.
Fax: 212- 530-5219.
Midtown Office: 375 Park Avenue, Suite 3601, 10152.
Telephone: 212-530-5800.
Fax: 212-530-0158.
Los Angeles, California Office: 601 South Figueroa Street, 90017.
Telephone: 213-892-4000.
Fax: 213-629-5063.
Washington, D.C. Office: International Square Building, Suite 1100, 1825 Eye Street, N.W., 20006.
Telephone: 202-835-7500.
Fax: 202-835-7586.
Tokyo, Japan Office: Fukoku Seimei Building, 2-2, Uchisaiwai-cho 2-chome, Chiyoda-ku, Tokyo 100-0011, Japan.
Telephone: 81-3-3504-1050.
Fax: 81-3-3595-2790; 81-3-3595-2840.
Hong Kong Office: 3007 Alexandra House, 16 Chater Road.
Telephone: 852-2971-4888.
Fax: 852-2840-0792; 852-2845-9046.
Singapore Office: 14-00 Caltex House, 30 Raffles Place, 048622.
Telephone: 65-428-2400.
Fax: 65-428-2500.
Moscow, Russia Office: 24/27 Sadovaya-Samotyochnaya, Moscow, 103051.
Telephone: 7-501-258-5015.
Fax: 7-501-258-5014.

PARTNER

Thomas B. Siebens (Not admitted in England)

(Not admitted to practice in English courts)

For Complete List of Firm Personnel, See General Section

For full biographical listings, see the Martindale-Hubbell Law Directory

MEXICO

GARZA GARCIA, NUEVO LEON,

American Lawyers in Garza Garcia

THOMPSON & KNIGHT L.L.P.

(Attorneys and Counselors)
Edificio Losoles PD-4, Av. Lázaro Cárdenas No. 2400 PTE San Pedro Garza Garcia, Garza Garcia, Nuevo Leon 66220
Telephone: (52-8) 363-0096
Telecopy: (52-8) 363-3067
URL: http://www.tklaw.com
Dallas, Texas Office: 1700 Pacific Avenue, Suite 3300, 75201.
Telephone: 214-969-1700.
Telecopy: 214-969-1751.
Telex: 732298.
Austin, Texas Office: 1200 San Jacinto Center, 98 San Jacinto Boulevard, 78701.
Telephone: 512-469-6100.
Telecopy: 512-469-6180.
Fort Worth, Texas Office: 801 Cherry Street, Suite 1600, 76102.
Telephone: 817-347-1700.
Telecopy: 817-347-1799.
Houston, Texas Office: Thompson Knight Brown Parker & Leahy L.L.P., 1200 Smith Street, Suite 3600.
Telephone: 713-654-8111.
Telecopier: 713-654-1871.

PARTNER

Michael C. Titens

For Complete List of Firm Personnel, See General Section

For full biographical listings, see the Martindale-Hubbell Law Directory

SPORTS AND ENTERTAINMENT LAW

MINNESOTA

*MINNEAPOLIS,** Hennepin Co.

ABDO AND ABDO, P.A. (AV)

710 Northstar West 625 Marquette Avenue, 55402
Telephone: 612-333-1526
Fax: 612-342-2608
Email: abdoabdo@aol.com *URL:* http://www.abdo.com.br

Robert P. Abdo	Daniel M. Satorius
Kenneth J. Abdo	Timothy C. Matson

Representative Client: Twin Cities Public Television; Independent Feature Project/North; Independent Television Services; Semisonic; Free Spirit Publishing; Jonny Lang; The Blenders; NPG's Records; Estate of Tiny Tim; Warner/Chappell Music, Inc.

For Complete List of Firm Personnel, See General Section

For full biographical listings, see the Martindale-Hubbell Law Directory

NEVADA

STATELINE, Douglas Co.

JOHN MASON PARTNERS, LTD. (AV)

195 U.S. Highway 50 Suite 200, 89449
Telephone: 775-588-6963
Fax: 775-588-8519
Mailing Address: P.O. Box 12337, Zephyr Cove, NV, 89448
Nashville, Tennessee Office: 1107 17th Avenue, South. 37212.
Telephone: 615-320-5150.
Facsimile: 615-320-5410.

John E. Mason	Joel A. Cherry (Not admitted in NV)
Deborah Lanora Wagnon (Not admitted in NV)	

For full biographical listings, see the Martindale-Hubbell Law Directory

NEW JERSEY

*NEWARK,** Essex Co.

SILLS CUMMIS RADIN TISCHMAN EPSTEIN & GROSS, A PROFESSIONAL CORPORATION (AV)

One Riverfront Plaza, 07102-5400
Telephone: 973-643-7000
Fax: 973-643-6500
Telex: 820630 Sillsbeck Nwk
Email: sillsmail@sillscummis.com *URL:* http://www.sillscummis.com
Atlantic City, New Jersey Office: 17 Gordon's Alley.
Telephone: 609-344-2800.
New York, N.Y. Office: 712 Fifth Avenue.
Telephone: 212-643-7000.
Washington, D.C. Office: 1800 K Street, N.W.
Telephone: 202-296-4750.

MEMBERS OF FIRM

Clive S. Cummis	James D. Toll (Resident at Atlantic City, N.J. Office)
Noah Bronkesh	Steven R. Kamen
Kenneth F. Oettle	

Eric D. Mann (Resident at Atlantic City, N.J. Office)	Paul P. Josephson

Representative Clients: Park Place Entertainment Corp.; Resorts International Hotel, Inc.; Claridge Hotel & Casino; Autotote Corp.

For Complete List of Firm Personnel, See General Section

For full biographical listings, see the Martindale-Hubbell Law Directory

WOODBRIDGE, Middlesex Co.

WILENTZ, GOLDMAN & SPITZER, A PROFESSIONAL CORPORATION (AV)

90 Woodbridge Center Drive Suite 900, Box 10, 07095
Telephone: 732-636-8000
Telecopier: 732-855-6117
URL: http://www.newjerseylaw.com
Eatontown, New Jersey Office: Meridian Center I, Two Industrial Way West, 07724.
Telephone: 732-542-4500.
Telecopier: 732-493-8387.
New York, New York Office: Wall Street Plaza, 88 Pine Street, 9th Floor, 10005.
Telephone: 212-267-3091.
Telecopier: 212-267-3828.

Brian J. Molloy	Jay J. Ziznewski
Roy H. Tanzman	Angelo J. Cifaldi

David P. Pepe

Representative Clients: Amerada Hess Corp.; Chevron, U.S.A.; Co-Steel Raritan; Cumberland Farms, Inc.; Middlesex County Utilities Authority; New Jersey Automobile Dealers Assn.; The Rouse Co.

For Complete List of Firm Personnel, See General Section

For full biographical listings, see the Martindale-Hubbell Law Directory

NEW YORK

*NEW YORK,** New York Co.

GOLDSTEIN & MORRIS, LLP (AV)

570 Lexington Avenue, 34th Floor, 10022
Telephone: 212-605-0918
Fax: 212-605-0919

Mark L. Goldstein	Francine J. Morris

ASSOCIATE

Andrea H. Stempel

For full biographical listings, see the Martindale-Hubbell Law Directory

MCGUIRE, KEHL & NEALON, LLP (AV)

230 Park Avenue, Suite 2830, 10169
Telephone: 212-557-0040
Telecopier: 212-953-0768

MEMBERS OF FIRM

Harold F. McGuire, Jr.	Jeffrey A. Kehl

Arthur V. Nealon

OF COUNSEL

Andrea Green	Shelley Sanders Kehl
Marion C. Katzive	Terri E. Simon

For full biographical listings, see the Martindale-Hubbell Law Directory

WHITE, FLEISCHNER & FINO (AV)

140 Broadway, 10005
Telephone: 212-487-9700
Telecopier: 212-487-9777
Email: infor@wff-law.com
Red Bank, New Jersey Office: 272 Broad Street.
Telephone: 732-530-7787.
Telecopier: 732-530-8552.

MEMBER OF FIRM

Allan P. White

Representative Clients: Markel Insurance Company; Lloyd's Syndicates.

For Complete List of Firm Personnel, See General Section

For full biographical listings, see the Martindale-Hubbell Law Directory

PENNSYLVANIA

*PHILADELPHIA,** Philadelphia Co.

REMICK MARTONE, A PROFESSIONAL CORPORATION (AV)

1608 Walnut Street, Suite 703, 19103
Telephone: 215-772-3010
Fax: 215-772-3017
URL: http://remick-martone.com
Hammonton, New Jersey Office: P.O. Box 1172. 110 Route 206, 08037.
Telephone: 609-567-4500.
Fax: 609-567-7524.

Lloyd Zane Remick
Lauren Remick Martone
Margaret Loud Charendoff
Marjorie Singer Ochroch
Jacqueline Borock
Ernest De Stefano
Gregory M. Pedicin (Not admitted in PA)
Charles Sovel
Paul A. Leodori

LEGAL SUPPORT PERSONNEL

Amanda Rae Gross

For full biographical listings, see the Martindale-Hubbell Law Directory

TENNESSEE

*NASHVILLE,** Davidson Co.

STEWART, ESTES & DONNELL (AV)

SunTrust Financial Center, 424 Church Street Suite 1401, 37219
Telephone: 615-244-6538
Telecopier: 615-256-8386

MEMBERS OF FIRM

H. Francis Stewart (1915-1991)
Robert L. (Larry) Estes
Thomas M. Donnell, Jr.
Philip M. Kirkpatrick
Stephen K. Heard
M. Reid Estes, Jr.
Jerry W. Carnes
Martin Douglas Holmes
Peter F. Klett
W. Stuart Scott
Jeffrey L. Peterson

ASSOCIATES

John Edward Anderson
Jeffrey M. Beemer
Jennifer A. Lawrence
Leah K. Shearin
Jennifer L. Novak
Andrew C. Matteson

For full biographical listings, see the Martindale-Hubbell Law Directory

TEXAS

*DALLAS,** Dallas Co.

HUGHES & LUCE, L.L.P. (AV)

A Registered Limited Liability Partnership including Professional Corporations
1717 Main Street, Suite 2800, 75201
Telephone: 214-939-5500
Fax: 214-939-6100; 214-939-5849
Email: H&L@hughesluce.com *URL:* http://www.hughesluce.com
Austin, Texas Office: 111 Congress, Suite 900.
Telephone: 512-482-6800.
Fax: 512-482-6859.
Houston, Texas Office: 1600 Smith Street, Suite 3550.
Telephone: 713-754-5200.
Fax: 713-754-5270.

MEMBERS OF FIRM

Kim Juanita Askew
Alan J. Bogdanow
Craig W. Budner
Allan B. Diamond
Jeff W. Dorrill
Scott C. Drablos
Deborah J. Eichner
Zammurad Hyatt Feroze
David Lee Fields
William B. Finkelstein
Stephen G. Gleboff
David N. Guedry
Kenneth G. Hawari
Kathryn G. Henkel
Daniel K. Hennessy
Glen J. Hettinger
John E. Howell
Vester T. Hughes, Jr.
Clifton T. Hutchinson
MaryAnn Joerres
Darrell E. Jordan
David H. Judson
David C. Kent
Jeffrey C. King
Paul M. Koning
David G. Luther, Jr.
James D. McCarthy
William A. McCormack
R. Matthew Molash
James A. Moomaw
Robert H. Mow, Jr. (P.C.)
Ross Clayton Mulford
Dudley W. Murrey
Gary G. Null
Cynthia Morgan Ohlenforst
Walter G. Pettey, III
Bobby M. Rubarts
Mark K. Sales
James W. Sargent
Dwight A. Shupe

(See Next Column)

MEMBERS OF FIRM (Continued)

David L. Sinak
Theodore Stevenson, III
Karen K. Suhre
J. Gregory Taylor
Elizabeth R. Turner
David Weitman

ASSOCIATES

James H. Billingsley
Julie Edwards Blend
James E. Cahill, III
Joseph M. Cox
Robert B. Hale
James W. Hryekewicz
Laura M. Kalesnik
Bart Sloan
Anthony Gorham Soards

OF COUNSEL

Paul A. Berry
Matthew C. Wood

For Complete List of Firm Personnel, See General Section

For full biographical listings, see the Martindale-Hubbell Law Directory

VIRGINIA

ALEXANDRIA, (Independent City)

CARTER & COLEMAN (AV)

602 Cameron Street, 22314
Telephone: 703-739-4200
Fax: 703-739-4210
Email: rcarter@cartercoleman.com *URL:* http://www.lawyers.com/carter&coleman
Washington, D.C. Office: 900 Seventeenth Street, N.W., Suite 900, 20006.
Telephone: 202-326-8600.
Fax: 202-289-0184.

Richard D. Carter
Douglas M. Coleman
David C. Simmons (Not admitted in VA)
James M. Loots (Not admitted in VA)

ASSOCIATES

Juliane C. Miller
Mercedes Madole (Not admitted in VA)
Paul A. Daniels

For full biographical listings, see the Martindale-Hubbell Law Directory

CANADA
NEWFOUNDLAND

*ST. JOHN'S,**

MCINNES COOPER (AV)

Barristers, Solicitors & Trade Mark Agents
Baine Johnston Centre, 5th Floor, 10 Fort William Place, P.O. Box 5939, A1C 5X4
Telephone: 709-722-8735
Telecopier: 709-722-1763
Email: mcrsj@mcrlaw.com *URL:* http://www.mcrlaw.com
Halifax, Nova Scotia Office: Summit Place, 1601 Lower Water Street, P.O. Box 730, B3J 2V1.
Telephone: 902-425-6500.
Fax: 902-425-6350. Email: mcrhfx@mcrlaw.com.
Moncton, New Brunswick Office: Place Moncton Place, 655 Main Street, P.O. Box 1368, E1C 8T6.
Telephone: 506-857-8970.
Fax: 506-857-4095. Email: mcrmctn@mcrlaw.com.
Charlottetown, Prince Edward Island Office: BDC Place, Suite 620, 119 Kent Street, C1A 1N3.
Telephone: 902-368-8473.
Fax: 902-368-8346. Email: mcrpei@mcrlaw.com.
Fredericton, New Brunswick Office: Suite 600, 570 Queen Street, P.O. Box 610.
Telephone: 506-458-8572.
Fax: 506-458-9903. Email: mcrfton@mcrlaw.com.

PARTNER

Deborah L. J. Hutchings

For Complete List of Firm Personnel, See General Section

For full biographical listings, see the Martindale-Hubbell Law Directory

CANADA
NOVA SCOTIA

*HALIFAX,** Regional Munic. of Halifax

McInnes Cooper (AV)

Barristers, Solicitors & Trade Mark Agents
Summit Place, 1601 Lower Water Street, P.O. Box 730, B3J 2V1
Telephone: 902-425-6500
Fax: 902-425-6350
Email: mcrhfx@mcrlaw.com *URL:* http://www.mcrlaw.com
St. John's, Newfoundland Office: Baine Johnston Centre, 5th Floor, 10 Fort William Place, P.O. Box 5939, A1C 5X4.
Telephone: 709-722-8735.
Telecopier: 709-722-1763. Email: mcrsj@mcrlaw.com.
Moncton, New Brunswick Office: Place Moncton Place, 655 Main Street, P.O. Box 1368, E1C 8T6.
Telephone: 506-857-8970.
Fax: 506-857-4095. Email: mcrmctn@mcrlaw.com.
Charlottetown, Prince Edward Island Office: BDC Place, Suite 620, 119 Kent Street, C1A 1N3.
Telephone: 902-368-8473.
Fax: 902-368-8346. Email: mcrpei@mcrlaw.com.
Fredericton, New Brunswick Office: Suite 600, 570 Queen Street, P.O. Box 610.
Telephone: 506-458-8572.
Fax: 506-458-9903. Email: mcrfton@mcrlaw.com.

PARTNER

G. Grant Machum

For Complete List of Firm Personnel, See General Section

For full biographical listings, see the Martindale-Hubbell Law Directory

CANADA
QUEBEC

*MONTREAL,** Montreal Dist.

Woods & Partners (AV)

2000 McGill College Avenue, Suite 1100, H3A 3H3
Telephone: 514-982-4545
Telecopier: 514-284-2046
Email: general@woods.qc.ca

MEMBERS OF FIRM

James A. Woods
Christian Immer
Julien Cools-Lartigue
Nathalie Chalifour
Christopher Lund Richter
Annie Galarneau
Sébastien Richemont
Kathleen Beaugé
Marjorie Delagrave

For full biographical listings, see the Martindale-Hubbell Law Directory

TAX LAW

MINNESOTA

*FERGUS FALLS,** Otter Tail Co.

David F. Lundeen (AV)

107 Court Street, 56537
Telephone: 218-736-4866
FAX: 218-736-7747
Email: dlundlaw@prtel.com

For full biographical listings, see the Martindale-Hubbell Law Directory

*HASTINGS,** Dakota Co.

Langlais & Schumacher, P.A. (AV)

Suite 13, 1303 South Frontage Road, 55033
Telephone: 651-438-3789
Fax: 651-438-3936
Email: langlais@minn.net *URL:* http://www.lawyers.com/langlais&schumacher

Richard J. Langlais
Jean M. Langlais
Leo F. Schumacher
Susan T. Steveken
Christopher W. Brownell

For full biographical listings, see the Martindale-Hubbell Law Directory

*MINNEAPOLIS,** Hennepin Co.

Martin & Associates, P.A. (AV)

1650 West 82nd Street, Suite 1460, 55431
Telephone: 612-885-5665
Fax: 612-885-5664
Email: mail@martinandassociates.com

Judith Martin Ventres

Michael J. Zitta
Richard William Van Sickle

For full biographical listings, see the Martindale-Hubbell Law Directory

*ST. PAUL,** Ramsey Co.

John Murray & Associates, Ltd. (AV)

Suite 920 Piper Jaffray Plaza, 444 Cedar Street, 55101
Telephone: 651-227-8820
Telecopier: 651-223-5332
Email: jmurray@abanet.org

John A. Murray

Reference: American National (Firstar) Bank, St. Paul.

For full biographical listings, see the Martindale-Hubbell Law Directory

MISSISSIPPI

*JACKSON,** Hinds Co.

Alston & Jones (AV)

A Professional Limited Liability Company
121 North State Street, P.O. Drawer 1532, 39215-1532
Telephone: 601-948-6882
Fax: 601-948-6902
Email: ARVS@Teclink.net

MEMBERS OF FIRM

Alex A. Alston, Jr.
Richard L. Jones
Sheldon G. Alston

OF COUNSEL

Beth C. Clay
Rowan H. Taylor

Counsel for: E.I. du Pont de Nemours Co.; Prudential Bache-Securities; Mississippi Baptist Foundation; Jostens, Inc.; Trustmark National Bank; Merchants & Farmers Bank; Georgia-Pacific Corp.; Dean Witter Reynolds, Inc.; Transcontinental Gas Pipeline Corp.; Hibernia National Bank.

For full biographical listings, see the Martindale-Hubbell Law Directory

Baker, Donelson, Bearman & Caldwell (AV)

Suite 500, 700 North State Street, 39202
Telephone: 601-351-2400
Telecopier: 601-351-2424
Email: info@bdbc.com *URL:* http://www.bakerdonelson.com
Memphis, Tennessee Office: 20th Floor, First Tennessee Building, 165 Madison, 38103.
Telephone: 901-526-2000.
Telecopier: 901-577-2303.
Nashville, Tennessee Office: 1700 Nashville City Center, 511 Union Street, 37219.
Telephone: 615-726-5600.
Telecopier: 615-726-0464.
Chattanooga, Tennessee Office: 1800 Republic Centre, 633 Chestnut Street, 37450-1800.
Telephone: 423-756-2010.
Telecopier: 423-756-3447.
Knoxville, Tennessee Office: 2200 Riverview Tower, 900 South Gay Street, 37901.
Telephone: 423-549-7000.
Telecopier: 423-525-8569.
Johnson City, Tennessee Office: SunTrust Bank Building, 207 Mockingbird Lane, P.O. Box 3038, 37602.
Telephone: 423-928-0181.
Telecopier: 423-928-5694; 423-928-3654; Kingsport: 423-246-6191.
Huntsville, Tennessee Office: 3 Courthouse Square, 37756.
Telephone: 423-663-2321.
Telecopier: 423-663-2111.
Washington, D.C. Office: Market Square, 801 Pennsylvania Avenue, N.W., 20004.
Telephone: 202-508-3400.
Telecopier: 202-508-3402.

MANAGING PARTNER

James K. Dossett, Jr.

PARTNER

William S. Painter

ASSOCIATES

Stacy E. Thomas
Jody Brian Martin
Charles W. Ferguson

OF COUNSEL

John B. Beard

For Complete List of Firm Personnel, See General Section

For full biographical listings, see the Martindale-Hubbell Law Directory

Copeland Cook Taylor & Bush, A Professional Association (AV)

200 Concourse, Suite 200, 1062 Highland Colony Parkway, P.O. Box 2132, 39225-2132
Telephone: 601-856-7200
Facsimile: 601-856-7626
Email: mail@cctb.com *URL:* http://www.cctb.com
Ridgeland, Mississippi Office: Post Office Box 6020, 39158.
Telephone: 601-856-7200.
Facsimile: 601-856-7626.

Charles G. Copeland
Thomas A. Cook
Glenn Gates Taylor
C. Glen Bush
Thomas C. Gerity
James T. Knight
James R. Moore, Jr.
J. Tucker Mitchell
Robert P. Thompson
Thomas R. Hudson
R. Nash Neyland
Michael W. Baxter
C. Ted Sanderson, Jr.
Monte L. Barton, Jr.
W. Shan Thompson
C. Dale Shearer
Robert C. Richardson
Lee Howell, III
John M. Breland
Jefferson P.W. Skelton
Patricia H. Cottingham
Samuel S. Goza
Amanda L. Baham
Samuel O. Morris, IV
Michelle C. Partridge
John E. Gough, Jr.
Victor Donald Hunt
Donald J. Blackwood, Jr.
Rhonda Lea McCullough

OF COUNSEL

James P. Knight, Jr.
Robert L. Goza

For full biographical listings, see the Martindale-Hubbell Law Directory

Watkins & Eager (AV)

A Professional Limited Liability Company
Suite 300 The Emporium Building, 400 East Capitol Street, P.O. Box 650, 39205
Telephone: 601-948-6470
Facsimile: 601-354-3623

MEMBERS OF FIRM

Jamie G. Houston, III
Frank J. Hammond, III

(See Next Column)

WATKINS & EAGER, *Jackson—Continued*

ASSOCIATES

Joe D. Nosef, III
Jesse M. Harrington

Representative Clients: Chevron U.S.A. Inc.; Shell Oil Co.; Trustmark National Bank; Kerr-McGee Chemical Corp.; The Black & Decker Corp.; Blossman Gas, Inc.; Pavco Industries, Inc.; Freide Goldman International, Inc.; Merchants & Marine Bank; Millsaps College.

For Complete List of Firm Personnel, See General Section

For full biographical listings, see the Martindale-Hubbell Law Directory

MISSOURI

KANSAS CITY, Jackson, Clay, Platte & Cass Cos.

A. GLENN SOWDERS, JR. (AV)

701 Plaza Center Building, 800 West 47th Street, 64112
Telephone: 816-531-6163
Fax: 816-753-6965
Email: agsowders@worldnet.att.net

References: Country Club Bank; Commerce Bank-Plaza.

For full biographical listings, see the Martindale-Hubbell Law Directory

SWANSON MIDGLEY, LLC (AV)

Crown Center, 2420 Pershing Road, Suite 400, 64108
Telephone: 816-842-6100
Fax: 816-842-0013
Email: mail@swansonmidgley.com *URL:* http://www.swansonmidgley.com
Overland Park, Kansas Office: Commerce Plaza I, 7th Floor, 7300 W. 110th Street.
Telephone: 913-317-2717.
FAX: 913-317-1505.

Robert R. Bartunek
George H. Gangwere, Jr.
Daniel V. Hiatt
Rodney V. Hipp

Counsel For: National Collegiate Athletic Assn.; Danka Business Systems; Physicians Reference Laboratory; Right Management Consultants; BSC Holding, Inc.; Lee Complete Vending; Taylor Cable Products.

For Complete List of Firm Personnel, See General Section

For full biographical listings, see the Martindale-Hubbell Law Directory

ST. LOUIS, (Independent City)

ARMSTRONG TEASDALE LLP (AV)

A Partnership including Professional Corporations
One Metropolitan Square, 63102-2740
Telephone: 314-621-5070
Facsimile: 314-621-5065
Twx: 910 761-2246
Cable: ATKV LAW
Email: armstrongteasdale@armstrongteasdale.com *URL:* http://www.armstrongteasdale.com
Kansas City, Missouri Office: 2345 Grand Boulevard, Suite 2000, 64108.
Telephone: 816-221-3420.
Facsimile: 816-221-0786.
Jefferson City, Missouri Office: 3405 W. Truman Blvd., Suite 210, 65109.
Telephone: 573-636-8394.
Washington, D.C. Office: 1747 Pennsylvania Avenue, N.W., Suite 300, 20006.
Telephone: 202-347-0259.
Belleville, Illinois Office: 23 South First Street, 62220.
Telephone: 618-397-4411.
Olathe, Kansas Office: 100 East Park, 66061.
Telephone: 913-345-0706.
Shanghai, China Office: A-T International Consultants, LLC, Suite 310, No. 12 Zhongshan Road (E1), Shanghai 200002 P.R.C.
Telephone: 86-21-6326-7001.
Facsimile: 86-21-6326-0626.

MEMBERS OF FIRM

John R. Barsanti, Jr., (P.C.)
Peter L. Clark (P.C.)
Scott Hunt
Robert Lewis Jackson (P.C.)
Philip G. Louis, Jr.
Larry M. Sewell (P.C.)

ASSOCIATES

Stephen C. Hartnett
Benjamin A. Trujillo

OF COUNSEL

Frederick O. Hanser (P.C.)

Representative Clients: ESCO Electronics; Clark Refining & Marketing; Manna Pro Corporation; Reliable Life Insurance Co.; Spartech Corporation.

For Complete List of Firm Personnel, See General Section

For full biographical listings, see the Martindale-Hubbell Law Directory

DANKENBRING GREIMAN OSTERHOLT & HOFFMANN, P.C. (AV)

Clayton Centre, Fifth Floor, 120 S. Central Avenue, 63105
Telephone: 314-863-7733
Fax: 314-862-4656
URL: http://www.dgohlaw.com

James R. Dankenbring
Gerald Phillip Greiman
Francis E. Pennington, III

James R. Loranger

For full biographical listings, see the Martindale-Hubbell Law Directory

THE KOHN PARTNERSHIP, L.P. (AV)

7820 Maryland Avenue, 63105
Telephone: 314-721-8888
Fax: 314-721-6609
Tucson, Arizona Office: 1200 North El Dorado Place, Suite H-810, 85715.
Telephone: 520-721-4921.
Fax: 520-722-5767.

Michael E. Kohn
Sidney Y. Kohn (Resident, Tucson, Arizona Office)
Thomas C. Piccioli (Not admitted in MO)

Jeff D. Figge

OF COUNSEL

Catherine Kriegshauser Kohn

For full biographical listings, see the Martindale-Hubbell Law Directory

KOHN, SHANDS, ELBERT, GIANOULAKIS & GILJUM, LLP (AV)

24th Floor, One Mercantile Center, 63101
Telephone: 314-241-3963
Telecopier: 314-241-2509
Email: attys@ksegg.com

Joseph P. Giljum

For full biographical listings, see the Martindale-Hubbell Law Directory

LEWIS, RICE & FINGERSH (AV)

A Limited Liability Company
500 North Broadway, Suite 2000, 63102-2147
Telephone: 314-444-7600
Telecopier: 314-241-6056
URL: http://www.lrf.com
Belleville, Illinois Office: 325 South High Street.
Telephone: 618-234-8636.
Leawood, Kansas Office: Suite 375, 8900 State Line Road.
Telephone: 913-381-8898.
Creve Coeur, Missouri Office: 700 Office Parkway, Suite 15.
Telephone: 314-569-2262.
Kansas City, Missouri Office: 1010 Walnut, Suite 500.
Telephone: 816-421-2500.
Washington, Missouri Office: 216 West Main, P.O. Box 1040.
Telephone: 636-239-7747.

RESIDENT MEMBERS

Henry H. Stern, Jr.
Bernard N. Frank
Lawrence H. Weltman
Robert N. Kahn
Lori W. Jones

For Complete List of Firm Personnel, See General Section

For full biographical listings, see the Martindale-Hubbell Law Directory

LOWENHAUPT & CHASNOFF, L.L.C. (AV)

10 South Broadway, Suite 600, 63102-1733
Telephone: 314-241-5950
Facsimile: 314-436-2667

Charles A. Lowenhaupt

For Complete List of Firm Personnel, See General Section

For full biographical listings, see the Martindale-Hubbell Law Directory

ROSENBLUM, GOLDENHERSH, SILVERSTEIN & ZAFFT, P.C. (AV)

Fourth Floor, 7733 Forsyth Boulevard, 63105
Telephone: 314-726-6868
Telecopier: 314-726-6786
Belleville, Illinois Office: 2 Park Place Professional Centre, 62221.
Telephone: 618-234-9900.
Columbia, Missouri Office: 3201 South Providence, Suite 101, 65205-4000.
Telephone: 573-441-8686.

Stanley M. Rosenblum
Robert S. Goldenhersh
Merle L. Silverstein
Gene M. Zafft
Carl C. Lang
Richard S. Bender
Michael A. Markenson
David V. Capes

(See Next Column)

ROSENBLUM, GOLDENHERSH, SILVERSTEIN & ZAFFT P.C.—*Continued*

Mark E. Goodman
Jay A. Nathanson
Richard Greenberg
Bennett S. Keller
Leonard D. Vines
Roger M. Herman
Thomas A. Duda
Paul G. Klug
Ira L. Blank
Ellen Levy Siwak
Joshua M. Schindler
Sanford J. Boxerman
Carl R. Desenberg
Scott H. Malin

Jeffrey Alan Cohen
Kristen L. Maly
Todd C. Brockmann
Marilyn Eichler Nathanson
Shelley H. Koren
Jared M. Minkoff

For full biographical listings, see the Martindale-Hubbell Law Directory

---

MONTANA

*BILLINGS,** Yellowstone Co.

BROWN LAW FIRM, P.C. (AV)

315 North 24th Street, P.O. Drawer 849, 59103-0849
Telephone: 406-248-2611
FAX: 406-248-3128
URL: http://www.brownfirm.com
Bozeman, Montana Office: 510 South 23rd Street.
Telephone: 406-587-8486.
Fax: 406-587-4524.

Angus B. Fulton
Timothy A. Filz

For Complete List of Firm Personnel, See General Section

For full biographical listings, see the Martindale-Hubbell Law Directory

CROWLEY, HAUGHEY, HANSON, TOOLE & DIETRICH, P.L.L.P. (AV)

500 Transwestern II, 490 North 31st Street, P.O. Box 2529, 59103
Telephone: 406-252-3441
Fax: 406-259-4159
Email: crowley@crowleylaw.com
Helena, Montana Office: IBM Building, 100 North Park Avenue, Suite 300, 59601.
Telephone: 406-449-4165.
Fax: 406-449-5149.
Kalispell, Montana Office: 431 1st Avenue West, 59901.
Telephone: 406-752-6644.
Fax: 406-752-5108.
Williston, North Dakota Office: 113 East Broadway, 58801.
Telephone: 701-572-2200.
Fax: 701-572-7072.

OF COUNSEL

John M. Dietrich
Myles J. Thomas

MEMBERS OF FIRM

David L. Johnson
Terry B. Cosgrove (Resident, Helena, Montana Office)
James P. Sites
Daniel N. McLean (Resident, Helena, Montana Office)
Robert G. Michelotti, Jr.
John R. Alexander
Eric K. Anderson
Scott M. Heard

Representative Clients: AT&T; Pacificorp; General Mills; Billings Clinic; United Grain Corporation; Deaconess Medical Center of Billings; Mid-Rivers Telephone Cooperative; United Parcel Service; Holly Sugar Corporation; MDM Broadcasting, Inc.

For Complete List of Firm Personnel, See General Section

For full biographical listings, see the Martindale-Hubbell Law Directory

*HELENA,** Lewis and Clark Co.

JOHN R. KLINE, P.C. (AV)

Arcade Building, Third Floor, 111 North Last Chance Gulch, P.O. Box 1705, 59624
Telephone: 406-442-8950
Fax: 406-442-9558

John R. Kline

*KALISPELL,** Flathead Co.

HASH & O'BRIEN, PLLP (AV)

Plaza West, 136 First Avenue, West, P.O. Box 1178, 59901
Telephone: 406-755-6919
Fax: 406-755-6911
Email: cmhash@digisys.net

(See Next Column)

MEMBERS OF FIRM

Charles L. Hash
Kenneth E. O'Brien
C. Mark Hash

General Counsel for: Glacier Bancorp, Inc; Glacier Bank, Eureka and Whitefish; First National Bank of Eureka; Vortex Fishing Systems.
Representative Clients: Western Surety Co.; Liberty Mutual Insurance Co.; Allstate Insurance Co.; Lincoln Electric Cooperative; Read Enterprises.
Reference: Glacier Bancorp, Inc.

For full biographical listings, see the Martindale-Hubbell Law Directory

---

NEBRASKA

*LINCOLN,** Lancaster Co.

CLINE, WILLIAMS, WRIGHT, JOHNSON & OLDFATHER (AV)

1900 U.S. Bank Building, 233 South 13th Street, 68508
Telephone: 402-474-6900
Fax: 402-474-5393
Email: postmaster@cline-law.com *URL:* http://www.cline-law.com
Omaha, Nebraska Office: Suite 720, One Pacific Place, 1125 South 103rd Street, 68124.
Telephone: 402-397-1700.
Fax: 402-397-1806.

ATTORNEYS

Allen L. Graves
Charles M. Pallesen, Jr.
Fredric H. Kauffman
Donald F. Burt
Alan E. Peterson
Stephen E. Gehring
Robert J. Routh
Kevin Colleran
L. Bruce Wright
James M. Bausch
Larry A. Holle
David R. Buntain
Stephen H. Nelsen
Michael C. Mueller
Lauren W. Wismer
Daniel R. Stogsdill
Scott D. Kelly
Terry R. Wittler
Pamela Hastings Carrier
Mark A. Christensen
Richard P. Garden, Jr.
Shawn D. Renner
John C. Miles
Mary Kay Frank
Thomas C. Huston
Sonya S. Ekart
Don R. Janssen
Susan Kubert Sapp
Kevin J. Schneider
Andrew D. Strotman
Jill Gossin Jensen
Rochelle A. Mullen
John L. Horan
Bryan S. Hatch
Steven C. Likes
Tracy A. Oldemeyer
Jolene M. Papa
Timothy G. Aschoff
Eric N. Bergquist
Janis J. Winterhof
Andrea Dylan Snowden

OF COUNSEL

Charles E. Wright
Richard P. Jeffries
Mary M. Campbell

RETIRED PARTNERS

Flavel A. Wright (Retired)
Warren C. Johnson (Retired)
Charles E. Oldfather (1927-1998)

Representative Clients: U.S. Bank National Association; University of Nebraska; Nebraska Medical Assn.; Saint Elizabeth Regional Medical Center; Media of Nebraska; Cargill Inc.; State Farm Insurance Cos.; Wal-Mart Stores, Inc.; Textron/Cushman; Isco, Inc.

For full biographical listings, see the Martindale-Hubbell Law Directory

*OMAHA,** Douglas Co.

DWYER, SMITH, GARDNER, LAZER, POHREN, ROGERS & FORREST (AV)

Suite 400, 8712 West Dodge Road, 68114
Telephone: 402-392-0101
Telefax: 402-392-1011
Email: dwyerlaw@dwyer-smith.com *URL:* http://www.dwyer-smith.com

MEMBERS OF FIRM

Robert V. Dwyer, Jr.
Paul J. Gardner
Bruce J. Goracke

Representative Clients: Nebraska Health System; The Community Hospital Association, McCook, Nebraska; Nebraska Hospital Association subsidiary Bio Electronics; Faith Regional Health Services, Norfolk, Nebraska; Western Nebraska Health Systems, Sidney, Nebraska.

For Complete List of Firm Personnel, See General Section

For full biographical listings, see the Martindale-Hubbell Law Directory

Omaha—Continued

Erickson & Sederstrom, P.C. (AV)

Regency Westpointe, 10330 Regency Parkway Drive, Suite 100, 68114-3761
Telephone: 402-397-2200
Fax: 402-390-7137
Lincoln, Nebraska Office: Suite 400, Cornhusker Plaza, 301 South 13th Street, 68508-2571.
Telephone: 402-476-1000.
Fax: 402-476-6167.

Samuel Earle Clark
William T. Foley
David C. Mussman

Representative Clients: Baker's Supermarkets; Bozell, Inc.; Hicks Construction Co., Inc.; Berkshire Hathaway, Inc.; Immanuel Medical Center; First Data Resources, Inc.; Lincoln General Hospital; Lincoln Electric System; Eli Lilly & Co.; Burkley Envelope Co.

For Complete List of Firm Personnel, See General Section

For full biographical listings, see the Martindale-Hubbell Law Directory

Fraser, Stryker, Vaughn, Meusey, Olson, Boyer & Bloch, P.C. (AV)

500 Energy Plaza, 409 South 17th Street, 68102
Telephone: 402-341-6000
Telecopier: 402-341-8290
Email: fraserstryker.com

Peter J. Vaughn
John K. Boyer
Kenneth W. Sharp

For Complete List of Firm Personnel, See General Section

For full biographical listings, see the Martindale-Hubbell Law Directory

Laughlin, Peterson & Lang (AV)

11306 Davenport Street, 68154
Telephone: 402-330-1900
Fax: 402-330-0936
Email: mlaugh43@aol.com

MEMBERS OF FIRM

Mark L. Laughlin
James E. Lang

Representative Clients: General Electric Capital Corp.; Dodge Land Co.; Security Mutual Life Insurance Co. of Lincoln, NE; Century Development Co.

For Complete List of Firm Personnel, See General Section

For full biographical listings, see the Martindale-Hubbell Law Directory

McGill, Gotsdiner, Workman & Lepp, P.C. (AV)

Suite 500 - First National Plaza, 11404 West Dodge Road, 68154
Telephone: 402-492-9200
Telecopier: 402-492-9222
Email: mgwl@mgwl.com

Stephen T. McGill (1932-1997)
Gary M. Gotsdiner

Representative Clients: Behlen Mfg. Co.; Bethesda Ministries; Lozier Corporation; Great Plains Communications, Inc.; Cryogenic Transportation, Inc.

For Complete List of Firm Personnel, See General Section

For full biographical listings, see the Martindale-Hubbell Law Directory

McGrath, North, Mullin & Kratz, P.C. (AV)

Suite 1400, One Central Park Plaza, 68102
Telephone: 402-341-3070
Fax: 402-341-0216

John E. North
David L. Hefflinger
Jeffrey J. Pirruccello
Randal M. Limbeck
James D. Wegner
Nicholas K. Niemann
Daniel C. Pape
Michael J. Weaver, Jr.
Thomas J. Kelley
Jennifer J. Sellers
Vicki L. Colwell

General Counsel for: ConAgra, Inc.; InaCom Corp.; Omaha Airport Authority; Physicians Mutual Insurance Co.; Supertel Hospitality, Inc.; Valmont Industries, Inc.
Representative Clients: Clarkson Hospital; Omaha Chamber of Commerce.
Insurance Clients: American Family Insurance Group; Blue Cross-Blue Shield of Nebraska.

For Complete List of Firm Personnel, See General Section

For full biographical listings, see the Martindale-Hubbell Law Directory

NEVADA

*LAS VEGAS,** Clark Co.

Jerome L. Blut Chartered (AV)

Third Floor, 302 East Carson Avenue, 89101
Telephone: 702-382-8840
Fax: 702-382-4800
Email: blutlaw@aol.com *URL:* http://www.lawyers.com/blutlaw

Jerome L. Blut

References: Wells Fargo Bank of Nevada; Nevada State Bank.

For full biographical listings, see the Martindale-Hubbell Law Directory

Edwards & Winterton, Chtd. (AV)

401 North Buffalo Drive, Suite 200, 89128
Telephone: 702-363-0317
Telecopier: 702-363-1630
Email: EOWW.LAW@worldnet.att.net

George T. Morse, III (1945-1996)
Douglas M. Edwards
David J. Winterton

Nazario J. Jureidini
Robert B. Gerard
Thomas E. Trojan
Chris A. Beecroft, Jr.

OF COUNSEL

Nicholas A. Boylan (Not admitted in NV)

For full biographical listings, see the Martindale-Hubbell Law Directory

Hale Lane Peek Dennison Howard and Anderson (AV)

Nevada Financial Center, 2300 West Sahara Avenue, Eighth Floor, Box 8, 89102
Telephone: 702-222-2500
Fax: 702-365-6940
Email: info@halelane.com
Reno, Nevada Office: 100 West Liberty Street, Tenth Floor, P.O. Box 3237.
Telephone: 775-327-3000.
Telefax: 775-786-6179.
Carson City, Nevada Office: 777 East William Street, Suite 200, P.O. Box 2620.
Telephone: 775-684-6000.
Telefax: 775-684-6001.

MEMBERS OF FIRM

Marilyn L. Skender (Resident, Reno, Nevada)
Robert C. Anderson (Resident, Reno, Nevada)
Matthew E. Woodhead

Representative Clients: Marnell Corrao Construction; Cashman Equipment Company; Juliett Corporation; Southwest Systems Corporation; Scolaris Warehouse Markets, Inc.

For Complete List of Firm Personnel, See General Section

For full biographical listings, see the Martindale-Hubbell Law Directory

McDonald Carano Wilson McCune Bergin Frankovich & Hicks LLP (AV)

Suite 1000, 2300 West Sahara Avenue, 89102
Telephone: 702-873-4100
Telecopier: 702-873-9966
URL: http://www.mcdonaldcarano.com
Reno, Nevada Office: 241 Ridge Street.
Telephone: 775-788-2000.
Telecopier: 775-788-2020.

MEMBER OF FIRM

Robert E. Armstrong

ASSOCIATE

Donald G. Martin

Representative Clients: Eldorado Hotel & Casino; Jackpot Enterprises, Inc.; James Hardie (USA), Inc.; Lambda Pharmaceuticals, Inc.; Primm Investment, Inc.; Zeni Drilling Company.

For Complete List of Firm Personnel, See General Section

For full biographical listings, see the Martindale-Hubbell Law Directory

Oshins & Associates, P.C. (AV)

Suite 170, 1645 Village Center Circle, 89134
Telephone: 702-341-6000
Fax: 702-341-6001
Email: Steveo@wizard.com
Email: Dickoshins@aol.com *URL:* http://firms.findlaw.com/oshins

Richard A. Oshins
Steven J. Oshins

For full biographical listings, see the Martindale-Hubbell Law Directory

*RENO,** Washoe Co.

Hale Lane Peek Dennison Howard and Anderson (AV)

100 West Liberty Street, Tenth Floor, P.O. Box 3237, 89505
Telephone: 775-327-3000
Telefax: 775-786-6179
Email: info@halelane.com
Las Vegas, Nevada Office: Nevada Financial Center, 2300 West Sahara Avenue, Eighth Floor, Box 8.
Telephone: 702-222-2500.
Fax: 702-365-6940.
Carson City, Nevada Office: 777 East William Street, Suite 200, P.O. Box 2620.
Telephone: 775-684-6000.
Telefax: 775-684-6001.

MEMBERS OF FIRM

Marilyn L. Skender
Robert C. Anderson
James L. Kelly
Matthew E. Woodhead

ASSOCIATES

Richard P. Schulze, III
Julia S. Gold (Not admitted in NV)

OF COUNSEL

Andrew Pearl

Representative Clients: Construction and Development: Caughlin Ranch General: Puliz Moving & Storage Co.; Scolari's Warehouse Markets, Inc.; Marnell Corrao Construction; Cashman Equipment Company; Juliett Corporation.

For Complete List of Firm Personnel, See General Section

For full biographical listings, see the Martindale-Hubbell Law Directory

McDonald Carano Wilson McCune Bergin Frankovich & Hicks LLP (AV)

241 Ridge Street, 89501
Telephone: 775-788-2000
Telecopier: 775-788-2020
URL: http://www.mcdonaldcarano.com
Las Vegas, Nevada Office: Suite 1000, 2300 West Sahara Avenue.
Telephone: 702-873-4100.
Telecopier: 702-873-9966.

MEMBERS OF FIRM

Robert E. Armstrong
John B. Galvin
Scott A. Swain

Representative Clients: Eldorado Hotel & Casino; Jackpot Enterprises, Inc.; James Hardie (USA), Inc..

For Complete List of Firm Personnel, See General Section

For full biographical listings, see the Martindale-Hubbell Law Directory

Walther, Key, Maupin, Oats, Cox & LeGoy, A Professional Corporation (AV)

Lakeside Professional Plaza, 3500 Lakeside Court, 89509
Telephone: 775-827-2000
Facsimile: 775-827-2185
Mailing Address: P.O. Box 30000, Reno, Nevada, 89520

Ernest J. Maupin
Fred L. Oats
L. Robert LeGoy, Jr.
W. Douglass Maupin
G. Barton Mowry
Procter J. Hug
Gustave J. Rossi
Robert A. Winkel
Kurt O. Hunsberger

Michaelle D. Rafferty

Representative Clients: Bank America of Nevada (Trust Dept.); Bechtel Corporations; Bill Pearce Olds, BMW, Volvo; Wells Fargo, N.A. (Trust Dept.); General Motors Acceptance Corp.; Nevada Realtors; Radiation Oncology Associates; The Ralph M. Parsons Corporation; Parsons Corporation; Reno Air, Inc.

For full biographical listings, see the Martindale-Hubbell Law Directory

NEW HAMPSHIRE

*CONCORD,** Merrimack Co.

Rath, Young and Pignatelli, Professional Association (AV)

One Capital Plaza, P.O. Box 1500, 03302-1500
Telephone: 603-226-2600
Telecopier: 603-226-2700; 228-2294; 225-9774
Email: ryp@rathlaw.com *URL:* http://www.rathlaw.com
Nashua, New Hampshire Office: The Glass Tower, 20 Trafalgar Square.
Telephone: 603-889-9952.
Telecopier: 603-595-7489.

Thomas D. Rath
William F. J. Ardinger
David L. Dubrow
Raquel S. Colby

For Complete List of Firm Personnel, See General Section

For full biographical listings, see the Martindale-Hubbell Law Directory

*MANCHESTER,** Hillsborough Co.

Sheehan Phinney Bass + Green, Professional Association (AV)

Hampshire Plaza, 1000 Elm Street, P.O. Box 3701, 03105-3701
Telephone: 603-668-0300
800-625-SPBG
Fax: 603-627-8121
Email: postmaster@sheehan.com *URL:* http://www.sheehan.com
Portsmouth, New Hampshire Office: Old City Hall, 126 Daniel Street.
Telephone: 603-433-2111.
Fax: 603-433-3126.
Concord, New Hampshire Office: 143 North Main Street.
Telephone: 603-223-2020.
Fax: 603-224-8899.

Kimon S. Zachos
Alan L. Reische
James T. Cain
Ann Meissner Flood

Representative Clients: Anheuser-Busch, Inc.; Bank of New Hampshire Corp.; The Elliot Hospital of Manchester; Granite State Packing Co.; Moore Business Forms, Inc.; New Hampshire College; New Hampshire Dental Service Corp.; New Hampshire Yankee Electric Corp.; Numerica Financial Corp.

For Complete List of Firm Personnel, See General Section

For full biographical listings, see the Martindale-Hubbell Law Directory

PORTSMOUTH, Rockingham Co.

Sheehan Phinney Bass + Green, Professional Association (AV)

Old City Hall, 126 Daniel Street, 03801
Telephone: 603-433-2111
Fax: 603-433-3126
Email: postmaster@sheehan.com *URL:* http://www.sheehan.com
Manchester, New Hampshire Office: Hampshire Plaza, 1000 Elm Street, P.O. Box 3701.
Telephone: 603-668-0300.
Fax: 603-627-8121.
Concord, New Hampshire Office: 143 North Main Street.
Telephone: 603-223-2020.
Fax: 603-224-8899.

Michael C. Harvell
Christopher Cole

For full biographical listings, see the Martindale-Hubbell Law Directory

NEW JERSEY

BAYONNE, Hudson Co.

Fitzpatrick & Waterman (AV)

90 West 40th Street, P.O. Box 1227, 07002
Telephone: 201-339-4000
800 BOND LAW
Secaucus, New Jersey Office: 400 Plaza Drive, P.O. Box 3159, 07096-3159.
Telephone: 201-865-9100.
Facsimile: 201-865-4805.

Harold F. Fitzpatrick

For full biographical listings, see the Martindale-Hubbell Law Directory

CHERRY HILL, Camden Co.

FLASTER/GREENBERG, P.C. (AV)

Commerce Center, 1810 Chapel Avenue West, Third Floor, 08002-4609
Telephone: 856-661-1900
Telecopier: 856-661-1919
Email: FIRM@FLASTERGREENBERG.COM *URL:* http://www.flastergreenberg.com

Richard J. Flaster
Stephen M. Greenberg
Laura B. Wallenstein
Allen P. Fineberg
Markley S. Roderick
Peter R. Spirgel
Alan H. Zuckerman
William S. Skinner
J. Philip Kirchner
Paul J. Russoniello
Carl S. Bisgaier
Steven B. Sacharow
E. Richard Dressel
Kenneth S. Goodkind
Frank H. Wisniewski
Alma L. Saravia

OF COUNSEL

Peter M. Dolinger
James J. Binns

Elizabeth J. Hampton
Jeffrey Herskowitz
Christopher E. Kaltenbach
Steven J. Abrams
Julie A. Williamson
Donna T. Urban
Amelia Carolla
Matthew Azoulay
Elaine J. Petruzziello (Not admitted in NJ)
Ann Marie Iannone
Pasquale Guglietta

LEGAL SUPPORT PERSONNEL

PARALEGALS

Ann Gorman
Patricia D'Alessio
Theresa Cooke
Rosemary Dunaif

For full biographical listings, see the Martindale-Hubbell Law Directory

FLORHAM PARK, Morris Co.

DRINKER BIDDLE & SHANLEY LLP (AV)

A Pennsylvania Limited Liability Partnership
500 Campus Drive, 07932-1047
Telephone: 973-360-1100
Fax: 973-285-1625; 360-9831
URL: http://www.dbr.com
Philadelphia, Pennsylvania Office: Drinker Biddle & Reath LLP, One Logan Square, 18th & Cherry Streets.
Telephone: 215-988-2700.
Telefax: 215-988-2757.
Cable Address: "Debemac."
Washington, D.C. Office: Drinker Biddle & Reath LLP, 1500 K Street, N.W., Suite 1100.
Telephone: 202-842-8800.
Telefax: 202-842-8465.
Princeton, New Jersey Office: Suite 300, 105 College Road East.
Telephone: 609-716-6500.
Telefax: 609-799-7000.
Berwyn, Pennsylvania Office: Drinker Biddle & Reath LLP, Suite 300, 1000 Westlakes Drive.
Telephone: 610-993-2200.
Telefax: 610-993-8585.
New York, New York Office: Drinker Biddle & Reath LLP, 89th Floor, One World Trade Center.
Telephone: 212-321-1812.
Telecopier: 1-212-466-0569.

John Kandravy
Kevin M. Kilcullen
Edward A. Gramigna, Jr.

COUNSEL

Joan M. Neri

Stephanie Mergel Hadley
Pasquale J. Rufolo
Diane M. Flynn
Joseph G. Dolan
Marianne Calabrese

For Complete List of Firm Personnel, See General Section

For full biographical listings, see the Martindale-Hubbell Law Directory

GEDNEY, SEAMAN & HILGENDORFF (AV)

248 Columbia Turnpike, P.O. Box 166, 07932-0166
Telephone: 973-377-9120
Fax: 973-377-9126
Morristown, New Jersey Office: 15 James Street.
Telephone: 973-539-3088.
Fax: 973-539-0163

MEMBERS OF FIRM

Stanley L. Gedney, Jr. (1889-1977)
Bradford C. Seaman (1898-1986)
Hugo A. Hilgendorff, Jr. (1914-1991)
Hugo A. Hilgendorff, III

ASSOCIATES

Peter B. Hilgendorff
George B. Wright

For full biographical listings, see the Martindale-Hubbell Law Directory

HACKENSACK, Bergen Co.

DEENER, FEINGOLD & STERN, A PROFESSIONAL CORPORATION (AV)

2 University Plaza, Suite 503, 07601
Telephone: 201-343-8788
Fax: 201-343-4640
Email: JeromeDeener@DeenerFeingold.com *URL:* http://www.lawyers.com/deenerfeingold&stern

Jerome A. Deener
Cal R. Feingold
Robert A. Stern
David M. Edelblum
Anthony M. Vizzoni

Debra T. Hirsch
Andrew M. Grumet
Ronen Gabbay

References: Hudson United Bank; Commerce Bank.

For full biographical listings, see the Martindale-Hubbell Law Directory

SHAPIRO & CROLAND (AV)

A Partnership including Professional Corporations
Continental Plaza II, 411 Hackensack Avenue, 07601
Telephone: 201-488-3900
Fax: 201-488-9481

Barry I. Croland, P.C.
Robert P. Shapiro, P.C.
Barry L. Baime
Jay Rubenstein
Kenneth S. Apfel
Kenneth S. Goldrich, P.C.
Bruce J. Ackerman
Stuart Reiser, P.C.
Meridith J. Bronson
John P. Di Iorio
David O. Marcus
Robert F. Green
Lizabeth Sarakin
David Torchin
Robin C. Bogan
Craig D. Spector

OF COUNSEL

Harvey R. Sorkow

Donald R. Sorkow (1930-1985)

Reference: Bank of New York-National Community Division.

For full biographical listings, see the Martindale-Hubbell Law Directory

HAMILTON SQUARE, Mercer Co.

HARRY HAUSHALTER (AV)

Lexington Square Commons, 2119 Route 33, Suite A, 08690
Telephone: 609-631-7388
Fax: 609-631-7329
Email: harry_haushalter@msn.com *URL:* http://www.lawyers.com/haushaltertaxlawyer

LEGAL SUPPORT PERSONNEL

Jeanie E. Riggio

For full biographical listings, see the Martindale-Hubbell Law Directory

LIBERTY CORNER, Somerset Co.

KALISON, MCBRIDE & JACKSON, P.A. (AV)

Liberty Corner Executive Center, 645 Martinsville Road, P.O. Box 814, 07938
Telephone: 908-647-4600
Telecopier: 908-647-6226

Michael J. Kalison
Andrew F. McBride III
Paul R. Murphy
John Zen Jackson
James V. Hetzel
James Acre Robertson, IV

Barry Liss
Sloane S. Belitz
Todd Schaper
Daniel R. Esposito
Alison Wholey Mynick
Jennifer Candace Weissman

OF COUNSEL

Wendy C. Tomey

LEGAL SUPPORT PERSONNEL

Susan R. Buchanan
Roman Bohoslawec

For full biographical listings, see the Martindale-Hubbell Law Directory

LIVINGSTON, Essex Co.

SKOLOFF & WOLFE, P.C. (AV)

293 Eisenhower Parkway, 07039
Telephone: 973-992-0900
Fax: 973-992-0301
Morristown, New Jersey Office: 10 Park Place.
Telephone: 973-267-3511.

Saul A. Wolfe
Robert F. Giancaterino
Heather A. Turnbull

(See Next Column)

SKOLOFF & WOLFE P.C.—*Continued*

Garry J. Roettger

For Complete List of Firm Personnel, See General Section

For full biographical listings, see the Martindale-Hubbell Law Directory

MONTCLAIR, Essex Co.

GARIPPA AND DAVENPORT, A PROFESSIONAL CORPORATION (AV)

66 Park Street, 07042
Telephone: 201-744-1688
Telecopier: 201-744-1641
Email: gd@taxappeal.com *URL:* http://www.taxappeal.com

John E. Garippa | Philip J. Giannuario
Seth I. Davenport | Gregory G. Lotz

Daniel J. Mulligan

For full biographical listings, see the Martindale-Hubbell Law Directory

*MORRISTOWN,** Morris Co.

ALAN R. ADLER (AV)

Suite 306, 10 Park Place, 07960
Telephone: 973-292-9212
Fax: 973-292-0878
URL: http://www.lawyers.com/alanradler

For full biographical listings, see the Martindale-Hubbell Law Directory

EDWARDS & ANTHOLIS, P.C. (AV)

22 Pine Street, 07960-6092
Telephone: 973-540-0050; 800-464-9608
Fax: 973-292-1889
Email: eandapc@aol.com *URL:* http://www.lawyers.com/eandapc

David F. Edwards (1908-1983) | John K. Antholis

For full biographical listings, see the Martindale-Hubbell Law Directory

*NEWARK,** Essex Co.

CARPENTER, BENNETT & MORRISSEY (AV)

Three Gateway Center, 17th Floor, 100 Mulberry Street, 07102-4079
Telephone: 973-622-7711
New York City: 212-943-6530
Telex: 139405
Telecopier: 973-622-5314
Email: cbm@carpben.com

MEMBERS OF FIRM

Laurence Reich | Francis X. O'Brien
John D. Goldsmith

OF COUNSEL

Warren Lloyd Lewis | Edward F. Day, Jr.

ASSOCIATES

Hans G. Polak | Mary B. Goldhirsch

Representative Clients: General Motors Corp.; E. I. du Pont de Nemours & Co.; Texaco Inc.; AT&T; ITT Industries, Inc.; International Flavors & Fragrances Inc.; Nabisco, Inc.; Rutgers, The State University of New Jersey; Prudential Insurance Company of America; Hartford Insurance Co.

For Complete List of Firm Personnel, See General Section

For full biographical listings, see the Martindale-Hubbell Law Directory

GREENBERG DAUBER EPSTEIN & TUCKER, A PROFESSIONAL CORPORATION (AV)

Suite 600, One Gateway Center, 07102-5311
Telephone: 973-643-3700
Facsimile: 973-643-1218
URL: http://www.greenbergdauber.com

Stanley A. Epstein

For Complete List of Firm Personnel, See General Section

For full biographical listings, see the Martindale-Hubbell Law Directory

HELLRING LINDEMAN GOLDSTEIN & SIEGAL LLP (AV)

One Gateway Center, 07102-5386
Telephone: 973-621-9020
Fax: 973-621-7406
Englewood, New Jersey Office: 32-40 North Dean Street.
Telephone: 201-871-3060.

(See Next Column)

Jonathan L. Goldstein | Charles Oransky
David N. Narciso

For Complete List of Firm Personnel, See General Section

For full biographical listings, see the Martindale-Hubbell Law Directory

LEVY, EHRLICH & PETRIELLO, A PROFESSIONAL CORPORATION (AV)

60 Park Place Suite 1016, 07102
Telephone: 973-643-0040
Telecopier: 973-596-1781
URL: http://www.lep-lawyers.com

Ira A. Levy | Alan Ehrlich

Representative Clients: Transamerica; General Electric; U.S. Department of HUD.
Reference: First Union Bank.

For Complete List of Firm Personnel, See General Section

For full biographical listings, see the Martindale-Hubbell Law Directory

MCCARTER & ENGLISH, LLP (AV)

Four Gateway Center, 100 Mulberry Street, P.O. Box 652, 07101-0652
Telephone: 973-622-4444
Telecopier: 973-624-7070
URL: http://www.mccarter.com
Cherry Hill, New Jersey Office: 1820 Chapel Avenue West, Suite 380.
Telephone: 609-662-8444.
Telecopier: 609-662-6203.
New York, New York Office: Suite 2247, One World Trade Center.
Telephone: 212-466-9018.
Telecopier: 212-432-6568.
Boca Raton, Florida Office: 2255 Glades Road, Suite 319-A.
Telephone: 561-994-6262.
Telecopier: 561-241-0798.
Wilmington, Delaware Office: Mellon Bank Center, 919 Market Street.
Telephone: 302-654-8010.
Telecopier: 302-654-0795.
Philadelphia, Pennsylvania Office: One Commerce Square, 2005 Market Street, Suite 3600.
Telephone: 215-557-7700.
Telecopier: 215-557-6544.

MEMBERS OF FIRM

John B. Brescher, Jr. | Stephen M. Vajtay, Jr.
Michael A. Guariglia | Mark A. Daniele
David A. Ludgin | Susan A. Feeney
Gary Duescher

OF COUNSEL

Peter C. Aslanides

COUNSEL

Beth Yingling | Phyllis Gutto

SPECIAL COUNSEL

Charles M. Costenbader

ASSOCIATE

Susan M. Mello

For Complete List of Firm Personnel, See General Section

For full biographical listings, see the Martindale-Hubbell Law Directory

MCMANIMON & SCOTLAND, L.L.C. (AV)

One Riverfront Plaza, 4th Floor, 07102-5311
Telephone: 973-622-1800
Fax: 973-622-7333; 973-622-3744

MEMBERS OF FIRM

Joseph P. Baumann, Jr. | Ronald J. Ianoale
John V. Cavaliere | Andrea L. Kahn
John B. Hall | Jeffrey G. Kramer
Glenn F. Scotland | Leslie G. London
Edward J. McManimon, III

OF COUNSEL

Norman M. Robertson | Carla J. Brundage

ASSOCIATES

Peter S. Crisafi | Kristin Dwyer Ganley
Sheila Newsome Maddox | Joseph C. Jasaitis
M. Frances Ciesla | Stephen N. Severud
Thomas J. Hastie, Jr.

LEGAL SUPPORT PERSONNEL

Helen Lysaght

PARALEGALS

Sandra Simoes

For full biographical listings, see the Martindale-Hubbell Law Directory

Newark—Continued

St. John & Wayne, L.L.C. (AV)

Two Penn Plaza East, 07105-2249
Telephone: 973-491-3600
Fax: 973-491-3555
Email: firm@nwk.stjohn-law.com *URL:* http://www.stjohn-law.com
Rochester, New York Office: St. John & Curtin, L.L.C., First Federal Plaza.
Telephone: 716-262-6780.
Fax: 716-262-6755.
New York, New York Office: Heron Tower, 70 East 55th. Street.
Telephone: 212-446-5000.
Fax: 212-446-5055.

Richard I. Bier
John J. Oberdorf

For Complete List of Firm Personnel, See General Section

For full biographical listings, see the Martindale-Hubbell Law Directory

Sills Cummis Radin Tischman Epstein & Gross, A Professional Corporation (AV)

One Riverfront Plaza, 07102-5400
Telephone: 973-643-7000
Fax: 973-643-6500
Telex: 820630 Sillsbeck Nwk
Email: sillsmail@sillscummis.com *URL:* http://www.sillscummis.com
Atlantic City, New Jersey Office: 17 Gordon's Alley.
Telephone: 609-344-2800.
New York, N.Y. Office: 712 Fifth Avenue.
Telephone: 212-643-7000.
Washington, D.C. Office: 1800 K Street, N.W.
Telephone: 202-296-4750.

MEMBERS OF FIRM

Lawrence S. Horn
Simon Levin
Alan E. Sherman
Robert J. Alter
Allan C. Bell
Richard J. Sapinski
Nathan E. Arnell

SENIOR COUNSEL

David Beck
Herbert L. Zuckerman

Brenda J. Rediess-Hoosein
Jacqueline Valouch
Michael S. Mirone

Representative Clients: Alpine Lace Brands, Inc.; Crown Travel, Inc.; ABC Tours; Dreyfus Corp.; Margaretten Financial Corp.; Unit Investment Management Co.; O'Brien Environment Energy, Inc.; Snia BPD, S.p.A and Sorin Biomedica, S.p.A.; White Systems, Inc.

For Complete List of Firm Personnel, See General Section

For full biographical listings, see the Martindale-Hubbell Law Directory

NORTH BERGEN, Hudson Co.

Edward Pesin A Professional Corporation (AV)

5-75th Street, 07047
Telephone: 201-868-0144
Fax: 201-453-1528

Edward Pesin

For full biographical listings, see the Martindale-Hubbell Law Directory

NORTH BRUNSWICK, Middlesex Co.

Borrus, Goldin, Foley, Vignuolo, Hyman, Stahl & Clarkin, A Professional Corporation (AV)

2875 U.S. Highway 1, Route 1 & Finnigans Lane, P.O. Box 7463, 08902
Telephone: 732-422-1000
Fax: 732-422-1016
Email: attys@borrus.com *URL:* http://www.borrus.com

Jack Borrus
Martin S. Goldin
David M. Foley
Anthony B. Vignuolo
Jeffrey M. Hyman
James E. Stahl
James F. Clarkin III
Eileen Mary Foley

Robert C. Nisenson
Rosalind Westlake
Lisa M. Vignuolo
Steven L. Fox
Peter A. Vignuolo
Gerald T. Foley (1903-1976)

Representative Clients: Summit Bank; R. J. Reynolds Tobacco Co.; K. Hovnanian Enterprises, Inc.; Johnson and Johnson; Foster Wheeler, Inc.; Hartz Mountain Industries; Middlesex County Vocational Services Commission; Borough of South Plainfield Board of Adjustment; U-Haul of Northern NJ.

For full biographical listings, see the Martindale-Hubbell Law Directory

ROSELAND, Essex Co.

Brach, Eichler, Rosenberg, Silver, Bernstein, Hammer & Gladstone, A Professional Corporation (AV)

101 Eisenhower Parkway, 07068
Telephone: 973-228-5700
Telecopier: 973-228-7852
Email: law@bracheichler.com *URL:* http://www.bracheichler.com

Stuart M. Gladstone
Brian R. Lenker
Robert C. Mignella
Stuart L. Pachman
David J. Ritter

Ann D. Stevens
Susan K. Dromsky-Reed
Dahesh D. Patel

OF COUNSEL

Henry N. Portner

COUNSEL

Dorothy G. Black (1927-1996)

Representative Clients: Eagle Work Clothes, Inc.; Howard Press; Isaac Hazan & Co.; I. Epstein, Inc.; Perlmart Shop-Rites; Silverline Building Products Corp.

For Complete List of Firm Personnel, See General Section

For full biographical listings, see the Martindale-Hubbell Law Directory

Mark Levin (AV)

5 Becker Farm Road, 4th Floor, 07068
Telephone: 973-740-9299

For full biographical listings, see the Martindale-Hubbell Law Directory

Walder, Sondak & Brogan, A Professional Corporation (AV)

5 Becker Farm Road, P.O. Box 901, 07068
Telephone: 973-992-5300
Telecopier: 973-992-1505; 992-1006
Email: general@wsbesqs.com *URL:* http://www.wsbesqs.com

Heather Grasz Suarez

OF COUNSEL

John H. Skarbnik

For Complete List of Firm Personnel, See General Section

For full biographical listings, see the Martindale-Hubbell Law Directory

SADDLE BROOK, Bergen Co.

Krugman & Kailes LLP (AV)

Park 80 West-Plaza Two, 07663-5835
Telephone: 201-845-3434; 212-695-3262
Telecopier: 201-845-9627
Email: counsel@krugmankailes.com
New York, New York Office: 99 Park Avenue, Suite 2200.
Telephone: 212-599-1060.
Telecopier: 212-599-6282.
London, England Office: 90 Fetter Lane, London EC4A-1PT.
Telephone: 011 (44) 171-421-7918.
Telecopier: 011 (44) 171-831-6407.

MEMBERS OF FIRM

Martin Krugman (1916-1994)
Howard Kailes
Thomas J. Goodwin
Ward C. Laracy
Robert I. Wexler
Alan H. Fox
Joy M. Mercer
Kerry B. Flowers

OF COUNSEL

James D. Krugman

COUNSEL

Judith S. Musicant

ASSOCIATES

Anne M. Wallace (Not admitted in NJ)
April A. Savoye
Lisa Ann Miller
Patrizia E. DeBari
David J. Hanley, Jr.
Anjana D. Patel
W. Mark O'Brien

For full biographical listings, see the Martindale-Hubbell Law Directory

SECAUCUS, Hudson Co.

Fitzpatrick & Waterman (AV)

400 Plaza Drive, P.O. Box 3159, 07096-3159
Telephone: 201-865-9100
800 BOND LAW
Facsimile: 201-865-4805
Bayonne, New Jersey Office: 90 West 40th Street, P.O. Box 1227, 07002.
Telephone: 201-339-4000; 1-800 BOND LAW.

(See Next Column)

FITZPATRICK & WATERMAN—*Continued*

Harold F. Fitzpatrick
Stephen P. Waterman

ASSOCIATES

Glenn C. Merritt
Jeanette M. Samra

OF COUNSEL

Michael J. Israels
Andre Shramenko

For full biographical listings, see the Martindale-Hubbell Law Directory

SUMMIT, Union Co.

BOURNE, NOLL & KENYON, A PROFESSIONAL CORPORATION (AV)

382 Springfield Avenue, P.O. Box 690, 07902-0690
Telephone: 908-277-2200
Facsimile: 908-277-6808

Cary R. Hardy
Charles R. Berman
Martin Rubashkin
Roger Mehner
James R. Ottobre
Lawrence A. Rudnick
John F. Kuntz

OF COUNSEL

Edward T. Kenyon
Robert B. Bourne

COUNSEL

Ellyn A. Draikiwicz

Jaime A. O'Brien
Timothy A. Kalas
Alan F. Schwarz
Ross W. Smith

For full biographical listings, see the Martindale-Hubbell Law Directory

TEANECK, Bergen Co.

ROSENBLUM, WOLF & LLOYD, A PROFESSIONAL CORPORATION (AV)

Glenpointe Centre East, 300 Frank W. Burr Boulevard, 07666
Telephone: 201-836-0400
Fax: 201-836-8365
Email: rwlnj@cs.com

Leo Rosenblum (1906-1990)
Edward G. Rosenblum
Nathan P. Wolf
John R. Lloyd

Reference: The Bank of New York, formerly National Community Bank.

For full biographical listings, see the Martindale-Hubbell Law Directory

WESTFIELD, Union Co.

LINDABURY, MCCORMICK & ESTABROOK, P.A. (AV)

53 Cardinal Drive, P.O. Box 2369, 07091
Telephone: 908-233-6800
Fax: 908-233-5078
New York, N.Y. Office: 26 Broadway, Suite 2300.
Telephone: 212-742-3390.
Fax: 212-269-5016.

John R. Blasi
James K. Estabrook
Robert S. Schwartz

Jany Sabins

OF COUNSEL

Kenneth L. Estabrook

Representative Clients: Furnished Upon Request.

For Complete List of Firm Personnel, See General Section

For full biographical listings, see the Martindale-Hubbell Law Directory

WEST ORANGE, Essex Co.

GOLDBERG, MUFSON & SPAR, A PROFESSIONAL CORPORATION (AV)

200 Executive Drive, 07052
Telephone: 973-736-0100
Telecopier: 973-736-0961
Email: gmspa@chelsea.ios.com

Leonard M. Goldberg
Michael R. Spar

For full biographical listings, see the Martindale-Hubbell Law Directory

HAUPTMAN & RICHMOND, P.A. (AV)

100 Executive Drive, Suite 330, 07052
Telephone: 973-731-1100
Fax: 973-731-1467
URL: http://www.lawyers.com/hauptman_richmond

(See Next Column)

Martin D. Hauptman
Harold N. Richmond

For full biographical listings, see the Martindale-Hubbell Law Directory

LAMPF, LIPKIND, PRUPIS, PETIGROW & LABUE, A PROFESSIONAL CORPORATION (AV)

80 Main Street, 07052
Telephone: 973-325-2100
New York: 212-349-1021
Fax: 973-325-2839
Email: administrator@llppl.com *URL:* http://www.llppl.com

William D. Lipkind
Stephen E. Lampf
Neil L. Prupis
Paul M. Petigrow
Anthony F. LaBue
Elizabeth Gasser
Andrew S. Berns
Grace D. Mack
Susan Fruchtman
Sheila W. Tarabour

Eric W. Olson
William J. Volonte
Lois S. Feldman
Adam M. Kaplan
Cathy S. Harvey

OF COUNSEL

Theodore I. Botter
Neil Oswald Eriksen
Theresa Borzelli

For full biographical listings, see the Martindale-Hubbell Law Directory

WOODBRIDGE, Middlesex Co.

GREENBAUM, ROWE, SMITH, RAVIN, DAVIS AND HIMMEL LLP (AV)

Metro Corporate Campus I, P.O. Box 5600, 07095-0988
Telephone: 732-549-5600
Fax: 732-549-1881 529
Email: info@greenbaumlaw.com *URL:* http://www.greenbaumlaw.com
Roseland, New Jersey Office: 6 Becker Farm Road.
Telephone: 973-535-1600.
Fax: 973-535-1698.

MEMBERS OF FIRM

Michael A. Backer
Martin L. Lepelstat
Thomas C. Senter
Michael K. Feinberg

ASSOCIATES

Allen V. Brown
James A. Mohoney
Dilip B. Patel
William D. Brick

For Complete List of Firm Personnel, See General Section

For full biographical listings, see the Martindale-Hubbell Law Directory

GREENBERG & SCHULMAN (AV)

90 Woodbridge Center Drive Suite 610, 07095-1142
Telephone: 732-636-8800
Fax: 732-636-8833
Email: greenyanks@aol.com *URL:* http://www.lawyers.com/g&slaw

Richard H. Greenberg
David M. Schulman

For full biographical listings, see the Martindale-Hubbell Law Directory

WILENTZ, GOLDMAN & SPITZER, A PROFESSIONAL CORPORATION (AV)

90 Woodbridge Center Drive Suite 900, Box 10, 07095
Telephone: 732-636-8000
Telecopier: 732-855-6117
URL: http://www.newjerseylaw.com
Eatontown, New Jersey Office: Meridian Center I, Two Industrial Way West, 07724.
Telephone: 732-542-4500.
Telecopier: 732-493-8387.
New York, New York Office: Wall Street Plaza, 88 Pine Street, 9th Floor, 10005.
Telephone: 212-267-3091.
Telecopier: 212-267-3828.

Robert C. Kautz
Steven P. Marshall

Helen C. Lee

Representative Clients: Amerada Hess Corp.; Chevron, U.S.A.; Middlesex County Utilities Authority; The Rouse Co.; New Jersey Arts Center at Newark Corp.; Eaton Vance Management; Goldman Sachs; Hilton Clothes, Inc.

For Complete List of Firm Personnel, See General Section

For full biographical listings, see the Martindale-Hubbell Law Directory

NEW MEXICO

*ALBUQUERQUE,** Bernalillo Co.

MILLER, STRATVERT & TORGERSON, P.A. (AV)

500 Marquette Avenue, N.W., Suite 1100, P.O. Box 25687, 87102
Telephone: 505-842-1950
Facsimile: 505-243-4408
Email: info@mstLAW.com *URL:* http://www.mstLAW.com
Farmington, New Mexico Office: 300 West Arrington, Suite 300, P.O. Box 869.
Telephone: 505-326-4521.
Facsimile: 505-325-5474.
Las Cruces, New Mexico Office: 500 South Main, Suite 800, P.O. Box 1209.
Telephone: 505-523-2481.
Facsimile: 505-526-2215.
Santa Fe, New Mexico Office: 150 Washington Avenue, Suite 300, P.O. Box 1986.
Telephone: 505-989-9614.
Facsimile: 505-989-9857.

Sharon P. Gross
Marte D. Lightstone
Joel T. Newton (Resident at Las Cruces Office)
Fred Schiller (Resident at Las Cruces Office)
Dean B. Cross (Resident at Las Cruces Office)

COUNSEL

Paul W. Robinson
Ralph Wm. Richards (Resident at Las Cruces Office)
Ross B. Perkal
James J. Widland
Bradley D. Tepper

For Complete List of Firm Personnel, See General Section

For full biographical listings, see the Martindale-Hubbell Law Directory

RODEY, DICKASON, SLOAN, AKIN & ROBB, P.A. (AV)

Albuquerque Plaza, Suite 2200, 201 Third Street, N.W., P.O. Box 1888, 87103-1888
Telephone: 505-765-5900
Fax: 505-768-7395
Email: info@rodey.com *URL:* http://www.rodey.com
Santa Fe, New Mexico Office: Suite 101 Marcy Plaza, 123 East Marcy Street, P.O. Box 1357, 87504-1357.
Telephone: 505-984-0100.
Fax: 505-989-9542.

Benjamin C. Roybal
Gary D. Eisenberg

COUNSEL

Jeffrey W. Loubet
Richard C. Minzner

For Complete List of Firm Personnel, See General Section

For full biographical listings, see the Martindale-Hubbell Law Directory

SWAIM & SCHRANDT, P.C. (AV)

4830 Juan Tabo Boulevard, N.E., Suite F, 87111
Telephone: 505-237-0064; 1-800-460-8670
Fax: 505-237-9440

Donald E. Swaim
Judith D. Schrandt

Tessa T. Davidson

For full biographical listings, see the Martindale-Hubbell Law Directory

TAX, ESTATE & BUSINESS LAW N.A. LLC (AV)

4217 Montgomery Boulevard, N.E., 87109
Telephone: 505-830-2200
Fax: 505-830-4400
Email: tsmidt2@aol.com

Thomas Smidt, II

LEGAL SUPPORT PERSONNEL

William T. Smith

For full biographical listings, see the Martindale-Hubbell Law Directory

JUDITH L. ZABEL, P.A. (AV)

2632 Mesilla Street, N.E., 87110
Telephone: 505-881-7241
Fax: 505-837-2141
Email: jlzabel@flash.net

Judith L. Zabel

For full biographical listings, see the Martindale-Hubbell Law Directory

*CLOVIS,** Curry Co.

TATUM & McDOWELL (AV)

Suite E, Sagebrush Professional Office Complex, 921 East 21st Street, P.O. Drawer 1270, 88101
Telephone: 505-762-7756
Fax: 505-769-1606

MEMBER OF FIRM

Edwin B. Tatum

Representative Clients: High Plains Federal Credit Union; Citizens Bank of Clovis; Clovis Feedyard, Inc.; Lewter Cattle Co.; ENMRSH, Inc.; PDRPIP, Inc.; Curry County Fertilizer, Inc.; Southwest Ag, Inc.

For Complete List of Firm Personnel, See General Section

For full biographical listings, see the Martindale-Hubbell Law Directory

*SANTA FE,** Santa Fe Co.

CATRON, CATRON & SAWTELL, A PROFESSIONAL ASSOCIATION (AV)

2006 Botulph Road, P.O. Box 788, 87504-0788
Telephone: 505-982-1947
Telecopier: 505-986-1013
Email: catronlaw@aol.com

Thomas B. Catron III
William A. Sawtell, Jr.
Fletcher R. Catron
Forrest S. Smith

LEGAL SUPPORT PERSONNEL

Peggy L. Feldt (Certified Public Accountant)

For Complete List of Firm Personnel, See General Section

For full biographical listings, see the Martindale-Hubbell Law Directory

NEW YORK

*ALBANY,** Albany Co.

ROBERT S. CATAPANO-FRIEDMAN, P.C. (AV)

744 Broadway, 12207
Telephone: 518-463-7501; 518-463-7502
Fax: 518-463-1948
Email: catapan@worldnet.att.net

Robert S. Catapano-Friedman

For full biographical listings, see the Martindale-Hubbell Law Directory

ISEMAN, CUNNINGHAM, RIESTER & HYDE, LLP (AV)

9 Thurlow Terrace, 12203
Telephone: 518-462-3000
Telecopier: 518-462-4199
Email: lawfirm@icrh.com *URL:* http://www.icrh.com
Canandaigua, New York Office: 37 East Gibson Street, P.O. Box 179, 14424.
Telephone: 716-394-1450.
Fax: 716-394-5121.

MEMBERS OF FIRM

Frederick C. Riester
Michael J. Cunningham
Robert Hall Iseman
Carol Ann Hyde
Linda J. Clark

Brian M. Culnan
Kihyun S. Kim
Richard A. Frankel
Stephanie E. Moriarty
Valerie R. Lape Handy
Marcia B. Smith
Ellen Gillerman Cox
Jennifer A. Grego
Cara E. Johnson

OF COUNSEL

Michael J. McNeil
Deborah A. Kirby

For full biographical listings, see the Martindale-Hubbell Law Directory

HOWARD M. KOFF, P.C. (AV)

Pieter Schulyer Building, 600 Broadway, 12207
Telephone: 518-463-5530
Telecopier: 518-463-0156

Howard M. Koff

For full biographical listings, see the Martindale-Hubbell Law Directory

NANCY M. SILLS (AV)

126 State Street, 12207-1606
Telephone: 518-436-4056
Fax: 518-436-1456

For full biographical listings, see the Martindale-Hubbell Law Directory

*BINGHAMTON,** Broome Co.

HINMAN, HOWARD & KATTELL, LLP (AV)

700 Security Mutual Building, 80 Exchange Street, P.O. Box 5250, 13902-5250
Telephone: 607-723-5341
Fax: 607-723-6605
Email: jworband@hhk.com *URL:* http://www.hhk.com
Norwich, New York Office: 48 Hale Street, 13815-2039.
Telephone: 607-334-5896.
Fax: 607-336-1628.
Oneonta, New York Office: 12 South Main Street, 13820-2542.
Telephone: 607-432-5331.
Fax: 607-432-2683.
New York, N.Y. Office: 500 5th Avenue, Suite 1725, 10110.
Telephone: 212-840-3017.
Fax: 212-840-2345.

MEMBERS OF FIRM

James W. Orband
Colin T. Naylor, III
Eugene E. Peckham
Wilbur D. Dahlgren
Allen J. Hall
Thomas A. Conlon, Jr.
C. Addison Keeler, Jr.

COUNSEL

Joseph P. Minnich, Jr.
Erik Edward Joh

SPECIAL COUNSEL

Frederick A. Griffen
Martin J. Kane

Representative Clients: The Chase Manhattan Bank; BSB Bank & Trust Co.; International Business Machines Corp.; Universal Instruments Corp.; Security Mutual Life Insurance Company of New York; Bell Atlantic; New York State Electric & Gas Corp.; Exxon Corp.; Wilber National Bank; Binghamton Giant Markets, Inc.

For Complete List of Firm Personnel, See General Section

For full biographical listings, see the Martindale-Hubbell Law Directory

BRONXVILLE, Westchester Co.

GRIFFIN, COOGAN & VENERUSO, P.C. (AV)

51 Pondfield Road, 10708
Telephone: 914-961-1300
Telecopier: 914-961-1476; 914-961-9385

William E. Griffin
James M. Coogan
James J. Veneruso

Daniel J. Griffin
Paul R. Herrick
Thomas G. Marzullo
William E. Sulzer (Not admitted in NY)

Approved Closing Attorneys: Hudson Valley Bank.

For full biographical listings, see the Martindale-Hubbell Law Directory

*BUFFALO,** Erie Co.

HODGSON, RUSS, ANDREWS, WOODS & GOODYEAR, LLP (AV)

A Registered Limited Liability Partnership including Professional Associations
One M & T Plaza, Suite 2000, 14203
Telephone: 716-856-4000
Fax: 716-849-0349
Email: info@hodgsonruss.com *URL:* www.hodgsonruss.com
Albany, New York Office: Three City Square, 12207.
Telephone: 518-465-2333.
Fax: 518-465-1567.
Boca Raton, Florida Office: Suite 400, 2000 Glades Road, 33431.
Telephone: 561-394-0500.
Fax: 561-394-3862.
Toronto, Ontario, Canada Office: 150 King Street West, Suite 2309, M5H 1J9, P.O. Box 30.
Telephone: 416-595-5100.
Fax: 416-595-5021.
New York, New York Office: 65 East 55th Street, 10th Floor, 10022.
Telephone: 212-751-4300.
Fax: 212-751-0928.
Gloversville, New York Office: 6 Fremont Street, 12078.
Telephone: 518-725-6347.
Fax: 518-773-7350.
Newark, New Jersey Office: One Gateway Center, Suite 2600, 07102.
Telephone: 973-645-0577.
Fax: 973-645-0551.

MEMBERS OF FIRM

(ALPHABETICALLY BY YEAR OF ADMISSION TO BAR)

Richard E. Heath (Boca Raton, Florida Office)
Paul R. Comeau
Todd M. Joseph
Dianne Bennett (President)
Richard F. Campbell
Daniel R. Sharpe
Richard W. Kaiser
Mark S. Klein
Alice Accola Joseffer
Thomas W. Nelson
Carol Anne Fitzsimmons (Newark, New Jersey & New York, N.Y. Offices)

(See Next Column)

MEMBERS OF FIRM

(ALPHABETICALLY BY YEAR OF ADMISSION TO BAR) (Continued)

Christopher L. Doyle
Michel Pierre Cassier
Alvan L. Bobrow (New York, N.Y. Office)
Peter K. Bradley

ASSOCIATES

(ALPHABETICALLY BY YEAR OF ADMISSION TO BAR)

Tim Sawers
James R. Maloney
Andrew B. Sabol
Leslie R. Kellogg
Brad A. Birmingham
Arthur K. Bartlett
Anita Coles Costello
James T. Ritzel

For Complete List of Firm Personnel, See General Section

For full biographical listings, see the Martindale-Hubbell Law Directory

PHILLIPS, LYTLE, HITCHCOCK, BLAINE & HUBER LLP (AV)

(Formerly Kenefick, Letchworth, Baldy, Phillips & Emblidge)
3400 HSBC Center, 14203
Telephone: 716-847-8400
Telecopier: 716-852-6100
Email: info@phillipslytle.com *URL:* http://www.phillipslytle.com
Jamestown, New York Office: 307 Chase Bank Building, 8 E. Third Street.
Telephone: 716-664-3906.
Telecopier: 716-664-4230.
Rochester, New York Office: 1400 First Federal Plaza.
Telephone: 716-238-2000.
Telecopier: 716-232-3141.
New York, New York Office: 437 Madison Avenue.
Telephone: 212-759-4888.
Telecopier: 212-308-9079.
Fredonia, New York Office: 11 East Main Street.
Telephone: 716-672-2164.
FAX: 716-672-7979.

OF COUNSEL

Thomas M. Barney
Arthur M. Sherwood

PARTNERS

Caroline Hassett Buerk
Edward M. Griffith, Jr.
James A. Locke
Martha L. Salzman
John C. Spitzmiller

ASSOCIATE

Maria K. Hadley (Not admitted in NY)

General Counsel for: Astronics Corp.; Bryant & Stratton Business Institute; Canisius College; Chase Manhattan Bank, N.A.; Columbus McKinnon Corp.
Local Counsel for: A.O. Smith Corp.; Allied Signal; Bethlehem Steel Corp.; Chrysler Motor Corp.; E.I. DuPont deNemours Co., Inc.

For Complete List of Firm Personnel, See General Section

For full biographical listings, see the Martindale-Hubbell Law Directory

EAST MEADOW, Nassau Co.

CERTILMAN BALIN ADLER & HYMAN, LLP (AV)

90 Merrick Avenue, 11554
Telephone: 516-296-7000
Telecopier: 516-296-7111
URL: http://www.cbah.com

MEMBERS OF FIRM

Ira J. Adler
Dale Allinson
Michael C. Axelrod
Herbert M. Balin
Bruce J. Bergman
Eileen O'Boyle Bitetto
Michael D. Brofman
Lewis J. Campanella
Morton L. Certilman
Robert J. Ciovacco
Brian J. Davis
Wayne G. Edwards
Joseph P. Famighetti
Howard R. Gladston
Murray Greenberg
Gavin C. Grusd
David Z. Herman
Richard Herzbach
M. Allan Hyman
Bernard Hyman
Donna-Marie Korth
Steven J. Kuperschmid
Jeffrey S. Lisabeth
Jaspreet S. Mayall
Richard J. McCord
Thomas J. McNamara
Michael F. O'Shea
Marilyn Price
Fred S. Skolnik
Louis Soloway
Harold Somer
Howard M. Stein
Brian K. Ziegler

OF COUNSEL

Daniel S. Cohan
Joseph N. Mondello

ASSOCIATES

Lawrence A. Altholtz
Meredith W. Ayres
Daniel J. Baker
Kimberly I. Berson
Scott B. Black
Brendan J. DeRiggi
Thomas M. Farrell
Mary C. Florentz
Candace Reid Gladstone
Harry P. Greenbaum
David E. Herold
Jodi S. Hoffman
James G. Kapralos
Linda P. Manfredi
Edward G. McCabe
Patrick McCormick

(See Next Column)

CERTILMAN BALIN ADLER & HYMAN LLP, *East Meadow—Continued*

ASSOCIATES (Continued)

Susan L. McWalters
Jothy Narendran
James A. Rose
Wayne J. Schaefer
Leslie H. Scharf
Afsheen Ashley Shah
Victor Spinnelli
Russell H. Stern
Robert G. Wilk

For full biographical listings, see the Martindale-Hubbell Law Directory

MELVILLE, Suffolk Co.

LAMB & BARNOSKY, LLP (AV)

534 Broadhollow Road-CS 9034, 11747-9034
Telephone: 631-694-2300
Telecopier: 631-694-2309
Email: thefirm@lambbarnosky.com *URL:* http://www.lambbarnosky.com

PARTNERS

Eugene R. Barnosky
Robert H. Cohen
Marcia Lyn Finkelstein
Michael J. Heller
Gary Holman
Scott M. Karson
P. L. Lamb
Arthur A. Lane
Joel M. Markowitz
Gerald P. Rosenberg
Patrice Dowd Shenn

OF COUNSEL

Louis E. Black
James F. Gesualdi
Howard W. Newman
Joseph J. Salvatore
Joseph H. Wishod

COUNSEL

Lloyd K. Chanin
Scott P. McBride

ASSOCIATES

Cathleen D. Allen
Catherine Healy Kanzler
Rita Fishman Sheena
Shari Lee Sugarman

For full biographical listings, see the Martindale-Hubbell Law Directory

MERRICK, Nassau Co.

JACK A. BENNARDO (AV)

2163 Merrick Avenue, P.O. Box 360, 11566
Telephone: 516-378-1110
Fax: 516-378-1252
Email: jablaw1@aol.com *URL:* http://www.lawyers.com/bennardolaw

For full biographical listings, see the Martindale-Hubbell Law Directory

NEW ROCHELLE, Westchester Co.

McGOVERN, CONNELLY & DAVIDSON (AV)

145 Huguenot Street, 10801
Telephone: 914-632-9300
Telecopier: 914-632-1615

MEMBERS OF FIRM

J. Raymond McGovern (1898-1974)
Frank H. Connelly, Sr. (1907-1989)
Harry G. Davidson (1912-1981)
Frank H. Connelly, Jr.
John A. Vasile
Francis B. Orlando
Margaret M. Fitzpatrick

Representative Clients: Capital Sports Inc.; City of New Rochelle; Halpern-Stillman, Inc.; Marine Midland Bank; Samson Management, Co.; The Rawlplug Co., Inc.; Pace Oldsmobile, Inc.; Flynn Burner Corp.

For full biographical listings, see the Martindale-Hubbell Law Directory

*NEW YORK,** New York Co.

BAKER BOTTS L.L.P. (AV)

599 Lexington Avenue, 10022-6030 and 30 Rockefeller Plaza, 10112-0228
Telephone: 212-705-5000
Fax: 212-705-5125 (599 Lexington Ave.)
Fax: 212-705-5020 (30 Rockeffeller Plaza)
Email: postmaster@bakerbotts.com *URL:* http://www.bakerbotts.com
Washington, D.C. Office: The Warner, 1299 Pennsylvania Avenue, N.W.
Telephone: 202-639-7700.
Austin, Texas Office: 1600 San Jacinto Center, 98 San Jacinto Boulevard.
Telephone: 512-322-2500.
Dallas, Texas Office: 2001 Ross Avenue.
Telephone: 214-953-6500.
Houston, Texas Office: One Shell Plaza, 910 Louisiana.
Telephone: 713-229-1234.
Moscow, Russia Office: 10 ul. Bolshaya Dimitrovka (formerly ul. Pushkinskaya), 103031.
Telephone: 7095/921-5300 (Local); 7095/929-7070 (International).
London, England Office: 45 Ludgate Hill.
Telephone: 0171-778-1400 (Local); 011-44-171-778-1400.
Baku, Azerbaijan Office: 6-10 Vagif Mustafa-zadeh Street, Third Floor, Icheri Sheher, 370004.
Telephone: 994-12-97-63-88 (Local); 011-994-12-97-63-88 (International).
Fax: 994-12-97-63-91 (Local); 011-994-12-97-63-61 (International).

(See Next Column)

OF COUNSEL

Robert S. Langley, Jr.

For Complete List of Firm Personnel, See General Section

For full biographical listings, see the Martindale-Hubbell Law Directory

BERLACK, ISRAELS & LIBERMAN LLP (AV)

120 West 45th Street, 10036
Telephone: 212-704-0100
Cable Address: "Berilib"
Telecopier: 212-704-0196
Email: info@berlack.com
Morristown, New Jersey Office: 65 Madison Avenue.
Telephone: 201-644-3400.
Telecopier: 201-644-3159.

MEMBERS OF FIRM

Harris Berlack (1946-1968)
Carlos L. Israels (1946-1969)
Kenneth R. Asher
Claude A. Baum
Scott M. Berman
Wade M. Boswell
Douglas E. Davidson
Alan N. Forman
Steven E. Greenbaum
Harvey M. Katz
James B. Liberman
Stuart Neuhauser
Robert D. Schmicker
Martin S. Siegel
Steven F. Wasserman
Edward S. Weisfelner

SENIOR ATTORNEYS

Andrew S. Dash
Erica M. Ryland

ASSOCIATES

John P. Biedermann
Anne M. Cunningham
Pauline Foley (Resident, Morristown, New Jersey Office)
Julie L. Friedberg (Resident, Morristown, New Jersey Office)
Emilio A. Galván
Linda B. Goebel
Louis Lombardo
Rachel F. Mayerson (Not admitted in NY)
Amy P. K. Motzenbecker (Resident, Morristown, New Jersey Office)
Antonio Peguero, Jr.
Elizabeth Quirk (Resident, Morristown, New Jersey Office)
Marcela M. Sanchez
Melissa Sarubbi

OF COUNSEL

Gerald W. Conway (Not admitted in NY; Resident, Morristown, New Jersey Office)
Marc B. Lasky (Resident, Morristown, New Jersey Office)

For full biographical listings, see the Martindale-Hubbell Law Directory

CURTIS, MALLET-PREVOST, COLT & MOSLE LLP (AV)

101 Park Avenue, 10178-0061
Telephone: 212-696-6000
Telecopier: 212-697-1559
Email: info@cm-p.com *URL:* http://www.cm-p.com
Washington, D.C. Office: Suite 1205L, 1801 K Street, N.W.
Telephone: 202-452-7373.
Telecopier: 202-452-7333.
Newark, New Jersey Office: One Gateway Center, Suite 403.
Telephone: 973-622-0605.
Telecopier: 973-622-5646.
Houston, Texas Office: 2 Houston Center, 909 Fannin Street, Suite 3725.
Telephone: 713-759-9555.
Telecopier: 713-759-0712.
Stamford, Connecticut Office: One Canterbury Green.
Telephone: 203-359-6200.
Telecopier: 203-328-2617.
Mexico City, D.F., Mexico Office: Curtis, Mallet-Prevost, Colt & Mosle, Ruben Dario 281, Piso 9, Col. Bosque de Chapultepec, 11530 Mexico, D.F.
Telephone: 525-282-0444.
Telecopier: 525-282-0637.
Paris, France Office: 15 rue d'Astorg, 75008.
Telephone: +33-1 42-66-39-10.
Telecopier: +33-1 42-66-39-62.
London, England Office: Two Throgmorton Avenue, EC2N 2DL.
Telephone: 0207-638-7957.
Telecopier: 0207-638-5512.
Frankfurt am Main 1, Germany Office: Staufenstrasse 42.
Telephone: +49-69-971-4420.
Telecopier: +49-69-17 33 99.
Muscat, Sultanate of Oman Office: Jewel Beach-134.
Telephone: 968-607-725.
Telecopier: 968-607-724.
Milan, Italy Office: Curtis, Mallet-Prevost & Gilioli, Piazzale Principessa Clotilde 8, 20121.
Telephone: +(39) 02 29 00 29 32.
Telefax: +(39) 02 65 75 969.

MEMBERS OF FIRM

Alan Berlin
Marco A. Blanco
William L. Bricker, Jr.
Eduardo A. Cukier
Jeffrey D. Mamorsky
Robert D. Whoriskey

(See Next Column)

CURTIS, MALLET-PREVOST, COLT & MOSLE LLP—*Continued*

COUNSEL

David B. Spanier

ASSOCIATES

Elizabeth E. Butler
John C. Dworkin
Mark Feldman
Jae W. Lee
Caryn B. Sobelman

For full biographical listings, see the Martindale-Hubbell Law Directory

---

FEINGOLD & ALPERT, L.L.P. (AV)

1330 Avenue of the Americas, 10019
Telephone: 212-582-8000
Fax: 212-582-8080
Email: MAIL@FEINGOLDALPERT.COM

Fred Feingold
Herbert H. Alpert
Mark E. Berg
Jonathan S. Brenner

ASSOCIATE

Mary Ann Amodeo

For full biographical listings, see the Martindale-Hubbell Law Directory

---

GIBNEY, ANTHONY & FLAHERTY, LLP (AV)

A Limited Liability Partnership including a Professional Corporation
665 Fifth Avenue, 10022
Telephone: 212-688-5151
Telecopier: 212-688-8315
URL: http://www.gibney.com

MEMBERS OF FIRM

Wilson J. Gibney (1917-1987)
Ralph F. Anthony (1917-1996)
John F. Flaherty
Barry Zalaznick
James H. McGivney
Frederick W. Anthony
Robert V. Okulski
Stephen F. Ruffino
Gerald J. Dunworth
Stephen J. O. Maltby
Kenneth N. Sacks
Brian W. Brokate
Pierre Cournot
Wm. Lee Kinnally, Jr.
Peter Cousins
Melville Southard, Jr.
Robert J. Costello
Heather J. McDonald
Joseph Di Cesare
Paul G. Kelly
Alan M. Weintraub
Melvyn H. Halper
Angelo E. P. Mazza
Beth M. Frenchman
John Macaluso
Marc Ragovin

ASSOCIATES

Pierre G. Bonnefil
Robert G. Kinnally
Kenneth D. Suzan
Ebonette Bates
Thao P. Nguyen

COUNSEL

Donald J. Williamson
Christopher Magrath
Richard L. Fisch
Stuart H. Brody
Paolo S. Grassi

For full biographical listings, see the Martindale-Hubbell Law Directory

---

HOFFINGER FRIEDLAND DOBRISH & STERN, P.C. (AV)

A Professional Corporation including Professional Corporations
110 East 59th Street, 10022-1392
Telephone: 212-421-4000
Telecopier: 212-223-3857

Jack S. Hoffinger
Lawrence N. Friedland
Robert Z. Dobrish (P.C.)
Stephen R. Stern (P.C.)
Samuel P. Ross
Warren R. Gleicher
Philip S. Ross

Michael J. Sherman
Fran Hoffinger
John H. Friedland
Lydia A. Milone
Devorah S. Weinschneider
Eric I. Wrubel
Nina S. Gross
Scott Lawrence D'Aloise

For full biographical listings, see the Martindale-Hubbell Law Directory

---

INGRAM YUZEK GAINEN CARROLL & BERTOLOTTI, LLP (AV)

250 Park Avenue, 10177
Telephone: 212-907-9600
Facsimile: 212-907-9681

MEMBERS OF FIRM

Ernest J. Bertolotti (1942-1999)
Daniel L. Carroll
Roger Cukras
David G. Ebert
Larry F. Gainen
Samuel W. Ingram, Jr.
Paulette Kendler
Steven Mastbaum
Shane O'Neill
Dean G. Yuzek

ASSOCIATES

Warren E. Barrows
Amy Bertolotti
Patricia Hewitt
Theodore M. Kakoyiannis
Jeanne F. Pucci
Leigh A. Roveda
Jennifer E. Schwartz
Paul H. Slaney

(See Next Column)

OF COUNSEL

Karin J. Barkhorn
Beverly L. Deickler
Mark E. Klein
Paulette Lemay Peters
Cory L. Weiss

For full biographical listings, see the Martindale-Hubbell Law Directory

---

KOSTELANETZ & FINK, LLP (AV)

530 Fifth Avenue, 22nd Floor, 10036
Telephone: 212-808-8100
Fax: 212-808-8108
Email: mail@kostelanetzfink.com

SENIOR COUNSEL

Boris Kostelanetz

MEMBERS OF FIRM

Robert S. Fink
Kevin M. Flynn
Bryan C. Skarlatos

COUNSEL

Norman Sinrich
Theodore F. Dickson
Caroline Rule
Brian C. Wille
William F. Cuozzi, III
Dawn Ngo

For full biographical listings, see the Martindale-Hubbell Law Directory

---

BUREAU FRANCIS LEFEBVRE (AV)

712 Fifth Avenue, 10019
Telephone: 212-246-8045
Fax: 212-246-2951
Email: clevintoff@bflny.com
Paris, France Office: 1-3, Villa Emile Bergerat, 92522 Neuilly-Sur-Seine, Cedex.
Telephone: +33-1 47 38 55 00.
Fax: +33-1 47 38 55 55. Email: central@bfl-avocats.com.
Barcelona, Spain Office: Rodes y Sala Bureau Francis Lefebvre, Calle Pau Casals 15-3, 08021, Barcelona.
Telephone: +34 93 241 37 40.
Fax: +34 93 209 89 96. Email: rodesysala@bam-bfl.com.
Berlin, Germany Office: Friedrichstrasse 200, D-10117 Berlin.
Telephone: +49 30 2233 11 00.
Fax: +49 30 2233 11 22. Email: bfl-berlin@berlin.sireco.net.
Brussels, Belgium Office: avenue Louise, 523, 1050 Bruxelles.
Telephone: +32-2 644 26 61.
Fax: +32-2 649 68 01. Email: bfl@skynet.be.
Bucharest, Romania Office: 4bd Natiunilor Unite, Bloc 106, sector 5, Bucharest.
Telephone: +40 1 335 15 40.
Fax: +40 1 335 08 74. Email: marcuc@ines.ro.
Buenos Aires, Argentina Office: Paraquay 1132, piso 4°, Buenos Aires, 1057 Capital Federal.
Telephone: +54 11.48.13.64.61.
Fax: +54 11.48.16. 06.08. Email: bfl@ba.net.
Casablanca, Morocco Office: 106 rue Abderrahman Sehraoui, Casablanca 2000.
Telephone: +(212) 2.26.19.92.
Fax: +(212) 2.26.37.61.
Düsseldorf, Germany Office: Immermannstrasse 15, 40210 Düsseldorf.
Telephone: +49 211 17 59 10.
Fax: +49 211 1 64 04 11. Email: bfl-duss@t-online.dc.
Madrid, Spain Office: Briones, Alonso y Martin Bureau Francis Lefebvre, Paseo de la Castellana 20, 28046 Madrid.
Telephone: +34 91 436 45 31.
Fax: +34 91 436 43 02. Email: bam@mx3.rodestb.cs.
Moscow, Russia Office: 10, Uspensky Pereoulok, 103006 Moscow.
Telephone: +7.502.221.49.03.
Fax: +7.095.299.30.24. Email: bflrus@co.ru.

RESIDENT PARTNERS

Carina Levintoff
Edouard Milhac (Not admitted in the United States)

RESIDENT ASSOCIATES

Francine L. Alfandary
Paul Bayle (Not admitted in the United States)

OF COUNSEL

John P. Lowe, Jr.

For full biographical listings, see the Martindale-Hubbell Law Directory

---

LOEB & LOEB LLP (AV)

A Limited Liability Partnership including Professional Corporations
345 Park Avenue, 10154-0037
Telephone: 212-407-4000
Facsimile: 212-407-4990
Email: info@loeb.com *URL:* http://www.loeb.com
Los Angeles, California Office: Suite 1800, 1000 Wilshire Boulevard, 90017-2475.
Telephone: 213-688-3400.
Facsimile: 213-688-3460.

(See Next Column)

LOEB & LOEB LLP, *New York—Continued*

Century City (Los Angeles), California Office: Suite 2200, 10100 Santa Monica Boulevard, Los Angeles, 90067-4164.
Telephone: 310-282-2000.
Facsimile: 310-282-2192.
Nashville, Tennessee Office: 45 Music Square West, 37203-3205.
Telephone: 615-749-8300.
Facsimile: 615-749-8308.
Rome, Italy Office: Piazza Digione 1, 00197.
Telephone: 011-3906-808-8456.
Facsimile: 011-3906-808-8288.

MEMBER OF FIRM

Jay Fenster

For Complete List of Firm Personnel, See General Section

For full biographical listings, see the Martindale-Hubbell Law Directory

GEORGE J. NOUMAIR, P.C. (AV)

200 Park Avenue, Suite 4514, 10166
Telephone: 212-822-3266
Fax: 212-822-3277

George J. Noumair
Michael T. Kiesel
John V. Thornton

For full biographical listings, see the Martindale-Hubbell Law Directory

PARKER CHAPIN LLP (AV)

Chrysler Building, 405 Lexington Avenue, 10017
Telephone: 212-704-6000
Telecopier: 212-704-6288
URL: http://www.parkerchapin.com
Great Neck, New York Office: 175 Great Neck Road.
Telephone: 516-482-4422.
Telecopier: 516-482-4469.
Hackensack, New Jersey: 190 Morre Street, Suite 307.
Telephone: 210-883-6400.
Telecopier: 210-883-6404.
Beverly Hills, California: 9454 Wilshire Boulevard.
Telephone: 310-288-8367.
Telecopier: 310-288-8365.

MEMBERS OF FIRM

Carol F. Burger
Brian R. Gallagher
Mark A. Limardo

SENIOR COUNSEL

Irving Rosenzweig

For Complete List of Firm Personnel, See General Section

For full biographical listings, see the Martindale-Hubbell Law Directory

SEIDMAN, SILVERMAN & SEIDMAN, P.C. (AV)

600 Third Avenue 33rd Floor, 10016-2001
Telephone: 212-922-1900

Irving P. Seidman
Lawrence H. Silverman
Brian William Seidman

Joseph M. Fein

For full biographical listings, see the Martindale-Hubbell Law Directory

STEIN RISO MANTEL HASPEL & JACOBS LLP (AV)

405 Lexington Avenue, 42nd Floor, 10174
Telephone: 212-599-1515
Fax: 212-599-6155
Email: email@srmhj.com
New City, New York Office: 254 South Main Street, 10956.
Telephone: 914-634-1010.
Fax: 914-634-8317.

Dennis L. Stein
Gerard A. Riso
Allan D. Mantel
Joseph J. Haspel
Neil I. Jacobs

Beth E. Spickler
Kevin M. McDonough

COUNSEL

Mark Ira Chinitz

For full biographical listings, see the Martindale-Hubbell Law Directory

STROOCK & STROOCK & LAVAN LLP (AV)

180 Maiden Lane, 10038-4982
Telephone: 212-806-5400
Telecopier: 212-806-6006
Telexes: Stroock, UT 177693 and Plastroock NYK 177077 (International)
Email: info@stroock.com *URL:* http://www.stroock.com
New York Conference Center: 767 Third Avenue, New York, N.Y., 10017-2023.
Telephones: 212-806-5767; 5768; 5769; 5770.
Telecopier: 212-421-6234. Email: info@stroock.com
Boston, Massachusetts Office: 100 Federal Street, Boston, MA., 02110-1813 .
Telephone: 617-482-6800.
Fax: 617-330-5111. Email: infoboston@stroock.com
Los Angeles, California Office: 2029 Century Park East, Suite 1800, Los Angeles, CA., 90067-3086.
Telephone: 310-556-5800.
Telecopier: 310-556-5959. Email: infola@stroock.com
Miami, Florida Office: First Union Financial Center, 200 South Biscayne Boulevard, Suite 3300, Miami, FL., 33131-2385.
Telephone: 305-358-9900.
Telecopier: 305-789-9302. Email: infomiami@stroock.com
Washington, D.C. Office: 1150 Seventeenth Street, N.W., Suite 600, Washington, D.C., 20036-4652.
Telephone: 202-452-9250.
Telecopier: 202-293-2293. Email: infodc@stroock.com

MEMBERS OF FIRM

Micah W. Bloomfield
Mayer Greenberg
Barbara D. Klippert
Jonathan S. Kusko
Mark A. Levy
Jeffrey D. Uffner

RETIRED PARTNER

Charles B. Hochman

Mark Eichler
Susan R. Friedman
Michael E. Lubin

For Complete List of Firm Personnel, See General Section

For full biographical listings, see the Martindale-Hubbell Law Directory

TODTMAN, NACHAMIE, SPIZZ & JOHNS, P.C. (AV)

425 Park Avenue, 10022
Telephone: 212-754-9400
Fax: 212-754-6262
Email: INFO@tnsj-law.com *URL:* http://www.tnsj-law.com
Paris, France Office: 3, rue du Faubourg Saint-Honoré 75008.
Telephone: +33-1 44-71-03-03.
Facsimile: +33-1 44-71-03-04.

Martin Todtman
Barton Nachamie
Alex Spizz
Peter A. Johns (Not admitted in United States)
Robert D. Tolz
Beth S. Barash
Arthur Goldstein
Perry L. Cohen
Mathew E. Hoffman
S. Timothy Ball
Scott S. Markowitz
Gilbert A. Samberg
Alan S. Liebman

Perri E. Frosch
Andrew L. Rosenberg
Richard S. Kanowitz
William A. Palomo
Felipe Montejo
Julie K. Horowitz
Matthew W. Woodruff

OF COUNSEL

Jack Newton Lerner
Harvey I. Sladkus

For full biographical listings, see the Martindale-Hubbell Law Directory

WACHTEL & MASYR, LLP (AV)

110 East 59th Street, 10022
Telephone: 212-909-9500
Telecopier: (212) 371-0320

MEMBERS OF FIRM

Robert W. Berend
Steven J. Cohen
William F. Dowling
Scott J. Lesser
Marvin J. Levine
Jesse Masyr
John H. Reichman
I. Frederick Shotkin
Jeffrey T. Strauss
William B. Wachtel
Morris Missry
Evan S. Weintraub
John W. McConnell
Brian G. Lustbader
Howard J. Goldman

OF COUNSEL

Walter Castore (Legal Consultant on the Laws of Italy)
Walter P. Stasiuk
Robert Stone
Vladimir Zlobinsky
Rosemary Ginty
Francesco Penta (Not admitted in United States)
Maurizio Ulrich-Bansa (Not admitted in United States)
Karen Binder

(See Next Column)

WACHTEL & MASYR LLP—*Continued*

ASSOCIATES

Aimee Cain
Michele D'Avolio
Howard I. Elman
Aaron D. Greenberg
Avram E. Posner
Allan Joseph Weiss
Anne F. McCaughey

For full biographical listings, see the Martindale-Hubbell Law Directory

WINTHROP, STIMSON, PUTNAM & ROBERTS (AV)

One Battery Park Plaza, 10004-1490
Telephone: 212-858-1000
Telex: 62854 WINSTIM
Telefax: 212-858-1500
URL: http://www.winstim.com
Stamford, Connecticut Office: Financial Centre, 695 East Main Street, P.O. Box 6760, 06904-6760.
Telephone: 203-348-2300.
Fax: 203-965-8226.
Washington, D.C. Office: 1133 Connecticut Avenue, N.W., 20036.
Telephone: 202-775-9800.
Fax: 202-833-8491.
Palm Beach, Florida Office: 125 Worth Avenue, Suite 310, 33480.
Telephone: 561-655-7297.
Fax: 561-833-6726.
London Office: 54 Lombard Street, London EC3V 9DH, England.
Telephone: 011-44207-648-9200.
Fax: 011-44207-283-1656.
Tokyo, Japan Office: 608 Atagoyama Bengoshi Building 6-7, Atago 1-chome, Minato-ku, Tokyo 105 Japan.
Telephone: 011-813-3437-9740.
Fax: 011-813-3437-9261.
Hong Kong, China Office: 2505 Asia Pacific Finance Tower, Citibank Plaza, 3 Garden Road, Central.
Telephone: 011-852-2530-3400.
Fax: 011-852-2530-3355.
Singapore Office: 6 Battery Road #38-01/B, Singapore 049909.
Telephone: 65-227-4700.
Fax: 65-227-4711.

NEW YORK OFFICE
MEMBERS OF FIRM

William C. Bowers
William L. Burke
James T. Chudy
Richard G. Cohen
Hugh M. Dougan
Lori S. Hoberman
Susan P. Serota

For Complete List of Firm Personnel, See General Section

For full biographical listings, see the Martindale-Hubbell Law Directory

*POUGHKEEPSIE,** Dutchess Co.

TEAHAN & CONSTANTINO (AV)

325 South Road, P.O. Box 1969, 12601
Telephone: 914-452-1834
Fax: 914-452-1421
Email: tandc@idsi.net *URL:* http://www.TCTaxPlan.com
Albany, New York Office: 125 Wolf Road, Suite 412, 12205.
Telephone: 518-435-0534;
Fax: 518-435-0546.

MEMBERS OF FIRM

Vincent L. Teahan
James P. Constantino

OF COUNSEL

Richard I. Cantor
Eliot D. Hawkins
Gina A. Gulotty

For full biographical listings, see the Martindale-Hubbell Law Directory

VAN DEWATER & VAN DEWATER (AV)

40 Garden Street, P.O. Box 112, 12602
Telephone: 914-452-5900
Fax: 914-452-5848
Pawling, New York Office: 243 Route 22, P.O. Box 668.
Telephone: 914-855-5900.
Fax: 914-855-5945.

MEMBERS OF FIRM

John B. Van DeWater (1892-1968)
Robert B. Van DeWater (1920-1990)
David D. Hagstrom
John K. Gifford
James E. Nelson
Craig T. Digilio
Gerard J. Comatos
Ronald C. Blass, Jr.

OF COUNSEL

Noel deCordova, Jr.
Edward VK. Cunningham, Jr.
James D. Benson
Susanna E. Bedell

ASSOCIATES

Rebecca Supple Mensch
Michael G. Hayes

Counsel for: J. D. Johnson Co., Inc.; The Fishkill National Bank; The Bank of the Hudson; Vassar Brothers Hospital.
Local Counsel for: Vassar College; Chemprene Div. of Witco Chemical Corp.; Gannett Satellite Information Network, Inc.

(See Next Column)

For full biographical listings, see the Martindale-Hubbell Law Directory

*ROCHESTER,** Monroe Co.

SHERRY S. KRAUS (AV)

513 Times Square Building, 45 Exchange Boulevard, 14614
Telephone: 716-262-3360
Fax: 716-262-2739

For full biographical listings, see the Martindale-Hubbell Law Directory

UNDERBERG & KESSLER LLP (AV)

1800 Chase Square, 14604
Telephone: 716-258-2800
Fax: 716-258-2821
Email: INFO@UNDERBERG-KESSLER.COM
Buffalo, New York Office: 1100 Main Place Tower. 14202.
Telephone: 716-848-9000.
Fax: 716-847-6004.

MEMBERS OF FIRM

Alan J. Underberg (1929-1998)
Irving L. Kessler
Michael J. Beyma
James A. Coniglio
Frank T. Crego
Robert W. Croessmann
John W. Crowe
Patrick L. Cusato
Michael C. Dwyer
Bernard A. Frank
Steven R. Gersz
Katherine Howk Karl
Lawrence P. Keller
Gordon J. Lipson
Anna E. Lynch
Robert F. Mechur
Paul V. Nunes
Terry M. Richman
J. David Sampson (Resident, Buffalo Office)
Sharon P. Stiller
Stephen H. Waite
Russell I. Zuckerman

OF COUNSEL

Andrew M. Greenstein

SENIOR ATTORNEYS

Duncan R. Farney
Ronald G. Hull

ASSOCIATES

James F. Armstrong (Resident, Buffalo Office)
Karen A. DiNardo
Lise C. Hamilton
Jeffrey D. Hummel
Paul F. Keneally
Ella L. Krzanowicz
Maureen E. Mulholland
Suzanne D. Nott
Kelly L. Odorisi
Thomas A. Rall

For full biographical listings, see the Martindale-Hubbell Law Directory

SCARSDALE, Westchester Co.

STANLEY E. BULUA, ATTORNEY AT LAW, LLC (AV)

670 White Plains Road, Suite 226, 10583
Telephone: 914-725-0909
Fax: 914-725-0987
Email: sbulua@sbulua-atty.com *URL:* http://www.lawyers.com/stanleyebulualaw

Stanley E. Bulua

Roberta S. Goodman

For full biographical listings, see the Martindale-Hubbell Law Directory

*SYRACUSE,** Onondaga Co.

COSTELLO COONEY & FEARON, LLP (AV)

Salina Place, 205 South Salina Street, 13202
Telephone: 315-422-1152
Fax: 315-422-1139
Email: ccf-law.com *URL:* http://www.ccf-law.com

MEMBERS OF FIRM

Warren W. Bader
Alicia S. Calagiovanni
Timothy J. Conan

General Counsel for: Auburn Memorial Hospital; Crouse Hospital; Health Services Association of Central New York; St. Joseph's Hospital Health Center.
Local Counsel for: Deere & Co.; New York Telephone Co.; Crum & Forster Insurance Co.; The Travelers Insurance Companies; Caterpillar, Inc.; Otis Elevator.

For Complete List of Firm Personnel, See General Section

For full biographical listings, see the Martindale-Hubbell Law Directory

HANCOCK & ESTABROOK, LLP (AV)

MONY Tower 1, P.O. Box 4976, 13221-4976
Telephone: 315-471-3151
Telecopier: 315-471-3167
Email: DBYRNE@HANCOCKLAW.COM
Albany, New York Office: Suite 505, 125 Wolf Road.
Telephone: 518-458-7660.
Telecopier: 518-458-7731.

(See Next Column)

HANCOCK & ESTABROOK LLP, *Syracuse—Continued*

MEMBERS OF FIRM

Gerald F. Stack
Jeffrey B. Andrus
Michael L. Corp
Marion Hancock Fish
Cora A. Alsante

Representative Clients: HSBC; Crucible Materials Corp.; Mobil Oil Corp.; Syracuse City School District; Metropolitan Development Assoc.; Metropolitan Life Insurance Co.; Amerada Hess Corp.; Cooper Industries, Inc.; Carrier Corp.; LeMoyne College; Conmed; Crouse Hospital; Chrysler Corporation; Ryder Transportation Services, Inc.

For Complete List of Firm Personnel, See General Section

For full biographical listings, see the Martindale-Hubbell Law Directory

*WHITE PLAINS,** Westchester Co.

GREENSPAN & GREENSPAN (AV)

34 South Broadway, Suite 605, 10601-4400
Telephone: 914-946-2500
Cable Address: "Gadlex"
Telecopier: 914-946-1432
Email: GandGEsqs@aol.com
Boca Raton, Florida Office: Greenspan & Kane, 301 Yamato Road, Suite 3160.
Telephone: 561-995-8140.
Oradell, New Jersey Office: 690 Kinderkamack Rd., 07649.
Telephone: 201-599-2849; 800-553-6009.

MEMBERS OF FIRM

Leon J. Greenspan
Michael E. Greenspan

For full biographical listings, see the Martindale-Hubbell Law Directory

SMITH, RANSCHT, CONNORS, MUTINO, NORDELL & SIRIGNANO, P.C. (AV)

235 Main Street, 10601
Telephone: 914-946-8800
Telecopier: 914-946-8861
Cable Address: "Smiran" White Plains, New York

James P. Connors, Jr.
Peter J. Mutino
Michael Nordell
George A. Sirignano, Jr.

Counsel for: Universal Builders Supply, Inc.; The Walter Karl Cos.; Hartsdale Canine Cemetery; Wise Components, Inc.; Facsimile Communications Industries, Inc.; Carlcraft Knit Sales, Inc.
Closing Attorney for: First Union Mortgage Corp.
Representative Client: United Airlines, Corporate Express, Inc.

For full biographical listings, see the Martindale-Hubbell Law Directory

JOHN E. WATKINS, JR. (AV)

175 Main Street, 10601
Telephone: 914-428-1292
Telecopier: 914-428-4104
Local 800 Service: 1-800-33WATKINS
Email: wat2kins@netcom.com *URL:* http://www.lawyers.com/johnewatkinsjr
New York, New York Office: 29 Broadway.
Telephone: 212-968-1500.

ASSOCIATE

Ira S. Levy

For full biographical listings, see the Martindale-Hubbell Law Directory

NORTH CAROLINA

*CHARLOTTE,** Mecklenburg Co.

BAILEY, PATTERSON, CADDELL, HART, MILLIKEN & BAILEY, P.A. (AV)

Suite 502, Cameron Brown Building, 301 South McDowell Street, 28204
Telephone: 704-333-8612
FAX: 704-333-5279
Email: BaileyPA8@aol.com

Allen A. Bailey
Michael A. Bailey
William J. Patterson
H. Morris Caddell, Jr.
Walter L. Hart, IV
Emery E. Milliken
Martha L. Ramsay
Helen Ruth Harwell

For full biographical listings, see the Martindale-Hubbell Law Directory

CAUDLE & SPEARS, P.A. (AV)

2600 Interstate Tower, 121 West Trade Street, 28202
Telephone: 704-377-1200
Telecopier: 704-338-5858
Email: caudlespears@caudlespears.com

(See Next Column)

Jeffrey L. Helms

Counsel for: Bituminous Casualty Corp.; Baumann Springs A.G.; The A. G. Boone Co.; Capitol Funds, Inc.; Consolidated Freightways; Employers Mutual Casualty Co.; Mark Oil Company, Inc.; Metromont Materials; Otis Elevator Co.; N.C. Farm Bureau Mutual Insurance Co.

For Complete List of Firm Personnel, See General Section

For full biographical listings, see the Martindale-Hubbell Law Directory

CULP ELLIOTT & CARPENTER, P.L.L.C. (AV)

A Professional Limited Liability Company
227 West Trade Street Suite 1500, 28202
Telephone: 704-372-6322
Telefax: 704-372-1474
URL: http://www.ceandc.com

William R. Culp, Jr., (P.A.)
W. Curtis Elliott, Jr.
John Joseph Carpenter
Paul M. Hattenhauer
Margaret R. K. Leinbach
Christopher E. Hannum
Jeffrey D. Barnes
Mark Louis Richardson

Chace D. Campbell
Stephen W. Martin
Virginia Leggett Stevenson (Not admitted in NC)
Melody Y. Malone
John E. Troxel
C. Shannon Elliotte

For full biographical listings, see the Martindale-Hubbell Law Directory

WOMBLE CARLYLE SANDRIDGE & RICE (AV)

A Professional Limited Liability Company
3300 One First Union Center, 301 South College Street, 28202-6025
Telephone: 704-331-4900
Fax: 704-331-4955
Email: lawyers@wcsr.com *URL:* http://www.wcsr.com
Winston-Salem, North Carolina Office: 200 West Second Street, P.O. Drawer 84.
Telephone: 336-721-3600.
Fax: 336-721-3660.
Raleigh, North Carolina Office: 2100 First Union Capitol Center, 150 Fayetteville Street Mall, P.O. Box 831.
Telephone: 919-755-2100.
Fax: 919-755-2150.
Research Triangle Park, North Carolina Office: 2505 Meridian Parkway, Suite 300 (Durham), 27713.
Telephone: 919-484-2300.
Fax: 919-484-2340.
Atlanta, Georgia Office: One Atlantic Center, 1201 West Peachtree Street, Suite 3500.
Telephone: 404-872-7000.
Fax: 404-888-7490.
Other Atlanta, Georgia Office: Suite 404, 2296 Henderson Mill Road, N.E.
Telephone: 770-492-9030.
Fax: 770-492-9609.
Washington, D.C. Office: 1120 Nineteenth Street, N.W., Eighth Floor.
Telephone: 202-857-4400.
Fax: 202-467-6910.
Greenville, South Carolina Office: 15 South Main Street, Suite 601, P.O. Box 10208.
Telephone: 864-255-5400.
Fax: 864-255-5440.

RESIDENT MEMBERS

Joe B. Cogdell, Jr.
J. Carlton Fleming
James E. Johnson, Jr.

Representative Clients: Childress Klein Properties, Inc.; Food Lion, Inc.; J.A. Jones Construction Co.; Parkdale Mills, Inc.; Pillowtex; Duke Power Co.; Bowles Hollowell Conner & Co.; ALLTEL Carolina, Inc.; Belk Store Services, Inc.; Philip Holzmann A.G.

For Complete List of Firm Personnel, See General Section

For full biographical listings, see the Martindale-Hubbell Law Directory

*GREENSBORO,** Guilford Co.

SCHOCH & WOODRUFF, L.L.P. (AV)

420 West Market Street, 27401
Telephone: 336-272-9122
Fax: 336-272-7991
Email: swlawgbo@bellsouth.net
High Point, North Carolina Office: 500 East Green Drive, P.O. Box 1893, 27261.
Telephone: 336-884-4151.
Telecopier: 336-883-7151.

Carolyn J. Woodruff

Anna E. Worley
Dwight G. Rodgers, Jr.

For full biographical listings, see the Martindale-Hubbell Law Directory

HIGH POINT, Guilford Co.

Schoch & Woodruff, L.L.P. (AV)

500 East Green Drive, P.O. Box 1893, 27261
Telephone: 336-884-4151
Telecopier: 336-883-7151
Email: swlawgbo@bellsouth.net
Greensboro, North Carolina Office: 420 West Market Street, 27401.
Telephone: 336-272-9122.
Telecopier: 336-272-7991.

MEMBERS OF FIRM

Arch K. Schoch (1909-1980)
Louise Rodes Schoch (1909-1995)
Arch K. Schoch IV

ASSOCIATE

Arch K. Schoch V

Representative Clients: Archdale Oil Co.; Classic Gallery, Inc.; Cramer Wood Products, Inc.; The High Point Enterprise, Inc.; Jones & Peacock Insurance, Inc.; Phillips Industries, Inc.; Piedmont Chemical Industries, Inc.

For full biographical listings, see the Martindale-Hubbell Law Directory

*RALEIGH,** Wake Co.

Womble Carlyle Sandridge & Rice (AV)

A Professional Limited Liability Company
2100 First Union Capitol Center, 150 Fayetteville Street Mall, P.O. Box 831, 27602
Telephone: 919-755-2100
Fax: 919-755-2150
Email: lawyers@wcsr.com *URL:* http://www.wcsr.com
Charlotte, North Carolina Office: 3300 One First Union Center, 301 South College Street.
Telephone: 704-331-4900.
Fax: 704-331-4955.
Winston-Salem, North Carolina Office: 200 West Second Street, P.O. Drawer 84.
Telephone: 336-721-3600.
Fax: 336-721-3660.
Research Triangle Park, North Carolina Office: 2505 Meridian Parkway, Suite 300 (Durham), 27713.
Telephone: 919-484-2300.
Fax: 919-484-2340.
Atlanta, Georgia Office: One Atlantic Center, 1201 West Peachtree Street, Suite 3500.
Telephone: 404-872-7000.
Fax: 404-888-7490.
Other Atlanta, Georgia Office: Suite 404, 2296 Henderson Mill Road, N.E.
Telephone: 770-492-9030.
Fax: 770-492-9609.
Washington, D.C. Office: 1120 Nineteenth Street, N.W., Eighth Floor.
Telephone: 202-857-4400.
Fax: 202-467-6910.
Greenville, South Carolina Office: 15 South Main Street, Suite 601, P.O. Box 10208.
Telephone: 864-255-5400.
Fax: 864-255-5440.

RESIDENT MEMBER

Frederick W. Rom

RESIDENT ASSOCIATE

Charles L. Becker

Representative Clients: Aetna Casualty and Surety Co., Inc.; ALSCO/AmeriMark Building Products, Inc.; Aoki Corporation America, Inc.; Hackney Brothers, Inc.; Lawyers Mutual Liability Insurance Company of North Carolina; Meredith College; Regency Park Corp.; Wachovia Bank, N.A.

For Complete List of Firm Personnel, See General Section

For full biographical listings, see the Martindale-Hubbell Law Directory

*WILMINGTON,** New Hanover Co.

Murchison, Taylor & Gibson, L.L.P. (AV)

16 North Fifth Avenue, 28401-4593
Telephone: 910-763-2426
Fax: 910-763-6561

MEMBERS OF FIRM

Wallace C. Murchison (Retired)
Joseph O. Taylor, Jr.
Frank B. Gibson, Jr.
Michael Murchison
Nancy M. Guyton
W. Berry Trice
G. Stephen Diab
James W. Latshaw

ASSOCIATE

Frances Youngblood Trask

Representative Clients: Bell South; Branch Banking & Trust Co.; General Electric Co.; Landfall Assn.; Landmark Organization, Inc.; Telechron, Inc.; Trustees, Employers-ILA Pension, Welfare and Vacation Fund; Worsley Cos., Inc.

(See Next Column)

For full biographical listings, see the Martindale-Hubbell Law Directory

*WINSTON-SALEM,** Forsyth Co.

Womble Carlyle Sandridge & Rice (AV)

A Professional Limited Liability Company
200 West Second Street, P.O. Drawer 84, 27102
Telephone: 336-721-3600
Fax: 336-721-3660
Email: lawyers@wcsr.com *URL:* http://www.wcsr.com
Charlotte, North Carolina Office: 3300 One First Union Center, 301 South College Street.
Telephone: 704-331-4900.
Fax: 704-331-4955.
Raleigh, North Carolina Office: 2100 First Union Capitol Center, 150 Fayetteville Street Mall, P.O. Box 831.
Telephone: 919-755-2100.
Fax: 919-755-2150.
Research Triangle Park, North Carolina Office: 2505 Meridian Parkway, Suite 300 (Durham), 27713.
Telephone: 919-484-2300.
Fax: 919-484-2340.
Atlanta, Georgia Office: One Atlantic Center, 1201 West Peachtree Street, Suite 3500.
Telephone: 404-872-7000.
Fax: 404-888-7490.
Other Atlanta, Georgia Office: Suite 404, 2296 Henderson Mill Road, N.E.
Telephone: 770-492-9030.
Fax: 770-492-9609.
Washington, D.C. Office: 1120 Nineteenth Street, N.W., Eighth Floor.
Telephone: 202-857-4400.
Fax: 202-467-6910.
Greenville, South Carolina Office: 15 South Main Street, Suite 601, P.O. Box 10208.
Telephone: 864-255-5400.
Fax: 864-255-5440.

RESIDENT MEMBERS

Linwood L. Davis
Murray C. Greason, Jr.
Michael D. Gunter
Greg L. Smith
C. Mark Wiley

RESIDENT ASSOCIATE

Neil G. O'Rourke

MEMBER OF COUNSEL

Ranlet S. Bell

Representative Clients: Brad Ragan, Inc.; Brenner Companies; Food Lion, Inc.; Hanes Companies, Inc.; North Carolina Baptist Hospitals, Inc.; R.J. Reynolds Tobacco Co.; Thomasville Furniture Industries, Inc.; Wachovia Corp.; Wake Forest University.

For Complete List of Firm Personnel, See General Section

For full biographical listings, see the Martindale-Hubbell Law Directory

NORTH DAKOTA

*BISMARCK,** Burleigh Co.

Pearce and Durick, PLLP (AV)

314 East Thayer Avenue, P.O. Box 400, 58502
Telephone: 701-223-2890
Fax: 701-223-7865
Email: law.office@pearce-durick.com *URL:* http://www.pearce-durick.com

MEMBERS OF FIRM

William P. Pearce
Lawrence Bender

Representative Clients: Amerada Hess Corp.; AMOCO Oil Co.; Conoco, Inc.; Dupont Inc.; IBM; MDU Resources Group, Inc.; Phillips Petroleum Co.; Northwest Airlines; Shell Oil Co.; Texaco, Inc.

For Complete List of Firm Personnel, See General Section

For full biographical listings, see the Martindale-Hubbell Law Directory

Tschider & Smith (AV)

A Partnership including Professional Corporations
Professional Building - Suite 200, 418 East Rosser Avenue, 58501
Telephone: 701-258-4000
Fax: 701-258-4001
Email: ssmith@tschider-smithlaw.com

MEMBERS OF FIRM

Morris A. Tschider (P.C.)
Sean O. Smith (P.C.)
David A. Tschider

Representative Clients: Agri Bank, FCB; Farm Credit Services of Mandan, FLCA; Farm Credit Services of Mandan, P.C.A.; Twin City Implement, Inc.; First Bank Bismarck; N.D. Independent Insurance Agents; Western Steel & Plumbing; Froelich Oil Co.; Bismarck Eagles; St. Alexius Medical Center.

(See Next Column)

TSCHIDER & SMITH, *Bismarck—Continued*

For full biographical listings, see the Martindale-Hubbell Law Directory

*FARGO,** Cass Co.

NILLES, HANSEN & DAVIES, LTD. (AV)

1800 Radisson Tower, P.O. Box 2626, 58108
Telephone: 701-237-5544
Facsimile: 701-280-0762
Williston, North Dakota Office: Energy Resource Building, 504 East Broadway, Suite 101, P.O. Box 1525.
Telephone: 701-572-5544.
Fax: 701-572-5561.

Russell F. Freeman — Harry M. Pippin

Representative Client: Burlington Northern.

For Complete List of Firm Personnel, See General Section

For full biographical listings, see the Martindale-Hubbell Law Directory

VOGEL, WEIR, BYE, HUNKE & McCORMICK, LTD. (AV)

502 First Avenue North, P.O. Box 1389, 58107
Telephone: 701-237-6983
Facsimile: 701-237-0847
Email: vogellaw@vogellaw.com *URL:* http://www.vogellaw.com

C. Nicholas Vogel — Maurice G. McCormick
Frank G. Gokey

Representative Clients: Associated General Contractors of North Dakota; Blue Shield of North Dakota; Cass County Electric Cooperative, Inc.; Clark Equipment Co.; Forum Communications Company; Merit Care Medical Group; Northern Improvement Co.; Dakota Clinic Ltd.; United Parcel Service; Gateway Chevrolet, Inc.

For Complete List of Firm Personnel, See General Section

For full biographical listings, see the Martindale-Hubbell Law Directory

OHIO

*AKRON,** Summit Co.

GOLDMAN & ROSEN, LTD. (AV)

12th Floor, One Cascade Plaza, 44308-1196
Telephone: 330-376-8336
Telecopier: 330-376-2522
Email: Goldman@Raex.com

Samuel Goldman — Michael B. Hendler
Bernard I. Rosen — Marc P. Gertz
George P. Tsarnas — Gary M. Rosen
Irving B. Sugerman

Thomas K. Seeker — Stacey Tsarnas Hackenberg

OF COUNSEL

Frank E. Steel, Jr. — Joseph F. Gorman

References: First National Bank of Ohio; National City Bank, Akron.

For full biographical listings, see the Martindale-Hubbell Law Directory

*CINCINNATI,** Hamilton Co.

FROST & JACOBS LLP (AV)

2500 PNC Center, 201 East Fifth Street, 45202
Telephone: 513-651-6800
Telecopier: 513-651-6981
URL: http://www.frojac.com
Columbus, Ohio Office: One Columbus, 10 West Broad Street, 43215.
Telephone: 614-464-1211.
Telecopier: 614-464-1737.
Lexington, Kentucky Office: 1100 Vine Center Tower, 333 West Vine Street, 40507.
Telephone: 606-254-1100.
Telecopier: 606-253-2990.
Middletown, Ohio Office: 400 First National Bank Building, 2 North Main Street, 45042.
Telephone: 513-422-2001.
Telecopier: 513-422-3010.
Frankfort, Kentucky Office: 201 W. Main Street, 40601.
Telephone: 502-223-1400.
Telecopier: 502-223-1410.

MEMBERS OF FIRM

James S. Wachs — Ruth R. Longenecker
Ronald E. Heinlen — Martin E. Mooney
T. Stephen Phillips — Patricia D. Laub
John H. Appel — William C. Strangfeld
Douglas D. Thomson

(See Next Column)

SENIOR ATTORNEYS

Barbara F. Applegarth — Michael K. Moyers
Daniel W. Scharff — Christopher DeLuca

ASSOCIATES

Bernard L. McKay — Kimberly D. Wright (Not admitted in OH)
Karen M. Ecker
Sylvius H. Von Saucken

OF COUNSEL

Jerry L. Cowan — Ljubomir Nacev
James A. Katsanis — (Not admitted in OH)

Representative Clients: Armco Inc.; Arthur Andersen & Co.; Catholic Healthcare Partners; Champion International; Cincinnati Bell Inc.; Cincinnati Machine; Federated Department Stores Inc.; Mercy Regional Health System-Greater Cincinnati; PNC Bank, National Association; Sencorp.

For Complete List of Firm Personnel, See General Section

For full biographical listings, see the Martindale-Hubbell Law Directory

KATZ, TELLER, BRANT & HILD A LEGAL PROFESSIONAL ASSOCIATION (AV)

2400 Chemed Center, 255 East Fifth Street, 45202-4724
Telephone: 513-721-4532
Telecopier: 513-721-7120
Email: corp@ktbh.com

Robert E. Brant — William F. Russo
Stephen C. Kisling — Suzanne Prieur Land

Joel S. Brant

OF COUNSEL

Joseph A. Brant

For Complete List of Firm Personnel, See General Section

For full biographical listings, see the Martindale-Hubbell Law Directory

KEATING, MUETHING & KLEKAMP, P.L.L. (AV)

1400 Provident Tower, One East Fourth Street, 45202
Telephone: 513-579-6400
Facsimile: 513-579-6457
URL: http://www.kmklaw.com

MEMBERS OF FIRM

Joseph P. Rouse — Joseph P. Mellen
J. Neal Gardner — Stephen M. Goodson
Timothy B. Matthews — Lisa Wintersheimer Michel
William J. Keating, Jr. — Laura S. Petrie

ASSOCIATES

Alan S. Fershtman — Christopher J. Skufca
Camille Kathleen Kushman

Representative Clients: American Financial Group; BP America Inc.; Chiquita Brands International, Inc.; Cintas Corporation; Comair Holdings, Inc.; Duke Realty Limited Partnership; LSI Industries Inc.; Mosler Inc.; Provident Financial Group Inc.

For Complete List of Firm Personnel, See General Section

For full biographical listings, see the Martindale-Hubbell Law Directory

PORTER & PORTER (AV)

2100 Fourth & Vine Tower, One West Fourth Street, 45202
Telephone: 513-621-3993
Fax: 513-621-1746

MEMBERS OF FIRM

Robert C. Porter, Jr. — Robert C. Porter, III

For full biographical listings, see the Martindale-Hubbell Law Directory

STRAUSS & TROY A LEGAL PROFESSIONAL ASSOCIATION (AV)

The Federal Reserve Building, 150 East Fourth Street, 45202-4018
Telephone: 513-621-2120
Telecopier: 513-241-8259
URL: http://www.strauss-troy.com
Northern Kentucky Office: Suite 1400, 50 East Rivercenter Boulevard, Covington, Kentucky, 41011.
Telephone: 513-621-8900; 513-621-2120.
Telecopier: 513-629-9444.

Mark H. Berliant — Claudia G. Allen
Larry A. Neuman — Marilyn J. Maag
Thomas C. Rink — Marshall K. Dosker (Resident, Covington, Kentucky Office)

Representative Clients: PNC Bank, N.A. (Ohio and Kentucky); Corporex Companies, Inc.; Mercantile Stores Co., Inc.; Star Bank, N.A. (Ohio and Kentucky).

For Complete List of Firm Personnel, See General Section

For full biographical listings, see the Martindale-Hubbell Law Directory

*CLEVELAND,** Cuyahoga Co.

ARTER & HADDEN LLP (AV)

1100 Huntington Building, 925 Euclid Avenue, 44115-1475
Telephone: 216-696-1100
Fax: 216-696-2645
Telex: 98-5384
URL: http://www.arterhadden.com
In Columbus, Ohio: Suite 1200, One Columbus, 10 West Broad Street. 43215-3422.
Telephone: 614-221-3155.
Fax: 614-221-0479.
In Dayton, Ohio: Kettering Tower, Suite 2310, 40 North Main Street. 45423.
Telephone: 937-223-4701.
Fax: 937-223-0170.
In Washington, D.C.: 1801 K Street, N.W., Suite 400K. 20006-3480.
Telephone: 202-775-7100.
Fax: 202-857-0172.
In Dallas, Texas: 1717 Main Street, Suite 4100. 75201-4605.
Telephone: 214-761-2100.
Fax: 214-741-7139.
In Los Angeles, California: 725 South Figueroa Street, Suite 3400. 90017.
Telephone: 213-430-3000.
Fax: 213-617-9255.
In Irvine, California: Five Park Plaza, Suite 1000, Jamboree Center, 92714.
Telephone: 949-252-7500.
Fax: 949-833-9604.
In Austin, Texas: 100 Congress Avenue, Suite 1800.
Telephone: 512-479-6403.
Fax: 512-469-5505.
In San Antonio, Texas: One Riverwalk Place, 700 North Saint Mary's Street, Suite 800, 78205.
Telephone: 210-805-8497.
Fax: 210-805-8519.
In San Francisco, California: Two Embarcadero Center, 5th Floor, 94111.
Telephone: 415-617-2100.
Fax: 415-912-3636.
In Sacramento, California: Wells Fargo Center, 400 Capitol Mall, Suite 900, 95814.
Telephone: 916-449-3917.
Fax: 916-449-8249.
In San Diego, California: 402 West Broadway, Sixth Floor, 92102.
Telephone: 619-238-0001.
Fax: 619-238-8333.
In Woodland Hills, California: 5959 Topanga Canyon Boulevard, Suite 244, 91367.
Telephone: 818-712-0036.
Fax: 818-346-6502.

MEMBERS OF FIRM

Brian W. FitzSimons
Michael F. Harris
Robert E. Glaser
Susan L. Racey
Robert B. Tomaro

RETIRED PARTNER

Charles W. Landefeld

OF COUNSEL

Bernard J. Smith
Ann H. Womer Benjamin

For Complete List of Firm Personnel, See General Section

For full biographical listings, see the Martindale-Hubbell Law Directory

BAKER & HOSTETLER LLP (AV)

3200 National City Center, 1900 East Ninth Street, 44114-3485
Telephone: 216-621-0200
Telecopier: 216-696-0740
TWX: 810 421 8375
RCA Telex: 215032
To contact an attorney on the Internet use first initial and surname followed by @baker-hostetler.com
URL: http://www.bakerlaw.com
In Cincinnati, Ohio: 312 Walnut Street, Suite 2650.
Telephone: 513-929-3400.
In Columbus, Ohio: Capitol Square, Suite 2100, 65 East State Street.
Telephone: 614-228-1541.
In Denver, Colorado: 303 East 17th Avenue, Suite 1100.
Telephone: 303-861-0600.
In Houston, Texas: 1000 Louisiana, Suite 2000.
Telephone: 713-751-1600.
In Beverly Hills, California: 9150 Wilshire Boulevard, Suite 205.
Telephone: 310-385-7500.
In Long Beach, California: 300 Oceangate, Suite 620.
Telephone: 562-432-2827.
In Los Angeles, California: 600 Wilshire Boulevard.
Telephone: 213-624-2400.
In Orlando, Florida: SunBank Center, Suite 2300, 200 South Orange Avenue.
Telephone: 407-649-4000.
In Washington, D.C.: Washington Square, Suite 1100, 1050 Connecticut Avenue, N.W.
Telephone: 202-861-1500.

(See Next Column)

OFFICE MANAGING PARTNER

Kenneth F. Snyder

PARTNERS

Paul H. Feinberg
David J. Strauss
Robert R. Galloway
Christopher J. Swift
Edward G. Ptaszek, Jr.
Alexander J. Szilvas
Hewitt B. Shaw, Jr.
William M. Toomajian

RETIRED PARTNERS

Sherman Dye
David R. Fullmer

For Complete List of Firm Personnel, See General Section

For full biographical listings, see the Martindale-Hubbell Law Directory

JONES, DAY, REAVIS & POGUE (AV)

North Point, 901 Lakeside Avenue, 44114
Telephone: 216-586-3939
Telecopier: 216-579-0212
Email: counsel@jonesday.com *URL:* http://www.jonesday.com
In Columbus, Ohio: 1900 Huntington Center.
Telephone: 614-469-3939.
Telecopier: 614-461-4198.
In Atlanta, Georgia: 3500 SunTrust Plaza, 303 Peachtree Street.
Telephone: 404-521-3939.
Telecopier: 404-581-8330.
In Brussels, Belgium: Avenue Louise 480, 7th Floor. B-1050 Brussels.
Telephone: 32-2-645-14-11.
Telecopier: 32-2-645-14-45.
In Chicago, Illinois: 77 West Wacker.
Telephone: 312-782-3939.
Telecopier: 312-782-8585.
In Dallas, Texas: 2727 North Harwood Street.
Telephone: 214-220-3939.
Telecopier: 214-969-5100.
In Frankfurt, Germany: Hochhaus am Park, Grüneburgweg 102, 60323 Frankfurt am Main.
Telephone: 49-69-9726-3939.
Telecopier: 49-69-9726-3993.
In Geneva, Switzerland: 20, rue de Candolle.
Telephone: 41-22-320-2339.
Telecopier: 41-22-320-1232.
In Hong Kong, China: 29th Floor, Entertainment Building, 30 Queen's Road Central.
Telephone: 852-2526-6895.
Telecopier: 852-2868-5871 or 852-2868-5699.
In Irvine, California: 5 Park Plaza, Suite 1100.
Telephone: 949-851-3939.
Telecopier: 949-553-7539.
In London, England: Bucklersbury House, 3 Queen Victoria Street.
Telephone: 44-171-236-3939.
Telecopier: 44-171-236-1113.
In Los Angeles, California: 555 West Fifth Street, Suite 4600.
Telephone: 213-489-3939.
Telecopier: 213-243-2539.
In New Delhi, India (Associate Office): Pathak & Associates (an associate firm of Jones, Day, Reavis & Pogue), 1st Floor, Dr. Gopal Das Bhaven, 28 Barakhamba Road.
Telephone: 91-11-373-8793; 91-11-335-7345.
Telecopier: 91-11-335-3761.
In New York, N.Y.: 599 Lexington Avenue.
Telephone: 212-326-3939.
Telecopier: 212-755-7306.
In Paris, France: 120, rue du Faubourg Saint-Honoré.
Telephone: 33-1-56-59-39-39.
Telecopier: 33-1-56-59-39-38
In Pittsburgh, Pennsylvania: 500 Grant Street, 31st Floor.
Telephone: 412-391-3939.
Telecopier: 412-394-7959.
In Riyadh, Saudi Arabia: The International Law Firm (In Association with Jones, Day, Reavis & Pogue), Sulaymaniyah, Prince Mishari IBN, Abdulaziz Street, P.O. Box 22166.
Telephone: (966-1) 462-8866.
Telecopier: (966-1) 462-9001.
In Shanghai, China: 2805 Kerry Centre, 1515 Nanjing Road West.
Telephone: 86-21-5298-6568.
Telecopier: 86-21-5298-6569.
In Sydney, Australia: Governor Phillip Tower, Level 38, 1 Farrer Place.
Telephone: 61-2-9210-6921.
Telecopier: 61-2-9210-6926.
In Taipei, Taiwan: 8th Floor, Tun Hwa South Road, Section 2.
Telephone: (886-2) 2704-6808.
Telecopier: (886-2) 2704-6791.
In Tokyo, Japan: Toranomon MT Building, 4th Floor, 10-3, Toranomon 3-Chome, Minato-ku, Tokyo 105, Japan.
Telephone: 81-3-3433-3939.
Telecopier: 81-3-5401-2725.
In Washington, D.C.: 51 Louisiana Avenue, N.W.
Telephone: 202-879-3939.
Telecopier: 202-626-1700.

(See Next Column)

JONES, DAY, REAVIS & POGUE, *Cleveland—Continued*

MEMBERS OF FIRM IN CLEVELAND

John L. Sterling
Kenneth E. Updegraft, Jr.
Kenneth G. Hochman
Jeffrey S. Leavitt
Michael J. Horvitz
John D. Currivan
Daniel C. Hagen
Richard P. Layman
Carl M. Jenks

COUNSEL

John C. Duffy, Jr.
Charles M. Steines
Kathleen Hohler
Ellen E. Halfon
Mary D. Maloney

ASSOCIATES

Lisa A. Roberts-Mamone
Edward Purnell
Robert J. Ringel
Julia Ann Renfro
Eric H. Mosier

For Complete List of Firm Personnel, See General Section

For full biographical listings, see the Martindale-Hubbell Law Directory

McCARTHY, LEBIT, CRYSTAL & HAIMAN CO., L.P.A. (AV)

1800 Midland Building, 101 Prospect Avenue, West, 44115
Telephone: 216-696-1422
Fax: 216-696-1210

Daniel R. McCarthy
Larry Crystal
John S. Seich
Kimon P. Karas

Douglas M. Nelson, II

For full biographical listings, see the Martindale-Hubbell Law Directory

McDONALD, HOPKINS, BURKE & HABER CO., L.P.A. (AV)

2100 Bank One Center, 600 Superior Avenue, E., 44114-2653
Telephone: 216-348-5400
Telecopier: 216-348-5474
Email: attorney@mhbh.com *URL:* http://www.mhbh.com

Patrick J. Berry
Jeffrey P. Consolo
Jerome W. Cook
Richard S. Cooper
Anthony J. DiVenere
Paul N. Edwards
Theodore J. Esborn
Steven L. Gardner
Carl J. Grassi
James A. Griffith
Jeffrey R. Huntsberger
Brian J. Jereb
Bernard L. Karr
Thomas W. Keen
Roger L. Kleinman
Joseph J. LoPresti, Jr.
Dan L. Makee
George L. McGaughey, Jr.
John T. Mulligan
Brian M. O'Neill
William J. O'Neill
Stephen T. Parisi
R. Jeffrey Pollock
Michael G. Riley
Shawn M. Riley
Albert N. Salvatore
Thomas C. Schrader
Roger L. Shumaker
Barbara J. Smith
James M. Stone
Dale R. Vlasek
Kenneth J. Walsh
John M. Wirtshafter
Jane Marie Pine Wood
Charles B. Zellmer

OF COUNSEL

John J. Monroe

Julie A. Callsen
Anne T. Corrigan
Steven A. Eisenberg
G. Andrew Gardner
Anuj Goswami
Donald E. Kacmar
David M. Kall
Jeffrey B. Keiper
Kevin J. Kessinger
Mark D. Klimek
Alan M. Koschik
Deviani M. Kuhar
Paul W. Linehan
Tyler L. Mathews
Jennifer A. Mills
Antoinette K. Palmer
Ketan K. Patel
Sharon Szolosi Regas
Douglas B. Schnee
Michele Smolin
Glenn D. Southworth
Michael R. Spreng

For full biographical listings, see the Martindale-Hubbell Law Directory

SPIETH, BELL, McCURDY & NEWELL CO., L.P.A. (AV)

2000 Huntington Building, 925 Euclid Avenue, 44115-1496
Telephone: 216-696-4700
Fax: 216-696-2706
Email: law@spiethbell.com

Patrick J. Amer
James M. Havach
John M. Slivka

Representative Clients: Cleveland Cavaliers; Nationwide Advertising Services, Inc.; Independent Steel Co.; The Tool-Die Engineering Co.; Dougherty-Hanna Resources Company.

For Complete List of Firm Personnel, See General Section

For full biographical listings, see the Martindale-Hubbell Law Directory

ULMER & BERNE LLP (AV)

Ninth Floor, Bond Court Building, 1300 East Ninth Street, 44114-1583
Telephone: 216-621-8400
FAX: 216-621-7488
Email: infocleveland@ulmer.com
Email: infocolumbus@ulmer.com *URL:* http://www.ulmer.com/
Columbus, Ohio Office: 88 East Broad Street, Suite 1980.
Telephone: 614-228-8400.
FAX: 614-228-8561.

MEMBERS OF FIRM

Lewis T. Barr
John C. Goheen
James A. Goldsmith
Ronald L. Kahn
Herbert B. Levine
Patricia A. Shlonsky

RETIRED MEMBER

William A. Edwards (Retired)

For Complete List of Firm Personnel, See General Section

For full biographical listings, see the Martindale-Hubbell Law Directory

WALTER & HAVERFIELD, P.L.L. (AV)

1300 Terminal Tower, 44113-2253
Telephone: 216-781-1212
Telecopier: 216-575-0911
Email: law@walterhav.com *URL:* http://www.walterhav.com
Columbus, Ohio Office: 88 East Broad Street.
Telephone: 614-898-1096.

MEMBERS OF FIRM

Charles R. Schaefer
Herbert L. Braverman
David W. Welty
Gary A. Zwick

ASSOCIATE

Mia M. Mounts

OF COUNSEL

Arthur P. Steinmetz

For Complete List of Firm Personnel, See General Section

For full biographical listings, see the Martindale-Hubbell Law Directory

WESTON HURD FALLON PAISLEY & HOWLEY L.L.P. (AV)

2500 Terminal Tower, 50 Public Square, 44113-2241
Telephone: 216-241-6602;
Ohio Toll Free: 800-336-4952
FAX: 216-621-8369
Email: Hurd2500@westonhurd.com

MEMBERS OF FIRM

Robert P. McManus
Christopher A. Anselmo

For Complete List of Firm Personnel, See General Section

For full biographical listings, see the Martindale-Hubbell Law Directory

*COLUMBUS,** Franklin Co.

BAKER & HOSTETLER LLP (AV)

Capitol Square, Suite 2100, 65 East State Street, 43215-4260
Telephone: 614-228-1541
Telecopier: 614-462-2616
To contact an attorney on the Internet use first initial and surname followed by @baker-hostetler.com
URL: http://www.bakerlaw.com
In Cleveland, Ohio: 3200 National City Center, 1900 East Ninth Street.
Telephone: 216-621-0200.
In Cincinnati, Ohio: 312 Walnut Street, Suite 2650.
Telephone: 513-929-3400.
In Denver, Colorado: 303 East 17th Avenue, Suite 1100.
Telephone: 303-861-0600.
In Houston, Texas: 1000 Louisiana, Suite 2000.
Telephone: 713-751-1600.
In Beverly Hills, California: 9150 Wilshire Boulevard, Suite 205.
Telephone: 310-385-7500.
In Long Beach, California: 300 Oceangate, Suite 620.
Telephone: 562-432-2827.
In Los Angeles, California: 600 Wilshire Boulevard.
Telephone: 213-624-2400.
In Orlando, Florida: SunBank Center, Suite 2300, 200 South Orange Avenue.
Telephone: 407-649-4000.
In Washington, D. C.: Washington Square, Suite 1100, 1050 Connecticut Avenue, N.W.
Telephone: 202-861-1500.

PARTNER

Edward J. Bernert

For Complete List of Firm Personnel, See General Section

For full biographical listings, see the Martindale-Hubbell Law Directory

Columbus—Continued

BRICKER & ECKLER LLP (AV)

100 South Third Street, 43215-4291
Telephone: 614-227-2300
Telecopy: 614-227-2390
Email: info@be.bricker.com *URL:* http://www.bricker.com

James A. Rutledge
Mark A. Engel
Jerry O. Allen
Gordon F. Litt

Mary Leslie Robins
Christine M. Poth

RETIRED

Charles F. Glander

Representative Clients: Mill's Pride; Ohio Farmers Insurance Company (Westfield Insurance); Boehringer Ingelheim Pharmaceuticals, Inc.; The Hertz Corporation; Hyatt Corporation; The McGraw-Hill Companies, Inc.; Pillsbury Co.; Morgan Stanley Dean Witter & Co.; Sears, Roebuck & Co.; USX Corporation.

For Complete List of Firm Personnel, See General Section

For full biographical listings, see the Martindale-Hubbell Law Directory

KEGLER, BROWN, HILL & RITTER (AV)

Capitol Square Suite 1800, 65 East State Street, 43215-4294
Telephone: 614-462-5400
Telecopier: 614-464-2634
Cable Address: "Law KBHR"
Telex: 246671
Email: info@kbhr.com *URL:* http://www.kbhr.com
Marion, Ohio Office: 250 Executive Drive, Suite B, P.O. Box 919.
Telephone: 614-387-3501.
Facsimile: 614-387-3630.

Edward C. Hertenstein
Charles J. Kegler
Paul D. Ritter, Jr.

Greg R. Grabovac
Todd M. Kegler

Representative Clients: Donato's Pizza, Inc.; Drug Emporium, Inc.; The Fishel Co.; Spenley Newspapers, Inc.; Warner Cable Communication, Inc.

For Complete List of Firm Personnel, See General Section

For full biographical listings, see the Martindale-Hubbell Law Directory

PORTER WRIGHT MORRIS & ARTHUR LLP (AV)

41 South High Street, 43215-6194
Telephone: 614-227-2000; (800-533-2794)
Fax: 614-227-2100
Email: cmh@porterwright.com *URL:* http://www.porterwright.com
Cincinnati, Ohio Office: 250 E. Fifth Street, Suite 2200, 45202-4199.
Telephones: 513-381-4700; (800-582-5813).
Fax: 513-421-0991. Internet: cvg@porterwright.com.
Cleveland, Ohio Office: 925 Euclid Avenue, Suite 1700, 44115-1483.
Telephones: 216-443-9000; (800-824-1980).
Fax: 216-443-9011. Internet: cle@porterwright.com.
Dayton, Ohio Office: One Dayton Centre, One South Main Street, Suite 1600, 45402-2028.
Telephones: 937-449-6810; (800-533-4434).
Fax: 937-449-6820. Internet: day@porterwright.com.
Naples, Florida Office: 5801 Pelican Bay Boulevard, Suite 300, 34108-2709.
Telephones: 941-593-2900; (800-876-7962).
Fax: 941-593-2990. Internet: apf@porterwright.com.
Washington, D.C. Office: 1667 K Street, N.W., Suite 1100, 20006-1605.
Telephones: 202-778-3000; (800-456-7962).
Fax: 202-778-3063. Internet: dca@porterwright.com.

MEMBERS OF FIRM
COLUMBUS, OHIO OFFICE

Jon M. Anderson
Diane K. Goulder
Paul A. Hanke
James M. Mattimoe
Michael T. Radcliffe
David A. Tumen

ASSOCIATES
COLUMBUS, OHIO OFFICE

M. Theresa Finneran
Kelly J. Fox

OF COUNSEL
COLUMBUS, OHIO OFFICE

Ronald W. Gabriel

For Complete List of Firm Personnel, See General Section

For full biographical listings, see the Martindale-Hubbell Law Directory

SCHOTTENSTEIN, ZOX & DUNN A LEGAL PROFESSIONAL ASSOCIATION (AV)

The Huntington Center, 41 South High Street, 43215
Telephone: 614-462-2700
Telecopier: 614-462-5135
Telex: 650 24 444 365
URL: http://www.szd.com
Cincinnati, Ohio Office: Bank One Towers, 8044 Montgomery Road, Suite 700, 45236-2926.
Telephone: 513-792-2730.
Cleveland, Ohio Office: One Cleveland Center, 1375 East 9th Street, Suite 950.
Telephone: 216-621-6501.
Fax: 216-621-6502.

Harvey Dunn
John Terakedis, Jr.
Fredrick L. Fisher
Richard W. Holz
Martin S. Rosenthal
Michael R. Becker
Terrence A. Grady
Thomas J. Sigmund
Phillip G. Lilly

William P. Zox
Marcus D. Dunn
J. Troy Terakedis
William J. Liss

Reference: Bank One of Columbus, N.A.

For Complete List of Firm Personnel, See General Section

For full biographical listings, see the Martindale-Hubbell Law Directory

VORYS, SATER, SEYMOUR AND PEASE LLP (AV)

52 East Gay Street, P.O. Box 1008, 43216-1008
Telephone: 614-464-6400
Telecopier: 614-464-6350
URL: http://www.vssp.com
Washington, D.C. Office: 1828 L Street, N.W., 20036-5109.
Telephone: 202-467-8800.
Telex: 440693.
Telecopier: 202-467-8900.
Cleveland, Ohio Office: 2100 One Cleveland Center, 1375 East Ninth Street, 44114-1724.
Telephone: 216-479-6100.
Telecopier: 216-479-6060.
Cincinnati, Ohio Office: Suite 2100, 221 East Fourth Street, P.O. Box 0236, 45201-0236.
Telephone: 513-723-4000.
Telecopier: 513-723-4056.
Alexandria, Virginia Office: 277 South Washington St., Suite 310, 22314.
Telephone: 703-549-4282.
Telecopier: 703-549-4492.

MEMBERS OF FIRM

Lawrence L. Fisher
George N. Corey
Ronald L. Rowland
Raymond D. Anderson
Aaron P. Rosenfeld
Robert G. Dykes
Anker M. Bell
Anthony C. Ciriaco
Dan L. Jaffe
David A. Swift
Mark E. Vannatta
Anthony L. Ehler
Kevin M. Czerwonka

OF COUNSEL

Carol Mahaffey
Colborn M. Addison
Richard Heer Oman
Richard R. Stedman

Local Counsel for: Honda of America Mfg., Inc.; The Limited, Inc.; Children's Hospital; Wendy's International, Inc.; The Ohio League of Financial Institutions; Abbott Laboratories; The Ohio State University; Ohio Petroleum Marketers Assoc.

For Complete List of Firm Personnel, See General Section

For full biographical listings, see the Martindale-Hubbell Law Directory

DUBLIN, Franklin Co.

BLAUGRUND, HERBERT & MARTIN, INCORPORATED (AV)

5455 Rings Road, Suite 500, 43017-7517
Telephone: 614-764-0681
Fax: 614-764-0774
Email: bhm@bhmlaw.net

Lawrence H. Cohen
Steven A. Martin

For full biographical listings, see the Martindale-Hubbell Law Directory

*TOLEDO,** Lucas Co.

DOYLE, LEWIS & WARNER (AV)

202 North Erie Street, P.O. Box 2168, 43603
Telephone: 419-248-1500
Fax: 419-248-2002
Email: dlw1@primenet.com

MEMBERS OF FIRM

Steven Timonere
Richard F. Ellenberger
Michael E. Hyrne
Michael A. Bruno
David W. Doerner

(See Next Column)

DOYLE, LEWIS & WARNER, *Toledo—Continued*

ASSOCIATES

Kevin A. Pituch
Maureen O. Atkins

Counsel for: Consolidated Rail Corp.; The Lakefront Dock & Railroad Terminal Co.; Prudential Insurance Co. of America; Equitable Life Assurance Society of the U.S.; Metropolitan Life Insurance Co.; Greyhound Lines; Fireman's Fund Insurance Cos.

For Complete List of Firm Personnel, See General Section

For full biographical listings, see the Martindale-Hubbell Law Directory

EASTMAN & SMITH LTD. (AV)

One Seagate, Twenty-Fourth Floor, P.O. Box 10032, 43699-0032
Telephone: 419-241-6000
Telecopier: 419-247-1777
Columbus, Ohio Office: 65 East State Street, Suite 1000, 43215.
Telephone: 614-460-3556.
Telecopier: 614-228-5371.

MEMBERS OF FIRM

Frank D. Jacobs
Morton Bobowick
John H. Boggs
Gary M. Harden
Mark C. Abramson
David C. Krock

OF COUNSEL

Gerald P. Moran

Representative Clients: Glass Tech, Inc.; The City of Wauseon; Swanton Local School District; Capital Bank, N.A.; Medicare Equipment Supply Co.; Riverside Hospital; Memorial Hospital; McGruder Hospital; Art Iron, Inc.; Commonwealth Construction Corp.; S & R Equipment Co., Inc.

For Complete List of Firm Personnel, See General Section

For full biographical listings, see the Martindale-Hubbell Law Directory

ROHRBACHERS, LIGHT, CRON, ZMUDA & TRIMBLE CO., L.P.A. (AV)

National City Bank Building 8th Floor, 405 Madison Avenue, 43604-1243
Telephone: 419-248-2600
Telecopier: 419-248-2614
URL: http://www.rlczt.com
URL: http://www.lawyers.com/rlcztcom

Vernon E. Rohrbacher (1920-1978)
David J. Rohrbacher
Matthew J. Rohrbacher
C. Randolph Light
Nicholas J. Cron
Gene A. Zmuda
J. Mark Trimble

Beverly J. St. Clair
Diane J. Knoblauch
Todd M. Zimmerman

OF COUNSEL

Brent B. Nicholson

LEGAL SUPPORT PERSONNEL

PARALEGAL

Anne E. Scott

For full biographical listings, see the Martindale-Hubbell Law Directory

OKLAHOMA

*NORMAN,** Cleveland Co.

KEVIN D. WATLEY (AV)

Suite 202-A, 224 West Gray Street, P.O. Box 922, 73070
Telephone: 405-321-5858

For full biographical listings, see the Martindale-Hubbell Law Directory

*OKLAHOMA CITY,** Oklahoma Co.

ANDREWS DAVIS LEGG BIXLER MILSTEN & PRICE, A PROFESSIONAL CORPORATION (AV)

500 West Main, Suite 500, 73102
Telephone: 405-272-9241
FAX: 405-235-8786
Email: andrewsdavis@andrewsdavis.com *URL:* http://www.andrewsdavis.com

James F. Davis
Sally A. Hasenfratz
Richard B. Kells, Jr.
Timothy M. Larason
Mark H. Price
William H. Whitehill, Jr.

OF COUNSEL

Keith T. Childers
Robert B. Milsten

For Complete List of Firm Personnel, See General Section

For full biographical listings, see the Martindale-Hubbell Law Directory

CONNER & WINTERS, A PROFESSIONAL CORPORATION (AV)

One Leadership Square, 211 North Robinson, Suite 1700, 73102-7101
Telephone: 405-272-5711
Facsimile: 405-232-2695
Email: postmaster@cwlaw.com
Tulsa, Oklahoma Office: 3700 First Place Tower, 15 East 5th Street, 74103-4344.
Telephone: 918-586-5711.
Facsimile: 918-586-8982.
Fayetteville, Arkansas Office: Conner & Winters, P.L.L.C., 100 West Center Street, Suite 200, 72701-6081.
Telephone: 501-582-5711.
Facsimile: 501-587-1426.
Washington, D.C. Office: 1050 Seventeenth Street, N.W., Suite 810, 20036-5503.
Telephone: 202-783-5711.
Facsimile: 202-783-5720.

Mark H. Bennett

Cecily H. Murray

For Complete List of Firm Personnel, See General Section

For full biographical listings, see the Martindale-Hubbell Law Directory

CROWE & DUNLEVY, A PROFESSIONAL CORPORATION (AV)

1800 Mid-America Tower, 20 North Broadway, 73102-8273
Telephone: 405-235-7700
Fax: 405-239-6651
Email: marketing@crowedunlevy.com *URL:* http://www.crowedunlevy.com
Tulsa, Oklahoma Office: 500 Kennedy Building, 321 South Boston Avenue, 74103-3313.
Telephone: 918-592-9800.
Fax: 918-592-9801.
Norman, Oklahoma Office: Crowe & Dunlevy, 2500 South McGee, Suite 140, 73072-6705.
Telephone: 405-321-7317.
Fax: 405-360-4002.

Allen D. Evans
James H. Holloman, Jr.
Cynda C. Ottaway
Reeder E. Ratliff
Roger A. Stong
Timothy E. Foley

Cynthia L. Andrews

OF COUNSEL

Terry R. Hanna

For Complete List of Firm Personnel, See General Section

For full biographical listings, see the Martindale-Hubbell Law Directory

HARTZOG CONGER & CASON, A PROFESSIONAL CORPORATION (AV)

1600 Bank of Oklahoma Plaza 201 Robert S. Kerr, 73102
Telephone: 405-235-7000
Facsimile: 405-235-7329

Larry D. Hartzog
J. William Conger
Len Cason
James C. Prince
Steven C. Davis
Joseph P. Hogsett
John D. Robertson
Kurt M. Rupert
Laura Haag McConnell
Linda G. Scoggins
Susan B. Shields
Ryan S. Wilson
Amy J. Sine
Jon H. Trudgeon
Charles E. Geister, III
Phillip G. Whaley
Armand Paliotta

J. Christian Guzzy
Stacey D. Spivey
Melissa Beeson Heindselman
Christin V. Adkins
Byron K. Linkous

OF COUNSEL

Kent F. Frates
Kenneth R. Davis
Alan Newman

For full biographical listings, see the Martindale-Hubbell Law Directory

MCAFEE & TAFT, A PROFESSIONAL CORPORATION (AV)

Tenth Floor, Two Leadership Square, 73102
Telephone: 405-235-9621
Facsimile: (405) 235-0439 (405) 232-2404
Email: mcafee@ionet.net *URL:* http://www.mcafee-taft.com

Kenneth E. McAfee (1903-1986)
Mark E. Burget
Steven P. Cole
Gary F. Fuller
Frank D. Hill
James Dudley Hyde
David J. Ketelsleger
Steven T. Ledgerwood
Dee A. Replogle, Jr.
John N. Schaefer
Scott W. Sewell
Joel D. Stafford

(See Next Column)

McAFEE & TAFT A PROFESSIONAL CORPORATION—*Continued*

OF COUNSEL
Richard G. Taft

Representative Clients: Bank of Oklahoma, N.A.; Fleming Companies, Inc.; Paine Webber Group, Inc.; Arthur Andersen & Co.; Exxon Corp.; St. Paul Fire & Marine Insurance Co.; Columbia/HCA Healthcare Corp.

For Complete List of Firm Personnel, See General Section

For full biographical listings, see the Martindale-Hubbell Law Directory

JOSEPH G. SHANNONHOUSE, IV (AV)

2800 Oklahoma Tower, 210 W. Park Avenue, 73102
Telephone: 405-235-8318
Fax: 405-235-9605

For full biographical listings, see the Martindale-Hubbell Law Directory

*TULSA,** Tulsa Co.

BARROW GADDIS GRIFFITH & GRIMM, A PROFESSIONAL CORPORATION (AV)

610 South Main, Suite 300, 74119-1248
Telephone: 918-584-1600
Fax: 918-585-2444
Email: EMAIL@BGGG.com *URL:* http://www.bggg.com

Allen E. Barrow, Jr.
Robert W. Gaddis
David W. Griffith
William R. Grimm
William E. Farrior
Nancy C. Pruitt
Wm. Brad Heckenkemper
J. Patrick Mensching, Jr.
Robert B. Sartin
L. Michele Nelson

Reference: NationsBank.

For full biographical listings, see the Martindale-Hubbell Law Directory

CONNER & WINTERS, A PROFESSIONAL CORPORATION (AV)

3700 First Place Tower, 15 East 5th Street, 74103-4344
Telephone: 918-586-5711
Fax: 918-586-8982
Email: postmaster@cwlaw.com
Oklahoma City, Oklahoma Office: One Leadership Square, 211 North Robinson, Suite 1700, 73102-7101.
Telephone: 405-272-5711.
Facsimile: 405-232-2695.
Fayetteville, Arkansas Office: Conner & Winters, P.L.L.C., 100 West Center Street, Suite 200, 72701-6081.
Telephone: 501-582-5711.
Facsimile: 501-587-1426.
Washington, D.C. Office: 1050 Seventeenth Street, N.W., Suite 810, 20036-5503.
Telephone: 202-783-5711.
Facsimile: 202-783-5720.

Henry G. Will
Steven W. McGrath
Martin R. Wing
Douglas M. Rather
Paul E. Braden
Gregory D. Renberg

Katherine Gallagher Coyle
Jonathan M. Cinocca

OF COUNSEL
Debbie L. Blackwell

For Complete List of Firm Personnel, See General Section

For full biographical listings, see the Martindale-Hubbell Law Directory

EAGLETON, EAGLETON AND HARRISON, INC. (AV)

Suite 1700, 320 South Boston Avenue, 74103-4706
Telephone: 918-584-0462
Fax: 918-584-3724
Email: eagleton@worldnet.att.net

E. John Eagleton
James R. Eagleton
Charles D. Harrison

OF COUNSEL
Norma Eagleton

For full biographical listings, see the Martindale-Hubbell Law Directory

JAMES, POTTS AND WULFERS, INC. (AV)

2828 Mid-Continent Tower, 401 South Boston Avenue, 74103-4016
Telephone: 918-584-0881
Fax: 918-584-4521

David F. James
Thomas G. Potts
David W. Wulfers

For full biographical listings, see the Martindale-Hubbell Law Directory

OREGON

*PORTLAND,** Multnomah Co.

BLACK HELTERLINE LLP (AV)

1200 Union Bank of California Tower, 707 S.W. Washington Street, 97205
Telephone: 503-224-5560
Telecopier: 503-224-6148
URL: http://www.bhlaw.com

MEMBER OF FIRM
Clarence H. Greenwood

ASSOCIATES
Joshua M. Barrett
Steven R. Lastomirsky

Representative Clients: Ataka Lumber America, Inc.; Union Bank of California, N.A.; ESCO Corp.; Georgia-Pacific Corp.; NACCO Materials Handling Group, Inc.; Northwest Copper Works, Inc.; Oregon Potato Company; Pope & Talbot, Inc.; The Sivers Companies; Willamette Industries, Inc.

For Complete List of Firm Personnel, See General Section

For full biographical listings, see the Martindale-Hubbell Law Directory

ROBERT G. BURT, P.C. (AV)

The 1515 Building, Suite 600, 1515 S.W. Fifth Avenue, 97201-5449
Telephone: 503-223-3600
Fax: 503-274-0778

Robert G. Burt

For full biographical listings, see the Martindale-Hubbell Law Directory

HAGEN, DYE, HIRSCHY & DILORENZO, P.C. (AV)

888 Southwest 5th Avenue Suite 1000, 97204
Telephone: 503-222-1812
Fax: 503-274-7979

Joseph T. Hagen
Jeffrey L. Dye
John A. Hirschy
John A. DiLorenzo, Jr.
Dana R. Taylor
Mark A. Golding
Kenneth A. Williams
John D. Parsons
David E. Grein

OF COUNSEL
Lewis B. Hampton

Adam S. Rittenberg
Michael E. Farnell
Aaron K. Stuckey
Joel L. Augee
Gretchen M. Ladd
Pamela R. Albee

LEGAL SUPPORT PERSONNEL
Kathryn J. Bell
Gail E. Kuechle
Linda M. Lufkin

For full biographical listings, see the Martindale-Hubbell Law Directory

HANNA, KERNS & STRADER, A PROFESSIONAL CORPORATION (AV)

300 Hoffman Columbia Plaza, 1300 S.W. Sixth Avenue, 97201
Telephone: 503-273-2700
FAX: 503-273-2712
Email: hkspdx@aol.com

Harry M. Hanna
Joseph J. Hanna, Jr.
Diane C. Kerns
Timothy R. Strader

For full biographical listings, see the Martindale-Hubbell Law Directory

KELL, ALTERMAN & RUNSTEIN, LLP (AV)

1001 S.W. Fifth Avenue, Suite 1800, 97204
Telephone: 503-222-3531
Telecopier: 503-227-2980
Email: kell@teleport.com

MEMBERS OF FIRM
Raymond M. Kell (1911-1991)
Clifford B. Alterman (1925-1995)
Ted E. Runstein
Lee Davis Kell
Wayne D. Palmer
Lloyd R. Summers
William D. Dickas
Gary P. Compa
Charles R. Williamson
Mary Ellen Page Farr
Eric Sogge
Thomas J. Matsuda
Thomas R. Rask, III
Nicholas S. Fish

Dana L. Barnes
Cory Larvik
Robert E. Kabacy
Robin M. Runstein

References: Union Bank of California, N.A. (Portland Branch); The Bank of Tokyo-Mitsubishi, Ltd. (Portland Branch); Bank of America (5th S. Main Branch).

For full biographical listings, see the Martindale-Hubbell Law Directory

PENNSYLVANIA

BLUE BELL, Montgomery Co.

KAPLIN STEWART MELOFF REITER & STEIN, PROFESSIONAL CORPORATION (AV)

350 Sentry Parkway, Building 640, P.O. Box 3037, 19422-0765
Telephone: 610-260-6000
Telecopier: 610-260-1240
Cherry Hill, New Jersey Office: 900 Dudley Avenue, #250, 08002-4426.
Telephone: 856-486-1044.
Fax: 856-486-1074.

MEMBERS OF FIRM

Maury B. Reiter
Barry A. Furman

ASSOCIATE

Matthew A. Cosenza

For full biographical listings, see the Martindale-Hubbell Law Directory

*ERIE,** Erie Co.

MARSH, SPAEDER, BAUR, SPAEDER & SCHAAF, LLP (AV)

Suite 300, 300 State Street, 16507
Telephone: 814-456-5301
Fax: 814-456-1112
Email: MSBSS@AOL.COM

MEMBERS OF FIRM

James E. Marsh, Sr. (1908-1988)
Ritchie T. Marsh (1870-1947)
John A. Spaeder (1902-1994)
Robert N. Spaeder (1915-1993)
Byron A. Baur (Retired)
Will J. Schaaf
Ritchie T. Marsh
William J. Schaaf
James E. Marsh, Jr.
John P. Eppinger
John C. Brydon
Thomas E. Kuhn
Thomas M. Lent
Francis J. Klemensic
John B. Fessler
Eugene C. Sundberg, Jr.
James R. Fryling
Donald F. Fessler, Jr.
Kurt L. Sundberg

Jeffrey Scibetta

Representative Clients: Borough of Edinboro; Cincinnati Insurance; Donegal Mutual Insurance Co.; Progressive Insurance; Erie Parking Authority; Home Insurance Co.; Marquette Savings Assn.; Motorists Insurance Co.; Northwest Savings Bank; Risk Enterprise and Management, Ltd.

For full biographical listings, see the Martindale-Hubbell Law Directory

*HARRISBURG,** Dauphin Co.

BARLEY, SNYDER, SENFT & COHEN, LLC (AV)

240 North Third Street, P.O. Box 1129, 17108
Telephone: 717-238-8263
Fax: 717-238-8278
Email: barley@barley.com *URL:* http://www.barley.com
Lancaster, Pennsylvania Office: 126 East King Street.
Telephone: 717-299-5201.
Fax: 717-291-4660.
York, Pennsylvania Office: 100 East Market Street.
Telephone: 717-846-8888.
Fax: 717-843-8492.
Chambersburg, Pennsylvania Office: 247 Lincoln Way East.
Telephone: 717-264-6494.
Fax: 717-264-1662.
Reading, Pennsylvania Office: 501 Washington Street.
Telephone: 610-376-6651.
Fax: 610-376-5243.
Hanover, Pennsylvania Office: 14 Center Square.
Telephone: 717-637-6239.
Fax: 717-637-5407.
Birdsboro, Pennsylvania Office: 115 E. Main Street.
Telephone: 610-582-2735.
Hamburg, Pennsylvania Office: 239 State Street.
Telephone: 610-562-3721.
Oley, Pennsylvania Office: Route 73 and Main Street.
Telephone: 610-987-6350.
Morgantown, Pennsylvania Office: Route 23.
Telephone: 610-286-5958.

MEMBERS OF FIRM

Harry J. Rubin
David R. Keller
Brian R. Ott
Michael S. Butler
Michael W. Davis

ASSOCIATE

Robert Freedenberg

(See Next Column)

RETIRED

H. Robert Lasday

Representative State Tax Clients: ABD. Inc.; American Home Products Corporation; Akzo America, Inc.; Combustion Engineering, Inc.; Conoco, Inc.; Dean Witter Reynolds, Inc.; E.I. DuPont de Nemours and Company; Ford Motor Company; General Public Utilities Corporation.

For full biographical listings, see the Martindale-Hubbell Law Directory

GOLDBERG, KATZMAN & SHIPMAN, P.C. (AV)

320 Market Street - Strawberry Square, P.O. Box 1268, 17108-1268
Telephone: 717-234-4161
Telecopier: 717-234-6808; 717-234-6810
Email: gks@gkslaw.com

Ronald M. Katzman
Neil Hendershot
Jesse Jay Cooper

Arnold B. Kogan

Reference: Fulton Bank.

For Complete List of Firm Personnel, See General Section

For full biographical listings, see the Martindale-Hubbell Law Directory

KEEFER WOOD ALLEN & RAHAL, LLP (AV)

210 Walnut Street, P.O. Box 11963, 17108-1963
Telephone: 717-255-8000
Telecopier: 717-255-8050
Email: info@keeferwood.com *URL:* http://www.keeferwood.com
Camp Hill, Pennsylvania Office: 415 Fallowfield Road.
Telephone: 717-612-5800.
Telecopier: 717-612-5805.

MEMBERS OF FIRM

N. David Rahal
Robert L. Weldon
John H. Enos, III
Donna S. Weldon
Jeffrey S. Stokes
Robert R. Church
R. Scott Shearer
Wayne M. Pecht

OF COUNSEL

Samuel C. Harry

SENIOR ATTORNEY

Bridget M. Whitley

ASSOCIATE

Allan J. Rossi

Representative Clients: ALCOA; American Standard Inc.; Caterpillar, Inc.; CSX Transportation; Hercules Inc.; IBM Corp.; Mellon Bank N.A.; PECO Energy Co.; Rockwell International Corp.; W. R. Grace & Co. - Conn.

For Complete List of Firm Personnel, See General Section

For full biographical listings, see the Martindale-Hubbell Law Directory

METTE, EVANS & WOODSIDE, A PROFESSIONAL CORPORATION (AV)

3401 North Front Street, P.O. Box 5950, 17110-0950
Telephone: 717-232-5000
Fax: 717-236-1816
Email: MEW@Mette.com *URL:* HTTP://WWW.METTE.COM

Howell C. Mette
Peter J. Ressler
Lloyd R. Persun
James A. Ulsh
Elyse E. Rogers
Jeffrey A. Ernico
Gary J. Heim
Thomas F. Smida

Vicky Ann Trimmer
Bradley A. Walker

Counsel for: The B. F. Goodrich Co.; MCI Telecommunications Corp.; Monongahela Power Co.; Community Banks; GTE Products Corp.; CBS/Westinghouse; Bell & Howell; Woolrich; 360 Communications.

For Complete List of Firm Personnel, See General Section

For full biographical listings, see the Martindale-Hubbell Law Directory

RHOADS & SINON LLP (AV)

One South Market Square, 12th Floor, P.O. Box 1146, 17108-1146
Telephone: 717-233-5731
Fax: 717-232-1459
Boca Raton, Florida Affiliated Office: Charles L. Sieck, 1700 South Dixie Highway, Suite 2-C.
Telephone: 561-395-5595.
Fax: 561-395-9497.
York, Pennsylvania Office: 15 North Cherry Lane, Suite 21.
Telephone: 717-843-1718.
Fax: 717-232-1459.

MEMBERS OF FIRM

Sherill T. Moyer
John P. Manbeck
Jack F. Hurley, Jr.
Drake D. Nicholas

(See Next Column)

RHOADS & SINON LLP—*Continued*

ASSOCIATES

Lori J. McElroy | Richard E. Artell

For Complete List of Firm Personnel, See General Section

For full biographical listings, see the Martindale-Hubbell Law Directory

*PHILADELPHIA,** Philadelphia Co.

BALLARD SPAHR ANDREWS & INGERSOLL, LLP (AV)

1735 Market Street, 51st Floor, 19103-7599
Telephone: 215-665-8500
Fax: 215-864-8999
URL: http://www.ballardspahr.com
Baltimore, Maryland Office: 300 East Lombard Street. 19th Floor.
Telephone: 410-528-5600.
Fax: 410-528-5650.
Camden, New Jersey Office: 800 Hudson Square, 5th Floor.
Telephone: 856-541-5577.
Fax: 856-541-8272.
Denver, Colorado Office: Seventeenth Street Plaza Building, Suite 2300, 1225 17th Street.
Telephone: 303-292-2400.
Fax: 303-296-3956.
Salt Lake City, Utah Office: One Utah Center, Suite 1200, 201 South Main Street.
Telephone: 801-531-3000.
Fax: 801-531-3001.
Voorhees, New Jersey Office: Suite 100, 1101 Laurel Oak Drive.
Telephone: 856-627-8555.
Fax: 856-627-1153.
Washington, D.C. Office: Suite 1000 South, 601 13th Street, N.W.
Telephone: 202-661-2200.
Fax: 202-661-2299.

Frederic L. Ballard, Jr.
Steven P. Berman
John M. Bernard
Rhonda Resnick Cohen
Robert E. McQuiston
Louis W. Ricker
Marilyn C. Sanborne
Paul J. Schneider
Wayne R. Strasbaugh
Regina O'Brien Thomas

OF COUNSEL

Kurt R. Anderson
Robert R. Batt
Deborah J. Zateeny

COUNSEL

Edward Ira Leeds

Roberta A. Barsotti
Michele Berman Golkow
Penny S. Indictor
W. Andrew Macan
Brian Michael Pinheiro
Sharmon Priaulx
Pedro A. Ramos
Kathleen M. Ranalli
Marla G. Roshkoff

For Complete List of Firm Personnel, See General Section

For full biographical listings, see the Martindale-Hubbell Law Directory

EPSTEIN, SHAPIRO & EPSTEIN (AV)

Fifteenth Floor, 1515 Market Street, 19102
Telephone: 215-563-1200
Telecopier: 215-564-5132
Email: Jeepsu@aol.com

MEMBERS OF FIRM

J. Earl Epstein
Boris Shapiro
Phyllis Horn Epstein

LEGAL SUPPORT PERSONNEL

Jacqueline Heffron (Paralegal)

For full biographical listings, see the Martindale-Hubbell Law Directory

FOX, ROTHSCHILD, O'BRIEN & FRANKEL, LLP (AV)

2000 Market Street, Tenth Floor, 19103-3291
Telephone: 215-299-2000
Cable Address: FROF
Fax: 215-299-2150
Email: frof@frof.com *URL:* http://www.frof.com
Atlantic City, New Jersey Office: CitiCenter Building, Suite 500, 1300 Atlantic Avenue, 08401.
Telephone: 609-348-4515.
Fax: 609-348-6834.
Doylestown, Pennsylvania Office: 102 North Main Street, P.O. Box 1589, 18901-0700.
Telephone: 215-345-7500.
Fax: 215-345-7507.
Exton, Pennsylvania Office: Eagleview Corporate Center, 760 Constitution Drive, Suite 104, P.O. Box 673, 19341-0673.
Telephone: 610-458-7500.
Fax: 610-458-7337.

(See Next Column)

Lansdale, Pennsylvania Office: 1250 South Broad Street, Suite 1000, P.O. Box 431, 19446.
Telephone: 215-699-6000.
Fax: 215-699-0231.
Sellersville, Pennsylvania Office: 64 North Main Street, 18960-0580.
Telephone: 215-257-3661.
Fax: 215-257-7999.
Trenton (Lawrenceville), New Jersey Office: Princeton Pike Corporate Center, 997 Lenox Drive, Building 3, 08648-2311.
Telephone: 609-896-3600.
Fax: 609-896-1469.
Voorhees, New Jersey Office: Laurelwood, Suite 103, 1103 Laurel Oak Road, 08043.
Telephone: 856-782-6000.
Fax: 856-346-9866.

MEMBERS OF FIRM

Alex Satinsky
Thomas A. Bell
Robert Perry Frankel
Steven C. Levitt (Not admitted in PA; Resident, Trenton (Lawrenceville), New Jersey Office)
Richard M. Kohn (Resident, Trenton (Lawrenceville), New Jersey Office)
Stephen P. Weiss
Victor Walcoff (Not admitted in PA; Resident, Trenton (Lawrenceville), New Jersey Office)
Albert R. Riviezzo (Resident, Exton, Pennsylvania Office)
Robin B. Matlin
Owen A. Knopping
Mark L. Silow
Norman Leibovitz
Gerald M. Hatfield
Barry Cooperberg (Resident, Lansdale, Pennsylvania Office)
Michael C. McBratnie (Resident, Exton, Pennsylvania Office)
Barbara R. Flacker

ASSOCIATES

Michael S. Bookbinder
Annamaria Vitelli

For Complete List of Firm Personnel, See General Section

For full biographical listings, see the Martindale-Hubbell Law Directory

MERVIN M. WILF, LTD. (AV)

3901 Mellon Bank Center, 1735 Market Street, 19103
Telephone: 215-994-1430; 215-568-4842
Facsimile: 215-994-1432
Email: mwilf@erols.com
Cambridge, Massachusetts Office: 2 Berkeley Place, 02138.
Telephone: 617-876-5200.

Mervin M. Wilf

A list of Representative Clients and References will be furnished upon request.

For full biographical listings, see the Martindale-Hubbell Law Directory

*PITTSBURGH,** Allegheny Co.

MARCUS & SHAPIRA LLP (AV)

35th Floor, One Oxford Centre, 301 Grant Street, 15219-6401
Telephone: 412-471-3490
Telecopier: 412-391-8758
Email: info@marcus-shapira.com *URL:* http://www.marcus-shapira.com

MEMBERS OF FIRM

Robert M. Barnes
Estelle F. Comay

For Complete List of Firm Personnel, See General Section

For full biographical listings, see the Martindale-Hubbell Law Directory

*READING,** Berks Co.

MOGEL, SPEIDEL, BOBB & KERSHNER, A PROFESSIONAL CORPORATION (AV)

520 Walnut Street, P.O. Box 8581, 19603-8581
Telephone: 610-376-1515
Telecopier: 610-372-8710

George B. Balmer (1902-1969)
Michael L. Mixell
George A. Kershner (1907-1969)
George M. Lutz
Carl F. Mogel (1919-1994)
Paul M. Yatron
Edwin H. Kershner
Stephen H. Price
Frederick R. Mogel
Kathryn K. Harenza

Sean J. O'Brien
Matthew Earl Glinn

OF COUNSEL

Harry W. Speidel
Donald K. Bobb
Henry A. Gass

Representative Clients: Great Valley Bank; Union Township, Berks County, Pennsylvania.

For full biographical listings, see the Martindale-Hubbell Law Directory

*WILKES-BARRE,** Luzerne Co.

ROSENN, JENKINS & GREENWALD, L.L.P. (AV)

15 South Franklin Street, 18711-0075
Telephone: 570-826-5600
Fax: 570-826-5640
Email: rjg@rjglaw.com *URL:* http://www.rjglaw.com
Hazleton, Pennsylvania Office: P.O. Box 618, 18201-0618.
Telephone: 570-455-7112.
Fax: 570-455-8304.

MEMBERS OF FIRM

Marshall S. Jacobson
Murray Ufberg
Alan S. Hollander
George F. Shovlin

ASSOCIATE

Thomas J. MacNeely

Representative Clients: C-TEC Corp.; Chicago Title Insurance Co.; Manufacturers & Traders Trust Company; Guard Insurance Group; May Department Stores Co.; Student Loan Marketing Assn. (Sallie Mae); Penn-State Geisinger Medical Center; Subaru of America, Inc.

For Complete List of Firm Personnel, See General Section

For full biographical listings, see the Martindale-Hubbell Law Directory

RHODE ISLAND

*PROVIDENCE,** Providence Co.

EDMUND C. BENNETT (AV)

50 South Main Street, 02903
Telephone: 401-421-1150
Facsimile: 401-521-4080
Email: ECBennett@worldnet.att.net *URL:* http://www.lawyers.com/ecblaw

For full biographical listings, see the Martindale-Hubbell Law Directory

EDWARDS & ANGELL, LLP (AV)

A Partnership including Professional Corporations
2800 BankBoston Plaza, 02903
Telephone: 401-274-9200
Telecopier: 401-276-6611
Cable Address: "Edwangle Providence"
Telex: 952001 "E A PVD"
Email: postmaster@ealaw.com *URL:* http://www.ealaw.com
Boston, Massachusetts Office: 101 Federal Street, 02110-1800.
Telephone: 617-439-4444.
Telecopier: 617-439-4170.
New York, New York Office: 750 Lexington Avenue, 10022-1200.
Telephone: 212-308-4411.
Telecopier: 212-308-4844.
Palm Beach, Florida Office: 250 Royal Palm Way, Suite 300, 33480-4356.
Telephone: 561-833-7700.
Telecopier: 561-655-8719.
Short Hills, New Jersey Office: 51 John F. Kennedy Parkway, 07078.
Telephone: 973-376-7700.
Telecopier: 973-376-3380.
Hartford, Connecticut Office: 90 State House Square, 06103-2715.
Telephone: 860-525-5065.
Telecopier: 860-527-4198.
Newport, Rhode Island Office: 130 Bellevue Avenue, 02840.
Telephone: 401-849-7800.
Telecopier: 401-849-7887.

MEMBERS OF FIRM

Alfred S. Lombardi
G. Scott Nebergall

For Complete List of Firm Personnel, See General Section

For full biographical listings, see the Martindale-Hubbell Law Directory

HINCKLEY, ALLEN & SNYDER LLP (AV)

1500 Fleet Center, 02903-2393
Telephone: 401-274-2000
Fax: 401-277-9600
Email: firm@haslaw.com *URL:* http://www.haslaw.com
Boston, Massachusetts Office: 28 State Street, 30th Floor.
Telephone: 617-345-9000.
Fax: 617-345-9020. URL: http://www.haslaw.com.

MEMBERS OF FIRM

Paula K. Andrews (Not admitted in RI)
David D. Barricelli
E. Jerome Batty
Jonathan Bell
Leon C. Boghossian III
Paul Bork (Not admitted in RI)
Stephen J. Carlotti
David Barry Connolly (Not admitted in RI)
Joseph P. Curran
Michael P. DeFanti
Eric F. Eisenberg (Not admitted in RI)
Malcolm Farmer, III
Margaret D. Farrell

(See Next Column)

MEMBERS OF FIRM (Continued)

Noel M. Field, Jr.
Pasco Gasbarro Jr.
Hugh J. Gorman, III (Not admitted in RI)
Alan P. Gottlieb (Not admitted in RI)
William R. Grimm
Paul A. Hedstrom (Not admitted in RI)
Richard L. E. Jocelyn
Joel Lewin (Not admitted in RI)
Doris Jami Licht
Sandra Matrone Mack
Matthew T. Marcello, III
Frederick P. McClure
Elizabeth Murdock Myers
Paul F. O'Donnell, III (Not admitted in RI)
H. Peter Olsen
Julianne Palumbo (Not admitted in RI)
John J. Pendergast, III
Gerald J. Petros
Richard H. Pierce
James O. Reavis
Jeremy Ritzenberg (Not admitted in RI)
Ralph J. Rivkind (Not admitted in RI)
David J. Rubin
Charles E. Schaub, Jr. (Not admitted in RI)
Douglas F. Seaver (Not admitted in RI)
Paul A. Silver
Herman Snyder (Not admitted in RI)
David R. Sullivan (Not admitted in RI)
Robert F. Sylvia (Not admitted in RI)
Howard E. Walker
Richard D. Wayne (Not admitted in RI)

ASSOCIATES

Jessica M. Bettencourt
Mark Bianchi
Alyssa V. Boss
Alexandra K. Callam
Clifford R. Cohen (Not admitted in RI)
Jane E. Cohen (Not admitted in RI)
Andrew D. Cummings (Not admitted in RI)
June E. Daniel
Josephine A. Giuffre (Not admitted in RI)
Kim Herman Goslant (Not admitted in RI)
Gloria Maria Gutierrez (Not admitted in RI)
Kelley Jordan-Price
Catherine S. Kim (Not admitted in RI)
Christopher W. Morog (Not admitted in RI)
Elena B. Olson (Not admitted in RI)
Joseph D. Whelan

OF COUNSEL

Willard Krasnow (Not admitted in RI)
Willard R. Pope (Not admitted in RI)
Bentley Tobin
Joachim A. Weissfeld

For Complete List of Firm Personnel, See General Section

For full biographical listings, see the Martindale-Hubbell Law Directory

PLOURDE & LEONARD, LTD. (AV)

One Citizens Plaza Suite 830, 02903
Telephone: 401-453-0550
Fax: 401-421-7806
Email: plourde_leonard@compuserve.com
Boston, Massachusetts Office: 171 Milk Street, Suite 25, 02109.
Telephone: 617-542-0600.
Fax: 617-426-3663.

Paul Plourde
Arthur J. Leonard

Richard Bogue
F. Moore McLaughlin, IV
Thomas J. Moylan
Jeffrey J. Wolfe

OF COUNSEL

Paul R. Merlino

LEGAL SUPPORT PERSONNEL

Mary G. Porcaro

For full biographical listings, see the Martindale-Hubbell Law Directory

REILLY LAW ASSOCIATES, INC. (AV)

1040 Turks Head Building, 02903
Telephone: 401-861-1120
Telecopier: 401-331-6187
Email: reillylaw1@aol.com

Charles J. Reilly

OF COUNSEL

Joseph D. Tudino
Thomas J. Reilly, Jr.

LEGAL SUPPORT PERSONNEL

Roger A. Francoeur
John G. Wood

For full biographical listings, see the Martindale-Hubbell Law Directory

SOUTH CAROLINA

*BEAUFORT,** Beaufort Co.

HARVEY & BATTEY, P.A. (AV)

1001 Craven Street, P.O. Drawer 1107, 29902
Telephone: 843-524-3109
Telefax: 843-524-6973

W. Brantley Harvey, Jr. E. Carew Rice, III

Approved Attorneys for: Lawyers Title Insurance Corp.; Chicago Title Insurance Corp.
Representative Clients: Nations Bank; First Bank, F.S.B.; Pleasant Point Plantation Associates; Century 21-Carolina Realty, Inc.; Lobeco Products, Inc.; Beaufort County Association of Realtors; The Fripp Company.

For Complete List of Firm Personnel, See General Section

For full biographical listings, see the Martindale-Hubbell Law Directory

*CHARLESTON,** Charleston Co.

EVANS, CARTER, KUNES & BENNETT, P.A. (AV)

115 Church Street, P.O. Box 369, 29402-0369
Telephone: 843-577-2300
Telefax: 843-577-2055
Email: eckb@eckb.com

George C. Evans
Robert M. Kunes
T. Heyward Carter, Jr.
Edward G. R. Bennett

Charlotte Nancie Quick
Graeme Philp
Chalmers W. Poston, Jr.
Susan A. Teschner

For full biographical listings, see the Martindale-Hubbell Law Directory

HAYNSWORTH, MARION, MCKAY & GUÉRARD, L.L.P. (AV)

134 Meeting Street, P.O. Box 1119, 29402
Telephone: 843-722-7606
Facsimile: 843-724-8016
Columbia, South Carolina Office: Suite 2400 Affinity Building, 1201 Main Street, P.O. Drawer 7157, 29202.
Telephone: 803-765-1818. Facsimile 803-765-2399.
Greenville, South Carolina Office: 75 Beattie Place, Eleventh Floor, P.O. Box 2048, 29602.
Telephone: 864-240-3200.
Facsimile: 864-240-3300.

MEMBER OF FIRM

Robert B. Pearlman

ASSOCIATE

M. Jean Lee

OF COUNSEL

Gus H. Pearlman

Counsel for: Fluor-Daniel Corp.; Greenville Hospital System; Baker Hospital; Roper Hospital; Silstar Corp. of America; Santee Cooper; Coward-Hund Construction Co.; Hogan, Mellow and Ladd.

For Complete List of Firm Personnel, See General Section

For full biographical listings, see the Martindale-Hubbell Law Directory

SLOTCHIVER & SLOTCHIVER, L.L.P. (AV)

44 State Street, 29401
Telephone: 803-577-6531
Facsimile: 803-577-0261
Email: slotchiver@charleston.net

MEMBERS OF FIRM

Irvin J. Slotchiver
Daniel S. Slotchiver
Stephen M. Slotchiver

For full biographical listings, see the Martindale-Hubbell Law Directory

SOLOMON, BUDMAN, STRICKER & SCHWARTZ, L.L.P. (AV)

Parkshore Centre, 1 Poston Road, Suite 395, P.O. Box 30280, 29417-0280
Telephone: 843-763-1118
Telecopier: 843-763-7518

A. Bernard Solomon
Michael A. Stricker
Donald J. Budman
Lester S. Schwartz

Local Counsel for: Lawyers Title Insurance Corp.

For full biographical listings, see the Martindale-Hubbell Law Directory

WARREN & SINKLER, L.L.P. (AV)

Suite 340 171 Church Street, P.O. Box 1254, 29402
Telephone: 843-577-0660
Fax: 843-577-6843
Email: law@warren-sinkler.com

(See Next Column)

MEMBERS OF FIRM

G. Dana Sinkler
Mark S. Sharpe
John H. Warren, III
Elizabeth W. Settle
Henry B. Fishburne, Jr.
Andrea Hall Duenas
Scott Y. Barnes
William O. Hanahan, III
Holly R. Jensen

For full biographical listings, see the Martindale-Hubbell Law Directory

*COLUMBIA,** Richland Co.

BARNES, ALFORD, STORK & JOHNSON, L.L.P. (AV)

1613 Main Street, P.O. Box 8448, 29202
Telephone: 803-799-1111
Telefax: 803-254-1335
Email: basj@basjlaw.com

OF COUNSEL

Alan J. Reyner
Roger A. Way, Jr.

Representative Clients: First Union National Bank; M.B. Kahn Construction Co., Inc.

For Complete List of Firm Personnel, See General Section

For full biographical listings, see the Martindale-Hubbell Law Directory

FINKEL & ALTMAN, L.L.C. (AV)

Suite 1800, 1201 Main Street, P.O. Box 1799, 29202
Telephone: 803-765-2935
Fax: 803-252-0786
Email: webmaster@finkellaw.com *URL:* http://www.finkellaw.com
Charleston, South Carolina Office: 12 Exchange Street, P.O. Box 225.
Telephone: 843-577-5460.
Fax: 843-577-5135.

Joseph Alton Bivens

COUNSEL

Elizabeth Rhodes

Representative Clients: Hewitt-Robins; 1st Union National Bank; Banc One Mortgage Co.; Motorola Communications & Electronics Corp.

For full biographical listings, see the Martindale-Hubbell Law Directory

NEXSEN PRUET JACOBS & POLLARD, LLP (AV)

1441 Main Street, 15th Floor, P.O. Drawer 2426, 29202
Telephone: 803-771-8900
Facsimile: 803-253-8277
Email: NPJP@NPJP.COM *URL:* HTTP://WWW.NPJP.COM
Charleston, South Carolina Office: 200 Meeting Street, Suite 301. P.O. Box 486.
Telephone: 803-577-9440.
Facsimile: 803-720-1777.
Greenville, South Carolina Office: 201 West McBee Avenue, Fourth Floor, P.O. Box 10648.
Telephone: 864-370-2211.
Facsimile: 864-282-1177.
Myrtle Beach, South Carolina Office: 2411 Oak Street, Suite 105.
Telephone: 843-445-9688.
Facsimile: 843-445-9949.
Charlotte, North Carolina Office: 212 South Tryon Street, Suite 1700.
Telephone: 704-339-0304.
Facsimile: 704-338-5377.

MEMBERS OF FIRM

J. James Duggan (Resident, Charleston, SC Office)
William G. Newsome, III
R. Kent Porth
Fred L. Kingsmore, Jr.
B. Joel Stoudenmire (Resident, Greenville, SC Office)

ASSOCIATE

John D. Watts, III (Resident, Greenville, SC Office)

For Complete List of Firm Personnel, See General Section

For full biographical listings, see the Martindale-Hubbell Law Directory

*GREENVILLE,** Greenville Co.

HAYNSWORTH, MARION, MCKAY & GUÉRARD, L.L.P. (AV)

75 Beattie Place, Eleventh Floor, P.O. Box 2048, 29602
Telephone: 864-240-3200
Facsimile: 864-240-3300
Columbia, South Carolina Office: Suite 2400 Affinity Building, 1201 Main Street, P.O. Drawer 7157, 29202
Telephone: 803-765-1818.
Facsimile: 803-765-2399.
Charleston, South Carolina Office: 134 Meeting Street, P.O. Box 1119, 29402.
Telephone: 843-722-7606.
Facsimile: 843-724-8016.

(See Next Column)

HAYNSWORTH, MARION, MCKAY & GUÉRARD L.L.P., *Greenville—Continued*

MEMBERS OF FIRM

Arthur Frazier McLean, III
Frank T. Davis, III

Counsel for: Fluor-Daniel Corp.; Synalloy Corp.; Greenville Hospital System.

For Complete List of Firm Personnel, See General Section

For full biographical listings, see the Martindale-Hubbell Law Directory

LEATHERWOOD WALKER TODD & MANN, P.C. (AV)

100 East Coffee Street, P.O. Box 87, 29602
Telephone: 864-242-6440
FAX: 864-240-2477
Email: leatherwood@lwtm.com *URL:* http://www.lwtm.com
Spartanburg, South Carolina Office: 1451 East Main Street, P.O. Box 3188.
Telephone: 864-582-4365.
Telefax: 864-583-8961.

J. Richard Kelly
Jack H. Tedards, Jr.
William L. Dennis
Richard L. Few, Jr.
J. Tod Hyche

Counsel for: John D. Hollingsworth on Wheels, Inc.; Canal Insurance Co.; Suitt Construction Co.; Platt Saco Lowell Corp.; The Litchfield Company of South Carolina; Textile Hall Corp.
Representative Client: Springs Industries, Inc.

For Complete List of Firm Personnel, See General Section

For full biographical listings, see the Martindale-Hubbell Law Directory

MERLINE & THOMAS, P.A. (AV)

812 East North Street, P.O. Box 10796, 29603
Telephone: 864-242-4080
Fax: 864-242-5758

David A. Merline
John R. Thomas
David A. Merline, Jr.
Keith G. Meacham
Randy E. Fisher
Robert E. August
Tommy D. Permenter, Jr.

LEGAL SUPPORT PERSONNEL

Mary S. Rose (Legal Administrator)

For full biographical listings, see the Martindale-Hubbell Law Directory

HILTON HEAD ISLAND, Beaufort Co.

RUTH & MACNEILLE, PROFESSIONAL ASSOCIATION (AV)

40 Pope Avenue, 29928
Telephone: 843-785-4251
Telex: 988944
Telecopier: 843-686-5404
Mailing Address: P.O. Box 5706, Hilton Head Island, SC, 29938
Bluffton, South Carolina Office: 7 Simmonsville Road, Suite 200.
Telephone: 803-815-5353.
Fax: 803-815-5354.

William A. Ruth

References: NationsBank of South Carolina, N.A.; Anchor Bank; Wachovia Bank, N.A.; Chicago Title Insurance Corp.; First American Title Insurance Co.

For full biographical listings, see the Martindale-Hubbell Law Directory

SOUTH DAKOTA

*SIOUX FALLS,** Minnehaha Co.

DAVENPORT, EVANS, HURWITZ & SMITH, L.L.P. (AV)

513 South Main Avenue, P.O. Box 1030, 57101-1030
Telephone: 605-336-2880
Telecopier: 605-335-3639
Email: lawyers@dehs.com

MEMBERS OF FIRM

David L. Knudson
Catherine A. Tanck

Counsel for: American Society of Composers, Authors and Publishers (A.S.C.A.P.); Continental Insurance Cos.; The First National Bank in Sioux Falls; Ford Motor Credit Co.; General Motors Corp.; The St. Paul Cos.; The Travelers.

For Complete List of Firm Personnel, See General Section

For full biographical listings, see the Martindale-Hubbell Law Directory

TENNESSEE

BRENTWOOD, Williamson Co.

THRAILKILL, HARRIS & WOOD, PLC (AV)

105 Westpark Drive, Suite 400, P.O. Box 2408, 37024-2408
Telephone: 615-376-3555
Fax: 615-376-3016

Larry T. Thrailkill
Christopher Harris
Steven K. Wood

Angela Humphreys Hamilton

For full biographical listings, see the Martindale-Hubbell Law Directory

*CHATTANOOGA,** Hamilton Co.

BAKER, DONELSON, BEARMAN & CALDWELL (AV)

1800 Republic Centre, 633 Chestnut Street, 37450-1800
Telephone: 423-756-2010
Telecopier: 423-756-3447
Email: info@bdbc.com *URL:* http://www.bakerdonelson.com
Memphis, Tennessee Office: 20th Floor, First Tennessee Building, 165 Madison, 38103.
Telephone: 901-526-2000.
Telecopier: 901-577-2303.
Nashville, Tennessee Office: 1700 Nashville City Center, 511 Union Street, 37219.
Telephone: 615-726-5600.
Telecopier: 615-726-0464.
Knoxville, Tennessee Office: 2200 Riverview Tower, 900 South Gay Street, 37901.
Telephone: 423-549-7000.
Telecopier: 423-525-8569.
Johnson City, Tennessee Office: SunTrust Bank Building, 207 Mockingbird Lane, P.O. Box 3038, 37602.
Telephone: 423-928-0181.
Telecopier: 423-928-5694; 423-928-3654; Kingsport: 423-246-6191.
Huntsville, Tennessee Office: 3 Courthouse Square, 37756.
Telephone: 423-663-2321.
Telecopier: 423-663-2111.
Washington, D.C. Office: Market Square, 801 Pennsylvania Avenue, N.W., 20004.
Telephone: 202-508-3400.
Telecopier: 202-508-3402.
Jackson, Mississippi Office: Suite 500, 700 North State Street, 39202.
Telephone: 601-351-2400.
Telecopier: 601-351-2424.

MANAGING PARTNER

Susan Elliott Rich

SHAREHOLDERS

Lewis R. Donelson, III
Howard H. Baker, Jr.
Thomas A. Caldwell
John C. Mooney
Thomas O. Helton
Richard B. Gossett
Carl E. Hartley
Virginia C. Love
Richard J. McAfee
John C. Harrison
Gladys Smith Mynatt
Louann Prater Smith
Kenneth C. Beckman
J. Porter Durham, Jr.
Joe A. Conner
Robert C. Divine

OF COUNSEL

Randall D. Van Dolson
Robert W. Sauser
H. Allen Corey
Micheline Kelly Johnson
Michael C. Mallen
Charles N. Jolly
Jo C. Dearing

ASSOCIATES

Russell W. Gray
Cameron S. Hill
Victoria S. Childres
James H. Levine
Roddy Bailey (Not admitted in TN)
Misty Smith Kelley
Alison Tuley (Not admitted in TN)

For full biographical listings, see the Martindale-Hubbell Law Directory

GEARHISER, PETERS, LOCKABY & TALLANT, PLLC (AV)

320 McCallie Avenue, 37402-2007
Telephone: 423-756-5171
Fax: 423-266-1605
Email: law@gplt.com

MEMBERS OF FIRM

Charles J. Gearhiser
R. Wayne Peters
Robert L. Lockaby, Jr.
Ralph E. Tallant, Jr.
Terry Atkin Cavett
Sam D. Elliott
Lane C. Avery
Wade K. Cannon

ASSOCIATES

Robin L. Miller
Christopher T. Varner
James C. Davey
Lee Ann Adams
Jeffrey H. Moore
Kevin T. Beck

(See Next Column)

GEARHISER, PETERS, LOCKABY & TALLANT PLLC—*Continued*

OF COUNSEL

Richard P. Jahn, Jr.

References: First Tennessee Bank; First American National Bank.

For full biographical listings, see the Martindale-Hubbell Law Directory

HUGH F. KENDALL, ATTORNEY, P.C. (AV)

Suite 305, Victorian Gardens, 6918 Shallowford Road, 37421-1783
Telephone: 423-499-9863
Telecopier: 423-894-0682
Email: hukendall@aol.com

Hugh F. Kendall

For full biographical listings, see the Martindale-Hubbell Law Directory

KINGSPORT, Sullivan Co.

HUNTER, SMITH & DAVIS, LLP (AV)

1212 North Eastman Road, P.O. Box 3740, 37664
Telephone: 423-378-8800
Telecopier: 423-378-8801
Email: info@hsdlaw.com *URL:* http://www.hsdlaw.com
Johnson City, Tennessee Office: Suite 500 First American Center, 208 Sunset Drive, 37604.
Telephone: 423-283-6300.
Telecopier: 423-283-6301.

MEMBERS OF FIRM

T. Arthur Scott, Jr.
William T. Wray, Jr.
William C. Argabrite

LEGAL SUPPORT PERSONNEL

James R. Bowles (CPA; CFP)

Representative Clients: Medical Laundry of Tri-Cities, Inc.; Publix Food Markets, Inc.; Industrial Gas & Supply, Inc.; Paty Lumber Co.; The Parks Group, L.L.C.; Moody Dunbar, Inc.; Holston Builders Supply, Inc.; Com-Net Construction Services, Inc.; JA Investments, L.L.C.

For Complete List of Firm Personnel, See General Section

For full biographical listings, see the Martindale-Hubbell Law Directory

*KNOXVILLE,** Knox Co.

BAKER, DONELSON, BEARMAN & CALDWELL (AV)

2200 Riverview Tower, 900 South Gay Street, 37901
Telephone: 423-549-7000
Telecopier: 423-525-8569
Email: info@bdbc.com *URL:* http://www.bakerdonelson.com
Memphis, Tennessee Office: 20th Floor, First Tennessee Building, 165 Madison, 38103.
Telephone: 901-526-2000.
Telecopier: 901-577-2303.
Nashville, Tennessee Office: 1700 Nashville City Center, 511 Union Street, 37219.
Telephone: 615-726-5600.
Telecopier: 615-726-0464.
Chattanooga, Tennessee Office: 1800 Republic Centre, 633 Chestnut Street, 37450-1800.
Telephone: 423-756-2010.
Telecopier: 423-756-3447.
Johnson City, Tennessee Office: SunTrust Bank Building, 207 Mockingbird Lane, P.O. Box 3038, 37602.
Telephone: 423-928-0181.
Telecopier: 423-928-5694; 423-928-3654; Kingsport: 423-246-6191.
Huntsville, Tennessee Office: 3 Courthouse Square, 37756.
Telephone: 423-663-2321.
Telecopier: 423-663-2111.
Washington, D.C. Office: Market Square, 801 Pennsylvania Avenue, N.W., 20004.
Telephone: 202-508-3400.
Telecopier: 202-508-3402.
Jackson, Mississippi Office: Suite 500, 700 North State Street, 39202.
Telephone: 601-351-2400.
Telecopier: 601-351-2424.

MANAGING PARTNER

Stephen E. Roth

PARTNERS

Lewis R. Donelson, III
Howard H. Baker, Jr.
Robert F. Worthington, Jr.
Robert G. McCullough
Richard B. Gossett
James A. McIntosh
Stephen G. Anderson
David E. Fielder
P. Edward Pratt
Mary Dillard Miller
Nelwyn W. Inman
Bruce C. Doeg
Kelli L. Thompson

(See Next Column)

ASSOCIATES

Wm. Gregory Hall, Jr.
Mary LeAnn Mynatt
Andrew L. Colocotronis
Clarence Risin
Richard D. Plumley
Jason I. Epstein
Suzanne Hefner Bauknight
David L. Morehous (Not admitted in TN)
H. Susanne Bales

For full biographical listings, see the Martindale-Hubbell Law Directory

EGERTON, MCAFEE, ARMISTEAD & DAVIS, P.C. (AV)

500 First American National Bank Center, P.O. Box 2047, 37901
Telephone: 423-546-0500
Fax: 423-525-5293
URL: http://emadlaw.com

William W. Davis
Joe M. McAfee
William E. McClamroch, III
Jonathan D. Reed

For full biographical listings, see the Martindale-Hubbell Law Directory

WAGNER, MYERS & SANGER, A PROFESSIONAL CORPORATION (AV)

1801 First Tennessee Plaza, P.O. Box 1308, 37901-1308
Telephone: 423-525-4600
Fax: 423-524-5731
Email: wms1801@usit.net

William C. Myers, Jr.
M. Douglas Campbell, Jr.

Representative Clients: Carolina Power & Light Co.; Cullman Electric Cooperative; Diversified Energy, Inc.; Fort Sanders Health Systems; Gatliff Coal Company, Inc.; Martin Marietta Energy Systems, Inc.; North American Rayon Corp.; Regal Cinemas, Inc.; Roddy Vending Co.; Skyline Coal Company.

For Complete List of Firm Personnel, See General Section

For full biographical listings, see the Martindale-Hubbell Law Directory

*MEMPHIS,** Shelby Co.

ARMSTRONG ALLEN PREWITT GENTRY JOHNSTON & HOLMES, PLLC (AV)

Brinkley Plaza, Suite 700, 80 Monroe Avenue, 38103-2467
Telephone: 901-523-8211
Facsimile: 901-524-4936
Little Rock, Arkansas Office: Suite 100, 100 Morgan Keegan Drive, 72202.
Telephone: 501-280-0100.
Facsimile: 501-280-0166.
Jackson, Mississippi Office: 2525 Lakeward Drive, Suite 200, 39216.
Telephone: 601-713-1192.
Facsimile: 601-713-2049.
Jackson, Tennessee Office: 464 North Parkway, Suite A, 38305.
Telephone: 901-660-2332.
Facsimile: 901-664-1109.

MEMBERS OF FIRM

Joseph Brent Walker
James Rogers (Josh) Hall, Jr.
James L. Pettis, III (Resident, Jackson, Mississippi Office)

For Complete List of Firm Personnel, See General Section

For full biographical listings, see the Martindale-Hubbell Law Directory

BAKER, DONELSON, BEARMAN & CALDWELL (AV)

20th Floor, First Tennessee Building, 165 Madison, 38103
Telephone: 901-526-2000
Telecopier: 901-577-2303
Email: info@bdbc.com *URL:* http://www.bakerdonelson.com
Nashville, Tennessee Office: 1700 Nashville City Center, 511 Union Street, 37219.
Telephone: 615-726-5600.
Telecopier: 615-726-0464.
Chattanooga, Tennessee Office: 1800 Republic Centre, 633 Chestnut Street, 37450-1800.
Telephone: 423-756-2010.
Telecopier: 423-756-3447.
Knoxville, Tennessee Office: 2200 Riverview Tower, 900 South Gay Street, 37901.
Telephone: 423-549-7000.
Telecopier: 423-525-8569.
Johnson City, Tennessee Office: SunTrust Bank Building, 207 Mockingbird Lane, P.O. Box 3038, 37602.
Telephone: 423-928-0181.
Telecopier: 423-928-5694; 423-928-3654; Kingsport: 423-246-6191.
Huntsville, Tennessee Office: 3 Courthouse Square, 37756.
Telephone: 423-663-2321.
Telecopier: 423-663-2111.
Washington, D.C. Office: Market Square, 801 Pennsylvania Avenue, N.W., 20004.
Telephone: 202-508-3400.
Telecopier: 202-508-3402.
Jackson, Mississippi Office: Suite 500, 700 North State Street, 39202.
Telephone: 601-351-2400.
Telecopier: 601-351-2424.

(See Next Column)

BAKER, DONELSON, BEARMAN & CALDWELL, *Memphis—Continued*

MANAGING PARTNER

Robert Mark Glover

SHAREHOLDERS

Lewis R. Donelson, III
Roy Keathley
David G. Williams
Leo Bearman, Jr.
Maurice Wexler
Frank L. Watson, Jr.
Robert Walker
Boyd L. Rhodes, Jr.
W. Michael Richards
John C. Speer
Charles T. Tuggle, Jr.
Larry E. Killebrew
Jerry Stauffer
Robert C. Liddon
William H.D. Fones, Jr.
William P. Kenworthy
Allan J. Wade
Gregory G. Fletcher
Charles C. Harrell
Stephen D. Goodwin
George T. Lewis, III
Ben C. Adams, Jr.
Eugene J. Podesta, Jr.
Sam B. Blair, Jr.
Carla Peacher-Ryan
Mary Aronov
Jill M. Steinberg
Matthew S. Heiter
Michael C. Patton
Janis Wild Kesser
Stephen William Ragland
Monique A. Nassar
Bradley E. Trammell
M. Clay Bethell
Desiree M. Franklin
R. Alan Pritchard, Jr.
Peter H. Kesser

OF COUNSEL

Frierson M. Graves, Jr.
Donald A. Malmo
Lynn Ackerman Landau
Paul E. Risner (Not admitted in TN)

ASSOCIATES

Paul R. O'Rourke
Anne B. Mathes
Elizabeth Einstman Chance
Frank L. Watson, III
W. Douglas Sweet
Wm. Scott Young
Mary Ann Jackson
Angela R. Merideth
Jackie G. Prester
David L. Bearman
Clarissa M. Cissell
Robert C. McConkey, III
Jennifer R. Keown
Brett T. Parks
Cedric C.Y. Tan
Lang Wiseman
Diane Schratz Holitik
D. Benjamin Bullen
Shannon M. Hernandez
Sylvia Monique Reed
Christopher G. Boling
Louise P. Gaerig
Lori Hackleman Patterson
Lea Hall Speed

For full biographical listings, see the Martindale-Hubbell Law Directory

EVANS & PETREE (AV)

81 Monroe Avenue, 38103
Telephone: 901-525-6781
Telecopier: 901-527-7756

MEMBERS OF FIRM

Marion G. Evans (1877-1957)
Jack Petree (1921-1973)
Charles Pittman Cobb (Retired)
Elwood L. Edwards (Retired)
W. Lytle Nichol IV
John W. McQuiston II
Ernest G. Kelly, Jr.
Michael C. Williams
Joseph W. Barnwell, Jr.
David C. Scruggs
Leonard C. Dunavant, Jr.
E. Woods Weathersby
C. Bradford Foster III
Andrew H. Raines
Frank N. Stockdale Carney
Paul F. T. Edwards
Percy H. Harvey
Katharine A. Jungkind
Scott A. Frick
Michael R. Marshall
Richard E.M. Nichol, Jr.

Karen Baim Reagler

For full biographical listings, see the Martindale-Hubbell Law Directory

HALE HEADRICK DEWEY & WOLF, PLLC (AV)

One Memphis Place, 200 Jefferson Avenue Suite 1450, 38103
Telephone: 901-523-1123
Fax: 901-523-7472
Nashville, Tennessee Office: Suntrust Bank Building, 201 Fourth Avenue North, Suite 1450, 37219.
Telephone: 615-843-5160.
Fax: 615-843-5165

Stephen P. Hale
S. Russell Headrick
H. Tucker Dewey
Herbert B. Wolf, Jr.
John S. Golwen

OF COUNSEL

Steven L. Gill

Jennifer Ziegenhorn
Wendy A. Geurin
John W. Campbell
Joseph M. Koury
Holly N. Knight
Charles S. Blatteis
Jennifer S. Kiesewetter
J. William Williams

For full biographical listings, see the Martindale-Hubbell Law Directory

WARING COX, PLC (AV)

Morgan Keegan Tower, 50 North Front Street, Suite 1300, 38103-1190
Telephone: 901-543-8000
Telecopy: 901-543-8030
Email: Desk@waringcox.com

Shellie G. McCain, Jr.
Douglas P. Quay
William T. Mays, Jr.
Robert C. Starnes

Representative Clients: Federal Express Corp.; Delta Life and Annuity.

For Complete List of Firm Personnel, See General Section

For full biographical listings, see the Martindale-Hubbell Law Directory

*NASHVILLE,** Davidson Co.

BAKER, DONELSON, BEARMAN & CALDWELL (AV)

1700 Nashville City Center, 511 Union Street, 37219
Telephone: 615-726-5600
Telecopier: 615-726-0464
Email: info@bdbc.com *URL:* http://www.bakerdonelson.com
Memphis, Tennessee Office: 20th Floor, First Tennessee Building, 165 Madison, 38103.
Telephone: 901-526-2000.
Telecopier: 901-577-2303.
Chattanooga, Tennessee Office: 1800 Republic Centre, 633 Chestnut Street, 37450-1800.
Telephone: 423-756-2010.
Telecopier: 423-756-3447.
Knoxville, Tennessee Office: 2200 Riverview Tower, 900 South Gay Street, 37901.
Telephone: 423-549-7000.
Telecopier: 423-525-8569.
Johnson City, Tennessee Office: SunTrust Bank Building, 207 Mockingbird Lane, P.O. Box 3038, 37602.
Telephone: 423-928-0181.
Telecopier: 423-928-5694; 423-928-3654; Kingsport: 423-246-6191.
Huntsville, Tennessee Office: 3 Courthouse Square, 37756.
Telephone: 423-663-2321.
Telecopier: 423-663-2111.
Washington, D.C. Office: Market Square, 801 Pennsylvania Avenue, N.W., 20004.
Telephone: 202-508-3400.
Telecopier: 202-508-3402.
Jackson, Mississippi Office: Suite 500, 700 North State Street, 39202.
Telephone: 601-351-2400.
Telecopier: 601-351-2424.

MANAGING PARTNER

Laurence M. Papel

SHAREHOLDERS

Lewis R. Donelson, III
Howard H. Baker, Jr.
Robert F. Worthington, Jr.
Robert G. McCullough
Richard D. Bird
Thomas O. Helton
Richard B. Gossett
Robert L. Baker
Robert G. McDowell
Carl E. Hartley
William S. Painter (Not admitted in TN)
John A. Gupton, III
Claudia W. Dickerson
James A. DeLanis
Richard G. Cowart
Kenneth P. Ezell, Jr.
James L. McElroy
Robert M. Steele
Gary C. Shockley
Randal S. Mashburn
Steven J. Eisen
John S. Hicks
J. Porter Durham, Jr.
M. Kevin Outterson
J. Steven Kirkham
John H. Rowland
Philip Stuart McSween
Thomas E. Bartrum (Not admitted in TN)

ASSOCIATES

Claire F. Miley
Barbara A. Rose
John F. Rogers, Jr.
Scott D. Carey
John M. Bryant, Jr.
Kenneth A. Weber
Darwin A. Hindman III
Ann Duncan Jarvis
Lawrence S. Eastwood, Jr.
Jonathan Cole
Christopher R. Kelly
Brigid T. Miller
Christy Tosh Crider
Kelley Taylor Oliver
Richard H. Stout
J. Adin Lara
Tonya Mitchem Grindon (Not admitted in TN)
Jennifer Lynch Butler

OF COUNSEL

Peter C. Ward (Not admitted in TN)
Thomas H. Holter (Not admitted in TN)
Christy F. Batts

For full biographical listings, see the Martindale-Hubbell Law Directory

BASS, BERRY & SIMS PLC (AV)

2700 First American Center, 37238-2700
Telephone: 615-742-6200
Telecopy: 615-742-6293
URL: http://www.bassberry.com
Knoxville, Tennessee Office: 1700 Riverview Tower, 900 S. Gay Street, 37902 and P.O. Box 1509, 37901-1509.
Telephone: 423-521-6200.
Telecopy: 423-521-6234.

(See Next Column)

BASS, BERRY & SIMS PLC—*Continued*

Memphis, Tennessee Office: 119 S. Main Street, Suite 500, 38103.
Telephone: 901-312-9100.
Fax: 901-312-9101.

MEMBERS OF FIRM

W. W. Berry
James C. Gooch
James W. Berry, Jr.
Richard H. Barry
Michael D. Sontag
Fritz Richter, III
James T. O'Hare

ASSOCIATES

Bryan W. Metcalf
Carter R. Brothers
Christopher L. May

Representative Clients: Ingram Industries; Service Merchandise, Inc.; First American Corp.; DeVlieg-Bullard, Inc.; Thomas Nelson, Inc.; CUC International, Inc.

For full biographical listings, see the Martindale-Hubbell Law Directory

CORBETT CROCKETT & LECKRONE (AV)

An Association of Attorneys including a Professional Corporation
Suite 1050, American Center, 3100 West End Avenue, 37203
Telephone: 615-383-0500
Facsimile: 615-383-5556
Email: counsel@ccllaw.com *URL:* http://www.lawyers.com/ccl

Joe Vaulx Crockett, III
James David Leckrone

For full biographical listings, see the Martindale-Hubbell Law Directory

D. JEFFERSON HERRING (AV)

The Pilcher Building, Suite 200, 144 Second Avenue North, 37201
Telephone: 615-259-9594
Fax: 615-259-9584

For full biographical listings, see the Martindale-Hubbell Law Directory

HOLTON HOWARD & GOODMAN, P.C. (AV)

424 Church Street, Suite 2700, 37219-2323
Telephone: 615-256-3338
Fax: 615-244-2104
Email: Plan@hohogoo.com

Richard D. Holton
Bryan Howard
Joe M. Goodman
William E. Blackstone

Mattison C. Painter
Brian C. Mayberry
Lucibeth Nave
Stephen C. Passen

Reference: SunTrust Bank, Nashville, N.A.

For full biographical listings, see the Martindale-Hubbell Law Directory

KING & BALLOW (AV)

Union Street Plaza, 315 Union Street, Suite 1100, 37201
Telephone: 615-259-3456
Fax: 615-254-7907
Email: lawfirm@king-ballow.com *URL:* http://www.king-ballow.com
San Diego, California Office: 2700 Symphony Towers, 750 B Street, 92101.
Telephone: 619-236-9401.
Fax: 619-236-9437.

MEMBERS OF FIRM

Frank S. King, Jr.
Robert L. Ballow
Larry D. Crabtree
Alan L. Marx
Paul H. Duvall (Resident, San Diego, California Office)
Mark E. Hunt
R. Brent Ballow

ASSOCIATES

Dorothy L. Starnes
Patrick M. Thomas
Stephen F. Peluso
Candace Ferrell-Bhavsar

Representative Clients: Garden State Newspapers, Inc., Woodbury, New Jersey; Gaylord Entertainment Company; Ingram Industries, Inc., Nashville, Tennessee; Opryland, Nashville, Tennessee; Parade Magazine, Inc., New York, New York; Sullivan Graphics, Inc., Nashville, Tennessee; Tribune Company, Chicago, Illinois.

For Complete List of Firm Personnel, See General Section

For full biographical listings, see the Martindale-Hubbell Law Directory

TEXAS

*AUSTIN,** Travis Co.

CANTEY & HANGER ROAN & AUTREY L.L.P. (AV)

200 First State Bank Tower, 400 West Fifteenth Street, 78701-4200
Telephone: 512-474-4200
FAX: 512-469-0470; 512-469-0474
Email: FIRM@ROAN-AUTREY.COM *URL:* http://www.Roan-Autrey.com
Fort Worth, Texas Office: Cantey & Hanger, 2100 Burnett Plaza, 801 Cherry Street.
Telephone: 817-877-2800, Metro Line: 429-3815.
Telex: 758631.
FAX: 877-2807. Email: cantey@onramp.net
Dallas, Texas Office: Cantey & Hanger, 3330 Harwood Center, 1999 Bryan Street.
Telephone: 214-978-4100.
FAX: 214-978-4150. Email: chdallas@onramp.net

Forrest C. Roan
Jeff W. Autrey
Stephen L. Phillips
Brian C. Newby
Julie K. Lane

OF COUNSEL

Tieman H. Dippel, Jr.

LEGAL SUPPORT PERSONNEL

Mary B. Jordan
Mary Perroni Blevins

For full biographical listings, see the Martindale-Hubbell Law Directory

OSBORNE, LOWE, HELMAN & SMITH, L.L.P. (AV)

301 Congress Avenue Suite 1900, 78701
Telephone: 512-469-7700
Fax: 512-469-7711
Email: olhslan@aol.com

MEMBERS OF FIRM

Duncan Elliott Osborne
Stephen Jody Helman
Derry W. Swanger
Jack E. Owen, Jr.
Leslie C. Giordani
Carolyn M. Beckett
Elizabeth Morgan Schurig
Elizabeth Gibson Deleery
Whitney Jade Fleming
Paul E. Williams
Gina Lambert

OF COUNSEL

Hugh S. Lowe
Paula Y. Smith

For full biographical listings, see the Martindale-Hubbell Law Directory

THOMPSON & KNIGHT L.L.P. (AV)

(Attorneys and Counselors)
1200 San Jacinto Center, 98 San Jacinto Boulevard, 78701
Telephone: 512-469-6100
Telecopy: 512-469-6180
URL: http://www.tklaw.com
Dallas, Texas Office: 1700 Pacific Avenue, Suite 3300, 75201.
Telephone: 214-969-1700.
Telecopy: 512-969-1751.
Telex: 732298.
Fort Worth, Texas Office: 801 Cherry Street, Suite 1600, 76102.
Telephone: 817-347-1700.
Telecopy: 817-347-1799.
Houston, Texas Office: Thompson Knight Brown Parker & Leahy L.L.P., 1200 Smith Street, Suite 3600, 77002-4595.
Telephone: 713-654-8111.
Telecopier: 713-654-1871.
San Pedro Garza Garcia, Nuevo León, Mexico Office: Edificio Losoles PD-4, Av. Lázaro Cárdenas No. 2400 Pte., C.P. 66220.
Telephone: (52-8) 363-0096.
Telecopy: (52-8) 363-3067.

PARTNER

Frank L. Hill

For Complete List of Firm Personnel, See General Section

For full biographical listings, see the Martindale-Hubbell Law Directory

*CORPUS CHRISTI,** Nueces Co.

PEARSON & PRICE, PLLC (AV)

Suite 1700, South Tower, 800 North Shoreline Boulevard, 78401
Telephone: 361-885-0077
Fax: 361-885-0288
Email: INFO@PEARSON-PRICE.COM *URL:* HTTP://WWW.PEARSON-PRICE.COM

Paul C. Pearson, III
Paul O. Price
Richard E. Flint

For full biographical listings, see the Martindale-Hubbell Law Directory

*DALLAS,** Dallas Co.

CALHOUN & STACY (AV)

Suite 5700 - Bank of America Plaza, 901 Main Street, 75202-3713
Telephone: 214-748-5000
Facsimile: 214-748-1421
Email: info@calhounstacy.com *URL:* http://www.calhounstacy.com

MEMBERS OF FIRM

Rees T. Bowen, III
LeAnn Wainscott Cross
David W. Elrod
Parker Nelson
Roy L. Stacy
Pamela J. Touchstone
Michael C. Wright

ASSOCIATES

David G. Allen
Joseph G. Barkate, Jr.
Scott S. Crocker
Sean P. Fitzgerald
Elizabeth Reding Gambrell
Leanne Capps Medford
Joel W. Reese
Barbara L. Wohlrabe

For Complete List of Firm Personnel, See General Section

For full biographical listings, see the Martindale-Hubbell Law Directory

CARRINGTON, COLEMAN, SLOMAN & BLUMENTHAL, L.L.P. (AV)

200 Crescent Court, Suite 1500, 75201
Telephone: 214-855-3000
Telecopy: 214-855-1333
Email: ccsb@ccsb.com *URL:* http://www.carringtoncoleman.com

MEMBER OF FIRM

Robert L. Blumenthal

For Complete List of Firm Personnel, See General Section

For full biographical listings, see the Martindale-Hubbell Law Directory

GODWIN WHITE & GRUBER, A PROFESSIONAL CORPORATION (AV)

Suite 2500, 901 Main Street, 75202-3714
Telephone: 214-939-4400
Fax: 214-760-7332

Bob J. Shelton
James G. Vetter, Jr.

For Complete List of Firm Personnel, See General Section

For full biographical listings, see the Martindale-Hubbell Law Directory

HUGHES & LUCE, L.L.P. (AV)

A Registered Limited Liability Partnership including Professional Corporations
1717 Main Street, Suite 2800, 75201
Telephone: 214-939-5500
Fax: 214-939-6100; 214-939-5849
Email: H&L@hughesluce.com *URL:* http://www.hughesluce.com
Austin, Texas Office: 111 Congress, Suite 900.
Telephone: 512-482-6800.
Fax: 512-482-6859.
Houston, Texas Office: 1600 Smith Street, Suite 3550.
Telephone: 713-754-5200.
Fax: 713-754-5270.

MEMBERS OF FIRM

Jeff W. Dorrill
Scott C. Drablos
Kathryn G. Henkel
Vester T. Hughes, Jr.
Ronald D. Kerridge
Cynthia Morgan Ohlenforst
David L. Sinak
Karen K. Suhre
Elizabeth R. Turner

ASSOCIATES

Bradley L. Adams
J. David Clark, Jr. (Not admitted in TX)
Lora G. Davis
Tracy Eaton
Paul J. Kardish
D. Alexander Ritchie
Matthew R. Schindel
Margaret Laurel Stephenson

For Complete List of Firm Personnel, See General Section

For full biographical listings, see the Martindale-Hubbell Law Directory

JACKSON WALKER L.L.P. (AV)

901 Main Street, Suite 6000, 75202-3797
Telephone: 214-953-6000
Fax: 214-953-5822
URL: http://www.jw.com
Austin, Texas Office: 100 Congress Avenue, Suite 1100.
Telephone: 512-236-2000.
Fax: 512-236-2002.
Fort Worth, Texas Office: 301 Commerce Street, Suite 2400.
Telephone: 817-334-7200.
Fax: 817-334-7290.

(See Next Column)

Houston, Texas Office: 1100 Louisiana, Suite 4200.
Telephone: 713-752-4200.
Fax: 713-752-4221.
Richardson, Texas Office: 2435 North Central Expressway, Suite 600.
Telephone: 972-671-2560.
Fax: 972-671-2566.
San Angelo, Texas Office: 225 West Beauregard Avenue.
Telephone: 915-481-2550.
Fax: 915-481-2552.
San Antonio, Texas Office: 112 E. Pecan Street, Suite 2100.
Telephone: 210-978-7700.
Fax: 210-978-7790.

MEMBERS OF FIRM

Larry L. Bean
Daniel G. Easley
James R. Griffin
R. Thomas Groves, Jr.
William H. Hornberger
Michael L. Kaufman
John J. Klein

Representative Clients Furnished Upon Request.

For Complete List of Firm Personnel, See General Section

For full biographical listings, see the Martindale-Hubbell Law Directory

JONES, DAY, REAVIS & POGUE (AV)

2727 North Harwood Street, 75201-1515
Telephone: 214-220-3939
Telecopier: 214-969-5100
Email: counsel@jonesday.com *URL:* http://www.jonesday.com
In Atlanta, Georgia: 3500 SunTrust Plaza, 303 Peachtree Street.
Telephone: 404-521-3939.
Telecopier: 404-581-8330.
In Brussels, Belgium: Avenue Louise 480, 7th Floor, B-1050 Brussels.
Telephone: 32-2-645-14-11.
Telecopier: 32-2-645-14-45.
In Chicago, Illinois: 77 West Wacker.
Telephone: 312-782-3939.
Telecopier: 312-782-8585.
In Cleveland, Ohio: North Point, 901 Lakeside Avenue.
Telephone: 216-586-3939.
Telecopier: 216-579-0212.
In Columbus, Ohio: 1900 Huntington Center.
Telephone: 614-469-3939.
Telecopier: 614-461-4198.
In Frankfurt, Germany: Hochhaus am Park, Grüneburgweg 102, 60323 Frankfurt am Main.
Telephone: 49-69-9726-3939.
Telecopier: 49-69-9726-3993.
In Geneva, Switzerland: 20, rue de Candolle.
Telephone: 41-22-320-2339.
Telecopier: 41-22-320-1232.
In Hong Kong: 29th Floor, Entertainment Building, 30 Queen's Road Central.
Telephone: 852-2526-6895.
Telecopier: 852-2868-5871.
In Irvine, California: 5 Park Plaza, Suite 1100.
Telephone: 949-851-3939.
Telecopier: 949-553-7539.
In London, England: Bucklersbury House, 3 Queen Victoria Street.
Telephone: 44-20-7236-3939.
Telecopier: 44-20-7236-1113.
In Los Angeles, California: 555 West Fifth Street, Suite 4600.
Telephone: 213-489-3939.
Telecopier: 213-243-2539.
In New York, New York: 599 Lexington Avenue.
Telephone: 212-326-3939.
Telecopier: 212-755-7306.
In Paris, France: 120, rue du Faubourg Saint-Honoré.
Telephone: 33-1-56-59-39-39.
Telecopier: 33-1-56-59-39-38
In Pittsburgh, Pennsylvania: 500 Grant Street, 31st Floor.
Telephone: 412-391-3939.
Telecopier: 412-394-7959.
Riyadh, Saudi Arabia: The International Law Firm (In Association with Jones, Day, Reavis & Pogue), Sulaymaniyah, Prince Mishari IBN, Addulaziz Street, P.O. Box 22166.
Telephone: (966-1) 462-8866.
Telecopier: (966-1) 462-9001.
In Shanghai, China: 2805 Kerry Centre, 1515 Nanjing Road West.
Telephone: 86-21-5298-6568.
Telecopier: 86-21-5298-6569.
In Sydney, Australia: Governor Phillip Tower, Level 38, 1 Farrer Place.
Telephone: 61-2-9210-6921.
Telecopier: 61-2-9210-6926.
In Taipei, Taiwan: 8th Floor, 2 Tun Hwa South Road, Section 2.
Telephone: (886-2) 2704-6808.
Telecopier: (886-2) 2704-6791.
In Tokyo, Japan: Toranomon 45 Mori Building, 3rd Floor, 1-5, Toranomon, 5-Chome, Minato-ku, Tokyo 105, Japan.
Telephone: 81-3-3433-3939.
Telecopier: 81-3-5401-2725.
In Washington, D.C.: 51 Louisiana Avenue, N.W.
Telephone: 202-879-3939.
Telecopier: 202-626-1700.

(See Next Column)

JONES, DAY, REAVIS & POGUE—*Continued*

MEMBERS OF FIRM IN DALLAS

James F. Carey
David E. Cowling
John T. McCafferty
Ronald G. Weitz
Dennis B. Drapkin
Alan S. Miller
Todd Wallace

OF COUNSEL

Richard A. Freling

COUNSEL

Robert D. Lochridge

ASSOCIATE

Charolette F. Noel

For Complete List of Firm Personnel, See General Section

For full biographical listings, see the Martindale-Hubbell Law Directory

KANE, RUSSELL, COLEMAN & LOGAN, A PROFESSIONAL CORPORATION (AV)

3700 Thanksgiving Tower, 1601 Elm Street, 75201-7207
Telephone: 214-777-4200
Fax: 214-777-4299
Email: krcl@krcl.com

Raymond J. Kane
David N. Condon
Gordon B. Russell
Karen A. Cox
Joseph M. Coleman
William D. Elliott
Michael A. Logan
Joseph A. Friedman
Patrick V. Stark
Robert N. LeMay
Kenneth W. Biermacher
Michael L. Atchley, II
Margaret M. McLeod Jordan

Terry Flett Barakis
Jaqluin M. Bickmore Lloyd
Harold R. Busch
Robert L. Manteuffel
Priscilla K. Davenport
David D. Ritter
Deborah A. DiMarco
Holly J. Roman
Evangelos J. Gegas (Not admitted in TX)
Jeffrey S. Seeburger
Jeffrey Charles Tasker
Shelli R. Inmon
Steven M. Thornton
Kenneth C. Johnston
Karin M. Zaner

For full biographical listings, see the Martindale-Hubbell Law Directory

KRAGE & JANVEY, L.L.P. (AV)

2001 Bryan Tower, Suite 2700, 75201-3059
Telephone: 214-969-7500
Telecopier: 214-220-0230

C. Clinton Davis, Jr.

Representative Client: Regal Capital Co.

For full biographical listings, see the Martindale-Hubbell Law Directory

MEADOWS, OWENS, COLLIER, REED, COUSINS & BLAU, L.L.P. (AV)

901 Main Street, Suite 3700, 75202-3725
Telephone: 214-744-3700; 800-451-0093
Fax: 214-747-3732
URL: http://www.meadowsowens.com

MEMBERS OF FIRM

Charles M. Meadows, Jr.
Charles W. Blau
Rodney J. Owens
George R. Bedell
Robert Don Collier
Michael E. McCue
David N. Reed
Fielder F. Nelms
Thomas G. Hineman
Joel N. Crouch
William R. Cousins, III
Alan K. Davis
Charles D. Pulman

ASSOCIATES

Patricia King Dorey
Sara E. Lankford
Robert M. Bolton
Sarah Q. Qureshi
M. Todd Welty
Bradley G. Korell
Josh O. Ungerman
Todd A. Kraft
Robyn A. Frohlin
Alan L. Stroud
Gregory A. Cardenas
Matthew D. Richards

For full biographical listings, see the Martindale-Hubbell Law Directory

SMITH, UNDERWOOD & PERKINS, A PROFESSIONAL CORPORATION (AV)

600 Two Lincoln Centre, 5420 LBJ Freeway, 75240
Telephone: 972-661-5114
Telecopier: 972-661-5691
Email: firm@suandp.com *URL:* http://www.suplaw.com

Timothy S. Perkins
G. Lynn Smith
David W. Ralston
William J. Underwood, Jr.

(See Next Column)

Christine A. McGuire
Ellen P. Stewart
Amy K. Ratzlaff
Todd W. Shadle
P. Theodore Stoinoff, II
Ruth C. Logan
Val C. Cronin
Christina L. Betanzos
Kent D. Williamson

For full biographical listings, see the Martindale-Hubbell Law Directory

THOMPSON & KNIGHT L.L.P. (AV)

(Attorneys and Counselors)
1700 Pacific Avenue Suite 3300, 75201
Telephone: 214-969-1700
Telecopy: 214-969-1751
Telex: 732 298
URL: http://www.tklaw.com
Austin, Texas Office: 1200 San Jacinto Center, 98 San Jacinto Boulevard, 78701.
Telephone: 512-469-6100.
Telecopy: 512-469-6180.
Fort Worth, Texas Office: 801 Cherry Street, Suite 1600, 76102.
Telephone: 817-347-1700.
Telecopy: 817-347-1799.
Houston, Texas Office: Thompson Knight Brown Parker & Leahy L.L.P., 1200 Smith Street, Suite 3600, 77002-4595.
Telephone: 713-654-8111.
Telecopier: 713-654-1871.
San Pedro Garza Garcia, Nuevo León, Mexico Office: Edificio Losoles PD-4, Av. Lázaro Cárdenas No. 2400 Pte., C.P. 66220.
Telephone: (52-8) 363-0096.
Telecopy: (52-8) 363-3067.

PARTNERS

George C. Chapman
John A. Mackintosh, Jr.

For Complete List of Firm Personnel, See General Section

For full biographical listings, see the Martindale-Hubbell Law Directory

*EL PASO,** El Paso Co.

KEMP, SMITH, DUNCAN & HAMMOND, A PROFESSIONAL CORPORATION (AV)

221 North Kansas, Suite 1700, 79901, P.O. Drawer 2800, 79999
Telephone: 915-533-4424
Fax: 915-546-5360
Email: ksdh@kempsmith.com *URL:* http://www.kempsmith.com
Austin, Texas Office: 816 Congress, Suite 1650.
Telephone: 512-320-5466.
Fax: 512-320-5431.

Allan M. Goldfarb
Gene Wolf
Mark Hedrick
Alfonso Soto, III

OF COUNSEL

Bruce Hallmark

Attorneys for: Security Capital Pacific Trust; Sun World Corporation.

For Complete List of Firm Personnel, See General Section

For full biographical listings, see the Martindale-Hubbell Law Directory

*FORT WORTH,** Tarrant Co.

BROUDE, SMITH & JENNINGS, P.C. (AV)

309 West Seventh Street Suite 1100, 76102
Telephone: 817-335-1615
Metro: 817-654-3505
Fax: 817-335-1603

John S. Broude
Cary L. Jennings
Steven M. Smith
Kathryn Durham McGlinchey
Jerry Betsill

OF COUNSEL

Janna Ward Clarke

LEGAL SUPPORT PERSONNEL

Laura deLagerheim (Paralegal).

For full biographical listings, see the Martindale-Hubbell Law Directory

CANTEY & HANGER (AV)

A Registered Limited Liability Partnership
2100 Burnett Plaza, 801 Cherry Street, 76102-6899
Telephone: 817-877-2800, Metro Line: 429-3815
Telex: 758631 FAX: 877-2807
Dallas
Email: cantey@onramp.net
Dallas, Texas Office: 3330 Harwood Center, 1999 Bryan Street.
Telephone: 214-978-4100.
FAX: 214-978-4150. Email: chdallas@onramp.net

(See Next Column)

CANTEY & HANGER, *Fort Worth—Continued*

Austin, Texas Office: Cantey & Hanger Roan & Autrey L.L.P., 200 First State Bank Tower, 400 West Fifteenth Street.
Telephone: 512-474-4200.
FAX: 512-469-0470; 512-469-0474. Email: FIRM@ROAN-AUTREY.COM

MEMBERS OF FIRM

Harry E. Bartel
Allan Howeth
Noel C. Ice
Kirk R. Manning

OF COUNSEL

Whitfield J. Collins
Diego O. Giordano
Warren W. Shipman III

ASSOCIATES

Michael G. Appleman
Jason D. Prather

Represent: General Motors Corp.; Miller Brewing Co.; The Medical Protective Co.; Texas Utilities Electric Co.; Bank of America, N.A.; Union Pacific Resources Company.

For Complete List of Firm Personnel, See General Section

For full biographical listings, see the Martindale-Hubbell Law Directory

DECKER, JONES, MCMACKIN, MCCLANE, HALL & BATES, A PROFESSIONAL CORPORATION (AV)

2500 Bank One Tower, 500 Throckmorton Street, 76102-3812
Telephone: 817-336-2400; Metro: 817-429-5260
Fax: 817-332-3043; 336-2181
Email: email@deckerjones.com *URL:* http://www.deckerjones.com

Daniel L. Bates
Robert W. Decker
Mark S. Dugan
Janet L. Hahn
Randy J. Hall
Raymond B. Kelly, III
John B. McClane
John W. McMackin
Charles B. Milliken
Gary M. Moates
Bradley H. Rice
Jeffrey W. Storie
James L. Stripling
Brian K. Yost
Tamera H. Bennett
Arthur F. Zobal
Geoffrey A. Mantooth

Representative Clients: Martin-Sprocket and Gear, Inc.; Williamson-Dickie Manufacturing Co.; MICA Corp.; Ibertech, Inc.; Harbison-Fischer Manufacturing Co.; Employers Insurance of Texas; American International Group; Medical Protective Co.; Redman Homes, Inc.; Liberty Mutual Insurance.

For full biographical listings, see the Martindale-Hubbell Law Directory

MICHENER, LARIMORE, SWINDLE, WHITAKER, FLOWERS, SAWYER, REYNOLDS & CHALK, L.L.P. (AV)

3500 City Center Tower II, 301 Commerce Street, 76102
Telephone: 817-335-4417
Telecopy: 817-335-6935

MEMBERS OF FIRM

John W. Michener, Jr.
Tom L. Larimore
Mack Ed Swindle
Wayne M. Whitaker
H. David Flowers
Jerry K. Sawyer
James G. Reynolds
John Allen Chalk, Sr.
Thomas S. Brandon, Jr.
Matthew P. McDonald
Clark R. Cowley
Thomas F. Harkins, Jr.
John A. Chalk, Jr.
Leslie Combs
Robert G. West
Theresa Brewton Lyons
Jonathan K. Henderson
David R. Childress
Harold S. Sparks, III
John M. Cummings
Melinda Watts Smith
Hunter T. McLean

For full biographical listings, see the Martindale-Hubbell Law Directory

THOMPSON & KNIGHT L.L.P. (AV)

(Attorneys and Counselors)
801 Cherry Street, Suite 1600, 76102
Telephone: 817-347-1700
Telecopy: 817-347-1799
URL: http://www.tklaw.com
Dallas, Texas Office: 1700 Pacific Avenue, Suite 3300, 75201.
Telephone: 214-969-1700.
Telecopy: 214-969-1751.
Telex: 732298.
Austin, Texas Office: 1200 San Jacinto Center, 98 San Jacinto Boulevard, 78701.
Telephone: 512-469-6100.
Telecopy: 512-469-6180.
Houston, Texas Office: Thompson Knight Brown Parker & Leahy L.L.P., 1200 Smith Street, Suite 3600, 77002-4595.
Telephone: 713-654-8111.
Telecopier: 713-654-1871.
San Pedro Garza Garcia, Nuevo León, Mexico Office: Edificio Losoles PD-4, Av. Lázaro Cárdenas No. 2400 Pte., C.P. 66220.
Telephone: (52-8) 363-0096.
Telecopy: (52-8) 363-3067.

(See Next Column)

PARTNER

R Gordon Appleman

For Complete List of Firm Personnel, See General Section

For full biographical listings, see the Martindale-Hubbell Law Directory

*HOUSTON,** Harris Co.

BAKER BOTTS L.L.P. (AV)

One Shell Plaza, 910 Louisiana, 77002
Telephone: 713-229-1234
Cable Address: "Boterlove"
Fax: 713-229-1522
Email: postmaster@bakerbotts.com *URL:* http://www.bakerbotts.com
Washington, D.C. Office: The Warner, 1299 Pennsylvania Avenue, N.W.
Telephone: 202-639-7700.
New York, New York Office: 599 Lexington Avenue.
Telephone: 212-705-5000.
Austin, Texas Office: 1600 San Jacinto Center, 98 San Jacinto Boulevard.
Telephone: 512-322-2500.
Dallas, Texas Office: 2001 Ross Avenue.
Telephone: 214-953-6500.
Moscow, Russia Office: 10 ul. Bolshaya Dimitrovka (formerly Pushkinskaya), 103031.
Telephone: 7095/921-5300 (Local); 7095/929-7070 (International).
London, England Office: 45 Ludgate Hill.
Telephone: 0171-778-1400 (Local); 011-44-171-778-1400 (International).
Baku, Azerbaijan Office: 6-10 Vagif Mustafa-zadeh Street, Third Floor, Icheri Sheher, 370004.
Telephone: 994-12-97-63-88 (Local); 011-994-12-97-63-88 (International).
Fax: 994-12-97-63-91 (Local); 011-994-12-97-63-91 (International)

MEMBERS OF FIRM

Stanley C. Beyer
Gerard A. Desrochers
Richard Allen Husseini
Gray Jennings
Gregory V. Nelson
John Edward Neslage
James R. Raborn
Stuart F. Schaffer
Gail Woodson Stewart
Benjamin G. Wells

RETIRED PARTNER

William C. Griffith

SPECIAL COUNSEL

Laura C. Higley
Tracee Kennedy Lewis

ASSOCIATES

Mark A. Bodron
Michael P. Bresson
Deidre Sullivan Brod
T. Chuck Campbell
J. Robert Fowler
Daniel Harris Kroll
Paul F. Perea
Lori McFarlin Troutman

For Complete List of Firm Personnel, See General Section

For full biographical listings, see the Martindale-Hubbell Law Directory

CORDRAY & GOODRICH, PROFESSIONAL CORPORATION (AV)

3306 Sul Ross, 77098-1808
Telephone: 713-630-0600
Facsimile: 713-630-0017

Howard F. Cordray, Jr.
Christopher M. Goodrich
Richard Alan Tomlin
Gregory A. Goodrich
Glynn D. Nance, Jr.

OF COUNSEL

Ellen M. Lang
Van A. Cates
Robert G. Bailey

For full biographical listings, see the Martindale-Hubbell Law Directory

GILLIS & SLOGAR (AV)

6905 Wells Fargo Plaza, 1000 Louisiana, 77002
Telephone: 713-951-9100
Telecopier: 713-951-9718
Email: gillisslogar@worldnet.att.net

Charles Michael Gillis
John Michael Slogar

OF COUNSEL

Randall W. Heinrich

For full biographical listings, see the Martindale-Hubbell Law Directory

THOMPSON KNIGHT BROWN PARKER & LEAHY L.L.P. (AV)

A Registered Limited Liability Partnership including Professional Corporations
(Attorneys and Counselors)
1200 Smith Street, Suite 3600, 77002-4595
Telephone: 713-654-8111
Telecopier: 713-654-1871
URL: http://www.tklaw.com
Dallas, Texas Office: Thompson & Knight L.L.P., 1700 Pacific Avenue, Suite 3300, 75201.
Telephone: 214-969-1700.
Telecopy: 214-969-1751.
Telex: 732298.

(See Next Column)

THOMPSON KNIGHT BROWN PARKER & LEAHY L.L.P.—*Continued*

Austin, Texas Office: Thompson & Knight L.L.P., 1200 San Jacinto Center, 98 San Jacinto Boulevard, 78701.
Telephone: 512-469-6100.
Telecopy: 512-469-6180.
Fort Worth, Texas Office: Thompson & Knight L.L.P., 801 Cherry Street, Suite 1600, 76102.
Telephone: 817-347-1700.
Telecopy: 817-347-1799.
San Pedro Garza Garcia, Nuevo León, Mexico Office: Thompson & Knight L.L.P., Edificio Losoles PD-4, Av. Lázaro Cárdenas No. 2400 PTE., C.P. 66220.
Telephone: (52-8) 363-0096.
Telecopy: (52-8) 363-3067.

PARTNER

Robert S. MacIntyre, Jr.

ASSOCIATE

W. Cameron McCulloch

For Complete List of Firm Personnel, See General Section

For full biographical listings, see the Martindale-Hubbell Law Directory

VINSON & ELKINS L.L.P. (AV)

2300 First City Tower, 1001 Fannin, 77002-6760
Telephone: 713-758-2222
Fax: 713-758-2346
Email: info@velaw.com *URL:* http://www.velaw.com
Austin, Texas Office: One American Center Suite 2700, 600 Congress Avenue, Austin, Texas, 78701-3200.
Telephone: 512-495-8400.
Fax: 512-495-8612.
Beijing, China Office: 20/F, Beijing Silver Tower, No. 2, Dong San Huan Bei Lu, Chaoyang District, 100027.
Telephone: +86-10-6410-6300.
Fax: +86-10-6410-6360.
Dallas, Texas Office: 3700 Trammell Crow Center, 2001 Ross Avenue, Dallas, Texas, 75201-2975.
Telephone: 214-220-7700.
Fax: 214-220-7716.
London, England Office: Regis House, 8th Floor, 45 King William Street, London, EC4R 9AN, England.
Telephone: (44-171) 618-6000.
Fax: (44-171) 618-6001.
Moscow, Russia Office: 16 Ulitsa Spiridonovka, Second Floor, 103001 Moscow, Russia.
Telephone: (7-095) 956-1995. Local
Fax: (7-095) 956-1996. U.S. Satellite
Fax: (212) 803-0142.
New York, N.Y. Office: 1325 Avenue of the Americas, 17th Floor, New York, N.Y., 10019.
Telephone: 917-206-8000.
Fax: 917-206-8100.
Singapore Office: 6 Battery Road, #39-01, Singapore, 049909.
Telephone: (65) 536-8300.
Fax: (65) 536-8311.
Washington, D.C. Office: The Willard Office Building, 1455 Pennsylvania Avenue, N.W., Washington, D.C., 20004-1008.
Telephone: 202-639-6500.
Fax: 202-639-6604.

MEMBERS OF FIRM

Charles L. Almond
Gary P. Amaon
Roger L. Beebe
Judith M. Blissard
Brian R. Bloom
Miriam M. (Dusty) Burke (Resident, Austin, Texas Office)
John E. Chapoton (Resident, Washington, D.C. Office)
Thomas Crichton, IV (Resident, Dallas, Texas Office)
Felicia A. Finston (Resident, Dallas, Texas Office)
George M. Gerachis
Steven H. Gerdes
R. Todd Greenwalt
Carol H. Jewett
Yolanda Chávez Knull
John W. Leggett
John E. Lynch
L. Price Manford
Thomas P. Marinis, Jr.
James S. Meyer (Resident, Dallas, Texas Office)
Garry M. Miles (Resident, Dallas, Texas Office)
Edward C. Osterberg, Jr.
Alan J. Robin
Glen A. Rosenbaum
Gary G. Short (Resident, Dallas, Texas Office)
Michael D. Thomson (Resident, Washington, D.C. Office)
Eric Viehman
Donald F. Wood (Resident, Austin, Texas Office)

HOUSTON OF COUNSEL

Karey Dubiel Dye
Stanley M. Johanson
James D. Penny
James David Pittman
Pamela Hays Stabler

AUSTIN OF COUNSEL

O. Wade Anderson
John D. Christian

DALLAS OF COUNSEL

Mark A. Cover
Carla N. Lindley
Geoffrey R. Polma

(See Next Column)

WASHINGTON, D.C. OF COUNSEL

Samuel B. Sterrett

ASSOCIATES

Tobey D. Blanton
Ronald F. Bradshaw (Resident, Austin, Texas Office)
Herman Mallory Caldwell
Charles H. Campbell, Jr. (Resident, Austin, Texas Office)
David C. D'Alessandro (Resident, Dallas, Texas Office)
Timothy J. Devetski
Katy Anne Drechsel
Debra J. Duncan (Resident, Washington, D.C. Office)
Charles Timothy Fenn
Jennifer K. Gray
Lisa J. Kaufman
Adam Miles Kramer
Matthew L. Larsen (Resident, Dallas, Texas Office)
Renn G. Neilson (Resident, Dallas, Texas Office)
David S. Peck (Resident, Dallas, Texas Office)
Laura Brodbeck Phillips (Resident, Washington, D.C. Office)
Cary D. Pugh (Resident, Washington, D.C. Office)
Mary J. Steichen (Resident, Dallas, Texas Office)
Ann K. Stewart (Resident, Dallas, Texas Office)
Jeanne Klinefelter Wilson

For Complete List of Firm Personnel, See General Section

For full biographical listings, see the Martindale-Hubbell Law Directory

IRVING, Dallas Co.

JOHN D. OWSEN, P.C. (AV)

4545 Fuller Drive, Suite 200, 75038-6530
Telephone: 972-719-9112
Fax: 972-719-9114
Email: owsen@lawyers.com *URL:* http://www.lawyers.com/owsen

John D. Owsen

For full biographical listings, see the Martindale-Hubbell Law Directory

*MIDLAND,** Midland Co.

LYNCH, CHAPPELL & ALSUP, A PROFESSIONAL CORPORATION (AV)

The Summit, Suite 700, 300 North Marienfeld, 79701
Telephone: 915-683-3351
Fax: 915-683-2587

Steven C. Lindgren
W. Scott Ryburn

Alan J. Brown

OF COUNSEL

Barbara J. Farish

Representative Clients: Tom Brown, Inc.; NationsBank of Texas, N.A.; Pioneer Natural Resources; Chevron U.S.A. Inc.; Norwest Bank Texas, Midland, N.A.; Wagner & Brown, Ltd.

For Complete List of Firm Personnel, See General Section

For full biographical listings, see the Martindale-Hubbell Law Directory

*SAN ANTONIO,** Bexar Co.

BENTON CLARK & TAYLOR, P.C. (AV)

105 South St. Marys Street, Suite 905, 78205
Telephone: 210-472-1800
Fax: 210-472-1872

Barry G. Benton
R. Christopher Clark
Richard M. Taylor, III

Phillip R. Hall

For full biographical listings, see the Martindale-Hubbell Law Directory

COX & SMITH INCORPORATED (AV)

112 East Pecan Street, Suite 1800, 78205-1521
Telephone: 210-554-5500
Fax: 210-226-8395
Email: info@coxsmith.com *URL:* http://www.coxsmith.com

William H. Lester, Jr.
Robert W. Nelson
R. Bradley Oxford
Harry W. Wolff, Jr.
Matthew S. Parkin
Joshua A. Sutin
Michael A. Tomberg (Not admitted in TX)

OF COUNSEL

Jack Guenther

For Complete List of Firm Personnel, See General Section

For full biographical listings, see the Martindale-Hubbell Law Directory

PAYNE, GATES, FARTHING & RADD P.C., *Norfolk—Continued*

Ronald M. Gates
Philip R. Farthing
Anthony F. Radd
Glen M. Robertson
Brian R. Dinning
Todd J. Preti
Marshall A. Winslow, Jr.

C. Arthur Robinson, II
Stephen E. Heretick
Raymond L. Hogge, Jr.

OF COUNSEL

Charles E. Payne

For full biographical listings, see the Martindale-Hubbell Law Directory

VANDEVENTER BLACK LLP (AV)

500 World Trade Center, 23510-1699
Telephone: 757-446-8600
Cable Address: "Hughsvan"
Telecopier: 757-446-8670
URL: http://www.vanblk.com
Kitty Hawk, North Carolina Office: 6 Juniper Trail.
Telephone: 252-261-5055.
Fax: 252-261-8444. E-Mail: nshearin@pinn.net.
London, England Office: Mitre House, 4th Floor, 12-14 Mitre Street.
Telephone: (0171) 623-2081.
Facsimile: (0171) 929-0043.

PARTNERS OF FIRM

Walter B. Martin, Jr.
Patrick W. Herman

For Complete List of Firm Personnel, See General Section

For full biographical listings, see the Martindale-Hubbell Law Directory

RICHMOND, (Independent City)

LECLAIR RYAN, A PROFESSIONAL CORPORATION (AV)

707 East Main Street, 11th Floor, 23219
Telephone: 804-783-2003
Facsmile: 804-783-2294
Email: email@leclairryan.com
Glen Allen, Virginia Office: 4201 Dominion Boulevard, Suite 200, 23060.
Telephone: 804-270-0070.
Facsimile: 804-270-4715.
Blacksburg, Virginia Office: 1872 Pratt Drive, Suite 1865, 24060.
Telephone: 540-961-2762.
Fax: 540-961-2781.
Norfolk, Virginia Office: 999 Waterside Drive, Suite 2025.
Telephone: 757-624-1454.
Facsimile: 757-624-3773.
Alexandria, Virginia Office: 225 Reinekers Lane, Suite 290, 22314.
Telephone: 703-684-8007.
Facsimile: 703-684-8075.
Charlottesville, Virginia Office: 108 S.E. Second Street, P.O. Box 2017, 22902.
Telephone: 804-971-7771.
Facsimile: 804-296-0905.

Marie D. Carter
Steven J. Keeler
Gary D. LeClair
Kurt Robert Magette
Andrew W. White

Nicholas J. Pace
Victoria J. Roberson

For full biographical listings, see the Martindale-Hubbell Law Directory

MCGUIRE, WOODS, BATTLE & BOOTHE LLP (AV)

One James Center, 901 East Cary Street, 23219-4030
Telephone: 804-775-1000
Fax: 804-775-1061
Email: info@mwbb.com *URL:* http://www.mwbb.com
Atlanta, Georgia Office: 285 Peachtree Center Avenue, N.E., Suite 2200, Marquis Tower Two, 30303-1234.
Telephone: 404-443-5500.
Fax: 404-443-5599.
Baltimore, Maryland Office: 7 Saint Paul Street, Suite 1000, 21202-1671.
Telephone: 410-659-4400.
Fax: 410-659-4599.
Charlotte, North Carolina Offices: 3700 Bank of America Plaza, 101 South Tryon Street, 28280.
Telephone: 704-373-8999.
Fax: 704-373-8990 and Bank of America Corporate Center, Suite 2900, 100 North Tryon Street, 28202.
Telephone: 704-373-8999.
Fax: 704-373-8935.
Charlottesville, Virginia Office: Court Square Building, 310 Fourth Street, N.E., Suite 300, P.O. Box 1288, 22902-1288.
Telephone: 804-977-2500.
Fax: 804-980-2222.
Chicago, Illinois Office: R.R. Donnelly Building, 77 West Wacker Drive, Suite 4500, 60601-1635.
Telephone: 312-849-3699.
Fax: 312-849-3690.

(See Next Column)

Jacksonville, Florida Office: 50 North Laura Street, 32202-3635.
Telephone: 904-798-3200.
Fax: 904-798-3207.
McLean, (Tysons Corner) Virginia Office: 1750 Tysons Boulevard, Suite 1800, 22102-3892.
Telephone: 703-712-5000.
Fax: 703-712-5050.
Norfolk, Virginia Office: World Trade Center, 101 West Main Street, Suite 9000, 23510-1655.
Telephone: 757-640-3700.
Fax: 757-640-3701. 23219-4030.
Washington, D.C. Office: Washington Square, 1050 Connecticut Avenue, N.W., Suite 1200, 20036-5317.
Telephone: 202-857-1700.
Fax: 202-857-1737.
Almaty, Republic of Kazakhstan Office: Park Palace, 41 Kazibek Bi Street, 2nd Floor, 480100.
Telephone: 7-3272-608-300.
Fax: 7-3272-608-305.
Brussels, Belgium Office: 250 Avenue Louise, Bte. 64, 1050.
Telephone: 32-2-629-42-11.
Fax: 32-2-629-42-22.
Moscow, Russia Office: Paveltskaya Square, 1 Valovaya Street, 7th Floor, 13054.
Telephone: 7-502-937-0774.
Fax: 7-502-937-0776.

MEMBERS OF FIRM

Dennis I. Belcher
James W. C. Canup
Jeffrey R. Capwell
W. Birch Douglass III
James P. McElligott Jr.
Robert G. McElroy
David N. Oakey
John Brad O'Grady
Martin B. Richards
Thomas P. Rohman
Thomas S. Word Jr.

RETIRED OF COUNSEL

Carle E. Davis
Thomas F. Dean

OF COUNSEL

Michele A. W. McKinnon

ASSOCIATES

Robert M. Cipolla
Paige G. Lester

For Complete List of Firm Personnel, See General Section

For full biographical listings, see the Martindale-Hubbell Law Directory

WILLIAMS, MULLEN, CLARK & DOBBINS, A PROFESSIONAL CORPORATION (AV)

Two James Center, 1021 East Cary Street, P.O. Box 1320, 23218-1320
Telephone: 804-643-1991
Fax: 804-783-6507
URL: http://www.wmcd.com
Newport News Office: Harbor Bank Center, Suite 210, One Old Oyster Point Road, 23602-7119.
Telephone: 757-249-5100.
Fax: 757-249-5109.
Virginia Beach Office: One Columbus Center, 23462-6763.
Telephone: 757-499-8800.
Fax: 757-473-0395.
Vienna Office: 1593 Spring Hill Road, Suite 510, 22182.
Telephone: 703-760-5200.
Fax: 703-748-0244.
Washington, D.C. Office: The Farragut Building, 900 17th Street, N.W., Suite 700, 20006.
Telephone: 202-293-0213.
Fax: 804-783-6507. Fax Within D.C.: 202-293-5939.
London, England Office: Blake Lodge, Bridge Lane, SW11 3AD.
Telephone: (011-44-71) 223-2756.
Fax: (011-44-71) 350-0156.
Riyadh, Saudi Arabia Affiliate Office: Saudi-American Legal Consultants Commercial Building #2, Diplomatic Quarter, P.O. Box 57270, 11574.
Telephone: (011-966-1) 488-1563.
Fax: (011-966-1) 488-0542.

David D. Addison
JoAnn Blair-Davis (Resident, Virginia Beach Office)
Theodore L. Chandler, Jr.
C. Richard Davis
Joseph A. Di Julio (Resident, Virginia Beach Office)
Thomas R. Frantz (Resident, Virginia Beach Office)
Randolph H. Lickey
Robert L. Musick, Jr.
Craig L. Rascoe
Robert M. Reed (Resident, Virginia Beach Office)

J. Conrad Garcia
M. Nicole Hanna (Resident, Virginia Beach Office)
William D. Perun, Jr.
Brian C. Purcell (Resident, Virginia Beach Office)

For Complete List of Firm Personnel, See General Section

For full biographical listings, see the Martindale-Hubbell Law Directory

VIENNA, Fairfax Co.

GARY & GOODMAN LIMITED (AV)

8500 Leesburg Pike, Suite 7000 (Tysons Corner), 22182
Telephone: 703-848-2828
Facsimile: 703-893-9276
Email: garygoodman@ggllaw.com

Stuart H. Gary

OF COUNSEL

George B. Delta

For full biographical listings, see the Martindale-Hubbell Law Directory

REES, BROOME & DIAZ, P.C. (AV)

Ninth Floor, 8133 Leesburg Pike, 22182
Telephone: 703-790-1911
Telecopier: 703-848-2530
Email: attorney@RBDlaw.com *URL:* http://www.rbdlaw.com

Jonathan J. Broome, Jr. | John F. Boland

For full biographical listings, see the Martindale-Hubbell Law Directory

WASHINGTON

*SEATTLE,** King Co.

BOELTER & ASSOCIATES (AV)

121 Lakeside Avenue, Suite 100, 98122
Telephone: 206-587-0000
Fax: 206-325-8973
URL: http://www.lawyers.com/boelterlaw

Arthur H. Boelter

ASSOCIATE

William R. Connors

For full biographical listings, see the Martindale-Hubbell Law Directory

CHICOINE & HALLETT, P.S. (AV)

Waterfront Place One, Suite 803, 1011 Western Avenue, 98104
Telephone: 206-223-0800
206-467-8170
URL: http://www.c-hlaw.com
Email: chicoine-hallett.com *URL:* http://www.lawyers.com/chattorneys

Robert J. Chicoine | Darrell D. Hallett

Larry N. Johnson | John M. Colvin

Scott A. Schumacher

For full biographical listings, see the Martindale-Hubbell Law Directory

LANE POWELL SPEARS LUBERSKY LLP (AV)

Limited Liability Partnership composed of Individuals and Professional Service Corporations
1420 Fifth Avenue, Suite 4100, 98101-2338
Telephone: 206-223-7000
Facsimile: 206-223-7107
Email: information@lanepowell.com *URL:* http://www.lanepowell.com
Other Offices at: Portland, Oregon; Anchorage, Alaska; Olympia and Mount Vernon, Washington; London, England.

MEMBERS OF FIRM

Thomas F. Grohman | Gary M. Kirk
Jim D. Johnston | Charles W. Riley, Jr.
Kenyon P. Kellogg | Gary P. Tober

COUNSEL

Ada Ko

ASSOCIATES

Daniel J. Caplinger | Masahiro "Max" Yoshimura

Representative Clients: AT&T; Cutter & Buck; Consolidated Freightways; Fred Hutchinson Cancer Research Center; The Home Depot; Mitsui & Co., Ltd.; Nordstrom, Inc.; Simpson Investment Co. and Affiliates; Texaco Inc.; Underwriters at Lloyds, London.

For Complete List of Firm Personnel, See General Section

For full biographical listings, see the Martindale-Hubbell Law Directory

PERKINS COIE LLP (AV)

Strategic Alliance with Russell & DuMoulin
1201 Third Avenue, Suite 4800, 98101-3099
Telephone: 206-583-8888
Facsimile: 206-583-8500
Email: perkins@perkinscoic.com *URL:* http://www.perkinscoie.com
Anchorage, Alaska: 1029 West Third Avenue, Suite 300, 99501-1970.
Telephone: 907-279-8561.
Facsimile: 907-276-3108.
Los Angeles, California: 1620 26th Street, 6th Floor, 90404.
Telephone: 310-788-9900.
Facsimile: 310-788-3399.
Menlo Park, California: 135 Commonwealth Drive, Suite 250, 94025-1105.
Telephone: 650-752-6000.
Facsimile: 650-752-6050.
San Francisco, California: 180 Townsend Street, 94107-1909.
Telephone: 415-781-3200.
Facsimile: 415-781-2525.
Denver, Colorado: World Trade Center, 1675 Broadway, Suite 2800, 80202-062.
Telephone: 303-571-6100.
Facsimile: 303-571-6111.
Washington, D.C.: 607 Fourteenth Street, N.W., 20005-2011.
Telephone: 202-628-6600.
Telex: 44-0277 PCSO.
Facsimile: 202-434-1690.
Boise, Idaho: 714 West State Street, 83702.
Telephone: 208-343-3434.
Facsimile: 208-343-3232.
Portland, Oregon: Suite 1500, 1211 Southwest Fifth Avenue.
Telephone: 503-727-2000.
Facsimile: 503-727-2222.
Bellevue, Washington: Suite 1800, One Bellevue Center, 411 - 108th Avenue N.E., 98004-5584.
Telephone: 425-453-6980.
Facsimile: 425-453-7350.
Spokane, Washington: North 221 Wall Street, Suite 600, 99201-0826.
Telephone: 509-624-2212.
Facsimile: 509-458-3399.
Hong Kong: 17/F, Standard Charter Bank Building, 4 Des Voeux Road.
Telephone: 852-2878-1177.
Facsimile: 852-2524-9988.
Taipei, Taiwan, R.O.C.: 8/F Cathay United Bank Tower, 85 Jen Ai Rd., Section 5.
Telephone: 886-2-2778-1177.
Facsimile: 886-2-2777-9898.
Canada: Strategic Alliance with Russell & DuMoulin, 1700-1075 West Georgia Street. Vancouver, British Columbia, V6E 3G2.
Telephone: 604-631-3131.

PARTNERS

George M. Beal II | James M. Hilton (P.S.)
Kurt Becker (Resident, Bellevue, Washington Office) | James R. Lisbakken
Richard L. Mull
Dori E. Lee Brewer | Alan D. Smith
Graham H. Fernald | Steven R. Yentzer
Robert Edward Giles (Managing Partner) | D. Michael Young

OF COUNSEL

Lorri A. Dunsmore | John T. Piper (P.S.)

Counsel for: The Boeing Company; Puget Sound Energy; US West; Amazon.-com; Louisiana-Pacific; Lloyds of London (Aviation); Weyerhauser.

For Complete List of Firm Personnel, See General Section

For full biographical listings, see the Martindale-Hubbell Law Directory

WEST VIRGINIA

*CHARLESTON,** Kanawha Co.

ALLEN GUTHRIE & MCHUGH (AV)

1300 Bank One Center, P.O. Box 3394, 25333
Telephone: 304-345-7250
Telecopier: 304-345-9941
Email: kagwv@kagww.com

Robert B. Allen | S. Benjamin Bryant

Teresa K. Thompson

For full biographical listings, see the Martindale-Hubbell Law Directory

Charleston—Continued

JACKSON & KELLY (AV)

1600 Laidley Tower, P.O. Box 553, 25322
Telephone: 304-340-1000
Fax: 304-340-1130
Email: info@jacksonkelly.com *URL:* http://www.jacksonkelly.com
Martinsburg, West Virginia Office: 300 Foxcroft Avenue, P.O. Box 1068.
Telephone: 304-263-8800.
Fax: 304-263-7110.
Morgantown, West Virginia Office: 6000 Hampton Center, P.O. Box 619.
Telephone: 304-599-3000.
Fax: 304-285-2040.
New Martinsville, West Virginia Office: 256 Russell Avenue, P.O. Box 68.
Telephone: 304-455-1751.
Fax: 304-455-6314.
Parkersburg, West Virginia Office: 412 Market Street, Suite 202, P.O. Box 1144.
Telephone: 304-424-3490.
Fax: 304-424-3499.
Fairmont, West Virginia Office: 1000 Technology Drive, Suite 1310.
Telephone: 304-368-2000.
Fax: 304-368-2020.
Lexington, Kentucky Office: 175 East Main Street, Suite 500, P.O. Box 2150.
Telephone: 606-255-9500.
Fax: 606-281-6478.
Washington, D. C. Office: 2401 Pennsylvania Avenue, N.W., Suite 400.
Telephone: 202-973-0200.
Fax: 202-973-0232.
Denver, Colorado Office: Suite 2710, 1660 Lincoln Street.
Telephone: 303-390-0003.
Fax: 303-390-0040.
Wheeling, West Virginia Office: 1144 Market Street.
Telephone: 304-233-4000.
Fax: 304-233-4077.

MEMBERS OF FIRM

Louis S. Southworth, II
Thomas G. Freeman, II
Michael D. Foster
Thomas N. McJunkin
Jeffrey J. Yost (Resident, Lexington, Kentucky Office)
Eric H. London (Morgantown, West Virginia Office)
Anthony J. Ferrise
John A. Mairs

ASSOCIATES

Patience Ann Alexander
Robert G. Tweel

Representative Clients: West Virginia Coal Assn.; One Valley Bancorp of West Virginia, Inc.; Go-Mart, Inc.; Associated Radiologists, Inc.; CONSOL Inc.

For Complete List of Firm Personnel, See General Section

For full biographical listings, see the Martindale-Hubbell Law Directory

*CLARKSBURG,** Harrison Co.

JOHNSON, SIMMERMAN & BROUGHTON, L.C. (AV)

Ogden Building, 203 West Main Street, 26301
Telephone: 304-624-6555; 304-623-4900
Telecopier: 304-623-4933
Mailing Address: P.O. Box 150, Clarksburg, West Virginia, 26302-0150

Charles G. Johnson
Frank E. Simmerman, Jr.
Marcia Allen Broughton
Bridget D. Furbee
Robin Queen Triplett

For full biographical listings, see the Martindale-Hubbell Law Directory

MCNEER, HIGHLAND, MCMUNN AND VARNER, L.C. (AV)

One Valley Bank Building, P.O. Drawer 2040, 26302-2040
Telephone: 304-626-1100
Facsimile: 304-623-3035
Martinsburg Office: 2520 Aikens Center, P.O. Box 2509.
Telephone: 304-264-4621.
Fax: 304-264-8623.
Parkersburg Office: 404 Market Street, Suite 204, P.O. Box 1507.
Telephone: 304-422-7193.
Facsimile: 304-422-7196.

C. David McMunn
J. Cecil Jarvis
James A. Varner
Robert W. Trumble (Resident, Martinsburg Office)
Catherine D. Munster
James N. Riley
Steven R. Bratke (Resident, Parkersburg Office)
Michael J. Novotny (Resident, Martinsburg Office)
Dennis M. Shreve
Geraldine S. Roberts
William F. Rohrbaugh (Resident, Martinsburg Office)
Gregory H. Schillace
Judy L. Shanholtz
Tiffany R. Durst
Gene W. Bailey, II

(See Next Column)

OF COUNSEL

James E. McNeer
Cecil B. Highland, Jr.
William L. Fury

Representative Clients: One Valley Bank of Clarksburg, National Assn.; Bruceton Bank; Harrison County Bank; Nationwide Mutual Insurance Cos.; Clarksburg Publishing Co.; C.I.T. Financial Services; State Automobile Mutual Insurance Co.; United Hospital Center, Inc.; West Virginia Coals, Inc.; Swanson Plating Co.

For full biographical listings, see the Martindale-Hubbell Law Directory

*WHEELING,** Ohio Co.

SCHRADER BYRD & COMPANION, PLLC (AV)

(A Professional Limited Liability Company)
The Maxwell Centre, 32-20th Street, Suite 500, P.O. Box 6336, 26003
Telephone: 304-233-3390
Fax: 304-233-2769
URL: http://www.schraderlaw.com
Martins Ferry, Ohio Office: 205 North Fifth Street, P.O. Box 309, 43935.
Telephone: 740-633-9976.
Fax: 740-633-0400.
Weirton, West Virginia Office: 3205 Pennsylvania Avenue, Suite 103, Penn Place, P.O. Box 2785, 26062.
Telephone: 304-723-2674.
Fax: 304-723-2876.

MEMBERS

Ray A. Byrd
James F. Companion
Frank X. Duff
Teresa Rieman-Camilletti
Yolonda G. Lambert
Daniel P. Fry (Resident Partner, Martins Ferry, Ohio Office)
James P. Mazzone (Resident Member, Weirton, West Virginia Office)
Sandra K. Law
D. Kevin Coleman

SPECIAL COUNSEL

Thomas B. Miller

ASSOCIATES

Denise D. Klug
Michael A. Adams
John Porco
Aimee Morgan Stern
Kimberly R. Wilson
Christopher J. Adams

OF COUNSEL

James A. Byrum, Jr.

General Counsel: Reynolds Memorial Hospital; WesBanco Bank-Elm Grove.
Representative Clients: American Cyanamid Company; Bank One; Matlack Systems, Inc.; Moutaineer Gas Co.; Ohio County Board of Education; PHICO Insurance Co.; Wheeling Hospital; Wheeling-Pittsburg Steel Corp.

For full biographical listings, see the Martindale-Hubbell Law Directory

WISCONSIN

*MADISON,** Dane Co.

NEIDER & BOUCHER, S.C. (AV)

440 Science Drive, P.O. Box 5510, 53705-0510
Telephone: 608-661-4500
Facsimile: 608-661-4510
URL: http://www.neiderboucher.com
URL: http://www.lawyers.com/neider&boucher-sc

Ronald C. Berman
Joseph W. Boucher
Charles E. Neider
Steven C. Underwood

Susan M. De Groot
Erik W. Ibele
Rana Kang
Cynthia L. Richson
Matthew L. Schemmel
Kent L. Schlienger
Dean T. Stange

OF COUNSEL

Ralph M. Cagle
Ronald R. Smith

For full biographical listings, see the Martindale-Hubbell Law Directory

*MILWAUKEE,** Milwaukee Co.

COOK & FRANKE S.C. (AV)

660 East Mason Street, 53202
Telephone: 414-271-5900
Facsimile: 414-271-2002

Thomas J. Drought
Margaret T. Lund
Brian R. Wanasek
Sandra J. Janssen
Ann M. Rieger
Jason R. Handal
Denasha A. Scott

(See Next Column)

COOK & FRANKE S.C.—*Continued*

OF COUNSEL

Joseph E. Tierney, Jr.

Representative Clients: Wisconsin Electric Power Co.; Payne & Dolan, Inc.; Bradley Center Corp.; Mr. and Mrs. Lloyd H. Pettit; Seidel Tanning Corp.; Bradley Family Foundation.

For Complete List of Firm Personnel, See General Section

For full biographical listings, see the Martindale-Hubbell Law Directory

DAVIS & KUELTHAU, S.C. (AV)

111 East Kilbourn Avenue, Suite 1400, 53202-6613
Telephone: 414-276-0200
Facsimile: 414-276-9369
Cable Address: "Shiplaw"
Email: info@daviskuelthau.com *URL:* http://www.daviskuelthau.com
Madison, Wisconsin Office: Ten East Doty Street, Suite 600, P.O. Box 1068, 53703.
Telephone: 608-280-8235.
Fax: 608-280-8231.
Sheboygan, Wisconsin Office: 605 North Eighth, Suite 610, P.O. Box 1287.
Telephone: 920-451-1461.
Fax: 920-451-1465.
Green Bay, Wisconsin Office: 414 East Walnut Street, Suite 240.
Telephone: 920-435-9378.
Fax: 920-435-9391.

Gregory J. Sell

For full biographical listings, see the Martindale-Hubbell Law Directory

DRINKA, LEVINE & MASSON, S.C. (AV)

2000 Milwaukee Center, 111 East Kilbourn Avenue, 53202-6618
Telephone: 414-291-6080
Fax: 414-291-6090
URL: http://www.lawyers.com/drinkalevine&masson

Judith A. Drinka
Micaela H. Levine
Grace M. Masson

For full biographical listings, see the Martindale-Hubbell Law Directory

FOLEY & LARDNER (AV)

Firstar Center, 777 East Wisconsin Avenue, 53202-5367
Telephone: 414-271-2400
Telex: 26-819 (Foley Lard Mil)
Facsimile: 414-297-4900
Email: foleylardner@worldnet.att.net *URL:* http://www.foleylardner.com
Los Angeles, California Office: 2029 Century Park East, 35th Floor.
Telephone: 310-277-2223.
Fax: 310-557-8475.
Sacramento, California Office: 300 Capitol Mall, Suite 1125.
Telephone: 916-443-8005.
Fax: 916-443-2240.
San Diego, California Office: 402 West Broadway, 23rd Floor.
Telephone: 619-234-6655.
Fax: 619-234-3510.
San Francisco, California Office: One Maritime Plaza, Sixth Floor.
Telephone: 415-434-4484.
Fax: 415-434-4507.
Denver, Colorado Office: 1999 Broadway, Suite 2560.
Telephone: 303-297-0260.
Fax: 303-297-0266.
Washington, D.C. Office: Washington Harbour, Suite 500, 3000 K Street, N.W.
Telephone: 202-672-5300.
Telex: 904136 (Foley Lard Wash).
Facsimile: 202-672-5399.
Jacksonville, Florida Office: The Greenleaf Building, 200 Laura Street. P.O. Box 240.
Telephone: 904-359-2000.
Facsimile: 904-359-8700.
Orlando, Florida Office: Suite 1800, 111 North Orange Avenue, P.O. Box 2193.
Telephone: 407-423-7656.
Facsimile: 407-648-1743.
Tallahassee, Florida Office: 300 East Park Avenue, P.O. Box 1454.
Telephone: 850-222-6100.
Facsimile: 850-561-6475.
Tampa, Florida Offices: Suite 2700, One Hundred N. Tampa Street, P.O. Box 3391.
Telephones: 813-229-2300; Pinellas County: 813-442-3296.
Facsimile: 813-221-4210.
West Palm Beach, Florida Office: Suite 200, Phillips Point East Tower, 777 South Flagler Drive.
Telephone: 561-655-5050.
Facsimile: 561-655-6925.
Chicago, Illinois Office: Suite 3300, One IBM Plaza, 330 N. Wabash Avenue.
Telephone: 312-755-1900.
Facsimile: 312-755-1925.

(See Next Column)

Annapolis, Maryland Office: Suite 102, 175 Admiral Cochrane Drive.
Telephone: 410-266-8077.
Telex: 899149 (Oldtownpat).
Facsimile: 410-266-8664.
Madison, Wisconsin Office: Verex Plaza, 150 East Gilman Street, P.O. Box 1497.
Telephone: 608-257-5035.
Facsimile: 608-258-4258.
Brussels, Belgium Office: Avenue Louise, 283.
Telephone: 32-2-646-2777.
Facsimile: 32-2-646-7574.

PARTNERS

Carl D. Fortner
Timothy C. Frautschi
Richard S. Gallagher
Marsha E. Huff
Jeffrey J. Jones
Jere D. McGaffey
Jamshed J. Patel
Ronald L. Walter
Lynette M. Zigman

For Complete List of Firm Personnel, See General Section

For full biographical listings, see the Martindale-Hubbell Law Directory

FRAZER SCHAPIRO & RICH, S.C. (AV)

1110 N. Old World Third Street, Suite 218, 53203
Telephone: 414-347-9500
Fax: 414-347-9455
URL: http://www.fsrlaw.net

Douglas H. Frazer
Karen M. Schapiro
Elizabeth G. Rich

For full biographical listings, see the Martindale-Hubbell Law Directory

MEISSNER TIERNEY FISHER & NICHOLS S.C. (AV)

The Milwaukee Center, 111 East Kilbourn Avenue, 19th Floor, 53202-6622
Telephone: 414-273-1300
Facsimile: 414-273-5840
URL: http://www.mtfn.com

Joseph E. Tierney III
Thomas J. Nichols
Randal J. Brotherhood

Michael A. Kallas
Jeffrey A. Ellis
Adam J. Tutaj

OF COUNSEL

Paul F. Meissner

For full biographical listings, see the Martindale-Hubbell Law Directory

MICHAEL BEST & FRIEDRICH LLP (AV)

100 East Wisconsin Avenue, 53202-4108
Telephone: 414-271-6560
Telecopier: 414-277-0656
Cable Address: "Mibef"
Email: info@mbf-law.com *URL:* http://www.mbf-law.com
Madison, Wisconsin Office: One South Pinckney Street, Firstar Plaza, P.O. Box 1806, 53701-1806.
Telephone: 608-257-3501.
Telecopier: 283-2275.
Manitowoc, Wisconsin Office: 1000 Maritime Drive, 54220.
Telephone: 920-686-2800.
Fax: 920-686-2810.
Chicago, Illinois Office: Michael Best & Friedrich LLC, 77 West Wacker Drive, Suite 4300, 60601-1635.
Telephone: 312-845-5800.
Telecopier: 312-845-5828.

PARTNERS

Frank J. Pelisek
Robert A. Schnur
Jerome H. Kringel
Robert J. Johannes
Timothy G. Schally
Bret A. Roge
Bartlett C. Petersen
Joseph A. Pickart
Paul R. Riegel

ASSOCIATES

Linda Sauser Moroney
E. Troy Blanchard

For Complete List of Firm Personnel, See General Section

For full biographical listings, see the Martindale-Hubbell Law Directory

QUARLES & BRADY LLP (AV)

411 East Wisconsin Avenue, 53202-4497
Telephone: 414-277-5000
Fax: 414-271-3552
URL: http://www.quarles.com
Madison, Wisconsin Office: Firstar Plaza, One South Pinckney Street, P.O. Box 2113, 53701-2113.
Telephone: 608-251-5000.
Fax: 608-251-9166.
West Palm Beach, Florida Office: 222 Lakeview Avenue, 4th Floor, 33401.
Telephone: 561-653-5000.
Fax: 561-653-5333.

(See Next Column)

QUARLES & BRADY LLP, *Milwaukee—Continued*

Naples, Florida Office: Barnett Center, 4501 Tamiami Trail North, Suite 300, 34103-3060.
Telephone: 941-262-5959.
Fax: 941-434-4999.
Phoenix, Arizona Office: One Camelback Building, One East Camelback Road, Suite 400, 85012-1649.
Telephone: 602-230-5500.
Fax: 602-230-5598.
Chicago, Illinois Office: Quarles & Brady LLC, Citicorp Center, 500 West Madison Street, Suite 3700.
Telephone: 312-715-5000.
Fax: 312-715-5155.

MEMBERS OF FIRM
(ALPHABETICALLY BY YEAR OF ADMISSION TO BAR)

Donald S. Taitelman
Peter J. Lettenberger
Gary H. Kline (Resident, Chicago, Illinois Office)
Thomas A. Polachek (Resident, Chicago, Illinois Office)
Thomas E. Chomicz (Resident, Chicago, Illinois Office)
Steven R. Duback
Thomas J. Phillips
Michael J. Conlan
James J. Gatziolis (Resident, Chicago, Illinois Office)
Janice E. Rodgers (Resident, Chicago, Illinois Office)
Thomas A. Simonis
David D. Wilmoth
Elizabeth G. Nowakowski
Sarah M. Linsley (Resident, Chicago, Illinois Office)
Patrick J. Bitterman (Resident, Chicago, Illinois Office)

OF COUNSEL
Dale L. Sorden

ASSOCIATES
Michael G. Galloway (Resident, Phoenix, Arizona Office)
Chris K. Gawart
Patricia A. Hintz
Stephen R. White
Susan Kubar (Resident, Naples, Florida Office)
David C. Swanson

For Complete List of Firm Personnel, See General Section

For full biographical listings, see the Martindale-Hubbell Law Directory

WALSH & KEATING, S.C. (AV)

1505 Wawatosa Avenue, 53213
Telephone: 414-257-9929
Fax: 414-257-9959
URL: http://www.lawyers.com/walshandkeating

Gerald S. Walsh
David C. Keating

ASSOCIATE
Peter J. Walsh

OF COUNSEL
Lloyd W. Herrold

Representative Clients: Immtech International, Inc.; Howard Precision Metals Inc.; James L. Callan Inc.; Milwaukee Chaplet & Mfg. Co., Inc.; Milwaukee Envelope, Inc.; Stearns Foundation, Inc.; Wausau Tile, Inc.; August Urbanek Investments, Inc.; Germantown Market Place, Inc.; Precision Metrology, Inc.

For full biographical listings, see the Martindale-Hubbell Law Directory

PUERTO RICO

SAN JUAN, San Juan Dist.

FIDDLER GONZÁLEZ & RODRÍGUEZ, LLP

254 Muñoz Rivera Avenue (Hato Rey), P.O. Box 363507, 00936-3507
Telephone: 787-753-3113
Telecopier: 787-759-3123
Email: fiddler@fgrlaw.com *URL:* http://www.fgrlaw.com

MEMBERS OF FIRM
Roberto B. Suárez
César Gómez Negrón

Representative Clients: The Chase Manhattan Bank, N.A.; Pfizer, Inc.; Merck & Co., Inc.; Bacardi Corp.; The Eastman Kodak Co.; Nestle S.A.; UPS; Banco Bilbao Vizcaya; Microsoft Corp.; Amgen, Inc.

For Complete List of Firm Personnel, See General Section

For full biographical listings, see the Martindale-Hubbell Law Directory

GOLDMAN ANTONETTI & CÓRDOVA

American International Plaza Fourteenth & Fifteenth Floors, 250 Muñoz Rivera Avenue (Hato Rey), P.O. Box 70364, 00936-0364
Telephone: 787-759-8000
Telecopiers: 787-767-9333 (Main)
787-767-9177 (Litigation Department)
787-767-8660 (Labor & Corporate Law Departments)
787-767-9325 (Tax & Environmental Law Departments)
URL: http://www.gaclaw.com

(See Next Column)

MEMBERS OF FIRM
Roberto Montalvo Carbia
Antonio Bauza-Santos

OF COUNSEL
Max Goldman

ASSOCIATES
Aida Barrios-Castellanos
Sara Vazquez
Rebeca Vargas-Ruiz

Representative Clients: Philip Morris; Borden, Inc.; Xerox Corp.; Crown Cork & Seal Co.; Forest Laboratories; Ferrero, Inc.

For Complete List of Firm Personnel, See General Section

For full biographical listings, see the Martindale-Hubbell Law Directory

MARTÍNEZ ODELL & CALABRIA

Banco Popular Center, 209 Muñoz Rivera Avenue, Suite 1600 (Hato Rey), P.O. Box 190998, 00919-0998
Telephone: 787-753-8914
Facsimile: 787-753-8402; 787-759-9075; 787-764-5664
Email: postmaster@mocpr.com

MEMBERS OF FIRM
Fred H. Martínez
Jose R. Cestero
Angel S. Ruiz-Rodriguez
Brunilda Rodríguez-Vélez
Ignacio M. Arbona-Arbona

OF COUNSEL
Jose L. Calabria

Representative Clients: Banco Popular de Puerto Rico; Daewoo Motor Corporation; Eckerd Corporation; Empresas Fonalledas; Hilton International; L'Aire Liquide, S.A.; Loctile Corporation; Lucent Technologies; Lutron Electronics Co., Inc.; Waste Management, Inc.

For Complete List of Firm Personnel, See General Section

For full biographical listings, see the Martindale-Hubbell Law Directory

BARRY A. WOODS

Capital Center Building, 239 Arterial Hostos, Suite 706, 00918-1476
Telephone: 787-759-8181
Fax: 787-751-3115
Email: baw@canibe.net/bawbat@cs.com

For full biographical listings, see the Martindale-Hubbell Law Directory

VIRGIN ISLANDS

*CHARLOTTE AMALIE, ST. THOMAS,** St. Thomas

GRUNERT STOUT & BRUCH

24-25 Kongensgade, P.O. Box 1030, 00804
Telephone: 340-774-1320
Fax: 340-774-7839
Email: gsbusvi@viaccess.net
Affiliated with: Solomon Pearl Blum & Quinn LLP, New York, New York and Denver, Colorado.

MEMBERS OF FIRM
John E. Stout
Susan Bruch Moorehead

ASSOCIATE
Gabriel J. Villegas

OF COUNSEL
William L. Blum

For full biographical listings, see the Martindale-Hubbell Law Directory

CANADA
ALBERTA

*CALGARY,** Calgary Jud. Dist.

PARLEE MCLAWS (AV)

3400 Petro-Canada Centre, 150 - 6th Avenue, SW, T2P 3Y7
Telephone: 403-294-7000
Telecopier: 403-265-8263
Email: lawyers@parlee.com *URL:* http://www.parlee.com
Edmonton, Alberta Office: 15th Floor Manulife Place, 10180 101st Street.
Telephone: 403-423-8500.
Telecopier: 403-423-2870.

MEMBER OF FIRM
Lindsay J. Holmes

(See Next Column)

PARLEE MCLAWS—*Continued*

ASSOCIATE

Seema S. Johal

For Complete List of Firm Personnel, See General Section

For full biographical listings, see the Martindale-Hubbell Law Directory

*EDMONTON,** Edmonton Jud. Dist.

PARLEE MCLAWS (AV)

15th Floor Manulife Place, 10180 101st Street, T5J 4K1
Telephone: 403-423-8500
Telecopier: 403-423-2870
Email: lawyers@parlee.com *URL:* http://www.parlee.com
Calgary, Alberta Office: 3400 Petro-Canada Centre, 150 - 6th Avenue, SW.
Telephone: 403-294-7000.
Telecopier: 403-265-8263.

MEMBER OF FIRM

John W. McClure

ASSOCIATE

George E. Flemming

For Complete List of Firm Personnel, See General Section

For full biographical listings, see the Martindale-Hubbell Law Directory

CANADA BRITISH COLUMBIA

*VANCOUVER,** Vancouver Co.

THORSTEINSSONS (AV)

27th Floor, Three Bentall Centre, 595 Burrard Street, P.O. Box 49123, V7X 1J2
Telephone: 604-689-1261
Toll Free 1-877-616-2200
Fax: 604-688-4711
Email: thor@thor.ca *URL:* http://www.thor.ca
Toronto, Ontario Office: P.O. Box 611, BCE Place, 36th Floor, 161 Bay Street, Toronto, Ontario, M5J 2S1.
Telephone: 416-864-0829.
Fax: 416-864-1106. Toll Free: 1-888-666-9998. Email: thor@thor.ca.
Website: http://www.thor.ca

Warren J. A. Mitchell, Q.C.
Leslie M. Little, Q.C.
Michael J. O'Keefe, Q.C.
Craig C. Sturrock
Charles E. Beil
Lorne A. Green
Steven M. Cook
John N. Gregory
David G. Thompson
John R. Owen
Douglas J. Powrie
Douglas H. Mathew
Ian J. Gamble
William R. Holmes
David R. Davies
Terry G. Barnett
David J. Christian
Paul J. Gibney
Thomas A. Bauer

ASSOCIATES

Thomas M. Boddez
Kerri L. Mooney
David R. Baxter
Paul S. Carenza
Karl A. Chowscano
Thomas J. Clearwater
Andrew B. Stewart
Gianpaolo Panusa
Samantha W. Mason
Michael W. Colborne
Mark W. Chu

For full biographical listings, see the Martindale-Hubbell Law Directory

CANADA MANITOBA

*WINNIPEG,** Eastern Jud. Dist.

AIKINS, MACAULAY & THORVALDSON (AV)

Thirtieth Floor, Commodity Exchange Tower, 360 Main Street, R3C 4G1
Telephone: 204-957-0050
Fax: 204-957-0840
Email: amt@aikins.com *URL:* http://www.aikins.com

MEMBERS OF FIRM

Bryan D. Klein
Joel A. Weinstein, Q.C.
Robert Gordon Sly
Frank Lavitt
Barbara M. Shields
Carmele N. Peter
Steven J. Kohn
Robert C. Lee
Rachel E. R. Margolis

(See Next Column)

Counsel for: Air Canada; Bank of Montreal; Boeing of Canada; Canada Safeway Limited; Canadian Medical Protective Assn.; The Great West Life Assurance Co.; John Labatt Limited; Russel Metals Inc.; Winnipeg Free Press.

For Complete List of Firm Personnel, See General Section

For full biographical listings, see the Martindale-Hubbell Law Directory

CANADA NEW BRUNSWICK

*FREDERICTON,** York Co.

COX HANSON O'REILLY MATHESON (AV)

(Formerly Hanson Hashey)
Suite 400, Phoenix Square, P.O. Box 310, E3B 4Y9
Telephone: 506-453-7771
Fax: 506-453-9600
Email: fredericton@coxhanson.ca *URL:* http://www.coxhanson.ca
Halifax, Nova Scotia Office: Suite 1100, Purdy's Wharf Tower 1, P.O. Box 2380 Station Central RPO, B3J 3E5.
Telephone: 902-421-6262.
Fax: 902-421-3130. E-Mail: halifax@coxhanson.ca
Saint John, New Brunswick Office: 1212-One Brunswick Square, 1 Germain St. E2L 4V1.
Telephone: 506-652-7771.
Fax: 506-632-9600.
St. John's, Newfoundland Office: Scotia Centre, 401-235 Water Street, A1C 1B6.
Telephone: 709-726-3321.
Fax: 709-726-2992. E-Mail: stjohns@coxhanson.ca
Charlottetown, Prince Edward Island Office: Queen Square, Suite 202, 119 Queen Street, P.O. Box 875, Station Central, C1A 7L9.
Telephone: 902-894-7051.
Fax: 902-368-3762. E-Mail: charlottetown@coxhanson.ca

MEMBERS OF FIRM

H. A. Hanson, Q.C. (1909-1985)
David T. Hashey, Q.C.
David M. Norman, Q.C.
J. Ian M. Whitcomb, Q.C.
John M. Hanson, Q.C.
Walter D. Vail, Q.C.
Michael E. Bowlin
John D. Larlee, Q.C.
Bruce D. Hatfield, Q.C.
Julian A. G. Dickson, Q.C.
Anne D. Wooder
Terrence J. Morrison
Lucie Richard
Catherine M. Bowlen
J. Marc Richard

ASSOCIATES

Amanda J. Frenette
Monika M. L. Zauhar
Jade A. Spalding
William E. Gould
Christopher R. DeLong
Deborah M. Power
Corinne A. Godbout
Marc-Antoine Chiasson

For full biographical listings, see the Martindale-Hubbell Law Directory

MCINNES COOPER (AV)

Suite 600, 570 Queen Street, P.O. Box 610, E3B 5A6
Telephone: 506-458-8572
Fax: 506-458-9903
Email: mcrfton@mcrlaw.com *URL:* http://www.mcrlaw.com
Halifax, Nova Scotia Office: Summit Place, 1601 Lower Water Street, P.O. Box 730, B3J 2V1.
Telephone: 902-425-6500.
Fax: 902-425-6350. Email: mcrhfx@mcrlaw.com.
St. John's, Newfoundland Office: Baine Johnston Centre, 5th Floor, 10 Fort William Place, P.O. Box 5939, A1C 5X4.
Telephone: 709-722-8735.
Telecopier: 709-722-1763. Email: mcrsj@mcrlaw.com.
Moncton, New Brunswick Office: Place Moncton Place, 655 Main Street, P.O. Box 1368, E1C 8T6.
Telephone: 506-857-8970.
Fax: 506-857-4095. Email: mcrmctn@mcrlaw.com.
Charlottetown, Prince Edward Island Office: BDC Place, Suite 620, 119 Kent Street, C1A 1N3.
Telephone: 902-368-8473.
Fax: 902-368-8346. Email: mcrpei@mcrlaw.com.

PARTNERS

Leonard T. Hoyt
Carol J. Downs

For Complete List of Firm Personnel, See General Section

For full biographical listings, see the Martindale-Hubbell Law Directory

*SAINT JOHN,** Saint John Co.

COX HANSON O'REILLY MATHESON (AV)

(Formerly Hanson Hashey)
1212-One Brunswick Square 1 Germain Street, E2L 4V1
Telephone: 506-652-7771
Telecopier: 506-632-9600
Email: stjohns@coxhanson.ca *URL:* http://www.coxhanson.ca
Fredericton, New Brunswick Office: Suite 400, Phoenix Square, P.O. Box 310, E3B 4Y9.
Telephone: 506-453-7771.
Fax: 506-453-9600.
Halifax, Nova Scotia Office: Suite 1100, Purdy's Wharf Tower 1, P.O. Box 2380 Station Central RPO, B3J 3E5.
Telephone: 902-421-6262.
Fax: 902-421-3130. E-Mail: halifax@coxhanson.ca
St. John's, Newfoundland Office: Scotia Centre, 401-235 Water Street, A1C 1B6.
Telephone: 709-726-3321.
Fax: 709-726-2992. E-Mail: stjohns@coxhanson.ca
Charlottetown, Prince Edward Island Office: Queen Square, Suite 202, 119 Queen Street, P.O. Box 875, Station Central, C1A 7L9.
Telephone: 902-894-7051.
Fax: 902-368-3762. E-Mail: charlottetown@coxhanson.ca

J. Ian M. Whitcomb, Q.C. (Resident)

For full biographical listings, see the Martindale-Hubbell Law Directory

CANADA
NEWFOUNDLAND

*ST. JOHN'S,**

McINNES COOPER (AV)

Barristers, Solicitors & Trade Mark Agents
Baine Johnston Centre, 5th Floor, 10 Fort William Place, P.O. Box 5939, A1C 5X4
Telephone: 709-722-8735
Telecopier: 709-722-1763
Email: mcrsj@mcrlaw.com *URL:* http://www.mcrlaw.com
Halifax, Nova Scotia Office: Summit Place, 1601 Lower Water Street, P.O. Box 730, B3J 2V1.
Telephone: 902-425-6500.
Fax: 902-425-6350. Email: mcrhfx@mcrlaw.com.
Moncton, New Brunswick Office: Place Moncton Place, 655 Main Street, P.O. Box 1368, E1C 8T6.
Telephone: 506-857-8970.
Fax: 506-857-4095. Email: mcrmctn@mcrlaw.com.
Charlottetown, Prince Edward Island Office: BDC Place, Suite 620, 119 Kent Street, C1A 1N3.
Telephone: 902-368-8473.
Fax: 902-368-8346. Email: mcrpei@mcrlaw.com.
Fredericton, New Brunswick Office: Suite 600, 570 Queen Street, P.O. Box 610.
Telephone: 506-458-8572.
Fax: 506-458-9903. Email: mcrfton@mcrlaw.com.

ASSOCIATE

William James O'Keefe

For Complete List of Firm Personnel, See General Section

For full biographical listings, see the Martindale-Hubbell Law Directory

CANADA
NOVA SCOTIA

*HALIFAX,** Regional Munic. of Halifax

McINNES COOPER (AV)

Barristers, Solicitors & Trade Mark Agents
Summit Place, 1601 Lower Water Street, P.O. Box 730, B3J 2V1
Telephone: 902-425-6500
Fax: 902-425-6350
Email: mcrhfx@mcrlaw.com *URL:* http://www.mcrlaw.com
St. John's, Newfoundland Office: Baine Johnston Centre, 5th Floor, 10 Fort William Place, P.O. Box 5939, A1C 5X4.
Telephone: 709-722-8735.
Telecopier: 709-722-1763. Email: mcrsj@mcrlaw.com.
Moncton, New Brunswick Office: Place Moncton Place, 655 Main Street, P.O. Box 1368, E1C 8T6.
Telephone: 506-857-8970.
Fax: 506-857-4095. Email: mcrmctn@mcrlaw.com.

(See Next Column)

Charlottetown, Prince Edward Island Office: BDC Place, Suite 620, 119 Kent Street, C1A 1N3.
Telephone: 902-368-8473.
Fax: 902-368-8346. Email: mcrpei@mcrlaw.com.
Fredericton, New Brunswick Office: Suite 600, 570 Queen Street, P.O. Box 610.
Telephone: 506-458-8572.
Fax: 506-458-9903. Email: mcrfton@mcrlaw.com.

PARTNER

Barry D. Horne

ASSOCIATES

Bruce S. Russell
Henry A. Visser
Matthew O'Halloran

For Complete List of Firm Personnel, See General Section

For full biographical listings, see the Martindale-Hubbell Law Directory

CANADA
ONTARIO

*OTTAWA,** Regional Munic. of Ottawa-Carleton

BORDEN ELLIOT SCOTT & AYLEN (AV)

1000-60 Rue Queen Street, K1P 5Y7
Telephone: 613-237-5160; 800-661-4237
General Facsimile: 613-230-8842
IP Dept. Facsimile: 613-787-3558
Email: ottinfo@scottaylen.com *URL:* http://www.borden.com
Toronto, Ontario Office: Borden & Elliot: Scotia Plaza, 40 King Street West.
Telephone: 416-367-6000.
Telecopier: 416-367-6749. Email: info @borden.com. URL: http://www.borden.com.

David W. Scott, Q.C.
Bernard G. Roach
William C. V. Johnson
Kent D. Howie

For full biographical listings, see the Martindale-Hubbell Law Directory

*TORONTO,** Regional Munic. of Toronto

BORDEN & ELLIOT (AV)

Barristers & Solicitors
Scotia Plaza, 40 King Street West, M5H 3Y4
Telephone: 416-367-6000
Telecopier: 416-367-6749
Email: info@borden.com *URL:* http://www.borden.com
Ottawa, Ontario Office: Borden Elliot Scott & Aylen, 1000-60 Rue Queen Street.
Telephone: 613-237-5160; 800-661-4237. General
Facsimile: 613-230-8842. IP Dept.
Facsimile: 613-787-3558. Email: ottinfo@scottaylen.com. URL: http://www.borden.com.

Terrance A. Sweeney

For Complete List of Firm Personnel, See General Section

For full biographical listings, see the Martindale-Hubbell Law Directory

DAVIES, WARD & BECK (AV)

1 First Canadian Place, M5X 1B1
Telephone: 416-863-0900
Fax: 416-863-0871
Email: info@dwb.com *URL:* http://www.dwb.com

PARTNERS AND ASSOCIATES

David A. Ward, Q.C.
Timothy G. Youdan
John A. Zinn
Colin Campbell
K. A. Siobhan Monaghan
Maureen Y. Berry
Geoffrey S. Turner
Claire M. C. Kennedy
David W. Smith, Q.C.
Ronald S. Wilson
John M. Ulmer
Neal H. Armstrong
R. Ian Crosbie
Catherine A. MacNeill
Jennifer A. Pfuetzner
Jennifer D. Howard
Domenic Marciano

For Complete List of Firm Personnel, See General Section

For full biographical listings, see the Martindale-Hubbell Law Directory

McDONALD & HAYDEN (AV)

One Queen Street East Suite 1500, M5C 2Y3
Telephone: 416-364-3100
Telecopier: 416-601-4100
Email: ddouglas@mchayden.on.ca *URL:* http://www.mchayden.on.ca

(See Next Column)

McDONALD & HAYDEN—*Continued*

MEMBERS OF FIRM

John G. McDonald, Q.C. (1922-1993)
Peter Reginald Hayden, Q.C.
David C. Nathanson, Q.C.
Marvin D. Demone
D. H. Jack
David R. Street
Clifford M. Goldlist
Wendy C. Posluns
Warren S. Rapoport
David H. Goldman
A. Richard Rodier
Mark Adilman
John D. Brunt
Kevin Cai
Jane Southren
Shea T. Small

ASSOCIATE

Bram J. Green

For full biographical listings, see the Martindale-Hubbell Law Directory

THORSTEINSSONS (AV Ⓣ)

P.O. Box 611, BCE Place, 36th Floor, 161 Bay Street, M5J 2S1
Telephone: 416-864-0829
Toll Free: 1-888-666-9998
Fax: 416-864-1106
Email: thor@thor.ca *URL:* http://www.thor.ca
Vancouver, British Columbia Office: 27th Floor, Three Bentall Centre, 595 Burrard Street, P.O. Box 49123, V7X 1J2.
Telephone: 604-689-1261.
Fax: 604-688-4711. Toll Free: 1-877-616-2200. Email: thor@thor.ca.
Website: http://www.thor.ca

Warren J. A. Mitchell, Q.C.
Michael J. O'Keefe, Q.C.
Lorne A. Green
Stephen W. Bowman
Steven M. Cook
John N. Gregory
John R. Owen
Douglas H. Mathew
Terry G. Barnett
Paul J. Gibney

ASSOCIATES

Kerri L. Mooney
Paul S. Carenza
Stephanie A. Wong
Michael W. Colborne
Vincenzo F. Imerti

For full biographical listings, see the Martindale-Hubbell Law Directory

CANADA QUEBEC

*MONTREAL,** Montreal Dist.

McMASTER GERVAIS (AV)

A General Partnership
1000 de La Gauchetière Street West, Suite 900, H3B 5H4
Telephone: 514-879-1212
Fax: 514-954-1905
Email: info@mcmastergervais.com *URL:* http://www.mcmastergervais.com

MEMBERS OF FIRM

Brian M. Schneiderman
François Morin
Charles P. Marquette
Virginia Chan
Joel M. Cabelli

For Complete List of Firm Personnel, See General Section

For full biographical listings, see the Martindale-Hubbell Law Directory

MENDELSOHN ROSENTZVEIG SHACTER (AV)

1000 Sherbrooke Street West, 27th Floor, H3A 3G4
Telephone: 514-987-5000
Telex: 05-27284 Colorlaw
Telecopier: 514-987-1213
Email: mrs@mrslaw.com *URL:* http://www.mrslaw.com

PARTNERS

S. Leon Mendelsohn, Q.C. (1902-1996)
Leo Rosentzveig, Q.C.
Manuel Shacter, Q.C.
Jack C. Shayne
William Levitt
Arthur A. Garvis
Edward E. Aronoff
L. Michael Blumenstein
Max Mendelsohn
Earl S. Cohen
Michael Garonce
Donald M. Devine
Richard S. Uditsky
Joel Weitzman
Ian R. Rudnikoff
Marc I. Leiter
L. B. Erdle
Fredric L. Carsley
Frank Zylberberg
Jules Brossard
David L. Rosentzveig
Judie K. Jokinen
Gilles Seguin
Martin Desrosiers
Andrew Etcovitch
Alain Breault
Jean Carrière
Henri M. Bybelezer
Louis Frédérick Côté
Sandra Abitan

(See Next Column)

ASSOCIATES

Carl M. Ravinsky
Catherine Muraz
Francine Wiseman
Joelle Sebag
Maria R. Battaglia
Keyvan Nassiry
Linda Schachter
Emmanuelle Saucier
Arnold Cohen
Aaron Makovka
Michel Rochefort
Céline Tessier
Sophie Crevier
Annick Joyal
Francis Desmarais
Nicolas J. Beugnot
Jean-François Brière
Marc-Antoine Deschamps
Philipp F. Duffy
Fred Purkey
Martin Sills
David Tardif-Latourelle

For full biographical listings, see the Martindale-Hubbell Law Directory

CANADA SASKATCHEWAN

*REGINA,** Regina Jud. Centre

MacPHERSON LESLIE & TYERMAN (AV)

1500-1874 Scarth Street, S4P 4E9
Telephone: 306-347-8000
Telecopier: 306-352-5250
Email: mltreg@mlt.com
Saskatoon, Saskatchewan Office: 1500-410 22nd Street East, S7K 5T6.
Telephone: 306-975-7100.
Telecopier: 306-975-7145.

MEMBERS OF FIRM

Alain J. Gaucher (Resident, Saskatoon Office)
Todd M. Rosenberg (Resident, Saskatoon Office)
Curtis R. Stewart (Resident, Saskatoon Office)

ASSOCIATE

Rachelle M. Verret

For Complete List of Firm Personnel, See General Section

For full biographical listings, see the Martindale-Hubbell Law Directory

ENGLAND

*LONDON,**

American Lawyers In London

JONES, DAY, REAVIS & POGUE

Bucklersbury House, 3 Queen Victoria Street, London EC4N 8NA
Telephone: 44-20-7236-3939
Telecopier: 44-20-7236-1113
Email: counsel@jonesday.com *URL:* http://www.jonesday.com
In Atlanta, Georgia: 3500 SunTrust Plaza, 303 Peachtree Street.
Telephone: 404-521-3939.
Telecopier: 404-581-8330.
In Brussels, Belgium: Avenue Louise 480, 7th Floor. B-1050 Brussels.
Telephone: 32-2-645-14-11.
Telecopier: 32-2-645-14-45.
In Chicago, Illinois: 77 West Wacker.
Telephone: 312-782-3939.
Telecopier: 312-782-8585.
In Cleveland, Ohio: North Point, 901 Lakeside Avenue.
Telephone: 216-586-3939.
Telecopier: 216-579-0212.
In Columbus, Ohio: 1900 Huntington Center.
Telephone: 614-469-3939.
Telecopier: 614-461-4198.
In Dallas, Texas: 2727 North Harwood Street.
Telephone: 214-220-3939.
Telecopier: 214-969-5100.
In Frankfurt, Germany: Hochhaus am Park, Grüneburgweg 102, 60323 Frankfurt am Main.
Telephone: 49-69-9726-3939.
Telecopier: 49-69-9726-3993.
In Geneva, Switzerland: 20, rue de Candolle.
Telephone: 41-22-320-2339.
Telecopier: 41-22-320-1232.
In Hong Kong: 29th Floor, Entertainment Building, 30 Queen's Road Central.
Telephone: 852-2526-6895.
Telecopier: 852-2868-5871.
In Irvine, California: 5 Park Plaza, Suite 1100.
Telephone: 949-851-3939.
Telecopier: 949-553-7539.
In Los Angeles, California: 555 West Fifth Street, Suite 4600.
Telephone: 213-489-3939.
Telecopier: 213-243-2539.

(See Next Column)

JONES, DAY, REAVIS & POGUE, *London—Continued*

In New York, New York: 599 Lexington Avenue.
Telephone: 212-326-3939.
Telecopier: 212-755-7306.
In Paris, France: 120, rue du Faubourg Saint-Honoré.
Telephone: 33-1-56-59-39-39.
Telecopier: 33-1-56-59-39-38
In Pittsburgh, Pennsylvania: 500 Grant Street, 31st Floor.
Telephone: 412-391-3939.
Telecopier: 412-394-7959.
In Riyadh, Saudi Arabia: The International Law Firm (In Association with Jones, Day, Reavis & Pogue), Sulaymaniyah, Prince Mishari IBN, Abdulaziz Street, P.O. Box 22166.
Telephone: (966-1) 462-8866.
Telecopier: (966-1 462-9001.
In Shanghai, China: 2805 Kerry Centre, 1515 Nanjing Road West.
Telephone: 86-21-5298-6568.
Telecopier: 86-21-5298-6569.
In Sydney, Australia: Governor Phillip Tower, Level 38, 1 Farrer Place.
Telephone: 61-2-9210-6921.
Telecopier: 61-2-9210-6926.
In Taipei, Taiwan: 8th Floor, 2 Tun Hwa South Road, Section 2.
Telephone: (886-2) 2704-6808.
Telecopier: (886-2) 2704-6791.
In Tokyo, Japan: Toranomon 45 Mori Building, 3rd Floor, 1-5, Toranomon 5-Chome, Minato-Ku, Tokyo 105, Japan.
Telephone: 81-3-3433-3939.
Telecopier: 81-3-5401-2725.
In Washington, D.C.: 51 Louisiana Avenue, N.W.
Telephone: 202-879-3939.
Telecopier: 202-626-1700.

MEMBERS OF FIRM IN LONDON

Stephen E. Fiamma (Not admitted in England)
Keith Featherstone

ASSOCIATES

Maryann Clemente (Not admitted in England)
Martin S. Rowley (Not admitted in England)

(Not admitted to practice in English courts)

For Complete List of Firm Personnel, See General Section

For full biographical listings, see the Martindale-Hubbell Law Directory

TOXIC TORTS

MISSISSIPPI

MADISON, Madison Co.

BELL & ASSOCIATES, P.A. (AV)

967 Madison Avenue, 39110
Telephone: 601-898-1111
Toll Free: 1-888-898-1600
Fax: 601-898-1102
Mailing Address: P.O. Box 890, Madison, Mississippi, 39130-0890
Email: JamesDBell@aol.com *URL:* http://www.lawyers.com/bell&associates

James D. Bell

Eduardo Alberto Flechas

For full biographical listings, see the Martindale-Hubbell Law Directory

MISSOURI

ST. LOUIS, (Independent City)

COFFEY & GRIESBACH (AV)

6202 Columbia Avenue, 63139
Telephone: 314-647-0033
Fax: 314-647-8231
Email: candg@I1.net *URL:* http://www.lawyers.com/c&g

Mary Coffey
Toni Griesbach

For full biographical listings, see the Martindale-Hubbell Law Directory

NEVADA

*LAS VEGAS,** Clark Co.

LEFEBVRE, BARRON & VIVONE, CHTD. (AV)

1404 South Jones Boulevard, 89146-1231
Telephone: 702-383-8668
Facsimile: 702-383-6828
Email: lb@coam.net

Alan J. Lefebvre
David L. Barron
Thomas J. Vivone
Raymond W. Holland
Michelle O. Tobler
William Howard Pruitt
Bradley V. Gibbons
Jared Casper
(Not admitted in NV)
Kevin S. Smith

LEGAL SUPPORT PERSONNEL

Jennifer L. Hageman

For full biographical listings, see the Martindale-Hubbell Law Directory

NEW JERSEY

HADDONFIELD, Camden Co.

WILBRAHAM, LAWLER & BUBA, A PROFESSIONAL CORPORATION (AV®)

24 Kings Highway West, 08033-2122
Telephone: 856-795-4422
Fax: 856-795-4699
Philadelphia, Pennsylvania Office: 1818 Market Street, Suite 3100.
Telephone: 215-564-4141.
Fax: 215-564-4385.
Wilmington, Delaware Office: Stoney Batter Office Building, 5301 Limestone Road, Suite 221.
Telephone: 302-234-8217.
Fax: 302-234-8218.

Edward J. Wilbraham
Michael J. Block
Mary S. Cook

For full biographical listings, see the Martindale-Hubbell Law Directory

MOORESTOWN, Burlington Co.

CHIERICI, CHIERICI & SMITH, A PROFESSIONAL CORPORATION (AV)

Blason Campus - III, 509 South Lenola Road Building Six, 08057-1561
Telephone: 856-234-6300
Fax: 856-234-9490

Donald R. Chierici, Jr.
Elizabeth Coleman Chierici
Julie C. Smith

Carolyn J. Kornas
Mark G. Esposito
Richard D. DiTomaso
Melvin McDowell
David J. Karbasian
Peter P. Sanchez
Donald R. Chierici, III

For full biographical listings, see the Martindale-Hubbell Law Directory

*MORRISTOWN,** Morris Co.

BAUMEISTER & SAMUELS, P.C. (AV®)

1776 On The Green, P.O. Box 1116, 07962-1116
Telephone: 973-267-6666
Telecopier: 973-605-1812
Email: BAUMSAM@AOL.COM
New York, N.Y. Office: One Exchange Plaza, 10006-3008.
Telephone: 212-363-1200.
Telecopier: 212-363-1346.

Michel F. Baumeister
Douglas A. Latto
(Not admitted in NJ)
Dorothea M. Capone

OF COUNSEL

Lynn F. Samuels
Robert S. Franklin
(Not admitted in NJ)
Marc Z. Edell

For full biographical listings, see the Martindale-Hubbell Law Directory

PARSIPPANY, Morris Co.

CUYLER BURK (AV)

Parsippany Corporate Center, Four Century Drive, 07054-4663
Telephone: 973-734-3200
Telex: 429071
Telecopier: 973-734-3201
Email: Main@Cuyler.com *URL:* http://www.cuyler.com
New York, New York Office: 350 Fifth Avenue, Suite 3304. 10018.
Telephone: 212-645-4039.

MEMBERS OF FIRM

Stephen D. Cuyler
Jo Ann Burk
Stefano Calogero
David L. Menzel
Peter Petrou
Richard A. Crooker
Michael J. Jones

COUNSEL

Anne M. Mohan
Frank J. Miele

ASSOCIATES

Jan C. Walker
Kathleen Jane Olear
Claudia L. Marchese
Mark G. Eliades
Kimberly A. Joel
Christy A. Ramunno
Catherine E. Youngman
Andrew K. Craig
Mark S. Winter
Thomas J. Castano
Hugo A. Hilgendorff, IV

LEGAL SUPPORT PERSONNEL

Frederick M. H. Currie, Jr.

For full biographical listings, see the Martindale-Hubbell Law Directory

*TOMS RIVER,** Ocean Co.

LOMELL, MUCCIFORI, ADLER, RAVASCHIERE, AMABILE & PEHLIVANIAN, A PROFESSIONAL CORPORATION (AV)

250 Washington Street, P.O. Box 787, 08754
Telephone: 732-349-2443
Fax: 732-349-6917
Email: thefirm@lomell.com *URL:* http://www.lomell.com

Herman A. Adler
Dominic Ravaschiere
John S. Pehlivanian
Ronald E. Prusek
Jeffrey R. Surenian
James M. McKenna
Teresa K. Gierla
Arthur F. Leyden, III

Marc S. Galella
Robyn A. Belluardo
Janet Zaorski Kalapos
James S. Braaten
Regina M. Butler
Paul J Capotorto

For Complete List of Firm Personnel, See General Section

For full biographical listings, see the Martindale-Hubbell Law Directory

NEW MEXICO

*ALBUQUERQUE,** Bernalillo Co.

BRANCH LAW FIRM (AV)

Including a Professional Association
2025 Rio Grande Boulevard, N.W., 87104
Telephone: 505-243-3500
Fax: 505-243-3534
New Mexico Toll Free: 1-800-562-3456
Nationwide Toll Free: 1-800-828-4LAW
Email: reception@branchlawfirm.com *URL:* http://www.branchlawfirm.com
Durango, Colorado Office: Suite 205, 102 East Eighth Street.
Telephone: 303-385-7671.
Houston, Texas Office: 808 Travis Street, Suite 1303.
Telephone: 800-243-3545.
Fax: 713-224-1622.

Turner W. Branch (P.A.)
Margaret Moses Branch

Arthur M. Solon
Daniel R. Swiss
Rebecca C. Branch
Justin K. Hall
James P. Lyle
Rhett D. Klok
Suzanne Lafleur Klok
Clyde DeMersseman
Shari D. Thieman

LEGAL SUPPORT PERSONNEL

Krisann Y. Matthes (Office Manager)
Jacqueline Adams
Amy Rigg
Shariesse McCannon
Judi Seff
Daphne Moore (Registered Nurse)
Yvette Rodarte
Shelly Hourani (Houston Office)

For full biographical listings, see the Martindale-Hubbell Law Directory

NEW YORK

*ALBANY,** Albany Co.

ISEMAN, CUNNINGHAM, RIESTER & HYDE, LLP (AV)

9 Thurlow Terrace, 12203
Telephone: 518-462-3000
Telecopier: 518-462-4199
Email: lawfirm@icrh.com *URL:* http://www.icrh.com
Canandaigua, New York Office: 37 East Gibson Street, P.O. Box 179, 14424.
Telephone: 716-394-1450.
Fax: 716-394-5121.

MEMBERS OF FIRM

Frederick C. Riester
Michael J. Cunningham
Robert Hall Iseman
Carol Ann Hyde
Linda J. Clark

Brian M. Culnan
Kihyun S. Kim
Richard A. Frankel
Stephanie E. Moriarty
Valerie R. Lape Handy
Marcia B. Smith
Ellen Gillerman Cox
Jennifer A. Grego
Cara E. Johnson

OF COUNSEL

Michael J. McNeil
Deborah A. Kirby

For full biographical listings, see the Martindale-Hubbell Law Directory

O'CONNOR, O'CONNOR, MAYBERGER & FIRST, P.C. (AV)

20 Corporate Woods Boulevard, 12211-0400
Telephone: 518-465-0400
Facsimile: 518-465-0015
Email: info@1stlaw.com *URL:* http://www.1stlaw.com

Michael J. O'Connor
Terence P. O'Connor
Dianne Bresee Mayberger
Dennis A. First
Michele M. Monserrate
Cynthia Ann Platt

Justin O. Corcoran
Michael P. Cavanagh
Christopher D. Drake
Eugene N. Sarfoh
Francis J. Brennan
Colleen D. Galligan

For full biographical listings, see the Martindale-Hubbell Law Directory

THORN AND GERSHON, LLP (AV)

5 Wembley Court, New Karner Road, P.O. Box 15054, 12212-5054
Telephone: 518-464-6770
Fax: 518-464-6778

(See Next Column)

MEMBERS OF FIRM

Richard M. Gershon
Arthur H. Thorn
Jeffrey J. Tymann
Maureen Sullivan Bonanni
Noreen J. Van Doren
Nancy Nicholson Bogan
Sheila Toborg

ASSOCIATES

Paul D. Jureller
Kristen H. Martin
William M. Hoblock
Kyle N. Kordich
Jennifer H. Goody

OF COUNSEL

Robert F. Doran

For full biographical listings, see the Martindale-Hubbell Law Directory

GARDEN CITY, Nassau Co.

L'ABBATE, BALKAN, COLAVITA & CONTINI, L.L.P. (AV)

1050 Franklin Avenue, 11530
Telephone: 516-294-8844
Telecopier: 516-294-8202; 742-6563
Email: law@labbatebalkan.com *URL:* http://www.labbatebalkan.com
Livingston, New Jersey Office: 7 Regent Street, Suite 711, 07039.
Telephone: 973-422-0422.
Telecopier: 973-422-0420.

MEMBERS OF FIRM

Donald R. L'Abbate
Anthony P. Colavita
Peter L. Contini
Monte E. Sokol
Douglas L. Pintauro
Richard P. Byrne
Jane M. Myers
Paula M. Gart
Anna M. DiLonardo
David B. Kosakoff
Lewis A. Bartell
Marian C. Rice
Ralph A. Catalano
Douglas R. Halstrom
Steven R. Goldstein
Gary Petropoulos
Domingo R. Gallardo
Mercedes Colwin

COUNSEL TO THE FIRM

Kenneth J. Balkan

SPECIAL COUNSEL

Arthur D. Bromberg (Resident, Livingston, New Jersey Office)
Jonathan M. Kuller (Resident, Livingston, New Jersey Office)

OF COUNSEL

Marianne S. Conklin
Joanne C. Watson
Marie Ann Hoenings

ASSOCIATES

Colleen M. Cronin
Wendy S. Van Dorn
Nicholas Toumbekis
Andrew Marc Warshauer
Michelle J. Simon
Annalee J. Cataldo-Barile
Martin A. Schwartzberg
Louis M. Goldberg
Scott Evan Kossove
Peter D. Rigelhaupt
Orin J. Ketyer
Anthony T. Battaglia
Christopher B. Block (Resident, Livingston, New Jersey Office)
James S. Montano (Resident, Livingston, New Jersey Office)
Maureen E. Scott
John D. McKenna
Michael B. Curan
Jeffrey E. Edelman (Resident, Livingston, New Jersey Office)
Matthew K. Flanagan
Claudia M. Kessler

A list of References and Representative Clients will be furnished upon request.

For full biographical listings, see the Martindale-Hubbell Law Directory

*NEW YORK,** New York Co.

BAUMEISTER & SAMUELS, P.C. (AV)

One Exchange Plaza, 10006-3008
Telephone: 212-363-1200
Telecopier: 212-363-1346
Email: BAUMSAM@AOL.COM
Morristown, New Jersey Office: 1776 On The Green, P.O. Box 1116, 07962-1116.
Telephone: 973-267-6666.
Telecopier: 973-605-1812.

Michel F. Baumeister
Douglas A. Latto
Dorothea M. Capone

OF COUNSEL

Lynn F. Samuels
Robert S. Franklin
Marc Z. Edell

For full biographical listings, see the Martindale-Hubbell Law Directory

LEDY-GURREN & BLUMENSTOCK, L.L.P. (AV)

150 East 52nd Street-30th Floor, 10022
Telephone: 212-753-4444
Fax: 212-753-1003
Email: ledygurren@aol.com

Nancy Ledy-Gurren
John U. H. Blumenstock
Deborah Bass
Daniel E. Siff

Elissa L. Shechter

(See Next Column)

LEDY-GURREN & BLUMENSTOCK L.L.P.—*Continued*

OF COUNSEL

Elizabeth Marion Young

For full biographical listings, see the Martindale-Hubbell Law Directory

OHRENSTEIN & BROWN, L.L.P. (AV)

One World Trade Center 85th Floor, 10048
Telephone: 212-682-4500
Facsimile: 212-839-0854
Garden City, New York Office: 1050 Franklin Avenue.
Telephone: 516-873-6334.
Telecopier: 516-873-8912.

MEMBERS OF FIRM

Manfred Ohrenstein
Michael D. Brown
Peter J. Biging
Joseph Francis Fields
Abraham E. Havkins
Geoffrey W. Heineman
Christopher B. Hitchcock
Andrew L. Margulis
Steven H. Rosenfeld
Abe M. Rychik
John R. Sachs, Jr.

COUNSEL

Anne J. Coploff
Stanley M. Kolber
Paul L. Dillon
Gail L. Ritzert

ASSOCIATES

Joseph G. Colbert
Jonathan A. Judd
Bennett R. Katz
Kenneth M. Labbate
Jennifer A. Lowitt
John A. McGrath
Tessie M. Perrini (Resident, Garden City, New York)
Jennifer R. Robinson
Sharon Portnof Russ
Philip Touitou
Carla Varriale
Brian D. Waller
Cristin L. Flynn
Jason A. Advocate
Timothy F. Finnerty (Resident, Garden City Office)
Michelle Maerov
Stacey Niditch
Brian A. Smith
Theresa Brennan Murphy
Thomas Brian Ferris (Resident at Garden City Office)

LEGAL SUPPORT PERSONNEL

Christine A. Maguire (Office Manager)

For full biographical listings, see the Martindale-Hubbell Law Directory

PAUL A. SCRUDATO (AV)

150 E. 52nd Street, Suite 2700, 10022
Telephone: 212-371-1153
Fax: 212-753-5044
Email: paulscrudato@ibm.net

For full biographical listings, see the Martindale-Hubbell Law Directory

SHANDELL, BLITZ, BLITZ, GLASS, BOOKSON & KERN, LLP (AV)

150 Broadway, 10038-4498
Telephone: 212-513-1300
Fax: 212-385-1916
Email: SBBGBK@aol.com

MEMBERS OF FIRM

Herman B. Glaser (1915-1994)
Richard E. Shandell
Bert A. Blitz
Arthur Blitz
Shoshana T. Bookson
Chet W. Kern

Mitchel H. Ashley
Fredrick A. Schulman

For full biographical listings, see the Martindale-Hubbell Law Directory

SMITH MAZURE DIRECTOR WILKINS YOUNG YAGERMAN & TARALLO, P.C. (AV)

111 John Street, 10038
Telephone: 212-964-7400
Fax: 212-374-1935 (Not for Legal Service)

Gerald Director
David E. Mazure
Stanley Wilkins
Nicholas Tarallo
Jacob J. Young
Mark S. Yagerman

Irwin D. Miller
Marc H. Pillinger
Michael K. Berman
John Kevin Reilly
Cary Maynard
Robert P. Siegel
John Colucci
Haydn J. Brill
Jeffrey T. Miller
Corey A. Tavel
Mark D. Levi
Howard S. Shafer
Peter H. Graber
Irwin Bloom
Michael S. Livow
Steven I. Brizel
Joel M. Simon
Frank J. Keenan
Melissa S. Romano
Paul L. LaClair
Constantine Vlavianos
Joseph A. Schwarzenberg
Stephanie Morfesis
Stacy I. Oberman

(See Next Column)

Dawn McNamara
David A. Glazer
Lara Jill Miller
Andrew J. Funk
Angela Lurie Milch
Seth M. Katz
Michael G. Brown
Christopher M. FitzPatrick
Neil Thomas Veilleux
Doris M. Carrasquillo
Alan C. Kelhoffer
Howard J. Snyder

For full biographical listings, see the Martindale-Hubbell Law Directory

WHITE, FLEISCHNER & FINO (AV)

140 Broadway, 10005
Telephone: 212-487-9700
Telecopier: 212-487-9777
Email: infor@wff-law.com
Red Bank, New Jersey Office: 272 Broad Street.
Telephone: 732-530-7787.
Telecopier: 732-530-8552.

MEMBER OF FIRM

James A. Robbins

For Complete List of Firm Personnel, See General Section

For full biographical listings, see the Martindale-Hubbell Law Directory

OHIO

*CLEVELAND,** Cuyahoga Co.

BONEZZI SWITZER MURPHY & POLITO CO. L.P.A. (AV)

Leader Building, Suite 1400, 526 Superior Avenue, 44114-1491
Telephone: 216-875-2767
Telecopier: 216-875-1570
Email: bsmp@bsmplaw.com

William D. Bonezzi
Donald H. Switzer
Patrick Joseph Murphy
John S. Polito
Steven J. Hupp

Susan M. Reinker
Kevin O. Kadlec
Edward E. Taber

Representative Clients: The Cleveland Clinic Foundation; Southwest General Health Center; Ashtabula County Medical Center; Mutual Assurance Company; The Doctors' Company; Kentucky Medical Insurance Company; Liberty Mutual Insurance Company; Kaiser Engineering; MMI Companies; Medical Inter-Insurance Exchange.

For full biographical listings, see the Martindale-Hubbell Law Directory

OKLAHOMA

*OKLAHOMA CITY,** Oklahoma Co.

DAY, EDWARDS, FEDERMAN, PROPESTER & CHRISTENSEN, P.C. (AV)

Suite 2900 Oklahoma Tower, 210 Park Avenue, 73102-5605
Telephone: 405-239-2121
Telecopier: 405-236-1012
URL: http://lawlinks.com/attys/ok/defpc.html

Joe E. Edwards
William B. Federman
Rodney J. Heggy

Stuart W. Emmons
Bill Powell Guest

Representative Clients: BancFirst; Bank One, Oklahoma City; Bank of America, N.A.; Bobby Joe Cudd Company; Delta Western Drilling Funds; Fluid Technologies; Federal Deposit Insurance Corp.; Community Bank, Binger; First National Bank and Trust Company of Weatherford; First State Bank & Trust Co., Hollis.

For Complete List of Firm Personnel, See General Section

For full biographical listings, see the Martindale-Hubbell Law Directory

*TULSA,** Tulsa Co.

RHODES, HIERONYMUS, JONES, TUCKER & GABLE, P.L.L.C. (AV)

Oneok Plaza, 100 West 5th Street, Suite 400, P.O. Box 21100, 74121-1100
Telephone: 918-582-1173
Fax: 918-592-3390
URL: http://www.rhodesokla.com

MEMBERS OF FIRM

William D. Perrine
Robert P. Redemann
Chris L. Rhodes, III
John H. Tucker
Harold C. Zuckerman

(See Next Column)

RHODES, HIERONYMUS, JONES, TUCKER & GABLE P.L.L.C., *Tulsa—Continued*

Representative Clients: American International Companies; Bechtel; Chubb Group of Insurance Companies; General Motors Corporation; Merrill, Lynch; Nissan Motor Corporation in U.S.A.; Pfizer, Inc.; Volkswagen of America, Volkswagen, A.G.; Zurich U.S.

For full biographical listings, see the Martindale-Hubbell Law Directory

OREGON

*PORTLAND,** Multnomah Co.

SWANSON, THOMAS & COON (AV)

American Bank Building, 621 S.W. Morrison, Suite 900, 97205-3892
Telephone: 503-228-5222
Fax: 503-273-9175
URL: http://www.stc-law.com

MEMBERS OF FIRM

Douglas A. Swanson
Raymond F. Thomas
James S. Coon

ASSOCIATES

Megan E. Glor
Alan Stuart Graf
Margaret F. Weddell

For full biographical listings, see the Martindale-Hubbell Law Directory

PENNSYLVANIA

BENSALEM, Bucks Co.

RUDOLPH, DORIAN, GOLDSTEIN, ROCHESTIE, WISNIEWSKI & TAYLOR, P.C. (AV)

Neshaminy Valley Commons, 2410 Bristol Road, 19020
Telephone: 215-750-7200
Fax: 215-750-9294
Email: admin@rudolphdorian.com *URL:* http://www.palaw.lawoffice.com
Philadelphia, Pennsylvania Office: 1818 Market Street, Suite 2300, 19103.
Telephone: 215-299-9900.
Fax: 215-299-9910.

Edward Rudolph
Harry A. Dorian, Jr.
Stephan H. Goldstein
Gary A. Rochestie
Mark A. Wisniewski
John J. Taylor
Jeffrey S. Orchinik
Kim A. Piermattei
Michael Parlow
Lawrence P. Kempner
Nancy M. Bonner

For full biographical listings, see the Martindale-Hubbell Law Directory

FORT WASHINGTON, Montgomery Co.

DALLER GREENBERG & DIETRICH, LLP (AV)

Valley Green Corporate Center, 7111 Valley Green Road, 19034
Telephone: 215-836-1100
Facsimile: 215-836-2845
URL: http://www.dallergreenberg.com
Haddon Heights, New Jersey Office: 2 White Horse Pike.
Telephone: 856-547-9068.
Facsimile: 856-547-2391.

PARTNERS

Morton F. Daller
Edward A. Greenberg
Gerhard P. Dietrich
Eileen M. Johnson
Dennis R. Callahan

ASSOCIATES

Tracy Canuso Nugent (Resident, Haddon Heights, New Jersey Office)
Catherine N. Walto
Mark S. Kirby
Marie Handrich Kramer
Alison R. Rohmer

For full biographical listings, see the Martindale-Hubbell Law Directory

*NORRISTOWN,** Montgomery Co.

MURPHY, OLIVER, CAIOLA & GOWEN, A PROFESSIONAL LAW CORPORATION (AV)

43 East Marshall Street, 19401-4828
Telephone: 610-272-4222; 610-279-3838
Fax: 610-272-2549; 610-275-0140
Email: molaw@injury-law.com *URL:* http://www.injury-law.com
Spring City, Pennsylvania Office: 500 S. Main Street, 19475.
Telephone: 610-948-3770.
Pottstown, Pennsylvania Office: 5 Sunnybrook Road, 19464.
Telephone: 610-323-3480.

(See Next Column)

West Chester, Pennsylvania Office: 1534 McDaniel Drive, Westtown Business Center, 19250.
Telephone: 610-272-4222.

James J. Oliver
Frank P. Murphy
Frank L. Caiola
Thomas L. Gowen, Jr.
Carla E. Connor
Barbara A. Barnes

John F. Haskins, Jr.
Cynthia Love Dengler
Carol A. Crisci

LEGAL SUPPORT PERSONNEL

Patricia A. Talese (Paralegal)
Kathleen Nicholson

For full biographical listings, see the Martindale-Hubbell Law Directory

*PHILADELPHIA,** Philadelphia Co.

ANAPOL, SCHWARTZ, WEISS, COHAN, FELDMAN AND SMALLEY, P.C. (AV)

1900 Delancey Place, 19103
Telephone: 215-735-1130
Fax: 215-735-2024
URL: http://www.aswc.net
Other Philadelphia, Pennsylvania Office: 1710 Spruce Street.
Fax: 215-735-2211.
Cherry Hill, New Jersey Office: 402 Park Boulevard, 08002.
Telephone: 1-609-427-9229.
Fax: 609-488-1396.
Fairless Hills, Pennsylvania Office: 920 Trenton Road.
Telephone: 215-945-6799.
Reading, Pennsylvania Office: 146 North 6th Street.
Telephone: 610-375-7488.
Media, Pennsylvania Office: 334 W. Front Street, 19063.
Telephone: 610-892-3714.

Alan Schwartz
Sol H. Weiss
Lawrence R. Cohan
Joel D. Feldman
Howard J. Levin
Bernard W. Smalley
Stanton Dubin
Margaret A. Barry
Stephen J. Pokiniewski, Jr.
Sidney M. Grobman
Nelson Levin

Nathaniel E.P. Ehrlich
Thomas R. Anapol
Miriam Benton Barish
Patrice A. Gillotti
Michele Lee Reed
Heather J. Lipson
Michelle L. Altenpohl
Lisa R. Schwartz
Kevin R. Marciano
Brian J. Taylor
Tobias L. Millrood
Tracy A. Finken

OF COUNSEL

Paul R. Anapol
Richard B. Schwartz (Resident, Other Philadelphia Office)
Mark F. Seltzer

Reference: Meridian Bank, Philadelphia, Pennsylvania.

For full biographical listings, see the Martindale-Hubbell Law Directory

GALFAND BERGER, LLP (AV)

1818 Market Street, 23rd Floor, 19103-3623
Telephone: 215-665-1600
Fax: 215-564-2262
Email: sdonaway@galfandberger.com *URL:* http://www.galfandberger.com

Richard M. Jurewicz
Peter M. Patton

For full biographical listings, see the Martindale-Hubbell Law Directory

HOLLSTEIN KEATING CATTELL JOHNSON & GOLDSTEIN, P.C. (AV)

Suite 1602 1608 Walnut Street, 19103
Telephone: 215-893-9488
Fax: 215-893-9480
Email: JFJ@HKCJG.com
Voorhees, New Jersey Office: 1016 Laurel Oak Road, Suite 2, 08043.
Telephone: 609-309-9000.
Fax: 609-309-0337.
Wilmington, Delaware Office: One Commerce Center, Suite 730, 12th and Orange Streets, 19801.
Telephone: 302-884-6700.
Fax: 302-573-2507.

Richard W. Hollstein
E. Michael Keating, III
Edward V. Cattell, Jr.
James W. Johnson
Stuart M. Goldstein (Resident, Voorhees, New Jersey Office)
Mark G. Lionetti
John E. Tyrrell
Lynne M. Parker (at Voorhees, New Jersey and Wilmington, Delaware Offices)
Paul F. Weisbein
James D. Lloyd
Nancy D. Wagman
Margaret M. Grasso

(See Next Column)

HOLLSTEIN KEATING CATTELL JOHNSON & GOLDSTEIN P.C.—*Continued*

LEGAL SUPPORT PERSONNEL

Nancy Hevener (Paralegal)
Libby Carrol (Paralegal)

For full biographical listings, see the Martindale-Hubbell Law Directory

HOWARD, BRENNER & NASS, P.C. (AV)

(Predecessor firm, George W. Howard, III, P.C.)
Suite 1700, 1608 Walnut Street, 19103
Telephone: 215-546-8200
Fax: 215-545-1591
Westmont, New Jersey Office: 212 Haddon Avenue, 08108.
Telephone: 609-427-9100.
Fax: 609-869-9881.

George W. Howard, III
David E. Brenner
Edward M. Nass
Richard P. Hackman

Robert J. O'Shea, Jr.
Thomas D. Summerville
Michael A. Cancelliere, Jr.
William Charles Bensley

Representative Clients: East Coast Credit; The Republic Bank; The Chestnut Hill Hospital; Heritage Bank; Jakes Bar and Grill; Critiques, Inc.; Mann and Fountain, Inc.; William Austin's Ltd.; Narbeth Presbyterian Church.

For full biographical listings, see the Martindale-Hubbell Law Directory

KELLEY, JASONS, McGUIRE & SPINELLI, L.L.P. (AV)

One Penn Center, Suite 1400, 1617 JFK Boulevard, 19103
Telephone: 215-854-0658
Fax: 215-854-8434; 215-854-0777
Marlton, New Jersey Office: One Greentree Centre, Suite 201, 08053.
Telephone: 609-988-5543.
Fax: 609-988-9165.
Wilmington, Delaware Office: 800 Delaware Avenue, P.O. Box 194, 19899.
Telephone: 302-652-8560.
Fax: 302-652-8405.

MEMBERS OF FIRM

John Patrick Kelley
Catherine N. Jasons
Joseph W. McGuire
Armand J. Della Porta, Jr.
Christopher N. Santoro
Robert N. Spinelli
Thomas P. Hanna
Thomas J. Johanson
Michael L. Turner
Richard L. Walker, II
Timothy McGowan

ASSOCIATES

Neal C. Glenn
W. Matthew Reber
Ann C. Lebowitz
Anthony J. Ryan

OF COUNSEL

Matthew D. Blum

For full biographical listings, see the Martindale-Hubbell Law Directory

KLEINBARD, BELL & BRECKER LLP (AV)

Suite 700, 1900 Market Street, 19103
Telephone: 215-568-2000
Facsimile: 215-568-0140
Montclair, New Jersey Office: 240 Claremont Avenue, 07042.
Telephone: 973-233-0600.
Facsimile: 973-233-9390.

Joseph S. Kleinbard (1905-1994)
Robert John Brecker (1916-1996)

COUNSEL TO THE FIRM

Arthur S. Keyser

MEMBERS OF FIRM

Paul E. Bomze
Murray I. Blackman
Howard J. Davis
Steven R. Waxman
Steven J. Engelmyer (Resident, Montclair Office)
David L. Hyman (Resident, Montclair Office)
Imogene E. Hughes
John P. Hickey
Jay R. Goldstein
Ralph J. Mauro
Thomas H. Speranza
Lisa E. Brody

ASSOCIATES

Mary Beth H. Gray
Eric J. Rothschild
Mary Vassallo Slinkard
Michael A. Frattone
Benjamin C. Graff (Not admitted in PA)
Ralph F. Salgado

COUNSEL

Joseph Bell

For full biographical listings, see the Martindale-Hubbell Law Directory

MARKS, O'NEILL, REILLY, O'BRIEN & COURTNEY, P.C. (AV)

1880 John F. Kennedy Boulevard Suite 1200, 19103
Telephone: 215-564-6688
Fax: 215-564-2526
Email: moro1@morocpa.com
Norristown, Pennsylvania Office: 411 Cherry Street.
Telephone: 215-277-7601.
Pittsburgh, Pennsylvania Office: 707 Grant Street, Gulf Tower, Suite 3200.
Telephone: 412-391-6171.
Fax: 412-391-8804.
Westmont, New Jersey Office: 216 Haddon Avenue, Suite 500.
Telephone: 856-858-6110.
Fax: 856-858-3687. E-Mail: moro1@morocnj.com
Wilmington, Delaware Office: 2004 Foulk Road, Suite 7.
Telephone: 302-475-5500.
Fax: 302-475-5584.

Jerome E. Marks
Joseph M. O'Neill
Vincent F. Reilly
Kevin J. O'Brien
Dawn R. Courtney
Sean Xavier Kelly
Gino P. Mecoli
John J. Repcheck (Resident, Pittsburgh Office)

David P. Helwig (Resident, Pittsburgh Office)
Maureen Murray-O'Toole
Patrick C. Lamb
Christine G. Boyle
Nancy E. Mancheski
Michael T. Hamilton
Kelly L. Bracken
Tracey Marie McDevitt
Sharon A. Connors (Resident, Westmont, New Jersey Office)
Malissa A. Richetti
Patricia M. Henrich
Judith H. Ring
Gary Weinberg (Resident, Westmont, New Jersey Office)
Lee J. Janiczek
Wendy D. Testa (Resident, Westmont, New Jersey Office)
Gary F. Sharlock (Resident, Pittsburgh Office)
Robert Dale Leidigh (Resident, Pittsburgh Office)
Joseph L. Orszulak, II (Resident, Pittsburgh Office)
Diane Beckman Carvell
Karen J. Stanzione
Michael A. Kosar
Susan D. Grant (Resident, Westmont, New Jersey Office)
Frances Wang-Deveney (Resident, Westmont, New Jersey)
Courtney E. Passin
Stephanie Victoria Shreibman
Megan Kochell D'Iorio (Resident, Wilmington, Delaware Office)
Megan Trocki Mantzavinos (Resident, Wilmington, Delaware Office)
Toni Anderson Moore
Natalie M. Nugent
Frank Gattuso
Michael A. Ring (Resident, Westmont, New Jersey Office)
Ann M. Madden (Not admitted in PA)
Matthew J. Zamites
Salvatore A. Clemente

LEGAL SUPPORT PERSONNEL

PARALEGALS

Gregory P. Sabo
Elisa LaRosa
Frances P. Rossi
Heather Feenan
Jerry Ezekiel
Steven Randisi
Sharon Williams
Melanie Gaskins

For full biographical listings, see the Martindale-Hubbell Law Directory

McCORMICK & PRIORE, P.C. (AV)

One Penn Square West, 30 S. 15th Street, Suite 1500, 19102
Telephone: 215-972-0161
Fax: 215-972-5580
Email: mccormick5@aol.com
Marlton, New Jersey Office: One Greentree Centre, Suite 201, 08053.
Telephone: 609-988-5452.
Fax: 609-596-8359.

David M. McCormick
Philip D. Priore
Stephen M. McManus

OF COUNSEL

Harry A. Short, Jr.

Wendy L. Schmidt-Levin
H. Joseph Byron
Michelle Nick Rossi
Christina A. Toriello
Jill Schneider
John P. Lock

LEGAL SUPPORT PERSONNEL

Deborah Stefan
Jane Coley

For full biographical listings, see the Martindale-Hubbell Law Directory

MYLOTTE, DAVID & FITZPATRICK (AV)

7 Penn Center, 1635 Market Street, 9th Floor, 19103
Telephone: 215-751-9450
Facsimile: 215-751-9918
Email: mylottedav@aol.com *URL:* http://www.mylottedavid.com
Voorhees, New Jersey Office: 306 W. Somerdale Road.
Telephone: 609-427-4411.
Wilkes-Barre, Pennsylvania Office: Suite 200, 15 Public Square.
Telephone: 570-824-7739.
Hazleton, Pennsylvania Office: 67 North Church Street.
Telephone: 570-454-5575.

(See Next Column)

MYLOTTE, DAVID & FITZPATRICK, *Philadelphia—Continued*

MEMBERS OF FIRM

Joseph P. Mylotte (1939-1991)
Edward J. David
Charles A. Fitzpatrick, III
John A. Fitzpatrick
Robert J. Gillespie, Jr. (Resident, Wilkes-Barre Office)
John C. Janos
Joseph R. Ferdinand (Resident, Hazleton Office)
Daniel A. Miscavige (Resident, Hazleton Office)
William C. McGovern
Bruce K. Anders (Resident, Wilkes-Barre Office)
Martin G. Malloy
Fredrick C. Hanselmann
Christine F. McCafferty
Joseph R. Baranko, Jr. (Resident, Hazleton Office)
Patrice S. O'Brien
Arthur B. Keppel
M. Susan Riley
Edward J. McCarthy
Brian J. Durkin
Kathleen Daily Mock
Peter P. O'Donnell (Resident, Wilkes-Barre Office)
Joseph Zola (Resident, Wilkes-Barre Office)
Brandon G. Johnson
James Hickey
Tyler Tomlinson
Adam D. Wilf
Justin P. McGlynn
James R. Scallion (Resident, Hazleton Office)
Christopher B. Slusser (Resident, Hazleton Office)
Helena M. Quinn
Michael G. Sabo
Sandra L. Jacques

Representative Clients: PENJERDEL Stores Mutual Assn.; Travelers Property & Casualty Co.; ABB C-E Services, Inc.; Lewis Environmental, Inc.; General Refactories, Co.

For full biographical listings, see the Martindale-Hubbell Law Directory

CLAYTON H. THOMAS, JR. (AV)

37th Floor, Bell Atlantic Tower Building, 1717 Arch Street, 19103-2793
Telephone: 215-994-5290
Fax: 215-994-5296

Benjamin Rose

For full biographical listings, see the Martindale-Hubbell Law Directory

WILBRAHAM, LAWLER & BUBA, A PROFESSIONAL CORPORATION (AV)

1818 Market Street, Suite 3100, 19103-3631
Telephone: 215-564-4141
Fax: 215-564-4385
Email: @wlbdeflaw.com
Haddonfield, New Jersey Office: 24 Kings Highway West.
Telephone: 856-795-4422.
Fax: 856-795-4699.
Wilmington, Delaware Office: Stoney Batter Office Building, 5301 Limestone Road, Suite 221.
Telephone: 302-234-8217.
Fax: 302-234-8218.

Edward J. Wilbraham
Robert B. Lawler
Barbara J. Buba
Michael J. Block

R. Erick Chizmar
Kevin J. Maginnis
InSook Kim
Sandra D. Terry-Crawford
John S. Howarth
David M. Maselli
Renee E. Berger
Edward T. Finch
Sean P. Buggy

OF COUNSEL

Walter J. Timby, Jr.
Daniel J. Allan

Representative Clients: GAF Corporation; Armstrong World Industries, Inc.; U.S. Gypsum Company; Georgia-Pacific Corporation; ARCO; Shell; Royal; AIG; Chubb; Keystone.

For full biographical listings, see the Martindale-Hubbell Law Directory

SOUTH CAROLINA

*CHARLESTON,** Charleston Co.

LEATH, BOUCH & CRAWFORD, L.L.P. (AV)

134 Meeting Street, P.O. Box 59, 29402-0059
Telephone: 843-937-8811
Fax: 843-937-0606
Columbia, South Carolina Office: 221 Pickens Street (29205), P.O. Box 5066, 29250.
Telephone: 803-254-0048.
Facsimile: 803-254-0063.

MEMBERS OF FIRM

W. Jefferson Leath, Jr.
Timothy W. Bouch
B. Lindsay Crawford, III

(See Next Column)

Linda J. Amason
Elizabeth Rice Polk (Resident, Columbia Office)

For full biographical listings, see the Martindale-Hubbell Law Directory

TENNESSEE

*MEMPHIS,** Shelby Co.

SMITH, SABBATINI & MCLEARY, PLLC (AV)

100 Peabody Place Suite 1250, 38103
Telephone: 901-312-5555
Fax: 901-312-5667
Mailing Address: P.O. Box 3582, Memphis, TN, 38173
URL: http://www.smithlawetal.com

Gary K. Smith
Robert L. Sabbatini
Harold W. McLeary, Jr.
William D. Domico
James F. Kyle
James T. McColgan, III
G. Edward Coleman, III
Bryant C. Witt

Representative Clients: Premier RRG Insurance; Illinois Central Railroad; Medical Assurance; Albertson's, Inc.; Med. Marc (Chiro Co.); Medical Protective Co.; Methodist Health Systems; Hartford Insurance Co.; Sentry Insurance; State Farm Insurance.

For full biographical listings, see the Martindale-Hubbell Law Directory

TEXAS

*AUSTIN,** Travis Co.

THOMPSON & KNIGHT L.L.P. (AV)

(Attorneys and Counselors)
1200 San Jacinto Center, 98 San Jacinto Boulevard, 78701
Telephone: 512-469-6100
Telecopy: 512-469-6180
URL: http://www.tklaw.com
Dallas, Texas Office: 1700 Pacific Avenue, Suite 3300, 75201.
Telephone: 214-969-1700.
Telecopy: 512-969-1751.
Telex: 732298.
Fort Worth, Texas Office: 801 Cherry Street, Suite 1600, 76102.
Telephone: 817-347-1700.
Telecopy: 817-347-1799.
Houston, Texas Office: Thompson Knight Brown Parker & Leahy L.L.P., 1200 Smith Street, Suite 3600, 77002-4595.
Telephone: 713-654-8111.
Telecopier: 713-654-1871.
San Pedro Garza Garcia, Nuevo León, Mexico Office: Edificio Losoles PD-4, Av. Lázaro Cárdenas No. 2400 Pte., C.P. 66220.
Telephone: (52-8) 363-0096.
Telecopy: (52-8) 363-3067.

PARTNERS

Eugene W. Brees, II
Frank L. Hill

For Complete List of Firm Personnel, See General Section

For full biographical listings, see the Martindale-Hubbell Law Directory

*CENTER,** Shelby Co.

FAIRCHILD, PRICE, THOMAS, HALEY & WILLINGHAM, L.L.P. (AV)

413 Shelbyville Street, P.O. Drawer 1719, 75935
Telephone: 409-598-2981
Fax: 409-598-7712
Email: wmthomas@fpthw.com
Nacogdoches, Texas Office: 1801 North Street, P. O. Box 631668, 75963-1668.
Telephone: 409-569-2327.
Fax: 409-569-7932. E-Mail: chaley@fpthw.com
Houston, Texas Office: 440 Louisiana Street, Suite 2110, 77002-4205.
Telephone: 713-426-1700.
Fax: 713-426-1717. E-Mail: mwillingham@fpthw.com

MEMBERS OF FIRM

John L. Price
W. Miller Thomas
C. Victor Haley
R. Mark Willingham
Ryan A. Beason (Resident at Houston Office)
Travis P. Clardy
David J. Fisher
Clayton H. Haley
Russell R. Smith
James A. Payne, Jr.

OF COUNSEL

Robert L. Fairchild

(See Next Column)

FAIRCHILD, PRICE, THOMAS, HALEY & WILLINGHAM L.L.P.—*Continued*

ASSOCIATES

David Edward Ash
Campbell Cox
Jefferson B. Davis
Thomas L. Cougill
Jeffrey Pierce Fultz
Matthew D. Mettauer

Representative Clients: AIG; Chubb Group of Insurance Companies; Continental National American Group (CNA); Fireman's Fund Insurance Company; Kemper Insurance Companies; Liberty Mutual Insurance Company; St. Paul Insurance Company.

For full biographical listings, see the Martindale-Hubbell Law Directory

*DALLAS,** Dallas Co.

THOMPSON & KNIGHT L.L.P. (AV)

(Attorneys and Counselors)
1700 Pacific Avenue Suite 3300, 75201
Telephone: 214-969-1700
Telecopy: 214-969-1751
Telex: 732 298
URL: http://www.tklaw.com
Austin, Texas Office: 1200 San Jacinto Center, 98 San Jacinto Boulevard, 78701.
Telephone: 512-469-6100.
Telecopy: 512-469-6180.
Fort Worth, Texas Office: 801 Cherry Street, Suite 1600, 76102.
Telephone: 817-347-1700.
Telecopy: 817-347-1799.
Houston, Texas Office: Thompson Knight Brown Parker & Leahy L.L.P., 1200 Smith Street, Suite 3600, 77002-4595.
Telephone: 713-654-8111.
Telecopier: 713-654-1871.
San Pedro Garza Garcia, Nuevo León, Mexico Office: Edificio Losoles PD-4, Av. Lázaro Cárdenas No. 2400 Pte., C.P. 66220.
Telephone: (52-8) 363-0096.
Telecopy: (52-8) 363-3067.

PARTNERS

G. Luke Ashley
P. Jefferson Ballew
Cheryl E. Diaz
Stephen S. Livingston
Joseph S. Pevsner
Stephen C. Schoettmer
Molly Steele
Dawn Marie Wright

For Complete List of Firm Personnel, See General Section

For full biographical listings, see the Martindale-Hubbell Law Directory

*FORT WORTH,** Tarrant Co.

DECKER, JONES, MCMACKIN, MCCLANE, HALL & BATES, A PROFESSIONAL CORPORATION (AV)

2500 Bank One Tower, 500 Throckmorton Street, 76102-3812
Telephone: 817-336-2400; Metro: 817-429-5260
Fax: 817-332-3043; 336-2181
Email: email@deckerjones.com *URL:* http://www.deckerjones.com

Daniel L. Bates
Robert W. Decker
Mark S. Dugan
Janet L. Hahn
Randy J. Hall
Raymond B. Kelly, III
John B. McClane
John W. McMackin
Charles B. Milliken
Gary M. Moates
Bradley H. Rice
Jeffrey W. Storie
James L. Stripling
Brian K. Yost
Tamera H. Bennett
Arthur F. Zobal
Geoffrey A. Mantooth

Representative Clients: Employers Insurance of Texas; American International Group; Medical Protective Co.; Redman Homes, Inc.; Liberty Mutual Insurance; Martin-Sprocket and Gear, Inc.; Williamson-Dickie Manufacturing Co.; Harbison-Fischer Manufacturing Co.; Royal Sun Alliance; Champion Homebuilders.

For full biographical listings, see the Martindale-Hubbell Law Directory

*HOUSTON,** Harris Co.

BURROW & PARROTT, L.L.P. (AV)

A Registered Limited Liability Partnership
3500 Chevron Tower, 1301 McKinney, 77010-3092
Telephone: 713-222-6333
Fax: 713-650-6333
Email: bpfirm@bpcd.com *URL:* http://www.lawyers.com/burrowlaw

David H. Burrow
Alice Oliver-Parrott

Philip Brashier
Randall R. Smidt

OF COUNSEL

Robert H. Walker

For full biographical listings, see the Martindale-Hubbell Law Directory

DAVIS, ORETSKY & GUILFOYLE, P.C. (AV)

1415 Louisiana, Suite 4200, 77002
Telephone: 713-659-1010
Facsimile: 713-659-1122
Email: doglawfirm@dog.pc *URL:* http://www.dogpc.com
Affiliated Law Firm: Wommack Law Firm, P.C., 7 West Way Court, Suite A, P.O. Box 420, Lake Jackson, Texas 77566.
Telephone: 409-297-9755. Houston
Telephone: 713-355-5737.
Fax: 409-297-9761. Email: wdm-george@computron.net.

Tom M. Davis, Jr.
Andrew S. Oretsky
Matthew C. Guilfoyle
Juliann H. Panagos
Curt M. Langley
George T. Wommack, Jr.
David C. Redford

M. Lucille Anderson
Kristin Bauer
Robert M. Browning
Paige Black Larrabee
Norman W. Peters, Jr.
Jonathan L. Phillips
William R. Pilat

For full biographical listings, see the Martindale-Hubbell Law Directory

FAIRCHILD, PRICE, THOMAS, HALEY & WILLINGHAM, L.L.P. (AV)

440 Louisiana Street, Suite 2110, 77002-4205
Telephone: 713-426-1700
Fax: 713-426-1717.
Email: mwillingham@fpthw.com
Center, Texas Office: 413 Shelbyville Street, P.O. Drawer 1719, 75935.
Telephone: 409-598-2981.
Fax: 409-598-7712. E-Mail: wmthomas@fpthw.com
Nacogdoches, Texas Office: 1801 North Street, P.O. Box 631668, 75963-1668.
Telephone: 409-569-2327.
Fax: 409-569-7932. E-Mail: chaley@fpthw.com

John L. Price
W. Miller Thomas
C. Victor Haley
R. Mark Willingham
Travis P. Clardy
David J. Fisher
Clayton H. Haley
Russell R. Smith
Ryan A. Beason

OF COUNSEL

Robert L. Fairchild

James A. Payne, Jr.
David Edward Ash
Campbell Cox
Jefferson B. Davis
Thomas L. Cougill
Jeffrey Pierce Fultz
Matthew D. Mettauer

Representative Clients: AIG; Chubb Group of Insurance Companies; Continental National American Group (CNA); Fireman's Fund Insurance Company; Kemper Insurance Companies; Liberty Mutual Insurance Company; St. Paul Insurance Company.

For full biographical listings, see the Martindale-Hubbell Law Directory

JOHNSON, FERGUSON & PIPKIN (AV)

4900 Woodway, Suite 1100, 77056
Telephone: 713-961-3730
Facsimile: 713-961-5438
Email: Johnsoned@johnsonassoc.com

Ned W. Johnson
Richard Y. Ferguson
John E. Pipkin
Clinton E. Phillips
William C. Nantz
Elizabeth Barnes Phillips
Catherine A. Dickerson

OF COUNSEL

James E. Brown, Jr.
Annelie Menke

For full biographical listings, see the Martindale-Hubbell Law Directory

RAMSEY & MURRAY, A PROFESSIONAL CORPORATION (AV)

10000 Memorial Drive, Suite 700, 77024-3412
Telephone: 713-613-5400
Fax: 713-613-5414

Ben Ramsey
John A. Murray, Jr.
Russell J. Ramsey
Mark Ramsey
Curtis D. Collette
Michael Stout Wright
Rick McRory

Joseph W. Gagnon
R. Russell Hollenbeck
Adrian V. Villacorta
Brenda Renee Ferguson

Representative Clients: Great Central Insurance Co.; Republic Insurance Co.

For full biographical listings, see the Martindale-Hubbell Law Directory

Houston—Continued

THOMPSON KNIGHT BROWN PARKER & LEAHY L.L.P. (AV)

A Registered Limited Liability Partnership including Professional Corporations
(Attorneys and Counselors)
1200 Smith Street, Suite 3600, 77002-4595
Telephone: 713-654-8111
Telecopier: 713-654-1871
URL: http://www.tklaw.com
Dallas, Texas Office: Thompson & Knight L.L.P., 1700 Pacific Avenue, Suite 3300, 75201.
Telephone: 214-969-1700.
Telecopy: 214-969-1751.
Telex: 732298.
Austin, Texas Office: Thompson & Knight L.L.P., 1200 San Jacinto Center, 98 San Jacinto Boulevard, 78701.
Telephone: 512-469-6100.
Telecopy: 512-469-6180.
Fort Worth, Texas Office: Thompson & Knight L.L.P., 801 Cherry Street, Suite 1600, 76102.
Telephone: 817-347-1700.
Telecopy: 817-347-1799.
San Pedro Garza Garcia, Nuevo León, Mexico Office: Thompson & Knight L.L.P., Edificio Losoles PD-4, Av. Lázaro Cárdenas No. 2400 PTE., C.P. 66220.
Telephone: (52-8) 363-0096.
Telecopy: (52-8) 363-3067.

PARTNERS

Gregory S. Meece
David R. Noteware

For Complete List of Firm Personnel, See General Section

For full biographical listings, see the Martindale-Hubbell Law Directory

*LONGVIEW,** Gregg Co.

ERSKINE & MCMAHON, L.L.P. (AV)

426 North Center Street, P.O. Box 3485, 75606
Telephone: 903-757-8435
1-800-544-5479
Fax: 903-757-9429
Email: brucek@erskine-mcmahon.com *URL:* http://www.lawyers.com/erskine-mcmahon

MEMBERS OF FIRM

Blake C. Erskine
Mark P. McMahon

Kathy D. Colvin
Dennis M. McKinney

For full biographical listings, see the Martindale-Hubbell Law Directory

*NACOGDOCHES,** Nacogdoches Co.

FAIRCHILD, PRICE, THOMAS, HALEY & WILLINGHAM, L.L.P. (AV)

1801 North Street, P.O. Box 631668, 75963-1668
Telephone: 409-569-2327
Fax: 409-569-7932.
Email: chaley@fpthw.com
Center, Texas Office: 413 Shelbyville Street, P.O. Drawer 1719, 75935.
Telephone: 409-598-2981.
Fax: 409-598-7712. E-Mail: wmthomas@fpthw.com
Houston, Texas Office: 440 Louisiana Street, Suite 2110, 77002-4205.
Telephone: 713-426-1700.
Fax: 713-426-1717. E-Mail: mwillingham@fpthw.com

John L. Price
W. Miller Thomas
C. Victor Haley
R. Mark Willingham
Travis P. Clardy
David J. Fisher
Clayton H. Haley
Russell R. Smith
Ryan A. Beason

OF COUNSEL

Robert L. Fairchild

James A. Payne, Jr.
David Edward Ash
Campbell Cox
Jefferson B. Davis
Thomas L. Cougill
Jeffrey Pierce Fultz
Matthew D. Mettauer

Representative Clients: AIG; Chubb Group of Insurance Companies; Continental National American Group (CNA); Fireman's Fund Insurance Company; Kemper Insurance Companies; Liberty Mutual Insurance Company; St. Paul Insurance Company.

For full biographical listings, see the Martindale-Hubbell Law Directory

*SAN ANTONIO,** Bexar Co.

O'CONNELL, BENJAMIN & COGHLAN, L.L.P. (AV)

153 Treeline Park, Suite 200, 78209
Telephone: 210-824-0009
Fax: 210-824-9429
Email: obcllp@oconben.com

Keith B. O'Connell
David P. Benjamin
G. Thomas Coghlan
Ernest F. Avery
Les Katona, Jr.
Dan Vana

Gayla S. Corley
Cathrin J. Martinez

For full biographical listings, see the Martindale-Hubbell Law Directory

UTAH

*SALT LAKE CITY,** Salt Lake Co.

VAN COTT, BAGLEY, CORNWALL & MCCARTHY, A PROFESSIONAL CORPORATION (AV)

50 South Main Street, Suite 1600, P.O. Box 45340, 84145-0340
Telephone: 801-532-3333
Telecopier: 801-534-0058
Email: info@vancott.com *URL:* http://www.vancott.com
Ogden, Utah Office: 2404 Washington Boulevard, Suite 900.
Telephone: 801-394-5783.
Park City, Utah Office: 2200 Park Avenue, Suite C200-A.
Telephone: 435-649-3889.

Jeremy M. Hoffman
H. Michael Keller
Kenneth W. Yeates

Justin Toth (Not admitted in UT)

For Complete List of Firm Personnel, See General Section

For full biographical listings, see the Martindale-Hubbell Law Directory

WEST VIRGINIA

HUNTINGTON, Cabell & Wayne Cos.

BAKER, LANCIANESE, CAMPBELL & CONATY (AV)

The River Tower, 1108 Third Avenue, Suite 300, 25701-1578
Telephone: 304-522-6906
Facsimile: 304-522-6910
Email: BLCC@BLCCLAW.COM *URL:* http://www.BLCCLAW.COM
Washington, D.C. Office: 1090 Vermont Avenue, N.W. Suite 800.
Telephone: 202-966-1500.
Fax: 202-966-7075. E-Mail: BLCC@BLCCLAW.COM.
Lexington, Kentucky Office: 2265 Harrodsburg Road, Suite 200, 40504-3517.
Telephone: 606-278-0297.
Fax: 206-278-0334. E-Mail: BLCC@BLCCLAW.COM.

Roy D. Baker, Jr.
Richard L. Lancianese
David L. Campbell
Brian P. Conaty
Janice P. Epperly

OF COUNSEL

Margaret M. Brizzolara (Not admitted in WV)

For full biographical listings, see the Martindale-Hubbell Law Directory

CANADA
BRITISH COLUMBIA

*VANCOUVER,** Vancouver Co.

SINGLETON URQUHART (AV)

1200 - 1125 Howe Street, V6Z 2K8
Telephone: 604-682-7474
Fax: 604-682-1283
Email: reception@singleton.com *URL:* http://www.singleton.com

John R. Singleton, Q.C.
Derek A. Brindle
Jeffery A. Hand
C. L. (Kate) Mclean

Representative Clients: ENCON Insurance Managers Inc.; Commonwealth Insurance Company; Allianz Canada; Municipal Insurance Association.

(See Next Column)

SINGLETON URQUHART—*Continued*

For Complete List of Firm Personnel, See General Section

For full biographical listings, see the Martindale-Hubbell Law Directory

CANADA
NOVA SCOTIA

*HALIFAX,** Regional Munic. of Halifax

McINNES COOPER (AV)

Barristers, Solicitors & Trade Mark Agents
Summit Place, 1601 Lower Water Street, P.O. Box 730, B3J 2V1
Telephone: 902-425-6500
Fax: 902-425-6350
Email: mcrhfx@mcrlaw.com *URL:* http://www.mcrlaw.com
St. John's, Newfoundland Office: Baine Johnston Centre, 5th Floor, 10 Fort William Place, P.O. Box 5939, A1C 5X4.
Telephone: 709-722-8735.
Telecopier: 709-722-1763. Email: mcrsj@mcrlaw.com.
Moncton, New Brunswick Office: Place Moncton Place, 655 Main Street, P.O. Box 1368, E1C 8T6.
Telephone: 506-857-8970.
Fax: 506-857-4095. Email: mcrmctn@mcrlaw.com.
Charlottetown, Prince Edward Island Office: BDC Place, Suite 620, 119 Kent Street, C1A 1N3.
Telephone: 902-368-8473.
Fax: 902-368-8346. Email: mcrpei@mcrlaw.com.
Fredericton, New Brunswick Office: Suite 600, 570 Queen Street, P.O. Box 610.
Telephone: 506-458-8572.
Fax: 506-458-9903. Email: mcrfton@mcrlaw.com.

PARTNER

George T. H. Cooper, Q.C.

For Complete List of Firm Personnel, See General Section

For full biographical listings, see the Martindale-Hubbell Law Directory

TRADEMARK, COPYRIGHT AND UNFAIR COMPETITION

(See also listings under Patent, Trademark, Copyright and Unfair Competition)

MISSOURI

ST. LOUIS, (Independent City)

DANKENBRING GREIMAN OSTERHOLT & HOFFMANN, P.C. (AV)

Clayton Centre, Fifth Floor, 120 S. Central Avenue, 63105
Telephone: 314-863-7733
Fax: 314-862-4656
URL: http://www.dgohlaw.com

James R. Dankenbring
Gerald Phillip Greiman
Francis E. Pennington, III

James R. Loranger
Michael A. Thorne

For full biographical listings, see the Martindale-Hubbell Law Directory

MONTANA

*BILLINGS,** Yellowstone Co.

CROWLEY, HAUGHEY, HANSON, TOOLE & DIETRICH, P.L.L.P. (AV)

500 Transwestern II, 490 North 31st Street, P.O. Box 2529, 59103
Telephone: 406-252-3441
Fax: 406-259-4159
Email: crowley@crowleylaw.com
Helena, Montana Office: IBM Building, 100 North Park Avenue, Suite 300, 59601.
Telephone: 406-449-4165.
Fax: 406-449-5149.
Kalispell, Montana Office: 431 1st Avenue West, 59901.
Telephone: 406-752-6644.
Fax: 406-752-5108.
Williston, North Dakota Office: 113 East Broadway, 58801.
Telephone: 701-572-2200.
Fax: 701-572-7072.

MEMBER OF FIRM

Mary Scrim Dyre (Resident, Kalispell, Montana Office)

Representative Clients: Montana Power Co.; First Interstate Bank of Commerce; MDU Resources Group, Inc.; Chevron U.S.A., Inc.; Noranda Minerals Corp.; United Parcel Service.
Insurance Clients: Farmers Insurance Group; New York Life Insurance Co.

For Complete List of Firm Personnel, See General Section

For full biographical listings, see the Martindale-Hubbell Law Directory

NEW JERSEY

*HACKENSACK,** Bergen Co.

KLAUBER & JACKSON (AV)

Continental Plaza, 411 Hackensack Avenue, 07601
Telephone: 201-487-5800
Telex: 133521
Fax: 201-343-1684; 343-7544
Email: kjiplaw@webspan.net
Email: 6261210@mcimail.com

MEMBER OF FIRM

David A. Jackson

ASSOCIATES

Michael D. Davis (Not admitted in NJ)
Donald J. Cox, Jr. (Not admitted in NJ)

OF COUNSEL

Stefan J. Klauber
Jack Matalon
Roger M. Rathbun

LEGAL SUPPORT PERSONNEL

Christine E. Dietzel (Patent Agent)
Michael A. Yamin (Patent Agent)

For full biographical listings, see the Martindale-Hubbell Law Directory

MOORESTOWN, Burlington Co.

ESTELLA S. GOLD (AV)

Blason II, 505 South Lenola Road, 08057
Telephone: 609-234-1004
Telecopier: 609-234-7836
Email: esglaw@aol.com

Representative Clients: South Jersey Processing, Inc.; OM Assn., Inc.

For full biographical listings, see the Martindale-Hubbell Law Directory

*NEWARK,** Essex Co.

McCARTER & ENGLISH, LLP (AV)

Four Gateway Center, 100 Mulberry Street, P.O. Box 652, 07101-0652
Telephone: 973-622-4444
Telecopier: 973-624-7070
URL: http://www.mccarter.com
Cherry Hill, New Jersey Office: 1820 Chapel Avenue West, Suite 380.
Telephone: 609-662-8444.
Telecopier: 609-662-6203.
New York, New York Office: Suite 2247, One World Trade Center.
Telephone: 212-466-9018.
Telecopier: 212-432-6568.
Boca Raton, Florida Office: 2255 Glades Road, Suite 319-A.
Telephone: 561-994-6262.
Telecopier: 561-241-0798.
Wilmington, Delaware Office: Mellon Bank Center, 919 Market Street.
Telephone: 302-654-8010.
Telecopier: 302-654-0795.
Philadelphia, Pennsylvania Office: One Commerce Square, 2005 Market Street, Suite 3600.
Telephone: 215-557-7700.
Telecopier: 215-557-6544.

MEMBERS OF FIRM

Charles R. Merrill
Roslyn S. Harrison
William J. Heller
Myrna L. Wigod

COUNSEL

Robert W. Smith

For Complete List of Firm Personnel, See General Section

For full biographical listings, see the Martindale-Hubbell Law Directory

PRINCETON, Mercer Co.

MATHEWS, COLLINS, SHEPHERD & GOULD, A PROFESSIONAL CORPORATION (AV)

100 Thanet Circle Suite 306, 08540
Telephone: 609-924-8555
Fax: 609-924-3036
Telex: 642948
Email: Attorneys@MathewsLaw.Com

H. Hume Mathews (1911-1989)
Bruce M. Collins
Robert G. Shepherd
Ronald Gould
Diane Dunn McKay
Glen E. Books
Brooks R. Bruneau
Anastasia P. Winslow
Todd A. Denys
Dr. Charles Joseph Brumlik (Not admitted in NJ)

Representative Clients: Novartis Corp.; Medtronic, Inc.; Stiefel Laboratories, Inc.; Celgene Corp.; Princeton University; Summit Bank; Church & Dwight, Inc.; Rutgers University; Genzyme.

For full biographical listings, see the Martindale-Hubbell Law Directory

WEST ORANGE, Essex Co.

ALPERT, BUTLER & SANDERS, P.C. (AV)

The Alpert Professional Building, 449 Mount Pleasant Avenue, 07052
Telephone: 973-325-1188
Fax: 973-325-3399
Email: mailbox@abslaw.com *URL:* http://www.abslaw.com
New York, New York Office: 509 Madison Avenue.
Telephone: 212-758-6958.
Fax: 212-758-2817.

Clark E. Alpert
David N. Butler
William D. Sanders

OF COUNSEL

Martin L. Bearg
Ted M. Rosen (Not admitted in NJ)

Elliot L. Lewis
Matthew J. Rice

LEGAL SUPPORT PERSONNEL

PARALEGAL

Robin S. Karpel

For full biographical listings, see the Martindale-Hubbell Law Directory

NEW YORK

*NEW YORK,** New York Co.

BAKER BOTTS L.L.P. (AV)

599 Lexington Avenue, 10022-6030 and 30 Rockefeller Plaza, 10112-0228
Telephone: 212-705-5000
Fax: 212-705-5125 (599 Lexington Ave.)
Fax: 212-705-5020 (30 Rockeffeller Plaza)
Email: postmaster@bakerbotts.com *URL:* http://www.bakerbotts.com
Washington, D.C. Office: The Warner, 1299 Pennsylvania Avenue, N.W.
Telephone: 202-639-7700.
Austin, Texas Office: 1600 San Jacinto Center, 98 San Jacinto Boulevard.
Telephone: 512-322-2500.
Dallas, Texas Office: 2001 Ross Avenue.
Telephone: 214-953-6500.
Houston, Texas Office: One Shell Plaza, 910 Louisiana.
Telephone: 713-229-1234.
Moscow, Russia Office: 10 ul. Bolshaya Dimitrovka (formerly ul. Pushkinskaya), 103031.
Telephone: 7095/921-5300 (Local); 7095/929-7070 (International).
London, England Office: 45 Ludgate Hill.
Telephone: 0171-778-1400 (Local); 011-44-171-778-1400.
Baku, Azerbaijan Office: 6-10 Vagif Mustafa-zadeh Street, Third Floor, Icheri Sheher, 370004.
Telephone: 994-12-97-63-88 (Local); 011-994-12-97-63-88 (International).
Fax: 994-12-97-63-91 (Local); 011-994-12-97-63-61 (International).

MEMBERS OF FIRM

Richard G. Berkley
Gary M. Butter
Richard S. Clark
Doreen Leavens Costa
Marta E. Delsignore
Russell H. Falconer
John A. Fogarty, Jr.
Bradley B. Geist
Lisa B. Kole
James J. Maune
John D. Murnane
Thomas R. Nesbitt, Jr.
Robert Neuner
Robert C. Scheinfeld
Rochelle K. Seide
Louis S. Sorell
Henry Tang

RETIRED FIRM MEMBERS

Frederick C. Carver
Dana M. Raymond
Arthur S. Tenser

OF COUNSEL

Joseph D. Garon
Ronald B. Hildreth
Francis J. Hone

ASSOCIATES

Paul D. Ackerman
Richard L. Blaylock
Anthony Giaccio
Robert L. Greenfeld
Steven R. Gustavson
Jeanne M. Hamburg
Samuel SungMok Lee (Not admitted in NY)
Dr. Janet M. MacLeod
Paul A. Ragusa
Paul J. Reilly
Neil P. Sirota
David W. Whealan
Karen Wuertz

For Complete List of Firm Personnel, See General Section

For full biographical listings, see the Martindale-Hubbell Law Directory

COBRIN & GITTES (AV)

750 Lexington Avenue, 10022
Telephone: 212-486-4000
Telecopier: 212-486-4007
Email: cgpats@ix.netcom.com

Peter T. Cobrin
Marvin S. Gittes
Richard M. Lehrer
David W. Denenberg

Robert J. Hess
Michael A. Adler
Gerald J. Cechony (Not admitted in NY)
Oren J. Warshavsky
Clyde Alvin Shuman
Lawrence E. Russ

Representative Clients: Northern Telecom, Inc.; DataPoint Corporation; Magnivision, Inc.; Atico; Global Direct Mail Corporation; MW; Oxigene, Inc.; Horphag Research, LTD.

For full biographical listings, see the Martindale-Hubbell Law Directory

COLUCCI & UMANS (AV)

Manhattan Tower, 101 East 52nd Street, 10022
Telephone: 212-935-5700
Facsimile: 212-935-5728
Telex: 661503 WUI
Email: emial@colucci-umans.com
Westchester County, Scarsdale, New York Office: 670 White Plains Road, Scarsdale.
Telephone: 914-472-1500.
Facsimile: 914-472-1551.

MEMBERS OF FIRM

Frank J. Colucci
Courtney Wilson Monahan

(See Next Column)

Thomas A. Kain
Raymond J. Glynn
W. Brant Mossop
Susan B. Jacobson
Gregory J. Colucci (Resident, Scarsdale Office)
Richard P. Jacobson
David M. Dahan
Katherine Beecher Carlburg
Kathleen M. McGann
Renée L. Duff (Resident, Scarsdale Office)

OF COUNSEL

Angelo Notaro

For full biographical listings, see the Martindale-Hubbell Law Directory

COOPER & DUNHAM LLP (AV)

1185 Avenue of the Americas, 10036
Telephone: 212-278-0400
Fax: 212-391-0525
Email: counsel@cooperdunham.com *URL:* http://www.cooperdunham.com

MEMBERS OF FIRM

Christopher C. Dunham
Norman H. Zivin
John P. White
William E. Pelton
Robert D. Katz
Peter J. Phillips
Wendy E. Miller
Ivan S. Kavrukov
Peter D. Murray
Jay H. Maioli
Robert B. G. Horowitz
Donald S. Dowden
Donna A. Tobin
Richard S. Milner
Albert Wai-Kit Chan

ASSOCIATES

Robert T. Maldonado
Elizabeth M. Wieckowski
Pedro C. Fernandez
Todd W. Evans
Michael F. Morano
Spencer H. Schneider
Paul Teng
Richard F. Jaworski
Gary J. Gershik
William Y. Lee (Not admitted in NY)
Raymond A. DiPerna

OF COUNSEL

Gerald W. Griffin
John R. Garber

LEGAL SUPPORT PERSONNEL

SCIENTIFIC ADVISORS

Jane M. Love
Alan D. Miller

For full biographical listings, see the Martindale-Hubbell Law Directory

FROSS ZELNICK LEHRMAN & ZISSU, P.C. (AV)

866 United Nations Plaza, 10017
Telephone: 212-813-5900
Facsimile: 212-813-5901
Email: fzlz@frosszelnick.com

Alvin Fross
Ronald J. Lehrman
Stephen Bigger
Michael I. Davis
Roger L. Zissu
Marie V. Driscoll
Richard Z. Lehv
Carol F. Simkin
Margaret Frenkel Goldstein
David W. Ehrlich
Susan Upton Douglass
Janet L. Hoffman
Peter J. Silverman
Lawrence Eli Apolzon
Barbara A. Solomon
Lisa Schilit Pearson
Mark D. Engelmann
Glenn M. Mitchell
Martin B. Schwimmer
Nadine H. Parker
Andrew N. Fredbeck

OF COUNSEL

Allan Zelnick

COUNSEL

James D. Silberstein

Georges Nahitchevansky
Rose Auslander
Patrick T. Perkins
Diane Marcovici Plaut
J. Allison Strickland
Gregory P. Gulia
Craig S. Mende
Michelle Pia Foxman
Robert A. Becker
David A. Cohen
Ronald E. Wiggins
Martha H. Kimes
Jennifer J. Mathews
Tamar Niv

For full biographical listings, see the Martindale-Hubbell Law Directory

GRAHAM, CAMPAIGN P.C. (AV)

The Bar Building, 36 West 44th Street, 10036-8178
Telephone: 212-354-5650
Cable Address: "Forbland"
Telex: 6502048313 MCI UW
MCI Mail: 204-8313
Telecopier: 212-354-6354
Email: gracam@aol.com *URL:* http://www.lawyers.com/trademarks

Andrew J. Graham (1911-1986)
William L. McGuire, Sr. (1926-1992)
H. John Campaign
John M. Keene
Charles H. Knull
Gail E. Nickols
William C. Wright

(See Next Column)

GRAHAM, CAMPAIGN P.C.—*Continued*

OF COUNSEL

Gerard H. Davis

For full biographical listings, see the Martindale-Hubbell Law Directory

JONES, DAY, REAVIS & POGUE (AV)

599 Lexington Avenue, 10022
Telephone: 212-326-3939
Telecopier: 212-755-7306
Email: counsel@jonesday.com *URL:* http://www.jonesday.com
In Atlanta, Georgia: 3500 SunTrust Plaza, 303 Peachtree Street.
Telephone: 404-521-3939.
Telecopier: 404-581-8330.
In Brussels, Belgium: Avenue Louise 480, 7th Floor, B-1050 Brussels.
Telephone: 32-2-645-14-11.
Telecopier: 32-2-645-14-45.
In Chicago, Illinois: 77 West Wacker.
Telephone: 312-782-3939.
Telecopier: 312-782-8585.
In Cleveland, Ohio: North Point, 901 Lakeside Avenue.
Telephone: 216-586-3939.
Telecopier: 216-579-0212.
In Columbus, Ohio: 1900 Huntington Center.
Telephone: 614-469-3939.
Telecopier: 614-461-4198.
In Dallas, Texas: 2727 North Harwood Street.
Telephone: 214-220-3939.
Telecopier: 214-969-5100.
In Frankfurt, Germany: Hochhaus am Park, Grüneburgweg 102, 60323 Frankfurt am Main.
Telephone: 49-69-9726-3939.
Telecopier: 49-69-9726-3993.
In Geneva, Switzerland: 20, rue de Candolle.
Telephone: 41-22-320-2339.
Telecopier: 41-22-320-1232.
In Hong Kong: 29th Floor, Entertainment Building, 30 Queen's Road Central.
Telephone: 852-2526-6895.
Telecopier: 852-2868-5871.
In Irvine, California: 5 Park Plaza, Suite 1100.
Telephone: 949-851-3939.
Telecopier: 949-553-7539.
In London, England: Bucklersbury House, 3 Queen Victoria Street.
Telephone: 44-20-7236-3939
Telecopier: 44-20-7236-1113.
In Los Angeles, California: 555 West Fifth Street, Suite 4600.
Telephone: 213-489-3939.
Telecopier: 213-243-2539.
In Paris, France: 120, rue du Faubourg Saint-Honoré.
Telephone: 33-1-56-59-39-39.
Telecopier: 33-1-56-59-39-38
In Pittsburgh, Pennsylvania: 500 Grant Street, 31st Floor.
Telephone: 412-391-3939.
Telecopier: 412-394-7959.
In Riyadh, Saudi Arabia: The International Law Firm (In Association with Jones, Day, Reavis & Pogue), Sulaymaniyah, Prince Mishari IBN, Abdulaziz Street, P.O. Box 22166.
Telephone: (966-1) 462-8866.
Telecopier: (966-1) 462-9001.
In Shanghai, China: 2805 Kerry Centre, 1515 Nanjing Road West.
Telephone: 86-21-5298-6568.
Telecopier: 86-21-5298-6569.
In Sydney, Australia: Governor Phillip Tower, Level 38, 1 Farrer Place.
Telephone: 61-2-9210-6921.
Telecopier: 61-2-9210-6926.
In Taipei, Taiwan: 8th Floor, 2 Tun Hwa South Road, Section 2.
Telephone: (886-2) 2704-6808.
Telecopier: (886-2) 2704-6791.
In Tokyo, Japan: Toranomon 45 Mori Building, 3rd Floor, 1-5, Toranomon 5-Chome, Minato-Ku, Tokyo 105, Japan.
Telephone: 81-3-3433-3939.
Telecopier: 81-3-5401-2725.
In Washington, D.C.: 51 Louisiana Avenue, N.W.
Telephone: 202-879-3939.
Telecopier: 202-626-1700.

MEMBER OF FIRM IN NEW YORK

Thomas V. Heyman

For Complete List of Firm Personnel, See General Section

For full biographical listings, see the Martindale-Hubbell Law Directory

LOEB & LOEB LLP (AV)

A Limited Liability Partnership including Professional Corporations
345 Park Avenue, 10154-0037
Telephone: 212-407-4000
Facsimile: 212-407-4990
Email: info@loeb.com *URL:* http://www.loeb.com
Los Angeles, California Office: Suite 1800, 1000 Wilshire Boulevard, 90017-2475.
Telephone: 213-688-3400.
Facsimile: 213-688-3460.
Century City (Los Angeles), California Office: Suite 2200, 10100 Santa Monica Boulevard, Los Angeles, 90067-4164.
Telephone: 310-282-2000.
Facsimile: 310-282-2192.
Nashville, Tennessee Office: 45 Music Square West, 37203-3205.
Telephone: 615-749-8300.
Facsimile: 615-749-8308.
Rome, Italy Office: Piazza Digione 1, 00197.
Telephone: 011-3906-808-8456.
Facsimile: 011-3906-808-8288.

MEMBERS OF FIRM

Kenneth B. Anderson
David H. Carlin
Marc Chamlin
William J. Marlow
Charles H. Miller
Terri J. Seligman
James D. Taylor
Michael P. Zweig

For Complete List of Firm Personnel, See General Section

For full biographical listings, see the Martindale-Hubbell Law Directory

MARSHALL LAW FIRM (AV)

1065 Avenue of the Americas, 10018
Telephone: 212-382-2044
Fax: 212-382-3610

Paul G. Marshall

ASSOCIATES

David E. Benjamin
Scott F. Brown
George T. Gilbert
Rebecca M. Heller
Francois Mobasser
Lawrence J. Studnicky, III

OF COUNSEL

Marilyn G. Haft

For full biographical listings, see the Martindale-Hubbell Law Directory

NIMS, HOWES, COLLISON, HANSEN & LACKERT (AV)

605 Third Avenue, Suite 3500, 10158
Telephone: 212-661-9700
Cable Address: "Nims"
Telex: 237665
Facsimile: 212-661-9213
Email: nims@nimslaw.com

MEMBERS OF FIRM

Oliver P. Howes, Jr.
William R. Hansen
Clark W. Lackert
Elizabeth Atkins
Thomas H. Curtin
Keith E. Sharkin
William J. Sapone

OF COUNSEL

Bert A. Collison
Karen P. Clancy
Irving N. Stein
August G. Maron, Jr.
Bruce J. Grossman
Robert P. Schwartz
Robert J. O'Hare
Robert E. Isner (1921-1993)

ASSOCIATES

Robert L. Powley
Edwin J. Lubin
Larry H. Tronco
Richard P. Georget

For full biographical listings, see the Martindale-Hubbell Law Directory

OTTERBOURG, STEINDLER, HOUSTON & ROSEN, P.C. (AV)

230 Park Avenue, 29th Floor, 10169
Telephone: 212-661-9100
Telecopier: 212-682-6104

GENERAL COUNSEL

Kurt J. Wolff

COUNSEL

Bernard Beitel

For Complete List of Firm Personnel, See General Section

For full biographical listings, see the Martindale-Hubbell Law Directory

New York—Continued

PENNIE & EDMONDS LLP (AV)

1155 Avenue of the Americas, 10036
Telephone: 212-790-9090
Facsimile: GI/GII/GIII (212) 869-9741
GIII (212) 869-8864
Email: pennie.com *URL:* http://www.pennie.com
Washington, D.C. Office: 1667 K Street, N.W.
Telephone: 202-496-4400.
Facsimile: 202-496-4444.
Palo Alto, California Office: 3300 Hillview Avenue.
Telephone: 650-493-4935.
Facsimile: 650-493-5556.

John C. Pennie (1858-1921)
Dean S. Edmonds (1879-1972)

MEMBERS OF FIRM

S. Leslie Misrock
Harry C. Jones, III
Berj A. Terzian
David Weild, III
Jonathan A. Marshall
Barry D. Rein
Stanton T. Lawrence, III
Charles E. Miller
Francis E. Morris
Gidon D. Stern
John J. Lauter
Brian M. Poissant
Brian D. Coggio
Charles E. McKenney
Philip T. Shannon
John M. Richardson
Rory J. Radding
Stephen J. Harbulak
Donald J. Goodell
James N. Palik
William G. Pecau
Joseph Diamante
Thomas E. Friebel
Laura A. Coruzzi
Jennifer Gordon
Jon R. Stark (Resident, Palo Alto, California Office)
James W. Dabney
Paul R. De Stefano (Resident, Palo Alto, California Office)
Allan A. Fanucci
Geraldine F. Baldwin
Victor N. Balancia
Peter D. Vogl
John J. Normile, Jr.
Catherine H. Stockell
Samuel B. Abrams
Thomas A. Canova
Steven I. Wallach
Jonathan E. Moskin
Adriane M. Antler
Paul J. Zegger (Resident, Washington, D.C. Office)
Edmond R. Bannon
Marcia H. Sundeen (Resident, Washington, D.C. Office)
Bruce J. Barker
Thomas G. Rowan
James G. Markey
Darren W. Saunders
Thomas D. Kohler (Resident, Palo Alto, California Office)
Scott D. Stimpson
William S. Galliani (Resident, Palo Alto, California Office)
Gary S. Williams (Resident, Palo Alto, California Office)
Ann L. Gisolfi
Scott B. Familant
Todd A. Wagner
Kelly D. Talcott

COUNSEL

Constance Golden
Ilene B. Tannen
Nancy A. Zoubek

ASSOCIATES

Wilma F. Triebwasser (Resident, Washington, D.C. Office)
Hailing Zhang
Mikhail Lotvin
Brian M. Rothery
Brian D. Siff
William J. Sipio
Alan Tenenbaum
F. Dominic Cerrito
Ronald M. Daignault
Jacqueline M. Lesser
Edward R. Gomez
Anthony M. Insogna
Joyce M. Ferraro
Garland T. Stephens
Michael J. Lyons (Resident, Palo Alto, California Office)
Maria E. Pasquale
Susan C. Shin
Troy R. Lester (Resident, Washington, D.C. Office)
Katharine E. Smith
Wendy A. Haller
Andrew J. Gray, IV (Resident, Palo Alto, California Office)
Carol M. Wilhelm
H.T. Than (Resident, Washington, D.C. Office)
Lester L. Levy (Resident, Palo Alto, California Office)
Bryan W. Butler (Resident, Palo Alto, California Office)
Gianni P. Servodidio
Kenneth L. Stein
John D. Garretson
Alan P. Force
Maria S. Kratzer
Karen G. Horowitz
Ognjan V. Shentov
Nongfan Zhu
Daniel Hansburg
Catharina Chin Eng
Stephen S. Rabinowitz
Nanda K. Alapati (Resident, Washington, D.C. Office)
Nathan P. Letts
Timothy E. DeMasi
Nikolaos Charles George
Carl P. Bretscher (Resident, Washington, D.C. Office)
Pablo Perhacs (Not admitted in NY)
Eric J. Fues (Resident, Washington, D.C. Office)
Jonathan L. Klein-Evans (Resident, Washington, D.C. Office)
Matthew E. Langer
Greg P. Roggin (Resident, Washington, D.C. Office)
Leo Merken
Kathleen Fowler (Resident, Palo Alto, California Office)
Lorri W. Jones (Resident, Washington, D.C. Office)
Nancy H. Lutz (Resident, Washington, D.C. Office)
Jeffrey A. Wolfson (Resident, Washington, D.C. Office)
Anne M. Coughlin
Caroline R. Clark
Margaret Bolce Brivanlou
Henry C. Lebowitz
Granetta M. Coleman (Resident, Washington, D.C. Office)
David R. Owens (Resident, Palo Alto, California Office)
Michèle A. Moser

(See Next Column)

ASSOCIATES (Continued)

Lavatus V. Powell
Steven D. Chin
Emil Bradley Gould (Resident, Washington, D.C. Office)
James S. McDonald (Resident, Palo Alto, California Office)
Andrew Sanders
George A. Senich
Scott Jacobson
John P. Mulgrew (Resident, Washington, D.C. Office)
Daniel L. Malone (Not admitted in NY)
Todd L. Krause
Philip H. Lee (Resident, Palo Alto, California Office)
Alexandra Haner
Brian T. Clarke (Resident, Palo Alto, California Office)
Peter L. Herridge (Not admitted in NY)
Claudia D.P. Zumbro
Ian Scott
Janet M. Skafar (Resident, Palo Alto, California Office)
Elizabeth S. Langston (Not admitted in NY)
Atulya Agarwal (Resident, Washington, D.C. Office)
Vivian S. Kuo (Resident, Washington, D.C. Office)
C. Edward Polk, Jr. (Resident, Washington, D.C. Office)
Anthony H. Kahng (Resident, Washington, D.C. Office)
Patrick M. Boucher
James A. DeFelice (Resident, Washington, D.C. Office)
Paul E. Dietze (Resident, Washington, D.C. Office)
Colleen M. Keegan (Not admitted in NY)
Lewis E. Hudnell III
Charles R. Richard (Resident, Washington, D.C. Office)
Steven D. Underwood
Keith A. Walter, Jr.
Gail H. Zarick
Julie M. Holloway (Resident, Palo Alto, California Office)
Serge Sira (Resident, Washington, D.C. Office)
Matthew J. Engle (Resident, Palo Alto, California Office)
Dion M. Bregman (Resident, Palo Alto, California Office)
Gary Zhang (Resident, Washington, D.C. Office)
Deborah J. Barnett
Margaret A. Pepper
Susie S. Cheng
Lawrence S. Graham
Youngtack Shim (Resident, Palo Alto, California Office)
Seth Alain Watkins (Resident, Washington, D.C. Office)
David Chan Lee (Resident, Washington, D.C. Office)
Ann M. Caviani Pease (Resident, Palo Alto, California Office)
Tracy L. Hurt (Resident, Palo Alto, California Office)
Birgit Millauer (Resident, Palo Alto, California Office)

For full biographical listings, see the Martindale-Hubbell Law Directory

PILIERO GOLDSTEIN JENKINS & SULLIVAN, LLP (AV)

292 Madison Avenue, 10017
Telephone: 212-213-8200
Fax: 212-685-2028
Email: lawyers@pgjhlaw.com *URL:* http://www.pgjhlaw.com
Carlstadt, New Jersey Office: One Palmer Terrace.
Telephone: 201-507-5157.
FAX: 201-507-5221.
Washington, D.C. Office: 888 17th Street, N.W., Suite 1100.
Telephone: 202-467-6991.
FAX: 202-467-6703.
San Francisco, California Office: 507 Howard Street, Suite 200.
Telephone: 415-281-3631.
Fax: 415-281-3630.

MEMBERS OF FIRM

Kimberlee S. Bogen
Edward J. Goldstein
Jon Mark Jenkins
Marc A. Lebowitz
Robert D. Piliero
George O. Richardson, III
Michael T. Sullivan

ASSOCIATES

Craig Avedisian
Rosemary G. Feit
Eric M. Kogan
Mariano Schwed

OF COUNSEL

Kenneth D. Arbeeny
Christopher P. Hall

For full biographical listings, see the Martindale-Hubbell Law Directory

SEIDMAN, SILVERMAN & SEIDMAN, P.C. (AV)

600 Third Avenue 33rd Floor, 10016-2001
Telephone: 212-922-1900

Irving P. Seidman
Lawrence H. Silverman
Brian William Seidman

Joseph M. Fein

For full biographical listings, see the Martindale-Hubbell Law Directory

SLADE & ASSOCIATES, P.C. (AV)

11 Vestry Street, 5th Floor, 10013
Telephone: 212-226-8787
Fax: 212-226-3619
URL: http://www.lawyers.com/slade&associatespc

Jeffrey C. Slade

Marianne Yen
Bridget Connolly

(See Next Column)

SLADE & ASSOCIATES P.C.—*Continued*

OF COUNSEL

Douglas E. Grover | Norman A. Bloch

For full biographical listings, see the Martindale-Hubbell Law Directory

*SYRACUSE,** Onondaga Co.

COSTELLO COONEY & FEARON, LLP (AV)

Salina Place, 205 South Salina Street, 13202
Telephone: 315-422-1152
Fax: 315-422-1139
Email: ccf-law.com *URL:* http://www.ccf-law.com

OF COUNSEL

Vincent A. O'Neil

General Counsel for: Auburn Memorial Hospital; Crouse Hospital; Health Services Association of Central New York; St. Joseph's Hospital Health Center.
Local Counsel for: Deere & Co.; New York Telephone Co.; Crum & Forster Insurance Co.; The Travelers Insurance Companies; Caterpillar, Inc.; Otis Elevator.

For Complete List of Firm Personnel, See General Section

For full biographical listings, see the Martindale-Hubbell Law Directory

UNIONDALE, Nassau Co.

LEHMAN & EILEN LLP (AV)

50 Charles Lindbergh Boulevard, Suite 505, 11553-3600
Telephone: 516-222-0888
Fax: 516-222-0948
Email: info@lehmaneilen.com *URL:* http://www.securitiesattys.com

MEMBERS OF FIRM

Bob E. Lehman | Howard S. Eilen

OF COUNSEL

Hank Gracin | Timothy P. Kebbe

ASSOCIATES

Stephanie G. Senzer
Maureen Ann Porette
Eva M. Possavino
Audrey Blain
Scott D. Stechman
Steven J. Pappas

For full biographical listings, see the Martindale-Hubbell Law Directory

NORTH CAROLINA

*DURHAM,** Durham Co.

MOORE & VAN ALLEN, PLLC (AV)

Suite 800, 2200 West Main Street, 27705
Telephone: 919-286-8000
Fax: 919-286-8199
URL: http://www.mvalaw.com
Charleston, South Carolina Office: 40 Calhoun Street, Suite 300.
Telephone: 843-579-7000.
Fax: 843-579-7099.
Charlotte, North Carolina Office: 100 North Tryon Street, Floor 47.
Telephone: 704-331-1000.
Fax: 704-331-1159.
Raleigh, North Carolina Office: One Hannover Square, Suite 1700, P.O. Box 26507.
Telephone: 919-821-6200.
Fax: 919-821-6500.

Dominic J. Chiantera | David A. Harlow

OF COUNSEL

William G. Dossé | William L. London, III

COUNSEL

Rita M.K. Purut

ASSOCIATES

Arlene D. Hanks
Michael G. Johnston
Laura Keohane
Scott W. Reid
Mark H. Webbink

For full biographical listings, see the Martindale-Hubbell Law Directory

OHIO

*CINCINNATI,** Hamilton Co.

KEATING, MUETHING & KLEKAMP, P.L.L. (AV)

1400 Provident Tower, One East Fourth Street, 45202
Telephone: 513-579-6400
Facsimile: 513-579-6457
URL: http://www.kmklaw.com

ASSOCIATE

Daniel B. Runk

OF COUNSEL

Patricia B. Hogan

Representative Clients: American Financial Group; BP America Inc.; Chiquita Brands International, Inc.; Cintas Corporation; Comair Holdings, Inc.; Duke Realty Limited Partnership; LSI Industries Inc.; Mosler Inc.; Provident Financial Group Inc.

For Complete List of Firm Personnel, See General Section

For full biographical listings, see the Martindale-Hubbell Law Directory

*CLEVELAND,** Cuyahoga Co.

BAKER & HOSTETLER LLP (AV)

3200 National City Center, 1900 East Ninth Street, 44114-3485
Telephone: 216-621-0200
Telecopier: 216-696-0740
TWX: 810 421 8375
RCA Telex: 215032
To contact an attorney on the Internet use first initial and surname followed by @baker-hostetler.com
URL: http://www.bakerlaw.com
In Cincinnati, Ohio: 312 Walnut Street, Suite 2650.
Telephone: 513-929-3400.
In Columbus, Ohio: Capitol Square, Suite 2100, 65 East State Street.
Telephone: 614-228-1541.
In Denver, Colorado: 303 East 17th Avenue, Suite 1100.
Telephone: 303-861-0600.
In Houston, Texas: 1000 Louisiana, Suite 2000.
Telephone: 713-751-1600.
In Beverly Hills, California: 9150 Wilshire Boulevard, Suite 205.
Telephone: 310-385-7500.
In Long Beach, California: 300 Oceangate, Suite 620.
Telephone: 562-432-2827.
In Los Angeles, California: 600 Wilshire Boulevard.
Telephone: 213-624-2400.
In Orlando, Florida: SunBank Center, Suite 2300, 200 South Orange Avenue.
Telephone: 407-649-4000.
In Washington, D.C.: Washington Square, Suite 1100, 1050 Connecticut Avenue, N.W.
Telephone: 202-861-1500.

PARTNERS

Bruce O. Baumgartner | Deborah A. Schaff Wilcox

For Complete List of Firm Personnel, See General Section

For full biographical listings, see the Martindale-Hubbell Law Directory

CALFEE, HALTER & GRISWOLD LLP (AV)

1400 McDonald Investment Center, 800 Superior Avenue, 44114-2688
Telephone: 216-622-8200
Telecopier: 216-241-0816
Telex: 980499
URL: http://www.calfee.com
Columbus, Ohio Office: 88 East Broad Street, Suite 1500.
Telephone: 614-321-1500.
Telecopier: 614-621-0010.

MEMBERS OF FIRM

Charles B. Lyon
John T. Wiedemann
Jeanne E. Longmuir
Mary E. Golrick
Daniel J. McMullen
John S. Cipolla

ASSOCIATES

Sean T. Moorhead
Sean P. Dunn
(Resident Columbus Office)
James A. Dimitrijevs
Nenad Pejic
June Rickey

SENIOR ATTORNEYS

Pamela A. Docherty
Tara A. Kastelic
James A. Rich
(Not admitted in OH)

For Complete List of Firm Personnel, See General Section

For full biographical listings, see the Martindale-Hubbell Law Directory

Cleveland—Continued

FAY, SHARPE, FAGAN, MINNICH & MCKEE, LLP (AV)

1100 Superior Avenue, Seventh Floor, 44114
Telephone: 216-861-5582
FAX: 216-241-1666
Email: fs@faysharpe.com *URL:* http://www.faysharpe.com

MEMBERS OF FIRM

Albert P. Sharpe, III
Christopher B. Fagan
Richard J. Minnich
James W. McKee
Patrick R. Roche
Thomas E. Kocovsky, Jr.
Timothy E. Nauman
Richard M. Klein
Jay F. Moldovanyi
Philip J. Moy, Jr.
Mark S. Svat
Joseph D. Dreher
Scott Andrew McCollister
Mark E. Bandy
Michael E. Hudzinski

ASSOCIATES

Sandra M. Koenig
Jude A. Fry
Colleen Flynn Goss
Brian E. Kondas
Steven M. Auvil
R. Scott Speroff
Steven M. Haas
John P. Cornely
Ann M. Skerry
James E. Scarbrough
W. Scott Harders
Brian G. Bembenick
Christopher P. Harris

OF COUNSEL

Sue Ellen Phillips

For full biographical listings, see the Martindale-Hubbell Law Directory

JANIK & FORBES (AV)

Building Two, 8223 Brecksville Road, 44141-1371
Telephone: 440-838-7600
Fax: 440-838-7601

MEMBERS OF FIRM

Steven G. Janik
Steven Forbes

For Complete List of Firm Personnel, See General Section

For full biographical listings, see the Martindale-Hubbell Law Directory

JONES, DAY, REAVIS & POGUE (AV)

North Point, 901 Lakeside Avenue, 44114
Telephone: 216-586-3939
Telecopier: 216-579-0212
Email: counsel@jonesday.com *URL:* http://www.jonesday.com
In Columbus, Ohio: 1900 Huntington Center.
Telephone: 614-469-3939.
Telecopier: 614-461-4198.
In Atlanta, Georgia: 3500 SunTrust Plaza, 303 Peachtree Street.
Telephone: 404-521-3939.
Telecopier: 404-581-8330.
In Brussels, Belgium: Avenue Louise 480, 7th Floor. B-1050 Brussels.
Telephone: 32-2-645-14-11.
Telecopier: 32-2-645-14-45.
In Chicago, Illinois: 77 West Wacker.
Telephone: 312-782-3939.
Telecopier: 312-782-8585.
In Dallas, Texas: 2727 North Harwood Street.
Telephone: 214-220-3939.
Telecopier: 214-969-5100.
In Frankfurt, Germany: Hochhaus am Park, Grüneburgweg 102, 60323 Frankfurt am Main.
Telephone: 49-69-9726-3939.
Telecopier: 49-69-9726-3993.
In Geneva, Switzerland: 20, rue de Candolle.
Telephone: 41-22-320-2339.
Telecopier: 41-22-320-1232.
In Hong Kong, China: 29th Floor, Entertainment Building, 30 Queen's Road Central.
Telephone: 852-2526-6895.
Telecopier: 852-2868-5871 or 852-2868-5699.
In Irvine, California: 5 Park Plaza, Suite 1100.
Telephone: 949-851-3939.
Telecopier: 949-553-7539.
In London, England: Bucklersbury House, 3 Queen Victoria Street.
Telephone: 44-171-236-3939.
Telecopier: 44-171-236-1113.
In Los Angeles, California: 555 West Fifth Street, Suite 4600.
Telephone: 213-489-3939.
Telecopier: 213-243-2539.
In New Delhi, India (Associate Office): Pathak & Associates (an associate firm of Jones, Day, Reavis & Pogue), 1st Floor, Dr. Gopal Das Bhaven, 28 Barakhamba Road.
Telephone: 91-11-373-8793; 91-11-335-7345.
Telecopier: 91-11-335-3761.
In New York, N.Y.: 599 Lexington Avenue.
Telephone: 212-326-3939.
Telecopier: 212-755-7306.
In Paris, France: 120, rue du Faubourg Saint-Honoré.
Telephone: 33-1-56-59-39-39.
Telecopier: 33-1-56-59-39-38

(See Next Column)

In Pittsburgh, Pennsylvania: 500 Grant Street, 31st Floor.
Telephone: 412-391-3939.
Telecopier: 412-394-7959.
In Riyadh, Saudi Arabia: The International Law Firm (In Association with Jones, Day, Reavis & Pogue), Sulaymaniyah, Prince Mishari IBN, Abdulaziz Street, P.O. Box 22166.
Telephone: (966-1) 462-8866.
Telecopier: (966-1) 462-9001.
In Shanghai, China: 2805 Kerry Centre, 1515 Nanjing Road West.
Telephone: 86-21-5298-6568.
Telecopier: 86-21-5298-6569.
In Sydney, Australia: Governor Phillip Tower, Level 38, 1 Farrer Place.
Telephone: 61-2-9210-6921.
Telecopier: 61-2-9210-6926.
In Taipei, Taiwan: 8th Floor, Tun Hwa South Road, Section 2.
Telephone: (886-2) 2704-6808.
Telecopier: (886-2) 2704-6791.
In Tokyo, Japan: Toranomon MT Building, 4th Floor, 10-3, Toranomon 3-Chome, Minato-ku, Tokyo 105, Japan.
Telephone: 81-3-3433-3939.
Telecopier: 81-3-5401-2725.
In Washington, D.C.: 51 Louisiana Avenue, N.W.
Telephone: 202-879-3939.
Telecopier: 202-626-1700.

MEMBERS OF FIRM IN CLEVELAND

Regan J. Fay
Kenneth R. Adamo
Robert Conley Kahrl
Robert P. Ducatman
Timothy J. O'Hearn

For Complete List of Firm Personnel, See General Section

For full biographical listings, see the Martindale-Hubbell Law Directory

RENNER, OTTO, BOISSELLE & SKLAR, P.L.L. (AV)

Nineteenth Floor, 1621 Euclid Avenue, 44115-2183
Telephone: 216-621-1113
Cable: "Oldpat"
Telex: 8104212034 Oldpat Clv
Fax: 216-621-6165
Email: mailroom@rennerotto.com

John F. Oberlin (1880-1971)
Edwin E. Donnelly, Jr. (1925-1976)

MEMBERS OF FIRM

John W. Renner
Donald L. Otto
Armand P. Boisselle
Warren A. Sklar
Neil A. DuChez
Don W. Bulson
Gordon D. Kinder
William C. Tritt
Jay R. Campbell
Mark D. Saralino

ASSOCIATES

Cynthia S. Murphy
Thomas W. Adams
Christopher B. Jacobs
Joseph J. Crimaldi
Jonathan A Platt
Paul R. Steffes

OF COUNSEL

Walter Maky
Charles S. Lynch (Not admitted in OH; Retired)

For full biographical listings, see the Martindale-Hubbell Law Directory

WESTON HURD FALLON PAISLEY & HOWLEY L.L.P. (AV)

2500 Terminal Tower, 50 Public Square, 44113-2241
Telephone: 216-241-6602;
Ohio Toll Free: 800-336-4952
FAX: 216-621-8369
Email: Hurd2500@westonhurd.com

MEMBERS OF FIRM

John S. Kluznik
Todd G. Jackson

ASSOCIATE

Jeremy R. Sayre

For Complete List of Firm Personnel, See General Section

For full biographical listings, see the Martindale-Hubbell Law Directory

*COLUMBUS,** Franklin Co.

KEGLER, BROWN, HILL & RITTER (AV)

Capitol Square Suite 1800, 65 East State Street, 43215-4294
Telephone: 614-462-5400
Telecopier: 614-464-2634
Cable Address: "Law KBHR"
Telex: 246671
Email: info@kbhr.com *URL:* http://www.kbhr.com
Marion, Ohio Office: 250 Executive Drive, Suite B, P.O. Box 919.
Telephone: 614-387-3501.
Facsimile: 614-387-3630.

James R. Eley
Gene W. Holliker
Robert G. Schuler
S. Martijn Steger
Shawnell Williams

(See Next Column)

KEGLER, BROWN, HILL & RITTER—*Continued*

COUNSEL

John L. Gray

Representative Clients: Borden, Inc.; Drug Emporium, Inc.; The Ohio State University.

For Complete List of Firm Personnel, See General Section

For full biographical listings, see the Martindale-Hubbell Law Directory

OREGON

*PORTLAND,** Multnomah Co.

MARGER, JOHNSON & McCOLLOM, P.C. (AV)

1030 S.W. Morrison Street, 97205
Telephone: 503-222-3613
FAX: 503-274-4622
Email: inquiry@techlaw.com *URL:* http://www.techlaw.com
Bend, Oregon Office: 777 N.W. Wall, Suite 308, 97702.
Telephone: 541-312-2500.
Fax: 541-312-8900.

Alexander C. Johnson, Jr.
Alan T. McCollom
Glenn C. Brown
Stephen S. Ford

Scott A. Schaffer
Joseph S. Makuch
Graciela G. Cowger
Hosoon Lee
Ariel S. Rogson
Gregory T. Kavounas
James E. Harris
James G. Stewart
Craig R. Rogers

LEGAL SUPPORT PERSONNEL

PARALEGAL

Kimberly A. Hubbell

OF COUNSEL

Jerome S. Marger

Representative Clients: Adidas; Advanced Power Technology; Analog Devices; Baker Hughes Inc.; Battelle Pacific Northwest Laboratories; Cisco Systems; Columbia Machine, Inc.; Elmers Restaurants, Inc.; Hanson Natural Resources Co.; Hewlett-Packard Co.

For full biographical listings, see the Martindale-Hubbell Law Directory

PENNSYLVANIA

*PHILADELPHIA,** Philadelphia Co.

PAUL & PAUL (AV)

2900 Two Thousand Market Street, 19103
Telephone: 215-568-4900
Cable Address: "Caveat"
Telex: 710-670-1352 Dex
Telecopier: 215-567-5057
Email: paulandpaul@compuserve.com

MEMBERS OF FIRM

James C. McConnon
John F. McNulty
Alex R. Sluzas

ASSOCIATES

Frank J. Bonini, Jr.
Paul A. Taufer
Gary A. Greene

For full biographical listings, see the Martindale-Hubbell Law Directory

VALLEY FORGE, Chester Co.

MICHAEL F. PETOCK (AV)

46 The Commons at Valley Forge, 1220 Valley Forge Road, P.O. Box 856, 19482-0856
Telephone: 610-935-8600; 215-922-5550
Fax: 610-933-9300
Email: MFP@iplaw-petock.com *URL:* http://www.IPLaw-petock.com

For full biographical listings, see the Martindale-Hubbell Law Directory

ZACHARY T. WOBENSMITH, III (AV)

86 The Commons at Valley Forge East, 1288 Valley Forge Road, P.O. Box 750, 19482-0750
Telephone: 610-935-9750
Telecopier: 610-935-0600
URL: http://www.lawyers.com/zachary&wobensmith

For full biographical listings, see the Martindale-Hubbell Law Directory

RHODE ISLAND

*PROVIDENCE,** Providence Co.

EDWARDS & ANGELL, LLP (AV)

A Partnership including Professional Corporations
2800 BankBoston Plaza, 02903
Telephone: 401-274-9200
Telecopier: 401-276-6611
Cable Address: "Edwangle Providence"
Telex: 952001 "E A PVD"
Email: postmaster@ealaw.com *URL:* http://www.ealaw.com
Boston, Massachusetts Office: 101 Federal Street, 02110-1800.
Telephone: 617-439-4444.
Telecopier: 617-439-4170.
New York, New York Office: 750 Lexington Avenue, 10022-1200.
Telephone: 212-308-4411.
Telecopier: 212-308-4844.
Palm Beach, Florida Office: 250 Royal Palm Way, Suite 300, 33480-4356.
Telephone: 561-833-7700.
Telecopier: 561-655-8719.
Short Hills, New Jersey Office: 51 John F. Kennedy Parkway, 07078.
Telephone: 973-376-7700.
Telecopier: 973-376-3380.
Hartford, Connecticut Office: 90 State House Square, 06103-2715.
Telephone: 860-525-5065.
Telecopier: 860-527-4198.
Newport, Rhode Island Office: 130 Bellevue Avenue, 02840.
Telephone: 401-849-7800.
Telecopier: 401-849-7887.

MEMBER OF FIRM

John E. Ottaviani

For Complete List of Firm Personnel, See General Section

For full biographical listings, see the Martindale-Hubbell Law Directory

HINCKLEY, ALLEN & SNYDER LLP (AV)

1500 Fleet Center, 02903-2393
Telephone: 401-274-2000
Fax: 401-277-9600
Email: firm@haslaw.com *URL:* http://www.haslaw.com
Boston, Massachusetts Office: 28 State Street, 30th Floor.
Telephone: 617-345-9000.
Fax: 617-345-9020. URL: http://www.haslaw.com.

MEMBERS OF FIRM

Paula K. Andrews (Not admitted in RI)
David D. Barricelli
E. Jerome Batty
Jonathan Bell
Paul Bork (Not admitted in RI)
Stephen J. Carlotti
David Barry Connolly (Not admitted in RI)
Joseph P. Curran
Michael P. DeFanti
Eric F. Eisenberg (Not admitted in RI)
Malcolm Farmer, III
Margaret D. Farrell
Hugh J. Gorman, III (Not admitted in RI)
Alan P. Gottlieb (Not admitted in RI)
William R. Grimm
Paul A. Hedstrom (Not admitted in RI)
Joel Lewin (Not admitted in RI)
Sandra Matrone Mack
Matthew T. Marcello, III
Elizabeth Murdock Myers
Paul F. O'Donnell, III (Not admitted in RI)
H. Peter Olsen
Gerald J. Petros
James O. Reavis
Jeremy Ritzenberg (Not admitted in RI)
Ralph J. Rivkind (Not admitted in RI)
David J. Rubin
Charles E. Schaub, Jr. (Not admitted in RI)
Herman Snyder (Not admitted in RI)
David R. Sullivan (Not admitted in RI)
Robert F. Sylvia (Not admitted in RI)
Howard E. Walker
John R. Allen (Retired)
Richard W. Billings (Retired)
Thomas J. Hogan (Retired)
Jacques V. Hopkins (Retired)
James A. Jackson (Retired)
James E. Keeley (Retired)
Robert F. Pickard (Retired)
Robert W. Shadd (Retired)
Richard F. Staples (Retired)
Edwin G. Torrance (Retired)

ASSOCIATES

Jessica M. Bettencourt
Mark Bianchi
Alyssa V. Boss
Alexandra K. Callam
Jane E. Cohen (Not admitted in RI)
Andrew D. Cummings (Not admitted in RI)
June E. Daniel
Kim Herman Goslant (Not admitted in RI)
Gloria Maria Gutierrez (Not admitted in RI)
Kelley Jordan-Price
Catherine S. Kim (Not admitted in RI)
Christopher W. Morog (Not admitted in RI)
Elena B. Olson (Not admitted in RI)
Joseph D. Whelan

(See Next Column)

HINCKLEY, ALLEN & SNYDER LLP, *Providence—Continued*

OF COUNSEL

Willard R. Pope (Not admitted in RI)
Bentley Tobin
Joachim A. Weissfeld

For Complete List of Firm Personnel, See General Section

For full biographical listings, see the Martindale-Hubbell Law Directory

VETTER & WHITE, INCORPORATED (AV)

20 Washington Place, 02903
Telephone: 401-421-3060
Telecopier: 401-272-6803
Email: vetlit@aol.com

Benjamin V. White, III
Gordon P. Cleary
Howard A. Merten, Jr.
Brooks R. Magratten

OF COUNSEL

George Vetter

Kimberly A. Simpson
Michael W. Long

For full biographical listings, see the Martindale-Hubbell Law Directory

TENNESSEE

*MEMPHIS,** Shelby Co.

ARMSTRONG ALLEN PREWITT GENTRY JOHNSTON & HOLMES, PLLC (AV)

Brinkley Plaza, Suite 700, 80 Monroe Avenue, 38103-2467
Telephone: 901-523-8211
Facsimile: 901-524-4936
Little Rock, Arkansas Office: Suite 100, 100 Morgan Keegan Drive, 72202.
Telephone: 501-280-0100.
Facsimile: 501-280-0166.
Jackson, Mississippi Office: 2525 Lakeward Drive, Suite 200, 39216.
Telephone: 601-713-1192.
Facsimile: 601-713-2049.
Jackson, Tennessee Office: 464 North Parkway, Suite A, 38305.
Telephone: 901-660-2332.
Facsimile: 901-664-1109.

MEMBERS OF FIRM

James B. McLaren, Jr.
Lucian T. Pera

Kathy Laughter Laizure

For Complete List of Firm Personnel, See General Section

For full biographical listings, see the Martindale-Hubbell Law Directory

*NASHVILLE,** Davidson Co.

CHERNAU, CHAFFIN & BURNSED, PLLC (AV)

SunTrust Center, 424 Church Street, Suite 1750, 37219-2305
Telephone: 615-244-5480
Fax: 615-242-7951
Email: CCBABSMITH@AOL.COM

MEMBERS OF FIRM

Louis Leftwich, Jr. (1910-1960)
Stanley M. Chernau
R. Garry Chaffin
Linda F. Burnsed
Amy Bryson Smith

Representative Clients: Dolly Parton Enterprises; Carl Perkins Music; Someday Baby, Inc. d/b/a/ A Child's Gift of Lullabyes; B & G Wholesalers, Inc.

For full biographical listings, see the Martindale-Hubbell Law Directory

KING & BALLOW (AV)

Union Street Plaza, 315 Union Street, Suite 1100, 37201
Telephone: 615-259-3456
Fax: 615-254-7907
Email: lawfirm@king-ballow.com *URL:* http://www.king-ballow.com
San Diego, California Office: 2700 Symphony Towers, 750 B Street, 92101.
Telephone: 619-236-9401.
Fax: 619-236-9437.

MEMBERS OF FIRM

Frank S. King, Jr.
Robert L. Ballow
R. Eddie Wayland
Alan L. Marx
Paul H. Duvall (Resident, San Diego, California Office)
Douglas R. Pierce
Mark E. Hunt

(See Next Column)

ASSOCIATES

Patrick M. Thomas
Lynn Morrow
D'Lesli M. Davis
Nels Jacobson

Representative Clients: John F. Blair Publishers, Winston-Salem, North Carolina; Cliffie Stone Productions, Los Angeles, California; Grant/Tribune Productions, Los Angeles, California; Hamilton House Entertainment Group, Oklahoma City, Oklahoma; Ingram Book Co., Nashville, TN; Menasha Ridge Press, Inc., Birmingham, Alabama; Opryland Music Group, Nashville, TN; Pelican Publishing, Gretna, Louisiana; SESAC, Inc., New York, New York; Scene Three, Inc., Nashville, TN.

For Complete List of Firm Personnel, See General Section

For full biographical listings, see the Martindale-Hubbell Law Directory

TUKE YOPP & SWEENEY, PLC (AV)

NationsBank Plaza Suite 1100, 414 Union Street, 37219
Telephone: 615-313-3300
Fax: 615-313-3310

MEMBERS OF FIRM

Robert D. Tuke
G. Michael Yopp
Matthew J. Sweeney, III
Lawrence C. Maxwell
Peter H. Curry
Barrett B. Sutton, Jr.
John W. Stone, III
Gary M. Brown
David J. White
Robert P. Felber, Jr.
Robb S. Harvey
Gerald F. Mace
Kathryn A. Stephenson
John C. Tishler

ASSOCIATES

W. Edward Ramage
Lisa L. Collins
Theresa M. Costonis
E. Blaine Sprouse
Warren A. Jasper
Mark W. Miller
Elizabeth A. Carnahan
Richard L. Pensinger

OF COUNSEL

Kenneth E. Douthat
William B. Drescher
Michael T. Folks (Not admitted in TN)
Larry D. Soderquist
Charles K. Grant

For full biographical listings, see the Martindale-Hubbell Law Directory

WYATT, TARRANT & COMBS (AV)

1500 Nashville City Center, 511 Union Street, 37219-1750
Telephone: 615-244-0020
Telecopier: 615-256-1726
URL: http://www.wyattfirm.com
Music Row Office: 29 Music Square East, Nashville, 37203.
Telephone: 615-255-6161.
Telecopier: 615-254-4490.
Hendersonville, Tennessee Office: 313 E. Main Street, Suite 1, Hendersonville, 37075.
Telephone: 615-822-8822.
Telecopier: 615-824-4684.
Memphis, Tennessee Office: Crescent Center, Suite 650, 6075 Poplar Avenue, Memphis, 38119.
Telephone: 901-537-1000.
Telecopier: 901-537-1010.
Tri-Cities, Tennessee Office: Northeast Tennessee Business Park, 10368 Wallace Alley Street, Suite 6, Kingsport, Tennessee, 37663.
Telephone: 423-279-1825.
Telecopier: 423-279-9357.
Louisville, Kentucky Office: Citizens Plaza.
Telephone: 502-589-5235.
Telecopier: 502-589-0309.
Lexington, Kentucky Office: 1700 Lexington Financial Center.
Telephone: 606-233-2012.
Telecopier: 606-259-0649.
Frankfort, Kentucky Office: The Taylor-Scott Building, 311 West Main Street.
Telephone: 502-223-2104.
Telecopier: 502-227-7681.
New Albany, Indiana Office: The Elsby Building, 117 East Spring Street,
Telephone: 812-945-3561.
Telecopier: 812-949-2524.

MEMBERS OF FIRM

W. Michael Milom (Resident, Music Row Office)
Christian A. Horsnell (Resident, Music Row Office)

ASSOCIATE

Grace H. Awh (Resident, Music Row Office)

COUNSEL

Robin Mitchell Joyce (Resident, Music Row Office)

Representative Clients: Brentwood Music, Inc.; CPL Publishing, Inc.; Morgan Music Group; REN Corp USA; Thomas Nelson, Inc.

For Complete List of Firm Personnel, See General Section

For full biographical listings, see the Martindale-Hubbell Law Directory

TEXAS

*AUSTIN,** Travis Co.

BAKER BOTTS L.L.P. (AV)

1600 San Jacinto Center, 98 San Jacinto Boulevard, 78701
Telephone: 512-322-2500
Fax: 512-322-2501
Email: postmaster@bakerbotts.com *URL:* http://www.bakerbotts.com
Houston, Texas Office: One Shell Plaza, 910 Louisiana.
Telephone: 713-229-1234.
Dallas, Texas Office: 2001 Ross Avenue.
Telephone: 214-953-6500.
Washington, D.C. Office: The Warner, 1299 Pennsylvania Avenue, N.W.
Telephone: 202-639-7700.
New York, New York Office: 599 Lexington Avenue.
Telephone: 212-705-5000.
Moscow, Russia Office: 10 ul. Bolshaya Dimitrovka (formerly Pushkinskaya), 103031.
Telephone: 7095/921-5300 (Local); 7501/929-7070 (International).
London, England Office: 45 Ludgate Hill.
Telephone: 0171-778-1400 (Local); 011-44-171-778-1400 (International).
Baku, Azerbaijan Office: 6-10 Vagif Mustafa-zadeh Street, Third Floor, Icheri Sheher, 370004.
Telephone: 994-12-97-63-88 (Local); 011-994-12-97-63-88 (International).
Fax: 994-12-97-63-61 (Local); 011-994-12-97-63-91 (International).

SPECIAL COUNSEL

Thomas R. Felger

ASSOCIATES

Robert W. Holland
Anna Conyers Kuhn
Ann Livingston
Scott T. Morris

For Complete List of Firm Personnel, See General Section

For full biographical listings, see the Martindale-Hubbell Law Directory

THOMPSON & KNIGHT L.L.P. (AV)

(Attorneys and Counselors)
1200 San Jacinto Center, 98 San Jacinto Boulevard, 78701
Telephone: 512-469-6100
Telecopy: 512-469-6180
URL: http://www.tklaw.com
Dallas, Texas Office: 1700 Pacific Avenue, Suite 3300, 75201.
Telephone: 214-969-1700.
Telecopy: 512-969-1751.
Telex: 732298.
Fort Worth, Texas Office: 801 Cherry Street, Suite 1600, 76102.
Telephone: 817-347-1700.
Telecopy: 817-347-1799.
Houston, Texas Office: Thompson Knight Brown Parker & Leahy L.L.P., 1200 Smith Street, Suite 3600, 77002-4595.
Telephone: 713-654-8111.
Telecopier: 713-654-1871.
San Pedro Garza Garcia, Nuevo León, Mexico Office: Edificio Losoles PD-4, Av. Lázaro Cárdenas No. 2400 Pte., C.P. 66220.
Telephone: (52-8) 363-0096.
Telecopy: (52-8) 363-3067.

PARTNERS

Debora Beck Alsup
Michael L. Bengtson
Jeffrey S. Boyd
Eugene W. Brees, II
Holly Claghorn
James E. Cousar
Frank L. Hill
Becky L. Jolin
James C. Morriss III
Regina C. Williams

ASSOCIATES

Kari Lavelle Arneil
Christine E. Burgess
Andrew A. Ingrum
Matthew J. Knifton
D'Ana Howard Mikeska
T. Christopher Pledger
Dale L. Roberts
Peter A. Vermillion

SENIOR ATTORNEY

Elizabeth A. Webb

OF COUNSEL

Raymond M. Galasso (Not admitted in TX)
Mark L. Murdock

For full biographical listings, see the Martindale-Hubbell Law Directory

*DALLAS,** Dallas Co.

BAKER BOTTS L.L.P. (AV)

2001 Ross Avenue, 75201
Telephone: 214-953-6500
Fax: 214-953-6503
Email: postmaster@bakerbotts.com *URL:* http://www.bakerbotts.com
Houston, Texas Office: One Shell Plaza, 910 Louisiana.
Telephone: 713-229-1234.
Washington, D.C. Office: The Warner, 1299 Pennsylvania Avenue, N.W.
Telephone: 202-639-7700.
Austin, Texas Office: 1600 San Jacinto Center, 98 San Jacinto Boulevard.
Telephone: 512-322-2500.

(See Next Column)

New York, New York Office: 599 Lexington Avenue.
Telephone: 212-705-5000.
Moscow, Russia Office: 10 ul. Bolshaya Dimitrovka (formerly Pushkinskaya), 103031.
Telephone: 7095/921-5300 (Local); 7095/929-7070.
London, England Office: 45 Ludgate Hill.
Telephone: 0171-778-1400 (Local); 011-44-171-778-1400 (International).
Baku, Azerbaijan Office: 6-10 Vagif Mustafa-zadeh Street, Third Floor, Icheri Sheher, 370004.
Telephone: 994-12-97-63-88 (Local); 011-994-12-97-63-88 (International).

MEMBERS OF FIRM

Robert M. Chiaviello, Jr.
Charles S. Fish
Robert W. Jordan
Kevin J. Meek
Jerry W. Mills

ASSOCIATES

Wei Wei Jeang
Jay B. Johnson (Not admitted in TX)
Christopher W. Kennerly
Douglas M. Kubehl
Barton Earl Showalter
Alexandra L. Siegel
Terry J. Stalford
Alfred Steiner
David G. Wille
Bradley P. Williams

For Complete List of Firm Personnel, See General Section

For full biographical listings, see the Martindale-Hubbell Law Directory

THOMPSON & KNIGHT L.L.P. (AV)

(Attorneys and Counselors)
1700 Pacific Avenue Suite 3300, 75201
Telephone: 214-969-1700
Telecopy: 214-969-1751
Telex: 732 298
URL: http://www.tklaw.com
Austin, Texas Office: 1200 San Jacinto Center, 98 San Jacinto Boulevard, 78701.
Telephone: 512-469-6100.
Telecopy: 512-469-6180.
Fort Worth, Texas Office: 801 Cherry Street, Suite 1600, 76102.
Telephone: 817-347-1700.
Telecopy: 817-347-1799.
Houston, Texas Office: Thompson Knight Brown Parker & Leahy L.L.P., 1200 Smith Street, Suite 3600, 77002-4595.
Telephone: 713-654-8111.
Telecopier: 713-654-1871.
San Pedro Garza Garcia, Nuevo León, Mexico Office: Edificio Losoles PD-4, Av. Lázaro Cárdenas No. 2400 Pte., C.P. 66220.
Telephone: (52-8) 363-0096.
Telecopy: (52-8) 363-3067.

PARTNERS

Jane Politz Brandt
Beverly Ray Burlingame
Frank Finn
Herbert J. Hammond
William J. Schuerger
Bruce S. Sostek
Peter J. Thoma

ASSOCIATES

Priscilla Lynn Dunckel
Anna E. Marple

For Complete List of Firm Personnel, See General Section

For full biographical listings, see the Martindale-Hubbell Law Directory

*FORT WORTH,** Tarrant Co.

DECKER, JONES, MCMACKIN, MCCLANE, HALL & BATES, A PROFESSIONAL CORPORATION (AV)

2500 Bank One Tower, 500 Throckmorton Street, 76102-3812
Telephone: 817-336-2400; Metro: 817-429-5260
Fax: 817-332-3043; 336-2181
Email: email@deckerjones.com *URL:* http://www.deckerjones.com

Daniel L. Bates
Robert W. Decker
Mark S. Dugan
Janet L. Hahn
Randy J. Hall
Raymond B. Kelly, III
John B. McClane
John W. McMackin
Charles B. Milliken
Gary M. Moates
Bradley H. Rice
Jeffrey W. Storie
James L. Stripling
Brian K. Yost
Tamera H. Bennett
Arthur F. Zobal
Geoffrey A. Mantooth

Representative Clients: Ibertech, Inc.; Akai Musical Instrument Corp.; Blackmon Mooring Steamatic, Inc.; Lubrication Engineers, Inc.; Martin-Sprocket and Gear, Inc.; Williamson-Dickie Manufacturing Co.; Harbison-Fischer Manufacturing Co.; Employers Insurance of Texas; American International Group.

For full biographical listings, see the Martindale-Hubbell Law Directory

UTAH

*SALT LAKE CITY,** Salt Lake Co.

Parsons, Davies, Kinghorn & Peters, P.C. (AV)

185 South State Street, Suite 700, 84111
Telephone: 801-363-4300
Facsimile: 801-363-4378
Email: Attorneys@pdkplaw.com

Glen E. Davies
Langdon T. Owen, Jr.
Ken P. Jones
David W. Scofield

For Complete List of Firm Personnel, See General Section

For full biographical listings, see the Martindale-Hubbell Law Directory

Van Cott, Bagley, Cornwall & McCarthy, A Professional Corporation (AV)

50 South Main Street, Suite 1600, P.O. Box 45340, 84145-0340
Telephone: 801-532-3333
Telecopier: 801-534-0058
Email: info@vancott.com *URL:* http://www.vancott.com
Ogden, Utah Office: 2404 Washington Boulevard, Suite 900.
Telephone: 801-394-5783.
Park City, Utah Office: 2200 Park Avenue, Suite C200-A.
Telephone: 435-649-3889.

David J. Smith

Stephen K. Christiansen
Tacy A. Hartman
Bradley M. Strassberg

For Complete List of Firm Personnel, See General Section

For full biographical listings, see the Martindale-Hubbell Law Directory

VERMONT

*BURLINGTON,** Chittenden Co.

Miller, Eggleston & Cramer, Ltd. (AV)

150 South Champlain Street, P.O. Box 1489, 05402-1489
Telephone: 802-864-0880
Telecopier: 802-864-0328

Victoria J. Brown

For Complete List of Firm Personnel, See General Section

For full biographical listings, see the Martindale-Hubbell Law Directory

VIRGINIA

ALEXANDRIA, (Independent City)

Burns, Doane, Swecker & Mathis, L.L.P. (AV)

Suite 500, 1737 King Street, 22314
Telephone: 703-836-6620
Facsimile: 703-836-2021; 703-836-7356; 703-836-3503; Group 4: 703-836-0028
Mailing Address: P.O. Box 1404, 22313-1404
Email: info@burnsdoane.com *URL:* http://www.burnsdoane.com
Redwood Shores, California Office: Suite 700, 333 Twin Dolphin Drive, Redwood Shores, 94065-1418.
Telephone: 650-622-2300.
Fax: 650-631-7600.
Research Triangle Park, North Carolina Office: P.O. Box 14846, Research Triangle Park, 27709-4846, 1009 Slater Road, Suite 210, Durham, 27703.
Telephone: 919-941-9240.
Facsimile: 919-941-1515.

James P. Burns (1896-1982)
Vernon H. Doane (1909-1960)
J. Preston Swecker (1904-1996)

MEMBERS OF FIRM

Robert S. Swecker
Platon N. Mandros
Benton S. Duffett, Jr.
Norman H. Stepno
Ronald L. Grudziecki (Admitted in District of Columbia; limited admission in Virginia)
Frederick G. Michaud, Jr.
Alan E. Kopecki
Regis E. Slutter
Samuel C. Miller, III
Robert G. Mukai
George A. Hovanec, Jr.
James A. LaBarre
E. Joseph Gess
R. Danny Huntington
Eric H. Weisblatt
James W. Peterson (Redwood Shores, California Office)
Teresa Stanek Rea (Not admitted in VA)

(See Next Column)

MEMBERS OF FIRM (Continued)

Robert E. Krebs (Redwood Shores, California Office)
Adrienne L. White
William C. Rowland
T. Gene Dillahunty (Redwood Shores, California Office)
Patrick C. Keane (Not admitted in VA)
B. Jefferson Boggs, Jr.
William H. Benz (Redwood Shores, California Office)
Peter K. Skiff
Richard J. McGrath
Matthew L. Schneider
Michael G. Savage (Research Triangle Park, North Carolina Office)
Gerald F. Swiss (Redwood Shores, California Office)
David M. Schlitz
Robert DeVos
B. Parker Livingston, Jr.
Bassam N. Ibrahim
Michael J. Ure (Redwood Shores, California Office)
Charles F. Wieland III
Bruce T. Wieder
Todd Ray Walters
Ronni S. Jillions
Harold R. Brown, III
Allen R. Baum (Research Triangle Park, North Carolina Office)
Steven M. DuBois
Brian P. O'Shaughnessy

COUNSEL

H. Jonathan Redway

OF COUNSEL

William L. Mathis
Peter H. Smolka
Roy H. Massengill
William A. Knoeller

ASSOCIATES

Kenneth B. Leffler
Leslie A. Mooi (Redwood Shores, California Office)
Donna M. Meuth
Charles H. Jew (Redwood Shores, California Office)
Robin L. Teskin
Richard C. Ekstrom
Fred W. Hathaway
Allan M. Soobert
Jonathan D. Baskin
Nhat D. Phan
Mark R. Kresloff (Not admitted in VA)
Matthew P. Blischak
Leslie J. Boley (Redwood Shores, California Office)
Barbara Webb Walker (Not admitted in VA)
Michael A. Wrenn
Jeffrey A. Hagenah (Redwood Shores, California Office)
Robert S. Babayi (Not admitted in VA)
Rel S. Ambrozy (Not admitted in VA)
Wendi L. Weinstein (Not admitted in VA)
Susan M. Dadio
Adam Jason Cermak
M. David Ream (Not admitted in VA)
Mary Ann Dillahunty (Redwood Shores, California Office)
Krishna Kalidindi (Not admitted in VA)
Cindy A. Lynch (Redwood Shores, California Office)
Curtis A. Evans (Not admitted in VA)
Kathleen Neuner Manne
Alan L. Whitehurst
S. Lloyd Smith (Not admitted in VA)
Scott W. Cummings
Khaled Shami (Redwood Shores, California Office)
Jennifer Pearson Wright (Research Triangle Park, North Carolina Office)
John J.G. Kim (Not admitted in VA)
David S. Bradin (Research Triangle Park, North Carolina Office)
Stephen W. Palan
Joseph P. O'Malley (Redwood Shores, California Office)
Iurie A. Schwartz (Not admitted in VA)
Chester L. Jordan, II (Not admitted in VA)
Elaine Papavasiliou (Not admitted in VA)
Rekha P. Bansal (Redwood Shores, California Office)
Jed W. Caven (Research Triangle Park, North Carolina Office)
Michael A. Springs (Research Triangle Park Office)
Robert L. Scott, II
Mark A. Rademacher (Not admitted in VA)
Malcolm K. McGowan
Michael B. Chernoff
Peter G. Korytnyk
Scott C. Richardson
Christine M. Szwerc (Not admitted in VA)
Mercedes K. Meyer (Not admitted in VA)
Mary B. Grant (Research Triangle Park, North Carolina Office)
Thomas E. Coverstone (Menlo Park, California Office)
Marcia R. Morton (Not admitted in VA)

LEGAL SUPPORT PERSONNEL

David M. Huntley
Brian C. Oakes
Bonnie D. Weiss
Dawn M. Gardner
Tony M. Cole
Victoria Hui-Ye Mah (Redwood Shores, California Office)
Samir Elamrani
Roger Lee
Patrick Stanzione
Douglas H. Pearson
Nicole E. Kinsey
Philip W. Marsh

PATENT AGENTS

Mary Katherine Baumeister
Susan E. Heminger (Redwood Shores, California Office)

For full biographical listings, see the Martindale-Hubbell Law Directory

Rogers & Killeen (AV)

Suite 400, 510 King Street, 22314
Telephone: 703-836-0400
Telex: 283843 LAWR UR
Cable Address: "LAWROGERS"
Facsimile: 703-836-1539
Email: ideas@randk.com

(See Next Column)

ROGERS & KILLEEN—*Continued*

MEMBERS OF FIRM

Joseph M. Killeen (1947-1998)
L. Lawton Rogers, III
Mark Charles Comtois
D. Joseph English
Patrick Dennis McPherson (Not admitted in VA)

ASSOCIATES

Howard N. Shipley
Patrick J. Wells (Not admitted in VA)
Donna D. King (Not admitted in VA)

For full biographical listings, see the Martindale-Hubbell Law Directory

*ARLINGTON,** Arlington Co.

HALEY BADER & POTTS P.L.C. (AV)

4350 North Fairfax Drive, Suite 900, 22203-1633
Telephone: 703-841-0606
Fax: 703-841-2345
Email: haleybp@haleybp.com *URL:* http://www.haleybp.com

MEMBERS OF FIRM

Andrew G. Haley (1904-1966)
Michael H. Bader
Henry A. Solomon
John Wells King
John M. Pelkey
John Crigler
Melodie A. Virtue
James E. Dunstan
Benjamin J. Lambiotte

Paul Ferguson
Lisa M. Patera
Julie M. Kearney
Adam R. Brownstein

OF COUNSEL

Theodore D. Kramer

For full biographical listings, see the Martindale-Hubbell Law Directory

*FAIRFAX,** (Ind. City; Seat of Fairfax Co.)

ODIN, FELDMAN & PITTLEMAN, P.C. (AV)

9302 Lee Highway, Suite 1100, 22031
Telephone: 703-218-2100
Facsimile: 703-218-2160
Email: OFP@OFPLAW.COM

Dexter S. Odin
Leslye S. Fenton
Kevin Thomas Oliveira

Thomas N. Tartaro

Representative Clients: Qwest Communications Corp.; Upper Occoquan Sewage Authority; James Martin & Co.; TechSpan, Inc.; Top Cow Productions, Inc.; The Hair Cuttery; F&M Bank-Northern Virginia; Stewart Title and Escrow, Inc.; Seaward International, Inc.; Capitol Building Supply, Inc.

For Complete List of Firm Personnel, See General Section

For full biographical listings, see the Martindale-Hubbell Law Directory

RICHMOND, (Independent City)

WILLIAMS, MULLEN, CLARK & DOBBINS, A PROFESSIONAL CORPORATION (AV)

Two James Center, 1021 East Cary Street, P.O. Box 1320, 23218-1320
Telephone: 804-643-1991
Fax: 804-783-6507
URL: http://www.wmcd.com
Newport News Office: Harbor Bank Center, Suite 210, One Old Oyster Point Road, 23602-7119.
Telephone: 757-249-5100.
Fax: 757-249-5109.
Virginia Beach Office: One Columbus Center, 23462-6763.
Telephone: 757-499-8800.
Fax: 757-473-0395.
Vienna Office: 1593 Spring Hill Road, Suite 510, 22182.
Telephone: 703-760-5200.
Fax: 703-748-0244.
Washington, D.C. Office: The Farragut Building, 900 17th Street, N.W., Suite 700, 20006.
Telephone: 202-293-0213.
Fax: 804-783-6507. Fax Within D.C.: 202-293-5939.
London, England Office: Blake Lodge, Bridge Lane, SW11 3AD.
Telephone: (011-44-71) 223-2756.
Fax: (011-44-71) 350-0156.
Riyadh, Saudi Arabia Affiliate Office: Saudi-American Legal Consultants Commercial Building #2, Diplomatic Quarter, P.O. Box 57270, 11574.
Telephone: (011-966-1) 488-1563.
Fax: (011-966-1) 488-0542.

Gregory P. Cirillo (Resident, Washington, D.C. Office)
Daniel B. Hassett (Resident, Washington, D.C. Office)
Dana D. McDaniel
Craig L. Mytelka (Resident, Virginia Beach Office)
Ian D. Titley

(*See Next Column*)

Bradford D. Bimson (Resident, Virginia Beach Office)
Megan E. Burns (Resident, Virginia Beach Office)
John F. Carroll, IV (Resident, Virginia Beach Office)

For Complete List of Firm Personnel, See General Section

For full biographical listings, see the Martindale-Hubbell Law Directory

WISCONSIN

*MADISON,** Dane Co.

LATHROP & CLARK, LLP (AV)

Suite 400, 740 Regent Street, P.O. Box 1507, 53701-1507
Telephone: 608-257-7766
FAX: 608-257-1507
URL: http://www.lathropclark.com
Poynette, Wisconsin Office: 111 North Main Street, P.O. Box 128.
Telephone: 608-635-4324.
FAX: 608-635-4690.
Lodi, Wisconsin Office: 108 Lodi Street, P.O. Box 256.
Telephone: 608-592-3877.
FAX: 608-592-5844.
Belleville, Wisconsin Office: 27 West Main.
Telephone: 608-424-3404.

MEMBERS OF FIRM

Theodore J. Long
Shelley J. Safer
Jill Weber Dean
Jeffry W. Smith
Heidi S. Tepp

Representative Clients: Westfalia-Surge, LLC; Penda Corporation; Metropolitan Life Insurance Co.; Cuna Mutual Insurance Group; Wisconsin Physicians Service Insurance Corp.; TriEnda Corp.; Auto Glass Specialists, Inc.; Highsmith Inc.; Persoft, Inc.

For Complete List of Firm Personnel, See General Section

For full biographical listings, see the Martindale-Hubbell Law Directory

NEIDER & BOUCHER, S.C. (AV)

440 Science Drive, P.O. Box 5510, 53705-0510
Telephone: 608-661-4500
Facsimile: 608-661-4510
URL: http://www.neiderboucher.com
URL: http://www.lawyers.com/neider&boucher-sc

Ronald C. Berman
Joseph W. Boucher
Charles E. Neider
Steven C. Underwood

Susan M. De Groot
Erik W. Ibele
Rana Kang
Cynthia L. Richson
Matthew L. Schemmel
Kent L. Schlienger
Dean T. Stange

OF COUNSEL

Ralph M. Cagle
Ronald R. Smith

For full biographical listings, see the Martindale-Hubbell Law Directory

STROUD, WILLINK & HOWARD, LLC (AV)

25 West Main Street, Suite 300, P.O. Box 2236, 53701
Telephone: 608-257-2281
Fax: 608-257-7643
Email: email@stroudlaw.com

MEMBERS OF FIRM

Ronald W. Todd
Robert R. Stroud
H. Dale Peterson
Carolyn A. Hegge
James F. Gebhart

ASSOCIATES

Sverre David Roang
Peter J. Richter
Norman D. Farnam

General Counsel For: American TV & Appliance of Madison, Wisconsin; Temperature Systems, Inc.; Ocotpus Car Washes; Goodmans Jewelers; Anchor Bank, SSB; J.H. Findorff & Son, Inc.; Rural Insurance Cos.; Wisconsin Farm Bureau Federation; Appleton Mills; The Wisconsin Cheeseman, Inc.

For Complete List of Firm Personnel, See General Section

For full biographical listings, see the Martindale-Hubbell Law Directory

McMaster Gervais, *Montreal—Continued*

MEMBERS OF FIRM

Timothy R. Carsley	Lionel J. Blanshay
Raymond Picard	Pierre Gattuso
Michael Patry	H. John Godber
Michael Bantey	Patrice Martin

Geneviève Bergeron

COUNSEL

Bartha M. Knoppers

For Complete List of Firm Personnel, See General Section

For full biographical listings, see the Martindale-Hubbell Law Directory

Pouliot, Mercure (AV)

CIBC Tower, 31st Floor, 1155 René-Lévesque Boulevard, West, H3B 3S6
Telephone: 514-875-5210
Telecopier: 514-875-4308
Email: POUMER@CEDEP.COM
Genève, Suisse Office: 8, Rue de la Rôtisserie, 1204 Geneva, Switzerland.
Telephone: +41 22-28 79 40.
Telecopier: +41 22-21 23 67.

MEMBERS OF FIRM

Georges A. Pouliot, Q.C.	Gilles Bertrand
Gilles Brunelle	Jean Larivière
Luc Gratton	Louis-Michel Tremblay
Brian Riordan	David I. Johnston
Pierre Paquet	Stéphane Hébert
Anne-Marie Gauthier	Jacques LeBel, Q.C.
Yvon Brizard	Joel A. Silcoff
Robert Tessier	Ronald M. Auclair
Daniel Gagné	Philippe Roy
Lilia Pouliot	Maxime B. Rhéaume
Marco Veilleux	Serge Desrochers
Alain Nadon	C. Keenan LaPierre
Jean H. Gagnon	Alain Bond
Richard Fontaine	Louis Coallier
Normand Royal	Nicole Chouinard

Stéphane Teasdale

ASSOCIATES

Micheline Perrault	Brent J. Muir
Caroline Lemoine	Louise Tremblay
Béatrice Arronis	Chantal Joubert
Yvan Nantel	Normand D'Amour
Sylvie Boulanger	Pascale Cloutier
Vincent Frenette	Eric Couture
Robert Cardin	Frédéric Chatel
Alexandre Henri	Mary-Lynn Breton

Alexandre Ajami

For full biographical listings, see the Martindale-Hubbell Law Directory

TRANSPORTATION LAW

MINNESOTA

*ST. PAUL,** Ramsey Co.

SPENCE, RICKE & THURMER, P.A. (AV)

Suite 600, Degree of Honor Building, 325 Cedar Street, 55101
Telephone: 651-223-8000
Fax: 651-223-8003
Email: meganr@srtpa.com

Thomas W. Spence
Megan Korfhage Ricke
Susan D. Thurmer

Patrick J. Sweeney
Timothy K. Masterson
Julius W. Gernes
Rodney A. Honkanen
Glenn Olander-Quamme
Scott H. Rauser

Representative Clients: Burlington Northern Sante Fe Railroad; Glacier Park Co.

For full biographical listings, see the Martindale-Hubbell Law Directory

MISSISSIPPI

BILOXI, Harrison Co.

BROWN, WATT & BUCHANAN, P.A. (AV)

115 Main Street, P.O. Box 1377, 39533-1377
Telephone: 228-374-2999
Telecopier: 228-435-7090
Email: mail@bwblaw.com *URL:* http://www.bwblaw.com
Pascagoula, Mississippi Office: 3112 Canty Street, P.O. Box 2220.
Telephone: 228-762-0035.
Fax: 228-762-0299.

Raymond L. Brown
W. Mark Edwards
W. Lee Watt
A. Kelly Sessoms, III
Patrick R. Buchanan
Alan K. Sudduth

Representative Clients: Canal Insurance; CSX Transportation, Inc.; Colonial Freight Systems; Sea-Land Services, Inc.; The Travelers Companies; USF&G Co.; Wausau Insurance.

For full biographical listings, see the Martindale-Hubbell Law Directory

*GULFPORT,** Harrison Co.

DUKES, DUKES, KEATING AND FANECA, P.A. (AV)

2909 13th Street, 6th Floor, P.O. Drawer W, 39501
Telephone: 228-868-1111
Fax: 228-863-2886
Email: ddkf@ddkf.com

Walter W. Dukes
Hugh D. Keating
Cy Faneca

For Complete List of Firm Personnel, See General Section

For full biographical listings, see the Martindale-Hubbell Law Directory

*PASCAGOULA,** Jackson Co.

BROWN, WATT & BUCHANAN, P.A. (AV)

3112 Canty Street, P.O. Box 2220, 39569-2220
Telephone: 228-762-0035
Telecopier: 228-762-0299
Email: mail@bwblaw.com *URL:* http://www.bwblaw.com
Biloxi, Mississippi Office: 115 Main Street, P.O. Box 1377.
Telephone: 228-374-2999.
Fax: 228-435-7090.

Raymond L. Brown
W. Mark Edwards
W. Lee Watt
A. Kelly Sessoms, III
Patrick R. Buchanan
Alan K. Sudduth

Representative Clients: Canal Insurance; CSX Transportation, Inc.; Colonial Freight Systems; Sea-Land Services, Inc.; The Travelers Companies; USF&G Co.; Wausau Insurance.

For full biographical listings, see the Martindale-Hubbell Law Directory

MISSOURI

KANSAS CITY, Jackson, Clay, Platte & Cass Cos.

THE LEWANDOWSKI LAW FIRM A PROFESSIONAL CORPORATION (AV)

9249 Ward Parkway, 64114
Telephone: 816-822-9600
Facsimile: 816-363-3900
Email: lewandowski@justicemail.com

Alex M. Lewandowski
Russell Powell

For full biographical listings, see the Martindale-Hubbell Law Directory

ST. LOUIS, (Independent City)

REBMAN WAGENER & LINHARES, P.C. (AV)

8000 Maryland Avenue, Suite 1060, 63105-3762
Telephone: 314-725-1118
Telecopier: 314-725-1026
URL: http://www.lawyers.com/rebman&wagener

Joseph E. Rebman
Jeffrey R. Wagener
Robert J. Linhares

For full biographical listings, see the Martindale-Hubbell Law Directory

MONTANA

*BILLINGS,** Yellowstone Co.

CROWLEY, HAUGHEY, HANSON, TOOLE & DIETRICH, P.L.L.P. (AV)

500 Transwestern II, 490 North 31st Street, P.O. Box 2529, 59103
Telephone: 406-252-3441
Fax: 406-259-4159
Email: crowley@crowleylaw.com
Helena, Montana Office: IBM Building, 100 North Park Avenue, Suite 300, 59601.
Telephone: 406-449-4165.
Fax: 406-449-5149.
Kalispell, Montana Office: 431 1st Avenue West, 59901.
Telephone: 406-752-6644.
Fax: 406-752-5108.
Williston, North Dakota Office: 113 East Broadway, 58801.
Telephone: 701-572-2200.
Fax: 701-572-7072.

MEMBER OF FIRM

Carolyn S. Ostby

Representative Clients: Montana Power Co.; First Interstate Bank of Commerce; MDU Resources Group, Inc.; Chevron U.S.A., Inc.; Noranda Minerals Corp.; United Parcel Service.
Insurance Clients: Farmers Insurance Group; New York Life Insurance Co.

For Complete List of Firm Personnel, See General Section

For full biographical listings, see the Martindale-Hubbell Law Directory

NEVADA

*LAS VEGAS,** Clark Co.

JOLLEY, URGA, WIRTH & WOODBURY (AV)

3800 Howard Hughes Parkway Suite 1600, 89109
Telephone: 702-699-7500
Facsimile: 702-699-7555
URL: http://www.juww.com
Boulder City, Nevada Office: Suite 105, 1000 Nevada Highway, 89005.
Telephone: 702-293-3674.

MEMBERS OF FIRM

William R. Urga
Brian E. Holthus

Representative Clients: Wells Fargo Bank and its predecessor, First Interstate Bank of Nevada; Nevada State Bank; Chicago Title Insurance Co.; Melvin Simon & Associates, Inc.; General Motors Acceptance Corp.; Toyota Motor Credit Corporation; Champion Home Builders Co.; Circus Circus Casinos, Inc.

For Complete List of Firm Personnel, See General Section

For full biographical listings, see the Martindale-Hubbell Law Directory

NEW JERSEY

*NEWARK,** Essex Co.

McCarter & English, LLP (AV)

Four Gateway Center, 100 Mulberry Street, P.O. Box 652, 07101-0652
Telephone: 973-622-4444
Telecopier: 973-624-7070
URL: http://www.mccarter.com
Cherry Hill, New Jersey Office: 1820 Chapel Avenue West, Suite 380.
Telephone: 609-662-8444.
Telecopier: 609-662-6203.
New York, New York Office: Suite 2247, One World Trade Center.
Telephone: 212-466-9018.
Telecopier: 212-432-6568.
Boca Raton, Florida Office: 2255 Glades Road, Suite 319-A.
Telephone: 561-994-6262.
Telecopier: 561-241-0798.
Wilmington, Delaware Office: Mellon Bank Center, 919 Market Street.
Telephone: 302-654-8010.
Telecopier: 302-654-0795.
Philadelphia, Pennsylvania Office: One Commerce Square, 2005 Market Street, Suite 3600.
Telephone: 215-557-7700.
Telecopier: 215-557-6544.

MEMBER OF FIRM

James H. Keale

OF COUNSEL

Thomas F. Daly

For Complete List of Firm Personnel, See General Section

For full biographical listings, see the Martindale-Hubbell Law Directory

Sills Cummis Radin Tischman Epstein & Gross, A Professional Corporation (AV)

One Riverfront Plaza, 07102-5400
Telephone: 973-643-7000
Fax: 973-643-6500
Telex: 820630 Sillsbeck Nwk
Email: sillsmail@sillscummis.com *URL:* http://www.sillscummis.com
Atlantic City, New Jersey Office: 17 Gordon's Alley.
Telephone: 609-344-2800.
New York, N.Y. Office: 712 Fifth Avenue.
Telephone: 212-643-7000.
Washington, D.C. Office: 1800 K Street, N.W.
Telephone: 202-296-4750.

MEMBERS OF FIRM

Clive S. Cummis
Kenneth F. Oettle

OF COUNSEL

Mitchel E. Ostrer

Paul P. Josephson

Representative Clients: Gray Line Worldwide Tours; Shortline Bus Company; Westates Airlines.

For Complete List of Firm Personnel, See General Section

For full biographical listings, see the Martindale-Hubbell Law Directory

*NEW BRUNSWICK,** Middlesex Co.

Watson, Stevens, Fiorilla & Rutter, LLP (AV)

A New Jersey Limited Liability Partnership
390 George Street, P.O. Box 1185, 08903-1185
Telephone: 732-545-2250
Fax: 732-214-0242
URL: http://www.wsfr.net
New York, N.Y. Office: 630 Third Avenue.
Telephone: 212-840-2700.

MEMBERS OF FIRM

John K. Fiorilla
Michael K. Rutter
Mark S. Stevens
Carol Ann Stevens

OF COUNSEL

Joseph Stevens

Leslie-Ann M. Justus
Christine A. Roy

Representative Clients: Consolidated Rail Corp. (Conrail); Transcontinental Gas Pipe Line Corp.; Norfolk Southern Corporation; CSX Transportation; The New York, Susquehanna and Western Railway Corporation; Morristown & Erie Railway, Inc.; KLLM, Inc.; Rhino Trucking, Inc.; Union Pacific Railroad; The Williams Companies, Inc.

For full biographical listings, see the Martindale-Hubbell Law Directory

SPRINGFIELD, Union Co.

Hardin, Kundla, McKeon, Poletto & Polifroni, P.A., A Professional Corporation (AV)

673 Morris Avenue, P.O. Box 730, 07081
Telephone: 973-912-5222
Fax: 973-912-9212
Email: info@HKMPP.com
New York, New York Office: 55 John Street, 10038.
Telephone: 212-571-0111.
Fax: 212-571-1117.

George R. Hardin
Robert L. Polifroni
Janet L. Poletto
Mark S. Kundla
John F. McKeon
James R. Greene
Nicea J. D'Annunzio
John Samuel Favate
Patrick J. Clare
Anna Marie Strand

Jeffrey A. Oshin
Joseph R. Lowicky
Tracy C. Forsyth
Joseph A. DeFuria
John G. Kilbride
Jeffrey H. Goldsmith
Jeffrey Roth
Nora J. Grimbergen
William C. Sullivan, Jr.
Paul Daly
V. Christopher Hirsch
Richard S. Reig
Sam A. Dotro
Brian K. Kaiser
David M. Steiner
Lani M. D'Agostino
Sheila A. Glackin
Michael S. Schwartz
Kirsten L. McCaw
Sanjoy Mukherjee
Louisa B. Sargent
Michael A. Cifelli
James J. A. Mulhall
Kevin M. Regan
Lisa D. Chanel
Maria-Milagros Herrero
Brian A. King
Christina Fichera Dente
Andrea L. Strack
Roger J. Imhof
John P. Monaghan
Stephen J. Donahue
Cindy L. Thompson
Lisa A. Ganzhorn

Representative Clients: Hertz Equipment Rental Corp.; Hertz Corp.; Mayflower Transit.

For full biographical listings, see the Martindale-Hubbell Law Directory

NEW YORK

*NEW YORK,** New York Co.

Badiak Will & Ruddy (AV)

Suite 1040, 120 Broadway, 10271
Telephone: 212-376-6767
Telecopier: 212-376-6777
Telex: 6716686 BANDW
Email: admiralaw@aol.com
North Miami Beach, Florida Office: Badiak, Will & Kallen, 17071 West Dixie Highway, P.O. Box 600550.
Telephone: 305-945-1851.

MEMBERS OF FIRM

Roman Badiak
Alfred J. Will
James J. Ruddy
John D. Kallen (Resident, North Miami, Florida Office)
David L. Maloof (1924-1992)

ASSOCIATES

Stephen A. Frank
Nicholas Kalfa
James P. Krauzlis
Martin L. Lindahl
Lisa A. Scognamillo
Deborah R. Reid

OF COUNSEL

Charles C. Goodenough

For full biographical listings, see the Martindale-Hubbell Law Directory

De Orchis, Walker & Corsa, LLP (AV)

One Battery Park Plaza, Second Floor, 10004-1480
Telephone: 212-344-4700
MCI Telex: 673-4608
Telefax: 212-509-7886
Email: DW&C@MCIMAIL.COM *URL:* http://www.marinelex.com
Union, New Jersey Office: 1495 Morris Avenue, P.O. Box 1718.
Telephone: 973-467-4740.
Telefax: 908-687-0255.
Stamford, Connecticut Office: 999 Summer Street.
Telephone: 203-323-9120.
Telefax: 203-323-9015.
Boston, Massachusetts Office: One Boston Place, 5th Floor, 02180.
Telephone: 617-619-3610.
Telefax: 617-619-3924.
Miami, Florida Office: De Orchis, Corsa & Hillerbrand, LLP, 2650 Biscayne Boulevard, 33137.
Telephone: 305-571-9200.
Telefax: 305-571-9250.

(See Next Column)

DE ORCHIS, WALKER & CORSA LLP—*Continued*

PARTNERS

LeRoy S. Corsa
Vincent M. De Orchis
Christopher H. Mansuy
Alexander V. Sansone
John A. Orzel
Michael E. Unger
Cary R. Wiener

ASSOCIATES

R. Brett Kelly
William E. Lakis
Marc I. Kunkin
Francesco A. Di Pietro

RESIDENT COUNSEL

M. E. De Orchis

OF COUNSEL

Ara A. Shimshidian
Bruce H. Neuman

For full biographical listings, see the Martindale-Hubbell Law Directory

MILBANK, TWEED, HADLEY & MCCLOY LLP (AV)

1 Chase Manhattan Plaza, 10005-1413
Telephone: 212-530-5000
Fax: 212-530-5219
Email: postmaster@milbank.com *URL:* http://www.milbank.com
Midtown Office: 375 Park Avenue, Suite 3601, 10152.
Telephone: 212-530-5800.
Fax: 212-530-0158.
Los Angeles, California Office: 601 South Figueroa Street, 30th Floor, 90017.
Telephone: 213-892-4000.
Fax: 213-629-5063.
Washington, D.C. Office: International Square Building, Suite 1100, 1825 Eye Street, N.W., 20006.
Telephone: 202-835-7500.
Fax: 202-835-7586.
Tokyo, Japan Office: Fukoku Seimei Building, 2-2, Uchisaiwai-cho 2-Chome, Chiyoda-ku, Tokyo 100-0011, Japan.
Telephone: 011-81-3-3504-1050.
Fax: 011-81-3-3595-2790, 011-81-3-3595-2840.
London, England Office: Dashwood House, 69 Old Broad Street, London EC2M 1QS.
Telephone: 011-44-207-448-3000.
Fax: 011-44-207-448-3029.
Hong Kong Office: 3007 Alexandra House, 16 Chater Road.
Telephone: 011-852-2971-4888.
Fax: 011-852-2840-0792; 011-852-2845-9046.
Singapore Office: 14-00 Caltex House, 30 Raffles Place, 048622.
Telephone: 011-65-428-2400.
Fax: 011-65-428-2500.
Moscow, Russia Office: 24/27 Sadovaya-Samotyochnya, Moscow, 103051.
Telephone: 011-7-501-258-5015.
Fax: 011-7-501-258-5014.

MEMBERS OF FIRM

W. Rogers Benson, Jr.
Drew S. Fine
Elliot Gewirtz
Young Joon Kim (Resident, Tokyo, Japan Office)
Elihu F. Robertson
Helfried J. Schwarz

OF COUNSEL

Fred W. Reinke (Resident, Washington, D.C. Office)

ASSOCIATES

Christopher L. Beers
Christine Luba Carver
James G. Hnat II
Robert S. Kim
Young Il Kim
Ariel Z. Kronman
Thomas C. Lee (Resident, Tokyo, Japan Office)
Alvin K. Leong
Zarrar Sehgal
Robert Sternthal
Susan A. Young (Resident, Tokyo, Japan Office)
Jay S. Zwerling

For Complete List of Firm Personnel, See General Section

For full biographical listings, see the Martindale-Hubbell Law Directory

SERKO & SIMON LLP (AV)

Suite 3371, 1 World Trade Center, 10048
Telephone: 212-775-0055
Facsimile: 212-839-9103
Email: serko-simon@customs-law.com *URL:* http://www.customs-law.com

MEMBERS OF FIRM

David Serko
Joel K. Simon
Daniel J. Gluck
Christopher M. Kane

SPECIAL COUNSEL

Melvyn N. Minsky

ASSOCIATES

Despina Keegan
Jerome L. Hanifin (Not admitted in NY)

OF COUNSEL-NEW YORK

David S. Chang
Rafael F. Castro-Lang (Not admitted in NY)

(See Next Column)

TECHNICAL ADVISORS

Joseph Raul
Martin L. Weiss

For full biographical listings, see the Martindale-Hubbell Law Directory

WATSON, FARLEY & WILLIAMS (AV)

380 Madison Avenue, 10017
Telephone: 212-922-2200
Telex: 6790626 WFWNY
Fax: 212-922-1512
Email: josborne@wfw.com *URL:* http://www.wfw.com
London, England Office: 15 Appold Street, London EC2A 2HB.
Telephone: (44 171) 814 8000.
Telex: 8955707 WFWLON G.
Fax: (44 171) 814 8141.
Paris, France Office: 47, rue de Monceau, 75008 Paris.
Telephone: (33 1) 53 83 12 12.
Telex: WFWPAR 651096 F.
Fax: (33 1) 45 61 09 01.
Athens, Greece Office: 5th Floor, Alassia Building, Defteras Merarchias 13, 185-35 Piraeus.
Telephone: (30 1) 422 3660.
Telex: 24 1311 WFWGR.
Fax: (30 1) 422 3664.
Singapore Office: 16 Collyer Quay, #12-02 Hitachi Tower, Singapore 049318.
Telephone: (65) 532-5335.
Fax: (65) 532-5454.
Moscow, Russia Office: 16/2 Tverskaya Ulitsa, Business Centre Bldg. 3, The Actor Gallery, Moscow 103009.
Telephone: 7502 237 7770 (international only); 7095 935 7770.
Fax: 7502 237 7771 (international only); 7095 935 7771.
Copenhagen, Denmark Office: Lille Kongensgade 20 DK-1074 Copenhagen K.
Telephone: (45 33) 91 33 03.
Fax: (45 33) 91 49 12.
Associated Office: Abbas F. Ghazzawi Law Firm, Saudi Arabia.

MEMBERS OF FIRM

Leo Chang
John S. Osborne, Jr.
Alfred E. Yudes, Jr.
Philip H. Spector
Richard L. Jarashow
William S. Haft
Christopher P. Belisle

For Complete List of Firm Personnel, See General Section

For full biographical listings, see the Martindale-Hubbell Law Directory

*WHITE PLAINS,** Westchester Co.

BOEGGEMAN, GEORGE, HODGES & CORDE, P.C. (AV)

11 Martine Avenue, 10606
Telephone: 914-761-2252
Telecopier: 914-761-5211
Email: boeggeman@bghc-law.com *URL:* http://www.bghc-law.com
Albany, New York Office: 46 Columbia Street, 12207-2716.
Telephone: 518-465-1100.
Fax: 518-465-1800.

George S. Hodges
Richard G. Corde
John J. Walsh, II
Harold L. Moroknek
Robert S. Ondrovic
Thomas A. Sica (Resident Managing Attorney, Albany Office)

Karen A.D. Jockimo
William M. Wingertzahn
Elizabeth C. Mirisola
Cynthia Dolan
Marcella M. Green
Paul A. Hurley
Leslie K. Arfine
John T. Holden
James J. Lofrese
Jeanne M. Hurley
Ira H. Lapp
Matt Randolph Belkin
Cynthia K. Messemer

OF COUNSEL

Joseph H. George
John E. Boeggeman (1919-1993)

Representative Clients: American Telephone & Telegraph; Anheuser-Busch Companies, Inc.; Lowe's Home Centers; Great Atlantic & Pacific Tea Company; Reliance National Insurance Company; Metropolitan Property & Casualty Insurance Company; Fisher Price, Inc.; CGU Insurance Company; United Services Automobile Association; New York Central Mutual Fire Insurance Company.

For full biographical listings, see the Martindale-Hubbell Law Directory

OHIO

*COLUMBUS,** Franklin Co.

BAKER & HOSTETLER LLP (AV)

Capitol Square, Suite 2100, 65 East State Street, 43215-4260
Telephone: 614-228-1541
Telecopier: 614-462-2616
To contact an attorney on the Internet use first initial and surname followed by @baker-hostetler.com
URL: http://www.bakerlaw.com
In Cleveland, Ohio: 3200 National City Center, 1900 East Ninth Street.
Telephone: 216-621-0200.
In Cincinnati, Ohio: 312 Walnut Street, Suite 2650.
Telephone: 513-929-3400.
In Denver, Colorado: 303 East 17th Avenue, Suite 1100.
Telephone: 303-861-0600.
In Houston, Texas: 1000 Louisiana, Suite 2000.
Telephone: 713-751-1600.
In Beverly Hills, California: 9150 Wilshire Boulevard, Suite 205.
Telephone: 310-385-7500.
In Long Beach, California: 300 Oceangate, Suite 620.
Telephone: 562-432-2827.
In Los Angeles, California: 600 Wilshire Boulevard.
Telephone: 213-624-2400.
In Orlando, Florida: SunBank Center, Suite 2300, 200 South Orange Avenue.
Telephone: 407-649-4000.
In Washington, D. C.: Washington Square, Suite 1100, 1050 Connecticut Avenue, N.W.
Telephone: 202-861-1500.

PARTNER

A. Charles Tell

RETIRED PARTNER

John P. McMahon

For Complete List of Firm Personnel, See General Section

For full biographical listings, see the Martindale-Hubbell Law Directory

BEERY & SPURLOCK CO., L.P.A. (AV)

275 East State Street, 43215
Telephone: 614-228-8575
FAX: 614-228-1408
Email: beeryspurlock@iwaynet.net *URL:* http://www.lawyers.com/beery&spurlock

Michael Spurlock
Eric W. Beery

OF COUNSEL

Paul F. Beery

Representative Clients: Central Parcel Express, Inc.; Comprehensive Logistics, Inc.; Dart Trucking, Inc.; Dunbar Armored, Inc.; Falcon Transport Co.; H.T.I.-Hall Trucking, Inc.; A.B.F. Freight Systems, Inc.; Greyhound Lines, Inc.; Landstar Ligon, Inc.; Victory Express, Inc.

For full biographical listings, see the Martindale-Hubbell Law Directory

*TOLEDO,** Lucas Co.

DOYLE, LEWIS & WARNER (AV)

202 North Erie Street, P.O. Box 2168, 43603
Telephone: 419-248-1500
Fax: 419-248-2002
Email: dlw1@primenet.com

MEMBERS OF FIRM

Steven Timonere
Richard F. Ellenberger
Michael E. Hyrne
Michael A. Bruno
David W. Doerner

ASSOCIATES

Kevin A. Pituch
Maureen O. Atkins

Counsel for: Consolidated Rail Corp.; The Lakefront Dock & Railroad Terminal Co.; Prudential Insurance Co. of America; Equitable Life Assurance Society of the U.S.; Metropolitan Life Insurance Co.; Greyhound Lines; Fireman's Fund Insurance Cos.

For Complete List of Firm Personnel, See General Section

For full biographical listings, see the Martindale-Hubbell Law Directory

OKLAHOMA

*OKLAHOMA CITY,** Oklahoma Co.

WILLIAM C. BOSTON, P.L.L.C. (AV)

4005 Northwest Expressway, Suite 600, 73116
Telephone: 405-848-0600
Telefax: 405-848-0655
Email: wcbfirm@ionet.net *URL:* http://www.okaircraftlaw.com

William C. Boston, Jr.

Scott D. McCreary
William Clayton Boston, III
Eric L. Johnson
Lisa Anne Drescher

OF COUNSEL

Donna M. Schmidt (Not admitted in OK)
Willis W. Luttrell (Not admitted in OK)
Joseph T. Brennan (Not admitted in OK)

For full biographical listings, see the Martindale-Hubbell Law Directory

*TULSA,** Tulsa Co.

RHODES, HIERONYMUS, JONES, TUCKER & GABLE, P.L.L.C. (AV)

Oneok Plaza, 100 West 5th Street, Suite 400, P.O. Box 21100, 74121-1100
Telephone: 918-582-1173
Fax: 918-592-3390
URL: http://www.rhodesokla.com

MEMBERS OF FIRM

Kevin D. Berry
Jo Anne Deaton
Richard M. Eldridge
E. D. Hieronymus (1908 -1994)
Bert M. Jones
William S. Leach
Michael W. McGivern
William D. Perrine
Mary Quinn-Cooper
Robert P. Redemann
David P. Reid
Chris L. Rhodes, III
Thomas E. Steichen
Catherine C. Taylor
John H. Tucker
Wilson T. White
Harold C. Zuckerman

Ann E. Allison
Steven K. Bunting
Robert P. Coffey, Jr.
J. Christopher Davis
Andrew D. Downing
Dana L. Gish
Kerry R. Lewis
Andrew L. Richardson
Michael F. Smith
Leslie J. Southerland
Kimberly E. West
Keith A. Wilkes

OF COUNSEL

George W. Gable (Retired Partner)
Larry J. Fulton
Kelly M. Greenough

Representative Clients: American International Companies; Bechtel; Chubb Group of Insurance Companies; General Motors Corporation; Merrill, Lynch; Nissan Motor Corporation in U.S.A.; Pfizer, Inc.; Volkswagen of America, Volkswagen, A.G.; Zurich U.S.

For full biographical listings, see the Martindale-Hubbell Law Directory

PENNSYLVANIA

*HARRISBURG,** Dauphin Co.

MANCKE, WAGNER, HERSHEY AND TULLY (AV)

2233 North Front Street, 17110
Telephone: 717-234-7051

MEMBERS OF FIRM

John B. Mancke
P. Richard Wagner
David E. Hershey
William T. Tully

For full biographical listings, see the Martindale-Hubbell Law Directory

MCNEES, WALLACE & NURICK (AV)

100 Pine Street, P.O. Box 1166, 17108-1166
Telephone: 717-232-8000
Fax: 717-237-5300
Email: info@mwn.com *URL:* http://www.mwn.com
Columbus, Ohio Office: 21 East State Street, Suite 1700, 43215.
Telephone: 614-469-8000.
Fax: 614-469-4653.
Washington, D.C. Office: 1200 G Street, N.W., 20005.
Telephone: 202-434-8991.
Fax: 202-434-8707.
Hazleton, Pennsylvania Office: 1 South Church Street, Suite 302, 18201.
Telephone: 570-455-8300.
Fax: 570-455-8390.

(See Next Column)

McNees, Wallace & Nurick—*Continued*

MEMBERS OF THE FIRM

James L. Fritz
Delano M. Lantz
Robert A. Mills
Lawrence R. Wieder

ASSOCIATE

Curtis N. Stambaugh

For Complete List of Firm Personnel, See General Section

For full biographical listings, see the Martindale-Hubbell Law Directory

*PHILADELPHIA,** Philadelphia Co.

Marvin I. Barish Law Offices A Professional Corporation (AV)

6th and Walnut Streets, Suite 801E, 19106-3308
Telephone: 215-923-8900; 800-233-7101
Email: mbarish@aol.com *URL:* http://www.lawyers.com/barishlawoffices
Cherry Hill, New Jersey Office: 1930 East Marlton Pike, Suite Q-38.
Telephone: 609-338-0550.

Marvin I. Barish

Gregory L. Nester

For full biographical listings, see the Martindale-Hubbell Law Directory

John Gerard Devlin & Associates, P.C. (AV)

1515 Market Street Suite 2010, 19102
Telephone: 215-564-6740
Telefax: 215-564-6732
Email: devlinlaw@aol.com
Allentown, Pennsylvania Office: The Sovereign Building, Executive Suite 103, 609 Hamilton Mall.
Telephone: 215-820-6422.
Westmont, New Jersey Office: 216 Haddon Avenue, Suite 103.
Telephone: 609-858-1690.
Fax: 609-858-8998.
East Brunswick, New Jersey Office: 190 Route 18, Suite 3000.
Telephone: 908-214-2621.
Fax: 908-246-2917.
Wilkes-Barre, Pennsylvania Office: Cross Creek Pointe, 1065 Hwy 315, Suite H.
Telephone: 610-820-6422.

John Gerard Devlin
James B. Corrigan, Jr.
Joseph T. Murphy, Jr.
Thomas Paschos
Michael Malarick
Suzanne Curran Murphy
Arthur F. Wheeler
Paul A. Lawless, Jr.

Representative Clients: Lloyds of London; Commercial Union; John Hancock Property and Casualty Insurance Co.; Wausau Insurance Co.; Hanseco Insurance Co.; American Family Insurance Co.; Liberty Mutual Insurance Co.; Linberg Adjustment Co.

For full biographical listings, see the Martindale-Hubbell Law Directory

McEldrew & Fullam, P.C. (AV)

Suite 5050 One Liberty Place, 19103
Telephone: 215-563-8300
800-223-3352
Fax: 215-563-6130
URL: http://www.lawyers.com/mceldrew&fullampc
New York, New York Office: McEldrew & Ressler, Suite 2101, 11 Pennsylvania Plaza, 10001.
Telephone: 212-695-6446.
Fax: 212-268-0287.

James J. McEldrew, III
Nancy H. Fullam

Marcella J. Schell
Carol L. Vassallo
Sallie Updyke Mundy
David Felderman

LEGAL SUPPORT PERSONNEL

Christine Doelp (Comptroller)

For full biographical listings, see the Martindale-Hubbell Law Directory

*PITTSBURGH,** Allegheny Co.

Howard F. Messer, P.C. (AV)

1404 Grant Building, 15219
Telephone: 412-281-7200
FAX: 412-765-0440
URL: http://www.lawyers.com/messerlaw

Howard F. Messer

Philip A. Fabiano

For full biographical listings, see the Martindale-Hubbell Law Directory

Pillar • Mulroy & Ferber, Professional Corporation (AV)

1106 Frick Building, 15219-6101
Telephone: 412-471-3300
Fax: 412-471-6068
URL: http://www.lawyers.com/pmf_law

John A. Pillar

Reference: Pittsburgh National Bank.

For full biographical listings, see the Martindale-Hubbell Law Directory

SOUTH CAROLINA

*COLUMBIA,** Richland Co.

Willoughby & Hoefer, P.A. (AV)

1022 Calhoun Street, Suite 302, P.O. Box 8416, 29202-8416
Telephone: 803-252-3300
Telecopier: 803-256-8062
Email: willhoef@sc-online.net

Mitchell M. Willoughby
Alvis J. Bynum, Jr.

Elizabeth Zeck
Paige Jones Gossett

Representative Clients: Superior Carriers, Inc.; Truckers Express, Inc.; Consolidated Freightways; Wills Trucking; Dart Transit.

For full biographical listings, see the Martindale-Hubbell Law Directory

*GREENVILLE,** Greenville Co.

Leatherwood Walker Todd & Mann, P.C. (AV)

100 East Coffee Street, P.O. Box 87, 29602
Telephone: 864-242-6440
FAX: 864-240-2477
Email: leatherwood@lwtm.com *URL:* http://www.lwtm.com
Spartanburg, South Carolina Office: 1451 East Main Street, P.O. Box 3188.
Telephone: 864-582-4365.
Telefax: 864-583-8961.

O. Doyle Martin
Joseph E. Major
Duke K. McCall, Jr.
Michael J. Giese
Samuel Wright Outten
Robert D. Moseley, Jr.

Kurt M. Rozelsky
Cathy H. Dunn
(Resident, Spartanburg Office)
William B. Swent

Representative Clients: Canal Insurance Co.; Roadway Express; Highlands Insurance Co.; Empire Fire & Marine Insurance Co.; Overnite Transportation Co.; Orion Specialty Group; John Deere Insurance Co.; Chubb & Sons Insurance Group; Pinnacle Insurance Co.; Vanliner Insurance Co.

For Complete List of Firm Personnel, See General Section

For full biographical listings, see the Martindale-Hubbell Law Directory

TENNESSEE

*NASHVILLE,** Davidson Co.

Cox, LeVan, Sprader & Patton, P.L.L.C. (AV)

172 Second Avenue, North Suite 214, 37201
Telephone: 615-843-0300
Telecopier: 615-843-0310
URL: http://www.lawyers.com/clsp

MEMBERS OF FIRM

Stephen E. Cox
Mark S. LeVan
Paul L. Sprader
C. Benton Patton

For full biographical listings, see the Martindale-Hubbell Law Directory

TEXAS

*AUSTIN,** Travis Co.

BURNS ANDERSON JURY & BRENNER, L.L.P. (AV)

A Limited Liability Partnership including a Professional Corporation
4807 Spicewood Springs Road, Building 4, P.O. Box 26300, 78755-6300
Telephone: 512-338-5322
Facsimile: 512-338-5363
Email: lmackey@bajb.com

Robert B. Burns, Jr. (P.C.)
Joe R. Anderson
Jeffrey R. Jury
David L. Brenner
Michael J. Donovan

Gilbert Atkinson
Arturo M. Aviles
Lea M. Burleson
Kenton P. Campbell
Cristina Mireles Cooper
Paul Gonzalez
Kristin Lee Lemke
Danielle M. Harsany
David L. Swanson

For full biographical listings, see the Martindale-Hubbell Law Directory

*DALLAS,** Dallas Co.

CALHOUN & STACY (AV)

Suite 5700 - Bank of America Plaza, 901 Main Street, 75202-3713
Telephone: 214-748-5000
Facsimile: 214-748-1421
Email: info@calhounstacy.com *URL:* http://www.calhounstacy.com

MEMBERS OF FIRM

Mark Alan Calhoun
Dennis D. Conder
LeAnn Wainscott Cross
David W. Elrod
Shannon B. Schuster
Roy L. Stacy
Michael C. Wright

ASSOCIATES

Joseph G. Barkate, Jr.
Scott S. Crocker
Sean P. Fitzgerald
Elizabeth Reding Gambrell
Leanne Capps Medford
Jonathan G. Polak
Joel W. Reese
Barbara L. Wohlrabe

For Complete List of Firm Personnel, See General Section

For full biographical listings, see the Martindale-Hubbell Law Directory

VIRGINIA

*ARLINGTON,** Arlington Co.

JACKSON & JESSUP, P.C. (AV)

3426 North Washington Boulevard, P.O. Box 1240, 22210
Telephone: 703-525-4050
Facsimile: 703-525-4054
Email: wpj@translaw.com

William P. Jackson, Jr.
Gerald E. Jessup (1911-1994)

References: Upon request.

For full biographical listings, see the Martindale-Hubbell Law Directory

NORFOLK, (Independent City)

DAVEY & BROGAN, P.C. (AV)

101 Granby Street, Suite 300, 23510
Telephone: 757-622-0100
Telecopier: 757-622-4924
Email: daveylaw@pilot.infi.net *URL:* http://www.lawyers.com/davey&associates

Philip N. Davey
Patrick M. Brogan
R. Arthur Jett, Jr.

Representative Clients: GRE Insurance Group; Marine Office of America Corp.; Spliethoff's Bevrachtingskantoor B.V.; W.F. Magann Corp.; The North of England Protecting and Indemnity Association Limited; Evergreen America Corporation; Sveriges Angfartygs Assurans Forening "The Swedish Club"; Mediterranean Shipping Co., S.A.
Reference: Crestar Bank.

For full biographical listings, see the Martindale-Hubbell Law Directory

WEST VIRGINIA

*CHARLESTON,** Kanawha Co.

JACKSON & KELLY (AV)

1600 Laidley Tower, P.O. Box 553, 25322
Telephone: 304-340-1000
Fax: 304-340-1130
Email: info@jacksonkelly.com *URL:* http://www.jacksonkelly.com
Martinsburg, West Virginia Office: 300 Foxcroft Avenue, P.O. Box 1068.
Telephone: 304-263-8800.
Fax: 304-263-7110.
Morgantown, West Virginia Office: 6000 Hampton Center, P.O. Box 619.
Telephone: 304-599-3000.
Fax: 304-285-2040.
New Martinsville, West Virginia Office: 256 Russell Avenue, P.O. Box 68.
Telephone: 304-455-1751.
Fax: 304-455-6314.
Parkersburg, West Virginia Office: 412 Market Street, Suite 202, P.O. Box 1144.
Telephone: 304-424-3490.
Fax: 304-424-3499.
Fairmont, West Virginia Office: 1000 Technology Drive, Suite 1310.
Telephone: 304-368-2000.
Fax: 304-368-2020.
Lexington, Kentucky Office: 175 East Main Street, Suite 500, P.O. Box 2150.
Telephone: 606-255-9500.
Fax: 606-281-6478.
Washington, D. C. Office: 2401 Pennsylvania Avenue, N.W., Suite 400.
Telephone: 202-973-0200.
Fax: 202-973-0232.
Denver, Colorado Office: Suite 2710, 1660 Lincoln Street.
Telephone: 303-390-0003.
Fax: 303-390-0040.
Wheeling, West Virginia Office: 1144 Market Street.
Telephone: 304-233-4000.
Fax: 304-233-4077.

MEMBERS OF FIRM

Thomas E. Potter
Michael A. Albert
Stephen R. Crislip
A. L. Emch
David Allen Barnette
Dennis C. Sauter
Thomas J. Hurney, Jr.
John Philip Melick
William J. Powell
David J. Hardy

ASSOCIATE

Maris E. McCambley

Representative Clients: United Parcel Service; Kanawha Valley Regional Transportation Authority; Central West Virginia Regional Airport Authority; Norfolk & Western Railway Co.; Savage Industries, Inc.; Beech Aircraft Corporation; Overnite Transportation Company; Lloyds of London Insurance Company.

For Complete List of Firm Personnel, See General Section

For full biographical listings, see the Martindale-Hubbell Law Directory

WISCONSIN

*MILWAUKEE,** Milwaukee Co.

WALTHER LAW OFFICES, S.C. (AV)

222 East Mason Street, 53202-3602
Telephone: 414-273-4400
Facsimile: 414-273-8381

Christopher D. Walther
Karla A. Walther

William H. Nehrkorn, II

Reference: Liberty Bank.

For full biographical listings, see the Martindale-Hubbell Law Directory

PUERTO RICO

SAN JUAN, San Juan Dist.

JIMÉNEZ, GRAFFAM & LAUSELL

Suite 505, Midtown Building, 421 Muñoz Rivera Avenue, Hato Rey, P.O. Box 366104, 00936-6104
Telephone: 787-767-1030; 767-1000; 767-1061; 767-1064
Telefax: 787-751-4068;
Cable: "Nezte"
RCA Telex: 325-2730
Email: manager@jgl.com *URL:* http://www.jgl.com

MEMBERS OF FIRM

William A. Graffam
Steven C. Lausell
J. Ramón Rivera-Morales
José Juan Torres-Escalera
Manolo T. Rodríguez-Bird

ASSOCIATES

Patricia A. Garrity
Isabel J. Vélez-Serrano
Edgardo A. Vega-López
Jorge F. Blasini
Ruy V. Díaz-Díaz

Representative Clients: Crowley Maritime Corp.; Sea-Land Service, Inc.; NYK Line, Inc.; Overnite Transportation Co.; Carnival Cruise Lines, Inc.; The Britannia Steamship Insurance Association.

For Complete List of Firm Personnel, See General Section

For full biographical listings, see the Martindale-Hubbell Law Directory

CANADA
NEW BRUNSWICK

*SAINT JOHN,** Saint John Co.

CLARK DRUMMIE (AV)

40 Wellington Row, P.O. Box 6850, E2L 4S3
Telephone: 506-633-3800
Telecopier (Automatic): 506-633-3811
Email: cd@nbnet.nb.ca

MEMBERS OF FIRM

Deno P. Pappas, Q.C.
W. Andrew LeMesurier

Reference: Royal Bank of Canada.

For Complete List of Firm Personnel, See General Section

For full biographical listings, see the Martindale-Hubbell Law Directory

CANADA
NOVA SCOTIA

*HALIFAX,** Regional Munic. of Halifax

MCINNES COOPER (AV)

Barristers, Solicitors & Trade Mark Agents
Summit Place, 1601 Lower Water Street, P.O. Box 730, B3J 2V1
Telephone: 902-425-6500
Fax: 902-425-6350
Email: mcrhfx@mcrlaw.com *URL:* http://www.mcrlaw.com
St. John's, Newfoundland Office: Baine Johnston Centre, 5th Floor, 10 Fort William Place, P.O. Box 5939, A1C 5X4.
Telephone: 709-722-8735.
Telecopier: 709-722-1763. Email: mcrsj@mcrlaw.com.
Moncton, New Brunswick Office: Place Moncton Place, 655 Main Street, P.O. Box 1368, E1C 8T6.
Telephone: 506-857-8970.
Fax: 506-857-4095. Email: mcrmctn@mcrlaw.com.
Charlottetown, Prince Edward Island Office: BDC Place, Suite 620, 119 Kent Street, C1A 1N3.
Telephone: 902-368-8473.
Fax: 902-368-8346. Email: mcrpei@mcrlaw.com.
Fredericton, New Brunswick Office: Suite 600, 570 Queen Street, P.O. Box 610.
Telephone: 506-458-8572.
Fax: 506-458-9903. Email: mcrfton@mcrlaw.com.

PARTNERS

George T. H. Cooper, Q.C.
Lawrence A. Freeman
James E. Gould, Q.C.
Wylie Spicer, Q.C.
John D. Stringer, Q.C.

For Complete List of Firm Personnel, See General Section

For full biographical listings, see the Martindale-Hubbell Law Directory

CANADA
QUEBEC

*MONTREAL,** Montreal Dist.

MCMASTER GERVAIS (AV)

A General Partnership
1000 de La Gauchetière Street West, Suite 900, H3B 5H4
Telephone: 514-879-1212
Fax: 514-954-1905
Email: info@mcmastergervais.com *URL:* http://www.mcmastergervais.com

MEMBERS OF FIRM

Sean J. Harrington
Robert E. Charbonneau
D. James Papadimitriou
Yvan Houle
Darren E.G. McGuire
Manon Gauthier
Georges R. Thibaudeau
P. Jeremy Bolger
Peter G. Pamel
Michael Bantey
Caroline Matte
Stéphane Pitre

COUNSEL

A. Stuart Hyndman, Q.C.

For Complete List of Firm Personnel, See General Section

For full biographical listings, see the Martindale-Hubbell Law Directory

JAPAN

*TOKYO,**

American Lawyers In Tokyo

MILBANK, TWEED, HADLEY & MCCLOY LLP

(Gaikokuho Jimu Bengoshi Jimusho)
Fukoku Seimei Building, 2-2, Uchisaiwai-cho 2-Chome, Chiyoda-ku, Tokyo 100-0011
Telephone: 81-3-3504-1050
Fax: 81-3-3595-2790; 81-3-3595-2840
Email: postmaster@milbank.com *URL:* http://www.milbank.com
New York, New York Office: 1 Chase Manhattan Plaza, 10005-1413.
Telephone: 212-530-5000.
Fax: 212-530-5219.
Midtown Office: 375 Park Avenue, Suite 3601, 10152.
Telephone: 212-530-5800.
Fax: 212-530-0158.
Los Angeles, California Office: 601 South Figueroa Street, 90017.
Telephone: 213-892-4000.
Fax: 213-629-5063.
Washington, D.C. Office: International Square Building, Suite 1100, 1825 Eye Street, N.W., 20006.
Telephone: 202-835-7500.
Fax: 202-835-7586.
London, England Office: Dashwood House, 69 Old Broad Street, London, EC2M 1QS.
Telephone: 44-207-448-3000.
Fax: 44-207-448-3029.
Hong Kong Office: 3007 Alexandra House, 16 Chater Road.
Telephone: 011-852-2971-4888.
Fax: 852-2840-0792; 852-2845-9046.
Singapore Office: 14-00 Caltex House, 30 Raffles Place, 048622.
Telephone: 65-428-2400.
Fax: 65-428-2500.
Moscow, Russia Office: 24/27 Sadovaya-Samotyochnya, Moscow, 103051.
Telephone: 7-501-258-5015.
Fax: 7-501-258-5014.

PARTNER

Young Joon Kim

ASSOCIATES

Thomas C. Lee (Not admitted in Japan)
Susan A. Young (Not admitted in Japan)

For Complete List of Firm Personnel, See General Section

For full biographical listings, see the Martindale-Hubbell Law Directory

TRUSTS AND ESTATES, WILLS AND PROBATE

MINNESOTA

*DULUTH,** St. Louis Co.

HANFT, FRIDE, O'BRIEN, HARRIES, SWELBAR & BURNS, P.A. (AV)
1000 U.S. Bank Place, 130 West Superior Street, 55802-2094
Telephone: 218-722-4766
Fax: 218-529-2401
Email: firm@hanftlaw.com

Gilbert W. Harries
Richard R. Burns
Jennifer L. Carey

Counsel for: Canadian National Railways; First Bank National Association; Great American Insurance Companies; Johnson-Wilson Constructors, Inc.; Minnesota Power; Murphy McGinnis Media, Inc.; Northern Minnesota Utilities; Oglebay Norton Co.; United States Fidelity and Guaranty Company; U.S. Insurance Group.

For Complete List of Firm Personnel, See General Section

For full biographical listings, see the Martindale-Hubbell Law Directory

*FERGUS FALLS,** Otter Tail Co.

DAVID F. LUNDEEN (AV)
107 Court Street, 56537
Telephone: 218-736-4866
FAX: 218-736-7747
Email: dlundlaw@prtel.com

For full biographical listings, see the Martindale-Hubbell Law Directory

*MINNEAPOLIS,** Hennepin Co.

ABDO AND ABDO, P.A. (AV)
710 Northstar West 625 Marquette Avenue, 55402
Telephone: 612-333-1526
Fax: 612-342-2608
Email: abdoabdo@aol.com *URL:* http://www.abdo.com.br

E. John Abdo (1912-1993)
Robert P. Abdo
Steven R. Hedges
Keith J. Broady
Kenneth J. Abdo
Timothy C. Matson

For Complete List of Firm Personnel, See General Section

For full biographical listings, see the Martindale-Hubbell Law Directory

HAGERTY, JOHNSON, ALBRIGHTSON & BEITZ, P.A. (AV)
Suite 901, 701 Fourth Avenue South, 55415
Telephone: 612-349-9000
Telecopier: 612-332-3751
Email: hjab@hjab.com

Edward S. Hagerty
David W. Johnson

Representative Clients: Augustana Care Foundation; Data-Metalcraft,Inc.; Distribution Alternatives, Inc.; Fidelity National Title Insurance Company of New York; Independent Fire Protection, Inc.; PaR Systems Corportion; Universal Hospital Services, Inc.; Nott Co.; Zinpro Corp.
Reference: Norwest Bank of Minnesota, N.A.

For full biographical listings, see the Martindale-Hubbell Law Directory

THOMAS G. LOVETT, JR. (AV)
100 South Fifth Street, Suite 2250, 55402
Telephone: 612-339-4567
Voice Mail: 612-573-4685
Fax: 612-349-6210
Email: LOVET001@tc.UMN.EDU

For full biographical listings, see the Martindale-Hubbell Law Directory

MANSFIELD TANICK & COHEN, P.A. (AV)
1560 International Centre, 900 Second Avenue South, 55402
Telephone: 612-339-4295
Fax: 612-339-3161
Email: tanick@mansfieldtanick.com *URL:* http://www.mansfieldtanick.com

Seymour J. Mansfield
Marshall H. Tanick
Earl H. Cohen
Robert A. Johnson
Teresa J. Ayling
Richard J. Fuller

Phillip J. Trobaugh
Debra S. Lepert
Ann M. Zewiske
V. John Ella

(See Next Column)

OF COUNSEL

James P. Cullen
Sholly A. Blustin

For full biographical listings, see the Martindale-Hubbell Law Directory

MARTIN & ASSOCIATES, P.A. (AV)
1650 West 82nd Street, Suite 1460, 55431
Telephone: 612-885-5665
Fax: 612-885-5664
Email: mail@martinandassociates.com

Judith Martin Ventres

Michael J. Zitta
Richard William Van Sickle

For full biographical listings, see the Martindale-Hubbell Law Directory

PARSINEN KAPLAN LEVY ROSBERG & GOTLIEB P.A. (AV)
100 South 5th Street Suite 1100, 55402-1298
Telephone: 612-333-2111
Fax: 612-333-6798

John Parsinen
Robert A. Levy
Sidney Kaplan
Jack A. Rosberg
David Gotlieb
Karen A. Ciegler Hansen
Joseph M. Sokolowski
Howard J. Rubin
David A. Orenstein
John C. Levy
Steven R. Katz
Kathleen Doar
Brian R. Martens
Rebecca J. McDaniel
Stephen M. Hickok
Ann Marks Sanford
Jude Anne Carluccio
Pamela A. Curran
David B. Gollin

Theresa M. Kowalski
Joan P. Kurlander
Bryan D. Biesterfeld
Daniel W. Eck
Nels E. Carlson
John Scott De Lanoy
Ann S. Grayson
Kimberley Ste. Marie Becker
Heidi E. Pergament

For full biographical listings, see the Martindale-Hubbell Law Directory

MISSISSIPPI

*BROOKHAVEN,** Lincoln Co.

ALLEN, ALLEN, BOERNER & BREELAND (AV)
214 Justice Street, P.O. Box 751, 39602-0751
Telephone: 601-833-4361
Fax: 601-833-6647
Email: aabblaw@tislink.com

Emmette P. Allen (1915-1999)
Robert O. Allen
William D. Boerner
Durwood J. Breeland

ASSOCIATE

Sally Burchfield Doty

For full biographical listings, see the Martindale-Hubbell Law Directory

*CLARKSDALE,** Coahoma Co.

HOLCOMB DUNBAR, A PROFESSIONAL ASSOCIATION (AV)
152 Delta Avenue, P.O. Box 368, 38614
Telephone: 601-627-2241
Facsimile: 601-627-9788
Email: mchaffin@clarksdale.com *URL:* http://www.holcombdunbar.com
Oxford, Mississippi Office: 1217 Jackson Avenue, P.O. Drawer 707, 38655.
Telephone: 601-234-8775.
Facsimile: 601-238-7552.
Southaven, Mississippi Office: Suite 1, 728 Goodman Road East, P.O. Box 190, 38671.
Telephone: 601-349-0664.
Facsimile: 601-349-2432.

William M. Chaffin
Michael K. Graves
Edward (Ted) P. Connell, Jr.

For Complete List of Firm Personnel, See General Section

For full biographical listings, see the Martindale-Hubbell Law Directory

*GREENWOOD,** Leflore Co.

FLOYD M. MELTON, JR. (AV)
107 1/2 East Market Street, P.O. Box 534, 38935-0534
Telephone: 601-453-8016
Fax: 601-453-0145

ASSOCIATE

Floyd M. Melton, III

For full biographical listings, see the Martindale-Hubbell Law Directory

*GULFPORT,** Harrison Co.

FRANKE, RAINEY & SALLOUM, PLLC (AV)

2605 14th Street, P.O. Drawer 460, 39502
Telephone: 228-868-7070
Telecopier: 228-868-7090
Email: frs@diversicomm.com

Paul M. Franke, Jr.
Paul B. Howell
William M. Rainey
Fredrick B. Feeney, II
Richard P. Salloum
Traci M. Castille
Donald P. Moore

Kaleel G. Salloum, Jr.
Brandi C. Schwartz
James C. Simpson, Jr.

For full biographical listings, see the Martindale-Hubbell Law Directory

MEADOWS RILEY LAW FIRM (AV)

1720 23rd Avenue, P.O. Box 550, 39502
Telephone: 601-864-4511
Telecopier: 601-868-2178

Joseph R. Meadows
Jerry D. Riley
Donnie D. Riley
Karen J. Young

Representative Clients: Bubba Oustalat Lincoln Mercury, Inc.; Lee Tractor Co. of Mississippi.
Reference: Hancock Bank.

For full biographical listings, see the Martindale-Hubbell Law Directory

NEWTON AND HOFF, L.L.P. (AV)

2019 23rd Avenue, P.O. Box 910, 39502-0910
Telephone: 228-863-8827
Fax: 228-868-6007
Email: newtonhoff@aol.com *URL:* http://www.newtonhoff.com

Paul M. Newton (Resident)
Frederick T. Hoff, Jr. (Resident)
Paul M. Newton, Jr. (Resident)

For full biographical listings, see the Martindale-Hubbell Law Directory

*JACKSON,** Hinds Co.

BAKER, DONELSON, BEARMAN & CALDWELL (AV)

Suite 500, 700 North State Street, 39202
Telephone: 601-351-2400
Telecopier: 601-351-2424
Email: info@bdbc.com *URL:* http://www.bakerdonelson.com
Memphis, Tennessee Office: 20th Floor, First Tennessee Building, 165 Madison, 38103.
Telephone: 901-526-2000.
Telecopier: 901-577-2303.
Nashville, Tennessee Office: 1700 Nashville City Center, 511 Union Street, 37219.
Telephone: 615-726-5600.
Telecopier: 615-726-0464.
Chattanooga, Tennessee Office: 1800 Republic Centre, 633 Chestnut Street, 37450-1800.
Telephone: 423-756-2010.
Telecopier: 423-756-3447.
Knoxville, Tennessee Office: 2200 Riverview Tower, 900 South Gay Street, 37901.
Telephone: 423-549-7000.
Telecopier: 423-525-8569.
Johnson City, Tennessee Office: SunTrust Bank Building, 207 Mockingbird Lane, P.O. Box 3038, 37602.
Telephone: 423-928-0181.
Telecopier: 423-928-5694; 423-928-3654; Kingsport: 423-246-6191.
Huntsville, Tennessee Office: 3 Courthouse Square, 37756.
Telephone: 423-663-2321.
Telecopier: 423-663-2111.
Washington, D.C. Office: Market Square, 801 Pennsylvania Avenue, N.W., 20004.
Telephone: 202-508-3400.
Telecopier: 202-508-3402.

MANAGING PARTNER
James K. Dossett, Jr.

PARTNER
Leonard C. Martin

OF COUNSEL
John B. Beard

For Complete List of Firm Personnel, See General Section

For full biographical listings, see the Martindale-Hubbell Law Directory

WATKINS & EAGER (AV)

A Professional Limited Liability Company
Suite 300 The Emporium Building, 400 East Capitol Street, P.O. Box 650, 39205
Telephone: 601-948-6470
Facsimile: 601-354-3623

MEMBERS OF FIRM

Jamie G. Houston, III
Frank J. Hammond, III
J. Grant Sellers

ASSOCIATES

Joe D. Nosef, III
Jesse M. Harrington

A list of Representative Clients and References will be furnished upon request.

For Complete List of Firm Personnel, See General Section

For full biographical listings, see the Martindale-Hubbell Law Directory

*MERIDIAN,** Lauderdale Co.

GLOVER, YOUNG, WALTON, PHILLIPS & TUCKER, PLLC (AV)

Jefferson Square Office Plaza, 1724-A 23rd Avenue, P.O. Box 5514, 39302-5514
Telephone: 601-693-1301
Telecopy: 601-693-1363
Email: gywptpsp@hotmail.com

H. Wingfield Glover, Jr.
P. Scott Phillips
Ralph E. Young, Jr.
H. Wingfield Glover, III
Ronnie L. Walton
Judson T. Tucker

Representative Clients: Alfa Insurance Companies; American States Insurance Co.; Deposit Guaranty National Bank; General Agents Insurance Company of America, Inc.; Great River Insurance; Jeff Anderson Regional Medical Center; Liberty National Life Insurance Co.; Mississippi Power Co.; State Auto Insurance Companies; Universal Underwriters.

For full biographical listings, see the Martindale-Hubbell Law Directory

*NATCHEZ,** Adams Co.

MULHEARN & MULHEARN (AV)

202 South Wall Street, P.O. Box 967, 39120
Telephone: 601-442-4808
Fax: 601-446-6224
Email: woodland@bkbank.com *URL:* http://www.lawyers.com/mulhearnlaw

MEMBERS OF FIRM

John E. Mulhearn (1910-1981)
John E. Mulhearn, Jr.

LEGAL SUPPORT PERSONNEL

Eva Ruth Seale
Judith A. Strickland

Representative Clients: Ashland Plantation; Exxon Corporation; Belle Oil, Inc.; Supermarket Operations, Inc.; Petron, Inc.; Concordia Bank & Trust Co.; Dunleith; J.M. Jones Lumber Co., Inc.; Southwest Mississippi Anesthesia P.A.; Paradise Foods, Inc.

For full biographical listings, see the Martindale-Hubbell Law Directory

TRULY, SMITH & LATHAM (AV)

100 South Pearl Street, P.O. Box 1307, 39121-1307
Telephone: 601-442-6495
Telecopier: 601-442-8874
URL: http://www.lawyers.com/trulysmith&latham

George Lawrence Adams (1913-1994)
R. Brent Forman (1917-1994)
E. C. Ward (1928-1994)

MEMBERS OF FIRM

William Marion Smith
Robert C. Latham

OF COUNSEL

Everette Truly

Representative Clients: Deposit Guaranty National Bank; Exxon U.S.A.; Mississippi Power & Light Co.; Southwest Mississippi Electric Power Assn.; South Central Bell Telephone Co.; Sears, Roebuck & Co.; American International Group; Kemper Insurance Co.

For full biographical listings, see the Martindale-Hubbell Law Directory

MISSOURI

BRANSON, Taney Co.

MOTLEY & MOTLEY (AV)

117 West Pacific, 65616
Telephone: 417-334-2166
FAX: 417-334-2168

(See Next Column)

MOTLEY & MOTLEY—*Continued*

MEMBERS OF FIRM

Marvin Motley | Thomas David Motley

Representative Client: Ozark Mountain Bank.

For full biographical listings, see the Martindale-Hubbell Law Directory

*JEFFERSON CITY,** Cole Co.

CARSON & COIL, P.C. (AV)

515 East High, P.O. Box 28, 65102
Telephone: 573-636-2177
Telecopier: 573-636-7119
Email: general@carsoncoil.com

Forrest P. Carson (1910-1981)
Cullen Coil (1907-1989)
Michael P. Riley
Ronald R. McMillin
Eugene G. Bushmann
James W. Gallaher
Lori J. Levine
Rudolph L. Veit
Michael Madsen
R. Max Humphreys
Mark A. Ludwig
Dana L. Frese
Edward C. Clausen
Carla G. Holste
Kent L. Brown
Douglas W. Hennon
Charles J. McPheeters

James W. "Jamie" Gallaher, Jr.

General Counsel for: Capital Reserve Life Insurance Co.; Missouri Farm Bureau; Healthcare Services Group.
Reference: Central Trust Bank.

For full biographical listings, see the Martindale-Hubbell Law Directory

KANSAS CITY, Jackson, Clay, Platte & Cass Cos.

SWANSON MIDGLEY, LLC (AV)

Crown Center, 2420 Pershing Road, Suite 400, 64108
Telephone: 816-842-6100
Fax: 816-842-0013
Email: mail@swansonmidgley.com *URL:* http://www.swansonmidgley.com
Overland Park, Kansas Office: Commerce Plaza I, 7th Floor, 7300 W. 110th Street.
Telephone: 913-317-2717.
FAX: 913-317-1505.

Robert R. Bartunek
George H. Gangwere, Jr.
Daniel V. Hiatt
Rodney V. Hipp
James H. McLarney

For Complete List of Firm Personnel, See General Section

For full biographical listings, see the Martindale-Hubbell Law Directory

LEE'S SUMMIT, Jackson Co.

CARL CHINNERY & ASSOCIATES, P.C. (AV)

200 S.E. Douglas Street, Suite 200, 64063-2375
Telephone: 816-525-2050

Carl L. Chinnery

Nancy E. Blackwell

OF COUNSEL

Elizabeth Unger Carlyle

LEGAL SUPPORT PERSONNEL

PARALEGALS

Jean Wehner Chinnery
Elaine K. Hanrahan
Alicia Hodges
Susan Breitenbach
Pam Kane
Virginia Galate
Alice Mistler

For full biographical listings, see the Martindale-Hubbell Law Directory

*ROCK PORT,** Atchison Co.

WALTER L. MULVANIA (AV)

213 South Main Street, 64482-1531
Telephone: 660-744-2575

Representative Clients: Genetic Seeds, Inc.; Stanton Grain, Inc.; Big Tarkio Drainage District; City of Fairfax, Mo.; Mo. Valley Agra Service; Iowa State Bank, Hamburg, Iowa.

For full biographical listings, see the Martindale-Hubbell Law Directory

ST. LOUIS, (Independent City)

JEROME R. MANDELSTAMM (AV)

Suite 1600, 1010 Market Street, 63101-2082
Telephone: 314-621-2261
Fax: 314-436-2303

For full biographical listings, see the Martindale-Hubbell Law Directory

NEWMAN, FREYMAN, KLEIN & GAMACHE, P.C. (AV)

7777 Bonhomme, 24th Floor, 63105
Telephone: 314-727-0220
Telecopier: 314-727-9246
URL: http://www.nfk-law.com

David B. Freyman | Janet L. Maltagliati

For full biographical listings, see the Martindale-Hubbell Law Directory

OTTSEN, MAUZÉ, LEGGAT & BELZ, L.C. (AV)

The Midvale Building, 112 South Hanley Road, 63105-3418
Telephone: 314-726-2800
Telecopier: 314-863-3821

Lamar E. Ottsen
James F. Mauzé
Robert B. Leggat, Jr.
W. Robert Leible
Thomas E. Pulliam

For full biographical listings, see the Martindale-Hubbell Law Directory

PAULE, CAMAZINE & BLUMENTHAL, A PROFESSIONAL CORPORATION (AV)

Sixth Floor, 165 North Meramec Avenue (Clayton), 63105
Telephone: 314-727-2266
Telecopier: 314-727-2101
Email: pcblaw@stlnet.com

Donald W. Paule
Stanley H. Chorlins
Joann N. Lynch Dyroff
Bernard W. Gerdelman
Heidi M. Ottsen

For full biographical listings, see the Martindale-Hubbell Law Directory

SCHRAMM & PINES, L.L.C. (AV)

Suite 950 The Bemiston Tower, 231 South Bemiston Avenue, 63105
Telephone: 314-721-5321
Telecopier: 314-721-0790

MEMBERS OF FIRM

Paul H. Schramm
M. Harvey Pines
Daniel R. Schramm

Timothy I. Nicholson | Dean A. Schramm

Reference: Magna Bank.

For full biographical listings, see the Martindale-Hubbell Law Directory

SIKESTON, Scott Co.

DRUMM & THORNTON (AV)

113 West North Street, P.O. Box 40, 63801
Telephone: 573-471-1207
Fax: 573-471-1050

MEMBERS OF FIRM

Manuel Drumm | Fred Howell Thornton, III

Representative Clients: Aetna Casualty & Surety Co.; Cameron Mutual Insurance Co.; Boyer Construction Co.

For full biographical listings, see the Martindale-Hubbell Law Directory

MONTANA

*BIG TIMBER,** Sweet Grass Co.

JOSEPHSON, LOVELL & DRINGMAN (AV)

115 West Second Avenue, P.O. Box 1047, 59011
Telephone: 406-932-5440
Fax: 406-932-5752
Email: josephsonlaw@mcn.net

Richard W. Josephson
R. Mark Josephson
Lance Lovell
Patrick N. Dringman
Page C. Dringman

(See Next Column)

JOSEPHSON, LOVELL & DRINGMAN, *Big Timber—Continued*

LEGAL SUPPORT PERSONNEL

Dawn M. Curry (Legal Assistant)
Barbara W. Cutchin (Legal Assistant)
Colleen A. Ellis (Legal Secretary)
Carmen Hodges (Legal Assistant)
Shirle Norquist (Legal Assistant)
Esther S. Pearce (Legal Assistant)
Lauren M. Rudd (Legal Secretary and Administrative Assistant)

OTHER STAFF

Bev Josephson (Accounting)
Gail Burmeister (Receptionist and Office Administrator)

For full biographical listings, see the Martindale-Hubbell Law Directory

*BILLINGS,** Yellowstone Co.

BROWN LAW FIRM, P.C. (AV)
315 North 24th Street, P.O. Drawer 849, 59103-0849
Telephone: 406-248-2611
FAX: 406-248-3128
URL: http://www.brownfirm.com
Bozeman, Montana Office: 510 South 23rd Street.
Telephone: 406-587-8486.
Fax: 406-587-4524.

Angus B. Fulton
Timothy A. Filz

For Complete List of Firm Personnel, See General Section

For full biographical listings, see the Martindale-Hubbell Law Directory

CROWLEY, HAUGHEY, HANSON, TOOLE & DIETRICH, P.L.L.P. (AV)
500 Transwestern II, 490 North 31st Street, P.O. Box 2529, 59103
Telephone: 406-252-3441
Fax: 406-259-4159
Email: crowley@crowleylaw.com
Helena, Montana Office: IBM Building, 100 North Park Avenue, Suite 300, 59601.
Telephone: 406-449-4165.
Fax: 406-449-5149.
Kalispell, Montana Office: 431 1st Avenue West, 59901.
Telephone: 406-752-6644.
Fax: 406-752-5108.
Williston, North Dakota Office: 113 East Broadway, 58801.
Telephone: 701-572-2200.
Fax: 701-572-7072.

OF COUNSEL

John M. Dietrich
Myles J. Thomas

MEMBERS OF FIRM

David L. Johnson
James P. Sites
Daniel N. McLean (Resident, Helena, Montana Office)
Robert G. Michelotti, Jr.
Eric K. Anderson
Scott M. Heard

Representative Clients: First Interstate Bank of Commerce, Trust Department.

For Complete List of Firm Personnel, See General Section

For full biographical listings, see the Martindale-Hubbell Law Directory

*BOZEMAN,** Gallatin Co.

KIRWAN & BARRETT, P.C. (AV)
215 West Mendenhall, P.O. Box 1348, 59771-1348
Telephone: 406-586-1553
Fax: 406-586-8971

Stephen M. Barrett

For full biographical listings, see the Martindale-Hubbell Law Directory

*HELENA,** Lewis and Clark Co.

JOHN R. KLINE, P.C. (AV)
Arcade Building, Third Floor, 111 North Last Chance Gulch, P.O. Box 1705, 59624
Telephone: 406-442-8950
Fax: 406-442-9558

John R. Kline

NEBRASKA

*BROKEN BOW,** Custer Co.

CARLOS E. SCHAPER LAW OFFICE (AV)
345 South 10th Avenue, P.O. Box 586, 68822
Telephone: 308-872-6481
Fax: 308-872-6385

William C. Schaper (1890-1977)

General Counsel for: Custer Federal Savings & Loan Assn., Broken Bow; United Nebraska Bank, Broken Bow, Nebraska; Jennie Malham Memorial Medical Center; Anselmo-Merna, Nebraska School Districts.
Local Counsel for: Federated Mutual Implement and Hardware Insurance Co.; Shield of Shelter Insurance Co.; John Hancock Mutual Life Insurance Co.; Prudential Life Insurance Co.; Massey-Ferguson, Inc.; F.D.I.C.; Resolution Trust Corporation.

For full biographical listings, see the Martindale-Hubbell Law Directory

*LINCOLN,** Lancaster Co.

CLINE, WILLIAMS, WRIGHT, JOHNSON & OLDFATHER (AV)
1900 U.S. Bank Building, 233 South 13th Street, 68508
Telephone: 402-474-6900
Fax: 402-474-5393
Email: postmaster@cline-law.com *URL:* http://www.cline-law.com
Omaha, Nebraska Office: Suite 720, One Pacific Place, 1125 South 103rd Street, 68124.
Telephone: 402-397-1700.
Fax: 402-397-1806.

ATTORNEYS

Allen L. Graves
Charles M. Pallesen, Jr.
Fredric H. Kauffman
Donald F. Burt
Alan E. Peterson
Stephen E. Gehring
Robert J. Routh
Kevin Colleran
L. Bruce Wright
James M. Bausch
Larry A. Holle
David R. Buntain
Stephen H. Nelsen
Michael C. Mueller
Lauren W. Wismer
Daniel R. Stogsdill
Scott D. Kelly
Terry R. Wittler
Pamela Hastings Carrier
Mark A. Christensen
Richard P. Garden, Jr.
Shawn D. Renner
John C. Miles
Mary Kay Frank
Thomas C. Huston
Sonya S. Ekart
Don R. Janssen
Susan Kubert Sapp
Kevin J. Schneider
Andrew D. Strotman
Jill Gossin Jensen
Rochelle A. Mullen
John L. Horan
Bryan S. Hatch
Steven C. Likes
Tracy A. Oldemeyer
Jolene M. Papa
Timothy G. Aschoff
Eric N. Bergquist
Janis J. Winterhof
Andrea Dylan Snowden

OF COUNSEL

Charles E. Wright
Richard P. Jeffries
Mary M. Campbell

RETIRED PARTNERS

Flavel A. Wright (Retired)
Warren C. Johnson (Retired)
Charles E. Oldfather (1927-1998)

Representative Clients: U.S. Bank National Association; University of Nebraska; Nebraska Medical Assn.; Saint Elizabeth Regional Medical Center; Media of Nebraska; Cargill Inc.; State Farm Insurance Cos.; Wal-Mart Stores, Inc.; Textron/Cushman; Isco, Inc.

For full biographical listings, see the Martindale-Hubbell Law Directory

ERICKSON & SEDERSTROM, P.C. (AV)
Suite 400, Cornhusker Plaza, 301 South 13th Street, 68508
Telephone: 402-476-1000
Fax: 402-476-6167
Omaha, Nebraska Office: Regency Westpointe, 10330 Regency Parkway Drive, Suite 100, 68114-3761.
Telephone: 402-397-2200.
Fax: 402-390-7137.

Charles D. Humble
Alan M. Wood

Representative Clients: Lincoln Electric System; Lincoln General Hospital; Nash Finch Co.; LinWeld, Inc.; Bryant Air Conditioning & Heating; Osco Drug; Citadel Communication; Douglas Theatres; Sioux City Foundry; American Honda.

For Complete List of Firm Personnel, See General Section

For full biographical listings, see the Martindale-Hubbell Law Directory

JOHNSON, FLODMAN, GUENZEL, ESKE & WIDGER (AV)
1227 Lincoln Mall, P.O. Box 81686, 68501-1686
Telephone: 402-475-4240
Fax: 402-475-0329
URL: http://www.linclaw.com

(See Next Column)

JOHNSON, FLODMAN, GUENZEL, ESKE & WIDGER—*Continued*

MEMBER OF FIRM
Steven E. Guenzel

Special Counsel: Nebraska Public Power District.
Representative Clients: Atlanta Casualty; Chubb/Pacific Indemnity Group; Citizens State Bank, Polk, Nebraska; Crum & Foster; Federated Rural Electric Insurance Corp.; Runza Drive-Inns of America; State Farm Insurance Cos.; Viking Insurance Company of Wisconsin.

For full biographical listings, see the Martindale-Hubbell Law Directory

WOLFE, SNOWDEN, HURD, LUERS & AHL (AV)

Suite 830, NBC Center, 68508-1424
Telephone: 402-474-1507
Fax: 402-474-3170

MEMBERS OF FIRM
Jack G. Wolfe
James A. Snowden
John C. Hurd
James B. Luers
Stephen L. Ahl
Dean J. Sitzmann

ASSOCIATES
Douglas L. Kluender
Thomas B. Wood

For full biographical listings, see the Martindale-Hubbell Law Directory

*OMAHA,** Douglas Co.

DWYER, SMITH, GARDNER, LAZER, POHREN, ROGERS & FORREST (AV)

Suite 400, 8712 West Dodge Road, 68114
Telephone: 402-392-0101
Telefax: 402-392-1011
Email: dwyerlaw@dwyer-smith.com *URL:* http://www.dwyer-smith.com

MEMBERS OF FIRM
Robert V. Dwyer, Jr.
Paul J. Gardner
John L. Apker
Bruce J. Goracke

For Complete List of Firm Personnel, See General Section

For full biographical listings, see the Martindale-Hubbell Law Directory

ERICKSON & SEDERSTROM, P.C. (AV)

Regency Westpointe, 10330 Regency Parkway Drive, Suite 100, 68114-3761
Telephone: 402-397-2200
Fax: 402-390-7137
Lincoln, Nebraska Office: Suite 400, Cornhusker Plaza, 301 South 13th Street, 68508-2571.
Telephone: 402-476-1000.
Fax: 402-476-6167.

Donald H. Erickson
Daniel D. Koukol
Wm. E. Morrow, Jr.
Soren S. Jensen
Daniel B. Kinnamon
Virgil K. Johnson
Charles V. Sederstrom, Jr.
Michael C. Washburn
John C. Brownrigg
Thomas J. Culhane
Richard J. Gilloon
Samuel Earle Clark
Gary L. Hoffman
J Russell Derr
Jerald L. Rauterkus
William T. Foley
David C. Mussman

Andrea M. Jahn
Kevin R. McManaman
Michelle B. Miller

OF COUNSEL
Lewis R. Leigh
Leo Eisenstatt
Roland J. Santoni

Representative Clients: Nebraska State Bank of Omaha; Berkshire Hathaway, Inc.; Bozell, Inc.; IBP, Inc. Quaker Oats Co.; United A-G Cooperative, Inc.; Immanuel Medical Center; Cornhusker Casualty Co.; Hartford Accident & Indemnity Co.; Mortgage Guaranty Insurance Corp. (MGIC).

For Complete List of Firm Personnel, See General Section

For full biographical listings, see the Martindale-Hubbell Law Directory

LAUGHLIN, PETERSON & LANG (AV)

11306 Davenport Street, 68154
Telephone: 402-330-1900
Fax: 402-330-0936
Email: mlaugh43@aol.com

MEMBERS OF FIRM
Mark L. Laughlin
Robert F. Peterson
James E. Lang

Representative Clients: General Electric Capital Corp.; Dodge Land Co.; Security Mutual Life Insurance Co. of Lincoln, NE; Century Development Co.

For full biographical listings, see the Martindale-Hubbell Law Directory

RASMUSSEN & MITCHELL (AV)

11605 Miracle Hills Drive, Suite 205, 68154
Telephone: 402-493-3300
Fax: 402-496-0766
Email: lawman000@aol.com *URL:* http://www.lawyers.com/rasmussen&mitchell

MEMBERS OF FIRM
Wayne S. Rasmussen
James S. Mitchell
Kathryn J. Derr
Shane M. Niebergall

For full biographical listings, see the Martindale-Hubbell Law Directory

NEVADA

*ELKO,** Elko Co.

WILSON AND BARROWS, LTD. (AV)

442 Court Street, 89801
Telephone: 775-738-7271
Fax: 775-738-5041
Email: R.Barrows@WilsonandBarrows.com *URL:* http://www.WilsonandBarrows.com

Richard G. Barrows

For Complete List of Firm Personnel, See General Section

For full biographical listings, see the Martindale-Hubbell Law Directory

*LAS VEGAS,** Clark Co.

ALBRIGHT, STODDARD, WARNICK & ALBRIGHT, A PROFESSIONAL CORPORATION (AV)

Quail Park I, Building D-4, 801 South Rancho Drive, 89106
Telephone: 702-384-7111
Fax: 702-384-0605
URL: http://www.aswalaw.com

G. Vern Albright
William H. Stoddard
Whitney B. Warnick
G. Mark Albright

D. Chris Albright
Tami C. Budo
Corey D. Randall (Not admitted in NV)

Representative Clients: Tokio Marine and Fire Insurance Co.; INAPRO, a CIGNA Co.; Nevada Ready Mix; North American Health Care, Inc. (Nursing Home); Royal Insurance; First Security Bank of Utah; Nevada Community Bank; Nationwide Insurance Co.; Liberty Mutual Insurance; CB Commercial.

For full biographical listings, see the Martindale-Hubbell Law Directory

ALVERSON, TAYLOR, MORTENSEN, NELSON & SANDERS (AV)

7401 West Charleston Boulevard, 89117
Telephone: 702-384-7000
FAX: 702-385-7000
Email: alverson@intermind.net
Reno, Nevada Office: 245 East Liberty, Suite 520, 89505.
Telephone: 775-329-0473.
Fax: 775-329-3303.

MEMBERS OF FIRM
J. Bruce Alverson
Eric K. Taylor
David J. Mortensen
Erven T. Nelson
LeAnn Sanders

OF COUNSEL
Jack C. Cherry
Kurt D. Anderson
Philip C. Van Alstyne

ASSOCIATES
Rebecca Hopkins Miller
Sandra Smagac
Victoria L. Nelson
Aaron D. Lovaas
Diane Obritsch
Michael A. Olsen
Randal D. Shimon
Catherine A. Olendorff
Monica L. Pierce
Gabriel D. Lither
Kurt R. Bonds
Darius F. Rafie
Mark J. King, IV
Shell L. Mercer
Carrie S. Bourdeau
Jason Lane Earnest
Nathan R. Reinmiller
Donn C. Alexander
Afshin Tadayon
Eric O. Freeman
Lindsay L. Stadtlander
Julie M. Sueoka

Representative Clients: Citibank (Nevada), N.A.; First Interstate Bank of Nevada; The CIT Group; Federal Deposit Insurance Corporation/Resolution Trust Corporation (TRTC); General Electric Company; St. Paul Fire & Marine Insurance Co.; The Doctors Company; University Medical Center of So. Nevada; Chubb Group of Insurance Companies.

For full biographical listings, see the Martindale-Hubbell Law Directory

Las Vegas—Continued

JEROME L. BLUT CHARTERED (AV)

Third Floor, 302 East Carson Avenue, 89101
Telephone: 702-382-8840
Fax: 702-382-4800
Email: blutlaw@aol.com *URL:* http://www.lawyers.com/blutlaw

Jerome L. Blut

References: Wells Fargo Bank of Nevada; Nevada State Bank.

For full biographical listings, see the Martindale-Hubbell Law Directory

JEFFREY L. BURR & ASSOCIATES (AV)

4455 South Pecos, 89121-5029
Telephone: 702-433-4455
Fax: 702-451-1853
Email: info@jeffreyburr.com *URL:* http://www.jeffreyburr.com
Other Las Vegas, Nevada Office: 1645 Village Center Circle, Suite 141, 89134.
Telephone: 702-254-4455.
Fax: 702-254-3330.

Jeffrey L. Burr

Mark Lee Dodds
Jeffrey C. Boyce
Brian C. Tanko

For full biographical listings, see the Martindale-Hubbell Law Directory

DENTON & LOPEZ (AV)

626 South Seventh Street, 89101
Telephone: 702-384-1723
Fax: 702-384-8019

Ralph L. Denton
Joseph A. Lopez, IV

Representative Clients: Shetakis Wholesalers, Inc.; TRW, Inc.; Leprechaun Mining & Chemical, Inc.; USA Hosts, Ltd; Experian Information Solutions, Inc.
Reference: Bank of America.

For full biographical listings, see the Martindale-Hubbell Law Directory

EDWARDS & WINTERTON, CHTD. (AV)

401 North Buffalo Drive, Suite 200, 89128
Telephone: 702-363-0317
Telecopier: 702-363-1630
Email: EOWW.LAW@worldnet.att.net

George T. Morse, III (1945-1996)
Douglas M. Edwards
David J. Winterton

Nazario J. Jureidini
Robert B. Gerard
Thomas E. Trojan
Chris A. Beecroft, Jr.

OF COUNSEL

Nicholas A. Boylan (Not admitted in NV)

For full biographical listings, see the Martindale-Hubbell Law Directory

HALE LANE PEEK DENNISON HOWARD AND ANDERSON (AV)

Nevada Financial Center, 2300 West Sahara Avenue, Eighth Floor, Box 8, 89102
Telephone: 702-222-2500
Fax: 702-365-6940
Email: info@halelane.com
Reno, Nevada Office: 100 West Liberty Street, Tenth Floor, P.O. Box 3237.
Telephone: 775-327-3000.
Telefax: 775-786-6179.
Carson City, Nevada Office: 777 East William Street, Suite 200, P.O. Box 2620.
Telephone: 775-684-6000.
Telefax: 775-684-6001.

MEMBERS OF FIRM

Steve Lane
Marilyn L. Skender (Resident, Reno, Nevada)
James L. Kelly (Resident, Reno, Nevada)
Matthew E. Woodhead

For Complete List of Firm Personnel, See General Section

For full biographical listings, see the Martindale-Hubbell Law Directory

LAW OFFICES JOHNSON & JOHNSON (AV)

530 South Fourth Street, 89101
Telephone: 702-384-2830
Fax: 702-385-3059
URL: http://www.lawyers.com/jjlawoffices
Email: dcjlaw@ix.netcom.com *URL:* http://www.johnsonlegal.com

Charles William Johnson
David Charles Johnson

Representative Clients: Wells Fargo Bank (Trust Department); Bank of America (Trust Department); Nevada State Bank (Trust Department).

(See Next Column)

For full biographical listings, see the Martindale-Hubbell Law Directory

JOLLEY, URGA, WIRTH & WOODBURY (AV)

3800 Howard Hughes Parkway Suite 1600, 89109
Telephone: 702-699-7500
Facsimile: 702-699-7555
URL: http://www.juww.com
Boulder City, Nevada Office: Suite 105, 1000 Nevada Highway, 89005.
Telephone: 702-293-3674.

MEMBERS OF FIRM

R. Gardner Jolley
Bruce L. Woodbury
Kathryn Stryker Wirth

ASSOCIATE

Gregory G. Gordon

Representative Clients: Wells Fargo Bank and its predecessor, First Interstate Bank of Nevada; Bank of America, Nevada; Nevada State Bank; First Security Trust Co.; First Nationwide Bank.

For Complete List of Firm Personnel, See General Section

For full biographical listings, see the Martindale-Hubbell Law Directory

KOLESAR & LEATHAM, CHARTERED (AV)

Norwest Bank Center, 3320 West Sahara Avenue, Suite 380, 89102
Telephone: 702-362-7800
Telecopier: 702-362-9472

Robert J. Kolesar
Kenneth A. Burns
Charles H. Miles, Jr.

Mark W. Patterson

For full biographical listings, see the Martindale-Hubbell Law Directory

JOHN PETER LEE, LTD. (AV)

830 Las Vegas Boulevard South, 89101
Telephone: 702-382-4044
Telecopier: 702-383-9950

John Peter Lee

Nancy L. Allf
Paul C. Ray
Timothy P. Thomas

For Complete List of Firm Personnel, See General Section

For full biographical listings, see the Martindale-Hubbell Law Directory

BRYAN A LOWE & ASSOCIATES A PROFESSIONAL LAW CORPORATION (AV)

4011 Meadows Lane, Suite 102, 89107
Telephone: 702-259-0002
Fax: 702-259-7774
Email: LoweAssoc@aol.com *URL:* http://www.lawyers.com/lowelaw
Boulder City, Nevada Office: 916 Nevada highway, Suite 6, 89005.
Telephone: 702-293-6888.

Bryan A. Lowe

Robert Winn
S. Craig Stone, II

Representative Client: Clark County Housing Authority.
References: Wells Fargo Bank, Trust Department; Bank of America, Trust Department; Clark County, Nevada, Public Administrator.

For full biographical listings, see the Martindale-Hubbell Law Directory

McDONALD CARANO WILSON McCUNE BERGIN FRANKOVICH & HICKS LLP (AV)

Suite 1000, 2300 West Sahara Avenue, 89102
Telephone: 702-873-4100
Telecopier: 702-873-9966
URL: http://www.mcdonaldcarano.com
Reno, Nevada Office: 241 Ridge Street.
Telephone: 775-788-2000.
Telecopier: 775-788-2020.

MEMBERS OF FIRM

Robert E. Armstrong
Scott A. Swain

ASSOCIATE

Donald G. Martin

Representative Clients: AT&T Communications of Nevada; Boomtown, Inc.; Boyd Gaming Corporation; Jackpot Enterprises, Inc.; Primm Investments, Inc.

For Complete List of Firm Personnel, See General Section

For full biographical listings, see the Martindale-Hubbell Law Directory

Las Vegas—Continued

MORSE & MOWBRAY, A PROFESSIONAL CORPORATION (AV)

Suite 1400 Bank of America Plaza, 300 South Fourth Street, 89101
Telephone: 702-384-6340
Telecopier: 702-384-4596
London, England Office: Lamb Building, Temple.
Telephone: 071-353-6701.

William R. Morse — John H. Mowbray
Harold M. Morse — Christopher H. Byrd
Kimberly A. Buchanan

For full biographical listings, see the Martindale-Hubbell Law Directory

OSHINS & ASSOCIATES, P.C. (AV)

Suite 170, 1645 Village Center Circle, 89134
Telephone: 702-341-6000
Fax: 702-341-6001
Email: Steveo@wizard.com
Email: Dickoshins@aol.com *URL:* http://firms.findlaw.com/oshins

Richard A. Oshins — Steven J. Oshins

For full biographical listings, see the Martindale-Hubbell Law Directory

PICO & MITCHELL (AV)

2000 South Eastern Avenue, 89104
Telephone: 702-457-9099
FAX: 702-457-8451
Email: lawyers@picomitchell.com

MEMBERS OF FIRM

James F. Pico — Christy Brad Escobar
Bert O. Mitchell — James R. Rosenberger
E. Breen Arntz

ASSOCIATES

Michelle Schwarz — Jill M. Chase
Rebecca L. Mastrangelo — Daniel E. Carvalho
Stephen H. Rogers

Representative Clients: Home Insurance Co.; State Farm Mutual Insurance Co.; Industrial Indemnity Insurance Co.; Great American Insurance Co.; Argonaut Insurance Cos.; Clark County Medical Society; Rose de Lima Hospital; Fairway Chevrolet; American States Insurance Co.; The Hartford Insurance Co.

For full biographical listings, see the Martindale-Hubbell Law Directory

SHIRINIAN & ROITMAN (AV)

333 North Rancho Drive, Suite 520, 89106
Telephone: 702-631-5650
Fax: 702-631-5603
Email: ashirinian@aol.com *URL:* http://www.lawyers.com/shirinian&roitman
San Francisco, California Office: 44 Montgomery Street, Suite 1500, 94104.
Telephone: 415-788-1771.
Fax: 415-788-1744.

Ara H. Shirinian — Howard Roitman

For full biographical listings, see the Martindale-Hubbell Law Directory

*RENO,** Washoe Co.

GUILD, RUSSELL, GALLAGHER & FULLER, LTD. (AV)

100 West Liberty, Suite 800, P.O. Box 2838, 89505
Telephone: 775-786-2366
Telecopier: 775-322-9105
Email: attorneys@grgflaw.com

Clark J. Guild (1887-1971) — C. David Russell
Clark J. Guild, Jr. — John K. Gallagher
Gary M. Fuller

Jason J. Freelin

Representative Clients: Caithness Resources, Inc.; Chevron USA, Inc.; Dickson Realty; DRGM Advertising Agency; Federal Deposit Insurance Corp.; Intermountain Power Project; Land Rover North America; Porsche Cars North America; Jones-West Ford; City of Los Angeles, Department of Water & Power; Metropolitan Water District of Southern California; Microsoft Corporation; 100 W. Liberty Ltd. Partnership.

For full biographical listings, see the Martindale-Hubbell Law Directory

HALE LANE PEEK DENNISON HOWARD AND ANDERSON (AV)

100 West Liberty Street, Tenth Floor, P.O. Box 3237, 89505
Telephone: 775-327-3000
Telefax: 775-786-6179
Email: info@halelane.com
Las Vegas, Nevada Office: Nevada Financial Center, 2300 West Sahara Avenue, Eighth Floor, Box 8.
Telephone: 702-222-2500.
Fax: 702-365-6940.

(See Next Column)

Carson City, Nevada Office: 777 East William Street, Suite 200, P.O. Box 2620.
Telephone: 775-684-6000.
Telefax: 775-684-6001.

MEMBERS OF FIRM

Steve Lane (Resident, Las Vegas, Nevada) — Marilyn L. Skender
James L. Kelly
Matthew E. Woodhead

ASSOCIATES

Richard P. Schulze, III — Julia S. Gold (Not admitted in NV)

OF COUNSEL

Andrew Pearl

For Complete List of Firm Personnel, See General Section

For full biographical listings, see the Martindale-Hubbell Law Directory

MCDONALD CARANO WILSON MCCUNE BERGIN FRANKOVICH & HICKS LLP (AV)

241 Ridge Street, 89501
Telephone: 775-788-2000
Telecopier: 775-788-2020
URL: http://www.mcdonaldcarano.com
Las Vegas, Nevada Office: Suite 1000, 2300 West Sahara Avenue.
Telephone: 702-873-4100.
Telecopier: 702-873-9966.

MEMBERS OF FIRM

Robert E. Armstrong — John B. Galvin
Scott A. Swain

ASSOCIATES

David F. Grove — Donald Gregory Martin

Representative Clients: AT&T Communications of Nevada; Associated General Contractors of America; Eldorado Hotel & Casino; Intermountain Federal Land Bank Association; James Hardie (USA), Inc. Scolari's Warehouse Markets; Shaver Construction; Time Oil Co. (Nevada Counsel); Sunstate Bank, ITT Small Business Finance Corporation; First Security Bank.

For Complete List of Firm Personnel, See General Section

For full biographical listings, see the Martindale-Hubbell Law Directory

WALTHER, KEY, MAUPIN, OATS, COX & LEGOY, A PROFESSIONAL CORPORATION (AV)

Lakeside Professional Plaza, 3500 Lakeside Court, 89509
Telephone: 775-827-2000
Facsimile: 775-827-2185
Mailing Address: P.O. Box 30000, Reno, Nevada, 89520

Steven T. Walther — G. Barton Mowry
Jon J. Key — Procter J. Hug
Ernest J. Maupin — Donald A. Lattin
Fred L. Oats — Gustave J. Rossi
C. Robert Cox — Robert A. Winkel
L. Robert LeGoy, Jr. — Kurt O. Hunsberger
Michael E. Malloy — Michael A. Nivinskus
W. Douglass Maupin — Christopher D. Jaime

Rick R. Hsu — Michaelle D. Rafferty

Representative Clients: Bank America of Nevada (Trust Dept.); Bechtel Corporations; Bill Pearce Olds, BMW, Volvo; Wells Fargo, N.A. (Trust Dept.); General Motors Acceptance Corp.; Nevada Realtors; Radiation Oncology Associates; The Ralph M. Parsons Corporation; Parsons Corporation; Reno Air, Inc.

For full biographical listings, see the Martindale-Hubbell Law Directory

WOODBURN AND WEDGE (AV)

One East First Street, Suite 1600, P.O. Box 2311, 89505
Telephone: 775-688-3000
Telecopier: 775-688-3088
Email: postmaster@woodburnlaw.com *URL:* http://www.woodburnlaw.com
Las Vegas, Nevada Office: Suite 700 Bank of America Plaza, 300 South Fourth Street.
Telephone: 702-387-1000.
Telecopier: 702-387-0024.

MEMBERS OF FIRM

James J. Halley — Lynne K. Jones
Don L. Ross

Representative Clients: Atlantic Richfield Co.; Sierra Pacific Power Co.; The Union Pacific Railroad Co.; Western Union Telegraph Co.; Bank of America; Cyprus Minerals Corp.; The Roman Catholic Bishop of Reno, A Corporation Sole; Shell Oil Co.

For full biographical listings, see the Martindale-Hubbell Law Directory

NEW HAMPSHIRE

*CONCORD,** Merrimack Co.

Douglas, Robinson, Leonard & Garvey, P.C. (AV)

6 Loudon Road Suite 502, 03301
Telephone: 603-224-1988
Fax: 603-229-1988
Email: drlg@grolen.com *URL:* http://www.lawyers.com/drl&glaw

Charles G. Douglas, III
Timothy I. Robinson
C. Kevin Leonard
Carolyn S. Garvey
Susanna G. Robinson

For full biographical listings, see the Martindale-Hubbell Law Directory

McDonald & Kanyuk, P.L.L.C. (AV)

9 Hills Avenue, Suite B, 03301
Telephone: 603-228-9900
Fax: 603-228-2802
Email: law@mckan.com *URL:* http://www.lawyers.com/mckan

Joseph F. McDonald, III
Amy K. Kanyuk

Joy V. Riddell

For full biographical listings, see the Martindale-Hubbell Law Directory

HAMPTON, Rockingham Co.

Casassa and Ryan (AV)

459 Lafayette Road, 03842
Telephone: 603-926-6336
Fax: 603-926-4127
Email: casassa@concentric.net

MEMBERS OF FIRM

H. Alfred Casassa
John J. Ryan
Peter J. Saari
Robert A. Casassa

ASSOCIATE

Daniel R. Hartley

General Counsel: Foss Manufacturing Company.
Representative Clients: Town of Hampton Falls; Town of North Hampton; Rye Beach Village District; Hampton School District; Susan Conway Enterprises; Wal-Mart Inc.

For Complete List of Firm Personnel, See General Section

For full biographical listings, see the Martindale-Hubbell Law Directory

*LACONIA,** Belknap Co.

Normandin, Cheney & O'Neil (AV)

Normandin Square, 213 Union Avenue, P.O. Box 575, 03247-0575
Telephone: 603-524-4380
Fax: 603-528-6831
Email: nco@lr.net

MEMBERS OF FIRM

Paul L. Normandin
John D. O'Shea, Jr.
Robert A. Dietz

ASSOCIATE

Susanne M. Weldon

Counsel for: Laconia Savings Bank; Lakes Region Mental Health Center; Laconia Airport Authority; Central New Hampshire Realty, Inc.; All Metals Industries, Inc.; Lakes Region Anesthesiology, P.A.
Representative Clients: Edwin C. Remick Foundation; Lela M. Lancaster Charitable Trust; Holy Trinity Foundation Trust.

For Complete List of Firm Personnel, See General Section

For full biographical listings, see the Martindale-Hubbell Law Directory

NEW JERSEY

BRIDGEWATER, Somerset Co.

William E. Ozzard (AV)

P.O. Box 8135, 08807
Telephone: 908-526-0700
Telecopier: 908-722-5707

For full biographical listings, see the Martindale-Hubbell Law Directory

CHERRY HILL, Camden Co.

Flaster/Greenberg, P.C. (AV)

Commerce Center, 1810 Chapel Avenue West, Third Floor, 08002-4609
Telephone: 856-661-1900
Telecopier: 856-661-1919
Email: FIRM@FLASTERGREENBERG.COM *URL:* http://www.flastergreenberg.com

Richard J. Flaster
Stephen M. Greenberg
Laura B. Wallenstein
Allen P. Fineberg
Markley S. Roderick
Peter R. Spirgel
Alan H. Zuckerman
William S. Skinner
J. Philip Kirchner
Paul J. Russoniello
Carl S. Bisgaier
Steven B. Sacharow
E. Richard Dressel
Kenneth S. Goodkind
Frank H. Wisniewski
Alma L. Saravia

OF COUNSEL

Peter M. Dolinger
James J. Binns

Elizabeth J. Hampton
Jeffrey Herskowitz
Christopher E. Kaltenbach
Steven J. Abrams
Julie A. Williamson
Donna T. Urban
Amelia Carolla
Matthew Azoulay
Elaine J. Petruzziello (Not admitted in NJ)
Ann Marie Iannone
Pasquale Guglietta

LEGAL SUPPORT PERSONNEL

PARALEGALS

Ann Gorman
Patricia D'Alessio
Theresa Cooke
Rosemary Dunaif

For full biographical listings, see the Martindale-Hubbell Law Directory

FLORHAM PARK, Morris Co.

Gedney, Seaman & Hilgendorff (AV)

248 Columbia Turnpike, P.O. Box 166, 07932-0166
Telephone: 973-377-9120
Fax: 973-377-9126
Morristown, New Jersey Office: 15 James Street.
Telephone: 973-539-3088.
Fax: 973-539-0163

MEMBERS OF FIRM

Stanley L. Gedney, Jr. (1889-1977)
Bradford C. Seaman (1898-1986)
Hugo A. Hilgendorff, Jr. (1914-1991)
Hugo A. Hilgendorff, III

ASSOCIATES

Peter B. Hilgendorff
George B. Wright

For full biographical listings, see the Martindale-Hubbell Law Directory

Hack, Piro, O'Day, Merklinger, Wallace & McKenna, P.A. (AV)

30 Columbia Turnpike, P.O. Box 941, 07932-0941
Telephone: 973-301-6500
Fax: 973-301-0094
Email: hpom@ix.netcom.com

John M. McKenna

Peter Nastasi

Representative Clients: Cenlar Federal Savings Bank; County Mortgage Company, Inc.; First Fidelity Bank, N.A., N.J.; Citicorp Mortgage, Inc.; Travelers Insurance Co.; State Farm Insurance Companies; Aetna Life & Casualty Co.

For Complete List of Firm Personnel, See General Section

For full biographical listings, see the Martindale-Hubbell Law Directory

*HACKENSACK,** Bergen Co.

Contant, Scherby & Atkins (AV)

33 Hudson Street, 07601
Telephone: 201-342-1070
Fax: 201-342-5213
Email: LawfirmCSA@aol.com *URL:* http://www.lawyers.com/csalaw

MEMBERS OF THE FIRM

John M. Contant (1907-1988)
Richard J. Contant
Michael L. Scherby
Bruce L. Atkins
Matthew S. Rogers
Andrew T. Fede
Brian T. Keane
Robert B. Hille

ASSOCIATES

Geraldine E. Beers
Suzanne J. Ryderman
Lisa R. Aljian
Christina A. Stoneburner
Sheila O'Shea

(See Next Column)

CONTANT, SCHERBY & ATKINS—*Continued*

OF COUNSEL

Fenster & Weiss, New City, New York

For full biographical listings, see the Martindale-Hubbell Law Directory

DEENER, FEINGOLD & STERN, A PROFESSIONAL CORPORATION (AV)

2 University Plaza, Suite 503, 07601
Telephone: 201-343-8788
Fax: 201-343-4640
Email: JeromeDeener@DeenerFeingold.com *URL:* http://www.lawyers.com/deenerfeingold&stern

Jerome A. Deener
Robert A. Stern
Cal R. Feingold
David M. Edelblum
Anthony M. Vizzoni

Debra T. Hirsch
Andrew M. Grumet
Ronen Gabbay

References: Hudson United Bank; Commerce Bank.

For full biographical listings, see the Martindale-Hubbell Law Directory

FERRO LABELLA LOGERFO & ZUCKER, A PROFESSIONAL CORPORATION (AV)

The Landmark Building, 27 Warren Street, 07601
Telephone: 201-489-9110
Fax: 201-489-5653

Michael J. Ferro, Jr.
Arthur P. Zucker
Rocco J. Labella
Sean M. Aylward
Michael F. Logerfo
Christopher L. Weiss

Rocio T. Aliaga
Melanie J. Scroble
E. Vicki Arians

Representative Clients: Summit Bank; CoreStates New Jersey National Bank; Bio Medic Corp.; Lab Products, Inc.; COSCO North Americas, Inc.; Thomas J. Lipton Co.

For full biographical listings, see the Martindale-Hubbell Law Directory

HOGAN, PALACE & SCULLY (AV)

20 Court Street, 07601
Telephone: 201-342-4422
Fax: 201-342-2554
Email: hpsnj@bellatlantic.net *URL:* http://www.lawyers.com/hogan&palace

MEMBERS OF FIRM

Thomas A. Hogan
Thomas W. Palace
Michael R. Scully

LEGAL SUPPORT PERSONNEL

Shannon S. Casey (Real Estate Paralegal)

Reference: Bergen Commercial Bank, New Jersey.

For full biographical listings, see the Martindale-Hubbell Law Directory

JONES AND JONES (AV)

45 Essex Street, 07601
Telephone: 201-487-3600
FAX: 201-487-2826
URL: http://www.lawyers.com/jonesjoneslaw

MEMBER OF FIRM

Graham O. Jones
Walter Henry Jones (1912-1982)
Vincent J. Massa, III

ASSOCIATE

Joyce Wilkins Pollison

OF COUNSEL

Walter Henry Jones, III

For full biographical listings, see the Martindale-Hubbell Law Directory

NICOLETTE & PERKINS, P.A. (AV)

3 University Plaza, Fifth Floor, 07601
Telephone: 201-488-9080
Telecopier: 201-488-5580
Email: nicoletteperkins@juno.com *URL:* http://www.lawyers.com/nicolette&perkins

David A. Nicolette, Jr.
Eric R. Perkins

Jeanette A. Odynski
Laura N. Keenan
Toni Marie McPhillips

For full biographical listings, see the Martindale-Hubbell Law Directory

PASHMAN STEIN, A PROFESSIONAL CORPORATION (AV)

45 Essex Street, 07601-5415
Telephone: 201-488-8200
Fax: 201-488-5556
Email: info@pashmanstein.com *URL:* http://www.lawyers.com/pashmanstein

Louis Pashman
Dennis T. Smith
Samuel J. Samaro
Michael S. Stein

Amy E. Whitteaker
John T. Whipple

SPECIAL COUNSEL

Morris Pashman

For full biographical listings, see the Martindale-Hubbell Law Directory

THURBER CAPPELL, L.L.C. (AV)

235 Main Street, Suite 300, 07601
Telephone: 201-488-0594
Telecopier: 201-488-5283
Email: thurblaw@aol.com *URL:* http://www.lawyers.com/thurber,cappell,law

Mary F. Thurber
Cynthia A. Cappell

ASSOCIATES

Allison Turley Madden
Anne Marie Fox

OF COUNSEL

Frank Huttle, III

For full biographical listings, see the Martindale-Hubbell Law Directory

LIBERTY CORNER, Somerset Co.

KALISON, MCBRIDE & JACKSON, P.A. (AV)

Liberty Corner Executive Center, 645 Martinsville Road, P.O. Box 814, 07938
Telephone: 908-647-4600
Telecopier: 908-647-6226

Michael J. Kalison
John Zen Jackson
Andrew F. McBride III
James V. Hetzel
Paul R. Murphy
James Acre Robertson, IV

Barry Liss
Daniel R. Esposito
Sloane S. Belitz
Alison Wholey Mynick
Todd Schaper
Jennifer Candace Weissman

OF COUNSEL

Wendy C. Tomey

LEGAL SUPPORT PERSONNEL

Susan R. Buchanan
Roman Bohoslawec

For full biographical listings, see the Martindale-Hubbell Law Directory

MONTCLAIR, Essex Co.

BOOTH, BATE, GRIECO AND BRIODY (AV)

Formerly Boyd, Dodd, Keer & Booth
31 Park Street, 07042
Telephone: 973-744-1900
Fax: 973-744-3803

John A. Booth (1901-1984)

MEMBERS OF FIRM

David S. Bate
Gloria E. Grieco
Thomas M. Briody

Counsel for: Annin & Co.; Borough of Essex Fells, New Jersey; The Florence and John Schumann Foundation; The International Foundation.

For full biographical listings, see the Martindale-Hubbell Law Directory

MOORESTOWN, Burlington Co.

FREDERICK W. HARDT (AV)

Suite 101, 300 Chester Avenue, P.O. Box 840, 08057-2512
Telephone: 609-234-4141
Fax: 609-273-8617

ASSOCIATE

Pamela A. Moy

For full biographical listings, see the Martindale-Hubbell Law Directory

*MORRISTOWN,** Morris Co.

PITNEY, HARDIN, KIPP & SZUCH LLP (AV)

P.O. Box 1945, 07962-1945
Telephone: 973-966-6300
New York City: 212-687-6000
Telex: 642014
Telecopier: 973-966-1550
URL: http://www.phks.com
New York, New York Office: 711 Third Avenue, 10017-4014.
Telephone: 212-687-6000.
Fax: 212-682-3485.

MEMBERS OF FIRM

Robert C. Neff
Richard Kahn
Mary Lou Parker
Kevin J. O'Donnell

OF COUNSEL

George A. Aguilar

COUNSEL

Jane H. Hardin
L. Allison Garde
Charles P. Abraham

ASSOCIATE

Jill Petroro

Representative Clients: Beacon Trust Company.

For Complete List of Firm Personnel, See General Section

For full biographical listings, see the Martindale-Hubbell Law Directory

*NEWARK,** Essex Co.

CARPENTER, BENNETT & MORRISSEY (AV)

Three Gateway Center, 17th Floor, 100 Mulberry Street, 07102-4079
Telephone: 973-622-7711
New York City: 212-943-6530
Telex: 139405
Telecopier: 973-622-5314
Email: cbm@carpben.com

MEMBERS OF FIRM

Laurence Reich
Francis X. O'Brien
John D. Goldsmith

OF COUNSEL

Warren Lloyd Lewis
Edward F. Day, Jr.

ASSOCIATES

Hans G. Polak
Mary B. Goldhirsch
Marny Lundy Solazzo

Reference: Summit Bank.

For Complete List of Firm Personnel, See General Section

For full biographical listings, see the Martindale-Hubbell Law Directory

HELLRING LINDEMAN GOLDSTEIN & SIEGAL LLP (AV)

One Gateway Center, 07102-5386
Telephone: 973-621-9020
Fax: 973-621-7406
Englewood, New Jersey Office: 32-40 North Dean Street.
Telephone: 201-871-3060.

Philip Lindeman, II
Joel D. Siegal
Charles Oransky
Judah I. Elstein
David N. Narciso

For Complete List of Firm Personnel, See General Section

For full biographical listings, see the Martindale-Hubbell Law Directory

LEVY, EHRLICH & PETRIELLO, A PROFESSIONAL CORPORATION (AV)

60 Park Place Suite 1016, 07102
Telephone: 973-643-0040
Telecopier: 973-596-1781
URL: http://www.lep-lawyers.com

Ira A. Levy
Alan Ehrlich

Representative Clients: Transamerica; General Electric; U.S. Department of HUD.
Reference: First Union Bank.

For Complete List of Firm Personnel, See General Section

For full biographical listings, see the Martindale-Hubbell Law Directory

McCARTER & ENGLISH, LLP (AV)

Four Gateway Center, 100 Mulberry Street, P.O. Box 652, 07101-0652
Telephone: 973-622-4444
Telecopier: 973-624-7070
URL: http://www.mccarter.com
Cherry Hill, New Jersey Office: 1820 Chapel Avenue West, Suite 380.
Telephone: 609-662-8444.
Telecopier: 609-662-6203.
New York, New York Office: Suite 2247, One World Trade Center.
Telephone: 212-466-9018.
Telecopier: 212-432-6568.
Boca Raton, Florida Office: 2255 Glades Road, Suite 319-A.
Telephone: 561-994-6262.
Telecopier: 561-241-0798.
Wilmington, Delaware Office: Mellon Bank Center, 919 Market Street.
Telephone: 302-654-8010.
Telecopier: 302-654-0795.
Philadelphia, Pennsylvania Office: One Commerce Square, 2005 Market Street, Suite 3600.
Telephone: 215-557-7700.
Telecopier: 215-557-6544.

MEMBERS OF FIRM

Rodney N. Houghton
David A. Ludgin
Myrna L. Wigod
Gerard G. Brew

OF COUNSEL

Peter C. Aslanides

COUNSEL

Beth Yingling
Phyllis Gutto

ASSOCIATES

Kimberly J. Hines
Michael R. Von Ohlen

For Complete List of Firm Personnel, See General Section

For full biographical listings, see the Martindale-Hubbell Law Directory

MEYNER AND LANDIS (AV)

One Gateway Center, Suite 2500, 07102-5311
Telephone: 973-624-2800
Fax: 973-624-0356
Email: attys@meyner.com *URL:* http://www.meyner.com

Robert B. Meyner (1908-1990)
Edwin C. Landis, Jr.
John N. Malyska
William J. Fiore
Anthony F. Siliato
Francis R. Perkins
Howard O. Thompson
Scott T. McCleary
Linda Townley Snyder
William H. Schmidt, Jr.
David B. Grantz

For full biographical listings, see the Martindale-Hubbell Law Directory

SILLS CUMMIS RADIN TISCHMAN EPSTEIN & GROSS, A PROFESSIONAL CORPORATION (AV)

One Riverfront Plaza, 07102-5400
Telephone: 973-643-7000
Fax: 973-643-6500
Telex: 820630 Sillsbeck Nwk
Email: sillsmail@sillscummis.com *URL:* http://www.sillscummis.com
Atlantic City, New Jersey Office: 17 Gordon's Alley.
Telephone: 609-344-2800.
New York, N.Y. Office: 712 Fifth Avenue.
Telephone: 212-643-7000.
Washington, D.C. Office: 1800 K Street, N.W.
Telephone: 202-296-4750.

MEMBERS OF FIRM

Simon Levin
Alan E. Sherman
Allan C. Bell
Nathan E. Arnell

SENIOR COUNSEL

David Beck
Herbert L. Zuckerman

Brenda J. Rediess-Hoosein
Jacqueline Valouch
Michael S. Mirone

Representative Clients: Beneficiaries; Corporate Fiduciaries; High Net Worth Individuals; Executives and Individual Professionals; Public Charities and Private Foundations; Religious Organizations; Educational Institutions.

For Complete List of Firm Personnel, See General Section

For full biographical listings, see the Martindale-Hubbell Law Directory

*NEWTON,** Sussex Co.

TRAPASSO, DOLAN & HOLLANDER (AV)

40 Park Place, P.O. Box 99, 07860
Telephone: 973-383-3233
Fax: 973-383-4922
Email: TDH@nac.net

MEMBERS OF FIRM

Albert P. Trapasso (1923-1990)
Frank A. Dolan (Retired)
Sanford Lloyd Hollander
Paul L. Abramo
David J. Weaver
William E. Hinkes

(See Next Column)

TRAPASSO, DOLAN & HOLLANDER—*Continued*

ASSOCIATE

John D. Williams

OF COUNSEL

Chester Kosarek

Representative Clients: Town of Newton; Green Township; Fredon Township; Borough of Ogdensburg; Hopatcong Board of Education; Newton Memorial Hospital; The Nature Conservancy; Sussex County Farm and Horse Show Association, Inc.; Andover Nursing Home; Newton Medical Building.
Reference: Newton Trust Company; Sussex County State Bank.

For full biographical listings, see the Martindale-Hubbell Law Directory

NORTH BERGEN, Hudson Co.

EDWARD PESIN A PROFESSIONAL CORPORATION (AV)

5-75th Street, 07047
Telephone: 201-868-0144
Fax: 201-453-1528

Edward Pesin

For full biographical listings, see the Martindale-Hubbell Law Directory

NORTH BRUNSWICK, Middlesex Co.

BORRUS, GOLDIN, FOLEY, VIGNUOLO, HYMAN, STAHL & CLARKIN, A PROFESSIONAL CORPORATION (AV)

2875 U.S. Highway 1, Route 1 & Finnigans Lane, P.O. Box 7463, 08902
Telephone: 732-422-1000
Fax: 732-422-1016
Email: attys@borrus.com *URL:* http://www.borrus.com

Jack Borrus
Martin S. Goldin
David M. Foley
Anthony B. Vignuolo
Jeffrey M. Hyman
James E. Stahl
James F. Clarkin III
Eileen Mary Foley

Robert C. Nisenson
Rosalind Westlake
Lisa M. Vignuolo
Steven L. Fox
Peter A. Vignuolo
Gerald T. Foley (1903-1976)

Representative Clients: Summit Bank; R. J. Reynolds Tobacco Co.; K. Hovnanian Enterprises, Inc.; Johnson and Johnson; Foster Wheeler, Inc.; Hartz Mountain Industries; Middlesex County Vocational Services Commission; Borough of South Plainfield Board of Adjustment; U-Haul of Northern NJ.

For full biographical listings, see the Martindale-Hubbell Law Directory

BUSCH AND BUSCH, LLP (AV)

215 North Center Drive, Commerce Center - U.S. #1 South, P.O. Box 7448, 08902-7448
Telephone: 732-821-2300
Telecopier: 732-821-5588
Email: busch@ifu.net

MEMBERS OF FIRM

Lewis D. Busch (1901-1986)
Henry Busch (Retired)
Malcolm R. Busch
Ronald J. Busch
Bertram E. Busch
Mark N. Busch
Leonard R. Busch
Steven F. Satz
Donald J. Sears

ASSOCIATE

Paul Alan VanBuskirk

Representative Clients: Utica Mutual Insurance Co.; New Brunswick Tomorrow; Township of South Brunswick; Township of Monroe, Board of Education; Township of East Brunswick; Minnesota Mutual Life Insurance Co.

For full biographical listings, see the Martindale-Hubbell Law Directory

NUTLEY, Essex Co.

ARTHUR S. HORN, P.A. (AV)

247 Franklin Avenue, 07110
Telephone: 973-235-1550
Fax: 973-235-1582

Arthur S. Horn

Reference: First Union Bank.

For full biographical listings, see the Martindale-Hubbell Law Directory

PRINCETON, Mercer Co.

BERGMAN & BARRETT (AV)

9 Tamarack Circle, Montgomery Knoll, U.S. Highway 206 North, P.O. Box 1273, 08542
Telephone: 609-921-1502
Fax: 609-683-0288

Edward J. Bergman
Michael T. Barrett

(See Next Column)

LEGAL SUPPORT PERSONNEL

Kelli E. Murphy (Paralegal)

For full biographical listings, see the Martindale-Hubbell Law Directory

STEELE R. CHADWELL (AV)

134 Nassau Street, 08542
Telephone: 609-924-8262
Fax: 609-921-9468
URL: http://www.lawyers.com/steelerchadwell

For full biographical listings, see the Martindale-Hubbell Law Directory

MASON, GRIFFIN & PIERSON, A PROFESSIONAL CORPORATION (AV)

101 Poor Farm Road, 08540
Telephone: 609-921-6543
Fax: 609-683-7978
Email: mgp@mgplaw.com *URL:* http://www.mgplaw.com
Flemington, New Jersey, Office: P.O. Box 2420, 151 Main Street, 08822.
Telephone: 908-782-2900.
Fax: 908-782-2428. Email: denilaw@erols.com.

Ralph S. Mason (1913-1988)
Craig H. Davis (1947-1997)
Gordon D. Griffin
Kester R. Pierson
Edwin W. Schmierer
Kristina Pike Hadinger
Donald B. Veix, Jr.
Charles F. Harris
Edmond M. Konin
Shawn M. Neufeld
Valerie L. Howe

Barbara J. Morgan
Christopher H. DeGrezia
F. Clifford Gibbons
Carleen M. Steward
Georgia M. Fraser

OF COUNSEL

William P. Deni, Sr.
Jules Farkas

Representative Clients: Connecticut Indemnity Company; Griffith Electric Supply Company, Inc.; Johnson Controls World Services, Inc.; The Pennington School; Township of Montgomery; Township of Princeton; Management Planning, Inc.

For full biographical listings, see the Martindale-Hubbell Law Directory

McCARTHY AND SCHATZMAN, P.A. (AV)

228 Alexander Street, P.O. Box 2329, 08543-2329
Telephone: 609-924-1199
Fax: 609-683-5251

John F. McCarthy, Jr.
Richard Schatzman
G. Christopher Baker
John F. McCarthy, III
Michael A. Spero
Barbara Strapp Nelson
W. Scott Stoner
James J. Britt, Jr.

Charly Gayden

Representative Clients: Trustees of Princeton University; Carnegie Center Associates; Merrill Lynch Pierce Fenner & Smith, Inc.; Calton Homes, Inc.

For full biographical listings, see the Martindale-Hubbell Law Directory

STARK & STARK, A PROFESSIONAL CORPORATION (AV)

Princeton Pike Corporate Center, P.O. Box 5315, 08543-5315
Telephone: 609-896-9060
Fax: 609-896-0629
Email: info@stark-stark.com *URL:* http://www.stark-stark.com

Steven L. Friedman
Elizabeth Walsh Kreger
Lewis J. Pepperman
Allen M. Silk

OF COUNSEL

Arthur L. Levy

Rosemary D. Durkin (Not admitted in NJ)

For full biographical listings, see the Martindale-Hubbell Law Directory

ROSELAND, Essex Co.

MARK LEVIN (AV)

5 Becker Farm Road, 4th Floor, 07068
Telephone: 973-740-9299

For full biographical listings, see the Martindale-Hubbell Law Directory

SADDLE BROOK, Bergen Co.

KRUGMAN & KAILES LLP (AV)

Park 80 West-Plaza Two, 07663-5835
Telephone: 201-845-3434; 212-695-3262
Telecopier: 201-845-9627
Email: counsel@krugmankailes.com
New York, New York Office: 99 Park Avenue, Suite 2200.
Telephone: 212-599-1060.
Telecopier: 212-599-6282.

(See Next Column)

KRUGMAN & KAILES LLP, *Saddle Brook—Continued*

London, England Office: 90 Fetter Lane, London EC4A-1PT.
Telephone: 011 (44) 171-421-7918.
Telecopier: 011 (44) 171-831-6407.

MEMBERS OF FIRM

Martin Krugman (1916-1994)
Howard Kailes
Thomas J. Goodwin
Ward C. Laracy
Robert I. Wexler
Alan H. Fox
Joy M. Mercer
Kerry B. Flowers

OF COUNSEL

James D. Krugman

COUNSEL

Judith S. Musicant

ASSOCIATES

Anne M. Wallace (Not admitted in NJ)
April A. Savoye
Lisa Ann Miller
Patrizia E. DeBari
David J. Hanley, Jr.
Anjana D. Patel
W. Mark O'Brien

For full biographical listings, see the Martindale-Hubbell Law Directory

*SOMERVILLE,** Somerset Co.

SCHACHTER, TROMBADORE, OFFEN, STANTON & PAVICS, A PROFESSIONAL CORPORATION (AV)

45 East High Street, P.O. Box 520, 08876-0520
Telephone: 908-722-5700
Fax: 908-722-8853

Richard J. Schachter
John J. Trombadore
Stephen M. Offen
Michael J. Stanton
Thomas A. Pavics

Timothy P. McKeown
Jerry S. D'Aniello

For full biographical listings, see the Martindale-Hubbell Law Directory

SPRINGFIELD, Union Co.

JARDINE & PAGANO, A PROFESSIONAL CORPORATION (AV)

11 Cleveland Place, 07081
Telephone: 201-467-1620
Fax: 201-467-5562
Email: jandp@interserv.com *URL:* http://www.lawyers.com/jandplaw

Thomas V. Jardine
Joseph R. Pagano

For full biographical listings, see the Martindale-Hubbell Law Directory

SUMMIT, Union Co.

BOURNE, NOLL & KENYON, A PROFESSIONAL CORPORATION (AV)

382 Springfield Avenue, P.O. Box 690, 07902-0690
Telephone: 908-277-2200
Facsimile: 908-277-6808

Cary R. Hardy
Charles R. Berman
Martin Rubashkin
Roger Mehner
James R. Ottobre
Lawrence A. Rudnick
John F. Kuntz

OF COUNSEL

Edward T. Kenyon
Robert B. Bourne

COUNSEL

Ellyn A. Draikiwicz

Jaime A. O'Brien
Timothy A. Kalas
Alan F. Schwarz
Ross W. Smith

For full biographical listings, see the Martindale-Hubbell Law Directory

*TRENTON,** Mercer Co.

SCHRAGGER, LAVINE & NAGY (AV)

Mountainview Office Park, 840 Bear Tavern Road, Suite 307, 08628
Telephone: 609-771-0700
Fax: 609-771-9535

Bruce M. Schragger
Raymond L. Nagy
James A. Schragger
Jonathan S. Robinson

OF COUNSEL

Henry C. Schragger
Alan S. Lavine
Frank P. Reiche
A. Jerome Moore

LEGAL SUPPORT PERSONNEL

Annemarie Saccani (Office Administrator)

Representative Clients: New Jersey Manufacturers Insurance Co.; Mercer County Community College; Mercer Mutual Insurance Co.; New Jersey Optometric Association; Allentown Caging; Dick Greenfield Dodge.

(See Next Column)

For Complete List of Firm Personnel, See General Section

For full biographical listings, see the Martindale-Hubbell Law Directory

VINELAND, Cumberland Co.

GRUCCIO, PEPPER GIOVINAZZI, DESANTO & FARNOLY, P.A. (AV)

817 Landis Avenue, P.O. Box 1501, 08362
Telephone: 856-691-0100
Fax: 856-692-4095
Email: Gruccio1@eticomm.net
Woodbury, New Jersey Office: 21 Delaware Street.
Telephone: 856-848-5558.
Fax: 856-384-1181.
Bridgeton, New Jersey Office: 120 West Broad Street.
Telephone: 856-459-3334.
Fax: 856-692-4095.

Lawrence Pepper, Jr.
Cosmo A. Giovinazzi, III

Stephen D. Barse

OF COUNSEL

Richard M. Milstead

Representative Clients: State Farm Mutual Automobile Insurance Cos.; United States Fidelity & Guaranty Co.; South Jersey Transportation Authority; County of Salem; County of Cape May; Cumberland Mutual Fire Insurance Co.; Farmers and Merchants National Bank of Bridgeton; Vineland Board of Education; Southern Intercounty Medical Association; Sun National Bank of N.J.

For Complete List of Firm Personnel, See General Section

For full biographical listings, see the Martindale-Hubbell Law Directory

WEST ORANGE, Essex Co.

GOLDBERG, MUFSON & SPAR, A PROFESSIONAL CORPORATION (AV)

200 Executive Drive, 07052
Telephone: 973-736-0100
Telecopier: 973-736-0961
Email: gmspa@chelsea.ios.com

Leonard M. Goldberg
Michael R. Spar

For full biographical listings, see the Martindale-Hubbell Law Directory

HAUPTMAN & RICHMOND, P.A. (AV)

100 Executive Drive, Suite 330, 07052
Telephone: 973-731-1100
Fax: 973-731-1467
URL: http://www.lawyers.com/hauptman_richmond

Martin D. Hauptman
Harold N. Richmond

For full biographical listings, see the Martindale-Hubbell Law Directory

LAMPF, LIPKIND, PRUPIS, PETIGROW & LABUE, A PROFESSIONAL CORPORATION (AV)

80 Main Street, 07052
Telephone: 973-325-2100
New York: 212-349-1021
Fax: 973-325-2839
Email: administrator@llppl.com *URL:* http://www.llppl.com

William D. Lipkind
Stephen E. Lampf
Neil L. Prupis
Paul M. Petigrow
Anthony F. LaBue
Elizabeth Gasser
Andrew S. Berns
Grace D. Mack
Susan Fruchtman
Sheila W. Tarabour

Eric W. Olson
William J. Volonte
Lois S. Feldman
Adam M. Kaplan
Cathy S. Harvey

OF COUNSEL

Theodore I. Botter
Neil Oswald Eriksen
Theresa Borzelli

For full biographical listings, see the Martindale-Hubbell Law Directory

WOODBRIDGE, Middlesex Co.

GREENBERG & SCHULMAN (AV)

90 Woodbridge Center Drive Suite 610, 07095-1142
Telephone: 732-636-8800
Fax: 732-636-8833
Email: greenyanks@aol.com *URL:* http://www.lawyers.com/g&slaw

Richard H. Greenberg
David M. Schulman

For full biographical listings, see the Martindale-Hubbell Law Directory

Woodbridge—Continued

WILENTZ, GOLDMAN & SPITZER, A PROFESSIONAL CORPORATION (AV)

90 Woodbridge Center Drive Suite 900, Box 10, 07095
Telephone: 732-636-8000
Telecopier: 732-855-6117
URL: http://www.newjerseylaw.com
Eatontown, New Jersey Office: Meridian Center I, Two Industrial Way West, 07724.
Telephone: 732-542-4500.
Telecopier: 732-493-8387.
New York, New York Office: Wall Street Plaza, 88 Pine Street, 9th Floor, 10005.
Telephone: 212-267-3091.
Telecopier: 212-267-3828.

Richard F. Lert
Stuart T. Cox, Jr.
Russell J. Fishkind

Linda Lashbrook
Nancy A. Slowe
Elizabeth Connolly Dell
Timothy J. Dengler

Representative Clients: Amerada Hess Corp.; Chevron, U.S.A. Inc.; Cumberland Farms, Inc.; Middlesex County Utilities Co.; New Jersey Automobile Dealers Assn.; Co-Steel Raritan; The Rouse Co.

For Complete List of Firm Personnel, See General Section

For full biographical listings, see the Martindale-Hubbell Law Directory

NEW MEXICO

*ALBUQUERQUE,** Bernalillo Co.

JAMES F. BECKLEY, P.A. (AV)

One Executive Center Suite A-400, 8500 Menaul Boulevard, N.E., P.O. Box 30868, 87190-0868
Telephone: 505-275-1222
1-800-213-1569
Fax: 505-275-7927
Email: JFBECKLEY@AOL.COM

James F. Beckley

Gaelle D. McConnell

For full biographical listings, see the Martindale-Hubbell Law Directory

KELEHER & MCLEOD, P.A. (AV)

201 Third Street, N.W., Suite 1200, P.O. Drawer AA, 87103
Telephone: 505-346-4646
Fax: 505-346-1370

William B. Keleher
Michael L. Keleher
Tracy J. Ahr

Claudia Gayheart Crawford
Evan S. Hobbs

Representative Client: First Security Bank.

For full biographical listings, see the Martindale-Hubbell Law Directory

KENNETH C. LEACH, P.C. (AV)

1110 Pennsylvania N.E., Suite A, 87110
Telephone: 505-243-3322
Fax: 505-242-1268
URL: http://www.lawyers.com/leachlaw

Kenneth C. Leach

Jonathan Reid Mowrer

LEGAL SUPPORT PERSONNEL

Wayne C. Edwards (CEO)
Virginia Bosworth (Paralegal)
Marilyn Alires Marsh (Paralegal)

For full biographical listings, see the Martindale-Hubbell Law Directory

MILLER, STRATVERT & TORGERSON, P.A. (AV)

500 Marquette Avenue, N.W., Suite 1100, P.O. Box 25687, 87102
Telephone: 505-842-1950
Facsimile: 505-243-4408
Email: info@mstLAW.com *URL:* http://www.mstLAW.com
Farmington, New Mexico Office: 300 West Arrington, Suite 300, P.O. Box 869.
Telephone: 505-326-4521.
Facsimile: 505-325-5474.

(See Next Column)

Las Cruces, New Mexico Office: 500 South Main, Suite 800, P.O. Box 1209.
Telephone: 505-523-2481.
Facsimile: 505-526-2215.
Santa Fe, New Mexico Office: 150 Washington Avenue, Suite 300, P.O. Box 1986.
Telephone: 505-989-9614.
Facsimile: 505-989-9857.

Seth V. Bingham (Resident at Farmington Office)
Dana M. Kyle (Resident at Las Cruces Office)
Sharon P. Gross
Fred Schiller (Resident at Las Cruces Office)
Joel T. Newton (Resident at Las Cruces Office)
Dean B. Cross (Resident at Las Cruces Office)

COUNSEL

Paul W. Robinson
James J. Widland
Ross B. Perkal
Bradley D. Tepper

For Complete List of Firm Personnel, See General Section

For full biographical listings, see the Martindale-Hubbell Law Directory

RODEY, DICKASON, SLOAN, AKIN & ROBB, P.A. (AV)

Albuquerque Plaza, Suite 2200, 201 Third Street, N.W., P.O. Box 1888, 87103-1888
Telephone: 505-765-5900
Fax: 505-768-7395
Email: info@rodey.com *URL:* http://www.rodey.com
Santa Fe, New Mexico Office: Suite 101 Marcy Plaza, 123 East Marcy Street, P.O. Box 1357, 87504-1357.
Telephone: 505-984-0100.
Fax: 505-989-9542.

Robert M. St. John
Gary D. Eisenberg
John P. Burton (Resident, Santa Fe Office)

COUNSEL

Jeffrey W. Loubet

For Complete List of Firm Personnel, See General Section

For full biographical listings, see the Martindale-Hubbell Law Directory

SWAIM & SCHRANDT, P.C. (AV)

4830 Juan Tabo Boulevard, N.E., Suite F, 87111
Telephone: 505-237-0064; 1-800-460-8670
Fax: 505-237-9440

Donald E. Swaim
Judith D. Schrandt

Tessa T. Davidson

For full biographical listings, see the Martindale-Hubbell Law Directory

TAX, ESTATE & BUSINESS LAW N.A. LLC (AV)

4217 Montgomery Boulevard, N.E., 87109
Telephone: 505-830-2200
Fax: 505-830-4400
Email: tsmidt2@aol.com

Thomas Smidt, II

LEGAL SUPPORT PERSONNEL

William T. Smith

For full biographical listings, see the Martindale-Hubbell Law Directory

TOMITA & SIMPSON, P.C. (AV)

4263 Montgomery Boulevard, N.E., Suite 210, 87109
Telephone: 505-883-4993
Fax: 505-883-4599
Email: admin@tomitasimpson.com *URL:* http://www.lawyers.com/tomita&simpson

Susan K. Tomita
Elizabeth E. Simpson

LEGAL SUPPORT PERSONNEL

Susan A. McEntee (Legal Assistant)

For full biographical listings, see the Martindale-Hubbell Law Directory

JUDITH L. ZABEL, P.A. (AV)

2632 Mesilla Street, N.E., 87110
Telephone: 505-881-7241
Fax: 505-837-2141
Email: jlzabel@flash.net

Judith L. Zabel

For full biographical listings, see the Martindale-Hubbell Law Directory

*CLOVIS,** Curry Co.

TATUM & McDOWELL (AV)

Suite E, Sagebrush Professional Office Complex, 921 East 21st Street, P.O. Drawer 1270, 88101
Telephone: 505-762-7756
Fax: 505-769-1606

MEMBER OF FIRM

Edwin B. Tatum

Representative Clients: ENMRSH, Inc.; Sunwest Bank of Clovis, N.A.; CitizensBank of Clovis; Retirement Ranch, Inc.; Curry County Abstract Co.; High Plains Credit Union; Senior Citizen Residence Center, Inc.; National Grain Sorghum Producers.
References: Citizens Bank of Clovis; NationsBank, N.A.

For Complete List of Firm Personnel, See General Section

For full biographical listings, see the Martindale-Hubbell Law Directory

*LAS CRUCES,** Dona Ana Co.

REEVES, CHAVEZ, GREENFIELD & WALKER, P.A. (AV)

300 South Water Street, P.O. Box 2769, 88004-2769
Telephone: 505-524-9617
Fax: 505-524-1954
Email: rcgw@zianet.com

B. James Reeves
Frank N. Chavez
Charlotte Greenfield
William A. Walker, Jr.
Kelly P. Albers
Joyce A. Montes
William R. Anderson
Carolyn J. Baca

Glenn D. Hall
CaraLyn Banks

For full biographical listings, see the Martindale-Hubbell Law Directory

*SANTA FE,** Santa Fe Co.

CATRON, CATRON & SAWTELL, A PROFESSIONAL ASSOCIATION (AV)

2006 Botulph Road, P.O. Box 788, 87504-0788
Telephone: 505-982-1947
Telecopier: 505-986-1013
Email: catronlaw@aol.com

Thomas B. Catron III
John S. Catron
William A. Sawtell, Jr.
Fletcher R. Catron
W. Anthony Sawtell
Forrest S. Smith

LEGAL SUPPORT PERSONNEL

Peggy L. Feldt (Certified Public Accountant)

For Complete List of Firm Personnel, See General Section

For full biographical listings, see the Martindale-Hubbell Law Directory

GERBER & BATEMAN, A PROFESSIONAL ASSOCIATION (AV)

417 East Palace Avenue, P.O. Box 2325, 87501
Telephone: 505-988-9646
Facsimile: 505-989-7335
Email: gb@swcp.com

Paul D. Gerber
Kenneth Bateman

Peter Burman

References: The First National Bank of Santa Fe; Century Bank.

For full biographical listings, see the Martindale-Hubbell Law Directory

SCHEUER, YOST & PATTERSON, A PROFESSIONAL CORPORATION (AV)

125 Lincoln Avenue, Suite 223, P.O. Drawer 9570, 87504
Telephone: 505-982-9911
505-989-7500
Fax: 505-982-1621
Email: firm@santafelawyers.com

Melvin T. Yost (Retired)
Ralph H. Scheuer
Mel E. Yost
John N. Patterson
Byron L. Treaster
Donald A. Walcott
Christopher M. Grimmer
Daniel J. Monte

OF COUNSEL

Reverdy Johnson

Representative Clients: Cyprus-AMAX, Inc.; Century Bank, FSB; School of American Research; GEICO; Los Alamos National Bank; St. John's College; Stewart Title Guaranty Co.; Sun Loan Companies; Territorial Abstract & Title Co.; Ticor Title Insurance Co.

For full biographical listings, see the Martindale-Hubbell Law Directory

WHITE, KOCH, KELLY & McCARTHY, A PROFESSIONAL ASSOCIATION (AV)

433 Paseo De Peralta, P.O. Box 787, 87504-0787
Telephone: 505-982-4374
ABA/NET: 1154
Fax: 505-982-0350; 984-8631
Email: WKKM@NM.NET

Sandra J. Brinck

OF COUNSEL

John M. Hickey

For Complete List of Firm Personnel, See General Section

For full biographical listings, see the Martindale-Hubbell Law Directory

NEW YORK

*ALBANY,** Albany Co.

NANCY M. SILLS (AV)

126 State Street, 12207-1606
Telephone: 518-436-4056
Fax: 518-436-1456

For full biographical listings, see the Martindale-Hubbell Law Directory

TABNER, RYAN AND KENIRY (AV)

26 Computer Drive West, P.O. Box 12605, 12212-2605
Telephone: 518-459-9000
Telecopier: 518-459-9165
Email: trk@tabnerryanandkeniry.com

MEMBERS OF FIRM

John W. Tabner
William F. Ryan, Jr.
William J. Keniry

OF COUNSEL

C. Theodore Carlson

ASSOCIATES

Eric N. Dratler
Jennifer K. Corona
Donald W. Biggs

Special Counsel for: Water and Sewer District for Towns of Colonie, Coxsackie, Guilderland, Johnstown, Queensbury, Rotterdam and Village Castleton.
References: FleetBank; Trustco Bank.

For full biographical listings, see the Martindale-Hubbell Law Directory

*AUBURN,** Cayuga Co.

CONTIGUGLIA & GIACONA (AV)

The Federal House, 7 William Street, 13021
Telephone: 315-253-9746
Fax: 315-253-0880

MEMBERS OF FIRM

Anthony J. Contiguglia (1897-1986)
Louis P. Contiguglia
Samuel P. Giacona

David A. Contiguglia

Representative Clients: Cayuga Bank; Cayuga Homesite Development Corp.; Homested Funding Corp.; Statewide Funding Corp.; American Residential Mortgage Corp.; GE Capital Home Equity Services; Commonwealth Mortgage Co., Inc.
References: Marine Midland Bank (Auburn Office); Cayuga Savings Bank; The Key Bank of Central New York.

For full biographical listings, see the Martindale-Hubbell Law Directory

*BATH,** Steuben Co.

COLE LAW OFFICES, P.C. (AV)

7 East Steuben Street, P.O. Box 232, 14810
Telephone: 607-776-3306
Fax: 607-776-4189
Email: RCole@LinkNY.Com
Hammondsport, New York Office: Railroad Station Depot, Water Street, P.O. Box 396, 14840.
Telephone: 607-569-2213.
Fax: 607-569-2214,

Robert H. Cole

(See Next Column)

COLE LAW OFFICES P.C.—*Continued*

Christine Valkenburgh | James H. Burns
William H. Reed

General Counsel for: Bath National Bank; Mercury Aircraft, Inc.
Local Counsel for: Equitable Life Assurance Society of the United States.
Reference: Bath National Bank.

For full biographical listings, see the Martindale-Hubbell Law Directory

*BUFFALO,** Erie Co.

BORINS, SETEL, SNITZER & BROWNSTEIN (AV)

710 Statler Towers, 14202-2907
Telephone: 716-854-5200
Fax: 716-854-5204

MEMBERS OF FIRM

Louis Borins (1908-1979) | Eugene M. Setel
Isadore Snitzer | Joel Brownstein

Reference: HSBC.

For full biographical listings, see the Martindale-Hubbell Law Directory

BROWN & KELLY, L.L.P. (AV)

1500 Liberty Building, 14202-3663
Telephone: 716-854-2620
Fax: 716-854-0082
Email: mail@brownkelly.com *URL:* http://www.brownkelly.com

MEMBERS OF FIRM

Thomas J. Kelly | Andrew D. Merrick
Rodney O. Personius | William P. Wiles
Frederick D. Turner | William D. Harrington
Paul Michael Hassett | Joseph M. Schnitter
Peter E. Klaasesz | Paula L. Feroleto
Donald B. Eppers | Daniel J. Marren
Lisa T. Sofferin

OF COUNSEL

Ogden R. Brown | Roland R. Benzow
Charles F. Harrington | Philip B. Abramowitz
James T. Duggan | Elizabeth R. O'Connor
Karen Cook Serotte | Catherine E. Marra

ASSOCIATES

David S. Zygaj | David O. Teach
Olney H. Clowe | Patricia S. Ciccarelli
Brian M. Melber | Susan J. Schmidt

For full biographical listings, see the Martindale-Hubbell Law Directory

*COOPERSTOWN,** Otsego Co.

GOZIGIAN, WASHBURN & CLINTON (AV)

Orange L. Van Horne (1907-1946)
Van Horne & Feury (1946-1970)
Van Horne, Feury & Gozigian (1970-1979)
Feury, Gozigian & Washburn (1979-1992)
201-204 Key Bank Building, P.O. Box 431, 13326
Telephone: 607-547-2522
Fax: 607-547-2845
Email: GozigianWC@aol.com

MEMBERS OF FIRM

Edward Gozigian | Philip L. Washburn
David J. Clinton

ASSOCIATE

E.W. Garo Gozigan

Counsel for: New York Central Mutual Insurance Co.
Local Counsel for: Key Bank, N.A.; Empire Farm Credit ACA.

For full biographical listings, see the Martindale-Hubbell Law Directory

EAST MEADOW, Nassau Co.

CERTILMAN BALIN ADLER & HYMAN, LLP (AV)

90 Merrick Avenue, 11554
Telephone: 516-296-7000
Telecopier: 516-296-7111
URL: http://www.cbah.com

MEMBERS OF FIRM

Ira J. Adler | Wayne G. Edwards
Dale Allinson | Joseph P. Famighetti
Michael C. Axelrod | Howard R. Gladston
Herbert M. Balin | Murray Greenberg
Bruce J. Bergman | Gavin C. Grusd
Eileen O'Boyle Bitetto | David Z. Herman
Michael D. Brofman | Richard Herzbach
Lewis J. Campanella | M. Allan Hyman
Morton L. Certilman | Bernard Hyman
Robert J. Ciovacco | Donna-Marie Korth
Brian J. Davis | Steven J. Kuperschmid

(See Next Column)

MEMBERS OF FIRM (Continued)

Jeffrey S. Lisabeth | Marilyn Price
Jaspreet S. Mayall | Fred S. Skolnik
Richard J. McCord | Louis Soloway
Thomas J. McNamara | Harold Somer
Michael F. O'Shea | Howard M. Stein
Brian K. Ziegler

OF COUNSEL

Daniel S. Cohan | Joseph N. Mondello

ASSOCIATES

Lawrence A. Altholtz | James G. Kapralos
Meredith W. Ayres | Linda P. Manfredi
Daniel J. Baker | Edward G. McCabe
Kimberly I. Berson | Patrick McCormick
Scott B. Black | Susan L. McWalters
Brendan J. DeRiggi | Jothy Narendran
Thomas M. Farrell | James A. Rose
Mary C. Florentz | Wayne J. Schaefer
Candace Reid Gladston | Leslie H. Scharf
Harry P. Greenbaum | Afsheen Ashley Shah
David E. Herold | Victor Spinnelli
Jodi S. Hoffman | Russell H. Stern
Robert G. Wilk

For full biographical listings, see the Martindale-Hubbell Law Directory

FARMINGDALE, Nassau Co.

CARMAN, CALLAHAN & INGHAM (AV)

Carman Building, 280 Main Street, 11735
Telephone: 516-249-3450
Telecopier: 516-249-3782

Willis B. Carman, Jr. | Michael F. Ingham
Robert M. Callahan | Gregory W. Carman, Jr.
James M. Carman

ASSOCIATE

Stephanie L. Boden

For full biographical listings, see the Martindale-Hubbell Law Directory

GARDEN CITY, Nassau Co.

MARK S. CHARWAT, P.C. (AV)

1305 Franklin Avenue, 11530
Telephone: 516-294-4300
Fax: 516-294-4322

Mark S. Charwat

ASSOCIATES

Deborah S. Barcham | Ilene D. Samuel

OF COUNSEL

Michael R. Klein

For full biographical listings, see the Martindale-Hubbell Law Directory

DASILVA, HILOWITZ & MCEVILY LLP (AV)

585 Stewart Avenue, 11530
Telephone: 516-222-0700
Fax: 516-222-0743

Willard H. DaSilva | Lynne S. Hilowitz
Charles J. McEvily

OF COUNSEL

Frank G. D'Angelo, Jr.

For full biographical listings, see the Martindale-Hubbell Law Directory

JONES & JONES (AV)

1000 Franklin Avenue Suite 302, 11530
Telephone: 516-747-1141
Fax: 516-741-5842
URL: http://www.lawyers.com/jones&joneslaw

MEMBERS OF FIRM

C. H. Tunnicliffe Jones (1900-1991) | Lawrence T. Jones

OF COUNSEL

Howard L. DeMott

Reference: Bank of New York, Long Island Region.

For full biographical listings, see the Martindale-Hubbell Law Directory

GLENS FALLS, Warren Co.

FITZGERALD MORRIS BAKER FIRTH (AV)

One Broad Street Plaza, P.O. Box 2017, 12801
Telephone: 518-745-1400
Fax: 518-745-1576
Email: info@fmbf-law.com

(See Next Column)

FITZGERALD MORRIS BAKER FIRTH, *Glens Falls—Continued*

Robert C. Morris
Peter D. FitzGerald
Peter A. Firth
Carl T. Baker
J. Mark Noordsy
Robert P. McNally
Laura V. Nield
Veronica Carrozza O'Dell

Bruce G. Carr
David Gregory Richardson
Kevin O'Shell

Representative Clients: Woodbury Development Group, Ltd.; Homequity; Glens Falls Cement Co., Inc.; Greater Glens Falls Development Corp.; Glens Falls Industrial Development Agency; Torrington Industries, Inc.; Whiteman Chevrolet, Inc.

For full biographical listings, see the Martindale-Hubbell Law Directory

HUNTINGTON, Suffolk Co.

SMYTH & LACK (AV)

143 Main Street, 11743
Telephone: 516-271-7500
Telecopier: 516-271-7504
URL: http://www.lawyers.com/smyth&lacklaw

MEMBERS OF FIRM

Vincent A. Smyth
James J. Lack

ASSOCIATES

Dana M. Barberis
Edmund J.M. Smyth
Karen E. Nora

Reference: Chemical Bank.

For full biographical listings, see the Martindale-Hubbell Law Directory

*ITHACA,** Tompkins Co.

WIGGINS AND MASSON, LLP (AV)

308 North Tioga Street, P.O. Box 399, 14851
Telephone: 607-272-0479
Telecopier: 607-273-0502
Email: law@wigginsandmasson.com *URL:* http://www.wigginsandmasson.com

MEMBERS OF FIRM

Walter J. Wiggins
Robin Abrahamson Masson
Erin E. McKinley
Lorraine Moynihan

Approved Attorneys for: Ticor Title Guaranty Corp.
References: Tompkins County Trust Co.

For full biographical listings, see the Martindale-Hubbell Law Directory

JAMESTOWN, Chautauqua Co.

ERICKSON, WEBB & SCOLTON (AV)

111 West Second Street, 14701
Telephone: 716-488-1178
Fax: 716-488-1448
Email: ews@netsync.net

MEMBERS OF FIRM

Alton R. Erickson (1904-1968)
Philip A. Erickson
Paul V. Webb, Jr.
Bruce S. Scolton
Lyle T. Hajdu

References: Marine Midland Bank, N.A.; Chase Manhattan Bank.

For full biographical listings, see the Martindale-Hubbell Law Directory

JERICHO, Nassau Co.

MARTIN, VAN DE WALLE, DONOHUE, MCGAHAN, CATALANO & FAIRGRIEVE (AV)

555 North Broadway, P.O. Box 350, 11753
Telephone: 516-681-3100
Telecopier: 516-681-5357

MEMBERS OF FIRM

Jules Martin (1928-1995)
Charles R. Van de Walle
Joseph A. Guarino (1946-1991)
Nicholas J. Donohue
James M. McGahan
Thomas C. Catalano, Jr.
Scott Fairgrieve
Michael Belitsis

ASSOCIATES

Randi M. Seidner
Laurie Ann Corallo

Representative Clients: Fidelity National Title Insurance Company of New York; Festo Corp.; First Investors Corp.; First Financial Savings Bank, S.L.A.; Chaminade High School; Oppenheimer Funds, Inc.; Old Republic National Title Insurance Company; New York State Land Title Association, Inc.; Chase Manhattan Mortgage Corp.; First Investors Corp.; Leo and Arnstein Agency; Jones Fund; Northeast Adjustment Co., Inc.; Cahse Manhattan Bank, N.A.; Capital Trading Corp.

For full biographical listings, see the Martindale-Hubbell Law Directory

*KINGSTON,** Ulster Co.

HOWARD C. ST. JOHN AND ASSOCIATES (AV)

P.O. Box 4380, 12402
Telephone: 914-338-4500
Fax: 914-338-0638

ASSOCIATES

Richard A. Anthony
Joseph L. Canino
John J. Cook
Michael Francis Jordan
J. Michael Bruhn, Jr.

General Counsel for: Ulster Savings Bank.
Representative Clients: Government Employees Insurance Co.; National Grange Insurance Co.; New York Central Mutual Fire Insurance Co.; AT&T (local counsel); Volkswagen of America, Inc. (local counsel); Inland Steel (local counsel).

For full biographical listings, see the Martindale-Hubbell Law Directory

LAKE SUCCESS, Nassau Co.

DIKMAN AND DIKMAN (AV)

5 Dakota Drive, Suite 208, 11042
Telephone: 516-354-2526
Fax: 516-354-2528
Jamaica, New York Office: 161-10 Jamaica Avenue, *Telephone:* 718-739-4830.

MEMBERS OF FIRM

Leo Dikman
David S. Dikman

Reference: Chase Manhattan Bank.

For full biographical listings, see the Martindale-Hubbell Law Directory

*LOCKPORT,** Niagara Co.

SACCA AND SACCA (AV)

102 East Avenue, 14094
Telephone: 716-434-5518
Fax: 716-434-8050
Email: gssacca@aol.com *URL:* http://www.lawyers.com/gsacca

MEMBERS OF FIRM

Stephen A. Sacca
Gerald Stephen Sacca

LEGAL SUPPORT PERSONNEL

Anna Marie Holman (Paralegal)
Lauree E. Chase (Paralegal)

Representative Clients: Lawyers Title Insurance Corp. (Virginia); Village of Wilson.
References: Manufacturers & Traders Trust Co.; Marine Midland Bank; Lockport Savings Bank.

For full biographical listings, see the Martindale-Hubbell Law Directory

MELVILLE, Suffolk Co.

LAMB & BARNOSKY, LLP (AV)

534 Broadhollow Road-CS 9034, 11747-9034
Telephone: 631-694-2300
Telecopier: 631-694-2309
Email: thefirm@lambbarnosky.com *URL:* http://www.lambbarnosky.com

PARTNERS

Eugene R. Barnosky
Robert H. Cohen
Marcia Lyn Finkelstein
Michael J. Heller
Gary Holman
Scott M. Karson
P. L. Lamb
Arthur A. Lane
Joel M. Markowitz
Gerald P. Rosenberg
Patrice Dowd Shenn

OF COUNSEL

Louis E. Black
James F. Gesualdi
Howard W. Newman
Joseph J. Salvatore
Joseph H. Wishod

COUNSEL

Lloyd K. Chanin
Scott P. McBride

ASSOCIATES

Cathleen D. Allen
Catherine Healy Kanzler
Rita Fishman Sheena
Shari Lee Sugarman

For full biographical listings, see the Martindale-Hubbell Law Directory

MERRICK, Nassau Co.

JACK A. BENNARDO (AV)

2163 Merrick Avenue, P.O. Box 360, 11566
Telephone: 516-378-1110
Fax: 516-378-1252
Email: jablaw1@aol.com *URL:* http://www.lawyers.com/bennardolaw

For full biographical listings, see the Martindale-Hubbell Law Directory

MIDDLETOWN, Orange Co.

MacVean, Lewis, Sherwin & McDermott, P.C. (AV)

34 Grove Street, P.O. Box 310, 10940
Telephone: 914-343-3000
Fax: 914-343-3866

Kenneth A. MacVean (1926-1999)
Kermit W. Lewis
Louis H. Sherwin
Paul T. McDermott
Jeffrey D. Sherwin
Thomas P. Clarke, Jr.
John M. Clancy

SENIOR TRIAL COUNSEL

George F. Roesch, III

Kevin F. Preston
Ferol Reed McDermott
Anthony R. LoBiondo
James V. Galvin

OF COUNSEL

Samuel W. Eager, Jr.

Counsel for: Orange County Trust Co.; Middletown Savings Bank; First Federal Savings & Loan Association of Middletown; Goshen Savings Bank; Advest Bank.

For full biographical listings, see the Martindale-Hubbell Law Directory

*MINEOLA,** Nassau Co.

Robert L. Clarey (AV)

96 Willis Avenue, 11501
Telephone: 516-747-6660
Voice Mail: 516-742-9116
Fax: 516-742-5278
URL: http://www.lawyers.com/clareylaw

For full biographical listings, see the Martindale-Hubbell Law Directory

John B. Dawson, Jr., P.C. (AV)

1565 Franklin Avenue, 11501
Telephone: 516-248-2131
Fax: 516-294-4866

John B. Dawson, Jr.

For full biographical listings, see the Martindale-Hubbell Law Directory

Hatter, Donovan & McFaul, LLP (AV)

47 Mineola Boulevard, 11501
Telephone: 516-873-8800
Fax: 516-873-1418
Email: law@hdmlaw.com
URL: http://www.hdmlaw.com

MEMBERS OF FIRM

James R. Hatter
Thomas J. Donovan
John M. McFaul

Lawrence J. Freeze, III

For full biographical listings, see the Martindale-Hubbell Law Directory

NEWBURGH, Orange Co.

Rider, Weiner, Frankel & Calhelha, P.C. (AV)

655 Little Britain Road, P.O. Box 2280, 12550
Telephone: 914-562-9100
Fax: 914-562-9126
Email: firm@rwfc.com *URL:* http://www.rwfc.com

M.J. Rider (1906-1968)
Elliott M. Weiner (1915-1990)
David L. Rider
Charles E. Frankel
Moacyr R. Calhelha
Maureen Crush
Michael J. Matsler

Donna M. Badura
Mark C. Taylor
Roderick E. de Ramon
Teri L. Shulman

OF COUNSEL

Craig F. Simon
David E. Tower

LEGAL SUPPORT PERSONNEL

Lynn W. Cybulski
Aliza S. D'Agati
Carol E. Garner

For full biographical listings, see the Martindale-Hubbell Law Directory

*NEW CITY,** Rockland Co.

Freeman, Loftus & Manley (AV)

4 Laurel Road, P.O. Box 629, 10956-0629
Telephone: 914-634-0888
Fax: 914-634-9312
Email: flmattys@aol.com

(See Next Column)

MEMBERS OF FIRM

James J. Freeman, Jr.
Patrick J. Loftus
Loring K. Manley

OF COUNSEL

James H. Bowers
Ira M. Emanuel
Albert J. Kaiser

For full biographical listings, see the Martindale-Hubbell Law Directory

*NEW YORK,** New York Co.

Berlack, Israels & Liberman LLP (AV)

120 West 45th Street, 10036
Telephone: 212-704-0100
Cable Address: "Berilib"
Telecopier: 212-704-0196
Email: info@berlack.com
Morristown, New Jersey Office: 65 Madison Avenue.
Telephone: 201-644-3400.
Telecopier: 201-644-3159.

MEMBERS OF FIRM

Harris Berlack (1946-1968)
Carlos L. Israels (1946-1969)
Kenneth R. Asher
Claude A. Baum
Scott M. Berman
Wade M. Boswell
Douglas E. Davidson
Alan N. Forman
Steven E. Greenbaum
Harvey M. Katz
James B. Liberman
Stuart Neuhauser
Robert D. Schmicker
Martin S. Siegel
Steven F. Wasserman
Edward S. Weisfelner

SENIOR ATTORNEYS

Andrew S. Dash
Erica M. Ryland

ASSOCIATES

John P. Biedermann
Anne M. Cunningham
Pauline Foley (Resident, Morristown, New Jersey Office)
Julie L. Friedberg (Resident, Morristown, New Jersey Office)
Emilio A. Galván
Linda B. Goebel
Louis Lombardo
Rachel F. Mayerson (Not admitted in NY)
Amy P. K. Motzenbecker (Resident, Morristown, New Jersey Office)
Antonio Peguero, Jr.
Elizabeth Quirk (Resident, Morristown, New Jersey Office)
Marcela M. Sanchez
Melissa Sarubbi

OF COUNSEL

Gerald W. Conway (Not admitted in NY; Resident, Morristown, New Jersey Office)
Marc B. Lasky (Resident, Morristown, New Jersey Office)

For full biographical listings, see the Martindale-Hubbell Law Directory

Mitchell B. Booth (AV)

City Spire, 156 West 56th Street, 10019
Telephone: 212-977-9500
Telecopier: 212-459-8947
Cable Address: "Boothlaws"

For full biographical listings, see the Martindale-Hubbell Law Directory

Brauner Baron Rosenzweig & Klein, L.L.P. (AV)

The Firm of Herman Goldman
61 Broadway, 10006
Telephone: 212-797-9100
Cable Address: "Goldenlaw"
Telecopier: (212) 797-9161
URL: http://www.braunerbaron.com

MEMBERS OF FIRM

Herman Goldman (1880-1968)
Herman M. Brauner (1903-1980)
Stanley Klein (1934-1998)
Raymond S. Baron (1916-1998)
Seymour H. Kligler (1920-1998)
Paul Bauman (1922-1999)
David A. Brauner
David R. Kay
Mel P. Barkan
Christopher C. Schwabacher
Roy M. Sparber
Alan Michigan
Howard L. Simon
Charles A. Damato
Alan Nisselson
Michael J. Clain
Francis P. Manfredi
Nina P. Silfen
Michael J. Weitzner

ASSOCIATES

Christopher L. Chin
Caroline H. Hahn
Stacy M. Modlin
Dina M. Friedman
Margaret A. M. Shearer
Son K. Le
Shalu Rastogi
Sharon I. Farman
Lawrence A. Dunn, Jr.

(See Next Column)

BRAUNER BARON ROSENZWEIG & KLEIN L.L.P., *New York—Continued*

OF COUNSEL

Jules M. Baron
Norman H. Sparber
Elias Rosenzweig
John J. Bennett, Jr.
Michael L. Goldstein
William L. Kadish
Jon D. Kaplon

For full biographical listings, see the Martindale-Hubbell Law Directory

CAPLIN & DRYSDALE, CHARTERED (AV)

399 Park Avenue 36th Floor, 10022
Telephone: 212-319-7125
Fax: 212-644-6755
Washington, D.C. Office: One Thomas Circle, N.W.
Telephone: 202-862-5000.
Fax: 202-429-3301.

Elihu Inselbuch

Rita C. Tobin

For full biographical listings, see the Martindale-Hubbell Law Directory

CARB, LURIA, COOK & KUFELD, LLP (AV)

521 Fifth Avenue, 10175
Telephone: 212-986-3131
Telecopier: 212-682-2682
Email: mail@carbluria.com *URL:* http://www.carbluria.com

MEMBERS OF FIRM

Alfred B. Carb (1902-1963)
George Cook, III (1915-1994)
William M. Kufeld (1922-1998)
Stephen A. Carb
Daniel Scheyer
Geoffrey P. Picket
Leonard H. Carter
Stephen J. Fallis
M. William Scherer
Linda T. Newman
Edwin A. Novak
Carol Wallis Duffy
James E. Schwartz
Kenneth Richter

ASSOCIATES

Jonathan K. Bright
Janet M. Joyce
Jay A. Lang
Peter L. Lese
Andrew G. Lipkin
David L. Paldy
Jeffrey A. Samuels

COUNSEL

Sydney A. Luria
Gerald J. Robinson

SPECIAL COUNSEL

David K. Ford

For full biographical listings, see the Martindale-Hubbell Law Directory

CURTIS, MALLET-PREVOST, COLT & MOSLE LLP (AV)

101 Park Avenue, 10178-0061
Telephone: 212-696-6000
Telecopier: 212-697-1559
Email: info@cm-p.com *URL:* http://www.cm-p.com
Washington, D.C. Office: Suite 1205L, 1801 K Street, N.W.
Telephone: 202-452-7373.
Telecopier: 202-452-7333.
Newark, New Jersey Office: One Gateway Center, Suite 403.
Telephone: 973-622-0605.
Telecopier: 973-622-5646.
Houston, Texas Office: 2 Houston Center, 909 Fannin Street, Suite 3725.
Telephone: 713-759-9555.
Telecopier: 713-759-0712.
Stamford, Connecticut Office: One Canterbury Green.
Telephone: 203-359-6200.
Telecopier: 203-328-2617.
Mexico City, D.F., Mexico Office: Curtis, Mallet-Prevost, Colt & Mosle, Ruben Dario 281, Piso 9, Col. Bosque de Chapultepec, 11530 Mexico, D.F.
Telephone: 525-282-0444.
Telecopier: 525-282-0637.
Paris, France Office: 15 rue d'Astorg, 75008.
Telephone: +33-1 42-66-39-10.
Telecopier: +33-1 42-66-39-62.
London, England Office: Two Throgmorton Avenue, EC2N 2DL.
Telephone: 0207-638-7957.
Telecopier: 0207-638-5512.
Frankfurt am Main 1, Germany Office: Staufenstrasse 42.
Telephone: +49-69-971-4420.
Telecopier: +49-69-17 33 99.
Muscat, Sultanate of Oman Office: Jewel Beach-134.
Telephone: 968-607-725.
Telecopier: 968-607-724.
Milan, Italy Office: Curtis, Mallet-Prevost & Gilioli, Piazzale Principessa Clotilde 8, 20121.
Telephone: +(39) 02 29 00 29 32.
Telefax: +(39) 02 65 75 969.

MEMBERS OF FIRM

J. Dinsmore Adams, Jr.
Robert W. Sheehan

(See Next Column)

COUNSEL

Morgan A. Casey, Jr.
Antoinette N. Ceisler
Miner D. Crary, Jr.

ASSOCIATES

Brian Bandler
Brendan P. Kearse

For full biographical listings, see the Martindale-Hubbell Law Directory

FREEDMAN AND FISH (AV)

260 Madison Avenue, 10016
Telephone: 212-481-0810
Fax: 212-213-0924
Email: fandf1985@aol.com *URL:* http://www.lawyers.com/freedmanandfish

MEMBERS OF FIRM

Robert M. Freedman
Daniel G. Fish
Barry I. Lutzky

ASSOCIATES

Allison Jill Busch
Sheryl R. Frishman
Lawrence I. Garbuz
Marcie G. Roth

For full biographical listings, see the Martindale-Hubbell Law Directory

GALLET DREYER & BERKEY, LLP (AV)

845 Third Avenue, 10022-6601
Telephone: 212-935-3131
Telecopier: 212-935-4514
Email: gdb@gdblaw.com *URL:* http://www.gdblaw.com

MEMBERS OF FIRM

Simon Gallet (1914-1974)
Stanley B. Dreyer
David L. Berkey
Ray Beckerman
Benjamin S. Klapper
Seymour D. Reich
Sidney Ingber
John W. Manning
Jerome S. Solomon
Harvey Schwartz
Perry L. Mintz

Beatrice Lesser
Morlan Ty Rogers
Christina M. Ambrosio
Jeffrey S. Harwin
Regina M. Marotti
Natasha Leigh Nordahl
Carole M. Bass

For full biographical listings, see the Martindale-Hubbell Law Directory

KOSTELANETZ & FINK, LLP (AV)

530 Fifth Avenue, 22nd Floor, 10036
Telephone: 212-808-8100
Fax: 212-808-8108
Email: mail@kostelanetzfink.com

SENIOR COUNSEL

Boris Kostelanetz

MEMBERS OF FIRM

Robert S. Fink
Kevin M. Flynn
Bryan C. Skarlatos

COUNSEL

Norman Sinrich
Theodore F. Dickson
Caroline Rule
Brian C. Wille
William F. Cuozzi, III
Dawn Ngo

For full biographical listings, see the Martindale-Hubbell Law Directory

LOEB & LOEB LLP (AV)

A Limited Liability Partnership including Professional Corporations
345 Park Avenue, 10154-0037
Telephone: 212-407-4000
Facsimile: 212-407-4990
Email: info@loeb.com *URL:* http://www.loeb.com
Los Angeles, California Office: Suite 1800, 1000 Wilshire Boulevard, 90017-2475.
Telephone: 213-688-3400.
Facsimile: 213-688-3460.
Century City (Los Angeles), California Office: Suite 2200, 10100 Santa Monica Boulevard, Los Angeles, 90067-4164.
Telephone: 310-282-2000.
Facsimile: 310-282-2192.
Nashville, Tennessee Office: 45 Music Square West, 37203-3205.
Telephone: 615-749-8300.
Facsimile: 615-749-8308.
Rome, Italy Office: Piazza Digione 1, 00197.
Telephone: 011-3906-808-8456.
Facsimile: 011-3906-808-8288.

MEMBERS OF FIRM

Jerome L. Levine
Bruce J. Wexler

SENIOR COUNSEL

Laurie S. Ruckel

(See Next Column)

LOEB & LOEB LLP—*Continued*

ASSOCIATE

Lynda C. Loigman

For Complete List of Firm Personnel, See General Section

For full biographical listings, see the Martindale-Hubbell Law Directory

MAZUR, CARP & RUBIN, P.C. (AV)

2 Park Avenue, 10016
Telephone: 212-686-7700
Telecopier: 212-532-1425
Email: mcrlaw@sprynet.com

Gerald I. Carp
Sayward Mazur
Gary L. Rubin
Ira M. Schulman

OF COUNSEL

Charles H. Weinberg

Thomas G. Draper, Jr.
Richard Raab
Frank L. Wagner

For full biographical listings, see the Martindale-Hubbell Law Directory

MORRISSEY & MORRISSEY, LLP (AV)

Brown Brothers Harriman Building, 63 Wall Street, Suite 1903, 10005-3001
Telephone: 212-809-0550
Fax: 212-809-2214
Email: morrissey@spacelab.net

MEMBERS OF FIRM

James J. Morrissey, Jr.
Sabrina E. Morrissey

Brenda M. Lynch
Martha Ketro

Reference: United States Trust Company.

For full biographical listings, see the Martindale-Hubbell Law Directory

NEUFELD & O'LEARY (AV)

Suite 527, 230 Park Avenue, 10169
Telephone: 212-986-0999
Telecopier: 212-986-6341
Long Island Office: Melville Law Center, 225 Old Country Road, Melville, New York, 11747.
Telephone: 516-549-1717.

MEMBERS OF FIRM

David S. J. Neufeld
Denis P. O'Leary

ASSOCIATES

Lisa Mendelson Hecht
Donald M. Spector
Peter J. Schancupp

OF COUNSEL

Edwin T. Broderick

For full biographical listings, see the Martindale-Hubbell Law Directory

OTTERBOURG, STEINDLER, HOUSTON & ROSEN, P.C. (AV)

230 Park Avenue, 29th Floor, 10169
Telephone: 212-661-9100
Telecopier: 212-682-6104

Daniel Wallen

COUNSEL

Bernard Beitel

For Complete List of Firm Personnel, See General Section

For full biographical listings, see the Martindale-Hubbell Law Directory

PARKER CHAPIN LLP (AV)

Chrysler Building, 405 Lexington Avenue, 10017
Telephone: 212-704-6000
Telecopier: 212-704-6288
URL: http://www.parkerchapin.com
Great Neck, New York Office: 175 Great Neck Road.
Telephone: 516-482-4422.
Telecopier: 516-482-4469.
Hackensack, New Jersey: 190 Morre Street, Suite 307.
Telephone: 210-883-6400.
Telecopier: 210-883-6404.
Beverly Hills, California: 9454 Wilshire Boulevard.
Telephone: 310-288-8367.
Telecopier: 310-288-8365.

MEMBER OF FIRM

Carol F. Burger

SENIOR COUNSEL

Seymour Levine

(See Next Column)

OF COUNSEL

Richard E. Schneyer

For Complete List of Firm Personnel, See General Section

For full biographical listings, see the Martindale-Hubbell Law Directory

PLUNKETT & JAFFE, P.C. (AV)

230 Park Avenue, Suite 1847, 10169
Telephone: 212-922-1800
Facsimile: 212-922-1819
Email: plunkettjaffe.com
White Plains, New York Office: 1 North Broadway.
Telephone: 914-948-7722.
Facsimile: 914-948-7603.
Albany, New York Office: 111 Washington Avenue.
Telephone: 518-462-1800.
Facsimile: 518-462-4875.

Justin E. Driscoll, III

OF COUNSEL

Susan Litwer

For Complete List of Firm Personnel, See General Section

For full biographical listings, see the Martindale-Hubbell Law Directory

JAY J. SANGERMAN & ASSOCIATES (AV)

60 East 42nd Street Suite 650, 10165
Telephone: 212-922-0711
Telephone Florida 561-989-9095
Fax: 212-922-0709
Email: law@sangerman.com *URL:* http://www.sangerman.com
Boca Raton, Florida Office: 4115 N.W. 60th Circle, 33496.
Telephone: 561-989-9095.
Fax: 561-989-9096.
Clifton, New Jersey Office: 4 Brighton Road, Suite 200, 07015.
Telephone: 973-778-3422.

For full biographical listings, see the Martindale-Hubbell Law Directory

WAGNER, DAVIS & GOLD, P.C. (AV)

99 Madison Avenue, 10016
Telephone: 212-481-9600
Telefax: 212-481-8245

Steven R. Wagner
Ronald Jay Gold
John R. Wagner
Bonnie Reid Berkow
William R. Fried

OF COUNSEL

Deborah Lynn Davis

Adam D. Finkelstein
Keith L. Woodside
Robert J. Patchen
Glen C. Rosenberg
Mikelle V. Lipsius (Not admitted in NY)

LEGAL SUPPORT PERSONNEL

Nicole J. Ottley (Paralegal)
Steven Henderson (Paralegal)
Tracey A. Lewis (Paralegal)
Karen Chin (Paralegal)
Daniel E. Glatter (Law Clerk)

For full biographical listings, see the Martindale-Hubbell Law Directory

WALLMAN, GREENBERG, GASMAN & McKNIGHT, LLP (AV)

350 Fifth Avenue, Suite 3000, 10118
Telephone: 212-695-6000
Fax: 212-695-6007

MEMBERS OF FIRM

Lester Wallman
Philip A. Greenberg
Gerald B. Gasman
Elaine McKnight
Donald R. Wall

OF COUNSEL

Clement Segal
Daniel E. Clement
Roy L. Jacobs
Frank J. Hariton

LEGAL SUPPORT PERSONNEL

Lisa Chiodi (Office Administrator)

For full biographical listings, see the Martindale-Hubbell Law Directory

ONEONTA, Otsego Co.

GETMAN LAW FIRM (AV)

16 Dietz Street, P.O. Box 613, 13820
Telephone: 607-432-3530
Fax: 607-432-3571
Email: getmanlw@wpe.com

Frank W. Getman
Michael F. Getman

References: Key Bank of New York; Wilber National Bank Oneonta, N.Y.

For full biographical listings, see the Martindale-Hubbell Law Directory

*PLATTSBURGH,** Clinton Co.

LEWIS, ROGERS & KUDRLE, P.C. (AV)

53 Court Street, 12901-2834
Telephone: 518-561-3700
Fax: 518-561-2080
Email: lrk@westelcom.com *URL:* http://www.lawyers.com/lrklaw

Clyde A. Lewis
Mark J. Rogers
Larry A. Kudrle
Harold A. Jerry (1893-1990)
Robert A. Lyon (1924-1982)

Attorneys for: Graystone Materials, Inc.; Plattsburgh Motor Service Inc.; The Development Corporation, Clinton County, New York.

For full biographical listings, see the Martindale-Hubbell Law Directory

*POUGHKEEPSIE,** Dutchess Co.

HANKIN, HANIG, STALL, CAPLICKI, REDL & CURTIN, LLP (AV)

319 Main Mall Rear, P.O. Box 911, 12602-0911
Telephone: 914-471-7177
FAX: 914-471-0105
Email: hhscrc@aol.com *URL:* http://www.hvlaw.com
Newburgh, New York Office: 6 Jeanne Drive, P.O. Box 7229, 12550.
Telephone: 914-566-8888.
Fax: 914-566-3886.
LaGrangeville, New York Office: Lexington Park, Route 55, P.O. Box 15, LaGrangeville, New York.
Telephone: 914-473-1200.

MEMBERS OF FIRM

Jerard S. Hankin
Joel D. Hanig
Todd S. Stall
Edmund V. Caplicki, Jr.
Frank E. Redl
Daniel F. Curtin

Lynn M. Smookler
David V. Hasin

For full biographical listings, see the Martindale-Hubbell Law Directory

TEAHAN & CONSTANTINO (AV)

325 South Road, P.O. Box 1969, 12601
Telephone: 914-452-1834
Fax: 914-452-1421
Email: tandc@idsi.net *URL:* http://www.TCTaxPlan.com
Albany, New York Office: 125 Wolf Road, Suite 412, 12205.
Telephone: 518-435-0534;
Fax: 518-435-0546.

MEMBERS OF FIRM

Vincent L. Teahan
James P. Constantino

OF COUNSEL

Richard I. Cantor
Eliot D. Hawkins
Gina A. Gulotty

For full biographical listings, see the Martindale-Hubbell Law Directory

PURCHASE, Westchester Co.

GIOFFRE & GIOFFRE, PROFESSIONAL CORPORATION (AV)

2900 Westchester Avenue Suite 206, 10577
Telephone: 914-696-3800
Fax: 914-696-3833

Bruno J. Gioffre
Lisa Gioffre Baird

Anthony B. Gioffre, III
Russell A. Giorno

Representative Clients: Sound Federal Savings & Loan Assn.; Port Chester Public Library; Rye Town Hilton Inn; Westchester Business Institute.

For full biographical listings, see the Martindale-Hubbell Law Directory

*RIVERHEAD,** Suffolk Co.

JOHN M. CZYGIER, JR. (AV)

214 Roanoke Avenue, P.O. Box 449, 11901-0449
Telephone: 516-727-2500
Facsimile: 516-727-2000

LEGAL SUPPORT PERSONNEL

Mary Anne Klipp (Office Manager)

For full biographical listings, see the Martindale-Hubbell Law Directory

*ROCHESTER,** Monroe Co.

LACY, KATZEN, RYEN & MITTLEMAN, LLP (AV)

The Granite Building, 130 East Main Street, 14604
Telephone: 716-454-5650
FAX: 716-454-6525
Email: MSS@Frontiernet.net
Charlotte, New York Office: 4292 Lake Avenue.
Telephone: 716-663-4543.

(See Next Column)

Hilton, New York Office: 20 Main Street.
Telephone: 716-392-2990.
Canandaigua, New York Office: 23 North Main Street.
Telephone: 716-394-5220.
Greece, New York Office: County Village Center, 110 Long Pond Road, Suite 214.
Telephone: 716-225-2470.
Fax: 716-225-5620.
Bergen, New York Office: 16 North Lake Street.
Telephone: 716-494-1382.
Ontario, New York Office: 1276 Ridge Road.
Telephone: 315-524-5000.
Roseland, New Jersey Office: 103 Eisenhower Parkway.
Telephone: 201-403-8001.
Penn Yan, New York Office: 116 Main Street, 2nd Floor, P.O. Box 439.
Telephone: 315-536-6281.

MEMBERS OF FIRM

Louis A. Ryen
Ronald A. Mittleman
Michael S. Schnittman
Peter T. Rodgers
Sally A. Smith
Karen Schaefer
Richard G. Curtis
Lawrence J. Schwind
David H. Walsh IV
David E. Anderson
Craig R. Welch
Christopher B. Mumford
Leslie W. Kernan, Jr.

COUNSEL

Leon Katzen
George F. Frey, Jr.
John J. Keigher
Paul A. Sandars, III

ASSOCIATES

David D. MacKnight
Nia J. Nichols
Terrance W. Emmens
Mark H. Stein
Denine K. Carr
Jacqueline M. Thomas
Stephen M. O'Neill
Jennifer Lynn Chadwick
William H. Drumm
Matthew A. Ryen
Roxanne A. Marvasti
Julie E. Meyer

General Counsel for: Village of Bergen, Bergen, New York; Village of Hilton, Hilton, New York; Byron-Bergen Central School District No. 1, Bergen, New York; Ferris Industries, Inc.; L. Woerner, Inc.d/b/a HCR.
Reference: The Chase Manhattan Bank, Rochester, N.Y.

For full biographical listings, see the Martindale-Hubbell Law Directory

LAWRENCE, WERNER, KESSELRING, SWARTOUT & BROWN, LLP (AV)

Formerly Suter Doyle Kesselring Lawrence & Werner
700 First Federal Plaza, 14614-1909
Telephone: 716-325-6446
Fax: 716-262-5185
Email: rochester@lwksb.com *URL:* http://www.lwksb.com
Canandaigua, New York Office: 23 Sly Street, 14424.
Telephone: 716-396-4000.
Fax: 716-396-1210. Email: canandaigua@lwksb.com.
Clifton Springs, New York: 26 East Main Street, P.O. Box 604, 14432.
Telephone: 315-462-3010.
Fax: 315-462-5039. Email: clifton_springs@lwksb.com

Paul J. Suter (1918-1989)

MEMBERS OF FIRM

Leo J. Kesselring
C. Bruce Lawrence
Christopher K. Werner
Colleen A. Brown
Steven H. Swartout
Mary Jo S. Korona

OF COUNSEL

James B. Doyle
Craig J. Doran
John F. Riley

ASSOCIATE

Jeffrey D. Graff

Representative Clients: Canandaigua National Bank; Hadlock Paint Company, Inc.; F.F. Thompson Health Systems, Inc.; Keuka College; Towns of Farmington and Gorham, NY; Toyota Motor Credit Corp.
References: Canandaigua National Bank; Fleet Bank, Rochester; National Association of Credit Manager, Rochester.

For full biographical listings, see the Martindale-Hubbell Law Directory

ROME, Oneida Co.

GRIFFITH LAW OFFICES (AV)

225 North Washington Street, 13440
Telephone: 315-336-6500
Fax: 315-336-6628
Email: griffi@aiusa.com *URL:* http://www.lawyers.com/griffith

MEMBER OF FIRM

Emlyn I. Griffith

Representative Clients: Alcan Aluminum Corporation; Camroden Associates, Inc.; C & H Plastics, Inc.; Covewood Mobile Park; D & H Asphalt Co., Inc.; Legendary Corp.; Statewide Funding Corp; Stonehedge Nursing Home.
Approved Attorneys for: The Title Guarantee Co.

For full biographical listings, see the Martindale-Hubbell Law Directory

Rome—Continued

PAUL L. PILECKAS (AV)

Professional Building, 217 North Washington Street, 13440
Telephone: 315-339-3020
Utica: 315-724-6381
Fax: 315-337-3876

Representative Clients: Don Davidson Motors, Inc.; Rome Rental, Inc.; West Electric, Inc.

For full biographical listings, see the Martindale-Hubbell Law Directory

ROSLYN HEIGHTS, Nassau Co.

NATISS, NATISS & GORDON, P.C. (AV)

277 Willis Avenue, 11577
Telephone: 516-621-0900
Telecopier: 516-621-1304
Email: MNatisslaw@aol.com

Marvin Natiss
Gary M. Natiss
Stacey Natiss Gordon

Sharon G. Haut

For full biographical listings, see the Martindale-Hubbell Law Directory

SALAMANCA, Cattaraugus Co.

BRADY, BROOKS & O'CONNELL, LLP (AV)

41 Main Street, P.O. Box 227, 14779
Telephone: 716-945-2000
Telecopier: 716-945-3566
Email: bbolaw@aol.com *URL:* http://www.lawyers.com/bbolaw
Randolph, New York Office: 165 Main Street.
Telephone: 716-358-6800.
Ellicottville, New York Office: 1887 Building, 1 Washington Street, P.O. Box 550.
Telephone: 716-699-8010.

MEMBERS OF FIRM

Thomas C. Brady
Kameron K. G. Brooks
Brian E. O'Connell, Jr.

Lori Pettit Rieman

For full biographical listings, see the Martindale-Hubbell Law Directory

SCARSDALE, Westchester Co.

GLORIA CROWLEY MARKUSON (AV)

Scarsdale Law Center Building, 185 Summerfield Street, 10583
Telephone: 914-472-5600
Fax: 914-472-5605
Email: rdm8@aol.com *URL:* http://www.lawyers.com/gloriacrowleymarkuson

Reference: Bank of New York, County Trust Region.

For full biographical listings, see the Martindale-Hubbell Law Directory

*SYRACUSE,** Onondaga Co.

ALDERMAN AND ALDERMAN (AV)

Suite 555 Empire Building, 472 South Salina Street, 13202
Telephone: 315-422-8131
Fax: 315-474-7507
Email: aldermanoffice@worldnet.att.net *URL:* http://www.lawyers.com/aldermanlaw

MEMBERS OF FIRM

Saul H. Alderman (1901-1985)
Bernard Samuels (1907-1985)
Edward B. Alderman
Richard B. Alderman

ASSOCIATE

Janet Jule Dougherty

LEGAL SUPPORT PERSONNEL

Judy M. Conger
Leticia A. Wicks
Tracy A. Esposito

Reference: First National of Rochester.

For full biographical listings, see the Martindale-Hubbell Law Directory

CARROLL, CARROLL, DAVIDSON & YOUNG, P.C. (AV)

The Galleries of Syracuse, Second Floor, 441 South Salina Street, 13202-0352
Telephone: 315-474-5356
Fax: 315-474-5451

Lee Carroll
John Benjamin Carroll (P.C.)
Eugene B. Young
J. Alexander Davidson

Woodruff L. Carroll
Sarkis L. Harootunian

For full biographical listings, see the Martindale-Hubbell Law Directory

DELANEY AND O'CONNOR LLP (AV)

Suite 275, Lincoln Center, 13202
Telephone: 315-476-8450
Telecopier: 315-476-8730
Email: deloco@dreamscape.com *URL:* http://www.dreamscape.com/deloco

MEMBERS OF FIRM

John M. DeLaney
Michael E. O'Connor
Denise P. Cambs

ASSOCIATES

Carol Currie Olech
Karin Sloan

For full biographical listings, see the Martindale-Hubbell Law Directory

LYNN LAW OFFICE (AV)

802 M & T Bank Building, 101 S. Salina Street, 13202
Telephone: 315-474-1267
Fax: 315-474-4514
Skaneateles, New York Office: 88 East Genesee Street.
Telephone: 315-685-1207.
Fax: 315-685-1047.

MEMBERS OF FIRM

William F. Lynn
Patricia A. Lynn-Ford
Thomas F. Shannon

For full biographical listings, see the Martindale-Hubbell Law Directory

MARTIN, MARTIN & WOODARD, LLP (AV)

Suite 300, One Lincoln Center, 13202-3010
Telephone: 315-478-2222
Fax: 315-478-4318

MEMBERS OF FIRM

Donald J. Martin
David P. Martin
Lee E. Woodard
Harold P. Goldberg
David M. Capriotti

ASSOCIATES

Wendy A. Kinsella
James T. Snyder
Daniel E. Dyer

For full biographical listings, see the Martindale-Hubbell Law Directory

*TROY,** Rensselaer Co.

MARTIN, SHUDT, WALLACE, DILORENZO & JOHNSON (AV)

The Dauchy Building, 279 River Street, P.O. Box 1530, 12181
Telephone: 518-272-6565
Fax: 518-272-5573
URL: http://www.estateplanning.com/martinlawfirm

Carl E. Martin (1902-1988)
Edwyn L. Shudt
Richard P. Wallace
Kirby W. DiLorenzo
Robert Wm. Johnson, III
James E. Prout
Frank C. Sarratori
Paul M. Macari

ASSOCIATES

Jennifer A. Cusack
Jaime B. Thomas
Matthew L. Hosford
Ronald J. Moss

OF COUNSEL

Thomas B. Hunt (Not admitted in NY)

For full biographical listings, see the Martindale-Hubbell Law Directory

VALATIE, Columbia Co.

BURNS F. BARFORD, JR. (AV)

1019 Kinderhook Street, 12184
Telephone: 518-758-7161
Facsimile: 518-758-9885

Counsel for: National Union Bank of Kinderhook.

For full biographical listings, see the Martindale-Hubbell Law Directory

*WARSAW,** Wyoming Co.

SMALLWOOD-COOK & SCHMIEDER (AV)

140 North Main Street, 14569-1103
Telephone: 716-786-2274
FAX: 716-786-2138
Email: smallwood@wycol.com

MEMBERS OF FIRM

Charlotte Smallwood-Cook
Jane A.C. Schmieder

Reference: Wyoming County Bank.

For full biographical listings, see the Martindale-Hubbell Law Directory

*WHITE PLAINS,** Westchester Co.

KENT, HAZZARD, JAEGER, GREER, WILSON & FAY (AV)
50 Main Street, 10606
Telephone: 914-948-4700
Telecopier: 914-948-4721
Email: KentHazz@aol.com

MEMBERS OF FIRM

Ralph S. Kent (1878-1949)
Lawrence S. Hazzard (1900-1958)
William J. Greer (1920-1994)
Mizell Wilson, Jr. (1927-1995)
Lawrence F. Fay
Robert D. Hazzard
Katharine Wilson Conroy

ASSOCIATE

John A. Verni

OF COUNSEL

Malcolm Wilson
Otto C. Jaeger
John R. Dinin
Harold L. Wood

Representative Client: The Bank of New York.
References: Bank of New York.

For full biographical listings, see the Martindale-Hubbell Law Directory

KURZMAN & EISENBERG, LLP (AV)
One North Broadway, 10601
Telephone: 914-285-9800
Fax: 914-285-9855
Email: ADMIN@KELAW.COM
New York, N.Y. Office: 99 Park Avenue.
Telephone: 212-671-1322.

MEMBERS OF FIRM

Robert G. Kurzman
Sam Eisenberg
Lee Harrison Corbin
Thomas B. Decea
Joel S. Lever
Stephen R. Levy
Jack S. Older
Alan John Rein
Robin A. Levitt Topol
Fred D. Weinstein

Ross J. Ellick
Michael H. Friedman
Katherine R. Steiner
Ilene B. Stern
Alfred S. Scope

OF COUNSEL

Judy B. Brownstein
Richard A. Danzig
Guy R. Fairstein
Elaine Fisher Haber
Elisa J. Lefkowitz

For full biographical listings, see the Martindale-Hubbell Law Directory

MARCUS, GOULD & SUSSMAN, LLP (AV)
222 Bloomingdale Road, 10605
Telephone: 914-683-0090
Telecopier: 914-683-0098
Email: firm@marcus-gould-sussman.com *URL:* http://www.lawyers.com/marcusgould&sussman

MEMBERS OF FIRM

Myron Marcus
Kenneth J. Gould
Marianne L. Sussman

References: Bennett, Kielson & Co.; Citibank, N.A.; Chemical Bank.

For full biographical listings, see the Martindale-Hubbell Law Directory

MCGOVERN AND DAWSON (AV)
50 Main Street, 10606
Telephone: 914-686-1055
Fax: 914-948-4721

MEMBERS OF FIRM

Joseph W. McGovern
Lawrence F. McGovern

OF COUNSEL

Philip C. McGovern

For full biographical listings, see the Martindale-Hubbell Law Directory

O'CONNOR, MCGUINNESS, CONTE, DOYLE & OLESON (AV)
One Barker Avenue, 10601
Telephone: 914-948-4500
Telecopier: 914-948-0645
Email: attys@omcdoc.com

MEMBERS OF FIRM

Dennis L. O'Connor (1913-1989)
Rocco Conte
Dennis T. Doyle
William S. Oleson
Richard C. Oleson
Dennis L. O'Connor, Jr.
William R. Watson
Kevin M. Loftus

ASSOCIATES

Louis K. Szarka
Montgomery Lee Effinger
Philomena Basuk
Debora J. Dillon
Daniel M. Miller
Peter Hyun Kim
James R. Callan
Dawn T. McConnell
George M. Lesnett
Robert Wolf

(See Next Column)

OF COUNSEL

Eugene J. McGuinness
Russell J. Hauck

Attorneys for: Insurance Company of North America; Allstate Insurance Co.; Continental Insurance Group; Government Employers Insurance Co.; Merchants Mutual Insurance Co.; Prudential Insurance Co.; Consolidated Rail Corp.; Medical Liability Mutual Insurance Co.; Colonial Penn Insurance Co.; G&W Electric Co.

For full biographical listings, see the Martindale-Hubbell Law Directory

POSNER, POSNER & ASSOCIATES, PC (AV)
399 Knollwood Road, 10603
Telephone: 914-948-6620
Telecopier: 914-948-0864
Email: relawyer@aol.com *URL:* http://www.lawyers.com/posner__posner&assoc

Henry A. Greenburg
Martin Louis Posner
Jane Y. Posner

Peter J. McCarthy
Karen Olson

References: Chemical Bank; Citibank.

For full biographical listings, see the Martindale-Hubbell Law Directory

ROGAN GUIDA & ORENSTEIN (AV)
235 Mamaroneck Avenue, 10605
Telephone: 1-888-WIN-WITH-US; 914-328-4480
Fax: 914-328-4479
URL: http://www.NYlawyers.com
Email: RoganGO@aol.com *URL:* http://www.lawyers.com/personalinjury

Jeffrey P. Rogan
Toni M. Guida
David L. Orenstein

Representative Clients: Recore One Mortgage Corp.; LEASCO; Pappas Enterprises Inc.; Steelcase, Inc.; Printing Center of Westchester Inc.; Corporate Imaging, Inc.; King Jolo's Flowers, Inc.; Systems Exchange, Inc.; Domus Realty.
Reference: Fleet Bank.

For full biographical listings, see the Martindale-Hubbell Law Directory

SMITH, RANSCHT, CONNORS, MUTINO, NORDELL & SIRIGNANO, P.C. (AV)
235 Main Street, 10601
Telephone: 914-946-8800
Telecopier: 914-946-8861
Cable Address: "Smiran" White Plains, New York

James P. Connors, Jr.
Peter J. Mutino
Michael Nordell
George A. Sirignano, Jr.

Counsel for: Universal Builders Supply, Inc.; The Walter Karl Cos.; Hartsdale Canine Cemetery; Wise Components, Inc.; Facsimile Communications Industries, Inc.; Carlcraft Knit Sales, Inc.
Closing Attorney for: First Union Mortgage Corp.
Representative Client: United Airlines, Corporate Express, Inc.

For full biographical listings, see the Martindale-Hubbell Law Directory

NORTH CAROLINA

*CHARLOTTE,** Mecklenburg Co.

DOZIER, MILLER, POLLARD & MURPHY (AV)
Cameron Brown Building, 301 South McDowell Street, Suite 700, 28204
Telephone: 704-372-6373
Fax: 704-347-0674
URL: http://www.dmpm.com

MEMBERS OF FIRM

W. Joseph Dozier, Jr.
R. Craig Miller, Jr.
Scott T. Pollard
Gary L. Murphy
William Patrick Hobson
Timothy H. Graham
George N. Miller
Richard S. Gordon
Thomas J. Falish
Kristin L. Smith

For full biographical listings, see the Martindale-Hubbell Law Directory

*DURHAM,** Durham Co.

MCPHERSON & ROCAMORA, PLLC (AV)
Suite 806 University Tower 3100 Tower Boulevard, 27707
Telephone: 919-493-0584
Facsimile: 919-493-0856
Email: mcestlaw@intrex.net

(See Next Column)

McPherson & Rocamora PLLC—*Continued*

William V. McPherson, Jr. Larry H. Rocamora

For full biographical listings, see the Martindale-Hubbell Law Directory

*GREENSBORO,** Guilford Co.

Alexander Ralston, Speckhard & Speckhard, L.L.P. (AV)

218 West Friendly Avenue, 27401
Telephone: 336-379-9302
Fax: 336-370-1232
URL: http://www.lawyers.com/aralston,speckhard

Donald K. Speckhard Stanley E. Speckhard

Representative Clients: Preferred Furniture Components, Inc.; Spring Financial Services, Inc.; Blazer Financial Services; Omega Sports, Inc.; Power & Heat Systems, Inc.; Branch & Company, P.A.; Acme Florist Supply, Inc.

For full biographical listings, see the Martindale-Hubbell Law Directory

Schell Bray Aycock Abel & Livingston P.L.L.C. (AV)

1500 Renaissance Plaza, 230 North Elm Street, P.O. Box 21847, 27420
Telephone: 336-370-8800
Fax: 336-370-8830
Email: Info@sbaal.com *URL:* http://www.sbaal.com

MEMBERS OF FIRM

Braxton Schell
Doris R. Bray
William P. Aycock, II
Michael R. Abel
Paul H. Livingston, Jr.
Thomas C. Watkins
Dan T. Barker, Jr.
Barbara R. Christy
John A. McLendon, Jr.

ASSOCIATES

Kathleen A. Kingsbury
Jacqueline E. Camp
A. Nicholas Purrington
Gregory M. Chabon
Jennifer Johnson
Eric M. Braun
Garland V. Gibbes

Representative Clients: The Breakers Palm Beach, Inc.; CBP Resources, Inc. (Carolina By-Products); Cone Mills Corp.; Cornwallis Development Co.; Kenan Transport Co.; Klaussner Furniture Industries, Inc.; North Carolina Trust Co.; Texfi Industries, Inc.; University of North Carolina at Chapel Hill Foundation, Inc.; Vanguard Cellular Systems, Inc.

For full biographical listings, see the Martindale-Hubbell Law Directory

*MORGANTON,** Burke Co.

Byrd, Byrd, Ervin, Whisnant, McMahon & Ervin, P.A. (AV)

One Northsquare, Post Office Drawer 1269, 28680
Telephone: 828-437-4220
Fax: 828-438-4517
Email: info@byrdlaw.com

Joe K. Byrd (Retired)
Robert B. Byrd
John W. Ervin, Jr.
C. Scott Whisnant
Lawrence D. McMahon, Jr.
Robert C. Ervin
Peggy McDaniel Saunders

Michelle C. Pritchard

For full biographical listings, see the Martindale-Hubbell Law Directory

*SYLVA,** Jackson Co.

Coward, Hicks & Siler, P.A. (AV)

705 West Main Street, 28779
Telephone: 828-586-2147
Fax: 828-586-2605
Franklin, North Carolina Office: 43 West Main Street, 28734.
Telephone: 828-524-6475.
Fax: 828-524-9833.
Cashiers, North Carolina Office: P.O. Box 1918, 28717.
Telephone: 828-743-2401.
Fax: 828-743-2403.

James Kent Coward (1929-1989)
Orville D. Coward
Ralph L. Hicks (Resident, Cashiers Office)
Robert F. Siler (Resident, Franklin Office)
Orville D. Coward, Jr. (Resident, Franklin Office)
J. K. Coward, Jr.
William H. Coward (Resident, Franklin Office)
Kimberly R. Coward (Resident, Cashiers Office)
Monty C. Beck (Resident, Franklin Office)
Richard K. Walker (Resident at Franklin Office)

Representative Clients: First Union National Bank; Wachovia Bank and Trust Co.; Haywood Savings and Loan Association; NationsBank of North Carolina; Cotton States Mutual Insurance Co.

For full biographical listings, see the Martindale-Hubbell Law Directory

*WILMINGTON,** New Hanover Co.

Matthew T. Dill (AV)

1430 Commonwealth Drive, Suite 206, 28403
Telephone: 910-256-9700
Telecopier: 910-256-2529
Mailing Address: P.O. Box 1226, Wrightsville Beach, North Carolina, 28480
Email: MTD@ISAAC.NET

References: Centura Bank; First Citizens Bank; First Union National Bank of North Carolina; Nations Bank of North Carolina, N.A.; Wachovia Bank of North Carolina, N.A.

For full biographical listings, see the Martindale-Hubbell Law Directory

Stevens, McGhee, Morgan, Lennon, O'Quinn & Toll (AV)

409 Wachovia Bank Building, 101 North Front Street, P.O. Drawer 59, 28402
Telephone: 910-763-3666
Fax: 910-251-9562
Email: smmlo@Wilmington.net

MEMBERS OF FIRM

John A. Stevens (1895-1990)
Karl W. McGhee (1923-1981)
Richard M. Morgan
Alton Y. Lennon
Robert A. O'Quinn
Alan E. Toll
J. Layne McNeill

ASSOCIATE

Maria D. McIntyre

Representative Clients: Hanover Iron Works, Inc.; Queensboro Steel Corp.; Star-News Newspapers Co.; The Pillsbury Co.; Wachovia Bank & Trust Co.; Wertheimer Bag Co.

For full biographical listings, see the Martindale-Hubbell Law Directory

*WINSTON-SALEM,** Forsyth Co.

Craige, Brawley, Liipfert & Walker, L.L.P. (AV)

500 West Fourth Street, Suite 200, P.O. Box 1666, 27102-1666
Telephone: 336-725-0583
Fax: 336-725-4677

MEMBERS OF FIRM

Cowles Liipfert
William W. Walker
B. Bailey Liipfert, III

ASSOCIATES

John A. Keiger
J. Laross Ketner
Robert A. Lefkowitz
Brent Wayne Stephens
Robert Martin Addison

Approved Attorneys for: Lawyers Title Insurance Corp.; Chicago Title Insurance Co.; Commonwealth Land Title Insurance Co.; First American Title Insurance Co.; Jefferson-Pilot Title Insurance Co.

For full biographical listings, see the Martindale-Hubbell Law Directory

Womble Carlyle Sandridge & Rice (AV)

A Professional Limited Liability Company
200 West Second Street, P.O. Drawer 84, 27102
Telephone: 336-721-3600
Fax: 336-721-3660
Email: lawyers@wcsr.com *URL:* http://www.wcsr.com
Charlotte, North Carolina Office: 3300 One First Union Center, 301 South College Street.
Telephone: 704-331-4900.
Fax: 704-331-4955.
Raleigh, North Carolina Office: 2100 First Union Capitol Center, 150 Fayetteville Street Mall, P.O. Box 831.
Telephone: 919-755-2100.
Fax: 919-755-2150.
Research Triangle Park, North Carolina Office: 2505 Meridian Parkway, Suite 300 (Durham), 27713.
Telephone: 919-484-2300.
Fax: 919-484-2340.
Atlanta, Georgia Office: One Atlantic Center, 1201 West Peachtree Street, Suite 3500.
Telephone: 404-872-7000.
Fax: 404-888-7490.
Other Atlanta, Georgia Office: Suite 404, 2296 Henderson Mill Road, N.E.
Telephone: 770-492-9030.
Fax: 770-492-9609.
Washington, D.C. Office: 1120 Nineteenth Street, N.W., Eighth Floor.
Telephone: 202-857-4400.
Fax: 202-467-6910.
Greenville, South Carolina Office: 15 South Main Street, Suite 601, P.O. Box 10208.
Telephone: 864-255-5400.
Fax: 864-255-5440.

(See Next Column)

WOMBLE CARLYLE SANDRIDGE & RICE, *Winston-Salem—Continued*

RESIDENT MEMBERS

Jean Taylor Adams
Elizabeth L. Quick
George A. Ragland

RESIDENT ASSOCIATES

C. Lynn Gargis
Sydney J. Warren

Representative Clients: Brad Ragan, Inc.; Brenner Companies; Food Lion, Inc.; Hanes Companies, Inc.; North Carolina Baptist Hospitals, Inc.; R.J. Reynolds Tobacco Co.; Thomasville Furniture Industries, Inc.; Wachovia Corp.; Wake Forest University.

For Complete List of Firm Personnel, See General Section

For full biographical listings, see the Martindale-Hubbell Law Directory

NORTH DAKOTA

*BISMARCK,** Burleigh Co.

TSCHIDER & SMITH (AV)

A Partnership including Professional Corporations
Professional Building - Suite 200, 418 East Rosser Avenue, 58501
Telephone: 701-258-4000
Fax: 701-258-4001
Email: ssmith@tschider-smithlaw.com

MEMBERS OF FIRM

Morris A. Tschider (P.C.)
Sean O. Smith (P.C.)
David A. Tschider

Representative Clients: Agri Bank, FCB; Farm Credit Services of Mandan, FLCA; Farm Credit Services of Mandan, P.C.A.; Twin City Implement, Inc.; First Bank Bismarck; N.D. Independent Insurance Agents; Western Steel & Plumbing; Froelich Oil Co.; Bismarck Eagles; St. Alexius Medical Center.

For full biographical listings, see the Martindale-Hubbell Law Directory

*FARGO,** Cass Co.

CONMY, FESTE, HUBBARD, CORWIN & BRUST, LTD. (AV)

200 Norwest Center, 406 Main Avenue, 58126
Telephone: 701-293-9911
Fax: 701-293-3133
URL: http://www.conmylaw.com

Charles A. Feste
Paul M. Hubbard
Wickham Corwin
Kim E. Brust
Michael M. Thomas
Robert J. Schultz
Nancy J. Morris

OF COUNSEL

Lauris N. Molbert
E. T. Conmy, Jr.

For full biographical listings, see the Martindale-Hubbell Law Directory

NILLES, HANSEN & DAVIES, LTD. (AV)

1800 Radisson Tower, P.O. Box 2626, 58108
Telephone: 701-237-5544
Facsimile: 701-280-0762
Williston, North Dakota Office: Energy Resource Building, 504 East Broadway, Suite 101, P.O. Box 1525.
Telephone: 701-572-5544.
Fax: 701-572-5561.

Timothy Q. Davies
Russell F. Freeman
Gregory B. Selbo
Andrew L. B. Noah

Representative Clients: U.S. Bank National Association; Northern Capital Trust.

For Complete List of Firm Personnel, See General Section

For full biographical listings, see the Martindale-Hubbell Law Directory

OHNSTAD TWICHELL, P.C. (AV)

15 Broadway, Suite 206, 58102
Telephone: 701-280-5801
Fax: 701-280-5803
West Fargo, North Dakota Office: 901 13th Avenue East, P.O. Box 458.
Telephone 701-282-3249.
Fax: 701-282-0825.
Hillsboro, North Dakota Office: West Caledonia Avenue, P.O. Box 220.
Telephone 701-436-5700.
Fax: 701-436-4025.
Mayville, North Dakota Office: 12 Third Street S.E., P.O. Box 547.
Telephone: 701-786-3251.
Fax: 701-786-4243.

(See Next Column)

Duane R. Breitling
Robert E. Rosenvold
(Resident, West Fargo Office)

Representative Clients: First National Bank North Dakota; Bank of North Dakota; Quality Boneless Beef; City of West Fargo; Bond Counsel for Cities of Fargo, Jamestown, West Fargo and Valley City; Industrial Indemnity Co.; Integrity Insurance Co.; Westchester Fire Insurance Co.

For Complete List of Firm Personnel, See General Section

For full biographical listings, see the Martindale-Hubbell Law Directory

VOGEL, WEIR, BYE, HUNKE & MCCORMICK, LTD. (AV)

502 First Avenue North, P.O. Box 1389, 58107
Telephone: 701-237-6983
Facsimile: 701-237-0847
Email: vogellaw@vogellaw.com *URL:* http://www.vogellaw.com

C. Nicholas Vogel

For Complete List of Firm Personnel, See General Section

For full biographical listings, see the Martindale-Hubbell Law Directory

OHIO

*AKRON,** Summit Co.

GOLDMAN & ROSEN, LTD. (AV)

12th Floor, One Cascade Plaza, 44308-1196
Telephone: 330-376-8336
Telecopier: 330-376-2522
Email: Goldman@Raex.com

Samuel Goldman
Bernard I. Rosen
George P. Tsarnas
Michael B. Hendler
Marc P. Gertz
Gary M. Rosen
Irving B. Sugerman

Thomas K. Seeker
Stacey Tsarnas Hackenberg

OF COUNSEL

Frank E. Steel, Jr.
Joseph F. Gorman

References: First National Bank of Ohio; National City Bank, Akron.

For full biographical listings, see the Martindale-Hubbell Law Directory

OLDHAM & DOWLING (AV)

195 South Main Street Suite 300, 44308
Telephone: 330-762-7377
Telecopier: 330-762-7390
Email: wdowling@oldham-dowling.com *URL:* http://www.lawyers.com/oldham&dowling

William M. Oldham
William D. Dowling, Jr.
Hamilton DeSaussure, Jr.
Martin R. Hulthen
Joseph K. Oldham
Raymond C. Mueller
Blake R. Gerney

Representative Clients: State Farm Mutual Automobile Insurance Co.; State Farm Mutual Fire Insurance Co.; Ohio Casualty Group Insurance Companies; Step II Corp.; WCI Steel Inc.; American States Insurance Co.; Taco Bell Corp.; May Company Department Stores; National City Bank, Masco.
Reference: Key Bank.

For full biographical listings, see the Martindale-Hubbell Law Directory

STARK & KNOLL CO., L.P.A. (AV)

76 South Main Street, Suite 1512, 44308-1824
Telephone: 330-376-3300
Telecopier: 330-376-6237
URL: http://www.stark-knoll.com

Michael L. Stark
Thomas G. Knoll
James L. Rench
Richard W. Burke
John K. Krajewski
John P. Susany
Jeffrey T. Knoll

Benjamin B. de Forest
Michael P. Morley
Ronald K. Starkey
Ralph R. Waszak, Jr.
Catherine Kemp Erisey
Aaron G. Lepp
Robert W. Spencer, Jr.
Mary Jo Lockshin

LEGAL SUPPORT PERSONNEL

Melissa L. Shinaberry
Diane Petrella
Teresa A. Corall

References: Bank One Akron; Society Bank of Akron.

For full biographical listings, see the Martindale-Hubbell Law Directory

*ATHENS,** Athens Co.

William A. Lavelle (AV)
207 Columbus Road, Suite B, 45701-5693
Telephone: 740-593-3348
Fax: 740-594-3343
URL: http://www.johnplavelle.com

For full biographical listings, see the Martindale-Hubbell Law Directory

*CHILLICOTHE,** Ross Co.

Cutright & Cutright (AV)
76 West Second Street, 45601
Telephone: 740-772-5595
Fax: 740-773-9261
Email: atlaw@bright.net

MEMBERS OF FIRM

James M. Cutright
James K. Cutright

Representative Clients: Citizens National Bank; Chivaho Federal Credit Union; Rockhold, Brown & Co. Bank; Litter Industries; Scioto Valley Mental Health Center; Paint Valley A.D.A.M.H.S. Board.
Approved Attorneys for: Lawyers Title Insurance Co.; Ohio Bar Title Insurance Co.; Chicago Title Insurance Co., Inc.

For full biographical listings, see the Martindale-Hubbell Law Directory

*CINCINNATI,** Hamilton Co.

Barrett & Weber A Legal Professional Association (AV)
500 Fourth & Walnut Centre, 105 East Fourth Street, 45202
Telephone: 513-721-2120
Facsimile: 513-721-2139

H. Patrick Weber

For full biographical listings, see the Martindale-Hubbell Law Directory

Goodman & Goodman A Legal Professional Association (AV)
123 East Fourth Street, 45202
Telephone: 513-621-1505; 1-800-494-4529
Fax: 513-621-6900
URL: http://www.goodlaw.com

Stanley Goodman
Ronald J. Goodman

For full biographical listings, see the Martindale-Hubbell Law Directory

Katz, Teller, Brant & Hild A Legal Professional Association (AV)
2400 Chemed Center, 255 East Fifth Street, 45202-4724
Telephone: 513-721-4532
Telecopier: 513-721-7120
Email: corp@ktbh.com

Reuven J. Katz
Robert E. Brant
Stephen C. Kisling
William F. Russo
Suzanne Prieur Land

Sheila K. Christie
Joel S. Brant

OF COUNSEL

Joseph A. Brant

For Complete List of Firm Personnel, See General Section
For full biographical listings, see the Martindale-Hubbell Law Directory

Porter & Porter (AV)
2100 Fourth & Vine Tower, One West Fourth Street, 45202
Telephone: 513-621-3993
Fax: 513-621-1746

MEMBERS OF FIRM

Robert C. Porter, Jr.
Robert C. Porter, III

For full biographical listings, see the Martindale-Hubbell Law Directory

*CLEVELAND,** Cuyahoga Co.

Baker & Hostetler LLP (AV)
3200 National City Center, 1900 East Ninth Street, 44114-3485
Telephone: 216-621-0200
Telecopier: 216-696-0740
TWX: 810 421 8375
RCA Telex: 215032
To contact an attorney on the Internet use first initial and surname followed by @baker-hostetler.com
URL: http://www.bakerlaw.com
In Cincinnati, Ohio: 312 Walnut Street, Suite 2650.
Telephone: 513-929-3400.

(See Next Column)

In Columbus, Ohio: Capitol Square, Suite 2100, 65 East State Street.
Telephone: 614-228-1541.
In Denver, Colorado: 303 East 17th Avenue, Suite 1100.
Telephone: 303-861-0600.
In Houston, Texas: 1000 Louisiana, Suite 2000.
Telephone: 713-751-1600.
In Beverly Hills, California: 9150 Wilshire Boulevard, Suite 205.
Telephone: 310-385-7500.
In Long Beach, California: 300 Oceangate, Suite 620.
Telephone: 562-432-2827.
In Los Angeles, California: 600 Wilshire Boulevard.
Telephone: 213-624-2400.
In Orlando, Florida: SunBank Center, Suite 2300, 200 South Orange Avenue.
Telephone: 407-649-4000.
In Washington, D.C.: Washington Square, Suite 1100, 1050 Connecticut Avenue, N.W.
Telephone: 202-861-1500.

PARTNERS

Oakley V. Andrews
Robert M. Brucken
Jane T. Haylor
Calvin B. Kirchick
Robert K. Lease
Kevin G. Robertson

ASSOCIATE

Stacey S. Staub

For Complete List of Firm Personnel, See General Section
For full biographical listings, see the Martindale-Hubbell Law Directory

Chattman, Gaines & Stern (AV)
1400 Renaissance Center, 1350 Euclid Avenue, 44115-1817
Telephone: 216-781-1700; 800-321-1700
Telecopier: 216-781-1972
Lorain, Ohio Office: 5300 Baumhart Road.
Telephone: 216-282-4598.
Fax: 216-960-1298.

Harold S. Stern
John J. Sutula
James M. Mackey
Ronald F. Wayne

John Patrick

For full biographical listings, see the Martindale-Hubbell Law Directory

Hennenberg & Associates (AV)
30100 Chagrin Boulevard, Suite 301, 44124-5704
Telephone: 216-765-9600
Fax: 216-765-8292
Email: Hennenberg@aol.com

Michael C. Hennenberg

ASSOCIATE

John A. Fatica

For full biographical listings, see the Martindale-Hubbell Law Directory

McDonald, Hopkins, Burke & Haber Co., L.P.A. (AV)
2100 Bank One Center, 600 Superior Avenue, E., 44114-2653
Telephone: 216-348-5400
Telecopier: 216-348-5474
Email: attorney@mhbh.com *URL:* http://www.mhbh.com

Patrick J. Berry
Jeffrey P. Consolo
Jerome W. Cook
Richard S. Cooper
Anthony J. DiVenere
Paul N. Edwards
Theodore J. Esborn
Steven L. Gardner
Carl J. Grassi
James A. Griffith
Jeffrey R. Huntsberger
Brian J. Jereb
Bernard L. Karr
Thomas W. Keen
Roger L. Kleinman
Joseph J. LoPresti, Jr.
Dan L. Makee
George L. McGaughey, Jr.
John T. Mulligan
Brian M. O'Neill
William J. O'Neill
Stephen T. Parisi
R. Jeffrey Pollock
Michael G. Riley
Shawn M. Riley
Albert N. Salvatore
Thomas C. Schrader
Roger L. Shumaker
Barbara J. Smith
James M. Stone
Dale R. Vlasek
Kenneth J. Walsh
John M. Wirtshafter
Jane Marie Pine Wood
Charles B. Zellmer

OF COUNSEL

John J. Monroe

Julie A. Callsen
Anne T. Corrigan
Steven A. Eisenberg
G. Andrew Gardner
Anuj Goswami
Donald E. Kacmar
David M. Kall
Jeffrey B. Keiper
Kevin J. Kessinger
Mark D. Klimek
Alan M. Koschik
Deviani M. Kuhar
Paul W. Linehan
Tyler L. Mathews

(See Next Column)

McDONALD, HOPKINS, BURKE & HABER CO. L.P.A., *Cleveland—Continued*

Jennifer A. Mills
Antoinette K. Palmer
Ketan K. Patel
Sharon Szolosi Regas
Douglas B. Schnee
Michele Smolin
Glenn D. Southworth
Michael R. Spreng

For full biographical listings, see the Martindale-Hubbell Law Directory

SEELEY, SAVIDGE AND EBERT A LEGAL PROFESSIONAL ASSOCIATION (AV)

800 Bank One Center, 600 Superior Avenue, East, 44114-2655
Telephone: 216-566-8200
Fax-Telecopier: 216-566-0213
URL: http://www.sse-law.com

Gary A. Ebert
William M. Fumich, Jr.

Andrew D. Bemer
Kathleen S. Grady
Michael E. Stinn

Reference: KeyBank.

For Complete List of Firm Personnel, See General Section

For full biographical listings, see the Martindale-Hubbell Law Directory

SPIETH, BELL, McCURDY & NEWELL CO., L.P.A. (AV)

2000 Huntington Building, 925 Euclid Avenue, 44115-1496
Telephone: 216-696-4700
Fax: 216-696-2706
Email: law@spiethbell.com

J. Donald Cairns
Patrick J. Amer
Rebecca Holloway Dent
James R. Bright
John M. Slivka
M. Elizabeth Monihan

For Complete List of Firm Personnel, See General Section

For full biographical listings, see the Martindale-Hubbell Law Directory

WALTER & HAVERFIELD, P.L.L. (AV)

1300 Terminal Tower, 44113-2253
Telephone: 216-781-1212
Telecopier: 216-575-0911
Email: law@walterhav.com *URL:* http://www.walterhav.com
Columbus, Ohio Office: 88 East Broad Street.
Telephone: 614-898-1096.

MEMBERS OF FIRM

Anthony J. Viola
Robert S. Horbaly
Herbert L. Braverman
David W. Welty
David P.N. Silk

ASSOCIATE

Teresa M. Beasley

OF COUNSEL

Arthur P. Steinmetz
J. Robert Malloy

For Complete List of Firm Personnel, See General Section

For full biographical listings, see the Martindale-Hubbell Law Directory

WEGMAN, HESSLER, VANDERBURG & O'TOOLE A LEGAL PROFESSIONAL ASSOCIATION (AV)

6055 Rockside Woods Boulevard, Suite 200, 44131
Telephone: 216-642-3342
Telecopier: 216-642-8826

Martin J. Wegman (1918-1977)
David J. Hessler
Keith A. Vanderburg
Peter A. Hessler
John K. O'Toole
David R. Knowles
John D. Kedzior
Steven E. Pryatel

Richard T. Coyne
Christopher A. Holecek
Jeffrey W. Krueger
David W. Herrington
Antoinette F. Gideon
David R. Button
Nathan E. Hessler
Lawrence S. Crowther
Derek Kaesgen
David M. Leneghan
Erin M. O'Toole
Elizabeth M. Woda
Dennis J. Siciliano
Tanja M. Holecek
Jeffrey A. Gorski
Diana Delmar Jancura
Anthony N. Palombo
Carl D. Gum, III
Patricia J. Haas

Reference: Key Bank of Cleveland.

For full biographical listings, see the Martindale-Hubbell Law Directory

*COLUMBUS,** Franklin Co.

CHESTER, WILLCOX AND SAXBE LLP (AV)

17 South High Street, Suite 900, 43215-3413
Telephone: 614-221-4000
Fax: 614-221-4012
Email: cwslaw.com

PARTNERS

Andrew J. Art
James J. Chester
John J. Chester
John J. Chester, Jr.
J. Richard Emens
J. Anthony Kington
Roderick H. Willcox
Beatrice E. Wolper

ASSOCIATE

Thomas H. Mallory, Jr.

Representative Clients: American Municipal Power-Ohio, Inc.; The Limited; Scioto Downs, Inc.; Tee Jaye's Country Place Restaurants.

For full biographical listings, see the Martindale-Hubbell Law Directory

KEGLER, BROWN, HILL & RITTER (AV)

Capitol Square Suite 1800, 65 East State Street, 43215-4294
Telephone: 614-462-5400
Telecopier: 614-464-2634
Cable Address: "Law KBHR"
Telex: 246671
Email: info@kbhr.com *URL:* http://www.kbhr.com
Marion, Ohio Office: 250 Executive Drive, Suite B, P.O. Box 919.
Telephone: 614-387-3501.
Facsimile: 614-387-3630.

Edward C. Hertenstein
Charles J. Kegler
Paul D. Ritter, Jr.
R. Douglas Wrightsel

Greg R. Grabovac
Todd M. Kegler

For Complete List of Firm Personnel, See General Section

For full biographical listings, see the Martindale-Hubbell Law Directory

KETCHAM & KETCHAM (AV)

Suite 1416, 50 West Broad Street, 43215
Telephone: 614-224-2176

MEMBERS OF FIRM

Victor A. Ketcham
Richard S. Ketcham

Reference: Key Bank.

For full biographical listings, see the Martindale-Hubbell Law Directory

HARVEY S. MINTON & ASSOCIATES (AV)

6641 North High Street, 43085-4038
Telephone: 614-848-9600
Telecopier: 614-848-9818
URL: http://www.lawyers.com/mintonlaw

OF COUNSEL

Richard E. Gombert
Rainer E. Steinhoff

For full biographical listings, see the Martindale-Hubbell Law Directory

SCHOTTENSTEIN, ZOX & DUNN A LEGAL PROFESSIONAL ASSOCIATION (AV)

The Huntington Center, 41 South High Street, 43215
Telephone: 614-462-2700
Telecopier: 614-462-5135
Telex: 650 24 444 365
URL: http://www.szd.com
Cincinnati, Ohio Office: Bank One Towers, 8044 Montgomery Road, Suite 700, 45236-2926.
Telephone: 513-792-2730.
Cleveland, Ohio Office: One Cleveland Center, 1375 East 9th Street, Suite 950.
Telephone: 216-621-6501.
Fax: 216-621-6502.

Harvey Dunn
John Terakedis, Jr.
Fredrick L. Fisher
Richard W. Holz
Martin S. Rosenthal
Michael R. Becker
Terrence A. Grady
Thomas J. Sigmund
Phillip G. Lilly
Missia H. Vaselaney (Resident, Cleveland Office)

William P. Zox
J. Troy Terakedis

Reference: Bank One of Columbus, N.A.

For Complete List of Firm Personnel, See General Section

For full biographical listings, see the Martindale-Hubbell Law Directory

*DAYTON,** Montgomery Co.

SEBALY, SHILLITO & DYER A LEGAL PROFESSIONAL ASSOCIATION (AV)

1300 Courthouse Plaza, NE, P.O. Box 220, 45402-0220
Telephone: 937-222-2500
Telefax: 937-222-6554; 222-8279
URL: http://www.ssdlaw.com

Martin A. Beyer
Daniel A. Brown
James A. Dyer
Gale S. Finley
John R. Glankler
Deborah D. Hunt
Michael P. Moloney
Jon M. Sebaly
Beverly F. Shillito
Jeffrey B. Shulman
Karl R. Ulrich
Lawrence S. Walter
Nita S. Yates

OF COUNSEL

William W. Lambert

Michael A. Booth
Robert E. Goff, Jr.
Leslie Blair Graden
Joseph V. Hatala
J. David Ruffner, II
Kendra F. Thompson

For full biographical listings, see the Martindale-Hubbell Law Directory

TYE AND TYE (AV)

A Legal Professional Association
5975 Kentshire Drive, 45440
Telephone: 937-291-8646
Telecopier: 937-291-8650
Email: tyelaw@erinet.com

MEMBERS OF FIRM

Rose R. Tye
Timothy N. Tye

References: National City Bank; Bank One, Dayton N.A.

For full biographical listings, see the Martindale-Hubbell Law Directory

DOVER, Tuscarawas Co.

MARIO D. CORSI (AV)

117 East Third Street, 44622
Telephone: 330-364-4414
Fax: 330-364-4472

References: The Huntington National Bank; Bank One of Dover.

For full biographical listings, see the Martindale-Hubbell Law Directory

DUBLIN, Franklin Co.

BLAUGRUND, HERBERT & MARTIN, INCORPORATED (AV)

5455 Rings Road, Suite 500, 43017-7517
Telephone: 614-764-0681
Fax: 614-764-0774
Email: bhm@bhmlaw.net

John S. Jones
Steven A. Martin
Sharon L. R. Miller

For full biographical listings, see the Martindale-Hubbell Law Directory

*EATON,** Preble Co.

BENNETT & BENNETT (AV)

Bennett Law Building, 200 West Main Street, 45320
Telephone: 937-456-5100; 456-4100
Fax: 937-456-4300; 456-7278

MEMBERS OF FIRM

Lloyd B. Bennett (1909-1983)
Herd L. Bennett
Gray W. Bennett

Representative Clients: The National Hummel Foundation and Museum; Star Bank NA, Eaton, Ohio; Eaton National Bank & Trust Co.; First National Bank of Southwestern Ohio; Brookville National Bank; Farm Credit Services of Mid-America, ACA; Miller's Super Markets, Inc.; Northedge Shopping Center, Inc.; Herman M. Brubaker Registered Holstein Cattle; The Eaton Foundation.

For Complete List of Firm Personnel, See General Section

For full biographical listings, see the Martindale-Hubbell Law Directory

PERRYSBURG, Wood Co.

LEATHERMAN, WITZLER, DOMBEY & HART (AV)

353 Elm Street, 43551
Telephone: 419-874-3536
Fax: 419-874-3899
Email: OURNET@GLASSCITY.NET *URL:* http://www.lawyers.com/lwdhlaw

(See Next Column)

MEMBERS OF FIRM

Wayne M. Leatherman
Philip L. Dombey
James H. Hart
T. Hamilton Noll
Kay L. Howard

Representative Clients: Craig Transportation Co.; Ed Schmidt Pontiac, Inc.; Perrysburg Township Trustees; Carlson Travel Co.; Village of Holland; Village of Haskins; Waterville Township Trustees; 577 Foundation.

For full biographical listings, see the Martindale-Hubbell Law Directory

*PORTSMOUTH,** Scioto Co.

JOHNSON & OLIVER, A LEGAL PROFESSIONAL ASSOCIATION (AV)

701 Sixth Street, P.O. Box 1505, 45662
Telephone: 740-354-4200
Telecopier: 740-353-2413

C. Clayton Johnson

Stephen L. Oliver

OF COUNSEL

Robert Kurt McCurdy

Representative Clients: OSCO Industries, Inc.; Citizens Deposit Bank and Trust; First National Bank of Lewis County, Kentucky; Home Federal Savings and Loan; McDonalds Corp.; National Maintenance & Repair, Inc.; McGinnis, Inc.
Approved Attorney for: Lawyers Title Insurance Co.

For full biographical listings, see the Martindale-Hubbell Law Directory

SWANTON, Fulton Co.

THE McQUADES CO., L.P.A. (AV)

Lincoln at Broadway, P.O. Box 237, 43558
Telephone: 419-826-0055
Fax: 419-825-3871
Email: mcquadelaw@cs.com *URL:* http://www.lawyers.com/mcquadelaw
Archbold, Ohio Office: 200 N. Defiance Street.
Telephone: 419-445-3755.
Whitehouse, Ohio Office: 6632 Providence Street.
Telephone: 419-877-0746.

Richard B. McQuade, Sr. (1912-1996)
Daniel P. McQuade
Colin J. McQuade

Alan J. Lehenbauer

For full biographical listings, see the Martindale-Hubbell Law Directory

*TOLEDO,** Lucas Co.

DOYLE, LEWIS & WARNER (AV)

202 North Erie Street, P.O. Box 2168, 43603
Telephone: 419-248-1500
Fax: 419-248-2002
Email: dlw1@primenet.com

MEMBERS OF FIRM

Steven Timonere
Richard F. Ellenberger
Michael E. Hyrne
Michael A. Bruno
David W. Doerner

ASSOCIATES

Kevin A. Pituch
Maureen O. Atkins

Counsel for: Consolidated Rail Corp.; The Lakefront Dock & Railroad Terminal Co.; Prudential Insurance Co. of America; Equitable Life Assurance Society of the U.S.; Metropolitan Life Insurance Co.; Greyhound Lines; Fireman's Fund Insurance Cos.

For Complete List of Firm Personnel, See General Section

For full biographical listings, see the Martindale-Hubbell Law Directory

EASTMAN & SMITH LTD. (AV)

One Seagate, Twenty-Fourth Floor, P.O. Box 10032, 43699-0032
Telephone: 419-241-6000
Telecopier: 419-247-1777
Columbus, Ohio Office: 65 East State Street, Suite 1000, 43215.
Telephone: 614-460-3556.
Telecopier: 614-228-5371.

MEMBERS OF FIRM

Frank D. Jacobs
Morton Bobowick
John H. Boggs
David C. Krock

ASSOCIATES

David A. Dennis
Nirakar C. Thakur

OF COUNSEL

Gerald P. Moran

For Complete List of Firm Personnel, See General Section

For full biographical listings, see the Martindale-Hubbell Law Directory

Toledo—Continued

MORAN & MORAN (AV)

626 Madison Avenue, Suite 300, 43604
Telephone: 419-241-8171
Fax: Available Upon Request

Peter L. Moran
Mary Beth Moran

Representative Clients: The Exchange Bank; Payak Insurance Agency; Monroe Pharmacy, Inc.
References: Society Bank; The Fifth Third Bank, Toledo, Ohio.

For Complete List of Firm Personnel, See General Section

For full biographical listings, see the Martindale-Hubbell Law Directory

SCHNORF & SCHNORF CO., L.P.A. A PROFESSIONAL CORPORATION (AV)

1400 National City Bank Building, 405 Madison Avenue, 43604
Telephone: 419-248-2646
Facsimile: 419-248-2889

Brandon G. Schnorf, Sr. (1904-1977)
David M. Schnorf
Christopher F. Parker
Johna M. Bella
Barry F. Hudgin

Local Counsel for: Universal Underwriters Group; Charter One Bank; Medical Mutual of Ohio; Bankers Multiple Line Insurance Company; National City Bank, Northwest; Charter One Bank.
Representative Clients: American Federation of Teachers, AFL-CIO; Ohio Federation of Teachers, AFL-CIO; Toledo Federation of Teachers, AFL-CIO; Hart Associates, Inc.

For full biographical listings, see the Martindale-Hubbell Law Directory

*WAPAKONETA,** Auglaize Co.

EDWARD STROEBEL (AV)

108 West Auglaize Street, P.O. Box 88, 45895
Telephone: 419-738-4417; 738-3222
Fax: 419-738-9758

*WOOSTER,** Wayne Co.

KENNEDY, CICCONETTI & KNOWLTON, L.P.A. (AV)

558 North Market Street, 44691-3406
Telephone: 330-262-7555
Telecopier: 330-264-5739

Charles A. Kennedy
Frank Cicconetti
David C. Knowlton
Michael G. Buytendyk

Reference: Wayne County National Bank.

For full biographical listings, see the Martindale-Hubbell Law Directory

OKLAHOMA

BLACKWELL, Kay Co.

JAMES R. RODGERS (AV)

105 North Main, P.O. Box 514, 74631
Telephone: 580-363-3684
Fax: 580-363-2434
URL: http://www.lawyers.com/rodgerslaw

William W. Rodgers (1907-1979)

For full biographical listings, see the Martindale-Hubbell Law Directory

*DUNCAN,** Stephens Co.

LEACH, SULLIVAN, SULLIVAN & WATKINS (AV)

921 Main Street, P.O. Box 160, 73534
Telephone: 580-255-8260
Telecopier: 580-255-5587
URL: http://www.leachsullivan.com

MEMBERS OF FIRM

William O. Leach (1919-1990)
Paul D. Sullivan
Patrick D. Sullivan
Michael P. Sullivan
Kent P. Sullivan
Jay B. Watkins
Scott P. Sullivan

Representative Clients: Citizens' Bank, Velma, Oklahoma; Leffler Construction Co.; Jackson Ranches, Inc.; Jackson Cattle Corp.; Legacy Bank; BancFirst of Marlow; L.A. Edwards Trust; John E. Jackson Trust; Interstate Petroleum Corp.; PaceCo Financial Services, Inc.

For full biographical listings, see the Martindale-Hubbell Law Directory

LAVERNE, Harper Co.

G. W. ARMOR (AV)

103 West Jayroe Street, P.O. Box 267, 73848
Telephone: 580-921-3335
Fax: 580-921-5720

*OKLAHOMA CITY,** Oklahoma Co.

ANDREWS DAVIS LEGG BIXLER MILSTEN & PRICE, A PROFESSIONAL CORPORATION (AV)

500 West Main, Suite 500, 73102
Telephone: 405-272-9241
FAX: 405-235-8786
Email: andrewsdavis@andrewsdavis.com *URL:* http://www.andrewsdavis.com

James F. Davis
Sally A. Hasenfratz
Richard B. Kells, Jr.
Mark H. Price

OF COUNSEL

Lynn O. Holloman

For Complete List of Firm Personnel, See General Section

For full biographical listings, see the Martindale-Hubbell Law Directory

F. SMITH BARNES, P.C. (AV)

1012 Northwest Grand Boulevard, 73118
Telephone: 405-848-1776
Fax: 405-840-1164

F. Smith Barnes

For full biographical listings, see the Martindale-Hubbell Law Directory

HARTZOG CONGER & CASON, A PROFESSIONAL CORPORATION (AV)

1600 Bank of Oklahoma Plaza 201 Robert S. Kerr, 73102
Telephone: 405-235-7000
Facsimile: 405-235-7329

Larry D. Hartzog
J. William Conger
Len Cason
James C. Prince
Steven C. Davis
Joseph P. Hogsett
John D. Robertson
Kurt M. Rupert
Laura Haag McConnell
Linda G. Scoggins
Susan B. Shields
Ryan S. Wilson
Amy J. Sine
Jon H. Trudgeon
Charles E. Geister, III
Phillip G. Whaley
Armand Paliotta

J. Christian Guzzy
Stacey D. Spivey
Melissa Beeson Heindselman
Christin V. Adkins
Byron K. Linkous

OF COUNSEL

Kent F. Frates
Kenneth R. Davis
Alan Newman

For full biographical listings, see the Martindale-Hubbell Law Directory

NASH, COHENOUR, KELLEY & HUNT, P.C. (AV)

Suite 101, 1001 Northwest 63rd Street, 73116
Telephone: 405-848-7170
Fax: 405-848-1442
Email: NCKHlaw@aol.com *URL:* http://www.law-n-okla.com

Rollin Nash, Jr.
Cynthia Cohenour

For full biographical listings, see the Martindale-Hubbell Law Directory

*STILLWATER,** Payne Co.

ELLIS & MORGAN (AV)

711 South Husband Street, P.O. Box 1507, 74076
Telephone: 405-743-3770
Fax: 405-743-3773

MEMBERS OF FIRM

Hal Wm. Ellis
Michael S. Morgan
Tracy Emmet Morgan
G. Michael Solomon

For full biographical listings, see the Martindale-Hubbell Law Directory

*TULSA,** Tulsa Co.

EAGLETON, EAGLETON AND HARRISON, INC. (AV)

Suite 1700, 320 South Boston Avenue, 74103-4706
Telephone: 918-584-0462
Fax: 918-584-3724
Email: eagleton@worldnet.att.net

(See Next Column)

EAGLETON, EAGLETON AND HARRISON INC.—*Continued*

E. John Eagleton
James R. Eagleton
Charles D. Harrison

OF COUNSEL

Norma Eagleton

For full biographical listings, see the Martindale-Hubbell Law Directory

JAMES, POTTS AND WULFERS, INC. (AV)

2828 Mid-Continent Tower, 401 South Boston Avenue, 74103-4016
Telephone: 918-584-0881
Fax: 918-584-4521

David F. James
Thomas G. Potts
David W. Wulfers

For full biographical listings, see the Martindale-Hubbell Law Directory

WILLIAM LEITER (AV)

320 South Boston, Suite 1107, 74103-4700
Telephone: 918-582-8535
Fax: 918-582-8537

For full biographical listings, see the Martindale-Hubbell Law Directory

SNEED LANG, P.C. (AV)

2300 Williams Center Tower II, Two West Second Street, 74103
Telephone: 918-583-3145
Telecopier: 918-582-0410

James C. Lang
D. Faith Orlowski
Brian S. Gaskill
G. Steven Stidham
Stephen R. McNamara
Thomas E. Black, Jr.
Robbie Emery Burke
Patrick O. Waddel
Randolph P. Stainer
Steven K. Balman
Brian T. Inbody
D. Michael McBride III

OF COUNSEL

James L. Sneed

Representative Clients: Amoco Production Co.; Bank One, Texas; Enron Corp.; Halliburton Energy Services; Helmerich & Payne, Inc.; Shell Oil Co.; State Farm Mutual Automobile Insurance Co.; The Williams Companies.

For full biographical listings, see the Martindale-Hubbell Law Directory

OREGON

*PORTLAND,** Multnomah Co.

ROBERT G. BURT, P.C. (AV)

The 1515 Building, Suite 600, 1515 S.W. Fifth Avenue, 97201-5449
Telephone: 503-223-3600
Fax: 503-274-0778

Robert G. Burt

For full biographical listings, see the Martindale-Hubbell Law Directory

HAGEN, DYE, HIRSCHY & DILORENZO, P.C. (AV)

888 Southwest 5th Avenue Suite 1000, 97204
Telephone: 503-222-1812
Fax: 503-274-7979

Joseph T. Hagen
Jeffrey L. Dye
John A. Hirschy
John A. DiLorenzo, Jr.
Dana R. Taylor
Mark A. Golding
Kenneth A. Williams
John D. Parsons
David E. Grein

OF COUNSEL

Lewis B. Hampton

Adam S. Rittenberg
Michael E. Farnell
Aaron K. Stuckey
Joel L. Augee
Gretchen M. Ladd
Pamela R. Albee

LEGAL SUPPORT PERSONNEL

Kathryn J. Bell
Gail E. Kuechle
Linda M. Lufkin

For full biographical listings, see the Martindale-Hubbell Law Directory

HANNA, KERNS & STRADER, A PROFESSIONAL CORPORATION (AV)

300 Hoffman Columbia Plaza, 1300 S.W. Sixth Avenue, 97201
Telephone: 503-273-2700
FAX: 503-273-2712
Email: hkspdx@aol.com

(See Next Column)

Harry M. Hanna
Joseph J. Hanna, Jr.
Diane C. Kerns
Timothy R. Strader

For full biographical listings, see the Martindale-Hubbell Law Directory

KELL, ALTERMAN & RUNSTEIN, LLP (AV)

1001 S.W. Fifth Avenue, Suite 1800, 97204
Telephone: 503-222-3531
Telecopier: 503-227-2980
Email: kell@teleport.com

MEMBERS OF FIRM

Raymond M. Kell (1911-1991)
Clifford B. Alterman (1925-1995)
Ted E. Runstein
Lee Davis Kell
Wayne D. Palmer
Lloyd R. Summers
William D. Dickas
Gary P. Compa
Charles R. Williamson
Mary Ellen Page Farr
Eric Sogge
Thomas J. Matsuda
Thomas R. Rask, III
Nicholas S. Fish

Dana L. Barnes
Cory Larvik
Robert E. Kabacy
Robin M. Runstein

References: Union Bank of California, N.A. (Portland Branch); The Bank of Tokyo-Mitsubishi, Ltd. (Portland Branch); Bank of America (5th S. Main Branch).

For full biographical listings, see the Martindale-Hubbell Law Directory

STAHANCYK, GEARING & RACKNER, P.C. (AV)

200 Jackson Tower, 806 S.W. Broadway, 97205-3304
Telephone: 503-222-9115
Facsimile: 503-222-4037
URL: http://www.stahancyk.com
Bend, Oregon Office: 141 N.W. Greenwood Avenue, Suite 100.
Telephone: 541-318-9115.
Fax: 541-318-9116.
Astoria, Oregon Office: 52 Commercial Street, 97103.
Telephone: 503-325-9117.

Jody L. Stahancyk
David C. Gearing
Laura E. Rackner

Joel J. Kent (Resident, Bend Office)
Brett E. Engel
Elizabeth M. Cline
Pierre L. Robert

For full biographical listings, see the Martindale-Hubbell Law Directory

*SALEM,** Marion Co.

ASHCROFT WILES, LLP (AV)

Formerly Rhoten, Rhoten & Speerstra
201 Pioneer Trust Building, 117 Commercial Street N.E., 97301
Telephone: 503-364-6734
Fax: 503-364-6735
Email: ashcroftwiles@uswest.net

MEMBERS OF FIRM

Lynn E. Ashcroft
David B. Wiles

ASSOCIATE

Mark Allen Ronning

OF COUNSEL

Timothy G. Bickler
J. Ray Rhoten (Retired)
Geo. A. Rhoten (1906-1988)
Sam F. Speerstra (1913-1994)

A list of representative clients will be furnished upon request.

For full biographical listings, see the Martindale-Hubbell Law Directory

PENNSYLVANIA

ABINGTON, Montgomery Co.

SMITH & JAKUBOWSKI (AV)

1330 Easton Road, 19001
Telephone: 215-572-5444
Fax: 215-572-6897
Philadelphia, Pennsylvania Office: 926 Public Ledger Building.
Telephone: 215-572-5444.

Joseph Michael Smith
John R. Jakubowski

Reference: Willow Grove Bank.

For full biographical listings, see the Martindale-Hubbell Law Directory

*ALLENTOWN,** Lehigh Co.

LITTNER, DESCHLER & LITTNER

(See Bethlehem)

NOONAN & PROKUP (AV)

526 Walnut Street, 18101
Telephone: 610-433-5211
Fax: 610-433-5219

MEMBERS OF FIRM

Charles T. Noonan
Michael Prokup
Thomas K. Noonan
Linda S. Noonan
Susan M. Noonan

For full biographical listings, see the Martindale-Hubbell Law Directory

RICHARD W. SHAFFER (AV)

740 Hamilton Mall, 18101
Telephone: 610-439-0800
Fax: 610-439-8852
Email: Rwspalaw@aol.com

LEGAL SUPPORT PERSONNEL

Barbara J. Nemes (Paralegal)

For full biographical listings, see the Martindale-Hubbell Law Directory

TALLMAN, HUDDERS & SORRENTINO, P.C. (AV)

Suite 300 The Paragon Centre, 1611 Pond Road, 18104
Telephone: 610-391-1800
Fax: 610-391-1805
Email: info@ths.com *URL:* http://www.thslaw.com

Robert G. Tallman
Matthew R. Sorrentino
John R. Hudders (Retired)
Paul McHale, Jr.
Donald H. Lipson
Barbara L. Hollenbach
Thomas C. Sadler, Jr.
Timothy J. Siegfried
Donald A. Zamborsky
Dolores A. Laputka
Oldrich Foucek, III
Scott B. Allinson

Michael E. Loomis
Jeffrey A. Durney
John K. Baker
Beverly J. Doneker
Laura J. Herzog
George C. Hlavac
Scott R. Lipson
Douglas G. Cappellini
Theodore J. Zeller, III
Ronnie F. Hess
Amy Kohler Howard

OF COUNSEL

Paul J. Schoff

For full biographical listings, see the Martindale-Hubbell Law Directory

BALA CYNWYD, Montgomery Co.

SUSAN M. HARMON (AV)

The GSB Building, One Belmont Avenue, Suite 605, 19004-1609
Telephone: 610-668-5160
Fax: 610-667-3706
Email: sharmon992@aol.com *URL:* http://www.lawyers.com/harmon__estate__planning

For full biographical listings, see the Martindale-Hubbell Law Directory

BETHLEHEM, Northampton Co.

LITTNER, DESCHLER & LITTNER (AV)

512 North New Street, P.O. Box 1407, 18016
Telephone: 610-865-6770
Fax: 610-865-6433

MEMBERS OF FIRM

Robert H. Littner
Michael C. Deschler
Robert V. Littner

For full biographical listings, see the Martindale-Hubbell Law Directory

BLUE BELL, Montgomery Co.

SAMUEL T. SWANSEN, P.C. (AV)

640 Sentry Parkway, Suite 104, 19422-2361
Telephone: 610-834-9810
Fax: 610-834-9812
URL: http://www.samswansen.com
Email: sam@samswansen.com *URL:* http://www.lawyers.com/samswansen

Samuel T. Swansen

For full biographical listings, see the Martindale-Hubbell Law Directory

*CARLISLE,** Cumberland Co.

FISHMAN & MORGENTHAL (AV)

95 Alexander Spring Road, 17013
Telephone: 717-249-6333
Fax: 717-249-7334
Email: info@carlislelaw.com *URL:* http://www.carlislelaw.com

MEMBERS OF FIRM

Steven J. Fishman
Roger M. Morgenthal

For full biographical listings, see the Martindale-Hubbell Law Directory

*EASTON,** Northampton Co.

FOX, OLDT & BROWN (AV)

Suite 508, First Union Bank Building, Six South Third Street, Center Square, 18042
Telephone: 610-258-6111
Fax: 610-253-4532
URL: http://www.lawyers.com/foxoldt&brown

MEMBERS OF FIRM

Charles L. Oldt
Robert C. Brown, Jr.

Counsel for: First Union National Bank; Easton Cemetery; Travelers Insurance Co.

For full biographical listings, see the Martindale-Hubbell Law Directory

LITTNER, DESCHLER & LITTNER

(See Bethlehem)

*HARRISBURG,** Dauphin Co.

GOLDBERG, KATZMAN & SHIPMAN, P.C. (AV)

320 Market Street - Strawberry Square, P.O. Box 1268, 17108-1268
Telephone: 717-234-4161
Telecopier: 717-234-6808; 717-234-6810
Email: gks@gkslaw.com

Ronald M. Katzman
Neil Hendershot

Arnold B. Kogan
John DeLorenzo

References: Fulton Bank; Dauphin Deposit Bank & Trust; Mellon Bank.

For Complete List of Firm Personnel, See General Section

For full biographical listings, see the Martindale-Hubbell Law Directory

METZGER, WICKERSHAM, KNAUSS & ERB, P.C. (AV)

3211 North Front Street, P.O. Box 5300, 17110-0300
Telephone: 717-238-8187
Telefax: 717-234-9478
Other Harrisburg, Pennsylvania Office: 4813 Jonestown Road, P.O. Box 5300, 17110-0300.
Telephone: 717-652-7020.

Maurice R. Metzger (1918-1980)
James F. Carl
F. Brewster Wickersham (1918-1974)
Edward E. Knauss, IV
Jered L. Hock
Edward E. Knauss, III (Retired)
Karl R. Hildabrand
Christian S. Erb, Jr.
Richard B. Druby
Robert E. Yetter
Steven P. Miner

Clark DeVere
Carrie L. Carroll

Representative Clients: Allstate Insurance Co.; Chubb Group of Insurance Companies; Fireman's Fund American Insurance Group; Liberty Mutual Insurance Co.; Crum & Forster; CNA Insurance; Prudential Insurance Co.

For full biographical listings, see the Martindale-Hubbell Law Directory

JENKINTOWN, Montgomery Co.

RICHARD W. STEVENS (AV)

One Jenkintown Station, 115 West Avenue, Suite 108, 19046-2031
Telephone: 215-887-4600
Fax: 215-887-4604
URL: http://www.lawyers.com/richardstevens

OF COUNSEL

Daniel B. Michie, Jr.

For full biographical listings, see the Martindale-Hubbell Law Directory

*MEDIA,** Delaware Co.

BEATTY, CRAMP, KAUFFMAN & LINCKE (AV)

215 North Olive Street, P.O. Box 901, 19063
Telephone: 610-565-8800
Fax: 610-565-8127
Email: BCKLLaw@aol.com

(See Next Column)

BEATTY, CRAMP, KAUFFMAN & LINCKE—*Continued*

MEMBERS OF FIRM

Lewis B. Beatty, Jr.
Joseph W. Kauffman
David J. Otis
David G. Blake
William P. Lincke
Natalie M. Habert
Peter W. Dicce

ASSOCIATES

Regina M. MacKenzie
Bereth K. Graeff
Daniel J. McCusker
Kelly A. Barnes

OF COUNSEL

John F. Cramp
Ralph B. D'Iorio
Robert C. Grasberger

Joseph R. Young (1921-1993)

Representative Clients: Delaware County School Employees Health and Welfare Trust.

For full biographical listings, see the Martindale-Hubbell Law Directory

---

*NORRISTOWN,** Montgomery Co.

MURPHY, OLIVER, CAIOLA & GOWEN, A PROFESSIONAL LAW CORPORATION (AV)

43 East Marshall Street, 19401-4828
Telephone: 610-272-4222; 610-279-3838
Fax: 610-272-2549; 610-275-0140
Email: molaw@injury-law.com *URL:* http://www.injury-law.com
Spring City, Pennsylvania Office: 500 S. Main Street, 19475.
Telephone: 610-948-3770.
Pottstown, Pennsylvania Office: 5 Sunnybrook Road, 19464.
Telephone: 610-323-3480.
West Chester, Pennsylvania Office: 1534 McDaniel Drive, Westtown Business Center, 19250.
Telephone: 610-272-4222.

James J. Oliver
Frank P. Murphy
Frank L. Caiola
Thomas L. Gowen, Jr.
Carla E. Connor
Barbara A. Barnes

John F. Haskins, Jr.
Cynthia Love Dengler
Carol A. Crisci

LEGAL SUPPORT PERSONNEL

Patricia A. Talese (Paralegal)
Kathleen Nicholson

For full biographical listings, see the Martindale-Hubbell Law Directory

---

*PHILADELPHIA,** Philadelphia Co.

ASTOR WEISS KAPLAN & ROSENBLUM, LLP (AV)

The Bellevue, 6th Floor, 200 South Broad Street, 19102
Telephone: 215-790-0100
Fax: 215-790-0509
Email: lawyers@astorweiss.com
Bala Cynwyd, Pennsylvania Office: 401 City Avenue, Suite 500.
Telephone: 610-667-8660.
Fax: 610-667-2783.

MEMBERS OF FIRM

Alvin M. Weiss (1936-1976)
Paul C. Astor
G. David Rosenblum
Arthur H. Kaplan
Barbara Oaks Silver
David S. Workman
David Gutin
David S. Mandel
Gerald J. Schorr

ASSOCIATES

Christopher P. Flannery
Janet G. Felgoise
Elizabeth F. Warner
Daniel A. Shabel
Frances F. Freedman

SPECIAL COUNSEL

Neil Hurowitz
Jerrold V. Moss
Robert P. Style

OF COUNSEL

Edward W. Silver

For full biographical listings, see the Martindale-Hubbell Law Directory

---

BALLARD SPAHR ANDREWS & INGERSOLL, LLP (AV)

1735 Market Street, 51st Floor, 19103-7599
Telephone: 215-665-8500
Fax: 215-864-8999
URL: http://www.ballardspahr.com
Baltimore, Maryland Office: 300 East Lombard Street. 19th Floor.
Telephone: 410-528-5600.
Fax: 410-528-5650.
Camden, New Jersey Office: 800 Hudson Square, 5th Floor.
Telephone: 856-541-5577.
Fax: 856-541-8272.

(See Next Column)

Denver, Colorado Office: Seventeenth Street Plaza Building, Suite 2300, 1225 17th Street.
Telephone: 303-292-2400.
Fax: 303-296-3956.
Salt Lake City, Utah Office: One Utah Center, Suite 1200, 201 South Main Street.
Telephone: 801-531-3000.
Fax: 801-531-3001.
Voorhees, New Jersey Office: Suite 100, 1101 Laurel Oak Drive.
Telephone: 856-627-8555.
Fax: 856-627-1153.
Washington, D.C. Office: Suite 1000 South, 601 13th Street, N.W.
Telephone: 202-661-2200.
Fax: 202-661-2299.

Beverly R. Budin
Mary G. Lawler
Benjamin R. Neilson
Bruce L. Castor
Ann T. Loftus
Marilyn C. Sanborne
Regina O'Brien Thomas

Robert R. Baron, Jr.
Ann Marie Ritchie
Roberta A. Barsotti
David L. Weinreb

For Complete List of Firm Personnel, See General Section

For full biographical listings, see the Martindale-Hubbell Law Directory

---

LESLIE J. CARSON, JR. (AV)

42 South 15th Street, Suite 1150, 19102
Telephone: 215-568-1980
Fax: 215-568-6882
Email: carsonles@aol.com
Overbrook, Pennsylvania Office: City Line and Lancaster Avenues, Philadelphia, Pennsylvania.

LEGAL SUPPORT PERSONNEL

Stacy K. Paramore

For full biographical listings, see the Martindale-Hubbell Law Directory

---

FURIA AND TURNER (AV)

1717 Rittenhouse Square, 19103-6109
Telephone: 215-985-4500
Telecopier: 215-985-2824
Email: rfuria1717@aol.com *URL:* http://www.lawyers.com/furiaandturner

MEMBER OF FIRM

Richard F. Furia

ASSOCIATE

Gina R. Furia

OF COUNSEL

Robert S. Esposito

For full biographical listings, see the Martindale-Hubbell Law Directory

---

GALFAND BERGER, LLP (AV)

1818 Market Street, 23rd Floor, 19103-3623
Telephone: 215-665-1600
Fax: 215-564-2262
Email: sdonaway@galfandberger.com *URL:* http://www.galfandberger.com

---

Norman M. Berger
Leanna Johannes Harman

For full biographical listings, see the Martindale-Hubbell Law Directory

---

LEDGEWOOD LAW FIRM, A PROFESSIONAL CORPORATION (AV)

1521 Locust Street, 19102
Telephone: 215-731-9450
FAX: 215-735-2513
Affiliated with: Whittlesey McDowell & Holtz, P.C. 46 W. Main St., Maple Shade, N.J.
Telephone: 609-482-5544.

Richard J. Abt
Kevin F. Berry
Jeffrey F. Brotman
Paula Baiman Brown
Lisa A. Ernst
Thomas B. Fiddler
Joseph B. Finlay, Jr.
Dennis A. Holtz
Sean Patrick Kirby
Michael W. Perner
J. Baur Whittlesey

Stacy C. Ruch
Michele R. Weisbaum

LEGAL SUPPORT PERSONNEL

Terri Dello Buono (Firm Administrator)
Victoria Jaret
Diane Vecchio
Lisa D. Schumm

For full biographical listings, see the Martindale-Hubbell Law Directory

Philadelphia—Continued

SCHUBERT, BELLWOAR, CAHILL & QUINN, A PROFESSIONAL CORPORATION (AV)

Two Penn Center, Suite 1400, 1500 John F. Kennedy Boulevard, 19102-1890
Telephone: 215-569-3535
Fax: 215-557-7426
Email: attorneys@sbcq.com
Haddon Township, New Jersey Office: 311 West Cuthbert Boulevard, 08108.
Telephone: 856-854-5757.

Thomas M. Schubert (1924-1989)
William E. Schubert, Jr. (1921-1998)
Harry J. J. Bellwoar, III
John P. Quinn
John J. Cahill, Jr.
Robert T. Lynch
Robert G. Bellwoar
John P. Gallagher
James O. Hausch
Deborah E. Kolodner
Richard T. Mulcahey, Jr.
James M. Tyler
Jan M. Ritchie

Joseph W. Cunningham
Michael S. Piotrowicz
Patricia Farrell Kerelo
Christopher B. Hogan
Kathleen M. O'Connell
Mark Pfeiffer
Eric A. Feldhake

OF COUNSEL

John D. Lucey, Jr.
Robert F. Blanck

For full biographical listings, see the Martindale-Hubbell Law Directory

MERVIN M. WILF, LTD. (AV)

3901 Mellon Bank Center, 1735 Market Street, 19103
Telephone: 215-994-1430; 215-568-4842
Facsimile: 215-994-1432
Email: mwilf@erols.com
Cambridge, Massachusetts Office: 2 Berkeley Place, 02138.
Telephone: 617-876-5200.

Mervin M. Wilf

A list of Representative Clients and References will be furnished upon request.

For full biographical listings, see the Martindale-Hubbell Law Directory

*PITTSBURGH,** Allegheny Co.

FECZKO AND SEYMOUR (AV)

520 Grant Building, 15219
Telephone: 412-261-4970
Fax: Available upon Request
Bethel Park, Pennsylvania Office: 3400 South Park Road.
Telephone: 412-833-5554.

MEMBERS OF FIRM

Albert G. Feczko, Jr.
Michael J. Seymour

ASSOCIATE

Michael D. Seymour

Reference: Pittsburgh National Bank.

For full biographical listings, see the Martindale-Hubbell Law Directory

MARCUS & SHAPIRA LLP (AV)

35th Floor, One Oxford Centre, 301 Grant Street, 15219-6401
Telephone: 412-471-3490
Telecopier: 412-391-8758
Email: info@marcus-shapira.com *URL:* http://www.marcus-shapira.com

MEMBERS OF FIRM

Elly Heller-Toig
Darlene M. Nowak

For Complete List of Firm Personnel, See General Section

For full biographical listings, see the Martindale-Hubbell Law Directory

PLOWMAN, SPIEGEL & LEWIS, P.C. (AV)

Second Floor, The Grant Building, 310 Grant Street, 15219-2201
Telephone: 412-471-8521
Fax: 412-471-4481

Mark A. Griffith
William A. Houston

Reference: Pittsburgh National Bank.

For Complete List of Firm Personnel, See General Section

For full biographical listings, see the Martindale-Hubbell Law Directory

*READING,** Berks Co.

MOGEL, SPEIDEL, BOBB & KERSHNER, A PROFESSIONAL CORPORATION (AV)

520 Walnut Street, P.O. Box 8581, 19603-8581
Telephone: 610-376-1515
Telecopier: 610-372-8710

George B. Balmer (1902-1969)
George A. Kershner (1907-1969)
Carl F. Mogel (1919-1994)
Edwin H. Kershner
Frederick R. Mogel
Michael L. Mixell
George M. Lutz
Paul M. Yatron
Stephen H. Price
Kathryn K. Harenza

Sean J. O'Brien
Matthew Earl Glinn

OF COUNSEL

Harry W. Speidel
Donald K. Bobb
Henry A. Gass

Representative Clients: Great Valley Bank; Union Township, Berks County, Pennsylvania.

For full biographical listings, see the Martindale-Hubbell Law Directory

*SCRANTON,** Lackawanna Co.

WELLES & MCGRATH (AV)

1117 Bank Towers, 321 Spruce Street, 18503
Telephone: 570-348-4951
Fax: 570-348-4954

MEMBERS OF FIRM

Charles H. Welles, Jr. (1876-1962)
Matthew D. Mackie (1897-1965)
Charles H. Welles (1907-1997)
Henry C. McGrath
Charles H. Welles, IV

Counsel For: Grange National Bank; Scranton Industrial Development Co.; Bear Creek Nursing Home; Northeastern Ob-Gyn Associates, P.C.; Metropolitan Life Insurance Co.; New Health Management Systems, Inc.; Chamberlin Insurance Inc.

For full biographical listings, see the Martindale-Hubbell Law Directory

SELINSGROVE, Snyder Co.

JOHN R. MOORE (AV)

719 North Market Street, 17870
Telephone: 570-374-8138
Fax: 570-374-7558
Email: moorelaw@sunlink.net *URL:* http://www.lawyers.com/jrmlaw

For full biographical listings, see the Martindale-Hubbell Law Directory

*SUNBURY,** Northumberland Co.

APFELBAUM, APFELBAUM & APFELBAUM (AV)

43 South Fifth Street, 17801
Telephone: 717-286-9421
Fax: 717-286-5349

MEMBERS OF FIRM

Sidney Apfelbaum
Jeffrey Apfelbaum
Michael Morris Apfelbaum

Counsel for: Weis Markets, Inc.; Sunbury Textile Mills, Inc.; Shikellamy School District; City of Sunbury; Borough of Northumberland; Central Builders Supply Co.; The Daily Item.
Agents for: Commonwealth Land Title Insurance Co.
Reference: Snyder County Trust Co.

For full biographical listings, see the Martindale-Hubbell Law Directory

*TUNKHANNOCK,** Wyoming Co.

FARR, DAVIS & FITZE (AV)

7 Marion Street, P.O. Box H, 18657
Telephone: 570-836-3185
Facsimile: 570-836-4991

MEMBERS OF FIRM

John B. Farr (1907-1995)
James E. Davis
Judd B. Fitze

Representative Clients: Community Bank & Trust Co.; Proctor & Gamble Paper Products Co.
Title Agents for: Commonwealth Land Title Insurance Co.
References: Mellon Bank, Tunkhannock, PA Office; First Union Bank (Tunkhannock, PA Office); Community Bank and Trust Co.; Grange National Bank of Wyoming County.

For full biographical listings, see the Martindale-Hubbell Law Directory

*WASHINGTON,** Washington Co.

Peacock Keller Ecker & Crothers, LLP (AV)

East Beau Building, 70 East Beau Street, 15301
Telephone: 724-222-4520
Telefax: 724-222-3318 ABA/NET ABA 34517
Email: peacock@cobweb.net
Waynesburg, Pennsylvania Office: 102 East High Street.
Telephone: 724-627-8331.
Telefax: 724-627-8025.

MEMBERS OF FIRM

Kenneth L. Baker
Richard J. Amrhein

ASSOCIATE

Susan Mondik Key

SENIOR COUNSEL

Davis G. Yohe

Representative Clients: Consolidation Coal Co.; Monongahela Valley Hospital, Inc.; Nationwide Insurance Co.; Family Health Council, Inc.; Cal-Ed Federal Credit Union; Marianna & Scenery Hill Telephone Co.; Maternal & Family Health Services, Inc.; Pennsylvania Hospital Insurance Company.

For Complete List of Firm Personnel, See General Section

For full biographical listings, see the Martindale-Hubbell Law Directory

*WEST CHESTER,** Chester Co.

Buckley, Nagle, Gentry, Brion, McGuire & Morris (AV)

304 North High Street, 19380
Telephone: 610-436-4400
Telecopier: 610-436-8305
URL: http://www.buckleynagle.com

MEMBERS OF FIRM

C. Barry Buckley
Ronald C. Nagle
W. Richard Gentry
Joseph E. Brion
Stephen P. McGuire
Anthony Morris
Jeffrey R. Sommer

ASSOCIATES

John T. Mannato
Kristin S. Camp
Donald F. Kohler, Jr.

For full biographical listings, see the Martindale-Hubbell Law Directory

Gawthrop, Greenwood & Halsted, A Professional Corporation (AV)

119 North High Street, P.O. Box 562, 19381-0562
Telephone: 610-696-8225
Fax: 610-344-0922
Email: gghlaw@gawthrop.com *URL:* http://www.gawthrop.com

John S. Halsted
Robert F. Adams
Kevin Holleran
George C. Zumbano
Mark L. Tunnell
Roger N. Huggins
Walter P. Eells

Andrew D.H. Rau
Jeffrey T. Baker
Miguel D. Pena

Counsel for: Chester County Hospital; Brandywine Hospital; First Union Corporation; Boy Scouts of America; Freedom Valley Girl Scout Council.

For full biographical listings, see the Martindale-Hubbell Law Directory

*WILKES-BARRE,** Luzerne Co.

Hourigan, Kluger & Quinn, A Professional Corporation (AV)

700 Mellon Bank Center, 8 West Market Street, 18701-1867
Telephone: 570-825-9401
FAX: 570-829-3460
Email: hkq@epix.net
Scranton, Pennsylvania Office: Suite 200, 434 Lackawanna Avenue.
Telephone: 570-346-8414.
Allentown, Pennsylvania Office: Sovereign Building, 609 Hamilton Mall.
Telephone: 610-437-1584.

Allan M. Kluger
Richard M. Goldberg
Richard S. Bishop (Resident, Scranton Office)
Joseph E. Kluger

For Complete List of Firm Personnel, See General Section

For full biographical listings, see the Martindale-Hubbell Law Directory

Rosenn, Jenkins & Greenwald, L.L.P. (AV)

15 South Franklin Street, 18711-0075
Telephone: 570-826-5600
Fax: 570-826-5640
Email: rjg@rjglaw.com *URL:* http://www.rjglaw.com
Hazleton, Pennsylvania Office: P.O. Box 618, 18201-0618.
Telephone: 570-455-7112.
Fax: 570-455-8304.

MEMBERS OF FIRM

Marshall S. Jacobson
Murray Ufberg
Alan S. Hollander
George F. Shovlin

ASSOCIATE

Thomas J. MacNeely

Representative Clients: C-TEC Corp.; Chicago Title Insurance Co.; Manufacturers & Traders Trust Company; Guard Insurance Group; May Department Stores Co.; Student Loan Marketing Assn. (Sallie Mae); Penn-State Geisinger Medical Center; Subaru of America, Inc.

For Complete List of Firm Personnel, See General Section

For full biographical listings, see the Martindale-Hubbell Law Directory

RHODE ISLAND

CRANSTON, Providence Co.

Taft & McSally (AV)

21 Garden City Drive, P.O. Box 20130, 02920
Telephone: 401-946-3800
Fax: 401-943-8859
Email: taftmcsally@ids.net

MEMBERS OF FIRM

James L. Taft (1901-1959)
Bernard F. McSally (1928-1978)
James L. Taft, Jr.

ASSOCIATES

Sarah Taft-Carter
John V. McGreen
Robert D. Murray
David H. Ferrara
Kenneth K. McKay, IV

LEGAL SUPPORT PERSONNEL

Mary T. Rochford

Representative Clients: General Motors Corp.; General Motors Acceptance Corp.; Providence Gas Co.; Fleet National Bank; Fleet Mortgage; Citizens Savings Bank; Rhode Island Hospital Trust National Bank; Town of Narragansett, Rhode Island (Bond Counsel); Brown Broadcasting Service, Inc.

For full biographical listings, see the Martindale-Hubbell Law Directory

*PROVIDENCE,** Providence Co.

Edmund C. Bennett (AV)

50 South Main Street, 02903
Telephone: 401-421-1150
Facsimile: 401-521-4080
Email: ECBennett@worldnet.att.net *URL:* http://www.lawyers.com/ecblaw

For full biographical listings, see the Martindale-Hubbell Law Directory

Hinckley, Allen & Snyder LLP (AV)

1500 Fleet Center, 02903-2393
Telephone: 401-274-2000
Fax: 401-277-9600
Email: firm@haslaw.com *URL:* http://www.haslaw.com
Boston, Massachusetts Office: 28 State Street, 30th Floor.
Telephone: 617-345-9000.
Fax: 617-345-9020. URL: http://www.haslaw.com.

MEMBERS OF FIRM

Leon C. Boghossian III
Noel M. Field, Jr.
Doris Jami Licht
Richard H. Pierce
James O. Reavis
Paul A. Silver

ASSOCIATES

Clifford R. Cohen (Not admitted in RI)
Lynn E. Riley

For Complete List of Firm Personnel, See General Section

For full biographical listings, see the Martindale-Hubbell Law Directory

SMITHFIELD, Providence Co.

Charles S. Sokoloff Incorporated (AV)

Eleven Thurber Boulevard, 02917-1859
Telephone: 401-233-2800; Toll Free: 888-SOKOLAW
Fax: 401-233-2890
URL: http://www.sokolawyer.com
Email: sokolaw@sokolawyer.com *URL:* http://www.lawyers.com/sokolaw

(See Next Column)

CHARLES S. SOKOLOFF INCORPORATED, *Smithfield—Continued*

Charles S. Sokoloff

Anne-Marie Krollman

For full biographical listings, see the Martindale-Hubbell Law Directory

WARWICK, Kent Co.

SJOBERG & VOTTA LAW OFFICES (AV)

200 Centerville Road, Suite 4, 02886-4339
Telephone: 401-737-9696
Telecopier: 401-737-9119
Email: sjoberg@erols.com

MEMBERS OF FIRM

Mark A. Sjoberg Paul J. Votta, Jr.

Approved Attorneys for: Commonwealth Land Title Insurance Company; Chicago Title Insurance Company; Mortgage Guaranty & Title Company; American Title Insurance Company; Lawyers Title Insurance Company.
Representative Clients: Citizens Bank; Chicago Title Insurance Company; Domestic Savings Bank.

For full biographical listings, see the Martindale-Hubbell Law Directory

WESTERLY, Washington Co.

ORSINGER & NARDONE (AV)

Narragansett Building, 53 High Street, P.O. Box 558, 02891-0558
Telephone: 401-596-2094
Telecopier: 401-596-4555

MEMBERS OF FIRM

Victor J. Orsinger William A. Nardone

ASSOCIATE

Jon D. Lallo

References: The Washington Trust Co.; Fleet National Bank.

For full biographical listings, see the Martindale-Hubbell Law Directory

SOUTH CAROLINA

*BEAUFORT,** Beaufort Co.

DAVIS, TUPPER & GRIMSLEY, L.L.P. (AV)

611 Bay Street, P.O. Box 2055, 29901-2055
Telephone: 843-524-1116
Facsimile: 843-524-1463
Email: DTGS@Hargray.com

MEMBERS OF FIRM

James A. Grimsley, III Virginia D. Meeks

For full biographical listings, see the Martindale-Hubbell Law Directory

HARVEY & BATTEY, P.A. (AV)

1001 Craven Street, P.O. Drawer 1107, 29902
Telephone: 843-524-3109
Telefax: 843-524-6973

W. Brantley Harvey, Jr. E. Carew Rice, III

Approved Attorneys for: Lawyers Title Insurance Corp.; Chicago Title Insurance Corp.
Representative Clients: Nations Bank; First Bank, F.S.B.; Pleasant Point Plantation Associates; Century 21-Carolina Realty, Inc.; Lobeco Products, Inc.; Beaufort County Association of Realtors; The Fripp Company.

For Complete List of Firm Personnel, See General Section

For full biographical listings, see the Martindale-Hubbell Law Directory

LEVIN & GILLEY (AV)

811 Craven Street, P.O. Box 2358, 29901-2358
Telephone: 843-522-9000
Fax: 843-524-8248
Email: dcg@hargray.com *URL:* http://www.lawyers.com/levinandgilley

Julian S. Levin Dewey C. Gilley, Jr.

Approved Attorneys for: Old Republic National Title Insurance Company.

For full biographical listings, see the Martindale-Hubbell Law Directory

*CHARLESTON,** Charleston Co.

EVANS, CARTER, KUNES & BENNETT, P.A. (AV)

115 Church Street, P.O. Box 369, 29402-0369
Telephone: 843-577-2300
Telefax: 843-577-2055
Email: eckb@eckb.com

(See Next Column)

George C. Evans Robert M. Kunes
T. Heyward Carter, Jr. Edward G. R. Bennett

Charlotte Nancie Quick Graeme Philp
Chalmers W. Poston, Jr. Susan A. Teschner

For full biographical listings, see the Martindale-Hubbell Law Directory

HAYNSWORTH, MARION, MCKAY & GUÉRARD, L.L.P. (AV)

134 Meeting Street, P.O. Box 1119, 29402
Telephone: 843-722-7606
Facsimile: 843-724-8016
Columbia, South Carolina Office: Suite 2400 Affinity Building, 1201 Main Street, P.O. Drawer 7157, 29202.
Telephone: 803-765-1818. Facsimile 803-765-2399.
Greenville, South Carolina Office: 75 Beattie Place, Eleventh Floor, P.O. Box 2048, 29602.
Telephone: 864-240-3200.
Facsimile: 864-240-3300.

MEMBER OF FIRM

Robert B. Pearlman

ASSOCIATE

M. Jean Lee

OF COUNSEL

Gus H. Pearlman

Counsel for: Healthsource of South Carolina; Allstate Insurance Co.; CSX Corp.; Lloyd's Underwriters; Coward-Hund Construction Co.; Charleston County; City of Hanahan; Duke Power Co.

For Complete List of Firm Personnel, See General Section

For full biographical listings, see the Martindale-Hubbell Law Directory

*COLUMBIA,** Richland Co.

RICHARDSON, PLOWDEN, CARPENTER & ROBINSON, P.A. (AV)

1600 Marion Street, P.O. Drawer 7788, 29202
Telephone: 803-771-4400
Telecopy: 803-779-0016
Email: atty@rpcrlaw.com *URL:* http://www.rpcrlaw.com
Myrtle Beach, South Carolina Office: 2103 B Farlow Street, P.O. Box 3646, 29578.
Telephone: 843-448-1008.
FAX: 843-448-1533.

Frederick A. Crawford

For Complete List of Firm Personnel, See General Section

For full biographical listings, see the Martindale-Hubbell Law Directory

ROGERS TOWNSEND & THOMAS, PC (AV)

1441 Main Street, 10th Floor, P.O. Box 100200, 29202-3200
Telephone: 803-771-7900
Fax: 803-254-6305; 343-7017; 343-7019
URL: http://www.rtt-law.com

Robert Bryan Barnes Samuel C. Waters
B. Michael Brackett W. Alex Weatherly, Jr.
Sherwood M. Cleveland Robert P. Wood
Harry B. Gregory, Jr. James C. Leventis
Clifford O. Koon, Jr. Richard M. Unger
Albert L. Moses Cheryl H. Fisher
Eugene F. Rogers D. Randolph Whitt
Robert J. Thomas Stacey Lynch Hewson
Joe W. Underwood Kendall R. Walker
Wm. Bert Brannon

Glen Paul Caulk Denis A. Brosnan, Jr.
Thomas McRoy Shelley, III Paul D. de Holczer

OF COUNSEL

James S. Guignard Gwendelyn Geidel

LEGAL SUPPORT PERSONNEL

Carol A. Cummings

For full biographical listings, see the Martindale-Hubbell Law Directory

TURNER, PADGET, GRAHAM & LANEY, P.A. (AV)

Seventeenth Floor, 1901 Main Street, P.O. Box 1473, 29202
Telephone: 803-254-2200
Telecopy: 803-799-3957
Florence, South Carolina Office: Fourth Floor, 1831 West Evans Street, P.O. Box 5478, 29502.
Telephone: 843-662-9008.
Fax: 843-667-0828.
Charleston, South Carolina Office: 21 Broad Street, 1st Floor, P.O. Box 836, 29402.
Telephone: 843-723-1622.
Fax: 843-577-3369.

(See Next Column)

TURNER, PADGET, GRAHAM & LANEY P.A.—*Continued*

R. Wayne Byrd (Resident, Florence, SC, Office)
David G. Fawcett

William O. Higgins

For Complete List of Firm Personnel, See General Section

For full biographical listings, see the Martindale-Hubbell Law Directory

*GREENVILLE,** Greenville Co.

DAN A. COLLINS & ASSOCIATES, P.A. (AV)

1154 Haywood Road, Suite B, P.O. Box 25726, 29616
Telephone: 864-281-0284
Telecopier: 864-281-0285
Email: collinsd@innova.net *URL:* http://www.lawyers.com/daclaw

Dan A. Collins

For full biographical listings, see the Martindale-Hubbell Law Directory

HAYNSWORTH, MARION, MCKAY & GUÉRARD, L.L.P. (AV)

75 Beattie Place, Eleventh Floor, P.O. Box 2048, 29602
Telephone: 864-240-3200
Facsimile: 864-240-3300
Columbia, South Carolina Office: Suite 2400 Affinity Building, 1201 Main Street, P.O. Drawer 7157, 29202
Telephone: 803-765-1818.
Facsimile: 803-765-2399.
Charleston, South Carolina Office: 134 Meeting Street, P.O. Box 1119, 29402.
Telephone: 843-722-7606.
Facsimile: 843-724-8016.

MEMBERS OF FIRM

Arthur Frazier McLean, III
Frank T. Davis, III

ASSOCIATE

Christina M. Condon

For Complete List of Firm Personnel, See General Section

For full biographical listings, see the Martindale-Hubbell Law Directory

MERLINE & THOMAS, P.A. (AV)

812 East North Street, P.O. Box 10796, 29603
Telephone: 864-242-4080
Fax: 864-242-5758

David A. Merline
John R. Thomas
David A. Merline, Jr.
Keith G. Meacham
Randy E. Fisher
Robert E. August
Tommy D. Permenter, Jr.

LEGAL SUPPORT PERSONNEL

Mary S. Rose (Legal Administrator)

For full biographical listings, see the Martindale-Hubbell Law Directory

C. LEWIS RASOR, JR. (AV)

Suite D, 245 East Broad Street, P.O. Box 8679, 29601
Telephone: 864-242-9094
Fax: 864-242-9095
Email: rasorlaw@bellsouth.net

For full biographical listings, see the Martindale-Hubbell Law Directory

CHARLES M. STUART, JR. (AV)

Suite F 862 South Pleasantburg Drive, 29607
Telephone: 864-232-5411
FAX: 864-232-5179

For full biographical listings, see the Martindale-Hubbell Law Directory

HILTON HEAD ISLAND, Beaufort Co.

RUTH & MACNEILLE, PROFESSIONAL ASSOCIATION (AV)

40 Pope Avenue, 29928
Telephone: 843-785-4251
Telex: 988944
Telecopier: 843-686-5404
Mailing Address: P.O. Box 5706, Hilton Head Island, SC, 29938
Bluffton, South Carolina Office: 7 Simmonsville Road, Suite 200.
Telephone: 803-815-5353.
Fax: 803-815-5354.

William A. Ruth

References: NationsBank of South Carolina, N.A.; Anchor Bank; Wachovia Bank, N.A.; Chicago Title Insurance Corp.; First American Title Insurance Co.

For full biographical listings, see the Martindale-Hubbell Law Directory

MYRTLE BEACH, Horry Co.

BELLAMY, RUTENBERG, COPELAND, EPPS, GRAVELY & BOWERS, P.A. (AV)

1000 29th Avenue North, P.O. Box 357, 29578
Telephone: 843-448-2400
Telecopier: 843-448-3022

Howell V. Bellamy, Jr.
John K. Rutenberg
John E. Copeland
Claude M. Epps, Jr.
David R. Gravely
Edward B. Bowers, Jr.
Bradley D. King
Henrietta U. Golding
M. Edwin Hinds, Jr.
Jill F. Griffith
Kathryn M. Cook
David B. Miller
C. Winfield Johnson, III
Sarah A. Johnson
Douglas M. Zayicek
Jeffrey W. King
Mary Anna Malpass
Martin Charles Dawsey

Representative Clients: Dargan Construction Co.; Coastal Federal Savings Bank; Sands Investments; Wachovia Bank of South Carolina; AVX Corp.; Bank of America; Parthenon Insurance Co.; Burroughs & Chapin Co.; International Paper Co.; Hospital Corporation of America.

For full biographical listings, see the Martindale-Hubbell Law Directory

JEFFCOAT, PIKE & NAPPIER, LLC (AV)

1601 North Oak Street, Suite 303, P.O. Box 3678, 29578
Telephone: 843-626-9000
Telecopier: 843-448-1914
Email: jpnlaw1@sccoast.net
North Myrtle Beach, South Carolina Office: 110 Ye Olde Kings Highway, P.O. Box 4360.
Telephone: 843-249-3581.
Telecopier: 843-249-6231.
Calabash, North Carolina Office: 9222-3 Beach Drive SW, P.O. Box 44000.
Telephone: 910-579-4050.
Facsimile: 910-579-2770.

Otis Allen Jeffcoat, III
Mark A. Nappier

ASSOCIATES

Patrick J. Reilly (Resident, North Myrtle Beach Office)
Melissa Johnson Emery
Eldon Donald Risher, III

OF COUNSEL

James C. Pike, Jr. (Resident, North Myrtle Beach Office)

For full biographical listings, see the Martindale-Hubbell Law Directory

SOUTH DAKOTA

LEAD, Lawrence Co.

FULLER, TELLINGHUISEN, GORDON & PERCY, P.C. (AV)

203 West Main Street, P.O. Box 898, 57754
Telephone: 605-584-2440
Fax: 605-584-1979
Email: leadlaw@mato.com
Spearfish, South Dakota Office: 132 East Illinois, 57783.
Telephone: 605-642-8080.
Fax: 605-642-1756. E-mail: spflaw@mato.com

A. P. Fuller
Roger A. Tellinghuisen
Bradley P. Gordon
Michelle Palmer Percy

Representative Clients: Homestake Mining Co.; Hotel Franklin & Gaming; Black Hills Novelty/Automatic Vending, Inc.; Northern Hills General Hospital; Lantis Enterprises, Inc.; Norwest Bank South Dakota N.A.; Lead-Deadwood Independent School District # 40-1; City of Lead.

For full biographical listings, see the Martindale-Hubbell Law Directory

*RAPID CITY,** Pennington Co.

BANGS, MCCULLEN, BUTLER, FOYE & SIMMONS, L.L.P. (AV)

818 St. Joseph Street, P.O. Box 2670, 57709
Telephone: 605-343-1040
Telecopier: 605-343-1503
URL: http://www.bangsmccullen.com

MEMBERS OF FIRM

Thomas H. Foye
Charles L. Riter
John H. Raforth

Representative Clients: Norwest Bank South Dakota, N.A., Rapid City, S.D.; Pete Lien & Sons; The Travelers Insurance Co.; Rapid City Regional Hospital; Dakota Steel & Supply Co.; Great American Insurance Co.; Fireman's Fund Insurance; United States Automobile Association; Moyle Petroleum; Rapid City Area School District 51-4.

For Complete List of Firm Personnel, See General Section

For full biographical listings, see the Martindale-Hubbell Law Directory

TENNESSEE

BRENTWOOD, Williamson Co.

THRAILKILL, HARRIS & WOOD, PLC (AV)

105 Westpark Drive, Suite 400, P.O. Box 2408, 37024-2408
Telephone: 615-376-3555
Fax: 615-376-3016

Larry T. Thrailkill
Christopher Harris
Steven K. Wood

Angela Humphreys Hamilton

For full biographical listings, see the Martindale-Hubbell Law Directory

*CHATTANOOGA,** Hamilton Co.

BAKER, DONELSON, BEARMAN & CALDWELL (AV)

1800 Republic Centre, 633 Chestnut Street, 37450-1800
Telephone: 423-756-2010
Telecopier: 423-756-3447
Email: info@bdbc.com *URL:* http://www.bakerdonelson.com
Memphis, Tennessee Office: 20th Floor, First Tennessee Building, 165 Madison, 38103.
Telephone: 901-526-2000.
Telecopier: 901-577-2303.
Nashville, Tennessee Office: 1700 Nashville City Center, 511 Union Street, 37219.
Telephone: 615-726-5600.
Telecopier: 615-726-0464.
Knoxville, Tennessee Office: 2200 Riverview Tower, 900 South Gay Street, 37901.
Telephone: 423-549-7000.
Telecopier: 423-525-8569.
Johnson City, Tennessee Office: SunTrust Bank Building, 207 Mockingbird Lane, P.O. Box 3038, 37602.
Telephone: 423-928-0181.
Telecopier: 423-928-5694; 423-928-3654; Kingsport: 423-246-6191.
Huntsville, Tennessee Office: 3 Courthouse Square, 37756.
Telephone: 423-663-2321.
Telecopier: 423-663-2111.
Washington, D.C. Office: Market Square, 801 Pennsylvania Avenue, N.W., 20004.
Telephone: 202-508-3400.
Telecopier: 202-508-3402.
Jackson, Mississippi Office: Suite 500, 700 North State Street, 39202.
Telephone: 601-351-2400.
Telecopier: 601-351-2424.

SHAREHOLDERS

Thomas A. Caldwell
Virginia C. Love

OF COUNSEL

Randall D. Van Dolson

For Complete List of Firm Personnel, See General Section

For full biographical listings, see the Martindale-Hubbell Law Directory

GEARHISER, PETERS, LOCKABY & TALLANT, PLLC (AV)

320 McCallie Avenue, 37402-2007
Telephone: 423-756-5171
Fax: 423-266-1605
Email: law@gplt.com

MEMBERS OF FIRM

Charles J. Gearhiser
R. Wayne Peters
Robert L. Lockaby, Jr.
Ralph E. Tallant, Jr.
Terry Atkin Cavett
Sam D. Elliott
Lane C. Avery
Wade K. Cannon

ASSOCIATES

Robin L. Miller
Christopher T. Varner
James C. Davey
Lee Ann Adams
Jeffrey H. Moore
Kevin T. Beck

OF COUNSEL

Richard P. Jahn, Jr.

References: First Tennessee Bank; First American National Bank.

For full biographical listings, see the Martindale-Hubbell Law Directory

HUGH F. KENDALL, ATTORNEY, P.C. (AV)

Suite 305, Victorian Gardens, 6918 Shallowford Road, 37421-1783
Telephone: 423-499-9863
Telecopier: 423-894-0682
Email: hukendall@aol.com

Hugh F. Kendall

For full biographical listings, see the Martindale-Hubbell Law Directory

WITT, GAITHER & WHITAKER, P.C. (AV)

1100 SunTrust Bank Building, 37402-2608
Telephone: 423-265-8881
Telefax: 423-266-4138; 423-756-5612

Philip B. Whitaker
John W. Murrey, III
Harold Alan Schwartz, Jr.
Philip B. Whitaker, Jr.
Jane K. Ricci

Representative Clients: The Baylor School; Chattanooga Bakery, Inc.; Coca-Cola Bottling Co. Consolidated; Crescent Hosiery Mills, Inc.; Girls Preparatory School; Masland Carpets, Inc.; Robbins & Bohr, Inc.; The Dixie Group, Inc.

For Complete List of Firm Personnel, See General Section

For full biographical listings, see the Martindale-Hubbell Law Directory

*CLARKSVILLE,** Montgomery Co.

RUNYON AND RUNYON, PLLC (AV)

301 Main Street, P.O. Box 1023, 37041-1023
Telephone: 931-647-3377
Fax: 931-551-3561
URL: http://www.lawyers.com/runyonandrunyon
Erin Office: 143 East Main.
Telephone: 931-289-5900.

MEMBERS OF FIRM

Charles V. Runyon (1886-1973)
Frank J. Runyon
Markley Runyon Gill
Frank J. Runyon, III
Raymond F. Runyon

Representative Clients: Clarksville Department of Electricity; St. Paul Insurance Co.; The Trane Co.; Aetna Life & Casualty Co.; Houston County; Union Planters Bank, National Association; Prudential Professional Realty.
Reference: First Union Bank, Clarksville.

For full biographical listings, see the Martindale-Hubbell Law Directory

JOHNSON CITY, Washington Co.

BRANDT AND BEESON, P.C. (AV)

206 Princeton Road, Suite 25, 37601
Telephone: 423-282-1981
Fax: 423-283-4778
Email: bnb@brandtbeeson.com

Frederic H. Brandt
D. R. Beeson, III
Jack L. Mayfield

For full biographical listings, see the Martindale-Hubbell Law Directory

WALTER LEE DAVIS, JR. A PROFESSIONAL CORPORATION (AV)

121 East Unaka Avenue, 37601-4697
Telephone: 423-929-7000
Fax: 423-926-3991
Email: info@davislaw.net

Walter Lee Davis, Jr.

René Riggs Gilliam
Jeannette C. Smith

For full biographical listings, see the Martindale-Hubbell Law Directory

*KNOXVILLE,** Knox Co.

EGERTON, MCAFEE, ARMISTEAD & DAVIS, P.C. (AV)

500 First American National Bank Center, P.O. Box 2047, 37901
Telephone: 423-546-0500
Fax: 423-525-5293
URL: http://emadlaw.com

William W. Davis
Joe M. McAfee
Lewis C. Foster, Jr.
William E. McClamroch, III
Jonathan D. Reed

Reese K. Thomas

Representative Clients: First American Trust Company; Home Federal Bank of Tennessee, F.S.B.; Carson Newman College; East Tennessee Foundation.

For full biographical listings, see the Martindale-Hubbell Law Directory

LEIBOWITZ & COHEN (AV)

608 Gay Street, S.W., 37902
Telephone: 423-637-1809
FAX: 423-637-9276

MEMBERS OF FIRM

Arnold G. Cohen
Lawrence P. Leibowitz

ASSOCIATE

Melissa A. Ashburn

(See Next Column)

LEIBOWITZ & COHEN—*Continued*

OF COUNSEL
Russell T. Greene

For full biographical listings, see the Martindale-Hubbell Law Directory

ANNE M. MCKINNEY, P.C. (AV)

Suite 700, Arnstein Building, 505 Market Street, 37902
Telephone: 423-525-8700
Fax: 423-521-4189
Email: amckinney@ammtaxlaw.com

Anne M. McKinney
Lisa Wolff Gammeltoft

Stacy Ann Ellison

OF COUNSEL
Gale Graham Allison

LEGAL SUPPORT PERSONNEL
Eugene E. Jones (Legal Assistant)
Theilia E. Payne (Legal Assistant)

For full biographical listings, see the Martindale-Hubbell Law Directory

*MEMPHIS,** Shelby Co.

ARMSTRONG ALLEN PREWITT GENTRY JOHNSTON & HOLMES, PLLC (AV)

Brinkley Plaza, Suite 700, 80 Monroe Avenue, 38103-2467
Telephone: 901-523-8211
Facsimile: 901-524-4936
Little Rock, Arkansas Office: Suite 100, 100 Morgan Keegan Drive, 72202.
Telephone: 501-280-0100.
Facsimile: 501-280-0166.
Jackson, Mississippi Office: 2525 Lakeward Drive, Suite 200, 39216.
Telephone: 601-713-1192.
Facsimile: 601-713-2049.
Jackson, Tennessee Office: 464 North Parkway, Suite A, 38305.
Telephone: 901-660-2332.
Facsimile: 901-664-1109.

MEMBERS OF FIRM
Elmore Holmes, III
Joseph Brent Walker
James Rogers (Josh) Hall, Jr.
James L. Pettis, III (Resident, Jackson, Mississippi Office)

For Complete List of Firm Personnel, See General Section

For full biographical listings, see the Martindale-Hubbell Law Directory

CAUSEY, CAYWOOD, TAYLOR, MCMANUS & BAILEY (AV)

A Professional Association, Not a Partnership
Suite 2400, 100 North Main Building, 38103
Telephone: 901-526-0206
Telecopier: 901-525-1540

James D. Causey
David E. Caywood
Daniel Loyd Taylor
John E. McManus

Craig B. Flood, II
Jean E. Markowitz
Amy R. Fulton
David Shepherd Walker
John N. Bean

For Complete List of Firm Personnel, See General Section

For full biographical listings, see the Martindale-Hubbell Law Directory

HARKAVY, SHAINBERG, KOSTEN, KAPLAN & DUNSTAN, PC (AV)

100 Peabody Place, Suite 1300, 38103
Telephone: 901-761-1263
Telecopier: 901-763-3340
Downtown Telecopier: 901-843-0864
Downtown Office: Memphis, Tennessee, 6060 Poplar Avenue, Suite 140, 38119.

MEMBERS AND ASSOCIATES
Ronald M. Harkavy
Raymond M. Shainberg
Alan L. Kosten
Michael D. Kaplan
Allen C. Dunstan
Neil Harkavy
Jerome A. Broadhurst
Alan M. Harkavy

OF COUNSEL
Ira D. Pruitt, Jr.
Laurie A. Cooper
G. Thomas McPherson

For full biographical listings, see the Martindale-Hubbell Law Directory

KRIVCHER MAGIDS PLC (AV)

International Place II, 6410 Poplar Avenue, Suite 300, 38119-4839
Telephone: 901-682-6431
Facsimile: 901-682-6453
Email: lawfirm@kmplc.com

(See Next Column)

Charles C. Cottam

ASSOCIATES
Rachel L. Hotze
Aubrey Lee Brown, Jr.

For Complete List of Firm Personnel, See General Section

For full biographical listings, see the Martindale-Hubbell Law Directory

ROSSIE, LUCKETT, PARKER & RIDDER, P.C. (AV)

675 Oakleaf Office Lane, Suite 200, 38117-4863
Telephone: 901-763-1800
Telecopier: 901-767-6514
Email: rlpr@rlpr.com

J. Richard Rossie
John H. Parker
William Martin Seiler

COUNSEL
Harry W. Laughlin, III

For Complete List of Firm Personnel, See General Section

For full biographical listings, see the Martindale-Hubbell Law Directory

*NASHVILLE,** Davidson Co.

D. JEFFERSON HERRING (AV)

The Pilcher Building, Suite 200, 144 Second Avenue North, 37201
Telephone: 615-259-9594
Fax: 615-259-9584

For full biographical listings, see the Martindale-Hubbell Law Directory

HOLTON HOWARD & GOODMAN, P.C. (AV)

424 Church Street, Suite 2700, 37219-2323
Telephone: 615-256-3338
Fax: 615-244-2104
Email: Plan@hohogoo.com

Richard D. Holton
Bryan Howard
Joe M. Goodman
William E. Blackstone

Mattison C. Painter
Brian C. Mayberry
Lucibeth Nave
Stephen C. Passen

Reference: SunTrust Bank, Nashville, N.A.

For full biographical listings, see the Martindale-Hubbell Law Directory

TEXAS

*ALICE,** Jim Wells Co.

WARBURTON, ADAMI, MCNEILL, PAISLEY & APPELL, P.C. (AV)

Norwest Bank Building, Fourth Floor, 601 East Main Street, P.O. Box 331, 78333-0331
Telephone: 361-668-8101
Fax: 361-668-8106
Beeville Office: 107 North Washington Street, P.O. Box 278, 78104-0278.
Telephone: 361-358-2525.
Fax: 361-358-2532.

Lawrence H. Warburton, Jr.
John G. "Buster" Adami, Jr.
Wallis D. McNeill, Jr.
Mark R. Paisley
R. Michael Appell

Representative Clients: Norwest Bank, Alice; Bowden Ford Lincoln Mercury Co.; Brooks County Independent School District; Jim Wells County; Lundells, Inc.; Brush County Bank; Mildred Talbert Estate; Ruth Moos Estate; John G. Kenedy Charitable Trust; San Diego Independent School District.

For full biographical listings, see the Martindale-Hubbell Law Directory

*AUSTIN,** Travis Co.

OSBORNE, LOWE, HELMAN & SMITH, L.L.P. (AV)

301 Congress Avenue Suite 1900, 78701
Telephone: 512-469-7700
Fax: 512-469-7711
Email: olhslan@aol.com

MEMBERS OF FIRM
Duncan Elliott Osborne
Stephen Jody Helman
Derry W. Swanger
Jack E. Owen, Jr.
Leslie C. Giordani
Carolyn M. Beckett
Elizabeth Morgan Schurig
Elizabeth Gibson Deleery
Whitney Jade Fleming
Paul E. Williams
Gina Lambert

(See Next Column)

OSBORNE, LOWE, HELMAN & SMITH L.L.P., *Austin—Continued*

OF COUNSEL

Hugh S. Lowe Paula Y. Smith

For full biographical listings, see the Martindale-Hubbell Law Directory

*CORPUS CHRISTI,** Nueces Co.

PEARSON & PRICE, PLLC (AV)

Suite 1700, South Tower, 800 North Shoreline Boulevard, 78401
Telephone: 361-885-0077
Fax: 361-885-0288
Email: INFO@PEARSON-PRICE.COM *URL:* HTTP://WWW.PEARSON-PRICE.COM

Paul C. Pearson, III Paul O. Price
Richard E. Flint

For full biographical listings, see the Martindale-Hubbell Law Directory

*DALLAS,** Dallas Co.

JOSEPH E. ASHMORE, JR., P.C. (AV)

Regency Plaza, 3710 Rawlins, Suite 1210, LB 84, 75219-4217
Telephone: 214-559-7202
Fax: 214-520-1550

Joseph E. Ashmore, Jr.

C. Gregory Shamoun Lori Ashmore Peters

For Complete List of Firm Personnel, See General Section

For full biographical listings, see the Martindale-Hubbell Law Directory

CALHOUN & STACY (AV)

Suite 5700 - Bank of America Plaza, 901 Main Street, 75202-3713
Telephone: 214-748-5000
Facsimile: 214-748-1421
Email: info@calhounstacy.com *URL:* http://www.calhounstacy.com

MEMBERS OF FIRM

Rees T. Bowen, III Parker Nelson

For Complete List of Firm Personnel, See General Section

For full biographical listings, see the Martindale-Hubbell Law Directory

CALLOWAY, NORRIS & BURDETTE (AV)

3811 Turtle Creek Boulevard, Suite 400, 75219
Telephone: 214-521-1520
Telecopier: 214-521-2201

MEMBERS OF FIRM

Chas. D. Turner (1888-1960)
J. Woodall Rodgers (1890-1961)
James R. Rodgers (1922-1992)
R.W. Calloway
John R. Norris III
Mary Clariday Burdette

For full biographical listings, see the Martindale-Hubbell Law Directory

GEARY, PORTER & DONOVAN, P.C. (AV)

One Bent Tree Tower, 16475 Dallas Parkway, Suite 500, 75001-6837
Telephone: 972-931-9901
Facsimile: 972-931-9208
Mailing Address: P.O. Box 700248, Dallas, Texas, 75370-0248
Email: firm@gpd.com *URL:* http://www.gpd.com

Emmett W. Berryman
Paul K. Braswell
Bruce W. Claycombe
Nancy L. DeLeon
Daniel P. Donovan
Jeffrey L. Fisher
Joseph W. Geary
Michael P. Geary
Troy S. Gilreath
Ronald D. Gray
David J. Kaplan
Catherine C. Kays
Laura M. Keith
Nicole T. LeBoeuf
Jeffrey T. Libby
Larry L. Martin
Gregory L. Miller
James T. Porter
Amy D. Reilly
Theodore J. Riney
Kim Alan Roberts
Bradley T. Sharpe
Thomas L. Staley
David M. Tatum

OF COUNSEL

Jerry L. Arnold
Susan Land Finnell
Henry M. Wade
Roger O. West

For full biographical listings, see the Martindale-Hubbell Law Directory

GODWIN WHITE & GRUBER, A PROFESSIONAL CORPORATION (AV)

Suite 2500, 901 Main Street, 75202-3714
Telephone: 214-939-4400
Fax: 214-760-7332

(See Next Column)

Bob J. Shelton James G. Vetter, Jr.

For Complete List of Firm Personnel, See General Section

For full biographical listings, see the Martindale-Hubbell Law Directory

THE HARTNETT LAW FIRM (AV)

A Partnership including a Professional Corporation
4900 Thanksgiving Tower, 1601 Elm Street, 75201
Telephone: 214-742-4655
Telecopier: 214-855-7857

MEMBERS OF FIRM

James J. Hartnett (P.C.)
Will Ford Hartnett
James J. Hartnett, Jr.
Jay David Hartnett

ASSOCIATES

R. Kevin Spencer Fred Hartnett

OF COUNSEL

Thomas R. Hartnett

For full biographical listings, see the Martindale-Hubbell Law Directory

HOLMES, WOODS & GARZA (AV)

Highland Park Place, Suite 550, 4514 Cole Avenue, L.B. 32, 75205
Telephone: 214-520-8100
Facsimile: 214-520-6565
Email: familylaw@texfamlaw.com *URL:* http://www.texasfamilylawyers.com
McKinney, Texas Office: 1700 Redbud Boulevard, Suite 190, 75070.
Telephone: 972-569-3166.
Facsimile: 972-569-3167. Email: familylaw@texfamlaw.com.
Houston, Texas Office: 2550 North Loop West, Suite 860, 77092.
Telephone: 713-812-1113.
Facsimile: 713-812-7819. Email: familylaw@texfamlaw.com.

MEMBERS OF FIRM

Robert E. Holmes Jr. Lisa G. Garza

ASSOCIATE

Brad M. LaMorgese

For full biographical listings, see the Martindale-Hubbell Law Directory

HUGHES & LUCE, L.L.P. (AV)

A Registered Limited Liability Partnership including Professional Corporations
1717 Main Street, Suite 2800, 75201
Telephone: 214-939-5500
Fax: 214-939-6100; 214-939-5849
Email: H&L@hughesluce.com *URL:* http://www.hughesluce.com
Austin, Texas Office: 111 Congress, Suite 900.
Telephone: 512-482-6800.
Fax: 512-482-6859.
Houston, Texas Office: 1600 Smith Street, Suite 3550.
Telephone: 713-754-5200.
Fax: 713-754-5270.

MEMBERS OF FIRM

Kathryn G. Henkel Vester T. Hughes, Jr.
Elizabeth R. Turner

ASSOCIATES

Bradley L. Adams Margaret Laurel Stephenson

For Complete List of Firm Personnel, See General Section

For full biographical listings, see the Martindale-Hubbell Law Directory

KRONEY • MINCEY, INC. (AV)

1210 Three Forest Plaza, 12221 Merit Drive, 75251
Telephone: 972-386-8500
FAX: 972-701-0307

Sabina R. Choudhry
H. Kate Hopkins
Robert H. Kroney
Donald P. Lan, Jr.
Taryn N. Milewski
James M. Mincey, Jr.
Stuart A. Morse

For full biographical listings, see the Martindale-Hubbell Law Directory

MEADOWS, OWENS, COLLIER, REED, COUSINS & BLAU, L.L.P. (AV)

901 Main Street, Suite 3700, 75202-3725
Telephone: 214-744-3700; 800-451-0093
Fax: 214-747-3732
URL: http://www.meadowsowens.com

(See Next Column)

MEADOWS, OWENS, COLLIER, REED, COUSINS & BLAU L.L.P.—*Continued*

MEMBERS OF FIRM

Charles M. Meadows, Jr.
Rodney J. Owens
Robert Don Collier
David N. Reed
Thomas G. Hineman
William R. Cousins, III
Charles W. Blau
George R. Bedell
Michael E. McCue
Fielder F. Nelms
Joel N. Crouch
Alan K. Davis
Charles D. Pulman

ASSOCIATES

Patricia King Dorey
Robert M. Bolton
M. Todd Welty
Josh O. Ungerman
Robyn A. Frohlin
Gregory A. Cardenas
Sara E. Lankford
Sarah Q. Qureshi
Bradley G. Korell
Todd A. Kraft
Alan L. Stroud
Matthew D. Richards

For full biographical listings, see the Martindale-Hubbell Law Directory

SMITH, UNDERWOOD & PERKINS, A PROFESSIONAL CORPORATION (AV)

600 Two Lincoln Centre, 5420 LBJ Freeway, 75240
Telephone: 972-661-5114
Telecopier: 972-661-5691
Email: firm@suandp.com *URL:* http://www.suplaw.com

Timothy S. Perkins
David W. Ralston
G. Lynn Smith
William J. Underwood, Jr.

Christine A. McGuire
Amy K. Ratzlaff
P. Theodore Stoinoff, II
Val C. Cronin
Ellen P. Stewart
Todd W. Shadle
Ruth C. Logan
Christina L. Betanzos
Kent D. Williamson

For full biographical listings, see the Martindale-Hubbell Law Directory

THOMPSON & KNIGHT L.L.P. (AV)

(Attorneys and Counselors)
1700 Pacific Avenue Suite 3300, 75201
Telephone: 214-969-1700
Telecopy: 214-969-1751
Telex: 732 298
URL: http://www.tklaw.com
Austin, Texas Office: 1200 San Jacinto Center, 98 San Jacinto Boulevard, 78701.
Telephone: 512-469-6100.
Telecopy: 512-469-6180.
Fort Worth, Texas Office: 801 Cherry Street, Suite 1600, 76102.
Telephone: 817-347-1700.
Telecopy: 817-347-1799.
Houston, Texas Office: Thompson Knight Brown Parker & Leahy L.L.P., 1200 Smith Street, Suite 3600, 77002-4595.
Telephone: 713-654-8111.
Telecopier: 713-654-1871.
San Pedro Garza Garcia, Nuevo León, Mexico Office: Edificio Losoles PD-4, Av. Lázaro Cárdenas No. 2400 Pte., C.P. 66220.
Telephone: (52-8) 363-0096.
Telecopy: (52-8) 363-3067.

PARTNERS

Barbara B. Ferguson
J. Mike Holt
P. Mike McCullough
William R. Mureiko
Rust E. Reid
James Y. Robb III
Terry L. Simmons

SENIOR ATTORNEY

Shawna L. Brown

ASSOCIATE

Susan G. Henry

For Complete List of Firm Personnel, See General Section

For full biographical listings, see the Martindale-Hubbell Law Directory

WINN, BEAUDRY & WINN, LLP (AV)

A Limited Liability Partnership including Professional Corporations
4200 Thanksgiving Tower, 1601 Elm Street, 75201-7203
Telephone: 214-969-0001
Fax: 214-969-0005
Email: wbw@airmail.net

Edward B. Winn (P.C.)
G. Ward Beaudry (P.C.)
David B. Winn (Retired)
Joel H. Whitney
Tiffany A. Self

OF COUNSEL

Wallace H. Savage
Stanley C. Simon

For full biographical listings, see the Martindale-Hubbell Law Directory

*DENTON,** Denton Co.

PHILIPS, HOPKINS, EAMES & COBB, P.C. (AV)

525 North Locust, P.O. Box 2027, 76202-2027
Telephone: 940-566-7010; Metro 940-243-0946
Facsimile: 940-898-0502
Email: dentonlaw.com

Lawrence C. Collister
William P. Philips, Jr.

OF COUNSEL

George Hopkins

Representative Clients: First Federal Bank of North Texas; First State Bank of Texas, Denton, Texas; Sanger Bank, Sanger, Texas; BankOne, Texas, N.A.; Provident Bank, Denton, Texas; Dentex Title Co., Denton, Texas.

For full biographical listings, see the Martindale-Hubbell Law Directory

ROBISON & ROBISON (AV)

120 North Austin, 76201
Telephone: 940-380-0911
Fax: 940-381-5024
Email: robison@iglobal.net *URL:* http://www.wld.com/firm/robison-robison/denton

Douglas M. Robison
Bonnie Jean Robison

For full biographical listings, see the Martindale-Hubbell Law Directory

*EL PASO,** El Paso Co.

MAYFIELD & PERRENOT, P.C. (AV)

221 N. Kansas, Suite 1600, P.O. Box 2039, 79950
Telephone: 915-533-2468
Telecopier: 915-533-0620
Email: mayper@1eagle1.com

Richard B. Perrenot
Roger C. Davie
James R. Dennis
Jeffery W. McElroy

Lisa M. Power
Shelly Weatherly
Marina Mata De La Garza

OF COUNSEL

Ellis O. Mayfield
James B. McIntyre

For full biographical listings, see the Martindale-Hubbell Law Directory

*FORT WORTH,** Tarrant Co.

BROUDE, SMITH & JENNINGS, P.C. (AV)

309 West Seventh Street Suite 1100, 76102
Telephone: 817-335-1615
Metro: 817-654-3505
Fax: 817-335-1603

John S. Broude
Steven M. Smith
Cary L. Jennings
Kathryn Durham McGlinchey
Jerry Betsill

OF COUNSEL

Janna Ward Clarke

LEGAL SUPPORT PERSONNEL

Laura deLagerheim (Paralegal).

For full biographical listings, see the Martindale-Hubbell Law Directory

DECKER, JONES, MCMACKIN, MCCLANE, HALL & BATES, A PROFESSIONAL CORPORATION (AV)

2500 Bank One Tower, 500 Throckmorton Street, 76102-3812
Telephone: 817-336-2400; Metro: 817-429-5260
Fax: 817-332-3043; 336-2181
Email: email@deckerjones.com *URL:* http://www.deckerjones.com

Daniel L. Bates
Robert W. Decker
Mark S. Dugan
Janet L. Hahn
Randy J. Hall
Raymond B. Kelly, III
John B. McClane
John W. McMackin
Charles B. Milliken
Gary M. Moates
Bradley H. Rice
Jeffrey W. Storie
James L. Stripling
Brian K. Yost
Tamera H. Bennett
Arthur F. Zobal
Geoffrey A. Mantooth

Representative Clients: Howell Instruments, Inc.; Martin-Sprocket and Gear, Inc.; Williamson-Dickie Manufacturing Co.; Harbison-Fischer Manufacturing Co.; Employers Insurance of Texas; American International Group; Medical Protective Co.; Redman Homes, Inc.; Liberty Mutual Insurance.

For full biographical listings, see the Martindale-Hubbell Law Directory

Fort Worth—Continued

THOMPSON & KNIGHT L.L.P. (AV)

(Attorneys and Counselors)
801 Cherry Street, Suite 1600, 76102
Telephone: 817-347-1700
Telecopy: 817-347-1799
URL: http://www.tklaw.com
Dallas, Texas Office: 1700 Pacific Avenue, Suite 3300, 75201.
Telephone: 214-969-1700.
Telecopy: 214-969-1751.
Telex: 732298.
Austin, Texas Office: 1200 San Jacinto Center, 98 San Jacinto Boulevard, 78701.
Telephone: 512-469-6100.
Telecopy: 512-469-6180.
Houston, Texas Office: Thompson Knight Brown Parker & Leahy L.L.P., 1200 Smith Street, Suite 3600, 77002-4595.
Telephone: 713-654-8111.
Telecopier: 713-654-1871.
San Pedro Garza Garcia, Nuevo León, Mexico Office: Edificio Losoles PD-4, Av. Lázaro Cárdenas No. 2400 Pte., C.P. 66220.
Telephone: (52-8) 363-0096.
Telecopy: (52-8) 363-3067.

PARTNER

R Gordon Appleman

For Complete List of Firm Personnel, See General Section

For full biographical listings, see the Martindale-Hubbell Law Directory

FRISCO, Collin & Denton Cos.

WINIKATES & WINIKATES (AV)

Prosper State Bank Building, 7700 Main Street, P.O. Box 249, 75034-0249
Telephone: 972-335-1122
Fax: 972-335-1125

MEMBERS OF FIRM

Charles J. Winikates
Charles J. Winikates, Jr.
Regina W. Mentesana
Frances A. Fazio

For full biographical listings, see the Martindale-Hubbell Law Directory

*GREENVILLE,** Hunt Co.

MORGAN AND GOTCHER (AV)

2610-A Stonewall Street, P.O. Box 556, 75403-0556
Telephone: 903-455-3183
Metro Tel: 903-450-8800
Fax: 903-454-4654
Email: jhmorgan@koyote.com

J. Harris Morgan
Holly H. Gotcher

Representative Clients: Huffines Enterprises; Greenville Independent School District; International Cassettes, Inc.; Universal Health Services, Inc.; Hunt County Appraisal District; Bank One Greenville; Citizens Bank of Royce City.

For full biographical listings, see the Martindale-Hubbell Law Directory

*HOUSTON,** Harris Co.

SALLY S. ANDREWS (AV)

Two Bering Place, 800 Bering Drive, Suite 200, 77057-2130
Telephone: 713-787-6648
Fax: 713-787-6182
Email: andrews_nelson@compuserve.com

For full biographical listings, see the Martindale-Hubbell Law Directory

BAKER BOTTS L.L.P. (AV)

One Shell Plaza, 910 Louisiana, 77002
Telephone: 713-229-1234
Cable Address: "Boterlove"
Fax: 713-229-1522
Email: postmaster@bakerbotts.com *URL:* http://www.bakerbotts.com
Washington, D.C. Office: The Warner, 1299 Pennsylvania Avenue, N.W.
Telephone: 202-639-7700.
New York, New York Office: 599 Lexington Avenue.
Telephone: 212-705-5000.
Austin, Texas Office: 1600 San Jacinto Center, 98 San Jacinto Boulevard.
Telephone: 512-322-2500.
Dallas, Texas Office: 2001 Ross Avenue.
Telephone: 214-953-6500.
Moscow, Russia Office: 10 ul. Bolshaya Dimitrovka (formerly Pushkinskaya), 103031.
Telephone: 7095/921-5300 (Local); 7095/929-7070 (International).
London, England Office: 45 Ludgate Hill.
Telephone: 0171-778-1400 (Local); 011-44-171-778-1400 (International).

(See Next Column)

Baku, Azerbaijan Office: 6-10 Vagif Mustafa-zadeh Street, Third Floor, Icheri Sheher, 370004.
Telephone: 994-12-97-63-88 (Local); 011-994-12-97-63-88 (International).
Fax: 994-12-97-63-91 (Local); 011-994-12-97-63-91 (International)

MEMBERS OF FIRM

S. Stacy Eastland
Ronald W. Kesterson
John W. Porter
Robert M. Weylandt

SENIOR COUNSEL

J. Thomas Eubank

SPECIAL COUNSEL

Margaret W. Brown
Kristine Dubiel Maclay

ASSOCIATES

Brian D. Cororve
Stephen T. Dyer
Jeffrey E. Raley

For Complete List of Firm Personnel, See General Section

For full biographical listings, see the Martindale-Hubbell Law Directory

BAYLESS & STOKES (AV)

2931 Ferndale Street, 77098
Telephone: 713-522-2224
Fax: 713-522-2218
Email: bayless@baylessstokes.com

MEMBER OF FIRM

Dalia Browning Stokes

ASSOCIATE

Spencer W. Creed

For full biographical listings, see the Martindale-Hubbell Law Directory

CENATIEMPO & DITTA, LLP (AV)

1550 Two Houston Center, 909 Fannin, 77010-1050
Telephone: 713-655-1550
Fax: 713-655-9635

MEMBERS OF FIRM

Michael J. Cenatiempo
Louis M. Ditta

ASSOCIATES

Ray J. Black, Jr.
Douglas R. McCullough

For full biographical listings, see the Martindale-Hubbell Law Directory

CORDRAY & GOODRICH, PROFESSIONAL CORPORATION (AV)

3306 Sul Ross, 77098-1808
Telephone: 713-630-0600
Facsimile: 713-630-0017

Howard F. Cordray, Jr.
Christopher M. Goodrich
Richard Alan Tomlin
Gregory A. Goodrich
Glynn D. Nance, Jr.

OF COUNSEL

Ellen M. Lang
Van A. Cates
Robert G. Bailey

For full biographical listings, see the Martindale-Hubbell Law Directory

HORRIGAN & GOEHRS, L.L.P. (AV)

1000 Two Houston Center, 909 Fannin, 77010-1003
Telephone: 713-659-4200
Fax: 713-659-3804
Email: lawyers@horrgoehrs.com

Joseph S. Horrigan
Linda C. Goehrs

ASSOCIATES

Sharon C. Stodghill
Julie McDaniel Dallison

Reference: Northern Trust Bank of Texas.

For full biographical listings, see the Martindale-Hubbell Law Directory

KORMEIER & WALTERS (AV)

8705 Katy Freeway, Suite 400, P.O. Box 6512, 77265-6512
Telephone: 713-973-2777
Telecopier: 713-984-1141
Email: kwlawyer.com *URL:* http://www.kwlawyer.com

Victor A. Kormeier, Jr.
Richard B. Walters

For full biographical listings, see the Martindale-Hubbell Law Directory

*LUBBOCK,** Lubbock Co.

CRENSHAW, DUPREE & MILAM, L.L.P. (AV)

Norwest Center, 1500 Broadway, 10th Floor, P.O. Box 1499, 79408-1499
Telephone: 806-762-5281
Fax: 806-762-3510
Email: attorney@cdmlaw.com

(See Next Column)

CRENSHAW, DUPREE & MILAM L.L.P.—*Continued*

Chas. C. Crenshaw (1886-1964) Geo. W. Dupree (1890-1973)
James H. Milam (1911-1994)

MEMBERS OF FIRM

Cecil C. Kuhne
John Crews
William J. Wade
Jack McCutchin, Jr.
W C Bratcher
Layton Z. Woodul
David R. Cobb
Robert L. Duncan
W. Chris Boyer
Robert L. Jones
Mark W. Harmon
Mark O. Blankenship
Charlotte D. Bingham

ASSOCIATES

Sheila M. Kidwell
Matt D. Matzner
Jeff R. Lashaway
Taylor L. Pope

OF COUNSEL

Tom S. Milam
William R. Moss

For full biographical listings, see the Martindale-Hubbell Law Directory

*SAN ANTONIO,** Bexar Co.

LAW OFFICES OF JAMES R. BASS, INC. (AV)

9002 Wurzbach Road, 78240
Telephone: 210-614-4444
Fax: 210-614-7737
Email: JBASSLAW@AOL.COM *URL:* http://www.lawyers.com/basslaw

James R. Bass

Michele Kay Jura

Reference: Frost National Bank.

For full biographical listings, see the Martindale-Hubbell Law Directory

BENTON CLARK & TAYLOR, P.C. (AV)

105 South St. Marys Street, Suite 905, 78205
Telephone: 210-472-1800
Fax: 210-472-1872

Barry G. Benton
R. Christopher Clark
Richard M. Taylor, III

Phillip R. Hall

For full biographical listings, see the Martindale-Hubbell Law Directory

COX & SMITH INCORPORATED (AV)

112 East Pecan Street, Suite 1800, 78205-1521
Telephone: 210-554-5500
Fax: 210-226-8395
Email: info@coxsmith.com *URL:* http://www.coxsmith.com

Paul H. Smith
Richard T. Brady
William H. Lester, Jr.
Robert W. Nelson
R. Bradley Oxford
Harry W. Wolff, Jr.
Allan G. Paterson, Jr.
Abigail G. Kampmann
Carl A. Werner
Matthew S. Parkin
Joshua A. Sutin

For Complete List of Firm Personnel, See General Section

For full biographical listings, see the Martindale-Hubbell Law Directory

GIBBS AND SCHWARTZMAN (AV)

A Partnership including Professional Corporations
5717 Northwest Parkway, Suite 101, 78249
Telephone: 210-690-8858
Fax: 210-690-0024
Email: union@unionresource.com

Larry W. Gibbs (P.C.)
Mark A. Schwartzman (P.C.)

For full biographical listings, see the Martindale-Hubbell Law Directory

SCHOENBAUM, CURPHY & SCANLAN, P.C. (AV)

NationsBank Plaza, Suite 1775, 300 Convent Street, 78205-3744
Telephone: 210-224-4491
Fax: 210-224-7983

Stanley Schoenbaum
R. James Curphy
William Scanlan, Jr.
Alfred G. Holcomb
Banks M. Smith
Darin N. Digby
Patricia Flora Sitchler
Emily Harrison Liljenwall

Stacey Alison Warnix

For full biographical listings, see the Martindale-Hubbell Law Directory

TEXARKANA, Bowie Co.

PATTON, HALTOM, ROBERTS, MCWILLIAMS & GREER, L.L.P. (AV)

A Registered Limited Liability Partnership including Professional Corporations
700 Hibernia National Bank Building, P.O. Box 1928, 75504-1928
Telephone: 903-794-3341
Fax: 903-792-6542; 903-792-0448
URL: http://www.pattonhaltom.com

William B. Roberts

For Complete List of Firm Personnel, See General Section

For full biographical listings, see the Martindale-Hubbell Law Directory

*WICHITA FALLS,** Wichita Co.

GIBSON, HOTCHKISS, ROACH & DAVENPORT (AV)

807 8th Street, 8th Floor, 76301
Telephone: 940-322-7856
Fax: 940-322-1204
Email: ed@ghrdlaw.com *URL:* http://www.lawyers.com/ghrdlaw

MEMBER OF FIRM

Erwin Davenport

Representative Clients: American National Bank, Wichita Falls; First National Bank of Bowie; Wichita Falls PCA; Bennett Production Co.; Red River Authority of Texas; Burcamp Steel Co.

For Complete List of Firm Personnel, See General Section

For full biographical listings, see the Martindale-Hubbell Law Directory

UTAH

*SALT LAKE CITY,** Salt Lake Co.

CALLISTER NEBEKER & MCCULLOUGH, A PROFESSIONAL CORPORATION (AV)

Gateway Tower East, Suite 900, 10 East South Temple, 84133
Telephone: 801-530-7300
Telecopier: 801-364-9127
Email: mjeaston@cnmlaw.com *URL:* http://www.cnmlaw.com

Leland S. McCullough
Craig F. McCullough
George E. Harris, Jr.
Damon E. Coombs
Laurie S. Hart
Douglas K. Cummings

David R. York
Lee S. McCullough, III

Representative Clients: Zions First National Bank Trust Department.

For Complete List of Firm Personnel, See General Section

For full biographical listings, see the Martindale-Hubbell Law Directory

KIRTON & MCCONKIE, A PROFESSIONAL CORPORATION (AV)

1800 Eagle Gate Tower, 60 East South Temple, 84111
Telephone: 801-328-3600
Telecopier: 801-321-4893

Lorin C. Barker
Fred D. Essig

For Complete List of Firm Personnel, See General Section

For full biographical listings, see the Martindale-Hubbell Law Directory

PARR WADDOUPS BROWN GEE & LOVELESS, A PROFESSIONAL CORPORATION (AV)

Suite 1300, 185 South State Street, 84111-1537
Telephone: 801-532-7840
Fax: 801-532-7750
URL: http://www.pwlaw.com

Kent H. Collins
Stephen M. Sargent

For Complete List of Firm Personnel, See General Section

For full biographical listings, see the Martindale-Hubbell Law Directory

PARSONS, DAVIES, KINGHORN & PETERS, P.C. (AV)

185 South State Street, Suite 700, 84111
Telephone: 801-363-4300
Facsimile: 801-363-4378
Email: Attorneys@pdkplaw.com

(See Next Column)

PARSONS, DAVIES, KINGHORN & PETERS P.C., *Salt Lake City—Continued*

John M. Parsons
Bill Thomas Peters
Langdon T. Owen, Jr.
John N. Brems
Ken P. Jones
John S. Bradley

For Complete List of Firm Personnel, See General Section

For full biographical listings, see the Martindale-Hubbell Law Directory

RAY, QUINNEY & NEBEKER, A PROFESSIONAL CORPORATION (AV)

79 South Main Street, Suite 400, P.O. Box 45385, 84145-0385
Telephone: 801-532-1500
Fax: 801-532-7543
Email: rqn@rqn.com *URL:* http://www.rqn.com
Provo, Utah Office: 92 North University Avenue, Suite 210, 84601-4420.
Telephone: 801-342-2400.
Fax: 801-375-8379.
Albuquerque, New Mexico Office: Suite 620, 40 First Plaza, N.W.
Telephone: 505-243-6665.
Fax: 505-764-9890.

Clark P. Giles
Narrvel E. Hall
Herbert C. Livsey
D. Jay Curtis
Gerald T. Snow
David K. Lauritzen
John R. Madsen
Calvin C. Curtis
Thomas A. Mecham

Representative Clients: First Security Bank, N.A.; Borden, Inc.; Salt Lake Organizing Committee for the Winter Olympic Games of 2002; Southern Pacific Transportation; Utah Power & Light Co.; Travelers Insurance Co.; U.S. West.

For Complete List of Firm Personnel, See General Section

For full biographical listings, see the Martindale-Hubbell Law Directory

STRONG & HANNI, A PROFESSIONAL CORPORATION (AV)

Sixth Floor Boston Building, 9 Exchange Place, 84111
Telephone: 801-532-7080
Fax: 801-596-1508
Email: pfishler@strongandhanni.com

Gordon R. Strong (1909-1969)
Glenn C. Hanni
Henry E. Heath
Philip R. Fishler
Roger H. Bullock
R. Scott Williams
Dennis M. Astill (Managing Partner)
Stuart H. Schultz
Paul M. Belnap
Stephen J. Trayner
Joseph J. Joyce
Bradley Wm. Bowen
Robert L. Janicki
Elizabeth L. Willey
H. Burt Ringwood
Peter H. Christensen
David R. Nielson

Kevin D. Swenson
Catherine M. Larson
Kristin Van Orman
Darren K. Nelson
Peter H. Barlow
Steven T. Densley
Jennifer C. Polley-Abramson
Shawn T. Welch

OF COUNSEL

Robert A. Burton

Representative Clients: State Farm Mutual Automobile Insurance Co.; Standard Accident Insurance Co.; United Services Automobile Assn.; Western Casualty & Surety Co.; Government Employees Insurance Co.; Guaranty Mutual Life Co.

For full biographical listings, see the Martindale-Hubbell Law Directory

VAN COTT, BAGLEY, CORNWALL & MCCARTHY, A PROFESSIONAL CORPORATION (AV)

50 South Main Street, Suite 1600, P.O. Box 45340, 84145-0340
Telephone: 801-532-3333
Telecopier: 801-534-0058
Email: info@vancott.com *URL:* http://www.vancott.com
Ogden, Utah Office: 2404 Washington Boulevard, Suite 900.
Telephone: 801-394-5783.
Park City, Utah Office: 2200 Park Avenue, Suite C200-A.
Telephone: 435-649-3889.

David E. Sloan
Stephen D. Swindle

Kevin L. Jones
Stephen R. Sloan

OF COUNSEL

David E. Salisbury

For Complete List of Firm Personnel, See General Section

For full biographical listings, see the Martindale-Hubbell Law Directory

VERMONT

BARRE, Washington Co.

OTTERMAN & ALLEN, P.C. (AV)

188 Washington Street, P.O. Box 473, 05641
Telephone: 802-479-2552

Harvey B. Otterman, Jr.
O. Fay Allen, Jr. (Retired)
David A. Otterman
Andrea L. Gallitano

Representative Clients: Fleet National Bank of Mass.; Bank of Boston; County of Orange; Benoit Electric, Inc.; Towns of Fairlee, Orange, West Fairlee, Groton, Topsham.

For full biographical listings, see the Martindale-Hubbell Law Directory

*BURLINGTON,** Chittenden Co.

GRAVEL AND SHEA, A PROFESSIONAL CORPORATION (AV)

Corporate Plaza, 76 St. Paul Street, P.O. Box 369, 05402-0369
Telephone: 802-658-0220
Fax: 802-658-1456

William G. Post, Jr.
Stephen P. Magowan

OF COUNSEL

Clarke A. Gravel
Charles T. Shea

For Complete List of Firm Personnel, See General Section

For full biographical listings, see the Martindale-Hubbell Law Directory

WALLINGFORD, Rutland Co.

CHRISTOPHER A. WEBBER, JR. (AV)

12 N. Main Street, P.O. Box 576, 05773
Telephone: 802-446-2446
Fax: 802-446-3356

For full biographical listings, see the Martindale-Hubbell Law Directory

VIRGINIA

ALEXANDRIA, (Independent City)

JOY S. CHAMBERS (AV)

201 North Fairfax Street, Suite 12, 22314
Telephone: 703-684-5477
Fax: 703-684-1045
Email: JOYS@WORLDWEB.NET *URL:* http://www.vitalaging.com

LEGAL SUPPORT PERSONNEL

Stacie Crookston (Paralegal and Office Manager)

For full biographical listings, see the Martindale-Hubbell Law Directory

E. MICHAEL PATURIS (AV)

Lee Street Square, 431 North Lee Street, 22314-2301
Telephone: 703-836-2501
Facsimile: 703-836-4487
Email: paturis@worldweb.net

For full biographical listings, see the Martindale-Hubbell Law Directory

GORDON P. PEYTON, P.C. (AV)

908 King Street, Suite 201, P.O. Box 25456, 22313
Telephone: 703-549-0200
Facsimile: 703-549-2370
Email: gpeyton.law@worldnet.att.net

Carl Budwesky (1891-1982)
Gordon P. Peyton

References: Burke & Herbert Bank & Trust Co.

For full biographical listings, see the Martindale-Hubbell Law Directory

*CHARLOTTESVILLE,** Charlottesville City Co.

ROBERT M. MUSSELMAN & ASSOCIATES (AV)

413 7th Street, N.E., P.O. Box 254, 22902
Telephone: 804-977-4500
Fax: 804-293-5727
Email: rmmesquire@aol.com

ASSOCIATES

Carolyn C. Musselman
Jonathan B. Burns
Douglas E. Little

(See Next Column)

ROBERT M. MUSSELMAN & ASSOCIATES—*Continued*

LEGAL SUPPORT PERSONNEL

Eleanor P. Carter (Legal Secretary and Real Estate Paralegal)
Faye M. McBurney (Legal Secretary and Bankruptcy Paralegal)

For full biographical listings, see the Martindale-Hubbell Law Directory

*EASTVILLE,** Northampton Co.

TANKARD AND GORDON (AV)

Court Green, P.O. Box 5, 23347-0005
Telephone: 757-678-5117
Fax: 757-678-7664
Email: lawyer@esva.net

MEMBERS OF FIRM

Baxley T. Tankard
Croxton Gordon

Representative Clients: Chesapeake Bay Bridge and Tunnel District; A & N Electric Cooperative; First Virginia Bank-Tidewater, Exmore, Virginia.
Approved Attorneys for: Lawyers Title Insurance Corp.; Ticor Title Insurance Co.

For full biographical listings, see the Martindale-Hubbell Law Directory

*FAIRFAX,** (Ind. City; Seat of Fairfax Co.)

DOHERTY & SHERIDAN, L.L.P. (AV)

8408 Arlington Boulevard, Suite 200, 22031
Telephone: 703-698-7700
Facsimile: 703-641-9645
Email: d&s.law@erols.com
Washington, D.C. Office: 1050 17th Street, Suite 1250, 20036-5510.
Bethesda, Maryland Office: 4701 Sangamore Road, Suite S-225, 20816.
Vero Beach, Florida Office: 1701 Highway AIA, Suite 220, 32963.

MEMBER OF FIRM

Cornelius H. Doherty, Jr.

For full biographical listings, see the Martindale-Hubbell Law Directory

MACKALL, MACKALL & GIBB, A PROFESSIONAL CORPORATION (AV)

4031 Chain Bridge Road, 22030
Telephone: 703-273-0320
Fax: 703-273-0267
Email: mackall@wizard.net

Henry C. Mackall
Douglass S. Mackall, III
Mary D. Wagaman

For full biographical listings, see the Martindale-Hubbell Law Directory

McCANDLISH & LILLARD, A PROFESSIONAL CORPORATION (AV)

Fair Oaks Plaza, 11350 Random Hills Road, Suite 500, 22030-7429
Telephone: 703-273-2288
Fax: 703-352-4300
Email: mccand@patriot.net *URL:* http://www.mccandlaw.com
Leesburg, Virginia Office: 305 Harrison Street, S.E., Third Floor.
Telephone: 703-737-0200.
Fax: 703-737-0165.

Robert J. McCandlish, Jr. (1909-1996)
Rothwell J. Lillard (1910-1989)
Jesse B. Wilson, III
Peter A. Arntson
Gary W. Brown
Randolph A. Sutliff
Robert H. J. Loftus
William McCauley Arnold
Stephen C. Price
Stephen K. Fox
Douglas J. Sanderson
R. Peyton Mahaffey
William L. Carey
John W. Farrell
Eric J. Berghold
Ralph M. Tener
Vicki L. Layman
Adam W. Smith

Daniel P. Lyon
Lawrence J. McClafferty
Brian R. Sanderson

For full biographical listings, see the Martindale-Hubbell Law Directory

FALLS CHURCH, (Independent City)

MALONEY & YURACHEK, P.C. (AV)

104 North Oak Street, 22046-3234
Telephone: 703-237-1470
Fax: 703-237-4328
URL: http://www.maloneylaw.com

James H. Maloney
Wendy B. Yurachek

For full biographical listings, see the Martindale-Hubbell Law Directory

NORFOLK, (Independent City)

GOLDBLATT, LIPKIN & COHEN, P.C. (AV)

Suite 300, 415 St. Paul's Boulevard, P.O. Box 3505, 23514
Telephone: 757-627-6225
Telefax: 757-622-3698

Paul M. Lipkin
Robert S. Cohen
Steven M. Legum
Mary G. Commander
Neal C. Schulwolf

For full biographical listings, see the Martindale-Hubbell Law Directory

PAYNE, GATES, FARTHING & RADD, P.C. (AV)

15th Floor, Dominion Tower, 999 Waterside Drive, Suite 1515, 23510-3309
Telephone: 757-640-1500
Facsimile: 757-627-6583
URL: http://www.paynegates.com

Ronald M. Gates
Philip R. Farthing
Anthony F. Radd
Glen M. Robertson
Brian R. Dinning
Todd J. Preti
Marshall A. Winslow, Jr.

C. Arthur Robinson, II
Stephen E. Heretick
Raymond L. Hogge, Jr.

OF COUNSEL

Charles E. Payne

For full biographical listings, see the Martindale-Hubbell Law Directory

*ORANGE,** Orange Co.

SHACKELFORD, HONENBERGER, THOMAS, WILLIS & GREGG, P.L.C. (AV)

149 West Main Street, P.O. Box 871, 22960
Telephone: 540-672-2711
Fax: 540-672-2714
Email: shtwg1@ns.gemlink.com
Culpeper, Virginia Office: 147 West Davis Street, P.O. Box 1002.
Telephone: 540-825-0305.

OF COUNSEL

Virginius R. Shackelford, Jr.

MEMBERS OF FIRM

Virginius R. Shackelford, III
Christopher J. Honenberger
Frank A. Thomas, III
Jere M. H. Willis, III (Resident, Culpeper, Virginia Office)
Sarah Collins Honenberger
Sean D. Gregg

For full biographical listings, see the Martindale-Hubbell Law Directory

RICHMOND, (Independent City)

LITTLE, PARSLEY & CLUVERIUS, P.C. (AV)

1300 Federal Reserve Bank Building, P.O. Box 555, 23218
Telephone: 804-644-4100
Facsimile: 804-644-0800
Email: admin@lpc-va.com

George B. Little
J. Terry Parsley
James K. Cluverius

Nathan McAdams Lord
Andrew M. Lohmann

Reference: Crestar Bank.

For full biographical listings, see the Martindale-Hubbell Law Directory

WILLIAMS, MULLEN, CLARK & DOBBINS, A PROFESSIONAL CORPORATION (AV)

Two James Center, 1021 East Cary Street, P.O. Box 1320, 23218-1320
Telephone: 804-643-1991
Fax: 804-783-6507
URL: http://www.wmcd.com
Newport News Office: Harbor Bank Center, Suite 210, One Old Oyster Point Road, 23602-7119.
Telephone: 757-249-5100.
Fax: 757-249-5109.
Virginia Beach Office: One Columbus Center, 23462-6763.
Telephone: 757-499-8800.
Fax: 757-473-0395.
Vienna Office: 1593 Spring Hill Road, Suite 510, 22182.
Telephone: 703-760-5200.
Fax: 703-748-0244.
Washington, D.C. Office: The Farragut Building, 900 17th Street, N.W., Suite 700, 20006.
Telephone: 202-293-0213.
Fax: 804-783-6507. Fax Within D.C.: 202-293-5939.

(See Next Column)

WILLIAMS, MULLEN, CLARK & DOBBINS A PROFESSIONAL CORPORATION, *Richmond—Continued*

London, England Office: Blake Lodge, Bridge Lane, SW11 3AD.
Telephone: (011-44-71) 223-2756.
Fax: (011-44-71) 350-0156.
Riyadh, Saudi Arabia Affiliate Office: Saudi-American Legal Consultants Commercial Building #2, Diplomatic Quarter, P.O. Box 57270, 11574.
Telephone: (011-966-1) 488-1563.
Fax: (011-966-1) 488-0542.

David D. Addison
C. Richard Davis
Robert L. Musick, Jr.
Craig L. Rascoe
Derek L. Smith
Julious P. Smith, Jr.
Fielding L. Williams, Jr.
Russell Alton Wright

Mark S. Shepard
John Henderson Turner III

For Complete List of Firm Personnel, See General Section

For full biographical listings, see the Martindale-Hubbell Law Directory

ROANOKE, Roanoke City Co.

WOOTEN & HART, A PROFESSIONAL CORPORATION (AV)

707 Building, Suite 300, P.O. Box 12247, 24024-2247
Telephone: 540-343-2451; 540-342-9672
Telecopier: 540-345-6417
URL: http://www.wootenhart.com

George W. Wooten
David B. Hart
L. Thompson Hanes
Susan A. Waddell
Bradley D. McGraw
John L. Cooley
Thomas W. Farrell
Paul C. Kuhnel
Peter D. Vieth

David W. Hearn
John Mark Cooley
Christopher W. Stevens
Elizabeth D. Guilbert
Eunice Park Austin

OF COUNSEL

M. Lanier Woodrum

Representative Clients: Wachovia Bank; St. Paul Insurance Cos.
Approved Attorneys for: Lawyers Title Insurance Corp.
Reference: First Union National Bank.

For full biographical listings, see the Martindale-Hubbell Law Directory

VIENNA, Fairfax Co.

REES, BROOME & DIAZ, P.C. (AV)

Ninth Floor, 8133 Leesburg Pike, 22182
Telephone: 703-790-1911
Telecopier: 703-848-2530
Email: attorney@RBDlaw.com *URL:* http://www.rbdlaw.com

Joel M. Birken
Raymond J. Diaz
Jonathan J. Broome, Jr.
John F. Boland
Michael L. O'Reilly
Henry F. Brandenstein, Jr.
Robert E. Scully, Jr.
Juan R. Cardenas
Bruce E. Titus
Peter S. Philbin
Andrew B. Golkow
William P. Daly, Jr.
Susan Richards Salen
Richard M. Ware, Jr.
Joseph F. Jackson
Mitchell N. Roth

Edward J. O'Connell, III
Henry Joseph Schuldinger
Robert A. Feisee
Nancy J. O'Reilly
Mark Patrick Graham
Marie Annette Buntua
Kenneth C. Germer
Michele Claire Meiners
William M. Vermette
Todd A. Sinkins
Mary Catherine H. Gibbs
James M. Rees (1941-1986)

For full biographical listings, see the Martindale-Hubbell Law Directory

SMOLEN & PLEVY P.C. (AV)

Seventh Floor 8045 Leesburg Pike, 22182
Telephone: 703-790-1900
Telecopier: 703-790-1754
Email: smolenplevy@smolenplevy.com

Jason D. Smolen
Alan B. Plevy
Daniel H. Ruttenberg

For full biographical listings, see the Martindale-Hubbell Law Directory

WASHINGTON

PULLMAN, Whitman Co.

AITKEN, SCHAUBLE, PATRICK, NEILL & RUFF (AV)

210 Downtown Professional Building, P.O. Box 307, 99163
Telephone: 509-334-3505
Fax: 509-334-5367
Colfax, Washington Office: North 209 Main Street.
Telephone: 509-397-3091.
St. John, Washington Office: Inland Empire Milling Co. Building, North 4th Park Street.
Telephone: 509-648-3346.

MEMBERS OF FIRM

Albert J. Schauble
Robert F. Patrick
Howard M. Neill
Linda Schauble-Ruff

OF COUNSEL

James D. McMannis (Retired)
Donald L. McMannis (Retired)

Representative Clients: Johnson Union Warehouse Co.; Bank of Pullman; Uniontown Coop.; St. John Grain Growers; Lamont Bank of St. John; Inland Empire Milling Co.
References: Seattle-First National Bank, Pullman Branch; Bank of Pullman; The U.S. Bank of Washington.

For full biographical listings, see the Martindale-Hubbell Law Directory

*SEATTLE,** King Co.

BRUCE R. MOEN (AV)

3050 Westin Building, 2001 Sixth Avenue, 98121-2522
Telephone: 206-441-1156
Fax: 206-441-6727
Email: moen@wolfenet.com *URL:* http://www.brmnet.com

For full biographical listings, see the Martindale-Hubbell Law Directory

WEST VIRGINIA

*CHARLESTON,** Kanawha Co.

JACKSON & KELLY (AV)

1600 Laidley Tower, P.O. Box 553, 25322
Telephone: 304-340-1000
Fax: 304-340-1130
Email: info@jacksonkelly.com *URL:* http://www.jacksonkelly.com
Martinsburg, West Virginia Office: 300 Foxcroft Avenue, P.O. Box 1068.
Telephone: 304-263-8800.
Fax: 304-263-7110.
Morgantown, West Virginia Office: 6000 Hampton Center, P.O. Box 619.
Telephone: 304-599-3000.
Fax: 304-285-2040.
New Martinsville, West Virginia Office: 256 Russell Avenue, P.O. Box 68.
Telephone: 304-455-1751.
Fax: 304-455-6314.
Parkersburg, West Virginia Office: 412 Market Street, Suite 202, P.O. Box 1144.
Telephone: 304-424-3490.
Fax: 304-424-3499.
Fairmont, West Virginia Office: 1000 Technology Drive, Suite 1310.
Telephone: 304-368-2000.
Fax: 304-368-2020.
Lexington, Kentucky Office: 175 East Main Street, Suite 500, P.O. Box 2150.
Telephone: 606-255-9500.
Fax: 606-281-6478.
Washington, D. C. Office: 2401 Pennsylvania Avenue, N.W., Suite 400.
Telephone: 202-973-0200.
Fax: 202-973-0232.
Denver, Colorado Office: Suite 2710, 1660 Lincoln Street.
Telephone: 303-390-0003.
Fax: 303-390-0040.
Wheeling, West Virginia Office: 1144 Market Street.
Telephone: 304-233-4000.
Fax: 304-233-4077.

MEMBERS OF FIRM

J. S. Francis (Resident, New Martinsville, West Virginia Office)
Louis S. Southworth, II
Thomas G. Freeman, II
Jeffrey J. Yost (Resident, Lexington, Kentucky Office)
Eric H. London (Morgantown, West Virginia Office)
Anthony J. Ferrise

ASSOCIATE

Patience Ann Alexander

For Complete List of Firm Personnel, See General Section

For full biographical listings, see the Martindale-Hubbell Law Directory

*CLARKSBURG,** Harrison Co.

JOHNSON, SIMMERMAN & BROUGHTON, L.C. (AV)

Ogden Building, 203 West Main Street, 26301
Telephone: 304-624-6555; 304-623-4900
Telecopier: 304-623-4933
Mailing Address: P.O. Box 150, Clarksburg, West Virginia, 26302-0150

Charles G. Johnson
Marcia Allen Broughton
Frank E. Simmerman, Jr.
Bridget D. Furbee
Robin Queen Triplett

For full biographical listings, see the Martindale-Hubbell Law Directory

MCNEER, HIGHLAND, MCMUNN AND VARNER, L.C. (AV)

One Valley Bank Building, P.O. Drawer 2040, 26302-2040
Telephone: 304-626-1100
Facsimile: 304-623-3035
Martinsburg Office: 2520 Aikens Center, P.O. Box 2509.
Telephone: 304-264-4621.
Fax: 304-264-8623.
Parkersburg Office: 404 Market Street, Suite 204, P.O. Box 1507.
Telephone: 304-422-7193.
Facsimile: 304-422-7196.

C. David McMunn
J. Cecil Jarvis
James A. Varner
Robert W. Trumble (Resident, Martinsburg Office)
Catherine D. Munster
James N. Riley
Steven R. Bratke (Resident, Parkersburg Office)
Michael J. Novotny (Resident, Martinsburg Office)
Dennis M. Shreve
Geraldine S. Roberts
William F. Rohrbaugh (Resident, Martinsburg Office)
Gregory H. Schillace
Judy L. Shanholtz
Tiffany R. Durst
Gene W. Bailey, II

OF COUNSEL

James E. McNeer
Cecil B. Highland, Jr.
William L. Fury

Representative Clients: One Valley Bank of Clarksburg, National Assn.; Bruceton Bank; Harrison County Bank; Nationwide Mutual Insurance Cos.; Clarksburg Publishing Co.; C.I.T. Financial Services; State Automobile Mutual Insurance Co.; United Hospital Center, Inc.; West Virginia Coals, Inc.; Swanson Plating Co.

For full biographical listings, see the Martindale-Hubbell Law Directory

HUNTINGTON, Cabell & Wayne Cos.

DAVID H. DAUGHERTY (AV)

401 10th Street, Suite 350, 25701
Telephone: 304-523-0131
Fax: 304-523-0132

For full biographical listings, see the Martindale-Hubbell Law Directory

WISCONSIN

*GREEN BAY,** Brown Co.

GEIMER LAW FIRM, S.C. (AV)

2301 Riverside Drive, 54301
Telephone: 414-432-4433
Fax: 414-432-4905

Robert H. Geimer

For full biographical listings, see the Martindale-Hubbell Law Directory

LAKE GENEVA, Walworth Co.

BRADEN & OLSON (AV)

716 Wisconsin Street, P.O. Box 940, 53147
Telephone: 414-248-6636
Fax: 414-248-2901
Email: bando@genevaonline.com

MEMBERS OF FIRM

Berwyn B. Braden
John O. Olson

ASSOCIATES

Christine Tomas
Daniel S. Draper

For full biographical listings, see the Martindale-Hubbell Law Directory

*MADISON,** Dane Co.

AXLEY BRYNELSON, LLP (AV)

(Formerly Brynelson, Herrick, Bucaida, Dorschel & Armstrong Including the former Easton & Assoc., S.C.)
2 East Mifflin Street, P.O. Box 1767, 53701-1767
Telephone: 608-257-5661
Fax: 608-257-5444
Email: law@axley.com *URL:* http://www.axley.com

MEMBERS OF FIRM

Daniel T. Hardy
Steven A. Brezinski

ASSOCIATE

Steven E. Grimm

For Complete List of Firm Personnel, See General Section

For full biographical listings, see the Martindale-Hubbell Law Directory

BALISLE & ROBERSON, S.C. (AV)

217 South Hamilton, Suite 302, P.O. Box 870, 53701-0870
Telephone: 608-259-8702
Fax: 608-259-0807
Email: office@mail.b-rlaw.com

Linda S. Balisle
Linda Roberson
Jane Dragisic Clark

ASSOCIATE

Sarah A. Davies

LEGAL SUPPORT PERSONNEL

Diana K. Fleming
Anne C. Harrington (Paralegal)
Laura M. Roenning (Paralegal)

For full biographical listings, see the Martindale-Hubbell Law Directory

NEIDER & BOUCHER, S.C. (AV)

440 Science Drive, P.O. Box 5510, 53705-0510
Telephone: 608-661-4500
Facsimile: 608-661-4510
URL: http://www.neiderboucher.com
URL: http://www.lawyers.com/neider&boucher-sc

Ronald C. Berman
Charles E. Neider
Joseph W. Boucher
Steven C. Underwood

Susan M. De Groot
Cynthia L. Richson
Erik W. Ibele
Matthew L. Schemmel
Rana Kang
Kent L. Schlienger
Dean T. Stange

OF COUNSEL

Ralph M. Cagle
Ronald R. Smith

For full biographical listings, see the Martindale-Hubbell Law Directory

STROUD, WILLINK & HOWARD, LLC (AV)

25 West Main Street, Suite 300, P.O. Box 2236, 53701
Telephone: 608-257-2281
Fax: 608-257-7643
Email: email@stroudlaw.com

MEMBERS OF FIRM

C. Vernon Howard
Robert J. Schwab
Robert R. Stroud
Carolyn A. Hegge
Joseph P. Bartol

OF COUNSEL

Seward Ritchey Stroud
Donald R. Stroud
Dale R. Thompson

ASSOCIATES

Sverre David Roang
Peter J. Richter
Norman D. Farnam

Representative Clients: William F. Vilas Estate; Wisconsin Farm Bereau Federation; Anchor Bank; SSB; The Wisconson Cheese; J.H. Findorff & Son, Inc.; Edward Kramer & Sons, Inc.; Hilldale Shopping Center; American T.V. & Appliance of Madison, Inc.; Demco, Inc.; Schoep's Ice Cream.

For Complete List of Firm Personnel, See General Section

For full biographical listings, see the Martindale-Hubbell Law Directory

*MILWAUKEE,** Milwaukee Co.

CHERNOV, STERN & KRINGS, S.C. (AV)

Suite 1275, Two Plaza East, 330 East Kilbourn Avenue, 53202
Telephone: 414-276-4080
Fax: 414-276-4152
Email: mail@chernovlaw.com *URL:* http://www.lawyers.com/chernovlaw

OF COUNSEL

Ben L. Chernov

For full biographical listings, see the Martindale-Hubbell Law Directory

Milwaukee—Continued

DAVIS & KUELTHAU, S.C. (AV)

111 East Kilbourn Avenue, Suite 1400, 53202-6613
Telephone: 414-276-0200
Facsimile: 414-276-9369
Cable Address: "Shiplaw"
Email: info@daviskuelthau.com *URL:* http://www.daviskuelthau.com
Madison, Wisconsin Office: Ten East Doty Street, Suite 600, P.O. Box 1068, 53703.
Telephone: 608-280-8235.
Fax: 608-280-8231.
Sheboygan, Wisconsin Office: 605 North Eighth, Suite 610, P.O. Box 1287.
Telephone: 920-451-1461.
Fax: 920-451-1465.
Green Bay, Wisconsin Office: 414 East Walnut Street, Suite 240.
Telephone: 920-435-9378.
Fax: 920-435-9391.

Dianne S. Cauble
Robert E. Kuelthau
Gregory J. Sell

OF COUNSEL

John G. Vergeront

Catherine M. Priebe Hertzberg

For full biographical listings, see the Martindale-Hubbell Law Directory

---

DRINKA, LEVINE & MASSON, S.C. (AV)

2000 Milwaukee Center, 111 East Kilbourn Avenue, 53202-6618
Telephone: 414-291-6080
Fax: 414-291-6090
URL: http://www.lawyers.com/drinkalevine&masson

Judith A. Drinka
Micaela H. Levine
Grace M. Masson

For full biographical listings, see the Martindale-Hubbell Law Directory

---

MEISSNER TIERNEY FISHER & NICHOLS S.C. (AV)

The Milwaukee Center, 111 East Kilbourn Avenue, 19th Floor, 53202-6622
Telephone: 414-273-1300
Facsimile: 414-273-5840
URL: http://www.mtfn.com

Joseph E. Tierney III
Thomas J. Nichols
Randal J. Brotherhood

OF COUNSEL

Paul F. Meissner

For full biographical listings, see the Martindale-Hubbell Law Directory

---

QUARLES & BRADY LLP (AV)

411 East Wisconsin Avenue, 53202-4497
Telephone: 414-277-5000
Fax: 414-271-3552
URL: http://www.quarles.com
Madison, Wisconsin Office: Firstar Plaza, One South Pinckney Street, P.O. Box 2113, 53701-2113.
Telephone: 608-251-5000.
Fax: 608-251-9166.
West Palm Beach, Florida Office: 222 Lakeview Avenue, 4th Floor, 33401.
Telephone: 561-653-5000.
Fax: 561-653-5333.
Naples, Florida Office: Barnett Center, 4501 Tamiami Trail North, Suite 300, 34103-3060.
Telephone: 941-262-5959.
Fax: 941-434-4999.
Phoenix, Arizona Office: One Camelback Building, One East Camelback Road, Suite 400, 85012-1649.
Telephone: 602-230-5500.
Fax: 602-230-5598.
Chicago, Illinois Office: Quarles & Brady LLC, Citicorp Center, 500 West Madison Street, Suite 3700.
Telephone: 312-715-5000.
Fax: 312-715-5155.

MEMBERS OF FIRM
(ALPHABETICALLY BY YEAR OF ADMISSION TO BAR)

Jeremy C. Shea (Resident, Madison Office)
Donald S. Taitelman
Peter J. Lettenberger
Henry J. Loos
David L. Kinnamon
Gary H. Kline (Resident, Chicago, Illinois Office)
Anthony W. Asmuth, III
Thomas E. Maloney (Resident, Naples, Florida Office)
Thomas A. Polachek (Resident, Chicago, Illinois Office)
Thomas E. Chomicz (Resident, Chicago, Illinois Office)
Steven R. Duback
John R. Maynard
James F. Daly
John H. Lhost
John T. Bannen
Patrick J. Goebel
Paul J. Tilleman

(See Next Column)

MEMBERS OF FIRM
(ALPHABETICALLY BY YEAR OF ADMISSION TO BAR) (Continued)

Sally C. Merrell
Kimberly Leach Johnson (Resident, Naples, Florida Office)
Kathleen A. Gray
Sarah M. Linsley (Resident, Chicago, Illinois Office)
Jeffrey L. Elverman
Patrick J. Bitterman (Resident, Chicago, Illinois Office)

OF COUNSEL

A. William Asmuth, Jr.
Dale L. Sorden
John S. Sammond (Resident, West Palm Beach, Florida Office)
David L. MacGregor

ASSOCIATES

Chris K. Gawart
Samara S. Holland (Resident, Naples, Florida Office)
Stephen R. White
Susan Kubar (Resident, Naples, Florida Office)

For Complete List of Firm Personnel, See General Section

For full biographical listings, see the Martindale-Hubbell Law Directory

---

WALSH & KEATING, S.C. (AV)

1505 Wawatosa Avenue, 53213
Telephone: 414-257-9929
Fax: 414-257-9959
URL: http://www.lawyers.com/walshandkeating

Gerald S. Walsh
David C. Keating

ASSOCIATE

Peter J. Walsh

OF COUNSEL

Lloyd W. Herrold

For full biographical listings, see the Martindale-Hubbell Law Directory

---

*OSHKOSH,** Winnebago Co.

CURTIS LAW OFFICE (AV)

2905 Universal Street, P.O. Box 2845, 54903-2845
Telephone: 920-233-1010
Fax: 920-233-8053
Email: osowski@execpc.com

Beth Driscoll Osowski

Reference: M & I Bank.

For full biographical listings, see the Martindale-Hubbell Law Directory

---

WYOMING

*BUFFALO,** Johnson Co.

KIRVEN & KIRVEN, P.C. (AV)

104 Fort Street, P.O. Box 640, 82834
Telephone: 307-684-2248
Fax: 307-684-2242
Email: tkirven@wyo.com

William J. Kirven (Retired)
Dennis M. Kirven
Timothy J. Kirven

Representative Clients: Texaco Inc.; Wyoming Bank and Trust Co.; Buffalo Federal Savings & Loan Assn.; Reeves Concrete Products; Gordon Ranch; Powder River Corporation Reservoir; TR Ranch; School District Coalition; City of Buffalo.

For full biographical listings, see the Martindale-Hubbell Law Directory

---

*CASPER,** Natrona Co.

BROWN, DREW & MASSEY, LLP (AV)

Casper Business Center, Suite 800, 123 West First Street, 82601-2486
Telephone: 307-234-1000
800-877-6755
Telefax: 307-265-8025
Email: brwndrew@coffey.com

MEMBERS OF FIRM

Morris R. Massey
Harry B. Durham, III
Thomas F. Reese
J. Kenneth Barbe
Courtney Robert Kepler

For Complete List of Firm Personnel, See General Section

For full biographical listings, see the Martindale-Hubbell Law Directory

*CHEYENNE,** Laramie Co.

HIRST & APPLEGATE, A PROFESSIONAL CORPORATION (AV)

1720 Carey Avenue, Suite 200, P.O. Box 1083, 82003-1083
Telephone: 307-632-0541
Telefax: 307-632-4999
Email: attorneys@hirstapplegate.com *URL:* http://hirstapplegate.com

James L. Applegate
Thomas G. Gorman
Thomas A. Nicholas III
Gary R. Scott
John J. Metzke
Dale W. Cottam

Richard A. Mincer
Misha E. Westby
Boyd M. McMaster
Ryan T. Schelhaas

Representative Clients: American Insurance Group; ARCO; Ford Motor Company; Scottsdale Insurance Co.; The Doctors Company; Copley Pharmaceutical, Inc.; Royal Insurance Co.; Wyoming Stock Growers Assn.; General Motors Corp.; Fassett-Nickel, Inc.
Reference: Norwest Bank Wyoming Cheyenne, N.A.

For full biographical listings, see the Martindale-Hubbell Law Directory

*CODY,** Park Co.

SIMPSON, KEPLER & EDWARDS, LC (AV)

1135 14th Street, P.O. Box 490, 82414
Telephone: 307-527-7891
Fax: 307-527-7897
Email: skeatty@wavecom.net

Milward L. Simpson (1897-1993)
Charles G. Kepler
William L. Simpson
Colin M. Simpson
Chris D. Edwards

OF COUNSEL

Alan K. Simpson

References: Community First National Bank-Cody; Shoshone-First National Bank; Jackson State Bank.

For full biographical listings, see the Martindale-Hubbell Law Directory

VIRGIN ISLANDS

*CHARLOTTE AMALIE, ST. THOMAS,** St. Thomas

GRUNERT STOUT & BRUCH

24-25 Kongensgade, P.O. Box 1030, 00804
Telephone: 340-774-1320
Fax: 340-774-7839
Email: gsbusvi@viaccess.net
Affiliated with: Solomon Pearl Blum & Quinn LLP, New York, New York and Denver, Colorado.

MEMBERS OF FIRM

John E. Stout
Susan Bruch Moorehead

ASSOCIATE

Gabriel J. Villegas

OF COUNSEL

William L. Blum

For full biographical listings, see the Martindale-Hubbell Law Directory

CANADA ALBERTA

*CALGARY,** Calgary Jud. Dist.

BENNETT JONES (AV)

4500 Bankers Hall East, 855-2nd Street S.W., T2P 4K7
Telephone: 403-298-3100
Facsimile: 403-265-7219
Email: firmwatch@bennettjones.ca *URL:* http://www.bennettjones.ca
Edmonton, Alberta Office: 1000, 10035-105 Street.
Telephone: 780-421-8133.
Facsimile: 780-421-7951.
Toronto, Ontario Office: 3400 1 First Canadian Place, P.O. Box 130.
Telephone: 416-863-1200.
Facsimile: 416-863-1716.

MEMBER OF FIRM

John C. Armstrong, Q.C.

For Complete List of Firm Personnel, See General Section

For full biographical listings, see the Martindale-Hubbell Law Directory

PARLEE MCLAWS (AV)

3400 Petro-Canada Centre, 150 - 6th Avenue, SW, T2P 3Y7
Telephone: 403-294-7000
Telecopier: 403-265-8263
Email: lawyers@parlee.com *URL:* http://www.parlee.com
Edmonton, Alberta Office: 15th Floor Manulife Place, 10180 101st Street.
Telephone: 403-423-8500.
Telecopier: 403-423-2870.

ASSOCIATES

Dennis J. Pelkie
Barbara E. Janzen
Alec N. Silenzi

For Complete List of Firm Personnel, See General Section

For full biographical listings, see the Martindale-Hubbell Law Directory

*EDMONTON,** Edmonton Jud. Dist.

PARLEE MCLAWS (AV)

15th Floor Manulife Place, 10180 101st Street, T5J 4K1
Telephone: 403-423-8500
Telecopier: 403-423-2870
Email: lawyers@parlee.com *URL:* http://www.parlee.com
Calgary, Alberta Office: 3400 Petro-Canada Centre, 150 - 6th Avenue, SW.
Telephone: 403-294-7000.
Telecopier: 403-265-8263.

ASSOCIATE

Christopher R. Head

For Complete List of Firm Personnel, See General Section

For full biographical listings, see the Martindale-Hubbell Law Directory

CANADA MANITOBA

*WINNIPEG,** Eastern Jud. Dist.

AIKINS, MACAULAY & THORVALDSON (AV)

Thirtieth Floor, Commodity Exchange Tower, 360 Main Street, R3C 4G1
Telephone: 204-957-0050
Fax: 204-957-0840
Email: amt@aikins.com *URL:* http://www.aikins.com

MEMBERS OF FIRM

A. Lorne Campbell, O.C., C.D., LL.D., D.C.L., Q.C.
Thomas P. Dooley
Joel A. Weinstein, Q.C.
E. Bruce Parker
Frank Lavitt
Herbert J. Peters
Carmele N. Peter
Robert L. Tyler
Barbara S. MacDonald
Steven J. Kohn
Robert C. Lee
Marla S. Singer

Counsel for: Air Canada; Bank of Montreal; Boeing of Canada; Canada Safeway Limited; Canadian Medical Protective Assn.; The Great West Life Assurance Co.; John Labatt Limited; Russel Metals Inc.; Winnipeg Free Press.

For Complete List of Firm Personnel, See General Section

For full biographical listings, see the Martindale-Hubbell Law Directory

CANADA NEW BRUNSWICK

*FREDERICTON,** York Co.

MCINNES COOPER (AV)

Suite 600, 570 Queen Street, P.O. Box 610, E3B 5A6
Telephone: 506-458-8572
Fax: 506-458-9903
Email: mcrfton@mcrlaw.com *URL:* http://www.mcrlaw.com
Halifax, Nova Scotia Office: Summit Place, 1601 Lower Water Street, P.O. Box 730, B3J 2V1.
Telephone: 902-425-6500.
Fax: 902-425-6350. Email: mcrhfx@mcrlaw.com.
St. John's, Newfoundland Office: Baine Johnston Centre, 5th Floor, 10 Fort William Place, P.O. Box 5939, A1C 5X4.
Telephone: 709-722-8735.
Telecopier: 709-722-1763. Email: mcrsj@mcrlaw.com.
Moncton, New Brunswick Office: Place Moncton Place, 655 Main Street, P.O. Box 1368, E1C 8T6.
Telephone: 506-857-8970.
Fax: 506-857-4095. Email: mcrmctn@mcrlaw.com.
Charlottetown, Prince Edward Island Office: BDC Place, Suite 620, 119 Kent Street, C1A 1N3.
Telephone: 902-368-8473.
Fax: 902-368-8346. Email: mcrpei@mcrlaw.com.

(See Next Column)

McInnes Cooper, *Fredericton—Continued*

PARTNERS

R. Bruce Eddy, Q.C. Carol J. Downs

For Complete List of Firm Personnel, See General Section

For full biographical listings, see the Martindale-Hubbell Law Directory

*SAINT JOHN,** Saint John Co.

Clark Drummie (AV)

40 Wellington Row, P.O. Box 6850, E2L 4S3
Telephone: 506-633-3800
Telecopier (Automatic): 506-633-3811
Email: cd@nbnet.nb.ca

MEMBERS OF FIRM

Donald F. MacGowan, Q.C. Terrence W. Hutchinson

Reference: Royal Bank of Canada.

For Complete List of Firm Personnel, See General Section

For full biographical listings, see the Martindale-Hubbell Law Directory

CANADA NOVA SCOTIA

*HALIFAX,** Regional Munic. of Halifax

McInnes Cooper (AV)

Barristers, Solicitors & Trade Mark Agents
Summit Place, 1601 Lower Water Street, P.O. Box 730, B3J 2V1
Telephone: 902-425-6500
Fax: 902-425-6350
Email: mcrhfx@mcrlaw.com *URL:* http://www.mcrlaw.com
St. John's, Newfoundland Office: Baine Johnston Centre, 5th Floor, 10 Fort William Place, P.O. Box 5939, A1C 5X4.
Telephone: 709-722-8735.
Telecopier: 709-722-1763. Email: mcrsj@mcrlaw.com.
Moncton, New Brunswick Office: Place Moncton Place, 655 Main Street, P.O. Box 1368, E1C 8T6.
Telephone: 506-857-8970.
Fax: 506-857-4095. Email: mcrmctn@mcrlaw.com.
Charlottetown, Prince Edward Island Office: BDC Place, Suite 620, 119 Kent Street, C1A 1N3.
Telephone: 902-368-8473.
Fax: 902-368-8346. Email: mcrpei@mcrlaw.com.
Fredericton, New Brunswick Office: Suite 600, 570 Queen Street, P.O. Box 610.
Telephone: 506-458-8572.
Fax: 506-458-9903. Email: mcrfton@mcrlaw.com.

PARTNERS

Lawrence J. Hayes, Q.C. Alan J. Stern, Q.C.
George T. H. Cooper, Q.C.

ASSOCIATES

Jeffrey R. Blucher Jennifer A. Healy
Matthew O'Halloran Kristi Sebalj

For Complete List of Firm Personnel, See General Section

For full biographical listings, see the Martindale-Hubbell Law Directory

CANADA ONTARIO

KITCHENER, Regional Munic. of Waterloo

Giffen Lee (AV)

50 Queen Street North, P.O. Box 2396, N2H 6M3
Telephone: 519-578-4150
Fax: 519-578-8740
Email: info@GiffenLeeLaw.com *URL:* http://www.GiffenLeeLaw.com

MEMBERS OF FIRM

J. Peter Giffen, Q.C. Brian R. Wagner
Bruce L. Lee Philip A. Garbutt
J. Scott Morley Daniel J. Fife

ASSOCIATES

(Ms.) Milena Protich Graham M. Bennett
Cindy L. Dickinson Mitra Golnaraghi
Edward J. Vanderkloet Donald C. Olson

For full biographical listings, see the Martindale-Hubbell Law Directory

*TORONTO,** Regional Munic. of Toronto

Borden & Elliot (AV)

Barristers & Solicitors
Scotia Plaza, 40 King Street West, M5H 3Y4
Telephone: 416-367-6000
Telecopier: 416-367-6749
Email: info@borden.com *URL:* http://www.borden.com
Ottawa, Ontario Office: Borden Elliot Scott & Aylen, 1000-60 Rue Queen Street.
Telephone: 613-237-5160; 800-661-4237. General
Facsimile: 613-230-8842. IP Dept.
Facsimile: 613-787-3558. Email: ottinfo@scottaylen.com. URL: http://www.borden.com.

W. Douglas R. Beamish

For Complete List of Firm Personnel, See General Section

For full biographical listings, see the Martindale-Hubbell Law Directory

CANADA PRINCE EDWARD ISLAND

*CHARLOTTETOWN,** Queen's Co.

McInnes Cooper (AV(T))

Barristers, Solicitors & Trade Mark Agents
BDC Place, Suite 620, 119 Kent Street, C1A 1N3
Telephone: 902-368-8473
Fax: 902-368-8346
Email: mcrpei@mcrlaw.com *URL:* http://www.mcrlaw.com
Halifax, Nova Scotia Office: Summit Place, 1601 Lower Water Street, P.O. Box 730, B3J 2V1.
Telephone: 902-425-6500.
Fax: 902-425-6350. Email: mcrhfx@mcrlaw.com.
St. John's, Newfoundland Office: Baine Johnston Centre, 5th Floor, 10 Fort William Place, P.O. Box 5939, A1C 5X4.
Telephone: 709-722-8735.
Telecopier: 709-722-1763. Email: mcrsj@mcrlaw.com.
Moncton, New Brunswick Office: Place Moncton Place, 655 Main Street, P.O. Box 1368, E1C 8T6.
Telephone: 506-857-8970.
Fax: 506-857-4095. Email: mcrmctn@mcrlaw.com.
Fredericton, New Brunswick Office: Suite 600, 570 Queen Street, P.O. Box 610.
Telephone: 506-458-8572.
Fax: 506-458-9903. Email: mcrfton@mcrlaw.com.

PARTNERS

Horace B. Carver, Q.C. Michele M. Murphy

For Complete List of Firm Personnel, See General Section

For full biographical listings, see the Martindale-Hubbell Law Directory

CANADA QUEBEC

*MONTREAL,** Montreal Dist.

McMaster Gervais (AV)

A General Partnership
1000 de La Gauchetière Street West, Suite 900, H3B 5H4
Telephone: 514-879-1212
Fax: 514-954-1905
Email: info@mcmastergervais.com *URL:* http://www.mcmastergervais.com

MEMBERS OF FIRM

William E. Stavert Paul R. Marchand
Marilyn Ann Piccini Roy Elana Weissbach
Avi Levy

For Complete List of Firm Personnel, See General Section

For full biographical listings, see the Martindale-Hubbell Law Directory

CANADA
SASKATCHEWAN

*REGINA,** Regina Jud. Centre

MacPherson Leslie & Tyerman (AV)

1500-1874 Scarth Street, S4P 4E9
Telephone: 306-347-8000
Telecopier: 306-352-5250
Email: mltreg@mlt.com
Saskatoon, Saskatchewan Office: 1500-410 22nd Street East, S7K 5T6.
Telephone: 306-975-7100.
Telecopier: 306-975-7145.

MEMBERS OF FIRM

Alain J. Gaucher (Resident, Saskatoon Office)
Eileen V. Libby
Curtis R. Stewart (Resident, Saskatoon Office)
Todd M. Rosenberg (Resident, Saskatoon Office)

ASSOCIATES

David B. Jahnke (Resident, Saskatoon Office)
Grant D. Marshak (Resident, Saskatoon Office)
Rachelle M. Verret

For Complete List of Firm Personnel, See General Section

For full biographical listings, see the Martindale-Hubbell Law Directory

WORKERS COMPENSATION

MINNESOTA

*MINNEAPOLIS,** Hennepin Co.

BORKON, RAMSTEAD, MARIANI & LETOURNEAU, LTD. (AV)
485 Northstar East, 608 Second Avenue, South, 55402
Telephone: 612-333-7155
Fax: 612-333-5956

Edward H. Borkon
John H. Ramstead
John D. Mariani
Dennis R. Letourneau
William M. Fishman
Howard S. Carp
Howard S. Marker
Lewis H. Seltz
Lorrie L. Bescheinen
Martin T. Montilino
Howard L. Bolter
Michael C. Van Berkom

OF COUNSEL
William Seltz

Reference: Norwest Bank, Minneapolis.

For full biographical listings, see the Martindale-Hubbell Law Directory

SIEBEN, GROSE, VON HOLTUM & CAREY, LTD. (AV)
900 Midwest Plaza East, 800 Marquette Avenue, 55402
Telephone: 612-333-4500
Fax: 612-333-5970
URL: http://www.know-your-rights.com
Fairfax, Minnesota Office: 117 South Park Street.
Telephone: 507-426-8211.
Fax: 507-426-8213.
Duluth, Minnesota Office: 612 U.S. Bank Place, 130 Superior Street West.
Telephone: 218-722-6848. Toll Free (Minnesota): 800-422-0612.
Fax: 218-722-6841.
Lakeville, Minnesota Office: Southfork Office Centre, Suite 105, 17645 Juniper Path, 55044.
Telephone: 612-898-1894.
Fax: 612-898-4147.

Mark G. Olive

David A. Stofferahn

For full biographical listings, see the Martindale-Hubbell Law Directory

MISSISSIPPI

BILOXI, Harrison Co.

BROWN, WATT & BUCHANAN, P.A. (AV)
115 Main Street, P.O. Box 1377, 39533-1377
Telephone: 228-374-2999
Telecopier: 228-435-7090
Email: mail@bwblaw.com *URL:* http://www.bwblaw.com
Pascagoula, Mississippi Office: 3112 Canty Street, P.O. Box 2220.
Telephone: 228-762-0035.
Fax: 228-762-0299.

Raymond L. Brown
W. Lee Watt
Patrick R. Buchanan
W. Mark Edwards
A. Kelly Sessoms, III
Alan K. Sudduth

General Counsel for: Mississippi Export Railroad Co.; Pascagoula Municipal Separate School District.
Representative Clients: United States Fidelity & Guaranty Co.; The Travelers Companies; The Home Insurance Co.; CSX Transportation, Inc.; Blue Cross-Blue Shield of Mississippi; Burlington Insurance Co.; Continental Insurance; Deere & Co.

For full biographical listings, see the Martindale-Hubbell Law Directory

*CLARKSDALE,** Coahoma Co.

HOLCOMB DUNBAR, A PROFESSIONAL ASSOCIATION (AV)
152 Delta Avenue, P.O. Box 368, 38614
Telephone: 601-627-2241
Facsimile: 601-627-9788
Email: mchaffin@clarksdale.com *URL:* http://www.holcombdunbar.com
Oxford, Mississippi Office: 1217 Jackson Avenue, P.O. Drawer 707, 38655.
Telephone: 601-234-8775.
Facsimile: 601-238-7552.
Southaven, Mississippi Office: Suite 1, 728 Goodman Road East, P.O. Box 190, 38671.
Telephone: 601-349-0664.
Facsimile: 601-349-2432.

(See Next Column)

William M. Chaffin
Michael K. Graves

Representative Clients: Union Planters Bank, National Association; Deposit Guaranty National Bank; Trustmark National Bank; Mississippi Power & Light Co.; Mississippi Valley Gas Co.; South Central Bell Telephone Co.; Southern Farm Bureau Casualty Insurance Co.; Bituminous Insurance Co.; State Farm Fire & Casualty Insurance Co.; Fireman's Fund Insurance Cos.

For Complete List of Firm Personnel, See General Section

For full biographical listings, see the Martindale-Hubbell Law Directory

*GREENWOOD,** Leflore Co.

UPSHAW, WILLIAMS, BIGGERS, BECKHAM & RIDDICK, LLP (AV)
309 Fulton Street, 38930
Telephone: 662-455-1613
Facsimile: 662-453-9245
Mailing Address: P.O. Drawer 8230, Greenwood, Mississippi, 38935-8230
Email: lexgwd@uwbbr.com
Jackson, Mississippi Office: Suite 300 Plaza One, 715 South Pear Orchard Road, P.O. Box 9147, 39286-9147.
Telephone: 601-978-1996.
Facsimile: 601-978-1949. Email: lexjax@uwbbr.com.

MEMBERS OF FIRM

James E. Upshaw
Roger C. Riddick (Resident, Jackson Office)
Robert S. Upshaw
Richard L. Kimmel

ASSOCIATES

Steven H. Funderburg (Resident, Jackson Office)
James K. Warrington
Cecil D. McClellan, III (Resident, Jackson Office)

OF COUNSEL
Ben L. Riddick (Resident, Jackson Office)

Representative Clients: United States Fidelity & Guaranty Co.; State Farm Mutual Automobile Insurance Co.; CNA Insurance Cos.; St. Paul Fire & Marine Insurance Co.; Travelers/Aetna Property and Casualty Corp.; Kemper Insurance Co.; Zurich-American Insurance Group; Risk Enterprise Management, Ltd.; Allstate Insurance Co.

For Complete List of Firm Personnel, See General Section

For full biographical listings, see the Martindale-Hubbell Law Directory

*GULFPORT,** Harrison Co.

ALLEN, VAUGHN, COBB & HOOD, P.A. (AV)
One Hancock Plaza, Suite 1209, P.O. Drawer 4108, 39502-4108
Telephone: 601-864-4011
Fax: 601-864-4852
Email: avchlaw@sunherald.infinet.com

Harry R. Allen
Thomas E. Vaughn
David L. Cobb
Billy W. Hood
Joy Lambert Phillips
Robert W. Atkinson
Benjamin U. Bowden
Richard B. Tubertini
Rodney Douglas Robinson
E. Colette Towles
David W. Crane
John A. Foxworth, Jr.

J. Adrian Smith
Michael J. Casano

OF COUNSEL
D. Knox White

LEGAL SUPPORT PERSONNEL
Kevin C. Stachowski (Paralegal)

For full biographical listings, see the Martindale-Hubbell Law Directory

DUKES, DUKES, KEATING AND FANECA, P.A. (AV)
2909 13th Street, 6th Floor, P.O. Drawer W, 39501
Telephone: 228-868-1111
Fax: 228-863-2886
Email: ddkf@ddkf.com

Walter W. Dukes
Phillip W. Jarrell

W. Edward Hatten, Jr.
Thomas William Busby
Trace D. McRaney

For Complete List of Firm Personnel, See General Section

For full biographical listings, see the Martindale-Hubbell Law Directory

FRANKE, RAINEY & SALLOUM, PLLC (AV)
2605 14th Street, P.O. Drawer 460, 39502
Telephone: 228-868-7070
Telecopier: 228-868-7090
Email: frs@diversicomm.com

(See Next Column)

FRANKE, RAINEY & SALLOUM PLLC, *Gulfport—Continued*

Paul M. Franke, Jr.
William M. Rainey
Richard P. Salloum
Paul B. Howell
Fredrick B. Feeney, II
Traci M. Castille
Donald P. Moore

Kaleel G. Salloum, Jr.
Brandi C. Schwartz
James C. Simpson, Jr.

For full biographical listings, see the Martindale-Hubbell Law Directory

BOYCE HOLLEMAN A PROFESSIONAL CORPORATION (AV)

1913 15th Street, P.O. Drawer 1030, 39502
Telephone: 228-863-3142; 1-800-863-3140
Telecopier: 228-863-9829
Email: boyce1913@aol.com

Boyce Holleman

Timothy C. Holleman
Leslie Dean Holleman
David J. "Jeff" White

References: Hancock Bank, Gulfport; Merchants Bank & Trust Co., Gulfport; Bank of Wiggins, Wiggins, Mississippi.

For full biographical listings, see the Martindale-Hubbell Law Directory

HOPKINS, CRAWLEY, BAGWELL & UPSHAW, P.L.L.C. (AV)

2701 24th Avenue, P.O. Box 1510, 39501-4941
Telephone: 228-864-2200
Mississippi and USA Wats: 1-800-421-3629
Fax: 228-868-9358; 228-863-4227
Email: Hopkins@MSLawyer.com
Jackson, Mississippi Office: 499 South President Street, Second Floor, Suite 1.
Telephone: 601-355-6510.
Fax: 601-355-6503. Email: TCrawley@MSLawyer.com.

MEMBERS OF FIRM

Alben N. Hopkins
Timothy D. Crawley
Douglas Bagwell
Jessica Sibley Upshaw
Thomas Alan Waller

ASSOCIATES

Raymond D. Carter
Kenneth S. Womack
Mary Benton-Shaw
Pat Sharkey Burke, Jr.
David E. Wilson
Laura Faye Paulk
Ronald C. Small
(Not admitted in MS)

Representative Clients: Coregis Group; General Cable Corp.; Insurance Company of North America; Liberty Mutual Insurance Group; Reliance Insurance Co.; USX Corp.; Employers Insurance of Wausau; American International Group (AIG); Quaker Chemical Corp.

For full biographical listings, see the Martindale-Hubbell Law Directory

*JACKSON,** Hinds Co.

UPSHAW, WILLIAMS, BIGGERS, BECKHAM & RIDDICK, LLP (AV)

Suite 300 Plaza One, 715 South Pear Orchard Road (Ridgeland), 39147
Telephone: 601-978-1996
Facsimile: 601-978-1949
Mailing Address: P.O. Box 9147, Jackson, Mississippi, 39286-9147
Email: lexjax@uwbbr.com
Greenwood, Mississippi Office: 309 Fulton Street, P.O. Drawer 8230, 38935-8230.
Telephone: 662-455-1613.
Facsimile: 662-453-9245. Email: lexgwd@uwbbr.com.

MEMBERS OF FIRM

James E. Upshaw
(Resident, Greenwood Office)
Roger C. Riddick
Robert S. Upshaw
(Resident, Greenwood Office)
Richard L. Kimmel
(Resident, Greenwood Office)

ASSOCIATES

Steven H. Funderburg
James K. Warrington
(Resident, Greenwood Office)
Cecil D. McClellan, III

OF COUNSEL

Ben L. Riddick

Representative Clients: United States Fidelity & Guaranty Co.; State Farm Mutual Automobile Insurance Co.; CNA Insurance Cos.; St. Paul Fire & Marine Insurance Co.; Travelers/Aetna Property and Casualty Corp.; Kemper Insurance Co.; Zurich-America Insurance Group; Risk Enterprise Management, Ltd.; Allstate Insurance Co.

For Complete List of Firm Personnel, See General Section

For full biographical listings, see the Martindale-Hubbell Law Directory

*MERIDIAN,** Lauderdale Co.

HAMILTON & LINDER (AV)

2713 Seventh Street, P.O. Box 1511, 39302-1511
Telephone: 601-693-5548
Fax: 601-693-2949
URL: http://www.lawyers.com/handllaw

MEMBERS OF FIRM

Joe Clay Hamilton
David H. Linder

ASSOCIATES

Will Parker
G. Richard Baker

For full biographical listings, see the Martindale-Hubbell Law Directory

*PASCAGOULA,** Jackson Co.

BROWN, WATT & BUCHANAN, P.A. (AV)

3112 Canty Street, P.O. Box 2220, 39569-2220
Telephone: 228-762-0035
Telecopier: 228-762-0299
Email: mail@bwblaw.com *URL:* http://www.bwblaw.com
Biloxi, Mississippi Office: 115 Main Street, P.O. Box 1377.
Telephone: 228-374-2999.
Fax: 228-435-7090.

Raymond L. Brown
W. Lee Watt
Patrick R. Buchanan
W. Mark Edwards
A. Kelly Sessoms, III
Alan K. Sudduth

General Counsel for: Mississippi Export Railroad Co.; Pascagoula Municipal Separate School District.
Representative Clients: United States Fidelity & Guaranty Co.; The Travelers Companies; The Home Insurance Co.; CSX Transportation, Inc.; Blue Cross-Blue Shield of Mississippi; Burlington Insurance Co.; Continental Insurance; Deere & Co.

For full biographical listings, see the Martindale-Hubbell Law Directory

COLINGO, WILLIAMS, HEIDELBERG, STEINBERGER & McELHANEY, P.A. (AV)

711 Delmas Avenue, P.O. Box 1407, 39568-1407
Telephone: 228-762-8021
FAX: 228-762-7589
Email: info@colingowilliams.com *URL:* http://www.ColingoWilliams.com

Karl R. Steinberger
Michael J. McElhaney, Jr.

Gina Bardwell Thompkins

Representative Clients: International Paper Co.; R.J. Reynolds; CBS Corp.; Kemper Group; Singing River Hospital System; Mississippi Gulf Coast Regional Wastewater Authority; Medical Assurance Company of Mississippi; Mutual Assurance of Alabama; Dole Food Co.

For full biographical listings, see the Martindale-Hubbell Law Directory

MISSOURI

*COLUMBIA,** Boone Co.

OLIVER, WALKER, WILSON & EHRHARDT, LLC (AV)

Suite 406, 401 Locust Street, P.O. Box 977, 65205
Telephone: 573-443-3134
Telecopier: 573-442-6323
Email: owwe@socket.net

MEMBERS OF FIRM

David A. Oliver
Roland P. Walker
Betty K. Wilson
Glen R. Ehrhardt
Cynthia Barchet
Ronald N. Sweet

Representative Clients: Aetna Insurance Co.; Allied Group; American Family Insurance Group; Safeco; CNA Insurance; Federated Insurance Co.; Old Republic; Shelter Insurance Cos.

For full biographical listings, see the Martindale-Hubbell Law Directory

*JEFFERSON CITY,** Cole Co.

CARSON & COIL, P.C. (AV)

515 East High, P.O. Box 28, 65102
Telephone: 573-636-2177
Telecopier: 573-636-7119
Email: general@carsoncoil.com

Forrest P. Carson (1910-1981)
Cullen Coil (1907-1989)
Michael P. Riley
Ronald R. McMillin
Eugene G. Bushmann
James W. Gallaher
Lori J. Levine
Rudolph L. Veit
Michael Madsen
R. Max Humphreys

(See Next Column)

CARSON & COIL P.C.—*Continued*

Mark A. Ludwig
Dana L. Frese
Edward C. Clausen
Carla G. Holste
Kent L. Brown
Douglas W. Hennon
Charles J. McPheeters
Paul T. Graham

Jack C. Hauser, Jr.

General Counsel for: Capital Reserve Life Insurance Co.; Missouri Farm Bureau; Healthcare Services Group.
Reference: Central Trust Bank.

For full biographical listings, see the Martindale-Hubbell Law Directory

KANSAS CITY, Jackson, Clay, Platte & Cass Cos.

MARK & BURKHEAD

(See Mission, Kansas)

ARTHUR H. STOUP & ASSOCIATES, P.C. (AV)

1710 Mercantile Tower, 1101 Walnut Street, 64106
Telephone: 816-474-0707; 417-887-3600
Fax: 816-474-0714; 417-887-3600
Email: Stoup@msn.com
Springfield, Missouri Office: 1949 East Sunshine, Suite 1-108.
Telephone: 417-887-3600.

Arthur H. Stoup

Stephen W. Nichols

For full biographical listings, see the Martindale-Hubbell Law Directory

RAYMORE, Cass Co.

HENSLEY & HENSLEY (AV)

401 West 58 Highway, P.O. Box 620, 64083
Telephone: 816-322-4466
Email: hensley8.@worldnet.att.net

MEMBERS OF FIRM

Kenneth C. Hensley
Teresa Hensley

Representative Clients: Farmers Bank of Northern Missouri; Corporate Dental Care, Inc.; Cole & Myers Oil Co.

For full biographical listings, see the Martindale-Hubbell Law Directory

ST. LOUIS, (Independent City)

ABELE & SANDERSON, L.L.C. (AV)

Suite 1024, 1015 Locust, 63101-1323
Telephone: 314-241-3123; 1-800-886-3123
Fax: 314-241-4361
Email: abelesand@aol.com *URL:* http://www.lawyers.com/abele&sanderson

Charles R. Abele
M. Melinda Sanderson

For full biographical listings, see the Martindale-Hubbell Law Directory

LYNN D. BARNETT (AV)

906 Olive, Suite 400, 63101
Telephone: 314-231-7171
Fax: 314-231-7209
URL: http://www.swb.net/LOBDC.Com

For full biographical listings, see the Martindale-Hubbell Law Directory

LAW OFFICES THOMAS M. BURKE, P.C. (AV)

Gateway One Building, 701 Market Street, Suite 1075, 63101
Telephone: 314-241-8200
Telecopier: 314-241-5890

Thomas M. Burke

Scott L. Kolker

For full biographical listings, see the Martindale-Hubbell Law Directory

EVANS & DIXON, L.L.C. (AV)

1200 Saint Louis Place, 200 North Broadway, 63102-2749
Telephone: 314-621-7755
URL: http://www.evans-dixon.com
Kansas City, Missouri Office: City Center Square, 1100 Main Street, Suite 2000, 64105-2119.
Telephone: 816-472-4600.
Edwardsville, Illinois Office: 17 Ginger Creek Meadows, P.O. Box 405. 62025-3508.
Telephone: 618-656-8505.
Leawood, Kansas Office: 8016 State Line Road, Suite 207. 66208-3713.
Telephone: 913-649-5386.

(See Next Column)

MEMBERS OF FIRM

Robert M. Evans
Edward M. Vokoun
James B. Kennedy
James A. Thoenen
Raymond J. Flunker
James M. Gallen
Robert E. Bidstrup
Bradley V. Spaunhorst
Robert N. Hendershot, II
William F. Ringer (Resident, Kansas City, Missouri Office)
Marilyn C. Phillips
David S. Ware
George T. Floros
Robert W. Haeckel
Michael F. Banahan
Betsy J. Levitt
Brian J. Fowler (Kansas City, Missouri and Leawood, Kansas Offices)
Thomas Clinkenbeard (Resident, Kansas City, Missouri Office)
Paul D. Larimore
Patrick A. Patterson
Timothy M. Tierney
Kim M. Parks

Mark R. Kornblum

ASSOCIATES

Scott C. Annunziata
Lynn M. Curtis (Resident, Kansas City, Missouri Office)
Kristan M. Dames
Jennifer K. Greene
Brent W. Halbleib
Rhonda J. Henry-Webb
Robert L. Hinson
Paul F. Keeven
Daniel J. Kertz
Carl Kessinger
Martin A. Klug
John Joseph Lee
Jay Lory
Kevin J. Marquitz
Jacqueline E. Moore
Terry J. Mort (Not admitted in MO)
Karen A. Mulroy
Cristina Clare Nolan
Jeffrey M. Proske
David J. Reynolds, Jr.
Michele G. Roy
Steven R. Sharp
Elizabeth S. Stumpf
Ethan Vaughan (Resident, Kansas City, Missouri Office)
Helen J.S. White (Not admitted in MO)
Betsy S. Willer

Attorneys for: Allstate Insurance Co.; Anheuser Busch, Inc.; Chrysler Corp.; Chubb & Son, Inc.; Kemper Insurance Group; Southwestern Bell Telephone Co.; Travelers Insurance Co.; Zurich Insurance Co.

For full biographical listings, see the Martindale-Hubbell Law Directory

ROBERTS, PERRYMAN, BOMKAMP & MEIVES, P.C. (AV)

Suite 2300, One Mercantile Center, 63101
Telephone: 314-421-1850
Cable Address: "Henrogo"
Telecopier: 314-421-4346
Email: rpbm@istnet.net
Belleville, Illinois Office: 23 Public Square, Suite 402.
Telephone: 618-277-9955.

Ted L. Perryman
J. Bradley Young
Michael P. McDonald, Jr.
Robert C. Anderson

James D. Maschoff

Reference: Boatmen's National Bank.

For full biographical listings, see the Martindale-Hubbell Law Directory

*SPRINGFIELD,** Greene Co.

HARRISON, TUCKER & HYDE, LLP (AV)

1121 South Glenstone, 65804
Telephone: 417-831-4046
Fax: 417-831-4989
Email: 100576.2300@compuserve.com

MEMBERS OF FIRM

Jeffrey H. Harrison
James D. Tucker
Kent O. Hyde
William C. Love
Brian E. Hamburg
Aaron P. Lyons

For full biographical listings, see the Martindale-Hubbell Law Directory

MONTANA

*BILLINGS,** Yellowstone Co.

CROWLEY, HAUGHEY, HANSON, TOOLE & DIETRICH, P.L.L.P. (AV)

500 Transwestern II, 490 North 31st Street, P.O. Box 2529, 59103
Telephone: 406-252-3441
Fax: 406-259-4159
Email: crowley@crowleylaw.com
Helena, Montana Office: IBM Building, 100 North Park Avenue, Suite 300, 59601.
Telephone: 406-449-4165.
Fax: 406-449-5149.
Kalispell, Montana Office: 431 1st Avenue West, 59901.
Telephone: 406-752-6644.
Fax: 406-752-5108.
Williston, North Dakota Office: 113 East Broadway, 58801.
Telephone: 701-572-2200.
Fax: 701-572-7072.

(See Next Column)

CROWLEY, HAUGHEY, HANSON, TOOLE & DIETRICH P.L.L.P., *Billings—Continued*

OF COUNSEL

Neil S. Keefer

MEMBERS OF FIRM

William J. Mattix
Jon T. Dyre (Resident, Kalispell, Montana Office)
Joe C. Maynard, Jr.

Representative Clients: Montana Power Co.; First Interstate Bank of Commerce; MDU Resources Group, Inc.; Chevron U.S.A., Inc.; Noranda Minerals Corp.; United Parcel Service.
Insurance Clients: Farmers Insurance Group; New York Life Insurance Co.

For Complete List of Firm Personnel, See General Section

For full biographical listings, see the Martindale-Hubbell Law Directory

NEBRASKA

*LINCOLN,** Lancaster Co.

REHM LAW FIRM, A PROFESSIONAL CORPORATION (AV)

1327 "H" Street, Suite 200, 68508
Telephone: 402-474-2300
Fax: 402-474-4716
Email: RR33224@navix.net *URL:* http://www.rehmlawfirm.com

Rod Rehm

Todd D. Bennett
Daniel A. Fix

OF COUNSEL

William R. Hoppner

For full biographical listings, see the Martindale-Hubbell Law Directory

*OMAHA,** Douglas Co.

MCGILL, GOTSDINER, WORKMAN & LEPP, P.C. (AV)

Suite 500 - First National Plaza, 11404 West Dodge Road, 68154
Telephone: 402-492-9200
Telecopier: 402-492-9222
Email: mgwl@mgwl.com

Robert L. Lepp
Mary L. Hewitt

Representative Clients: Metz Baking Co.; Mutual of Omaha; Sentry Insurance Co.

For Complete List of Firm Personnel, See General Section

For full biographical listings, see the Martindale-Hubbell Law Directory

NEVADA

*LAS VEGAS,** Clark Co.

CROCKETT & MYERS, LTD. A PROFESSIONAL CORPORATION (AV)

700 South Third Street, 89101
Telephone: 702-382-6711
Fax: 702-384-8102
Email: cmlegal@wizard.com *URL:* http://www.lawyers.com/c&mlaw

OF COUNSEL

Gerald M. Welt

Reference: American Bank of Commerce.

For full biographical listings, see the Martindale-Hubbell Law Directory

GREENMAN, GOLDBERG, RABY & MARTINEZ, PROFESSIONAL CORPORATION (AV)

601 South Ninth Street, 89101-7012
Telephone: 702-384-1616
FAX: 702-384-2990

John A. Greenman
Aubrey Goldberg
Paul E. Raby
Gabriel A. Martinez

Michael J. Ryan
Lisa M. Anderson
John R. Gordon

For full biographical listings, see the Martindale-Hubbell Law Directory

THORNDAL, ARMSTRONG, DELK, BALKENBUSH & EISINGER, A PROFESSIONAL CORPORATION (AV)

1100 East Bridger Avenue, P.O. Box 2070, 89125-2070
Telephone: 702-366-0622
Fax: 702-366-0327
Email: info@thorndal.com *URL:* http://www.thorndal.com
Reno, Nevada Office: Suite 200, 888 West Second Street.
Telephone: 775-786-2882.
Fax: 775-786-8004.
Elko, Nevada Office: 919 Idaho Street, P.O. Box 5508.
Telephone: 775-777-3011.
Fax: 775-786-8004.

John L. Thorndal
James G. Armstrong
Craig R. Delk
Stephen C. Balkenbush (Resident, Reno Office)
Paul F. Eisinger
Charles Lee Burcham (Resident, Reno Office)
Brian K. Terry
Brent Thomas Kolvet (Resident, Reno Office)
Blair C. Parker
William R. Killip, Jr.
Robert F. Balkenbush (Resident, Reno Office)

Michael E. Sullivan (Resident, Reno Office)
Philip Goodhart
Deborah L. Elsasser
James J. Jackson
Gavin C. Jangard
R. Scott Rasmussen
Christopher J. Curtis
Alyssa A. Martini
Susan E. Frasca
Daniel D. Norr
David P. Lane
William R. Jones
Katherine F. Bobier (Resident, Reno Office)
C. Scott Wormsley
Renee E. Jensen
Thierry V. Barkley (Resident, Reno Office)

Representative Clients: Public Agency Compensation Trust; Reliance Insurance Co., Inc.; Cybercomp; Cigna; Health South Corp.; Cashman Equipment Co.; Bechtel Nevada Corp.; Kiewit Construction Group; EG&G Special Projects, Inc.; Randstad North America.

For full biographical listings, see the Martindale-Hubbell Law Directory

*RENO,** Washoe Co.

MCDONALD CARANO WILSON MCCUNE BERGIN FRANKOVICH & HICKS LLP (AV)

241 Ridge Street, 89501
Telephone: 775-788-2000
Telecopier: 775-788-2020
URL: http://www.mcdonaldcarano.com
Las Vegas, Nevada Office: Suite 1000, 2300 West Sahara Avenue.
Telephone: 702-873-4100.
Telecopier: 702-873-9966.

MEMBERS OF FIRM

Larry R. Hicks
Timothy E. Rowe

ASSOCIATES

Anthony D. Guenther
Judy P. Osgood

Representative Clients: AT&T Communications of Nevada; Associated General Contractors of America; Eldorado Hotel & Casino; Intermountain Federal Land Bank Association; James Hardie (USA), Inc. Scolari's Warehouse Markets; Time Oil Co. (Nevada Counsel); Nevada State Bank; GE Capital Small Business Finance Corporation; FirstSecurity Bank.

For Complete List of Firm Personnel, See General Section

For full biographical listings, see the Martindale-Hubbell Law Directory

NEW JERSEY

FLORHAM PARK, Morris Co.

HACK, PIRO, O'DAY, MERKLINGER, WALLACE & MCKENNA, P.A. (AV)

30 Columbia Turnpike, P.O. Box 941, 07932-0941
Telephone: 973-301-6500
Fax: 973-301-0094
Email: hpom@ix.netcom.com

Joseph V. Wallace
John T. West

Carol A. Rankin

For Complete List of Firm Personnel, See General Section

For full biographical listings, see the Martindale-Hubbell Law Directory

*HACKENSACK,** Bergen Co.

HEIN, SMITH, BEREZIN, MALOOF & JACOBS, L.L.C. (AV)

Court Plaza East, 19 Main Street, 07601-7023
Telephone: 201-487-7400
Telecopier: 201-487-4228
Email: counsel@heinsmith.com

MEMBER OF FIRM

Sidney Berezin

ASSOCIATE

Eileen P. Mulroy

Representative Clients: Bergen County Joint Municipal Insurance Fund; Commercial General Union Insurance Cos. of New York; Crawford & Co.; Health Care Insurance Co.; Princeton Insurance Co.; St. Paul Fire & Marine Insurance Co.; Pro Mutual Insurance Company; NJ Cure.
Reference: Summit Bank.

For Complete List of Firm Personnel, See General Section

For full biographical listings, see the Martindale-Hubbell Law Directory

LIVINGSTON, Essex Co.

PHILIP M. LUSTBADER & DAVID LUSTBADER A PROFESSIONAL CORPORATION (AV)

615 West Mount Pleasant Avenue, 07039
Telephone: 973-740-1000
Fax: 973-740-1520
URL: http://www.lawyers.com/lustbader,law

Philip M. Lustbader — David Lustbader

John L. Riordan, Jr. — James S. Colavito

For full biographical listings, see the Martindale-Hubbell Law Directory

*NEWARK,** Essex Co.

CARPENTER, BENNETT & MORRISSEY (AV)

Three Gateway Center, 17th Floor, 100 Mulberry Street, 07102-4079
Telephone: 973-622-7711
New York City: 212-943-6530
Telex: 139405
Telecopier: 973-622-5314
Email: cbm@carpben.com

MEMBERS OF FIRM

Anthony C. Famulari — Michael J. Greenwood

ASSOCIATES

Glenn F. Corbett — Robert L. Ghelli

Representative Clients: General Motors Corp.; Lucent Technologies, Inc.; Anheuser-Busch, Inc.; The New York Times Co.; Roadway Express, Inc.; BP Chemicals Inc.; Owen-Illinois; Schindler Elevator Corp.; International Specialty Products; New Jersey Self-Insurers Guaranty Assn.

For Complete List of Firm Personnel, See General Section

For full biographical listings, see the Martindale-Hubbell Law Directory

PRINCETON, Mercer Co.

BERGMAN & BARRETT (AV)

9 Tamarack Circle, Montgomery Knoll, U.S. Highway 206 North, P.O. Box 1273, 08542
Telephone: 609-921-1502
Fax: 609-683-0288

Edward J. Bergman — Michael T. Barrett

LEGAL SUPPORT PERSONNEL

Kelli E. Murphy (Paralegal)

For full biographical listings, see the Martindale-Hubbell Law Directory

STARK & STARK, A PROFESSIONAL CORPORATION (AV)

Princeton Pike Corporate Center, P.O. Box 5315, 08543-5315
Telephone: 609-896-9060
Fax: 609-896-0629
Email: info@stark-stark.com *URL:* http://www.stark-stark.com

Godfrey W. Harper, III — Arthur H. Kravitz
John A. Sakson

Vicki W. Beyer — Samuel M. Gaylord

For full biographical listings, see the Martindale-Hubbell Law Directory

*TOMS RIVER,** Ocean Co.

LOMELL, MUCCIFORI, ADLER, RAVASCHIERE, AMABILE & PEHLIVANIAN, A PROFESSIONAL CORPORATION (AV)

250 Washington Street, P.O. Box 787, 08754
Telephone: 732-349-2443
Fax: 732-349-6917
Email: thefirm@lomell.com *URL:* http://www.lomell.com

Herman A. Adler — Jeffrey R. Surenian
Dominic Ravaschiere — James M. McKenna
John S. Pehlivanian — Teresa K. Gierla
Ronald E. Prusek — Arthur F. Leyden, III

Marc S. Galella — James S. Braaten
Robyn A. Belluardo — Regina M. Butler
Janet Zaorski Kalapos — Paul J Capotorto

Representative Clients: Commercial Union Insurance; Kemper Insurance Co.; The Ohio Casualty Insurance Co.; Royal Insurance Co.; US Fidelity & Guaranty Co.; Warwick Group; Zurich-American Insurance Company; Jersey Central Power & Light Co.; Asbury Park Press; Coco Cola Foods Company.

For Complete List of Firm Personnel, See General Section

For full biographical listings, see the Martindale-Hubbell Law Directory

STARKEY, KELLY, BLANEY & WHITE (AV)

2 Hooper Avenue, 08753
Telephone: 732-240-3600
Fax: 732-240-3777
Brick, New Jersey Office: 459 Jack Martin Boulevard, 08724.
Telephone: 732-840-5900.
Fax: 732-840-5901.
Manasquan, New Jersey Office: 23 Route 71, 08736.
Telephone: 732-223-7328.
Fax: 732-240-3777.

MEMBERS OF FIRM

Charles E. Starkey — William V. Kelly
James M. Blaney

ASSOCIATES

Natalie Pouch — Scott W. Kenneally
Anthony Mancuso — Susan K. White
Robert A. Bauer — Brent D. Miller

Representative Clients: Hartford Insurance Co.; New Jersey Education Assn.; New Jersey Psychiatric Assn.; Ocean County Utilities Authority; Brick Township Municipal Utilities Authority; Manasquan River Regional Sewerage Authority; Hanover Insurance Co.; John Hancock Insurance Co.; Rider Inc. Co.

For full biographical listings, see the Martindale-Hubbell Law Directory

NEW YORK

*ALBANY,** Albany Co.

BUCKLEY, MENDLESON & CRISCIONE, P.C. (AV)

29 Wards Lane, 12204-2013
Telephone: 518-449-3107; 427-7521
Fax: 518-449-3108
Email: INFO@BMC-LAW.COM

James E. Buckley — Ira Mendleson, III
John J. Criscione

Brendan G. Quinn — Karen R. Arndt
Cherie Indelicato — Maureen N. Tighe
John M. Oliver

Reference: Key Bank of New York.

For full biographical listings, see the Martindale-Hubbell Law Directory

SULLIVAN, CUNNINGHAM, KEENAN, MRAZ & LEMIRE (AV)

152 Central Avenue, 12206
Telephone: 518-434-1022
Fax: 518-434-2304
Email: complaw@empireone.net

William J. Sullivan (1904-1980)

MEMBERS OF FIRM

John J. Cunningham — Mary J. Mraz
Michael J. Keenan — Christopher R. Lemire

(See Next Column)

SULLIVAN, CUNNINGHAM, KEENAN, MRAZ & LEMIRE, *Albany—Continued*

ASSOCIATES

Michael D. Violando
Nannette R. Kelleher
Michael Rosenblum

Reference: Trustco Bank.

For full biographical listings, see the Martindale-Hubbell Law Directory

*BUFFALO,** Erie Co.

WILLIAMS & WILLIAMS (AV)

237 Main Street Suite 1400, 14203
Telephone: 716-856-8200
Fax: 716-856-0559
Email: wmswmsfirm@aol.com

Mark W. Kerwood
Roger J. Edel
Mary Meyer Russo

Robert D. Leary
Lynette M. Gohr
Ellen Shanahan Becker
Boyd L. Earl
Wayne D. Schiffhauer
Julie A. Houghtaling
Melissa A. Day
Dawn M. Netzel
Christina M. Hassler

OF COUNSEL

Clyde M. Williams
Paul D. Williams (1910-1993)

A List of Representative Clients and References will be furnished upon request.

For full biographical listings, see the Martindale-Hubbell Law Directory

PALMYRA, Wayne Co.

FOLEY & FOLEY (AV)

235 East Main Street, P.O. Box 211, 14522
Telephone: 315-597-6611
Fax: 315-597-8920
Email: JFOLEY12@MSN.COM

MEMBERS OF FIRM

James F. Foley
Ann Firestine Foley

Reference: Marine Midland Bank (Palmyra Office).

For full biographical listings, see the Martindale-Hubbell Law Directory

*SYRACUSE,** Onondaga Co.

SMITH, SOVIK, KENDRICK & SUGNET, P.C. (AV)

250 South Clinton Street, Suite 600, 13202-1252
Telephone: 315-474-2911
Fax: 315-474-6015
URL: http://www.smithsovik.com

John Timothy Smith (1902-1964)
Nelson J. Smith (1923-1967)
Martin F. Kendrick (1917-1983)
Laurence Sovik (1904-1998)
Laurence F. Sovik
William E. Sugnet (Retired)
James A. O'Shea
James D. Lantier
Michael P. Ringwood
Peter J. Cambs
Kevin E. Hulslander
Thomas N. Kaufmann
Daniel A. Bronk
Steven W. Williams
Mary Kendrick-Gaffney
James W. Cunningham

Thomas P. Roerden
Robert P Cahalan
Denis J. Bastible
G. John Flemma
Theresa N. C. McCorry

OF COUNSEL

Gary A. Hall

For full biographical listings, see the Martindale-Hubbell Law Directory

*WHITE PLAINS,** Westchester Co.

HOFFMAN, WACHTELL, KOSTER & MAIER (AV)

399 Knollwood Road, 10603
Telephone: 914-682-8000
FAX: 914-682-1512
URL: http://www.lawyers.com/hwk&mlaw

MEMBERS OF FIRM

Lee A. Hoffman, Jr.
Marc J. Wachtell
Eric D. Koster
Lynn J. Maier

Representative Clients: CIGNA; Georgia Pacific Corporation; American States Insurance; Crawford & Company; Markel Underwriters, Special Fund Conservation Comm., individual client/claimants.

For full biographical listings, see the Martindale-Hubbell Law Directory

NORTH CAROLINA

*ASHEVILLE,** Buncombe Co.

ELMORE, ELMORE & WILLIAMS, P.A. (AV)

53 North Market Street, 28801
Telephone: 828-253-1492
Fax: 828-253-9648
Email: eewlaw@wnc.com *URL:* http://www.lawyers.com/elmore-elmore-williams

Bruce A. Elmore
Bruce A. Elmore, Jr.
Reed G. Williams

For full biographical listings, see the Martindale-Hubbell Law Directory

CARY, Wake Co.

BROOKS, STEVENS & POPE, P.A. (AV)

2000 Regency Parkway, Suite 150, P.O. Box 1870, 27511-8507
Telephone: 919-481-9103
Fax: 919-481-9137
Email: attys@bsp-pa.com *URL:* http://www.bsp-pa.com

David Victor Brooks
Robert H. Stevens, Jr.
Daniel Carter Pope, Jr.
Jane Kestenbaum
Michael C. Sigmon
Kathlyn Corbett Hobbs
Robert S. Welch

Amy K. Whinery
Ashley B. White
Paul F. Toland
Joy H. Brewer
John Abb Payne
Alicia M. Benson
Matthew P. Blake
Matthew John Dixon

OF COUNSEL

Archie W. Futrell, III
Cathy A. Hinton Pope

Representative Clients: AMR Corp.; Duke Energy Corp.; GAB Robins; Key Risk Management; North Carolina League of Municipalities; Lumbermen's Underwriting Alliance; State Farm Insurance Co.; RSK Co.; U.S. Airways.

For full biographical listings, see the Martindale-Hubbell Law Directory

*CHARLOTTE,** Mecklenburg Co.

TIM L. HARRIS AND ASSOCIATES (AV)

4000 Tuckaseegee Road, 28208
Telephone: 704-392-4111
Fax: 704-391-1905
URL: http://www.timharris.com
Gastonia, North Carolina Office: 616 Cox Road. P.O. Box 249.
Telephone: 704-864-3409.
Fax: 704-853-1040.
Monroe, North Carolina Office: 3513 Highway 74 West, Suite E.
Telephone: 704-283-9200.
Fax: 704-392-9695.
Concord, North Carolina Office: 435 Church Street.
Telephone: 704-795-9317.
Fax: 704-795-5738

MEMBERS OF FIRM

Tim L. Harris
Jerry Neil Ragan (Resident, Gastonia Office)

ASSOCIATE

Rebecca L. Thomas (Resident)

For full biographical listings, see the Martindale-Hubbell Law Directory

*GREENSBORO,** Guilford Co.

ALEXANDER RALSTON, SPECKHARD & SPECKHARD, L.L.P. (AV)

218 West Friendly Avenue, 27401
Telephone: 336-379-9302
Fax: 336-370-1232
URL: http://www.lawyers.com/aralston,speckhard

Donald K. Speckhard
Stanley E. Speckhard

Representative Clients: Preferred Furniture Components, Inc.; Spring Financial Services, Inc.; Blazer Financial Services; Omega Sports, Inc.; Power & Heat Systems, Inc.; Branch & Company, P.A.; Acme Florist Supply, Inc.

For full biographical listings, see the Martindale-Hubbell Law Directory

BURTON & SUE, L.L.P. (AV)

419 North Elm Street, P.O. Box 20083, 27420
Telephone: 336-275-0512
Facsimile: 336-378-1390

MEMBERS OF FIRM

Gary K. Sue
Walter K. Burton

(See Next Column)

BURTON & SUE L.L.P.—*Continued*

ASSOCIATES

James D Secor, III
William T. Corbett, Jr.
William L. Hill
Kurt A. Seeber

For full biographical listings, see the Martindale-Hubbell Law Directory

CLIFFORD CLENDENIN O'HALE & JONES, L.L.P. (AV)

415 West Friendly Avenue, 27401
Telephone: 336-378-1212
Fax: 336-333-9820
Email: ccojcd@nr.infi.net

MEMBER OF FIRM

Harry H. Clendenin, III

For full biographical listings, see the Martindale-Hubbell Law Directory

*NEW BERN,** Craven Co.

KELLUM & JONES, P.A. (AV)

219 Broad Street, P.O. Box 866, 28563
Telephone: 919-633-2550
Fax: 919-633-4623
Jacksonville, North Carolina Office: 445-L Western Boulevard.
Telephone: 910-455-4546.
Fax: 910-455-2422.

John W. Beaman (1911-1984)
Norman B. Kellum, Jr.
Douglas M. Jones

Michael E. Garland
John T. Briggs
T. Russell Peterman, Jr.
Russell L. Needell
J. Kevin Jones

For full biographical listings, see the Martindale-Hubbell Law Directory

*RALEIGH,** Wake Co.

LEWIS & ROBERTS, P.L.L.C. (AV)

1305 Navaho Drive, Suite 400, 27609-7482
Telephone: 919-981-0191
888-981-0939
Facsimile: 919-981-0199
Mailing Address: P.O. Box 17529, Raleigh, N.C., 27619-7529
Rock Hill, South Carolina Office: 448 Lakeshore Parkway, Suite 200.
Telephone: 803-324-8118.
Facsimile: 803-324-2093.

Richard M. Lewis
James A. Roberts, III
Steven M. Rudisill (Resident, Rock Hill, South Carolina Office)
Winston L. Page, Jr.
Timothy S. Riordan
Jack Spain Holmes
Daniel K. Bryson
John D. Elvers
A. Graham Shirley
Brian D. Lake
John H. Ruocchio
Robert L. Pratt
Garth Hinsdale White (Resident, Rock Hill, South Carolina Office)
Devin Ferree Thomas
James T. Johnson
Daniel T. Tower

For full biographical listings, see the Martindale-Hubbell Law Directory

MICHAELS, JONES, MARTIN, PARRIS & TESSENER LAW OFFICES, PLLC (AV)

Suite 200, 410 Glenwood Avenue, 27603
Telephone: 919-821-0005
Fax: 919-832-7426
URL: http://www.michaelsandjones.com
Durham, North Carolina Office: University Tower, Suite 526, 27707.
Telephone: 919-544-3000.
Wilmington, North Carolina Office: 1213 Culbreth Drive, Suite 104, 28405.
Telephone: 910-256-4005.
Charlotte, North Carolina Office: 301 South McDowell Street, Suite 400.
Telephone: 1-800-662-1234.

Paul J. Michaels
John Alan Jones
Gregory M. Martin
E. Spencer Parris
Hoyt G. Tessener
Kenneth B. Oettinger
H. Forest Horne, Jr.
Gary W. Jackson
Tamara R. Nance
John Michael Riley
Monique M. Peebles
Sandra W. Mitterling
Gabriel F. Jiménez (Not admitted in NC)
Ronald L. Pressley

For full biographical listings, see the Martindale-Hubbell Law Directory

TEAGUE, CAMPBELL, DENNIS & GORHAM, L.L.P. (AV)

1621 Midtown Place, 27609
Telephone: 919-873-0166
Facsimile: 919-873-1814
URL: http://www.tcdg.com
Lumberton, North Carolina Office: 408 North Chestnut Street, P.O. Box 1424.
Telephone: 910-738-8534.

MEMBERS OF FIRM

C. Woodrow Teague
George W. Dennis III
Henry W. Gorham
Dayle A. Flammia
Linda Stephens
Thomas M. Clare
Robert C. Kerner, Jr.
John A. Tomei
Bruce Alan Hamilton
George H. Pender

ASSOCIATES

Donald F. Lively
Bryan T. Simpson
J. Matthew Little
Gregory M. Willis
Mallory A. Taylor
Jan N. Pittman
Kurt F. Hausler
John R. Green, Jr.
Melissa R. Garrell
Heather L. Aberle

LEGAL SUPPORT PERSONNEL

William H. Stephenson

Representative Clients: AIG; CIGNA; CNA Insurance Co.; Sedgwick CMS; Zurich US Insurance Group; Wausau Insurance Companies; Fireman's Fund Insurance Co.; Great American Insurance Co.; Ohio Casualty Group; USF&G.

For full biographical listings, see the Martindale-Hubbell Law Directory

YATES, MCLAMB & WEYHER, L.L.P. (AV)

One Hannover Square, 421 Fayetteville Street Mall, Suite 1200, 27601
Telephone: 919-835-0900
Fax: 919-835-0910
Mailing Address: P.O. Box 2889, 27602-2889

MEMBERS OF FIRM

R. Scott Brown
Derek M. Crump
Dan J. McLamb
John W. Minier
Rodney E. Pettey
O. Craig Tierney, Jr.
Andrew A. Vanore, III
Kirk G. Warner
Barbara B. Weyher
Joseph W. Yates, III (Retired)

ASSOCIATES

Virginia Green Adams
Michael J. Byrne
Hunt K. Choi
Barry S. Cobb
Renee Billings Crawford
Susan T. Fountain
Gwenda L. Laws
Michael E. McDaniel
Travis K. Morton
Shirley Maring Pruitt
Beth Y. Smoot
Diane S. Tilley
Michael W. Washburn

OF COUNSEL

Michael C. Hurley

Representative Clients: Employer's Insurance of Wausau; The Travelers; Universal Underwriters Insurance Co.; St. Paul Insurance Cos.

For full biographical listings, see the Martindale-Hubbell Law Directory

*WILMINGTON,** New Hanover Co.

STEPHEN E. CULBRETH (AV)

514 Chestnut Street, P.O. Box 446, 28402
Telephone: 910-763-3416
Facsimile: 910-763-9975
Email: culbreth@wilmington.net *URL:* http://www.lawyers.com/culbrethlaw

For full biographical listings, see the Martindale-Hubbell Law Directory

*WINSTON-SALEM,** Forsyth Co.

BENNETT & GUTHRIE, P.L.L.C. (AV)

3334 Healy Drive, Suite 203, 27103-1476
Telephone: 336-765-3121
Fax: 336-765-8622

Richard V. Bennett
Rodney A. Guthrie
Stanley P. Dean

Kevin J. Williams

Representative Clients: American Continental Insurance Company; Commercial Union Insurance Company; Integon Insurance; Kentucky Medical Insurance Company; Medtronic, Inc.; Montgomery Mutual Insurance Company; Novant Health, Inc.; Pennsylvania Lumberman's Mutual Insurance Company; St. Paul Fire & Marine Insurance Company; Zurich Insurance Company.

For full biographical listings, see the Martindale-Hubbell Law Directory

OHIO

*CINCINNATI,** Hamilton Co.

CLEMENTS, MAHIN & COHEN (AV)

708 Walnut Street, Suite 600, 45202-4009
Telephone: 513-721-6500
Facsimile: 513-763-6415

MEMBERS OF FIRM

William E. Clements
Edward Cohen

For full biographical listings, see the Martindale-Hubbell Law Directory

FINKELMEIER & FARRELL (AV)

36 East Seventh Street, Suite 1660, 45202-4461
Telephone: 513-621-9921
Fax: 513-621-9923

Louis J. Finkelmeier
William I. Farrell

For full biographical listings, see the Martindale-Hubbell Law Directory

KEPLEY, GILLIGAN & EYRICH A LEGAL PROFESSIONAL ASSOCIATION (AV)

525 Vine Street, Suite 2200, 45202
Telephone: 513-241-5540; 621-1045
Fax: 513-241-8111; 621-0038

Augustine Giglio

Representative Clients and References furnished upon request.

For full biographical listings, see the Martindale-Hubbell Law Directory

*CLEVELAND,** Cuyahoga Co.

DUVIN, CAHN & HUTTON A LEGAL PROFESSIONAL ASSOCIATION (AV)

Erieview Tower, 20th Floor, 1301 East Ninth Street, 44114
Telephone: 216-696-7600
Facsimile: 216-696-2038
Email: attorneys@duvin.com *URL:* http://www.duvinlaw.com
Southfield, Michigan Office: 26211 Central Park Boulevard, Suite 500, 48076.
Telephone: 248-945-1977.
Fax: 248-945-1162.

Robert P. Duvin
Stephen J. Cahn
Lee J. Hutton
Marc J. Bloch
Andrew C. Meyer
Martin S. List
Craig M. Brown
Frank W. Buck
Neal B. Wainblat
Kenneth B. Stark
Martin T. Wymer
Robert M. Wolff
Steven W. Albert
Stephen J. Sferra
Christine C. Covey
Richard C. Hubbard, III
Jon M. Dileno
Suellen Oswald
David A. Posner
Janette McCarthy Louard

Lisa Froimson Mann
David W. Neel
Kathleen M. Kordeleski
Michael T. Pearson
Kenneth D. Schwartz
Brett S. Krantz
Barry Y. Freeman
Bradley A. Sherman
Jonathan S. Forman
Mark F. Humenik
Robert C. Pivonka
Fredrick W Englehart
Jonathan T. Hyman
Latha M. Srinivasan
Shannon K. Patton

OF COUNSEL

Mark V. Webber

Representative Clients: Ameritech; Lincoln Electric; Cleveland-Akron-Canton Supermarket Industry; Cleveland Clinic Foundation; The Scott Fetzer Co.; LTV Steel Company; Electronic Data Systems Corporation; Steris; AVI Foodsystem; Ohio Turnpike Commission.

For full biographical listings, see the Martindale-Hubbell Law Directory

NURENBERG, PLEVIN, HELLER & MCCARTHY CO., L.P.A. (AV)

1370 Ontario Street First Floor, 44113-1792
Telephone: 216-621-2300; Toll Free: 1-800-562-7438
Fax: 216-771-2242
Email: nphm@nphm.com *URL:* http://www.nphm.com

A. H. Dudnik (1905-1963)
S. F. Komito (1902-1984)
Marshall I. Nurenberg
Leon M. Plevin
Maurice L. Heller
John J. McCarthy
Thomas Mester
Harlan M. Gordon
David M. Paris
Richard L. Demsey
Jamie R. Lebovitz
William S. Jacobson
Jeffrey A. Leikin

(See Next Column)

Robin J. Peterson
Robert S. Zeller
Ellen M. McCarthy
J. Charles Ruiz-Bueno
Kathleen J. St. John
Jonathan D. Mester
Brenda M. Johnson

Reference: Society Key Corp.

For full biographical listings, see the Martindale-Hubbell Law Directory

STEWART AND DE CHANT CO., L.P.A. (AV)

The Atrium Office Plaza-Suite 850, 668 Euclid Avenue, 44114-3060
Telephone: 216-781-2258
Fax: 216-781-8210
Email: INFO@STEWARTDECHANT.COM *URL:* http://www.STEWARTdeChant.COM

Lawrence E. Stewart
Thomas H. De Chant
Fred Wendel III
Scott E. Stewart
Samuel V. Butcher
Lawrence C. Davison
Matthew T. Brady

Reference: Keybank (Main Office).

For full biographical listings, see the Martindale-Hubbell Law Directory

*COLUMBUS,** Franklin Co.

BRICKER & ECKLER LLP (AV)

100 South Third Street, 43215-4291
Telephone: 614-227-2300
Telecopy: 614-227-2390
Email: info@be.bricker.com *URL:* http://www.bricker.com

Charles D. Smith

Nelson M. Reid
Bobbie S. Sprader

Representative Clients: NFIB (Ohio); Kraft Foods; Hill's Pride.

For Complete List of Firm Personnel, See General Section

For full biographical listings, see the Martindale-Hubbell Law Directory

PHILIP J. FULTON & ASSOCIATES (AV)

Two Nationwide Plaza, Suite 225, 280 North High Street, 43215
Telephone: 614-224-3838
Fax: 614-224-3933
Email: phil@fultonlaw.com

William A. Thorman III
Lori Burns Painter

For full biographical listings, see the Martindale-Hubbell Law Directory

*DAYTON,** Montgomery Co.

E. S. GALLON & ASSOCIATES (AV)

40 West Fourth Street Centre Suite 2200, 45402
Telephone: 937-586-3100; 800-998-4374
Fax: 937-586-3200
URL: http://www.esgallon.com

MEMBERS OF FIRM

Jack A. Cervay
David A. Saphire
Joseph R. Ebenger
Joan B. Brenner
James D. Dennis
James R. Piercy
Richard M. Malone
Kyle D. Martin
Natalie J. Tackett

ASSOCIATE

David R. Salyer

For full biographical listings, see the Martindale-Hubbell Law Directory

DUBLIN, Franklin Co.

BLAUGRUND, HERBERT & MARTIN, INCORPORATED (AV)

5455 Rings Road, Suite 500, 43017-7517
Telephone: 614-764-0681
Fax: 614-764-0774
Email: bhm@bhmlaw.net

Sharon Cason-Adams

For full biographical listings, see the Martindale-Hubbell Law Directory

EASTLAKE, Lake Co.

JANE P. WILSON & ASSOCIATES CO., L.P.A. (AV)

Centre Plaza South, 35350 Curtis Boulevard, Suite 350, 44095-4063
Telephone: 440-954-9390
Fax: 440-954-9389
Email: WILSONLPA@aol.com *URL:* http://www.lawyers.com/janepwilson

Jane P. Wilson

(See Next Column)

JANE P. WILSON & ASSOCIATES CO., L.P.A.—*Continued*

Graig E. Kluge

Representative Clients: Apex Paper Box; Bailey Controls; Florida Panthers Hockey Club; Lexington Connector Seals; Magic American Corporation; PepsiCo.; Perkins Family Restaurants; Plastech, Inc.; R.M.I. Titanium Company; Sterling Tenatronics.

For full biographical listings, see the Martindale-Hubbell Law Directory

MIDDLETOWN, Butler Co.

CASPER AND CASPER (AV)

615 Gas & Electric Building, One North Main Street, P.O. Box 510, 45042
Telephone: 513-424-2401;
Cincinnati: 513-381-7096;
Dayton: 937-224-1222;
Hamilton: 513-892-2560
Fax: 513-424-0622

I. A. Casper (1910-1981)
Jack A. Casper (1912-1996)
Arthur Brandeis Casper
E. Jeffrey Casper
Douglas W. Casper
Sanford I. Casper
Ronald M. Kabakoff
Rebecca L. Wilkinson
Patrick W. Allen
Barbara L. Strady
Margaret Halnon McCollum
Mark A. Summers
Megan Richards
Nicole C. Allbritain
William P. Allen

For full biographical listings, see the Martindale-Hubbell Law Directory

*TOLEDO,** Lucas Co.

EASTMAN & SMITH LTD. (AV)

One Seagate, Twenty-Fourth Floor, P.O. Box 10032, 43699-0032
Telephone: 419-241-6000
Telecopier: 419-247-1777
Columbus, Ohio Office: 65 East State Street, Suite 1000, 43215.
Telephone: 614-460-3556.
Telecopier: 614-228-5371.

MEMBERS OF FIRM

Patrick J. Johnson
John T. Landwehr
Robert J. Gilmer, Jr.
Thomas A. Dixon
Thomas J. Gibney

ASSOCIATES

Margaret A. Mattimoe
Michael J. Spisak
Katharine M. Thomas
Natacha M. Vincent-Kolcun

Counsel for: Chrysler Corp.; Marathon Oil; Envirosafe Service of Ohio, Inc.; Glasstech, Inc.; Toledo-Lucas County Port Authority; Huntington National Bank; Capital Bank, N.A.; Riverside Hospital; The Travelers Group; The Hartford Insurance Group.

For Complete List of Firm Personnel, See General Section

For full biographical listings, see the Martindale-Hubbell Law Directory

OKLAHOMA

*ARDMORE,** Carter Co.

HARRY L. BICKFORD LAW OFFICE (AV)

29 B Street, S.W., P.O. Box 1027, 73402
Telephone: 580-223-5566
Fax: 580-226-1893
Email: bickford@brightok.net

Local Counsel: Ultramar Diamond Shamrock Corporation (Total Petroleum, Inc. and Total Pipeline Corporation); The Williams Companies, Inc.; Williams Pipe Line Company.
References: American National Bank of Ardmore; BancFirst; Citizens National Bank & Trust Company.

For full biographical listings, see the Martindale-Hubbell Law Directory

*OKLAHOMA CITY,** Oklahoma Co.

CROWE & DUNLEVY, A PROFESSIONAL CORPORATION (AV)

1800 Mid-America Tower, 20 North Broadway, 73102-8273
Telephone: 405-235-7700
Fax: 405-239-6651
Email: marketing@crowedunlevy.com *URL:* http://www.crowedunlevy.com
Tulsa, Oklahoma Office: 500 Kennedy Building, 321 South Boston Avenue, 74103-3313.
Telephone: 918-592-9800.
Fax: 918-592-9801.

(See Next Column)

Norman, Oklahoma Office: Crowe & Dunlevy, 2500 South McGee, Suite 140, 73072-6705.
Telephone: 405-321-7317.
Fax: 405-360-4002.

Arlen E. Fielden

For Complete List of Firm Personnel, See General Section

For full biographical listings, see the Martindale-Hubbell Law Directory

DAY, EDWARDS, FEDERMAN, PROPESTER & CHRISTENSEN, P.C. (AV)

Suite 2900 Oklahoma Tower, 210 Park Avenue, 73102-5605
Telephone: 405-239-2121
Telecopier: 405-236-1012
URL: http://lawlinks.com/attys/ok/defpc.html

D. Wade Christensen

Nick C. Linholm
Gary L. Farnum

Representative Clients: Accord Human Resources; Allied Group Insurance; Anchor Claims Management; Casualty Reciprocal Exchange; Consolidated Benefits Resources; Crawford & Company; Cunningham Lindsey Claims Management; Employer's Mutual Companies; Equitable Plan Services; Gallagher Bassett Services.

For Complete List of Firm Personnel, See General Section

For full biographical listings, see the Martindale-Hubbell Law Directory

MCCAFFREY & TAWWATER (AV)

Suite 1950, One Leadership Square, 211 North Robinson, 73102-7124
Telephone: 405-235-2900
Fax: 405-231-2818
URL: http://www.mccaffreytawwater.com
Other Oklahoma City, Oklahoma Office: 3015 N.W. 59th, 73112.

MEMBERS OF FIRM

George J. McCaffrey
Larry A. Tawwater

ASSOCIATES

Jo Lynn Slama
Loren F. Gibson
Steven R. Davis
Piper E. John
David B. Custar

For full biographical listings, see the Martindale-Hubbell Law Directory

*TULSA,** Tulsa Co.

BEST & SHARP, A PROFESSIONAL CORPORATION (AV)

Oneok Plaza, 100 W. 5th, Suite 808, 74103-4225
Telephone: 918-582-1234
Fax: 918-585-9447
Email: Webmaster@BestSharp.com *URL:* http://www.BestSharp.com

Malcom D. Smith, Jr.

For full biographical listings, see the Martindale-Hubbell Law Directory

BOONE, SMITH, DAVIS, HURST & DICKMAN, A PROFESSIONAL CORPORATION (AV)

500 Oneok Plaza, 100 West 5th Street, 74103
Telephone: 918-587-0000
Fax: 918-599-9317
URL: http://www.boonesmith.com

Byron V. Boone (1908-1988)
Teresa Meinders Burkett
John A. Burkhardt
Paul J. Cleary
Reuben Davis
J. Jerry Dickman
Monica Goodman
David J. Hyman
William C. Kellough
Donald A. Lepp
Mary Lohrke
Kimberly Lambert Love
Scott R. Rowland
Frederic N. (Nick) Schneider III
Jeffrey R. Schoborg
Stephen Schuller
L. K. Smith
Paul E. Swain III

OF COUNSEL

Edwin S. Hurst
Lloyd G. Minter

Representative Clients: American Airlines; BP Amoco Corp.; Chevron U.S.A., Inc.; Ford Motor Co.; Hillcrest Medical Center; PricewaterhouseCoopers; Phillips Petroleum Co.; The Boeing Company; Sears, Roebuck & Co.; World Publishing Co; Whirlpool Corp.

For full biographical listings, see the Martindale-Hubbell Law Directory

Tulsa—Continued

CROWE & DUNLEVY, A PROFESSIONAL CORPORATION (AV)

500 Kennedy Building, 321 South Boston Avenue, 74103-3313
Telephone: 918-592-9800
Fax: 918-592-9801
Email: marketing@crowedunlevy.com *URL:* http://www.crowedunlevy.com
Oklahoma City, Oklahoma Office: 1800 Mid-America Tower, 20 North Broadway, 73102-8273.
Telephone: 405-235-7700.
Fax: 405-239-6651.
Norman, Oklahoma Office: Crowe & Dunlevy, 2500 South McGee, Suite 140, 73072-6705.
Telephone: 405-321-7317.
Fax: 405-360-4002.

Madalene A. B. Witterholt

For Complete List of Firm Personnel, See General Section

For full biographical listings, see the Martindale-Hubbell Law Directory

---

FRASIER, FRASIER & HICKMAN (AV)

1700 Southwest Boulevard, 74107
Telephone: 918-584-4724
Fax: 918-583-5637
Email: frasier@tulsa.com *URL:* http://www.frasierlaw.com

MEMBERS OF FIRM

Thomas Dee Frasier
James E. Frasier
Steven R. Hickman
John W. Flippo
Everett R. Bennett, Jr.
Jerry L. Franks, Jr.
Robert A. Flynn
Frank Frasier, III

ASSOCIATE

Gary G. Brasel
George M. Miles

References: Community State Bank, Tulsa, Oklahoma; American Exchange Bank, Tulsa, Oklahoma; The Bank of Oklahoma, Tulsa, Oklahoma.

For full biographical listings, see the Martindale-Hubbell Law Directory

---

RHODES, HIERONYMUS, JONES, TUCKER & GABLE, P.L.L.C. (AV)

Oneok Plaza, 100 West 5th Street, Suite 400, P.O. Box 21100, 74121-1100
Telephone: 918-582-1173
Fax: 918-592-3390
URL: http://www.rhodesokla.com

MEMBERS OF FIRM

Kevin D. Berry
Jo Anne Deaton
Richard M. Eldridge
E. D. Hieronymus (1908 -1994)
Bert M. Jones
William S. Leach
Michael W. McGivern
William D. Perrine
Mary Quinn-Cooper
Robert P. Redemann
David P. Reid
Chris L. Rhodes, III
Thomas E. Steichen
Catherine C. Taylor
John H. Tucker
Wilson T. White
Harold C. Zuckerman

Ann E. Allison
Steven K. Bunting
Robert P. Coffey, Jr.
J. Christopher Davis
Andrew D. Downing
Dana L. Gish
Kerry R. Lewis
Andrew L. Richardson
Michael F. Smith
Leslie J. Southerland
Kimberly E. West
Keith A. Wilkes

OF COUNSEL

George W. Gable (Retired Partner)
Larry J. Fulton
Kelly M. Greenough

Representative Clients: American International Companies; Bechtel; Chubb Group of Insurance Companies; General Motors Corporation; Merrill, Lynch; Nissan Motor Corporation in U.S.A.; Pfizer, Inc.; Volkswagen of America, Volkswagen, A.G.; Zurich U.S.

For full biographical listings, see the Martindale-Hubbell Law Directory

---

OREGON

*PORTLAND,** Multnomah Co.

RONALD W. ATWOOD, P.C. (AV)

925 Yeon Building, 522 S.W. Fifth Avenue, 97204
Telephone: 503-525-0963
Fax: 503-525-0966
Email: ratwood@europa.com *URL:* http://www.lawyers.com/atwoodlaw

Ronald W. Atwood

For full biographical listings, see the Martindale-Hubbell Law Directory

SATHER, BYERLY & HOLLOWAY, LLP (AV)

621 Southwest Morrison Street, Suite 650, 97205
Telephone: 503-225-5858
Fax: 503-721-9272
Email: sbh@teleport.com *URL:* http://www.teleport.com/~sbh/sbh.htm

Deborah L. Sather
Bruce L. Byerly
Ronald C. Holloway
Krishna Balasubramani
Tracy J. White
Constance Lynn Wold

For full biographical listings, see the Martindale-Hubbell Law Directory

---

SWANSON, THOMAS & COON (AV)

American Bank Building, 621 S.W. Morrison, Suite 900, 97205-3892
Telephone: 503-228-5222
Fax: 503-273-9175
URL: http://www.stc-law.com

MEMBERS OF FIRM

Douglas A. Swanson
Raymond F. Thomas
James S. Coon

ASSOCIATES

Megan E. Glor
Alan Stuart Graf
Margaret F. Weddell

For full biographical listings, see the Martindale-Hubbell Law Directory

---

WALLACE, KLOR & MANN, P.C. (AV)

1500 Koin Center, 222 Southwest Columbia, 97201
Telephone: 503-224-8949
FAX: 503-224-0410
URL: http://www.wallaceklor.com
Seattle, Washington Office: 4200 Two Union Square, 601 Union Street, 98101-4000.
Telephone: 206-223-1176.
Fax: 206-467-2884.

Schuyler T. Wallace, Jr.
John L. Klor
Lawrence E. Mann

Edward S. McGlone, III
Leah D. Sideras
Linda Conratt
Jeffery Howard Capener

For full biographical listings, see the Martindale-Hubbell Law Directory

---

PENNSYLVANIA

BLUE BELL, Montgomery Co.

KELLEY & MURPHY (AV)

Union Meeting Corporate Center V, Suite 160 925 Harvest Drive, 19422
Telephone: 215-643-6500
Fax: 215-643-8356
Cable Address: "BIGTIME"
Email: kmlaw@counsel.com

Joseph T. Kelley, Jr.
Patrick G. Murphy
Joseph T. Kelley, III

LEGAL SUPPORT PERSONNEL

Marianne Rowen
Tanja M.Z. Barron

For full biographical listings, see the Martindale-Hubbell Law Directory

DOWNINGTOWN, Chester Co.

WUSINICH AND BROGAN (AV)

537 West Uwchlan Avenue, Suite 200, P.O. Box 478, 19335-0478
Telephone: 610-594-1600
Fax: 610-594-6518
Email: info@wusinichbrogon.com *URL:* http://www.wusinichbrogan.com
Reading, Pennsylvania Office: 522 Washington Street.
Telephone: 610-373-8550.
West Chester, Pennsylvania Office: Nineteen South High Street.
Telephone: 610-436-6280.

MEMBERS OF FIRM

Joseph F. Wusinich, III
Dennis D. Brogan
John J. Stanzione

Louis Aurely, III
David V. Grow
Edward C. Sweeney

For full biographical listings, see the Martindale-Hubbell Law Directory

*GREENSBURG,** Westmoreland Co.

BELDEN, BELDEN, PERSIN & JOHNSTON (AV)

Belden Building, 117 North Main Street, 15601
Telephone: 724-834-0300
Fax: 724-834-1307

(See Next Column)

BELDEN, BELDEN, PERSIN & JOHNSTON—*Continued*

MEMBERS OF FIRM

H. Reginald Belden (1907-1993)
Dennis N. Persin
H. Reginald Belden, Jr.
Robert I. Johnston

ASSOCIATES

John K. Greiner
Jeffrey D. Monzo

Represent: GenCorp.; Moore & Morford, Inc.; Standard Steel; Equipment Finance Co.; The Home Insurance Co.; Westmoreland Museum of Art; Grange Mutual Insurance Co.; Bell Telephone of Pennsylvania; Coregil Group; Westmoreland County.

For full biographical listings, see the Martindale-Hubbell Law Directory

*HARRISBURG,** Dauphin Co.

THOMAS, THOMAS & HAFER, LLP (AV)

305 North Front Street, 6th Floor, P.O. Box 999, 17108
Telephone: 717-237-7100
Fax: 717-237-7105
Verify: 717-255-7642
Bethlehem, Pennsylvania Office: 12 East Market Street, P.O. Box 1172, 12016.
Telephone: 610-868-1675.
Fax: 610-868-1702.

MEMBERS OF FIRM

Joseph P. Hafer
James K. Thomas, II
Robertson B. Taylor
Jeffrey B. Rettig
Peter J. Curry
R. Burke McLemore, Jr.
Edward H. Jordan, Jr.
C. Kent Price
Randall G. Gale
David L. Schwalm
Peter J. Speaker
Douglas B. Marcello
Paul J. Dellasega

OF COUNSEL

James K. Thomas

Timothy I. Mark
Daniel J. Gallagher
Robert A. Taylor
Sarah W. Arosell
Eugene N. McHugh
Stephen E. Geduldig
Karen S. Coates
Gary T. Lathrop
Todd B. Narvol
James J. Dodd-o
Kenneth A. Rapp
Kevin C. McNamara
Brooks R. Foland
John Flounlacker
John M. Popilock
Michele J. Thorp

Representative Clients: Aetna Casualty & Surety Co.; Bethlehem Steel Corp.; Commercial Union Insurance Companies; Geisinger Medical Center; Hartford Insurance Group; Liberty Mutual Insurance Co.; Pennsylvania Hospital Insurance Co.; Pennsylvania Medical Society Liability Insurance Co.; UGI Corp.; Weis Markets, Inc.

For full biographical listings, see the Martindale-Hubbell Law Directory

*PHILADELPHIA,** Philadelphia Co.

CHRISTINA J. BARBIERI & ASSOCIATES (AV)

1518 Walnut Street, 13th Floor, 19102
Telephone: 215-772-3020;
800-844-3467
Fax: 215-772-1908

ASSOCIATES

Michael C. Bauerle
Catherine Tanaka Surbeck
Eric S. Borjeson
Richard W. Rosenblitt

LEGAL SUPPORT PERSONNEL

Theresa M. Skay (Paralegal)

For full biographical listings, see the Martindale-Hubbell Law Directory

FURIA AND TURNER (AV)

1717 Rittenhouse Square, 19103-6109
Telephone: 215-985-4500
Telecopier: 215-985-2824
Email: rfuria1717@aol.com *URL:* http://www.lawyers.com/furiaandturner

MEMBER OF FIRM

James M. Turner, Jr.

ASSOCIATES

Gina R. Furia
Donna DiPietro-Gerace

For full biographical listings, see the Martindale-Hubbell Law Directory

GALFAND BERGER, LLP (AV)

1818 Market Street, 23rd Floor, 19103-3623
Telephone: 215-665-1600
Fax: 215-564-2262
Email: sdonaway@galfandberger.com *URL:* http://www.galfandberger.com

Marc S. Jacobs

Jean H. Chey
Michael W. McGurrin
Kelly F. Melcher
Thomas J. O'Brien

For full biographical listings, see the Martindale-Hubbell Law Directory

GOLDFEIN & JOSEPH, A PROFESSIONAL CORPORATION (AV)

1600 Market Street 33rd Floor, 19103-7288
Telephone: 215-979-8200
Fax: 215-979-8201
URL: http://www.goldfeinlaw.com
Princeton, New Jersey Office: Princeton Metro Center, Suite 115, 5 Vaughn Drive.
Telephone: 609-520-0400.
Fax: 609-520-1450.
Wilmington, Delaware Office: PNC Bank Center, Suite 1110, P.O. Box 2206, 222 Delaware Avenue.
Telephone: 302-656-3301.
Fax: 302-656-0643.
New York, New York Office: 150 Broadway, Suite 1212, 10038.
Telephone: 212-791-0340.
Fax: 212-791-0347.

Edward B. Joseph
Fredric L. Goldfein
E. Chandler Hosmer, III
David C. Weinberg
Bernard L. Levinthal
Roseann Lynn Brenner
Gary H. Kaplan
John A. Turlik

Michael A. Billotti
Medford J. Brown, III
Robert P. Coleman
Robert T. Connor
Charles D. Cooper
Kelly A. Costello
Lawrence E. Currier
Janet E. Golup
Christine Renee Guiliano
David M. Katzenstein
Matthew A Kelly, III
Deborah M. Knight
Pamela A. Post
Thomas M. Savon
Julie M. Sebring (Not admitted in PA)
Robert M. Stroh
Marc R. Wilner
Anthony F. Zabicki, Jr.

For full biographical listings, see the Martindale-Hubbell Law Directory

MARKS, O'NEILL, REILLY, O'BRIEN & COURTNEY, P.C. (AV)

1880 John F. Kennedy Boulevard Suite 1200, 19103
Telephone: 215-564-6688
Fax: 215-564-2526
Email: moro1@morocpa.com
Norristown, Pennsylvania Office: 411 Cherry Street.
Telephone: 215-277-7601.
Pittsburgh, Pennsylvania Office: 707 Grant Street, Gulf Tower, Suite 3200.
Telephone: 412-391-6171.
Fax: 412-391-8804.
Westmont, New Jersey Office: 216 Haddon Avenue, Suite 500.
Telephone: 856-858-6110.
Fax: 856-858-3687. E-Mail: moro1@morocnj.com
Wilmington, Delaware Office: 2004 Foulk Road, Suite 7.
Telephone: 302-475-5500.
Fax: 302-475-5584.

Jerome E. Marks
Joseph M. O'Neill
Vincent F. Reilly
Kevin J. O'Brien
Dawn R. Courtney
Sean Xavier Kelly
Gino P. Mecoli
John J. Repcheck (Resident, Pittsburgh Office)

David P. Helwig (Resident, Pittsburgh Office)
Maureen Murray-O'Toole
Patrick C. Lamb
Christine G. Boyle
Nancy E. Mancheski
Michael T. Hamilton
Kelly L. Bracken
Tracey Marie McDevitt
Sharon A. Connors (Resident, Westmont, New Jersey Office)
Malissa A. Richetti
Patricia M. Henrich
Judith H. Ring
Gary Weinberg (Resident, Westmont, New Jersey Office)
Lee J. Janiczek
Wendy D. Testa (Resident, Westmont, New Jersey Office)
Gary F. Sharlock (Resident, Pittsburgh Office)
Robert Dale Leidigh (Resident, Pittsburgh Office)
Joseph L. Orszulak, II (Resident, Pittsburgh Office)
Diane Beckman Carvell
Karen J. Stanzione
Michael A. Kosar
Susan D. Grant (Resident, Westmont, New Jersey Office)
Frances Wang-Deveney (Resident, Westmont, New Jersey)
Courtney E. Passin
Stephanie Victoria Shreibman
Megan Kochell D'Iorio (Resident, Wilmington, Delaware Office)
Megan Trocki Mantzavinos (Resident, Wilmington, Delaware Office)
Toni Anderson Moore
Natalie M. Nugent
Frank Gattuso
Michael A. Ring (Resident, Westmont, New Jersey Office)
Ann M. Madden (Not admitted in PA)
Matthew J. Zamites
Salvatore A. Clemente

(See Next Column)

MARKS, O'NEILL, REILLY, O'BRIEN & COURTNEY P.C., *Philadelphia—Continued*

LEGAL SUPPORT PERSONNEL

PARALEGALS

Gregory P. Sabo
Elisa LaRosa
Frances P. Rossi
Heather Feenan
Jerry Ezekiel
Steven Randisi
Sharon Williams
Melanie Gaskins

For full biographical listings, see the Martindale-Hubbell Law Directory

MULVEY & FLANAGAN, P.C. (AV)

1520 Locust Street, 10th Floor, 19102
Telephone: 215-731-0100
Fax: 215-731-0180
Email: mulvey@ix.netcom.com *URL:* http://www.lawyers.com/mflaw

W. Michael Mulvey
Michael J. Flanagan
Maureen Hope Flanagan
Michael G. Dryden
Richard R. Budney, Jr.

For full biographical listings, see the Martindale-Hubbell Law Directory

RALPH D. SAMUEL & CO. A PROFESSIONAL CORPORATION (AV)

225 South 15th Street, Suite 1776, 19102
Telephone: 215-893-9992
Fax: 215-893-9996
Email: RalphSamuel@lawmine.com *URL:* http://www.lawyers.com/ralphdsamuellaw

Ralph David Samuel
Lynn Malmgren

For full biographical listings, see the Martindale-Hubbell Law Directory

CLAYTON H. THOMAS, JR. (AV)

37th Floor, Bell Atlantic Tower Building, 1717 Arch Street, 19103-2793
Telephone: 215-994-5290
Fax: 215-994-5296

Benjamin Rose

For full biographical listings, see the Martindale-Hubbell Law Directory

*PITTSBURGH,** Allegheny Co.

CAROSELLI, BEACHLER, MCTIERNAN & CONBOY, LLC (AV)

312 Boulevard of Allies, 8th Floor, 15222
Telephone: 412-391-9860
Pennsylvania Only: 1-800-222-8816
Nationally: 1-800-554-5864
Fax: 412-391-7453
URL: http://www.cbmclaw.com

MEMBERS OF FIRM

William R. Caroselli
Edwin H. Beachler
John W. McTiernan
G. Timothy Conboy
Thomas G. Smith
Craig E. Coleman
David A. McGowan
Catherine A. Baxter

ASSOCIATES

Daniel Bricmont
John J. Gaughan
William A. Penrod
Kevin W. Lee
Susan A. Meredith
Joanna P. Papazekos
Kelly L. Enders
Michael Brady Dodd

For full biographical listings, see the Martindale-Hubbell Law Directory

DAVIES MCFARLAND & CARROLL, P.C. (AV)

One Gateway Center, Tenth Floor, 15222
Telephone: 412-281-0737
Email: firm@dmcpc.com

Edward A. McFarland
James M. Poerio
C. Robert Keenan III
Christopher Pierson
Robert P. Walter
Susan Valerie Mason

Representative Clients: Motorists Insurance Cos.; Cincinnati Insurance Co.; GAB Robins North America; Nabisco Brands, Inc.; Marriott Corp.; May Department Stores; Municipal Risk Management; Food Lion, Inc.; The Home Depot, Inc.; John Deere Insurance Co.

For Complete List of Firm Personnel, See General Section

For full biographical listings, see the Martindale-Hubbell Law Directory

MARCUS & SHAPIRA LLP (AV)

35th Floor, One Oxford Centre, 301 Grant Street, 15219-6401
Telephone: 412-471-3490
Telecopier: 412-391-8758
Email: info@marcus-shapira.com *URL:* http://www.marcus-shapira.com

MEMBER OF FIRM

Sylvester A. Beozzo

ASSOCIATE

Susan H. Snively

For Complete List of Firm Personnel, See General Section

For full biographical listings, see the Martindale-Hubbell Law Directory

*SCRANTON,** Lackawanna Co.

LENAHAN & DEMPSEY, A PROFESSIONAL CORPORATION (AV)

116 North Washington Avenue, 18503-0234
Telephone: 717-346-2097; 1-888-LENAHAN
Fax: 717-346-1174
Mailing Address: P.O. Box 234, Scranton, Pennsylvania, 18501-0234

John R. Lenahan, Sr. (1915-1998)
William J. Dempsey (Of Counsel)
John R. Lenahan, Jr.
Joseph P. Lenahan
Kathleen A. Lenahan
David E. Heisler
Timothy G. Lenahan
Matthew D. Dempsey

Alan P. Schoen
Brian J. Lenahan
Diane Hepford Lenahan
George E. Mehalchick
Brian Yeager
Thomas R. Daniels
Terrence E. Dempsey
Christine S. Mayernick-Lezinski
John M. Mulcahey
Margaret M. Dempsey
Lisa G. Wilson

Representative Insurance Clients: Allstate Insurance Co.; America Security Insurance Co.; Metropolitan Casualty Insurance Co.; Aetna Insurance Co.; Pennsylvania National Insurance Group; Kemper Insurance Group; American Mutual Insurance Cos.; American States Insurance, Co.

For full biographical listings, see the Martindale-Hubbell Law Directory

MUNLEY, MUNLEY & CARTWRIGHT, P.C. (AV)

205 Madison Avenue, 18503
Telephone: 570-346-7401
Fax: 570-346-3452
URL: http://www.lawyers.com/mmclaw
Email: lawyers@munley.com *URL:* http://www.munley.com

Robert W. Munley
James Christopher Munley
Daniel W. Munley
Robert W. Munley, III

Reference: First National Bank of Jermyn.

For full biographical listings, see the Martindale-Hubbell Law Directory

O'MALLEY & HARRIS, P.C. (AV)

345 Wyoming Avenue, 18503
Telephone: 570-348-3711
Fax: 570-348-4092
Email: ohpc@epix.net *URL:* http://www.ohpclaw.com
Stroudsburg, Pennsylvania Office: 111 North Seventh Street.
Telephone: 570-421-2252; 570-422-1280.
FAX: 570-422-1281. Email: cerato@ptdprolog.net.
Wilkes-Barre, Pennsylvania Office: 61 North Washington Street.
Telephone: 570-829-3232.
FAX: 570-829-4418. Email: ohpcwb@epix.net.
Williamsport, Pennsylvania Office: 321 Pine Street, Suite 308.
Telephone: 570-323-4380.

Eugene Nogi (1905-1975)
Henry Nogi (1900-1976)
Russell J. O'Malley, Sr. (1904-1993)
Norman Harris (1907-1998)
William H. Amesbury (Resident, Wilkes-Barre Office)
Paul A. Barrett
Matthew P. Barrett
J. Scott Brady (Resident, Wilkes-Barre Office)
Lori J. Cerato (Resident, Stroudsburg Office)
Bruce L. Coyer
John Q. Durkin
Gerald J. Hanchulak
Richard K. Hodges
Timothy J. Holland (Resident, Wilkes-Barre Office)
John F. Kennedy (Resident, Wilkes-Barre Office)
Daniel Morgan
Michael Perry
James M. Tressler
Joseph Timothy Healey
A. Ruth Whalen (Resident, Wilkes-Barre Office)

Representative Clients: Pennsylvania Hospital Insurance Co.; MMI Systems Agency, Inc.; State Farm Insurance Company; ITT Specialty Risk Services; St. Paul Fire & Marine Insurance Co.; Chubb Group of Insurance Companies; Geisingen System Services; Princeton Insurance Company; Northeastern Pennsylvania Physicians Organization; Catholic Healthcare Partners.

For full biographical listings, see the Martindale-Hubbell Law Directory

Scranton—Continued

O'MALLEY & LANGAN A PROFESSIONAL CORPORATION (AV)

Mulberry Professional Plaza, Suite 203, 426 Mulberry Street, 18503
Telephone: 570-344-COMP (2667)
Fax: 570-344-6199
Email: OandL@AOL.COM *URL:* http://www.omalleylangan.com
Pittston, Pennsylvania Office: 9 North Main Street, P.O. Box 664.
Telephone: 570-883-1321.
Fax: 570-883-1250.

Todd J. O'Malley
Gerard W. Langan, Jr.
Mary D. Walsh-Dempsey
Mary Anne O. Lucas
Thomas E. Lucas, Jr.
Christina T. Novajosky
Michael J. Vazquez, Jr.
Michael J. Kenny

For full biographical listings, see the Martindale-Hubbell Law Directory

SCANLON, HOWLEY, SCANLON & DOHERTY (AV)

321 Spruce Street, 10th Floor, 18503
Telephone: 570-346-7651
Fax: 570-344-1542

MEMBERS OF FIRM

James M. Howley
James M. Scanlon
James A. Doherty, Jr.
Thomas R. Nealon
Thomas B. Helbig
Patrick R. Casey

Counsel for: CNA Insurance Company; The Medical Protective Co.; Harleysville Insurance Co.; The Procter & Gamble Co.; Prudential-Bach Securities, Inc.; Zurich-American Insurance Co.; The Keystone Coca-Cola Bottling Co.; The Home Insurance Co.; The Travelers Insurance Co.; Utica First Ins. Co.

For full biographical listings, see the Martindale-Hubbell Law Directory

*WILLIAMSPORT,** Lycoming Co.

MITCHELL, MITCHELL, GRAY & GALLAGHER, A PROFESSIONAL CORPORATION (AV)

10 West Third Street, 17701-6513
Telephone: 570-323-8404
Fax: 570-323-8585
Email: mmggpc@csrlink.net

Jacob Neafie Mitchell (1919-1996)
C. Edward S. Mitchell
Richard A. Gray
Robert A. Gallagher
Gary L. Weber
Bret J. Southard

Darryl R. Wishard

For full biographical listings, see the Martindale-Hubbell Law Directory

RHODE ISLAND

*PROVIDENCE,** Providence Co.

HINCKLEY, ALLEN & SNYDER LLP (AV)

1500 Fleet Center, 02903-2393
Telephone: 401-274-2000
Fax: 401-277-9600
Email: firm@haslaw.com *URL:* http://www.haslaw.com
Boston, Massachusetts Office: 28 State Street, 30th Floor.
Telephone: 617-345-9000.
Fax: 617-345-9020. URL: http://www.haslaw.com.

MEMBERS OF FIRM

Paula K. Andrews (Not admitted in RI)
David D. Barricelli
Jonathan Bell
Paul Bork (Not admitted in RI)
Stephen J. Carlotti
Joseph P. Curran
Michael P. DeFanti
Eric F. Eisenberg (Not admitted in RI)
Malcolm Farmer, III
Margaret D. Farrell
Hugh J. Gorman, III (Not admitted in RI)
William R. Grimm
Richard L. E. Jocelyn
Joel Lewin (Not admitted in RI)
Sandra Matrone Mack
Matthew T. Marcello, III
Frederick P. McClure
Elizabeth Murdock Myers
Paul F. O'Donnell, III (Not admitted in RI)
H. Peter Olsen
Julianne Palumbo (Not admitted in RI)
John J. Pendergast, III
Gerald J. Petros
James O. Reavis
Jeremy Ritzenberg (Not admitted in RI)
Ralph J. Rivkind (Not admitted in RI)
Charles E. Schaub, Jr. (Not admitted in RI)
Douglas F. Seaver (Not admitted in RI)
Herman Snyder (Not admitted in RI)
David R. Sullivan (Not admitted in RI)
Robert F. Sylvia (Not admitted in RI)
Howard E. Walker
Richard D. Wayne (Not admitted in RI)

(See Next Column)

ASSOCIATES

Jessica M. Bettencourt
Mark Bianchi
Alexandra K. Callam
Jane E. Cohen (Not admitted in RI)
Andrew D. Cummings (Not admitted in RI)
June E. Daniel
Kelley Jordan-Price
Catherine S. Kim (Not admitted in RI)
Christopher W. Morog (Not admitted in RI)
Elena B. Olson (Not admitted in RI)
Joseph D. Whelan

OF COUNSEL

Willard Krasnow (Not admitted in RI)
Bentley Tobin
Joachim A. Weissfeld

For Complete List of Firm Personnel, See General Section

For full biographical listings, see the Martindale-Hubbell Law Directory

SOUTH CAROLINA

*ANDERSON,** Anderson Co.

CHAPMAN, BYRHOLDT & YON (AV)

117 West Benson Street, P.O. Box 2506, 29622
Telephone: 864-225-1411
Fax: 864-231-9131

MEMBER OF FIRM

V. Laniel Chapman

For full biographical listings, see the Martindale-Hubbell Law Directory

*CHARLESTON,** Charleston Co.

URICCHIO, HOWE, KRELL, JACOBSON, TOPOREK & THEOS, P.A. (AV)

17 1/2 Broad Street, 29401
Telephone: 803-723-7491
1-800-899-1683
Fax: 803-577-4179
Mailing Address: P.O. Box 399, Charleston, S.C., 29402-0399
Email: uricchio@ix.netcom.com

Paul N. Uricchio, Jr.
Arthur G. Howe
Barry Krell
Carl H. Jacobson
Alan David Toporek
Jerry N. Theos
Gregory Daulton Keith

For full biographical listings, see the Martindale-Hubbell Law Directory

*COLUMBIA,** Richland Co.

BARNES, ALFORD, STORK & JOHNSON, L.L.P. (AV)

1613 Main Street, P.O. Box 8448, 29202
Telephone: 803-799-1111
Telefax: 803-254-1335
Email: basj@basjlaw.com

Weldon R. Johnson
Kay Gaffney Crowe
L. Elaine Mozingo

Melody Lynn James
Andrea C. Pope

Representative Clients: Travelers/Aetna; Cigna; CNA; St. Paul; Fireman's Fund; Stirling Cooke; Berkshire Hathaway; Reliance Ins. Co.

For Complete List of Firm Personnel, See General Section

For full biographical listings, see the Martindale-Hubbell Law Directory

HOWSER, NEWMAN & BESLEY, L.L.C. (AV)

1508 Washington Street, P.O. Box 12009, 29211
Telephone: 803-758-6000
Fax: 803-758-4445
Email: rdhowser@hnblaw.com

R. Davis Howser
James P. Newman, Jr.
William G. Besley
Benjamin D. McCoy

Kelley S. Shull
Andrew E. Haselden
Janet Brooks

Representative Clients: American Modern Home Company; Clayton Homes; CNA Risk Management Group; DPIC Companies, Inc.; Horace Mann Insurance Company; Zurich Companies; Selective Insurance Company; South Carolina School Boards Insurance Trust; State Auto Insurance Company; Utica National Insurance Group.

For full biographical listings, see the Martindale-Hubbell Law Directory

Columbia—Continued

LEE, EADON, ISGETT AND POPWELL, P.A. (AV)

1314 Lincoln Street, P.O. Box 1505, 29202
Telephone: 803-799-9811; 1-800-882-0742
Telecopier: 803-779-8572
URL: http://www.lawyers.com/leeeadonisgett&popwell

Luther M. Lee (1923-1996)
Sherod H. Eadon, Jr.
Christopher C. Isgett
Gary W. Popwell, Jr.

Gerald E. Reardon

For full biographical listings, see the Martindale-Hubbell Law Directory

McANGUS, GOUDELOCK & COURIE, L.L.C. (AV)

1517 Hampton Street, P.O. Box 12519 Capitol Station, 29211-2519
Telephone: 803-779-2300
Telecopier: 803-748-0526
Email: mgc@mgclaw.com *URL:* http://www.mgclaw.com
Charlotte, North Carolina Office: 6101 Carnegie Boulevard, Suite 510. P.O. Box 30307, 28230.
Telephone: 704-940-2300.
Telecopier: 704-643-2376.

MEMBERS OF FIRM

W. Hugh McAngus
J. Russell Goudelock, II
James R. Courie
Yolanda C. Courie
Scott B. Garrett
Sterling G. Davies

ASSOCIATES

George D. Gallagher
Anne Marie Partin
A. Mundi Moss
Richard Daniel Addison
Louise M. Boylston
Sean A. Scoopmire
G. Thomas Chase

For full biographical listings, see the Martindale-Hubbell Law Directory

ROGERS TOWNSEND & THOMAS, PC (AV)

1441 Main Street, 10th Floor, P.O. Box 100200, 29202-3200
Telephone: 803-771-7900
Fax: 803-254-6305; 343-7017; 343-7019
URL: http://www.rtt-law.com

Harry B. Gregory, Jr.

Thomas McRoy Shelley, III

For Complete List of Firm Personnel, See General Section

For full biographical listings, see the Martindale-Hubbell Law Directory

TURNER, PADGET, GRAHAM & LANEY, P.A. (AV)

Seventeenth Floor, 1901 Main Street, P.O. Box 1473, 29202
Telephone: 803-254-2200
Telecopy: 803-799-3957
Florence, South Carolina Office: Fourth Floor, 1831 West Evans Street, P.O. Box 5478, 29502.
Telephone: 843-662-9008.
Fax: 843-667-0828.
Charleston, South Carolina Office: 21 Broad Street, 1st Floor, P.O. Box 836, 29402.
Telephone: 843-723-1622.
Fax: 843-577-3369.

Arthur E. Justice, Jr. (Resident, Florence, SC, Office)
Vernon F. Dunbar
Michael E. Chase
Walter H. Barefoot (Resident, Florence, SC Office)

Michael C. Abbott (Resident, Florence, SC, Office)
Cynthia C. Dooley

For Complete List of Firm Personnel, See General Section

For full biographical listings, see the Martindale-Hubbell Law Directory

GREENVILLE,* Greenville Co.

CLARKSON, FORTSON, WALSH & RHENEY, P.A. (AV)

117 Manly Street, P.O. Box 6186, 29606
Telephone: 864-232-4400
Fax: 864-235-4399
Email: cfwr@cfwr.com

Rebecca R. Wray
Samuel C. Weldon

For full biographical listings, see the Martindale-Hubbell Law Directory

HAYNSWORTH, MARION, McKAY & GUÉRARD, L.L.P. (AV)

75 Beattie Place, Eleventh Floor, P.O. Box 2048, 29602
Telephone: 864-240-3200
Facsimile: 864-240-3300
Columbia, South Carolina Office: Suite 2400 Affinity Building, 1201 Main Street, P.O. Drawer 7157, 29202
Telephone: 803-765-1818.
Facsimile: 803-765-2399.
Charleston, South Carolina Office: 134 Meeting Street, P.O. Box 1119, 29402.
Telephone: 843-722-7606.
Facsimile: 843-724-8016.

MEMBERS OF FIRM

William E. Shaughnessy
Richard B. Kale, Jr.
David Hill Keller
Jeffrey S. Jones

ASSOCIATES

Harold J. Willson, Jr.
Tracy Welsh Tiddy
Jeffrey R. Gilbert
Thomas M. Sears, Jr.

Representative Clients: Liberty Mutual Insurance Company; Travelers Insurance Company; Hartford Accident & Indemnity Co.; Kemper Insurance Company; Michelin Tire Corporation; Fluor Daniel; Sedgwick James of the Carolinas; Hewitt, Coleman & Assoc.; Greenville County; Palmetto Hospital Trust; Greenville Hospital System.

For Complete List of Firm Personnel, See General Section

For full biographical listings, see the Martindale-Hubbell Law Directory

KATHRYN WILLIAMS, P.A. (AV)

619 North Main Street, P.O. Box 10693, 29603
Telephone: 864-235-6254
Fax: 864-233-6591

Kathryn Williams

LEGAL SUPPORT PERSONNEL

Barbara Kamb

For full biographical listings, see the Martindale-Hubbell Law Directory

LORIS, Horry Co.

STEVENS LAW FIRM, P.C. (AV)

3341 Broad Street P.O. Drawer 127, 29569-0127
Telephone: 843-756-7652
Fax: 843-756-3785
E-Mail: RUMMPOLE@AOL.COM
Email: JPKLAW@AOL.COM

James P. Stevens, Jr.
Jonathan P. Kresken

For full biographical listings, see the Martindale-Hubbell Law Directory

SPARTANBURG,* Spartanburg Co.

EDWARDS, BALLARD, BISHOP, STURM, CLARK & KEIM, P.A. (AV)

International Center, Suite 400, 101 North Pine Street, P.O. Box 5398, 29304-5398
Telephone: 864-542-8612
Fax: 864-542-8712
Email: lawfirm@ebbsck.com
Winston-Salem, North Carolina Office: Edwards, Ballard, Clark, Barrett and Carlson, P.A., 380 Knollwood, Suite 730, P.O. Box 1708. 27102-1708.
Telephone: 336-750-0707.
Fax: 336-750-0711.

James F. Edwards, Jr.
Wade E. Ballard
Michael W. Bishop
Kevin W. Sturm
Terry A. Clark (Resident Partner, Edwards, Ballard, Clark, Barrett and Carlson, P.A., Winston-Salem, North Carolina)
Thomas H. Keim, Jr.
Karen M. Tyner
Roger G. Chandler
Patrick L. Cont

S. Clay Keim
Krishna Y. McVey
W. Allen Myrick, Jr.
Penny Correll Wofford

Representative Clients: Texfi Industries, Inc.; Coca-Cola Bottling Co. Consolidated; Kobe Copper Products, Inc.; Van Waters & Rogers, Inc.; Spartanburg Steel Products, Inc.; Century Furniture Co.; Grimes Aerospace Corp.; Sulzer Ruti, Inc.; Comm/Scope, Inc.; South Carolina Insurance Reserve Fund.

For full biographical listings, see the Martindale-Hubbell Law Directory

HARRISON, WHITE, SMITH, HAYES & COGGINS, P.A. (AV)

178 West Main Street, 29306
Telephone: 864-542-2990
Fax: 864-542-2994

(See Next Column)

HARRISON, WHITE, SMITH, HAYES & COGGINS P.A.—*Continued*

Benjamin C. Harrison
John B. White, Jr.
J. Mark Hayes, II
Danny R. Smith
Donald C. Coggins, Jr.

For full biographical listings, see the Martindale-Hubbell Law Directory

SOUTH DAKOTA

LEAD, Lawrence Co.

FULLER, TELLINGHUISEN, GORDON & PERCY, P.C. (AV)

203 West Main Street, P.O. Box 898, 57754
Telephone: 605-584-2440
Fax: 605-584-1979
Email: leadlaw@mato.com
Spearfish, South Dakota Office: 132 East Illinois, 57783.
Telephone: 605-642-8080.
Fax: 605-642-1756. E-mail: spflaw@mato.com

A. P. Fuller
Roger A. Tellinghuisen
Bradley P. Gordon
Michelle Palmer Percy

Representative Clients: Homestake Mining Co.; Hotel Franklin & Gaming; Black Hills Novelty/Automatic Vending, Inc.; Northern Hills General Hospital; Lantis Enterprises, Inc.; Norwest Bank South Dakota N.A.; Lead-Deadwood Independent School District # 40-1; City of Lead.

For full biographical listings, see the Martindale-Hubbell Law Directory

TENNESSEE

*CHATTANOOGA,** Hamilton Co.

SUMMERS & WYATT, P.C. (AV)

500 Lindsay Street, 37402
Telephone: 423-265-2385
Fax: 423-266-5211
Email: summers@voy.net

Jerry H. Summers
Thomas L. Wyatt
Jeffrey W. Rufolo
Jimmy F. Rodgers, Jr.

For full biographical listings, see the Martindale-Hubbell Law Directory

*CLEVELAND,** Bradley Co.

JENNE, SCOTT & JENNE (AV)

260 Ocoee Street, P.O. Box 161, 37364-0161
Telephone: 423-476-5506
Fax: 423-476-5058
Email: MichaelJenne@mindspring.com

MEMBERS OF FIRM

Roger E. Jenne
Robert A. Scott (1940-1984)
Michael E. Jenne

For full biographical listings, see the Martindale-Hubbell Law Directory

KINGSPORT, Sullivan Co.

HAWKINS, MOODY, BINGHAM, MILLER & ASSOCIATES, P.C. (AV)

1397 East Center Street, 37664
Telephone: 423-246-9100
Fax: 423-246-9282

William W. Hawkins (1929-1997)
Edgar G. Moody
John S. Bingham
J. David Miller

For full biographical listings, see the Martindale-Hubbell Law Directory

SHINE & MASON LAW OFFICE (AV)

Suite 201, 433 East Center Street, 37660
Telephone: 423-246-8433
Fax: 423-246-7464
Email: shimas@mounet.com

MEMBERS OF FIRM

D. Bruce Shine
Donald F. Mason, Jr.

Reference: Citizens Bank, Kingsport, TN.

For full biographical listings, see the Martindale-Hubbell Law Directory

*KNOXVILLE,** Knox Co.

EGERTON, MCAFEE, ARMISTEAD & DAVIS, P.C. (AV)

500 First American National Bank Center, P.O. Box 2047, 37901
Telephone: 423-546-0500
Fax: 423-525-5293
URL: http://emadlaw.com

Lewis C. Foster, Jr.
Barry K. Maxwell
Rockforde D. King

Wesley L. Hatmaker

Representative Clients: Baptist Hospital of East Tennessee; National American Insurance Co.; The Hartford Mutual Insurance Company; Mr. Gattis's Inc.; Pharmacist Mutual Insurance Co.; National Association of Employors; Lumberman's Underwriting Alliance; Royal Insurance.

For full biographical listings, see the Martindale-Hubbell Law Directory

WIMBERLY LAWSON & SEALE, PLLC (AV)

Suite 601, NationsBank Center, 550 Main Avenue, P.O. Box 2231, 37901-2231
Telephone: 423-546-1000
Telefax: 423-546-1001
Email: wls@wls-law.com
Cookeville, Tennessee Office: 524 Kentucky Road, P.O. Box 655.
Telephone: 931-372-9123.
Telefax: 931-372-9181.
Morristown, Tennessee Office: 929 West First North Street, P.O. Box 1066.
Telephone: 423-587-6870.
Telefax: 423-587-1479.
Nashville, Tennessee Office: 3200 West End Avenue, Suite 500.
Telephone: 615-783-2190.
Telefax: 615-783-1606.
Affiliated Firms:
Atlanta, Georgia Office: Wimberly, Lawson, Steckel, Nelson & Schneider, P.C., Suite 400, Lenox Towers, 3400 Peachtree Street, N.E.
Telephone: 404-365-0900.
Fax: 404-261-3707. E-Mail: wl@wimlaw.com.
Fernandina Beach, Florida Office: Wimberly, Lawson & Leggio, P.O. Box 1128.
Telephone: 904-277-2222.
Fax: 904-277-6598.
Greenville, South Carolina Office: Wimberly, Lawson Daniels & Brandon, Overlook Executive Park, 109 Laurens Road, Building 4, Suite A.
Telephone: 864-242-9484.
Fax: 864-242-6833. E-Mail: mldjr@aol.com.

Philip J. Lawson
William R. Seale
Gary W. Wright
Ronald G. Daves
Mark C. Travis
G. Gerard Jabaley
Jeffrey C. Taylor

ASSOCIATES

George R. Arrants, Jr.
Fredrick J. Bissinger
J. Timothy Bobo
Kelly A. Campbell
Joseph J. Doherty
Kevin M. Dorris
Robert Durham
Robert S. Hahn
Stephanie J. Weber Hale
J. Eric Harrison
Mary Moffatt Helms
Jeffrey G. Jones
Robin M. King
Jerome D. Pinn
Scott M. Robbins
Henry E. Sledge, Jr.
Lisa A. Temple
Patty K. Wheeler

For full biographical listings, see the Martindale-Hubbell Law Directory

*MEMPHIS,** Shelby Co.

ALLEN, SCRUGGS, SOSSAMAN & THOMPSON, P.C. (AV)

813 Ridge Lake Boulevard, Suite 300, 38120-9409
Telephone: 901-763-4200
Facsimile: 901-684-1768
Mailing Address: P.O. Box 17349, Memphis, TN, 38187-0349
Email: asstlaw@asstlaw.com

James M. Simpson
Kirk A. Caraway
Charles R. Keckler, III
M. Blake Barton

For full biographical listings, see the Martindale-Hubbell Law Directory

ARMSTRONG ALLEN PREWITT GENTRY JOHNSTON & HOLMES, PLLC (AV)

Brinkley Plaza, Suite 700, 80 Monroe Avenue, 38103-2467
Telephone: 901-523-8211
Facsimile: 901-524-4936
Little Rock, Arkansas Office: Suite 100, 100 Morgan Keegan Drive, 72202.
Telephone: 501-280-0100.
Facsimile: 501-280-0166.
Jackson, Mississippi Office: 2525 Lakeward Drive, Suite 200, 39216.
Telephone: 601-713-1192.
Facsimile: 601-713-2049.

(See Next Column)

BRAULT, PALMER, GROVE, ZIMMERMAN, WHITE & STEINHILBER, *Fairfax—Continued*

MEMBERS OF FIRM

Adelard L. Brault (Emeritus)
Thomas C. Palmer, Jr. (Resident, Manassas Office)
Edward H. Grove, III
Michael L. Zimmerman
Bruce D. White
August W. Steinhilber, III

ASSOCIATES

Jack A. Robbins, Jr. (Resident, Manassas Office)
C. Mark Whittington
Craig J. Franco
Bobby Puri (Resident, Manassas Office)

Representative Clients: Alamo Rent-A-Car, Inc.; CNA Insurance Companies; E.I. du Pont de Nemours and Company; Erie Insurance Group; Fidelity & Deposit Company of Maryland; Hanover Insurance Company; Harleysville Insurance Companies; Home Insurance Company; J.B. Hunt Transport, Inc.; Kemper Insurance Group.

For full biographical listings, see the Martindale-Hubbell Law Directory

*MANASSAS,** Prince William Co.

McCARTHY & MASSEY, P.C. (AV)

9315 Center Street, Suite 104, 20110
Telephone: 703-330-2726; Metro: 703-551-2146
Fax: 703-330-2429

Tara M. McCarthy
Joyce A. Naumann Massey

Susan L. Mitchell
Marian L. Beckett

For full biographical listings, see the Martindale-Hubbell Law Directory

NORFOLK, (Independent City)

GOLDBLATT, LIPKIN & COHEN, P.C. (AV)

Suite 300, 415 St. Paul's Boulevard, P.O. Box 3505, 23514
Telephone: 757-627-6225
Telefax: 757-622-3698

Mary G. Commander

For full biographical listings, see the Martindale-Hubbell Law Directory

RICHMOND, (Independent City)

MALONEY, HUENNEKENS, PARKS, GECKER & PARSONS, A PROFESSIONAL CORPORATION (AV)

Bank of America Center, 1111 East Main Street, Suite 800, 23219-3103
Telephone: 804-644-0313
Telecopier: 804-783-6192

Malcolm Parks
Joel G. Clarke

Ruth E. Nathanson

Reference: First Union National Bank.

For Complete List of Firm Personnel, See General Section

For full biographical listings, see the Martindale-Hubbell Law Directory

ROANOKE, Roanoke City Co.

WOOTEN & HART, A PROFESSIONAL CORPORATION (AV)

707 Building, Suite 300, P.O. Box 12247, 24024-2247
Telephone: 540-343-2451; 540-342-9672
Telecopier: 540-345-6417
URL: http://www.wootenhart.com

George W. Wooten
David B. Hart
L. Thompson Hanes
Susan A. Waddell
Bradley D. McGraw
John L. Cooley
Thomas W. Farrell
Paul C. Kuhnel
Peter D. Vieth

David W. Hearn
John Mark Cooley
Christopher W. Stevens
Elizabeth D. Guilbert
Eunice Park Austin

OF COUNSEL

M. Lanier Woodrum

Representative Clients: Wachovia Bank; St. Paul Insurance Cos.
Approved Attorneys for: Lawyers Title Insurance Corp.
Reference: First Union National Bank.

For full biographical listings, see the Martindale-Hubbell Law Directory

WASHINGTON

MOSES LAKE, Grant Co.

CALBOM & SCHWAB, P.S.C. (AV)

1240 South Pioneer Way, P.O. Drawer 1429, 98837
Telephone: 509-765-1851
Toll Free: 1-800-497-1755
Fax: 509-766-2727
Wenatchee, Kennewick, Chelan, Brewster, Ellensburg
URL: http://www.calbomschwab.com
Wenatchee, Washington Office: 819 N. Miller.
Telephone: 509-662-5677.
Kennewick, Washington Office: 118 Vista Way.
Telephone: 509-736-0866.
Chelan, Washington Office: 127 E. Woodin Avenue.
Telephone: 509-682-4364.
Brewster, Washington Office: 102 S. Bridge Street.
Telephone: 509-689-2615.
Ellensburg, Washington Office: 1633 Vantage Highway.
Telephone: 509-962-6080.

G. Joe Schwab
John E. Calbom (1925-1995)
David L. Lybbert
Kathleen G. Kilcullen
Jeffrey Schwab

LEGAL SUPPORT PERSONNEL

PARALEGALS

Jeff Parkinson
Jane V. King
Gracie Ortiz

Reference: Seattle-First National Bank, Moses Lake Branch.

For full biographical listings, see the Martindale-Hubbell Law Directory

WEST VIRGINIA

*CHARLESTON,** Kanawha Co.

JACKSON & KELLY (AV)

1600 Laidley Tower, P.O. Box 553, 25322
Telephone: 304-340-1000
Fax: 304-340-1130
Email: info@jacksonkelly.com *URL:* http://www.jacksonkelly.com
Martinsburg, West Virginia Office: 300 Foxcroft Avenue, P.O. Box 1068.
Telephone: 304-263-8800.
Fax: 304-263-7110.
Morgantown, West Virginia Office: 6000 Hampton Center, P.O. Box 619.
Telephone: 304-599-3000.
Fax: 304-285-2040.
New Martinsville, West Virginia Office: 256 Russell Avenue, P.O. Box 68.
Telephone: 304-455-1751.
Fax: 304-455-6314.
Parkersburg, West Virginia Office: 412 Market Street, Suite 202, P.O. Box 1144.
Telephone: 304-424-3490.
Fax: 304-424-3499.
Fairmont, West Virginia Office: 1000 Technology Drive, Suite 1310.
Telephone: 304-368-2000.
Fax: 304-368-2020.
Lexington, Kentucky Office: 175 East Main Street, Suite 500, P.O. Box 2150.
Telephone: 606-255-9500.
Fax: 606-281-6478.
Washington, D. C. Office: 2401 Pennsylvania Avenue, N.W., Suite 400.
Telephone: 202-973-0200.
Fax: 202-973-0232.
Denver, Colorado Office: Suite 2710, 1660 Lincoln Street.
Telephone: 303-390-0003.
Fax: 303-390-0040.
Wheeling, West Virginia Office: 1144 Market Street.
Telephone: 304-233-4000.
Fax: 304-233-4077.

MEMBERS OF FIRM

John L. McClaugherty
Robert J. Busse
Allen R. Prunty
George E. Roeder, III (Resident, Morgantown, West Virginia Office)
Jeff Chandler Woods
A. Stuart Bennett (Resident, Lexington, Kentucky Office)
Timothy E. Huffman
Natalie D. Brown (Resident, Lexington, Kentucky Office)
Mary Jane Curran (Resident, Fairmont, West Virginia Office)
Bradley A. Crouser
Melissa Mize Robinson

(See Next Column)

JACKSON & KELLY—*Continued*

ASSOCIATES

Lucinda Fluharty Fitch (Resident, Wheeling, West Virginia Office)
Christopher Kenneth Robertson (Resident, Martinsburg, West Virginia Office)
Kathy L. Snyder (Resident, Morgantown, West Virginia Office)

Representative Clients: CONSOL, Inc.; Union Carbide Corporation; Wheeling-Pittsburgh Steel Corp.; ACF Industries, Inc.; United Parcel Service; Pittston Coal Management Company; Rhone-Poulenc Ag Co.; Zeigler Coal Holding Company; Shoney's, Inc.; Wal-Mart Stores, Inc.

For Complete List of Firm Personnel, See General Section

For full biographical listings, see the Martindale-Hubbell Law Directory

*CLARKSBURG,** Harrison Co.

MCNEER, HIGHLAND, MCMUNN AND VARNER, L.C. (AV)

One Valley Bank Building, P.O. Drawer 2040, 26302-2040
Telephone: 304-626-1100
Facsimile: 304-623-3035
Martinsburg Office: 2520 Aikens Center, P.O. Box 2509.
Telephone: 304-264-4621.
Fax: 304-264-8623.
Parkersburg Office: 404 Market Street, Suite 204, P.O. Box 1507.
Telephone: 304-422-7193.
Facsimile: 304-422-7196.

C. David McMunn
J. Cecil Jarvis
James A. Varner
Robert W. Trumble (Resident, Martinsburg Office)
Catherine D. Munster
James N. Riley
Steven R. Bratke (Resident, Parkersburg Office)
Michael J. Novotny (Resident, Martinsburg Office)
Dennis M. Shreve
Geraldine S. Roberts
William F. Rohrbaugh (Resident, Martinsburg Office)
Gregory H. Schillace
Judy L. Shanholtz
Tiffany R. Durst
Gene W. Bailey, II

OF COUNSEL

James E. McNeer
Cecil B. Highland, Jr.
William L. Fury

Representative Clients: One Valley Bank of Clarksburg, National Assn.; Bruceton Bank; Harrison County Bank; Nationwide Mutual Insurance Cos.; Clarksburg Publishing Co.; C.I.T. Financial Services; State Automobile Mutual Insurance Co.; United Hospital Center, Inc.; West Virginia Coals, Inc.; Swanson Plating Co.

For full biographical listings, see the Martindale-Hubbell Law Directory

*PRINCETON,** Mercer Co.

GIBSON, LEFLER & ASSOCIATES (AV)

1345 Mercer Street, 24740
Telephone: 304-425-8276
800-742-3545

MEMBERS OF FIRM

Michael F. Gibson
Derrick W. Lefler

LEGAL SUPPORT PERSONNEL

NURSE PARALEGAL

Melody Lambert, RN-RLNC

SOCIAL SECURITY PARALEGAL

Nancy Belcher

PERSONAL INJURY PARALEGAL

Kathy Richards

WORKERS COMPENSATION PARALEGAL

Carol Hylton

MEDICAL NEGLIGENCE PARALEGAL

Deborah Frye

For full biographical listings, see the Martindale-Hubbell Law Directory

SANDERS, AUSTIN, SWOPE & FLANIGAN (AV)

Hunter Park, 320 Courthouse Road, 24740-2421
Telephone: 304-425-8125
FAX: 304-425-4155
Email: sasf@inetone.net

MEMBERS OF FIRM

Hartley Sanders (1879-1952)
Lane O. Austin
Derek C. Swope
William H. Sanders, III
William B. Flanigan
Gregory S. Prudich

ASSOCIATES

S. Paige Burress
Omar J. Aboulhosn

(See Next Column)

OF COUNSEL

William H. Sanders, II

References: First Community Bank-Princeton; One Valley Bank-Princeton.

For full biographical listings, see the Martindale-Hubbell Law Directory

WISCONSIN

BROOKFIELD, Waukesha Co.

NELSON, DRIES, CONNELL & KRAMER, S.C. (AV)

150 North Sunnyslope Road, Suite 305, 53005
Telephone: 262-789-5880
Facsimile: 262-789-5888
Email: ndck@execpc.com

Christine K. Nelson
Craig W. Nelson
Robert W. Connell
Mark R. Kramer
Kurt R. Anderson

For full biographical listings, see the Martindale-Hubbell Law Directory

*MILWAUKEE,** Milwaukee Co.

KASDORF, LEWIS & SWIETLIK, S.C. (AV)

1551 South 108th Street, 53214
Telephone: 414-257-1055
Facsimile: 414-257-3759
Green Bay, Wisconsin Office: 727 East Walnut Street, 54301.
Telephone: 920-436-0304.
Wausau, Wisconsin Office: 2100 Stewart Avenue, Suite 230, 54401.
Telephone: 715-848-9250.
Facsimile: 715-849-2017.

James P. Reardon
Werner E. Scherr
Terrance E. Davczyk
Jeff Schmeckpeper
Gregory J. Cook
Michael J. Cieslewicz
Michael A. Mesirow
Joseph J. Ferris
James J. Kriva
David L. Styer
Robert J. Lauer
James M. Ryan
Robert P. Ochowicz

Michael C. Frohman
Charles G. Maris
Vicki L. Arrowood
Michael S. Murray
Peter J. Eckardt (Resident)
Christine D. Esser
Thomas A. Cabush
John K. Garofani
Bonni D. Fredrick
Christopher A. Duesing
Daniel W. Varline (Resident, Wausau Office)
Jerome A. Long (Resident, Wausau Office)

OF COUNSEL

Clifford C. Kasdorf
John M. Swietlik
Hugh E. Russell
Patti J. Kurth

Representative Clients: Allstate Insurance Co.; State Farm Mutual Automobile; Liberty Mutual Insurance Co.; Shelby Mutual Insurance Co.; Government Employees Insurance Co.
Reference: M & I Marshall & Ilsley Bank.

For full biographical listings, see the Martindale-Hubbell Law Directory

SENECZKO LAW OFFICES, S.C. (AV)

Associated Bank Building, Suite 200, 10701 West National Avenue, 53227
Telephone: 414-321-5959
Fax: 414-321-1404
Email: seneczko@excepc.com

Alan E. Seneczko

For full biographical listings, see the Martindale-Hubbell Law Directory

*OSHKOSH,** Winnebago Co.

CURTIS LAW OFFICE (AV)

2905 Universal Street, P.O. Box 2845, 54903-2845
Telephone: 920-233-1010
Fax: 920-233-8053
Email: osowski@execpc.com

Scott C. Woldt

Reference: M & I Bank.

For full biographical listings, see the Martindale-Hubbell Law Directory

CANADA NEWFOUNDLAND

*ST. JOHN'S,**

McINNES COOPER (AV)

Barristers, Solicitors & Trade Mark Agents
Baine Johnston Centre, 5th Floor, 10 Fort William Place, P.O. Box 5939, A1C 5X4
Telephone: 709-722-8735
Telecopier: 709-722-1763
Email: mcrsj@mcrlaw.com *URL:* http://www.mcrlaw.com
Halifax, Nova Scotia Office: Summit Place, 1601 Lower Water Street, P.O. Box 730, B3J 2V1.
Telephone: 902-425-6500.
Fax: 902-425-6350. Email: mcrhfx@mcrlaw.com.
Moncton, New Brunswick Office: Place Moncton Place, 655 Main Street, P.O. Box 1368, E1C 8T6.
Telephone: 506-857-8970.
Fax: 506-857-4095. Email: mcrmctn@mcrlaw.com.
Charlottetown, Prince Edward Island Office: BDC Place, Suite 620, 119 Kent Street, C1A 1N3.
Telephone: 902-368-8473.
Fax: 902-368-8346. Email: mcrpei@mcrlaw.com.
Fredericton, New Brunswick Office: Suite 600, 570 Queen Street, P.O. Box 610.
Telephone: 506-458-8572.
Fax: 506-458-9903. Email: mcrfton@mcrlaw.com.

PARTNER

Denis J. Mahoney

For Complete List of Firm Personnel, See General Section

For full biographical listings, see the Martindale-Hubbell Law Directory

CANADA NOVA SCOTIA

*HALIFAX,** Regional Munic. of Halifax

McINNES COOPER (AV)

Barristers, Solicitors & Trade Mark Agents
Summit Place, 1601 Lower Water Street, P.O. Box 730, B3J 2V1
Telephone: 902-425-6500
Fax: 902-425-6350
Email: mcrhfx@mcrlaw.com *URL:* http://www.mcrlaw.com
St. John's, Newfoundland Office: Baine Johnston Centre, 5th Floor, 10 Fort William Place, P.O. Box 5939, A1C 5X4.
Telephone: 709-722-8735.
Telecopier: 709-722-1763. Email: mcrsj@mcrlaw.com.
Moncton, New Brunswick Office: Place Moncton Place, 655 Main Street, P.O. Box 1368, E1C 8T6.
Telephone: 506-857-8970.
Fax: 506-857-4095. Email: mcrmctn@mcrlaw.com.
Charlottetown, Prince Edward Island Office: BDC Place, Suite 620, 119 Kent Street, C1A 1N3.
Telephone: 902-368-8473.
Fax: 902-368-8346. Email: mcrpei@mcrlaw.com.
Fredericton, New Brunswick Office: Suite 600, 570 Queen Street, P.O. Box 610.
Telephone: 506-458-8572.
Fax: 506-458-9903. Email: mcrfton@mcrlaw.com.

PARTNERS

Eric Durnford, Q.C.
Malcolm D. Boyle
John H. (Jack) Graham

ASSOCIATES

Paul McLean
Rebecca Saturley

For Complete List of Firm Personnel, See General Section

For full biographical listings, see the Martindale-Hubbell Law Directory

CANADA QUEBEC

*MONTREAL,** Montreal Dist.

McMASTER GERVAIS (AV)

A General Partnership
1000 de La Gauchetière Street West, Suite 900, H3B 5H4
Telephone: 514-879-1212
Fax: 514-954-1905
Email: info@mcmastergervais.com *URL:* http://www.mcmastergervais.com

MEMBER OF FIRM

Rosaire S. Houde

For Complete List of Firm Personnel, See General Section

For full biographical listings, see the Martindale-Hubbell Law Directory

CANADA SASKATCHEWAN

*REGINA,** Regina Jud. Centre

MacPHERSON LESLIE & TYERMAN (AV)

1500-1874 Scarth Street, S4P 4E9
Telephone: 306-347-8000
Telecopier: 306-352-5250
Email: mltreg@mlt.com
Saskatoon, Saskatchewan Office: 1500-410 22nd Street East, S7K 5T6.
Telephone: 306-975-7100.
Telecopier: 306-975-7145.

MEMBERS OF FIRM

Leonard D. Andrychuk
Robert G. Richards, Q.C.

For Complete List of Firm Personnel, See General Section

For full biographical listings, see the Martindale-Hubbell Law Directory